AMERiCAN BUSiNESS LOCATiONS DiRECTORY

AMERiCAN BUSiNESS LOCATiONS DiRECTORY

FIRST EDITION

volume

4

south

Alabama • Arkansas • Delaware • District of Columbia • Florida • Georgia • Kentucky
Louisiana • Maryland • Mississippi • North Carolina • Oklahoma • Puerto Rico
South Carolina • Tennessee • Texas • Virgin Islands • Virginia • West Virginia

Valerie J. Webster, Editor
Lia M. Watson, Associate Editor

Gale Research

An ITP Information/Reference Group Company

Changing the Way the World Learns

NEW YORK • LONDON • BONN • BOSTON • DETROIT
MADRID • MELBOURNE • MEXICO CITY • PARIS
SINGAPORE • TOKYO • TORONTO • WASHINGTON
ALBANY NY • BELMONT CA • CINCINNATI OH

Valerie J. Webster, *Editor*

Lia M. Watson, *Associate Editor*

Amy K. Barrett, Deborah S. Fennell, Carol T. Gaffke, Scott F. Heil, Catherine L. Johnson, *Assistant Editors*

Donald P. Boyden, *Managing Editor*

Susan E. Edgar, Christine A. Kesler, Kathleen E. Maki, Jane A. Malonis, *Contributing Editors*

Donna Craft, Stefanie Scarlett, *Contributing Associate Editors*

Andrew Guy Malonis, Gary Oudersluys, *Research Specialists*

Theresa Rocklin, *Manager, Technical Support Services*

Neil S. Yee, *Senior Programmer*

Mary Beth Trimper, *Production Director*

Shanna Heilveil, *Production Assistant*

Benita L. Spight, *Manager, Data Entry Services*

Gwendolyn Tucker, *Data Entry Supervisor*

Beverly Jendrowski, *Senior Data Entry Associate*

LeSandra C. Davis, Edgar C. Jackson, Arlene Kevonian, Francis L. Monroe, and Constance Wells, *Data Entry Associates*

Barbara Yarrow, *Graphic Services Supervisor*

Michelle Dimercurio, *Art Director*

Yolanda Latham, *Desktop Publisher*

∞™ This book is printed on acid-free paper that meets the minimum requirements of the American National Standard for Information Sciences—Permanence Paper for Printed Library Materials, ANSI Z39.48-1984.

♻ This book is printed on recycled paper that meets Environmental Protection Agency standards.

ISBN 0-8103-8368-3 (5-volume set)

ISBN 0-8103-8369-1 (Volume 1)

ISBN 0-8103-8370-5 (Volume 2)

ISBN 0-8103-8371-3 (Volume 3)

ISBN 0-8103-8372-1 (Volume 4)

ISBN 0-7976-0802-5 (Volume 5)

Printed in the United States of America

 Gale Research Inc., an International Thomson Publishing Company.

ITP logo is a trademark under license.

Contents

Volume 4: South

Contents

Volume 1: West

Contents

Volume 2 : Midwest

Contents

Volume 3: Northeast

Contents

Volume 5: Parent List with Company Names

Highlights

Use *American Business Locations Directory* for these key business applications:

- ► Sales and marketing executives can identify new customers, locate new suppliers, assess market potential, and assign sales territories.

- ► Consultants can identify local companies in their area of expertise

- ► Job seekers can target specific locations of major corporations

- ► Students can obtain local and regional company information for assignments and to prepare for job interviews

Powerful features of *American Business Locations Directory*:

- ► Almost 100,000 sites for the most important 1000 service and industrial companies are identified and linked back to their parent company

- ► Detailed entries include address and contact information for each site, corporate affiliations, employee counts, sales figures, and company or location type

- ► Individual regional volumes provide key coverage of local sites

- ► Cumulative index volume brings together under the parent headquarters all of that companies sites nationwide

- ► Volume specific SIC and alphabetical indexes work with the geographic main body arrangement to provide precise access to the site and parent company listings

For more information about the content and uses of *American Business Locations Directory*, please refer to the **Introduction** and the **User's Guide** sections on the following pages.

Introduction

American Business Locations Directory fills an important information void left by other reference products that cover U.S. business. *American Business Locations Directory* doesn't stop with just listing the parent headquarters, but continues on to identify and locate individual manufacturing plants, branch offices, R&D centers, divisions, subsidiaries, and other sites throughout the U.S. and then links them back to their parent.

American Business Locations Directory provides this unique coverage for the 1,000 most important industrial and service companies in the U.S. as identified by Fortune magazine in their annual Fortune Industrial 500 and Fortune Service 500 Companies rankings.

Arrangement

American Business Locations Directory's regional arrangement provides the geographic access to the information needed by sales professionals, market researchers, job seekers, and students for their business applications.

The SIC and alphabetic indexes contained in each volume provide convenient access to the sites listed in that volume, while the valuable fifth volume gathers all sites together under each parent company.

Volume coverage is as follows:

Volume 1: The West. Includes Alaska, Arizona, California, Colorado, Hawaii, Idaho, Montana, Nevada, New Mexico, Oregon, Utah, Washington, and Wyoming.

Volume 2: The Midwest. Includes Illinois, Indiana, Iowa, Kansas, Michigan, Minnesota, Missouri, Nebraska, North Dakota, Ohio, South Dakota, and Wisconsin.

Volume 3: The Northeast. Includes Connecticut, Maine, Massachusetts, New Hampshire, New Jersey, New York, Pennsylvania, Rhode Island, and Vermont.

Volume 4: The South. Includes Alabama, Arkansas, Delaware, District of Columbia, Florida, Georgia, Kentucky, Louisiana, Maryland, Mississippi, North Carolina, Oklahoma, Puerto Rico, South Carolina, Tennessee, Texas, Virgin Islands, Virginia, and West Virginia.

Volume 5: Parent List with Company Names. Consists of a single volume listing all parent companies alphabetically and all associated companies alphabetically under the parent.

Entry Content

American Business Locations Directory entries contain up to eight types of information.

- ▶   Company name, address and phone number.
- ▶   Ultimate parent name.
- ▶   Location and/or company type (i.e. plant, subsidiary).
- ▶   Officer name.
- ▶   SIC.
- ▶   Employee count.
- ▶   Financial information in millions.
- ▶   Fortune rankings (ultimate parent listings only).

Indexes Help Users Locate Target Companies

- ▶   **SIC Index** provides access to entries using the U.S. government's Standard Industrial Classification Codes (see pages xv through xxxi for code definitions).

- ▶   **Company Name Index** provides a complete alphabetic listing of entries in each volume.

Method of Compilation

The information presented in *American Business Locations Directory* was identified and complied through extensive research that involved contacting the companies listed, reviewing annual reports and 10k's, searching government databases, scanning periodical literature, analyzing Gale's company databases, and other original research.

Acknowledgements

Fortune Industrial 500 and Fortune Service 500 lists are © 1993 Time Inc. All rights reserved. Reprinted by permission of the publisher.

Comments Welcome

We welcome comments on this edition of *American Business Locations Directory* as well as suggestions for future editions. Please contact:

Editors
American Business Locations Directory
Gale Research Inc.
835 Penobscot Bldg.
Detroit, MI 48226-4094
Phone: (313)961-2242
Toll-free: (800)347-4253

User's Guide

Entries in *American Business Locations Directory* are arranged alphabetically by company name under the city and state in which they are located.

Each volume contains the following tools designed to help users find companies by specific Standard Industrial Classification Codes and Parent/Subsidiary relationships:

▶ **SIC Index**

▶ **Parent/Subsidiary Index**

Entries and indexes are alphabetized word by word, as opposed to letter by letter. Thus, "Bell Gardens' appears before "Bellflower." In most cases, company names consisting of a person's name are listed according to the surname. In the case of well-known names, brand names, and trade names, entries are listed according to the first name. For example, Thomas Hodgson & Sons Inc. appears under "H," while Walt Disney Co. appears under "W."

Sample Entry

The following fabricated entry illustrates the types of information that may be found in a typical entry. For demonstrative purposes, each type of information has been numbered; an explanation of the numbered items is presented after the sample entry. The length and detail of each entry varies according to the availability of information and the interest level of the companies contacted.

1. ★330★
2. **Watson Brothers Automotive Services**
3. Automotive Glass Div.
4. 9902 Hubbell
   Detroit, MI 48227
   (313)836-4144
5. **Fax:** (313)836-4113; (800)836-6000
6. **Location Type:** Plant.
7. **Company Type:** Subsidiary.
8. **Officer:** Ken Watson, President & CEO.
9. **Ultimate Parent:** U.S. Motor Co.
10. **SIC:** 1793—Glass & Glazing Work; 7536—Automotive Glass Replacement Shops.
11. **Employee Count:** 25.
12. **Sales:** 12 M.
13. **Fortune Service 500:** Ranking 225.

Explanation of Sample Entry

1. **Entry Number:** Entries are numbered sequentially starting with 1. Entry numbers, not page numbers, are cited in the Company Index and the Parent/Subsidiary Index.

2. **Company Name:** Companies are listed under their legal names.

3. **Division Name.**

4. **Address and Phone Number.**

5. **Fax, Toll-free, and Telex.**

6. **Location Type:** This refers to the company's location. The most common company location types are branch offices, plants, and regional offices.

7. **Company Type:** This refers to company ownership. The most common company types listed are headquarters, division, and subsidiary.

8. **Officer Information:** Lists the names of executive officers and their corporate titles.

9. **Ultimate Parent:** Provides the name of the ultimate parent company.

10. **Standard Industrial Classification Code:** Identifies the company by industry.

11. **Employee Count:** Includes the total number of employees figure for up to three years. Other employee-specific information may be provided as well.

12. **Financial Information:** Includes revenue, revenue type, revenue year, and fiscal year end. Figures are in millions.

13. **Media Rank:** Notes the company's status if included on media lists, such as the Fortune Service 500, as well from which list the information was gathered.

Standard Industrial Classification (SIC) Codes Alphabetic Listing

Abrasive Products   3291
Accident & Health Insurance   6321
Accounting, Auditing & Bookkeeping   8721
Adhesives & Sealants   2891
Adjustment & Collection Services   7322
Administration of Educational Programs   9411
Administration of General Economic Programs   9611
Administration of Public Health Programs   9431
Administration of Social and Manpower Programs   9441
Administration of Veterans' Affairs   9451
Advertising Agencies   7311
Advertising Nec   7319
Agricultural Chemicals Nec   2879
Air & Gas Compressors   3563
Air Courier Services   4513
Air Transportation—Nonscheduled   4522
Air Transportation—Scheduled   4512
Air, Water & Solid Waste Management   9511
Aircraft   3721
Aircraft Engines & Engine Parts   3724
Aircraft Parts & Equipment Nec   3728
Airports, Flying Fields & Services   4581
Alkalies & Chlorine   2812
Aluminum Die-Castings   3363
Aluminum Extruded Products   3354
Aluminum Foundries   3365
Aluminum Rolling & Drawing Nec   3355
Aluminum Sheet, Plate & Foil   3353
Ammunition Except for Small Arms   3483
Amusement & Recreation Nec   7999
Amusement Parks   7996
Analytical Instruments   3826
Animal & Marine Fats & Oils   2077
Animal Aquaculture   0273
Animal Specialties Nec   0279
Animal Specialty Services   0752
Anthracite Mining   1231
Apartment Building Operators   6513
Apparel & Accessories Nec   2389
Apparel Belts   2387
Architectural Metal Work   3446
Architectural Services   8712
Armature Rewinding Shops   7694
Asbestos Products   3292
Asphalt Felts & Coatings   2952
Asphalt Paving Mixtures & Blocks   2951
Automatic Vending Machines   3581
Automobile & Home Supply Stores   5531
Automobile Exhaust System Repair Shops   7533
Automobile Parking   7521
Automobiles & Other Motor Vehicles   5012
Automotive & Apparel Trimmings   2396
Automotive Dealers Nec   5599
Automotive Glass Replacement Shops   7536

Automotive Repair Shops Nec   7539
Automotive Services Nec   7549
Automotive Stampings   3465
Automotive Transmission Repair Shops   7537
Bags—Plastics, Laminated & Coated   2673
Bags—Uncoated Paper & Multiwall   2674
Ball & Roller Bearings   3562
Bank Holding Companies   6712
Barber Shops   7241
Beauty Shops   7231
Beef Cattle Except Feedlots   0212
Beef Cattle Feedlots   0211
Beer & Ale   5181
Beet Sugar   2063
Berry Crops   0171
Biological Products Except Diagnostic   2836
Bituminous Coal & Lignite—Surface   1221
Bituminous Coal—Underground   1222
Blankbooks & Looseleaf Binders   2782
Blast Furnaces & Steel Mills   3312
Blowers & Fans   3564
Boat Building & Repairing   3732
Boat Dealers   5551
Bolts, Nuts, Rivets & Washers   3452
Book Printing   2732
Book Publishing   2731
Book Stores   5942
Bookbinding & Related Work   2789
Books, Periodicals & Newspapers   5192
Botanical & Zoological Gardens   8422
Bottled & Canned Soft Drinks   2086
Bowling Centers   7933
Bras, Girdles & Allied Garments   2342
Bread, Cake & Related Products   2051
Brick & Structural Clay Tile   3251
Brick, Stone & Related Materials   5032
Bridge, Tunnel & Elevated Highway   1622
Broadwoven Fabric Mills—Cotton   2211
Broadwoven Fabric Mills—Manmade   2221
Broadwoven Fabric Mills—Wool   2231
Broiler, Fryer & Roaster Chickens   0251
Brooms & Brushes   3991
Building Maintenance Services Nec   7349
Burial Caskets   3995
Bus Charter Service Except Local   4142
Bus Terminal & Service Facilities   4173
Business & Secretarial Schools   8244
Business Associations   8611
Business Consulting Services Nec   8748
Business Services Nec   7389
Cable & Other Pay Television Services   4841
Calculating & Accounting Equipment   3578
Camera & Photographic Supply Stores   5946
Candy & Other Confectionery Products   2064

Standard Industrial Classification (SIC) Codes
Numeric Listing

01—Agricultural Production—Crops

0111	Wheat
0112	Rice
0115	Corn
0116	Soybeans
0119	Cash Grains Nec
0131	Cotton
0132	Tobacco
0133	Sugarcane & Sugar Beets
0134	Irish Potatoes
0139	Field Crops Except Cash Grains Nec
0161	Vegetables & Melons
0171	Berry Crops
0172	Grapes
0173	Tree Nuts
0174	Citrus Fruits
0175	Deciduous Tree Fruits
0179	Fruits & Tree Nuts Nec
0181	Ornamental Nursery Products
0182	Food Crops Grown Under Cover
0191	General Farms—Primarily Crop

02—Agricultural Production—Livestock

0211	Beef Cattle Feedlots
0212	Beef Cattle Except Feedlots
0213	Hogs
0214	Sheep & Goats
0219	General Livestock Nec
0241	Dairy Farms
0251	Broiler, Fryer & Roaster Chickens
0252	Chicken Eggs
0253	Turkeys & Turkey Eggs
0254	Poultry Hatcheries
0259	Poultry & Eggs Nec
0271	Fur-Bearing Animals & Rabbits
0272	Horses & Other Equines
0273	Animal Aquaculture
0279	Animal Specialties Nec
0291	General Farms—Primarily Animal

07—Agricultural Services

0711	Soil Preparation Services
0721	Crop Planting, Cultivating & Protecting
0722	Crop Harvesting
0723	Crop Preparation Services for Market
0724	Cotton Ginning
0741	Veterinary Services—Livestock
0742	Veterinary Services—Specialties
0751	Livestock Services
0752	Animal Specialty Services
0761	Farm Labor Contractors
0762	Farm Management Services
0781	Landscape Counseling & Planning
0782	Lawn & Garden Services
0783	Ornamental Shrub & Tree Services

08—Forestry

0811	Timber Tracts
0831	Forest Products
0851	Forestry Services

09—Fishing, Hunting & Trapping

0912	Finfish
0913	Shellfish
0919	Miscellaneous Marine Products
0921	Fish Hatcheries & Preserves
0971	Hunting, Trapping & Game Propagation

10—Metal Mining

1011	Iron Ores
1021	Copper Ores
1031	Lead & Zinc Ores
1041	Gold Ores
1044	Silver Ores
1061	Ferroalloy Ores Except Vanadium
1081	Metal Mining Services
1094	Uranium, Radium & Vanadium Ores
1099	Metal Ores Nec

12—Coal Mining

1221	Bituminous Coal & Lignite—Surface
1222	Bituminous Coal—Underground
1231	Anthracite Mining
1241	Coal Mining Services

13—Oil & Gas Extraction

1311	Crude Petroleum & Natural Gas
1321	Natural Gas Liquids
1381	Drilling Oil & Gas Wells
1382	Oil & Gas Exploration Services
1389	Oil & Gas Field Services Nec

14—Nonmetallic Minerals Except Fuels

1411	Dimension Stone
1422	Crushed & Broken Limestone
1423	Crushed & Broken Granite
1429	Crushed & Broken Stone Nec
1442	Construction Sand & Gravel
1446	Industrial Sand

2369	Girls'/Children's Outerwear Nec
2371	Fur Goods
2381	Fabric Dress & Work Gloves
2384	Robes & Dressing Gowns
2385	Waterproof Outerwear
2386	Leather & Sheep-Lined Clothing
2387	Apparel Belts
2389	Apparel & Accessories Nec
2391	Curtains & Draperies
2392	Housefurnishings Nec
2393	Textile Bags
2394	Canvas & Related Products
2395	Pleating & Stitching
2396	Automotive & Apparel Trimmings
2397	Schiffli Machine Embroideries
2399	Fabricated Textile Products Nec

24—Lumber & Wood Products

2411	Logging
2421	Sawmills & Planing Mills—General
2426	Hardwood Dimension & Flooring Mills
2429	Special Product Sawmills Nec
2431	Millwork
2434	Wood Kitchen Cabinets
2435	Hardwood Veneer & Plywood
2436	Softwood Veneer & Plywood
2439	Structural Wood Members Nec
2441	Nailed Wood Boxes & Shook
2448	Wood Pallets & Skids
2449	Wood Containers Nec
2451	Mobile Homes
2452	Prefabricated Wood Buildings
2491	Wood Preserving
2493	Reconstituted Wood Products
2499	Wood Products Nec

25—Furniture & Fixtures

2511	Wood Household Furniture
2512	Upholstered Household Furniture
2514	Metal Household Furniture
2515	Mattresses & Bedsprings
2517	Wood T.V. and Radio Cabinets
2519	Household Furniture Nec
2521	Wood Office Furniture
2522	Office Furniture Except Wood
2531	Public Building & Related Furniture
2541	Wood Partitions & Fixtures
2542	Partitions & Fixtures Except Wood
2591	Drapery Hardware, Blinds & Shades
2599	Furniture & Fixtures Nec

26—Paper & Allied Products

2611	Pulp Mills
2621	Paper Mills
2631	Paperboard Mills
2652	Setup Paperboard Boxes
2653	Corrugated & Solid Fiber Boxes
2655	Fiber Cans, Drums & Similar Products
2656	Sanitary Food Containers
2657	Folding Paperboard Boxes
2671	Paper Coated & Laminated—Packaging
2672	Coated & Laminated Paper Nec
2673	Bags—Plastics, Laminated & Coated
2674	Bags—Uncoated Paper & Multiwall
2675	Die-Cut Paper & Board
2676	Sanitary Paper Products
2677	Envelopes
2678	Stationery Products
2679	Converted Paper Products Nec

27—Printing & Publishing

2711	Newspapers
2721	Periodicals
2731	Book Publishing
2732	Book Printing
2741	Miscellaneous Publishing
2752	Commercial Printing—Lithographic
2754	Commercial Printing—Gravure
2759	Commercial Printing Nec
2761	Manifold Business Forms
2771	Greeting Cards
2782	Blankbooks & Looseleaf Binders
2789	Bookbinding & Related Work
2791	Typesetting
2796	Platemaking Services

28—Chemicals & Allied Products

2812	Alkalies & Chlorine
2813	Industrial Gases
2816	Inorganic Pigments
2819	Industrial Inorganic Chemicals Nec
2821	Plastics Materials & Resins
2822	Synthetic Rubber
2823	Cellulosic Manmade Fibers
2824	Organic Fibers—Noncellulosic
2833	Medicinals & Botanicals
2834	Pharmaceutical Preparations
2835	Diagnostic Substances
2836	Biological Products Except Diagnostic
2841	Soap & Other Detergents
2842	Polishes & Sanitation Goods
2843	Surface Active Agents
2844	Toilet Preparations
2851	Paints & Allied Products
2861	Gum & Wood Chemicals
2865	Cyclic Crudes & Intermediates
2869	Industrial Organic Chemicals Nec
2873	Nitrogenous Fertilizers
2874	Phosphatic Fertilizers
2875	Fertilizers—Mixing Only
2879	Agricultural Chemicals Nec
2891	Adhesives & Sealants
2892	Explosives
2893	Printing Ink
2895	Carbon Black
2899	Chemical Preparations Nec

29—Petroleum & Coal Products

2911	Petroleum Refining
2951	Asphalt Paving Mixtures & Blocks
2952	Asphalt Felts & Coatings
2992	Lubricating Oils & Greases
2999	Petroleum & Coal Products Nec

30—Rubber & Miscellaneous Plastics Products

3011	Tires & Inner Tubes
3021	Rubber & Plastics Footwear
3052	Rubber & Plastics Hose & Belting
3053	Gaskets, Packing & Sealing Devices
3061	Mechanical Rubber Goods
3069	Fabricated Rubber Products Nec
3081	Unsupported Plastics Film & Sheet
3082	Unsupported Plastics Profile Shapes
3083	Laminated Plastics Plate & Sheet
3084	Plastics Pipe
3085	Plastics Bottles
3086	Plastics Foam Products

3559	Special Industry Machinery Nec
3561	Pumps & Pumping Equipment
3562	Ball & Roller Bearings
3563	Air & Gas Compressors
3564	Blowers & Fans
3565	Packaging Machinery
3566	Speed Changers, Drives & Gears
3567	Industrial Furnaces & Ovens
3568	Power Transmission Equipment Nec
3569	General Industrial Machinery Nec
3571	Electronic Computers
3572	Computer Storage Devices
3575	Computer Terminals
3577	Computer Peripheral Equipment Nec
3578	Calculating & Accounting Equipment
3579	Office Machines Nec
3581	Automatic Vending Machines
3582	Commercial Laundry Equipment
3585	Refrigeration & Heating Equipment
3586	Measuring & Dispensing Pumps
3589	Service Industry Machinery Nec
3592	Carburetors, Pistons, Rings & Valves
3593	Fluid Power Cylinders & Actuators
3594	Fluid Power Pumps & Motors
3596	Scales & Balances Except Laboratory
3599	Industrial Machinery Nec

36—Electronic & Other Electrical Equipment

3612	Transformers Except Electronic
3613	Switchgear & Switchboard Apparatus
3621	Motors & Generators
3624	Carbon & Graphite Products
3625	Relays & Industrial Controls
3629	Electrical Industrial Apparatus Nec
3631	Household Cooking Equipment
3632	Household Refrigerators & Freezers
3633	Household Laundry Equipment
3634	Electric Housewares & Fans
3635	Household Vacuum Cleaners
3639	Household Appliances Nec
3641	Electric Lamps
3643	Current-Carrying Wiring Devices
3644	Noncurrent-Carrying Wiring Devices
3645	Residential Lighting Fixtures
3646	Commercial Lighting Fixtures
3647	Vehicular Lighting Equipment
3648	Lighting Equipment Nec
3651	Household Audio & Video Equipment
3652	Prerecorded Records & Tapes
3661	Telephone & Telegraph Apparatus
3663	Radio & T.V. Communications Equipment
3669	Communications Equipment Nec
3671	Electron Tubes
3672	Printed Circuit Boards
3674	Semiconductors & Related Devices
3675	Electronic Capacitors
3676	Electronic Resistors
3677	Electronic Coils & Transformers
3678	Electronic Connectors
3679	Electronic Components Nec
3691	Storage Batteries
3692	Primary Batteries—Dry & Wet
3694	Engine Electrical Equipment
3695	Magnetic & Optical Recording Media
3699	Electrical Equipment & Supplies Nec

37—Transportation Equipment

3711	Motor Vehicles & Car Bodies
3713	Truck & Bus Bodies
3714	Motor Vehicle Parts & Accessories

3715	Truck Trailers
3716	Motor Homes
3721	Aircraft
3724	Aircraft Engines & Engine Parts
3728	Aircraft Parts & Equipment Nec
3731	Ship Building & Repairing
3732	Boat Building & Repairing
3743	Railroad Equipment
3751	Motorcycles, Bicycles & Parts
3761	Guided Missiles & Space Vehicles
3764	Space Propulsion Units & Parts
3769	Space Vehicle Equipment Nec
3792	Travel Trailers & Campers
3795	Tanks & Tank Components
3799	Transportation Equipment Nec

38—Instruments & Related Products

3812	Search & Navigation Equipment
3821	Laboratory Apparatus & Furniture
3822	Environmental Controls
3823	Process Control Instruments
3824	Fluid Meters & Counting Devices
3825	Instruments to Measure Electricity
3826	Analytical Instruments
3827	Optical Instruments & Lenses
3829	Measuring & Controlling Devices Nec
3841	Surgical & Medical Instruments
3842	Surgical Appliances & Supplies
3843	Dental Equipment & Supplies
3844	X-Ray Apparatus & Tubes
3845	Electromedical Equipment
3851	Ophthalmic Goods
3861	Photographic Equipment & Supplies
3873	Watches, Clocks, Watchcases & Parts

39—Miscellaneous Manufacturing Industries

3911	Jewelry & Precious Metal
3914	Silverware & Plated Ware
3915	Jewelers' Materials & Lapidary Work
3931	Musical Instruments
3942	Dolls & Stuffed Toys
3944	Games, Toys & Children's Vehicles
3949	Sporting & Athletic Goods Nec
3951	Pens & Mechanical Pencils
3952	Lead Pencils & Art Goods
3953	Marking Devices
3955	Carbon Paper & Inked Ribbons
3961	Costume Jewelry
3965	Fasteners, Buttons, Needles & Pins
3991	Brooms & Brushes
3993	Signs & Advertising Displays
3995	Burial Caskets
3996	Hard Surface Floor Coverings Nec
3999	Manufacturing Industries Nec

40—Railroad Transportation

4011	Railroads—Line-Haul Operating
4013	Switching & Terminal Services

41—Local & Interurban Passenger Transit

4111	Local & Suburban Transit
4119	Local Passenger Transportation Nec
4121	Taxicabs
4131	Intercity & Rural Bus Transportation
4141	Local Bus Charter Service
4142	Bus Charter Service Except Local
4151	School Buses
4173	Bus Terminal & Service Facilities

42—Trucking & Warehousing

4212	Local Trucking Without Storage
4213	Trucking Except Local
4214	Local Trucking With Storage
4215	Courier Services Except by Air
4221	Farm Product Warehousing & Storage
4222	Refrigerated Warehousing & Storage
4225	General Warehousing & Storage
4226	Special Warehousing & Storage Nec
4231	Trucking Terminal Facilities

43—U.S. Postal Service

| 4311 | U.S. Postal Service |

44—Water Transportation

4412	Deep Sea Foreign Transportation of Freight
4424	Deep Sea Domestic Transportation of Freight
4432	Freight Transportation on the Great Lakes
4449	Water Transportation of Freight Nec
4481	Deep Sea Passenger Transportation Except Ferry
4482	Ferries
4489	Water Passenger Transportation Nec
4491	Marine Cargo Handling
4492	Towing & Tugboat Services
4493	Marinas
4499	Water Transportation Services Nec

45—Transportation by Air

4512	Air Transportation—Scheduled
4513	Air Courier Services
4522	Air Transportation—Nonscheduled
4581	Airports, Flying Fields & Services

46—Pipelines Except Natural Gas

4612	Crude Petroleum Pipelines
4613	Refined Petroleum Pipelines
4619	Pipelines Nec

47—Transportation Services

4724	Travel Agencies
4725	Tour Operators
4729	Passenger Transportation Arrangement Nec
4731	Freight Transportation Arrangement
4741	Rental of Railroad Cars
4783	Packing & Crating
4785	Inspection & Fixed Facilities
4789	Transportation Services Nec

48—Communications

4812	Radiotelephone Communications
4813	Telephone Communications Except Radiotelephone
4822	Telegraph & Other Communications
4832	Radio Broadcasting Stations
4833	Television Broadcasting Stations
4841	Cable & Other Pay Television Services
4899	Communications Services Nec

49—Electric, Gas & Sanitary Services

4911	Electric Services
4922	Natural Gas Transmission
4923	Gas Transmission & Distribution
4924	Natural Gas Distribution
4925	Gas Production & Distribution Nec
4931	Electric & Other Services Combined
4932	Gas & Other Services Combined
4939	Combination Utility Nec

4941	Water Supply
4952	Sewerage Systems
4953	Refuse Systems
4959	Sanitary Services Nec
4961	Steam & Air-Conditioning Supply
4971	Irrigation Systems

50—Wholesale Trade—Durable Goods

5012	Automobiles & Other Motor Vehicles
5013	Motor Vehicle Supplies & New Parts
5014	Tires & Tubes
5015	Motor Vehicle Parts—Used
5021	Furniture
5023	Homefurnishings
5031	Lumber, Plywood & Millwork
5032	Brick, Stone & Related Materials
5033	Roofing, Siding & Insulation
5039	Construction Materials Nec
5043	Photographic Equipment & Supplies
5044	Office Equipment
5045	Computers, Peripherals & Software
5046	Commercial Equipment Nec
5047	Medical & Hospital Equipment
5048	Ophthalmic Goods
5049	Professional Equipment Nec
5051	Metals Service Centers & Offices
5052	Coal, Other Minerals & Ores
5063	Electrical Apparatus & Equipment
5064	Electrical Appliances—Television & Radio
5065	Electronic Parts & Equipment NEC
5072	Hardware
5074	Plumbing & Hydronic Heating Supplies
5075	Warm Air Heating & Air-Conditioning
5078	Refrigeration Equipment & Supplies
5082	Construction & Mining Machinery
5083	Farm & Garden Machinery
5084	Industrial Machinery & Equipment
5085	Industrial Supplies
5087	Service Establishment Equipment
5088	Transportation Equipment & Supplies
5091	Sporting & Recreational Goods
5092	Toys & Hobby Goods & Supplies
5093	Scrap & Waste Materials
5094	Jewelry & Precious Stones
5099	Durable Goods Nec

51—Wholesale Trade—Nondurable Goods

5111	Printing & Writing Paper
5112	Stationery & Office Supplies
5113	Industrial & Personal Service Paper
5122	Drugs, Proprietaries & Sundries
5131	Piece Goods & Notions
5136	Men's/Boys' Clothing
5137	Women's/Children's Clothing
5139	Footwear
5141	Groceries—General Line
5142	Packaged Frozen Foods
5143	Dairy Products Except Dried or Canned
5144	Poultry & Poultry Products
5145	Confectionery
5146	Fish & Seafoods
5147	Meats & Meat Products
5148	Fresh Fruits & Vegetables
5149	Groceries & Related Products Nec
5153	Grain & Field Beans
5154	Livestock
5159	Farm-Product Raw Materials Nec
5162	Plastics Materials & Basic Shapes
5169	Chemicals & Allied Products Nec
5171	Petroleum Bulk Stations & Terminals

5172 Petroleum Products Nec
5181 Beer & Ale
5182 Wines & Distilled Beverages
5191 Farm Supplies
5192 Books, Periodicals & Newspapers
5193 Flowers & Florists' Supplies
5194 Tobacco & Tobacco Products
5198 Paints, Varnishes & Supplies
5199 Nondurable Goods Nec

52—Building Materials & Garden Supplies

5211 Lumber & Other Building Materials
5231 Paint, Glass & Wallpaper Stores
5251 Hardware Stores
5261 Retail Nurseries & Garden Stores
5271 Mobile Home Dealers

53—General Merchandise Stores

5311 Department Stores
5331 Variety Stores
5399 Miscellaneous General Merchandise Store

54—Food Stores

5411 Grocery Stores
5421 Meat & Fish Markets
5431 Fruit & Vegetable Markets
5441 Candy, Nut & Confectionery Stores
5451 Dairy Products Stores
5461 Retail Bakeries
5499 Miscellaneous Food Stores

55—Automotive Dealers & Service Stations

5511 New & Used Car Dealers
5521 Used Car Dealers
5531 Automobile & Home Supply Stores
5541 Gasoline Service Stations
5551 Boat Dealers
5561 Recreational Vehicle Dealers
5571 Motorcycle Dealers
5599 Automotive Dealers Nec

56—Apparel & Accessory Stores

5611 Men's & Boys' Clothing Stores
5621 Women's Clothing Stores
5632 Women's Accessory & Specialty Stores
5641 Children's & Infants' Wear Stores
5651 Family Clothing Stores
5661 Shoe Stores
5699 Miscellaneous Apparel & Accessory Stores

57—Furniture & Homefurnishings Stores

5712 Furniture Stores
5713 Floor Covering Stores
5714 Drapery & Upholstery Stores
5719 Miscellaneous Home Furnishings Stores
5722 Household Appliance Stores
5731 Radio, Television & Electronics Stores
5734 Computer & Software Stores
5735 Record & Prerecorded Tape Stores
5736 Musical Instruments Stores

58—Eating & Drinking Places

5812 Eating Places
5813 Drinking Places

59—Miscellaneous Retail

5912 Drug Stores & Proprietary Stores
5921 Liquor Stores
5932 Used Merchandise Stores
5941 Sporting Goods & Bicycle Shops
5942 Book Stores
5943 Stationery Stores
5944 Jewelry Stores
5945 Hobby, Toy & Game Shops
5946 Camera & Photographic Supply Stores
5947 Gift, Novelty & Souvenir Shops
5948 Luggage & Leather Goods Stores
5949 Sewing, Needlework & Piece Goods
5961 Catalog & Mail-Order Houses
5962 Merchandising Machine Operators
5963 Direct Selling Establishments
5983 Fuel Oil Dealers
5984 Liquefied Petroleum Gas Dealers
5989 Fuel Dealers Nec
5992 Florists
5993 Tobacco Stores & Stands
5994 News Dealers & Newsstands
5995 Optical Goods Stores
5999 Miscellaneous Retail Stores Nec

60—Depository Institutions

6011 Federal Reserve Banks
6019 Central Reserve Depository Nec
6021 National Commercial Banks
6022 State Commercial Banks
6029 Commercial Banks Nec
6035 Federal Savings Institutions
6036 Savings Institutions Except Federal
6061 Federal Credit Unions
6062 State Credit Unions
6081 Foreign Banks—Branches & Agencies
6082 Foreign Trade & International Banks
6091 Nondeposit Trust Facilities
6099 Functions Related to Deposit Banking

61—Nondepository Institutions

6111 Federal & Federally-Sponsored Credit
6141 Personal Credit Institutions
6153 Short-Term Business Credit
6159 Miscellaneous Business Credit Institutions
6162 Mortgage Bankers & Correspondents
6163 Loan Brokers

62—Security & Commodity Brokers

6211 Security Brokers & Dealers
6221 Commodity Contracts Brokers & Dealers
6231 Security & Commodity Exchanges
6282 Investment Advice
6289 Security & Commodity Services Nec

63—Insurance Carriers

6311 Life Insurance
6321 Accident & Health Insurance
6324 Hospital & Medical Service Plans
6331 Fire, Marine & Casualty Insurance
6351 Surety Insurance
6361 Title Insurance
6371 Pension, Health & Welfare Funds
6399 Insurance Carriers Nec

64—Insurance Agents, Brokers & Service

6411   Insurance Agents, Brokers & Service

65—Real Estate

6512   Nonresidential Building Operators
6513   Apartment Building Operators
6514   Dwelling Operators Except Apartments
6515   Mobile Home Site Operators
6517   Railroad Property Lessors
6519   Real Property Lessors Nec
6531   Real Estate Agents & Managers
6541   Title Abstract Offices
6552   Subdividers & Developers Nec
6553   Cemetery Subdividers & Developers

67—Holding & Other Investment Offices

6712   Bank Holding Companies
6719   Holding Companies Nec
6722   Management Investment—Open-End
6726   Investment Offices Nec
6732   Educational & Religious Trusts
6733   Trusts Nec
6792   Oil Royalty Traders
6794   Patent Owners & Lessors
6798   Real Estate Investment Trusts
6799   Investors Nec

70—Hotels & Other Lodging Places

7011   Hotels & Motels
7021   Rooming & Boarding Houses
7032   Sporting & Recreational Camps
7033   Trailer Parks & Campsites
7041   Membership-Basis Organization Hotels

72—Personal Services

7211   Power Laundries—Family & Commercial
7212   Garment Pressing & Cleaners' Agents
7213   Linen Supply
7215   Coin-Operated Laundries & Cleaning
7216   Dry Cleaning Plants Except Rug
7217   Carpet & Upholstery Cleaning
7218   Industrial Launderers
7219   Laundry & Garment Services Nec
7221   Photographic Studios—Portrait
7231   Beauty Shops
7241   Barber Shops
7251   Shoe Repair & Shoeshine Parlors
7261   Funeral Services & Crematories
7291   Tax Return Preparation Services
7299   Miscellaneous Personal Services Nec

73—Business Services

7311   Advertising Agencies
7312   Outdoor Advertising Services
7313   Radio, T.V. & Publisher Representatives
7319   Advertising Nec
7322   Adjustment & Collection Services
7323   Credit Reporting Services
7331   Direct Mail Advertising Services
7334   Photocopying & Duplicating Services
7335   Commercial Photography
7336   Commercial Art & Graphic Design
7338   Secretarial & Court Reporting
7342   Disinfecting & Pest Control Services
7349   Building Maintenance Services Nec
7352   Medical Equipment Rental
7353   Heavy Construction Equipment Rental

7359   Equipment Rental & Leasing Nec
7361   Employment Agencies
7363   Help Supply Services
7371   Computer Programming Services
7372   Prepackaged Software
7373   Computer Integrated Systems Design
7374   Data Processing & Preparation
7375   Information Retrieval Services
7376   Computer Facilities Management
7377   Computer Rental & Leasing
7378   Computer Maintenance & Repair
7379   Computer Related Services Nec
7381   Detective & Armored Car Services
7382   Security Systems Services
7383   News Syndicates
7384   Photofinishing Laboratories
7389   Business Services Nec

75—Automobile Repair, Services & Parking

7513   Truck Rental & Leasing Without Drivers
7514   Passenger Car Rental
7515   Passenger Car Leasing
7519   Utility Trailer Rental
7521   Automobile Parking
7532   Top & Body Repair & Paint Shops
7533   Automobile Exhaust System Repair Shops
7534   Tire Retreading & Repair Shops
7536   Automotive Glass Replacement Shops
7537   Automotive Transmission Repair Shops
7538   General Automotive Repair Shops
7539   Automotive Repair Shops Nec
7542   Car Washes
7549   Automotive Services Nec

76—Miscellaneous Repair Services

7622   Radio & T.V. Repair
7623   Refrigeration Services Repair
7629   Electrical Repair Shops Nec
7631   Watch, Clock & Jewelry Repair
7641   Reupholstery & Furniture Repair
7692   Welding Repair
7694   Armature Rewinding Shops
7699   Repair Services Nec

78—Motion Pictures

7812   Motion Picture & Video Production
7819   Services Allied to Motion Pictures
7822   Motion Picture & Tape Distribution
7829   Motion Picture Distribution Services
7832   Motion Picture Theaters Except Drive-In
7833   Drive-In Motion Picture Theaters
7841   Video Tape Rental

79—Amusement & Recreation Services

7911   Dance Studios, Schools & Halls
7922   Theatrical Producers & Services
7929   Entertainers & Entertainment Groups
7933   Bowling Centers
7941   Sports Clubs, Managers & Promoters
7948   Racing Including Track Operations
7991   Physical Fitness Facilities
7992   Public Golf Courses
7993   Coin-Operated Amusement Devices
7996   Amusement Parks
7997   Membership Sports & Recreation Clubs
7999   Amusement & Recreation Nec

80—Health Services

8011	Offices & Clinics of Medical Doctors
8021	Offices & Clinics of Dentists
8031	Offices of Osteopathic Physicians
8041	Offices & Clinics of Chiropractors
8042	Offices & Clinics of Optometrists
8043	Offices & Clinics of Podiatrists
8049	Offices of Health Practitioners Nec
8051	Skilled Nursing Care Facilities
8052	Intermediate Care Facilities
8059	Nursing & Personal Care Nec
8062	General Medical & Surgical Hospitals
8063	Psychiatric Hospitals
8069	Specialty Hospitals Except Psychiatric
8071	Medical Laboratories
8072	Dental Laboratories
8082	Home Health Care Services
8092	Kidney Dialysis Centers
8093	Specialty Outpatient Facilities Nec
8099	Health & Allied Services Nec

81—Legal Services

8111	Legal Services

82—Educational Services

8211	Elementary & Secondary Schools
8221	Colleges & Universities
8222	Junior Colleges
8231	Libraries
8243	Data Processing Schools
8244	Business & Secretarial Schools
8249	Vocational Schools Nec
8299	Schools & Educational Services Nec

83—Social Services

8322	Individual & Family Services
8331	Job Training & Related Services
8351	Child Day Care Services
8361	Residential Care
8399	Social Services Nec

84—Museums, Botanical & Zoological Gardens

8412	Museums & Art Galleries
8422	Botanical & Zoological Gardens

86—Membership Organizations

8611	Business Associations
8621	Professional Organizations
8631	Labor Organizations
8641	Civic & Social Associations
8651	Political Organizations
8661	Religious Organizations
8699	Membership Organizations Nec

87—Engineering & Management Services

8711	Engineering Services
8712	Architectural Services
8713	Surveying Services
8721	Accounting, Auditing & Bookkeeping
8731	Commercial Physical Research
8732	Commercial Nonphysical Research
8733	Noncommercial Research Organizations
8734	Testing Laboratories
8741	Management Services
8742	Management Consulting Services
8743	Public Relations Services
8744	Facilities Support Services
8748	Business Consulting Services Nec

88—Private Households

8811	Private Households

89—Services Not Elsewhere Classified

8999	Services Nec

91—Executive, Legislative & General

9111	Executive Offices
9121	Legislative Bodies
9131	Executive and Legislative Combined
9199	General Government Nec

92—Justice, Public Order & Safety

9211	Courts
9221	Police Protection
9222	Legal Counsel & Prosecution
9223	Correctional Institutions
9224	Fire Protection
9229	Public Order & Safety Nec

93—Finance, Taxation & Monetary Policy

9311	Finance, Taxation & Monetary Policy

94—Administration of Human Resources

9411	Administration of Educational Programs
9431	Administration of Public Health Programs
9441	Administration of Social and Manpower Programs
9451	Administration of Veterans' Affairs

95—Environmental Quality & Housing

9511	Air, Water & Solid Waste Management
9512	Land, Mineral and Wildlife Conservation
9531	Housing Programs
9532	Urban & Community Development

96—Administration of Economic Programs

9611	Administration of General Economic Programs
9621	Regulation & Administration of Transportation
9631	Regulation & Administration of Utilities
9641	Regulation of Agricultural Marketing
9651	Regulation of Miscellaneous Commercial Sectors
9661	Space Research & Technology

97—National Security & International Affairs

9711	National Security
9721	International Affairs

99—Nonclassifiable Establishments

9999	Nonclassifiable Establishments

AMERiCAN BUSiNESS LOCATiONS DiRECTORY

ALABAMA

Abbeville

★ 54951 ★ **Piggly Wiggly**
W Washington
Abbeville, AL 36310
(205)585-2789
Ultimate Parent: Bruno's. **SIC:** 5411—
Grocery Stores.

Adamsville

★ 54952 ★ **Zippy Mart Inc. No. 515**
3616 Main St.
Adamsville, AL 35005
(205)674-1307
Ultimate Parent: Crown Central Petroleum Corp. **SIC:** 5411—Grocery Stores.

Alabaster

★ 54953 ★ **AmSouth Bank**
1235 1st Ave. W
Alabaster, AL 35007-9783
(205)663-0165
Location Type: Branch office. **Ultimate Parent:** AmSouth Bancorp. **SIC:** 6021—National Commercial Banks.

★ 54954 ★ **Kentucky Fried Chicken**
3536 Hwy. 31 S
Alabaster, AL 35007
(205)663-6158
Ultimate Parent: Pepsico. **SIC:** 5812—
Eating Places.

★ 54955 ★ **McDonalds Restaurant**
1499 1st St. N
Alabaster, AL 35007
(205)664-3761
Ultimate Parent: McDonald's.
SIC: 5812—Eating Places.

★ 54956 ★ **Ryder Truck Rental**
3510 Hwy. 31
Alabaster, AL 35007
(205)664-0515
Ultimate Parent: Ryder System. **SIC:** 7359—Equipment Rental & Leasing Nec.

★ 54957 ★ **Wal Mart Discount City**
Us 31 S
Alabaster, AL 35007
(205)663-6925
Ultimate Parent: Wal-Mart Stores, Inc. **SIC:** 5311—Department Stores.

Alberta

★ 54958 ★ **First Alabama Bank**
25013 State St.
Alberta, AL 36530
(205)986-5396
Location Type: Branch office. **Ultimate Parent:** First Alabama Bancshares. **SIC:** 6021—National Commercial Banks.

Albertville

★ 54959 ★ **Bowater Inc.**
Hwy. 431 N
Albertville, AL 35950
(205)878-8202
Ultimate Parent: Bowater. **SIC:** 2421—Sawmills & Planing Mills—General; 2611—Pulp Mills; 2679—Converted Paper Products Nec.

★ 54960 ★ **Bowater Inc.**
Southern Div.
8357 US Hwy. 431 N
Albertville, AL 35950-1019
(205)878-8202
Officer: Woodlands Oprns. **Ultimate Parent:** Bowater. **SIC:** 2611—Pulp Mills;

0811—Timber Tracts; 5099—Durable Goods Nec.

★ 54961 ★ **Bowater Lumber Co.**
660 Industrial Blvd.
Albertville, AL 35950-4073
(205)878-7987
Location Type: Branch office. **Officer:** Ben Rooke. **Ultimate Parent:** Bowater. **SIC:** 2621—Paper Mills; 2421—Sawmills & Planing Mills—General; 2611—Pulp Mills; 5031—Lumber, Plywood & Millwork.

★ 54962 ★ **Bowater Lumber Co.**
660 Industrial Blvd.
Albertville, AL 35950
(205)878-7987
Ultimate Parent: Bowater. **SIC:** 2421—Sawmills & Planing Mills—General; 2611—Pulp Mills; 2679—Converted Paper Products Nec.

★ 54963 ★ **First Alabama Bank**
116 W. Sand Mountain Dr.
Albertville, AL 35950
(205)878-4616
Ultimate Parent: First Alabama Bancshares. **SIC:** 6099—Functions Related to Deposit Banking.

★ 54964 ★ **First Alabama Bank**
509 Baltimore Ave.
Albertville, AL 35950-2415
(205)878-4616
Location Type: Branch office. **Ultimate Parent:** First Alabama Bancshares.

★ 54965 ★ **First Alabama Bank**
116 Sand Mountain Dr.
Albertville, AL 35950-1710
(205)878-4616
Location Type: Branch office. **Officer:** Lowell D. Galloway, President. **Ultimate Parent:** First Alabama Bancshares. **SIC:** 6021—National Commercial Banks.

★ 54966 ★ **Hudson Farms Inc.**
Railroad Ave.
Albertville, AL 35950
Ultimate Parent: Hudson Foods. **SIC:** 2048—Prepared Feeds Nec.

★ 54967 ★ **Hudson Foods Inc.**
6600 Hwy. 431
Albertville, AL 35950
Ultimate Parent: Hudson Foods. **SIC:** 2015—Poultry Slaughtering & Processing.

★ 54968 ★ **Mueller Co.**
956 Industrial Blvd.
Albertville, AL 35950
(205)878-7930
Officer: Lloyd W. Darnell, President.
Ultimate Parent: Tyco International. **SIC:** 3321—Gray & Ductile Iron Foundries; 3429—Hardware Nec; 3491—Industrial Valves.

★ 54969 ★ **Pizza Hut**
Albertville, AL 35950
(205)891-1551
Ultimate Parent: Pepsico. **SIC:** 5812—
Eating Places.

★ 54970 ★ **Radio Shack**
911 Hwy. 431 S
Albertville, AL 35950
(205)878-0613
Company Type: Division. **Ultimate Parent:** Tandy Corp. **SIC:** 5099—Durable Goods Nec; 5731—Radio, Television & Electronics Stores.

★ 54971 ★ **Trailways Bus Station**
Sampson Cir.
Albertville, AL 35950
(205)878-0871
Ultimate Parent: Greyhound Lines Inc. **SIC:** 4131—Intercity & Rural Bus Transportation.

Alex City

★ 54972 ★ **Kentucky Fried Chicken**
280 By Pass
Alex City, AL 35010
(205)329-1611
Ultimate Parent: Pepsico. **SIC:** 5812—
Eating Places.

★ 54973 ★ **Wal Mart**
1102 Hwy. 280 Bypass
Alex City, AL 35010
(205)329-3286
Ultimate Parent: Wal-Mart Stores, Inc. **SIC:** 5311—Department Stores.

Alexander City

★ 54974 ★ **First Alabama Bank**
201 Commerce Dr.
Alexander City, AL 35010-2661
(205)234-2561
Location Type: Branch office. **Ultimate Parent:** First Alabama Bancshares. **SIC:** 6021—National Commercial Banks.

★ 54975 ★ **Mary Kay Cosmetics**
303 University Cir.
Alexander City, AL 35010
(205)234-5150
Ultimate Parent: Mary Kay Cosmetics. **SIC:** 5999—Miscellaneous Retail Stores Nec.

★ 54976 ★ **Russell**
1 Lee St.
Alexander City, AL 35010
(205)329-4000
Company Type: Headquarters. **Officer:** John C. Adams. **Employee Count:** 16640. **Sales:** 931 M. **Fortune 500:** Largest U.S. Industrial Corporations: Ranking 374.

★ 54977 ★ **Russell Corp.**
PO Box 272
Alexander City, AL 35010
(205)329-4000 Fax: (205)329-4474
Officer: John C. Adams, CEO. **Ultimate Parent:** Russell. **Employee Count:** 16594. **Sales:** 931 M.

★ 54978 ★ **Russell Corp.**
1 Lee St.
Alexander City, AL 35010
(205)329-4000
Ultimate Parent: Russell. **SIC:** 2253—Knit Outerwear Mills; 2281—Yarn Spinning Mills; 2282—Throwing & Winding Mills.

★ 54979 ★ **Russell Corp.**
Lee St. PO Box 272
Alexander City, AL 35010
Ultimate Parent: Russell. **SIC:** 2281—Yarn Spinning Mills; 2221—Broadwoven Fabric Mills—Manmade; 2211—Broadwoven Fabric Mills—Cotton; 2329—Men's/Boys' Clothing Nec; 2259—Knitting Mills Nec; 2269—Finishing Plants Nec.

★ 54980 ★ **Russell Corp.**
Lee St.
Alexander City, AL 35010
Ultimate Parent: Russell. **SIC:** 2281—Yarn Spinning Mills; 2221—Broadwoven Fabric Mills—Manmade; 2257—Weft Knit Fabric Mills.

★ 54981 ★ **Ryder Truck Rental**
108 Lee St.
Alexander Cy, AL 35010
(205)329-3608
Ultimate Parent: Ryder System. **SIC:** 7513—Truck Rental & Leasing Without Drivers.

Aliceville

★ 54982 ★ **Burlington Northern Railroa**
3 Ave. NW
Aliceville, AL 35442
(205)373-2242
Ultimate Parent: Burlington Northern. **SIC:** 4011—Railroads—Line-Haul Operating.

★ 54983 ★ **Piggly Wiggly**
1 Ave. St. NE
Aliceville, AL 35442
(205)373-6396
Ultimate Parent: Bruno's. **SIC:** 5812—
Eating Places.

★ 54984 ★ **Texaco Mini Mart**
Hwy. 17 N
Aliceville, AL 35442
(205)373-2811
Ultimate Parent: Texaco. **SIC:** 5411—
Grocery Stores.

Andalusia

★ 54985 ★ **Coca-Cola Bottling Co.**
239 Church St.
Andalusia, AL 36420
(205)222-4168
Ultimate Parent: Coca-Cola Enterprises. **SIC:** 2086—Bottled & Canned Soft Drinks; 5149—Groceries & Related Products Nec.

★ 54986 ★ **Commercial Bank**
200 Church St.
Andalusia, AL 36420
(205)222-2423
Ultimate Parent: First Virginia Banks Inc. **SIC:** 6022—State Commercial Banks.

★ 54987 ★ **First Alabama Bank**
200 Church St.
Andalusia, AL 36420-3702
(205)222-2423
Location Type: Branch office. **Officer:** Joseph A. Bratton, President, CEO, & Chairman of the Board. **Ultimate Parent:** First Alabama Bancshares. **SIC:** 6021—National Commercial Banks.

★ 54988 ★ **Pizza Hut**
Hwy. 84 E
Andalusia, AL 36420
(205)222-4106
Ultimate Parent: Pepsico. **SIC:** 5812—
Eating Places.

Anniston

★ 54989 ★ **Allied Signal**
Anniston, AL 36201
(205)835-4100
Ultimate Parent: Allied-Signal Inc. **SIC:** 3724—Aircraft Engines & Engine Parts.

★ 54990 ★ **Allied-Signal Airline Services Inc.**
1 Cliff Garrett Dr.
Anniston, AL 36201
Ultimate Parent: Allied-Signal Inc. **SIC:** 3728—Aircraft Parts & Equipment Nec.

★ 54991 ★ **Allied Signal Inc.**
Anniston, AL 36201
(205)835-4100
Ultimate Parent: Allied-Signal Inc. **SIC:** 3724—Aircraft Engines & Engine Parts.

★ 54992 ★ **Allied-Signal Inc.**
Garrett Airline Repair
1 Cliff Garrett Dr.
Anniston, AL 36201
Ultimate Parent: Allied-Signal Inc. **SIC:** 3728—Aircraft Parts & Equipment Nec.

★ 54993 ★ **Anchor Metals Inc.
Steel Structures Group**
1008 Glen Addie Ave.
Anniston, AL 36201
Ultimate Parent: Thomas & Betts. **SIC:**
3441—Fabricated Structural Metal.

★ 54994 ★ **Colonial Pipeline**
1604 Hale St.
Anniston, AL 36203
(205)831-2951
Ultimate Parent: Colonial Pipeline. **SIC:**
4922—Natural Gas Transmission.

★ 54995 ★ **First Alabama Bank**
Quintard Mall
Anniston, AL 36203
(205)236-1890
Ultimate Parent: First Alabama
Bancshares. **SIC:** 6022—State Commercial
Banks.

★ 54996 ★ **First Alabama Bank**
5510 McClellan Blvd.
Anniston, AL 36201-4647
(205)231-1312
Location Type: Branch office. **Ultimate
Parent:** First Alabama Bancshares. **SIC:**
6021—National Commercial Banks.

★ 54997 ★ **First Alabama Bank**
1031 Quintard Ave.
Anniston, AL 36202-5703
(205)236-1890
Location Type: Branch office. **Officer:**
John P. Wheeler, President & CEO.
Ultimate Parent: First Alabama
Bancshares. **SIC:** 6021—National
Commercial Banks.

★ 54998 ★ **FMC Corp.**
2101 W. 10th St.
Anniston, AL 36201
(205)237-2841
Officer: Dennis Wagner, Manager. **Ultimate
Parent:** FMC. **SIC:** 3325—Steel Foundries
Nec; 3398—Metal Heat Treating; 3462—
Iron & Steel Forgings.

★ 54999 ★ **FMC Corp., Anniston
Plant**
2101 W. 10th St.
Anniston, AL 36201
Location Type: Plant. **Ultimate Parent:**
FMC. **SIC:** 3462—Iron & Steel Forgings;
3324—Steel Investment Foundries; 3325—
Steel Foundries Nec.

★ 55000 ★ **Garrett Airlines
Repair**
1 Cliff Garrett Dr.
Anniston, AL 36203
(205)835-4100
Ultimate Parent: Allied-Signal Inc. **SIC:**
4581—Airports, Flying Fields & Services.

★ 55001 ★ **Hertz Rent-A-Car**
End S. Barry St.
Anniston, AL 36203
(205)831-3712
Ultimate Parent: Hertz. **SIC:** 7514—
Passenger Car Rental.

★ 55002 ★ **Kentucky Fried
Chicken**
216 Tomahawk Trl
Anniston, AL 36206
(205)820-5640
Ultimate Parent: Pepsico. **SIC:** 5812—
Eating Places.

★ 55003 ★ **Kentucky Fried
Chicken**
609 Snow St.
Anniston, AL 36203
(205)831-9576
Ultimate Parent: Pepsico. **SIC:** 5812—
Eating Places.

★ 55004 ★ **Mead Ink Products**
104 National Dr.
Anniston, AL 36201
Ultimate Parent: Mead. **SIC:** 2741—
Miscellaneous Publishing.

★ 55005 ★ **Monsanto Anniston
Empl Crdt Un**
300 Al Hwy. 202
Anniston, AL 36201-5300
(205)237-0651
Ultimate Parent: Monsanto. **SIC:** 6061—
Federal Credit Unions.

★ 55006 ★ **Monsanto Co.**
300 Birmingham Hwy.
Anniston, AL 36201-5300
(205)231-8400
Company Type: Branch. **Officer:** Bill Defer.
Ultimate Parent: Monsanto. **SIC:** 2819—
Industrial Inorganic Chemicals Nec; 2899—
Chemical Preparations Nec.

★ 55007 ★ **Pizza Hut**
202 Hamric Dr. E
Anniston, AL 36203
(205)831-7721
Ultimate Parent: Pepsico. **SIC:** 5812—
Eating Places.

★ 55008 ★ **Pizza Hut**
322 E. Blue Mountain Rd.
Anniston, AL 36201
(205)237-3251
Ultimate Parent: Pepsico. **SIC:** 5812—
Eating Places.

★ 55009 ★ **Radio Shack**
3118 Mcclellan Blvd.
Anniston, AL 36201
(205)236-3720
Company Type: Division. **Ultimate Parent:**
Tandy Corp. **SIC:** 5065—Electronic Parts &
Equipment Nec.

★ 55010 ★ **Radio Shack**
Quintard Mall
Anniston, AL 36203
(205)831-5020
Company Type: Division. **Ultimate Parent:**
Tandy Corp. **SIC:** 5731—Radio, Television
& Electronics Stores.

★ 55011 ★ **Rmc Corp. Anniston
Plant**
2101 W.12th St.
Anniston, AL 36201
Ultimate Parent: FMC. **SIC:** 3462—Iron &
Steel Forgings; 3324—Steel Investment
Foundries; 3325—Steel Foundries Nec.

★ 55012 ★ **Ryder Truck Rental**
720 Quintard Ave.
Anniston, AL 36201
(205)237-6403
Ultimate Parent: Ryder System. **SIC:**
7359—Equipment Rental & Leasing Nec.

★ 55013 ★ **Ryder Truck Rental**
5700 Pelham Rd.
Anniston, AL 36206
(205)237-6403
Ultimate Parent: Ryder System. **SIC:**
7359—Equipment Rental & Leasing Nec.

★ 55014 ★ **Stop & Shop Store**
Hwy. 78
Anniston, AL 36203
(205)236-0323
Ultimate Parent: Stop & Shop.

★ 55015 ★ **Taco Bell**
620 Quintard Dr.
Anniston, AL 36203
(205)831-1629
Ultimate Parent: Pepsico. **SIC:** 5812—
Eating Places.

★ 55016 ★ **Texaco**
1531 Quintard Ave.
Anniston, AL 36201
(205)237-1262
Ultimate Parent: Texaco. **SIC:** 5541—
Gasoline Service Stations.

★ 55017 ★ **Thomas & Betts
Anchor Metals Steel Structures
Group**
1008 Glen Addie Ave.
Anniston, AL 36201
Ultimate Parent: Thomas & Betts. **SIC:**
3441—Fabricated Structural Metal; 3479—
Metal Coating & Allied Services.

★ 55018 ★ **Wal Mart**
5560 McClellan Blvd.
Anniston, AL 36206
Ultimate Parent: Wal-Mart Stores, Inc. **SIC:**
5311—Department Stores.

Arab

★ 55019 ★ **Dana Corp.**
Arab Hydraulic Plant
218 Arad Thompson Rd. NE
Arab, AL 35016
(205)586-8152
Ultimate Parent: Dana Corp. **SIC:** 3469—

Metal Stampings Nec; 3599—Industrial
Machinery Nec.

★ 55020 ★ **Dana Corp. Arab
Hydraulics**
104 Arad Thompson Rd. PO Box C
Arab, AL 35016
Ultimate Parent: Dana Corp. **SIC:** 3499—
Fabricated Metal Products Nec; 3593—Fluid
Power Cylinders & Actuators.

★ 55021 ★ **Dana Corp. Arab
Hydraulics**
PO Box C
Arab, AL 35016
Ultimate Parent: Dana Corp. **SIC:** 3593—
Fluid Power Cylinders & Actuators; 3499—
Fabricated Metal Products Nec.

★ 55022 ★ **Dana Corp. Arab
Hydraulics Plant**
218 Arad Thompson Rd. NE PO Box C
Arab, AL 35016
Ultimate Parent: Dana Corp. **SIC:** 3499—
Fabricated Metal Products Nec; 3593—Fluid
Power Cylinders & Actuators.

★ 55023 ★ **Eaton Corp.**
300 8th Ave. SE
Arab, AL 35016
(205)586-6061
Ultimate Parent: Eaton Corp. **SIC:** 3613—
Switchgear & Switchboard Apparatus;
3625—Relays & Industrial Controls.

★ 55024 ★ **Eaton Corp.**
Aerospace & Commercial Controls Div.
Eight Ave., SE
PO Box 97
Arab, AL 35016
(205)586-6061
Company Type: Division. **Location Type:**
Plant. **Ultimate Parent:** Eaton Corp. **SIC:**
3643—Current-Carrying Wiring Devices.

★ 55025 ★ **First Alabama Bank**
1090 N. Brindlee Mountain Pky.
Arab, AL 35016-1016
(205)586-8166
Location Type: Branch office. **Ultimate
Parent:** First Alabama Bancshares. **SIC:**
6021—National Commercial Banks.

★ 55026 ★ **Pizza Hut**
Hwy. 231 Northgate Dr.
Arab, AL 35016
(205)586-2511
Ultimate Parent: Pepsico. **SIC:** 5812—
Eating Places.

★ 55027 ★ **Trailway Bus Station**
Arab Byp
Arab, AL 35016
(205)586-8929
Ultimate Parent: Greyhound Lines Inc. **SIC:**
4131—Intercity & Rural Bus Transportation.

★ 55028 ★ **Wrangler**
510 4th St. SE
Arab, AL 35016
(205)586-4271
Location Type: Plant. **Officer:** Terry
Ramsey, Plant Manager. **Ultimate Parent:**
VF Corp. **SIC:** 2325—Men's/Boys' Trousers
& Slacks.

Ardmore

★ 55029 ★ **Bankers Trust of
Madison**
Hwy. 251 & 6th Ave.
Ardmore, AL 35739
(205)423-4444
Location Type: Branch office. **Ultimate
Parent:** Bankers Trust New York Corp. **SIC:**
6022—State Commercial Banks; 6021—
National Commercial Banks; 6141—
Personal Credit Institutions; 6162—
Mortgage Bankers & Correspondents.

Ariton

★ 55030 ★ **Sloss Industries Corp.
Ariton Facility**
Hwy. 51
Ariton, AL 36311
Ultimate Parent: Walter Industries, Inc.
SIC: 2869—Industrial Organic Chemicals
Nec.

Ashland

★ 55031 ★ **Russell Corp.**
Hwy. 77 N
Ashland, AL 36251
(205)354-7114
Officer: Robert Crist, Manager. **Ultimate
Parent:** Russell. **SIC:** 2329—Men's/Boys'
Clothing Nec.

★ 55032 ★ **Tyson Foods Inc.**
PO Box 458-Old Lineville Hwy.
Ashland, AL 36251
Ultimate Parent: Tyson Foods, Inc. **SIC:**
2000—Food & Kindred Products.

★ 55033 ★ **Tyson Foods Inc.**
PO Box 458-Old Lineville Hwy.
Ashland, AL 36251
Ultimate Parent: Tyson Foods, Inc. **SIC:**
2000—Food & Kindred Products.

★ 55034 ★ **Tyson Foods Inc.**
Old Lineville Hwy.
Ashland, AL 36251
(205)354-2155
Officer: Tommy Waters, Manager. **Ultimate
Parent:** Tyson Foods, Inc. **SIC:** 2015—
Poultry Slaughtering & Processing.

Athens

★ 55035 ★ **Cast Products Inc.**
1202 PO Box
Athens, AL 35611
(205)233-1500
Ultimate Parent: Harvard Industries. **SIC:**
5051—Metals Service Centers & Offices.

★ 55036 ★ **ConAgra Broiler Co.**
1004 E. Pryor St.
Athens, AL 35611
(205)232-3993
Company Type: Division. **Location Type:**
Plant. **Officer:** Buck Kornemann, Plant
Manager. **Ultimate Parent:** Conagra.

★ 55037 ★ **Eaton Corp.**
200 E. Elm St.
Athens, AL 35611
(205)232-8300
Location Type: Plant. **Officer:** Robert
Robillard, Plant Manager. **Ultimate Parent:**
Eaton Corp. **SIC:** 3613—Switchgear &
Switchboard Apparatus.

★ 55038 ★ **Eaton Corp.**
200 E. Elm St.
Athens, AL 35611
(205)232-8300
Location Type: Plant. **Ultimate Parent:**
Eaton Corp. **SIC:** 3822—Environmental
Controls.

★ 55039 ★ **First Alabama Bank**
1106 E. Hobbs St.
Athens, AL 35611-2323
(205)232-4500
Location Type: Branch office. **Ultimate
Parent:** First Alabama Bancshares. **SIC:**
6021—National Commercial Banks.

★ 55040 ★ **First Alabama Bank**
201 W. Green St.
Athens, AL 35611-2542
(205)232-4500
Location Type: Branch office. **Officer:**
Terrell A. McCormick, President & CEO.
Ultimate Parent: First Alabama
Bancshares. **SIC:** 6021—National
Commercial Banks.

★ 55041 ★ **Kentucky Fried
Chicken**
Hwy. 72 W
Athens, AL 35611
(205)232-8033
Ultimate Parent: Pepsico. **SIC:** 5812—
Eating Places.

★ 55042 ★ **Magnetek**
315 E. Elm St.
Athens, AL 35611
Ultimate Parent: Magnetek Inc. **SIC:**
3612—Transformers Except Electronic.

★ 55043 ★ **Magnetek Jefferson
Electric**
315 E. Elm St.
Athens, AL 35611
Ultimate Parent: Magnetek Inc. **SIC:**
3612—Transformers Except Electronic.

★ 55044 ★   Mutual of New York
303 N. Ghouston
Athens, AL 35611
(205)232-6669
Ultimate Parent: Mutual of New York. SIC: 6411—Insurance Agents, Brokers & Service.

★ 55045 ★   Pizza Hut
207 Hwy. 31 N
Athens, AL 35611
(205)233-1812
Ultimate Parent: Pepsico. SIC: 5812—Eating Places.

★ 55046 ★   Sara Lee Corp.
222 NE MacArthur Dr.
Athens, AL 35611
(205)232-4201
Company Type: Division. Ultimate Parent: Sara Lee Corp.

★ 55047 ★   Sweet Sue Kitchens
Mcarthur Dr.
Athens, AL 35611
Ultimate Parent: Sara Lee Corp. SIC: 2032—Canned Specialties.

★ 55048 ★   Sweet Sue Kitchens Inc.
Sweet Sue Dr.
PO Box 1107
Athens, AL 35611
(205)232-4201 Fax: (205)232-9631
Company Type: Division. Officer: Larry Ruiter, Vice President of Operations. Ultimate Parent: Sara Lee Corp. SIC: 2013—Sausages & Other Prepared Meats.

Atmore

★ 55049 ★   American Family Life Assurance
1112 S. Pensacola Ave.
Atmore, AL 36502
(205)368-5713
Ultimate Parent: American Family Life Assurance Co. SIC: 6411—Insurance Agents, Brokers & Service.

★ 55050 ★   Exxon Co. USA
Wawbeck Tower Rd.
Atmore, AL 36502
(205)368-8137
Officer: Duane E. Miller, Manager. Ultimate Parent: Exxon. SIC: 2911—Petroleum Refining.

★ 55051 ★   Piggly Wiggly
Adams Plz.
Atmore, AL 36502
(205)368-9168
Ultimate Parent: Bruno's. SIC: 5411—Grocery Stores.

★ 55052 ★   Pizza Hut
1827 S. Main St.
Atmore, AL 36502
(205)368-5646
Ultimate Parent: Pepsico. SIC: 5812—Eating Places.

★ 55053 ★   Vanity Fair Mills Inc.
Kelly Blvd.
Atmore, AL 36502
(205)368-2171
Officer: Vance Perry, Plant Manager. Ultimate Parent: VF Corp. SIC: 2341—Women's/Children's Underwear; 2342—Bras, Girdles & Allied Garments.

Attalla

★ 55054 ★   Dean Sausage Co.
501 Pleasant Valley Rd.
Attalla, AL 35954
(205)538-6082
Officer: Marsye Dean Lancaster, President. Ultimate Parent: Dean Foods. SIC: 2013—Sausages & Other Prepared Meats.

★ 55055 ★   Kentucky Fried Chicken
500 Cherry St.
Attalla, AL 35954
(205)538-5880
Ultimate Parent: Pepsico. SIC: 5812—Eating Places.

★ 55056 ★   Piggly Wiggly
422 4th Ave. NW
Attalla, AL 35954
(205)538-5850
Ultimate Parent: Bruno's. SIC: 5912—Drug Stores & Proprietary Stores.

★ 55057 ★   Pizza Hut
620 Cleveland Ave.
Attalla, AL 35954
(205)538-1235
Ultimate Parent: Pepsico. SIC: 5812—Eating Places.

★ 55058 ★   Tyson Feed Mill
Hwy. 278 W. & Carnes Chapel Rd.
Attalla, AL 35954
Ultimate Parent: Tyson Foods, Inc. SIC: 2048—Prepared Feeds Nec.

★ 55059 ★   Wal Mart
Alabama Hwy.
Attalla, AL 35954
(205)538-2611
Ultimate Parent: Wal-Mart Stores, Inc. SIC: 5912—Drug Stores & Proprietary Stores.

Auburn

★ 55060 ★   First Alabama Bank
165 N. College St.
Auburn, AL 36830
(205)821-5664
Ultimate Parent: First Alabama Bancshares. SIC: 6022—State Commercial Banks.

★ 55061 ★   Gayfers
Village
Auburn, AL 36830
(205)821-0290
Ultimate Parent: Mercantile Stores. SIC: 7231—Beauty Shops.

★ 55062 ★   Kentucky Fried Chicken
1550 Opelika Rd.
Auburn, AL 36830
(205)821-7507
Ultimate Parent: Pepsico. SIC: 5812—Eating Places.

★ 55063 ★   Kroger Co.
300 N. Dean Rd.
Auburn, AL 36830
(205)821-1325
Ultimate Parent: Kroger. SIC: 5411—Grocery Stores.

★ 55064 ★   Lane Bryant
43 Village Mall
Auburn, AL 36830
(205)821-9490
Ultimate Parent: Limited. SIC: 5651—Family Clothing Stores.

★ 55065 ★   Mary Kay Cosmetics
605 S. Gay St.
Auburn, AL 36830
(205)821-2371
Ultimate Parent: Mary Kay Cosmetics. SIC: 5999—Miscellaneous Retail Stores Nec.

★ 55066 ★   Master Lock Co.
300 Webster Rd.
Auburn, AL 36830
(205)826-3300
Officer: Dan Strittmater, President. Ultimate Parent: American Brands Inc. SIC: 2431—Millwork; 3429—Hardware Nec.

★ 55067 ★   Piggly Wiggly
2065 E. University Dr.
Auburn, AL 36830
(205)887-8652
Ultimate Parent: Bruno's. SIC: 5411—Grocery Stores.

★ 55068 ★   Pizza Hut
806 Opelika Rd.
Auburn, AL 36830
(205)821-1811
Ultimate Parent: Pepsico. SIC: 5812—Eating Places.

★ 55069 ★   Pizza Hut
334 W. Magnolia Ave.
Auburn, AL 36830
(205)821-7507
Ultimate Parent: Pepsico. SIC: 5812—Eating Places.

★ 55070 ★   Radio Shack
19 Village Mall
Auburn, AL 36830
(205)821-4612
Company Type: Division. Ultimate Parent: Tandy Corp. SIC: 5065—Electronic Parts & Equipment Nec.

★ 55071 ★   Sterwin Laboratories Inc.
Birmingham Hwy.
Auburn, AL 36830
(205)887-7036
Ultimate Parent: Imcera Group. SIC: 2836—Biological Products Except Diagnostic.

★ 55072 ★   Taco Bell
271 S. Gay St.
Auburn, AL 36830
(205)821-2019
Ultimate Parent: Pepsico. SIC: 5812—Eating Places.

★ 55073 ★   Vermont American Corp.
155 Alabama St.
Auburn, AL 36830
Ultimate Parent: Emerson Electric Co. Inc.

Bay Minette

★ 55074 ★   First Alabama Bank
101 Hand Ave.
Bay Minette, AL 36507-4822
(205)937-5581
Location Type: Branch office. Officer: Ron A. Shaddix, President & CEO. Ultimate Parent: First Alabama Bancshares. SIC: 6021—National Commercial Banks.

★ 55075 ★   International Paper
100 Dickman Rd.
Bay Minette, AL 36507
Ultimate Parent: International Paper Co. SIC: 2653—Corrugated & Solid Fiber Boxes.

★ 55076 ★   Piggly Wiggly
6 Plaza Shopping Ctr.
Bay Minette, AL 36507
(205)937-7865
Ultimate Parent: Bruno's. SIC: 5411—Grocery Stores.

★ 55077 ★   Pizza Hut
D Olive
Bay Minette, AL 36507
(205)937-6714
Ultimate Parent: Pepsico. SIC: 5812—Eating Places.

Bayou La Batre

★ 55078 ★   First Alabama Bank
188 S. Wintzell Ave.
Bayou La Batre, AL 36509-2411
(205)824-2131
Location Type: Branch office. Ultimate Parent: First Alabama Bancshares. SIC: 6021—National Commercial Banks.

Belk

★ 55079 ★   Georgia Pacific Corp.
Hwy. 96 W
Belk, AL 35545
Location Type: Plant. Officer: Robert Wilkerson, Plant Manager. Ultimate Parent: Georgia-Pacific. SIC: 2421—Sawmills & Planing Mills—General.

★ 55080 ★   Georgia Pacific Corp.
Belk, AL 35545
(205)932-3243
Location Type: Plant. Officer: Robert Wilkerson, Plant Manager. Ultimate Parent: Georgia-Pacific. SIC: 2421—Sawmills & Planing Mills—General.

Bellamy

★ 55081 ★   Georgia Pacific Corp.
1 Pine St.
Bellamy, AL 36901
(205)392-5221
Location Type: Plant. Officer: Shelton Roberts, Manager. Ultimate Parent: Georgia-Pacific. SIC: 2421—Sawmills & Planing Mills—General.

Bessemer

★ 55082 ★   American General Finance
615 9th Ave. N
Bessemer, AL 35020-5368
(205)428-6237
Location Type: Branch office. Officer: Janice E. Hyde. Ultimate Parent: American General Corp. SIC: 6141—Personal Credit Institutions; 6162—Mortgage Bankers & Correspondents.

★ 55083 ★   American General Finance Inc.
615 9th Ave. N
Bessemer, AL 35020-5368
(205)428-6237
Location Type: Branch office. Officer: Janice E. Hyde. Ultimate Parent: American General Corp. SIC: 6141—Personal Credit Institutions; 6162—Mortgage Bankers & Correspondents.

★ 55084 ★   American Steel Corp.
1355 Industrial Blvd.
Bessemer, AL 35023
(205)426-1701
Ultimate Parent: National Steel. SIC: 5051—Metals Service Centers & Offices.

★ 55085 ★   AmSouth Bank
1801 2nd Ave. N
Bessemer, AL 35020-0823
(205)424-5910
Location Type: Branch office. Officer: Don C. Edge. Ultimate Parent: AmSouth Bancorp. SIC: 6021—National Commercial Banks; 6153—Short-Term Business Credit; 6162—Mortgage Bankers & Correspondents; 6141—Personal Credit Institutions.

★ 55086 ★   Baxter Healthcare
5950 Greenwood Pky.
Bessemer, AL 35023
(205)424-7040
Ultimate Parent: Baxter International. SIC: 5047—Medical & Hospital Equipment.

★ 55087 ★   First Alabama Bank
330 19th St. N
Bessemer, AL 35020-0821
(205)326-7666
Location Type: Branch office. Ultimate Parent: First Alabama Bancshares. SIC: 6021—National Commercial Banks.

★ 55088 ★   First Alabama Bank of Birmi
731 9th Ave. N
Bessemer, AL 35020
(205)326-7658
Ultimate Parent: First Alabama Bancshares.

★ 55089 ★   First Alabama Bank of Birmingham
330 19th St. N
Bessemer, AL 35020
(205)326-7666
Ultimate Parent: First Alabama Bancshares. SIC: 6022—State Commercial Banks.

★ 55090 ★   Firstfed Bancorp Inc.
1630 4th Ave. N
Bessemer, AL 35020-5711
(205)428-8472
Officer: R. A. Coats, Chairman. Ultimate Parent: Firstfed Financial Corp. SIC: 6712—Bank Holding Companies; 6035—Federal Savings Institutions. Employee Count: 34. Sales: 8626000 M.

★ 55091 ★   Greyhound Bus Lines
1718 4th Ave. N
Bessemer, AL 35020
(205)425-3914
Ultimate Parent: Greyhound Lines Inc. SIC: 4111—Local & Suburban Transit; 4131—Intercity & Rural Bus Transportation; 4173—Bus Terminal & Service Facilities.

★ 55092 ★   Griffin Wheel Co.
2100 Griffin Dr.
Bessemer, AL 35020
(205)424-3920
Officer: Aubrey F. Arnett, President. Ultimate Parent: Amsted Industries Inc. SIC: 3312—Blast Furnaces & Steel Mills; 3325—Steel Foundries Nec.

★ 55093 ★ **Griffin Wheel Co.**
2100 Wheel Dr.
Bessemer, AL 35020
(205)424-3920
Ultimate Parent: Amsted Industries Inc.
SIC: 3325—Steel Foundries Nec.

★ 55094 ★ **Griffin Wheel Co.**
Bessemer Plant
2100 Griffin Wheel Dr.
Bessemer, AL 35020
Location Type: Plant. **Ultimate Parent:**
Amsted Industries Inc. **SIC:** 3325—Steel
Foundries Nec.

★ 55095 ★ **Harbison Walker
Refractories Dresser Industries Inc.**
300 North 32nd St.
Bessemer, AL 35020
Ultimate Parent: Dresser Industries Inc.
SIC: 3255—Clay Refractories.

★ 55096 ★ **Kentucky Fried
Chicken**
1818 9th Ave. N
Bessemer, AL 35020
(205)428-0360
Ultimate Parent: Pepsico. **SIC:** 5812—
Eating Places.

★ 55097 ★ **Kentucky Fried
Chicken**
654 Bessemer Super Hwy.
Bessemer, AL 35020
(205)425-5812
Ultimate Parent: Pepsico. **SIC:** 5812—
Eating Places.

★ 55098 ★ **McDonalds
Restaurants**
911 9th Ave. SW
Bessemer, AL 35023
(205)426-9261
Ultimate Parent: McDonald's.
SIC: 5812—Eating Places.

★ 55099 ★ **Pizza Hut**
829 8th St. N
Bessemer, AL 35020
(205)426-1204
Ultimate Parent: Pepsico. **SIC:** 5812—
Eating Places.

★ 55100 ★ **Pizza Hut**
3044 Warrior River Rd.
Bessemer, AL 35023
(205)491-4889
Ultimate Parent: Pepsico. **SIC:** 5812—
Eating Places.

★ 55101 ★ **Radio Shack**
Westlake Mall
Bessemer, AL 35020
(205)426-4151
Company Type: Division. **Ultimate Parent:**
Tandy Corp. **SIC:** 5731—Radio, Television
& Electronics Stores.

★ 55102 ★ **Radio Shack**
113 Hueytown Plz.
Bessemer, AL 35023
(205)491-4490
Company Type: Division. **Ultimate Parent:**
Tandy Corp. **SIC:** 5731—Radio, Television
& Electronics Stores.

★ 55103 ★ **Taco Bell**
1001 9th Ave. N
Bessemer, AL 35020
(205)424-4867
Ultimate Parent: Pepsico. **SIC:** 5812—
Eating Places.

★ 55104 ★ **Texaco Food Mart**
2801 9th Ave. N
Bessemer, AL 35020
(205)426-0544
Ultimate Parent: Texaco. **SIC:** 5411—
Grocery Stores.

★ 55105 ★ **Texaco Self Serv**
900 9th Ave. N
Bessemer, AL 35020
(205)424-2230
Ultimate Parent: Texaco. **SIC:** 5541—
Gasoline Service Stations.

★ 55106 ★ **Texaco Self Service**
900 9th Ave. SW
Bessemer, AL 35023
(205)424-2230
Ultimate Parent: Texaco. **SIC:** 5541—
Gasoline Service Stations.

★ 55107 ★ **Trinity Industries Inc.**
5th Ave. 24th St.
Bessemer, AL 35020
Ultimate Parent: Trinity Industries. **SIC:**
3743—Railroad Equipment.

★ 55108 ★ **Zippy Mart Inc. No.
516**
531 4th Ave. SW
Bessemer, AL 35023
(205)426-2680
Ultimate Parent: Crown Central Petroleum
Corp. **SIC:** 5411—Grocery Stores.

Birmingham

★ 55109 ★ **ABM Graphics**
217 Oxmoor Cir.
Birmingham, AL 35209
(205)942-9796
Company Type: Subsidiary. **Location
Type:** Branch office. **Officer:** David
MacKintosh, President. **Ultimate Parent:**
Alco Standard Corp. **SIC:** 3663—Radio &
T.V. Communications Equipment; 5044—
Office Equipment; 5999—Miscellaneous
Retail Stores Nec.

★ 55110 ★ **Ace Hardware**
2304 Ctr. Point Pky.
Birmingham, AL 35215
(205)854-1310
Ultimate Parent: Ace Hardware. **SIC:**
5251—Hardware Stores.

★ 55111 ★ **Ace Hardware**
1215 Forestdale Blvd.
Birmingham, AL 35214
(205)798-3013
Ultimate Parent: Ace Hardware. **SIC:**
5251—Hardware Stores.

★ 55112 ★ **Advanced Medical
Systems Inc.**
2714 19th Pl S
Birmingham, AL 35209
(205)879-5467
Ultimate Parent: Standard Register. **SIC:**
5047—Medical & Hospital Equipment.

★ 55113 ★ **Advanced Medical
Systems Inc.**
6 Office Park Cir.
Birmingham, AL 35223
(205)879-5467
Ultimate Parent: Standard Register. **SIC:**
5047—Medical & Hospital Equipment;
5049—Professional Equipment Nec.

★ 55114 ★ **Air Products &
Chemicals Inc.**
6 Office Park Circle
Birmingham, AL 35223-2512
(205)870-5603
Ultimate Parent: Air Products & Chemicals,
Inc. **SIC:** 5169—Chemicals & Allied
Products Nec.

★ 55115 ★ **Allied-Signal**
1327 Erie St.
Birmingham, AL 35224
Ultimate Parent: Allied-Signal Inc. **SIC:**
2865—Cyclic Crudes & Intermediates.

★ 55116 ★ **Allied-Signal Corp.**
1327 Erie St.
Birmingham, AL 35224-2305
(205)787-8605
Officer: J. Wes Wade. **Ultimate Parent:**
Allied-Signal Inc. **SIC:** 2899—Chemical
Preparations Nec.

★ 55117 ★ **Allied-Signal Inc.**
1327 Erie St.
Birmingham, AL 35224
(205)787-8605
Officer: William Hightower, Plant Manager.
Ultimate Parent: Allied-Signal Inc. **SIC:**
2865—Cyclic Crudes & Intermediates.

★ 55118 ★ **Allied-Signal Inc.**
1327 Erie St.
Birmingham, AL 35224
(205)787-8605
Officer: William Hightower, Plant Manager.
Ultimate Parent: Allied-Signal Inc. **SIC:**
2865—Cyclic Crudes & Intermediates.

★ 55119 ★ **Allied-Signal Inc.**
1327 Erie St.
Birmingham, AL 35224
Ultimate Parent: Allied-Signal Inc. **SIC:**
2865—Cyclic Crudes & Intermediates.

★ 55120 ★ **American Family Life
Assurance**
300 Vestavia Pky. 2300
Birmingham, AL 35216
Ultimate Parent: American Family Life
Assurance Co. **SIC:** 6411—Insurance
Agents, Brokers & Service.

★ 55121 ★ **American General
Finance**
1984 Forestdale Blvd.
Birmingham, AL 35214-2049
(205)798-0080
Ultimate Parent: American General Corp.
SIC: 6141—Personal Credit Institutions;
6162—Mortgage Bankers &
Correspondents.

★ 55122 ★ **American General
Finance**
786 Green Springs Hwy.
Birmingham, AL 35209-4915
(205)942-4915
Location Type: Branch office. **Officer:**
Michelle Y. Gillian. **Ultimate Parent:**
American General Corp. **SIC:** 6141—
Personal Credit Institutions; 6162—
Mortgage Bankers & Correspondents.

★ 55123 ★ **American General
Finance Inc.**
1984 Forestdale Blvd.
Birmingham, AL 35214-2049
(205)798-0080
Location Type: Branch office. **Ultimate
Parent:** American General Corp. **SIC:**
6141—Personal Credit Institutions; 6162—
Mortgage Bankers & Correspondents.

★ 55124 ★ **American General
Finance Inc.**
2110 7th Ave. S
Birmingham, AL 35233-3106
(205)251-8121
Location Type: Branch office. **Officer:** G.
Edward Glanton. **Ultimate Parent:**
American General Corp. **SIC:** 6141—
Personal Credit Institutions.

★ 55125 ★ **American General
Finance Inc.**
786 Green Springs Hwy.
Birmingham, AL 35209-4915
(205)942-4915
Location Type: Branch office. **Officer:**
Michelle Y. Gillian. **Ultimate Parent:**
American General Corp. **SIC:** 6141—
Personal Credit Institutions; 6162—
Mortgage Bankers & Correspondents.

★ 55126 ★ **American Steel Corp.**
801 30th St. N
Birmingham, AL 35203
(205)323-3151
Ultimate Parent: National Steel. **SIC:**
5051—Metals Service Centers & Offices.

★ 55127 ★ **AmSouth Bancorp**
1900 5th Ave. N
Birmingham, AL 35203-2610
(205)320-5120
Company Type: Headquarters. **Officer:**
William A. Powell Jr., President. **SIC:**
6021—National Commercial Banks.
Employee Count: 5177. **Sales:** 12547 M.
Fortune Service 500: Ranking 50.

★ 55128 ★ **AmSouth
Bancorporation**
PO Box 11007
Birmingham, AL 35288
Company Type: Headquarters. **Ultimate
Parent:** AmSouth Bancorp.

★ 55129 ★ **AmSouth
Bancorporation**
1900 5th Ave. N, Ste., 1400
Birmingham, AL 35203
(205)320-7151
Company Type: Headquarters. **Officer:**
John W. Woods, Chairman of the Board &
CEO. **Ultimate Parent:** AmSouth Bancorp.
SIC: 6712—Bank Holding Companies.
Employee Count: 4600.

★ 55130 ★ **AmSouth Bank NA**
1900 5th Ave. N, Ste. 1400
PO Box 11007
Birmingham, AL 35203
(205)320-7151
Company Type: Subsidiary. **Officer:** John
W. Woods, Chairman of the Board & CEO.
Ultimate Parent: AmSouth Bancorp. **SIC:**
6021—National Commercial Banks.
Employee Count: 4300.

★ 55131 ★ **AmSouth Bank, N.A.**
4400 7th Ave.
Birmingham, AL 35224
(205)716-1945
Location Type: Branch office. **Ultimate
Parent:** AmSouth Bancorp. **SIC:** 6035—
Federal Savings Institutions; 6099—
Functions Related to Deposit Banking;
6111—Federal & Federally-Sponsored
Credit; 6153—Short-Term Business Credit;
6162—Mortgage Bankers &
Correspondents; 6163—Loan Brokers;
6282—Investment Advice.

★ 55132 ★ **AmSouth Bank, N.A.**
2653 Valleydale Rd.
Birmingham, AL 35244
(205)716-1960
Location Type: Branch office. **Ultimate
Parent:** AmSouth Bancorp. **SIC:** 6035—
Federal Savings Institutions; 6099—
Functions Related to Deposit Banking;
6111—Federal & Federally-Sponsored
Credit; 6153—Short-Term Business Credit;
6162—Mortgage Bankers &
Correspondents; 6163—Loan Brokers;
6282—Investment Advice.

★ 55133 ★ **AmSouth Bank, N.A.**
5428 1st Ave. N
Birmingham, AL 35212
(205)716-1950
Location Type: Branch office. **Ultimate
Parent:** AmSouth Bancorp. **SIC:** 6035—
Federal Savings Institutions; 6099—
Functions Related to Deposit Banking;
6111—Federal & Federally-Sponsored
Credit; 6153—Short-Term Business Credit;
6162—Mortgage Bankers &
Correspondents; 6163—Loan Brokers;
6282—Investment Advice.

★ 55134 ★ **AmSouth Bank, N.A.**
2100 6th Ave. S
Birmingham, AL 35233
(205)716-1245
Location Type: Branch office. **Ultimate
Parent:** AmSouth Bancorp. **SIC:** 6035—
Federal Savings Institutions; 6099—
Functions Related to Deposit Banking;
6111—Federal & Federally-Sponsored
Credit; 6153—Short-Term Business Credit;
6162—Mortgage Bankers &
Correspondents; 6163—Loan Brokers;
6282—Investment Advice.

★ 55135 ★ **AmSouth Bank, N.A.**
1900 University Blvd.
Birmingham, AL 35233
(205)716-1280
Location Type: Branch office. **Ultimate
Parent:** AmSouth Bancorp. **SIC:** 6035—
Federal Savings Institutions; 6099—
Functions Related to Deposit Banking;
6111—Federal & Federally-Sponsored
Credit; 6153—Short-Term Business Credit;
6162—Mortgage Bankers &
Correspondents; 6163—Loan Brokers;
6282—Investment Advice.

★ 55136 ★ **AmSouth Bank, N.A.**
3390 Morgan Dr.
Birmingham, AL 35243
(205)716-1215
Location Type: Branch office. **Ultimate
Parent:** AmSouth Bancorp. **SIC:** 6035—
Federal Savings Institutions; 6099—
Functions Related to Deposit Banking;
6111—Federal & Federally-Sponsored
Credit; 6153—Short-Term Business Credit;
6162—Mortgage Bankers &
Correspondents; 6163—Loan Brokers;
6282—Investment Advice.

★ 55137 ★ **AmSouth Bank, N.A.**
9178 Parkway E
Birmingham, AL 35206
(205)716-1235
Location Type: Branch office. **Ultimate
Parent:** AmSouth Bancorp. **SIC:** 6035—
Federal Savings Institutions; 6099—
Functions Related to Deposit Banking;
6111—Federal & Federally-Sponsored
Credit; 6153—Short-Term Business Credit;
6162—Mortgage Bankers &
Correspondents; 6163—Loan Brokers;
6282—Investment Advice.

★ **55138** ★ **AmSouth Bank, N.A.**
2930 27th St. N
Birmingham, AL 35207
(205)716-1205
Location Type: Branch office. **Ultimate Parent:** AmSouth Bancorp. **SIC:** 6035—Federal Savings Institutions; 6099—Functions Related to Deposit Banking; 6111—Federal & Federally-Sponsored Credit; 6153—Short-Term Business Credit; 6162—Mortgage Bankers & Correspondents; 6163—Loan Brokers; 6282—Investment Advice.

★ **55139** ★ **AmSouth Bank, N.A.**
1901 6th Ave. N, Ste. 100
Birmingham, AL 35203
(205)581-7444
Location Type: Branch office. **Ultimate Parent:** AmSouth Bancorp. **SIC:** 6035—Federal Savings Institutions; 6099—Functions Related to Deposit Banking; 6111—Federal & Federally-Sponsored Credit; 6153—Short-Term Business Credit; 6162—Mortgage Bankers & Correspondents; 6163—Loan Brokers; 6282—Investment Advice.

★ **55140** ★ **AmSouth Bank, N.A.**
102 Inverness Plz.
Birmingham, AL 35242
(205)716-1170
Location Type: Branch office. **Ultimate Parent:** AmSouth Bancorp. **SIC:** 6035—Federal Savings Institutions; 6099—Functions Related to Deposit Banking; 6111—Federal & Federally-Sponsored Credit; 6153—Short-Term Business Credit; 6162—Mortgage Bankers & Correspondents; 6163—Loan Brokers; 6282—Investment Advice.

★ **55141** ★ **AmSouth Bank, N.A.**
200 Corporate Ridge N
Birmingham, AL 35242
(205)980-1525
Location Type: Branch office. **Ultimate Parent:** AmSouth Bancorp. **SIC:** 6035—Federal Savings Institutions; 6099—Functions Related to Deposit Banking; 6111—Federal & Federally-Sponsored Credit; 6153—Short-Term Business Credit; 6162—Mortgage Bankers & Correspondents; 6163—Loan Brokers; 6282—Investment Advice.

★ **55142** ★ **AmSouth Bank, N.A.**
1304 Tomahawk Rd.
Birmingham, AL 35214
(205)716-1075
Location Type: Branch office. **Ultimate Parent:** AmSouth Bancorp. **SIC:** 6035—Federal Savings Institutions; 6099—Functions Related to Deposit Banking; 6111—Federal & Federally-Sponsored Credit; 6153—Short-Term Business Credit; 6162—Mortgage Bankers & Correspondents; 6163—Loan Brokers; 6282—Investment Advice.

★ **55143** ★ **AmSouth Bank, N.A.**
17 N. 70th St.
Birmingham, AL 35203
(205)320-7105
Location Type: Branch office. **Ultimate Parent:** AmSouth Bancorp. **SIC:** 6035—Federal Savings Institutions; 6099—Functions Related to Deposit Banking; 6111—Federal & Federally-Sponsored Credit; 6153—Short-Term Business Credit; 6162—Mortgage Bankers & Correspondents; 6163—Loan Brokers; 6282—Investment Advice.

★ **55144** ★ **AmSouth Bank, N.A.**
1809 Avenue E
Birmingham, AL 35218
(205)716-1065
Location Type: Branch office. **Ultimate Parent:** AmSouth Bancorp. **SIC:** 6035—Federal Savings Institutions; 6099—Functions Related to Deposit Banking; 6111—Federal & Federally-Sponsored Credit; 6153—Short-Term Business Credit; 6162—Mortgage Bankers & Correspondents; 6163—Loan Brokers; 6282—Investment Advice.

★ **55145** ★ **AmSouth Bank, N.A.**
2249 Bessemer Rd.
Birmingham, AL 35208
(205)716-1105
Location Type: Branch office. **Ultimate Parent:** AmSouth Bancorp. **SIC:** 6035—Federal Savings Institutions; 6099—

Functions Related to Deposit Banking; 6111—Federal & Federally-Sponsored Credit; 6153—Short-Term Business Credit; 6162—Mortgage Bankers & Correspondents; 6163—Loan Brokers; 6282—Investment Advice.

★ **55146** ★ **AmSouth Bank, N.A.**
2268 Brewster Rd.
Birmingham, AL 35235
(205)716-1015
Location Type: Branch office. **Ultimate Parent:** AmSouth Bancorp. **SIC:** 6035—Federal Savings Institutions; 6099—Functions Related to Deposit Banking; 6111—Federal & Federally-Sponsored Credit; 6153—Short-Term Business Credit; 6162—Mortgage Bankers & Correspondents; 6163—Loan Brokers; 6282—Investment Advice.

★ **55147** ★ **AmSouth Bank, N.A.**
833 Dennison Ave. SW
Birmingham, AL 35211
(205)581-7307
Location Type: Branch office. **Ultimate Parent:** AmSouth Bancorp. **SIC:** 6035—Federal Savings Institutions; 6099—Functions Related to Deposit Banking; 6111—Federal & Federally-Sponsored Credit; 6153—Short-Term Business Credit; 6162—Mortgage Bankers & Correspondents; 6163—Loan Brokers; 6282—Investment Advice.

★ **55148** ★ **AmSouth Bank, N.A.**
3179 Green Valley Rd.
Birmingham, AL 35293
(205)715-2855
Location Type: Branch office. **Ultimate Parent:** AmSouth Bancorp. **SIC:** 6035—Federal Savings Institutions; 6099—Functions Related to Deposit Banking; 6111—Federal & Federally-Sponsored Credit; 6153—Short-Term Business Credit; 6162—Mortgage Bankers & Correspondents; 6163—Loan Brokers; 6282—Investment Advice.

★ **55149** ★ **AmSouth Bank, N.A.**
251 Century Plz.
Birmingham, AL 35210
(205)716-1050
Location Type: Branch office. **Ultimate Parent:** AmSouth Bancorp. **SIC:** 6035—Federal Savings Institutions; 6111—Federal & Federally-Sponsored Credit; 6099—Functions Related to Deposit Banking; 6153—Short-Term Business Credit; 6162—Mortgage Bankers & Correspondents; 6163—Loan Brokers; 6282—Investment Advice.

★ **55150** ★ **AmSouth Bank N.A.**
PO Box 11007
Birmingham, AL 35228
(205)326-5120
Officer: John W. Woods, Chairman, President & CEO. **Ultimate Parent:** AmSouth Bancorp. **SIC:** 6035—Federal Savings Institutions; 6099—Functions Related to Deposit Banking; 6111—Federal & Federally-Sponsored Credit; 6153—Short-Term Business Credit; 6153—Short-Term Business Credit; 6162—Mortgage Bankers & Correspondents; 6163—Loan Brokers; 6163—Loan Brokers; 6282—Investment Advice.

★ **55151** ★ **AmSouth Bank, N.A.**
1533 Montclair Rd.
Birmingham, AL 35210
(205)711-1025
Location Type: Branch office. **Ultimate Parent:** AmSouth Bancorp. **SIC:** 6035—Federal Savings Institutions; 6099—Functions Related to Deposit Banking; 6111—Federal & Federally-Sponsored Credit; 6153—Short-Term Business Credit; 6162—Mortgage Bankers & Correspondents; 6163—Loan Brokers; 6282—Investment Advice.

★ **55152** ★ **AmSouth Bank North America**
1900 5th Ave. N
Birmingham, AL 35288-0001
(205)326-5120
Officer: John W. Woods, Chairman of the Board & President. **Ultimate Parent:** AmSouth Bancorp. **SIC:** 6022—State Commercial Banks; 6162—Mortgage Bankers & Correspondents; 7359—Equipment Rental & Leasing Nec; 6211—

Security Brokers & Dealers. **Employee Count:** 4476.

★ **55153** ★ **AmSouth Financial Corp.**
John A. Hand Bldg.
1st Ave., 20th Fl.
North & 20th St.
Birmingham, AL 35203
(205)326-5780
Company Type: Subsidiary. **Officer:** Jack G. Harp, President. **Ultimate Parent:** AmSouth Bancorp. **SIC:** 6141—Personal Credit Institutions. **Employee Count:** 9.

★ **55154** ★ **AmSouth Investment Services Inc.**
1900 5th Ave. N
Birmingham, AL 35203-2610
(205)581-7585
Officer: Wilbur Brown, President. **Ultimate Parent:** AmSouth Bancorp. **SIC:** 6211—Security Brokers & Dealers. **Employee Count:** 40. **Sales:** 3 M.

★ **55155** ★ **AmSouth Mortgage Co.**
15 20th St. S
Birmingham, AL 35233-2017
(205)326-4600
Officer: Michael L. Padalino, President & CEO. **Ultimate Parent:** AmSouth Bancorp. **SIC:** 6162—Mortgage Bankers & Correspondents. **Employee Count:** 452.

★ **55156** ★ **AmSouth Mortgage Co.**
500 John A. Hand Bldg.
1st Ave. N. & 20th
Birmingham, AL 35203
(205)326-4600
Company Type: Subsidiary. **Officer:** Michael L. Padalino, President. **Ultimate Parent:** AmSouth Bancorp. **SIC:** 6021—National Commercial Banks. **Employee Count:** 362.

★ **55157** ★ **APAC**
700 37th St. S.
Birmingham, AL 35222
(205)252-3456
Officer: Tim Mullendore, President. **Ultimate Parent:** Ashland Oil. **SIC:** 2951—Asphalt Paving Mixtures & Blocks.

★ **55158** ★ **Bama Food Products**
3900 Vanderbilt Rd.
Birmingham, AL 35217
(205)849-3205 **Fax:** (205)849-3250
Company Type: Division. **Location Type:** Headquarters. **Officer:** Joe LeDuc, Plant Manager. **Ultimate Parent:** Borden, Inc. **SIC:** 2033—Canned Fruits & Vegetables; 2035—Pickles, Sauces & Salad Dressings; 2099—Food Preparations Nec.

★ **55159** ★ **Banana Republic**
155 Riverchase Pky. E
Birmingham, AL 35244
(205)985-0052
Ultimate Parent: GAP. **SIC:** 5651—Family Clothing Stores.

★ **55160** ★ **Bell Atl Syst Leasing International**
2 Metroplex Dr., Ste. 111
Birmingham, AL 35209-6800
(205)870-1680
Officer: William L. Valentz. **Ultimate Parent:** Bell Atlantic Corp. **SIC:** 7377—Computer Rental & Leasing; 7353—Heavy Construction Equipment Rental.

★ **55161** ★ **Bell Atlantic Business System Services**
120 Summit Pky. Ste. 208
Birmingham, AL 35209-4719
(205)942-8878
Officer: Larry Williams. **Ultimate Parent:** Bell Atlantic Corp. **SIC:** 4813—Telephone Communications Except Radiotelephone; 4812—Radiotelephone Communications; 7378—Computer Maintenance & Repair; 6159—Miscellaneous Business Credit Institutions; 2741—Miscellaneous Publishing; 6719—Holding Companies Nec.

★ **55162** ★ **Bellsouth Adv & Publishing Corp. ALA**
400 Chase Park S
Birmingham, AL 35244-2820
(205)987-6500
Officer: Pamela C. Reed. **Ultimate Parent:** BellSouth Corp. **SIC:** 2759—Commercial Printing Nec.

★ **55163** ★ **Bellsouth Communications**
3000 Galleria Office Bldg., Rm. 1750
Birmingham, AL 35244
(205)985-6213
Location Type: Branch office. **Officer:** Florence Tisdale. **Ultimate Parent:** BellSouth Corp. **SIC:** 5065—Electronic Parts & Equipment Nec.

★ **55164** ★ **Bellsouth Communications**
135 Goodrich Dr.
Birmingham, AL 35217-1465
(205)856-4200
Officer: Doug Holcomb. **Ultimate Parent:** BellSouth Corp. **SIC:** 5065—Electronic Parts & Equipment Nec.

★ **55165** ★ **BellSouth Mobility**
3800 Colonnade Pky., Ste. 150
Birmingham, AL 35243-2351
(205)969-7600
Location Type: Branch office. **Officer:** Sarah Relfe. **Ultimate Parent:** BellSouth Corp. **SIC:** 5065—Electronic Parts & Equipment Nec; 4812—Radiotelephone Communications.

★ **55166** ★ **BellSouth Services Inc.**
3535 Colonnade Pky.
Birmingham, AL 35243-2358
(205)977-1392
Location Type: Branch office. **Officer:** Hugh B. Jacks. **Ultimate Parent:** BellSouth Corp. **SIC:** 8741—Management Services; 5999—Miscellaneous Retail Stores Nec.

★ **55167** ★ **Birmingham Coca-Cola**
4600 East Lake Blvd.
Birmingham, AL 35217
Ultimate Parent: Coca-Cola Bottling Consol. **SIC:** 2086—Bottled & Canned Soft Drinks.

★ **55168** ★ **Birmingham Coca-Cola Bottling Co.**
4600 E. Lake Blvd.
Birmingham, AL 35217
Ultimate Parent: Coca-Cola Bottling Consol. **SIC:** 2086—Bottled & Canned Soft Drinks.

★ **55169** ★ **Brookwood Medical Center**
2010 Brookwood Medical Ctr. Dr.
Birmingham, AL 35209
(205)877-1000
Officer: Gregory Burfitt, President & Executive Director. **Ultimate Parent:** American Medical Holdings. **SIC:** 8062—General Medical & Surgical Hospitals.

★ **55170** ★ **Brownell Electro Inc.**
3028 7th Ave. S
Birmingham, AL 35233
(205)322-3374
Location Type: Branch office. **Ultimate Parent:** Avnet. **SIC:** 5063—Electrical Apparatus & Equipment.

★ **55171** ★ **Bruno's Inc. Birmingham**
800 Lakeshore Pky.
Birmingham, AL 35211
(205)940-9400 **Fax:** (205)940-9568
Officer: Ronald G. Bruno. **Ultimate Parent:** Bruno's. **Employee Count:** 26486. **Sales:** 2872 M.

★ **55172** ★ **Bruno's Inc.**
800 Lakeshore Pky.
Birmingham, AL 35211-4447
(205)940-9400
Officer: Joseph S. Bruno, Chairman. **Ultimate Parent:** Bruno's. **SIC:** 5411—Grocery Stores; 5912—Drug Stores & Proprietary Stores. **Employee Count:** 26486. **Sales:** 2872327000 M.

★ **55173** ★ **Bruno's Inc.**
800 Lakeshore Pky.
Birmingham, AL 35211
(205)940-9400
Company Type: Headquarters. **Officer:** Ronald G. Bruno. **Fortune Service 500:** Ranking 44.

★ 55174 ★ Bruno's Inc.
800 Lakeshore Pky.
PO Box 2486
Birmingham, AL 35201-2486
(205)940-9400
Company Type: Headquarters. Officer: Ronald G. Bruno, Chairman, President, & CEO. Ultimate Parent: Bruno's. Employee Count: 23000.

★ 55175 ★ Burlington Air Express
25 Municipal Airport
Birmingham, AL 35212
(205)595-9240
Ultimate Parent: Pittston. SIC: 4513—Air Courier Services.

★ 55176 ★ Burlington Northern Railroa
441 Finley Blvd.
Birmingham, AL 35204
(205)320-3640
Ultimate Parent: Burlington Northern. SIC: 4013—Switching & Terminal Services.

★ 55177 ★ Burlington Northern Railroa
30 18th St. S
Birmingham, AL 35233
(205)320-2821
Ultimate Parent: Burlington Northern. SIC: 4011—Railroads—Line-Haul Operating.

★ 55178 ★ Capco Pipe Co. Inc.
450 Century Pk. S
Birmingham, AL 35226-3910
(205)978-6100
Company Type: Branch. Officer: S. C. Parris. Ultimate Parent: Asarco. SIC: 3084—Plastics Pipe; 2821—Plastics Materials & Resins; 3089—Plastics Products Nec; 3272—Concrete Products Nec; 3292—Asbestos Products; 3498—Fabricated Pipe & Fittings; 3999—Manufacturing Industries Nec; 5074—Plumbing & Hydronic Heating Supplies.

★ 55179 ★ Capco Pipe Co. Inc.
450 Central Park S., Ste. 200B
Birmingham, AL 35226
(205)978-6100
Officer: Sam C. Parris, President & CEO. Ultimate Parent: Asarco. SIC: 3084—Plastics Pipe; 3272—Concrete Products Nec. Employee Count: 250. Sales: 57.7 M.

★ 55180 ★ Capco Pipe Co. Inc.
1400 20th St. S.
Birmingham, AL 35255
(205)933-7281
Company Type: Subsidiary. Officer: S.C. Parris, President & CEO. Ultimate Parent: Asarco. SIC: 3292—Asbestos Products; 3272—Concrete Products Nec; 2821—Plastics Materials & Resins.

★ 55181 ★ Casual Corner
244 Century Plz.
Birmingham, AL 35210
(205)591-8791
Ultimate Parent: United States Shoe. SIC: 5651—Family Clothing Stores.

★ 55182 ★ Casual Corner
244 Riverchase Pky. E
Birmingham, AL 35244
(205)985-3222
Ultimate Parent: United States Shoe. SIC: 5651—Family Clothing Stores.

★ 55183 ★ Casual Corner
739 Brookwood Village
Birmingham, AL 35209
(205)879-2307
Ultimate Parent: United States Shoe. SIC: 5621—Women's Clothing Stores; 5651—Family Clothing Stores.

★ 55184 ★ Champion International Corp.
621 Lorna Sq.
Birmingham, AL 35216
(205)979-9902
Ultimate Parent: Champion International. SIC: 6519—Real Property Lessors Nec.

★ 55185 ★ Chicago Title Insurance
Ticor
1 Perimeter Park S
Birmingham, AL 35243-2327
(205)969-0731
Ultimate Parent: Alleghany Corp. SIC:

6361—Title Insurance; 1743—Terrazzo, Tile, Marble & Mosaic Work.

★ 55186 ★ Cincinnati Insurance Co.
1616 6th Ave. N
Birmingham, AL 35203
(205)251-7765
Ultimate Parent: Cincinnati Financial. SIC: 6411—Insurance Agents, Brokers & Service.

★ 55187 ★ Circuit City
1688 Montgomery Hwy.
Birmingham, AL 35216
(205)823-5566
Ultimate Parent: Circuit City Stores. SIC: 5722—Household Appliance Stores.

★ 55188 ★ Circuit City
7720 Ludington Ln.
Birmingham, AL 35210
(205)956-0671
Ultimate Parent: Circuit City Stores. SIC: 5722—Household Appliance Stores.

★ 55189 ★ Circus World
162 Century Plz.
Birmingham, AL 35210
(205)592-7766
Ultimate Parent: Melville. SIC: 5945—Hobby, Toy & Game Shops.

★ 55190 ★ Circus World
137 Riverchase Pky. E
Birmingham, AL 35244
(205)985-0905
Ultimate Parent: Melville. SIC: 5945—Hobby, Toy & Game Shops.

★ 55191 ★ Circus World
736 Brookwood Village
Birmingham, AL 35209
(205)879-6230
Ultimate Parent: Melville. SIC: 5945—Hobby, Toy & Game Shops.

★ 55192 ★ Citgo
1030 24th St. N
Birmingham, AL 35203
(205)254-9513
Ultimate Parent: Citgo Petroleum. SIC: 5541—Gasoline Service Stations.

★ 55193 ★ Citgo Petroleum Corp.
2200 25th St. SW
Birmingham, AL 35211
(205)925-6641
Ultimate Parent: Citgo Petroleum. SIC: 1311—Crude Petroleum & Natural Gas; 5172—Petroleum Products Nec.

★ 55194 ★ City National Bank
1600 Forestdale Plz.
Birmingham, AL 35214
(205)328-4490
Ultimate Parent: City National Corp. SIC: 6029—Commercial Banks Nec.

★ 55195 ★ City National Bank
1034 Montgomery Hwy.
Birmingham, AL 35216
(205)328-4490
Ultimate Parent: City National Corp. SIC: 6029—Commercial Banks Nec.

★ 55196 ★ Coast to Coast Express
726 16th Ave. W
Birmingham, AL 35204
(205)324-6535
Ultimate Parent: Servistar Corp. SIC: 4213—Trucking Except Local.

★ 55197 ★ Compass Bancshares
15 S. 20th St.
Birmingham, AL 35233
(205)933-3000
Company Type: Headquarters. Officer: D. Paul Jones Jr. Employee Count: 3771. Fortune Service 500: Ranking 76.

★ 55198 ★ Compass Bank
1151 Bankhead Hwy.
Birmingham, AL 35204-1328
(205)933-3190
Location Type: Branch office. Ultimate Parent: Compass Bancshares.

★ 55199 ★ Compass Bank
201 State Farm Pky.
Birmingham, AL 35209
(205)558-5462
Location Type: Branch office. Ultimate Parent: Compass Bancshares.

★ 55200 ★ Compass Bank
9246 Parkway E
Birmingham, AL 35206-5513
(205)933-3230
Location Type: Branch office. Ultimate Parent: Compass Bancshares.

★ 55201 ★ Compass Bank
5990 Chalkville Mountain Rd.
Birmingham, AL 35235
(205)558-5552
Location Type: Branch office. Ultimate Parent: Compass Bancshares.

★ 55202 ★ Compass Bank
505 N. 20th St.
Birmingham, AL 35203
(205)933-3206
Location Type: Branch office. Ultimate Parent: Compass Bancshares.

★ 55203 ★ Compass Bank
1916 Forestdale Blvd.
Birmingham, AL 35214-1328
(205)933-3955
Location Type: Branch office. Ultimate Parent: Compass Bancshares.

★ 55204 ★ Compass Bank
1675 Ctr. Point Pky.
Birmingham, AL 35215
(205)558-5390
Location Type: Branch office. Ultimate Parent: Compass Bancshares.

★ 55205 ★ Compass Bank
1694 Montclair Rd.
Birmingham, AL 35210-2496
(205)933-3200
Location Type: Branch office. Ultimate Parent: Compass Bancshares.

★ 55206 ★ Compass Bank
15 S. 20th St.
Birmingham, AL 35233
(205)933-3000 Telex: 59877
Location Type: Branch office. Officer: D. Paul Jones Jr., Chairman & CEO. Ultimate Parent: Compass Bancshares.

★ 55207 ★ Compass Bank
PO Box 10566
Birmingham, AL 35296
Location Type: Branch office. Ultimate Parent: Compass Bancshares.

★ 55208 ★ Conagra Foodservice Companies
155 Cleage Dr.
Birmingham, AL 35217
Ultimate Parent: Conagra. SIC: 2000—Food & Kindred Products.

★ 55209 ★ Continental Group Inc.
140 Citation Ct
Birmingham, AL 35209
(205)942-6320
Ultimate Parent: Continental Assurance Co. Inc. SIC: 5085—Industrial Supplies.

★ 55210 ★ Courtyard by Marriott
500 Shades Creek Pky.
Birmingham, AL 35209
(205)879-0400
Ultimate Parent: Marriott International. SIC: 7011—Hotels & Motels.

★ 55211 ★ Delta Air Lines
1535 Montgomery Hwy.
Birmingham, AL 35216
(205)328-2000
Ultimate Parent: Delta Air Lines, Inc.

★ 55212 ★ Delta Air Lines
2001 Park Pl
Birmingham, AL 35203
(205)328-2000
Ultimate Parent: Delta Air Lines, Inc. SIC: 4724—Travel Agencies.

★ 55213 ★ Delta Air Lines
Municipal Airport
Birmingham, AL 35212
(205)599-3128
Ultimate Parent: Delta Air Lines, Inc. SIC: 4512—Air Transportation—Scheduled; 4729—Passenger Transportation Arrangement Nec.

★ 55214 ★ Delta Air Lines
Municipal Airport
Birmingham, AL 35212
(205)599-3128
Ultimate Parent: Delta Air Lines, Inc. SIC: 4512—Air Transportation—Scheduled; 4729—Passenger Transportation Arrangement Nec.

★ 55215 ★ Delta Air Lines Inc.
2001 Park Pl
Birmingham, AL 35203
(205)328-2000
Ultimate Parent: Delta Air Lines, Inc. SIC: 4724—Travel Agencies.

★ 55216 ★ Delta Air Systems Corp.
244 Goodwin Crest Dr.
Birmingham, AL 35209
(205)945-9201
Ultimate Parent: Delta Air Lines, Inc. SIC: 7389—Business Services Nec; 7300—Business Services.

★ 55217 ★ Delta Air Systems Corp.
3100 6th Ave. S
Birmingham, AL 35233
(205)251-8460
Ultimate Parent: Delta Air Lines, Inc. SIC: 5075—Warm Air Heating & Air-Conditioning.

★ 55218 ★ Dexter Corp.
Midland Div.
90 Carson Rd.
Birmingham, AL 35215
Company Type: Division. Ultimate Parent: Dexter Corp. SIC: 2851—Paints & Allied Products; 2821—Plastics Materials & Resins.

★ 55219 ★ Dexter Corp.
Packaging Products Div.
90 Carson Rd.
Birmingham, AL 35215
Company Type: Division. Ultimate Parent: Dexter Corp. SIC: 2851—Paints & Allied Products; 2821—Plastics Materials & Resins.

★ 55220 ★ Dexter Packaging Products
90 Carson Rd. N
Birmingham, AL 35215
(205)854-5454
Officer: William G. Daniel Jr., Manager. Ultimate Parent: Dexter Corp. SIC: 2851—Paints & Allied Products; 3554—Paper Industries Machinery; 2821—Plastics Materials & Resins.

★ 55221 ★ Diebold Inc.
190 W. Valley Ave.
Birmingham, AL 35209
(205)942-6183
Ultimate Parent: Diebold, Inc. SIC: 5046—Commercial Equipment Nec.

★ 55222 ★ Diebold Inc.
2192 Parkway Lake Dr. F
Birmingham, AL 35244
Ultimate Parent: Diebold, Inc.

★ 55223 ★ Digital Equipment Corp.
2 Riverchase Pky. S
Birmingham, AL 35244
(205)988-5433
Ultimate Parent: Digital Equipment Corp. SIC: 5734—Computer & Software Stores; 8661—Religious Organizations.

★ 55224 ★ Digital Equipment Corp.
2 Perimeter Park S
Birmingham, AL 35243
(205)969-5500
Ultimate Parent: Digital Equipment Corp. SIC: 5046—Commercial Equipment Nec; 7373—Computer Integrated Systems Design.

★ 55225 ★ Diversified Claim Services
2718 20th St. S
Birmingham, AL 35209-3111
(205)879-3111
Ultimate Parent: Aon Corp. SIC: 7381—Detective & Armored Car Services.

★ 55226 ★　Dixie Insurance Co.
2204 Lakeshore Dr.
Birmingham, AL 35209
(205)870-4000
Company Type: Subsidiary. **Officer:** James C. Sullivan, President. **Ultimate Parent:** American Financial. **SIC:** 6331—Fire, Marine & Casualty Insurance.

★ 55227 ★　Durr-Fillauer Medical Inc.
107 Walter Davis Dr.
Birmingham, AL 35209
(205)942-8721
Ultimate Parent: Bergen Brunswig Corp. **SIC:** 5047—Medical & Hospital Equipment.

★ 55228 ★　E. R. Carpenter Co. Inc.
165 Goodrich Dr.
Birmingham, AL 35217
Ultimate Parent: Carpenter. **SIC:** 3086—Plastics Foam Products.

★ 55229 ★　Eckerd Drug Co.
2020 Cahaba Rd.
Birmingham, AL 35223
(205)870-8254
Ultimate Parent: Eckerd Corp. **SIC:** 5431—Fruit & Vegetable Markets; 5912—Drug Stores & Proprietary Stores.

★ 55230 ★　Emery Worldwide
Municipal Airport
Birmingham, AL 35212
(205)328-5057
Ultimate Parent: Consolidated Freightways. **SIC:** 4731—Freight Transportation Arrangement.

★ 55231 ★　E.R. Carpenter Co. Inc.
165 Goodrich Dr.
Birmingham, AL 35217
Ultimate Parent: Carpenter. **SIC:** 3086—Plastics Foam Products.

★ 55232 ★　Evodex
90 Carson Rd.
Birmingham, AL 35215
Ultimate Parent: Dexter Corp. **SIC:** 2851—Paints & Allied Products.

★ 55233 ★　Exxon Corp.
201 Vulcan Rd.
Birmingham, AL 35209
(205)945-1889
Ultimate Parent: Exxon. **SIC:** 5541—Gasoline Service Stations.

★ 55234 ★　Fairfield Inn by Marriott
155 Vulcan Rd.
Birmingham, AL 35209
(205)945-9600
Ultimate Parent: Marriott International. **SIC:** 7011—Hotels & Motels.

★ 55235 ★　First Alabama Bancshares
417 N. 20th St.
Birmingham, AL 35203
(205)326-7540
Company Type: Headquarters. **Officer:** J. Stanley Mackin. **Fortune Service 500:** Ranking 57.

★ 55236 ★　First Alabama Bancshares, Inc.
PO Box 10247
Birmingham, AL 35202
Location Type: Branch office. **Ultimate Parent:** First Alabama Bancshares.

★ 55237 ★　First Alabama Bank
1531 25th St. N
Birmingham, AL 35234-2800
(205)326-7685
Location Type: Branch office. **Ultimate Parent:** First Alabama Bancshares.

★ 55238 ★　First Alabama Bank
298 W. Valley Ave.
Birmingham, AL 35209-3624
(205)290-5301
Location Type: Branch office. **Ultimate Parent:** First Alabama Bancshares.

★ 55239 ★　First Alabama Bank
7508 1st Ave. N
Birmingham, AL 35206-4220
(205)326-7927
Location Type: Branch office. **Ultimate Parent:** First Alabama Bancshares.

★ 55240 ★　First Alabama Bank
417 N. 20th St.
Birmingham, AL 35203-3203
(205)326-7148
Location Type: Branch office. **Ultimate Parent:** First Alabama Bancshares.

★ 55241 ★　First Alabama Bank
417 20th St. N
Birmingham, AL 35203-3203
(205)832-8011
Company Type: Subsidiary. **Officer:** J. Stanley Mackin, Chairman of the Board & CEO. **Ultimate Parent:** First Alabama Bancshares. **SIC:** 6022—State Commercial Banks; 6722—Management Investment—Open-End. **Employee Count:** 4201.

★ 55242 ★　First Alabama Bank
3313 Lorna Rd.
Birmingham, AL 35216
(205)326-7970
Ultimate Parent: First Alabama Bancshares. **SIC:** 6035—Federal Savings Institutions.

★ 55243 ★　First Alabama Bank
9700 Parkway E
Birmingham, AL 35215
(205)326-7541
Ultimate Parent: First Alabama Bancshares. **SIC:** 6022—State Commercial Banks.

★ 55244 ★　First Alabama Bank
7703 Crestwood Blvd. F600
Birmingham, AL 35210
(205)326-7558
Ultimate Parent: First Alabama Bancshares. **SIC:** 6022—State Commercial Banks.

★ 55245 ★　First Alabama Bank
475 Green Springs Hwy.
Birmingham, AL 35209
(205)326-7351
Ultimate Parent: First Alabama Bancshares. **SIC:** 6022—State Commercial Banks.

★ 55246 ★　First Alabama Bank
832 19th St. S
Birmingham, AL 35205
(205)326-7477
Ultimate Parent: First Alabama Bancshares. **SIC:** 6022—State Commercial Banks.

★ 55247 ★　First Alabama Bank
948 20th St. S
Birmingham, AL 35205
(205)326-7514
Ultimate Parent: First Alabama Bancshares. **SIC:** 6022—State Commercial Banks.

★ 55248 ★　First Alabama Bank of Birmi
529 Montgomery Hwy.
Birmingham, AL 35216
(205)326-7364
Ultimate Parent: First Alabama Bancshares. **SIC:** 6022—State Commercial Banks.

★ 55249 ★　First Alabama Bank of Birmi
1651 Montgomery Hwy.
Birmingham, AL 35216
(205)326-7357
Ultimate Parent: First Alabama Bancshares. **SIC:** 6022—State Commercial Banks.

★ 55250 ★　First Alabama Bank of Birmi
2020 Ctr. Point Rd.
Birmingham, AL 35215
(205)326-7531
Ultimate Parent: First Alabama Bancshares. **SIC:** 6022—State Commercial Banks.

★ 55251 ★　First Alabama Bank of Birmi
2721 Culver Rd.
Birmingham, AL 35223
(205)326-7471
Ultimate Parent: First Alabama Bancshares. **SIC:** 6022—State Commercial Banks.

★ 55252 ★　First Alabama Bank of Birmi
3121 3rd Ave. S
Birmingham, AL 35233
(205)326-7591
Ultimate Parent: First Alabama Bancshares. **SIC:** 6022—State Commercial Banks.

★ 55253 ★　First Alabama Bank of Birmi
3172 Cahaba Rd.
Birmingham, AL 35223
(205)326-7574
Ultimate Parent: First Alabama Bancshares. **SIC:** 6022—State Commercial Banks.

★ 55254 ★　First Alabama Bank Birmingh
1013 Vanderbilt Rd.
Birmingham, AL 35234
(205)326-7651
Ultimate Parent: First Alabama Bancshares. **SIC:** 6022—State Commercial Banks.

★ 55255 ★　First Alabama Bank Birmingh
234 W. Valley Ave.
Birmingham, AL 35209
(205)326-7301
Ultimate Parent: First Alabama Bancshares. **SIC:** 6022—State Commercial Banks.

★ 55256 ★　First Alabama Bank Birmingh
529 Montgomery Hwy.
Birmingham, AL 35216
(205)945-7364
Ultimate Parent: First Alabama Bancshares. **SIC:** 6022—State Commercial Banks.

★ 55257 ★　First Alabama Bank Birmingh
1651 Montgomery Hwy.
Birmingham, AL 35216
(205)945-7357
Ultimate Parent: First Alabama Bancshares. **SIC:** 6022—State Commercial Banks.

★ 55258 ★　First Alabama Bank Birmingh
2250 Bessemer Rd.
Birmingham, AL 35208
(205)326-7582
Ultimate Parent: First Alabama Bancshares. **SIC:** 6022—State Commercial Banks.

★ 55259 ★　First Alabama Bank Birmingh
475 Green Springs Hwy.
Birmingham, AL 35209
(205)945-7351
Ultimate Parent: First Alabama Bancshares. **SIC:** 6022—State Commercial Banks.

★ 55260 ★　First Alabama Bank Birmingh
1531 25th St. N
Birmingham, AL 35234
(205)326-7685
Ultimate Parent: First Alabama Bancshares. **SIC:** 6022—State Commercial Banks.

★ 55261 ★　First Alabama Bank Birmingh
3121 3rd Ave. S
Birmingham, AL 35233
(205)326-7592
Ultimate Parent: First Alabama Bancshares. **SIC:** 6022—State Commercial Banks.

★ 55262 ★　First Alabama Bank of Birmingham
417 20th St. N
Birmingham, AL 35203
(205)326-7148
Ultimate Parent: First Alabama Bancshares. **SIC:** 6022—State Commercial Banks.

★ 55263 ★　First Commercial Bank
501 21st St. S
Birmingham, AL 35203
(205)868-4964
Location Type: Branch office. **Ultimate Parent:** Synovus Financial Corp. **SIC:** 6021—National Commercial Banks.

★ 55264 ★　First Commercial Bank
9324 Parkway E
Birmingham, AL 35215-8304
(205)868-1120
Location Type: Branch office. **Ultimate Parent:** Synovus Financial Corp. **SIC:** 6021—National Commercial Banks.

★ 55265 ★　First Commercial Bank
300 N. 21st St.
Birmingham, AL 35203-3326
(205)868-4850
Location Type: Branch office. **Ultimate Parent:** Synovus Financial Corp. **SIC:** 6021—National Commercial Banks.

★ 55266 ★　First Commercial Bank
100 Inverness Corners
Birmingham, AL 35242-3760
(205)868-4929
Location Type: Branch office. **Ultimate Parent:** Synovus Financial Corp. **SIC:** 6021—National Commercial Banks.

★ 55267 ★　First Commercial Bank
3329 Oak Hill Dr.
Birmingham, AL 35216-5409
(205)868-4975
Location Type: Branch office. **Ultimate Parent:** Synovus Financial Corp. **SIC:** 6021—National Commercial Banks.

★ 55268 ★　First Commercial Bank
44 Church St.
Birmingham, AL 35213-3702
(205)868-4868
Location Type: Branch office. **Ultimate Parent:** Synovus Financial Corp. **SIC:** 6021—National Commercial Banks.

★ 55269 ★　First Commercial Bank
2000 SouthBridge Pky.
Birmingham, AL 35209-1303
(205)879-2800 **Fax:** (205)868-4832
Location Type: Branch office. **Ultimate Parent:** Synovus Financial Corp. **SIC:** 6021—National Commercial Banks.

★ 55270 ★　First Commercial Bank
PO Box 11746
Birmingham, AL 35202-1746
Location Type: Branch office. **Ultimate Parent:** Synovus Financial Corp. **SIC:** 6021—National Commercial Banks.

★ 55271 ★　First Commercial Bank
550 Montgomery Hwy.
Birmingham, AL 35216
(205)978-4400
Location Type: Branch office. **Ultimate Parent:** Synovus Financial Corp. **SIC:** 6021—National Commercial Banks.

★ 55272 ★　First Security Mortgage Cor
200 Office Park Dr.
Birmingham, AL 35223
(205)870-8980
Ultimate Parent: First Security Corp. **SIC:** 6162—Mortgage Bankers & Correspondents.

★ 55273 ★　FMP-Rauma Co.
104 Inverness Ctr. Pl.
Birmingham, AL 35242-4869
(205)995-0190
Company Type: Division. **Officer:** Gerry L. Albertson, President. **Ultimate Parent:** CBI Industries, Inc. **SIC:** 3443—Fabricated Plate Work—Boiler Shops; 3554—Paper Industries Machinery. **Employee Count:** 200. **Sales:** 24 M.

★ 55274 ★ The Gap
178 Riverchase Pky. E
Birmingham, AL 35244
(205)985-0501
Ultimate Parent: GAP. SIC: 5651—Family
Clothing Stores.

★ 55275 ★ The Gap
160 Century Plz.
Birmingham, AL 35210
(205)592-4604
Ultimate Parent: GAP. SIC: 5611—Men's &
Boys' Clothing Stores.

★ 55276 ★ Gap Stores Inc
160 Century Plz.
Birmingham, AL 35210
(205)592-4604
Ultimate Parent: GAP. SIC: 5611—Men's &
Boys' Clothing Stores.

★ 55277 ★ General American Life
Insur
1025 Montgomery Hwy.
Birmingham, AL 35216
(205)979-3176
Ultimate Parent: General American Life.
SIC: 6411—Insurance Agents, Brokers &
Service.

★ 55278 ★ General Electric Co.
1500 Mims Ave. SW
Birmingham, AL 35211
(205)925-3103
Officer: Jim Rogers, Manager. Ultimate
Parent: General Electric. SIC: 3599—
Industrial Machinery Nec.

★ 55279 ★ Greyhound Bus Lines
2719 19th St. S
Birmingham, AL 35209
(205)870-3113
Ultimate Parent: Greyhound Lines Inc. SIC:
4131—Intercity & Rural Bus Transportation;
4215—Courier Services Except by Air.

★ 55280 ★ Hertz Rent-A-Car
Municipal Airport
Birmingham, AL 35212
(205)591-6090
Ultimate Parent: Hertz. SIC: 7514—
Passenger Car Rental.

★ 55281 ★ Hill-Rom Co. Inc.
1 Riverchase Pky. S
Birmingham, AL 35244
(205)987-9105
Ultimate Parent: Hillenbrand Industries.
SIC: 5049—Professional Equipment Nec.

★ 55282 ★ Hit or Miss
400 Palisades Blvd.
Birmingham, AL 35209
(205)870-0357
Ultimate Parent: TJX. SIC: 5651—Family
Clothing Stores.

★ 55283 ★ Hit or Miss No 327
1668 Montgomery Hwy.
Birmingham, AL 35216
(205)979-0307
Ultimate Parent: TJX. SIC: 5651—Family
Clothing Stores.

★ 55284 ★ Industrial Systems
132 Stratford Cir.
Birmingham, AL 35209-4329
(205)871-0916
Ultimate Parent: Ball Corp. SIC: 5063—
Electrical Apparatus & Equipment.

★ 55285 ★ Jiffy Lube
9640 Parkway E
Birmingham, AL 35215
(205)836-9031
Ultimate Parent: Pennzoil. SIC: 7539—
Automotive Repair Shops Nec.

★ 55286 ★ Jiffy Lube
International
321 Palisades Blvd.
Birmingham, AL 35209
(205)870-5736
Ultimate Parent: Pennzoil. SIC: 7538—
General Automotive Repair Shops.

★ 55287 ★ Kaiser Aluminum &
Chemical
1810 Decatur Hwy.
Birmingham, AL 35207
(205)841-4308
Ultimate Parent: Maxxam. SIC: 5023—
Homefurnishings.

★ 55288 ★ Kay-Bee Toy & Hobby
260 Riverchase Pky. E
Birmingham, AL 35244
(205)985-3089
Ultimate Parent: Melville. SIC: 5945—
Hobby, Toy & Game Shops.

★ 55289 ★ Kay Bee Toy&Hobby
Shop
Western Hill Mall
Birmingham, AL 35228
(205)925-2588
Ultimate Parent: Melville. SIC: 5945—
Hobby, Toy & Game Shops.

★ 55290 ★ Kelly Assisted Living
Servi
120 Summit Pky.
Birmingham, AL 35209
(205)942-4076
Ultimate Parent: Kelly Services. SIC:
8082—Home Health Care Services.

★ 55291 ★ Kentucky Fried
Chicken
2113 Old Rocky Ridge Rd.
Birmingham, AL 35216
Ultimate Parent: Pepsico. SIC: 5812—
Eating Places.

★ 55292 ★ Kentucky Fried
Chicken
828 Green Springs Hwy.
Birmingham, AL 35209
(205)942-7651
Ultimate Parent: Pepsico. SIC: 5812—
Eating Places.

★ 55293 ★ Kentucky Fried
Chicken
26 N
Birmingham, AL 35228
(205)328-1304
Ultimate Parent: Pepsico. SIC: 5812—
Eating Places.

★ 55294 ★ Kentucky Fried
Chicken
1653 Ctr. Point Pky.
Birmingham, AL 35215
(205)854-4698
Ultimate Parent: Pepsico. SIC: 5812—
Eating Places.

★ 55295 ★ Kentucky Fried
Chicken
7909 Crestwood Blvd.
Birmingham, AL 35210
(205)967-7177
Ultimate Parent: Pepsico. SIC: 5812—
Eating Places.

★ 55296 ★ Kentucky Fried
Chicken
1718 3rd Ave. W
Birmingham, AL 35208
(205)787-2009
Ultimate Parent: Pepsico. SIC: 5812—
Eating Places; 8742—Management
Consulting Services.

★ 55297 ★ Kentucky Fried
Chicken
1928 Bessemer Rd.
Birmingham, AL 35208
(205)787-5233
Ultimate Parent: Pepsico. SIC: 5812—
Eating Places.

★ 55298 ★ Kentucky Fried
Chicken
940 20th St. S
Birmingham, AL 35205
(205)854-4698
Ultimate Parent: Pepsico. SIC: 5812—
Eating Places.

★ 55299 ★ Kentucky Fried
Chicken
1800 20th Street Ensley
Birmingham, AL 35218
Ultimate Parent: Pepsico. SIC: 5812—
Eating Places.

★ 55300 ★ Kids R US
1723 Montgomery Hwy. S
Birmingham, AL 35244
(205)988-8336
Ultimate Parent: Toys "R" US. SIC: 5651—
Family Clothing Stores.

★ 55301 ★ Lane Bryant
230 Century Plz.
Birmingham, AL 35210
(205)592-2775
Ultimate Parent: Limited. SIC: 5651—
Family Clothing Stores.

★ 55302 ★ Lane Bryant
763 Brookwood Village
Birmingham, AL 35209
(205)879-0766
Ultimate Parent: Limited. SIC: 5651—
Family Clothing Stores.

★ 55303 ★ Lane Bryant
132 Riverchase Pky. E
Birmingham, AL 35244
(205)985-3080
Ultimate Parent: Limited. SIC: 5651—
Family Clothing Stores.

★ 55304 ★ Lane Bryant
1808 2nd Ave. N
Birmingham, AL 35203
(205)251-3287
Ultimate Parent: Limited. SIC: 5651—
Family Clothing Stores.

★ 55305 ★ Lapp Insulator Co.
3 Riverchase Pky. S
Birmingham, AL 35244
(205)985-9526
Ultimate Parent: Great American
Management & Investment. SIC: 1742—
Plastering, Drywall & Insulation.

★ 55306 ★ Lerner Shop
7728 Eastwood Mall
Birmingham, AL 35210
(205)595-1541
Ultimate Parent: Limited. SIC: 5621—
Women's Clothing Stores; 5651—Family
Clothing Stores.

★ 55307 ★ Lerner Shop
134 Riverchase Pky. E
Birmingham, AL 35244
(205)985-0352
Ultimate Parent: Limited. SIC: 5651—
Family Clothing Stores.

★ 55308 ★ The Limited
Riverchase Pky. E
Birmingham, AL 35244
(205)985-0717
Ultimate Parent: Limited. SIC: 5651—
Family Clothing Stores.

★ 55309 ★ The Limited
Brookwood Village
Birmingham, AL 35209
(205)871-8286
Ultimate Parent: Limited. SIC: 5621—
Women's Clothing Stores; 5651—Family
Clothing Stores.

★ 55310 ★ The Limited Express
114 Riverchase Pky. E
Birmingham, AL 35244
(205)985-0026
Ultimate Parent: Limited. SIC: 5651—
Family Clothing Stores.

★ 55311 ★ Macy's Riverchase
Galleria
2400 Riverchase Galleria
Birmingham, AL 35244-2311
(205)985-3883
Officer: John Proft. Ultimate Parent: R. H.
Macy. SIC: 5311—Department Stores.

★ 55312 ★ Marathon Petroleum
Co.
2704 28th St. SW
Birmingham, AL 35211
(205)925-7037
Ultimate Parent: USX Corp. SIC: 2911—
Petroleum Refining; 5172—Petroleum
Products Nec.

★ 55313 ★ Marshalls
1709 Montgomery Hwy. S
Birmingham, AL 35244
(205)733-8399
Ultimate Parent: Melville. SIC: 5311—
Department Stores.

★ 55314 ★ Mary Kay Cosmetics
3582 Springhill Rd.
Birmingham, AL 35223
(205)967-5258
Ultimate Parent: Mary Kay Cosmetics. SIC:
5999—Miscellaneous Retail Stores Nec.

★ 55315 ★ Mary Kay Cosmetics
307 Heath Dr.
Birmingham, AL 35242
(205)967-5618
Ultimate Parent: Mary Kay Cosmetics. SIC:
5999—Miscellaneous Retail Stores Nec.

★ 55316 ★ Mary Kay Cosmetics
5201 Rock Ridge Pl.
Birmingham, AL 35210
(205)699-8820
Ultimate Parent: Mary Kay Cosmetics. SIC:
5999—Miscellaneous Retail Stores Nec.

★ 55317 ★ Mary Kay Cosmetics
2509 Mallard Sq.
Birmingham, AL 35216
(205)823-6598
Ultimate Parent: Mary Kay Cosmetics. SIC:
5999—Miscellaneous Retail Stores Nec.

★ 55318 ★ Mary Kay Cosmetics
820 Sylvia Dr.
Birmingham, AL 35209
(205)871-2953
Ultimate Parent: Mary Kay Cosmetics. SIC:
5999—Miscellaneous Retail Stores Nec.

★ 55319 ★ Massachusetts Mutual
Life Insurance
813 Shades Creek Pky.
Birmingham, AL 35209
(205)879-0180
Ultimate Parent: Massacuetts Mutual Life.
SIC: 6411—Insurance Agents, Brokers &
Service.

★ 55320 ★ McDonalds Office
124 Summit Pky.
Birmingham, AL 35242
(205)942-0451
Ultimate Parent: McDonald's.
SIC: 7389—Business Services Nec.

★ 55321 ★ Microage
2140 11th Ave. S
Birmingham, AL 35205
(205)933-0100
Ultimate Parent: MicroAge. SIC: 7373—
Computer Integrated Systems Design.

★ 55322 ★ Motion Industries Inc.
Alton Rd.
PO Box 1477
Birmingham, AL 35201
(205)956-1122 Fax: (205)951-3841
Company Type: Subsidiary. Ultimate
Parent: Genuine Parts.

★ 55323 ★ Motion Industries Inc.
1605 Alton Rd.
Birmingham, AL 35210-3770
(205)956-1122
Officer: Michael S. Gaffney, President &
Chief Executive Officer. Ultimate Parent:
Genuine Parts. SIC: 5085—Industrial
Supplies. Employee Count: 2600. Sales:
654000000 M.

★ 55324 ★ Motion Industries
Midwest, Inc.
1605 Alton Rd.
Birmingham, AL 35210
(205)956-1122
Officer: Michael S. Gaffney, President.
Ultimate Parent: Genuine Parts. SIC:
3714—Motor Vehicle Parts & Accessories.

★ 55325 ★ New York Life
Birmingham General Office
104 Inverness Ctr., Ste. 500
Birmingham, AL 35242
(205)995-1122 Fax: (205)995-0078
Officer: Linda C. Bell, Manager. Ultimate
Parent: New York Life.

★ 55326 ★ Northwest Airlines
Inc.
Municipal Airport
Birmingham, AL 35212
(205)592-9619
Ultimate Parent: NWA. SIC: 4512—Air
Transportation—Scheduled.

★ 55327 ★ Otis Elevator Co.
3728 4th Ave. S
Birmingham, AL 35222
(205)591-7200
Ultimate Parent: United Technologies. SIC:
3534—Elevators & Moving Stairways;
5084—Industrial Machinery & Equipment.

★ 55328 ★ **Pappagallo**
2803 Cahaba Rd.
Birmingham, AL 35223
(205)870-0470
Ultimate Parent: United States Shoe. **SIC:**
5621—Women's Clothing Stores; 5661—
Shoe Stores.

★ 55329 ★ **Petite Sophisticate**
234 Riverchase Pky. E
Birmingham, AL 35244
(205)985-0329
Ultimate Parent: United States Shoe. **SIC:**
5651—Family Clothing Stores.

★ 55330 ★ **Petite Sophisticate**
715 Brookwood Village
Birmingham, AL 35209
(205)871-6019
Ultimate Parent: United States Shoe. **SIC:**
5651—Family Clothing Stores.

★ 55331 ★ **Piggly Wiggly**
1675 Tuscaloosa Ave. SW
Birmingham, AL 35211
(205)925-6744
Ultimate Parent: Bruno's. **SIC:** 5411—
Grocery Stores.

★ 55332 ★ **Piggly Wiggly**
1500 31st St. SW
Birmingham, AL 35221
(205)925-9513
Ultimate Parent: Bruno's. **SIC:** 5411—
Grocery Stores.

★ 55333 ★ **Piggly Wiggly**
2305 6th Ave. N
Birmingham, AL 35203
(205)925-9513
Ultimate Parent: Bruno's. **SIC:** 5411—
Grocery Stores.

★ 55334 ★ **Piggly Wiggly**
3000 Montgomery Hwy.
Birmingham, AL 35209
(205)879-0884
Ultimate Parent: Bruno's. **SIC:** 5499—
Miscellaneous Food Stores.

★ 55335 ★ **Piggly Wiggly**
5401 1st Ave. N
Birmingham, AL 35212
(205)592-8303
Ultimate Parent: Bruno's. **SIC:** 5411—
Grocery Stores.

★ 55336 ★ **Piggly Wiggly**
Alabama Distribution
2500 13th St. W
Birmingham, AL 35208
(205)788-3343
Ultimate Parent: Bruno's. **SIC:** 5141—
Groceries—General Line.

★ 55337 ★ **Pizza Hut**
1109 Forestdale Blvd.
Birmingham, AL 35214
(205)798-7723
Ultimate Parent: Pepsico. **SIC:** 5812—
Eating Places.

★ 55338 ★ **Pizza Hut**
1568 Cooper Hill Rd.
Birmingham, AL 35210
(205)956-5200
Ultimate Parent: Pepsico. **SIC:** 5812—
Eating Places.

★ 55339 ★ **Pizza Hut**
1919 28th Ave. S
Birmingham, AL 35209
(205)978-8073
Ultimate Parent: Pepsico. **SIC:** 5812—
Eating Places.

★ 55340 ★ **Pizza Hut**
14 Green Springs Hwy.
Birmingham, AL 35209
(205)942-1815
Ultimate Parent: Pepsico. **SIC:** 5812—
Eating Places.

★ 55341 ★ **Pizza Hut**
1713 10th Ave. S
Birmingham, AL 35205
(205)933-2517
Ultimate Parent: Pepsico. **SIC:** 5812—
Eating Places.

★ 55342 ★ **Pizza Hut**
9921 Parkway E
Birmingham, AL 35215
(205)854-0094
Ultimate Parent: Pepsico. **SIC:** 5812—
Eating Places.

★ 55343 ★ **Pizza Hut**
23 24th Ave. NW
Birmingham, AL 35215
(205)853-8353
Ultimate Parent: Pepsico. **SIC:** 5812—
Eating Places.

★ 55344 ★ **Pizza Hut**
3748 Lorna Rd.
Birmingham, AL 35216
(205)987-0568
Ultimate Parent: Pepsico. **SIC:** 5812—
Eating Places.

★ 55345 ★ **Pizza Hut**
5400 1st Ave. N
Birmingham, AL 35212
(205)595-2228
Ultimate Parent: Pepsico. **SIC:** 5812—
Eating Places.

★ 55346 ★ **Pizza Hut**
2531 Rocky Ridge Rd.
Birmingham, AL 35243
(205)978-8000
Ultimate Parent: Pepsico. **SIC:** 5812—
Eating Places.

★ 55347 ★ **Pizza Hut**
1805 Ctr. Point Pky.
Birmingham, AL 35215
(205)978-8000
Ultimate Parent: Pepsico. **SIC:** 5812—
Eating Places.

★ 55348 ★ **Pizza Hut**
195 E. Valley Ave. W
Birmingham, AL 35209
(205)978-8070
Ultimate Parent: Pepsico. **SIC:** 5812—
Eating Places.

★ 55349 ★ **Pizza Hut**
2931 Columbiana Rd.
Birmingham, AL 35216
(205)979-2394
Ultimate Parent: Pepsico. **SIC:** 5812—
Eating Places.

★ 55350 ★ **Pizza Hut**
3173 Green Valley Rd.
Birmingham, AL 35243
(205)978-8067
Ultimate Parent: Pepsico. **SIC:** 5812—
Eating Places.

★ 55351 ★ **Pizza Hut**
1301 Bessemer Rd.
Birmingham, AL 35208
(205)923-0047
Ultimate Parent: Pepsico. **SIC:** 5812—
Eating Places.

★ 55352 ★ **Pizza Hut**
1301 Bessemer Super Hwy.
Birmingham, AL 35228
(205)923-0047
Ultimate Parent: Pepsico. **SIC:** 5812—
Eating Places.

★ 55353 ★ **Principal Mutual Life**
Insurance
1025 Montgomery Hwy.
Birmingham, AL 35216
(205)822-7205
Ultimate Parent: Principal Mutual Life. **SIC:**
6411—Insurance Agents, Brokers &
Service.

★ 55354 ★ **Radio Shack**
602 Brookwood Village
Birmingham, AL 35209
(205)870-9919
Company Type: Division. **Ultimate Parent:**
Tandy Corp. **SIC:** 7373—Computer
Integrated Systems Design.

★ 55355 ★ **Radio Shack**
Western Hill Mall
Birmingham, AL 35228
(205)923-0028
Company Type: Division. **Ultimate Parent:**
Tandy Corp. **SIC:** 5065—Electronic Parts &
Equipment Nec.

★ 55356 ★ **Radio Shack**
220 31st St. S
Birmingham, AL 35233
(205)780-2340
Company Type: Division. **Ultimate Parent:**
Tandy Corp. **SIC:** 5065—Electronic Parts &
Equipment Nec.

★ 55357 ★ **Radio Shack**
Midfield Park Shopping Ctr.
Birmingham, AL 35228
(205)923-0888
Company Type: Division. **Ultimate Parent:**
Tandy Corp. **SIC:** 5731—Radio, Television
& Electronics Stores.

★ 55358 ★ **Radio Shack**
2009 2nd Ave. N
Birmingham, AL 35210
(205)324-9737
Company Type: Division. **Ultimate Parent:**
Tandy Corp. **SIC:** 5065—Electronic Parts &
Equipment Nec.

★ 55359 ★ **Radio Shack**
292 Riverchase Pky. E
Birmingham, AL 35244
(205)985-0930
Company Type: Division. **Ultimate Parent:**
Tandy Corp. **SIC:** 5065—Electronic Parts &
Equipment Nec.

★ 55360 ★ **Radio Shack**
300 Vestavia Office Park 1400
Birmingham, AL 35216
Company Type: Division. **Ultimate Parent:**
Tandy Corp. **SIC:** 5065—Electronic Parts &
Equipment Nec.

★ 55361 ★ **Radio Shack**
5372 Oporto Madrid Blvd. S
Birmingham, AL 35210
(205)591-5516
Company Type: Division. **Ultimate Parent:**
Tandy Corp. **SIC:** 5065—Electronic Parts &
Equipment Nec.

★ 55362 ★ **Radio Shack**
9140 Parkway E
Birmingham, AL 35206
(205)833-5833
Company Type: Division. **Ultimate Parent:**
Tandy Corp. **SIC:** 5065—Electronic Parts &
Equipment Nec.

★ 55363 ★ **Radio Shack**
116 Green Springs Hwy.
Birmingham, AL 35209
(205)942-4425
Company Type: Division. **Ultimate Parent:**
Tandy Corp. **SIC:** 5065—Electronic Parts &
Equipment Nec.

★ 55364 ★ **Radio Shack**
1409 Montgomery Hwy.
Birmingham, AL 35216
(205)822-8001
Company Type: Division. **Ultimate Parent:**
Tandy Corp. **SIC:** 5731—Radio, Television
& Electronics Stores.

★ 55365 ★ **Radio Shack**
2338 Ctr. Pt Pky.
Birmingham, AL 35215
(205)856-0991
Company Type: Division. **Ultimate Parent:**
Tandy Corp. **SIC:** 5063—Electrical
Apparatus & Equipment; 5065—Electronic
Parts & Equipment Nec.

★ 55366 ★ **Radio Shack**
209 Century Plz.
Birmingham, AL 35210
(205)591-7465
Company Type: Division. **Ultimate Parent:**
Tandy Corp. **SIC:** 5065—Electronic Parts &
Equipment Nec.

★ 55367 ★ **Radio Shack**
2200 31st St. W
Birmingham, AL 35208
(205)780-2340
Company Type: Division. **Ultimate Parent:**
Tandy Corp. **SIC:** 5065—Electronic Parts &
Equipment Nec.

★ 55368 ★ **Reliance Electric Co.**
3100 Pinson Valley Pky.
Birmingham, AL 35217
(205)841-8377
Officer: Gene Angle, Manager. **Ultimate**
Parent: Reliance Electric. **SIC:** 3621—
Motors & Generators.

★ 55369 ★ **Reliance Insurance**
Co.
11 W. Oxmoor Rd.
Birmingham, AL 35209
(205)942-4384
Ultimate Parent: Reliance Group Holdings.
SIC: 6411—Insurance Agents, Brokers &
Service.

★ 55370 ★ **Reliance Insurance**
Co.
1 Perimeter Park S
Birmingham, AL 35243
(205)967-1856
Ultimate Parent: Reliance Group Holdings.
SIC: 6411—Insurance Agents, Brokers &
Service.

★ 55371 ★ **Richards S P Co.**
204 Industrial Dr.
Birmingham, AL 35211
(205)945-8846
Ultimate Parent: Genuine Parts. **SIC:**
5044—Office Equipment; 5112—Stationery
& Office Supplies.

★ 55372 ★ **RJ Reynolds Tobacco**
Co.
3588 Lorna Ridge Dr.
Birmingham, AL 35216
(205)822-9570
Ultimate Parent: RJR Nabisco Holdings.
SIC: 5993—Tobacco Stores & Stands.

★ 55373 ★ **Rust International Inc.**
100 Corporate Pky.
Birmingham, AL 35242
(205)995-7878 **Fax:** (205)995-7777
Officer: Rodney C. Gilbert, CEO. **Ultimate**
Parent: WMX Technologies, Inc. **Sales:**
1535 M.

★ 55374 ★ **Ryder Truck Rental**
3 Riverchase Pky. S
Birmingham, AL 35244
(205)988-9111
Ultimate Parent: Ryder System. **SIC:**
7514—Passenger Car Rental.

★ 55375 ★ **Ryder Truck Rental**
830070 PO Box
Birmingham, AL 35283
(205)841-8777
Ultimate Parent: Ryder System. **SIC:**
7359—Equipment Rental & Leasing Nec;
7513—Truck Rental & Leasing Without
Drivers.

★ 55376 ★ **Ryder Truck Rental**
721 Montgomery Hwy.
Birmingham, AL 35216
(205)979-1277
Ultimate Parent: Ryder System. **SIC:**
7359—Equipment Rental & Leasing Nec.

★ 55377 ★ **Ryder Truck Rental**
2032 Green Springs Hwy. S
Birmingham, AL 35205
(205)328-8270
Ultimate Parent: Ryder System. **SIC:**
7359—Equipment Rental & Leasing Nec.

★ 55378 ★ **Ryder Truck Rental**
3145 Lorna Rd.
Birmingham, AL 35216
(205)823-7140
Ultimate Parent: Ryder System. **SIC:**
7359—Equipment Rental & Leasing Nec.

★ 55379 ★ **Ryder Truck Rental**
2749 Crestwood Blvd.
Birmingham, AL 35210
(205)956-6415
Ultimate Parent: Ryder System. **SIC:**
7359—Equipment Rental & Leasing Nec.

★ 55380 ★ **Ryder Truck Rental**
402 28th St. S
Birmingham, AL 35233
(205)956-5636
Ultimate Parent: Ryder System. **SIC:**
7513—Truck Rental & Leasing Without
Drivers.

★ 55381 ★ **Ryder Truck Rental**
275 Snow Dr.
Birmingham, AL 35209
(205)841-8777
Ultimate Parent: Ryder System. **SIC:**
7513—Truck Rental & Leasing Without
Drivers.

★ 55382 ★ **Ryder Truck Rental**
Body Shop
3109 5th Ave. S
Birmingham, AL 35233
(205)849-3345
Ultimate Parent: Ryder System. **SIC:**
7532—Top & Body Repair & Paint Shops.

★ 55383 ★ **Safeco Insurance Co. of America**
450 Century Park S
Birmingham, AL 35226
(205)822-6622
Ultimate Parent: Safeco. **SIC:** 6411—
Insurance Agents, Brokers & Service.

★ 55384 ★ **Safety Kleen Corp.**
1002 Hoke Ave.
Birmingham, AL 35217
(205)744-9170
Ultimate Parent: Safety-Kleen. **SIC:** 5013—
Motor Vehicle Supplies & New Parts.

★ 55385 ★ **Sam's Wholesale Club**
3900 Kilgore Memorial Dr.
Birmingham, AL 35210
(205)956-3987
Ultimate Parent: Wal-Mart Stores, Inc. **SIC:**
5311—Department Stores.

★ 55386 ★ **Service Merchandise**
7736 Eastwood Mall
Birmingham, AL 35210
(205)592-6960
Ultimate Parent: Service Merchandise Co.,
Inc. **SIC:** 5944—Jewelry Stores.

★ 55387 ★ **Service Merchandise**
Loehmanns Vlg. Shopping Ctr.
Birmingham, AL 35244
(205)988-5410
Ultimate Parent: Service Merchandise Co.,
Inc. **SIC:** 5944—Jewelry Stores.

★ 55388 ★ **Shell Oil Co.**
120 Summit Pky.
Birmingham, AL 35209
(205)942-0824
Ultimate Parent: Shell Oil Co. **SIC:** 2911—
Petroleum Refining.

★ 55389 ★ **Sloan Paper Co.**
170 Cleage Dr. No. 108
Birmingham, AL 35217-1461
(205)781-2644
Officer: Thomas R. Snader. **Ultimate
Parent:** Alco Standard Corp. **SIC:** 5111—
Printing & Writing Paper.

★ 55390 ★ **Sloan Paper Co. Inc.**
120 Cleage Dr. No. 108
Birmingham, AL 35217-1461
Officer: C.R. Hester. **Ultimate Parent:** Alco
Standard Corp. **SIC:** 2621—Paper Mills.

★ 55391 ★ **Sloss Industries Corp.
Birmingham Facility**
3500 35th Ave. North
Birmingham, AL 35207
Ultimate Parent: Walter Industries, Inc.
SIC: 3312—Blast Furnaces & Steel Mills;
2869—Industrial Organic Chemicals Nec.

★ 55392 ★ **Southtrust Corp.**
420 N. 20th St.
Birmingham, AL 35203
(205)254-5000 **Fax:** (205)254-6688
Company Type: Headquarters. **Officer:**
Wallace D. Malone Jr. **Employee Count:**
7033. **Sales:** 1102 M. **Fortune Service
500:** Ranking 42.

★ 55393 ★ **Southtrust Securities Inc.**
112 20th St. N
Birmingham, AL 35203
(205)254-5321
Ultimate Parent: Southtrust Corp. **SIC:**
6722—Management Investment—
Open-End.

★ 55394 ★ **Standard Fire Insurance Co.**
Court S
Birmingham, AL 35209
(205)870-5400
Ultimate Parent: Aetna Life & Casualty.
SIC: 6399—Insurance Carriers Nec.

★ 55395 ★ **Steiner Bank**
9420 Parkway E
Birmingham, AL 35215
(205)833-7600
Location Type: Branch office. **Ultimate
Parent:** Union Planters Corp. **SIC:** 6021—
National Commercial Banks.

★ 55396 ★ **Steiner Bank**
1920 3rd Ave. N
Birmingham, AL 35203-3578
(205)323-7181
Location Type: Branch office. **Ultimate**

Parent: Union Planters Corp. **SIC:** 6021—
National Commercial Banks.

★ 55397 ★ **Sterling Advertising**
2906 Crescent Ave.
Birmingham, AL 35209
(205)870-0390
Ultimate Parent: Lowe's. **SIC:** 7311—
Advertising Agencies; 8743—Public
Relations Services.

★ 55398 ★ **Stevens Graphics Inc.**
100 W. Oxmoor Rd.
Birmingham, AL 35209-6329
Ultimate Parent: BellSouth Corp. **SIC:**
2752—Commercial Printing—Lithographic.

★ 55399 ★ **Stone Container Corp.**
3200 Pinson Valley Pky.
Birmingham, AL 35217
(205)853-5796
Officer: William Ellis, Manager. **Ultimate
Parent:** Stone Container Corp. **SIC:** 2631—
Paperboard Mills.

★ 55400 ★ **Stonewall Insurance Co.**
PO Box 1688
2204 Lakeshore Dr.
Birmingham, AL 35201-1688
(205)879-5357
Company Type: Subsidiary. **Officer:**
Ronald F. Johnson, President. **Ultimate
Parent:** American Financial. **SIC:** 6331—
Fire, Marine & Casualty Insurance.
Employee Count: 320. **Sales:** 20421000
M.

★ 55401 ★ **T J Maxx**
1125 Huffman Rd.
Birmingham, AL 35215
(205)856-2300
Ultimate Parent: TJX. **SIC:** 5311—
Department Stores.

★ 55402 ★ **T J Maxx**
1646 Montgomery Hwy.
Birmingham, AL 35216
(205)822-8255
Ultimate Parent: TJX. **SIC:** 5311—
Department Stores; 5651—Family Clothing
Stores.

★ 55403 ★ **T J Maxx**
7517 Crestwood Blvd.
Birmingham, AL 35210
(205)592-8011
Ultimate Parent: TJX. **SIC:** 5311—
Department Stores.

★ 55404 ★ **Taco Bell**
2520 Rocky Ridge Rd.
Birmingham, AL 35243
(205)979-4737
Ultimate Parent: Pepsico. **SIC:** 5812—
Eating Places.

★ 55405 ★ **Taco Bell**
2418 Spring Hwy.
Birmingham, AL 35213
(205)942-0254
Ultimate Parent: Pepsico. **SIC:** 5812—
Eating Places.

★ 55406 ★ **Taco Bell**
9509 Parkway E
Birmingham, AL 35215
(205)836-2476
Ultimate Parent: Pepsico. **SIC:** 5812—
Eating Places.

★ 55407 ★ **Taco Bell**
1801 Pinson Valley Pky.
Birmingham, AL 35217
(205)849-7464
Ultimate Parent: Pepsico. **SIC:** 5812—
Eating Places.

★ 55408 ★ **Taco Bell**
1457 Montgomery Hwy.
Birmingham, AL 35216
(205)823-2750
Ultimate Parent: Pepsico. **SIC:** 5812—
Eating Places.

★ 55409 ★ **Taco Bell**
381 Palisades Blvd.
Birmingham, AL 35209
(205)871-5219
Ultimate Parent: Pepsico. **SIC:** 2241—
Narrow Fabric Mills.

★ 55410 ★ **Taco Bell**
1101 Forestdale Blvd.
Birmingham, AL 35214
(205)956-5251
Ultimate Parent: Pepsico. **SIC:** 5812—
Eating Places.

★ 55411 ★ **Taco Bell**
J Riverchs Gllr Home
Birmingham, AL 35244
(205)985-0815
Ultimate Parent: Pepsico. **SIC:** 5812—
Eating Places.

★ 55412 ★ **Taco Bell**
100 Bessemer Super Hwy.
Birmingham, AL 35228
(205)925-0039
Ultimate Parent: Pepsico. **SIC:** 5812—
Eating Places.

★ 55413 ★ **Taco Bell**
1910 Ctr. Point Pky.
Birmingham, AL 35215
(205)853-7216
Ultimate Parent: Pepsico. **SIC:** 5812—
Eating Places.

★ 55414 ★ **Taco Bell**
3501 Avenue E
Birmingham, AL 35218
(205)780-1255
Ultimate Parent: Pepsico. **SIC:** 5812—
Eating Places.

★ 55415 ★ **Taco Bell**
2300 Bessemer Rd.
Birmingham, AL 35208
(205)785-7223
Ultimate Parent: Pepsico. **SIC:** 5812—
Eating Places.

★ 55416 ★ **Taco Bell**
7630 1st Ave. N
Birmingham, AL 35206
(205)833-8312
Ultimate Parent: Pepsico. **SIC:** 5812—
Eating Places.

★ 55417 ★ **Taco Bell**
1700 5th Ave. S
Birmingham, AL 35233
(205)324-1392
Ultimate Parent: Pepsico. **SIC:** 5812—
Eating Places.

★ 55418 ★ **Taco Bell Executive Office**
200 Century Park S
Birmingham, AL 35226
(205)979-5773
Ultimate Parent: Pepsico. **SIC:** 5812—
Eating Places.

★ 55419 ★ **Texaco Food Mart**
2529 28th St. SW
Birmingham, AL 35211
Ultimate Parent: Texaco. **SIC:** 5411—
Grocery Stores.

★ 55420 ★ **Texaco Inc.**
3020 12th Ave. N
Birmingham, AL 35234
(205)251-7417
Ultimate Parent: Texaco. **SIC:** 5172—
Petroleum Products Nec.

★ 55421 ★ **Texaco Refining & Marketing**
2529 28th St. SW
Birmingham, AL 35211
(205)925-3660
Ultimate Parent: Texaco. **SIC:** 2911—
Petroleum Refining.

★ 55422 ★ **Texaco Self Serve**
6620 Weibel Dr.
Birmingham, AL 35228
(205)854-2483
Ultimate Parent: Texaco. **SIC:** 5541—
Gasoline Service Stations.

★ 55423 ★ **Texaco Self-Service**
5117 10th Ave. N
Birmingham, AL 35212
(205)591-7341
Ultimate Parent: Texaco. **SIC:** 5541—
Gasoline Service Stations.

★ 55424 ★ **Texaco Self Service**
9871 Parkway E
Birmingham, AL 35215
(205)854-2483
Ultimate Parent: Texaco. **SIC:** 5541—
Gasoline Service Stations.

★ 55425 ★ **Texaco Self Service**
290 W. Valley Ave.
Birmingham, AL 35209
(205)942-9099
Ultimate Parent: Texaco. **SIC:** 5541—
Gasoline Service Stations.

★ 55426 ★ **Texaco Self Service**
1604 Forestdale Blvd.
Birmingham, AL 35214
(205)791-0107
Ultimate Parent: Texaco. **SIC:** 5541—
Gasoline Service Stations.

★ 55427 ★ **Thermacote-Welco**
708 5th Ave. N
Birmingham, AL 35203
(205)323-3080
Ultimate Parent: Foster Wheeler Corp.
SIC: 5084—Industrial Machinery &
Equipment.

★ 55428 ★ **Ticor Title Insurance**
1 Perimeter Park S, Ste. 100N
Birmingham, AL 35243-2338
(205)879-0561
Location Type: Branch office. **Ultimate
Parent:** Alleghany Corp. **SIC:** 6361—Title
Insurance.

★ 55429 ★ **Torrington Co. the**
1855 Data Dr.
Birmingham, AL 35244
(205)987-4966
Ultimate Parent: Ingersoll-Rand. **SIC:**
3562—Ball & Roller Bearings.

★ 55430 ★ **Torrington Co.**
100 Century Park S
Birmingham, AL 35226
(205)822-2994
Ultimate Parent: Ingersoll-Rand. **SIC:**
3562—Ball & Roller Bearings; 5085—
Industrial Supplies.

★ 55431 ★ **Toys R US**
1715 Montgomery Hwy. S
Birmingham, AL 35244
(205)733-1551
Ultimate Parent: Toys "R" US. **SIC:** 5945—
Hobby, Toy & Game Shops.

★ 55432 ★ **Toys R US**
7701 Ludington Ln.
Birmingham, AL 35210
(205)956-8303
Ultimate Parent: Toys "R" US. **SIC:** 5641—
Children's & Infants' Wear Stores; 5945—
Hobby, Toy & Game Shops.

★ 55433 ★ **Trailways Bu System**
3324 Independence Dr.
Birmingham, AL 35209
(205)871-3065
Ultimate Parent: Greyhound Lines Inc.

★ 55434 ★ **Trailways Inc.**
2324 5th Ave. N
Birmingham, AL 35203
(205)323-1678
Ultimate Parent: Greyhound Lines Inc. **SIC:**
4173—Bus Terminal & Service Facilities.

★ 55435 ★ **Union Camp Corp.**
School Supplies Div.
3300 Pinson Valley Pky.
Birmingham, AL 35217
(205)853-7032
Company Type: Division. **Officer:** Mackie
Horton, President. **Ultimate Parent:** Union
Camp Corp. **SIC:** 2678—Stationery
Products; 2679—Converted Paper Products
Nec.

★ 55436 ★ **Union Oil Co. of California Inc.**
1537 Mims Ave. SW
Birmingham, AL 35211
(205)925-7055
Ultimate Parent: Unocal Corp. **SIC:** 5172—
Petroleum Products Nec.

★ 55437 ★ **Unisys Corp.**
2340 Woodcrest Pl
Birmingham, AL 35209
(205)870-3853
Ultimate Parent: Unisys Corp. **SIC:** 7373—
Computer Integrated Systems Design.

★ 55438 ★ United Brake Systems Inc.
2809 8th Ave. N
Birmingham, AL 35203
(205)324-4551
Ultimate Parent: Echlin. SIC: 5531—Automobile & Home Supply Stores.

★ 55439 ★ United Brake Systems Inc.
229 26th Ave. W
Birmingham, AL 35204
(205)324-4551
Ultimate Parent: Echlin. SIC: 3714—Motor Vehicle Parts & Accessories.

★ 55440 ★ United Parcel Service
118 Citation Ct
Birmingham, AL 35209
(205)942-3441
Ultimate Parent: United Parcel Service of America. SIC: 4212—Local Trucking Without Storage; 4215—Courier Services Except by Air.

★ 55441 ★ United Parcel Service Air
34 Municipal Airport
Birmingham, AL 35212
(205)942-3441
Ultimate Parent: United Parcel Service of America. SIC: 4513—Air Courier Services.

★ 55442 ★ US Fidelity
15 20th St. S
Birmingham, AL 35233
(205)250-6100
Ultimate Parent: USF&G Corp. SIC: 6411—Insurance Agents, Brokers & Service.

★ 55443 ★ US Gypsum Co.
2015 Vanderbilt Rd.
Birmingham, AL 35234
(205)849-0156
Ultimate Parent: USG Corp. SIC: 5039—Construction Materials Nec.

★ 55444 ★ USG Interiors Inc.
2015 Vanderbilt Rd.
Birmingham, AL 35234
(205)849-0156
Officer: L.M. King, Manager. Ultimate Parent: USG Corp. SIC: 3086—Plastics Foam Products; 3296—Mineral Wool.

★ 55445 ★ Van Waters & Rogers Inc.
131 W. Oxmoor Rd. 127
Birmingham, AL 35209
(205)942-0244
Ultimate Parent: Univar Corp. SIC: 2899—Chemical Preparations Nec.

★ 55446 ★ Victoria's Secret
116 Riverchase Pky. E
Birmingham, AL 35244
(205)985-0029
Ultimate Parent: Limited. SIC: 5651—Family Clothing Stores.

★ 55447 ★ Vulcan Materials Co.
2101 Pinson Valley Pky.
Birmingham, AL 35217
(205)849-7451
Officer: Jim Bailey, Manager. Ultimate Parent: Vulcan Materials Co. SIC: 3281—Cut Stone & Stone Products; 3295—Minerals—Ground or Treated; 3296—Mineral Wool.

★ 55448 ★ Vulcan Materials Co.
1 Metroplex Dr.
Birmingham, AL 35209
(205)877-3000
Company Type: Headquarters. Officer: Herbert A. Sklenar. Employee Count: 6320. Sales: 1133.5 M. Fortune 500: Largest U.S. Industrial Corporations: Ranking 338.

★ 55449 ★ Wal Mart
2000 Forestdale Blvd.
Birmingham, AL 35214
(205)798-9721
Ultimate Parent: Wal-Mart Stores, Inc. SIC: 5399—Miscellaneous General Merchandise Store.

★ 55450 ★ Wal Mart
1855 Montgomery Hwy. S
Birmingham, AL 35244
(205)733-0303
Ultimate Parent: Wal-Mart Stores, Inc. SIC: 5311—Department Stores.

★ 55451 ★ Wal Mart (Cafeteria)
1189 Huffman Rd.
Birmingham, AL 35215
(205)853-0711
Ultimate Parent: Wal-Mart Stores, Inc. SIC: 5812—Eating Places.

★ 55452 ★ Waldenbooks
7748 Crestwood Blvd.
Birmingham, AL 35210
(205)956-6032
Ultimate Parent: K-Mart. SIC: 5942—Book Stores.

★ 55453 ★ Wall Street Journal
2940 4th Ave. S
Birmingham, AL 35233
(205)326-6206
Ultimate Parent: Dow Jones. SIC: 2711—Newspapers.

★ 55454 ★ Western Auto Supply Co.
1627 Forestdale Blvd.
Birmingham, AL 35214
(205)798-7071
Ultimate Parent: Sears Roebuck & Co. SIC: 5531—Automobile & Home Supply Stores.

★ 55455 ★ Western Auto Supply Co.
34 Phillips Dr.
Birmingham, AL 35228
(205)322-8767
Ultimate Parent: Sears Roebuck & Co. SIC: 5531—Automobile & Home Supply Stores.

★ 55456 ★ Western Auto Supply Co.
6435 1st Ave. N
Birmingham, AL 35212
(205)595-8331
Ultimate Parent: Sears Roebuck & Co. SIC: 5531—Automobile & Home Supply Stores.

★ 55457 ★ Wheeling Machine Products
2504 2nd St. W
Birmingham, AL 35204
(205)322-2044
Ultimate Parent: Cooper Industries. SIC: 3599—Industrial Machinery Nec.

★ 55458 ★ Wilson Brands Corp.
1221 2nd Ave. N.
Birmingham, AL 35203
Ultimate Parent: Doskocil. SIC: 2013—Sausages & Other Prepared Meats.

★ 55459 ★ Woodhaven Foods
1421 Robinwood Cir.
Birmingham, AL 35217
(205)849-7927
Ultimate Parent: ARA Group. SIC: 5141—Groceries—General Line; 5812—Eating Places.

★ 55460 ★ Xerox Business Services
1000 Urban Ctr. Pky.
Birmingham, AL 35242
(205)970-4600
Officer: Bill Sims, Manager. Ultimate Parent: Xerox Corp. SIC: 3663—Radio & T.V. Communications Equipment; 3861—Photographic Equipment & Supplies.

★ 55461 ★ Zep Manuf Co.
146 W. Valley Ave.
Birmingham, AL 35209
(205)942-9704
Ultimate Parent: National Service Industries. SIC: 5087—Service Establishment Equipment.

★ 55462 ★ Zippy Mart Inc.
2601 Warrior Rd.
Birmingham, AL 35208
(205)781-4741
Ultimate Parent: Crown Central Petroleum Corp. SIC: 5411—Grocery Stores.

Blountsville

★ 55463 ★ First Alabama Bank
Main St. S
Blountsville, AL 35031
(205)429-4161
Location Type: Branch office. Ultimate Parent: First Alabama Bancshares. SIC: 6021—National Commercial Banks.

★ 55464 ★ Tyson Foods, Inc.
Hwy. 231 N
Blountsville, AL 35031
(205)429-2421
Officer: Wade Hankinson, Manager. Ultimate Parent: Tyson Foods, Inc. SIC: 2015—Poultry Slaughtering & Processing.

★ 55465 ★ Tyson Foods Inc. Blountsville Plant
Hwy. 231 South
Blountsville, AL 35031
Ultimate Parent: Tyson Foods, Inc. SIC: 2000—Food & Kindred Products.

Boaz

★ 55466 ★ Cooper Industries Inc. Wagner Brake Subsidiary
300 Wagner Dr.
Boaz, AL 35957-1064
Ultimate Parent: Cooper Industries. SIC: 3714—Motor Vehicle Parts & Accessories.

★ 55467 ★ Gold Kist Inc. Poultry
Gold Kist St.
Boaz, AL 35957
Ultimate Parent: Gold Kist. SIC: 2000—Food & Kindred Products.

★ 55468 ★ Kentucky Fried Chicken
Hwy. 431 S
Boaz, AL 35957
(205)593-3331
Ultimate Parent: Pepsico. SIC: 5812—Eating Places.

★ 55469 ★ Kitchen Collection Inc.
315 S. Mac Clesky St.
Boaz, AL 35957
(205)593-2766
Ultimate Parent: Nacco Industries. SIC: 1521—Single-Family Housing Construction.

★ 55470 ★ Liz Claiborne
214 S. McCleskey St. 1
Boaz, AL 35957
(205)593-1255
Ultimate Parent: Liz Claiborne. SIC: 5651—Family Clothing Stores.

★ 55471 ★ Parker Hannifin
301 Wagner Dr.
Boaz, AL 35957
Ultimate Parent: Parker Hannifin. SIC: 3494—Valves & Pipe Fittings Nec; 3451—Screw Machine Products.

★ 55472 ★ Parker Hannifin Corp. Icd
301 Wagner Dr.
Boaz, AL 35957
Ultimate Parent: Parker Hannifin. SIC: 3451—Screw Machine Products; 3462—Iron & Steel Forgings; 3463—Nonferrous Forgings; 3471—Plating & Polishing.

★ 55473 ★ Piggly Wiggly
306 E. Mill Ave.
Boaz, AL 35957
(205)593-5279
Ultimate Parent: Bruno's. SIC: 5912—Drug Stores & Proprietary Stores.

★ 55474 ★ Pizza Hut
845 Us 431 N
Boaz, AL 35957
(205)593-1070
Ultimate Parent: Pepsico. SIC: 5812—Eating Places.

★ 55475 ★ Ryder Truck Rental
300 N. Main St.
Boaz, AL 35957
(205)582-0143
Ultimate Parent: Ryder System. SIC: 7513—Truck Rental & Leasing Without Drivers.

★ 55476 ★ Taco Bell
225 Us 431 N
Boaz, AL 35957
(205)593-8889
Ultimate Parent: Pepsico. SIC: 5812—Eating Places.

★ 55477 ★ Texaco Service Station
Hwy. 69
Boaz, AL 35957
(205)582-6973
Ultimate Parent: Texaco. SIC: 5531—Automobile & Home Supply Stores.

★ 55478 ★ Tyson Foods
513 Henderson Rd.
Boaz, AL 35957
(205)593-9548
Officer: Bill Bollinger, Plant Manager. Ultimate Parent: Tyson Foods, Inc. SIC: 2015—Poultry Slaughtering & Processing.

Brent

★ 55479 ★ Union Camp Corp.
227 Rural Route 1
Brent, AL 35034
(205)926-4289
Ultimate Parent: Union Camp Corp. SIC: 2411—Logging.

Brewton

★ 55480 ★ Coast to Coast
128 Mildred St.
Brewton, AL 36426
(205)867-7029
Ultimate Parent: Servistar Corp. SIC: 5251—Hardware Stores.

★ 55481 ★ Greyhound Bus Lines
207 Saint Nicholas Ave.
Brewton, AL 36426
(205)867-3824
Ultimate Parent: Greyhound Lines Inc. SIC: 4173—Bus Terminal & Service Facilities.

★ 55482 ★ Kentucky Fried Chicken
K Mart Shopping Ctr.
Brewton, AL 36426
(205)867-6957
Ultimate Parent: Pepsico. SIC: 5812—Eating Places.

★ 55483 ★ Piggly Wiggly
Hwy. 31 S
Brewton, AL 36426
(205)867-7909
Ultimate Parent: Bruno's. SIC: 5411—Grocery Stores.

★ 55484 ★ Taco Bell
1600 Douglas Ave.
Brewton, AL 36426
(205)867-9356
Ultimate Parent: Pepsico. SIC: 5812—Eating Places.

Bridgeport

★ 55485 ★ Jacobs Manufacturing Co.
Edmonds Ave.
Bridgeport, AL 35740
(205)495-2261
Officer: H. G. Jacobs Jr., President. Ultimate Parent: Danaher Corp. SIC: 3321—Gray & Ductile Iron Foundries; 3325—Steel Foundries Nec.

Brilliant

★ 55486 ★ Texaco Station
Rural Route 1
Brilliant, AL 35548
(205)465-9484
Ultimate Parent: Texaco. SIC: 5541—Gasoline Service Stations.

Birmingham

★ 55487 ★ Pitney Bowes Facsimile Systems
4100 Colonnade Pky., Ste. 100
Brimingham, AL 35243
(205)967-7477
Officer: Larry Otto, Manager. Ultimate Parent: Pitney Bowes. SIC: 3663—Radio & T.V. Communications Equipment.

Brundidge

★ 55488 ★ Greyhound Bus Lines
N Main
Brundidge, AL 36010
(205)735-2826
Ultimate Parent: Greyhound Lines Inc. SIC:
4111—Local & Suburban Transit.

Bucks

★ 55489 ★ Hoechst-Celanese
Corp.
Hwy. 43 N. PO Box 64
Bucks, AL 36512
Ultimate Parent: Hoechst Celanese Corp.
SIC: 2819—Industrial Inorganic Chemicals
Nec; 2869—Industrial Organic Chemicals
Nec; 2873—Nitrogenous Fertilizers.

★ 55490 ★ Hoechst Celanese
Corp. Virginia Chemicals Co.
Hwy. 43 North, PO Box 64
Bucks, AL 36512-0064
Ultimate Parent: Hoechst Celanese Corp.
SIC: 2819—Industrial Inorganic Chemicals
Nec; 2869—Industrial Organic Chemicals
Nec.

Burkville

★ 55491 ★ GE Plastics-Burkville
Operation
One Plastics Dr.
Burkville, AL 36752
Ultimate Parent: General Electric. SIC:
2821—Plastics Materials & Resins.

★ 55492 ★ General Electric Co.
1 Plastics Dr.
Burkville, AL 36752
(205)832-5627
Officer: Ken Woodring, Manager. Ultimate
Parent: General Electric. SIC: 3089—
Plastics Products Nec.

Butler

★ 55493 ★ Ace Hardware of
Butler Inc.
231 W. Pushmataha St.
Butler, AL 36904
(205)459-2777
Ultimate Parent: Ace Hardware. SIC:
5211—Lumber & Other Building Materials.

★ 55494 ★ Coast to Coast Auto
230 Riderwood Dr.
Butler, AL 36904
(205)459-2940
Ultimate Parent: Servistar Corp. SIC:
5531—Automobile & Home Supply Stores.

★ 55495 ★ First Alabama Bank
132 S. Mulberry
Butler, AL 36904-2524
(205)459-3051
Location Type: Branch office. Officer:
William A. Evans, President & CEO.
Ultimate Parent: First Alabama
Bancshares. SIC: 6021—National
Commercial Banks.

★ 55496 ★ Piggly Wiggly
W Pushmataha
Butler, AL 36904
(205)459-2797
Ultimate Parent: Bruno's. SIC: 5411—
Grocery Stores.

★ 55497 ★ Vanity Fair Mills Inc.
403 Vanity Fair Ave.
Butler, AL 36904
(205)459-2421
Officer: Doyle King, President. Ultimate
Parent: VF Corp. SIC: 2341—
Women's/Children's Underwear; 2342—
Bras, Girdles & Allied Garments.

Cahaba Heights

★ 55498 ★ First Alabama Bank
3172 Cahaba Heights Plz.
Cahaba Heights, AL 35203
(205)326-7574
Location Type: Branch office. Ultimate
Parent: First Alabama Bancshares. SIC:
6021—National Commercial Banks.

Calera

★ 55499 ★ Vulcan Materials Co.
1614 Hwy. 84
Calera, AL 35040
(205)668-2492
Officer: Ray Greene, Manager. Ultimate
Parent: Vulcan Materials Co. SIC: 3295—
Minerals—Ground or Treated.

Camden

★ 55500 ★ Radio Shack
217 Claiborne St.
Camden, AL 36726
(205)682-9131
Company Type: Division. Ultimate Parent:
Tandy Corp. SIC: 5731—Radio, Television
& Electronics Stores.

Carbon Hill

★ 55501 ★ First National Bank of
Jasper
US 78 & Sycamore St.
Carbon Hill, AL 35549
(205)924-4431
Location Type: Branch office. Officer:
Steven Key, Manager. Ultimate Parent:
Synovus Financial Corp. SIC: 6021—
National Commercial Banks.

Center Point

★ 55502 ★ First Alabama Bank
2020 Ctr. Point Rd.
Center Point, AL 35215-4624
(205)326-7531
Location Type: Branch office. Ultimate
Parent: First Alabama Bancshares. SIC:
6021—National Commercial Banks.

Centre

★ 55503 ★ First Alabama Bank
470 Cedar Bluff Rd.
Centre, AL 35960
(205)927-5521
Location Type: Branch office. Ultimate
Parent: First Alabama Bancshares. SIC:
6021—National Commercial Banks.

★ 55504 ★ First Alabama Bank
110 W. Main St.
Centre, AL 35960-1324
(205)927-5521
Location Type: Branch office. Officer: Tim
S. Williams, President & CEO. Ultimate
Parent: First Alabama Bancshares. SIC:
6021—National Commercial Banks.

★ 55505 ★ Piggly Wiggly
W Main Shopping Ctr.
Centre, AL 35960
(205)927-5661
Ultimate Parent: Bruno's. SIC: 5421—Meat
& Fish Markets.

Chapman

★ 55506 ★ Union Camp Corp.
U.S. Hwy. 31
Chapman, AL 36015
Ultimate Parent: Union Camp Corp. SIC:
2421—Sawmills & Planing Mills—General;
2436—Softwood Veneer & Plywood; 2411—
Logging.

★ 55507 ★ Union Camp Corp.
PO Box 38
Chapman, AL 36015
(205)376-2241
Officer: N. Floyd McGowin Jr., President.
Ultimate Parent: Union Camp Corp. SIC:
2411—Logging; 2421—Sawmills & Planing
Mills—General; 2436—Softwood Veneer &
Plywood.

★ 55508 ★ Union Camp Corp.
Chapman, AL 36015
(205)376-2241
Ultimate Parent: Union Camp Corp. SIC:
5211—Lumber & Other Building Materials.

Chatom

★ 55509 ★ Piggly Wiggly
Chatom, AL 36518
(205)847-2470
Ultimate Parent: Bruno's. SIC: 5421—Meat
& Fish Markets.

★ 55510 ★ Rockland React-Rite
Inc.
Hwy. 17 S.
Chatom, AL 36518
Ultimate Parent: Interface Inc. SIC: 2869—
Industrial Organic Chemicals Nec.

Chickasaw

★ 55511 ★ Coastal Mobile
Refining Co.
200 Viaduct Rd.
Chickasaw, AL 36611-0526
Ultimate Parent: Coastal Corp. SIC:
2911—Petroleum Refining.

★ 55512 ★ Pfizer Specialty
Minerals Inc.
Paper Mill Rd.
Chickasaw, AL 36611
Ultimate Parent: Pfizer. SIC: 2819—
Industrial Inorganic Chemicals Nec.

★ 55513 ★ Union Carbide Corp.
Molecular Sieve Plant
Linde Dr.
Chickasaw, AL 36611
Ultimate Parent: Union Carbide Corp. SIC:
2819—Industrial Inorganic Chemicals Nec.

Childersburg

★ 55514 ★ Kentucky Fried
Chicken
Hwy. 280
Childersburg, AL 35044
(205)378-5121
Ultimate Parent: Pepsico. SIC: 5812—
Eating Places.

Chunchula

★ 55515 ★ Unocal Corp.
12303 Roberts Rd.
Chunchula, AL 36521
(205)675-6180
Officer: Tim Noack, Manager. Ultimate
Parent: Unocal Corp.

Citronelle

★ 55516 ★ First Alabama Bank
7850 State St.
Citronelle, AL 36522-2427
(205)866-5516
Location Type: Branch office. Ultimate
Parent: First Alabama Bancshares. SIC:
6021—National Commercial Banks.

★ 55517 ★ Piggly Wiggly
Us Hwy. 45
Citronelle, AL 36522
(205)866-5705
Ultimate Parent: Bruno's. SIC: 5411—
Grocery Stores.

Clanton

★ 55518 ★ Ace Hardware &
Building Sup
202 6th St. S
Clanton, AL 35045
(205)755-5500
Ultimate Parent: Ace Hardware. SIC:
5251—Hardware Stores.

★ 55519 ★ First Alabama Bank
102 7th St. S
Clanton, AL 35045
(205)755-9660
Ultimate Parent: First Alabama
Bancshares.

★ 55520 ★ First Alabama Bank
101 7th St.
Clanton, AL 35045-3431
(205)785-9660
Location Type: Branch office. Ultimate
Parent: First Alabama Bancshares. SIC:
6021—National Commercial Banks.

★ 55521 ★ Greyhound Bus Lines
500 7th St. N
Clanton, AL 35045
(205)755-2310
Ultimate Parent: Greyhound Lines Inc. SIC:
4111—Local & Suburban Transit.

Clayton

★ 55522 ★ Louisiana Pacific
Corp.
White Oak Station
Clayton, AL 36016
(205)775-3201
Ultimate Parent: Louisiana-Pacific. SIC:
2221—Broadwoven Fabric Mills—Manmade.

★ 55523 ★ Louisiana-Pacific
Corp. Eufaula Mdf Mill
White Oak Station Rd.
Clayton, AL 36016
Ultimate Parent: Louisiana-Pacific. SIC:
2400—Lumber & Wood Products.

★ 55524 ★ Louisiana-Pacific Mdf
White Oak Station Rd.
Clayton, AL 36016
Ultimate Parent: Louisiana-Pacific. SIC:
2400—Lumber & Wood Products.

Columbia

★ 55525 ★ Russell Corp.
Hwy. 95 N
Columbia, AL 36319
(205)696-4434
Ultimate Parent: Russell. SIC: 2322—
Men's/Boys' Underwear & Nightwear;
2399—Fabricated Textile Products Nec.

Columbiana

★ 55526 ★ First Alabama Bank
Davis Plz. Shopping Ctr.
College St.
Columbiana, AL 35051
(205)669-4123
Location Type: Branch office. Ultimate
Parent: First Alabama Bancshares. SIC:
6021—National Commercial Banks.

Coosa Pines

★ 55527 ★ US Pulp & Newsprint
Alabama Rte. 235
Coosa Pines, AL 35044-0555
Ultimate Parent: Kimberly-Clark. SIC:
2611—Pulp Mills; 2621—Paper Mills.

Cordova

★ 55528 ★ Electro Mechanical
Devices Inc.
RR 2 Box 138
Cordova, AL 35550-9696
(205)648-9076
Officer: James Roberts. Ultimate Parent:
Ametek Inc. SIC: 3599—Industrial
Machinery Nec; 3625—Relays & Industrial
Controls; 7629—Electrical Repair Shops
Nec.

★ 55529 ★ First Alabama Bank
106 Mill St.
Cordova, AL 35550-1490
(205)483-9228
Location Type: Branch office. Ultimate
Parent: First Alabama Bancshares. SIC:
6021—National Commercial Banks.

★ 55530 ★ First National Bank of
Jasper
125 Main St.
Cordova, AL 35550
(205)483-9231
Location Type: Branch office. Officer:
Phillip H. Stover, Manager. Ultimate
Parent: Synovus Financial Corp. SIC:
6021—National Commercial Banks.

Cottonton

★ 55531 ★ Mead Coated Board
Inc.
Alabama Hwy. 165 S
Cottonton, AL 36868-0940
Ultimate Parent: Mead. SIC: 2631—
Paperboard Mills.

Courtland

★ 55532 ★ **Champion International Corp.**
316 Tennessee
Courtland, AL 35618
(205)637-2781
Ultimate Parent: Champion International.
SIC: 0811—Timber Tracts.

★ 55533 ★ **Champion International Corp. Courtland Mill**
County Line Rd.
Courtland, AL 35618
Ultimate Parent: Champion International.
SIC: 2621—Paper Mills.

★ 55534 ★ **Champion International Corp. Courtland Mill**
PO Box 189
Courtland, AL 35618
Ultimate Parent: Champion International.
SIC: 2621—Paper Mills.

★ 55535 ★ **Champion International Courtland Mill**
Rd. 29
Courtland, AL 35618
Ultimate Parent: Champion International.
SIC: 2621—Paper Mills.

★ 55536 ★ **Piggly Wiggly**
Spring Creek Rd.
Courtland, AL 35618
(205)637-2056
Ultimate Parent: Bruno's. **SIC:** 5411—Grocery Stores.

Cullman

★ 55537 ★ **BFI Waste Systems**
16 Patton St.
Cullman, AL 35057-0226
(205)734-6230
Ultimate Parent: Browning-Ferris Industries. **SIC:** 4953—Refuse Systems.

★ 55538 ★ **Bowater Inc.**
South Div.
411 Schwaiger Rd.
Cullman, AL 35055-0333
(205)739-0530
Ultimate Parent: Bowater. **SIC:** 2611—Pulp Mills; 0811—Timber Tracts; 6552—Subdividers & Developers Nec.

★ 55539 ★ **Champion International Corp.**
410 1st Ave. SE
Cullman, AL 35055
(205)739-6041
Ultimate Parent: Champion International.
SIC: 2411—Logging.

★ 55540 ★ **Coast to Coast**
1603 3rd St. SE
Cullman, AL 35055
(205)739-6978
Ultimate Parent: Servistar Corp. **SIC:** 4841—Cable & Other Pay Television Services.

★ 55541 ★ **First Alabama Bank**
100 PO Box
Cullman, AL 35055
(205)734-1040
Ultimate Parent: First Alabama Bancshares. **SIC:** 6099—Functions Related to Deposit Banking.

★ 55542 ★ **First Alabama Bank**
1553 3rd St. NE
Cullman, AL 35055
(205)737-8842
Ultimate Parent: First Alabama Bancshares. **SIC:** 6022—State Commercial Banks.

★ 55543 ★ **First Alabama Bank**
711 2nd Ave. SW
Cullman, AL 35055-4291
(205)734-1040
Location Type: Branch office. **Officer:** Larry O. Holt, President & CEO. **Ultimate Parent:** First Alabama Bancshares. **SIC:** 6021—National Commercial Banks.

★ 55544 ★ **First Federal S & L**
1616 2nd Ave. SW
Cullman, AL 35055-5313
(205)737-9552
Ultimate Parent: Bancorp Hawaii. **SIC:** 6021—National Commercial Banks.

★ 55545 ★ **Kentucky Fried Chicken**
S Cullman Shopping Ctr.
Cullman, AL 35055
(205)734-6958
Ultimate Parent: Pepsico. **SIC:** 5812—Eating Places.

★ 55546 ★ **Nicholson File**
2125 Second Ave. SW
Cullman, AL 35055
Ultimate Parent: Cooper Industries. **SIC:** 3423—Hand & Edge Tools Nec.

★ 55547 ★ **Piggly Wiggly**
106 2nd Ave. NE
Cullman, AL 35055
(205)734-4731
Ultimate Parent: Bruno's. **SIC:** 5411—Grocery Stores.

★ 55548 ★ **Pizza Hut**
1310 2nd Ave. NW
Cullman, AL 35055
(205)734-1010
Ultimate Parent: Pepsico. **SIC:** 5812—Eating Places.

★ 55549 ★ **Radio Shack**
1652 Town Sq.
Cullman, AL 35055
(205)739-0768
Company Type: Division. **Ultimate Parent:** Tandy Corp. **SIC:** 5731—Radio, Television & Electronics Stores.

★ 55550 ★ **Ryder Truck Rental**
2147 3rd Ave. SE
Cullman, AL 35055
(205)734-6636
Ultimate Parent: Ryder System. **SIC:** 7513—Truck Rental & Leasing Without Drivers.

★ 55551 ★ **Ryder Truck Rental**
504 2nd Ave. NW
Cullman, AL 35055
(205)739-5194
Ultimate Parent: Ryder System. **SIC:** 7359—Equipment Rental & Leasing Nec.

★ 55552 ★ **Taco Bell**
1669 Cherokee Ave. SW
Cullman, AL 35055
(205)739-1889
Ultimate Parent: Pepsico. **SIC:** 5812—Eating Places.

★ 55553 ★ **Tyson Feed Mill**
2011 Old Hanceville Hwy.
Cullman, AL 35056-1144
Ultimate Parent: Tyson Foods, Inc. **SIC:** 2048—Prepared Feeds Nec.

★ 55554 ★ **Tyson Foods Inc.**
2460 3rd Ave. SE
Cullman, AL 35055
(205)734-7100
Officer: Davis Lee, Manager. **Ultimate Parent:** Tyson Foods, Inc. **SIC:** 2048—Prepared Feeds Nec.

★ 55555 ★ **Tyson Foods Inc. Tyson Feed Mill**
2011 Old Hanceville Hwy.
Cullman, AL 35056-1144
Ultimate Parent: Tyson Foods, Inc. **SIC:** 2048—Prepared Feeds Nec.

★ 55556 ★ **Wal Mart Discount City**
1604 Town Sq.
Cullman, AL 35055
(205)734-8141
Ultimate Parent: Wal-Mart Stores, Inc. **SIC:** 5311—Department Stores.

★ 55557 ★ **Wal Mart Distribution Center**
2200 7th Ave. SW
Cullman, AL 35055
(205)739-0763
Ultimate Parent: Wal-Mart Stores, Inc. **SIC:** 5311—Department Stores.

Dadeville

★ 55558 ★ **Piggly Wiggly**
104 E. Lafayette St.
Dadeville, AL 36853
(205)825-6233
Ultimate Parent: Bruno's. **SIC:** 5411—Grocery Stores.

★ 55559 ★ **Piggly Wiggly**
513 N. Spring St.
Dadeville, AL 36853
Ultimate Parent: Bruno's. **SIC:** 5421—Meat & Fish Markets.

★ 55560 ★ **Russell Corp.**
Hwy. 280
Dadeville, AL 36853
(205)825-9615
Officer: Tony Johnson, Manager. **Ultimate Parent:** Russell. **SIC:** 2322—Men's/Boys' Underwear & Nightwear; 2399—Fabricated Textile Products Nec.

Daleville

★ 55561 ★ **Coca Cola Bottling Co.**
Newton Hwy.
Daleville, AL 36322
(205)598-4804
Ultimate Parent: Coca-Cola Enterprises. **SIC:** 4225—General Warehousing & Storage.

★ 55562 ★ **Kentucky Fried Chicken**
Hwy. 145
Daleville, AL 36322
(205)598-2811
Ultimate Parent: Pepsico. **SIC:** 5812—Eating Places.

★ 55563 ★ **Piggly Wiggly**
Hwy. 134
Daleville, AL 36322
(205)598-2311
Ultimate Parent: Bruno's. **SIC:** 5812—Eating Places.

Daphne

★ 55564 ★ **Citgo Quick Mart**
2504 Us Hwy. 98
Daphne, AL 36526
(205)621-9514
Ultimate Parent: Citgo Petroleum. **SIC:** 5411—Grocery Stores.

★ 55565 ★ **First Alabama Bank**
28509 US Hwy. 98
Daphne, AL 36526
(205)626-6718
Location Type: Branch office. **Ultimate Parent:** First Alabama Bancshares. **SIC:** 6021—National Commercial Banks.

★ 55566 ★ **Gayfers Department Str**
Jubilee Plz.
Daphne, AL 36526
(205)626-6031
Ultimate Parent: Mercantile Stores.

★ 55567 ★ **Miles**
Cutter Biological Division
5500 Bayline Dr.
Daphne, AL 36526
(205)626-5326
Ultimate Parent: Miles. **SIC:** 2834—Pharmaceutical Preparations; 8099—Health & Allied Services Nec.

★ 55568 ★ **Pizza Hut**
28751 Hwy. 98
Daphne, AL 36526
(205)626-6063
Ultimate Parent: Pepsico. **SIC:** 5812—Eating Places.

★ 55569 ★ **Ryder Truck Rental**
Hwy. 98
Daphne, AL 36526
(205)626-5855
Ultimate Parent: Ryder System.

Decatur

★ 55570 ★ **Air Products & Chemicals**
Rte. 1 Box 59-A
Decatur, AL 35601-9730
(205)353-6310
Location Type: Branch office. **Officer:** Mark Watkins. **Ultimate Parent:** Air Products & Chemicals, Inc. **SIC:** 2813—Industrial Gases.

★ 55571 ★ **Air Products & Chemicals Inc.**
Ipsco St. NW
Decatur, AL 35601
(205)353-6310
Officer: Mark Watkins, Manager. **Ultimate Parent:** Air Products & Chemicals, Inc. **SIC:** 2813—Industrial Gases.

★ 55572 ★ **Air Products & Chemicals Inc.**
Ipsco Street, NW
Decatur, AL 35602
Ultimate Parent: Air Products & Chemicals, Inc. **SIC:** 2813—Industrial Gases.

★ 55573 ★ **American General Finance**
1602 Beltline Rd. SE
Decatur, AL 35601-1660
(205)353-1660
Location Type: Branch office. **Ultimate Parent:** American General Corp. **SIC:** 6141—Personal Credit Institutions; 6162—Mortgage Bankers & Correspondents.

★ 55574 ★ **American General Finance Inc.**
1602 Beltline Rd. SE
Decatur, AL 35601-1660
(205)353-1660
Location Type: Branch office. **Ultimate Parent:** American General Corp. **SIC:** 6141—Personal Credit Institutions; 6162—Mortgage Bankers & Correspondents.

★ 55575 ★ **Atlas Cylinder**
1021 Brook St.
Decatur, AL 35602
Ultimate Parent: Parker Hannifin. **SIC:** 3593—Fluid Power Cylinders & Actuators.

★ 55576 ★ **Business Systems**
517 Bradley St. SW
Decatur, AL 35601-6379
(205)350-0892
Ultimate Parent: Avery Dennison Corp. **SIC:** 5049—Professional Equipment Nec.

★ 55577 ★ **Decatur Aluminum Co.**
Tuscumbia Hwy., No. 20
Decatur, AL 35601
(205)353-1550
Company Type: Subsidiary. **Officer:** H. Vest, Vice President. **Ultimate Parent:** Banta Corp. **SIC:** 3353—Aluminum Sheet, Plate & Foil; 3355—Aluminum Rolling & Drawing Nec. **Employee Count:** 175.

★ 55578 ★ **First Alabama Bank**
1833 Beltline Hwy. SW
Decatur, AL 35601-5506
(205)355-1511
Location Type: Branch office. **Ultimate Parent:** First Alabama Bancshares. **SIC:** 6021—National Commercial Banks.

★ 55579 ★ **First Alabama Bank**
1940 6th Ave.
Gateway Shopping Ctr.
Decatur, AL 35601
(205)355-1511
Location Type: Branch office. **Ultimate Parent:** First Alabama Bancshares. **SIC:** 6021—National Commercial Banks.

★ 55580 ★ **First Alabama Bank**
108 4th Ave. NE
Decatur, AL 35602
(205)355-1511
Location Type: Branch office. **Ultimate Parent:** First Alabama Bancshares. **SIC:** 6021—National Commercial Banks.

★ 55581 ★ **First American Bank**
237 Johnston St. SE
Decatur, AL 35601-2515
(205)350-6111
Officer: Dan M. David, President. **Ultimate Parent:** First American Bank. **SIC:** 6022—State Commercial Banks. **Employee Count:** 75.

★ 55582 ★ **Fruehauf Trailer Corp.**
Tuscumbia Hwy., No. 20
Decatur, AL 35601
(205)353-1550
Company Type: Affiliate. **Location Type:** Plant. **Officer:** Ed Kenyon, Plant Manager. **Ultimate Parent:** Terex Corp. **SIC:** 3715—Truck Trailers. **Employee Count:** 310.

★ 55583 ★ Fruehauf Trailer Corp.
PO Box 608
Decatur, AL 35602-0608
(205)353-1550
Location Type: Branch office. **Officer:** J.
M. Moore. **Ultimate Parent:** Terex Corp.
SIC: 3354—Aluminum Extruded Products.

★ 55584 ★ Fruehauf Trailer Corp.
Tuscumbia Hwy. 20 W.
Decatur, AL 35601
(205)353-1550
Company Type: Affiliate. **Location Type:**
Plant. **Officer:** Ed Kenyon, Plant Manager.
Ultimate Parent: Terex Corp. **SIC:** 3715—
Truck Trailers. **Employee Count:** 310.

★ 55585 ★ GE
Appliances Manufacturing Division
2328 Point Mallard Dr.
Decatur, AL 35601
(205)552-1305
Officer: Tom Boehme, Manager. **Ultimate
Parent:** General Electric. **SIC:** 3632—
Household Refrigerators & Freezers.

★ 55586 ★ General Electric Co.
2328 Eighth Street, SE
Decatur, AL 35601
Ultimate Parent: General Electric. **SIC:**
3632—Household Refrigerators & Freezers.

★ 55587 ★ Giant Foods of
Decatur
115 6th Ave. NE
Decatur, AL 35601
(205)355-2952
Ultimate Parent: Giant Food. **SIC:** 5411—
Grocery Stores.

★ 55588 ★ Goodyear Tire &
Rubber Co.
500 19th Ave. SE
Decatur, AL 35601
Ultimate Parent: Goodyear Tire & Rubber.
SIC: 2296—Tire Cord & Fabrics.

★ 55589 ★ Goodyear Tire &
Rubber Co.
500 - 19th Ave. SE
Decatur, AL 35601
Ultimate Parent: Goodyear Tire & Rubber.
SIC: 2296—Tire Cord & Fabrics.

★ 55590 ★ Goodyear Tire &
Rubber Co.
500 - 19th Avenue, SE
Decatur, AL 35601
Ultimate Parent: Goodyear Tire & Rubber.
SIC: 2296—Tire Cord & Fabrics.

★ 55591 ★ Greyhound Bus Lines
215 Grant St. SE
Decatur, AL 35601
(205)353-5554
Ultimate Parent: Greyhound Lines Inc. **SIC:**
4131—Intercity & Rural Bus Transportation.

★ 55592 ★ Hispan Corp.
3300 Mallard Fox Dr. NW
Decatur, AL 35609
Ultimate Parent: Hercules. **SIC:** 2824—
Organic Fibers—Noncellulosic.

★ 55593 ★ Jim Dandy Co. Inc.
1200 Market St. SE
Decatur, AL 35601
Ultimate Parent: Pet. **SIC:** 2000—Food &
Kindred Products; 2047—Dog & Cat Food.

★ 55594 ★ Kroger Co
Beltline Rd. SW
Decatur, AL 35601
(205)350-9770
Ultimate Parent: Kroger. **SIC:** 5411—
Grocery Stores.

★ 55595 ★ Kroger Financial
Cetner
1101 Beltline Rd. SE
Decatur, AL 35601
(205)353-2220
Ultimate Parent: Kroger. **SIC:** 6411—
Insurance Agents, Brokers & Service.

★ 55596 ★ Lerner Shop
Beltline
Decatur, AL 35601
(205)350-6592
Ultimate Parent: Limited. **SIC:** 5621—
Women's Clothing Stores.

★ 55597 ★ Monsanto Co.
PO Box 2204
Decatur, AL 35609-2204
(205)552-2011
Officer: Peter Clarke. **Ultimate Parent:**
Monsanto. **SIC:** 2819—Industrial Inorganic
Chemicals Nec.

★ 55598 ★ Monsanto Co.
Courtland Hwy.
Decatur, AL 35601
Ultimate Parent: Monsanto. **SIC:** 2824—
Organic Fibers—Noncellulosic; 2869—
Industrial Organic Chemicals Nec.

★ 55599 ★ Monsanto Co.
Chemical Group
Courtland Hwy.
Decatur, AL 35609-2204
Company Type: Division. **Ultimate Parent:**
Monsanto. **SIC:** 2824—Organic Fibers—
Noncellulosic; 2869—Industrial Organic
Chemicals Nec.

★ 55600 ★ Morton International
Inc.
PO Box 2238
Decatur, AL 35609-2238
(205)355-5440
Company Type: Branch. **Officer:** Gerald
W. Kelly. **Ultimate Parent:** Morton
International. **SIC:** 2851—Paints & Allied
Products; 3479—Metal Coating & Allied
Services.

★ 55601 ★ Pepsi-Cola Bottling
Co.
Ipsco Rd.
Decatur, AL 35601
(205)353-8334
Officer: Rodger Shabel, Manager. **Ultimate
Parent:** Pepsico. **SIC:** 2086—Bottled &
Canned Soft Drinks.

★ 55602 ★ Pizza Hut
1805 Beltline Rd. SW
Decatur, AL 35601
(205)350-4015
Ultimate Parent: Pepsico. **SIC:** 5812—
Eating Places.

★ 55603 ★ Pizza Hut
1318 6th Ave.
Decatur, AL 35601
(205)355-9010
Ultimate Parent: Pepsico. **SIC:** 5812—
Eating Places.

★ 55604 ★ Spartan Express Inc.
2538 Central Pky. SW
Decatur, AL 35601
(205)355-4477
Ultimate Parent: Roadway Services. **SIC:**
4212—Local Trucking Without Storage.

★ 55605 ★ Taco Bell
1807 Beltline Rd. SW
Decatur, AL 35601
(205)350-0147
Ultimate Parent: Pepsico. **SIC:** 5812—
Eating Places.

★ 55606 ★ Taco Bell
2116 6th Ave. SE
Decatur, AL 35601
(205)350-1128
Ultimate Parent: Pepsico. **SIC:** 5812—
Eating Places.

★ 55607 ★ 3M Co.
State Dock Rd.
Decatur, AL 35601
(205)552-6010
Company Type: Branch. **Officer:** Jim King.
Ultimate Parent: Minnesota Mining & Mfg.
SIC: 2899—Chemical Preparations Nec.

★ 55608 ★ Trailways Bus System
215 Grant St. SE
Decatur, AL 35601
(205)353-2611
Ultimate Parent: Greyhound Lines Inc.

★ 55609 ★ Union Camp Corp.
Ipsco St.
Decatur, AL 35601
Ultimate Parent: Union Camp Corp. **SIC:**
2653—Corrugated & Solid Fiber Boxes.

★ 55610 ★ Union Camp Corp.
Decatur
Decatur, AL 35601
(205)355-7610
Ultimate Parent: Union Camp Corp. **SIC:**
5113—Industrial & Personal Service Paper.

★ 55611 ★ Vickers
250 Courtland Rd.
Decatur, AL 35603
(205)353-2001
Officer: Rick Smith, Manager. **Ultimate
Parent:** Trinova Corp. **SIC:** 3443—
Fabricated Plate Work—Boiler Shops;
3593—Fluid Power Cylinders & Actuators.

★ 55612 ★ Wal Mart Discount
City
1682 Beltline Rd. SW
Decatur, AL 35601
(205)355-7775
Ultimate Parent: Wal-Mart Stores, Inc. **SIC:**
5311—Department Stores.

Demopolis

★ 55613 ★ Borden Inc.
Chemical
Lock & Dam Rd.
Demopolis, AL 36732
Company Type: Division. **Ultimate Parent:**
Borden, Inc. **SIC:** 2821—Plastics Materials
& Resins; 2869—Industrial Organic
Chemicals Nec.

★ 55614 ★ Borden Packaging &
Industrial Products
Lock & Dam Rd.
Demopolis, AL 36732
(205)289-0840
Officer: Kim B. Townsend, Manager.
Ultimate Parent: Borden, Inc. **SIC:** 2821—
Plastics Materials & Resins; 2869—
Industrial Organic Chemicals Nec.

★ 55615 ★ First Alabama Bank
501 S. Cedar Ave.
Demopolis, AL 36732-2235
(205)289-4040
Location Type: Branch office. **Ultimate
Parent:** First Alabama Bancshares. **SIC:**
6021—National Commercial Banks.

★ 55616 ★ Lafarge Corp.
Arcola Rd.
Demopolis, AL 36732
Ultimate Parent: Lafarge. **SIC:** 3241—
Cement—Hydraulic.

★ 55617 ★ Mary Kay Cosmetics
1725 Mauvilla Dr.
Demopolis, AL 36732
(205)289-2515
Ultimate Parent: Mary Kay Cosmetics. **SIC:**
5999—Miscellaneous Retail Stores Nec.

★ 55618 ★ Systech Corp.
Arcola Rd.
Demopolis, AL 36732
Ultimate Parent: Lafarge. **SIC:** 3241—
Cement—Hydraulic.

★ 55619 ★ Systech
Environmental Corp.
Arcola Rd.
Demopolis, AL 36732
Ultimate Parent: Lafarge. **SIC:** 3241—
Cement—Hydraulic.

★ 55620 ★ Wal Mart
1614 Hwy. 80 E
Demopolis, AL 36732
(205)289-3212
Ultimate Parent: Wal-Mart Stores, Inc. **SIC:**
5311—Department Stores.

Dolomite

★ 55621 ★ Texaco Express Lube
1607 Valley Rd.
Dolomite, AL 35061
(205)744-4141
Ultimate Parent: Texaco.

Dora

★ 55622 ★ First National Bank of
Jasper
US 78 & Dora Rd.
Dora, AL 35062
(205)648-3287
Location Type: Branch office. **Officer:**
Betty Sargent, Vice President. **Ultimate**

Parent: Synovus Financial Corp. **SIC:**
6021—National Commercial Banks.

Dothan

★ 55623 ★ Ace Hardware
2541 SW Ross Clark Cir.
Dothan, AL 36301
(205)792-4121
Ultimate Parent: Ace Hardware. **SIC:**
5251—Hardware Stores.

★ 55624 ★ American Family Life
Assurance
3110 Wesley Way
Dothan, AL 36301
(205)792-4800
Ultimate Parent: American Family Life
Assurance Co. **SIC:** 6411—Insurance
Agents, Brokers & Service.

★ 55625 ★ AmSouth Bank NA
400 W. Main St.
Dothan, AL 36301
(205)793-3000
Company Type: Branch. **Officer:** James E.
Conway, President. **Ultimate Parent:**
AmSouth Bancorp. **SIC:** 6021—National
Commercial Banks.

★ 55626 ★ Borden Inc.
Dairy Division
100 W. Powell Rd.
Dothan, AL 36301
Company Type: Division. **Ultimate Parent:**
Borden, Inc. **SIC:** 2024—Ice Cream &
Frozen Desserts.

★ 55627 ★ Borden Inc. Dairy
604 N. Oates St.
Dothan, AL 36301
Ultimate Parent: Borden, Inc. **SIC:** 2024—
Ice Cream & Frozen Desserts.

★ 55628 ★ Borden Inc. Diary
100 West Powell St.
Dothan, AL 36303
Ultimate Parent: Borden, Inc. **SIC:** 2024—
Ice Cream & Frozen Desserts.

★ 55629 ★ Borden Inc.
Refrigerated Products
604 N. Oates St.
Dothan, AL 36302
Ultimate Parent: Borden, Inc. **SIC:** 2024—
Ice Cream & Frozen Desserts.

★ 55630 ★ Circus World
3625 NW Ross Clark Cir.
Dothan, AL 36303
(205)792-4526
Ultimate Parent: Melville. **SIC:** 5945—
Hobby, Toy & Game Shops.

★ 55631 ★ City National Bank
400 W. Main St.
Dothan, AL 36301
(205)793-3000
Ultimate Parent: City National Corp. **SIC:**
6022—State Commercial Banks.

★ 55632 ★ City National Bank of
Dotha
1900 Montgomery Hwy.
Dothan, AL 36303
(205)794-7501
Ultimate Parent: City National Corp. **SIC:**
6022—State Commercial Banks.

★ 55633 ★ City National Bank of
Dotha
1625 Ashford Hwy.
Dothan, AL 36301
(205)794-7501
Ultimate Parent: City National Corp. **SIC:**
6022—State Commercial Banks.

★ 55634 ★ Coast to Coast
Coatings
Hwy. 84 E
Dothan, AL 36301
(205)793-9238
Ultimate Parent: Servistar Corp. **SIC:**
3479—Metal Coating & Allied Services.

★ 55635 ★ Coca Cola Bottling
Co.
308 N. Saint Andrews St.
Dothan, AL 36303
(205)792-3116
Ultimate Parent: Coca-Cola Enterprises.
SIC: 2086—Bottled & Canned Soft Drinks;
5149—Groceries & Related Products Nec.

★ 55636 ★ **First Alabama Bank**
1144 SE Ross Clark Cir.
Dothan, AL 36301
(205)677-2561
Ultimate Parent: First Alabama
Bancshares. **SIC:** 6022—State Commercial
Banks.

★ 55637 ★ **First Alabama Bank**
Porter Square Shopping Ctr.
826 W. Main St.
Dothan, AL 36301-1448
(205)677-2500
Location Type: Branch office. **Officer:**
Boyd F. Horn Jr., President & CEO.
Ultimate Parent: First Alabama
Bancshares. **SIC:** 6021—National
Commercial Banks.

★ 55638 ★ **First Alabama Bank**
822 S. Oates St.
Dothan, AL 36301-3544
(205)677-2520
Location Type: Branch office. **Ultimate
Parent:** First Alabama Bancshares. **SIC:**
6021—National Commercial Banks.

★ 55639 ★ **First Alabama Bank**
1824 Montgomery Hwy.
Dothan, AL 36303-3203
(205)677-2540
Location Type: Branch office. **Ultimate
Parent:** First Alabama Bancshares. **SIC:**
6021—National Commercial Banks.

★ 55640 ★ **First Alabama Bank**
1144 Ross Clark Cir. SE
Dothan, AL 36301-5748
(205)677-2560
Location Type: Branch office. **Ultimate
Parent:** First Alabama Bancshares. **SIC:**
6021—National Commercial Banks.

★ 55641 ★ **First Alabama Bank**
4201 Ross Clark Cir. NW
Dothan, AL 36303-5837
(205)677-2580
Location Type: Branch office. **Ultimate
Parent:** First Alabama Bancshares. **SIC:**
6021—National Commercial Banks.

★ 55642 ★ **First Alabama Bank**
3201 Ross Clark Cir. NW
Dothan, AL 36303-3039
(205)677-2400
Location Type: Branch office. **Ultimate
Parent:** First Alabama Bancshares. **SIC:**
6021—National Commercial Banks.

★ 55643 ★ **First Alabama Bank of
Dotha**
822 S. Oates St.
Dothan, AL 36301
(205)677-2520
Ultimate Parent: First Alabama
Bancshares. **SIC:** 6022—State Commercial
Banks.

★ 55644 ★ **First Alabama Bank of
Dotha**
826 W. Main St.
Dothan, AL 36301
(205)677-2500
Ultimate Parent: First Alabama
Bancshares. **SIC:** 6022—State Commercial
Banks.

★ 55645 ★ **First Alabama Bank of
Dotha**
1824 Montgomery Hwy.
Dothan, AL 36303
(205)677-2540
Ultimate Parent: First Alabama
Bancshares. **SIC:** 6022—State Commercial
Banks.

★ 55646 ★ **First Alabama Bank of
Dotha**
3201 NW Ross Clark Cir.
Dothan, AL 36303
(205)677-2400
Ultimate Parent: First Alabama
Bancshares. **SIC:** 6022—State Commercial
Banks.

★ 55647 ★ **First Alabama Bank
Dothan**
620 Hodgesville Rd.
Dothan, AL 36301
(205)794-0411
Ultimate Parent: First Alabama
Bancshares. **SIC:** 6022—State Commercial
Banks.

★ 55648 ★ **Footaction**
3625 NW Ross Clark Cir.
Dothan, AL 36303
(205)794-8265
Ultimate Parent: Melville. **SIC:** 5661—Shoe
Stores.

★ 55649 ★ **Gayfers**
3625 NW Ross Clark Cir.
Dothan, AL 36303
(205)794-3300
Ultimate Parent: Mercantile Stores. **SIC:**
5651—Family Clothing Stores.

★ 55650 ★ **General Electric Co.**
737 Hodgesville Rd.
Dothan, AL 36301
(205)671-3475
Officer: Al Veres, Manager. **Ultimate
Parent:** General Electric. **SIC:** 3621—
Motors & Generators.

★ 55651 ★ **Golden Peanut**
805 E. Newton St.
Dothan, AL 36303-4759
(205)712-1263
Officer: Roy J. Roberts. **Ultimate Parent:**
Archer Daniels Midland Co. **SIC:** 5159—
Farm-Product Raw Materials Nec; 0139—
Field Crops Except Cash Grains Nec;
2076—Vegetable Oil Mills Nec.

★ 55652 ★ **Greyhound Bus Lines**
213 S. Foster St.
Dothan, AL 36301
(205)792-1191
Ultimate Parent: Greyhound Lines Inc. **SIC:**
4111—Local & Suburban Transit.

★ 55653 ★ **Hertz Rent-A-Car**
Flight Line Dr.
Dothan, AL 36303
(205)983-4514
Ultimate Parent: Hertz. **SIC:** 7514—
Passenger Car Rental.

★ 55654 ★ **Kentucky Fried
Chicken**
103 NE Ross Clark Cir.
Dothan, AL 36303
(205)792-6474
Ultimate Parent: Pepsico. **SIC:** 5812—
Eating Places.

★ 55655 ★ **Lerner Shop**
3625 NW Ross Clark Cir.
Dothan, AL 36303
(205)794-3626
Ultimate Parent: Limited. **SIC:** 5651—
Family Clothing Stores.

★ 55656 ★ **Meadow Gold Dairy**
604 N. Oates St.
Dothan, AL 36303
(205)792-1181
Officer: Jack Spangler, Manager. **Ultimate
Parent:** Borden, Inc. **SIC:** 2024—Ice Cream
& Frozen Desserts.

★ 55657 ★ **Pappagallo**
109 Westgate Pky.
Dothan, AL 36303
(205)793-4335
Ultimate Parent: United States Shoe. **SIC:**
5621—Women's Clothing Stores; 5651—
Family Clothing Stores.

★ 55658 ★ **Petite Sophisticate**
3625 NW Ross Clark Cir.
Dothan, AL 36303
(205)794-6616
Ultimate Parent: United States Shoe. **SIC:**
5651—Family Clothing Stores.

★ 55659 ★ **Piggly Wiggly**
3108 NW Ross Clark Cir.
Dothan, AL 36303
(205)794-8602
Ultimate Parent: Bruno's. **SIC:** 5411—
Grocery Stores; 5992—Florists.

★ 55660 ★ **Piggly Wiggly**
925 Honeysuckle Rd.
Dothan, AL 36301
(205)793-6526
Ultimate Parent: Bruno's. **SIC:** 5411—
Grocery Stores.

★ 55661 ★ **Pizza Hut**
1912 SE Ross Clark Cir.
Dothan, AL 36301
(205)792-9884
Ultimate Parent: Pepsico. **SIC:** 5812—
Eating Places.

★ 55662 ★ **Pizza Hut**
3455 NW Ross Clark Cir.
Dothan, AL 36303
(205)794-4373
Ultimate Parent: Pepsico. **SIC:** 5812—
Eating Places.

★ 55663 ★ **Radio Shack**
Southview Shopping Ctr.
Dothan, AL 36301
(205)792-6682
Company Type: Division. **Ultimate Parent:**
Tandy Corp. **SIC:** 5065—Electronic Parts &
Equipment Nec.

★ 55664 ★ **Radio Shack**
3489 NW Ross Clark Cir.
Dothan, AL 36303
(205)792-0123
Company Type: Division. **Ultimate Parent:**
Tandy Corp. **SIC:** 5731—Radio, Television
& Electronics Stores.

★ 55665 ★ **Radio Shack**
3625 NW Ross Clark Cir.
Dothan, AL 36303
(205)792-6682
Company Type: Division. **Ultimate Parent:**
Tandy Corp. **SIC:** 5731—Radio, Television
& Electronics Stores.

★ 55666 ★ **Rite Aid**
3625 NW Ross Clark Cir. 4
Dothan, AL 36303
(205)794-9924
Ultimate Parent: Rite Aid. **SIC:** 5912—Drug
Stores & Proprietary Stores.

★ 55667 ★ **Ryder Truck Rental**
301 NE Ross Clark Cir.
Dothan, AL 36303
(205)794-8774
Ultimate Parent: Ryder System. **SIC:**
7513—Truck Rental & Leasing Without
Drivers.

★ 55668 ★ **Ryder Truck Rental**
2209 Montgomery Hwy.
Dothan, AL 36303
(205)792-3041
Ultimate Parent: Ryder System.

★ 55669 ★ **Shell Food Mart**
Rr 1
Dothan, AL 36301
(205)793-1412
Ultimate Parent: Shell Oil Co. **SIC:** 5541—
Gasoline Service Stations.

★ 55670 ★ **Shell Service Ctr**
800 W. Main St.
Dothan, AL 36301
(205)792-7298
Ultimate Parent: Shell Oil Co. **SIC:** 5541—
Gasoline Service Stations.

★ 55671 ★ **Taco Bell**
3625 NW Ross Clark Cir.
Dothan, AL 36303
(205)794-0515
Ultimate Parent: Pepsico. **SIC:** 5812—
Eating Places.

★ 55672 ★ **Trailways Bus
Systems**
130 S. Saint Andrews St.
Dothan, AL 36301
(205)792-7286
Ultimate Parent: Greyhound Lines Inc. **SIC:**
4131—Intercity & Rural Bus Transportation.

★ 55673 ★ **United Parcel Service**
2812 Montgomery Hwy.
Dothan, AL 36303
(205)794-2116
Ultimate Parent: United Parcel Service of
America. **SIC:** 4215—Courier Services
Except by Air.

★ 55674 ★ **Wal Mart Discount
City**
Northside
Dothan, AL 36303
(205)793-3099
Ultimate Parent: Wal-Mart Stores, Inc. **SIC:**
5311—Department Stores.

★ 55675 ★ **Waldenbooks**
3625 NW Ross Clark Cir.
Dothan, AL 36303
(205)792-4554
Ultimate Parent: K-Mart. **SIC:** 5942—Book
Stores.

Elba

★ 55676 ★ **Piggly Wiggly**
Northwood Plz.
Elba, AL 36323
(205)897-2294
Ultimate Parent: Bruno's. **SIC:** 5141—
Groceries—General Line.

Elkmont

★ 55677 ★ **First Alabama Bank
Athens**
Fort Hampton Rd.
Elkmont, AL 35620
(205)732-4255
Ultimate Parent: First Alabama
Bancshares. **SIC:** 6029—Commercial Banks
Nec.

Ensley

★ 55678 ★ **First Alabama Bank**
2010 Ave. F
Ensley, AL 35218
(205)326-7926
Location Type: Branch office. **Ultimate
Parent:** First Alabama Bancshares.

Enterprise

★ 55679 ★ **Big Bear Super
Market**
505 N. Main St.
Enterprise, AL 36330
(205)347-7351
Ultimate Parent: Penn Traffic. **SIC:** 5411—
Grocery Stores.

★ 55680 ★ **Casual Corner**
560 Meadowbrook Mall
Enterprise, AL 36330
(205)842-5515
Ultimate Parent: United States Shoe. **SIC:**
5651—Family Clothing Stores.

★ 55681 ★ **Conagra Broiler Co.**
Hwy. 14 PO Box 1276
Enterprise, AL 36330
Ultimate Parent: Conagra. **SIC:** 2015—
Poultry Slaughtering & Processing; 2077—
Animal & Marine Fats & Oils.

★ 55682 ★ **Conagra Feed Mill**
208 Middlebrook St.
Enterprise, AL 36330
Ultimate Parent: Conagra. **SIC:** 2048—
Prepared Feeds Nec.

★ 55683 ★ **First Alabama Bank**
621 Boll Weevil Cir., Ste. 37
Enterprise, AL 36330-2078
(205)347-0502
Location Type: Branch office. **Ultimate
Parent:** First Alabama Bancshares. **SIC:**
6021—National Commercial Banks.

★ 55684 ★ **First Alabama Bank**
110 E. College St.
Enterprise, AL 36330-2531
(205)347-0502
Location Type: Branch office. **Officer:** W.
Brett Morgan, President & CEO. **Ultimate
Parent:** First Alabama Bancshares. **SIC:**
6021—National Commercial Banks.

★ 55685 ★ **The Gap**
345 Meadowbrook Mall
Enterprise, AL 36330
(205)842-2929
Ultimate Parent: GAP. **SIC:** 5651—Family
Clothing Stores.

★ 55686 ★ **Greyhound Bus Lines**
2028 18th St.
Enterprise, AL 36330
(205)486-7663
Ultimate Parent: Greyhound Lines Inc. **SIC:**
4131—Intercity & Rural Bus Transportation.

★ 55687 ★ **Kay Bee Toy & Hobby**
650 Meadowbrook Massachusetts
Enterprise, AL 36330
(205)842-2375
Ultimate Parent: Melville. **SIC:** 5945—
Hobby, Toy & Game Shops.

★ 55688 ★ **Mary Kay Cosmetics**
810 Dixie Dr.
Enterprise, AL 36330
(205)347-4186
Ultimate Parent: Mary Kay Cosmetics. **SIC:**
5999—Miscellaneous Retail Stores Nec.

★ 55689 ★ **Piggly Wiggly**
Geneva Hwy.
Enterprise, AL 36330
(205)347-6722
Ultimate Parent: Bruno's. **SIC:** 5411—
Grocery Stores.

★ 55690 ★ **Pizza Hut**
1010 Rucker Blvd.
Enterprise, AL 36330
(205)347-7441
Ultimate Parent: Pepsico. **SIC:** 5812—
Eating Places.

★ 55691 ★ **Radio Shack**
600 Us 84 Byp
Enterprise, AL 36330
(205)347-1604
Company Type: Division. **Ultimate Parent:**
Tandy Corp. **SIC:** 5065—Electronic Parts &
Equipment Nec.

★ 55692 ★ **Radio Shack**
Morgan Sq.
Enterprise, AL 36330
(205)347-4079
Company Type: Division. **Ultimate Parent:**
Tandy Corp. **SIC:** 5731—Radio, Television
& Electronics Stores.

★ 55693 ★ **Rite-Aid**
110 Meadowbrook Dr.
Enterprise, AL 36330
(205)842-6089
Ultimate Parent: Rite Aid. **SIC:** 5912—Drug
Stores & Proprietary Stores.

★ 55694 ★ **Rite Aid Pharmacy**
913 Morgan Sq.
Enterprise, AL 36330
(205)347-3491
Ultimate Parent: Rite Aid. **SIC:** 5912—Drug
Stores & Proprietary Stores.

★ 55695 ★ **Ryder Truck Rental**
Westgate Shopping Ctr.
Enterprise, AL 36330
(205)393-3526
Ultimate Parent: Ryder System. **SIC:**
7359—Equipment Rental & Leasing Nec.

★ 55696 ★ **Ryder Truck Rental**
659 Us 84 Byp
Enterprise, AL 36330
(205)347-5606
Ultimate Parent: Ryder System. **SIC:**
7513—Truck Rental & Leasing Without
Drivers; 7539—Automotive Repair Shops
Nec.

★ 55697 ★ **Trailway Bus Station**
913 Morgan Sq.
Enterprise, AL 36330
(205)347-4385
Ultimate Parent: Greyhound Lines Inc. **SIC:**
4173—Bus Terminal & Service Facilities.

★ 55698 ★ **Trailways Bus Station**
502 E. Park Ave.
Enterprise, AL 36330
(205)347-6322
Ultimate Parent: Greyhound Lines Inc. **SIC:**
4131—Intercity & Rural Bus Transportation.

★ 55699 ★ **United Parcel Service**
PO Box 1424
Enterprise, AL 36331
(205)492-3782
Ultimate Parent: United Parcel Service of
America. **SIC:** 4215—Courier Services
Except by Air.

★ 55700 ★ **Waldenbooks**
640 Meadowbrook Mall
Enterprise, AL 36330
(205)842-3203
Ultimate Parent: K-Mart. **SIC:** 5942—Book
Stores.

Eufaula

★ 55701 ★ **Mini Mart**
Cobbs Ford Rd.
Eufaula, AL 36027
(205)285-3180
Ultimate Parent: Kroger. **SIC:** 5411—
Grocery Stores.

★ 55702 ★ **Mutual of New York**
1135 S. Eufaula Ave.
Eufaula, AL 36027
(205)687-5255
Ultimate Parent: Mutual of New York. **SIC:**
6411—Insurance Agents, Brokers &
Service.

★ 55703 ★ **Ryder Truck Rental**
599 S. Eufaula Ave.
Eufaula, AL 36027
(205)687-2116
Ultimate Parent: Ryder System. **SIC:**
7513—Truck Rental & Leasing Without
Drivers.

Eutaw

★ 55704 ★ **Greyhound Bus Depot**
104 Main St.
Eutaw, AL 35462
(205)372-4508
Ultimate Parent: Greyhound Lines Inc. **SIC:**
4111—Local & Suburban Transit.

Evergreen

★ 55705 ★ **First Alabama Bank**
119 E. Front St.
Evergreen, AL 36401
(205)578-3410
Location Type: Branch office. **Ultimate
Parent:** First Alabama Bancshares. **SIC:**
6021—National Commercial Banks.

★ 55706 ★ **First Alabama Bank
Conecuh**
E Front
Evergreen, AL 36401
(205)578-3410
Ultimate Parent: First Alabama
Bancshares. **SIC:** 6022—State Commercial
Banks.

★ 55707 ★ **Greyhound Bus Stop**
Belleville
Evergreen, AL 36401
(205)578-1150
Ultimate Parent: Greyhound Lines Inc. **SIC:**
4111—Local & Suburban Transit.

★ 55708 ★ **Kentucky Fried
Chicken**
Hwy. 83
Evergreen, AL 36401
(205)578-4060
Ultimate Parent: Pepsico. **SIC:** 5812—
Eating Places.

★ 55709 ★ **Louisiana Pacific
Corp.**
Owassa Rd.
Evergreen, AL 36401
(205)578-3131
Ultimate Parent: Louisiana-Pacific. **SIC:**
5031—Lumber, Plywood & Millwork.

★ 55710 ★ **Piggly Wiggly**
107 Mcghee St.
Evergreen, AL 36401
(205)578-3844
Ultimate Parent: Bruno's. **SIC:** 5411—
Grocery Stores.

Fairfield

★ 55711 ★ **AmSouth Bank**
4607 Gary Ave.
Fairfield, AL 35064-1341
(205)326-5846
Location Type: Branch office. **Officer:**
Donald F. Oakley. **Ultimate Parent:**
AmSouth Bancorp. **SIC:** 6021—National
Commercial Banks.

★ 55712 ★ **First Alabama Bank**
43 Western Hills Mall
Fairfield, AL 35064
(205)326-7551
Ultimate Parent: First Alabama
Bancshares. **SIC:** 6022—State Commercial
Banks.

★ 55713 ★ **Harbison-Walker
Refractories Dresser Industries Inc.**
Pleasant Grove Rd.
Fairfield, AL 35064
Ultimate Parent: Dresser Industries Inc.
SIC: 3255—Clay Refractories.

★ 55714 ★ **Lerner Shop**
24 Western Hills Mall
Fairfield, AL 35064
(205)923-0346
Ultimate Parent: Limited. **SIC:** 5651—
Family Clothing Stores.

★ 55715 ★ **Radio Shack**
6 Western Hill Mall
Fairfield, AL 35064
(205)923-0028
Company Type: Division. **Ultimate Parent:**
Tandy Corp. **SIC:** 5731—Radio, Television
& Electronics Stores.

★ 55716 ★ **Ryder Truck Rental**
4025 Commerce Ave.
Fairfield, AL 35064
(205)849-3388
Ultimate Parent: Ryder System. **SIC:**
7513—Truck Rental & Leasing Without
Drivers.

★ 55717 ★ **Uss Fairfield Works
Fairfield Works**
5700 Valley Rd. PO Box 599
Fairfield, AL 35064
Ultimate Parent: USX Corp. **SIC:** 3312—
Blast Furnaces & Steel Mills.

★ 55718 ★ **USX Fairfield Works**
Valley Rd.
PO Box 599
Fairfield, AL 35064
Ultimate Parent: USX Corp. **SIC:** 3312—
Blast Furnaces & Steel Mills.

★ 55719 ★ **Vulcan Materials Co.**
No. 8 Rd.
Fairfield, AL 35064
(205)781-3671
Officer: Doug Lawson, Manager. **Ultimate
Parent:** Vulcan Materials Co. **SIC:** 2879—
Agricultural Chemicals Nec; 3295—
Minerals—Ground or Treated.

★ 55720 ★ **Wal Mart Discount
City**
7100 Weibel Dr.
Fairfield, AL 35064
(205)786-8228
Ultimate Parent: Wal-Mart Stores, Inc. **SIC:**
5311—Department Stores.

Fairhope

★ 55721 ★ **First Alabama Bank**
98 S. Greeno Rd.
Fairhope, AL 36532-2048
(205)928-9226
Location Type: Branch office. **Ultimate
Parent:** First Alabama Bancshares. **SIC:**
6021—National Commercial Banks.

★ 55722 ★ **First Alabama Bank**
107 N. Section St.
Fairhope, AL 36532-2048
(205)928-6060
Location Type: Branch office. **Ultimate
Parent:** First Alabama Bancshares. **SIC:**
6021—National Commercial Banks.

★ 55723 ★ **Kentucky Fried
Chicken**
96 Plantation Pointe
Fairhope, AL 36532
(205)928-9331
Ultimate Parent: Pepsico. **SIC:** 5812—
Eating Places.

★ 55724 ★ **Pizza Hut**
241 S. Greeno Rd.
Fairhope, AL 36532
(205)928-1145
Ultimate Parent: Pepsico. **SIC:** 5812—
Eating Places.

★ 55725 ★ **Rohr Aero Service
Inc.**
16150 Greeno Rd.
Fairhope, AL 36532
(205)928-3220
Ultimate Parent: Rohr. **SIC:** 5088—
Transportation Equipment & Supplies.

★ 55726 ★ **World Book**
Childcraft
913 Plantation Blvd.
Fairhope, AL 36532-2949
(205)928-3333
Officer: Ray Clark. **Ultimate Parent:**
Berkshire Hathaway. **SIC:** 5963—Direct
Selling Establishments; 5942—Book Stores.

Fayette

★ 55727 ★ **American Olean Tile
Co.**
Fayette Industrial Park PO Box 659
Fayette, AL 35555-0659
Ultimate Parent: Armstrong World
Industries. **SIC:** 3251—Brick & Structural
Clay Tile.

★ 55728 ★ **Arvin Industries Inc.**
800 Columbus St. E
Fayette, AL 35555
(205)932-6735
Officer: G. Smith, President. **Ultimate
Parent:** Arvin Industries Inc. **SIC:** 3714—
Motor Vehicle Parts & Accessories.

★ 55729 ★ **Arvin North American
Automotive**
800 E. Columbus St.
Fayette, AL 35555
Ultimate Parent: Arvin Industries Inc. **SIC:**
3714—Motor Vehicle Parts & Accessories.

★ 55730 ★ **Computer Associates**
115 W. Columbus St.
Fayette, AL 35555
(205)932-7601
Ultimate Parent: Computer Associates
International.

★ 55731 ★ **Kentucky Fried
Chicken**
Hwy. 43 N
Fayette, AL 35555
(205)932-4715
Ultimate Parent: Pepsico. **SIC:** 5812—
Eating Places.

★ 55732 ★ **Pizza Hut**
Town
Fayette, AL 35555
(205)932-8621
Ultimate Parent: Pepsico. **SIC:** 5812—
Eating Places.

Flomaton

★ 55733 ★ **Greyhound Bus
Station**
202 Hwy. 31 N
Flomaton, AL 36441
(205)296-5204
Ultimate Parent: Greyhound Lines Inc. **SIC:**
4111—Local & Suburban Transit.

Florala

★ 55734 ★ **Piggly Wiggly**
404 S. 2nd St.
Florala, AL 36442
(205)858-3444
Ultimate Parent: Bruno's. **SIC:** 5411—
Grocery Stores.

Florence

★ 55735 ★ **Coca Cola Bottling
Co.**
895 PO Box
Florence, AL 35631
(205)764-5921
Ultimate Parent: Coca-Cola Enterprises.
SIC: 5149—Groceries & Related Products
Nec.

★ 55736 ★ **First Federal S & L**
102 S. Court St.
Florence, AL 35630-5678
(205)764-7131
Company Type: Headquarters. **Officer:**
Charles Frederick Jr. **Ultimate Parent:**
Bancorp Hawaii. **SIC:** 6035—Federal
Savings Institutions; 6021—National
Commercial Banks; 6162—Mortgage
Bankers & Correspondents; 6512—
Nonresidential Building Operators.

★ 55737 ★ **Imc Fertilizer Inc.**
Corner Commerce & Union St.
Florence, AL 35631
Ultimate Parent: IMC Fertilizer Group. **SIC:**
2874—Phosphatic Fertilizers.

★ 55738 ★ **Kmart**
3612 Cloverdale Rd.
Florence, AL 35633
(205)764-2388
Ultimate Parent: K-Mart. **SIC:** 5651—
Family Clothing Stores.

★ **56344** ★ **Hussmann Corp.**
101 Smothers Rd.
Montgomery, AL 36117
Ultimate Parent: Whitman Corp. **SIC:**
3585—Refrigeration & Heating Equipment.

★ **56345** ★ **IDS Financial Services Inc.**
2000 Interstate Park Dr., Ste. 20
Montgomery, AL 36109-5414
(205)277-3850
Ultimate Parent: American Express Co.
SIC: 6211—Security Brokers & Dealers;
6282—Investment Advice; 6289—Security &
Commodity Services Nec.

★ **56346** ★ **Jiffy Lube**
4131 Atlanta Hwy.
Montgomery, AL 36109
(205)279-6157
Ultimate Parent: Pennzoil. **SIC:** 7539—
Automotive Repair Shops Nec.

★ **56347** ★ **Kentucky Fried Chicken**
4220 Mobile Hwy.
Montgomery, AL 36108
(205)281-8981
Ultimate Parent: Pepsico. **SIC:** 5812—
Eating Places.

★ **56348** ★ **Kimball Furniture Reproductions**
1919 Bell St.
Montgomery, AL 36195
Ultimate Parent: Kimball International Inc.
SIC: 2512—Upholstered Household
Furniture.

★ **56349** ★ **Kimball Furniture Reproductions Inc.**
1919 Bell St.
Montgomery, AL 36195
Ultimate Parent: Kimball International Inc.
SIC: 2512—Upholstered Household
Furniture; 2426—Hardwood Dimension &
Flooring Mills; 2511—Wood Household
Furniture.

★ **56350** ★ **Lane Bryant**
5501 Atlanta Hwy.
Montgomery, AL 36117
(205)272-5782
Ultimate Parent: Limited. **SIC:** 5651—
Family Clothing Stores.

★ **56351** ★ **Lane Bryant**
E South Blvd.
Montgomery, AL 36111
(205)281-2408
Ultimate Parent: Limited. **SIC:** 5651—
Family Clothing Stores.

★ **56352** ★ **Lerner Shop**
E South Blvd.
Montgomery, AL 36111
(205)288-8014
Ultimate Parent: Limited. **SIC:** 5651—
Family Clothing Stores.

★ **56353** ★ **The Limited Express**
E South Blvd.
Montgomery, AL 36111
(205)281-5661
Ultimate Parent: Limited. **SIC:** 5651—
Family Clothing Stores.

★ **56354** ★ **Manpower, Inc.**
124 Interstate Park Dr.
Montgomery, AL 36109
(205)271-0052
Ultimate Parent: Manpower, Inc. **SIC:**
7361—Employment Agencies.

★ **56355** ★ **McDonalds**
2615 E. S. Blvd.
Montgomery, AL 36116
(205)288-4841
Ultimate Parent: McDonald's.
SIC: 5812—Eating Places.

★ **56356** ★ **Montgomery Food Processing Inc.**
4530 Mobile Hwy.
Montgomery, AL 36108
Ultimate Parent: Chiquita Brands
International. **SIC:** 2011—Meat Packing
Plants.

★ **56357** ★ **New York Life Montgomery General Office**
Southeastern Agencies
500 Interstate Park Dr., Ste. 509
Montgomery, AL 36109
(205)244-1696 **Fax:** (205)244-0092
Officer: William P. Horton, General
Manager. **Ultimate Parent:** New York Life.

★ **56358** ★ **O-I Brockway Glass Inc.**
Plant 13
3480 Lower Wetumpka Rd.
Montgomery, AL 36110
Location Type: Plant. **Ultimate Parent:**
Owens-Illinois. **SIC:** 3221—Glass
Containers.

★ **56359** ★ **Otis Elevator Co.**
207 Montgomery St.
Montgomery, AL 36104
(205)262-0671
Ultimate Parent: United Technologies. **SIC:**
1796—Installing Building Equipment Nec.

★ **56360** ★ **Owens-Brockway Glass Container**
3480 Lower Wetumpka Rd.
Montgomery, AL 36110
Ultimate Parent: Owens-Illinois. **SIC:**
3221—Glass Containers.

★ **56361** ★ **Palletizers**
3101 Old Hayneville Rd.
Montgomery, AL 36108
(205)269-2355
Company Type: Division. **Ultimate Parent:**
Litton Industries. **SIC:** 3537—Industrial
Trucks & Tractors.

★ **56362** ★ **Pappagallo**
1717 Carter Hill Rd.
Montgomery, AL 36106
(205)834-2778
Ultimate Parent: United States Shoe. **SIC:**
5661—Shoe Stores.

★ **56363** ★ **Pepsi-Cola Seven-Up Bottling**
820 Air Base Blvd.
Montgomery, AL 36108
(205)265-0581
Officer: Mike Bruemmer, Manager.
Ultimate Parent: Pepsico. **SIC:** 2086—
Bottled & Canned Soft Drinks.

★ **56364** ★ **Pizza Hut**
6035 Atlanta Hwy.
Montgomery, AL 36117
(205)277-5045
Ultimate Parent: Pepsico. **SIC:** 5812—
Eating Places.

★ **56365** ★ **Pizza Hut**
3378 Norman Bridge Rd.
Montgomery, AL 36105
(205)265-6000
Ultimate Parent: Pepsico. **SIC:** 5812—
Eating Places.

★ **56366** ★ **Pizza Hut**
7828 Vaughn Rd.
Montgomery, AL 36116
(205)270-1482
Ultimate Parent: Pepsico. **SIC:** 5812—
Eating Places.

★ **56367** ★ **Pizza Hut**
2600 Spruce St.
Montgomery, AL 36107
(205)269-1234
Ultimate Parent: Pepsico. **SIC:** 5812—
Eating Places.

★ **56368** ★ **Pizza Hut**
3030 Woodley Rd.
Montgomery, AL 36116
(205)265-6000
Ultimate Parent: Pepsico. **SIC:** 5812—
Eating Places.

★ **56369** ★ **Pizza Hut**
2520 Lower Wetumpka Rd.
Montgomery, AL 36110
(205)264-6564
Ultimate Parent: Pepsico. **SIC:** 5812—
Eating Places.

★ **56370** ★ **Premark International**
2765 W. Gunter Park Dr.
Montgomery, AL 36109
Ultimate Parent: Premark International.
SIC: 3585—Refrigeration & Heating
Equipment.

★ **56371** ★ **Radio Shack**
Eastbrook Shopping Ctr.
Montgomery, AL 36109
(205)279-8500
Company Type: Division. **Ultimate Parent:**
Tandy Corp. **SIC:** 5812—Eating Places.

★ **56372** ★ **Radio Shack**
E South Blvd.
Montgomery, AL 36111
(205)286-0704
Company Type: Division. **Ultimate Parent:**
Tandy Corp. **SIC:** 5065—Electronic Parts &
Equipment Nec.

★ **56373** ★ **Russell Corp.**
1 Retail Dr.
Montgomery, AL 36110
(205)288-1515
Officer: Jerry Leadbetter, Manager.
Ultimate Parent: Russell. **SIC:** 2322—
Men's/Boys' Underwear & Nightwear;
2399—Fabricated Textile Products Nec.

★ **56374** ★ **Ryder Truck Rental**
145 Eastdale Rd. S
Montgomery, AL 36117
(205)279-0539
Ultimate Parent: Ryder System. **SIC:**
7513—Truck Rental & Leasing Without
Drivers.

★ **56375** ★ **Ryder Truck Rental**
3900 Mobile Hwy.
Montgomery, AL 36108
(205)281-0450
Ultimate Parent: Ryder System. **SIC:**
7513—Truck Rental & Leasing Without
Drivers.

★ **56376** ★ **Safeco Insurance Co. of America**
2820 Fairlane Dr.
Montgomery, AL 36116
(205)277-1845
Ultimate Parent: Safeco. **SIC:** 6411—
Insurance Agents, Brokers & Service.

★ **56377** ★ **Safety Kleen Corp.**
3001 Day St.
Montgomery, AL 36108
Ultimate Parent: Safety-Kleen. **SIC:** 5013—
Motor Vehicle Supplies & New Parts.

★ **56378** ★ **Service Merchandise**
2270 E. S. Blvd.
Montgomery, AL 36116
(205)288-5940
Ultimate Parent: Service Merchandise Co.,
Inc. **SIC:** 5961—Catalog & Mail-Order
Houses.

★ **56379** ★ **Southern Controls**
3511 Wetumpka Hwy.
Montgomery, AL 36110
(205)277-5030
Ultimate Parent: Eckerd Corp. **SIC:** 3674—
Semiconductors & Related Devices.

★ **56380** ★ **Southern Cotton Oil**
1720 Bell St.
Montgomery, AL 36104-2936
(205)263-4747
Officer: Jack Lowry. **Ultimate Parent:**
Archer Daniels Midland Co. **SIC:** 2074—
Cottonseed Oil Mills; 5159—Farm-Product
Raw Materials Nec.

★ **56381** ★ **Sterling Bank**
4121 Carmichael Rd., Ste. 100
Montgomery, AL 36106
(205)279-7800
Location Type: Branch office. **Officer:** W.
Alan Worrell, Chairman of the Board, CEO,
& President. **Ultimate Parent:** Synovus
Financial Corp. **SIC:** 6021—National
Commercial Banks.

★ **56382** ★ **Sterling Bank**
PO Box 230849
Montgomery, AL 36123-0849
(205)279-7800 **Fax:** (205)244-4432
Location Type: Branch office. **Ultimate
Parent:** Synovus Financial Corp. **SIC:**
6021—National Commercial Banks.

★ **56383** ★ **T J Maxx**
2741 Eastern Blvd.
Montgomery, AL 36117
(205)271-4151
Ultimate Parent: TJX. **SIC:** 5311—
Department Stores.

★ **56384** ★ **Texaco**
520 Hunter Loop
Montgomery, AL 36108
(205)264-3439
Ultimate Parent: Texaco. **SIC:** 2911—
Petroleum Refining.

★ **56385** ★ **Texaco Gas Mart**
4020 Troy Hwy.
Montgomery, AL 36116
(205)281-8267
Ultimate Parent: Texaco. **SIC:** 5541—
Gasoline Service Stations.

★ **56386** ★ **Thermal Components Group**
2760 Gunter Park Dr. W
Montgomery, AL 36109
(205)277-1810 **Fax:** (205)271-4210
Company Type: Subsidiary. **Officer:** John
Marshall, President. **Ultimate Parent:**
Insilco Corp.

★ **56387** ★ **Thermal Components Inc.**
2760 Gunter Park Dr. W
Montgomery, AL 36109
Ultimate Parent: Insilco Corp. **SIC:** 3585—
Refrigeration & Heating Equipment.

★ **56388** ★ **Thermal Components Inc.**
2760 Gunter Park Drive, West
Montgomery, AL 36109
Ultimate Parent: Insilco Corp. **SIC:** 3585—
Refrigeration & Heating Equipment.

★ **56389** ★ **Trinity Industries**
Structural Steel Div. No. 32
1401 N. Decatur St.
Montgomery, AL 36104-2201
Company Type: Division. **Ultimate Parent:**
Trinity Industries. **SIC:** 3441—Fabricated
Structural Metal.

★ **56390** ★ **Trinity Industries**
Trinity Structural Div.
1401 N. Decatur St.
Montgomery, AL 36195-2201
Company Type: Division. **Ultimate Parent:**
Trinity Industries. **SIC:** 3441—Fabricated
Structural Metal.

★ **56391** ★ **Trinity Industries Inc. Plant 32**
1401 N.Decatur St.
Montgomery, AL 36195-2201
Ultimate Parent: Trinity Industries. **SIC:**
3441—Fabricated Structural Metal.

★ **56392** ★ **Trinity Industries, Plant 77**
Structural Steel Div.
1085 Parker St.
Montgomery, AL 36108
Ultimate Parent: Trinity Industries. **SIC:**
3441—Fabricated Structural Metal.

★ **56393** ★ **Trinity Industries Transport**
1340 N. Decatur St.
Montgomery, AL 36104
(205)269-0038
Ultimate Parent: Trinity Industries. **SIC:**
4213—Trucking Except Local; 5084—
Industrial Machinery & Equipment.

★ **56394** ★ **US Fidelity & Gu**
5931 Carmichael Rd.
Montgomery, AL 36117
(205)279-9325
Ultimate Parent: USF&G Corp. **SIC:**
6411—Insurance Agents, Brokers &
Service.

★ **56395** ★ **Vapor Corp.**
2740 Gunter Park Dr. W
Montgomery, AL 36109
Ultimate Parent: Brunswick Corp. **SIC:**
3585—Refrigeration & Heating Equipment;
3444—Sheet Metal Work; 3449—
Miscellaneous Metal Work.

★ **56396** ★ **Westinghouse Electric Corp.**
Thermo King Corp.
2740 Gunter Park Dr. W.
Montgomery, AL 36109
Ultimate Parent: Westinghouse Electric
Corp. **SIC:** 3585—Refrigeration & Heating
Equipment.

Moulton

★ 56397 ★ Piggly Wiggly
Hwy. 157
Moulton, AL 35650
(205)974-9814
Ultimate Parent: Bruno's. SIC: 5411—Grocery Stores.

★ 56398 ★ Piggly Wiggly
22747 Al Hwy. 24 24
Moulton, AL 35650
(205)974-0266
Ultimate Parent: Bruno's. SIC: 5411—Grocery Stores.

Mountain Brook

★ 56399 ★ First Alabama Bank
2721 Culver Rd.
Mountain Brook, AL 35223-2313
(205)326-7471
Location Type: Branch office. Ultimate Parent: First Alabama Bancshares. SIC: 6021—National Commercial Banks.

Mulga

★ 56400 ★ Lyondell Petrochemical Comp
Birmingport
Mulga, AL 35118
(205)436-3641
Ultimate Parent: Lyondell Petrochemical Co. SIC: 5172—Petroleum Products Nec.

★ 56401 ★ Union Oil Co. of California
2112 11th Ave. S
Mulga, AL 35118
(205)251-7676
Ultimate Parent: Unocal Corp. SIC: 5171—Petroleum Bulk Stations & Terminals.

Munford

★ 56402 ★ First Alabama Bank Talladeg
Hwy. 21 S
Munford, AL 36268
(205)358-4801
Ultimate Parent: First Alabama Bancshares. SIC: 6022—State Commercial Banks.

Muscle Shoals

★ 56403 ★ Occidental Chemical Corp.
1000 N. Wilson Dam Rd.
Muscle Shoals, AL 35661-1300
Ultimate Parent: Occidental Petroleum Corp. SIC: 2812—Alkalies & Chlorine.

★ 56404 ★ Reynolds Metals Co. Alloys Plant
3509 E. 2nd St.
Muscle Shoals, AL 35661
Ultimate Parent: Reynolds Metals Co. SIC: 3353—Aluminum Sheet, Plate & Foil.

★ 56405 ★ Reynolds Metals Co. Listerhill Reduction
3401 E. 2nd St.
Muscle Shoals, AL 35661-1257
Ultimate Parent: Reynolds Metals Co. SIC: 3334—Primary Aluminum.

North Port

★ 56406 ★ First Alabama Bank
2001 Bridge Ave.
North Port, AL 35476-3901
(205)345-3610
Location Type: Branch office. Ultimate Parent: First Alabama Bancshares. SIC: 6021—National Commercial Banks.

Northport

★ 56407 ★ Hertz Rent-A-Car Licensee
Municipal Airport
Northport, AL 35476
(205)759-5204
Ultimate Parent: Hertz. SIC: 7514—Passenger Car Rental.

★ 56408 ★ Piggly Wiggly Corp.
17405 Northwood Lake
Northport, AL 35476
(205)345-1307
Ultimate Parent: Bruno's. SIC: 5411—Grocery Stores.

★ 56409 ★ Pizza Hut
2500 US 82 Bypass
Northport, AL 35476
(205)339-3545
Ultimate Parent: Pepsico. SIC: 5812—Eating Places.

Notasulga

★ 56410 ★ First Alabama Bank
113 Main St.
Notasulga, AL 36866
(205)257-3101
Location Type: Branch office. Ultimate Parent: First Alabama Bancshares. SIC: 6021—National Commercial Banks.

Oakman

★ 56411 ★ First National Bank of Jasper
Main & Market Sts.
Oakman, AL 35579
(205)622-3156
Location Type: Branch office. Officer: Marie Rutledge, Manager. Ultimate Parent: Synovus Financial Corp. SIC: 6021—National Commercial Banks.

Oneonta

★ 56412 ★ First Alabama Bank
201 1st Ave. E
Oneonta, AL 35121-1710
(205)274-2343
Location Type: Branch office. Officer: Hoy L. Taylor, President & CEO. Ultimate Parent: First Alabama Bancshares. SIC: 6021—National Commercial Banks.

★ 56413 ★ Wal Mart
Bham Hwy.
Oneonta, AL 35121
(205)625-3640
Ultimate Parent: Wal-Mart Stores, Inc. SIC: 5311—Department Stores.

★ 56414 ★ Wrangler
402 Blue Bell St.
Oneonta, AL 35121
(205)625-3111
Officer: Benny Bellenger, Manager. Ultimate Parent: VF Corp. SIC: 2325—Men's/Boys' Trousers & Slacks; 2326—Men's/Boys' Work Clothing.

Opelika

★ 56415 ★ Ace Hardware Co.
1703 W. End Ct
Opelika, AL 36801
(205)749-1484
Ultimate Parent: Ace Hardware. SIC: 5251—Hardware Stores.

★ 56416 ★ First Alabama Bank Lee Cnty
601 Avenue a
Opelika, AL 36801
(205)749-5664
Ultimate Parent: First Alabama Bancshares. SIC: 6029—Commercial Banks Nec.

★ 56417 ★ Flowers Baking Co.
101 Simmons St.
Opelika, AL 36801
(205)749-8257
Officer: Calvin W. Rhodes, President. Ultimate Parent: Flowers Industries. SIC: 2051—Bread, Cake & Related Products.

★ 56418 ★ Flowers Baking Co. of Opelika Inc.
101 Simmons St.
PO Box 2548
Opelika, AL 36801-2548
(205)749-8257 Fax: (205)749-0835
Company Type: Subsidiary. Officer: Calvin Rhodes, President. Ultimate Parent: Flowers Industries.

★ 56419 ★ Greyhound Bus Lines
517 S. 10th St.
Opelika, AL 36801
(205)745-4201
Ultimate Parent: Greyhound Lines Inc. SIC: 4131—Intercity & Rural Bus Transportation.

★ 56420 ★ Kroger Company Food Store
1515 2nd Ave.
Opelika, AL 36801
(205)749-5645
Ultimate Parent: Kroger.

★ 56421 ★ Kroger Drugs
1515 2nd Ave.
Opelika, AL 36801
(205)749-9096
Ultimate Parent: Kroger. SIC: 5912—Drug Stores & Proprietary Stores.

★ 56422 ★ Pizza Hut
3611 Pepperell Pky.
Opelika, AL 36801
(205)749-7111
Ultimate Parent: Pepsico. SIC: 5812—Eating Places.

★ 56423 ★ Radio Shack
1515 2nd Ave.
Opelika, AL 36801
(205)749-6278
Company Type: Division. Ultimate Parent: Tandy Corp. SIC: 5731—Radio, Television & Electronics Stores.

★ 56424 ★ Ryder Truck Rental
100 Rocket Ave.
Opelika, AL 36801
(205)749-9925
Ultimate Parent: Ryder System. SIC: 7359—Equipment Rental & Leasing Nec.

★ 56425 ★ Ryder Truck Rental
3700 Pepperell Pky.
Opelika, AL 36801
(205)749-5536
Ultimate Parent: Ryder System. SIC: 7359—Equipment Rental & Leasing Nec.

★ 56426 ★ Texaco Service Center Inc.
300 S. 6th St.
Opelika, AL 36801
(205)749-3326
Ultimate Parent: Texaco. SIC: 5541—Gasoline Service Stations; 7539—Automotive Repair Shops Nec.

★ 56427 ★ Union Camp Corp.
W.C. Davis Industrial Pk.
Opelika, AL 36801
(205)749-6281
Officer: Jim McMillan, Manager. Ultimate Parent: Union Camp Corp. SIC: 2211—Broadwoven Fabric Mills—Cotton; 2611—Pulp Mills.

★ 56428 ★ Union Camp Corp.
4230 PO Box
Opelika, AL 36803
(205)749-6281
Ultimate Parent: Union Camp Corp. SIC: 5031—Lumber, Plywood & Millwork.

★ 56429 ★ Union Camp Corp.
W C Daveis Indl Park
Opelika, AL 36801
(205)749-3313
Ultimate Parent: Union Camp Corp. SIC: 2421—Sawmills & Planing Mills—General.

★ 56430 ★ United Parcel Service
800 Fox Run Pky.
Opelika, AL 36801
(205)749-0674
Ultimate Parent: United Parcel Service of America. SIC: 4215—Courier Services Except by Air.

★ 56431 ★ Wal Mart
Rural Route 4
Opelika, AL 36801
(205)749-2074
Ultimate Parent: Wal-Mart Stores, Inc. SIC: 5311—Department Stores.

★ 56432 ★ West Point Pepperell
2401-B 1st Ave.
Opelika, AL 36801
Location Type: Plant. Ultimate Parent: West Point Stevens. SIC: 2269—Finishing Plants Nec.

★ 56433 ★ West Point Pepperell
Grifftex Chemicals
1900 Cunningham Dr.
Opelika, AL 36801
Ultimate Parent: West Point Stevens. SIC: 2299—Textile Goods Nec.

Opp

★ 56434 ★ Piggly Wiggly
408 N. Main St.
Opp, AL 36467
(205)493-6309
Ultimate Parent: Bruno's. SIC: 5411—Grocery Stores.

★ 56435 ★ Pizza Hut
Hwy. 331 S
Opp, AL 36467
(205)493-4543
Ultimate Parent: Pepsico. SIC: 5812—Eating Places.

Oxford

★ 56436 ★ Allied-Signal Inc.
1 Cliff Garrett Dr.
Oxford, AL 36203

Officer: Patrick Flaherty, Manager. Ultimate Parent: Allied-Signal Inc. SIC: 3724—Aircraft Engines & Engine Parts; 3728—Aircraft Parts & Equipment Nec.

★ 56437 ★ Allied-Signal Inc.

Oxford, AL 36203
(205)835-4100
Officer: Patrick Flaherty, Manager. Ultimate Parent: Allied-Signal Inc. SIC: 3724—Aircraft Engines & Engine Parts; 3728—Aircraft Parts & Equipment Nec.

★ 56438 ★ Atlanta Coca-Cola Bottling Co. Oxford Al Plant
701 Hamric Dr.
Oxford, AL 36203
Ultimate Parent: Coca-Cola Enterprises. SIC: 2086—Bottled & Canned Soft Drinks.

★ 56439 ★ First Alabama Bank
825 Quintard Dr.
Oxford, AL 36203
(205)231-1308
Location Type: Branch office. Ultimate Parent: First Alabama Bancshares. SIC: 6021—National Commercial Banks.

★ 56440 ★ Tyson Foods Inc.
1520 McPherson St.
Oxford, AL 36203
(205)831-4381
Officer: Kenton Keith, Manager. Ultimate Parent: Tyson Foods, Inc. SIC: 2015—Poultry Slaughtering & Processing;

★ 56441 ★ Tyson Foods Inc.
1520 McPherson St. PO Box 3428
Oxford, AL 36203
Ultimate Parent: Tyson Foods, Inc.

Ozark

★ 56442 ★ Delta Air Lines
Ozark Manor
Ozark, AL 36360
(205)221-1212
Ultimate Parent: Delta Air Lines, Inc.

★ 56443 ★ Delta Air Lines Inc.
Ozark Manor
Ozark, AL 36360
(205)221-1212
Ultimate Parent: Delta Air Lines, Inc.

★ 56444 ★ Golden Peanut Co.
PO Box 160
Ozark, AL 36361-0160
(205)774-2671
Officer: Bo Stowers. Ultimate Parent: Archer Daniels Midland Co. SIC: 2068—Salted & Roasted Nuts & Seeds.

★ 56445 ★ Pizza Hut
977 E. Andrews Ave.
Ozark, AL 36360
(205)774-2131
Ultimate Parent: Pepsico. SIC: 5812—Eating Places.

Parrish

★ 56446 ★ **Piggly Wiggly**
Parrish, AL 35580
(205)686-7708
Ultimate Parent: Bruno's. **SIC:** 5411—
Grocery Stores.

Pelham

★ 56447 ★ **First Alabama Bank**
Southgate Village
US Hwy. 31
Pelham, AL 35124
(205)326-7940
Location Type: Branch office. **Ultimate
Parent:** First Alabama Bancshares. **SIC:**
6021—National Commercial Banks.

★ 56448 ★ **First Alabama Bank**
2964 US Hwy. 31 S
Pelham, AL 35124
(205)663-0723
Location Type: Branch office. **Ultimate
Parent:** First Alabama Bancshares. **SIC:**
6021—National Commercial Banks.

★ 56449 ★ **Greyhound Bus Lines**
Hwy. 31 S
Pelham, AL 35124
(205)663-6597
Ultimate Parent: Greyhound Lines Inc.

★ 56450 ★ **Radio Shack**
Pelham Plz.
Pelham, AL 35124
(205)663-0523
Company Type: Division. **Ultimate Parent:**
Tandy Corp. **SIC:** 5065—Electronic Parts &
Equipment Nec.

Pell City

★ 56451 ★ **Citgo Food Mart**
38 Cogswell Ave.
Pell City, AL 35125
(205)884-3246
Ultimate Parent: Citgo Petroleum. **SIC:**
5411—Grocery Stores.

★ 56452 ★ **Radio Shack**
401 Martin St. S
Pell City, AL 35125
(205)338-2329
Company Type: Division. **Ultimate Parent:**
Tandy Corp. **SIC:** 5065—Electronic Parts &
Equipment Nec.

Pennington

★ 56453 ★ **First Alabama Bank**
Hwys. 14 & 156
Pennington, AL 36916
(205)654-2535
Location Type: Branch office. **Ultimate
Parent:** First Alabama Bancshares. **SIC:**
6021—National Commercial Banks.

★ 56454 ★ **First Alabama Bank**
190 PO Box
Pennington, AL 36916
(205)654-2535
Ultimate Parent: First Alabama
Bancshares. **SIC:** 6099—Functions Related
to Deposit Banking.

★ 56455 ★ **James River Corp.
Naheola Mill**
HC 66 Box 315
Pennington, AL 36916-9499
Ultimate Parent: James River Corp. of
Virginia. **SIC:** 2611—Pulp Mills; 2621—
Paper Mills; 2631—Paperboard Mills;
2679—Converted Paper Products Nec.

Phenix City

★ 56456 ★ **CB&T Bank of Russell
County**
1806 Stadium Dr.
Phenix City, AL 36867
(205)291-3437
Location Type: Branch office. **Officer:**
Peggy Lauder, Manager. **Ultimate Parent:**
Synovus Financial Corp. **SIC:** 6021—
National Commercial Banks.

★ 56457 ★ **CB&T Bank of Russell
County**
910 13th St.
Phenix City, AL 36867-5452
(205)297-7000 **Fax:** (205)291-3378
Location Type: Branch office. **Officer:**
Sammy Howard, President, CEO, &
Marketing. **Ultimate Parent:** Synovus
Financial Corp. **SIC:** 6021—National
Commercial Banks.

★ 56458 ★ **CB&T Bank of Russell
County**
1413 280 Bypass
Phenix City, AL 36867
(205)291-3401
Location Type: Branch office. **Officer:**
Eddie Lowe, Vice President. **Ultimate
Parent:** Synovus Financial Corp. **SIC:**
6021—National Commercial Banks.

★ 56459 ★ **CB&T Bank of Russell
County**
PO Box 2400
Phenix City, AL 36868-2400
(205)297-7000 **Fax:** (205)291-3378
Location Type: Branch office. **Ultimate
Parent:** Synovus Financial Corp. **SIC:**
6021—National Commercial Banks.

★ 56460 ★ **First Alabama Bank**
1837 Stadium Dr.
Phenix City, AL 36867
(205)297-3674
Ultimate Parent: First Alabama
Bancshares. **SIC:** 6022—State Commercial
Banks.

★ 56461 ★ **First Alabama Bank**
1200 Broad St.
Phenix City, AL 36867
(205)298-3674
Ultimate Parent: First Alabama
Bancshares. **SIC:** 6022—State Commercial
Banks.

★ 56462 ★ **Kentucky Fried
Chicken**
1001 13th St.
Phenix City, AL 36867
(205)298-2918
Ultimate Parent: Pepsico. **SIC:** 5812—
Eating Places.

★ 56463 ★ **Piggly Wiggly**
1837 Stadium Dr.
Phenix City, AL 36867
(205)297-7410
Ultimate Parent: Bruno's. **SIC:** 5411—
Grocery Stores.

★ 56464 ★ **Piggly Wiggly**
433 RR 1
Phenix City, AL 36867
(205)298-8070
Ultimate Parent: Bruno's. **SIC:** 5411—
Grocery Stores.

★ 56465 ★ **Piggly Wiggly**
512 13th St.
Phenix City, AL 36867
(205)291-0846
Ultimate Parent: Bruno's. **SIC:** 5411—
Grocery Stores.

★ 56466 ★ **Piggly Wiggly**
3808 Summerville Rd.
Phenix City, AL 36867
(205)298-2445
Ultimate Parent: Bruno's. **SIC:** 5411—
Grocery Stores.

★ 56467 ★ **Piggly Wiggly**
Ladonia Sq.
Phenix City, AL 36867
(205)298-2182
Ultimate Parent: Bruno's. **SIC:** 5411—
Grocery Stores.

★ 56468 ★ **Piggly Wiggly**
1116 28th Pl
Phenix City, AL 36867
(205)297-7486
Ultimate Parent: Bruno's. **SIC:** 5411—
Grocery Stores.

★ 56469 ★ **Piggly Wiggly**
3745 US Hwy. 80
Phenix City, AL 36867
(205)291-3343
Ultimate Parent: Bruno's. **SIC:** 5411—
Grocery Stores.

★ 56470 ★ **Pizza Hut**
1106 US 280 Bypass
Phenix City, AL 36867
(205)298-3115
Ultimate Parent: Pepsico. **SIC:** 5812—
Eating Places.

★ 56471 ★ **Radio Shack**
1109 Phenix Sq.
Phenix City, AL 36867
(205)297-2465
Company Type: Division. **Ultimate Parent:**
Tandy Corp. **SIC:** 5731—Radio, Television
& Electronics Stores.

★ 56472 ★ **Shell Food Mart**
US 280 Bypass
Phenix City, AL 36867
(205)291-3026
Ultimate Parent: Shell Oil Co. **SIC:** 5541—
Gasoline Service Stations.

★ 56473 ★ **Southern Phenix
Textiles Inc.**
Broad St. Extension
Phenix City, AL 36867
Ultimate Parent: Johnson & Johnson. **SIC:**
2211—Broadwoven Fabric Mills—Cotton.

★ 56474 ★ **Southern Phenix
Textiles Inc.**
Broad St. Ext. PO Box 1108
Phenix City, AL 36867
Ultimate Parent: Johnson & Johnson. **SIC:**
2211—Broadwoven Fabric Mills—Cotton.

★ 56475 ★ **Wal Mart Discount
City**
800 22nd St.
Phenix City, AL 36867
(205)291-1700
Ultimate Parent: Wal-Mart Stores, Inc. **SIC:**
5311—Department Stores.

★ 56476 ★ **Witco Corp.**
1500 E. State Docks Rd.
Phenix City, AL 36869
(205)297-3675
Officer: Ken Wilder, Manager. **Ultimate
Parent:** Witco Corp. **SIC:** 2895—Carbon
Black.

★ 56477 ★ **Witco Corp.**
Concarb
1500 E. State Docks Rd. PO Box 1327
Phenix City, AL 36869
Ultimate Parent: Witco Corp. **SIC:** 2895—
Carbon Black.

★ 56478 ★ **Witco Corp.**
Concarb
State Docks Rd. PO Box 1327
Phenix City, AL 36867
Ultimate Parent: Witco Corp. **SIC:** 2895—
Carbon Black.

Pheonix City

★ 56479 ★ **Fieldcrest Cannon**
500 Fontaine Rd.
Pheonix City, AL 36869
(205)297-8465
Officer: Carl Williams, Plant Manager.
Ultimate Parent: Fieldcrest Cannon. **SIC:**
2269—Finishing Plants Nec.

Phil Campbell

★ 56480 ★ **Piggly Wiggly**
Phil Campbell, AL 35581
(205)993-5827
Ultimate Parent: Bruno's. **SIC:** 5411—
Grocery Stores.

Piedmont

★ 56481 ★ **Radio Shack**
613 N. Main St.
Piedmont, AL 36272
(205)447-9048
Company Type: Division. **Ultimate Parent:**
Tandy Corp.

★ 56482 ★ **Springs Industries,
Inc.**
100 Springs Dr.
Piedmont, AL 36272
(205)447-3156
Officer: Joe Formby, Plant Manager.
Ultimate Parent: Springs Industries. **SIC:**
2261—Finishing Plants—Cotton; 2392—
Housefurnishings Nec.

Pleasant Grove

★ 56483 ★ **City National Bank**
95 PO Box
Pleasant Grove, AL 35127
(205)328-4490
Ultimate Parent: City National Corp. **SIC:**
6029—Commercial Banks Nec.

Point Clear

★ 56484 ★ **Pappagallo**
Hwy. 98
Point Clear, AL 36564
(205)928-5983
Ultimate Parent: United States Shoe. **SIC:**
5661—Shoe Stores.

Prattville

★ 56485 ★ **Big Bear Store**
234 S. Chestnut St.
Prattville, AL 36067
(205)365-6741
Ultimate Parent: Penn Traffic. **SIC:** 5411—
Grocery Stores.

★ 56486 ★ **First Alabama Bank**
612 S. Memorial Dr.
Prattville, AL 36067-4932
(205)365-6353
Location Type: Branch office. **Ultimate
Parent:** First Alabama Bancshares. **SIC:**
6021—National Commercial Banks.

★ 56487 ★ **First Alabama Bank**
1901 Cobbs Ford Rd.
Prattville, AL 36066-5533
(205)361-9743
Location Type: Branch office. **Ultimate
Parent:** First Alabama Bancshares. **SIC:**
6021—National Commercial Banks.

★ 56488 ★ **First Alabama Bank**
1901 E. Main St.
Prattville, AL 36066
(205)361-9743
Ultimate Parent: First Alabama
Bancshares. **SIC:** 6022—State Commercial
Banks.

★ 56489 ★ **Jiffy Lube**
1672 E. Main St.
Prattville, AL 36066
(205)365-2524
Ultimate Parent: Pennzoil. **SIC:** 5172—
Petroleum Products Nec.

★ 56490 ★ **Pizza Hut**
311 S. Memorial Dr.
Prattville, AL 36067
(205)365-1299
Ultimate Parent: Pepsico. **SIC:** 5812—
Eating Places.

★ 56491 ★ **Prattville Mfg. Inc.**
101 Echlin Blvd.
Prattville, AL 36067
Ultimate Parent: Echlin. **SIC:** 3714—Motor
Vehicle Parts & Accessories.

★ 56492 ★ **Ring Around
Products**
Reynolds Mill Rd.
Prattville, AL 36067
(205)365-5971
Ultimate Parent: Occidental Petroleum
Corp. **SIC:** 5961—Catalog & Mail-Order
Houses.

★ 56493 ★ **Union Camp Corp.**
100 Jensen Rd.
Prattville, AL 36067
Ultimate Parent: Union Camp Corp. **SIC:**
2631—Paperboard Mills; 2611—Pulp Mills;
2861—Gum & Wood Chemicals.

★ 56494 ★ **Wal Mart**
206 Poplar St.
Prattville, AL 36066
(205)361-0337
Ultimate Parent: Wal-Mart Stores, Inc. **SIC:**
5311—Department Stores.

Priceville

★ 56495 ★ **First Alabama Bank**
Hwy. 67 E. & Bethel Rd.
Priceville, AL 35602
(205)355-1511
Location Type: Branch office. **Ultimate
Parent:** First Alabama Bancshares. **SIC:**
6021—National Commercial Banks.

Quinton

★ 56496 ★ **Mary Kay Cosmetics**
207 Coral Way
Quinton, AL 35130
(205)393-2913
Ultimate Parent: Mary Kay Cosmetics. **SIC:**
5999—Miscellaneous Retail Stores Nec.

Red Bay

★ 56497 ★ **Wrangler**
315 Hospital Rd.
Red Bay, AL 35582
(205)356-9521
Officer: Steve Hardman, Manager. **Ultimate
Parent:** VF Corp. **SIC:** 2325—Men's/Boys'
Trousers & Slacks; 2329—Men's/Boys'
Clothing Nec.

Reform

★ 56498 ★ **Trailways Bus Station**
205 1st Ave. W
Reform, AL 35481
(205)375-2265
Ultimate Parent: Greyhound Lines Inc. **SIC:**
4131—Intercity & Rural Bus Transportation.

Roanoke

★ 56499 ★ **Commercial Bank**
20 N. Main St.
Roanoke, AL 36274
(205)863-4151
Ultimate Parent: First Virginia Banks Inc.
SIC: 6022—State Commercial Banks.

★ 56500 ★ **Kentucky Fried
Chicken**
809 E. Main St.
Roanoke, AL 36274
(205)863-8964
Ultimate Parent: Pepsico. **SIC:** 5812—
Eating Places.

★ 56501 ★ **Piggly Wiggly**
109 N. Main St.
Roanoke, AL 36274
(205)863-6712
Ultimate Parent: Bruno's. **SIC:** 5411—
Grocery Stores.

Robertsdale

★ 56502 ★ **First Alabama Bank**
22070 Hwy. 59
Robertsdale, AL 36567
(205)947-2522
Location Type: Branch office. **Ultimate
Parent:** First Alabama Bancshares. **SIC:**
6021—National Commercial Banks.

★ 56503 ★ **Sun Diamond
Growers**
2 Campbell St.
Robertsdale, AL 36567
(205)947-2011
Ultimate Parent: Sun-Diamond Growers.
SIC: 5441—Candy, Nut & Confectionery
Stores.

★ 56504 ★ **Vanity Fair Mills Inc.**
2251 Palmer St.
Robertsdale, AL 36567
(205)947-2982
Officer: Delores Sturma, Manager. **Ultimate
Parent:** VF Corp. **SIC:** 2341—
Women's/Children's Underwear; 2342—
Bras, Girdles & Allied Garments.

Rogersville

★ 56505 ★ **First Alabama Bank**
205 E. Lee St.
Rogersville, AL 35652
(205)247-5436
Location Type: Branch office. **Ultimate
Parent:** First Alabama Bancshares. **SIC:**
6021—National Commercial Banks.

★ 56506 ★ **Piggly Wiggly**
202 E. Lee
Rogersville, AL 35652
(205)247-3303
Ultimate Parent: Bruno's. **SIC:** 5411—
Grocery Stores.

Russellville

★ 56507 ★ **Golden Poultry Co.**
County Hwy. No. 44
Russellville, AL 35653
Ultimate Parent: Gold Kist. **SIC:** 2015—
Poultry Slaughtering & Processing.

★ 56508 ★ **Kentucky Fried
Chicken**
Hwy. 43
Russellville, AL 35653
(205)332-5526
Ultimate Parent: Pepsico. **SIC:** 5812—
Eating Places.

★ 56509 ★ **Piggly Wiggly**
314 Jackson Ave. S
Russellville, AL 35653
(205)332-3535
Ultimate Parent: Bruno's. **SIC:** 5411—
Grocery Stores.

★ 56510 ★ **Pizza Hut**
Hwy. 43 Bypass
Russellville, AL 35653
(205)332-4583
Ultimate Parent: Pepsico. **SIC:** 5812—
Eating Places.

★ 56511 ★ **Radio Shack**
1110 Hwy. 43 Byp SE
Russellville, AL 35653
(205)332-6861
Company Type: Division. **Ultimate Parent:**
Tandy Corp. **SIC:** 7622—Radio & T.V.
Repair; 7622—Radio & T.V. Repair.

Samson

★ 56512 ★ **Piggly Wiggly**
4 S. East St.
Samson, AL 36477
(205)898-2152
Ultimate Parent: Bruno's. **SIC:** 5411—
Grocery Stores.

Saraland

★ 56513 ★ **First Alabama Bank**
23 S. Hwy.
Saraland, AL 36571-2801
(205)675-4663
Location Type: Branch office. **Officer:**
Beverly Vickers, Manager. **Ultimate Parent:**
First Alabama Bancshares. **SIC:** 6021—
National Commercial Banks.

★ 56514 ★ **First Alabama Bank**
1025 S. Hwy. 43
Saraland, AL 36571-3683
(205)690-1171
Location Type: Branch office. **Ultimate
Parent:** First Alabama Bancshares. **SIC:**
6021—National Commercial Banks.

★ 56515 ★ **L L & E Petroleum
Marketing Inc.**
Industrial Pky.
Saraland, AL 36571
Ultimate Parent: Louisiana Land &
Exploration.

★ 56516 ★ **L L & E Petroleum
Mtg. Inc.**
Industrial Pky.
Saraland, AL 36571
Ultimate Parent: Louisiana Land &
Exploration. **SIC:** 2900—Petroleum & Coal
Products.

★ 56517 ★ **LI & E Petroleum Mtg.
Inc.**
Industrial Pky.
Saraland, AL 36571
Ultimate Parent: Louisiana Land &
Exploration. **SIC:** 2911—Petroleum Refining.

★ 56518 ★ **LI&E Petroleum
Marketing Inc. Mobile Refinery**
400 Industrial Pky. Hwy. 158 E.
Saraland, AL 36571
Ultimate Parent: Louisiana Land &
Exploration. **SIC:** 2911—Petroleum Refining.

★ 56519 ★ **Sonoco Semi-Bulk
Packaging**
200 Jacintoport Blvd.
Saraland, AL 36571
(205)675-2925
Officer: Kevin Mitchell, Plant Manager.
Ultimate Parent: Sonoco Products. **SIC:**
2655—Fiber Cans, Drums & Similar

Products; 3412—Metal Barrels, Drums &
Pails.

Scottsboro

★ 56520 ★ **Fieldcrest Cannon**
2601 E. Willow St.
Scottsboro, AL 35768
(205)259-1222
Officer: Timothy Edwards, Manager.
Ultimate Parent: Fieldcrest Cannon.

★ 56521 ★ **Goodyear Tire &
Rubber Co.**
Goodyear Blvd. Rte. 9 Box 66
Scottsboro, AL 35768
Ultimate Parent: Goodyear Tire & Rubber.
SIC: 2824—Organic Fibers—Noncellulosic;
2296—Tire Cord & Fabrics.

★ 56522 ★ **Pizza Hut**
3311 S. Broad St.
Scottsboro, AL 35768
(205)259-0893
Ultimate Parent: Pepsico. **SIC:** 5812—
Eating Places.

★ 56523 ★ **Scottsboro Rug Mill**
2601 E. Willow Rd.
PO Box 610
Scottsboro, AL 35768
Ultimate Parent: Fieldcrest Cannon. **SIC:**
2221—Broadwoven Fabric Mills—Manmade.

★ 56524 ★ **Taco Bell**
308 County Park Rd.
Scottsboro, AL 35768
(205)259-1473
Ultimate Parent: Pepsico. **SIC:** 5812—
Eating Places.

Selma

★ 56525 ★ **First Alabama Bank**
608 Highland Ave.
Selma, AL 36701-4924
(205)875-1770
Location Type: Branch office. **Ultimate
Parent:** First Alabama Bancshares. **SIC:**
6021—National Commercial Banks.

★ 56526 ★ **First Alabama Bank**
101 Church St.
Selma, AL 36701-4610
(205)875-2201
Location Type: Branch office. **Officer:** G.
Carlton Baker, President & CEO. **Ultimate
Parent:** First Alabama Bancshares. **SIC:**
6021—National Commercial Banks.

★ 56527 ★ **First Alabama Bank**
479 PO Box
Selma, AL 36701
(205)875-2201
Ultimate Parent: First Alabama
Bancshares. **SIC:** 6099—Functions Related
to Deposit Banking.

★ 56528 ★ **First Alabama Bank of
Selma**
609 Highland Ave.
Selma, AL 36701
(205)875-1770
Ultimate Parent: First Alabama
Bancshares. **SIC:** 6022—State Commercial
Banks.

★ 56529 ★ **First Alabama Bank
Slema**
Craig a F B
Selma, AL 36701
(205)875-9363
Ultimate Parent: First Alabama
Bancshares. **SIC:** 6022—State Commercial
Banks.

★ 56530 ★ **Greyhound Bus Lines**
434 Broad St.
Selma, AL 36701
(205)874-4503
Ultimate Parent: Greyhound Lines Inc. **SIC:**
4111—Local & Suburban Transit; 4131—
Intercity & Rural Bus Transportation.

★ 56531 ★ **Hammermill Papers
Riverdale Plant**
River Rd.
Selma, AL 36702
Ultimate Parent: International Paper Co.
SIC: 2611—Pulp Mills; 2621—Paper Mills.

★ 56532 ★ **International Paper
Hammermill Riverdale Mill**
10130 River Rd. PO Box 1409
Selma, AL 36702-1409
Ultimate Parent: International Paper Co.
SIC: 2611—Pulp Mills; 2621—Paper Mills.

★ 56533 ★ **Pepsi-Cola Bottling
Co.**
1400 W. Highland Ave.
Selma, AL 36701
(205)875-2616
Officer: Jim Brannick, Manager. **Ultimate
Parent:** Pepsico. **SIC:** 2086—Bottled &
Canned Soft Drinks.

★ 56534 ★ **Piggly Wiggly**
212 Highland Ave.
Selma, AL 36701
(205)875-7158
Ultimate Parent: Bruno's. **SIC:** 5411—
Grocery Stores.

★ 56535 ★ **Radio Shack**
1391 Highland Ave.
Selma, AL 36701
(205)872-9423
Company Type: Division. **Ultimate Parent:**
Tandy Corp. **SIC:** 5731—Radio, Television
& Electronics Stores.

★ 56536 ★ **Radio Shack**
12 Martin Luther King St.
Selma, AL 36701
(205)875-2974
Company Type: Division. **Ultimate Parent:**
Tandy Corp. **SIC:** 5731—Radio, Television
& Electronics Stores.

★ 56537 ★ **Ryder Truck Rental**
2230 Mulberry Ave.
Selma, AL 36701
(205)874-8889
Ultimate Parent: Ryder System. **SIC:**
7513—Truck Rental & Leasing Without
Drivers.

★ 56538 ★ **Ryder Truck Rental**
537 Broad St.
Selma, AL 36701
(205)872-3200
Ultimate Parent: Ryder System. **SIC:**
7359—Equipment Rental & Leasing Nec.

★ 56539 ★ **Taco Bell**
303 Highland Ave.
Selma, AL 36701
(205)872-6034
Ultimate Parent: Pepsico. **SIC:** 5812—
Eating Places.

★ 56540 ★ **United Parcel Service**
314 Old Montgomery Rd.
Selma, AL 36701
(205)875-1554
Ultimate Parent: United Parcel Service of
America. **SIC:** 4215—Courier Services
Except by Air.

★ 56541 ★ **Wal Mart Discount
Store**
212 Highland Ave.
Selma, AL 36701
(205)872-3469
Ultimate Parent: Wal-Mart Stores, Inc. **SIC:**
5311—Department Stores.

Semmes

★ 56542 ★ **First Alabama Bank**
9001 Moffat Rd.
Semmes, AL 36575
(205)649-5201
Location Type: Branch office. **Ultimate
Parent:** First Alabama Bancshares. **SIC:**
6021—National Commercial Banks.

Sheffield

★ 56543 ★ **Air Products &
Chemicals Inc.**
200 River Rd.
Sheffield, AL 35661-1237
(205)381-0542
Location Type: Branch office. **Officer:**
Jerrold L. Davis. **Ultimate Parent:** Air
Products & Chemicals, Inc. **SIC:** 2813—
Industrial Gases; 5047—Medical & Hospital
Equipment; 5169—Chemicals & Allied
Products Nec.

★ 56544 ★   **Alabama Reclamation Plant**
Ford Rd.
Sheffield, AL 35660
Ultimate Parent: Reynolds Metals Co. **SIC:** 3341—Secondary Nonferrous Metals.

★ 56545 ★   **Alabama Reclamation Plant**
Ford Road, PO Box 120
Sheffield, AL 35660
Ultimate Parent: Reynolds Metals Co. **SIC:** 3341—Secondary Nonferrous Metals.

★ 56546 ★   **Alabama Reclamation Plant Alabama Reclamation Plant**
Ford Rd.
Sheffield, AL 35660
Ultimate Parent: Reynolds Metals Co. **SIC:** 3341—Secondary Nonferrous Metals.

★ 56547 ★   **Avon Products Inc.**
301 N. Montgomery Ave.
Sheffield, AL 35660
(205)381-4673
Ultimate Parent: Avon Products, Inc. **SIC:** 5999—Miscellaneous Retail Stores Nec.

★ 56548 ★   **Exxon Products**
1314 E. 21st St.
Sheffield, AL 35660
(205)381-0511
Ultimate Parent: Exxon. **SIC:** 5172—Petroleum Products Nec.

★ 56549 ★   **First Federal S & L**
1027 Avalon Ave.
Sheffield, AL 35661-2401
(205)381-7720
Company Type: Branch. **Officer:** Brenda Crittenden. **Ultimate Parent:** Bancorp Hawaii. **SIC:** 6035—Federal Savings Institutions; 6021—National Commercial Banks.

★ 56550 ★   **Greyhound Bus Lines**
1112 S. Jackson Hwy.
Sheffield, AL 35660
(205)383-7628
Ultimate Parent: Greyhound Lines Inc. **SIC:** 4131—Intercity & Rural Bus Transportation.

★ 56551 ★   **Kroger Groc**
1306 Woodward Ave.
Sheffield, AL 35661
(205)386-7677
Ultimate Parent: Kroger. **SIC:** 5411—Grocery Stores.

★ 56552 ★   **Kroger Groc**
Towne Plz.
Sheffield, AL 35660
(205)383-2428
Ultimate Parent: Kroger. **SIC:** 5411—Grocery Stores.

★ 56553 ★   **Occidental Chemical Corp.**
Wilson Dam Rd.
PO Box 1000
Sheffield, AL 35660
Ultimate Parent: Occidental Petroleum Corp. **SIC:** 2812—Alkalies & Chlorine.

★ 56554 ★   **Otis Elevator Co.**
101 W. 3rd St.
Sheffield, AL 35660
(205)381-0878
Ultimate Parent: United Technologies. **SIC:** 1796—Installing Building Equipment Nec.

★ 56555 ★   **Reynolds Metal Co. Alloys Plant**
East 2nd St.
Sheffield, AL 35660
Ultimate Parent: Reynolds Metals Co. **SIC:** 3353—Aluminum Sheet, Plate & Foil.

★ 56556 ★   **Reynolds Metals Co.**
East 2nd St.
Sheffield, AL 35660
Ultimate Parent: Reynolds Metals Co. **SIC:** 3253—Ceramic Wall & Floor Tile.

★ 56557 ★   **Reynolds Metals Co.**
Ford Rd.
Sheffield, AL 35660
(205)386-4800
Ultimate Parent: Reynolds Metals Co. **SIC:** 3341—Secondary Nonferrous Metals; 3399—Primary Metal Products Nec.

★ 56558 ★   **Reynolds Metals Co. Alabama Reclamation Plant**
Ford Rd.
Sheffield, AL 35660
Ultimate Parent: Reynolds Metals Co. **SIC:** 3341—Secondary Nonferrous Metals.

★ 56559 ★   **Reynolds Metals Co. Alloys Plant**
East 2nd St.
Sheffield, AL 35660
Ultimate Parent: Reynolds Metals Co. **SIC:** 3353—Aluminum Sheet, Plate & Foil.

★ 56560 ★   **Reynolds Metals Co. Listerhill Reduction**
East 2nd St.
Sheffield, AL 35660
Ultimate Parent: Reynolds Metals Co. **SIC:** 3334—Primary Aluminum.

★ 56561 ★   **Reynolds Metals Co. Listerhill Reduction**
East Second St.
Sheffield, AL 35660
Ultimate Parent: Reynolds Metals Co. **SIC:** 3334—Primary Aluminum.

★ 56562 ★   **Reynolds Metals Co. Sheffield Plant**
501 W. 20th Ave.
Sheffield, AL 35660
Ultimate Parent: Reynolds Metals Co. **SIC:** 3253—Ceramic Wall & Floor Tile.

★ 56563 ★   **Southern Reclamation Co.**
River Rd.
Sheffield, AL 35660
Ultimate Parent: Reynolds Metals Co. **SIC:** 5051—Metals Service Centers & Offices.

★ 56564 ★   **Texaco Food Mart No 6**
532 E. 2nd St.
Sheffield, AL 35660
(205)383-7525
Ultimate Parent: Texaco. **SIC:** 5411—Grocery Stores.

★ 56565 ★   **Texaco Mart**
1409 Woodward Ave.
Sheffield, AL 35661
(205)381-9694
Ultimate Parent: Texaco. **SIC:** 5541—Gasoline Service Stations.

★ 56566 ★   **Wal Mart**
519 Southgate Mall
Sheffield, AL 35660
(205)386-7375
Ultimate Parent: Wal-Mart Stores, Inc. **SIC:** 5311—Department Stores.

Shelby

★ 56567 ★   **Piggly Wiggly**
2652 Valleydale Rd.
Shelby, AL 35143
(205)991-5146
Ultimate Parent: Bruno's. **SIC:** 5411—Grocery Stores.

Silas

★ 56568 ★   **James River Corp.-Naheola Mill**
Rte. 114
Silas, AL 36919
Ultimate Parent: James River Corp. of Virginia. **SIC:** 2611—Pulp Mills; 2621—Paper Mills.

Somerville

★ 56569 ★   **Exxon**
Hwy. 6736
Somerville, AL 35670
(205)778-8748
Ultimate Parent: Exxon. **SIC:** 5411—Grocery Stores.

Spanish Fort

★ 56570 ★   **First Alabama Bank**
6470 Spanish Fort Blvd.
Spanish Fort, AL 36527
(205)626-0900
Location Type: Branch office. **Ultimate Parent:** First Alabama Bancshares. **SIC:** 6021—National Commercial Banks.

Steele

★ 56571 ★   **Culp Smelting & Refining Co.**
Brogdon Rd. Rte. 1 PO Box 455
Steele, AL 35987
Ultimate Parent: Leggett & Platt Inc. **SIC:** 3341—Secondary Nonferrous Metals.

Stevenson

★ 56572 ★   **Mead Containerboard**
Hwy. 72 E.
Stevenson, AL 35772
Ultimate Parent: Mead. **SIC:** 2631—Paperboard Mills.

★ 56573 ★   **Shaw Industries Inc.**
2nd St.
Stevenson, AL 35772
(205)437-2263
Officer: Joe R. Hart, Manager. **Ultimate Parent:** Shaw Industries, Inc. **SIC:** 2281—Yarn Spinning Mills; 2282—Throwing & Winding Mills.

Sulligent

★ 56574 ★   **Piggly Wiggly**
Sulligent, AL 35586
(205)698-8428
Ultimate Parent: Bruno's. **SIC:** 5411—Grocery Stores.

Sylacauga

★ 56575 ★   **Avondale Mills Inc.**
900 Avondale Ave.
Sylacauga, AL 35150-1899
Ultimate Parent: M.A.Hanna. **SIC:** 2211—Broadwoven Fabric Mills—Cotton; 2261—Finishing Plants—Cotton; 2281—Yarn Spinning Mills.

★ 56576 ★   **City National Bank**
126 N. Broadway Ave.
Sylacauga, AL 35150
(205)245-2281
Ultimate Parent: City National Corp. **SIC:** 6141—Personal Credit Institutions.

★ 56577 ★   **City National Bank**
Talladega Hwy.
Sylacauga, AL 35150
(205)245-2033
Ultimate Parent: City National Corp. **SIC:** 6022—State Commercial Banks.

★ 56578 ★   **City National Bank Mignon Branch**
1010 Talladega Hwy.
Sylacauga, AL 35150-1653
(205)245-2033
Company Type: Branch. **Officer:** Gordon Buyles, Manager. **Ultimate Parent:** City National Corp. **SIC:** 6021—National Commercial Banks.

★ 56579 ★   **City National Bank Sylacauga**
126 N. Broadway Ave.
Sylacauga, AL 35150-2524
(205)245-2281
Company Type: Headquarters. **Officer:** Gordon R. Boyles, President. **Ultimate Parent:** City National Corp. **SIC:** 6021—National Commercial Banks; 6141—Personal Credit Institutions; 6162—Mortgage Bankers & Correspondents.

★ 56580 ★   **City National Bank of Sylacauga**
PO Box 420
Sylacauga, AL 35150-0420
Company Type: Subsidiary. **Ultimate Parent:** Citicorp.

★ 56581 ★   **City National Bank of Sylacauga**
1010 N. Talladega Hwy.
Sylacauga, AL 35150-2162
(205)245-2033
Company Type: Subsidiary. **Location Type:** Branch office. **Officer:** Keith Weldon, Manager. **Ultimate Parent:** Citicorp. **SIC:** 6021—National Commercial Banks.

★ 56582 ★   **City National Bank of Sylacauga**
126 N. Broadway Ave.
Sylacauga, AL 35150-2524
(205)245-2281 **Fax:** (205)208-6190
Company Type: Subsidiary. **Location Type:** Headquarters. **Officer:** Gordon R. Boyles, President & CEO. **Ultimate Parent:** Citicorp. **SIC:** 6021—National Commercial Banks.

★ 56583 ★   **City National Corp.**
126 N. Broadway Ave.
Sylacauga, AL 35150-2554
(205)245-2281
Company Type: Subsidiary. **Location Type:** Headquarters. **Officer:** W.T Campbell Jr., Chairman & CEO. **Ultimate Parent:** Citicorp. **SIC:** 6021—National Commercial Banks.

★ 56584 ★   **City National Corp.**
PO Box 420
Sylacauga, AL 35150-0420
Company Type: Subsidiary. **Location Type:** Headquarters. **Ultimate Parent:** Citicorp.

★ 56585 ★   **Coca Cola Bottling Co.**
Talladega Hwy.
Sylacauga, AL 35150
(205)245-5681
Ultimate Parent: Coca-Cola Enterprises. **SIC:** 5149—Groceries & Related Products Nec.

★ 56586 ★   **First Federal S & L**
126 N. Norton Ave.
Sylacauga, AL 35150-2400
(205)845-4365
Company Type: Headquarters. **Officer:** Donald C. Stroup. **Ultimate Parent:** Bancorp Hawaii. **SIC:** 6035—Federal Savings Institutions; 6021—National Commercial Banks; 6162—Mortgage Bankers & Correspondents.

★ 56587 ★   **Pizza Hut**
511 W. Fort Williams St.
Sylacauga, AL 35150
(205)245-7073
Ultimate Parent: Pepsico. **SIC:** 5812—Eating Places.

★ 56588 ★   **Radio Shack**
1314 Talladega Hwy.
Sylacauga, AL 35150
(205)249-0080
Company Type: Division. **Ultimate Parent:** Tandy Corp. **SIC:** 5571—Motorcycle Dealers.

★ 56589 ★   **Russell Corp.**
Birmingham Ave.
Sylacauga, AL 35150
(205)682-1286
Ultimate Parent: Russell. **SIC:** 2322—Men's/Boys' Underwear & Nightwear; 2399—Fabricated Textile Products Nec.

★ 56590 ★   **Trailways Bus Station**
111 W. 1st St.
Sylacauga, AL 35150
(205)245-4357
Ultimate Parent: Greyhound Lines Inc. **SIC:** 4131—Intercity & Rural Bus Transportation.

Talladega

★ 56591 ★   **AmSouth Bank National Association**
409 Battle St.
Talladega, AL 35160-2423
(205)362-8784
Location Type: Branch office. **Officer:** Johnny Dutton. **Ultimate Parent:** AmSouth Bancorp. **SIC:** 6022—State Commercial Banks; 6021—National Commercial Banks.

★ 56592 ★   **First Alabama Bank**
215 W. North St.
Talladega, AL 35160-2033
(205)362-2238
Location Type: Branch office. **Officer:** Curtis C. Lackey, President. **Ultimate Parent:** First Alabama Bancshares. **SIC:** 6021—National Commercial Banks.

★ 56593 ★ **First Federal S & L**
North & Spring Sts.
Talladega, AL 35160
(205)362-6101
Company Type: Branch. **Officer:** Stanley Mitchell. **Ultimate Parent:** Bancorp Hawaii. **SIC:** 6035—Federal Savings Institutions; 6021—National Commercial Banks; 6141—Personal Credit Institutions; 6162—Mortgage Bankers & Correspondents.

★ 56594 ★ **Kentucky Fried Chicken**
819 Battle St. E
Talladega, AL 35160
(205)362-5681
Ultimate Parent: Pepsico. **SIC:** 5812—Eating Places; 5812—Eating Places.

★ 56595 ★ **Mary Kay Cosmetics**
RR 7
Talladega, AL 35160
(205)362-7362
Ultimate Parent: Mary Kay Cosmetics. **SIC:** 5999—Miscellaneous Retail Stores Nec.

★ 56596 ★ **Mary Kay Cosmetics**
Talladega, AL 35160
(205)362-6984
Ultimate Parent: Mary Kay Cosmetics. **SIC:** 5999—Miscellaneous Retail Stores Nec.

★ 56597 ★ **Pizza Hut**
710 Battle St. E
Talladega, AL 35160
(205)362-4050
Ultimate Parent: Pepsico. **SIC:** 5812—Eating Places.

★ 56598 ★ **Radio Shack**
5 Talladega Plz.
Talladega, AL 35160
(205)362-6761
Company Type: Division. **Ultimate Parent:** Tandy Corp. **SIC:** 5065—Electronic Parts & Equipment Nec.

★ 56599 ★ **Ryder Truck Rental**
310 Coosa St. E
Talladega, AL 35160
(205)362-7848
Ultimate Parent: Ryder System. **SIC:** 7513—Truck Rental & Leasing Without Drivers.

★ 56600 ★ **Trailways Bus Station**
216 Battle St. E
Talladega, AL 35160
(205)362-2512
Ultimate Parent: Greyhound Lines Inc. **SIC:** 4131—Intercity & Rural Bus Transportation; 4173—Bus Terminal & Service Facilities.

★ 56601 ★ **United Parcel Service**
144 East St. N
Talladega, AL 35160
(205)362-6104
Ultimate Parent: United Parcel Service of America. **SIC:** 4215—Courier Services Except by Air.

★ 56602 ★ **United Parcel Service**
144 East St. N
Talladega, AL 35160
(205)362-6104
Ultimate Parent: United Parcel Service of America. **SIC:** 4215—Courier Services Except by Air.

★ 56603 ★ **Wal Mart Discount City**
135 Westgate Apts.
Talladega, AL 35160
(205)362-0130
Ultimate Parent: Wal-Mart Stores, Inc. **SIC:** 5311—Department Stores.

Tarrant City

★ 56604 ★ **Maxwell House Coffee Co.**
140 Goodrich Dr.
Tarrant City, AL 35217
Ultimate Parent: Philip Morris. **SIC:** 3479—Metal Coating & Allied Services; 3400—Fabricated Metal Products.

Theodore

★ 56605 ★ **Air Products & Chemicals**
5660 Willis Rd.
Theodore, AL 36582
(205)653-6366
Ultimate Parent: Air Products & Chemicals, Inc. **SIC:** 3559—Special Industry Machinery Nec; 5084—Industrial Machinery & Equipment.

★ 56606 ★ **Kerr-Mcgee Chemical Corp.**
Rangeline Rd. PO Box 629
Theodore, AL 36590
Ultimate Parent: Kerr-McGee. **SIC:** 2816—Inorganic Pigments.

Thomaston

★ 56607 ★ **Burlington Northern Railroad**
Thomaston, AL 36783
(205)627-3408
Ultimate Parent: Burlington Northern. **SIC:** 4011—Railroads—Line-Haul Operating.

Thomasville

★ 56608 ★ **First Alabama Bank**
121 Hwy. 43 SW
Thomasville, AL 36784-1625
(205)636-5828
Location Type: Branch office. **Ultimate Parent:** First Alabama Bancshares. **SIC:** 6021—National Commercial Banks.

★ 56609 ★ **Greyhound Bus Lines Inc.**
Hwy. 43 S
Thomasville, AL 36784
(205)636-4480
Ultimate Parent: Greyhound Lines Inc. **SIC:** 4131—Intercity & Rural Bus Transportation.

★ 56610 ★ **Radio Shack**
538 Hwy. 43 N
Thomasville, AL 36784
(205)636-5634
Company Type: Division. **Ultimate Parent:** Tandy Corp. **SIC:** 5731—Radio, Television & Electronics Stores.

Thorsby

★ 56611 ★ **First Alabama Bank Chilton**
Hwy. 31
Thorsby, AL 35171
(205)646-3323
Ultimate Parent: First Alabama Bancshares. **SIC:** 6022—State Commercial Banks.

★ 56612 ★ **Union Camp Corp.**
Hwy. 231
Thorsby, AL 35171
(205)646-3346
Ultimate Parent: Union Camp Corp. **SIC:** 2436—Softwood Veneer & Plywood.

★ 56613 ★ **Union Camp Corp.**
Us 31 South
Thorsby, AL 35171
Ultimate Parent: Union Camp Corp. **SIC:** 2436—Softwood Veneer & Plywood.

★ 56614 ★ **Union Camp Corp.**
U.S. 31, South
Thorsby, AL 35171
Ultimate Parent: Union Camp Corp. **SIC:** 2436—Softwood Veneer & Plywood.

Trinity

★ 56615 ★ **First Alabama Bank**
Hwy. 20 W. & Seneca Dr.
Trinity, AL 35673-9309
(205)355-1511
Location Type: Branch office. **Ultimate Parent:** First Alabama Bancshares. **SIC:** 6021—National Commercial Banks.

★ 56616 ★ **Mini Mart**
Hwy. 24
Trinity, AL 35673
(205)350-4412
Ultimate Parent: Kroger. **SIC:** 5411—Grocery Stores.

Troy

★ 56617 ★ **First Alabama Bank**
1225 US Hwy. 231 & Franklin Dr.
Troy, AL 36081-4123
(205)566-2270
Location Type: Branch office. **Ultimate Parent:** First Alabama Bancshares. **SIC:** 6021—National Commercial Banks.

★ 56618 ★ **First Alabama Bank**
613 Park St.
Troy, AL 36081-4123
(205)566-2270
Location Type: Branch office. **Ultimate Parent:** First Alabama Bancshares. **SIC:** 6021—National Commercial Banks.

★ 56619 ★ **First Alabama Bank**
63 S. Court Sq.
Troy, AL 36081-2609
(205)566-2270
Location Type: Branch office. **Officer:** H. Leon Hilyer, President & CEO. **Ultimate Parent:** First Alabama Bancshares. **SIC:** 6021—National Commercial Banks.

★ 56620 ★ **Greyhound Bus Lines**
909 S. Brundidge St.
Troy, AL 36081
(205)566-0941
Ultimate Parent: Greyhound Lines Inc. **SIC:** 4142—Bus Charter Service Except Local.

★ 56621 ★ **Texaco Auto Service**
909 S. Brundidge St.
Troy, AL 36081
(205)566-6176
Ultimate Parent: Texaco. **SIC:** 7538—General Automotive Repair Shops.

Trussville

★ 56622 ★ **Ball Corp.**
Metal Decorating & Service Div.
5051 Gardinale St.
Trussville, AL 35173-1878
Company Type: Division. **Ultimate Parent:** Ball Corp. **SIC:** 3479—Metal Coating & Allied Services.

★ 56623 ★ **Ball Corp.**
Metal Decorating & Service Div.
5051 Gardinale St.
Trussville, AL 35173
Company Type: Division. **Ultimate Parent:** Ball Corp. **SIC:** 3479—Metal Coating & Allied Services.

★ 56624 ★ **Ball Corp.**
Metal Decorating & Service Div.
5051 Gardinale St.
Trussville, AL 35173
Company Type: Division. **Ultimate Parent:** Ball Corp. **SIC:** 3479—Metal Coating & Allied Services.

★ 56625 ★ **Ball Metal Decorating**
PO Box 446
Trussville, AL 35173-0446
(205)655-8845
Officer: David Wayne. **Ultimate Parent:** Ball Corp. **SIC:** 2800—Chemicals & Allied Products.

★ 56626 ★ **Ball Metal Decorating & Service**
5051 Cardinal St.
Trussville, AL 35173
(205)655-8845
Officer: David Wayne, Manager. **Ultimate Parent:** Ball Corp. **SIC:** 2752—Commercial Printing—Lithographic; 3542—Machine Tools—Metal Forming Types; 3555—Printing Trades Machinery.

★ 56627 ★ **First Alabama Bank**
305 Main St.
Trussville, AL 35173-1452
(205)326-7924
Location Type: Branch office. **Ultimate Parent:** First Alabama Bancshares. **SIC:** 6021—National Commercial Banks.

★ 56628 ★ **Gold Kist Inc. Poultry**
7200 Will Pond Rd.
Trussville, AL 35173
Ultimate Parent: Gold Kist. **SIC:** 2015—Poultry Slaughtering & Processing; 2077—Animal & Marine Fats & Oils.

★ 56629 ★ **Pizza Hut**
2211 Valley Rd.
Trussville, AL 35173
(205)655-3676
Ultimate Parent: Pepsico. **SIC:** 5812—Eating Places.

Tuscaloosa

★ 56630 ★ **American Family Life Assurance**
2324 University Blvd. E
Tuscaloosa, AL 35404
(205)556-1855
Ultimate Parent: American Family Life Assurance Co. **SIC:** 6411—Insurance Agents, Brokers & Service.

★ 56631 ★ **Bank of Tuscaloosa**
6800 Hwy. 69 S
Tuscaloosa, AL 35405
(205)391-1020
Location Type: Branch office. **Officer:** Don Gardiner, Vice President. **Ultimate Parent:** First Alabama Bancshares. **SIC:** 6021—National Commercial Banks.

★ 56632 ★ **Bank of Tuscaloosa**
2209 9th St., Ste. 300
Tuscaloosa, AL 35401-2370
(205)345-6200 **Fax:** (205)345-5853
Location Type: Branch office. **Officer:** James B. Flemming, Chairman of the Board, CEO, & President. **Ultimate Parent:** Synovus Financial Corp. **SIC:** 6021—National Commercial Banks.

★ 56633 ★ **Bank of Tuscaloosa**
205 McFarland Cir. N
Tuscaloosa, AL 35406-1800
(205)391-1082
Location Type: Branch office. **Officer:** Sally Brown, Manager. **Ultimate Parent:** Synovus Financial Corp. **SIC:** 6021—National Commercial Banks.

★ 56634 ★ **Bell South Mobility**
1351 McFarland Blvd. E
Tuscaloosa, AL 35405-1201
(205)750-2020
Ultimate Parent: BellSouth Corp. **SIC:** 5065—Electronic Parts & Equipment Nec.

★ 56635 ★ **Borden Inc.**
Dairy
1712 16th St.
Tuscaloosa, AL 35401
Company Type: Division. **Ultimate Parent:** Borden, Inc. **SIC:** 2026—Fluid Milk.

★ 56636 ★ **Borden Inc.**
Dairy
1712 16th St.
Tuscaloosa, AL 35401
Company Type: Division. **Ultimate Parent:** Borden, Inc. **SIC:** 2026—Fluid Milk.

★ 56637 ★ **Casual Corner**
105 University Blvd. E
Tuscaloosa, AL 35401
(205)553-9653
Ultimate Parent: United States Shoe. **SIC:** 5651—Family Clothing Stores.

★ 56638 ★ **Circus World Toy Stores**
Mac Farland
Tuscaloosa, AL 35401
(205)758-3064
Ultimate Parent: Melville. **SIC:** 5945—Hobby, Toy & Game Shops.

★ 56639 ★ **Exxon**
724 Skyland Blvd. E
Tuscaloosa, AL 35405
(205)758-2924
Ultimate Parent: Exxon. **SIC:** 5541—Gasoline Service Stations.

★ 56640 ★ **Exxon Co. USA**
2501 6th St.
Tuscaloosa, AL 35401
(205)345-3051
Ultimate Parent: Exxon. **SIC:** 5541—Gasoline Service Stations.

★ 56641 ★ **First Alabama bank**
2001 Bridge Ave.
Tuscaloosa, AL 35476
(205)345-4610
Location Type: Branch office. **Ultimate Parent:** First Alabama Bancshares. **SIC:** 6021—National Commercial Banks.

★ 56642 ★ First Alabama Bank
1549 McFarland Blvd. N
Tuscaloosa, AL 35406
(205)345-4610
Location Type: Branch office. Ultimate
Parent: First Alabama Bancshares. SIC:
6021—National Commercial Banks.

★ 56643 ★ First Alabama Bank
McFarland Blvd. & 15th St.
Tuscaloosa, AL 35405
(205)345-4610
Location Type: Branch office. Ultimate
Parent: First Alabama Bancshares. SIC:
6021—National Commercial Banks.

★ 56644 ★ First Alabama Bank
504 Paul Bryant Dr.
Tuscaloosa, AL 35401
(205)345-4610
Location Type: Branch office. Ultimate
Parent: First Alabama Bancshares. SIC:
6021—National Commercial Banks.

★ 56645 ★ First Alabama Bank
LeLand Shopping Ctr.
2601 University BLvd. E
Tuscaloosa, AL 35404
(205)345-4610
Location Type: Branch office. Ultimate
Parent: First Alabama Bancshares. SIC:
6021—National Commercial Banks.

★ 56646 ★ First Alabama Bank
1225 Skyland Blvd. E
Tuscaloosa, AL 35405-4234
(205)345-4610
Location Type: Branch office. Ultimate
Parent: First Alabama Bancshares. SIC:
6021—National Commercial Banks.

★ 56647 ★ First Alabama Bank
2222 9th St.
Tuscaloosa, AL 35401-2318
(205)345-4610
Location Type: Branch office. Officer:
Chuck Sittason, President. Ultimate Parent:
First Alabama Bancshares. SIC: 6021—
National Commercial Banks.

★ 56648 ★ First Alabama Bank
Hwy. 216
Tuscaloosa, AL 35444
(205)345-4610
Location Type: Branch office. Ultimate
Parent: First Alabama Bancshares. SIC:
6021—National Commercial Banks.

★ 56649 ★ First Alabama Bank
2509 PO Box
Tuscaloosa, AL 35401
(205)345-4610
Ultimate Parent: First Alabama
Bancshares. SIC: 6099—Functions Related
to Deposit Banking.

★ 56650 ★ First Alabama Bank of
Tusca
1701 McFarland Blvd. E
Tuscaloosa, AL 35405
(205)345-4610
Ultimate Parent: First Alabama
Bancshares. SIC: 6022—State Commercial
Banks.

★ 56651 ★ First Alabama Bank of
Tusca
Leland Shopping Ctr.
Tuscaloosa, AL 35404
(205)345-4610
Ultimate Parent: First Alabama
Bancshares. SIC: 6022—State Commercial
Banks.

★ 56652 ★ First Choice, Inc.
26 Brentwood
Tuscaloosa, AL 35404
(205)349-4444
Ultimate Parent: Bindley-Western
Industries, Inc.

★ 56653 ★ First National Bank of
Tuscaloosa
2330 University Blvd.
Tuscaloosa, AL 35403
(205)345-5000
Company Type: Subsidiary. Officer:
George S. Shirley, Chairman of the Board &
President. Ultimate Parent: AmSouth
Bancorp. SIC: 6021—National Commercial
Banks. Employee Count: 250.

★ 56654 ★ First National Bank of
Tusk
2506 University Blvd. E
Tuscaloosa, AL 35404
(205)345-5000
Ultimate Parent: AmSouth Bancorp. SIC:
6022—State Commercial Banks.

★ 56655 ★ Gayfers Department
Store
Mac Farland
Tuscaloosa, AL 35401
(205)759-2000
Ultimate Parent: Mercantile Stores.

★ 56656 ★ Greyhound Bus Lines
2520 9th St.
Tuscaloosa, AL 35401
(205)758-6651
Ultimate Parent: Greyhound Lines Inc. SIC:
4111—Local & Suburban Transit; 4131—
Intercity & Rural Bus Transportation.

★ 56657 ★ Hardin's Bakery
546 15th St.
Tuscaloosa, AL 35401
(205)752-5586
Officer: A. Royce Kirkland, President.
Ultimate Parent: Flowers Industries. SIC:
2051—Bread, Cake & Related Products.

★ 56658 ★ Hardin's Bakery Inc.
546 15th St.
PO Box 1458
Tuscaloosa, AL 35403
(205)752-5586 Fax: (205)752-1780
Company Type: Subsidiary. Officer: Royce
Kirkland, President. Ultimate Parent:
Flowers Industries.

★ 56659 ★ Kentucky Fried
Chicken
2517 11th St.
Tuscaloosa, AL 35401
(205)725-6739
Ultimate Parent: Pepsico. SIC: 5812—
Eating Places.

★ 56660 ★ Kentucky Fried
Chicken
1930 24th Ave.
Tuscaloosa, AL 35401
(205)758-7436
Ultimate Parent: Pepsico. SIC: 5812—
Eating Places.

★ 56661 ★ Lerner Shop
138 University Blvd. E
Tuscaloosa, AL 35401
(205)556-4476
Ultimate Parent: Limited. SIC: 5651—
Family Clothing Stores.

★ 56662 ★ The Limited
103 University Blvd. E
Tuscaloosa, AL 35401
(205)553-8100
Ultimate Parent: Limited. SIC: 5621—
Women's Clothing Stores; 5651—Family
Clothing Stores.

★ 56663 ★ Mary Kay Cosmetics
70 Cedar Knolls
Tuscaloosa, AL 35405
(205)556-7700
Ultimate Parent: Mary Kay Cosmetics.

★ 56664 ★ Mutual of New York
2315 9th St.
Tuscaloosa, AL 35401
(205)752-0494
Ultimate Parent: Mutual of New York. SIC:
6411—Insurance Agents, Brokers &
Service.

★ 56665 ★ Pepsi-Cola Bottling
Co.
912 29th Ave.
Tuscaloosa, AL 35401
(205)345-6001
Location Type: Plant. Officer: Tim
Shuman, Plant Manager. Ultimate Parent:
Pepsico. SIC: 2086—Bottled & Canned Soft
Drinks.

★ 56666 ★ Piggly Wiggly
1721 24th Ave.
Tuscaloosa, AL 35401
(205)758-7130
Ultimate Parent: Bruno's. SIC: 5411—
Grocery Stores.

★ 56667 ★ Piggly Wiggly
638 Skyland Blvd. E
Tuscaloosa, AL 35405
(205)752-3562
Ultimate Parent: Bruno's. SIC: 5411—
Grocery Stores.

★ 56668 ★ Pizza Hut
2815 University Blvd. E
Tuscaloosa, AL 35404
(205)556-4511
Ultimate Parent: Pepsico. SIC: 5812—
Eating Places.

★ 56669 ★ Pizza Hut
702 Skyland Blvd. E
Tuscaloosa, AL 35405
(205)758-6617
Ultimate Parent: Pepsico. SIC: 5812—
Eating Places.

★ 56670 ★ Radio Shack
Meadowbrook Mall
Tuscaloosa, AL 35401
(205)752-7111
Company Type: Division. Ultimate Parent:
Tandy Corp. SIC: 5065—Electronic Parts &
Equipment Nec.

★ 56671 ★ Radio Shack
Mac Farland
Tuscaloosa, AL 35401
(205)345-0805
Company Type: Division. Ultimate Parent:
Tandy Corp. SIC: 5065—Electronic Parts &
Equipment Nec.

★ 56672 ★ Radio Shack
12 Mac Farland Mall
Tuscaloosa, AL 35405
(205)345-0805
Company Type: Division. Ultimate Parent:
Tandy Corp. SIC: 5065—Electronic Parts &
Equipment Nec.

★ 56673 ★ Ryder Truck Rental
5402 Kauloosa Ave.
Tuscaloosa, AL 35405
(205)345-2181
Ultimate Parent: Ryder System. SIC:
7359—Equipment Rental & Leasing Nec.

★ 56674 ★ Ryder Truck Rental
149 Skyland Blvd.
Tuscaloosa, AL 35405
(205)752-7086
Ultimate Parent: Ryder System. SIC:
7359—Equipment Rental & Leasing Nec.

★ 56675 ★ Ryder Truck Rental
2541 Old Kaulton Rd.
Tuscaloosa, AL 35401
(205)758-8375
Ultimate Parent: Ryder System. SIC:
7513—Truck Rental & Leasing Without
Drivers.

★ 56676 ★ Taco Bell
405 15th St. E
Tuscaloosa, AL 35401
(205)752-6962
Ultimate Parent: Pepsico. SIC: 5812—
Eating Places; 7241—Barber Shops.

★ 56677 ★ Texaco Self Serv
808 15th St. E
Tuscaloosa, AL 35405
(205)758-0612
Ultimate Parent: Texaco. SIC: 5541—
Gasoline Service Stations.

★ 56678 ★ Trailways Bus System
711 S. L B Wallace Blvd.
Tuscaloosa, AL 35401
(205)758-4494
Ultimate Parent: Greyhound Lines Inc. SIC:
4131—Intercity & Rural Bus Transportation.

★ 56679 ★ Wal Mart
Bama Masschstts
Tuscaloosa, AL 35405
(205)759-5491
Ultimate Parent: Wal-Mart Stores, Inc. SIC:
5311—Department Stores.

★ 56680 ★ Wal Mart Discount
City
Wood Sq.
Tuscaloosa, AL 35405
(205)752-1591
Ultimate Parent: Wal-Mart Stores, Inc. SIC:
5311—Department Stores.

★ 56681 ★ Waldenbooks
167 University Blvd. E
Tuscaloosa, AL 35401
(205)556-0983
Ultimate Parent: K-Mart. SIC: 5942—Book
Stores.

★ 56682 ★ Waldenbooks
1701 Mcfarland Blvd. E
Tuscaloosa, AL 35405
(205)556-0983
Ultimate Parent: K-Mart. SIC: 5942—Book
Stores.

Tuscumbia

★ 56683 ★ Golden Poultry Co.
Feedmill
Hwy. 72 W.
Tuscumbia, AL 35674
Ultimate Parent: Gold Kist. SIC: 2048—
Prepared Feeds Nec.

Tuskegee

★ 56684 ★ Big Bear
270 W. Lee St.
Tuskegee, AL 36083
(205)727-3410
Ultimate Parent: Penn Traffic. SIC: 5411—
Grocery Stores.

★ 56685 ★ Greyhound Bus Depot
203 E. Martin L King Hwy.
Tuskegee, AL 36083
(205)727-1290
Ultimate Parent: Greyhound Lines Inc. SIC:
4173—Bus Terminal & Service Facilities.

Union Springs

★ 56686 ★ American National
Bank
104 E. Hardaway Ave.
Union Springs, AL 36089-1607
(205)738-2080
Officer: J. H. Williamson, President.
Ultimate Parent: First Chicago Corp. SIC:
6022—State Commercial Banks; 6021—
National Commercial Banks. Employee
Count: 6.

★ 56687 ★ Piggly Wiggly
293 PO Box
Union Springs, AL 36089
Ultimate Parent: Bruno's. SIC: 5411—
Grocery Stores.

Valley

★ 56688 ★ Eckerd Drug Co.
3418 20th Ave.
Valley, AL 36854
(205)768-2112
Ultimate Parent: Eckerd Corp. SIC: 5912—
Drug Stores & Proprietary Stores.

★ 56689 ★ Kentucky Fried
Chicken
3006 20th Ave.
Valley, AL 36854
(205)768-2311
Ultimate Parent: Pepsico. SIC: 5812—
Eating Places.

★ 56690 ★ Radio Shack
2918 20th Ave.
Valley, AL 36854
(205)768-2440
Company Type: Division. Ultimate Parent:
Tandy Corp. SIC: 5065—Electronic Parts &
Equipment Nec.

★ 56691 ★ West Point Pepperell
River Rd.
Valley, AL 36854
Location Type: Plant. Ultimate Parent:
West Point Stevens. SIC: 2211—
Broadwoven Fabric Mills—Cotton.

★ 56692 ★ West Point Pepperell
201 Blvd.
Valley, AL 36854
Location Type: Plant. Ultimate Parent:
West Point Stevens. SIC: 2211—
Broadwoven Fabric Mills—Cotton.

★ 56693 ★   West Point Pepperell
201 Blvd.
Valley, AL 36854
(205)392-9197

Location Type:
Plant. Ultimate Parent: West Point
Stevens. SIC: 2211—Broadwoven Fabric
Mills—Cotton.

★ 56694 ★   West Point Pepperell
I-85 Valley-Huguley Exit
Valley, AL 36854
Ultimate Parent: West Point Stevens. SIC:
2211—Broadwoven Fabric Mills—Cotton.

★ 56695 ★   West Point Pepperell
River Rd.
Valley, AL 36854
Location Type: Plant. Ultimate Parent:
West Point Stevens. SIC: 2211—
Broadwoven Fabric Mills—Cotton.

Valley Head

★ 56696 ★   Shaw Industries Inc.
Hwy. 117
Valley Head, AL 35989
(205)635-6243
Officer: Rick Morgan, Manager. Ultimate
Parent: Shaw Industries, Inc. SIC: 2281—
Yarn Spinning Mills.

Vernon

★ 56697 ★   Citizens State Bank
211 W. Columbus St.
Vernon, AL 35592
(205)695-9162
Ultimate Parent: Liberty National Bancorp.
SIC: 6022—State Commercial Banks.

★ 56698 ★   Emerson Electric Co.
E. L. Wiegnd Div.
Yellow Creek Rd.
Vernon, AL 35592-1439
Company Type: Division. Ultimate Parent:
Emerson Electric Co. Inc. SIC: 5063—

Electrical Apparatus & Equipment; 3567—
Industrial Furnaces & Ovens; 3629—
Electrical Industrial Apparatus Nec; 3639—
Household Appliances Nec.

★ 56699 ★   Marathon Equipment
Co.
County Hwy. 9 S
Vernon, AL 35592
(205)695-9105
Officer: Grant Fenner, President. Ultimate
Parent: Dover Corp. SIC: 3469—Metal
Stampings Nec; 3589—Service Industry
Machinery Nec.

★ 56700 ★   Southland Royalty
Co.
Vernon, Al 35592
(205)695-9129
Ultimate Parent: Burlington Resources.
SIC: 5191—Farm Supplies.

★ 56701 ★   Southland Royalty
Co.
Vernon, AL 35592
(205)695-9129
Ultimate Parent: Burlington Resources.
SIC: 5191—Farm Supplies.

Vestavia Hills

★ 56702 ★   First Alabama Bank
529 Montgomery Hwy.
Vestavia Hills, AL 35216-1807
(205)290-5364
Location Type: Branch office. Ultimate
Parent: First Alabama Bancshares. SIC:
6021—National Commercial Banks.

Vinemont

★ 56703 ★   Exxon Distributor
Rr 15
Vinemont, AL 35179
(205)734-7718
Ultimate Parent: Exxon. SIC: 1311—Crude
Petroleum & Natural Gas.

Wetumpka

★ 56704 ★   Pizza Hut
820 SE Main St.
Wetumpka, AL 36092
(205)567-2014
Ultimate Parent: Pepsico. SIC: 5812—
Eating Places.

Wilsonville

★ 56705 ★   Clean Coal Research
Center
Hwy. 25 N.
Wilsonville, AL 35186
Ultimate Parent: Southern. SIC: 2999—
Petroleum & Coal Products Nec.

★ 56706 ★   Clean Coal Research
Center Southern Co. Services Inc.
Hwy. 25 N.
Wilsonville, AL 35186
Ultimate Parent: Southern. SIC: 2999—
Petroleum & Coal Products Nec.

Winfield

★ 56707 ★   Burlington Northern
Railroa
10 St.
Winfield, AL 35594
(205)487-6505
Ultimate Parent: Burlington Northern. SIC:
4011—Railroads—Line-Haul Operating.

★ 56708 ★   Greyhound Bus Lines
110 W. Frisco Ave.
Winfield, AL 35594
(205)487-2140
Ultimate Parent: Greyhound Lines Inc. SIC:
4111—Local & Suburban Transit.

★ 56709 ★   Piggly Wiggly
17 1st St. E
Winfield, AL 35594
(205)487-6480
Ultimate Parent: Bruno's. SIC: 5411—
Grocery Stores.

★ 56710 ★   Piggly Wiggly
Winfield, AL 35594
(205)487-4341
Ultimate Parent: Bruno's. SIC: 5411—
Grocery Stores.

Wylam

★ 56711 ★   First National Bank of
Birmingham Alabama
4400 7th Ave.
PO Box 11007
Wylam, AL 35224
(205)326-5986
Company Type: Subsidiary. Officer: Betty
S. McGee, Manager. Ultimate Parent:
AmSouth Bancorp. SIC: 6021—National
Commercial Banks.

York

★ 56712 ★   First Alabama Bank
582 4th Ave.
York, AL 36925
(205)392-5551
Ultimate Parent: First Alabama
Bancshares. SIC: 6022—State Commercial
Banks.

★ 56713 ★   Texaco Food Mart
U S. Hwy. 80
York, AL 36925
(205)392-9197
Ultimate Parent: Texaco. SIC: 5541—
Gasoline Service Stations.

ARKANSAS

Alma

★ 56714 ★ Kentucky Fried
Chicken
Hwy. 71 N
Alma, AR 72921
(501)632-4151
Ultimate Parent: Pepsico. SIC: 5812—
Eating Places.

★ 56715 ★ Wal Mart Discount
City
Hwy. 64
Alma, AR 72921
(501)632-4585
Ultimate Parent: Wal-Mart Stores, Inc. SIC:
5311—Department Stores; 7538—General
Automotive Repair Shops.

Arkadelphia

★ 56716 ★ Coast to Coast
705 Main St.
Arkadelphia, AR 71923
(501)246-2851
Ultimate Parent: Servistar Corp. SIC:
5722—Household Appliance Stores.

★ 56717 ★ Kentucky Fried
Chicken
921 Clinton St.
Arkadelphia, AR 71923
(501)246-6149
Ultimate Parent: Pepsico. SIC: 5812—
Eating Places.

★ 56718 ★ Piggly Wiggly
810 Main St.
Arkadelphia, AR 71923
(501)246-4336
Ultimate Parent: Bruno's. SIC: 5411—
Grocery Stores.

★ 56719 ★ Piggly Wiggly
2701 Pine St.
Arkadelphia, AR 71923
(501)246-4641
Ultimate Parent: Bruno's. SIC: 5411—
Grocery Stores.

★ 56720 ★ Pizza Hut
Hwy. 67 N
Arkadelphia, AR 71923
(501)246-5895
Ultimate Parent: Pepsico. SIC: 5812—
Eating Places.

★ 56721 ★ Superior Federal
Bank, FSB
702 Caddo
Arkadelphia, AR 71923-5916
(501)246-4547
Company Type: Subsidiary. Location
Type: Branch office. Ultimate Parent:
Boatmen's Bancshares. SIC: 6021—
National Commercial Banks.

★ 56722 ★ Trailways Bus Station
10th
Arkadelphia, AR 71923
(501)246-5861
Ultimate Parent: Greyhound Lines Inc. SIC:
4131—Intercity & Rural Bus Transportation.

★ 56723 ★ Wal Mart Discount
City
2727 Caddo St.
Arkadelphia, AR 71923
(501)246-2459
Ultimate Parent: Wal-Mart Stores, Inc. SIC:
5311—Department Stores.

Arkansas City

★ 56724 ★ Potlatch Corp.
Hwy. 4
Arkansas City, AR 71630
(501)222-6310
Ultimate Parent: Potlatch. SIC: 2621—
Paper Mills.

Armorel

★ 56725 ★ Nucor-Yamato Steel
Co.
Hwy. 18 E. River Landing
Armorel, AR 72310
Ultimate Parent: Nucor Corp. SIC: 3312—
Blast Furnaces & Steel Mills.

Ash Flat

★ 56726 ★ Pizza Hut
Jct 62
Ash Flat, AR 72513
(501)994-7304
Ultimate Parent: Pepsico. SIC: 5812—
Eating Places.

Ashdown

★ 56727 ★ Georgia Pacific Corp.
Hwy. 71 S
Ashdown, AR 71822
(501)898-2711
Officer: Roger Brear, Manager. Ultimate
Parent: Georgia-Pacific. SIC: 2611—Pulp
Mills; 2621—Paper Mills.

★ 56728 ★ Kentucky Fried
Chicken
Hwy. 71 S
Ashdown, AR 71822
(501)898-3131
Ultimate Parent: Pepsico. SIC: 5812—
Eating Places.

★ 56729 ★ Pizza Hut
Hwy. 71 S
Ashdown, AR 71822
(501)898-5119
Ultimate Parent: Pepsico. SIC: 5812—
Eating Places.

Asher

★ 56730 ★ Borden Inc.
Dairy
7900 Asher Ave.
Asher, AR 72204
Company Type: Division. Ultimate Parent:
Borden, Inc. SIC: 2026—Fluid Milk.

Atkins

★ 56731 ★ Atkins Pickle Co.
602 SE 1st St.
Atkins, AR 72823
(501)641-2966
Officer: Robert Horrocks Jr., Manager.
Ultimate Parent: Dean Foods. SIC: 2035—
Pickles, Sauces & Salad Dressings.

★ 56732 ★ Conagra Frozen
Foods
Hwy. 64 E. PO Box 218
Atkins, AR 72823
Ultimate Parent: Conagra. SIC: 2048—
Prepared Feeds Nec.

★ 56733 ★ Green Bay Food Co.
PO Box 158
Atkins, AR
(501)641-2966 Fax: (501)641-1319
Location Type: Plant. Officer: Biff
Horrocks, Plant Manager. Ultimate Parent:
Dean Foods. SIC: 2035—Pickles, Sauces &
Salad Dressings.

★ 56734 ★ Green Bay Food Co.
Atkins Plant
602 SE 1st St.
Atkins, AR 72823
Ultimate Parent: Dean Foods. SIC: 2035—
Pickles, Sauces & Salad Dressings.

Augusta

★ 56735 ★ Itw Paslode
Hwy. 33B S.
Augusta, AR 72006
Ultimate Parent: Illinois Tool Works. SIC:
3496—Miscellaneous Fabricated Wire
Products.

Bald Knob

★ 56736 ★ Citizens State Bank
110 S. Elm
Bald Knob, AR 72010
(501)724-3241
Ultimate Parent: Liberty National Bancorp.
SIC: 6022—State Commercial Banks;
6029—Commercial Banks Nec.

★ 56737 ★ Piggly Wiggly
Hwy. 367
Bald Knob, AR 72010
(501)724-3285
Ultimate Parent: Bruno's. SIC: 5411—
Grocery Stores.

★ 56738 ★ Trailways Bus Station
Hwy. Ave.
Bald Knob, AR 72010
(501)724-5893
Ultimate Parent: Greyhound Lines Inc. SIC:
4131—Intercity & Rural Bus Transportation.

Barfield

★ 56739 ★ Nucor-Yamato Steel
Co.
Hwy. 18 East of Armorel
Barfield, AR 72310
Ultimate Parent: Nucor Corp. SIC: 3312—
Blast Furnaces & Steel Mills.

Batesville

★ 56740 ★ Arkansas Eastman
Co.
State Hwy. 394
Batesville, AR 72503
Ultimate Parent: Eastman Kodak. SIC:
2865—Cyclic Crudes & Intermediates.

★ 56741 ★ Arkansas Eastman
Co.
Hwy. 394 S
Batesville, AR 72501
(501)698-1811
Officer: Ronald Spillers, President.
Ultimate Parent: Eastman Kodak. SIC:
2899—Chemical Preparations Nec.

★ 56742 ★ Coast to Coast
Hardware
2400 Harrison St.
Batesville, AR 72501
(501)793-5668
Ultimate Parent: Servistar Corp. SIC:
5251—Hardware Stores.

★ 56743 ★ Coca Cola Bottling
Co.
College St. E
Batesville, AR 72501
(501)793-3320
Ultimate Parent: Coca-Cola Enterprises.
SIC: 2086—Bottled & Canned Soft Drinks.

★ 56744 ★ ConAgra Frozen
Foods
1810 St. Louis St.
Batesville, AR 72501
(501)793-8700 Fax: (501)793-8735
Company Type: Division. Officer: Tate
Lawrence, Plant Manager. Ultimate Parent:
Conagra.

★ 56745 ★ Conagra Frozen
Foods Cooking Plant
1810 St. Louis St. PO Box 2127
Batesville, AR 72501
Ultimate Parent: Conagra. SIC: 2038—
Frozen Specialties Nec.

★ 56746 ★ Conagra Frozen
Foods Cooking Plant
1810 St. Louis St.
Batesville, AR 72503
Ultimate Parent: Conagra. SIC: 2048—
Prepared Feeds Nec.

★ 56747 ★ Conagra Frozen
Foods Feed Mill
1810 St. Louis St.
Batesville, AR 72501
Ultimate Parent: Conagra. SIC: 2048—
Prepared Feeds Nec.

★ 56748 ★ Conagra Frozen
Foods Feedmill
1810 Saint Louis PO Box 2127
Batesville, AR 72503
Ultimate Parent: Conagra. SIC: 2048—
Prepared Feeds Nec.

★ 56749 ★ Conagra Frozen
Foods Processing Plant
1810 St. Louis St. PO Box 2127
Batesville, AR 72501
Ultimate Parent: Conagra. SIC: 2015—
Poultry Slaughtering & Processing.

★ 56750 ★ Diversitech General
Dba Gencorp Automotive
200 General St.
Batesville, AR 72503-2237
Ultimate Parent: Gencorp. SIC: 3069—
Fabricated Rubber Products Nec.

★ 56751 ★ Diversitech General
Inc. Dba Gencorp Automotive
200 General St.
Batesville, AR 72503-2237
Ultimate Parent: Gencorp. SIC: 3069—
Fabricated Rubber Products Nec.

★ 56752 ★ Eastman Kodak Co.
Arkansas Eastman Co.
State Hwy. 394
Batesville, AR 72501
Company Type: Division. Ultimate Parent:
Eastman Kodak. SIC: 2865—Cyclic Crudes
& Intermediates.

★ 56753 ★ Eastman Kodak Co.
Arkansas Eastman Div.
State Hwy. 394
Batesville, AR 72503
Company Type: Division. Ultimate Parent:
Eastman Kodak. SIC: 2865—Cyclic Crudes
& Intermediates; 2869—Industrial Organic
Chemicals Nec.

★ 56754 ★ Exxon Co.
Hwy. 167 St. N
Batesville, AR 72501
(501)793-7644
Ultimate Parent: Exxon. SIC: 5171—
Petroleum Bulk Stations & Terminals.

★ 56755 ★ Gencorp Automotive
Dba Gencorp Automotive
200 General St.
Batesville, AR 72501
Ultimate Parent: Gencorp. SIC: 3069—
Fabricated Rubber Products Nec.

★ 56756 ★ Gencorp Automotive
Inc. Dba Gencorp Automotive
200 General St.
Batesville, AR 72501
Ultimate Parent: Gencorp. SIC: 3061—
Mechanical Rubber Goods.

★ 56757 ★ **Hertz Rent-A-Car**
167 S. Hwy.
Batesville, AR 72501
(501)251-2678
Ultimate Parent: Hertz. **SIC:** 7514—
Passenger Car Rental.

★ 56758 ★ **Kroger Pharmacy**
425 St. Louis
Batesville, AR 72501
(501)793-6883
Ultimate Parent: Kroger. **SIC:** 5411—
Grocery Stores.

★ 56759 ★ **Pepsi-Cola Bottling Co.**
1125 Batesville Blvd.
Batesville, AR 72501
(501)251-2519
Officer: Brett Dingler, Manager. **Ultimate Parent:** Pepsico. **SIC:** 2086—Bottled &
Canned Soft Drinks.

★ 56760 ★ **Pizza Hut**
St Louis Bates
Batesville, AR 72501
(501)793-5779
Ultimate Parent: Pepsico. **SIC:** 5812—
Eating Places; 5812—Eating Places.

★ 56761 ★ **Professional Dental Inc.**
633 Lawrence St.
Batesville, AR 72501
(501)698-2113
Officer: Bob Lemon, President. **Ultimate Parent:** Bausch & Lomb Inc. **SIC:** 3843—
Dental Equipment & Supplies.

★ 56762 ★ **Ryder Truck Rental**
1308 E. Main St.
Batesville, AR 72501
(501)698-1228
Ultimate Parent: Ryder System. **SIC:**
2653—Corrugated & Solid Fiber Boxes.

★ 56763 ★ **Wal Mart Discount Cities**
20 Harrison
Batesville, AR 72501
(501)793-9821
Ultimate Parent: Wal-Mart Stores, Inc. **SIC:**
5311—Department Stores.

★ 56764 ★ **White Rodgers Co.**
2895 Harrison St.
Batesville, AR 72501
Ultimate Parent: Emerson Electric Co. Inc.
SIC: 3822—Environmental Controls.

Bauxite

★ 56765 ★ **Aluminum Co. of America**
PO Box 300
Bauxite, AR 72011
(501)776-4677
Ultimate Parent: Aluminum Co. of America-
-Alcoa. **SIC:** 2819—Industrial Inorganic
Chemicals Nec.

Beaver

★ 56766 ★ **Quotron Systems**
Hwy. 62 E
Beaver, AR 72613
(501)253-7446
Ultimate Parent: Citicorp.

Beebe

★ 56767 ★ **Coast to Coast**
115 N. Main St.
Beebe, AR 72012
(501)882-5314
Ultimate Parent: Servistar Corp. **SIC:**
5531—Automobile & Home Supply Stores.

★ 56768 ★ **Pizza Hut**
Hwy. 31 N
Beebe, AR 72012
(501)882-6444
Ultimate Parent: Pepsico. **SIC:** 5812—
Eating Places.

★ 56769 ★ **Texaco Food Mart**
Hwy. 64
Beebe, AR 72012
(501)882-3119
Ultimate Parent: Texaco. **SIC:** 5411—
Grocery Stores.

Benton

★ 56770 ★ **ACI**
1912 Dale
Benton, AR 72015
Ultimate Parent: Adolph Coors. **SIC:**
3269—Pottery Products Nec.

★ 56771 ★ **Aluminum Co. of America**
Hwy. 88
Benton, AR 72015
(501)778-3644
Ultimate Parent: Aluminum Co. of America-
-Alcoa. **SIC:** 3334—Primary Aluminum.

★ 56772 ★ **J.M. Huber**
Solem Ind.
1217 River St.
Benton, AR 72015
Company Type: Division. **Ultimate Parent:**
J. M. Huber. **SIC:** 2800—Chemicals & Allied
Products.

★ 56773 ★ **Pizza Hut**
1209 Old Hot Springs Rd.
Benton, AR 72015
(501)778-3661
Ultimate Parent: Pepsico. **SIC:** 5812—
Eating Places.

★ 56774 ★ **Radio Shack**
1205 Military Rd.
Benton, AR 72015
(501)778-8499
Company Type: Division. **Ultimate Parent:**
Tandy Corp. **SIC:** 5065—Electronic Parts &
Equipment Nec.

★ 56775 ★ **Solem Industries Inc.**
1217 River St.
Benton, AR 72015
Ultimate Parent: J. M. Huber. **SIC:** 2800—
Chemicals & Allied Products.

★ 56776 ★ **Superior Federal Bank, FSB**
609 N. Main St.
Benton, AR 72015
(501)778-1158
Location Type: Branch office. **Ultimate Parent:** Boatmen's Bancshares. **SIC:**
6021—National Commercial Banks.

★ 56777 ★ **Superior Federal Bank, FSB**
601 N. East St.
Benton, AR 72015-0537
(501)778-7402
Location Type: Branch office. **Officer:** Sue
Spivey, Manager. **Ultimate Parent:**
Boatmen's Bancshares. **SIC:** 6021—
National Commercial Banks.

★ 56778 ★ **Taco Bell**
1704 Military Rd.
Benton, AR 72015
(501)778-4826
Ultimate Parent: Pepsico. **SIC:** 5812—
Eating Places.

★ 56779 ★ **Texaco Distbtr**
302 E. Hazel St.
Benton, AR 72015
(501)778-1518
Ultimate Parent: Texaco.

★ 56780 ★ **Texaco-Nrthrn Oil**
302 E. Hazel St.
Benton, AR 72015
(501)847-4537
Ultimate Parent: Texaco.

★ 56781 ★ **Wal Mart**
Military Plz.
Benton, AR 72015
(501)778-3623
Ultimate Parent: Wal-Mart Stores, Inc. **SIC:**
5311—Department Stores.

★ 56782 ★ **Wal Mart**
1516 Military Rd.
Benton, AR 72015
(501)776-1355
Ultimate Parent: Wal-Mart Stores, Inc. **SIC:**
5399—Miscellaneous General Merchandise
Store.

★ 56783 ★ **Wal Mart Pharmacy**
Military Plz.
Benton, AR 72015
(501)778-5041
Ultimate Parent: Wal-Mart Stores, Inc. **SIC:**
5912—Drug Stores & Proprietary Stores.

Bentonville

★ 56784 ★ **Exxon**
3601 Moberly Ln.
Bentonville, AR 72712
(501)273-7476
Ultimate Parent: Exxon. **SIC:** 5411—
Grocery Stores; 5734—Computer &
Software Stores.

★ 56785 ★ **Kentucky Fried Chicken**
Hwy. 71 N
Bentonville, AR 72712
(501)273-5714
Ultimate Parent: Pepsico. **SIC:** 5812—
Eating Places.

★ 56786 ★ **Kraft Inc.**
507 SE E. St.
Bentonville, AR 72712
Ultimate Parent: Philip Morris. **SIC:** 2022—
Cheese—Natural & Processed.

★ 56787 ★ **McDonalds**
200 N. Hwy. 71
Bentonville, AR 72712
(501)273-7705
Ultimate Parent: McDonald's.

★ 56788 ★ **Radio Shack**
222 N. Hwy. 71
Bentonville, AR 72712
(501)273-2213
Company Type: Division. **Ultimate Parent:**
Tandy Corp. **SIC:** 5731—Radio, Television
& Electronics Stores.

★ 56789 ★ **Ryder Truck Rental**
Northwest 1st
Bentonville, AR 72712
(501)273-7796
Ultimate Parent: Ryder System. **SIC:**
5113—Industrial & Personal Service Paper.

★ 56790 ★ **Tyson Foods of Bentonville**
801 SE 8th
Bentonville, AR 72712
Ultimate Parent: Tyson Foods, Inc. **SIC:**
2000—Food & Kindred Products.

★ 56791 ★ **Tyson Foods Inc.**
801 SE 8th St.
Bentonville, AR 72712
(501)273-3321
Ultimate Parent: Tyson Foods, Inc. **SIC:**
2015—Poultry Slaughtering & Processing.

★ 56792 ★ **Tyson Foods Inc. of Bentonville**
801 SE 8th
Bentonville, AR 72712
Ultimate Parent: Tyson Foods, Inc. **SIC:**
2000—Food & Kindred Products.

★ 56793 ★ **Tyson Foods Inc. Krispy Kitchens**
801 SE 8th
Bentonville, AR 72712
Ultimate Parent: Tyson Foods, Inc. **SIC:**
2000—Food & Kindred Products.

★ 56794 ★ **Wal Mart**
Hwy. 71 N
Bentonville, AR 72712
(501)273-2461
Ultimate Parent: Wal-Mart Stores, Inc. **SIC:**
5311—Department Stores.

★ 56795 ★ **Wal Mart Properties Inc.**
701 S. Walton Blvd.
Bentonville, AR 72712
(501)273-4260
Ultimate Parent: Wal-Mart Stores, Inc. **SIC:**
5399—Miscellaneous General Merchandise
Store.

★ 56796 ★ **Wal Mart Properties Inc.**
116 PO Box
Bentonville, AR 72712
(501)273-7741
Ultimate Parent: Wal-Mart Stores, Inc. **SIC:**
6512—Nonresidential Building Operators.

★ 56797 ★ **Wal-Mart Stores, Inc.**
702 SW 8th St.
Bentonville, AR 72716
(501)273-4000 **Fax:** (501)273-8650
Company Type: Headquarters. **Officer:**
David D. Glass, CEO. **Employee Count:**
520000. **Sales:** 67344.6 M. **Fortune
Service 500:** Ranking 1.

Bergman

★ 56798 ★ **Tyson Foods Inc.
Bergman Feed Mill**
Ash St. & Railroad PO Box 56
Bergman, AR 72615
Ultimate Parent: Tyson Foods, Inc. **SIC:**
2048—Prepared Feeds Nec.

Berryville

★ 56799 ★ **Tyson Foods Inc.**
110 W. Freeman Ave.
Berryville, AR 72616
(501)423-2164
Officer: Hoy Slaughter, Manager. **Ultimate
Parent:** Tyson Foods, Inc. **SIC:** 2015—
Poultry Slaughtering & Processing; 2033—
Canned Fruits & Vegetables.

★ 56800 ★ **Tyson Foods Inc. of Berryville**
110 W. Freeman
Berryville, AR 72616
Ultimate Parent: Tyson Foods, Inc. **SIC:**
2000—Food & Kindred Products.

★ 56801 ★ **Tyson Foods Inc. Berryville**
110 W. Freeman
Berryville, AR 72616
Ultimate Parent: Tyson Foods, Inc. **SIC:**
2000—Food & Kindred Products.

Blytheville

★ 56802 ★ **Ball Corp.**
400 W. McHaney St.
Blytheville, AR 72315
Officer: Ronnie Russell, Plant Manager.
Ultimate Parent: Ball Corp. **SIC:** 3411—
Metal Cans.

★ 56803 ★ **Borg Warner Automotive**
4149 E. State Hwy. 18
Blytheville, AR 72315
(501)763-0830
Ultimate Parent: Borg Warner Automotive.
SIC: 3592—Carburetors, Pistons, Rings &
Valves; 3694—Engine Electrical Equipment.

★ 56804 ★ **Freeport Mcmoran**
Agrico Chemical Co. Div.
Arkansas Hwy. 18 & Mississippi River
Blytheville, AR 72315-9613
Company Type: Division. **Ultimate Parent:**
Freeport-McMoran. **SIC:** 2873—Nitrogenous
Fertilizers.

★ 56805 ★ **Greyhound Bus Lines**
109 N. 5th St.
Blytheville, AR 72315
(501)763-4441
Ultimate Parent: Greyhound Lines Inc. **SIC:**
4111—Local & Suburban Transit.

★ 56806 ★ **Heekin Can, Inc.**
PO Box 928
Blytheville, AR 72316-0928
(501)763-8821
Officer: Bobby Thornton. **Ultimate Parent:**
Ball Corp. **SIC:** 3411—Metal Cans.

★ 56807 ★ **Kentucky Fried Chicken**
Hwy. I 55
Blytheville, AR 72315
(501)762-2333
Ultimate Parent: Pepsico. **SIC:** 5812—
Eating Places.

★ 56808 ★ **Magnetek Inc.**
RT 1 Box 35
Blytheville, AR 72315-9802
(501)763-7898
Officer: Phil Partin. **Ultimate Parent:**
Magnetek Inc. **SIC:** 3612—Transformers
Except Electronic; 5063—Electrical
Apparatus & Equipment.

★ 56809 ★ **Magnetek Universal Manufacturing**
Rte. 1, Box 35, Industrial Dr.
Blytheville, AR 72315
Ultimate Parent: Magnetek Inc. **SIC:**
3612—Transformers Except Electronic.

★ 56810 ★ **Nucor Steel Arkansas**
7301 E. County Rd. 142
Blytheville, AR 72315
Ultimate Parent: Nucor Corp. **SIC:** 3312—
Blast Furnaces & Steel Mills; 3312—Blast
Furnaces & Steel Mills.

★ 56811 ★ **Nucor-Yamato Steel Co.**
5929 E. State Hwy. 18
Blytheville, AR 72316
Ultimate Parent: Nucor Corp. **SIC:** 3312—
Blast Furnaces & Steel Mills.

★ 56812 ★ **Nucor-Yamato Steel Co.**
PO Box 1228
Blytheville, AR 72316
(501)762-5500 **Fax:** (501)762-1130
Officer: Daniel DiMicco, Vice President &
General Manager. **Ultimate Parent:** Nucor
Corp.

★ 56813 ★ **Pizza Hut**
111 N. Division St.
Blytheville, AR 72315
(501)762-2224
Ultimate Parent: Pepsico. **SIC:** 5812—
Eating Places.

★ 56814 ★ **Randall Textron Inc.**
505 W. John McHaney Rd.
Blytheville, AR 72315
Ultimate Parent: Textron. **SIC:** 3469—
Metal Stampings Nec; 3471—Plating &
Polishing; 3499—Fabricated Metal Products
Nec.

★ 56815 ★ **Randall Textron Inc.**
505 W. McHaney Rd.
Blytheville, AR 72316-1048
Ultimate Parent: Textron. **SIC:** 7600—
Miscellaneous Repair Services.

★ 56816 ★ **Ryder Truck Rental**
Hwy. I 55
Blytheville, AR 72315
(501)763-3182
Ultimate Parent: Ryder System. **SIC:**
5113—Industrial & Personal Service Paper.

Booneville

★ 56817 ★ **Exxon Co. USA**
67 W. Main St.
Booneville, AR 72927
(501)675-4020
Ultimate Parent: Exxon. **SIC:** 5541—
Gasoline Service Stations.

★ 56818 ★ **Kentucky Fried Chicken**
Hwy. 10 E
Booneville, AR 72927
(501)675-2216
Ultimate Parent: Pepsico. **SIC:** 5812—
Eating Places.

Brinkley

★ 56819 ★ **Greyhound Bus Lines**
100 S. Main St.
Brinkley, AR 72021
(501)734-4624
Ultimate Parent: Greyhound Lines Inc. **SIC:**
4131—Intercity & Rural Bus Transportation.

★ 56820 ★ **Kentucky Fried Chicken**
3 N. Main
Brinkley, AR 72021
(501)734-2818
Ultimate Parent: Pepsico. **SIC:** 5812—
Eating Places.

★ 56821 ★ **Pizza Hut**
Pinecrest Shopping Ctr.
Brinkley, AR 72021
(501)734-1351
Ultimate Parent: Pepsico. **SIC:** 5812—
Eating Places.

★ 56822 ★ **Superior Federal Bank, FSB**
311 W. Cedar
Brinkley, AR 72021
(501)734-1598
Location Type: Branch office. **Officer:** Pat
Young, Manager. **Ultimate Parent:**
Boatmen's Bancshares. **SIC:** 6021—
National Commercial Banks.

Bryant

★ 56823 ★ **Jefferson Smurfit Corp.**
W-Exit 123
Bryant, AR 72022
(501)847-2905
Ultimate Parent: Jefferson Smurfit Corp.
SIC: 2653—Corrugated & Solid Fiber
Boxes.

★ 56824 ★ **Pizza Hut**
Reynolds & Puckett Rds.
Bryant, AR 72022
(501)847-4818
Ultimate Parent: Pepsico. **SIC:** 5812—
Eating Places.

Bull Shoals

★ 56825 ★ **Mary Kay Cosmetics**
PO Box 458
Bull Shoals, AR 72619
(501)445-4366
Ultimate Parent: Mary Kay Cosmetics.

Cabot

★ 56826 ★ **McDonalds Hamburgers**
1001 W. Main St.
Cabot, AR 72023
(501)843-5559
Ultimate Parent: McDonald's.

Camden

★ 56827 ★ **Brunswick Corp.**
PO Box 3163
Camden, AR 71701
(501)574-2800
Officer: Jim Fuller, Manager. **Ultimate
Parent:** Brunswick Corp. **SIC:** 3489—
Ordnance & Accessories Nec; 3761—
Guided Missiles & Space Vehicles.

★ 56828 ★ **Coca Cola Bottling Co.**
250 PO Box
Camden, AR 71701
(501)231-6434
Ultimate Parent: Coca-Cola Enterprises.
SIC: 5149—Groceries & Related Products
Nec.

★ 56829 ★ **Exxon**
Rr 5
Camden, AR 71701
(501)836-2265
Ultimate Parent: Exxon.

★ 56830 ★ **First Federal S & L**
208 Cardinal Shopping Ctr.
Camden, AR 71701
(501)231-6741
Company Type: Branch. **Ultimate Parent:**
Bancorp Hawaii. **SIC:** 6035—Federal
Savings Institutions.

★ 56831 ★ **GE Capital Railcar Service**
148 Ouachita 220
Camden, AR 71701
(501)574-0930
Officer: William O. Benefiel, Manager.
Ultimate Parent: General Electric. **SIC:**
3743—Railroad Equipment.

★ 56832 ★ **Greyhound Bus Line**
353 Jefferson St. SW
Camden, AR 71701
(501)836-2004
Ultimate Parent: Greyhound Lines Inc. **SIC:**
4111—Local & Suburban Transit.

★ 56833 ★ **International Paper Camden Facility**
1944 Adams Ave. PO Box 2045
Camden, AR 71701
Ultimate Parent: International Paper Co.
SIC: 2611—Pulp Mills; 2621—Paper Mills;
2674—Bags—Uncoated Paper & Multiwall.

★ 56834 ★ **International Paper Co. Camden Mill**
1944 Adams Ave., PO Box 2045
Camden, AR 71701
Ultimate Parent: International Paper Co.
SIC: 2611—Pulp Mills; 2621—Paper Mills.

★ 56835 ★ **Kroger Co.**
Ark Hwy. 4 Spur
Camden, AR 71701
(501)836-3101
Ultimate Parent: Kroger. **SIC:** 5411—
Grocery Stores.

★ 56836 ★ **Loral Vought Systems**
Hwy. 274
Highland Industrial Park
Camden, AR 71701
(501)574-0200
Company Type: Subsidiary. **Ultimate
Parent:** Loral Corp. **SIC:** 3728—Aircraft
Parts & Equipment Nec; 3711—Motor
Vehicles & Car Bodies; 3761—Guided
Missiles & Space Vehicles.

★ 56837 ★ **Loral Vought Systems Corp.**
Missiles & Electronics Div.
Walton Rd. Highland Industrial Park
Camden, AR 71701
Company Type: Division. **Ultimate Parent:**
Loral Corp. **SIC:** 3999—Manufacturing
Industries Nec.

★ 56838 ★ **Piggly Wiggly**
Cardinal Shopping Ctr.
Camden, AR 71701
(501)231-5985
Ultimate Parent: Bruno's. **SIC:** 5411—
Grocery Stores.

★ 56839 ★ **Pizza Hut**
Garden Oaks Shopping Ctr.
Camden, AR 71701
(501)836-6421
Ultimate Parent: Pepsico. **SIC:** 5812—
Eating Places.

★ 56840 ★ **Radio Shack**
106 N. Adams Ave.
Camden, AR 71701
(501)836-6937
Company Type: Division. **Ultimate Parent:**
Tandy Corp. **SIC:** 5731—Radio, Television
& Electronics Stores.

★ 56841 ★ **Shell Super Stop**
Hwy. 4 Bypass
Camden, AR 71701
(501)836-9416
Ultimate Parent: Shell Oil Co. **SIC:** 5541—
Gasoline Service Stations.

Canden

★ 56842 ★ **Sonoco Products Co.**
700 Carr Rd.
Canden, AR 71701
(501)574-1250
Officer: Sam F. Richey Jr., Plant Manager.
Ultimate Parent: Sonoco Products. **SIC:**
2655—Fiber Cans, Drums & Similar
Products.

Carlisle

★ 56843 ★ **Coast to Coast Home & Auto**
Hwy. 70
Carlisle, AR 72024
(501)552-3821
Ultimate Parent: Servistar Corp. **SIC:**
5531—Automobile & Home Supply Stores.

★ 56844 ★ **Superior Federal Bank, FSB**
Main & Williams
Carlisle, AR 72024
(501)552-7521
Location Type: Branch office. **Officer:** Pat
Hogan, Manager. **Ultimate Parent:**
Boatmen's Bancshares. **SIC:** 6021—
National Commercial Banks.

Charleston

★ 56845 ★ **Tyson Foods Bloomer Plant**
27711 Hwy. 22
Charleston, AR 72933
(501)965-2242
Officer: Allan Sturdivant, Manager.
Ultimate Parent: Tyson Foods, Inc. **SIC:**
2015—Poultry Slaughtering & Processing.

Clarendon

★ 56846 ★ **Greyhound Bus Line**
5th
Clarendon, AR 72029
(501)747-5221
Ultimate Parent: Greyhound Lines Inc. **SIC:**
4131—Intercity & Rural Bus Transportation.

★ 56847 ★ **Piper/Casepro**
Hwy. 79 E
Clarendon, AR 72029
Ultimate Parent: Texas Industries. **SIC:**
3496—Miscellaneous Fabricated Wire
Products; 3499—Fabricated Metal Products
Nec; 3799—Transportation Equipment Nec;
2441—Nailed Wood Boxes & Shook;
3446—Architectural Metal Work; 3569—
General Industrial Machinery Nec.

Clarksville

★ 56848 ★ **Kim Products**
PO Box 528
Clarksville, AR 72830
(501)754-6313
Location Type: Facility. **Officer:** Jerry
Coffee, Plant Manager. **Ultimate Parent:**
H.J. Heinz. **SIC:** 2038—Frozen Specialties
Nec.

★ 56849 ★ **Piggly Wiggly**
Hwy. 103 S
Clarksville, AR 72830
(501)754-3900
Ultimate Parent: Bruno's. **SIC:** 5411—
Grocery Stores.

★ 56850 ★ **Pizza Hut**
Hwy. 103 S
Clarksville, AR 72830
(501)754-6900
Ultimate Parent: Pepsico. **SIC:** 5812—
Eating Places.

★ 56851 ★ **Ryder Truck Rental**
I Hwy. 103 40th
Clarksville, AR 72830
(501)754-3119
Ultimate Parent: Ryder System. **SIC:**
7359—Equipment Rental & Leasing Nec.

★ 56852 ★ **Trailways Bus Depot**
Runner
Clarksville, AR 72830
(501)754-7550
Ultimate Parent: Greyhound Lines Inc. **SIC:**
4131—Intercity & Rural Bus Transportation.

★ 56853 ★ **Tyson Foods Inc.**
200 East Cheery
Clarksville, AR 72830
Ultimate Parent: Tyson Foods, Inc. **SIC:**
2000—Food & Kindred Products

★ 56854 ★ **Tyson Foods Inc.**
200 E. Cherry St.
Clarksville, AR 72830
(501)754-3586
Officer: Ken Nelson, Manager. **Ultimate
Parent:** Tyson Foods, Inc. **SIC:** 2015—
Poultry Slaughtering & Processing.

Clinton

★ 56855 ★ **Belden Wire & Cable**
Factory Rd. - Box H
Clinton, AR 72031
Ultimate Parent: Cooper Industries. **SIC:**
3357—Nonferrous Wiredrawing & Insulating.

★ 56856 ★ **Cooper Industries**
Belden Div.
Quality Dr.
Clinton, AR 72031-0908
Company Type: Division. **Ultimate Parent:**
Cooper Industries. **SIC:** 3643—
Current-Carrying Wiring Devices; 3399—
Primary Metal Products Nec.

★ 56857 ★ **Cooper Industries Inc.**
Belden Div.
Quality Dr.
Clinton, AR 72031-0908
Company Type: Division. **Ultimate Parent:**
Cooper Industries. **SIC:** 3643—
Current-Carrying Wiring Devices.

★ 56858 ★ **Pizza Hut**
N Hwy. 65 Bypass
Clinton, AR 72031
(501)745-4828
Ultimate Parent: Pepsico. **SIC:** 5812—
Eating Places.

Conway

★ 56859 ★ **Ace Hardware Store**
1006 Garland St.
Conway, AR 72032
(501)329-5150
Ultimate Parent: Ace Hardware.

★ 56860 ★ **First State Bank & Trust Co.**
712 Court St.
Conway, AR 72032
(501)327-0053
Ultimate Parent: Michigan National Corp.
SIC: 6022—State Commercial Banks.

★ 56861 ★ **FMC Corp.**
309 Exchange Ave.
Conway, AR 72032
(501)327-4433
Officer: Ron Hill, Manager. **Ultimate
Parent:** FMC. **SIC:** 3559—Special Industry
Machinery Nec; 3825—Instruments to
Measure Electricity.

★ 56862 ★ **FMC Corp., Conway Plant**
Industrial Pk. Exchange Ave.
Conway, AR 72032
Location Type: Plant. **Ultimate Parent:**
FMC. **SIC:** 3559—Special Industry
Machinery Nec; 3549—Metalworking
Machinery Nec.

★ 56863 ★ **Kay Bee Toys**
Hwy. 65 N
Conway, AR 72032
(501)327-6946
Ultimate Parent: Melville. **SIC:** 5945—
Hobby, Toy & Game Shops.

★ 56864 ★ **Kentucky Fried Chicken**
W Oak St.
Conway, AR 72032
(501)327-0951
Ultimate Parent: Pepsico. **SIC:** 5812—
Eating Places.

★ 56865 ★ **Kroger Company**
100 Oak St.
Conway, AR 72032
(501)329-2557
Ultimate Parent: Kroger. **SIC:** 5411—
Grocery Stores.

★ 56866 ★ **Kroger Pharmacy**
Faulkner Plz.
Conway, AR 72032
(501)327-4441
Ultimate Parent: Kroger. **SIC:** 5912—Drug
Stores & Proprietary Stores.

★ 56867 ★ **Piggly Wiggly**
2125 Hwy. 64 W
Conway, AR 72032
(501)327-2975
Ultimate Parent: Bruno's. **SIC:** 5411—
Grocery Stores.

★ 56868 ★ **Pizza Hut**
1076 Harkrider St.
Conway, AR 72032
(501)327-1396
Ultimate Parent: Pepsico. **SIC:** 5812—
Eating Places.

★ 56869 ★ **Radio Shack**
100 Oak St.
Conway, AR 72032
(501)327-2485
Company Type: Division. **Ultimate Parent:**
Tandy Corp. **SIC:** 5731—Radio, Television
& Electronics Stores.

★ 56870 ★ **Ryder Truck Rental**
1000 Nabco Ave.
Conway, AR 72032
(501)327-5556
Ultimate Parent: Ryder System. **SIC:**
7353—Heavy Construction Equipment
Rental.

★ 56871 ★ **Sico Inc.**
100 Exchange Ave.
Conway, AR 72032
(501)327-6728
Ultimate Parent: American Life. **SIC:**
2511—Wood Household Furniture.

★ 56872 ★ **Taco Bell**
W Oak St.
Conway, AR 72032
(501)329-5090
Ultimate Parent: Pepsico. **SIC:** 5812—
Eating Places.

★ 56873 ★ **Texaco Inc.**
E Robbins
Conway, AR 72032
(501)327-2782
Ultimate Parent: Texaco. **SIC:** 5541—
Gasoline Service Stations.

★ 56874 ★ **Trailways Bus System**
1015 Harkrider St.
Conway, AR 72032
(501)329-3166
Ultimate Parent: Greyhound Lines Inc. **SIC:**
4131—Intercity & Rural Bus Transportation.

★ 56875 ★ **Union Camp Corp.**
730 Enterprise Ave.
Conway, AR 72032
(501)329-9456
Officer: Gil Becker, Manager. **Ultimate
Parent:** Union Camp Corp. **SIC:** 2672—
Coated & Laminated Paper Nec; 2752—
Commercial Printing—Lithographic; 2759—
Commercial Printing Nec.

★ 56876 ★ **United Parcel Service**
Halter Rd.
Conway, AR 72032
(501)329-8416
Ultimate Parent: United Parcel Service of
America. **SIC:** 4215—Courier Services
Except by Air.

★ 56877 ★ **Wal Mart**
Hwy. 65 N
Conway, AR 72032
(501)327-5799
Ultimate Parent: Wal-Mart Stores, Inc. **SIC:**
5311—Department Stores.

Crossett

★ 56878 ★ **Ashley Drew & Northern Railway**
PO Box 757
Crossett, AR 71635
(501)567-8028 **Fax:** (501)364-9355
Company Type: Subsidiary. **Ultimate
Parent:** Georgia Gulf.

★ 56879 ★ **Bemis Co.**
1401 W. 3rd Ave.
Crossett, AR 71635
(501)364-2103
Officer: Billy Abraugh, Manager. **Ultimate
Parent:** Bemis Co., Inc. **SIC:** 2673—Bags-
Plastics, Laminated & Coated; 2674—
Bags—Uncoated Paper & Multiwall.

★ 56880 ★ **Fordyce & Princeton Railroad**
Plywood Mill Rd.
Crossett, AR 71635
(501)567-8028 **Fax:** (501)364-9355
Company Type: Subsidiary. **Ultimate
Parent:** Georgia Gulf.

★ 56881 ★ **Georgia-Pacific Corp. Paper Operations**
Paper Mill Rd.
Crossett, AR 71635
Ultimate Parent: Georgia-Pacific. **SIC:**
2611—Pulp Mills.

★ 56882 ★ **Georgia-Pacific Corp. Paper Ops.**
Paper Mill Rd.
Crossett, AR 71635
Ultimate Parent: Georgia-Pacific. **SIC:**
2611—Pulp Mills.

★ 56883 ★ **Georgia-Pacific Corp. Plywood**
Hwy. 82
Crossett, AR 71635
Ultimate Parent: Georgia-Pacific. **SIC:**
2436—Softwood Veneer & Plywood.

★ 56884 ★ **Georgia Pacific Resins Inc.**
Hwy. 82
Crossett, AR 71635
Ultimate Parent: Georgia-Pacific. **SIC:**
2821—Plastics Materials & Resins; 2869—
Industrial Organic Chemicals Nec.

★ 56885 ★ **Georgia-Pacific Resins Inc. Resins**
Hwy. 82 Papermill Rd. Hwy. 82
Crossett, AR 71635
Ultimate Parent: Georgia-Pacific. **SIC:**
2436—Softwood Veneer & Plywood.

★ 56886 ★ **Radio Shack**
205 Main St.
Crossett, AR 71635
(501)364-5989
Company Type: Division. **Ultimate Parent:**
Tandy Corp. **SIC:** 5731—Radio, Television
& Electronics Stores.

Danville

★ 56887 ★ **Superior Federal Bank, FSB**
Cleveland & Hwy. 10 E
Danville, AR 72833
(501)495-2321
Location Type: Branch office. **Officer:**
Betty Parish, Manager. **Ultimate Parent:**
Boatmen's Bancshares. **SIC:** 6021—
National Commercial Banks.

Dardanelle

★ 56888 ★ **Pizza Hut**
507 Union St.
Dardanelle, AR 72834
(501)229-3517
Ultimate Parent: Pepsico. **SIC:** 5812—
Eating Places.

★ 56889 ★ **Tyson Foods Inc.**
6th & Locust St.
Dardanelle, AR 72834
(501)229-3357
Officer: Randy Milam, Manager. **Ultimate
Parent:** Tyson Foods, Inc. **SIC:** 2015—
Poultry Slaughtering & Processing; 2048—
Prepared Feeds Nec.

★ 56890 ★ **Tyson Foods Inc. Dardanelle Complex**
6th & Locust St.
Dardanelle, AR 72834
Ultimate Parent: Tyson Foods, Inc. **SIC:**
2015—Poultry Slaughtering & Processing;
2048—Prepared Feeds Nec.

De Queen

★ 56891 ★ **Exxon Co.**
815 S. Rockefeller
De Queen, AR 71832
(501)642-3455
Ultimate Parent: Exxon. **SIC:** 5172—
Petroleum Products Nec.

★ 56892 ★ **Piggly Wiggly**
Town Shopping Ctr. N
De Queen, AR 71832
(501)642-2726
Ultimate Parent: Bruno's. **SIC:** 5411—
Grocery Stores.

★ 56893 ★ **Pilgrim's Pride Corp.**
123 W. Park
De Queen, AR 71832
Ultimate Parent: Pilgrim's Pride Corp. **SIC:**
2000—Food & Kindred Products.

★ 56894 ★ **Pilgrim's Pride Corp.**
Dequeen Processing
123 W. Park St.
De Queen, AR 71832
Company Type: Division. **Ultimate Parent:**
Pilgrim's Pride Corp. **SIC:** 2015—Poultry
Slaughtering & Processing.

★ 56895 ★ **Pizza Hut**
71 N
De Queen, AR 71832
(501)642-4321
Ultimate Parent: Pepsico. **SIC:** 5812—
Eating Places.

★ 56896 ★ **Ryder Truck Rental**
Hwy. 70
De Queen, AR 71832
(501)642-6025
Ultimate Parent: Ryder System. **SIC:**
7359—Equipment Rental & Leasing Nec.

★ 56897 ★ **Wal Mart**
Jct Us 70 71
De Queen, AR 71832
(501)642-2794
Ultimate Parent: Wal-Mart Stores, Inc. **SIC:**
5331—Variety Stores.

★ 56898 ★ **Weyerhaeuser Co.**
1000 S. Treating Plant Rd.
De Queen, AR 71832
(501)642-1344
Officer: W. L. Gregory, Manager. **Ultimate
Parent:** Weyerhaeuser Co. **SIC:** 2421—
Sawmills & Planing Mills—General; 2491—
Wood Preserving.

★ 56899 ★ **Weyerhaeuser Co. Wood Treating Plant**
Treating Plant Rd.
De Queen, AR 71832
Ultimate Parent: Weyerhaeuser Co. **SIC:**
2491—Wood Preserving.

★ 56900 ★ **Weyerhaeuser Wood Treating Plant**
PO Box 387
De Queen, AR 71832
Location Type: Plant. **Ultimate Parent:**
Weyerhaeuser Co. **SIC:** 2491—Wood
Preserving.

De Valls Bluff

★ 56901 ★ **Sun Refining & Marketing Co.**
Hwy. 70 W
De Valls Bluff, AR 72041
(501)998-2615
Ultimate Parent: Sun. **SIC:** 5722—
Household Appliance Stores.

De Witt

★ 56902 ★ **Kroger Co. Inc**
Hwy. 1
De Witt, AR 72042
(501)946-2095
Ultimate Parent: Kroger. **SIC:** 5411—
Grocery Stores.

Delaplaine

★ 56903 ★ **Corning Grain Drying Co.**
Delaplaine, AR 72425
(501)857-3582
Ultimate Parent: Riceland Foods. **SIC:**
2044—Rice Milling.

Dierks

★ 56904 ★ **Exxon**
S Main St.
Dierks, AR 71833
(501)286-3117
Ultimate Parent: Exxon. **SIC:** 5531—
Automobile & Home Supply Stores.

★ 56905 ★ **Northrop Aircraft Inc.**
Dierks, AR 71833
(501)286-2444
Ultimate Parent: Northrop Corp. **SIC:**
4581—Airports, Flying Fields & Services.

★ 56906 ★ **Weyerhaeuser Co.**
Hwy. 70 E.
Dierks, AR 71833
Ultimate Parent: Weyerhaeuser Co. **SIC:**
2421—Sawmills & Planing Mills—General;
2436—Softwood Veneer & Plywood.

★ 56907 ★ **Weyerhaeuser Co.**
Hwy. 70
Dierks, AR
(501)286-2193
Officer: Ron Endicott, Manager. **Ultimate
Parent:** Weyerhaeuser Co. **SIC:** 2411—
Logging; 2421—Sawmills & Planing Mills—
General; 2436—Softwood Veneer &
Plywood.

Dumas

★ **56908** ★ **Belden Automotive Wire & Cable**
Brookhaven St.
Dumas, AR 71639
Ultimate Parent: Cooper Industries. **SIC:** 3714—Motor Vehicle Parts & Accessories.

★ **56909** ★ **Belden Automotive Wire & Cable**
S. Main St.
Dumas, AR 71639
Ultimate Parent: Cooper Industries. **SIC:** 3357—Nonferrous Wiredrawing & Insulating.

★ **56910** ★ **Belden Automotive Wire & Cable**
South Main St.
Dumas, AR 71639
Ultimate Parent: Cooper Industries. **SIC:** 3357—Nonferrous Wiredrawing & Insulating.

★ **56911** ★ **Hussmann Corp.**
Hwy. 65 South
Dumas, AR 71639
Ultimate Parent: Whitman Corp. **SIC:** 3585—Refrigeration & Heating Equipment.

★ **56912** ★ **Kentucky Fried Chicken**
Hwy. 65 S
Dumas, AR 71639
(501)382-6300
Ultimate Parent: Pepsico. **SIC:** 5812—Eating Places.

★ **56913** ★ **Mini Mart**
401 W. Waterman St.
Dumas, AR 71639
(501)382-2030
Ultimate Parent: Kroger. **SIC:** 5411—Grocery Stores.

★ **56914** ★ **Riceland Foods Inc.**
Rte. 1
Dumas, AR 71639
(501)673-5500
Officer: Stewart E. Jessup, Chairman. **Ultimate Parent:** Riceland Foods. **SIC:** 2044—Rice Milling; 2075—Soybean Oil Mills; 2079—Edible Fats & Oils Nec.

★ **56915** ★ **Ryder Truck Rental**
Hwy. 165 N
Dumas, AR 71639
(501)382-6239
Ultimate Parent: Ryder System. **SIC:** 7359—Equipment Rental & Leasing Nec.

East Camden

★ **56916** ★ **Atlantic Research Corp.**
Walton Rd. Highland Industrial Park
East Camden, AR 71701-1036
Ultimate Parent: Sequa Corp. **SIC:** 3761—Guided Missiles & Space Vehicles; 3764—Space Propulsion Units & Parts.

★ **56917** ★ **Atlantic Research Corp.**
Arkansas Propulsion
Highland Industrial Park Walton Rd.
East Camden, AR 71701-1036
Ultimate Parent: Sequa Corp. **SIC:** 3764—Space Propulsion Units & Parts.

★ **56918** ★ **Brunswick**
Defense Div.
Bldg. 5SH-1 Walton Rd.
East Camden, AR 71701
Ultimate Parent: Brunswick Corp. **SIC:** 3761—Guided Missiles & Space Vehicles.

★ **56919** ★ **Brunswick Composites**
Defense Div.
Hwy. 274 E. Walton Rd., Bldg. 5-SH-1
East Camden, AR 71701
Ultimate Parent: Brunswick Corp. **SIC:** 3761—Guided Missiles & Space Vehicles.

★ **56920** ★ **Brunswick Corp.**
Defense Div.
Hwy. 274 E. Walton Rd.,Bldg. 5 SH-1
East Camden, AR 71701
Ultimate Parent: Brunswick Corp. **SIC:** 3761—Guided Missiles & Space Vehicles.

★ **56921** ★ **Brunswick Corp.**
Defense Division
Building 5-Sh-1 Walton Rd.
East Camden, AR 71701
Ultimate Parent: Brunswick Corp. **SIC:** 3761—Guided Missiles & Space Vehicles.

★ **56922** ★ **General Dynamics**
204 Quachita 212 Park
East Camden, AR 71701
Ultimate Parent: General Dynamics. **SIC:** 3761—Guided Missiles & Space Vehicles.

★ **56923** ★ **General Dynamics**
Rte. 4 Airport Industrial Park
East Camden, AR 71701
Ultimate Parent: General Dynamics. **SIC:** 3761—Guided Missiles & Space Vehicles.

★ **56924** ★ **Hughes Missile Sys. Co.**
204 Quachita 212 Park
East Camden, AR 71701
Ultimate Parent: General Dynamics. **SIC:** 3761—Guided Missiles & Space Vehicles.

El Dorado

★ **56925** ★ **Arkansas Chemicals Inc.**
Hwy. 15 South Newell
El Dorado, AR 71730
Ultimate Parent: Great Lakes Chemical. **SIC:** 2819—Industrial Inorganic Chemicals Nec.

★ **56926** ★ **Arkansas Chemicals Inc.**
Hwy. 15, Newell
El Dorado, AR 71730
Ultimate Parent: Great Lakes Chemical. **SIC:** 2819—Industrial Inorganic Chemicals Nec.

★ **56927** ★ **Columbian Chemicals Co.**
713 Industrial Rd.
El Dorado, AR 71730
Ultimate Parent: Phelps Dodge. **SIC:** 2895—Carbon Black.

★ **56928** ★ **Columbian Chemicals Co.**
Industrial Rd.
El Dorado, AR 71731-0299
Ultimate Parent: Phelps Dodge. **SIC:** 2895—Carbon Black.

★ **56929** ★ **Conagra Broiler**
295 Feed Mill Rd.
El Dorado, AR 71730
Ultimate Parent: Conagra. **SIC:** 2048—Prepared Feeds Nec.

★ **56930** ★ **Conagra Broiler Co.**
1810 Southwest Ave.
El Dorado, AR 71730
Ultimate Parent: Conagra. **SIC:** 2015—Poultry Slaughtering & Processing; 2077—Animal & Marine Fats & Oils.

★ **56931** ★ **ConAgra Broiler Co.**
PO Box 1758
El Dorado, AR 71730
Ultimate Parent: Conagra. **SIC:** 2048—Prepared Feeds Nec.

★ **56932** ★ **ConAgra Broiler Co.**
422 N. Washington St.

El Dorado, AR 71731
(501)863-1600
Company Type: Division. **Officer:** Pat Cauley, Executive Vice President of Personnel. **Ultimate Parent:** Conagra.

★ **56933** ★ **ConAgra Broiler Co.**
PO Box 1997
El Dorado, AR 71730
(501)863-1600 **Fax:** (501)863-1793
Officer: George R. Haefner, President. **Ultimate Parent:** Conagra.

★ **56934** ★ **ConAgra Poultry Co.**
PO Box 1997
El Dorado, AR 71730
(501)863-1600 **Fax:** (501)863-1793
Officer: George R. Haefner, President & COO. **Ultimate Parent:** Conagra.

★ **56935** ★ **ConAgra Poultry Co.**
422 N. Washington St.
El Dorado, AR 71730
Company Type: Division. **Location Type:** Headquarters. **Officer:** Bob Womack, President & COO. **Ultimate Parent:** Conagra.

★ **56936** ★ **Cooper Industrial Products**
Prescolite Dr.
El Dorado, AR 71730
Ultimate Parent: Cooper Tire & Rubber Co. Inc. **SIC:** 3069—Fabricated Rubber Products Nec; 3061—Mechanical Rubber Goods; 3053—Gaskets, Packing & Sealing Devices.

★ **56937** ★ **Cooper Tire & Rubber Co.**
Engineered Products Div.
166 Cooper Dr.
El Dorado, AR 71730
Company Type: Division. **Ultimate Parent:** Cooper Tire & Rubber Co. Inc. **SIC:** 3069—Fabricated Rubber Products Nec; 3061—Mechanical Rubber Goods; 3053—Gaskets, Packing & Sealing Devices.

★ **56938** ★ **Copper Industrial Products**
Prescolite Dr.
El Dorado, AR 71730
Ultimate Parent: Cooper Tire & Rubber Co. Inc. **SIC:** 3069—Fabricated Rubber Products Nec; 3061—Mechanical Rubber Goods; 3053—Gaskets, Packing & Sealing Devices.

★ **56939** ★ **Copper Tire & Rubber Co.**
Engineered Products Div.
166 Cooper Dr.
El Dorado, AR 71730
Company Type: Division. **Ultimate Parent:** Cooper Tire & Rubber Co. Inc. **SIC:** 3069—Fabricated Rubber Products Nec; 3061—Mechanical Rubber Goods; 3053—Gaskets, Packing & Sealing Devices.

★ **56940** ★ **Deltic Farm & Timber Co., Inc.**
200 Peach St.
El Dorado, AR 71730
(501)864-6562
Officer: Ron L. Pearce, President. **Ultimate Parent:** Murphy Oil.

★ **56941** ★ **Exxon Food Mart 5**
2109 Junction City Rd.
El Dorado, AR 71730
(501)862-3488
Ultimate Parent: Exxon.

★ **56942** ★ **First Financial Bank a Fsb**
315 W. Main St.
El Dorado, AR 71730
(501)863-7000
Ultimate Parent: First Financial Corp. **SIC:** 6036—Savings Institutions Except Federal.

★ **56943** ★ **Georgia Pacific Corp.**
5369 Junction City Hwy.
El Dorado, AR 71730
(501)862-7904
Officer: Randall Green, Manager. **Ultimate Parent:** Georgia-Pacific. **SIC:** 2421—Sawmills & Planing Mills—General; 2426—Hardwood Dimension & Flooring Mills.

★ **56944** ★ **Great Lakes Chemical Co. El Dorado-Main Plant**
Hwy. 15 South
El Dorado, AR 71731
Ultimate Parent: Great Lakes Chemical. **SIC:** 2819—Industrial Inorganic Chemicals Nec; 2869—Industrial Organic Chemicals Nec.

★ **56945** ★ **Great Lakes Chemical Co. El Dorado Plant**

El Dorado, AR
Ultimate Parent: Great Lakes Chemical. **SIC:** 2819—Industrial Inorganic Chemicals Nec; 2869—Industrial Organic Chemicals Nec.

★ **56946** ★ **Great Lakes Chemical Corp. El Dorado Plant**

El Dorado, AR
Ultimate Parent: Great Lakes Chemical. **SIC:** 2819—Industrial Inorganic Chemicals

Nec; 2869—Industrial Organic Chemicals Nec.

★ **56947** ★ **Great Lakes Chemical Corp. South Plant**
324 Southfield Cutoff
El Dorado, AR 71730
Ultimate Parent: Great Lakes Chemical. **SIC:** 2869—Industrial Organic Chemicals Nec; 2819—Industrial Inorganic Chemicals Nec.

★ **56948** ★ **Great Lakes Chemical Corp., South Plant**
Rte. 7, Box 529
El Dorado, AR 71730
Location Type: Plant. **Ultimate Parent:** Great Lakes Chemical. **SIC:** 2869—Industrial Organic Chemicals Nec; 2819—Industrial Inorganic Chemicals Nec.

★ **56949** ★ **Hertz Rent-A-Car**
401 N. West Ave.
El Dorado, AR 71730
(501)862-6649
Ultimate Parent: Hertz.

★ **56950** ★ **Kentucky Fried Chicken**
427 W. Hillsboro St.
El Dorado, AR 71730
(501)862-1763
Ultimate Parent: Pepsico. **SIC:** 5812—Eating Places; 5812—Eating Places.

★ **56951** ★ **Kroger**
2202 N. West Ave.
El Dorado, AR 71730
(501)862-5602
Ultimate Parent: Kroger. **SIC:** 5411—Grocery Stores.

★ **56952** ★ **Kroger Delicatessen**
Mellor Park Mall
El Dorado, AR 71730
(501)863-8581
Ultimate Parent: Kroger. **SIC:** 5411—Grocery Stores.

★ **56953** ★ **Murphy Oil**
200 Peach St.
El Dorado, AR 71730
(501)862-6411
Company Type: Headquarters. **Officer:** Jack W. McNutt. **Employee Count:** 1803. **Sales:** 1637 M. **Fortune 500:** Largest U.S. Industrial Corporations: Ranking 262.

★ **56954** ★ **Murphy Oil Corp.**
200 Peach St.
El Dorado, AR 71730
(501)862-6411 **Fax:** (501)862-9057 **Telex:** 536210
Officer: Jack W. McNutt, President & CEO. **Ultimate Parent:** Murphy Oil. **Employee Count:** 1787.

★ **56955** ★ **Murphy Oil USA, Inc.**
200 Peach St.
El Dorado, AR 71730
(501)864-6446
Officer: H. A. Fox Jr., President. **Ultimate Parent:** Murphy Oil.

★ **56956** ★ **Pizza Hut**
615 E. Hillsboro St.
El Dorado, AR 71730
(501)862-5821
Ultimate Parent: Pepsico. **SIC:** 5812—Eating Places.

★ **56957** ★ **Prescolite**
Industrial Rd. & Prescolite Dr.
El Dorado, AR 71731-0151
Ultimate Parent: Hanson Industries. **SIC:** 3646—Commercial Lighting Fixtures; 3363—Aluminum Die-Castings; 3469—Metal Stampings Nec.

★ **56958** ★ **Professional Food Systems**
PO Box 1627
El Dorado, AR 71730
(501)863-1773 **Fax:** (501)863-1750
Officer: Rolan Brevard, President. **Ultimate Parent:** Conagra.

★ **56959** ★ **Taco Bell**
2137 N. West Ave.
El Dorado, AR 71730
(501)862-7079
Ultimate Parent: Pepsico. **SIC:** 5812—Eating Places.

★ 56960 ★   **Texaco Petroleum**
208 S. Mosby Ave.
El Dorado, AR 71730
(501)863-3051
Ultimate Parent: Texaco.

★ 56961 ★   **Trailways Bus Station**
340 W. Hillsboro St.
El Dorado, AR 71730
(501)863-7107
Ultimate Parent: Greyhound Lines Inc. **SIC:**
4111—Local & Suburban Transit; 4173—
Bus Terminal & Service Facilities.

★ 56962 ★   **Wal Mart Discount City**
2115 N. West Ave.
El Dorado, AR 71730
(501)863-4043
Ultimate Parent: Wal-Mart Stores, Inc. **SIC:**
5311—Department Stores.

Eldorado

★ 56963 ★   **Arkansas Chemicals Inc.**
3940 Haynesville Hwy.
Eldorado, AR 71730
(501)862-4973 **Fax:** (501)862-4964
Company Type: Subsidiary. **Officer:**
Emerson Kampen, President. **Ultimate Parent:** Great Lakes Chemical. **SIC:** 2819—
Industrial Inorganic Chemicals Nec.

Emerson

★ 56964 ★   **Willamette Industries, Inc.**
RR 1
Emerson, AR 71740
(501)547-2955
Ultimate Parent: Willamette Industries, Inc.
SIC: 5211—Lumber & Other Building
Materials.

★ 56965 ★   **Willamette Industries Inc.**
Emerson
Hwy. 79 South
Emerson, AR 71740
Ultimate Parent: Willamette Industries, Inc.
SIC: 2436—Softwood Veneer & Plywood;
2421—Sawmills & Planing Mills—General.

England

★ 56966 ★   **Superior Federal Bank, FSB**
100 Stuttgart Hwy.
England, AR 72046
(501)842-2535
Location Type: Branch office. **Officer:** Pat
Hogan, Manager. **Ultimate Parent:**
Boatmen's Bancshares. **SIC:** 6021—
National Commercial Banks.

Fayetteville

★ 56967 ★   **Air Products & Chemicals Inc.**
2865 N. Hwy. 112
Fayetteville, AR 72703-7407
(501)442-9191
Ultimate Parent: Air Products & Chemicals,
Inc. **SIC:** 5085—Industrial Supplies; 5047—
Medical & Hospital Equipment; 5169—
Chemicals & Allied Products Nec.

★ 56968 ★   **Air Products & Chemicals, Inc.**
PO Box 1672
Fayetteville, AR 72702
(501)442-9191
Ultimate Parent: Air Products & Chemicals,
Inc. **SIC:** 2813—Industrial Gases; 5084—
Industrial Machinery & Equipment.

★ 56969 ★   **American Family Life Assurance**
125 E. Township St.
Fayetteville, AR 72703
(501)442-3770
Ultimate Parent: American Family Life
Assurance Co. **SIC:** 6411—Insurance
Agents, Brokers & Service.

★ 56970 ★   **Campbell Soup Co.**
1100 W. 15th St.
PO Box G
Fayetteville, AR 72702
(501)443-3451
Location Type: Plant. **Officer:** P. J.

Brewer, Plant Manager. **Ultimate Parent:**
Campbell Soup.

★ 56971 ★   **Campbell Soup Co.**
Swanson Div.
1100 W. 15th St.
Fayetteville, AR 72701
Company Type: Division. **Ultimate Parent:**
Campbell Soup. **SIC:** 2015—Poultry
Slaughtering & Processing; 2038—Frozen
Specialties Nec.

★ 56972 ★   **Carpenter Paper Co.**
1733 Carolyn Dr.
Fayetteville, AR 72701-2512
(501)521-8819
Ultimate Parent: Alco Standard Corp.

★ 56973 ★   **Casual Corner**
Northwest Arkansas M
Fayetteville, AR 72701
(501)443-7142
Ultimate Parent: United States Shoe. **SIC:**
5621—Women's Clothing Stores.

★ 56974 ★   **Danaher Tool Group Fayetteville Ar. Operation**
2900 City Lake Rd.
Fayetteville, AR 72703
Ultimate Parent: Danaher Corp. **SIC:**
3423—Hand & Edge Tools Nec.

★ 56975 ★   **Digital Equipment Corporati**
4171 N. Crossover Rd.
Fayetteville, AR 72703
(501)221-4636
Ultimate Parent: Digital Equipment Corp.
SIC: 7373—Computer Integrated Systems
Design.

★ 56976 ★   **Emery Worldwide**
Hwy. 71 S
Fayetteville, AR 72701
(501)443-0901
Ultimate Parent: Consolidated Freightways.
SIC: 4731—Freight Transportation
Arrangement.

★ 56977 ★   **Fayetteville Freezer**
2700 South School
Fayetteville, AR 72701
Ultimate Parent: Tyson Foods, Inc. **SIC:**
2000—Food & Kindred Products.

★ 56978 ★   **First Choice, Inc.**
4171 N. Crossover Rd.
Fayetteville, AR 72703
(501)442-7044
Ultimate Parent: Bindley-Western
Industries, Inc. **SIC:** 5149—Groceries &
Related Products Nec.

★ 56979 ★   **Herider Farms Inc.**
404 W. 15th St.
Fayetteville, AR 72701-6401
(501)442-4966
Company Type: Subsidiary. **Officer:**
Francis A. Duvernois, Chairman of the
Board. **Ultimate Parent:** Campbell Soup.
SIC: 0251—Broiler, Fryer & Roaster
Chickens; 0253—Turkeys & Turkey Eggs.
Employee Count: 90. **Sales:** 80 M.

★ 56980 ★   **Kay Bee Toy&Hobby Shop**
2100 Green Acres Rd.
Fayetteville, AR 72703
(501)521-5421
Ultimate Parent: Melville. **SIC:** 5945—
Hobby, Toy & Game Shops.

★ 56981 ★   **Kentucky Fried Chicken**
2117 W. 6th St.
Fayetteville, AR 72701
(501)442-0416
Ultimate Parent: Pepsico. **SIC:** 5812—
Eating Places.

★ 56982 ★   **Kentucky Fried Chicken**
514 N. College Ave.
Fayetteville, AR 72701
(501)442-5481
Ultimate Parent: Pepsico. **SIC:** 5812—
Eating Places.

★ 56983 ★   **Mini Mart No 3**
2229 E. Hwy. 16
Fayetteville, AR 72703
(501)521-1199
Ultimate Parent: Kroger. **SIC:** 5411—
Grocery Stores.

★ 56984 ★   **New York Life Fort Smith Sales Office**
Arkansas General Office
101 W. Mountain, Ste. 200
5000 Rodgers Ave.
Fayetteville, AR 72703
(501)443-0200
Ultimate Parent: New York Life.

★ 56985 ★   **Otis Elevator Co.**
632 W. Dickson St.
Fayetteville, AR 72701
(501)521-5750
Ultimate Parent: United Technologies. **SIC:**
3534—Elevators & Moving Stairways.

★ 56986 ★   **Pizza Hut**
2325 N. College Ave.
Fayetteville, AR 72703
(501)521-2992
Ultimate Parent: Pepsico. **SIC:** 5812—
Eating Places.

★ 56987 ★   **Pizza Hut**
847 PO Box
Fayetteville, AR 72702
Ultimate Parent: Pepsico. **SIC:** 5812—
Eating Places.

★ 56988 ★   **Pizza Hut**
Northwest Arkansas Plz.
Fayetteville, AR 72701
(501)521-0891
Ultimate Parent: Pepsico. **SIC:** 5812—
Eating Places.

★ 56989 ★   **Radio Shack**
1702 N. College Ave.
Fayetteville, AR 72703
(501)442-6151
Company Type: Division. **SIC:** 5065—
Electronic Parts & Equipment Nec.
Ultimate Parent: Tandy Corp.

★ 56990 ★   **Ryder Truck Rental**
2408 N. College Ave.
Fayetteville, AR 72703
(501)521-5944
Ultimate Parent: Ryder System. **SIC:**
7359—Equipment Rental & Leasing Nec.

★ 56991 ★   **Ryder Truck Rental**
313 W. Dickson St.
Fayetteville, AR 72701
(501)521-5944
Ultimate Parent: Ryder System. **SIC:**
7359—Equipment Rental & Leasing Nec.

★ 56992 ★   **Standard Register Co.**
3655 S. School St.
Fayetteville, AR 72701
(501)521-6900
Officer: W. H. Bequette, Manager. **Ultimate
Parent:** Standard Register. **SIC:** 2761—
Manifold Business Forms.

★ 56993 ★   **Superior Federal Bank, FSB**
2552 W. 6th St.
Fayetteville, AR 72701-7656
(501)442-4787
Location Type: Branch office. **Officer:**
Catherine Chaufty, Manager. **Ultimate
Parent:** Boatmen's Bancshares. **SIC:**
6021—National Commercial Banks.

★ 56994 ★   **Superior Federal Bank, FSB**
Northwest Plz. Mall
4201 N. College
Fayetteville, AR 72701-5183
(501)521-0020
Location Type: Branch office. **Officer:** Lee
Munyon, Manager. **Ultimate Parent:**
Boatmen's Bancshares. **SIC:** 6021—
National Commercial Banks.

★ 56995 ★   **Taco Bell**
2055 W. 6th St.
Fayetteville, AR 72701
(501)521-2538
Ultimate Parent: Pepsico. **SIC:** 5812—
Eating Places.

★ 56996 ★   **Taco Bell**
1772 N. College Ave.
Fayetteville, AR 72703
(501)442-6570
Ultimate Parent: Pepsico. **SIC:** 5812—
Eating Places.

★ 56997 ★   **Tyson Foods Inc.**
2615 S. School Ave.
Fayetteville, AR 72701
(501)521-2561
Officer: Mike Group, Plant Manager.
Ultimate Parent: Tyson Foods, Inc. **SIC:**
2015—Poultry Slaughtering & Processing.

★ 56998 ★   **Tyson Foods Inc.**
2700 S. School Ave.
Fayetteville, AR 72701
(501)521-2561
Ultimate Parent: Tyson Foods, Inc. **SIC:**
2099—Food Preparations Nec.

★ 56999 ★   **Tyson Foods Inc.**
Entree Div.
2615 S. School
Fayetteville, AR 72701
Company Type: Division. **Ultimate Parent:**
Tyson Foods, Inc. **SIC:** 2038—Frozen
Specialties Nec.

★ 57000 ★   **Tyson's of Fayetteville Entree**
2615 S. School Ave.
Fayetteville, AR 72701
(501)521-0677
Officer: Mike Rush, Plant Manager.
Ultimate Parent: Tyson Foods, Inc. **SIC:**
2038—Frozen Specialties Nec.

★ 57001 ★   **Wal Mart**
W Hwy. 62 Bypass
Fayetteville, AR 72701
(501)521-7222
Ultimate Parent: Wal-Mart Stores, Inc. **SIC:**
5311—Department Stores.

★ 57002 ★   **Wal Mart Pharmacy**
Hwy. P
Fayetteville, AR 72701
(501)521-4350
Ultimate Parent: Wal-Mart Stores, Inc. **SIC:**
5912—Drug Stores & Proprietary Stores.

★ 57003 ★   **Wal Mart Pharmacy**
College Rd.
Fayetteville, AR 72701
(501)443-9267
Ultimate Parent: Wal-Mart Stores, Inc. **SIC:**
5912—Drug Stores & Proprietary Stores.

Fordyce

★ 57004 ★   **Ace Hardware&Furniture Inc.**
113 W. 2nd St.
Fordyce, AR 71742
(501)352-3668
Ultimate Parent: Ace Hardware. **SIC:**
5211—Lumber & Other Building Materials.

★ 57005 ★   **Georgia Pacific Corp.**
600 W. College St.
Fordyce, AR 71742
(501)352-6100
Officer: Larry Livingston, Manager.
Ultimate Parent: Georgia-Pacific. **SIC:**
2421—Sawmills & Planing Mills—General.

Foreman

★ 57006 ★   **Mobil Bulk Plant**
Foreman, AR 71836
(501)542-7267
Ultimate Parent: Mobil. **SIC:** 5172—
Petroleum Products Nec.

★ 57007 ★   **Mobil Pipe Line Co.**
Foreman, AR 71836
(501)542-6221
Company Type: Branch. **Ultimate Parent:**
Mobil. **SIC:** 4612—Crude Petroleum
Pipelines.

Forrest City

★ 57008 ★   **Greyhound Bus Lines**
1004 E. Broadway St.
Forrest City, AR 72335
(501)633-1402
Ultimate Parent: Greyhound Lines Inc. **SIC:**
4111—Local & Suburban Transit.

★ 57009 ★   **Kentucky Fried Chicken**
737 N. Washington St.
Forrest City, AR 72335
(501)633-6616
Ultimate Parent: Pepsico. **SIC:** 5812—
Eating Places.

★ 57010 ★   McDonalds
2301 N. Washington St.
Forrest City, AR 72335
(501)633-4146
Ultimate Parent: McDonald's.
SIC: 5812—Eating Places.

★ 57011 ★   Pizza Hut
2023 N. Washington St.
Forrest City, AR 72335
(501)633-9118
Ultimate Parent: Pepsico. SIC: 5812—
Eating Places.

★ 57012 ★   Radio Shack
955 N. Washington St.
Forrest City, AR 72335
(501)633-8169
Company Type: Division. Ultimate Parent:
Tandy Corp. SIC: 5731—Radio, Television
& Electronics Stores.

★ 57013 ★   Ryder Truck Rental
Hwy. I 40
Forrest City, AR 72335
(501)633-2970
Ultimate Parent: Ryder System. SIC:
7513—Truck Rental & Leasing Without
Drivers.

★ 57014 ★   Wal Mart Discount
Cities
Hwy. 1 N
Forrest City, AR 72335
(501)633-7340
Ultimate Parent: Wal-Mart Stores, Inc. SIC:
5311—Department Stores.

Fort Smith

★ 57015 ★   ABF Cartage, Inc.
1000 S. 21st St.
PO Box 48
Fort Smith, AR 72902
(501)785-6141
Company Type: Subsidiary. Ultimate
Parent: Arkansas Best. SIC: 4213—
Trucking Except Local.

★ 57016 ★   ABF Freight System
(BC) Ltd.
1000 S. 21st St.
PO Box 48
Fort Smith, AR 72902
(501)785-6141
Company Type: Subsidiary. Ultimate
Parent: Arkansas Best.

★ 57017 ★   ABF Freight System,
Inc.
301 S. 11th St.
Fort Smith, AR 72902
(501)785-8700 Fax: (501)785-8783
Company Type: Subsidiary. Ultimate
Parent: Arkansas Best. SIC: 4213—
Trucking Except Local.

★ 57018 ★   Ace Hardware
1200 S. 54th St.
Fort Smith, AR 72903
(501)452-4440
Ultimate Parent: Ace Hardware.

★ 57019 ★   Air Products &
Chemicals, Inc.
PO Box 252
Fort Smith, AR 72902
(501)782-7218
Ultimate Parent: Air Products & Chemicals,
Inc. SIC: 2813—Industrial Gases; 5084—
Industrial Machinery & Equipment.

★ 57020 ★   Air Products &
Chemicals Inc.
622 Divison St.
Fort Smith, AR 72904-5950
(501)782-7218
Officer: Billy Kennedy. Ultimate Parent: Air
Products & Chemicals, Inc. SIC: 5085—
Industrial Supplies.

★ 57021 ★   American Family Life
Assurance
2120 S. Waldron Rd.
Fort Smith, AR 72903
(501)452-6311
Ultimate Parent: American Family Life
Assurance Co. SIC: 6411—Insurance
Agents, Brokers & Service.

★ 57022 ★   Arkansas Best
1000 S. 21st St.
Fort Smith, AR 72901-4098
(501)785-6000
Company Type: Headquarters. SIC:
4213—Trucking Except Local; 7534—Tire
Retreading & Repair Shops; 5531—
Automobile & Home Supply Stores; 7374—
Data Processing & Preparation; 6512—
Nonresidential Building Operators.

★ 57023 ★   Arkansas Best Corp.
PO Box 48
Fort Smith, AR 72901-4008
                             Fax: (501)785-6009
Location Type: Headquarters. Officer:
Robert A. Young III. Ultimate Parent:
Arkansas Best. SIC: 4213—Trucking Except
Local; 3011—Tires & Inner Tubes; 4212—
Local Trucking Without Storage; 5531—
Automobile & Home Supply Stores; 6061—
Federal Credit Unions; 6552—Subdividers &
Developers Nec; 6719—Holding Companies
Nec; 7374—Data Processing & Preparation;
7379—Computer Related Services Nec;
7534—Tire Retreading & Repair Shops;
2511—Wood Household Furniture; 2512—
Upholstered Household Furniture; 3011—
Tires & Inner Tubes.

★ 57024 ★   Arkansas Best Corp.
PO Box 48
Fort Smith, AR 72902
Company Type: Headquarters. Ultimate
Parent: Arkansas Best.

★ 57025 ★   Avon Products Inc.
3017 S. 100th St.
Fort Smith, AR 72903
(501)452-5345
Ultimate Parent: Avon Products, Inc. SIC:
5999—Miscellaneous Retail Stores Nec.

★ 57026 ★   Ball Corp.
8307 Ball Rd.
Fort Smith, AR 72903
(501)646-8293
Ultimate Parent: Ball Corp. SIC: 3089—
Plastics Products Nec.

★ 57027 ★   Ball Corp. Plastics
8307 Ball Rd.
Fort Smith, AR 72903-8435
(501)646-8293
Location Type: Branch office. Officer: Kyle
Dejaeger. Ultimate Parent: Ball Corp.

★ 57028 ★   Beverly Enterprises
PO Box 3324
Fort Smith, AR 72913
(501)452-6712 Fax: (501)452-5131
Company Type: Headquarters. Officer:
David R. Banks, Chairman; President &
CEO. Ultimate Parent: Beverly Enterprises.
Employee Count: 93000.

★ 57029 ★   Beverly Enterprises
120 S. Waldron Rd.
Fort Smith, AR 72403
(501)452-6712
Company Type: Headquarters. Officer:
David R. Banks. Employee Count: 89000.
Sales: 2871 M. Fortune Service 500:
Ranking 44.

★ 57030 ★   Beverly Enterprises
Medical Equipment Corp.
1200 S. Waldron Rd. Ste. 155
Fort Smith, AR 72903-2569
(501)452-6712
Company Type: Subsidiary. Officer: David
R. Banks, President. Ultimate Parent:
Beverly Enterprises. SIC: 5047—Medical &
Hospital Equipment. Sales: 45 M.

★ 57031 ★   Beverly Manor of
Portsmouth
1200 S. Waldron Rd., Ste. .155
Fort Smith, AR 72903
(501)452-6712 Fax: (501)452-5131
Officer: David R. Banks, CEO. Ultimate
Parent: Beverly Enterprises. Employee
Count: 9300. Sales: 2886 M.

★ 57032 ★   Borden City Foods,
Inc.
24 N. C St.
Fort Smith, AR 72901
(501)785-4428
Officer: Milton Smallwood, Owner. Ultimate
Parent: Borden, Inc. SIC: 2015—Poultry
Slaughtering & Processing.

★ 57033 ★   Butler Paper
5400 S. 66th St.
Fort Smith, AR 72903-6560
(501)646-4701
Officer: Kent D. Sheridan. Ultimate Parent:
Alco Standard Corp. SIC: 5113—Industrial
& Personal Service Paper; 5111—Printing &
Writing Paper.

★ 57034 ★   Butler Paper
5400 S. 66th St.
Fort Smith, AR 72903-6560
(501)646-4701
Officer: Kent D. Sheridan. Ultimate Parent:
Alco Standard Corp. SIC: 5113—Industrial
& Personal Service Paper; 5111—Printing &
Writing Paper.

★ 57035 ★   Casual Corner
5111 Central Mall N
Fort Smith, AR 72903
(501)452-3012
Ultimate Parent: United States Shoe. SIC:
5651—Family Clothing Stores.

★ 57036 ★   City National Bank
Hwy. 71 S.
Fort Smith, AR 72916
Company Type: Branch. Ultimate Parent:
City National Corp. SIC: 6022—State
Commercial Banks.

★ 57037 ★   City National Bank
1222 Rogers Ave.
Fort Smith, AR 72901-2678
(501)785-2811
Company Type: Headquarters. Officer:
Connie Stevenson, Senior Vice President.
Ultimate Parent: City National Corp. SIC:
6022—State Commercial Banks; 6099—
Functions Related to Deposit Banking;
6141—Personal Credit Institutions; 6211—
Security Brokers & Dealers.

★ 57038 ★   City National Bank
Central Mall
Fort Smith, AR 72903
Company Type: Branch. Ultimate Parent:
City National Corp. SIC: 6022—State
Commercial Banks; 6021—National
Commercial Banks.

★ 57039 ★   City National Bank
7000 Rogers Ave.
Fort Smith, AR 72903
(501)452-7930
Ultimate Parent: City National Corp. SIC:
6022—State Commercial Banks.

★ 57040 ★   City National Bank
S. Hwy. 71
Fort Smith, AR 72903
(501)646-1677
Ultimate Parent: City National Corp. SIC:
6022—State Commercial Banks.

★ 57041 ★   City National Bank
Hwy. 71 S
Fort Smith, AR 72901
(501)646-1677
Ultimate Parent: City National Corp. SIC:
6022—State Commercial Banks.

★ 57042 ★   City National Bank
5111 Central Mall N
Fort Smith, AR 72903
(501)452-1188
Location Type: Branch office. Ultimate
Parent: City National Corp. SIC: 6022—
State Commercial Banks.

★ 57043 ★   City National Bank of
Fort
3117 Grand Ave.
Fort Smith, AR 72904
(501)785-0023
Ultimate Parent: City National Corp. SIC:
6022—State Commercial Banks.

★ 57044 ★   Data-Tronics Corp.
900 Rogers Ave.
Fort Smith, AR 72901
(501)784-8400 Fax: (501)785-6009
Company Type: Subsidiary. Ultimate
Parent: Arkansas Best. SIC: 7374—Data
Processing & Preparation.

★ 57045 ★   Data-Tronics Corp.
PO Box 305
Fort Smith, AR 72902-0305
(501)784-8400
Location Type: Branch office. Officer: J. A.
Yarbrough. Ultimate Parent: Arkansas
Best. SIC: 7374—Data Processing &

Preparation; 7379—Computer Related
Services Nec.

★ 57046 ★   Data-Tronics Corp.
100 S. 10th St.
Fort Smith, AR 72901-3793
(501)784-8400
Company Type: Subsidiary. Ultimate
Parent: Arkansas Best. SIC: 7374—Data
Processing & Preparation.

★ 57047 ★   Diebold Inc.
7423 Hwy. 271 S
Fort Smith, AR 72903
(501)646-8036
Ultimate Parent: Diebold, Inc. SIC: 1731—
Electrical Work.

★ 57048 ★   E. R. Carpenter Co.
Inc.
201 N. 2nd St.
Fort Smith, AR 72901
Ultimate Parent: Carpenter. SIC: 3086—
Plastics Foam Products.

★ 57049 ★   Exxon
5720 Rogers Ave.
Fort Smith, AR 72903
(501)452-0877
Ultimate Parent: Exxon.

★ 57050 ★   Exxon
1549 N. Greenwood Ave.
Fort Smith, AR 72901
(501)783-9857
Ultimate Parent: Exxon. SIC: 5541—
Gasoline Service Stations.

★ 57051 ★   Exxon
4622 Old Greenwood Rd.
Fort Smith, AR 72903
(501)648-1091
Ultimate Parent: Exxon. SIC: 5541—
Gasoline Service Stations.

★ 57052 ★   Gencorp Polymer
Prods.
3333 S. Zero St.
Fort Smith, AR 72906
Ultimate Parent: Gencorp. SIC: 3082—
Unsupported Plastics Profile Shapes.

★ 57053 ★   Gencorp Polymer
Products
3333 S. Zero St.
Fort Smith, AR 72903
(501)646-4535
Officer: Jack Faulkner, Manager. Ultimate
Parent: Gencorp. SIC: 3053—Gaskets,
Packing & Sealing Devices; 3089—Plastics
Products Nec.

★ 57054 ★   H. J. Baker & Bro. Inc.
1717 Ballman Rd.
Fort Smith, AR 72901
Ultimate Parent: H.J. Heinz. SIC: 2048—
Prepared Feeds Nec.

★ 57055 ★   Hertz Rent-A-Car
End Municipal Airport
Fort Smith, AR 72903
(501)646-7823
Ultimate Parent: Hertz. SIC: 7514—
Passenger Car Rental.

★ 57056 ★   IBM Corp.
120 N. 13th St.
Fort Smith, AR 72901
(501)441-1300
Ultimate Parent: IBM.

★ 57057 ★   Inland Container
Corp. No. 33
4500 Newlon Rd.
Fort Smith, AR 72904
Ultimate Parent: Temple-Inland. SIC:
2653—Corrugated & Solid Fiber Boxes.

★ 57058 ★   James River Corp.
Dixie Products Group
4411 Midland Blvd.
Fort Smith, AR 72904
Ultimate Parent: James River Corp. of
Virginia. SIC: 2600—Paper & Allied
Products.

★ 57059 ★   James River Paper
Co. Dixie Products
4411 Midland Blvd.
Fort Smith, AR 72904
Ultimate Parent: James River Corp. of
Virginia. SIC: 2679—Converted Paper
Products Nec.

★ 57060 ★ **James River Paper Co. Inc. Dixie Products**
4411 Midland Blvd.
Fort Smith, AR 72904
Ultimate Parent: James River Corp. of Virginia. **SIC:** 2656—Sanitary Food Containers.

★ 57061 ★ **Kay-Bee Toy & Hobby Shop**
5111 Central Mall N
Fort Smith, AR 72903
(501)452-5607
Ultimate Parent: Melville. **SIC:** 5945—Hobby, Toy & Game Shops.

★ 57062 ★ **Kentucky Fried Chicken**
1601 Hwy. 71 S
Fort Smith, AR 72901
(501)646-7133
Ultimate Parent: Pepsico. **SIC:** 5812—Eating Places.

★ 57063 ★ **Kentucky Fried Chicken**
Rogers Ave.
Fort Smith, AR 72901
(501)782-0230
Ultimate Parent: Pepsico. **SIC:** 5812—Eating Places.

★ 57064 ★ **Kentucky Fried Chicken**
7719 Rogers Ave.
Fort Smith, AR 72903
(501)452-6900
Ultimate Parent: Pepsico. **SIC:** 5812—Eating Places.

★ 57065 ★ **Kentucky Fried Chicken**
4207 Grand Ave.
Fort Smith, AR 72904
(501)785-4998
Ultimate Parent: Pepsico. **SIC:** 5812—Eating Places.

★ 57066 ★ **Land Marine Cargo Inc.**
1000 S. 21st St.
Fort Smith, AR 72902
(501)785-6000 **Fax:** (501)785-6009
Company Type: Subsidiary. **Ultimate Parent:** Arkansas Best.

★ 57067 ★ **Lane Bryant**
5111 Central Mall N
Fort Smith, AR 72903
(501)452-5716
Ultimate Parent: Limited. **SIC:** 5651—Family Clothing Stores.

★ 57068 ★ **Liberty Mutual Insurance Co.**
104 N. 16th St.
Fort Smith, AR 72901
(501)785-2260
Ultimate Parent: Liberty Mutual Group. **SIC:** 6411—Insurance Agents, Brokers & Service.

★ 57069 ★ **The Limited**
1200 S. 54th St.
Fort Smith, AR 72903
(501)452-6707
Ultimate Parent: Limited.

★ 57070 ★ **Okla Homer Smith Furniture Co. Inc.**
416 South 5th St.
Fort Smith, AR 72901
Ultimate Parent: Gerber Products. **SIC:** 2511—Wood Household Furniture.

★ 57071 ★ **Osco Drug**
5201 Rogers Ave.
Fort Smith, AR 72903
(501)452-1196
Ultimate Parent: American Stores.

★ 57072 ★ **Osco Drug**
5111 Central Mall N
Fort Smith, AR 72903
(501)452-1195
Ultimate Parent: American Stores. **SIC:** 5912—Drug Stores & Proprietary Stores.

★ 57073 ★ **Osco Drug**
4000 N. O St.
Fort Smith, AR 72904
(501)783-1137
Ultimate Parent: American Stores. **SIC:** 5912—Drug Stores & Proprietary Stores.

★ 57074 ★ **Otis Elevator Co.**
1311 S. 11th St.
Fort Smith, AR 72901
(501)782-5487
Ultimate Parent: United Technologies. **SIC:** 3534—Elevators & Moving Stairways.

★ 57075 ★ **Owens Corning Fiberglas**
PO Box 1387
Fort Smith, AR 72902
(501)646-8000
Ultimate Parent: Owens-Corning. **SIC:** 5131—Piece Goods & Notions.

★ 57076 ★ **Owens Corning Fiberglas Corp.**
5000 Planters Rd.
Fort Smith, AR 72903
Ultimate Parent: Owens-Corning. **SIC:** 3229—Pressed & Blown Glass Nec.

★ 57077 ★ **Owens-Corning Fiberglas Corp.**
5520 Planters Rd.
Fort Smith, AR 72916
(501)646-8000
Officer: Newt Holloway, Manager. **Ultimate Parent:** Owens-Corning. **SIC:** 3296—Mineral Wool.

★ 57078 ★ **Owens-Corning Fiberglass**
Roofing Mat Plant
5520 Planters Rd. Industrial Park S.
Fort Smith, AR 72916
Location Type: Plant. **Ultimate Parent:** Owens-Corning. **SIC:** 3229—Pressed & Blown Glass Nec.

★ 57079 ★ **Payless Cashways Inc.**
3300 Briar Cliff Ave.
Fort Smith, AR 72903
(501)646-6200
Ultimate Parent: Payless Cashways. **SIC:** 5039—Construction Materials Nec.

★ 57080 ★ **Penn Mutual Life Insurance Co.**
6200 Free Ferry Rd.
Fort Smith, AR 72903
(501)452-1893
Ultimate Parent: Penn Mutual Life. **SIC:** 6411—Insurance Agents, Brokers & Service.

★ 57081 ★ **Pepsi-Cola Co.**
3701 S. Zero St.
Fort Smith, AR 72906
Ultimate Parent: Pepsico. **SIC:** 2086—Bottled & Canned Soft Drinks.

★ 57082 ★ **Pharmacy Corp. of America**
1200 S. Waldron Rd., Ste. 155
Fort Smith, AR 72903-2569
(501)452-6712
Company Type: Subsidiary. **Officer:** David Banks, Chairman of the Board & CEO. **Ultimate Parent:** Betz Laboratories Inc. **SIC:** 5912—Drug Stores & Proprietary Stores. **Employee Count:** 1400. **Sales:** 170 M.

★ 57083 ★ **Pizza Hut**
4700 Rogers Ave.
Fort Smith, AR 72903
(501)452-2361
Ultimate Parent: Pepsico. **SIC:** 5812—Eating Places.

★ 57084 ★ **Pizza Hut**
1813 Grand Ave.
Fort Smith, AR 72901
Ultimate Parent: Pepsico. **SIC:** 5812—Eating Places.

★ 57085 ★ **Pizza Hut**
1323 Hwy. 71 S
Fort Smith, AR 72901
(501)646-2196
Ultimate Parent: Pepsico. **SIC:** 5812—Eating Places.

★ 57086 ★ **Quanex Co.**
Macsteel Division
4700 Planters Rd.
Fort Smith, AR 72916
(501)646-0223
Ultimate Parent: Quanex. **SIC:** 3312—Blast Furnaces & Steel Mills.

★ 57087 ★ **Quanex Corp.**
Macsteel Div.
5225 Planters Rd.
Fort Smith, AR 72916-9549
Ultimate Parent: Quanex. **SIC:** 3312—Blast Furnaces & Steel Mills; 3398—Metal Heat Treating.

★ 57088 ★ **Quanex Corp.**
Macsteel Div.
4700 Planters Rd.
Fort Smith, AR 72902
Ultimate Parent: Quanex. **SIC:** 3312—Blast Furnaces & Steel Mills; 3398—Metal Heat Treating; 3313—Electrometallurgical Products.

★ 57089 ★ **Radio Shack**
155 Phoenix Village Sq.
Fort Smith, AR 72901
(501)646-0380
Company Type: Division. **Ultimate Parent:** Tandy Corp. **SIC:** 5065—Electronic Parts & Equipment Nec.

★ 57090 ★ **Radio Shack**
2101 Rogers Ave.
Fort Smith, AR 72901
(501)785-2417
Company Type: Division. **Ultimate Parent:** Tandy Corp. **SIC:** 5712—Furniture Stores.

★ 57091 ★ **Radio Shack**
Central Mall
Fort Smith, AR 72903
(501)452-1182
Company Type: Division. **Ultimate Parent:** Tandy Corp. **SIC:** 5065—Electronic Parts & Equipment Nec.

★ 57092 ★ **Riverside Furniture**
Plant 4
406 S. E St.
Fort Smith, AR 72901
Location Type: Plant. **Ultimate Parent:** Arkansas Best. **SIC:** 2512—Upholstered Household Furniture.

★ 57093 ★ **Riverside Furniture**
Plant 1
301 South E. St.
Fort Smith, AR 72901
Location Type: Plant. **Ultimate Parent:** Arkansas Best. **SIC:** 2512—Upholstered Household Furniture.

★ 57094 ★ **Riverside Furniture**
Plants 2, 6, & 7
1400 S. 6th St.
Fort Smith, AR 72901
Location Type: Plant. **Ultimate Parent:** Arkansas Best. **SIC:** 2512—Upholstered Household Furniture.

★ 57095 ★ **Riverside Furniture Corp.**
1400 S. 6th St.
Fort Smith, AR 72901-4398
(501)785-8100
Company Type: Subsidiary. **Location Type:** Headquarters. **Officer:** Howard T. Spradlin. **Ultimate Parent:** Arkansas Best. **SIC:** 2511—Wood Household Furniture; 2512—Upholstered Household Furniture; 2519—Household Furniture Nec; 2521—Wood Office Furniture; 2522—Office Furniture Except Wood.

★ 57096 ★ **Ryder Truck Rental**
3315 Cavanaugh Rd.
Fort Smith, AR 72903
(501)646-6111
Ultimate Parent: Ryder System. **SIC:** 7513—Truck Rental & Leasing Without Drivers.

★ 57097 ★ **Ryder Truck Rental**
3616 Towson Ave.
Fort Smith, AR 72901
(501)782-1593
Ultimate Parent: Ryder System. **SIC:** 7359—Equipment Rental & Leasing Nec.

★ 57098 ★ **Ryder Truck Rental**
3740 Midland Blvd.
Fort Smith, AR 72904
(501)782-9757
Ultimate Parent: Ryder System. **SIC:** 7359—Equipment Rental & Leasing Nec.

★ 57099 ★ **Sam's Wholesale Club**
7700 Rogers Ave.
Fort Smith, AR 72903
(501)484-5454
Ultimate Parent: Wal-Mart Stores, Inc.

★ 57100 ★ **Taco Bell**
4910 Towson Ave.
Fort Smith, AR 72901
(501)646-9623
Ultimate Parent: Pepsico. **SIC:** 5812—Eating Places.

★ 57101 ★ **Taco Bell**
4710 Rogers Ave.
Fort Smith, AR 72903
(501)452-5202
Ultimate Parent: Pepsico. **SIC:** 5812—Eating Places.

★ 57102 ★ **Taco Bell**
7910 Rogers Ave.
Fort Smith, AR 72903
(501)484-7534
Ultimate Parent: Pepsico.

★ 57103 ★ **Taco Bell**
915 N. Greenwood Ave.
Fort Smith, AR 72901
(501)783-0202
Ultimate Parent: Pepsico. **SIC:** 5812—Eating Places.

★ 57104 ★ **This End Up Furn Co.**
5111 Central Mall N
Fort Smith, AR 72903
(501)452-5616
Ultimate Parent: Melville. **SIC:** 5712—Furniture Stores.

★ 57105 ★ **Toys R US**
5609 Rogers Ave.
Fort Smith, AR 72903
(501)484-0002
Ultimate Parent: Toys "R" US.

★ 57106 ★ **Trane Co.**
4811 S. Zero St.
Fort Smith, AR 72903
Ultimate Parent: American Standard. **SIC:** 3585—Refrigeration & Heating Equipment.

★ 57107 ★ **Trane Co.**
4811 South Zero St.
Fort Smith, AR 72903
Ultimate Parent: American Standard. **SIC:** 3585—Refrigeration & Heating Equipment.

★ 57108 ★ **Trans State Lines, Inc.**
6815 Jenny Lind Ave.
Fort Smith, AR 72903-7496
(501)648-4400
Ultimate Parent: Arkansas Best. **SIC:** 4213—Trucking Except Local; 5531—Automobile & Home Supply Stores.

★ 57109 ★ **Treadco, Inc.**
1000 S. 21st St.
PO Box 48
Fort Smith, AR 72902
(501)785-6000 **Fax:** (501)785-6009
Company Type: Subsidiary. **Ultimate Parent:** Arkansas Best. **SIC:** 7534—Tire Retreading & Repair Shops.

★ 57110 ★ **Tyson Foods Inc.**
PO Box 4130
Fort Smith, AR 72914
(501)783-8996
Ultimate Parent: Tyson Foods, Inc. **SIC:** 2034—Dehydrated Fruits, Vegetables & Soups.

★ 57111 ★ **Tyson Foods Inc.**
1610 Midland Blvd.
Fort Smith, AR 72901
(501)893-8996
Officer: Jim Gregory, Manager. **Ultimate Parent:** Tyson Foods, Inc. **SIC:** 2015—Poultry Slaughtering & Processing; 2048—Prepared Feeds Nec.

★ 57112 ★ **Underwriters Adjusting Co.**
1318 N. B St.
Fort Smith, AR 72901
(501)782-6157
Ultimate Parent: Continental. **SIC:** 6411—Insurance Agents, Brokers & Service.

★ 57113 ★   **Unisys Corp.**
1800 N. 50th St.
Fort Smith, AR 72904
Ultimate Parent: Unisys Corp.

★ 57114 ★   **United Parcel Service**
6715 S. 28th St.
Fort Smith, AR 72903
(501)648-0280
Ultimate Parent: United Parcel Service of
America. **SIC:** 4215—Courier Services
Except by Air.

★ 57115 ★   **Wal Mart Auto Ctr**
5609 Rogers Ave.
Fort Smith, AR 72903
(501)452-3850
Ultimate Parent: Wal-Mart Stores, Inc.

★ 57116 ★   **Wal Mart Discount
Cities**
1401 Hwy. 71 S
Fort Smith, AR 72901
(501)646-6382
Ultimate Parent: Wal-Mart Stores, Inc. **SIC:**
5311—Department Stores; 7342—
Disinfecting & Pest Control Services.

★ 57117 ★   **Wal Mart Discount
Cities**
2600 Midland Blvd.
Fort Smith, AR 72904
(501)785-5964
Ultimate Parent: Wal-Mart Stores, Inc. **SIC:**
7342—Disinfecting & Pest Control Services.

★ 57118 ★   **Wal Mart Discount
Cities**
5609 Rogers Ave.
Fort Smith, AR 72903
(501)452-3695
Ultimate Parent: Wal-Mart Stores, Inc. **SIC:**
5912—Drug Stores & Proprietary Stores.

★ 57119 ★   **Whirlpool Corp.**
6400 Jenny Lind Ave.
Fort Smith, AR 72903
(501)648-2000
Officer: Al Holaday, Vice President.
Ultimate Parent: Whirlpool Corp. **SIC:**
3632—Household Refrigerators & Freezers.

Glenwood

★ 57120 ★   **Mobil Pipe Line Co.**
Glenwood, AR 71943
(501)356-3533
Company Type: Branch. **Ultimate Parent:**
Mobil. **SIC:** 4612—Crude Petroleum
Pipelines.

Grannis

★ 57121 ★   **Tyson Foods Inc.**
Hwy. 71 N
Grannis, AR 71944
(501)385-2331
Officer: Mike Baker, Manager. **Ultimate
Parent:** Tyson Foods, Inc. **SIC:** 2015—
Poultry Slaughtering & Processing.

Green Forest

★ 57122 ★   **Tyson Foods, Inc.**
601 E. 6th St.
Green Forest, AR 72638
(501)438-5211
Ultimate Parent: Tyson Foods, Inc. **SIC:**
5144—Poultry & Poultry Products; 2015—
Poultry Slaughtering & Processing.

Greenbrier

★ 57123 ★   **First State Bank &
Trust Co.**
Hwy. 65
Greenbrier, AR 72058
(501)679-2156
Ultimate Parent: Michigan National Corp.
SIC: 6022—State Commercial Banks.

Gurdon

★ 57124 ★   **International Paper
Co.**
Gurdon Wood Products
Hwy. 67 North, PO Box 440
Gurdon, AR 71743
Company Type: Division. **Officer:** Philip R.
Freer. **Ultimate Parent:** International Paper

Co. **SIC:** 2421—Sawmills & Planing Mills—
General.

★ 57125 ★   **International Paper
Gurdon Wood Products**
Hwy. 67 N. PO Box 440
Gurdon, AR 71743-0440
Ultimate Parent: International Paper Co.
SIC: 2421—Sawmills & Planing Mills—
General.

★ 57126 ★   **Piggly Wiggly**
506 E. Main St.
Gurdon, AR 71743
(501)353-2818
Ultimate Parent: Bruno's. **SIC:** 5411—
Grocery Stores.

H Spg Nat Pk

★ 57127 ★   **Pizza Hut**
202 Airport Rd.
H Spg Nat Pk, AR 71913
(501)623-5417
Ultimate Parent: Pepsico. **SIC:** 5812—
Eating Places.

★ 57128 ★   **Radio Shack**
Hot Spring Mall
H Spg Nat Pk, AR 71901
(501)525-3711
Company Type: Division. **Ultimate Parent:**
Tandy Corp. **SIC:** 5065—Electronic Parts &
Equipment Nec.

★ 57129 ★   **Radio Shack**
5701 Central Ave.
H Spg Nat Pk, AR 71913
(501)525-3711
Company Type: Division. **Ultimate Parent:**
Tandy Corp. **SIC:** 5731—Radio, Television
& Electronics Stores.

★ 57130 ★   **Radio Shack**
3419 Central Ave.
H Spg Nat Pk, AR 71913
(501)623-3478
Company Type: Division. **Ultimate Parent:**
Tandy Corp. **SIC:** 5735—Record &
Prerecorded Tape Stores.

★ 57131 ★   **Radio Shack**
4423 Central Ave.
H Spg Nat Pk, AR 71913
(501)624-7073
Company Type: Division. **Ultimate Parent:**
Tandy Corp. **SIC:** 5731—Radio, Television
& Electronics Stores.

★ 57132 ★   **Ryder Truck Rental**
2128 Spring St.
H Spg Nat Pk, AR 71901
(501)623-3806
Ultimate Parent: Ryder System. **SIC:**
7359—Equipment Rental & Leasing Nec;
7513—Truck Rental & Leasing Without
Drivers.

★ 57133 ★   **Taco Bell**
3995 Central Ave.
H Spg Nat Pk, AR 71913
(501)623-5610
Ultimate Parent: Pepsico. **SIC:** 5812—
Eating Places.

★ 57134 ★   **Taco Bell**
1000 Albert Pike
H Spg Nat Pk, AR 71913
(501)321-4395
Ultimate Parent: Pepsico. **SIC:** 5812—
Eating Places.

Harrisburg

★ 57135 ★   **ACME Frame
Products**
RR 2 Box 131
Harrisburg, AR 72432-9648
(501)578-2486
Location Type: Branch office. **Ultimate
Parent:** American Greetings. **SIC:** 2499—
Wood Products Nec.

Harrison

★ 57136 ★   **Emerson Electric Co.**
White-Rodger Div.
303 N. Industrial Park Rd.
Harrison, AR 72601
Company Type: Division. **Ultimate Parent:**
Emerson Electric Co. Inc. **SIC:** 3639—
Household Appliances Nec; 3444—Sheet

Metal Work; 3451—Screw Machine
Products.

★ 57137 ★   **First Federal S & L**
200 W. Stephenson Ave.
Harrison, AR 72601-4299
(501)741-7641
Company Type: Headquarters. **Officer:**
Larry J. Brandt. **Ultimate Parent:** Bancorp
Hawaii. **SIC:** 6035—Federal Savings
Institutions; 6021—National Commercial
Banks; 6141—Personal Credit Institutions.

★ 57138 ★   **McKesson**
Service Merchandising Div.
PO Box 790
Harrison, AR 72601
(501)741-3425 **Fax:** (501)365-3206
Company Type: Division. **Officer:** Frank
Conner, President. **Ultimate Parent:**
McKesson.

★ 57139 ★   **Modern Business
Systems**
502 Security Bank Plz.
Harrison, AR 72601
(501)741-3655
Ultimate Parent: Alco Standard Corp. **SIC:**
5999—Miscellaneous Retail Stores Nec;
5044—Office Equipment.

★ 57140 ★   **Pizza Hut**
1164 N. Hwy. 62-65
Harrison, AR 72601
(501)741-5354
Ultimate Parent: Pepsico. **SIC:** 5812—
Eating Places.

★ 57141 ★   **Trailways Bus Center**
221 E. Ridge Ave.
Harrison, AR 72601
(501)741-3000
Ultimate Parent: Greyhound Lines Inc. **SIC:**
8111—Legal Services.

★ 57142 ★   **Wal Mart**
Hwy. Bypass P
Harrison, AR 72601
(501)741-1511
Ultimate Parent: Wal-Mart Stores, Inc. **SIC:**
5531—Automobile & Home Supply Stores.

★ 57143 ★   **Wal Mart**
Hwy. 62 Bypass
Harrison, AR 72601
(501)741-9496
Ultimate Parent: Wal-Mart Stores, Inc. **SIC:**
5311—Department Stores.

★ 57144 ★   **Wal Mart Pharmacy**
Hwy. 62 Bypass
Harrison, AR 72601
(501)741-2327
Ultimate Parent: Wal-Mart Stores, Inc. **SIC:**
5912—Drug Stores & Proprietary Stores.

★ 57145 ★   **Wal Mart Shoes**
Hwy. 62 Bypass P
Harrison, AR 72601
(501)741-4844
Ultimate Parent: Wal-Mart Stores, Inc. **SIC:**
5541—Gasoline Service Stations; 8211—
Elementary & Secondary Schools.

★ 57146 ★   **White-Rodgers**
303 N. Industrial Park Rd.
Harrison, AR 72601
Company Type: Division. **Ultimate Parent:**
Emerson Electric Co. Inc. **SIC:** 3639—
Household Appliances Nec; 3444—Sheet
Metal Work; 3451—Screw Machine
Products.

★ 57147 ★   **White-Rodgers
Harrison Air**
303 N. Industrial Park Rd.
Harrison, AR 72601
Company Type: Division. **Ultimate Parent:**
Emerson Electric Co. Inc. **SIC:** 3639—
Household Appliances Nec; 3444—Sheet
Metal Work; 3451—Screw Machine
Products.

Heber Springs

★ 57148 ★   **Aeroquip Corp.**
Hwy. 337
Heber Springs, AR 72543-0392
Ultimate Parent: Trinova Corp. **SIC:**
3585—Refrigeration & Heating Equipment.

★ 57149 ★   **Aeroquip Corp.**
Libby Rd.
Heber Springs, AR 72543
Ultimate Parent: Trinova Corp. **SIC:**
3585—Refrigeration & Heating Equipment.

★ 57150 ★   **Kentucky Fried
Chicken**
112 Main
Heber Springs, AR 72543
(501)362-5509
Ultimate Parent: Pepsico. **SIC:** 5812—
Eating Places.

★ 57151 ★   **Pizza Hut**
Hwy. 25 N
Heber Springs, AR 72543
(501)362-2772
Ultimate Parent: Pepsico. **SIC:** 5812—
Eating Places.

★ 57152 ★   **Rohr Ind. Inc.**
424 Industrial Park Dr.
Heber Springs, AR 72543
Ultimate Parent: Rohr. **SIC:** 3728—Aircraft
Parts & Equipment Nec.

★ 57153 ★   **Rohr Industries Inc.**
5201 Hwy. 210 E.
Heber Springs, AR 72543
Ultimate Parent: Rohr. **SIC:** 3728—Aircraft
Parts & Equipment Nec.

★ 57154 ★   **Rohr Industries Inc.**
424 Industrial Park Dr.
Heber Springs, AR 72543
(501)362-9500
Location Type: Plant. **Officer:** Greg Peters,
Manager. **Ultimate Parent:** Rohr. **SIC:**
3724—Aircraft Engines & Engine Parts;
3728—Aircraft Parts & Equipment Nec.

★ 57155 ★   **Skil Corp.**
2 Bolton Sullivan Dr.
Heber Springs, AR 72543
Ultimate Parent: Emerson Electric Co. Inc.
SIC: 3546—Power-Driven Handtools.

Helena

★ 57156 ★   **Kroger Co.**
590 Oakland Ave.
Helena, AR 72342
(501)338-7100
Ultimate Parent: Kroger. **SIC:** 5411—
Grocery Stores.

Hope

★ 57157 ★   **Kentucky Fried
Chicken**
Hwy. 29 N. I30
Hope, AR 71801
(501)777-8677
Ultimate Parent: Pepsico. **SIC:** 5812—
Eating Places.

★ 57158 ★   **Pilgrim's Pride Corp.**
Hope Feed Mill
Hwy. 29 S.
Hope, AR 71801
Company Type: Division. **Ultimate Parent:**
Pilgrim's Pride Corp. **SIC:** 2048—Prepared
Feeds Nec.

★ 57159 ★   **Texaco Inc.
Distributor**
711 N. Main St.
Hope, AR 71801
(501)777-4440
Ultimate Parent: Texaco.

★ 57160 ★   **Trailways Bus Station**
4th
Hope, AR 71801
(501)777-3822
Ultimate Parent: Greyhound Lines Inc. **SIC:**
4131—Intercity & Rural Bus Transportation.

Hot Springs

★ 57161 ★   **Capezio Factory
Direct**
5332 Central Ave.
Hot Springs, AR 71913
(501)525-5799
Ultimate Parent: United States Shoe.

★ 57162 ★ **Dr. Pepper Bottling Co.**
321 Market St.
Hot Springs, AR 71901
(501)623-1024
Officer: Van H. Lyell Jr., President.
Ultimate Parent: Dr. Pepper/Seven-Up.
SIC: 2086—Bottled & Canned Soft Drinks.

★ 57163 ★ **Kentucky Fried Chicken**
114 Airport Rd.
Hot Springs, AR 71913
Ultimate Parent: Pepsico. **SIC:** 5812—
Eating Places.

★ 57164 ★ **Kroger Pharmacy**
3423 Central Ave.
Hot Springs, AR 71913
(501)922-4313
Ultimate Parent: Kroger.

★ 57165 ★ **Kroger Pharmacy**
3341 Central Ave.
Hot Springs, AR 71913
(501)624-5542
Ultimate Parent: Kroger.

★ 57166 ★ **Wal Mart Discount City**
200 Airport Rd.
Hot Springs, AR 71913
(501)624-5384
Ultimate Parent: Wal-Mart Stores, Inc. **SIC:**
5311—Department Stores.

★ 57167 ★ **Weyerhaeuser Co.**
810 Whittington Ave.
Hot Springs, AR 71901
(501)624-8121
Officer: Jim Olmedo, Vice President.
Ultimate Parent: Weyerhaeuser Co. **SIC:**
2411—Logging; 2611—Pulp Mills.

Hot Springs National Park

★ 57168 ★ **Exxon**
Hwy. 70 E
Hot Springs National Park, AR 71902
(501)262-3341
Ultimate Parent: Exxon. **SIC:** 5812—Eating
Places.

★ 57169 ★ **Hertz Rent-A-Car**
625 Airport Rd.
Hot Springs National Park, AR 71913
(501)623-7591
Ultimate Parent: Hertz. **SIC:** 7514—
Passenger Car Rental.

★ 57170 ★ **Hertz Rent-A-Car Licensee**
Memorial Airport
Hot Springs National Park, AR 71901
(501)623-7591
Ultimate Parent: Hertz. **SIC:** 7514—
Passenger Car Rental.

★ 57171 ★ **Kentucky Fried Chicken**
3716 Central Ave.
Hot Springs National Park, AR 71913
(501)624-6363
Ultimate Parent: Pepsico. **SIC:** 5812—
Eating Places.

★ 57172 ★ **Kroger Co**
3700 Central Ave.
Hot Springs National Park, AR 71913
(501)624-0259
Ultimate Parent: Kroger. **SIC:** 5411—
Grocery Stores.

★ 57173 ★ **Kroger Co**
201 Airport Rd.
Hot Springs National Park, AR 71913
(501)624-3649
Ultimate Parent: Kroger. **SIC:** 5461—Retail
Bakeries.

★ 57174 ★ **Lerner Shop**
Hot Spring Mall
Hot Springs National Park, AR 71901
(501)525-4653
Ultimate Parent: Limited. **SIC:** 5621—
Women's Clothing Stores.

★ 57175 ★ **Lerner Shop**
5701 Central Ave.
Hot Springs National Park, AR 71913
(501)525-4653
Ultimate Parent: Limited. **SIC:** 5651—
Family Clothing Stores.

★ 57176 ★ **National Park Medical Center**
1910 Malvevne Ave.
Hot Springs National Park, AR 71901
(501)321-1000
Officer: Warner Kass, Executive Director.
Ultimate Parent: American Medical
Holdings. **SIC:** 8062—General Medical &
Surgical Hospitals.

★ 57177 ★ **Payless Shoesource**
3011 Central Ave.
Hot Springs National Park, AR 71913
(501)624-7007
Ultimate Parent: May Department Stores.
SIC: 5661—Shoe Stores.

★ 57178 ★ **Piggly Wiggly**
Malvern
Hot Springs National Park, AR 71901
(501)623-4381
Ultimate Parent: Bruno's. **SIC:** 5411—
Grocery Stores.

★ 57179 ★ **Piggly Wiggly**
2272 Malvern Rd.
Hot Springs National Park, AR 71901
(501)623-4831
Ultimate Parent: Bruno's. **SIC:** 5411—
Grocery Stores.

★ 57180 ★ **Piggly Wiggly**
899 Park Ave.
Hot Springs National Park, AR 71901
(501)623-8767
Ultimate Parent: Bruno's. **SIC:** 5411—
Grocery Stores.

★ 57181 ★ **Piggly Wiggly**
1268 PO Box
Hot Springs National Park, AR 71902
(501)623-5353
Ultimate Parent: Bruno's. **SIC:** 5411—
Grocery Stores.

★ 57182 ★ **Pizza Hut**
108 Crawford Dr.
Hot Springs National Park, AR 71913
(501)624-5041
Ultimate Parent: Pepsico. **SIC:** 5812—
Eating Places.

★ 57183 ★ **Pizza Hut**
K Mart Shopping Ctr.
Hot Springs National Park, AR 71901
(501)624-5041
Ultimate Parent: Pepsico. **SIC:** 5812—
Eating Places.

★ 57184 ★ **Super Saver**
910 Albert Pike
Hot Springs National Park, AR 71913
(501)624-9363
Ultimate Parent: Wal-Mart Stores, Inc. **SIC:**
5411—Grocery Stores.

★ 57185 ★ **Wal Mart**
3407 Central Ave.
Hot Springs National Park, AR 71913
(501)623-7605
Ultimate Parent: Wal-Mart Stores, Inc. **SIC:**
5311—Department Stores.

★ 57186 ★ **Wal Mart Pharmacy**
Hwy. 7 S
Hot Springs National Park, AR 71901
(501)623-7689
Ultimate Parent: Wal-Mart Stores, Inc. **SIC:**
5912—Drug Stores & Proprietary Stores.

★ 57187 ★ **Wal Mart Pharmacy**
200 Airport Rd.
Hot Springs National Park, AR 71913
(501)624-0142
Ultimate Parent: Wal-Mart Stores, Inc. **SIC:**
5912—Drug Stores & Proprietary Stores.

★ 57188 ★ **Waldenbooks**
5701 Central Ave.
Hot Springs National Park, AR 71913
(501)525-1305
Ultimate Parent: K-Mart. **SIC:** 5942—Book
Stores.

★ 57189 ★ **Waldenbooks**
Hot Spring Mall
Hot Springs National Park, AR 71901
(501)525-1305
Ultimate Parent: K-Mart. **SIC:** 5942—Book
Stores.

★ 57190 ★ **Walgreen Drug Stores**
524 Central Ave.
Hot Springs National Park, AR 71901
(501)623-8855
Ultimate Parent: Walgreen Co. **SIC:**
5912—Drug Stores & Proprietary Stores.

★ 57191 ★ **Walgreen Drug Stores**
1933 Albert Pike
Hot Springs National Park, AR 71913
(501)624-5589
Ultimate Parent: Walgreen Co. **SIC:**
5912—Drug Stores & Proprietary Stores.

Huntsville

★ 57192 ★ **Air Products & Chemicals Inc.**
Huntsville, AR 72740
(501)738-1090
Ultimate Parent: Air Products & Chemicals,
Inc. **SIC:** 5085—Industrial Supplies.

★ 57193 ★ **Armour Swift-Eckrich**
1200 N. College St.
PO Box 665
Huntsville, AR 72740
(501)738-2151
Company Type: Division. **Location Type:**
Plant. **Officer:** Randy Counts, Plant
Manager. **Ultimate Parent:** Conagra.

★ 57194 ★ **Wal Mart Discount City**
E Lee St.
Huntsville, AR 72740
(501)738-2001
Ultimate Parent: Wal-Mart Stores, Inc. **SIC:**
5311—Department Stores.

Jacksonville

★ 57195 ★ **Mary Kay Cosmetics**
Sales
1509 Dogwood Dr.
Jacksonville, AR 72076
(501)982-4052
Ultimate Parent: Mary Kay Cosmetics. **SIC:**
5999—Miscellaneous Retail Stores Nec.

★ 57196 ★ **McDonalds**
2030 N. 1st St.
Jacksonville, AR 72076
(501)982-4939
Ultimate Parent: McDonald's.

★ 57197 ★ **Osco Drug Inc.**
105 Gregory Pl
Jacksonville, AR 72076
(501)982-2125
Ultimate Parent: American Stores. **SIC:**
5912—Drug Stores & Proprietary Stores.

★ 57198 ★ **Pizza Hut**
1910 Marshall Rd.
Jacksonville, AR 72076
(501)985-2575
Ultimate Parent: Pepsico.

★ 57199 ★ **Pizza Hut**
501 S. James St.
Jacksonville, AR 72076
(501)982-9111
Ultimate Parent: Pepsico. **SIC:** 5812—
Eating Places.

★ 57200 ★ **Radio Shack**
104 Gregory Pl
Jacksonville, AR 72076
(501)982-1186
Company Type: Division. **Ultimate Parent:**
Tandy Corp. **SIC:** 5065—Electronic Parts &
Equipment Nec.

★ 57201 ★ **Ryder Truck Rental**
1310 John Hardin Dr.
Jacksonville, AR 72076
(501)982-4776
Ultimate Parent: Ryder System. **SIC:**
4214—Local Trucking With Storage.

★ 57202 ★ **Stone Container Corp.**
1031 Redmond Rd.
Jacksonville, AR 72076
(501)982-1573
Officer: Bill Flynn, Manager. **Ultimate
Parent:** Stone Container Corp. **SIC:** 2673—
Bags—Plastics, Laminated & Coated;
2674—Bags—Uncoated Paper & Multiwall.

★ 57203 ★ **Taco Bell**
505 S. James St.
Jacksonville, AR 72076
(501)982-9172
Ultimate Parent: Pepsico. **SIC:** 5812—
Eating Places.

Jones Mills

★ 57204 ★ **Hot Spring Continuous Rolling Plant**
US Hwy. 270
Jones Mills, AR 72105
Ultimate Parent: Reynolds Metals Co. **SIC:**
3353—Aluminum Sheet, Plate & Foil.

★ 57205 ★ **Reynolds Metal Co. Malvern Cable Plant**
U. S. Hwy. 270 E.
Jones Mills, AR 72105
Ultimate Parent: Reynolds Metals Co. **SIC:**
3357—Nonferrous Wiredrawing & Insulating.

★ 57206 ★ **Reynolds Metals Co.**
Hwy. 270
Jones Mills, AR 72105
(501)844-2000
Officer: Charlie Keene, Manager. **Ultimate
Parent:** Reynolds Metals Co. **SIC:** 3353—
Aluminum Sheet, Plate & Foil.

★ 57207 ★ **Reynolds Metals Co. Hot Spring Cont. Rolling Plant**
U.S. Hwy. 270
Jones Mills, AR 72105
Ultimate Parent: Reynolds Metals Co. **SIC:**
3353—Aluminum Sheet, Plate & Foil.

★ 57208 ★ **Reynolds Metals Co. Malvern Cable Plant**
US Hwy. 270 E
Jones Mills, AR 72105
Ultimate Parent: Reynolds Metals Co. **SIC:**
3357—Nonferrous Wiredrawing & Insulating.

Jonesboro

★ 57209 ★ **ADM Milling Co. Otwell**
18811 Southwest Dr.
Jonesboro, AR 72401
(501)935-2441
Ultimate Parent: Archer Daniels Midland
Co. **SIC:** 5149—Groceries & Related
Products Nec.

★ 57210 ★ **Casual Corner**
1901 S. Caraway Rd.
Jonesboro, AR 72401
(501)932-0886
Ultimate Parent: United States Shoe. **SIC:**
5621—Women's Clothing Stores; 5651—
Family Clothing Stores.

★ 57211 ★ **Dana Corp.**
4929 Krueger Dr.
Jonesboro, AR 72401
(501)972-8100
Company Type: Subsidiary. **Ultimate
Parent:** Dana Corp. **SIC:** 3714—Motor
Vehicle Parts & Accessories.

★ 57212 ★ **Dana Corp.**
Spicer Transmission Div.
4929 Krueger Dr.
Jonesboro, AR 72401
Company Type: Division. **Ultimate Parent:**
Dana Corp. **SIC:** 3714—Motor Vehicle Parts
& Accessories.

★ 57213 ★ **Dana Corp.**
Spicer Transmission Div. Gear Plant
4929 Krueger Dr.
Jonesboro, AR 72401
Company Type: Division. **Location Type:**
Plant. **Ultimate Parent:** Dana Corp. **SIC:**
3714—Motor Vehicle Parts & Accessories.

★ 57214 ★ **Dana Corp.**
Spicer Transmission Div. Jonesboro Gear
Plant
4929 Krueger Dr.
Jonesboro, AR 72401
Company Type: Division. **Location Type:**
Plant. **Ultimate Parent:** Dana Corp. **SIC:**
3714—Motor Vehicle Parts & Accessories.

★ 57215 ★ **Federal Express Corp.**
2712 Phillips Dr.
Jonesboro, AR 72401
(501)238-5355
Ultimate Parent: Federal Express. **SIC:**
7389—Business Services Nec.

★ 57216 ★　FMC
Agricultural Machinery Div.
5601 E. Highland Dr.
Jonesboro, AR 72401-6810
Company Type: Division. **Ultimate Parent:**
FMC. **SIC:** 3523—Farm Machinery &
Equipment.

★ 57217 ★　FMC Corp.
5601 E. Highland Dr.
Jonesboro, AR 72401
(501)935-1970
Officer: Fred Strater, Manager. **Ultimate
Parent:** FMC. **SIC:** 3523—Farm Machinery
& Equipment.

★ 57218 ★　FMC Corp.
Agricultural Machinery Div.
5601 E. Highland Dr.
Jonesboro, AR 72401
Company Type: Division. **Ultimate Parent:**
FMC. **SIC:** 3523—Farm Machinery &
Equipment.

★ 57219 ★　General Electric Co.
101 Gee St.
Jonesboro, AR 72401
Ultimate Parent: General Electric. **SIC:**
3621—Motors & Generators.

★ 57220 ★　General Electric Co.
101 N. Gee St.
Jonesboro, AR 72401
(501)932-7491
Officer: Ray Finecy, Manager. **Ultimate
Parent:** General Electric. **SIC:** 3621—
Motors & Generators; 3699—Electrical
Equipment & Supplies Nec.

★ 57221 ★　Hertz Rent-A-Car
Lindberg Dr.
Jonesboro, AR 72401
(501)932-0221
Ultimate Parent: Hertz. **SIC:** 7514—
Passenger Car Rental.

★ 57222 ★　Kay Bee Toy & Hobby
1901 S. Caraway Rd.
Jonesboro, AR 72401
(501)935-6965
Ultimate Parent: Melville. **SIC:** 3944—
Games, Toys & Children's Vehicles.

★ 57223 ★　Kentucky Fried
Chicken
1600 S. Caraway Rd.
Jonesboro, AR 72401
(501)935-3864
Ultimate Parent: Pepsico. **SIC:** 5812—
Eating Places.

★ 57224 ★　Kentucky Fried
Chicken
139 Southwest Dr.
Jonesboro, AR 72401
(501)935-1650
Ultimate Parent: Pepsico. **SIC:** 5812—
Eating Places.

★ 57225 ★　Lincoln
2601 Commerce Dr.
Jonesboro, AR 72401
Ultimate Parent: Pentair. **SIC:** 3569—
General Industrial Machinery Nec.

★ 57226 ★　Payless Shoesource
1518 S. Caraway Rd.
Jonesboro, AR 72401
(501)935-9097
Ultimate Parent: May Department Stores.
SIC: 5661—Shoe Stores.

★ 57227 ★　Pepsi-Cola Bottling
Co.
1301 Aggie Rd.
Jonesboro, AR 72401
(501)932-6649
Officer: Chris Conger, Manager. **Ultimate
Parent:** Pepsico. **SIC:** 2086—Bottled &
Canned Soft Drinks.

★ 57228 ★　Radio Shack
1901 S. Caraway Rd.
Jonesboro, AR 72401
(501)972-6280
Company Type: Division. **SIC:** 5065—
Electronic Parts & Equipment Nec.
Tandy Corp. **Ultimate Parent:**

★ 57229 ★　Riceland Foods Inc.
216 N. Gee St.
Jonesboro, AR 72401
(501)932-7433
Officer: Rick Rorex, Manager. **Ultimate
Parent:** Riceland Foods. **SIC:** 2044—Rice

Milling; 2075—Soybean Oil Mills; 2079—
Edible Fats & Oils Nec.

★ 57230 ★　Ryder Truck Rental
900 W. Johnson Ave.
Jonesboro, AR 72401
(501)935-1222
Ultimate Parent: Ryder System. **SIC:**
7513—Truck Rental & Leasing Without
Drivers.

★ 57231 ★　Taco Bell
S Caraway Rd.
Jonesboro, AR 72401
(501)932-9039
Ultimate Parent: Pepsico. **SIC:** 5812—
Eating Places.

★ 57232 ★　United Parcel Service
S Hwy. 49
Jonesboro, AR 72401
(501)932-4088
Ultimate Parent: United Parcel Service of
America. **SIC:** 4215—Courier Services
Except by Air.

★ 57233 ★　United Parcel Service
S Hwy. 49
Jonesboro, AR 72401
(501)482-8853
Ultimate Parent: United Parcel Service of
America. **SIC:** 4215—Courier Services
Except by Air.

★ 57234 ★　United Parcel Service
S. Hwy. 49
Jonesboro, AR 72401
(501)932-4088
Ultimate Parent: United Parcel Service of
America. **SIC:** 4215—Courier Services
Except by Air.

★ 57235 ★　Wal Mart Discount
Pharmacy
1843 E. Highland Dr.
Jonesboro, AR 72401
(501)972-1838
Ultimate Parent: Wal-Mart Stores, Inc. **SIC:**
5912—Drug Stores & Proprietary Stores.

★ 57236 ★　Waldenbooks
1901 S. Caraway Rd.
Jonesboro, AR 72401
(501)972-5004
Ultimate Parent: K-Mart. **SIC:** 5942—Book
Stores.

Knobel

★ 57237 ★　ADM Milling
Knobel, AR 72435
(501)259-3244
Ultimate Parent: Archer Daniels Midland
Co. **SIC:** 5153—Grain & Field Beans;
1490—Miscellaneous Nonmetallic Minerals.

Lake Village

★ 57238 ★　Farm Fresh Catfish
Co.
PO Box 348
Lake Village, AR 71653
(501)265-5394
Company Type: Subsidiary. **Location
Type:** Plant. **Officer:** Herbert Hodges, Plant
Manager. **Ultimate Parent:** Hormel Foods.
SIC: 2091—Canned & Cured Fish &
Seafoods; 2092—Fresh or Frozen Prepared
Fish.

★ 57239 ★　Farm Fresh Catfish
Co.
Bill Young Rd.
Lake Village, AR 71653
(501)265-3571
Ultimate Parent: Hormel Foods. **SIC:**
0921—Fish Hatcheries & Preserves.

★ 57240 ★　First State Bank &
Trust Co.
216 Main St.
Lake Village, AR 71653
(501)265-5366
Ultimate Parent: Michigan National Corp.
SIC: 6081—Foreign Banks—Branches &
Agencies.

★ 57241 ★　Mobil Oil Products
St Mart St.
Lake Village, AR 71653
(501)265-2460
Ultimate Parent: Mobil. **SIC:** 5172—
Petroleum Products Nec.

Lewisville

★ 57242 ★　Greyhound Bus Lines
210 W. 2nd
Lewisville, AR 71845
(501)921-5770
Ultimate Parent: Greyhound Lines Inc. **SIC:**
4142—Bus Charter Service Except Local.

Lincoln

★ 57243 ★　Latco, Inc.- Pro AG
17850 W. Hwy. 62
Lincoln, AR 72744
(501)824-3282
Officer: James Latta, Owner. **Ultimate
Parent:** Universal Corp. **SIC:** 3441—
Fabricated Structural Metal.

Little Rock

★ 57244 ★　ALLTEL Arkansas Inc.
PO Box 2177
Little Rock, AR 72203
(501)661-8000
Ultimate Parent: ALLTEL Corp. **SIC:**
4812—Radiotelephone Communications.

★ 57245 ★　ALLTEL Corp.
1 Allied Dr.
Little Rock, AR 72202
(501)661-8000 **Fax:** (501)664-3469
Company Type: Headquarters. **Officer:**
Joe T. Ford. **SIC:** 4812—Radiotelephone
Communications; 6719—Holding
Companies Nec; 3661—Telephone &
Telegraph Apparatus; 5065—Electronic
Parts & Equipment Nec; 2741—
Miscellaneous Publishing; 4899—
Communications Services Nec; 4911—
Electric Services; 4813—Telephone
Communications Except Radiotelephone.
Employee Count: 14864. **Sales:** 2342 M.
Fortune Service 500: Ranking 63.

★ 57246 ★　ALLTEL Corp.
Telephone
1 Allied Dr.
Little Rock, AR 72202
Company Type: Subsidiary. **Ultimate
Parent:** ALLTEL Corp.

★ 57247 ★　ALLTEL Finance
Corp.
1 Allied Dr.
Little Rock, AR 72203
(501)661-8000
Company Type: Subsidiary. **Ultimate
Parent:** ALLTEL Corp. **SIC:** 6159—
Miscellaneous Business Credit Institutions.

★ 57248 ★　ALLTEL Mobile
Communications Inc.
2 Financial Centre
10825 Financial Pky., Ste. 401
Little Rock, AR 72211
(501)661-8500
Company Type: Subsidiary. **Ultimate
Parent:** ALLTEL Corp. **SIC:** 4812—
Radiotelephone Communications.

★ 57249 ★　ALLTEL Services Inc.
1 Allied Dr.
PO Box 2177
Little Rock, AR 72203
(501)661-8000
Company Type: Subsidiary. **Ultimate
Parent:** ALLTEL Corp. **SIC:** 4812—
Radiotelephone Communications.

★ 57250 ★　Archer Daniels
Midland Co.
PO Box 30
Little Rock, AR 72203-0030
(501)372-0277
Officer: Rick Benware. **Ultimate Parent:**
Archer Daniels Midland Co. **SIC:** 2075—
Soybean Oil Mills.

★ 57251 ★　Archer Daniels
Midland Co.
E 9th & Bond St.
Little Rock, AR 72203
(501)372-0277
Officer: Mark Bemis, Manager. **Ultimate
Parent:** Archer Daniels Midland Co. **SIC:**
2074—Cottonseed Oil Mills; 2075—Soybean
Oil Mills.

★ 57252 ★　Arkansas Power &
Light Co.
425 W. Capitol Ave., 40th Fl.
Little Rock, AR 72201-3439
(501)377-4000
Company Type: Subsidiary. **Officer:** Jerry
L. Maulden, Chairman of the Board & CEO.
Ultimate Parent: Entergy. **SIC:** 4911—
Electric Services. **Employee Count:** 3170.

★ 57253 ★　Ask. Coca-Cola
Bottling Co.
7000 I 30
Little Rock, AR 72209
Ultimate Parent: Coca-Cola Bottling
Consol. **SIC:** 2086—Bottled & Canned Soft
Drinks.

★ 57254 ★　AT&T
7600 Interstate 30
Little Rock, AR 72209
(501)569-5100
Officer: Elizabeth Elrod, Manager. **Ultimate
Parent:** AT&T. **SIC:** 3571—Electronic
Computers; 3575—Computer Terminals;
3577—Computer Peripheral Equipment Nec.

★ 57255 ★　AT&T
PO Box 8912
Little Rock, AR 72219-8912
(501)562-4411
Location Type: Branch office. **Officer:** J. J.
Eishenhauer. **Ultimate Parent:** AT&T. **SIC:**
3575—Computer Terminals; 3571—
Electronic Computers; 3577—Computer
Peripheral Equipment Nec.

★ 57256 ★　Avon Products Inc.
Boyle Bldg.
Little Rock, AR 72201
(501)372-0406
Ultimate Parent: Avon Products, Inc. **SIC:**
5999—Miscellaneous Retail Stores Nec.

★ 57257 ★　Baxter Hospital
Supplies
5800 Lindsey Rd.
Little Rock, AR 72206-3820
(501)790-0556
Officer: Curt Kramer. **Ultimate Parent:**
Baxter International. **SIC:** 5047—Medical &
Hospital Equipment.

★ 57258 ★　Best Foods Grocery
Products Group
8500 Frazier Pke.
Little Rock, AR 72203
(501)490-1441
Company Type: Division. **Location Type:**
Plant. **Officer:** Horace Childress, Plant
Manager. **Ultimate Parent:** CPC
International.

★ 57259 ★　BFI-Model Fill Landfill
3817 Mabelvale Pke.
Little Rock, AR 72204-7953
(501)562-0070
Ultimate Parent: Browning-Ferris
Industries. **SIC:** 4953—Refuse Systems.

★ 57260 ★　Borden Inc.
Dairy
7900 Asher St.
Little Rock, AR 72204
Company Type: Division. **Ultimate Parent:**
Borden, Inc. **SIC:** 2026—Fluid Milk.

★ 57261 ★　Borden Inc.
Grocery & Specialty Products
7900 Asher Ave.
Little Rock, AR 72204
Ultimate Parent: Borden, Inc. **SIC:** 2026—
Fluid Milk.

★ 57262 ★　Brownell Electro Inc.
Little Rock Corp. Ctr.
7501 I-30, Ste. 15
Little Rock, AR 72209
(501)562-2061
Location Type: Branch office. **Ultimate
Parent:** Avnet. **SIC:** 5063—Electrical
Apparatus & Equipment.

★ 57263 ★　Burlington Coat
Factory
9101 W. Markham St.
Little Rock, AR 72205-2260
(501)223-3868
Location Type: Branch office. **Officer:**
Elwin Jones. **Ultimate Parent:** Burlington
Industries, Equity. **SIC:** 5311—Department
Stores; 5651—Family Clothing Stores.

★ 57264 ★   Charles Schwab Inc.
303 W. Capitol Ave.
Little Rock, AR 72201
(501)374-0644
Ultimate Parent: Charles Schwab Corp.

★ 57265 ★   Coca-Cola Bottling
Co. of Arkansas
7000 I-30
Little Rock, AR 72209-3175
(501)569-2700
Officer: Donald R. Keough, Chairman.
Ultimate Parent: Coca-Cola Enterprises.
SIC: 2086—Bottled & Canned Soft Drinks.
Employee Count: 350.

★ 57266 ★   Coca Cola U S a Fnt
Sales
Univ
Little Rock, AR 72201
(501)666-9165
Ultimate Parent: Coca-Cola. SIC: 2086—
Bottled & Canned Soft Drinks.

★ 57267 ★   Continental Express
Inc.
1701 S. Shackleford Rd.
Little Rock, AR 72211-4386
(501)224-3378
Company Type: Division. Officer: Edward
M. Harvey, Chairman of the Board, CEO.
Ultimate Parent: Coastal Corp. SIC:
4213—Trucking Except Local. Employee
Count: 300. Sales: 28 M.

★ 57268 ★   Delta Air Lines
200 N. Bowman Rd.
Little Rock, AR 72211
(501)221-1266
Ultimate Parent: Delta Air Lines, Inc.

★ 57269 ★   Delta Air Lines
1 Airport Rd.
Little Rock, AR 72202
(501)374-7654
Ultimate Parent: Delta Air Lines, Inc. SIC:
4512—Air Transportation—Scheduled.

★ 57270 ★   Delta Air Lines
Municipal Airport
Little Rock, AR 72202
(501)374-2040
Ultimate Parent: Delta Air Lines, Inc. SIC:
4512—Air Transportation—Scheduled.

★ 57271 ★   Delta Air Lines Inc.
1 Airport Rd.
Little Rock, AR 72202
(501)374-7654
Ultimate Parent: Delta Air Lines, Inc. SIC:
4512—Air Transportation—Scheduled.

★ 57272 ★   D.H. Holmes Co.
Limited, Inc.
1600 Cantrell Rd.
Little Rock, AR 72201-1110
(501)376-5200
Company Type: Subsidiary. Ultimate
Parent: Dillard Department Stores. SIC:
5311—Department Stores.

★ 57273 ★   Digital Equipment
Corporati
1701 Centerview Dr. 100
Little Rock, AR 72211
(501)221-4609
Ultimate Parent: Digital Equipment Corp.
SIC: 7372—Prepackaged Software.

★ 57274 ★   Dillard Department
Stores
1600 Cantrell Rd.
Little Rock, AR 72203
(501)376-5200
Company Type: Headquarters. Officer:
William T. Dillard Sr., CEO. Employee
Count: 35536. Sales: 5131 M. Fortune
Service 500: Ranking 27.

★ 57275 ★   Dillard Department
Stores
Park
Little Rock, AR 72205
(501)660-1301
Ultimate Parent: Dillard Department Stores.
SIC: 5311—Department Stores.

★ 57276 ★   Dillard Department
Stores
Little Rock Division
6th & Main St.
Little Rock, AR 72201
(501)376-5808
Officer: Mike Dillard, Chairman of the

Board. Ultimate Parent: Dillard Department
Stores. SIC: 5311—Department Stores.

★ 57277 ★   Dillard Department
Stores, Inc.
P O Box 486
Little Rock, AR 72203
Company Type: Headquarters. Ultimate
Parent: Dillard Department Stores.

★ 57278 ★   Dillard Investment
Co., Inc.
1600 Cantrell Rd.
Little Rock, AR 72201-1110
(501)376-5200
Officer: William T. Dillard, Chairman.
Ultimate Parent: Dillard Department Stores.
SIC: 6153—Short-Term Business Credit.
Employee Count: 5.

★ 57279 ★   Dillard Travel Inc.
1600 Cantrell Rd.
Little Rock, AR 72201-1110
(501)376-5369
Company Type: Subsidiary. Officer:
William T. Dillard Sr., Chairman of the
Board. Ultimate Parent: Dillard Department
Stores. SIC: 4724—Travel Agencies.
Employee Count: 260. Sales: 67000000
M.

★ 57280 ★   Dillards
6 Main St.
Little Rock, AR 72203
(501)376-5201
Ultimate Parent: Dillard Department Stores.
SIC: 5311—Department Stores.

★ 57281 ★   Emery Worldwide
Adams Field
Little Rock, AR 72202
(501)372-7366
Ultimate Parent: Consolidated Freightways.
SIC: 4512—Air Transportation—Scheduled.

★ 57282 ★   Fred Meyers Co. Inc.
Tower Bldg.
Little Rock, AR 72201
(501)372-1800
Ultimate Parent: Fred Meyer. SIC: 7381—
Detective & Armored Car Services.

★ 57283 ★   Fred Meyers Co. Inc.
Tower Bldg.
Little Rock, AR 72201
(501)372-1800
Ultimate Parent: Fred Meyer. SIC: 7381—
Detective & Armored Car Services.

★ 57284 ★   Fruehauf Trailer Corp.
2300 W. 60th St.
Little Rock, AR 72209-2509
(501)562-4680
Location Type: Branch office. Officer: Ned
Armstead. Ultimate Parent: Terex Corp.
SIC: 5013—Motor Vehicle Supplies & New
Parts; 5012—Automobiles & Other Motor
Vehicles.

★ 57285 ★   Georgia-Pacific Corp.
Hwy. 165 South PO Box 15370
Little Rock, AR 72231-5370
Ultimate Parent: Georgia-Pacific. SIC:
2499—Wood Products Nec.

★ 57286 ★   Greyhound Bus Lines
200 E. Markham St.
Little Rock, AR 72201
(501)372-3296
Ultimate Parent: Greyhound Lines Inc. SIC:
4131—Intercity & Rural Bus Transportation.

★ 57287 ★   Hewlett Packard Co.
111 N. Fillmore St.
Little Rock, AR 72205
(501)376-1844
Ultimate Parent: Hewlett-Packard. SIC:
5047—Medical & Hospital Equipment.

★ 57288 ★   IBM Corp.
401 W. Capitol Ave.
Little Rock, AR 72201
(501)370-2300
Ultimate Parent: IBM. SIC: 5099—Durable
Goods Nec.

★ 57289 ★   Kroger Co
6420 Asher Ave.
Little Rock, AR 72204
(501)565-0188
Ultimate Parent: Kroger. SIC: 5912—Drug
Stores & Proprietary Stores.

★ 57290 ★   Kroger Company
8824 Geyer Springs Rd.
Little Rock, AR 72209
(501)568-2330
Ultimate Parent: Kroger. SIC: 5411—
Grocery Stores.

★ 57291 ★   Kroger Food Stores
14000 Cantrell Rd.
Little Rock, AR 72212
(501)225-6006
Ultimate Parent: Kroger.

★ 57292 ★   Linens N Things
9100 N. Rodney Parham Rd.
Little Rock, AR 72212
(501)227-5751
Ultimate Parent: Melville.

★ 57293 ★   Mobil Oil Corp.
9001 W. Markham St.
Little Rock, AR 72205
(501)227-9786
Ultimate Parent: Mobil. SIC: 5541—
Gasoline Service Stations.

★ 57294 ★   New York Life
Arkansas General Office
10810 Executive Ctr. Dr., Ste. 101
Little Rock, AR 72211
(501)223-1600 Fax: (501)223-1646
Officer: Thomas Kelly Gilder, Manager.
Ultimate Parent: New York Life.

★ 57295 ★   Pizza Hut
6801 Cantrell Rd.
Little Rock, AR 72207
(501)666-2900
Ultimate Parent: Pepsico. SIC: 7389—
Business Services Nec.

★ 57296 ★   Pizza Hut
11410 W. Markham St.
Little Rock, AR 72211
(501)221-1515
Ultimate Parent: Pepsico.

★ 57297 ★   Pizza Hut
912 I 30
Little Rock, AR 72209
(501)372-7065
Ultimate Parent: Pepsico. SIC: 5812—
Eating Places.

★ 57298 ★   Pizza Hut
1810 S. University Ave.
Little Rock, AR 72204
(501)663-4433
Ultimate Parent: Pepsico. SIC: 5812—
Eating Places.

★ 57299 ★   Porocel Corp.
10,000 Arch St.
Little Rock, AR 72206
Ultimate Parent: Engelhard Corp. SIC:
2819—Industrial Inorganic Chemicals Nec.

★ 57300 ★   Radio Shack
10720 Parham R
Little Rock, AR 72205
(501)227-4109
Company Type: Division. Ultimate Parent:
Tandy Corp. SIC: 5065—Electronic Parts &
Equipment Nec.

★ 57301 ★   Radio Shack
Markham Manor Apts
Little Rock, AR 72211
(501)224-2994
Company Type: Division. Ultimate Parent:
Tandy Corp. SIC: 5065—Electronic Parts &
Equipment Nec.

★ 57302 ★   Radio Shack
Markham Sq.
Little Rock, AR 72205
(501)224-2994
Company Type: Division. Ultimate Parent:
Tandy Corp. SIC: 5065—Electronic Parts &
Equipment Nec.

★ 57303 ★   Radio Shack
5820 Asher Ave.
Little Rock, AR 72204
(501)666-0101
Company Type: Division. Ultimate Parent:
Tandy Corp. SIC: 5065—Electronic Parts &
Equipment Nec.

★ 57304 ★   Radio Shack
300 S. University Ave.
Little Rock, AR 72205
(501)663-2870
Company Type: Division. Ultimate Parent:

Tandy Corp. SIC: 5065—Electronic Parts &
Equipment Nec.

★ 57305 ★   Ryder Truck Rental
3000 W. 68th St.
Little Rock, AR 72209
(501)562-9334
Ultimate Parent: Ryder System. SIC:
7513—Truck Rental & Leasing Without
Drivers.

★ 57306 ★   Ryder Truck Rental
Roosevelt Rd.
Little Rock, AR 72206
(501)374-5030
Ultimate Parent: Ryder System. SIC:
7513—Truck Rental & Leasing Without
Drivers.

★ 57307 ★   Ryder Truck Rental
3300 S. Polk St.
Little Rock, AR 72204
(501)568-2381
Ultimate Parent: Ryder System.

★ 57308 ★   Ryder Truck Rental
9302 Hwy. I 30
Little Rock, AR 72209
(501)562-9316
Ultimate Parent: Ryder System.

★ 57309 ★   Ryder Truck Rental
7325 Kanis Rd.
Little Rock, AR 72204
(501)223-8460
Ultimate Parent: Ryder System.

★ 57310 ★   Ryder Truck Rental
7400 Cantrell Rd.
Little Rock, AR 72207
(501)663-9592
Ultimate Parent: Ryder System.

★ 57311 ★   Smith Fiberglass
Products Inc.
2700 W. 65th St.
Little Rock, AR 72209-8592
Ultimate Parent: A. O. Smith. SIC: 3089—
Plastics Products Nec.

★ 57312 ★   Smoky Hollow Foods
3200 Woodrow St.
Little Rock, AR 72203-3377
Ultimate Parent: Sara Lee Corp. SIC:
2013—Sausages & Other Prepared Meats.

★ 57313 ★   Systematics
Information Services Inc.
4001 Rodney Parham Rd.
Little Rock, AR 72212
(501)220-5100
Company Type: Subsidiary. Ultimate
Parent: ALLTEL Corp. SIC: 7372—
Prepackaged Software; 7374—Data
Processing & Preparation.

★ 57314 ★   Texaco Express Lub
6021 W. 12th St.
Little Rock, AR 72204
(501)666-2451
Ultimate Parent: Texaco.

★ 57315 ★   Texaco Slf Sv&Fd
2620 W. 65th St.
Little Rock, AR 72209
(501)565-3864
Ultimate Parent: Texaco.

★ 57316 ★   3M Co.
PO Box 165860
Little Rock, AR 72216-5860
(501)490-1509
Officer: Dean Skaer. Ultimate Parent:
Minnesota Mining & Mfg. SIC: 3295—
Minerals—Ground or Treated.

★ 57317 ★   Trailways Bus System
Markham
Little Rock, AR 72201
(501)372-1871
Ultimate Parent: Greyhound Lines Inc. SIC:
4111—Local & Suburban Transit.

★ 57318 ★   Underwriters
Adjusting Co.
Prospect
Little Rock, AR 72201
(501)661-9880
Ultimate Parent: Continental. SIC: 6411—
Insurance Agents, Brokers & Service.

★ 57319 ★   Waldenbooks
11108 N. Rodney Parham Rd.
Little Rock, AR 72212
(501)223-9640
Ultimate Parent: K-Mart. **SIC:** 5942—Book
Stores.

★ 57320 ★   Watco Inc.
11519 Kanis Rd.
Little Rock, AR 72211
(501)225-6891
Ultimate Parent: Eastman Kodak. **SIC:**
5199—Nondurable Goods Nec; 5169—
Chemicals & Allied Products Nec.

★ 57321 ★   Xerox Corp.
10801 Executive Center, Ste. 100
Little Rock, AR 72211
(501)221-6600
Officer: Nord Foster, Manager. **Ultimate
Parent:** Xerox Corp. **SIC:** 3663—Radio &
T.V. Communications Equipment.

Lonoke

★ 57322 ★   Coast to Coast
318 Jacuzzi Ln.
Lonoke, AR 72086
(501)676-2064
Ultimate Parent: Servistar Corp. **SIC:**
5941—Sporting Goods & Bicycle Shops.

★ 57323 ★   Remington Arms Co.
1 H 40 & Remington Rd.
Lonoke, AR 72086
(501)676-3161
Officer: Paul Otto, President. **Ultimate
Parent:** E.I. DuPont De Nemours. **SIC:**
3482—Small Arms Ammunition.

Lowell

★ 57324 ★   Hunt Transport Inc/J
B
Hwy. 71 N
Lowell, AR 72745
(501)751-1700
Ultimate Parent: IDS Life. **SIC:** 4213—
Trucking Except Local.

★ 57325 ★   J. B. Hunt Transport
615 J.B. Hunt Dr.
Lowell, AR 72745
(501)820-0000
Company Type: Headquarters. **Officer:** J.
Kirk Thompson. **Employee Count:** 10476.
Fortune Service 500: Ranking 30.

★ 57326 ★   J B Hunt Transport
Services Inc.
615 J B Hunt Corporate Dr.
PO Box 130
Lowell, AR 72745
(501)820-0000 **Fax:** (501)820-8397
Company Type: Headquarters. **Officer:**
J.B. Hunt, Chairman. **Ultimate Parent:** J. B.
Hunt Transport. **Employee Count:** 11000.
Sales: 900 illion M.

Mabelvale

★ 57327 ★   Pizza Hut
10500 Shannon Hills Dr.
Mabelvale, AR 72103
(501)455-2121
Ultimate Parent: Pepsico.

Magnolia

★ 57328 ★   Arco Oil & Gas Co.
Eldorado Hwy.
Magnolia, AR 71753
(501)234-2924
Ultimate Parent: Atlantic Richfield Co., Inc.
SIC: 1311—Crude Petroleum & Natural
Gas.

★ 57329 ★   Dow Chemical Co.
Hwy. 132 S
Magnolia, AR 71753
Ultimate Parent: Dow Chemical Co. USA.
SIC: 2819—Industrial Inorganic Chemicals
Nec.

★ 57330 ★   Ethyl Corp.
Hwy. 132 W.
Magnolia, AR 71753
Ultimate Parent: Ethyl. **SIC:** 2819—
Industrial Inorganic Chemicals Nec; 2869—
Industrial Organic Chemicals Nec.

★ 57331 ★   Ethyl Corp.
Rte. 79 S.
Magnolia, AR 71753
Ultimate Parent: Ethyl. **SIC:** 2869—
Industrial Organic Chemicals Nec.

★ 57332 ★   Greyhound Bus Lines
1326 N. Vine St.
Magnolia, AR 71753
(501)234-2100
Ultimate Parent: Greyhound Lines Inc. **SIC:**
4131—Intercity & Rural Bus Transportation.

★ 57333 ★   Kroger Deli&Bakery
Hwy. 82
Magnolia, AR 71753
(501)234-4571
Ultimate Parent: Kroger. **SIC:** 5411—
Grocery Stores.

★ 57334 ★   Ryder Truck Rental
Haynesville Hwy.
Magnolia, AR 71753
(501)234-3428
Ultimate Parent: Ryder System. **SIC:**
7513—Truck Rental & Leasing Without
Drivers.

★ 57335 ★   Ryder Truck Rental
2113 N. Vine St.
Magnolia, AR 71753
(501)234-6000
Ultimate Parent: Ryder System. **SIC:**
7389—Business Services Nec.

★ 57336 ★   Shell Super Stop
Hwy. 79 Bypass
Magnolia, AR 71753
(501)234-8468
Ultimate Parent: Shell Oil Co. **SIC:** 5812—
Eating Places.

★ 57337 ★   Wal Mart Discount
Cities
Hwy. 82 N
Magnolia, AR 71753
(501)234-6500
Ultimate Parent: Wal-Mart Stores, Inc. **SIC:**
5311—Department Stores.

★ 57338 ★   Wal Mart Pharmacy
Hwy. 82 N
Magnolia, AR 71753
(501)234-5421
Ultimate Parent: Wal-Mart Stores, Inc. **SIC:**
5912—Drug Stores & Proprietary Stores.

Malvern

★ 57339 ★   Exxon Car Care
538 E. Page Ave.
Malvern, AR 72104
(501)337-4141
Ultimate Parent: Exxon.

★ 57340 ★   Kentucky Fried
Chicken
Hwy. 270 W
Malvern, AR 72104
(501)337-1722
Ultimate Parent: Pepsico. **SIC:** 5812—
Eating Places.

★ 57341 ★   Pizza Hut
1400 E. Page Ave.
Malvern, AR 72104
(501)337-9549
Ultimate Parent: Pepsico.

★ 57342 ★   Ryder Truck Rental
329 E. Page Ave.
Malvern, AR 72104
(501)337-0017
Ultimate Parent: Ryder System.

★ 57343 ★   Wal Mart Pharmacy
1400 E. Page Ave.
Malvern, AR 72104
(501)337-1170
Ultimate Parent: Wal-Mart Stores, Inc. **SIC:**
5912—Drug Stores & Proprietary Stores.

★ 57344 ★   Willamette Industries,
Inc.
Malvern
Rte. 3 Gifford Community
Malvern, AR 72104
Ultimate Parent: Willamette Industries, Inc.
SIC: 2493—Reconstituted Wood Products.

★ 57345 ★   Williamette Industries
Inc.
Malvern
Rte. 3 Gifford Community
Malvern, AR 72104
Ultimate Parent: Willamette Industries, Inc.
SIC: 2499—Wood Products Nec.

Mammoth Spg

★ 57346 ★   Radio Shack
277 Main St.
Mammoth Spg, AR 72554
(501)625-3830
Company Type: Division. **Ultimate Parent:**
Tandy Corp. **SIC:** 5719—Miscellaneous
Home Furnishings Stores.

Marion

★ 57347 ★   Wal Mart Disc
300 S. Service Rd.
Marion, AR 72364
(501)732-1757
Ultimate Parent: Wal-Mart Stores, Inc.

Marked Tree

★ 57348 ★   Trailways Bus System
50 Frisco St.
Marked Tree, AR 72365
(501)358-2484
Ultimate Parent: Greyhound Lines Inc. **SIC:**
5912—Drug Stores & Proprietary Stores.

Marshall

★ 57349 ★   Superior Federal
Bank, FSB
Hwy. 65 N
Marshall, AR 72650-0919
(501)448-3166
Location Type: Branch office. **Officer:**
Leada Horton, Manager. **Ultimate Parent:**
Boatmen's Bancshares. **SIC:** 6021—
National Commercial Banks.

Marvell

★ 57350 ★   Texaco Inc.
Main
Marvell, AR 72366
(501)829-2481
Ultimate Parent: Texaco. **SIC:** 5171—
Petroleum Bulk Stations & Terminals.

★ 57351 ★   Texaco Stop & Co.
Hwy. 49 E
Marvell, AR 72366
(501)829-3661
Ultimate Parent: Texaco.

Marysville

★ 57352 ★   Great Lakes Chemical
Co. (West Plant)
Union County Rd. 10
Marysville, AR 71730
Ultimate Parent: Great Lakes Chemical.
SIC: 2819—Industrial Inorganic Chemicals
Nec.

★ 57353 ★   Great Lakes Chemical
Corp. Marysville Plant
Union County Rd. 10
Marysville, AR 71730
Ultimate Parent: Great Lakes Chemical.
SIC: 2819—Industrial Inorganic Chemicals
Nec.

Maumelle

★ 57354 ★   Carrier Corp.
100 Murphy Dr.
Maumelle, AR 72118
Ultimate Parent: United Technologies. **SIC:**
3585—Refrigeration & Heating Equipment.

Mayflower

★ 57355 ★   First State Bank &
Trust Co.
US 365
Mayflower, AR 72106
(501)470-1326
Ultimate Parent: Michigan National Corp.
SIC: 6022—State Commercial Banks.

Mc Gehee

★ 57356 ★   Kentucky Fried
Chicken
Hwy. 65
Mc Gehee, AR 71654
(501)222-3120
Ultimate Parent: Pepsico. **SIC:** 5812—
Eating Places.

★ 57357 ★   Potlatch Corp.
Hwy. 4 Near Rohwer
Mc Gehee, AR 71654
Ultimate Parent: Potlatch. **SIC:** 2631—
Paperboard Mills.

★ 57358 ★   Radio Shack
227 Hwy. 65 N
Mc Gehee, AR 71654
(501)222-5543
Company Type: Division. **Ultimate Parent:**
Tandy Corp. **SIC:** 5734—Computer &
Software Stores.

★ 57359 ★   Trailways Bus System
300 S. 1st St.
Mc Gehee, AR 71654
(501)222-3770
Ultimate Parent: Greyhound Lines Inc. **SIC:**
4131—Intercity & Rural Bus Transportation.

McCrory

★ 57360 ★   American Greetings
Corp.
Rte. 2
McCrory, AR 72101-9802
(501)731-2552
Ultimate Parent: American Greetings. **SIC:**
2771—Greeting Cards.

★ 57361 ★   American Greetings
Inc.
Hwy. 64B
McCrory, AR 72101
(501)731-2552
Ultimate Parent: American Greetings. **SIC:**
5112—Stationery & Office Supplies.

McGehee

★ 57362 ★   Potlatch Corp.
Hwy. 4
McGehee, AR 71654-0727
Ultimate Parent: Potlatch. **SIC:** 2631—
Paperboard Mills.

Mena

★ 57363 ★   Coast to Coast
813 Mena St.
Mena, AR 71953
(501)394-3456
Ultimate Parent: Servistar Corp. **SIC:**
5941—Sporting Goods & Bicycle Shops.

★ 57364 ★   Exxon
Hwy. 71 N
Mena, AR 71953
(501)394-1193
Ultimate Parent: Exxon. **SIC:** 5541—
Gasoline Service Stations.

★ 57365 ★   Kentucky Fried
Chicken
Northside Shopping Ctr.
Mena, AR 71953
(501)394-5482
Ultimate Parent: Pepsico. **SIC:** 5812—
Eating Places.

★ 57366 ★   Pizza Hut
Northside Shopping C
Mena, AR 71953
(501)394-5952
Ultimate Parent: Pepsico. **SIC:** 5812—
Eating Places.

★ 57367 ★   US Electrical Motors
401 N. Morrow
Mena, AR 71953
Ultimate Parent: Emerson Electric Co. Inc.
SIC: 3621—Motors & Generators.

★ 57368 ★   US Electrical Motors
401 N. Morrow
Mena, AR 71953
Ultimate Parent: Emerson Electric Co. Inc.
SIC: 3621—Motors & Generators.

★ 57369 ★ Wal Mart Discount
Cities
Northside Shopping Ctr.
Mena, AR 71953
(501)394-5050
Ultimate Parent: Wal-Mart Stores, Inc. SIC:
5311—Department Stores.

Monticello

★ 57370 ★ Burlington Industries
Inc.
235 E. Shelton Ave.
Monticello, AR 71655
(501)367-6251
Officer: John Ware, President. Ultimate
Parent: Burlington Industries, Equity. SIC:
2273—Carpets & Rugs; 2281—Yarn
Spinning Mills; 2399—Fabricated Textile
Products Nec.

★ 57371 ★ Coast to Coast
300 N. Bailey St.
Monticello, AR 71655
(501)367-6875
Ultimate Parent: Servistar Corp. SIC:
5531—Automobile & Home Supply Stores.

★ 57372 ★ Coca Cola Bottling
Co.
Hwy. 81
Monticello, AR 71655
(501)367-9771
Ultimate Parent: Coca-Cola Enterprises.
SIC: 2086—Bottled & Canned Soft Drinks;
5149—Groceries & Related Products Nec.

★ 57373 ★ Coca-Cola Bottling
Co. of South Arkansas
Hwy. 4 & 81
Monticello, AR 71655
Ultimate Parent: Coca-Cola Bottling
Consol. SIC: 2000—Food & Kindred
Products.

★ 57374 ★ Taco Bell
177 S. Hwy. 81
Monticello, AR 71655
(501)367-9229
Ultimate Parent: Pepsico. SIC: 5812—
Eating Places; 5812—Eating Places.

★ 57375 ★ Trailways
334 E. Gaines St.
Monticello, AR 71655
(501)367-3546
Ultimate Parent: Greyhound Lines Inc. SIC:
4131—Intercity & Rural Bus Transportation.

Morrilton

★ 57376 ★ Coca Cola Bottling
Co. of Ar
Hwy. 64 E
Morrilton, AR 72110
(501)354-2416
Ultimate Parent: Coca-Cola Enterprises.
SIC: 5149—Groceries & Related Products
Nec.

★ 57377 ★ Coca-Cola Bottling
Co. of Arkansas
Broadway & Crestlinger Ave.
Morrilton, AR 72110
Ultimate Parent: Coca-Cola Bottling
Consol. SIC: 2086—Bottled & Canned Soft
Drinks.

★ 57378 ★ Kroger Delicatessen
Hwy. 9 N
Morrilton, AR 72110
(501)354-3248
Ultimate Parent: Kroger. SIC: 5411—
Grocery Stores.

★ 57379 ★ Piggly Wiggly
100 S. Saint Joseph St.
Morrilton, AR 72110
(501)354-1700
Ultimate Parent: Bruno's. SIC: 5411—
Grocery Stores.

★ 57380 ★ Ryder Truck Rental
Hwy. 9 N
Morrilton, AR 72110
(501)354-1104
Ultimate Parent: Ryder System. SIC:
7359—Equipment Rental & Leasing Nec.

Mountain Home

★ 57381 ★ Aeroquip Corp.
Hwy. 201 S
Mountain Home, AR 72653
(501)425-6051
Officer: Jim Thurman, Manager. Ultimate
Parent: Trinova Corp. SIC: 3052—Rubber
& Plastics Hose & Belting.

★ 57382 ★ Aeroquip Corp.
Hwy. 201 S.
Mountain Home, AR 72653
Ultimate Parent: Trinova Corp. SIC:
3052—Rubber & Plastics Hose & Belting.

★ 57383 ★ Aeroquip Corp.
Rte. 2
Mountain Home, AR 72653-9802
Ultimate Parent: Trinova Corp. SIC:
3052—Rubber & Plastics Hose & Belting.

★ 57384 ★ Baxter Healthcare
Corp.
1900 N. Hwy. 201
Mountain Home, AR 72653-2433
(501)424-5200
Location Type: Branch office. Officer: Jim
Venters. Ultimate Parent: Baxter
International. SIC: 3841—Surgical &
Medical Instruments; 5122—Drugs,
Proprietaries & Sundries.

★ 57385 ★ Coast to Coast Store
339 Hwy. 62 E
Mountain Home, AR 72653
(501)425-4254
Ultimate Parent: Servistar Corp. SIC:
5251—Hardware Stores.

★ 57386 ★ First Federal S & L
Hwy. 62 E
Mountain Home, AR 72653
(501)425-6061
Company Type: Branch. Officer: Jerry
Jones. Ultimate Parent: Bancorp Hawaii.
SIC: 6035—Federal Savings Institutions;
6021—National Commercial Banks; 6141—
Personal Credit Institutions.

★ 57387 ★ Kentucky Fried
Chicken
College Plz.
Mountain Home, AR 72653
(501)425-2200
Ultimate Parent: Pepsico. SIC: 5812—
Eating Places.

★ 57388 ★ Pizza Hut
NE Us 62
Mountain Home, AR 72653
(501)425-6081
Ultimate Parent: Pepsico. SIC: 5812—
Eating Places.

★ 57389 ★ Radio Shack
Wal Wert Shopping Ctr.
Mountain Home, AR 72653
(501)425-7616
Company Type: Division. Ultimate Parent:
Tandy Corp. SIC: 5065—Electronic Parts &
Equipment Nec.

★ 57390 ★ Ryder Truck Rental
Hwy. 5 N
Mountain Home, AR 72653
(501)425-4413
Ultimate Parent: Ryder System.

★ 57391 ★ Shell Service Ctr
157 S. Main St.
Mountain Home, AR 72653
(501)425-8586
Ultimate Parent: Shell Oil Co. SIC: 7384—
Photofinishing Laboratories.

★ 57392 ★ Wal Mart
NE Us 62
Mountain Home, AR 72653
(501)425-6218
Ultimate Parent: Wal-Mart Stores, Inc. SIC:
5311—Department Stores.

★ 57393 ★ Wal Mart Pharmacy
NE Us 62
Mountain Home, AR 72653
(501)425-7733
Ultimate Parent: Wal-Mart Stores, Inc. SIC:
5912—Drug Stores & Proprietary Stores.

Mountain Pine

★ 57394 ★ Weyerhaeuser Co.
1st & Main
Mountain Pine, AR 71956
(501)767-7235
Officer: H. Ray Henry, Manager. Ultimate
Parent: Weyerhaeuser Co. SIC: 2421—
Sawmills & Planing Mills—General; 2436—
Softwood Veneer & Plywood.

★ 57395 ★ Weyerhaeuser Co.
Hwy. 227 N
Mountain Pine, AR 71956
Ultimate Parent: Weyerhaeuser Co. SIC:
2421—Sawmills & Planing Mills—General;
2436—Softwood Veneer & Plywood; 2430—
Millwork, Plywood & Structural Members.

Mountain View

★ 57396 ★ Kentucky Fried
Chicken
Rural Route 72
Mountain View, AR 72560
(501)269-3900
Ultimate Parent: Pepsico. SIC: 5812—
Eating Places.

Mountainburg

★ 57397 ★ Mary Kay Cosmetics
RR 1
Mountainburg, AR 72946
(501)369-4379
Ultimate Parent: Mary Kay Cosmetics. SIC:
5999—Miscellaneous Retail Stores Nec.

Mulberry

★ 57398 ★ Piggly Wiggly
Mulberry, AR 72947
(501)997-8181
Ultimate Parent: Bruno's. SIC: 5411—
Grocery Stores.

Murfreesboro

★ 57399 ★ Piggly Wiggly
Murfreesboro, AR 71958
(501)285-3216
Ultimate Parent: Bruno's. SIC: 5411—
Grocery Stores.

★ 57400 ★ Trailways Inc.
Murfreesboro, AR 71958
(501)285-2421
Ultimate Parent: Greyhound Lines Inc.

N Little Rock

★ 57401 ★ Exxon
2724 Central Airport Rd.
N Little Rock, AR 72117
(501)945-1421
Ultimate Parent: Exxon. SIC: 4231—
Trucking Terminal Facilities.

★ 57402 ★ Funk Manufacturing
Inc/O D
3006 E. Washington Ave.
N Little Rock, AR 72114
(501)945-4304
Ultimate Parent: Deere. SIC: 3429—
Hardware Nec.

★ 57403 ★ Jiffy Lube
5110 J F Kennedy Blvd.
N Little Rock, AR 72116
(501)758-7076
Ultimate Parent: Pennzoil. SIC: 7539—
Automotive Repair Shops Nec.

★ 57404 ★ Kay-Bee Toy & Hobby
Inc.
3929 Mccain Blvd.
N Little Rock, AR 72116
(501)753-2593
Ultimate Parent: Melville. SIC: 5945—
Hobby, Toy & Game Shops.

★ 57405 ★ Kentucky Fried
Chicken
4308 E. Broadway St.
N Little Rock, AR 72117
(501)945-2119
Ultimate Parent: Pepsico. SIC: 5812—
Eating Places.

★ 57406 ★ Kentucky Fried
Chicken
7117 J F Kennedy Blvd.
N Little Rock, AR 72116
(501)835-5570
Ultimate Parent: Pepsico. SIC: 5812—
Eating Places.

★ 57407 ★ Kentucky Fried
Chicken
4511 Camp Robinson Rd.
N Little Rock, AR 72118
(501)758-9577
Ultimate Parent: Pepsico. SIC: 5812—
Eating Places.

★ 57408 ★ Kentucky Fried
Chicken
613 E. Broadway St.
N Little Rock, AR 72114
(501)372-7807
Ultimate Parent: Pepsico. SIC: 5812—
Eating Places.

★ 57409 ★ Kroger Co. Inc.
1302 Pike Ave.
N Little Rock, AR 72114
(501)375-4638
Ultimate Parent: Kroger. SIC: 5411—
Grocery Stores.

★ 57410 ★ Kroger Co. No 642
6929 J F Kennedy Blvd.
N Little Rock, AR 72116
(501)835-0400
Ultimate Parent: Kroger. SIC: 5411—
Grocery Stores.

★ 57411 ★ Kroger Food Stores
2649 Pike Ave.
N Little Rock, AR 72114
(501)835-6530
Ultimate Parent: Kroger.

★ 57412 ★ Lerner Shop
3929 Mccain Blvd.
N Little Rock, AR 72116
(501)753-1602
Ultimate Parent: Limited. SIC: 5651—
Family Clothing Stores.

★ 57413 ★ The Limited
Mccain Blvd.
N Little Rock, AR 72116
(501)753-8733
Ultimate Parent: Limited. SIC: 5651—
Family Clothing Stores.

★ 57414 ★ The Limited
3929 Mccain Blvd.
N Little Rock, AR 72116
(501)753-8733
Ultimate Parent: Limited.

★ 57415 ★ Osco Drug
3929 Mccain Blvd.
N Little Rock, AR 72116
(501)758-3936
Ultimate Parent: American Stores. SIC:
5912—Drug Stores & Proprietary Stores.

★ 57416 ★ Pizza Hut
4704 Camp Robinson Rd.
N Little Rock, AR 72118
(501)758-5185
Ultimate Parent: Pepsico. SIC: 5812—
Eating Places; 5812—Eating Places.

★ 57417 ★ Pizza Hut
3701 Warden Rd.
N Little Rock, AR 72116
(501)758-4355
Ultimate Parent: Pepsico.

★ 57418 ★ Ppg Industries Inc.
1320 Henderson St.
N Little Rock, AR 72114
(501)372-4164
Ultimate Parent: PPG Industries Inc.

★ 57419 ★ Radio Shack
2632 Pike Ave.
N Little Rock, AR 72114
(501)758-7765
Company Type: Division. Ultimate Parent:
Tandy Corp. SIC: 5731—Radio, Television
& Electronics Stores.

★ 57420 ★ Radio Shack
3929 Mccain Blvd.
N Little Rock, AR 72116
(501)758-5357
Company Type: Division. Ultimate Parent:
Tandy Corp. SIC: 5065—Electronic Parts &
Equipment Nec.

★ 57421 ★   Ring Around
Products Inc.
13 Cedar Ct
N Little Rock, AR 72116
(501)375-0214
Ultimate Parent: Occidental Petroleum
Corp. SIC: 5191—Farm Supplies.

★ 57422 ★   Ryder Truck Rental
7121 J F Kennedy Blvd.
N Little Rock, AR 72116
(501)835-0653
Ultimate Parent: Ryder System. SIC:
7359—Equipment Rental & Leasing Nec.

★ 57423 ★   Taco Bell
3929 Mccain Blvd.
N Little Rock, AR 72116
(501)753-5502
Ultimate Parent: Pepsico.

★ 57424 ★   Taco Bell
2531 Jacksonville Hwy.
N Little Rock, AR 72117
(501)945-5760
Ultimate Parent: Pepsico. SIC: 5812—
Eating Places.

★ 57425 ★   Taco Bell
4307 E. Broadway St.
N Little Rock, AR 72117
(501)945-5509
Ultimate Parent: Pepsico. SIC: 5812—
Eating Places.

★ 57426 ★   Taco Bell
7201 J F Kennedy Blvd.
N Little Rock, AR 72116
(501)835-3357
Ultimate Parent: Pepsico. SIC: 5812—
Eating Places.

★ 57427 ★   Taco Bell
4324 Camp Robinson Rd.
N Little Rock, AR 72118
(501)753-6746
Ultimate Parent: Pepsico. SIC: 5812—
Eating Places.

★ 57428 ★   Taco Bell
400 E. Broadway St.
N Little Rock, AR 72114
(501)372-3715
Ultimate Parent: Pepsico. SIC: 5812—
Eating Places.

★ 57429 ★   Texaco Fastop
4800 Macarthur Dr.
N Little Rock, AR 72118
(501)753-5512
Ultimate Parent: Texaco. SIC: 5541—
Gasoline Service Stations.

★ 57430 ★   Texaco Slf Sv&Fd
2428 Wildwood Ave.
N Little Rock, AR 72116
(501)835-7090
Ultimate Parent: Texaco.

★ 57431 ★   This End Up-Furniture
Co.
3929 Mccain Blvd.
N Little Rock, AR 72116
(501)753-4958
Ultimate Parent: Melville. SIC: 2599—
Furniture & Fixtures Nec.

★ 57432 ★   Union Bank
103 E. Kiehl Ave.
N Little Rock, AR 72120
(501)835-8035
Ultimate Parent: Union Bank. SIC: 5947—
Gift, Novelty & Souvenir Shops.

★ 57433 ★   Victoria's Secret
3929 Mccain Blvd.
N Little Rock, AR 72116
(501)753-9944
Ultimate Parent: Limited. SIC: 5651—
Family Clothing Stores.

★ 57434 ★   Wal Mart Discount
Cities
3801 Camp Robinson Rd.
N Little Rock, AR 72118
(501)753-3003
Ultimate Parent: Wal-Mart Stores, Inc. SIC:
5311—Department Stores.

★ 57435 ★   Wal Mart Discount
City
6929 J F Kennedy Blvd.
N Little Rock, AR 72116
(501)835-0186
Ultimate Parent: Wal-Mart Stores, Inc. SIC:

5399—Miscellaneous General Merchandise
Store.

★ 57436 ★   Waldenbooks
Mac Cain
N Little Rock, AR 72116
(501)758-5447
Ultimate Parent: K-Mart. SIC: 5942—Book
Stores.

★ 57437 ★   Western Auto Supply
Co.
105 E. Pershing Blvd.
N Little Rock, AR 72114
(501)758-1583
Ultimate Parent: Sears Roebuck & Co.
SIC: 5531—Automobile & Home Supply
Stores.

N. Little Rock

★ 57438 ★   Molex Inc.
801 Murphy Dr.
N. Little Rock, AR 72113-6190
(501)851-4296
Company Type: Headquarters. Ultimate
Parent: Molex. SIC: 3678—Electronic
Connectors; 3357—Nonferrous Wiredrawing
& Insulating; 3643—Current-Carrying Wiring
Devices; 3679—Electronic Components
Nec.

Nashville

★ 57439 ★   Citizens State Bank
420 S. Main St.
Nashville, AR 71852
(501)845-4451
Ultimate Parent: Liberty National Bancorp.
SIC: 6022—State Commercial Banks;
6141—Personal Credit Institutions.

★ 57440 ★   Pilgrim's Pride Corp.
Nashville Feed Mill
200 E. Sheppart
Nashville, AR 71852
Company Type: Division. Ultimate Parent:
Pilgrim's Pride Corp. SIC: 2048—Prepared
Feeds Nec.

★ 57441 ★   Pizza Hut
Mineral Spring Hwy.
Nashville, AR 71852
(501)845-1127
Ultimate Parent: Pepsico. SIC: 5812—
Eating Places.

★ 57442 ★   Trailways Bus Station
115 W. Sypert St.
Nashville, AR 71852
(501)845-4255
Ultimate Parent: Greyhound Lines Inc. SIC:
4131—Intercity & Rural Bus Transportation.

★ 57443 ★   Tyson Foods Inc.
100 E. Cassidy
Nashville, AR 71852
Ultimate Parent: Tyson Foods, Inc. SIC:
2015—Poultry Slaughtering & Processing.

★ 57444 ★   Tyson Foods Inc.
Nashville Feed Mill
Hwy. 27 S. Toland Heights Industrial Park
Nashville, AR 71852
Ultimate Parent: Tyson Foods, Inc. SIC:
2048—Prepared Feeds Nec.

★ 57445 ★   Tyson of Nashville
100 E. Cassidy
Nashville, AR 71852
Ultimate Parent: Tyson Foods, Inc. SIC:
2000—Food & Kindred Products.

★ 57446 ★   Wal Mart Discount
Cities
Southpark Shopping Ctr.
Nashville, AR 71852
(501)845-2434
Ultimate Parent: Wal-Mart Stores, Inc. SIC:
5311—Department Stores.

Newport

★ 57447 ★   Capital Wire & Cable
7301 Victory Blvd.
Newport, AR 72112
Ultimate Parent: General Cable Corp. SIC:
3357—Nonferrous Wiredrawing & Insulating.

★ 57448 ★   Exxon Co. USA
Hwy. 67 N
Newport, AR 72112
(501)523-2672
Ultimate Parent: Exxon. SIC: 5172—
Petroleum Products Nec.

★ 57449 ★   Kentucky Fried
Chicken
110 3rd St.
Newport, AR 72112
(501)523-6323
Ultimate Parent: Pepsico. SIC: 5812—
Eating Places.

★ 57450 ★   Pizza Hut
Village
Newport, AR 72112
(501)523-8961
Ultimate Parent: Pepsico. SIC: 5812—
Eating Places.

★ 57451 ★   Pizza Hut
Hwy. 57
Newport, AR 72112
(501)523-2045
Ultimate Parent: Pepsico. SIC: 5812—
Eating Places.

North Little Rock

★ 57452 ★   ADM Milling Co. Inc.
8th & N. Beech St.
North Little Rock, AR 72114
(501)374-9782
Ultimate Parent: Archer Daniels Midland
Co. SIC: 5149—Groceries & Related
Products Nec.

★ 57453 ★   Archer Daniels
Southern Cotton Oil Co.
324 Buckeye
North Little Rock, AR 72119
Company Type: Division. Ultimate Parent:
Archer Daniels Midland Co. SIC: 2074—
Cottonseed Oil Mills; 2075—Soybean Oil
Mills.

★ 57454 ★   Citgo
3701 John F Kennedy Blvd.
North Little Rock, AR 72116
(501)753-9503
Ultimate Parent: Citgo Petroleum. SIC:
5541—Gasoline Service Stations.

★ 57455 ★   Dillard Department
Stores
3929 McCain Blvd., Ste. 4k
North Little Rock, AR 72116
(501)376-5200
Ultimate Parent: Dillard Department Stores.
SIC: 5311—Department Stores.

★ 57456 ★   First American
National Bank
4610 Camp Robinson Rd.
North Little Rock, AR 72118
(501)758-8445
Ultimate Parent: First American Corp. SIC:
6022—State Commercial Banks.

★ 57457 ★   First American
National Bank
3811 MacArthur Dr.
North Little Rock, AR 72118
(501)758-8447
Ultimate Parent: First American Corp. SIC:
6022—State Commercial Banks.

★ 57458 ★   First American
National Bank
4610 Camp Robinson Rd.
North Little Rock, AR 72118
(501)758-8445
Ultimate Parent: First American Corp. SIC:
6022—State Commercial Banks.

★ 57459 ★   First American
National Bank
3811 MacArthur Dr.
North Little Rock, AR 72118
(501)758-8447
Ultimate Parent: First American Corp. SIC:
6022—State Commercial Banks.

★ 57460 ★   First American
National Bank
120 Main St.
North Little Rock, AR 72114
(501)370-4400
Ultimate Parent: First American Corp. SIC:
6022—State Commercial Banks; 6022—
State Commercial Banks.

★ 57461 ★   First American
National Bank
MacCain
North Little Rock, AR 72116
(501)758-8446
Ultimate Parent: First American Corp. SIC:
6022—State Commercial Banks.

★ 57462 ★   First American
National Bank
Rose City Shopping Ctr.
North Little Rock, AR 72114
(501)945-2314
Ultimate Parent: First American Corp. SIC:
6022—State Commercial Banks.

★ 57463 ★   Georgia Pacific Corp.
Hwy. 165 S
North Little Rock, AR 72117
(501)945-7171
Officer: Jack Mizinski, Manager. Ultimate
Parent: Georgia-Pacific. SIC: 2493—
Reconstituted Wood Products; 2499—Wood
Products Nec.

★ 57464 ★   Georgia-Pacific Corp.
Hwy. 165 S. PO Box 15370
North Little Rock, AR 72117
Ultimate Parent: Georgia-Pacific. SIC:
2499—Wood Products Nec.

★ 57465 ★   Goergia Pacific Corp.
Hwy. 165 S
North Little Rock, AR 72117
(501)945-7171
Officer: Jack Mizinski, Manager. Ultimate
Parent: Georgia-Pacific. SIC: 2493—
Reconstituted Wood Products; 2499—Wood
Products Nec.

★ 57466 ★   Kroger Co. the
44 Camp Robinson
North Little Rock, AR 72118
(501)758-6360
Ultimate Parent: Kroger. SIC: 5912—Drug
Stores & Proprietary Stores.

★ 57467 ★   Manpower, Inc.
2001 Fendley Dr.
North Little Rock, AR 72114
(501)771-2806
Ultimate Parent: Manpower, Inc. SIC:
7363—Help Supply Services.

★ 57468 ★   Mary Kay Cosmetics
5813 Elk River Rd.
North Little Rock, AR 72116
(501)835-0832
Ultimate Parent: Mary Kay Cosmetics. SIC:
5999—Miscellaneous Retail Stores Nec.

★ 57469 ★   Maybelline USA
PO Box 3392, I-40 at Galoway
North Little Rock, AR 72117-3392
Ultimate Parent: Schering-Plough Corp.
SIC: 2844—Toilet Preparations.

★ 57470 ★   Payless Shoesource
4316 Camp Robinson Rd.
North Little Rock, AR 72118
(501)753-6786
Ultimate Parent: May Department Stores.
SIC: 5661—Shoe Stores.

★ 57471 ★   Service Merchandise
4201 E. Mccain Blvd.
North Little Rock, AR 72117
(501)945-4856
Ultimate Parent: Service Merchandise Co.,
Inc. SIC: 5399—Miscellaneous General
Merchandise Store; 5944—Jewelry Stores.

★ 57472 ★   Southern Co.
1201 N. Cypress St.
North Little Rock, AR 72114
(501)376-6333
Officer: Norma Childers, Manager. Ultimate
Parent: Southern. SIC: 3569—General
Industrial Machinery Nec.

★ 57473 ★   Southern Cotton Oil
Co.
PO Box 5727
North Little Rock, AR 72119-5727
(501)945-1414
Officer: Jerry Johnson. Ultimate Parent:
Archer Daniels Midland Co. SIC: 2074—
Cottonseed Oil Mills; 2044—Rice Milling.

★ 57474 ★ Southern Cotton Oil
Co.
324 Buckeye St.
North Little Rock, AR 72119
Ultimate Parent: Archer Daniels Midland
Co. SIC: 2074—Cottonseed Oil Mills;
2075—Soybean Oil Mills.

★ 57475 ★ Southern Cotton Oil
Co. Inc.
324 N. Buckeye St.
North Little Rock, AR 72114
(501)945-1414
Officer: Steve Hill, Manager. Ultimate
Parent: Archer Daniels Midland Co. SIC:
2044—Rice Milling; 2074—Cottonseed Oil
Mills; 2075—Soybean Oil Mills.

★ 57476 ★ Superwood Corp.
Hwy. 165 South
North Little Rock, AR 72117
Ultimate Parent: Georgia-Pacific. SIC:
2499—Wood Products Nec.

★ 57477 ★ Target Stores
4000 McCain Blvd.
North Little Rock, AR 72116
(501)771-4220
Company Type: Subsidiary. Ultimate
Parent: Dayton Hudson. SIC: 5311—
Department Stores.

★ 57478 ★ Tyson Foods Inc.
3800 Progress
North Little Rock, AR 72114
Ultimate Parent: Tyson Foods, Inc. SIC:
2000—Food & Kindred Products.

★ 57479 ★ Tyson Foods Inc. N.
Litle Rock Plant
3800 Progress St.
North Little Rock, AR 72114
Ultimate Parent: Tyson Foods, Inc. SIC:
2015—Poultry Slaughtering & Processing.

Osceola

★ 57480 ★ American Greetings
Corp.
PO Box 488
Osceola, AR 72370-0488
(501)563-5221
Location Type: Branch office. Ultimate
Parent: American Greetings. SIC: 2771—
Greeting Cards; 2679—Converted Paper
Products Nec; 5112—Stationery & Office
Supplies.

★ 57481 ★ American Greetings
Corp.
Rfd 1 Crompton Rd.
Osceola, AR 72370-0488
Ultimate Parent: American Greetings. SIC:
2771—Greeting Cards.

★ 57482 ★ Fruit of the Loom Inc.
Arkansas
1425 Crompton Rd.
Osceola, AR 72370
Ultimate Parent: Fruit of the Loom. SIC:
2322—Men's/Boys' Underwear & Nightwear.

★ 57483 ★ Greyhound Bus Lines
Hwy. I 55
Osceola, AR 72370
(501)563-6241
Ultimate Parent: Greyhound Lines Inc. SIC:
4111—Local & Suburban Transit.

★ 57484 ★ Piggly Wiggly
1200 W. Johnson
Osceola, AR 72370
(501)563-5479
Ultimate Parent: Bruno's. SIC: 5411—
Grocery Stores.

★ 57485 ★ Wal Mart Pharmacy
Hwy. 140 W
Osceola, AR 72370
(501)563-6633
Ultimate Parent: Wal-Mart Stores, Inc. SIC:
5912—Drug Stores & Proprietary Stores.

Ozark

★ 57486 ★ Piggly Wiggly
1910 W. Commercial St.
Ozark, AR 72949
(501)667-4366
Ultimate Parent: Bruno's. SIC: 5411—
Grocery Stores.

★ 57487 ★ Pizza Hut
Hyw W. 64
Ozark, AR 72949
(501)667-4741
Ultimate Parent: Pepsico. SIC: 5812—
Eating Places.

Paragould

★ 57488 ★ Boston Industrial
Products
201 Dana Dr.
Paragould, AR 72450
(501)239-4051
Ultimate Parent: Dana Corp. SIC: 3052—
Rubber & Plastics Hose & Belting; 3053—
Gaskets, Packing & Sealing Devices;
3069—Fabricated Rubber Products Nec.

★ 57489 ★ Boston Industrial
Products
Dana Dr.
Paragould, AR 72450
Ultimate Parent: Dana Corp. SIC: 3052—
Rubber & Plastics Hose & Belting.

★ 57490 ★ Dana Corp.
Boston Industrial Products Div.
Dana Dr.
Paragould, AR 72450
Company Type: Division. Ultimate Parent:
Dana Corp. SIC: 3052—Rubber & Plastics
Hose & Belting; 3053—Gaskets, Packing &
Sealing Devices; 3061—Mechanical Rubber
Goods; 3069—Fabricated Rubber Products
Nec.

★ 57491 ★ Emerson Electric Co.
Pekin & Scott Streets
Paragould, AR 72450
Ultimate Parent: Emerson Electric Co. Inc.
SIC: 3621—Motors & Generators.

★ 57492 ★ Kentucky Fried
Chicken
Linwood Dr.
Paragould, AR 72450
(501)239-8155
Ultimate Parent: Pepsico. SIC: 5812—
Eating Places.

★ 57493 ★ Kroger's
121 Medical Dr.
Paragould, AR 72450
(501)239-3321
Ultimate Parent: Kroger. SIC: 5411—
Grocery Stores.

★ 57494 ★ Monroe Auto
Equipment Co.
1601 Hwy. 49b
Paragould, AR 72450
Ultimate Parent: Tenneco Inc. SIC: 3714—
Motor Vehicle Parts & Accessories.

★ 57495 ★ Monroe Auto
Equipment Co.
Hwy. 49-B North
Paragould, AR 72450
Ultimate Parent: Tenneco Inc. SIC: 3714—
Motor Vehicle Parts & Accessories.

★ 57496 ★ Sunbeam Outdoor
Products
1600 Jones Rd.
Paragould, AR 72450
(501)236-8731
Officer: Mark Broadway, Plant Manager.
Ultimate Parent: Sunbeam/Oster. SIC:
3631—Household Cooking Equipment.

★ 57497 ★ Sunbean Outdoor
Prods.
1600 Jones Rd.
Paragould, AR 72450
Ultimate Parent: Sunbeam/Oster. SIC:
3300—Primary Metal Industries.

★ 57498 ★ Wal Mart
Paragould Plz.
Paragould, AR 72450
(501)236-8548
Ultimate Parent: Wal-Mart Stores, Inc. SIC:
5311—Department Stores.

Paris

★ 57499 ★ Kentucky Fried
Chicken
507 E. Walnut St.
Paris, AR 72855
(501)963-6526
Ultimate Parent: Pepsico. SIC: 5812—
Eating Places.

★ 57500 ★ Superior Federal
Bank, FSB
3rd & Walnut
Paris, AR 72855
(501)963-3038
Location Type: Branch office. Officer:
Kathy Schulterman, Manager. Ultimate
Parent: Boatmen's Bancshares. SIC:
6021—National Commercial Banks.

★ 57501 ★ Tyson Foods Inc.
309 S. Elm
Paris, AR 72855
Ultimate Parent: Tyson Foods, Inc. SIC:
2048—Prepared Feeds Nec.

★ 57502 ★ Tyson Foods Inc.
PO Box 584
Paris, AR 72855
(501)963-3857
Officer: Bill Hardcastle, Manager. Ultimate
Parent: Tyson Foods, Inc. SIC: 2048—
Prepared Feeds Nec.

★ 57503 ★ Tyson Foods Inc.
109 S. Elm St.
Paris, AR 72855
(501)963-3092
Officer: Bill Hardcastle, Manager. Ultimate
Parent: Tyson Foods, Inc. SIC: 2015—
Poultry Slaughtering & Processing; 2048—
Prepared Feeds Nec.

Pea Ridge

★ 57504 ★ Pizza Hut
Pea Ridge, AR 72751
(501)451-8175
Ultimate Parent: Pepsico. SIC: 5812—
Eating Places.

Pearcy

★ 57505 ★ Diebold Inc.
110 Ranchero Dr.
Pearcy, AR 71964
(501)767-1104
Ultimate Parent: Diebold, Inc. SIC: 5044—
Office Equipment.

Piggott

★ 57506 ★ Magee Co.
PO Box 55
Piggott, AR 72454
Ultimate Parent: Tandy Corp. SIC: 2499—
Wood Products Nec.

★ 57507 ★ Magee Co.
S. Garfield
Piggott, AR 72454
Ultimate Parent: Tandy Corp. SIC: 2499—
Wood Products Nec.

Pine Bluff

★ 57508 ★ Brighton Corp.
4505 Emmett Sanders Rd.
Pine Bluff, AR 71611
(501)535-7617
Officer: Gordon Whitaker, Manager.
Ultimate Parent: American Express Co.
SIC: 3443—Fabricated Plate Work—Boiler
Shops.

★ 57509 ★ Central Moloney
Transformer Div.
2400 W. 6th St.
Pine Bluff, AR 71601
Company Type: Division. Ultimate Parent:
Coltec Industries. SIC: 3612—Transformers
Except Electronic.

★ 57510 ★ Central Moloney
Transformer Components
Operation
5500 Jefferson Pky.
Pine Bluff, AR 71602
Ultimate Parent: Coltec Industries. SIC:
3089—Plastics Products Nec.

★ 57511 ★ Clark Printing Co.
421 W. Barraque St.
Pine Bluff, AR 71601
(501)534-8803
Ultimate Parent: Terex.

★ 57512 ★ Coca-Cola Bottling
Co. of so
205 E. 2nd Ave.
Pine Bluff, AR 71601
(501)534-0621
Ultimate Parent: Coca-Cola Enterprises.
SIC: 2086—Bottled & Canned Soft Drinks;
5046—Commercial Equipment Nec.

★ 57513 ★ Exxon
1900 University Dr.
Pine Bluff, AR 71601
(501)534-9329
Ultimate Parent: Exxon. SIC: 5541—
Gasoline Service Stations.

★ 57514 ★ Gaylord Container
Corp.
1701 Jefferson Pky.
Pine Bluff, AR 71602
Ultimate Parent: Gaylord Container. SIC:
2621—Paper Mills.

★ 57515 ★ Gaylord Container
Corp.
500 McFadden Rd.
Pine Bluff, AR 71602
Ultimate Parent: Gaylord Container. SIC:
2621—Paper Mills.

★ 57516 ★ Gaylord Container
Corp. Formerly Known as Mid-
America
500 McFadden Rd.
Pine Bluff, AR 71602
Ultimate Parent: Gaylord Container. SIC:
2621—Paper Mills.

★ 57517 ★ Greyhound Bus
Station
221 W. 4th Ave.
Pine Bluff, AR 71601
(501)535-1020
Ultimate Parent: Greyhound Lines Inc. SIC:
4111—Local & Suburban Transit; 4131—
Intercity & Rural Bus Transportation; 4173—
Bus Terminal & Service Facilities.

★ 57518 ★ Hoover Treated Wood
Prods. Inc.
Dixie Wood Dr.
Pine Bluff, AR 71611
Ultimate Parent: Ply Gem. SIC: 2491—
Wood Preserving.

★ 57519 ★ Hoover Treated Wood
Products
Dixie Wood Dr.
Pine Bluff, AR 71611
Ultimate Parent: Ply Gem. SIC: 2491—
Wood Preserving.

★ 57520 ★ International Paper
Co. Pine Bluff Mill
PO Box 7069
Pine Bluff, AR 71611
Ultimate Parent: International Paper Co.
SIC: 2611—Pulp Mills; 2621—Paper Mills.

★ 57521 ★ International Paper -
Pine Bluff Mill
Fairfield Rd.
Pine Bluff, AR 71611
Ultimate Parent: International Paper Co.
SIC: 2611—Pulp Mills; 2621—Paper Mills.

★ 57522 ★ Kay Bee Toys &
Hobby Shop
2901 Pines Mall
Pine Bluff, AR 71601
(501)535-5912
Ultimate Parent: Melville. SIC: 5945—
Hobby, Toy & Game Shops.

★ 57523 ★ Kentucky Fried
Chicken
2707 W. 28th Ave.
Pine Bluff, AR 71603
(501)534-8000
Ultimate Parent: Pepsico. SIC: 5812—
Eating Places.

★ 57524 ★ Kroger Store No 542
Jefferson Sq.
Pine Bluff, AR 71601
(501)535-5596
Ultimate Parent: Kroger. SIC: 5411—
Grocery Stores.

★ 57525 ★ **Mary Kay Cosmetics**
3211 S. Tennessee St.
Pine Bluff, AR 71601
(501)541-0026
Ultimate Parent: Mary Kay Cosmetics. **SIC:**
5999—Miscellaneous Retail Stores Nec.

★ 57526 ★ **Mid America Packaging Inc.**
Viking Rd.
Pine Bluff, AR 71602
(501)541-5120
Officer: Fred Donisi, Manager. **Ultimate Parent:** Gaylord Container. **SIC:** 2631—
Paperboard Mills; 2673—Bags—Plastics,
Laminated & Coated; 2674—Bags—
Uncoated Paper & Multiwall.

★ 57527 ★ **Pizza Hut**
2203 E. Harding Ave.
Pine Bluff, AR 71601
(501)535-4450
Ultimate Parent: Pepsico. **SIC:** 5812—
Eating Places.

★ 57528 ★ **Radio Shack**
809 W. 6th Ave.
Pine Bluff, AR 71601
(501)536-5717
Company Type: Division. **Ultimate Parent:**
Tandy Corp. **SIC:** 5731—Radio, Television
& Electronics Stores.

★ 57529 ★ **Radio Shack**
2901 Pnes Mall Dr.
Pine Bluff, AR 71603
(501)536-2132
Company Type: Division. **Ultimate Parent:**
Tandy Corp. **SIC:** 5065—Electronic Parts &
Equipment Nec.

★ 57530 ★ **Shell Gas Station**
1519 S. Cherry St.
Pine Bluff, AR 71601
(501)534-7966
Ultimate Parent: Shell Oil Co. **SIC:** 5541—
Gasoline Service Stations.

★ 57531 ★ **Taco Bell**
103 N. Blake St.
Pine Bluff, AR 71601
(501)536-7531
Ultimate Parent: Pepsico. **SIC:** 5812—
Eating Places.

★ 57532 ★ **Trailways Bus Systems**
4th
Pine Bluff, AR 71601
(501)535-8330
Ultimate Parent: Greyhound Lines Inc. **SIC:**
4142—Bus Charter Service Except Local.

★ 57533 ★ **Tyson Foods Inc.**
2201 W. 2nd St.
Pine Bluff, AR 71601
Ultimate Parent: Tyson Foods, Inc. **SIC:**
2015—Poultry Slaughtering & Processing.

★ 57534 ★ **Tyson Foods Inc.**
5505 Jefferson Pky.
Pine Bluff, AR 71602
(501)247-9127
Officer: Donnie King, Manager. **Ultimate Parent:** Tyson Foods, Inc. **SIC:** 2015—
Poultry Slaughtering & Processing.

★ 57535 ★ **Tyson Foods Inc. Feed Mill**
4211 Emmitt Sanders Rd.
Pine Bluff, AR 71601
Ultimate Parent: Tyson Foods, Inc. **SIC:**
2048—Prepared Feeds Nec.

★ 57536 ★ **Tyson Foods Inc. Pine Bluff Feed Mill**
Emmitt Sanders Rd.
Pine Bluff, AR 71603
Ultimate Parent: Tyson Foods, Inc. **SIC:**
2048—Prepared Feeds Nec.

★ 57537 ★ **Tyson Foods Inc. Pine Bluff Further Processing**
5505 Jefferson Pky.
Pine Bluff, AR 71602
Ultimate Parent: Tyson Foods, Inc. **SIC:**
2015—Poultry Slaughtering & Processing.

★ 57538 ★ **Wal Mart Discount**
2901 Pines Mall Dr.
Pine Bluff, AR 71601
(501)536-8927
Ultimate Parent: Wal-Mart Stores, Inc.

★ 57539 ★ **Wal Mart Discount City**
2901 Pines Mall
Pine Bluff, AR 71601
(501)535-4516
Ultimate Parent: Wal-Mart Stores, Inc. **SIC:**
5311—Department Stores.

★ 57540 ★ **Wheeling-Machine Products Cooper Industries**
5411 Industrial Dr. South
Pine Bluff, AR 71602
Ultimate Parent: Cooper Industries. **SIC:**
3494—Valves & Pipe Fittings Nec.

Pocahontas

★ 57541 ★ **Kentucky Fried Chicken**
Bettis
Pocahontas, AR 72455
(501)892-4692
Ultimate Parent: Pepsico. **SIC:** 5812—
Eating Places.

★ 57542 ★ **Magee Co.**
Hwy. 67 South
Pocahontas, AR 72455
Ultimate Parent: Tandy Corp. **SIC:** 2499—
Wood Products Nec.

★ 57543 ★ **Pizza Hut**
N Hwy. 67
Pocahontas, AR 72455
(501)892-4558
Ultimate Parent: Pepsico. **SIC:** 5812—
Eating Places.

★ 57544 ★ **Trailways Bus Station**
511 S. Bettis St.
Pocahontas, AR 72455
(501)892-4271
Ultimate Parent: Greyhound Lines Inc. **SIC:**
4131—Intercity & Rural Bus Transportation.

★ 57545 ★ **Wal Mart Discount Cities**
Hwy. 62 W
Pocahontas, AR 72455
(501)892-4536
Ultimate Parent: Wal-Mart Stores, Inc. **SIC:**
5311—Department Stores.

★ 57546 ★ **Walker Manufacturing Co.**
Hwy. 67 S
Pocahontas, AR 72455
(501)892-9626
Ultimate Parent: Tenneco Inc. **SIC:** 2599—
Furniture & Fixtures Nec.

★ 57547 ★ **Waterloo Industries Inc.**
Hwy. 304
Pocahontas, AR 72455
Ultimate Parent: American Brands Inc.
SIC: 3499—Fabricated Metal Products Nec.

★ 57548 ★ **Waterloo Industries Inc.**
PO Box 1048
Pocahontas, AR 72455-1048
(501)892-4586
Location Type: Branch office. **Officer:** Ray
Campbell. **Ultimate Parent:** American
Brands Inc. **SIC:** 3089—Plastics Products
Nec; 2542—Partitions & Fixtures Except
Wood; 2599—Furniture & Fixtures Nec;
3499—Fabricated Metal Products Nec;
5084—Industrial Machinery & Equipment.

★ 57549 ★ **Waterloo Industries Inc.**
1612 Hwy. 304 E
Pocahontas, AR 72455
(501)892-4586
Officer: Ray Campbell, Manager. **Ultimate Parent:** American Brands Inc. **SIC:** 3499—
Fabricated Metal Products Nec.

Prairie Grove

★ 57550 ★ **Magnetek Universal Electric**
424 S. Baggett St.
Prairie Grove, AR 72753
Ultimate Parent: Magnetek Inc. **SIC:**
3621—Motors & Generators.

Prescott

★ 57551 ★ **Pizza Hut**
E N
Prescott, AR 71857
(501)887-2678
Ultimate Parent: Pepsico.

★ 57552 ★ **Pizza Hut**
E N. 1st
Prescott, AR 71857
(501)887-6871
Ultimate Parent: Pepsico. **SIC:** 5812—
Eating Places.

Rector

★ 57553 ★ **Ace Hardware&Farm Supply**
S Main
Rector, AR 72461
(501)595-3577
Ultimate Parent: Ace Hardware. **SIC:**
5251—Hardware Stores.

★ 57554 ★ **Bank of Rector**
400 Main St.
Rector, AR 72461
(501)595-3591
Location Type: Branch office. **Officer:**
Ronald L. Benson, President. **Ultimate Parent:** Union Planters Corp. **SIC:** 6021—
National Commercial Banks.

★ 57555 ★ **Bank of Rector**
PO Box 7
Rector, AR 72461-0007
(501)595-3591
Location Type: Branch office. **Ultimate Parent:** Union Planters Corp. **SIC:** 6021—
National Commercial Banks.

Rison

★ 57556 ★ **Sun Refining & Marketing Co.**
103 W. 2nd
Rison, AR 71665
(501)325-6211
Ultimate Parent: Sun. **SIC:** 5984—
Liquefied Petroleum Gas Dealers.

★ 57557 ★ **Tyson Foods Inc.**
Hwy. 79 S
Rison, AR 71665
(501)325-6225
Officer: Don Tyson, Owner. **Ultimate Parent:** Tyson Foods, Inc. **SIC:** 2426—
Hardwood Dimension & Flooring Mills.

Rogers

★ 57558 ★ **Butler Paper Co.**
808 N. 24th St.
Rogers, AR 72756-2118
(501)636-7075
Location Type: Branch office. **Ultimate Parent:** Alco Standard Corp. **SIC:** 5111—
Printing & Writing Paper.

★ 57559 ★ **Butler Paper Co.**
808 N. 24th St.
Rogers, AR 72756-2118
(501)636-7075
Location Type: Branch office. **Ultimate Parent:** Alco Standard Corp. **SIC:** 5111—
Printing & Writing Paper.

★ 57560 ★ **Chick-N-Quick**
PO Box 988
Rogers, AR 72756
Ultimate Parent: Tyson Foods, Inc. **SIC:**
2000—Food & Kindred Products.

★ 57561 ★ **Coca Cola Bottling Co.**
215 W. Poplar St.
Rogers, AR 72756
(501)636-3123
Ultimate Parent: Coca-Cola Enterprises.
SIC: 5149—Groceries & Related Products
Nec.

★ 57562 ★ **Crane Co.**
1201 N. 8th St.
Rogers, AR 72756
Ultimate Parent: Crane. **SIC:** 3491—
Industrial Valves.

★ 57563 ★ **First Brands Corp.**
1700 N. 13th St.
Rogers, AR 72756
(501)636-2845
Ultimate Parent: Shaw Industries, Inc. **SIC:**
2673—Bags—Plastics, Laminated &
Coated; 3081—Unsupported Plastics Film &
Sheet.

★ 57564 ★ **Foam Molding Co. of Arkansas**
2503 Water Tower Rd.
Rogers, AR 72756
Ultimate Parent: H.J. Heinz. **SIC:** 3000—
Rubber & Miscellaneous Plastics Products.

★ 57565 ★ **Hudson Foods**
1225 Hudson Rd.
Rogers, AR 72756
(501)636-1100
Company Type: Headquarters. **Officer:**
James T. Hudson. **Sales:** 920.5 M. **Fortune 500:** Largest U.S. Industrial Corporations:
Ranking 375.

★ 57566 ★ **Hudson Foods Inc.**
1225 Hudson Rd.
Rogers, AR 72756
(501)636-1100 **Fax:** (501)631-5400
Company Type: Headquarters. **Officer:**
James T. Hudson, Chairman & CEO.
Ultimate Parent: Hudson Foods.

★ 57567 ★ **Pizza Hut**
921 S. 8th St.
Rogers, AR 72756
(501)636-4021
Ultimate Parent: Pepsico.

★ 57568 ★ **Pizza Hut**
1900 W. Walnut St.
Rogers, AR 72756
(501)631-2393
Ultimate Parent: Pepsico.

★ 57569 ★ **Radio Shack**
917 W. Walnut St.
Rogers, AR 72756
(501)636-3160
Company Type: Division. **Ultimate Parent:**
Tandy Corp. **SIC:** 5731—Radio, Television
& Electronics Stores.

★ 57570 ★ **Taco Bell**
608 S. 8th St.
Rogers, AR 72756
(501)631-7484
Ultimate Parent: Pepsico.

★ 57571 ★ **Tyson Distribution Center**
400 W. Olrich St.
Rogers, AR 72756
Ultimate Parent: Tyson Foods, Inc. **SIC:**
2000—Food & Kindred Products.

★ 57572 ★ **Tyson Food Chick'n Quick**
400 W. Olrich St.
Rogers, AR 72756
Ultimate Parent: Tyson Foods, Inc. **SIC:**
2000—Food & Kindred Products.

★ 57573 ★ **Tyson Foods Inc.**
212 E. Elm St.
Rogers, AR 72756
Ultimate Parent: Tyson Foods, Inc. **SIC:**
2015—Poultry Slaughtering & Processing.

★ 57574 ★ **Tyson Garrett Plant**
212 East Elm
Rogers, AR 72756
Ultimate Parent: Tyson Foods, Inc. **SIC:**
2000—Food & Kindred Products.

★ 57575 ★ **Tyson's Chick'n Quick**
400 W. Olrich St.
Rogers, AR 72756
(501)636-7251
Officer: Ron Howard, Manager. **Ultimate Parent:** Tyson Foods, Inc. **SIC:** 2015—
Poultry Slaughtering & Processing; 2038—
Frozen Specialties Nec.

★ 57576 ★ **Tyson's & ORG Rogers**
212 E. Elm St.
Rogers, AR 72756
(501)636-1620
Officer: Frank Richert, Manager. **Ultimate Parent:** Tyson Foods, Inc. **SIC:** 2015—
Poultry Slaughtering & Processing.

★ 57577 ★   Wal Mart
2110 W. Walnut St.
Rogers, AR 72756
(501)636-3222
Ultimate Parent: Wal-Mart Stores, Inc. **SIC:**
5999—Miscellaneous Retail Stores Nec.

★ 57578 ★   Wal Mart Tire & Auto
Ctr
Walnut Plz.
Rogers, AR 72756
(501)636-6392
Ultimate Parent: Wal-Mart Stores, Inc. **SIC:**
7538—General Automotive Repair Shops.

Russellville

★ 57579 ★   ConAgra Frozen
Foods
Hwy. 64 E
PO Box 250
Russellville, AR 72801
(501)968-2535
Company Type: Division. **Officer:** Ray
George, Plant Manager. **Ultimate Parent:**
Conagra.

★ 57580 ★   Dana Corp. Camshaft
Plant
2301 E. 16th St.
Russellville, AR 72801
Ultimate Parent: Dana Corp. **SIC:** 3714—
Motor Vehicle Parts & Accessories.

★ 57581 ★   Dow Chemical Co.
Lock & Dam Rd.
Russellville, AR 72801
Ultimate Parent: Dow Chemical Co. USA.
SIC: 3499—Fabricated Metal Products Nec;
3479—Metal Coating & Allied Services.

★ 57582 ★   Dow Chemical Co.
USA
Lock & Dam Rd.
Russellville, AR 72801
Ultimate Parent: Dow Chemical Co. USA.
SIC: 3499—Fabricated Metal Products Nec;
3479—Metal Coating & Allied Services.

★ 57583 ★   Dow Chemical USA
Lock & Dam Rd. Rte. 1 Box 116
Russellville, AR 72801
Ultimate Parent: Dow Chemical Co. USA.
SIC: 3559—Special Industry Machinery
Nec.

★ 57584 ★   The Limited
3103 W. Main Pl
Russellville, AR 72801
(501)968-5763
Ultimate Parent: Limited. **SIC:** 5999—
Miscellaneous Retail Stores Nec.

★ 57585 ★   Pizza Hut
1312 N. Ark
Russellville, AR 72801
(501)968-2672
Ultimate Parent: Pepsico. **SIC:** 5812—
Eating Places.

★ 57586 ★   Riverside Furniture
PO Box 1379
Russellville, AR 72811-1379
(501)968-4922
Officer: Gary Binz. **Ultimate Parent:**
Arkansas Best. **SIC:** 2426—Hardwood
Dimension & Flooring Mills.

★ 57587 ★   Russellville
Distribution Center
1000 East Main St.
Russellville, AR 72801
Ultimate Parent: Tyson Foods, Inc. **SIC:**
4222—Refrigerated Warehousing &
Storage.

★ 57588 ★   Ryder Truck Rental
Hwy. 64 E
Russellville, AR 72801
(501)968-2643
Ultimate Parent: Ryder System. **SIC:**
7359—Equipment Rental & Leasing Nec.

★ 57589 ★   Saint Mary's Medical
Center
1808 W. Main St.
Russellville, AR 72801
(501)968-2841
Officer: Jerry D. Marbry, Executive Director.
Ultimate Parent: American Medical
Holdings. **SIC:** 8062—General Medical &
Surgical Hospitals.

★ 57590 ★   Taco Bell
1308 N. Arkansas Ave.
Russellville, AR 72801
(501)968-7444
Ultimate Parent: Pepsico. **SIC:** 3732—Boat
Building & Repairing.

★ 57591 ★   Texaco Inc.
Hwy. I 40
Russellville, AR 72801
(501)968-5719
Ultimate Parent: Texaco. **SIC:** 5541—
Gasoline Service Stations.

★ 57592 ★   Trailways Bus System
119 E. Main St.
Russellville, AR 72801
(501)968-3317
Ultimate Parent: Greyhound Lines Inc. **SIC:**
4131—Intercity & Rural Bus Transportation.

★ 57593 ★   Tyson Foods Inc.
Tyler Rd. Plant
PO Box 847
Russellville, AR 72801
Ultimate Parent: Tyson Foods, Inc. **SIC:**
2015—Poultry Slaughtering & Processing.

★ 57594 ★   Tyson Foods Inc.
Tyler Road Plant
· Tyler Rd.
Russellville, AR 72801
Ultimate Parent: Tyson Foods, Inc. **SIC:**
2000—Food & Kindred Products.

★ 57595 ★   Tyson Valley
Distribution Center
Hwy. 64 East
Russellville, AR 72801
Ultimate Parent: Tyson Foods, Inc. **SIC:**
4222—Refrigerated Warehousing &
Storage.

★ 57596 ★   Wal Mart Self Serve
Sta.
Hwy. 64 E
Russellville, AR 72801
(501)968-6810
Ultimate Parent: Wal-Mart Stores, Inc. **SIC:**
5541—Gasoline Service Stations.

Saffell

★ 57597 ★   Mobil Pipe Line Co.
Saffell, AR 72572
(501)528-3581
Company Type: Branch. **Ultimate Parent:**
Mobil. **SIC:** 4612—Crude Petroleum
Pipelines.

Scranton

★ 57598 ★   River Valley By-
Products
Hwy. 109 S. & 393 W.
Scranton, AR 72863
Ultimate Parent: Tyson Foods, Inc. **SIC:**
2047—Dog & Cat Food; 2048—Prepared
Feeds Nec; 2077—Animal & Marine Fats &
Oils.

★ 57599 ★   River Valley By-
Products
PO Box 376
Scranton, AR 72863
Ultimate Parent: Tyson Foods, Inc. **SIC:**
2047—Dog & Cat Food; 2048—Prepared
Feeds Nec; 2076—Vegetable Oil Mills Nec.

Searcy

★ 57600 ★   Ace Hardware
119 W. Arch Ave.
Searcy, AR 72143
(501)268-3515
Ultimate Parent: Ace Hardware. **SIC:**
5231—Paint, Glass & Wallpaper Stores.

★ 57601 ★   Central Arkansas
Hospital
1200 S. Main
Searcy, AR 72143
(501)268-7171
Officer: David Lafoon, Executive Director.
Ultimate Parent: American Medical
Holdings. **SIC:** 8062—General Medical &
Surgical Hospitals.

★ 57602 ★   Coast to Coast
Trucking Inc.
Hwy. 67 S
Searcy, AR 72143
(501)268-7129
Ultimate Parent: Servistar Corp. **SIC:**
4213—Trucking Except Local.

★ 57603 ★   Kentucky Fried
Chicken
119 W. Market Ave.
Searcy, AR 72143
(501)268-7930
Ultimate Parent: Pepsico. **SIC:** 5812—
Eating Places.

★ 57604 ★   Kentucky Fried
Chicken
Hwy. 64 W
Searcy, AR 72143
(501)268-3607
Ultimate Parent: Pepsico. **SIC:** 5812—
Eating Places.

★ 57605 ★   Kroger Delicatessen
1401 E. Race Ave.
Searcy, AR 72143
(501)268-5138
Ultimate Parent: Kroger. **SIC:** 5411—
Grocery Stores.

★ 57606 ★   Pizza Hut
1513 W. Pleasure Ave.
Searcy, AR 72143
(501)268-4276
Ultimate Parent: Pepsico. **SIC:** 5812—
Eating Places.

★ 57607 ★   Pizza Hut
2841 E. Race Ave.
Searcy, AR 72143
(501)268-5868
Ultimate Parent: Pepsico. **SIC:** 5812—
Eating Places.

★ 57608 ★   Ryder Truck Rental
1210 E. Race Ave.
Searcy, AR 72143
(501)268-0543
Ultimate Parent: Ryder System. **SIC:**
5113—Industrial & Personal Service Paper;
7359—Equipment Rental & Leasing Nec.

★ 57609 ★   Speed Queen Co.
200 Queens Way
Searcy, AR 72143
Ultimate Parent: Raytheon Co. **SIC:**
3633—Household Laundry Equipment.

★ 57610 ★   Vickers
400 E. Lincoln Ave.
Searcy, AR 72143
(501)268-5854
Officer: Dennis Hadden, Manager. **Ultimate
Parent:** Trinova Corp. **SIC:** 3492—Fluid
Power Valves & Hose Fittings; 3494—
Valves & Pipe Fittings Nec.

★ 57611 ★   Vickers Inc.
400 Lincoln Ave.
Searcy, AR 72143
Ultimate Parent: Trinova Corp. **SIC:**
3492—Fluid Power Valves & Hose Fittings.

Sheridan

★ 57612 ★   Rohr Ind. Inc.
Hwy. 270 E.
Sheridan, AR 72150
Ultimate Parent: Rohr. **SIC:** 3728—Aircraft
Parts & Equipment Nec.

★ 57613 ★   Rohr Industries Inc.
PO Box 488
Sheridan, AR 72150
(501)942-8100
Officer: Bob Gordon, Manager. **Ultimate
Parent:** Rohr. **SIC:** 3724—Aircraft Engines
& Engine Parts.

★ 57614 ★   Stone Container Corp.
Blake Rd.
Sheridan, AR 72150
(501)942-2151
Officer: Talbott Young, Manager. **Ultimate
Parent:** Stone Container Corp. **SIC:** 2671—
Paper Coated & Laminated—Packaging;
2674—Bags—Uncoated Paper & Multiwall;
3089—Plastics Products Nec.

Siloam Spring

★ 57615 ★   Carpenter Paper Co.
620 E. Granite St.
Siloam Spring, AR 72761-3730
(501)524-3799
Ultimate Parent: Alco Standard Corp. **SIC:**
5113—Industrial & Personal Service Paper.

★ 57616 ★   Carpenter Paper Co.
620 E. Granite St.
Siloam Spring, AR 72761-3730
(501)524-3799
Ultimate Parent: Alco Standard Corp. **SIC:**
5113—Industrial & Personal Service Paper.

Siloam Springs

★ 57617 ★   Coast to Coast
725 S. Mount Olive St.
Siloam Springs, AR 72761
(501)524-8761
Ultimate Parent: Servistar Corp. **SIC:**
5261—Retail Nurseries & Garden Stores;
5261—Retail Nurseries & Garden Stores.

★ 57618 ★   Kentucky Fried
Chicken
Hwy. 68 Bypass W
Siloam Springs, AR 72761
(501)524-6321
Ultimate Parent: Pepsico. **SIC:** 5812—
Eating Places.

★ 57619 ★   La-Z-Boy Arkansas
PO Box 578
Siloam Springs, AR 72761
(501)524-6491 **Fax:** (501)524-9464
Officer: Richard B. Swiderski, Vice
President. **Ultimate Parent:** La-Z-Boy Chair.

★ 57620 ★   La-Z-Boy Chair Co.
1445 E. Tahlequah
Siloam Springs, AR 72761
Ultimate Parent: La-Z-Boy Chair. **SIC:**
2512—Upholstered Household Furniture.

★ 57621 ★   La-Z-Boy Chair Co.
Chair Co.
501 N. Lincoln
Siloam Springs, AR 72761
Ultimate Parent: La-Z-Boy Chair. **SIC:**
2512—Upholstered Household Furniture.

★ 57622 ★   Radio Shack
Highland Park Manor
Siloam Springs, AR 72761
(501)524-5617
Company Type: Division. **Ultimate Parent:**
Tandy Corp. **SIC:** 5731—Radio, Television
& Electronics Stores.

★ 57623 ★   Superior Federal
Bank, FSB
916 Hwy. 412 W
Siloam Springs, AR 72761
(501)524-8505
Location Type: Branch office. **Officer:**
Jeneen Hubbard, Manager. **Ultimate
Parent:** Boatmen's Bancshares. **SIC:**
6021—National Commercial Banks.

★ 57624 ★   Wal Mart Drug Stores
Hwy. 68 Bypo Ave.
Siloam Springs, AR 72761
(501)524-3156
Ultimate Parent: Wal-Mart Stores, Inc. **SIC:**
5912—Drug Stores & Proprietary Stores.

Smackover

★ 57625 ★   Ace Hardware
204 E. 8th St.
Smackover, AR 71762
(501)725-3002
Ultimate Parent: Ace Hardware.

Spingdale

★ 57626 ★   Tyson Foods, Inc.
2210 W. Oaklawn Dr.
Spingdale, AR
(501)290-4000
Company Type: Headquarters. **Officer:**
Leland E. Tollett. **Employee Count:** 50385.
Sales: 4704.4 M. Fortune 500: Largest
U.S. Industrial Corporations: Ranking 110.

Springdale

★ 57627 ★   Burlington Northern Railroa
107 E. Emma Ave.
Springdale, AR 72764
(501)751-5763
Ultimate Parent: Burlington Northern. **SIC:** 4011—Railroads—Line-Haul Operating.

★ 57628 ★   Danaher Tool Group
1609 S. Old Missouri Rd.
Springdale, AR 72764
(501)751-8500
Ultimate Parent: Danaher Corp. **SIC:** 3423—Hand & Edge Tools Nec.

★ 57629 ★   Easco Hand Tools Inc.
1609 N. Old Missouri Rd.
Springdale, AR 72764
Ultimate Parent: Danaher Corp. **SIC:** 3423—Hand & Edge Tools Nec.

★ 57630 ★   Emery Worldwide
2200 Hwy. 265 S
Springdale, AR 72764
(501)756-8070
Ultimate Parent: Consolidated Freightways.

★ 57631 ★   Exxon Food Mart
4765 W. Sunset St.
Springdale, AR 72764
(501)750-2440
Ultimate Parent: Exxon. **SIC:** 5411—Grocery Stores.

★ 57632 ★   Heekin Can Inc.
1200 Crutcher St.
Springdale, AR 72764
(501)751-4666
Officer: Harold Barron, Plant Manager.
Ultimate Parent: Ball Corp. **SIC:** 3411—Metal Cans.

★ 57633 ★   Heekin Can Inc.
PO Box H
Springdale, AR 72765-2033
(501)751-4666
Officer: Harold Barron. **Ultimate Parent:** Ball Corp. **SIC:** 3411—Metal Cans.

★ 57634 ★   Hiland Dairy Co.
508 Huntsville
Springdale, AR 72764
(501)751-4712
Ultimate Parent: Prairie Farms Dairy Inc.
SIC: 5451—Dairy Products Stores.

★ 57635 ★   Hudson Foods Inc.
1521 Ford Ave.
Springdale, AR 72765
Ultimate Parent: Hudson Foods. **SIC:** 2000—Food & Kindred Products.

★ 57636 ★   Kentucky Fried Chicken
600 S. Thompson St.
Springdale, AR 72764
(501)751-8241
Ultimate Parent: Pepsico. **SIC:** 5812—Eating Places.

★ 57637 ★   Kentucky Fried Chicken
2610 W. Sunset St.
Springdale, AR 72764
(501)756-0565
Ultimate Parent: Pepsico. **SIC:** 5812—Eating Places.

★ 57638 ★   NCR Corp.
Springdale, AR 72764
(501)751-3507
Ultimate Parent: AT&T. **SIC:** 5045—Computers, Peripherals & Software.

★ 57639 ★   Pepsi-Cola Bottling Co.
707 E. Robinson Ave.
Springdale, AR 72764
(501)751-1900
Officer: Wayne Sutton, Manager. **Ultimate Parent:** Pepsico. **SIC:** 2086—Bottled & Canned Soft Drinks.

★ 57640 ★   Pizza Hut
Hwy. 68 W
Springdale, AR 72764
(501)751-8400
Ultimate Parent: Pepsico. **SIC:** 5812—Eating Places.

★ 57641 ★   Radio Shack
906 W. Sunset St.
Springdale, AR 72764
(501)751-3060
Company Type: Division. **Ultimate Parent:** Tandy Corp. **SIC:** 5734—Computer & Software Stores.

★ 57642 ★   Ryder Truck Rental
Hwy. 68 E
Springdale, AR 72764
(501)751-0340
Ultimate Parent: Ryder System. **SIC:** 7359—Equipment Rental & Leasing Nec.

★ 57643 ★   Sam's Wholesale Club
2200 S. Pleasant St.
Springdale, AR 72764
(501)756-5923
Ultimate Parent: Wal-Mart Stores, Inc.

★ 57644 ★   Sterwin Labs Imc
3408 W. Sunset
Springdale, AR 72762
(501)751-7464
Ultimate Parent: Imcera Group.

★ 57645 ★   Tyson E. Feed Mill
401 Jeff Brown Rd.
Springdale, AR 72764
Ultimate Parent: Tyson Foods, Inc. **SIC:** 2048—Prepared Feeds Nec.

★ 57646 ★   Tyson Foods Cornish Plant
671 N. Randall-Wobbe Ln.
Springdale, AR 72764
Ultimate Parent: Tyson Foods, Inc. **SIC:** 2015—Poultry Slaughtering & Processing.

★ 57647 ★   Tyson Foods Feed Mill
3801 Johnson Rd.
Springdale, AR 72762
(501)756-4241
Officer: Marty Perry, Executive Director.
Ultimate Parent: Tyson Foods, Inc. **SIC:** 2048—Prepared Feeds Nec.

★ 57648 ★   Tyson Foods Inc.
Berry St.
Springdale, AR 72764
(501)756-4316
Officer: Ted Burnett, Manager. **Ultimate Parent:** Tyson Foods, Inc. **SIC:** 2015—Poultry Slaughtering & Processing; 2048—Prepared Feeds Nec.

★ 57649 ★   Tyson Foods Inc.
647 Randall Rd.
Springdale, AR 72764
(501)756-4291
Officer: Jerry Phillips, Manager. **Ultimate Parent:** Tyson Foods, Inc. **SIC:** 2015—Poultry Slaughtering & Processing.

★ 57650 ★   Tyson Foods Inc.
600 N. Berry St.
Springdale, AR 72764
Ultimate Parent: Tyson Foods, Inc. **SIC:** 2000—Food & Kindred Products.

★ 57651 ★   Tyson Foods Inc.
PO Box
Springdale, AR 72765
(501)751-4545
Ultimate Parent: Tyson Foods, Inc. **SIC:** 6512—Nonresidential Building Operators.

★ 57652 ★   Tyson Foods Inc.
2210 Oaklawn
Springdale, AR 72762
(501)756-4000
Ultimate Parent: Tyson Foods, Inc.

★ 57653 ★   Tyson Foods, Inc.-Berry St. Plant
600 N. Berry St.
Springdale, AR 72764
Location Type: Plant. **Ultimate Parent:** Tyson Foods, Inc. **SIC:** 2015—Poultry Slaughtering & Processing.

★ 57654 ★   Tyson Foods Inc. Cornish Plant-Protein
Randall Rd.
Springdale, AR 72764
Ultimate Parent: Tyson Foods, Inc. **SIC:** 2048—Prepared Feeds Nec; 2047—Dog & Cat Food; 2077—Animal & Marine Fats & Oils.

★ 57655 ★   Tyson Foods Inc.
2210 W. Oaklawn Dr.
Springdale, AR 72764-6999
(501)290-4000
Officer: Don Tyson, Chairman. **Ultimate Parent:** Tyson Foods, Inc. **SIC:** 2015—Poultry Slaughtering & Processing; 2011—Meat Packing Plants; 2013—Sausages & Other Prepared Meats; 2032—Canned Specialties; 2092—Fresh or Frozen Prepared Fish. **Employee Count:** 47950. **Sales:** 4168840000 M.

★ 57656 ★   Tyson Foods Longhaul Shop
490 Creek St.
Springdale, AR 72764
Ultimate Parent: Tyson Foods, Inc. **SIC:** 4212—Local Trucking Without Storage.

★ 57657 ★   Tyson Johnson Rd. Mill
3801 Johnson Rd.
Springdale, AR 72764
Ultimate Parent: Tyson Foods, Inc. **SIC:** 2048—Prepared Feeds Nec.

★ 57658 ★   Wal Mart Pharmacy
Pleasant
Springdale, AR 72764
(501)756-0860
Ultimate Parent: Wal-Mart Stores, Inc. **SIC:** 5912—Drug Stores & Proprietary Stores.

Stephens

★ 57659 ★   Marathon Petroleum Co.
Stephens, AR 71764
(501)786-5435
Ultimate Parent: USX Corp. **SIC:** 1382—Oil & Gas Exploration Services.

Stuttgart

★ 57660 ★   Kinder-Harris, Inc.
PO Box 1900
Stuttgart, AR 72160
(501)673-1518 **Fax:** (501)673-1518
Officer: David B. Kossove, President & CEO. **Ultimate Parent:** J.C. Penney.

★ 57661 ★   Kroger Delicatessen
2116 S. Main St.
Stuttgart, AR 72160
(501)673-6846
Ultimate Parent: Kroger. **SIC:** 5411—Grocery Stores.

★ 57662 ★   Piggly Wiggly
2104 S. Buerkle St.
Stuttgart, AR 72160
(501)673-8101
Ultimate Parent: Bruno's. **SIC:** 5411—Grocery Stores.

★ 57663 ★   Pizza Hut
2108 S. Main St.
Stuttgart, AR 72160
(501)673-1521
Ultimate Parent: Pepsico. **SIC:** 5812—Eating Places.

★ 57664 ★   Potlatch Corp.
Townsend Unit
Hwy. 79 E
Stuttgart, AR 72160
Ultimate Parent: Potlatch. **SIC:** 2431—Millwork; 2426—Hardwood Dimension & Flooring Mills.

★ 57665 ★   Radio Shack
215 E. Michigan St.
Stuttgart, AR 72160
(501)673-1136
Company Type: Division. **Ultimate Parent:** Tandy Corp. **SIC:** 5731—Radio, Television & Electronics Stores.

★ 57666 ★   Riceland Foods
2120 S. Park Ave.
Stuttgart, AR 72160
(501)673-5521
Company Type: Headquarters. **Officer:** Richard E. Bell. **Employee Count:** 1850. **Sales:** 683 M. **Fortune 500:** Largest U.S. Industrial Corporations: Ranking 462.

★ 57667 ★   Riceland Foods Inc.
2120 S. Park Ave.
Stuttgart, AR 72160
(501)673-5500 **Fax:** (501)673-3366
Officer: Tommy Hillman, CEO. **Ultimate**

Parent: Riceland Foods. **Employee Count:** 1848. **Sales:** 692 M.

★ 57668 ★   Riceland Foods Inc. Soybean Plant
Hwy. 79 & Park Ave.
Stuttgart, AR 72160
Ultimate Parent: Riceland Foods. **SIC:** 2075—Soybean Oil Mills.

★ 57669 ★   Riceland Foods Soybean Plant
PO Box 927
Stuttgart, AR 72160
Ultimate Parent: Riceland Foods. **SIC:** 2075—Soybean Oil Mills.

★ 57670 ★   Ryder Truck Rental
Hwy. 79 W
Stuttgart, AR 72160
(501)673-2196
Ultimate Parent: Ryder System. **SIC:** 7513—Truck Rental & Leasing Without Drivers.

Texarkana

★ 57671 ★   Cooper Tire Co.
3500 E. Washington Rd.
Texarkana, AR 75502
Ultimate Parent: Cooper Tire & Rubber Co. Inc. **SIC:** 3011—Tires & Inner Tubes.

★ 57672 ★   Cooper Tire Co.
Cooper Tire & Rubber Co. Div.
3500 E. Washington Rd. 3500 E. Washington Rd.
Texarkana, AR 75502
Company Type: Division. **Ultimate Parent:** Cooper Tire & Rubber Co. Inc. **SIC:** 3011—Tires & Inner Tubes.

★ 57673 ★   Cooper Tire & Rubber Co.
Rte. 12, PO Box 252
Texarkana, AR 75502
Ultimate Parent: Cooper Tire & Rubber Co. Inc. **SIC:** 3011—Tires & Inner Tubes.

★ 57674 ★   Cooper Tire&Rubber
3500 Washington St.
Texarkana, AR 75502
(501)773-4502
Ultimate Parent: Cooper Tire & Rubber Co. Inc.

★ 57675 ★   E. R. Carpenter Co.
41 Globe Union Ave.
Texarkana, AR 75502
Ultimate Parent: Carpenter. **SIC:** 3086—Plastics Foam Products.

★ 57676 ★   Flowers Baking Co. of Texarkana Inc.
7 Jim Walters Dr.
PO Box 2427
Texarkana, AR 75502
(501)773-7523 **Fax:** (501)772-2174
Company Type: Subsidiary. **Officer:** Debbie Engeldowl, Vice President/General Manager. **Ultimate Parent:** Flowers Industries.

★ 57677 ★   McDonalds Restaurant
711 E. 7th St.
Texarkana, AR 75502
(501)772-5172
Ultimate Parent: McDonald's.

★ 57678 ★   Mobil Oil Co.
1221 Dudley St.
Texarkana, AR 75502
(501)773-3313
Ultimate Parent: Mobil.

★ 57679 ★   Rockwell International Corp.
30 Globe Ave.
Texarkana, AR 75502
Ultimate Parent: Rockwell International Corp. **SIC:** 3479—Metal Coating & Allied Services.

★ 57680 ★   Ryder Truck Rental
101 East St.
Texarkana, AR 75502
(501)773-1233
Ultimate Parent: Ryder System. **SIC:** 5113—Industrial & Personal Service Paper.

★ 57681 ★ **Ryder Truck Rental**
5104 Garland St.
Texarkana, AR 75502
(501)774-3129
Ultimate Parent: Ryder System.

★ 57682 ★ **Trailways Restaurnat**
401 Wood St.
Texarkana, AR 75502
(501)774-9485
Ultimate Parent: Greyhound Lines Inc. **SIC:**
5812—Eating Places.

Thornton

★ 57683 ★ **Mary Kay Cosmetics**
Thornton, AR 71766
(501)352-2210
Ultimate Parent: Mary Kay Cosmetics. **SIC:**
5999—Miscellaneous Retail Stores Nec.

Trumann

★ 57684 ★ **Kentucky Fried Chicken**
Hwy. 63
Trumann, AR 72472
(501)483-2212
Ultimate Parent: Pepsico. **SIC:** 5812—
Eating Places.

★ 57685 ★ **Parker Hannifin Corp.**
301 Parker Industrial Dr.
Trumann, AR 72472
Ultimate Parent: Parker Hannifin. **SIC:**
3714—Motor Vehicle Parts & Accessories.

★ 57686 ★ **Pizza Hut**
Hwy. 63 S
Trumann, AR 72472
(501)483-2233
Ultimate Parent: Pepsico. **SIC:** 5812—
Eating Places.

★ 57687 ★ **Radio Shack**
Hwy. 69 W
Trumann, AR 72472
(501)483-5384
Company Type: Division. **Ultimate Parent:**
Tandy Corp. **SIC:** 5731—Radio, Television
& Electronics Stores.

Van Buren

★ 57688 ★ **Capco Pipe Co.**
603 S. 28th St.
Van Buren, AR 72956
(501)474-2393
Officer: Jim Barber, Manager. **Ultimate
Parent:** Asarco. **SIC:** 3292—Asbestos
Products.

★ 57689 ★ **Capco Pipe Co. Inc.**
603 S. 28th St.
Van Buren, AR 72956-6117
(501)474-2393
Company Type: Branch. **Officer:** Bruce
Klomfas. **Ultimate Parent:** Asarco. **SIC:**
3084—Plastics Pipe; 3292—Asbestos
Products; 5074—Plumbing & Hydronic
Heating Supplies.

★ 57690 ★ **Mary Kay Cosmetics**
4805 Alma Hwy.
Van Buren, AR 72956
(501)474-3621
Ultimate Parent: Mary Kay Cosmetics. **SIC:**
7231—Beauty Shops.

★ 57691 ★ **Pizza Hut**
2414 Alma Hwy.
Van Buren, AR 72956
(501)474-1132
Ultimate Parent: Pepsico. **SIC:** 5812—
Eating Places.

★ 57692 ★ **Radio Shack**
Alma Hwy.
Van Buren, AR 72956
(501)474-1496
Company Type: Division. **Ultimate Parent:**
Tandy Corp. **SIC:** 5065—Electronic Parts &
Equipment Nec.

★ 57693 ★ **Ryder Truck Rental**
59 N. Van Buren
Van Buren, AR 72956
(501)474-7797
Ultimate Parent: Ryder System. **SIC:**
7359—Equipment Rental & Leasing Nec.

★ 57694 ★ **Taco Bell**
3003 Alma Hwy.
Van Buren, AR 72956
(501)471-5309
Ultimate Parent: Pepsico. **SIC:** 5812—
Eating Places.

★ 57695 ★ **Texaco Express Lube**
1818 E. Main St.
Van Buren, AR 72956
(501)471-8700
Ultimate Parent: Texaco. **SIC:** 7539—
Automotive Repair Shops Nec.

★ 57696 ★ **Tyson Foods Inc.**
802 South 28th St.
Van Buren, AR 72956
Ultimate Parent: Tyson Foods, Inc. **SIC:**
2000—Food & Kindred Products.

★ 57697 ★ **Tyson Foods Inc.**
802 S. 28th St.
Van Buren, AR 72956
(501)474-7041
Officer: Don Thompson, President.
Ultimate Parent: Tyson Foods, Inc. **SIC:**
2015—Poultry Slaughtering & Processing.

★ 57698 ★ **Union Camp Corp.**
621 S. 28th St.
Van Buren, AR 72956
(501)474-5055
Ultimate Parent: Union Camp Corp.

★ 57699 ★ **Wal Mart Discount
Cities**
Cloverleaf Plz.
Van Buren, AR 72956
(501)474-3449
Ultimate Parent: Wal-Mart Stores, Inc. **SIC:**
5311—Department Stores.

Vilonia

★ 57700 ★ **First State Bank &
Trust Co.**
Hwy. 64
Vilonia, AR 72173
(501)796-2500
Ultimate Parent: Michigan National Corp.
SIC: 6022—State Commercial Banks.

Waldron

★ 57701 ★ **Tyson Foods**
End of Fir St.
Waldron, AR 72958
Ultimate Parent: Tyson Foods, Inc. **SIC:**
2015—Poultry Slaughtering & Processing;
2048—Prepared Feeds Nec.

★ 57702 ★ **Tyson Foods Inc.**
10 Fir St.
Waldron, AR 72958
Ultimate Parent: Tyson Foods, Inc. **SIC:**
2015—Poultry Slaughtering & Processing.

★ 57703 ★ **Tyson Foods Inc.**
End of Fir St.
Waldron, AR 72958-0460
Ultimate Parent: Tyson Foods, Inc. **SIC:**
2000—Food & Kindred Products; 2048—
Prepared Feeds Nec.

★ 57704 ★ **Tyson Foods Inc.**
Waldron, AR 72958
(501)637-2121
Officer: Randy Milam, Manager. **Ultimate
Parent:** Tyson Foods, Inc. **SIC:** 2015—
Poultry Slaughtering & Processing.

★ 57705 ★ **Wal Mart Auto Repair**
Hwy. 71 Bypass
Waldron, AR 72958
(501)637-2284
Ultimate Parent: Wal-Mart Stores, Inc. **SIC:**
7538—General Automotive Repair Shops.

Walnut Ridge

★ 57706 ★ **Douglas/Quikut**
Hwy. 67 N
Walnut Ridge, AR 72476
(501)886-6774
Company Type: Division. **Ultimate Parent:**
Berkshire Hathaway.

★ 57707 ★ **Skil Dremel Corp.**
Skil Dr.
Walnut Ridge, AR 72476
Ultimate Parent: Emerson Electric Co. Inc.
SIC: 3546—Power-Driven Handtools.

★ 57708 ★ **Wal Mart**
Hwy. 67 N
Walnut Ridge, AR 72476
(501)886-2483
Ultimate Parent: Wal-Mart Stores, Inc. **SIC:**
5311—Department Stores.

Warren

★ 57709 ★ **Pizza Hut**
105 W. Central St.
Warren, AR 71671
(501)226-6741
Ultimate Parent: Pepsico. **SIC:** 5812—
Eating Places.

★ 57710 ★ **Potlatch Corp.**
810 W. Pine St.
Warren, AR 71671
(501)226-2611
Ultimate Parent: Potlatch. **SIC:** 5031—
Lumber, Plywood & Millwork.

★ 57711 ★ **Potlatch Corp.**
Southern Unit
810 W. Pine St.
Warren, AR 71671
Company Type: Division. **Ultimate Parent:**
Potlatch. **SIC:** 2421—Sawmills & Planing
Mills—General.

Weiner

★ 57712 ★ **ADM Milling Co.**
Hwy. 49 S.
Weiner, AR 72479
(501)684-7444
Officer: Phil Stratton, Manager. **Ultimate
Parent:** Archer Daniels Midland Co. **SIC:**
2044—Rice Milling.

West Helena

★ 57713 ★ **Kentucky Fried
Chicken**
Hwy. 49 Bypass
West Helena, AR 72390
(501)572-9334
Ultimate Parent: Pepsico. **SIC:** 5812—
Eating Places.

★ 57714 ★ **Pizza Hut**
Tri County Shopping Ctr.
West Helena, AR 72390
(501)572-2579
Ultimate Parent: Pepsico. **SIC:** 5812—
Eating Places.

★ 57715 ★ **Wal Mart Discount
Pharmacy**
Tri County Plz.
West Helena, AR 72390
(501)572-6741
Ultimate Parent: Wal-Mart Stores, Inc. **SIC:**
5441—Candy, Nut & Confectionery Stores.

West Memphis

★ 57716 ★ **Belcher Co. of
Tennessee**
1281 S. 8th St.
West Memphis, AR 72301
Ultimate Parent: Coastal Corp. **SIC:**
2992—Lubricating Oils & Greases; 3085—
Plastics Bottles.

★ 57717 ★ **Boise Cascade Corp.**
Container
1235 N. 7th St.
West Memphis, AR 72301
Location Type: Plant. **Ultimate Parent:**
Boise Cascade. **SIC:** 2653—Corrugated &
Solid Fiber Boxes.

★ 57718 ★ **Canners of Eastern
Arkansas Inc.**
1400 Rainer Rd.
West Memphis, AR 72301
Ultimate Parent: Coca-Cola Enterprises.
SIC: 2086—Bottled & Canned Soft Drinks.

★ 57719 ★ **Citgo Petroleum Corp.**
1281 S. 8th St.
West Memphis, AR 72301
(501)732-4390
Ultimate Parent: Citgo Petroleum.

★ 57720 ★ **Coastal Unilube Inc.**
310 Mid Continent Plz.
West Memphis, AR 72301-1749
(501)735-0020
Company Type: Subsidiary. **Officer:**

Kenneth O. Johnson, Chairman of the
Board. **Ultimate Parent:** Coastal Corp. **SIC:**
5172—Petroleum Products Nec; 2992—
Lubricating Oils & Greases; 2899—
Chemical Preparations Nec; 3085—Plastics
Bottles. **Employee Count:** 450. **Sales:** 100
M.

★ 57721 ★ **Coastal Unilube Inc.**
1200 S. 8th St.
West Memphis, AR 72301
Ultimate Parent: Coastal Corp. **SIC:**
2992—Lubricating Oils & Greases; 3085—
Plastics Bottles.

★ 57722 ★ **Coastal Unilube Inc.**
915 E. Jefferson St.
West Memphis, AR 72301
Ultimate Parent: Coastal Corp. **SIC:**
2992—Lubricating Oils & Greases.

★ 57723 ★ **Coastal Unilube Inc.**
1000 Jefferson St.
West Memphis, AR 72301
Ultimate Parent: Coastal Corp. **SIC:**
2992—Lubricating Oils & Greases.

★ 57724 ★ **Kentucky Fried
Chicken**
314 N. Missouri St.
West Memphis, AR 72301
(501)735-6711
Ultimate Parent: Pepsico. **SIC:** 5812—
Eating Places.

★ 57725 ★ **Kroger**
209 Shoppingway Blvd.
West Memphis, AR 72301
(501)732-2111
Ultimate Parent: Kroger.

★ 57726 ★ **Kroger's**
209 Shoppingway Blvd.
West Memphis, AR 72301
(501)732-2110
Ultimate Parent: Kroger. **SIC:** 5411—
Grocery Stores.

★ 57727 ★ **McDonalds**
3901 Petro Dr.
West Memphis, AR 72301
(501)735-6881
Ultimate Parent: McDonald's.

★ 57728 ★ **Pappagallo**
712 N. Missouri St.
West Memphis, AR 72301
(501)732-5046
Ultimate Parent: United States Shoe. **SIC:**
5661—Shoe Stores.

★ 57729 ★ **Payless Shoesource**
111 N. Missouri St.
West Memphis, AR 72301
(501)735-7119
Ultimate Parent: May Department Stores.
SIC: 5632—Women's Accessory &
Specialty Stores.

★ 57730 ★ **Pizza Hut**
1105 N. Missouri St.
West Memphis, AR 72301
(501)735-7607
Ultimate Parent: Pepsico. **SIC:** 5812—
Eating Places.

★ 57731 ★ **Radio Shack**
Holiday Plz.
West Memphis, AR 72301
(501)735-3943
Company Type: Division. **Ultimate Parent:**
Tandy Corp. **SIC:** 5065—Electronic Parts &
Equipment Nec.

★ 57732 ★ **Radio Shack**
6 Holiday Plz.
West Memphis, AR 72301
(501)735-8119
Company Type: Division. **Ultimate Parent:**
Tandy Corp. **SIC:** 7373—Computer
Integrated Systems Design.

★ 57733 ★ **Ryder Truck Rental**
100 W. Broadway St.
West Memphis, AR 72301
(501)732-6650
Ultimate Parent: Ryder System. **SIC:**
7513—Truck Rental & Leasing Without
Drivers.

★ 57734 ★ **Ryder Truck Rental**
100 W. Broadway St.
West Memphis, AR 72301
(501)732-5697
Ultimate Parent: Ryder System.

★ 57735 ★ **Safety Kleen Corp.**
309 Mound City Rd.
West Memphis, AR 72301
(501)449-4303 (501)735-3119
Ultimate Parent: Texaco. **SIC:** 7538—
General Automotive Repair Shops. **Ultimate Parent:** Safety-Kleen. **SIC:** 5013—Motor
Vehicle Supplies & New Parts.

★ 57736 ★ **Taco Bell**
1219 N. Missouri St.
West Memphis, AR 72301
Ultimate Parent: Pepsico. **SIC:** 5812—
Eating Places.

★ 57737 ★ **Wal Mart**
300 S. Service Rd.
West Memphis, AR 72301
(501)732-3460
Ultimate Parent: Wal-Mart Stores, Inc. **SIC:**
5311—Department Stores.

★ 57738 ★ **Walgreen Drug Stores**
West Memphis, AR 72301
(501)735-8999
Ultimate Parent: Walgreen Co. **SIC:**
5912—Drug Stores & Proprietary Stores.

★ 57739 ★ **Walgreen Drug Stores**
2 Holiday Plz.
West Memphis, AR 72301
(501)735-8996
Ultimate Parent: Walgreen Co. **SIC:**
5912—Drug Stores & Proprietary Stores.

Wheatley

★ 57740 ★ **Shell Super Stop**
I Us 78 N. 40
Wheatley, AR 72392
(501)457-2300
Ultimate Parent: Shell Oil Co.

Wynne

★ 57741 ★ **Kentucky Fried Chicken**
Bridges
Wynne, AR 72396
(501)238-9111
Ultimate Parent: Pepsico. **SIC:** 5812—
Eating Places.

★ 57742 ★ **McDonalds of Wynne**
N Falls Blvd.
Wynne, AR 72396
(501)238-8811
Ultimate Parent: McDonald's.
SIC: 5812—Eating Places.

★ 57743 ★ **Piggly Wiggly**
Oakwood Shopping Ctr.
Wynne, AR 72396
(501)238-3414
Ultimate Parent: Bruno's. **SIC:** 5411—
Grocery Stores.

★ 57744 ★ **Radio Shack**
669 N. Falls Blvd.
Wynne, AR 72396
(501)238-7440
Company Type: Division. **Ultimate Parent:**
Tandy Corp. **SIC:** 5731—Radio, Television
& Electronics Stores.

★ 57745 ★ **Shell Super Stop**
115 S. Falls Blvd.
Wynne, AR 72396
(501)238-4255
Ultimate Parent: Shell Oil Co. **SIC:** 5411—
Grocery Stores.

★ 57746 ★ **Texaco Auto Service**
1005 S. Falls Blvd.
Wynne, AR 72396
(501)238-7176
Ultimate Parent: Texaco. **SIC:** 5541—
Gasoline Service Stations.

Yellville

★ 57747 ★ **Texaco 62**
Yellville, AR 72687
(501)449-4303
Ultimate Parent: Texaco. **SIC:** 7538—
General Automotive Repair Shops.

DELAWARE

Bear

★ 57748 ★ **Bank of Delaware**
230 Fox Hunt Dr.
Bear, DE 19701
(302)733-7470
Location Type: Branch office. **Ultimate Parent:** PNC Bank Corp. **SIC:** 6021—National Commercial Banks.

★ 57749 ★ **Beneficial National Bank**
Rtes. 7 & 40
Bear, DE 19701
(302)425-2383
Location Type: Branch office. **Officer:** Catherine Kehler, Manager. **Ultimate Parent:** Beneficial. **SIC:** 6021—National Commercial Banks.

★ 57750 ★ **Beneficial National Bank**
Rte. 7 & 40
Bear, DE 19701-9807
(302)792-9807
Location Type: Branch office. **Ultimate Parent:** Beneficial. **SIC:** 6022—State Commercial Banks.

Bethany Beach

★ 57751 ★ **Baltimore Trust Co.**
Pennsylvania Ave.
Bethany Beach, DE 19975
(302)436-8236
Location Type: Branch office. **Officer:** Clayton L. Ringler, Senior Vice President. **Ultimate Parent:** Mercantile Bankshares Corp. **SIC:** 6021—National Commercial Banks.

Bridgeville

★ 57752 ★ **Baltimore Trust Co.**
100 Laws St.
Bridgeville, DE 19933-1199
(302)337-8263
Location Type: Branch office. **Officer:** Ralph A. Mills, Assistant Vice President. **Ultimate Parent:** Mercantile Bankshares Corp. **SIC:** 6021—National Commercial Banks.

★ 57753 ★ **Mary Kay Cosmetics**
Redden Rd.
Bridgeville, DE 19933
(302)337-8484
Ultimate Parent: Mary Kay Cosmetics. **SIC:** 5999—Miscellaneous Retail Stores Nec.

★ 57754 ★ **Pet Poultry Products Inc.**
Railroad Ave.
Bridgeville, DE 19933
(302)337-8223
Ultimate Parent: Pet. **SIC:** 2015—Poultry Slaughtering & Processing.

Camden

★ 57755 ★ **Camdel Metals Corp.**
Drawer "F"
Camden, DE 19934
(302)697-9521
Company Type: Subsidiary. **Officer:** Millard V. Vaughn, Division Manager. **Ultimate Parent:** Handy & Harman.

★ 57756 ★ **Camdel Metals Corp.**
Rte. 10 Vepco Industrial Park
Camden, DE 19934
Ultimate Parent: Handy & Harman. **SIC:** 3317—Steel Pipe & Tubes.

Camden Wy

★ 57757 ★ **Blazer Financial Services**
2114 N. Dupont Hwy.
Camden Wy, DE 19934
(302)697-9571
Ultimate Parent: Great Western Financial Corp. **SIC:** 6141—Personal Credit Institutions.

Claymont

★ 57758 ★ **Allied-Signal Inc.**
6100 Philadelphia Pike
Claymont, DE 19703
Ultimate Parent: Allied-Signal Inc. **SIC:** 2819—Industrial Inorganic Chemicals Nec; 2869—Industrial Organic Chemicals Nec.

★ 57759 ★ **Allied-Signal, Inc.**
PO Box 607
Claymont, DE 19703-0607
(302)791-6703
Officer: Mr. Thomas J. Silverio. **Ultimate Parent:** Allied-Signal Inc. **SIC:** 2899—Chemical Preparations Nec.

★ 57760 ★ **Bank of Delaware**
691 Naaman's Rd.
Claymont, DE 19703-2309
(302)429-1643
Location Type: Branch office. **Ultimate Parent:** PNC Bank Corp. **SIC:** 6021—National Commercial Banks.

★ 57761 ★ **Eaton Kenway Inc.**
706 Philadelphia Pike
Claymont, DE 19703
(302)764-8010
Ultimate Parent: Eaton Corp. **SIC:** 5084—Industrial Machinery & Equipment.

★ 57762 ★ **Eckerd Drugs**
Philadelphia Pke.
Claymont, DE 19703
(302)798-9529
Ultimate Parent: Eckerd Corp. **SIC:** 5912—Drug Stores & Proprietary Stores.

★ 57763 ★ **GSC Leasing Dr.**
1302 Society Dr.
Claymont, DE 19703
(302)655-6454
Company Type: Joint venture. **Ultimate Parent:** Lukens. **SIC:** 4741—Rental of Railroad Cars.

★ 57764 ★ **Radio Shack**
Northtowne Plz.
Claymont, DE 19703
(302)798-5312
Company Type: Division. **Ultimate Parent:** Tandy Corp. **SIC:** 5065—Electronic Parts & Equipment Nec.

★ 57765 ★ **Rite Aid**
Tri Statemall
Claymont, DE 19703
(302)798-9967
Ultimate Parent: Rite Aid. **SIC:** 5912—Drug Stores & Proprietary Stores.

★ 57766 ★ **Rite Aid**
Foulk Naamansrd
Claymont, DE 19703
(302)475-3334
Ultimate Parent: Rite Aid.

Dagsboro

★ 57767 ★ **Mellon Bank(DE) NA**
Main & Clayton Sts.
Dagsboro, DE 19939-9781
(302)732-3610
Location Type: Branch office. **Ultimate Parent:** Mellon Bank Corp. **SIC:** 6021—National Commercial Banks.

Delaware City

★ 57768 ★ **Air Products & Chemicals Inc.**
Governor Lea Rd.
Delaware City, DE 19706
(302)653-4131
Location Type: Branch office. **Ultimate Parent:** Air Products & Chemicals, Inc. **SIC:** 5169—Chemicals & Allied Products Nec.

★ 57769 ★ **Georgia Gulf Corp.**
River Rd.
Delaware City, DE 19706
(302)834-8117
Officer: David Di Piero, Manager. **Ultimate Parent:** Georgia Gulf. **SIC:** 2812—Alkalies & Chlorine; 2821—Plastics Materials & Resins.

★ 57770 ★ **Georgia Gulf Corp.**
1685 River Rd.
Delaware City, DE 19706
Ultimate Parent: Georgia Gulf. **SIC:** 2821—Plastics Materials & Resins.

★ 57771 ★ **Georgia Gulf Corp.**
PO Box 610
Delaware City, DE 19706
(302)836-2110
Ultimate Parent: Georgia Gulf. **SIC:** 2821—Plastics Materials & Resins.

★ 57772 ★ **Occidental Chemical Corp.**
River Rd.
Delaware City, DE 19706-0550
Ultimate Parent: Occidental Petroleum Corp. **SIC:** 2812—Alkalies & Chlorine.

★ 57773 ★ **Star Enterprise Delaware City Refinery**
2000 Wrangle Hill Rd.
Delaware City, DE 19706
Ultimate Parent: Texaco. **SIC:** 2911—Petroleum Refining.

★ 57774 ★ **Texaco Delaware City Plant**
2000 Wrangle Hill Rd.
Delaware City, DE 19706
Ultimate Parent: Texaco. **SIC:** 2911—Petroleum Refining.

Dover

★ 57775 ★ **ACME Markets**
Rte. 13
Dover, DE 19901
(302)674-8308
Officer: Mr. Craig Austin. **Ultimate Parent:** American Stores. **SIC:** 5411—Grocery Stores.

★ 57776 ★ **ACME Markets**
Dover Downs Shopping Ctr.
Dover, DE 19901
(302)674-8307
Ultimate Parent: American Stores. **SIC:** 5411—Grocery Stores.

★ 57777 ★ **Acme Markets**
1103 S. Central Ave.
Dover, DE 19901
(302)875-9951
Ultimate Parent: American Stores. **SIC:** 5411—Grocery Stores.

★ 57778 ★ **Acme Markets**
1001 N. Dupont Hwy.
Dover, DE 19901
(302)674-9953
Ultimate Parent: American Stores. **SIC:** 5411—Grocery Stores.

★ 57779 ★ **American General Finance**
105 S. Dupont Hwy.
Dover, DE 19901-7432
(302)678-2950
Ultimate Parent: American General Corp. **SIC:** 6141—Personal Credit Institutions; 6162—Mortgage Bankers & Correspondents.

★ 57780 ★ **American General Finance Inc.**
105 S. Dupont Hwy.
Dover, DE 19901-7432
(302)678-2950
Location Type: Branch office. **Ultimate Parent:** American General Corp. **SIC:** 6141—Personal Credit Institutions; 6162—Mortgage Bankers & Correspondents.

★ 57781 ★ **Bank of Delaware**
87 Greentree Dr.
Greentree Village Shopping Center
Dover, DE 19901
(302)735-2160
Location Type: Branch office. **Ultimate Parent:** PNC Bank Corp. **SIC:** 6021—National Commercial Banks.

★ 57782 ★ **Bank of Delaware**
505 N. DuPont Hwy.
Dover, DE 19901
(302)735-2380
Location Type: Branch office. **Ultimate Parent:** PNC Bank Corp. **SIC:** 6021—National Commercial Banks.

★ 57783 ★ **Bank of Delaware**
315 The Plz.
Dover, DE 19901
(302)735-2300
Location Type: Branch office. **Ultimate Parent:** PNC Bank Corp. **SIC:** 6021—National Commercial Banks.

★ 57784 ★ **Beneficial Delaware Inc.**
Leisure World Shopping Ctr.
Dover, DE 19901
(302)678-1606
Ultimate Parent: Beneficial. **SIC:** 6141—Personal Credit Institutions; 6162—Mortgage Bankers & Correspondents.

★ 57785 ★ **Beneficial National Bank**
405 S. New St.
Dover, DE 19901-6715
(302)425-2373
Location Type: Branch office. **Ultimate Parent:** Beneficial. **SIC:** 6021—National Commercial Banks.

★ 57786 ★ **Blazer Financial Services**
31 W. Loockerman St.
Dover, DE 19901
Ultimate Parent: Great Western Financial Corp. **SIC:** 6141—Personal Credit Institutions.

★ 57787 ★ **Casual Corner**
Dover
Dover, DE 19901
(302)734-1040
Ultimate Parent: United States Shoe. **SIC:** 5621—Women's Clothing Stores.

★ 57788 ★ **Equitable Life Insurance Co.**
675 PO Box
Dover, DE 19903
Ultimate Parent: American General Corp. **SIC:** 6411—Insurance Agents, Brokers & Service.

★ 57789 ★ **General Foods USA**
W. North St.
Dover, DE 19901
Ultimate Parent: Philip Morris. **SIC:** 2099—Food Preparations Nec.

★ 57790 ★ **Greyhound Bus Lines**
1465 S. Governors Ave.
Dover, DE 19901
(302)734-3372
Ultimate Parent: Greyhound Lines Inc. **SIC:** 4131—Intercity & Rural Bus Transportation.

★ 57791 ★ **Hertz Rent-A-Car**
Hwy. 10
Dover, DE 19901
(302)697-0299
Ultimate Parent: Hertz. **SIC:** 7514—
Passenger Car Rental.

★ 57792 ★ **Mary Kay Cosmetics**
106 Applewood Dr.
Dover, DE 19901
(302)697-9567
Ultimate Parent: Mary Kay Cosmetics.

★ 57793 ★ **Mellon Bank (DE) NA**
Rodney Village Shopping Ctr.
Dover, DE 19901-7046
(302)734-0285
Location Type: Branch office. **Ultimate
Parent:** Mellon Bank Corp. **SIC:** 6021—
National Commercial Banks.

★ 57794 ★ **Mellon Bank (DE) NA**
Rte. 8 & Dover Kenton Rd.
Dover, DE 19901-9808
(302)734-0231
Location Type: Branch office. **Ultimate
Parent:** Mellon Bank Corp. **SIC:** 6021—
National Commercial Banks.

★ 57795 ★ **Mellon Bank (DE) NA**
8 Loockerman
Dover, DE 19901-7381
(302)734-0206
Location Type: Branch office. **Ultimate
Parent:** Mellon Bank Corp. **SIC:** 6021—
National Commercial Banks.

★ 57796 ★ **Mellon Bank DE NA**
Dover AFB
Dover, DE 19902-5000
(302)734-0281
Location Type: Branch office. **Ultimate
Parent:** Mellon Bank Corp. **SIC:** 6021—
National Commercial Banks.

★ 57797 ★ **Northwestern Mutual
Life**
1679 S. Dupont Hwy.
Dover, DE 19901
(302)734-8777
Ultimate Parent: Northwestern Mutual Life.
SIC: 6411—Insurance Agents, Brokers &
Service.

★ 57798 ★ **Playtex Apparel Inc.**
Ridgley St.
Dover, DE 19901
Ultimate Parent: Sara Lee Corp. **SIC:**
2241—Narrow Fabric Mills.

★ 57799 ★ **PPG Industries Inc.**
PO Box 656
Dover, DE 19903
(302)678-9800
Officer: R. C. Austin, Manager. **Ultimate
Parent:** PPG Industries Inc. **SIC:** 2851—
Paints & Allied Products; 3991—Brooms &
Brushes.

★ 57800 ★ **Radio Shack**
Edgehill Shopping Ctr.
Dover, DE 19901
(302)734-5223
Company Type: Division. **Ultimate Parent:**
Tandy Corp. **SIC:** 5046—Commercial
Equipment Nec.

★ 57801 ★ **Radio Shack**
Rodney Village Shopping Ctr.
Dover, DE 19901
(302)674-3374
Company Type: Division. **Ultimate Parent:**
Tandy Corp. **SIC:** 5065—Electronic Parts &
Equipment Nec.

★ 57802 ★ **Radio Shack**
Blue Hen Mall
Dover, DE 19901
(302)674-0974
Company Type: Division. **Ultimate Parent:**
Tandy Corp. **SIC:** 5065—Electronic Parts &
Equipment Nec.

★ 57803 ★ **Radio Shack**
Dover
Dover, DE 19901
(302)734-0196
Company Type: Division. **Ultimate Parent:**
Tandy Corp. **SIC:** 5065—Electronic Parts &
Equipment Nec.

★ 57804 ★ **Radio Shack**
Rodney Village Shopping Ctr.
Dover, DE 19901
(302)674-3374
Company Type: Division. **Ultimate Parent:**
Tandy Corp. **SIC:** 5065—Electronic Parts &
Equipment Nec.

★ 57805 ★ **Radio Shack**
Edgehill Shopping Ctr.
Dover, DE 19901
(302)734-5223
Company Type: Division. **Ultimate Parent:**
Tandy Corp. **SIC:** 5046—Commercial
Equipment Nec.

★ 57806 ★ **Radio Shack**
Blue Hen Mall
Dover, DE 19901
(302)674-0974
Company Type: Division. **Ultimate Parent:**
Tandy Corp. **SIC:** 5065—Electronic Parts &
Equipment Nec.

★ 57807 ★ **Radio Shack**
Dover
Dover, DE 19901
(302)734-0196
Company Type: Division. **Ultimate Parent:**
Tandy Corp. **SIC:** 5065—Electronic Parts &
Equipment Nec.

★ 57808 ★ **Scott Paper Co.**
Hazlettville Rd.
Dover, DE 19901
Ultimate Parent: Scott Paper Co. **SIC:**
2621—Paper Mills.

★ 57809 ★ **Thrift Drug**
Rodney Village Shopping Ctr.
Dover, DE 19901
(302)734-5266
Ultimate Parent: J.C. Penney. **SIC:** 5049—
Professional Equipment Nec.

★ 57810 ★ **Thrift Drug**
Edgehill Shopping Ctr.
Dover, DE 19901
(302)674-2945
Ultimate Parent: J.C. Penney. **SIC:** 5049—
Professional Equipment Nec.

★ 57811 ★ **Waldenbooks**
Dover
Dover, DE 19901
(302)674-8775
Ultimate Parent: K-Mart. **SIC:** 5942—Book
Stores.

★ 57812 ★ **Waldenbooks**
Blue Hen Mall
Dover, DE 19901
(302)736-6888
Ultimate Parent: K-Mart. **SIC:** 5942—Book
Stores.

Elsmere

★ 57813 ★ **Bank of Delaware**
2203 Kirkwood Hwy.
Elsmere, DE 19805-4903
(302)429-1196
Location Type: Branch office. **Ultimate
Parent:** PNC Bank Corp. **SIC:** 6021—
National Commercial Banks.

Farmington

★ 57814 ★ **United Parcel Service**
Us 13
Farmington, DE 19942

Ultimate Parent: United Parcel Service of
America.

★ 57815 ★ **United Parcel Service**

Farmington, DE
(302)398-4452
Ultimate Parent: United Parcel Service of
America.

Fenwick Island

★ 57816 ★ **Baltimore Trust Co.**
Farmington St.
Fenwick Island, DE 19944
(302)436-8236
Location Type: Branch office. **Officer:** Geri
Cobb, Assistant Vice President. **Ultimate
Parent:** Mercantile Bankshares Corp. **SIC:**
6021—National Commercial Banks.

Georgetown

★ 57817 ★ **McDonald's
Hamburgers**
Rural Route 113
Georgetown, DE 19947
(302)856-6101
Ultimate Parent: McDonald's. **SIC:** 5812—
Eating Places.

★ 57818 ★ **Mellon Bank (DE) NA**
13 The Circle
Georgetown, DE 19947
(302)856-4231 **Telex:** '
Location Type: Branch office. **Ultimate
Parent:** Mellon Bank Corp. **SIC:** 6021—
National Commercial Banks.

Greenville

★ 57819 ★ **Bank of Delaware**
3840 Kennett Pke.
Greenville, DE 19807-2389
(302)429-1167
Location Type: Branch office. **Ultimate
Parent:** PNC Bank Corp. **SIC:** 6021—
National Commercial Banks.

Harrington

★ 57820 ★ **JCPenney National
Bank**
7 Commerce St.
Harrington, DE 19952
(302)398-3232 **Fax:** (302)398-9728
Officer: Ted L. Spurlock, Chairman.
Ultimate Parent: J.C. Penney.

Hartly

★ 57821 ★ **Delta Air Lines**
Hartly, DE 19953
(302)492-3600
Ultimate Parent: Delta Air Lines, Inc. **SIC:**
4729—Passenger Transportation
Arrangement Nec.

Henry Clay

★ 57822 ★ **Bank of Delaware**
DuPont Experimental Sta.
Henry Clay, DE 19898
(302)429-2062
Location Type: Branch office. **Ultimate
Parent:** PNC Bank Corp. **SIC:** 6021—
National Commercial Banks.

Hockessin

★ 57823 ★ **Bank of Delaware**
Yorklyn Rd. & Rte. 41
Hockessin, DE 19707
(302)429-1153
Location Type: Branch office. **Ultimate
Parent:** PNC Bank Corp. **SIC:** 6021—
National Commercial Banks.

Laurel

★ 57824 ★ **American General
Finance**
1128 S. Central Ave.
Laurel, DE 19956-1418
(302)875-2251
Location Type: Branch office. **Ultimate
Parent:** American General Corp. **SIC:**
6141—Personal Credit Institutions; 6162—
Mortgage Bankers & Correspondents.

★ 57825 ★ **American General
Finance Inc.**
1128 S. Central Ave.
Laurel, DE 19956-1418
(302)875-2251
Location Type: Branch office. **Ultimate
Parent:** American General Corp. **SIC:**
6141—Personal Credit Institutions; 6162—
Mortgage Bankers & Correspondents.

★ 57826 ★ **Mellon Bank (DE) NA**
Delaware Ave. & Market St.
Laurel, DE 19956
(302)875-5901
Location Type: Branch office. **Ultimate
Parent:** Mellon Bank Corp. **SIC:** 6021—
National Commercial Banks.

Lewes

★ 57827 ★ **Barcroft Co.**
40 Cape Henlopen Dr.
Lewes, DE 19958
Ultimate Parent: Rhone-Poulenc Rorer.
SIC: 2834—Pharmaceutical Preparations.

★ 57828 ★ **Mellon Bank (DE) NA**
131 2nd St.
Lewes, DE 19958
(302)856-4296
Location Type: Branch office. **Ultimate
Parent:** Mellon Bank Corp. **SIC:** 6021—
National Commercial Banks.

★ 57829 ★ **New York Life
Insurance**
633 PO Box
Lewes, DE 19958
(302)674-9104
Ultimate Parent: New York Life. **SIC:**
6411—Insurance Agents, Brokers &
Service.

Middletown

★ 57830 ★ **Acme Markets**
19 W. Green St.
Middletown, DE 19709
(302)378-4070
Ultimate Parent: American Stores. **SIC:**
5411—Grocery Stores.

★ 57831 ★ **Bank of Delaware**
Middletown Shopping Ctr.
Middletown, DE 19709
(302)378-4441
Location Type: Branch office. **Ultimate
Parent:** PNC Bank Corp. **SIC:** 6021—
National Commercial Banks.

★ 57832 ★ **Hercules Inc.**
Middletown Industrial Park
Middletown, DE 19709
Ultimate Parent: Hercules. **SIC:** 2821—
Plastics Materials & Resins.

★ 57833 ★ **Johnson Controls Inc.**
700 N. Broad St., Rm. 1
Middletown, DE 19709
Ultimate Parent: Johnson & Johnson. **SIC:**
3691—Storage Batteries.

★ 57834 ★ **Johnson Controls Inc.**
Battery Group
700 N. Broad St.
Middletown, DE 19709
Ultimate Parent: Johnson & Johnson. **SIC:**
3691—Storage Batteries.

Milford

★ 57835 ★ **Acme Markets**
696 N. Du Pont Blvd.
Milford, DE 19963
(302)422-7554
Ultimate Parent: American Stores. **SIC:**
5411—Grocery Stores.

★ 57836 ★ **American General
Finance**
907 N. Dupont Blvd.
Milford, DE 19963-1072
(302)424-1300
Ultimate Parent: American General Corp.
SIC: 6141—Personal Credit Institutions;
6162—Mortgage Bankers &
Correspondents.

★ 57837 ★ **American General
Finance Inc.**
907 N. Dupont Blvd.
Milford, DE 19963-1072
(302)424-1300
Location Type: Branch office. **Ultimate
Parent:** American General Corp. **SIC:**
6141—Personal Credit Institutions; 6162—
Mortgage Bankers & Correspondents.

★ 57838 ★ **Bank of Delaware**
Milford Village Shopping Ctr.
Milford, DE 19963-1793
(302)422-1015
Location Type: Branch office. **Ultimate
Parent:** PNC Bank Corp. **SIC:** 6021—
National Commercial Banks.

★ 57839 ★   Bank of Delaware
117 S. Walnut St.
Milford, DE 19963-1955
(302)422-1000
Location Type: Branch office. **Ultimate Parent:** PNC Bank Corp. **SIC:** 6021—National Commercial Banks.

★ 57840 ★   Blazer Financial Services
26 N. Walnut St.
Milford, DE 19963
(302)422-9661
Ultimate Parent: Great Western Financial Corp. **SIC:** 6141—Personal Credit Institutions.

★ 57841 ★   Conagra
Delmarva Div.
Rehoboth Hwy.
Milford, DE 19963
(302)422-6681
Company Type: Division. **Location Type:** Plant. **Officer:** Wayne Jones, Plant Manager. **Ultimate Parent:** Conagra.

★ 57842 ★   Conagra Broiler Co. Milford Processing Plant
255 N. Rehoboth Blvd. PO Box 183
Milford, DE 19963
Ultimate Parent: Conagra. **SIC:** 2015—Poultry Slaughtering & Processing.

★ 57843 ★   Radio Shack
Milford Shopping Ctr.
Milford, DE 19963
(302)422-5596
Company Type: Division. **Ultimate Parent:** Tandy Corp. **SIC:** 5065—Electronic Parts & Equipment Nec.

★ 57844 ★   Radio Shack
Milford Shopping Ctr.
Milford, DE 19963
(302)422-5596
Company Type: Division. **Ultimate Parent:** Tandy Corp. **SIC:** 5065—Electronic Parts & Equipment Nec.

★ 57845 ★   Ryder Truck Rental Inc.
1921 Causey St.
Milford, DE 19963
(302)422-7820
Ultimate Parent: Ryder System. **SIC:** 7513—Truck Rental & Leasing Without Drivers.

Millsboro

★ 57846 ★   First Omni Bank, NA
PO Box 900
Millsboro, DE 19966-0900
Location Type: Branch office. **Ultimate Parent:** First Maryland Bancorp. **SIC:** 6021—National Commercial Banks.

★ 57847 ★   First Omni Bank NA
499 Mitchell Rd.
Millsboro, DE 19966-9404
(302)934-9232 **Fax:** (302)934-2926
Location Type: Branch office. **Ultimate Parent:** First Maryland Bancorp. **SIC:** 6021—National Commercial Banks.

★ 57848 ★   First Omni Bank National as
499 Mitchell St.
Millsboro, DE 19966
(302)934-9232
Ultimate Parent: First Maryland Bancorp. **SIC:** 6021—National Commercial Banks.

★ 57849 ★   Sterwin Laboratories
Millsboro, DE 19966
(302)934-9274
Ultimate Parent: Imcera Group. **SIC:** 5083—Farm & Garden Machinery.

★ 57850 ★   Vlasic Foods Inc.
PO Box 625
Millsboro, DE 19966
Ultimate Parent: Campbell Soup. **SIC:** 2035—Pickles, Sauces & Salad Dressings.

★ 57851 ★   Vlasic Foods Inc.
Rte. 331 South
Millsboro, DE 19966
Ultimate Parent: Campbell Soup. **SIC:** 2035—Pickles, Sauces & Salad Dressings.

★ 57852 ★   Vlasic Foods, Inc.
Rte. 331 S
PO Box 625
Millsboro, DE 19966-0625
(302)934-8061
Company Type: Subsidiary. **Location Type:** Plant. **Officer:** Stan Zielinski, Plant Manager. **Ultimate Parent:** Campbell Soup.

New Castle

★ 57853 ★   Air Products & Chemicals Inc.
755 Governor Lea Rd.
New Castle, DE 19720-5512
(302)836-2509
Location Type: Branch office. **Ultimate Parent:** Air Products & Chemicals, Inc. **SIC:** 2813—Industrial Gases.

★ 57854 ★   Air Products & Chemicals, Inc.
PO Box 432
New Castle, DE 19720
(302)836-2509
Officer: John Denton, Manager. **Ultimate Parent:** Air Products & Chemicals, Inc. **SIC:** 2813—Industrial Gases.

★ 57855 ★   Bank of Delaware
1 Penn Mart Ctr.
New Castle, DE 19720-4206
(302)429-1254
Location Type: Branch office. **Ultimate Parent:** PNC Bank Corp. **SIC:** 6021—National Commercial Banks.

★ 57856 ★   Beneficial National Bank
2080 New Castle Ave.
New Castle, DE 19720-2777
(302)425-2366
Location Type: Branch office. **Ultimate Parent:** Beneficial. **SIC:** 6021—National Commercial Banks.

★ 57857 ★   Beneficial National Bank
Crossroad Shopping Ctr. Rte. 9
New Castle, DE 19720
(302)792-4725
Location Type: Branch office. **Officer:** Robert Merritt. **Ultimate Parent:** Beneficial. **SIC:** 6022—State Commercial Banks.

★ 57858 ★   Blazer Financial Services
2076 New Castle Ave.
New Castle, DE 19720
(302)655-6311
Ultimate Parent: Great Western Financial Corp. **SIC:** 6141—Personal Credit Institutions.

★ 57859 ★   Boatman's Bank of Delaware
2 Read's Way, Ste. 120
New Castle, DE 19720-1617
(302)323-1444 **Fax:** (302)323-1128
Location Type: Branch office. **Ultimate Parent:** Boatmen's Bancshares.

★ 57860 ★   Boatmen's Bank of Delaware
2 Reads Way
New Castle, DE 19720
(302)323-1444
Ultimate Parent: Boatmen's Bancshares. **SIC:** 6022—State Commercial Banks.

★ 57861 ★   Citibank Delaware
1 Penns Way
New Castle, DE 19720-2408
(302)323-3800 **Fax:** (302)323-4691
Location Type: Branch office. **Officer:** Richard Freytag, President. **Ultimate Parent:** Citicorp. **SIC:** 6022—State Commercial Banks.

★ 57862 ★   Citicorp Holdings, Inc.
1 Penns Way
New Castle, DE 19720
(302)323-3100
Location Type: Branch office. **Ultimate Parent:** Citicorp.

★ 57863 ★   Eckerd Drugs
Basin Dr.
New Castle, DE 19720
(302)328-4173
Ultimate Parent: Eckerd Corp. **SIC:** 5912—Drug Stores & Proprietary Stores.

★ 57864 ★   First National Bank of Atlanta
77 Read's Way
New Castle, DE 19720-1602
(302)324-3805 **Fax:** (302)323-9199
Location Type: Branch office. **Officer:** Jerry D. Craft, President. **Ultimate Parent:** Wachovia Corp. **SIC:** 6021—National Commercial Banks.

★ 57865 ★   Herman Miller Inc.
72 W. 5th St.
New Castle, DE 19720-5016
(302)322-6040
Ultimate Parent: Herman Miller. **SIC:** 2599—Furniture & Fixtures Nec; 5021—Furniture.

★ 57866 ★   Hertz Rent-A-Car
Greater Wilmington
New Castle, DE 19720
(302)328-5155
Ultimate Parent: Hertz. **SIC:** 7514—Passenger Car Rental.

★ 57867 ★   James River Corp
Advance Film Div.
River Rd. & Grantham Ln.
New Castle, DE 19720
Company Type: Division. **Ultimate Parent:** James River Corp. of Virginia. **SIC:** 3081—Unsupported Plastics Film & Sheet; 2759—Commercial Printing Nec.

★ 57868 ★   James River Corp.
Advanced Film Div.
River Rd. & Grantham Ln.
New Castle, DE 19720
Company Type: Division. **Ultimate Parent:** James River Corp. of Virginia. **SIC:** 3081—Unsupported Plastics Film & Sheet; 2759—Commercial Printing Nec.

★ 57869 ★   Luhens Development Corp.
91 Lukens Dr., Ste. 7
New Castle, DE 19720
(302)429-8444
Company Type: Subsidiary. **Ultimate Parent:** Lukens. **SIC:** 6531—Real Estate Agents & Managers.

★ 57870 ★   Mellon Bank (DE) NA
130 N. DuPont Hwy.
New Castle, DE 19720
(302)322-0525
Location Type: Branch office. **Ultimate Parent:** Mellon Bank Corp. **SIC:** 6021—National Commercial Banks.

★ 57871 ★   Mellon Bank, NA
130 N. DuPont Hwy.
New Castle, DE 19720
(302)322-0525
Location Type: Branch office. **Officer:** Wesley E. Thawley, Manager. **Ultimate Parent:** Mellon Bank Corp. **SIC:** 6021—National Commercial Banks.

★ 57872 ★   Radio Shack
New Castle Sq.
New Castle, DE 19720
(302)322-4360
Company Type: Division. **Ultimate Parent:** Tandy Corp. **SIC:** 5065—Electronic Parts & Equipment Nec.

★ 57873 ★   Rhone-Poulenc Performance Resins & Coatings
58 Pyles Ln.
New Castle, DE 19720
Ultimate Parent: Rhone-Poulenc Rorer. **SIC:** 2821—Plastics Materials & Resins; 2851—Paints & Allied Products.

★ 57874 ★   Ryder Truck Rental Inc.
RR 13
New Castle, DE 19720
(302)328-6405
Ultimate Parent: Ryder System. **SIC:** 7359—Equipment Rental & Leasing Nec.

★ 57875 ★   Sponser's Plan Asset Management, Inc.
44 Forrester Ave.
New Castle, DE 19720
(302)323-9788
Company Type: Subsidiary. **Ultimate Parent:** Lukens. **SIC:** 6159—Miscellaneous Business Credit Institutions.

★ 57876 ★   Thrift Drug
330 New Castle so
New Castle, DE 19720
(302)322-1708
Ultimate Parent: J.C. Penney. **SIC:** 5912—Drug Stores & Proprietary Stores.

★ 57877 ★   United Missouri Bank, USA
2 Read's Way, Ste. 211
New Castle, DE 19720-1620
(302)322-6666 **Fax:** (302)323-1367
Location Type: Branch office. **Ultimate Parent:** United Missouri Bancshares. **SIC:** 6021—National Commercial Banks.

★ 57878 ★   Wilmington Plant
58 Pyles Ln.
New Castle, DE 19720
Ultimate Parent: Rhone-Poulenc Rorer. **SIC:** 2821—Plastics Materials & Resins; 2851—Paints & Allied Products.

Newar

★ 57879 ★   Bank of Delaware
25 Castle Mall
Newar, DE 19713-3407
(302)733-7172
Location Type: Branch office. **Ultimate Parent:** PNC Bank Corp. **SIC:** 6021—National Commercial Banks.

Newark

★ 57880 ★   ACME Markets
263-67 Elkton Rd.
Newark, DE 19711
(302)453-2330
Officer: Mr. Bob Drewen. **Ultimate Parent:** American Stores. **SIC:** 5411—Grocery Stores.

★ 57881 ★   ACME Markets
Rte. 273 & Chapman Rd.
Newark, DE 19711
(302)738-9509
Officer: Mr. John Donahue. **Ultimate Parent:** American Stores. **SIC:** 5411—Grocery Stores.

★ 57882 ★   Acme Markets
Newark Shopping Ctr.
Newark, DE 19711
(302)366-9349
Ultimate Parent: American Stores. **SIC:** 5411—Grocery Stores.

★ 57883 ★   Acme Markets
64 Welsh Tract Rd. 207
Newark, DE 19713
(302)836-9380
Ultimate Parent: American Stores.

★ 57884 ★   Air Products & Chemicals Inc.
202 Lena Ct.
Newark, DE 19711-3784
(302)368-7497
Location Type: Branch office. **Ultimate Parent:** Air Products & Chemicals, Inc. **SIC:** 5169—Chemicals & Allied Products Nec.

★ 57885 ★   AMCE Markets Inc.
1 University Plz.
Newark, DE 19702-1549
(302)738-9509
Ultimate Parent: American Stores. **SIC:** 5411—Grocery Stores.

★ 57886 ★   American General Finance
13 Chestnut Hill Plz.
Newark, DE 19713-2701
(302)368-8507
Location Type: Branch office. **Officer:** Mr. Jim Batty. **Ultimate Parent:** American General Corp. **SIC:** 6141—Personal Credit Institutions; 6162—Mortgage Bankers & Correspondents.

★ 57887 ★   American General Finance Inc.
13 Chestnut Hill Plz.
Newark, DE 19713-2701
(302)368-8507
Location Type: Branch office. **Officer:** Mr. Jim Batty. **Ultimate Parent:** American General Corp. **SIC:** 6141—Personal Credit Institutions; 6162—Mortgage Bankers & Correspondents.

★ 57888 ★   AMP-AKZO Corp.
710 Dawson Dr.
Newark, DE 19713-3414
(302)292-6240
Officer: Mr. Edward J. Grosso Jr. **Ultimate Parent:** AMP Inc. **SIC:** 3671—Electron Tubes.

★ 57889 ★   Automatic Data Processing
Prestbury Sq., Ste. 7
Newark, DE 19713-2608
(302)652-0908
Officer: Mr. Keven Dolan. **Ultimate Parent:** Automatic Data Processing, Inc. **SIC:** 7374—Data Processing & Preparation.

★ 57890 ★   Avon Products Inc.
2100 Ogletown Rd.
Newark, DE 19711-5431
(302)453-7788
Ultimate Parent: Avon Products, Inc. **SIC:** 5122—Drugs, Proprietaries & Sundries; 2844—Toilet Preparations; 5999—Miscellaneous Retail Stores Nec.

★ 57891 ★   Avon Sales & Distribution Branch
2100 Ogletown Rd.
Newark, DE 19711
(302)453-7700
Officer: Charles H. Google, Area Vice President. **Ultimate Parent:** Avon Products, Inc. **SIC:** 5122—Drugs, Proprietaries & Sundries.

★ 57892 ★   Bank of Delaware
425 New London Rd.
Newark, DE 19711-7009
(302)733-7182
Location Type: Branch office. **Ultimate Parent:** PNC Bank Corp. **SIC:** 6021—National Commercial Banks.

★ 57893 ★   Bank of Delaware
15 Polly Drummond Ctr.
Newark, DE 19711-4859
(302)733-7201
Location Type: Branch office. **Ultimate Parent:** PNC Bank Corp. **SIC:** 6021—National Commercial Banks.

★ 57894 ★   Bank of Delaware
201 Newark Shopping Ctr.
Newark, DE 19711-7316
(302)733-7208
Location Type: Branch office. **Ultimate Parent:** PNC Bank Corp. **SIC:** 6021—National Commercial Banks.

★ 57895 ★   Beneficial Delaware Inc.
1450 Capitol Tr.
Newark, DE 19711-5714
(302)456-1602
Ultimate Parent: Beneficial. **SIC:** 6141—Personal Credit Institutions; 6162—Mortgage Bankers & Correspondents.

★ 57896 ★   Beneficial Mortgage Corp.
Christian Executive Campus
Newark, DE 19713
(302)731-2500
Ultimate Parent: Beneficial. **SIC:** 6162—Mortgage Bankers & Correspondents.

★ 57897 ★   Beneficial Mortgage Corp.
200 Continental Dr.
Newark, DE 19714
(302)451-7500 **Fax:** (302)451-7581
Location Type: Branch office. **Ultimate Parent:** Beneficial.

★ 57898 ★   Beneficial National Bank
15 Possum Pk. Mall
Newark, DE 19711-5539
(302)425-2391
Location Type: Branch office. **Ultimate Parent:** Beneficial. **SIC:** 6021—National Commercial Banks.

★ 57899 ★   Blazer Financial Services
860 Peoples Plz.
Newark, DE 19702
(302)368-8793
Ultimate Parent: Great Western Financial Corp. **SIC:** 6141—Personal Credit Institutions.

★ 57900 ★   BNY Holdings (Delaware) Corp.
White Clay Ctr.
Rte. 273
Newark, DE 19711
(302)451-7400 **Fax:** (302)454-6170
Company Type: Subsidiary. **Location Type:** Branch office. **Officer:** Robert H. Burke, President. **Ultimate Parent:** Bank of New York Co. **SIC:** 6712—Bank Holding Companies.

★ 57901 ★   Casual Corner
Christiana Mall
Newark, DE 19702
(302)366-7480
Ultimate Parent: United States Shoe. **SIC:** 5621—Women's Clothing Stores.

★ 57902 ★   Eckerd Drugs
RR 1
Newark, DE 19702
(302)737-4440
Ultimate Parent: Eckerd Corp. **SIC:** 5912—Drug Stores & Proprietary Stores.

★ 57903 ★   Equitable Life Insurance Co.
126 E. Main St.
Newark, DE 19711
(302)368-8571
Ultimate Parent: American General Corp. **SIC:** 6411—Insurance Agents, Brokers & Service.

★ 57904 ★   FMC Corp.
1301 Ogletown Rd.
Newark, DE 19711
(302)451-0100
Officer: James Cronin, Manager. **Ultimate Parent:** FMC. **SIC:** 2812—Alkalies & Chlorine; 2879—Agricultural Chemicals Nec; 2834—Pharmaceutical Preparations.

★ 57905 ★   Fmc Corp. Newark
1301 Ogletown Rd.
Newark, DE 19711-5496
Ultimate Parent: FMC. **SIC:** 2869—Industrial Organic Chemicals Nec.

★ 57906 ★   Fmc Corp.-Newark De.
1301 Ogletown Rd.
Newark, DE 19711-5496
Ultimate Parent: FMC. **SIC:** 2869—Industrial Organic Chemicals Nec.

★ 57907 ★   Fmc Corp. Newark Delaware Plant
1301 Ogletown Rd.
Newark, DE 19711-5496
Ultimate Parent: FMC. **SIC:** 2869—Industrial Organic Chemicals Nec.

★ 57908 ★   The Gap
Christiana Mall
Newark, DE 19702
(302)366-7424
Ultimate Parent: GAP. **SIC:** 5611—Men's & Boys' Clothing Stores.

★ 57909 ★   Gaylord Container Corp.
1001 Ogletown Rd.
Newark, DE 19711
(302)737-6000
Officer: Tim Coffey, Manager. **Ultimate Parent:** Gaylord Container. **SIC:** 2652—Setup Paperboard Boxes.

★ 57910 ★   Gaylords National Corp.
Chestnut Hill Shopping Ctr.
Newark, DE 19711
(302)731-9105
Ultimate Parent: TJX. **SIC:** 5311—Department Stores.

★ 57911 ★   J P Morgan Services
500 Stanton Christiana Rd.
Newark, DE 19713-2107
(302)992-1000
Officer: Mr. Daominique Landi. **Ultimate Parent:** J.P. Morgan & Co. **SIC:** 6035—Federal Savings Institutions.

★ 57912 ★   James River Corp.
Curtis Div.
225 Paper Mill Rd.
Newark, DE 19711
Company Type: Division. **Ultimate Parent:** James River Corp. of Virginia. **SIC:** 2621—Paper Mills.

★ 57913 ★   James River Corp.
Curtis Div.
225 Paper Mill Rd.
Newark, DE 19711
Company Type: Division. **Ultimate Parent:** James River Corp. of Virginia. **SIC:** 2621—Paper Mills.

★ 57914 ★   James River Paper Co. Inc.
Curtis Div.
225 Paper Mill Rd.
Newark, DE 19711
Company Type: Division. **Ultimate Parent:** James River Corp. of Virginia. **SIC:** 2621—Paper Mills.

★ 57915 ★   Macy's
501 Christiana Mall
Newark, DE 19702-3298
(302)366-5800
Officer: Ms. Lois Sessa. **Ultimate Parent:** R. H. Macy. **SIC:** 5311—Department Stores.

★ 57916 ★   MBNA
400 Christiana Rd.
Newark, DE 19713
(302)456-8588
Company Type: Headquarters. **Officer:** Alfred Lerner. **Fortune Service 500:** Ranking 74.

★ 57917 ★   MBNA America Bank, NA
400 Christiana Rd.
Newark, DE 19713-4236
(302)456-8588 **Fax:** (302)456-8541
Location Type: Branch office. **Ultimate Parent:** MBNA. **SIC:** 6021—National Commercial Banks.

★ 57918 ★   MBNA Corp.
400 Christiana Rd.
Newark, DE 19713
(302)456-8588 **Fax:** (302)456-8541
Location Type: Branch office. **Ultimate Parent:** MBNA.

★ 57919 ★   McDonald's Hamburgers
815 S. College Ave.
Newark, DE 19713
(302)738-7857
Ultimate Parent: McDonald's. **SIC:** 5812—Eating Places.

★ 57920 ★   Mellon Bank (DE) NA
University of Delaware Campus
Newark, DE 19716
(302)456-7106
Location Type: Branch office. **Ultimate Parent:** Mellon Bank Corp. **SIC:** 6021—National Commercial Banks.

★ 57921 ★   Mellon Bank (DE) NA
40 Chestnut Hill Plz.
Newark, DE 19713-2210
(302)456-7110
Location Type: Branch office. **Ultimate Parent:** Mellon Bank Corp. **SIC:** 6021—National Commercial Banks.

★ 57922 ★   Mellon Bank (DE) NA
126 E. Main St.
Newark, DE 19711
(302)456-7100
Location Type: Branch office. **Ultimate Parent:** Mellon Bank Corp. **SIC:** 6021—National Commercial Banks.

★ 57923 ★   Newark Assembly Plant
550 S. College Ave.
Newark, DE 19714-6040
Ultimate Parent: Chrysler Corp. **SIC:** 3711—Motor Vehicles & Car Bodies.

★ 57924 ★   Newark Assembly Plant
550 South College Ave.
Newark, DE 19714
Ultimate Parent: Chrysler Corp. **SIC:** 3711—Motor Vehicles & Car Bodies.

★ 57925 ★   Petite Sophisticate
Christiana Mall
Newark, DE 19702
(302)738-9095
Ultimate Parent: United States Shoe. **SIC:** 5621—Women's Clothing Stores.

★ 57926 ★   Radio Shack
Universal Plz.
Newark, DE 19711
(302)737-4840
Company Type: Division. **Ultimate Parent:** Tandy Corp. **SIC:** 5065—Electronic Parts & Equipment Nec.

★ 57927 ★   Radio Shack
Castle Mall
Newark, DE 19713
(302)737-5702
Company Type: Division. **Ultimate Parent:** Tandy Corp. **SIC:** 5065—Electronic Parts & Equipment Nec.

★ 57928 ★   Radio Shack
Christiana Mall
Newark, DE 19702
(302)366-7407
Company Type: Division. **Ultimate Parent:** Tandy Corp. **SIC:** 5065—Electronic Parts & Equipment Nec.

★ 57929 ★   Rite Aid
245 Elkton Rd.
Newark, DE 19711
(302)368-1614
Ultimate Parent: Rite Aid. **SIC:** 5912—Drug Stores & Proprietary Stores.

★ 57930 ★   Ryder Truck Rental Inc.
1005 S. College Ave.
Newark, DE 19713
(302)731-8357
Ultimate Parent: Ryder System. **SIC:** 7359—Equipment Rental & Leasing Nec.

★ 57931 ★   Ryder Truck Rental Inc.
1400 Kirkwood Hwy.
Newark, DE 19711
(302)738-5614
Ultimate Parent: Ryder System. **SIC:** 7359—Equipment Rental & Leasing Nec.

★ 57932 ★   Shell Food Mart
1148 Christiana Rd.
Newark, DE 19713
(302)454-7544
Ultimate Parent: Shell Oil Co.

★ 57933 ★   Toys R US
10 Geoffrey Dr.
Newark, DE 19713
(302)731-4556
Ultimate Parent: Toys "R" US. **SIC:** 5945—Hobby, Toy & Game Shops.

★ 57934 ★   Westvaco Corp.
2000 Ogletown Rd.
Newark, DE 19711
(302)453-7200
Ultimate Parent: WestVaco Corp. **SIC:** 5113—Industrial & Personal Service Paper.

★ 57935 ★   Westvaco Corp.
Folding Carton
2000 Ogletown Rd.
Newark, DE 19711
Ultimate Parent: WestVaco Corp. **SIC:** 2600—Paper & Allied Products.

★ 57936 ★   WestVaco Corp.
Folding Carton Div.
2000 Ogletown Rd.
Newark, DE 19711
(302)453-7200
Company Type: Division. **Location Type:** Plant. **Officer:** Frank Alcamo, Plant Manager. **Ultimate Parent:** WestVaco Corp. **SIC:** 2652—Setup Paperboard Boxes; 2657—Folding Paperboard Boxes.

Newcastle

★ 57937 ★   Rite Aid
Crossroads Shopping. Ctr.
Newcastle, DE 19720
(302)652-9986
Ultimate Parent: Rite Aid. **SIC:** 5912—Drug Stores & Proprietary Stores.

★ 57938 ★   Rite Aid
Penn Mart Shopping. Ctr.
Newcastle, DE 19720
(302)328-9681
Ultimate Parent: Rite Aid. **SIC:** 5912—Drug Stores & Proprietary Stores.

Odessa

★ 57939 ★   Bank of Delaware
Main St. & 2nd
Odessa, DE 19730
(302)378-9801
Location Type: Branch office. **Ultimate Parent:** PNC Bank Corp. **SIC:** 6021—National Commercial Banks.

Ogletown

★ 57940 ★   Bank of Delaware
Stanton-Ogletown Rd.
Ogletown, DE 19713
(302)733-7192
Location Type: Branch office. **Ultimate Parent:** PNC Bank Corp. **SIC:** 6021—National Commercial Banks.

★ 57941 ★   Bank of Delaware
University Plaza Shopping Ctr.
Ogletown, DE 19711-7942
(302)733-7168
Location Type: Branch office. **Ultimate Parent:** PNC Bank Corp. **SIC:** 6021—National Commercial Banks.

Rehoboth Beach

★ 57942 ★   Baltimore Trust Co.
Hwy. 1
Rehoboth Beach, DE 19971-2600
(302)227-2600
Location Type: Branch office. **Officer:** Jim Barr, Assistant Vice President. **Ultimate Parent:** Mercantile Bankshares Corp. **SIC:** 6021—National Commercial Banks.

★ 57943 ★   Bank of Delaware
Rte. 1 & Sea Air Ave.
Rehoboth Beach, DE 19971-9523
(302)227-5010
Location Type: Branch office. **Ultimate Parent:** PNC Bank Corp. **SIC:** 6021—National Commercial Banks.

★ 57944 ★   Food Lion
Rural Route 1
Rehoboth Beach, DE 19971
(302)227-5756
Ultimate Parent: Food Lion. **SIC:** 5411—Grocery Stores.

★ 57945 ★   Food Lion Inc.
Rural Route 1
Rehoboth Beach, DE 19971
(302)227-5756
Ultimate Parent: Food Lion. **SIC:** 5411—Grocery Stores.

★ 57946 ★   Mellon Bank (DE) NA
41 Rehoboth Ave.
Rehoboth Beach, DE 19971-2190
(302)226-1001
Location Type: Branch office. **Ultimate Parent:** Mellon Bank Corp. **SIC:** 6021—National Commercial Banks.

★ 57947 ★   Mellon Bank (DE) NA
Ocean Bay Mart Shopping Ctr.
Rehoboth Beach, DE 19971
(302)226-1004
Location Type: Branch office. **Ultimate Parent:** Mellon Bank Corp. **SIC:** 6021—National Commercial Banks.

★ 57948 ★   New York Life Insurance
PO Box 851
Rehoboth Beach, DE 19971
(302)645-0144
Ultimate Parent: New York Life. **SIC:** 6411—Insurance Agents, Brokers & Service.

Seaford

★ 57949 ★   Bank of Delaware
300 High St.
Seaford, DE 19973-9920
(302)629-5006
Location Type: Branch office. **Ultimate Parent:** PNC Bank Corp. **SIC:** 6021—National Commercial Banks.

★ 57950 ★   Bank of Delaware
1200 Stein Hwy.
Seaford, DE 19973-1151
(302)629-5000
Location Type: Branch office. **Ultimate Parent:** PNC Bank Corp. **SIC:** 6021—National Commercial Banks.

★ 57951 ★   Mellon Bank (DE) NA
Nylon Capital Shopping Ctr.
Seaford, DE 19973-1147
(302)629-3912
Location Type: Branch office. **Ultimate Parent:** Mellon Bank Corp. **SIC:** 6021—National Commercial Banks.

★ 57952 ★   Radio Shack
Nylon Capitol Shopping Ctr.
Seaford, DE 19973
(302)629-9420
Company Type: Division. **Ultimate Parent:** Tandy Corp. **SIC:** 5065—Electronic Parts & Equipment Nec.

★ 57953 ★   Rite Aid
Ames Seaford Shoppingce
Seaford, DE 19973
(302)629-9986
Ultimate Parent: Rite Aid. **SIC:** 5912—Drug Stores & Proprietary Stores.

★ 57954 ★   Thrift Drug
411 W. Stein Hwy.
Seaford, DE 19973
(302)629-6686
Ultimate Parent: J.C. Penney. **SIC:** 5049—Professional Equipment Nec.

Selbyville

★ 57955 ★   Baltimore Trust Co.
1 W. Church St.
Selbyville, DE 19975
(302)436-8236 **Fax:** (302)436-4263
Location Type: Branch office. **Officer:** Robert E. Dickerson, Chairman of the Board, President & CEO. **Ultimate Parent:** Mercantile Bankshares Corp. **SIC:** 6021—National Commercial Banks.

★ 57956 ★   Baltimore Trust Co.
PO Box 470
Selbyville, DE 19975-0470
(302)436-8236 **Fax:** (302)436-4263
Location Type: Branch office. **Officer:** Robert E. Dickerson, Chairman of the Board, President & CEO. **Ultimate Parent:** Mercantile Bankshares Corp. **SIC:** 6021—National Commercial Banks.

Smyrna

★ 57957 ★   American General Finance
37 E. Glenwood Ave.
Smyrna, DE 19977-1423
(302)653-8591
Ultimate Parent: American General Corp. **SIC:** 6141—Personal Credit Institutions; 6162—Mortgage Bankers & Correspondents.

★ 57958 ★   American General Finance Inc.
37 E. Glenwood Ave.
Smyrna, DE 19977-1423
(302)653-8591
Location Type: Branch office. **Ultimate Parent:** American General Corp. **SIC:** 6141—Personal Credit Institutions; 6162—Mortgage Bankers & Correspondents.

★ 57959 ★   Bank of Delaware
7 S. Main St.
Smyrna, DE 19977-9901
(302)653-2475
Location Type: Branch office. **Ultimate Parent:** PNC Bank Corp. **SIC:** 6021—National Commercial Banks.

★ 57960 ★   Mellon Bank (DE) NA
5 W. Commerce St.
Smyrna, DE 19977
(302)653-9245
Location Type: Branch office. **Ultimate Parent:** Mellon Bank Corp. **SIC:** 6021—National Commercial Banks.

★ 57961 ★   Radio Shack
Smyrna Shopping Ctr.
Smyrna, DE 19977
(302)653-5645
Company Type: Division. **Ultimate Parent:** Tandy Corp. **SIC:** 5065—Electronic Parts & Equipment Nec.

★ 57962 ★   Radio Shack
Smyrna Shopping Ctr.
Smyrna, DE 19977
(302)653-5645
Company Type: Division. **Ultimate Parent:** Tandy Corp. **SIC:** 5065—Electronic Parts & Equipment Nec.

Talleyville

★ 57963 ★   Beneficial National Bank
Talleyville Pke.
Talleyville, DE 19803-1716
(302)429-1453
Location Type: Branch office. **Ultimate Parent:** Beneficial. **SIC:** 6021—National Commercial Banks.

Wilimington

★ 57964 ★   Eaton Administration Corp.
PO Box 8985
1105 N. Market St.
Wilimington, DE 19899
(302)652-3319
Company Type: Subsidiary. **Ultimate Parent:** Eaton Corp.

Wilmington

★ 57965 ★   ACME Markets
Limestone & New Linden Ave. Pke.
Wilmington, DE 19808
(302)997-9947
Officer: Mr. Bill Kirk. **Ultimate Parent:** American Stores. **SIC:** 5411—Grocery Stores.

★ 57966 ★   ACME Markets
Foulk & Naamans Rd.
Wilmington, DE 19810
(302)475-4618
Officer: Mr. Joe Kelly. **Ultimate Parent:** American Stores. **SIC:** 5411—Grocery Stores.

★ 57967 ★   ACME Markets
1401 N. DuPont St.
Wilmington, DE 19806-4029
(302)658-0575
Officer: Mr. Dave Kauffman. **Ultimate Parent:** American Stores. **SIC:** 5411—Grocery Stores.

★ 57968 ★   Acme Markets
Concord Pike/Murphy Rd.
Wilmington, DE 19803
(302)654-1803
Ultimate Parent: American Stores. **SIC:** 5411—Grocery Stores.

★ 57969 ★   Acme Markets
1308 Centerville Rd.
Wilmington, DE 19808
(302)994-9987
Ultimate Parent: American Stores. **SIC:** 5411—Grocery Stores.

★ 57970 ★   ACME Markets
1308 Centerville Rd.
Wilmington, DE 19808-6220
(302)994-3660
Location Type: Branch office. **Officer:** Mr. Steve Tolmie. **Ultimate Parent:** American Stores. **SIC:** 5411—Grocery Stores.

★ 57971 ★   ACME Markets Inc.
Concord Mall
Murphy Rd.
Wilmington, DE 19803
(302)654-1803
Location Type: Branch office. **Officer:** Mr. John McKeon. **Ultimate Parent:** American Stores. **SIC:** 5411—Grocery Stores.

★ 57972 ★   ACME Markets Inc.
Concord Mall
Murphy Rd.
Wilmington, DE 19803
(302)654-1803
Location Type: Branch office. **Officer:** Mr. John McKeon. **Ultimate Parent:** American Stores. **SIC:** 5411—Grocery Stores.

★ 57973 ★   ADP Automatic Data Processing
201 N. Walnut St., Ste. 901
Wilmington, DE 19801-3999
(302)571-0820
Officer: Mr. Jim Sullivan. **Ultimate Parent:** Automatic Data Processing, Inc. **SIC:** 7374—Data Processing & Preparation; 6719—Holding Companies Nec.

★ 57974 ★   AIG Marketing Inc.
505 Carr Rd.
Wilmington, DE 19809-2865
(302)761-3000
Officer: J. Ernest Hansen, President. **Ultimate Parent:** American International Group, Inc. **SIC:** 6411—Insurance Agents, Brokers & Service. **Employee Count:** 217.

★ 57975 ★   ALG Life Insurance Co.
1 Alco Plz.
Wilmington, DE 19801
(302)594-2000
Officer: Robert O'Connell, President. **Ultimate Parent:** American International Group, Inc. **SIC:** 6311—Life Insurance. **Employee Count:** 250.

★ 57976 ★   American Express Centurion Bank
301 N. Walnut St.
Wilmington, DE 19801
(302)576-4600
Location Type: Branch office. **Ultimate Parent:** American Express Co.

★ 57977 ★   American Express Credit Corp.
1 Rodney Sq.
Wilmington, DE 19801
(302)594-3350
Company Type: Subsidiary. **Ultimate Parent:** American Express Co. **SIC:** 6153—Short-Term Business Credit.

★ 57978 ★   American Express Credit Corp.
One Rodney Sq.
Wilmington, DE 19801
(302)594-3360 **Fax:** (302)571-9128
Location Type: Branch office. **Officer:** Vincent P. Lisanke, President & CEO. **Ultimate Parent:** American Express Co. **SIC:** 6021—National Commercial Banks.

★ 57979 ★   American Express Credit Corp.
1 Rodney Sq., Ste. 8
Wilmington, DE 19801-3350
(302)594-3350
Location Type: Branch office. **Officer:** Vincent P. Lisanke, President & CEO. **Ultimate Parent:** American Express Co. **SIC:** 6153—Short-Term Business Credit. **Employee Count:** 65.

★ 57980 ★   American Life
600 King St.
Wilmington, DE 19899
(302)594-2000
Company Type: Headquarters. **Officer:** R. Kendall Nottingham. **Fortune Service 500:** Ranking 40.

★ 57981 ★   American Life Insurance
Concord
Wilmington, DE 19801
(302)478-6478
Ultimate Parent: American Life. **SIC:** 6411—Insurance Agents, Brokers & Service.

★ 57982 ★   American Life Insurance Co.
12 St.
Wilmington, DE 19801
(302)655-7381
Ultimate Parent: American Life. **SIC:** 6399—Insurance Carriers Nec.

★ 57983 ★   Ametek Corp.
Haveg Div.
900 Greenbank Rd.
Wilmington, DE 19808-5998
(302)995-0400
Company Type: Division. **Location Type:** Branch office. **Officer:** Dudley Barton. **Ultimate Parent:** Ametek Inc. **SIC:** 2295—Coated Fabrics—Not Rubberized; 2262—Finishing Plants—Manmade; 2821—Plastics Materials & Resins; 3083—Laminated Plastics Plate & Sheet; 3084—Plastics Pipe; 3089—Plastics Products Nec; 3229—Pressed & Blown Glass Nec; 3443—Fabricated Plate Work—Boiler Shops; 3499—Fabricated Metal Products Nec; 3769—Space Vehicle Equipment Nec.

★ 57984 ★   **Ametek Inc.**
Haveg Division
900 Greenbank Rd.
Wilmington, DE 19808
(302)995-0400 **Fax:** (302)995-0491
Company Type: Subsidiary. **Officer:** H.
Dudley Barton, Vice President & General
Manager. **Ultimate Parent:** Ametek Inc.

★ 57985 ★   **Ametek, Inc.**
Heaveg Div.
900 Greenbank Rd.
Wilmington, DE 19808
Company Type: Division. **Ultimate Parent:**
Ametek Inc. **SIC:** 3083—Laminated Plastics
Plate & Sheet; 2241—Narrow Fabric Mills;
2262—Finishing Plants—Manmade; 2821—
Plastics Materials & Resins.

★ 57986 ★   **Aqualon Co.**
Hercules Plaza
Wilmington, DE 19894
(302)594-5000 **Fax:** (302)594-5400
Company Type: Subsidiary. **Officer:**
Dominick DiDonna, Vice President &
General Manager. **Ultimate Parent:**
Hercules.

★ 57987 ★   **Armstrong Cork
Finance Corp.**
300 Delaware Ave.
Wilmington, DE 19899
(302)652-7940
Company Type: Subsidiary. **Ultimate
Parent:** Armstrong World Industries. **SIC:**
6719—Holding Companies Nec.

★ 57988 ★   **Armstrong Ventures,
Inc.**
300 Delaware Ave.
Wilmington, DE 19899
Company Type: Subsidiary. **Ultimate
Parent:** Armstrong World Industries. **SIC:**
6159—Miscellaneous Business Credit
Institutions.

★ 57989 ★   **Armstrong World
Industries (DE), Inc.**
300 Delaware Ave.
Wilmington, DE 19899
(302)652-7940
Company Type: Subsidiary. **Ultimate
Parent:** Armstrong World Industries. **SIC:**
6719—Holding Companies Nec.

★ 57990 ★   **Bank of Delaware**
1009 Union St.
Wilmington, DE 19805-2752
(302)429-1761
Location Type: Branch office. **Ultimate
Parent:** PNC Bank Corp. **SIC:** 6021—
National Commercial Banks.

★ 57991 ★   **Bank of Delaware**
201 N. Union St.
Wilmington, DE 19805-3429
(302)429-1624
Location Type: Branch office. **Ultimate
Parent:** PNC Bank Corp. **SIC:** 6021—
National Commercial Banks.

★ 57992 ★   **Bank of Delaware**
4111 Concord Pke.
Wilmington, DE 19803-1401
(302)429-1453
Location Type: Branch office. **Ultimate
Parent:** PNC Bank Corp. **SIC:** 6021—
National Commercial Banks.

★ 57993 ★   **Bank of Delaware**
5325 Limestone Rd.
Wilmington, DE 19808-1222
(302)429-2800
Ultimate Parent: PNC Bank Corp. **SIC:**
6021—National Commercial Banks.

★ 57994 ★   **Bank of Delaware**
901 Market St.
Wilmington, DE 19801-3022
(302)429-1321
Location Type: Branch office. **Ultimate
Parent:** PNC Bank Corp. **SIC:** 6021—
National Commercial Banks.

★ 57995 ★   **Bank of Delaware**
4323 Governor Printz Blvd.
Wilmington, DE 19802-1705
(302)429-1244
Location Type: Branch office. **Officer:**
Jamie Lane, Manager. **Ultimate Parent:**
PNC Bank Corp. **SIC:** 6021—National
Commercial Banks.

★ 57996 ★   **Bank of Delaware**
300 Delaware Ave.
Wilmington, DE 19801-1653
(302)429-1353
Location Type: Branch office. **Ultimate
Parent:** PNC Bank Corp. **SIC:** 6021—
National Commercial Banks.

★ 57997 ★   **Bank of Delaware**
Midway Shopping Ctr.
Wilmington, DE 19808
(302)429-1535
Location Type: Branch office. **Ultimate
Parent:** PNC Bank Corp. **SIC:** 6021—
National Commercial Banks.

★ 57998 ★   **Bank of Delaware**
1704 Marsh Rd.
Wilmington, DE 19803-4600
(302)429-1740
Location Type: Branch office. **Ultimate
Parent:** PNC Bank Corp. **SIC:** 6021—
National Commercial Banks.

★ 57999 ★   **Bank of Delaware**
519 Market St.
Wilmington, DE 19801-3004
(302)429-1331
Location Type: Branch office. **Ultimate
Parent:** PNC Bank Corp. **SIC:** 6021—
National Commercial Banks.

★ 58000 ★   **Bank of Delaware**
222 Delaware Ave.
Wilmington, DE 19801-1621
(302)429-1011
Location Type: Branch office. **Ultimate
Parent:** PNC Bank Corp. **SIC:** 6021—
National Commercial Banks.

★ 58001 ★   **Bank of Delaware**
PO Box 791
Wilmington, DE 19899
Location Type: Branch office. **Ultimate
Parent:** PNC Bank Corp. **SIC:** 6021—
National Commercial Banks.

★ 58002 ★   **Bankers Trust**
1001 Jefferson St.
Wilmington, DE 19801-1447
(302)594-4400
Location Type: Branch office. **Officer:**
James Stalkamp. **Ultimate Parent:** Bankers
Trust New York Corp. **SIC:** 6022—State
Commercial Banks; 6021—National
Commercial Banks.

★ 58003 ★   **Bankers Trust
Delaware**
1001 N. Jefferson St., 5th Fl.
Wilmington, DE 19801-1447
(302)594-4400
Company Type: Subsidiary. **Officer:**
George J. Vojta, Chairman of the Board.
Ultimate Parent: Bankers Trust New York
Corp. **SIC:** 6021—National Commercial
Banks. **Employee Count:** 185.

★ 58004 ★   **Bell Atlantic Capital
Funding Corp.**
501 Carr Rd., Ste. 201
Wilmington, DE 19809
Company Type: Subsidiary. **Ultimate
Parent:** Bell Atlantic Corp.

★ 58005 ★   **Bell Atlantic Capital
Investments, Inc.**
501 Carr Rd., Ste. 201
Wilmington, DE 19801
Company Type: Subsidiary. **Ultimate
Parent:** Bell Atlantic Corp.

★ 58006 ★   **Bell Atlantic Financial
Services**
1001 Jefferson Plz., 5th Fl.
Wilmington, DE 19801
(302)429-8000
Company Type: Subsidiary. **Ultimate
Parent:** Bell Atlantic Corp.

★ 58007 ★   **Bell Atlantic Financial
Svs.**
501 Carr Rd. Ste. 201
Wilmington, DE 19809-2863
(302)761-4200
Officer: Joseph Purcell. **Ultimate Parent:**
Bell Atlantic Corp. **SIC:** 6159—
Miscellaneous Business Credit Institutions.

★ 58008 ★   **Bell Atlantic
Investments, Inc.**
501 Carr Rd., Ste. 201
Wilmington, DE 19809
Company Type: Subsidiary. **Ultimate
Parent:** Bell Atlantic Corp.

★ 58009 ★   **Bell Atlantic Mobile
Systems**
502 First State Blvd.
Wilmington, DE 19804-3746
(302)633-1000
Officer: Robin Smith. **Ultimate Parent:** Bell
Atlantic Corp. **SIC:** 4813—Telephone
Communications Except Radiotelephone;
5065—Electronic Parts & Equipment Nec.

★ 58010 ★   **Bell Atlantic Network
Funding Corp.**
501 Carr Rd., Ste. 201
Wilmington, DE 19809
Company Type: Subsidiary. **Ultimate
Parent:** Bell Atlantic Corp.

★ 58011 ★   **Bell Atlantic New
Zealand Investments, Inc.**
501 Carr Rd., Ste. 201
Wilmington, DE
Company Type: Subsidiary. **Ultimate
Parent:** Bell Atlantic Corp.

★ 58012 ★   **Bell atlantic Financial
Services**
501 Carr Rd., Ste. 201
Wilmington, DE 19809-2863
(302)761-4200
Company Type: Subsidiary. **Officer:** Janet
Garrity, President. **Ultimate Parent:** Bell
Atlantic Corp. **SIC:** 8741—Management
Services. **Sales:** 48 M.

★ 58013 ★   **Bencharge Credit
Service of America, Inc.**
400 Bellevue Pky.
Wilmington, DE 19809
(302)792-0800
Company Type: Subsidiary. **Officer:** Ross
N. Longfield, President. **Ultimate Parent:**
Beneficial. **SIC:** 6141—Personal Credit
Institutions.

★ 58014 ★   **Beneficial**
301 N. Walnut St.
Wilmington, DE 19801
(302)425-2500
Company Type: Headquarters. **Officer:**
Finn M. W. Caspersen. **Employee Count:**
8200. **Fortune Service 500:** Ranking 31.

★ 58015 ★   **Beneficial Corp.**
PO Box 911
Wilmington, DE 19899-0911
(302)798-0800
Location Type: Headquarters. **Officer:** Finn
M. W. Caspersen. **Ultimate Parent:**
Beneficial. **SIC:** 6719—Holding Companies
Nec; 6021—National Commercial Banks;
6035—Federal Savings Institutions; 6141—
Personal Credit Institutions; 6162—
Mortgage Bankers & Correspondents;
6351—Surety Insurance; 6552—Subdividers
& Developers Nec.

★ 58016 ★   **Beneficial Corp.**
301 N. Walnut St.
Wilmington, DE 19801
(302)425-2500
Officer: Finn M. W. Caspersen, CEO.
Ultimate Parent: Beneficial.

★ 58017 ★   **Beneficial Corp.**
400 Bellevue Pky.
Wilmington, DE 19899
(302)798-0800
Location Type: Branch office. **Officer:** Finn
M.W. Caspersen, Chairman of the Board &
CEO. **Ultimate Parent:** Beneficial. **SIC:**
6021—National Commercial Banks.

★ 58018 ★   **Beneficial
Management Corp. of America &
Affiliated Corp.**
1100 Carr Rd.
Wilmington, DE 19809
(302)798-0800
Company Type: Subsidiary. **Ultimate
Parent:** Beneficial.

★ 58019 ★   **Beneficial National
Bank**
400 Bellevue Pky.
Wilmington, DE 19809
(302)798-0800
Company Type: Subsidiary. **Officer:** James
H. Gilliam Jr., Chm. Bd. **Ultimate Parent:**
Beneficial. **SIC:** 6022—State Commercial
Banks; 6021—National Commercial Banks.
Sales: 190600000 M.

★ 58020 ★   **Beneficial National
Bank**
400 Bellevue Pky.
Wilmington, DE 19809-3706
(302)792-4600
Company Type: Subsidiary. **Officer:** James
H. Gilliam Jr., Chairman of the Board.
Ultimate Parent: Beneficial. **SIC:** 6021—
National Commercial Banks. **Employee
Count:** 165.

★ 58021 ★   **Beneficial National
Bank**
301 N. Walnut St.
Wilmington, DE 19801
(302)425-2000
Location Type: Branch office. **Ultimate
Parent:** Beneficial. **SIC:** 6021—National
Commercial Banks.

★ 58022 ★   **Beneficial National
Bank**
1800 W. 4th St.
Wilmington, DE 19805-3499
(302)425-2378
Location Type: Branch office. **Officer:**
John Reale Jr., Manager. **Ultimate Parent:**
Beneficial. **SIC:** 6021—National Commercial
Banks.

★ 58023 ★   **Beneficial National
Bank**
PO Box 1551
Wilmington, DE 19899-1551
Location Type: Branch office. **Ultimate
Parent:** Beneficial. **SIC:** 6021—National
Commercial Banks.

★ 58024 ★   **Beneficial National
Bank**
1300 Market St.
Wilmington, DE 19801-1136
(302)425-2387
Location Type: Branch office. **Officer:** Joe
Atz, Manager. **Ultimate Parent:** Beneficial.
SIC: 6021—National Commercial Banks.

★ 58025 ★   **Beneficial National
Bank USA**
1405 Foulk Rd.
Wilmington, DE 19803
(302)478-9056
Company Type: Subsidiary. **Ultimate
Parent:** Beneficial. **SIC:** 6021—National
Commercial Banks.

★ 58026 ★   **Beneficial National
Bank USA**
PO Box 7494
Wilmington, DE 19803
Company Type: Subsidiary. **Ultimate
Parent:** Beneficial. **SIC:** 6021—National
Commercial Banks.

★ 58027 ★   **Beneficial National
Bank USA**
400 Bellevue Pky.
Wilmington, DE 19809
(302)798-0800
Company Type: Subsidiary. **Officer:** Ross
N. Longfield, Presisent & CEO. **Ultimate
Parent:** Beneficial. **SIC:** 6153—Short-Term
Business Credit.

★ 58028 ★   **Beneficial National
Bank USA**
1405 Foulk Rd., Ste. 100
Wilmington, DE 19803-2756
(302)478-9056
Company Type: Subsidiary. **Officer:** Ross
N. Longfield, President & CEO. **Ultimate
Parent:** Beneficial. **SIC:** 7389—Business
Services Nec. **Employee Count:** 503.
Sales: 16 M.

★ 58029 ★   **Beneficial National
Bank-USA**
1405 Foulk Rd.
Wilmington, DE 19803-2765
(302)478-9056
Ultimate Parent: Beneficial. **SIC:** 6021—
National Commercial Banks.

★ 58030 ★   **Casual Corner**
Concord Mall
Wilmington, DE 19803
(302)478-5800
Ultimate Parent: United States Shoe. **SIC:**
5621—Women's Clothing Stores; 5946—
Camera & Photographic Supply Stores.

★ 58031 ★ Chase Manhatten Bank (USA)
1 Chase Manhatten Plz.
802 Delaware Ave.
Wilmington, DE 19801-1398
(302)575-5000 Telex: 628-32723
Location Type: Branch office. Ultimate Parent: Chase Manhattan Corp. SIC: 6022—State Commercial Banks.

★ 58032 ★ Chase Manhatten Bank (USA)
PO Box 15018
Wilmington, DE 19850-5018
Ultimate Parent: Chase Manhattan Corp. SIC: 6022—State Commercial Banks.

★ 58033 ★ Chase Manhatten Overseas Banking Corp.
802 Delaware Ave.
Wilmington, DE 19801-1300
(302)575-5923 Fax: (302)429-0456 Telex: 1561738
Location Type: Branch office. Ultimate Parent: Chase Manhattan Corp.

★ 58034 ★ Chase Manhatten Overseas Banking Corp.
PO Box 15371
Wilmington, DE 19850
Location Type: Branch office. Ultimate Parent: Chase Manhattan Corp.

★ 58035 ★ Chemical Bank Delaware
1201 Market St.
Wilmington, DE 19801-1160
(302)428-3300 Fax: (302)654-3008 Telex: RCA 244984
Location Type: Branch office. Ultimate Parent: Chemical Banking Corp.

★ 58036 ★ Chemical Bank Delaware
1201 N. Market St. 9th Fl.
Wilmington, DE 19801-1147
(302)428-3300
Company Type: Subsidiary. Officer: Richard J. Nolan Jr., President. Ultimate Parent: Chemical Banking Corp. SIC: 6022—State Commercial Banks. Employee Count: 148.

★ 58037 ★ Church Street Capital Corp.
Wilmington Trust Ctr.
1100 N. Market St., Ste. 780
Wilmington, DE 19801
(302)654-0416
Company Type: Subsidiary. Officer: William S. Lee, President. Ultimate Parent: Duke Power. SIC: 6726—Investment Offices Nec. Sales: 19818456 M.

★ 58038 ★ Cigna Holdings Inc.
1 Beaver Valley Rd.
Wilmington, DE 19803-1115
(302)479-6000
Company Type: Subsidiary. Officer: Paul B. Lukens, Ch. Bd. & President. Ultimate Parent: Cigna Corp. SIC: 6311—Life Insurance; 6321—Accident & Health Insurance; 6331—Fire, Marine & Casualty Insurance; 6512—Nonresidential Building Operators; 6514—Dwelling Operators Except Apartments; 6282—Investment Advice. Employee Count: 24260.

★ 58039 ★ Cigna Worldwide Insurance Co. Inc.
1 Beaver Valley Rd.
Wilmington, DE 19803-1115
(302)479-6000
Company Type: Subsidiary. Officer: Virginia Hollis, President. Ultimate Parent: Cigna Corp. SIC: 6311—Life Insurance; 6331—Fire, Marine & Casualty Insurance. Employee Count: 40.

★ 58040 ★ Collective Federal Savings Bank
2201 Silverside Rd.
Wilmington, DE 19810
Company Type: Subsidiary. Location Type: Branch office. Ultimate Parent: Collective Bancorp. SIC: 6021—National Commercial Banks; 6035—Federal Savings Institutions.

★ 58041 ★ Collective Mortgage Service
5301 Limestone Rd.
Wilmington, DE 19808
(302)239-1900
Ultimate Parent: Collective Bancorp. SIC:

6162—Mortgage Bankers & Correspondents.

★ 58042 ★ Columbia Atlantic Trading Corp.
20 Montchanin Rd.
Wilmington, DE 19807
Officer: L. Michael Bridges, President. Ultimate Parent: Columbia Gas System.

★ 58043 ★ Columbia Gas System
20 Montchanin Rd.
Wilmington, DE 19807
(302)429-5000
Company Type: Headquarters. Officer: John H. Croom. Fortune Service 500: Ranking 37.

★ 58044 ★ Columbia Gas System Service Corp.
20 Montchanin Rd.
Wilmington, DE 19807
(302)429-5211
Officer: John H. Croom, Chairman, President & CEO. Ultimate Parent: Columbia Gas System.

★ 58045 ★ Columbia LNG Corp.
20 Montchanin Rd.
Wilmington, DE 19807
Officer: L. Michael Bridges, President & CEO. Ultimate Parent: Columbia Gas System.

★ 58046 ★ Congen Properties Inc.
1 Beaver Valley Rd.
Wilmington, DE 19803-1115
(302)479-6000
Company Type: Subsidiary. Officer: John A. Scott, President. Ultimate Parent: Cigna Corp. SIC: 6512—Nonresidential Building Operators; 6514—Dwelling Operators Except Apartments. Employee Count: 20. Sales: 1 M.

★ 58047 ★ Corestates Bank Of Delaware NA
1523 Concord Pke.
Wilmington, DE 19803-3612
(302)594-1704
Company Type: Subsidiary. Officer: Blair McNeill, Chairman of the Board. Ultimate Parent: Corestates Financial Corp. SIC: 6153—Short-Term Business Credit. Employee Count: 400.

★ 58048 ★ Dauphin Investment Co.
103 Springer Bldg.
341 Silverside Rd.
Wilmington, DE 19805
(302)478-6160
Company Type: Division. Officer: Christopher Jennings, President. Ultimate Parent: Dauphin Deposit Corp. SIC: 6282—Investment Advice.

★ 58049 ★ Delaware American Life Insurance Co.
12th & Market Sts.
Wilmington, DE 19801
(302)428-3800
Officer: Paul A. Finkel, President Domestic Life Companies. Ultimate Parent: American International Group, Inc. SIC: 6311—Life Insurance.

★ 58050 ★ Delaware American Life Insurance Co.
600 N. King St.
Wilmington, DE 19801-3708
(302)594-2000
Officer: Robert O'Connell, President. Ultimate Parent: American International Group, Inc. SIC: 6311—Life Insurance. Employee Count: 3.

★ 58051 ★ Diamond State Telephone Co.
911 Tatnall St.
Wilmington, DE 19801
(302)571-1571 Fax: (302)571-1585
Company Type: Subsidiary. Officer: Carolyn S. Burger, President & CEO. Ultimate Parent: Bell Atlantic Corp. SIC: 4813—Telephone Communications Except Radiotelephone. Employee Count: 1000. Sales: 240000000 M.

★ 58052 ★ The Diamond State Telephone Co. Inc.
901 N. Tatnall St., Ste. 2
Wilmington, DE 19801-1644
(302)571-1571
Company Type: Subsidiary. Officer: Carolyn S. Burger, President & CEO. Ultimate Parent: Bell Atlantic Corp. SIC: 4813—Telephone Communications Except Radiotelephone. Employee Count: 981. Sales: 234 M.

★ 58053 ★ Diamond State Telephone Co. The
300 Delaware Ave.
Wilmington, DE 19801-1608
(302)576-5312
Location Type: Branch office. Officer: Carolyn S. Burger. Ultimate Parent: Bell Atlantic Corp. SIC: 4813—Telephone Communications Except Radiotelephone.

★ 58054 ★ Digital Equipment Corp.
1 Pike Creek Ctr.
Wilmington, DE 19808
(302)995-2111
Ultimate Parent: Digital Equipment Corp. SIC: 7374—Data Processing & Preparation.

★ 58055 ★ E.I. DuPont De Nemours
1007 Market St.
Wilmington, DE 19898
(302)774-1000
Company Type: Headquarters. Officer: Edgar S. Wollard Jr. Employee Count: 114000. Sales: 32 M. Fortune 500: Largest U.S. Industrial Corporations: Ranking 10.

★ 58056 ★ Eaton International Corp.
The Corp. Trust Company
100 W. 10th St.
Wilmington, DE 19801
(302)658-7581 Fax: (302)792-9680
Company Type: Subsidiary. Officer: Patrick X. Donovan, President. Ultimate Parent: Eaton Corp. SIC: 3492—Fluid Power Valves & Hose Fittings; 3317—Steel Pipe & Tubes; 3542—Machine Tools—Metal Forming Types; 3625—Relays & Industrial Controls.

★ 58057 ★ Eckerd Drugs
2005 Concord Pke.
Wilmington, DE 19803
(302)655-8866
Ultimate Parent: Eckerd Corp. SIC: 5912—Drug Stores & Proprietary Stores.

★ 58058 ★ Encoat-North Arlington, Inc.
Corporate Trust Ctr.
1209 Orange Street
Wilmington, DE 19801
Company Type: Subsidiary. Ultimate Parent: Lukens. SIC: 3479—Metal Coating & Allied Services.

★ 58059 ★ Equitable Life Insurance Co.
2502 Silverside Rd.
Wilmington, DE 19810
(302)478-4466
Ultimate Parent: American General Corp. SIC: 6411—Insurance Agents, Brokers & Service.

★ 58060 ★ FCC National Bank
300 N. King St.
Wilmington, DE 19801-2550
(302)594-8530
Company Type: Subsidiary. Officer: Scott Marks Jr., Chairman of the Board, Senior Vice President. Ultimate Parent: First Chicago Corp. SIC: 7389—Business Services Nec. Employee Count: 1943. Sales: 43.5 M.

★ 58061 ★ FCC National Bank
1 Gateway Ctr.
300 King St.
Wilmington, DE 19801
(302)594-8606 Fax: (302)888-6754 Telex: 722462
Location Type: Branch office. Ultimate Parent: First Chicago Corp. SIC: 6021—National Commercial Banks.

★ 58062 ★ First National Bank of Atlanta
PO Box 12485
Wilmington, DE 19850-2485
Location Type: Branch office. Ultimate Parent: Wachovia Corp. SIC: 6021—National Commercial Banks.

★ 58063 ★ Gap the
Concord Mall
Wilmington, DE 19803
(302)478-9640
Ultimate Parent: GAP.

★ 58064 ★ Georgia Pacific Corp.
Wilmington Marine Terminal
Wilmington, DE 19899
(302)658-7221
Officer: Robert Lindsey, Manager. Ultimate Parent: Georgia-Pacific. SIC: 3275—Gypsum Products.

★ 58065 ★ Greyhound Bus Lines
318 N. Market St.
Wilmington, DE 19801
(302)655-6111
Ultimate Parent: Greyhound Lines Inc. SIC: 4111—Local & Suburban Transit.

★ 58066 ★ Hercules
Hercules Plz.
Wilmington, DE 19894
(302)594-5000
Company Type: Headquarters. Officer: Thomas L. Gossage. Employee Count: 14083. Fortune 500: Largest U.S. Industrial Corporations: Ranking 168.

★ 58067 ★ Hercules Aerospace Co.
Hercules Plaza
Wilmington, DE 19894
(302)594-5000 Fax: (302)594-5400
Company Type: Subsidiary. Officer: Richard Schwartz, President. Ultimate Parent: Hercules.

★ 58068 ★ Hercules Chemical Specialty Co.
Hercules Plaza
Wilmington, DE 19894
(302)594-5000 Fax: (302)594-5400
Company Type: Subsidiary. Officer: C. Doyle Miller, President. Ultimate Parent: Hercules.

★ 58069 ★ Hercules Food & Functional Products Co.
Hercules Plaza
Wilmington, DE 19894
(302)594-5000 Fax: (302)594-5400
Company Type: Subsidiary. Officer: Thomas G. Tepas, President. Ultimate Parent: Hercules.

★ 58070 ★ Hercules Inc.
Hercules Plaza
Wilmington, DE 19894
(302)594-5000 Fax: (302)594-5400
Company Type: Headquarters. Officer: Thomas L. Gossage, Chairman, President & CEO. Ultimate Parent: Hercules. Employee Count: 15419.

★ 58071 ★ Hercules Inc. Hercules Research Center
Hercules Rd. & Rte. 48
Wilmington, DE 19803-1599
Ultimate Parent: Hercules. SIC: 2821—Plastics Materials & Resins.

★ 58072 ★ Hercules Inc. Research Center
500 Hercules Rd.
Wilmington, DE 19808-1599
Ultimate Parent: Hercules. SIC: 2821—Plastics Materials & Resins.

★ 58073 ★ Hercules Inc. Research Center
Rte. 48 & Hercules Rd.
Wilmington, DE 19894
Ultimate Parent: Hercules. SIC: 2821—Plastics Materials & Resins.

★ 58074 ★ Hercules Material Co.
Hercules Plaza
Wilmington, DE 19894
(302)594-5000 Fax: (302)594-5400
Company Type: Subsidiary. Officer: Vincent J. Corbo, President. Ultimate Parent: Hercules.

★ 58075 ★ **INA Financial Corp.**
1 Beaver Valley Rd.
Wilmington, DE 19803-1115
(302)792-5100 (302)479-6000
Officer: John Klinge, Manager. **Ultimate
Parent:** Xerox Corp. **SIC:** 3663—Radio &
T.V. Communications Equipment. **Company
Type:** Subsidiary. **Officer:** Bill Hartman,
President & Treasurer. **Ultimate Parent:**
Cigna Corp. **SIC:** 6331—Fire, Marine &
Casualty Insurance; 6321—Accident &
Health Insurance; 6351—Surety Insurance;
6411—Insurance Agents, Brokers &
Service. **Employee Count:** 18000.

★ 58076 ★ **J P Morgan Delaware**
902 Market St.
Wilmington, DE 19801
(302)651-2323
Company Type: Branch. **Officer:** John
Field. **Ultimate Parent:** J.P. Morgan & Co.
SIC: 6733—Trusts Nec; 6021—National
Commercial Banks; 6022—State
Commercial Banks; 6719—Holding
Companies Nec.

★ 58077 ★ **J. Schoeneman Wiltex**
9 Vandever Ave.
Wilmington, DE 19802-0000
Ultimate Parent: West Point Stevens. **SIC:**
2329—Men's/Boys' Clothing Nec.

★ 58078 ★ **Liberty Mutual
Insurance Co.**
7473 PO Box
Wilmington, DE 19803
(302)478-9600
Ultimate Parent: Liberty Mutual Group.
SIC: 6411—Insurance Agents, Brokers &
Service.

★ 58079 ★ **Lubrizol Corp.**
3411 Silverside Rd.
Wilmington, DE 19810
(302)478-3676
Ultimate Parent: Lubrizol. **SIC:** 5169—
Chemicals & Allied Products Nec.

★ 58080 ★ **McDonald's
Hamburgers**
101 New Rd.
Wilmington, DE 19805
(302)656-2010
Ultimate Parent: McDonald's. **SIC:** 5812—
Eating Places.

★ 58081 ★ **Mellon Bank (DE) NA**
Maryland Ave. & Germany Dr.
Wilmington, DE 19804
(302)421-2248
Location Type: Branch office. **Ultimate
Parent:** Mellon Bank Corp. **SIC:** 6021—
National Commercial Banks.

★ 58082 ★ **Mellon Bank (DE) NA**
301 N. Market St. E
Wilmington, DE 19801
(302)421-2261
Location Type: Branch office. **Ultimate
Parent:** Mellon Bank Corp. **SIC:** 6021—
National Commercial Banks.

★ 58083 ★ **Mellon Bank (DE) NA**
1620 Marsh Rd.
Wilmington, DE 19803
(302)477-1205
Location Type: Branch office. **Ultimate
Parent:** Mellon Bank Corp. **SIC:** 6021—
National Commercial Banks.

★ 58084 ★ **Mellon Bank (DE) NA**
16th & DuPont St.
Wilmington, DE 19806
(302)421-2240
Location Type: Branch office. **Ultimate
Parent:** Mellon Bank Corp. **SIC:** 6021—
National Commercial Banks.

★ 58085 ★ **Mellon Bank (DE) NA**
4435 Kirkwood Hwy.
Wilmington, DE 19808
(302)633-4500
Location Type: Branch office. **Ultimate**

Parent: Mellon Bank Corp. **SIC:** 6021—
National Commercial Banks.

★ 58086 ★ **Mellon Bank (DE) NA**
10th & Market St.
Wilmington, DE 19801
(302)995-5700
Location Type: Branch office. **Ultimate
Parent:** Mellon Bank Corp. **SIC:** 6021—
National Commercial Banks.

★ 58087 ★ **Mellon Bank (DE) NA**
4735 Concord Pke.
Wilmington, DE 19803
(302)477-1200
Location Type: Branch office. **Ultimate
Parent:** Mellon Bank Corp. **SIC:** 6021—
National Commercial Banks.

★ 58088 ★ **Monsanto Co.**
3519 Silverside Rd.
Wilmington, DE 19810-4909
(302)479-9646
Ultimate Parent: Monsanto. **SIC:** 5169—
Chemicals & Allied Products Nec.

★ 58089 ★ **New York Life
Insurance Co.**
300 Delaware Ave.
Wilmington, DE 19801
(302)656-9491
Ultimate Parent: New York Life. **SIC:**
6411—Insurance Agents, Brokers &
Service.

★ 58090 ★ **New York Life
Wilmington General Office**
Northeasten Agencies
Bank of Delaware Bldg.
300 Delaware Ave., Ste. 900
Wilmington, DE 19801
(302)656-9491 **Fax:** (302)656-3183
Officer: Jon Walton, General Manager.
Ultimate Parent: New York Life.

★ 58091 ★ **Noramco of Delaware
Inc.**
500 Old Swedes Landing Rd.
Wilmington, DE 19801
Ultimate Parent: Johnson & Johnson. **SIC:**
2833—Medicinals & Botanicals.

★ 58092 ★ **Pepsi-Cola Bottling
Co.**
3501 Governor Printz Blvd.
Wilmington, DE 19802
(302)764-6770
Officer: Lynn Nowicki, Manager. **Ultimate
Parent:** Pepsico. **SIC:** 2086—Bottled &
Canned Soft Drinks.

★ 58093 ★ **PNC National Bank**
103 Bellevue Pky.
Wilmington, DE 19809
(302)791-1200 **Fax:** (302)791-2106
Location Type: Branch office. **Ultimate
Parent:** PNC Bank Corp. **SIC:** 6021—
National Commercial Banks.

★ 58094 ★ **PNC National Bank**
PO Box 8836
Wilmington, DE 19899
Location Type: Branch office. **Ultimate
Parent:** PNC Bank Corp.

★ 58095 ★ **Prodair Corp.**
1105 N. Market St., Ste. 1300
Wilmington, DE 19801
(302)658-5183
Company Type: Subsidiary. **Officer:** James
Christy, President. **Ultimate Parent:** Air
Products & Chemicals, Inc. **SIC:** 6719—
Holding Companies Nec.

★ 58096 ★ **Radio Shack**
Branmar
Wilmington, DE 19810
(302)475-4800
Company Type: Division. **Ultimate Parent:**
Tandy Corp. **SIC:** 5065—Electronic Parts &
Equipment Nec.

★ 58097 ★ **Radio Shack**
Pike Creek Shopping Ctr.
Wilmington, DE 19808
(302)995-1373
Company Type: Division. **Ultimate Parent:**
Tandy Corp. **SIC:** 5065—Electronic Parts &
Equipment Nec.

★ 58098 ★ **Radio Shack**
Kirkwood
Wilmington, DE 19808
(302)999-7670
Company Type: Division. **Ultimate Parent:**
Tandy Corp. **SIC:** 5065—Electronic Parts &
Equipment Nec.

★ 58099 ★ **Radio Shack**
Concord Mall
Wilmington, DE 19803
(302)478-7467
Company Type: Division. **Ultimate Parent:**
Tandy Corp. **SIC:** 5731—Radio, Television
& Electronics Stores.

★ 58100 ★ **Rite Aid**
634 S. Marylandave
Wilmington, DE 19804
(302)994-3473
Ultimate Parent: Rite Aid. **SIC:** 5912—Drug
Stores & Proprietary Stores.

★ 58101 ★ **Rite Aid**
801 N. Marketst
Wilmington, DE 19801
(302)655-7432
Ultimate Parent: Rite Aid. **SIC:** 5912—Drug
Stores & Proprietary Stores.

★ 58102 ★ **Rite Aid**
2080 Naamansrd
Wilmington, DE 19810
(302)475-4690
Ultimate Parent: Rite Aid. **SIC:** 5912—Drug
Stores & Proprietary Stores.

★ 58103 ★ **Rite Aid**
14 Dupontave
Wilmington, DE 19809
(302)652-9053
Ultimate Parent: Rite Aid. **SIC:** 5912—Drug
Stores & Proprietary Stores.

★ 58104 ★ **Rite Aid**
1716 Marshrd
Wilmington, DE 19810
(302)478-9811
Ultimate Parent: Rite Aid. **SIC:** 5912—Drug
Stores & Proprietary Stores.

★ 58105 ★ **Rite Aid**
1306 Centervillerd
Wilmington, DE 19808
(302)994-2575
Ultimate Parent: Rite Aid. **SIC:** 5912—Drug
Stores & Proprietary Stores.

★ 58106 ★ **Rite Aid**
5 W. 8th St.
Wilmington, DE 19801
(302)654-1252
Ultimate Parent: Rite Aid.

★ 58107 ★ **Ryder Truck Rental
Inc.**
6605 Gov Printz Blvd.
Wilmington, DE 19809
(302)798-1471
Ultimate Parent: Ryder System. **SIC:**
7513—Truck Rental & Leasing Without
Drivers.

★ 58108 ★ **Ryder Truck Rental
Inc.**
1 Dunlinden Dr.
Wilmington, DE 19808
(302)994-0416
Ultimate Parent: Ryder System. **SIC:**
7389—Business Services Nec.

★ 58109 ★ **Service Merchandise**
Midway Shopping Ctr.
Wilmington, DE 19801
(302)999-7691
Ultimate Parent: Service Merchandise Co.,
Inc.

★ 58110 ★ **Shaw Co/Benjamin F**
2 Mill Rd.
Wilmington, DE 19804
(302)658-7181
Ultimate Parent: Blount Inc. **SIC:** 3498—
Fabricated Pipe & Fittings.

★ 58111 ★ **Shell Petroleum Inc.**
1100 N. Market St.
Wilmington, DE 19801
(302)658-5704
Ultimate Parent: Shell Oil Co.

★ 58112 ★ **Slocomb Industries
Inc.**
900 W. 30th St.
Wilmington, DE 19802-2931
(302)762-4445
Officer: Leon F. Slocomb Jr., President.
Ultimate Parent: Collins & Aikman Group.
SIC: 3089—Plastics Products Nec.
Employee Count: 150. **Sales:** 15.6 M.

★ 58113 ★ **Southland Corp.**
1113 N. Market St.
Wilmington, DE 19801
(302)999-1346
Ultimate Parent: Southland Corp.

★ 58114 ★ **Thrift Drug**
Concord Mall
Wilmington, DE 19803
(302)478-5108
Ultimate Parent: J.C. Penney. **SIC:** 7299—
Miscellaneous Personal Services Nec.

★ 58115 ★ **Thrift Drug**
Prices Corner Shopping Ctr.
Wilmington, DE 19808
(302)994-4935
Ultimate Parent: J.C. Penney. **SIC:** 5049—
Professional Equipment Nec.

★ 58116 ★ **TriStar Capital Corp.**
20 Montchanin Rd.
Wilmington, DE 19807
Officer: William F. Morse, President.
Ultimate Parent: Columbia Gas System.

★ 58117 ★ **TriStar Ventures
Corp.**
20 Montchanin Rd.
Wilmington, DE 19807
Officer: Bartholomew F. Cranston,
President. **Ultimate Parent:** Columbia Gas
System.

★ 58118 ★ **United Missouri Bank,
USA**
PO Box 15351
Wilmington, DE 19850-5351
Location Type: Branch office. **Ultimate
Parent:** United Missouri Bancshares. **SIC:**
6021—National Commercial Banks.

★ 58119 ★ **Waldenbooks**
Concord Mall
Wilmington, DE 19803
(302)478-5509
Ultimate Parent: K-Mart. **SIC:** 5942—Book
Stores.

★ 58120 ★ **Xerox Corp.**
200 Bellevue Pky., 3rd Fl.
Wilmington, DE 19809
(302)792-5100
Officer: John Klinge, Manager. **Ultimate
Parent:** Xerox Corp. **SIC:** 3663—Radio &
T.V. Communications Equipment.

DISTRICT OF COLUMBIA

Washignton

★ 58121 ★ **Smith Barney Harris Upham & Co.**
1850 K St. NW
Washignton, DC 20006-2213
(202)862-2800
Ultimate Parent: Automatic Data Processing, Inc. **SIC:** 6211—Security Brokers & Dealers.

Washington

★ 58122 ★ **Acme Markets**
275 Park Ave.
Washington, DC 20019
(202)399-8792
Ultimate Parent: American Stores. **SIC:** 5947—Gift, Novelty & Souvenir Shops.

★ 58123 ★ **ADP Network Services**
1333 New Hampshire Ave. NW
Washington, DC 20036-1500
(202)833-1468
Ultimate Parent: Automatic Data Processing, Inc. **SIC:** 7374—Data Processing & Preparation.

★ 58124 ★ **Aerojet Electrosystems Co.**
1025 Conn Ave. NW
Washington, DC
(202)828-6835
Ultimate Parent: Gencorp.

★ 58125 ★ **Aerojet Ordnance Co.**
1025 Conn Ave. NW
Washington, DC
(202)828-6855
Ultimate Parent: Gencorp.

★ 58126 ★ **Amdahl Corp.**
5335 Wisconsin Ave. NW
Washington, DC
(202)362-7772
Ultimate Parent: Amdahl Corp.

★ 58127 ★ **Ameritech Services Inc.**
1050 17th St. NW
Washington, DC 20036
(202)785-2824
Ultimate Parent: AT&T.

★ 58128 ★ **Asarco Inc.**
1600 M St. NW
Washington, DC 20036-3208
(202)857-1028
Officer: E. Romagnoli. **Ultimate Parent:** Asarco. **SIC:** 1481—Nonmetallic Minerals Services.

★ 58129 ★ **August Max Woman**
529 14th St. NW
Washington, DC 20045
(202)347-0108
Ultimate Parent: United States Shoe.

★ 58130 ★ **Avon Products Inc.**
638 Otis Pl. NW
Washington, DC 20010-1702
Location Type: Headquarters. **Ultimate Parent:** Avon Products, Inc. **SIC:** 2844—Toilet Preparations; 3961—Costume Jewelry; 5122—Drugs, Proprietaries & Sundries; 5999—Miscellaneous Retail Stores Nec.

★ 58131 ★ **Baker Hughes Inc.**
816 Conn Ave. NW
Washington, DC
(202)785-8093
Ultimate Parent: Baker Hughes.

★ 58132 ★ **Banana Republic**
3200 M St. NW
Washington, DC 20007
(202)333-2554
Ultimate Parent: GAP.

★ 58133 ★ **Banana Republic**
601 13th St. NW
Washington, DC 20005
(202)638-2724
Ultimate Parent: GAP.

★ 58134 ★ **Banana Republic**
529 14th St. NW
Washington, DC 20045
(202)783-1400
Ultimate Parent: GAP.

★ 58135 ★ **Baxter International**
Washington D.C. Government Affairs Office
1667 K St. NW, Ste. 710
Washington, DC 20006
(202)223-4016 **Fax:** (202)296-7177
Officer: David J. Aho, Vice President Government Relations. **Ultimate Parent:** Baxter International.

★ 58136 ★ **Bear Stearns Fiduciary Services Inc.**
805 15th St. NW
Washington, DC 20005
Ultimate Parent: Bear Stearns. **SIC:** 6341—Insurance & Diversified Financial Companies; 6211—Security Brokers & Dealers.

★ 58137 ★ **Bear, Stearns Fiduciary Services Inc.**
805 15th St. NW, Ste. 1120
Washington, DC 20005
(202)898-2260
Company Type: Subsidiary. **Officer:** Francis X. Lilly, President. **Ultimate Parent:** Bear Stearns. **SIC:** 6371—Pension, Health & Welfare Funds.

★ 58138 ★ **Bellsouth Corp.**
1133 21st St. NW
Washington, DC 20036
(202)463-4100
Ultimate Parent: BellSouth Corp.

★ 58139 ★ **Browning Ferris Industries**
2020 Fairview Ave. NE
Washington, DC 20002-1612
(202)526-4057
Ultimate Parent: Browning-Ferris Industries. **SIC:** 4953—Refuse Systems.

★ 58140 ★ **Business Week-Corporate Circul**
1200 G St. NW
Washington, DC 20005
(202)383-3707
Ultimate Parent: McGraw-Hill.

★ 58141 ★ **Business Week Editorial**
1200 G St. NW
Washington, DC 20005
(202)383-2100
Ultimate Parent: McGraw-Hill.

★ 58142 ★ **Casual Corner**
1017 Connecticut Ave. NW
Washington, DC 20036
(202)659-8344
Ultimate Parent: United States Shoe.

★ 58143 ★ **Casual Corner**
408 L'enfant Ctr. SW
Washington, DC 20024
(202)554-5240
Ultimate Parent: United States Shoe.

★ 58144 ★ **Casual Corner**
3222 M St. NW
Washington, DC 20007
(202)342-1926
Ultimate Parent: United States Shoe.

★ 58145 ★ **Casual Corner**
1331 Pennsylvania Ave. NW
Washington, DC 20004
(202)737-9280
Ultimate Parent: United States Shoe.

★ 58146 ★ **Casual Corner**
1905 M St. NW
Washington, DC 20036
(202)857-4280
Ultimate Parent: United States Shoe.

★ 58147 ★ **Central & South West Services**
801 Pa Ave. NW
Washington, DC
(202)628-0886
Ultimate Parent: Central Fidelity Bank.

★ 58148 ★ **Chesapeake & Patomac Telephone Co.**
1710 H St. NW
Washington, DC 20006
(202)392-9900 **Fax:** (202)887-9195
Company Type: Subsidiary. **Officer:** Delano E. Lewis, President & CEO. **Ultimate Parent:** Bell Atlantic Corp.

★ 58149 ★ **Chesapeake & Potomac Tel Co.**
2055 L St. NW
Washington, DC 20036-4905
(202)392-9900
Location Type: Branch office. **Officer:** Delano E. Lewis. **Ultimate Parent:** Bell Atlantic Corp. **SIC:** 4813—Telephone Communications Except Radiotelephone; 2741—Miscellaneous Publishing.

★ 58150 ★ **The Chesapeake & Potomac Telephone Co.**
1710 H St. NW
Washington, DC 20006-4601
(202)392-1234
Company Type: Subsidiary. **Officer:** Delano E. Lewis, President & CEO. **Ultimate Parent:** Bell Atlantic Corp. **SIC:** 4813—Telephone Communications Except Radiotelephone; 8721—Accounting, Auditing & Bookkeeping; 2741—Miscellaneous Publishing. **Employee Count:** 2900. **Sales:** 537 M.

★ 58151 ★ **Citibank Federal Savings Bank**
1775 Pennsylvania Ave. NW
Washington, DC 20006-4605
(202)857-6700
Location Type: Branch office. **Ultimate Parent:** Citicorp. **SIC:** 6021—National Commercial Banks; 6035—Federal Savings Institutions.

★ 58152 ★ **Citibank Federal Savings Bank**
1001 Pennsylvania Ave. NW
Washington, DC 20004-2505
(202)857-6930
Location Type: Branch office. **Ultimate Parent:** Citicorp. **SIC:** 6021—National Commercial Banks; 6035—Federal Savings Institutions.

★ 58153 ★ **Citibank Federal Savings Bank**
5250 MacArthur Blvd.
Washington, DC 20016-2540
(202)857-6890
Location Type: Branch office. **Ultimate Parent:** Citicorp. **SIC:** 6021—National Commercial Banks; 6035—Federal Savings Institutions.

★ 58154 ★ **Citibank Federal Savings Bank**
1544 Benning Rd. NE
Washington, DC 20002-4695
(202)857-4180
Location Type: Branch office. **Ultimate Parent:** Citicorp. **SIC:** 6021—National Commercial Banks; 6035—Federal Savings Institutions.

★ 58155 ★ **Citibank Federal Savings Bank**
1829 Connecticut Ave. NW
Washington, DC 20009-5702
(202)429-8313
Location Type: Branch office. **Ultimate Parent:** Citicorp. **SIC:** 6021—National Commercial Banks; 6035—Federal Savings Institutions.

★ 58156 ★ **Citibank Federal Savings Bank**
5001 Wisconsin NW
Washington, DC 20016-4109
(202)857-6860
Location Type: Branch office. **Ultimate Parent:** Citicorp. **SIC:** 6021—National Commercial Banks; 6035—Federal Savings Institutions.

★ 58157 ★ **Citibank Federal Savings Bank**
2901 M St. NW
Washington, DC 20007-3714
(202)857-6990
Location Type: Branch office. **Ultimate Parent:** Citicorp. **SIC:** 6021—National Commercial Banks; 6035—Federal Savings Institutions.

★ 58158 ★ **Citibank Federal Savings Bank**
600 Pennsylvania Ave. SE
Washington, DC 20003-4316
(202)857-4191
Location Type: Branch office. **Ultimate Parent:** Citicorp. **SIC:** 6021—National Commercial Banks; 6035—Federal Savings Institutions.

★ 58159 ★ **Citibank Federal Savings Bank**
1400 G. St. NW
Washington, DC 20005-2001
(202)857-6988
Location Type: Branch office. **Ultimate Parent:** Citicorp. **SIC:** 6021—National Commercial Banks; 6035—Federal Savings Institutions.

★ 58160 ★ **Citibank Federal Savings Bank**
5700 Connecticut Ave. NW
Washington, DC 20015-2991
(202)857-6887
Location Type: Branch office. **Ultimate Parent:** Citicorp. **SIC:** 6021—National Commercial Banks; 6035—Federal Savings Institutions.

★ 58161 ★ **Citibank Federal Savings Bank**
3800 12th St. NE
Washington, DC 20017-2695
(202)857-6970
Location Type: Branch office. **Ultimate Parent:** Citicorp. **SIC:** 6021—National Commercial Banks; 6035—Federal Savings Institutions.

★ 58162 ★ **Citibank Federal Savings Bank**
1901 Wisconsin Ave. NW
Washington, DC 20007
(202)828-7640
Location Type: Branch office. **Ultimate Parent:** Citicorp. **SIC:** 6021—National Commercial Banks; 6035—Federal Savings Institutions.

★ 58163 ★ **Citibank Federal Savings Bank**
1000 Connecticut Ave. NW
Washington, DC 20036-5302
(202)857-6877
Location Type: Branch office. **Ultimate Parent:** Citicorp. **SIC:** 6021—National Commercial Banks; 6035—Federal Savings Institutions.

★ 58164 ★　Citibank Federal
Savings Bank
3917 Minnesota Ave. NE
Washington, DC 20019-2662
(202)429-7737
Location Type: Branch office. **Ultimate
Parent:** Citicorp. **SIC:** 6021—National
Commercial Banks; 6035—Federal Savings
Institutions.

★ 58165 ★　Citibank Federal
Savings Bank
1090 Vermont Ave. NW
Washington, DC 20005-4905
(202)857-6895
Location Type: Branch office. **Ultimate
Parent:** Citicorp. **SIC:** 6021—National
Commercial Banks; 6035—Federal Savings
Institutions.

★ 58166 ★　Citibank Federal
Savings Bank
1751 Columbia Rd. NW
Washington, DC 20009
(202)828-2903
Location Type: Branch office. **Ultimate
Parent:** Citicorp. **SIC:** 6021—National
Commercial Banks; 6035—Federal Savings
Institutions.

★ 58167 ★　Colonial Pipeline Co.
401 Farragt NE
Washington, DC 20011
(202)529-8332
Ultimate Parent: Colonial Pipeline.

★ 58168 ★　Columbia First Bank,
A Federal Savings Bank
2000 L St. NW
Washington, DC 20036-4983
(202)879-7140
Location Type: Branch office. **Ultimate
Parent:** Columbia First Bank, FSB. **SIC:**
6021—National Commercial Banks; 6035—
Federal Savings Institutions.

★ 58169 ★　Columbia First Bank,
A Federal Savings Bank
1900 Pennsylvania Ave. NW
Washington, DC 20006-3303
(202)879-7182
Location Type: Branch office. **Ultimate
Parent:** Columbia First Bank, FSB. **SIC:**
6021—National Commercial Banks; 6035—
Federal Savings Institutions.

★ 58170 ★　Columbia First Bank,
A Federal Savings Bank
5005 New Hampshire Ave. NW
Washington, DC 20011-4117
(202)879-7210
Location Type: Branch office. **Ultimate
Parent:** Columbia First Bank, FSB. **SIC:**
6021—National Commercial Banks; 6035—
Federal Savings Institutions.

★ 58171 ★　Columbia First Bank,
A Federal Savings Bank
1800 M St. NW
Washington, DC 20036-5859
(202)879-7150
Location Type: Branch office. **Ultimate
Parent:** Columbia First Bank, FSB. **SIC:**
6021—National Commercial Banks; 6035—
Federal Savings Institutions.

★ 58172 ★　Columbia First Bank,
A Federal Savings Bank
3216 Pennsylvania Ave. SE
Washington, DC 20020-3716
(202)879-7232
Location Type: Branch office. **Ultimate
Parent:** Columbia First Bank, FSB. **SIC:**
6021—National Commercial Banks; 6035—
Federal Savings Institutions.

★ 58173 ★　Columbia First Bank,
A Federal Savings Bank
4857 Massachusetts Ave. NW
Washington, DC 20016-2094
(202)879-7192
Location Type: Branch office. **Ultimate
Parent:** Columbia First Bank, FSB. **SIC:**
6021—National Commercial Banks; 6035—
Federal Savings Institutions.

★ 58174 ★　Columbia First Bank,
A Federal Savings Bank
4340 Connecticut Ave. NW
Washington, DC 20008-2315
(202)879-7201
Location Type: Branch office. **Ultimate
Parent:** Columbia First Bank, FSB. **SIC:**
6021—National Commercial Banks; 6035—
Federal Savings Institutions.

★ 58175 ★　Columbia First Bank,
A Federal Savings Bank
1700 Pennsylvania Ave. NW
Washington, DC 20006-4762
(202)879-7172
Location Type: Branch office. **Ultimate
Parent:** Columbia First Bank, FSB. **SIC:**
6021—National Commercial Banks; 6035—
Federal Savings Institutions.

★ 58176 ★　Columbia First Bank,
A Federal Savings Bank
1101 15th St. NW
Washington, DC 20005-5064
(202)879-7133
Location Type: Branch office. **Ultimate
Parent:** Columbia First Bank, FSB. **SIC:**
6021—National Commercial Banks; 6035—
Federal Savings Institutions.

★ 58177 ★　Columbia First Bank,
A Federal Savings Bank
615 12th St. NW
Washington, DC 20001-4584
(202)879-7122
Location Type: Branch office. **Ultimate
Parent:** Columbia First Bank, FSB. **SIC:**
6021—National Commercial Banks; 6035—
Federal Savings Institutions.

★ 58178 ★　Columbia First Bank,
A Federal Savings Bank
5025 Wisconsin Ave. NW
Washington, DC 20016-4121
(202)879-7223
Location Type: Branch office. **Ultimate
Parent:** Columbia First Bank, FSB. **SIC:**
6021—National Commercial Banks; 6035—
Federal Savings Institutions.

★ 58179 ★　Columbia First Bank,
A Federal Savings Bank
5701 Connecticut Ave. NW
Washington, DC 20015
(202)686-4660
Location Type: Branch office. **Ultimate
Parent:** Columbia First Bank, FSB. **SIC:**
6021—National Commercial Banks; 6035—
Federal Savings Institutions.

★ 58180 ★　Columbia First Bank,
A Federal Savings Bank
303 Pennsylvania Ave. SE
Washington, DC 20003-1176
(202)544-5780
Location Type: Branch office. **Ultimate
Parent:** Columbia First Bank, FSB. **SIC:**
6021—National Commercial Banks; 6035—
Federal Savings Institutions.

★ 58181 ★　Compaq Computer
Corp.
1300 I St. NW
Washington, DC 20005
(202)962-3830
Ultimate Parent: Compaq Computer.

★ 58182 ★　Crestar Bank, NA
3435 Connecticut Ave. NW
Washington, DC 20008-1307
(800)451-2435
Location Type: Branch office. **Officer:**
Maria Randall, Branch Officer. **Ultimate
Parent:** Crestar Financial Corp. **SIC:**
6021—National Commercial Banks.

★ 58183 ★　Crestar Bank, NA
5601 Thirs St. NE
Washington, DC 20011-2596
(800)451-2435
Location Type: Branch office. **Officer:**
Cheryl Penick, Branch Officer. **Ultimate
Parent:** Crestar Financial Corp. **SIC:**
6021—National Commercial Banks.

★ 58184 ★　Crestar Bank, NA
965 L'Enfant Plaza North SW
Washington, DC 20024-2194
(800)451-2435
Location Type: Branch office. **Officer:**
Mario Benitez, Branch Officer. **Ultimate
Parent:** Crestar Financial Corp. **SIC:**
6021—National Commercial Banks.

★ 58185 ★　Crestar Bank, NA
1111 Connecticut Ave. NW
Washington, DC 20036-4301
(800)451-2435
Location Type: Branch office. **Officer:**
Steward Smith, Branch Officer. **Ultimate
Parent:** Crestar Financial Corp. **SIC:**
6021—National Commercial Banks.

★ 58186 ★　Crestar Bank, NA
5000 Connecticut Ave. NW
Washington, DC 20008-2070
(800)451-2435
Location Type: Branch office. **Officer:**
Jean Pommerening, Branch Officer.
Ultimate Parent: Crestar Financial Corp.
SIC: 6021—National Commercial Banks.

★ 58187 ★　Crestar Bank, NA
4900 Massachusetts Ave. NW
Washington, DC 20016-4358
(800)451-2435
Location Type: Branch office. **Officer:**
Catherine Saunders, Branch Officer.
SIC: 6021—National Commercial Banks.

★ 58188 ★　Crestar Bank, NA
1369 Connecticut Ave. NW
Washington, DC 20036-1894
(800)451-2435
Location Type: Branch office. **Officer:**
Georgann Romaye, Manager. **Ultimate
Parent:** Crestar Financial Corp. **SIC:**
6021—National Commercial Banks.

★ 58189 ★　Crestar Bank, NA
300 Pennsylvania Ave. SE
Washington, DC 20003-1192
(800)451-2435
Location Type: Branch office. **Officer:**
Todd W. Miller, Assistant Vice President.
Ultimate Parent: Crestar Financial Corp.
SIC: 6021—National Commercial Banks.

★ 58190 ★　Crestar Bank, NA
1340 Good Hope Rd. SE
Washington, DC 20020-6995
(800)451-2435
Location Type: Branch office. **Officer:**
Steward Henderson, Branch Officer.
Ultimate Parent: Crestar Financial Corp.
SIC: 6021—National Commercial Banks.

★ 58191 ★　Crestar Bank, NA
445 11th St. NW
Washington, DC 20004-1389
(800)451-2435
Location Type: Branch office. **Officer:**
Lillian Lockette, Branch Officer. **Ultimate
Parent:** Crestar Financial Corp. **SIC:**
6021—National Commercial Banks.

★ 58192 ★　Crestar Bank, NA
1300 L St.
Washington, DC 20005-4107
(800)451-2435
Location Type: Branch office. **Officer:**
Ronald Westbrook, Manager. **Ultimate
Parent:** Crestar Financial Corp. **SIC:**
6021—National Commercial Banks.

★ 58193 ★　Crestar Bank, NA
18th & Columbia Rd. NW
Washington, DC 20009
(800)451-2435
Location Type: Branch office. **Officer:**
Guillermo Fuentes, Branch Officer. **Ultimate
Parent:** Crestar Financial Corp. **SIC:**
6021—National Commercial Banks.

★ 58194 ★　Crestar Bank, NA
1 Indiana Ave. NW
Washington, DC 20001-2199
(800)451-2435
Location Type: Branch office. **Officer:** Patti
Zindler, Assistant Vice President. **Ultimate
Parent:** Crestar Financial Corp. **SIC:**
6021—National Commercial Banks.

★ 58195 ★　Crestar Bank, NA
1700 K St. NW
Washington, DC 20006-3817
(800)451-2435
Location Type: Branch office. **Officer:**
Yolanda Scott-Boone, Vice President.
Ultimate Parent: Crestar Financial Corp.
SIC: 6021—National Commercial Banks.

★ 58196 ★　Crestar Bank, NA
3440 Wisconsin Ave. NW
Washington, DC 20016-3009
(800)451-2435
Location Type: Branch office. **Officer:**
Katheyn Kinney, Assistant Vice President.
Ultimate Parent: Crestar Financial Corp.
SIC: 6021—National Commercial Banks.

★ 58197 ★　Crestar Bank, NA
2929 M St. NW
Washington, DC 20007-3714
(800)451-2435
Location Type: Branch office. **Officer:**
Tami Boland, Manager. **Ultimate Parent:**
Crestar Financial Corp. **SIC:** 6021—National
Commercial Banks.

★ 58198 ★　Crestar Bank, NA
3301 New Mexico Ave. NW
Washington, DC 20016-3622
(800)451-2435
Location Type: Branch office. **Officer:**
Susan K. Amatangelo, Assistant Vice
President. **Ultimate Parent:** Crestar
Financial Corp. **SIC:** 6021—National
Commercial Banks.

★ 58199 ★　Crestar Bank, NA
410 Rhode Island Ave. NE
Washington, DC 20002-1295
(800)451-2435
Location Type: Branch office. **Officer:** J,
Mitchell Krebs, Assistant Vice President.
Ultimate Parent: Crestar Financial Corp.
SIC: 6021—National Commercial Banks.

★ 58200 ★　Crestar Bank, NA
825 Capitol St. NE
Washington, DC 20002-4277
(800)451-2435
Location Type: Branch office. **Officer:** Ada
G. Nealy, Assistant Vice President. **Ultimate
Parent:** Crestar Financial Corp. **SIC:**
6021—National Commercial Banks.

★ 58201 ★　Crestar Bank, NA
Mercury Bldg.
1925 K St. NW
Washington, DC 20020-5147
(800)451-2435
Location Type: Branch office. **Officer:** Amy
L. MacKay, Assistant Vice President.
Ultimate Parent: Crestar Financial Corp.
SIC: 6021—National Commercial Banks.

★ 58202 ★　Crestar Bank, NA
1225 Connecticut Ave. NW
Washington, DC 20036-2616
(800)451-2435
Location Type: Branch office. **Officer:**
Georgann Ramage, Assistant Vice
President. **Ultimate Parent:** Crestar
Financial Corp. **SIC:** 6021—National
Commercial Banks.

★ 58203 ★　Crestar Bank, NA
5025 Wisconsin Ave.
Washington, DC 20016
(800)451-2435
Location Type: Branch office. **Officer:**
Robert Ward, Branch Officer. **Ultimate
Parent:** Crestar Financial Corp. **SIC:**
6021—National Commercial Banks.

★ 58204 ★　Crestar Bank, NA
1750 New York Ave. NW
Washington, DC 20006-5301
(800)451-2435
Location Type: Branch office. **Officer:**
Nancy Y. Cree, Assistant Vice President.
Ultimate Parent: Crestar Financial Corp.
SIC: 6021—National Commercial Banks.

★ 58205 ★　Crestar Bank NA
15th & New York Ave. NW
Washington, DC 20042-0002
(202)879-6000
Company Type: Subsidiary. **Ultimate
Parent:** Crestar Financial Corp. **SIC:**
6022—State Commercial Banks.

★ 58206 ★　Crestar Bank, NA
15th St. & New York Ave. NW
Washington, DC 20005
(202)879-6000
Location Type: Branch office. **Officer:**
William C. Harris, President, CEO, and
Chairman of the Board. **Ultimate Parent:**
Crestar Financial Corp. **SIC:** 6021—National
Commercial Banks.

★ 58207 ★　Crestar Securities
Corp.
1445 Ny Ave. NW
Washington, DC
(202)879-6127
Ultimate Parent: Crestar Financial Corp.

★ 58208 ★　Crestview Bank, NA
6422 Georgia Ave. NW
Washington, DC 20012-2995
(800)451-2435
Location Type: Branch office. **Officer:** Inez
Cannon, Branch Officer. **Ultimate Parent:**
Crestar Financial Corp. **SIC:** 6021—National
Commercial Banks.

★ 58209 ★   Danaher Corp.
1250 24th St. NW, Ste. 800
Washington, DC 20037-1124
(202)828-0850
Company Type: Headquarters. Officer:
Steven M. Rales, Ch. Bd. Ultimate Parent:
Danaher Corp. SIC: 3423—Hand & Edge
Tools Nec; 3714—Motor Vehicle Parts &
Accessories; 3559—Special Industry
Machinery Nec; 3519—Internal Combustion
Engines Nec; 3823—Process Control
Instruments; 3579—Office Machines Nec;
3089—Plastics Products Nec; 3451—Screw
Machine Products; 3452—Bolts, Nuts,
Rivets & Washers; 6719—Holding
Companies Nec; 6531—Real Estate Agents
& Managers; 6162—Mortgage Bankers &
Correspondents. Employee Count: 7296.
Sales: 955 M.

★ 58210 ★   Danaher Corp.
1250 24th St. NW
Washington, DC 20037
(202)828-0850
Company Type: Headquarters. Officer:
George Sherman. Sales: 1067 M. Fortune
500: Largest U.S. Industrial Corporations:
Ranking 353.

★ 58211 ★   Delta Air Lines
1629 K St. NW
Washington, DC 20006
(202)296-9860
Ultimate Parent: Delta Air Lines, Inc.

★ 58212 ★   Detroit Edison Co.
601 13th St. NW
Washington, DC 20005
(202)347-8420
Ultimate Parent: Detroit Edison Co.

★ 58213 ★   Detroit Edison Co. the
601 13th St. NW
Washington, DC 20005
(202)347-8420
Ultimate Parent: Detroit Edison Co.

★ 58214 ★   Digital Equipment
Corp.
1331 Pa Ave. NW
Washington, DC 20004
(202)383-5600
Ultimate Parent: Digital Equipment Corp.

★ 58215 ★   Digital Equipment
Corp.
1825 I St. NW
Washington, DC 20006
(202)429-9200
Ultimate Parent: Digital Equipment Corp.

★ 58216 ★   Dow Jones Capital
Markets Report (Washington
Bureau)
1025 Connecticut Ave., NW
Ste., 800
Washington, DC 20036
(202)862-9200 Fax: (202)862-9266
Company Type: Subsidiary. Ultimate
Parent: Dow Jones.

★ 58217 ★   Dow Jones News
Service (Washington Bureau)
1025 Connecticut Ave. NW, Ste. 800
Washington, DC 20036
Company Type: Subsidiary. Ultimate
Parent: Dow Jones.

★ 58218 ★   Drake Beam Morin
Inc.
1828 L St. NW
Washington, DC 20036
(202)466-6090
Ultimate Parent: Harcourt General.

★ 58219 ★   El Paso Natural Gas
Co.
601 13th St. NW
Washington, DC 20005
(202)662-4300
Ultimate Parent: Burlington Northern.

★ 58220 ★   Electronic Warfare
Systems
490 L'Engant Plz. E, SW No. 8206
Washington, DC 20024-2179
(202)554-2570
Company Type: Division. Ultimate Parent:
Litton Industries.

★ 58221 ★   Eli Lilly & Co.
1901 L St. NW
Washington, DC 20036
(202)955-5350
Ultimate Parent: Eli Lilly.

★ 58222 ★   Emc
1825 Q St. NW
Washington, DC 20009
(202)232-4597
Ultimate Parent: EMC.

★ 58223 ★   Enron Gas Marketing
750 17th St. NW
Washington, DC 20006
(202)828-9113
Ultimate Parent: Enron.

★ 58224 ★   Exxon Co.
5521 Connecticut Ave. NW
Washington, DC 20015
(202)966-6448
Ultimate Parent: Exxon.

★ 58225 ★   Exxon Co.
Washington, DC
(202)347-1215
Ultimate Parent: Exxon.

★ 58226 ★   Exxon Co.
5030 Conn Ave. NW
Washington, DC
(202)364-6374
Ultimate Parent: Exxon.

★ 58227 ★   Exxon Co.
Washington, DC
(202)347-1215
Ultimate Parent: Exxon.

★ 58228 ★   Exxon Corp.
1899 L St. NW
Washington, DC 20036
(202)862-0200
Ultimate Parent: Exxon.

★ 58229 ★   Exxon Service Station
4244 Wisconsin Ave. NW
Washington, DC 20016
(202)364-6372
Ultimate Parent: Exxon.

★ 58230 ★   Exxon Service Station
5501 S. Dakota Ave. NE
Washington, DC 20011
(202)832-6220
Ultimate Parent: Exxon.

★ 58231 ★   Exxon Service Station
2708 Virginia Ave. NW
Washington, DC 20037
(202)338-7739
Ultimate Parent: Exxon.

★ 58232 ★   Exxon Service Station
3201 Pa Ave. SE
Washington, DC 20020
(202)581-7254
Ultimate Parent: Exxon.

★ 58233 ★   Exxon Service Station
3103 Rhode Island Ave. NE
Washington, DC 20018
(202)526-9811
Ultimate Parent: Exxon.

★ 58234 ★   Exxon Service Station
4866 Mass Ave. NW
Washington, DC
(202)364-6370
Ultimate Parent: Exxon.

★ 58235 ★   Exxon Service Station
339 Pa Ave. SE
Washington, DC 20003
(202)547-4054
Ultimate Parent: Exxon.

★ 58236 ★   Exxon Service Station
1 Florida Ave. NE
Washington, DC 20002
(202)635-1659
Ultimate Parent: Exxon.

★ 58237 ★   Exxon Service Station
5230 Ga Ave. NW
Washington, DC
(202)234-0026
Ultimate Parent: Exxon.

★ 58238 ★   Fairfield Inn by
Marriott
333 Jefferson Davis Hwy.
Washington, DC
(202)628-4200
Ultimate Parent: Marriott International.

★ 58239 ★   Federal Home Loan
Mortgage Cor
1101 Pa Ave.
Washington, DC
(202)639-8126
Ultimate Parent: Federal Home Loan
Mortgage.

★ 58240 ★   Federal National
Mortgage Asso
3900 Wisconsin Ave. NW
Washington, DC 20016
(202)752-7630
Ultimate Parent: Federal National Mortgage
Association.

★ 58241 ★   Federal National
Mortgage Association
3900 Wisconsin Ave. NW
Washington, DC 20016
(202)752-7000
Company Type: Headquarters. Officer:
James A. Johnson. Fortune Service 500:
Ranking 1.

★ 58242 ★   Federal Systems
Group Inc.
1717 K St. NW
Washington, DC 20006
(202)293-2727
Ultimate Parent: Apple Computer.

★ 58243 ★   Fhp Inc.
1225 19th St. NW
Washington, DC 20036
(202)223-5718
Ultimate Parent: FHP International.

★ 58244 ★   First American Bank
740 15th St. NW
Washington, DC 20005
(202)637-6100
Ultimate Parent: First American Corp.

★ 58245 ★   First American Corp.
15th & H Sts. NW
Washington, DC 20005
(202)383-1400
Officer: Nicholas De B Katzenbach,
Chairman of the Board & Trustee. Ultimate
Parent: First American Corp. SIC: 6022—
State Commercial Banks; 6021—National
Commercial Banks. Employee Count:
3666.

★ 58246 ★   First National Bank of
Maryland, DC
555 13th St. NW
Washington, DC 20004-1109
(202)737-3060 Fax: (202)737-6813
Location Type: Branch office. Ultimate
Parent: First Maryland Bancorp. SIC:
6021—National Commercial Banks.

★ 58247 ★   First Union National
Bank of Washington
927 15th St. NW
Washington, DC 20005
(202)624-0400 Fax: (202)628-0832
Company Type: Subsidiary. Officer:
Joseph L. Marlone, President & CEO.
Ultimate Parent: First Union Corp. SIC:
6021—National Commercial Banks.
Employee Count: 40.

★ 58248 ★   First Union National
Bank of Washington DC
1300 Eye St.
Washington, DC 20005-3306
(202)637-0630
Location Type: Branch office. Ultimate
Parent: First Union Corp. SIC: 6021—
National Commercial Banks.

★ 58249 ★   First Union National
Bank of Washington DC
5345 Wisconsin Ave.
Washington, DC 20015
(202)637-0600
Location Type: Branch office. Ultimate
Parent: First Union Corp. SIC: 6021—
National Commercial Banks.

★ 58250 ★   First Union National
Bank of Washington DC
4910 Massachusetts Ave.
Washington, DC 20016-4300
(202)637-2897
Location Type: Branch office. Ultimate
Parent: First Union Corp. SIC: 6021—
National Commercial Banks.

★ 58251 ★   First Union National
Bank of Washington DC
20 Chevy Chase Cir. NW
Washington, DC 20015-2912
(202)637-2949
Location Type: Branch office. Ultimate
Parent: First Union Corp. SIC: 6021—
National Commercial Banks.

★ 58252 ★   First Union National
Bank of Washington DC
502 23rd St. NW
Washington, DC 20037-2899
(202)637-2506
Location Type: Branch office. Ultimate
Parent: First Union Corp. SIC: 6021—
National Commercial Banks.

★ 58253 ★   First Union National
Bank of Washington DC
1055 Thomas Jefferson St. NW
Washington, DC 20007-5202
(202)637-2502
Location Type: Branch office. Ultimate
Parent: First Union Corp. SIC: 6021—
National Commercial Banks.

★ 58254 ★   First Union National
Bank of Washington DC
417 6th St. NW
Washington, DC 20001-2734
(202)637-2527
Location Type: Branch office. Ultimate
Parent: First Union Corp. SIC: 6021—
National Commercial Banks.

★ 58255 ★   First Union National
Bank of Washington DC
320 Riggs Rd. NE
Washington, DC 20011-2534
(202)637-2522
Location Type: Branch office. Ultimate
Parent: First Union Corp. SIC: 6021—
National Commercial Banks.

★ 58256 ★   First Union National
Bank of Washington DC
509 7th St. NW
Washington, DC 20004-1694
(202)634-2513
Location Type: Branch office. Ultimate
Parent: First Union Corp. SIC: 6021—
National Commercial Banks.

★ 58257 ★   First Union National
Bank of Washington DC
1701 Pennsylvania Ave. NW
Washington, DC 20006-5801
(202)637-2511
Location Type: Branch office. Ultimate
Parent: First Union Corp. SIC: 6021—
National Commercial Banks.

★ 58258 ★   First Union National
Bank of Washington DC
3200 Pennsylvania Ave. SE
Washington, DC 20020-3715
(202)637-2518
Location Type: Branch office. Ultimate
Parent: First Union Corp. SIC: 6021—
National Commercial Banks.

★ 58259 ★   First Union National
Bank of Washington DC
1301 Pennsylvania Ave. NW
Washington, DC 20004-1701
(202)637-2503
Location Type: Branch office. Ultimate
Parent: First Union Corp. SIC: 6021—
National Commercial Banks.

★ 58260 ★   First Union National
Bank of Washington DC
600 Maryland Ave. SW
Washington, DC 20024-2520
(202)637-2524
Location Type: Branch office. Ultimate
Parent: First Union Corp. SIC: 6021—
National Commercial Banks.

★ 58261 ★   First Union National
Bank of Washington DC
444 N. Capitol St. NW
Washington, DC 20001-1512
(202)637-2510
Location Type: Branch office. Ultimate
Parent: First Union Corp. SIC: 6021—
National Commercial Banks.

★ 58262 ★   **First Union National Bank of Washington DC**
2301 M St. NW
Washington, DC 20007-1427
(202)637-2525
Location Type: Branch office. **Ultimate Parent:** First Union Corp. **SIC:** 6021—National Commercial Banks.

★ 58263 ★   **First Union National Bank of Washington DC**
5201 MacArthur Blvd. NW
Washington, DC 20016-2500
(202)637-2515
Location Type: Branch office. **Ultimate Parent:** First Union Corp. **SIC:** 6021—National Commercial Banks.

★ 58264 ★   **First Union National Bank of Washington DC**
1800 K St. NW
Washington, DC 20006-2674
(202)637-2508
Location Type: Branch office. **Ultimate Parent:** First Union Corp. **SIC:** 6021—National Commercial Banks.

★ 58265 ★   **First Union National Bank of Washington DC**
1919 M St. NW
Washington, DC 20036-3507
(202)637-2516
Location Type: Branch office. **Ultimate Parent:** First Union Corp. **SIC:** 6021—National Commercial Banks.

★ 58266 ★   **First Union National Bank of Washington DC**
1123 15th St. NW
Washington, DC 20005-2702
(202)637-2519
Location Type: Branch office. **Ultimate Parent:** First Union Corp. **SIC:** 6021—National Commercial Banks.

★ 58267 ★   **First Union National Bank of Washington DC**
1325 G St. NW
Washington, DC 20005-3104
(202)637-2512
Location Type: Branch office. **Ultimate Parent:** First Union Corp. **SIC:** 6021—National Commercial Banks.

★ 58268 ★   **First Union National Bank of Washington DC**
4250 Connecticut Ave. NW
Washington, DC 20008-1173
(202)637-2526
Location Type: Branch office. **Ultimate Parent:** First Union Corp. **SIC:** 6021—National Commercial Banks.

★ 58269 ★   **First Union National Bank of Washington DC**
1100 Connecticut Ave. NW
Washington, DC 20036-4103
(202)637-2505
Location Type: Branch office. **Ultimate Parent:** First Union Corp. **SIC:** 6021—National Commercial Banks.

★ 58270 ★   **First Union National Bank of Washington DC**
2810 Bladensburg Rd. NE
Washington, DC 20018-4101
(202)637-2523
Location Type: Branch office. **Ultimate Parent:** First Union Corp. **SIC:** 6021—National Commercial Banks.

★ 58271 ★   **First Union National Bank of Washington DC**
3700 Calvert St. NW
Washington, DC 20007-1898
(202)637-2514
Location Type: Branch office. **Ultimate Parent:** First Union Corp. **SIC:** 6021—National Commercial Banks.

★ 58272 ★   **First Union National Bank of Washington DC**
400 Virginia St. NW
Washington, DC 20007
(202)637-2517
Location Type: Branch office. **Ultimate Parent:** First Union Corp. **SIC:** 6021—National Commercial Banks.

★ 58273 ★   **First Union National Bank of Washington DC**
740 15th St. NW
Washington, DC 20005-7648
(202)637-6100
Location Type: Branch office. **Ultimate Parent:** First Union Corp. **SIC:** 6021—National Commercial Banks.

★ 58274 ★   **First Union National Bank of Washington DC**
3301 New Mexico Ave. NW
Washington, DC 20016-3622
(202)537-8620
Location Type: Branch office. **Ultimate Parent:** First Union Corp. **SIC:** 6021—National Commercial Banks.

★ 58275 ★   **First Union National Bank of Washington DC**
2010 Rhode Island Ave. NE
Washington, DC 20018-2835
(202)537-8640
Location Type: Branch office. **Ultimate Parent:** First Union Corp. **SIC:** 6021—National Commercial Banks.

★ 58276 ★   **First Union National Bank of Washington DC**
1899 L St. NW
Washington, DC 20036-3804
(202)624-0488
Location Type: Branch office. **Ultimate Parent:** First Union Corp. **SIC:** 6021—National Commercial Banks.

★ 58277 ★   **First Union National Bank of Washington DC**
4301 Connecticut Ave. NW
Washington, DC 20008-2304
(202)537-8660
Location Type: Branch office. **Ultimate Parent:** First Union Corp. **SIC:** 6021—National Commercial Banks.

★ 58278 ★   **First Union National Bank of Washington DC**
7824 Eastern Ave. NW
Washington, DC 20012-1399
(202)624-0466
Location Type: Branch office. **Ultimate Parent:** First Union Corp. **SIC:** 6021—National Commercial Banks.

★ 58279 ★   **First Union National Bank of Washington DC**
1425 K St. NW
Washington, DC 20005-2304
(800)677-3778 **Fax:** (202)628-0832
Location Type: Branch office. **Ultimate Parent:** First Union Corp. **SIC:** 6021—National Commercial Banks.

★ 58280 ★   **Food & Services Management**
Marriott Dr.
Washington, DC 20058
Officer: Daniel P. Howells, Executive Vice President & General Manager. **Ultimate Parent:** Marriott International.

★ 58281 ★   **Foster Wheeler Enviresponse Inc.**
1225 I St. NW
Washington, DC 20005
(202)682-4786
Ultimate Parent: Foster Wheeler Corp.

★ 58282 ★   **The Gap**
2000 Pa Ave. NW
Washington, DC 20006
(202)429-6862
Ultimate Parent: GAP.

★ 58283 ★   **The Gap**
1267 Wis Ave. NW
Washington, DC
(202)333-2657
Ultimate Parent: GAP.

★ 58284 ★   **Gap Kids**
2000 Pa Ave. NW
Washington, DC 20006
(202)429-8711
Ultimate Parent: GAP.

★ 58285 ★   **The Gap Store**
4455 Conn Ave. NW
Washington, DC
(202)364-3535
Ultimate Parent: GAP.

★ 58286 ★   **Gap Stores**
1120 Connecticut Ave. NW
Washington, DC
(202)429-0691
Ultimate Parent: GAP.

★ 58287 ★   **Gap Stores the District Store**
1120 Conn Ave. NW
Washington, DC
(202)429-0691
Ultimate Parent: GAP.

★ 58288 ★   **Geico**
1 Geico Plaza
Washington, DC 20076
(202)986-2500
Company Type: Headquarters. **Officer:** William B. Snyder.

★ 58289 ★   **Geico Corp.**
1 Geico Plz.
Washington, DC 20076
(202)986-3000
Officer: William B. Snyder, Chairman of the Board & CEO. **Ultimate Parent:** Geico. **SIC:** 6331—Fire, Marine & Casualty Insurance; 6321—Accident & Health Insurance; 6311—Life Insurance; 6141—Personal Credit Institutions. **Employee Count:** 7703.

★ 58290 ★   **Geico Indemnity Co., Inc.**
1 Geico Plz.
Washington, DC 20047
(202)986-3000
Company Type: Subsidiary. **Officer:** Edward H. Utley, Chairman of the Board & CEO. **Ultimate Parent:** Geico. **SIC:** 6331—Fire, Marine & Casualty Insurance. **Employee Count:** 288.

★ 58291 ★   **General Mills Inc.**
1101 Pa Ave. NW
Washington, DC 20004
(202)737-8200
Ultimate Parent: General Mills.

★ 58292 ★   **Government Employees Insurance Co.**
1 Geico Plz.
Washington, DC 20046
(202)986-2500
Company Type: Subsidiary. **Officer:** William B. Snyder, Chairman of the Board. **Ultimate Parent:** Geico. **SIC:** 6331—Fire, Marine & Casualty Insurance; 6141—Personal Credit Institutions. **Employee Count:** 6535.

★ 58293 ★   **Greyhound Bus Lines**
1008 10th St. NW
Washington, DC 20001
(202)289-5141
Ultimate Parent: Greyhound Lines Inc.

★ 58294 ★   **Greyhound Bus Lines**
1005 1st St. NW
Washington, DC 20001
(202)289-5155
Ultimate Parent: Greyhound Lines Inc.

★ 58295 ★   **Greyhound Bus Lines**
1345 Ny Ave. NE
Washington, DC
(202)289-5191
Ultimate Parent: Greyhound Lines Inc.

★ 58296 ★   **Hamilton Insurance Co. Inc.**
5101 Wisconsin Ave. NW
Washington, DC 20016-4120
(202)537-8930
Company Type: Subsidiary. **Ultimate Parent:** Figgie International. **SIC:** 6331—Fire, Marine & Casualty Insurance.

★ 58297 ★   **Harman International Industries Inc.**
1101 Pennsylvania Ave. NW
Washington, DC 20004-2514
(202)393-1101
Officer: Sidney Harman, Chairman of the Board & CEO. **Ultimate Parent:** Harmen International Industries. **SIC:** 3651—Household Audio & Video Equipment. **Employee Count:** 4600. **Sales:** 604 M.

★ 58298 ★   **Harmen International Industries**
1101 Pennsylvania Ave. NW
Washington, DC 20004
(202)393-1101
Company Type: Headquarters. **Officer:** Sidney Harmen. **Employee Count:** 4710. **Sales:** 665 M. **Fortune 500:** Largest U.S. Industrial Corporations: Ranking 469.

★ 58299 ★   **Herman Miller Inc.**
3050 K St. NW
Washington, DC 20007-5108
(202)342-3840
Ultimate Parent: Herman Miller. **SIC:** 5021—Furniture.

★ 58300 ★   **Hertz Rent-A-Car Rental Statio**
901 11th St. NW
Washington, DC 20001
(202)628-6174
Ultimate Parent: Hertz. **SIC:** 7514—Passenger Car Rental.

★ 58301 ★   **Hit or Miss**
1331 Pennsylvania Ave. NW
Washington, DC 20004
(202)347-0280
Ultimate Parent: TJX.

★ 58302 ★   **Hit or Miss**
900 19th St. NW
Washington, DC 20006
(202)785-3089
Ultimate Parent: TJX.

★ 58303 ★   **Host Marriott**
10400 Fernwood Rd.
Washington, DC 20058
(202)380-9000
Company Type: Headquarters. **Officer:** Stephen F. Bollenbach. **Fortune Service 500:** Ranking 86.

★ 58304 ★   **Host Marriott Corp.**
10400 Fernwood Rd.
Washington, DC 20058
(202)380-9000
Company Type: Headquarters. **Officer:** Richard E. Marriott, Chairman. **Ultimate Parent:** Host Marriott. **Sales:** 1000000000 M.

★ 58305 ★   **Hot Shoppes Cafeterias & Restaurants**
Marriott Dr.
Washington, DC 20058
Company Type: Division. **Ultimate Parent:** Marriott International.

★ 58306 ★   **IDS Financial Services Inc.**
569 Division Ave. NE
Washington, DC 20019-5455
(202)895-4334
Ultimate Parent: American Express Co. **SIC:** 6211—Security Brokers & Dealers.

★ 58307 ★   **Illinois Power**
919 18th St. NW
Washington, DC 20006
(202)466-6535
Ultimate Parent: Illinois Power.

★ 58308 ★   **Interface Flooring Systems Inc.**
300 D St. SW
Washington, DC 20024
(202)863-0020
Ultimate Parent: Interface Inc.

★ 58309 ★   **Jostens Learning Corp.**
Washington, DC
(202)575-0054
Ultimate Parent: Jostens.

★ 58310 ★   **Kaiser Aluminum&Chemical Corp.**
900 17th St. NW
Washington, DC 20006
(202)296-5474
Ultimate Parent: Maxxam.

★ 58311 ★   **Leucadia National Corp.**
1819 L St. NW
Washington, DC 20036
(202)785-3280
Ultimate Parent: Leucadia National.

★ 58312 ★   **Lord & Taylor**
5255 Western Ave. NW
Washington, DC 20015
(202)362-7814
Ultimate Parent: May Department Stores.

★ 58313 ★ Louisiana Land & Exploration
655 15th St. NW
Washington, DC
(202)639-4027
Ultimate Parent: Louisiana Land & Exploration.

★ 58314 ★ Loyola Fsb Farragut North
1801 L St. NW
Washington, DC
(202)775-8774
Ultimate Parent: Loyola Capital Corp.

★ 58315 ★ LTV Corp.
1025 Thomas Jefferson St. NW
Washington, DC 20007
(202)625-3340
Ultimate Parent: LTV.

★ 58316 ★ Mail-Well Envelopes
1 Cascade Dr. Allenton
Washington, DC
(202)393-0057
Ultimate Parent: Georgia-Pacific.

★ 58317 ★ Marriott/Fairfield Inn
Marriott Dr.
Washington, DC 20098
Company Type: Division. Officer: J. W. Marriott Jr., Chairman of the Board.
Ultimate Parent: Marriott International. SIC: 7011—Hotels & Motels.

★ 58318 ★ Marriott Hotels
1221 22nd St. NW
Washington, DC 20037
(202)872-1500
Ultimate Parent: Marriott International.

★ 58319 ★ Marriott Hotels
6711 Democracy Blvd.
Washington, DC
(202)897-5600
Ultimate Parent: Marriott International.

★ 58320 ★ Marriott Hotels, Resorts, & Suites
1 Marriott Dr.
Washington, DC 20058
Company Type: Subsidiary. Officer: William R. Tiefel, President. Ultimate Parent: Marriott International. SIC: 7011—Hotels & Motels.

★ 58321 ★ Marriott Hotels Resorts Suites
1221 22nd St. NW
Washington, DC 20037
(202)872-1500
Ultimate Parent: Marriott International.

★ 58322 ★ Marriott International
Marriott Dr.
Washington, DC 20058
(202)380-3000
Company Type: Headquarters. Officer: J. Willard Marriott Jr. Fortune Service 500: Ranking 13.

★ 58323 ★ Marriott International, Inc.
Marriott Dr.
Washington, DC 20058
Telex: 89597
Company Type: Headquarters. Officer: J. W. Marriott Jr., President & Chairman of the Board. Ultimate Parent: Marriott International. SIC: 5812—Eating Places; 7011—Hotels & Motels.

★ 58324 ★ Martin Marietta Air Traffic Systems
475 School St., SW
Washington, DC 20024
(202)646-2000
Officer: Brian N. Etheridge, Vice President.
Ultimate Parent: Martin Marietta.

★ 58325 ★ Martin Marietta Corp. Air Traff
475 School St. SW
Washington, DC 20024
(202)646-2000
Ultimate Parent: Martin Marietta.

★ 58326 ★ Martin Marietta Corp. En
600 Md Ave. SW
Washington, DC
(202)479-0254
Ultimate Parent: Martin Marietta.

★ 58327 ★ Martin Marietta Corp. Washingto
499 S. Cap St.
Washington, DC
(202)488-1969
Ultimate Parent: Martin Marietta.

★ 58328 ★ Mary Kay Cosmetics Independent
3424 Summit Ct NE
Washington, DC 20018
(202)526-6722
Ultimate Parent: Mary Kay Cosmetics.

★ 58329 ★ Mary Kay Cosmetics Independent
4530 Conn Ave. NW
Washington, DC
(202)966-5313
Ultimate Parent: Mary Kay Cosmetics.

★ 58330 ★ Matson Navigation Co.
444 N. Cap St.
Washington, DC
(202)737-1473
Ultimate Parent: Alexander & Baldwin Inc.

★ 58331 ★ McDonald's Call-In
911 E. St. NW
Washington, DC 20004
(202)347-1488
Ultimate Parent: McDonald's.

★ 58332 ★ McDonald's Hamburgers
1916 M St. NW
Washington, DC 20036
(202)296-8839
Ultimate Parent: McDonald's.

★ 58333 ★ McDonald's Hamburgers
625 Pennsylvania Ave. SE
Washington, DC 20003
(202)547-2784
Ultimate Parent: McDonald's.

★ 58334 ★ McDonald's Hamburgers
1635 Benng Rd. NE
Washington, DC
(202)397-1190
Ultimate Parent: McDonald's.

★ 58335 ★ McDonald's Hamburgers
3407 Connecticut Ave. NW
Washington, DC
(202)537-1486
Ultimate Parent: McDonald's.

★ 58336 ★ McDonald's Hamburgers
750 17th St. NW
Washington, DC 20006
(202)828-8311
Ultimate Parent: McDonald's.

★ 58337 ★ McDonald's Hamburgers
1901 9th St. NE
Washington, DC 20001
(202)832-9225
Ultimate Parent: McDonald's.

★ 58338 ★ McDonald's Hamburgers
2328 Georgia Ave. NW
Washington, DC 20001
(202)387-2111
Ultimate Parent: McDonald's.

★ 58339 ★ McDonald's Hamburgers
555 13th St. NW
Washington, DC 20004
(202)638-5933
Ultimate Parent: McDonald's.

★ 58340 ★ McDonald's Hamburgers
Union Station
Washington, DC
(202)408-5014
Ultimate Parent: McDonald's.

★ 58341 ★ McDonald's Hamburgers
2 I St. SE
Washington, DC 20003
(202)479-0518
Ultimate Parent: McDonald's.

★ 58342 ★ McDonald's Hamburgers
169 M St. SE
Washington, DC 20003
(202)889-3085
Ultimate Parent: McDonald's.

★ 58343 ★ McDonald's Hamburgers
Rhode Island Ave. & 4th
Washington, DC
(202)526-3138
Ultimate Parent: McDonald's.

★ 58344 ★ McDonald's Hamburgers
4323 Wisconsin Ave. NW
Washington, DC
(202)363-3955
Ultimate Parent: McDonald's.

★ 58345 ★ McDonald's Hamburgers
2481 18th St. NW
Washington, DC 20009
(202)332-1805
Ultimate Parent: McDonald's.

★ 58346 ★ McDonald's Hamburgers
1539 Pennsylvania Ave. SE
Washington, DC 20003
(202)543-0467
Ultimate Parent: McDonald's.

★ 58347 ★ McDonald's Hamburgers
1401 K St. NW
Washington, DC 20005
(202)737-1652
Ultimate Parent: McDonald's.

★ 58348 ★ McDonald's Hamburgers
2228 New York Ave. NE
Washington, DC 20002
(202)526-6131
Ultimate Parent: McDonald's.

★ 58349 ★ McDonald's Hamburgers
2529 Goodhope Rd. SE
Washington, DC 20020
(202)582-5220
Ultimate Parent: McDonald's.

★ 58350 ★ McDonald's Hamburgers
5300 Wisconsin Ave. NW
Washington, DC
(202)244-1122
Ultimate Parent: McDonald's.

★ 58351 ★ McDonald's Hamburgers
1229 New York Ave. NW
Washington, DC
(202)347-0047
Ultimate Parent: McDonald's.

★ 58352 ★ McDonald's Hamburgers
4950 South Dakota Ave. NE
Washington, DC
(202)529-5126
Ultimate Parent: McDonald's.

★ 58353 ★ McDonald's Hamburgers
4301 Nannie Helen Burroughs
Washington, DC
(202)399-1396
Ultimate Parent: McDonald's.

★ 58354 ★ McDonald's Hamburgers
75 New York Ave. NE
Washington, DC
(202)789-0276
Ultimate Parent: McDonald's.

★ 58355 ★ McDonald's Hamburgers
1909 K St. NW
Washington, DC 20006
(202)293-2087
Ultimate Parent: McDonald's.

★ 58356 ★ McDonald's Hamburgers
2705 Martin Luther King Jr. Ave. SE
Washington, DC 20032
(202)561-7581
Ultimate Parent: McDonald's.

★ 58357 ★ McDonald's Hamburgers
5948 Georgia Ave. NW
Washington, DC
(202)722-1104
Ultimate Parent: McDonald's.

★ 58358 ★ McDonald's Hamburgers
7425 Georgia Ave. NW
Washington, DC 20012
(202)882-6372
Ultimate Parent: McDonald's.

★ 58359 ★ McDonald's Hamburgers
1619 17th St. NW
Washington, DC 20009
(202)234-9327
Ultimate Parent: McDonald's.

★ 58360 ★ McDonald's Hamburgers
1101 Connecticut Ave. NW
Washington, DC 20036
(202)331-0447
Ultimate Parent: McDonald's.

★ 58361 ★ MCI Communications
1801 Penn. Ave. NW
Washington, DC
(202)872-1600
Company Type: Headquarters. Officer: Bert C. Roberts Jr., CEO. Employee Count: 36235. Sales: 11921 M. Fortune Service 500: Ranking 4.

★ 58362 ★ MCI Communications Corp.
1801 Pennsylvania Ave., NW
Washington, DC 20006
(202)872-1600 Fax: (202)887-2443
Officer: Bert C. Roberts Jr., Chairman of the Board & CEO. Ultimate Parent: MCI Communications. Employee Count: 30000.

★ 58363 ★ Meredith Corp.
Washington, DC
(202)223-2406
Ultimate Parent: Meredith.

★ 58364 ★ Microsoft Corp.
5335 Wisconsin Ave. NW
Washington, DC 20015
(202)364-4266
Ultimate Parent: Microsoft.

★ 58365 ★ Midsouth Corp.
1250 24th St. NW
Washington, DC 20037
(202)466-0510
Ultimate Parent: Kansas City South Industries.

★ 58366 ★ Mobil Electronic Association
2101 L St. NW
Washington, DC 20037
(202)828-2270
Ultimate Parent: Mobil.

★ 58367 ★ Mobil Oil Corp.
1250 H St. NW
Washington, DC 20005
(202)862-1300
Ultimate Parent: Mobil.

★ 58368 ★ Mobil Oil Corp.
3445 Fairfld Rd. Balto Md
Washington, DC
(202)628-1363
Ultimate Parent: Mobil.

★ 58369 ★ Monsanto Co.
700 14th St. NW Fl. 1100
Washington, DC 20005-2010
(202)783-2460
Company Type: Branch. Officer: Thomas M. Helscher. Ultimate Parent: Monsanto. SIC: 5169—Chemicals & Allied Products Nec.

★ 58370 ★ National Steel Corp.
1575 I St. NW
Washington, DC 20005
(202)638-7707
Ultimate Parent: National Intergroup.

★ 58371 ★ Nationsbank-Dc Area Branch Ofc
5301 Wisconsin Ave. NW
Washington, DC 20015
(202)955-8840
Ultimate Parent: Nationsbank Corp.

★ 58372 ★ **Nationsbank-Dc Area Branch Ofc**
1090 Vermongt Ave.
Washington, DC
(202)955-8850
Ultimate Parent: Nationsbank Corp.

★ 58373 ★ **Nationsbank-Dc Area Branch Ofc**
1729 Wisconsin Ave. NW
Washington, DC 20007
(202)955-8835
Ultimate Parent: Nationsbank Corp.

★ 58374 ★ **Nationsbank-Dc Area Branch Ofc**
666 Pennsylvania Ave. SE
Washington, DC 20003
(202)955-8860
Ultimate Parent: Nationsbank Corp.

★ 58375 ★ **Nationsbank-Dc Area Branch Ofc**
1001 Pennsylvania Ave. NW
Washington, DC 20004
(202)955-8880
Ultimate Parent: Nationsbank Corp.

★ 58376 ★ **Nationsbank-Dc Area Branch Ofc**
961 H Street NE
Washington, DC 20002
(202)955-8198
Ultimate Parent: Nationsbank Corp.

★ 58377 ★ **Nationsbank-Dc Area Branch Ofc**
1818 L St. NW
Washington, DC 20036
(202)955-8845
Ultimate Parent: Nationsbank Corp.

★ 58378 ★ **Nationsbank-Dc Area Branch Ofc**
601 13th St. NW
Washington, DC 20005
(202)637-5406
Ultimate Parent: Nationsbank Corp.

★ 58379 ★ **Nationsbank-Dc Area Branch Ofc**
4400 Connecticut Ave. NW
Washington, DC 20008
(202)955-8830
Ultimate Parent: Nationsbank Corp.

★ 58380 ★ **NationsBank of DC, NA**
1001 Pennsylvania Ave. NW
Washington, DC 20004
(202)955-8880
Location Type: Branch office. **Ultimate Parent:** Nationsbank Corp. **SIC:** 6021—National Commercial Banks.

★ 58381 ★ **NationsBank of DC, NA**
1090 Vermont Ave. NW
Washington, DC 20005
(202)955-8850
Location Type: Branch office. **Ultimate Parent:** Nationsbank Corp. **SIC:** 6021—National Commercial Banks.

★ 58382 ★ **NationsBank of DC, NA**
601 13th St. NW, Ste. 200 S
Washington, DC 20004
(202)955-8790
Location Type: Branch office. **Ultimate Parent:** Nationsbank Corp. **SIC:** 6021—National Commercial Banks.

★ 58383 ★ **NationsBank of DC, NA**
1818 L St. NW
Washington, DC 20036
(202)955-8845
Location Type: Branch office. **Ultimate Parent:** Nationsbank Corp. **SIC:** 6021—National Commercial Banks.

★ 58384 ★ **NationsBank of DC, NA**
1729 Wisconsin Ave. NW
Washington, DC 20007
(202)955-8835
Location Type: Branch office. **Ultimate Parent:** Nationsbank Corp. **SIC:** 6021—National Commercial Banks.

★ 58385 ★ **NationsBank of DC, NA**
961 H St. NE
Washington, DC 20002
(202)955-8893
Location Type: Branch office. **Ultimate Parent:** Nationsbank Corp. **SIC:** 6021—National Commercial Banks.

★ 58386 ★ **NationsBank of DC, NA**
1350 Connecticut Ave. NW
Washington, DC 20036
(202)955-8992
Location Type: Branch office. **Ultimate Parent:** Nationsbank Corp. **SIC:** 6021—National Commercial Banks.

★ 58387 ★ **NationsBank of DC, NA**
5301 Wisconsin Ave. NW
Washington, DC 20016
(202)955-8840
Location Type: Branch office. **Ultimate Parent:** Nationsbank Corp.

★ 58388 ★ **NationsBank of DC, NA**
666 Pennsylvania Ave. SE
Washington, DC 20003
(202)955-8860
Location Type: Branch office. **Ultimate Parent:** Nationsbank Corp. **SIC:** 6021—National Commercial Banks.

★ 58389 ★ **NationsBank of DC, NA**
4400 Connecticut Ave. NW
Washington, DC 20008
(202)955-8830
Location Type: Branch office. **Ultimate Parent:** Nationsbank Corp. **SIC:** 6021—National Commercial Banks.

★ 58390 ★ **NationsBank of DC, NA**
3131 Mt. Pleasant NW
Washington, DC 20010
(202)955-8974
Location Type: Branch office. **Ultimate Parent:** Nationsbank Corp. **SIC:** 6021—National Commercial Banks.

★ 58391 ★ **NationsBank of DC, NA**
2100 Martin Luther King, Jr. Ave. SE
Washington, DC 20020
(202)955-8980
Location Type: Branch office. **Ultimate Parent:** Nationsbank Corp. **SIC:** 6021—National Commercial Banks.

★ 58392 ★ **NationsBank of DC, NA**
1801 K St. NW
Washington, DC 20006
(202)955-8810 **Telex:** MCI6844406
Location Type: Branch office. **Officer:** J. H. Chanler, President & CEO. **Ultimate Parent:** Nationsbank Corp. **SIC:** 6021—National Commercial Banks.

★ 58393 ★ **Nationsbankdc Area Branch Ofc**
1801 K Street NW
Washington, DC 20006
(202)955-8810
Ultimate Parent: Nationsbank Corp.

★ 58394 ★ **Natural Gas Pipeline Co. of Ame**
1747 Pa Ave. NW
Washington, DC
(202)783-7000
Ultimate Parent: Occidental Petroleum Corp.

★ 58395 ★ **New York Life Insurance Co. Fede**
1001 Pa Ave. NW
Washington, DC 20004
(202)783-4484
Ultimate Parent: New York Life.

★ 58396 ★ **New York State Electric & Gas**
601 Pa Ave. NW
Washington, DC
(202)783-5521
Ultimate Parent: New York State Electric & Gas.

★ 58397 ★ **North American Van Lines Agenc**
Wash Dc
Washington, DC
(202)529-6424
Ultimate Parent: Norfolk Southern.

★ 58398 ★ **Occidental International Corp.**
1747 Pennsylvania Ave., NW, Ste. 375
Washington, DC 20006
(202)857-3000 **Fax:** (202)857-3030
Officer: Mel H. Fischer, President. **Ultimate Parent:** Occidental Petroleum Corp.

★ 58399 ★ **Occupational Health Services Inc.**
Washington, DC
(202)857-0467
Ultimate Parent: Foundation Health Corp.

★ 58400 ★ **Oryx Energy Co.**
1212 Ny Ave. NW
Washington, DC
(202)682-1212
Ultimate Parent: Oryx Energy.

★ 58401 ★ **Owens-Corning Fiberglass Corp.**
1225 I St. NW
Washington, DC 20005
(202)682-4785
Ultimate Parent: Owens-Corning.

★ 58402 ★ **Pacific Gas & Electric Co.**
1726 M St. NW
Washington, DC
(202)466-7980
Ultimate Parent: Pacific Gas & Electric.

★ 58403 ★ **Pacific Telesis Group Washington**
1275 Pa Ave. NW
Washington, DC 20004
(202)383-6400
Ultimate Parent: Pacific Telesis Group.

★ 58404 ★ **Personal Systems**
6029 Dix St. NE
Washington, DC 20019
(202)398-5989
Ultimate Parent: IBM.

★ 58405 ★ **Pinnacle West Capital Corporate**
1735 I St. NW
Washington, DC 20006
(202)293-2655
Ultimate Parent: Pinnacle West Capital.

★ 58406 ★ **Pitney Bowes**
901 E. St. NW
Washington, DC 20004
(202)223-2230
Officer: Mary Seifried, Vice President. **Ultimate Parent:** Pitney Bowes. **SIC:** 2759—Commercial Printing Nec.

★ 58407 ★ **Potomac Capital Investment Corp.**
900 19th St. NW
Washington, DC 20006
(202)775-4620
Ultimate Parent: Potomac Electric Power.

★ 58408 ★ **Potomac Electric Power**
1900 Pennsylvania Ave. NW
Washington, DC 20068
(202)872-2000
Company Type: Headquarters. **Officer:** Edward F. Mitchell. **Employee Count:** 4893. **Fortune Service 500:** Ranking 39.

★ 58409 ★ **Prudential Securities Inc.**
815 Connecticut Ave. NW 3
Washington, DC 20006
(202)872-6500
Ultimate Parent: Prudential of America.

★ 58410 ★ **Qualtec Quality Service Inc.**
1155 Conn Ave. NW
Washington, DC
(202)429-6644
Ultimate Parent: FPL Group.

★ 58411 ★ **Qualtec Quality Services**
801 Pa Ave. NW
Washington, DC
(202)638-3608
Ultimate Parent: FPL Group.

★ 58412 ★ **Radio Shack**
3222 M St. NW
Washington, DC 20007
(202)965-7440
Company Type: Division. **Ultimate Parent:** Tandy Corp.

★ 58413 ★ **Radio Shack**
1150 Connecticut Ave. NW
Washington, DC 20036
(202)833-3355
Company Type: Division. **Ultimate Parent:** Tandy Corp.

★ 58414 ★ **Radio Shack**
3222 M St. NW
Washington, DC 20007
(202)965-7440
Company Type: Division. **Ultimate Parent:** Tandy Corp.

★ 58415 ★ **Radio Shack**
4608 Wisconsin Ave. NW
Washington, DC 20016
(202)363-2541
Company Type: Division. **Ultimate Parent:** Tandy Corp.

★ 58416 ★ **Radio Shack**
1100 15th St. NW
Washington, DC 20005
(202)296-2311
Company Type: Division. **Ultimate Parent:** Tandy Corp.

★ 58417 ★ **Radio Shack**
1528 Benning Rd. NE
Washington, DC 20002
(202)397-3090
Company Type: Division. **Ultimate Parent:** Tandy Corp.

★ 58418 ★ **Radio Shack**
1345 F St. NW
Washington, DC 20004
(202)737-6055
Company Type: Division. **Ultimate Parent:** Tandy Corp.

★ 58419 ★ **Radio Shack**
401 M St. NW
Washington, DC
(202)488-4544
Company Type: Division. **Ultimate Parent:** Tandy Corp.

★ 58420 ★ **Radio Shack**
4608 Wisconsin Ave. NW
Washington, DC 20016
(202)363-2541
Company Type: Division. **Ultimate Parent:** Tandy Corp.

★ 58421 ★ **Radio Shack**
1345 F St. NW
Washington, DC 20004
(202)737-6055
Company Type: Division. **Ultimate Parent:** Tandy Corp.

★ 58422 ★ **Radio Shack**
401 M St. NW
Washington, DC
(202)488-4544
Company Type: Division. **Ultimate Parent:** Tandy Corp.

★ 58423 ★ **Radio Shack**
1528 Benning Rd. NE
Washington, DC 20002
(202)397-3090
Company Type: Division. **Ultimate Parent:** Tandy Corp.

★ 58424 ★ **Radio Shack**
1150 Connecticut Ave. NW
Washington, DC 20036
(202)833-3355
Company Type: Division. **Ultimate Parent:** Tandy Corp.

★ 58425 ★ **Radio Shack**
1100 15th St. NW
Washington, DC 20005
(202)296-2311
Company Type: Division. **Ultimate Parent:** Tandy Corp.

★ 58426 ★   Radio Shack
Div. of Tandy
4250 Conn Ave. NW
Washington, DC
(202)537-0600
Company Type: Division. Ultimate Parent:
Tandy Corp.

★ 58427 ★   Radio Shack
Div. of Tandy Corp.
1835 K St. NW
Washington, DC 20006
(202)293-0585
Company Type: Division. Ultimate Parent:
Tandy Corp.

★ 58428 ★   Residence Inn by
Marriott
1000 29th St. NW
Washington, DC 20007
(202)298-1600
Ultimate Parent: Marriott International.

★ 58429 ★   Riggs National Bank
Washington 301 Seven
Washington, DC
(202)835-6000
Ultimate Parent: Riggs National Corp.

★ 58430 ★   Riggs National Bank
of Washington
Washington, DC
(202)835-6422
Location Type: Branch office. Ultimate
Parent: Riggs National Corp.

★ 58431 ★   Riggs National Bank
of Washington
800 H St., NE
Washington, DC 20002-3698
(202)624-3304
Location Type: Branch office. Ultimate
Parent: Riggs National Corp. SIC: 6021—
National Commercial Banks.

★ 58432 ★   Riggs National Bank
of Washington
1201 Wisconsin Ave., NW
Washington, DC 20007-3221
(202)835-5580
Location Type: Branch office. Ultimate
Parent: Riggs National Corp. SIC: 6021—
National Commercial Banks.

★ 58433 ★   Riggs National Bank
of Washington
1800 M St., NW
Washington, DC 20036-5802
(202)835-5560
Location Type: Branch office. Officer:
Larry Walsh, Manager. Ultimate Parent:
Riggs National Corp. SIC: 6021—National
Commercial Banks.

★ 58434 ★   Riggs National Bank
of Washington
4249 Wisconsin Ave., NW
Washington, DC 20016-2187
(202)835-5650
Location Type: Branch office. Ultimate
Parent: Riggs National Corp. SIC: 6021—
National Commercial Banks.

★ 58435 ★   Riggs National Bank
of Washington
1750 Pennsylvania Ave., NW
Washington, DC 20006-4503
(202)835-5605
Location Type: Branch office. Ultimate
Parent: Riggs National Corp. SIC: 6021—
National Commercial Banks.

★ 58436 ★   Riggs National Bank
of Washington
37th & O Sts., NW
Washington, DC 20057
(202)835-4908
Location Type: Branch office. Ultimate
Parent: Riggs National Corp. SIC: 6021—
National Commercial Banks.

★ 58437 ★   Riggs National Bank
of Washington
7th St. & Florida Ave., NE
Washington, DC 20002
(202)835-5660
Location Type: Branch office. Ultimate
Parent: Riggs National Corp. SIC: 6021—
National Commercial Banks.

★ 58438 ★   Riggs National Bank
of Washington
3400 International Dr., NW
Washington, DC 20008-3006
(202)835-5030
Location Type: Branch office. Officer:
Joseph Goheen, Vice President. Ultimate
Parent: Riggs National Corp. SIC: 6021—
National Commercial Banks.

★ 58439 ★   Riggs National Bank
of Washington
2000 Martin Luther King, Jr. Ave., SE
Washington, DC 20020-7000
(202)624-3643
Location Type: Branch office. Ultimate
Parent: Riggs National Corp. SIC: 6021—
National Commercial Banks.

★ 58440 ★   Riggs National Bank
of Washington
17th & H Sts., NW
Washington, DC 20006
(202)835-5250
Location Type: Branch office. Ultimate
Parent: Riggs National Corp. SIC: 6021—
National Commercial Banks.

★ 58441 ★   Riggs National Bank
of Washington
935 L'Enfant Plz. North, SW
Washington, DC 20024-2193
(202)835-5665
Location Type: Branch office. Ultimate
Parent: Riggs National Corp. SIC: 6021—
National Commercial Banks.

★ 58442 ★   Riggs National Bank
of Washington
1779 Columbia Rd., NW
Washington, DC 20009-2897
(202)835-5700
Location Type: Branch office. Ultimate
Parent: Riggs National Corp. SIC: 6021—
National Commercial Banks.

★ 58443 ★   Riggs National Bank
of Washington
1348 4th St., NE
Washington, DC 20002-7098
(202)835-5690
Location Type: Branch office. Ultimate
Parent: Riggs National Corp. SIC: 6021—
National Commercial Banks.

★ 58444 ★   Riggs National Bank
of Washington
1919 Pennsylvania Ave., NW
Washington, DC 20006-3404
(202)624-3333
Location Type: Branch office. Officer:
Sheldon Brown, Manager. Ultimate Parent:
Riggs National Corp. SIC: 6021—National
Commercial Banks.

★ 58445 ★   Riggs National Bank
of Washington
3300 14th St., NW
Washington, DC 20010-2399
(202)835-5720
Location Type: Branch office. Officer:
Rosa Valentine, Manager. Ultimate Parent:
Riggs National Corp. SIC: 6021—National
Commercial Banks.

★ 58446 ★   Riggs National Bank
of Washington
7601 Georgia Ave., NW
Washington, DC 20012-1695
(202)624-3313
Location Type: Branch office. Officer:
Kathryn Clay, Vice President. Ultimate
Parent: Riggs National Corp. SIC: 6021—
National Commercial Banks.

★ 58447 ★   Riggs National Bank
of Washington
833 7th St., NW
Washington, DC 20001-3767
(202)835-5735
Location Type: Branch office. Officer:
Jacqueline Hawkins, Manager. Ultimate
Parent: Riggs National Corp. SIC: 6021—
National Commercial Banks.

★ 58448 ★   Riggs National Bank
of Washington
4801 Massachusetts Ave., NW
Washington, DC 20016-2069
(202)835-5765
Location Type: Branch office. Ultimate
Parent: Riggs National Corp. SIC: 6021—
National Commercial Banks.

★ 58449 ★   Riggs National Bank
of Washington
4100 S. Capital St., SE
Washington, DC 20032-1390
(202)835-5750
Location Type: Branch office. Officer:
Maggie Bethea, Vice President. Ultimate
Parent: Riggs National Corp. SIC: 6021—
National Commercial Banks.

★ 58450 ★   Riggs National Bank
of Washington
1120 Vermont Ave., NW
Washington, DC 20005-3523
(202)835-6400
Location Type: Branch office. Ultimate
Parent: Riggs National Corp. SIC: 6021—
National Commercial Banks.

★ 58451 ★   Riggs National Bank
of Washington
1300 New York Ave., NW
Washington, DC 20005-4710
(202)835-5427
Location Type: Branch office. Officer:
Lynne Watson, Manager. Ultimate Parent:
Riggs National Corp. SIC: 6021—National
Commercial Banks.

★ 58452 ★   Riggs National Bank
of Washington
1875 Connecticut Ave., NW
Washington, DC 20009-5728
(202)835-5795
Location Type: Branch office. Officer:
Maria Lamont, Vice President. Ultimate
Parent: Riggs National Corp. SIC: 6021—
National Commercial Banks.

★ 58453 ★   Riggs National Bank
of Washington
1920 L St. NW
Washington, DC 20036-5004
(202)835-5780
Location Type: Branch office. Ultimate
Parent: Riggs National Corp. SIC: 6021—
National Commercial Banks.

★ 58454 ★   Riggs National Bank
of Washington
301 7th St., NW
Washington, DC 20007-5108
(202)835-6000
Location Type: Branch office. Officer:
James Nelson, Manager. Ultimate Parent:
Riggs National Corp. SIC: 6021—National
Commercial Banks.

★ 58455 ★   Riggs National Bank
of Washington
3050 K St. NW, Ste. 120
Washington, DC 20007-5108
(202)835-4900
Location Type: Branch office. Ultimate
Parent: Riggs National Corp. SIC: 6021—
National Commercial Banks.

★ 58456 ★   Riggs National Bank
of Washington
26th & M Sts. NW
Washington, DC 20037
(202)835-4939
Location Type: Branch office. Ultimate
Parent: Riggs National Corp. SIC: 6021—
National Commercial Banks.

★ 58457 ★   Riggs National Bank
of Washington
2600 Virginia Ave., NW
Washington, DC 20037-1905
(202)835-5845
Location Type: Branch office. Ultimate
Parent: Riggs National Corp. SIC: 6021—
National Commercial Banks.

★ 58458 ★   Riggs National Bank
of Washington
5252 Wisconsin Ave. NW
Washington, DC 20015-2062
(202)835-5765
Location Type: Branch office. Ultimate
Parent: Riggs National Corp. SIC: 6021—
National Commercial Banks.

★ 58459 ★   Riggs National Corp.
1503 Pennsylvania Ave. NW
Washington, DC 20005
(202)835-6000 Fax: (202)835-4009
Company Type: Headquarters. Officer:
Joseph L. Allbritton, CEO. Employee
Count: 1667. Sales: 369 M. Fortune
Service 500: Ranking 94.

★ 58460 ★   Rite Aid
1501 K St. NW
Washington, DC
(202)638-5226
Ultimate Parent: Rite Aid.

★ 58461 ★   Rite Aid
5720 Georgia Ave. NW
Washington, DC
(202)722-5251
Ultimate Parent: Rite Aid.

★ 58462 ★   Rite Aid
15th & L Sts NW
Washington, DC
(202)296-7737
Ultimate Parent: Rite Aid.

★ 58463 ★   Rite Aid
1815 Connecticut Ave.
Washington, DC 20009
(202)745-9115
Ultimate Parent: Rite Aid.

★ 58464 ★   Rite Aid
801 H St. NE
Washington, DC 20002
(202)675-2555
Ultimate Parent: Rite Aid.

★ 58465 ★   Rite Aid
2907 Martin Luther King Jr.
Washington, DC 20032
(202)574-9173
Ultimate Parent: Rite Aid.

★ 58466 ★   Rite Aid
15th & L Sts NW
Washington, DC
(202)296-6171
Ultimate Parent: Rite Aid.

★ 58467 ★   Salomon Brothers
Inc.
1455 Pa Ave. NW
Washington, DC 20004
(202)879-4100
Ultimate Parent: Salomon, Inc.

★ 58468 ★   Schuller International
Inc-Man
1625 K St. NW
Washington, DC 20006
(202)785-4940
Ultimate Parent: Manville Corp. SIC:
9721—International Affairs.

★ 58469 ★   Schwab & Co. Inc/
Charles
1722 I St. NW
Washington, DC 20006
(202)638-2500
Ultimate Parent: Charles Schwab Corp.

★ 58470 ★   Seabury & Smith
1255 23rd St. NW
Washington, DC 20037
(202)296-8030
Ultimate Parent: Marsh & McLennan.

★ 58471 ★   Shell Oil Co.
1401 I St. NW
Washington, DC 20005
(202)466-1405
Ultimate Parent: Shell Oil Co.

★ 58472 ★   Signet Bank, NA
2119 Bladensburg Rd.
Washington, DC 20018-1484
(202)351-5720
Company Type: Subsidiary. Location
Type: Branch office. Officer: Doris
Harrison, Mgr. Ultimate Parent: Signet
Banking Corp. SIC: 6021—National
Commercial Banks.

★ 58473 ★   Signet Bank, NA
1505 Maryland Ave. NE
Washington, DC 20002-7696
(202)388-4350
Company Type: Subsidiary. Location
Type: Branch office. Officer: Tracy Davis,
Mgr. Ultimate Parent: Signet Banking Corp.
SIC: 6021—National Commercial Banks.

★ 58474 ★   Signet Bank, NA
1400 Montana Ave. NE
Washington, DC 20018-3403
(202)452-5829
Company Type: Subsidiary. Location
Type: Branch office. Officer: Blanche
Peebles McNeil, Mgr. Ultimate Parent:
Signet Banking Corp. SIC: 6021—National
Commercial Banks.

★ 58475 ★　Signet Bank, NA
1850 K St. NW
Washington, DC 20006-2213
(202)452-5825
Company Type: Subsidiary. **Location Type:** Branch office. **Officer:** Ruthie Campbell, Mgr. **Ultimate Parent:** Signet Banking Corp. **SIC:** 6021—National Commercial Banks.

★ 58476 ★　Signet Bank, NA
3940 Minnesota Ave. NE
Washington, DC 20019-2691
(202)452-5800
Company Type: Subsidiary. **Location Type:** Branch office. **Officer:** Sabrina Butler, Mgr. **Ultimate Parent:** Signet Banking Corp. **SIC:** 6021—National Commercial Banks.

★ 58477 ★　Signet Bank, NA
2801 Georgia Ave. NW
Washington, DC 20001-3818
(202)452-5810
Company Type: Subsidiary. **Location Type:** Branch office. **Officer:** Antoinette Redding, Mgr. **Ultimate Parent:** Signet Banking Corp. **SIC:** 6021—National Commercial Banks.

★ 58478 ★　Signet Bank, NA
1287 4th St. NE
Washington, DC 20002-7012
(202)542-5680
Company Type: Subsidiary. **Location Type:** Branch office. **Officer:** Sharon Jones, Mgr. **Ultimate Parent:** Signet Banking Corp. **SIC:** 6021—National Commercial Banks.

★ 58479 ★　Signet Bank, NA
1800 G St. NW
Washington, DC 20006-4407
(202)452-5640
Company Type: Subsidiary. **Location Type:** Branch office. **Officer:** San Juan Bailey, Mgr. **Ultimate Parent:** Signet Banking Corp. **SIC:** 6021—National Commercial Banks.

★ 58480 ★　Signet Bank, NA
4841 Massachusetts Ave. NW
Washington, DC 20016-2070
(202)452-5700
Company Type: Subsidiary. **Location Type:** Branch office. **Officer:** Laura Medigovich, Mgr. **Ultimate Parent:** Signet Banking Corp. **SIC:** 6021—National Commercial Banks.

★ 58481 ★　Signet Bank, NA
620 Michigan Ave. NE
Washington, DC 20064
(202)452-5720
Company Type: Subsidiary. **Location Type:** Branch office. **Officer:** Sheila Wells, Mgr. **Ultimate Parent:** Signet Banking Corp. **SIC:** 6021—National Commercial Banks.

★ 58482 ★　Signet Bank, NA
1850 M St. NW
Washington, DC 20036-3307
(202)331-5646
Company Type: Subsidiary. **Location Type:** Branch office. **Officer:** Connie Karpowich, Mgr. **Ultimate Parent:** Signet Banking Corp. **SIC:** 6021—National Commercial Banks.

★ 58483 ★　Signet Bank, NA
215 Pennsylvania Ave. SE
Washington, DC 20003-1155
(202)331-2100
Company Type: Subsidiary. **Location Type:** Branch office. **Officer:** Betty Wang, Mgr. **SIC:** 6021—National Commercial Banks.

★ 58484 ★　Signet Bank, NA
1510 K St. NW
Washington, DC 20005-1205
(202)331-5693
Company Type: Subsidiary. **Location Type:** Branch office. **Officer:** Millie Axell, Mgr. **Ultimate Parent:** Signet Banking Corp. **SIC:** 6021—National Commercial Banks.

★ 58485 ★　Signet Bank, NA
1350 F St. NW
Washington, DC 20004-1101
(202)331-5710
Company Type: Subsidiary. **Location Type:** Branch office. **Officer:** Margaret L. Knight, Mgr. **Ultimate Parent:** Signet Banking Corp. **SIC:** 6021—National Commercial Banks.

★ 58486 ★　Signet Bank, NA
5025 Connecticut Ave. NW
Washington, DC 20008-2024
(202)331-5740
Company Type: Subsidiary. **Location Type:** Branch office. **Officer:** Felicia Cotton, Mgr. **Ultimate Parent:** Signet Banking Corp. **SIC:** 6021—National Commercial Banks.

★ 58487 ★　Signet Bank, NA
400 7th St. NW
Washington, DC 20004-2206
(202)331-5004
Company Type: Subsidiary. **Location Type:** Branch office. **Officer:** Sherry Asrarieh, Mgr. **Ultimate Parent:** Signet Banking Corp. **SIC:** 6021—National Commercial Banks.

★ 58488 ★　Signet Bank, NA
1130 Connecticut Ave. NW
Washington, DC 20036-3904
(202)825-8400 **Fax:** (202)223-4857
Company Type: Subsidiary. **Location Type:** Branch office. **Officer:** G. Patrick Clancy, Chairman, President, & CEO. **Ultimate Parent:** Signet Banking Corp. **SIC:** 6021—National Commercial Banks.

★ 58489 ★　Smith Barney Harris Upham & Co.
1776 I St. NW
Washington, DC 20006-3700
(202)857-5444
Officer: E. Joseph West. **Ultimate Parent:** Automatic Data Processing, Inc. **SIC:** 6211—Security Brokers & Dealers; 6221—Commodity Contracts Brokers & Dealers.

★ 58490 ★　Solar Turbines Inc.
1730 Pa Ave. NW
Washington, DC 20006
(202)783-1833
Ultimate Parent: Caterpillar.

★ 58491 ★　Southern California Edison Co.
1001 Pa Ave. NW
Washington, DC 20004
(202)393-3075
Ultimate Parent: Scecorp.

★ 58492 ★　Southern California Gas Co.
1150 Connecticut Ave. NW
Washington, DC 20036
(202)822-3700
Ultimate Parent: Pacific Enterprises.

★ 58493 ★　Southern International Corp.
1285 4th St. NE
Washington, DC 20002
(202)543-3130
Ultimate Parent: Southern.

★ 58494 ★　Structure
Chevy Chase Paviln
Washington, DC
(202)362-2054
Ultimate Parent: Limited.

★ 58495 ★　Structure Tone Interior Design
1001 Pa Ave. NW
Washington, DC 20004
(202)638-2901
Ultimate Parent: Limited.

★ 58496 ★　Student Loan Marketing Association
1050 Thomas Jefferson St. NW
Washington, DC 20007
(202)333-8000 **Fax:** (202)298-3160
Company Type: Headquarters. **Officer:** Lawrence A. Hough, CEO. **Employee Count:** 4510. **Sales:** 2418 M. **Fortune Service 500:** Ranking 13.

★ 58497 ★　Student Loan Marketing Association
1050 Thomas Jefferson St.
Washington, DC 20007
(202)965-7700
Ultimate Parent: Student Loan Marketing Association.

★ 58498 ★　Student Loan Marketing Association
1055 Thomas Jefferson NW
Washington, DC 20007
(202)333-8000
Ultimate Parent: Student Loan Marketing Association.

★ 58499 ★　Syscon Corp.
1000 Thomas Jefferson St.
Washington, DC 20007-3835
(202)342-4000 **Fax:** (202)342-4449
Company Type: Subsidiary. **Officer:** Nils Ericson, President & COO. **Ultimate Parent:** Harnischfeger Industries. **SIC:** 7371—Computer Programming Services; 7372—Prepackaged Software; 7374—Data Processing & Preparation. **Employee Count:** 1600. **Sales:** 235 M.

★ 58500 ★　Syscon Services Inc.
2828 Pennsylvania Ave. NW
Washington, DC 20007-3719
(202)342-4900
Company Type: Subsidiary. **Officer:** James Perriello, President. **Ultimate Parent:** Harnischfeger Industries. **SIC:** 7371—Computer Programming Services; 7379—Computer Related Services Nec; 7376—Computer Facilities Management. **Employee Count:** 400. **Sales:** 27 M.

★ 58501 ★　Tesoro Petroleum Corp.
1800 K St. NW
Washington, DC 20006
(202)775-8840
Ultimate Parent: Tesoro Petroleum Corp.

★ 58502 ★　Texas Instruments Government
1455 Pennsylvania Ave. NW
Washington, DC 20004
(202)628-3133
Ultimate Parent: Texas Instruments.

★ 58503 ★　Texas Utilities Services Inc.
1825 K St. NW
Washington, DC 20006
(202)822-9745
Ultimate Parent: Texas Utilities.

★ 58504 ★　TheChesapeake & Potomac Telephone Co.
1710 "H" St.
Washington, DC 20006
(202)392-3701
Company Type: Subsidiary. **Officer:** Delamo E. Lewis, Pres. & CEO. **Ultimate Parent:** Bell Atlantic Corp. **SIC:** 4812—Radiotelephone Communications. **Employee Count:** 3580. **Sales:** 509600000 M.

★ 58505 ★　Trans World Airlines
808 17th St. NW
Washington, DC 20006
(202)737-7400
Ultimate Parent: Trans World Airlines.

★ 58506 ★　Trans World Airlines
1601 K St. NW
Washington, DC 20006
(202)737-7400
Ultimate Parent: Trans World Airlines.

★ 58507 ★　Trans World Airlines, Inc.
Washington, DC 20006
(202)859-2525
Ultimate Parent: Trans World Airlines.

★ 58508 ★　Trans World Airlines, Inc.
808 17th St. NW
Washington, DC 20006
(202)457-4750
Ultimate Parent: Trans World Airlines.

★ 58509 ★　Union Oil Co. of California
1050 Conneticut Ave. NW
Washington, DC
(202)659-7600
Ultimate Parent: Unocal Corp.

★ 58510 ★　United Technologies Auto
1401 1 St. NW, 600
Washington, DC 20005
(202)336-7400
Officer: William Paul, Senior Vice President. **Ultimate Parent:** United Technologies. **SIC:** 3721—Aircraft.

★ 58511 ★　Utility Fuels Inc.
1050 17th St. NW
Washington, DC 20036
(202)467-5040
Ultimate Parent: Houston Industries.

★ 58512 ★　Vickers Inc.
450 5th St. NW
Washington, DC
(202)783-1859
Ultimate Parent: Trinova Corp.

★ 58513 ★　Waldenbooks
Georgetown
Washington, DC 20007
(202)333-3033
Ultimate Parent: K-Mart.

★ 58514 ★　Waldenbooks Wa Spring Valley S
1700 Pa Ave. NW
Washington, DC 20006
(202)362-6329
Ultimate Parent: K-Mart.

★ 58515 ★　Waldenbooks Wa Stores Spring V
1700 Pa Ave. NW
Washington, DC 20006
(202)362-6329
Ultimate Parent: K-Mart.

★ 58516 ★　Wall Street Journal
1025 Connecticut Avenue
Washington, DC 20036
(202)862-9200
Ultimate Parent: Dow Jones.

★ 58517 ★　Wall Street Journal
1025 Connecticut Ave. NW, No. 800
Washington, DC 20036
(202)862-9200
Officer: Al Hunt, Manager. **Ultimate Parent:** Dow Jones. **SIC:** 2711—Newspapers.

★ 58518 ★　Washington Post
1150 15th St. NW
Washington, DC 20071
(202)334-6000
Company Type: Headquarters. **Officer:** Donald E. Graham. **Sales:** 1498.2 M. **Fortune 500:** Largest U.S. Industrial Corporations: Ranking 279.

★ 58519 ★　Washington Post Newspaper
1150 15th St. NW Fl. 7
Washington, DC 20005
(202)334-6000
Officer: Thomas H. Ferguson, President. **Ultimate Parent:** Washington Post. **SIC:** 2711—Newspapers; 2721—Periodicals; 2759—Commercial Printing Nec.

★ 58520 ★　Western Union International
26 Broadway New York Ny
Washington, DC
(202)628-5155
Ultimate Parent: MCI Communications.

★ 58521 ★　Wichita Eagle-Beacon the
529 14th St. NW
Washington, DC 20045
(202)383-6000
Ultimate Parent: Knight-Ridder.

★ 58522 ★　Wusa-Tv Channel Job Inquiries
4100 Wis Ave. NW
Washington, DC
(202)895-5895
Ultimate Parent: Gannett.

★ 58523 ★　WUSA-TV Channel 9
4001 Brandywine St. NW
Washington, DC 20016
(202)364-3900
Ultimate Parent: Gannett.

★ 58524 ★　WUSA-TV Channel 9
4100 Wisconsin Ave. NW
Washington, DC
(202)895-5500
Ultimate Parent: Gannett.

★ 58525 ★　WUSA-TV Channel 9 Community Affairs
4100 Wis Ave. NW
Washington, DC
(202)895-5810
Ultimate Parent: Gannett.

★ 58526 ★　WUSA-TV Channel 9 News
4100 Wis Ave. NW
Washington, DC
(202)895-5700
Ultimate Parent: Gannett.

★ 58527 ★　WUSA-TV Channel 9
Personnel
4100 Wis Ave. NW
Washington, DC
(202)473-8666 **Fax:** (202)785-9344 (202)
895-5884
Officer: Barbara Braboy, Group Claims
Director. **Ultimate Parent:** New York Life.
Ultimate Parent: Gannett.

★ 58528 ★　Wusa-Tv Channel 9
Program Info
4100 Wis Ave. NW
Washington, DC
(202)895-5800
Ultimate Parent: Gannett.

★ 58529 ★　Wusa-Tv Channel 9
Sales
4100 Wis Ave. NW
Washington, DC
(202)895-5938
Ultimate Parent: Gannett.

Washinton

★ 58530 ★　**New York Life World
Bank Group Claims Office**
Eastern Group Claims Region
World Bank Bldg.
1818 H St. NW, Room N105
Washinton, DC 20433
(202)473-8666 **Fax:** (202)785-9344
Officer: Barbara Braboy, Group Claims
Director. **Ultimate Parent:** New York Life.

FLORIDA

Alachua

★ 58532 ★ Pizza Hut
1750 W. Martin Luther King
Alachua, FL 32615
(904)462-5900
Ultimate Parent: Pepsico. SIC: 5812—
Eating Places.

Altamonte Spg

★ 58533 ★ Burdines Optical
Altamonte
Altamonte Spg, FL 32701
(407)830-2398
Ultimate Parent: Federated Department
Stores. SIC: 5995—Optical Goods Stores.

★ 58534 ★ Burdines Travel
Bureau
Altamonte
Altamonte Spg, FL 32701
(407)834-5454
Ultimate Parent: Federated Department
Stores. SIC: 7999—Amusement &
Recreation Nec.

★ 58535 ★ Circus World Toy
Store Inc.
66 Altamonte Mall
Altamonte Spg, FL 32701
(407)834-7887
Ultimate Parent: Melville. SIC: 5945—
Hobby, Toy & Game Shops.

★ 58536 ★ Coca Cola U S a
921 Douglas Ave.
Altamonte Spg, FL 32714
(407)774-1574
Ultimate Parent: Coca-Cola. SIC: 2086—
Bottled & Canned Soft Drinks.

★ 58537 ★ Jiffy Lube
420 State Hwy. 434
Altamonte Spg, FL 32714
(407)788-2585
Ultimate Parent: Pennzoil. SIC: 7549—
Automotive Services Nec.

★ 58538 ★ Kentucky Fried
Chicken
100 E. Altamonte Dr.
Altamonte Spg, FL 32701
(407)834-3121
Ultimate Parent: Pepsico. SIC: 5812—
Eating Places.

★ 58539 ★ Lane Bryant
705 Altamonte Mall
Altamonte Spg, FL 32701
(407)831-8200
Ultimate Parent: Limited. SIC: 5621—
Women's Clothing Stores.

★ 58540 ★ Lerner Shop
451 E. Altamonte Dr. 331
Altamonte Spg, FL 32701
(407)331-0840
Ultimate Parent: Limited. SIC: 5621—
Women's Clothing Stores.

★ 58541 ★ The Limited
20 Altamonte Mall
Altamonte Spg, FL 32701
(407)339-4752
Ultimate Parent: Limited. SIC: 5651—
Family Clothing Stores.

★ 58542 ★ The Limited Express
451 E. Altamonte Dr.
Altamonte Spg, FL 32701
(407)830-5225
Ultimate Parent: Limited. SIC: 5621—
Women's Clothing Stores.

★ 58543 ★ Mobil Mart
201 E. Altamonte Dr.
Altamonte Spg, FL 32701
(407)862-5906
Ultimate Parent: Mobil. SIC: 5541—
Gasoline Service Stations.

★ 58544 ★ Mobil Oil No H Four-D
901 E. Altamonte Dr.
Altamonte Spg, FL 32701
(407)682-5912
Ultimate Parent: Mobil. SIC: 5541—
Gasoline Service Stations.

★ 58545 ★ Radio Shack
140 E. Altamonte Dr.
Altamonte Spg, FL 32701
(407)831-0081
Company Type: Division. Ultimate Parent:
Tandy Corp. SIC: 5731—Radio, Television
& Electronics Stores.

★ 58546 ★ Taco Bell
3352 State Rd. 436 NW
Altamonte Spg, FL 32714
(407)774-9300
Ultimate Parent: Pepsico. SIC: 5812—
Eating Places.

★ 58547 ★ Transamerica
Occidental Life Inc.
395 Douglas Ave.
Altamonte Spg, FL 32714
(407)788-8336
Ultimate Parent: Transamerica Occidental
Life Insurance. SIC: 6411—Insurance
Agents, Brokers & Service.

Altamonte Springs

★ 58548 ★ American Family Life
Assurance
405 Douglas Ave.
Altamonte Springs, FL 32714
(407)788-3565
Ultimate Parent: American Family Life
Assurance Co. SIC: 6411—Insurance
Agents, Brokers & Service.

★ 58549 ★ Barnett Bank of
Central Florida, NA
460 E. Altamonte Dr.
Altamonte Springs, FL 32701
(407)263-6000
Company Type: Subsidiary. Location
Type: Branch office. Officer: Mike
McCarthy, Manager. Ultimate Parent:
Barnett Banks. SIC: 6021—National
Commercial Banks.

★ 58550 ★ Bindley-Western
Industries, Inc.
Charise Charles Division
285 Central Pkwy., Ste. 1704
Altamonte Springs, FL 32714
(407)869-7001 Fax: (407)869-8700
Company Type: Subsidiary. Officer:
Michael R. Visnich, Chief Executive Officer.
Ultimate Parent: Bindley-Western
Industries, Inc.

★ 58551 ★ Casual Corner
104 Altamonte Mall
Altamonte Springs, FL 32701
(407)831-9686
Ultimate Parent: United States Shoe. SIC:
5621—Women's Clothing Stores.

★ 58552 ★ Circuit City
1140 E. Altamonte Dr.
Altamonte Springs, FL 32701
(407)339-2228
Ultimate Parent: Circuit City Stores. SIC:
5719—Miscellaneous Home Furnishings
Stores.

★ 58553 ★ Citgo Petroleum Corp.
Altamonte
Altamonte Springs, FL 32701
(407)331-4148
Ultimate Parent: Citgo Petroleum. SIC:
5172—Petroleum Products Nec.

★ 58554 ★ First Union National
Bank of Florida
351 State Rd.
Altamonte Springs, FL 32714-2186
(407)744-3620
Location Type: Branch office. Ultimate
Parent: First Union Corp. SIC: 6021—
National Commercial Banks.

★ 58555 ★ First Union National
Bank Of Florida
1030 Montgomery Rd.
Altamonte Springs, FL 32714-3110
(407)657-3110
Location Type: Branch office. Ultimate
Parent: First Union Corp. SIC: 6021—
National Commercial Banks.

★ 58556 ★ The Gap
97 Altamonte Mall
Altamonte Springs, FL 32701
(407)831-6880
Ultimate Parent: GAP. SIC: 5651—Family
Clothing Stores.

★ 58557 ★ Lens Crafters
451 E. Altamonte Dr.
Altamonte Springs, FL 32701
(407)830-7448
Ultimate Parent: United States Shoe. SIC:
5999—Miscellaneous Retail Stores Nec.

★ 58558 ★ Linens N Things
995 W. US Hwy. 436
Altamonte Springs, FL 32714
(407)774-0604
Ultimate Parent: Melville.

★ 58559 ★ Maison Blanche
Altamonte Mall
Altamonte Springs, FL 32701
(407)830-1211
Ultimate Parent: Mercantile Stores. SIC:
5311—Department Stores.

★ 58560 ★ Owens Corning
Fiberglas
222 S. Westmonte Dr.
Altamonte Springs, FL 32714
(407)788-0870
Ultimate Parent: Owens-Corning. SIC:
5131—Piece Goods & Notions.

★ 58561 ★ Petite Sophisticate
451 E. Altamonte Dr. 483
Altamonte Springs, FL 32701
(407)830-9550
Ultimate Parent: United States Shoe. SIC:
5621—Women's Clothing Stores.

★ 58562 ★ Pizza Hut
3346 State Rd. 436 NW
Altamonte Springs, FL 32714
(407)774-3373
Ultimate Parent: Pepsico. SIC: 5812—
Eating Places.

★ 58563 ★ Savings of America, A
Division of Home Savings of
America
450 E. Altamonte Springs Dr.
Altamonte Springs, FL 32701-4602
(407)331-8647
Company Type: Division. Location Type:
Branch office. Ultimate Parent: H. F.
Ahmanson. SIC: 6021—National
Commercial Banks.

★ 58564 ★ Taylor Rental Corp.
506 State Hwy. 434
Altamonte Springs, FL 32714
(407)682-5500
Ultimate Parent: Stanley Works. SIC:
1711—Plumbing, Heating & Air-
Conditioning.

★ 58565 ★ Waldenbooks
67 Altamonte Mall
Altamonte Springs, FL 32701
(407)831-3030
Ultimate Parent: K-Mart. SIC: 5942—Book
Stores.

★ 58566 ★ Walgreen Co.
343 Whooping Loop
Altamonte Springs, FL 32701
(407)834-4337
Ultimate Parent: Walgreen Co. SIC:
5912—Drug Stores & Proprietary Stores.

Apollo Beach

★ 58567 ★ Barnett Bank of
Tampa
203 Apollo Beach Blvd.
Apollo Beach, FL 33572-2251
(813)645-3227
Company Type: Subsidiary. Location
Type: Branch office. Officer: Harriet Morris,
Office Manager. Ultimate Parent: Barnett
Banks. SIC: 6022—State Commercial
Banks.

Apopka

★ 58568 ★ Barnett Bank of
Central Florida, NA
33 E. Main St.
Apopka, FL 32703-5256
(407)889-1100
Company Type: Subsidiary. Location
Type: Branch office. Officer: David Rankin,
Manager. Ultimate Parent: Barnett Banks.
SIC: 6021—National Commercial Banks.

★ 58569 ★ Barnett Bank of
Central Florida, NA
555 S. Hunt Club Blvd.
Apopka, FL 32703-4959
(407)263-6030
Company Type: Subsidiary. Location
Type: Branch office. Officer: Bob Johnson,
Manager. Ultimate Parent: Barnett Banks.
SIC: 6021—National Commercial Banks.

★ 58570 ★ First Union Bank of
Florida
2488 Sermoran Blvd.
Apopka, FL 32703-5800
(407)884-3200
Location Type: Branch office. Ultimate
Parent: First Union Corp. SIC: 6021—
National Commercial Banks.

★ 58571 ★ Greyhound Bus Lines
316 W. Main St.
Apopka, FL 32712
(407)886-3521
Ultimate Parent: Greyhound Lines Inc. SIC:
4822—Telegraph & Other Communications.

★ 58572 ★ Kentucky Fried
Chicken
256 E. Main St.
Apopka, FL 32703
(407)886-0171
Ultimate Parent: Pepsico. SIC: 5812—
Eating Places.

★ 58573 ★ Litton Industries, Inc.
Laser Systems
2787 S. Orange Blossom Trail
Apopka, FL 32703-4397
(407)295-4010
Company Type: Division. Officer: Al Bran,
Chairman-Litton System. Ultimate Parent:
Litton Industries. SIC: 3669—
Communications Equipment Nec.

★ 58574 ★ McDonalds
Restaurants
233 E. Main St.
Apopka, FL 32703
(407)886-0822
Ultimate Parent: McDonald's.
SIC: 5812—Eating Places.

★ 58575 ★   **Radio Shack**
600 S. Hunt Club Blvd.
Apopka, FL 32703
(407)788-2852
Company Type: Division. **Ultimate Parent:** Tandy Corp. **SIC:** 5734—Computer & Software Stores.

★ 58576 ★   **Rite Aid Pharmacy**
827 Semoran Blvd.
Apopka, FL 32703
(407)886-6464
Ultimate Parent: Rite Aid. **SIC:** 5912—Drug Stores & Proprietary Stores.

★ 58577 ★   **Ryder Truck Rental**
2327 Semoran Blvd.
Apopka, FL 32703
(407)889-0977
Ultimate Parent: Ryder System. **SIC:** 7359—Equipment Rental & Leasing Nec.

★ 58578 ★   **Walgreen Drug Stores**
534 S. Hunt Club Blvd.
Apopka, FL 32703
(407)869-1020
Ultimate Parent: Walgreen Co. **SIC:** 5912—Drug Stores & Proprietary Stores.

Arcadia

★ 58579 ★   **Barnett Bank of Highlands County**
1409 E. Oak St.
Arcadia, FL 33821
(813)494-1300
Company Type: Subsidiary. **Location Type:** Branch office. **Officer:** Katie Taylor, Vice President. **Ultimate Parent:** Barnett Banks. **SIC:** 6022—State Commercial Banks.

★ 58580 ★   **Central Moloney Inc. Arcadia**
211 West Palmetto St.
Arcadia, FL 33821
Ultimate Parent: Coltec Industries. **SIC:** 3612—Transformers Except Electronic.

★ 58581 ★   **Central Moloney Transformer Arcadia**
211 W. Palmetto St.
Arcadia, FL 33821
Ultimate Parent: Coltec Industries. **SIC:** 3612—Transformers Except Electronic.

★ 58582 ★   **First of America Bank**
34 West Oak St.
Arcadia, FL 33821
(813)494-1212
Location Type: Branch office. **Ultimate Parent:** First of America Bank Corp. **SIC:** 6021—National Commercial Banks.

★ 58583 ★   **Frist of America Bank**
34 W. Oak St.
Arcadia, FL 33821
(813)494-1212
Location Type: Branch office. **Ultimate Parent:** First of America Bank Corp. **SIC:** 6021—National Commercial Banks.

★ 58584 ★   **Kentucky Fried Chicken**
161 S. Brevard Ave.
Arcadia, FL 33821
(813)494-0737
Ultimate Parent: Pepsico. **SIC:** 5812—Eating Places.

★ 58585 ★   **Pizza Hut**
916 E. Oak St.
Arcadia, FL 33821
(813)993-1193
Ultimate Parent: Pepsico. **SIC:** 5812—Eating Places.

★ 58586 ★   **Trailways Bus System**
202 N. Brevard Ave.
Arcadia, FL 33821
(813)494-1315
Ultimate Parent: Greyhound Lines Inc. **SIC:** 4142—Bus Charter Service Except Local.

Archer

★ 58587 ★   **Barnett Bank of Alachua County, NA**
400 Cottonwood Ctr.
Archer, FL 32618-9407
(904)338-6542
Company Type: Subsidiary. **Location Type:** Branch office. **Officer:** Mary

Copeland, Assistant Vice President.
Ultimate Parent: Barnett Banks. **SIC:** 6021—National Commercial Banks.

Atlantic Beach

★ 58588 ★   **Business Systems Services**
376 Ahern St.
Atlantic Beach, FL 32233-5248
(904)246-4603
Ultimate Parent: Avery Dennison Corp. **SIC:** 7371—Computer Programming Services.

Atlantis

★ 58589 ★   **Barnett Bank of Palm Beach County**
100 JFK Cir.
Atlantis, FL 33462-6699
(407)433-2424
Company Type: Subsidiary. **Location Type:** Branch office. **Officer:** Doug Barto, Manager. **Ultimate Parent:** Barnett Banks. **SIC:** 6022—State Commercial Banks.

Auburndale

★ 58590 ★   **Barnett Bank of Polk County**
300 Havendale Blvd.
Auburndale, FL 33823-4537
(813)297-1435
Company Type: Subsidiary. **Location Type:** Branch office. **Officer:** Raymond Epperson, Vice President. **Ultimate Parent:** Barnett Banks. **SIC:** 6022—State Commercial Banks.

★ 58591 ★   **Coca-Cola**
602 Mckean St.
Auburndale, FL 33823
Ultimate Parent: Coca-Cola. **SIC:** 2080—Beverages.

★ 58592 ★   **Coca-Cola Foods**
602 Mckean St.
Auburndale, FL 33823
Ultimate Parent: Coca-Cola. **SIC:** 2080—Beverages.

★ 58593 ★   **Coca-Cola Foods Auburndale**
602 Mckean St.
Auburndale, FL 33823
Ultimate Parent: Coca-Cola. **SIC:** 2037—Frozen Fruits & Vegetables.

★ 58594 ★   **Coca-Cola Foods Auburndale Facility**
602 Mckean St.
Auburndale, FL 33823
Ultimate Parent: Coca-Cola. **SIC:** 2037—Frozen Fruits & Vegetables; 2033—Canned Fruits & Vegetables; 5142—Packaged Frozen Foods; 4213—Trucking Except Local.

★ 58595 ★   **Dial Corp.**
909 Magnolia Ave.
Auburndale, FL 33823-4008
Ultimate Parent: Dial Corp. **SIC:** 2800—Chemicals & Allied Products.

★ 58596 ★   **First Union National Bank of Florida**
220 Magnolia Ave.
Auburndale, FL 33823
(813)967-6648
Location Type: Branch office. **Ultimate Parent:** First Union Corp. **SIC:** 6021—National Commercial Banks.

★ 58597 ★   **Fleetwood Homes**
700 S. Bartow Ave.
Auburndale, FL 33823
(813)967-7575
Officer: Bill Finley, Manager. **Ultimate Parent:** Fleetwood Enterprises, Inc. **SIC:** 2451—Mobile Homes.

★ 58598 ★   **Fleetwood Homes of Florida Inc. No. 70**
700 S. Bartow Ave. PO Box 1405
Auburndale, FL 33823
Ultimate Parent: Fleetwood Enterprises, Inc. **SIC:** 2451—Mobile Homes.

★ 58599 ★   **Kentucky Fried Chicken**
1442 PO Box
Auburndale, FL 33823
(813)967-9830
Ultimate Parent: Pepsico. **SIC:** 5812—Eating Places.

★ 58600 ★   **Owens-Corning Fiberglas Corp.**
211 Sandra Jackson Rd.
Auburndale, FL 33823
Ultimate Parent: Owens-Corning. **SIC:** 3000—Rubber & Miscellaneous Plastics Products.

★ 58601 ★   **Radio Shack**
337 Havendale Blvd.
Auburndale, FL 33823
(813)967-2972
Company Type: Division. **Ultimate Parent:** Tandy Corp. **SIC:** 5731—Radio, Television & Electronics Stores.

★ 58602 ★   **Taylor Building Products of**
1307 PO Box
Auburndale, FL 33823
(813)967-7544
Ultimate Parent: Mascotech, Inc. **SIC:** 2431—Millwork.

★ 58603 ★   **Universal Forest Products, Inc.**
105 Progress Rd.
Auburndale, FL 33823
(813)965-2566
Officer: Kevin O'Neill, Manager. **Ultimate Parent:** Universal Forest Products. **SIC:** 2421—Sawmills & Planing Mills—General; 2439—Structural Wood Members Nec; 2491—Wood Preserving.

★ 58604 ★   **Walgreen Drug Stores**
325 Havendale Blvd.
Auburndale, FL 33823
(813)965-2591
Ultimate Parent: Walgreen Co. **SIC:** 4833—Television Broadcasting Stations; 5912—Drug Stores & Proprietary Stores.

Avon Park

★ 58605 ★   **Barnett Bank of Highlands County**
299 US Hwy. 27 S
Avon Park, FL 33825-3440
(813)452-1215
Company Type: Subsidiary. **Location Type:** Branch office. **Officer:** Donna Vinson, Vice President. **Ultimate Parent:** Barnett Banks. **SIC:** 6022—State Commercial Banks.

★ 58606 ★   **Greyhound Bus Terminal**
1023 W. Palmetto St.
Avon Park, FL 33825
(813)453-7755
Ultimate Parent: Greyhound Lines Inc. **SIC:** 4173—Bus Terminal & Service Facilities.

★ 58607 ★   **Huntington Federal Savings Bank**
825 W. Main St.
Avon Park, FL 33825-3632
(813)453-6671
Location Type: Branch office. **Ultimate Parent:** Huntington Bancshares. **SIC:** 6021—National Commercial Banks.

★ 58608 ★   **Kentucky Fried Chicken**
201 Us 27 N
Avon Park, FL 33825
(813)453-7120
Ultimate Parent: Pepsico. **SIC:** 5812—Eating Places.

★ 58609 ★   **Pizza Hut**
310 Us 27 N
Avon Park, FL 33825
(813)452-5101
Ultimate Parent: Pepsico. **SIC:** 5812—Eating Places.

★ 58610 ★   **Radio Shack**
804 Us 27 S
Avon Park, FL 33825
(813)453-4116
Company Type: Division. **Ultimate Parent:** Tandy Corp. **SIC:** 5065—Electronic Parts & Equipment Nec; 5731—Radio, Television & Electronics Stores.

★ 58611 ★   **Stop & Shop**
562 PO Box
Avon Park, FL 33825
(813)453-5103
Ultimate Parent: Stop & Shop. **SIC:** 5411—Grocery Stores.

★ 58612 ★   **Walgreen Drug Store**
1028 Us 27 S
Avon Park, FL 33825
(813)453-0220
Ultimate Parent: Walgreen Co. **SIC:** 5912—Drug Stores & Proprietary Stores.

Baco Raton

★ 58613 ★   **Chase Manhatten Bank of Florida, NA**
5355 Town Ctr. Rd., St. 402
Baco Raton, FL 33486
(407)347-7008
Location Type: Branch office. **Ultimate Parent:** Chase Manhattan Corp. **SIC:** 6021—National Commercial Banks.

★ 58614 ★   **Comerica Bank & Trust, FSB**
1800 Corporate Blvd. NW, Ste. 100
Baco Raton, FL 33431
(407)994-6801 **Fax:** (407)994-6333
Location Type: Branch office. **Ultimate Parent:** Comerica Bank. **SIC:** 6021—National Commercial Banks.

Baker

★ 58615 ★   **Louisiana Pacific Corp.**
Us 90 W
Baker, FL 32531
(904)557-5331
Ultimate Parent: Louisiana-Pacific. **SIC:** 2421—Sawmills & Planing Mills—General.

Baldwin

★ 58616 ★   **Southern Wood Piedmont Co.**
900 N. Ctr. St.
Baldwin, FL 32234
Ultimate Parent: ITT Rayonier Inc. **SIC:** 2491—Wood Preserving.

Barefoot Bay

★ 58617 ★   **First Union National Bank of Florida**
947 Barefoot Blvd.
Barefoot Bay, FL 32976
(407)664-7100
Location Type: Branch office. **Ultimate Parent:** First Union Corp. **SIC:** 6021—National Commercial Banks.

Barton

★ 58618 ★   **Farmland Hydr L.P.**
Hwy. 640
Barton, FL 33830
(813)533-1141 **Fax:** (813)533-8793
Company Type: Subsidiary. **Officer:** Merle Farris, Vice President of Operations. **Ultimate Parent:** Farmland Industries.

★ 58619 ★   **First Union National Bank of Florida**
205 S. Broadway
Barton, FL 33830-4604
(813)533-7106
Location Type: Branch office. **Ultimate Parent:** First Union Corp. **SIC:** 6021—National Commercial Banks.

Bartow

★ 58620 ★   **Ace Hardware Store**
290 E. Main St.
Bartow, FL 33830
(813)533-4169
Ultimate Parent: Ace Hardware. **SIC:** 5992—Florists.

★ 58621 ★   **Ametek Corp.**
US Gauge Div.
450 Polk St.
Bartow, FL 33830
Company Type: Division. **Ultimate Parent:** Ametek Inc. **SIC:** 3499—Fabricated Metal Products Nec.

★ 58622 ★ Ametek Inc.
450 Polk St.
Bartow, FL 33830
(813)534-1504
Ultimate Parent: Ametek Inc. SIC: 3545—
Machine Tool Accessories.

★ 58623 ★ Ametek Inc.
US Gauge Div.
450 W. Polk St.
Bartow, FL 33830
Company Type: Division. Ultimate Parent:
Ametek Inc. SIC: 3823—Process Control
Instruments.

★ 58624 ★ Ametek US Gauge
PO Box 1959
Bartow, FL 33830-1959
(813)534-1504
Location Type: Branch office. Officer:
Patrick O'Connor. Ultimate Parent: Ametek
Inc. SIC: 3499—Fabricated Metal Products
Nec; 3812—Search & Navigation
Equipment; 3824—Fluid Meters & Counting
Devices; 3829—Measuring & Controlling
Devices Nec; 5084—Industrial Machinery &
Equipment.

★ 58625 ★ Cf Chemicals Inc.
Bonnie Mine Rd.
Bartow, FL 33830
Ultimate Parent: CF Industries. SIC:
2874—Phosphatic Fertilizers.

★ 58626 ★ IMC Development
Corp.
PO Box 2620
Bartow, FL 33830
(813)533-1121 Fax: (813)534-3916
Company Type: Subsidiary. Officer: James
D. Speir, President. Ultimate Parent: IMC
Fertilizer Group.

★ 58627 ★ IMC Fertilizer Inc.
PO Box 867
Bartow, FL 33830
(813)533-1121 Fax: (813)534-3916
Company Type: Subsidiary. Officer:
Wendell F. Bueche, President. Ultimate
Parent: IMC Fertilizer Group.

★ 58628 ★ Kentucky Fried
Chicken
1492 N. Broadway Ave.
Bartow, FL 33830
(813)533-5120
Ultimate Parent: Pepsico. SIC: 5812—
Eating Places.

★ 58629 ★ Ryder Truck Rental
Us 17 S
Bartow, FL 33830
(813)533-4762
Ultimate Parent: Ryder System. SIC:
7513—Truck Rental & Leasing Without
Drivers.

★ 58630 ★ Seminole Fertilizer
Corp.
Hwy. 60 W.
Bartow, FL 33830
Ultimate Parent: Tosco Corp. SIC: 2874—
Phosphatic Fertilizers.

★ 58631 ★ US Agri-Chemicals
Bartow Facility
Rte. 60 West
Bartow, FL 33830
Ultimate Parent: USX Corp. SIC: 2874—
Phosphatic Fertilizers.

★ 58632 ★ US Agri-Chemicals
Bartow Plant
Hwy. 60
Bartow, FL 33830
Ultimate Parent: USX Corp. SIC: 2874—
Phosphatic Fertilizers; 2873—Nitrogenous
Fertilizers.

★ 58633 ★ Wal Mart Discount
City
1350 N. Broadway Ave.
Bartow, FL 33830
(813)533-0541
Ultimate Parent: Wal-Mart Stores, Inc. SIC:
6512—Nonresidential Building Operators.

★ 58634 ★ Walgreen
155 E. Van Fleet Dr.
Bartow, FL 33830
(813)533-3669
Ultimate Parent: Walgreen Co. SIC:
5912—Drug Stores & Proprietary Stores.

★ 58635 ★ W.R. Grace & Co.
Bartow Chemical Complex
Hwy. 60 W.
Bartow, FL 33830
Company Type: Division. Ultimate Parent:
W. R. Grace. SIC: 2874—Phosphatic
Fertilizers.

Bay Harbor Islands

★ 58636 ★ Barnett Bank of South
Florida, NA
1108 Kane Concourse
Bay Harbor Islands, FL 33154-2095
(305)899-4100
Company Type: Subsidiary. Location
Type: Branch office. Officer: Neil Stickler,
Manager. Ultimate Parent: Barnett Banks.
SIC: 6021—National Commercial Banks.

Bayonet Point

★ 58637 ★ Barnett Bank of
Pasco County
6901 State Rd. 52
Bayonet Point, FL 34667-6704
(813)861-8476
Company Type: Subsidiary. Location
Type: Branch office. Officer: Diane M.
White, Manager. Ultimate Parent: Barnett
Banks. SIC: 6022—State Commercial
Banks.

★ 58638 ★ Barnett Bank of
Pasco County
7419 State Rd. 52
Bayonet Point, FL 34667-6714
(813)861-8494
Company Type: Subsidiary. Location
Type: Branch office. Officer: Patricia
Trapnell, Manager. Ultimate Parent:
Barnett Banks. SIC: 6022—State
Commercial Banks.

★ 58639 ★ World S&L, A Federal
S&L
7839 State Rd. 52
Bayonet Point, FL 34667-6722
(813)868-2176
Location Type: Branch office. Ultimate
Parent: Golden West Financial Corp. SIC:
6021—National Commercial Banks.

Bellaire Bluffs

★ 58640 ★ First of America Bank
200 N. Indian Rocks
Bellaire Bluffs, FL 34640
(813)586-5463
Location Type: Branch office. Ultimate
Parent: First of America Bank Corp. SIC:
6021—National Commercial Banks.

Belle Glade

★ 58641 ★ Asgrow Florida Co.
425 NW Ave. L
Belle Glade, FL 33430-0280
Ultimate Parent: Upjohn Co. SIC: 2879—
Agricultural Chemicals Nec.

★ 58642 ★ Barnett Bank of Lake
Okeechobee
915 S. Main St.
Belle Glade, FL 33430-4995
(407)996-8291
Company Type: Subsidiary. Location
Type: Branch office. Officer: Hattie Ruth
Bennett, Vice President. Ultimate Parent:
Barnett Banks. SIC: 6022—State
Commercial Banks.

★ 58643 ★ First Union National
Bank of Florida
41 SW Ave. B
Belle Glade, FL 33430-3496
(407)996-2067
Location Type: Branch office. Ultimate
Parent: First Union Corp. SIC: 6021—
National Commercial Banks.

★ 58644 ★ Kentucky Fried
Chicken
101 S. Main St.
Belle Glade, FL 33430
(407)996-7783
Ultimate Parent: Pepsico. SIC: 5812—
Eating Places.

★ 58645 ★ Kentucky Fried
Chicken
800 W. Canal St. S
Belle Glade, FL 33430
(407)996-7300
Ultimate Parent: Pepsico. SIC: 5812—
Eating Places.

★ 58646 ★ QO Chemicals Inc.
Belle Glade Plant
1602 W. Sugarhouse Rd.
Belle Glade, FL 33430
Ultimate Parent: Great Lakes Chemical.
SIC: 2869—Industrial Organic Chemicals
Nec.

Belleair Bluff

★ 58647 ★ First Union National
Bank of Florida
2515 West Bay Dr.
Belleair Bluff, FL 33540-2621
(813)538-4584
Location Type: Branch office. Ultimate
Parent: First Union Corp. SIC: 6021—
National Commercial Banks.

Belleair Bluffs

★ 58648 ★ AmSouth Bank of
Florida
2845 W. Bay Dr.
Belleair Bluffs, FL 34640
(813)462-2474
Location Type: Branch office. Ultimate
Parent: AmSouth Bancorp. SIC: 6022—
State Commercial Banks.

★ 58649 ★ Barnett Bank of
Pinellas County
125 N. Indian Rocks
Belleair Bluffs, FL 34640-1796
(813)539-9000
Company Type: Subsidiary. Location
Type: Branch office. Officer: Andrew
Craske, Manager. Ultimate Parent: Barnett
Banks. SIC: 6022—State Commercial
Banks.

★ 58650 ★ First of America Bank
205 N. Indian Rocks
Belleair Bluffs, FL 34640
(813)586-5463
Location Type: Branch office. Ultimate
Parent: First of America Bank Corp. SIC:
6021—National Commercial Banks.

★ 58651 ★ Fortune Bank, A
Savings Bank
100-G Indian Rocks Rd. N
Belleair Bluffs, FL 34640-1770
(813)581-1851
Location Type: Branch office. Officer:
Janis Marino, Manager. Ultimate Parent:
Fortune Bancorp.

Belleview

★ 58652 ★ Ace Hardware
5940 SE Hames Rd.
Belleview, FL 32620
(904)245-5777
Ultimate Parent: Ace Hardware. SIC:
5251—Hardware Stores.

★ 58653 ★ AmSouth Bank of
Florida
10697 SE Hwy. 441
Belleview, FL 34420-2801
(904)245-5106
Ultimate Parent: AmSouth Bancorp. SIC:
6022—State Commercial Banks.

★ 58654 ★ Barnett Bank of
Marion County, NA
5222 SE Abshier Blvd.
Belleview, FL 34421-3917
(904)620-1111
Company Type: Subsidiary. Location
Type: Branch office. Officer: Didi Baron,
Manager. Ultimate Parent: Barnett Banks.
SIC: 6021—National Commercial Banks.

★ 58655 ★ California Federal
Bank, AFSB
10990 SE Hwy. 441
Belleview, FL 34420
(904)245-0134
Location Type: Branch office. Officer:
Danielle Combs, Manager. Ultimate Parent:
California Federal Bank.

★ 58656 ★ Pizza Hut
10738 SE US 441
Belleview, FL 34420
(904)245-3639
Ultimate Parent: Pepsico. SIC: 5812—
Eating Places.

★ 58657 ★ Walgreen
10369 SE US Hwy. 441 301
Belleview, FL 34420
(904)245-0177
Ultimate Parent: Walgreen Co.

Beverly Hills

★ 58658 ★ AmSouth Bank of
Florida
State Rd. 491
Beverly Hills, FL 34465
(904)746-2221
Location Type: Branch office. Ultimate
Parent: AmSouth Bancorp. SIC: 6022—
State Commercial Banks.

★ 58659 ★ Barnett Bank of the
Suncoast, NA
3505 N. Lecanto Hwy.
Beverly Hills, FL 32665-3544
(904)795-8165
Company Type: Subsidiary. Location
Type: Branch office. Officer: Donna Boire,
Manager. Ultimate Parent: Barnett Banks.
SIC: 6021—National Commercial Banks.

Big Pine Key

★ 58660 ★ Barnett Bank of the
Keys
US Hwy. 1, Mile Marker 30.5
Big Pine Key, FL 33043-9757
(305)292-3903
Company Type: Subsidiary. Location
Type: Branch office. Officer: John North,
Manager. Ultimate Parent: Barnett Banks.
SIC: 6022—State Commercial Banks.

Blountstown

★ 58661 ★ Ace Hardware
405 Main St.
Blountstown, FL 32424
(904)762-3228
Ultimate Parent: Ace Hardware. SIC:
5211—Lumber & Other Building Materials.

★ 58662 ★ Radio Shack
244 N. Main St.
Blountstown, FL 32424
(904)674-8111
Company Type: Division. Ultimate Parent:
Tandy Corp. SIC: 5912—Drug Stores &
Proprietary Stores.

★ 58663 ★ Trailways Bus System
512 W. Central Ave.
Blountstown, FL 32424
(904)674-5714
Ultimate Parent: Greyhound Lines Inc. SIC:
4131—Intercity & Rural Bus Transportation.

Boca Raton

★ 58664 ★ American Savings of
FL FSB
9020 Kimberly Blvd.
Boca Raton, FL 33434-2823
(407)482-1114
Location Type: Branch office. Officer:
Kathryn B. Monk. Ultimate Parent:
American Savings of Florida. SIC: 6035—
Federal Savings Institutions; 6021—National
Commercial Banks.

★ 58665 ★ American Savings of
Florida
1377 W. Palmetto Park Rd.
Boca Raton, FL 33486-3314
(407)392-6960
Ultimate Parent: American Savings of
Florida. SIC: 6035—Federal Savings
Institutions; 6021—National Commercial
Banks.

★ **58666** ★ **American Savings of Florida, FSB**
9020 Kimberly Blvd.
Boca Raton, FL 33434-2823
(407)482-1114
Location Type: Branch office. **Officer:** Steve Goldstein, Manager. **Ultimate Parent:** American Savings of Florida. **SIC:** 6035—Federal Savings Institutions; 6211—Security Brokers & Dealers.

★ **58667** ★ **American Savings of Florida, FSB**
1377 W. Palmetto Park Rd.
Boca Raton, FL 33486-3345
(407)392-6960
Location Type: Branch office. **Officer:** Matthew Kennedy, Managers. **Ultimate Parent:** American Savings of Florida. **SIC:** 6035—Federal Savings Institutions; 6211—Security Brokers & Dealers.

★ **58668** ★ **Ameritech Plastics**
532 77th St. NW
Boca Raton, FL 33487
(407)997-5455
Officer: Rex M. Johnson, President. **Ultimate Parent:** Ameritech. **SIC:** 3089—Plastics Products Nec.

★ **58669** ★ **AMP Inc.**
2500 N. Military Tr., Ste. 320
Boca Raton, FL 33431-6342
(407)997-7005
Location Type: Branch office. **Officer:** Paul Farrell. **Ultimate Parent:** AMP Inc. **SIC:** 5065—Electronic Parts & Equipment Nec.

★ **58670** ★ **Banana Republic**
370 Camino Gardens Blvd.
Boca Raton, FL 33432
(407)394-9867
Ultimate Parent: GAP. **SIC:** 5651—Family Clothing Stores.

★ **58671** ★ **Banana Republic**
360 Town Ctr.
Boca Raton, FL 33431
(407)338-3490
Ultimate Parent: GAP. **SIC:** 5651—Family Clothing Stores.

★ **58672** ★ **Barnett Bank of Palm Beach County**
5455 N. Federal Hwy.
Boca Raton, FL 33487
(407)393-2588
Company Type: Subsidiary. **Location Type:** Branch office. **Officer:** Vicki Allman, Manager. **Ultimate Parent:** Barnett Banks. **SIC:** 6022—State Commercial Banks.

★ **58673** ★ **Barnett Bank of Palm Beach County**
1000 N. Federal Hwy.
Boca Raton, FL 33432-2742
(407)393-2500
Company Type: Subsidiary. **Location Type:** Branch office. **Officer:** Warren Hulburt, Manager. **Ultimate Parent:** Barnett Banks. **SIC:** 6022—State Commercial Banks.

★ **58674** ★ **Barnett Bank of Palm Beach County**
4199 N. Federal Hwy.
Boca Raton, FL 33431-4528
(407)393-2530
Company Type: Subsidiary. **Location Type:** Branch office. **Officer:** Donn Londeree, Manager. **Ultimate Parent:** Barnett Banks. **SIC:** 6022—State Commercial Banks.

★ **58675** ★ **Barnett Bank of Palm Beach County**
7024 Palmetto Park Rd.
Boca Raton, FL 33433-3411
(407)393-2592
Company Type: Subsidiary. **Location Type:** Branch office. **Officer:** Jason Yao, Manager. **Ultimate Parent:** Barnett Banks. **SIC:** 6022—State Commercial Banks.

★ **58676** ★ **Barnett Bank of Palm Beach County**
23123 State Rd. No. 7
Boca Raton, FL 33428-5407
(407)393-2580
Company Type: Subsidiary. **Location Type:** Branch office. **Officer:** Albert Ellis, Manager. **Ultimate Parent:** Barnett Banks. **SIC:** 6022—State Commercial Banks.

★ **58677** ★ **Barnett Bank of Palm Beach County**
2250 Glades Rd.
Boca Raton, FL 33431-7399
(407)391-7400
Company Type: Subsidiary. **Location Type:** Branch office. **Officer:** Susan Anderson, Manager. **Ultimate Parent:** Barnett Banks. **SIC:** 6022—State Commercial Banks.

★ **58678** ★ **Barnett Bank of Palm Beach County**
20431 US Hwy. 441
Boca Raton, FL 33498-6741
(407)393-2550
Company Type: Subsidiary. **Location Type:** Branch office. **Officer:** Kaela Lerner, Manager. **Ultimate Parent:** Barnett Banks. **SIC:** 6022—State Commercial Banks.

★ **58679** ★ **Barnett Bank of Palm Beach County**
5030 Champion Blvd.
Boca Raton, FL 33496
(407)241-1942
Company Type: Subsidiary. **Location Type:** Branch office. **Officer:** Eva Roth, Manager. **Ultimate Parent:** Barnett Banks. **SIC:** 6022—State Commercial Banks.

★ **58680** ★ **Barnett Bank of Palm Beach County**
9080 Kimberly Blvd.
Boca Raton, FL 33434-2862
(407)488-5550
Company Type: Subsidiary. **Location Type:** Branch office. **Officer:** Susan DeWitt, Manager. **Ultimate Parent:** Barnett Banks. **SIC:** 6022—State Commercial Banks.

★ **58681** ★ **Barnett Bank of Palm Beach County**
21060 St. Andrews Blvd.
Boca Raton, FL 33433-2499
(407)393-2560
Company Type: Subsidiary. **Location Type:** Branch office. **Officer:** Glen Romm, Manager. **Ultimate Parent:** Barnett Banks. **SIC:** 6022—State Commercial Banks.

★ **58682** ★ **California Federal Bank**
7301 W. Palmetto Park Rd.
Boca Raton, FL 33433
(407)368-3637
Ultimate Parent: California Federal Bank. **SIC:** 6099—Functions Related to Deposit Banking.

★ **58683** ★ **California Federal Bank, AFSB**
7301 W. Palmetto Pk. Rd.
Boca Raton, FL 33433-3458
(407)368-3638
Location Type: Branch office. **Ultimate Parent:** California Federal Bank.

★ **58684** ★ **California Federal Bank, AFSB**
2200 W. Glades Rd.
Boca Raton, FL 33431
(407)392-2570
Location Type: Branch office. **Ultimate Parent:** California Federal Bank. **SIC:** 6021—National Commercial Banks.

★ **58685** ★ **Casi-Rusco**
1155 Broken Sound Pkwy NW
Boca Raton, FL 33487
(407)998-6100 **Fax:** (407)994-6572
Company Type: Subsidiary. **Officer:** David A. Schuldt, President. **Ultimate Parent:** Figgie International.

★ **58686** ★ **Casi-Rusco**
1155 NW Broken Sound Pky.
Boca Raton, FL 33487
(407)997-9699
Officer: David Schuldt, President. **Ultimate Parent:** Figgie International. **SIC:** 3625—Relays & Industrial Controls.

★ **58687** ★ **Casi-Rusco Inc.**
1155 NW Broken Sound Pky.
Boca Raton, FL 33487-3526
(407)998-6100
Company Type: Subsidiary. **Ultimate Parent:** Figgie International. **SIC:** 3577—Computer Peripheral Equipment Nec; 8731—Commercial Physical Research; 7373—Computer Integrated Systems Design; 8742—Management Consulting Services.

★ **58688** ★ **Casual Corner**
277 Town Ctr.
Boca Raton, FL 33431
(407)392-0996
Ultimate Parent: United States Shoe. **SIC:** 5651—Family Clothing Stores.

★ **58689** ★ **Chemical Bank Florida**
4800 N. Federal Hwy.
Boca Raton, FL 33431-5145
(407)393-6694
Location Type: Branch office. **Ultimate Parent:** Chemical Banking Corp. **SIC:** 6021—National Commercial Banks.

★ **58690** ★ **Citibak, FSB**
7400 W. Camino Real, Ste. 130
Boca Raton, FL 33433-5586
(407)392-1203
Location Type: Branch office. **Ultimate Parent:** Citicorp. **SIC:** 6021—National Commercial Banks.

★ **58691** ★ **Citizens Federal Bank, AFSB**
9060 Kimberly Rd., Ste. 42
Boca Raton, FL 33434
(407)482-6655
Location Type: Branch office. **Officer:** Mara Greenberg, Manager. **Ultimate Parent:** CSF Holdings. **SIC:** 6021—National Commercial Banks.

★ **58692** ★ **Comerica Trust Co. of Florid**
1900 Corporate Blvd. NW
Boca Raton, FL 33431
(407)994-6800
Ultimate Parent: Comerica Bank. **SIC:** 6022—State Commercial Banks.

★ **58693** ★ **Continental Illinois Trust Co. of Florida, NA**
1 Boco Pl., Ste. 337 W
2255 Glades Rd.
Boca Raton, FL 33431
(407)997-0900 **Fax:** (407)997-1611
Company Type: Subsidiary. **Location Type:** Branch office. **Ultimate Parent:** Continental Bank Corp. **SIC:** 6021—National Commercial Banks.

★ **58694** ★ **Delta Business Systems**
951 Broken Sound Pky. NW, No. 200
Boca Raton, FL 33487
(407)655-7661
Officer: Rick Soluri, Manager. **Ultimate Parent:** Alco Standard Corp. **SIC:** 3663—Radio & T.V. Communications Equipment.

★ **58695** ★ **Express**
Town Ctr.
Boca Raton, FL 33432
(407)338-0622
Ultimate Parent: Limited. **SIC:** 5651—Family Clothing Stores.

★ **58696** ★ **First of America Bank**
9136 W. Glades Rd.
Boca Raton, FL 33434
(407)487-1000
Location Type: Branch office. **Ultimate Parent:** First of America Bank Corp. **SIC:** 6021—National Commercial Banks.

★ **58697** ★ **First Union National Bank of Florida**
651 NW 13th St.
Boca Raton, FL 33486-2499
(407)338-6031
Location Type: Branch office. **SIC:** 6021—National Commercial Banks.

★ **58698** ★ **First Union National Bank of Florida**
6653 Jog Rd.
Boca Raton, FL 33496
(407)338-3991
Location Type: Branch office. **Ultimate Parent:** First Union Corp. **SIC:** 6021—National Commercial Banks.

★ **58699** ★ **First Union National Bank of Florida**
1 Town Ctr. Cir., Rm. 334
Boca Raton, FL 33486
(407)338-3960
Location Type: Branch office. **Ultimate Parent:** First Union Corp. **SIC:** 6021—National Commercial Banks.

★ **58700** ★ **First Union National Bank of Florida**
77 E. Camino Rd.
Boca Raton, FL 33432
(407)338-3986
Location Type: Branch office. **Ultimate Parent:** First Union Corp. **SIC:** 6021—National Commercial Banks.

★ **58701** ★ **First Union National Bank of Florida**
5355 Town Ctr. Rd., Ste. 101
Boca Raton, FL 33486
(407)338-3991
Location Type: Branch office. **Ultimate Parent:** First Union Corp. **SIC:** 6021—National Commercial Banks.

★ **58702** ★ **First Union National Bank of Florida**
9190 Glades Rd.
Boca Raton, FL 33434-3998
(407)483-6063
Location Type: Branch office. **Ultimate Parent:** First Union Corp. **SIC:** 6021—National Commercial Banks.

★ **58703** ★ **First Union National Bank of Florida**
7009 Beracusa Way
Boca Raton, FL 33433-4299
(407)338-6000
Location Type: Branch office. **Ultimate Parent:** First Union Corp. **SIC:** 6021—National Commercial Banks.

★ **58704** ★ **First Union National Bank of Florida**
3601 N. Federal Hwy.
Boca Raton, FL 33431
(407)338-6043
Location Type: Branch office. **Ultimate Parent:** First Union Corp. **SIC:** 6021—National Commercial Banks.

★ **58705** ★ **The Gap**
355 Town Ctr.
Boca Raton, FL 33431
(407)394-5584
Ultimate Parent: GAP. **SIC:** 5699—Miscellaneous Apparel & Accessory Stores.

★ **58706** ★ **W. R. Grace**
1 Town Ctr. Rd.
Boca Raton, FL 33486
(407)362-2000
Company Type: Headquarters. **Officer:** J. P. Boluc. **Employee Count:** 40900. **Sales:** 5737 M. **Fortune 500:** Largest U.S. Industrial Corporations: Ranking 94.

★ **58707** ★ **Great Western Bank**
20441 State Rd. 7
Boca Raton, FL 33498
(407)483-7400
Ultimate Parent: Great Western Financial Corp. **SIC:** 6099—Functions Related to Deposit Banking.

★ **58708** ★ **Great Western Bank**
23060 Sandalfoot Plz.
Boca Raton, FL 33428
(407)482-9610
Ultimate Parent: Great Western Financial Corp. **SIC:** 6022—State Commercial Banks.

★ **58709** ★ **Great Western Bank**
5950 Glades Rd.
Boca Raton, FL 33431
Ultimate Parent: Great Western Financial Corp. **SIC:** 6099—Functions Related to Deposit Banking.

★ **58710** ★ **Greyhound Bus**
Boca
Boca Raton, FL 33432
(407)395-6696
Ultimate Parent: Greyhound Lines Inc. **SIC:** 4131—Intercity & Rural Bus Transportation.

★ **58711** ★ **Hit or Miss**
1924 NE 5th Ave.
Boca Raton, FL 33431
(407)394-0516
Ultimate Parent: TJX. **SIC:** 5699—Miscellaneous Apparel & Accessory Stores.

★ **58712** ★ **Human Affairs International**
7601 N. Federal Hwy.
Boca Raton, FL 33487
(407)994-3601
Ultimate Parent: Aetna Life & Annuity. **SIC:** 8322—Individual & Family Services; 8742—Management Consulting Services.

★ 58713 ★   IBM Corp.
1000 NW 51st Street
Boca Raton, FL 33431
(407)982-7067
Ultimate Parent: IBM.

★ 58714 ★   IBM Corp.
PO Box 1328
Boca Raton, FL 33429
(407)443-6804
Ultimate Parent: IBM.

★ 58715 ★   **International Business Machines Corp.**
1000 NW 51st St.
Boca Raton, FL 33431
Ultimate Parent: IBM. **SIC:** 3500—Industrial Machinery & Equipment.

★ 58716 ★   **Lane Bryant**
132 Town Ctr.
Boca Raton, FL 33431
(407)392-8450
Ultimate Parent: Limited. **SIC:** 5651—Family Clothing Stores.

★ 58717 ★   **Lerner Shop**
112 Town Ctr.
Boca Raton, FL 33431
(407)368-0554
Ultimate Parent: Limited. **SIC:** 5651—Family Clothing Stores.

★ 58718 ★   **The Limited**
Town Ctr. Mall
Boca Raton, FL 33432
(407)391-6651
Ultimate Parent: Limited. **SIC:** 5621—Women's Clothing Stores.

★ 58719 ★   **Maison Blanche**
Town Ctr.
Boca Raton, FL 33432
(407)338-3310
Ultimate Parent: Mercantile Stores. **SIC:** 5944—Jewelry Stores.

★ 58720 ★   **Mary Kay Cosmetics**
7667 Courtyard Run W
Boca Raton, FL 33433
(407)392-0759
Ultimate Parent: Mary Kay Cosmetics. **SIC:** 5999—Miscellaneous Retail Stores Nec.

★ 58721 ★   **Mima**
1081 Holand Dr.
Boca Raton, FL 33487
(407)241-8222 **Fax:** (407)241-6186
Company Type: Subsidiary. **Officer:** Arno Proctor, Vice President & General Manager. **Ultimate Parent:** Illinois Tool Works.

★ 58722 ★   **NBD Bank, FSB**
1515 N. Federal Hwy., Ste. 100
Boca Raton, FL 33432
(407)392-3098
Location Type: Branch office. **Ultimate Parent:** NBD Bancorp. **SIC:** 6021—National Commercial Banks.

★ 58723 ★   **NBD Trust Co. of Florida, NA**
1515 N. Federal Hwy., Ste. 10
Boca Raton, FL 33432-1953
(407)368-3971
Location Type: Branch office. **Ultimate Parent:** NBD Bancorp. **SIC:** 6021—National Commercial Banks.

★ 58724 ★   **New York Life Boca Raton**
Southeastern Agencies
777 Yamato Rd., Room 310
Boca Raton, FL 33487
(407)994-8211
Ultimate Parent: New York Life.

★ 58725 ★   **Pappagallo**
Town Ctr. Mall
Boca Raton, FL 33431
(407)395-2127
Ultimate Parent: United States Shoe. **SIC:** 5621—Women's Clothing Stores.

★ 58726 ★   **Petite Sophisticate**
6000 Glades Rd.
Boca Raton, FL 33431
(407)393-7197
Ultimate Parent: United States Shoe. **SIC:** 5621—Women's Clothing Stores.

★ 58727 ★   **Pizza Hut**
23233 State Rd. 7
Boca Raton, FL 33428
(407)483-4735
Ultimate Parent: Pepsico. **SIC:** 5812—Eating Places.

★ 58728 ★   **Pizza Hut**
642 Congress Ave.
Boca Raton, FL 33431
(407)994-3490
Ultimate Parent: Pepsico. **SIC:** 6531—Real Estate Agents & Managers.

★ 58729 ★   **Pizza Hut**
1180 N. Federal Hwy.
Boca Raton, FL 33432
(407)391-4333
Ultimate Parent: Pepsico. **SIC:** 5812—Eating Places.

★ 58730 ★   **Pizza Hut**
331 51st St.
Boca Raton, FL 33431
(407)241-4221
Ultimate Parent: Pepsico. **SIC:** 5812—Eating Places.

★ 58731 ★   **Publix Super Market**
150 S. Federal Hwy.
Boca Raton, FL 33432
(407)427-2602
Ultimate Parent: Publix Super Markets. **SIC:** 5461—Retail Bakeries.

★ 58732 ★   **Publix Super Market**
1968 N. Federal Hwy.
Boca Raton, FL 33432
(407)395-5515
Ultimate Parent: Publix Super Markets. **SIC:** 5411—Grocery Stores.

★ 58733 ★   **Publix Super Markets**
1968 N. Federal Hwy.
Boca Raton, FL 33432
(407)395-5515
Ultimate Parent: Publix Super Markets. **SIC:** 5411—Grocery Stores.

★ 58734 ★   **Radio Shack**
101 Town Ctr.
Boca Raton, FL 33431
(407)391-5354
Company Type: Division. **Ultimate Parent:** Tandy Corp. **SIC:** 5731—Radio, Television & Electronics Stores.

★ 58735 ★   **Radio Shack**
1918 NE 5th Ave.
Boca Raton, FL 33431
(407)395-2663
Company Type: Division. **Ultimate Parent:** Tandy Corp. **SIC:** 5731—Radio, Television & Electronics Stores.

★ 58736 ★   **Radio Shack**
Town Ctr. Mall
Boca Raton, FL 33432
(407)391-5354
Company Type: Division. **Ultimate Parent:** Tandy Corp. **SIC:** 5731—Radio, Television & Electronics Stores.

★ 58737 ★   **Radio Shack**
252 N. Federal Hwy.
Boca Raton, FL 33432
(407)368-1466
Company Type: Division. **Ultimate Parent:** Tandy Corp. **SIC:** 5731—Radio, Television & Electronics Stores.

★ 58738 ★   **Rite Aid Disc Pharmacies**
11427 W. Palmetto Park Rd.
Boca Raton, FL 33428
(407)483-1335
Ultimate Parent: Rite Aid. **SIC:** 5912—Drug Stores & Proprietary Stores.

★ 58739 ★   **Ryder Truck Rental**
9900 SW 18th St.
Boca Raton, FL 33428
(407)483-3972
Ultimate Parent: Ryder System. **SIC:** 7389—Business Services Nec.

★ 58740 ★   **Ryder Truck Rental**
3600 NW 2nd Ave.
Boca Raton, FL 33431
(407)392-3341
Ultimate Parent: Ryder System. **SIC:** 7389—Business Services Nec.

★ 58741 ★   **Savings of America, A Division of Home Savings of America, FSB**
9035 LaFontana Blvd.
Boca Raton, FL 33434-5699
(407)488-9300
Company Type: Division. **Location Type:** Branch office. **Ultimate Parent:** H. F. Ahmanson. **SIC:** 6021—National Commercial Banks.

★ 58742 ★   **Shell Station & Car Wash**
21290 Saint Andrews Blvd.
Boca Raton, FL 33433
(407)395-3123
Ultimate Parent: Shell Oil Co. **SIC:** 5541—Gasoline Service Stations.

★ 58743 ★   **Stop & Shop Food Store Inc.**
5999 N. Federal Hwy.
Boca Raton, FL 33487
(407)997-7351
Ultimate Parent: Stop & Shop. **SIC:** 5411—Grocery Stores.

★ 58744 ★   **T J Maxx**
8903 Glades Rd.
Boca Raton, FL 33434
(407)479-4035
Ultimate Parent: TJX. **SIC:** 5932—Used Merchandise Stores.

★ 58745 ★   **Taco Bell**
23073 Sandalfoot Plz.
Boca Raton, FL 33428
(407)488-2255
Ultimate Parent: Pepsico. **SIC:** 5812—Eating Places.

★ 58746 ★   **Unisys Corp.**
7700 W. Camino Real
Boca Raton, FL 33433
(407)750-5800
Ultimate Parent: Unisys Corp. **SIC:** 3599—Industrial Machinery Nec.

★ 58747 ★   **Variable Annuity Life Insurance**
399 Camino Gardens Blvd.
Boca Raton, FL 33432
(407)833-1035
Ultimate Parent: American General Corp. **SIC:** 6411—Insurance Agents, Brokers & Service.

★ 58748 ★   **Variable Annuity Life Insurance Co.**
399 Camino Gardens Blvd.
Boca Raton, FL 33432
(407)833-1035
Ultimate Parent: American General Corp. **SIC:** 6411—Insurance Agents, Brokers & Service.

★ 58749 ★   **W. R. Grace & Co.**
1 Town Ctr. Rd.
Boca Raton, FL 33486-1010
(407)362-2000 **Fax:** (407)362-2193
Company Type: Headquarters. **Officer:** J. P. Bolduc, President & CEO. **Ultimate Parent:** W. R. Grace. **Employee Count:** 44000.

★ 58750 ★   **W. R. Grace & Co. Inc.**
Connecticut
1 Town Ctr. Rd.
Boca Raton, FL 33486-1010
(407)362-2000
Company Type: Subsidiary. **Officer:** J. Peter Grace, Chairman of the Board & Chief Executive Officer. **Ultimate Parent:** W. R. Grace. **SIC:** 3081—Unsupported Plastics Film & Sheet; 2891—Adhesives & Sealants. **Employee Count:** 1300. **Sales:** 6.1000000 M.

★ 58751 ★   **Walgreen Drug Stores**
21290 Saint Andrews Blvd.
Boca Raton, FL 33433
(407)368-5588
Ultimate Parent: Walgreen Co. **SIC:** 5912—Drug Stores & Proprietary Stores.

★ 58752 ★   **Walgreen Drug Stores**
Shadowood Sq.
Boca Raton, FL 33432
(407)487-2100
Ultimate Parent: Walgreen Co. **SIC:** 5912—Drug Stores & Proprietary Stores.

★ 58753 ★   **Walgreen Drug Stores**
9851 Glades Rd.
Boca Raton, FL 33434
(407)487-2100
Ultimate Parent: Walgreen Co. **SIC:** 5912—Drug Stores & Proprietary Stores.

★ 58754 ★   **World S&L, A Federal S&L**
7032 W. Palmetto Park Rd.
Boca Raton, FL 33433
(407)338-7800
Location Type: Branch office. **Ultimate Parent:** Golden West Financial Corp. **SIC:** 6021—National Commercial Banks.

★ 58755 ★   **World S&L, A Federal S&L**
3005 Yamato Rd.
Boca Raton, FL 33434
(407)241-8066
Location Type: Branch office. **Ultimate Parent:** Golden West Financial Corp.

★ 58756 ★   **World S&L, A Federal S&L**
9162 Glades Rd.
Boca Raton, FL 33434-3999
(407)482-6290
Location Type: Branch office. **Ultimate Parent:** Golden West Financial Corp. **SIC:** 6021—National Commercial Banks.

★ 58757 ★   **W.R. Grace**
InterAmerican Division
1 Town Ctr. Rd.
Boca Raton, FL 33416
(407)362-2000 **Fax:** (407)362-2701
Company Type: Subsidiary. **Officer:** Antonio R. Ferre, President. **Ultimate Parent:** W. R. Grace.

Bonifay

★ 58758 ★   **Mini Mart&Service**
St Johns Rd.
Bonifay, FL 32425
(904)547-2724
Ultimate Parent: Kroger. **SIC:** 5411—Grocery Stores.

Bonita Springs

★ 58759 ★   **Kentucky Fried Chicken**
28 Bonita Beach Rd.
Bonita Springs, FL 33923
(813)597-4103
Ultimate Parent: Pepsico. **SIC:** 5812—Eating Places.

★ 58760 ★   **Mobil Oil Corp.**
28175 Tamiami Trl
Bonita Springs, FL 33923
(813)947-9202
Ultimate Parent: Mobil. **SIC:** 5599—Automotive Dealers Nec.

★ 58761 ★   **Radio Shack**
28441 Tamiami Trl
Bonita Springs, FL 33923
(813)947-2488
Company Type: Division. **Ultimate Parent:** Tandy Corp. **SIC:** 5065—Electronic Parts & Equipment Nec.

Boynton Beach

★ 58762 ★   **Barnett Bank of Palm Beach County**
3603 Woolbright Rd.
Boynton Beach, FL 33436-7297
(407)736-7560
Company Type: Subsidiary. **Location Type:** Branch office. **Officer:** Gail Richter, Manager. **Ultimate Parent:** Barnett Banks. **SIC:** 6022—State Commercial Banks.

★ 58763 ★   **Barnett Bank of Palm Beach County**
4793 N. Congress Ave.
Boynton Beach, FL 33462-5837
(407)433-2497
Company Type: Subsidiary. **Location Type:** Branch office. **Officer:** Michael Koons, Manager. **Ultimate Parent:** Barnett Banks. **SIC:** 6022—State Commercial Banks.

★ 58764 ★　Barnett Bank of Palm Beach County
114 N. Federal Hwy.
Boynton Beach, FL 33435-4197
(407)736-7500
Company Type: Subsidiary. Location Type: Branch office. Officer: Keith Girten, Manager. Ultimate Parent: Barnett Banks. SIC: 6022—State Commercial Banks.

★ 58765 ★　Barnett Bank of Palm Beach County
105 N. Congress Ave.
Boynton Beach, FL 33436-4260
(407)736-7555
Company Type: Subsidiary. Location Type: Branch office. Officer: Donald Zyto, Manager. Ultimate Parent: Barnett Banks. SIC: 6022—State Commercial Banks.

★ 58766 ★　California Federal Bank, AFSB
289 N. Congress Ave.
Boynton Beach, FL 33426-4297
(407)737-2020
Location Type: Branch office. Officer: Patty Lusignan, Manager. Ultimate Parent: California Federal Bank. SIC: 6021—National Commercial Banks.

★ 58767 ★　California Federal Bank, AFSB
1600 S. Federal Hwy.
Boynton Beach, FL 33435
(407)734-2323
Location Type: Branch office. Ultimate Parent: California Federal Bank. SIC: 6021—National Commercial Banks.

★ 58768 ★　Casual Corner
349 Boynton Beach Mall
Boynton Beach, FL 33435
(407)736-7641
Ultimate Parent: United States Shoe. SIC: 5651—Family Clothing Stores.

★ 58769 ★　Citizens Federal Bank, AFSB
145 N. Congress Ave.
Boynton Beach, FL
(407)732-6400
Location Type: Branch office. Officer: Linda Farina, Manager. Ultimate Parent: CSF Holdings. SIC: 6021—National Commercial Banks.

★ 58770 ★　Express
823 W. Boynton Beach Blvd.
Boynton Beach, FL 33426
(407)736-8266
Ultimate Parent: Limited. SIC: 5651—Family Clothing Stores.

★ 58771 ★　First Union National Bank of Florida
11060 S. Military Trl.
Boynton Beach, FL 33436-7298
(407)533-7618
Location Type: Branch office. Ultimate Parent: First Union Corp. SIC: 6021—National Commercial Banks.

★ 58772 ★　First Union National Bank of Florida
4600 N. Ocean Blvd.
Boynton Beach, FL 33435-7388
(407)272-1297
Location Type: Branch office. Ultimate Parent: First Union Corp. SIC: 6021—National Commercial Banks.

★ 58773 ★　First Union National Bank of Florida
3619 S. Federal Hwy.
Boynton Beach, FL 33435-8697
(407)736-7625
Location Type: Branch office. Ultimate Parent: First Union Corp. SIC: 6021—National Commercial Banks.

★ 58774 ★　First Union National Bank of Florida
200 N. Congress Ave.
Boynton Beach, FL 33238-4290
(407)533-7750
Location Type: Branch office. Ultimate Parent: First Union Corp. SIC: 6021—National Commercial Banks.

★ 58775 ★　The Gap
355 Boynton Bch Mall
Boynton Beach, FL 33435
(407)736-9288
Ultimate Parent: GAP. SIC: 5651—Family Clothing Stores.

★ 58776 ★　Great Western Bank
901 S. Federal Hwy.
Boynton Beach, FL 33435
(407)732-8183
Ultimate Parent: Great Western Financial Corp. SIC: 6022—State Commercial Banks.

★ 58777 ★　Great Western Bank
555 N. Congress Ave.
Boynton Beach, FL 33426
(407)738-6900
Ultimate Parent: Great Western Financial Corp. SIC: 6531—Real Estate Agents & Managers.

★ 58778 ★　Greyhound Bus Station
112 S. Federal Hwy.
Boynton Beach, FL 33435
(407)732-2301
Ultimate Parent: Greyhound Lines Inc. SIC: 4131—Intercity & Rural Bus Transportation; 4173—Bus Terminal & Service Facilities.

★ 58779 ★　Hit or Miss
340 N. Congress Ave.
Boynton Beach, FL 33426
(407)734-6026
Ultimate Parent: TJX. SIC: 5621—Women's Clothing Stores.

★ 58780 ★　Kay-Bee Toy & Hobby
495 Boynton Beach Mall
Boynton Beach, FL 33435
(407)736-4875
Ultimate Parent: Melville. SIC: 5945—Hobby, Toy & Game Shops.

★ 58781 ★　Kentucky Fried Chicken
131 E. Boynton Beach Blvd.
Boynton Beach, FL 33435
(407)369-3822
Ultimate Parent: Pepsico. SIC: 5812—Eating Places.

★ 58782 ★　Lane Bryant
161 Boynton Beach Mall
Boynton Beach, FL 33435
(407)736-4424
Ultimate Parent: Limited. SIC: 5651—Family Clothing Stores.

★ 58783 ★　Lerner Shop
801 N. Congress Ave.
Boynton Beach, FL 33426
(407)736-3551
Ultimate Parent: Limited. SIC: 5621—Women's Clothing Stores.

★ 58784 ★　Lerner Shop
233 Boynton Beach Mall
Boynton Beach, FL 33435
(407)736-3551
Ultimate Parent: Limited. SIC: 5651—Family Clothing Stores.

★ 58785 ★　The Limited
817 W. Boynton Beach Blvd.
Boynton Beach, FL 33426
(407)736-2234
Ultimate Parent: Limited. SIC: 5651—Family Clothing Stores.

★ 58786 ★　Petite Sophisticate
801 N. Congress Ave.
Boynton Beach, FL 33426
(407)734-0803
Ultimate Parent: United States Shoe. SIC: 5651—Family Clothing Stores.

★ 58787 ★　Pizza Hut
2011 S. Federal Hwy.
Boynton Beach, FL 33435
(407)734-2400
Ultimate Parent: Pepsico. SIC: 5812—Eating Places.

★ 58788 ★　Radio Shack
139 N. Congress Ave.
Boynton Beach, FL 33435
(407)734-3567
Company Type: Division. Ultimate Parent: Tandy Corp. SIC: 5731—Radio, Television & Electronics Stores.

★ 58789 ★　Radio Shack
1618 S. Federal Hwy.
Boynton Beach, FL 33435
(407)732-8874
Company Type: Division. Ultimate Parent: Tandy Corp. SIC: 5065—Electronic Parts & Equipment Nec; 5731—Radio, Television & Electronics Stores.

★ 58790 ★　Rite Aid Pharmacy
552 SE 15th Ave.
Boynton Beach, FL 33435
(407)732-7416
Ultimate Parent: Rite Aid. SIC: 5912—Drug Stores & Proprietary Stores.

★ 58791 ★　Ryder Truck Rental
3653 S. Federal Hwy.
Boynton Beach, FL 33435
(407)736-1601
Ultimate Parent: Ryder System. SIC: 7513—Truck Rental & Leasing Without Drivers.

★ 58792 ★　Savings of America, A Division of Home Savings of America, FSB
127 N. Congress Ave.
Boynton Beach, FL 33436-4292
(407)736-8880
Location Type: Branch office. Ultimate Parent: H. F. Ahmanson. SIC: 6021—National Commercial Banks.

★ 58793 ★　Sermatech International Inc.
507 Industrial Way
Boynton Beach, FL 33426
Ultimate Parent: Teleflex. SIC: 3479—Metal Coating & Allied Services.

★ 58794 ★　United Parcel Service
4010 Thor Dr.
Boynton Beach, FL 33426
(407)734-7071
Ultimate Parent: United Parcel Service of America. SIC: 4215—Courier Services Except by Air.

★ 58795 ★　United Parcel Service
4010 Thor Dr.
Boynton Beach, FL 33426
(407)734-7071
Ultimate Parent: United Parcel Service of America. SIC: 4215—Courier Services Except by Air.

★ 58796 ★　Victoria's Secret
811 W. Boynton Beach Blvd.
Boynton Beach, FL 33426
(407)736-2203
Ultimate Parent: Limited. SIC: 5651—Family Clothing Stores.

★ 58797 ★　Waldenbooks
467 Boynton Bch Mall
Boynton Beach, FL 33435
(407)736-5531
Ultimate Parent: K-Mart. SIC: 5942—Book Stores.

★ 58798 ★　Walgreen
483 Boynton Beach Mall
Boynton Beach, FL 33435
(407)736-6008
Ultimate Parent: Walgreen Co. SIC: 5912—Drug Stores & Proprietary Stores.

Bradenton

★ 58799 ★　Ace Hardware
641 44th Ave. W
Bradenton, FL 34207
Ultimate Parent: Ace Hardware. SIC: 5251—Hardware Stores.

★ 58800 ★　Albertson's Liquor Store
7417 Manatee Ave. W
Bradenton, FL 34209
(813)794-3350
Ultimate Parent: Albertson's Inc. SIC: 5921—Liquor Stores.

★ 58801 ★　Albertson's Southco
3620 1st St.
Bradenton, FL 34208
(813)747-7781
Ultimate Parent: Albertson's Inc. SIC: 5411—Grocery Stores.

★ 58802 ★　Barnett Bank of Manatee County, NA
4311 Manatee Ave. W
Bradenton, FL 34209
(813)775-8889
Company Type: Subsidiary. Location Type: Branch office. Officer: R. Wayne Smith, Senior Vice President. Ultimate Parent: Barnett Banks. SIC: 6021—National Commercial Banks.

★ 58803 ★　Barnett Bank of Manatee County, NA
4545 14th St. W
Bradenton, FL 34207-1426
(813)775-8889
Company Type: Subsidiary. Location Type: Branch office. Officer: Gail Staib, Vice President. Ultimate Parent: Barnett Banks. SIC: 6021—National Commercial Banks.

★ 58804 ★　Barnett Bank of Manatee County, NA
5315 39th St. E
Bradenton, FL 34209-6705
(813)775-8889
Company Type: Subsidiary. Location Type: Branch office. Officer: Ruby Mulzer, Assistant Vice President. Ultimate Parent: Barnett Banks. SIC: 6021—National Commercial Banks.

★ 58805 ★　Barnett Bank of Manatee County, NA
6160 14th St. W
Bradenton, FL 34207-4601
(813)755-8889
Company Type: Subsidiary. Location Type: Branch office. Officer: Ben Hatcher, Senior Vice President. Ultimate Parent: Barnett Banks. SIC: 6021—National Commercial Banks.

★ 58806 ★　Barnett Bank of Manatee County, NA
3401 Cortez Rd. W
Bradenton, FL 34210-3102
(813)775-8889
Company Type: Subsidiary. Location Type: Branch office. Officer: George Najmy, Assistant Vice President. Ultimate Parent: Barnett Banks. SIC: 6021—National Commercial Banks.

★ 58807 ★　Barnett Bank of Manatee County, NA
7459 Manatee Ave. W
Bradenton, FL 34209-3444
(813)755-8889
Company Type: Subsidiary. Location Type: Branch office. Officer: Mary Hellhake, Assistant Vice President. Ultimate Parent: Barnett Banks. SIC: 6021—National Commercial Banks.

★ 58808 ★　Barnett Bank of Manatee County, NA
9416 Cortez Rd. W
Bradenton, FL 34210-2005
(813)755-8889
Company Type: Subsidiary. Location Type: Branch office. Officer: Linda Johns, Assistant Vice President. Ultimate Parent: Barnett Banks. SIC: 6021—National Commercial Banks.

★ 58809 ★　Barnett Bank of Manatee County, NA
4303 1st St.
Bradenton, FL 34208-4448
(813)755-8889
Company Type: Subsidiary. Location Type: Branch office. Officer: Otto Walter, Assistant Vice President. Ultimate Parent: Barnett Banks. SIC: 6021—National Commercial Banks.

★ 58810 ★　Barnett Bank of Manatee County, NA
4302 State Rd. 64 E
Bradenton, FL 34208-9678
(813)755-8889
Company Type: Subsidiary. Location Type: Branch office. Officer: Raymond Sleeth, Manager. Ultimate Parent: Barnett Banks. SIC: 6021—National Commercial Banks.

★ 58811 ★　Barnett Bank of Manatee County, NA
1001 3rd Ave. W
PO Box 9390
Bradenton, FL 34206-9390
(813)755-8889 Fax: (813)747-9056
Company Type: Subsidiary. Location Type: Branch office. Officer: Kenneth W. Oden, Chairman, President & CEO. Ultimate Parent: Barnett Banks. SIC: 6021—National Commercial Banks.

★ 58812 ★   Casual Corner
303 Us 301 Blvd. W
Bradenton, FL 34205
(813)748-4660
Ultimate Parent: United States Shoe. **SIC:**
5651—Family Clothing Stores.

★ 58813 ★   Express
3 Us 301 Blvd. W. 87
Bradenton, FL 34205
(813)747-4508
Ultimate Parent: Limited. **SIC:** 5651—
Family Clothing Stores.

★ 58814 ★   First of America Bank
3818 W. Manatee Ave.
Bradenton, FL 34205
(813)746-4263
Location Type: Branch office. **Ultimate
Parent:** First of America Bank Corp. **SIC:**
6021—National Commercial Banks.

★ 58815 ★   First of America Bank
7419 W. Manatee ave.
Bradenton, FL 34209
(813)794-0799
Location Type: Branch office. **Ultimate
Parent:** First of America Bank Corp. **SIC:**
6021—National Commercial Banks.

★ 58816 ★   First of America Bank
4215 W. Cortez Rd.
Bradenton, FL 34210
(813)753-5647
Location Type: Branch office. **Ultimate
Parent:** First of America Bank Corp. **SIC:**
6021—National Commercial Banks.

★ 58817 ★   First of America Bank
617 W. Cortez Rd.
Bradenton, FL 34207
(813)766-8711
Location Type: Branch office. **Ultimate
Parent:** First of America Bank Corp. **SIC:**
6021—National Commercial Banks.

★ 58818 ★   First Union National
Bank of Florida
5810 Manatee Ave. W
Bradenton, FL 34209-2541
(813)753-3960
Location Type: Branch office. **Ultimate
Parent:** First Union Corp. **SIC:** 6021—
National Commercial Banks.

★ 58819 ★   First Union National
Bank of Florida
920 Manatee Ave. W
Bradenton, FL 34205-8658
(813)745-7400
Location Type: Branch office. **Ultimate
Parent:** First Union Corp. **SIC:** 6021—
National Commercial Banks.

★ 58820 ★   First Union National
Bank of Florida
6285 14th St. W
Bradenton, FL 34207-4611
(813)753-3960
Location Type: Branch office. **Ultimate
Parent:** First Union Corp. **SIC:** 6021—
National Commercial Banks.

★ 58821 ★   First Union National
Bank of Florida
1416 51st Ave. E
Bradenton, FL 34203
(813)798-2693
Location Type: Branch office. **Ultimate
Parent:** First Union Corp. **SIC:** 6021—
National Commercial Banks.

★ 58822 ★   First Union National
Bank of Florida
1700 59th St. W
Bradenton, FL 34209-4666
(813)798-2630
Location Type: Branch office. **Ultimate
Parent:** First Union Corp. **SIC:** 6021—
National Commercial Banks.

★ 58823 ★   First Union National
Bank of Florida
7500 Cortez Rd. W
Bradenton, FL 34210-2409
(813)798-2686
Location Type: Branch office. **Ultimate
Parent:** First Union Corp. **SIC:** 6021—
National Commercial Banks.

★ 58824 ★   Flowers Baking Co. of
Bradenton Inc.
PO Box 20539
Bradenton, FL 34203-0539
(813)758-5656 **Fax:** (813)758-0937
Company Type: Subsidiary. **Officer:** John
L. Coate Sr., President. **Ultimate Parent:**
Flowers Industries.

★ 58825 ★   Footaction USA
303 Us Hwy. 301 Blvd. W
Bradenton, FL 34205
(813)746-1444
Ultimate Parent: Melville. **SIC:** 5661—Shoe
Stores.

★ 58826 ★   Jiffy Lube
2605 Cortez Rd. W
Bradenton, FL 34207
(813)756-4511
Ultimate Parent: Pennzoil.

★ 58827 ★   Kentucky Fried
Chicken
525 1st St.
Bradenton, FL 34208
(813)746-7393
Ultimate Parent: Pepsico. **SIC:** 5812—
Eating Places.

★ 58828 ★   Kentucky Fried
Chicken
8004 Cortez Rd. W
Bradenton, FL 34210
(813)794-3790
Ultimate Parent: Pepsico. **SIC:** 5812—
Eating Places.

★ 58829 ★   Kids-R-US
904 43rd St. W
Bradenton, FL 34209
(813)747-4904
Ultimate Parent: Toys "R" US. **SIC:** 5945—
Hobby, Toy & Game Shops; 8351—Child
Day Care Services.

★ 58830 ★   Lane Bryant
303 Us Hwy. 301 Blvd. W
Bradenton, FL 34205
(813)748-3049
Ultimate Parent: Limited. **SIC:** 5651—
Family Clothing Stores.

★ 58831 ★   Lerner Shop
303 Us Hwy. 301 Blvd. W. 457461
Bradenton, FL 34205
Ultimate Parent: Limited. **SIC:** 5651—
Family Clothing Stores.

★ 58832 ★   Lerner Shop
617 Desoto Sq.
Bradenton, FL 34210
(813)748-1544
Ultimate Parent: Limited. **SIC:** 5621—
Women's Clothing Stores.

★ 58833 ★   The Limited
303 Us Hwy. 301 Blvd. W
Bradenton, FL 34205
(813)749-1685
Ultimate Parent: Limited. **SIC:** 5621—
Women's Clothing Stores.

★ 58834 ★   McDonalds
Restaurants
3631 Cortez Rd. W
Bradenton, FL 34210
(813)756-9882
Ultimate Parent: McDonald's.
SIC: 5812—Eating Places.

★ 58835 ★   McDonalds
Restaurants
4711 14th St. W
Bradenton, FL 34207
(813)755-9595
Ultimate Parent: McDonald's.
SIC: 5812—Eating Places.

★ 58836 ★   Mcduff Electronics
4708 Cortez Rd. W
Bradenton, FL 34210
(813)794-6625
Ultimate Parent: Tandy Corp. **SIC:** 5719—
Miscellaneous Home Furnishings Stores.

★ 58837 ★   Mcduff Electronics
303 Us Hwy. 301 Blvd. W
Bradenton, FL 34205
(813)748-1636
Ultimate Parent: Tandy Corp. **SIC:** 5719—
Miscellaneous Home Furnishings Stores.

★ 58838 ★   Oshkosh
Trailer Div.
1512 38th Ave. E.
Bradenton, FL 34206
Company Type: Division. **Ultimate Parent:**
Oshkosh Truck. **SIC:** 3715—Truck Trailers.

★ 58839 ★   Pizza Hut
4903 14th St. W
Bradenton, FL 34207
(813)756-0667
Ultimate Parent: Pepsico. **SIC:** 5812—
Eating Places.

★ 58840 ★   Pizza Hut
2811 Manatee Ave. W
Bradenton, FL 34205
(813)749-0198
Ultimate Parent: Pepsico. **SIC:** 5812—
Eating Places.

★ 58841 ★   Pizza Hut
5627 14th St. W
Bradenton, FL 34207
(813)753-2238
Ultimate Parent: Pepsico. **SIC:** 5812—
Eating Places.

★ 58842 ★   Pizza Hut
5105 Manatee Ave. W
Bradenton, FL 34209
(813)794-6675
Ultimate Parent: Pepsico. **SIC:** 5812—
Eating Places.

★ 58843 ★   Publix Super Market
6124 14th St. W
Bradenton, FL 34207
(813)755-3797
Ultimate Parent: Publix Super Markets.
SIC: 5411—Grocery Stores.

★ 58844 ★   Publix Super Market
5584 Cortez Rd. W
Bradenton, FL 34210
(813)794-1930
Ultimate Parent: Publix Super Markets.
SIC: 5411—Grocery Stores.

★ 58845 ★   Publix Super Market
3909 Manatee Ave. W
Bradenton, FL 34205
(813)748-1334
Ultimate Parent: Publix Super Markets.
SIC: 5411—Grocery Stores.

★ 58846 ★   Publix Super Market
1005 Cortez Rd. W
Bradenton, FL 34207
(813)755-6315
Ultimate Parent: Publix Super Markets.
SIC: 5411—Grocery Stores.

★ 58847 ★   Radio Shack
5713 Manatee Ave. W
Bradenton, FL 34209
(813)792-2860
Company Type: Division. **Ultimate Parent:**
Tandy Corp. **SIC:** 5719—Miscellaneous
Home Furnishings Stores.

★ 58848 ★   Radio Shack
303 Us 301 Blvd. W
Bradenton, FL 34205
(813)748-3255
Company Type: Division. **Ultimate Parent:**
Tandy Corp. **SIC:** 5731—Radio, Television
& Electronics Stores.

★ 58849 ★   Rite-Aid Pharmacy
5730 14th St. W
Bradenton, FL 34207
(813)751-9736
Ultimate Parent: Rite Aid. **SIC:** 5912—Drug
Stores & Proprietary Stores.

★ 58850 ★   Ryder Truck Rental
3215 1st St.
Bradenton, FL 34208
(813)746-4769
Ultimate Parent: Ryder System. **SIC:**
7513—Truck Rental & Leasing Without
Drivers.

★ 58851 ★   Savings of America, A
Division of Home Savings of
America, FSB
7380 Manatee Ave. W
Bradenton, FL 34209
(813)794-1999
Location Type: Branch office. **Ultimate
Parent:** H. F. Ahmanson. **SIC:** 6021—
National Commercial Banks.

★ 58852 ★   Savings of America, A
Division of Home Savings of
America, FSB
497 Cortez Rd. W
Bradenton, FL 34207-1544
(813)753-7518
Location Type: Branch office. **Ultimate
Parent:** H. F. Ahmanson. **SIC:** 6021—
National Commercial Banks.

★ 58853 ★   Tropicana Products
Inc.
1001 13th Ave. East
PO Box 338
Bradenton, FL 34206
(813)747-4461
Company Type: Division. **Location Type:**
Facility. **Ultimate Parent:** J.E. Seagram &
Sons, Inc. **SIC:** 2033—Canned Fruits &
Vegetables.

★ 58854 ★   United Parcel Service
929 26th Ave. E
Bradenton, FL 34208
(813)748-2859
Ultimate Parent: United Parcel Service of
America. **SIC:** 4215—Courier Services
Except by Air.

★ 58855 ★   Wal Mart
815 Cortez Rd. W
Bradenton, FL 34207
(813)753-6751
Ultimate Parent: Wal-Mart Stores, Inc. **SIC:**
5311—Department Stores.

★ 58856 ★   Wal Mart Discount
City
6305 Manatee Ave. W
Bradenton, FL 34209
(813)795-1512
Ultimate Parent: Wal-Mart Stores, Inc. **SIC:**
5331—Variety Stores.

★ 58857 ★   Waldenbooks
303 Us Hwy. 301 Blvd. W. Apt
Bradenton, FL 34205
(813)747-7405
Ultimate Parent: K-Mart. **SIC:** 5942—Book
Stores.

★ 58858 ★   Walgreen
4425 14th St. W
Bradenton, FL 34207
(813)755-8528
Ultimate Parent: Walgreen Co. **SIC:**
5999—Miscellaneous Retail Stores Nec.

★ 58859 ★   Walgreen Drug Stores
5574 Cortez Rd. W
Bradenton, FL 34210
(813)792-3613
Ultimate Parent: Walgreen Co. **SIC:**
5999—Miscellaneous Retail Stores Nec.

★ 58860 ★   Walgreen Drug Stores
3915 Manatee Ave. W
Bradenton, FL 34205
(813)748-6086
Ultimate Parent: Walgreen Co. **SIC:**
5912—Drug Stores & Proprietary Stores.

★ 58861 ★   Walgreen Drug Stores
6112 14th St. W
Bradenton, FL 34207
(813)755-8526
Ultimate Parent: Walgreen Co. **SIC:**
5912—Drug Stores & Proprietary Stores.

Bradenton Beach

★ 58862 ★   Walgreen Drug Stores
3248 E. Bay Dr.
Bradenton Beach, FL 34217
(813)778-0461
Ultimate Parent: Walgreen Co. **SIC:**
5912—Drug Stores & Proprietary Stores.

Brandon

★ 58863 ★   Ace
Hardware&Locksmith
Rural Route 574
Brandon, FL 33511
(813)681-7790
Ultimate Parent: Ace Hardware. **SIC:**
5251—Hardware Stores.

★ 58864 ★ Barnett Bank of
Tampa
947 Lithia Pinecrest Rd.
Brandon, FL 33511-6120
(813)685-3628
Company Type: Subsidiary. **Location
Type:** Branch office. **Officer:** John Giroux,
Assistant Vice President. **Ultimate Parent:**
Barnett Banks. **SIC:** 6022—State
Commercial Banks.

★ 58865 ★ Barnett Bank of
Tampa
300 S. Parsons
Brandon, FL 33511-5229
(813)685-2941
Company Type: Subsidiary. **Location
Type:** Branch office. **Officer:** Doug Russell,
Vice President. **Ultimate Parent:** Barnett
Banks. **SIC:** 6022—State Commercial
Banks.

★ 58866 ★ Beneficial Savings
Bank FSB
930 W. Brandon Blvd.
Brandon, FL 33511-4906
Location Type: Branch office. **Ultimate
Parent:** Beneficial. **SIC:** 6022—State
Commercial Banks.

★ 58867 ★ Chase Home
Mortgage Corp.
710 Oakfield Dr.
Brandon, FL 33511
(813)681-7791
Ultimate Parent: Chase Manhattan Corp.
SIC: 6162—Mortgage Bankers &
Correspondents.

★ 58868 ★ Delta Air Lines
1903 Princeton Lakes Dr.
Brandon, FL 33511
(813)286-5000
Ultimate Parent: Delta Air Lines, Inc.

★ 58869 ★ First Union National
Bank of Florida
110 W. Bloomingdale Ave.
Brandon, FL 33511-5713
(813)276-6026
Location Type: Branch office. **Ultimate
Parent:** First Union Corp. **SIC:** 6021—
National Commercial Banks.

★ 58870 ★ Fleet Finance Inc.
768 W. Lumsden Rd.
Brandon, FL 33511
Ultimate Parent: Fleet Financial Group.
SIC: 6062—State Credit Unions; 6141—
Personal Credit Institutions.

★ 58871 ★ Frist Union National
Bank of Florida
510 Oakfield Dr.
Brandon, FL 33511-5713
(813)276-6188
Location Type: Branch office. **Ultimate
Parent:** First Union Corp. **SIC:** 6021—
National Commercial Banks.

★ 58872 ★ Great Western Bank
1015 Providence Rd.
Brandon, FL 33511
(813)654-1006
Ultimate Parent: Great Western Financial
Corp. **SIC:** 6159—Miscellaneous Business
Credit Institutions.

★ 58873 ★ Hit or Miss
2468 W. Brandon Blvd.
Brandon, FL 33511
(813)689-9490
Ultimate Parent: TJX. **SIC:** 5651—Family
Clothing Stores.

★ 58874 ★ McDonalds
Restaurants
Rural Route 584
Brandon, FL 33511
(813)685-3118
Ultimate Parent: McDonald's.
SIC: 5812—Eating Places.

★ 58875 ★ Piggly Wiggly
1007 PO Box
Brandon, FL 33509
Ultimate Parent: Bruno's. **SIC:** 5411—
Grocery Stores.

★ 58876 ★ Pizza Hut
1200 W. Brandon Blvd.
Brandon, FL 33511
(813)685-7453
Ultimate Parent: Pepsico. **SIC:** 5812—
Eating Places.

★ 58877 ★ Publix Super Market
1945 W. Lumsden Rd.
Brandon, FL 33511
(813)685-2900
Ultimate Parent: Publix Super Markets.
SIC: 5411—Grocery Stores.

★ 58878 ★ Publix Super Market
525 W. Brandon Blvd.
Brandon, FL 33511
(813)689-1275
Ultimate Parent: Publix Super Markets.
SIC: 5411—Grocery Stores.

★ 58879 ★ Radio Shack
746 W. Brandon Blvd.
Brandon, FL 33511
(813)685-7208
Company Type: Division. **Ultimate Parent:**
Tandy Corp. **SIC:** 5065—Electronic Parts &
Equipment Nec; 5731—Radio, Television &
Electronics Stores.

★ 58880 ★ Ryder Truck Rental
301 W. Brandon Blvd.
Brandon, FL 33511
(813)689-5598
Ultimate Parent: Ryder System. **SIC:**
7513—Truck Rental & Leasing Without
Drivers.

★ 58881 ★ Universal Data
Systems
911 S. Parsons Ave.
Brandon, FL 33511
(813)684-0615
Ultimate Parent: Motorola Inc. **SIC:** 7374—
Data Processing & Preparation.

★ 58882 ★ Walgreen Drug Stores
911 S. Lithia Pinecrest Rd.
Brandon, FL 33511
(813)689-6716
Ultimate Parent: Walgreen Co. **SIC:**
5912—Drug Stores & Proprietary Stores;
7384—Photofinishing Laboratories.

Brooksville

★ 58883 ★ AmSouth Bank of
Florida
1290 S. Broad St.
Brooksville, FL 34601-3194
(904)796-5106
Location Type: Branch office. **Ultimate
Parent:** AmSouth Bancorp. **SIC:** 6022—
State Commercial Banks.

★ 58884 ★ AmSouth Bank of
Florida
201 N. Howell Ave.
Brooksville, FL 34601-2099
(904)796-6751
Location Type: Branch office. **Ultimate
Parent:** AmSouth Bancorp. **SIC:** 6022—
State Commercial Banks.

★ 58885 ★ Barnett Bank of the
Suncoast, NA
US 41 & State Rd. 700
Brooksville, FL 34601
(904)796-1106
Company Type: Subsidiary. **Location
Type:** Branch office. **Officer:** Vernon Hall,
Manager. **Ultimate Parent:** Barnett Banks.
SIC: 6021—National Commercial Banks.

★ 58886 ★ Barnett Bank of the
Suncoast, NA
9223 Cortez Blvd.
Brooksville, FL 34613-6318
(904)596-8888
Company Type: Subsidiary. **Location
Type:** Branch office. **Officer:** H. M. Shirley
Jr., Chairman of the Board, President, &
CEO. **Ultimate Parent:** Barnett Banks. **SIC:**
6021—National Commercial Banks.

★ 58887 ★ Barnett Bank of the
Suncoast, NA
1362 W. US 41 Hwy. S
Brooksville, FL 34601-3118
(904)596-8840
Company Type: Subsidiary. **Location
Type:** Branch office. **Officer:** Pete Franztis,
Manager. **Ultimate Parent:** Barnett Banks.
SIC: 6021—National Commercial Banks.

★ 58888 ★ Food Lion
4221 Mariner Blvd.
Brooksville, FL 34609
(904)688-1771
Ultimate Parent: Food Lion. **SIC:** 5411—
Grocery Stores.

★ 58889 ★ Food Lion Inc.
4221 Mariner Blvd.
Brooksville, FL 34609
(904)688-1771
Ultimate Parent: Food Lion. **SIC:** 5411—
Grocery Stores.

★ 58890 ★ Greyhound Bus
Station
512 S. Broad St.
Brooksville, FL 34601
(904)796-3068
Ultimate Parent: Greyhound Lines Inc. **SIC:**
4173—Bus Terminal & Service Facilities.

★ 58891 ★ Kentucky Fried
Chicken
1145 Us 41 S
Brooksville, FL 34601
(904)796-4124
Ultimate Parent: Pepsico. **SIC:** 5812—
Eating Places.

★ 58892 ★ Mary Kay Cosmetics
27111 Thorncrest Ave.
Brooksville, FL 34602
(904)796-5736
Ultimate Parent: Mary Kay Cosmetics.

★ 58893 ★ Pizza Hut
1170 Us 41 S
Brooksville, FL 34601
(904)796-4040
Ultimate Parent: Pepsico. **SIC:** 5812—
Eating Places.

★ 58894 ★ Radio Shack
63 S. Court
Brooksville, FL 34610
(904)796-6032
Company Type: Division. **Ultimate Parent:**
Tandy Corp. **SIC:** 5065—Electronic Parts &
Equipment Nec.

★ 58895 ★ Radio Shack
S Us 41
Brooksville, FL 34601
(904)796-6032
Company Type: Division. **Ultimate Parent:**
Tandy Corp. **SIC:** 5731—Radio, Television
& Electronics Stores.

★ 58896 ★ Rite Aid Discount
Pharmacy
4207 Mariner Blvd.
Brooksville, FL 34609
(904)688-1832
Ultimate Parent: Rite Aid. **SIC:** 5912—Drug
Stores & Proprietary Stores.

★ 58897 ★ Texaco
20200 Cortez Blvd.
Brooksville, FL 34601
(904)796-9181
Ultimate Parent: Texaco. **SIC:** 5411—
Grocery Stores.

★ 58898 ★ Walgreen
1344 Us 41 S
Brooksville, FL 34601
(904)799-9543
Ultimate Parent: Walgreen Co. **SIC:**
5331—Variety Stores.

★ 58899 ★ Walgreen Drug Stores
1344 S. Us Hwy. 41
Brooksville, FL 34610
(904)799-9543
Ultimate Parent: Walgreen Co. **SIC:**
5912—Drug Stores & Proprietary Stores.

Bushnell

★ 58900 ★ AmSouth Bank of
Florida
900 N. Main St.
Bushnell, FL 33513
(904)793-2225
Location Type: Branch office. **Ultimate
Parent:** AmSouth Bancorp. **SIC:** 6022—
State Commercial Banks.

★ 58901 ★ First Union National
Bank of Florida
107 Bushnell Rd.
Bushnell, FL 33513
(904)793-0300
Location Type: Branch office. **Ultimate
Parent:** First Union Corp. **SIC:** 6021—
National Commercial Banks.

★ 58902 ★ Wal Mart Discount
Cities
1010 N. Main St.
Bushnell, FL 33513
(904)793-1300
Ultimate Parent: Wal-Mart Stores, Inc. **SIC:**
5311—Department Stores.

Callahan

★ 58903 ★ Anchor Savings Bank,
FSB
305 S. Kings Rd.
Callahan, FL 32011-9582
(904)879-2613
Location Type: Branch office. **Officer:** Sam
Murrow, Manager. **Ultimate Parent:** Anchor
Bancorp. **SIC:** 6021—National Commercial
Banks; 6035—Federal Savings Institutions;
6211—Security Brokers & Dealers.

★ 58904 ★ Anchor Savings Bank
FSB
305 Kings Rd. S
Callahan, FL 32011
(904)879-2613
Ultimate Parent: Anchor Bancorp. **SIC:**
6099—Functions Related to Deposit
Banking; 6159—Miscellaneous Business
Credit Institutions.

★ 58905 ★ Barnett Bank of
Nassau County
300 1st Ave. E
Callahan, FL 32011-9709
(904)879-1410
Company Type: Subsidiary. **Location
Type:** Branch office. **Officer:** Roswitha
Abels, Vice President. **Ultimate Parent:**
Barnett Banks. **SIC:** 6022—State
Commercial Banks.

★ 58906 ★ First Union National
Bank of Florida
401 S. King Rd.
Callahan, FL 32011-9102
(904)879-3510
Location Type: Branch office. **Ultimate
Parent:** First Union Corp. **SIC:** 6021—
National Commercial Banks.

Cantonment

★ 58907 ★ Barnett Bank of West
Florida
400 Hwy. 29 S.
Cantonment, FL 32533-1411
(904)968-1508
Location Type: Branch office. **Ultimate
Parent:** Barnett Banks. **SIC:** 6021—National
Commercial Banks.

★ 58908 ★ Champion
International Corp.
375 Muscogee Rd.
Cantonment, FL 32533
(904)968-2121
Ultimate Parent: Champion International.
SIC: 2679—Converted Paper Products Nec.

★ 58909 ★ James River Corp.
610 Chemstrand Rd.
Cantonment, FL 32533
Ultimate Parent: James River Corp. of
Virginia. **SIC:** 2297—Nonwoven Fabrics.

★ 58910 ★ Monsanto Co.
3000 Old Chemstrand Rd.
Cantonment, FL 32533
Ultimate Parent: Monsanto. **SIC:** 2824—
Organic Fibers—Noncellulosic; 2869—
Industrial Organic Chemicals Nec; 2821—
Plastics Materials & Resins; 2865—Cyclic
Crudes & Intermediates.

★ 58911 ★ Piggly Wiggly
Muscogee Rd.
Cantonment, FL 32533
(904)968-9519
Ultimate Parent: Bruno's. **SIC:** 5411—
Grocery Stores.

Cape Canaveral

★ 58912 ★ First Union National
Bank of Florida
7800 Astronaut Blvd.
Cape Canaveral, FL 32920-3799
(407)639-5244
Location Type: Branch office. **Ultimate
Parent:** First Union Corp. **SIC:** 6021—
National Commercial Banks.

★ 58913 ★　First Union National Bank of Florida
111 George J. King Blvd.
Cape Canaveral, FL 32920-3301
(407)639-5293
Location Type: Branch office. **Ultimate Parent:** First Union Corp. **SIC:** 6021—National Commercial Banks.

★ 58914 ★　General Dynamics Corp. Space Sys.
Hangar J Receiving
Cape Canaveral, FL 32899
Ultimate Parent: General Dynamics. **SIC:** 3761—Guided Missiles & Space Vehicles.

★ 58915 ★　Martin Marietta Space Launch Systems
Titan Iv Warehouse
Cape Canaveral, FL 32920
Ultimate Parent: Martin Marietta. **SIC:** 3761—Guided Missiles & Space Vehicles.

Cape Canavral

★ 58916 ★　General Dynamics Services C
710 Mullett Rd.
Cape Canaval, FL 32920
(407)783-1236
Ultimate Parent: General Dynamics. **SIC:** 8731—Commercial Physical Research.

★ 58917 ★　Unisys Corp.
8105 Canaveral Blvd.
Cape Canaval, FL 32920
(407)783-0667
Ultimate Parent: Unisys Corp. **SIC:** 5044—Office Equipment.

Cape Coral

★ 58918 ★　First of America Bank
717 Cape Coral Pkwy.
Cape Coral, FL 33904
(813)549-1611
Location Type: Branch office. **Ultimate Parent:** First of America Bank Corp. **SIC:** 6021—National Commercial Banks.

★ 58919 ★　First Federal S & L
521 Del Prado Blvds.
Cape Coral, FL 33990-2611
(813)772-7775
Company Type: Branch. **Officer:** Michael T. Meszaros. **Ultimate Parent:** Bancorp Hawaii. **SIC:** 6035—Federal Savings Institutions; 6021—National Commercial Banks.

★ 58920 ★　First Union National Bank of Florida
2307 Del Prado Blvd.
Cape Coral, FL 33990-4696
(813)574-1776
Location Type: Branch office. **Ultimate Parent:** First Union Corp. **SIC:** 6021—National Commercial Banks.

★ 58921 ★　First Union National Bank of Florida
1625 Cape Coral Pky. SE
Cape Coral, FL 33904-9010
(813)549-5030
Location Type: Branch office. **Ultimate Parent:** First Union Corp. **SIC:** 6021—National Commercial Banks.

★ 58922 ★　Fortune Bank, ASB
1821 DelPrado Blvd.
Cape Coral, FL 33990-4539
(813)574-5444
Location Type: Branch office. **Ultimate Parent:** Fortune Bancorp. **SIC:** 6021—National Commercial Banks.

★ 58923 ★　Frist of America Bank
717 Cape Coral Parkway
Cape Coral, FL 33904
(813)549-1611
Location Type: Branch office. **Ultimate Parent:** First of America Bank Corp. **SIC:** 6021—National Commercial Banks.

★ 58924 ★　McDonalds of Cape Coral
1715 Del Prado Blvd.
Cape Coral, FL 33904
(813)945-2555
Ultimate Parent: McDonald's. **SIC:** 5812—Eating Places.

★ 58925 ★　Radio Shack
1343 SE 47th Ter
Cape Coral, FL 33904
(813)542-5680
Company Type: Division. **Ultimate Parent:** Tandy Corp. **SIC:** 5065—Electronic Parts & Equipment Nec.

★ 58926 ★　Ryder Truck Rental
928 SE 13th Pl
Cape Coral, FL 33990
(813)772-1112
Ultimate Parent: Ryder System. **SIC:** 7513—Truck Rental & Leasing Without Drivers.

Casselberry

★ 58927 ★　Barnett Bank of Central Florida, NA
5300 S. US Hwy. 17-92
Casselberry, FL 32707
(407)263-6010
Company Type: Subsidiary. **Location Type:** Branch office. **Officer:** Jerry Baker, Manager. **Ultimate Parent:** Barnett Banks. **SIC:** 6021—National Commercial Banks.

★ 58928 ★　Barnett Bank of Central Florida, NA
1001 Red Bug Lake Rd.
Casselberry, FL 32707-5719
(407)263-6040
Company Type: Subsidiary. **Location Type:** Branch office. **Officer:** Mary Owen, Manager. **Ultimate Parent:** Barnett Banks. **SIC:** 6021—National Commercial Banks.

★ 58929 ★　Builders Square
204 E. State Rd. 436
Casselberry, FL 32730
(407)830-1060
Company Type: Subsidiary. **Ultimate Parent:** K-Mart. **SIC:** 5039—Construction Materials Nec.

★ 58930 ★　Builders Square
204 Semoran Blvd.
Casselberry, FL 32707
(407)830-1060
Company Type: Subsidiary. **Ultimate Parent:** K-Mart. **SIC:** 1521—Single-Family Housing Construction.

★ 58931 ★　Exxon Car Wash
105 Hwy. 17
Casselberry, FL 32730
(407)831-5433
Ultimate Parent: Exxon. **SIC:** 7542—Car Washes.

★ 58932 ★　First Union Natonal Bank of Florida
1391 E. Semoran Blvd.
Casselberry, FL 32707
(407)657-3105
Location Type: Branch office. **Ultimate Parent:** First Union Corp. **SIC:** 6021—National Commercial Banks.

★ 58933 ★　Jiffy Lube
2289 Semoran Way
Casselberry, FL 32707
(407)671-6769
Ultimate Parent: Pennzoil. **SIC:** 7549—Automotive Services Nec.

★ 58934 ★　Kentucky Fried Chicken
1410 Semoran Blvd.
Casselberry, FL 32707
(407)678-1333
Ultimate Parent: Pepsico. **SIC:** 5812—Eating Places.

★ 58935 ★　Kentucky Fried Chicken
5650 S. Dixie Hwy. NE
Casselberry, FL 32707
(407)831-6500
Ultimate Parent: Pepsico. **SIC:** 5812—Eating Places.

★ 58936 ★　Mellon Financial Service Corp.
1486 Semoran Blvd.
Casselberry, FL 32707
(407)671-7312
Ultimate Parent: Mellon Bank Corp. **SIC:** 6141—Personal Credit Institutions.

★ 58937 ★　Pennzoil Ten Minute Oil Change
1 Purlieu Pl
Casselberry, FL 32707
(407)671-6289
Ultimate Parent: Pennzoil. **SIC:** 5172—Petroleum Products Nec.

★ 58938 ★　Personal Performance Consultants
754 Lake Kathryn Cir.
Casselberry, FL 32707
(407)699-8145
Ultimate Parent: Medco Containment Services. **SIC:** 8742—Management Consulting Services.

★ 58939 ★　Pizza Hut
Hwy. 1792 Building
Casselberry, FL 32707
(407)831-2404
Ultimate Parent: Pepsico. **SIC:** 5812—Eating Places.

★ 58940 ★　Radio Shack
Butler Plz.
Casselberry, FL 32707
(407)671-4321
Company Type: Division. **Ultimate Parent:** Tandy Corp. **SIC:** 5731—Radio, Television & Electronics Stores.

★ 58941 ★　Safety Kleen Corp.
180835 PO Box
Casselberry, FL 32718
(407)830-6906
Ultimate Parent: Safety-Kleen. **SIC:** 7538—General Automotive Repair Shops.

★ 58942 ★　Sam's Wholesale Club
355 E. State Rd. 436
Casselberry, FL 32730
(407)260-8109
Ultimate Parent: Wal-Mart Stores, Inc. **SIC:** 5099—Durable Goods Nec.

★ 58943 ★　Taco Bell
1410 Semoran Blvd.
Casselberry, FL 32707
(407)657-5077
Ultimate Parent: Pepsico. **SIC:** 5812—Eating Places.

★ 58944 ★　Wal Mart
1241 Semoran Blvd.
Casselberry, FL 32707
(407)679-0377
Ultimate Parent: Wal-Mart Stores, Inc. **SIC:** 5399—Miscellaneous General Merchandise Store.

★ 58945 ★　Walgreen Drug Stores
1448 State Rd. 436
Casselberry, FL 32707
(407)678-6161
Ultimate Parent: Walgreen Co. **SIC:** 5912—Drug Stores & Proprietary Stores.

★ 58946 ★　Wells Fargo Guard Services
400 State Rd. 436
Casselberry, FL 32707
(407)331-9611
Ultimate Parent: Borg Warner Automotive. **SIC:** 7381—Detective & Armored Car Services.

Century

★ 58947 ★　Piggly Wiggly
Pensacola Hwy.
Century, FL 32535
(904)256-3228
Ultimate Parent: Bruno's. **SIC:** 5411—Grocery Stores.

Charlotte Harbor

★ 58948 ★　Barnett Bank of Southwest Florida
23081 Harbor View Rd.
Charlotte Harbor, FL 33980
(813)951-4800
Company Type: Subsidiary. **Location Type:** Branch office. **Officer:** Jeff Parlier, Manager. **Ultimate Parent:** Barnett Banks. **SIC:** 6021—National Commercial Banks.

★ 58949 ★　Frist Union National Bank of Florida
4369 Tamiami Trl.
Charlotte Harbor, FL 33908-2118
(813)627-6235
Location Type: Branch office. **Ultimate Parent:** First Union Corp. **SIC:** 6021—National Commercial Banks.

Chattahoochie

★ 58950 ★　Quincy State Bank
35 Jefferson St.
Chattahoochie, FL 32324-1415
(904)663-4392
Company Type: Subsidiary. **Location Type:** Branch office. **Officer:** Edna Brown, Mgr. **Ultimate Parent:** Synovus Financial Corp. **SIC:** 6021—National Commercial Banks.

Chiefland

★ 58951 ★　Greyhound Bus Lines
N Hwy. 19
Chiefland, FL 32626
(904)493-4954
Ultimate Parent: Greyhound Lines Inc. **SIC:** 4131—Intercity & Rural Bus Transportation.

★ 58952 ★　Wal Mart Discount Cities
2202 N. Young Blvd.
Chiefland, FL 32626
(904)493-0709
Ultimate Parent: Wal-Mart Stores, Inc. **SIC:** 5311—Department Stores.

Chipley

★ 58953 ★　First Union National Bank of Florida
208 E. Jackson Ave. E
Chipley, FL 32428-1930
(904)638-0570
Location Type: Branch office. **Ultimate Parent:** First Union Corp. **SIC:** 6021—National Commercial Banks.

★ 58954 ★　Greyhound Bus Lines
801 Us 90
Chipley, FL 32428
(904)638-1922
Ultimate Parent: Greyhound Lines Inc. **SIC:** 4111—Local & Suburban Transit.

Citrus Springs

★ 58955 ★　Barnett Bank of the Suncoast, NA
10241 N. Florida Ave.
Citrus Springs, FL 32630
(904)465-0034
Company Type: Subsidiary. **Location Type:** Branch office. **Officer:** Art Krueger, Manager. **Ultimate Parent:** Barnett Banks. **SIC:** 6021—National Commercial Banks.

Clair Mel City

★ 58956 ★　Safety Kleen Corp.
5309 24th Ave. S
Clair Mel City, FL 33619
(813)626-1203
Ultimate Parent: Safety-Kleen. **SIC:** 5087—Service Establishment Equipment.

★ 58957 ★　Sybra Inc.
3014 N. Us Hwy. 301 900
Clair Mel City, FL 33619
(813)621-8595
Ultimate Parent: Valhi Inc.

Clearwater

★ 58958 ★　Advanced Medical Systems
21967 Us Hwy. 19 N
Clearwater, FL 34625
(813)530-3242
Ultimate Parent: Standard Register. **SIC:** 7372—Prepackaged Software.

★ 58959 ★　Air Products & Chemicals, Inc.
3255 US Hwy. 19 N
Clearwater, FL 34621
(813)787-2005
Ultimate Parent: Air Products & Chemicals, Inc. **SIC:** 5199—Nondurable Goods Nec.

★ 58960 ★ **American Savings of Florida**
1866 Us Hwy. 19 N
Clearwater, FL 34625
(813)726-8556
Ultimate Parent: American Savings of Florida. **SIC:** 6099—Functions Related to Deposit Banking.

★ 58961 ★ **AmSouth Bank of Florida**
2475 Sunset Point Rd.
Clearwater, FL 34625
(813)462-1308
Location Type: Branch office. **Ultimate Parent:** AmSouth Bancorp. **SIC:** 6022—State Commercial Banks.

★ 58962 ★ **AmSouth Bank of Florida**
1350 W. Bay Dr.
Clearwater, FL 34640
(813)462-1200
Location Type: Branch office. **Ultimate Parent:** AmSouth Bancorp. **SIC:** 6022—State Commercial Banks.

★ 58963 ★ **AmSouth Bank of Florida**
13501 Icot Blvd.
Clearwater, FL 34620
(813)462-1264
Location Type: Branch office. **Ultimate Parent:** AmSouth Bancorp. **SIC:** 6022—State Commercial Banks.

★ 58964 ★ **AmSouth Bank of Florida**
2175 Nursery Rd.
Clearwater, FL 34624
(813)462-1245
Location Type: Branch office. **Ultimate Parent:** AmSouth Bancorp. **SIC:** 6022—State Commercial Banks.

★ 58965 ★ **AmSouth Bank of Florida**
2201 Drew St.
Clearwater, FL 34625
(813)462-1185
Location Type: Branch office. **Ultimate Parent:** AmSouth Bancorp.

★ 58966 ★ **AmSouth Bank of Florida**
3021 Enterprise Rd.
Clearwater, FL 34619
(813)462-1271
Location Type: Branch office. **Ultimate Parent:** AmSouth Bancorp. **SIC:** 6022—State Commercial Banks.

★ 58967 ★ **AmSouth Bank of Florida**
400 Cleveland St.
PO Box 179
Clearwater, FL 34617-0179
(813)441-9611
Location Type: Branch office. **Officer:** Alfred W. Swan Jr., President. **Ultimate Parent:** AmSouth Bancorp. **SIC:** 6022—State Commercial Banks; 6035—Federal Savings Institutions; 6282—Investment Advice.

★ 58968 ★ **Barnett Bank of Pinellas County**
1911 N. Belcher Rd.
Clearwater, FL 34623-1593
(813)539-9011
Company Type: Subsidiary. **Location Type:** Branch office. **Officer:** Stayce Clayman, Manager. **Ultimate Parent:** Barnett Banks. **SIC:** 6022—State Commercial Banks.

★ 58969 ★ **Barnett Bank of Pinellas County**
423 Mandalay Ave.
Clearwater, FL 34630-2097
(813)539-9010
Company Type: Subsidiary. **Location Type:** Branch office. **Officer:** Judy Stokely, Manager. **Ultimate Parent:** Barnett Banks. **SIC:** 6022—State Commercial Banks.

★ 58970 ★ **Barnett Bank of Pinellas County**
1499 Gulf-To-Bay Blvd.
Clearwater, FL 34615-5325
(813)539-9020
Company Type: Subsidiary. **Location Type:** Branch office. **Officer:** Kathryn Kegarise, Manager. **Ultimate Parent:**

Barnett Banks. **SIC:** 6022—State Commercial Banks.

★ 58971 ★ **Barnett Bank of Pinellas County**
122 Island Way
Clearwater, FL 34630-2216
(813)539-9021
Company Type: Subsidiary. **Location Type:** Branch office. **Officer:** Karen Amyx, Manager. **Ultimate Parent:** Barnett Banks. **SIC:** 6022—State Commercial Banks.

★ 58972 ★ **Barnett Bank of Pinellas County**
2751 Regency Oaks Blvd.
Clearwater, FL 34619
(813)539-9311
Company Type: Subsidiary. **Location Type:** Branch office. **Officer:** Carol Meyer, Manager. **Ultimate Parent:** Barnett Banks. **SIC:** 6022—State Commercial Banks.

★ 58973 ★ **Barnett Bank of Pinellas County**
600 Cleveland St.
Clearwater, FL 34615-4101
(813)539-9091
Company Type: Subsidiary. **Location Type:** Branch office. **Officer:** Mike Neville, Manager. **Ultimate Parent:** Barnett Banks. **SIC:** 6022—State Commercial Banks.

★ 58974 ★ **Barnett Bank of Pinellas County**
1610 S. Missouri Ave.
Clearwater, FL 34616-1287
(813)539-9366
Company Type: Subsidiary. **Location Type:** Branch office. **Officer:** Patricia Sieg, Vice President. **Ultimate Parent:** Barnett Banks. **SIC:** 6022—State Commercial Banks.

★ 58975 ★ **Barnett Bank of Pinellas County**
2200 Belleair Rd.
Clearwater, FL 34624-2734
(813)539-9685
Company Type: Subsidiary. **Location Type:** Branch office. **Officer:** Laura Pesci, Manager. **Ultimate Parent:** Barnett Banks. **SIC:** 6022—State Commercial Banks.

★ 58976 ★ **Barnett Bank of Pinellas County**
2150 Cleveland St.
Clearwater, FL 34625-3211
(813)539-9181
Company Type: Subsidiary. **Location Type:** Branch office. **Officer:** Melissa Ransdell, Manager. **Ultimate Parent:** Barnett Banks. **SIC:** 6022—State Commercial Banks.

★ 58977 ★ **Barnett Bank of Pinellas County**
15201 Roosevelt Blvd.
Clearwater, FL 34620-3532
(813)539-9180
Company Type: Subsidiary. **Location Type:** Branch office. **Officer:** Mike Corrigan, Manager. **Ultimate Parent:** Barnett Banks. **SIC:** 6022—State Commercial Banks.

★ 58978 ★ **Barnett Bank of Pinellas County**
3000 Enterprise Rd. E
Clearwater, FL 34619-1303
(813)539-9713
Company Type: Subsidiary. **Location Type:** Branch office. **Officer:** Carol Meyer, Vice President. **Ultimate Parent:** Barnett Banks. **SIC:** 6022—State Commercial Banks.

★ 58979 ★ **Barnett Bank of Pinellas County**
1261 Gulf Blvd., Ste. 128
Clearwater, FL 34630
(813)539-9815
Company Type: Subsidiary. **Location Type:** Branch office. **Officer:** Judy Stokely, Manager. **Ultimate Parent:** Barnett Banks. **SIC:** 6022—State Commercial Banks.

★ 58980 ★ **California Federal Bank, AFSB**
1810 N. Belcher Rd.
Clearwater, FL 34625
(813)442-4422
Location Type: Branch office. **Ultimate Parent:** California Federal Bank. **SIC:** 6021—National Commercial Banks.

★ 58981 ★ **California Federal Bank, AFSB**
2519 McMullen Booth Rd.
Clearwater, FL 34621-4152
(813)725-3644
Location Type: Branch office. **Ultimate Parent:** California Federal Bank. **SIC:** 6021—National Commercial Banks.

★ 58982 ★ **Casual Corner**
527 Countryside Mall
Clearwater, FL 34621
(813)796-1071
Ultimate Parent: United States Shoe. **SIC:** 5651—Family Clothing Stores.

★ 58983 ★ **Chase Manhatten Bank of Florida, NA**
28100 US 19 N
Clearwater, FL 34621-2619
(813)785-0179
Location Type: Branch office. **Ultimate Parent:** Chase Manhattan Corp. **SIC:** 6021—National Commercial Banks.

★ 58984 ★ **Circuit City**
23656 Us Hwy. 19 N
Clearwater, FL 34625
(813)726-2899
Ultimate Parent: Circuit City Stores. **SIC:** 5719—Miscellaneous Home Furnishings Stores.

★ 58985 ★ **Citibank, FSB**
28050 US Hwy. 19 N, Ste. 101
Clearwater, FL 34621-2600
(813)791-5556
Location Type: Branch office. **Ultimate Parent:** Citicorp. **SIC:** 6021—National Commercial Banks; 6035—Federal Savings Institutions.

★ 58986 ★ **Citizens Federal Bank, AFSB**
140 Island Way
Clearwater, FL 34630
(813)442-1133
Location Type: Branch office. **Ultimate Parent:** CSF Holdings.

★ 58987 ★ **Citizens Federal Bank, AFSB**
23684 US Hwy. 19 N.
Clearwater, FL 34625
(813)725-9606
Ultimate Parent: CSF Holdings. **SIC:** 6021—National Commercial Banks.

★ 58988 ★ **Coast to Coast Exteriors**
1872 Draw St.
Clearwater, FL 34625
(813)461-4120
Ultimate Parent: Servistar Corp.

★ 58989 ★ **Cole Engineering Corp.**
1201 Cedar St.
Clearwater, FL 34615
(813)726-5556
Ultimate Parent: Giant Food. **SIC:** 1521—Single-Family Housing Construction.

★ 58990 ★ **Comerica Bank & Trust, FSB**
26133 US Hwy. 19 N.
Clearwater, FL 34623-2015
(813)799-6880
Location Type: Branch office. **Ultimate Parent:** Comerica Bank. **SIC:** 6021—National Commercial Banks.

★ 58991 ★ **Eckerd Corp.**
PO Box 4689
Clearwater, FL 34618
(813)399-6000 **Fax:** (813)399-6119
Company Type: Headquarters. **Officer:** Stewart Turley, Chairman & CEO. **Ultimate Parent:** Eckerd Corp. **Employee Count:** 325000.

★ 58992 ★ **Federal Express Corp.**
12415 Automobile Blvd.
Clearwater, FL 34622
(813)821-1256
Ultimate Parent: Federal Express. **SIC:** 7389—Business Services Nec.

★ 58993 ★ **First of America**
2539 Countryside Blvd.
Clearwater, FL 34621
(813)797-6808
Location Type: Branch office. **Ultimate Parent:** First of America Bank Corp. **SIC:** 6021—National Commercial Banks.

★ 58994 ★ **First of America Bank**
2201 Drew St.
Clearwater, FL 34625
(813)797-6556
Location Type: Branch office. **Ultimate Parent:** First of America Bank Corp. **SIC:** 6021—National Commercial Banks.

★ 58995 ★ **First of America Bank**
2539 Countryside Blvd.
Clearwater, FL 34621
(813)797-6808
Location Type: Branch office. **Ultimate Parent:** First of America Bank Corp. **SIC:** 6021—National Commercial Banks.

★ 58996 ★ **First Union National Bank of Florida**
5005 Ulmerton Rd.
Clearwater, FL 34620-4040
(813)892-7403
Location Type: Branch office. **Ultimate Parent:** First Union Corp. **SIC:** 6021—National Commercial Banks.

★ 58997 ★ **First Union National Bank of Florida**
5250 E. Bay Dr.
Clearwater, Fl 34624
(813)538-4545
Location Type: Branch office. **Ultimate Parent:** First Union Corp. **SIC:** 6021—National Commercial Banks.

★ 58998 ★ **First Union National Bank of Florida**
1545 S. Belcher Rd.
Clearwater, FL 34624-7607
(813)538-4580
Location Type: Branch office. **Ultimate Parent:** First Union Corp. **SIC:** 6021—National Commercial Banks.

★ 58999 ★ **First Union National Bank of Florida**
1401 S. Fort Harrison Ave.
Clearwater, FL 34616
(813)538-4560
Location Type: Branch office. **Ultimate Parent:** First Union Corp. **SIC:** 6021—National Commercial Banks.

★ 59000 ★ **First Union National Bank of Florida**
500 Clearwater Mall
US Hwy. 19 N
Clearwater, FL 34624-7306
(813)538-4565
Location Type: Branch office. **Ultimate Parent:** First Union Corp. **SIC:** 6021—National Commercial Banks.

★ 59001 ★ **First Union National Bank of Florida**
2580 N. McMullen Booth Rd.
Clearwater, FL 34621
(813)538-4524
Location Type: Branch office. **Ultimate Parent:** First Union Corp. **SIC:** 6021—National Commercial Banks.

★ 59002 ★ **First Union National Bank of Florida**
28163 US Hwy. 19 N
Clearwater, FL 34621-2638
(813)538-4460
Location Type: Branch office. **Ultimate Parent:** First Union Corp. **SIC:** 6021—National Commercial Banks.

★ 59003 ★ **First Union National Bank of Florida**
2140 Gulf-to-Bay Blvd.
Clearwater, FL 34625-3921
(813)538-4488
Location Type: Branch office. **Ultimate Parent:** First Union Corp. **SIC:** 6021—National Commercial Banks.

★ 59004 ★ **Fortune Bancorp**
16120 US 19 N
Clearwater, FL 34624
(813)538-1000
Company Type: Headquarters. **Officer:** John R. Torell III. **Fortune Service 500:** Ranking 39.

★ 59005 ★   Fortune Bancorp Inc.
16120 U.S. 19 N
Clearwater, FL 34624
(813)538-1000
Officer: John R. Torell III, Chairman.
Ultimate Parent: Fortune Bancorp. **SIC:**
6712—Bank Holding Companies; 6036—
Savings Institutions Except Federal.
Employee Count: 798. **Sales:** 220757000
M.

★ 59006 ★   Fortune Bancorp. Inc.
PO Box 6100
Clearwater, FL 34618-6100
(813)538-1000
Location Type: Branch office. **Ultimate
Parent:** Fortune Bancorp. **SIC:** 6021—
National Commercial Banks.

★ 59007 ★   Fortune Bancorp, Inc.
16120 US Hwy. 19 N
Clearwater, FL 34624-6895
(813)538-1000
Location Type: Branch office. **Ultimate
Parent:** Fortune Bancorp. **SIC:** 6021—
National Commercial Banks.

★ 59008 ★   Fortune
Bancorporation
16120 US Hwy. 19 N.
Clearwater, FL 34624-5748
(813)538-1000
Officer: John R. Torell III, Ch. Bd. CEO.
Ultimate Parent: Fortune Bancorp. **SIC:**
6036—Savings Institutions Except Federal.
Employee Count: 798.

★ 59009 ★   Fortune Bank
16120 US Hwy. 19 N.
Clearwater, FL 34624-5748
(813)538-1000
Company Type: Subsidiary. **Officer:** John
R. Torell III, Ch. Bd. CEO. **Ultimate Parent:**
Fortune Bancorp. **SIC:** 6035—Federal
Savings Institutions. **Employee Count:** 735.

★ 59010 ★   Fortune Bank, ASB
2575 Countryside Blvd.
Clearwater, FL 34621-3413
(813)796-4497
Location Type: Facility. **Officer:** Scott
Sawyer, Manager. **Ultimate Parent:** Fortune
Bancorp. **SIC:** 6021—National Commercial
Banks.

★ 59011 ★   Fortune Bank, ASB
5200 E. Bay Dr.
Clearwater, FL 34624-5764
(813)535-5527
Location Type: Facility. **Ultimate Parent:**
Fortune Bancorp. **SIC:** 6021—National
Commercial Banks.

★ 59012 ★   Fortune Bank, ASB
655 S. Belcher Rd.
Clearwater, FL 34624-6392
(813)796-0488
Location Type: Facility. **Ultimate Parent:**
Fortune Bancorp. **SIC:** 6021—National
Commercial Banks.

★ 59013 ★   Fortune Bank, ASB
2551 Sunset Point Rd.
Clearwater, FL 34625-0196
(813)796-0196
Location Type: Facility. **Ultimate Parent:**
Fortune Bancorp. **SIC:** 6021—National
Commercial Banks.

★ 59014 ★   Fortune Bank, ASB
1500 Belleair Rd.
Clearwater, FL 34616-2399
(813)441-8451
Location Type: Branch office. **Ultimate
Parent:** Fortune Bancorp. **SIC:** 6021—
National Commercial Banks.

★ 59015 ★   Fortune Bank, ASB
475 Poinsettia Ave.
Clearwater, FL 34630-2049
(813)461-3344
Location Type: Branch office. **Ultimate
Parent:** Fortune Bancorp. **SIC:** 6021—
National Commercial Banks.

★ 59016 ★   Fortune Bank, ASB
606 Chestnut St.
Clearwater, FL 34616
(813)447-0600
Location Type: Branch office. **Officer:** Bill
English, Manager. **Ultimate Parent:** Fortune
Bancorp. **SIC:** 6021—National Commercial
Banks.

★ 59017 ★   The Gap
159 Clearwater Mall
Clearwater, FL 34624
(813)796-8062
Ultimate Parent: GAP. **SIC:** 5651—Family
Clothing Stores.

★ 59018 ★   Hercules Defense
Electronics Systems Inc.
13133 34th St.
Clearwater, FL 34622
Ultimate Parent: Hercules. **SIC:** 3812—
Search & Navigation Equipment.

★ 59019 ★   Hit or Miss
733 Countryside Mall
Clearwater, FL 34621
(813)797-5181
Ultimate Parent: TJX. **SIC:** 5651—Family
Clothing Stores.

★ 59020 ★   Hit or Miss
15525 Us Hwy. 19 N
Clearwater, FL 34624
(813)530-3112
Ultimate Parent: TJX. **SIC:** 5699—
Miscellaneous Apparel & Accessory Stores.

★ 59021 ★   Home Depot Inc.
2351 N. Us Hwy. 19
Clearwater, FL 34623
(813)797-8755
Ultimate Parent: Home Depot. **SIC:** 5211—
Lumber & Other Building Materials.

★ 59022 ★   Honeywell Inc.
13350 U.S. Hwy. 19 N.
Clearwater, FL 34624-7290
Ultimate Parent: Honeywell. **SIC:** 3812—
Search & Navigation Equipment.

★ 59023 ★   Honeywell Inc.
13350 Us Hwy. 19
Clearwater, FL 34624-7290
Ultimate Parent: Honeywell. **SIC:** 3769—
Space Vehicle Equipment Nec; 3674—
Semiconductors & Related Devices.

★ 59024 ★   Jiffy Lube
901 S. Missouri Ave.
Clearwater, FL 34616
(813)441-9133
Ultimate Parent: Pennzoil. **SIC:** 7539—
Automotive Repair Shops Nec.

★ 59025 ★   Kentucky Fried
Chicken
1280 S. Missouri Ave.
Clearwater, FL 34616
(813)446-0161
Ultimate Parent: Pepsico. **SIC:** 5812—
Eating Places; 5812—Eating Places.

★ 59026 ★   Kentucky Fried
Chicken
1960 Gulf to Bay Blvd.
Clearwater, FL 34625
(813)446-5935
Ultimate Parent: Pepsico. **SIC:** 5812—
Eating Places.

★ 59027 ★   Lane Bryant
541 Countryside Mall
Clearwater, FL 34621
(813)791-1398
Ultimate Parent: Limited. **SIC:** 5651—
Family Clothing Stores.

★ 59028 ★   Lerner Shop
327 Countryside Mall
Clearwater, FL 34621
(813)796-1266
Ultimate Parent: Limited. **SIC:** 5621—
Women's Clothing Stores.

★ 59029 ★   The Limited
171 Clearwater Mall
Clearwater, FL 34624
(813)799-4409
Ultimate Parent: Limited. **SIC:** 5621—
Women's Clothing Stores.

★ 59030 ★   The Limited Express
831 Countryside Mall
Clearwater, FL 34621
(813)796-2681
Ultimate Parent: Limited. **SIC:** 5949—
Sewing, Needlework & Piece Goods.

★ 59031 ★   Linens N Things
15525 Us Hwy. 19 N
Clearwater, FL 34624
(813)535-4090
Ultimate Parent: Melville. **SIC:** 5719—
Miscellaneous Home Furnishings Stores.

★ 59032 ★   Maison Blanche
Countryside Mall
Clearwater, FL 34621
(813)796-2242
Ultimate Parent: Mercantile Stores. **SIC:**
5311—Department Stores.

★ 59033 ★   Mary Kay Cosmetics
1682 Linwood Dr.
Clearwater, FL 34615
(813)442-6101
Ultimate Parent: Mary Kay Cosmetics.

★ 59034 ★   McDonald's
Restaurants
1885 N. Us 19
Clearwater, FL 34625
(813)796-1912
Ultimate Parent: McDonald's.
SIC: 5812—Eating Places.

★ 59035 ★   Petite Sophisticate
329 Countryside Mall
Clearwater, FL 34621
(813)797-2283
Ultimate Parent: United States Shoe. **SIC:**
5651—Family Clothing Stores.

★ 59036 ★   Piggly Wiggly
1661 Gulf to Bay Blvd.
Clearwater, FL 34615
(813)442-5243
Ultimate Parent: Bruno's. **SIC:** 5411—
Grocery Stores.

★ 59037 ★   Pizza Hut
397 S. Us 19
Clearwater, FL 34625
(813)797-6707
Ultimate Parent: Pepsico. **SIC:** 5812—
Eating Places.

★ 59038 ★   Pizza Hut
2140 Drew St.
Clearwater, FL 34625
(813)442-0185
Ultimate Parent: Pepsico. **SIC:** 5812—
Eating Places.

★ 59039 ★   Publix Super Market
1856 Us Hwy. 19 N
Clearwater, FL 34625
(813)799-1110
Ultimate Parent: Publix Super Markets.
SIC: 5411—Grocery Stores.

★ 59040 ★   Publix Super Market
2160 Us Hwy. 19 S
Clearwater, FL 34624
(813)531-1479
Ultimate Parent: Publix Super Markets.
SIC: 5411—Grocery Stores.

★ 59041 ★   Publix Super Markets
1856 Us Hwy. 19 N
Clearwater, FL 34625
(813)799-1110
Ultimate Parent: Publix Super Markets.
SIC: 5411—Grocery Stores.

★ 59042 ★   Radio Shack
2601 Us 19 N. 455
Clearwater, FL 34621
(813)446-3776
Company Type: Division. **Ultimate Parent:**
Tandy Corp. **SIC:** 5731—Radio, Television
& Electronics Stores.

★ 59043 ★   Radio Shack
455 Countryside Mall
Clearwater, FL 34621
(813)796-1235
Company Type: Division. **Ultimate Parent:**
Tandy Corp. **SIC:** 5065—Electronic Parts &
Equipment Nec.

★ 59044 ★   Radio Shack
1865 N. Highland Ave.
Clearwater, FL 34615
(813)447-8624
Company Type: Division. **Ultimate Parent:**
Tandy Corp. **SIC:** 5731—Radio, Television
& Electronics Stores.

★ 59045 ★   Rite Aid Drugs
1478 S. Belcher Rd.
Clearwater, FL 34624
(813)531-1416
Ultimate Parent: Rite Aid. **SIC:** 5912—Drug
Stores & Proprietary Stores.

★ 59046 ★   Savings of America, A
Division of Home Savings of
America, FSB
25749 US Hwy. 19 N
Clearwater, FL 34623-2040
(813)797-1994
Location Type: Branch office. **Ultimate
Parent:** H. F. Ahmanson. **SIC:** 6021—
National Commercial Banks.

★ 59047 ★   Service Merchandise
139 Us Hwy. 19 N
Clearwater, FL 34625
(813)797-6100
Ultimate Parent: Service Merchandise Co.,
Inc. **SIC:** 5944—Jewelry Stores.

★ 59048 ★   Taco Bell
2552 E. Bay Dr.
Clearwater, FL 34624
(813)531-8655
Ultimate Parent: Pepsico. **SIC:** 5812—
Eating Places.

★ 59049 ★   Tech Data Corp.
5350 Tech Data Dr.
Clearwater, FL 34620-3134
(813)539-7429 Fax: (813)538-7050
Company Type: Headquarters. **Officer:**
Steven A. Raymond, CEO. **Employee
Count:** 1350. **Sales:** 1532.4 M. **Fortune
Service 500:** Ranking 95.

★ 59050 ★   Toys R US
2486 Us Hwy. 19 N
Clearwater, FL 34623
(813)797-5222
Ultimate Parent: Toys "R" US. **SIC:** 5945—
Hobby, Toy & Game Shops.

★ 59051 ★   Victoria's Secret
211 Countryside Mall
Clearwater, FL 34621
(813)791-1003
Ultimate Parent: Limited. **SIC:** 5651—
Family Clothing Stores.

★ 59052 ★   Victoria's Secret
505 Us Hwy. 19 S
Clearwater, FL 34624
(813)726-3782
Ultimate Parent: Limited. **SIC:** 5699—
Miscellaneous Apparel & Accessory Stores.

★ 59053 ★   Waldenbooks
136 Clearwater Mall
Clearwater, FL 34624
(813)796-1407
Ultimate Parent: K-Mart. **SIC:** 5942—Book
Stores.

★ 59054 ★   Walgreen Drug Stores
1704 Clearwater Largo Rd.
Clearwater, FL 34616
(813)586-4116
Ultimate Parent: Walgreen Co. **SIC:**
5912—Drug Stores & Proprietary Stores.

★ 59055 ★   Walgreen Drugs
1685 Gulf to Bay Blvd.
Clearwater, FL 34615
(813)441-8604
Ultimate Parent: Walgreen Co. **SIC:**
5912—Drug Stores & Proprietary Stores.

Clermont

★ 59056 ★   First Union National
Bank of Florida
726 E. Hwy. 50
Clermont, FL 34711-3197
(904)394-4015
Location Type: Branch office. **Ultimate
Parent:** First Union Corp. **SIC:** 6021—
National Commercial Banks.

★ 59057 ★   Pizza Hut
750 State Hwy. 50 E
Clermont, FL 34711
(904)394-5526
Ultimate Parent: Pepsico. **SIC:** 5812—
Eating Places.

★ 59058 ★   Publix Super Market
660 E. Hwy. 50
Clermont, FL 34711
(904)394-2107
Ultimate Parent: Publix Super Markets.
SIC: 5411—Grocery Stores.

Clewiston

★ 59059 ★   Everglades Sugar Refinery Inc.
State Rd. 832
Clewiston, FL 33440
Ultimate Parent: Savannah Foods & Industries, Inc. **SIC:** 2062—Cane Sugar Refining.

★ 59060 ★   Kentucky Fried Chicken
110 S. WC Owen Ave.
Clewiston, FL 33440
(813)983-8373
Ultimate Parent: Pepsico. **SIC:** 5812—Eating Places.

★ 59061 ★   Rite Aid
949 W. Sugarland Hwy.
Clewiston, FL 33440
(813)983-2162
Ultimate Parent: Rite Aid. **SIC:** 5912—Drug Stores & Proprietary Stores.

★ 59062 ★   South Central Florida Railroad
900 W.C. Owen
Clewiston, FL 33440
(813)983-3163
Company Type: Subsidiary. **Ultimate Parent:** Lukens. **SIC:** 4011—Railroads—Line-Haul Operating.

★ 59063 ★   Stop & Shop
215 W. Ventura Ave.
Clewiston, FL 33440
(813)983-4616
Ultimate Parent: Stop & Shop. **SIC:** 5199—Nondurable Goods Nec.

Clg Pkwy

★ 59064 ★   Pulte Home Corp.
3350 NW 53rd St.
Clg Pkwy, FL 33919
(813)486-6500
Ultimate Parent: Pulte. **SIC:** 1521—Single-Family Housing Construction.

Cocoa

★ 59065 ★   Barnett Bank of Central Florida, NA
430 Brevard Ave.
Cocoa, FL 32922-7989
(407)633-1100
Company Type: Subsidiary. **Location Type:** Branch office. **Officer:** Bill Taylor, Manager. **Ultimate Parent:** Barnett Banks. **SIC:** 6021—National Commercial Banks.

★ 59066 ★   Citgo Mini Mart
4601 W. King St.
Cocoa, FL 32926
(407)631-6181
Ultimate Parent: Citgo Petroleum. **SIC:** 5411—Grocery Stores.

★ 59067 ★   EG & G Florida (Cocoa)
410 High Point Dr.
Cocoa, FL 32926
(407)639-3530 **Fax:** (407)639-0228
Company Type: Subsidiary. **Officer:** James R. Dubay, Manager. **Ultimate Parent:** EG & G.

★ 59068 ★   First Union National Bank of Florida
834 N. Cocoa Ave.
Cocoa, FL 32922-7587
(407)639-5328
Location Type: Branch office. **Ultimate Parent:** First Union Corp. **SIC:** 6021—National Commercial Banks.

★ 59069 ★   Publix Super Market
1131 Byrd Plz.
Cocoa, FL 32922
(407)636-3111
Ultimate Parent: Publix Super Markets. **SIC:** 5411—Grocery Stores.

★ 59070 ★   Publix Super Markets
1131 Byrd Plz.
Cocoa, FL 32922
(407)636-3111
Ultimate Parent: Publix Super Markets. **SIC:** 5411—Grocery Stores.

★ 59071 ★   Radio Shack
1149 Byrd Plz.
Cocoa, FL 32922
(407)632-2340
Company Type: Division. **Ultimate Parent:** Tandy Corp. **SIC:** 5731—Radio, Television & Electronics Stores.

★ 59072 ★   Radio Shack
1149 Byrd Plz.
Cocoa, FL 32922
(407)632-3774
Company Type: Division. **Ultimate Parent:** Tandy Corp. **SIC:** 7373—Computer Integrated Systems Design.

★ 59073 ★   Ryder Truck Rental
3525 N. Us Hwy. 1
Cocoa, FL 32926
(407)636-6424
Ultimate Parent: Ryder System. **SIC:** 7513—Truck Rental & Leasing Without Drivers.

★ 59074 ★   Ryder Truck Rental
1609 N. Us Hwy. 1
Cocoa, FL 32922
(407)636-6422
Ultimate Parent: Ryder System. **SIC:** 7539—Automotive Repair Shops Nec.

★ 59075 ★   Shell Self Serve Food Mart
5 N. Cocoa Blvd.
Cocoa, FL 32922
(407)631-0245
Ultimate Parent: Shell Oil Co. **SIC:** 5541—Gasoline Service Stations.

★ 59076 ★   Walgreen Drug Stores
1155 Byrd Plz.
Cocoa, FL 32922
(407)636-6720
Ultimate Parent: Walgreen Co. **SIC:** 5912—Drug Stores & Proprietary Stores.

Cocoa Beach

★ 59077 ★   Ace Hardware
705 N. Atlantic Ave.
Cocoa Beach, FL 32931
(407)783-5810
Ultimate Parent: Ace Hardware. **SIC:** 5251—Hardware Stores.

★ 59078 ★   Barnett Bank of Central Florida, NA
150 Cocoa Isles Blvd.
Cocoa Beach, FL 32931-3061
(407)799-2400
Company Type: Subsidiary. **Location Type:** Branch office. **Officer:** Vilma Williams, Manager. **Ultimate Parent:** Barnett Banks. **SIC:** 6021—National Commercial Banks.

★ 59079 ★   Cape Canaveral Air Force Station
PO Box 321399
Cocoa Beach, FL 32932-1399
Ultimate Parent: Martin Marietta. **SIC:** 9999—Nonclassifiable Establishments.

★ 59080 ★   First Union National Bank of Florida
1205 N. Atlantic Ave.
Cocoa Beach, FL 32931-3196
(407)639-5210
Location Type: Branch office. **Ultimate Parent:** First Union Corp. **SIC:** 6021—National Commercial Banks.

★ 59081 ★   General Dynamics Space Systems
PO Box 320999
Cocoa Beach, FL 32932
(407)853-6011
Officer: Richard F. Gibb, Vice President. **Ultimate Parent:** General Dynamics. **SIC:** 3761—Guided Missiles & Space Vehicles.

★ 59082 ★   Pizza Hut
179 E. Cocoa Beach Causeway
Cocoa Beach, FL 32931
(407)783-2780
Ultimate Parent: Pepsico. **SIC:** 5812—Eating Places.

★ 59083 ★   Radio Shack
110 Canaveral Plz.
Cocoa Beach, FL 32931
(407)783-5360
Company Type: Division. **Ultimate Parent:** Tandy Corp. **SIC:** 5731—Radio, Television & Electronics Stores.

★ 59084 ★   Ryder Truck Rental
2411 S. Atlantic Ave.
Cocoa Beach, FL 32931
(407)783-6694
Ultimate Parent: Ryder System. **SIC:** 7513—Truck Rental & Leasing Without Drivers.

★ 59085 ★   Walgreen
4150 N. Atlantic Ave.
Cocoa Beach, FL 32931
(407)799-9110
Ultimate Parent: Walgreen Co. **SIC:** 5912—Drug Stores & Proprietary Stores.

Coconut Creek

★ 59086 ★   American Savings of Florida, FSB
4901 Coconut Creek Pky.
Coconut Creek, FL 33063-3998
(305)975-8936
Location Type: Branch office. **Officer:** Sherry Rienas, Manager. **Ultimate Parent:** American Savings of Florida. **SIC:** 6035—Federal Savings Institutions; 6211—Security Brokers & Dealers.

★ 59087 ★   Barnett Bank of Broward County, NA
4829-31 Coconut Creek Pky.
Coconut Creek, FL 33063
(305)975-0711
Company Type: Subsidiary. **Location Type:** Branch office. **Officer:** Georgia Lee, Manager. **Ultimate Parent:** Barnett Banks. **SIC:** 6021—National Commercial Banks.

★ 59088 ★   California Federal Bank, AFSB
4803 Coconut Creek Pky.
Coconut Creek, FL 33063-3903
(305)979-6804
Location Type: Branch office. **Ultimate Parent:** California Federal Bank. **SIC:** 6021—National Commercial Banks.

★ 59089 ★   Citibank, NA
4807 Coconut Creek Pky.
Coconut Creek, FL 33063-3903
(305)975-7233
Location Type: Branch office. **Ultimate Parent:** Citicorp. **SIC:** 6021—National Commercial Banks.

Cooper City

★ 59090 ★   Barnett Bank of Broward County, NA
5504 S. Flamingo Rd.
Cooper City, FL 33330-2728
(305)434-4441
Company Type: Subsidiary. **Location Type:** Branch office. **Officer:** Marty Masters, Manager. **Ultimate Parent:** Barnett Banks. **SIC:** 6021—National Commercial Banks.

★ 59091 ★   First Union National Bank of Florida
2603 N. Hiatus Rd.
Cooper City, FL 33026
(305)985-3664
Location Type: Branch office. **Ultimate Parent:** First Union Corp. **SIC:** 6021—National Commercial Banks.

Coral Gables

★ 59092 ★   American Savings of Florida, FSB
2401 Ponce de Leon Blvd.
Coral Gables, FL 33134-6016
(305)448-6030
Location Type: Branch office. **Officer:** William Bell, Manager. **Ultimate Parent:** American Savings of Florida. **SIC:** 6035—Federal Savings Institutions; 6211—Security Brokers & Dealers.

★ 59093 ★   Barnett Bank of South Florida, NA
1500 S. Dixie Hwy.
Coral Gables, FL 33146-3033
(305)663-5100
Company Type: Subsidiary. **Location Type:** Branch office. **Officer:** Arden Habay, Manager. **Ultimate Parent:** Barnett Banks. **SIC:** 6021—National Commercial Banks.

★ 59094 ★   Barnett Bank of South Florida, NA
550 Biltmore Way
Coral Gables, FL 33134-5730
(305)663-5100
Company Type: Subsidiary. **Location Type:** Branch office. **Officer:** Mayling Exposito, Manager. **Ultimate Parent:** Barnett Banks. **SIC:** 6021—National Commercial Banks.

★ 59095 ★   Barnett Bank of South Florida, NA
2600 Douglas Rd.
Coral Gables, FL 33177
(305)663-5100
Company Type: Subsidiary. **Location Type:** Branch office. **Officer:** Frank Lopez, Manager. **Ultimate Parent:** Barnett Banks. **SIC:** 6021—National Commercial Banks.

★ 59096 ★   California Federal Bank, AFSB
221 Aragon Ave.
Coral Gables, FL 33134-5056
(305)445-9700
Location Type: Branch office. **Ultimate Parent:** California Federal Bank. **SIC:** 6021—National Commercial Banks.

★ 59097 ★   Chase Manhatten Bank of Florida, NA
5 Alhambra
Coral Gables, FL 33134
(305)443-2217
Location Type: Branch office. **Officer:** Alice Brightbill, Manager. **Ultimate Parent:** Chase Manhattan Corp.

★ 59098 ★   Citibank (Florida), NA
1190 S. Dixie Hwy.
Coral Gables, FL 33146-2960
(305)662-9625
Location Type: Branch office. **Officer:** Steve Evans, Manager. **Ultimate Parent:** Citicorp. **SIC:** 6021—National Commercial Banks.

★ 59099 ★   Citibank, FSB
396 Alhambra
Coral Gables, FL 33134-7703
(305)460-8695
Location Type: Branch office. **Ultimate Parent:** Citicorp.

★ 59100 ★   First Union National Bank of Florida
2100 Ponce De Leon Blvd.
Coral Gables, FL 33134-5200
(305)447-6200
Location Type: Branch office. **Ultimate Parent:** First Union Corp. **SIC:** 6021—National Commercial Banks.

★ 59101 ★   First Union National Bank of Florida
169 Miracle Mile
Coral Gables, FL 33134-5412
(305)460-6000
Location Type: Branch office. **Ultimate Parent:** First Union Corp. **SIC:** 6021—National Commercial Banks.

★ 59102 ★   New York Life Miami General Office
Southeastern Agencies
2333 Ponce De Leon Blvd., Ste. 700
Coral Gables, FL 33134
(305)441-2225 **Fax:** (305)441-1755
Officer: Olga F. Jondahl, General Manager. **Ultimate Parent:** New York Life.

★ 59103 ★   Phelps Dodge International Corp.
2121 Ponce de Leon Blvd.
Coral Gables, FL 33134
(305)447-4306 **Fax:** (305)447-4337
Officer: Manuel J. Iraola, President. **Ultimate Parent:** Phelps Dodge.

★ 59104 ★   Savings of America, A Division of Home Savings of America, FSB
301 Miracle Mile
Coral Gables, FL 33134-5863
(305)448-3502
Company Type: Division. **Location Type:** Branch office. **Ultimate Parent:** H. F. Ahmanson. **SIC:** 6021—National Commercial Banks.

★ 59105 ★   **Xerox Corp.**
800 S. Douglas Rd.
Coral Gables, FL 33134
(305)447-6000
Officer: Marlene Williams, Manager.
Ultimate Parent: Xerox Corp. **SIC:** 3663—Radio & T.V. Communications Equipment.

Coral Springs

★ 59106 ★   **American Savings of Florida, FSB**
10385 Royal Palm Blvd.
Coral Springs, FL 33065-4817
(305)341-0900
Location Type: Branch office. **Officer:** Carol Deluca, Manager. **Ultimate Parent:** American Savings of Florida. **SIC:** 6035—Federal Savings Institutions; 6211—Security Brokers & Dealers.

★ 59107 ★   **Barnett Bank of Broward County, NA**
10425 W. Sample Rd.
Coral Springs, FL 33065-3924
(305)753-9300
Company Type: Subsidiary. **Location Type:** Branch office. **Officer:** Treena Crumpler, Manager. **Ultimate Parent:** Barnett Banks. **SIC:** 6021—National Commercial Banks.

★ 59108 ★   **Barnett Bank of Broward County, NA**
8357 W. Atlantic Blvd.
Coral Springs, FL 33065
(305)753-4104
Company Type: Subsidiary. **Location Type:** Branch office. **Officer:** Steven Brown, Manager. **Ultimate Parent:** Barnett Banks. **SIC:** 6021—National Commercial Banks.

★ 59109 ★   **Barnett Bank of Broward County, NA**
3001 N. University Dr.
Coral Springs, FL 33065-5080
(305)979-6098
Company Type: Subsidiary. **Location Type:** Branch office. **Officer:** Mary Purdy, Manager. **Ultimate Parent:** Barnett Banks. **SIC:** 6021—National Commercial Banks.

★ 59110 ★   **California Federal Bank, AFSB**
1260 University Dr.
Coral Springs, FL 33071
(305)753-8855
Location Type: Branch office. **Ultimate Parent:** California Federal Bank.

★ 59111 ★   **Citibank, FSB**
8264 Wiles Rd.
Coral Springs, FL 33067
(305)344-4922
Location Type: Branch office. **Ultimate Parent:** Citicorp. **SIC:** 6021—National Commercial Banks; 6035—Federal Savings Institutions.

★ 59112 ★   **Citibank, FSB**
1201 University Dr.
Coral Springs, FL 33071
(305)344-5100
Location Type: Branch office. **Ultimate Parent:** Citicorp. **SIC:** 6021—National Commercial Banks; 6035—Federal Savings Institutions.

★ 59113 ★   **First Union National Bank of Florida**
3300 University Dr.
Coral Springs, FL 33065-4126
(305)755-6005
Location Type: Branch office. **Ultimate Parent:** First Union Corp. **SIC:** 6021—National Commercial Banks.

★ 59114 ★   **First Union National Bank of Florida**
1950 University Dr.
Coral Springs, FL 33701-6064
(305)786-7236
Location Type: Branch office. **Ultimate Parent:** First Union Corp. **SIC:** 6021—National Commercial Banks.

★ 59115 ★   **Great Western Bank**
8901 W. Atlantic Blvd.
Coral Springs, FL 33071
(305)755-8992
Ultimate Parent: Great Western Financial Corp. **SIC:** 6099—Functions Related to Deposit Banking.

★ 59116 ★   **New Industrial Techniques, Inc.**
12325 W. Sample Rd.
Coral Springs, FL 33065
(305)752-5200 **Fax:** (305)752-4163
Company Type: Subsidiary. **Officer:** C. L. Shute, Vice President & General Manager.
Ultimate Parent: Handy & Harman. **SIC:** 3499—Fabricated Metal Products Nec.

★ 59117 ★   **Westinghouse Electric Corp.**
4300 Coral Ridge Dr.
Coral Springs, FL 33065
Ultimate Parent: Westinghouse Electric Corp. **SIC:** 3613—Switchgear & Switchboard Apparatus.

Corel Gables

★ 59118 ★   **Rohm & Haas Co. Latin America**
2600 SW 37th Ave.
Corel Gables, FL 33134
(305)447-3600
Ultimate Parent: Rohm & Haas. **SIC:** 2899—Chemical Preparations Nec.

Cottondale

★ 59119 ★   **Golden Peanut Co.**
3151 Main St.
Cottondale, FL 32431-4341
(904)352-4341
Ultimate Parent: Archer Daniels Midland Co. **SIC:** 5159—Farm-Product Raw Materials Nec.

Crescent City

★ 59120 ★   **Barnett Bank of the St. Johns**
1 N. Summit St.
Crescent City, FL 32112-2505
(904)698-1125
Company Type: Subsidiary. **Location Type:** Branch office. **Officer:** David Ott, Manager. **Ultimate Parent:** Barnett Banks. **SIC:** 6022—State Commercial Banks.

★ 59121 ★   **Barnett Bank of the St. Johns**
917 N. Summit St.
Crescent City, FL 32112-1724
(904)698-1096
Company Type: Subsidiary. **Location Type:** Branch office. **Ultimate Parent:** Barnett Banks. **SIC:** 6022—State Commercial Banks.

Crestview

★ 59122 ★   **American Family Life Assurance**
820 Ferdon Blvd.
Crestview, FL 32536
(904)682-0972
Ultimate Parent: American Family Life Assurance Co. **SIC:** 6411—Insurance Agents, Brokers & Service.

★ 59123 ★   **First National Bank & Trust**
885 S. Ferdon Blvd.
Crestview, FL 32536
(904)682-3351
Ultimate Parent: Society Corp. **SIC:** 6021—National Commercial Banks; 6022—State Commercial Banks.

★ 59124 ★   **Kentucky Fried Chicken**
511 Ferdon
Crestview, FL 32536
(904)682-2310
Ultimate Parent: Pepsico. **SIC:** 5812—Eating Places.

★ 59125 ★   **Russell Corp.**
5680 John Givens Rd.
Crestview, FL 32536
(904)682-1286
Ultimate Parent: Russell. **SIC:** 2253—Knit Outerwear Mills; 2329—Men's/Boys' Clothing Nec.

★ 59126 ★   **Ryder Truck Rental**
422 E. Pnes Ave.
Crestview, FL 32536
(904)682-9460
Ultimate Parent: Ryder System. **SIC:** 1521—Single-Family Housing Construction.

★ 59127 ★   **Ryder Truck Rental**
302 E. Us 90
Crestview, FL 32536
(904)682-6681
Ultimate Parent: Ryder System. **SIC:** 7513—Truck Rental & Leasing Without Drivers.

Cross City

★ 59128 ★   **Georgia Pacific Corp.**
US Hwy. 19 S
Cross City, FL 32628
(904)498-3355
Officer: George Bowen, Manager. **Ultimate Parent:** Georgia-Pacific. **SIC:** 2421—Sawmills & Planing Mills—General; 2491—Wood Preserving; 2611—Pulp Mills.

★ 59129 ★   **Piggly Wiggly**
Hwy. 19
Cross City, FL 32628
(904)498-3479
Ultimate Parent: Bruno's. **SIC:** 5411—Grocery Stores.

Crystal River

★ 59130 ★   **Barnett Bank of the Suncoast, NA**
1500 N. Meadowcrest Blvd.
Crystal River, FL 34429-8735
(904)795-8100
Company Type: Subsidiary. **Location Type:** Branch office. **Officer:** Kathy Frank, Regulation Manager. **Ultimate Parent:** Barnett Banks. **SIC:** 6021—National Commercial Banks.

★ 59131 ★   **First Union National Bank of Florida**
821 SE US Hwy. 19
Crystal River, FL 34429-4811
(904)795-2301
Location Type: Branch office. **Ultimate Parent:** First Union Corp. **SIC:** 6021—National Commercial Banks.

★ 59132 ★   **Great Western Bank**
517 NE 5th St.
Crystal River, FL 32629
(904)795-6031
Ultimate Parent: Great Western Financial Corp. **SIC:** 6159—Miscellaneous Business Credit Institutions.

★ 59133 ★   **Greyhound Bus Lines Inc.**
200 NE Hwy. 19
Crystal River, FL 34429
(904)795-4445
Ultimate Parent: Greyhound Lines Inc. **SIC:** 4111—Local & Suburban Transit.

★ 59134 ★   **Mary Kay Cosmetics**
Southeast Ct. 1st
Crystal River, FL 34429
(904)795-5576
Ultimate Parent: Mary Kay Cosmetics. **SIC:** 5999—Miscellaneous Retail Stores Nec.

★ 59135 ★   **Walgreen Drugs**
1631 S. Suncoast Blvd.
Crystal River, FL 34429
(904)563-1003
Ultimate Parent: Walgreen Co. **SIC:** 5912—Drug Stores & Proprietary Stores.

Crytal River

★ 59136 ★   **AmSouth Bank of Florida**
7647 W. Gulf to Lake Hwy.
Crytal River, FL 34429
(904)795-2000
Location Type: Branch office. **Ultimate Parent:** AmSouth Bancorp. **SIC:** 6022—State Commercial Banks.

Dade City

★ 59137 ★   **Barnett Bank of Pasco County**
1880 US Hwy. 301 S
Dade City, FL 33525-6015
(813)783-0850
Company Type: Subsidiary. **Location Type:** Branch office. **Officer:** Curt Leuschner, Manager. **Ultimate Parent:** Barnett Banks. **SIC:** 6022—State Commercial Banks.

★ 59138 ★   **First Union National Bank of Florida**
401 E. Meridian Ave.
Dade City, FL 33525-3823
(904)521-6220
Location Type: Branch office. **Ultimate Parent:** First Union Corp. **SIC:** 6021—National Commercial Banks.

★ 59139 ★   **Greyhound Bus Lines**
511 E. Pineapple Ave.
Dade City, FL 33525
(904)567-5368
Ultimate Parent: Greyhound Lines Inc. **SIC:** 4111—Local & Suburban Transit.

★ 59140 ★   **Humana Medical Plan**
103 E. Meridian Ave.
Dade City, FL 33525
(904)567-1129
Ultimate Parent: Humana. **SIC:** 8011—Offices & Clinics of Medical Doctors.

★ 59141 ★   **Kentucky Fried Chicken**
504 Willingham Ave.
Dade City, FL 33525
(904)567-5580
Ultimate Parent: Pepsico. **SIC:** 5812—Eating Places.

★ 59142 ★   **Pizza Hut**
810 Us 98 N
Dade City, FL 33525
(904)567-7791
Ultimate Parent: Pepsico. **SIC:** 5812—Eating Places.

★ 59143 ★   **Texaco Inc.**
1504 S. Us Hwy. 301
Dade City, FL 33525
(904)567-6103
Ultimate Parent: Texaco. **SIC:** 5172—Petroleum Products Nec.

★ 59144 ★   **Wal Mart Discount City**
1804 S. Us Hwy. 301
Dade City, FL 33525
(904)567-1551
Ultimate Parent: Wal-Mart Stores, Inc. **SIC:** 5331—Variety Stores.

Dania

★ 59145 ★   **Barnett Bank of Broward County, NA**
1991 Stirling Rd.
Dania, FL 33004-2101
(305)922-7501
Company Type: Subsidiary. **Location Type:** Branch office. **Officer:** David Rosendahl, Manager. **Ultimate Parent:** Barnett Banks. **SIC:** 6021—National Commercial Banks.

★ 59146 ★   **Citibank, NA**
255 E. Dania Beach Blvd.
Dania, FL 33004-3098
(305)599-5555 **Fax:** (305)599-5618 **Telex:** 51-4311
Location Type: Branch office. **Ultimate Parent:** Citicorp. **SIC:** 6021—National Commercial Banks.

★ 59147 ★   **Coast to Coast Communications Inc.**
419 S. Federal Hwy.
Dania, FL 33004
(305)371-2690
Ultimate Parent: Servistar Corp.

★ 59148 ★   **Kentucky Fried Chicken**
506 S. Federal Hwy.
Dania, FL 33004
(305)921-4750
Ultimate Parent: Pepsico. **SIC:** 5812—Eating Places.

★ 59149 ★   **Pizza Hut**
1300 S. Federal Hwy.
Dania, FL 33004
(305)920-2377
Ultimate Parent: Pepsico. **SIC:** 5812—Eating Places.

Datona Beach Shores

★ 59150 ★ **Barnett Bank of Volusia County**
12 N. Hwy. 17-92
Datona Beach Shores, FL 32713
(407)668-4438
Location Type: Branch office. **Ultimate Parent:** Barnett Banks. **SIC:** 6022—State Commercial Banks.

Davenport

★ 59151 ★ **McDonald's Restaurant**
5825 Us 27 N
Davenport, FL 33837
(813)424-2269
Ultimate Parent: McDonald's.
SIC: 5812—Eating Places.

★ 59152 ★ **Walt Disney World**
1706 County Rd. 547 W
Davenport, FL 33837
(813)560-7881
Ultimate Parent: Walt Disney Co.

Davie

★ 59153 ★ **American Savings of Florida, FSB**
8890 State Rd. 84
Davie, FL 33324-4409
(305)474-3900
Location Type: Branch office. **Officer:** Ledger Kellrer, Manager. **Ultimate Parent:** American Savings of Florida. **SIC:** 6035—Federal Savings Institutions; 6211—Security Brokers & Dealers.

★ 59154 ★ **Barnett Bank of Broward County, NA**
6300 Stirling Rd.
Davie, FL 33024
(305)474-3900
Company Type: Subsidiary. **Location Type:** Branch office. **Officer:** John Naclerio, Manager. **Ultimate Parent:** Barnett Banks. **SIC:** 6021—National Commercial Banks.

★ 59155 ★ **Citibank, FSB**
184549 S. University Dr.
Davie, FL 33324
(305)475-9007
Location Type: Branch office. **Ultimate Parent:** Citicorp. **SIC:** 6021—National Commercial Banks.

★ 59156 ★ **Citibank, NA**
6497 Stirling Rd.
Davie, FL 33314-7126
(305)791-2804
Location Type: Branch office. **Ultimate Parent:** Citicorp. **SIC:** 6021—National Commercial Banks.

★ 59157 ★ **First Union National Bank of Florida**
4150 SW 64th Ave.
Davie, FL 33314-3490
(305)467-5571
Location Type: Branch office. **Ultimate Parent:** First Union Corp. **SIC:** 6021—National Commercial Banks.

★ 59158 ★ **First Union National Bank of Florida**
3575 S. University Dr.
Davie, FL 33328
(305)468-2811
Location Type: Branch office. **Ultimate Parent:** First Union Corp. **SIC:** 6021—National Commercial Banks.

★ 59159 ★ **Reddy Ice**
5050 SW 51st St.
Davie, FL 33314
Ultimate Parent: Southland Corp. **SIC:** 2097—Manufactured Ice.

★ 59160 ★ **Tesco Hi-Lift Inc.**
3400 SW 46th Ave.
Davie, FL 33314
(305)791-9470
Officer: Charles Traficant II, President. **Ultimate Parent:** Dover Corp. **SIC:** 3356—Nonferrous Rolling & Drawing Nec; 3713—Truck & Bus Bodies; 3714—Motor Vehicle Parts & Accessories.

Daytona Beach

★ 59161 ★ **ABF Freight System Inc.**
460 Walker St.
Daytona Beach, FL 32117-2688
(904)2572005
Ultimate Parent: Arkansas Best. **SIC:** 4212—Local Trucking Without Storage.

★ 59162 ★ **Albertson's Food Center**
814 Nova Rd.
Daytona Beach, FL 32117
(904)238-1390
Ultimate Parent: Albertson's Inc. **SIC:** 5411—Grocery Stores.

★ 59163 ★ **Albertson's Food Centers**
3803 S. Nova Rd.
Daytona Beach, FL 32119
(904)788-4845
Ultimate Parent: Albertson's Inc. **SIC:** 5411—Grocery Stores.

★ 59164 ★ **Barnett Bank of Volusia County**
1025 International Speedway Dr.
Daytona Beach, FL 32114-3416
(904)257-3626
Company Type: Subsidiary. **Location Type:** Branch office. **Officer:** Shirley Killough, Senior Vice President. **Ultimate Parent:** Barnett Banks. **SIC:** 6022—State Commercial Banks.

★ 59165 ★ **Barnett Bank of Volusia County**
1550 S. Clyde Morris Blvd.
Daytona Beach, FL 32114-5127
(904)258-3650
Company Type: Subsidiary. **Location Type:** Branch office. **Officer:** Michael Lacey, Vice President. **Ultimate Parent:** Barnett Banks. **SIC:** 6022—State Commercial Banks.

★ 59166 ★ **Barnett Bank of Volusia County**
200 S. Palmetto Ave.
Daytona Beach, FL 32114-4314
(904)258-3700
Location Type: Branch office. **Ultimate Parent:** Barnett Banks. **SIC:** 6021—National Commercial Banks.

★ 59167 ★ **Barnett Bank of Volusia County**
2315 Beville Rd.
Daytona Beach, FL 32119-8723
(904)258-3600
Location Type: Branch office. **Ultimate Parent:** Barnett Banks.

★ 59168 ★ **Casual Corner**
554 Volusia Mall
Daytona Beach, FL 32114
(904)255-6583
Ultimate Parent: United States Shoe. **SIC:** 5651—Family Clothing Stores.

★ 59169 ★ **Circus World**
208 Volusia Mall
Daytona Beach, FL 32114
(904)258-0436
Ultimate Parent: Melville. **SIC:** 5945—Hobby, Toy & Game Shops.

★ 59170 ★ **Delta Air Freight**
614 Midway Ave.
Daytona Beach, FL 32114
(904)252-3331
Ultimate Parent: Delta Air Lines, Inc. **SIC:** 4513—Air Courier Services.

★ 59171 ★ **Delta Air Lines**
220 S. Ridgewood Ave. 130
Daytona Beach, FL 32114
(904)252-1197
Ultimate Parent: Delta Air Lines, Inc. **SIC:** 4512—Air Transportation—Scheduled.

★ 59172 ★ **Delta Air Lines**
760 Terminal Dr.
Daytona Beach, FL 32114
(904)252-5115
Ultimate Parent: Delta Air Lines, Inc. **SIC:** 4512—Air Transportation—Scheduled.

★ 59173 ★ **Digital Equipment Corp.**
1901 Mason Ave.
Daytona Beach, FL 32117
(904)257-1182
Ultimate Parent: Digital Equipment Corp. **SIC:** 7374—Data Processing & Preparation.

★ 59174 ★ **First Union National Bank of Florida**
828 White St.
Daytona Beach, FL 32117-4607
(904)254-7220
Location Type: Branch office. **Ultimate Parent:** First Union Corp. **SIC:** 6021—National Commercial Banks.

★ 59175 ★ **First Union National Bank of Florida**
1302 International Speedway Blvd.
Daytona Beach, FL 32114
(904)254-1803
Location Type: Branch office. **Ultimate Parent:** First Union Corp. **SIC:** 6021—National Commercial Banks.

★ 59176 ★ **First Union National Bank of Florida**
130 N. Ridgewood Ave.
Daytona Beach, FL 32114
(904)254-1780
Location Type: Branch office. **Ultimate Parent:** First Union Corp. **SIC:** 6021—National Commercial Banks.

★ 59177 ★ **First Union National Bank of Florida**
1300 Beville Rd.
Daytona Beach, FL 32114-5747
(904)254-7232
Location Type: Branch office. **Ultimate Parent:** First Union Corp. **SIC:** 6021—National Commercial Banks.

★ 59178 ★ **First Union National Bank of Florida**
2310 S. Ridgewood Ave.
Daytona Beach, FL 32119
(904)254-1820
Location Type: Branch office. **Ultimate Parent:** First Union Corp. **SIC:** 6021—National Commercial Banks.

★ 59179 ★ **Food Lion**
1603 Nova Rd.
Daytona Beach, FL 32117
(904)253-4764
Ultimate Parent: Food Lion. **SIC:** 5411—Grocery Stores.

★ 59180 ★ **Foot Action**
380 Volusia Mall
Daytona Beach, FL 32114
(904)257-6468
Ultimate Parent: Melville. **SIC:** 5661—Shoe Stores.

★ 59181 ★ **The Gap**
120 Volusia Mall
Daytona Beach, FL 32114
(904)258-1070
Ultimate Parent: GAP. **SIC:** 5651—Family Clothing Stores.

★ 59182 ★ **General Electric Simulation & Control Systems**
1800 Volusia Ave.
Daytona Beach, FL 32114
Ultimate Parent: General Electric. **SIC:** 3600—Electronic & Other Electrical Equipment.

★ 59183 ★ **Great Western Bank**
1128 Beville Rd.
Daytona Beach, FL 32114
(904)636-1731
Ultimate Parent: Great Western Financial Corp. **SIC:** 6062—State Credit Unions.

★ 59184 ★ **Hertz Rent-A-Car**
918 S. Atlantic Ave.
Daytona Beach, FL 32118
(904)253-4177
Ultimate Parent: Hertz. **SIC:** 7514—Passenger Car Rental.

★ 59185 ★ **Hertz Rent-A-Car**
620 Midway Ave.
Daytona Beach, FL 32114
(904)255-3681
Ultimate Parent: Hertz. **SIC:** 7514—Passenger Car Rental.

★ 59186 ★ **Jiffy Lube**
201 N. Nova Rd.
Daytona Beach, FL 32114
(904)257-5733
Ultimate Parent: Pennzoil. **SIC:** 7539—Automotive Repair Shops Nec.

★ 59187 ★ **Kentucky Fried Chicken**
2433 N. Atlantic Ave.
Daytona Beach, FL 32118
(904)672-6616
Ultimate Parent: Pepsico. **SIC:** 5812—Eating Places.

★ 59188 ★ **Kentucky Fried Chicken**
2424 S. Ridgewood Ave.
Daytona Beach, FL 32119
(904)761-2132
Ultimate Parent: Pepsico. **SIC:** 5812—Eating Places.

★ 59189 ★ **Kentucky Fried Chicken**
1035 Dunlawton Ave.
Daytona Beach, FL 32127
(904)760-1835
Ultimate Parent: Pepsico. **SIC:** 5812—Eating Places.

★ 59190 ★ **Lane Bryant**
124 Volusia Mall
Daytona Beach, FL 32114
(904)258-0479
Ultimate Parent: Limited. **SIC:** 5651—Family Clothing Stores.

★ 59191 ★ **The Limited**
116 Volusia Mall
Daytona Beach, FL 32114
(904)255-5763
Ultimate Parent: Limited. **SIC:** 5651—Family Clothing Stores.

★ 59192 ★ **Marshalls**
1808 Volusia Ave.
Daytona Beach, FL 32114
(904)258-8855
Ultimate Parent: Melville. **SIC:** 5311—Department Stores.

★ 59193 ★ **Mobil Service Center**
1501 Ridgewood Ave.
Daytona Beach, FL 32117
(904)677-8080
Ultimate Parent: Mobil. **SIC:** 5541—Gasoline Service Stations.

★ 59194 ★ **Mobil Service Station**
790 N. Nova Rd.
Daytona Beach, FL 32114
(904)257-6911
Ultimate Parent: Mobil. **SIC:** 5541—Gasoline Service Stations.

★ 59195 ★ **Otis Elevator Co.**
2090 S. Nova Rd.
Daytona Beach, FL 32119
(904)761-8062
Ultimate Parent: United Technologies. **SIC:** 1796—Installing Building Equipment Nec.

★ 59196 ★ **Pepsi-Cola Co.**
860 Bellevue Ave.
Daytona Beach, FL 32114
(904)252-2507
Ultimate Parent: Pepsico. **SIC:** 2086—Bottled & Canned Soft Drinks.

★ 59197 ★ **Pizza Hut**
3790 S. Nova Rd.
Daytona Beach, FL 32119
(904)756-3490
Ultimate Parent: Pepsico. **SIC:** 5812—Eating Places.

★ 59198 ★ **Pizza Hut**
1844 S. Ridgewood Ave.
Daytona Beach, FL 32119
(904)767-4481
Ultimate Parent: Pepsico. **SIC:** 5812—Eating Places.

★ 59199 ★ **Pizza Hut**
831 Ridgewood Ave.
Daytona Beach, FL 32117
(904)252-0077
Ultimate Parent: Pepsico. **SIC:** 5812—Eating Places.

★ 59200 ★ **Pizza Hut**
500 S. Atlantic Ave.
Daytona Beach, FL 32118
(904)255-7234
Ultimate Parent: Pepsico. **SIC:** 5812—
Eating Places.

★ 59201 ★ **Pizza Hut**
102 Dunlawton Blvd.
Daytona Beach, FL 32127
(904)788-3554
Ultimate Parent: Pepsico. **SIC:** 5812—
Eating Places.

★ 59202 ★ **Pizza Hut**
2310 Volusia Ave.
Daytona Beach, FL 32114
(904)252-2020
Ultimate Parent: Pepsico. **SIC:** 5812—
Eating Places.

★ 59203 ★ **Publix Super Market**
2455 Bellair Plz.
Daytona Beach, FL 32118
(904)677-5150
Ultimate Parent: Publix Super Markets.
SIC: 5411—Grocery Stores.

★ 59204 ★ **Publix Super Market**
2014 S. Ridgewood Ave.
Daytona Beach, FL 32119
(904)767-1721
Ultimate Parent: Publix Super Markets.
SIC: 5411—Grocery Stores.

★ 59205 ★ **Publix Super Market**
3821 S. Nova Rd.
Daytona Beach, FL 32127
(904)788-2220
Ultimate Parent: Publix Super Markets.
SIC: 5411—Grocery Stores; 5461—Retail
Bakeries.

★ 59206 ★ **Radio Shack**
532 Volusia Mall
Daytona Beach, FL 32114
(904)258-5552
Company Type: Division. **Ultimate Parent:**
Tandy Corp. **SIC:** 5065—Electronic Parts &
Equipment Nec.

★ 59207 ★ **Radio Shack**
2579 N. Atlantic Ave.
Daytona Beach, FL 32118
(904)672-3595
Company Type: Division. **Ultimate Parent:**
Tandy Corp. **SIC:** 5731—Radio, Television
& Electronics Stores.

★ 59208 ★ **Radio Shack**
2400 S. Ridgewood Ave.
Daytona Beach, FL 32119
(904)767-8373
Company Type: Division. **Ultimate Parent:**
Tandy Corp. **SIC:** 5731—Radio, Television
& Electronics Stores.

★ 59209 ★ **Ryder Truck Rental**
429 Beville Rd.
Daytona Beach, FL 32119
Ultimate Parent: Ryder System. **SIC:**
7359—Equipment Rental & Leasing Nec;
7513—Truck Rental & Leasing Without
Drivers.

★ 59210 ★ **Ryder Truck Rental**
1544 Ridgewood Ave.
Daytona Beach, FL 32117
(904)672-5507
Ultimate Parent: Ryder System. **SIC:**
7513—Truck Rental & Leasing Without
Drivers.

★ 59211 ★ **Ryder Truck Rental**
1630 S. Seagrave St.
Daytona Beach, FL 32119
(904)767-4821
Ultimate Parent: Ryder System. **SIC:**
7539—Automotive Repair Shops Nec.

★ 59212 ★ **Service Merchandise**
260 Jimmy Ann Dr.
Daytona Beach, FL 32114
(904)253-4433
Ultimate Parent: Service Merchandise Co.,
Inc. **SIC:** 5961—Catalog & Mail-Order
Houses.

★ 59213 ★ **Shell Food Mart**
1001 Dunlawton Ave.
Daytona Beach, FL 32127
(904)756-2931
Ultimate Parent: Shell Oil Co. **SIC:** 5541—
Gasoline Service Stations.

★ 59214 ★ **Simulation &
Automated Systems**
1800 Volusia Ave.
Daytona Beach, FL 32118
Officer: Peter L. Kujawski, General
Manager. **Ultimate Parent:** Martin Marietta.

★ 59215 ★ **Taco Bell**
2375 S. Ridgewood Ave.
Daytona Beach, FL 32119
(904)788-8990
Ultimate Parent: Pepsico. **SIC:** 5812—
Eating Places.

★ 59216 ★ **Taco Bell**
158 Ridgewood Ave.
Daytona Beach, FL 32117
(904)252-5834
Ultimate Parent: Pepsico. **SIC:** 5812—
Eating Places.

★ 59217 ★ **Texaco Gas Station &
Food M**
600 Volusia Ave.
Daytona Beach, FL 32114
(904)253-8466
Ultimate Parent: Texaco. **SIC:** 5541—
Gasoline Service Stations.

★ 59218 ★ **Texaco Mini Mart Ii**
740 N. Ridgewood Ave.
Daytona Beach, FL 32114
(904)253-9085
Ultimate Parent: Texaco. **SIC:** 5411—
Grocery Stores; 5999—Miscellaneous Retail
Stores Nec.

★ 59219 ★ **Thom Mcan Shoes**
1700 Volusia Ave.
Daytona Beach, FL 32114
(904)252-4637
Ultimate Parent: Melville. **SIC:** 5661—Shoe
Stores.

★ 59220 ★ **Thom Mcan Shoes**
2675 N. Atlantic Ave.
Daytona Beach, FL 32118
(904)677-9815
Ultimate Parent: Melville. **SIC:** 5661—Shoe
Stores.

★ 59221 ★ **Trailways Bus System**
910 Volusia Ave.
Daytona Beach, FL 32114
(904)253-0692
Ultimate Parent: Greyhound Lines Inc. **SIC:**
4142—Bus Charter Service Except Local.

★ 59222 ★ **United Media
Productions Inc.**
2700 S. Ridgewood Ave.
Daytona Beach, FL 32119
(904)761-2358
Ultimate Parent: E.W. Scripps Co. **SIC:**
7389—Business Services Nec.

★ 59223 ★ **United Parcel Service**
425 Fentress Blvd.
Daytona Beach, FL 32114
(904)432-8686
Ultimate Parent: United Parcel Service of
America. **SIC:** 4215—Courier Services
Except by Air; 5521—Used Car Dealers.

★ 59224 ★ **Wal Mart**
S Nova Rd.
Daytona Beach, FL 32127
(904)756-2711
Ultimate Parent: Wal-Mart Stores, Inc. **SIC:**
5399—Miscellaneous General Merchandise
Store.

★ 59225 ★ **Walgreen**
4015 S. Nova Rd.
Daytona Beach, FL 32127
(904)756-0030
Ultimate Parent: Walgreen Co. **SIC:**
5912—Drug Stores & Proprietary Stores.

★ 59226 ★ **Walgreen Co.**
2435 N. Atlantic Ave.
Daytona Beach, FL 32118
(904)672-2008
Ultimate Parent: Walgreen Co. **SIC:**
5999—Miscellaneous Retail Stores Nec.

★ 59227 ★ **Walgreen Drug Stores**
2580 S. Atlantic Ave.
Daytona Beach, FL 32118
(904)788-4511
Ultimate Parent: Walgreen Co. **SIC:**
5912—Drug Stores & Proprietary Stores.

★ 59228 ★ **Walgreen Drug Stores**
550 Volusia Mall
Daytona Beach, FL 32114
(904)252-4734
Ultimate Parent: Walgreen Co. **SIC:**
5912—Drug Stores & Proprietary Stores.

★ 59229 ★ **Walgreen Drug Stores**
1549 Nova Rd.
Daytona Beach, FL 32117
(904)252-2769
Ultimate Parent: Walgreen Co. **SIC:**
5912—Drug Stores & Proprietary Stores.

★ 59230 ★ **Walgreen Drug Stores**
2318 S. Ridgewood Ave.
Daytona Beach, FL 32119
(904)767-8442
Ultimate Parent: Walgreen Co. **SIC:**
5912—Drug Stores & Proprietary Stores.

★ 59231 ★ **Walgreen Drug Stores**
2435 N. Atlantic Ave.
Daytona Beach, FL 32118
(904)677-5200
Ultimate Parent: Walgreen Co. **SIC:**
5912—Drug Stores & Proprietary Stores.

★ 59232 ★ **Walgreen Drug Stores**
180 N. Beach St.
Daytona Beach, FL 32114
(904)252-8558
Ultimate Parent: Walgreen Co. **SIC:**
5912—Drug Stores & Proprietary Stores.

Daytona Beach Shores

★ 59233 ★ **Barnett Bank of
Volusia County**
3046 S. Atlantic Ave.
Daytona Beach Shores, FL 32118-6102
(904)258-3615
Company Type: Subsidiary. **Location
Type:** Branch office. **Officer:** Charlyse
Roberts, Vice President. **Ultimate Parent:**
Barnett Banks. **SIC:** 6022—State
Commercial Banks.

★ 59234 ★ **Barnett Banks of
Volusia County**
3046 S. Atlantic Ave.
Daytona Beach Shores, FL 32118-6102
(904)258-3615
Location Type: Branch office. **Ultimate
Parent:** Barnett Banks. **SIC:** 6022—State
Commercial Banks.

Daytonna Beach

★ 59235 ★ **First Union National
Bank of Florida**
444 Seabreeze Blvd.
Daytonna Beach, FL 32118-3995
(904)254-7240
Location Type: Branch office. **Ultimate
Parent:** First Union Corp. **SIC:** 6021—
National Commercial Banks.

De Bary

★ 59236 ★ **Barnett Bank of
Volusia County**
23 N. 17-92 S.
De Bary, FL 32713
(407)668-4438
Company Type: Subsidiary. **Location
Type:** Branch office. **Officer:** Lorraine
Morris, Assistant Vice President & Retail
Banking Manager. **Ultimate Parent:** Barnett
Banks. **SIC:** 6022—State Commercial
Banks.

★ 59237 ★ **Radio Shack**
840 Deltona Blvd.
De Bary, FL 32713
(407)574-6498
Company Type: Division. **Ultimate Parent:**
Tandy Corp. **SIC:** 5731—Radio, Television
& Electronics Stores.

De Funiak Spg

★ 59238 ★ **Champion
International Corp.**
1111 N. 9th St.
De Funiak Spg, FL 32433
(904)892-2948
Ultimate Parent: Champion International.
SIC: 5099—Durable Goods Nec.

★ 59239 ★ **Ryder Truck Rental**
W Hwy. 90
De Funiak Spg, FL 32433
(904)892-4666
Ultimate Parent: Ryder System. **SIC:**
7359—Equipment Rental & Leasing Nec.

De Funiak Spring

★ 59240 ★ **Piggly Wiggly**
10th
De Funiak Spring, FL 32433
(904)892-7711
Ultimate Parent: Bruno's. **SIC:** 5411—
Grocery Stores.

De Funiak Springs

★ 59241 ★ **Barnett Bank of
Northwest Florida**
401 W. Nelson Ave.
De Funiak Springs, FL 32433-1534
(904)892-3231
Company Type: Subsidiary. **Location
Type:** Branch office. **Officer:** Rachel
Thomas, Vice President. **Ultimate Parent:**
Barnett Banks. **SIC:** 6022—State
Commercial Banks.

★ 59242 ★ **Greyhound Bus Lines**
107 Freeport Rd.
De Funiak Springs, FL 32433
(904)892-2232
Ultimate Parent: Greyhound Lines Inc. **SIC:**
4142—Bus Charter Service Except Local.

★ 59243 ★ **Louisiana Pacific
Corp.**
Glendale Hwy.
De Funiak Springs, FL 32433
(904)892-3175
Ultimate Parent: Louisiana-Pacific. **SIC:**
2421—Sawmills & Planing Mills—General.

★ 59244 ★ **Pizza Hut**
RR 6
De Funiak Springs, FL 32433
(904)892-7226
Ultimate Parent: Pepsico. **SIC:** 5812—
Eating Places.

★ 59245 ★ **Shell Oil Co.**
RR 6
De Funiak Springs, FL 32433
(904)892-6197
Ultimate Parent: Shell Oil Co. **SIC:** 5541—
Gasoline Service Stations.

De Land

★ 59246 ★ **Ardmore Farms Inc.**
1915 N. Woodland Blvd.
De Land, FL 32720
Ultimate Parent: Quaker Oats. **SIC:**
2037—Frozen Fruits & Vegetables.

★ 59247 ★ **Barnett Bank of
Volusia County**
230 N. Woodland Blvd.
PO Box 2077
De Land, FL 32721-2077
(904)822-4800 **Fax:** (904)822-4938
Company Type: Subsidiary. **Location
Type:** Branch office. **Officer:** Lowell E.
Renfroe, Chairman, President & CEO.
Ultimate Parent: Barnett Banks. **SIC:**
6022—State Commercial Banks.

★ 59248 ★ **Barnett Bank of
Volusia County**
2599 S. Woodland Blvd.
De Land, FL 32720-8639
(904)734-5118
Company Type: Subsidiary. **Location
Type:** Branch office. **Officer:** Gail Kurth,
Assistant Vice President. **Ultimate Parent:**
Barnett Banks. **SIC:** 6022—State
Commercial Banks.

★ 59249 ★ **Brunswick Corp.**
Defense Div.
2000 Brunswick Ln.
De Land, FL 32724
Company Type: Division. **Ultimate Parent:**
Brunswick Corp. **SIC:** 3483—Ammunition
Except for Small Arms.

★ 59250 ★   Brunswick Corp.
Technetics Division
2000 Brunswick Ln.
De Land, FL 32724
Ultimate Parent: Brunswick Corp. **SIC:**
3496—Miscellaneous Fabricated Wire
Products.

★ 59251 ★   Kentucky Fried
Chicken
844 E. New York Ave.
De Land, FL 32724
(904)734-3216
Ultimate Parent: Pepsico. **SIC:** 5812—
Eating Places.

★ 59252 ★   Kentucky Fried
Chicken
1408 N. Woodland Blvd.
De Land, FL 32720
(904)734-3216
Ultimate Parent: Pepsico. **SIC:** 5812—
Eating Places.

★ 59253 ★   Mutual of New York
St Johns Rd.
De Land, FL 32720
(904)734-5211
Ultimate Parent: Mutual of New York. **SIC:**
6311—Life Insurance.

★ 59254 ★   Pizza Hut
2199 S. Woodland Blvd.
De Land, FL 32720
(904)736-7666
Ultimate Parent: Pepsico. **SIC:** 5812—
Eating Places.

★ 59255 ★   Pizza Hut
1403 N. Woodland Blvd.
De Land, FL 32720
(904)734-0516
Ultimate Parent: Pepsico. **SIC:** 5812—
Eating Places.

★ 59256 ★   Radio Shack
Goodies Plz.
De Land, FL 32720
(904)736-7662
Company Type: Division. **Ultimate Parent:**
Tandy Corp. **SIC:** 5719—Miscellaneous
Home Furnishings Stores; 5731—Radio,
Television & Electronics Stores.

★ 59257 ★   Rite Aid
1738 S. Woodland Blvd.
De Land, FL 32720
(904)738-2681
Ultimate Parent: Rite Aid. **SIC:** 5912—Drug
Stores & Proprietary Stores.

★ 59258 ★   Rite Aid Pharmacy
1384 S. Woodland Blvd.
De Land, FL 32720
(904)738-9820
Ultimate Parent: Rite Aid. **SIC:** 5912—Drug
Stores & Proprietary Stores.

★ 59259 ★   Sherwood Medical
Co.
2010 International Speedway Blvd.
De Land, FL 32724-8707
Ultimate Parent: American Home Products.
SIC: 3841—Surgical & Medical Instruments.

★ 59260 ★   Technetics Corp.
Technetics Div.
1600 Industrial Dr.
De Land, FL 32724
Company Type: Division. **Ultimate Parent:**
Brunswick Corp. **SIC:** 3496—Miscellaneous
Fabricated Wire Products.

★ 59261 ★   United Van Lines Inc.
1600 Lexington Ave.
De Land, FL 32724
(904)734-1232
Ultimate Parent: Unigroup. **SIC:** 7389—
Business Services Nec.

★ 59262 ★   Walgreen Drug Stores
1560 N. Woodland Blvd.
De Land, FL 32720
(904)734-4251
Ultimate Parent: Walgreen Co. **SIC:**
5912—Drug Stores & Proprietary Stores.

Deerfield

★ 59263 ★   Eckerd Corp.
Eckerd Drug Co.
824 S. Military Trial
Deerfield, FL 33442
(305)428-2830
Company Type: Headquarters. **Officer:**
Thomas Kaplin, Vice President. **Ultimate
Parent:** Eckerd Corp. **SIC:** 5912—Drug
Stores & Proprietary Stores.

Deerfield Beach

★ 59264 ★   American Savings of
FL FSB
1950 W. Hillsboro Blvd.
Deerfield Beach, FL 33442-1488
(305)428-2350
Location Type: Branch office. **Ultimate
Parent:** American Savings of Florida. **SIC:**
6035—Federal Savings Institutions; 6021—
National Commercial Banks; 6162—
Mortgage Bankers & Correspondents.

★ 59265 ★   American Savings of
Florida, FSB
1950 W. Hillsboro Blvd.
Deerfield Beach, FL 33442-1488
(305)428-2350
Location Type: Branch office. **Officer:**
Barbara Bloom, Manager. **Ultimate Parent:**
American Savings of Florida. **SIC:** 6035—
Federal Savings Institutions; 6211—Security
Brokers & Dealers.

★ 59266 ★   Anchor Savings Bank,
FSB
1327 S. Military Trl.
Deerfield Beach, FL 33442-7666
(305)426-6660
Location Type: Branch office. **Officer:** Tara
Prasad, Manager. **Ultimate Parent:** Anchor
Bancorp. **SIC:** 6021—National Commercial
Banks; 6035—Federal Savings Institutions;
6211—Security Brokers & Dealers; 6141—
Personal Credit Institutions; 6162—
Mortgage Bankers & Correspondents.

★ 59267 ★   Arrow/Kierulff
Electronics
400 Fairview Dr.
Deerfield Beach, FL 33441
(305)429-8200
Company Type: Division. **Location Type:**
Distribution center. **Officer:** Pete Germino,
General Manager. **Ultimate Parent:** Arrow
Electronics. **SIC:** 5065—Electronic Parts &
Equipment Nec.

★ 59268 ★   Barnett Bank of
Broward County, NA
1630 W. Hillsboro Blvd.
Deerfield Beach, FL 33441
(305)427-4522
Company Type: Subsidiary. **Location
Type:** Branch office. **Officer:** Joanne
Bowers, Manager. **Ultimate Parent:** Barnett
Banks. **SIC:** 6021—National Commercial
Banks.

★ 59269 ★   Barnett Bank of
Broward County, NA
77 N. Federal Hwy.
Deerfield Beach, FL 33441-3699
(305)428-4500
Company Type: Subsidiary. **Location
Type:** Branch office. **Officer:** Garrie
Fanning, Manager. **Ultimate Parent:**
Barnett Banks. **SIC:** 6021—National
Commercial Banks.

★ 59270 ★   Barnett Bank of
Broward County, NA
1886 W. Hillsboro Blvd.
Deerfield Beach, FL 33442-1492
(305)426-4200
Company Type: Subsidiary. **Location
Type:** Branch office. **Officer:** Jill Geraci,
Manager. **Ultimate Parent:** Barnett Banks.
SIC: 6021—National Commercial Banks.

★ 59271 ★   Barnett Bank of
Broward County, NA
3311 W. Hillsboro Blvd.
Deerfield Beach, FL 33441
(305)428-2400
Company Type: Subsidiary. **Location
Type:** Branch office. **Officer:** Carlen
Whitbourne, Manager. **Ultimate Parent:**
Barnett Banks. **SIC:** 6021—National
Commercial Banks.

★ 59272 ★   Bell Atlantic Tricon
Leasing
800 Fairway Dr.
Deerfield Beach, FL 33441-1828
(305)422-1900
Officer: Jeffrey Silverstein. **Ultimate
Parent:** Bell Atlantic Corp. **SIC:** 6159—
Miscellaneous Business Credit Institutions.

★ 59273 ★   California Federal
Bank, AFSB
1856 W. Hillsboro Blvd. Ste. A
Deerfield Beach, FL 33441
(305)426-5150
Location Type: Branch office. **Officer:**
Rhonda Bilsker, Manager. **Ultimate Parent:**
California Federal Bank. **SIC:** 6021—
National Commercial Banks.

★ 59274 ★   Citibank, FSB
3660 W. Hillsboro Blvd.
Deerfield Beach, FL 33442-9405
(305)427-4422
Location Type: Branch office. **Ultimate
Parent:** Citicorp. **SIC:** 6021—National
Commercial Banks.

★ 59275 ★   Citibank, NA
10 Fairway Dr.
Deerfield Beach, FL 33441-1801
(305)421-1015
Location Type: Branch office. **Ultimate
Parent:** Citicorp. **SIC:** 6021—National
Commercial Banks.

★ 59276 ★   Citizens Federal
Bank, AFSB
1862 W. Hillsboro Blvd.
Deerfield Beach, FL 33442-1469
(305)428-3022
Location Type: Branch office. **Officer:**
Brenda Greenberg, Manager. **Ultimate
Parent:** CSF Holdings.

★ 59277 ★   First Union National
Bank of Florida
3668 W. Hillsborn Blvd.
Deerfield Beach, FL 33442-1263
(305)426-6200
Location Type: Branch office. **Ultimate
Parent:** First Union Corp. **SIC:** 6021—
National Commercial Banks.

★ 59278 ★   First Union National
Bank of Florida
1007 S. Federal Hwy.
Deerfield Beach, FL 33441-7096
(305)426-6200
Location Type: Branch office. **Ultimate
Parent:** First Union Corp. **SIC:** 6021—
National Commercial Banks.

★ 59279 ★   Hit or Miss
1089 S. Federal Hwy.
Deerfield Beach, FL 33441
(305)421-9821
Ultimate Parent: TJX. **SIC:** 5621—
Women's Clothing Stores.

★ 59280 ★   Hit or Miss
3876 W. Hillsboro Blvd.
Deerfield Beach, FL 33442
(305)426-5231
Ultimate Parent: TJX. **SIC:** 5621—
Women's Clothing Stores.

★ 59281 ★   Kentucky Fried
Chicken
3349 W. Hillsboro Blvd.
Deerfield Beach, FL 33442
(305)481-2494
Ultimate Parent: Pepsico. **SIC:** 5812—
Eating Places.

★ 59282 ★   Kentucky Fried
Chicken
535 S. Federal Hwy.
Deerfield Beach, FL 33441
(305)427-9147
Ultimate Parent: Pepsico. **SIC:** 5812—
Eating Places.

★ 59283 ★   Linens 'n Things
3888 W. Hillsboro Blvd.
Deerfield Beach, FL 33442
(305)480-6622
Ultimate Parent: Melville. **SIC:** 5719—
Miscellaneous Home Furnishings Stores.

★ 59284 ★   Publix Deerfield
Beach Facility
777 SW 12th Ave.
Deerfield Beach, FL 33411
Ultimate Parent: Publix Super Markets.
SIC: 2024—Ice Cream & Frozen Desserts;

2026—Fluid Milk; 2086—Bottled & Canned
Soft Drinks.

★ 59285 ★   Radio Shack
3350 W. Hillsboro Blvd.
Deerfield Beach, FL 33442
(305)428-4442
Company Type: Division. **Ultimate Parent:**
Tandy Corp. **SIC:** 5065—Electronic Parts &
Equipment Nec.

★ 59286 ★   Radio Shack
730 S. Federal Hwy.
Deerfield Beach, FL 33441
(305)421-8923
Company Type: Division. **Ultimate Parent:**
Tandy Corp. **SIC:** 5065—Electronic Parts &
Equipment Nec.

★ 59287 ★   Ryder Truck Rental
S Federal Hwy.
Deerfield Beach, FL 33441
(305)429-9966
Ultimate Parent: Ryder System. **SIC:**
7389—Business Services Nec.

★ 59288 ★   Ryder Truck Rental
2 Ave.
Deerfield Beach, FL 33441
(305)426-4555
Ultimate Parent: Ryder System. **SIC:**
7513—Truck Rental & Leasing Without
Drivers.

★ 59289 ★   Savings of America, A
Division of Home Savings of
America
3325 W. Hillsboro Blvd.
Deerfield Beach, FL 33442-9477
(305)428-2300
Company Type: Division. **Location Type:**
Branch office. **Ultimate Parent:** H. F.
Ahmanson. **SIC:** 6021—National
Commercial Banks.

★ 59290 ★   Walgreen Drug Stores
1325 S. Military Trl.
Deerfield Beach, FL 33442
(305)421-4109
Ultimate Parent: Walgreen Co. **SIC:**
5912—Drug Stores & Proprietary Stores.

★ 59291 ★   Walgreen Drug Stores
289 S. Federal Hwy.
Deerfield Beach, FL 33441
(305)481-2991
Ultimate Parent: Walgreen Co. **SIC:**
7389—Business Services Nec.

★ 59292 ★   Walgreen Drug Stores
3768 W. Hillsboro Blvd.
Deerfield Beach, FL 33442
(305)360-7603
Ultimate Parent: Walgreen Co. **SIC:**
7389—Business Services Nec.

★ 59293 ★   Westinghouse
Electric Corp.
580 S. Military Trl.
Deerfield Beach, FL 33441
Ultimate Parent: Westinghouse Electric
Corp. **SIC:** 3613—Switchgear &
Switchboard Apparatus.

DeLand

★ 59294 ★   Barnett Bank of
Volusia County
PO Box 2077
DeLand, FL 32721-2077
Location Type: Branch office. **Ultimate
Parent:** Barnett Banks.

★ 59295 ★   Barnett Bank of
Volusia County
3101 N. Woodland Blvd.
DeLand, FL 32721-1108
(904)738-5782
Location Type: Branch office. **Ultimate
Parent:** Barnett Banks. **SIC:** 6022—State
Commercial Banks.

★ 59296 ★   Barnett Banks of
Volusia County
2599 S. Woodland Blvd.
DeLand, FL 32720-8639
(904)734-5118
Location Type: Branch office. **Ultimate
Parent:** Barnett Banks. **SIC:** 6022—State
Commercial Banks.

★ 59297 ★   Brunswick Corp.
2000 Brunswick Ln.
DeLand, FL 32724
(904)736-1700
Officer: Hank Lattanzi, Manager. Ultimate Parent: Brunswick Corp. SIC: 2211—Broadwoven Fabric Mills—Cotton; 2865—Cyclic Crudes & Intermediates; 3569—General Industrial Machinery Nec.

Deland

★ 59298 ★   Brunswick Corp.
Defense Div.
2000 Brunswick Ln.
Deland, FL 32724-2001
(904)736-1700
Location Type: Branch office. Officer: Hank Lattanzi. Ultimate Parent: Brunswick Corp. SIC: 3812—Search & Navigation Equipment.

DeLand

★ 59299 ★   Citizens Federal Bank, AFSB
901 N. Woodland Blvd.
DeLand, FL 32720-2790
(904)738-2666
Location Type: Branch office. Ultimate Parent: CSF Holdings. SIC: 6021—National Commercial Banks.

Deland

★ 59300 ★   Coast Federal Bank
2595 S. Woodland Blvd.
Deland, FL 32720
Ultimate Parent: Coast Savings Financial. SIC: 6159—Miscellaneous Business Credit Institutions.

DeLand

★ 59301 ★   First Union National Bank of Florida
1045 Williamsburg Rd.
DeLand, FL 32720-1449
(904)822-5450
Location Type: Branch office. Ultimate Parent: First Union Corp. SIC: 6021—National Commercial Banks.

★ 59302 ★   First Union National Bank of Florida
131 E. New York Ave.
DeLand, FL 32724-5565
(904)822-5400
Location Type: Branch office. Ultimate Parent: First Union Corp. SIC: 6021—National Commercial Banks.

Delray Beach

★ 59303 ★   Ace Hardware
50 SE 6th Ave.
Delray Beach, FL 33483
(407)278-1144
Ultimate Parent: Ace Hardware. SIC: 5084—Industrial Machinery & Equipment.

★ 59304 ★   American Savings of Florida
Kings Point Prof Bldg.
Delray Beach, FL 33446
(407)499-0120
Ultimate Parent: American Savings of Florida. SIC: 6099—Functions Related to Deposit Banking.

★ 59305 ★   American Savings of Florida
7385 W. Atlantic Ave.
Delray Beach, FL 33446
(407)496-5400
Ultimate Parent: American Savings of Florida. SIC: 6035—Federal Savings Institutions.

★ 59306 ★   American Savings of Florida, FSB
6646 W. Atlantic Ave.
Delray Beach, FL 33446-1616
(407)499-0120
Location Type: Branch office. Officer: Michelle Garelick, Manager. Ultimate Parent: American Savings of Florida. SIC: 6035—Federal Savings Institutions; 6211—Security Brokers & Dealers.

★ 59307 ★   American Savings of Florida, FSB
7385 W. Atlantic Ave.
Delray Beach, FL 33446-1303
(407)496-5400
Location Type: Branch office. Officer: Jean Whelan, Manager. Ultimate Parent: American Savings of Florida. SIC: 6035—Federal Savings Institutions; 5211—Lumber & Other Building Materials.

★ 59308 ★   Barnett Bank of Palm Beach County
7215 W. Atlantic Ave.
Delray Beach, FL 33446
(407)272-2734
Company Type: Subsidiary. Location Type: Branch office. Officer: Cindy Hollenberger, Manager. Ultimate Parent: Barnett Banks. SIC: 6022—State Commercial Banks.

★ 59309 ★   Barnett Bank of Palm Beach County
551 SE 8th St.
Delray Beach, FL 33483-5183
(407)243-1937
Company Type: Subsidiary. Location Type: Branch office. Officer: Raymond Lanzi, Manager. Ultimate Parent: Barnett Banks. SIC: 6022—State Commercial Banks.

★ 59310 ★   Barnett Bank of Palm Beach County
4650 W. Atlantic Ave.
Delray Beach, FL 33445-3889
(407)243-1958
Company Type: Subsidiary. Location Type: Branch office. Officer: John Morris, Manager. Ultimate Parent: Barnett Banks. SIC: 6022—State Commercial Banks.

★ 59311 ★   Barnett Bank of Palm Beach County
1001 E. Atlantic Ave.
Delray Beach, FL 33483-6909
(407)243-1928
Company Type: Subsidiary. Location Type: Branch office. Officer: Jeffrey Smith, Manager. Ultimate Parent: Barnett Banks. SIC: 6022—State Commercial Banks.

★ 59312 ★   Bi-Lo Grocery & Deli
926 W. Atlantic Ave.
Delray Beach, FL 33444
(407)243-9623
Ultimate Parent: Penn Traffic.

★ 59313 ★   California Federal Bank, AFSB
1002 E. Atlantic Ave.
Delray Beach, FL 33483-6910
(407)272-3611
Location Type: Branch office. Ultimate Parent: California Federal Bank. SIC: 6035—Federal Savings Institutions.

★ 59314 ★   Citibank, FSB
4071 W. Atlantic Ave.
Delray Beach, FL 33445-3904
(407)498-2600
Location Type: Branch office. Ultimate Parent: Citicorp. SIC: 6021—National Commercial Banks.

★ 59315 ★   Citibank, FSB
355 E. Lincoln Blvd., Ste. 10-12
Delray Beach, FL 33483-5043
(407)272-5699
Location Type: Branch office. Ultimate Parent: Citicorp. SIC: 6021—National Commercial Banks.

★ 59316 ★   First Union National Bank of Florida
4899 W. Atlantic Blvd.
Delray Beach, FL 33445-3840
(407)498-0700
Location Type: Branch office. Ultimate Parent: First Union Corp. SIC: 6021—National Commercial Banks.

★ 59317 ★   First Union National Bank of Florida
1660 S. Congress Ave.
Delray Beach, FL 33445-6328
(407)338-6015
Location Type: Branch office. Ultimate Parent: First Union Corp. SIC: 6021—National Commercial Banks.

★ 59318 ★   Greyhound Bus Lines
402 SE 6th Ave.
Delray Beach, FL 33483
(407)272-6447
Ultimate Parent: Greyhound Lines Inc. SIC: 4131—Intercity & Rural Bus Transportation.

★ 59319 ★   Hertz Rent-A-Car
1161 E. Atlantic Ave.
Delray Beach, FL 33483
(407)276-0324
Ultimate Parent: Hertz. SIC: 7539—Automotive Repair Shops Nec.

★ 59320 ★   Kentucky Fried Chicken
2222 N. Federal Hwy.
Delray Beach, FL 33483
(407)278-5333
Ultimate Parent: Pepsico. SIC: 5812—Eating Places.

★ 59321 ★   Marshalls Department Store
1600 S. Federal Hwy.
Delray Beach, FL 33483
(407)272-4971
Ultimate Parent: Melville. SIC: 5311—Department Stores.

★ 59322 ★   Mobil Oil Corp.
3199 S. Federal Hwy.
Delray Beach, FL 33483
(407)272-0360
Ultimate Parent: Mobil. SIC: 5599—Automotive Dealers Nec.

★ 59323 ★   Mobil Oil Corp.
4990 Linton Blvd.
Delray Beach, FL 33445
(407)496-4932
Ultimate Parent: Mobil. SIC: 5599—Automotive Dealers Nec.

★ 59324 ★   Mobil Oil Corp.
13555 Military Trl
Delray Beach, FL 33484
(407)495-2799
Ultimate Parent: Mobil. SIC: 5541—Gasoline Service Stations.

★ 59325 ★   Pappagallo
430 E. Atlantic Ave.
Delray Beach, FL 33483
(407)276-6906
Ultimate Parent: United States Shoe. SIC: 5661—Shoe Stores.

★ 59326 ★   Publix Super Market
314 NE 2nd Ave.
Delray Beach, FL 33444
(407)276-5214
Ultimate Parent: Publix Super Markets. SIC: 5411—Grocery Stores.

★ 59327 ★   Radio Shack
1528 S. Federal Hwy.
Delray Beach, FL 33483
(407)272-6011
Company Type: Division. Ultimate Parent: Tandy Corp. SIC: 5731—Radio, Television & Electronics Stores.

★ 59328 ★   Radio Shack
4951 Delray Sq.
Delray Beach, FL 33444
(407)498-8853
Company Type: Division. Ultimate Parent: Tandy Corp. SIC: 5731—Radio, Television & Electronics Stores.

★ 59329 ★   Rite Aid Discount Pharmacie
3065 S. Federal Hwy.
Delray Beach, FL 33483
(407)276-3668
Ultimate Parent: Rite Aid. SIC: 5912—Drug Stores & Proprietary Stores.

★ 59330 ★   Ryder Truck Rental
2706 N. Federal Hwy.
Delray Beach, FL 33483
(407)278-9277
Ultimate Parent: Ryder System. SIC: 5541—Gasoline Service Stations.

★ 59331 ★   Savings of America, A Div. of Home Savings of America, FSB
1500 S. Federa Hwy.
Delray Beach, FL 33483-5091
(407)272-1501
Location Type: Branch office. Ultimate Parent: H. F. Ahmanson. SIC: 6021—National Commercial Banks.

★ 59332 ★   Walt Disney World
1305 Poinsettia Dr.
Delray Beach, FL 33444
(407)345-7767
Ultimate Parent: Walt Disney Co.

Deltona

★ 59333 ★   Barnett Bank of Volusia County
1260 Deltona Blvd.
Deltona, FL 32725
(407)860-0251
Location Type: Branch office. Ultimate Parent: Barnett Banks. SIC: 6022—State Commercial Banks.

★ 59334 ★   Citizens Federal Bank, AFSB
1200 Deltona Blvd., Ste. 41
Deltona, FL 32725-6397
(407)574-5217
Location Type: Branch office. Ultimate Parent: CSF Holdings. SIC: 6021—National Commercial Banks.

★ 59335 ★   First Union National Bank of Florida
1235 A Providence Blvd.
Deltona, FL 32725-7362
(407)574-8631
Location Type: Branch office. Ultimate Parent: First Union Corp. SIC: 6021—National Commercial Banks.

★ 59336 ★   First Union National Bank of Florida
1130 Deltona Blvd.
Deltona, FL 32725-6363
(407)574-7200
Location Type: Branch office. Ultimate Parent: First Union Corp. SIC: 6021—National Commercial Banks.

Destin

★ 59337 ★   Ace Hardware
235 Main St.
Destin, FL 32541
(904)837-6915
Ultimate Parent: Ace Hardware. SIC: 5251—Hardware Stores.

★ 59338 ★   AmSouth Bank of Florida
5050 Hwy., 98 E
Destin, FL 32541
(904)833-8250
Location Type: Branch office. Ultimate Parent: AmSouth Bancorp. SIC: 6022—State Commercial Banks.

★ 59339 ★   AmSouth Bank of Florida
1100 Hwy., 98 E
Destin, FL 32541
(904)444-1000
Location Type: Branch office. Officer: Debbie Patzig, Manager. Ultimate Parent: AmSouth Bancorp. SIC: 6022—State Commercial Banks.

★ 59340 ★   AmSouth Bank of Florida
100 Main St.
Destin, FL 32541-2502
(904)837-2191
Location Type: Branch office. Officer: Walter Givhan, President. Ultimate Parent: AmSouth Bancorp. SIC: 6022—State Commercial Banks.

★ 59341 ★   Barnett Bank of Northwest Florida
1014 Hwy. 98 E
Destin, FL 32541-2910
(904)837-0066
Company Type: Subsidiary. Location Type: Branch office. Officer: Michael Locht, Vice President. Ultimate Parent: Barnett Banks. SIC: 6022—State Commercial Banks.

★ 59342 ★   Deer Park Spring Water Co., Inc.
4 Commerce Pk.
Destin, FL 32541
(904)837-1244
Ultimate Parent: Clorox Co. SIC: 5149—Groceries & Related Products Nec.

★ 59343 ★ **First National Bank & Trust**
Us 98
Destin, FL 32541
(904)837-9171
Ultimate Parent: Society Corp. **SIC:** 6022—State Commercial Banks.

★ 59344 ★ **First Union National Bank of Florida**
5490 Hwy. 90 E
Destin, FL 32541-4205
(904)837-5555
Location Type: Branch office. **Ultimate Parent:** First Union Corp. **SIC:** 6021—National Commercial Banks.

★ 59345 ★ **McDonalds Restaurant**
711 Hwy. 98 E
Destin, FL 32541
(904)863-2792
Ultimate Parent: McDonald's. **SIC:** 5812—Eating Places.

★ 59346 ★ **Payroll Data Service Inc.**
316 Mountain Dr.
Destin, FL 32541
(904)837-2978
Ultimate Parent: Automatic Data Processing, Inc. **SIC:** 7374—Data Processing & Preparation; 8721—Accounting, Auditing & Bookkeeping.

★ 59347 ★ **Pizza Hut**
1027 Us 98 E
Destin, FL 32541
(904)654-1835
Ultimate Parent: Pepsico. **SIC:** 5812—Eating Places.

★ 59348 ★ **Pizza Hut**
5099 Hwy. 98 E
Destin, FL 32541
(904)837-4755
Ultimate Parent: Pepsico. **SIC:** 5812—Eating Places.

★ 59349 ★ **Ryder Truck Rental**
3 Okeechobee Ct
Destin, FL 32541
(904)837-0612
Ultimate Parent: Ryder System. **SIC:** 7513—Truck Rental & Leasing Without Drivers.

★ 59350 ★ **Transamerica Occidental Life Insurance**
Destin, FL 32541
(904)837-8210
Ultimate Parent: Transamerica Occidental Life Insurance. **SIC:** 6411—Insurance Agents, Brokers & Service.

Dowling Park

★ 59351 ★ **Barnett Bank of North Central Florida**
Hwy. 136
Dowling Park, FL 32060
(904)364-5000
Company Type: Subsidiary. **Location Type:** Branch office. **Officer:** Betty Fortner, Manager. **Ultimate Parent:** Barnett Banks. **SIC:** 6022—State Commercial Banks.

Dundee

★ 59352 ★ **Barnett Bank of Polk County**
229 US Hwy. 27 S
Dundee, FL 33838-4140
(813)297-1466
Company Type: Subsidiary. **Location Type:** Branch office. **Ultimate Parent:** Barnett Banks. **SIC:** 6022—State Commercial Banks.

★ 59353 ★ **First Union National Bank of Florida**
124 Dundee Rd.
Dundee, FL 33838
(813)421-3401
Location Type: Branch office. **Ultimate Parent:** First Union Corp. **SIC:** 6021—National Commercial Banks.

Dunedin

★ 59354 ★ **AmSouth Bank of Florida**
1478 Main St.
Dunedin, FL 34698
(813)462-1126
Location Type: Branch office. **Ultimate Parent:** AmSouth Bancorp. **SIC:** 6022—State Commercial Banks.

★ 59355 ★ **Barnett Bank of Pinellas County**
2046 Bayshore Blvd.
Dunedin, FL 34698
(813)539-9692
Company Type: Subsidiary. **Location Type:** Branch office. **Ultimate Parent:** Barnett Banks. **SIC:** 6022—State Commercial Banks.

★ 59356 ★ **Barnett Bank of Pinellas County**
1160 County Rd. 70
Dunedin, FL 34698-5631
(813)539-9184
Company Type: Subsidiary. **Location Type:** Branch office. **Officer:** Lynne Marshall, Manager. **Ultimate Parent:** Barnett Banks. **SIC:** 6022—State Commercial Banks.

★ 59357 ★ **Coca-Cola Foods Food Service Group**
427 San Christopher Dr.
Dunedin, FL 34698-0979
Ultimate Parent: Coca-Cola. **SIC:** 2033—Canned Fruits & Vegetables; 2037—Frozen Fruits & Vegetables.

★ 59358 ★ **Coca-Cola Foods Foodservice Product Group**
427 San Christopher Dr.
Dunedin, FL 34698
Ultimate Parent: Coca-Cola. **SIC:** 2080—Beverages.

★ 59359 ★ **First of America Bank**
912 Curlew Rd.
Dunedin, FL 34698
(813)736-6751
Location Type: Branch office. **Ultimate Parent:** First of America Bank Corp. **SIC:** 6021—National Commercial Banks.

★ 59360 ★ **First Union NAtional Bank of Florida**
2100 Main St.
Dunedin, FL 34698-5699
(813)538-4580
Location Type: Branch office. **Ultimate Parent:** First Union Corp. **SIC:** 6021—National Commercial Banks.

★ 59361 ★ **First Union National Bank of Florida**
2494 Bayshore Blvd.
Dunedin, FL 34698-2002
(813)538-4535
Location Type: Branch office. **Ultimate Parent:** First Union Corp. **SIC:** 6021—National Commercial Banks.

★ 59362 ★ **Fortuen Bank, ASB**
1042 Main St.
Dunedin, FL 34698-3201
(813)733-9354
Location Type: Branch office. **Ultimate Parent:** Fortune Bancorp. **SIC:** 6022—State Commercial Banks.

★ 59363 ★ **Kentucky Fried Chicken**
956 Patricia Ave.
Dunedin, FL 34698
(813)734-2217
Ultimate Parent: Pepsico. **SIC:** 5812—Eating Places.

★ 59364 ★ **Piggly Wiggly**
950 Patricia Ave.
Dunedin, FL 34698
(813)734-2147
Ultimate Parent: Bruno's. **SIC:** 5411—Grocery Stores.

★ 59365 ★ **Pizza Hut**
1452 Main St.
Dunedin, FL 34698
(813)736-6771
Ultimate Parent: Pepsico. **SIC:** 5812—Eating Places.

★ 59366 ★ **Publix Super Market**
902 Curlew Rd.
Dunedin, FL 34698
(813)733-4173
Ultimate Parent: Publix Super Markets. **SIC:** 5411—Grocery Stores.

★ 59367 ★ **Savings of America, A Division of Home Savings of America, FSB**
1483 Main St.
Dunedin, FL 34698
(813)734-4411
Company Type: Division. **Location Type:** Branch office. **Ultimate Parent:** H. F. Ahmanson. **SIC:** 6021—National Commercial Banks.

★ 59368 ★ **Walgreen Drug Stores**
934 Curlew Rd.
Dunedin, FL 34698
(813)733-9373
Ultimate Parent: Walgreen Co. **SIC:** 5912—Drug Stores & Proprietary Stores.

Dunnellon

★ 59369 ★ **Ace Hardware Co.**
Roosevelt Blvd.
Dunnellon, FL 32630
(904)746-3664
Ultimate Parent: Ace Hardware. **SIC:** 5251—Hardware Stores.

★ 59370 ★ **AmSouth Bank of Florida**
301 E. Pennsylvania Ave.
Dunnellon, FL 34432
Location Type: Branch office. **Ultimate Parent:** AmSouth Bancorp. **SIC:** 6022—State Commercial Banks.

★ 59371 ★ **Barnett Bank of Marion County, NA**
498 N. Williams St.
Dunnellon, FL 34432-9369
(904)620-1111
Company Type: Subsidiary. **Location Type:** Branch office. **Officer:** V. David Roland, Vice President. **Ultimate Parent:** Barnett Banks. **SIC:** 6021—National Commercial Banks.

★ 59372 ★ **California Federal Bank**
1643 N. Us Hwy. 41
Dunnellon, FL 32630
(904)489-2222
Ultimate Parent: California Federal Bank. **SIC:** 6099—Functions Related to Deposit Banking.

★ 59373 ★ **California Federal Bank, AFSB**
11392 N. Williams St.
Dunnellon, FL 34432
(904)489-2222
Location Type: Branch office. **Ultimate Parent:** California Federal Bank. **SIC:** 6021—National Commercial Banks; 6035—Federal Savings Institutions.

Eagle Lake

★ 59374 ★ **First National Bank of Florida**
300 US Hwy. 175
Eagle Lake, FL 33839-4646
(813)294-4500
Location Type: Branch office. **Ultimate Parent:** First Union Corp. **SIC:** 6021—National Commercial Banks.

Eastpoint

★ 59375 ★ **Greyhound Bus Station**
16 Madison St.
Eastpoint, FL 32328
(904)663-4454
Ultimate Parent: Greyhound Lines Inc. **SIC:** 4142—Bus Charter Service Except Local.

Edgewater

★ 59376 ★ **Barnett Bank of Volusia County**
1900 S. Ridgewood Ave.
Edgewater, FL 32141
(904)423-6997
Location Type: Branch office. **Ultimate**
Parent: Barnett Banks. **SIC:** 6022—State Commercial Banks.

★ 59377 ★ **First Union National Bank of Florida**
1813 S. Ridgewood Ave.
Edgewater, FL 32141
(904)423-4525
Location Type: Branch office. **Ultimate Parent:** First Union Corp. **SIC:** 6021—National Commercial Banks.

★ 59378 ★ **Ryder Truck Rental**
402 N. Ridgewood Ave.
Edgewater, FL 32132
(904)428-5622
Ultimate Parent: Ryder System. **SIC:** 7513—Truck Rental & Leasing Without Drivers.

★ 59379 ★ **Ryder Truck Rental**
411 S. Old County Rd.
Edgewater, FL 32132
(904)427-8371
Ultimate Parent: Ryder System. **SIC:** 7513—Truck Rental & Leasing Without Drivers.

Eglin AFB

★ 59380 ★ **Vaguard Bank & Trust Co.**
Memorial Lake Trl.
Eglin AFB, FL 32542
(904)729-5500
Company Type: Subsidiary. **Location Type:** Branch office. **Officer:** Richard Dalehite, Mgr. **Ultimate Parent:** Synovus Financial Corp. **SIC:** 6021—National Commercial Banks.

★ 59381 ★ **Vanguard Bank & Trust Co.**
Georgia Ave.
Eglin AFB, FL 32542
(904)729-5500
Company Type: Subsidiary. **Location Type:** Branch office. **Officer:** Richard Dalehite, Mgr. **Ultimate Parent:** Synovus Financial Corp. **SIC:** 6021—National Commercial Banks.

El Jobean

★ 59382 ★ **First of America Bank**
1379 McCall Rd.
El Jobean, FL 33981
(813)697-6000
Location Type: Branch office. **Ultimate Parent:** First of America Bank Corp. **SIC:** 6021—National Commercial Banks.

Elfers

★ 59383 ★ **Barnett Bank of Pasco County**
6121 State Rd. 54
Elfers, FL 34653-6004
(813)847-7130
Company Type: Subsidiary. **Location Type:** Branch office. **Officer:** Kathleen Colontonio, Manager. **Ultimate Parent:** Barnett Banks. **SIC:** 6022—State Commercial Banks.

★ 59384 ★ **Barnett Bank of Pasco County**
4041 Rowan Rd.
Elfers, FL 34680
(813)847-7331
Company Type: Subsidiary. **Location Type:** Branch office. **Officer:** Cathleen L. Alred, Manager. **Ultimate Parent:** Barnett Banks. **SIC:** 6022—State Commercial Banks.

Ellenton

★ 59385 ★ **Barnett Bank of Manatee County, NA**
6102 US Hwy. 301 N
Ellenton, FL 34222-3030
(813)755-8889
Company Type: Subsidiary. **Location Type:** Branch office. **Officer:** Jacqueline Peebles, Vice President. **Ultimate Parent:** Barnett Banks. **SIC:** 6021—National Commercial Banks.

★ 59386 ★ **First of America Bank**
3815 Hwy. 301
Ellenton, FL 34222
(813)722-6671
Location Type: Branch office. **Ultimate Parent:** First of America Bank Corp. **SIC:** 6021—National Commercial Banks.

★ 59387 ★ **First of America Bank**
7112 N. Hwy. 301
Ellenton, FL 34222
(813)729-3853
Location Type: Branch office. **Ultimate Parent:** First of America Bank Corp. **SIC:** 6021—National Commercial Banks.

★ 59388 ★ **First of America Bank**
7112 N. Hwy. 301
Ellenton, FL 34222
(813)729-3853
Location Type: Branch office. **Ultimate Parent:** First of America Bank Corp. **SIC:** 6021—National Commercial Banks.

★ 59389 ★ **First of America Bank**
3815 Hwy. 301
Ellenton, FL 34222
(813)722-6671
Location Type: Branch office. **Ultimate Parent:** First of America Bank Corp. **SIC:** 6021—National Commercial Banks.

Englewood

★ 59390 ★ **Barnett Bank of Southwest Florida**
1865 Englewood Rd.
Englewood, FL 34223-4298
(813)951-4800
Company Type: Subsidiary. **Location Type:** Branch office. **Officer:** Gretchen Dudash, Manager. **Ultimate Parent:** Barnett Banks. **SIC:** 6021—National Commercial Banks.

★ 59391 ★ **Barnett Bank of Southwest Florida**
1785 McCall Rd.
Englewood, FL 34223
(813)951-4800
Company Type: Subsidiary. **Location Type:** Branch office. **Officer:** Robert Torrington, Manager. **Ultimate Parent:** Barnett Banks. **SIC:** 6021—National Commercial Banks.

★ 59392 ★ **Barnett Bank of Southwest Florida**
333 S. Indiana Ave.
Englewood, FL 34233-3786
(813)951-4800
Company Type: Subsidiary. **Location Type:** Branch office. **Officer:** Beth Harrison, Manager. **Ultimate Parent:** Barnett Banks. **SIC:** 6021—National Commercial Banks.

★ 59393 ★ **First of America Bank**
2 S. Indiana Ave.
Englewood, FL 34223
(813)474-9555
Location Type: Branch office. **Ultimate Parent:** First of America Bank Corp. **SIC:** 6021—National Commercial Banks.

★ 59394 ★ **First Union National Bank of Florida**
1831 S. McCall
Englewood, FL 34223
(813)474-9347
Location Type: Branch office. **Ultimate Parent:** First Union Corp. **SIC:** 6021—National Commercial Banks.

★ 59395 ★ **First Union National Bank of Florida**
1805 Englewood Rd.
Englewood, FL 34223-1822
(813)474-3221
Location Type: Branch office. **Ultimate Parent:** First Union Corp. **SIC:** 6021—National Commercial Banks.

Eustis

★ 59396 ★ **Barnett Bank of Lake County, NA**
200 S. Eustis St.
Eustis, FL 32726-4114
(904)589-5000
Company Type: Subsidiary. **Location Type:** Branch office. **Officer:** John Tench, Vice President. **Ultimate Parent:** Barnett

Banks. **SIC:** 6021—National Commercial Banks.

★ 59397 ★ **Barnett Bank of Lake County, NA**
100 N. Bay St.
PO Box 1560
Umatilla
Eustis, FL 32784-1560
(904)589-5000 **Fax:** (904)589-5266
Company Type: Subsidiary. **Location Type:** Branch office. **Officer:** Don D. Roberts, Chairman, President & CEO. **Ultimate Parent:** Barnett Banks. **SIC:** 6021—National Commercial Banks.

★ 59398 ★ **First Union National Bank of FLorida**
21 N. Grove St.
Eustis, FL
Location Type: Branch office. **Ultimate Parent:** First Union Corp. **SIC:** 6021—National Commercial Banks.

★ 59399 ★ **First Union National Bank of Florida**
50 W. Ardice Ave.
Eustis, FL 32726
(904)589-7100
Company Type: Subsidiary. **Location Type:** Branch office. **Ultimate Parent:** First Union Corp. **SIC:** 6021—National Commercial Banks.

★ 59400 ★ **Lowe's**
901 Us 441 W
Eustis, FL 32726
(904)589-6881
Ultimate Parent: Lowe's. **SIC:** 5039—Construction Materials Nec.

★ 59401 ★ **Pizza Hut**
1597 State Rd.
Eustis, FL 32726
(904)357-5577
Ultimate Parent: Pepsico. **SIC:** 5812—Eating Places.

★ 59402 ★ **Rite Aid Drugs**
415 N. Grove St.
Eustis, FL 32726
(904)589-9715
Ultimate Parent: Rite Aid. **SIC:** 5912—Drug Stores & Proprietary Stores.

Fern Park

★ 59403 ★ **AmSouth Bank of Florida**
780 S. Hwy. 17-92
Fern Park, FL 32720
(407)331-1961
Location Type: Branch office. **Ultimate Parent:** AmSouth Bancorp. **SIC:** 6022—State Commercial Banks.

Fernandina

★ 59404 ★ **Itt Rayonier**
4 N. 2nd St.
Fernandina, FL 32034
(904)261-5705
Ultimate Parent: ITT Rayonier Inc. **SIC:** 2611—Pulp Mills.

★ 59405 ★ **Sherwin Williams Paint Stor**
1892 S. 14th St.
Fernandina, FL 32034
(904)277-3800
Ultimate Parent: Sherwin-Williams Co. **SIC:** 5231—Paint, Glass & Wallpaper Stores.

Fernandina Beach

★ 59406 ★ **Barnett Bank of Nassau County**
520 Centre St.
PO Box 476
Fernandina Beach, FL 32034-0476
(904)321-1000 **Fax:** (904)321-1092
Company Type: Subsidiary. **Location Type:** Branch office. **Officer:** Dian S. Williams, Chairman, President & CEO. **Ultimate Parent:** Barnett Banks. **SIC:** 6022—State Commercial Banks.

★ 59407 ★ **Barnett Bank of Nassau County**
1810 S. 8th St.
Fernandina Beach, FL 32034-3061
(904)261-6811
Company Type: Subsidiary. **Location**

Type: Branch office. **Officer:** Charmaine Woodward, Manager. **Ultimate Parent:** Barnett Banks. **SIC:** 6022—State Commercial Banks.

★ 59408 ★ **First Coast Community Bank**
PO Box 1739
Fernandina Beach, FL 32035-1739
(904)277-4400 **Fax:** (904)277-8025
Location Type: Branch office. **Officer:** James M. Townsend, Chairman of the Board, President & CEO. **Ultimate Parent:** Synovus Financial Corp. **SIC:** 6021—National Commercial Banks.

★ 59409 ★ **First Union National Bank of Florida**
1950 S. 8th St.
Fernandina Beach, FL 32034-3060
(904)227-1925
Company Type: Subsidiary. **Location Type:** Branch office. **Ultimate Parent:** First Union Corp. **SIC:** 6021—National Commercial Banks.

★ 59410 ★ **First Union National Bank of Florida**
402 Centre St.
Fernandina Beach, FL 32034-4243
(904)277-1900
Company Type: Subsidiary. **Location Type:** Branch office. **Ultimate Parent:** First Union Corp. **SIC:** 6021—National Commercial Banks.

★ 59411 ★ **Food Lion**
2132 Sadler Rd.
Fernandina Beach, FL 32034
(904)261-0043
Ultimate Parent: Food Lion. **SIC:** 5411—Grocery Stores.

★ 59412 ★ **Kentucky Fried Chicken**
819 Courson Rd.
Fernandina Beach, FL 32034
(904)261-2135
Ultimate Parent: Pepsico. **SIC:** 5812—Eating Places.

★ 59413 ★ **Pizza Hut**
200 Adams Rd.
Fernandina Beach, FL 32034
(904)261-6661
Ultimate Parent: Pepsico. **SIC:** 5812—Eating Places.

★ 59414 ★ **Taco Bell**
311 Centre St. 205
Fernandina Beach, FL 32034
(904)277-2263
Ultimate Parent: Pepsico. **SIC:** 5812—Eating Places.

★ 59415 ★ **Wal Mart**
1757 S. 8th St.
Fernandina Beach, FL 32034
(904)261-5306
Ultimate Parent: Wal-Mart Stores, Inc. **SIC:** 5912—Drug Stores & Proprietary Stores.

Fernandino Beach

★ 59416 ★ **First Coast Community Bank**
1900 S. 14th St.
Fernandina Beach, FL 32035-1739
(904)277-4400 **Fax:** (904)277-8025
Location Type: Branch office. **Officer:** James M. Townsend, Chairman of the Board, President & CEO. **Ultimate Parent:** Synovus Financial Corp. **SIC:** 6021—National Commercial Banks.

Flagler Beach

★ 59417 ★ **Barnett Bank of Volusia County**
323 Moody Blvd.
Flagler Beach, FL 32136-3512
(904)439-2326
Location Type: Branch office. **Ultimate Parent:** Barnett Banks. **SIC:** 6022—State Commercial Banks.

★ 59418 ★ **Pizza Hut**
611 Hwy. A1a
Flagler Beach, FL 32136
(904)439-3120
Ultimate Parent: Pepsico. **SIC:** 5812—Eating Places.

Foot Meyers

★ 59419 ★ **First of America Bank**
1920 Colonial Blvd.
Foot Meyers, FL 33907
(813)936-4711
Location Type: Branch office. **Ultimate Parent:** First of America Bank Corp. **SIC:** 6021—National Commercial Banks.

For Lauderdale

★ 59420 ★ **First Union National Bank of Florida**
100 NE 3rd Ave.
For Lauderdale, FL 33301
(305)467-5106
Company Type: Subsidiary. **Location Type:** Branch office. **Ultimate Parent:** First Union Corp. **SIC:** 6021—National Commercial Banks.

For Myers

★ 59421 ★ **First Union National Bank of Florida**
15650 San Carlos Blvd.
For Myers, FL 33908-3315
(813)433-2021
Company Type: Subsidiary. **Location Type:** Branch office. **Ultimate Parent:** First Union Corp. **SIC:** 6021—National Commercial Banks.

Fort Lauderda

★ 59422 ★ **Walgreen Drug Stores**
Sunset Sq.
Fort Lauderda, FL 33322
(305)741-2771
Ultimate Parent: Walgreen Co. **SIC:** 7389—Business Services Nec.

Fort Lauderdale

★ 59423 ★ **Ace Hardware**
1380 Weston Rd.
Fort Lauderdale, FL 33326
(305)384-1118
Ultimate Parent: Ace Hardware. **SIC:** 5099—Durable Goods Nec.

★ 59424 ★ **Ace Hardware Store**
4343 N. Andrews Ave.
Fort Lauderdale, FL 33309
(305)566-2961
Ultimate Parent: Ace Hardware. **SIC:** 5251—Hardware Stores.

★ 59425 ★ **Advanced Micro Devices Inc.**
4740 N. State Rd. 7
Fort Lauderdale, FL 33319
(305)484-8600
Ultimate Parent: Advanced Micro Devices Inc. **SIC:** 5199—Nondurable Goods Nec.

★ 59426 ★ **Airborne Freight Corp.**
2009 NW 70th Ave.
Fort Lauderdale, FL 33313
(305)525-0416
Ultimate Parent: Airborne Freight Corp. **SIC:** 4512—Air Transportation—Scheduled.

★ 59427 ★ **Albertson's Food Centers**
7100 N. University Dr.
Fort Lauderdale, FL 33321
(305)720-1995
Ultimate Parent: Albertson's Inc. **SIC:** 5411—Grocery Stores.

★ 59428 ★ **Allied Signal Aerospace**
2100 NW 62nd St.
Fort Lauderdale, FL 33309
(305)928-2100
Ultimate Parent: Allied-Signal Inc. **SIC:** 3829—Measuring & Controlling Devices Nec.

★ 59429 ★ **Allied-Signal Aerospace Co.**
Garrett Hydraulics
2150 NW 62nd St.
Fort Lauderdale, FL 33309
Ultimate Parent: Allied-Signal Inc. **SIC:** 3728—Aircraft Parts & Equipment Nec.

★ 59430 ★ **Allied-Signal Inc.**
Aerospace Controls & Accessories
2150 NW 62nd St.
Fort Lauderdale, FL 33309
Ultimate Parent: Allied-Signal Inc. **SIC:**
3728—Aircraft Parts & Equipment Nec.

★ 59431 ★ **Allied-Signal Inc.**
Bendix-King Air Transport
2100 NW 62nd St.
Fort Lauderdale, FL 33309
Ultimate Parent: Allied-Signal Inc. **SIC:**
3812—Search & Navigation Equipment.

★ 59432 ★ **Allied-Signal Inc.**
Bendix Transport Avionics
2100 NW 62nd St.
Fort Lauderdale, FL 33309
Ultimate Parent: Allied-Signal Inc. **SIC:**
3812—Search & Navigation Equipment.

★ 59433 ★ **Amerada Hess Corp.**
1501 SE 20th St.
Fort Lauderdale, FL 33316
(305)522-3643
Ultimate Parent: Amerada Hess. **SIC:**
5172—Petroleum Products Nec.

★ 59434 ★ **American General**
Finance
2511 S. University Dr.
Fort Lauderdale, FL 33324-5819
(305)474-1990
Location Type: Branch office. **Ultimate**
Parent: American General Corp. **SIC:**
6141—Personal Credit Institutions; 6162—
Mortgage Bankers & Correspondents.

★ 59435 ★ **American General**
Finance
6306 NW 9th Ave.
Fort Lauderdale, FL 33309-2020
(305)938-9201
Ultimate Parent: American General Corp.
SIC: 6141—Personal Credit Institutions;
6162—Mortgage Bankers &
Correspondents.

★ 59436 ★ **American General**
Finance
7305 W. Orlando Park Blvd.
Fort Lauderdale, FL 33319-4959
(305)748-3101
Location Type: Branch office. **Ultimate**
Parent: American General Corp. **SIC:**
6141—Personal Credit Institutions; 6162—
Mortgage Bankers & Correspondents.

★ 59437 ★ **American General**
Finance Inc.
7305 W. Orlando Park Blvd.
Fort Lauderdale, FL 33319-4959
(305)748-3101
Location Type: Branch office. **Ultimate**
Parent: American General Corp. **SIC:**
6141—Personal Credit Institutions; 6162—
Mortgage Bankers & Correspondents.

★ 59438 ★ **American General**
Finance Inc.
2511 S. University Dr.
Fort Lauderdale, FL 33324-5819
(305)474-1990
Location Type: Branch office. **Ultimate**
Parent: American General Corp. **SIC:**
6141—Personal Credit Institutions; 6162—
Mortgage Bankers & Correspondents.

★ 59439 ★ **American General**
Finance Inc.
6306 NW 9th Ave.
Fort Lauderdale, FL 33309-2020
(305)938-9201
Location Type: Branch office. **Ultimate**
Parent: American General Corp. **SIC:**
6141—Personal Credit Institutions; 6162—
Mortgage Bankers & Correspondents.

★ 59440 ★ **American Savings of**
Florida
4111 W. Commercial Blvd.
Fort Lauderdale, FL 33319
(305)485-5540
Ultimate Parent: American Savings of
Florida. **SIC:** 6099—Functions Related to
Deposit Banking.

★ 59441 ★ **Anchor Glass**
Container Corp.
200 E. Las Olas Blvd.
Fort Lauderdale, FL 33301
(305)767-2100
Company Type: Headquarters. **Officer:**
Roger Schiple, CEO. **Sales:** 1126 M.

Fortune 500: Largest U.S. Industrial
Corporations: Ranking 340.

★ 59442 ★ **Arnet Computer**
3343 W. Commercial Blvd., Ste. 107
Fort Lauderdale, FL 33309
(305)730-9110
Location Type: Branch office. **Ultimate**
Parent: Avnet. **SIC:** 5045—Computers,
Peripherals & Software; 7379—Computer
Related Services Nec.

★ 59443 ★ **Banana Republic**
2562 E. Sunrise Blvd.
Fort Lauderdale, FL 33304
(305)564-5880
Ultimate Parent: GAP. **SIC:** 5611—Men's &
Boys' Clothing Stores.

★ 59444 ★ **Barnett Bank of**
Broward County, NA
1625 N. Commerce Pky.
Fort Lauderdale, FL 33326
(305)389-1100
Company Type: Subsidiary. **Location**
Type: Branch office. **Officer:** Pauline
D'Ambrosio, Manager. **Ultimate Parent:**
Barnett Banks. **SIC:** 6021—National
Commercial Banks.

★ 59445 ★ **Barnett Bank of**
Broward County, NA
8401 W. Oakland Park Blvd.
Fort Lauderdale, FL 33432
(305)741-2400
Company Type: Subsidiary. **Location**
Type: Branch office. **Officer:** Larry McAteer,
Manager. **Ultimate Parent:** Barnett Banks.
SIC: 6021—National Commercial Banks.

★ 59446 ★ **Barnett Bank of**
Broward County, NA
910 SE 17th St.
Fort Lauderdale, FL 33316-2993
(305)765-1663
Company Type: Subsidiary. **Location**
Type: Branch office. **Officer:** Pat Chong,
Manager. **Ultimate Parent:** Barnett Banks.
SIC: 6021—National Commercial Banks.

★ 59447 ★ **Barnett Bank of**
Broward County, NA
888 NW 62nd St.
Fort Lauderdale, FL 33310
(305)928-1920
Company Type: Subsidiary. **Location**
Type: Branch office. **Officer:** Terry Metz,
Manager. **Ultimate Parent:** Barnett Banks.
SIC: 6021—National Commercial Banks.

★ 59448 ★ **Barnett Bank of**
Broward County, NA
2455 E. Sunrise Blvd.
Fort Lauderdale, FL 33304-3116
(305)765-1770
Company Type: Subsidiary. **Location**
Type: Branch office. **Officer:** Fred
Livingston, Manager. **Ultimate Parent:**
Barnett Banks. **SIC:** 6021—National
Commercial Banks.

★ 59449 ★ **Barnett Bank of**
Broward County, NA
2929 E. Commercial Blvd.
Fort Lauderdale, FL 33308-4214
(305)797-0577
Company Type: Subsidiary. **Location**
Type: Branch office. **Officer:** Steve
Charlassier, Manager. **Ultimate Parent:**
Barnett Banks. **SIC:** 6021—National
Commercial Banks.

★ 59450 ★ **Barnett Bank of**
Broward County, NA
6825 N. Powerline Rd.
Fort Lauderdale, FL 33309-2192
(305)973-1412
Company Type: Subsidiary. **Location**
Type: Branch office. **Officer:** Mary St.
Pierre, Manager. **Ultimate Parent:** Barnett
Banks. **SIC:** 6021—National Commercial
Banks.

★ 59451 ★ **Barnett Bank of**
Broward County, NA
3030 Davie Blvd.
Fort Lauderdale, FL 33310
(305)797-0515
Company Type: Subsidiary. **Location**
Type: Branch office. **Officer:** Ralph
Sanchez, Manager. **Ultimate Parent:**
Barnett Banks. **SIC:** 6021—National
Commercial Banks.

★ 59452 ★ **Barnett Bank of**
Broward County, NA
4790 N. State Rd. 7
Fort Lauderdale, FL 33319-5860
(305)733-7500
Company Type: Subsidiary. **Location**
Type: Branch office. **Officer:** Bruce Austin,
Manager. **Ultimate Parent:** Barnett Banks.
SIC: 6021—National Commercial Banks.

★ 59453 ★ **Barnett Bank of**
Broward County, NA
3430 Galt Ocean Mile
Fort Lauderdale, FL 33308-7003
(305)566-8881
Company Type: Subsidiary. **Location**
Type: Branch office. **Officer:** Margaret
Rodriguez, Manager. **Ultimate Parent:**
Barnett Banks. **SIC:** 6021—National
Commercial Banks.

★ 59454 ★ **Barnett Bank of**
Broward County, NA
1 E. Broward Blvd.
Fort Lauderdale, FL 33301
(305)765-1656 **Fax:** (305)765-1526
Company Type: Subsidiary. **Location**
Type: Branch office. **Officer:** Richard A.
Anderson, Chairman, President & CEO.
Ultimate Parent: Barnett Banks. **SIC:**
6021—National Commercial Banks.

★ 59455 ★ **Barnett Bank of**
Broward County, NA
2800 E. Oakland Park Blvd.
Fort Lauderdale, FL 33306-1879
(305)561-4100
Company Type: Subsidiary. **Location**
Type: Branch office. **Officer:** Gary Turner,
Manager. **Ultimate Parent:** Barnett Banks.
SIC: 6021—National Commercial Banks.

★ 59456 ★ **BCT International Inc.**
3000 NE 30th Pl., 5th Fl.
Fort Lauderdale, FL 33306
(305)564-5302
Officer: William A. Wilkerson, Chairman.
Ultimate Parent: Boise Cascade. **SIC:**
2759—Commercial Printing Nec.

★ 59457 ★ **Broward Hurricane**
Panel Co.
450 W. McNab Rd.
Fort Lauderdale, FL 33309
(305)974-3300
Ultimate Parent: Doskocil. **SIC:** 3444—
Sheet Metal Work; 3448—Prefabricated
Metal Buildings; 3449—Miscellaneous Metal
Work.

★ 59458 ★ **Browning-Ferris**
Industries
2380 College Ave.
Fort Lauderdale, FL 33317-7190
(305)525-1227
Ultimate Parent: Browning-Ferris
Industries. **SIC:** 4953—Refuse Systems.

★ 59459 ★ **Burdines**
2314 E. Sunrise Blvd.
Fort Lauderdale, FL 33304
(305)537-2494
Ultimate Parent: Federated Department
Stores. **SIC:** 5311—Department Stores.

★ 59460 ★ **Burdines**
1212 SW 18th St.
Fort Lauderdale, FL 33315
(305)537-2222
Ultimate Parent: Federated Department
Stores.

★ 59461 ★ **California Federal**
Bank
3099 N. State Rd. 7
Fort Lauderdale, FL 33313
(305)497-1900
Ultimate Parent: California Federal Bank.

★ 59462 ★ **California Federal**
Bank
3676 N. Federal Hwy.
Fort Lauderdale, FL 33308
(305)537-5632
Ultimate Parent: California Federal Bank.
SIC: 6099—Functions Related to Deposit
Banking.

★ 59463 ★ **California Federal**
Bank, AFSB
2400 E. Commercial Blvd.
Fort Lauderdale, FL 33308
(305)493-9700
Location Type: Branch office. **Ultimate**
Parent: California Federal Bank.

★ 59464 ★ **California Federal**
Bank, AFSB
3600 N. Federal Hwy.
Fort Lauderdale, FL 33308-6293
(305)566-9705
Location Type: Branch office. **Ultimate**
Parent: California Federal Bank. **SIC:**
6021—National Commercial Banks; 6035—
Federal Savings Institutions.

★ 59465 ★ **California Federal**
Bank, AFSB
2400 SE 17th St.
Fort Lauderdale, FL 33316-3180
(305)522-3776
Location Type: Branch office. **Ultimate**
Parent: California Federal Bank.

★ 59466 ★ **Centex Rooney**
Construction Co., Inc.
6300 NW 5th Way
Fort Lauderdale, FL 33309
(305)565-2771 **Fax:** (305)565-9566
Officer: Bob L. Moss, President & CEO.
Ultimate Parent: Centex.

★ 59467 ★ **Centex-Rooney**
Enterprises, Inc.
6300 NW 5th Way
Fort Lauderdale, FL 33309
(305)771-7122 **Fax:** (305)938-3007
Officer: Bob L. Moss, President, CEO &
COO. **Ultimate Parent:** Centex.

★ 59468 ★ **Chase Manhatten**
Bank of Florida, NA
200 E. Las Olas Blvd., Ste. 100
Fort Lauderdale, FL 33301
(305)356-5125
Location Type: Branch office. **Officer:**
Harriett Robkin, Manager. **Ultimate Parent:**
Chase Manhattan Corp. **SIC:** 6021—
National Commercial Banks.

★ 59469 ★ **Circuit City Inc.**
801 S. University Dr.
Fort Lauderdale, FL 33324
(305)424-7600
Ultimate Parent: Circuit City Stores. **SIC:**
5999—Miscellaneous Retail Stores Nec.

★ 59470 ★ **Circuit City Stores**
Inc.
801 S. University Dr.
Fort Lauderdale, FL 33324
(305)424-7600
Ultimate Parent: Circuit City Stores. **SIC:**
5999—Miscellaneous Retail Stores Nec.

★ 59471 ★ **Citgo Petroleum Corp.**
800 SE 28th St.
Fort Lauderdale, FL 33316
(305)525-6742
Ultimate Parent: Citgo Petroleum. **SIC:**
5172—Petroleum Products Nec.

★ 59472 ★ **Citgo Quick Mart**
1199 S. Federal Hwy.
Fort Lauderdale, FL 33316
(305)463-0852
Ultimate Parent: Citgo Petroleum. **SIC:**
5541—Gasoline Service Stations.

★ 59473 ★ **Citibank (Florida), NA**
190 E. Broward Blvd.
Fort Lauderdale, FL 33301-2079
(305)463-7204
Location Type: Branch office. **Ultimate**
Parent: Citicorp. **SIC:** 6021—National
Commercial Banks.

★ 59474 ★ **Citizens Federal Bank**
1100 W. McNab Rd.
Fort Lauderdale, FL 33309-1116
(305)979-6600
Officer: Charles B. Stuzin, Chairmand of
the Board & President. **Ultimate Parent:**
CSF Holdings. **SIC:** 6035—Federal Savings
Institutions. **Employee Count:** 881.

★ 59475 ★ **City National Bank of**
Florida
25 W. Flagler St.
Fort Lauderdale, FL 33301
(305)525-5533
Ultimate Parent: City National Corp. **SIC:**
6021—National Commercial Banks.

★ 59476 ★ **Coast to Coast Cr**
Servs Inc.
5200 NW 33rd Ave.
Fort Lauderdale, FL 33309
(305)484-9696
Ultimate Parent: Servistar Corp. **SIC:**
7323—Credit Reporting Services.

★ 59477 ★   Coast to Coast Credit
Servs
2880 W. Oakland Park Blvd.
Fort Lauderdale, FL 33311
(305)484-9696
Ultimate Parent: Servistar Corp. SIC:
6411—Insurance Agents, Brokers &
Service; 7322—Adjustment & Collection
Services.

★ 59478 ★   Comerica Bank &
Trust, FSB
5401 N. Federal Hwy.
Fort Lauderdale, FL 33308
(305)771-6700
Location Type: Branch office. Officer: Sara
Yarick, Manager. Ultimate Parent:
Comerica Bank.

★ 59479 ★   Delta Air Lines
611 E. Las Olas Blvd.
Fort Lauderdale, FL 33301
(305)763-2211
Ultimate Parent: Delta Air Lines, Inc. SIC:
4512—Air Transportation—Scheduled.

★ 59480 ★   Delta Air Lines Inc.
611 E. Las Olas Blvd.
Fort Lauderdale, FL 33301
(305)763-2211
Ultimate Parent: Delta Air Lines, Inc. SIC:
4512—Air Transportation—Scheduled.

★ 59481 ★   Donzi Marine Inc.
2740 NW 29th Ter
Fort Lauderdale, FL 33311
(305)486-3111
Ultimate Parent: Outboard Marine. SIC:
3732—Boat Building & Repairing.

★ 59482 ★   Emery Worldwide
7675 NW 12th Ct
Fort Lauderdale, FL 33322
(305)523-6482
Ultimate Parent: Consolidated Freightways.
SIC: 4212—Local Trucking Without Storage.

★ 59483 ★   Executive Airlines Inc.
850 SW 34th St.
Fort Lauderdale, FL 33315
(305)944-2230
Ultimate Parent: AMR Corp. SIC: 4522—
Air Transportation—Nonscheduled.

★ 59484 ★   First Union National
Bank of Florida
633 S. Federal Hwy.
Fort Lauderdale, FL 33301-3132
(305)467-4100
Company Type: Subsidiary. Location
Type: Branch office. Ultimate Parent: First
Union Corp. SIC: 6021—National
Commercial Banks.

★ 59485 ★   First Union National
Bank of Florida
2419 E. Commercial Blvd., Ste. 101
Fort Lauderdale, FL 33308-4042
(305)467-5564
Company Type: Subsidiary. Location
Type: Branch office. Ultimate Parent: First
Union Corp. SIC: 6021—National
Commercial Banks.

★ 59486 ★   First Union National
Bank of Florida
6245 N. Federal Hwy.
Fort Lauderdale, FL 33308
(305)492-4504
Company Type: Subsidiary. Location
Type: Branch office. Ultimate Parent: First
Union Corp. SIC: 6021—National
Commercial Banks.

★ 59487 ★   First Union National
Bank of Florida
3600 N. Ocean Blvd.
Fort Lauderdale, FL 33308-6497
(305)468-2840
Company Type: Subsidiary. Location
Type: Branch office. Ultimate Parent: First
Union Corp. SIC: 6021—National
Commercial Banks.

★ 59488 ★   First Union National
Bank of Florida
800 W. Cypress Creek Rd.
Fort Lauderdale, FL 33309-2039
(305)468-2830
Company Type: Subsidiary. Location
Type: Branch office. Ultimate Parent: First
Union Corp. SIC: 6021—National
Commercial Banks.

★ 59489 ★   First Union National
Bank of Florida
1700 W. Commercial Blvd.
Fort Lauderdale, FL 33309-3014
(305)772-2870
Company Type: Subsidiary. Location
Type: Branch office. Ultimate Parent: First
Union Corp. SIC: 6021—National
Commercial Banks.

★ 59490 ★   First Union National
Bank of Florida
2577 E. Sunrise Blvd.
Fort Lauderdale, FL 33304-3203
(305)468-2820
Company Type: Subsidiary. Location
Type: Branch office. Ultimate Parent: First
Union Corp. SIC: 6021—National
Commercial Banks.

★ 59491 ★   First Union National
Bank of Florida
1710 S. Andrews Ave.
Fort Lauderdale, FL 33316-2576
(305)467-5380
Company Type: Subsidiary. Location
Type: Branch office. Ultimate Parent: First
Union Corp. SIC: 6021—National
Commercial Banks.

★ 59492 ★   First Union National
Bank of Florida
2903 Stirling Rd.
Fort Lauderdale, FL 33312-6524
(305)985-3540
Company Type: Subsidiary. Location
Type: Branch office. Ultimate Parent: First
Union Corp. SIC: 6021—National
Commercial Banks.

★ 59493 ★   First Union National
Bank of Florida
3300 N. Federal Hwy.
Fort Lauderdale, FL 33306-1035
(305)467-5255
Company Type: Subsidiary. Location
Type: Branch office. Ultimate Parent: First
Union Corp. SIC: 6021—National
Commercial Banks.

★ 59494 ★   First Union National
Bank of Florida
1100 W. State Rd. 84
Fort Lauderdale, FL 33315-2499
(305)467-5525
Company Type: Subsidiary. Location
Type: Branch office. Ultimate Parent: First
Union Corp. SIC: 6021—National
Commercial Banks.

★ 59495 ★   First Union National
Bank of Florida
200 E. Broward Blvd.
Fort Lauderdale, FL 33301
(305)467-5106
Company Type: Subsidiary. Location
Type: Branch office. Ultimate Parent: First
Union Corp. SIC: 6021—National
Commercial Banks.

★ 59496 ★   The Gap
321 N. University Dr.
Fort Lauderdale, FL 33324
(305)474-3749
Ultimate Parent: GAP. SIC: 5699—
Miscellaneous Apparel & Accessory Stores.

★ 59497 ★   GE Medical Systems
5101 NW 21st Ave., No. 210
Fort Lauderdale, FL 33309
(305)486-8300
Officer: Alfredo Arguello, Manager. SIC:
3844—X-Ray Apparatus & Tubes.
Ultimate Parent: General Electric. SIC:
3844—X-Ray Apparatus & Tubes.

★ 59498 ★   Greyhound Bus Lines
6229 N. Federal Hwy.
Fort Lauderdale, FL 33308
(305)491-1122
Ultimate Parent: Greyhound Lines Inc. SIC:
4111—Local & Suburban Transit.

★ 59499 ★   Greyhound Bus Lines
515 NE 3rd St.
Fort Lauderdale, FL 33301
(305)764-6621
Ultimate Parent: Greyhound Lines Inc. SIC:
4111—Local & Suburban Transit.

★ 59500 ★   Harris
Computer Systems Div.
2101 W. Cypress Creek Rd.
Fort Lauderdale, FL 33309-1892
Company Type: Division. Ultimate Parent:
Harris. SIC: 3674—Semiconductors &

Related Devices; 3571—Electronic
Computers.

★ 59501 ★   Harris
Computer Systems Division
2101 W. Cypress Creek Rd.
Fort Lauderdale, FL 33309
(305)974-1700 Fax: (305)977-5580
Company Type: Subsidiary. Officer: E.
Courtney Siegel, Vice President & General
Manager. Ultimate Parent: Harris.

★ 59502 ★   Harris Corp.
Computer Systems Div.
2101 W. Cypress Creek Rd.
Fort Lauderdale, FL 33309-1892
Company Type: Division. Ultimate Parent:
Harris. SIC: 3571—Electronic Computers.

★ 59503 ★   Hertz Rent-A-Car
4250 SW 14th Ave.
Fort Lauderdale, FL 33315
(305)940-6092
Ultimate Parent: Hertz. SIC: 7539—
Automotive Repair Shops Nec.

★ 59504 ★   Hertz Rent-A-Car
1711 N. University Dr.
Fort Lauderdale, FL 33322
(305)472-0740
Ultimate Parent: Hertz. SIC: 7514—
Passenger Car Rental.

★ 59505 ★   Hertz Rent-A-Car
1615 N. Federal Hwy.
Fort Lauderdale, FL 33305
(305)561-8100
Ultimate Parent: Hertz. SIC: 7514—
Passenger Car Rental.

★ 59506 ★   Hertz Rent-A-Car
Fort Lauderdale-Hollywood
Fort Lauderdale, FL 33315
(305)359-5281
Ultimate Parent: Hertz. SIC: 7539—
Automotive Repair Shops Nec.

★ 59507 ★   Hewlett-Packard Co.
5900 N. Andrews Ave.
Fort Lauderdale, FL 33309
(305)938-9800
Ultimate Parent: Hewlett-Packard. SIC:
5099—Durable Goods Nec.

★ 59508 ★   Hit or Miss
3200 N. Federal Hwy.
Fort Lauderdale, FL 33306
(305)565-8484
Ultimate Parent: TJX. SIC: 5621—
Women's Clothing Stores.

★ 59509 ★   Hit or Miss
7143 W. Broward Blvd.
Fort Lauderdale, FL 33317
(305)587-9616
Ultimate Parent: TJX. SIC: 5621—
Women's Clothing Stores.

★ 59510 ★   Home Depot Inc.
2300 S. University Dr.
Fort Lauderdale, FL 33324
(305)476-9600
Ultimate Parent: Home Depot. SIC: 5211—
Lumber & Other Building Materials.

★ 59511 ★   Jiffy Lube
7404 N. Pine Island Rd.
Fort Lauderdale, FL 33321
(305)720-1390
Ultimate Parent: Pennzoil. SIC: 7538—
General Automotive Repair Shops.

★ 59512 ★   Jiffy Lube
5390 N. State Rd. 7
Fort Lauderdale, FL 33319
(305)485-5823
Ultimate Parent: Pennzoil. SIC: 7538—
General Automotive Repair Shops.

★ 59513 ★   Jiffy Lube of Sunrise
4359 N. University Dr.
Fort Lauderdale, FL 33351
(305)748-5354
Ultimate Parent: Pennzoil. SIC: 7538—
General Automotive Repair Shops.

★ 59514 ★   Johnson Controls Inc.
8650 NW 58th St.
Fort Lauderdale, FL 33321
(305)525-7480
Ultimate Parent: Johnson Controls Inc.
SIC: 5063—Electrical Apparatus &
Equipment.

★ 59515 ★   Jostens Learning
Corporatio
4901 NW 17th Way
Fort Lauderdale, FL 33309
(305)491-3481
Ultimate Parent: Jostens. SIC: 8999—
Services Nec.

★ 59516 ★   Kentucky Fried
Chicken
3061 W. Sunrise Blvd.
Fort Lauderdale, FL 33311
(305)584-2288
Ultimate Parent: Pepsico. SIC: 5812—
Eating Places.

★ 59517 ★   Kentucky Fried
Chicken
4200 SW 64th Ave.
Fort Lauderdale, FL 33314
(305)584-1066
Ultimate Parent: Pepsico. SIC: 5812—
Eating Places.

★ 59518 ★   Kentucky Fried
Chicken
2101 W. Oakland Park Blvd.
Fort Lauderdale, FL 33311
(305)739-5629
Ultimate Parent: Pepsico. SIC: 5812—
Eating Places.

★ 59519 ★   Kentucky Fried
Chicken
2600 N. State Rd. 7
Fort Lauderdale, FL 33313
(305)731-4538
Ultimate Parent: Pepsico. SIC: 5812—
Eating Places.

★ 59520 ★   Kitchen Collection
Inc.
10064 Griffin Rd.
Fort Lauderdale, FL 33328
(305)434-2890
Ultimate Parent: Nacco Industries. SIC:
5719—Miscellaneous Home Furnishings
Stores.

★ 59521 ★   Kmart Automotive
Center
8050 W. Oakland Park Blvd.
Fort Lauderdale, FL 33351
(305)741-6130
Ultimate Parent: K-Mart. SIC: 5531—
Automobile & Home Supply Stores.

★ 59522 ★   Lane Bryant
2462 E. Sunrise Blvd.
Fort Lauderdale, FL 33304
Ultimate Parent: Limited. SIC: 5621—
Women's Clothing Stores.

★ 59523 ★   Lens Crafters
321 N. University Dr.
Fort Lauderdale, FL 33324
(305)370-6040
Ultimate Parent: United States Shoe. SIC:
5999—Miscellaneous Retail Stores Nec.

★ 59524 ★   The Limited
321 N. University Dr.
Fort Lauderdale, FL 33324
(305)370-2661
Ultimate Parent: Limited. SIC: 5621—
Women's Clothing Stores.

★ 59525 ★   The Limited
2336 E. Sunrise Blvd.
Fort Lauderdale, FL 33304
(305)565-9433
Ultimate Parent: Limited. SIC: 5621—
Women's Clothing Stores.

★ 59526 ★   Macy's Close-Out
12801 W. Sunrise Blvd.
Fort Lauderdale, FL 33323
(305)846-8050
Ultimate Parent: R. H. Macy. SIC: 5311—
Department Stores.

★ 59527 ★   Marathon Oil Co.
Port
Fort Lauderdale, FL 33316
(305)525-4717
Ultimate Parent: USX Corp. SIC: 5172—
Petroleum Products Nec.

★ 59528 ★   Marathon Oil Co.
Port
Fort Lauderdale, FL 33316
(305)525-4717
Ultimate Parent: USX Corp. SIC: 5172—
Petroleum Products Nec.

★ 59529 ★　Mary Kay Cosmestics
5701 NE 19th Ter
Fort Lauderdale, FL 33308
(305)938-0572
Ultimate Parent: Mary Kay Cosmetics.

★ 59530 ★　McDonalds
1600 S. State Rd. 7
Fort Lauderdale, FL 33317
(305)587-2182
Ultimate Parent: McDonald's.
SIC: 5812—Eating Places.

★ 59531 ★　McDonalds
1351 S. University Dr.
Fort Lauderdale, FL 33324
(305)475-0289
Ultimate Parent: McDonald's.
SIC: 5812—Eating Places.

★ 59532 ★　McDonalds
4398 N. State Rd. 7
Fort Lauderdale, FL 33319
(305)739-8040
Ultimate Parent: McDonald's.
SIC: 5812—Eating Places.

★ 59533 ★　McDonalds
1630 S. Federal Hwy.
Fort Lauderdale, FL 33316
(305)527-1204
Ultimate Parent: McDonald's.
SIC: 5812—Eating Places.

★ 59534 ★　McDonalds
1352 E. Commercial Blvd.
Fort Lauderdale, FL 33334
(305)771-7171
Ultimate Parent: McDonald's.
SIC: 5812—Eating Places.

★ 59535 ★　McDonalds
Restaurant
2300 W. Sunrise Blvd.
Fort Lauderdale, FL 33311
(305)791-3526
Ultimate Parent: McDonald's.
SIC: 5812—Eating Places.

★ 59536 ★　McDonalds
Restaurant
929 NW 62nd St.
Fort Lauderdale, FL 33309
(305)491-6363
Ultimate Parent: McDonald's.
SIC: 5812—Eating Places.

★ 59537 ★　McDonalds
Restaurant
265 W. Oakland Park Blvd.
Fort Lauderdale, FL 33311
(305)565-8881
Ultimate Parent: McDonald's.
SIC: 5812—Eating Places.

★ 59538 ★　Mellon Financial
Services Corp.
4330 N. State Rd. 7
Fort Lauderdale, FL 33319
(305)735-7640
Ultimate Parent: Mellon Bank Corp. SIC:
6141—Personal Credit Institutions.

★ 59539 ★　Mobil Oil Corp-10 Aer
15988 W. State Rd. 84
Fort Lauderdale, FL 33326
(305)389-0150
Ultimate Parent: Mobil. SIC: 5599—
Automotive Dealers Nec.

★ 59540 ★　Mobil Oil Corp.
8810 W. State Rd. 84
Fort Lauderdale, FL 33324
(305)473-1824
Ultimate Parent: Mobil. SIC: 5411—
Grocery Stores.

★ 59541 ★　Mobil Oil Corp.
2626 E. Oakland Park Blvd.
Fort Lauderdale, FL 33306
(305)563-0331
Ultimate Parent: Mobil. SIC: 5172—
Petroleum Products Nec.

★ 59542 ★　Mobil Oil Corp.
3101 N. Dixie Hwy.
Fort Lauderdale, FL 33334
(305)561-0215
Ultimate Parent: Mobil. SIC: 5541—
Gasoline Service Stations.

★ 59543 ★　Mobil Service Center
1799 N. University Dr.
Fort Lauderdale, FL 33322
(305)472-5449
Ultimate Parent: Mobil. SIC: 5599—
Automotive Dealers Nec; 7538—General
Automotive Repair Shops.

★ 59544 ★　Mutual of New York
3015 N. Ocean Blvd.
Fort Lauderdale, FL 33308
(305)564-3755
Ultimate Parent: Mutual of New York. SIC:
6411—Insurance Agents, Brokers &
Service.

★ 59545 ★　New England
Mutual Life Insurance
1040 Bayview Dr.
Fort Lauderdale, FL 33304
(305)566-4341
Ultimate Parent: New England Mutual Life.
SIC: 6411—Insurance Agents, Brokers &
Service.

★ 59546 ★　New England
Mutual Life Insurance
3801 N. University Dr.
Fort Lauderdale, FL 33351
(305)741-8302
Ultimate Parent: New England Mutual Life.
SIC: 6311—Life Insurance.

★ 59547 ★　New York Life Fort
Lauderdale General Office
Southeastern Agencies
2400 E. Commercial Blvd. 5th Fl.
Fort Lauderdale, FL 33308
(305)772-5200 Fax: (305)491-2101
Officer: Allan L. Howard, General Manager.
Ultimate Parent: New York Life.

★ 59548 ★　North Ridgef Medical
Center
5757 N. Dixy Hwy.
Fort Lauderdale, FL 33334
(305)776-6000
Officer: Don Stegman, Executive Director.
Ultimate Parent: American Medical
Holdings. SIC: 8062—General Medical &
Surgical Hospitals.

★ 59549 ★　Northwest Airlines
Inc.
8050 W. Sunrise Blvd.
Fort Lauderdale, FL 33322
(305)475-2533
Ultimate Parent: NWA. SIC: 4729—
Passenger Transportation Arrangement
Nec.

★ 59550 ★　Northwest Airlines
Inc.
2727 E. Oakland Park Blvd.
Fort Lauderdale, FL 33306
(305)563-1033
Ultimate Parent: NWA. SIC: 4724—Travel
Agencies.

★ 59551 ★　Pappagallo
8000 W. Broward Blvd.
Fort Lauderdale, FL 33388
(305)940-0935
Ultimate Parent: United States Shoe. SIC:
5661—Shoe Stores.

★ 59552 ★　Petite Sophisticate
2332 E. Sunrise Blvd.
Fort Lauderdale, FL 33304
(305)563-0907
Ultimate Parent: United States Shoe. SIC:
5621—Women's Clothing Stores.

★ 59553 ★　Pizza Hut
3890 W. Commercial Blvd.
Fort Lauderdale, FL 33309
(305)731-8970
Ultimate Parent: Pepsico. SIC: 5812—
Eating Places.

★ 59554 ★　Pizza Hut
2759 W. Oakland Park Blvd.
Fort Lauderdale, FL 33311
(305)486-7555
Ultimate Parent: Pepsico. SIC: 5812—
Eating Places.

★ 59555 ★　Pizza Hut
1239 S. Federal Hwy.
Fort Lauderdale, FL 33316
(305)523-1153
Ultimate Parent: Pepsico. SIC: 5812—
Eating Places.

★ 59556 ★　Pizza Hut
7580 W. Commercial Blvd.
Fort Lauderdale, FL 33319
(305)741-0077
Ultimate Parent: Pepsico. SIC: 5812—
Eating Places.

★ 59557 ★　Pizza Hut
1651 N. State Rd. 7
Fort Lauderdale, FL 33313
(305)739-0377
Ultimate Parent: Pepsico. SIC: 5812—
Eating Places.

★ 59558 ★　Pizza Hut
1330 Riverland Rd.
Fort Lauderdale, FL 33312
(305)581-5010
Ultimate Parent: Pepsico. SIC: 5812—
Eating Places.

★ 59559 ★　Pizza Hut
3924 Davie Blvd.
Fort Lauderdale, FL 33312
(305)792-9002
Ultimate Parent: Pepsico. SIC: 5812—
Eating Places.

★ 59560 ★　Pizza Hut
4096 N. Andrews Ave.
Fort Lauderdale, FL 33309
(305)565-5965
Ultimate Parent: Pepsico. SIC: 5812—
Eating Places.

★ 59561 ★　Publix Super Market
6989 W. Broward Blvd.
Fort Lauderdale, FL 33317
(305)587-4002
Ultimate Parent: Publix Super Markets.
SIC: 5411—Grocery Stores.

★ 59562 ★　Publix Super Market
10155 W. Oakland Park Blvd.
Fort Lauderdale, FL 33351
(305)748-5300
Ultimate Parent: Publix Super Markets.
SIC: 5411—Grocery Stores.

★ 59563 ★　Publix Super Market
8245 N. Pine Island Rd.
Fort Lauderdale, FL 33321
(305)726-1990
Ultimate Parent: Publix Super Markets.
SIC: 5411—Grocery Stores.

★ 59564 ★　Publix Super Market
4701 S. University Dr.
Fort Lauderdale, FL 33328
(305)434-6202
Ultimate Parent: Publix Super Markets.
SIC: 5411—Grocery Stores.

★ 59565 ★　Publix Super Market
3400 N. Federal Hwy.
Fort Lauderdale, FL 33306
(305)564-9612
Ultimate Parent: Publix Super Markets.
SIC: 5411—Grocery Stores.

★ 59566 ★　Publix Super Market
4703 N. Ocean Blvd.
Fort Lauderdale, FL 33308
(305)942-8822
Ultimate Parent: Publix Super Markets.
SIC: 5411—Grocery Stores.

★ 59567 ★　Publix Super Market
931 E. Commercial Blvd.
Fort Lauderdale, FL 33334
(305)772-0290
Ultimate Parent: Publix Super Markets.
SIC: 5411—Grocery Stores.

★ 59568 ★　Publix Super Market
2633 N. Dixie Hwy.
Fort Lauderdale, FL 33334
(305)566-8379
Ultimate Parent: Publix Super Markets.
SIC: 5411—Grocery Stores.

★ 59569 ★　Publix Super Markets
2633 N. Dixie Hwy.
Fort Lauderdale, FL 33334
(305)566-8379
Ultimate Parent: Publix Super Markets.
SIC: 5411—Grocery Stores.

★ 59570 ★　Publix Super Markets
10155 W. Oakland Park Blvd.
Fort Lauderdale, FL 33351
(305)748-5300
Ultimate Parent: Publix Super Markets.
SIC: 5411—Grocery Stores.

★ 59571 ★　Publix Super Markets
4701 S. University Dr.
Fort Lauderdale, FL 33328
(305)434-6202
Ultimate Parent: Publix Super Markets.
SIC: 5411—Grocery Stores.

★ 59572 ★　Publix Super Markets
931 E. Commercial Blvd.
Fort Lauderdale, FL 33334
(305)772-0290
Ultimate Parent: Publix Super Markets.
SIC: 5411—Grocery Stores.

★ 59573 ★　Publix Super Markets
6989 W. Broward Blvd.
Fort Lauderdale, FL 33317
(305)587-4002
Ultimate Parent: Publix Super Markets.
SIC: 5411—Grocery Stores.

★ 59574 ★　Publix Super Markets
8245 N. Pine Island Rd.
Fort Lauderdale, FL 33321
(305)726-1990
Ultimate Parent: Publix Super Markets.
SIC: 5411—Grocery Stores.

★ 59575 ★　Publix Super Markets
3400 N. Federal Hwy.
Fort Lauderdale, FL 33306
(305)564-9612
Ultimate Parent: Publix Super Markets.
SIC: 5411—Grocery Stores.

★ 59576 ★　Publix Super Markets
4703 N. Ocean Blvd.
Fort Lauderdale, FL 33308
(305)942-8822
Ultimate Parent: Publix Super Markets.
SIC: 5411—Grocery Stores.

★ 59577 ★　Radio Shack
8918 W. State Rd. 84
Fort Lauderdale, FL 33324
(305)370-7548
Company Type: Division. Ultimate Parent:
Tandy Corp. SIC: 5734—Computer &
Software Stores.

★ 59578 ★　Radio Shack
8253 W. Sunrise Blvd.
Fort Lauderdale, FL 33322
(305)473-5517
Company Type: Division. Ultimate Parent:
Tandy Corp. SIC: 5734—Computer &
Software Stores.

★ 59579 ★　Radio Shack
5500 W. Oakland Park Blvd.
Fort Lauderdale, FL 33313
(305)733-6432
Company Type: Division. Ultimate Parent:
Tandy Corp. SIC: 5731—Radio, Television
& Electronics Stores.

★ 59580 ★　Radio Shack
971 W. State Rd. 84
Fort Lauderdale, FL 33315
(305)522-6850
Company Type: Division. Ultimate Parent:
Tandy Corp. SIC: 5065—Electronic Parts &
Equipment Nec.

★ 59581 ★　Radio Shack
1348 SW 17th Ave.
Fort Lauderdale, FL 33312
(305)467-2313
Company Type: Division. Ultimate Parent:
Tandy Corp. SIC: 5731—Radio, Television
& Electronics Stores.

★ 59582 ★　Radio Shack
3201 W. Commercial Blvd. 230
Fort Lauderdale, FL 33309
Company Type: Division. Ultimate Parent:
Tandy Corp. SIC: 5734—Computer &
Software Stores.

★ 59583 ★　Radio Shack
4850 S. State Rd. 7
Fort Lauderdale, FL 33314
(305)791-7754
Company Type: Division. Ultimate Parent:
Tandy Corp. SIC: 5065—Electronic Parts &
Equipment Nec.

★ 59584 ★　Radio Shack
4637 S. University Dr.
Fort Lauderdale, FL 33328
(305)434-5829
Company Type: Division. Ultimate Parent:
Tandy Corp. SIC: 5065—Electronic Parts &
Equipment Nec.

★ 59585 ★   Radio Shack
1431 NW 40th Ave.
Fort Lauderdale, FL 33313
(305)587-1666
Company Type: Division. **Ultimate Parent:** Tandy Corp. **SIC:** 5065—Electronic Parts & Equipment Nec.

★ 59586 ★   Radio Shack
238 NW 49th Ave.
Fort Lauderdale, FL 33317
(305)792-8310
Company Type: Division. **Ultimate Parent:** Tandy Corp. **SIC:** 5065—Electronic Parts & Equipment Nec.

★ 59587 ★   Radio Shack
4411 N. Federal Hwy.
Fort Lauderdale, FL 33308
(305)771-3587
Company Type: Division. **Ultimate Parent:** Tandy Corp. **SIC:** 5065—Electronic Parts & Equipment Nec.

★ 59588 ★   Radio Shack
5405 N. University Dr.
Fort Lauderdale, FL 33351
(305)741-9414
Company Type: Division. **Ultimate Parent:** Tandy Corp. **SIC:** 5734—Computer & Software Stores.

★ 59589 ★   Radio Shack
Galleria
Fort Lauderdale, FL 33304
(305)565-0704
Company Type: Division. **Ultimate Parent:** Tandy Corp. **SIC:** 5065—Electronic Parts & Equipment Nec.

★ 59590 ★   Radio Shack
920 N. Federal Hwy.
Fort Lauderdale, FL 33304
(305)764-8805
Company Type: Division. **Ultimate Parent:** Tandy Corp. **SIC:** 5734—Computer & Software Stores.

★ 59591 ★   Radio Shack
2724 E. Commercial Blvd.
Fort Lauderdale, FL 33308
(305)771-5985
Company Type: Division. **Ultimate Parent:** Tandy Corp. **SIC:** 5734—Computer & Software Stores.

★ 59592 ★   Radio Shack
Broward Mall
Fort Lauderdale, FL 33324
(305)473-9775
Company Type: Division. **Ultimate Parent:** Tandy Corp. **SIC:** 5065—Electronic Parts & Equipment Nec.

★ 59593 ★   Radio Shack
2741 Davie Blvd.
Fort Lauderdale, FL 33312
(305)584-6232
Company Type: Division. **Ultimate Parent:** Tandy Corp. **SIC:** 5065—Electronic Parts & Equipment Nec.

★ 59594 ★   Radio Shack
5589 N. University Dr.
Fort Lauderdale, FL 33351
(305)741-9498
Company Type: Division. **Ultimate Parent:** Tandy Corp. **SIC:** 5065—Electronic Parts & Equipment Nec.

★ 59595 ★   Rite Aid Discount Pharmacie
6441 Stirling Rd.
Fort Lauderdale, FL 33314
(305)583-9815
Ultimate Parent: Rite Aid. **SIC:** 5912—Drug Stores & Proprietary Stores.

★ 59596 ★   Rite Aid Discount Pharms
Pine Plz.
Fort Lauderdale, FL 33321
(305)749-8106
Ultimate Parent: Rite Aid. **SIC:** 5912—Drug Stores & Proprietary Stores.

★ 59597 ★   Rite Aid Discount Pharms
3857 W. Broward Blvd.
Fort Lauderdale, FL 33312
(305)587-3920
Ultimate Parent: Rite Aid. **SIC:** 5912—Drug Stores & Proprietary Stores.

★ 59598 ★   Rite Aid 2012
2355 NE 26th St.
Fort Lauderdale, FL 33305
(305)565-5606
Ultimate Parent: Rite Aid. **SIC:** 5999—Miscellaneous Retail Stores Nec.

★ 59599 ★   Ryder Truck Rental
6600 W. State Rd. 84
Fort Lauderdale, FL 33317
(305)475-8900
Ultimate Parent: Ryder System. **SIC:** 7513—Truck Rental & Leasing Without Drivers.

★ 59600 ★   Ryder Truck Rental
3535 SW 46th Ave.
Fort Lauderdale, FL 33314
(305)581-5552
Ultimate Parent: Ryder System. **SIC:** 7359—Equipment Rental & Leasing Nec.

★ 59601 ★   Ryder Truck Rental
3350 Davie Blvd.
Fort Lauderdale, FL 33312
(305)583-6598
Ultimate Parent: Ryder System. **SIC:** 7359—Equipment Rental & Leasing Nec.

★ 59602 ★   Ryder Truck Rental
130 W. State Rd. 84
Fort Lauderdale, FL 33315
(305)467-6668
Ultimate Parent: Ryder System. **SIC:** 7359—Equipment Rental & Leasing Nec.

★ 59603 ★   Ryder Truck Rental
1309 W. Sunrise Blvd.
Fort Lauderdale, FL 33311
(305)524-2702
Ultimate Parent: Ryder System. **SIC:** 7359—Equipment Rental & Leasing Nec.

★ 59604 ★   Ryder Truck Rental
591 SW 27th Ave.
Fort Lauderdale, FL 33312
(305)583-4649
Ultimate Parent: Ryder System. **SIC:** 7359—Equipment Rental & Leasing Nec.

★ 59605 ★   Ryder Truck Rental
3990 W. Oakland Park Blvd.
Fort Lauderdale, FL 33311
(305)486-4555
Ultimate Parent: Ryder System. **SIC:** 7359—Equipment Rental & Leasing Nec.

★ 59606 ★   Ryder Truck Rental
5500 N. State Rd. 7
Fort Lauderdale, FL 33319
(305)781-2044
Ultimate Parent: Ryder System. **SIC:** 7359—Equipment Rental & Leasing Nec.

★ 59607 ★   Ryder Truck Rental
1020 NE 4th Ave.
Fort Lauderdale, FL 33304
(305)764-1196
Ultimate Parent: Ryder System. **SIC:** 7359—Equipment Rental & Leasing Nec.

★ 59608 ★   Savings of America, A Division of Home Savings of America, FSB
3710 N. Ocean Blvd.
Fort Lauderdale, FL 33308-6400
(305)564-8099
Company Type: Subsidiary. **Location Type:** Branch office. **Officer:** Linda Peets, Mgr. **Ultimate Parent:** H. F. Ahmanson. **SIC:** 6021—National Commercial Banks.

★ 59609 ★   Savings of America, A Division of Home Savings of America, FSB
4875 N. Federal Hwy.
Fort Lauderdale, FL 33308-4610
(305)771-3600
Company Type: Subsidiary. **Location Type:** Branch office. **Officer:** Carol Peddycord, Mgr. **Ultimate Parent:** H. F. Ahmanson. **SIC:** 6021—National Commercial Banks.

★ 59610 ★   Sears Roebuck & Co.
901 N. Federal Hwy.
Fort Lauderdale, FL 33304
(305)779-1382
Officer: Jim Suomi, Manager. **Ultimate Parent:** Sears Roebuck & Co. **SIC:** 3499—Fabricated Metal Products Nec.

★ 59611 ★   Service Merchandise
1801 S. University Dr.
Fort Lauderdale, FL 33324
(305)474-6500
Ultimate Parent: Service Merchandise Co., Inc. **SIC:** 5961—Catalog & Mail-Order Houses.

★ 59612 ★   Southland Corp.
3841 N. Andrews Ave.
Fort Lauderdale, FL 33309
(305)563-4284
Ultimate Parent: Southland Corp. **SIC:** 2097—Manufactured Ice.

★ 59613 ★   Sunbeam/Oster
200 E. Los Olas Blvd.
Fort Lauderdale, FL 33301
(305)767-2100
Company Type: Headquarters. **Officer:** Roger W. Schipke. **Employee Count:** 10500. **Sales:** 1066 M. **Fortune 500:** Largest U.S. Industrial Corporations: Ranking 354.

★ 59614 ★   T J Maxx
3120 N. Federal Hwy.
Fort Lauderdale, FL 33306
(305)563-0313
Ultimate Parent: TJX. **SIC:** 5621—Women's Clothing Stores.

★ 59615 ★   Taco Bell
7625 W. Commercial Blvd.
Fort Lauderdale, FL 33351
(305)726-8186
Ultimate Parent: Pepsico. **SIC:** 5812—Eating Places.

★ 59616 ★   Taco Bell
1650 S. State Rd. 7
Fort Lauderdale, FL 33317
(305)581-3349
Ultimate Parent: Pepsico. **SIC:** 5812—Eating Places.

★ 59617 ★   Tektronix Inc.
2745 NW 62nd St.
Fort Lauderdale, FL 33309
(305)973-9300
Ultimate Parent: Tektronix, Inc. **SIC:** 1731—Electrical Work.

★ 59618 ★   Texaco
4401 NW 31st Ave.
Fort Lauderdale, FL 33309
(305)484-5886
Ultimate Parent: Texaco. **SIC:** 5541—Gasoline Service Stations.

★ 59619 ★   Texaco Inc.
13012 PO Box
Fort Lauderdale, FL 33316
(305)686-4811
Ultimate Parent: Texaco. **SIC:** 5172—Petroleum Products Nec.

★ 59620 ★   Thom Mcan Shoe Stores
4050 W. Broward Blvd.
Fort Lauderdale, FL 33317
(305)583-9740
Ultimate Parent: Melville. **SIC:** 5661—Shoe Stores.

★ 59621 ★   Thom Mcan Shoe Stores
2400 E. Sunrise Blvd.
Fort Lauderdale, FL 33304
(305)564-9307
Ultimate Parent: Melville. **SIC:** 5661—Shoe Stores.

★ 59622 ★   Thom Mcan Shoe Stores
3180 N. Federal Hwy.
Fort Lauderdale, FL 33306
(305)566-9347
Ultimate Parent: Melville. **SIC:** 5699—Miscellaneous Apparel & Accessory Stores.

★ 59623 ★   Total Auto Care
1008 W. Oakland Park Blvd.
Fort Lauderdale, FL 33311
(305)561-0770
Ultimate Parent: Total Petroleum Inc. **SIC:** 5046—Commercial Equipment Nec.

★ 59624 ★   TRW Inc. Redi Property Data
1700 NW 66th Ave.
Fort Lauderdale, FL 33313
Ultimate Parent: TRW, Inc. **SIC:** 2752—Commercial Printing—Lithographic.

★ 59625 ★   Waldenbooks
Broward Mall
Fort Lauderdale, FL 33324
(305)472-4825
Ultimate Parent: K-Mart. **SIC:** 5942—Book Stores.

★ 59626 ★   Waldenbooks & More
3396 N. University Dr.
Fort Lauderdale, FL 33351
(305)572-1504
Ultimate Parent: K-Mart. **SIC:** 5942—Book Stores.

★ 59627 ★   Walgreen
2711 W. Sunrise Blvd.
Fort Lauderdale, FL 33311
(305)797-9771
Ultimate Parent: Walgreen Co. **SIC:** 5399—Miscellaneous General Merchandise Store.

★ 59628 ★   Walgreen
5101 NW 21st Ave. 530
Fort Lauderdale, FL 33309
(305)739-2802
Ultimate Parent: Walgreen Co. **SIC:** 5912—Drug Stores & Proprietary Stores.

★ 59629 ★   Walgreen
5001 N. Dixie Hwy.
Fort Lauderdale, FL 33334
(305)772-4206
Ultimate Parent: Walgreen Co. **SIC:** 5999—Miscellaneous Retail Stores Nec.

★ 59630 ★   Walgreen Drug Stores
Sunrise Sunset Shopping C
Fort Lauderdale, FL 33304
(305)741-2771
Ultimate Parent: Walgreen Co. **SIC:** 5912—Drug Stores & Proprietary Stores.

★ 59631 ★   Walgreen Drug Stores
959 W. State Rd. 84
Fort Lauderdale, FL 33315
(305)525-8269
Ultimate Parent: Walgreen Co. **SIC:** 5912—Drug Stores & Proprietary Stores.

★ 59632 ★   Walgreen Drug Stores
5101 NW 21st Ave.
Fort Lauderdale, FL 33309
(305)922-1554
Ultimate Parent: Walgreen Co. **SIC:** 5912—Drug Stores & Proprietary Stores.

★ 59633 ★   Walgreen Drug Stores
1805 S. University Dr.
Fort Lauderdale, FL 33324
(305)475-9375
Ultimate Parent: Walgreen Co. **SIC:** 5912—Drug Stores & Proprietary Stores.

★ 59634 ☆   Walgreen Drug Stores
10153 W. Oakland Park Blvd.
Fort Lauderdale, FL 33351
(305)748-5002
Ultimate Parent: Walgreen Co. **SIC:** 5912—Drug Stores & Proprietary Stores.

★ 59635 ★   Walgreen Drug Stores
Coral Ridge Shopping Plz.
Fort Lauderdale, FL 33306
(305)565-2705
Ultimate Parent: Walgreen Co. **SIC:** 5912—Drug Stores & Proprietary Stores.

★ 59636 ★   Walgreen Drug Stores
Lauderhill Mall
Fort Lauderdale, FL 333*3
(305)587-1670
Ultimate Parent: Walgreen Co. **SIC:** 5912—Drug Stores & Proprietary Stores.

★ 59637 ★   Walgreen Drug Stores
761 SE 17th St.
Fort Lauderdale, FL 33316
(305)467-5445
Ultimate Parent: Walgreen Co. **SIC:** 7389—Business Services Nec.

★ 59638 ★   Walgreen Drug Stores
4455 N. State Rd. 7
Fort Lauderdale, FL 33319
(305)485-6702
Ultimate Parent: Walgreen Co. **SIC:** 7389—Business Services Nec.

★ 59639 ★   Walgreen Drug Stores
1030 NE 15th Ave.
Fort Lauderdale, FL 33304
(305)524-3555
Ultimate Parent: Walgreen Co. **SIC:** 7389—Business Services Nec.

★ 59640 ★ **Walgreen Drug Stores**
4319 N. Ocean Dr.
Fort Lauderdale, FL 33308
(305)776-1199
Ultimate Parent: Walgreen Co. **SIC:**
5912—Drug Stores & Proprietary Stores.

★ 59641 ★ **West American Insurance Co.**
4101 N. Andrews Ave.
Fort Lauderdale, FL 33309
(305)563-3486
Ultimate Parent: Ohio Casualty. **SIC:**
6411—Insurance Agents, Brokers & Service.

★ 59642 ★ **Wilson Foods Corp.**
2530 W. Oakland Park Blvd.
Fort Lauderdale, FL 33311
(305)949-8935
Ultimate Parent: Doskocil. **SIC:** 5147—Meats & Meat Products.

★ 59643 ★ **Winston Carpet**
909 E. Las Olas Blvd.
Fort Lauderdale, FL 33301
(305)462-7735
Ultimate Parent: Shaw Industries, Inc. **SIC:**
5713—Floor Covering Stores.

★ 59644 ★ **Xerox Corp.**
1 E. Broward Blvd., Ste. 9
Fort Lauderdale, FL 33301
(305)728-2400
Officer: Marlene Williams, Manager.
Ultimate Parent: Xerox Corp. **SIC:** 3663—Radio & T.V. Communications Equipment.

★ 59645 ★ **Zenger-Miller**
4620 N. State Rd. 7
Fort Lauderdale, FL 33319
(305)731-6373
Ultimate Parent: Times Mirror Co. **SIC:**
8742—Management Consulting Services.

Fort Meade

★ 59646 ★ **Alcoa**
Hwy. 630 2 Miles W. of Fort Meade
Fort Meade, FL 33841
Ultimate Parent: Aluminum Co. of America--Alcoa. **SIC:** 2819—Industrial Inorganic Chemicals Nec.

★ 59647 ★ **Aluminum Co. of America**
PO Box 896
Fort Meade, FL 33841-0896
(813)285-8101
Officer: Takashi Fujioka. **Ultimate Parent:**
Aluminum Co. of America–Alcoa. **SIC:**
2819—Industrial Inorganic Chemicals Nec.

★ 59648 ★ **Aluminum Co. of America**
PO Box 896
Fort Meade, FL 33841-0896
(813)285-8101
Officer: Takashi Fujioka. **Ultimate Parent:**
Aluminum Co. of America–Alcoa. **SIC:**
2819—Industrial Inorganic Chemicals Nec.

★ 59649 ★ **First Union National Bank of Florida**
18 E. Broadway
Fort Meade, FL 33841-2902
(813)285-9351
Company Type: Subsidiary. **Location Type:** Branch office. **Ultimate Parent:** First Union Corp. **SIC:** 6021—National Commercial Banks.

★ 59650 ★ **Imc Fertilizer**
2690 Brook Rd. N
Fort Meade, FL 33841
(813)533-1135
Ultimate Parent: IMC Fertilizer Group.

★ 59651 ★ **United Parcel Service**
711 E. Broadway St.
Fort Meade, FL 33841
(813)285-8774
Ultimate Parent: United Parcel Service of America. **SIC:** 7389—Business Services Nec.

★ 59652 ★ **United Parcel Service**
711 E. Broadway St.
Fort Meade, FL 33841
(813)285-8774
Ultimate Parent: United Parcel Service of America. **SIC:** 7389—Business Services Nec.

★ 59653 ★ **US Agri-Chemicals Fort Meade Chemical Plant**
3225 S.R. 630
Fort Meade, FL 33841
Ultimate Parent: USX Corp. **SIC:** 2874—Phosphatic Fertilizers.

★ 59654 ★ **US Agri-Chemicals Ft. Meade Facility**
3225 S.R. 630
Fort Meade, FL 33841
Ultimate Parent: USX Corp. **SIC:** 2874—Phosphatic Fertilizers.

Fort Meyers

★ 59655 ★ **Anchor Savings Bank, FSB**
15600-15 San Carlos Blvd.
Fort Meyers, FL 33908-2564
(813)433-7747
Location Type: Branch office. **Officer:**
Sandra Allen, Assistant Treasurer. **Ultimate Parent:** Anchor Bancorp. **SIC:** 6021—National Commercial Banks; 6035—Federal Savings Institutions; 6211—Security Brokers & Dealers; 6141—Personal Credit Institutions; 6162—Mortgage Bankers & Correspondents.

★ 59656 ★ **First of America Bank**
12453 Cleveland Ave.
Fort Meyers, FL 33907
Location Type: Branch office. **Ultimate Parent:** First of America Bank Corp. **SIC:**
6021—National Commercial Banks.

Fort Myers

★ 59657 ★ **Ace Hardware**
3700 Fowler St.
Fort Myers, FL 33901
(813)936-7863
Ultimate Parent: Ace Hardware. **SIC:**
5251—Hardware Stores.

★ 59658 ★ **Ace Hardware Marine Eqot**
121 Del Prado Blvd. S
Fort Myers, FL 33990
(813)574-6336
Ultimate Parent: Ace Hardware. **SIC:**
5251—Hardware Stores.

★ 59659 ★ **American Family Life Assurance**
12370 New Brittany Blvd.
Fort Myers, FL 33907
(813)939-7510
Ultimate Parent: American Family Life Assurance Co. **SIC:** 6411—Insurance Agents, Brokers & Service.

★ 59660 ★ **Amtran**
2149 McGregor Blvd.
Fort Myers, FL 33901
(813)337-1777
Ultimate Parent: Amtran. **SIC:** 4119—Local Passenger Transportation Nec.

★ 59661 ★ **APAC**
12030 Alice Rd.
Fort Myers, FL 33913
(813)267-7767
Officer: Joel Chambers, Manager. **Ultimate Parent:** Ashland Oil. **SIC:** 2951—Asphalt Paving Mixtures & Blocks; 3531—Construction Machinery.

★ 59662 ★ **Bagel Bites**
5521 Division Dr.
Fort Myers, FL 33905
(813)694-3663
Company Type: Subsidiary. **Location Type:** Facility. **Officer:** Robert Mosher, Plant Manager. **Ultimate Parent:** H.J. Heinz. **SIC:** 2038—Frozen Specialties Nec.

★ 59663 ★ **Barnett Bank of Lee County, NA**
1533 Cape Coral Pky. W
Fort Myers, FL 33914
(813)549-4400
Company Type: Subsidiary. **Location Type:** Branch office. **Officer:** Charles Nash, Manager. **Ultimate Parent:** Barnett Banks. **SIC:** 6021—National Commercial Banks.

★ 59664 ★ **Barnett Bank of Lee County, NA**
13650 6 Mile Cypress Park
Fort Myers, FL 33912
(813)768-5556
Company Type: Subsidiary. **Location Type:** Branch office. **Officer:** Gail Mulford, Manager. **Ultimate Parent:** Barnett Banks. **SIC:** 6021—National Commercial Banks.

★ 59665 ★ **Barnett Bank of Lee County, NA**
5 Del Prado Blvd.
Fort Myers, FL 33904
(813)772-3133
Company Type: Subsidiary. **Location Type:** Branch office. **Officer:** Ellen Ebben, Manager. **Ultimate Parent:** Barnett Banks. **SIC:** 6021—National Commercial Banks.

★ 59666 ★ **Barnett Bank of Lee County, NA**
13901 N. Cleveland Ave.
Fort Myers, FL 33903
(813)995-6661
Company Type: Subsidiary. **Location Type:** Branch office. **Officer:** Mark Stramel, Manager. **Ultimate Parent:** Barnett Banks. **SIC:** 6021—National Commercial Banks.

★ 59667 ★ **Barnett Bank of Lee County, NA**
9860 Stringfellow Rd.
Fort Myers, FL 33956
(813)283-2200
Company Type: Subsidiary. **Location Type:** Branch office. **Officer:** Linda Barbe, Manager. **Ultimate Parent:** Barnett Banks. **SIC:** 6021—National Commercial Banks.

★ 59668 ★ **Barnett Bank of Lee County, NA**
1707 Del Prado
Fort Myers, FL 33990
(813)574-7136
Company Type: Subsidiary. **Location Type:** Branch office. **Officer:** Donna Orstrom, Manager. **Ultimate Parent:** Barnett Banks. **SIC:** 6021—National Commercial Banks.

★ 59669 ★ **Barnett Bank of Lee County, NA**
1360 Homestead Rd. N
Fort Myers, FL 33936
(813)369-5855
Company Type: Subsidiary. **Location Type:** Branch office. **Officer:** Jim Kane, Manager. **Ultimate Parent:** Barnett Banks. **SIC:** 6021—National Commercial Banks.

★ 59670 ★ **Barnett Bank of Lee County, NA**
1800 N. Tamiami Trl.
Fort Myers, FL 33903
(813)995-5800
Company Type: Subsidiary. **Location Type:** Branch office. **Ultimate Parent:** Barnett Banks. **SIC:** 6021—National Commercial Banks.

★ 59671 ★ **Barnett Bank of Lee County, NA**
9020 Bonita Beach Rd.
Fort Myers, FL 33923
(813)947-1500
Company Type: Subsidiary. **Location Type:** Branch office. **Officer:** Marie Comeau, Manager. **Ultimate Parent:** Barnett Banks. **SIC:** 6021—National Commercial Banks.

★ 59672 ★ **Barnett Bank of Lee County, NA**
2000 Main St.
Fort Myers, FL 33901
(813)936-6666
Company Type: Subsidiary. **Location Type:** Branch office. **Officer:** Julie Richards, Vice President & Manager. **Ultimate Parent:** Barnett Banks. **SIC:** 6021—National Commercial Banks.

★ 59673 ★ **Barnett Bank of Lee County, NA**
926 Cape Coral Pky.
Fort Myers, FL 33904
(813)549-1011
Company Type: Subsidiary. **Location Type:** Branch office. **Officer:** Todd Rinehoizt, Manager. **Ultimate Parent:** Barnett Banks. **SIC:** 6021—National Commercial Banks.

★ 59674 ★ **Barnett Bank of Lee County, NA**
16690 San Carlos Blvd.
Fort Myers, FL 33908-2570
(813)275-2194
Company Type: Subsidiary. **Location Type:** Branch office. **Officer:** Sarah Woodby, Manager. **Ultimate Parent:** Barnett Banks. **SIC:** 6021—National Commercial Banks.

★ 59675 ★ **Barnett Bank of Lee County, NA**
1366 Colonial Blvd.
Fort Myers, FL 33907-1023
(813)275-2183
Company Type: Subsidiary. **Location Type:** Branch office. **Officer:** Bryan Hughes, Manager. **Ultimate Parent:** Barnett Banks. **SIC:** 6021—National Commercial Banks.

★ 59676 ★ **Barnett Bank of Lee County, NA**
3210 Cleveland Ave.
Fort Myers, FL 33901-7199
(813)936-6666
Company Type: Subsidiary. **Location Type:** Branch office. **Officer:** Beverly Jacob, Assistant Vice President & Manager. **Ultimate Parent:** Barnett Banks. **SIC:** 6021—National Commercial Banks.

★ 59677 ★ **Barnett Bank of Lee County, NA**
14490 S. Palm Beach Blvd.
Fort Myers, FL 33905-2323
(813)275-2365
Company Type: Subsidiary. **Location Type:** Branch office. **Officer:** Mala Simonvelli, Manager. **Ultimate Parent:** Barnett Banks. **SIC:** 6021—National Commercial Banks.

★ 59678 ★ **Barnett Bank of Lee County, NA**
12381 Cleveland Ave.
Fort Myers, FL 33907-3850
(813)936-8188
Company Type: Subsidiary. **Location Type:** Branch office. **Officer:** Mike Drohan, Vice President & Manager. **Ultimate Parent:** Barnett Banks. **SIC:** 6021—National Commercial Banks.

★ 59679 ★ **Barnett Bank of Lee County, NA**
8681 Cypress Lake Dr.
Fort Myers, FL 33919
(813)482-0541
Company Type: Subsidiary. **Location Type:** Branch office. **Officer:** Pete D'Alessandro, Vice President & Manager. **Ultimate Parent:** Barnett Banks. **SIC:** 6021—National Commercial Banks.

★ 59680 ★ **Barnett Bank of Lee County, NA**
17120 San Carlos Blvd.
Fort Myers, FL 33907
(813)466-3800
Company Type: Subsidiary. **Location Type:** Branch office. **Officer:** Robert Brown, Assistant Vice President & Manager. **Ultimate Parent:** Barnett Banks. **SIC:** 6021—National Commercial Banks.

★ 59681 ★ **Barnett Bank of Lee County, NA**
7050 Winkler Rd.
Fort Myers, FL 33907
(813)482-5543
Company Type: Subsidiary. **Location Type:** Branch office. **Officer:** Pete D'Alessandro, Vice President & Manager. **Ultimate Parent:** Barnett Banks. **SIC:** 6021—National Commercial Banks.

★ 59682 ★ **Barnett Bank of Lee County, NA**
11691 Gateway Blvd.
Fort Myers, FL 33913-7907
(813)768-2343
Company Type: Subsidiary. **Location Type:** Branch office. **Officer:** Gail Mulford, Manager. **Ultimate Parent:** Barnett Banks. **SIC:** 6021—National Commercial Banks.

★ 59683 ★   **Barnett Bank of Lee County, NA**
18875 S. Tamiami Trl.
Fort Myers, FL 33908-4701
(813)267-1700
Company Type: Subsidiary. **Location Type:** Branch office. **Officer:** Sal Maniscalco, Manager. **Ultimate Parent:** Barnett Banks. **SIC:** 6021—National Commercial Banks.

★ 59684 ★   **Barnett Bank of Lee County, NA**
2000 Main St., Box 338
Fort Myers, FL 33902-0338
(813)936-6666 **Fax:** (813)275-2390
Company Type: Subsidiary. **Location Type:** Branch office. **Officer:** Allan L. McLeod Jr., President & CEO. **Ultimate Parent:** Barnett Banks. **SIC:** 6021—National Commercial Banks.

★ 59685 ★   **Burdines**
Edison Mall
Fort Myers, FL 33901
(813)939-6311
Ultimate Parent: Federated Department Stores. **SIC:** 5311—Department Stores.

★ 59686 ★   **Burdines Optical Dept**
Edison Mall
Fort Myers, FL 33901
(813)939-6324
Ultimate Parent: Federated Department Stores. **SIC:** 5995—Optical Goods Stores.

★ 59687 ★   **California Federal Bank, FSB**
7050 Winkler Rd. SW
Fort Myers, FL 33919-7038
(813)482-5700
Location Type: Branch office. **Ultimate Parent:** California Federal Bank. **SIC:** 6021—National Commercial Banks.

★ 59688 ★   **Casual Corner**
Edison
Fort Myers, FL 33901
(813)939-3515
Ultimate Parent: United States Shoe. **SIC:** 5621—Women's Clothing Stores.

★ 59689 ★   **Casual Corner**
34 Edison Mall
Fort Myers, FL 33901
(813)939-4515
Ultimate Parent: United States Shoe. **SIC:** 5651—Family Clothing Stores.

★ 59690 ★   **Circus World**
90 Edison Mall
Fort Myers, FL 33901
(813)275-4533
Ultimate Parent: Melville. **SIC:** 5945—Hobby, Toy & Game Shops.

★ 59691 ★   **Coast to Coast Fence Co.**
839 Miramar St.
Fort Myers, FL 33904
(813)549-8866
Ultimate Parent: Servistar Corp. **SIC:** 1799—Special Trade Contractors Nec.

★ 59692 ★   **Delta Air Cargo**
16000 Chamberlin Pky.
Fort Myers, FL 33913
(813)768-3200
Ultimate Parent: Delta Air Lines, Inc. **SIC:** 4513—Air Courier Services.

★ 59693 ★   **Delta Air Lines**
1811 College Pky.
Fort Myers, FL 33919
(813)337-1020
Ultimate Parent: Delta Air Lines, Inc. **SIC:** 4724—Travel Agencies.

★ 59694 ★   **Delta Air Lines**
7290 College Pky.
Fort Myers, FL 33907
(813)337-1020
Ultimate Parent: Delta Air Lines, Inc. **SIC:** 4729—Passenger Transportation Arrangement Nec.

★ 59695 ★   **Digital Equipment Corp.**
2830 Winkler Ave.
Fort Myers, FL 33916
(813)286-6660
Ultimate Parent: Digital Equipment Corp. **SIC:** 7373—Computer Integrated Systems Design.

★ 59696 ★   **First Union National Bank of Florida**
13000 S. Cleveland Ave.
Fort Myers, FL 33907-7778
(813)433-2265
Company Type: Subsidiary. **Location Type:** Branch office. **Ultimate Parent:** First Union Corp. **SIC:** 6021—National Commercial Banks.

★ 59697 ★   **First Union National Bank of Florida**
2301 McGregor Blvd.
Fort Myers, FL 33901-3388
(813)433-2428
Company Type: Subsidiary. **Location Type:** Branch office. **Ultimate Parent:** First Union Corp. **SIC:** 6021—National Commercial Banks.

★ 59698 ★   **Fortune Bank, ASB**
13499 US Hwy. 41 S., Ste. 243
Fort Myers, FL 33907-3831
(813)482-4464
Location Type: Branch office. **Officer:** Carol Osterhout, Manager. **Ultimate Parent:** Fortune Bancorp.

★ 59699 ★   **The Gap**
111 Edison Mall
Fort Myers, FL 33901
(813)939-4466
Ultimate Parent: GAP. **SIC:** 5651—Family Clothing Stores.

★ 59700 ★   **Great Western Bank**
8595 College Pky. 69
Fort Myers, FL 33919
(813)489-2993
Ultimate Parent: Great Western Financial Corp. **SIC:** 6022—State Commercial Banks.

★ 59701 ★   **Great Western Bank**
1342 Colonial Blvd.
Fort Myers, FL 33907
(813)936-5110
Ultimate Parent: Great Western Financial Corp. **SIC:** 6035—Federal Savings Institutions; 6159—Miscellaneous Business Credit Institutions.

★ 59702 ★   **Greyhound Bus Terminal**
2275 S. Cleveland Ave.
Fort Myers, FL 33901
(813)334-1011
Ultimate Parent: Greyhound Lines Inc. **SIC:** 4131—Intercity & Rural Bus Transportation.

★ 59703 ★   **Harper Brothers, Inc.**
14860 6 Mile
Fort Myers, FL 33912
(813)481-2350 **Fax:** (813)481-9131
Ultimate Parent: Delta Woodside Industries. **SIC:** 1611—Highway & Street Construction; 1422—Crushed & Broken Limestone; 1499—Miscellaneous Nonmetallic Minerals; 1629—Heavy Construction Nec.

★ 59704 ★   **Harts Dairy**
2330 Anderson Ave.
Fort Myers, FL 33901
Ultimate Parent: Dean Foods. **SIC:** 2026—Fluid Milk.

★ 59705 ★   **Hertz Rent-A-Car**
16000 Chamberlin Pky.
Fort Myers, FL 33913
(813)768-3100
Ultimate Parent: Hertz. **SIC:** 7514—Passenger Car Rental.

★ 59706 ★   **IBM Corp.**
9600 S. Tamiami Trl
Fort Myers, FL 33903
(813)939-9600
Ultimate Parent: IBM. **SIC:** 5046—Commercial Equipment Nec.

★ 59707 ★   **Kelly Assisted Living Servi**
2830 Winkler Ave.
Fort Myers, FL 33916
(813)936-8292
Ultimate Parent: Kelly Services. **SIC:** 8099—Health & Allied Services Nec.

★ 59708 ★   **Kentucky Fried Chicken**
4722 Palm Beach Blvd.
Fort Myers, FL 33905
(813)694-1425
Ultimate Parent: Pepsico. **SIC:** 5499—Miscellaneous Food Stores.

★ 59709 ★   **Kentucky Fried Chicken**
12250 S. Cleveland Ave.
Fort Myers, FL 33907
(813)936-1020
Ultimate Parent: Pepsico. **SIC:** 5812—Eating Places.

★ 59710 ★   **Kentucky Fried Chicken**
6757 N. Cleveland Ave.
Fort Myers, FL 33903
(813)997-1313
Ultimate Parent: Pepsico. **SIC:** 5812—Eating Places.

★ 59711 ★   **Kentucky Fried Chicken**
4336 Palm Beach Blvd.
Fort Myers, FL 33905
(813)694-2145
Ultimate Parent: Pepsico. **SIC:** 5812—Eating Places.

★ 59712 ★   **Kentucky Fried Chicken**
4409 Del Prado Blvd. S
Fort Myers, FL 33904
(813)945-2922
Ultimate Parent: Pepsico. **SIC:** 5812—Eating Places.

★ 59713 ★   **Kentucky Fried Chicken**
16037 Kelly Blvd.
Fort Myers, FL 33901
(813)466-8530
Ultimate Parent: Pepsico. **SIC:** 5812—Eating Places.

★ 59714 ★   **Kmart**
Coralwood
Fort Myers, FL 33904
(813)574-7447
Ultimate Parent: K-Mart. **SIC:** 5912—Drug Stores & Proprietary Stores.

★ 59715 ★   **T. G. Lee Foods**
3579 Work Dr.
Fort Myers, FL 33916
(813)334-1114
Officer: Danny Lennartz, Manager. **Ultimate Parent:** Dean Foods. **SIC:** 2024—Ice Cream & Frozen Desserts; 2026—Fluid Milk.

★ 59716 ★   **Lerner Shop**
132 Edison Mall
Fort Myers, FL 33901
(813)936-4740
Ultimate Parent: Limited. **SIC:** 5651—Family Clothing Stores.

★ 59717 ★   **The Limited**
44 Edison Mall
Fort Myers, FL 33901
(813)936-4668
Ultimate Parent: Limited. **SIC:** 5651—Family Clothing Stores.

★ 59718 ★   **Mary Kay Cosmetics**
12811 Kenwood Ln.
Fort Myers, FL 33907
(813)936-9193
Ultimate Parent: Mary Kay Cosmetics. **SIC:** 5999—Miscellaneous Retail Stores Nec.

★ 59719 ★   **Mary Kay Cosmetics**
Sales Div.
473 Juanita Ave. SW
Fort Myers, FL 33908
(813)466-8022
Ultimate Parent: Mary Kay Cosmetics. **SIC:** 5999—Miscellaneous Retail Stores Nec.

★ 59720 ★   **McDonalds**
15455 Mcgregor Blvd.
Fort Myers, FL 33908
(813)433-5111
Ultimate Parent: McDonald's. **SIC:** 5812—Eating Places.

★ 59721 ★   **McDonalds of Fort Myers**
8550 S. Cleveland Ave.
Fort Myers, FL 33907
(813)939-5756
Ultimate Parent: McDonald's. **SIC:** 5812—Eating Places.

★ 59722 ★   **McDonalds of Miners Plaza**
12290 S. Cleveland Ave.
Fort Myers, FL 33907
(813)936-5494
Ultimate Parent: McDonald's. **SIC:** 5812—Eating Places.

★ 59723 ★   **Mobil Gas Station**
12255 S. Cleveland Ave.
Fort Myers, FL 33907
(813)936-3556
Ultimate Parent: Mobil. **SIC:** 5541—Gasoline Service Stations.

★ 59724 ★   **Mobil Mart**
1206 Cape Coral Pky. E
Fort Myers, FL 33904
(813)945-4661
Ultimate Parent: Mobil.

★ 59725 ★   **Northwest Airlines Inc.**
Southwest Florida Re
Fort Myers, FL 33901
(813)768-2232
Ultimate Parent: NWA. **SIC:** 4512—Air Transportation—Scheduled.

★ 59726 ★   **Omni Business Systems, Inc.**
5850 Corporation Cir.
Fort Myers, FL 33905
(813)693-7575
Officer: Terry Smith, Manager. **Ultimate Parent:** Alco Standard Corp. **SIC:** 3663—Radio & T.V. Communications Equipment.

★ 59727 ★   **Omni Business Systems, Inc.**
5850 Corporation Cir.
Fort Myers, FL 33905
(813)693-7575
Officer: Terry Smith, Manager. **Ultimate Parent:** Alco Standard Corp. **SIC:** 3663—Radio & T.V. Communications Equipment.

★ 59728 ★   **Otis Elevator Co.**
2243 Peck St.
Fort Myers, FL 33901
(813)334-8144
Ultimate Parent: United Technologies. **SIC:** 1796—Installing Building Equipment Nec.

★ 59729 ★   **Pappagallo**
Bell Tower
Fort Myers, FL 33907
(813)433-2102
Ultimate Parent: United States Shoe. **SIC:** 5621—Women's Clothing Stores.

★ 59730 ★   **Pappagallo**
Bell Tower Shopping Ctr.
Fort Myers, FL 33908
(813)433-2102
Ultimate Parent: United States Shoe. **SIC:** 5621—Women's Clothing Stores.

★ 59731 ★ * **Petite Sophisticate**
115 Edison Mall
Fort Myers, FL 33901
(813)275-9888
Ultimate Parent: United States Shoe. **SIC:** 5651—Family Clothing Stores.

★ 59732 ★   **Pizza Hut**
12377 S. Cleveland Ave.
Fort Myers, FL 33907
(813)275-5999
Ultimate Parent: Pepsico. **SIC:** 5812—Eating Places.

★ 59733 ★   **Pizza Hut**
15501 McGregor Blvd.
Fort Myers, FL 33908
(813)482-7030
Ultimate Parent: Pepsico. **SIC:** 5812—Eating Places.

★ 59734 ★   **Pizza Hut**
11498 S. Cleveland Ave.
Fort Myers, FL 33907
(813)936-4871
Ultimate Parent: Pepsico. **SIC:** 5812—Eating Places.

★ 59735 ★   **Pizza Hut**
9151 Palm Beach Blvd.
Fort Myers, FL 33905
(813)693-5400
Ultimate Parent: Pepsico. **SIC:** 5812—Eating Places.

★ 59736 ★   Pizza Hut
3706 S. Cleveland Ave.
Fort Myers, FL 33901
(813)936-8333
Ultimate Parent: Pepsico. SIC: 5812—
Eating Places.

★ 59737 ★   Pizza Hut
5466 N. Tamiami Trl.
Fort Myers, FL 33903
(813)936-4871
Ultimate Parent: Pepsico. SIC: 5812—
Eating Places.

★ 59738 ★   Pizza Hut
6807 North Dr.
Fort Myers, FL 33905
(813)997-5151
Ultimate Parent: Pepsico. SIC: 5812—
Eating Places.

★ 59739 ★   Pizza Hut
13190 N. Cleveland Ave.
Fort Myers, FL 33903
(813)997-5151
Ultimate Parent: Pepsico. SIC: 5812—
Eating Places.

★ 59740 ★   Pizza Hut
16521 N. Cleveland Ave.
Fort Myers, FL 33903
(813)489-1577
Ultimate Parent: Pepsico. SIC: 5812—
Eating Places.

★ 59741 ★   Publix Super Market
15600 Gulf Pt Sq.
Fort Myers, FL 33908
(813)482-3144
Ultimate Parent: Publix Super Markets.
SIC: 5411—Grocery Stores.

★ 59742 ★   Publix Super Market
6444 Us 41 N
Fort Myers, FL 33903
(813)997-5045
Ultimate Parent: Publix Super Markets.
SIC: 5461—Retail Bakeries.

★ 59743 ★   Publix Super Market
13821 N. Cleveland Ave.
Fort Myers, FL 33903
(813)997-5111
Ultimate Parent: Publix Super Markets.
SIC: 5411—Grocery Stores.

★ 59744 ★   Publix Super Market
1016 Cape Coral Pky. E
Fort Myers, FL 33904
(813)542-2117
Ultimate Parent: Publix Super Markets.
SIC: 5411—Grocery Stores; 5461—Retail
Bakeries.

★ 59745 ★   Publix Super Markets
6444 Us 41 N
Fort Myers, FL 33903
(813)997-5045
Ultimate Parent: Publix Super Markets.
SIC: 5461—Retail Bakeries.

★ 59746 ★   Publix Super Markets
15600 Gulf Pt Sq.
Fort Myers, FL 33908
(813)482-3144
Ultimate Parent: Publix Super Markets.
SIC: 5411—Grocery Stores.

★ 59747 ★   Radio Shack
4023 Palm Beach Blvd.
Fort Myers, FL 33916
(813)694-8883
Company Type: Division. Ultimate Parent:
Tandy Corp. SIC: 5731—Radio, Television
& Electronics Stores.

★ 59748 ★   Radio Shack
18911 S. Tamiami Trl
Fort Myers, FL 33908
(813)267-1235
Company Type: Division. Ultimate Parent:
Tandy Corp. SIC: 5734—Computer &
Software Stores.

★ 59749 ★   Radio Shack
74 Edison Mall
Fort Myers, FL 33901
(813)936-7087
Company Type: Division. Ultimate Parent:
Tandy Corp. SIC: 5734—Computer &
Software Stores.

★ 59750 ★   Radio Shack
15271 Mcgregor Blvd. 9-10
Fort Myers, FL 33908
(813)482-5370
Company Type: Division. Ultimate Parent:
Tandy Corp. SIC: 5065—Electronic Parts &
Equipment Nec.

★ 59751 ★   Radio Shack
7101 Cypress Lake Dr. 20
Fort Myers, FL 33907
(813)481-5656
Company Type: Division. Ultimate Parent:
Tandy Corp. SIC: 5065—Electronic Parts &
Equipment Nec.

★ 59752 ★   Radio Shack
Gulf Pt Sq.
Fort Myers, FL 33907
(813)482-5370
Company Type: Division. Ultimate Parent:
Tandy Corp. SIC: 5065—Electronic Parts &
Equipment Nec.

★ 59753 ★   Radio Shack
172 Edison Mall
Fort Myers, FL 33901
(813)939-3534
Company Type: Division. Ultimate Parent:
Tandy Corp. SIC: 7373—Computer
Integrated Systems Design.

★ 59754 ★   Radio Shack
5738 Corporation Cir.
Fort Myers, FL 33905
(813)693-1291
Company Type: Division. Ultimate Parent:
Tandy Corp. SIC: 5731—Radio, Television
& Electronics Stores.

★ 59755 ★   Rite Aid
15600 Gulf Pt Sq.
Fort Myers, FL 33908
(813)482-3868
Ultimate Parent: Rite Aid. SIC: 5912—Drug
Stores & Proprietary Stores.

★ 59756 ★   Rite Aid
4123 Palm Beach Blvd.
Fort Myers, FL 33916
(813)694-2124
Ultimate Parent: Rite Aid. SIC: 5912—Drug
Stores & Proprietary Stores.

★ 59757 ★   Rite Aid
15600 Gulf Points Sq.
Fort Myers, FL 33908
(813)482-3717
Ultimate Parent: Rite Aid. SIC: 5912—Drug
Stores & Proprietary Stores.

★ 59758 ★   Rite Aid Discount
Pharmacie
Island Park Shopping
Fort Myers, FL 33908
(813)433-9985
Ultimate Parent: Rite Aid. SIC: 5912—Drug
Stores & Proprietary Stores.

★ 59759 ★   Rite Aid Pharmacy
16520 N. Cleveland Ave.
Fort Myers, FL 33903
(813)433-2110
Ultimate Parent: Rite Aid. SIC: 5912—Drug
Stores & Proprietary Stores.

★ 59760 ★   Ryder Truck Rental
15415 Pine Ridge Rd.
Fort Myers, FL 33908
(813)433-5335
Ultimate Parent: Ryder System. SIC:
7389—Business Services Nec.

★ 59761 ★   Ryder Truck Rental
2200 Rockfill Rd.
Fort Myers, FL 33916
(813)334-2157
Ultimate Parent: Ryder System. SIC:
7513—Truck Rental & Leasing Without
Drivers; 7513—Truck Rental & Leasing
Without Drivers.

★ 59762 ★   Savings of America
A Div. of Home Savings of America, FSB
12370 S. Cleveland Ave.
Fort Myers, FL 33907-3751
(813)939-5655
Company Type: Subsidiary. Location
Type: Branch office. Officer: Tammy
Barbur, Mgr. Ultimate Parent: H. F.
Ahmanson. SIC: 6021—National
Commercial Banks.

★ 59763 ★   Taco Bell
2847 S. Cleveland Ave.
Fort Myers, FL 33901
(813)334-4204
Ultimate Parent: Pepsico. SIC: 5812—
Eating Places.

★ 59764 ★   Taco Bell
12851 S. Cleveland Ave.
Fort Myers, FL 33907
(813)939-5919
Ultimate Parent: Pepsico. SIC: 5812—
Eating Places.

★ 59765 ★   Taco Bell
9020 S. Tamiami
Fort Myers, FL 33903
(813)939-5919
Ultimate Parent: Pepsico. SIC: 5812—
Eating Places.

★ 59766 ★   Taco Bell
Fort Myers, FL 33912
(813)768-2018
Ultimate Parent: Pepsico. SIC: 5023—
Homefurnishings.

★ 59767 ★   Toys R US
2160 Colonial Blvd.
Fort Myers, FL 33907
(813)275-8697
Ultimate Parent: Toys "R" US. SIC: 5092—
Toys & Hobby Goods & Supplies; 5641—
Children's & Infants' Wear Stores; 5945—
Hobby, Toy & Game Shops.

★ 59768 ★   Trailways Bus System
2275 S. Cleveland Ave.
Fort Myers, FL 33901
(813)334-8238
Ultimate Parent: Greyhound Lines Inc. SIC:
4731—Freight Transportation Arrangement.

★ 59769 ★   Trans World Airlines
16000 Chamberlin Pky.
Fort Myers, FL 33913
(813)768-3712
Ultimate Parent: Trans World Airlines. SIC:
4512—Air Transportation—Scheduled.

★ 59770 ★   US Fidelity
1614 Colonial Blvd.
Fort Myers, FL 33907
Ultimate Parent: USF&G Corp. SIC:
6411—Insurance Agents, Brokers &
Service.

★ 59771 ★   Vision Energy
2619 Katherine St.
Fort Myers, FL 33901
(813)332-7422
Ultimate Parent: Becton Dickinson. SIC:
5984—Liquefied Petroleum Gas Dealers;
5984—Liquefied Petroleum Gas Dealers.

★ 59772 ★   Wal Mart
7101 Cypress Lake Dr.
Fort Myers, FL 33907
(813)433-7700
Ultimate Parent: Wal-Mart Stores, Inc. SIC:
5311—Department Stores.

★ 59773 ★   Wal Mart Discount
City
N Cleveland Ave.
Fort Myers, FL 33903
(813)997-2112
Ultimate Parent: Wal-Mart Stores, Inc. SIC:
5311—Department Stores.

★ 59774 ★   Waldenbooks
Edison
Fort Myers, FL 33901
(813)936-5117
Ultimate Parent: K-Mart. SIC: 5942—Book
Stores.

★ 59775 ★   Walgreen
15271 McGregor Blvd.
Fort Myers, FL 33908
(813)489-2223
Ultimate Parent: Walgreen Co.

★ 59776 ★   Walgreen Drug Stores
7070 College Pky.
Fort Myers, FL 33907
(813)939-1179
Ultimate Parent: Walgreen Co. SIC:
5912—Drug Stores & Proprietary Stores.

★ 59777 ★   Walgreen Drug Stores
6434 N. Cleveland Ave.
Fort Myers, FL 33903
(813)997-5424
Ultimate Parent: Walgreen Co. SIC:
5912—Drug Stores & Proprietary Stores.

★ 59778 ★   Walgreen Drug Stores
1717 Del Prado Blvd.
Fort Myers, FL 33904
(813)574-1928
Ultimate Parent: Walgreen Co. SIC:
5912—Drug Stores & Proprietary Stores.

★ 59779 ★   Walgreen Drug Stores
15335 McGregor Blvd.
Fort Myers, FL 33908
(813)489-3400
Ultimate Parent: Walgreen Co. SIC:
5912—Drug Stores & Proprietary Stores.

★ 59780 ★   Walgreen Drugs
162 Edison Mall
Fort Myers, FL 33901
(813)936-8119
Ultimate Parent: Walgreen Co. SIC:
5912—Drug Stores & Proprietary Stores.

Fort Myers Beach

★ 59781 ★   Kentucky Fried
Chicken
17220 San Carlos Blvd.
Fort Myers Beach, FL 33931
(813)454-3444
Ultimate Parent: Pepsico. SIC: 6531—Real
Estate Agents & Managers.

★ 59782 ★   Publix Super Market
28 San Carlos Blvd.
Fort Myers Beach, FL 33931
(813)482-3144
Ultimate Parent: Publix Super Markets.
SIC: 5411—Grocery Stores.

★ 59783 ★   Publix Super Markets
28 San Carlos Blvd.
Fort Myers Beach, FL 33931
(813)482-3144
Ultimate Parent: Publix Super Markets.
SIC: 5411—Grocery Stores.

Fort Myers Fl

★ 59784 ★   Publix Super Market
1631 Del Prado Blvd.
Fort Myers Fl, FL 33904
(813)574-3713
Ultimate Parent: Publix Super Markets.
SIC: 5461—Retail Bakeries.

★ 59785 ★   Publix Super Markets
1631 Del Prado Blvd.
Fort Myers Fl, FL 33904
(813)574-3713
Ultimate Parent: Publix Super Markets.
SIC: 5461—Retail Bakeries.

Fort Pierce

★ 59786 ★   Barnett Bank of the
Treasure Coast
5345 Sunshine Pky. & Feeder Rd.
Fort Pierce, FL 34951
(407)340-5451
Company Type: Subsidiary. Location
Type: Branch office. Officer: Betty Lollio,
Assistant Vice President & Office Manager.
Ultimate Parent: Barnett Banks. SIC:
6021—National Commercial Banks.

★ 59787 ★   Barnett Bank of the
Treasure Coast
2421 S. US Hwy. No. 1
Fort Pierce, FL 34982-5921
(407)340-5440
Company Type: Subsidiary. Location
Type: Branch office. Officer: Carolyn
Elkins, Assistant Vice President. Ultimate
Parent: Barnett Banks. SIC: 6021—National
Commercial Banks.

★ 59788 ★   Barnett Bank of the
Treasure Coast
4950 S. US Hwy. No. 1
Fort Pierce, FL 34982
(407)340-5430
Company Type: Subsidiary. Location
Type: Branch office. Officer: Tina
Nicholson, Assistant Vice President & Office
Manager. Ultimate Parent: Barnett Banks.
SIC: 6021—National Commercial Banks.

★ 59789 ★   Casual Corner
4128 Okeechobee Rd.
Fort Pierce, FL 34947
(407)461-2718
Ultimate Parent: United States Shoe. SIC:
5651—Family Clothing Stores.

★ 59790 ★   Circus World
4208 Okeechobee Rd.
Fort Pierce, FL 34947
(407)461-0654
Ultimate Parent: Melville. SIC: 5945—
Hobby, Toy & Game Shops.

★ 59791 ★   Citgo Service Station
1311 25th St.
Fort Pierce, FL 34947
(407)464-9224
Ultimate Parent: Citgo Petroleum. SIC:
6513—Apartment Building Operators.

★ 59792 ★   Coast to Coast
Carriers
330 Dixon Dr.
Fort Pierce, FL 34982
(407)461-1044
Ultimate Parent: Servistar Corp. SIC:
7539—Automotive Repair Shops Nec.

★ 59793 ★   Coast to Coast
Pressure Clg
2492 SE Marius St.
Fort Pierce, FL 34952
(407)468-6603
Ultimate Parent: Servistar Corp. SIC:
7349—Building Maintenance Services Nec.

★ 59794 ★   First National Bank &
Trust
7177 S. Federal Hwy.
Fort Pierce, FL 34952
(407)879-0222
Ultimate Parent: Society Corp. SIC: 6022—
State Commercial Banks.

★ 59795 ★   First Union National
Bank of Florida
4915 S. US Hwy. 1
Fort Pierce, FL 34950-5924
(407)461-2270
Company Type: Subsidiary. Location
Type: Branch office. Ultimate Parent: First
Union Corp. SIC: 6021—National
Commercial Banks.

★ 59796 ★   First Union National
Bank of Florida
501 Orange Ave.
Fort Pierce, FL 34950-4243
(407)467-2200
Company Type: Subsidiary. Location
Type: Branch office. Ultimate Parent: First
Union Corp. SIC: 6021—National
Commercial Banks.

★ 59797 ★   First Union National
Bank of Florida
2470 First Blvd.
Fort Pierce, FL 34950-4873
(407)467-2261
Company Type: Subsidiary. Location
Type: Branch office. Ultimate Parent: First
Union Corp. SIC: 6021—National
Commercial Banks.

★ 59798 ★   Omni Business
Systems, Inc.
2801 Industrial Ave. 2
Fort Pierce, FL 34946
(407)464-8733
Officer: Ron McCurdy, Manager. Ultimate
Parent: Alco Standard Corp. SIC: 3663—
Radio & T.V. Communications Equipment.

★ 59799 ★   Pizza Hut
2947 S. 4th St.
Fort Pierce, FL 34982
(407)465-3346
Ultimate Parent: Pepsico. SIC: 5812—
Eating Places.

★ 59800 ★   Pizza Hut
131 N. 2nd St. Bldg. N
Fort Pierce, FL 34950
(407)466-6685
Ultimate Parent: Pepsico. SIC: 5812—
Eating Places.

★ 59801 ★   Pizza Hut
3500 Okeechobee Rd.
Fort Pierce, FL 34947
(407)465-8700
Ultimate Parent: Pepsico. SIC: 5812—
Eating Places.

★ 59802 ★   Publix Super Market
2569 S. 4th St.
Fort Pierce, FL 34982
(407)464-3255
Ultimate Parent: Publix Super Markets.
SIC: 5411—Grocery Stores.

★ 59803 ★   Radio Shack
10081 S. Federal Hwy.
Fort Pierce, FL 34982
(407)335-5668
Company Type: Division. Ultimate Parent:
Tandy Corp. SIC: 5731—Radio, Television
& Electronics Stores.

★ 59804 ★   Radio Shack
4210 Okeechobee Rd.
Fort Pierce, FL 34947
(407)466-2330
Company Type: Division. Ultimate Parent:
Tandy Corp. SIC: 5065—Electronic Parts &
Equipment Nec.

★ 59805 ★   Radio Shack
2930 S. 4th St.
Fort Pierce, FL 34982
(407)464-6762
Company Type: Division. Ultimate Parent:
Tandy Corp. SIC: 5731—Radio, Television
& Electronics Stores.

★ 59806 ★   Radio Shack
3223 S. Federal Hwy.
Fort Pierce, FL 34982
(407)466-2200
Company Type: Division. Ultimate Parent:
Tandy Corp. SIC: 7373—Computer
Integrated Systems Design.

★ 59807 ★   Rite Aid
2563 S. 4th St.
Fort Pierce, FL 34982
(407)465-7600
Ultimate Parent: Rite Aid. SIC: 5912—Drug
Stores & Proprietary Stores.

★ 59808 ★   Ryder Truck Rental
5000 S. Federal Hwy.
Fort Pierce, FL 34982
(407)466-5397
Ultimate Parent: Ryder System. SIC:
7513—Truck Rental & Leasing Without
Drivers.

★ 59809 ★   Ryder Truck Rental
4501 S. Us Hwy. 1
Fort Pierce, FL 34982
(407)465-6534
Ultimate Parent: Ryder System. SIC:
7539—Automotive Repair Shops Nec.

★ 59810 ★   Ryder Truck Rental
2421 N. Federal Hwy.
Fort Pierce, FL 34946
(407)464-5910
Ultimate Parent: Ryder System. SIC:
7513—Truck Rental & Leasing Without
Drivers.

★ 59811 ★   Savings of America, A
Division of Home Savings of
America, FSB
2597 S. US Hwy. 1
Fort Pierce, FL 34982-5982
(407)466-6660
Company Type: Subsidiary. Location
Type: Branch office. Officer: Joyce Kyker,
Mgr. Ultimate Parent: H. F. Ahmanson.
SIC: 6021—National Commercial Banks.

★ 59812 ★   Service Merchandise
2912 S. 4th St.
Fort Pierce, FL 34982
(407)466-5200
Ultimate Parent: Service Merchandise Co.,
Inc. SIC: 5311—Department Stores.

★ 59813 ★   Sherwin Williams
Paint Stor
2014 S. 4th St.
Fort Pierce, FL 34950
(407)464-3422
Ultimate Parent: Sherwin-Williams Co. SIC:
5231—Paint, Glass & Wallpaper Stores.

★ 59814 ★   Superior Pools
Products Inc.
704 Farmers Market Rd.
Fort Pierce, FL 34982
(407)461-1262
Ultimate Parent: Olin Corp. SIC: 5099—
Durable Goods Nec.

★ 59815 ★   United Parcel Service
3203 Oleander Ave.
Fort Pierce, FL 34982
(407)465-8403
Ultimate Parent: United Parcel Service of
America. SIC: 4215—Courier Services
Except by Air.

★ 59816 ★   Walgreen Drug Store
6682 S. Federal Hwy.
Fort Pierce, FL 34952
(407)466-8188
Ultimate Parent: Walgreen Co. SIC:
5912—Drug Stores & Proprietary Stores.

★ 59817 ★   Washington Inventory
Servic
7440 S. Federal Hwy.
Fort Pierce, FL 34952
(407)340-4410
Ultimate Parent: Huffy. SIC: 8721—
Accounting, Auditing & Bookkeeping.

Fort Walton Beach

★ 59818 ★   Aero Technical
Services
630 Anchors St.
Fort Walton Beach, FL 32548
Ultimate Parent: Sequa Corp. SIC: 7699—
Repair Services Nec.

★ 59819 ★   Air Products &
Chemicals, Inc.
922 Skipper Ave.
Fort Walton Beach, FL 32547
(904)862-5214
Ultimate Parent: Air Products & Chemicals,
Inc. SIC: 5084—Industrial Machinery &
Equipment.

★ 59820 ★   Albertson's
600 Eglin Pky. NE
Fort Walton Beach, FL 32547-2832
(904)864-4440
Officer: Bennie Dalzell. Ultimate Parent:
Albertson's Inc. SIC: 5411—Grocery Stores;
6311—Life Insurance; 5912—Drug Stores &
Proprietary Stores.

★ 59821 ★   AmSouth Bank of
Florida
212 NW Racetrack Rd.
Fort Walton Beach, FL 32547
(904)833-8260
Location Type: Branch office. Ultimate
Parent: AmSouth Bancorp. SIC: 6022—
State Commercial Banks.

★ 59822 ★   AmSouth Bank of
Florida
25 NE Beal Pky.
Fort Walton Beach, FL 32548
(904)244-7265
Location Type: Branch office. Officer:
Brian K. James, President. Ultimate
Parent: AmSouth Bancorp. SIC: 6022—
State Commercial Banks.

★ 59823 ★   Barnett Bank of
Northwest Florida
99 Racetrack Rd.
Fort Walton Beach, FL 32547-1802
(904)862-5438
Company Type: Subsidiary. Location
Type: Branch office. Officer: Charles Pick,
Manager. Ultimate Parent: Barnett Banks.
SIC: 6022—State Commercial Banks.

★ 59824 ★   Barnett Bank of
Northwest Florida
189 Eglin Pky. NE
PO Drawer 2947
Fort Walton Beach, FL 32549-2947
(904)729-4100 Fax: (904)729-4448
Company Type: Subsidiary. Location
Type: Branch office. Officer: Freddy G.
Carr, Chairman of the Board, President &
CEO. Ultimate Parent: Barnett Banks. SIC:
6022—State Commercial Banks.

★ 59825 ★   First National Bank &
Trust
29 Eglin Pky. NE
Fort Walton Beach, FL 32548
(904)243-7111
Ultimate Parent: Society Corp. SIC: 6021—
National Commercial Banks.

★ 59826 ★   First National Bank &
Trust
448 Eglin Pky. NE
Fort Walton Beach, FL 32547
(904)863-1177
Ultimate Parent: Society Corp.

★ 59827 ★   Gayfers
Santa Rosa Mall
Fort Walton Beach, FL 32548
(904)244-7111
Ultimate Parent: Mercantile Stores. SIC:
5311—Department Stores.

★ 59828 ★   Kmart Pharmacy
200 Irwin Ave. NE
Fort Walton Beach, FL 32548
(904)244-7143
Ultimate Parent: K-Mart. SIC: 5912—Drug
Stores & Proprietary Stores.

★ 59829 ★   Lerner Shop
Santa Rosa Mall
Fort Walton Beach, FL 32548
(904)244-2313
Ultimate Parent: Limited. SIC: 5621—
Women's Clothing Stores.

★ 59830 ★   Mary Kay Cosmetics
709 Trowbridge Ave.
Fort Walton Beach, FL 32547
(904)863-9350
Ultimate Parent: Mary Kay Cosmetics. SIC:
5999—Miscellaneous Retail Stores Nec.

★ 59831 ★   McDonalds
Hamburgers
11 Racetrack Rd. NE
Fort Walton Beach, FL 32547
(904)863-2792
Ultimate Parent: McDonald's.
SIC: 5812—Eating Places.

★ 59832 ★   Pepsi-Cola Bottling
Co.
43 Jet Dr. NW
Fort Walton Beach, FL 32548
(904)243-3932
Officer: Ike Beasley, Manager. Ultimate
Parent: Pepsico. SIC: 2086—Bottled &
Canned Soft Drinks.

★ 59833 ★   Pizza Hut
421 Racetrack Rd. NE
Fort Walton Beach, FL 32547
(904)863-4470
Ultimate Parent: Pepsico. SIC: 5812—
Eating Places.

★ 59834 ★   Pizza Hut
141 Miracle Strip Pky. SW
Fort Walton Beach, FL 32548
(904)244-2824
Ultimate Parent: Pepsico. SIC: 5812—
Eating Places.

★ 59835 ★   Pizza Hut
432 Racetrack Rd. NE
Fort Walton Beach, FL 32547
(904)862-0423
Ultimate Parent: Pepsico. SIC: 5812—
Eating Places.

★ 59836 ★   Radio Shack
5 Fort Walton Sq.
Fort Walton Beach, FL 32548
(904)243-5502
Company Type: Division. Ultimate Parent:
Tandy Corp. SIC: 5731—Radio, Television
& Electronics Stores.

★ 59837 ★   Rite Aide Drugs
10 Fort Walton Sq.
Fort Walton Beach, FL 32548
(904)249-9838
Ultimate Parent: Rite Aid. SIC: 5912—Drug
Stores & Proprietary Stores.

★ 59838 ★   Ryder Truck Rental
620 Beal Pky. NW
Fort Walton Beach, FL 32548
(904)862-5060
Ultimate Parent: Ryder System. SIC:
7513—Truck Rental & Leasing Without
Drivers.

★ 59839 ★   Taco Bell
65 Eglin Pky. NE
Fort Walton Beach, FL 32548
(904)664-2200
Ultimate Parent: Pepsico. SIC: 5812—
Eating Places.

★ 59840 ★ Texaco Food Mart
901 Beal Pky. NW
Fort Walton Beach, FL 32547
(904)862-5841
Ultimate Parent: Texaco. SIC: 5411—
Grocery Stores.

★ 59841 ★ Trailways Bus System
105 Chestnut Ave. SE
Fort Walton Beach, FL 32548
(904)243-6156
Ultimate Parent: Greyhound Lines Inc. SIC:
4111—Local & Suburban Transit.

★ 59842 ★ United Parcel Service
219 Santa Rosa St. SW
Fort Walton Beach, FL 32548
(904)244-2653
Ultimate Parent: United Parcel Service of
America. SIC: 4215—Courier Services
Except by Air.

★ 59843 ★ Vaguard Bank & Trust
Co.
815 Beal Pky.
Fort Walton Beach, FL 32548-1955
(904)664-9575
Company Type: Subsidiary. Location
Type: Branch office. Officer: Kathleenn
Pritchard, Mgr. Ultimate Parent: Synovus
Financial Corp. SIC: 6021—National
Commercial Banks.

Frnandina Beach

★ 59844 ★ Ace Hardware
1350 PO Box
Frnandina Beach, FL 32034
(904)261-6291
Ultimate Parent: Ace Hardware. SIC:
5251—Hardware Stores.

Frostproof

★ 59845 ★ Citrus Hill
Manufacturing Co.
100 E. 6th St.
Frostproof, FL 33843
Ultimate Parent: Procter & Gamble Co.
SIC: 2037—Frozen Fruits & Vegetables.

★ 59846 ★ Citrus Hill Mfg. Co.
100 E. 6th St.
Frostproof, FL 33843
Ultimate Parent: Procter & Gamble Co.
SIC: 2037—Frozen Fruits & Vegetables.

Ft. Lauderdale

★ 59847 ★ American Savings of
FL FSB
3001 N. University Dr.
Ft. Lauderdale, FL 33322-1610
(305)741-3606
Location Type: Branch office. Officer:
Rollin L. Parker. Ultimate Parent: American
Savings of Florida. SIC: 6035—Federal
Savings Institutions; 6021—National
Commercial Banks; 6162—Mortgage
Bankers & Correspondents.

★ 59848 ★ American Savings of
FL FSB
8980 W. State Rd. 84
Ft. Lauderdale, FL 33324-4409
(305)474-3900
Location Type: Branch office. Officer:
Peggy H. Fernandez. Ultimate Parent:
American Savings of Florida. SIC: 6035—
Federal Savings Institutions; 6021—National
Commercial Banks.

★ 59849 ★ American Savings of
Florida
8237 NW 88th Ave.
Ft. Lauderdale, FL 33321-1541
(305)722-5944
Ultimate Parent: American Savings of
Florida. SIC: 6035—Federal Savings
Institutions; 6021—National Commercial
Banks.

★ 59850 ★ BancBoston Mortgage
Corp.
3230 W. Commercial Blvd.
Ft. Lauderdale, FL 33309-3400
(305)733-5200
Ultimate Parent: Bank of Boston Corp.
SIC: 6141—Personal Credit Institutions;
6162—Mortgage Bankers &
Correspondents.

★ 59851 ★ Bell Atlantic Bus
Systems Svc.
6500 NW 12th Ave.
Ft. Lauderdale, FL 33309-1146
(305)771-4044
Ultimate Parent: Bell Atlantic Corp. SIC:
7378—Computer Maintenance & Repair.

★ 59852 ★ Bell Atlantic Tricon
Lease Corp.
4500 N. State Rd. 7
Ft. Lauderdale, FL 33319-5882
(305)426-9828
Ultimate Parent: Bell Atlantic Corp. SIC:
4813—Telephone Communications Except
Radiotelephone; 4812—Radiotelephone
Communications; 7378—Computer
Maintenance & Repair; 6159—
Miscellaneous Business Credit Institutions;
2741—Miscellaneous Publishing; 6719—
Holding Companies Nec.

★ 59853 ★ Hamilton Hallmark
6801 NW 15th Way
Ft. Lauderdale, FL 33309
(305)767-6377
Location Type: Branch office. Ultimate
Parent: Avnet. SIC: 5065—Electronic Parts
& Equipment Nec.

★ 59854 ★ McArthur Dairy Inc.
1101 N. State, Road 7
Ft. Lauderdale, FL 33313
(305)583-4340
Officer: Michael McDonald, Manager.
Ultimate Parent: Dean Foods. SIC: 2024—
Ice Cream & Frozen Desserts.

★ 59855 ★ Sunbeam Oster Co.
Inc.
200 E. Las Olas Blvd., Ste. 2100
Ft. Lauderdale, FL 33301-2248
(305)767-2100
Officer: Michael G. Lederman, CEO.
Ultimate Parent: Sunbeam/Oster.
Employee Count: 9400. Sales: 1066 M.

★ 59856 ★ Time Electronics
5200 NW 33rd Ave., Ste. 214
Ft. Lauderdale, FL 33309
(305)484-7778
Location Type: Branch office. Ultimate
Parent: Avnet. SIC: 5065—Electronic Parts
& Equipment Nec.

Gainesville

★ 59857 ★ Barnett Bank of
Alachua County, NA
1961 N. Main St.
Gainesville, FL 32609-3648
(904)338-6534
Company Type: Subsidiary. Location
Type: Branch office. Officer: Mike Mynatt,
Vice President. Ultimate Parent: Barnett
Banks. SIC: 6021—National Commercial
Banks.

★ 59858 ★ Barnett Bank of
Alachua County, NA
7606 Newberry Rd.
Gainesville, FL 32606-6726
(904)338-6548
Company Type: Subsidiary. Location
Type: Branch office. Officer: Marina Rojas,
Vice President. Ultimate Parent: Barnett
Banks. SIC: 6021—National Commercial
Banks.

★ 59859 ★ Barnett Bank of
Alachua County, NA
1116 W. University Ave.
Gainesville, FL 32601-5110
(904)338-6545
Company Type: Subsidiary. Location
Type: Branch office. Officer: Kathy Koebke,
Assistant Vice President. Ultimate Parent:
Barnett Banks. SIC: 6021—National
Commercial Banks.

★ 59860 ★ Barnett Bank of
Alachua County, NA
2627 NW 43rd St.
PO Box 147047
Gainesville, FL 32614-7047
(904)338-6601 Fax: (904)376-6382
Company Type: Subsidiary. Officer: Mark
D. Walker, President & CEO. Ultimate
Parent: Barnett Banks. SIC: 6021—National
Commercial Banks.

★ 59861 ★ Barnett Bank of
Alachua County, NA
2815 NW 13th St.
Gainesville, FL 32609-2861
(904)338-6670
Company Type: Subsidiary. Location
Type: Branch office. Officer: Lori Harrison,
Manager. Ultimate Parent: Barnett Banks.
SIC: 6021—National Commercial Banks.

★ 59862 ★ BFI Waste Systems
5002 SW 41st Blvd.
Gainesville, FL 32608-4929
(904)375-3908
Location Type: Branch office. Ultimate
Parent: Browning-Ferris Industries. SIC:
4953—Refuse Systems; 9111—Executive
Offices.

★ 59863 ★ Burdines Department
Store
6671 W. Newberry Rd.
Gainesville, FL 32605
(904)333-2321
Ultimate Parent: Federated Department
Stores. SIC: 5311—Department Stores.

★ 59864 ★ Burdines Travel
Bureau
Oaks Mall
Gainesville, FL 32601
(904)375-6065
Ultimate Parent: Federated Department
Stores. SIC: 4724—Travel Agencies.

★ 59865 ★ Career Image
6677 W. Newberry Rd.
Gainesville, FL 32605
(904)331-8416
Ultimate Parent: United States Shoe. SIC:
5651—Family Clothing Stores.

★ 59866 ★ Circus World
6463 W. Newberry Rd.
Gainesville, FL 32605
(904)331-1508
Ultimate Parent: Melville. SIC: 5945—
Hobby, Toy & Game Shops.

★ 59867 ★ Collective Mortgage
Service
2831 NW 41st St.
Gainesville, FL 32606
(904)373-0222
Ultimate Parent: Collective Bancorp. SIC:
6162—Mortgage Bankers &
Correspondents.

★ 59868 ★ Exxon Service Center
3325 W. University Ave.
Gainesville, FL 32607
(904)372-8436
Ultimate Parent: Exxon. SIC: 5541—
Gasoline Service Stations.

★ 59869 ★ First Union National
Bank of Florida
104 Main St.
Gainesville, FL 32601-3337
(904)335-3300
Location Type: Branch office. Ultimate
Parent: First Union Corp. SIC: 6021—
National Commercial Banks.

★ 59870 ★ First Union National
Bank of Florida
3501 W. University Ave.
Gainesville, FL 32607-2404
(904)335-3353
Location Type: Branch office. Ultimate
Parent: First Union Corp. SIC: 6021—
National Commercial Banks.

★ 59871 ★ First Union National
Bank of Florida
4210 NW 37th Pl., Ste. 100
Gainesville, FL 32602
(904)335-3450
Location Type: Branch office. Ultimate
Parent: First Union Corp. SIC: 6021—
National Commercial Banks.

★ 59872 ★ First Union National
Bank of Florida
3505 SW Archer Rd.
Gainesville, FL 32608-2410
(904)335-3460
Location Type: Branch office. Ultimate
Parent: First Union Corp. SIC: 6021—
National Commercial Banks.

★ 59873 ★ First Union National
Bank of Florida
1200 NW 23rd Blvd.
Gainesville, FL 32609-5149
(904)335-3470
Location Type: Branch office. Ultimate
Parent: First Union Corp. SIC: 6021—
National Commercial Banks.

★ 59874 ★ First Union National
Bank of Florida
5270 NW 34th St.
Gainesville, FL 32605-1154
(904)335-3491
Location Type: Branch office. Ultimate
Parent: First Union Corp. SIC: 6021—
National Commercial Banks.

★ 59875 ★ First Union National
Bank of Florida
3838 NW 13th St.
Gainesville, FL 32601-2178
(904)335-3433
Location Type: Branch office. Ultimate
Parent: First Union Corp. SIC: 6021—
National Commercial Banks.

★ 59876 ★ First Union National
Bank of Florida
US Hwy. 90 & Haffye St.
Gainesville, FL 32331-9501
(904)948-2122
Location Type: Branch office. Ultimate
Parent: First Union Corp. SIC: 6021—
National Commercial Banks.

★ 59877 ★ Food Lion
4100 NW 22nd Dr.
Gainesville, FL 32605
(904)371-2733
Ultimate Parent: Food Lion. SIC: 5411—
Grocery Stores.

★ 59878 ★ Food Lion Inc.
4100 NW 22nd Dr.
Gainesville, FL 32605
(904)371-2733
Ultimate Parent: Food Lion. SIC: 5411—
Grocery Stores.

★ 59879 ★ Greyhound Bus
Terminal
516 SW 4th Ave.
Gainesville, FL 32601
(904)376-5252
Ultimate Parent: Greyhound Lines Inc. SIC:
4111—Local & Suburban Transit; 4173—
Bus Terminal & Service Facilities.

★ 59880 ★ Hertz Rent-A-Car
Northeast Ave. 39th
Gainesville, FL 32601
(904)373-8444
Ultimate Parent: Hertz. SIC: 7514—
Passenger Car Rental.

★ 59881 ★ IBM Corp.
2511 NW 41st St.
Gainesville, FL 32606
(904)376-4535
Ultimate Parent: IBM. SIC: 5999—
Miscellaneous Retail Stores Nec.

★ 59882 ★ Jiffy Lube
2310 SW Archer Rd.
Gainesville, FL 32608
(904)371-1784
Ultimate Parent: Pennzoil.

★ 59883 ★ Jiffy Lube
1921 N. Main St.
Gainesville, FL 32609
(904)371-6958
Ultimate Parent: Pennzoil.

★ 59884 ★ Johnson Controls Inc.
4445 SW 35th Ter
Gainesville, FL 32608
(904)335-3933
Ultimate Parent: Johnson Controls Inc.
SIC: 8711—Engineering Services.

★ 59885 ★ Kentucky Fried
Chicken
3525 SW Archer Rd.
Gainesville, FL 32608
(904)375-7899
Ultimate Parent: Pepsico. SIC: 5812—
Eating Places.

★ 59886 ★　Kentucky Fried
Chicken
1502 N. Main St.
Gainesville, FL 32601
(904)373-5700
Ultimate Parent: Pepsico. SIC: 5812—
Eating Places.

★ 59887 ★　Kentucky Fried
Chicken
114 SW 34th St.
Gainesville, FL 32607
(904)372-3649
Ultimate Parent: Pepsico. SIC: 5812—
Eating Places.

★ 59888 ★　Kentucky Fried
Chicken
1231 E. University Ave.
Gainesville, FL 32601
(904)372-2984
Ultimate Parent: Pepsico. SIC: 5812—
Eating Places.

★ 59889 ★　Lane Bryant
Oaks Mall
Gainesville, FL 32601
(904)374-4213
Ultimate Parent: Limited. SIC: 5621—
Women's Clothing Stores.

★ 59890 ★　Lane Bryant
6678 W. Newberry Rd.
Gainesville, FL 32605
(904)331-4213
Ultimate Parent: Limited. SIC: 5651—
Family Clothing Stores.

★ 59891 ★　Lerner Shop
2546 NW 13th St.
Gainesville, FL 32609
(904)378-8836
Ultimate Parent: Limited. SIC: 5651—
Family Clothing Stores; 5651—Family
Clothing Stores.

★ 59892 ★　Mary Kay Cosmetics
2514 NW 31st Ter.
Gainesville, FL 32605
(904)378-7788
Ultimate Parent: Mary Kay Cosmetics. SIC:
5999—Miscellaneous Retail Stores Nec.

★ 59893 ★　Massachusetts Mutual
Life Insurance
2727 NW 43rd St.
Gainesville, FL 32606
(904)373-3970
Ultimate Parent: Massasucetts Mutual Life.
SIC: 6411—Insurance Agents, Brokers &
Service.

★ 59894 ★　Metal Container Corp.
5909 NW 18th Dr.
Gainesville, FL 32606
Officer: Joseph L. Waters. Ultimate
Parent: Anheuser-Busch. SIC: 3411—Metal
Cans.

★ 59895 ★　Metal Container Corp.
5909 NW 18th Dr.
Gainesville, FL 32606-1639
(904)378-8800
Officer: Joseph J. Waters. Ultimate
Parent: Ball Corp. SIC: 3411—Metal Cans.

★ 59896 ★　Pennzoil Products
4460 SW 35th Ter
Gainesville, FL 32608
(904)378-2468
Ultimate Parent: Pennzoil. SIC: 2911—
Petroleum Refining.

★ 59897 ★　Pepsi-Cola Bottling
Co.
1950 NE 27th Ave.
Gainesville, FL 32609
(904)376-0722
Officer: Ronaldo Swilley, Manager.
Ultimate Parent: Pepsico. SIC: 2086—
Bottled & Canned Soft Drinks.

★ 59898 ★　Petite Sophisticate
6601 W. Newberry Rd.
Gainesville, FL 32605
(904)331-4632
Ultimate Parent: United States Shoe. SIC:
5651—Family Clothing Stores.

★ 59899 ★　Pizza Hut
2320 NW 43rd St.
Gainesville, FL 32606
(904)373-6699
Ultimate Parent: Pepsico. SIC: 5812—
Eating Places.

★ 59900 ★　Pizza Hut
7545 W. Newberry Rd.
Gainesville, FL 32606
(904)332-4383
Ultimate Parent: Pepsico. SIC: 5812—
Eating Places.

★ 59901 ★　Pizza Hut
3511 SW Archer Rd.
Gainesville, FL 32608
(904)376-1681
Ultimate Parent: Pepsico. SIC: 5812—
Eating Places.

★ 59902 ★　Pizza Hut
2109 NW 13th St.
Gainesville, FL 32609
(904)372-5295
Ultimate Parent: Pepsico. SIC: 5812—
Eating Places.

★ 59903 ★　Pizza Hut
2320 SW Archer Rd.
Gainesville, FL 32608
(904)374-4440
Ultimate Parent: Pepsico. SIC: 5812—
Eating Places.

★ 59904 ★　Pizza Hut
Newberry Rd.
Gainesville, FL 32601
(904)373-4383
Ultimate Parent: Pepsico. SIC: 5812—
Eating Places.

★ 59905 ★　Publix Super Market
1200 NW 76th Blvd.
Gainesville, FL 32606
(904)332-0661
Ultimate Parent: Publix Super Markets.
SIC: 5411—Grocery Stores.

★ 59906 ★　Publix Super Market
1014 N. Main St.
Gainesville, FL 32601
(904)372-3614
Ultimate Parent: Publix Super Markets.
SIC: 5411—Grocery Stores.

★ 59907 ★　Publix Super Markets
1200 NW 76th Blvd.
Gainesville, FL 32606
(904)332-0661
Ultimate Parent: Publix Super Markets.
SIC: 5411—Grocery Stores.

★ 59908 ★　Radio Shack
6461 W. Newberry Rd.
Gainesville, FL 32605
(904)331-7217
Company Type: Division. Ultimate Parent:
Tandy Corp. SIC: 5719—Miscellaneous
Home Furnishings Stores.

★ 59909 ★　Radio Shack
2 NW 16th Ave.
Gainesville, FL 32601
(904)375-2336
Company Type: Division. Ultimate Parent:
Tandy Corp. SIC: 5731—Radio, Television
& Electronics Stores.

★ 59910 ★　Radio Shack
3224 SW 35th Blvd.
Gainesville, FL 32608
(904)375-2426
Company Type: Division. Ultimate Parent:
Tandy Corp. SIC: 5731—Radio, Television
& Electronics Stores.

★ 59911 ★　Radio Shack
2627 NW 13th St.
Gainesville, FL 32609
(904)373-1396
Company Type: Division. Ultimate Parent:
Tandy Corp. SIC: 5065—Electronic Parts &
Equipment Nec.

★ 59912 ★　Radio Shack
3315 SW Archer Rd.
Gainesville, FL 32608
(904)375-7062
Company Type: Division. Ultimate Parent:
Tandy Corp. SIC: 5065—Electronic Parts &
Equipment Nec.

★ 59913 ★　Radio Shack
Oaks Mall
Gainesville, FL 32601
(904)377-7217
Company Type: Division. Ultimate Parent:
Tandy Corp. SIC: 5046—Commercial
Equipment Nec.

★ 59914 ★　Rite Aid Drugs
4130 NW 16th Blvd.
Gainesville, FL 32605
(904)377-4306
Ultimate Parent: Rite Aid. SIC: 5912—Drug
Stores & Proprietary Stores.

★ 59915 ★　Rite Aid Store
Number Two Z
2504 NW 13th St.
Gainesville, FL 32609
(904)374-9542
Ultimate Parent: Rite Aid. SIC: 5912—Drug
Stores & Proprietary Stores.

★ 59916 ★　Ryder Truck Rental
4545 NW 13th St.
Gainesville, FL 32609
(904)372-1310
Ultimate Parent: Ryder System. SIC:
7389—Business Services Nec.

★ 59917 ★　Ryder Truck Rental
35 SE 16th Ave.
Gainesville, FL 32601
(904)373-3397
Ultimate Parent: Ryder System. SIC:
7359—Equipment Rental & Leasing Nec;
7513—Truck Rental & Leasing Without
Drivers.

★ 59918 ★　Service Merchandise
7111 NW 10th Pl
Gainesville, FL 32605
(904)331-7700
Ultimate Parent: Service Merchandise Co.,
Inc. SIC: 5399—Miscellaneous General
Merchandise Store.

★ 59919 ★　T J Maxx
1103 NW 76th Blvd.
Gainesville, FL 32606
(904)332-9917
Ultimate Parent: TJX. SIC: 5311—
Department Stores.

★ 59920 ★　Taco Bell
7400 W. Newberry Rd.
Gainesville, FL 32605
(904)332-1238
Ultimate Parent: Pepsico. SIC: 5812—
Eating Places.

★ 59921 ★　Taco Bell
3408 SW Archer Rd.
Gainesville, FL 32608
(904)372-0453
Ultimate Parent: Pepsico. SIC: 5812—
Eating Places.

★ 59922 ★　Texaco
1206 W. University Ave.
Gainesville, FL 32601
(904)375-3161
Ultimate Parent: Texaco. SIC: 5411—
Grocery Stores.

★ 59923 ★　Victoria's Secret
6419 W. Newberry Rd. B8
Gainesville, FL 32605
(904)331-5232
Ultimate Parent: Limited. SIC: 5651—
Family Clothing Stores.

★ 59924 ★　Wal Mart
2649 NW 13th St.
Gainesville, FL 32609
(904)378-0619
Ultimate Parent: Wal-Mart Stores, Inc. SIC:
5311—Department Stores.

★ 59925 ★　Wells Fargo Guard
Service
3131 NW 13th St.
Gainesville, FL 32609
(904)378-5788
Ultimate Parent: Borg Warner Automotive.
SIC: 7381—Detective & Armored Car
Services.

Gibsonton

★ 59926 ★　Agrico Chemical Co.
US Hwy.
Gibsonton, FL 33534
(813)677-8404
Ultimate Parent: Freeport-McMoran. SIC:
4491—Marine Cargo Handling.

Golden Gate

★ 59927 ★　Barnett Bank of
Naples
5101 Golden Gate Pky.
Golden Gate, FL 33999-7672
(813)263-1392
Company Type: Subsidiary. Location
Type: Branch office. Officer: Pamela G.
Johnson, Assistant Vice President. Ultimate
Parent: Barnett Banks. SIC: 6022—State
Commercial Banks.

Goldenrod

★ 59928 ★　Barnett Bank of
Central Florida, NA
7605 Aloma Ave.
Goldenrod, FL 32792
(407)646-3402
Company Type: Subsidiary. Location
Type: Branch office. Officer: Dave Hood,
Manager. Ultimate Parent: Barnett Banks.
SIC: 6021—National Commercial Banks.

Grant

★ 59929 ★　Zippy Mart Inc.
143 S. Us 1
Grant, FL 32949
(407)724-1377
Ultimate Parent: Crown Central Petroleum
Corp. SIC: 5411—Grocery Stores.

Green Springs

★ 59930 ★　Stevens Graphics
Business
1286 Harbor Rd.
Green Springs, FL 32043-8729
(904)284-1206
Officer: Tom Stubbs. Ultimate Parent:
BellSouth Corp. SIC: 2759—Commercial
Printing Nec.

Green Cove Springs

★ 59931 ★　First Union National
Bank of Florida
425 N. Orange Ave.
Green Cove Springs, FL 32043-2913
(904)284-5681
Location Type: Branch office. Ultimate
Parent: First Union Corp. SIC: 6021—
National Commercial Banks.

★ 59932 ★　Kentucky Fried
Chicken
422 Orange Ave. S
Green Cove Springs, FL 32043
(904)264-3813
Ultimate Parent: Pepsico. SIC: 5812—
Eating Places.

Gulf Breeze

★ 59933 ★　AmSouth Bank of
Florida
3373 Gulf Breeze Pky.
Gulf Breeze, FL 32566
(904)444-1071
Location Type: Branch office. Ultimate
Parent: AmSouth Bancorp. SIC: 6022—
State Commercial Banks.

★ 59934 ★　AmSouth Bank of
Florida
60 Northclife Dr.
Gulf Breeze, FL 32561-4495
(904)444-1065
Location Type: Branch office. Ultimate
Parent: AmSouth Bancorp. SIC: 6022—
State Commercial Banks.

★ 59935 ★　Barnett Bank of West
Florida
400 Gulf Breeze Pky.
Gulf Breeze, FL 32561-4464
(904)732-0271
Location Type: Branch office. Ultimate
Parent: Barnett Banks. SIC: 6021—National
Commercial Banks.

★ 59936 ★　Exxon Co. USA
103 Nightingale Ln.
Gulf Breeze, FL 32561
(904)932-5124
Ultimate Parent: Exxon. SIC: 5172—
Petroleum Products Nec.

★ 59937 ★ **Great Western Bank**
1177 Gulf Breeze Pky.
Gulf Breeze, FL 32561
(904)435-3034
Ultimate Parent: Great Western Financial
Corp. **SIC:** 6099—Functions Related to
Deposit Banking.

★ 59938 ★ **Pizza Hut**
2787 Gulf Breeze Pky.
Gulf Breeze, FL 32561
(904)934-1980
Ultimate Parent: Pepsico. **SIC:** 5812—
Eating Places.

Gulfport

★ 59939 ★ **AmSouth Bank of Florida**
5728 Gulfport Blvd. S
Gulfport, FL 33707-4835
(813)462-5101
Location Type: Branch office. **Ultimate
Parent:** AmSouth Bancorp. **SIC:** 6022—
State Commercial Banks.

★ 59940 ★ **Fortune Bank, ASB**
4901 Gulfport Blvd. S
Gulfport, FL 33707-4939
(813)321-9117
Location Type: Branch office. **Officer:**
Elizabeth Scarlett, Manager. **Ultimate
Parent:** Fortune Bancorp. **SIC:** 6021—
National Commercial Banks.

Haines City

★ 59941 ★ **Barnett Bank of Polk County**
Haines City Mall
631 W. US 92
Haines City, FL 33844
(813)422-5908
Company Type: Subsidiary. **Location
Type:** Branch office. **Officer:** JoAnn
Quadrozzi, Manager. **Ultimate Parent:**
Barnett Banks. **SIC:** 6022—State
Commercial Banks.

★ 59942 ★ **Barnett Bank of Polk County**
905 E. Hinson Ave.
Haines City, FL 33844-5247
(813)297-1425
Company Type: Subsidiary. **Location
Type:** Branch office. **Officer:** J. Theron
Stangry, Vice President. **Ultimate Parent:**
Barnett Banks. **SIC:** 6022—State
Commercial Banks.

★ 59943 ★ **Big Bear**
1305 Us 17-92 W
Haines City, FL 33844
(813)422-3412
Ultimate Parent: Penn Traffic. **SIC:** 5521—
Used Car Dealers.

★ 59944 ★ **First Union National Bank of Florida**
519 Jones Ave.
Haines City, FL 33844-4208
(813)422-6421
Location Type: Branch office. **Ultimate
Parent:** First Union Corp. **SIC:** 6021—
National Commercial Banks.

★ 59945 ★ **First Union National Bank of Florida**
1591 US Hwy. 27 S
Haines City, FL 33844-8666
(813)421-3452
Location Type: Branch office. **Ultimate
Parent:** First Union Corp. **SIC:** 6021—
National Commercial Banks.

★ 59946 ★ **Fleetwood Homes of Fl. Inc. 33**
1603 Grove Ave.
Haines City, FL 33844
Inc. **SIC:** 3711—Motor Vehicles & Car
Bodies.

★ 59947 ★ **Fleetwood Homes Florida Inc.**
1603 Grove Ave.
Haines City, FL 33844
(813)422-7591
Officer: Phill Tanner, Manager. **Ultimate
Parent:** Fleetwood Enterprises, Inc. **SIC:**
2451—Mobile Homes.

★ 59948 ★ **Fleetwood Motor Homes of Florida Inc.**
1603 Grove Ave. PO Box 37
Haines City, FL 33844
Ultimate Parent: Fleetwood Enterprises,
Inc. **SIC:** 2451—Mobile Homes.

★ 59949 ★ **Greyhound Bus Station**
802 Ingraham Ave.
Haines City, FL 33844
(813)422-6245
Ultimate Parent: Greyhound Lines Inc. **SIC:**
4131—Intercity & Rural Bus Transportation.

★ 59950 ★ **Kentucky Fried Chicken**
1100 Us 27 N
Haines City, FL 33844
(813)422-0090
Ultimate Parent: Pepsico. **SIC:** 5812—
Eating Places.

★ 59951 ★ **Pizza Hut**
127 W. Hinson Ave.
Haines City, FL 33844
(813)422-5945
Ultimate Parent: Pepsico. **SIC:** 5812—
Eating Places.

★ 59952 ★ **Radio Shack**
1170 Us Hwy. 27 N
Haines City, FL 33844
Company Type: Division. **Ultimate Parent:**
Tandy Corp. **SIC:** 7629—Electrical Repair
Shops Nec.

★ 59953 ★ **Ryder Truck Rental**
505 Us 17-92 W
Haines City, FL 33844
(813)422-7183
Ultimate Parent: Ryder System. **SIC:**
7513—Truck Rental & Leasing Without
Drivers.

★ 59954 ★ **Texaco Food Mart**
501 Us 17-92 N
Haines City, FL 33844
(813)421-4822
Ultimate Parent: Texaco. **SIC:** 5411—
Grocery Stores.

★ 59955 ★ **Texaco Food Mart**
7110 State Rd. 544 E
Haines City, FL 33844
(813)421-4724
Ultimate Parent: Texaco. **SIC:** 5411—
Grocery Stores.

★ 59956 ★ **Wal Mart Discount Cities**
1150 Us Hwy. 27 N
Haines City, FL 33844
(813)533-0541
Ultimate Parent: Wal-Mart Stores, Inc. **SIC:**
5912—Drug Stores & Proprietary Stores.

Hallandale

★ 59957 ★ **American Savings of FL FSB**
2500 E. Hallandale Beach Blvd.
Hallandale, FL 33009-4833
(305)458-4666
Company Type: Branch. **Ultimate Parent:**
American Savings of Florida. **SIC:** 6035—
Federal Savings Institutions; 6021—National
Commercial Banks.

★ 59958 ★ **Barnett Bank of Broward County, NA**
801 E. Hallandale Beach Blvd.
Hallandale, FL 33009-4486
(305)457-1137
Company Type: Subsidiary. **Location
Type:** Branch office. **Officer:** Nancy Jones,
Manager. **Ultimate Parent:** Barnett Banks.
SIC: 6021—National Commercial Banks.

★ 59959 ★ **City National Bank of Florida**
1995 E. Hallandale Beach Blvd.
Hallandale, FL 33009-4708
(305)454-5000
Company Type: Branch. **Officer:** Eugene
Yagle, Vice President. **Ultimate Parent:**
City National Corp. **SIC:** 6022—State
Commercial Banks; 6141—Personal Credit
Institutions; 6211—Security Brokers &
Dealers.

★ 59960 ★ **Kentucky Fried Chicken**
850 W. Hallandale Beach Blvd.
Hallandale, FL 33009
(305)454-7179
Ultimate Parent: Pepsico. **SIC:** 5812—
Eating Places.

★ 59961 ★ **Linens N Things Inc.**
1470 E. Hallandale Beach Blvd.
Hallandale, FL 33009
(305)458-4661
Ultimate Parent: Melville. **SIC:** 5719—
Miscellaneous Home Furnishings Stores.

★ 59962 ★ **McDonalds**
1011 W. Hallandale Beach Blvd.
Hallandale, FL 33009
(305)454-7921
Ultimate Parent: McDonald's.
SIC: 5812—Eating Places.

★ 59963 ★ **Radio Shack**
1725 E. Hallandale Beach Blvd.
Hallandale, FL 33009
(305)454-9718
Company Type: Division. **Ultimate Parent:**
Tandy Corp. **SIC:** 5065—Electronic Parts &
Equipment Nec.

★ 59964 ★ **Rite Aid Disc Pharmacies**
1065 W. Hallandale Beach Blvd.
Hallandale, FL 33009
(305)458-6121
Ultimate Parent: Rite Aid. **SIC:** 5912—Drug
Stores & Proprietary Stores.

★ 59965 ★ **Ryder Truck Rental**
Hallandale, FL 33009
(305)923-7482
Ultimate Parent: Ryder System. **SIC:**
7389—Business Services Nec.

★ 59966 ★ **Walgreen Drug Stores**
1000 W. Hallandale Beach Blvd.
Hallandale, FL 33009
(305)456-3990
Ultimate Parent: Walgreen Co. **SIC:**
7389—Business Services Nec.

Hallendale

★ 59967 ★ **American Savings of Florida, FSB**
2500 E. Hallandale Beach Blvd.
Hallendale, FL 33009-4817
(305)458-4666
Location Type: Branch office. **Officer:**
Sheryl Wolfman, Manager. **Ultimate Parent:**
American Savings of Florida. **SIC:** 6035—
Federal Savings Institutions; 6211—Security
Brokers & Dealers.

Havana

★ 59968 ★ **Piggly Wiggly**
Hwy. 27
Havana, FL 32333
(904)539-6904
Ultimate Parent: Bruno's. **SIC:** 5411—
Grocery Stores.

★ 59969 ★ **Quincy State Bank**
201 S. Main St.
Havana, FL 32333-1658
(904)539-8114
Company Type: Subsidiary. **Location
Type:** Branch office. **Officer:** George T.
Rude, Mgr. **Ultimate Parent:** Synovus
Financial Corp. **SIC:** 6021—National
Commercial Banks.

Hawthorne

★ 59970 ★ **Georgia Pacific Corp.**
Gordon Chapel Rd.
Hawthorne, FL 32640
(904)481-4311
Officer: Wayne Richardson, Manager.
Ultimate Parent: Georgia-Pacific. **SIC:**
2435—Hardwood Veneer & Plywood;
2491—Wood Preserving.

★ 59971 ★ **Georgia-Pacific Corp. Hawthorne Plywood**
Gordon Chapel Rd.
Hawthorne, FL 32460
Ultimate Parent: Georgia-Pacific. **SIC:**
2436—Softwood Veneer & Plywood.

★ 59972 ★ **Kentucky Fried Chicken**
Keystone Hts
Hawthorne, FL 32640
(904)473-2445
Ultimate Parent: Pepsico. **SIC:** 5812—
Eating Places.

★ 59973 ★ **Texaco Corp.**
N Hwy. 301
Hawthorne, FL 32640
(904)481-2253
Ultimate Parent: Texaco. **SIC:** 5541—
Gasoline Service Stations.

Hialeah

★ 59974 ★ **Barnett Bank of South Florida, NA**
1 E. 49th St.
Hialeah, FL 33013-1896
(305)825-5900
Company Type: Subsidiary. **Location
Type:** Branch office. **Officer:** Placido
Martinez, Manager. **Ultimate Parent:**
Barnett Banks. **SIC:** 6021—National
Commercial Banks.

★ 59975 ★ **Barnett Bank of South Florida, NA**
101 Hialeah Dr.
Hialeah, FL 33010-5299
(305)883-2400
Company Type: Subsidiary. **Location
Type:** Branch office. **Officer:** Albert Perez,
Manager. **Ultimate Parent:** Barnett Banks.
SIC: 6021—National Commercial Banks.

★ 59976 ★ **Barnett Bank of South Florida, NA**
8210 NW 103rd St.
Hialeah, FL 33016-2200
(305)883-2400
Company Type: Subsidiary. **Location
Type:** Branch office. **Officer:** Mory
Rodriguez, Manager. **Ultimate Parent:**
Barnett Banks. **SIC:** 6021—National
Commercial Banks.

★ 59977 ★ **Boise Cascade**
Office Products Division
5400 NW 163rd St.
Hialeah, FL 33014
(305)620-9100
Ultimate Parent: Boise Cascade. **SIC:**
5112—Stationery & Office Supplies.

★ 59978 ★ **Casual Corner Inc.**
1645 W. 49th St.
Hialeah, FL 33012
(305)557-1598
Ultimate Parent: United States Shoe. **SIC:**
5621—Women's Clothing Stores.

★ 59979 ★ **Citgo**
1598 W. 68th St.
Hialeah, FL 33014
(305)821-0281
Ultimate Parent: Citgo Petroleum. **SIC:**
5599—Automotive Dealers Nec.

★ 59980 ★ **Citgo Quick Mart**
50 SE 8th Ave.
Hialeah, FL 33010
(305)888-2747
Ultimate Parent: Citgo Petroleum. **SIC:**
5541—Gasoline Service Stations.

★ 59981 ★ **Citizens Federal Bank, FSB**
401 W. 49th St.
Hialeah, FL 33012-3690
(305)557-4477
Location Type: Branch office. **Officer:**
Barbara Moreno, Manager. **Ultimate
Parent:** CSF Holdings. **SIC:** 6021—National
Commercial Banks.

★ 59982 ★ **Citizens Federal Bank, FSB**
400 Hialeah Dr.
Hialeah, FL 33010-5394
(305)884-6111
Location Type: Branch office. **Ultimate
Parent:** CSF Holdings. **SIC:** 6021—National
Commercial Banks.

★ 59983 ★ **Express**
1665 W. 49th St.
Hialeah, FL 33012
(305)556-5054
Ultimate Parent: Limited. **SIC:** 5621—
Women's Clothing Stores.

★ 59984 ★   **First Union National Bank of Florida**
1225 W. 68th St.
Hialeah, FL 33014-4570
(305)795-2975
Location Type: Branch office. **Ultimate Parent:** First Union Corp. **SIC:** 6021—National Commercial Banks.

★ 59985 ★   **First Union National Bank of Florida**
1900 W. 49th St.
Hialeah, FL 33012-2989
(305)364-2450
Location Type: Branch office. **Ultimate Parent:** First Union Corp. **SIC:** 6021—National Commercial Banks.

★ 59986 ★   **Grand Union Co**
1000 W. 36th Pl
Hialeah, FL 33012
(305)949-5724
Ultimate Parent: Grand Union Holdings Corp. **SIC:** 5141—Groceries—General Line.

★ 59987 ★   **Greyhound Bus Lines**
93 W. Okeechobee Rd.
Hialeah, FL 33010
(305)885-1413
Ultimate Parent: Greyhound Lines Inc. **SIC:** 4212—Local Trucking Without Storage.

★ 59988 ★   **International Computer Service**
585 NW 161st St.
Hialeah, FL 33014
(305)949-7674
Location Type: Branch office. **Officer:** Jerome Godin. **Ultimate Parent:** American International Group, Inc. **SIC:** 7384—Photofinishing Laboratories.

★ 59989 ★   **International Computer Service Inc.**
6001 NW 153rd St., Ste. 140
Hialeah, FL 33014-2447
(305)558-0052
Location Type: Branch office. **Officer:** Timothy Morgan. **Ultimate Parent:** American International Group, Inc. **SIC:** 7374—Data Processing & Preparation; 5734—Computer & Software Stores; 7336—Commercial Art & Graphic Design; 7389—Business Services Nec.

★ 59990 ★   **Jiffy Lube of Hialeah**
4100 W. 12th Ave.
Hialeah, FL 33012
(305)362-9572
Ultimate Parent: Pennzoil. **SIC:** 7538—General Automotive Repair Shops.

★ 59991 ★   **Kelly Springfield Tire**
1143 W. 68th St.
Hialeah, FL 33014
(305)633-6359
Ultimate Parent: Goodyear Tire & Rubber. **SIC:** 5531—Automobile & Home Supply Stores.

★ 59992 ★   **Kentucky Fried Chicken**
444 Hialeah Dr.
Hialeah, FL 33010
(305)888-7022
Ultimate Parent: Pepsico. **SIC:** 5812—Eating Places.

★ 59993 ★   **Kentucky Fried Chicken**
1325 E. 4th Ave.
Hialeah, FL 33010
(305)888-7632
Ultimate Parent: Pepsico. **SIC:** 5812—Eating Places.

★ 59994 ★   **Kentucky Fried Chicken**
444 Hialeah Dr.
Hialeah, FL 33010
(305)888-6946
Ultimate Parent: Pepsico. **SIC:** 5812—Eating Places.

★ 59995 ★   **Kentucky Fried Chicken**
14411 Commerce Way 250
Hialeah, FL 33016
(305)558-6150
Ultimate Parent: Pepsico. **SIC:** 5812—Eating Places.

★ 59996 ★   **Lerner Shop**
1705 W. 49th St.
Hialeah, FL 33012
(305)823-1391
Ultimate Parent: Limited. **SIC:** 5621—Women's Clothing Stores.

★ 59997 ★   **The Limited**
1675 W. 49th St.
Hialeah, FL 33012
(305)557-7641
Ultimate Parent: Limited. **SIC:** 5621—Women's Clothing Stores.

★ 59998 ★   **Mary Kay Cosmetics**
3205 W. 16th Ave.
Hialeah, FL 33012
(305)556-1927
Ultimate Parent: Mary Kay Cosmetics. **SIC:** 5999—Miscellaneous Retail Stores Nec.

★ 59999 ★   **Palmetto General Hospital**
2001 W. 68th St.
Hialeah, FL 33016
(305)823-5000
Officer: Edward Tudanger, Executive Director. **Ultimate Parent:** American Medical Holdings. **SIC:** 8062—General Medical & Surgical Hospitals.

★ 60000 ★   **Pizza Hut**
4975 W. 12th Ave.
Hialeah, FL 33012
(305)556-0741
Ultimate Parent: Pepsico. **SIC:** 5812—Eating Places.

★ 60001 ★   **Pizza Hut**
8390 W. 12th Ave.
Hialeah, FL 33014
(305)556-0051
Ultimate Parent: Pepsico. **SIC:** 5812—Eating Places.

★ 60002 ★   **Pizza Hut**
1801 E. 4th Ave.
Hialeah, FL 33010
(305)883-0050
Ultimate Parent: Pepsico. **SIC:** 5812—Eating Places.

★ 60003 ★   **Porter Cable Corp.**
16375 NW 57th Ave.
Hialeah, FL 33014
(305)624-2523
Ultimate Parent: Pentair. **SIC:** 7699—Repair Services Nec.

★ 60004 ★   **Pulte Home Corp.**
14100 Palmetto Expy.
Hialeah, FL 33016
(305)556-0764
Ultimate Parent: Pulte. **SIC:** 6552—Subdividers & Developers Nec.

★ 60005 ★   **Radio Shack**
1150 W. 49th St.
Hialeah, FL 33012
(305)821-6656
Company Type: Division. **Ultimate Parent:** Tandy Corp. **SIC:** 5065—Electronic Parts & Equipment Nec.

★ 60006 ★   **Radio Shack**
Westland Mall
Hialeah, FL 33012
(305)825-4191
Company Type: Division. **Ultimate Parent:** Tandy Corp. **SIC:** 5065—Electronic Parts & Equipment Nec.

★ 60007 ★   **Radio Shack**
1550 W. 84th St.
Hialeah, FL 33014
(305)558-2401
Company Type: Division. **Ultimate Parent:** Tandy Corp. **SIC:** 5734—Computer & Software Stores.

★ 60008 ★   **Ryder Truck Rental**
5801 NW 151st St.
Hialeah, FL 33014
(305)558-7467
Ultimate Parent: Ryder System. **SIC:** 7513—Truck Rental & Leasing Without Drivers.

★ 60009 ★   **Service Merchandise**
1700 W. 49th St.
Hialeah, FL 33012
(305)556-1400
Ultimate Parent: Service Merchandise Co., Inc. **SIC:** 5961—Catalog & Mail-Order Houses.

★ 60010 ★   **Shell Service Station**
4002 W. 12th Ave.
Hialeah, FL 33012
(305)825-7888
Ultimate Parent: Shell Oil Co. **SIC:** 5541—Gasoline Service Stations.

★ 60011 ★   **Taco Bell**
555 Hialeah Dr.
Hialeah, FL 33010
(305)883-4675
Ultimate Parent: Pepsico. **SIC:** 5812—Eating Places.

★ 60012 ★   **Texaco**
7701 NW 103rd St.
Hialeah, FL 33016
(305)822-4367
Ultimate Parent: Texaco. **SIC:** 5541—Gasoline Service Stations.

★ 60013 ★   **Thom Mcan**
Westland Mall
Hialeah, FL 33012
(305)558-9295
Ultimate Parent: Melville. **SIC:** 5661—Shoe Stores.

★ 60014 ★   **3M & D Inc.**
790 W. 27th St.
Hialeah, FL 33010-1216
(305)885-9866
Ultimate Parent: Minnesota Mining & Mfg. **SIC:** 5136—Men's/Boys' Clothing.

★ 60015 ★   **Toys R US**
500 W. 49th St.
Hialeah, FL 33012
(305)557-6704
Ultimate Parent: Toys "R" US. **SIC:** 5641—Children's & Infants' Wear Stores.

★ 60016 ★   **Victoria's Secret**
1695 W. 49th St.
Hialeah, FL 33012
(305)821-1372
Ultimate Parent: Limited. **SIC:** 5699—Miscellaneous Apparel & Accessory Stores.

★ 60017 ★   **Waldenbooks**
Westland Mall
Hialeah, FL 33012
(305)823-9032
Ultimate Parent: K-Mart. **SIC:** 5942—Book Stores.

★ 60018 ★   **Walgreen Drug Stores**
500 W. 49th St.
Hialeah, FL 33012
(305)557-4623
Ultimate Parent: Walgreen Co. **SIC:** 5912—Drug Stores & Proprietary Stores.

★ 60019 ★   **Walt Disney World**
1671 W. 37th Ave.
Hialeah, FL 33012
(305)828-1885
Ultimate Parent: Walt Disney Co. **SIC:** 7389—Business Services Nec.

★ 60020 ★   **Walt Disney World**
1140 W. 50th St.
Hialeah, FL 33012
(305)828-3611
Ultimate Parent: Walt Disney Co.

★ 60021 ★   **ZEP Manufacturing Co.**
5551 NW 159th St.
Hialeah, FL 33014
(305)624-8488
Officer: Bert Slater, Manager. **Ultimate Parent:** National Service Industries. **SIC:** 2842—Polishes & Sanitation Goods; 2899—Chemical Preparations Nec; 3589—Service Industry Machinery Nec.

Hialeah Gdns

★ 60022 ★   **Radio Shack**
15464 NW 77th Ct
Hialeah Gdns, FL 33016
(305)822-8892
Company Type: Division. **Ultimate Parent:** Tandy Corp. **SIC:** 5734—Computer & Software Stores.

★ 60023 ★   **Rite Aid Discount Pharmacie**
15490 NW 77th Ct
Hialeah Gdns, FL 33016
(305)821-9106
Ultimate Parent: Rite Aid. **SIC:** 5912—Drug Stores & Proprietary Stores.

High Springs

★ 60024 ★   **Barnett Bank of Alachua County, NA**
35 N. Main St.
High Springs, FL 32615
(904)454-1067
Company Type: Subsidiary. **Location Type:** Branch office. **Officer:** Jackie Terry, Assistant Vice President. **Ultimate Parent:** Barnett Banks. **SIC:** 6021—National Commercial Banks.

Hobe Sound

★ 60025 ★   **Ace Hardware Stores**
100 N. Old Dixie Hwy.
Hobe Sound, FL 33455
(407)746-4611
Ultimate Parent: Ace Hardware. **SIC:** 5211—Lumber & Other Building Materials.

★ 60026 ★   **Barnett Bank of Martin County, NA**
11900 S. Federal Hwy.
Hobe Sound, FL 33455-5321
(407)221-3500 **Fax:** (407)288-9739
Company Type: Subsidiary. **Location Type:** Branch office. **Officer:** David M. Strickland, President & CEO. **Ultimate Parent:** Barnett Banks. **SIC:** 6021—National Commercial Banks.

Holiday

★ 60027 ★   **AmSouth Bank of Florida**
2338 US Hwy. 19 N
Holiday, FL 34691-3995
(813)937-5173
Location Type: Branch office. **Ultimate Parent:** AmSouth Bancorp. **SIC:** 6022—State Commercial Banks.

★ 60028 ★   **Barnett Bank of Pasco County**
2865 US Hwy. 19
Holiday, FL 34691-2709
(813)847-7114
Company Type: Subsidiary. **Location Type:** Branch office. **Officer:** George Grover, Manager. **Ultimate Parent:** Barnett Banks. **SIC:** 6022—State Commercial Banks.

★ 60029 ★   **Barnett Bank of Pasco County**
4539 Bartlet Rd.
Holiday, FL 34690-5533
(813)847-7250
Company Type: Subsidiary. **Location Type:** Branch office. **Officer:** Melanie Bancroft, Manager. **Ultimate Parent:** Barnett Banks. **SIC:** 6022—State Commercial Banks.

★ 60030 ★   **Citizens Federal Bank, FSB**
1714 US Hwy. 19
Holiday, FL 34691
(813)937-6183
Location Type: Branch office. **Ultimate Parent:** CSF Holdings.

Hollandale

★ 60031 ★   **Savings of America, FSB**
Home Savings of America
1401-B E. Hollandale Beach Blvd.
Hollandale, FL 33009-4624
(305)456-3600
Location Type: Branch office. **Officer:** Guy Peets, Manager. **Ultimate Parent:** H. F. Ahmanson. **SIC:** 6021—National Commercial Banks.

Holly Hill

★ 60032 ★   **Citizens Federal Bank, FSB**
237 Riverside Dr.
Holly Hill, FL 32117-4933
(904)253-5666
Location Type: Branch office. **Officer:** Karen Bloodworth, Manager. **Ultimate Parent:** CSF Holdings. **SIC:** 6021—National Commercial Banks.

Hollywood

★ 60033 ★   American General Finance
8376 Pines Blvd.
Hollywood, FL 33024-6616
(305)433-7700
Ultimate Parent: American General Corp.
SIC: 6141—Personal Credit Institutions; 6162—Mortgage Bankers & Correspondents.

★ 60034 ★   American General Finance Inc.
8376 Pines Blvd.
Hollywood, FL 33024-6616
(305)433-7700
Location Type: Branch office. **Ultimate Parent:** American General Corp. **SIC:** 6141—Personal Credit Institutions; 6162—Mortgage Bankers & Correspondents.

★ 60035 ★   American Savings of FL FSB
1653 N. Hiatus Rd.
Hollywood, FL 33026-2129
(305)432-8044
Location Type: Branch office. **Ultimate Parent:** American Savings of Florida. **SIC:** 6035—Federal Savings Institutions.

★ 60036 ★   American Savings of FL FSB
4555 Sheridan St.
Hollywood, FL 33021-3515
(305)966-0870
Location Type: Branch office. **Ultimate Parent:** American Savings of Florida. **SIC:** 6035—Federal Savings Institutions; 6021—National Commercial Banks.

★ 60037 ★   American Savings of Florida
294 S. Flamingo Rd.
Hollywood, FL 33027-1769
(305)435-7272
Location Type: Branch office. **Ultimate Parent:** American Savings of Florida. **SIC:** 6035—Federal Savings Institutions; 6021—National Commercial Banks.

★ 60038 ★   American Savings of Florida, FSB
5361 Sheridan St.
Hollywood, FL 33021-3587
(305)966-0870
Location Type: Branch office. **Ultimate Parent:** American Savings of Florida. **SIC:** 6035—Federal Savings Institutions; 6211—Security Brokers & Dealers.

★ 60039 ★   Barnett Bank of Broward County, NA
2655 N. 60th Ave.
Hollywood, FL 33021-2702
(305)963-8395
Company Type: Subsidiary. **Location Type:** Branch office. **Officer:** Jackie Lungi, Manager. **Ultimate Parent:** Barnett Banks. **SIC:** 6021—National Commercial Banks.

★ 60040 ★   Barnett Bank of Broward County, NA
4080 S. Ocean Dr.
Hollywood, FL 33019
(305)454-7501
Company Type: Subsidiary. **Location Type:** Branch office. **Officer:** Denise Casale, Manager. **Ultimate Parent:** Barnett Banks. **SIC:** 6021—National Commercial Banks.

★ 60041 ★   Barnett Bank of Broward County, NA
1900 Tyler St.
Hollywood, FL 33021
(305)921-3839
Company Type: Subsidiary. **Location Type:** Branch office. **Officer:** Andres Pintaluga, Manager. **Ultimate Parent:** Barnett Banks. **SIC:** 6021—National Commercial Banks.

★ 60042 ★   Barnett Bank of Broward County, NA
3509 N. Ocean Dr.
Hollywood, FL 33019-3807
(305)925-7800
Company Type: Subsidiary. **Location Type:** Branch office. **Officer:** Alice Prestia, Manager. **Ultimate Parent:** Barnett Banks. **SIC:** 6021—National Commercial Banks.

★ 60043 ★   Burdines
Hollywood Fashion Ctr.
Hollywood, FL 33021
(305)985-2399
Ultimate Parent: Federated Department Stores. **SIC:** 5311—Department Stores.

★ 60044 ★   Burdines
1120 SW 86th Ave.
Hollywood, FL 33025
(305)985-2211
Ultimate Parent: Federated Department Stores.

★ 60045 ★   Burdines Beauty Salon
2823 Jackson St.
Hollywood, FL 33020
(305)940-4421
Ultimate Parent: Federated Department Stores. **SIC:** 5995—Optical Goods Stores.

★ 60046 ★   Burdines Department Store
1240 SW 86th Ave.
Hollywood, FL 33025
(305)825-7202
Ultimate Parent: Federated Department Stores.

★ 60047 ★   California Federal Bank, FSB
4601 Sheridan St.
Hollywood, FL 33021-3412
(305)981-8400
Location Type: Branch office. **Officer:** William Duesler, Manager. **Ultimate Parent:** California Federal Bank. **SIC:** 6021—National Commercial Banks.

★ 60048 ★   Casual Corner
250 Hollywood Mall
Hollywood, FL 33021
(305)981-3506
Ultimate Parent: United States Shoe. **SIC:** 5621—Women's Clothing Stores.

★ 60049 ★   Circus World Toys
Hollywood Fash Ctr.
Hollywood, FL 33021
(305)981-8455
Ultimate Parent: Melville. **SIC:** 5945—Hobby, Toy & Game Shops.

★ 60050 ★   Citibank (Florida), NA
3440 Hollywood Blvd.
Hollywood, FL 33021-6927
(305)962-0477
Location Type: Branch office. **Ultimate Parent:** Citicorp. **SIC:** 6021—National Commercial Banks.

★ 60051 ★   Citibank, FSB
3800 S. Ocean Dr.
Hollywood, FL 33019-2927
(305)457-8005
Location Type: Branch office. **Ultimate Parent:** Citicorp. **SIC:** 6021—National Commercial Banks.

★ 60052 ★   Citizens Federal Bank, FSB
4008 S. Ocean Dr.
Hollywood, FL 33019-3010
(305)456-7166
Location Type: Branch office. **Officer:** JoAnne DePrima, Manager. **Ultimate Parent:** CSF Holdings. **SIC:** 6021—National Commercial Banks.

★ 60053 ★   Coca-Cola Botting Co. of Miami
3350 Pembroke Rd.
Hollywood, FL 33021
Ultimate Parent: Coca-Cola Enterprises. **SIC:** 2086—Bottled & Canned Soft Drinks.

★ 60054 ★   Coca-Cola Bottling Co. of Miami
3350 Pembroke Rd.
Hollywood, FL 33021
Ultimate Parent: Coca-Cola Enterprises. **SIC:** 2086—Bottled & Canned Soft Drinks.

★ 60055 ★   Coca-Cola Bottling Co. of Miami Inc.
3350 Pembroke Rd.
Hollywood, FL 33021
Ultimate Parent: Coca-Cola Enterprises. **SIC:** 2086—Bottled & Canned Soft Drinks.

★ 60056 ★   Coca-Cola Bottling of Miami Inc.
3350 Pembroke Rd.
Hollywood, FL 33021
Ultimate Parent: Coca-Cola Enterprises. **SIC:** 2086—Bottled & Canned Soft Drinks.

★ 60057 ★   First Union National Bank of Florida
1600 S. Federal Hwy.
Hollywood, FL 33028-6346
(305)985-3621
Location Type: Branch office. **Ultimate Parent:** First Union Corp. **SIC:** 6021—National Commercial Banks.

★ 60058 ★   First Union National Bank of Florida
3325 Hollywood Blvd.
Hollywood, FL 33021-6971
(305)985-2130
Location Type: Branch office. **Ultimate Parent:** First Union Corp. **SIC:** 6021—National Commercial Banks.

★ 60059 ★   First Union National Bank of Florida
6015 Washington St.
Hollywood, FL 33023-1366
(305)985-3565
Location Type: Branch office. **Ultimate Parent:** First Union Corp. **SIC:** 6021—National Commercial Banks.

★ 60060 ★   Florida Coca-Cola Bottling Co.
3350 Pembroke Rd.
Hollywood, FL 33021-8320
(305)985-5000
Officer: Oscar Munoz, CEO. **Ultimate Parent:** Coca-Cola Enterprises. **SIC:** 2086—Bottled & Canned Soft Drinks. **Employee Count:** 2500.

★ 60061 ★   The Gap
101 S. State Rd. 7
Hollywood, FL 33023
(305)987-5980
Ultimate Parent: GAP. **SIC:** 5611—Men's & Boys' Clothing Stores.

★ 60062 ★   Gap Stores Inc.
101 S. State Rd. 7
Hollywood, FL 33023
(305)987-5980
Ultimate Parent: GAP. **SIC:** 5611—Men's & Boys' Clothing Stores.

★ 60063 ★   Greyhound Bus Lines
1707 Tyler St.
Hollywood, FL 33020
(305)922-8228
Ultimate Parent: Greyhound Lines Inc. **SIC:** 4111—Local & Suburban Transit.

★ 60064 ★   Hit or Miss
8040 Pines Blvd.
Hollywood, FL 33024
(305)435-9820
Ultimate Parent: TJX. **SIC:** 5621—Women's Clothing Stores.

★ 60065 ★   Jiffy Lube of Davie
3221 N. University Dr.
Hollywood, FL 33024
(305)437-9217
Ultimate Parent: Pennzoil. **SIC:** 7538—General Automotive Repair Shops.

★ 60066 ★   Jiffy Lube of Pembroke
8329 Pines Blvd.
Hollywood, FL 33024
(305)437-8525
Ultimate Parent: Pennzoil. **SIC:** 7538—General Automotive Repair Shops.

★ 60067 ★   Johnson Controls Inc.
200 Oakwood Ln.
Hollywood, FL 33020
(305)921-8500
Ultimate Parent: Johnson Controls Inc. **SIC:** 7623—Refrigeration Services Repair.

★ 60068 ★   Kentucky Fried Chicken
5951 Sheridan St.
Hollywood, FL 33021
(305)963-5226
Ultimate Parent: Pepsico. **SIC:** 5812—Eating Places.

★ 60069 ★   Kentucky Fried Chicken
6090 Miramar Pky.
Hollywood, FL 33023
(305)987-7806
Ultimate Parent: Pepsico. **SIC:** 5812—Eating Places.

★ 60070 ★   Kentucky Fried Chicken
1836 N. University Dr.
Hollywood, FL 33024
(305)432-6560
Ultimate Parent: Pepsico. **SIC:** 5812—Eating Places.

★ 60071 ★   Kentucky Fried Chicken
5959 Hollywood Blvd.
Hollywood, FL 33021
(305)983-0456
Ultimate Parent: Pepsico. **SIC:** 5812—Eating Places.

★ 60072 ★   Lane Bryant
Hollywood Fash Ctr.
Hollywood, FL 33021
(305)961-3585
Ultimate Parent: Limited. **SIC:** 5621—Women's Clothing Stores.

★ 60073 ★   Lerner Shop
3201 Hollywood Blvd.
Hollywood, FL 33021
(305)987-6020
Ultimate Parent: Limited. **SIC:** 5621—Women's Clothing Stores.

★ 60074 ★   Lerner Shop
101 S. State Rd. 7
Hollywood, FL 33023
(305)961-5084
Ultimate Parent: Limited. **SIC:** 5621—Women's Clothing Stores.

★ 60075 ★   Mary Kay Cosmetics
2020 NW 107th Ave.
Hollywood, FL 33026
(305)435-3131
Ultimate Parent: Mary Kay Cosmetics. **SIC:** 5999—Miscellaneous Retail Stores Nec.

★ 60076 ★   Matco Tools Dist
6725 W. Dogwood Dr.
Hollywood, FL 33023
(305)964-3769
Ultimate Parent: Danaher Corp.

★ 60077 ★   Mini Mart Supplies
223622 PO Box
Hollywood, FL 33022
(305)962-1517
Ultimate Parent: Kroger.

★ 60078 ★   Mobil Oil Corp.
12351 Taft St.
Hollywood, FL 33026
(305)432-7577
Ultimate Parent: Mobil. **SIC:** 5599—Automotive Dealers Nec.

★ 60079 ★   Mobil Oil Corp.
200 S. Flamingo Rd.
Hollywood, FL 33027
(305)437-3634
Ultimate Parent: Mobil. **SIC:** 5599—Automotive Dealers Nec.

★ 60080 ★   Pizza Hut
2040 N. University Dr.
Hollywood, FL 33024
(305)432-5906
Ultimate Parent: Pepsico. **SIC:** 5812—Eating Places.

★ 60081 ★   Pizza Hut
2404 N. University Dr.
Hollywood, FL 33024
(305)432-0033
Ultimate Parent: Pepsico. **SIC:** 5812—Eating Places.

★ 60082 ★   Pizza Hut
7996 Miramar Pky.
Hollywood, FL 33023
(305)983-3882
Ultimate Parent: Pepsico. **SIC:** 5812—Eating Places.

★ 60083 ★   Pizza Hut
2311 N. 60th Ave.
Hollywood, FL 33021
(305)987-6450
Ultimate Parent: Pepsico. **SIC:** 5812—Eating Places.

★ 60084 ★ **Publix Super Market**
1657 N. Hiatus Rd.
Hollywood, FL 33026
(305)432-1505
Ultimate Parent: Publix Super Markets.
SIC: 5411—Grocery Stores.

★ 60085 ★ **Publix Super Market**
1735 E. Young Cir.
Hollywood, FL 33020
(305)922-1531
Ultimate Parent: Publix Super Markets.
SIC: 5411—Grocery Stores.

★ 60086 ★ **Publix Super Market**
9951 Miramar Pky.
Hollywood, FL 33025
(305)437-6124
Ultimate Parent: Publix Super Markets.
SIC: 5411—Grocery Stores.

★ 60087 ★ **Publix Super Markets**
9951 Miramar Pky.
Hollywood, FL 33025
(305)437-6124
Ultimate Parent: Publix Super Markets.
SIC: 5411—Grocery Stores.

★ 60088 ★ **Radio Shack**
Univ
Hollywood, FL 33024
(305)432-0745
Company Type: Division. **Ultimate Parent:**
Tandy Corp. **SIC:** 5065—Electronic Parts &
Equipment Nec.

★ 60089 ★ **Radio Shack**
3399 Sheridan St.
Hollywood, FL 33021
(305)963-0330
Company Type: Division. **Ultimate Parent:**
Tandy Corp. **SIC:** 5731—Radio, Television
& Electronics Stores.

★ 60090 ★ **Radio Shack**
6609 Taft St.
Hollywood, FL 33024
(305)961-0661
Company Type: Division. **Ultimate Parent:**
Tandy Corp. **SIC:** 5065—Electronic Parts &
Equipment Nec.

★ 60091 ★ **Radio Shack**
6870 Miramar Pky.
Hollywood, FL 33023
(305)966-5560
Company Type: Division. **Ultimate Parent:**
Tandy Corp. **SIC:** 5065—Electronic Parts &
Equipment Nec.

★ 60092 ★ **Ryder Truck Rental**
62 N. University Dr.
Hollywood, FL 33024
(305)437-5136
Ultimate Parent: Ryder System. **SIC:**
7389—Business Services Nec.

★ 60093 ★ **Ryder Truck Rental**
1211 N. State Rd. 7
Hollywood, FL 33021
(305)981-7855
Ultimate Parent: Ryder System. **SIC:**
7359—Equipment Rental & Leasing Nec.

★ 60094 ★ **Savings of America,
FSB**
Home Savings of America
1701 E. Young Cir.
Hollywood, FL 33020-6824
(305)923-4705
Location Type: Branch office. **Officer:**
Joann Palacino, Manager. **Ultimate Parent:**
H. F. Ahmanson. **SIC:** 6021—National
Commercial Banks.

★ 60095 ★ **Saxon Paper**
Florida
3501 Commerce Pky.
Hollywood, FL 33025-3918
Location Type: Branch office. **Officer:**
Gene Press. **Ultimate Parent:** Alco
Standard Corp. **SIC:** 5111—Printing &
Writing Paper; 5084—Industrial Machinery &
Equipment; 5112—Stationery & Office
Supplies; 5113—Industrial & Personal
Service Paper.

★ 60096 ★ **Service Merchandise**
1951 S. State Rd. 7
Hollywood, FL 33023
(305)963-5200
Ultimate Parent: Service Merchandise Co.,
Inc. **SIC:** 5944—Jewelry Stores.

★ 60097 ★ **Taco Bell**
48 N. University Dr.
Hollywood, FL 33024
(305)437-1090
Ultimate Parent: Pepsico. **SIC:** 5812—
Eating Places.

★ 60098 ★ **Taco Bell**
6519 Taft St.
Hollywood, FL 33024
(305)963-1738
Ultimate Parent: Pepsico. **SIC:** 5812—
Eating Places.

★ 60099 ★ **Thom Mcan Shoe**
Hollywood Fash Ctr.
Hollywood, FL 33021
(305)966-2103
Ultimate Parent: Melville. **SIC:** 5661—Shoe
Stores.

★ 60100 ★ **Toys R US**
500 S. State Rd. 7
Hollywood, FL 33023
(305)981-2992
Ultimate Parent: Toys "R" US. **SIC:** 5941—
Sporting Goods & Bicycle Shops.

★ 60101 ★ **Trailways Bus System**
210 S. Federal Hwy.
Hollywood, FL 33020
(305)923-8238
Ultimate Parent: Greyhound Lines Inc. **SIC:**
4131—Intercity & Rural Bus Transportation.

★ 60102 ★ **Unijax Sloan Paper**
3501 Commerce Pky.
Hollywood, FL 33025
(305)436-0700
Officer: Gene Marin, Manager. **Ultimate
Parent:** Alco Standard Corp. **SIC:** 2759—
Commercial Printing Nec.

★ 60103 ★ **Waldenbooks**
85 Hollywood Fashion Ctr.
Hollywood, FL 33023
(305)961-3657
Ultimate Parent: K-Mart. **SIC:** 5999—
Miscellaneous Retail Stores Nec.

★ 60104 ★ **Walgreen**
Hollywood Fashion Ctr.
Hollywood, FL 33023
(305)962-4181
Ultimate Parent: Walgreen Co. **SIC:**
5912—Drug Stores & Proprietary Stores.

★ 60105 ★ **Walgreen Drug Stores**
6971 Taft St.
Hollywood, FL 33024
(305)989-8900
Ultimate Parent: Walgreen Co. **SIC:**
5912—Drug Stores & Proprietary Stores.

★ 60106 ★ **Walgreen Drug Stores**
2855 Stirling Rd.
Hollywood, FL 33020
(305)981-1102
Ultimate Parent: Walgreen Co. **SIC:**
7389—Business Services Nec.

★ 60107 ★ **Walgreen Drug Stores**
890 N. State Rd. 7
Hollywood, FL 33021
(305)962-0228
Ultimate Parent: Walgreen Co. **SIC:**
7389—Business Services Nec.

★ 60108 ★ **Walgreen Drug Stores**
3352 S. University Dr.
Hollywood, FL 33025
(305)437-9442
Ultimate Parent: Walgreen Co. **SIC:**
7389—Business Services Nec.

★ 60109 ★ **Walgreen Drug Stores**
1723 E. Young Cir.
Hollywood, FL 33020
(305)922-1554
Ultimate Parent: Walgreen Co. **SIC:**
7389—Business Services Nec.

Holmes Beach

★ 60110 ★ **Barnett Bank of
Manatee County, NA**
699 Manatee Ave. W
Holmes Beach, FL 34217-1922
(813)755-8889
Company Type: Subsidiary. **Location
Type:** Branch office. **Officer:** Charles
Robinson, Assistant Vice President.
Ultimate Parent: Barnett Banks. **SIC:**
6021—National Commercial Banks.

★ 60111 ★ **First of America Bank**
603 W. Manatee Ave.
Holmes Beach, FL 34217
(813)778-0705
Location Type: Branch office. **Ultimate
Parent:** First of America Bank Corp. **SIC:**
6021—National Commercial Banks.

★ 60112 ★ **First Union National
Bank of Florida**
5327 Gulf Dr.
Holmes Beach, FL 34217-1799
(813)798-2704
Location Type: Branch office. **SIC:** 6021—
National Commercial Banks.

Homestead

★ 60113 ★ **Barnett Bank of South
Florida, NA**
850 Homestead Blvd.
Homestead, FL 33030
(305)246-7400
Company Type: Subsidiary. **Location
Type:** Branch office. **Officer:** David
Cunigan, Manager. **Ultimate Parent:**
Barnett Banks. **SIC:** 6021—National
Commercial Banks.

★ 60114 ★ **Greyhound Bus
Station**
5 NE 3rd Rd.
Homestead, FL 33030
(305)247-2040
Ultimate Parent: Greyhound Lines Inc. **SIC:**
4111—Local & Suburban Transit; 4173—
Bus Terminal & Service Facilities.

★ 60115 ★ **Jiffy Lube**
26990 S. Dixie Hwy.
Homestead, FL 33032
(305)245-6719
Ultimate Parent: Pennzoil. **SIC:** 7538—
General Automotive Repair Shops.

★ 60116 ★ **Kentucky Fried
Chicken**
232 SE 1st Ave.
Homestead, FL 33034
(305)247-0688
Ultimate Parent: Pepsico. **SIC:** 5812—
Eating Places.

★ 60117 ★ **Mary Kay Cosmetics**
23701 SW 167th Ave.
Homestead, FL 33031
(305)247-3823
Ultimate Parent: Mary Kay Cosmetics.

★ 60118 ★ **Pizza Hut**
27101 S. Federal Hwy.
Homestead, FL 33032
(305)245-7341
Ultimate Parent: Pepsico. **SIC:** 5812—
Eating Places.

★ 60119 ★ **Radio Shack**
367 S. Homestead Blvd.
Homestead, FL 33030
(305)245-3557
Company Type: Division. **Ultimate Parent:**
Tandy Corp. **SIC:** 5065—Electronic Parts &
Equipment Nec.

★ 60120 ★ **Radio Shack**
28909 Old Dixie Hwy.
Homestead, FL 33033
(305)245-7891
Company Type: Division. **Ultimate Parent:**
Tandy Corp. **SIC:** 5065—Electronic Parts &
Equipment Nec.

★ 60121 ★ **Rite Aid Drugs**
230 NE 8th St.
Homestead, FL 33030
(305)248-0022
Ultimate Parent: Rite Aid. **SIC:** 5912—Drug
Stores & Proprietary Stores.

★ 60122 ★ **Ryder Truck Rental**
23655 S. Old Dixie Hwy.
Homestead, FL 33032
(305)258-2247
Ultimate Parent: Ryder System. **SIC:**
7359—Equipment Rental & Leasing Nec.

★ 60123 ★ **Thom Mcan Shoe
Store**
937 N. Homestead Blvd.
Homestead, FL 33030
(305)247-9844
Ultimate Parent: Melville. **SIC:** 5661—Shoe
Stores.

Homosassa

★ 60124 ★ **AmSouth Bank of
Florida**
4556 S. Suncoast Blvd.
Homosassa, FL 34446
(305)247-5541
Location Type: Branch office. **Ultimate
Parent:** AmSouth Bancorp. **SIC:** 6022—
State Commercial Banks.

★ 60125 ★ **Pizza Hut**
4845 S. Suncoast Blvd.
Homosassa, FL 34446
(904)628-1234
Ultimate Parent: Pepsico. **SIC:** 5812—
Eating Places.

★ 60126 ★ **Radio Shack**
4520 S. Suncoast Blvd.
Homosassa, FL 34446
(904)628-3666
Company Type: Division. **Ultimate Parent:**
Tandy Corp. **SIC:** 5731—Radio, Television
& Electronics Stores.

Homosassa Springs

★ 60127 ★ **Barnett Bank of the
Suncoast, NA**
4395 S. Suncoast Blvd.
Homosassa Springs, FL 34446-7500
(904)628-3276
Company Type: Subsidiary. **Location
Type:** Branch office. **Officer:** Marie Straight,
Manager. **Ultimate Parent:** Barnett Banks.
SIC: 6021—National Commercial Banks.

★ 60128 ★ **Walgreen Drug Stores**
4546 S. Suncoast Blvd.
Homosassa Springs, FL 34447
(904)628-3484
Ultimate Parent: Walgreen Co. **SIC:**
5912—Drug Stores & Proprietary Stores.

Hudson

★ 60129 ★ **Barnett Bank of
Pasco County**
14207 Fivay Rd.
Hudson, FL 34667-7108
(813)861-8483
Company Type: Subsidiary. **Location
Type:** Branch office. **Officer:** Robert Upton,
Manager. **Ultimate Parent:** Barnett Banks.
SIC: 6022—State Commercial Banks.

★ 60130 ★ **Barnett Bank of
Pasco County**
18934 US Hwy. 19
Hudson, FL 34667-6651
(813)861-8569
Company Type: Subsidiary. **Location
Type:** Branch office. **Officer:** Hazel D.
Dilger, Manager. **Ultimate Parent:** Barnett
Banks. **SIC:** 6022—State Commercial
Banks.

★ 60131 ★ **First of America Bank**
14166 N. US 19
Hudson, FL 34667
(813)852-5471
Location Type: Branch office. **Ultimate
Parent:** First of America Bank Corp. **SIC:**
6021—National Commercial Banks.

★ 60132 ★ **Fortune Bank, ASB**
7512 State Rd. 52
Hudson, FL 34667-6798
(813)868-9457
Location Type: Branch office. **Officer:**
Frances Lamoureux, Manager. **Ultimate
Parent:** Fortune Bancorp. **SIC:** 6021—
National Commercial Banks.

★ 60133 ★ **Fortune Bank, ASB**
14212 US Hwy. 19 N
Hudson, FL 34667-1169
(813)868-9530
Location Type: Branch office. **Ultimate
Parent:** Fortune Bancorp. **SIC:** 6021—
National Commercial Banks.

Immokalee

★ 60134 ★ **First National Bank &
Trust**
29 Lake Trafford Rd.
Immokalee, FL 33934
(813)657-6161
Ultimate Parent: Society Corp. **SIC:** 6022—
State Commercial Banks.

Indialantic

★ 60135 ★   First Union National
Bank of Florida
1060 N. A1A
Indialantic, FL 32903-2909
(407)984-7446
Location Type: Branch office. Ultimate
Parent: First Union Corp. SIC: 6021—
National Commercial Banks.

Indian Harbour Beach

★ 60136 ★   Barnett Bank of
Central Florida, NA
202 E. Eau Gallie Blvd.
Indian Harbour Beach, FL 32937-3525
(407)777-4122
Company Type: Subsidiary. Location
Type: Branch office. Officer: Neal Johnson,
Manager. Ultimate Parent: Barnett Banks.
SIC: 6021—National Commercial Banks.

★ 60137 ★   First Union National
Bank of Florida
276 E. Eau Gallie Blvd.
Indian Harbour Beach, FL 32937-4235
(407)777-2760
Location Type: Branch office. Ultimate
Parent: First Union Corp. SIC: 6021—
National Commercial Banks.

★ 60138 ★   First Union National
Bank of Florida
1901 S. Patrick Dr.
Indian Harbour Beach, FL 32937-4487
(407)984-7466
Location Type: Branch office. Ultimate
Parent: First Union Corp. SIC: 6021—
National Commercial Banks.

Indian Rocks

★ 60139 ★   Mary Kay Cosmetics
Resident St.
Indian Rocks, FL 34635
(813)595-1914
Ultimate Parent: Mary Kay Cosmetics. SIC:
5999—Miscellaneous Retail Stores Nec.

Indian Shores

★ 60140 ★   AmSouth Bank of
Florida
18395 Gulf Blvd.
Indian Shores, FL 34635-2001
(813)462-5105
Location Type: Branch office. Ultimate
Parent: AmSouth Bancorp. SIC: 6022—
State Commercial Banks.

Indiantown

★ 60141 ★   First Bank
15588 SW Warfield Blvd.
Indiantown, FL 34956
(407)597-2181
Ultimate Parent: Shawmut National Corp.
SIC: 6099—Functions Related to Deposit
Banking.

★ 60142 ★   Imc Fertilizer Inc.
17250 SW Railroad Ave.
Indiantown, FL 34956
Ultimate Parent: IMC Fertilizer Group. SIC:
2875—Fertilizers—Mixing Only.

Inverness

★ 60143 ★   AmSouth Bank of
Florida
2875 E. Gulf to Lake Hwy.
Inverness, FL 34453
(904)344-3183
Location Type: Branch office. Ultimate
Parent: AmSouth Bancorp. SIC: 6022—
State Commercial Banks.

★ 60144 ★   AmSouth Bank of
Florida
301 US Hwy. 41, S
Inverness, FL 34450
(904)726-9022
Location Type: Branch office. Ultimate
Parent: AmSouth Bancorp. SIC: 6022—
State Commercial Banks.

★ 60145 ★   Barnett Bank of the
Suncoast, NA
2709 E. Gulf to Lake Hwy.
Inverness, FL 34453-3216
(904)795-8100
Company Type: Subsidiary. Location
Type: Branch office. Officer: Ben Branch,
Manager. Ultimate Parent: Barnett Banks.
SIC: 6021—National Commercial Banks.

★ 60146 ★   Barnett Bank of the
Suncoast, NA
S. Main & Highland
Inverness, FL 34450-4855
(904)726-3663
Company Type: Subsidiary. Location
Type: Branch office. Officer: Art Krueger,
Manager. Ultimate Parent: Barnett Banks.
SIC: 6021—National Commercial Banks.

★ 60147 ★   Barnett Bank of the
Suncoast, NA
1077 US Hwy. 41 N
Inverness, FL 34452-3964
(904)726-3663
Company Type: Subsidiary. Location
Type: Branch office. Officer: Art Krueger,
Manager. Ultimate Parent: Barnett Banks.
SIC: 6021—National Commercial Banks.

★ 60148 ★   California Federal
Bank, FSB
1488 Hwy. 41 N.
Inverness, FL 34450
(904)726-3919
Location Type: Branch office. Ultimate
Parent: California Federal Bank. SIC:
6021—National Commercial Banks.

★ 60149 ★   First of America Bank
211 E. Highland Blvd.
Inverness, FL 34452
(904)344-8800
Location Type: Branch office. Ultimate
Parent: First of America Bank Corp. SIC:
6021—National Commercial Banks.

★ 60150 ★   Kentucky Fried
Chicken
1110 Hwy. 41 N
Inverness, FL 34450
(904)726-7007
Ultimate Parent: Pepsico. SIC: 5812—
Eating Places.

★ 60151 ★   Pizza Hut
940 W. Main St.
Inverness, FL 34450
(904)726-4880
Ultimate Parent: Pepsico. SIC: 5812—
Eating Places.

★ 60152 ★   Walgreen
1510 Hwy. 41 N
Inverness, FL 34450
(904)344-2198
Ultimate Parent: Walgreen Co. SIC:
5912—Drug Stores & Proprietary Stores.

Islamorada

★ 60153 ★   Barnett Bank of the
Keys
81541 Old Hwy.
Islamorada, FL 33036-9761
(305)292-3904
Company Type: Subsidiary. Location
Type: Branch office. Officer: Marcy
Tangen, Manager. Ultimate Parent: Barnett
Banks. SIC: 6022—State Commercial
Banks.

★ 60154 ★   Greyhound Bus Lines
Islamorada, FL 33036
(305)664-9694
Ultimate Parent: Greyhound Lines Inc. SIC:
4131—Intercity & Rural Bus Transportation.

Jacksonville

★ 60155 ★   Delta Business
Systems
8081 Phillips Hwy., No. 19
Jacksonville, FL 32256
(904)731-3227
Officer: Brian King, President. Ultimate
Parent: Alco Standard Corp. SIC: 3663—
Radio & T.V. Communications Equipment.

Jacksonville

★ 60156 ★   Ace Hardware
12548 San Jose Blvd.
Jacksonville, FL 32223
(904)268-9597
Ultimate Parent: Ace Hardware. SIC:
5261—Retail Nurseries & Garden Stores.

★ 60157 ★   Ace Hardware Garner
2245 N. Main St.
Jacksonville, FL 32206
(904)354-8251
Ultimate Parent: Ace Hardware. SIC:
5251—Hardware Stores.

★ 60158 ★   Ace Hardware Proctor
525 3rd St. N
Jacksonville, FL 32250
(904)249-5622
Ultimate Parent: Ace Hardware. SIC:
5261—Retail Nurseries & Garden Stores.

★ 60159 ★   Adcom Wire Co.
925 N. Ln. Ave.
Jacksonville, FL 32254
Ultimate Parent: Leggett & Platt Inc. SIC:
3315—Steel Wire & Related Products;
3479—Metal Coating & Allied Services;
3315—Steel Wire & Related Products;
3479—Metal Coating & Allied Services.

★ 60160 ★   Air Products &
Chemicals Inc.
5837 W. 5th St.
Jacksonville, FL 32254-1509
(904)786-2662
Location Type: Branch office. Ultimate
Parent: Air Products & Chemicals, Inc. SIC:
5169—Chemicals & Allied Products Nec;
7699—Repair Services Nec.

★ 60161 ★   Airborne Freight
Corp.
Jacksonville, FL 32229
(904)757-2455
Ultimate Parent: Airborne Freight Corp.
SIC: 4512—Air Transportation—Scheduled.

★ 60162 ★   Allied-Signal
Aerospace Co.
Engine Controls
7575 Baymeadows Way
Jacksonville, FL 32256
Ultimate Parent: Allied-Signal Inc. SIC:
3724—Aircraft Engines & Engine Parts;
3728—Aircraft Parts & Equipment Nec.

★ 60163 ★   Amerada Hess Corp.
2617 Hecksher Dr.
Jacksonville, FL 32226-2719
(904)757-4498
Location Type: Branch office. Ultimate
Parent: Amerada Hess. SIC: 5172—
Petroleum Products Nec; 2911—Petroleum
Refining.

★ 60164 ★   American General
Finance
10909 Atlantic Blvd. Rm 8
Jacksonville, FL 32225-2933
(904)642-2225
Officer: Ted Smith. Ultimate Parent:
American General Corp. SIC: 6141—
Personal Credit Institutions; 6162—
Mortgage Bankers & Correspondents.

★ 60165 ★   American General
Finance
9850 San Jose Blvd.
Jacksonville, FL 32257-5457
(904)824-4093
Officer: Isabella McManus. Ultimate
Parent: American General Corp. SIC:
6141—Personal Credit Institutions; 6162—
Mortgage Bankers & Correspondents.

★ 60166 ★   American General
Finance
1036 Dunn Ave.
Jacksonville, FL 32218-4830
(904)751-2100
Ultimate Parent: American General Corp.
SIC: 6141—Personal Credit Institutions;
6162—Mortgage Bankers &
Correspondents.

★ 60167 ★   American General
Finance
9550 Regency Sq. Blvd.
Jacksonville, FL 32225-8101
(904)721-8225
Ultimate Parent: American General Corp.
SIC: 6141—Personal Credit Institutions;

6162—Mortgage Bankers &
Correspondents.

★ 60168 ★   American General
Finance
1400 Cassat Ave.
Jacksonville, FL 32205-7244
(904)389-1184
Location Type: Branch office. Officer:
Chuck Gross. Ultimate Parent: American
General Corp. SIC: 6141—Personal Credit
Institutions; 6162—Mortgage Bankers &
Correspondents.

★ 60169 ★   American General
Finance
4345 10th S. University Blvd.
Jacksonville, FL 32216
(904)737-2404
Ultimate Parent: American General Corp.
SIC: 6141—Personal Credit Institutions;
6162—Mortgage Bankers &
Correspondents.

★ 60170 ★   American General
Finance Inc.
10909 Atlantic Blvd. Rm 8
Jacksonville, FL 32225-2933
(904)642-2225
Location Type: Branch office. Officer: Ted
Smith. Ultimate Parent: American General
Corp. SIC: 6141—Personal Credit
Institutions; 6162—Mortgage Bankers &
Correspondents.

★ 60171 ★   American General
Finance Inc.
9850 San Jose Blvd.
Jacksonville, FL 32257-5457
(904)824-4093
Location Type: Branch office. Officer:
Isabella McManus. Ultimate Parent:
American General Corp. SIC: 6141—
Personal Credit Institutions; 6162—
Mortgage Bankers & Correspondents.

★ 60172 ★   American General
Finance Inc.
1036 Dunn Ave.
Jacksonville, FL 32218-4830
(904)751-2100
Location Type: Branch office. Ultimate
Parent: American General Corp. SIC:
6141—Personal Credit Institutions; 6162—
Mortgage Bankers & Correspondents.

★ 60173 ★   American General
Finance Inc.
9550 Regency Sq. Blvd.
Jacksonville, FL 32225-8101
(904)721-8225
Location Type: Branch office. Ultimate
Parent: American General Corp. SIC:
6141—Personal Credit Institutions; 6162—
Mortgage Bankers & Correspondents.

★ 60174 ★   American General
Finance Inc.
1400 Cassat Ave.
Jacksonville, FL 32205-7244
(904)389-1184
Location Type: Branch office. Officer:
Chuck Gross. Ultimate Parent: American
General Corp. SIC: 6141—Personal Credit
Institutions; 6162—Mortgage Bankers &
Correspondents.

★ 60175 ★   American General
Finance Inc.
4345 10th S. University Blvd.
Jacksonville, FL 32216
(904)737-2404
Location Type: Branch office. Ultimate
Parent: American General Corp. SIC:
6141—Personal Credit Institutions; 6162—
Mortgage Bankers & Correspondents.

★ 60176 ★   American General
Group Insurance Co. of Florida
1301 Gulf Life Dr.
Jacksonville, FL 32207
(904)390-0000
Officer: Howard L. Korn, Chairman & CEO.
Ultimate Parent: American General Corp.
SIC: 6311—Life Insurance; 6321—Accident
& Health Insurance.

★ 60177 ★   American Transtech
Inc.
8000 Baymeadows Way
Jacksonville, FL 32216
(904)636-1000 Fax: (904)731-5202
Officer: Monica Mehan, President & CEO.
Ultimate Parent: AT&T. SIC: 6289—
Security & Commodity Services Nec.

★ 60178 ★ **American Transtech Inc.**
8000 Baymeadows Way
Jacksonville, FL 32216
(904)636-1000 **Fax:** (904)731-5202
Company Type: Subsidiary. **Officer:** Monica M. Mehan, President & CEO.
Ultimate Parent: AT&T.

★ 60179 ★ **Anchor Glass Container Corp.**
2121 Huron St.
Jacksonville, FL 32254
(904)786-1010
Officer: Ken Troup, Manager. **Ultimate Parent:** Anchor Glass Container Corp. **SIC:** 3221—Glass Containers.

★ 60180 ★ **Anchor Mortgage Services Inc.**
8659 Paypine Rd.
Jacksonville, FL 32256-7577
(904)828-2400
Ultimate Parent: Anchor Bancorp. **SIC:** 6162—Mortgage Bankers & Correspondents.

★ 60181 ★ **Anchor Savings Bank F S B**
924 Beach Blvd.
Jacksonville, FL 32250
(904)249-5643
Ultimate Parent: Anchor Bancorp. **SIC:** 6035—Federal Savings Institutions.

★ 60182 ★ **Anheuser-Busch Inc.**
111 Busch Dr.
Jacksonville, FL 32218-5595
Ultimate Parent: Anheuser-Busch. **SIC:** 2082—Malt Beverages.

★ 60183 ★ **AT & T Family Federal Credit Union**
8787 Baypine Rd.
Jacksonville, FL 32256
(904)954-8571
Location Type: Branch office. **Officer:** Lana Sebosky, Manager. **Ultimate Parent:** AT&T. **SIC:** 6061—Federal Credit Unions.

★ 60184 ★ **AT&T Universal Card Services**
8787 Baypine Rd.
Jacksonville, FL 32256
(904)443-7500 **Fax:** (904)443-8790
Company Type: Subsidiary. **Officer:** David K. Hunt, President. **Ultimate Parent:** AT&T.

★ 60185 ★ **AT&T Universal Card Services Corp.**
8775 Baypine Rd.
Jacksonville, FL 32258
Officer: David K. Hunt, President & CEO.
Ultimate Parent: AT&T.

★ 60186 ★ **Austill Packaging**
3389 Powers Ave.
Jacksonville, FL 32207-8013
Ultimate Parent: Jefferson Smurfit Corp.
SIC: 2754—Commercial Printing—Gravure.

★ 60187 ★ **Austill Packaging Inc.**
3389 Powers Ave.
Jacksonville, FL 32207-8013
Ultimate Parent: Jefferson Smurfit Corp.
SIC: 2754—Commercial Printing—Gravure.

★ 60188 ★ **B. F. Goodrich Aerospace Epp**
6061 B. F. Goodrich Blvd.
Jacksonville, FL 32226-3409
Ultimate Parent: B.F. Goodrich. **SIC:** 3069—Fabricated Rubber Products Nec.

★ 60189 ★ **Banana Republic**
2 Independent Dr.
Jacksonville, FL 32202
(904)353-8119
Ultimate Parent: GAP. **SIC:** 5699—Miscellaneous Apparel & Accessory Stores.

★ 60190 ★ **BancBoston Mortgage Corp.**
7310 Baymeadows Way
Jacksonville, FL 32256-6833
(904)281-3000
Company Type: Subsidiary. **Officer:** Joe K. Pickett, CEO & Chairman of the Board.
Ultimate Parent: Bank of Boston Corp.
SIC: 6162—Mortgage Bankers & Correspondents. **Employee Count:** 1100.

★ 60191 ★ **Barnett Bank of Jacksonville, NA**
7254 103rd St.
Jacksonville, FL 32210
(904)573-1301
Company Type: Affiliate. **Location Type:** Branch office. **Ultimate Parent:** Barnett Banks. **SIC:** 6021—National Commercial Banks.

★ 60192 ★ **Barnett Bank of Jacksonville, NA**
6622 Southpoint Dr. S
Jacksonville, FL 32217
(904)296-3260
Company Type: Subsidiary. **Location Type:** Branch office. **Ultimate Parent:** Barnett Banks. **SIC:** 6021—National Commercial Banks.

★ 60193 ★ **Barnett Bank of Jacksonville, NA**
50 W. State St.
Jacksonville, FL 32202
(904)791-7432
Company Type: Affiliate. **Location Type:** Branch office. **Ultimate Parent:** Barnett Banks. **SIC:** 6021—National Commercial Banks.

★ 60194 ★ **Barnett Bank of Jacksonville, NA**
14288 Beach Blvd.
Jacksonville, FL 32216
(904)223-9204
Company Type: Affiliate. **Location Type:** Branch office. **Ultimate Parent:** Barnett Banks. **SIC:** 6021—National Commercial Banks.

★ 60195 ★ **Barnett Bank of Jacksonville, NA**
11790 San Jose Blvd.
Jacksonville, FL 32223
(904)292-2700
Company Type: Affiliate. **Location Type:** Branch office. **Ultimate Parent:** Barnett Banks. **SIC:** 6021—National Commercial Banks.

★ 60196 ★ **Barnett Bank of Jacksonville, NA**
3535 University Blvd. W
Jacksonville, FL 32217
(904)791-7313
Company Type: Affiliate. **Location Type:** Branch office. **Ultimate Parent:** Barnett Banks. **SIC:** 6021—National Commercial Banks.

★ 60197 ★ **Barnett Bank of Jacksonville, NA**
2011 San Marco Blvd.
Jacksonville, FL 32223
(904)346-4350
Company Type: Affiliate. **Location Type:** Branch office. **Ultimate Parent:** Barnett Banks. **SIC:** 6021—National Commercial Banks.

★ 60198 ★ **Barnett Bank of Jacksonville, NA**
4500 Wabash Ave.
Jacksonville, FL 32210
(904)381-4340
Company Type: Affiliate. **Location Type:** Branch office. **Ultimate Parent:** Barnett Banks. **SIC:** 6021—National Commercial Banks.

★ 60199 ★ **Barnett Bank of Jacksonville, NA**
11140 Beach Blvd.
Jacksonville, FL 32216
(904)565-2611
Company Type: Affiliate. **Location Type:** Branch office. **Ultimate Parent:** Barnett Banks. **SIC:** 6021—National Commercial Banks.

★ 60200 ★ **Barnett Bank of Jacksonville, NA**
9550 Regency Square Blvd.
Jacksonville, FL 32211
(904)791-7212
Company Type: Affiliate. **Location Type:** Branch office. **Ultimate Parent:** Barnett Banks. **SIC:** 6021—National Commercial Banks.

★ 60201 ★ **Barnett Bank of Jacksonville, NA**
859 Blanding Blvd.
Jacksonville, FL 32073
(904)276-1806
Company Type: Affiliate. **Location Type:** Branch office. **Ultimate Parent:** Barnett Banks. **SIC:** 6021—National Commercial Banks.

★ 60202 ★ **Barnett Bank of Jacksonville, NA**
29 Blanding Blvd.
Jacksonville, FL 32073
(904)264-1111
Company Type: Affiliate. **Location Type:** Branch office. **Ultimate Parent:** Barnett Banks. **SIC:** 6021—National Commercial Banks.

★ 60203 ★ **Barnett Bank of Jacksonville, NA**
631 State Rd. A1A
Jacksonville, FL 32083
(904)285-4260
Company Type: Affiliate. **Location Type:** Branch office. **Ultimate Parent:** Barnett Banks. **SIC:** 6021—National Commercial Banks.

★ 60204 ★ **Barnett Bank of Jacksonville, NA**
1055 Dunn Ave.
Jacksonville, FL 32218
(904)791-7212
Company Type: Affiliate. **Location Type:** Branch office. **Ultimate Parent:** Barnett Banks. **SIC:** 6021—National Commercial Banks.

★ 60205 ★ **Barnett Bank of Jacksonville, NA**
10445 San Jose Blvd.
Jacksonville, FL 32217
(904)292-2727
Company Type: Affiliate. **Location Type:** Branch office. **Ultimate Parent:** Barnett Banks. **SIC:** 6021—National Commercial Banks.

★ 60206 ★ **Barnett Bank of Jacksonville, NA**
7770 Normandy Blvd.
Jacksonville, FL 32221
(904)693-5101
Company Type: Affiliate. **Location Type:** Branch office. **Ultimate Parent:** Barnett Banks. **SIC:** 6021—National Commercial Banks.

★ 60207 ★ **Barnett Bank of Jacksonville, NA**
500 3rd St.
Jacksonville, FL 32233
(904)249-6701
Company Type: Affiliate. **Location Type:** Branch office. **Ultimate Parent:** Barnett Banks. **SIC:** 6021—National Commercial Banks.

★ 60208 ★ **Barnett Bank of Jacksonville, NA**
840 S. Edgewood Ave.
Jacksonville, FL 32205
(904)791-7126
Company Type: Affiliate. **Location Type:** Branch office. **Ultimate Parent:** Barnett Banks. **SIC:** 6021—National Commercial Banks.

★ 60209 ★ **Barnett Bank of Jacksonville, NA**
NAS Jacksonville
Jacksonville, FL 32212
(904)573-1310
Company Type: Affiliate. **Location Type:** Branch office. **Ultimate Parent:** Barnett Banks. **SIC:** 6021—National Commercial Banks.

★ 60210 ★ **Barnett Bank of Jacksonville, NA**
2710 Blanding Blvd.
Jacksonville, FL 32086
(904)282-3724
Company Type: Affiliate. **Location Type:** Branch office. **Ultimate Parent:** Barnett Banks. **SIC:** 6021—National Commercial Banks.

★ 60211 ★ **Barnett Bank of Jacksonville, NA**
5859 Moncrief Rd.
Jacksonville, FL 32209
(904)766-4181
Company Type: Affiliate. **Location Type:** Branch office. **Ultimate Parent:** Barnett Banks. **SIC:** 6021—National Commercial Banks.

★ 60212 ★ **Barnett Bank of Jacksonville, NA**
2285 Kingsley Ave.
Jacksonville, FL 32073
(904)272-6500
Company Type: Affiliate. **Location Type:** Branch office. **Ultimate Parent:** Barnett Banks. **SIC:** 6021—National Commercial Banks.

★ 60213 ★ **Barnett Bank of Jacksonville, NA**
10560 St. Augustine Rd.
Jacksonville, FL 32217
(904)292-2711
Company Type: Affiliate. **Location Type:** Branch office. **Ultimate Parent:** Barnett Banks. **SIC:** 6021—National Commercial Banks.

★ 60214 ★ **Barnett Bank of Jacksonville, NA**
1315 S. 3rd St.
Jacksonville, FL 32250
(904)241-3600
Company Type: Affiliate. **Location Type:** Branch office. **Ultimate Parent:** Barnett Banks. **SIC:** 6021—National Commercial Banks.

★ 60215 ★ **Barnett Bank of Jacksonville, NA**
425 State Rd. 13 N
Jacksonville, FL 32259
(904)287-3631
Company Type: Affiliate. **Location Type:** Branch office. **Ultimate Parent:** Barnett Banks. **SIC:** 6021—National Commercial Banks.

★ 60216 ★ **Barnett Bank of Jacksonville, NA**
1300 Cooks Ln.
Jacksonville, FL 32043
(904)284-1744
Company Type: Affiliate. **Location Type:** Branch office. **Ultimate Parent:** Barnett Banks. **SIC:** 6021—National Commercial Banks.

★ 60217 ★ **Barnett Bank of Jacksonville, NA**
13170 Atlantic Blvd.
Jacksonville, FL 32225
(904)221-8382
Company Type: Affiliate. **Location Type:** Branch office. **Ultimate Parent:** Barnett Banks. **SIC:** 6021—National Commercial Banks.

★ 60218 ★ **Barnett Bank of Jacksonville, NA**
5560 Ft. Caroline Rd.
Jacksonville, FL 32211
(904)745-4800
Company Type: Affiliate. **Location Type:** Branch office. **Ultimate Parent:** Barnett Banks. **SIC:** 6021—National Commercial Banks.

★ 60219 ★ **Barnett Bank of Jacksonville, NA**
5156-2 Norwood Ave.
Jacksonville, FL 32209
(904)766-4191
Company Type: Affiliate. **Location Type:** Branch office. **Ultimate Parent:** Barnett Banks. **SIC:** 6021—National Commercial Banks.

★ 60220 ★ **Barnett Bank of Jacksonville, NA**
9971 Baymeadows Rd.
Jacksonville, FL 32256
(904)565-2602
Company Type: Affiliate. **Location Type:** Branch office. **Ultimate Parent:** Barnett Banks. **SIC:** 6021—National Commercial Banks.

★ 60221 ★ Barnett Bank of Jacksonville, NA
50 Laura St.
PO Box 990
Jacksonville, FL 32231-3099
(904)791-7500 Telex: 4450012
Company Type: Affiliate. Location Type: Headquarters. Officer: Andrew B. Cheney, President & CEO. Ultimate Parent: Barnett Banks. SIC: 6021—National Commercial Banks.

★ 60222 ★ Barnett Bank of Jacksonville, NA
2709 Monument Rd.
Jacksonville, FL 32225
(904)565-2621
Company Type: Affiliate. Location Type: Branch office. Ultimate Parent: Barnett Banks. SIC: 6021—National Commercial Banks.

★ 60223 ★ Barnett Banks
50 N. Laura St.
Jacksonville, FL 32202
(904)791-7720
Company Type: Headquarters. Officer: Charles E. Rice. Fortune Service 500: Ranking 21.

★ 60224 ★ Barnett Banks Inc.
50 N. Laura St.
Jacksonville, FL 32202-3638
(904)791-7720 Fax: (904)791-7166
Officer: Charles E. Rice, CEO. Ultimate Parent: Barnett Banks. Employee Count: 22179. Sales: 3132 M.

★ 60225 ★ Barnett Banks Trust Co., NA
9000 Southside Blvd., Bldg. 100
Jacksonville, FL 32256-0708
(904)464-3650 Fax: (904)464-3680
Location Type: Branch office. Ultimate Parent: Barnett Banks. SIC: 6021—National Commercial Banks.

★ 60226 ★ Barnett Banks Trust Co., NA
PO Box 40200
Jacksonville, FL 32203-0200
Location Type: Branch office. Ultimate Parent: Barnett Banks. SIC: 6021—National Commercial Banks.

★ 60227 ★ Bell Atlantic Bus Systems Svc.
6800 Southpoint Pky.
Jacksonville, FL 32216-6219
(904)296-1037
Ultimate Parent: Bell Atlantic Corp. SIC: 7378—Computer Maintenance & Repair.

★ 60228 ★ Bellinger Shipyard
13911 Atlantic Blvd.
Jacksonville, FL 32225-3299
(904)221-0981
Location Type: Branch office. Officer: Ken R. Debusk. Ultimate Parent: Banta Corp. SIC: 3731—Ship Building & Repairing; 3325—Steel Foundries Nec; 3732—Boat Building & Repairing.

★ 60229 ★ Beneficial Mgmt Corp.
933 University Blvd. N.
Jacksonville, FL 32211-5529
(904)743-4725
Ultimate Parent: Beneficial. SIC: 6141—Personal Credit Institutions.

★ 60230 ★ Bethelhem Steel Corp. Sales OFC
9428 Baymeadows Rd.
Jacksonville, FL 32256-0190
(904)731-5490
Ultimate Parent: Bethlehem Steel Corp. SIC: 3312—Blast Furnaces & Steel Mills.

★ 60231 ★ Betz PaperChem, Inc.
7510 Bay Meadows Way
Jacksonville, FL 32256-7524
(904)733-7110
Company Type: Subsidiary. Officer: Donald M. Loop, President. Ultimate Parent: Betz Laboratories Inc. SIC: 5169—Chemicals & Allied Products Nec; 2899—Chemical Preparations Nec. Employee Count: 410. Sales: 180 M.

★ 60232 ★ BF Goodrich Co.
6061 BF Goodrich Blvd.
Jacksonville, FL 32226
Ultimate Parent: B.F. Goodrich. SIC: 3069—Fabricated Rubber Products Nec.

★ 60233 ★ Browning Ferris Industries Florida Inc.
7580 Phillips Hwy.
Jacksonville, FL 32256-6810
(904)731-3440
Location Type: Branch office. Officer: Brad G. Gardner. Ultimate Parent: Browning-Ferris Industries. SIC: 4953—Refuse Systems; 4212—Local Trucking Without Storage.

★ 60234 ★ Burlington Air Express
853558 Baymeadows Rd.
Jacksonville, FL 32216
(904)730-2344
Ultimate Parent: Pittston. SIC: 4513—Air Courier Services.

★ 60235 ★ Burlington Coat Factory Warehouse
8195 Arlington Expy.
Jacksonville, FL 32211-6243
(904)724-9487
Location Type: Branch office. Officer: Rick L. Wise. Ultimate Parent: Burlington Industries, Equity. SIC: 4225—General Warehousing & Storage; 5661—Shoe Stores.

★ 60236 ★ Career Image
274 Regency Sq.
Jacksonville, FL 32225
(904)725-4734
Ultimate Parent: United States Shoe. SIC: 5651—Family Clothing Stores.

★ 60237 ★ Casual Corner
10300 Southside Blvd.
Jacksonville, FL 32256
(904)363-2478
Ultimate Parent: United States Shoe. SIC: 5699—Miscellaneous Apparel & Accessory Stores.

★ 60238 ★ Casual Corner
4427 Roosevelt Blvd.
Jacksonville, FL 32210
(904)387-1631
Ultimate Parent: United States Shoe. SIC: 5621—Women's Clothing Stores.

★ 60239 ★ Champion International Corp.
7785 Baymeadows Way
Jacksonville, FL 32256
(904)731-4550
Ultimate Parent: Champion International. SIC: 5211—Lumber & Other Building Materials.

★ 60240 ★ Champion International Corp.
435 Clark Rd.
Jacksonville, FL 32218
(904)766-5399
Ultimate Parent: Champion International. SIC: 5099—Durable Goods Nec.

★ 60241 ★ Champion International Corp.
109 Halsema Rd. S
Jacksonville, FL 32220
(904)786-4155
Ultimate Parent: Champion International. SIC: 2421—Sawmills & Planing Mills—General.

★ 60242 ★ Chase Home Mortgage Corp.
3100 University Blvd. S
Jacksonville, FL 32216
(904)724-9000
Ultimate Parent: Chase Manhattan Corp. SIC: 1521—Single-Family Housing Construction.

★ 60243 ★ Circuit City
9998 Atlantic Blvd.
Jacksonville, FL 32225
(904)725-9517
Ultimate Parent: Circuit City Stores. SIC: 7622—Radio & T.V. Repair.

★ 60244 ★ Circuit City Superstore
6155 Youngerman Cir.
Jacksonville, FL 32244
(904)778-8255
Ultimate Parent: Circuit City Stores. SIC: 5731—Radio, Television & Electronics Stores.

★ 60245 ★ Coast to Coast Cap Co.
4851 Rosselle St.
Jacksonville, FL 32205
(904)374-3700
Ultimate Parent: Servistar Corp. SIC: 5199—Nondurable Goods Nec.

★ 60246 ★ Coast to Coast Cap Co.
2750 Lane Ave. N
Jacksonville, FL 32205
(904)781-5862
Ultimate Parent: Servistar Corp. SIC: 5199—Nondurable Goods Nec.

★ 60247 ★ Coast to Coast Express
3335 Edgewood Ave. N
Jacksonville, FL 32205
(904)354-7575
Ultimate Parent: Servistar Corp. SIC: 4213—Trucking Except Local.

★ 60248 ★ CSX Technology Inc.
550 Water St.
Jacksonville, FL 32202-5157
(904)359-3106
Company Type: Subsidiary. Officer: George F. Sekely, President. Ultimate Parent: CSX Corp. SIC: 7371—Computer Programming Services; 7374—Data Processing & Preparation. Employee Count: 940. Sales: 245 M.

★ 60249 ★ CSX Transportation Inc.
500 Water St.
Jacksonville, FL 32202
(904)359-3100 Fax: (904)359-7674
Officer: Alvin R. Carpenter, President & CEO. Ultimate Parent: CSX Corp.

★ 60250 ★ Customized Transportation Inc.
9485 Regency Square Blvd., N Ste. 500
Jacksonville, FL 32225
(904)721-2104 Fax: (904)721-7088
Officer: William C. Bender, President. Ultimate Parent: CSX Corp.

★ 60251 ★ D-Graphics Inc.
3389 Powers Ave.
Jacksonville, FL 32207-8013
Ultimate Parent: Jefferson Smurfit Corp. SIC: 2754—Commercial Printing—Gravure.

★ 60252 ★ Delta Air Cargo
13906 Thomas Imeson Ave.
Jacksonville, FL 32218
(904)741-2600
Ultimate Parent: Delta Air Lines, Inc. SIC: 4513—Air Courier Services.

★ 60253 ★ Delta Air Lines
2400 Yankee Clipper Dr.
Jacksonville, FL 32218
(904)741-2611
Ultimate Parent: Delta Air Lines, Inc. SIC: 4512—Air Transportation—Scheduled.

★ 60254 ★ Delta Air Lines
Independent
Jacksonville, FL 32202
(904)398-3011
Ultimate Parent: Delta Air Lines, Inc. SIC: 4512—Air Transportation—Scheduled.

★ 60255 ★ Delta Air Lines
2232 Gulf Life Tower
Jacksonville, FL 32207
(904)398-3011
Ultimate Parent: Delta Air Lines, Inc. SIC: 7922—Theatrical Producers & Services.

★ 60256 ★ Delta Air Lines Inc.
Independent
Jacksonville, FL 32202
(904)398-3011
Ultimate Parent: Delta Air Lines, Inc. SIC: 4512—Air Transportation—Scheduled.

★ 60257 ★ Delta Business Systems
8081 Phillips Hwy., No. 19
Jacksonville, FL 32256
(904)731-3227
Officer: Brian King, President. Ultimate Parent: Alco Standard Corp. SIC: 3663—Radio & T.V. Communications Equipment.

★ 60258 ★ Deluxe Check Printers
3044 Mercury Rd. S
Jacksonville, FL 32207
Ultimate Parent: Deluxe Corp. SIC: 2782—Blankbooks & Looseleaf Binders; 2752—Commercial Printing—Lithographic.

★ 60259 ★ Deluxe Check Printers Inc.
3044 Mercury Rd. S
Jacksonville, FL 32207
Ultimate Parent: Deluxe Corp. SIC: 2782—Blankbooks & Looseleaf Binders; 2752—Commercial Printing—Lithographic.

★ 60260 ★ Diebold Inc.
853521 Baymeadows Rd.
Jacksonville, FL 32216
(904)731-1344
Ultimate Parent: Diebold, Inc. SIC: 7382—Security Systems Services.

★ 60261 ★ Diebold Inc.
5913 Saint Augustine Rd.
Jacksonville, FL 32207
(904)731-1344
Ultimate Parent: Diebold, Inc. SIC: 5046—Commercial Equipment Nec.

★ 60262 ★ Digital Equipment Corporati
7775 Baymeadows Way 105
Jacksonville, FL 32256
(904)733-8800
Ultimate Parent: Digital Equipment Corp. SIC: 5099—Durable Goods Nec.

★ 60263 ★ Digital Equipment Corp.
6620 Southpoint Dr. S
Jacksonville, FL 32216
(904)354-4005
Ultimate Parent: Digital Equipment Corp. SIC: 5734—Computer & Software Stores.

★ 60264 ★ Duracell International Inc.
8021 Bayberry Rd.
Jacksonville, FL 32256
(904)733-7308
Ultimate Parent: Duracell International Inc. SIC: 5531—Automobile & Home Supply Stores.

★ 60265 ★ Durr-Fillauer Medical Inc.
7501 Phillips Hwy.
Jacksonville, FL 32256
(904)733-5765
Ultimate Parent: Bergen Brunswig Corp. SIC: 5047—Medical & Hospital Equipment.

★ 60266 ★ Emery Worldwide
Airport Rd.
Jacksonville, FL 32218
(904)757-2391
Ultimate Parent: Consolidated Freightways. SIC: 4512—Air Transportation—Scheduled.

★ 60267 ★ Express Ltd.
2 Independent Dr.
Jacksonville, FL 32202
(904)354-6962
Ultimate Parent: Limited. SIC: 5621—Women's Clothing Stores.

★ 60268 ★ Fastening Systems Inc.
11315 St. Johns Industrial Pky.
Jacksonville, FL 32246
(904)641-8909
Ultimate Parent: Black & Decker Corp. SIC: 5082—Construction & Mining Machinery; 5085—Industrial Supplies.

★ 60269 ★ First Trust Savings Bank, FSB
10601-36 San Jose Blvd.
Jacksonville, FL 32237-6255
(904)262-5555 Fax: (904)262-4118
Location Type: Branch office. Officer: James S. Follon, Chairman of the Board, President & CEO. Ultimate Parent: Huntington Bancshares. SIC: 6021—National Commercial Banks.

★ 60270 ★ First Union National Bank of Florida
4328 Blanding Blvd.
Jacksonville, FL 32210
(904)361-7386
Location Type: Branch office. Ultimate Parent: First Union Corp. SIC: 6021—National Commercial Banks.

★ 60271 ★   First Union National
Bank of Florida
1601 Main St.
Jacksonville, FL 32206
(904)361-7317
Location Type: Branch office. Ultimate
Parent: First Union Corp. SIC: 6021—
National Commercial Banks.

★ 60272 ★   First Union National
Bank of Florida
7991 Normandy Blvd.
Jacksonville, FL 32221
(904)783-8447
Location Type: Branch office. Ultimate
Parent: First Union Corp. SIC: 6021—
National Commercial Banks.

★ 60273 ★   First Union National
Bank of Florida
12222 San Jose Blvd.
Jacksonville, FL 32223
(904)361-5740
Location Type: Branch office. Ultimate
Parent: First Union Corp. SIC: 6021—
National Commercial Banks.

★ 60274 ★   First Union National
Bank of Florida
4348 Southpoint Blvd., Ste. 100
Jacksonville, FL 32216
(904)361-5501
Location Type: Branch office. Ultimate
Parent: First Union Corp. SIC: 6021—
National Commercial Banks.

★ 60275 ★   First Union National
Bank of Florida
380 S. Edgewood Ave.
Jacksonville, FL 32205-3785
(904)361-2091
Location Type: Branch office. Ultimate
Parent: First Union Corp. SIC: 6021—
National Commercial Banks.

★ 60276 ★   First Union National
Bank of Florida
1200 Gulf Life Dr.
Jacksonville, FL 32207-9092
(904)391-7600
Location Type: Branch office. Ultimate
Parent: First Union Corp. SIC: 6021—
National Commercial Banks.

★ 60277 ★   First Union National
Bank of Florida
9661 San Jose Blvd.
Jacksonville, FL 32257-5433
(904)361-4413
Location Type: Branch office. Ultimate
Parent: First Union Corp. SIC: 6021—
National Commercial Banks.

★ 60278 ★   First Union National
Bank of Florida
9700 Baymeadows Rd.
Jacksonville, FL 32256-7985
(904)361-4406
Location Type: Branch office. Ultimate
Parent: First Union Corp. SIC: 6021—
National Commercial Banks.

★ 60279 ★   First Union National
Bank of Florida
803 Lomax St.
Jacksonville, FL 32204-3901
(904)366-2140
Location Type: Branch office. Ultimate
Parent: First Union Corp. SIC: 6021—
National Commercial Banks.

★ 60280 ★   First Union National
Bank of Florida
6530 St. Augustine Rd.
Jacksonville, FL 32217
(904)366-2140
Location Type: Branch office. Ultimate
Parent: First Union Corp. SIC: 6021—
National Commercial Banks.

★ 60281 ★   First Union National
Bank of Florida
3650 Phillips Hwy.
Jacksonville, FL 32207
(904)361-5271
Location Type: Branch office. Ultimate
Parent: First Union Corp. SIC: 6021—
National Commercial Banks.

★ 60282 ★   First Union National
Bank of Florida
9850 Regency Square Blvd.
Jacksonville, FL 32225
(904)367-5498
Location Type: Branch office. Ultimate
Parent: First Union Corp. SIC: 6021—
National Commercial Banks.

★ 60283 ★   First Union National
Bank of Florida
4206 San Juan Ave.
Jacksonville, FL 32210
(904)361-7950
Location Type: Branch office. Ultimate
Parent: First Union Corp. SIC: 6021—
National Commercial Banks.

★ 60284 ★   First Union National
Bank of Florida
1004 N. Edgewood Ave.
Jacksonville, FL 32205
(904)783-2221
Location Type: Branch office. Ultimate
Parent: First Union Corp. SIC: 6021—
National Commercial Banks.

★ 60285 ★   First Union National
Bank of Florida
1471 Monument Rd.
Jacksonville, FL 32211
(904)642-7501
Location Type: Branch office. Ultimate
Parent: First Union Corp. SIC: 6021—
National Commercial Banks.

★ 60286 ★   First Union National
Bank of Florida
6545 Normandy Blvd.
Jacksonville, FL 32205
(904)361-7469
Location Type: Branch office. Ultimate
Parent: First Union Corp. SIC: 6021—
National Commercial Banks.

★ 60287 ★   First Union National
Bank of Florida
3627 University Blvd. S, Ste. 100
Jacksonville, FL 32216
(904)367-5865
Location Type: Branch office. Ultimate
Parent: First Union Corp. SIC: 6021—
National Commercial Banks.

★ 60288 ★   First Union National
Bank of Florida
7101 Merrill Rd.
Jacksonville, FL 32211
(904)743-4842
Location Type: Branch office. Ultimate
Parent: First Union Corp. SIC: 6021—
National Commercial Banks.

★ 60289 ★   First Union National
Bank of Florida
4617 San Juan Ave.
Jacksonville, FL 32210
(904)361-2535
Location Type: Branch office. Ultimate
Parent: First Union Corp. SIC: 6021—
National Commercial Banks.

★ 60290 ★   First Union National
Bank of Florida
10600 San Jose Blvd.
Jacksonville, FL 32257-6211
(904)262-6402
Location Type: Branch office. Ultimate
Parent: First Union Corp. SIC: 6021—
National Commercial Banks.

★ 60291 ★   First Union National
Bank of Florida
214 Hogan St.
Jacksonville, FL 32202
(904)361-1944
Location Type: Branch office. Ultimate
Parent: First Union Corp. SIC: 6021—
National Commercial Banks.

★ 60292 ★   First Union National
Bank of Florida
1336 Edgewood Ave. W
Jacksonville, FL 32208
(904)361-7416
Location Type: Branch office. Ultimate
Parent: First Union Corp. SIC: 6021—
National Commercial Banks.

★ 60293 ★   First Union National
Bank of Florida
5592 Norwood Ave.
Jacksonville, FL 32208-5085
(901)361-2135
Location Type: Branch office. Ultimate
Parent: First Union Corp. SIC: 6021—
National Commercial Banks.

★ 60294 ★   First Union National
Bank of Florida
13166 Atlantic Blvd.
Jacksonville, FL 32225
(904)361-5720
Location Type: Branch office. Ultimate
Parent: First Union Corp. SIC: 6021—
National Commercial Banks.

★ 60295 ★   First Union National
Bank of Florida
225 Water St.
Jacksonville, FL 32202
(904)361-2265
Location Type: Branch office. Ultimate
Parent: First Union Corp. SIC: 6021—
National Commercial Banks.

★ 60296 ★   First Union National
Bank of Florida
300 Clay St.
Jacksonville, FL 32202
(904)361-2489
Location Type: Branch office. Ultimate
Parent: First Union Corp. SIC: 6021—
National Commercial Banks.

★ 60297 ★   First Union National
Bank of Florida
840 University Blvd. N
Jacksonville, FL 32211
(904)361-7770
Location Type: Branch office. Ultimate
Parent: First Union Corp. SIC: 6021—
National Commercial Banks.

★ 60298 ★   First Union National
Bank of Florida
8715 Baymeadows Rd.
Jacksonville, FL 32256
(904)739-4665
Location Type: Branch office. Ultimate
Parent: First Union Corp. SIC: 6021—
National Commercial Banks.

★ 60299 ★   First Union National
Bank of Florida
11415 Beach Blvd.
Jacksonville, FL 32216
(904)361-5288
Location Type: Branch office. Ultimate
Parent: First Union Corp. SIC: 6021—
National Commercial Banks.

★ 60300 ★   First Union National
Bank of Florida
PO Box 2080
Jacksonville, FL 32231
Company Type: Subsidiary. Officer: John
A. Michell III, Chairman of the Board.
Ultimate Parent: First Union Corp. SIC:
6021—National Commercial Banks; 6162—
Mortgage Bankers & Correspondents;
6712—Bank Holding Companies.

★ 60301 ★   Fist Trust Savings
Bank, FSB
PO Box 23280
Jacksonville, FL 32241-3280
(904)262-5555 Fax: (904)262-4118
Location Type: Branch office. Officer:
James S. Follon, Chairman of the Board,
President & CEO. Ultimate Parent:
Huntington Bancshares. SIC: 6021—
National Commercial Banks.

★ 60302 ★   Flagstar Co.
Volume Services
1145 E. Adams St.
Jacksonville, FL 32202
(904)354-3620
Ultimate Parent: Flagstar Co. SIC: 5812—
Eating Places.

★ 60303 ★   Florida Coca-Cola
Bottling Co.
1411 Huron St.
Jacksonville, FL 32205
Ultimate Parent: Coca-Cola Enterprises.
SIC: 2086—Bottled & Canned Soft Drinks.

★ 60304 ★   Flowers Baking Co.
2261 W. 30th St.
Jacksonville, FL 32209
(904)354-3771
Officer: Ray McDaniel, President. Ultimate

Parent: Flowers Industries. SIC: 2051—
Bread, Cake & Related Products.

★ 60305 ★   Flowers Baking Co. of
Jacksonville Inc.
2261 W. 30th St.
PO Box 12579
Jacksonville, FL 32209
(904)354-3771 Fax: (904)634-4829
Company Type: Subsidiary. Officer: Ray
McDaniel, President. Ultimate Parent:
Flowers Industries.

★ 60306 ★   FMC Corp.
1200 Talleyrand Ave.
Jacksonville, FL 32206
(904)353-9041
Location Type: Plant. Officer: Frank
Siwajek, Plant Manager. Ultimate Parent:
FMC. SIC: 2879—Agricultural Chemicals
Nec.

★ 60307 ★   Fmc Corp.
Jacksonville Plant
1200 Talleyrand Ave.
Jacksonville, FL 32206
Ultimate Parent: FMC. SIC: 2879—
Agricultural Chemicals Nec.

★ 60308 ★   Food Lion
6855 Wilson Blvd.
Jacksonville, FL 32210
(904)777-0301
Ultimate Parent: Food Lion. SIC: 5411—
Grocery Stores.

★ 60309 ★   Food Lion
5150 Timuquana Rd.
Jacksonville, FL 32210
(904)778-0966
Ultimate Parent: Food Lion. SIC: 5411—
Grocery Stores.

★ 60310 ★   Food Lion
7200 Normandy Blvd.
Jacksonville, FL 32205
(904)783-9970
Ultimate Parent: Food Lion. SIC: 5411—
Grocery Stores.

★ 60311 ★   Food Lion
6271 Saint Augustine Rd.
Jacksonville, FL 32217
(904)737-5088
Ultimate Parent: Food Lion. SIC: 5411—
Grocery Stores.

★ 60312 ★   Food Lion
1680 Dunn Ave. 8
Jacksonville, FL 32218
(904)757-0522
Ultimate Parent: Food Lion. SIC: 5411—
Grocery Stores.

★ 60313 ★   Food Lion Inc.
6855 Wilson Blvd.
Jacksonville, FL 32210
(904)777-0301
Ultimate Parent: Food Lion. SIC: 5411—
Grocery Stores.

★ 60314 ★   FPL Group
700 Universe Blvd.
Jacksonville, FL 32202
(904)791-7720
Company Type: Headquarters. Officer:
James L. Broadhead. Fortune Service 500:
Ranking 21.

★ 60315 ★   The Gap
2 Independent Dr.
Jacksonville, FL 32202
(904)634-8907
Ultimate Parent: GAP. SIC: 5651—Family
Clothing Stores.

★ 60316 ★   The Gap
Regency Sq.
Jacksonville, FL 32211
(904)724-6914
Ultimate Parent: GAP. SIC: 5611—Men's &
Boys' Clothing Stores.

★ 60317 ★   Gap Stores
Regency Sq.
Jacksonville, FL 32211
(904)724-6914
Ultimate Parent: GAP. SIC: 5611—Men's &
Boys' Clothing Stores.

★ 60318 ★　GATX Logistics Inc.
1301 Gulf Line Dr., Ste. 1800
Jacksonville, FL 32207
(904)396-3984 Fax: (904)396-3984
Company Type: Subsidiary. Officer:
William S. Elston, President & CEO.
Ultimate Parent: GATX Corp.

★ 60319 ★　GE Electrical
Distribution
10 Van Dyck Rd.
Jacksonville, FL 32218
(904)757-2600
Officer: Paul Steele, Manager. Ultimate
Parent: General Electric. SIC: 3599—
Industrial Machinery Nec.

★ 60320 ★　Greyhound Bus Lines
5333 Lenox Ave.
Jacksonville, FL 32205
(904)786-4323
Ultimate Parent: Greyhound Lines Inc. SIC:
4173—Bus Terminal & Service Facilities.

★ 60321 ★　Greyhound Bus Lines
8030 Phillips Hwy. Ste. 16
Jacksonville, FL 32256
(904)737-7011
Ultimate Parent: Greyhound Lines Inc. SIC:
4131—Intercity & Rural Bus Transportation.

★ 60322 ★　Greyhound Bus
Station
10 N. Pearl St.
Jacksonville, FL 32202
Ultimate Parent: Greyhound Lines Inc. SIC:
4131—Intercity & Rural Bus Transportation;
4173—Bus Terminal & Service Facilities.

★ 60323 ★　Hertz Rent-A-Car
2400 Yankee Clipper Dr.
Jacksonville, FL 32218
(904)741-2151
Ultimate Parent: Hertz. SIC: 7514—
Passenger Car Rental.

★ 60324 ★　Hertz Rent-A-Car
304 N. Pearl St.
Jacksonville, FL 32202
(904)354-5474
Ultimate Parent: Hertz. SIC: 7514—
Passenger Car Rental.

★ 60325 ★　Hertz Rent-A-Car
Jacksonville
Jacksonville, FL 32229
(904)757-2151
Ultimate Parent: Hertz. SIC: 7514—
Passenger Car Rental.

★ 60326 ★　Hewlett Packard Co.
Inc.
4080 Woodcock Dr.
Jacksonville, FL 32207
(904)398-0663
Ultimate Parent: Hewlett-Packard. SIC:
3571—Electronic Computers.

★ 60327 ★　Hit or Miss
Regency Ct
Jacksonville, FL 32211
(904)725-9946
Ultimate Parent: TJX. SIC: 5621—
Women's Clothing Stores.

★ 60328 ★　Hit or Miss
600131 Argyle Forest Blvd.
Jacksonville, FL 32244
(904)777-0557
Ultimate Parent: TJX. SIC: 5651—Family
Clothing Stores.

★ 60329 ★　Hit or Miss Clothes
9308 Arlington Expy.
Jacksonville, FL 32225
(904)725-4633
Ultimate Parent: TJX. SIC: 5651—Family
Clothing Stores.

★ 60330 ★　Home Depot Inc. the
9355 Atlantic Blvd.
Jacksonville, FL 32225
(904)724-5921
Ultimate Parent: Home Depot. SIC: 5251—
Hardware Stores.

★ 60331 ★　Jacksonville Coca-
Cola Bottling Co.
1411 Huron St.
Jacksonville, FL 32205
Ultimate Parent: Coca-Cola Enterprises.

★ 60332 ★　Jacksonville
Shipyards Inc.
750 East Bay St.
Jacksonville, FL 32203
(904)798-3700
Company Type: Subsidiary. Officer: Roger
Palmer, President & CEO. Ultimate Parent:
Banta Corp. SIC: 3731—Ship Building &
Repairing. Employee Count: 705.

★ 60333 ★　Jacksonville
Shipyards, Inc.
Electro Lube Devices
5502 Shawland Rd.
Jacksonville, FL 32205
(904)786-0784
Company Type: Subsidiary. Officer: Arnold
P. McIlwan, President. Ultimate Parent:
Banta Corp. SIC: 3731—Ship Building &
Repairing.

★ 60334 ★　Jacksonville
Shipyards, Inc.-Electro Lube
Devices
5502 Shawland Rd.
Jacksonville, FL 32205
(904)786-0784
Company Type: Subsidiary. Officer: Arnold
P. McIlwan, President. Ultimate Parent:
Banta Corp. SIC: 3731—Ship Building &
Repairing.

★ 60335 ★　Jacksonville
Shipyards, Inc.-Key Houston &
Bellinger
13911 Atlantic Blvd.
Jacksonville, FL 32225
(904)241-0633
Company Type: Subsidiary. Officer: A. P.
McIlwain, President. Ultimate Parent: Banta
Corp. SIC: 3731—Ship Building &
Repairing.

★ 60336 ★　Jacksonville Welder
Sup
2312 Edwards Ave.
Jacksonville, FL 32205
(904)388-0561
Ultimate Parent: Praxair. SIC: 5084—
Industrial Machinery & Equipment.

★ 60337 ★　Jefferson Smurfit
Corp.
1915 Wigmore St.
Jacksonville, FL 32206
Ultimate Parent: Jefferson Smurfit Corp.
SIC: 2630—Paperboard Mills.

★ 60338 ★　Jefferson Smurfit
Corp.
Containerboard Mill Div.
1915 Wigmore St.
Jacksonville, FL 32206
Company Type: Division. Ultimate Parent:
Jefferson Smurfit Corp. SIC: 2631—
Paperboard Mills.

★ 60339 ★　Jiffy Lube
4821 Blanding Blvd.
Jacksonville, FL 32210
(904)722-1701
Ultimate Parent: Pennzoil.

★ 60340 ★　Jiffy Lube
2837 Townsend Blvd.
Jacksonville, FL 32211
(904)744-3402
Ultimate Parent: Pennzoil. SIC: 7539—
Automotive Repair Shops Nec.

★ 60341 ★　Jiffy Lube
8379 Baymeadows Rd.
Jacksonville, FL 32256
(904)731-3989
Ultimate Parent: Pennzoil. SIC: 7539—
Automotive Repair Shops Nec.

★ 60342 ★　Jsc/Cca D-Graphics
3389 Powers Ave.
Jacksonville, FL 32207-8013
Ultimate Parent: Jefferson Smurfit Corp.
SIC: 2754—Commercial Printing—Gravure.

★ 60343 ★　Kaiser Aluminum &
Chemical
5301 W. 5th St.
Jacksonville, FL 32205
(904)786-5432
Ultimate Parent: Maxxam. SIC: 3411—
Metal Cans.

★ 60344 ★　Kentucky Fried
Chicken
3714 Beach Blvd.
Jacksonville, FL 32207
(904)388-2441
Ultimate Parent: Pepsico. SIC: 5812—
Eating Places.

★ 60345 ★　Kentucky Fried
Chicken
3930 University Blvd. W
Jacksonville, FL 32217
(904)737-2252
Ultimate Parent: Pepsico. SIC: 5812—
Eating Places.

★ 60346 ★　Kentucky Fried
Chicken
1556 Whitlock Ave.
Jacksonville, FL 32211
(904)389-7643
Ultimate Parent: Pepsico. SIC: 5812—
Eating Places.

★ 60347 ★　Kentucky Fried
Chicken
6630 N. Main St.
Jacksonville, FL 32208
(904)764-7941
Ultimate Parent: Pepsico. SIC: 5812—
Eating Places.

★ 60348 ★　Kentucky Fried
Chicken
3430 University Blvd. S
Jacksonville, FL 32216
(904)398-3339
Ultimate Parent: Pepsico. SIC: 5812—
Eating Places.

★ 60349 ★　Kentucky Fried
Chicken
1007 Lane Ave. S
Jacksonville, FL 32205
(904)783-3947
Ultimate Parent: Pepsico. SIC: 5812—
Eating Places.

★ 60350 ★　Kentucky Fried
Chicken
1909 N. Main St.
Jacksonville, FL 32206
(904)354-7062
Ultimate Parent: Pepsico. SIC: 5812—
Eating Places.

★ 60351 ★　Kentucky Fried
Chicken
1142 Dunn Ave.
Jacksonville, FL 32218
(904)757-4454
Ultimate Parent: Pepsico. SIC: 5812—
Eating Places.

★ 60352 ★　Kentucky Fried
Chicken
2258 Edgewood Ave. W
Jacksonville, FL 32209
(904)765-2788
Ultimate Parent: Pepsico. SIC: 5812—
Eating Places.

★ 60353 ★　Kentucky Fried
Chicken
8761 Baymeadows Rd.
Jacksonville, FL 32256
(904)737-9724
Ultimate Parent: Pepsico. SIC: 5812—
Eating Places.

★ 60354 ★　Kentucky Fried
Chicken
334 Beach Blvd.
Jacksonville, FL 32250
(904)246-8444
Ultimate Parent: Pepsico. SIC: 5812—
Eating Places.

★ 60355 ★　Kentucky Fried
Chicken
7276 103rd St.
Jacksonville, FL 32210
(904)772-9449
Ultimate Parent: Pepsico. SIC: 5812—
Eating Places.

★ 60356 ★　Kentucky Fried
Chicken
10400 Atlantic Blvd.
Jacksonville, FL 32225
(904)642-0967
Ultimate Parent: Pepsico. SIC: 5812—
Eating Places.

★ 60357 ★　Kentucky Fried
Chicken
2260 Mayport Rd.
Jacksonville, FL 32233
(904)241-4412
Ultimate Parent: Pepsico. SIC: 5812—
Eating Places.

★ 60358 ★　Label Systems
International
836 Mamie Rd.
Jacksonville, FL 32205-4742
(904)786-9131
Officer: Don Copeland. Ultimate Parent:
Avery Dennison Corp. SIC: 2679—
Converted Paper Products Nec.

★ 60359 ★　Land-Marine Cargo
Inc.
PO Box 51527
Jacksonville, FL 32240-1527
(904)241-0333
Ultimate Parent: Arkansas Best. SIC:
4212—Local Trucking Without Storage.

★ 60360 ★　Lens Crafters
50 E. Regency Sq.
Jacksonville, FL 32225
(904)724-7702
Ultimate Parent: United States Shoe. SIC:
5995—Optical Goods Stores.

★ 60361 ★　Lens Crafters
9551 Atlantic Blvd.
Jacksonville, FL 32225
(904)721-7521
Ultimate Parent: United States Shoe. SIC:
5995—Optical Goods Stores.

★ 60362 ★　Lerner Shop
4461 Roosevelt Blvd.
Jacksonville, FL 32210
(904)387-6861
Ultimate Parent: Limited. SIC: 5621—
Women's Clothing Stores; 5651—Family
Clothing Stores.

★ 60363 ★　Lerner Shop
3576 Blanding Blvd.
Jacksonville, FL 32210
(904)771-7333
Ultimate Parent: Limited. SIC: 5621—
Women's Clothing Stores; 5651—Family
Clothing Stores.

★ 60364 ★　Lerner Shop
40 Regency Sq.
Jacksonville, FL 32225
(904)721-2088
Ultimate Parent: Limited. SIC: 5651—
Family Clothing Stores.

★ 60365 ★　Liberty Mutual
Insurance Co.
3986 Boulevard Ctr. Dr.
Jacksonville, FL 32207
(904)398-3061
Ultimate Parent: Liberty Mutual Group.
SIC: 6411—Insurance Agents, Brokers &
Service.

★ 60366 ★　The Limited
181 Regency Sq.
Jacksonville, FL 32225
(904)724-5515
Ultimate Parent: Limited. SIC: 5651—
Family Clothing Stores.

★ 60367 ★　Manpower, Inc.
7933 Baymeadows Way
Jacksonville, FL 32256
(904)731-1869
Ultimate Parent: Manpower, Inc. SIC:
7363—Help Supply Services.

★ 60368 ★　Manpower, Inc.
8101 Southside Blvd.
Jacksonville, FL 32256
(904)645-7690
Ultimate Parent: Manpower, Inc. SIC:
7363—Help Supply Services.

★ 60369 ★　Manpower, Inc.
7033 Commonwealth Ave.
Jacksonville, FL 32220
(904)783-9400
Ultimate Parent: Manpower, Inc. SIC:
7361—Employment Agencies.

★ 60370 ★　Manpower, Inc.
8647 Baypine Rd.
Jacksonville, FL 32256
(904)733-0136
Ultimate Parent: Manpower, Inc. SIC:
7363—Help Supply Services.

★ 60371 ★   Mark Vii
Transportation
2121-B Corporate Sq.
Jacksonville, FL 32216
(904)727-7006
Ultimate Parent: MNX.

★ 60372 ★   Mark Vii
Transportation
9951 Atlantic Blvd.
Jacksonville, FL 32225
(904)724-5112
Ultimate Parent: MNX. SIC: 4213—
Trucking Except Local.

★ 60373 ★   Maxwell House Coffee
Co.
735 E. Bay St.
Jacksonville, FL 32203
Ultimate Parent: Philip Morris. SIC: 2095—
Roasted Coffee.

★ 60374 ★   Maxwell House Coffee
Co.
International Div.
735 E. Bay St.
Jacksonville, FL 32203
Company Type: Division. Ultimate Parent:
Philip Morris. SIC: 2095—Roasted Coffee.

★ 60375 ★   Metal Container Corp.
1100 Ellis Rd. S
Jacksonville, FL 32205-6219
(904)695-7600
Officer: William McClarnand. Ultimate
Parent: Ball Corp. SIC: 3411—Metal Cans.

★ 60376 ★   Metal Container Corp.
1100 N. Ellis Rd.
Jacksonville, FL 32205-6275
Ultimate Parent: Anheuser-Busch. SIC:
3411—Metal Cans.

★ 60377 ★   Metal Container Corp.
1100 N. Ellis Rd.
Jacksonville, FL 32205-6275
Ultimate Parent: Anheuser-Busch. SIC:
3411—Metal Cans.

★ 60378 ★   Mobil Gas Station
5430 Avenue B
Jacksonville, FL 32209
(904)768-3479
Ultimate Parent: Mobil. SIC: 5541—
Gasoline Service Stations.

★ 60379 ★   Mobil Oil Corp.
1974 Talleyrand Ave.
Jacksonville, FL 32206
(904)358-1385
Ultimate Parent: Mobil. SIC: 5171—
Petroleum Bulk Stations & Terminals.

★ 60380 ★   Nalco Chemical Co.
2121 Corporate Sq.
Jacksonville, FL 32216
(904)724-3788
Ultimate Parent: Nalco Chemical Co. SIC:
5074—Plumbing & Hydronic Heating
Supplies; 5169—Chemicals & Allied
Products Nec.

★ 60381 ★   New York Life
Jackson General Office
Southeastern Agencies
50 N. Laura St., Ste. 1900
Jacksonville, FL 32202
(904)632-5600 Fax: (904)632-5620
Officer: Brad L. Willson, General Manager.
Ultimate Parent: New York Life.

★ 60382 ★   Oaks at Baymeadows
the
8401 Southside Blvd.
Jacksonville, FL 32256
(904)642-0857
Ultimate Parent: Connecticut General Life.
SIC: 6513—Apartment Building Operators.

★ 60383 ★   Otis Elevator Co.
4801 Executive Park Ct N. 210
Jacksonville, FL 32216
Ultimate Parent: United Technologies. SIC:
5084—Industrial Machinery & Equipment.

★ 60384 ★   Owens Corning
Fiberglas
1035 Talleyrand Ave.
Jacksonville, FL 32206
(904)353-7361
Ultimate Parent: Owens-Corning. SIC:
5039—Construction Materials Nec; 5131—
Piece Goods & Notions.

★ 60385 ★   Owens-Corning
Fiberglass
Roofing Plant
1035 Talleyrand Ave.
Jacksonville, FL 32206
Location Type: Plant. Ultimate Parent:
Owens-Corning. SIC: 2952—Asphalt Felts &
Coatings.

★ 60386 ★   Pappagallo
Regency Sq.
Jacksonville, FL 32211
(904)721-3762
Ultimate Parent: United States Shoe. SIC:
5621—Women's Clothing Stores.

★ 60387 ★   Pennzoil Co.
6319 Powers Ave.
Jacksonville, FL 32217
(904)737-3426
Ultimate Parent: Pennzoil. SIC: 2911—
Petroleum Refining.

★ 60388 ★   Pepsi-Cola Bottling
Co.
5829 Pepsi Pl.
Jacksonville, FL 32216
(904)737-3774
Officer: Scott Toth, President. Ultimate
Parent: Pepsico. SIC: 2086—Bottled &
Canned Soft Drinks.

★ 60389 ★   Petite Sophisticate
10300 Southside Blvd.
Jacksonville, FL 32256
(904)363-8380
Ultimate Parent: United States Shoe. SIC:
5699—Miscellaneous Apparel & Accessory
Stores.

★ 60390 ★   Petite Sophisticate
290 Regency Sq.
Jacksonville, FL 32225
(904)725-2311
Ultimate Parent: United States Shoe. SIC:
5651—Family Clothing Stores.

★ 60391 ★   Pitney Bowes
3740 St. Johns Bluff Rd. S
Jacksonville, FL 32224
(904)464-0500
Officer: John Zupancic, Vice President.
Ultimate Parent: Pitney Bowes. SIC:
3554—Paper Industries Machinery.

★ 60392 ★   Pizza Hut
5102 Timuquana Rd.
Jacksonville, FL 32210
(904)725-2222
Ultimate Parent: Pepsico. SIC: 5812—
Eating Places.

★ 60393 ★   Pizza Hut
4311 University Blvd. S
Jacksonville, FL 32216
(904)733-9650
Ultimate Parent: Pepsico. SIC: 5812—
Eating Places.

★ 60394 ★   Pizza Hut
5421 Roosevelt Blvd.
Jacksonville, FL 32210
(904)389-5966
Ultimate Parent: Pepsico. SIC: 5812—
Eating Places.

★ 60395 ★   Pizza Hut
9703 San Jose Blvd.
Jacksonville, FL 32257
(904)268-0066
Ultimate Parent: Pepsico. SIC: 5812—
Eating Places.

★ 60396 ★   Pizza Hut
6037 Merrill Rd.
Jacksonville, FL 32211
(904)744-5566
Ultimate Parent: Pepsico. SIC: 5812—
Eating Places.

★ 60397 ★   Pizza Hut
7939 Normandy Blvd.
Jacksonville, FL 32221
(904)783-3229
Ultimate Parent: Pepsico. SIC: 5812—
Eating Places.

★ 60398 ★   Pizza Hut
670 Edgewood Ave. N
Jacksonville, FL 32205
(904)387-2449
Ultimate Parent: Pepsico. SIC: 5812—
Eating Places.

★ 60399 ★   Pizza Hut
9300 Lem Turner Rd.
Jacksonville, FL 32208
(904)765-4427
Ultimate Parent: Pepsico. SIC: 5812—
Eating Places.

★ 60400 ★   Pizza Hut
8490 Baymeadows Rd.
Jacksonville, FL 32256
(904)731-8125
Ultimate Parent: Pepsico. SIC: 5812—
Eating Places.

★ 60401 ★   Pizza Hut
8560 Beach Blvd.
Jacksonville, FL 32216
(904)641-3066
Ultimate Parent: Pepsico. SIC: 5812—
Eating Places.

★ 60402 ★   Pizza Hut
7750 Atlantic Blvd.
Jacksonville, FL 32211
(904)724-3382
Ultimate Parent: Pepsico. SIC: 5812—
Eating Places.

★ 60403 ★   Pizza Hut
6501 Arlington Expy. B111
Jacksonville, FL 32211
Ultimate Parent: Pepsico. SIC: 5812—
Eating Places.

★ 60404 ★   Pizza Hut
815 Atlantic Blvd.
Jacksonville, FL 32233
(904)246-7443
Ultimate Parent: Pepsico. SIC: 5812—
Eating Places.

★ 60405 ★   Pizza Hut
7403 103rd St.
Jacksonville, FL 32210
(904)778-4363
Ultimate Parent: Pepsico. SIC: 5812—
Eating Places.

★ 60406 ★   Pizza Hut
975 3rd St. S
Jacksonville, FL 32250
(904)241-7266
Ultimate Parent: Pepsico. SIC: 5812—
Eating Places.

★ 60407 ★   Pizza Hut
Jacksonville, FL 32211
(904)724-5822
Ultimate Parent: Pepsico. SIC: 6159—
Miscellaneous Business Credit Institutions.

★ 60408 ★   Pizza Hut
853546 Baymeadows Rd.
Jacksonville, FL 32216
(904)731-7166
Ultimate Parent: Pepsico. SIC: 5812—
Eating Places.

★ 60409 ★   Pizza Hut
2771 Monument Rd. 13
Jacksonville, FL 32225
Ultimate Parent: Pepsico. SIC: 5812—
Eating Places.

★ 60410 ★   Pizza Hut
7556 103rd St.
Jacksonville, FL 32210
(904)778-1803
Ultimate Parent: Pepsico. SIC: 5812—
Eating Places.

★ 60411 ★   Pizza Hut
7897 Normandy Blvd.
Jacksonville, FL 32221
(904)786-1977
Ultimate Parent: Pepsico. SIC: 5812—
Eating Places.

★ 60412 ★   Pizza Hut
1141 Dunn Ave.
Jacksonville, FL 32218
(904)751-3700
Ultimate Parent: Pepsico. SIC: 5812—
Eating Places.

★ 60413 ★   Publix Super Market
4399 Roosevelt Blvd.
Jacksonville, FL 32210
(904)388-7694
Ultimate Parent: Publix Super Markets.
SIC: 5411—Grocery Stores.

★ 60414 ★   Publix Super Market
8159 Arlington Expy.
Jacksonville, FL 32211
(904)721-1321
Ultimate Parent: Publix Super Markets.
SIC: 5411—Grocery Stores.

★ 60415 ★   Publix Super Market
3600 University Blvd. W
Jacksonville, FL 32217
(904)733-4582
Ultimate Parent: Publix Super Markets.
SIC: 5411—Grocery Stores.

★ 60416 ★   Publix Super Market
1100 Dunn Ave.
Jacksonville, FL 32218
(904)751-1980
Ultimate Parent: Publix Super Markets.
SIC: 5411—Grocery Stores.

★ 60417 ★   Publix Super Market
10601 San Jose Blvd.
Jacksonville, FL 32257
(904)268-5512
Ultimate Parent: Publix Super Markets.
SIC: 5411—Grocery Stores.

★ 60418 ★   Publix Super Market
5858 Atlantic Blvd.
Jacksonville, FL 32207
(904)724-2784
Ultimate Parent: Publix Super Markets.
SIC: 5411—Grocery Stores.

★ 60419 ★   Publix Super Market
9964 Baymeadows Rd.
Jacksonville, FL 32216
(904)641-2435
Ultimate Parent: Publix Super Markets.
SIC: 5411—Grocery Stores.

★ 60420 ★   Publix Super Market
7628 103rd St.
Jacksonville, FL 32210
(904)777-3122
Ultimate Parent: Publix Super Markets.
SIC: 5411—Grocery Stores.

★ 60421 ★   Publix Super Markets
4399 Roosevelt Blvd.
Jacksonville, FL 32210
(904)388-7694
Ultimate Parent: Publix Super Markets.
SIC: 5411—Grocery Stores.

★ 60422 ★   Radio Shack
580815 Normandy Blvd.
Jacksonville, FL 32205
(904)786-0833
Company Type: Division. Ultimate Parent:
Tandy Corp. SIC: 7373—Computer
Integrated Systems Design.

★ 60423 ★   Radio Shack
4419 Roosevelt Blvd.
Jacksonville, FL 32210
(904)388-4926
Company Type: Division. Ultimate Parent:
Tandy Corp. SIC: 5731—Radio, Television
& Electronics Stores.

★ 60424 ★   Radio Shack
700131 Merrill Rd.
Jacksonville, FL 32211
(904)743-8537
Company Type: Division. Ultimate Parent:
Tandy Corp. SIC: 5731—Radio, Television
& Electronics Stores.

★ 60425 ★   Radio Shack
7915 Normandy Blvd.
Jacksonville, FL 32221
(904)783-2087
Company Type: Division. Ultimate Parent:
Tandy Corp. SIC: 5731—Radio, Television
& Electronics Stores.

★ 60426 ★   Radio Shack
738 Edgewood Ave. N
Jacksonville, FL 32205
(904)389-0495
Company Type: Division. Ultimate Parent:
Tandy Corp. SIC: 5065—Electronic Parts &
Equipment Nec.

★ 60427 ★   Radio Shack
5566 Fort Caroline Rd.
Jacksonville, FL 32211
(904)744-3311
Company Type: Division. Ultimate Parent:
Tandy Corp. SIC: 5731—Radio, Television
& Electronics Stores.

★ 60428 ★ Radio Shack
5671 Beach Blvd.
Jacksonville, FL 32207
(904)398-8167
Company Type: Division. Ultimate Parent: Tandy Corp. SIC: 5065—Electronic Parts & Equipment Nec; 5731—Radio, Television & Electronics Stores.

★ 60429 ★ Radio Shack
1036 Dunn Ave. 50
Jacksonville, FL 32218
(904)751-2662
Company Type: Division. Ultimate Parent: Tandy Corp. SIC: 5719—Miscellaneous Home Furnishings Stores.

★ 60430 ★ Radio Shack
3944 3rd St. S
Jacksonville, FL 32250
(904)249-0666
Company Type: Division. Ultimate Parent: Tandy Corp. SIC: 5731—Radio, Television & Electronics Stores.

★ 60431 ★ Radio Shack
9378 Arlington Expy. 315
Jacksonville, FL 32225
Company Type: Division. Ultimate Parent: Tandy Corp. SIC: 5734—Computer & Software Stores.

★ 60432 ★ Radio Shack
9378 Arlington Expy. 315
Jacksonville, FL 32225
Company Type: Division. Ultimate Parent: Tandy Corp. SIC: 5046—Commercial Equipment Nec; 7372—Prepackaged Software.

★ 60433 ★ Radio Shack
9378 Arlington Expy. 315
Jacksonville, FL 32225
Company Type: Division. Ultimate Parent: Tandy Corp. SIC: 7372—Prepackaged Software.

★ 60434 ★ Radio Shack
12200 San Jose Blvd. 6
Jacksonville, FL 32223
(904)264-3681
Company Type: Division. Ultimate Parent: Tandy Corp. SIC: 5065—Electronic Parts & Equipment Nec.

★ 60435 ★ Radio Shack
4489 Roosevelt Blvd.
Jacksonville, FL 32210
(904)384-9568
Company Type: Division. Ultimate Parent: Tandy Corp. SIC: 7371—Computer Programming Services.

★ 60436 ★ Radio Shack
532 Atlantic Blvd.
Jacksonville, FL 32266
(904)249-4615
Company Type: Division. Ultimate Parent: Tandy Corp. SIC: 1711—Plumbing, Heating & Air-Conditioning.

★ 60437 ★ Rhone-Poulenc Specialty Chemicals Co.
5930 Soutel Dr.
Jacksonville, FL 32219
Ultimate Parent: Rhone-Poulenc Rorer. SIC: 2869—Industrial Organic Chemicals Nec; 2899—Chemical Preparations Nec.

★ 60438 ★ Richards S P Co.
5501 Commonwealth Ave.
Jacksonville, FL 32205
(904)786-0604
Ultimate Parent: Genuine Parts. SIC: 5942—Book Stores.

★ 60439 ★ Ryder Truck Rental
6555 103rd St.
Jacksonville, FL 32210
(904)772-9983
Ultimate Parent: Ryder System. SIC: 7513—Truck Rental & Leasing Without Drivers.

★ 60440 ★ Ryder Truck Rental
3302 W. 20th St.
Jacksonville, FL 32205
(904)786-1868
Ultimate Parent: Ryder System. SIC: 7359—Equipment Rental & Leasing Nec.

★ 60441 ★ Ryder Truck Rental
2015 E. 21st St.
Jacksonville, FL 32206
(904)356-4261
Ultimate Parent: Ryder System. SIC: 7359—Equipment Rental & Leasing Nec.

★ 60442 ★ Ryder Truck Rental
9711 Beach Blvd.
Jacksonville, FL 32246
Ultimate Parent: Ryder System. SIC: 7389—Business Services Nec.

★ 60443 ★ Ryder Truck Rental
2940 Strickland St.
Jacksonville, FL 32205
(904)389-2364
Ultimate Parent: Ryder System. SIC: 7359—Equipment Rental & Leasing Nec; 7513—Truck Rental & Leasing Without Drivers.

★ 60444 ★ Ryder Truck Rental
8686 Phillips Hwy.
Jacksonville, FL 32256
(904)733-7077
Ultimate Parent: Ryder System. SIC: 7513—Truck Rental & Leasing Without Drivers.

★ 60445 ★ Ryder Truck Rental
771 Cesery Blvd.
Jacksonville, FL 32211
(904)724-7574
Ultimate Parent: Ryder System. SIC: 4214—Local Trucking With Storage.

★ 60446 ★ Ryder Truck Rental
4909 Blanding Blvd.
Jacksonville, FL 32210
(904)771-1214
Ultimate Parent: Ryder System. SIC: 7513—Truck Rental & Leasing Without Drivers.

★ 60447 ★ Ryder Truck Rental
5201 Norwood Ave.
Jacksonville, FL 32208
(904)764-5772
Ultimate Parent: Ryder System. SIC: 7513—Truck Rental & Leasing Without Drivers.

★ 60448 ★ Ryder Truck Rental
2512 Commonwealth Ave.
Jacksonville, FL 32205
(904)384-5951
Ultimate Parent: Ryder System. SIC: 7359—Equipment Rental & Leasing Nec.

★ 60449 ★ Ryder Truck Rental
1187 Lane Ave. S
Jacksonville, FL 32205
(904)786-6656
Ultimate Parent: Ryder System. SIC: 7359—Equipment Rental & Leasing Nec.

★ 60450 ★ Ryder Truck Rental
5402 Beach Blvd.
Jacksonville, FL 32207
(904)398-2998
Ultimate Parent: Ryder System. SIC: 7513—Truck Rental & Leasing Without Drivers.

★ 60451 ★ Safety Kleen Corp.
6030 Richard St.
Jacksonville, FL 32216
(904)737-5699
Ultimate Parent: Safety-Kleen. SIC: 5013—Motor Vehicle Supplies & New Parts.

★ 60452 ★ Sam's Wholesale Club
5119 Normandy Blvd.
Jacksonville, FL 32205
(904)786-1125
Ultimate Parent: Wal-Mart Stores, Inc. SIC: 5651—Family Clothing Stores.

★ 60453 ★ Sam's Wholesale Club
10690 Beach Blvd.
Jacksonville, FL 32246
Ultimate Parent: Wal-Mart Stores, Inc. SIC: 5099—Durable Goods Nec.

★ 60454 ★ Scm Glidco Organics Corp.
601 Crestwood St.
Jacksonville, FL 32208
Ultimate Parent: Hanson Industries. SIC: 2869—Industrial Organic Chemicals Nec.

★ 60455 ★ Seminole Kraft Corp.
9469 Eastport Rd.
Jacksonville, FL 32218
Ultimate Parent: Stone Container Corp. SIC: 2621—Paper Mills; 2631—Paperboard Mills.

★ 60456 ★ Service Merchandise
600125 Argyle Forest Blvd.
Jacksonville, FL 32244
(904)777-3020
Ultimate Parent: Service Merchandise Co., Inc. SIC: 5311—Department Stores.

★ 60457 ★ Service Merchandise
9400 Atlantic Blvd. 100
Jacksonville, FL 32225
Ultimate Parent: Service Merchandise Co., Inc. SIC: 5399—Miscellaneous General Merchandise Store.

★ 60458 ★ Stop & Shop
345 E. 3rd St.
Jacksonville, FL 32206
(904)355-8719
Ultimate Parent: Stop & Shop. SIC: 5411—Grocery Stores.

★ 60459 ★ Stop & Shop
2039 W. 12th St.
Jacksonville, FL 32209
(904)354-6347
Ultimate Parent: Stop & Shop. SIC: 5411—Grocery Stores.

★ 60460 ★ Taco Bell
5940 Atlantic Blvd.
Jacksonville, FL 32207
(904)725-6626
Ultimate Parent: Pepsico. SIC: 5812—Eating Places.

★ 60461 ★ Taco Bell
5905 Merrill Rd.
Jacksonville, FL 32211
(904)744-7697
Ultimate Parent: Pepsico. SIC: 5812—Eating Places.

★ 60462 ★ Taco Bell
5084 Normandy Blvd.
Jacksonville, FL 32205
(904)781-6623
Ultimate Parent: Pepsico. SIC: 5812—Eating Places.

★ 60463 ★ Taco Bell
3860 University Blvd. W
Jacksonville, FL 32217
(904)731-8678
Ultimate Parent: Pepsico. SIC: 5812—Eating Places.

★ 60464 ★ Taco Bell
1319 Dunn Ave.
Jacksonville, FL 32218
(904)757-8919
Ultimate Parent: Pepsico. SIC: 5812—Eating Places.

★ 60465 ★ Taco Bell
3101 Emerson St.
Jacksonville, FL 32207
(904)398-6090
Ultimate Parent: Pepsico. SIC: 5812—Eating Places.

★ 60466 ★ Taco Bell
9341 Atlantic Blvd.
Jacksonville, FL 32225
(904)724-5246
Ultimate Parent: Pepsico. SIC: 5812—Eating Places.

★ 60467 ★ Taco Bell
8331 Baymeadows Rd.
Jacksonville, FL 32256
(904)731-0748
Ultimate Parent: Pepsico. SIC: 5812—Eating Places.

★ 60468 ★ Taco Bell
210 3rd St.
Jacksonville, FL 32233
(904)241-9919
Ultimate Parent: Pepsico. SIC: 5812—Eating Places.

★ 60469 ★ Taco Bell
240 3rd St. N
Jacksonville, FL 32250
(904)241-4440
Ultimate Parent: Pepsico. SIC: 5812—Eating Places.

★ 60470 ★ Taco Bell
7331 103rd St.
Jacksonville, FL 32210
(904)777-3626
Ultimate Parent: Pepsico. SIC: 5812—Eating Places.

★ 60471 ★ Texaco
4261 Roosevelt Blvd.
Jacksonville, FL 32210
(904)389-9222
Ultimate Parent: Texaco. SIC: 5541—Gasoline Service Stations.

★ 60472 ★ Texaco
1612 Saint Johns Bluff Rd. N
Jacksonville, FL 32225
(904)292-4400
Ultimate Parent: Texaco.

★ 60473 ★ Texaco Express Lube
10430 Atlantic Blvd.
Jacksonville, FL 32225
(904)642-7720
Ultimate Parent: Texaco. SIC: 5172—Petroleum Products Nec.

★ 60474 ★ Texaco Express Lube
5917 Roosevelt Blvd.
Jacksonville, FL 32244
(904)777-0187
Ultimate Parent: Texaco. SIC: 5541—Gasoline Service Stations.

★ 60475 ★ Texaco Inc.
3529 Talleyrand Ave.
Jacksonville, FL 32206
(904)356-2613
Ultimate Parent: Texaco. SIC: 5172—Petroleum Products Nec.

★ 60476 ★ Title Insur Co. of Minn Titl
120 E. Forsyth St.
Jacksonville, FL 32202
(904)354-7112
Ultimate Parent: Old Republic International. SIC: 6411—Insurance Agents, Brokers & Service.

★ 60477 ★ Toys R US
9600 Atlantic Blvd.
Jacksonville, FL 32225
(904)721-7829
Ultimate Parent: Toys "R" US. SIC: 5945—Hobby, Toy & Game Shops.

★ 60478 ★ Trailways Bus System
410 W. Duval St.
Jacksonville, FL 32202
(904)354-8543
Ultimate Parent: Greyhound Lines Inc. SIC: 4111—Local & Suburban Transit.

★ 60479 ★ Trinity Industries Inc.
11934 West Beaver St.
Jacksonville, FL 32220
Ultimate Parent: Trinity Industries. SIC: 3443—Fabricated Plate Work—Boiler Shops.

★ 60480 ★ Underwriters Adjusting Co.
4161 Carmichael Ave.
Jacksonville, FL 32207
(904)396-4967
Ultimate Parent: Continental. SIC: 6411—Insurance Agents, Brokers & Service.

★ 60481 ★ Underwriters Adjusting Co.
4811 Beach Blvd.
Jacksonville, FL 32207
(904)396-5133
Ultimate Parent: Continental.

★ 60482 ★ Unijax, Inc.
7785 Baymeadows Way, Ste. 200
Jacksonville, FL 32216
(904)733-7770
Company Type: Division. Ultimate Parent: Alco Standard Corp. SIC: 5111—Printing & Writing Paper; 5112—Stationery & Office Supplies; 5113—Industrial & Personal Service Paper; 5141—Groceries—General Line; 5162—Plastics Materials & Basic Shapes; 2677—Envelopes; 2675—Die-Cut Paper & Board; 5169—Chemicals & Allied Products Nec.

★ 60483 ★   **Union Camp Corp.**
2051 Lane Ave. N
Jacksonville, FL 32254
(904)783-2180
Officer: John Baggett, Manager. **Ultimate Parent:** Union Camp Corp. **SIC:** 2844—Toilet Preparations; 2861—Gum & Wood Chemicals; 2899—Chemical Preparations Nec.

★ 60484 ★   **Union Oil Co. of California**
2101 Heckscher Dr.
Jacksonville, FL 32226
(904)757-1726
Ultimate Parent: Unocal Corp. **SIC:** 5172—Petroleum Products Nec.

★ 60485 ★   **Union Oil Co. of California**
6406 103rd St.
Jacksonville, FL 32210
(904)778-4240
Ultimate Parent: Unocal Corp. **SIC:** 5541—Gasoline Service Stations.

★ 60486 ★   **United Parcel Service**
13850 Thomas Ave.
Jacksonville, FL 32218
(904)741-4520
Ultimate Parent: United Parcel Service of America. **SIC:** 7389—Business Services Nec.

★ 60487 ★   **United Parcel Service**
8285 Western Way
Jacksonville, FL 32256
(904)398-5272
Ultimate Parent: United Parcel Service of America. **SIC:** 4212—Local Trucking Without Storage.

★ 60488 ★   **US Fidelity & Gu**
3225 University Blvd. S
Jacksonville, FL 32216
(904)721-0705
Ultimate Parent: USF&G Corp. **SIC:** 6512—Nonresidential Building Operators.

★ 60489 ★   **US Gypsum Co.**
6825 Evergreen Ave.
Jacksonville, FL 32208
(904)768-2501
Ultimate Parent: USG Corp. **SIC:** 5039—Construction Materials Nec.

★ 60490 ★   **Vera Imported Parts Corp.**
8019 Bayberry Rd.
Jacksonville, FL 32256
(904)731-8800
Ultimate Parent: Collins & Aikman Group. **SIC:** 2893—Printing Ink.

★ 60491 ★   **Victoria's Secret**
2 Independent Dr.
Jacksonville, FL 32202
(904)354-8026
Ultimate Parent: Limited. **SIC:** 5699—Miscellaneous Apparel & Accessory Stores.

★ 60492 ★   **Vistakon Inc.**
1417 San Marco Blvd.
Jacksonville, FL 32207
Ultimate Parent: Johnson & Johnson. **SIC:** 3800—Instruments & Related Products.

★ 60493 ★   **Vistakon Inc.**
5985 Richard St.
Jacksonville, FL 32217
Ultimate Parent: Johnson & Johnson. **SIC:** 3851—Ophthalmic Goods.

★ 60494 ★   **Vistakon Johnson & Johnson Vision Products**
1417 San Marco Blvd.
Jacksonville, FL 32207
Ultimate Parent: Johnson & Johnson. **SIC:** 3851—Ophthalmic Goods.

★ 60495 ★   **Wal Mart**
6830 Normandy Blvd.
Jacksonville, FL 32205
(904)786-0390
Ultimate Parent: Wal-Mart Stores, Inc. **SIC:** 5311—Department Stores.

★ 60496 ★   **Wal Mart**
10991 San Jose Blvd.
Jacksonville, FL 32223
(904)260-4402
Ultimate Parent: Wal-Mart Stores, Inc. **SIC:** 5311—Department Stores.

★ 60497 ★   **Wal Mart Discount Cities**
6767 103rd St.
Jacksonville, FL 32210
(904)772-0011
Ultimate Parent: Wal-Mart Stores, Inc. **SIC:** 5311—Department Stores.

★ 60498 ★   **Waldenbooks**
Gateway Shopping
Jacksonville, FL 32208
(904)765-5957
Ultimate Parent: K-Mart. **SIC:** 5192—Books, Periodicals & Newspapers.

★ 60499 ★   **Walgreen**
Gateway Shopping Ctr.
Jacksonville, FL 32208
(904)764-4586
Ultimate Parent: Walgreen Co. **SIC:** 5912—Drug Stores & Proprietary Stores.

★ 60500 ★   **Walgreen**
3548 Blanding Blvd.
Jacksonville, FL 32210
(904)778-8821
Ultimate Parent: Walgreen Co. **SIC:** 5999—Miscellaneous Retail Stores Nec.

★ 60501 ★   **Walgreen Drug Store**
1666 University Blvd. W
Jacksonville, FL 32217
(904)636-0777
Ultimate Parent: Walgreen Co. **SIC:** 5912—Drug Stores & Proprietary Stores.

★ 60502 ★   **Walgreen Drug Stores**
3548 Blanding Blvd.
Jacksonville, FL 32210
(904)778-4076
Ultimate Parent: Walgreen Co. **SIC:** 5912—Drug Stores & Proprietary Stores.

★ 60503 ★   **Walgreen Drug Stores**
2771 Monument Rd.
Jacksonville, FL 32225
(904)646-1708
Ultimate Parent: Walgreen Co. **SIC:** 5912—Drug Stores & Proprietary Stores.

★ 60504 ★   **Walgreen Drug Stores**
7628 103rd St.
Jacksonville, FL 32210
(904)777-3100
Ultimate Parent: Walgreen Co. **SIC:** 5912—Drug Stores & Proprietary Stores.

★ 60505 ★   **Walgreen Drug Stores**
977 Atlantic Blvd.
Jacksonville, FL 32233
(904)247-1950
Ultimate Parent: Walgreen Co. **SIC:** 5912—Drug Stores & Proprietary Stores.

★ 60506 ★   **Walgreen Drug Stores**
Regency Sq.
Jacksonville, FL 32211
(904)724-6185
Ultimate Parent: Walgreen Co. **SIC:** 5912—Drug Stores & Proprietary Stores.

★ 60507 ★   **Washington Inventory Servic**
7933 Baymeadows Way
Jacksonville, FL 32256
(904)733-0381
Ultimate Parent: Huffy. **SIC:** 8721—Accounting, Auditing & Bookkeeping.

★ 60508 ★   **Waste Management Inc.**
4710 Dignan St.
Jacksonville, FL 32254
(904)388-8561
Officer: Bryan Johnson, Manager. **Ultimate Parent:** WMX Technologies, Inc. **SIC:** 3589—Service Industry Machinery Nec.

★ 60509 ★   **Wells Fargo Guard Services**
372840 Phillips Hwy.
Jacksonville, FL 32207
(904)398-7272
Ultimate Parent: Borg Warner Automotive. **SIC:** 7381—Detective & Armored Car Services.

★ 60510 ★   **Weyerhaeuser Paper Co.**
6821 Southpoint Dr. N
Jacksonville, FL 32216
(904)733-4166
Ultimate Parent: Weyerhaeuser Co. **SIC:** 5111—Printing & Writing Paper.

★ 60511 ★   **Winn-Dixie Stores, Inc.**
5050 Edgewood Ct.
Jacksonville, FL 32254
(904)783-5000 **Fax:** (904)783-5294
Company Type: Headquarters. **Officer:** A. Dano Davis. **Employee Count:** 105000. **Sales:** 10831.5 M. **Fortune Service 500:** Ranking 11.

★ 60512 ★   **Witco Corp.**
Kendall-Amalie
3101 Talleyrand Ave.
Jacksonville, FL 32206
Ultimate Parent: Witco Corp. **SIC:** 2992—Lubricating Oils & Greases.

★ 60513 ★   **Xerox Corp.**
4655 Salisbury Rd.
Jacksonville, FL 32256
(904)281-2000
Officer: Dan Costello, Manager. **Ultimate Parent:** Xerox Corp. **SIC:** 3663—Radio & T.V. Communications Equipment.

★ 60514 ★   **Xomed Inc.**
6743 Southpoint Dr. N
Jacksonville, FL 32216-6218
(904)296-9600
Location Type: Branch office. **Officer:** William P. Cusick. **Ultimate Parent:** Bristol-Myers Squibb. **SIC:** 3841—Surgical & Medical Instruments; 2833—Medicinals & Botanicals; 3842—Surgical Appliances & Supplies; 5047—Medical & Hospital Equipment.

★ 60515 ★   **Xomed-Treace Inc.**
6743 Southpoint Dr. N.
Jacksonville, FL 32216
Ultimate Parent: Bristol-Myers Squibb. **SIC:** 3841—Surgical & Medical Instruments.

★ 60516 ★   **Zippy Mart Inc.**
6299 Powers Ave.
Jacksonville, FL 32217
(904)739-1356
Ultimate Parent: Crown Central Petroleum Corp. **SIC:** 5719—Miscellaneous Home Furnishings Stores.

Jacksonville Beach

★ 60517 ★   **Anchor Savings Bank, FSB**
924 Beach Blvd.
Jacksonville Beach, FL 32240-4300
(904)249-5643
Location Type: Branch office. **Officer:** Judy Trocchia, Assistant Treasurer. **Ultimate Parent:** Anchor Bancorp. **SIC:** 6021—National Commercial Banks; 6035—Federal Savings Institutions; 6211—Security Brokers & Dealers.

★ 60518 ★   **First Union National Bank of Florida**
3740 S. 3rd St.
Jacksonville Beach, FL 32250
(904)361-2153
Location Type: Branch office. **Ultimate Parent:** First Union Corp. **SIC:** 6021—National Commercial Banks.

★ 60519 ★   **First Union National Bank of Florida**
222 N. 2nd St.
Jacksonville Beach, FL 32250-6949
(904)361-2323
Location Type: Branch office. **Ultimate Parent:** First Union Corp. **SIC:** 6021—National Commercial Banks.

Jasper

★ 60520 ★   **Barnett Bank of North Central Florida**
105 2nd Ave. NE
Jasper, FL 32052
(904)792-2251
Company Type: Subsidiary. **Location Type:** Branch office. **Officer:** George McKnight, Assistant Vice President. **Ultimate Parent:** Barnett Banks. **SIC:** 6022—State Commercial Banks.

★ 60521 ★   **Kentucky Fried Chicken**
Us 129 N
Jasper, FL 32052
(904)792-2784
Ultimate Parent: Pepsico. **SIC:** 5812—Eating Places.

Jaxville Beach

★ 60522 ★   **Kentucky Fried Chicken**
626 Atlantic Blvd.
Jaxville Beach, FL 32266
(904)241-0544
Ultimate Parent: Pepsico. **SIC:** 5812—Eating Places.

Jay

★ 60523 ★   **Exxon Co. USA**
Oil Plant Rd.
Jay, FL 32565
(904)975-6892
Officer: Bill Miller, Manager. **Ultimate Parent:** Exxon. **SIC:** 2911—Petroleum Refining.

Jensen Beach

★ 60524 ★   **Ace Hardware**
1140 NE Jensen Beach Blvd.
Jensen Beach, FL 34957
(407)334-4626
Ultimate Parent: Ace Hardware. **SIC:** 5251—Hardware Stores.

★ 60525 ★   **First Union National Bank of Florida**
1939 NE Jensen Beach Blvd.
Jensen Beach, FL 34954
(407)221-4540
Location Type: Branch office. **Ultimate Parent:** First Union Corp. **SIC:** 6021—National Commercial Banks.

★ 60526 ★   **First Union National Bank of Florida**
3405 NW Federal Hwy.
Jensen Beach, FL 34957-4439
(407)692-0968
Location Type: Branch office. **Ultimate Parent:** First Union Corp. **SIC:** 6021—National Commercial Banks.

★ 60527 ★   **Mary Kay Cosmetics**
9801 S. Ocean Dr.
Jensen Beach, FL 34957
(407)229-2104
Ultimate Parent: Mary Kay Cosmetics.

Juno Beach

★ 60528 ★   **First Union National Bank of Florida**
951 US Hwy. 1
Juno Beach, FL 33408-3897
(407)838-5275
Location Type: Branch office. **Ultimate Parent:** First Union Corp. **SIC:** 6021—National Commercial Banks.

Jupiter

★ 60529 ★   **Albertson's**
95 US, Hwy. 1 S
Jupiter, FL 33477
(407)575-2262
Ultimate Parent: Albertson's Inc. **SIC:** 5411—Grocery Stores.

★ 60530 ★   **Albertson's Pharmacy**
95 US Hwy. 1 S
Jupiter, FL 33477
(407)575-2626
Ultimate Parent: Albertson's Inc. **SIC:** 5912—Drug Stores & Proprietary Stores.

★ 60531 ★   **Barnett Bank of Palm Beach County**
6410 W. Indiantown Rd.
Jupiter, FL 33458-3956
(407)747-4080
Company Type: Subsidiary. **Location Type:** Branch office. **Officer:** Julie Dunn, Manager. **Ultimate Parent:** Barnett Banks. **SIC:** 6022—State Commercial Banks.

★ 60532 ★   **Barnett Bank of Palm Beach County**
51 S. US Hwy. 1
Jupiter, FL 33477-5117
(407)747-4061
Company Type: Subsidiary. **Location Type:** Branch office. **Officer:** Valerie Verner-Bentel, Manager. **Ultimate Parent:** Barnett Banks. **SIC:** 6022—State Commercial Banks.

★ **60533** ★ **Coast to Coast Real Estate**
196 Tequesta Dr.
Jupiter, FL 33469
(407)575-2616
Ultimate Parent: Servistar Corp. **SIC:** 6531—Real Estate Agents & Managers.

★ **60534** ★ **First Bank**
3720 Freshwater Dr.
Jupiter, FL 33477
(407)655-5270
Ultimate Parent: Shawmut National Corp.

★ **60535** ★ **First Union National Bank of Florida**
100 US Hwy. 1
Jupiter, FL 33458
(407)746-6600
Location Type: Branch office. **Ultimate Parent:** First Union Corp. **SIC:** 6021—National Commercial Banks.

★ **60536** ★ **First Union National Bank of Florida**
1360 US Hwy. 1
Jupiter, FL 33469-3237
(407)838-4980
Location Type: Branch office. **Ultimate Parent:** First Union Corp. **SIC:** 6021—National Commercial Banks.

★ **60537** ★ **First Union National Bank of Florida**
6735 W. Indiantown Rd.
Jupiter, FL 33458
(407)838-5291
Location Type: Branch office. **Ultimate Parent:** First Union Corp. **SIC:** 6021—National Commercial Banks.

★ **60538** ★ **First Union National Bank of Florida**
200 Admirals Cove Blvd.
Jupiter, FL 33477
(407)838-5240
Location Type: Branch office. **Ultimate Parent:** First Union Corp. **SIC:** 6021—National Commercial Banks.

★ **60539** ★ **Great Western Bank**
101 Us 1 N
Jupiter, FL 33477
(407)747-3608
Ultimate Parent: Great Western Financial Corp.

★ **60540** ★ **Greyhound Bus Lines**
1500 N. Us 1
Jupiter, FL 33469
(407)746-4324
Ultimate Parent: Greyhound Lines Inc. **SIC:** 4131—Intercity & Rural Bus Transportation.

★ **60541** ★ **Jonathan's Landing Inc.**
Clubhouse
Jupiter, FL 33477
(407)747-7600
Ultimate Parent: Aluminum Co. of America-Alcoa. **SIC:** 7997—Membership Sports & Recreation Clubs.

★ **60542** ★ **Kentucky Fried Chicken**
6700 W. Indiantown Rd.
Jupiter, FL 33458
(407)575-7225
Ultimate Parent: Pepsico. **SIC:** 5812—Eating Places.

★ **60543** ★ **Mobil Mart**
151 Us 1 S
Jupiter, FL 33477
(407)575-0950
Ultimate Parent: Mobil. **SIC:** 5541—Gasoline Service Stations.

★ **60544** ★ **Peco Inc.**
1200 S. Ocean Dr.
Jupiter, FL 33458
(407)746-2760
Ultimate Parent: Peco. **SIC:** 1531—Operative Builders.

★ **60545** ★ **Pizza Hut**
145 W. Indiantown Rd.
Jupiter, FL 33458
(407)575-4295
Ultimate Parent: Pepsico. **SIC:** 5812—Eating Places.

★ **60546** ★ **Publix Super Market**
105 N. Us 1
Jupiter, FL 33469
(407)746-8773
Ultimate Parent: Publix Super Markets. **SIC:** 5411—Grocery Stores.

★ **60547** ★ **Radio Shack**
75 E. Indiantown Rd.
Jupiter, FL 33469
(407)746-4090
Company Type: Division. **Ultimate Parent:** Tandy Corp. **SIC:** 5731—Radio, Television & Electronics Stores.

★ **60548** ★ **Radio Shack**
75 E. Indiantown Rd.
Jupiter, FL 33477
(407)746-4091
Company Type: Division. **Ultimate Parent:** Tandy Corp. **SIC:** 7373—Computer Integrated Systems Design.

★ **60549** ★ **Rite Aid Discount Pharmacie**
608 Us Hwy. 1
Jupiter, FL 33469
(407)747-9806
Ultimate Parent: Rite Aid. **SIC:** 5912—Drug Stores & Proprietary Stores.

★ **60550** ★ **Rite-Aid Pharmacy**
6689 W. Indiantown Rd.
Jupiter, FL 33458
(407)743-1736
Ultimate Parent: Rite Aid. **SIC:** 5912—Drug Stores & Proprietary Stores.

★ **60551** ★ **Rite Aid Pharmacy**
79 N. Us Hwy. 1
Jupiter, FL 33477
(407)747-6067
Ultimate Parent: Rite Aid. **SIC:** 5912—Drug Stores & Proprietary Stores.

★ **60552** ★ **Taco Bell**
738 E. Indiantown Rd.
Jupiter, FL 33477
(407)575-0733
Ultimate Parent: Pepsico. **SIC:** 5812—Eating Places.

★ **60553** ★ **United Technologies Optical**
17900 Beeline Hwy.
Jupiter, FL 33478
(407)775-4000
Officer: Ronald Freeman, Manager. **Ultimate Parent:** United Technologies. **SIC:** 3769—Space Vehicle Equipment Nec.

★ **60554** ★ **Walgreen Drug Stores**
4050 S. Us Hwy. 1
Jupiter, FL 33477
(407)627-8308
Ultimate Parent: Walgreen Co. **SIC:** 5912—Drug Stores & Proprietary Stores.

★ **60555** ★ **Walgreen Drugs**
6370 W. Indiantown Rd.
Jupiter, FL 33458
(407)744-6665
Ultimate Parent: Walgreen Co. **SIC:** 5912—Drug Stores & Proprietary Stores.

Kennedy Space Center

★ **60556** ★ **EG & G Florida**
PO Box 21267
Kennedy Space Center
Kennedy Space Center, FL 32815
(407)867-7295 **Fax:** (407)867-2217
Company Type: Subsidiary. **Officer:** James R. Dubay, Manager. **Ultimate Parent:** EG & G.

★ **60557** ★ **Srb Assembly & Refurbishment Facility**
L6-247
Kennedy Space Center, FL 32899-0001
Ultimate Parent: United Technologies. **SIC:** 3769—Space Vehicle Equipment Nec.

★ **60558** ★ **United Technologies Corp. Srb Assembly & Refurb. Fac.**
L6-247
Kennedy Space Center, FL 32899-0001
Ultimate Parent: United Technologies. **SIC:** 3769—Space Vehicle Equipment Nec.

★ **60559** ★ **Vehicle Assembly Building**
K6-848
Kennedy Space Center, FL 32899
Ultimate Parent: United Technologies. **SIC:** 3769—Space Vehicle Equipment Nec.

Kenneth City

★ **60560** ★ **First Union National Bank of Georgia**
5825 54th Ave. N
Kenneth City, FL 33709-1901
(813)892-2068
Location Type: Branch office. **Ultimate Parent:** First Union Corp. **SIC:** 6021—National Commercial Banks.

★ **60561** ★ **Rite Aid Pharmacy**
5800 54th Ave. N
Kenneth City, FL 33709
Ultimate Parent: Rite Aid. **SIC:** 5912—Drug Stores & Proprietary Stores.

Key Biscayne

★ **60562** ★ **Barnett Bank of South Florida, NA**
260 Crandon Blvd.
Key Biscayne, FL 33149
(305)350-7100
Company Type: Subsidiary. **Location Type:** Branch office. **Officer:** Olga Rodriguez, Manager. **Ultimate Parent:** Barnett Banks. **SIC:** 6021—National Commercial Banks.

★ **60563** ★ **Citibank, FSB**
84 Crandon Blvd.
Key Biscayne, FL 33149-1438
(305)361-2213
Location Type: Branch office. **Ultimate Parent:** Citicorp. **SIC:** 6021—National Commercial Banks.

Key Largo

★ **60564** ★ **Barnett Bank of the Keys**
99551 Overseas Hwy.
Key Largo, FL 33037-4370
(305)292-3912
Company Type: Subsidiary. **Location Type:** Branch office. **Officer:** Deborah Orlos, Manager. **Ultimate Parent:** Barnett Banks. **SIC:** 6022—State Commercial Banks.

★ **60565** ★ **Barnett Bank of South Florida, NA**
31 Ocean Reef Dr., Ste. C-100
Key Largo, FL 33037-4370
(305)246-7486
Company Type: Subsidiary. **Location Type:** Branch office. **Officer:** Rosa Gossman, Manager. **Ultimate Parent:** Barnett Banks. **SIC:** 6021—National Commercial Banks.

★ **60566** ★ **First Union National Bank of Florida**
100,000 Overseas Hwy.
Key Largo, FL 33037
(305)451-4477
Location Type: Branch office. **Ultimate Parent:** First Union Corp. **SIC:** 6021—National Commercial Banks.

★ **60567** ★ **Pizza Hut**
99020 Us Hwy. 1
Key Largo, FL 33037
(305)451-0945
Ultimate Parent: Pepsico. **SIC:** 5812—Eating Places.

★ **60568** ★ **Walgreen Drug Stores**
10340 Federal Hwy.
Key Largo, FL 33037
(305)451-2512
Ultimate Parent: Walgreen Co. **SIC:** 7389—Business Services Nec.

Key West

★ **60569** ★ **Barnett Bank of the Keys**
510 Southard St.
Key West, FL 33040
(305)292-3808
Company Type: Subsidiary. **Location Type:** Branch office. **Officer:** Charles A. Bradford Jr., Assistant Vice President &

Office Manager. **Ultimate Parent:** Barnett Banks. **SIC:** 6022—State Commercial Banks.

★ **60570** ★ **Barnett Bank of the Keys**
1010 Kennedy Dr.
PO Box 1299
Key West, FL 33040-4061
(305)292-3860 **Fax:** (305)292-3847
Company Type: Subsidiary. **Location Type:** Branch office. **Officer:** Harry L. Woolley Jr., President & CEO. **Ultimate Parent:** Barnett Banks. **SIC:** 6022—State Commercial Banks.

★ **60571** ★ **Coca Cola Bottling Co.**
101 Simonton St.
Key West, FL 33040
(305)296-6643
Ultimate Parent: Coca-Cola Enterprises. **SIC:** 5812—Eating Places.

★ **60572** ★ **First Union National Bank of Florida**
3131 Northside Dr.
Key West, FL 33040-4122
(305)292-6606
Location Type: Branch office. **Ultimate Parent:** First Union Corp. **SIC:** 6021—National Commercial Banks.

★ **60573** ★ **First Union National Bank of Florida**
422 Front St.
Key West, FL 33040-6698
(305)292-6603
Location Type: Branch office. **Ultimate Parent:** First Union Corp. **SIC:** 6021—National Commercial Banks.

★ **60574** ★ **Greyhound Bus Lines**
615 Duval St.
Key West, FL 33040
(305)296-9072
Ultimate Parent: Greyhound Lines Inc. **SIC:** 4111—Local & Suburban Transit.

★ **60575** ★ **Hertz Rent-A-Car**
2516 N. Roosevelt Blvd.
Key West, FL 33040
(305)294-1039
Ultimate Parent: Hertz. **SIC:** 7514—Passenger Car Rental.

★ **60576** ★ **National Projects Inc.**
5090 W. Junior College Rd.
Key West, FL 33040
Ultimate Parent: Morrison Knudsen. **SIC:** 1541—Industrial Buildings & Warehouses.

★ **60577** ★ **Pizza Hut**
1980 N. Roosevelt Blvd.
Key West, FL 33040
(305)296-2431
Ultimate Parent: Pepsico. **SIC:** 5812—Eating Places.

★ **60578** ★ **Radio Shack**
Key Plz.
Key West, FL 33040
(305)294-3984
Company Type: Division. **Ultimate Parent:** Tandy Corp. **SIC:** 5065—Electronic Parts & Equipment Nec.

★ **60579** ★ **Strunk Lumberyard Inc.**
120 Simonton St.
Key West, FL 33040-6627
(305)296-9091
Officer: Edward Strunk, President. **Ultimate Parent:** Ace Hardware. **SIC:** 5211—Lumber & Other Building Materials; 5251—Hardware Stores. **Employee Count:** 28.

Keystone Heights

★ **60580** ★ **First Union National Bank of Florida**
405 Lawrence Blvd.
Keystone Heights, FL 32656-9222
(904)473-4952
Location Type: Branch office. **Ultimate Parent:** First Union Corp. **SIC:** 6021—National Commercial Banks.

Kissimmee

★ 60581 ★   AmSouth Bank of
Florida
4595 W. Irlo Bronson Memorial Hwy.
Kissimmee, FL 34741
(407)396-4225
Location Type: Branch office. Ultimate
Parent: AmSouth Bancorp. SIC: 6022—
State Commercial Banks.

★ 60582 ★   Barnett Bank of
Central Florida, NA
3305 S. Orange Blossom Trl.
Kissimmee, FL 34746
(407)846-2871
Company Type: Subsidiary. Location
Type: Branch office. Officer: Laurie Sirrell,
Manager. Ultimate Parent: Barnett Banks.
SIC: 6021—National Commercial Banks.

★ 60583 ★   Barnett Bank of
Central Florida, NA
35 Dover Plum Ctr.
Kissimmee, FL 34759-3436
(407)870-1175
Company Type: Subsidiary. Location
Type: Branch office. Officer: Gary Dillard,
Manager. Ultimate Parent: Barnett Banks.
SIC: 6021—National Commercial Banks.

★ 60584 ★   Barnett Bank of
Central Florida, NA
400 W. Emmett St.
Kissimmee, FL 34741-3604
(407)846-2871
Company Type: Subsidiary. Location
Type: Branch office. Officer: Michael Pate,
Manager. Ultimate Parent: Barnett Banks.
SIC: 6021—National Commercial Banks.

★ 60585 ★   Barnett Bank of
Central Florida, NA
1703 W. Vine St.
Kissimmee, FL 34741-4093
(407)870-1100
Company Type: Subsidiary. Location
Type: Branch office. Officer: Don Rhodes,
Manager. Ultimate Parent: Barnett Banks.
SIC: 6021—National Commercial Banks.

★ 60586 ★   Barnett Bank of
Central Florida, NA
2000 Dart Blvd.
Kissimmee, FL 34743
(407)348-6363
Company Type: Subsidiary. Location
Type: Branch office. Officer: Diane Watton,
Manager. Ultimate Parent: Barnett Banks.
SIC: 6021—National Commercial Banks.

★ 60587 ★   First Union National
Bank of Florida
1700 W. Vine St.
Kissimmee, FL 34741-4057
(407)846-3030
Location Type: Branch office. Ultimate
Parent: First Union Corp. SIC: 6021—
National Commercial Banks.

★ 60588 ★   Hertz Rent-A-Car
7491 W. Coast Pky.
Kissimmee, FL 34746
(407)396-2800
Ultimate Parent: Hertz. SIC: 7514—
Passenger Car Rental.

★ 60589 ★   Jiffy Lube
109 E. Vine St.
Kissimmee, FL 34744
(407)870-0790
Ultimate Parent: Pennzoil.

★ 60590 ★   Kentucky Fried
Chicken
1907 W. Vine St.
Kissimmee, FL 34741
(407)847-5231
Ultimate Parent: Pepsico. SIC: 5812—
Eating Places.

★ 60591 ★   Lane Bryant
3831 W. Vine St.
Kissimmee, FL 34741
(407)870-9119
Ultimate Parent: Limited. SIC: 5621—
Women's Clothing Stores.

★ 60592 ★   Marriott Ownership
Resorts
3367 W. Vine St.
Kissimmee, FL 34741
(407)933-1448
Ultimate Parent: Marriott International. SIC:
6531—Real Estate Agents & Managers.

★ 60593 ★   McDonalds
Restaurants
7627 W. Irlo Bronson Memoria
Kissimmee, FL 34746
(407)396-1536
Ultimate Parent: McDonald's.
SIC: 5812—Eating Places.

★ 60594 ★   McDonalds
Restaurants
8530 W. Irlo Bronson Memoria
Kissimmee, FL 34746
(407)396-8082
Ultimate Parent: McDonald's.
SIC: 5812—Eating Places.

★ 60595 ★   Pizza Hut
1000 W. Vine St.
Kissimmee, FL 34741
(407)846-3702
Ultimate Parent: Pepsico. SIC: 5812—
Eating Places.

★ 60596 ★   Pizza Hut
1313 E. Vine St.
Kissimmee, FL 34744
(407)846-1118
Ultimate Parent: Pepsico. SIC: 5812—
Eating Places.

★ 60597 ★   Pizza Hut
4957 W. Irlo Bronson Memoria
Kissimmee, FL 34746
(407)396-7273
Ultimate Parent: Pepsico. SIC: 5812—
Eating Places.

★ 60598 ★   Publix Super Market
3227 S. Bermuda Ave.
Kissimmee, FL 34746
(407)933-0067
Ultimate Parent: Publix Super Markets.
SIC: 5411—Grocery Stores.

★ 60599 ★   Publix Super Markets
3227 S. Bermuda Ave.
Kissimmee, FL 34746
(407)933-0067
Ultimate Parent: Publix Super Markets.
SIC: 5411—Grocery Stores.

★ 60600 ★   Rite Aid
1526 W. Vine St.
Kissimmee, FL 34741
(407)846-4539
Ultimate Parent: Rite Aid. SIC: 5912—Drug
Stores & Proprietary Stores.

★ 60601 ★   Rite Aid Pharmacy
2507 Boggy Creek Rd.
Kissimmee, FL 34744
(407)348-9063
Ultimate Parent: Rite Aid. SIC: 5912—Drug
Stores & Proprietary Stores.

★ 60602 ★   Taco Bell
1550 W. Vine St.
Kissimmee, FL 34741
(407)847-8111
Ultimate Parent: Pepsico. SIC: 5812—
Eating Places.

★ 60603 ★   Texaco
120 S. Bermuda Ave.
Kissimmee, FL 34741
(407)847-5066
Ultimate Parent: Texaco. SIC: 5541—
Gasoline Service Stations.

★ 60604 ★   Texaco Food Mart
1205 W. Vine St.
Kissimmee, FL 34741
(407)847-8685
Ultimate Parent: Texaco. SIC: 5411—
Grocery Stores.

★ 60605 ★   Texaco Food Mart
400 N. Main St.
Kissimmee, FL 34744
(407)846-6804
Ultimate Parent: Texaco. SIC: 5411—
Grocery Stores.

★ 60606 ★   Texaco No 411
1078 S. Hoagland Blvd.
Kissimmee, FL 34741
(407)846-1519
Ultimate Parent: Texaco. SIC: 5541—
Gasoline Service Stations.

★ 60607 ★   Walgreen Drugs
1003 W. Vine St.
Kissimmee, FL 34741
(407)847-4222
Ultimate Parent: Walgreen Co. SIC:
5912—Drug Stores & Proprietary Stores.

La Belle

★ 60608 ★   Radio Shack
350 Hickpochee Ave.
La Belle, FL 33935
(813)675-2672
Company Type: Division. Ultimate Parent:
Tandy Corp. SIC: 5065—Electronic Parts &
Equipment Nec.

Lake Alfred

★ 60609 ★   First Union National
Bank of Florida
120 S. Lakeshore Way
Lake Alfred, FL 33850-2746
(813)956-1133
Location Type: Branch office. Ultimate
Parent: First Union Corp. SIC: 6021—
National Commercial Banks.

Lake Buena Vista

★ 60610 ★   Disney Development
Co.
PO Box 22771
Lake Buena Vista, FL 32830
(407)827-1900
Officer: Peter S. Rummell, President.
Ultimate Parent: Walt Disney Co.

★ 60611 ★   Reedy Creek Energy
Services Inc.
PO Box 10000
Lake Buena Vista, FL 32830
(407)824-4024 Fax: (407)824-4529
Officer: Judson C. Green, President.
Ultimate Parent: Walt Disney Co.

★ 60612 ★   Reedy Creek Energy
Services Inc.
5300 Ctr. Dr.
Lake Buena Vista, FL 32830
(407)824-4024
Company Type: Subsidiary. Officer:
Judson Green, President. Ultimate Parent:
Walt Disney Co. SIC: 7363—Help Supply
Services. Employee Count: 340. Sales: 12
M.

★ 60613 ★   Vista Insurance Inc.
PO Box 10000
Lake Buena Vista, FL 32830
(407)824-4080 Fax: (407)824-4529
Officer: Rosemary Fitzgerald, Manager.
Ultimate Parent: Walt Disney Co.

★ 60614 ★   Walt Disney World
Co.
PO Box 10000
Lake Buena Vista, FL 32830
(407)824-2222 Fax: (407)824-4529
Officer: Judson C. Green, President.
Ultimate Parent: Walt Disney Co.

★ 60615 ★   Walt Disney World
Co. Facilities Support
Facilities Way
Lake Buena Vista, FL 32830-1000
Ultimate Parent: Walt Disney Co. SIC:
3999—Manufacturing Industries Nec.

Lake City

★ 60616 ★   Anchor Savings Bank
F S B
1865 PO Box
Lake City, FL 32056
Ultimate Parent: Anchor Bancorp. SIC:
6159—Miscellaneous Business Credit
Institutions.

★ 60617 ★   Barnett Bank of North
Central Florida
3000 S. 1st St.
Lake City, FL 32055
(904)752-8943
Company Type: Subsidiary. Location
Type: Branch office. Officer: Don
Winkleman, Vice President. Ultimate
Parent: Barnett Banks. SIC: 6022—State
Commercial Banks.

★ 60618 ★   Barnett Bank of North
Central Florida
US Hwy. 90 W
Lake City, FL 32055
(904)752-8943
Company Type: Subsidiary. Location
Type: Branch office. Officer: John Burley,
Vice President. Ultimate Parent: Barnett
Banks. SIC: 6022—State Commercial
Banks.

★ 60619 ★   Barnett Bank of North
Central Florida
150 W. Madison St.
PO Drawer 1058
Lake City, FL 32055-1058
(904)752-8943 Fax: (904)752-1759
Company Type: Subsidiary. Location
Type: Branch office. Officer: Joe R.
Williams, Chairman, President & CEO.
Ultimate Parent: Barnett Banks. SIC:
6022—State Commercial Banks.

★ 60620 ★   Georgia Pacific Corp.
Hwy. 100 & Price Creek Rd.
Lake City, FL 32056
(904)752-7412
Officer: James R. Dunlap, Manager.
Ultimate Parent: Georgia-Pacific. SIC:
2452—Prefabricated Wood Buildings;
2491—Wood Preserving.

★ 60621 ★   Greyhound Bus
Center
301 S. Marion St.
Lake City, FL 32055
(904)752-3232
Ultimate Parent: Greyhound Lines Inc. SIC:
4131—Intercity & Rural Bus Transportation;
4173—Bus Terminal & Service Facilities;
4212—Local Trucking Without Storage.

★ 60622 ★   IBM Corp.
511 S. Marion St.
Lake City, FL 32055
(904)755-0017
Ultimate Parent: IBM. SIC: 5734—
Computer & Software Stores.

★ 60623 ★   Kentucky Fried
Chicken
Rural Route 13
Lake City, FL 32055
(904)752-1123
Ultimate Parent: Pepsico. SIC: 5812—
Eating Places.

★ 60624 ★   Pizza Hut
Rural Route 13
Lake City, FL 32055
(904)752-9172
Ultimate Parent: Pepsico. SIC: 5812—
Eating Places.

★ 60625 ★   Pizza Hut
2715 W. Hwy. 90
Lake City, FL 32055
(904)752-3896
Ultimate Parent: Pepsico. SIC: 5812—
Eating Places.

★ 60626 ★   Radio Shack
69 Rural Route 13
Lake City, FL 32055
(904)755-2683
Company Type: Division. Ultimate Parent:
Tandy Corp. SIC: 5731—Radio, Television
& Electronics Stores.

★ 60627 ★   Rite Aid
71 PO Box
Lake City, FL 32056
(904)752-9925
Ultimate Parent: Rite Aid. SIC: 5912—Drug
Stores & Proprietary Stores.

★ 60628 ★   Rite Aid Discount
Phrmcy
Gleason Mall Hwy. 90
Lake City, FL 32055
(904)752-9565
Ultimate Parent: Rite Aid. SIC: 5912—Drug
Stores & Proprietary Stores.

★ 60629 ★   Taco Bell
Gleason S. Corner Mall
Lake City, FL 32055
(904)755-9673
Ultimate Parent: Pepsico. SIC: 5812—
Eating Places.

119

★ 60630 ★   Taco Bell
Us 90 W
Lake City, FL 32055
(904)755-4675
Ultimate Parent: Pepsico. SIC: 5812—
Eating Places.

★ 60631 ★   Texaco Food Mart
Rural Route 13
Lake City, FL 32055
(904)752-0609
Ultimate Parent: Texaco. SIC: 5411—
Grocery Stores.

★ 60632 ★   Total Auto Care
451 S. 1st St.
Lake City, FL 32055
(904)752-7080
Ultimate Parent: Total Petroleum Inc. SIC:
7538—General Automotive Repair Shops.

★ 60633 ★   Trailways Bus Station
2665 Us 90 W
Lake City, FL 32055
(904)755-4144
Ultimate Parent: Greyhound Lines Inc. SIC:
4173—Bus Terminal & Service Facilities.

★ 60634 ★   United Parcel Service
Rural Route 7
Lake City, FL 32055
(904)432-8686
Ultimate Parent: United Parcel Service of
America. SIC: 4215—Courier Services
Except by Air.

★ 60635 ★   United Parcel Service
RR 7
Lake City, FL 32055
(904)432-8686
Ultimate Parent: United Parcel Service of
America. SIC: 4215—Courier Services
Except by Air.

★ 60636 ★   Wal Mart
Rural Route 13
Lake City, FL 32055
(904)755-6304
Ultimate Parent: Wal-Mart Stores, Inc. SIC:
5311—Department Stores.

Lake Mary

★ 60637 ★   Ace Hardware
641 W. Lake Mary Blvd.
Lake Mary, FL 32746
(407)330-6589
Ultimate Parent: Ace Hardware. SIC:
5251—Hardware Stores.

★ 60638 ★   Arrow/Kierulff
Electronics
37 Skylkine Dr., Ste. 3101-3
Lake Mary, FL 32746
(407)333-9300
Company Type: Division. Location Type:
Distribution center. Officer: Tom Paone,
General Manager. Ultimate Parent: Arrow
Electronics. SIC: 5065—Electronic Parts &
Equipment Nec.

★ 60639 ★   Taco Bell
621 W. Lake Mary Blvd.
Lake Mary, FL 32746
(407)321-8720
Ultimate Parent: Pepsico. SIC: 5812—
Eating Places.

Lake Panasoffkee

★ 60640 ★   First Union National
Bank of Florida
Hwy. 470
Lake Panasoffkee, FL 33538-9749
(904)793-5792
Location Type: Branch office. Ultimate
Parent: First Union Corp. SIC: 6021—
National Commercial Banks.

Lake Placid

★ 60641 ★   Barnett Bank of
Highlands County
421 Central Ave.
Lake Placid, FL 33852-5595
(813)465-5900
Company Type: Subsidiary. Location
Type: Branch office. Officer: David Veley,
Vice President. Ultimate Parent: Barnett
Banks. SIC: 6022—State Commercial
Banks.

★ 60642 ★   First of America Bank
199 N. Hwy. 27
Lake Placid, FL 33852
(813)465-4834
Location Type: Branch office. Ultimate
Parent: First of America Bank Corp. SIC:
6021—National Commercial Banks.

★ 60643 ★   Georgia Pacific Corp.
400 State Rd. 70 W
Lake Placid, FL 33852
(813)465-3413
Officer: Donald C. Hune, Manager.
Ultimate Parent: Georgia-Pacific. SIC:
2653—Corrugated & Solid Fiber Boxes.

★ 60644 ★   Greyhound Bus
Station
3 N. Magnolia St.
Lake Placid, FL 33852
(813)465-0110
Ultimate Parent: Greyhound Lines Inc. SIC:
4173—Bus Terminal & Service Facilities.

★ 60645 ★   Huntington, FSB
State Rd. 621 E. & US Hwy. 27 N.
Lake Placid, FL 33852
(813)465-2512
Location Type: Branch office. Officer:
Mary Birge, Manager. Ultimate Parent:
Huntington Bancshares. SIC: 6021—
National Commercial Banks.

★ 60646 ★   Kentucky Fried
Chicken
Hwy. 27 S
Lake Placid, FL 33852
(813)465-7373
Ultimate Parent: Pepsico. SIC: 5812—
Eating Places.

★ 60647 ★   Pizza Hut
1400 Us 27 S
Lake Placid, FL 33852
(813)465-5401
Ultimate Parent: Pepsico. SIC: 5812—
Eating Places.

★ 60648 ★   Radio Shack
142 S. Main St.
Lake Placid, FL 33852
(813)465-1591
Company Type: Division. Ultimate Parent:
Tandy Corp. SIC: 5065—Electronic Parts &
Equipment Nec.

★ 60649 ★   Rite Aid Drugs
100 Placid Dr.
Lake Placid, FL 33852
(813)465-9958
Ultimate Parent: Rite Aid. SIC: 5912—Drug
Stores & Proprietary Stores.

★ 60650 ★   Ryder Truck Rental
824 Us Hwy. 27 S
Lake Placid, FL 33852
(813)465-9577
Ultimate Parent: Ryder System. SIC:
2679—Converted Paper Products Nec.

Lake Wales

★ 60651 ★   Barnett Bank of Polk
County
1100 State Rd. 60 E
Lake Wales, FL 33853-4362
(813)297-1465
Company Type: Subsidiary. Location
Type: Branch office. Officer: Annemaria
Grunholzer, Manager. Ultimate Parent:
Barnett Banks. SIC: 6022—State
Commercial Banks.

★ 60652 ★   First Union National
Bank of Florida
149 E. Stuart Ave.
Lake Wales, FL 33853-4127
(813)676-2521
Location Type: Branch office. Ultimate
Parent: First Union Corp. SIC: 6021—
National Commercial Banks.

★ 60653 ★   Food Lion
2039 State Hwy. 60 E
Lake Wales, FL 33853
(813)676-6375
Ultimate Parent: Food Lion. SIC: 5411—
Grocery Stores.

★ 60654 ★   Greyhound Bus Lines
245 E. Bullard Ave.
Lake Wales, FL 33853
(813)676-2315
Ultimate Parent: Greyhound Lines Inc. SIC:

2026—Fluid Milk; 4131—Intercity & Rural
Bus Transportation.

★ 60655 ★   Kentucky Fried
Chicken
885 State Hwy. 60 W
Lake Wales, FL 33853
(813)676-8085
Ultimate Parent: Pepsico. SIC: 5812—
Eating Places.

★ 60656 ★   Pizza Hut
326 State Rd. 60 E
Lake Wales, FL 33853
(813)676-7512
Ultimate Parent: Pepsico. SIC: 5812—
Eating Places.

★ 60657 ★   Radio Shack
638 State Rd. 60 W
Lake Wales, FL 33853
(813)676-1076
Company Type: Division. Ultimate Parent:
Tandy Corp. SIC: 5731—Radio, Television
& Electronics Stores.

★ 60658 ★   Radio Shack
638 Lake Wales Estates
Lake Wales, FL 33853
(813)676-0777
Company Type: Division. Ultimate Parent:
Tandy Corp. SIC: 5731—Radio, Television
& Electronics Stores.

★ 60659 ★   Walgreen Drugs
1320 Orange Grove Shopping Plz.
Lake Wales, FL 33853
(813)676-7986
Ultimate Parent: Walgreen Co. SIC:
5912—Drug Stores & Proprietary Stores.

Lake Worth

★ 60660 ★   Ace Hardware
7343 Lake Worth Rd.
Lake Worth, FL 33467
(407)964-0555
Ultimate Parent: Ace Hardware. SIC:
5251—Hardware Stores.

★ 60661 ★   Ace Hardware
1212 W. Lantana Rd.
Lake Worth, FL 33462
(407)585-0247
Ultimate Parent: Ace Hardware. SIC:
5251—Hardware Stores.

★ 60662 ★   American Savings of
Florida
6350 Lake Worth Rd.
Lake Worth, FL 33463-3006
(407)642-6119
Ultimate Parent: American Savings of
Florida. SIC: 6035—Federal Savings
Institutions; 6021—National Commercial
Banks.

★ 60663 ★   American Savings of
Florida, FSB
6350 Lake Worth Rd.
Lake Worth, FL 33463-3090
(407)642-6119
Location Type: Branch office. Officer: Gail
Mancuso, Manager. Ultimate Parent:
American Savings of Florida. SIC: 6035—
Federal Savings Institutions; 6211—Security
Brokers & Dealers.

★ 60664 ★   Barnett Bank of Palm
Beach County
3716 S. Military Trl.
Lake Worth, FL 33463-3492
(407)433-2450
Company Type: Subsidiary. Location
Type: Branch office. Officer: Lou Marotta,
Manager. Ultimate Parent: Barnett Banks.
SIC: 6022—State Commercial Banks.

★ 60665 ★   Barnett Bank of Palm
Beach County
14 N. Federal Hwy.
Lake Worth, FL 33460-3840
(407)582-2544
Company Type: Subsidiary. Location
Type: Branch office. Officer: John Gaston,
Manager. Ultimate Parent: Barnett Banks.
SIC: 6022—State Commercial Banks.

★ 60666 ★   Barnett Bank of Palm
Beach County
6360 Lantana Rd.
Lake Worth, FL 33467
(407)641-7020
Company Type: Subsidiary. Location

Type: Branch office. Officer: Barbara
Pearce, Manager. Ultimate Parent: Barnett
Banks. SIC: 6022—State Commercial
Banks.

★ 60667 ★   Barnett Bank of Palm
Beach County
7281 Lake Worth Rd.
Lake Worth, FL 33467-2593
(407)433-2442
Company Type: Subsidiary. Location
Type: Branch office. Officer: Anna
Billingsley, Manager. Ultimate Parent:
Barnett Banks. SIC: 6022—State
Commercial Banks.

★ 60668 ★   First Union National
Bank of Florida
114 N. J St.
Lake Worth, FL 33460-3398
(407)533-7770
Location Type: Branch office. Ultimate
Parent: First Union Corp. SIC: 6021—
National Commercial Banks.

★ 60669 ★   First Union National
Bank of Florida
4148 Jog Rd.
Lake Worth, FL 33467-4037
(407)838-5355
Location Type: Branch office. Ultimate
Parent: First Union Corp. SIC: 6021—
National Commercial Banks.

★ 60670 ★   Fist Union National
Bank of Florida
3345 S. Congress Ave.
Lake Worth, FL 33467
(407)641-5000
Location Type: Branch office. Ultimate
Parent: First Union Corp. SIC: 6021—
National Commercial Banks.

★ 60671 ★   Great Western Bank
6710 Forest Hill Blvd.
Lake Worth, FL 33463
(407)642-0600
Ultimate Parent: Great Western Financial
Corp. SIC: 6099—Functions Related to
Deposit Banking.

★ 60672 ★   Great Western Bank
6350 Lantana Rd.
Lake Worth, FL 33463
(407)964-9919
Ultimate Parent: Great Western Financial
Corp. SIC: 6099—Functions Related to
Deposit Banking.

★ 60673 ★   Great Western Bank
2601 10th Ave. N
Lake Worth, FL 33461
(407)964-6400
Ultimate Parent: Great Western Financial
Corp. SIC: 6035—Federal Savings
Institutions.

★ 60674 ★   Great Western Bank
1300 W. Lantana Rd.
Lake Worth, FL 33462
(407)964-6400
Ultimate Parent: Great Western Financial
Corp. SIC: 6022—State Commercial Banks.

★ 60675 ★   Great Western Bank
200 Lake Ave.
Lake Worth, FL 33460
(407)964-6400
Ultimate Parent: Great Western Financial
Corp. SIC: 6022—State Commercial Banks.

★ 60676 ★   Greyhound Bus Lines
20 S. Federal Hwy.
Lake Worth, FL 33460
(407)582-1488
Ultimate Parent: Greyhound Lines Inc. SIC:
4131—Intercity & Rural Bus Transportation.

★ 60677 ★   Hit or Miss
6786 Forest Hill Blvd.
Lake Worth, FL 33463
(407)641-3361
Ultimate Parent: TJX. SIC: 5621—
Women's Clothing Stores.

★ 60678 ★   Kentucky Fried
Chicken
4507 Lake Worth Rd.
Lake Worth, FL 33463
(407)968-2461
Ultimate Parent: Pepsico. SIC: 5812—
Eating Places.

★ 60679 ★ Kentucky Fried Chicken
1222 W. Lantana Rd.
Lake Worth, FL 33462
(407)582-9881
Ultimate Parent: Pepsico. SIC: 5812—Eating Places.

★ 60680 ★ Mary Kay Cosmetics
7173 St. Andrews Rd.
Lake Worth, FL 33467
(407)967-5992
Ultimate Parent: Mary Kay Cosmetics. SIC: 5999—Miscellaneous Retail Stores Nec.

★ 60681 ★ Mary Kay Cosmetics
4283 Sussex Ave.
Lake Worth, FL 33461
(407)964-4366
Ultimate Parent: Mary Kay Cosmetics. SIC: 5999—Miscellaneous Retail Stores Nec.

★ 60682 ★ Mobil Oil
5960 S. Military Trl
Lake Worth, FL 33463
(407)969-3753
Ultimate Parent: Mobil. SIC: 5541—Gasoline Service Stations.

★ 60683 ★ Mobil Oil Corp.
7795 Lake Worth Rd.
Lake Worth, FL 33467
(407)969-0038
Ultimate Parent: Mobil. SIC: 5599—Automotive Dealers Nec.

★ 60684 ★ Mobil Oil Corp.
3000 Jog Rd.
Lake Worth, FL 33467
(407)968-6886
Ultimate Parent: Mobil. SIC: 2911—Petroleum Refining.

★ 60685 ★ Pizza Hut
6170 Congress Ave.
Lake Worth, FL 33462
(407)967-6733
Ultimate Parent: Pepsico. SIC: 5812—Eating Places.

★ 60686 ★ Pizza Hut
4891 Lake Worth Rd.
Lake Worth, FL 33463
(407)968-6211
Ultimate Parent: Pepsico. SIC: 5812—Eating Places.

★ 60687 ★ Pizza Hut
2764 Congress Ave.
Lake Worth, FL 33461
(407)965-6857
Ultimate Parent: Pepsico. SIC: 5812—Eating Places.

★ 60688 ★ Publix Super Market
1700 Congress Ave.
Lake Worth, FL 33461
(407)965-8700
Ultimate Parent: Publix Super Markets. SIC: 5411—Grocery Stores.

★ 60689 ★ Publix Super Markets
1700 Congress Ave.
Lake Worth, FL 33461
(407)965-8700
Ultimate Parent: Publix Super Markets. SIC: 5411—Grocery Stores.

★ 60690 ★ Radio Shack
1385 S. Dixie Hwy.
Lake Worth, FL 33462
(407)582-3196
Company Type: Division. Ultimate Parent: Tandy Corp. SIC: 5731—Radio, Television & Electronics Stores.

★ 60691 ★ Radio Shack
1906 Lake Worth Rd.
Lake Worth, FL 33461
(407)588-6767
Company Type: Division. Ultimate Parent: Tandy Corp. SIC: 5065—Electronic Parts & Equipment Nec; 5731—Radio, Television & Electronics Stores.

★ 60692 ★ Radio Shack
7159 Lake Worth Rd.
Lake Worth, FL 33467
(407)968-3667
Company Type: Division. Ultimate Parent: Tandy Corp. SIC: 5065—Electronic Parts & Equipment Nec; 5731—Radio, Television & Electronics Stores.

★ 60693 ★ Radio Shack
6204 Congress Ave.
Lake Worth, FL 33462
(407)965-7747
Company Type: Division. Ultimate Parent: Tandy Corp. SIC: 5065—Electronic Parts & Equipment Nec.

★ 60694 ★ Rite Aid
4517 Lake Worth Rd.
Lake Worth, FL 33463
(407)964-1864
Ultimate Parent: Rite Aid. SIC: 5912—Drug Stores & Proprietary Stores.

★ 60695 ★ Rite Aide Drug Store
214 N. Dixie Hwy.
Lake Worth, FL 33460
(407)586-2771
Ultimate Parent: Rite Aid. SIC: 5912—Drug Stores & Proprietary Stores.

★ 60696 ★ Ryder Truck Rental
S Dixie Hwy.
Lake Worth, FL 33460
(407)588-1419
Ultimate Parent: Ryder System. SIC: 7389—Business Services Nec.

★ 60697 ★ Savings of America
Home Savings of America, FSB
6905 Lake Worth Rd.
Lake Worth, FL 33467-2994
(407)965-6900
Location Type: Branch office. Officer: Lorraine Gray, Manager. Ultimate Parent: H. F. Ahmanson. SIC: 6021—National Commercial Banks.

★ 60698 ★ Shell Gas Station
1845 Hypoluxo Rd.
Lake Worth, FL 33462
(407)588-4320
Ultimate Parent: Shell Oil Co. SIC: 5541—Gasoline Service Stations.

★ 60699 ★ Texaco Royal Mart
6729 S. Military Trl.
Lake Worth, FL 33463
(407)642-6910
Ultimate Parent: Texaco. SIC: 5541—Gasoline Service Stations.

★ 60700 ★ Walgreen Drug Stores
6308 Lantana Rd.
Lake Worth, FL 33463
(407)969-2412
Ultimate Parent: Walgreen Co. SIC: 7389—Business Services Nec.

★ 60701 ★ Walgreen Drug Stores
6400 Lake Worth Rd.
Lake Worth, FL 33463
(407)965-2180
Ultimate Parent: Walgreen Co. SIC: 5912—Drug Stores & Proprietary Stores.

★ 60702 ★ Walgreen Drug Stores
1688 Congress Ave.
Lake Worth, FL 33461
(407)968-6206
Ultimate Parent: Walgreen Co. SIC: 7384—Photofinishing Laboratories.

Lakeland

★ 60703 ★ Ace Hardware
6285 PO Box
Lakeland, FL 33807
Ultimate Parent: Ace Hardware. SIC: 5251—Hardware Stores.

★ 60704 ★ Advanced Seperation Technologies Inc.
5315 Great Oak Dr.
Lakeland, FL 33801
(813)687-4460
Company Type: Subsidiary. Officer: Dudley E. Bryant, President;CEO. Ultimate Parent: Florida Progress.

★ 60705 ★ Barnett Bank of Polk County
3305 Lakeland Hills
Lakeland, FL 33805-1975
(813)680-5710
Company Type: Subsidiary. Location Type: Branch office. Officer: Mary Barrett, Manager. Ultimate Parent: Barnett Banks. SIC: 6022—State Commercial Banks.

★ 60706 ★ Barnett Bank of Polk County
1011 State Rd. 540 A
Lakeland, FL 33813
(813)680-5710
Company Type: Subsidiary. Location Type: Branch office. Officer: Keely Stewart, Manager. Ultimate Parent: Barnett Banks. SIC: 6022—State Commercial Banks.

★ 60707 ★ Barnett Bank of Polk County
2211 S. Florida Ave.
Lakeland, FL 33803-7226
(813)680-5710
Company Type: Subsidiary. Location Type: Branch office. Officer: Abby Howard Murphy, Manager. Ultimate Parent: Barnett Banks. SIC: 6022—State Commercial Banks.

★ 60708 ★ Barnett Bank of Polk County
1275 Oakbridge Pky.
Lakeland, FL 33803
(813)680-5710
Company Type: Subsidiary. Location Type: Branch office. Officer: Laura Hagan, Manager. Ultimate Parent: Barnett Banks. SIC: 6022—State Commercial Banks.

★ 60709 ★ Barnett Bank of Polk County
2536 US Hwy. 92 E
Lakeland, FL 33801-2652
(813)680-5981
Company Type: Subsidiary. Location Type: Branch office. Officer: Bruce Stephenson, Manager. Ultimate Parent: Barnett Banks. SIC: 6022—State Commercial Banks.

★ 60710 ★ Barnett Bank of Polk County
3635 S. Florida Ave.
Lakeland, FL 33803-4867
(813)680-5980
Company Type: Subsidiary. Location Type: Branch office. Officer: Faye Sanders, Vice President. Ultimate Parent: Barnett Banks. SIC: 6022—State Commercial Banks.

★ 60711 ★ Barnett Bank of Polk County
4330 US Hwy. 98 N
Lakeland, FL 33809-3821
(813)680-5966
Company Type: Subsidiary. Location Type: Branch office. Officer: Lisa Sprunger, Manager. Ultimate Parent: Barnett Banks. SIC: 6022—State Commercial Banks.

★ 60712 ★ Barnett Bank of Polk County
6990 S. Florida Ave.
Lakeland, FL 33813-3315
(813)680-5982
Company Type: Subsidiary. Location Type: Branch office. Officer: Jeff Hoch, Manager. Ultimate Parent: Barnett Banks. SIC: 6022—State Commercial Banks.

★ 60713 ★ Barnett Bank of Polk County
5015 S. Florida Ave.
Lakeland, FL 33813-2168
(813)680-5984
Company Type: Subsidiary. Location Type: Branch office. Officer: Jill Deka, Manager. Ultimate Parent: Barnett Banks. SIC: 6022—State Commercial Banks.

★ 60714 ★ Barnett Bank of Polk County
331 S. Florida Ave.
PO Box 427
Lakeland, FL 33802-0427
(813)688-1166 Fax: (813)680-5782
Company Type: Subsidiary. Location Type: Branch office. Officer: Bob Barbree, Chairman of the Board, President, & CEO. Ultimate Parent: Barnett Banks. SIC: 6022—State Commercial Banks.

★ 60715 ★ Barnett Bank of Polk County
101 N. Wabash Ave.
Lakeland, FL 33801-7368
(813)680-5984
Company Type: Subsidiary. Location Type: Branch office. Officer: Sandy Dobson, Manager. Ultimate Parent: Barnett Banks. SIC: 6022—State Commercial Banks.

★ 60716 ★ BFI Waste Systems
3939 US Hwy. 98 S
Lakeland, FL 33813
(813)858-3825
Officer: Brooke Meares, Manager. Ultimate Parent: Browning-Ferris Industries. SIC: 3589—Service Industry Machinery Nec.

★ 60717 ★ Bowater Communications Papers
5120 Great Oak Dr.
Lakeland, FL 33801-3180
(813)688-5529
Officer: Chuck Dierckx. Ultimate Parent: Bowater. SIC: 2621—Paper Mills.

★ 60718 ★ Circus World Toy Store
3800 Us Hwy. 98 N. 888
Lakeland, FL 33809
(813)858-0606
Ultimate Parent: Melville. SIC: 5945—Hobby, Toy & Game Shops.

★ 60719 ★ Express Ltd.
3800 Us Hwy. 98 N
Lakeland, FL 33809
(813)859-3583
Ultimate Parent: Limited. SIC: 5651—Family Clothing Stores.

★ 60720 ★ First Union National Bank of Florida
113 S. Tennessee Ave.
Lakeland, FL 33801-4637
(813)499-1000
Location Type: Branch office. Ultimate Parent: First Union Corp. SIC: 6021—National Commercial Banks.

★ 60721 ★ First Union National Bank of Florida
1414 S. Combee Rd.
Lakeland, FL 33801-7102
(813)499-1050
Location Type: Branch office. Ultimate Parent: First Union Corp. SIC: 6021—National Commercial Banks.

★ 60722 ★ First Union National Bank of Florida
2105 New Tampa Hwy.
Lakeland, FL 33801-7364
(813)499-1075
Location Type: Branch office. Ultimate Parent: First Union Corp.

★ 60723 ★ First Union National Bank of Florida
4405 S. Florida Ave.
Lakeland, FL 33813-2119
(813)499-1060
Location Type: Branch office. Ultimate Parent: First Union Corp. SIC: 6021—National Commercial Banks.

★ 60724 ★ First Union National Bank of Florida
6108 N. US Hwy. 97
Lakeland, FL 33809-3276
(813)499-1070
Location Type: Branch office. Ultimate Parent: First Union Corp. SIC: 6021—National Commercial Banks.

★ 60725 ★ Fleetwood Motor Homes of Florida Inc.
2433 Az Park Rd.
Lakeland, FL 33802
Ultimate Parent: Fleetwood Enterprises, Inc. SIC: 3711—Motor Vehicles & Car Bodies.

★ 60726 ★ Fleetwood Motor Homes of Florida Inc.
2433 Az Park Rd. PO Drawer F
Lakeland, FL 33802
Ultimate Parent: Fleetwood Enterprises, Inc. SIC: 2451—Mobile Homes.

★ 60727 ★ Florida Tile Industries Inc.
Florida Tile Div.
400 Kathleen Rd.
Lakeland, FL 33801
Ultimate Parent: Premark International. SIC: 3253—Ceramic Wall & Floor Tile.

★ 60728 ★ FMC Corp.
Fairway Ave.
Lakeland, FL 33801
(813)683-5411
Officer: Robert Blackwell, Manager. Ultimate Parent: FMC. SIC: 3556—Food Products Machinery.

★ 60729 ★   Fmc Corp. Lakeland
Facility
Fairway Ave.
Lakeland, FL 33802-1708
Ultimate Parent: FMC. SIC: 2899—
Chemical Preparations Nec.

★ 60730 ★   Fmc Corp. Lakeland
Plant
Fairway Ave.
Lakeland, FL 33801
Ultimate Parent: FMC. SIC: 2899—
Chemical Preparations Nec.

★ 60731 ★   Great Western Bank
16282 S. Florida Ave.
Lakeland, FL 33803
(813)682-3340
Ultimate Parent: Great Western Financial
Corp. SIC: 6022—State Commercial Banks.

★ 60732 ★   Greyhound Bus Lines
430 S. Missouri Ave.
Lakeland, FL 33801
(813)686-5601
Ultimate Parent: Greyhound Lines Inc. SIC:
4111—Local & Suburban Transit.

★ 60733 ★   Hertz Rent-A-Car
2101 S. Florida Ave.
Lakeland, FL 33803
(813)683-4727
Ultimate Parent: Hertz. SIC: 7514—
Passenger Car Rental.

★ 60734 ★   Intertrade Corp.
Lakeland, FL 33802
(813)687-3993
Ultimate Parent: FMC. SIC: 5083—Farm &
Garden Machinery.

★ 60735 ★   Juice Bowl Prods.
Inc.
2090 Bartow Hwy.
Lakeland, FL 33802
Ultimate Parent: Campbell Soup. SIC:
2086—Bottled & Canned Soft Drinks.

★ 60736 ★   Juice Bowl Products
Inc.
2090 Bartow Hwy. U.S. 98 South
Lakeland, FL 33802
Ultimate Parent: Campbell Soup. SIC:
2086—Bottled & Canned Soft Drinks.

★ 60737 ★   Juice Bowl Products
Inc.
2090 Bartow Rd.
Lakeland, FL 33801
(813)665-5517
Officer: Hani Badawi, Vice President.
Ultimate Parent: Dean Foods. SIC: 2033—
Canned Fruits & Vegetables; 2037—Frozen
Fruits & Vegetables.

★ 60738 ★   Kentucky Fried
Chicken
5208 S. Florida Ave.
Lakeland, FL 33813
(813)644-4199
Ultimate Parent: Pepsico. SIC: 5812—
Eating Places.

★ 60739 ★   Kentucky Fried
Chicken
3450 Us 98 N
Lakeland, FL 33809
(813)858-6059
Ultimate Parent: Pepsico. SIC: 5812—
Eating Places.

★ 60740 ★   Kentucky Fried
Chicken
727 E. Memorial Blvd.
Lakeland, FL 33801
(813)688-2111
Ultimate Parent: Pepsico. SIC: 5812—
Eating Places.

★ 60741 ★   Kentucky Fried
Chicken
2914 S. Florida Ave.
Lakeland, FL 33803
(813)688-4734
Ultimate Parent: Pepsico. SIC: 5812—
Eating Places.

★ 60742 ★   Lakeland Indl. Center
& Bakery & Bakery
3045 New Tampa Hwy.
Lakeland, FL 33802
Ultimate Parent: Publix Super Markets.
SIC: 2024—Ice Cream & Frozen Desserts;
2026—Fluid Milk; 2086—Bottled & Canned
Soft Drinks; 2051—Bread, Cake & Related

Products; 2052—Cookies & Crackers;
2099—Food Preparations Nec.

★ 60743 ★   Lane Bryant
3800 Us Hwy. 98 N. 558
Lakeland, FL 33809
(813)859-4166
Ultimate Parent: Limited. SIC: 5621—
Women's Clothing Stores.

★ 60744 ★   Lerner Shop
198 Lakeland Sq.
Lakeland, FL 33813
(813)858-6925
Ultimate Parent: Limited. SIC: 5651—
Family Clothing Stores.

★ 60745 ★   The Limited
3800 Us Hwy. 98 N. 740
Lakeland, FL 33809
(813)858-0778
Ultimate Parent: Limited. SIC: 5621—
Women's Clothing Stores.

★ 60746 ★   Maison Blanche
600 Lakeland Sq.
Lakeland, FL 33809
(813)859-2000
Ultimate Parent: Mercantile Stores. SIC:
5311—Department Stores.

★ 60747 ★   Marshalls Department
Store
3615 S. Florida Ave. 410
Lakeland, FL 33803
(813)647-3316
Ultimate Parent: Melville. SIC: 5311—
Department Stores.

★ 60748 ★   Mary Kay Cosmetics
1104 Bartow Rd. I103
Lakeland, FL 33801
(813)687-8651
Ultimate Parent: Mary Kay Cosmetics.

★ 60749 ★   McDonalds
Restaurants
2606 Us Hwy. 92 E
Lakeland, FL 33801
(813)665-1464
Ultimate Parent: McDonald's.
SIC: 5812—Eating Places.

★ 60750 ★   McDonalds
Restaurants
3420 Us Hwy. 98 N
Lakeland, FL 33809
(813)858-3009
Ultimate Parent: McDonald's.
SIC: 5812—Eating Places.

★ 60751 ★   McDonalds
Restaurants
2735 S. Florida Ave.
Lakeland, FL 33803
(813)682-1688
Ultimate Parent: McDonald's.
SIC: 5812—Eating Places.

★ 60752 ★   McDonalds
Restaurants
4721 S. Florida Ave.
Lakeland, FL 33813
(813)644-2205
Ultimate Parent: McDonald's.
SIC: 5812—Eating Places.

★ 60753 ★   Mervyn's
100 Lakeland Sq.
Lakeland, FL 33809
(813)859-6544
Ultimate Parent: Dayton Hudson. SIC:
5311—Department Stores.

★ 60754 ★   Mobil Oil Inc.
3440 Us 98 N
Lakeland, FL 33809
(813)858-5718
Ultimate Parent: Mobil. SIC: 5541—
Gasoline Service Stations.

★ 60755 ★   Mpi Inc.
1070 County Line Rd.
Lakeland, FL 33801
Ultimate Parent: Leggett & Platt Inc. SIC:
3086—Plastics Foam Products.

★ 60756 ★   Mutual of New York
4953 Southfork Dr.
Lakeland, FL 33813
(813)646-5074
Ultimate Parent: Mutual of New York. SIC:
6411—Insurance Agents, Brokers &
Service.

★ 60757 ★   Ncr Corp.
1200 Us Hwy. 98 S. 5
Lakeland, FL 33801
(813)688-7734
Ultimate Parent: AT&T. SIC: 7699—Repair
Services Nec.

★ 60758 ★   Owens-Brockway
Glass Container Inc.
2222 W. Bella Vista Rd.
Lakeland, FL 33809
Ultimate Parent: Owens-Illinois. SIC:
3221—Glass Containers.

★ 60759 ★   Owens-Illinois Glass
Container Inc.
Plant 16
2222 W. Bella Vista Rd.
Lakeland, FL 33809
Location Type: Plant. Ultimate Parent:
Owens-Illinois. SIC: 3221—Glass
Containers.

★ 60760 ★   Petite Sophisticate
392 Lakeland Sq.
Lakeland, FL 33809
(813)859-5487
Ultimate Parent: United States Shoe. SIC:
5651—Family Clothing Stores.

★ 60761 ★   Piggly Wiggly
Us 98 N
Lakeland, FL 33805
(813)858-3869
Ultimate Parent: Bruno's. SIC: 5411—
Grocery Stores.

★ 60762 ★   Pizza Hut
3121 Us 98 S
Lakeland, FL 33803
(813)666-1029
Ultimate Parent: Pepsico. SIC: 5812—
Eating Places.

★ 60763 ★   Pizza Hut
735 E. Memorial Blvd.
Lakeland, FL 33801
(813)686-1151
Ultimate Parent: Pepsico. SIC: 5812—
Eating Places.

★ 60764 ★   Pizza Hut
3919 S. Florida Ave.
Lakeland, FL 33813
(813)644-0598
Ultimate Parent: Pepsico. SIC: 5812—
Eating Places.

★ 60765 ★   Pizza Hut
1919 New Tampa Hwy.
Lakeland, FL 33801
(813)688-7311
Ultimate Parent: Pepsico. SIC: 5812—
Eating Places.

★ 60766 ★   Pizza Hut
2116 E. State Rd. 540A
Lakeland, FL 33813
(813)644-3151
Ultimate Parent: Pepsico. SIC: 5812—
Eating Places.

★ 60767 ★   Publix Super Market
3029 New Tampa Hwy.
Lakeland, FL 33801
(813)688-7150
Ultimate Parent: Publix Super Markets.
SIC: 5411—Grocery Stores.

★ 60768 ★   Publix Super Market
6767 Us 98 N
Lakeland, FL 33809
(813)858-4466
Ultimate Parent: Publix Super Markets.
SIC: 5411—Grocery Stores.

★ 60769 ★   Publix Super Market
1617 Us Hwy. 98 S
Lakeland, FL 33801
(813)682-0131
Ultimate Parent: Publix Super Markets.
SIC: 5411—Grocery Stores.

★ 60770 ★   Publix Super Market
407 PO Box
Lakeland, FL 33802
(813)686-1188
Ultimate Parent: Publix Super Markets.
SIC: 6512—Nonresidential Building
Operators.

★ 60771 ★   Publix Super Markets
3029 New Tampa Hwy.
Lakeland, FL 33801
(813)688-7150
Ultimate Parent: Publix Super Markets.
SIC: 5411—Grocery Stores.

★ 60772 ★   Publix Super Markets
1936 George Jenkins Blvd.
Lakeland, FL 33801
(813)688-1188
Company Type: Headquarters. Officer:
Howard M. Jenkins. Employee Count:
82000. Sales: 7473 M. Fortune Service
500: Ranking 21.

★ 60773 ★   Radio Shack
3133 Us 98 N
Lakeland, FL 33805
(813)682-3810
Company Type: Division. Ultimate Parent:
Tandy Corp. SIC: 5065—Electronic Parts &
Equipment Nec.

★ 60774 ★   Radio Shack
2810 S. Florida Ave.
Lakeland, FL 33809
(813)688-6049
Company Type: Division. Ultimate Parent:
Tandy Corp. SIC: 5719—Miscellaneous
Home Furnishings Stores.

★ 60775 ★   Radio Shack
4790 S. Florida Ave.
Lakeland, FL 33813
(813)644-3655
Company Type: Division. Ultimate Parent:
Tandy Corp. SIC: 5065—Electronic Parts &
Equipment Nec; 5731—Radio, Television &
Electronics Stores.

★ 60776 ★   Radio Shack
Lakeland Mall
Lakeland, FL 33801
(813)688-2998
Company Type: Division. Ultimate Parent:
Tandy Corp. SIC: 5731—Radio, Television
& Electronics Stores.

★ 60777 ★   Radio Shack
120 Lakeland Sq.
Lakeland, FL 33809
(813)859-6876
Company Type: Division. Ultimate Parent:
Tandy Corp. SIC: 5731—Radio, Television
& Electronics Stores.

★ 60778 ★   Radio Shack
1525 Bartow Rd.
Lakeland, FL 33801
(813)683-8858
Company Type: Division. Ultimate Parent:
Tandy Corp. SIC: 7629—Electrical Repair
Shops Nec.

★ 60779 ★   Rite Aid Drugs
3555 S. Florida Ave.
Lakeland, FL 33803
(813)646-2973
Ultimate Parent: Rite Aid. SIC: 5912—Drug
Stores & Proprietary Stores.

★ 60780 ★   Ryder Truck Rental
Rural Route 33a
Lakeland, FL 33809
(813)665-7321
Ultimate Parent: Ryder System. SIC:
7513—Truck Rental & Leasing Without
Drivers; 7514—Passenger Car Rental.

★ 60781 ★   Ryder Truck Rental
3310 Swindell Rd.
Lakeland, FL 33805
Ultimate Parent: Ryder System. SIC:
7359—Equipment Rental & Leasing Nec.

★ 60782 ★   Sam's Wholesale
Club
1140 Lakeland Mall
Lakeland, FL 33801
(813)686-6191
Ultimate Parent: Wal-Mart Stores, Inc. SIC:
5099—Durable Goods Nec.

★ 60783 ★   Service Merchandise
4015 Us Hwy. 98 N
Lakeland, FL 33809
(813)859-1421
Ultimate Parent: Service Merchandise Co.,
Inc. SIC: 5399—Miscellaneous General
Merchandise Store.

★ 60784 ★ Super Saver Warehouse Foods
2435 Us 98 N
Lakeland, FL 33805
(813)687-4769
Ultimate Parent: Wal-Mart Stores, Inc. SIC: 5411—Grocery Stores.

★ 60785 ★ Taco Bell
3601 S. Florida Ave.
Lakeland, FL 33803
(813)646-4207
Ultimate Parent: Pepsico. SIC: 5812—Eating Places.

★ 60786 ★ Texaco Food Mart
1605 E. Edgewood Dr.
Lakeland, FL 33803
(813)682-2065
Ultimate Parent: Texaco. SIC: 5411—Grocery Stores.

★ 60787 ★ Texaco Inc.
1145 N. Galloway Rd.
Lakeland, FL 33809
(813)682-9126
Ultimate Parent: Texaco. SIC: 5541—Gasoline Service Stations.

★ 60788 ★ Texaco 134
3801 Us Hwy. 98 N
Lakeland, FL 33809
(813)858-9018
Ultimate Parent: Texaco. SIC: 5541—Gasoline Service Stations.

★ 60789 ★ This End Up
640 Lakeland Sq.
Lakeland, FL 33809
(813)858-7200
Ultimate Parent: Melville. SIC: 5712—Furniture Stores.

★ 60790 ★ Union Bank
4825 Us Hwy. 98 N
Lakeland, FL 33809
(813)499-1055
Ultimate Parent: Union Bank. SIC: 6099—Functions Related to Deposit Banking.

★ 60791 ★ Victoria's Secret
3800 Us Hwy. 98 N. 746
Lakeland, FL 33809
(813)858-7586
Ultimate Parent: Limited. SIC: 5699—Miscellaneous Apparel & Accessory Stores.

★ 60792 ★ Wal Mart Discount Cities
3600 N. US Hwy 98
Lakeland, FL 33809
(813)859-3626
Ultimate Parent: Wal-Mart Stores, Inc. SIC: 5399—Miscellaneous General Merchandise Store.

★ 60793 ★ Wal Mart Discount City
4315 S. Florida Ave.
Lakeland, FL 33813
(813)644-0677
Ultimate Parent: Wal-Mart Stores, Inc. SIC: 5311—Department Stores.

★ 60794 ★ Wal Mart Discount Pharmacy
3600 Us Hwy. 98 N
Lakeland, FL 33809
(813)859-3772
Ultimate Parent: Wal-Mart Stores, Inc. SIC: 5912—Drug Stores & Proprietary Stores.

★ 60795 ★ Waldenbooks
470 Lakeland Sq.
Lakeland, FL 33809
(813)859-6875
Ultimate Parent: K-Mart. SIC: 5942—Book Stores.

★ 60796 ★ Walgreen Drug Stores
6210 Us Hwy. 98 N
Lakeland, FL 33809
(813)858-3834
Ultimate Parent: Walgreen Co. SIC: 5912—Drug Stores & Proprietary Stores.

★ 60797 ★ Walgreen Drug Stores
4241 S. Florida Ave.
Lakeland, FL 33813
(813)644-7539
Ultimate Parent: Walgreen Co. SIC: 5912—Drug Stores & Proprietary Stores.

★ 60798 ★ Walgreen Drug Stores
6848 S. Florida Ave.
Lakeland, FL 33813
(813)647-1541
Ultimate Parent: Walgreen Co. SIC: 5912—Drug Stores & Proprietary Stores.

★ 60799 ★ Walgreen Drug Stores
2637 S. Florida Ave.
Lakeland, FL 33803
(813)686-4159
Ultimate Parent: Walgreen Co. SIC: 5912—Drug Stores & Proprietary Stores.

★ 60800 ★ Western Auto Supply Co. No. 3
3245 S. Florida Ave.
Lakeland, FL 33803
(813)644-7571
Ultimate Parent: Sears Roebuck & Co. SIC: 5531—Automobile & Home Supply Stores.

Lakewood

★ 60801 ★ First Union National Bank of Florida
1400 W. State Rd. 434
Lakewood, FL 32750
(407)262-7360
Location Type: Branch office. Ultimate Parent: First Union Corp. SIC: 6021—National Commercial Banks.

Land O' Lakes

★ 60802 ★ Barnett Bank of Pasco County
21725 Village Lakes Shopping Ctr.
Land O' Lakes, FL 34639-5198
(813)783-0841
Company Type: Subsidiary. Location Type: Branch office. Officer: Valerie Miller, Manager. Ultimate Parent: Barnett Banks. SIC: 6022—State Commercial Banks.

Lantana

★ 60803 ★ Costco Wholesale Corp.
Southeast Division
1875 W. Lantana Rd.
Lantana, FL 33462
(407)533-0446 Fax: (407)582-5789
Officer: Roger A. Campbell, Vice President of Operations. Ultimate Parent: Costco Wholesale Corp.

★ 60804 ★ First Union National Bank of Florida
1500 W. Lantana Rd.
Lantana, FL 33460-1592
(407)533-7690
Location Type: Branch office. Ultimate Parent: First Union Corp. SIC: 6021—National Commercial Banks.

★ 60805 ★ First Union National Bank of Florida
6164 S. Congress Ave.
Lantana, FL 33463
(407)533-7660
Location Type: Branch office. Ultimate Parent: First Union Corp. SIC: 6021—National Commercial Banks.

Largo

★ 60806 ★ Ace Hardware
863 W. Bay Dr.
Largo, FL 34640
(813)586-5451
Ultimate Parent: Ace Hardware. SIC: 5251—Hardware Stores.

★ 60807 ★ Air Products & Chemicals, Inc.
7900 118th Ave.
Largo, FL 34643
(813)544-3949
Ultimate Parent: Air Products & Chemicals, Inc. SIC: 8099—Health & Allied Services Nec.

★ 60808 ★ Albertson's Pharmacy
13031 Walsingham Rd.
Largo, FL 34644
(813)593-0740
Ultimate Parent: Albertson's Inc. SIC: 5912—Drug Stores & Proprietary Stores.

★ 60809 ★ Ametek Inc.
Mansfield & Green
8600 Sommerset Dr.
Largo, FL 34643
(813)536-7831 Fax: (813)539-6882
Company Type: Subsidiary. Officer: Donald L. Whitehead, Vice President & General Manager. Ultimate Parent: Ametek Inc.

★ 60810 ★ Ametek Inc.
Mansfield & Green
PO Box 1982
Largo, FL 34649-1982
(813)536-7831
Company Type: Division. Officer: Don Whitehead. Ultimate Parent: Ametek Inc. SIC: 3829—Measuring & Controlling Devices Nec.

★ 60811 ★ AMP Inc.
230 Commerce Dr., N
Largo, FL 34640
(813)586-2631
Officer: Charlotte Stafford, Manager. Ultimate Parent: AMP Inc. SIC: 3544—Special Dies, Tools, Jigs & Fixtures.

★ 60812 ★ AmSouth Bank of Florida
12020 Seminole Blvd.
Largo, FL 34648
(813)462-1168
Location Type: Branch office. Ultimate Parent: AmSouth Bancorp. SIC: 6022—State Commercial Banks.

★ 60813 ★ Anchor Savings
2075 Seminole Blvd.
Largo, FL 34648-1712
(813)586-6660
Location Type: Branch office. Officer: Heather Lane. Ultimate Parent: Anchor Bancorp. SIC: 6035—Federal Savings Institutions; 6021—National Commercial Banks.

★ 60814 ★ Anchor Savings Bank
7300 Park St.
Largo, FL 34647-4601
(813)393-7555
Location Type: Branch office. Ultimate Parent: Anchor Bancorp. SIC: 6035—Federal Savings Institutions; 6021—National Commercial Banks.

★ 60815 ★ Anchor Savings Bank
2075 Seminole Blvd.
Largo, FL 34648
(813)586-6660
Ultimate Parent: Anchor Bancorp. SIC: 6022—State Commercial Banks.

★ 60816 ★ AT&T Paradyne
8545 126th Ave. N
PO Box 2826
Largo, FL 34649-2826
(813)530-2000 Fax: (813)530-8228
Company Type: Subsidiary. Officer: John J. Mitcham, President. Ultimate Parent: AT&T.

★ 60817 ★ AT&T Paradyne Corp.
8545 126th Ave.
Largo, FL 34649
(813)530-2000 (800)482-3333 Telex: 8108660432
Officer: John J. Miteham, President & CEO. Ultimate Parent: AT&T. SIC: 3577—Computer Peripheral Equipment Nec; 3579—Office Machines Nec. Employee Count: 2400. Sales: 600568000 M.

★ 60818 ★ AT&T Paradyne Corp.
8545 126th Ave.
Largo, FL 34643-1502
(813)530-2000
Location Type: Branch office. Officer: John Mitcham. Ultimate Parent: AT&T. SIC: 3571—Electronic Computers; 3577—Computer Peripheral Equipment Nec; 3579—Office Machines Nec; 3661—Telephone & Telegraph Apparatus; 3663—Radio & T.V. Communications Equipment; 5065—Electronic Parts & Equipment Nec; 7374—Data Processing & Preparation.

★ 60819 ★ Barnett Bank of Pinellas County
13075 Walshingham Rd.
Largo, FL 34644-3514
(813)539-9168
Company Type: Subsidiary. Location Type: Branch office. Officer: Bob Vermont,

Manager. Ultimate Parent: Barnett Banks. SIC: 6022—State Commercial Banks.

★ 60820 ★ Barnett Bank of Pinellas County
10900 Seminole Blvd.
Largo, FL 34648
(813)892-1694
Company Type: Subsidiary. Location Type: Branch office. Officer: Keith Felton, Manager. Ultimate Parent: Barnett Banks. SIC: 6022—State Commercial Banks.

★ 60821 ★ Barnett Bank of Pinellas County
13625 Belcher Rd.
Largo, FL 34641-4021
(813)539-9553
Company Type: Subsidiary. Location Type: Branch office. Officer: Cynthia Weller, Manager. Ultimate Parent: Barnett Banks. SIC: 6022—State Commercial Banks.

★ 60822 ★ Barnett Bank of Pinellas County
1150 8th Ave. SW
Largo, FL 34640-3174
(813)539-9179
Company Type: Subsidiary. Location Type: Branch office. Officer: Andrew Craske, Manager. Ultimate Parent: Barnett Banks. SIC: 6022—State Commercial Banks.

★ 60823 ★ Baxter Health Care
7511 114th Ave.
Largo, FL 34643
(813)541-6411
Officer: Gus Azel, Manager. Ultimate Parent: Baxter International. SIC: 3841—Surgical & Medical Instruments.

★ 60824 ★ Baxter Healthcare Corp.
PO Box 1230
Largo, FL 34649-1230
(813)541-6411
Officer: Ron Eshmann. Ultimate Parent: Baxter International. SIC: 3841—Surgical & Medical Instruments.

★ 60825 ★ Baxter Healthcare Corp.
7511 114 Ave. N
Largo, FL 34643
Ultimate Parent: Baxter International. SIC: 3841—Surgical & Medical Instruments.

★ 60826 ★ Builders Square Inc.
1215 Missouri Ave. N
Largo, FL 34640
(813)585-3599
Company Type: Subsidiary. Ultimate Parent: K-Mart. SIC: 5082—Construction & Mining Machinery.

★ 60827 ★ California Federal Bank, FSB
7490 Bryan Dairy Rd.
Largo, FL 34647
(813)541-7738
Location Type: Branch office. Officer: Deborah Rowe, Manager. Ultimate Parent: California Federal Bank. SIC: 6021—National Commercial Banks.

★ 60828 ★ California Federal Bank, FSB
2100 E. Bay Dr.
Largo, FL 34641
(813)586-1178
Location Type: Branch office. Ultimate Parent: California Federal Bank. SIC: 6021—National Commercial Banks.

★ 60829 ★ Eckerd Corp.
8333 Bryan Dairy Rd.
Largo, FL 34647
(813)399-6000
Company Type: Headquarters. Officer: John E. Davies, CEO. Ultimate Parent: Eckerd Corp. SIC: 5912—Drug Stores & Proprietary Stores; 7384—Photofinishing Laboratories. Sales: 8,957,000 M.

★ 60830 ★ Eckerd Corp.
8333 Bryan Dairy Rd.
Largo, FL 34647
Company Type: Headquarters. Ultimate Parent: Eckerd Corp.

★ 60831 ★ **Eckerd Corp.**
8333 Bryan Dairy Rd.
Largo, FL 34647
(813)399-6000
Ultimate Parent: Eckerd Corp. **SIC:** 3851—
Ophthalmic Goods.

★ 60832 ★ **Eckerd Corp.**
8333 Bryan Dairy Rd.
Largo, FL 34647
(813)399-6000
Company Type: Headquarters. **Officer:**
Stewart Turley. **Employee Count:** 24100.
Sales: 4190.5 M. **Fortune Service 500:**
Ranking 31.

★ 60833 ★ **Eckerd Corp.**
Eckerd Drug Co.
8333 Bryan Dairy Rd.
Largo, FL 34647
(813)397-7461
Company Type: Headquarters. **Officer:**
Les Reagin, Senior Vice President. **Ultimate
Parent:** Eckerd Corp. **SIC:** 5912—Drug
Stores & Proprietary Stores.

★ 60834 ★ **Jack Eckerd Corp.**
8333 Bryan Dairy Rd.
Largo, FL 34647-1230
(813)397-7461
Ultimate Parent: Eckerd Corp. **SIC:** 5912—
Drug Stores & Proprietary Stores; 7384—
Photofinishing Laboratories; 5995—Optical
Goods Stores; 8742—Management
Consulting Services; 4225—General
Warehousing & Storage.

★ 60835 ★ **Eckerd Drug Co.**
8333 Bryan Dairy Rd.
Largo, FL 34647
(813)399-6000
Ultimate Parent: Eckerd Corp.

★ 60836 ★ **Eckerd Express Photo**
8333 Bryan Dairy Rd.
Largo, FL 34647
(813)399-6000
Company Type: Subsidiary. **Officer:** Tim
Burger, President. **Ultimate Parent:** Eckerd
Corp.

★ 60837 ★ **Eckerd Vision Group**
8333 Bryan Dairy Rd.
Largo, FL 34647
(813)399-6000
Company Type: Subsidiary. **Officer:**
Richard W. Roberson, President. **Ultimate
Parent:** Eckerd Corp.

★ 60838 ★ **Fortune Bank, ASB**
9701 Starkey Rd.
Largo, FL 34647-2210
Location Type: Branch office. **Ultimate
Parent:** Fortune Bancorp. **SIC:** 6021—
National Commercial Banks.

★ 60839 ★ **General Electric Ndd
Pinellas Plant**
7887 Bryan Dairy Rd.
Largo, FL 34649
Ultimate Parent: General Electric. **SIC:**
3679—Electronic Components Nec; 9711—
National Security.

★ 60840 ★ **Great Western Bank**
8000 Seminole Mall
Largo, FL 34642
(813)393-7588
Ultimate Parent: Great Western Financial
Corp. **SIC:** 6159—Miscellaneous Business
Credit Institutions.

★ 60841 ★ **Hit or Miss**
710 Ulmerton Rd. E
Largo, FL 34641
(813)585-1493
Ultimate Parent: TJX. **SIC:** 5621—
Women's Clothing Stores.

★ 60842 ★ **Kentucky Fried
Chicken**
8880 Ulmerton Rd. E
Largo, FL 34641
(813)530-4376
Ultimate Parent: Pepsico. **SIC:** 5812—
Eating Places.

★ 60843 ★ **Kentucky Fried
Chicken**
13677 Walsingham Rd.
Largo, FL 34644
(813)595-1220
Ultimate Parent: Pepsico. **SIC:** 5812—
Eating Places.

★ 60844 ★ **Linvatec**
11311 Concept Blvd.
Largo, FL 34643-4908
(813)392-6464
Location Type: Branch office. **Officer:**
George Kempfell. **Ultimate Parent:**
Bristol-Myers Squibb. **SIC:** 3842—Surgical
Appliances & Supplies; 3841—Surgical &
Medical Instruments; 5999—Miscellaneous
Retail Stores Nec; 8011—Offices & Clinics
of Medical Doctors.

★ 60845 ★ **Linvatec Corp.**
11311 Concept Blvd.
Largo, FL 34643
(813)392-6464 **Fax:** (813)399-2603
Company Type: Subsidiary. **Officer:**
George P. Kempsell, President. **Ultimate
Parent:** Bristol-Myers Squibb.

★ 60846 ★ **Martin Marietta
Speciality Co.**
US Doe Pinellas Plant
7887 Bryan Dairy Rd.
Largo, FL 34643
Location Type: Plant. **Ultimate Parent:**
Martin Marietta. **SIC:** 3679—Electronic
Components Nec; 9711—National Security.

★ 60847 ★ **Martin Marietta
Specialty Components, Inc.**
PO Box 2908
Largo, FL 34649-2908
(813)541-8263
Officer: Dr. Charles A. Hall, President.
Ultimate Parent: Martin Marietta.

★ 60848 ★ **Matco Tools**
10447 109th St.
Largo, FL 34648
(813)799-4539
Ultimate Parent: Danaher Corp.

★ 60849 ★ **Pizza Hut**
1 Southern Commercial Ctr.
Largo, FL 34643
(813)585-3937
Ultimate Parent: Pepsico. **SIC:** 5812—
Eating Places.

★ 60850 ★ **Pizza Hut**
14450 Walsingham Rd.
Largo, FL 34644
(813)595-9436
Ultimate Parent: Pepsico. **SIC:** 5812—
Eating Places.

★ 60851 ★ **Pizza Hut**
12512 Starkey Rd.
Largo, FL 34643
(813)581-3182
Ultimate Parent: Pepsico. **SIC:** 5812—
Eating Places.

★ 60852 ★ **Pizza Hut**
2750 W. Bay Dr.
Largo, FL 34640
(813)581-6182
Ultimate Parent: Pepsico. **SIC:** 5812—
Eating Places.

★ 60853 ★ **Pizza Hut**
2745 E. Bay Dr.
Largo, FL 34641
(813)535-0761
Ultimate Parent: Pepsico. **SIC:** 5812—
Eating Places.

★ 60854 ★ **Publix Super Market**
16 Bardmoor Villge Shopping Mall
Largo, FL 34647
(813)393-7517
Ultimate Parent: Publix Super Markets.
SIC: 5411—Grocery Stores.

★ 60855 ★ **Publix Super Market**
857 W. Bay Dr.
Largo, FL 34640
(813)585-3855
Ultimate Parent: Publix Super Markets.
SIC: 5411—Grocery Stores.

★ 60856 ★ **Publix Super Market**
9330 Oakhurst Rd.
Largo, FL 34646
(813)596-3121
Ultimate Parent: Publix Super Markets.
SIC: 5411—Grocery Stores.

★ 60857 ★ **Publix Super Market**
12022 Indian Rocks Rd. S
Largo, FL 34644
(813)595-2514
Ultimate Parent: Publix Super Markets.
SIC: 5411—Grocery Stores.

★ 60858 ★ **Publix Super Markets**
9330 Oakhurst Rd.
Largo, FL 34646
(813)596-3121
Ultimate Parent: Publix Super Markets.
SIC: 5411—Grocery Stores.

★ 60859 ★ **Publix Super Markets**
857 W. Bay Dr.
Largo, FL 34640
(813)585-3855
Ultimate Parent: Publix Super Markets.
SIC: 5411—Grocery Stores.

★ 60860 ★ **Radio Shack**
12905 Walsingham Rd.
Largo, FL 34644
(813)596-6103
Company Type: Division. **Ultimate Parent:**
Tandy Corp. **SIC:** 5065—Electronic Parts &
Equipment Nec.

★ 60861 ★ **Radio Shack**
885 W. Bay Dr.
Largo, FL 34640
(813)581-5214
Company Type: Division. **Ultimate Parent:**
Tandy Corp. **SIC:** 5731—Radio, Television
& Electronics Stores.

★ 60862 ★ **Ryder Truck Rental**
13010 Walsingham Rd.
Largo, FL 34644
(813)593-1736
Ultimate Parent: Ryder System. **SIC:**
7389—Business Services Nec.

★ 60863 ★ **Service Merchandise**
310 Ulmerton Rd. E
Largo, FL 34641
(813)584-4476
Ultimate Parent: Service Merchandise Co.,
Inc. **SIC:** 5311—Department Stores.

★ 60864 ★ **Taco Bell**
2795 Ulmerton Rd. E
Largo, FL 34641
(813)535-7666
Ultimate Parent: Pepsico. **SIC:** 5812—
Eating Places.

★ 60865 ★ **Texaco No 320**
2400 E. Bay Dr.
Largo, FL 34641
(813)531-6362
Ultimate Parent: Texaco. **SIC:** 5541—
Gasoline Service Stations.

★ 60866 ★ **Varian Associates**
12360 66th St. V2
Largo, FL 34643
(813)539-1590
Ultimate Parent: Varian Associates, Inc.
SIC: 5084—Industrial Machinery &
Equipment.

★ 60867 ★ **Walgreen Drug Stores**
2900 W. Bay Dr.
Largo, FL 34640
(813)585-1488
Ultimate Parent: Walgreen Co. **SIC:**
5912—Drug Stores & Proprietary Stores.

★ 60868 ★ **Walgreen Drug Stores**
13020 66th St.
Largo, FL 34643
(813)530-4732
Ultimate Parent: Walgreen Co. **SIC:**
5912—Drug Stores & Proprietary Stores.

★ 60869 ★ **Walgreen Drug Stores**
13845 Walsingham Rd.
Largo, FL 34644
(813)596-6143
Ultimate Parent: Walgreen Co. **SIC:**
5912—Drug Stores & Proprietary Stores.

★ 60870 ★ **Western Auto Supply
Co.**
13015 Seminole Blvd.
Largo, FL 34648
Ultimate Parent: Sears Roebuck & Co.
SIC: 5531—Automobile & Home Supply
Stores.

Lauderdale Lakes

★ 60871 ★ **California Federal
Bank, FSB**
3099 N. State Rd.
Lauderdale Lakes, FL 33313-1995
(305)497-1900
Location Type: Branch office. **Officer:**
JoAnna Vitale, Manager. **Ultimate Parent:**

California Federal Bank. **SIC:** 6021—
National Commercial Banks.

★ 60872 ★ **First Union National
Bank of Florida**
4850 W. Oakland Park Blvd.
Lauderdale Lakes, FL 33313-7260
(305)467-5222
Location Type: Branch office. **Ultimate
Parent:** First Union Corp. **SIC:** 6021—
National Commercial Banks.

Lauderhill

★ 60873 ★ **American Savings of
Florida, FSB**
5581 Oakland Park Blvd.
Lauderhill, FL 33313-1480
(305)485-0207
Location Type: Branch office. **Officer:**
Jayne Kennedy, Manager. **Ultimate Parent:**
American Savings of Florida. **SIC:** 6035—
Federal Savings Institutions; 6211—Security
Brokers & Dealers.

★ 60874 ★ **California Federal
Bank, FSB**
5518 W. Oakland Park Blvd.
Lauderhill, FL 33313-1412
(305)485-9600
Location Type: Branch office. **Officer:** Etta
Waltzer, Manager. **Ultimate Parent:**
California Federal Bank. **SIC:** 6021—
National Commercial Banks.

★ 60875 ★ **First Union National
Bank of Florida**
3990 NW 16th St.
Lauderhill, FL 33313
(305)467-5514
Location Type: Branch office. **Ultimate
Parent:** First Union Corp. **SIC:** 6021—
National Commercial Banks.

Leesburg

★ 60876 ★ **Barnett Bank of Lake
County, NA**
10715 US Hwy. 441
Leesburg, FL 34788
(904)589-5000
Company Type: Subsidiary. **Location
Type:** Branch office. **Officer:** Barbara
Hurley, Vice President. **Ultimate Parent:**
Barnett Banks. **SIC:** 6021—National
Commercial Banks.

★ 60877 ★ **Barnett Bank of Lake
County, NA**
Southside Shopping Ctr.
S. Hwy. 27
Leesburg, FL 34789
(904)589-5000
Company Type: Subsidiary. **Location
Type:** Branch office. **Officer:** Ben
Seabrook, Vice President. **Ultimate Parent:**
Barnett Banks. **SIC:** 6021—National
Commercial Banks.

★ 60878 ★ **Barnett Bank of Lake
County, NA**
401 N. 14th St.
Leesburg, FL 34748-4825
(904)589-5000
Company Type: Subsidiary. **Location
Type:** Branch office. **Officer:** Ben
Seabrook, Manager. **Ultimate Parent:**
Barnett Banks. **SIC:** 6021—National
Commercial Banks.

★ 60879 ★ **Barnett Bank of Lake
County, NA**
1711 N. 14th St.
Leesburg, FL 34748
(904)589-5000
Company Type: Subsidiary. **Location
Type:** Branch office. **Officer:** Ben
Seabrook, Vice President. **Ultimate Parent:**
Barnett Banks. **SIC:** 6021—National
Commercial Banks.

★ 60880 ★ **Coca Cola Bottling
Co.**
110 County Rd. 468
Leesburg, FL 34748
(904)787-5531
Ultimate Parent: Coca-Cola Enterprises.
SIC: 2086—Bottled & Canned Soft Drinks.

★ 60881 ★ Coca-Cola Foods
11 Cloud St.
Leesburg, FL 34748
Ultimate Parent: Coca-Cola. SIC: 2080—
Beverages.

★ 60882 ★ Coca-Cola Foods
Leesburg
11 Cloud St.
Leesburg, FL 34748
Ultimate Parent: Coca-Cola. SIC: 2037—
Frozen Fruits & Vegetables.

★ 60883 ★ First Union National
Bank of Florida
400 North Blvd.
Leesburg, FL 34748-5247
(904)787-1222
Location Type: Branch office. Ultimate
Parent: First Union Corp. SIC: 6021—
National Commercial Banks.

★ 60884 ★ Lerner Shop
7246 S. Us Hwy. 441
Leesburg, FL 34748
(904)728-1118
Ultimate Parent: Limited. SIC: 5651—
Family Clothing Stores.

★ 60885 ★ Rite Aid
1413 S. 14th St.
Leesburg, FL 34748
(904)787-8556
Ultimate Parent: Rite Aid. SIC: 5912—Drug
Stores & Proprietary Stores.

★ 60886 ★ Ryder Truck Rental
32813 S. Us 441
Leesburg, FL 34788
(904)326-8711
Ultimate Parent: Ryder System. SIC:
7513—Truck Rental & Leasing Without
Drivers.

★ 60887 ★ Taco Bell
1103 N. 14th St.
Leesburg, FL 34748
(904)326-3005
Ultimate Parent: Pepsico. SIC: 5812—
Eating Places.

★ 60888 ★ Walgreen Drug Stores
701 N. 14th St.
Leesburg, FL 34748
(904)326-2355
Ultimate Parent: Walgreen Co. SIC:
5912—Drug Stores & Proprietary Stores.

★ 60889 ★ Wolverine Gasket Co.
PO Box 895038 PO Box 895038
Leesburg, FL 34788
Ultimate Parent: Eagle-Picher Industries
Inc. SIC: 3053—Gaskets, Packing & Sealing
Devices; 2675—Die-Cut Paper & Board.

★ 60890 ★ Wolverine Gasket Co.
10825 County Rd. PO Box 895038
Leesburg, FL 34788
Ultimate Parent: Eagle-Picher Industries
Inc. SIC: 3053—Gaskets, Packing & Sealing
Devices.

Lehigh Acres

★ 60891 ★ Citizens Federal
Bank, FSB
1328 Homestead Rd. N.
Lehigh Acres, FL 33936-6024
(813)369-6184
Location Type: Branch office. Officer:
Mary Hedrick, Manager. Ultimate Parent:
CSF Holdings. SIC: 6021—National
Commercial Banks.

★ 60892 ★ Exxon
1365 Lee Blvd.
Lehigh Acres, FL 33936
(813)369-1090
Ultimate Parent: Exxon. SIC: 6211—
Security Brokers & Dealers.

★ 60893 ★ First of America Bank
1300 Homstead Rd.
Lehigh Acres, FL 33936
(813)369-5821
Location Type: Branch office. Ultimate
Parent: First of America Bank Corp. SIC:
6021—National Commercial Banks.

★ 60894 ★ First Union National
Bank of Florida
1130 Homestead Rd.
Lehigh Acres, FL 33936-6092
(813)369-2175
Location Type: Branch office. Ultimate
Parent: First Union Corp. SIC: 6021—
National Commercial Banks.

★ 60895 ★ Pizza Hut
27 Homestead Rd.
Lehigh Acres, FL 33936
(813)368-6665
Ultimate Parent: Pepsico. SIC: 5812—
Eating Places.

★ 60896 ★ Walgreen
1149 Homestead Rd. W
Lehigh Acres, FL 33936
(813)368-6655
Ultimate Parent: Walgreen Co. SIC:
5912—Drug Stores & Proprietary Stores.

Lessburg

★ 60897 ★ First Union National
Bank of Florida
2271 N. Citrus Blvd.
Lessburg, FL 34748
(904)728-3656
Location Type: Branch office. Ultimate
Parent: First Union Corp. SIC: 6021—
National Commercial Banks.

Lghthouse Point

★ 60898 ★ Pizza Hut
440 E. Sample Rd.
Lghthouse Point, FL 33064
(305)942-8227
Ultimate Parent: Pepsico. SIC: 8748—
Business Consulting Services Nec.

Lighthouse Point

★ 60899 ★ Barnett Bank of
Broward County, NA
2850 N. Federal Hwy.
Lighthouse Point, FL 33064-6897
(305)786-3340
Company Type: Subsidiary. Location
Type: Branch office. Officer: Sandy Singer,
Manager. Ultimate Parent: Barnett Banks.
SIC: 6021—National Commercial Banks.

★ 60900 ★ California Federal
Bank, FSB
3260 N. Federal Hwy.
Lighthouse Point, FL 33064-6784
(305)782-8600
Location Type: Branch office. Ultimate
Parent: California Federal Bank. SIC:
6021—National Commercial Banks.

★ 60901 ★ Coast to Coast
512 N. Federal Hwy.
Lighthouse Point, FL 33062
(305)732-2233
Ultimate Parent: Servistar Corp. SIC:
5812—Eating Places.

★ 60902 ★ Exxon
3601 N. Dixie Hwy.
Lighthouse Point, FL 33064
(305)946-3530
Ultimate Parent: Exxon. SIC: 5541—
Gasoline Service Stations.

★ 60903 ★ First Union National
Bank of Florida
3550 N. Federal Hwy.
Lighthouse Point, FL 33064-6682
(305)786-6100
Location Type: Branch office. Ultimate
Parent: First Union Corp. SIC: 6021—
National Commercial Banks.

★ 60904 ★ Jiffy Lube
3207 N. Federal Hwy.
Lighthouse Point, FL 33064
(305)942-3911
Ultimate Parent: Pennzoil. SIC: 7538—
General Automotive Repair Shops.

Lisbon

★ 60905 ★ Eagle-Picher
Industries Inc.
Wolverine Gasket Div.
C.R. 44 PO Box 895038
Lisbon, FL 34788
Company Type: Division. Ultimate Parent:
Eagle-Picher Industries Inc. SIC: 3053—
Gaskets, Packing & Sealing Devices;
3479—Metal Coating & Allied Services.

Live Oak

★ 60906 ★ ALLTEL Florida
206 White Ave. SE
PO Box 550
Live Oak, FL 32060
(904)362-2400
Ultimate Parent: ALLTEL Corp. SIC:
4812—Radiotelephone Communications.

★ 60907 ★ Anchor Savings Bank
1562 Ohio Ave. S
Live Oak, FL 32060
(904)362-5411
Ultimate Parent: Anchor Bancorp. SIC:
6035—Federal Savings Institutions.

★ 60908 ★ Barnett Bank of North
Central Florida
201 S. Ohio Ave.
Live Oak, FL 32060
(904)364-5000
Company Type: Subsidiary. Location
Type: Branch office. Officer: Betsy Burch,
Vice President. Ultimate Parent: Barnett
Banks. SIC: 6022—State Commercial
Banks.

★ 60909 ★ Fleet Finance Inc.
534 Howard St. E
Live Oak, FL 32060
(904)362-1242
Ultimate Parent: Fleet Financial Group.
SIC: 6062—State Credit Unions; 6141—
Personal Credit Institutions.

★ 60910 ★ Food Lion
1429 Ohio Ave. N
Live Oak, FL 32060
(904)364-4099
Ultimate Parent: Food Lion. SIC: 5411—
Grocery Stores.

★ 60911 ★ Gold Kist Inc. Feed
Mill
Hwy. 90 W
Live Oak, FL 32060
Ultimate Parent: Gold Kist. SIC: 2048—
Prepared Feeds Nec.

★ 60912 ★ Gold Kist Inc. Poultry
Hwy. 90 W.
Live Oak, FL 32060
Ultimate Parent: Gold Kist. SIC: 2015—
Poultry Slaughtering & Processing; 2077—
Animal & Marine Fats & Oils.

★ 60913 ★ Greyhound Bus
Station
330 Howard St. W
Live Oak, FL 32060
(904)362-1819
Ultimate Parent: Greyhound Lines Inc. SIC:
4111—Local & Suburban Transit.

★ 60914 ★ Hudson's
514 Howard St. E
Live Oak, FL 32060
(904)362-6696
Ultimate Parent: Dayton Hudson. SIC:
5411—Grocery Stores.

★ 60915 ★ Kentucky Fried
Chicken
823 Ohio Ave. S
Live Oak, FL 32060
(904)362-4455
Ultimate Parent: Pepsico. SIC: 5812—
Eating Places.

★ 60916 ★ Pizza Hut
625 Ohio Ave. S
Live Oak, FL 32060
(904)364-1123
Ultimate Parent: Pepsico. SIC: 5812—
Eating Places.

★ 60917 ★ Publix Super Market
1528 Ohio Ave. S
Live Oak, FL 32060
(904)362-7144
Ultimate Parent: Publix Super Markets.
SIC: 5411—Grocery Stores.

★ 60918 ★ Publix Super Markets
1528 Ohio Ave. S
Live Oak, FL 32060
(904)362-7144
Ultimate Parent: Publix Super Markets.
SIC: 5411—Grocery Stores.

★ 60919 ★ Rite Aid
839 Pinewood Dr. SW
Live Oak, FL 32060
(904)362-5183
Ultimate Parent: Rite Aid. SIC: 5912—Drug
Stores & Proprietary Stores.

★ 60920 ★ Ryder Truck Rental
517 Howard St. W
Live Oak, FL 32060
(904)364-1402
Ultimate Parent: Ryder System. SIC:
7513—Truck Rental & Leasing Without
Drivers.

★ 60921 ★ Texaco Food Mart
Us 129 N
Live Oak, FL 32060
(904)364-1770
Ultimate Parent: Texaco. SIC: 5411—
Grocery Stores.

Lk Panasoffke

★ 60922 ★ Texaco Auto Truck
Stop
Hwy. 470
Lk Panasoffke, FL 33538
(904)793-4001
Ultimate Parent: Texaco. SIC: 5541—
Gasoline Service Stations.

Longboat Key

★ 60923 ★ Barnett Bank of
Southwest Florida
10 Avenue of the Flowers
Longboat Key, FL 34228-3134
(813)951-4800
Company Type: Subsidiary. Location
Type: Branch office. Officer: Sandy Tull,
Manager. Ultimate Parent: Barnett Banks.
SIC: 6021—National Commercial Banks.

Longwood

★ 60924 ★ Ace Hardware
404 Wild Oak Cir.
Longwood, FL 32779
Ultimate Parent: Ace Hardware. SIC:
5099—Durable Goods Nec.

★ 60925 ★ Ace Hardware
170 Sanlando Springs Rd. W
Longwood, FL 32750
(407)339-4883
Ultimate Parent: Ace Hardware. SIC:
5251—Hardware Stores.

★ 60926 ★ Barnett Bank of
Central Florida, NA
1145 W. State Rd. 434
Longwood, FL 32750-5107
(407)263-6050
Company Type: Subsidiary. Location
Type: Branch office. Officer: Brian Overby,
Manager. Ultimate Parent: Barnett Banks.
SIC: 6021—National Commercial Banks.

★ 60927 ★ Barnett Bank of
Central Florida, NA
2601 State Rd. 434
Longwood, FL 32779
(407)263-6020
Company Type: Subsidiary. Location
Type: Branch office. Officer: Janet
Sommer, Area Manager. Ultimate Parent:
Barnett Banks. SIC: 6021—National
Commercial Banks.

★ 60928 ★ Burdines
1051 Bennett Dr.
Longwood, FL 32750
(407)830-2370
Ultimate Parent: Federated Department
Stores. SIC: 5712—Furniture Stores.

★ 60929 ★ First Union National Bank of Florida
900 Fox Valley Dr., Ste. 101
Longwood, FL 32779-2551
(407)774-3610
Location Type: Branch office. **Ultimate Parent:** First Union Corp. **SIC:** 6021—National Commercial Banks.

★ 60930 ★ First Union National Bank of Florida
120 S. US Hwy. 17-92
Longwood, FL 32750
(407)830-8666
Location Type: Branch office. **Ultimate Parent:** First Union Corp. **SIC:** 6021—National Commercial Banks.

★ 60931 ★ First Union National Bank of Florida
2101 W. State Rd. 434
Longwood, FL 32779-4958
(407)774-3600
Location Type: Branch office. **Ultimate Parent:** First Union Corp. **SIC:** 6021—National Commercial Banks.

★ 60932 ★ Kentucky Fried Chicken
385 Us Hwy. 17
Longwood, FL 32750
(407)695-9666
Ultimate Parent: Pepsico. **SIC:** 5812—Eating Places.

★ 60933 ★ Mary Kay Cosmet Ind Sls Dir
177 Post
Longwood, FL 32750
(407)831-7318
Ultimate Parent: Mary Kay Cosmetics. **SIC:** 5999—Miscellaneous Retail Stores Nec.

★ 60934 ★ Mary Kay Cosmetics
134 Wisteria Dr.
Longwood, FL 32779
(407)869-0781
Ultimate Parent: Mary Kay Cosmetics. **SIC:** 5963—Direct Selling Establishments.

★ 60935 ★ Mobil Oil
100 Sanlando Springs Rd. W
Longwood, FL 32750
(407)332-1770
Ultimate Parent: Mobil. **SIC:** 5541—Gasoline Service Stations.

★ 60936 ★ Mobil Oil Corp.
2170 State Rd. 434 W
Longwood, FL 32779
(407)862-2211
Ultimate Parent: Mobil. **SIC:** 7373—Computer Integrated Systems Design.

★ 60937 ★ Mobil Oil Corp.
1999 State Rd. 434 W
Longwood, FL 32750
(407)260-2128
Ultimate Parent: Mobil. **SIC:** 5541—Gasoline Service Stations.

★ 60938 ★ Nalco Chemical Co.
2180 State Road 434 W. 1140
Longwood, FL 32779
Ultimate Parent: Nalco Chemical Co. **SIC:** 5199—Nondurable Goods Nec.

★ 60939 ★ Pappagallo
Longwood Village Shopping Ctr.
Longwood, FL 32750
(407)831-1064
Ultimate Parent: United States Shoe. **SIC:** 5621—Women's Clothing Stores.

★ 60940 ★ Parker Hannifin Corp.
Rac Div.
777 Bennett Dr.
Longwood, FL 32750
Company Type: Division. **Ultimate Parent:** Parker Hannifin. **SIC:** 3400—Fabricated Metal Products.

★ 60941 ★ Pennzoil Products Co.
520728 PO Box
Longwood, FL 32752
(407)834-7366
Ultimate Parent: Pennzoil. **SIC:** 5172—Petroleum Products Nec.

★ 60942 ★ Pennzoil Products Co.
520728 PO Box
Longwood, FL 32752
(407)834-7366
Ultimate Parent: Pennzoil. **SIC:** 5172—Petroleum Products Nec.

★ 60943 ★ Pizza Hut
241 Hunt Club Blvd.
Longwood, FL 32779
(407)788-4550
Ultimate Parent: Pepsico. **SIC:** 5812—Eating Places.

★ 60944 ★ Pizza Hut
Rural Route 434
Longwood, FL 32779
(407)862-1028
Ultimate Parent: Pepsico. **SIC:** 5812—Eating Places.

★ 60945 ★ Publix Super Market
1801 S. R W
Longwood, FL 32750
(407)834-1626
Ultimate Parent: Publix Super Markets. **SIC:** 5411—Grocery Stores.

★ 60946 ★ Publix Super Markets
1801 S. R W
Longwood, FL 32750
(407)834-1626
Ultimate Parent: Publix Super Markets. **SIC:** 5411—Grocery Stores.

★ 60947 ★ Radio Shack
969 Sanlando Springs Rd. W
Longwood, FL 32750
(407)767-2943
Company Type: Division. **Ultimate Parent:** Tandy Corp. **SIC:** 5065—Electronic Parts & Equipment Nec.

★ 60948 ★ Radio Shack
State Rd. 434
Longwood, FL 32750
(407)339-2914
Company Type: Division. **Ultimate Parent:** Tandy Corp. **SIC:** 5065—Electronic Parts & Equipment Nec.

★ 60949 ★ Taco Bell
1090 Hwy. 434 W
Longwood, FL 32750
(407)830-9066
Ultimate Parent: Pepsico. **SIC:** 5812—Eating Places.

★ 60950 ★ Ungermann-Bass Inc.
2170 State Rd. 434 W
Longwood, FL 32779
(407)682-5390
Ultimate Parent: Tandem. **SIC:** 7373—Computer Integrated Systems Design.

Lutz

★ 60951 ★ Barnett Bank of Tampa
18501 US Hwy. 41 N
Lutz, FL 33549-4456
(813)225-8623
Company Type: Subsidiary. **Location Type:** Branch office. **Officer:** Mike Mashke, Office Manager. **Ultimate Parent:** Barnett Banks. **SIC:** 6022—State Commercial Banks.

★ 60952 ★ Kids R US
2704 Lake Fern Rd. W
Lutz, FL 33549
(813)949-1795
Ultimate Parent: Toys "R" US. **SIC:** 8351—Child Day Care Services.

★ 60953 ★ Kids R US
2704 Lake Fern Rd. W
Lutz, FL 33549
(813)949-1795
Ultimate Parent: Toys "R" US. **SIC:** 8351—Child Day Care Services.

★ 60954 ★ Rite Aid Pharmacy
Rural Route 3
Lutz, FL 33549
(813)977-9590
Ultimate Parent: Rite Aid. **SIC:** 5912—Drug Stores & Proprietary Stores.

Lynn Haven

★ 60955 ★ Allied-Signal Inc.
Bendix Friction Materials
1006 Arthur Dr. PO Box 1250
Lynn Haven, FL 32444
Ultimate Parent: Allied-Signal Inc. **SIC:** 3069—Fabricated Rubber Products Nec.

★ 60956 ★ Piggly Wiggly
617 Ohio Ave.
Lynn Haven, FL 32444
(904)265-5957
Ultimate Parent: Bruno's. **SIC:** 5411—Grocery Stores.

★ 60957 ★ Stock Equipment Co.
10 Arthur Dr.
Lynn Haven, FL 32444
Ultimate Parent: General Signal. **SIC:** 3596—Scales & Balances Except Laboratory; 3535—Conveyors & Conveying Equipment.

Mac Dill Air Force Base

★ 60958 ★ Barnett Bank of Tampa
925 N. Boundary Rd.
Mac Dill Air Force Base, FL 33608
(813)832-0044
Company Type: Subsidiary. **Location Type:** Branch office. **Officer:** Jim Webb, Manager. **Ultimate Parent:** Barnett Banks. **SIC:** 6022—State Commercial Banks.

Macclenny

★ 60959 ★ Anchor Savings Bank F S B
595 S. 6th St.
Macclenny, FL 32063
(904)259-2245
Ultimate Parent: Anchor Bancorp. **SIC:** 6099—Functions Related to Deposit Banking.

★ 60960 ★ Exxon Truck Stop
Hwy. 228
Macclenny, FL 32063
(904)259-6088
Ultimate Parent: Exxon. **SIC:** 7538—General Automotive Repair Shops.

MacClenny

★ 60961 ★ Kentucky Fried Chicken
Hwy. 121 S
MacClenny, FL 32063
(904)259-6079
Ultimate Parent: Pepsico. **SIC:** 5812—Eating Places.

★ 60962 ★ Wal Mart Discount Cities
1160 S. 6th St.
MacClenny, FL 32063
(904)259-4760
Ultimate Parent: Wal-Mart Stores, Inc. **SIC:** 5311—Department Stores.

Madeira Beach

★ 60963 ★ Barnett Bank of Pinellas County
201 150th Ave.
Madeira Beach, FL 33708
(813)892-1320
Company Type: Subsidiary. **Location Type:** Branch office. **Officer:** Tina Gilmore, Manager. **Ultimate Parent:** Barnett Banks. **SIC:** 6022—State Commercial Banks.

★ 60964 ★ Citibank, FSB
652 E. Welch
Madeira Beach, FL 33708-2812
(813)391-9703
Location Type: Branch office. **Ultimate Parent:** Citicorp. **SIC:** 6021—National Commercial Banks.

★ 60965 ★ First Union National Bank of Florida
710 Madeira Beach Cswy.
Madeira Beach, FL 33708-2896
(813)892-2023
Location Type: Branch office. **Ultimate Parent:** First Union Corp. **SIC:** 6021—National Commercial Banks.

Madison

★ 60966 ★ First Union National Bank of Florida
400 W. Base St.
Madison, FL 32340-2004
(904)973-8700
Location Type: Branch office. **Ultimate**

Parent: First Union Corp. **SIC:** 6021—National Commercial Banks.

★ 60967 ★ Greyhound Bus Lines
615 E. Base St.
Madison, FL 32340
(904)973-6220
Ultimate Parent: Greyhound Lines Inc.

★ 60968 ★ Sale James J III
317 S. Range St.
Madison, FL 32340-2343
(904)973-2343
Officer: James J. Sale III, Owner. **Ultimate Parent:** Ace Hardware. **SIC:** 5251—Hardware Stores; 5722—Household Appliance Stores. **Employee Count:** 4.

★ 60969 ★ Texaco
110 State Rd. 53
Madison, FL 32340
(904)973-8611
Ultimate Parent: Texaco.

Maitland

★ 60970 ★ Advanced Micro Devices Inc.
Packwood
Maitland, FL 32751
(407)645-1957
Ultimate Parent: Advanced Micro Devices Inc. **SIC:** 5065—Electronic Parts & Equipment Nec.

★ 60971 ★ ,Albertson's
1051 Winderley Pl.
Maitland, FL 32751
Ultimate Parent: Albertson's Inc. **SIC:** 5411—Grocery Stores; 7359—Equipment Rental & Leasing Nec.

★ 60972 ★ American Credit Services
1051 Winderley Pl
Maitland, FL 32751
(407)660-2255
Ultimate Parent: Rochester Community Savings Bank. **SIC:** 6531—Real Estate Agents & Managers.

★ 60973 ★ Barnett Bank of Central Florida, NA
105 N. Maitland Ave.
Maitland, FL 32751-5509
(407)646-3432
Company Type: Subsidiary. **Location Type:** Branch office. **Officer:** Robert Quinlan, Manager. **Ultimate Parent:** Barnett Banks. **SIC:** 6021—National Commercial Banks.

★ 60974 ★ Coast to Coast Collection
2020 Fairbank St.
Maitland, FL 32751
(407)629-4414
Ultimate Parent: Servistar Corp. **SIC:** 8049—Offices of Health Practitioners Nec.

★ 60975 ★ Crestar Mortgage Corp.
851 Trafalgar Ct
Maitland, FL 32751
(407)660-0523
Ultimate Parent: Crestar Financial Corp. **SIC:** 6162—Mortgage Bankers & Correspondents.

★ 60976 ★ Donnelley Directory
500 Winderley Pl
Maitland, FL 32751
(407)875-6000
Ultimate Parent: R. R. Donnelley & Sons. **SIC:** 2741—Miscellaneous Publishing.

★ 60977 ★ First Union National Bank of Florida
301 S. Orlando Ave.
Maitland, FL 32751-5669
(407)646-1600
Location Type: Branch office. **Ultimate Parent:** First Union Corp. **SIC:** 6021—National Commercial Banks.

★ 60978 ★ General American Life Insurance C
2301 Maitland Ctr. Pky.
Maitland, FL 32751
(407)660-2770
Ultimate Parent: General American Life. **SIC:** 6411—Insurance Agents, Brokers & Service.

★ 60979 ★   **John Hancock Property & Cas**
851 Trafalgar Ct
Maitland, FL 32751
(407)660-0161
Ultimate Parent: John Hancock Mutual Life. **SIC:** 6411—Insurance Agents, Brokers & Service.

★ 60980 ★   **Kentucky Fried Chicken**
385 Us 17-92
Maitland, FL 32751
(407)695-9666
Ultimate Parent: Pepsico. **SIC:** 5812—Eating Places.

★ 60981 ★   **Mary Kay Cosmetics**
331 N. Maitland Ave.
Maitland, FL 32751
(407)629-4122
Ultimate Parent: Mary Kay Cosmetics. **SIC:** 5999—Miscellaneous Retail Stores Nec.

★ 60982 ★   **Norwest Mortgage Inc.**
100 E. Sybelia Ave.
Maitland, FL 32751
(407)628-3831
Ultimate Parent: Norwest Corp. **SIC:** 6141—Personal Credit Institutions.

★ 60983 ★   **Pizza Hut**
2335 Temple Trl.
Maitland, FL 32751
(407)628-3868
Ultimate Parent: Pepsico. **SIC:** 5812—Eating Places.

★ 60984 ★   **Pulte Home Corp. I C M Mortg**
2250 Lucien Way 250
Maitland, FL 32751
Ultimate Parent: Pulte.

★ 60985 ★   **Tektronix Inc.**
151 Southhall Ln. 170
Maitland, FL 32751
Ultimate Parent: Tektronix, Inc. **SIC:** 5099—Durable Goods Nec.

★ 60986 ★   **Texaco**
555 Winderley Pl
Maitland, FL 32751
Ultimate Parent: Texaco. **SIC:** 5541—Gasoline Service Stations.

★ 60987 ★   **Transamerica Occidental Life Inc.**
113 Hidden Oak Dr.
Maitland, FL 32751
(407)869-9887
Ultimate Parent: Transamerica Occidental Life Insurance. **SIC:** 6411—Insurance Agents, Brokers & Service.

★ 60988 ★   **Universal Data Systems**
100 E. Sybelia Ave.
Maitland, FL 32751
(407)539-1229
Ultimate Parent: Motorola Inc. **SIC:** 7372—Prepackaged Software.

★ 60989 ★   **Western Life Insurance Co.**
800 Trafalgar Ct
Maitland, FL 32751
(407)645-1113
Ultimate Parent: Westcorp. **SIC:** 6411—Insurance Agents, Brokers & Service.

Malabar

★ 60990 ★   **Harris Corp. Ess Malabar**
2800 Jordan Rd.
Malabar, FL 32950
Ultimate Parent: Harris. **SIC:** 3669—Communications Equipment Nec.

★ 60991 ★   **Harris Corp. GSS**
2800 Jordan Rd.
Malabar, FL 32905
Ultimate Parent: Harris. **SIC:** 3600—Electronic & Other Electrical Equipment.

Marathon

★ 60992 ★   **Barnett Bank of the Keys**
6090 Overseas Hwy.
Marathon, FL 33050-2723
(305)292-3905
Company Type: Subsidiary. **Location Type:** Branch office. **Officer:** Sherry Tallman, Manager. **Ultimate Parent:** Barnett Banks. **SIC:** 6022—State Commercial Banks.

★ 60993 ★   **Ryder Truck Rental**
6303 Overseas Hwy.
Marathon, FL 33050
(305)743-8708
Ultimate Parent: Ryder System. **SIC:** 7513—Truck Rental & Leasing Without Drivers.

★ 60994 ★   **Walgreen Drug Store**
10996 Overseas Hwy.
Marathon, FL 33050
(305)743-6923
Ultimate Parent: Walgreen Co. **SIC:** 5912—Drug Stores & Proprietary Stores.

Marco Island

★ 60995 ★   **Barnett Bank of Naples**
614 Bald Eagle Dr.
Marco Island, FL 33937-2777
(813)263-1381
Company Type: Subsidiary. **Location Type:** Branch office. **Officer:** Don A. Schnell, Vice President. **Ultimate Parent:** Barnett Banks. **SIC:** 6022—State Commercial Banks.

★ 60996 ★   **Citibank, FSB**
5610 W. Sample Rd.
Marco Island, FL 33073-3455
(305)968-4381
Location Type: Branch office. **Ultimate Parent:** Citicorp. **SIC:** 6021—National Commercial Banks.

★ 60997 ★   **Hertz Rent-A-Car**
400 S. Collier Blvd.
Marco Island, FL 33937
(813)394-3322
Ultimate Parent: Hertz. **SIC:** 7514—Passenger Car Rental.

Margate

★ 60998 ★   **American Savings of Florida, FSB**
7220 W. Atlantic Blvd.
Margate, FL 33063-4214
(305)973-0880
Location Type: Branch office. **Officer:** Siman Passi, Manager. **Ultimate Parent:** American Savings of Florida. **SIC:** 6035—Federal Savings Institutions; 6211—Security Brokers & Dealers.

★ 60999 ★   **Barnett Bank of Broward County, NA**
5590 W. Sample Rd.
Margate, FL 33093
(305)968-4500
Company Type: Subsidiary. **Location Type:** Branch office. **Officer:** Robert Falzarano, Manager. **Ultimate Parent:** Barnett Banks. **SIC:** 6021—National Commercial Banks.

★ 61000 ★   **Barnett Bank of Broward County, NA**
550 Main Blvd.
Margate, FL 33309
(305)979-6065
Company Type: Subsidiary. **Location Type:** Branch office. **Officer:** Tom Vincett, Manager. **Ultimate Parent:** Barnett Banks. **SIC:** 6021—National Commercial Banks.

★ 61001 ★   **First Union National Bank of Florida**
911 N. State Rd. 7
Margate, FL 33063-3685
(305)786-6140
Location Type: Branch office. **Ultimate Parent:** First Union Corp. **SIC:** 6021—National Commercial Banks.

★ 61002 ★   **Savings of America**
Home Savings of America, FSB
400 N. State Rd. 7
Margate, FL 33063-4593
(305)974-1000
Location Type: Branch office. **Officer:** Joan Schafer, Manager. **Ultimate Parent:** H. F. Ahmanson. **SIC:** 6021—National Commercial Banks.

Marianna

★ 61003 ★   **Greyhound Bus Terminal**
208 N. Caledonia St.
Marianna, FL 32446
(904)482-4561
Ultimate Parent: Greyhound Lines Inc. **SIC:** 4111—Local & Suburban Transit; 4173—Bus Terminal & Service Facilities.

★ 61004 ★   **Kentucky Fried Chicken**
1011 W. Lafayette St.
Marianna, FL 32446
(904)526-2438
Ultimate Parent: Pepsico. **SIC:** 5812—Eating Places.

★ 61005 ★   **Piggly Wiggly**
W Lafayette
Marianna, FL 32446
(904)482-2006
Ultimate Parent: Bruno's. **SIC:** 5411—Grocery Stores.

★ 61006 ★   **Pizza Hut**
305 S. Pennsylvania Ave.
Marianna, FL 32446
(904)482-4720
Ultimate Parent: Pepsico. **SIC:** 5812—Eating Places.

★ 61007 ★   **Pizza Hut**
219 W. Lafayette St.
Marianna, FL 32446
(904)526-2545
Ultimate Parent: Pepsico. **SIC:** 5812—Eating Places.

★ 61008 ★   **Russell Corp.**
4215 W. Kelson Ave.
Marianna, FL 32446
(904)526-3695
Ultimate Parent: Russell. **SIC:** 2321—Men's/Boys' Shirts.

★ 61009 ★   **Russell Corp.**
3521 Russell Rd.
Marianna, FL 32446
(904)482-5799
Ultimate Parent: Russell. **SIC:** 2329—Men's/Boys' Clothing Nec.

★ 61010 ★   **Russell Corp.**
3529 Russell Rd.
Marianna, FL 32446
(904)526-3661
Officer: Tom Casady, Manager. **Ultimate Parent:** Russell. **SIC:** 2253—Knit Outerwear Mills; 2321—Men's/Boys' Shirts; 2389—Apparel & Accessories Nec.

★ 61011 ★   **Russell Corp. D.C. & Ind. Park**
102 Russell Rd.
Marianna, FL 32446
Ultimate Parent: Russell. **SIC:** 2399—Fabricated Textile Products Nec; 2329—Men's/Boys' Clothing Nec.

★ 61012 ★   **Wal Mart**
2800 State Hwy. 71
Marianna, FL 32446
(904)526-5744
Ultimate Parent: Wal-Mart Stores, Inc. **SIC:** 5311—Department Stores.

Mary Esther

★ 61013 ★   **AmSouth Bank of Florida**
420 Mary Esther Cutoff
Santa Rosa Mall
Mary Esther, FL 32569-1606
(904)444-1000
Location Type: Branch office. **Officer:** Aggie Bass, Manager. **Ultimate Parent:** AmSouth Bancorp. **SIC:** 6022—State Commercial Banks.

★ 61014 ★   **Casual Corner**
300 Mary Esther Cut Off 51
Mary Esther, FL 32569
(904)244-9168
Ultimate Parent: United States Shoe. **SIC:** 5651—Family Clothing Stores.

★ 61015 ★   **Circus World**
300 Mary Esther Cut Off 32
Mary Esther, FL 32569
(904)243-7713
Ultimate Parent: Melville. **SIC:** 5945—Hobby, Toy & Game Shops.

★ 61016 ★   **First National Bank & Trust**
230 Mary Esther Cut Off
Mary Esther, FL 32569
(904)244-7635
Ultimate Parent: Society Corp. **SIC:** 6022—State Commercial Banks.

★ 61017 ★   **Lane Bryant**
300 Mary Esther Cut Off 40
Mary Esther, FL 32569
(904)243-3376
Ultimate Parent: Limited. **SIC:** 5651—Family Clothing Stores.

★ 61018 ★   **Lerner Shop**
300 Mary Esther Cut Off 86
Mary Esther, FL 32569
(904)244-2313
Ultimate Parent: Limited. **SIC:** 5651—Family Clothing Stores.

★ 61019 ★   **The Limited**
300 Mary Esther Cut Off 71
Mary Esther, FL 32569
(904)243-4997
Ultimate Parent: Limited. **SIC:** 5651—Family Clothing Stores.

★ 61020 ★   **Parker Properties**
15 Driftwood
Mary Esther, FL 32569
(904)244-0858
Ultimate Parent: Parker Hannifin. **SIC:** 1521—Single-Family Housing Construction.

★ 61021 ★   **Pizza Hut**
550 Mary Esther Cut Off
Mary Esther, FL 32569
(904)243-8727
Ultimate Parent: Pepsico. **SIC:** 5812—Eating Places.

★ 61022 ★   **Radio Shack**
300 Mary Esther Cut Off 74
Mary Esther, FL 32569
(904)244-3224
Company Type: Division. **Ultimate Parent:** Tandy Corp. **SIC:** 5065—Electronic Parts & Equipment Nec.

★ 61023 ★   **Taco Bell**
300 Mary Esther Cut Off 9
Mary Esther, FL 32569
(904)243-7808
Ultimate Parent: Pepsico. **SIC:** 5812—Eating Places.

★ 61024 ★   **Vanguard Bank & Trust Co.**
302 Mary Esther Blvd.
Mary Esther, FL 32569-2264
(904)664-9565
Company Type: Subsidiary. **Location Type:** Branch office. **Officer:** Kim Cox, Mgr. **Ultimate Parent:** Synovus Financial Corp. **SIC:** 6021—National Commercial Banks.

★ 61025 ★   **Wal Mart**
546 Mary Esther Cut Off
Mary Esther, FL 32569
(904)243-0484
Ultimate Parent: Wal-Mart Stores, Inc. **SIC:** 5311—Department Stores.

★ 61026 ★   **Waldenbooks**
251 Mary Esther Cut Off
Mary Esther, FL 32569
(904)244-3899
Ultimate Parent: K-Mart. **SIC:** 5942—Book Stores.

Meadows Village

★ 61027 ★   **Exxon Co. USA**
1960 21st St.
Meadows Village, FL 34234
(813)955-6277
Ultimate Parent: Exxon. **SIC:** 5172—Petroleum Products Nec.

★ 61028 ★   **Kentucky Fried Chicken**
4195 N. Tamiami Trl.
Meadows Village, FL 34234
(813)355-3234
Ultimate Parent: Pepsico. **SIC:** 5812—Eating Places.

★ 61029 ★   **Pizza Hut**
2901 N. Tamiami Trl.
Meadows Village, FL 34234
(813)355-8541
Ultimate Parent: Pepsico. **SIC:** 5812—Eating Places.

Medley

★ 61030 ★   **Parkson Aeration & Fiberglass Corp. Inc.**
9770 NW 91st. Ct.
Medley, FL 33178-1427
Ultimate Parent: Johnson & Johnson. **SIC:** 3089—Plastics Products Nec.

Melbourne

★ 61031 ★   **Ace Hardware**
1008 Hwy. A1a A1a
Melbourne, FL 32937
(407)777-0777
Ultimate Parent: Ace Hardware. **SIC:** 5251—Hardware Stores.

★ 61032 ★   **Ace Hardware**
1008 Atlantic Ave.
Melbourne, FL 32951
(407)777-0777
Ultimate Parent: Ace Hardware. **SIC:** 5251—Hardware Stores.

★ 61033 ★   **Albertson's**
961 E. Eau Gallie Blvd.
Melbourne, FL 32937
(407)777-9000
Ultimate Parent: Albertson's Inc. **SIC:** 5311—Department Stores.

★ 61034 ★   **Albertson's Pharmacy**
900 S. Babcock St.
Melbourne, FL 32901
(407)724-5830
Ultimate Parent: Albertson's Inc. **SIC:** 5912—Drug Stores & Proprietary Stores.

★ 61035 ★   **Barnett Bank of Central Florida, NA**
1109 E. New Haven
Melbourne, FL 32901-5438
(407)723-2511
Company Type: Subsidiary. **Location Type:** Branch office. **Officer:** Guy Lombardo, Manager. **Ultimate Parent:** Barnett Banks. **SIC:** 6021—National Commercial Banks.

★ 61036 ★   **Barnett Bank of Central Florida, NA**
3303 Sunfree Blvd.
Melbourne, FL 32940-7516
(407)259-4761
Company Type: Subsidiary. **Location Type:** Branch office. **Officer:** Joyce Chen, Manager. **Ultimate Parent:** Barnett Banks. **SIC:** 6021—National Commercial Banks.

★ 61037 ★   **Barnett Bank of Central Florida, NA**
950 S. Apollo Blvd.
Melbourne, FL 32901-1973
(407)725-1211
Company Type: Subsidiary. **Location Type:** Branch office. **Officer:** Wayne Gilmore, Manager. **Ultimate Parent:** Barnett Banks. **SIC:** 6021—National Commercial Banks.

★ 61038 ★   **Barnett Bank of Central Florida, NA**
2453 N. Wickham Rd.
Melbourne, FL 32935-8299
(407)259-4774
Company Type: Subsidiary. **Location Type:** Branch office. **Officer:** Susan Newton, Manager. **Ultimate Parent:** Barnett Banks. **SIC:** 6021—National Commercial Banks.

★ 61039 ★   **Burdines Department Store**
1700 W. New Haven Ave.
Melbourne, FL 32904
(407)676-9311
Ultimate Parent: Federated Department Stores. **SIC:** 5311—Department Stores.

★ 61040 ★   **Business Systems & Software**
816 E. New Haven Ave.
Melbourne, FL 32901-5433
(407)727-1774
Ultimate Parent: Avery Dennison Corp. **SIC:** 7371—Computer Programming Services.

★ 61041 ★   **Casual Corner**
Melbourne
Melbourne, FL 32901
(407)729-6488
Ultimate Parent: United States Shoe. **SIC:** 5621—Women's Clothing Stores.

★ 61042 ★   **Collins General Aviation**
305 North Dr. PO Box 1060
Melbourne, FL 32902
Ultimate Parent: Rockwell International Corp. **SIC:** 3812—Search & Navigation Equipment.

★ 61043 ★   **Collins General Aviation**
305 North Dr.
Melbourne, FL 32901
Ultimate Parent: Rockwell International Corp. **SIC:** 3812—Search & Navigation Equipment.

★ 61044 ★   **Collins General Aviation**
1100 West Hibiscus Blvd.
Melbourne, FL 32901
Ultimate Parent: Rockwell International Corp. **SIC:** 3679—Electronic Components Nec.

★ 61045 ★   **Delta Air Cargo**
720 Air Cargo Pl
Melbourne, FL 32901
(407)676-2468
Ultimate Parent: Delta Air Lines, Inc. **SIC:** 4513—Air Courier Services.

★ 61046 ★   **Delta Air Lines**
1050 Joe Walker Rd.
Melbourne, FL 32901
(407)676-2470
Ultimate Parent: Delta Air Lines, Inc. **SIC:** 4512—Air Transportation—Scheduled.

★ 61047 ★   **Delta Air Lines Inc.**
1050 Joe Walker Rd.
Melbourne, FL 32901
(407)676-2470
Ultimate Parent: Delta Air Lines, Inc. **SIC:** 4512—Air Transportation—Scheduled.

★ 61048 ★   **Dictaphone Corp.**
3900 W. Sarno Rd.
Melbourne, FL 32935
Ultimate Parent: Pitney Bowes. **SIC:** 3669—Communications Equipment Nec.

★ 61049 ★   **Digital Equipment Corporati**
1333 Gateway Dr.
Melbourne, FL 32901
(407)676-7400
Ultimate Parent: Digital Equipment Corp. **SIC:** 7373—Computer Integrated Systems Design.

★ 61050 ★   **Digital Equipment Corp.**
50 E. Woodlake Dr.
Melbourne, FL 32905
(407)676-4775
Ultimate Parent: Digital Equipment Corp. **SIC:** 3571—Electronic Computers.

★ 61051 ★   **Dolphin Construction Co.**
5435 N. Harbor City Blvd.
Melbourne, FL 32940
(407)242-9881
Ultimate Parent: Texas Industries.

★ 61052 ★   **Dolphin Construction Co. Inc.**
1600 S. Babcock St.
Melbourne, FL 32901
(407)725-1368
Ultimate Parent: Texas Industries. **SIC:** 1521—Single-Family Housing Construction.

★ 61053 ★   **Exxon**
1346 A Hwy. 1a
Melbourne, FL 32951
(407)773-6601
Ultimate Parent: Exxon. **SIC:** 5541—Gasoline Service Stations.

★ 61054 ★   **First Union National Bank of Florida**
1400 Sarno Rd.
Melbourne, FL 32901-5296
(407)984-7455
Location Type: Branch office. **Ultimate Parent:** Barnett Bank of Alachua County, NA. **SIC:** 6021—National Commercial Banks.

★ 61055 ★   **First Union National Bank of Florida**
1441 N. Harbor City Blvd.
Melbourne, FL 32935-6554
(407)984-7480
Location Type: Branch office. **Ultimate Parent:** First Union Corp. **SIC:** 6021—National Commercial Banks.

★ 61056 ★   **First Union National Bank of Georgia**
700 Babcock St.
Melbourne, FL 32901-1472
(407)984-7401
Location Type: Branch office. **Ultimate Parent:** First Union Corp. **SIC:** 6021—National Commercial Banks.

★ 61057 ★   **Grumman**
Melbourne Systems Division
2000 W. Nasa Blvd.
Melbourne, FL 32901
(407)951-5000 **Fax:** (407)951-6876
Company Type: Subsidiary. **Officer:** Martin E. D Dandridge, President. **Ultimate Parent:** Grumman.

★ 61058 ★   **Harris**
1025 W. Nasa Blvd.
Melbourne, FL 32919
(407)727-9100
Company Type: Headquarters. **Officer:** John T. Hartley. **Employee Count:** 28300. **Sales:** 3099 M. **Fortune 500:** Largest U.S. Industrial Corporations: Ranking 157.

★ 61059 ★   **Harris**
Air Traffic Control Systems Division
PO Box 91000
Melbourne, FL 32902
(407)727-4000 **Fax:** (407)727-5811
Company Type: Subsidiary. **Officer:** David E. Halley, Vice President & General Manager. **Ultimate Parent:** Harris.

★ 61060 ★   **Harris**
Controls Division
407 John Rodes Blvd.
Melbourne, FL 32934
(407)242-4000 **Fax:** (407)242-4071
Company Type: Subsidiary. **Officer:** Roland J. Valdes, Vice President & General Manager. **Ultimate Parent:** Harris.

★ 61061 ★   **Harris**
Electronic Systems Division
PO Box 96000
Melbourne, FL 32902
(407)727-4000 **Fax:** (407)729-2244
Company Type: Subsidiary. **Officer:** Lewis M. King, Vice President & General Manager. **Ultimate Parent:** Harris.

★ 61062 ★   **Harris**
Government Aerospace Systems Division
PO Box 94000
Melbourne, FL 32902
(407)727-4000 **Fax:** (407)727-5118
Company Type: Subsidiary. **Officer:** Charles J. Herbert, Vice President & General Manager. **Ultimate Parent:** Harris.

★ 61063 ★   **Harris**
Government Communication System Division
PO Box 91000
Melbourne, FL 32902
(407)727-4000 **Fax:** (407)727-6304
Company Type: Subsidiary. **Officer:** Harry

L. Deffebach, Vice President & General Manager. **Ultimate Parent:** Harris.

★ 61064 ★   **Harris**
Information System Division
PO Box 98000
Melbourne, FL 32902
(407)984-5500 **Fax:** (407)984-6323
Company Type: Subsidiary. **Officer:** R. Phillip Henderson, Vice President & General Manager. **Ultimate Parent:** Harris.

★ 61065 ★   **Harris Corp.**
1025 W. NASA Blvd.
Melbourne, FL 32919
(407)727-9100 **Fax:** (407)727-9344
Company Type: Headquarters. **Officer:** John T. Hartley, Chairman & CEO. **Ultimate Parent:** Harris. **Employee Count:** 28000.

★ 61066 ★   **Harris Technical Services**
PO Box 37
Melbourne, FL 32902
(407)729-7272 **Fax:** (407)729-3955
Company Type: Subsidiary. **Officer:** Richard E. Meccarielli, Vice President. **Ultimate Parent:** Harris.

★ 61067 ★   **Hewlett Packard Co.**
255 East Dr.
Melbourne, FL 32904
(407)729-0704
Ultimate Parent: Hewlett-Packard. **SIC:** 5099—Durable Goods Nec.

★ 61068 ★   **Hit or Miss**
1551 W. New Haven Ave.
Melbourne, FL 32904
(407)723-2311
Ultimate Parent: TJX. **SIC:** 5651—Family Clothing Stores.

★ 61069 ★   **IBM Corp.**
6767 N. Wickham Rd. 400
Melbourne, FL 32940
(407)259-1707
Ultimate Parent: IBM. **SIC:** 5099—Durable Goods Nec.

★ 61070 ★   **Inacomp Computer Centers**
104 S. Harbor City Blvd. B
Melbourne, FL 32901
Ultimate Parent: Beneficial. **SIC:** 7373—Computer Integrated Systems Design.

★ 61071 ★   **Jiffy Lube**
1991 N. Wickham Rd.
Melbourne, FL 32935
(407)259-7946
Ultimate Parent: Pennzoil.

★ 61072 ★   **Kay Bee Toy&Hobby Shop**
Melbourne Sq.
Melbourne, FL 32901
(407)724-8044
Ultimate Parent: Melville. **SIC:** 5945—Hobby, Toy & Game Shops.

★ 61073 ★   **Kentucky Fried Chicken**
2120 W. New Haven Ave.
Melbourne, FL 32904
(407)724-2209
Ultimate Parent: Pepsico. **SIC:** 5812—Eating Places.

★ 61074 ★   **Kentucky Fried Chicken**
A Hwy. 1
Melbourne, FL 32937
(407)773-7677
Ultimate Parent: Pepsico. **SIC:** 5812—Eating Places.

★ 61075 ★   **Kentucky Fried Chicken**
4901 Babcock St. NE
Melbourne, FL 32905
(407)951-2795
Ultimate Parent: Pepsico. **SIC:** 5812—Eating Places.

★ 61076 ★   **The Limited**
1700 W. New Haven Ave.
Melbourne, FL 32904
(407)676-0040
Ultimate Parent: Limited. **SIC:** 5621—Women's Clothing Stores; 5651—Family Clothing Stores.

★ 61077 ★   **Marshalls Department Store**
1541 W. New Haven Ave.
Melbourne, FL 32904
(407)729-9334
Ultimate Parent: Melville. SIC: 5311—Department Stores.

★ 61078 ★   **Mary Kay Cosmetics**
240 Cinnamon Dr.
Melbourne, FL 32937
(407)777-4306
Ultimate Parent: Mary Kay Cosmetics.

★ 61079 ★   **McDonalds Restaurants**
1179 Malabar Rd. NE
Melbourne, FL 32907
(407)727-2714
Ultimate Parent: McDonald's. SIC: 5812—Eating Places.

★ 61080 ★   **Mobil Station**
1705 Palm Bay Rd. NE
Melbourne, FL 32905
(407)725-0666
Ultimate Parent: Mobil. SIC: 5541—Gasoline Service Stations.

★ 61081 ★   **Omni Business Systems**
205 S. Wickham Rd.
Melbourne, FL 32904-1133
(407)242-3050
Ultimate Parent: Alco Standard Corp. SIC: 7373—Computer Integrated Systems Design.

★ 61082 ★   **Omni Business Systems, Inc.**
2725 Ctr. Pl.
Melbourne, FL 32940
(407)242-3050
Officer: Eugene Boyd, Owner. Ultimate Parent: Alco Standard Corp. SIC: 3663—Radio & T.V. Communications Equipment.

★ 61083 ★   **Pennzoil Ten Minute Oil Change**
2990 W. New Haven Ave.
Melbourne, FL 32904
(407)676-7595
Ultimate Parent: Pennzoil.

★ 61084 ★   **Pizza Hut**
1180 N. Hwy. A1a
Melbourne, FL 32903
(407)773-6526
Ultimate Parent: Pepsico. SIC: 5812—Eating Places.

★ 61085 ★   **Pizza Hut**
1630 S. Wickham Rd.
Melbourne, FL 32904
(407)676-2012
Ultimate Parent: Pepsico. SIC: 5812—Eating Places.

★ 61086 ★   **Pizza Hut**
4850 Babcock St. NE
Melbourne, FL 32905
(407)723-1006
Ultimate Parent: Pepsico. SIC: 5812—Eating Places.

★ 61087 ★   **Pizza Hut**
152 N. Harbor City Blvd.
Melbourne, FL 32935
(407)254-4454
Ultimate Parent: Pepsico. SIC: 5812—Eating Places.

★ 61088 ★   **Pizza Hut**
1180 Hwy. 1A
Melbourne, FL 32937
(407)773-6526
Ultimate Parent: Pepsico. SIC: 5812—Eating Places.

★ 61089 ★   **Prints Plus**
1700 W. New Haven Ave.
Melbourne, FL 32904
(407)723-9996
Ultimate Parent: Melville. SIC: 5719—Miscellaneous Home Furnishings Stores.

★ 61090 ★   **Publix Super Market**
2120 Sarno Rd.
Melbourne, FL 32935
(407)254-8446
Ultimate Parent: Publix Super Markets. SIC: 5411—Grocery Stores.

★ 61091 ★   **Publix Super Market**
2261 W. New Haven Ave.
Melbourne, FL 32904
(407)676-1441
Ultimate Parent: Publix Super Markets. SIC: 5411—Grocery Stores.

★ 61092 ★   **Publix Super Market**
4711 Babcock St. NE 17
Melbourne, FL 32905
(407)724-4724
Ultimate Parent: Publix Super Markets. SIC: 5411—Grocery Stores.

★ 61093 ★   **Publix Super Market**
1401 S. Babcock St.
Melbourne, FL 32901
(407)723-4841
Ultimate Parent: Publix Super Markets. SIC: 5411—Grocery Stores.

★ 61094 ★   **Publix Super Markets**
2120 Sarno Rd.
Melbourne, FL 32935
(407)254-8446
Ultimate Parent: Publix Super Markets. SIC: 5411—Grocery Stores.

★ 61095 ★   **Publix Super Markets**
2261 W. New Haven Ave.
Melbourne, FL 32904
(407)676-1441
Ultimate Parent: Publix Super Markets. SIC: 5411—Grocery Stores.

★ 61096 ★   **Publix Super Markets**
4711 Babcock St. NE 17
Melbourne, FL 32905
(407)724-4724
Ultimate Parent: Publix Super Markets. SIC: 5411—Grocery Stores.

★ 61097 ★   **Publix Super Markets**
1401 S. Babcock St.
Melbourne, FL 32901
(407)723-4841
Ultimate Parent: Publix Super Markets. SIC: 5411—Grocery Stores.

★ 61098 ★   **Radio Shack**
4600 Dixie Hwy. NE 19
Melbourne, FL 32905
(407)725-4580
Company Type: Division. Ultimate Parent: Tandy Corp. SIC: 5719—Miscellaneous Home Furnishings Stores.

★ 61099 ★   **Radio Shack**
1270 N. Wickham Rd. 44
Melbourne, FL 32935
(407)259-7224
Company Type: Division. Ultimate Parent: Tandy Corp. SIC: 5734—Computer & Software Stores.

★ 61100 ★   **Radio Shack**
404 S. Babcock St.
Melbourne, FL 32901
(407)724-1263
Company Type: Division. Ultimate Parent: Tandy Corp. SIC: 5099—Durable Goods Nec.

★ 61101 ★   **Raytheon Service Co.**
1275 S. Patrick Dr.
Melbourne, FL 32937
(407)777-3490
Ultimate Parent: Raytheon Co.

★ 61102 ★   **Rite Aid Disc Pharmacies**
2116 Sarno Rd.
Melbourne, FL 32935
(407)254-9934
Ultimate Parent: Rite Aid. SIC: 5912—Drug Stores & Proprietary Stores.

★ 61103 ★   **Rite Aid Discount Pharmacy**
7175 N. Wickham Rd.
Melbourne, FL 32940
(407)254-4230
Ultimate Parent: Rite Aid. SIC: 5122—Drugs, Proprietaries & Sundries.

★ 61104 ★   **Rite Aid Pharmacy**
3160 W. New Haven Ave.
Melbourne, FL 32904
(407)984-0981
Ultimate Parent: Rite Aid. SIC: 5912—Drug Stores & Proprietary Stores.

★ 61105 ★   **Rockwell International Corp.**
Collins General Aviation Div.
1100 W. Hibiscus Blvd.
Melbourne, FL 32901
Company Type: Division. Ultimate Parent: Rockwell International Corp. SIC: 3679—Electronic Components Nec.

★ 61106 ★   **Ryder Truck Rental**
460 S. Harbor City Blvd.
Melbourne, FL 32901
(407)768-1071
Ultimate Parent: Ryder System. SIC: 7513—Truck Rental & Leasing Without Drivers.

★ 61107 ★   **Taco Bell**
2035 W. New Haven Ave.
Melbourne, FL 32904
(407)723-2235
Ultimate Parent: Pepsico. SIC: 5812—Eating Places.

★ 61108 ★   **Taco Bell**
2150 Harris Ave. NE
Melbourne, FL 32905
(407)724-8826
Ultimate Parent: Pepsico. SIC: 5812—Eating Places.

★ 61109 ★   **Taco Bell**
421 S. Babcock St.
Melbourne, FL 32901
(407)727-8344
Ultimate Parent: Pepsico. SIC: 5812—Eating Places.

★ 61110 ★   **Texaco**
1115 S. Wickham Rd.
Melbourne, FL 32904
(407)768-2724
Ultimate Parent: Texaco. SIC: 5411—Grocery Stores.

★ 61111 ★   **This End Up Furniture**
1700 W. New Haven Ave.
Melbourne, FL 32904
(407)984-8504
Ultimate Parent: Melville. SIC: 5712—Furniture Stores.

★ 61112 ★   **Tj Maxx**
1344 S. Babcock St.
Melbourne, FL 32901
(407)984-3836
Ultimate Parent: TJX. SIC: 5651—Family Clothing Stores.

★ 61113 ★   **United Parcel Service**
2725 Kirby Ave. NE
Melbourne, FL 32905
(407)783-6661
Ultimate Parent: United Parcel Service of America. SIC: 4215—Courier Services Except by Air.

★ 61114 ★   **Wal Mart**
3990 S. Babcock St.
Melbourne, FL 32901
(407)943-2715
Ultimate Parent: Wal-Mart Stores, Inc. SIC: 5311—Department Stores.

★ 61115 ★   **Waldenbooks**
1700 W. New Haven Ave. 239
Melbourne, FL 32904
(407)676-2800
Ultimate Parent: K-Mart. SIC: 5942—Book Stores.

★ 61116 ★   **Waldenbooks**
Melbourne
Melbourne, FL 32903
(407)676-2800
Ultimate Parent: K-Mart. SIC: 5942—Book Stores.

★ 61117 ★   **Walgreen**
4700 Babcock St. NE 14
Melbourne, FL 32905
(407)676-3556
Ultimate Parent: Walgreen Co. SIC: 5912—Drug Stores & Proprietary Stores.

★ 61118 ★   **Walgreen Drug Stores**
1700 W. New Haven Ave.
Melbourne, FL 32904
(407)725-2115
Ultimate Parent: Walgreen Co. SIC: 5912—Drug Stores & Proprietary Stores.

★ 61119 ★   **Walgreen Drug Stores**
3100 Lake Washington Rd.
Melbourne, FL 32934
(407)254-7744
Ultimate Parent: Walgreen Co. SIC: 5912—Drug Stores & Proprietary Stores.

★ 61120 ★   **Walgreen Drug Stores**
1305 S. Babcock St.
Melbourne, FL 32901
(407)723-4177
Ultimate Parent: Walgreen Co. SIC: 5912—Drug Stores & Proprietary Stores.

★ 61121 ★   **Walgreen Drug Stores**
260 E. Eau Gallie Blvd.
Melbourne, FL 32937
(407)777-0595
Ultimate Parent: Walgreen Co. SIC: 5912—Drug Stores & Proprietary Stores.

★ 61122 ★   **Zippy Mart Inc.**
930 N. Hwy. 1
Melbourne, FL 32905
(407)724-5851
Ultimate Parent: Crown Central Petroleum Corp. SIC: 5411—Grocery Stores.

★ 61123 ★   **Zippy Mart Inc.**
595 Wickham Rd.
Melbourne, FL 32901
(407)727-1085
Ultimate Parent: Crown Central Petroleum Corp. SIC: 5411—Grocery Stores.

Melbourne Beach

★ 61124 ★   **Systems Engineering Associates International**
440 Sandy Key
Melbourne Beach, FL 32951-2724
(407)951-2128
Ultimate Parent: Ball Corp. SIC: 7371—Computer Programming Services; 8742—Management Consulting Services.

Melbourne Fl

★ 61125 ★   **Ryder Truck Rental**
1101 Palm Bay
Melbourne Fl, FL 32905
(407)725-4267
Ultimate Parent: Ryder System. SIC: 7389—Business Services Nec.

Melrose

★ 61126 ★   **Avon Products, Inc.**
Melrose, FL 32666
(904)475-2467
Ultimate Parent: Avon Products, Inc. SIC: 5999—Miscellaneous Retail Stores Nec.

Merritt

★ 61127 ★   **Mapco Express**
405 E. Michigan Causeway
Merritt, FL 32952
(407)453-3270
Ultimate Parent: Mapco. SIC: 5411—Grocery Stores.

Merritt is

★ 61128 ★   **The Gap**
205 Merritt Sq.
Merritt is, FL 32952
(407)453-0370
Ultimate Parent: GAP. SIC: 5651—Family Clothing Stores.

★ 61129 ★   **Publix Super Market**
239 Crockett Blvd.
Merritt is, FL 32953
(407)452-5757
Ultimate Parent: Publix Super Markets. SIC: 5411—Grocery Stores.

★ 61130 ★   **Radio Shack**
777 E. M I Cswy
Merritt is, FL 32952
(407)452-7734
Company Type: Division. Ultimate Parent: Tandy Corp. SIC: 5063—Electrical Apparatus & Equipment.

★ 61131 ★ Radio Shack
777 E. Merritt Island Cswy
Merritt is, FL 32952
(407)254-3690
Company Type: Division. Ultimate Parent:
Tandy Corp. SIC: 1542—Nonresidential
Construction Nec.

★ 61132 ★ Radio Shack
700 E. M I Cswy
Merritt is, FL 32952
(407)459-0145
Company Type: Division. Ultimate Parent:
Tandy Corp. SIC: 7373—Computer
Integrated Systems Design.

★ 61133 ★ Taco Bell
410 N. Courtenay Pky.
Merritt is, FL 32953
(407)459-1968
Ultimate Parent: Pepsico. SIC: 5812—
Eating Places.

★ 61134 ★ Texaco Oil Co.
536 N. Courtenay Pky.
Merritt is, FL 32953
(407)453-1733
Ultimate Parent: Texaco. SIC: 5541—
Gasoline Service Stations.

★ 61135 ★ Texaco Service
Station
2600 N. Courtenay Pky.
Merritt is, FL 32953
(407)452-1398
Ultimate Parent: Texaco. SIC: 5541—
Gasoline Service Stations.

Merritt Island

★ 61136 ★ Ace Hardware
1005 N. Courtenay Pky.
Merritt Island, FL 32953
(407)452-3484
Ultimate Parent: Ace Hardware. SIC:
5251—Hardware Stores; 7349—Building
Maintenance Services Nec.

★ 61137 ★ Barnett Bank of
Central Florida, NA
15 E. Merritt Island Causeway
Merritt Island, FL 32952-3656
(407)453-2200
Company Type: Subsidiary. Location
Type: Branch office. Officer: Larry Roselle,
Manager. Ultimate Parent: Barnett Banks.
SIC: 6021—National Commercial Banks.

★ 61138 ★ Burdines
Merrittana Dr.
Merritt Island, FL 32952
(407)454-1114
Ultimate Parent: Federated Department
Stores. SIC: 5599—Automotive Dealers
Nec.

★ 61139 ★ Casual Corner
777 E. MI Causeway
Merritt Island, FL 32952
(407)453-1929
Ultimate Parent: United States Shoe. SIC:
5651—Family Clothing Stores.

★ 61140 ★ First Union National
Bank of Florida
100 S. Sykes Creek Pky.
Merritt Island, FL 32952-3512
(407)439-5220
Location Type: Branch office. Ultimate
Parent: Barnett Bank of Alachua County,
NA. SIC: 6021—National Commercial
Banks.

★ 61141 ★ Kentucky Fried
Chicken
500 E. Merritt Island Causeway
Merritt Island, FL 32952
Ultimate Parent: Pepsico. SIC: 5812—
Eating Places.

★ 61142 ★ Lane Bryant
777 E. Merritt Island Causeway
Merritt Island, FL 32952
(407)454-4055
Ultimate Parent: Limited. SIC: 5651—
Family Clothing Stores.

★ 61143 ★ Pizza Hut
185 N. Courtenay Pky.
Merritt Island, FL 32953
(407)453-1390
Ultimate Parent: Pepsico. SIC: 5812—
Eating Places.

★ 61144 ★ Sea Ray Boats Inc.
350 Sea Ray Dr.
Merritt Island, FL 32953
Ultimate Parent: Brunswick Corp. SIC:
3732—Boat Building & Repairing.

★ 61145 ★ Sea Ray Boats Inc.
100 Sea Ray Dr.
Merritt Island, FL 32953
Ultimate Parent: Brunswick Corp. SIC:
3732—Boat Building & Repairing.

★ 61146 ★ Sea Ray Boats Inc.
Product Development
200 Sea Ray Dr.
Merritt Island, FL 32953
Ultimate Parent: Brunswick Corp. SIC:
3732—Boat Building & Repairing.

★ 61147 ★ Wal Mart Discount
City
323 E. Merritt Island Causeway
Merritt Island, FL 32952
(407)452-4340
Ultimate Parent: Wal-Mart Stores, Inc. SIC:
5331—Variety Stores.

★ 61148 ★ Wal Mart Discount
City
323 E. MI Causeway
Merritt Island, FL 32952
(407)452-4493
Ultimate Parent: Wal-Mart Stores, Inc. SIC:
5311—Department Stores.

★ 61149 ★ Waldenbooks
777 E. MI Causeway
Merritt Island, FL 32952
(407)452-0855
Ultimate Parent: K-Mart. SIC: 5942—Book
Stores.

★ 61150 ★ Walgreen Drug Stores
777 E. MI Causeway
Merritt Island, FL 32952
(407)452-5610
Ultimate Parent: Walgreen Co. SIC:
5912—Drug Stores & Proprietary Stores.

Miami

★ 61151 ★ Ace Hardware
2398 S. Dixie Hwy.
Miami, FL 33133
(305)854-3035
Ultimate Parent: Ace Hardware. SIC:
8111—Legal Services.

★ 61152 ★ Alcoa Inter-America,
Inc.
396 Alhambra Circle, Ste. 2
Miami, FL 33134-5007
(305)445-8544
Officer: R.T. McCrachen, President.
Ultimate Parent: Aluminum Co. of America-
-Alcoa. SIC: 5051—Metals Service Centers
& Offices. Employee Count: 35.

★ 61153 ★ Alcoa Inter-America,
Inc.
396 Alhambra Cir., Ste. 2
Miami, FL 33134-5007
(305)445-8544
Officer: R.T. McCrachen, President.
Ultimate Parent: Aluminum Co. of America-
-Alcoa. SIC: 5051—Metals Service Centers
& Offices. Employee Count: 35.

★ 61154 ★ American Brokerage
Co.
7001 NW 25th St.
Miami, FL 33122
(305)591-3957
Ultimate Parent: Phoenix Home Life
Mutual. SIC: 4731—Freight Transportation
Arrangement.

★ 61155 ★ American Brokerage
Co. Inc.
7150 NW 50th St.
Miami, FL 33166
(305)591-3957
Ultimate Parent: Phoenix Home Life
Mutual. SIC: 0919—Miscellaneous Marine
Products.

★ 61156 ★ American Express
Bank International
1221 Brickell Ave., 8th Fl.
Miami, FL 33131
(305)350-7750
Company Type: Subsidiary. Location
Type: Branch office. Officer: Sergio J.
Masvidal, General Manager. Ultimate

Parent: American Express Co. SIC: 6021—
National Commercial Banks.

★ 61157 ★ American Savings of
FL FSB
12855 N. Kendall Dr.
Miami, FL 33186-1707
(305)386-5033
Location Type: Branch office. Ultimate
Parent: American Savings of Florida. SIC:
6035—Federal Savings Institutions; 6021—
National Commercial Banks.

★ 61158 ★ American Savings of
FL FSB
2925 Aventura Blvd.
Miami, FL 33180-3124
(305)932-4630
Location Type: Branch office. Ultimate
Parent: American Savings of Florida. SIC:
6035—Federal Savings Institutions; 6021—
National Commercial Banks; 6162—
Mortgage Bankers & Correspondents.

★ 61159 ★ American Savings of
FL FSB
12155 Biscayne Blvd.
Miami, FL 33181
(305)895-5428
Location Type: Branch office. Ultimate
Parent: American Savings of Florida. SIC:
6035—Federal Savings Institutions; 6021—
National Commercial Banks.

★ 61160 ★ American Savings of
FL FSB
17801 NW 2nd Ave.
Miami, FL 33169-5029
(305)653-5353
Location Type: Branch office. Officer:
Stephen D. Taylor. Ultimate Parent:
American Savings of Florida. SIC: 6035—
Federal Savings Institutions; 6021—National
Commercial Banks; 6162—Mortgage
Bankers & Correspondents.

★ 61161 ★ American Savings of
FL FSB
2401 Ponce De Leon Blvd.
Miami, FL 33134-6016
(305)448-6030
Location Type: Branch office. Ultimate
Parent: American Savings of Florida. SIC:
6035—Federal Savings Institutions; 6021—
Personal Credit Institutions; 6162—
Mortgage Bankers & Correspondents.

★ 61162 ★ American Savings of
Florida
1802 NE Miami Gardens Dr.
Miami, FL 33179-5036
(305)956-9798
Ultimate Parent: American Savings of
Florida. SIC: 6035—Federal Savings
Institutions; 6021—National Commercial
Banks.

★ 61163 ★ American Savings of
Florida
200 71st St.
Miami, FL 33141-3210
(305)861-3783
Location Type: Branch office. Ultimate
Parent: American Savings of Florida. SIC:
6035—Federal Savings Institutions; 6021—
National Commercial Banks.

★ 61164 ★ American Savings of
Florida
17066 Collins Ave.
Miami, FL 33160-3642
(305)949-9596
Ultimate Parent: American Savings of
Florida. SIC: 6035—Federal Savings
Institutions; 6021—National Commercial
Banks.

★ 61165 ★ American Savings of
Florida
333 Arthur Godfrey Rd.
Miami, FL 33140-3608
(305)534-4344
Ultimate Parent: American Savings of
Florida. SIC: 6035—Federal Savings
Institutions; 6021—National Commercial
Banks.

★ 61166 ★ American Savings of
Florida
17801 NW 2nd Ave.
Miami, FL 33169
(305)653-5353
Company Type: Headquarters. Officer:

Stephen D. Taylor. Fortune Service 500:
Ranking 34.

★ 61167 ★ American Savings of
Florida FSB
12855 N. Kendall Dr.
Miami, FL 33186-1707
(305)386-5033
Location Type: Branch office. Officer: Alex
Gonzalez, Manager. Ultimate Parent:
American Savings of Florida. SIC: 6035—
Federal Savings Institutions; 6211—Security
Brokers & Dealers.

★ 61168 ★ American Savings of
Florida, FSB
17801 NW 2nd Ave.
Miami, FL 33169-5089
(305)770-2400
Location Type: Branch office. Officer:
Deloris Coleman, Manager. Ultimate
Parent: American Savings of Florida. SIC:
6035—Federal Savings Institutions; 6211—
Security Brokers & Dealers.

★ 61169 ★ Automated
Instruments Corp.
1361 SW 22nd St.
Miami, FL 33145
(305)858-1954
Ultimate Parent: United States Surgical
Corp. SIC: 5049—Professional Equipment
Nec.

★ 61170 ★ Banana Republic
9700 Collins Ave. 246
Miami, FL 33154
(305)864-3661
Ultimate Parent: GAP. SIC: 5699—
Miscellaneous Apparel & Accessory Stores.

★ 61171 ★ Bank of Boston
905 S. Bayshore Dr.
Miami, FL 33131
(305)375-0050
Ultimate Parent: Bank of Boston Corp.

★ 61172 ★ Bank of Boston
International
800 Brickell Plz.
Miami, FL 33131-2904
(305)377-0751
Location Type: Branch office. Officer:
Ignacio Riveira. Ultimate Parent: Bank of
Boston Corp. SIC: 6081—Foreign Banks-
Branches & Agencies; 5099—Durable
Goods Nec; 6021—National Commercial
Banks; 6022—State Commercial Banks;
6153—Short-Term Business Credit; 6282—
Investment Advice.

★ 61173 ★ Bank of Boston
International
800 Brickell Ave., Ste. 1500
Miami, FL 33131-2971
(305)530-2400
Company Type: Subsidiary. Officer:
Stewart E. Sutin, President. Ultimate
Parent: Bank of Boston Corp. SIC: 6082—
Foreign Trade & International Banks.
Employee Count: 63.

★ 61174 ★ Bank of Boston
International
800 Brickell Ave.
Miami, FL 33131
(305)377-0751
Ultimate Parent: Bank of Boston Corp.
SIC: 6022—State Commercial Banks;
6029—Commercial Banks Nec.

★ 61175 ★ Bank of New York
International Inc.
701 Brickell Ave., 11th Fl.
PO Box 013390
Miami, FL 33131
(305)372-7300 Fax: (305)372-7450 Telex:
515641
Company Type: Subsidiary. Officer: J. C.
Bocot, Chairman. Ultimate Parent: Bank of
New York Co.

★ 61176 ★ Bank of New York
Trust Co. of Florida National
Association
701 Brickell Ave., 11th Fl.
Miami, FL 33131-2822
(305)372-7444 Fax: (305)372-7383
Company Type: Subsidiary. Officer:
Richard G. Jackson, President & CEO of
Marketing. Ultimate Parent: Bank of New
York Co. SIC: 6021—National Commercial
Banks.

★ 61177 ★   Bank of Tokyo Ltd.
2100 Ponce DeLeon Blvd.
Miami, FL 33134-5214
(305)445-2100
Company Type: Subsidiary. Ultimate
Parent: Bank of Tokyo Trust. SIC: 6021—
National Commercial Banks.

★ 61178 ★   Bankers Trust
International
1 Biscayne Tower
Miami, FL 33131
(305)371-2664
Ultimate Parent: Bankers Trust New York
Corp. SIC: 6021—National Commercial
Banks.

★ 61179 ★   Barnett Bank of South
Florida, NA
13780 SW 88th St.
Miami, FL 33186-1388
(305)663-6100
Company Type: Subsidiary. Location
Type: Branch office. Officer: Victor
Hernandez, Manager. Ultimate Parent:
Barnett Banks. SIC: 6021—National
Commercial Banks.

★ 61180 ★   Barnett Bank of South
Florida, NA
13730 SW 8th St.
Miami, FL 33184-3000
(305)553-7900
Company Type: Subsidiary. Location
Type: Branch office. Officer: Jorge Perez,
Manager. Ultimate Parent: Barnett Banks.
SIC: 6021—National Commercial Banks.

★ 61181 ★   Barnett Bank of South
Florida, NA
6262 Sunset Dr.
Miami, FL 33143-4891
(305)663-5100
Company Type: Subsidiary. Location
Type: Branch office. Officer: Cheryl Martin,
Manager. Ultimate Parent: Barnett Banks.
SIC: 6021—National Commercial Banks.

★ 61182 ★   Barnett Bank of South
Florida, NA
5350 W. Flagler St.
Miami, FL 33134-1148
(305)553-7900
Company Type: Subsidiary. Location
Type: Branch office. Officer: Alex Carrasco,
Manager. Ultimate Parent: Barnett Banks.
SIC: 6021—National Commercial Banks.

★ 61183 ★   Barnett Bank of South
Florida, NA
13593 S. Dixie Hwy.
Miami, FL 33156-6588
(305)663-5100
Company Type: Subsidiary. Location
Type: Branch office. Officer: Denise King-
Smith, Manager. Ultimate Parent: Barnett
Banks. SIC: 6021—National Commercial
Banks.

★ 61184 ★   Barnett Bank of South
Florida, NA
8585 Coral Way
Miami, FL 33155-2335
(305)663-7900
Company Type: Subsidiary. Location
Type: Branch office. Officer: Ray Gonzalez,
Manager. Ultimate Parent: Barnett Banks.
SIC: 6021—National Commercial Banks.

★ 61185 ★   Barnett Bank of South
Florida, NA
150 W. Flagler St.
Miami, FL 33131-1536
(305)350-7100
Company Type: Subsidiary. Location
Type: Branch office. Officer: Oddulio
Piedra, Manager. Ultimate Parent: Barnett
Banks. SIC: 6021—National Commercial
Banks.

★ 61186 ★   Barnett Bank of South
Florida, NA
20295 NW 2nd Ave.
Miami, FL 33169-2511
(305)889-4100
Company Type: Subsidiary. Location
Type: Branch office. Officer: Mindy Seger,
Manager. Ultimate Parent: Barnett Banks.
SIC: 6021—National Commercial Banks.

★ 61187 ★   Barnett Bank of South
Florida, NA
18400 NW 67th Ave.
Miami, FL 33015-3411
(305)883-2400
Company Type: Subsidiary. Location
Type: Branch office. Officer: Cheryl
Thomas, Manager. Ultimate Parent:
Barnett Banks. SIC: 6021—National
Commercial Banks.

★ 61188 ★   Barnett Bank of South
Florida, NA
7760 W. Flagler St.
Miami, FL 33144-2395
(305)553-7900
Company Type: Subsidiary. Location
Type: Branch office. Officer: Rick Garcia,
Manager. Ultimate Parent: Barnett Banks.
SIC: 6021—National Commercial Banks.

★ 61189 ★   Barnett Bank of South
Florida, NA
7380 SW 152nd Ave.
Miami, FL 33193-2307
(305)663-5100
Company Type: Subsidiary. Location
Type: Branch office. Officer: Kathy
Huaroto, Manager. Ultimate Parent: Barnett
Banks. SIC: 6021—National Commercial
Banks.

★ 61190 ★   Barnett Bank of South
Florida, NA
7900 NE 2nd Ave.
Miami, FL 33138-4424
(305)663-5100
Company Type: Subsidiary. Location
Type: Branch office. Officer: Dottie Stewart,
Manager. Ultimate Parent: Barnett Banks.
SIC: 6021—National Commercial Banks.

★ 61191 ★   Barnett Bank of South
Florida, NA
8180 NW 36th St.
Miami, FL 33166-6650
(305)883-2400
Company Type: Subsidiary. Location
Type: Branch office. Officer: Bernie
Adrover, Manager. Ultimate Parent: Barnett
Banks. SIC: 6021—National Commercial
Banks.

★ 61192 ★   Barnett Bank of South
Florida, NA
10315 Hammocks Blvd.
Miami, FL 33196-2623
(305)663-5100
Company Type: Subsidiary. Location
Type: Branch office. Officer: Sonya
Fernandez, Manager. Ultimate Parent:
Barnett Banks. SIC: 6021—National
Commercial Banks.

★ 61193 ★   Barnett Bank of South
Florida, NA
13701 SW 152nd St.
Miami, FL 33177-1106
(305)663-5100
Company Type: Subsidiary. Location
Type: Branch office. Officer: Cheryl Wolf,
Manager. Ultimate Parent: Barnett Banks.
SIC: 6021—National Commercial Banks.

★ 61194 ★   Barnett Bank of South
Florida, NA
9101 S. Dixie Hwy.
Miami, FL 33156-2946
(305)663-5100
Company Type: Subsidiary. Location
Type: Branch office. Officer: John Coffey,
Manager. Ultimate Parent: Barnett Banks.
SIC: 6021—National Commercial Banks.

★ 61195 ★   Barnett Bank of South
Florida, NA
240 Biscayne Blvd.
Miami, FL 33131-2302
(305)663-5100
Company Type: Subsidiary. Location
Type: Branch office. Officer: Cecilia Rivero,
Manager. Ultimate Parent: Barnett Banks.
SIC: 6021—National Commercial Banks.

★ 61196 ★   Barnett Bank of South
Florida, NA
4020 SW 67th Ave.
Miami, FL 33155-4700
(305)663-5100
Company Type: Subsidiary. Location
Type: Branch office. Officer: Luis Cornide,
Manager. Ultimate Parent: Barnett Banks.
SIC: 6021—National Commercial Banks.

★ 61197 ★   Barnett Bank of South
Florida, NA
701 Brickell Ave.
PO Box 450310
Miami, FL 33245-0310
(305)350-1832 Fax: (305)350-7005 Telex:
160047
Company Type: Subsidiary. Location
Type: Branch office. Officer: William R.
Myers, President & CEO. Ultimate Parent:
Barnett Banks. SIC: 6021—National
Commercial Banks.

★ 61198 ★   Barnett Bank of South
Florida, NA
Miami International Airport
Miami, FL 33159
(305)883-2400
Company Type: Subsidiary. Location
Type: Branch office. Officer: Treva
Gillespie, Manager. Ultimate Parent:
Barnett Banks. SIC: 6021—National
Commercial Banks.

★ 61199 ★   Baxter Diagnostics
Inc.
9750 NW 25th St.
Miami, FL 33172
(305)592-2311
Officer: Lee Flowers, Manager. Ultimate
Parent: Baxter International. SIC: 3821—
Laboratory Apparatus & Furniture; 3841—
Surgical & Medical Instruments.

★ 61200 ★   Baxter Diagnostics
Inc.
1851 Delaware Pky.
Miami, FL 33125
(305)633-6461
Officer: Ken Nelson, Manager. Ultimate
Parent: Baxter International. SIC: 3821—
Laboratory Apparatus & Furniture.

★ 61201 ★   Baxter Diagnostics
Inc.
Dade Div.
9750 NW 25th St.
Miami, FL 33172
(305)592-2311 (800)327-1572 Fax:
(305)591-5552
Company Type: Division. Officer: King
Nelson, President. Ultimate Parent: Baxter
International. SIC: 3841—Surgical &
Medical Instruments; 5047—Medical &
Hospital Equipment.

★ 61202 ★   Baxter Healthcare
Corp. Dade
1851 Delaware Pky.
Miami, FL 33125-1113
(305)633-6461
Location Type: Branch office. Officer:
George Patterson. Ultimate Parent: Baxter
International. SIC: 2835—Diagnostic
Substances; 3821—Laboratory Apparatus &
Furniture; 5049—Professional Equipment
Nec.

★ 61203 ★   Baxter International
Baxter Diagnostics Div.
9750 NW 25th St.
Miami, FL 33172-2297
(305)592-2311
Company Type: Division. Location Type:
Branch office. Officer: George M. Darnell.
Ultimate Parent: Baxter International. SIC:
2835—Diagnostic Substances; 2836—
Biological Products Except Diagnostic;
3821—Laboratory Apparatus & Furniture;
3841—Surgical & Medical Instruments;
5047—Medical & Hospital Equipment;
5049—Professional Equipment Nec.

★ 61204 ★   Boeing Co.
7270 NW 12th St.
Miami, FL 33126
(305)593-1747
Ultimate Parent: Boeing. SIC: 3721—
Aircraft.

★ 61205 ★   Borden Inc.
Dairy
17707 NW Miami Ct.
Miami, FL 33169
Company Type: Division. Ultimate Parent:
Borden, Inc. SIC: 5143—Dairy Products
Except Dried or Canned; 2026—Fluid Milk;
2024—Ice Cream & Frozen Desserts.

★ 61206 ★   Borden Inc.
Dairy
17707 NW Miami Ct.
Miami, FL 33169
Company Type: Division. Ultimate Parent:
Borden, Inc. SIC: 5143—Dairy Products

Except Dried or Canned; 2026—Fluid Milk;
2024—Ice Cream & Frozen Desserts.

★ 61207 ★   Borden Inc.
Dairy Div.
17707 NW Miami Ct.
Miami, FL 33169
(305)652-4411
Company Type: Division. Officer: Jim Elsy,
Manager. Ultimate Parent: Borden, Inc.
SIC: 2024—Ice Cream & Frozen Desserts;
2026—Fluid Milk.

★ 61208 ★   Borden Inc. Grocery
& Speciality Prds.
17707 NW Miami Ct.
Miami, FL 33169
Ultimate Parent: Borden, Inc. SIC: 2026—
Fluid Milk; 2024—Ice Cream & Frozen
Desserts.

★ 61209 ★   Brownell Electro Inc.
6850 NW 74th Ave.
Miami, FL 33166
(305)884-3197
Location Type: Branch office. Ultimate
Parent: Avnet. SIC: 5063—Electrical
Apparatus & Equipment.

★ 61210 ★   Burdines
2490 Coral Way 5
Miami, FL 33145
Ultimate Parent: Federated Department
Stores. SIC: 5399—Miscellaneous General
Merchandise Store.

★ 61211 ★   Burdines
Department Store Division
7100 NW 32nd Ave.
Miami, FL 33147
Ultimate Parent: Federated Department
Stores. SIC: 5311—Department Stores.

★ 61212 ★   Burdines Department
Store
7100 NW 32nd Ave.
Miami, FL 33147
Ultimate Parent: Federated Department
Stores. SIC: 8249—Vocational Schools Nec.

★ 61213 ★   Burdines Department
Stores
Dadeland Mall
Miami, FL 33156
(305)662-3364
Ultimate Parent: Federated Department
Stores. SIC: 5661—Shoe Stores.

★ 61214 ★   Burdines Dept Store
10785 SW 108th Ave.
Miami, FL 33176
(305)662-3306
Ultimate Parent: Federated Department
Stores.

★ 61215 ★   Burdines Portrait
Studio
7303 Dadeland Mall
Miami, FL 33156
(305)662-3924
Ultimate Parent: Federated Department
Stores. SIC: 7221—Photographic Studios—
Portrait.

★ 61216 ★   Burdines Portrait
Studio
7100 NW 32nd Ave.
Miami, FL 33147
Ultimate Parent: Federated Department
Stores. SIC: 7221—Photographic Studios—
Portrait.

★ 61217 ★   Burdines Store Bty
Salon
163 St. Shopping Ctr.
Miami, FL 33162
(305)940-4421
Ultimate Parent: Federated Department
Stores. SIC: 7231—Beauty Shops.

★ 61218 ★   Burdines Travel
2490 Coral Way 5
Miami, FL 33145
Ultimate Parent: Federated Department
Stores. SIC: 4724—Travel Agencies.

★ 61219 ★   Butler Paper
255 NE 181st St.
Miami, FL 33162-1095
(305)652-3770
Location Type: Branch office. Officer:
Peter Garberding. Ultimate Parent: Alco
Standard Corp. SIC: 5113—Industrial &
Personal Service Paper; 5085—Industrial
Supplies.

★ 61220 ★ C S F Holdings Inc.
1221 Brickell Ave.
Miami, FL 33131-3261
(305)577-0400
Officer: Charles B. Stuzin, Chairman of the Board & President. **Ultimate Parent:** CSF Holdings. **SIC:** 6035—Federal Savings Institutions. **Employee Count:** 834.

★ 61221 ★ California Federal Bank, AFSB
6901 SW 117th Ave.
Miami, FL 33183-2800
(305)598-0350
Location Type: Branch office. **Officer:** Barrington Wright, Manager. **Ultimate Parent:** California Federal Bank. **SIC:** 6021—National Commercial Banks.

★ 61222 ★ Capezio Dance Theatre Shop
13821 S. Dixie Hwy.
Miami, FL 33176
(305)251-3937
Ultimate Parent: United States Shoe. **SIC:** 5699—Miscellaneous Apparel & Accessory Stores.

★ 61223 ★ Carnival Cruise Lines
3655 NW 87th Ave.
Miami, FL 33178-2428
(305)599-2600
Company Type: Headquarters. **Officer:** Michael M. Arison. **SIC:** 7999—Amusement & Recreation Nec; 4724—Travel Agencies. **Employee Count 500:** Ranking 25.

★ 61224 ★ Casual Corner
1215 NW 163rd St.
Miami, FL 33169
(305)944-4332
Ultimate Parent: United States Shoe. **SIC:** 5621—Women's Clothing Stores.

★ 61225 ★ Chase Bank International
2 S. Biscayne Blvd., 22nd Fl.
Miami, FL 33131
(305)579-9400 **Fax:** (305)374-0679 **Telex:** 152199
Company Type: Subsidiary. **Location Type:** Branch office. **Ultimate Parent:** Chase Manhattan Corp. **SIC:** 6021—National Commercial Banks.

★ 61226 ★ Chase Home Mortgage Corp.
9555 N. Kendall Dr.
Miami, FL 33176
(305)271-4045
Ultimate Parent: Chase Manhattan Corp. **SIC:** 6162—Mortgage Bankers & Correspondents.

★ 61227 ★ Chase Manhatten Bank of Florida, NA
1 Biscayne Tower
2 Biscayne Blvd.
Miami, FL 33131
(800)835-3786
Company Type: Subsidiary. **Location Type:** Branch office. **Officer:** Peter Sanchez, Manager. **Ultimate Parent:** Chase Manhattan Corp.

★ 61228 ★ Chromalloy Castings Miami Corp.
4701 NW 77th Ave.
Miami, FL 33166
Ultimate Parent: Sequa Corp. **SIC:** 3324—Steel Investment Foundries.

★ 61229 ★ Cigna Dental Health of Florida Inc.
1525 NW 167th St.
Miami, FL 33169-5131
(305)620-9922
Company Type: Subsidiary. **Officer:** Zayra Calderon, Ch. Bd. **Ultimate Parent:** Cigna Corp. **SIC:** 6411—Insurance Agents, Brokers & Service. **Employee Count:** 55.

★ 61230 ★ Cigna Dental Health Inc.
1525 NW 167th St.
Miami, FL 33169-5131
(305)620-9922
Company Type: Subsidiary. **Officer:** Lawrence P. English, Ch. Bd. **Ultimate Parent:** Cigna Corp. **SIC:** 6324—Hospital & Medical Service Plans. **Employee Count:** 276.

★ 61231 ★ Cigna Dental Health of Texas Inc.
1525 NW 167th St.
Miami, FL 33169-5131
(305)620-9922
Company Type: Subsidiary. **Officer:** Zayra F. Calderon, Ch. Bd. President. **Ultimate Parent:** Cigna Corp. **SIC:** 6411—Insurance Agents, Brokers & Service. **Employee Count:** 2.

★ 61232 ★ Circus World
Cutler Ridge Shopping
Miami, FL 33189
(305)251-3500
Ultimate Parent: Melville. **SIC:** 5945—Hobby, Toy & Game Shops.

★ 61233 ★ Citgo Service Station
2701 Salzedo St.
Miami, FL 33134
(305)445-2183
Ultimate Parent: Citgo Petroleum. **SIC:** 5541—Gasoline Service Stations.

★ 61234 ★ Citibank Federal Savings Bank
1 Citicorp Savings Plaza
Miami, FL 33178
(305)599-5450
Company Type: Subsidiary. **Officer:** John Ream, Chairman of the Board & CEO. **Ultimate Parent:** Citicorp. **SIC:** 6035—Federal Savings Institutions.

★ 61235 ★ Citibank Florida NA
8750 Doral Blvd.
Miami, FL 33178-2402
(305)599-5555
Company Type: Subsidiary. **Officer:** John K. Ream, Chairman of the Board & CEO. **Ultimate Parent:** Citicorp. **SIC:** 6021—National Commercial Banks. **Employee Count:** 1100.

★ 61236 ★ Citibank (Florida), NA
1401 Brickell Ave.
Miami, FL 33131
(305)374-1797
Location Type: Branch office. **Officer:** Regi Garcia, Manager. **Ultimate Parent:** Citicorp.

★ 61237 ★ Citibank (Florida), NA
120 S. Biscayne Blvd.
Miami, FL 33131
(305)530-3242
Location Type: Branch office. **Officer:** Ed Slagle, Manager. **Ultimate Parent:** Citicorp. **SIC:** 6021—National Commercial Banks.

★ 61238 ★ Citibank (Floride), NA
1627 NW 27th Ave.
Miami, FL 33125-2139
(305)635-0062
Location Type: Branch office. **Officer:** Peter Gonzalez, Manager. **Ultimate Parent:** Citicorp. **SIC:** 6021—National Commercial Banks.

★ 61239 ★ Citibank, FSB
8750 Doral Blvd.
Miami, FL 33178-2402
(305)599-5999
Location Type: Branch office. **Ultimate Parent:** Citicorp. **SIC:** 6021—National Commercial Banks.

★ 61240 ★ Citibank, FSB
1099 NW 14th St.
Miami, FL 33136-2139
(305)324-1061
Location Type: Branch office. **Ultimate Parent:** Citicorp. **SIC:** 6021—National Commercial Banks.

★ 61241 ★ Citibank, FSB
1790 Biscayne Blvd.
Miami, FL 33132-1179
(305)577-3097
Location Type: Branch office. **Ultimate Parent:** Citicorp. **SIC:** 6021—National Commercial Banks.

★ 61242 ★ Citibank, FSB
260 E. Plz.
Miami, FL 33147-4746
(305)691-5123
Location Type: Branch office. **Ultimate Parent:** Citicorp. **SIC:** 6021—National Commercial Banks.

★ 61243 ★ Citibank, FSB
1600 Coral Way
Miami, FL 33145-2852
(305)856-2990
Location Type: Branch office. **Ultimate Parent:** Citicorp. **SIC:** 6021—National Commercial Banks.

★ 61244 ★ Citibank, FSB
7795 W. Flagler St., Ste. 46-47
Miami, FL 33144
(305)261-0292
Location Type: Branch office. **Ultimate Parent:** Citicorp. **SIC:** 6021—National Commercial Banks.

★ 61245 ★ Citibank International
1 SE 3rd. Ave., 28th Fl.
Miami, FL 33131-1704
(305)377-6800 **Telex:** 51-9136
Location Type: Branch office. **Ultimate Parent:** Citicorp.

★ 61246 ★ Citizens Federal Bank, FSB
11205 S. Dixie Hwy.
Miami, FL 33156-4447
(305)235-6661
Location Type: Branch office. **Officer:** Wendy Compton, Manager. **Ultimate Parent:** CSF Holdings.

★ 61247 ★ Citizens Federal Bank, FSB
1221 Brickell Ave., 16th Fl.
Miami, FL 33131-3012
(305)577-0400
Location Type: Branch office. **Ultimate Parent:** CSF Holdings. **SIC:** 6021—National Commercial Banks.

★ 61248 ★ Citizens Federal Bank, FSB
13969 SW 88th St.
Miami, FL 33186-4097
(305)382-3900
Location Type: Branch office. **Ultimate Parent:** CSF Holdings.

★ 61249 ★ Citizens Federal Bank, FSB
999 Brickell Ave.
Miami, FL 33131-3012
(305)577-0430
Location Type: Branch office. **Officer:** Teresa Fett, Manager. **Ultimate Parent:** CSF Holdings. **SIC:** 6021—National Commercial Banks.

★ 61250 ★ City National Bank
6975 SE 87th Ave.
Miami, FL 33173-2594
(305)279-1990
Company Type: Branch. **Ultimate Parent:** City National Corp. **SIC:** 6021—National Commercial Banks; 6141—Personal Credit Institutions.

★ 61251 ★ City National Bank
13400 Biscayne Blvd.
Miami, FL 33181-2019
(305)947-6101
Company Type: Branch. **Officer:** Gwen Abell, Vice President. **Ultimate Parent:** City National Corp. **SIC:** 6021—National Commercial Banks; 6022—State Commercial Banks; 6141—Personal Credit Institutions.

★ 61252 ★ City National Bank
2701 S. Le Jeune Rd.
Miami, FL 33134-5896
(305)445-1941
Company Type: Branch. **Officer:** Marilyn Steffen, Vice President. **Ultimate Parent:** City National Corp. **SIC:** 6021—National Commercial Banks; 6022—State Commercial Banks.

★ 61253 ★ City National Bank
1 Biscayne Tower
Miami, FL 33131
Company Type: Branch. **Ultimate Parent:** City National Corp.

★ 61254 ★ City National Bank
801 Brickell Ave.
Miami, FL 33131-2900
(305)577-7400
Company Type: Branch. **Ultimate Parent:** City National Corp.

★ 61255 ★ City National Bank
111 NW 1st. St.
Miami, FL 33128-1901
(305)577-7223
Company Type: Branch. **Ultimate Parent:** City National Corp. **SIC:** 6021—National Commercial Banks.

★ 61256 ★ City National Bank of Fl
1 Biscayne Tower
Miami, FL 33131
(305)577-7277
Ultimate Parent: City National Corp. **SIC:** 6099—Functions Related to Deposit Banking.

★ 61257 ★ City National Bank of Fl
111 NW 1st St.
Miami, FL 33128
(305)577-7223
Ultimate Parent: City National Corp. **SIC:** 6099—Functions Related to Deposit Banking.

★ 61258 ★ City National Bank of Flori
801 Brickell Ave.
Miami, FL 33131
(305)577-7400
Ultimate Parent: City National Corp. **SIC:** 6099—Functions Related to Deposit Banking.

★ 61259 ★ City National Bank of Florida
524 Arthur Godfrey Rd.
Miami, FL 33140-3528
(305)534-4041
Company Type: Branch. **Officer:** Marcy Jurkowitz, Vice President. **Ultimate Parent:** City National Corp. **SIC:** 6021—National Commercial Banks; 6022—State Commercial Banks; 6211—Security Brokers & Dealers.

★ 61260 ★ City National Bank of Miami
2701 S. Le Jeune Rd.
Miami, FL 33134
(305)447-1806
Ultimate Parent: City National Corp. **SIC:** 6099—Functions Related to Deposit Banking.

★ 61261 ★ City National Bank of Miami
8784 Sunset Dr.
Miami, FL 33173
(305)279-1990
Ultimate Parent: City National Corp. **SIC:** 6022—State Commercial Banks.

★ 61262 ★ City National Bank of Miami
25 W. Flagler St.
Miami, FL 33130
(305)577-7333
Ultimate Parent: City National Corp. **SIC:** 6022—State Commercial Banks.

★ 61263 ★ Clark Equipment Co.
2199 Ponce De Leon Blvd.
Miami, FL 33134
(305)447-1648
Ultimate Parent: Clark Equipment Co. **SIC:** 5082—Construction & Mining Machinery.

★ 61264 ★ Coast to Coast Sfd Sales Inc.
10689 N. Kendall Dr.
Miami, FL 33176
(305)279-7229
Ultimate Parent: Servistar Corp. **SIC:** 5146—Fish & Seafoods.

★ 61265 ★ Coast to Coast Travel
1111 S. Bayshore Dr.
Miami, FL 33131
(305)371-7273
Ultimate Parent: Servistar Corp. **SIC:** 4724—Travel Agencies.

★ 61266 ★ Coastal Fuels Marketing, Inc.
8700 W. Flagler St.
Miami, FL 33174
(305)551-5200 **Fax:** (305)551-5366
Officer: Dan J. Hill, Chairman & CEO. **Ultimate Parent:** Coastal Corp.

★ 61267 ★   Coastal Fuels Marketing Inc.
8700 W. Flagler St.
Miami, FL 33174-2428
(305)551-5200
Company Type: Subsidiary. **Officer:** Dan J. Hill, Chairman of the Board, CEO. **Ultimate Parent:** Coastal Corp. **SIC:** 5172—Petroleum Products Nec; 5983—Fuel Oil Dealers. **Employee Count:** 250. **Sales:** 1 M.

★ 61268 ★   ConAgra Latin America
9100 S. Dadeland Blvd., Ste. 1603
Miami, FL 33156
(305)670-1388 **Fax:** (305)670-1391
Officer: Thomas L. Manuel, Managing Director. **Ultimate Parent:** Conagra.

★ 61269 ★   Costco Wholesale
9191 SW 137th Ave.
Miami, FL 33186
(305)386-7350
Ultimate Parent: Costco Wholesale Corp. **SIC:** 5999—Miscellaneous Retail Stores Nec.

★ 61270 ★   CSF Holdings
1221 Brickell Ave.
Miami, FL 33131
(305)979-6600
Company Type: Headquarters. **Officer:** Charles B. Stuzin. **Employee Count:** 719. **Fortune Service 500:** Ranking 21.

★ 61271 ★   CSF Holdings, Inc.
1221 Brickell Ave.
Miami, FL 33131-3012
(305)979-6600 **Fax:** (305)978-5436
Location Type: Branch office. **Officer:** Charles Stuzin, President, Chairman, & CEO. **Ultimate Parent:** CSF Holdings. **SIC:** 6021—National Commercial Banks.

★ 61272 ★   Delta Air Lines
345 Minola Dr.
Miami, FL 33166
(305)359-1850
Ultimate Parent: Delta Air Lines, Inc.

★ 61273 ★   Delta Air Lines
Miami
Miami, FL 33159
(305)526-4700
Ultimate Parent: Delta Air Lines, Inc. **SIC:** 4212—Local Trucking Without Storage; 4513—Air Courier Services.

★ 61274 ★   Delta Air Lines
202 SE 1st St.
Miami, FL 33131
(305)448-7000
Ultimate Parent: Delta Air Lines, Inc. **SIC:** 4724—Travel Agencies.

★ 61275 ★   Delta Air Lines Inc.
Miami
Miami, FL 33159
(305)526-4700
Ultimate Parent: Delta Air Lines, Inc. **SIC:** 4212—Local Trucking Without Storage; 4513—Air Courier Services.

★ 61276 ★   Delta Air Lines Inc.
202 SE 1st St.
Miami, FL 33131
(305)448-7000
Ultimate Parent: Delta Air Lines, Inc. **SIC:** 4724—Travel Agencies.

★ 61277 ★   Delta Business Systems
799 Brickell Plz.
Miami, FL 33131
(305)758-7604
Officer: Ramzi Erdini, Manager. **Ultimate Parent:** Alco Standard Corp. **SIC:** 3663—Radio & T.V. Communications Equipment.

★ 61278 ★   Digital Equipment Corp.
18425 NW 2nd Ave.
Miami, FL 33169
(305)652-1841
Ultimate Parent: Digital Equipment Corp. **SIC:** 5046—Commercial Equipment Nec.

★ 61279 ★   Electro Mechanical Services
12302 SW 99th St.
Miami, FL 33186-2545
(305)270-0956
Officer: Edgar Sierra. **Ultimate Parent:** Ametek Inc. **SIC:** 3443—Fabricated Plate

Work—Boiler Shops; 3469—Metal Stampings Nec; 5084—Industrial Machinery & Equipment; 5087—Service Establishment Equipment.

★ 61280 ★   Federal Metals Co.
2782 NW North River Dr.
Miami, FL 33142-7025
(305)633-9054
Officer: Max Undorfer Jr. **Ultimate Parent:** Asarco. **SIC:** 5051—Metals Service Centers & Offices; 4953—Refuse Systems; 5093—Scrap & Waste Materials.

★ 61281 ★   Federated Dept Stores
6465 SW 126th St.
Miami, FL 33156
(305)577-1567
Ultimate Parent: Dillard Department Stores.

★ 61282 ★   Ferro Corp.
1020 NW 163rd Dr.
Miami, FL 33169
(305)621-1407
Ultimate Parent: Ferro Corp. **SIC:** 2221—Broadwoven Fabric Mills—Manmade.

★ 61283 ★   First Union National Bank of Florida
4995 NW. 72nd Ave.
Miami, FL 33166
(305)795-2960
Location Type: Branch office. **Ultimate Parent:** First Union Corp. **SIC:** 6021—National Commercial Banks.

★ 61284 ★   First Union National Bank of Florida
18601 NW 27th Ave.
Miami, FL 33056-3192
(305)623-4300
Location Type: Branch office. **Ultimate Parent:** First Union Corp. **SIC:** 6021—National Commercial Banks.

★ 61285 ★   First Union National Bank of Florida
One First Union Financial Ctr.
Miami, FL 33131
(305)375-7594
Location Type: Branch office. **Ultimate Parent:** Barnett Bank of Alachua County, NA. **SIC:** 6021—National Commercial Banks.

★ 61286 ★   First Union National Bank of Florida
5880 Bird Rd.
Miami, FL 33155
(305)663-6167
Location Type: Branch office. **Ultimate Parent:** First Union Corp. **SIC:** 6021—National Commercial Banks.

★ 61287 ★   First Union National Bank of Florida
8201 NW 36th St.
Miami, FL 33166-6679
(305)597-5800
Location Type: Branch office. **Ultimate Parent:** First Union Corp. **SIC:** 6021—National Commercial Banks.

★ 61288 ★   First Union National Bank of Florida
10781 W. Flagler St.
Miami, FL 33174-1400
(305)229-2030
Location Type: Branch office. **Ultimate Parent:** First Union Corp. **SIC:** 6021—National Commercial Banks.

★ 61289 ★   First Union National Bank of Florida
8390 NW 27th Ave.
Miami, FL 33147-4151
(305)795-2811
Location Type: Branch office. **Ultimate Parent:** First Union Corp. **SIC:** 6021—National Commercial Banks.

★ 61290 ★   First Union National Bank of Florida
12200 SW 8th St.
Miami, FL 33184-1599
(305)229-2050
Location Type: Branch office. **Ultimate Parent:** First Union Corp. **SIC:** 6021—National Commercial Banks.

★ 61291 ★   First Union National Bank of Florida
6707 NW 186M St.
Miami, FL 33015-3395
(305)623-4360
Location Type: Branch office. **Ultimate Parent:** First Union Corp. **SIC:** 6021—National Commercial Banks.

★ 61292 ★   First Union National Bank of Florida
7100 N. Kendall Dr.
Miami, FL 33156-7839
(305)663-2200
Location Type: Branch office. **Ultimate Parent:** First Union Corp. **SIC:** 6021—National Commercial Banks.

★ 61293 ★   First Union National Bank of Florida
14801 SW Dixie Hwy.
Miami, FL 33176-7989
(305)253-9900
Location Type: Branch office. **Ultimate Parent:** First Union Corp. **SIC:** 6021—National Commercial Banks.

★ 61294 ★   First Union National Bank of Florida
10815 Sunset Dr.
Miami, FL 33173-2797
(305)595-4334
Location Type: Branch office. **Ultimate Parent:** First Union Corp. **SIC:** 6021—National Commercial Banks.

★ 61295 ★   First Union National Bank of Florida
5620 SW 137th Ave.
Miami, FL 33183-1102
(305)387-7505
Location Type: Branch office. **Ultimate Parent:** First Union Corp. **SIC:** 6021—National Commercial Banks.

★ 61296 ★   First Union National Bank of Florida
1699 Coral Way
Miami, FL 33145-2895
(305)285-3000
Location Type: Branch office. **Ultimate Parent:** First Union Corp. **SIC:** 6021—National Commercial Banks.

★ 61297 ★   First Union National Bank of Florida
10651 N. Kendall Dr.
Miami, FL 33176-1539
(305)229-2040
Location Type: Branch office. **Ultimate Parent:** First Union Corp. **SIC:** 6021—National Commercial Banks.

★ 61298 ★   First Union National Bank of Florida
627 SW 27th Ave.
Miami, FL 33135-2993
(305)789-3880
Location Type: Branch office. **Ultimate Parent:** First Union Corp. **SIC:** 6021—National Commercial Banks.

★ 61299 ★   First Union National Bank of Florida
2665 S. Bayshore Dr.
Miami, FL 33133-5401
(305)460-6065
Location Type: Branch office. **Ultimate Parent:** First Union Corp. **SIC:** 6021—National Commercial Banks.

★ 61300 ★   First Union National Bank of Florida
13700 N. Kendall Dr.
Miami, FL 33186-1392
(305)263-1060
Location Type: Branch office. **Ultimate Parent:** First Union Corp. **SIC:** 6021—National Commercial Banks.

★ 61301 ★   First Union National Bank of Florida
8701 Bird Rd.
Miami, FL 33165-5407
(305)229-2060
Location Type: Branch office. **Ultimate Parent:** First Union Corp. **SIC:** 6021—National Commercial Banks.

★ 61302 ★   First Union National Bank of Florida
100 E. Flager St.
Miami, FL 33131
(305)789-6840
Location Type: Branch office. **Ultimate Parent:** First Union Corp. **SIC:** 6021—National Commercial Banks.

★ 61303 ★   First Union National Bank of Florida
8686 Coral Way
Miami, FL 33155
(305)229-2000
Location Type: Branch office. **Ultimate Parent:** First Union Corp. **SIC:** 6021—National Commercial Banks.

★ 61304 ★   First Union National Bank of Florida
7200 NW 19th St.
Miami, FL 33126-1211
(305)594-0744
Location Type: Branch office. **Ultimate Parent:** First Union Corp. **SIC:** 6021—National Commercial Banks.

★ 61305 ★   First Union National Bank of Florida
11115 SW 132nd Ave.
Miami, FL 33186
(305)229-2000
Location Type: Branch office. **Ultimate Parent:** First Union Corp. **SIC:** 6021—National Commercial Banks.

★ 61306 ★   First Union National Bank of Florida
169 SW 8th St.
Miami, FL 33130
(305)229-2000
Location Type: Branch office. **Ultimate Parent:** First Union Corp. **SIC:** 6021—National Commercial Banks.

★ 61307 ★   First Union National Bank of Florida
11401 SW 40th St.
Miami, FL 33165-3338
(305)263-1133
Location Type: Branch office. **Ultimate Parent:** First Union Corp. **SIC:** 6021—National Commercial Banks.

★ 61308 ★   First Union National Bank of Florida
800 Brickell Ave.
Miami, FL 33131-2914
(305)789-3900
Location Type: Branch office. **Ultimate Parent:** First Union Corp. **SIC:** 6021—National Commercial Banks.

★ 61309 ★   First Union National Bank of Florida
9301 NW 7th Ave.
Miami, FL 33150-2093
(305)795-2800
Location Type: Branch office. **Ultimate Parent:** First Union Corp. **SIC:** 6021—National Commercial Banks.

★ 61310 ★   First Union National Bank of Florida
8601 S. Dixie Hwy.
Miami, FL 33143-7828
(305)663-6114
Location Type: Branch office. **Ultimate Parent:** First Union Corp. **SIC:** 6021—National Commercial Banks.

★ 61311 ★   Fleet Financial Group
Denrich Leasing Div.
8325 NW 53rd St., Ste. 101
Miami, FL 33166
(305)477-0390
Company Type: Subsidiary. **Ultimate Parent:** Fleet Financial Group. **SIC:** 7359—Equipment Rental & Leasing Nec.

★ 61312 ★   Flowers Baking Co.
17800 NW Miami Ct.
Miami, FL 33169
(305)652-3416
Officer: A. Craig White, President. **Ultimate Parent:** Flowers Industries. **SIC:** 2051—Bread, Cake & Related Products.

★ 61313 ★ Flowers Baking Co. of Miami Inc.
17800 NE Miami Ct.
PO Box 693483
Miami, FL 33269-0483
(305)652-3416 Fax: (305)770-1886
Company Type: Subsidiary. Officer: Craig White, President. Ultimate Parent: Flowers Industries.

★ 61314 ★ Foster Production Corp.
11333 S. Dixie Hwy.
Miami, FL 33156
(305)661-1264
Ultimate Parent: H. B. Fuller. SIC: 5712—Furniture Stores.

★ 61315 ★ The Gap
20505 S. Dixie Hwy.
Miami, FL 33189
(305)253-2640
Ultimate Parent: GAP. SIC: 5699—Miscellaneous Apparel & Accessory Stores.

★ 61316 ★ Garrett Airlines Service
8410 NW 53rd Ter.
Miami, FL 33166
(305)591-8547
Ultimate Parent: Allied-Signal Inc. SIC: 5088—Transportation Equipment & Supplies.

★ 61317 ★ Georgia Pacific Corp.
3201 NW 110th St.
Miami, FL 33167
(305)688-6603
Officer: Jim Knight, Manager. Ultimate Parent: Georgia-Pacific. SIC: 3275—Gypsum Products.

★ 61318 ★ Greyhound Bus Lines
17344 Perrine Ave.
Miami, FL 33157
(305)251-2459
Ultimate Parent: Greyhound Lines Inc. SIC: 4111—Local & Suburban Transit.

★ 61319 ★ Greyhound Bus Lines
2300 Salzedo St.
Miami, FL 33134
(305)443-1664
Ultimate Parent: Greyhound Lines Inc. SIC: 4212—Local Trucking Without Storage.

★ 61320 ★ Greyhound Bus Lines
1622 Collins Ave.
Miami, FL 33139
(305)538-0381
Ultimate Parent: Greyhound Lines Inc. SIC: 4111—Local & Suburban Transit.

★ 61321 ★ Greyhound Bus Lines
950 NE 2nd Ave.
Miami, FL 33132
(305)374-7222
Ultimate Parent: Greyhound Lines Inc. SIC: 4131—Intercity & Rural Bus Transportation.

★ 61322 ★ Greyhound Bus Lines
100 Biscayne Blvd.
Miami, FL 33132
(305)377-0744
Ultimate Parent: Greyhound Lines Inc. SIC: 4131—Intercity & Rural Bus Transportation.

★ 61323 ★ Greyhound Bus Lines
16250 Biscayne Blvd.
Miami, FL 33160
(305)945-0801
Ultimate Parent: Greyhound Lines Inc. SIC: 4131—Intercity & Rural Bus Transportation.

★ 61324 ★ Harris Space Systems
4801 NW 37th Ave.
Miami, FL 33142
(305)633-5733
Ultimate Parent: Harris. SIC: 5599—Automotive Dealers Nec.

★ 61325 ★ Hercules
Simmonds Precision Products Division
8075 NW 53rd St.
Miami, FL 33166
(305)593-1801
Ultimate Parent: Hercules. SIC: 7629—Electrical Repair Shops Nec.

★ 61326 ★ Hertz Rent-A-Car
944 Biscayne Blvd.
Miami, FL 33132
(305)377-4601
Ultimate Parent: Hertz. SIC: 7514—Passenger Car Rental.

★ 61327 ★ Hertz Rent Car
350 Ocean Dr.
Miami, FL 33149
(305)361-8225
Ultimate Parent: Hertz. SIC: 7514—Passenger Car Rental.

★ 61328 ★ Hertz Rent Car
638 Crandon Blvd.
Miami, FL 33149
(305)361-1054
Ultimate Parent: Hertz. SIC: 7514—Passenger Car Rental.

★ 61329 ★ Hit or Miss
7795 W. Flagler St.
Miami, FL 33144
(305)262-4755
Ultimate Parent: TJX. SIC: 5621—Women's Clothing Stores.

★ 61330 ★ Hit or Miss
1205 NE 163rd St.
Miami, FL 33162
(305)945-9422
Ultimate Parent: TJX. SIC: 5621—Women's Clothing Stores.

★ 61331 ★ Howard Industries Inc.
8130 NW 74th Ave.
Miami, FL 33166-7402
(305)888-1521
Officer: Marvin J. Zuckerman, President. Ultimate Parent: Collins & Aikman Group. SIC: 3442—Metal Doors, Sash & Trim. Employee Count: 140. Sales: 9.4 M.

★ 61332 ★ IDS Financial Services Inc.
9485 Sunset Dr.
Miami, FL 33173-3214
(305)271-3201
Ultimate Parent: American Express Co. SIC: 6211—Security Brokers & Dealers; 6282—Investment Advice.

★ 61333 ★ Israel Discount Bank Ltd
14 NE 1st Ave.
Miami, FL 33132
(305)579-9200
Ultimate Parent: Israel Discount Bank. SIC: 6099—Functions Related to Deposit Banking.

★ 61334 ★ IVAX
8800 NW 36th St.
Miami, FL 33178
(305)590-2200
Company Type: Headquarters. Officer: Phillip Frost. Sales: 645.3 M. Fortune 500: Largest U.S. Industrial Corporations: Ranking 483.

★ 61335 ★ Jiffy Lube
3841 Bird Rd.
Miami, FL 33146
(305)444-8214
Ultimate Parent: Pennzoil. SIC: 7538—General Automotive Repair Shops.

★ 61336 ★ Jiffy Lube Miami Shores
8787 Biscayne Blvd.
Miami, FL 33138
(305)756-0300
Ultimate Parent: Pennzoil. SIC: 7538—General Automotive Repair Shops.

★ 61337 ★ Kay Bee Toy&Hobby Shop
1603 NW 107th Ave.
Miami, FL 33172
(305)594-3630
Ultimate Parent: Melville. SIC: 5945—Hobby, Toy & Game Shops.

★ 61338 ★ Kay Bee Toy&Hobby Shop
1421 NE 163rd St.
Miami, FL 33162
(305)947-4418
Ultimate Parent: Melville. SIC: 5945—Hobby, Toy & Game Shops.

★ 61339 ★ Kentucky Fried Chicken
8760 SW 24th St.
Miami, FL 33165
(305)226-6132
Ultimate Parent: Pepsico. SIC: 5812—Eating Places.

★ 61340 ★ Kentucky Fried Chicken
5915 SW 8th St.
Miami, FL 33144
(305)264-1485
Ultimate Parent: Pepsico. SIC: 5812—Eating Places.

★ 61341 ★ Kentucky Fried Chicken
16851 S. Dixie Hwy.
Miami, FL 33157
(305)251-6142
Ultimate Parent: Pepsico. SIC: 5812—Eating Places.

★ 61342 ★ Kentucky Fried Chicken
3595 SW 22nd St.
Miami, FL 33145
(305)446-7928
Ultimate Parent: Pepsico. SIC: 5812—Eating Places.

★ 61343 ★ Kentucky Fried Chicken
2220 NW 36th St.
Miami, FL 33142
(305)638-1364
Ultimate Parent: Pepsico. SIC: 5812—Eating Places.

★ 61344 ★ Kentucky Fried Chicken
441 NW 84th St.
Miami, FL 33150
(305)835-0516
Ultimate Parent: Pepsico. SIC: 5812—Eating Places.

★ 61345 ★ Kentucky Fried Chicken
100 Crandon Blvd.
Miami, FL 33149
(305)361-1704
Ultimate Parent: Pepsico. SIC: 5812—Eating Places.

★ 61346 ★ Kentucky Fried Chicken
16200 NE Miami Garden Dr.
Miami, FL 33160
(305)947-7056
Ultimate Parent: Pepsico. SIC: 5812—Eating Places.

★ 61347 ★ Kentucky Fried Chicken
11725 S. Dixie Hwy.
Miami, FL 33156
(305)238-3401
Ultimate Parent: Pepsico. SIC: 5812—Eating Places.

★ 61348 ★ Kentucky Fried Chicken
20500 S. Dixie Hwy.
Miami, FL 33189
(305)235-1724
Ultimate Parent: Pepsico. SIC: 5812—Eating Places.

★ 61349 ★ Kentucky Fried Chicken
1990 NE 123rd St.
Miami, FL 33181
(305)891-3523
Ultimate Parent: Pepsico. SIC: 5812—Eating Places.

★ 61350 ★ Kentucky Fried Chicken
1190 NW 62nd St.
Miami, FL 33150
(305)751-5389
Ultimate Parent: Pepsico. SIC: 5812—Eating Places.

★ 61351 ★ Kentucky Fried Chicken
8791 Bird Rd.
Miami, FL 33165
(305)266-6111
Ultimate Parent: Pepsico. SIC: 5812—Eating Places.

★ 61352 ★ Knight-Ridder
1 Herald Plz.
Miami, FL 33132
(305)376-3800
Company Type: Headquarters. Officer: James K. Batten. Employee Count: 20420. Sales: 2451 M. Fortune 500: Largest U.S. Industrial Corporations: Ranking 190.

★ 61353 ★ Lane Bryant
7513 Dadeland Mall
Miami, FL 33156
(305)661-5313
Ultimate Parent: Limited. SIC: 5621—Women's Clothing Stores.

★ 61354 ★ Lane Bryant
1601 Biscayne Blvd.
Miami, FL 33132
(305)372-1118
Ultimate Parent: Limited. SIC: 5621—Women's Clothing Stores.

★ 61355 ★ Lane Bryant
19575 Biscayne Blvd.
Miami, FL 33180
(305)935-4280
Ultimate Parent: Limited. SIC: 5621—Women's Clothing Stores.

★ 61356 ★ Lerner Shop
7427 Dadeland Mall
Miami, FL 33156
(305)666-3475
Ultimate Parent: Limited. SIC: 5621—Women's Clothing Stores.

★ 61357 ★ Lerner Shop
30 E. Flagler St.
Miami, FL 33131
(305)374-4913
Ultimate Parent: Limited. SIC: 5621—Women's Clothing Stores.

★ 61358 ★ Lerner Shop
Biscayne
Miami, FL 33138
(305)754-8272
Ultimate Parent: Limited. SIC: 5621—Women's Clothing Stores.

★ 61359 ★ Liberty Mutual Insurance Cos
8420 NW 52nd St.
Miami, FL 33166
(305)592-0370
Ultimate Parent: Liberty Mutual Group. SIC: 6411—Insurance Agents, Brokers & Service.

★ 61360 ★ The Limited
19501 Biscayne Blvd.
Miami, FL 33180
(305)932-7356
Ultimate Parent: Limited. SIC: 5621—Women's Clothing Stores.

★ 61361 ★ The Limited
3301 Coral Way
Miami, FL 33145
(305)446-8306
Ultimate Parent: Limited. SIC: 5621—Women's Clothing Stores.

★ 61362 ★ The Limited Express
Cutler Ridge Shopping
Miami, FL 33189
(305)235-2867
Ultimate Parent: Limited. SIC: 5621—Women's Clothing Stores.

★ 61363 ★ Long Mile Rubber Co.
3760 NW 54 St.
Miami, FL 33142
Ultimate Parent: Goodyear Tire & Rubber. SIC: 3011—Tires & Inner Tubes.

★ 61364 ★ Maison Blanche
Aventura
Miami, FL 33180
(305)935-3376
Ultimate Parent: Mercantile Stores. SIC: 5632—Women's Accessory & Specialty Stores.

★ 61365 ★ Marshalls Inc.
13619 S. Dixie Hwy.
Miami, FL 33176
(305)253-3962
Ultimate Parent: Melville. SIC: 5311—Department Stores.

★ 61366 ★ Mary Kay Cosmetics
500 W. Park Dr.
Miami, FL 33172
(305)559-5444
Ultimate Parent: Mary Kay Cosmetics.

★ 61367 ★ Mary Kay Cosmetics
135 SW 114th Ave.
Miami, FL 33174
(305)554-6662
Ultimate Parent: Mary Kay Cosmetics. SIC: 5999—Miscellaneous Retail Stores Nec.

★ 61368 ★ **Mary Kay Cosmetics**
8370 W. Flagler St.
Miami, FL 33144
(305)559-5444
Ultimate Parent: Mary Kay Cosmetics. **SIC:** 5999—Miscellaneous Retail Stores Nec.

★ 61369 ★ **Mary Kay Cosmetics**
8570 SW 124th St.
Miami, FL 33156
(305)233-1386
Ultimate Parent: Mary Kay Cosmetics. **SIC:** 5999—Miscellaneous Retail Stores Nec.

★ 61370 ★ **McArthur Dairy, Inc.**
6851 NE 2nd Ave.
Miami, FL 33138-5503
Ultimate Parent: Dean Foods. **SIC:** 2026—Fluid Milk.

★ 61371 ★ **McDonalds Restaurant**
7901 Bird Rd.
Miami, FL 33155
(305)264-1244
Ultimate Parent: McDonald's. **SIC:** 5812—Eating Places.

★ 61372 ★ **McDonalds Restaurant**
100 S. Miami Ave.
Miami, FL 33130
(305)358-0300
Ultimate Parent: McDonald's. **SIC:** 5812—Eating Places.

★ 61373 ★ **McDonald's Restaurants**
3200 S. Dixie Hwy.
Miami, FL 33133
(305)448-0531
Ultimate Parent: McDonald's. **SIC:** 5812—Eating Places.

★ 61374 ★ **McDonalds Restaurants**
9850 SW 8th St.
Miami, FL 33174
(305)223-8687
Ultimate Parent: McDonald's. **SIC:** 5812—Eating Places.

★ 61375 ★ **Mellon Financial Service Corp.**
10417 SW 40th St.
Miami, FL 33165
(305)221-6070
Ultimate Parent: Mellon Bank Corp. **SIC:** 6141—Personal Credit Institutions.

★ 61376 ★ **Mellon Financial Services Corp.**
839 NW 119th St.
Miami, FL 33168
(305)556-2090
Ultimate Parent: Mellon Bank Corp. **SIC:** 6162—Mortgage Bankers & Correspondents.

★ 61377 ★ **Merisel Latin America**
2010 NW 84th Ave.
Miami, FL 33122
(305)591-6803 **Fax:** (305)599-7015
Officer: Cliff Dyer, President. **Ultimate Parent:** Merisel.

★ 61378 ★ **Miami Elevator Co.**
7481 NW 66th St.
Miami, FL 33168
(305)592-7722
Officer: Bob Rogers, Vice President. **Ultimate Parent:** Dover Corp. **SIC:** 3534—Elevators & Moving Stairways.

★ 61379 ★ **Miami Elevator Co. Inc.**
7481 NW 66th St.
Miami, FL 33166-2801
(305)592-7723
Company Type: Subsidiary. **Ultimate Parent:** Dover Corp. **SIC:** 5084—Industrial Machinery & Equipment.

★ 61380 ★ **Mini Mart Edwards Amoco**
1698 NW 79th St.
Miami, FL 33147
(305)693-8250
Ultimate Parent: Amoco Corp. **SIC:** 5541—Gasoline Service Stations.

★ 61381 ★ **New England Mutual Life Insurance**
10300 Sunset Dr.
Miami, FL 33173
(305)598-1177
Ultimate Parent: New England Mutual Life. **SIC:** 6411—Insurance Agents, Brokers & Service.

★ 61382 ★ **Northwest Airlines Inc.**
Miami
Miami, FL 33159
(305)526-4020
Ultimate Parent: NWA. **SIC:** 4512—Air Transportation—Scheduled.

★ 61383 ★ **Northwest Airlines Inc.**
325 SE 1st St.
Miami, FL 33131
(305)377-0311
Ultimate Parent: NWA. **SIC:** 4724—Travel Agencies.

★ 61384 ★ **Otis Elevator Co.**
1151 NW 159th Dr.
Miami, FL 33169
(305)621-0899
Ultimate Parent: United Technologies. **SIC:** 1796—Installing Building Equipment Nec.

★ 61385 ★ **Otis Elevator Co.**
1330 NE 1st Ct
Miami, FL 33132
(305)373-7303
Ultimate Parent: United Technologies. **SIC:** 1796—Installing Building Equipment Nec.

★ 61386 ★ **Pappagallo**
2338 E. Sunrise Blvd.
Miami, FL 33133
(305)945-7450
Ultimate Parent: United States Shoe. **SIC:** 5621—Women's Clothing Stores.

★ 61387 ★ **Pappagallo**
Dadeland Mall
Miami, FL 33156
(305)666-7915
Ultimate Parent: United States Shoe. **SIC:** 5661—Shoe Stores.

★ 61388 ★ **Pepsi-Cola Bottlers of Miami**
7777 NW 41st St.
Miami, FL 33166
(305)592-1980
Officer: A. David Velez, Manager. **Ultimate Parent:** Pepsico. **SIC:** 2086—Bottled & Canned Soft Drinks.

★ 61389 ★ **Petite Sophisticate**
1601 Biscayne Blvd.
Miami, FL 33132
(305)375-0882
Ultimate Parent: United States Shoe. **SIC:** 5621—Women's Clothing Stores.

★ 61390 ★ **Piggly Wiggly**
3400 NW 74th Ave.
Miami, FL 33122
(305)299-0061
Ultimate Parent: Bruno's. **SIC:** 5411—Grocery Stores.

★ 61391 ★ **Pizza Hut**
10795 SW 72nd St.
Miami, FL 33173
(305)274-6690
Ultimate Parent: Pepsico. **SIC:** 5812—Eating Places.

★ 61392 ★ **Pizza Hut**
10600 SW 8th St.
Miami, FL 33174
(305)554-7020
Ultimate Parent: Pepsico. **SIC:** 5812—Eating Places.

★ 61393 ★ **Pizza Hut**
5731 NW 36th St.
Miami, FL 33166
(305)871-3179
Ultimate Parent: Pepsico. **SIC:** 5812—Eating Places.

★ 61394 ★ **Pizza Hut**
15900 SW 104th Ct
Miami, FL 33157
Ultimate Parent: Pepsico. **SIC:** 5812—Eating Places.

★ 61395 ★ **Pizza Hut**
8900 Biscayne Blvd.
Miami, FL 33138
(305)754-3366
Ultimate Parent: Pepsico. **SIC:** 5812—Eating Places.

★ 61396 ★ **Pizza Hut**
13185 Biscayne Blvd.
Miami, FL 33181
(305)893-1349
Ultimate Parent: Pepsico. **SIC:** 5812—Eating Places.

★ 61397 ★ **Pizza Hut**
18285 NW 68th Ave.
Miami, FL 33166
(305)556-5027
Ultimate Parent: Pepsico. **SIC:** 5812—Eating Places.

★ 61398 ★ **Pizza Hut**
2882 NW 79th Ave.
Miami, FL 33122
(305)670-3054
Ultimate Parent: Pepsico. **SIC:** 5812—Eating Places.

★ 61399 ★ **Pizza Hut**
475 S. Dixie Hwy.
Miami, FL 33146
(305)666-6977
Ultimate Parent: Pepsico. **SIC:** 5812—Eating Places.

★ 61400 ★ **Polaroid Corp.**
2655 N. Le Jeune Rd.
Miami, FL 33142
(305)445-5200
Ultimate Parent: Polaroid. **SIC:** 5043—Photographic Equipment & Supplies.

★ 61401 ★ **Publix Super Market**
2270 SW 27th Ave.
Miami, FL 33145
(305)445-9661
Ultimate Parent: Publix Super Markets. **SIC:** 5411—Grocery Stores.

★ 61402 ★ **Publix Super Market**
3801 W. Flagler St.
Miami, FL 33134
(305)649-2626
Ultimate Parent: Publix Super Markets. **SIC:** 5411—Grocery Stores.

★ 61403 ★ **Publix Super Market**
9041 SW 107th Ave.
Miami, FL 33176
(305)271-5941
Ultimate Parent: Publix Super Markets. **SIC:** 5411—Grocery Stores.

★ 61404 ★ **Publix Super Market**
8680 SW 24th St.
Miami, FL 33155
(305)221-8051
Ultimate Parent: Publix Super Markets. **SIC:** 5411—Grocery Stores.

★ 61405 ★ **Publix Super Market**
19820 NW 2nd Ave.
Miami, FL 33169
(305)652-6070
Ultimate Parent: Publix Super Markets. **SIC:** 5411—Grocery Stores.

★ 61406 ★ **Publix Super Market**
18485 S. Dixie Hwy.
Miami, FL 33157
Ultimate Parent: Publix Super Markets. **SIC:** 5411—Grocery Stores.

★ 61407 ★ **Publix Super Market**
6876 Collins Ave.
Miami, FL 33141
(305)868-4065
Ultimate Parent: Publix Super Markets. **SIC:** 5461—Retail Bakeries.

★ 61408 ★ **Publix Super Market**
693430 PO Box
Miami, FL 33269
(305)689-0310
Ultimate Parent: Publix Super Markets. **SIC:** 5411—Grocery Stores.

★ 61409 ★ **Publix Super Market**
13820 SW 88th St.
Miami, FL 33186
(305)385-0203
Ultimate Parent: Publix Super Markets. **SIC:** 5461—Retail Bakeries.

★ 61410 ★ **Publix Super Market**
9050 Biscayne Blvd.
Miami, FL 33138
(305)758-3849
Ultimate Parent: Publix Super Markets. **SIC:** 5411—Grocery Stores.

★ 61411 ★ **Publix Super Market**
18485 S. Dixie Hwy. D-Plza
Miami, FL 33157
Ultimate Parent: Publix Super Markets. **SIC:** 5411—Grocery Stores; 5731—Radio, Television & Electronics Stores.

★ 61412 ★ **Publix Super Market**
2952 Aventura Blvd.
Miami, FL 33180
(305)931-4810
Ultimate Parent: Publix Super Markets. **SIC:** 5411—Grocery Stores.

★ 61413 ★ **Publix Super Markets**
19820 NW 2nd Ave.
Miami, FL 33169
(305)652-6070
Ultimate Parent: Publix Super Markets. **SIC:** 5411—Grocery Stores.

★ 61414 ★ **Publix Super Markets**
9041 SW 107th Ave.
Miami, FL 33176
(305)271-5941
Ultimate Parent: Publix Super Markets. **SIC:** 5411—Grocery Stores.

★ 61415 ★ **Publix Super Markets**
8680 SW 24th St.
Miami, FL 33155
(305)221-8051
Ultimate Parent: Publix Super Markets. **SIC:** 5411—Grocery Stores.

★ 61416 ★ **Publix Super Markets**
18485 S. Dixie Hwy.
Miami, FL 33157
Ultimate Parent: Publix Super Markets. **SIC:** 5411—Grocery Stores.

★ 61417 ★ **Publix Super Markets**
6876 Collins Ave.
Miami, FL 33141
(305)868-4065
Ultimate Parent: Publix Super Markets. **SIC:** 5461—Retail Bakeries.

★ 61418 ★ **Publix Super Markets**
2270 SW 27th Ave.
Miami, FL 33145
(305)445-9661
Ultimate Parent: Publix Super Markets. **SIC:** 5411—Grocery Stores.

★ 61419 ★ **Publix Super Markets**
3801 W. Flagler St.
Miami, FL 33134
(305)649-2626
Ultimate Parent: Publix Super Markets. **SIC:** 5411—Grocery Stores.

★ 61420 ★ **Radio Shack**
1610 Washington Ave.
Miami, FL 33139
(305)673-8703
Company Type: Division. **Ultimate Parent:** Tandy Corp. **SIC:** 5065—Electronic Parts & Equipment Nec.

★ 61421 ★ **Radio Shack**
19211 SW 118th Ct
Miami, FL 33177
(305)254-3343
Company Type: Division. **Ultimate Parent:** Tandy Corp.

★ 61422 ★ **Radio Shack**
10811 SW 78th Ave.
Miami, FL 33156
Company Type: Division. **Ultimate Parent:** Tandy Corp. **SIC:** 5046—Commercial Equipment Nec.

★ 61423 ★ **Radio Shack**
1250 S. Dixie Hwy.
Miami, FL 33146
(305)666-2016
Company Type: Division. **Ultimate Parent:** Tandy Corp. **SIC:** 5734—Computer & Software Stores.

★ 61424 ★   Radio Shack
20761 S. Dixie Hwy.
Miami, FL 33189
(305)238-2518
Company Type: Division. **Ultimate Parent:** Tandy Corp. **SIC:** 5046—Commercial Equipment Nec.

★ 61425 ★   Radio Shack
135 Miracle Mile
Miami, FL 33134
(305)445-6064
Company Type: Division. **Ultimate Parent:** Tandy Corp. **SIC:** 5734—Computer & Software Stores.

★ 61426 ★   Radio Shack
1455 NW 107th Ave.
Miami, FL 33172
(305)594-0804
Company Type: Division. **Ultimate Parent:** Tandy Corp. **SIC:** 5065—Electronic Parts & Equipment Nec.

★ 61427 ★   Radio Shack
8680 Bird Rd.
Miami, FL 33155
(305)552-6497
Company Type: Division. **Ultimate Parent:** Tandy Corp. **SIC:** 5734—Computer & Software Stores.

★ 61428 ★   Radio Shack
1601 Biscayne Blvd.
Miami, FL 33132
(305)374-6433
Company Type: Division. **Ultimate Parent:** Tandy Corp. **SIC:** 5065—Electronic Parts & Equipment Nec.

★ 61429 ★   Radio Shack
15 SE 2nd Ave.
Miami, FL 33131
(305)374-7304
Company Type: Division. **Ultimate Parent:** Tandy Corp. **SIC:** 5065—Electronic Parts & Equipment Nec.

★ 61430 ★   Radio Shack
8020 NW 5th Ave.
Miami, FL 33150
(305)758-7491
Company Type: Division. **Ultimate Parent:** Tandy Corp. **SIC:** 5065—Electronic Parts & Equipment Nec.

★ 61431 ★   Radio Shack
5763 NW 7th Ave.
Miami, FL 33127
(305)261-5437
Company Type: Division. **Ultimate Parent:** Tandy Corp. **SIC:** 5065—Electronic Parts & Equipment Nec.

★ 61432 ★   Radio Shack
1680 NE Miami Gardens Dr.
Miami, FL 33179
(305)949-7070
Company Type: Division. **Ultimate Parent:** Tandy Corp. **SIC:** 5731—Radio, Television & Electronics Stores.

★ 61433 ★   Radio Shack
234 NW 199th St.
Miami, FL 33169
(305)652-6939
Company Type: Division. **Ultimate Parent:** Tandy Corp. **SIC:** 5731—Radio, Television & Electronics Stores.

★ 61434 ★   Radio Shack
135 Miracle Mile
Miami, FL 33134
Company Type: Division. **Ultimate Parent:** Tandy Corp. **SIC:** 5065—Electronic Parts & Equipment Nec.

★ 61435 ★   Radio Shack
1746 NE 163rd St.
Miami, FL 33162
(305)940-2625
Company Type: Division. **Ultimate Parent:** Tandy Corp. **SIC:** 5065—Electronic Parts & Equipment Nec.

★ 61436 ★   Radio Shack
8573 Coral Way
Miami, FL 33155
(305)264-1147
Company Type: Division. **Ultimate Parent:** Tandy Corp. **SIC:** 5065—Electronic Parts & Equipment Nec.

★ 61437 ★   Radio Shack
7551 Dadeland Mall
Miami, FL 33156
(305)666-3296
Company Type: Division. **Ultimate Parent:** Tandy Corp. **SIC:** 5065—Electronic Parts & Equipment Nec.

★ 61438 ★   Radio Shack
1339 Biscayne Blvd.
Miami, FL 33132
(305)374-6727
Company Type: Division. **Ultimate Parent:** Tandy Corp. **SIC:** 5731—Radio, Television & Electronics Stores.

★ 61439 ★   Ralph Wilson Plastics Co.
1331 NW 82nd Ave.
Miami, FL 33126
(305)477-8121
Officer: Ron Zingaro, Manager. **Ultimate Parent:** Premark International. **SIC:** 3083—Laminated Plastics Plate & Sheet; 3089—Plastics Products Nec; 3553—Woodworking Machinery.

★ 61440 ★   Ralston Purina International
2801 Ponce De Leon Blvd.
Miami, FL 33134
(305)446-8621
Ultimate Parent: Ralston Purina. **SIC:** 5153—Grain & Field Beans.

★ 61441 ★   Republic New York Trust Co.
2954 Aventura Blvd.
Miami, FL 33180
(305)931-7202
Ultimate Parent: Republic New York Corp. **SIC:** 6029—Commercial Banks Nec.

★ 61442 ★   Rite Aid Discount Pharm
11721 S. Dixie Hwy.
Miami, FL 33156
(305)235-7961
Ultimate Parent: Rite Aid. **SIC:** 5912—Drug Stores & Proprietary Stores.

★ 61443 ★   Rite Aid Discount Pharmacie
744 Lincoln Rd.
Miami, FL 33139
(305)672-3511
Ultimate Parent: Rite Aid. **SIC:** 5912—Drug Stores & Proprietary Stores.

★ 61444 ★   Rite Aid Discount Pharmacie
735 NW 119th St.
Miami, FL 33168
(305)687-9658
Ultimate Parent: Rite Aid. **SIC:** 5912—Drug Stores & Proprietary Stores.

★ 61445 ★   Rite Aid Discount Pharms
998 SW 67th Ave.
Miami, FL 33144
(305)264-6848
Ultimate Parent: Rite Aid. **SIC:** 5912—Drug Stores & Proprietary Stores.

★ 61446 ★   Ryder System
3500 NW 82nd Ave.
Miami, FL 33166
(305)593-3726
Company Type: Headquarters. **Officer:** M. Anthony Burns. **Employee Count:** 37949. **Fortune Service 500:** Ranking 11.

★ 61447 ★   Ryder Systems Inc.
3600 NW 82nd Ave.
Miami, FL 33166
(305)593-3726 **Fax:** (305)593-3336
Officer: M. Anthony Burns, CEO. **Ultimate Parent:** Ryder System. **Employee Count:** 41695. **Sales:** 4217 M.

★ 61448 ★   Ryder Truck Rental
200 SW 57th Ave.
Miami, FL 33144
(305)642-6707
Ultimate Parent: Ryder System. **SIC:** 7389—Business Services Nec.

★ 61449 ★   Ryder Truck Rental
3600 NW 82nd Ave.
Miami, FL 33166
(305)593-3066
Ultimate Parent: Ryder System. **SIC:** 7513—Truck Rental & Leasing Without Drivers.

★ 61450 ★   Ryder Truck Rental
18494 S. Dixie Hwy.
Miami, FL 33157
(305)233-8092
Ultimate Parent: Ryder System. **SIC:** 7389—Business Services Nec.

★ 61451 ★   Ryder Truck Rental
6789 Biscayne Blvd.
Miami, FL 33138
(305)754-7128
Ultimate Parent: Ryder System. **SIC:** 7389—Business Services Nec.

★ 61452 ★   Ryder Truck Rental
7227 NW 74th Ave.
Miami, FL 33166
(305)884-3440
Ultimate Parent: Ryder System. **SIC:** 4214—Local Trucking With Storage.

★ 61453 ★   Ryder Truck Rental
3001 NW 87th Ave.
Miami, FL 33172
(305)592-8021
Ultimate Parent: Ryder System. **SIC:** 7359—Equipment Rental & Leasing Nec.

★ 61454 ★   Ryder Truck Rental
12380 SW 8th St.
Miami, FL 33184
(305)220-1771
Ultimate Parent: Ryder System. **SIC:** 7513—Truck Rental & Leasing Without Drivers.

★ 61455 ★   Ryder Truck Rental
10601 S. Dixie Hwy.
Miami, FL 33156
(305)665-6411
Ultimate Parent: Ryder System. **SIC:** 7538—General Automotive Repair Shops.

★ 61456 ★   Saxon Paper-Florida
1867 N.W. 72nd Ave.
Miami, FL 33126
(305)592-6650
Company Type: Division. **Ultimate Parent:** Alco Standard Corp. **SIC:** 5111—Printing & Writing Paper.

★ 61457 ★   Schering Lab
13900 SW 57th Ln.
Miami, FL 33183
(305)760-9113
Ultimate Parent: Schering-Plough Corp. **SIC:** 5199—Nondurable Goods Nec.

★ 61458 ★   Service Merchandise
16051 S. Dixie Hwy.
Miami, FL 33157
(305)255-0020
Ultimate Parent: Service Merchandise Co., Inc. **SIC:** 5961—Catalog & Mail-Order Houses.

★ 61459 ★   Service Merchandise
2424 S. Dixie Hwy.
Miami, FL 33133
(305)856-2612
Ultimate Parent: Service Merchandise Co., Inc. **SIC:** 7389—Business Services Nec.

★ 61460 ★   Shell Co.
7895 W. Flagler St.
Miami, FL 33144
(305)264-9787
Ultimate Parent: Shell Oil Co. **SIC:** 5541—Gasoline Service Stations.

★ 61461 ★   Simmonds Precision Products
6405 NW 36th St.
Miami, FL 33166
(305)871-5560
Ultimate Parent: Hercules. **SIC:** 7629—Electrical Repair Shops Nec.

★ 61462 ★   Smith Barney Harris Upham & Co.
20801 Biscayne Blvd.
Miami, FL 33180-1430
(305)932-4250
Company Type: Branch. **Officer:** Henry T. Tramazzo. **Ultimate Parent:** Automatic Data Processing, Inc. **SIC:** 6211—Security Brokers & Dealers.

★ 61463 ★   Smith Barney Harris Upham & Co.
1 SE 3rd Ave.
Miami, FL 33131-1704
(305)358-7750
Company Type: Branch. **Officer:** Jay Spieler. **Ultimate Parent:** Automatic Data Processing, Inc. **SIC:** 6211—Security Brokers & Dealers; 6221—Commodity Contracts Brokers & Dealers.

★ 61464 ★   Specialty Products of America
9112 NW 105th Way
Miami, FL 33178-1222
(305)885-6236
Ultimate Parent: Avery Dennison Corp. **SIC:** 2842—Polishes & Sanitation Goods.

★ 61465 ★   Sports Authority
11910 N. Kendall Dr.
Miami, FL 33186
(305)270-9762
Ultimate Parent: K-Mart. **SIC:** 5999—Miscellaneous Retail Stores Nec.

★ 61466 ★   Star Market Inc.
1541 Washington Ave.
Miami, FL 33139
(305)672-0166
Ultimate Parent: American Stores. **SIC:** 5411—Grocery Stores.

★ 61467 ★   System Devices & Supplies Inc.
9500 N.W. 41st St.
Miami, FL 33178
Company Type: Subsidiary. **Officer:** Lawrence Court, President. **Ultimate Parent:** Alco Standard Corp. **SIC:** 5044—Office Equipment; 7359—Equipment Rental & Leasing Nec.

★ 61468 ★   T J Maxx
7200 SW 117th Ave.
Miami, FL 33183
(305)271-1443
Ultimate Parent: TJX. **SIC:** 5311—Department Stores.

★ 61469 ★   Taco Bell
6740 SW 8th St.
Miami, FL 33144
(305)261-4772
Ultimate Parent: Pepsico. **SIC:** 5812—Eating Places.

★ 61470 ★   Taco Bell
3595 Biscayne Blvd.
Miami, FL 33137
(305)576-5832
Ultimate Parent: Pepsico. **SIC:** 5812—Eating Places.

★ 61471 ★   Taco Bell
710 NW 37th Ave.
Miami, FL 33125
(305)541-8767
Ultimate Parent: Pepsico. **SIC:** 5812—Eating Places.

★ 61472 ★   Tandy Corp.
2757 W. Flagler St.
Miami, FL 33135
(305)642-6110
Ultimate Parent: Tandy Corp. **SIC:** 5199—Nondurable Goods Nec.

★ 61473 ★   Tektronix Inc.
2745 NW 62nd St.
Miami, FL 33147
(305)947-6053
Ultimate Parent: Tektronix, Inc. **SIC:** 5065—Electronic Parts & Equipment Nec.

★ 61474 ★   Ten Minute Oil Change
17225 S. Dixie Hwy.
Miami, FL 33157
(305)233-7180
Ultimate Parent: Pennzoil. **SIC:** 7538—General Automotive Repair Shops.

★ 61475 ★   Texaco Latin Amer W African
2121 Ponce De Leon Blvd.
Miami, FL 33134
(305)446-2231
Ultimate Parent: Texaco. **SIC:** 5172—Petroleum Products Nec.

★ 61476 ★   This End Up Furniture
19575 Biscayne Blvd.
Miami, FL 33180
(305)931-4027
Ultimate Parent: Melville. **SIC:** 5712—Furniture Stores.

★ 61477 ★ Thom Mcan
1453 NE 163rd St.
Miami, FL 33162
(305)940-5360
Ultimate Parent: Melville. SIC: 5661—Shoe
Stores.

★ 61478 ★ Thom Mcan Shoe
Store
Midway Mall
Miami, FL 33133
(305)261-5952
Ultimate Parent: Melville. SIC: 5699—
Miscellaneous Apparel & Accessory Stores.

★ 61479 ★ Toys R US
19525 S. Dixie Hwy.
Miami, FL 33157
(305)233-6122
Ultimate Parent: Toys "R" US. SIC: 3944—
Games, Toys & Children's Vehicles.

★ 61480 ★ Toys R US
1645 NW 107th Ave.
Miami, FL 33172
(305)593-1517
Ultimate Parent: Toys "R" US. SIC: 5641—
Children's & Infants' Wear Stores.

★ 61481 ★ Trailways Bus System
99 NE 4th St.
Miami, FL 33132
(305)371-5185
Ultimate Parent: Greyhound Lines Inc. SIC:
4212—Local Trucking Without Storage.

★ 61482 ★ Trailways Bus
Systems
4101 NW 27th Ave.
Miami, FL 33142
(305)634-6523
Ultimate Parent: Greyhound Lines Inc. SIC:
4131—Intercity & Rural Bus Transportation.

★ 61483 ★ Trane Co.
8929 Western Way
Miami, FL 33256
(305)363-6088
Ultimate Parent: American Standard. SIC:
5075—Warm Air Heating & Air-Conditioning.

★ 61484 ★ Trane Co.
7415 NW 19th St.
Miami, FL 33126
(305)522-2214
Ultimate Parent: American Standard. SIC:
5075—Warm Air Heating & Air-Conditioning.

★ 61485 ★ Travel Publications
Inc.
1 Lincoln Rd.
Miami, FL 33139
(305)531-8116
Ultimate Parent: Reader's Digest
Association. SIC: 2721—Periodicals.

★ 61486 ★ Underwriters
Adjusting Co.
5757 NW 11th St.
Miami, FL 33126
(305)261-1020
Ultimate Parent: Continental. SIC: 6411—
Insurance Agents, Brokers & Service.

★ 61487 ★ Unijax Inc.
8150 76th Ave. NW
Miami, FL 33166
(305)885-4711
Officer: Robert Bates, Manager. Ultimate
Parent: Alco Standard Corp. SIC: 2677—
Envelopes; 2759—Commercial Printing Nec.

★ 61488 ★ Unijax Inc.
8150 76th Ave. NW
Miami, FL 33166
(305)885-4711
Officer: Robert Bates, Manager. Ultimate
Parent: Alco Standard Corp. SIC: 2677—
Envelopes; 2759—Commercial Printing Nec.

★ 61489 ★ Union Oil Co. of
California
3900 NW 79th Ave.
Miami, FL 33166
(305)592-3555
Ultimate Parent: Unocal Corp. SIC: 5172—
Petroleum Products Nec.

★ 61490 ★ United Parcel Service
1395 NW 167th St.
Miami, FL 33169
(305)659-3166
Ultimate Parent: United Parcel Service of
America. SIC: 4212—Local Trucking
Without Storage.

★ 61491 ★ US Gypsum Co.
1190 NE 163rd St.
Miami, FL 33162
(305)949-3436
Ultimate Parent: USG Corp. SIC: 5039—
Construction Materials Nec.

★ 61492 ★ Victoria's Secret
401 Biscayne Blvd.
Miami, FL 33132
(305)374-8030
Ultimate Parent: Limited. SIC: 5699—
Miscellaneous Apparel & Accessory Stores.

★ 61493 ★ Waldenbooks
Miracle Mile
Miami, FL 33134
(305)448-7888
Ultimate Parent: K-Mart. SIC: 5942—Book
Stores.

★ 61494 ★ Waldenbooks
Omni International
Miami, FL 33132
(305)358-5764
Ultimate Parent: K-Mart. SIC: 5942—Book
Stores.

★ 61495 ★ Waldenbooks
Mayfair Dr.
Miami, FL 33133
(305)448-0261
Ultimate Parent: K-Mart. SIC: 5942—Book
Stores.

★ 61496 ★ Waldenbooks
Miami
Miami, FL 33126
(305)594-0703
Ultimate Parent: K-Mart. SIC: 5942—Book
Stores.

★ 61497 ★ Waldenbooks
Cutler Ridge Shopping
Miami, FL 33189
(305)252-1053
Ultimate Parent: K-Mart. SIC: 5942—Book
Stores.

★ 61498 ★ Waldenbooks
Kendale
Miami, FL 33183
(305)385-5477
Ultimate Parent: K-Mart. SIC: 5942—Book
Stores.

★ 61499 ★ Waldenbooks
Aventura
Miami, FL 33161
(305)937-1371
Ultimate Parent: K-Mart. SIC: 5199—
Nondurable Goods Nec.

★ 61500 ★ Walgreen Discount
Store
6595 NW 36th St.
Miami, FL 33166
(305)587-1444
Ultimate Parent: Walgreen Co. SIC:
6531—Real Estate Agents & Managers.

★ 61501 ★ Walgreen Drug Stores
8550 Coral Way
Miami, FL 33155
(305)221-5013
Ultimate Parent: Walgreen Co. SIC:
7389—Business Services Nec.

★ 61502 ★ Walgreen Drug Stores
11 Northside Plz.
Miami, FL 33147
(305)691-0751
Ultimate Parent: Walgreen Co. SIC:
5912—Drug Stores & Proprietary Stores.

★ 61503 ★ Walgreen Drug Stores
7941 NE 5th Ave.
Miami, FL 33138
(305)759-4441
Ultimate Parent: Walgreen Co. SIC:
7384—Photofinishing Laboratories.

★ 61504 ★ Walgreen Drug Stores
12256 SW 8th St.
Miami, FL 33184
(305)226-1616
Ultimate Parent: Walgreen Co. SIC:
5912—Drug Stores & Proprietary Stores.

★ 61505 ★ Walgreen Drug Stores
Midway
Miami, FL 33144
(305)261-2213
Ultimate Parent: Walgreen Co. SIC:
7384—Photofinishing Laboratories.

★ 61506 ★ Walgreen Drug Stores
9380 Miller Rd.
Miami, FL 33165
(305)274-3033
Ultimate Parent: Walgreen Co. SIC:
5999—Miscellaneous Retail Stores Nec.

★ 61507 ★ Walgreen Drug Stores
200 E. Flagler St.
Miami, FL 33131
(305)373-8401
Ultimate Parent: Walgreen Co. SIC:
7384—Photofinishing Laboratories.

★ 61508 ★ Walgreen Drug Stores
19923 NW 2nd Ave.
Miami, FL 33169
(305)653-7850
Ultimate Parent: Walgreen Co. SIC:
5912—Drug Stores & Proprietary Stores.

★ 61509 ★ Walgreen Drug Stores
7342 SW 117th Ave.
Miami, FL 33183
(305)595-3326
Ultimate Parent: Walgreen Co. SIC:
5912—Drug Stores & Proprietary Stores.

★ 61510 ★ Walgreen Drug Stores
12295 Biscayne Blvd.
Miami, FL 33181
(305)893-7093
Ultimate Parent: Walgreen Co. SIC:
5999—Miscellaneous Retail Stores Nec.

★ 61511 ★ Walgreen Drug Stores
1341 NE 163rd St.
Miami, FL 33162
(305)947-3513
Ultimate Parent: Walgreen Co. SIC:
5912—Drug Stores & Proprietary Stores.

★ 61512 ★ Wall Street Journal
2100 Ponce De Leon Blvd.
Miami, FL 33134
(305)448-3236
Ultimate Parent: Dow Jones. SIC: 2711—
Newspapers.

★ 61513 ★ Wall Street Journal
1190 NE 163rd St.
Miami, FL 33162
(305)947-0581
Ultimate Parent: Dow Jones. SIC: 2711—
Newspapers.

★ 61514 ★ WCIX-TV
8900 NW 18th Terrace
Miami, FL 33172
(305)593-0606
Company Type: Division. Officer: Allen Y.
Shaklan, Vice President & General
Manager. Ultimate Parent: CBS. SIC:
4833—Television Broadcasting Stations.

★ 61515 ★ Wells Fargo Guard
Service Inc.
16300 NE 19th Ave.
Miami, FL 33162
(305)949-1444
Ultimate Parent: Borg Warner Automotive.
SIC: 7381—Detective & Armored Car
Services.

★ 61516 ★ Wrangler
35 NE 17th St.
Miami, FL 33132
(305)371-9222
Ultimate Parent: VF Corp. SIC: 5611—
Men's & Boys' Clothing Stores.

★ 61517 ★ Xeroc Corp.
7843 NW 15th St.
Miami, FL 33126
(305)591-7330
Officer: Liz Parnes, Manager. Ultimate
Parent: Xerox Corp. SIC: 2752—
Commercial Printing—Lithographic; 2759—
Commercial Printing Nec.

Miami Beach

★ 61518 ★ American Savings of
FL FSB
1200 Lincoln Rd.
Miami Beach, FL 33139-2315
(305)673-0281
Location Type: Branch office. Ultimate
Parent: American Savings of Florida. SIC:
6035—Federal Savings Institutions; 6021—
National Commercial Banks.

★ 61519 ★ American Savings of
Florida
1200 Lincoln Rd.
Miami Beach, FL 33139
Ultimate Parent: American Savings of
Florida. SIC: 6099—Functions Related to
Deposit Banking.

★ 61520 ★ American Savings of
Florida, FSB
17066 Collins Ave.
Miami Beach, FL 33160-3642
(305)949-9596
Location Type: Branch office. Officer:
Carole Connell, Manager. Ultimate Parent:
American Savings of Florida. SIC: 6035—
Federal Savings Institutions; 6211—Security
Brokers & Dealers.

★ 61521 ★ American Savings of
Florida, FSB
333 Arthur Godfrey Rd.
Miami Beach, FL 33140-3680
(305)534-4344
Location Type: Branch office. Officer:
Clara Valera, Manager. Ultimate Parent:
American Savings of Florida. SIC: 6035—
Federal Savings Institutions; 6211—Security
Brokers & Dealers.

★ 61522 ★ American Savings of
Florida, FSB
200 71st St.
Miami Beach, FL 33141-3210
(305)861-3783
Location Type: Branch office. Officer:
Susan Ferbin, Manager. Ultimate Parent:
American Savings of Florida. SIC: 6035—
Federal Savings Institutions; 6211—Security
Brokers & Dealers.

★ 61523 ★ American Savings of
Florida, FSB
1200 Lincoln Rd.
Miami Beach, FL 33139-2396
(305)673-0281
Location Type: Branch office. Officer: Inge
Weloff, Manager. Ultimate Parent:
American Savings of Florida. SIC: 6035—
Federal Savings Institutions; 6211—Security
Brokers & Dealers.

★ 61524 ★ Barnett Bank of South
Florida, NA
1414 Alton Rd.
Miami Beach, FL 33139-3895
(305)350-7500
Company Type: Subsidiary. Location
Type: Branch office. Officer: Jose Alonso,
Manager. Ultimate Parent: Barnett Banks.
SIC: 6021—National Commercial Banks.

★ 61525 ★ Barnett Bank of South
Florida, NA
420 Lincoln Rd. Mall
Miami Beach, FL 33139-2488
(305)531-5841
Company Type: Subsidiary. Location
Type: Branch office. Officer: Patty Callinan,
Vice President. Ultimate Parent: Barnett
Banks. SIC: 6021—National Commercial
Banks.

★ 61526 ★ Barnett Bank of South
Florida, NA
360 41st St.
Miami Beach, FL 33140-3666
(305)350-7500
Company Type: Subsidiary. Location
Type: Branch office. Officer: Michael
Goldberg, Manager. Ultimate Parent:
Barnett Banks. SIC: 6021—National
Commercial Banks.

★ 61527 ★ Citibank FSB
401 Arthur Godfrey Rd.
Miami Beach, FL 33140-3585
(305)538-1569
Location Type: Branch office. Ultimate
Parent: Citicorp. SIC: 6021—National
Commercial Banks.

★ 61528 ★ Citibank, FSB
160 Lincoln Rd.
Miami Beach, FL 33139-2098
(305)532-2979
Location Type: Branch office. Ultimate
Parent: Citicorp.

★ 61529 ★   Citizens Federal Bank, FSB
2203 Collins Ave.
Miami Beach, FL 33139-1798
(305)532-5550
Location Type: Branch office. **Officer:** Hilda Alfonso, Manager. **Ultimate Parent:** CSF Holdings. **SIC:** 6021—National Commercial Banks.

★ 61530 ★   Savings of America
Home Savings of America, FSB
555 Arthur Godfrey Rd.
Miami Beach, FL 33140-3509
(305)531-3411
Location Type: Branch office. **Ultimate Parent:** H. F. Ahmanson. **SIC:** 6021—National Commercial Banks.

★ 61531 ★   Savings of America
Home Savings of America, FSB
1901 Alton Rd.
Miami Beach, FL 33139-1534
(305)534-7364
Location Type: Branch office. **Officer:** Lewis Delmas, Manager. **Ultimate Parent:** H. F. Ahmanson. **SIC:** 6021—National Commercial Banks.

Miami Lakes

★ 61532 ★   Barnett Bank of South Florida, NA
15400 NW 77 Ct.
Miami Lakes, FL 33016-5803
(305)825-5900
Company Type: Subsidiary. **Location Type:** Branch office. **Officer:** Janette Davis, Manager. **Ultimate Parent:** Barnett Banks. **SIC:** 6021—National Commercial Banks.

★ 61533 ★   Barnett Bank of South Florida, NA
16320 NW 57th Ave.
Miami Lakes, FL 33014-6184
(305)825-5900
Company Type: Subsidiary. **Location Type:** Branch office. **Officer:** Don Streaker, Manager. **Ultimate Parent:** Barnett Banks. **SIC:** 6021—National Commercial Banks.

★ 61534 ★   Cd Medical Inc.
14600 NW 60th Ave.
Miami Lakes, FL 33014-9308
Ultimate Parent: Dow Chemical Co. USA. **SIC:** 3999—Manufacturing Industries Nec.

★ 61535 ★   First Union National Bank of Florida
15615 NW 67th Ave.
Miami Lakes, FL 33014-2124
(305)823-4499
Location Type: Branch office. **Ultimate Parent:** First Union Corp. **SIC:** 6021—National Commercial Banks.

Miami Shores

★ 61536 ★   Barnett Bank of South Florida, NA
9190 Biscayne Blvd.
Miami Shores, FL 33138-3297
(305)899-4100
Company Type: Subsidiary. **Location Type:** Branch office. **Officer:** Randall Holts, Manager. **Ultimate Parent:** Barnett Banks. **SIC:** 6021—National Commercial Banks.

★ 61537 ★   Savings of America
Home Savings of America, FSB
9899 NE 2nd Ave.
Miami Shores, FL 33138-2300
(305)751-0700
Location Type: Branch office. **Officer:** Kellie Begley, Manager. **Ultimate Parent:** H. F. Ahmanson. **SIC:** 6021—National Commercial Banks.

Miami Springs

★ 61538 ★   First Union National Bank of Florida
4299 NW 36th St.
Miami Springs, FL 33166-7345
(305)883-4020
Location Type: Branch office. **Ultimate Parent:** First Union Corp. **SIC:** 6021—National Commercial Banks.

Middleburg

★ 61539 ★   First Union National Bank of Florida
2465 Blanding Blvd.
Middleburg, FL 32068
(904)278-1463
Location Type: Branch office. **Ultimate Parent:** First Union Corp. **SIC:** 6021—National Commercial Banks.

Milton

★ 61540 ★   Air Products & Chemicals, Inc.
PO Box 467
Milton, FL 32572-0467
(904)994-5511
Officer: Martin Ferris. **Ultimate Parent:** Air Products & Chemicals, Inc. **SIC:** 2875—Fertilizers—Mixing Only; 2899—Chemical Preparations Nec.

★ 61541 ★   Air Products & Chemicals, Inc.
4575 Hwy. 90
Milton, FL 32571
(904)994-5511
Officer: Brian Gibbia, Manager. **Ultimate Parent:** Air Products & Chemicals, Inc. **SIC:** 2821—Plastics Materials & Resins; 2869—Industrial Organic Chemicals Nec; 2873—Nitrogenous Fertilizers.

★ 61542 ★   Air Products & Chemicals, Inc.
1401 US Hwy. 90 W
Milton, FL 32571
(904)994-5511
Ultimate Parent: Air Products & Chemicals, Inc. **SIC:** 2899—Chemical Preparations Nec.

★ 61543 ★   American Cyanamid Co.
1801 Cyanamid Rd.
Milton, FL 32571-2757
(904)994-5311
Officer: Ken Bunkowski. **Ultimate Parent:** American Cyanamid Co. **SIC:** 2824—Organic Fibers—Noncellulosic.

★ 61544 ★   AmSouth Bank of Florida
523 SE Caroline St.
Milton, FL 32570-4963
(904)444-1046
Location Type: Branch office. **Officer:** Tammy Williams, Manager. **Ultimate Parent:** AmSouth Bancorp. **SIC:** 6022—State Commercial Banks.

★ 61545 ★   Barnett Bank of West Florida
6204 Hwy. 90
Milton, FL
(904)432-0271
Location Type: Branch office. **Ultimate Parent:** Barnett Banks. **SIC:** 6021—National Commercial Banks.

★ 61546 ★   Barnett Bank of West Florida
306 Stewart St.
Milton, FL 32570-4226
(904)623-3666
Location Type: Branch office. **Ultimate Parent:** Barnett Banks. **SIC:** 6021—National Commercial Banks.

★ 61547 ★   Greyhound Bus Depot
202 Clara St.
Milton, FL 32570
(904)623-3300
Ultimate Parent: Greyhound Lines Inc. **SIC:** 4111—Local & Suburban Transit; 4173—Bus Terminal & Service Facilities.

★ 61548 ★   Kentucky Fried Chicken
417 Caroline St. SW
Milton, FL 32570
(904)623-4400
Ultimate Parent: Pepsico. **SIC:** 5812—Eating Places.

★ 61549 ★   Piggly Wiggly
4025 Us 90 E
Milton, FL 32571
(904)994-7050
Ultimate Parent: Bruno's. **SIC:** 5411—Grocery Stores.

★ 61550 ★   Pizza Hut
705 Us 90 W
Milton, FL 32570
(904)623-5853
Ultimate Parent: Pepsico. **SIC:** 5812—Eating Places.

★ 61551 ★   Radio Shack
422 Caroline St. SW
Milton, FL 32570
(904)623-2829
Company Type: Division. **Ultimate Parent:** Tandy Corp. **SIC:** 5731—Radio, Television & Electronics Stores.

Mims

★ 61552 ★   AmSouth Bank of Florida
2350 N. US Hwy. 1
Mims, FL 32754-3846
(407)268-2022
Location Type: Branch office. **Ultimate Parent:** AmSouth Bancorp. **SIC:** 6022—State Commercial Banks.

★ 61553 ★   Praxair Inc.
2801 Hammock Rd.
Mims, FL 32754-5681
Ultimate Parent: Praxair. **SIC:** 2813—Industrial Gases.

★ 61554 ★   Union Carbide Corp.
Linde Div.
2801 Hammock Rd.
Mims, FL 32754-0008
Company Type: Division. **Ultimate Parent:** Union Carbide Corp. **SIC:** 2813—Industrial Gases.

★ 61555 ★   Union Carbide Ind. Gases Inc.
Linde Div.
2801 Hammock Rd.
Mims, FL 32754-5681
Company Type: Division. **Ultimate Parent:** Union Carbide Corp. **SIC:** 2813—Industrial Gases.

★ 61556 ★   Union Carbide Industrial Gases Inc.
2801 Hammock Rd.
Mims, FL 32754-5681
Ultimate Parent: Union Carbide Corp. **SIC:** 2813—Industrial Gases.

Miramar

★ 61557 ★   Barnett Bank of Broward County, NA
7950 Miramar Pkwy.
Miramar, FL 33023-5895
(305)981-2600
Company Type: Subsidiary. **Location Type:** Branch office. **Officer:** Richard Schnappauf, Manager. **Ultimate Parent:** Barnett Banks. **SIC:** 6021—National Commercial Banks.

★ 61558 ★   First Union National Bank of Florida
6810 Miramar Pkwy.
Miramar, FL 33023-6090
(305)985-2180
Location Type: Branch office. **Ultimate Parent:** First Union Corp. **SIC:** 6021—National Commercial Banks.

Moore Haven

★ 61559 ★   Barnett Bank of Lake Okeechobee
515 Ave. I
Moore Haven, FL 33471-9730
(813)946-0131
Company Type: Subsidiary. **Location Type:** Branch office. **Officer:** Yvonne Bakich, Vice President. **Ultimate Parent:** Barnett Banks. **SIC:** 6022—State Commercial Banks.

Mount Dora

★ 61560 ★   Albertson's
3200 US, Hwy. 441 W
Mount Dora, FL 32757
(904)383-0400
Ultimate Parent: Albertson's Inc. **SIC:** 5411—Grocery Stores.

★ 61561 ★   Barnett Bank of Lake County, NA
2799 Old Hwy. 441
Mount Dora, FL 32757-3536
(904)589-5000
Company Type: Subsidiary. **Location Type:** Branch office. **Officer:** Bob Phillips, Vice President. **Ultimate Parent:** Barnett Banks. **SIC:** 6021—National Commercial Banks.

★ 61562 ★   Barnett Bank of Lake County, NA
163 N. 5th Ave.
Mount Dora, FL 32757-5547
(904)589-5000
Company Type: Subsidiary. **Location Type:** Branch office. **Officer:** Bob Phillips, Vice President. **Ultimate Parent:** Barnett Banks. **SIC:** 6021—National Commercial Banks.

★ 61563 ★   Delta Air Lines
106 W. Us Hwy. 441
Mount Dora, FL 32757
(904)393-4700
Ultimate Parent: Delta Air Lines, Inc. **SIC:** 7841—Video Tape Rental.

★ 61564 ★   First Union National Bank of Florida
600 N. Donnelly St.
Mount Dora, FL 32757
(904)383-7151
Location Type: Branch office. **Ultimate Parent:** First Union Corp. **SIC:** 6021—National Commercial Banks.

★ 61565 ★   Greyhound Bus Lines
796 PO Box
Mount Dora, FL 32757
(904)383-2537
Ultimate Parent: Greyhound Lines Inc. **SIC:** 4131—Intercity & Rural Bus Transportation.

★ 61566 ★   Kentucky Fried Chicken
3300 Us 441 W
Mount Dora, FL 32757
(904)383-4411
Ultimate Parent: Pepsico. **SIC:** 5812—Eating Places.

★ 61567 ★   Microage
110 W. 5th Ave.
Mount Dora, FL 32757
Ultimate Parent: MicroAge. **SIC:** 7373—Computer Integrated Systems Design.

★ 61568 ★   Radio Shack
3160 Us 441 W
Mount Dora, FL 32757
(904)385-5488
Company Type: Division. **Ultimate Parent:** Tandy Corp. **SIC:** 5731—Radio, Television & Electronics Stores.

★ 61569 ★   Wal Mart
17030 Us Hwy. 441
Mount Dora, FL 32757
Ultimate Parent: Wal-Mart Stores, Inc. **SIC:** 5311—Department Stores.

Mulberry

★ 61570 ★   Agrico Chemical Co.
Mulberry, FL 33860
(813)428-1314
Ultimate Parent: Freeport-McMoran.

★ 61571 ★   Agrico Chemical Co. S. Pierce
County Rd. 630 PO Box 1110
Mulberry, FL 33860
Ultimate Parent: Freeport-McMoran. **SIC:** 2874—Phosphatic Fertilizers.

★ 61572 ★   Agrico Chemical Co. S. Pierce
State Rd. 630 (PO Box 1110)
Mulberry, FL 33860-1100
Ultimate Parent: Freeport-McMoran. **SIC:** 2874—Phosphatic Fertilizers.

★ 61573 ★   Imc Fertilizer Inc.
2151 State Hwy. 60 W.
Mulberry, FL 33860
Ultimate Parent: IMC Fertilizer Group. **SIC:** 2875—Fertilizers—Mixing Only.

★ 61574 ★   IMC Fertilizer Inc.
New Wales Operation
Hwy. 640 & County Line Rd.
Mulberry, FL 33860
Ultimate Parent: IMC Fertilizer Group. SIC:
2874—Phosphatic Fertilizers; 2819—
Industrial Inorganic Chemicals Nec; 2048—
Prepared Feeds Nec.

★ 61575 ★   Industrial & Specialty
Chemicals Plant
P O Box 646
Old Hwy. 60 W.
Mulberry, FL 33860
(813)425-1195
Ultimate Parent: Maxxam. SIC: 2819—
Industrial Inorganic Chemicals Nec.

★ 61576 ★   Kaiser Aluminum &
Chemical
State Rd. 60 W
Mulberry, FL 33860
(813)425-1195
Ultimate Parent: Maxxam. SIC: 5169—
Chemicals & Allied Products Nec.

★ 61577 ★   Westvaco Corp.
State Rd. 60 E
Mulberry, FL 33860
(813)425-3043
Ultimate Parent: WestVaco Corp. SIC:
2869—Industrial Organic Chemicals Nec.

★ 61578 ★   Westvaco Corp.
Chemicals
Hwy. 60 E. PO Box 237
Mulberry, FL 33860
Ultimate Parent: WestVaco Corp. SIC:
2843—Surface Active Agents; 2861—Gum
& Wood Chemicals.

★ 61579 ★   Westvaco Corp.
Chemicals
Hwy. 60 E. POBox 237
Mulberry, FL 33860
Ultimate Parent: WestVaco Corp. SIC:
2843—Surface Active Agents; 2861—Gum
& Wood Chemicals.

★ 61580 ★   Westvaco Corp.
Chemicals
4800 Hwy. 60 E. Hwy. 60 E.
Mulberry, FL 33860
Company Type: Division. Location Type:
Plant. Ultimate Parent: WestVaco Corp.
SIC: 2843—Surface Active Agents; 2861—
Gum & Wood Chemicals.

★ 61581 ★   Westvaco Corp.
Chemical
4800 Hwy. 60 E
Mulberry, FL 33860
(813)425-5502
Ultimate Parent: WestVaco Corp. SIC:
2841—Soap & Other Detergents; 2869—
Industrial Organic Chemicals Nec.

Murdock

★ ɩ 32 ★   First of America Bank
1600 Tamiami Trail
Murdock, FL 33948
(813)627-3322
Location Type: Branch office. Ultimate
Parent: First of America Bank Corp. SIC:
6021—National Commercial Banks.

N Bay Village

★ 61583 ★   Pizza Hut
6724 Collins Ave.
N Bay Village, FL 33141
(305)861-8900
Ultimate Parent: Pepsico. SIC: 5812—
Eating Places.

★ 61584 ★   Radio Shack
6804 Collins Ave.
N Bay Village, FL 33141
(305)866-2990
Company Type: Division. Ultimate Parent:
Tandy Corp. SIC: 5734—Computer &
Software Stores.

★ 61585 ★   Ryder Truck Rental
331 69th St.
N Bay Village, FL 33141
(305)866-2889
Ultimate Parent: Ryder System. SIC:
7389—Business Services Nec.

N Fort Myers

★ 61586 ★   IBM Corp.
4210 Metro Pky.
N Fort Myers, FL 33916
(813)939-9600
Ultimate Parent: IBM. SIC: 5046—
Commercial Equipment Nec.

★ 61587 ★   Mobil
4101 Hancock Bridge Pky.
N Fort Myers, FL 33903
(813)997-2856
Ultimate Parent: Mobil. SIC: 5541—
Gasoline Service Stations.

★ 61588 ★   Mobil Marts
501 Pine Island Rd.
N Fort Myers, FL 33903
(813)995-4995
Ultimate Parent: Mobil. SIC: 5599—
Automotive Dealers Nec.

★ 61589 ★   Radio Shack
13860 N. Cleveland Ave.
N Fort Myers, FL 33903
(813)997-5799
Company Type: Division. Ultimate Parent:
Tandy Corp. SIC: 5719—Miscellaneous
Home Furnishings Stores.

★ 61590 ★   Radio Shack
4150 Hancock Bridge Pky. 2
N Fort Myers, FL 33903
(813)656-3523
Company Type: Division. Ultimate Parent:
Tandy Corp. SIC: 5719—Miscellaneous
Home Furnishings Stores.

N Miami Beach

★ 61591 ★   American Savings of
Florida
12155 Biscayne Blvd.
N Miami Beach, FL 33181
(305)895-5428
Ultimate Parent: American Savings of
Florida. SIC: 6099—Functions Related to
Deposit Banking.

★ 61592 ★   City National Bank of
Fl
13400 Biscayne Blvd.
N Miami Beach, FL 33181
(305)947-6101
Ultimate Parent: City National Corp. SIC:
6099—Functions Related to Deposit
Banking.

★ 61593 ★   McDonalds
127 NE 167th St.
N Miami Beach, FL 33162
(305)653-3363
Ultimate Parent: McDonald's.
SIC: 5812—Eating Places.

★ 61594 ★   Radio Shack
Promenade
N Miami Beach, FL 33162
(305)390-3011
Company Type: Division. Ultimate Parent:
Tandy Corp. SIC: 5734—Computer &
Software Stores.

N. Fort Meyers

★ 61595 ★   First of America Bank
14487 N. Cleveland
N. Fort Meyers, FL 33903
(813)997-1175
Location Type: Branch office. Ultimate
Parent: First of America Bank Corp. SIC:
6021—National Commercial Banks.

Naples

★ 61596 ★   Allied-Signal
Aerospace Co.
3581 Mercantile Ave.
Naples, FL 33942
(813)643-3013
Officer: James S. Divon, President.
Ultimate Parent: Allied-Signal Inc. SIC:
3599—Industrial Machinery Nec.

★ 61597 ★   Allied-Signal
Aerospace Co.
3581 Mercantile Ave.
Naples, FL 33942
(813)643-3013
Officer: James S. Divon, President.
Ultimate Parent: Allied-Signal Inc. SIC:
3599—Industrial Machinery Nec.

★ 61598 ★   Allied-Signal
Aerospace Co.
Engine Controls
3581 Mercantile Ave.
Naples, FL 33942
Ultimate Parent: Allied-Signal Inc. SIC:
3724—Aircraft Engines & Engine Parts;
3728—Aircraft Parts & Equipment Nec.

★ 61599 ★   Anchor Savings Bank
811 Vanderbilt Beach Rd.
Naples, FL 33963
(813)598-1001
Ultimate Parent: Anchor Bancorp. SIC:
6022—State Commercial Banks.

★ 61600 ★   Anchor Savings Bank,
FSB
811 Vanderbilt Beach Rd.
Naples, FL 33963-8708
(813)598-1001
Location Type: Branch office. Officer:
Rainer Olbrich, Assistant Treasurer.
Ultimate Parent: Anchor Bancorp. SIC:
6021—National Commercial Banks; 6035—
Federal Savings Institutions; 6211—Security
Brokers & Dealers; 6141—Personal Credit
Institutions; 6162—Mortgage Bankers &
Correspondents.

★ 61601 ★   Barnett Bank of
Naples
7305 Radio Rd.
Naples, FL 33942
(813)263-5591
Company Type: Subsidiary. Location
Type: Branch office. Officer: Lorenzo
Williams, Manager. Ultimate Parent:
Barnett Banks. SIC: 6022—State
Commercial Banks.

★ 61602 ★   Barnett Bank of
Naples
11120 Tamiami Trl. N
Naples, FL 33963
(813)263-5516
Company Type: Subsidiary. Location
Type: Branch office. Officer: Edward Baker,
Manager. Ultimate Parent: Barnett Banks.
SIC: 6022—State Commercial Banks.

★ 61603 ★   Barnett Bank of
Naples
385 14th Ave. S
Naples, FL 33940-7218
(813)263-1316
Company Type: Subsidiary. Location
Type: Branch office. Officer: Doris Rhoden,
Assistant Vice President. Ultimate Parent:
Barnett Banks. SIC: 6022—State
Commercial Banks.

★ 61604 ★   Barnett Bank of
Naples
3285 Tamiami Trl. E
Naples, FL 33962-5786
(813)263-1325
Company Type: Subsidiary. Location
Type: Branch office. Officer: William
Grauel, Senior Vice President. Ultimate
Parent: Barnett Banks. SIC: 6022—State
Commercial Banks.

★ 61605 ★   Barnett Bank of
Naples
120 Moorings Park Dr.
Naples, FL 33942-2188
(813)263-1395
Company Type: Subsidiary. Location
Type: Branch office. Officer: Nancy Kee,
Assistant Vice President. Ultimate Parent:
Barnett Banks. SIC: 6022—State
Commercial Banks.

★ 61606 ★   Barnett Bank of
Naples
1901 9th St. N
Naples, FL 33940-4804
(813)263-1340
Company Type: Subsidiary. Location
Type: Branch office. Officer: Pat Paris,
Manager. Ultimate Parent: Barnett Banks.
SIC: 6022—State Commercial Banks.

★ 61607 ★   Barnett Bank of
Naples
4898 Davis Blvd.
Naples, FL 33942-5338
(813)263-5565
Company Type: Subsidiary. Location
Type: Branch office. Officer: George E.
Roberts, Vice President. Ultimate Parent:
Barnett Banks. SIC: 6022—State
Commercial Banks.

★ 61608 ★   Barnett Bank of
Naples
4501 N. Tamiami Trl.
Naples, FL 33940-3060
(813)263-1313
Company Type: Subsidiary. Location
Type: Branch office. Officer: John
Cammarata, Vice President. Ultimate
Parent: Barnett Banks. SIC: 6022—State
Commercial Banks.

★ 61609 ★   Barnett Bank of
Naples
4957 Rattlesnake Hammock Rd.
Naples, FL 33962
(813)774-5219
Company Type: Subsidiary. Location
Type: Branch office. Officer: Tannya
Houtchens, Assistant Vice President.
Ultimate Parent: Barnett Banks. SIC:
6022—State Commercial Banks.

★ 61610 ★   Barnett Bank of
Naples
5475 Airport Pulling Rd.
Naples, FL 33942-2004
(813)263-5580
Company Type: Subsidiary. Location
Type: Branch office. Officer: Shannon D.
Marks, Assistant Vice President. Ultimate
Parent: Barnett Banks. SIC: 6022—State
Commercial Banks.

★ 61611 ★   Barnett Bank of
Naples
796 5th Ave. S
PO Box 413008
Naples, FL 33941-3008
(813)643-8200 Fax: (813)263-5544 Telex:
5109518530
Company Type: Subsidiary. Location
Type: Branch office. Officer: James E.
Loskill, Manager. Ultimate Parent: Barnett
Banks. SIC: 6022—State Commercial
Banks.

★ 61612 ★   Casual Corner
1822 9th St. N
Naples, FL 33940
(813)262-6000
Ultimate Parent: United States Shoe. SIC:
5651—Family Clothing Stores.

★ 61613 ★   Cincinnati Insurance
Co.
290 Ridge Dr.
Naples, FL 33963
(813)598-2533
Ultimate Parent: Cincinnati Financial. SIC:
6411—Insurance Agents, Brokers &
Service.

★ 61614 ★   Cincinnati Insurance
Co.
2900 14th St. N
Naples, FL 33940
(813)262-1658
Ultimate Parent: Cincinnati Financial. SIC:
6411—Insurance Agents, Brokers &
Service.

★ 61615 ★   Circus World
1902 9th St. N
Naples, FL 33940
(813)263-0059
Ultimate Parent: Melville. SIC: 5945—
Hobby, Toy & Game Shops.

★ 61616 ★   Citizens Federal
Bank, FSB
4315 Tamiami Trail N.
Naples, FL 33940-3190
(813)263-2461
Location Type: Branch office. Officer:
Marlene Martell, Manager. Ultimate Parent:
CSF Holdings.

★ 61617 ★   Comerica Bank Trust,
FSB
5551 Ridgewood Dr., Ste. 100
Naples, FL 33431
(813)597-4441
Location Type: Branch office. Ultimate
Parent: Comerica Bank. SIC: 6021—
National Commercial Banks.

★ 61618 ★   First Union National
Bank of Florida
4691 Tamiami Trl. N.
Naples, FL 33940
(813)434-4172
Location Type: Branch office. Ultimate
Parent: First Union Corp. SIC: 6021—
National Commercial Banks.

★ 61619 ★ First Union National
Bank of Florida
4915 Rattlesnake Hammock Rd.
Naples, FL 33962-6959
(813)434-4155
Location Type: Branch office. **Ultimate Parent:** First Union Corp. **SIC:** 6021—National Commercial Banks.

★ 61620 ★ First Union National
Bank of Florida
2829 Tamiami Trl. N.
Naples, FL 33940-4486
(813)434-4151
Location Type: Branch office. **Ultimate Parent:** First Union Corp. **SIC:** 6021—National Commercial Banks.

★ 61621 ★ First Union National
Bank of Florida
1100 5th Ave. S.
Naples, FL 33940-6407
(813)434-4110
Location Type: Branch office. **Ultimate Parent:** First Union Corp. **SIC:** 6021—National Commercial Banks.

★ 61622 ★ Fleet Trust Co. of
Florida, NA
5811 Pelican Bay Blvd., Ste. 300
Naples, FL 33963-2710
(813)592-5454 **Fax:** (813)592-6995
Location Type: Headquarters. **Officer:** Scott E. Alexander, Pres./CEO. **Ultimate Parent:** Fleet Financial Group. **SIC:** 6021—National Commercial Banks.

★ 61623 ★ Fleet Trust Co. of
Florida, NA
425 8th St. S
Naples, FL 33940
(813)263-5454
Company Type: Subsidiary. **Ultimate Parent:** Fleet Financial Group. **SIC:** 6091—Nondeposit Trust Facilities.

★ 61624 ★ Fortune Bank, ASB
2400 Tamiami Trail N
Naples, FL 33940-4405
(813)261-0030
Location Type: Branch office. **Officer:** Mary Agnew, Manager. **Ultimate Parent:** Fortune Bancorp. **SIC:** 6021—National Commercial Banks.

★ 61625 ★ Fortune Bank, ASB
405 8th St. S
Naples, FL 33940-6607
(813)263-1600
Location Type: Branch office. **Officer:** Susan Baker, Manager. **Ultimate Parent:** Fortune Bancorp.

★ 61626 ★ Fortune Bank, ASB
5325 Airport Pulling Rd. N
Naples, FL 33942-2011
(813)598-1004
Location Type: Branch office. **Ultimate Parent:** Fortune Bancorp. **SIC:** 6021—National Commercial Banks.

★ 61627 ★ Fortune Bank, ASB
8801 Tamiami Trail E.
Naples, FL 33962-3347
(813)775-4999
Location Type: Branch office. **Officer:** Karen Davis, Manager. **Ultimate Parent:** Fortune Bancorp. **SIC:** 6021—National Commercial Banks.

★ 61628 ★ Greyhound Bus Lines
2669 Davis Blvd.
Naples, FL 33942
(813)774-6522
Ultimate Parent: Greyhound Lines Inc. **SIC:** 4141—Local Bus Charter Service.

★ 61629 ★ Hertz Rent-A-Car
550 Terminal Dr.
Naples, FL 33942
(813)643-1515
Ultimate Parent: Hertz. **SIC:** 7514—Passenger Car Rental.

★ 61630 ★ Hertz Rent-A-Car
Naples Municipal Airport
Naples, FL 33940
(813)774-1617
Ultimate Parent: Hertz. **SIC:** 7514—Passenger Car Rental.

★ 61631 ★ Huntington, FSB
600 5th Ave. S, Ste. 101
Naples, FL 33940
(813)263-4447
Location Type: Branch office. **Ultimate Parent:** Huntington Bancshares. **SIC:** 6021—National Commercial Banks.

★ 61632 ★ Huntington Trust Co.
400 5th Ave. S
Naples, FL 33940
(813)263-3398
Ultimate Parent: Huntington Bancshares. **SIC:** 6022—State Commercial Banks.

★ 61633 ★ Huntington Trust Co.
of Florida, NA
600 5th Ave. S., Ste. 201
Naples, FL 33940
(813)263-3398 **Fax:** (813)263-1973
Location Type: Headquarters. **Officer:** Gail S. T. Webster, President. **Ultimate Parent:** Huntington Bancshares. **SIC:** 6021—National Commercial Banks.

★ 61634 ★ Kentucky Fried
Chicken
2248 Tamiami Trl. E
Naples, FL 33962
(813)774-2641
Ultimate Parent: Pepsico. **SIC:** 5812—Eating Places.

★ 61635 ★ Kentucky Fried
Chicken
1891 County Rd. 951 S
Naples, FL 33999
(813)455-1883
Ultimate Parent: Pepsico. **SIC:** 5812—Eating Places.

★ 61636 ★ Kentucky Fried
Chicken
1905 State Rd. 951
Naples, FL 33999
(813)455-8183
Ultimate Parent: Pepsico. **SIC:** 5812—Eating Places.

★ 61637 ★ Kentucky Fried
Chicken
2800 9th St. N
Naples, FL 33940
(813)261-1409
Ultimate Parent: Pepsico. **SIC:** 5812—Eating Places.

★ 61638 ★ The Limited Express
1720 9th St. N
Naples, FL 33940
(813)262-3449
Ultimate Parent: Limited. **SIC:** 5651—Family Clothing Stores.

★ 61639 ★ Maison Blanche
Department S
1798 9th St. N
Naples, FL 33940
(813)261-4100
Ultimate Parent: Mercantile Stores. **SIC:** 5311—Department Stores.

★ 61640 ★ Marshall & Ilsley
Trust Com
800 Laurel Oak Dr.
Naples, FL 33963
(813)597-2933
Ultimate Parent: Marshall & Ilsley Corp. **SIC:** 6022—State Commercial Banks.

★ 61641 ★ Marshall & Ilsley
Trust Co. of Florida
800 Laurel Oak Dr.
Ste. 101
Naples, FL 33963-2737
(813)597-2933 **Fax:** (813)598-2029
Company Type: Subsidiary. **Location Type:** Branch office. **Officer:** Robert J. Fiddes, President. **Ultimate Parent:** Marshall & Ilsley Corp. **SIC:** 6021—National Commercial Banks.

★ 61642 ★ Mary Kay Cosmetics
763 17th Ave. S
Naples, FL 33940
Ultimate Parent: Mary Kay Cosmetics.

★ 61643 ★ Massachusetts Mutual
Life Insurance
2500 9th St. N
Naples, FL 33940
(813)649-5222
Ultimate Parent: Massasucetts Mutual Life. **SIC:** 6411—Insurance Agents, Brokers & Service.

★ 61644 ★ Massachusetts Mutual
Life Insurance
5811 Pelican Bay Blvd.
Naples, FL 33963
(813)598-9962
Ultimate Parent: Massasucetts Mutual Life. **SIC:** 6411—Insurance Agents, Brokers & Service.

★ 61645 ★ Mobil Oil Corp.
2495 Pine Ridge Rd.
Naples, FL 33942
(813)597-6404
Ultimate Parent: Mobil. **SIC:** 5599—Automotive Dealers Nec.

★ 61646 ★ Mutual of New York
1010 28th Ave. N
Naples, FL 33940
(813)261-6669
Ultimate Parent: Mutual of New York. **SIC:** 6411—Insurance Agents, Brokers & Service.

★ 61647 ★ National City Trust
Co.
4085 Tamiami Trl. N
Ste. B103
Naples, FL 33940-6627
(813)649-6336
Company Type: Subsidiary. **Location Type:** Branch office. **Officer:** Donald A. Jones, Mgr. **Ultimate Parent:** National City Corp. **SIC:** 6021—National Commercial Banks.

★ 61648 ★ National City Trust
Co.
Collier Pl. 1, 3003 Tamiami Trl. N
Ste. 100
Naples, FL 33940-2714
(813)263-3555
Company Type: Subsidiary. **Location Type:** Branch office. **Ultimate Parent:** National City Corp. **SIC:** 6021—National Commercial Banks.

★ 61649 ★ NBD Bank, FSB
4901 Tamiami Trl. W
Naples, FL 33940
(813)434-0330
Location Type: Branch office. **Officer:** Gene Hunt, Manager. **Ultimate Parent:** NBD Bancorp. **SIC:** 6021—National Commercial Banks.

★ 61650 ★ NBD Trust Co. of
Florida, NA
4901 Tamiami Trl. W
Naples, FL 33940-3010
(813)434-2400
Location Type: Branch office. **Officer:** Richard J. Peck, Vice President. **Ultimate Parent:** NBD Bancorp. **SIC:** 6021—National Commercial Banks.

★ 61651 ★ Pizza Hut
3010 Tamiami Trl. E
Naples, FL 33962
(813)775-3352
Ultimate Parent: Pepsico. **SIC:** 5812—Eating Places.

★ 61652 ★ Pizza Hut
675 9th St. N
Naples, FL 33940
(813)261-8818
Ultimate Parent: Pepsico. **SIC:** 5812—Eating Places.

★ 61653 ★ Publix Super Market
4860 Davis Blvd.
Naples, FL 33942
(813)775-8800
Ultimate Parent: Publix Super Markets. **SIC:** 5411—Grocery Stores.

★ 61654 ★ Publix Super Market
701 Vanderbilt Beach Rd.
Naples, FL 33940
(813)597-2138
Ultimate Parent: Publix Super Markets. **SIC:** 5411—Grocery Stores.

★ 61655 ★ Publix Super Market
1981 9th St. N
Naples, FL 33940
(813)262-1401
Ultimate Parent: Publix Super Markets. **SIC:** 5411—Grocery Stores.

★ 61656 ★ Publix Super Market
871 Vanderbilt Beach Rd.
Naples, FL 33963
(813)597-2138
Ultimate Parent: Publix Super Markets. **SIC:** 5411—Grocery Stores.

★ 61657 ★ Publix Super Markets
701 Vanderbilt Beach Rd.
Naples, FL 33940
(813)597-2138
Ultimate Parent: Publix Super Markets. **SIC:** 5411—Grocery Stores.

★ 61658 ★ Publix Super Markets
Inc.
4860 Davis Blvd.
Naples, FL 33942
(813)775-8800
Ultimate Parent: Publix Super Markets. **SIC:** 5411—Grocery Stores.

★ 61659 ★ Radio Shack
1998 9th St. N
Naples, FL 33940
(813)261-5331
Company Type: Division. **Ultimate Parent:** Tandy Corp. **SIC:** 5065—Electronic Parts & Equipment Nec.

★ 61660 ★ Radio Shack
Gulf Gate Shopping Ctr.
Naples, FL 33942
(813)774-7811
Company Type: Division. **Ultimate Parent:** Tandy Corp. **SIC:** 5065—Electronic Parts & Equipment Nec.

★ 61661 ★ Rite Aid
4857 Golden Gate Pky.
Naples, FL 33999
(813)455-9975
Ultimate Parent: Rite Aid. **SIC:** 5912—Drug Stores & Proprietary Stores.

★ 61662 ★ Rite-Aid Pharmacy
778 9th St. N
Naples, FL 33940
(813)263-9934
Ultimate Parent: Rite Aid. **SIC:** 5912—Drug Stores & Proprietary Stores.

★ 61663 ★ Rite Aid Pharmacy
5401 Airport Pulling Rd. N
Naples, FL 33942
(813)597-9900
Ultimate Parent: Rite Aid. **SIC:** 5912—Drug Stores & Proprietary Stores.

★ 61664 ★ Savings of America
Home Savings of America, FSB
900 Neopolitan Way
Naples, FL 33940-8191
(813)434-6444
Location Type: Branch office. **Officer:** Cathy Lytell, Manager. **Ultimate Parent:** H. F. Ahmanson. **SIC:** 6021—National Commercial Banks.

★ 61665 ★ Taco Bell
2224 Tamiami Trl E
Naples, FL 33962
(813)774-6402
Ultimate Parent: Pepsico. **SIC:** 5812—Eating Places.

★ 61666 ★ This End Up
1956 9th St. N
Naples, FL 33940
(813)434-0881
Ultimate Parent: Melville. **SIC:** 5712—Furniture Stores.

★ 61667 ★ Trailways Bus System
2669 Davis Blvd.
Naples, FL 33942
(813)793-1102
Ultimate Parent: Greyhound Lines Inc. **SIC:** 1521—Single-Family Housing Construction.

★ 61668 ★ Underwriters
Adjusting Co.
580 Neapolitan Way
Naples, FL 33940
(813)262-3121
Ultimate Parent: Continental. **SIC:** 6411—Insurance Agents, Brokers & Service.

★ 61669 ★ Walgreen
4673 Tamiami Trl.
Naples, FL 33940
(813)649-6500
Ultimate Parent: Walgreen Co. **SIC:** 5331—Variety Stores.

★ 61670 ★   Walgreen Pharmacy
1915 9th St. N
Naples, FL 33940
(813)263-0117
Ultimate Parent: Walgreen Co. SIC:
5912—Drug Stores & Proprietary Stores.

New Port Rich

★ 61671 ★   Texaco Food Mart 119
9008 State Rd. 52
New Port Rich, FL 34654
(813)868-9727
Ultimate Parent: Texaco. SIC: 5541—
Gasoline Service Stations.

New Port Richey

★ 61672 ★   Ace Hardware
4411 Grand Blvd.
New Port Richey, FL 34652-5403
(813)842-9136
Ultimate Parent: Ace Hardware. SIC:
5999—Miscellaneous Retail Stores Nec;
5211—Lumber & Other Building Materials;
5231—Paint, Glass & Wallpaper Stores;
5261—Retail Nurseries & Garden Stores.

★ 61673 ★   Anchor Savings Bank
4124 Little Rd.
New Port Richey, FL 34655
(813)376-5233
Ultimate Parent: Anchor Bancorp. SIC:
6159—Miscellaneous Business Credit
Institutions.

★ 61674 ★   Anchor Savings Bank,
FSB
4124 Little Rd.
New Port Richey, FL 34655-1721
(813)376-5233
Location Type: Branch office. Officer:
Lenora Rowe, Assistant Vice President.
Ultimate Parent: Anchor Bancorp. SIC:
6021—National Commercial Banks; 6035—
Federal Savings Institutions; 6211—Security
Brokers & Dealers.

★ 61675 ★   Barnett Bank of
Pasco County
1452 7 Springs Blvd.
New Port Richey, FL 34655-5636
(813)847-7171
Company Type: Subsidiary. Location
Type: Branch office. Officer: Maria Potter,
Manager. Ultimate Parent: Barnett Banks.
SIC: 6022—State Commercial Banks.

★ 61676 ★   Barnett Bank of
Pasco County
6128 US Hwy. 19
New Port Richey, FL 34652-2526
(813)847-7149
Company Type: Subsidiary. Location
Type: Branch office. Officer: Marc
Bowman, Manager. Ultimate Parent:
Barnett Banks. SIC: 6022—State
Commercial Banks.

★ 61677 ★   Barnett Bank of
Pasco County
8928 State Rd. 54
New Port Richey, FL 34653-6425
(813)847-7107
Company Type: Subsidiary. Location
Type: Branch office. Officer: Kathleen
Dedomenico, Manager. Ultimate Parent:
Barnett Banks. SIC: 6022—State
Commercial Banks.

★ 61678 ★   Barnett Bank of
Pasco County
4918 Floramar Ter.
New Port Richey, FL 34652-3300
(813)847-7382
Company Type: Subsidiary. Location
Type: Branch office. Officer: Beverly
Shuler, Manager. Ultimate Parent: Barnett
Banks. SIC: 6022—State Commercial
Banks.

★ 61679 ★   Barnett Bank of
Pasco County
4526 US Hwy. 19
New Port Richey, FL 34652-4940
(813)847-7321
Company Type: Subsidiary. Location
Type: Branch office. Officer: Edwin
Hancock, Manager. Ultimate Parent:
Barnett Banks. SIC: 6022—State
Commercial Banks.

★ 61680 ★   Coast to Coast Bail
Bond
1056 PO Box
New Port Richey, FL 34656
(813)842-4220
Ultimate Parent: Servistar Corp. SIC:
7299—Miscellaneous Personal Services
Nec.

★ 61681 ★   First of America Bank
5245 US Hwy. 19
New Port Richey, FL 34652
(813)848-8912
Location Type: Branch office. Ultimate
Parent: First of America Bank Corp. SIC:
6021—National Commercial Banks.

★ 61682 ★   First of America Bank
3535 US Hwy. 19
New Port Richey, FL 34652
(813)817-0250
Location Type: Branch office. Ultimate
Parent: First of America Bank Corp. SIC:
6021—National Commercial Banks.

★ 61683 ★   First Union National
Bank of Florida
6604 Massachusetts Ave.
New Port Richey, FL 34653-2794
(813)848-0314
Location Type: Branch office. Ultimate
Parent: First Union Corp. SIC: 6021—
National Commercial Banks.

★ 61684 ★   First Union National
Bank of Florida
5312 State Rd. 54
New Port Richey, FL 34652
(813)849-2151
Location Type: Branch office. Ultimate
Parent: First Union Corp. SIC: 6021—
National Commercial Banks.

★ 61685 ★   First Union National
Bank of Florida
8423 Ridge Rd.
New Port Richey, FL 34654-4410
(813)848-6242
Location Type: Branch office. Ultimate
Parent: First Union Corp. SIC: 6021—
National Commercial Banks.

★ 61686 ★   Fortuen Bank, ASB
3535 US Hwy. 19
New Port Richey, FL 34652-6256
(813)845-0355
Location Type: Branch office. Ultimate
Parent: Fortune Bancorp. SIC: 6021—
National Commercial Banks.

★ 61687 ★   Fortune Bank, ASB
4010 Little Rd.
New Port Richey, FL 34655-1719
(813)376-1799
Location Type: Branch office. Officer: Lisa
Saksar, Manager. Ultimate Parent: Fortune
Bancorp. SIC: 6021—National Commercial
Banks.

★ 61688 ★   McDonalds
Restaurants
9121 Little Rd.
New Port Richey, FL 34654
(813)862-7482
Ultimate Parent: McDonald's.
SIC: 5812—Eating Places.

★ 61689 ★   Pall Land & Marine
10540 Ridge Rd.
New Port Richey, FL 34654
(813)849-9999 Fax: (813)848-5719
Officer: Charles R. Grimm, President.
Ultimate Parent: Pall.

★ 61690 ★   Pall Land & Marine
Corp.
10540 Ridge Rd.
New Port Richey, FL 34654
Ultimate Parent: Pall. SIC: 3720—Aircraft
& Parts.

★ 61691 ★   Pall Land & Marine
Corp.
7070 Moon Lake Rd.
New Port Richey, FL 34654
Ultimate Parent: Pall. SIC: 3720—Aircraft
& Parts.

★ 61692 ★   Texaco Food Mart
4015 Little Rd.
New Port Richey, FL 34655
(813)376-2891
Ultimate Parent: Texaco. SIC: 5541—
Gasoline Service Stations.

★ 61693 ★   Walgreen Drug Stores
7227 County Rd. 54
New Port Richey, FL 34653
(813)376-5064
Ultimate Parent: Walgreen Co. SIC:
5912—Drug Stores & Proprietary Stores.

★ 61694 ★   Walgreen Drug Stores
9143 Little Rd.
New Port Richey, FL 34654
(813)862-8526
Ultimate Parent: Walgreen Co. SIC:
5912—Drug Stores & Proprietary Stores.

New Smyrna

★ 61695 ★   Exxon Food Mart
330 Otter Blvd.
New Smyrna, FL 32168
Ultimate Parent: Exxon. SIC: 5411—
Grocery Stores.

★ 61696 ★   Radio Shack
1964 State Rd. 44
New Smyrna, FL 32168
(904)427-7237
Company Type: Division. Ultimate Parent:
Tandy Corp. SIC: 5719—Miscellaneous
Home Furnishings.

★ 61697 ★   Texaco Food Mart
1208 S. Atlantic Ave.
New Smyrna, FL 32169
(904)427-2326
Ultimate Parent: Texaco. SIC: 5541—
Gasoline Service Stations.

New Smyrna Beach

★ 61698 ★   Barnett Bank of
Volusia County
763 3rd. Ave.
New Smyrna Beach, FL 32169-3101
(904)427-1909
Location Type: Branch office. Ultimate
Parent: Barnett Banks. SIC: 6021—National
Commercial Banks.

★ 61699 ★   Barnett Bank of
Volusia County
111 N. Causeway
New Smyrna Beach, FL 32169-5303
(904)423-2206
Location Type: Branch office. Officer:
Edward Bennett, Manager. Ultimate
Parent: Barnett Banks. SIC: 6021—National
Commercial Banks.

★ 61700 ★   Barnett Bank of
Volusia County
1880 State Rd. 44
New Smyrna Beach, FL 32168-8343
(904)426-0030
Location Type: Branch office. Ultimate
Parent: Barnett Banks. SIC: 6021—National
Commercial Banks.

★ 61701 ★   First Union National
Bank of Florida
401 S. Dixie Frwy.
New Smyrna Beach, FL 32169
(904)423-2400
Location Type: Branch office. Ultimate
Parent: First Union Corp. SIC: 6021—
National Commercial Banks.

★ 61702 ★   First Union National
Bank of Florida
1791 State Rd. 44
New Smyrna Beach, FL 32168
(904)423-4511
Location Type: Branch office. Ultimate
Parent: First Union Corp. SIC: 6021—
National Commercial Banks.

★ 61703 ★   First Union National
Bank of Florida
1650 S. Atlantic Ave.
New Smyrna Beach, FL 32169-3118
(904)423-4541
Location Type: Branch office. Ultimate
Parent: First Union Corp. SIC: 6021—
National Commercial Banks.

★ 61704 ★   Publix Super Markets
765 E. 3rd Ave.
New Smyrna Beach, FL 32169
(904)428-6465
Ultimate Parent: Publix Super Markets.
SIC: 5411—Grocery Stores.

Newberry

★ 61705 ★   Ace Hardware
195 W. Central Ave.
Newberry, FL 32669
(904)472-2525
Ultimate Parent: Ace Hardware. SIC:
5992—Florists.

★ 61706 ★   Barnett Bank of
Alachua County, NA
300 N. Main St.
Newberry, FL 32669
(904)338-6543
Company Type: Subsidiary. Location
Type: Branch office. Officer: Don Davis,
Assistant Vice President. Ultimate Parent:
Barnett Banks. SIC: 6021—National
Commercial Banks.

Niceville

★ 61707 ★   AmSouth Bank of
Florida
1003-A John Sims Pky.
Niceville, FL 32578-2201
(904)444-1000
Location Type: Branch office. Officer:
Shelli Brown, Manager. Ultimate Parent:
AmSouth Bancorp. SIC: 6022—State
Commercial Banks.

★ 61708 ★   Barnett Bank of
Northwest Florida
701 John Sims Pky.
Niceville, FL 32578-2031
(904)729-4100
Company Type: Subsidiary. Location
Type: Branch office. Ultimate Parent:
Barnett Banks. SIC: 6022—State
Commercial Banks.

★ 61709 ★   Barnett Bank of
Northwest Florida
4500 Hwy. 20 E
Niceville, FL 32578-9755
(904)897-4506
Company Type: Subsidiary. Location
Type: Branch office. Officer: Maria Harris,
Assistant Vice President. Ultimate Parent:
Barnett Banks. SIC: 6022—State
Commercial Banks.

★ 61710 ★   Kentucky Fried
Chicken
205 John C Sims Pky.
Niceville, FL 32578
(904)678-6606
Ultimate Parent: Pepsico. SIC: 5812—
Eating Places.

★ 61711 ★   Mary Kay Cosmetics
105 21st St.
Niceville, FL 32578
(904)678-7646
Ultimate Parent: Mary Kay Cosmetics. SIC:
5999—Miscellaneous Retail Stores Nec.

★ 61712 ★   Mary Kay Cosmetics
Representatives
304 N. Cedar Ave.
Niceville, FL 32578
(904)678-8563
Ultimate Parent: Mary Kay Cosmetics. SIC:
7322—Adjustment & Collection Services.

★ 61713 ★   McDonalds
117 W. John Sims Pky.
Niceville, FL 32578
(904)678-1844
Ultimate Parent: McDonald's.
SIC: 5812—Eating Places.

★ 61714 ★   Piggly Wiggly
597 John C Sims Pky.
Niceville, FL 32578
(904)678-6557
Ultimate Parent: Bruno's. SIC: 5812—
Eating Places.

★ 61715 ★   Pizza Hut
1037 E. John Sims Pky.
Niceville, FL 32578
(904)678-7776
Ultimate Parent: Pepsico. SIC: 5812—
Eating Places.

★ 61716 ★   Radio Shack
1009 E. John Sims Pky.
Niceville, FL 32578
(904)678-4933
Company Type: Division. Ultimate Parent:
Tandy Corp. SIC: 5731—Radio, Television
& Electronics Stores.

★ 61717 ★ **Russell Corp.**
100 Hart St.
Niceville, FL 32578
(904)678-2212
Officer: Ron Templeton, Manager. **Ultimate Parent:** Russell. **SIC:** 2221—Broadwoven Fabric Mills—Manmade.

★ 61718 ★ **Ryder Truck Rental**
600 E. John Sims Pky.
Niceville, FL 32578
(904)678-8976
Ultimate Parent: Ryder System. **SIC:** 7513—Truck Rental & Leasing Without Drivers.

★ 61719 ★ **Twin Cities Hospital**
510 Crestview Ave.
Niceville, FL 32578
(904)678-4131
Ultimate Parent: Hospital Corp. of America. **SIC:** 8062—General Medical & Surgical Hospitals.

★ 61720 ★ **Vanguard Bank & Trust Co.**
Palm Plz.
Niceville, FL 32578
(904)729-5500
Company Type: Subsidiary. **Location Type:** Branch office. **Officer:** Patricia Ramsden, Mgr. **Ultimate Parent:** Synovus Financial Corp. **SIC:** 6021—National Commercial Banks.

★ 61721 ★ **Vanguard Bank & Trust Co.**
4400 Hwy. 20 E
Niceville, FL 32578-9735
(904)729-5500
Company Type: Subsidiary. **Location Type:** Branch office. **Officer:** Lenise Braziel, Mgr. **Ultimate Parent:** Synovus Financial Corp. **SIC:** 6021—National Commercial Banks.

Nichols

★ 61722 ★ **Mobil Mining & Minerals**
PO Box 311
Nichols, FL 33863-0311
(813)425-6200
Officer: R. E. Schulz. **Ultimate Parent:** Mobil. **SIC:** 2819—Industrial Inorganic Chemicals Nec; 5191—Farm Supplies.

No Palm Beach

★ 61723 ★ **Pizza Hut**
12100 Us Hwy. 1 A
No Palm Beach, FL 33408
Ultimate Parent: Pepsico. **SIC:** 5812—Eating Places.

Nokomis

★ 61724 ★ **Barnett Bank of Southwest Florida**
1099 N. Tamiami Trl.
Nokomis, FL 34275-2163
(813)951-4800
Company Type: Subsidiary. **Location Type:** Branch office. **Officer:** Carrie Santostasi, Manager. **Ultimate Parent:** Barnett Banks. **SIC:** 6021—National Commercial Banks.

★ 61725 ★ **Kentucky Fried Chicken**
700 Tamiami Trl. N
Nokomis, FL 34275
(813)488-8545
Ultimate Parent: Pepsico. **SIC:** 5812—Eating Places.

★ 61726 ★ **Publix Super Market**
1091 Tamiami Trl N
Nokomis, FL 34275
(813)484-8461
Ultimate Parent: Publix Super Markets. **SIC:** 5411—Grocery Stores.

North Bay Village

★ 61727 ★ **City National Bank**
300 71st St.
North Bay Village, FL 33141
(305)866-6861
Ultimate Parent: City National Corp. **SIC:** 6099—Functions Related to Deposit Banking.

North Fort Myers

★ 61728 ★ **First Union National Bank of Florida**
3405 Hancock Bridge Pky.
North Fort Myers, FL 33903-7004
(813)997-1776
Location Type: Branch office. **Officer:** Bridgit Sue McCorkie, Mgr. **Ultimate Parent:** First Union Corp. **SIC:** 6021—National Commercial Banks.

★ 61729 ★ **Taco Bell**
13170 N. Cleveland Ave.
North Fort Myers, FL 33903
(813)656-3616
Ultimate Parent: Pepsico. **SIC:** 5812—Eating Places.

North Miami

★ 61730 ★ **American Savings of Florida, FSB**
12155 Biscayne Blvd.
North Miami, FL 33181-2711
(305)895-5428
Location Type: Branch office. **Officer:** Nora Bauer, Manager. **Ultimate Parent:** American Savings of Florida. **SIC:** 6035—Federal Savings Institutions; 6211—Security Brokers & Dealers.

★ 61731 ★ **Barnett Bank of South Florida, NA**
11755 Biscayne Blvd.
North Miami, FL 33138
(305)899-4100
Company Type: Subsidiary. **Location Type:** Branch office. **Officer:** Becky Medina, Manager. **Ultimate Parent:** Barnett Banks. **SIC:** 6021—National Commercial Banks.

★ 61732 ★ **Barnett Bank of South Florida, NA**
13450 W. Dixie Hwy.
North Miami, FL 33161-4139
(305)899-4100
Company Type: Subsidiary. **Location Type:** Branch office. **Officer:** Maricarmen Coman, Manager. **Ultimate Parent:** Barnett Banks. **SIC:** 6021—National Commercial Banks.

★ 61733 ★ **Barnett Bank of South Florida, NA**
2875 NE 191st St.
North Miami, FL 33180-2803
(305)899-4100
Company Type: Subsidiary. **Location Type:** Branch office. **Officer:** Jeannine Romaine, Manager. **Ultimate Parent:** Barnett Banks. **SIC:** 6021—National Commercial Banks.

★ 61734 ★ **First Union National Bank of Florida**
18545 Biscayne Blvd.
North Miami, FL 33180
(305)597-5800
Location Type: Branch office. **Ultimate Parent:** First Union Corp. **SIC:** 6021—National Commercial Banks.

★ 61735 ★ **First Union National Bank of Florida**
12550 Biscayne Blvd.
North Miami, FL 33181-2541
(305)795-2900
Location Type: Branch office. **Ultimate Parent:** First Union Corp. **SIC:** 6021—National Commercial Banks.

★ 61736 ★ **Sparkletts Water Sys. Aqua Vend**
1998 NE 148th St.
North Miami, FL 33181
Ultimate Parent: McKesson. **SIC:** 7389—Business Services Nec.

★ 61737 ★ **Sparkletts Water Systems Aquavend**
1998 NE 148th St.
North Miami, FL 33181
Ultimate Parent: McKesson. **SIC:** 7389—Business Services Nec.

★ 61738 ★ **Sparkletts Water Sytems Aquavend**
1998 NE 148th St.
North Miami, FL 33181
Ultimate Parent: McKesson. **SIC:** 7389—Business Services Nec.

North Miami Beach

★ 61739 ★ **American Savings of Florida, FSB**
1802 NE Miami Gardens Dr.
North Miami Beach, FL 33179-5036
(305)956-9798
Location Type: Branch office. **Officer:** Mardi Larson, Manager. **Ultimate Parent:** American Savings of Florida. **SIC:** 6035—Federal Savings Institutions; 6211—Security Brokers & Dealers.

★ 61740 ★ **American Savings of Florida, FSB**
2925 Aventura Blvd.
North Miami Beach, FL 33180-3104
(305)932-4630
Location Type: Branch office. **Officer:** Rod Alonso, Manager. **Ultimate Parent:** American Savings of Florida. **SIC:** 6035—Federal Savings Institutions; 6211—Security Brokers & Dealers.

★ 61741 ★ **Barnett Bank of South Florida, NA**
18201 NE 19th Ave.
North Miami Beach, FL 33162-1684
(305)899-4100
Company Type: Subsidiary. **Location Type:** Branch office. **Officer:** Margaret Slaton, Manager. **Ultimate Parent:** Barnett Banks. **SIC:** 6021—National Commercial Banks.

★ 61742 ★ **Barnett Bank of South Florida, NA**
800 N. Miami Beach Rd.
North Miami Beach, FL 33162-3701
(305)956-9798
Company Type: Subsidiary. **Location Type:** Branch office. **Officer:** Gary Sciba, Manager. **Ultimate Parent:** Barnett Banks. **SIC:** 6021—National Commercial Banks.

★ 61743 ★ **Citibank, FSB**
3495 NE 163rd St.
North Miami Beach, FL 33160-4400
(305)947-1536
Location Type: Branch office. **Officer:** Katherine Corbett, Manager. **Ultimate Parent:** Citicorp. **SIC:** 6021—National Commercial Banks.

★ 61744 ★ **Savings of America**
Home Savings of America, FSB
3050 Aventura Blvd.
North Miami Beach, FL 33180-3110
(305)932-6435
Location Type: Branch office. **Officer:** Cheryl A. Smith, Manager. **Ultimate Parent:** H. F. Ahmanson. **SIC:** 6021—National Commercial Banks.

North Palm Beach

★ 61745 ★ **Barnett Bank of Palm Beach County**
401 Northlake Blvd.
North Palm Beach, FL 33408-5481
(407)863-9800
Company Type: Subsidiary. **Location Type:** Branch office. **Officer:** Robin Henderson, Manager. **Ultimate Parent:** Barnett Banks. **SIC:** 6022—State Commercial Banks.

★ 61746 ★ **Barnett Bank of Palm Beach County**
11011 US Hwy. 1
North Palm Beach, FL 33408
(407)845-3202
Company Type: Subsidiary. **Location Type:** Branch office. **Officer:** James Hall, Manager. **Ultimate Parent:** Barnett Banks. **SIC:** 6022—State Commercial Banks.

★ 61747 ★ **Barnett Bank of Palm Beach County**
1224 US Hwy. 1
North Palm Beach, FL 33408-3539
(407)845-3435
Company Type: Subsidiary. **Location Type:** Branch office. **Officer:** James Hall, Manager. **Ultimate Parent:** Barnett Banks. **SIC:** 6022—State Commercial Banks.

★ 61748 ★ **California Federal Bank, FSB**
1201 N. US Hwy. 1, Ste. 1
North Palm Beach, FL 33408-3546
(407)694-1667
Location Type: Branch office. **Ultimate**
Parent: California Federal Bank. **SIC:** 6021—National Commercial Banks.

★ 61749 ★ **First Union National Bank of Florida**
11710 US Hwy. 1
North Palm Beach, FL 33408
(407)838-5648
Location Type: Branch office. **Ultimate Parent:** First Union Corp. **SIC:** 6021—National Commercial Banks.

★ 61750 ★ **First Union National Bank of Florida**
500 S. US Hwy. 1
North Palm Beach, FL 33408-5467
(407)838-5312
Location Type: Branch office. **Ultimate Parent:** First Union Corp. **SIC:** 6021—National Commercial Banks.

★ 61751 ★ **NBD Bank, FSB**
11300 US Hwy. 1, Ste. 100
North Palm Beach, FL 33408
(407)624-4728
Location Type: Branch office. **Officer:** Sally Yerex, Manager. **Ultimate Parent:** NBD Bancorp. **SIC:** 6021—National Commercial Banks.

★ 61752 ★ **NBD Trust Co. of Florida, NA**
11300 US Hwy. 1, Ste. 101
North Palm Beach, FL 33408-3289
(407)627-9400 **Fax:** (407)627-9408
Location Type: Branch office. **Officer:** Frederick H. Gravelle, President. **Ultimate Parent:** NBD Bancorp. **SIC:** 6021—National Commercial Banks.

North Port

★ 61753 ★ **Barnett Bank of Southwest Florida**
14299 S. Tamiami Trl.
North Port, FL 34287
(813)951-4800
Company Type: Subsidiary. **Location Type:** Branch office. **Officer:** Ron Monck, Manager. **Ultimate Parent:** Barnett Banks. **SIC:** 6021—National Commercial Banks.

★ 61754 ★ **First of America Bank**
13605 Tamiami Trail
North Port, FL 34287
(813)426-1101
Location Type: Branch office. **Ultimate Parent:** First of America Bank Corp. **SIC:** 6021—National Commercial Banks.

★ 61755 ★ **First Union National Bank of Florida**
13675 S. Tamiami Trl.
North Port, FL 34287-2061
(813)426-1161
Location Type: Branch office. **Ultimate Parent:** First Union Corp. **SIC:** 6021—National Commercial Banks.

North Redington Beach

★ 61756 ★ **Barnett Bank of Pinellas County**
17101 Gulf Blvd.
North Redington Beach, FL 33708-1471
(813)892-1212
Company Type: Subsidiary. **Location Type:** Branch office. **Officer:** John Lee, Manager. **Ultimate Parent:** Barnett Banks. **SIC:** 6022—State Commercial Banks.

Northwest Smyrna Beach

★ 61757 ★ **Food Lion**
95 N. Causeway
Northwest Smyrna Beach, FL 32169
(904)423-0625
Ultimate Parent: Food Lion. **SIC:** 5411—Grocery Stores.

★ 61758 ★ **Publix Super Market**
765 E. 3rd Ave.
Northwest Smyrna Beach, FL 32169
(904)428-6465
Ultimate Parent: Publix Super Markets. **SIC:** 5411—Grocery Stores.

★ 61759 ★ **Wal Mart**
1998 State Rd. 44
Northwest Smyrna Beach, FL 32168
(904)427-5767
Ultimate Parent: Wal-Mart Stores, Inc. **SIC:** 5331—Variety Stores.

★ 61760 ★ **Walgreen**
1914 State Rd. 44
Northwest Smyrna Beach, FL 32168
(904)428-1556
Ultimate Parent: Walgreen Co. **SIC:**
5912—Drug Stores & Proprietary Stores.

★ 61761 ★ **Walgreen Pharmacy**
1914 State Rd. 44
Northwest Smyrna Beach, FL 32168
(904)428-1558
Ultimate Parent: Walgreen Co. **SIC:**
5912—Drug Stores & Proprietary Stores.

Nw Prt Richey

★ 61762 ★ **Ryder Truck Rental**
7322 Us 19
Nw Prt Richey, FL 34652
(813)842-4744
Ultimate Parent: Ryder System. **SIC:**
7513—Truck Rental & Leasing Without
Drivers.

Nw Smyrna Beach

★ 61763 ★ **Champion**
International Corp.
Rural Route 1
Nw Smyrna Beach, FL 32168
(904)428-2563
Ultimate Parent: Champion International.
SIC: 5111—Printing & Writing Paper.

Ocala

★ 61764 ★ **Ace Hardware, Inc.**
110 NW 10th St.
Ocala, FL 34475
(904)732-0115
Ultimate Parent: Ace Hardware. **SIC:**
5251—Hardware Stores.

★ 61765 ★ **AmSouth Bank of**
Florida
1030 SE 17th St.
Ocala, FL 34471-3912
(904)732-3806
Location Type: Branch office. **Ultimate**
Parent: AmSouth Bancorp. **SIC:** 6022—
State Commercial Banks.

★ 61766 ★ **AmSouth Bank of**
Florida
9351 Maricamp Rd.
Ocala, FL 34472-2476
(904)687-2174
Location Type: Branch office. **Ultimate**
Parent: AmSouth Bancorp. **SIC:** 6022—
State Commercial Banks.

★ 61767 ★ **AmSouth Bank of**
Florida
406 E. Silver Springs Blvd.
Ocala, FL 34470-5828
(904)629-9800
Location Type: Branch office. **Ultimate**
Parent: AmSouth Bancorp. **SIC:** 6022—
State Commercial Banks.

★ 61768 ★ **AmSouth Bank of**
Florida
2800 E. Silver Springs Blvd.
Ocala, FL 34470-7004
(904)368-6700
Location Type: Branch office. **Ultimate**
Parent: AmSouth Bancorp. **SIC:** 6022—
State Commercial Banks.

★ 61769 ★ **AmSouth Bank of**
Florida
8721 SW State Rd. 200
Ocala, FL 34476-7729
(904)854-7662
Location Type: Branch office. **Ultimate**
Parent: AmSouth Bancorp. **SIC:** 6022—
State Commercial Banks.

★ 61770 ★ **AmSouth Bank of**
Florida
2734 NE Jacksonville Rd.
Ocala, FL 34470-3745
(904)622-6233
Location Type: Branch office. **Ultimate**
Parent: AmSouth Bancorp. **SIC:** 6022—
State Commercial Banks.

★ 61771 ★ **AmSouth Bank of**
Florida
3232 SW College Rd.
Ocala, FL 34474-4412
(904)237-1194
Location Type: Branch office. **Ultimate**
Parent: AmSouth Bancorp. **SIC:** 6022—
State Commercial Banks.

★ 61772 ★ **Avon Products Inc.**
5978 SE 68th St.
Ocala, FL 32672
(904)624-2683
Ultimate Parent: Avon Products, Inc. **SIC:**
5999—Miscellaneous Retail Stores Nec.

★ 61773 ★ **Barnett Bank of**
Marion County, NA
2326 E. Silver Springs Blvd.
Ocala, FL 34470-6911
(904)620-1111
Company Type: Subsidiary. **Location**
Type: Branch office. **Officer:** Betty
McMillan, Vice President. **Ultimate Parent:**
Barnett Banks. **SIC:** 6021—National
Commercial Banks.

★ 61774 ★ **Barnett Bank of**
Marion County, NA
1899 SE Baseline Rd.
Ocala, FL 34472
(904)620-1111
Company Type: Subsidiary. **Location**
Type: Branch office. **Officer:** Shirley Bradt,
Assistant Vice President. **Ultimate Parent:**
Barnett Banks. **SIC:** 6021—National
Commercial Banks.

★ 61775 ★ **Barnett Bank of**
Marion County, NA
1120 SE 17th St.
Ocala, FL 34471
(904)620-1111
Company Type: Subsidiary. **Location**
Type: Branch office. **Officer:** Lola
Campbell, Vice President. **Ultimate Parent:**
Barnett Banks. **SIC:** 6021—National
Commercial Banks.

★ 61776 ★ **Barnett Bank of**
Marion County, NA
128 Marion Oaks Blvd., Ste. 105
Ocala, FL 34473
(904)620-1111
Company Type: Subsidiary. **Location**
Type: Branch office. **Officer:** Vicki Kain,
Assistant Vice President. **Ultimate Parent:**
Barnett Banks. **SIC:** 6021—National
Commercial Banks.

★ 61777 ★ **Barnett Bank of**
Marion County, NA
2540 NE 35th St.
Ocala, FL 34470-8700
(904)620-1111
Company Type: Subsidiary. **Location**
Type: Branch office. **Officer:** Kirk
VanMeter, Assistant Vice President.
Ultimate Parent: Barnett Banks. **SIC:**
6021—National Commercial Banks.

★ 61778 ★ **Barnett Bank of**
Marion County, NA
9305 Maricamp Rd.
Ocala, FL 34472
(904)620-1111
Company Type: Subsidiary. **Location**
Type: Branch office. **Officer:** Mary Jones,
Manager. **Ultimate Parent:** Barnett Banks.
SIC: 6021—National Commercial Banks.

★ 61779 ★ **Barnett Bank of**
Marion County, NA
7975 SW State Rd. 200
Ocala, FL 34476-7049
(904)620-1111
Company Type: Subsidiary. **Location**
Type: Branch office. **Officer:** Marti
Reckdenwald, Vice President. **Ultimate**
Parent: Barnett Banks. **SIC:** 6021—National
Commercial Banks.

★ 61780 ★ **Barnett Bank of**
Marion County, NA
35 SE 1st Ave.
PO Box 550
Ocala, FL 34478-0550
(904)620-1111 **Fax:** (904)732-2212
Company Type: Subsidiary. **Location**
Type: Branch office. **Officer:** Richard L.
Andrews, Chairman, President & CEO.
Ultimate Parent: Barnett Banks. **SIC:**
6021—National Commercial Banks.

★ 61781 ★ **Barnett Bank of**
Marion County, NA
3120 SW 34th Ave.
Ocala, FL 34474
(904)620-1111
Company Type: Subsidiary. **Location**
Type: Branch office. **Officer:** Jean Imes,
Manager. **Ultimate Parent:** Barnett Banks.
SIC: 6021—National Commercial Banks.

★ 61782 ★ **Baxter International**
Scientific Products Division
601 SW 33rd Ave.
Ocala, FL 32674
(904)732-3480
Ultimate Parent: Baxter International. **SIC:**
5049—Professional Equipment Nec.

★ 61783 ★ **California Federal**
Bank, FSB
3101 SW 34th Ave.
Ocala, FL 34474
(904)854-0030
Location Type: Branch office. **Ultimate**
Parent: California Federal Bank. **SIC:**
6021—National Commercial Banks.

★ 61784 ★ **California Federal**
Bank, FSB
25 E. Silver Springs Blvd.
Ocala, FL 34470
(904)732-7283
Location Type: Branch office. **Officer:**
Kerry Bond, Manager. **Ultimate Parent:**
California Federal Bank. **SIC:** 6021—
National Commercial Banks.

★ 61785 ★ **California Federal**
Bank, FSB
2444 E. Sliver Springs Blvd.
Ocala, FL 34470
(904)629-0036
Location Type: Branch office. **Ultimate**
Parent: California Federal Bank.

★ 61786 ★ **Citgo Service Center**
1001 S. Pine Ave.
Ocala, FL 34474
(904)867-0810
Ultimate Parent: Citgo Petroleum. **SIC:**
5541—Gasoline Service Stations.

★ 61787 ★ **Citgo Service Station**
18 S. Pine Ave.
Ocala, FL 34474
(904)732-2402
Ultimate Parent: Citgo Petroleum. **SIC:**
5541—Gasoline Service Stations.

★ 61788 ★ **Citizens Federal**
Bank, FSB
3504 E. Silver Springs Blvd.
Ocala, FL 34470
(904)629-6629
Location Type: Branch office. **Ultimate**
Parent: CSF Holdings. **SIC:** 6021—National
Commercial Banks.

★ 61789 ★ **Citizens Federal**
Bank, FSB
3101 SW 34th Ave., Ste. 600
Ocala, FL 34474
(904)237-1278
Location Type: Branch office. **Officer:**
Mary Gainor, Manager. **Ultimate Parent:**
CSF Holdings. **SIC:** 6021—National
Commercial Banks.

★ 61790 ★ **Clairson International**
Corp.
720 SW 17th St.
Ocala, FL 34474-3542
(904)351-6100
Company Type: Subsidiary. **Officer:**
Robert Zriny, President. **Ultimate Parent:**
Emerson Electric Co. Inc. **SIC:** 3496—
Miscellaneous Fabricated Wire Products.
Employee Count: 518. **Sales:** 36 M.

★ 61791 ★ **Coast to Coast Realty**
& Inv
1322 NE 10th Ave.
Ocala, FL 32670
(904)629-5511
Ultimate Parent: Servistar Corp. **SIC:**
6531—Real Estate Agents & Managers.

★ 61792 ★ **Coca-Cola Bottling**
Co.
2870 NE 24th St.
Ocala, FL 32670
(904)622-7218
Ultimate Parent: Coca-Cola Enterprises.
SIC: 5085—Industrial Supplies.

★ 61793 ★ **Dayco Products Inc.**
3100 Maricamp Rd.
Ocala, FL 34471
Ultimate Parent: Mark IV Industries. **SIC:**
3052—Rubber & Plastics Hose & Belting.

★ 61794 ★ **First Union National**
Bank of Florida
8300 SW 100th St.
Ocala, FL 34481
(904)873-5000
Location Type: Branch office. **Ultimate**
Parent: First Union Corp. **SIC:** 6021—
National Commercial Banks.

★ 61795 ★ **First Union National**
Bank of Florida
3201 SW College Rd.
Ocala, FL 34474
(904)873-5010
Location Type: Branch office. **Ultimate**
Parent: First Union Corp. **SIC:** 6021—
National Commercial Banks.

★ 61796 ★ **First Union National**
Bank of Florida
3541 SE Maricamp Rd.
Ocala, FL 34471
(904)620-7150
Location Type: Branch office. **Ultimate**
Parent: First Union Corp. **SIC:** 6021—
National Commercial Banks.

★ 61797 ★ **First Union National**
Bank of Florida
109 W. Silver Springs Blvd.
Ocala, FL 34475
(904)620-7100
Location Type: Branch office. **Ultimate**
Parent: First Union Corp. **SIC:** 6021—
National Commercial Banks.

★ 61798 ★ **First Union National**
Bank of Florida
3617 NE 7th St.
Ocala, FL 34470
(904)620-7135
Location Type: Branch office. **Ultimate**
Parent: First Union Corp. **SIC:** 6021—
National Commercial Banks.

★ 61799 ★ **Food Lion**
4901 NE Silver Springs Blvd.
Ocala, FL 34470
(904)236-0046
Ultimate Parent: Food Lion. **SIC:** 5411—
Grocery Stores.

★ 61800 ★ **Georgia Pacific Corp.**
1201 SW 17th St.
Ocala, FL 34474
(904)732-0001
Officer: Randall Graham, Manager.
Ultimate Parent: Georgia-Pacific. **SIC:**
2439—Structural Wood Members Nec.

★ 61801 ★ **Georgia-Pacific Corp.**
Ocala Wood-I-Beam
1201 SW 17th St.
Ocala, FL 34474
Ultimate Parent: Georgia-Pacific. **SIC:**
2439—Structural Wood Members Nec.

★ 61802 ★ **Greyhound Bus Lines**
512 N. Magnolia Ave.
Ocala, FL 34475
(904)732-2677
Ultimate Parent: Greyhound Lines Inc. **SIC:**
4111—Local & Suburban Transit; 4131—
Intercity & Rural Bus Transportation.

★ 61803 ★ **Kentucky Fried**
Chicken
1607 S. Pine Ave.
Ocala, FL 34474
(904)629-7964
Ultimate Parent: Pepsico. **SIC:** 5812—
Eating Places.

★ 61804 ★ **Lerner Shop**
26 S. Magnolia Ave.
Ocala, FL 34474
(904)732-6683
Ultimate Parent: Limited. **SIC:** 5621—
Women's Clothing Stores.

★ 61805 ★ **Martin Marietta**
Electronics Information & Missile
Systems
498 Oak Rd.
Ocala, FL 34472
Ultimate Parent: Martin Marietta. **SIC:**
3672—Printed Circuit Boards; 3761—
Guided Missiles & Space Vehicles; 3812—
Search & Navigation Equipment.

★ 61806 ★   **Martin Marietta Missile Systems**
Building 7 Ocala
5312 SW 6th Pl. Ocala Airport Comerce Ctr.
Ocala, FL 34474
Company Type: Division. **Ultimate Parent:** Martin Marietta. **SIC:** 3812—Search & Navigation Equipment.

★ 61807 ★   **Martin Marietta Ocala Operations**
498 Oak Rd.
Ocala, FL 34472
Ultimate Parent: Martin Marietta. **SIC:** 3761—Guided Missiles & Space Vehicles; 3769—Space Vehicle Equipment Nec; 7372—Prepackaged Software.

★ 61808 ★   **Mary Kay Cosmetics**
2402 SE 15th St.
Ocala, FL 34471
(904)622-7663
Ultimate Parent: Mary Kay Cosmetics. **SIC:** 5999—Miscellaneous Retail Stores Nec.

★ 61809 ★   **Mutual of New York**
10227 SW 82nd Ter
Ocala, FL 32676
(904)237-4934
Ultimate Parent: Mutual of New York. **SIC:** 6411—Insurance Agents, Brokers & Service.

★ 61810 ★   **Napa Auto Parts**
320 10th St. NW
Ocala, FL 32678
Ultimate Parent: Genuine Parts. **SIC:** 3714—Motor Vehicle Parts & Accessories.

★ 61811 ★   **Pizza Hut**
1316 E. Silver Springs Blvd.
Ocala, FL 34470
(904)629-2197
Ultimate Parent: Pepsico. **SIC:** 5812—Eating Places.

★ 61812 ★   **Pizza Hut**
2327 S. Pine Ave.
Ocala, FL 34471
(904)622-3714
Ultimate Parent: Pepsico. **SIC:** 5812—Eating Places.

★ 61813 ★   **Publix Super Market**
1901 E. Silver Springs Blvd.
Ocala, FL 34470
(904)622-3188
Ultimate Parent: Publix Super Markets. **SIC:** 5411—Grocery Stores.

★ 61814 ★   **Publix Super Market**
3450 NE Silver Springs Blvd.
Ocala, FL 34470
(904)732-1625
Ultimate Parent: Publix Super Markets. **SIC:** 5411—Grocery Stores.

★ 61815 ★   **Publix Super Markets**
1901 E. Silver Springs Blvd.
Ocala, FL 32670
(904)622-3188
Ultimate Parent: Publix Super Markets. **SIC:** 5411—Grocery Stores.

★ 61816 ★   **Radio Shack**
3100 SW College Rd.
Ocala, FL 34474
(904)237-3913
Company Type: Division. **Ultimate Parent:** Tandy Corp. **SIC:** 5731—Radio, Television & Electronics Stores; 5734—Computer & Software Stores.

★ 61817 ★   **Radio Shack**
1805 E. Silver Springs Blvd.
Ocala, FL 34470
(904)629-3144
Company Type: Division. **Ultimate Parent:** Tandy Corp. **SIC:** 5719—Miscellaneous Home Furnishings Stores.

★ 61818 ★   **Radio Shack**
3100 SW College Rd.
Ocala, FL 34474
(904)854-1089
Company Type: Division. **Ultimate Parent:** Tandy Corp. **SIC:** 7377—Computer Rental & Leasing.

★ 61819 ★   **Radio Shack**
426 S. Pine Ave.
Ocala, FL 34471
(904)622-8218
Company Type: Division. **Ultimate Parent:**

Tandy Corp. **SIC:** 5065—Electronic Parts & Equipment Nec.

★ 61820 ★   **Ryder Truck Rental**
1139 E. Silver Springs Blvd.
Ocala, FL 34470
(904)622-4228
Ultimate Parent: Ryder System. **SIC:** 7389—Business Services Nec.

★ 61821 ★   **Ryder Truck Rental**
2216 N. Magnolia Ave.
Ocala, FL 34475
(904)732-4222
Ultimate Parent: Ryder System. **SIC:** 7359—Equipment Rental & Leasing Nec; 7513—Truck Rental & Leasing Without Drivers.

★ 61822 ★   **Stop & Shop Pawn**
4422 W. Hwy. 40
Ocala, FL 32675
(904)351-3450
Ultimate Parent: Stop & Shop. **SIC:** 5999—Miscellaneous Retail Stores Nec.

★ 61823 ★   **Texaco**
3825 W. Silver Springs Blvd.
Ocala, FL 34475
(904)629-5319
Ultimate Parent: Texaco. **SIC:** 5541—Gasoline Service Stations.

★ 61824 ★   **Trailways Bus Lines**
1224 N. Magnolia Ave.
Ocala, FL 34475
(904)622-4132
Ultimate Parent: Greyhound Lines Inc. **SIC:** 4131—Intercity & Rural Bus Transportation.

★ 61825 ★   **Walgreen**
3233 SE Maricamp Rd.
Ocala, FL 34471
(904)694-4812
Ultimate Parent: Walgreen Co. **SIC:** 5912—Drug Stores & Proprietary Stores.

★ 61826 ★   **Walgreen**
3233 SE 24th St.
Ocala, FL 34471
(904)694-4182
Ultimate Parent: Walgreen Co. **SIC:** 5912—Drug Stores & Proprietary Stores.

★ 61827 ★   **Walgreen Drug Stores**
608 S. Pine Ave.
Ocala, FL 34471
(904)622-3291
Ultimate Parent: Walgreen Co. **SIC:** 5912—Drug Stores & Proprietary Stores.

★ 61828 ★   **Walgreen Drug Stores**
3100 SW College Rd.
Ocala, FL 34474
(904)237-1211
Ultimate Parent: Walgreen Co. **SIC:** 5999—Miscellaneous Retail Stores Nec.

Ocean Ridge

★ 61829 ★   **Barnett Bank of Palm Beach County**
5112 N. Ocean Blvd.
Ocean Ridge, FL 33435-7031
(407)243-1976
Company Type: Subsidiary. **Location Type:** Branch office. **Officer:** Glenda Agonis, Manager. **Ultimate Parent:** Barnett Banks. **SIC:** 6022—State Commercial Banks.

Ocoee

★ 61830 ★   **AmSouth Bank of Florida**
252 N. Apopka Hwy.
Ocoee, FL 34761
(407)656-2400
Location Type: Branch office. **Ultimate Parent:** AmSouth Bancorp. **SIC:** 6022—State Commercial Banks.

★ 61831 ★   **AmSouth Bank of Florida**
1550 McGuire Rd.
Ocoee, FL 34761-2982
(407)656-2420
Location Type: Branch office. **Ultimate Parent:** AmSouth Bancorp. **SIC:** 6022—State Commercial Banks.

★ 61832 ★   **Barnett Bank of Central Florida, NA**
2665 W. Hwy. 50
Ocoee, FL 34761-2977
(407)646-3593
Company Type: Subsidiary. **Location Type:** Branch office. **Officer:** Rodney Jolly, Manager. **Ultimate Parent:** Barnett Banks. **SIC:** 6021—National Commercial Banks.

★ 61833 ★   **Food Lion**
425 W. Silver Star Rd.
Ocoee, FL 34761
(407)877-0097
Ultimate Parent: Food Lion. **SIC:** 5411—Grocery Stores.

★ 61834 ★   **Food Lion Inc.**
425 W. Silver Star Rd.
Ocoee, FL 34761
(407)877-0097
Ultimate Parent: Food Lion. **SIC:** 5411—Grocery Stores.

★ 61835 ★   **Piggly Wiggly**
2750 State Rd. 50 W
Ocoee, FL 34761
(407)656-8180
Ultimate Parent: Bruno's. **SIC:** 5411—Grocery Stores.

★ 61836 ★   **Pizza Hut**
2754 Hwy. 50
Ocoee, FL 34761
(407)656-0696
Ultimate Parent: Pepsico. **SIC:** 5812—Eating Places.

★ 61837 ★   **Radio Shack**
2659 State Rd. 50 W
Ocoee, FL 34761
(407)656-6638
Company Type: Division. **Ultimate Parent:** Tandy Corp. **SIC:** 5731—Radio, Television & Electronics Stores.

★ 61838 ★   **Rite Aid Discount Drugs**
425 W. Silver Star Rd. 21
Ocoee, FL 34761
(407)656-9908
Ultimate Parent: Rite Aid. **SIC:** 5912—Drug Stores & Proprietary Stores.

★ 61839 ★   **Sysco Food Service**
200 Story Rd.
Ocoee, FL 34761
(407)877-8500
Ultimate Parent: Sysco. **SIC:** 5149—Groceries & Related Products Nec.

Okeechobee

★ 61840 ★   **Barnett Bank of Lake Okeechobee**
3261 US Hwy. 441 S
Okeechobee, FL 34974-6238
(813)357-4200
Company Type: Subsidiary. **Location Type:** Branch office. **Officer:** Mary Jean Harrell, Vice President. **Ultimate Parent:** Barnett Banks. **SIC:** 6022—State Commercial Banks.

★ 61841 ★   **Barnett Bank of Lake Okeechobee**
205 N. Parrott Ave.
PO Box 218
Okeechobee, FL 34973-0218
(813)357-4200 **Fax:** (813)357-4292
Company Type: Subsidiary. **Location Type:** Branch office. **Officer:** Richard D. Coleman, Chairman, President & CEO. **Ultimate Parent:** Barnett Banks. **SIC:** 6022—State Commercial Banks.

★ 61842 ★   **Barnett Bank of Lake Okeechobee**
3182 US Hwy. 441 SE
Okeechobee, FL 34974-6252
(813)357-4200
Company Type: Subsidiary. **Location Type:** Branch office. **Officer:** Carol Crews, Assistant Vice President. **Ultimate Parent:** Barnett Banks. **SIC:** 6022—State Commercial Banks.

★ 61843 ★   **Pizza Hut**
2795 Hwy. 441 S
Okeechobee, FL 34974
(813)763-8818
Ultimate Parent: Pepsico. **SIC:** 5812—Eating Places.

★ 61844 ★   **Radio Shack**
415 NE Park St.
Okeechobee, FL 34972
(813)763-3197
Company Type: Division. **Ultimate Parent:** Tandy Corp. **SIC:** 5731—Radio, Television & Electronics Stores.

Oldsmar

★ 61845 ★   **AmSouth Bank of Florida**
3132 Tampa Rd.
Oldsmar, FL 34677-2289
(813)462-2482
Location Type: Branch office. **Ultimate Parent:** AmSouth Bancorp. **SIC:** 6022—State Commercial Banks.

★ 61846 ★   **Barnett Bank of Pinellas County**
200 Oakleaf Blvd.
Oldsmar, FL 34677
(813)539-9327
Company Type: Subsidiary. **Location Type:** Branch office. **Officer:** Karen Coultas, Manager. **Ultimate Parent:** Barnett Banks. **SIC:** 6022—State Commercial Banks.

★ 61847 ★   **First Union National Bank of Florida**
3180 Tampa Rd.
Oldsmar, FL 34677
(813)538-4521
Location Type: Branch office. **Ultimate Parent:** First Union Corp. **SIC:** 6021—National Commercial Banks.

★ 61848 ★   **Paramax Systems Corp. Clearwater**
3655 Tampa Rd.
Oldsmar, FL 34677
Ultimate Parent: Unisys Corp. **SIC:** 3571—Electronic Computers.

★ 61849 ★   **Unisys Clearwater**
3655 Tampa Rd.
Oldsmar, FL 34677
Ultimate Parent: Unisys Corp. **SIC:** 3571—Electronic Computers.

★ 61850 ★   **Unisys Clearwater**
3655 State Rd. 584
Oldsmar, FL 34677
Ultimate Parent: Unisys Corp. **SIC:** 3699—Electrical Equipment & Supplies Nec.

★ 61851 ★   **Unisys Corp.**
3655 TampaRd.
Oldsmar, FL 34677
(813)855-5711
Officer: John Parish, executive Director. **Ultimate Parent:** Unisys Corp. **SIC:** 3571—Electronic Computers; 3679—Electronic Components Nec.

★ 61852 ★   **Westinghouse Electric**
110 Douglas Rd. E
Oldsmar, FL 34677
(813)855-4621
Officer: Steve Marcum, Manager. **Ultimate Parent:** Westinghouse Electric Corp. **SIC:** 3671—Electron Tubes.

★ 61853 ★   **Westinghouse Electric Corp.**
110 Douglas Rd. PO Box 819
Oldsmar, FL 34677
Ultimate Parent: Westinghouse Electric Corp. **SIC:** 3629—Electrical Industrial Apparatus Nec; 3625—Relays & Industrial Controls.

★ 61854 ★   **Westinghouse Electric Corp.**
Electrical Components
110 Douglas Rd. E. PO Box 819
Oldsmar, FL 34677
Ultimate Parent: Westinghouse Electric Corp. **SIC:** 3629—Electrical Industrial Apparatus Nec; 3625—Relays & Industrial Controls.

Olympia Heights

★ 61855 ★   Radio Shack
Concord Shopping Ctr.
Olympia Heights, FL 33165
(305)223-4566
Company Type: Division. Ultimate Parent:
Tandy Corp. SIC: 5734—Computer &
Software Stores.

Olympia Hgts

★ 61856 ★   United Parcel Service
13420 SW 36th St.
Olympia Hgts, FL 33175
(305)599-6405
Ultimate Parent: United Parcel Service of
America.

Oneco

★ 61857 ★   Barnett Bank of
Manatee County, NA
1608 53rd Ave. E
Oneco, FL 34264
(813)755-8889
Company Type: Subsidiary. Location
Type: Branch office. Officer: Susan Kruse,
Assistant Vice President. Ultimate Parent:
Barnett Banks. SIC: 6021—National
Commercial Banks.

Opa Locka

★ 61858 ★   First Union National
Bank of Florida
13100 NW 27th Ave.
Opa Locka, FL 33054
(305)795-2940
Location Type: Branch office. Ultimate
Parent: First Union Corp. SIC: 6021—
National Commercial Banks.

★ 61859 ★   Kentucky Fried
Chicken
13620 NW 27th Ave.
Opa Locka, FL 33054
(305)685-8677
Ultimate Parent: Pepsico. SIC: 5812—
Eating Places.

★ 61860 ★   Kentucky Fried
Chicken
17701 NW 27th Ave.
Opa Locka, FL 33056
(305)620-1341
Ultimate Parent: Pepsico. SIC: 5812—
Eating Places.

★ 61861 ★   Mobil Servcie Station
4701 NW 167th St.
Opa Locka, FL 33055
(305)624-6484
Ultimate Parent: Mobil. SIC: 7538—
General Automotive Repair Shops.

★ 61862 ★   Pizza Hut
4837 NW 183rd St.
Opa Locka, FL 33055
(305)620-7277
Ultimate Parent: Pepsico. SIC: 5812—
Eating Places.

★ 61863 ★   Texaco Oil Company
4701 NW 183rd St.
Opa Locka, FL 33055
(305)625-8094
Ultimate Parent: Texaco. SIC: 5541—
Gasoline Service Stations.

Opa-Locka

★ 61864 ★   Knoll International
Holdings
Foamex LP
3805 NW 132nd St.
Opa-Locka, FL 33054
Ultimate Parent: Foamex. SIC: 3086—
Plastics Foam Products.

★ 61865 ★   Knoll International
Holdings
Foamex L.P.
3805 NW 132 St.
Opa-Locka, FL 33054
Ultimate Parent: Foamex. SIC: 3086—
Plastics Foam Products.

★ 61866 ★   Radio Shack
16867 NW 57th Ave.
Opa-Locka, FL 33055
(305)625-3672
Company Type: Division. Ultimate Parent:
Tandy Corp. SIC: 5065—Electronic Parts &
Equipment Nec.

★ 61867 ★   Ryder Truck Rental
16495 NW 27th Ave.
Opa-Locka, FL 33054
(305)625-7625
Ultimate Parent: Ryder System. SIC:
7359—Equipment Rental & Leasing Nec.

Orange City

★ 61868 ★   Barnett Banks of
Volusia County
2461 Enterprise Rd.
Orange City, FL 32763-7901
(904)775-6446
Location Type: Branch office. Ultimate
Parent: Barnett Banks. SIC: 6021—National
Commercial Banks.

★ 61869 ★   California Federal
Bank
1229 Providence Blvd.
Orange City, FL 32725
(407)574-8660
Ultimate Parent: California Federal Bank.
SIC: 6099—Functions Related to Deposit
Banking.

★ 61870 ★   Delta Air Lines
1349 Montoya Dr.
Orange City, FL 32738
(407)574-0587
Ultimate Parent: Delta Air Lines, Inc.

★ 61871 ★   T. G. Lee Foods, Inc.
1675 State Rd.
PO Box 741126
Orange City, FL 32774-1126
Location Type: Plant. Ultimate Parent:
Dean Foods.

★ 61872 ★   T.G. Lee Foods, Inc.
1675 State Rd.
PO Box 741126
Orange City, FL 32774-1126
(904)775-6700
Company Type: Subsidiary. Officer: Daryl
Mahan, VP Finance. Ultimate Parent: Dean
Foods.

★ 61873 ★   T. G. Lee Foods
1675 State Rd. 472
Orange City, FL 32763
(904)775-9931
Officer: Tommy Hamm, Manager. Ultimate
Parent: Dean Foods. SIC: 2033—Canned
Fruits & Vegetables.

★ 61874 ★   T. G. Lee Lifestyle
1675 State Rd. 472
Orange City, FL 32763
(904)775-6700
Officer: Howard Dean, Chairman. Ultimate
Parent: Dean Foods. SIC: 2026—Fluid Milk.

★ 61875 ★   T. G. Lee Foods Inc.
1675 State Rd. 472
Orange City, FL 32763
Ultimate Parent: Dean Foods. SIC: 2026—
Fluid Milk.

★ 61876 ★   T.G. Lee Foods Inc.
1675 State Rd. 472
Orange City, FL 32763-1126
Ultimate Parent: Dean Foods. SIC: 2026—
Fluid Milk.

Orange Park

★ 61877 ★   Anchor/Lithkemko
Inc.
50 Industrial Loop N.
Orange Park, FL 32073
Ultimate Parent: International Paper Co.
SIC: 2819—Industrial Inorganic Chemicals
Nec.

★ 61878 ★   Circus World
48 Orange Park Mall
Orange Park, FL 32073
(904)269-0895
Ultimate Parent: Melville. SIC: 5945—
Hobby, Toy & Game Shops.

★ 61879 ★   Exxon Co.
1728 Kingsley Ave.
Orange Park, FL 32073
(904)269-3223
Ultimate Parent: Exxon. SIC: 5172—
Petroleum Products Nec.

★ 61880 ★   First Union National
Bank of Florida
450 Park Ave.
Orange Park, FL 32073
(904)278-1471
Location Type: Branch office. Ultimate
Parent: First Union Corp. SIC: 6021—
National Commercial Banks.

★ 61881 ★   First Union National
Bank of Florida
1567 Kingsley Ave.
Orange Park, FL 32073-4599
(904)278-1400
Location Type: Branch office. Ultimate
Parent: Barnett Bank of Alachua County,
NA. SIC: 6021—National Commercial
Banks.

★ 61882 ★   First Union National
Bank of Florida
400 Blanding Blvd.
Orange Park, FL 32073-5085
(904)278-1404
Location Type: Branch office. Ultimate
Parent: First Union Corp. SIC: 6021—
National Commercial Banks.

★ 61883 ★   First Union National
Bank of Florida
920 Blanding Blvd.
Orange Park, FL 32065-6206
(904)278-1448
Location Type: Branch office. Ultimate
Parent: First Union Corp. SIC: 6021—
National Commercial Banks.

★ 61884 ★   Food Lion
700 Blanding Blvd. 1
Orange Park, FL 32065
(904)272-0071
Ultimate Parent: Food Lion. SIC: 5411—
Grocery Stores.

★ 61885 ★   Food Lion
1670 Wells Rd. 103
Orange Park, FL 32073
(904)264-5909
Ultimate Parent: Food Lion. SIC: 5411—
Grocery Stores.

★ 61886 ★   The Gap
125 Orange Park Mall
Orange Park, FL 32073
(904)269-7215
Ultimate Parent: GAP. SIC: 5651—Family
Clothing Stores.

★ 61887 ★   Kay Bee Toys
82 Orange Park Mall
Orange Park, FL 32073
(904)269-6771
Ultimate Parent: Melville. SIC: 5945—
Hobby, Toy & Game Shops.

★ 61888 ★   Kentucky Fried
Chicken
1206 Park Ave.
Orange Park, FL 32073
(904)264-5323
Ultimate Parent: Pepsico. SIC: 5812—
Eating Places.

★ 61889 ★   Lane Bryant
13 Orange Park Mall
Orange Park, FL 32073
(904)269-4225
Ultimate Parent: Limited. SIC: 5651—
Family Clothing Stores.

★ 61890 ★   Lens Crafters
Orange Park Mall
Orange Park, FL 32073
(904)264-2888
Ultimate Parent: United States Shoe. SIC:
5999—Miscellaneous Retail Stores Nec.

★ 61891 ★   The Limited
10 Orange Park Mall
Orange Park, FL 32073
(904)269-3908
Ultimate Parent: Limited. SIC: 5651—
Family Clothing Stores.

★ 61892 ★   Petite Sophisticate
67 Orange Park Mall
Orange Park, FL 32073
(904)264-2203
Ultimate Parent: United States Shoe. SIC:
5651—Family Clothing Stores.

★ 61893 ★   Pizza Hut
1532 Kingsley Ave.
Orange Park, FL 32073
(904)264-4512
Ultimate Parent: Pepsico. SIC: 5812—
Eating Places.

★ 61894 ★   Pizza Hut
644 Park Ave.
Orange Park, FL 32073
(904)264-5631
Ultimate Parent: Pepsico. SIC: 5812—
Eating Places.

★ 61895 ★   Radio Shack
6 Old Orange Park Rd.
Orange Park, FL 32073
(904)269-2316
Company Type: Division. Ultimate Parent:
Tandy Corp. SIC: 5731—Radio, Television
& Electronics Stores.

★ 61896 ★   Ryder Truck Rental
231 Blanding Blvd.
Orange Park, FL 32073
(904)264-1345
Ultimate Parent: Ryder System. SIC:
7513—Truck Rental & Leasing Without
Drivers.

★ 61897 ★   Shell Oil Service
Station
46 Blanding Blvd.
Orange Park, FL 32073
(904)272-6106
Ultimate Parent: Shell Oil Co. SIC: 5541—
Gasoline Service Stations.

★ 61898 ★   Taco Bell
1249 Park Ave.
Orange Park, FL 32073
(904)269-9246
Ultimate Parent: Pepsico. SIC: 5812—
Eating Places.

★ 61899 ★   Toys R US
1972 Wells Rd.
Orange Park, FL 32073
(904)276-5492
Ultimate Parent: Toys "R" US. SIC: 5945—
Hobby, Toy & Game Shops.

★ 61900 ★   Wal Mart Plaza
661 Blanding Blvd.
Orange Park, FL 32073
(904)272-0036
Ultimate Parent: Wal-Mart Stores, Inc. SIC:
6512—Nonresidential Building Operators.

Orlanda

★ 61901 ★   First Union National
Bank of Florida
7204 Sand Lake Rd.
Orlanda, FL 32818
(407)469-5800
Location Type: Branch office. Ultimate
Parent: First Union Corp. SIC: 6021—
National Commercial Banks.

Orlando

★ 61902 ★   Air Products &
Chemicals Co.
8300 Exchange Dr.
Orlando, FL 32809
(407)859-5141
Ultimate Parent: Air Products & Chemicals,
Inc. SIC: 5169—Chemicals & Allied
Products Nec.

★ 61903 ★   Air Products &
Chemicals Inc.
8300 Exchange Dr.
Orlando, FL 32809
Ultimate Parent: Air Products & Chemicals,
Inc. SIC: 2813—Industrial Gases.

★ 61904 ★   Airborne Freight
Corp.
5400 Mccoy Rd.
Orlando, FL 32812
(407)855-1090
Ultimate Parent: Airborne Freight Corp.
SIC: 4212—Local Trucking Without Storage.

★ **61905** ★ **Airfoil Textron Inc.**
2287 Premier Row
Orlando, FL 32809
Ultimate Parent: Textron. **SIC:** 3724—
Aircraft Engines & Engine Parts.

★ **61906** ★ **Albertson's Inc.**
Florida Div.
PO Box 547100
602 Courtland St., Ste. 150
Orlando, FL 32854
Company Type: Division. **Officer:** Don
Dennis, Division Manager. **Ultimate Parent:**
Albertson's Inc. **SIC:** 5411—Grocery Stores.

★ **61907** ★ **Albertson's Inc.**
Southern Regional Office
PO Box 547100
602 Courtland St., Ste. 150
Orlando, FL 32854
(407)628-5858
Company Type: Division. **Officer:** R. Bruce
Gordon, Legal Vice President. **Ultimate
Parent:** Albertson's Inc. **SIC:** 5411—
Grocery Stores.

★ **61908** ★ **American General
Finance**
5214 W. Colonial Dr.
Orlando, FL 32808-7695
(407)299-0950
Location Type: Branch office. **Officer:** Dan
Poskevich. **Ultimate Parent:** American
General Corp. **SIC:** 6141—Personal Credit
Institutions; 6162—Mortgage Bankers &
Correspondents.

★ **61909** ★ **American General
Finance**
3660 Maguire Blvd., Ste. 100
Orlando, FL 32803-3059
(407)895-3555
Location Type: Branch office. **Ultimate
Parent:** American General Corp. **SIC:**
6141—Personal Credit Institutions; 6162—
Mortgage Bankers & Correspondents.

★ **61910** ★ **American General
Finance Inc.**
5214 W. Colonial Dr.
Orlando, FL 32808-7695
(407)299-0950
Location Type: Branch office. **Officer:** Dan
Poskevich. **Ultimate Parent:** American
General Corp. **SIC:** 6141—Personal Credit
Institutions; 6162—Mortgage Bankers &
Correspondents.

★ **61911** ★ **American General
Finance Inc.**
6220 S. Orange Blossom Trail SW
Orlando, FL 32809-4630
(407)855-3470
Location Type: Branch office. **Officer:**
Anne Montgomery. **Ultimate Parent:**
American General Corp. **SIC:** 6141—
Personal Credit Institutions; 6162—
Mortgage Bankers & Correspondents.

★ **61912** ★ **American General
Finance Inc.**
3660 Maguire Blvd., Ste. 100
Orlando, FL 32803-3059
(407)895-3555
Location Type: Branch office. **Ultimate
Parent:** American General Corp. **SIC:**
6141—Personal Credit Institutions; 6162—
Mortgage Bankers & Correspondents.

★ **61913** ★ **AmSouth Bank of
Florida**
5404 Silver Star Rd.
Orlando, FL 32808-4406
(407)246-8970
Location Type: Branch office. **Ultimate
Parent:** AmSouth Bancorp. **SIC:** 6022—
State Commercial Banks.

★ **61914** ★ **AmSouth Bank of
Florida**
5401 Kirkman Rd.
Orlando, FL 32819-7937
(407)351-0330
Location Type: Branch office. **Ultimate
Parent:** AmSouth Bancorp. **SIC:** 6022—
State Commercial Banks.

★ **61915** ★ **AmSouth Bank of
Florida**
500 E. Michigan St.
Orlando, FL 32806-4606
(407)246-8960
Location Type: Branch office. **Ultimate
Parent:** AmSouth Bancorp. **SIC:** 6022—
State Commercial Banks.

★ **61916** ★ **AmSouth Bank of
Florida**
305 N. Palmetto Ave.
Orlando, FL 32801-1603
(407)649-9460
Ultimate Parent: AmSouth Bancorp. **SIC:**
6022—State Commercial Banks.

★ **61917** ★ **AmSouth Bank of
Florida**
10537 E. Colonial Dr.
Orlando, FL 32817-4427
(407)246-8940
Location Type: Branch office. **Ultimate
Parent:** AmSouth Bancorp. **SIC:** 6022—
State Commercial Banks.

★ **61918** ★ **AmSouth Bank of
Florida**
1874 S. Semoran Blvd.
Orlando, FL 32822
(407)246-8980
Location Type: Branch office. **Ultimate
Parent:** AmSouth Bancorp. **SIC:** 6022—
State Commercial Banks.

★ **61919** ★ **AmSouth Bank of
Florida**
65 N. Orange Ave.
Orlando, FL 32801
(407)656-2400
Location Type: Branch office. **Ultimate
Parent:** AmSouth Bancorp. **SIC:** 6022—
State Commercial Banks.

★ **61920** ★ **At&T Microelectronics**
9333 S. John Young Pky.
Orlando, FL 32819-8698
Ultimate Parent: AT&T. **SIC:** 3674—
Semiconductors & Related Devices.

★ **61921** ★ **Barnett Bank of
Central Florida**
800 John Young Pky.
Orlando, FL 32804-8099
(407)420-2720
Company Type: Subsidiary. **Location
Type:** Branch office. **Officer:** Nadine Aulin,
Manager. **Ultimate Parent:** Barnett Banks.
SIC: 6021—National Commercial Banks.

★ **61922** ★ **Barnett Bank of
Central Florida, NA**
390 N. Orange Ave.
Orlando, FL 32801
(407)420-2894
Company Type: Subsidiary. **Location
Type:** Branch office. **Officer:** Nancy Sellers,
Manager. **Ultimate Parent:** Barnett Banks.
SIC: 6021—National Commercial Banks.

★ **61923** ★ **Barnett Bank of
Central Florida, NA**
2293 Sandlake Rd.
Orlando, FL 32809-7637
(407)646-3502
Company Type: Subsidiary. **Location
Type:** Branch office. **Officer:** Jim Glaze,
Manager. **Ultimate Parent:** Barnett Banks.
SIC: 6021—National Commercial Banks.

★ **61924** ★ **Barnett Bank of
Central Florida, NA**
7682 Dr. Phillips Dr.
Orlando, FL 32819
(407)244-7007
Company Type: Subsidiary. **Location
Type:** Branch office. **Officer:** Mike Hively,
Manager. **Ultimate Parent:** Barnett Banks.
SIC: 6021—National Commercial Banks.

★ **61925** ★ **Barnett Bank of
Central Florida, NA**
500 S. Goldenrod Rd.
Orlando, FL 32822-8199
(407)658-3891
Company Type: Subsidiary. **Location
Type:** Branch office. **Officer:** Susan
Reynolds, Manager. **Ultimate Parent:**
Barnett Banks. **SIC:** 6021—National
Commercial Banks.

★ **61926** ★ **Barnett Bank of
Central Florida, NA**
3117 E. Colonial Dr.
Orlando, FL 32803-5176
(407)420-2710
Company Type: Subsidiary. **Location
Type:** Branch office. **Ultimate Parent:**
Barnett Banks. **SIC:** 6021—National
Commercial Banks.

★ **61927** ★ **Barnett Bank of
Central Florida, NA**
2893 S. Orange Ave.
Orlando, FL 32806-5495
(407)236-5216
Company Type: Subsidiary. **Location
Type:** Branch office. **Officer:** Diana Cook,
Manager. **Ultimate Parent:** Barnett Banks.
SIC: 6021—National Commercial Banks.

★ **61928** ★ **Barnett Bank of
Central Florida, NA**
1700 S. Semoran Blvd.
Orlando, FL 32822-2999
(407)420-2741
Company Type: Subsidiary. **Location
Type:** Branch office. **Officer:** Gail Chandler,
Area Manager. **Ultimate Parent:** Barnett
Banks. **SIC:** 6021—National Commercial
Banks.

★ **61929** ★ **Barnett Bank of
Central Florida, NA**
11800 Research Pky.
Orlando, FL 32822
(407)658-3881
Company Type: Subsidiary. **Location
Type:** Branch office. **Officer:** Scott
Calloway, Manager. **Ultimate Parent:**
Barnett Banks. **SIC:** 6021—National
Commercial Banks.

★ **61930** ★ **Barnett Bank of
Central Florida, NA**
2501 N. Orange Ave., Ste. 127 S
Orlando, FL 32804-4640
(407)646-3446
Company Type: Subsidiary. **Location
Type:** Branch office. **Officer:** Darlene Peter,
Manager. **Ultimate Parent:** Barnett Banks.
SIC: 6021—National Commercial Banks.

★ **61931** ★ **Barnett Bank of
Central Florida, NA**
4725 Kirkman Rd.
Orlando, FL 32811-3656
(407)420-2760
Company Type: Subsidiary. **Location
Type:** Branch office. **Officer:** Craig Hazen,
Area Manager. **Ultimate Parent:** Barnett
Banks. **SIC:** 6021—National Commercial
Banks.

★ **61932** ★ **Barnett Bank of
Central Florida, NA**
10900 Orangewood Blvd.
Orlando, FL 32821-7954
(407)420-2774
Company Type: Subsidiary. **Location
Type:** Branch office. **Officer:** Harsha
Ramayya, Manager. **Ultimate Parent:**
Barnett Banks. **SIC:** 6021—National
Commercial Banks.

★ **61933** ★ **Barnett Bank of
Central Florida, NA**
5655 N. Orange Blossom Trl.
Orlando, FL 32810
(407)646-3567
Company Type: Subsidiary. **Location
Type:** Branch office. **Officer:** Marcie
Simmons, Manager. **Ultimate Parent:**
Barnett Banks. **SIC:** 6021—National
Commercial Banks.

★ **61934** ★ **Barnett Bank of
Central Florida, NA**
201 S. Orange Ave.
Orlando, FL 32801-3413
(407)420-2800
Company Type: Subsidiary. **Location
Type:** Branch office. **Officer:** Alexander van
den Berg, Area Manager. **Ultimate Parent:**
Barnett Banks. **SIC:** 6021—National
Commercial Banks.

★ **61935** ★ **Barnett Bank of
Central Florida, NA**
2051 Central Florida Pky.
Orlando, FL 32821-8902
(407)646-3573
Company Type: Subsidiary. **Location
Type:** Branch office. **Officer:** Larry Lee,
Manager. **Ultimate Parent:** Barnett Banks.
SIC: 6021—National Commercial Banks.

★ **61936** ★ **Beneficial Savings
Bank, FSB**
PO Box 140396
Orlando, FL 32803
Location Type: Branch office. **Ultimate
Parent:** Beneficial.

★ **61937** ★ **Beneficial Savings
Bank, FSB**
400 N. Bumby Ave.
Orlando, FL 32803-6090
(407)896-0774 **Fax:** (407)894-7099
Location Type: Branch office. **Ultimate
Parent:** Beneficial. **SIC:** 6021—National
Commercial Banks.

★ **61938** ★ **Bindley Western Drug
Co.**
Florida
2600 Titan Row
Orlando, FL 32809
(407)438-0500 **Fax:** (407)438-2771
Company Type: Subsidiary. **Officer:** J
Joshua Ramsteck, Division Manager.
Ultimate Parent: Bindley-Western
Industries, Inc.

★ **61939** ★ **Borden Inc.**
Dairy Division
1600 W. Gore St.
Orlando, FL 32805
Company Type: Division. **Ultimate Parent:**
Borden, Inc. **SIC:** 2024—Ice Cream &
Frozen Desserts.

★ **61940** ★ **Brownell Electro Inc.**
307 27th St.
Orlando, FL 32806
(305)843-6770
Location Type: Branch office. **Ultimate
Parent:** Avnet. **SIC:** 5063—Electrical
Apparatus & Equipment.

★ **61941** ★ **Burdines Home
Cleaning Service**
26 Plover Ave.
Orlando, FL 32825
(407)273-8280
Ultimate Parent: Federated Department
Stores. **SIC:** 7217—Carpet & Upholstery
Cleaning.

★ **61942** ★ **Burdines Travel
Bureau**
3505 E. Colonial Dr.
Orlando, FL 32803
(407)896-1901
Ultimate Parent: Federated Department
Stores. **SIC:** 4729—Passenger
Transportation Arrangement Nec.

★ **61943** ★ **Business Systems
Design Inc.**
12242 Gray Birch Cir.
Orlando, FL 32832-5705
(407)381-2205
Officer: Richard Slater. **Ultimate Parent:**
Avery Dennison Corp. **SIC:** 7371—
Computer Programming Services.

★ **61944** ★ **Casual Corner**
83 Colonial Plz.
Orlando, FL 32803
(407)894-2267
Ultimate Parent: United States Shoe. **SIC:**
5651—Family Clothing Stores.

★ **61945** ★ **Casual Corner**
580 Florida Mall
Orlando, FL 32809
(407)851-2103
Ultimate Parent: United States Shoe. **SIC:**
5651—Family Clothing Stores.

★ **61946** ★ **Centex-Great
Southwest Corp.**
9423 Tradeport Dr.
Orlando, FL 32827-5361
(407)856-7619 **Fax:** (407)856-8755
Officer: John D. Jeniec, President & CEO.
Ultimate Parent: Centex.

★ **61947** ★ **Chase Home
Mortgage Corp.**
605 E. Robinson St.
Orlando, FL 32801
(407)896-7082
Ultimate Parent: Chase Manhattan Corp.
SIC: 6141—Personal Credit Institutions.

★ **61948** ★ **Circuit City**
7915 S. Orange Blossom Trl.
Orlando, FL 32809
(407)850-3918
Ultimate Parent: Circuit City Stores. **SIC:**
5722—Household Appliance Stores.

★ 61949 ★   Circus World
284 Florida Mall
Orlando, FL 32809
(407)859-5922
Ultimate Parent: Melville. SIC: 5945—
Hobby, Toy & Game Shops.

★ 61950 ★   Circus World Toy Stores
Orlando
Orlando, FL 32803
(407)896-2711
Ultimate Parent: Melville. SIC: 5945—
Hobby, Toy & Game Shops.

★ 61951 ★   Citgo Petroleum Corp.
3111 E. Colonial Dr.
Orlando, FL 32803
(407)896-8152
Ultimate Parent: Citgo Petroleum. SIC:
5541—Gasoline Service Stations.

★ 61952 ★   Coast to Coast Limousine
700 E. Washington St.
Orlando, FL 32801
Ultimate Parent: Servistar Corp. SIC:
4119—Local Passenger Transportation Nec;
4119—Local Passenger Transportation Nec.

★ 61953 ★   Coast to Coast Sales Inc.
1320 N. Semoran Blvd.
Orlando, FL 32807
(407)273-2292
Ultimate Parent: Servistar Corp. SIC:
5199—Nondurable Goods Nec.

★ 61954 ★   Coca-Cola Bottling Co. Orlando
2900 Mercy Dr.
Orlando, FL 32808
Ultimate Parent: Coca-Cola Enterprises.
SIC: 2086—Bottled & Canned Soft Drinks.

★ 61955 ★   Coca Cola U S a
7598 Currency Dr.
Orlando, FL 32809
(407)856-0990
Ultimate Parent: Coca-Cola. SIC: 5149—
Groceries & Related Products Nec.

★ 61956 ★   Continental Industries Inc.
5151 Adanson St.
Orlando, FL 32804
(407)629-1594
Ultimate Parent: Handy & Harman. SIC:
6552—Subdividers & Developers Nec.

★ 61957 ★   Costco Wholesale
937 Sand Lake Rd.
Orlando, FL 32809
(407)857-3700
Ultimate Parent: Costco Wholesale Corp.
SIC: 5399—Miscellaneous General
Merchandise Store.

★ 61958 ★   Costco Wholesale
440 Kennedy Blvd.
Orlando, FL 32810
(407)660-1995
Ultimate Parent: Costco Wholesale Corp.
SIC: 4225—General Warehousing &
Storage.

★ 61959 ★   Delta Air Lines
3101 Maguire Blvd.
Orlando, FL 32803
(407)896-0374
Ultimate Parent: Delta Air Lines, Inc. SIC:
4512—Air Transportation—Scheduled.

★ 61960 ★   Delta Business Systems
4150 N. John Young Pky.
Orlando, FL 32804-7180
(407)299-7180
Location Type: Branch office. Officer:
Bryan King, President. Ultimate Parent:
Alco Standard Corp. SIC: 3663—Radio &
T.V. Communications Equipment; 7378—
Computer Maintenance & Repair; 5044—
Office Equipment; 5999—Miscellaneous
Retail Stores Nec; 6512—Nonresidential
Building Operators.

★ 61961 ★   Delta Business Systems
4150 John Young Pky.
Orlando, FL 32804
(407)299-7180
Company Type: Division. Officer: Bryan
King, President. Ultimate Parent: Alco
Standard Corp. SIC: 7378—Computer

Maintenance & Repair. Employee Count:
406. Sales: 21 M.

★ 61962 ★   Diebold Inc.
1130 S. Rio Grande Ave.
Orlando, FL 32805
(407)841-1772
Ultimate Parent: Diebold, Inc. SIC: 5046—
Commercial Equipment Nec.

★ 61963 ★   Eckerd Corp.
Eckerd Drug Co.
8201 Chancellor Dr.
Orlando, FL 32862
(407)858-4000
Company Type: Headquarters. Officer:
Jerry Stettner, Vice President. Ultimate
Parent: Eckerd Corp. SIC: 5912—Drug
Stores & Proprietary Stores.

★ 61964 ★   Exxon Shop
8099 S. Orange Ave.
Orlando, FL 32809
(407)855-0846
Ultimate Parent: Exxon. SIC: 5411—
Grocery Stores.

★ 61965 ★   Fairfield Inn by Marriott
1850 W. Landstreet Rd.
Orlando, FL 32809
(407)240-8400
Ultimate Parent: Marriott International. SIC:
7011—Hotels & Motels.

★ 61966 ★   Federal Express Corp.
5850 T G Lee Blvd.
Orlando, FL 32822
(407)855-6513
Ultimate Parent: Federal Express. SIC:
4215—Courier Services Except by Air.

★ 61967 ★   Federal Express Corp.
201 S. Orange Ave.
Orlando, FL 32801
(407)841-8631
Ultimate Parent: Federal Express. SIC:
4215—Courier Services Except by Air;
4513—Air Courier Services.

★ 61968 ★   Federal Express Corp.
635 29th St.
Orlando, FL 32805
(407)425-5793
Ultimate Parent: Federal Express. SIC:
7389—Business Services Nec.

★ 61969 ★   Federal Home Life Insurance Co. Inc.
6277 Sea Harbor Dr.
Orlando, FL 32887-0001
(407)345-2600
Company Type: Subsidiary. Officer:
Frederick M. Dawson, Chairman of the
Board & CEO. Ultimate Parent: Harcourt
General. SIC: 6211—Security Brokers &
Dealers; 6321—Accident & Health
Insurance. Employee Count: 617. Sales:
327 M.

★ 61970 ★   First Union National Bank of Florida
4549 Hoffner Ave.
Orlando, FL 32812-2334
(407)649-5426
Location Type: Branch office. Ultimate
Parent: First Union Corp. SIC: 6021—
National Commercial Banks.

★ 61971 ★   First Union National Bank of Florida
3900 Silver Star Rd.
Orlando, FL 32808-4676
(407)649-5169
Location Type: Branch office. Ultimate
Parent: First Union Corp. SIC: 6021—
National Commercial Banks.

★ 61972 ★   First Union National Bank of Florida
8120 Lake Underhill Rd.
Orlando, FL 32825-3519
(407)649-5611
Location Type: Branch office. Ultimate
Parent: First Union Corp. SIC: 6021—
National Commercial Banks.

★ 61973 ★   First Union National Bank of Florida
4012 Curry Ford Rd.
Orlando, FL 32806-2703
(407)649-5189
Location Type: Branch office. Ultimate
Parent: First Union Corp. SIC: 6021—
National Commercial Banks.

★ 61974 ★   First Union National Bank of Florida
1001 Lee Rd.
Orlando, FL 32810-5801
(407)539-7060
Location Type: Branch office. Ultimate
Parent: First Union Corp. SIC: 6021—
National Commercial Banks.

★ 61975 ★   First Union National Bank of Florida
6306 W. Colonial Dr.
Orlando, FL 32818-6818
(407)649-5607
Location Type: Branch office. Ultimate
Parent: First Union Corp. SIC: 6021—
National Commercial Banks.

★ 61976 ★   First Union National Bank of Florida
7336 E. Curry Ford Rd.
Orlando, FL 32822-7997
(407)649-5602
Location Type: Branch office. Ultimate
Parent: First Union Corp. SIC: 6021—
National Commercial Banks.

★ 61977 ★   First Union National Bank of Florida
4709 S. Orange Rd.
Orlando, FL 32806-6928
(407)649-5426
Location Type: Branch office. Ultimate
Parent: First Union Corp. SIC: 6021—
National Commercial Banks.

★ 61978 ★   First Union National Bank of Florida
798 N. Semoran Blvd.
Orlando, FL 32807-3447
(407)649-5781
Location Type: Branch office. Ultimate
Parent: First Union Corp. SIC: 6021—
National Commercial Banks.

★ 61979 ★   First Union National Bank of Florida
10375 Orangewood Blvd.
Orlando, FL 32821-8239
(407)649-5360
Location Type: Branch office. Ultimate
Parent: First Union Corp. SIC: 6021—
National Commercial Banks.

★ 61980 ★   First Union National Bank of Florida
2300 W. Oak Ridge Rd.
Orlando, FL 32809-3777
(407)649-5759
Location Type: Branch office. Ultimate
Parent: First Union Corp. SIC: 6021—
National Commercial Banks.

★ 61981 ★   First Union National Bank of Florida
1000 Universal Studios Plz.
Orlando, FL 32819
(407)649-5790
Location Type: Branch office. Ultimate
Parent: First Union Corp. SIC: 6021—
National Commercial Banks.

★ 61982 ★   First Union National Bank of Florida
3500 W. Colonial Dr.
Orlando, FL 32808-7902
(407)649-5771
Location Type: Branch office. Ultimate
Parent: First Union Corp. SIC: 6021—
National Commercial Banks.

★ 61983 ★   First Union National Bank of Florida
20 N. Orange
Orlando, FL 32802-2414
(407)649-2265
Location Type: Branch office. Ultimate
Parent: First Union Corp. SIC: 6021—
National Commercial Banks.

★ 61984 ★   First Union National Bank of Florida
7950 S. Orange Blossom Trl.
Orlando, FL 32809
(407)649-5158
Location Type: Branch office. Ultimate
Parent: First Union Corp. SIC: 6021—
National Commercial Banks.

★ 61985 ★   First Union National Bank of Florida
800 N. Magnolia Ave.
Orlando, FL 32803-3250
(407)649-5580
Location Type: Branch office. Ultimate
Parent: First Union Corp. SIC: 6021—
National Commercial Banks.

★ 61986 ★   Florida Coca-Cola Bottling Co.
2900 Mercy Dr.
Orlando, FL 32808
Ultimate Parent: Coca-Cola Enterprises.
SIC: 2086—Bottled & Canned Soft Drinks.

★ 61987 ★   Flowers Baking Co.
2424 Orlando Central Pky.
Orlando, FL 32809
(407)855-8888
Officer: Jim Matthews, President. Ultimate
Parent: Flowers Industries. SIC: 2051—
Bread, Cake & Related Products.

★ 61988 ★   Flowers Baking Co. of Orlando Inc.
2424 Orlando Central Pky.
Orlando, FL 32809
(407)855-8888 Fax: (407)857-0549
Officer: Jim Matthews, President. Ultimate
Parent: Flowers Industries.

★ 61989 ★   FMC Corp.
7300 Presidents Dr.
Orlando, FL 32809
(407)851-3377
Officer: Jerry Sibley, Manager. Ultimate
Parent: FMC. SIC: 3724—Aircraft Engines
& Engine Parts.

★ 61990 ★   Fmc Corp. Orlando
7300 Presidents Dr.
Orlando, FL 32809
Ultimate Parent: FMC. SIC: 3537—
Industrial Trucks & Tractors; 3713—Truck &
Bus Bodies.

★ 61991 ★   The Gap
3483 E. Colonial Dr.
Orlando, FL 32803
(407)895-0138
Ultimate Parent: GAP. SIC: 5699—
Miscellaneous Apparel & Accessory Stores.

★ 61992 ★   The Gap
65 Colonial Plz.
Orlando, FL 32803
(407)896-5579
Ultimate Parent: GAP. SIC: 5651—Family
Clothing Stores.

★ 61993 ★   The Gap Kids
8001 S. Orange Blossom Trl. 441
Orlando, FL 32809
Ultimate Parent: GAP. SIC: 5641—
Children's & Infants' Wear Stores.

★ 61994 ★   General American Life Insurance
315 E. Robinson St. 275
Orlando, FL 32801
(407)841-8138
Ultimate Parent: General American Life.
SIC: 6159—Miscellaneous Business Credit
Institutions.

★ 61995 ★   General American Life Insurance
2438 Lawton Rd.
Orlando, FL 32803
(407)896-0281
Ultimate Parent: General American Life.
SIC: 6162—Mortgage Bankers &
Correspondents.

★ 61996 ★   General Mills Restaurants Inc.
5900 Lake Ellenor Dr.
Orlando, FL 32809-4639
(407)851-0370
Company Type: Subsidiary. Officer:
Ronald N. Magruder, President of Olive
Garden. Ultimate Parent: General Mills.
SIC: 5812—Eating Places. Employee
Count: 90000. Sales: 2500 M.

★ 61997 ★   Great Western Bank
1389 Florida Mall Ave.
Orlando, FL 32809
(407)240-5858
Ultimate Parent: Great Western Financial
Corp. SIC: 6159—Miscellaneous Business
Credit Institutions.

★ 61998 ★ **Great Western Bank**
7575 Drive Phillips Blvd.
Orlando, FL 32819
(407)351-0017
Ultimate Parent: Great Western Financial
Corp. **SIC:** 6099—Functions Related to
Deposit Banking.

★ 61999 ★ **Harcourt Brace & Co.**
6277 Sea Harbor Dr.
Orlando, FL 32887
(407)345-2000 **Fax:** (407)345-8338
Company Type: Subsidiary. **Officer:**
Richard T. Morgan, President & CEO.
Ultimate Parent: Harcourt General.

★ 62000 ★ **Harcourt Brace
Insurance Co.**
6277 Sea Harbor Dr.
Orlando, FL 32887
(407)345-2600 **Fax:** (407)345-9354
Company Type: Subsidiary. **Officer:**
Frederick M. Dawson, Chairman & CEO.
Ultimate Parent: Harcourt General.

★ 62001 ★ **Harvest Life
Insurance Co.**
4805 Sand Lake Rd.
Orlando, FL 32819
(407)345-2000
Ultimate Parent: Harcourt General. **SIC:**
6311—Life Insurance.

★ 62002 ★ **Harvest Life
Insurance Co. Inc.**
6277 Sea Harbor Dr.
Orlando, FL 32887-0001
(407)345-2600
Company Type: Subsidiary. **Officer:**
Frederick M. Dawson, Chairman of the
Board & CEO. **Ultimate Parent:** Harcourt
General. **SIC:** 6311—Life Insurance.
Employee Count: 400.

★ 62003 ★ **Hertz Rent-A-Car**
8425 Bear Rd.
Orlando, FL 32827
(407)859-8400
Ultimate Parent: Hertz. **SIC:** 7514—
Passenger Car Rental.

★ 62004 ★ **Hertz Rent-A-Car**
Bay Lake
Orlando, FL 32808
(407)824-3632
Ultimate Parent: Hertz. **SIC:** 7539—
Automotive Repair Shops Nec.

★ 62005 ★ **Hertz Rent-A-Car**
8001 International Dr.
Orlando, FL 32819
(407)345-8121
Ultimate Parent: Hertz. **SIC:** 7539—
Automotive Repair Shops Nec.

★ 62006 ★ **Hertz Rent-A-Car**
520 N. Semoran Blvd.
Orlando, FL 32807
(407)281-0010
Ultimate Parent: Hertz. **SIC:** 7514—
Passenger Car Rental.

★ 62007 ★ **Hit or Miss**
4632 E. Colonial Dr.
Orlando, FL 32803
(407)898-2540
Ultimate Parent: TJX. **SIC:** 5621—
Women's Clothing Stores.

★ 62008 ★ **Hit or Miss Womens
Apparel**
5401 W. Oak Ridge Rd.
Orlando, FL 32819
(407)351-9737
Ultimate Parent: TJX. **SIC:** 5621—
Women's Clothing Stores.

★ 62009 ★ **Holt Rinehart &
Winston Inc.**
6277 Sea Harbor Dr.
Orlando, FL 32887-0001
(407)345-2000
Company Type: Subsidiary. **Officer:**
Richard T. Morgan, Chairman of the Board.
Ultimate Parent: Harcourt General. **SIC:**
2731—Book Publishing; 2741—
Miscellaneous Publishing; 2721—
Periodicals. **Employee Count:** 250. **Sales:**
28.1 (est) M.

★ 62010 ★ **Howmedica Inc.**
2462 Sand Lake Rd.
Orlando, FL 32809
(407)859-0192
Ultimate Parent: Pfizer. **SIC:** 3841—
Surgical & Medical Instruments.

★ 62011 ★ **IBM Corp.**
315 E. Robinson St.
Orlando, FL 32801
(407)849-9160
Ultimate Parent: IBM. **SIC:** 5099—Durable
Goods Nec.

★ 62012 ★ **Jiffy Lube**
1355 S. Semoran Blvd.
Orlando, FL 32807
(407)273-4994
Ultimate Parent: Pennzoil. **SIC:** 5541—
Gasoline Service Stations; 7539—
Automotive Repair Shops Nec.

★ 62013 ★ **Jiffy Lube**
5619 W. Colonial Dr.
Orlando, FL 32808
(407)293-0605
Ultimate Parent: Pennzoil.

★ 62014 ★ **Jiffy Lube**
60934 S. Orange Blossom Trl.
Orlando, FL 32821
(407)851-9302
Ultimate Parent: Pennzoil. **SIC:** 7538—
General Automotive Repair Shops.

★ 62015 ★ **Jiffy Lube Oil Change**
6034 S. Orange Blossom Trl
Orlando, FL 32809
(407)851-9302
Ultimate Parent: Pennzoil.

★ 62016 ★ **Johnson Controls Inc.**
4433 Parkbreeze Ct
Orlando, FL 32808
(407)291-1971
Ultimate Parent: Johnson Controls Inc.
SIC: 3822—Environmental Controls; 5063—
Electrical Apparatus & Equipment.

★ 62017 ★ **Kay Bee Toy & Hobby**
756 Florida Mall
Orlando, FL 32809
(407)859-4822
Ultimate Parent: Melville. **SIC:** 5945—
Hobby, Toy & Game Shops.

★ 62018 ★ **Kentucky Fried
Chicken**
4863 W. Colonial Dr.
Orlando, FL 32808
(407)299-1810
Ultimate Parent: Pepsico. **SIC:** 5812—
Eating Places.

★ 62019 ★ **Kentucky Fried
Chicken**
5912 S. Orange Blossom Trl
Orlando, FL 32809
(407)851-3920
Ultimate Parent: Pepsico. **SIC:** 5812—
Eating Places.

★ 62020 ★ **Kentucky Fried
Chicken**
4439 S. Semoran Blvd.
Orlando, FL 32822
(407)273-9105
Ultimate Parent: Pepsico. **SIC:** 5812—
Eating Places.

★ 62021 ★ **Kentucky Fried
Chicken**
2298 S. Orange Ave.
Orlando, FL 32806
(407)425-1836
Ultimate Parent: Pepsico. **SIC:** 5812—
Eating Places.

★ 62022 ★ **Kentucky Fried
Chicken**
104 S. Orange Blossom Trl
Orlando, FL 32805
(407)422-0421
Ultimate Parent: Pepsico. **SIC:** 5812—
Eating Places.

★ 62023 ★ **Kentucky Fried
Chicken**
444 N. Bumby Ave.
Orlando, FL 32803
(407)894-0431
Ultimate Parent: Pepsico. **SIC:** 5812—
Eating Places.

★ 62024 ★ **Kentucky Fried
Chicken**
104 S. Orange Ave.
Orlando, FL 32801
(407)422-0421
Ultimate Parent: Pepsico. **SIC:** 5812—
Eating Places.

★ 62025 ★ **Kentucky Fried
Chicken**
6217 International Dr.
Orlando, FL 32819
(407)352-9203
Ultimate Parent: Pepsico. **SIC:** 5812—
Eating Places.

★ 62026 ★ **Kentucky Fried
Chicken**
9879 International Dr.
Orlando, FL 32819
(407)352-5499
Ultimate Parent: Pepsico. **SIC:** 5812—
Eating Places.

★ 62027 ★ **Knoll International
Holdings**
Foames L.P.
1351 Gemini Blvd.
Orlando, FL 32837
Ultimate Parent: Foamex. **SIC:** 3086—
Plastics Foam Products.

★ 62028 ★ **Kroger/Nicholas**
6051 Conroy Rd.
Orlando, FL 32811
(407)363-4550
Ultimate Parent: Kroger.

★ 62029 ★ **Lane Bryant**
3443 E. Colonial Dr.
Orlando, FL 32803
(407)894-1311
Ultimate Parent: Limited. **SIC:** 5699—
Miscellaneous Apparel & Accessory Stores.

★ 62030 ★ **Lane Bryant**
Colonial Plz.
Orlando, FL 32803
(407)894-8441
Ultimate Parent: Limited. **SIC:** 5621—
Women's Clothing Stores.

★ 62031 ★ **Lane Bryant**
8001 S. Orange Blossom Trl
Orlando, FL 32809
(407)857-5900
Ultimate Parent: Limited. **SIC:** 5621—
Women's Clothing Stores.

★ 62032 ★ **T. G. Lee Foods Inc.**
315 N. Bumby Ave.
Orlando, FL 32803-6029
(407)894-4941
Company Type: Subsidiary. **Officer:**
William D. Fischer, President. **Ultimate
Parent:** Dean Foods.

★ 62033 ★ **T. G. Lee Foods**
315 N. Bumby Ave.
Orlando, FL 32803
(407)894-4941
Officer: Howard M. Dean, President.
Ultimate Parent: Dean Foods. **SIC:** 2024—
Ice Cream & Frozen Desserts; 2026—Fluid
Milk.

★ 62034 ★ **Lens Crafters**
22 Colonial Plz.
Orlando, FL 32803
(407)898-3580
Ultimate Parent: United States Shoe. **SIC:**
5995—Optical Goods Stores.

★ 62035 ★ **Lerner Shop**
69 E. Colonial Dr.
Orlando, FL 32801
(407)896-9555
Ultimate Parent: Limited. **SIC:** 5621—
Women's Clothing Stores.

★ 62036 ★ **Lerner Shop**
3287 E. Colonial Dr.
Orlando, FL 32803
(407)896-2421
Ultimate Parent: Limited. **SIC:** 5621—
Women's Clothing Stores; 5651—Family
Clothing Stores.

★ 62037 ★ **Lerner Shop**
5239 W. Colonial Dr.
Orlando, FL 32808
(407)295-0371
Ultimate Parent: Limited. **SIC:** 5651—
Family Clothing Stores.

★ 62038 ★ **Linens N Things**
4316 E. Colonial Dr.
Orlando, FL 32803
(407)898-0140
Ultimate Parent: Melville. **SIC:** 5949—
Sewing, Needlework & Piece Goods.

★ 62039 ★ **Linens N Things**
5425 International Dr.
Orlando, FL 32819
(407)352-0712
Ultimate Parent: Melville. **SIC:** 5719—
Miscellaneous Home Furnishings Stores.

★ 62040 ★ **Liquid Carbonic
Specialty Gas Corp.**
403 Zell Dr.
Orlando, FL 32824
Ultimate Parent: CBI Industries, Inc. **SIC:**
2813—Industrial Gases.

★ 62041 ★ **Loral Instrumentation**
12443 Research Pky. 306
Orlando, FL 32826
(407)658-0807
Ultimate Parent: Loral Corp. **SIC:** 5063—
Electrical Apparatus & Equipment.

★ 62042 ★ **Magic Chef Inc.**
1125 Intermodal Way
Orlando, FL 32824
(407)857-3639
Ultimate Parent: Maytag. **SIC:** 5064—
Electrical Appliances—Television & Radio.

★ 62043 ★ **Magnetek National
Electric Coil Inc.**
625 W. Pine St.
Orlando, FL 32805
Ultimate Parent: Magnetek Inc. **SIC:**
3621—Motors & Generators.

★ 62044 ★ **Martin Marietta Corp.
Electonic Systems Co.**
12506 E. Lake Underhill Rd.
Orlando, FL 32862-8007
Ultimate Parent: Martin Marietta. **SIC:**
3761—Guided Missiles & Space Vehicles;
3769—Space Vehicle Equipment Nec;
7372—Prepackaged Software.

★ 62045 ★ **Martin Marietta
Electronic Systems**
12506 Lake Underhill Dr.
Orlando, FL 32862-8007
Ultimate Parent: Martin Marietta. **SIC:**
3769—Space Vehicle Equipment Nec;
3812—Search & Navigation Equipment.

★ 62046 ★ **Martin Marietta
Electronics & Missiles**
PO Box 55587
Orlando, FL 32855-5837
(407)356-2000 **Fax:** (407)356-2010
Officer: Joseph D. Antinucci, President.
Ultimate Parent: Martin Marietta.

★ 62047 ★ **Martin Marietta
Electronics Systems Co.**
12506 E. Lake Underhill Rd.
Orlando, FL 32862-8007
Ultimate Parent: Martin Marietta. **SIC:**
3761—Guided Missiles & Space Vehicles;
3769—Space Vehicle Equipment Nec;
7372—Prepackaged Software.

★ 62048 ★ **Martin Marietta
Missile Systems**
5600 Sand Lake Rd.
Orlando, FL 32855
Ultimate Parent: Martin Marietta. **SIC:**
3761—Guided Missiles & Space Vehicles;
3812—Search & Navigation Equipment.

★ 62049 ★ **Martin Marietta
Missile Systems**
4600 Sand Lake Rd.
Orlando, FL 32855
Ultimate Parent: Martin Marietta. **SIC:**
3761—Guided Missiles & Space Vehicles;
3769—Space Vehicle Equipment Nec;
7372—Prepackaged Software.

★ 62050 ★ **Martin Marietta
Missile Systems Co.**
4600 Sand Lake Rd.
Orlando, FL 32855-5837
Ultimate Parent: Martin Marietta. **SIC:**
3761—Guided Missiles & Space Vehicles;
3769—Space Vehicle Equipment Nec;
7372—Prepackaged Software.

★ 62051 ★   Martin Marietta
Ordnance Systems, Inc.
PO Box 55587
Orlando, FL 32855-5837
(407)356-4101
Officer: Linda S. Hudson, Vice President.
Ultimate Parent: Martin Marietta.

★ 62052 ★   Martin Marietta
Technologies Inc.
5600 Sand Lake Rd.
Orlando, FL 32855-5837
Ultimate Parent: Martin Marietta. SIC:
3761—Guided Missiles & Space Vehicles;
3812—Search & Navigation Equipment.

★ 62053 ★   Mary Kay Cosmetics
5406 Chenault Ave.
Orlando, FL 32809
(407)855-3466
Ultimate Parent: Mary Kay Cosmetics. SIC:
5999—Miscellaneous Retail Stores Nec.

★ 62054 ★   Mary Kay Cosmetics
5231 Merimont Ct.
Orlando, FL 32808
Ultimate Parent: Mary Kay Cosmetics. SIC:
5999—Miscellaneous Retail Stores Nec.

★ 62055 ★   McDonald's
Restaurants
4 Gardenia
Orlando, FL 32813
(407)629-1282
Ultimate Parent: McDonald's.
SIC: 5812—Eating Places.

★ 62056 ★   McDonalds
Restaurants
2601 W. Colonial Dr.
Orlando, FL 32804
(407)293-9410
Ultimate Parent: McDonald's.
SIC: 5812—Eating Places.

★ 62057 ★   McDonalds
Restaurants
6820 N. Orange Blossom Trl
Orlando, FL 32810
(407)291-7352
Ultimate Parent: McDonald's.
SIC: 5812—Eating Places.

★ 62058 ★   McDonalds
Restaurants
12305 University Blvd.
Orlando, FL 32817
(407)658-0579
Ultimate Parent: McDonald's.
SIC: 5812—Eating Places.

★ 62059 ★   McDonalds
Restaurants
3613 Mccoy Rd.
Orlando, FL 32812
(407)859-0431
Ultimate Parent: McDonald's.
SIC: 5812—Eating Places.

★ 62060 ★   Mobil Corp.
6750 Forest City Rd.
Orlando, FL 32810
(407)291-3942
Ultimate Parent: Mobil. SIC: 5541—
Gasoline Service Stations.

★ 62061 ★   Mobil Mart (Mobil Oil
Corp)
7995 S. Orange Blossom Trl
Orlando, FL 32809
(407)240-3932
Ultimate Parent: Mobil. SIC: 5411—
Grocery Stores.

★ 62062 ★   Mobil Oil
5490 S. Kirkman Rd.
Orlando, FL 32819
(407)859-6359
Ultimate Parent: Mobil. SIC: 5541—
Gasoline Service Stations.

★ 62063 ★   Mobil Oil Corp.
7601 E. Colonial Dr.
Orlando, FL 32807
(407)281-8193
Ultimate Parent: Mobil. SIC: 5541—
Gasoline Service Stations.

★ 62064 ★   Mobil Service
5900 S. Orange Blossom Trl
Orlando, FL 32809
(407)855-8314
Ultimate Parent: Mobil. SIC: 5541—
Gasoline Service Stations.

★ 62065 ★   Monarch Industries
Inc.
717 S. Kirkman Rd.
Orlando, FL 32811
(407)291-1557
Ultimate Parent: Avery Dennison Corp.
SIC: 5084—Industrial Machinery &
Equipment.

★ 62066 ★   NCR Corp.
2700 S. Orange Ave.
Orlando, FL 32806-5409
(407)841-7823
Location Type: Branch office. Officer:
George Papageorgiou. Ultimate Parent:
AT&T. SIC: 5145—Confectionery; 7374—
Data Processing & Preparation.

★ 62067 ★   New England Mutual
Life Insurance
1111 S. Orange Ave.
Orlando, FL 32806
(407)843-3430
Ultimate Parent: New England Mutual Life.
SIC: 6411—Insurance Agents, Brokers &
Service.

★ 62068 ★   New York Life
Orlando General Office
Southeastern Agencies
Maitland Summitt Park
1950 Summitt Park Dr., 2nd Fl.
Orlando, FL 32810
(407)660-5600 Fax: (407)237-6223
Officer: William C Gallagher, General
Manager. Ultimate Parent: New York Life.

★ 62069 ★   Olive Garden
5900 Lake Ellenor Dr.
Orlando, FL 32809
(407)851-0370 Fax: (407)850-5290
Company Type: Subsidiary. Ultimate
Parent: General Mills.

★ 62070 ★   Orlando Coca-Cola
Bottling Co.
2900 Mercy Dr.
Orlando, FL 32808
Ultimate Parent: Coca-Cola Enterprises.
SIC: 2086—Bottled & Canned Soft Drinks.

★ 62071 ★   Otis Elevator Co.
4639 Parkway Commerce Blvd.
Orlando, FL 32808
(407)298-7033
Ultimate Parent: United Technologies. SIC:
5084—Industrial Machinery & Equipment.

★ 62072 ★   Pactel Paging
5125 Adanson St.
Orlando, FL 32804
(407)690-2300
Ultimate Parent: Pacific Telesis Group.
SIC: 5099—Durable Goods Nec; 4812—
Radiotelephone Communications.

★ 62073 ★   Penn Mutual Life
Insurance Co.
723 E. Colonial Dr.
Orlando, FL 32803
(407)898-2626
Ultimate Parent: Penn Mutual Life. SIC:
6411—Insurance Agents, Brokers &
Service.

★ 62074 ★   Pepsi-Cola Bottling
Co.
1700 Directors Row
Orlando, FL 32809
(407)826-5900
Officer: Dennis DeCarlo, Manager.
Ultimate Parent: Pepsico. SIC: 2086—
Bottled & Canned Soft Drinks.

★ 62075 ★   Pepsi-Cola Bottling
Co.
PO Box 13889
Orlando, FL 32859
(407)857-3300
Officer: Dennis DeCarlo, Manager.
Ultimate Parent: Pepsico. SIC: 2086—
Bottled & Canned Soft Drinks.

★ 62076 ★   Perkin Elmer Corp.
5750 Major Blvd.
Orlando, FL 32819
(407)351-6335
Ultimate Parent: Perkin-Elmer. SIC: 5046—
Commercial Equipment Nec.

★ 62077 ★   Personal Performance
Consultants
1200 Hillcrest St.
Orlando, FL 32803
(407)898-5561
Ultimate Parent: Medco Containment
Services. SIC: 8742—Management
Consulting Services.

★ 62078 ★   Petite Sophisticate
576 Florida Mall
Orlando, FL 32809
(407)857-5919
Ultimate Parent: United States Shoe. SIC:
5651—Family Clothing Stores.

★ 62079 ★   Petite Sophisticate
3383 E. Colonial Dr.
Orlando, FL 32803
(407)897-3515
Ultimate Parent: United States Shoe. SIC:
5621—Women's Clothing Stores.

★ 62080 ★   Piggly Wiggly
11672 E. Colonial Dr.
Orlando, FL 32817
(407)282-5050
Ultimate Parent: Bruno's. SIC: 5411—
Grocery Stores.

★ 62081 ★   Pitney Bowes
Facsimile Systems
4390 35th St.
Orlando, FL 32811
(407)423-2898
Officer: Ray Howard, Manager. Ultimate
Parent: Pitney Bowes. SIC: 3663—Radio &
T.V. Communications Equipment.

★ 62082 ★   Pizza Hut
4205 Curry Ford Rd.
Orlando, FL 32806
(407)895-5415
Ultimate Parent: Pepsico. SIC: 5812—
Eating Places.

★ 62083 ★   Pizza Hut
4096 W. Colonial Dr.
Orlando, FL 32808
(407)293-0333
Ultimate Parent: Pepsico. SIC: 5813—
Drinking Places.

★ 62084 ★   Pizza Hut
2215 W. Oak Ridge Rd.
Orlando, FL 32809
(407)851-6164
Ultimate Parent: Pepsico. SIC: 5812—
Eating Places.

★ 62085 ★   Pizza Hut
10002 University Blvd.
Orlando, FL 32817
(407)679-7575
Ultimate Parent: Pepsico. SIC: 5812—
Eating Places.

★ 62086 ★   Pizza Hut
810 W. Colonial Dr.
Orlando, FL 32804
(407)425-8801
Ultimate Parent: Pepsico. SIC: 5812—
Eating Places.

★ 62087 ★   Pizza Hut
4240 S. Semoran Blvd.
Orlando, FL 32822
(407)380-3444
Ultimate Parent: Pepsico. SIC: 5812—
Eating Places.

★ 62088 ★   Pizza Hut
6325 Silver Star Rd.
Orlando, FL 32818
(407)298-2100
Ultimate Parent: Pepsico. SIC: 5812—
Eating Places.

★ 62089 ★   Pizza Hut
8128 S. Orange Blossom Trl.
Orlando, FL 32809
(407)855-2287
Ultimate Parent: Pepsico. SIC: 5812—
Eating Places.

★ 62090 ★   Pizza Hut
883 S. Semoran Blvd.
Orlando, FL 32807
(407)886-1729
Ultimate Parent: Pepsico. SIC: 5812—
Eating Places.

★ 62091 ★   Pizza Hut
1621 S. Orange Ave.
Orlando, FL 32806
(407)425-2442
Ultimate Parent: Pepsico. SIC: 5812—
Eating Places.

★ 62092 ★   Pizza Hut
8015 S. Orange Ave.
Orlando, FL 32809
(407)855-8688
Ultimate Parent: Pepsico. SIC: 5812—
Eating Places.

★ 62093 ★   Pizza Hut
5110 N. Lane
Orlando, FL 32808
(407)291-9222
Ultimate Parent: Pepsico. SIC: 5812—
Eating Places.

★ 62094 ★   Pizza Hut
1400 S. Crystal Lake Dr.
Orlando, FL 32806
(407)425-4841
Ultimate Parent: Pepsico. SIC: 5813—
Drinking Places.

★ 62095 ★   Pizza Hut
700 Maguire Blvd.
Orlando, FL 32803
(407)898-2960
Ultimate Parent: Pepsico. SIC: 5812—
Eating Places.

★ 62096 ★   Pizza Hut
3100 N. Alafaya Trl.
Orlando, FL 32826
(407)277-2433
Ultimate Parent: Pepsico. SIC: 5812—
Eating Places.

★ 62097 ★   Pizza Hut
7685 E. Colonial Dr.
Orlando, FL 32807
(407)282-6828
Ultimate Parent: Pepsico. SIC: 5812—
Eating Places.

★ 62098 ★   Pizza Hut
820 Lee Rd.
Orlando, FL 32810
(407)645-3455
Ultimate Parent: Pepsico. SIC: 5813—
Drinking Places.

★ 62099 ★   Pizza Hut
5801 Conroy Rd.
Orlando, FL 32811
(407)297-7676
Ultimate Parent: Pepsico. SIC: 5812—
Eating Places.

★ 62100 ★   Ppg Industries Inc.
1705 S. Division Ave.
Orlando, FL 32805
(407)425-6657
Ultimate Parent: PPG Industries Inc. SIC:
1793—Glass & Glazing Work.

★ 62101 ★   Publix Super Market
483 S. Chickasaw Trl
Orlando, FL 32825
(407)275-5507
Ultimate Parent: Publix Super Markets.
SIC: 5411—Grocery Stores.

★ 62102 ★   Publix Super Market
7653 S. Orange Blossom Trl
Orlando, FL 32809
(407)857-0083
Ultimate Parent: Publix Super Markets.
SIC: 5411—Grocery Stores.

★ 62103 ★   Publix Super Market
10115 University Blvd.
Orlando, FL 32817
(407)657-6777
Ultimate Parent: Publix Super Markets.
SIC: 5411—Grocery Stores.

★ 62104 ★   Publix Super Market
7915 S. Orange Ave.
Orlando, FL 32809
(407)855-5823
Ultimate Parent: Publix Super Markets.
SIC: 5411—Grocery Stores.

★ 62105 ★   Publix Super Market
6135 Silver Star Rd.
Orlando, FL 32808
(407)298-0636
Ultimate Parent: Publix Super Markets.
SIC: 5411—Grocery Stores.

★ 62106 ★　Publix Super Market
2724 N. Hiawassee Rd.
Orlando, FL 32818
(407)298-5013
Ultimate Parent: Publix Super Markets.
SIC: 5411—Grocery Stores.

★ 62107 ★　Publix Super Market
5800 N. Orange Blossom Trl
Orlando, FL 32810
(407)297-0097
Ultimate Parent: Publix Super Markets.
SIC: 5411—Grocery Stores.

★ 62108 ★　Publix Super Market
2418 E. Colonial Dr.
Orlando, FL 32803
(407)894-4121
Ultimate Parent: Publix Super Markets.
SIC: 5411—Grocery Stores.

★ 62109 ★　Publix Super Market
300 E. Michigan St.
Orlando, FL 32806
(407)843-9285
Ultimate Parent: Publix Super Markets.
SIC: 5411—Grocery Stores.

★ 62110 ★　Publix Super Market
Conway Cir.
Orlando, FL 32806
(407)275-9161
Ultimate Parent: Publix Super Markets.
SIC: 5411—Grocery Stores.

★ 62111 ★　Publix Super Market
4402 Curry Ford Rd.
Orlando, FL 32812
(407)275-1961
Ultimate Parent: Publix Super Markets.
SIC: 5411—Grocery Stores.

★ 62112 ★　Publix Super Market
5132 W. Colonial Dr.
Orlando, FL 32808
(407)658-1869
Ultimate Parent: Publix Super Markets.
SIC: 5411—Grocery Stores.

★ 62113 ★　Publix Super Markets
10115 University Blvd.
Orlando, FL 32817
(407)657-6777
Ultimate Parent: Publix Super Markets.
SIC: 5411—Grocery Stores.

★ 62114 ★　Publix Super Markets
2724 N. Hiawassee Rd.
Orlando, FL 32818
(407)298-5013
Ultimate Parent: Publix Super Markets.
SIC: 5411—Grocery Stores.

★ 62115 ★　Publix Super Markets
5800 N. Orange Blossom Trl
Orlando, FL 32810
(407)297-0097
Ultimate Parent: Publix Super Markets.
SIC: 5411—Grocery Stores.

★ 62116 ★　Publix Super Markets
4402 Curry Ford Rd.
Orlando, FL 32812
(407)275-1961
Ultimate Parent: Publix Super Markets.
SIC: 5411—Grocery Stores.

★ 62117 ★　Publix Super Markets
6135 Silver Star Rd.
Orlando, FL 32808
(407)298-0636
Ultimate Parent: Publix Super Markets.
SIC: 5411—Grocery Stores.

★ 62118 ★　Publix Super Markets
7915 S. Orange Ave.
Orlando, FL 32809
(407)855-5823
Ultimate Parent: Publix Super Markets.
SIC: 5411—Grocery Stores.

★ 62119 ★　Publix Super Markets
Conway Cir.
Orlando, FL 32806
(407)275-9161
Ultimate Parent: Publix Super Markets.
SIC: 5411—Grocery Stores.

★ 62120 ★　Publix Super Markets
300 E. Michigan St.
Orlando, FL 32806
(407)843-9285
Ultimate Parent: Publix Super Markets.
SIC: 5411—Grocery Stores.

★ 62121 ★　Publix Super Markets
2418 E. Colonial Dr.
Orlando, FL 32803
(407)894-4121
Ultimate Parent: Publix Super Markets.
SIC: 5411—Grocery Stores.

★ 62122 ★　Radio Shack
2139 W. Colonial Dr.
Orlando, FL 32804
(407)425-7413
Company Type: Division. Ultimate Parent:
Tandy Corp. SIC: 5731—Radio, Television
& Electronics Stores.

★ 62123 ★　Radio Shack
2372 W. Oak Ridge Rd.
Orlando, FL 32809
(407)857-2185
Company Type: Division. Ultimate Parent:
Tandy Corp. SIC: 5063—Electrical
Apparatus & Equipment; 5731—Radio,
Television & Electronics Stores.

★ 62124 ★　Radio Shack
7905 S. Orange Blossom Trl
Orlando, FL 32809
(407)855-8034
Company Type: Division. Ultimate Parent:
Tandy Corp. SIC: 5731—Radio, Television
& Electronics Stores.

★ 62125 ★　Radio Shack
743 S. Semoran Blvd.
Orlando, FL 32807
(407)273-2119
Company Type: Division. Ultimate Parent:
Tandy Corp. SIC: 5731—Radio, Television
& Electronics Stores.

★ 62126 ★　Radio Shack
2979 E. Colonial Dr.
Orlando, FL 32803
(407)894-4391
Company Type: Division. Ultimate Parent:
Tandy Corp. SIC: 5065—Electronic Parts &
Equipment Nec.

★ 62127 ★　Radio Shack
748 Florida Mall
Orlando, FL 32809
(407)859-1811
Company Type: Division. Ultimate Parent:
Tandy Corp. SIC: 5065—Electronic Parts &
Equipment Nec.

★ 62128 ★　Radio Shack
8510 S. Orange Blossom Trl
Orlando, FL 32809
(407)894-0570
Company Type: Division. Ultimate Parent:
Tandy Corp. SIC: 5999—Miscellaneous
Retail Stores Nec; 7373—Computer
Integrated Systems Design.

★ 62129 ★　Radio Shack
3405 E. Colonial Dr.
Orlando, FL 32803
(407)894-4502
Company Type: Division. Ultimate Parent:
Tandy Corp. SIC: 5731—Radio, Television
& Electronics Stores.

★ 62130 ★　RAM Mobile Data
3504 Lake Lynda Dr.
Orlando, FL 32817-1484
(407)382-2368
Ultimate Parent: BellSouth Corp. SIC:
5065—Electronic Parts & Equipment Nec.

★ 62131 ★　Red Lobster USA
5900 Lake Ellenor Dr.
Orlando, FL 32809
(407)851-0370 Fax: (407)850-5290
Company Type: Subsidiary. Ultimate
Parent: General Mills.

★ 62132 ★　Reliance Insurance
Co.
615 E. Princeton St.
Orlando, FL 32803
(407)898-5611
Ultimate Parent: Reliance Group Holdings.
SIC: 6411—Insurance Agents, Brokers &
Service.

★ 62133 ★　Rite Aid Discount
Pharmacy
2641 N. Hiawassee Rd.
Orlando, FL 32818
(407)295-5762
Ultimate Parent: Rite Aid. SIC: 5912—Drug
Stores & Proprietary Stores.

★ 62134 ★　Rite Aid Discount
Pharmacy
2450 S. Orange Ave.
Orlando, FL 32806
(407)422-7811
Ultimate Parent: Rite Aid. SIC: 5912—Drug
Stores & Proprietary Stores.

★ 62135 ★　Rite-Aid Pharmacy
2716 N. Pine Hills Rd.
Orlando, FL 32808
(407)293-9865
Ultimate Parent: Rite Aid. SIC: 5912—Drug
Stores & Proprietary Stores.

★ 62136 ★　Ryder Truck Rental
2920 E. Robinson St.
Orlando, FL 32803
(407)898-4158
Ultimate Parent: Ryder System. SIC:
7513—Truck Rental & Leasing Without
Drivers.

★ 62137 ★　Ryder Truck Rental
4542 N. Orange Blossom Trl
Orlando, FL 32804
(407)898-4158
Ultimate Parent: Ryder System. SIC:
7539—Automotive Repair Shops Nec.

★ 62138 ★　Ryder Truck Rental
1816 W. Gore St.
Orlando, FL 32805
(407)849-0761
Ultimate Parent: Ryder System. SIC:
7539—Automotive Repair Shops Nec.

★ 62139 ★　Sea World of Florida,
Inc.
7007 Sea World Dr.
Orlando, FL 32821
(407)351-3600 Fax: (407)345-5268
Company Type: Subsidiary. Officer:
William Davis, President. Ultimate Parent:
Agway Inc. SIC: 7996—Amusement Parks.
Employee Count: 1100.

★ 62140 ★　Sealy Mattress Co.
11220 Space Blvd.
Orlando, FL 32837
(407)855-8523
Officer: Lou Sammartano, Manager.
Ultimate Parent: Sealy. SIC: 2515—
Mattresses & Bedsprings.

★ 62141 ★　Service Merchandise
901 W. Landstreet Rd.
Orlando, FL 32824
(407)856-2600
Ultimate Parent: Service Merchandise Co.,
Inc. SIC: 4226—Special Warehousing &
Storage Nec.

★ 62142 ★　Shell Oil Co.
1512 W. Colonial Dr.
Orlando, FL 32804
(407)422-4486
Ultimate Parent: Shell Oil Co. SIC: 5172—
Petroleum Products Nec.

★ 62143 ★　Sherwin-Williams Co.
2150 Sand Lake Rd.
Orlando, FL 32809
(407)859-4260
Officer: J.A. Samples, Manager. Ultimate
Parent: Sherwin-Williams Co. SIC: 2851—
Paints & Allied Products.

★ 62144 ★　Sonoco Products Co.
1854 Central Florida Pky.
Orlando, FL 32821
Ultimate Parent: Sonoco Products. SIC:
3499—Fabricated Metal Products Nec.

★ 62145 ★　Southland Corp.
1300 Lee Rd.
Orlando, FL 32810
(407)295-3076
Ultimate Parent: Southland Corp. SIC:
5411—Grocery Stores.

★ 62146 ★　Southland Corp.
3430 N. Orange Blossom Trl
Orlando, FL 32804
(407)298-5777
Ultimate Parent: Southland Corp. SIC:
5411—Grocery Stores.

★ 62147 ★　Southland Corp.
5389 Conroy Rd.
Orlando, FL 32811
(407)425-1531
Ultimate Parent: Southland Corp. SIC:
5411—Grocery Stores.

★ 62148 ★　Stanley Door Systems
7600 Kingspointe Pky.
Orlando, FL 32819
(407)363-0577
Officer: Linda Meyer, Manager. Ultimate
Parent: Stanley Works. SIC: 2431—
Millwork.

★ 62149 ★　Stone Container Corp.
4364 SW 34th St.
Orlando, FL 32811
(407)843-1300
Officer: Richard Roberts, Plant Manager.
Ultimate Parent: Stone Container Corp.
SIC: 3559—Special Industry Machinery
Nec.

★ 62150 ★　Sunoco Products Co.
1854 Central Florida Pky.
Orlando, FL 32837
(407)851-5800
Officer: Dean Miller, Manager. Ultimate
Parent: Sonoco Products. SIC: 2655—Fiber
Cans, Drums & Similar Products; 3411—
Metal Cans; 3412—Metal Barrels, Drums &
Pails.

★ 62151 ★　T. G. Lee Foods Inc.
315 N. Bumby St.
Orlando, FL 32803-6025
Ultimate Parent: Dean Foods. SIC: 2026—
Fluid Milk.

★ 62152 ★　T. G. Lee Foods Inc.
315 North Bay Ave.
Orlando, FL 32803-6025
Ultimate Parent: Dean Foods. SIC: 2026—
Fluid Milk.

★ 62153 ★　Taco Bell
2107 W. Colonial Dr.
Orlando, FL 32804
(407)422-7664
Ultimate Parent: Pepsico. SIC: 5812—
Eating Places.

★ 62154 ★　Taco Bell
1501 Lee Rd.
Orlando, FL 32810
(407)299-1929
Ultimate Parent: Pepsico. SIC: 5812—
Eating Places.

★ 62155 ★　Taco Bell
6127 S. Orange Blossom Trl
Orlando, FL 32809
(407)859-3900
Ultimate Parent: Pepsico. SIC: 5812—
Eating Places.

★ 62156 ★　Taco Bell
4225 E. Colonial Dr.
Orlando, FL 32803
(407)896-7940
Ultimate Parent: Pepsico. SIC: 5812—
Eating Places.

★ 62157 ★　Taco Bell
7853 E. Colonial Dr.
Orlando, FL 32807
(407)277-7543
Ultimate Parent: Pepsico. SIC: 5812—
Eating Places.

★ 62158 ★　Tektronix Inc.
3657 Maguire Blvd.
Orlando, FL 32803
(407)894-3911
Ultimate Parent: Tektronix, Inc. SIC:
5049—Professional Equipment Nec.

★ 62159 ★　Texaco
3200 S. Conway Rd.
Orlando, FL 32812
(407)275-3631
Ultimate Parent: Texaco. SIC: 5541—
Gasoline Service Stations.

★ 62160 ★　Texaco
827 W. Lancaster Rd.
Orlando, FL 32809
(407)857-2465
Ultimate Parent: Texaco. SIC: 5411—
Grocery Stores.

★ 62161 ★　Texaco
9555 E. Colonial Dr.
Orlando, FL 32817
(407)273-3555
Ultimate Parent: Texaco. SIC: 5541—
Gasoline Service Stations.

★ 62162 ★ **Texaco Food Mart**
1544 E. Ridgewood St.
Orlando, FL 32803
(407)258-3409
Ultimate Parent: Texaco. **SIC:** 5999—
Miscellaneous Retail Stores Nec.

★ 62163 ★ **Texaco Inc.**
3555 Maguire Blvd.
Orlando, FL 32803
(407)894-2731
Ultimate Parent: Texaco. **SIC:** 5171—
Petroleum Bulk Stations & Terminals.

★ 62164 ★ **T.G. Lee Foods Inc.**
315 North Bumby St.
Orlando, FL 32803-6025
Ultimate Parent: Dean Foods. **SIC:** 2026—
Fluid Milk.

★ 62165 ★ **This End Up**
3201 E. Colonial Dr.
Orlando, FL 32803
(407)898-2921
Ultimate Parent: Melville. **SIC:** 5712—
Furniture Stores.

★ 62166 ★ **This End Up Furniture**
908 Florida Mall
Orlando, FL 32809
(407)851-8451
Ultimate Parent: Melville. **SIC:** 5712—
Furniture Stores.

★ 62167 ★ **This End Up Furniture**
2011 Viscount Row
Orlando, FL 32809
Ultimate Parent: Melville. **SIC:** 5712—
Furniture Stores.

★ 62168 ★ **Thom Mcan Shoe
Store**
3485 E. Colonial Dr.
Orlando, FL 32803
(407)894-1389
Ultimate Parent: Melville. **SIC:** 5661—Shoe
Stores.

★ 62169 ★ **Thom Mcan Shoes**
3485 W. Colonial Dr.
Orlando, FL 32808
Ultimate Parent: Melville. **SIC:** 5661—Shoe
Stores.

★ 62170 ★ **Time Electronics**
4203 Vineland Rd., Ste. K7
Orlando, FL 32811
(407)841-6565
Location Type: Branch office. **Ultimate
Parent:** Avnet. **SIC:** 5065—Electronic Parts
& Equipment Nec.

★ 62171 ★ **Toys R US**
12323 S. Orange Ave.
Orlando, FL 32824
(407)826-0896
Ultimate Parent: Toys "R" US. **SIC:** 5699—
Miscellaneous Apparel & Accessory Stores.

★ 62172 ★ **Trailways Bus System**
30 N. Hughey Ave.
Orlando, FL 32801
(407)422-7107
Ultimate Parent: Greyhound Lines Inc. **SIC:**
4131—Intercity & Rural Bus Transportation;
4212—Local Trucking Without Storage.

★ 62173 ★ **United Parcel Service**
598027 PO Box
Orlando, FL 32859
(407)339-3500
Ultimate Parent: United Parcel Service of
America. **SIC:** 4212—Local Trucking
Without Storage.

★ 62174 ★ **United Parcel
Services Inc.**
598027 PO Box
Orlando, FL 32859
(407)339-3500
Ultimate Parent: United Parcel Service of
America. **SIC:** 4212—Local Trucking
Without Storage.

★ 62175 ★ **Valentec Dayron**
333 Maquire Blvd.
Orlando, FL 32814
Ultimate Parent: Insilco Corp. **SIC:** 3489—
Ordnance & Accessories Nec.

★ 62176 ★ **Valentec Dayron Inc.**
333 Maguire Blvd.
Orlando, FL 32803
Ultimate Parent: Insilco Corp. **SIC:** 3489—
Ordnance & Accessories Nec.

★ 62177 ★ **Valentec International
Corp.**
Valentec Dayron Div.
333 Maguire Blvd.
Orlando, FL 32803
Company Type: Division. **Ultimate Parent:**
Insilco Corp. **SIC:** 3489—Ordnance &
Accessories Nec.

★ 62178 ★ **Victoria's Secret**
8001 S. Orange Blossom Trl
Orlando, FL 32809
(407)859-9983
Ultimate Parent: Limited. **SIC:** 5699—
Miscellaneous Apparel & Accessory Stores.

★ 62179 ★ **Wal Mart Discount
City**
10749 E. Colonial Dr.
Orlando, FL 32817
(407)281-8941
Ultimate Parent: Wal-Mart Stores, Inc. **SIC:**
5331—Variety Stores.

★ 62180 ★ **Waldenbooks**
79 Colonial Plz.
Orlando, FL 32803
(407)896-2272
Ultimate Parent: K-Mart. **SIC:** 5942—Book
Stores.

★ 62181 ★ **Waldenbooks**
732 Florida Mall
Orlando, FL 32809
(407)859-8787
Ultimate Parent: K-Mart. **SIC:** 5942—Book
Stores.

★ 62182 ★ **Walgreen Drug Stores**
7669 S. Orange Blossom Trl.
Orlando, FL 32809
(407)856-1807
Ultimate Parent: Walgreen Co. **SIC:**
5912—Drug Stores & Proprietary Stores.

★ 62183 ★ **Walgreen Drug Stores**
5340 Silver Star Rd.
Orlando, FL 32808
(407)298-6360
Ultimate Parent: Walgreen Co. **SIC:**
5912—Drug Stores & Proprietary Stores.

★ 62184 ★ **Walgreen Drug Stores**
4608 E. Michigan St.
Orlando, FL 32812
(407)281-6892
Ultimate Parent: Walgreen Co. **SIC:**
5912—Drug Stores & Proprietary Stores.

★ 62185 ★ **Walgreen Drug Stores**
503 S. Chickasaw Trl.
Orlando, FL 32825
(407)658-1038
Ultimate Parent: Walgreen Co. **SIC:**
5912—Drug Stores & Proprietary Stores.

★ 62186 ★ **Walgreen Drug Stores**
2410 E. Colonial Dr.
Orlando, FL 32803
(407)894-5361
Ultimate Parent: Walgreen Co. **SIC:**
5912—Drug Stores & Proprietary Stores.

★ 62187 ★ **Walgreen Drug Stores**
4578 S. Kirkman Rd.
Orlando, FL 32811
(407)293-8398
Ultimate Parent: Walgreen Co. **SIC:**
5912—Drug Stores & Proprietary Stores.

★ 62188 ★ **Wall Street Journal**
8251 Presidents Dr.
Orlando, FL 32809
(407)857-2600
Officer: Edward Gareau, Manager.
Ultimate Parent: Dow Jones. **SIC:** 2711—
Newspapers; 2759—Commercial Printing
Nec.

★ 62189 ★ **Walt Disney Travel
Co. Inc.**
7100 Municipal Dr.
Orlando, FL 32819-8912
(407)363-6300
Company Type: Subsidiary. **Officer:** Jack
Lindquist, Chairman of the Board. **Ultimate
Parent:** Walt Disney Co. **SIC:** 4725—Tour
Operators; 4724—Travel Agencies.
Employee Count: 347. **Sales:** 54 M.

★ 62190 ★ **Walt Disney World**
3105 E. Washington St.
Orlando, FL 32803
(407)824-5752
Ultimate Parent: Walt Disney Co.

★ 62191 ★ **Walt Disney World
Co.**
1375 N. Buena Vista Ave.
Orlando, FL 32818-5901
Company Type: Subsidiary. **Officer:** Frank
Wells, Chairman of the Board, CEO.
Ultimate Parent: Walt Disney Co. **SIC:**
7996—Amusement Parks; 7011—Hotels &
Motels; 5947—Gift, Novelty & Souvenir
Shops. **Employee Count:** 32000. **Sales:** 3
M.

★ 62192 ★ **Webber Farms Inc.**
3716 Silver Star Rd.
Orlando, FL 32808
(407)293-2250
Ultimate Parent: Conagra. **SIC:** 5147—
Meats & Meat Products.

★ 62193 ★ **Westinghouse
Electric**
4400 N. Alafaya Trl.
Orlando, FL 32826
(407)281-2000
Officer: Frank Bakos, Vice President.
Ultimate Parent: Westinghouse Electric
Corp. **SIC:** 3569—General Industrial
Machinery Nec.

★ 62194 ★ **World Book, Inc.**
1310 W. Colonial Dr.
Orlando, FL 32804
(407)423-3181
Ultimate Parent: Berkshire Hathaway. **SIC:**
5942—Book Stores.

Ormond Beach

★ 62195 ★ **Barnett Bank of
Volusia County**
902 S. Atlantic Ave.
Ormond Beach, FL 32176-7859
(904)258-3652
Location Type: Branch office. **Ultimate
Parent:** Barnett Banks. **SIC:** 6021—National
Commercial Banks.

★ 62196 ★ **Barnett Bank of
Volusia County**
1280 Ocean Shore Blvd.
Ormond Beach, FL 32176-3620
(904)258-3670
Location Type: Branch office. **Ultimate
Parent:** Barnett Banks.

★ 62197 ★ **Barnett Bank of
Volusia County**
299 N. Nova Rd.
Ormond Beach, FL 32174-9497
(904)258-3658
Location Type: Branch office. **Ultimate
Parent:** Barnett Banks. **SIC:** 6021—National
Commercial Banks.

★ 62198 ★ **Barnett Bank of
Volusia County**
4 N. Beach St.
Ormond Beach, FL 32174-5602
(904)258-3600
Location Type: Branch office. **Ultimate
Parent:** Barnett Banks. **SIC:** 6021—National
Commercial Banks.

★ 62199 ★ **Barnett Bank of
Volusia County**
200 E. Granada Blvd.
Ormond Beach, FL 32176-6631
(904)258-3600
Location Type: Branch office. **Officer:** Jack
Wiles, Manager. **Ultimate Parent:** Barnett
Banks. **SIC:** 6021—National Commercial
Banks.

★ 62200 ★ **Citizens Federal
Bank, FSB**
193 E. Granada Blvd.
Ormond Beach, FL 32176-6663
(904)673-5351
Location Type: Branch office. **Officer:**
Kathy Gianos, Manager. **Ultimate Parent:**
CSF Holdings. **SIC:** 6021—National
Commercial Banks.

★ 62201 ★ **First Union National
Bank of Florida**
155 E. Granada Blvd.
Ormond Beach, FL 32176-6663
(904)254-7020
Location Type: Branch office. **Ultimate
Parent:** First Union Corp. **SIC:** 6021—
National Commercial Banks.

★ 62202 ★ **First Union National
Bank of Florida**
1100 W. Granada Rd.
Ormond Beach, FL 32174-9103
(904)254-7270
Location Type: Branch office. **Ultimate
Parent:** First Union Corp. **SIC:** 6021—
National Commercial Banks.

★ 62203 ★ **First Union National
Bank of Florida**
1210 Ocean Shore Blvd.
Ormond Beach, FL 32176
(904)254-7278
Location Type: Branch office. **Ultimate
Parent:** First Union Corp. **SIC:** 6021—
National Commercial Banks.

★ 62204 ★ **Food Lion**
101 E. Granada Blvd.
Ormond Beach, FL 32176
(904)677-6167
Ultimate Parent: Food Lion. **SIC:** 5411—
Grocery Stores.

★ 62205 ★ **Kelly Assisted Living
Servi**
770 W. Granada Blvd.
Ormond Beach, FL 32174
(904)252-1004
Ultimate Parent: Kelly Services. **SIC:**
8322—Individual & Family Services.

★ 62206 ★ **Kentucky Fried
Chicken**
195 W. Granada Blvd.
Ormond Beach, FL 32174
(904)257-1167
Ultimate Parent: Pepsico. **SIC:** 5812—
Eating Places.

★ 62207 ★ **Pizza Hut**
432 S. Atlantic Ave.
Ormond Beach, FL 32176
(904)677-0161
Ultimate Parent: Pepsico. **SIC:** 5812—
Eating Places.

★ 62208 ★ **Publix Super Market**
220 N. Nova Rd.
Ormond Beach, FL 32174
(904)677-0344
Ultimate Parent: Publix Super Markets.
SIC: 5411—Grocery Stores.

★ 62209 ★ **Radio Shack**
320 N. Nova Rd.
Ormond Beach, FL 32174
(904)672-3872
Company Type: Division. **Ultimate Parent:**
Tandy Corp. **SIC:** 5731—Radio, Television
& Electronics Stores.

★ 62210 ★ **Rite-Aid**
120 S. Nova Rd.
Ormond Beach, FL 32174
(904)673-4050
Ultimate Parent: Rite Aid. **SIC:** 5912—Drug
Stores & Proprietary Stores.

★ 62211 ★ **Ryder Truck Rental**
1188 N. Us Hwy. 1
Ormond Beach, FL 32174
(904)672-6316
Ultimate Parent: Ryder System. **SIC:**
7389—Business Services Nec.

★ 62212 ★ **Walgreen Drug Stores**
205 E. Granada Blvd.
Ormond Beach, FL 32176
(904)672-1013
Ultimate Parent: Walgreen Co. **SIC:**
5912—Drug Stores & Proprietary Stores.

Osprey

★ 62213 ★ **First of America Bank**
1300 S. Tamiami Trail
Osprey, FL 34229
(813)966-9515
Location Type: Branch office. **Ultimate
Parent:** First of America Bank Corp.

Oviedo

★ 62214 ★   Barnett Bank of Central Florida, NA
20 Alexandria Blvd.
Oviedo, FL 32765-6296
(407)646-3535
Company Type: Subsidiary. **Location Type:** Branch office. **Officer:** Vickie Eastham, Assistant Vice President. **Ultimate Parent:** Barnett Banks. **SIC:** 6021—National Commercial Banks.

★ 62215 ★   Great Western Bank
3 Alafaya Woods Blvd.
Oviedo, FL 32765
(407)365-1800
Ultimate Parent: Great Western Financial Corp. **SIC:** 6159—Miscellaneous Business Credit Institutions.

★ 62216 ★   Texaco Food Mart
1045 E. Broadway St.
Oviedo, FL 32765
(407)366-1761
Ultimate Parent: Texaco. **SIC:** 5541—Gasoline Service Stations.

Pace

★ 62217 ★   Air Products & Chemicals, Inc.
4575 Hwy. 90 E
Pace, FL 32571
Ultimate Parent: Air Products & Chemicals, Inc. **SIC:** 2873—Nitrogenous Fertilizers; 2869—Industrial Organic Chemicals Nec; 2865—Cyclic Crudes & Intermediates.

★ 62218 ★   Air Products & Chemicals Inc.
4575 East Hwy. 90
Pace, FL 32571
Ultimate Parent: Air Products & Chemicals, Inc. **SIC:** 2873—Nitrogenous Fertilizers; 2869—Industrial Organic Chemicals Nec; 2821—Plastics Materials & Resins; 2865—Cyclic Crudes & Intermediates.

★ 62219 ★   Air Products & Chemicals Inc.
E. Hwy. 90
Pace, FL 32571
Ultimate Parent: Air Products & Chemicals, Inc. **SIC:** 2873—Nitrogenous Fertilizers; 2869—Industrial Organic Chemicals Nec; 2821—Plastics Materials & Resins; 2865—Cyclic Crudes & Intermediates.

★ 62220 ★   Barnett Bank of West Florida
3895 Hwy. 90
Pace, FL 32571
(904)994-5301
Location Type: Branch office. **Ultimate Parent:** Barnett Banks. **SIC:** 6021—National Commercial Banks.

Pahokee

★ 62221 ★   Coca Cola Bottling Co.
246 E. Main St.
Pahokee, FL 33476
(407)924-5264
Ultimate Parent: Coca-Cola Enterprises. **SIC:** 5812—Eating Places.

★ 62222 ★   First Union National Bank of Florida
323 Bacom Point Rd.
Pahokee, FL 33476
(407)924-7145
Location Type: Branch office. **Ultimate Parent:** First Union Corp. **SIC:** 6021—National Commercial Banks.

Palatka

★ 62223 ★   Ace Hardware
Hwy. 19
Palatka, FL 32177
(904)328-7781
Ultimate Parent: Ace Hardware. **SIC:** 5063—Electrical Apparatus & Equipment.

★ 62224 ★   Barnett Bank of the St. Johns
620 S. Hwy. 19
Palatka, FL 32177-3945
(904)328-4627
Company Type: Subsidiary. **Location**

Type: Branch office. **Officer:** Suzanne Brown, Manager. **Ultimate Parent:** Barnett Banks. **SIC:** 6022—State Commercial Banks.

★ 62225 ★   First Union National Bank of Florida
200 Reid St.
Palatka, FL 32177
(904)329-1150
Location Type: Branch office. **Ultimate Parent:** First Union Corp. **SIC:** 6021—National Commercial Banks.

★ 62226 ★   First Union National Bank of Florida
400 Hwy. 19 N.
Palatka, FL 32177-2449
Location Type: Branch office. **Ultimate Parent:** First Union Corp. **SIC:** 6021—National Commercial Banks.

★ 62227 ★   Georgia-Pacific Corp.
State Rd. 216
Palatka, FL 32177
Ultimate Parent: Georgia-Pacific. **SIC:** 2611—Pulp Mills; 2621—Paper Mills.

★ 62228 ★   Georgia-Pacific Corp.
State Rd. 216 PO Box 919
Palatka, FL 32178
Ultimate Parent: Georgia-Pacific. **SIC:** 2611—Pulp Mills; 2621—Paper Mills; 2400—Lumber & Wood Products.

Palm Bay

★ 62229 ★   Ace Hardware of Palm Bay
6715 Babcock St. SE
Palm Bay, FL 32909
(407)729-6690
Ultimate Parent: Ace Hardware. **SIC:** 5251—Hardware Stores.

★ 62230 ★   Barnett Bank of Central Florida, NA
4600 Dixie Hwy. NE
Palm Bay, FL 32905-6087
(407)984-1502
Company Type: Subsidiary. **Location Type:** Branch office. **Officer:** Carolyn Young, Manager. **Ultimate Parent:** Barnett Banks. **SIC:** 6021—National Commercial Banks.

★ 62231 ★   Barnett Bank of Central Florida, NA
4710 Babcock St. NE
Palm Bay, FL 32905-2840
(407)723-8652
Company Type: Subsidiary. **Location Type:** Branch office. **Officer:** Cindy Robbins, Area Manager. **Ultimate Parent:** Barnett Banks. **SIC:** 6021—National Commercial Banks.

★ 62232 ★   Barnett Bank of Central Florida, NA
1151 Malabar Rd. NE
Palm Bay, FL 32907-3281
(407)676-2544
Company Type: Subsidiary. **Location Type:** Branch office. **Officer:** Carol Rodier, Manager. **Ultimate Parent:** Barnett Banks. **SIC:** 6021—National Commercial Banks.

★ 62233 ★   First Union National Bank of Florida
2200 Harris Ave. NE
Palm Bay, FL 32905-4107
(407)984-7425
Location Type: Branch office. **Ultimate Parent:** First Union Corp. **SIC:** 6021—National Commercial Banks.

★ 62234 ★   First Union National Bank of Florida
5240 Babcock St. NE
Palm Bay, FL 32905-4615
(407)984-3443
Location Type: Branch office. **Ultimate Parent:** First Union Corp. **SIC:** 6021—National Commercial Banks.

★ 62235 ★   Harris Corp.
Semiconductor Palm Bay
Palm Bay Rd.
Palm Bay, FL 32905
Company Type: Division. **Ultimate Parent:** Harris. **SIC:** 3674—Semiconductors & Related Devices.

★ 62236 ★   Harris Corp. Electronic Sys. Sector
2400 Palm Bay Rd. NE
Palm Bay, FL 32905
Ultimate Parent: Harris. **SIC:** 3669—Communications Equipment Nec.

★ 62237 ★   Harris Corp. Electronic System Sector
2400 Palm Bay Rd. NE
Palm Bay, FL 32905
Ultimate Parent: Harris. **SIC:** 3669—Communications Equipment Nec.

★ 62238 ★   Harris Corp. Government Systems Sector
2400 Palm Bay Rd. NE
Palm Bay, FL 32905
Ultimate Parent: Harris. **SIC:** 3669—Communications Equipment Nec.

★ 62239 ★   Harris Corp. GSS
2400 Palm Bay Rd. NE
Palm Bay, FL 32905
Ultimate Parent: Harris. **SIC:** 3600—Electronic & Other Electrical Equipment.

★ 62240 ★   Harris Corp. Semiconductor
2401 Palm Bay Rd.
Palm Bay, FL 32905
Ultimate Parent: Harris. **SIC:** 3674—Semiconductors & Related Devices.

★ 62241 ★   Harris Corp. Semiconductor Palm Bay
2401 Palm Bay Rd.
Palm Bay, FL 32905
Ultimate Parent: Harris. **SIC:** 3674—Semiconductors & Related Devices.

★ 62242 ★   Harris Corp. Semiconductor Sector
2401 Palm Bay Rd.
Palm Bay, FL 32905
Ultimate Parent: Harris. **SIC:** 3674—Semiconductors & Related Devices.

★ 62243 ★   Pizza Hut
5270 Babcock St. NE
Palm Bay, FL 32905
Ultimate Parent: Pepsico. **SIC:** 5812—Eating Places.

★ 62244 ★   Storage Tek Printer Operations
2725 Kirby Ave. NE
Palm Bay, FL 32905
(407)728-3111
Officer: Dick Radesi, Manager. **Ultimate Parent:** Storage Technology. **SIC:** 3571—Electronic Computers.

Palm Beach

★ 62245 ★   Bank of Boston-Florida
450 Royal Palm Way
Palm Beach, FL 33480-4139
(407)832-3399
Location Type: Branch office. **Officer:** Michael Engelbrecht. **Ultimate Parent:** Bank of Boston Corp. **SIC:** 6091—Nondeposit Trust Facilities; 6021—National Commercial Banks; 6282—Investment Advice.

★ 62246 ★   Bank of Boston-Florida N.A.
450 Royal Palm Way
Palm Beach, FL 33480-4139
(305)832-3399
Company Type: Subsidiary. **Location Type:** Branch office. **Officer:** Michael Engelbrecht. **Ultimate Parent:** Bank of Boston Corp. **SIC:** 6091—Nondeposit Trust Facilities; 6021—National Commercial Banks; 6282—Investment Advice.

★ 62247 ★   Barnett Bank of Palm Beach County
140 N. County Rd.
Palm Beach, FL 33480-3989
(407)835-6591
Company Type: Subsidiary. **Location Type:** Branch office. **Officer:** Susan Schupp, Manager. **Ultimate Parent:** Barnett Banks. **SIC:** 6022—State Commercial Banks.

★ 62248 ★   Chase Manhatten Bank of Florida, NA
218 Royal Palm Way
Palm Beach, FL 33480-4396
(407)659-6704
Location Type: Branch office. **Ultimate Parent:** Chase Manhattan Corp. **SIC:** 6021—National Commercial Banks.

★ 62249 ★   Chemical Bank Florida, SB
251 Royal Palm Way
Palm Beach, FL 33480-4310
(407)838-8700 **Fax:** (407)655-3659 **Telex:** 216362
Location Type: Branch office. **Ultimate Parent:** Chemical Banking Corp. **SIC:** 6021—National Commercial Banks.

★ 62250 ★   Citibank, FSB
400 Royal Palm Way
Palm Beach, FL 33480-4614
(407)659-5252
Location Type: Branch office. **Ultimate Parent:** Citicorp. **SIC:** 6021—National Commercial Banks.

★ 62251 ★   Citicorp Trust, NA
140 Royal Palm Way
Palm Beach, FL 33480-4204
(407)659-7028 **Fax:** (407)655-3128
Location Type: Branch office. **Ultimate Parent:** Citicorp.

★ 62252 ★   First Union National Bank of Florida
2875 S. Ocean Blvd.
Palm Beach, FL 33480-5590
(407)582-1273
Location Type: Branch office. **Ultimate Parent:** First Union Corp. **SIC:** 6021—National Commercial Banks.

★ 62253 ★   First Union National Bank of Florida
254 Sunrise Ave.
Palm Beach, FL 33480-3813
(407)655-1291
Location Type: Branch office. **Ultimate Parent:** First Union Corp. **SIC:** 6021—National Commercial Banks.

★ 62254 ★   First Union National Bank of Florida
9055 Ibis Blvd.
Palm Beach, FL 33412
(407)820-1247
Location Type: Branch office. **Ultimate Parent:** First Union Corp. **SIC:** 6021—National Commercial Banks.

★ 62255 ★   First Union National Bank of Florida
255 S. County Rd.
Palm Beach, FL 33480-4289
(407)665-7111
Location Type: Branch office. **Ultimate Parent:** First Union Corp. **SIC:** 6021—National Commercial Banks.

★ 62256 ★   First Union National Bank of Florida
411 S. County Rd.
Palm Beach, FL 33480-4420
(407)838-5680
Location Type: Branch office. **Ultimate Parent:** First Union Corp. **SIC:** 6021—National Commercial Banks.

★ 62257 ★   First Union National Bank of Florida
40 Coconut Row
Palm Beach, FL 33480-4072
(407)838-5564
Location Type: Branch office. **Ultimate Parent:** First Union Corp. **SIC:** 6021—National Commercial Banks.

★ 62258 ★   Hertz Rent-A-Car
231 Royal Poinciana Way
Palm Beach, FL 33480
(407)659-6435
Ultimate Parent: Hertz. **SIC:** 7514—Passenger Car Rental.

★ 62259 ★   Morgan Trust Co. of Florida, NA
109 Royal Palm Way
Palm Beach, FL 33480-4308
(407)838-4600 **Fax:** (407)833-5881
Location Type: Headquarters. **Officer:** David B. Robb. **Ultimate Parent:** J.P. Morgan & Co. **SIC:** 6021—National Commercial Banks.

★ 62260 ★   Publix Super Market
265 Sunset Ave.
Palm Beach, FL 33480
(407)832-2379
Ultimate Parent: Publix Super Markets.
SIC: 5411—Grocery Stores; 5461—Retail
Bakeries.

★ 62261 ★   Radio Shack
400 N. Lake Trl
Palm Beach, FL 33480
(407)845-2429
Company Type: Division. **Ultimate Parent:**
Tandy Corp. **SIC:** 5734—Computer &
Software Stores.

Palm Beach Garden

★ 62262 ★   First Union National
Bank of Florida
4480 Northlake Blvd.
Palm Beach Garden, FL 33410-6250
(407)838-5644
Location Type: Branch office. **Ultimate
Parent:** First Union Corp. **SIC:** 6021—
National Commercial Banks.

Palm Beach Gardens

★ 62263 ★   Barnett Bank of Palm
Beach County
8900 N. Military Dr.
Palm Beach Gardens, FL 33410
(407)845-3011
Company Type: Subsidiary. **Location
Type:** Branch office. **Officer:** Valerie
Vernal-Bentel, Manager. **Ultimate Parent:**
Barnett Banks. **SIC:** 6022—State
Commercial Banks.

★ 62264 ★   Barnett Bank of Palm
Beach County
7100 Fairway Dr.
Palm Beach Gardens, FL 33418-3777
(407)845-3417
Company Type: Subsidiary. **Location
Type:** Branch office. **Officer:** Stuart Weise,
Manager. **Ultimate Parent:** Barnett Banks.
SIC: 6022—State Commercial Banks.

★ 62265 ★   Barnett Bank of Palm
Beach County
2525 PGA Blvd.
Palm Beach Gardens, FL 33410-2997
(407)845-3417
Company Type: Subsidiary. **Location
Type:** Branch office. **Officer:** Steven Hood,
Manager. **Ultimate Parent:** Barnett Banks.
SIC: 6022—State Commercial Banks.

★ 62266 ★   Barnett Bank of Palm
Beach County
5560 PGA Blvd.
Palm Beach Gardens, FL 33418-3998
(407)845-3623
Company Type: Subsidiary. **Location
Type:** Branch office. **Officer:** Jay Crews,
Manager. **Ultimate Parent:** Barnett Banks.
SIC: 6022—State Commercial Banks.

★ 62267 ★   Barnett Bank of Palm
Beach County
4501 PGA Blvd.
Palm Beach Gardens, FL 33410
(407)626-7800
Company Type: Subsidiary. **Location
Type:** Branch office. **Officer:** Kristin Kutcel,
Manager. **Ultimate Parent:** Barnett Banks.
SIC: 6022—State Commercial Banks.

★ 62268 ★   Citibank, FSB
11521 US Hwy. 1
Palm Beach Gardens, FL 33408-3087
(407)627-1002
Location Type: Branch office. **Ultimate
Parent:** Citicorp. **SIC:** 6021—National
Commercial Banks.

★ 62269 ★   Comerica Bank &
Trust, FSB
2401 PGA Blvd.
Palm Beach Gardens, FL 33410-3566
(407)694-0455
Location Type: Branch office. **Ultimate
Parent:** Comerica Bank. **SIC:** 6021—
National Commercial Banks.

★ 62270 ★   First Union National
Bank of Florida
4440 PGA Blvd. & Military Trl.
Palm Beach Gardens, FL
(407)838-5500
Location Type: Branch office. **Ultimate

Parent:** First Union Corp. **SIC:** 6021—
National Commercial Banks.

★ 62271 ★   First Union National
Bank of Florida
7102 Fairway Dr.
Palm Beach Gardens, FL 33410
(407)838-5306
Location Type: Branch office. **Ultimate
Parent:** First Union Corp. **SIC:** 6021—
National Commercial Banks.

★ 62272 ★   The Gap
3101 PGA Blvd.
Palm Beach Gardens, FL 33410
(407)624-1810
Ultimate Parent: GAP. **SIC:** 5699—
Miscellaneous Apparel & Accessory Stores.

★ 62273 ★   Palm Beach Gardens
Medical Center
3360 Burns Rd.
Palm Beach Gardens, FL 33410
(407)622-1411
Officer: Arlen Reynolds, Executive Director.
Ultimate Parent: American Medical
Holdings. **SIC:** 8062—General Medical &
Surgical Hospitals.

★ 62274 ★   Sts-Klock
4215 Burns Rd.
Palm Beach Gardens, FL 33410
Ultimate Parent: Teleflex. **SIC:** 3398—
Metal Heat Treating.

★ 62275 ★   Sysco Food Services
3931 RCA Blvd.
Palm Beach Gardens, FL 33410
(407)622-1225
Ultimate Parent: Sysco. **SIC:** 5141—
Groceries—General Line.

Palm City

★ 62276 ★   Barnett Bank of
Martin County, NA
3720 SW Martin Downs Blvd.
Palm City, FL 34990
(407)288-9670
Company Type: Subsidiary. **Location
Type:** Branch office. **Officer:** Jamie Irvin,
Manager. **Ultimate Parent:** Barnett Banks.
SIC: 6021—National Commercial Banks.

★ 62277 ★   First Union National
Bank of Florida
3501 SW Corporate Pky.
Palm City, FL 34990
(407)221-4480
Location Type: Branch office. **Ultimate
Parent:** First Union Corp. **SIC:** 6021—
National Commercial Banks.

★ 62278 ★   First Union National
Bank of Florida
2740 SW Mapp Rd.
Palm City, FL 34990-2720
(407)221-4550
Location Type: Branch office. **Ultimate
Parent:** First Union Corp. **SIC:** 6021—
National Commercial Banks.

★ 62279 ★   Publix Super Market
3066 SW Martin Downs Blvd.
Palm City, FL 34990
(407)288-1500
Ultimate Parent: Publix Super Markets.
SIC: 5411—Grocery Stores.

★ 62280 ★   Walgreen Drug Stores
3078 SW Martin Downs Blvd.
Palm City, FL 34990
(407)288-0103
Ultimate Parent: Walgreen Co. **SIC:**
5912—Drug Stores & Proprietary Stores.

★ 62281 ★   Walgreen Pharmacy
3078 SW Martin Downs Blvd.
Palm City, FL 34990
(407)288-0105
Ultimate Parent: Walgreen Co. **SIC:**
5912—Drug Stores & Proprietary Stores.

Palm Coast

★ 62282 ★   Barnett Bank of
Volusia County
2 Old Kings Rd.
Palm Coast, FL 32137-8226
(904)445-5166
Location Type: Branch office. **Ultimate
Parent:** Barnett Banks. **SIC:** 6021—National
Commercial Banks.

★ 62283 ★   Barnett Bank of
Volusia County
100 Flagler Plz. Dr.
Palm Coast, FL 32137
(904)439-0113
Location Type: Branch office. **Ultimate
Parent:** Barnett Banks. **SIC:** 6021—National
Commercial Banks.

★ 62284 ★   First Union National
Bank of Florida
222 Palm Coast Pky.
Palm Coast, FL 32137-8217
(904)445-2175
Location Type: Branch office. **Ultimate
Parent:** First Union Corp.

★ 62285 ★   Publix Super Market
298 Palm Coast Pky. W
Palm Coast, FL 32137
(904)445-1430
Ultimate Parent: Publix Super Markets.
SIC: 5411—Grocery Stores.

★ 62286 ★   Sea Ray Boats Florida
Corp.
PO Box 420010
Palm Coast, FL 32142-0010
(904)439-3401
Officer: Dennis Wilson. **Ultimate Parent:**
Brunswick Corp. **SIC:** 3732—Boat Building
& Repairing.

Palm Harbor

★ 62287 ★   AmSouth Bank of
Florida
1027 Nebraska Ave.
Palm Harbor, FL 34683-4030
(813)462-5106
Location Type: Branch office. **Ultimate
Parent:** AmSouth Bancorp. **SIC:** 6022—
State Commercial Banks.

★ 62288 ★   AmSouth Bank of
Florida
33805 US Hwy. 19 N
Palm Harbor, FL 34684-2641
(813)462-1387
Location Type: Branch office. **Ultimate
Parent:** AmSouth Bancorp. **SIC:** 6022—
State Commercial Banks.

★ 62289 ★   Barnett Bank of
Pinellas County
4000 Lake St. George St.
Palm Harbor, FL 34684
(813)539-9185
Company Type: Subsidiary. **Location
Type:** Branch office. **Officer:** Joe Ritchie,
Vice President. **Ultimate Parent:** Barnett
Banks. **SIC:** 6022—State Commercial
Banks.

★ 62290 ★   Barnett Bank of
Pinellas County
2660 Alt 19 N
Palm Harbor, FL 34683
(813)539-9761
Company Type: Subsidiary. **Location
Type:** Branch office. **Officer:** Mary Lou
Stewart, Manager. **Ultimate Parent:** Barnett
Banks. **SIC:** 6022—State Commercial
Banks.

★ 62291 ★   Barnett Bank of
Pinellas County
1300 State Rd. 584
Palm Harbor, FL 34683-5646
(813)539-9129
Company Type: Subsidiary. **Location
Type:** Branch office. **Officer:** Joani Kelter,
Manager. **Ultimate Parent:** Barnett Banks.
SIC: 6022—State Commercial Banks.

★ 62292 ★   Barnett Bank of
Pinellas County
30569 US Hwy. 19 N
Palm Harbor, FL 34684-4415
(813)539-9178
Company Type: Subsidiary. **Location
Type:** Branch office. **Officer:** Delores
Mayfield, Manager. **Ultimate Parent:**
Barnett Banks. **SIC:** 6022—State
Commercial Banks.

★ 62293 ★   Barnett Bank of
Pinellas County
2650 W. Lake Rd.
Palm Harbor, FL 34684
(813)539-9777
Company Type: Subsidiary. **Location
Type:** Branch office. **Officer:** Fred Miller,

Manager. **Ultimate Parent:** Barnett Banks.
SIC: 6022—State Commercial Banks.

★ 62294 ★   Barnett Bank of
Pinellas County
37026 US Hwy. 19th N
Palm Harbor, FL 34683-1109
(813)539-9669
Company Type: Subsidiary. **Location
Type:** Branch office. **Officer:** Madelyn
Wicker, Manager. **Ultimate Parent:** Barnett
Banks. **SIC:** 6022—State Commercial
Banks.

★ 62295 ★   Barnett Bank of
Pinellas County
33715 US Hwy. 19 N
Palm Harbor, FL 34684-2696
(813)539-9726
Company Type: Subsidiary. **Location
Type:** Branch office. **Officer:** Fred Miller,
Manager. **Ultimate Parent:** Barnett Banks.
SIC: 6022—State Commercial Banks.

★ 62296 ★   Citizens Federal
Bank, FSB
33295 US Hwy. 19 N.
Palm Harbor, FL 34684-2639
(813)785-7628
Location Type: Branch office. **Officer:**
Linda Young, Manager. **Ultimate Parent:**
CSF Holdings. **SIC:** 6021—National
Commercial Banks.

★ 62297 ★   First Union National
Bank of Florida
35320 US Hwy. 19 N.
Palm Harbor, FL 34684-1931
(813)538-4495
Location Type: Branch office. **Ultimate
Parent:** First Union Corp. **SIC:** 6021—
National Commercial Banks.

★ 62298 ★   Fortune Bank, ASB
34650 US Hwy. 19 N
Palm Harbor, FL 34684-1929
(813)785-8827
Location Type: Branch office. **Officer:**
George Keim, Manager. **Ultimate Parent:**
Fortune Bancorp. **SIC:** 6021—National
Commercial Banks.

★ 62299 ★   Fortune Bank, ASB
3430 E. Lake Rd., Ste. 1
Palm Harbor, FL 34685-2412
(813)786-3345
Location Type: Branch office. **Officer:**
Judith Maroff, Manager. **Ultimate Parent:**
Fortune Bancorp. **SIC:** 6021—National
Commercial Banks.

★ 62300 ★   Fortune Bank, SB
2323 Curlew Rd.
Palm Harbor, FL 34683-6830
(813)786-8844
Location Type: Branch office. **Ultimate
Parent:** Fortune Bancorp. **SIC:** 6021—
National Commercial Banks.

★ 62301 ★   Mobil Oil Corporation
1198 Us 19 S
Palm Harbor, FL 34683
(813)785-9189
Ultimate Parent: Mobil. **SIC:** 5541—
Gasoline Service Stations.

Palm Springs

★ 62302 ★   Barnett Bank of Palm
Beach County
3320 S. Congress Ave.
Palm Springs, FL 33461-3098
(407)433-2433
Company Type: Subsidiary. **Location
Type:** Branch office. **Officer:** Earl Haywood,
Manager. **Ultimate Parent:** Barnett Banks.
SIC: 6022—State Commercial Banks.

★ 62303 ★   First Union National
Bank of Florida
3345 S. Congress Ave.
Palm Springs, FL 33461-3095
(407)533-7730
Location Type: Branch office. **Ultimate
Parent:** First Union Corp. **SIC:** 6021—
National Commercial Banks.

★ 62304 ★   Jiffy Lube
6696 NW 186th St.
Palm Springs, FL 33015
(305)822-7356
Ultimate Parent: Pennzoil. **SIC:** 7538—
General Automotive Repair Shops.

★ 62305 ★   Pizza Hut
7696 NW 186th St.
Palm Springs, FL 33015
(305)825-8322
Ultimate Parent: Pepsico. SIC: 5812—
Eating Places.

Palmetto

★ 62306 ★   Barnett Bank of
Manatee County, NA
1001 10th St. W
Palmetto, FL 34221-4133
(813)755-8889
Company Type: Subsidiary. Location
Type: Branch office. Officer: Paula Potter,
Manager. Ultimate Parent: Barnett Banks.
SIC: 6021—National Commercial Banks.

★ 62307 ★   Exxon
3500 Us Hwy. 41 N
Palmetto, FL 34221
(813)722-9350
Ultimate Parent: Exxon. SIC: 5541—
Gasoline Service Stations.

★ 62308 ★   First of America Bank
600 W. 8th Ave.
Palmetto, FL 34221
(813)723-5320
Location Type: Branch office. Ultimate
Parent: First of America Bank Corp. SIC:
6021—National Commercial Banks.

★ 62309 ★   Kentucky Fried
Chicken
1210 8th Ave. W
Palmetto, FL 34221
(813)722-0354
Ultimate Parent: Pepsico. SIC: 5812—
Eating Places.

★ 62310 ★   Magnetek
2001 US Hwy. 301 Ste. 100
Palmetto, FL 34221-6513
(813)729-5606
Officer: Tommy Walters. Ultimate Parent:
Magnetek Inc. SIC: 3677—Electronic Coils
& Transformers; 5999—Miscellaneous Retail
Stores Nec; 7699—Repair Services Nec.

★ 62311 ★   Magnetek Ohio
Transformer
Brandenton Plant
2001 US Hwy. 301 N. Ste. 100
Palmetto, FL 34221
Company Type: Division. Ultimate Parent:
Magnetek Inc. SIC: 3612—Transformers
Except Electronic.

Panama City

★ 62312 ★   Ace Hardware
3215 State Hwy. 77
Panama City, FL 32405
(904)763-3915
Ultimate Parent: Ace Hardware. SIC:
5251—Hardware Stores.

★ 62313 ★   AmSouth Bank of
Florida
1000 Delwood Beach Rd.
Panama City, FL 32408-7289
(904)785-3416
Location Type: Branch office. Officer:
Sonya Richbourg, Manager. Ultimate
Parent: AmSouth Bancorp. SIC: 6022—
State Commercial Banks.

★ 62314 ★   AmSouth Bank of
Florida
6916 Hwy. 98 W
Panama City, FL 32407-5412
(904)784-6601
Location Type: Branch office. Officer:
Carla A. Gross, Manager. Ultimate Parent:
AmSouth Bancorp. SIC: 6022—State
Commercial Banks.

★ 62315 ★   AmSouth Bank of
Florida
2208 State Ave.
Panama City, FL 32405
(904)784-3416
Location Type: Branch office. Officer:
Sherita Williams, Manager. Ultimate
Parent: AmSouth Bancorp. SIC: 6022—
State Commercial Banks.

★ 62316 ★   AmSouth Bank of
Florida
12720 Middle Beach Rd.
Panama City, FL 32407-2915
(904)785-3416
Location Type: Branch office. Officer:
Joyce Dean, Manager. Ultimate Parent:
AmSouth Bancorp. SIC: 6022—State
Commercial Banks.

★ 62317 ★   AmSouth Bank of
Florida
2711 W. 15th St.
Panama City, FL 32401-1366
(904)785-3416
Location Type: Branch office. Officer: Sara
Park, Manager. Ultimate Parent: AmSouth
Bancorp. SIC: 6022—State Commercial
Banks.

★ 62318 ★   Arizona Chemical Co.
2 Everitt Ave. PO Box 2447
Panama City, FL 32401
Ultimate Parent: International Paper Co.
SIC: 2861—Gum & Wood Chemicals;
2899—Chemical Preparations Nec.

★ 62319 ★   Casual Corner
2170 E. Cove Blvd. N
Panama City, FL 32405
(904)769-3566
Ultimate Parent: United States Shoe. SIC:
5651—Family Clothing Stores.

★ 62320 ★   First Union National
Bank of Florida
200 S. Arnold Rd.
Panama City, FL 32407
(904)235-6050
Location Type: Branch office. Ultimate
Parent: First Union Corp. SIC: 6021—
National Commercial Banks.

★ 62321 ★   First Union National
Bank of Florida
1002 W. 23rd. St.
Panama City, FL 32405-5314
(904)747-3975
Location Type: Branch office. Ultimate
Parent: First Union Corp. SIC: 6021—
National Commercial Banks.

★ 62322 ★   Greyhound Bus Lines
310 W. 5th St.
Panama City, FL 32401
(904)785-7861
Ultimate Parent: Greyhound Lines Inc. SIC:
4212—Local Trucking Without Storage.

★ 62323 ★   Greyhound Bus
Station
13498 Us 98a W
Panama City, FL 32407
(904)235-2915
Ultimate Parent: Greyhound Lines Inc. SIC:
4131—Intercity & Rural Bus Transportation.

★ 62324 ★   Hertz Rent-A-Car
9450 Thomas Dr.
Panama City, FL 32408
(904)234-6515
Ultimate Parent: Hertz. SIC: 7514—
Passenger Car Rental.

★ 62325 ★   Kentucky Fried
Chicken
3002 Us 98 W
Panama City, FL 32405
(904)763-9701
Ultimate Parent: Pepsico. SIC: 5812—
Eating Places.

★ 62326 ★   Kentucky Fried
Chicken
1200 W. 23rd St.
Panama City, FL 32405
(904)784-2570
Ultimate Parent: Pepsico. SIC: 5812—
Eating Places.

★ 62327 ★   Kentucky Fried
Chicken
427 S. Tyndall Pky.
Panama City, FL 32404
(904)784-0777
Ultimate Parent: Pepsico. SIC: 5812—
Eating Places.

★ 62328 ★   Kentucky Fried
Chicken
10272 US 98A W
Panama City, FL 32407
(904)235-2879
Ultimate Parent: Pepsico. SIC: 5812—
Eating Places.

★ 62329 ★   Lerner Shop
2160 N. Cove Blvd.
Panama City, FL 32405
(904)769-1883
Ultimate Parent: Limited. SIC: 5651—
Family Clothing Stores.

★ 62330 ★   Louisiana Pacific
Corp.
Bay
Panama City, FL 32405
(904)234-6692
Ultimate Parent: Louisiana-Pacific. SIC:
2421—Sawmills & Planing Mills—General.

★ 62331 ★   Manpower, Inc.
700 W. 23rd St.
Panama City, FL 32405
(904)769-1619
Ultimate Parent: Manpower, Inc. SIC:
7361—Employment Agencies.

★ 62332 ★   Mary Kay Cosmetics
3210 Douglas Rd.
Panama City, FL 32405
(904)763-9925
Ultimate Parent: Mary Kay Cosmetics. SIC:
5999—Miscellaneous Retail Stores Nec.

★ 62333 ★   McDonalds
648 Florida Ave.
Panama City, FL 32401
(904)769-1397
Ultimate Parent: McDonald's.
SIC: 5812—Eating Places.

★ 62334 ★   McDonalds No 6574
10628 W. Hwy. 98
Panama City, FL 32407
(904)234-6096
Ultimate Parent: McDonald's.
SIC: 5812—Eating Places.

★ 62335 ★   Panama City Coca
Cola Btlg
238 W. 5th St.
Panama City, FL 32401
(904)785-6171
Ultimate Parent: Coca-Cola Bottling
Consol. SIC: 5149—Groceries & Related
Products Nec.

★ 62336 ★   Pennzoil Swifty Lube
Center
309 E. 23nd St.
Panama City, FL 32405
(904)784-1157
Ultimate Parent: Pennzoil. SIC: 5172—
Petroleum Products Nec.

★ 62337 ★   Piggly Wiggly
2401 E. 5th St.
Panama City, FL 32401
(904)763-1221
Ultimate Parent: Bruno's. SIC: 5499—
Miscellaneous Food Stores.

★ 62338 ★   Pizza Hut
7721 US 98A W
Panama City, FL 32407
(904)235-4191
Ultimate Parent: Pepsico. SIC: 5812—
Eating Places.

★ 62339 ★   Pizza Hut
14323 US 98A W
Panama City, FL 32407
(904)234-9284
Ultimate Parent: Pepsico. SIC: 5812—
Eating Places.

★ 62340 ★   Pizza Hut
222 S. Tyndall Pky.
Panama City, FL 32404
(904)769-7494
Ultimate Parent: Pepsico. SIC: 5812—
Eating Places.

★ 62341 ★   Pizza Hut
1815 State Hwy. 77 N
Panama City, FL 32405
(904)265-4200
Ultimate Parent: Pepsico. SIC: 5812—
Eating Places.

★ 62342 ★   Pizza Hut
221 E. 23rd St.
Panama City, FL 32405
(904)769-2219
Ultimate Parent: Pepsico. SIC: 5812—
Eating Places.

★ 62343 ★   Pizza Hut
8776 Thomas Dr.
Panama City, FL 32408
(904)234-3677
Ultimate Parent: Pepsico. SIC: 5812—
Eating Places.

★ 62344 ★   Pizza Hut
14324 W. Hwy. 98 a
Panama City, FL 32413
(904)234-9284
Ultimate Parent: Pepsico. SIC: 5812—
Eating Places.

★ 62345 ★   Radio Shack
Panama
Panama City, FL 32405
(904)763-6915
Company Type: Division. Ultimate Parent:
Tandy Corp. SIC: 5065—Electronic Parts &
Equipment Nec.

★ 62346 ★   Rite Aid
2142 N. Cove Blvd.
Panama City, FL 32405
(904)769-7343
Ultimate Parent: Rite Aid. SIC: 5912—Drug
Stores & Proprietary Stores.

★ 62347 ★   Ryder Truck Rental
6146 Us 98 E
Panama City, FL 32404
(904)871-6262
Ultimate Parent: Ryder System. SIC:
7513—Truck Rental & Leasing Without
Drivers.

★ 62348 ★   Ryder Truck Rental
1421 Harrison Ave.
Panama City, FL 32401
(904)785-8608
Ultimate Parent: Ryder System. SIC:
5113—Industrial & Personal Service Paper.

★ 62349 ★   Shell Food Mart
2900 W. 23rd St.
Panama City, FL 32405
(904)769-7761
Ultimate Parent: Shell Oil Co. SIC: 5541—
Gasoline Service Stations.

★ 62350 ★   Shell Food Mart
2708 E. 15th St.
Panama City, FL 32405
(904)769-7818
Ultimate Parent: Shell Oil Co. SIC: 5411—
Grocery Stores.

★ 62351 ★   Stone Container Corp.
1 S. Everitt Ave.
Panama City, FL 32401
(904)785-4311
Officer: Jack Prescott, Manager. Ultimate
Parent: Stone Container Corp. SIC: 2611—
Pulp Mills; 2621—Paper Mills; 2631—
Paperboard Mills.

★ 62352 ★   Taco Bell
2875 W. 23rd St.
Panama City, FL 32405
(904)763-1555
Ultimate Parent: Pepsico. SIC: 5812—
Eating Places.

★ 62353 ★   Textron Marine
Systems
8109 Us 98 W
Panama City, FL 32407
(904)234-2292
Ultimate Parent: Textron. SIC: 5088—
Transportation Equipment & Supplies.

★ 62354 ★   Trailways Bus System
917 Harrison Ave.
Panama City, FL 32401
(904)785-6111
Ultimate Parent: Greyhound Lines Inc. SIC:
4131—Intercity & Rural Bus Transportation.

★ 62355 ★   Trailways Bus
Systems
601 Dogwood St.
Panama City, FL 32407
(904)234-9138
Ultimate Parent: Greyhound Lines Inc. SIC:
4131—Intercity & Rural Bus Transportation.

★ 62356 ★   Wal Mart
513 W. 23rd St.
Panama City, FL 32405
(904)785-0307
Ultimate Parent: Wal-Mart Stores, Inc. SIC:
5311—Department Stores.

★ 62357 ★   Wal Mart
330 S. Tyndall Pky.
Panama City, FL 32404
Ultimate Parent: Wal-Mart Stores, Inc. SIC:
5311—Department Stores.

★ 62358 ★   Waldenbooks
Panama City Mall
Panama City, FL 32405
(904)769-5839
Ultimate Parent: K-Mart. SIC: 5942—Book
Stores.

Panama City Beach

★ 62359 ★   First Union National
Bank of Florida
6706 W. Hwy. 98
Panama City Beach, FL 32407-5408
(904)235-6001
Location Type: Branch office. Ultimate
Parent: First Union Corp. SIC: 6021—
National Commercial Banks.

Parrish

★ 62360 ★   Turner Food Corp.
Rodgers Rd.
Parrish, FL 34219
(813)776-2661
Ultimate Parent: FPL Group. SIC: 0174—
Citrus Fruits.

Patrick Air Force Base

★ 62361 ★   Barnett Bank of
Central Florida, NA
1364 S. Patrick Dr.
Patrick Air Force Base, FL 32925
(407)784-5830
Company Type: Subsidiary. Location
Type: Branch office. Officer: Lou Vail,
Manager. Ultimate Parent: Barnett Banks.
SIC: 6021—National Commercial Banks.

Pembroke Pines

★ 62362 ★   American Savings of
Florida, FSB
10480 Taft St.
Pembroke Pines, FL 33026-2819
(305)431-2311
Location Type: Branch office. Officer:
Diane Neer, Manager. Ultimate Parent:
American Savings of Florida. SIC: 6035—
Federal Savings Institutions; 6211—Security
Brokers & Dealers.

★ 62363 ★   American Savings of
Florida, FSB
294 S. Flamingo Rd.
Pembroke Pines, FL 33027-1721
(305)435-7272
Location Type: Branch office. Ultimate
Parent: American Savings of Florida. SIC:
6035—Federal Savings Institutions; 6211—
Security Brokers & Dealers.

★ 62364 ★   Barnett Bank of
Broward County, NA
80 S. Flamingo Rd.
Pembroke Pines, FL 33027-1719
(305)437-8000
Company Type: Subsidiary. Location
Type: Branch office. Officer: John Mannix,
Manager. Ultimate Parent: Barnett Banks.
SIC: 6021—National Commercial Banks.

★ 62365 ★   Barnett Bank of
Broward County, NA
8020 Pines Blvd.
Pembroke Pines, FL 33026
(305)435-9883
Company Type: Subsidiary. Location
Type: Branch office. Officer: Terry Benson,
Manager. Ultimate Parent: Barnett Banks.
SIC: 6021—National Commercial Banks.

★ 62366 ★   Barnett Bank of
Broward County, NA
150 SW 136th Ave.
Pembroke Pines, FL 33028-1001
(305)435-1991
Company Type: Subsidiary. Location
Type: Branch office. Officer: Pat Waicek,
Manager. Ultimate Parent: Barnett Banks.
SIC: 6021—National Commercial Banks.

★ 62367 ★   California Federal
Bank, FSB
10050 Pines Blvd.
Pembroke Pines, FL 33024-6137
(305)435-4114
Location Type: Branch office. Officer:
Robin Yablonsky, Manager. Ultimate
Parent: California Federal Bank. SIC:
6021—National Commercial Banks.

★ 62368 ★   Citizens Federal
Bank, FSB
502 N. University Dr.
Pembroke Pines, FL 33082
(305)432-5450
Location Type: Branch office. Officer: Lisa
Hoffmeyer, Manager. Ultimate Parent: CSF
Holdings. SIC: 6021—National Commercial
Banks.

★ 62369 ★   First Union National
Bank of Florida
199 N. University Dr.
Pembroke Pines, FL 33025
(305)985-3511
Location Type: Branch office. Ultimate
Parent: First Union Corp. SIC: 6021—
National Commercial Banks.

★ 62370 ★   Jiffy Lube of
Hallandale
9000 Sheridan St. 158
Pembroke Pines, FL 33024
Ultimate Parent: Pennzoil. SIC: 7538—
General Automotive Repair Shops.

★ 62371 ★   Mobil
4090 State Rd. 7
Pembroke Pines, FL 33024
(305)989-2848
Ultimate Parent: Mobil. SIC: 5541—
Gasoline Service Stations.

★ 62372 ★   Savings of America
Home Savings of America, FSB
12440 SW Pines Blvd.
Pembroke Pines, FL 33027-1734
(305)432-6900
Location Type: Branch office. Officer:
Corinne Bozio, Manager. Ultimate Parent:
H. F. Ahmanson. SIC: 6021—National
Commercial Banks.

★ 62373 ★   Savings of America
Home Savings of America, FSB
702 N. University Dr.
Pembroke Pines, FL 33024-3610
(305)432-5105
Location Type: Branch office. Officer:
Constance Hunt. Ultimate Parent: H. F.
Ahmanson. SIC: 6021—National
Commercial Banks.

Pempano Beach

★ 62374 ★   Citibank (Florida), NA
990 N. Federal Hwy.
Pempano Beach, FL 33062-4318
(305)781-2223
Location Type: Branch office. Ultimate
Parent: Citicorp. SIC: 6021—National
Commercial Banks.

Pennsacola

★ 62375 ★   Borden Inc.
Dairy
3501 N. Alcniaz St.
Pennsacola, FL 32503
Company Type: Division. Ultimate Parent:
Borden, Inc. SIC: 2026—Fluid Milk.

Pensacola

★ 62376 ★   Ace Hardware 3141 a
1907 E. Olive Rd.
Pensacola, FL 32514
(904)476-1733
Ultimate Parent: Ace Hardware. SIC:
5261—Retail Nurseries & Garden Stores.

★ 62377 ★   Air Products &
Chemicals, Inc.
3535 N. Palafox St.
Pensacola, FL 32505
(904)432-1406
Ultimate Parent: Air Products & Chemicals,
Inc. SIC: 5084—Industrial Machinery &
Equipment.

★ 62378 ★   Albertson's Pharmacy
4525 Mobile Hwy.
Pensacola, FL 32506
(904)455-0344
Ultimate Parent: Albertson's Inc. SIC:
5912—Drug Stores & Proprietary Stores.

★ 62379 ★   American Family Life
Assur
701 W. Nine Mile Rd.
Pensacola, FL 32534
(904)476-9642
Ultimate Parent: American Family Life
Assurance Co. SIC: 6411—Insurance
Agents, Brokers & Service.

★ 62380 ★   American Family Life
Assurance
6702 Plantation Rd.
Pensacola, FL 32504
(904)478-5001
Ultimate Parent: American Family Life
Assurance Co. SIC: 6411—Insurance
Agents, Brokers & Service.

★ 62381 ★   American Family Life
Assurance
701 W. Nine Mile Rd.
Pensacola, FL 32534
(904)476-9642
Ultimate Parent: American Family Life
Assurance Co. SIC: 6411—Insurance
Agents, Brokers & Service.

★ 62382 ★   AmSouth Bank of
Florida
575 N. Navy Blvd.
Pensacola, FL 32507-2011
(904)444-1069
Location Type: Branch office. Ultimate
Parent: AmSouth Bancorp. SIC: 6022—
State Commercial Banks.

★ 62383 ★   AmSouth Bank of
Florida
8094 N. Davis Hwy.
Pensacola, FL 32514-7576
(904)444-1068
Location Type: Branch office. Ultimate
Parent: AmSouth Bancorp. SIC: 6022—
State Commercial Banks.

★ 62384 ★   AmSouth Bank of
Florida
3300 N. Pace Blvd.
Pensacola, FL 32505-5141
(904)444-1067
Location Type: Branch office. Ultimate
Parent: AmSouth Bancorp. SIC: 6022—
State Commercial Banks.

★ 62385 ★   AmSouth Bank of
Florida
4 E. 9 Mile Rd.
Pensacola, FL 32534-3133
(904)444-1063
Location Type: Branch office. Ultimate
Parent: AmSouth Bancorp. SIC: 6022—
State Commercial Banks.

★ 62386 ★   AmSouth Bank of
Florida
8022 Lillian Hwy.
Pensacola, FL 32506-3746
(904)444-1064
Location Type: Branch office. Ultimate
Parent: AmSouth Bancorp. SIC: 6022—
State Commercial Banks.

★ 62387 ★   AmSouth Bank of
Florida
5100 N. 9th Ave.
Pensacola, FL 32504-8735
(904)444-1061
Location Type: Branch office. Ultimate
Parent: AmSouth Bancorp. SIC: 6022—
State Commercial Banks.

★ 62388 ★   AmSouth Bank of
Florida
7130 N. 9th Ave.
Pensacola, FL 32504-6616
(904)444-1062
Location Type: Branch office. Ultimate
Parent: AmSouth Bancorp. SIC: 6022—
State Commercial Banks.

★ 62389 ★   AmSouth Bank of
Florida
70 N. Baylen St.
PO Box 12790
Pensacola, FL 32575-2790
(904)444-1000 Fax: (904)438-4603
Company Type: Subsidiary. Officer: Alfred
W. Swan Jr., President. Ultimate Parent:
AmSouth Bancorp. SIC: 6022—State
Commercial Banks.

★ 62390 ★   AmSouth Bank of
Florida
4505 Saufley Field Rd.
Pensacola, FL 32526-1717
(909)444-1060
Location Type: Branch office. Ultimate
Parent: AmSouth Bancorp. SIC: 6022—
State Commercial Banks.

★ 62391 ★   Armstrong World
Industries Inc.
300 S. Myrick St.
Pensacola, FL 32501
Ultimate Parent: Armstrong World
Industries. SIC: 2679—Converted Paper
Products Nec.

★ 62392 ★   Armstrong
Worldindustries Inc.
300 S. Myrick St.
Pensacola, FL 32505
Ultimate Parent: Armstrong World
Industries. SIC: 2600—Paper & Allied
Products.

★ 62393 ★   Bank of Pensacola
1898 E. 9th Mile Rd.
Pensacola, FL 32514-5751
(904)474-2187
Company Type: Subsidiary. Location
Type: Branch office. Officer: R. Randall
Kealer, Mgr. Ultimate Parent: Synovus
Financial Corp. SIC: 6021—National
Commercial Banks.

★ 62394 ★   Bank of Pensacola
400 W. Garden St.
Pensacola, FL 32501-4731
(904)436-7800
Company Type: Subsidiary. Location
Type: Branch office. Officer: Patricia M.
Thompson, Mgr. Ultimate Parent: Synovus
Financial Corp. SIC: 6021—National
Commercial Banks.

★ 62395 ★   Bank of Pensacola
University of West Florida, Commons Bldg.
Pensacola, FL 32514-5751
(904)474-2187
Company Type: Subsidiary. Location
Type: Branch office. Officer: Diane
Norwood, Mgr. Ultimate Parent: Synovus
Financial Corp. SIC: 6021—National
Commercial Banks.

★ 62396 ★   Bank of Pensacola
7150 N. 9th Ave.
PO Box 12966
Pensacola, FL 32591-2966
(904)494-7800 Fax: (904)494-7821
Company Type: Subsidiary. Location
Type: Branch office. Officer: W. Luther
Taylor, Chairman, President, & CEO.
Ultimate Parent: Synovus Financial Corp.
SIC: 6021—National Commercial Banks.

★ 62397 ★   Bank South NA/
Pensacola Main Office
213 S. Palafox St.
Pensacola, FL 32501
(904)456-5722
Company Type: Subsidiary. Location
Type: Branch office. Officer: Eric
Nickelsen, President. Ultimate Parent:
Bank South Corp. SIC: 6021—National
Commercial Banks.

★ 62398 ★   Barnett Bank of West
Florida
100 W. Garden St.
Pensacola, FL 32501-5661
(904)432-0271 Fax: (904)444-0402
Location Type: Branch office. Ultimate
Parent: Barnett Banks. SIC: 6021—National
Commercial Banks.

★ 62399 ★   Barnett Bank of West
Florida
13039 Sorrento Rd.
Pensacola, FL 32507-8703
(904)432-0271
Location Type: Branch office. Ultimate
Parent: Barnett Banks. SIC: 6021—National
Commercial Banks.

★ 62400 ★   Barnett Bank of West
Florida
PO Box 1192
Pensacola, FL 32595-1192
Location Type: Branch office. Ultimate
Parent: Barnett Banks. SIC: 6021—National
Commercial Banks.

★ **62401** ★ **Barnett Bank of West Florida**
206 New Warrington Rd.
Pensacola, FL 32506
Location Type: Branch office. **Ultimate Parent:** Barnett Banks. **SIC:** 6021—National Commercial Banks.

★ **62402** ★ **Barnett Bank of West Florida**
31 E. 9 Mile Rd.
Pensacola, FL 32534-3136
Location Type: Branch office. **Ultimate Parent:** Barnett Banks. **SIC:** 6021—National Commercial Banks.

★ **62403** ★ **Barnett Bank of West Florida**
5041 Bayou Blvd.
Pensacola, FL 32503
Location Type: Branch office. **Ultimate Parent:** Barnett Banks. **SIC:** 6021—National Commercial Banks.

★ **62404** ★ **Barnett Bank of West Florida**
6727 N. Davis Hwy.
Pensacola, FL 32504-6380
Location Type: Branch office. **Ultimate Parent:** Barnett Banks. **SIC:** 6021—National Commercial Banks.

★ **62405** ★ **Barnett Bank of West Florida**
8187 W. Fairfield Dr.
Pensacola, FL 32506
(904)457-0796
Location Type: Branch office. **Ultimate Parent:** Barnett Banks. **SIC:** 6021—National Commercial Banks.

★ **62406** ★ **Barnett Bank of West Florida**
213 S. Pala Fox St.
Pensacola, FL 32501-5886
(904)444-3350
Location Type: Branch office. **Ultimate Parent:** Barnett Banks. **SIC:** 6021—National Commercial Banks.

★ **62407** ★ **Barnett Bank of West Florida**
4240 W. Fairfield Dr.
Pensacola, FL 32506
(904)453-2300
Location Type: Branch office. **Ultimate Parent:** Barnett Banks. **SIC:** 6021—National Commercial Banks.

★ **62408** ★ **Barnett Bank of West Florida**
312 E. 9 Mile Rd.
Pensacola, FL
(904)479-3126
Location Type: Branch office. **Ultimate Parent:** Barnett Banks. **SIC:** 6021—National Commercial Banks.

★ **62409** ★ **Beneficial Florida Inc.**
6600 N. Davis Hwy.
Pensacola, FL 32504-6302
(904)478-6430
Officer: Howard R. Mayne. **Ultimate Parent:** Beneficial. **SIC:** 6141—Personal Credit Institutions; 6162—Mortgage Bankers & Correspondents; 7291—Tax Return Preparation Services.

★ **62410** ★ **Builders Square**
1412 W. Fairfield Dr.
Pensacola, FL 32501
(904)438-1227
Company Type: Subsidiary. **Ultimate Parent:** K-Mart. **SIC:** 5039—Construction Materials Nec.

★ **62411** ★ **Burlington Northern Railroa**
271 S. Pace Blvd.
Pensacola, FL 32501
(904)433-4686
Ultimate Parent: Burlington Northern. **SIC:** 4011—Railroads—Line-Haul Operating; 4119—Local Passenger Transportation Nec.

★ **62412** ★ **Business Systems Group**
4900 Bayou Blvd.
Pensacola, FL 32503-2525
(904)484-4297
Ultimate Parent: Avery Dennison Corp. **SIC:** 7371—Computer Programming Services.

★ **62413** ★ **Casual Corner**
5100 N. 9th Ave.
Pensacola, FL 32504
(904)476-1720
Ultimate Parent: United States Shoe. **SIC:** 5651—Family Clothing Stores.

★ **62414** ★ **Circuit City**
6121 N. Davis Hwy.
Pensacola, FL 32504
(904)479-2633
Ultimate Parent: Circuit City Stores. **SIC:** 5722—Household Appliance Stores.

★ **62415** ★ **Coast to Coast Auto Sales**
3901 N. Pace Blvd.
Pensacola, FL 32505
(904)434-7433
Ultimate Parent: Servistar Corp.

★ **62416** ★ **Coast to Coast Car Sales**
792 Van Pelt Ln.
Pensacola, FL 32505
Ultimate Parent: Servistar Corp. **SIC:** 5521—Used Car Dealers.

★ **62417** ★ **Collective Mortgage Service**
5401 Corporate Woods Dr.
Pensacola, FL 32504
(904)477-0032
Ultimate Parent: Collective Bancorp. **SIC:** 6162—Mortgage Bankers & Correspondents.

★ **62418** ★ **Delta Air Lines**
2430 Airport Blvd.
Pensacola, FL 32504
(904)435-7969
Ultimate Parent: Delta Air Lines, Inc. **SIC:** 4512—Air Transportation—Scheduled.

★ **62419** ★ **Digital Equipment Corporati**
4700 Bayou Blvd.
Pensacola, FL 32503
(904)478-8017
Ultimate Parent: Digital Equipment Corp. **SIC:** 5046—Commercial Equipment Nec; 5734—Computer & Software Stores.

★ **62420** ★ **Engineering Research Assoc**
616 Univ Blvd.
Pensacola, FL 32504
(904)476-1750
Ultimate Parent: E-Systems Inc. **SIC:** 8999—Services Nec.

★ **62421** ★ **Engineering Research Associ**
6425 Pensacola Blvd.
Pensacola, FL 32505
(904)476-1750
Ultimate Parent: E-Systems Inc. **SIC:** 8711—Engineering Services.

★ **62422** ★ **Exxon Co. USA**
PO Box 12159
Pensacola, FL 32590
(904)477-8240
Officer: B. W. Evans, Manager. **Ultimate Parent:** Exxon. **SIC:** 2911—Petroleum Refining.

★ **62423** ★ **Federal Express Corp.**
5903 N. W. St.
Pensacola, FL 32505
(904)478-1455
Ultimate Parent: Federal Express. **SIC:** 7389—Business Services Nec.

★ **62424** ★ **First Union National Bank of Florida**
2400 W. Cervantes St.
Pensacola, FL 32505-7168
(904)434-7421
Location Type: Branch office. **Ultimate Parent:** First Union Corp. **SIC:** 6021—National Commercial Banks.

★ **62425** ★ **First Union National Bank of Florida**
810 Scenic Hwy.
Pensacola, FL 32503-6832
(904)434-2146
Location Type: Branch office. **Ultimate Parent:** First Union Corp. **SIC:** 6021—National Commercial Banks.

★ **62426** ★ **First Union National Bank of Florida**
235 E. Nine Mile Rd.
Pensacola, FL 32501
(904)434-6684
Location Type: Branch office. **Ultimate Parent:** First Union Corp. **SIC:** 6021—National Commercial Banks.

★ **62427** ★ **First Union National Bank of Florida**
4441 Bayou Blvd.
Pensacola, FL 32503-2601
(904)469-4263
Location Type: Branch office. **Ultimate Parent:** First Union Corp. **SIC:** 6021—National Commercial Banks.

★ **62428** ★ **First Union National Bank of Florida**
6425 Mobile Hwy.
Pensacola, FL 32526
(904)944-6262
Location Type: Branch office. **Ultimate Parent:** First Union Corp. **SIC:** 6021—National Commercial Banks.

★ **62429** ★ **First Union National Bank of Florida**
5650 N. Pensacola Blvd.
Pensacola, FL 32505-2550
(904)474-0927
Location Type: Branch office. **Ultimate Parent:** First Union Corp. **SIC:** 6021—National Commercial Banks.

★ **62430** ★ **First Union National Bank of Florida**
21 New Warrington Rd.
Pensacola, FL 32506
(904)453-7215
Location Type: Branch office. **Ultimate Parent:** First Union Corp. **SIC:** 6021—National Commercial Banks.

★ **62431** ★ **Gayfers Cordova Mall**
5100 N. 9th Ave.
Pensacola, FL 32504
(904)477-6100
Ultimate Parent: Mercantile Stores. **SIC:** 5311—Department Stores.

★ **62432** ★ **Great Western Bank**
5600 N. 9th Ave.
Pensacola, FL 32504
Ultimate Parent: Great Western Financial Corp. **SIC:** 6022—State Commercial Banks.

★ **62433** ★ **Great Western Bank**
6677 N. Davis Hwy.
Pensacola, FL 32504
(904)435-3032
Ultimate Parent: Great Western Financial Corp. **SIC:** 6099—Functions Related to Deposit Banking.

★ **62434** ★ **Great Western Bank**
251 W. Garden St.
Pensacola, FL 32501
(904)435-3000
Ultimate Parent: Great Western Financial Corp. **SIC:** 6022—State Commercial Banks.

★ **62435** ★ **Hit or Miss**
6601 N. Davis Hwy.
Pensacola, FL 32504
(904)477-8034
Ultimate Parent: TJX. **SIC:** 5651—Family Clothing Stores.

★ **62436** ★ **Hudson's**
122 PO Box
Pensacola, FL 32591
(904)432-5721
Ultimate Parent: Dayton Hudson.

★ **62437** ★ **Hygeia Coca-Cola Bottling Co.**
7330 N. Davis Hwy.
Pensacola, FL 32514
Ultimate Parent: Coca-Cola Bottling Consol. **SIC:** 2086—Bottled & Canned Soft Drinks.

★ **62438** ★ **Kentucky Fried Chicken**
6704 N. 9th Ave.
Pensacola, FL 32504
(904)476-0918
Ultimate Parent: Pepsico. **SIC:** 5812—Eating Places.

★ **62439** ★ **Kentucky Fried Chicken**
13 Gulf Beach Hwy.
Pensacola, FL 32507
(904)455-0088
Ultimate Parent: Pepsico. **SIC:** 5812—Eating Places.

★ **62440** ★ **Kentucky Fried Chicken**
4365 W. Fairfield Dr.
Pensacola, FL 32505
(904)455-7262
Ultimate Parent: Pepsico. **SIC:** 5812—Eating Places.

★ **62441** ★ **Kentucky Fried Chicken**
60 W. Nine Mile Rd.
Pensacola, FL 32534
(904)478-1310
Ultimate Parent: Pepsico. **SIC:** 5812—Eating Places.

★ **62442** ★ **Kentucky Fried Chicken**
4101 Mobile Hwy.
Pensacola, FL 32506
(904)455-9421
Ultimate Parent: Pepsico. **SIC:** 5812—Eating Places.

★ **62443** ★ **Lane Bryant**
5100 N. 9th Ave.
Pensacola, FL 32504
(904)479-3420
Ultimate Parent: Limited. **SIC:** 5651—Family Clothing Stores.

★ **62444** ★ **Lane Bryant**
7 Univ Mall
Pensacola, FL 32504
(904)474-0392
Ultimate Parent: Limited. **SIC:** 5651—Family Clothing Stores.

★ **62445** ★ **Lerner Shop**
Cordova
Pensacola, FL 32504
(904)477-5707
Ultimate Parent: Limited. **SIC:** 5621—Women's Clothing Stores.

★ **62446** ★ **The Limited**
5100 N. 9th Ave.
Pensacola, FL 32504
(904)478-0321
Ultimate Parent: Limited. **SIC:** 5651—Family Clothing Stores.

★ **62447** ★ **The Limited Express**
5100 N. 9th Ave.
Pensacola, FL 32504
(904)478-7755
Ultimate Parent: Limited. **SIC:** 5651—Family Clothing Stores.

★ **62448** ★ **Mary Kay Cosmetics**
6639 Flagler Dr.
Pensacola, FL 32503
(904)477-0549
Ultimate Parent: Mary Kay Cosmetics. **SIC:** 5999—Miscellaneous Retail Stores Nec.

★ **62449** ★ **Mobil Station**
18279 PO Box
Pensacola, FL 32523
(904)477-5077
Ultimate Parent: Mobil. **SIC:** 5531—Automobile & Home Supply Stores.

★ **62450** ★ **Monsanto Co.**
PO Box 12830
Pensacola, FL 32575-2830
(904)968-7000
Officer: L. F. Hebert. **Ultimate Parent:** Monsanto. **SIC:** 2821—Plastics Materials & Resins.

★ **62451** ★ **Monsanto Employees Cr Union**
220 E. 9 Mile Rd.
Pensacola, FL 32534-3145
(904)479-9601
Company Type: Headquarters. **Officer:** Gerald McArthur. **Ultimate Parent:** Monsanto. **SIC:** 6061—Federal Credit Unions; 6141—Personal Credit Institutions.

★ 62452 ★ New England Mutl
Life Insurance C
3 W. Garden St.
Pensacola, FL 32501
(904)433-2696
Ultimate Parent: New England Mutual Life.
SIC: 6411—Insurance Agents, Brokers &
Service.

★ 62453 ★ Otis Elevator Co.
3960 W. Navy Blvd. 19
Pensacola, FL 32507
(904)456-0883
Ultimate Parent: United Technologies. SIC:
1796—Installing Building Equipment Nec.

★ 62454 ★ Pacer Industries Inc.
9101 Ely St.
Pensacola, FL 32514-7011
(904)476-0907
Company Type: Subsidiary. Officer: Bill
Henehan, Controller. Ultimate Parent:
Echlin. SIC: 3429—Hardware Nec; 3592—
Carburetors, Pistons, Rings & Valves;
3714—Motor Vehicle Parts & Accessories.
Employee Count: 540. Sales: 76 M.

★ 62455 ★ Petite Sophisticate
34 Univ Mall
Pensacola, FL 32504
(904)479-1362
Ultimate Parent: United States Shoe. SIC:
5651—Family Clothing Stores.

★ 62456 ★ Pizza Hut
121 Boone St.
Pensacola, FL 32505
(904)477-3508
Ultimate Parent: Pepsico. SIC: 5812—
Eating Places.

★ 62457 ★ Pizza Hut
2 N. Old Corry Field Rd.
Pensacola, FL 32507
(904)455-2269
Ultimate Parent: Pepsico. SIC: 5812—
Eating Places.

★ 62458 ★ Pizza Hut
7154 N. Davis Hwy.
Pensacola, FL 32504
(904)478-1402
Ultimate Parent: Pepsico. SIC: 5812—
Eating Places.

★ 62459 ★ Pizza Hut
104 Entrance Rd.
Pensacola, FL 32507
(904)453-4500
Ultimate Parent: Pepsico. SIC: 5812—
Eating Places.

★ 62460 ★ Pizza Hut
5660 Pensacola Blvd.
Pensacola, FL 32505
(904)477-1375
Ultimate Parent: Pepsico. SIC: 5812—
Eating Places.

★ 62461 ★ Pizza Hut
2 E. Nine Mile Rd.
Pensacola, FL 32534
(904)476-6253
Ultimate Parent: Pepsico. SIC: 5812—
Eating Places.

★ 62462 ★ Pizza Hut
5470 Mobile Hwy.
Pensacola, FL 32526
(904)944-1118
Ultimate Parent: Pepsico. SIC: 5812—
Eating Places.

★ 62463 ★ Radio Shack
38 Univ Mall
Pensacola, FL 32504
(904)478-3288
Company Type: Division. Ultimate Parent:
Tandy Corp. SIC: 5731—Radio, Television
& Electronics Stores.

★ 62464 ★ Radio Shack
8187 W. Fairfield Dr.
Pensacola, FL 32506
(904)455-2025
Company Type: Division. Ultimate Parent:
Tandy Corp. SIC: 5065—Electronic Parts &
Equipment Nec; 5731—Radio, Television &
Electronics Stores.

★ 62465 ★ Radio Shack
5100 N. 9th Ave.
Pensacola, FL 32504
(904)477-5676
Company Type: Division. Ultimate Parent:

Tandy Corp. SIC: 5731—Radio, Television
& Electronics Stores.

★ 62466 ★ Radio Shack
400 N. Navy Blvd. 8
Pensacola, FL 32507
(904)453-3069
Company Type: Division. Ultimate Parent:
Tandy Corp. SIC: 5065—Electronic Parts &
Equipment Nec; 5731—Radio, Television &
Electronics Stores.

★ 62467 ★ Radio Shack
Ensley Sq.
Pensacola, FL 32514
(904)478-6928
Company Type: Division. Ultimate Parent:
Tandy Corp. SIC: 5065—Electronic Parts &
Equipment Nec.

★ 62468 ★ Ryder Truck Rental
4980 Mobile Hwy.
Pensacola, FL 32506
(904)456-0189
Ultimate Parent: Ryder System. SIC:
5113—Industrial & Personal Service Paper.

★ 62469 ★ Ryder Truck Rental
8000 Pensacola Blvd.
Pensacola, FL 32534
(904)477-9852
Ultimate Parent: Ryder System. SIC:
7359—Equipment Rental & Leasing Nec;
7513—Truck Rental & Leasing Without
Drivers.

★ 62470 ★ Ryder Truck Rental
3225 N. L St.
Pensacola, FL 32505
(904)432-0025
Ultimate Parent: Ryder System. SIC:
7389—Business Services Nec.

★ 62471 ★ Sam's Wholesale
Club
1250 Airport Blvd.
Pensacola, FL 32504
Ultimate Parent: Wal-Mart Stores, Inc. SIC:
5141—Groceries—General Line.

★ 62472 ★ Service Merchandise
7303 Plantation Rd.
Pensacola, FL 32504
(904)478-5252
Ultimate Parent: Service Merchandise Co.,
Inc. SIC: 5399—Miscellaneous General
Merchandise Store.

★ 62473 ★ Stop & Shop Liquors
4510 Mobile Hwy.
Pensacola, FL 32506
(904)456-3993
Ultimate Parent: Stop & Shop. SIC: 5921—
Liquor Stores.

★ 62474 ★ Systems Research
Laboratories
33 N. Navy Blvd.
Pensacola, FL 32507
(904)455-1555
Ultimate Parent: Arvin Industries Inc. SIC:
8731—Commercial Physical Research.

★ 62475 ★ T J Maxx
6601 N. Davis Hwy.
Pensacola, FL 32504
(904)478-0509
Ultimate Parent: TJX. SIC: 5651—Family
Clothing Stores.

★ 62476 ★ Taco Bell
Rural Route 3
Pensacola, FL 32534
(904)474-0376
Ultimate Parent: Pepsico. SIC: 5812—
Eating Places.

★ 62477 ★ Taco Bell
2111 W. Fairfield Dr.
Pensacola, FL 32505
(904)432-9729
Ultimate Parent: Pepsico. SIC: 5812—
Eating Places.

★ 62478 ★ Taco Bell
8088 N. Davis Hwy.
Pensacola, FL 32514
(904)479-1290
Ultimate Parent: Pepsico. SIC: 5812—
Eating Places.

★ 62479 ★ Taco Bell
1025 N. Navy Blvd.
Pensacola, FL 32507
(904)455-7896
Ultimate Parent: Pepsico. SIC: 5812—
Eating Places.

★ 62480 ★ Taco Bell
5076 Bayou Blvd.
Pensacola, FL 32503
(904)477-6300
Ultimate Parent: Pepsico. SIC: 5812—
Eating Places.

★ 62481 ★ Tektronix Inc.
6425 Pensacola Blvd.
Pensacola, FL 32505
(904)476-1897
Ultimate Parent: Tektronix, Inc. SIC:
5049—Professional Equipment Nec.

★ 62482 ★ Toys R US
5065 N. 9th Ave.
Pensacola, FL 32504
(904)479-3776
Ultimate Parent: Toys "R" US. SIC: 5945—
Hobby, Toy & Game Shops.

★ 62483 ★ Trailways Bus System
301 N. Baylen St.
Pensacola, FL 32501
(904)433-5047
Ultimate Parent: Greyhound Lines Inc. SIC:
4131—Intercity & Rural Bus Transportation.

★ 62484 ★ Underwriters
Adjusting Co.
River Rd.
Pensacola, FL 32507
(904)492-1461
Ultimate Parent: Continental. SIC: 6411—
Insurance Agents, Brokers & Service.

★ 62485 ★ Victoria's Secret
5100 N. 9th Ave.
Pensacola, FL 32504
(904)479-2681
Ultimate Parent: Limited. SIC: 5651—
Family Clothing Stores.

★ 62486 ★ Wal Mart
8970 Pensacola Blvd.
Pensacola, FL 32534
(904)484-3771
Ultimate Parent: Wal-Mart Stores, Inc. SIC:
5311—Department Stores.

★ 62487 ★ Wal Mart
6325 N. Davis Hwy.
Pensacola, FL 32504
(904)479-2181
Ultimate Parent: Wal-Mart Stores, Inc. SIC:
5912—Drug Stores & Proprietary Stores.

★ 62488 ★ Western Auto Supply
Co.
Town Plz.
Pensacola, FL 32505
(904)438-4464
Ultimate Parent: Sears Roebuck & Co.
SIC: 5531—Automobile & Home Supply
Stores.

★ 62489 ★ Western Auto Supply
Co. Dela
4170 Barrancas Ave.
Pensacola, FL 32507
(904)455-5459
Ultimate Parent: Sears Roebuck & Co.
SIC: 5531—Automobile & Home Supply
Stores.

★ 62490 ★ Westinghouse
Electric
8301 Scenic Hwy.
Pensacola, FL 32514
(904)474-4011
Officer: Bernie Smelstoys, Manager.
Ultimate Parent: Westinghouse Electric
Corp. SIC: 3443—Fabricated Plate Work—
Boiler Shops; 3511—Turbines & Turbine
Generator Sets; 3599—Industrial Machinery
Nec.

★ 62491 ★ Westinghouse
Electric Corp.
Pensacola
8301 Scenic Hwy.
Pensacola, FL 32514-7810
Location Type: Plant. Ultimate Parent:
Westinghouse Electric Corp. SIC: 3443—
Fabricated Plate Work—Boiler Shops.

★ 62492 ★ Xerox Corp.
4455 Bayou Blvd, Ste. A
Pensacola, FL 32503
(904)477-8225
Officer: Steve Mogg, Manager. Ultimate
Parent: Xerox Corp. SIC: 3663—Radio &
T.V. Communications Equipment.

Pensacola Fl

★ 62493 ★ Williams Brothers
Engineering
Tow Way
Pensacola Fl, FL 32508
(904)457-1197
Ultimate Parent: Fluor. SIC: 1521—
Single-Family Housing Construction.

Perrine

★ 62494 ★ Barnett Bank of South
Florida, NA
18341 S. Dixie Hwy.
Perrine, FL 33157-5560
(305)246-7400
Company Type: Subsidiary. Location
Type: Branch office. Officer: Gail Meyers,
Manager. Ultimate Parent: Barnett Banks.
SIC: 6021—National Commercial Banks.

★ 62495 ★ First Union National
Bank of Florida
19455 S. Dixie Hwy.
Perrine, FL 33157-7605
(305)663-6147
Location Type: Branch office. Ultimate
Parent: First Union Corp. SIC: 6021—
National Commercial Banks.

Perry

★ 62496 ★ Ace Hardware
805 S. Jefferson St.
Perry, FL 32347
(904)584-2411
Ultimate Parent: Ace Hardware. SIC:
5251—Hardware Stores.

★ 62497 ★ Buckeye Cellulose
Corp.
Rte. 3 Box 260 Hwy. 30
Perry, FL 32347
Ultimate Parent: Procter & Gamble Co.
SIC: 2611—Pulp Mills.

★ 62498 ★ Buckeye Cellulose
Corp.
Rte. 3 Box 260 (Hwy. 30)
Perry, FL 32347
Ultimate Parent: Procter & Gamble Co.
SIC: 2611—Pulp Mills.

★ 62499 ★ First Union National
Bank of Florida
200 W. Main St.
Perry, FL 32347-2658
(904)584-6745
Location Type: Branch office. Ultimate
Parent: First Union Corp. SIC: 6021—
National Commercial Banks.

★ 62500 ★ Kentucky Fried
Chicken
2100 S. Byron Butler Pky.
Perry, FL 32347
(904)584-7914
Ultimate Parent: Pepsico. SIC: 5812—
Eating Places.

★ 62501 ★ Pizza Hut
2199 S. Byron Butler Pky.
Perry, FL 32347
(904)584-7480
Ultimate Parent: Pepsico. SIC: 5812—
Eating Places.

★ 62502 ★ Procter & Gamble
Cellulose Co.
Hwy. 30 E. Box 260
Perry, FL 32347-9512
Ultimate Parent: Procter & Gamble Co.
SIC: 2611—Pulp Mills.

★ 62503 ★ Procter & Gamble
Cellulose Co.
Rte. 3 Box 260
Perry, FL 32347-9512
Ultimate Parent: Procter & Gamble Co.
SIC: 2611—Pulp Mills.

★ 62504 ★ **Procter & Gamble Cellulose Co.**
Hwy. 30 Rte. 3 Box 260
Perry, FL 32347
Ultimate Parent: Procter & Gamble Co.
SIC: 2611—Pulp Mills.

★ 62505 ★ **Ryder Truck Rental**
1612 S. Dixie Hwy.
Perry, FL 32347
(904)584-6025
Ultimate Parent: Ryder System. **SIC:** 7359—Equipment Rental & Leasing Nec; 7513—Truck Rental & Leasing Without Drivers.

Pierce

★ 62506 ★ **Tropicana Products Inc.**
Glades Rd.
Pierce, FL 33450
(407)465-2030
Company Type: Division. **Location Type:** Facility. **Officer:** Tris Chapman, Plant Manager. **Ultimate Parent:** J.E. Seagram & Sons, Inc.

Pinellas Park

★ 62507 ★ **Ace Hardware**
7680 49th St.
Pinellas Park, FL 34665
(813)541-4607
Ultimate Parent: Ace Hardware. **SIC:** 5251—Hardware Stores.

★ 62508 ★ **Aircraft Porous Media Inc.**
6301 49th St. N.
Pinellas Park, FL 34665-5798
Ultimate Parent: Pall. **SIC:** 3728—Aircraft Parts & Equipment Nec.

★ 62509 ★ **Aircraft Porous Media, Inc.**
6301 49th St., N
Pinellas Park, FL 34665-5798
(813)522-3111 **Fax:** (813)522-0711
Officer: Joseph Campolong, President. **Ultimate Parent:** Pall.

★ 62510 ★ **Barnett Bank of Pinellas County**
10200 66th St.
Pinellas Park, FL 34666-2303
(813)892-1673
Company Type: Subsidiary. **Location Type:** Branch office. **Officer:** Jeff McDowell, Manager. **Ultimate Parent:** Barnett Banks. **SIC:** 6022—State Commercial Banks.

★ 62511 ★ **Barnett Bank of Pinellas County**
7694 49th St. N
Pinellas Park, FL 34665-3438
(813)892-1288
Company Type: Subsidiary. **Location Type:** Branch office. **Officer:** Gene Evans, Manager. **Ultimate Parent:** Barnett Banks. **SIC:** 6022—State Commercial Banks.

★ 62512 ★ **Beneficial Savings Bank**
6479 102nd Ave.
Pinellas Park, FL 34666-3027
(813)545-0982
Location Type: Branch office. **Ultimate Parent:** Beneficial. **SIC:** 6022—State Commercial Banks.

★ 62513 ★ **Casual Corner**
7200 Us 19 N
Pinellas Park, FL 34665
(813)525-5880
Ultimate Parent: United States Shoe. **SIC:** 5651—Family Clothing Stores.

★ 62514 ★ **Chase Manhatten Bank of Florida, NA**
6700 66th St. N
Pinellas Park, FL 34665-5051
(813)546-3591
Location Type: Branch office. **Officer:** Patricia Hamp, Manager. **Ultimate Parent:** Chase Manhattan Corp. **SIC:** 6021—National Commercial Banks.

★ 62515 ★ **Circus World Toy Store**
7200 Us 19 N
Pinellas Park, FL 34665
(813)525-0112
Ultimate Parent: Melville. **SIC:** 5945—Hobby, Toy & Game Shops.

★ 62516 ★ **Citizens Federal Bank, FSB**
9103 US Hwy. 19 N.
Pinellas Park, FL 34666-5406
(813)576-3499
Location Type: Branch office. **Officer:** Pat Stephens, Manager. **Ultimate Parent:** CSF Holdings. **SIC:** 6021—National Commercial Banks.

★ 62517 ★ **First of America Bank**
4501 Mainlands Blvd.
Pinellas Park, FL 34666
(813)676-8928
Location Type: Branch office. **Ultimate Parent:** First of America Bank Corp.

★ 62518 ★ **Foot Action U S a**
7200 Us 19 N
Pinellas Park, FL 34665
(813)525-8895
Ultimate Parent: Melville. **SIC:** 5661—Shoe Stores.

★ 62519 ★ **Fortune Bank, SB**
4325 Park Blvd.
Pinellas Park, FL 34665-4620
(813)547-1525
Location Type: Branch office. **Ultimate Parent:** Fortune Bancorp. **SIC:** 6021—National Commercial Banks.

★ 62520 ★ **The Gap**
7200 Us Hwy. 19 N
Pinellas Park, FL 34665
(813)526-3396
Ultimate Parent: GAP. **SIC:** 5651—Family Clothing Stores.

★ 62521 ★ **Kentucky Fried Chicken**
6595 Park Blvd.
Pinellas Park, FL 34665
(813)544-2345
Ultimate Parent: Pepsico. **SIC:** 5812—Eating Places.

★ 62522 ★ **Mobil Mart**
10195 66th St.
Pinellas Park, FL 34666
(813)546-6697
Ultimate Parent: Mobil. **SIC:** 5411—Grocery Stores.

★ 62523 ★ **Molex-ETC Inc.**
4650 62nd Ave. N
Pinellas Park, FL 34665
(813)521-2700 **Fax:** (813)528-1010
Officer: Edwin W. Parkinson, President. **Ultimate Parent:** Molex.

★ 62524 ★ **Payless Shoesource**
7200 US 19 N
Pinellas Park, FL 34665
(813)527-7420
Ultimate Parent: May Department Stores. **SIC:** 5661—Shoe Stores.

★ 62525 ★ **Pizza Hut**
8070 49th St.
Pinellas Park, FL 34665
(813)530-0511
Ultimate Parent: Pepsico. **SIC:** 5812—Eating Places.

★ 62526 ★ **Pizza Hut**
6575 Park Blvd.
Pinellas Park, FL 34665
(813)541-4418
Ultimate Parent: Pepsico. **SIC:** 5812—Eating Places.

★ 62527 ★ **Publix Super Market**
7580 49th St.
Pinellas Park, FL 34665
(813)544-1439
Ultimate Parent: Publix Super Markets. **SIC:** 5411—Grocery Stores.

★ 62528 ★ **Taco Bell**
4394 Park Blvd.
Pinellas Park, FL 34665
(813)541-4729
Ultimate Parent: Pepsico. **SIC:** 5812—Eating Places.

★ 62529 ★ **Waldenbooks**
7200 Us Hwy. 19 N. 636
Pinellas Park, FL 34665
(813)522-7709
Ultimate Parent: K-Mart. **SIC:** 5942—Book Stores.

★ 62530 ★ **Walgreen Drug Stores**
7450 66th St.
Pinellas Park, FL 34665
(813)546-3586
Ultimate Parent: Walgreen Co. **SIC:** 5912—Drug Stores & Proprietary Stores.

Pinellas Pk.

★ 62531 ★ **Macy's Close-Out**
4100 Pk. Blvd.
Pinellas Pk., FL 34665-3639
(813)547-8868
Ultimate Parent: R. H. Macy. **SIC:** 5311—Department Stores.

★ 62532 ★ **Molex-Etc Inc.**
4820 Pk. Blvd.
Pinellas Pk., FL 34665-3534
(813)541-4651
Company Type: Branch. **Ultimate Parent:** Molex. **SIC:** 3678—Electronic Connectors.

Plant City

★ 62533 ★ **Ace Hardware P P**
Park Plz.
Plant City, FL 33565
(813)541-4607
Ultimate Parent: Ace Hardware. **SIC:** 5072—Hardware.

★ 62534 ★ **Alumax Extrusions Inc.**
1650 Alumax Circle Industrial Park
Plant City, FL 33566
Ultimate Parent: Alumax Inc. **SIC:** 3354—Aluminum Extruded Products.

★ 62535 ★ **Asgrow Florida Co.**
4144 Hwy. 39 N.
Plant City, FL 33566
Ultimate Parent: Upjohn Co. **SIC:** 2879—Agricultural Chemicals Nec.

★ 62536 ★ **Avon Products Business Office**
111 E. Reynolds St.
Plant City, FL 33566-3351
(813)754-5572
Ultimate Parent: Avon Products, Inc. **SIC:** 8331—Job Training & Related Services; 5999—Miscellaneous Retail Stores Nec.

★ 62537 ★ **Barnett Bank of Tampa**
105 S. Wheeler St.
Plant City, FL 33566-5449
(813)752-6161
Company Type: Subsidiary. **Location Type:** Branch office. **Officer:** Barbara Gomez, Manager. **Ultimate Parent:** Barnett Banks. **SIC:** 6022—State Commercial Banks.

★ 62538 ★ **Barnett Bank of Tampa**
2309 Jim Redman Pky.
Plant City, FL 33566
(813)752-7787
Company Type: Subsidiary. **Location Type:** Branch office. **Officer:** Dale Royse, Vice President. **Ultimate Parent:** Barnett Banks. **SIC:** 6022—State Commercial Banks.

★ 62539 ★ **California Federal Bank**
6521 102nd Ave.
Plant City, FL 33565
(813)541-7738
Ultimate Parent: California Federal Bank. **SIC:** 6022—State Commercial Banks.

★ 62540 ★ **Casual Corner**
346 Pinellas Sq.
Plant City, FL 33565
(813)525-5880
Ultimate Parent: United States Shoe. **SIC:** 5621—Women's Clothing Stores.

★ 62541 ★ **Central Phosphates Inc.**
10609 NOrth Hwy. 39 N.
Plant City, FL 33566
Ultimate Parent: CF Industries. **SIC:** 2874—Phosphatic Fertilizers.

★ 62542 ★ **Central Phosphates Inc.**
10609 Hwy. 39 N.
Plant City, FL 33566
Ultimate Parent: CF Industries. **SIC:** 2874—Phosphatic Fertilizers.

★ 62543 ★ **Fleetwood Homes**
3804 Sydney Rd.
Plant City, FL 33567
(813)754-1884
Officer: Neil Scarborough, Manager. **Ultimate Parent:** Fleetwood Enterprises, Inc. **SIC:** 2451—Mobile Homes.

★ 62544 ★ **Food Lion**
1803 J L Redman Pky.
Plant City, FL 33566
(813)752-2826
Ultimate Parent: Food Lion. **SIC:** 5411—Grocery Stores.

★ 62545 ★ **Foot Action No 8036**
7200 Us 19
Plant City, FL 33565
(813)525-8895
Ultimate Parent: Melville. **SIC:** 5661—Shoe Stores.

★ 62546 ★ **Imc Fertilizer Inc. Plant City Uranium Recovery**
Hwy. 39 Hillsborough/Pasco County Line
Plant City, FL 33566
Ultimate Parent: IMC Fertilizer Group. **SIC:** 1094—Uranium, Radium & Vanadium Ores.

★ 62547 ★ **Imc Fertilizer Inc. Plant City Uranium Recovery**
Hwy. 39 & Hillsborough Pasco County
Plant City, FL 33566
Ultimate Parent: IMC Fertilizer Group. **SIC:** 1094—Uranium, Radium & Vanadium Ores.

★ 62548 ★ **Kentucky Fried Chicken**
6595 Park Blvd. N
Plant City, FL 33565
(813)544-2345
Ultimate Parent: Pepsico. **SIC:** 5812—Eating Places.

★ 62549 ★ **Kentucky Fried Chicken**
2305 S. Collins St.
Plant City, FL 33566
(813)752-0437
Ultimate Parent: Pepsico. **SIC:** 5812—Eating Places.

★ 62550 ★ **Lane Bryant**
7200 34th St. N
Plant City, FL 33565
(813)527-5374
Ultimate Parent: Limited. **SIC:** 5621—Women's Clothing Stores.

★ 62551 ★ **Pizza Hut**
1050 62nd Ave. N
Plant City, FL 33565
(813)521-4631
Ultimate Parent: Pepsico. **SIC:** 5812—Eating Places.

★ 62552 ★ **Plant City Steel Co.**
PO Drawer A
Plant City, FL 33564-9001
(813)752-1133 **Fax:** (813)754-7683
Company Type: Subsidiary. **Officer:** Moore Tappan Jr., President. **Ultimate Parent:** Harsco.

★ 62553 ★ **Publix Super Markets**
7580 49th St. N
Plant City, FL 33565
(813)544-1439
Ultimate Parent: Publix Super Markets. **SIC:** 5812—Eating Places.

★ 62554 ★ **Radio Shack**
802 Pinellas Sq.
Plant City, FL 33565
(813)526-3798
Company Type: Division. **Ultimate Parent:** Tandy Corp. **SIC:** 5065—Electronic Parts & Equipment Nec.

★ 62555 ★   **Russell Associates Inc.**
St N
Plant City, FL 33565
(813)526-1134
Ultimate Parent: Pall. **SIC:** 5088—
Transportation Equipment & Supplies.

★ 62556 ★   **Texaco**
703 S. Alexander St.
Plant City, FL 33566
(813)752-2515
Ultimate Parent: Texaco. **SIC:** 5411—
Grocery Stores.

★ 62557 ★   **Texaco**
2210 N. Park Rd.
Plant City, FL 33566
(813)754-3613
Ultimate Parent: Texaco. **SIC:** 5541—
Gasoline Service Stations.

★ 62558 ★   **Wal Mart Pharmacy**
2602 J L Redman Pky.
Plant City, FL 33566
Ultimate Parent: Wal-Mart Stores, Inc. **SIC:**
5912—Drug Stores & Proprietary Stores.

★ 62559 ★   **Waldenbooks**
Pinellas Sq.
Plant City, FL 33565
(813)522-7709
Ultimate Parent: K-Mart. **SIC:** 5942—Book
Stores.

★ 62560 ★   **Western Auto Supply Co.**
7561 49th St. N
Plant City, FL 33565
(813)544-1451
Ultimate Parent: Sears Roebuck & Co.
SIC: 5531—Automobile & Home Supply
Stores.

Plant City

★ 62561 ★   **Walker Manufacturing**
6545 44th St. N
Plant City Fl, FL 33565
(813)522-2195
Ultimate Parent: Tenneco Inc. **SIC:** 7622—
Radio & T.V. Repair.

Plantation

★ 62562 ★   **Barnett Bank of Broward County, NA**
300 S. Pine Island Rd.
Plantation, FL 33324-2619
(305)475-0733
Company Type: Subsidiary. **Location Type:** Branch office. **Officer:** Roy Binger,
Manager. **Ultimate Parent:** Barnett Banks.
SIC: 6021—National Commercial Banks.

★ 62563 ★   **Barnett Bank of Broward County, NA**
8190 W. Sunrise Blvd.
Plantation, FL 33318
(305)797-0589
Company Type: Subsidiary. **Location Type:** Branch office. **Officer:** Richard Plund,
Manager. **Ultimate Parent:** Barnett Banks.
SIC: 6021—National Commercial Banks.

★ 62564 ★   **Barnett Bank of Broward County, NA**
491 NW 40th Ave.
Plantation, FL 33310
(305)797-0584
Company Type: Subsidiary. **Location Type:** Branch office. **Officer:** Neville
Stewart, Manager. **Ultimate Parent:** Barnett
Banks. **SIC:** 6021—National Commercial
Banks.

★ 62565 ★   **California Federal Bank, FSB**
8181 W. Broward Blvd.
Plantation, FL 33324-2049
(305)473-2666
Location Type: Branch office. **Officer:**
Mark Sollenberger, Manager. **Ultimate
Parent:** California Federal Bank. **SIC:**
6021—National Commercial Banks.

★ 62566 ★   **Deluxe Check Printers**
6531 NW 18th Ct.
Plantation, FL 33313
Ultimate Parent: Deluxe Corp. **SIC:** 2782—
Blankbooks & Looseleaf Binders; 2752—
Commercial Printing—Lithographic.

★ 62567 ★   **Deluxe Check Printers Inc.**
6531 NW 18th Ct.
Plantation, FL 33313
Ultimate Parent: Deluxe Corp. **SIC:** 2782—
Blankbooks & Looseleaf Binders; 2752—
Commercial Printing—Lithographic.

★ 62568 ★   **First Union National Bank of Florida**
1191 S. University Dr.
Plantation, FL 33324
(305)467-5210
Location Type: Branch office. **Ultimate
Parent:** First Union Corp. **SIC:** 6021—
National Commercial Banks.

★ 62569 ★   **First Union National Bank of Florida**
50 SW 84th Ave.
Plantation, FL 33324-2713
(305)468-2800
Location Type: Branch office. **Ultimate
Parent:** First Union Corp. **SIC:** 6021—
National Commercial Banks.

★ 62570 ★   **First Union National Bank of Florida**
1790 N. Pine Island Rd.
Plantation, FL 33322-5246
(305)467-5560
Location Type: Branch office. **Ultimate
Parent:** First Union Corp. **SIC:** 6021—
National Commercial Banks.

★ 62571 ★   **Motorola Inc.**
Portable Products Div.
8000 W. Sunrise Blvd.
Plantation, FL 33322
Company Type: Division. **Ultimate Parent:**
Motorola Inc. **SIC:** 3600—Electronic & Other
Electrical Equipment; 3679—Electronic
Components Nec; 3471—Plating &
Polishing.

Plymouth

★ 62572 ★   **Coca-Cola Foods Plymouth**
2651 Orange Ave.
Plymouth, FL 32768
Ultimate Parent: Coca-Cola. **SIC:** 2080—
Beverages.

★ 62573 ★   **Coca-Cola Foods Plymouth Chilled Juice**
2659 Orange Ave.
Plymouth, FL 32768
Ultimate Parent: Coca-Cola. **SIC:** 2033—
Canned Fruits & Vegetables.

★ 62574 ★   **Coca-Cola Foods Special Products Dept.**
2501 Orange Ave.
Plymouth, FL 32768
Ultimate Parent: Coca-Cola. **SIC:** 2087—
Flavoring Extracts & Syrups Nec.

★ 62575 ★   **Coca-Cola Plymouth**
2659 Orange Ave.
Plymouth, FL 32768
Ultimate Parent: Coca-Cola. **SIC:** 2080—
Beverages; 2037—Frozen Fruits &
Vegetables.

★ 62576 ★   **Crown Cork & Seal Co. Inc.**
Metals Div.
Hwy. 441 & State Rte. 437
Plymouth, FL 32768
Company Type: Division. **Ultimate Parent:**
Crown Cork & Seal. **SIC:** 3411—Metal
Cans.

★ 62577 ★   **Southland**
S Hermit Smith Rd.
Plymouth, FL 32768
(407)889-4181
Ultimate Parent: Southland Corp. **SIC:**
0181—Ornamental Nursery Products.

Polk City

★ 62578 ★   **Agrico Chemical Co.**
Fort Green Rd.
Polk City, FL 33868
(813)428-2055
Ultimate Parent: Freeport-McMoran.

Pompano Beach

★ 62579 ★   **Ace Hardware Margate**
5825 Margate Blvd.
Pompano Beach, FL 33063
(305)972-1711
Ultimate Parent: Ace Hardware. **SIC:**
5251—Hardware Stores.

★ 62580 ★   **Ace Hardware&Lumber**
1101 S. Federal Hwy.
Pompano Beach, FL 33062
(305)942-3955
Ultimate Parent: Ace Hardware. **SIC:**
5251—Hardware Stores.

★ 62581 ★   **American Savings of FL FSB**
10385 Royal Palm Blvd.
Pompano Beach, FL 33065-4817
(305)341-0900
Location Type: Branch office. **Officer:**
Mark G. Mathosian. **Ultimate Parent:**
American Savings of Florida. **SIC:** 6035—
Federal Savings Institutions; 6021—National
Commercial Banks.

★ 62582 ★   **American Savings of FL FSB**
7220 W. Atlantic Blvd.
Pompano Beach, FL 33063-4205
(305)973-0880
Location Type: Branch office. **Ultimate
Parent:** American Savings of Florida. **SIC:**
6035—Federal Savings Institutions; 6021—
National Commercial Banks.

★ 62583 ★   **American Savings of FL FSB**
4901 Coconut Creek Pky.
Pompano Beach, FL 33063-3998
(305)975-8936
Location Type: Branch office. **Ultimate
Parent:** American Savings of Florida. **SIC:**
6021—National Commercial Banks.

★ 62584 ★   **Barnett Bank of Broward County, NA**
101 S. Oceanside Blvd.
Pompano Beach, FL 33062-5699
(305)786-3371
Company Type: Subsidiary. **Location
Type:** Branch office. **Officer:** Ray Wolowicz,
Manager. **Ultimate Parent:** Barnett Banks.
SIC: 6021—National Commercial Banks.

★ 62585 ★   **Barnett Bank of Broward County, NA**
1101 E. Atlantic Blvd.
Pompano Beach, FL 33060-7495
(305)786-3305
Company Type: Subsidiary. **Location
Type:** Branch office. **Officer:** Randy
Gaffney, Manager. **Ultimate Parent:** Barnett
Banks. **SIC:** 6021—National Commercial
Banks.

★ 62586 ★   **Barnett Bank of Broward County, NA**
900 W. Sample Rd.
Pompano Beach, FL 33064-2018
(305)979-6082
Company Type: Subsidiary. **Location
Type:** Branch office. **Officer:** Pat Lee,
Manager. **Ultimate Parent:** Barnett Banks.
SIC: 6021—National Commercial Banks.

★ 62587 ★   **Burdines Portrait Studio**
1200 NE 23rd St.
Pompano Beach, FL 33064
(305)946-1551
Ultimate Parent: Federated Department
Stores. **SIC:** 7221—Photographic Studios—
Portrait.

★ 62588 ★   **California Federal Bank, FSB**
1201 S. Ocean Blvd.
Pompano Beach, FL 33062-6696
(305)781-4860
Location Type: Branch office. **Ultimate
Parent:** California Federal Bank. **SIC:**
6021—National Commercial Banks.

★ 62589 ★   **Casual Corner**
1177 N. University Dr.
Pompano Beach, FL 33071
(305)755-6899
Ultimate Parent: United States Shoe. **SIC:**
5699—Miscellaneous Apparel & Accessory
Stores.

★ 62590 ★   **Casual Corner**
Pompano Fashion Sq.
Pompano Beach, FL 33062
(305)782-8150
Ultimate Parent: United States Shoe. **SIC:**
5621—Women's Clothing Stores.

★ 62591 ★   **Citibank, FSB**
20 Oceanside Shopping Ctr.
Pompano Beach, FL 33062-5790
(305)942-9501
Location Type: Branch office. **Ultimate
Parent:** Citicorp. **SIC:** 6021—National
Commercial Banks.

★ 62592 ★   **Coast to Coast Contractors**
426 E. Sample Rd.
Pompano Beach, FL 33064
(305)782-6577
Ultimate Parent: Servistar Corp. **SIC:**
5211—Lumber & Other Building Materials.

★ 62593 ★   **Dyno Merchandise Corp.**
1571 W. Copans Rd., Ste. 105
Pompano Beach, FL 33064
(305)791-2910 **Fax:** (305)972-0305
Officer: John Feinberg, President. **Ultimate
Parent:** Conagra.

★ 62594 ★   **First Union National Bank of Florida**
2400 E. Atlantic Blvd.
Pompano Beach, FL 33062-5299
(305)786-7210
Location Type: Branch office. **Ultimate
Parent:** First Union Corp. **SIC:** 6021—
National Commercial Banks.

★ 62595 ★   **First Union National Bank of Florida**
199 N. Ocean Blvd.
Pompano Beach, FL 33062-5741
(305)786-2690
Location Type: Branch office. **Ultimate
Parent:** First Union Corp. **SIC:** 6021—
National Commercial Banks.

★ 62596 ★   **First Union National Bank of Florida**
400 E. Sample Rd.
Pompano Beach, FL 33064
(305)786-6170
Location Type: Branch office. **Ultimate
Parent:** First Union Corp. **SIC:** 6021—
National Commercial Banks.

★ 62597 ★   **First Union National Bank of Florida**
351 S. Cypress Rd.
Pompano Beach, FL 33060-7159
(305)786-2690
Location Type: Branch office. **Ultimate
Parent:** First Union Corp. **SIC:** 6021—
National Commercial Banks.

★ 62598 ★   **The Gap**
9541 W. Atlantic Blvd.
Pompano Beach, FL 33071
(305)753-7802
Ultimate Parent: GAP. **SIC:** 5699—
Miscellaneous Apparel & Accessory Stores.

★ 62599 ★   **Greyhound Bus Lines**
2190 NE 4th St.
Pompano Beach, FL 33062
(305)946-7067
Ultimate Parent: Greyhound Lines Inc. **SIC:**
4131—Intercity & Rural Bus Transportation.

★ 62600 ★   **Hertz Rent-A-Car Dba**
1436 S. Powerline Rd.
Pompano Beach, FL 33069
Ultimate Parent: Hertz. **SIC:** 5148—Fresh
Fruits & Vegetables; 7514—Passenger Car
Rental.

★ 62601 ★   **Kay Bee Toy & Hobby Shop**
9469 W. Atlantic Blvd.
Pompano Beach, FL 33071
(305)752-8114
Ultimate Parent: Melville. **SIC:** 5945—
Hobby, Toy & Game Shops.

★ 62602 ★   **Kay Bee Toy&Hobby Shop**
Pompano Fashion Sq.
Pompano Beach, FL 33062
(305)786-0662
Ultimate Parent: Melville. **SIC:** 5945—
Hobby, Toy & Game Shops.

★ **62603** ★　**Kmart Sporting Goods**
2421 N. Federal Hwy.
Pompano Beach, FL 33064
(305)781-2580
Ultimate Parent: K-Mart. **SIC:** 5941—Sporting Goods & Bicycle Shops.

★ **62604** ★　**Kroger Wesco Foods Co.**
3970 NW 108th Dr.
Pompano Beach, FL 33065
(305)752-8855
Ultimate Parent: Kroger. **SIC:** 5148—Fresh Fruits & Vegetables.

★ **62605** ★　**Lerner Shop**
Pompano Fashion Sq.
Pompano Beach, FL 33062
(305)946-7744
Ultimate Parent: Limited. **SIC:** 5621—Women's Clothing Stores.

★ **62606** ★　**The Limited**
Pompano Fashion Sq.
Pompano Beach, FL 33062
(305)781-6089
Ultimate Parent: Limited. **SIC:** 5621—Women's Clothing Stores.

★ **62607** ★　**Marshalls Inc.**
1401 S. Federal Hwy.
Pompano Beach, FL 33062
(305)785-4801
Ultimate Parent: Melville. **SIC:** 5311—Department Stores.

★ **62608** ★　**Mary Kay Cosmetics**
3767 NW 35th St.
Pompano Beach, FL 33066
(305)979-8260
Ultimate Parent: Mary Kay Cosmetics.

★ **62609** ★　**Mary Kay Cosmetics**
8852 NW 56th St.
Pompano Beach, FL 33067
(305)755-3670
Ultimate Parent: Mary Kay Cosmetics.

★ **62610** ★　**McDonalds of Coral Springs**
7751 W. Sample Rd.
Pompano Beach, FL 33065
(305)752-6710
Ultimate Parent: McDonald's. **SIC:** 5812—Eating Places.

★ **62611** ★　**McDonalds Restaurant**
950 Atlantic Blvd.
Pompano Beach, FL 33069
(305)975-0072
Ultimate Parent: McDonald's. **SIC:** 5812—Eating Places.

★ **62612** ★　**Media Networks Inc.**
2640 NW 17th Ln.
Pompano Beach, FL 33064
(305)940-0414
Ultimate Parent: Minnesota Mining & Mfg. **SIC:** 7313—Radio, T.V. & Publisher Representatives.

★ **62613** ★　**Parkson Corp.**
231 SW 12th Ave.
Pompano Beach, FL 33069
(305)975-0072
Ultimate Parent: Johnson & Johnson. **SIC:** 3443—Fabricated Plate Work—Boiler Shops.

★ **62614** ★　**Pizza Hut**
1309 N. University Dr.
Pompano Beach, FL 33071
(305)344-4433
Ultimate Parent: Pepsico. **SIC:** 5812—Eating Places.

★ **62615** ★　**Pizza Hut**
2621 N. Riverside Dr.
Pompano Beach, FL 33062
(305)781-0652
Ultimate Parent: Pepsico. **SIC:** 5146—Fish & Seafoods.

★ **62616** ★　**Pizza Hut**
1875 N. State Rd. 7
Pompano Beach, FL 33063
(305)972-2211
Ultimate Parent: Pepsico. **SIC:** 5812—Eating Places.

★ **62617** ★　**Pizza Hut**
3003 N. Federal Hwy.
Pompano Beach, FL 33064
(305)781-7845
Ultimate Parent: Pepsico. **SIC:** 5812—Eating Places.

★ **62618** ★　**Publix Super Market**
693 S. Cypress Rd.
Pompano Beach, FL 33060
(305)942-0110
Ultimate Parent: Publix Super Markets. **SIC:** 5411—Grocery Stores.

★ **62619** ★　**Publix Super Market**
7230 W. Atlantic Blvd.
Pompano Beach, FL 33063
(305)979-2555
Ultimate Parent: Publix Super Markets. **SIC:** 5411—Grocery Stores.

★ **62620** ★　**Publix Super Market**
2511 E. Atlantic Blvd.
Pompano Beach, FL 33062
(305)942-8818
Ultimate Parent: Publix Super Markets. **SIC:** 5411—Grocery Stores.

★ **62621** ★　**Publix Super Market**
3700 N. Federal Hwy.
Pompano Beach, FL 33064
(305)941-1810
Ultimate Parent: Publix Super Markets. **SIC:** 5411—Grocery Stores.

★ **62622** ★　**Publix Super Markets**
3700 N. Federal Hwy.
Pompano Beach, FL 33064
(305)941-1810
Ultimate Parent: Publix Super Markets. **SIC:** 5411—Grocery Stores.

★ **62623** ★　**Publix Super Markets**
2511 E. Atlantic Blvd.
Pompano Beach, FL 33062
(305)942-8818
Ultimate Parent: Publix Super Markets. **SIC:** 5411—Grocery Stores.

★ **62624** ★　**Publix Super Markets**
7230 W. Atlantic Blvd.
Pompano Beach, FL 33063
(305)979-2555
Ultimate Parent: Publix Super Markets. **SIC:** 5411—Grocery Stores.

★ **62625** ★　**Publix Super Markets**
693 S. Cypress Rd.
Pompano Beach, FL 33060
(305)942-0110
Ultimate Parent: Publix Super Markets. **SIC:** 5411—Grocery Stores.

★ **62626** ★　**Radio Shack**
5443 W. Atlantic Blvd.
Pompano Beach, FL 33063
(305)971-4291
Company Type: Division. **Ultimate Parent:** Tandy Corp. **SIC:** 5731—Radio, Television & Electronics Stores.

★ **62627** ★　**Radio Shack**
960 N. Federal Hwy.
Pompano Beach, FL 33062
(305)781-8571
Company Type: Division. **Ultimate Parent:** Tandy Corp. **SIC:** 5065—Electronic Parts & Equipment Nec.

★ **62628** ★　**Radio Shack**
Pompano Fashion Sq.
Pompano Beach, FL 33062
(305)782-3082
Company Type: Division. **Ultimate Parent:** Tandy Corp. **SIC:** 5731—Radio, Television & Electronics Stores.

★ **62629** ★　**Rite Aid Drugs**
Cypress Plz.
Pompano Beach, FL 33060
(305)941-2333
Ultimate Parent: Rite Aid. **SIC:** 5912—Drug Stores & Proprietary Stores.

★ **62630** ★　**Royal Manufacturing Inc.**
2601 Gateway Dr.
Pompano Beach, FL 33069
(305)491-4264
Ultimate Parent: Delta Woodside Industries. **SIC:** 7389—Business Services Nec.

★ **62631** ★　**Ryder Truck Rental**
991 E. Sample Rd.
Pompano Beach, FL 33064
(305)942-4573
Ultimate Parent: Ryder System. **SIC:** 7359—Equipment Rental & Leasing Nec.

★ **62632** ★　**Ryder Truck Rental**
3860 NW 118th Ave.
Pompano Beach, FL 33065
(305)752-6953
Ultimate Parent: Ryder System. **SIC:** 7359—Equipment Rental & Leasing Nec.

★ **62633** ★　**Ryder Truck Rental**
Atlantic Univ
Pompano Beach, FL 33071
(305)975-0587
Ultimate Parent: Ryder System.

★ **62634** ★　**Savings of America**
Home Savings of America, FSB
225 N. Federal Hwy.
Pompano Beach, FL 33062-4308
(305)941-5000
Location Type: Branch office. **Officer:** Stephanie Ferguson, Manager. **Ultimate Parent:** H. F. Ahmanson. **SIC:** 6021—National Commercial Banks.

★ **62635** ★　**Savings of America**
Home Savings of America, FSB
2770 W. Atlantic Blvd.
Pompano Beach, FL 33069-2595
(305)974-1122
Location Type: Branch office. **Officer:** Joyce Lione, Manager. **Ultimate Parent:** H. F. Ahmanson. **SIC:** 6021—National Commercial Banks.

★ **62636** ★　**Savings of America**
Home Savings of America, FSB
3885 N. Federal Hwy.
Pompano Beach, FL 33064-6659
(305)781-0200
Location Type: Branch office. **Officer:** James Fudally, Manager. **Ultimate Parent:** H. F. Ahmanson. **SIC:** 6021—National Commercial Banks.

★ **62637** ★　**Tandy Consumer Service**
1951 W. Copans Rd. 2-6
Pompano Beach, FL 33064
Ultimate Parent: Tandy Corp. **SIC:** 8732—Commercial Nonphysical Research.

★ **62638** ★　**W. R. Grace & Co.**
Connecticut Construction Products Div.
1200 NW 15th Ave.
Pompano Beach, FL 33069
Company Type: Division. **Ultimate Parent:** W. R. Grace. **SIC:** 2899—Chemical Preparations Nec.

★ **62639** ★　**Waldenbooks**
10 N. Federal Hwy.
Pompano Beach, FL 33062
(305)782-4858
Ultimate Parent: K-Mart. **SIC:** 5942—Book Stores.

★ **62640** ★　**Waldenbooks**
Pompano Fashion Sq.
Pompano Beach, FL 33062
(305)946-9168
Ultimate Parent: K-Mart. **SIC:** 5199—Nondurable Goods Nec.

★ **62641** ★　**Walgreen Drug Stores**
5365 W. Atlantic Blvd.
Pompano Beach, FL 33063
(305)977-0191
Ultimate Parent: Walgreen Co. **SIC:** 7389—Business Services Nec.

★ **62642** ★　**Walgreen Drug Stores**
3555 N. Federal Hwy.
Pompano Beach, FL 33064
(305)941-4211
Ultimate Parent: Walgreen Co. **SIC:** 5912—Drug Stores & Proprietary Stores.

★ **62643** ★　**Walgreen Drug Stores**
3133 N. State Rd.
Pompano Beach, FL 33064
(305)979-9081
Ultimate Parent: Walgreen Co. **SIC:** 5912—Drug Stores & Proprietary Stores.

★ **62644** ★　**Walgreen Drug Stores**
4911 Coconut Creek Pky.
Pompano Beach, FL 33063
(305)975-0552
Ultimate Parent: Walgreen Co. **SIC:** 5912—Drug Stores & Proprietary Stores.

★ **62645** ★　**Walgreen Drug Stores**
437 E. Atlantic Blvd.
Pompano Beach, FL 33060
(305)942-1501
Ultimate Parent: Walgreen Co. **SIC:** 5912—Drug Stores & Proprietary Stores.

★ **62646** ★　**W.R. Grace & Co.**
Construction Products Div.
1200 NW 15th Ave.
Pompano Beach, FL 33069
Company Type: Division. **Ultimate Parent:** W. R. Grace. **SIC:** 2899—Chemical Preparations Nec; 3295—Minerals—Ground or Treated.

★ **62647** ★　**W.R. Grace & Co.-Conn. Cpd**
1200 NW 15th Ave.
Pompano Beach, FL 33069
Ultimate Parent: W. R. Grace. **SIC:** 2899—Chemical Preparations Nec; 3295—Minerals—Ground or Treated.

Ponte Vedra

★ **62648** ★　**Food Lion**
880 Us Hwy. A1a N
Ponte Vedra, FL 32082
(904)285-8106
Ultimate Parent: Food Lion. **SIC:** 5499—Miscellaneous Food Stores.

★ **62649** ★　**Food Lion Inc.**
880 Us Hwy. A1a N
Ponte Vedra, FL 32082
(904)285-8106
Ultimate Parent: Food Lion. **SIC:** 5499—Miscellaneous Food Stores.

Ponte Vedra Beach

★ **62650** ★　**First Union National Bank of Florida**
700 TPC Blvd.
Ponte Vedra Beach, FL 32082
(904)361-5850
Location Type: Branch office. **Ultimate Parent:** First Union Corp. **SIC:** 6021—National Commercial Banks.

★ **62651** ★　**Mary Kay Cosmetics**
111 Solano Rd.
Ponte Vedra Beach, FL 32082
(904)285-4609
Ultimate Parent: Mary Kay Cosmetics. **SIC:** 5999—Miscellaneous Retail Stores Nec.

Port Charlotte

★ **62652** ★　**APAC**
19300 Peachland Blvd.
Port Charlotte, FL 33948
(813)625-1300
Officer: Bryan Peacock, Manager. **Ultimate Parent:** Ashland Oil. **SIC:** 2951—Asphalt Paving Mixtures & Blocks.

★ **62653** ★　**Barnett Bank of Southwest Florida**
1930 Tamiami Trl. S
Port Charlotte, FL 33948-1047
(813)951-4800
Company Type: Subsidiary. **Location Type:** Branch office. **Officer:** John Burrows, Manager. **Ultimate Parent:** Barnett Banks. **SIC:** 6021—National Commercial Banks.

★ **62654** ★　**Barnett Bank of Southwest Florida**
21175 Olean Blvd.
Port Charlotte, FL 33949
(813)951-4800
Company Type: Subsidiary. **Location Type:** Branch office. **Officer:** Jeff Reynolds, Manager. **Ultimate Parent:** Barnett Banks. **SIC:** 6021—National Commercial Banks.

★ **62655** ★　**Citizens Federal Bank, FSB**
4200 -P Tamiami Trail
Port Charlotte, FL 33952-9233
(813)627-0709
Location Type: Branch office. **Officer:** Terri Blackmore. **Ultimate Parent:** CSF Holdings. **SIC:** 6021—National Commercial Banks.

★ 62656 ★ **First of America Bank**
3524-D Tamiami Trail
Port Charlotte, FL 33952
(813)629-3477
Location Type: Branch office. **Ultimate Parent:** First of America Bank Corp. **SIC:** 6021—National Commercial Banks.

★ 62657 ★ **Fortune Bank, SB**
2100 Forrest Nelson Blvd.
Port Charlotte, FL 33952-2129
(813)625-9866
Location Type: Branch office. **Officer:** Kevin Lingard, Manager. **Ultimate Parent:** Fortune Bancorp. **SIC:** 6021—National Commercial Banks.

★ 62658 ★ **Savings of America**
Home Savings of America, FSB
3340 Tamiami Trl.
Port Charlotte, FL 33952-8075
(813)627-6440
Location Type: Branch office. **Officer:** Ray Jasica, Mgr. **Ultimate Parent:** Brooks Foods. **SIC:** 6021—National Commercial Banks.

Port Orange

★ 62659 ★ **Barnett Bank of Volusia County**
4425 Ridgewood Ave.
Port Orange, FL 32127-4515
(904)258-3611
Location Type: Branch office. **Ultimate Parent:** Barnett Banks. **SIC:** 6021—National Commercial Banks.

★ 62660 ★ **Barnett Bank of Volusia County**
1058 Dunlawton Ave.
Port Orange, FL 32127-4950
(904)258-3664
Location Type: Branch office. **Ultimate Parent:** Barnett Banks. **SIC:** 6021—National Commercial Banks.

★ 62661 ★ **Barnett Bank of Volusia County**
3809 Nova Rd.
Port Orange, FL 32119-4201
(904)258-3663
Location Type: Branch office. **Ultimate Parent:** Barnett Banks. **SIC:** 6021—National Commercial Banks.

★ 62662 ★ **First Union National Bank of Florida**
3860 S. Nova Rd.
Port Orange, FL 32119-9272
(904)254-7273
Location Type: Branch office. **Ultimate Parent:** First Union Corp. **SIC:** 6021—National Commercial Banks.

★ 62663 ★ **First Union National Bank of Florida**
4076 S. Ridgewood Ave.
Port Orange, FL 32127-4501
(904)254-7027
Location Type: Branch office. **Ultimate Parent:** First Union Corp. **SIC:** 6021—National Commercial Banks.

Port Richey

★ 62664 ★ **AmSouth Bank of Florida**
6435 Ridge Rd.
Port Richey, FL 34668-6749
(813)847-5786
Location Type: Branch office. **Ultimate Parent:** AmSouth Bancorp. **SIC:** 6022—State Commercial Banks.

★ 62665 ★ **Barnett Bank of Pasco County**
6514 Ridge Rd.
Port Richey, FL 34668-6853
(813)847-7255
Company Type: Subsidiary. **Location Type:** Branch office. **Officer:** Jacob Smith, Manager. **Ultimate Parent:** Barnett Banks. **SIC:** 6022—State Commercial Banks.

★ 62666 ★ **Barnett Bank of Pasco County**
10220 US Hwy. 19
Port Richey, FL 34668
(813)861-8700 **Fax:** (813)861-8576
Company Type: Subsidiary. **Location Type:** Branch office. **Officer:** Kendall L. Spencer, Chairman, President & CEO.

Ultimate Parent: Barnett Banks. **SIC:** 6022—State Commercial Banks.

★ 62667 ★ **Barnett Bank of Pasco County**
8338 Embassy Blvd.
Port Richey, FL 34668-5118
(813)861-8413
Company Type: Subsidiary. **Location Type:** Branch office. **Officer:** Carolyn Kindt, Manager. **Ultimate Parent:** Barnett Banks. **SIC:** 6022—State Commercial Banks.

★ 62668 ★ **California Federal Bank**
9116 Us Hwy. 19
Port Richey, FL 34668
(813)848-0076
Ultimate Parent: California Federal Bank. **SIC:** 6159—Miscellaneous Business Credit Institutions.

★ 62669 ★ **California Federal Bank, FSB**
9116 US Hwy. 19 N.
Port Richey, FL 34668
(813)848-0076
Location Type: Branch office. **Officer:** Penny Gardner, Manager. **Ultimate Parent:** California Federal Bank. **SIC:** 6021—National Commercial Banks.

★ 62670 ★ **Circuit City**
6325 Tacoma Dr.
Port Richey, FL 34668
(813)847-4088
Ultimate Parent: Circuit City Stores. **SIC:** 5719—Miscellaneous Home Furnishings Stores.

★ 62671 ★ **First Union National Bank of Florida**
10934 US Hwy. 19 N.
Port Richey, FL 34668-2596
(813)869-5100
Location Type: Branch office. **Ultimate Parent:** First Union Corp. **SIC:** 6021—National Commercial Banks.

★ 62672 ★ **First Union National Bank of Florida**
9332 US Hwy. 19
Port Richey, FL 34668-4794
(813)842-9727
Location Type: Branch office. **Ultimate Parent:** First Union Corp. **SIC:** 6021—National Commercial Banks.

★ 62673 ★ **Fortune Bank, SB**
6424 Embassy Blvd.
Port Richey, FL 34668-4799
(813)848-6666
Location Type: Branch office. **Officer:** Russell Smith, Manager. **Ultimate Parent:** Fortune Bancorp. **SIC:** 6021—National Commercial Banks.

★ 62674 ★ **Home Depot Inc.**
10017 Us Hwy. 19
Port Richey, FL 34668
(813)869-2711
Ultimate Parent: Home Depot. **SIC:** 5251—Hardware Stores.

★ 62675 ★ **Hudson's**
6703 Seaview Blvd.
Port Richey, FL 34667
(813)869-8489
Ultimate Parent: Dayton Hudson.

★ 62676 ★ **Hudson's**
16206 Tree Line Dr.
Port Richey, FL 34667
(813)846-6250
Ultimate Parent: Dayton Hudson.

★ 62677 ★ **Kentucky Fried Chicken**
9406 Us Hwy. 19
Port Richey, FL 34668
(813)849-2041
Ultimate Parent: Pepsico. **SIC:** 5812—Eating Places.

★ 62678 ★ **Mary Kay Cosmetics**
7308 Grand Pine Dr.
Port Richey, FL 34667
(813)868-4320
Ultimate Parent: Mary Kay Cosmetics. **SIC:** 6531—Real Estate Agents & Managers.

★ 62679 ★ **Pizza Hut**
10633 Us Hwy. 19
Port Richey, FL 34668
(813)862-4084
Ultimate Parent: Pepsico. **SIC:** 5812—Eating Places.

★ 62680 ★ **Savings of America**
Home Savings of America, FSB
9446 US Hwy. 19 N
Port Richey, FL 34668-4623
(813)845-3033
Location Type: Branch office. **Officer:** Frank Carmen, Manager. **Ultimate Parent:** H. F. Ahmanson. **SIC:** 6021—National Commercial Banks.

★ 62681 ★ **Service Merchandise**
10340 Us Hwy. 19
Port Richey, FL 34668
(813)868-8849
Ultimate Parent: Service Merchandise Co., Inc. **SIC:** 5399—Miscellaneous General Merchandise Store.

★ 62682 ★ **Wal Mart Discount City**
Embassy Xi
Port Richey, FL 34668
(813)846-9504
Ultimate Parent: Wal-Mart Stores, Inc. **SIC:** 5611—Men's & Boys' Clothing Stores.

★ 62683 ★ **World Savings & Loan**
7839 State Rd. 52
Port Richey, FL 34667
(813)868-2176
Ultimate Parent: Golden West Financial Corp. **SIC:** 6159—Miscellaneous Business Credit Institutions.

Port Richey F

★ 62684 ★ **Coast to Coast Home & Auto**
7101 State Hwy. 52 Ave.
Port Richey F, FL 34667
(813)868-1809
Ultimate Parent: Servistar Corp. **SIC:** 5941—Sporting Goods & Bicycle Shops.

Port St Lucie

★ 62685 ★ **First National Bank & Trust**
7177 S. Us Hwy. 1
Port St Lucie, FL 34952
(407)335-2000
Ultimate Parent: Society Corp. **SIC:** 6099—Functions Related to Deposit Banking.

★ 62686 ★ **Great Western Bank**
130 S. Entrada Ave.
Port St Lucie, FL 34952
Ultimate Parent: Great Western Financial Corp. **SIC:** 6022—State Commercial Banks.

★ 62687 ★ **Great Western Bank Mtge Ofc**
905 E. Prima Vis
Port St Lucie, FL 34952
(407)879-2306
Ultimate Parent: Great Western Financial Corp. **SIC:** 6159—Miscellaneous Business Credit Institutions.

★ 62688 ★ **Mobil Oil Service Sta**
1090 SE Pt St.
Port St Lucie, FL 34984
(407)335-4125
Ultimate Parent: Mobil. **SIC:** 5599—Automotive Dealers Nec.

★ 62689 ★ **Pizza Hut**
10401 S. Federal Hwy.
Port St Lucie, FL 34952
(407)337-2227
Ultimate Parent: Pepsico. **SIC:** 5812—Eating Places.

★ 62690 ★ **Publix Super Market**
6666 S. Federal Hwy.
Port St Lucie, FL 34952
(407)466-3331
Ultimate Parent: Publix Super Markets. **SIC:** 5411—Grocery Stores.

★ 62691 ★ **Walgreen Drug Stores**
1169 SE Port Saint Lucie Blvd.
Port St Lucie, FL 34952
(407)335-4370
Ultimate Parent: Walgreen Co. **SIC:** 7389—Business Services Nec.

Port St. Joe

★ 62692 ★ **Arizona Chemical**
Hwy. 98 PO Box 947
Port St. Joe, FL 32456
Ultimate Parent: International Paper Co. **SIC:** 2861—Gum & Wood Chemicals.

★ 62693 ★ **Arizona Chemical Co. Sylvachem Corp.**
PO Box 947 - Hwy. 98
Port St. Joe, FL 32456
Ultimate Parent: International Paper Co. **SIC:** 2861—Gum & Wood Chemicals.

★ 62694 ★ **Sylvachem Corp.**
Hwy. 98 PO Box 947
Port St. Joe, FL 32456
Ultimate Parent: International Paper Co. **SIC:** 2861—Gum & Wood Chemicals.

Port St. Lucie

★ 62695 ★ **Barnett Bank of the Treasure Coast**
9110 SE Port St. Lucie Blvd.
Port St. Lucie, FL 34952
(407)340-5480
Company Type: Subsidiary. **Location Type:** Branch office. **Officer:** Fran Stein, Vice President & Office Manager. **Ultimate Parent:** Barnett Banks. **SIC:** 6022—State Commercial Banks.

★ 62696 ★ **Barnett Bank of the Treasure Coast**
2300 SE Midport Rd.
Port St. Lucie, FL 34952-4898
(407)340-5420
Company Type: Subsidiary. **Location Type:** Branch office. **Officer:** Louise Baker, Vice President. **Ultimate Parent:** Barnett Banks. **SIC:** 6021—National Commercial Banks.

★ 62697 ★ **Barnett Bank of the Treasure Coast**
900 E. Prima Vista Blvd.
PO Box 857220
Port St. Lucie, FL 34985
(407)340-5200 **Fax:** (407)340-5462
Company Type: Subsidiary. **Location Type:** Branch office. **Officer:** Sam E. Davis III, Chairman, President & CEO. **Ultimate Parent:** Barnett Banks. **SIC:** 6022—State Commercial Banks.

★ 62698 ★ **First Union National Bank of Florida**
9520 S. US Hwy. 1
Port St. Lucie, FL 34952-4294
(407)335-9500
Location Type: Branch office. **Ultimate Parent:** First Union Corp. **SIC:** 6021—National Commercial Banks.

Pt Charlotte

★ 62699 ★ **Lane Bryant**
1441 Tamiami Trl
Pt Charlotte, FL 33953
(813)625-7702
Ultimate Parent: Limited. **SIC:** 5731—Radio, Television & Electronics Stores.

★ 62700 ★ **Radio Shack**
Promenades Mall
Pt Charlotte, FL 33952
(813)625-1144
Company Type: Division. **Ultimate Parent:** Tandy Corp. **SIC:** 5065—Electronic Parts & Equipment Nec.

Punta Gorda

★ 62701 ★ **American Family Life Assurance**
422 E. Ann St.
Punta Gorda, FL 33950
(813)639-7002
Ultimate Parent: American Family Life Assurance Co. **SIC:** 6411—Insurance Agents, Brokers & Service.

★ 62702 ★ Coast to Coast Builders
162 Buckeye Ave. NW
Punta Gorda, FL 33952
(813)629-4748
Ultimate Parent: Servistar Corp. **SIC:**
7231—Beauty Shops.

★ 62703 ★ Coast to Coast Realty
4055 Tamiami Trl
Punta Gorda, FL 33952
(813)627-0877
Ultimate Parent: Servistar Corp. **SIC:**
6531—Real Estate Agents & Managers.

★ 62704 ★ Exxon
2331 Tamiami Trl.
Punta Gorda, FL 33950
(813)639-5727
Ultimate Parent: Exxon. **SIC:** 5541—
Gasoline Service Stations.

★ 62705 ★ First of America Bank
1121 Bal Harbor Blvd.
Punta Gorda, FL 33950
(813)639-5553
Location Type: Branch office. **Ultimate
Parent:** First of America Bank Corp. **SIC:**
6021—National Commercial Banks.

★ 62706 ★ First of America Bank
401 Taylor St.
Punta Gorda, FL 33950
(813)639-1500
Location Type: Branch office. **Ultimate
Parent:** First of America Bank Corp. **SIC:**
6021—National Commercial Banks.

★ 62707 ★ First Union National Bank of Florida
314 Taylor St.
Punta Gorda, FL 33950-4899
(813)639-3151
Location Type: Branch office. **Ultimate
Parent:** First Union Corp. **SIC:** 6021—
National Commercial Banks.

★ 62708 ★ Fortune Bank
2100 Forrest Nelson Blvd.
Punta Gorda, FL 33952
(813)625-9866
Ultimate Parent: Fortune Bancorp. **SIC:**
6035—Federal Savings Institutions.

★ 62709 ★ Greyhound Bus Lines
3265 Tamiami Trl.
Punta Gorda, FL 33952
(813)629-4808
Ultimate Parent: Greyhound Lines Inc. **SIC:**
4111—Local & Suburban Transit.

★ 62710 ★ Kentucky Fried Chicken
4635 Tamiami Trl.
Punta Gorda, FL 33980
(813)625-1200
Ultimate Parent: Pepsico. **SIC:** 5812—
Eating Places.

★ 62711 ★ Mary Kay Cosmetics
25188 Mariane
Punta Gorda, FL 33950
(813)637-3773
Ultimate Parent: Mary Kay Cosmetics.

★ 62712 ★ Mobil Service Center
305 Tamiami Trl
Punta Gorda, FL 33950
(813)639-7681
Ultimate Parent: Mobil. **SIC:** 5541—
Gasoline Service Stations.

★ 62713 ★ Payless Shoesource
1441 Tamiami Trl.
Punta Gorda, FL 33948
(813)624-4080
Ultimate Parent: May Department Stores.
SIC: 5661—Shoe Stores.

★ 62714 ★ Pizza Hut
3068 Tamiami Trl.
Punta Gorda, FL 33950
(813)629-4322
Ultimate Parent: Pepsico. **SIC:** 5812—
Eating Places.

★ 62715 ★ Progressive Insurance Agency
158 Catskill St. NE
Punta Gorda, FL 33952
(813)625-4800
Ultimate Parent: Progressive. **SIC:** 6411—
Insurance Agents, Brokers & Service.

★ 62716 ★ Publix Super Market
2150 Tamiami Trl
Punta Gorda, FL 33948
(813)629-3345
Ultimate Parent: Publix Super Markets.
SIC: 5411—Grocery Stores.

★ 62717 ★ Radio Shack
1441 Tamiami Trl
Punta Gorda, FL 33948
(813)629-9726
Company Type: Division. **Ultimate Parent:**
Tandy Corp. **SIC:** 5065—Electronic Parts &
Equipment Nec.

★ 62718 ★ Radio Shack
Promenades Shopping Ctr.
Punta Gorda, FL 33950
(813)625-1144
Company Type: Division. **Ultimate Parent:**
Tandy Corp. **SIC:** 5065—Electronic Parts &
Equipment Nec.

★ 62719 ★ Rite Aid Drug Store
1125 Bal Harbor Blvd.
Punta Gorda, FL 33950
Ultimate Parent: Rite Aid. **SIC:** 5912—Drug
Stores & Proprietary Stores.

★ 62720 ★ Rite Aid Pharmacy
1825 Tamiami Trl
Punta Gorda, FL 33948
(813)627-9303
Ultimate Parent: Rite Aid. **SIC:** 5912—Drug
Stores & Proprietary Stores.

★ 62721 ★ Ryder Truck Rental
1158 Market Cir.
Punta Gorda, FL 33953
(813)627-5866
Ultimate Parent: Ryder System. **SIC:**
5113—Industrial & Personal Service Paper.

★ 62722 ★ Turner Foods Corp.
25450 Airport Rd.
Punta Gorda, FL 33950-5746
(813)639-2410
Company Type: Subsidiary. **Officer:** John
C. Norris, President. **Ultimate Parent:** FPL
Group. **SIC:** 0174—Citrus Fruits; 0921—
Fish Hatcheries & Preserves; 6531—Real
Estate Agents & Managers; 8711—
Engineering Services. **Employee Count:**
258. **Sales:** 46.4 M.

★ 62723 ★ Victoria's Secret
1441 Tamiami Trl
Punta Gorda, FL 33948
(813)743-8887
Ultimate Parent: Limited. **SIC:** 5651—
Family Clothing Stores.

★ 62724 ★ Waldenbooks
1441 Tamiami Trl.
Punta Gorda, FL 33948
(813)743-3340
Ultimate Parent: K-Mart. **SIC:** 5942—Book
Stores.

★ 62725 ★ Walgreen Drug Stores
4265 Tamiami Trl.
Punta Gorda, FL 33980
(813)625-4169
Ultimate Parent: Walgreen Co. **SIC:**
5912—Drug Stores & Proprietary Stores;
5921—Liquor Stores.

★ 62726 ★ Walker Manufacturing
4419 Conway Blvd.
Punta Gorda, FL 33952
(813)627-0781
Ultimate Parent: Tenneco Inc. **SIC:** 2434—
Wood Kitchen Cabinets.

Quincy

★ 62727 ★ Barnett Bank of Tallahassee
1321 W. Jefferson St.
Quincy, FL 32351-2127
(904)875-4545
Company Type: Subsidiary. **Location
Type:** Branch office. **Officer:** Greg Suber,
Manager. **Ultimate Parent:** Barnett Banks.
SIC: 6022—State Commercial Banks.

★ 62728 ★ Barnett Bank of Tallahassee
24 N. Adams St.
Quincy, FL 32351-2402
(904)627-7156
Company Type: Subsidiary. **Location
Type:** Branch office. **Officer:** Greg Suber,
Branch Manager. **Ultimate Parent:** Barnett

Banks. **SIC:** 6022—State Commercial
Banks.

★ 62729 ★ Kentucky Fried Chicken
1307 W. Jefferson St.
Quincy, FL 32351
(904)627-8700
Ultimate Parent: Pepsico. **SIC:** 5812—
Eating Places.

★ 62730 ★ Mary Kay Cosmetics
342 PO Box
Quincy, FL 32351
(904)627-6710
Ultimate Parent: Mary Kay Cosmetics.

★ 62731 ★ Pizza Hut
Quincy Plz.
Quincy, FL 32351
(904)875-2828
Ultimate Parent: Pepsico. **SIC:** 5812—
Eating Places.

★ 62732 ★ Quincy State Bank
1607 W. Jefferson St.
Quincy, FL 32351-2133
(904)875-1001
Company Type: Subsidiary. **Location
Type:** Branch office. **Officer:** Almeta E.
Leverett, Mgr. **Ultimate Parent:** Synovus
Financial Corp. **SIC:** 6021—National
Commercial Banks.

★ 62733 ★ Quincy State Bank
4 E. Washington
PO Box 700
Quincy, FL 32353-0700
(904)875-1000 **Fax:** (904)875-5544
Company Type: Subsidiary. **Location
Type:** Branch office. **Officer:** W.C. Branson,
President & CEO. **Ultimate Parent:**
Synovus Financial Corp. **SIC:** 6021—
National Commercial Banks.

★ 62734 ★ Wilsons
18 E. Washington St.
Quincy, FL 32351
(904)627-6123
Ultimate Parent: Melville. **SIC:** 5311—
Department Stores.

Redington Shores

★ 62735 ★ First Union National Bank of Florida
17985 Gulf Blvd.
Redington Shores, FL 33708-1198
(813)392-4585
Location Type: Branch office. **Ultimate
Parent:** First Union Corp. **SIC:** 6021—
National Commercial Banks.

Riverview

★ 62736 ★ Barnett Bank of Tampa
9810 US Hwy. 301
Riverview, FL 33569-5800
(813)671-2261
Company Type: Subsidiary. **Location
Type:** Branch office. **Officer:** Rebecca Leto,
Office Manager. **Ultimate Parent:** Barnett
Banks. **SIC:** 6022—State Commercial
Banks.

Riviera Beach

★ 62737 ★ Barnett Bank of Palm Beach County
2001 Broadway
Riviera Beach, FL 33404-5669
(407)845-3517
Company Type: Subsidiary. **Location
Type:** Branch office. **Officer:** Keith Mosely,
Manager. **Ultimate Parent:** Barnett Banks.
SIC: 6022—State Commercial Banks.

★ 62738 ★ First Union National Bank of Florida
7289 Garden Rd., Ste. 101
Riviera Beach, FL 33404
(407)838-5345
Location Type: Branch office. **Ultimate
Parent:** First Union Corp. **SIC:** 6021—
National Commercial Banks.

★ 62739 ★ Miami Elevator Co.
7567 Central Industrial Dr.
Riviera Beach, FL 33404
(407)842-5761
Officer: Michael Thomas, Manager.

Ultimate Parent: Dover Corp. **SIC:** 3534—
Elevators & Moving Stairways.

★ 62740 ★ PCI Industries Inc.
1661 Old Dixie Hwy.
Riviera Beach, FL 33419
Ultimate Parent: RPM, Inc. **SIC:** 2891—
Adhesives & Sealants.

★ 62741 ★ Pepsi-Cola Bottling Co.
7305 Garden Rd.
Riviera Beach, FL 33404
(407)848-1000
Officer: Richard Caudill, President.
Ultimate Parent: Pepsico. **SIC:** 2086—
Bottled & Canned Soft Drinks.

Rockledge

★ 62742 ★ Barnett Bank of Central Florida, NA
234 Barton Blvd.
Rockledge, FL 32955-2851
(407)633-1100
Company Type: Subsidiary. **Location
Type:** Branch office. **Officer:** Tony Gamble,
Manager. **Ultimate Parent:** Barnett Banks.
SIC: 6021—National Commercial Banks.

★ 62743 ★ Coast to Coast Suppliers Inc.
566 Barton Blvd.
Rockledge, FL 32955
(407)636-2321
Ultimate Parent: Servistar Corp. **SIC:**
5085—Industrial Supplies.

★ 62744 ★ First Union National Bank of Florida
201 Barton Blvd.
Rockledge, FL 32955-2705
(407)639-5200
Location Type: Branch office. **Ultimate
Parent:** First Union Corp. **SIC:** 6021—
National Commercial Banks.

★ 62745 ★ Harris Space Systems Corp.
295 Barnes Blvd.
Rockledge, FL 32955
(407)633-3800 **Fax:** (407)633-3900
Company Type: Subsidiary. **Officer:**
William McCaslin, Vice President & General
Manager. **Ultimate Parent:** Harris.

★ 62746 ★ Mercury Powerboats
259 Gus Hipp Blvd.
Rockledge, FL 32955
Ultimate Parent: Brunswick Corp. **SIC:**
3732—Boat Building & Repairing.

★ 62747 ★ Pizza Hut
1172 Us 1 S
Rockledge, FL 32955
(407)636-1855
Ultimate Parent: Pepsico. **SIC:** 5812—
Eating Places.

★ 62748 ★ Ryder Truck Rental
480 Barnes Blvd.
Rockledge, FL 32955
(407)631-6116
Ultimate Parent: Ryder System. **SIC:**
7513—Truck Rental & Leasing Without
Drivers.

★ 62749 ★ United Parcel Service
1646 Barrett Dr.
Rockledge, FL 32955
(407)633-6667
Ultimate Parent: United Parcel Service of
America. **SIC:** 4215—Courier Services
Except by Air.

★ 62750 ★ Zippy Mart Inc.
193 Barton Ave.
Rockledge, FL 32955
(407)636-4511
Ultimate Parent: Crown Central Petroleum
Corp. **SIC:** 5411—Grocery Stores.

Rotonda West

★ 62751 ★ Mary Kay Cosmetics
151 Mark Twain Ln.
Rotonda West, FL 33947
(813)697-3220
Ultimate Parent: Mary Kay Cosmetics.

Rotunda

★ 62752 ★   First of America Bank
699 W. Rotunda Blvd.
Rotunda, FL 33947
(813)697-5541
Location Type: Branch office. **Ultimate Parent:** First of America Bank Corp. **SIC:** 6021—National Commercial Banks.

Royal Palm Beach

★ 62753 ★   Barnett Bank of Palm Beach County
11601 Okeechobee Blvd.
Royal Palm Beach, FL 33411
(407)641-7010
Company Type: Subsidiary. **Location Type:** Branch office. **Officer:** Lori Tavoletti, Manager. **Ultimate Parent:** Barnett Banks. **SIC:** 6022—State Commercial Banks.

★ 62754 ★   First Union National Bank of Florida
665 Royal Palm Beach Blvd.
Royal Palm Beach, FL 33411-7631
(407)838-4967
Location Type: Branch office. **Ultimate Parent:** First Union Corp. **SIC:** 6021—National Commercial Banks.

★ 62755 ★   First Union National Bank of Florida
11707 Okeechobee Blvd.
Royal Palm Beach, FL 33411-1699
(407)793-8300
Location Type: Branch office. **Ultimate Parent:** First Union Corp. **SIC:** 6021—National Commercial Banks.

Ruskin

★ 62756 ★   Barnett Bank of Tampa
502 N. Hwy. 41
Ruskin, FL 33570-3767
(813)645-3277
Company Type: Subsidiary. **Location Type:** Branch office. **Officer:** Tod Pukas, Assistant Vice President. **Ultimate Parent:** Barnett Banks. **SIC:** 6022—State Commercial Banks.

★ 62757 ★   Exxon Co. USA
Hwy. 41 S
Ruskin, FL 33570
(813)247-7360
Ultimate Parent: Exxon. **SIC:** 5983—Fuel Oil Dealers.

★ 62758 ★   Kentucky Fried Chicken
1025 Tamiami Trl. N
Ruskin, FL 33570
(813)645-3656
Ultimate Parent: Pepsico. **SIC:** 5812—Eating Places.

★ 62759 ★   Pizza Hut
1010 Tamiami Trl. N
Ruskin, FL 33570
(813)645-8421
Ultimate Parent: Pepsico. **SIC:** 5812—Eating Places.

★ 62760 ★   Walgreen Drug Stores
2519 MacMullen Booth Rd. N
Ruskin, FL 33572
(813)726-8891
Ultimate Parent: Walgreen Co. **SIC:** 5912—Drug Stores & Proprietary Stores.

★ 62761 ★   Western Auto Supply Co.
505 Tamiami Trl N
Ruskin, FL 33570
(813)645-1494
Ultimate Parent: Sears Roebuck & Co. **SIC:** 5531—Automobile & Home Supply Stores.

Safety Harbor

★ 62762 ★   Fortune Bank, SB
601 Main St.
Safety Harbor, FL 34695-3552
(813)725-2541
Location Type: Branch office. **Officer:** Edd Bales, Manager. **Ultimate Parent:** Fortune Bancorp. **SIC:** 6021—National Commercial Banks.

Sanford

★ 62763 ★   Ace Hareware
207 E. 25th St.
Sanford, FL 32771-4412
(407)321-0885
Location Type: Branch office. **Officer:** Bob Parcell. **Ultimate Parent:** Ace Hardware. **SIC:** 5984—Liquefied Petroleum Gas Dealers; 5251—Hardware Stores; 5999—Miscellaneous Retail Stores Nec.

★ 62764 ★   Barnett Bank of Central Florida, NA
3094 Orlando Dr.
Sanford, FL 32773
(407)646-3557
Company Type: Subsidiary. **Location Type:** Branch office. **Officer:** Sharon Michaels, Manager. **Ultimate Parent:** Barnett Banks. **SIC:** 6021—National Commercial Banks.

★ 62765 ★   Computer Assoc
165 Lakeside Cir.
Sanford, FL 32773
(407)660-9559
Ultimate Parent: Computer Associates International. **SIC:** 7389—Business Services Nec.

★ 62766 ★   First Union National Bank of Florida
1601 S. French Ave.
Sanford, FL 32771-3379
(407)330-7250
Location Type: Branch office. **Ultimate Parent:** First Union Corp. **SIC:** 6021—National Commercial Banks.

★ 62767 ★   First Union National Bank of Florida
101 E. 1st St.
Sanford, FL 32771-1350
(407)330-7289
Location Type: Branch office. **Officer:** James Young. **Ultimate Parent:** First Union Corp. **SIC:** 6021—National Commercial Banks.

★ 62768 ★   Kmart Discount Stores
3101 Hwy. 17
Sanford, FL 32771
(407)323-5760
Ultimate Parent: K-Mart. **SIC:** 5311—Department Stores.

★ 62769 ★   Mobil Tech Inc.
300 Northstar Ct.
Sanford, FL 32771-6673
(407)324-8100
Officer: Dave Foederer. **Ultimate Parent:** Mobil. **SIC:** 3711—Motor Vehicles & Car Bodies; 5012—Automobiles & Other Motor Vehicles.

★ 62770 ★   Pilgrim Farms, Inc.
325 Rand Yard Rd.
Sanford, FL 32771
(407)323-7760 **Fax:** (407)322-7890
Location Type: Plant. **Officer:** Bill Lloyd, Plant Manager. **Ultimate Parent:** Dean Foods. **SIC:** 2035—Pickles, Sauces & Salad Dressings.

★ 62771 ★   Pizza Hut
3852 Hwy. 1792
Sanford, FL 32771
(407)321-3840
Ultimate Parent: Pepsico. **SIC:** 5812—Eating Places.

★ 62772 ★   Pizza Hut
2002 S. French Ave.
Sanford, FL 32771
(407)323-8266
Ultimate Parent: Pepsico. **SIC:** 5812—Eating Places.

★ 62773 ★   Publix Super Market
1080 State St.
Sanford, FL 32773
(407)322-9581
Ultimate Parent: Publix Super Markets. **SIC:** 5411—Grocery Stores.

★ 62774 ★   Publix Super Markets
1080 State St.
Sanford, FL 32773
(407)322-9581
Ultimate Parent: Publix Super Markets. **SIC:** 5411—Grocery Stores.

★ 62775 ★   Radio Shack
3687 S. Orlando Dr.
Sanford, FL 32773
(407)322-6999
Company Type: Division. **Ultimate Parent:** Tandy Corp. **SIC:** 5719—Miscellaneous Home Furnishings Stores; 7629—Electrical Repair Shops Nec.

★ 62776 ★   Radio Shack
209 N. Country Club Rd.
Sanford, FL 32771
(407)322-5010
Company Type: Division. **Ultimate Parent:** Tandy Corp. **SIC:** 5734—Computer & Software Stores.

★ 62777 ★   Rite Aid Discount Pharmacy
2483 S. Airport Blvd.
Sanford, FL 32771
(407)321-6790
Ultimate Parent: Rite Aid. **SIC:** 5912—Drug Stores & Proprietary Stores.

★ 62778 ★   Rite Aid Discount Pharmacy
2438 S. French Ave.
Sanford, FL 32771
(407)322-8270
Ultimate Parent: Rite Aid. **SIC:** 5912—Drug Stores & Proprietary Stores.

★ 62779 ★   Ryder Truck Rental
3651 S. Sanford Ave.
Sanford, FL 32773
(407)323-5310
Ultimate Parent: Ryder System. **SIC:** 7513—Truck Rental & Leasing Without Drivers.

★ 62780 ★   Ryder Truck Rental
3159 Hwy. 1792
Sanford, FL 32771
(407)322-0201
Ultimate Parent: Ryder System. **SIC:** 7359—Equipment Rental & Leasing Nec.

★ 62781 ★   Taco Bell
2700 S. Orlando Dr.
Sanford, FL 32773
(407)321-4767
Ultimate Parent: Pepsico. **SIC:** 5812—Eating Places.

★ 62782 ★   Texaco Food Mart
1208 S. Park Ave.
Sanford, FL 32771
(407)321-1889
Ultimate Parent: Texaco. **SIC:** 5411—Grocery Stores.

★ 62783 ★   3M Advertising
2687 S. Design Ct.
Sanford, FL 32773-8120
(407)330-3999
Officer: John O'keefe. **Ultimate Parent:** Minnesota Mining & Mfg. **SIC:** 3993—Signs & Advertising Displays; 7312—Outdoor Advertising Services.

★ 62784 ★   Trailways Bus Systems
1002 S. French Ave.
Sanford, FL 32771
(407)322-4520
Ultimate Parent: Greyhound Lines Inc. **SIC:** 4142—Bus Charter Service Except Local.

Sanibel

★ 62785 ★   Johnson Controls Inc.
507 PO Box
Sanibel, FL 33957
(813)472-4240
Ultimate Parent: Johnson Controls Inc.

Sarasota

★ 62786 ★   APAC
1451 Myrtle St.
Sarasota, FL 34234
(813)355-7178
Officer: E.K. Richardson, President. **Ultimate Parent:** Ashland Oil. **SIC:** 2951—Asphalt Paving Mixtures & Blocks.

★ 62787 ★   Bank of Boston-Florida
2033 Main St. 2D Fl.
Sarasota, FL 34237-6056
Location Type: Branch office. **Officer:** Richard Angelotti. **Ultimate Parent:** Bank of Boston Corp. **SIC:** 6022—State Commercial

Banks; 6091—Nondeposit Trust Facilities; 6282—Investment Advice; 6282—Investment Advice.

★ 62788 ★   Barnett Bank of Manatee County, NA
8498 Lockwood Ridge Rd.
Sarasota, FL 34243
(813)755-8889
Company Type: Subsidiary. **Location Type:** Branch office. **Officer:** Karen Robinson, Assistant Vice President. **Ultimate Parent:** Barnett Banks. **SIC:** 6021—National Commercial Banks.

★ 62789 ★   Barnett Bank of Southwest Florida
3550 S. Tamiami Trl.
Sarasota, FL 34239-6092
(813)951-4800
Company Type: Subsidiary. **Location Type:** Branch office. **Officer:** Ellen Stevens, Manager. **Ultimate Parent:** Barnett Banks. **SIC:** 6021—National Commercial Banks.

★ 62790 ★   Barnett Bank of Southwest Florida
3300 N. Tamiami Trl.
Sarasota, FL 34234-5398
(813)355-7691
Company Type: Subsidiary. **Location Type:** Branch office. **Officer:** Tom McClean, Manager. **Ultimate Parent:** Barnett Banks. **SIC:** 6021—National Commercial Banks.

★ 62791 ★   Barnett Bank of Southwest Florida
3600 Bee Ridge Rd.
Sarasota, FL 34233-1001
(813)951-4800
Company Type: Subsidiary. **Location Type:** Branch office. **Officer:** David Boehn, Manager. **Ultimate Parent:** Barnett Banks. **SIC:** 6021—National Commercial Banks.

★ 62792 ★   Barnett Bank of Southwest Florida
30 Blvd. of Presidents
Sarasota, FL 34236-1305
(813)951-4800
Company Type: Subsidiary. **Location Type:** Branch office. **Officer:** Mary King, Manager. **Ultimate Parent:** Barnett Banks. **SIC:** 6021—National Commercial Banks.

★ 62793 ★   Barnett Bank of Southwest Florida
5140 Ocean Blvd.
Sarasota, FL 34242-1637
(813)951-4800
Company Type: Subsidiary. **Location Type:** Branch office. **Officer:** Gary MacDonald, Manager. **Ultimate Parent:** Barnett Banks. **SIC:** 6022—State Commercial Banks.

★ 62794 ★   Barnett Bank of Southwest Florida
1237 Stickney Point Rd.
Sarasota, FL 34242
(813)951-4800
Company Type: Subsidiary. **Location Type:** Branch office. **Officer:** Val Hadley, Manager. **Ultimate Parent:** Barnett Banks. **SIC:** 6022—State Commercial Banks.

★ 62795 ★   Barnett Bank of Southwest Florida
935 N. Beneva Rd.
Sarasota, FL 34232-1338
(813)951-4800
Company Type: Subsidiary. **Location Type:** Branch office. **Officer:** Rick Patrick, Manager. **Ultimate Parent:** Barnett Banks. **SIC:** 6021—National Commercial Banks.

★ 62796 ★   Barnett Bank of Southwest Florida
8055 Beneva Rd.
Sarasota, FL 34238-2999
(813)951-4800
Company Type: Subsidiary. **Location Type:** Branch office. **Officer:** Mike Freeman, Manager. **Ultimate Parent:** Barnett Banks. **SIC:** 6021—National Commercial Banks.

★ 62797 ★ Barnett Bank of Southwest Florida
240 S. Pineapple Ave.
PO Box 1478
Sarasota, FL 34230-1478
(813)951-4800 Fax: (813)951-4476
Company Type: Subsidiary. Location Type: Branch office. Officer: Rebecca S. Allen, President & CEO. Ultimate Parent: Barnett Banks. SIC: 6022—State Commercial Banks.

★ 62798 ★ Barnett Bank of Southwest Florida
3930 Cattlemen Rd.
Sarasota, FL 34233-5002
(813)951-4800
Company Type: Subsidiary. Location Type: Branch office. Officer: Jennifer Means, Manager. Ultimate Parent: Barnett Banks. SIC: 6021—National Commercial Banks.

★ 62799 ★ Bausch & Lomb Inc.
2040 Whitfield Ave.
Sarasota, FL 34243
(813)756-5521
Officer: David Radeke, Manager. Ultimate Parent: Bausch & Lomb Inc. SIC: 3827—Optical Instruments & Lenses; 3851—Ophthalmic Goods.

★ 62800 ★ California Federal Bank, FSB
1950 S. Tamiami Trail
Sarasota, FL 34239-3603
(813)366-1063
Location Type: Branch office. Ultimate Parent: California Federal Bank. SIC: 6021—National Commercial Banks.

★ 62801 ★ California Federal Bank, FSB
8292 S. Tamiami Trail
Sarasota, FL 34238-2931
(813)966-3655
Location Type: Branch office. Officer: Jerry Schmidt, Manager. Ultimate Parent: California Federal Bank. SIC: 6021—National Commercial Banks.

★ 62802 ★ Casual Corner
38 Sarasota Sq.
Sarasota, FL 34231
(813)921-5545
Ultimate Parent: United States Shoe. SIC: 5651—Family Clothing Stores.

★ 62803 ★ Citizens Federal Bank, FSB
501 N. Beneva Rd., Ste. 300
Sarasota, FL 34232
(813)957-0373
Location Type: Branch office. Ultimate Parent: CSF Holdings. SIC: 6021—National Commercial Banks.

★ 62804 ★ Citizens Federal Bank, FSB
4914 S. Tamiami Trail
Sarasota, FL 34231-3633
(813)923-1491
Location Type: Branch office. Ultimate Parent: CSF Holdings. SIC: 6021—National Commercial Banks.

★ 62805 ★ Coast to Coast Mortgage Ser
2080 Ringling Blvd.
Sarasota, FL 34237
(813)365-7340
Ultimate Parent: Servistar Corp. SIC: 6162—Mortgage Bankers & Correspondents.

★ 62806 ★ Continental Express Airline
6400 S. Tamiami Trl
Sarasota, FL 34231
(813)355-8831
Ultimate Parent: Continental Airlines. SIC: 4512—Air Transportation—Scheduled.

★ 62807 ★ Continental Illinois Trust Co. of Florida, NA
1819 Main St., Ste. 1204
Sarasota, FL 34236-5984
(813)953-4644
Location Type: Branch office. Ultimate Parent: Continental Bank Corp. SIC: 6021—National Commercial Banks.

★ 62808 ★ Dana Corp.
4675 Clark Rd.
Sarasota, FL 34233
(813)924-1284
Company Type: Subsidiary. Ultimate Parent: Dana Corp. SIC: 3494—Valves & Pipe Fittings Nec.

★ 62809 ★ Dana Corp.
Mobile Fluid Controls Div.
4675 Clark Rd.
Sarasota, FL 34233
Company Type: Division. Ultimate Parent: Dana Corp. SIC: 3494—Valves & Pipe Fittings Nec.

★ 62810 ★ Dana Corp.
Mobile Fluid Controls Div.
4675 Clark Rd.
Sarasota, FL 34233
Company Type: Division. Ultimate Parent: Dana Corp. SIC: 3494—Valves & Pipe Fittings Nec.

★ 62811 ★ Delta Air Lines
6400 S. Tamiami Trl.
Sarasota, FL 34231
(813)922-2205
Ultimate Parent: Delta Air Lines, Inc. SIC: 4512—Air Transportation—Scheduled.

★ 62812 ★ Donzi Marine
8161 15th St. E.
Sarasota, FL 34243
Ultimate Parent: Outboard Marine. SIC: 3732—Boat Building & Repairing.

★ 62813 ★ Donzi Marine
7110 21st St. E.
Sarasota, FL 34243
Ultimate Parent: Outboard Marine. SIC: 3732—Boat Building & Repairing.

★ 62814 ★ Eaton Corp.
2250 Whitfield Ave.
Sarasota, FL 34243
(813)758-7726
Officer: George LaChapelle, Manager. Ultimate Parent: Eaton Corp. SIC: 3613—Switchgear & Switchboard Apparatus; 3812—Search & Navigation Equipment.

★ 62815 ★ Eaton Corp.
Aerospace Commercial Controls Div.
2250 Whitfield Ave. Manatee Plant
Sarasota, FL 34243-9703
Company Type: Division. Ultimate Parent: Eaton Corp. SIC: 3625—Relays & Industrial Controls.

★ 62816 ★ Eaton Corp.
Aerospace & Commercial Controls Div.
2250 Whitfield Ave., E
Sarasota, FL 33243
(813)758-7721
Company Type: Division. Location Type: Plant. Officer: George LaChapolle, Plant Manager. Ultimate Parent: Eaton Corp. SIC: 3643—Current-Carrying Wiring Devices.

★ 62817 ★ Eaton Corp.
Florida Commercial Controls Div.
2250 Whitfield Ave. Manatee Plant
Sarasota, FL 34243-9703
Company Type: Division. Ultimate Parent: Eaton Corp. SIC: 3625—Relays & Industrial Controls.

★ 62818 ★ First of America Bank
6160 N. Lockwood Ridge
Sarasota, FL 34243
(813)379-1235
Location Type: Branch office. Ultimate Parent: First of America Bank Corp. SIC: 6021—National Commercial Banks.

★ 62819 ★ First of America Bank
4902 S. Tamiami Trail
Sarasota, FL 34231
Location Type: Branch office. Ultimate Parent: First of America Bank Corp. SIC: 6021—National Commercial Banks.

★ 62820 ★ First of America Bank
3982 Bec Bridge Rd.
Sarasota, FL 34231
(813)923-5841
Location Type: Branch office. Ultimate Parent: First of America Bank Corp.

★ 62821 ★ First of America Bank
2207 Gulfgate Dr.
Sarasota, FL 34231
(813)923-3617
Location Type: Branch office. Ultimate Parent: First of America Bank Corp. SIC: 6021—National Commercial Banks.

★ 62822 ★ First of America Bank
4059 Cattlemen Rd.
Sarasota, FL 34233
(813)379-1215
Location Type: Branch office. Ultimate Parent: First of America Bank Corp.

★ 62823 ★ First of America Bank
5292 Presidential Sq.
Sarasota, FL 34235
(813)379-1225
Location Type: Branch office. Ultimate Parent: First of America Bank Corp. SIC: 6021—National Commercial Banks.

★ 62824 ★ First of America Bank
1520 Ringling Rd.
Sarasota, FL 34236
(813)379-1210
Location Type: Branch office. Ultimate Parent: First of America Bank Corp.

★ 62825 ★ First Union National Bank of Florida
6076 N. Lockwood Ridge Rd.
Sarasota, FL 34243
(813)361-5780
Location Type: Branch office. Officer: Chris Graham Mgr. Ultimate Parent: First Union Corp. SIC: 6021—National Commercial Banks.

★ 62826 ★ First Union National Bank of Florida
1819 Main St.
Sarasota, FL 34236
(813)361-5737
Location Type: Branch office. Ultimate Parent: First Union Corp. SIC: 6021—National Commercial Banks.

★ 62827 ★ First Union National Bank of Florida
300 Madison Dr.
Sarasota, FL 34236-1399
(813)361-5849
Location Type: Branch office. Ultimate Parent: First Union Corp. SIC: 6021—National Commercial Banks.

★ 62828 ★ First Union National Bank of Florida
8595 S. Tamiami Trl.
Sarasota, FL 34238-5794
(813)361-5794
Location Type: Branch office. Officer: Jan Smutz Mgr. Ultimate Parent: First Union Corp. SIC: 6021—National Commercial Banks.

★ 62829 ★ First Union National Bank of Florida
3601 Bee Ridge Rd.
Sarasota, FL 34241
(813)361-5843
Location Type: Branch office. Ultimate Parent: First Union Corp. SIC: 6021—National Commercial Banks.

★ 62830 ★ First Union National Bank of Florida
5810 Midnight Pass Rd.
Sarasota, FL 34231-2196
(813)361-5838
Location Type: Branch office. Ultimate Parent: First Union Corp. SIC: 6021—National Commercial Banks.

★ 62831 ★ First Union National Bank of Florida
120 S. Tamiami Trl.
Sarasota, FL 34239-2203
(813)361-5708
Location Type: Branch office. Ultimate Parent: First Union Corp. SIC: 6021—National Commercial Banks.

★ 62832 ★ Firstar Trust Co. of Florida, NA
1800 Second St.
Ste. 901
Sarasota, FL 34236
(813)951-0901
Company Type: Subsidiary. Location Type: Branch office. Officer: Donald B. Griswold, Mgr. Ultimate Parent: Firstar Corp. SIC: 6021—National Commercial Banks.

★ 62833 ★ Fortune Bank, ASB
935 N. Beneva Rd.
Sarasota, FL 34232-1338
(813)954-0580
Location Type: Branch office. Ultimate Parent: Fortune Bancorp.

★ 62834 ★ Fortune Bank, SB
2353 Stickney Pt. Rd.
Sarasota, FL 33702-4115
(813)923-4189
Location Type: Branch office. Ultimate Parent: Fortune Bancorp. SIC: 6021—National Commercial Banks.

★ 62835 ★ Fortune Bank, SB
4280 Bee Ridge Rd.
Sarasota, FL 34233-1326
(813)377-0846
Location Type: Branch office. Ultimate Parent: Fortune Bancorp. SIC: 6021—National Commercial Banks.

★ 62836 ★ The Gap
51 Sarasota Sq.
Sarasota, FL 34231
(813)922-4462
Ultimate Parent: GAP. SIC: 5651—Family Clothing Stores.

★ 62837 ★ Hertz Rent-A-Car
6400 S. Tamiami Trl
Sarasota, FL 34231
(813)355-8848
Ultimate Parent: Hertz. SIC: 7514—Passenger Car Rental.

★ 62838 ★ Hit or Miss
170 Gulf Gate Mall
Sarasota, FL 34231
(813)924-0794
Ultimate Parent: TJX. SIC: 5621—Women's Clothing Stores.

★ 62839 ★ Kentucky Fried Chicken
8990 Us 301
Sarasota, FL 34243
(813)753-1217
Ultimate Parent: Pepsico. SIC: 5812—Eating Places.

★ 62840 ★ Kentucky Fried Chicken
5020 Fruitville Rd.
Sarasota, FL 34232
(813)378-4811
Ultimate Parent: Pepsico. SIC: 5812—Eating Places.

★ 62841 ★ Loral Data Systems
6000 Fruitville Rd.
Sarasota, FL 34232
(813)371-0811 Fax: (813)378-1893
Company Type: Division. Ultimate Parent: Loral Corp. SIC: 3812—Search & Navigation Equipment.

★ 62842 ★ Loral Fairchild Corp.
Loral Data Systems Div.
6000 Fruitville Rd.
Sarasota, FL 34232
Company Type: Division. Ultimate Parent: Loral Corp. SIC: 3679—Electronic Components Nec; 3672—Printed Circuit Boards.

★ 62843 ★ Marshalls Department Store
350 Gulf Gate Mall
Sarasota, FL 34231
(813)921-6641
Ultimate Parent: Melville. SIC: 5311—Department Stores.

★ 62844 ★ Mary Kay Cosmetics
420 Beach Rd.
Sarasota, FL 34242
(813)349-5676
Ultimate Parent: Mary Kay Cosmetics.

★ 62845 ★ Massachusetts Mutual Life Insurance
1345 Main St.
Sarasota, FL 34236
(813)951-1689
Ultimate Parent: Massasucetts Mutual Life. SIC: 6411—Insurance Agents, Brokers & Service.

Corp. SIC: 6021—National Commercial Banks.

★ 62846 ★   **NBD Bank, FSB**
1778 Main St.
Sarasota, FL 34236
(813)366-1736
Location Type: Branch office. **Officer:**
Monique Tremblay. **Ultimate Parent:** NBD
Bancorp. **SIC:** 6021—National Commercial
Banks.

★ 62847 ★   **Norwest Mortgage
Inc.**
1800 2nd St.
Sarasota, FL 34236
(813)954-0153
Ultimate Parent: Norwest Corp. **SIC:**
6162—Mortgage Bankers &
Correspondents.

★ 62848 ★   **Omc Chris Craft**
8161 15th St. E.
Sarasota, FL 34243
Ultimate Parent: Outboard Marine. **SIC:**
3732—Boat Building & Repairing.

★ 62849 ★   **Omc Chris Craft**
7110 21st St. E.
Sarasota, FL 34243
Ultimate Parent: Outboard Marine. **SIC:**
3732—Boat Building & Repairing.

★ 62850 ★   **Omc Chris Craft Inc.**
8161 15th St. E.
Sarasota, FL 34243
Ultimate Parent: Outboard Marine. **SIC:**
3732—Boat Building & Repairing.

★ 62851 ★   **Omc Chris Craft Inc.**
7110 21st St. E.
Sarasota, FL 34243
Ultimate Parent: Outboard Marine. **SIC:**
3732—Boat Building & Repairing.

★ 62852 ★   **Omc Inc.**
Boat Development Center
7921 15th St. E.
Sarasota, FL 34243
Company Type: Division. **Ultimate Parent:**
Outboard Marine. **SIC:** 3732—Boat Building
& Repairing.

★ 62853 ★   **OMC Recreational
Boat Group**
8161 15th St. E
Sarasota, FL 34243
(813)351-4900 **Fax:** (813)351-8974
Officer: John T. Keim, President. **Ultimate
Parent:** Outboard Marine.

★ 62854 ★   **Petite Sophisticate**
10 Sarasota Sq.
Sarasota, FL 34231
(813)921-6683
Ultimate Parent: United States Shoe. **SIC:**
5651—Family Clothing Stores.

★ 62855 ★   **Pizza Hut**
3564 17th St.
Sarasota, FL 34235
(813)365-3574
Ultimate Parent: Pepsico. **SIC:** 5812—
Eating Places.

★ 62856 ★   **Pizza Hut**
1615 S. Tamiami Trl.
Sarasota, FL 34239
(813)954-0118
Ultimate Parent: Pepsico. **SIC:** 5812—
Eating Places.

★ 62857 ★   **Radio Shack**
4850 S. Tamiami Trl
Sarasota, FL 34231
(813)924-4529
Company Type: Division. **Ultimate Parent:**
Tandy Corp. **SIC:** 5731—Radio, Television
& Electronics Stores.

★ 62858 ★   **Radio Shack**
13 Sarasota Sq.
Sarasota, FL 34231
(813)922-4248
Company Type: Division. **Ultimate Parent:**
Tandy Corp. **SIC:** 5731—Radio, Television
& Electronics Stores.

★ 62859 ★   **Radio Shack**
3680 Bee Ridge Rd.
Sarasota, FL 34233
(813)922-0800
Company Type: Division. **Ultimate Parent:**
Tandy Corp. **SIC:** 5731—Radio, Television
& Electronics Stores.

★ 62860 ★   **Radio Shack**
8364 Lockwood Ridge Rd.
Sarasota, FL 34243
Company Type: Division. **Ultimate Parent:**
Tandy Corp. **SIC:** 7373—Computer
Integrated Systems Design.

★ 62861 ★   **Savings of America**
Home Savings of America, FSB
2891 S. Tamiami Trl.
Sarasota, FL 34239-5143
(813)365-4922
Location Type: Branch office. **Officer:**
Karen Berthoff, Mgr. **Ultimate Parent:**
Brooks Foods. **SIC:** 6021—National
Commercial Banks.

★ 62862 ★   **Teleflex Inc.**
1816 57th St.
Sarasota, FL 34243-2297
Ultimate Parent: Teleflex. **SIC:** 3699—
Electrical Equipment & Supplies Nec.

★ 62863 ★   **Unisys Corp.**
1970 Landings Blvd.
Sarasota, FL 34231
(813)923-5886
Ultimate Parent: Unisys Corp. **SIC:** 7373—
Computer Integrated Systems Design.

★ 62864 ★   **Vision Energy**
3333 N. Washington Blvd.
Sarasota, FL 34234-6260
Officer: Larry Wheeler. **Ultimate Parent:**
Bell Atlantic Corp. **SIC:** 4924—Natural Gas
Distribution; 5722—Household Appliance
Stores; 5984—Liquefied Petroleum Gas
Dealers.

★ 62865 ★   **Walgreen**
3506 Clark Rd.
Sarasota, FL 34231
(813)923-2885
Ultimate Parent: Walgreen Co. **SIC:**
5999—Miscellaneous Retail Stores Nec.

★ 62866 ★   **Walgreen Drug Stores**
100 S. Gate Shopping Plz.
Sarasota, FL 34239
(813)955-9960
Ultimate Parent: Walgreen Co. **SIC:**
5912—Drug Stores & Proprietary Stores.

★ 62867 ★   **Walgreen Drug Stores**
25 Gulf Gate Mall
Sarasota, FL 34231
(813)922-1588
Ultimate Parent: Walgreen Co. **SIC:**
5912—Drug Stores & Proprietary Stores.

Sarasota Sq

★ 62868 ★   **Publix Super Market**
6123 Sawyer Rd.
Sarasota Sq, FL 34238
(813)923-4929
Ultimate Parent: Publix Super Markets.
SIC: 5411—Grocery Stores.

Saratoga

★ 62869 ★   **First of America Bank**
8444 S. Tamiami Trail
Saratoga, FL 34231
(813)966-3671
Location Type: Branch office. **Ultimate
Parent:** First of America Bank Corp. **SIC:**
6021—National Commercial Banks.

Satellite Beach

★ 62870 ★   **First Union National
Bank of Florida**
1090 Hwy. A1A
Satellite Beach, FL 32937-2339
(407)984-5040
Location Type: Branch office. **Ultimate
Parent:** First Union Corp. **SIC:** 6021—
National Commercial Banks.

Sebastian

★ 62871 ★   **Barnett Bank of the
Treasure Coast**
710 S. Fleming St.
Sebastian, FL 32958-4141
(407)770-3872
Company Type: Subsidiary. **Location
Type:** Branch office. **Officer:** Jim Joines,
Assistant Vice President & Office Manager.
Ultimate Parent: Barnett Banks. **SIC:**
6022—State Commercial Banks.

★ 62872 ★   **Barnett Bank of the
Treasure Coast**
13555 US Hwy. No. 1
Sebastian, FL 32958-3289
(407)770-3840
Company Type: Subsidiary. **Location
Type:** Branch office. **Officer:** Barbara Tilton,
Vice President. **Ultimate Parent:** Barnett
Banks. **SIC:** 6022—State Commercial
Banks.

★ 62873 ★   **First Union National
Bank of Florida**
1524 US Hwy. 1
Sebastian, FL 32958-3831
(407)589-0001
Location Type: Branch office. **Ultimate
Parent:** First Union Corp. **SIC:** 6021—
National Commercial Banks.

★ 62874 ★   **Publix Super Market**
13435 Us Hwy. 1
Sebastian, FL 32958
(407)589-5110
Ultimate Parent: Publix Super Markets.
SIC: 5411—Grocery Stores.

★ 62875 ★   **Publix Super Markets**
13435 Us Hwy. 1
Sebastian, FL 32958
(407)589-5110
Ultimate Parent: Publix Super Markets.
SIC: 5411—Grocery Stores.

★ 62876 ★   **Walgreen Drug Stores**
13415 Us Hwy. 1
Sebastian, FL 32958
(407)589-6455
Ultimate Parent: Walgreen Co. **SIC:**
5912—Drug Stores & Proprietary Stores.

Sebring

★ 62877 ★   **Barnett Bank of
Highlands County**
2715 Fairmount Dr.
Sebring, FL 33870-1699
(813)382-5355
Company Type: Subsidiary. **Location
Type:** Branch office. **Officer:** Stuart
Swanson, Vice President. **Ultimate Parent:**
Barnett Banks. **SIC:** 6022—State
Commercial Banks.

★ 62878 ★   **Barnett Bank of
Highlands County**
231 S. Ridgewood Dr.
PO Box 1947
Sebring, FL 33871-1947
(813)385-1515
Company Type: Subsidiary. **Location
Type:** Branch office. **Officer:** James L.
Ridley, Chairman, President & CEO.
Ultimate Parent: Barnett Banks. **SIC:**
6022—State Commercial Banks.

★ 62879 ★   **Barnett Bank of
Highlands County**
2838 Southgate
Sebring, FL 33870
(813)382-5360
Company Type: Subsidiary. **Location
Type:** Branch office. **Officer:** Johnnie
Franklin, Manager. **Ultimate Parent:** Barnett
Banks. **SIC:** 6022—State Commercial
Banks.

★ 62880 ★   **First Union National
Bank of Florida**
228 N. Ridgewood Dr.
Sebring, FL 33870-7203
(813)385-5101
Location Type: Branch office. **Ultimate
Parent:** First Union Corp. **SIC:** 6021—
National Commercial Banks.

★ 62881 ★   **First Union National
Bank of Florida**
3635 US Hwy. 27 N.
Sebring, FL 33870-1698
(813)471-5246
Location Type: Branch office. **Ultimate
Parent:** First Union Corp. **SIC:** 6021—
National Commercial Banks.

★ 62882 ★   **Greyhound Bus Lines**
3655 PO Box
Sebring, FL 33871
(813)385-7741
Ultimate Parent: Greyhound Lines Inc. **SIC:**
4111—Local & Suburban Transit.

★ 62883 ★   **Greyhound Bus Lines**
4700 Us 27 S
Sebring, FL 33870
(813)385-7741
Ultimate Parent: Greyhound Lines Inc. **SIC:**
4131—Intercity & Rural Bus Transportation;
4173—Bus Terminal & Service Facilities.

★ 62884 ★   **Huntington, FSB**
Southgate Shopping Ctr.
2934 US Hwy. 27 S.
Sebring, FL 33870
(813)385-2549
Location Type: Branch office. **Officer:**
Cindy Townsend, Manager. **Ultimate
Parent:** Huntington Bancshares. **SIC:**
6021—National Commercial Banks.

★ 62885 ★   **Huntington, FSB**
2821 US Hwy. 27 N
Sebring, FL 33872
(813)688-7192
Location Type: Branch office. **Officer:**
Tonja Weed, Manager. **Ultimate Parent:**
Huntington Bancshares. **SIC:** 6021—
National Commercial Banks.

★ 62886 ★   **Huntington, FSB**
6226 US Hwy. 98
Sebring, FL 33870-2320
(813)655-0177
Location Type: Branch office. **Officer:**
Tracy Lehman, Manager. **Ultimate Parent:**
Huntington Bancshares. **SIC:** 6021—
National Commercial Banks.

★ 62887 ★   **Huntington, FSB**
2631 US Hwy. 27 S
Sebring, FL 33870-2320
(813)385-1514
Location Type: Branch office. **Officer:**
Cindy Townsend, Manager. **Ultimate
Parent:** Huntington Bancshares. **SIC:**
6021—National Commercial Banks.

★ 62888 ★   **Huntington, FSB**
126 W. Ctr.
Sebring, FL 33870-1787
(813)385-1551 **Fax:** (813)385-5250
Location Type: Headquarters. **Officer:**
Lawrence J. Price, Chairman, President &
CEO. **Ultimate Parent:** Huntington
Bancshares. **SIC:** 6021—National
Commercial Banks.

★ 62889 ★   **Kentucky Fried
Chicken**
3317 Us 27 S
Sebring, FL 33870
(813)385-0442
Ultimate Parent: Pepsico. **SIC:** 5812—
Eating Places.

★ 62890 ★   **Mary Kay Cosmetics**
Moon Ranch Rd.
Sebring, FL 33871
(813)385-5658
Ultimate Parent: Mary Kay Cosmetics.

★ 62891 ★   **Pizza Hut**
2109 Us 27 S
Sebring, FL 33870
(813)385-1075
Ultimate Parent: Pepsico. **SIC:** 5812—
Eating Places.

★ 62892 ★   **Publix Super Market**
2824 Southgate Shopping Ctr.
Sebring, FL 33870
(813)385-0196
Ultimate Parent: Publix Super Markets.
SIC: 5411—Grocery Stores.

★ 62893 ★   **Radio Shack**
Lakeview Terrace Apt
Sebring, FL 33870
(813)385-3055
Company Type: Division. **Ultimate Parent:**
Tandy Corp. **SIC:** 5065—Electronic Parts &
Equipment Nec.

★ 62894 ★   **Ryder Truck Rental**
6820 Us 27 N
Sebring, FL 33870
(813)453-5354
Ultimate Parent: Ryder System. **SIC:**
4214—Local Trucking With Storage.

★ 62895 ★   **Texaco Food Mart**
629 N. Ridgewood Dr.
Sebring, FL 33870
(813)382-0001
Ultimate Parent: Texaco. **SIC:** 5411—
Grocery Stores.

★ 62896 ★   Wal Mart
3525 Us Hwy. 27 N
Sebring, FL 33870
Ultimate Parent: Wal-Mart Stores, Inc. **SIC:**
5399—Miscellaneous General Merchandise
Store.

Seffner

★ 62897 ★   Barnett Bank of
Tampa
816 State Rd. 574
Seffner, FL 33584-5186
(813)681-1336
Company Type: Subsidiary. **Location
Type:** Branch office. **Officer:** Arlene
Messer, Office Manager. **Ultimate Parent:**
Barnett Banks. **SIC:** 6022—State
Commercial Banks.

★ 62898 ★   Kentucky Fried
Chicken
Rural Route 2
Seffner, FL 33584
(813)681-8666
Ultimate Parent: Pepsico. **SIC:** 5812—
Eating Places.

★ 62899 ★   Radio Shack
Rural Route 2
Seffner, FL 33584
(813)681-6127
Company Type: Division. **Ultimate Parent:**
Tandy Corp. **SIC:** 5731—Radio, Television
& Electronics Stores.

★ 62900 ★   Ryder Truck Rental
2004 S. Parsons Ave.
Seffner, FL 33584
(813)689-8361
Ultimate Parent: Ryder System. **SIC:**
7513—Truck Rental & Leasing Without
Drivers.

Seminole

★ 62901 ★   Barnett Bank of
Pinellas County
8999 Park Blvd.
Seminole, FL 34647-4302
(813)892-1138
Company Type: Subsidiary. **Location
Type:** Branch office. **Officer:** Bill Reid,
Manager. **Ultimate Parent:** Barnett Banks.
SIC: 6022—State Commercial Banks.

★ 62902 ★   Barnett Bank of
Pinellas County
9130 Oakhurst Rd.
Seminole, FL 34646-2109
(813)539-9183
Company Type: Subsidiary. **Location
Type:** Branch office. **Officer:** Brenda
Williams, Manager. **Ultimate Parent:**
Barnett Banks. **SIC:** 6022—State
Commercial Banks.

★ 62903 ★   Barnett Bank of
Pinellas County
7405 Seminole Blvd.
Seminole, FL 34642-5427
(813)892-1684
Company Type: Subsidiary. **Location
Type:** Branch office. **Officer:** Melanie
Slaght, Manager. **Ultimate Parent:** Barnett
Banks. **SIC:** 6022—State Commercial
Banks.

★ 62904 ★   Barnett Bank of
Pinellas County
8333 Seminole Blvd.
Seminole, FL 34642
(813)892-1330
Company Type: Subsidiary. **Location
Type:** Branch office. **Officer:** Melanie
Slaght, Manager. **Ultimate Parent:** Barnett
Banks. **SIC:** 6022—State Commercial
Banks.

★ 62905 ★   First Union National
Bank of Florida
13099 Park Blvd.
Seminole, FL 34646-3640
(813)939-7531
Location Type: Branch office. **Ultimate
Parent:** First Union Corp. **SIC:** 6021—
National Commercial Banks.

★ 62906 ★   First Union National
Bank of Florida
8800 Park Blvd.
Seminole, FL 34647-4335
(813)892-7490
Location Type: Branch office. **Ultimate
Parent:** First Union Corp. **SIC:** 6021—
National Commercial Banks.

★ 62907 ★   First Union National
Bank of Florida
7700 Seminole Blvd.
Seminole, FL 34642
(813)399-3500
Location Type: Branch office. **Ultimate
Parent:** First Union Corp. **SIC:** 6021—
National Commercial Banks.

★ 62908 ★   Fortune Bank, ASB
7800 113th St. N
Seminole, FL 34642-4699
(813)397-1491
Location Type: Branch office. **Ultimate
Parent:** Fortune Bancorp. **SIC:** 6021—
National Commercial Banks.

★ 62909 ★   Fortune Bank, ASB
9398 Oakhurst Rd.
Seminole, FL 34646-2198
(813)595-8390
Location Type: Branch office. **Officer:**
Denise Bishop, Manager. **Ultimate Parent:**
Fortune Bancorp. **SIC:** 6021—National
Commercial Banks.

Shalimar

★ 62910 ★   AmSouth Bank of
Florida
1248 N. Eglin Pky.
Shalimar, FL 32579-1298
(904)444-1000
Location Type: Branch office. **Officer:**
Kathy Jones, Manager. **Ultimate Parent:**
AmSouth Bancorp. **SIC:** 6022—State
Commercial Banks.

★ 62911 ★   Barnett Bank of
Northwest Florida
1246 Eglin Pky.
Shalimar, FL 32579-1207
(904)651-3161
Company Type: Subsidiary. **Location
Type:** Branch office. **Officer:** Amy Brown,
Assistant Vice President. **Ultimate Parent:**
Barnett Banks. **SIC:** 6022—State
Commercial Banks.

★ 62912 ★   Hertz Rent-A-Car
US 85
Shalimar, FL 32579
(904)651-0612
Ultimate Parent: Hertz. **SIC:** 7514—
Passenger Car Rental.

★ 62913 ★   Mary Kay Cosmetics
26 Bayview Dr.
Shalimar, FL 32579
(904)651-1361
Ultimate Parent: Mary Kay Cosmetics. **SIC:**
5999—Miscellaneous Retail Stores Nec.

★ 62914 ★   Northrop Corp.
60 2nd St.
Shalimar, FL 32579
(904)651-1414
Ultimate Parent: Northrop Corp. **SIC:**
3761—Guided Missiles & Space Vehicles.

Silver Springs

★ 62915 ★   AmSouth Bank of
Florida
Rte. 2, Box 504
Silver Springs, FL 34488
(904)625-1166
Location Type: Branch office. **Ultimate
Parent:** AmSouth Bancorp. **SIC:** 6022—
State Commercial Banks.

★ 62916 ★   Barnett Bank of
Marion County, NA
15825 NE State Rd. 40
Silver Springs, FL 34489-9063
(904)620-1111
Company Type: Subsidiary. **Location
Type:** Branch office. **Officer:** Beverly
Yandle, Manager. **Ultimate Parent:** Barnett
Banks. **SIC:** 6021—National Commercial
Banks.

★ 62917 ★   Barnett Bank of
Marion County, NA
5431 NE Silver Springs Blvd.
Silver Springs, FL 34489
(904)620-1111
Company Type: Subsidiary. **Location
Type:** Branch office. **Officer:** Claudia
Porcelli, Manager. **Ultimate Parent:** Barnett
Banks. **SIC:** 6021—National Commercial
Banks.

Singer Island

★ 62918 ★   Barnett Bank of Palm
Beach County
2655 N. Ocean Dr.
Singer Island, FL 33404
(407)845-3430
Company Type: Subsidiary. **Location
Type:** Branch office. **Officer:** Jamie Neal,
Manager. **Ultimate Parent:** Barnett Banks.
SIC: 6022—State Commercial Banks.

Smyrna Beach

★ 62919 ★   Kentucky Fried
Chicken
823 E. 3rd Ave.
Smyrna Beach, FL 32169
(904)427-1181
Ultimate Parent: Pepsico. **SIC:** 5812—
Eating Places.

★ 62920 ★   Pizza Hut
1616 S. Dixie Fwy.
Smyrna Beach, FL 32168
(904)427-6282
Ultimate Parent: Pepsico. **SIC:** 5812—
Eating Places.

South Miami

★ 62921 ★   California Federal
Bank, FSB
1530 Pinehurst Dr.
South Miami, FL 34606-4500
(904)686-0601
Location Type: Branch office. **Ultimate
Parent:** California Federal Bank. **SIC:**
6021—National Commercial Banks.

★ 62922 ★   Citizens Federal
Bank, FSB
7377 Spring Hill Dr.
South Miami, FL 34606-4300
(904)683-7558
Location Type: Branch office. **Officer:**
Marjorie Berry, Manager. **Ultimate Parent:**
CSF Holdings. **SIC:** 6021—National
Commercial Banks.

★ 62923 ★   First Union National
Bank of Florida
7220 SW 5th Ave.
South Miami, FL 33143-5311
(305)663-6155
Location Type: Branch office. **Ultimate
Parent:** First Union Corp. **SIC:** 6021—
National Commercial Banks.

South Pasadena

★ 62924 ★   Barnett Bank of
Pinellas County
985 Pasadena Ave. S
South Pasadena, FL 33707-2093
(813)892-1186
Company Type: Subsidiary. **Location
Type:** Branch office. **Officer:** Lisa Massrula,
Manager. **Ultimate Parent:** Barnett Banks.
SIC: 6022—State Commercial Banks.

Spring Hill

★ 62925 ★   AmSouth Bank of
Florida
11234 Spring Hill Dr.
Spring Hill, FL 34609-4650
(904)686-1022
Location Type: Branch office. **Ultimate
Parent:** AmSouth Bancorp. **SIC:** 6022—
State Commercial Banks.

★ 62926 ★   AmSouth Bank of
Florida
7255 Forest Oak Blvd.
Spring Hill, FL 34606-2395
(904)686-1001
Location Type: Branch office. **Ultimate
Parent:** AmSouth Bancorp. **SIC:** 6022—
State Commercial Banks.

★ 62927 ★   AmSouth Bank of
Florida
6023 Spring Hill Dr.
Spring Hill, FL 34606-4628
(904)683-3002
Location Type: Branch office. **Ultimate
Parent:** AmSouth Bancorp. **SIC:** 6022—
State Commercial Banks.

★ 62928 ★   Barnett Bank of the
Suncoast, NA
7539 Spring Hill Blvd.
Spring Hill, FL 34606-4350
(904)686-1057
Company Type: Subsidiary. **Location
Type:** Branch office. **Ultimate Parent:**
Barnett Banks. **SIC:** 6021—National
Commercial Banks.

★ 62929 ★   Barnett Bank of the
Suncoast, NA
1300 Pinehurst Dr.
Spring Hill, FL 34606-4551
(904)683-5434
Company Type: Subsidiary. **Location
Type:** Branch office. **Officer:** Larry Fredrick,
Manager. **Ultimate Parent:** Barnett Banks.
SIC: 6021—National Commercial Banks.

★ 62930 ★   Barnett Bank of the
Suncoast, NA
7165 Mariner Blvd.
Spring Hill, FL 34609-1048
(904)596-8118
Company Type: Subsidiary. **Location
Type:** Branch office. **Officer:** Chris
Pippenger, Manager. **Ultimate Parent:**
Barnett Banks. **SIC:** 6021—National
Commercial Banks.

★ 62931 ★   Barnett Bank of the
Suncoast, NA
11050 Spring Hill Dr.
Spring Hill, FL 34608-5093
(904)686-5450
Company Type: Subsidiary. **Location
Type:** Branch office. **Officer:** Steve
Emerson, Vice President. **Ultimate Parent:**
Barnett Banks. **SIC:** 6021—National
Commercial Banks.

★ 62932 ★   Barnett Bank of the
Suncoast, NA
7347 Forest Oaks Blvd.
Spring Hill, FL 34606-2404
(904)596-8880
Company Type: Subsidiary. **Location
Type:** Branch office. **Officer:** Bill Andryusky,
Manager. **Ultimate Parent:** Barnett Banks.
SIC: 6021—National Commercial Banks.

★ 62933 ★   California Federal
Bank
19 Springhill Dr.
Spring Hill, FL 34606
(904)686-0601
Ultimate Parent: California Federal Bank.
SIC: 6099—Functions Related to Deposit
Banking.

★ 62934 ★   Fortune Bank, ASB
1500 Pinehurst Dr.
Spring Hill, FL 34606-4555
(904)683-6385
Location Type: Branch office. **Officer:**
Diana Bartlett, Manager. **Ultimate Parent:**
Fortune Bancorp. **SIC:** 6021—National
Commercial Banks.

★ 62935 ★   Kentucky Fried
Chicken
1135 Commercial Way
Spring Hill, FL 34606
(904)683-8467
Ultimate Parent: Pepsico. **SIC:** 5812—
Eating Places.

★ 62936 ★   Wal Mart Discount
Cities
3021 Commercial Way
Spring Hill, FL 34606
(904)686-0744
Ultimate Parent: Wal-Mart Stores, Inc. **SIC:**
5311—Department Stores.

St Augstn Beach

★ 62937 ★   Radio Shack
1803 K-Mart Plz.
St Augstn Beach, FL 32086
(904)824-4188
Company Type: Division. **Ultimate Parent:**
Tandy Corp. **SIC:** 5719—Miscellaneous
Home Furnishings Stores.

St Augustine

★ 62938 ★ Anchor Savings Bank F S B
1965 State Road 3
St Augustine, FL 32084
Ultimate Parent: Anchor Bancorp. **SIC:** 6022—State Commercial Banks.

★ 62939 ★ Borden Inc.
Wise Foods
4455 A Ave.
St Augustine, FL 32095
(904)829-9085
Company Type: Division. **Ultimate Parent:** Borden, Inc. **SIC:** 2096—Potato Chips & Similar Snacks.

★ 62940 ★ Food Lion
RR 4
St Augustine, FL 32086
(904)794-9910
Ultimate Parent: Food Lion. **SIC:** 5411—Grocery Stores.

★ 62941 ★ Kentucky Fried Chicken
2300 N. Ponce De Leon Blvd.
St Augustine, FL 32084
(904)824-2048
Ultimate Parent: Pepsico. **SIC:** 5812—Eating Places.

★ 62942 ★ Kentucky Fried Chicken
103 Anastasia Blvd.
St Augustine, FL 32084
(904)824-1684
Ultimate Parent: Pepsico. **SIC:** 5812—Eating Places.

★ 62943 ★ Lerner Shop
19 Ponce De Leon Ave.
St Augustine, FL 32084
(904)797-4743
Ultimate Parent: Limited. **SIC:** 5651—Family Clothing Stores.

★ 62944 ★ Lerner Shop
Ponce De Leon Mall
St Augustine, FL 32086
(904)797-4743
Ultimate Parent: Limited. **SIC:** 5651—Family Clothing Stores.

★ 62945 ★ McDonalds Hamburgers
State Rd. 16 I95
St Augustine, FL 32084
(904)824-8646
Ultimate Parent: McDonald's. **SIC:** 7299—Miscellaneous Personal Services Nec.

★ 62946 ★ Pizza Hut
80 Vilano Rd.
St Augustine, FL 32095
(904)824-8705
Ultimate Parent: Pepsico. **SIC:** 5812—Eating Places.

★ 62947 ★ Pizza Hut
Rural Route 4
St Augustine, FL 32086
(904)829-5659
Ultimate Parent: Pepsico. **SIC:** 5812—Eating Places.

★ 62948 ★ Pizza Hut
Us 312
St Augustine, FL 32084
(904)829-5659
Ultimate Parent: Pepsico. **SIC:** 5812—Eating Places.

★ 62949 ★ Pizza Hut
1200 N. Ponce De Leon Blvd.
St Augustine, FL 32084
(904)824-4451
Ultimate Parent: Pepsico. **SIC:** 5812—Eating Places.

★ 62950 ★ Pizza Hut
2 Dufferin St.
St Augustine, FL 32084
(904)829-3463
Ultimate Parent: Pepsico. **SIC:** 5812—Eating Places.

★ 62951 ★ Professional Accounting Ser
92 Coquina Ave.
St Augustine, FL 32084
(904)825-2331
Ultimate Parent: Olsten. **SIC:** 8721—Accounting, Auditing & Bookkeeping.

★ 62952 ★ Publix Super Market
1795 Mart Plz.
St Augustine, FL 32086
(904)824-8338
Ultimate Parent: Publix Super Markets. **SIC:** 5411—Grocery Stores.

★ 62953 ★ Publix Super Market
Hwy. 1
St Augustine, FL 32084
(904)824-8338
Ultimate Parent: Publix Super Markets. **SIC:** 5411—Grocery Stores.

★ 62954 ★ Publix Super Markets
Hwy. 1
St Augustine, FL 32084
(904)824-8338
Ultimate Parent: Publix Super Markets. **SIC:** 5411—Grocery Stores.

★ 62955 ★ Radio Shack
Hwy. 1
St Augustine, FL 32084
(904)824-2475
Company Type: Division. **Ultimate Parent:** Tandy Corp. **SIC:** 5065—Electronic Parts & Equipment Nec.

★ 62956 ★ Ryder Truck Rental
Rural Route 4
St Augustine, FL 32086
(904)797-7910
Ultimate Parent: Ryder System. **SIC:** 7513—Truck Rental & Leasing Without Drivers.

★ 62957 ★ Texaco Station
Rural Route 4
St Augustine, FL 32086
(904)826-0387
Ultimate Parent: Texaco. **SIC:** 5541—Gasoline Service Stations.

★ 62958 ★ Waldenbooks
Ponce De Leon Mall
St Augustine, FL 32086
(904)797-4013
Ultimate Parent: K-Mart. **SIC:** 5942—Book Stores.

★ 62959 ★ Waldenbooks
Hwy. 1
St Augustine, FL 32084
(904)797-4013
Ultimate Parent: K-Mart. **SIC:** 5942—Book Stores.

★ 62960 ★ Walgreen Drugs
Ponce De Leon Mall
St Augustine, FL 32086
(904)797-5300
Ultimate Parent: Walgreen Co. **SIC:** 5912—Drug Stores & Proprietary Stores.

St Pete

★ 62961 ★ Walgreen Drug Stores
3350 Central Ave.
St Pete, FL 33712
Ultimate Parent: Walgreen Co. **SIC:** 5912—Drug Stores & Proprietary Stores.

St Petersburg

★ 62962 ★ Ace Hardware
7680 49th St. N
St Petersburg, FL 33709
(813)541-4607
Ultimate Parent: Ace Hardware. **SIC:** 5072—Hardware.

★ 62963 ★ Ace Hardware
N East Shopping Ctr.
St Petersburg, FL 33704
(813)898-3141
Ultimate Parent: Ace Hardware. **SIC:** 5251—Hardware Stores.

★ 62964 ★ American Savings of Florida
2240 62nd Ave. S
St Petersburg, FL 33712
(813)864-1556
Ultimate Parent: American Savings of Florida. **SIC:** 6159—Miscellaneous Business Credit Institutions.

★ 62965 ★ Burdines
1400 66th St. N
St Petersburg, FL 33710
(813)381-7525
Ultimate Parent: Federated Department Stores. **SIC:** 4724—Travel Agencies.

★ 62966 ★ California Federal Bank
5275 34th St. S
St Petersburg, FL 33711
(813)864-1553
Ultimate Parent: California Federal Bank. **SIC:** 6035—Federal Savings Institutions.

★ 62967 ★ Circuit City
2066 Tyrone Blvd. N
St Petersburg, FL 33710
(813)347-1881
Ultimate Parent: Circuit City Stores. **SIC:** 5722—Household Appliance Stores.

★ 62968 ★ Circus World
6901 22nd Ave. N
St Petersburg, FL 33710
(813)344-3635
Ultimate Parent: Melville. **SIC:** 5945—Hobby, Toy & Game Shops.

★ 62969 ★ Delta Air Lines
431 1st Ave. N
St Petersburg, FL 33701
(813)894-1861
Ultimate Parent: Delta Air Lines, Inc. **SIC:** 4724—Travel Agencies.

★ 62970 ★ Delta Air Lines Inc.
431 1st Ave. N
St Petersburg, FL 33701
(813)894-1861
Ultimate Parent: Delta Air Lines, Inc. **SIC:** 4724—Travel Agencies.

★ 62971 ★ First of America Bank
3609 49th St.
St Petersburg, FL 33710
(813)525-6021
Location Type: Branch office. **Ultimate Parent:** First of America Bank Corp. **SIC:** 6021—National Commercial Banks.

★ 62972 ★ First of America Bank
7700 N. 9th St.
St Petersburg, FL 33710
(813)576-9660
Location Type: Branch office. **Ultimate Parent:** First of America Bank Corp. **SIC:** 6021—National Commercial Banks.

★ 62973 ★ Food Lion
2900 34th St. S
St Petersburg, FL 33711
(813)867-2099
Ultimate Parent: Food Lion. **SIC:** 5411—Grocery Stores.

★ 62974 ★ Graphic Packing Corp.
7901 4th St. N
St Petersburg, FL 33702
(813)577-4903
Ultimate Parent: Adolph Coors. **SIC:** 5113—Industrial & Personal Service Paper.

★ 62975 ★ Hertz Rent-A-Car
7800 Blind Pass Rd.
St Petersburg, FL 33706
(813)360-1631
Ultimate Parent: Hertz. **SIC:** 7514—Passenger Car Rental.

★ 62976 ★ Home Depot Inc
1725 34th St. N
St Petersburg, FL 33713
(813)527-1482
Ultimate Parent: Home Depot. **SIC:** 5211—Lumber & Other Building Materials.

★ 62977 ★ Jackson National Life Insur
9400 4th St. N
St Petersburg, FL 33702
(813)576-2200
Ultimate Parent: Jackson National Life. **SIC:** 6411—Insurance Agents, Brokers & Service.

★ 62978 ★ Jackson National Life Insurance C
9800 4th St. N
St Petersburg, FL 33702
(813)576-2220
Ultimate Parent: Jackson National Life. **SIC:** 6411—Insurance Agents, Brokers & Service.

★ 62979 ★ Jiffy Lube
5767 Central Ave.
St Petersburg, FL 33710
(813)384-5823
Ultimate Parent: Pennzoil. **SIC:** 7539—Automotive Repair Shops Nec.

★ 62980 ★ Jiffy Lube
7025 Seminole Blvd.
St Petersburg, FL 33708
(813)393-9703
Ultimate Parent: Pennzoil. **SIC:** 5541—Gasoline Service Stations.

★ 62981 ★ Kelly Assisted Living Servi
300 31st St. N
St Petersburg, FL 33713
(813)327-5961
Ultimate Parent: Kelly Services. **SIC:** 8099—Health & Allied Services Nec.

★ 62982 ★ Kentucky Fried Chicken
7200 Seminole Blvd.
St Petersburg, FL 33708
(813)391-1769
Ultimate Parent: Pepsico. **SIC:** 5812—Eating Places.

★ 62983 ★ Kentucky Fried Chicken
2186 Tyrone Blvd. N
St Petersburg, FL 33710
(813)345-5379
Ultimate Parent: Pepsico. **SIC:** 5812—Eating Places.

★ 62984 ★ Kentucky Fried Chicken
2430 34th St. S
St Petersburg, FL 33711
(813)327-8267
Ultimate Parent: Pepsico. **SIC:** 5812—Eating Places.

★ 62985 ★ Kentucky Fried Chicken
1760 9th St. S
St Petersburg, FL 33701
(813)825-0792
Ultimate Parent: Pepsico. **SIC:** 5812—Eating Places.

★ 62986 ★ Kentucky Fried Chicken
770 34th St. N
St Petersburg, FL 33713
(813)323-5016
Ultimate Parent: Pepsico. **SIC:** 5812—Eating Places.

★ 62987 ★ Kmart Store
3951 34th St. S
St Petersburg, FL 33711
(813)867-9142
Ultimate Parent: K-Mart. **SIC:** 7538—General Automotive Repair Shops.

★ 62988 ★ Kmart Tire & Service Center
4340 13th Ave. N
St Petersburg, FL 33713
(813)867-9142
Ultimate Parent: K-Mart.

★ 62989 ★ Lane Bryant
6901 22nd Ave. N. 854
St Petersburg, FL 33710
(813)344-5735
Ultimate Parent: Limited. **SIC:** 5621—Women's Clothing Stores; 5651—Family Clothing Stores.

★ 62990 ★ Lens Crafters
2092 Tyrone Blvd. N
St Petersburg, FL 33710
(813)343-4334
Ultimate Parent: United States Shoe. **SIC:** 5995—Optical Goods Stores.

★ 62991 ★ **Lerner Shop**
6901 22nd Ave. N
St Petersburg, FL 33710
(813)384-2032
Ultimate Parent: Limited. **SIC:** 5651—
Family Clothing Stores; 5651—Family
Clothing Stores.

★ 62992 ★ **Lerner Shop**
3275 Central Ave.
St Petersburg, FL 33713
(813)327-3439
Ultimate Parent: Limited. **SIC:** 5651—
Family Clothing Stores.

★ 62993 ★ **The Limited Express**
6901 22nd Ave. N
St Petersburg, FL 33710
(813)343-8311
Ultimate Parent: Limited. **SIC:** 5651—
Family Clothing Stores.

★ 62994 ★ **Marshalls Department Store**
2036 66th St. N
St Petersburg, FL 33710
(813)347-1170
Ultimate Parent: Melville. **SIC:** 5311—
Department Stores.

★ 62995 ★ **McDonalds Restaurants**
4595 34th St. S
St Petersburg, FL 33711
(813)866-2370
Ultimate Parent: May Department Stores.
SIC: 5812—Eating Places.

★ 62996 ★ **McDonalds Restaurants**
10771 Gulf Blvd.
St Petersburg, FL 33706
(813)360-6110
Ultimate Parent: McDonald's.
SIC: 5812—Eating Places.

★ 62997 ★ **McDonalds Restaurants**
650 150th Ave.
St Petersburg, FL 33708
(813)392-6302
Ultimate Parent: McDonald's.
SIC: 5812—Eating Places.

★ 62998 ★ **Mobil Mart**
7398 Seminole Blvd.
St Petersburg, FL 33708
(813)391-4274
Ultimate Parent: Mobil. **SIC:** 7542—Car
Washes.

★ 62999 ★ **Mobil Oil Corporation**
8900 Park St. N
St Petersburg, FL 33709
(813)397-1749
Ultimate Parent: Mobil. **SIC:** 7538—
General Automotive Repair Shops.

★ 63000 ★ **Penn Mutual Life Insurance**
5320 Gulfport Blvd. S
St Petersburg, FL 33707
(813)321-3400
Ultimate Parent: Penn Mutual Life. **SIC:**
6411—Insurance Agents, Brokers &
Service.

★ 63001 ★ **Petite Sophisticate**
6901 22nd Ave. N
St Petersburg, FL 33710
(813)343-6298
Ultimate Parent: United States Shoe. **SIC:**
5651—Family Clothing Stores.

★ 63002 ★ **Pizza Hut**
2875 Tyrone Blvd. N
St Petersburg, FL 33710
(813)344-3670
Ultimate Parent: Pepsico. **SIC:** 5812—
Eating Places.

★ 63003 ★ **Pizza Hut**
9099 4th St. N
St Petersburg, FL 33702
(813)579-4037
Ultimate Parent: Pepsico. **SIC:** 5812—
Eating Places.

★ 63004 ★ **Pizza Hut**
8380 Seminole Blvd.
St Petersburg, FL 33708
(813)397-1485
Ultimate Parent: Pepsico. **SIC:** 5812—
Eating Places.

★ 63005 ★ **Pizza Hut**
2620 4th St. N
St Petersburg, FL 33704
(813)894-5137
Ultimate Parent: Pepsico. **SIC:** 5812—
Eating Places.

★ 63006 ★ **Pizza Hut**
4001 4th St. N
St Petersburg, FL 33703
(813)821-5317
Ultimate Parent: Pepsico. **SIC:** 5812—
Eating Places.

★ 63007 ★ **Pizza Hut**
2551 34th St. S
St Petersburg, FL 33711
(813)327-2590
Ultimate Parent: Pepsico. **SIC:** 5812—
Eating Places.

★ 63008 ★ **Pizza Hut**
6876 46th Ave. N
St Petersburg, FL 33709
(813)545-3298
Ultimate Parent: Pepsico. **SIC:** 5812—
Eating Places.

★ 63009 ★ **Pizza Hut**
1590 34th St. N
St Petersburg, FL 33713
(813)321-2351
Ultimate Parent: Pepsico. **SIC:** 5812—
Eating Places.

★ 63010 ★ **Pizza Hut**
2236 62nd Ave. S
St Petersburg, FL 33712
(813)867-0820
Ultimate Parent: Pepsico. **SIC:** 5812—
Eating Places.

★ 63011 ★ **Pizza Hut**
2325 28th St. N
St Petersburg, FL 33713
(813)321-9064
Ultimate Parent: Pepsico. **SIC:** 5812—
Eating Places.

★ 63012 ★ **Publix Super Market**
5295 34th St. S
St Petersburg, FL 33711
(813)864-4250
Ultimate Parent: Publix Super Markets.
SIC: 5461—Retail Bakeries.

★ 63013 ★ **Publix Super Market**
7701 9th St. N
St Petersburg, FL 33702
(813)577-5885
Ultimate Parent: Publix Super Markets.
SIC: 5411—Grocery Stores.

★ 63014 ★ **Publix Super Market**
7044 22nd Ave. N
St Petersburg, FL 33710
(813)384-2261
Ultimate Parent: Publix Super Markets.
SIC: 5411—Grocery Stores.

★ 63015 ★ **Publix Super Market**
1700 34th St. N
St Petersburg, FL 33713
(813)323-4800
Ultimate Parent: Publix Super Markets.
SIC: 5411—Grocery Stores; 5812—Eating
Places.

★ 63016 ★ **Publix Super Market**
662 Madeira Beach Cswy
St Petersburg, FL 33708
(813)393-5471
Ultimate Parent: Publix Super Markets.
SIC: 5411—Grocery Stores.

★ 63017 ★ **Publix Super Market**
6850 Gulfport Blvd. S
St Petersburg, FL 33707
(813)345-9347
Ultimate Parent: Publix Super Markets.
SIC: 5411—Grocery Stores.

★ 63018 ★ **Publix Super Markets**
1700 34th St. N
St Petersburg, FL 33713
(813)323-4800
Ultimate Parent: Publix Super Markets.
SIC: 5411—Grocery Stores; 5812—Eating
Places.

★ 63019 ★ **Publix Super Markets**
7044 22nd Ave. N
St Petersburg, FL 33710
(813)384-2261
Ultimate Parent: Publix Super Markets.
SIC: 5411—Grocery Stores.

★ 63020 ★ **Publix Super Markets**
7701 9th St. N
St Petersburg, FL 33702
(813)577-5885
Ultimate Parent: Publix Super Markets.
SIC: 5411—Grocery Stores.

★ 63021 ★ **Radio Shack**
7901 9th St. N
St Petersburg, FL 33702
Company Type: Division. **Ultimate Parent:**
Tandy Corp. **SIC:** 5046—Commercial
Equipment Nec.

★ 63022 ★ **Radio Shack**
4370 6th St. S
St Petersburg, FL 33705
(813)895-4557
Company Type: Division. **Ultimate Parent:**
Tandy Corp. **SIC:** 5719—Miscellaneous
Home Furnishings Stores; 5731—Radio,
Television & Electronics Stores.

★ 63023 ★ **Radio Shack**
11221 78th Ave. N
St Petersburg, FL 33702
(813)397-8019
Company Type: Division. **Ultimate Parent:**
Tandy Corp. **SIC:** 7389—Business Services
Nec.

★ 63024 ★ **Radio Shack**
182 37th Ave. N
St Petersburg, FL 33704
(813)823-1420
Company Type: Division. **Ultimate Parent:**
Tandy Corp. **SIC:** 5719—Miscellaneous
Home Furnishings Stores; 5719—
Miscellaneous Home Furnishings Stores;
5731—Radio, Television & Electronics
Stores.

★ 63025 ★ **Radio Shack**
3717 49th St. N
St Petersburg, FL 33710
(813)525-3129
Company Type: Division. **Ultimate Parent:**
Tandy Corp. **SIC:** 7629—Electrical Repair
Shops Nec.

★ 63026 ★ **Radio Shack**
6901 22d Ave. N
St Petersburg, FL 33710
(813)381-2839
Company Type: Division. **Ultimate Parent:**
Tandy Corp. **SIC:** 5719—Miscellaneous
Home Furnishings Stores.

★ 63027 ★ **Radio Shack**
1879 34th St. N
St Petersburg, FL 33713
(813)327-3740
Company Type: Division. **Ultimate Parent:**
Tandy Corp. **SIC:** 5731—Radio, Television
& Electronics Stores.

★ 63028 ★ **Radio Shack**
7901 Gateway Mall
St Petersburg, FL 33702
(813)577-5959
Company Type: Division. **Ultimate Parent:**
Tandy Corp. **SIC:** 5065—Electronic Parts &
Equipment Nec; 5731—Radio, Television &
Electronics Stores.

★ 63029 ★ **Radio Shack**
7901 9th St. N
St Petersburg, FL 33702
Company Type: Division. **Ultimate Parent:**
Tandy Corp. **SIC:** 7373—Computer
Integrated Systems Design.

★ 63030 ★ **Rite Aid Drugs Store**
6901 22nd Ave. N
St Petersburg, FL 33710
(813)345-9236
Ultimate Parent: Rite Aid. **SIC:** 5912—Drug
Stores & Proprietary Stores.

★ 63031 ★ **Rite Aid Pharmacy**
7201 Seminole Blvd.
St Petersburg, FL 33708
(813)391-9618
Ultimate Parent: Rite Aid. **SIC:** 5912—Drug
Stores & Proprietary Stores.

★ 63032 ★ **Ryder Truck Rental**
1701 5th Ave. N
St Petersburg, FL 33713
(813)443-0635
Ultimate Parent: Ryder System. **SIC:**
7513—Truck Rental & Leasing Without
Drivers.

★ 63033 ★ **Ryder Truck Rental**
401 34th St. S
St Petersburg, FL 33711
(813)323-7883
Ultimate Parent: Ryder System.

★ 63034 ★ **Schwab Charles & Co. Inc.**
1301 66th St. N
St Petersburg, FL 33710
(813)384-4700
Ultimate Parent: Charles Schwab Corp.
SIC: 6211—Security Brokers & Dealers.

★ 63035 ★ **Taco Bell**
5600 66th St. N
St Petersburg, FL 33709
(813)545-1694
Ultimate Parent: Pepsico. **SIC:** 5812—
Eating Places.

★ 63036 ★ **Talquin Corp.**
260 1st Ave. S
St Petersburg, FL 33701
(813)895-1802
Ultimate Parent: Florida Progress. **SIC:**
6531—Real Estate Agents & Managers;
6552—Subdividers & Developers Nec.

★ 63037 ★ **Toys R US**
1900 Tyrone Blvd. N
St Petersburg, FL 33710
(813)347-7272
Ultimate Parent: Toys "R" US. **SIC:** 5945—
Hobby, Toy & Game Shops.

★ 63038 ★ **Trailways Bus System**
105 2nd St. S
St Petersburg, FL 33701
(813)823-3140
Ultimate Parent: Greyhound Lines Inc. **SIC:**
4724—Travel Agencies.

★ 63039 ★ **U S Bancorp Inc.**
1700 66th St. N
St Petersburg, FL 33710
(813)527-5811
Ultimate Parent: U.S. Bancorp. **SIC:**
6022—State Commercial Banks.

★ 63040 ★ **Unisys Corp.**
286 107th Ave.
St Petersburg, FL 33706
(813)360-5838
Ultimate Parent: Unisys Corp. **SIC:** 3579—
Office Machines Nec.

★ 63041 ★ **United Parcel Service**
5700 126th Ave.
St Petersburg, FL 33706
(813)571-8020
Ultimate Parent: United Parcel Service of
America.

★ 63042 ★ **United Parcel Service**
2900 44th Ave. N
St Petersburg, FL 33714
(813)526-0647
Ultimate Parent: United Parcel Service of
America. **SIC:** 4215—Courier Services
Except by Air.

★ 63043 ★ **Walgreen Drug Stores**
5400 9th St. N
St Petersburg, FL 33703
(813)527-7293
Ultimate Parent: Walgreen Co. **SIC:**
5912—Drug Stores & Proprietary Stores.

★ 63044 ★ **Walgreen Drug Stores**
945 62nd Ave. S
St Petersburg, FL 33705
(813)867-2149
Ultimate Parent: Walgreen Co. **SIC:**
5912—Drug Stores & Proprietary Stores.

★ 63045 ★ **Walgreen Drug Stores**
875 9th St. N
St Petersburg, FL 33701
Ultimate Parent: Walgreen Co. **SIC:**
5912—Drug Stores & Proprietary Stores.

★ 63046 ★   **Walgreen Drug Stores**
890 49th St. N
St Petersburg, FL 33710
(813)327-7718
Ultimate Parent: Walgreen Co. SIC: 5912—Drug Stores & Proprietary Stores.

St. Augustine

★ 63047 ★   **Barnett Bank of the St. Johns**
60 Cathedral Pl.
St. Augustine, FL 32084-4418
(904)797-1159
Company Type: Subsidiary. Location Type: Branch office. Officer: Wayne Solana, Senior Vice President. Ultimate Parent: Barnett Banks. SIC: 6022—State Commercial Banks.

★ 63048 ★   **Barnett Bank of the St. Johns**
1600 S. Ponce de Leon Blvd.
St. Augustine, FL 32084-2605
(904)797-1260
Company Type: Subsidiary. Location Type: Branch office. Officer: Meredith W. Colee, Vice President. Ultimate Parent: Barnett Banks. SIC: 6022—State Commercial Banks.

★ 63049 ★   **Barnett Bank of the St. Johns**
500 Anastasia Blvd.
St. Augustine, FL 32084-4511
(904)797-1157
Company Type: Subsidiary. Location Type: Branch office. Officer: Ingrid Guier, Manager. Ultimate Parent: Barnett Banks. SIC: 6022—State Commercial Banks.

★ 63050 ★   **Barnett Bank of the St. Johns**
4305 US Hwy. 1 S
St. Augustine, FL 32086-7278
(904)797-1202
Company Type: Subsidiary. Location Type: Branch office. Officer: Janet Dugger, Manager. Ultimate Parent: Barnett Banks. SIC: 6022—State Commercial Banks.

★ 63051 ★   **Barnett Bank of the St. Johns**
709 Ponce de Leon Blvd.
St. Augustine, FL 32084-4225
(904)797-1123
Company Type: Subsidiary. Location Type: Branch office. Officer: Michael Palmer, Manager. Ultimate Parent: Barnett Banks. SIC: 6022—State Commercial Banks.

★ 63052 ★   **Barnett Bank of the St. Johns**
3750 A1A S
St. Augustine, FL 32084-6725
(904)797-1250
Company Type: Subsidiary. Location Type: Branch office. Officer: Sharil Burney, Manager. Ultimate Parent: Barnett Banks. SIC: 6022—State Commercial Banks.

★ 63053 ★   **Barnett Bank of the St. Johns**
2155 Old Moultrie Rd.
PO Drawer 1929
St. Augustine, FL 32085-1929
(904)797-1100
Company Type: Subsidiary. Location Type: Branch office. Officer: William F. Young, Chairman, President & CEO. Ultimate Parent: Barnett Banks. SIC: 6022—State Commercial Banks.

★ 63054 ★   **Emc**
5255 Porter Road
St. Augustine, FL 32095
(904)824-9709
Ultimate Parent: EMC.

★ 63055 ★   **First Union National Bank of Florida**
1919 US Hwy. 1 S. & State Rd. 312
St. Augustine, FL 32084
(904)824-7550
Location Type: Branch office. Ultimate Parent: First Union Corp. SIC: 6021—National Commercial Banks.

★ 63056 ★   **First Union National Bank of Florida**
4285 US Hwy. 1
St. Augustine, FL 32084-7096
(904)824-7542
Location Type: Branch office. Ultimate Parent: First Union Corp. SIC: 6021—National Commercial Banks.

★ 63057 ★   **First Union National Bank of Florida**
24 Cathedral Pl.
St. Augustine, FL 32084
(904)824-7500
Location Type: Branch office. Ultimate Parent: First Union Corp. SIC: 6021—National Commercial Banks.

★ 63058 ★   **Grumman Corp. St. Augustine**
5000 U.S. Hwy. 1 N.
St. Augustine, FL 32095
Ultimate Parent: Grumman. SIC: 3721—Aircraft.

★ 63059 ★   **Grumman St. Augustine Corp.**
5000 U. S. 1 N.
St. Augustine, FL 32095
Ultimate Parent: Grumman. SIC: 3721—Aircraft.

★ 63060 ★   **Grumman St. Augustine Corp.**
5000 N. U.S. Hwy. 1
St. Augustine, FL 32085-3447
Ultimate Parent: Grumman. SIC: 3721—Aircraft.

★ 63061 ★   **Grumman St. Augustine Corp.**
5000 US Hwy. 1 N.
St. Augustine, FL 32095-6200
(904)825-3300
Company Type: Subsidiary. Ultimate Parent: Grumman. SIC: 3728—Aircraft Parts & Equipment Nec. Employee Count: 1100. Sales: 80 M.

★ 63062 ★   **Kentucky Fried Chicken**
1805 Mart Plz.
St. Augustine, FL 32086
(904)829-6019
Ultimate Parent: Pepsico. SIC: 5812—Eating Places.

★ 63063 ★   **Wise Foods**
4455 Ave. A
St. Augustine, FL 32095
(904)829-9085
Officer: Frank Pamies, Manager. Ultimate Parent: Borden, Inc. SIC: 2099—Food Preparations Nec.

St. Augustine Beach

★ 63064 ★   **Anchor Savings Bank, FSB**
1965 State Rd. 3
St. Augustine Beach, FL 32084-6509
(904)471-2424
Location Type: Branch office. Officer: Keith Couchman, Assistant Treasurer. Ultimate Parent: Anchor Bancorp. SIC: 6021—National Commercial Banks; 6035—Federal Savings Institutions; 6211—Security Brokers & Dealers.

St. Cloud

★ 63065 ★   **Barnett Bank of Central Florida, NA**
4300 W. 13th St.
St. Cloud, FL 34769-6700
(407)892-2009
Company Type: Subsidiary. Location Type: Branch office. Officer: Sean Bower, Manager. Ultimate Parent: Barnett Banks. SIC: 6021—National Commercial Banks.

★ 63066 ★   **Kentucky Fried Chicken**
2733 13th St.
St. Cloud, FL 34769
(407)892-6650
Ultimate Parent: Pepsico. SIC: 5812—Eating Places.

★ 63067 ★   **Mercury Marine**
1000 Robinson Ave.
St. Cloud, FL 34769
(407)892-2121
Officer: Larry Rink, Manager. Ultimate Parent: Brunswick Corp. SIC: 3089—Plastics Products Nec; 3679—Electronic Components Nec; 3732—Boat Building & Repairing.

★ 63068 ★   **Mercury Marine Plant 7**
1000 Robinson Ave.
St. Cloud, FL 34769
Ultimate Parent: Brunswick Corp. SIC: 3679—Electronic Components Nec; 3089—Plastics Products Nec.

★ 63069 ★   **Pizza Hut**
2818 13th St.
St. Cloud, FL 34769
(407)892-2110
Ultimate Parent: Pepsico. SIC: 5812—Eating Places.

★ 63070 ★   **Publix Super Market**
4049 13th St.
St. Cloud, FL 34769
(407)957-1334
Ultimate Parent: Publix Super Markets. SIC: 5411—Grocery Stores.

★ 63071 ★   **Wal Mart**
4271 13th St.
St. Cloud, FL 34769
(407)957-4343
Ultimate Parent: Wal-Mart Stores, Inc. SIC: 5311—Department Stores.

St. Marks

★ 63072 ★   **Olin Corp.**
Hwy. 98 & State Rd. 363
St. Marks, FL 32355
(904)925-6111
Officer: D. E. Findley, Executive Director. Ultimate Parent: Olin Corp. SIC: 2819—Industrial Inorganic Chemicals Nec; 3823—Process Control Instruments.

★ 63073 ★   **Olin Corp.**
US 98 & State Rte. 363
St. Marks, FL 32355-0222
Ultimate Parent: Olin Corp. SIC: 2892—Explosives.

St. Peterburg

★ 63074 ★   **California Federal Bank, FSB**
5275 34th St. S.
St. Peterburg, FL 33711-4517
(813)864-1553
Location Type: Branch office. Ultimate Parent: California Federal Bank. SIC: 6021—National Commercial Banks.

St. Petersburg

★ 63075 ★   **Ace Hardware**
Crossroads Shopping Ctr.
St. Petersburg, FL 33710
(813)345-9341
Ultimate Parent: Ace Hardware. SIC: 5251—Hardware Stores.

★ 63076 ★   **AmSouth Bank of Florida**
6025 4th St. N
St. Petersburg, FL 33703-1419
(813)462-5103
Location Type: Branch office. Ultimate Parent: AmSouth Bancorp. SIC: 6022—State Commercial Banks.

★ 63077 ★   **AmSouth Bank of Florida**
3399 66th St. N
St. Petersburg, FL 33710
(813)462-5104
Location Type: Branch office. Ultimate Parent: AmSouth Bancorp. SIC: 6022—State Commercial Banks.

★ 63078 ★   **AmSouth Bank of Florida**
5901 Sun Blvd.
St. Petersburg, FL 33715-1160
(813)462-5102
Location Type: Branch office. Ultimate Parent: AmSouth Bancorp. SIC: 6022—State Commercial Banks.

★ 63079 ★   **Anchor Savings Bank**
7301 9th St. N.
St. Petersburg, FL 33702-5201
(813)522-7775
Location Type: Branch office. Officer: Rick Dizilinski. Ultimate Parent: Anchor Bancorp. SIC: 6021—National Commercial Banks; 6022—State Commercial Banks.

★ 63080 ★   **Anchor Savings Bank**
6850 Central Ave.
St. Petersburg, FL 33707-1211
(813)347-7283
Location Type: Branch office. Officer: Lloyd D. Lance, President. Ultimate Parent: Anchor Bancorp. SIC: 6035—Federal Savings Institutions; 6159—Miscellaneous Business Credit Institutions; 6036—Savings Institutions Except Federal. Employee Count: 40.

★ 63081 ★   **Arnet Computer**
3247 Tech Dr. N
St. Petersburg, FL 33716
(813)573-5524
Location Type: Branch office. Ultimate Parent: Avnet. SIC: 5044—Office Equipment; 7379—Computer Related Services Nec.

★ 63082 ★   **Barnett Bank of Pinellas County**
2145 34th St. N
St. Petersburg, FL 33713-3609
(813)892-1201
Company Type: Subsidiary. Location Type: Branch office. Officer: Bijan Helalet, Manager. Ultimate Parent: Barnett Banks. SIC: 6022—State Commercial Banks.

★ 63083 ★   **Barnett Bank of Pinellas County**
2116 4th St. N
St. Petersburg, FL 33704-4312
(813)892-1175
Company Type: Subsidiary. Location Type: Branch office. Officer: Mary Jones, Manager. Ultimate Parent: Barnett Banks. SIC: 6022—State Commercial Banks.

★ 63084 ★   **Barnett Bank of Pinellas County**
1135 62nd Ave. N
St. Petersburg, FL 33702-7497
(813)892-1215
Company Type: Subsidiary. Location Type: Branch office. Officer: Myra Shipman, Manager. Ultimate Parent: Barnett Banks. SIC: 6022—State Commercial Banks.

★ 63085 ★   **Barnett Bank of Pinellas County**
2800 54th Ave. S
St. Petersburg, FL 33712-4610
(813)892-1131
Company Type: Subsidiary. Location Type: Branch office. Officer: Claudia Johnson, Vice President. Ultimate Parent: Barnett Banks. SIC: 6022—State Commercial Banks.

★ 63086 ★   **Barnett Bank of Pinellas County**
666 6th St. S
St. Petersburg, FL 33701
(813)892-1110
Company Type: Subsidiary. Location Type: Branch office. Officer: Nancy Johnson, Manager. Ultimate Parent: Barnett Banks. SIC: 6022—State Commercial Banks.

★ 63087 ★   **Barnett Bank of Pinellas County**
2808 58th St. S
St. Petersburg, FL 33707-5305
(813)892-1645
Company Type: Subsidiary. Location Type: Branch office. Officer: Pamela Schumacher, Manager. Ultimate Parent: Barnett Banks. SIC: 6022—State Commercial Banks.

★ 63088 ★   **Barnett Bank of Pinellas County**
5701 38th Ave. N
St. Petersburg, FL 33710-1996
(813)892-1608
Company Type: Subsidiary. Location Type: Branch office. Officer: Dorothy Tadder, Manager. Ultimate Parent: Barnett Banks. SIC: 6022—State Commercial Banks.

★ 63089 ★ Barnett Bank of
Pinellas County
1300 66th St. S
St. Petersburg, FL 33710-5594
(813)892-1114
Company Type: Subsidiary. Location
Type: Branch office. Officer: Jeanie
Benfield, Manager. Ultimate Parent:
Barnett Banks. SIC: 6022—State
Commercial Banks.

★ 63090 ★ Barnett Bank of
Pinellas County
3100 Central Ave.
St. Petersburg, FL 33712-1095
(813)892-1100
Company Type: Subsidiary. Location
Type: Branch office. Officer: Mark Raible,
Vice President. Ultimate Parent: Barnett
Banks. SIC: 6022—State Commercial
Banks.

★ 63091 ★ Barnett Bank of
Pinellas County
4250 6th St. S
St. Petersburg, FL 33705-4499
(813)892-1636
Company Type: Subsidiary. Location
Type: Branch office. Officer: Lee Johnson,
Manager. Ultimate Parent: Barnett Banks.
SIC: 6022—State Commercial Banks.

★ 63092 ★ Barnett Bank of
Pinellas County
301 38th Ave. N
St. Petersburg, FL 33704-1393
(813)892-1182
Company Type: Subsidiary. Location
Type: Branch office. Officer: Linda Garner,
Manager. Ultimate Parent: Barnett Banks.
SIC: 6022—State Commercial Banks.

★ 63093 ★ Barnett Bank of
Pinellas County
6100 4th St. N
St. Petersburg, FL 33703-1498
(813)892-1192
Company Type: Subsidiary. Location
Type: Branch office. Officer: Tish
McQuillen, Manager. Ultimate Parent:
Barnett Banks. SIC: 6022—State
Commercial Banks.

★ 63094 ★ Barnett Bank of
Pinellas County
8181 54th Ave. N
St. Petersburg, FL 33709-1095
(813)892-1626
Company Type: Subsidiary. Location
Type: Branch office. Officer: Frank
Buetzow, Manager. Ultimate Parent:
Barnett Banks. SIC: 6022—State
Commercial Banks.

★ 63095 ★ Barnett Bank of
Pinellas County
200 Central Ave.
PO Box 12288
St. Petersburg, FL 33733-2288
(813)892-1703 Fax: (813)823-7023
Company Type: Subsidiary. Location
Type: Branch office. Officer: Stephen G.
Zahorian, President & CEO. Ultimate
Parent: Barnett Banks. SIC: 6022—State
Commercial Banks.

★ 63096 ★ Barnett Bank of
Pinellas County
6201 Central Ave.
St. Petersburg, FL 33710-8431
(813)892-1618
Company Type: Subsidiary. Location
Type: Branch office. Officer: Sherri
Teague, Manager. Ultimate Parent: Barnett
Banks. SIC: 6022—State Commercial
Banks.

★ 63097 ★ Chase Manhatten
Bank of Florida, NA
240 1st Ave. S
St. Petersburg, FL 33701-4306
(813)894-0202
Location Type: Branch office. Officer:
Michael Brown, Manager. Ultimate Parent:
Chase Manhattan Corp. SIC: 6021—
National Commercial Banks.

★ 63098 ★ Citizens Federal
Bank, FSB
5505 Park St. N.
St. Petersburg, FL 33709-6319
(813)545-8777
Location Type: Branch office. Officer:
Peggy Rooney, Manager. Ultimate Parent:

CSF Holdings. SIC: 6021—National
Commercial Banks.

★ 63099 ★ E-Systems
ECI Div.
1501 72nd St. N
St. Petersburg, FL 33710
(813)381-2000
Company Type: Division. Officer: Terry
Heil, Manager. Ultimate Parent: E-Systems
Inc. SIC: 3663—Radio & T.V.
Communications Equipment; 3669—
Communications Equipment Nec.

★ 63100 ★ E-Systems Inc.
C. M. Div.
2501 72nd St. N
St. Petersburg, FL 33710
Company Type: Division. Ultimate Parent:
E-Systems Inc. SIC: 3663—Radio & T.V.
Communications Equipment.

★ 63101 ★ E-Systems Inc.
C.M. Div.
7400 22nd Ave. N
St. Petersburg, FL 33710
Company Type: Division. Ultimate Parent:
E-Systems Inc. SIC: 3663—Radio & T.V.
Communications Equipment.

★ 63102 ★ E-Systems Inc.
ECI Div.
1501 72nd St. N.
St. Petersburg, FL 33710
Company Type: Division. Ultimate Parent:
E-Systems Inc. SIC: 3663—Radio & T.V.
Communications Equipment.

★ 63103 ★ E-Systems Inc.
ECI Division
1501 72nd St. N
POB 12448
St. Petersburg, FL 33733-2248
(813)381-2000 Fax: (813)343-1295
Company Type: Subsidiary. Officer: James
C. Garrett, Vice President/General Manager.
Ultimate Parent: E-Systems Inc.

★ 63104 ★ Electric Fuels Corp.
PO Box 15208
St. Petersburg, FL 33733
(813)824-6600 Fax: (813)824-6601
Company Type: Subsidiary. Officer:
Richard D. Keller, President:CEO. Ultimate
Parent: Florida Progress.

★ 63105 ★ First of America
1065 N. 58th St.
St. Petersburg, FL 33710
(813)384-3310
Location Type: Branch office. Ultimate
Parent: First of America Bank Corp. SIC:
6021—National Commercial Banks.

★ 63106 ★ First of America Bank
5901 Sun Boulevard
St. Petersburg, FL 33715
(813)864-1852
Location Type: Branch office. Ultimate
Parent: First of America Bank Corp. SIC:
6021—National Commercial Banks.

★ 63107 ★ First of America Bank
2100 N. 66th St.
St. Petersburg, FL 33710
Location Type: Branch office. Ultimate
Parent: First of America Bank Corp. SIC:
6021—National Commercial Banks.

★ 63108 ★ First Union National
Bank of Florida
3805 Gulf Blvd.
St. Petersburg, FL 33706-3951
(813)892-7470
Location Type: Branch office. Ultimate
Parent: First Union Corp. SIC: 6021—
National Commercial Banks.

★ 63109 ★ First Union National
Bank of Florida
3095 54th Ave. S.
St. Petersburg, FL 33712-4613
(813)892-2034
Location Type: Branch office. Ultimate
Parent: First Union Corp. SIC: 6021—
National Commercial Banks.

★ 63110 ★ First Union National
Bank of Florida
1000 Tyrone Blvd.
St. Petersburg, FL 33710-6300
(813)892-7441
Location Type: Branch office. Ultimate
Parent: First Union Corp. SIC: 6021—
National Commercial Banks.

★ 63111 ★ First Union National
Bank of Florida
410 Central Ave.
St. Petersburg, FL 33701-3809
(813)892-7100
Location Type: Branch office. Ultimate
Parent: First Union Corp. SIC: 6021—
National Commercial Banks.

★ 63112 ★ First Union National
Bank of Florida
3637 4th St. N
St. Petersburg, FL 33704-1335
(813)892-2029
Location Type: Branch office. Ultimate
Parent: First Union Corp. SIC: 6021—
National Commercial Banks.

★ 63113 ★ First Union National
Bank of Florida
9655 4th St. N
St. Petersburg, FL 33702-2528
(813)892-7409
Location Type: Branch office. Ultimate
Parent: First Union Corp. SIC: 6021—
National Commercial Banks.

★ 63114 ★ First Union National
Bank of Florida
3131 66th St. N.
St. Petersburg, FL 33710-3115
(813)892-7433
Location Type: Branch office. Ultimate
Parent: First Union Corp. SIC: 6021—
National Commercial Banks.

★ 63115 ★ Florida Power Corp.
3201 34th St.
St. Petersburg, FL 33713
(813)866-5151 Fax: (813)866-4390
Company Type: Subsidiary. Officer: Allen
J. Keesler Jr., President:CEO. Ultimate
Parent: Florida Progress.

★ 63116 ★ Florida Progress
1 Progress Plaza
St. Petersburg, FL 33701
(813)824-6400
Company Type: Headquarters. Officer:
Jack B. Critchfield. Fortune Service 500:
Ranking 42.

★ 63117 ★ Florida Progress
Corp.
1 Progress Plz.
St. Petersburg, FL 33701
(813)824-6400 Fax: (813)824-6536
Company Type: Headquarters. Officer:
Jack B. Critchfield, Chariman:CEO.
Ultimate Parent: Florida Progress.
Employee Count: 7826. Sales:
Exceed5Billion M.

★ 63118 ★ Fortuen Bank, SB
903 Tyrone Blvd. N
St. Petersburg, FL 33710-6332
(813)345-8633
Location Type: Branch office. Officer: Paul
Appleby, Manager. Ultimate Parent:
Fortune Bancorp. SIC: 6021—National
Commercial Banks.

★ 63119 ★ Fortune Bank, SB
3463 22nd Ave. N
St. Petersburg, FL 33713-3654
(813)321-9205
Location Type: Branch office. Ultimate
Parent: Fortune Bancorp. SIC: 6021—
National Commercial Banks.

★ 63120 ★ Fortune Bank, SB
3505 4th St. N
St. Petersburg, FL 33704
(813)822-6454
Location Type: Branch office. Officer:
Nancy Yost, Manager. Ultimate Parent:
Fortune Bancorp. SIC: 6021—National
Commercial Banks.

★ 63121 ★ Fortune Bank, SB
6901 22nd Ave. N
St. Petersburg, FL 33710-3930
(813)345-7411
Location Type: Branch office. Officer:
Linda Reid, Manager. Ultimate Parent:
Fortune Bancorp. SIC: 6021—National
Commercial Banks.

★ 63122 ★ Fortune Bank, SB
2240 62nd Ave. S
St. Petersburg, FL 33712-5347
(813)864-1556
Location Type: Branch office. Officer:
Susan Klemme, Manager. Ultimate Parent:

Fortune Bancorp. SIC: 6021—National
Commercial Banks.

★ 63123 ★ Fortune Bank, SB
260 1st Ave. S
St. Petersburg, FL 33701-4307
(813)895-2885
Location Type: Branch office. Ultimate
Parent: Fortune Bancorp. SIC: 6021—
National Commercial Banks.

★ 63124 ★ Fortune Bank, SB
8250 9th St. N
St. Petersburg, FL 33702-4115
(813)576-1194
Location Type: Branch office. Officer:
Helen Papolas, Manager. Ultimate Parent:
Fortune Bancorp. SIC: 6021—National
Commercial Banks.

★ 63125 ★ Fortune Bank, SB
6800 Gulfport Blvd., Ste. 101
St. Petersburg, FL 33707-2194
(813)384-3166
Location Type: Branch office. Ultimate
Parent: Fortune Bancorp. SIC: 6021—
National Commercial Banks.

★ 63126 ★ Honeywell Inc.
11601 Roosevelt Blvd.
St. Petersburg, FL 33716
Ultimate Parent: Honeywell. SIC: 3812—
Search & Navigation Equipment.

★ 63127 ★ Leeds & Northrup
Instruments
3000 Old Roosevelt Blvd.
St. Petersburg, FL 33716
(813)573-1155
Officer: Rick Pohlman, Manager. Ultimate
Parent: General Signal. SIC: 3823—
Process Control Instruments.

★ 63128 ★ Molex-Etc Inc.
2375 72nd St. N
St. Petersburg, FL 33710
Ultimate Parent: Molex. SIC: 3678—
Electronic Connectors.

★ 63129 ★ Olin Ordance Div.
10101 9th St. N
St. Petersburg, FL 33716
(813)578-8100 Fax: (813)578-8119
Officer: Angelo A. Catani, President.
Ultimate Parent: Olin Corp.

★ 63130 ★ Progress Credit Corp.
PO Box 33042
St. Petersburg, FL 33733
(813)824-6760 Fax: (813)824-6536
Company Type: Subsidiary. Officer: Darryl
A. Le Clair, President. Ultimate Parent:
Florida Progress.

★ 63131 ★ Publix Super Markets
5295 34th St. S
St. Petersburg, FL 33711
(813)864-4250
Ultimate Parent: Publix Super Markets.
SIC: 5461—Retail Bakeries; 5411—Grocery
Stores.

★ 63132 ★ RFD Inc.
11300 9th St. North
St. Petersburg, FL 33716
Ultimate Parent: Sequa Corp. SIC: 3663—
Radio & T.V. Communications Equipment.

★ 63133 ★ Savings of America
Home Savings of America, FSB
4100 4th St. N
St. Petersburg, FL 33703-5700
(813)521-5700
Location Type: Branch office. Officer:
Beverly McCutcheon, Mgr. Ultimate Parent:
H.F. Ahmanson. SIC: 6021—National
Commercial Banks.

★ 63134 ★ Sparkletts Water Sys.
Aqua Vend
4059 7th Terrace S.
St. Petersburg, FL 33711
Ultimate Parent: McKesson. SIC: 7389—
Business Services Nec.

★ 63135 ★ Sparkletts Water
Systems Aquavend
4059 Seventh Terrace S.
St. Petersburg, FL 33711
Ultimate Parent: McKesson. SIC: 7389—
Business Services Nec.

★ 63136 ★ Sparkletts Water
Sytems Aqua Vend
4059 Seventh Terrace S.
St. Petersburg, FL 33711
Ultimate Parent: McKesson. SIC: 7389—
Business Services Nec.

★ 63137 ★ Walgreen
674 Welch Causeway
St. Petersburg, FL 33708
(813)391-9795
Ultimate Parent: Walgreen Co. SIC:
5999—Miscellaneous Retail Stores Nec.

St. Petersburg Beach

★ 63138 ★ Barnett Bank of
Pinellas County
7500 Gulf Blvd.
St. Petersburg Beach, FL 33706-1810
(813)892-1172
Company Type: Subsidiary. Location
Type: Branch office. Officer: Joann Cahill,
Manager. Ultimate Parent: Barnett Banks.
SIC: 6022—State Commercial Banks.

★ 63139 ★ Barnett Bank of
Pinellas County
4105 Gulf Blvd.
St. Petersburg Beach, FL 33706-3826
(813)539-1267
Company Type: Subsidiary. Location
Type: Branch office. Officer: Dean Dancer,
Manager. Ultimate Parent: Barnett Banks.
SIC: 6022—State Commercial Banks.

★ 63140 ★ First Union National
Bank of Florida
400 Corey Ave.
St. Petersburg Beach, FL 33706-1969
(813)892-2018
Location Type: Branch office. Ultimate
Parent: First Union Corp. SIC: 6021—
National Commercial Banks.

★ 63141 ★ Fortune Bank, ASB
4811 Gulf Blvd.
St. Petersburg Beach, FL 33706-2481
(813)367-7891
Location Type: Branch office. Officer:
Diana Hathaway, Manager. Ultimate
Parent: Fortune Bancorp. SIC: 6021—
National Commercial Banks.

Starke

★ 63142 ★ Ace Hardware &
Garden Cente
1101 S. Walnut St.
Starke, FL 32091
(904)964-4642
Ultimate Parent: Ace Hardware. SIC:
5251—Hardware Stores.

★ 63143 ★ First Union National
Bank of Florida
105 W. Jefferson St.
Starke, FL 32091-3218
(904)964-7050
Location Type: Branch office. Ultimate
Parent: First Union Corp. SIC: 6021—
National Commercial Banks.

★ 63144 ★ First Union National
Bank of Florida
841 S. Walnut St.
Starke, FL 32091-4401
(904)964-7050
Location Type: Branch office. Ultimate
Parent: First Union Corp. SIC: 6021—
National Commercial Banks.

★ 63145 ★ Food Lion
1475 S. Walnut St.
Starke, FL 32091
(904)964-3771
Ultimate Parent: Food Lion. SIC: 5411—
Grocery Stores.

★ 63146 ★ Greyhound Bus Lines
238 E. Washington St.
Starke, FL 32091
(904)964-6090
Ultimate Parent: Greyhound Lines Inc. SIC:
4111—Local & Suburban Transit; 4173—
Bus Terminal & Service Facilities.

★ 63147 ★ Greyhound Bus
Station
1475 S. Walnut St.
Starke, FL 32091
(904)964-8787
Ultimate Parent: Greyhound Lines Inc. SIC:
4131—Intercity & Rural Bus Transportation.

★ 63148 ★ Kentucky Fried
Chicken
1595 N. Temple Ave.
Starke, FL 32091
(904)964-5126
Ultimate Parent: Pepsico. SIC: 5812—
Eating Places.

★ 63149 ★ Mary Kay Cosmetic
Indpnt Sl
819 S. Walnut St.
Starke, FL 32091
(904)964-7882
Ultimate Parent: Mary Kay Cosmetics. SIC:
5999—Miscellaneous Retail Stores Nec.

★ 63150 ★ Pizza Hut
915 N. Temple Ave.
Starke, FL 32091
(904)964-8700
Ultimate Parent: Pepsico. SIC: 5812—
Eating Places.

★ 63151 ★ Shell Oil Co.
213 S. Cherry St.
Starke, FL 32091
(904)964-7022
Ultimate Parent: Shell Oil Co. SIC: 5983—
Fuel Oil Dealers.

★ 63152 ★ Taco Bell
840 S. Walnut St.
Starke, FL 32091
(904)964-3883
Ultimate Parent: Pepsico. SIC: 5812—
Eating Places.

★ 63153 ★ Texaco Food Mart
210 S. Temple Ave.
Starke, FL 32091
(904)964-2368
Ultimate Parent: Texaco. SIC: 5411—
Grocery Stores.

★ 63154 ★ Wal Mart
1371 S. Walnut St.
Starke, FL 32091
(904)964-3286
Ultimate Parent: Wal-Mart Stores, Inc. SIC:
5399—Miscellaneous General Merchandise
Store.

Stuart

★ 63155 ★ Barnett Bank of
Martin County, NA
3727 SE Ocean Blvd.
Stuart, FL 34996-6738
(407)288-9625
Company Type: Subsidiary. Location
Type: Branch office. Officer: Wade
Jacobson, Manager. Ultimate Parent:
Barnett Banks. SIC: 6021—National
Commercial Banks.

★ 63156 ★ Barnett Bank of
Martin County, NA
900 S. Federal Hwy.
Stuart, FL 34994-3733
(407)288-9655
Company Type: Subsidiary. Location
Type: Branch office. Officer: Karen
Pachete, Manager. Ultimate Parent:
Barnett Banks. SIC: 6021—National
Commercial Banks.

★ 63157 ★ Barnett Bank of
Martin County, NA
1991 S. Federal Hwy.
Stuart, FL 34994-3915
(407)288-9645
Company Type: Subsidiary. Location
Type: Branch office. Officer: Jane Rollins,
Manager. Ultimate Parent: Barnett Banks.
SIC: 6021—National Commercial Banks.

★ 63158 ★ Barnett Bank of
Martin County, NA
1778 NE Jensen Beach Blvd.
Stuart, FL 34957
(407)288-9685
Company Type: Subsidiary. Location
Type: Branch office. Officer: George Haley,
Manager. Ultimate Parent: Barnett Banks.
SIC: 6021—National Commercial Banks.

★ 63159 ★ Barnett Bank of
Martin County, NA
1010 NW Federal Hwy.
Stuart, FL 34994-1021
(407)288-9665
Company Type: Subsidiary. Location
Type: Branch office. Officer: Pam
Applegate, Manager. Ultimate Parent:
Barnett Banks. SIC: 6021—National
Commercial Banks.

★ 63160 ★ Barnett Bank of
Martin County, NA
5805 SE Federal Hwy.
Stuart, FL 34997-7869
(407)288-9635
Company Type: Subsidiary. Location
Type: Branch office. Officer: Patricia
Montanez, Manager. Ultimate Parent:
Barnett Banks. SIC: 6021—National
Commercial Banks.

★ 63161 ★ Casual Corner
3444 S. Federal Hwy.
Stuart, FL 34997
(407)692-0290
Ultimate Parent: United States Shoe. SIC:
5651—Family Clothing Stores.

★ 63162 ★ First National Bank &
Trust
4392 NE Ocean Blvd.
Stuart, FL 34996
(407)287-4000
Ultimate Parent: Society Corp. SIC: 6022—
State Commercial Banks.

★ 63163 ★ First Union National
Bank of Florida
5547 SE Federal Hwy.
Stuart, FL 34997-6641
(407)221-4570
Location Type: Branch office. Ultimate
Parent: First Union Corp. SIC: 6021—
National Commercial Banks.

★ 63164 ★ First Union National
Bank of Florida
200 SW Monterey Rd.
Stuart, FL 34994-4697
(407)221-4510
Location Type: Branch office. Ultimate
Parent: First Union Corp. SIC: 6021—
National Commercial Banks.

★ 63165 ★ First Union National
Bank of Florida
595 NE Ocean Blvd.
Stuart, FL 34996-1697
(407)221-4530
Location Type: Branch office. Ultimate
Parent: First Union Corp. SIC: 6021—
National Commercial Banks.

★ 63166 ★ First Union National
Bank of Florida
301 E. Ocean Blvd.
Stuart, FL 34994-2236
(407)221-4400
Location Type: Branch office. Ultimate
Parent: First Union Corp. SIC: 6021—
National Commercial Banks.

★ 63167 ★ Foot Action U S a
3020 S. Federal Hwy.
Stuart, FL 34994
(407)692-0063
Ultimate Parent: Melville. SIC: 5661—Shoe
Stores.

★ 63168 ★ Great Western Bank
2101 E. Ocean Blvd.
Stuart, FL 34996
(407)283-7560
Ultimate Parent: Great Western Financial
Corp. SIC: 6099—Functions Related to
Deposit Banking.

★ 63169 ★ Greyhound Bus Depot
757 SE Monterey Rd.
Stuart, FL 34994
(407)287-7777
Ultimate Parent: Greyhound Lines Inc. SIC:
4173—Bus Terminal & Service Facilities.

★ 63170 ★ Grumman Corp.
Aircraft Systems Div.
Witham Field
Stuart, FL 34995
Company Type: Division. Ultimate Parent:
Grumman. SIC: 3721—Aircraft.

★ 63171 ★ Hertz Rent-A-Car
3089 SE Dixie Hwy.
Stuart, FL 34997
(407)287-2120
Ultimate Parent: Hertz. SIC: 7514—
Passenger Car Rental.

★ 63172 ★ Lane Bryant
3240 S. Federal Hwy.
Stuart, FL 34997
(407)692-1379
Ultimate Parent: Limited. SIC: 5651—
Family Clothing Stores.

★ 63173 ★ Lerner Shop
3158 S. Federal Hwy.
Stuart, FL 34994
(407)692-1575
Ultimate Parent: Limited. SIC: 5651—
Family Clothing Stores.

★ 63174 ★ The Limited
3166 S. Federal Hwy.
Stuart, FL 34994
(407)692-1300
Ultimate Parent: Limited. SIC: 5651—
Family Clothing Stores.

★ 63175 ★ The Limited Express
3162 S. Federal Hwy.
Stuart, FL 34994
(407)692-2338
Ultimate Parent: Limited. SIC: 5651—
Family Clothing Stores.

★ 63176 ★ Petite Sophisticate
3228 S. Federal Hwy.
Stuart, FL 34997
(407)692-2703
Ultimate Parent: United States Shoe. SIC:
5651—Family Clothing Stores.

★ 63177 ★ Pizza Hut
1540 S. Federal Hwy.
Stuart, FL 34994
Ultimate Parent: Pepsico. SIC: 5812—
Eating Places.

★ 63178 ★ Ryder Truck Rental
1219 Dixie Cut Off Rd.
Stuart, FL 34994
(407)286-2224
Ultimate Parent: Ryder System. SIC:
7513—Truck Rental & Leasing Without
Drivers.

★ 63179 ★ Shawmut National
Trust Co.
819 S. Federal Hwy.
Stuart, FL 34994-2938
(407)283-6404 Fax: (407)286-1649
Location Type: Branch office. Officer:
Luther H. Hodge, Pres & CEO. Ultimate
Parent: Shawmut National Corp. SIC:
6021—National Commercial Banks.

★ 63180 ★ This End Up Furniture
Co.
3308 S. Federal Hwy.
Stuart, FL 34997
(407)692-9457
Ultimate Parent: Melville. SIC: 5712—
Furniture Stores.

★ 63181 ★ Victoria's Secret
3080 S. Federal Hwy.
Stuart, FL 34994
(407)692-2196
Ultimate Parent: Limited. SIC: 5651—
Family Clothing Stores.

★ 63182 ★ Waldenbooks
3152 S. Federal Hwy.
Stuart, FL 34994
(407)692-9615
Ultimate Parent: K-Mart. SIC: 5942—Book
Stores.

★ 63183 ★ Walgreen Drug Stores
2300 SE Ocean Blvd.
Stuart, FL 34996
(407)283-0991
Ultimate Parent: Walgreen Co. SIC:
5912—Drug Stores & Proprietary Stores;
5921—Liquor Stores.

Summerland Key

★ 63184 ★ Barnett Bank of the Keys
US 1 & Westshore Dr.
Summerland Key, FL 33042-9543
(305)292-3902
Company Type: Subsidiary. **Location Type:** Branch office. **Officer:** Debra LeBlanc, Manager. **Ultimate Parent:** Barnett Banks. **SIC:** 6022—State Commercial Banks.

Sun City

★ 63185 ★ Citizens Federal Bank, FSB
102 S. Pebble Blvd.
Sun City, FL 33573-5719
(813)634-5594
Location Type: Branch office. **Officer:** Karin Graziano, Manager. **Ultimate Parent:** CSF Holdings. **SIC:** 6021—National Commercial Banks.

Sun City Center

★ 63186 ★ Barnett Bank of Tampa
902 Pebble Beach Blvd.
Sun City Center, FL 33573-5336
(813)634-9239
Company Type: Subsidiary. **Location Type:** Branch office. **Officer:** John Cregier, Vice President. **Ultimate Parent:** Barnett Banks. **SIC:** 6022—State Commercial Banks.

★ 63187 ★ First Union National Bank of Florida
1502 Sun City Ctr. Plz.
Sun City Center, FL 33573-5304
(813)633-2228
Location Type: Branch office. **Ultimate Parent:** First Union Corp. **SIC:** 6021—National Commercial Banks.

Sunrise

★ 63188 ★ American Savings of Florida
5581 W. Oakland Park Blvd.
Sunrise, FL 33313
(305)485-0207
Ultimate Parent: American Savings of Florida. **SIC:** 6099—Functions Related to Deposit Banking.

★ 63189 ★ American Savings of Florida, FSB
3001 N. University Dr.
Sunrise, FL 33322-1610
(305)741-3606
Location Type: Branch office. **Officer:** Al Lettera, Manager. **Ultimate Parent:** American Savings of Florida. **SIC:** 6035—Federal Savings Institutions; 6211—Security Brokers & Dealers.

★ 63190 ★ American Savings of Florida, FSB
10077 W. Oakland Park Blvd.
Sunrise, FL 33351-6119
(305)748-5222
Location Type: Branch office. **Officer:** Marie Monte, Manager. **Ultimate Parent:** American Savings of Florida. **SIC:** 6035—Federal Savings Institutions; 6211—Security Brokers & Dealers.

★ 63191 ★ Barnett Bank of Broward County, NA
10001 W. Oakland Park Blvd.
Sunrise, FL 33351-6927
(305)742-2602
Company Type: Subsidiary. **Location Type:** Branch office. **Officer:** Jeanne McIntyre, Vice President. **Ultimate Parent:** Barnett Banks. **SIC:** 6021—National Commercial Banks.

★ 63192 ★ California Federal Bank, FSB
3000 N. University Dr.
Sunrise, FL 33322
(305)741-1400
Location Type: Branch office. **Ultimate Parent:** California Federal Bank. **SIC:** 6021—National Commercial Banks.

★ 63193 ★ First Union National Bank of Florida
11 Weston Rd.
Sunrise, FL 33326-1110
(305)384-8400
Location Type: Branch office. **Ultimate Parent:** First Union Corp.

★ 63194 ★ Gribetz International, Inc.
13800 N.W. 4th St.
Sunrise, FL 33325
(305)846-0300 **Fax:** (305)846-0381
Officer: Michael Gribetz, Chairman. **Ultimate Parent:** Leggett & Platt Inc.

★ 63195 ★ Pizza Hut
2934 N. State Rd. 7
Sunrise, FL 33313
(305)484-1330
Ultimate Parent: Pepsico. **SIC:** 5812—Eating Places.

★ 63196 ★ Publix Super Market
6041 W. Sunrise Blvd.
Sunrise, FL 33313
(305)581-4393
Ultimate Parent: Publix Super Markets. **SIC:** 5411—Grocery Stores.

★ 63197 ★ Publix Super Markets
6041 W. Sunrise Blvd.
Sunrise, FL 33313
(305)581-4393
Ultimate Parent: Publix Super Markets. **SIC:** 5411—Grocery Stores.

★ 63198 ★ Rite Aid Discount Pharmacie
6033 W. Sunrise Blvd.
Sunrise, FL 33313
(305)584-0767
Ultimate Parent: Rite Aid. **SIC:** 5912—Drug Stores & Proprietary Stores.

★ 63199 ★ Savings of America
Home Savings of America, FSB
2300 N. University Dr.
Sunrise, FL 33322-3098
(305)741-8100
Location Type: Branch office. **Officer:** Mike Cannone. **Ultimate Parent:** H. F. Ahmanson. **SIC:** 6021—National Commercial Banks.

★ 63200 ★ Stop & Shop Food Store
4120 NW 21st St.
Sunrise, FL 33313
(305)731-0977
Ultimate Parent: Stop & Shop. **SIC:** 5411—Grocery Stores.

Surfside

★ 63201 ★ Citibank, FSB
9525 Harding Ave.
Surfside, FL 33154-2539
(305)864-3020
Location Type: Branch office. **Ultimate Parent:** Citicorp. **SIC:** 6021—National Commercial Banks.

★ 63202 ★ Savings of America
Home Savings of America, FSB
9526 Harding Ave.
Surfside, FL 33154-2502
Location Type: Branch office. **Ultimate Parent:** H. F. Ahmanson. **SIC:** 6021—National Commercial Banks.

Tallahassee

★ 63203 ★ American Family Life Assurance
1391 Timberlane Rd.
Tallahassee, FL 32312
(904)893-6400
Ultimate Parent: American Family Life Assurance Co. **SIC:** 6411—Insurance Agents, Brokers & Service.

★ 63204 ★ American General Finance
220 W. Tharpe St.
Tallahassee, FL 32303-5595
(904)386-5154
Officer: Frank Markiewcz. **Ultimate Parent:** American General Corp. **SIC:** 6141—Personal Credit Institutions; 6162—Mortgage Bankers & Correspondents.

★ 63205 ★ American General Finance Inc.
220 W. Tharpe St.
Tallahassee, FL 32303-5595
(904)386-5154
Location Type: Branch office. **Officer:** Frank Markiewcz. **Ultimate Parent:** American General Corp. **SIC:** 6141—Personal Credit Institutions; 6162—Mortgage Bankers & Correspondents.

★ 63206 ★ AmSouth Bank of Florida
3425 Thomasville Rd.
Tallahassee, FL 32308
(904)894-2370
Location Type: Branch office. **Ultimate Parent:** AmSouth Bancorp. **SIC:** 6022—State Commercial Banks.

★ 63207 ★ AmSouth Bank of Florida
3102 Mayhan Dr.
Tallahassee, FL 32308
(904)878-0948
Location Type: Branch office. **Ultimate Parent:** AmSouth Bancorp. **SIC:** 6022—State Commercial Banks.

★ 63208 ★ Anchor Savings Bank F S B
111 Ocala Rd.
Tallahassee, FL 32304
(904)575-6651
Ultimate Parent: Anchor Bancorp.

★ 63209 ★ Anchor Savings Bank F S B
111 S. Monroe St.
Tallahassee, FL 32301
(904)561-8100
Ultimate Parent: Anchor Bancorp. **SIC:** 6035—Federal Savings Institutions.

★ 63210 ★ Anchor Savings Bank FSB
345 S. Magnolia Dr.
Tallahassee, FL 32301-2968
(904)656-3361
Location Type: Branch office. **Ultimate Parent:** Anchor Bancorp. **SIC:** 6035—Federal Savings Institutions.

★ 63211 ★ Barnett Bank of Tallahassee
215 S. Monroe St.
Tallahassee, FL 32301
Company Type: Subsidiary. **Location Type:** Branch office. **Officer:** Candi Pace, Branch Manager. **Ultimate Parent:** Barnett Banks. **SIC:** 6022—State Commercial Banks.

★ 63212 ★ Barnett Bank of Tallahassee
3003 Mahan Dr.
Tallahassee, FL 32308
Company Type: Subsidiary. **Location Type:** Branch office. **Officer:** Ruby Johnson, Branch Manager. **Ultimate Parent:** Barnett Banks. **SIC:** 6022—State Commercial Banks.

★ 63213 ★ Barnett Bank of Tallahassee
803 Lake Bradford Rd.
Tallahassee, FL 32304-4730
Company Type: Subsidiary. **Location Type:** Branch office. **Officer:** Kathy Rudd, Branch Manager. **Ultimate Parent:** Barnett Banks. **SIC:** 6022—State Commercial Banks.

★ 63214 ★ Barnett Bank of Tallahassee
3516 Thomasville Rd.
Tallahassee, FL 32308
Company Type: Subsidiary. **Location Type:** Branch office. **Officer:** Jeri Hunter, Branch Manager. **Ultimate Parent:** Barnett Banks. **SIC:** 6022—State Commercial Banks.

★ 63215 ★ Barnett Bank of Tallahassee
2930 Apalachee Pky.
Tallahassee, FL 32301
Company Type: Subsidiary. **Location Type:** Branch office. **Officer:** Renee Seal, Branch Manager. **Ultimate Parent:** Barnett Banks. **SIC:** 6022—State Commercial Banks.

★ 63216 ★ Barnett Bank of Tallahassee
600 N. Monroe St.
Tallahassee, FL 32301
Company Type: Branch office. **Officer:** Candi Pace, Branch Manager. **Ultimate Parent:** Barnett Banks. **SIC:** 6022—State Commercial Banks.

★ 63217 ★ Barnett Bank of Tallahassee
2262 N. Monroe St.
Tallahassee, FL 32303
Company Type: Subsidiary. **Location Type:** Branch office. **Officer:** Judy McEachern, Branch Manager. **Ultimate Parent:** Barnett Banks. **SIC:** 6022—State Commercial Banks.

★ 63218 ★ Barnett Bank of Tallahassee
315 S. Calhoun
Box 5257
Tallahassee, FL 32314-5257
(904)561-1700 **Fax:** (904)561-1740
Company Type: Subsidiary. **Location Type:** Branch office. **Officer:** B. P. Crosby, Chairman, President & CEO. **Ultimate Parent:** Barnett Banks. **SIC:** 6022—State Commercial Banks.

★ 63219 ★ Butler Paper
3406 W. Tharpe St.
Tallahassee, FL 32303-1149
(904)576-1161
Location Type: Branch office. **Officer:** Lute McEwen. **Ultimate Parent:** Alco Standard Corp. **SIC:** 5113—Industrial & Personal Service Paper; 5111—Printing & Writing Paper.

★ 63220 ★ Casual Corner
1020 Governors Dr.
Tallahassee, FL 32301
(904)878-8635
Ultimate Parent: United States Shoe. **SIC:** 5651—Family Clothing Stores.

★ 63221 ★ Circus World
1054 Governors Dr.
Tallahassee, FL 32301
(904)877-1279
Ultimate Parent: Melville. **SIC:** 5945—Hobby, Toy & Game Shops.

★ 63222 ★ City National Bank
2375 Centerville Rd.
Tallahassee, FL 32308-4317
(904)841-1301
Company Type: Branch. **Officer:** Gerald A. Basford, Manager. **Ultimate Parent:** City National Corp. **SIC:** 6021—National Commercial Banks.

★ 63223 ★ City National Bank
3255 Mahan Dr.
Tallahassee, FL 32308-5536
(904)841-1302
Company Type: Branch. **Officer:** Deborah G. Chaves, Manager. **Ultimate Parent:** City National Corp. **SIC:** 6021—National Commercial Banks.

★ 63224 ★ City National Bank
1031 Governors Dr.
Tallahassee, FL 32301-4504
(904)841-1303
Company Type: Branch. **Officer:** Tonia Baxter, Line Manager. **Ultimate Parent:** City National Corp. **SIC:** 6021—National Commercial Banks.

★ 63225 ★ City National Bank
1801 Apalachee Pky.
Tallahassee, FL 32301
(904)877-2191
Ultimate Parent: City National Corp.

★ 63226 ★ Colonial Pipeline Co.
1560 Capital Cir. NW 11
Tallahassee, FL 32303
(904)575-7227
Ultimate Parent: Colonial Pipeline. **SIC:** 4619—Pipelines Nec.

★ 63227 ★ Delta Air Cargo
3236 Capital Cir. SW
Tallahassee, FL 32310
(904)575-7008
Ultimate Parent: Delta Air Lines, Inc. **SIC:** 4522—Air Transportation—Nonscheduled.

★ 63228 ★   Delta Air Lines
Tallahassee Regional Airport
Tallahassee, FL 32310
(904)575-3221
Ultimate Parent: Delta Air Lines, Inc. **SIC:**
4512—Air Transportation—Scheduled.

★ 63229 ★   Delta Air Lines
Municipal
Tallahassee, FL 32304
(904)575-7008
Ultimate Parent: Delta Air Lines, Inc. **SIC:**
4512—Air Transportation—Scheduled.

★ 63230 ★   Delta Air Lines
2574 Seagate Dr.
Tallahassee, FL 32301
(904)656-2631
Ultimate Parent: Delta Air Lines, Inc. **SIC:**
4512—Air Transportation—Scheduled.

★ 63231 ★   Delta Air Lines
Municipal Airport
Tallahassee, FL 32304
(904)575-7008
Ultimate Parent: Delta Air Lines, Inc. **SIC:**
4512—Air Transportation—Scheduled.

★ 63232 ★   Delta Air Lines Inc.
2574 Seagate Dr.
Tallahassee, FL 32301
(904)656-2631
Ultimate Parent: Delta Air Lines, Inc. **SIC:**
4512—Air Transportation—Scheduled.

★ 63233 ★   Diebold Inc.
3305 Capital Cir. NE
Tallahassee, FL 32308
(904)386-8807
Ultimate Parent: Diebold, Inc. **SIC:** 7382—
Security Systems Services.

★ 63234 ★   Digital Equipment
Corp.
2640 Mitchum Dr.
Tallahassee, FL 32308
(904)656-2900
Ultimate Parent: Digital Equipment Corp.
SIC: 7373—Computer Integrated Systems
Design.

★ 63235 ★   Donnelley Directory
Tallahassee, FL 32308
(904)422-3300
Ultimate Parent: R. R. Donnelley & Sons.

★ 63236 ★   Electronic Data
Systems Corp.
315 S. Calhoun St.
Tallahassee, FL 32301
(904)224-0024
Ultimate Parent: Electronic Data Systems.
SIC: 7373—Computer Integrated Systems
Design.

★ 63237 ★   First Union National
Bank of Florida
3400 S. Monroe St.
Tallahassee, FL 32301-7298
(904)425-2565
Location Type: Branch office. **Ultimate
Parent:** First Union Corp. **SIC:** 6021—
National Commercial Banks.

★ 63238 ★   First Union National
Bank of Florida
1500 Apalachee Pkwy
Governors Square Mall
Tallahassee, FL 32301-3017
(904)425-2501
Location Type: Branch office. **Ultimate
Parent:** First Union Corp. **SIC:** 6021—
National Commercial Banks.

★ 63239 ★   First Union National
Bank of Florida
3121 Mahan Dr.
Tallahassee, FL 32308-5507
(904)425-6036
Location Type: Branch office. **Ultimate
Parent:** First Union Corp. **SIC:** 6021—
National Commercial Banks.

★ 63240 ★   First Union National
Bank of Florida
101 N. Monroe St.
Tallahassee, FL 32301-1546
(904)425-6060
Location Type: Branch office. **Ultimate
Parent:** First Union Corp. **SIC:** 6021—
National Commercial Banks.

★ 63241 ★   First Union National
Bank of Florida
3529 Thomasville Rd.
Tallahassee, FL 32308-3458
(904)425-6030
Location Type: Branch office. **Ultimate
Parent:** First Union Corp. **SIC:** 6021—
National Commercial Banks.

★ 63242 ★   Food Lion
4500 W. Shannon Lakes Dr.
Tallahassee, FL 32308
(904)668-0447
Ultimate Parent: Food Lion. **SIC:** 5411—
Grocery Stores.

★ 63243 ★   The Gap
1049 Governors Dr.
Tallahassee, FL 32301
(904)878-8143
Ultimate Parent: GAP. **SIC:** 5651—Family
Clothing Stores.

★ 63244 ★   Hertz Rent-A-Car
Municipal
Tallahassee, FL 32304
(904)576-1154
Ultimate Parent: Hertz. **SIC:** 7514—
Passenger Car Rental.

★ 63245 ★   Kentucky Fried
Chicken
1583 Apalachee Pky.
Tallahassee, FL 32301
(904)877-7620
Ultimate Parent: Pepsico. **SIC:** 5812—
Eating Places.

★ 63246 ★   Kentucky Fried
Chicken
3519 Thomasville Rd.
Tallahassee, FL 32308
(904)893-5540
Ultimate Parent: Pepsico. **SIC:** 5812—
Eating Places.

★ 63247 ★   Kentucky Fried
Chicken
1603 W. Tennessee St.
Tallahassee, FL 32304
(904)224-4313
Ultimate Parent: Pepsico. **SIC:** 5812—
Eating Places.

★ 63248 ★   Kentucky Fried
Chicken
2530 S. Monroe St.
Tallahassee, FL 32301
(904)878-2574
Ultimate Parent: Pepsico. **SIC:** 5812—
Eating Places.

★ 63249 ★   Lane Bryant
206 Tallahassee Mall
Tallahassee, FL 32303
(904)385-7708
Ultimate Parent: Limited. **SIC:** 5651—
Family Clothing Stores.

★ 63250 ★   Lerner Shop
2012 Governor Sq. S
Tallahassee, FL 32301
(904)878-7650
Ultimate Parent: Limited. **SIC:** 5651—
Family Clothing Stores.

★ 63251 ★   The Limited
2020 Governor's Sq.
Tallahassee, FL 32301
(904)877-5104
Ultimate Parent: Limited. **SIC:** 5651—
Family Clothing Stores; 5651—Family
Clothing Stores.

★ 63252 ★   Mutual of New York
2111 N. Monroe St.
Tallahassee, FL 32303
(904)386-3833
Ultimate Parent: Mutual of New York. **SIC:**
6411—Insurance Agents, Brokers &
Service.

★ 63253 ★   Otis Elevator Co.
1408 Capital Cir. NE
Tallahassee, FL 32308
(904)222-0545
Ultimate Parent: United Technologies. **SIC:**
5084—Industrial Machinery & Equipment.

★ 63254 ★   Pepsi-Cola Co.
3919 W. Pensacola St.
Tallahassee, FL 32304
(904)574-0281
Officer: Al Huggins, Manager. **Ultimate**

Parent: Pepsico. **SIC:** 2086—Bottled &
Canned Soft Drinks.

★ 63255 ★   Pizza Hut
3521 N. Monroe St.
Tallahassee, FL 32303
(904)562-2500
Ultimate Parent: Pepsico. **SIC:** 5812—
Eating Places.

★ 63256 ★   Pizza Hut
1705 Apalachee Pky.
Tallahassee, FL 32301
(904)942-2272
Ultimate Parent: Pepsico. **SIC:** 5812—
Eating Places.

★ 63257 ★   Pizza Hut
3470 Thomasville Rd.
Tallahassee, FL 32308
(904)893-3617
Ultimate Parent: Pepsico. **SIC:** 5812—
Eating Places.

★ 63258 ★   Pizza Hut
2258 N. Monroe St.
Tallahassee, FL 32303
(904)385-7636
Ultimate Parent: Pepsico. **SIC:** 5812—
Eating Places; 7641—Reupholstery &
Furniture Repair.

★ 63259 ★   Publix Super Market
1719 Apalachee Pky.
Tallahassee, FL 32301
(904)877-7171
Ultimate Parent: Publix Super Markets.
SIC: 5411—Grocery Stores; 5461—Retail
Bakeries.

★ 63260 ★   Radio Shack
1964 W. Tennessee St.
Tallahassee, FL 32304
(904)575-2355
Company Type: Division. **Ultimate Parent:**
Tandy Corp. **SIC:** 5065—Electronic Parts &
Equipment Nec.

★ 63261 ★   Radio Shack
2525 S. Monroe St.
Tallahassee, FL 32301
(904)224-4287
Company Type: Division. **Ultimate Parent:**
Tandy Corp. **SIC:** 5065—Electronic Parts &
Equipment Nec.

★ 63262 ★   Radio Shack
3491 Thomasville Rd. 3
Tallahassee, FL 32308
(904)668-7960
Company Type: Division. **Ultimate Parent:**
Tandy Corp. **SIC:** 5063—Electrical
Apparatus & Equipment.

★ 63263 ★   Radio Shack
2415 N. Monroe St.
Tallahassee, FL 32303
(904)385-7504
Company Type: Division. **Ultimate Parent:**
Tandy Corp. **SIC:** 5065—Electronic Parts &
Equipment Nec; 5731—Radio, Television &
Electronics Stores.

★ 63264 ★   Radio Shack
2529 S. Adams St.
Tallahassee, FL 32301
(904)222-4440
Company Type: Division. **Ultimate Parent:**
Tandy Corp. **SIC:** 5046—Commercial
Equipment Nec.

★ 63265 ★   Radio Shack
1707 Apalachee Pky.
Tallahassee, FL 32301
(904)877-6695
Company Type: Division. **Ultimate Parent:**
Tandy Corp. **SIC:** 5065—Electronic Parts &
Equipment Nec; 5731—Radio, Television &
Electronics Stores.

★ 63266 ★   Radio Shack
Tallahassee
Tallahassee, FL 32302
(904)385-7284
Company Type: Division. **Ultimate Parent:**
Tandy Corp. **SIC:** 5999—Miscellaneous
Retail Stores Nec.

★ 63267 ★   Radio Shack
1500 Apalachee Pky.
Tallahassee, FL 32301
(904)877-9804
Company Type: Division. **Ultimate Parent:**
Tandy Corp. **SIC:** 5065—Electronic Parts &
Equipment Nec.

★ 63268 ★   Richman Brothers Co.
the
Tallahassee Mall
Tallahassee, FL 32308
(904)385-1224
Ultimate Parent: Woolworth Corp. **SIC:**
5611—Men's & Boys' Clothing Stores.

★ 63269 ★   Ryder Truck Rental
3425 W. Tharpe St.
Tallahassee, FL 32303
(904)576-7123
Ultimate Parent: Ryder System. **SIC:**
7359—Equipment Rental & Leasing Nec;
7513—Truck Rental & Leasing Without
Drivers.

★ 63270 ★   Sam's Wholesale
Club
3221 N. Monroe St.
Tallahassee, FL 32303
(904)562-5959
Ultimate Parent: Wal-Mart Stores, Inc. **SIC:**
5099—Durable Goods Nec.

★ 63271 ★   Service Merchandise
2410 Allen Rd.
Tallahassee, FL 32312
(904)385-8161
Ultimate Parent: Service Merchandise Co.,
Inc. **SIC:** 5399—Miscellaneous General
Merchandise Store.

★ 63272 ★   Taco Bell
1218 N. Monroe St.
Tallahassee, FL 32303
(904)224-4873
Ultimate Parent: Pepsico. **SIC:** 5812—
Eating Places.

★ 63273 ★   Taco Bell
1964 W. Tennessee St. 2
Tallahassee, FL 32304
(904)222-0650
Ultimate Parent: Pepsico. **SIC:** 5812—
Eating Places.

★ 63274 ★   Taco Bell
1935 Apalachee Pky.
Tallahassee, FL 32301
(904)878-5559
Ultimate Parent: Pepsico. **SIC:** 5812—
Eating Places.

★ 63275 ★   Tallahassee State
Bank
3471 Thomasville Rd.
Tallahassee, FL 32308
(904)893-1600
Company Type: Subsidiary. **Location
Type:** Branch office. **Officer:** George
Williams, Mgr. **Ultimate Parent:** Synovus
Financial Corp. **SIC:** 6021—National
Commercial Banks.

★ 63276 ★   Tallahassee State
Bank
2720 W. Tennessee St.
PO Box 2275
Tallahassee, FL 32304-2840
(904)576-1182 **Fax:** (904)575-4958
Company Type: Subsidiary. **Location
Type:** Branch office. **Officer:** W. Booker
Moore, President & CEO. **Ultimate Parent:**
Synovus Financial Corp. **SIC:** 6021—
National Commercial Banks.

★ 63277 ★   Tallahassee State
Bank
601 N. Monroe
Tallahassee, FL 32301
(904)224-8494
Company Type: Subsidiary. **Location
Type:** Branch office. **Officer:** W. Booker
Moore, Mgr. **Ultimate Parent:** Synovus
Financial Corp.

★ 63278 ★   Talquin Corp.
2941 Brandemere Dr.
Tallahassee, FL 32312
(904)385-5224
Ultimate Parent: Florida Progress. **SIC:**
6531—Real Estate Agents & Managers.

★ 63279 ★   Texaco Food Mart
2828 N. Monroe St.
Tallahassee, FL 32303
(904)385-2026
Ultimate Parent: Texaco. **SIC:** 5411—
Grocery Stores.

★ 63280 ★ **Toys R US**
1625 Apalachee Pky.
Tallahassee, FL 32301
(904)656-5701
Ultimate Parent: Toys "R" US. **SIC:** 5945—Hobby, Toy & Game Shops.

★ 63281 ★ **Trailways Bus System**
324 N. Adams St.
Tallahassee, FL 32301
(904)224-3101
Ultimate Parent: Greyhound Lines Inc. **SIC:** 4142—Bus Charter Service Except Local.

★ 63282 ★ **Transamerica Occidental Life Insurance**
1625 Centerville Rd.
Tallahassee, FL 32308
(904)386-9498
Ultimate Parent: Transamerica Occidental Life Insurance. **SIC:** 6411—Insurance Agents, Brokers & Service.

★ 63283 ★ **United Parcel Service**
3735 Hartsfield Rd.
Tallahassee, FL 32303
(904)432-8686
Ultimate Parent: United Parcel Service of America. **SIC:** 4215—Courier Services Except by Air.

★ 63284 ★ **US Marine/Bayliner**
4755 Capital Circle Way
Tallahassee, FL 32303
Ultimate Parent: Brunswick Corp. **SIC:** 3732—Boat Building & Repairing.

★ 63285 ★ **Victoria's Secret**
2027 Governor Sq. S
Tallahassee, FL 32301
(904)878-8542
Ultimate Parent: Limited. **SIC:** 5651—Family Clothing Stores.

★ 63286 ★ **Wal Mart Corp.**
4400 W. Tennessee St.
Tallahassee, FL 32304
(904)574-3588
Ultimate Parent: Wal-Mart Stores, Inc. **SIC:** 5399—Miscellaneous General Merchandise Store.

★ 63287 ★ **Walgreen Drug Stores**
Tallahassee
Tallahassee, FL 32302
(904)385-7377
Ultimate Parent: Walgreen Co. **SIC:** 5812—Eating Places.

★ 63288 ★ **Walgreen Drug Stores**
3111 Mahan Dr. 12
Tallahassee, FL 32308
(904)656-7482
Ultimate Parent: Walgreen Co. **SIC:** 5912—Drug Stores & Proprietary Stores.

★ 63289 ★ **Walgreen Drug Stores**
536 Tallahassee Mall
Tallahassee, FL 32303
(904)385-7141
Ultimate Parent: Walgreen Co. **SIC:** 5912—Drug Stores & Proprietary Stores.

★ 63290 ★ **Xerox Corp.**
311 S. Calhoun St.
Tallahassee, FL 32301
(904)842-3110
Officer: Jesse Hill, Manager. **Ultimate Parent:** Xerox Corp. **SIC:** 3663—Radio & T.V. Communications Equipment.

Tallevast

★ 63291 ★ **Donzi Marine**
7000 Old Bradenton Rd.
Tallevast, FL 34243
Ultimate Parent: Outboard Marine. **SIC:** 3732—Boat Building & Repairing.

★ 63292 ★ **Loral American Beryllium**
1600 Tallevast Rd.
Tallevast, FL 34243
(813)355-8141 **Fax:** (813)351-3960
Officer: George M. Allen Jr., President.
Ultimate Parent: Loral Corp.

★ 63293 ★ **Loral American Beryllium Corp.**
1600 Tallevast Rd.
Tallevast, FL 34270
Ultimate Parent: Loral Corp. **SIC:** 3499—Fabricated Metal Products Nec.

Tamarac

★ 63294 ★ **American Savings of Florida, FSB**
8237 NW 88th Ave.
Tamarac, FL 33321-1541
(305)722-5944
Location Type: Branch office. **Officer:** Barbara Bernstein, Manager. **Ultimate Parent:** American Savings of Florida. **SIC:** 6035—Federal Savings Institutions; 6211—Security Brokers & Dealers.

★ 63295 ★ **Barnett Bank of Broward County, NA**
8200 N. University Dr.
Tamarac, FL 33321-1710
(305)726-8000
Company Type: Subsidiary. **Location Type:** Branch office. **Officer:** Liz Domke, Manager. **Ultimate Parent:** Barnett Banks. **SIC:** 6021—National Commercial Banks.

★ 63296 ★ **California Federal Bank, FSB**
7001 N. University Dr.
Tamarac, FL 33321-2976
(305)722-0200
Location Type: Branch office. **Ultimate Parent:** California Federal Bank. **SIC:** 6021—National Commercial Banks.

★ 63297 ★ **California Federal Bank, FSB**
5900 Rock Island Rd.
Tamarac, FL 33319-2500
(305)973-8607
Location Type: Branch office. **Ultimate Parent:** California Federal Bank. **SIC:** 6021—National Commercial Banks.

★ 63298 ★ **Citibank, FSB**
6848 N. University Dr.
Tamarac, FL 33321-4089
(305)722-8675
Location Type: Branch office. **Ultimate Parent:** Citicorp. **SIC:** 6021—National Commercial Banks.

★ 63299 ★ **First Union National Bank of Florida**
7201 W. McNab Rd.
Tamarac, FL 33321-5307
(305)786-6196
Location Type: Branch office. **Ultimate Parent:** First Union Corp. **SIC:** 6021—National Commercial Banks.

★ 63300 ★ **Savings of America**
Home Savings of America, FSB
5200 N. State Rd. 7
Tamarac, FL 33319-3391
(305)735-1440
Location Type: Branch office. **Officer:** Deryck Mattar, Manager. **Ultimate Parent:** H. F. Ahmanson. **SIC:** 6021—National Commercial Banks.

Tampa

★ 63301 ★ **ABF Freight System Inc.**
7801 Industrial Ln.
Tampa, FL 33637-6740
(813)989-2460
Location Type: Branch office. **Officer:** Herman Dooley. **Ultimate Parent:** Arkansas Best. **SIC:** 4212—Local Trucking Without Storage.

★ 63302 ★ **Ace Hardware & Locksmith**
Rural Route 6
Tampa, FL 33637
(813)988-3488
Ultimate Parent: Ace Hardware. **SIC:** 5251—Hardware Stores.

★ 63303 ★ **ADP-Automatic Data Processing**
Tampa International Airport
Tampa, FL 33607
(813)875-6640
Ultimate Parent: Automatic Data Processing, Inc. **SIC:** 7374—Data Processing & Preparation.

★ 63304 ★ **Air Products & Chemicals, Inc.**
2610 Tampa Blvd. E
Tampa, FL 33619
(813)621-2477
Ultimate Parent: Air Products & Chemicals, Inc. **SIC:** 5084—Industrial Machinery & Equipment; 5169—Chemicals & Allied Products Nec.

★ 63305 ★ **Airborne Freight Corp.**
4617 N. Westshore Blvd.
Tampa, FL 33614
(813)683-6982
Ultimate Parent: Airborne Freight Corp. **SIC:** 4512—Air Transportation—Scheduled.

★ 63306 ★ **AMBAC Indemnity Corp.**
8875 Hidden River Pky.
Tampa, FL 33637-1005
(813)229-1506
Ultimate Parent: AMBAC Inc. **SIC:** 6211—Security Brokers & Dealers.

★ 63307 ★ **Amerada Hess Corp.**
10001 N. Florida Ave.
Tampa, FL 33612
(813)933-3163
Ultimate Parent: Amerada Hess. **SIC:** 5541—Gasoline Service Stations.

★ 63308 ★ **America West Airlines**
Tampa International Airport
Tampa, FL 33607
(813)276-4217
Ultimate Parent: America West Airlines. **SIC:** 4512—Air Transportation—Scheduled.

★ 63309 ★ **American Financial Corp. of Tampa**
3903 Northdale Blvd.
Tampa, FL 33624-1864
(813)968-6436
Company Type: Division. **Officer:** Robert O. Blomquist, Chairman of the Board. **Ultimate Parent:** Integra Financial. **SIC:** 6163—Loan Brokers; 6162—Mortgage Bankers & Correspondents.

★ 63310 ★ **American General Finance**
5035 E. Busch Blvd.
Tampa, FL 33617-5301
(813)988-7383
Location Type: Branch office. **Officer:** Joe Goddard. **Ultimate Parent:** American General Corp. **SIC:** 6141—Personal Credit Institutions; 6162—Mortgage Bankers & Correspondents.

★ 63311 ★ **American General Finance**
9280 Bay Plz. Blvd.
Tampa, FL 33619-4414
(813)664-1400
Ultimate Parent: American General Corp. **SIC:** 6141—Personal Credit Institutions.

★ 63312 ★ **American General Finance**
1323 W. Busch Blvd.
Tampa, FL 33612-7709
(813)935-4555
Location Type: Branch office. **Officer:** Deanna Hames. **Ultimate Parent:** American General Corp. **SIC:** 6141—Personal Credit Institutions; 6162—Mortgage Bankers & Correspondents.

★ 63313 ★ **American General Finance**
6301 Memorial Hwy.
Tampa, FL 33615-4537
(813)885-7402
Ultimate Parent: American General Corp. **SIC:** 6141—Personal Credit Institutions; 6162—Mortgage Bankers & Correspondents.

★ 63314 ★ **American General Finance**
5201 W. Kennedy Blvd., Ste. 200
Tampa, FL 33609-1800
(813)876-2299
Location Type: Branch office. **Officer:** Cheryl Story. **Ultimate Parent:** American General Corp. **SIC:** 6141—Personal Credit Institutions; 6162—Mortgage Bankers & Correspondents.

★ 63315 ★ **American General Finance Inc.**
5035 E. Busch Blvd.
Tampa, FL 33617-5301
(813)988-7383
Location Type: Branch office. **Officer:** Joe Goddard. **Ultimate Parent:** American General Corp. **SIC:** 6141—Personal Credit Institutions; 6162—Mortgage Bankers & Correspondents.

★ 63316 ★ **American General Finance Inc.**
9280 Bay Plz. Blvd.
Tampa, FL 33619-4414
(813)664-1400
Location Type: Branch office. **Ultimate Parent:** American General Corp. **SIC:** 6141—Personal Credit Institutions.

★ 63317 ★ **American General Finance Inc.**
1323 W. Busch Blvd.
Tampa, FL 33612-7709
(813)935-4555
Location Type: Branch office. **Officer:** Deanna Hames. **Ultimate Parent:** American General Corp. **SIC:** 6141—Personal Credit Institutions; 6162—Mortgage Bankers & Correspondents.

★ 63318 ★ **American General Finance Inc.**
6301 Memorial Hwy.
Tampa, FL 33615-4537
(813)885-7402
Location Type: Branch office. **Ultimate Parent:** American General Corp. **SIC:** 6141—Personal Credit Institutions; 6162—Mortgage Bankers & Correspondents.

★ 63319 ★ **American General Finance Inc.**
5201 W. Kennedy Blvd., Ste. 200
Tampa, FL 33609-1800
(813)876-2299
Location Type: Branch office. **Officer:** Cheryl Story. **Ultimate Parent:** American General Corp. **SIC:** 6141—Personal Credit Institutions; 6162—Mortgage Bankers & Correspondents.

★ 63320 ★ **American Savings of Florida**
12002 Anderson Rd.
Tampa, FL 33625-5682
(813)968-1464
Ultimate Parent: American Savings of Florida. **SIC:** 6141—Personal Credit Institutions.

★ 63321 ★ **American Savings of Florida**
13188 N. Dale
Tampa, FL 33618
(813)962-4211
Officer: Judy Woodworth. **Ultimate Parent:** American Savings of Florida. **SIC:** 6141—Personal Credit Institutions; 6162—Mortgage Bankers & Correspondents.

★ 63322 ★ **Anchor Glass Container Corp.**
4343 Anchor Plz.
Tampa, FL 33634
(813)870-6120
Ultimate Parent: Anchor Glass Container Corp. **SIC:** 3229—Pressed & Blown Glass Nec.

★ 63323 ★ **Anchor Mortgage Services Inc.**
11790 N. Dale Mabry Hwy.
Tampa, FL 33618-3504
(813)969-0990
Officer: Stan Marine. **Ultimate Parent:** Anchor Bancorp. **SIC:** 6141—Personal Credit Institutions; 6162—Mortgage Bankers & Correspondents.

★ 63324 ★ **Anchor Savings Bank**
11790 N. Dale Mabry Hwy.
Tampa, FL 33618
Ultimate Parent: Anchor Bancorp. **SIC:** 6035—Federal Savings Institutions.

★ 63325 ★ **Anchor Savings Bank**
Sun
11790 N. Dale Marby Hwy.
Tampa, FL 33618-3504
Company Type: Division. **Location Type:** Branch office. **Officer:** Stephen N. Roberts. **Ultimate Parent:** Anchor Bancorp. **SIC:** 6035—Federal Savings Institutions; 6021—National Commercial Banks.

★ 63326 ★ **Anchor Savings Bank FSB**
1740 N. Dale Marby Dr.
Tampa, FL 33618
(813)969-0861
Location Type: Branch office. **Officer:** Gary Williams. **Ultimate Parent:** Anchor Bancorp. **SIC:** 6035—Federal Savings Institutions.

★ 63327 ★ **Anchor Savings Bank, FSB**
11790 N. Dale Mabry Hwy.
Tampa, FL 33618-3504
(813)969-0790
Location Type: Branch office. **Officer:** Gary Williams, Assistant Vice President. **Ultimate Parent:** Anchor Bancorp. **SIC:** 6021—National Commercial Banks; 6035—Federal Savings Institutions; 6211—Security Brokers & Dealers.

★ 63328 ★ **Anheuser-Busch Inc.**
3000 E. Busch Blvd.
Tampa, FL 33612
Ultimate Parent: Anheuser-Busch. **SIC:** 2082—Malt Beverages.

★ 63329 ★ **Ball Metal Container**
4700 E. Whiteway Dr.
Tampa, FL 33617-3424
(813)980-6073
Officer: Gary Fields. **Ultimate Parent:** Ball Corp. **SIC:** 3411—Metal Cans.

★ 63330 ★ **Ball Metal Container Group**
4700 E. Whiteway Dr.
Tampa, FL 33617
(813)980-6073
Officer: Gary Fields, Manager. **Ultimate Parent:** Ball Corp. **SIC:** 3411—Metal Cans.

★ 63331 ★ **Ball Metal Container Operations**
4700 Whiteway Dr.
Tampa, FL 33617
Ultimate Parent: Ball Corp. **SIC:** 3411—Metal Cans.

★ 63332 ★ **Ball Packaging Products Group Tampa Can Plant**
4700 Whiteway Dr.
Tampa, FL 33617
Ultimate Parent: Ball Corp. **SIC:** 3411—Metal Cans.

★ 63333 ★ **Banana Republic**
720 S. Village Cir.
Tampa, FL 33606
(813)253-3005
Ultimate Parent: GAP. **SIC:** 5651—Family Clothing Stores.

★ 63334 ★ **BancBoston Mortgage Corp.**
3550 W. Busch Blvd. Ste. 100
Tampa, FL 33618-4461
(813)932-7690
Officer: Wynette Griffin. **Ultimate Parent:** Bank of Boston Corp. **SIC:** 6141—Personal Credit Institutions; 6162—Mortgage Bankers & Correspondents.

★ 63335 ★ **Barnett Bank of Tampa**
5370 Ehrlich Rd.
Tampa, FL 33625
(813)225-2290
Company Type: Subsidiary. **Location Type:** Branch office. **Officer:** Linda Moghal, Manager. **Ultimate Parent:** Barnett Banks. **SIC:** 6022—State Commercial Banks.

★ 63336 ★ **Barnett Bank of Tampa**
8320 Hanley Rd.
Tampa, FL 33634-2280
(813)885-4776
Company Type: Subsidiary. **Location Type:** Branch office. **Officer:** Greg Parkes, Assistant Vice President. **Ultimate Parent:** Barnett Banks. **SIC:** 6022—State Commercial Banks.

★ 63337 ★ **Barnett Bank of Tampa**
2208 Fowler Ave.
Tampa, FL 33612-5526
(813)225-8795
Company Type: Subsidiary. **Location Type:** Branch office. **Officer:** Page Aspinwall, Manager. **Ultimate Parent:** Barnett Banks. **SIC:** 6022—State Commercial Banks.

★ 63338 ★ **Barnett Bank of Tampa**
16002 N. Dale Mabry Hwy.
Tampa, FL 33618-1330
(813)958-8505
Company Type: Subsidiary. **Location Type:** Branch office. **Officer:** Patricia Ashton, Vice President. **Ultimate Parent:** Barnett Banks. **SIC:** 6022—State Commercial Banks.

★ 63339 ★ **Barnett Bank of Tampa**
4825 S. Manhattan
Tampa, FL 33611-2335
(813)225-8050
Company Type: Subsidiary. **Location Type:** Branch office. **Officer:** Teresa Stinson, Office Manager. **Ultimate Parent:** Barnett Banks. **SIC:** 6022—State Commercial Banks.

★ 63340 ★ **Barnett Bank of Tampa**
1501 S. Church Ave.
Tampa, FL 33629-5822
(813)251-1828
Company Type: Subsidiary. **Location Type:** Branch office. **Officer:** Chris Stewart, Assistant Vice President. **Ultimate Parent:** Barnett Banks. **SIC:** 6022—State Commercial Banks.

★ 63341 ★ **Barnett Bank of Tampa**
4825 W. Kennedy Blvd.
Tampa, FL 33609-2593
(813)286-4700
Company Type: Subsidiary. **Location Type:** Branch office. **Officer:** Rene Alfonso, Manager. **Ultimate Parent:** Barnett Banks. **SIC:** 6022—State Commercial Banks.

★ 63342 ★ **Barnett Bank of Tampa**
12098 Anderson Rd.
Tampa, FL 33625-5682
(813)264-2070
Company Type: Subsidiary. **Location Type:** Branch office. **Officer:** Pam Ford, Office Manager. **Ultimate Parent:** Barnett Banks. **SIC:** 6022—State Commercial Banks.

★ 63343 ★ **Barnett Bank of Tampa**
8706 W. Hillsborough
Tampa, FL 33615-3705
(813)886-3291
Company Type: Subsidiary. **Location Type:** Branch office. **Officer:** David Newcombe, Manager. **Ultimate Parent:** Barnett Banks. **SIC:** 6022—State Commercial Banks.

★ 63344 ★ **Barnett Bank of Tampa**
15302 Amberly Dr.
Tampa, FL 33647-2143
(813)977-9993
Company Type: Subsidiary. **Location Type:** Branch office. **Officer:** Karen Johnson, Manager. **Ultimate Parent:** Barnett Banks. **SIC:** 6022—State Commercial Banks.

★ 63345 ★ **Barnett Bank of Tampa**
4545 N. Himes Ave.
Tampa, FL 33614-7310
(813)872-9346
Company Type: Subsidiary. **Location Type:** Branch office. **Officer:** Earl Kagler, Manager. **Ultimate Parent:** Barnett Banks. **SIC:** 6022—State Commercial Banks.

★ 63346 ★ **Barnett Bank of Tampa**
9601 Martin Luther King Blvd. E
Tampa, FL 33610-7408
(813)626-6427
Company Type: Subsidiary. **Location Type:** Branch office. **Officer:** Neil Pressley, Manager. **Ultimate Parent:** Barnett Banks. **SIC:** 6022—State Commercial Banks.

★ 63347 ★ **Barnett Bank of Tampa**
13502 N. Florida Ave.
Tampa, FL 33613-3213
(813)225-2275
Company Type: Subsidiary. **Location Type:** Branch office. **Officer:** Terry McFatter, Assistant Vice President. **Ultimate Parent:** Barnett Banks. **SIC:** 6022—State Commercial Banks.

★ 63348 ★ **Barnett Bank of Tampa**
1933 E. Hillsborough Ave.
Tampa, FL 33610-8281
(813)239-1702
Company Type: Subsidiary. **Location**

Barnett Banks. **SIC:** 6022—State Commercial Banks.

★ 63349 ★ **Barnett Bank of Tampa**
6925 56th St.
Tampa, FL 33617-8714
(813)225-8882
Company Type: Subsidiary. **Location Type:** Branch office. **Officer:** Sara Luciene, Vice President. **Ultimate Parent:** Barnett Banks. **SIC:** 6022—State Commercial Banks.

★ 63350 ★ **Barnett Bank of Tampa**
4600 W. Cypress St.
Tampa, FL 33607-4025
(813)225-4500
Company Type: Subsidiary. **Location Type:** Branch office. **Officer:** John Acosta, Vice President. **Ultimate Parent:** Barnett Banks. **SIC:** 6022—State Commercial Banks.

★ 63351 ★ **Barnett Bank of Tampa**
3804 S. Manhattan Ave.
Tampa, FL 33608
(813)839-8421
Company Type: Subsidiary. **Location Type:** Branch office. **Officer:** Nancy Gibbs, Manager. **Ultimate Parent:** Barnett Banks. **SIC:** 6022—State Commercial Banks.

★ 63352 ★ **Barnett Bank of Tampa**
10301 N. Dale Mabry Hwy.
Tampa, FL 33618-4499
(813)961-8749
Company Type: Subsidiary. **Location Type:** Branch office. **Officer:** Suzanne Rodman, Office Manager. **Ultimate Parent:** Barnett Banks. **SIC:** 6022—State Commercial Banks.

★ 63353 ★ **Barnett Bank of Tampa**
601 W. Platt St.
Tampa, FL 33606-2247
(813)254-1744
Company Type: Subsidiary. **Location Type:** Branch office. **Officer:** Mike Gottesman, Manager. **Ultimate Parent:** Barnett Banks. **SIC:** 6022—State Commercial Banks.

★ 63354 ★ **Barnett Bank of Tampa**
2700 W. Dr. Martin Luther King Dr.
Tampa, FL 33607
(813)879-7500
Company Type: Subsidiary. **Location Type:** Branch office. **Officer:** Doris Wise, Vice President. **Ultimate Parent:** Barnett Banks. **SIC:** 6022—State Commercial Banks.

★ 63355 ★ **Barnett Bank of Tampa**
3615 Gandy Blvd. W
Tampa, FL 33611-2607
(813)832-0372
Company Type: Subsidiary. **Location Type:** Branch office. **Officer:** Emma Wiseman, Manager. **Ultimate Parent:** Barnett Banks. **SIC:** 6022—State Commercial Banks.

★ 63356 ★ **Barnett Bank of Tampa**
15001 N. Florida Ave.
Tampa, FL 33613-1235
(813)962-8557
Company Type: Subsidiary. **Location Type:** Branch office. **Officer:** Sherlyn Richardson, Vice President. **Ultimate Parent:** Barnett Banks. **SIC:** 6022—State Commercial Banks.

★ 63357 ★ **Barnett Bank of Tampa**
13868 N. Dale Mabry Hwy.
Tampa, FL 33618-2437
(813)961-1277
Company Type: Subsidiary. **Location Type:** Branch office. **Officer:** Maida Blanco, Manager. **Ultimate Parent:** Barnett Banks. **SIC:** 6022—State Commercial Banks.

★ 63358 ★ **Barnett Bank of Tampa**
111 Madison St.
Tampa, FL 33602-4706
(813)224-1111
Company Type: Subsidiary. **Location Type:** Branch office. **Officer:** Wally Blount, Manager. **Ultimate Parent:** Barnett Banks. **SIC:** 6022—State Commercial Banks.

★ 63359 ★ **Barnett Bank of Tampa**
1701 E. 7th Ave.
Tampa, FL 33605-3805
(813)225-7545
Company Type: Subsidiary. **Location Type:** Branch office. **Officer:** Dan De La Cruz, Manager. **Ultimate Parent:** Barnett Banks. **SIC:** 6022—State Commercial Banks.

★ 63360 ★ **Barnett Bank of Tampa**
101 E. Kennedy Blvd.
PO Box 30014
Tampa, FL 33630-3014
(813)225-8111 **Fax:** (813)225-8715
Company Type: Subsidiary. **Location Type:** Branch office. **Officer:** James W. Ivey, President & CEO. **Ultimate Parent:** Barnett Banks. **SIC:** 6022—State Commercial Banks.

★ 63361 ★ **Bausch & Lomb Inc.**
Pharmaceutical Div.
Hidden River Pky.
Tampa, FL 33637
(813)972-7705
Company Type: Division. **Ultimate Parent:** Bausch & Lomb Inc. **SIC:** 2834—Pharmaceutical Preparations. **Employee Count:** 200.

★ 63362 ★ **Bausch & Lomb Pharmaceuticals Inc.**
205 Kelsey Ln.
Tampa, FL 33619
(813)972-7705 **Fax:** (813)972-0529
Company Type: Subsidiary. **Officer:** Thomas M. Riedhammer, Division President. **Ultimate Parent:** Bausch & Lomb Inc.

★ 63363 ★ **Bell Atlantic Bus System Svc.**
8176 Woodland Ctr. Blvd.
Tampa, FL 33614-2418
(813)882-0606
Officer: Paul Kelley. **Ultimate Parent:** Bell Atlantic Corp. **SIC:** 7378—Computer Maintenance & Repair; 5112—Stationery & Office Supplies.

★ 63364 ★ **Bell Atlantic Tricon Lease Corp.**
5401 W. Kennedy Blvd.
Tampa, FL 33609-2428
(813)286-7466
Ultimate Parent: Bell Atlantic Corp. **SIC:** 6141—Personal Credit Institutions; 6159—Miscellaneous Business Credit Institutions.

★ 63365 ★ **Beneficial Savings Bank, FSB**
777 S. Harbour Island Blvd., Ste. 125
Tampa, FL 33602-5701
(813)229-8546
Location Type: Branch office. **Ultimate Parent:** Beneficial. **SIC:** 6021—National Commercial Banks.

★ 63366 ★ **Beneficial Savings Bank, FSB**
777 S. Harbour Island Blvd., Ste. 877
Tampa, FL 33602-5729
(813)222-0488
Company Type: Subsidiary. **Ultimate Parent:** Beneficial. **SIC:** 6035—Federal Savings Institutions. **Employee Count:** 27.

★ 63367 ★ **Borden Inc.**
Dairy
4010 N. Lois Ave.
Tampa, FL 33614
Company Type: Division. **Ultimate Parent:** Borden, Inc. **SIC:** 2024—Ice Cream & Frozen Desserts.

★ 63368 ★ **Borden Inc.**
Dairy
4010 N. Lois Ave.
Tampa, FL 33614
Company Type: Division. **Ultimate Parent:** Borden, Inc. **SIC:** 2024—Ice Cream & Frozen Desserts.

★ 63369 ★ **Builders Square**
11309 N. Nebraska Ave.
Tampa, FL 33612
(813)972-1778
Company Type: Subsidiary. **Ultimate Parent:** K-Mart. **SIC:** 5039—Construction Materials Nec.

★ 63370 ★ **Burdines Department Store**
3149 W. Euclid Ave.
Tampa, FL 33629
(813)286-7527
Ultimate Parent: Federated Department Stores.

★ 63371 ★ **Burlington Northern Railroa**
1111 N. Westshore Blvd.
Tampa, FL 33607
(813)877-7463
Ultimate Parent: Burlington Northern. **SIC:** 4011—Railroads—Line-Haul Operating.

★ 63372 ★ **Busch Gardens**
PO Box 9158
Tampa, FL 33674
(813)987-5283
Officer: Joseph Fincher, General Manager. **Ultimate Parent:** Anheuser-Busch. **SIC:** 7996—Amusement Parks.

★ 63373 ★ **California Federal Bank**
1155 S. Dale Mabry Hwy. 14
Tampa, FL 33629
Ultimate Parent: California Federal Bank. **SIC:** 6099—Functions Related to Deposit Banking.

★ 63374 ★ **California Federal Bank**
1315 S. Dale Mabry Hwy.
Tampa, FL 33629
Ultimate Parent: California Federal Bank. **SIC:** 6022—State Commercial Banks.

★ 63375 ★ **California Federal Bank, FSB**
1315 S. Dale Mabry Hwy.
Tampa, FL 33629-5052
(813)254-4519
Location Type: Branch office. **Officer:** Grace Barnes, Manager. **Ultimate Parent:** California Federal Bank. **SIC:** 6021—National Commercial Banks.

★ 63376 ★ **California Federal Bank, FSB**
13188 N. Dale Mabry Hwy.
Tampa, FL 33618-2406
(813)968-6188
Location Type: Branch office. **Ultimate Parent:** California Federal Bank. **SIC:** 6021—National Commercial Banks.

★ 63377 ★ **California Federal Bank, FSB**
4830 W. Kennedy Blvd., Ste. 150
Tampa, FL 33609-2517
(813)287-8852
Location Type: Branch office. **Officer:** Robert Dane, Manager. **Ultimate Parent:** California Federal Bank. **SIC:** 6021—National Commercial Banks.

★ 63378 ★ **Casual Corner**
328 Westshore Plz.
Tampa, FL 33609
(813)286-0280
Ultimate Parent: United States Shoe. **SIC:** 5621—Women's Clothing Stores; 5651—Family Clothing Stores.

★ 63379 ★ **Casual Corner**
2146 University Sq.
Tampa, FL 33612
(813)977-7600
Ultimate Parent: United States Shoe. **SIC:** 5621—Women's Clothing Stores.

★ 63380 ★ **Casual Corner**
3302 W. Tampa Bay Blvd.
Tampa, FL 33607
(813)872-8571
Ultimate Parent: United States Shoe. **SIC:** 5651—Family Clothing Stores.

★ 63381 ★ **Casual Corners**
2399 E. Lake Ave.
Tampa, FL 33610
(813)621-3710
Ultimate Parent: United States Shoe. **SIC:** 5651—Family Clothing Stores.

★ 63382 ★ **Cf Industries Inc.**
2520 N. Guy Verger Blvd.
Tampa, FL 33605
(813)247-5531
Ultimate Parent: CF Industries. **SIC:** 4214—Local Trucking With Storage.

★ 63383 ★ **Chase Home Mortgage Corp.**
10008 N. Dale Mabry Hwy.
Tampa, FL 33618
(813)962-1868
Ultimate Parent: Chase Manhattan Corp. **SIC:** 6141—Personal Credit Institutions.

★ 63384 ★ **Chase Home Mortgage Corp.**
5006 E. Longboat Blvd.
Tampa, FL 33615
(813)881-2430
Ultimate Parent: Chase Manhattan Corp.

★ 63385 ★ **Chase Home Mortgage Corp.**
5006 E. Longboat Blvd.
Tampa, FL 33615
(813)881-2430
Ultimate Parent: Chase Manhattan Corp.

★ 63386 ★ **Chase Home Mortgage Corp.**
4915 Independence Pky.
Tampa, FL 33634
(813)881-2000 **Fax:** (813)881-2066
Location Type: Branch office. **Ultimate Parent:** Chase Manhattan Corp.

★ 63387 ★ **Chase Manhatten Bank of Florida, NA**
4915 Independence Pky.
Tampa, FL 33634-7540
(813)823-5880 **Fax:** (813)541-9165 **Telex:** 441412
Location Type: Branch office. **Ultimate Parent:** Chase Manhattan Corp. **SIC:** 6021—National Commercial Banks.

★ 63388 ★ **Chromalloy Castings Tampa Corp.**
7030 Anderson Rd.
Tampa, FL 33634
Ultimate Parent: Sequa Corp. **SIC:** 3724—Aircraft Engines & Engine Parts.

★ 63389 ★ **Cigna Health Plan of Florida Inc.**
2502 N. Rocky Point Dr.
Tampa, FL 33607-1421
(813)281-1000
Company Type: Subsidiary. **Officer:** Bradley Arms, President. **Ultimate Parent:** Cigna Corp. **SIC:** 6324—Hospital & Medical Service Plans; 8011—Offices & Clinics of Medical Doctors. **Employee Count:** 414.

★ 63390 ★ **Circus World**
1160 E. Lake Ave.
Tampa, FL 33605
(813)621-8338
Ultimate Parent: Melville. **SIC:** 5945—Hobby, Toy & Game Shops.

★ 63391 ★ **Circus World Toy Stores Inc.**
2148 University Sq.
Tampa, FL 33612
(813)971-6041
Ultimate Parent: Melville. **SIC:** 5945—Hobby, Toy & Game Shops.

★ 63392 ★ **Circus World Toys Store**
282 Westshore Plz.
Tampa, FL 33609
(813)876-0190
Ultimate Parent: Melville. **SIC:** 5945—Hobby, Toy & Game Shops.

★ 63393 ★ **Circus World Toys Store**
5701 E. Hillsborough Ave.
Tampa, FL 33610
(813)621-8338
Ultimate Parent: Melville. **SIC:** 5945—Hobby, Toy & Game Shops.

★ 63394 ★ **Clorox Co., Tampa Plant**
3601 E. Columbus Dr.
Tampa, FL 33605
Ultimate Parent: Clorox Co. **SIC:** 2842—Polishes & Sanitation Goods; 3085—Plastics Bottles.

★ 63395 ★ **Coast to Coast Express**
1801 N. 52nd St.
Tampa, FL 33619
(813)248-1278
Ultimate Parent: Servistar Corp. **SIC:** 4213—Trucking Except Local.

★ 63396 ★ **Coast to Coast Transmission**
1105 S. Us Hwy. 41
Tampa, FL 33619
(813)671-3787
Ultimate Parent: Servistar Corp.

★ 63397 ★ **Collective Mortgage Service**
4511 N. Himes Ave.
Tampa, FL 33614
(813)875-3914
Ultimate Parent: Collective Bancorp. **SIC:** 6162—Mortgage Bankers & Correspondents.

★ 63398 ★ **ConAgra Shrimp Co./ Singleton Seafood Co.**
PO Box 2819
Tampa, FL 33601
(813)241-1500 **Fax:** (813)247-2019
Officer: Jesse Gonzalez, President. **Ultimate Parent:** Conagra.

★ 63399 ★ **Delta Air Lines**
5201 W. Kennedy Blvd.
Tampa, FL 33609
(813)286-1800
Ultimate Parent: Delta Air Lines, Inc. **SIC:** 4512—Air Transportation—Scheduled; 4729—Passenger Transportation Arrangement Nec.

★ 63400 ★ **Delta Air Lines**
2 Tampa City Ctr.
Tampa, FL 33602
(813)879-5800
Ultimate Parent: Delta Air Lines, Inc. **SIC:** 4512—Air Transportation—Scheduled.

★ 63401 ★ **Delta Air Lines**
Tampa International Airport St.
Tampa, FL 33607
(813)286-1800
Ultimate Parent: Delta Air Lines, Inc. **SIC:** 4512—Air Transportation—Scheduled.

★ 63402 ★ **Delta Air Lines Inc.**
2 Tampa City Ctr.
Tampa, FL 33602
(813)879-5800
Ultimate Parent: Delta Air Lines, Inc. **SIC:** 4512—Air Transportation—Scheduled.

★ 63403 ★ **Delta Business Systems**
5440 Beaumont Central Bldg., No. 400
Tampa, FL 33634
(813)888-7710
Officer: Dave Albert, Manager. **Ultimate Parent:** Alco Standard Corp.

★ 63404 ★ **Delta Business Systems**
5440 Beaumont Central Bldg., No. 400
Tampa, FL 33634
(813)888-7710
Officer: Dave Albert, Manager. **Ultimate Parent:** Alco Standard Corp.

★ 63405 ★ **Deluxe Check Printers Inc.**
7705 Cheri Ct.
Tampa, FL 33634
Ultimate Parent: Deluxe Corp. **SIC:** 2782—Blankbooks & Looseleaf Binders; 2752—Commercial Printing—Lithographic.

★ 63406 ★ **Deluxe Check Printers Inc.**
5004 Cheri Ct.
Tampa, FL 33634
Ultimate Parent: Deluxe Corp. **SIC:** 2782—Blankbooks & Looseleaf Binders; 2752—Commercial Printing—Lithographic.

★ 63407 ★ **Deposit Guaranty Mortgage C**
4401 W. Kennedy Blvd.
Tampa, FL 33609
(813)287-2269
Ultimate Parent: Deposit Guaranty Corp. **SIC:** 6162—Mortgage Bankers & Correspondents.

★ 63408 ★ **Dun & Bradstreet**
Dun & Bradstreet Plan Services, Inc.
3501 Frontage Rd.
Tampa, FL 33607
(813)289-1000 **Fax:** (813)289-7937
Company Type: Headquarters. **Officer:** Trevor G. Smith, Chairman of the Board. **Ultimate Parent:** Dun & Bradstreet. **SIC:** 6411—Insurance Agents, Brokers & Service; 7372—Prepackaged Software.

★ 63409 ★ **Dun & Bradstreet Pension Services, Inc.**
3501 Frontage Rd.
Tampa, FL 33607
(813)289-1000 **Fax:** (813)287-7937
Company Type: Subsidiary. **Officer:** Clifford L. Bateman, President. **Ultimate Parent:** Dun & Bradstreet. **SIC:** 6411—Insurance Agents, Brokers & Service.

★ 63410 ★ **Dun & Bradstreet Plan Services**
3501 Frontage Rd.
Tampa, FL 33607
(813)289-1000
Company Type: Subsidiary. **Officer:** Clifford L. Bateman, President & CEO. **Ultimate Parent:** Dun & Bradstreet. **SIC:** 6411—Insurance Agents, Brokers & Service.

★ 63411 ★ **Dupont Publishing**
2502 N. Rocky Point Dr.
Tampa, FL 33607
(813)281-5656
Officer: Steve Chapman, President. **Ultimate Parent:** E.I. DuPont De Nemours. **SIC:** 2721—Periodicals.

★ 63412 ★ **Durr-Fillauer Medical Inc.**
4933 Tampa Blvd. W
Tampa, FL 33602
(813)885-7947
Ultimate Parent: Bergen Brunswig Corp. **SIC:** 5047—Medical & Hospital Equipment.

★ 63413 ★ **Emery Worldwide**
Tampa
Tampa, FL 33622
(813)883-3720
Ultimate Parent: Consolidated Freightways. **SIC:** 4731—Freight Transportation Arrangement.

★ 63414 ★ **Exxon**
10002 N. Florida Ave.
Tampa, FL 33612
(813)933-2200
Ultimate Parent: Exxon. **SIC:** 5541—Gasoline Service Stations.

★ 63415 ★ **Exxon Co. USA**
5010 W. Kennedy Blvd.
Tampa, FL 33609
(813)282-0919
Ultimate Parent: Exxon. **SIC:** 5599—Automotive Dealers Nec.

★ 63416 ★ **Exxon Gas**
2605 N. 50th St.
Tampa, FL 33619
(813)248-3415
Ultimate Parent: Exxon. **SIC:** 5541—Gasoline Service Stations.

★ 63417 ★ **First Union National Bank of Florida**
5144 E. Busch Blvd.
Tampa, FL 33617-5306
(813)276-6141
Location Type: Branch office. **Ultimate Parent:** First Union Corp. **SIC:** 6021—National Commercial Banks.

★ 63418 ★ **First Union National Bank of Florida**
5880 E. Fowler Ave.
Tampa, FL 33612-5507
(813)276-6096
Location Type: Branch office. **Ultimate Parent:** First Union Corp. **SIC:** 6021—National Commercial Banks.

★ 63419 ★ **First Union National Bank of Florida**
8125 W. Hillsborough Ave.
Tampa, FL 33615-4195
(813)276-6163
Location Type: Branch office. **Ultimate Parent:** First Union Corp. **SIC:** 6021—National Commercial Banks.

★ 63420 ★   First Union National
Bank of Florida
4203 Gandy Blvd.
Tampa, FL 33611-3403
(813)276-6050
Location Type: Branch office. **Ultimate Parent:** First Union Corp. **SIC:** 6021—National Commercial Banks.

★ 63421 ★   First Union National
Bank of Florida
13003 N. Dale Mabry Hwy.
Tampa, FL 33618-2818
(813)276-6201
Location Type: Branch office. **Ultimate Parent:** First Union Corp. **SIC:** 6021—National Commercial Banks.

★ 63422 ★   First Union National
Bank of Florida
1500 S. Dale Mabry Hwy.
Tampa, FL 33629-5893
(813)276-6128
Location Type: Branch office. **Ultimate Parent:** First Union Corp. **SIC:** 6021—National Commercial Banks.

★ 63423 ★   First Union National
Bank of Florida
1770 N. 50th St.
Tampa, FL 33619-3104
(813)276-6128
Location Type: Branch office. **Ultimate Parent:** First Union Corp. **SIC:** 6021—National Commercial Banks.

★ 63424 ★   First Union National
Bank of Florida
7920 Gunn Hwy.
Tampa, FL 33526-6023
(813)276-6023
Location Type: Branch office. **Ultimate Parent:** First Union Corp. **SIC:** 6021—National Commercial Banks.

★ 63425 ★   First Union National
Bank of Florida
214 S. Hyde Park Ave.
Tampa, FL 33606-1932
(813)276-6165
Location Type: Branch office. **Ultimate Parent:** First Union Corp. **SIC:** 6021—National Commercial Banks.

★ 63426 ★   First Union National
Bank of Florida
12650 N. Dale Mabry Hwy.
Tampa, FL 33618-2409
(813)276-6128
Location Type: Branch office. **Ultimate Parent:** First Union Corp. **SIC:** 6021—National Commercial Banks.

★ 63427 ★   First Union National
Bank of Florida
2009 E. Fowler Ave.
Tampa, FL 33612-6275
(813)276-6020
Location Type: Branch office. **Ultimate Parent:** First Union Corp. **SIC:** 6021—National Commercial Banks.

★ 63428 ★   First Union National
Bank of Florida
4950 W. Kennedy Blvd.
Tampa, FL 33609-1828
(813)276-6035
Location Type: Branch office. **Ultimate Parent:** First Union Corp. **SIC:** 6021—National Commercial Banks.

★ 63429 ★   First Union National
Bank of Florida
202 W. Bearss Ave.
Tampa, FL 33613-1210
(813)961-0921
Location Type: Branch office. **Ultimate Parent:** First Union Corp. **SIC:** 6021—National Commercial Banks.

★ 63430 ★   First Union National
Bank of Florida
12002 Anderson Rd.
Tampa, FL 33625
(813)276-6087
Location Type: Branch office. **Ultimate Parent:** First Union Corp. **SIC:** 6021—National Commercial Banks.

★ 63431 ★   First Union National
Bank of Florida
100 S. Ashley Dr.
Tampa, FL 33602-5348
(813)276-6000
Location Type: Branch office. **Ultimate Parent:** First Union Corp. **SIC:** 6021—National Commercial Banks.

★ 63432 ★   Florida Coca-Cola
Bottling Co.
9102 Sabal Industrial Blvd.
Tampa, FL 33619
Ultimate Parent: Coca-Cola Enterprises. **SIC:** 2086—Bottled & Canned Soft Drinks.

★ 63433 ★   Foamex L.P.
Curon
3119 Queen Palm Dr.
Tampa, FL 33619
Ultimate Parent: Foamex. **SIC:** 3086—Plastics Foam Products.

★ 63434 ★   Foot Action U S a
2244 University Sq.
Tampa, FL 33612
(813)972-3329
Ultimate Parent: Melville. **SIC:** 5941—Sporting Goods & Bicycle Shops.

★ 63435 ★   Fortune Bank, ASB
13944 N. Dale Mabry Hwy.
Tampa, FL 33618-2463
(813)962-2704
Location Type: Branch office. **Officer:** Bruce Burgin, Manager. **Ultimate Parent:** Fortune Bancorp.

★ 63436 ★   Fortune Bank, ASB
3902 Henderson Blvd.
Tampa, FL 34629-5016
(813)254-6071
Location Type: Branch office. **Ultimate Parent:** Fortune Bancorp. **SIC:** 6021—National Commercial Banks.

★ 63437 ★   GAF Corp.
5138 Madison Ave.
Tampa, FL 33619
(813)248-6202
Officer: Scott Norrington, Manager. **Ultimate Parent:** GAF Corp. **SIC:** 2952—Asphalt Felts & Coatings.

★ 63438 ★   The Gap
117 Westshore Plz.
Tampa, FL 33609
(813)286-1440
Ultimate Parent: GAP. **SIC:** 5651—Family Clothing Stores; 5651—Family Clothing Stores.

★ 63439 ★   The Gap
703 S. Dakota Ave.
Tampa, FL 33606
(813)251-3300
Ultimate Parent: GAP. **SIC:** 5611—Men's & Boys' Clothing Stores.

★ 63440 ★   The Gap
2027 Tampa Bay Ctr. Mall
Tampa, FL 33607
(813)876-3416
Ultimate Parent: GAP. **SIC:** 5651—Family Clothing Stores.

★ 63441 ★   The Gap
2118 University Sq.
Tampa, FL 33612
(813)977-9902
Ultimate Parent: GAP. **SIC:** 5611—Men's & Boys' Clothing Stores; 5651—Family Clothing Stores.

★ 63442 ★   General Electric Co.
4710 Eisenhower Blvd.
Tampa, FL 33634
(813)884-8455
Officer: Steve Pulliam, Manager. **Ultimate Parent:** General Electric. **SIC:** 3844—X-Ray Apparatus & Tubes.

★ 63443 ★   Georgia Pacific Corp.
815 S. 56th St.
Tampa, FL 33619
(813)621-1351
Officer: Rod Shelton, Manager. **Ultimate Parent:** Georgia-Pacific. **SIC:** 3275—Gypsum Products.

★ 63444 ★   Greyhound Bus Lines
4524 Oak Fair Blvd.
Tampa, FL 33610
(813)621-8677
Ultimate Parent: Greyhound Lines Inc. **SIC:** 4131—Intercity & Rural Bus Transportation.

★ 63445 ★   GTE Communications
Corp.
1907 N. US Hwy. 301
Tampa, FL 33619-2639
(813)623-4000
Company Type: Subsidiary. **Officer:** Gerald K. Dinsmore, President. **Ultimate Parent:** GTE. **SIC:** 5999—Miscellaneous Retail Stores Nec; 7629—Electrical Repair Shops Nec; 7359—Equipment Rental & Leasing Nec. **Employee Count:** 844. **Sales:** 81.6 M.

★ 63446 ★   GTE Data Services
Inc.
1 E. Telecom Pky.
Tampa, FL 33637-0902
(813)978-4000
Company Type: Subsidiary. **Officer:** Don A. Hayes, President. **Ultimate Parent:** GTE. **SIC:** 7374—Data Processing & Preparation.

★ 63447 ★   GTE Florida Inc.
1 Tampa City Ctr.
Tampa, FL 33602-5182
(813)224-4011
Company Type: Subsidiary. **Officer:** Gerald K. Dinsmore, President. **Ultimate Parent:** GTE. **SIC:** 4813—Telephone Communications Except Radiotelephone; 6519—Real Property Lessors Nec; 8721—Accounting, Auditing & Bookkeeping; 5065—Electronic Parts & Equipment Nec; 7629—Electrical Repair Shops Nec. **Employee Count:** 8850. **Sales:** 1.2 M.

★ 63448 ★   GTE Florida Inc.
1 Tampa City Ctr.
201 N. Franklin St.
Tampa, FL 33602
(813)224-4011 **Fax:** (813)221-3293
Company Type: Subsidiary. **Ultimate Parent:** GTE. **SIC:** 4812—Radiotelephone Communications.

★ 63449 ★   GTE Leasing Corp.
1 Tampa City Ctr.
201 N. Franklin St.
Tampa, FL 33602-5813
(813)229-6000 **Fax:** (813)229-3988
Company Type: Subsidiary. **Ultimate Parent:** GTE. **SIC:** 7374—Data Processing & Preparation.

★ 63450 ★   GTE Leasing Corp.
201 N. Franklin St.
Tampa, FL 33602-5187
(813)229-6000
Company Type: Subsidiary. **Officer:** Richard L. Shumate, President & Treasurer. **Ultimate Parent:** GTE. **SIC:** 7359—Equipment Rental & Leasing Nec. **Employee Count:** 81. **Sales:** 30.8 M.

★ 63451 ★   GTE South Inc.
1 Tampa City Ctr.
Tampa, FL 33602-5182
(813)224-4011
Company Type: Subsidiary. **Officer:** Gerald K. Dinsmore, President & CEO. **Ultimate Parent:** GTE. **SIC:** 4813—Telephone Communications Except Radiotelephone; 6519—Real Property Lessors Nec; 8721—Accounting, Auditing & Bookkeeping; 5065—Electronic Parts & Equipment Nec. **Employee Count:** 6238. **Sales:** 974 M.

★ 63452 ★   GTE South Inc.
1 Tampa City Center
201 N. Franklin St.
Tampa, FL 33602
Company Type: Subsidiary. **Ultimate Parent:** GTE. **SIC:** 4812—Radiotelephone Communications.

★ 63453 ★   GTE Telecom Inc.
100 S. Ashley St.
Tampa, FL 33602
Company Type: Subsidiary. **Ultimate Parent:** GTE. **SIC:** 4812—Radiotelephone Communications.

★ 63454 ★   GTE Telecom Inc.
100 S. Ashley St.
Tampa, FL 33602
Company Type: Subsidiary. **Ultimate Parent:** GTE.

★ 63455 ★   Harbour Island, Inc.
1 Tampa City Ctr.
Tampa, FL 33602
(813)228-0712
Company Type: Subsidiary. **Officer:** Gerald L. Holm, COO. **Ultimate Parent:** Beneficial. **SIC:** 6552—Subdividers & Developers Nec. **Employee Count:** 6.

★ 63456 ★   Hertz Rent-A-Car
7748 Adamo Dr.
Tampa, FL 33619
(813)621-6583
Ultimate Parent: Hertz. **SIC:** 7514—Passenger Car Rental.

★ 63457 ★   Hoechst Roussel
Pharmaceuti
3550 W. Busch Blvd.
Tampa, FL 33618
(813)933-8115
Ultimate Parent: Hoechst Celanese Corp. **SIC:** 2834—Pharmaceutical Preparations.

★ 63458 ★   Honeywell Inc. Dcpd
10901 Malcolm Mckinley Dr.
Tampa, FL 33612
Ultimate Parent: Honeywell. **SIC:** 3600—Electronic & Other Electrical Equipment.

★ 63459 ★   Household Mortgage
Services
3550 W. Busch Blvd. 210
Tampa, FL 33618
(813)932-8565
Ultimate Parent: Household International. **SIC:** 6162—Mortgage Bankers & Correspondents.

★ 63460 ★   IBM Corp.
3350 W. Hillsborough Ave.
Tampa, FL 33614
(813)878-4890
Ultimate Parent: IBM.

★ 63461 ★   Jiffy Lube
7202 W. Hillsborough Ave.
Tampa, FL 33634
(813)888-8949
Ultimate Parent: Pennzoil. **SIC:** 7539—Automotive Repair Shops Nec.

★ 63462 ★   Jiffy Lube
8303 N. Dale Mabry Hwy.
Tampa, FL 33614
(813)932-0740
Ultimate Parent: Pennzoil. **SIC:** 5541—Gasoline Service Stations.

★ 63463 ★   Jiffy Lube
10150 N. Florida Ave.
Tampa, FL 33612
(813)935-1433
Ultimate Parent: Pennzoil. **SIC:** 5541—Gasoline Service Stations.

★ 63464 ★   Johnson Controls Inc.
Battery Group
10215 N. 30th St.
Tampa, FL 33612
Ultimate Parent: Johnson Controls Inc. **SIC:** 3691—Storage Batteries.

★ 63465 ★   Kay Bee Toys &
Hobby
3302 Tampa Bay Ctr. Nit 1000
Tampa, FL 33607
(813)873-7015
Ultimate Parent: Melville. **SIC:** 5945—Hobby, Toy & Game Shops.

★ 63466 ★   Kentucky Fried
Chicken
2420 W. Kennedy Blvd.
Tampa, FL 33609
(813)254-4527
Ultimate Parent: Pepsico. **SIC:** 5812—Eating Places.

★ 63467 ★   Kentucky Fried
Chicken
8160 Woodland Ctr. Blvd.
Tampa, FL 33614
(813)626-1057
Ultimate Parent: Pepsico. **SIC:** 5812—Eating Places.

★ 63468 ★   Kentucky Fried
Chicken
7605 W. Hillsborough Ave.
Tampa, FL 33615
(813)884-4372
Ultimate Parent: Pepsico. **SIC:** 5812—Eating Places.

★ 63469 ★ Kentucky Fried Chicken
1611 N. Nebraska Ave.
Tampa, FL 33602
(813)273-0980
Ultimate Parent: Pepsico. **SIC:** 5812—Eating Places.

★ 63470 ★ Kentucky Fried Chicken
4402 W. Gandy Blvd.
Tampa, FL 33611
(813)837-5391
Ultimate Parent: Pepsico. **SIC:** 5812—Eating Places.

★ 63471 ★ Kentucky Fried Chicken
5310 N. Florida Ave.
Tampa, FL 33603
(813)237-1519
Ultimate Parent: Pepsico. **SIC:** 5812—Eating Places.

★ 63472 ★ Kentucky Fried Chicken
9202 N. Florida Ave.
Tampa, FL 33612
(813)935-6000
Ultimate Parent: Pepsico. **SIC:** 5812—Eating Places.

★ 63473 ★ Kentucky Fried Chicken
4302 N. Armenia Ave.
Tampa, FL 33607
(813)872-0282
Ultimate Parent: Pepsico. **SIC:** 5812—Eating Places.

★ 63474 ★ Kentucky Fried Chicken
8550 N. Dale Mabry Hwy.
Tampa, FL 33614
(813)933-4667
Ultimate Parent: Pepsico. **SIC:** 5812—Eating Places.

★ 63475 ★ Kentucky Fried Chicken
3509 E. Busch Blvd.
Tampa, FL 33612
(813)988-3370
Ultimate Parent: Pepsico. **SIC:** 5812—Eating Places.

★ 63476 ★ Kentucky Fried Chicken
3801 Henderson Blvd.
Tampa, FL 33629
(813)877-1000
Ultimate Parent: Pepsico. **SIC:** 5812—Eating Places.

★ 63477 ★ Kentucky Fried Chicken
1733 N. 50th St.
Tampa, FL 33619
(813)248-6936
Ultimate Parent: Pepsico. **SIC:** 5812—Eating Places.

★ 63478 ★ Key Bank of Fla
2727 W. Buffalo Ave.
Tampa, FL 33607
(813)933-7851
Ultimate Parent: Keycorp. **SIC:** 6022—State Commercial Banks.

★ 63479 ★ Lane Bryant
2258 University Sq.
Tampa, FL 33612
(813)971-7951
Ultimate Parent: Limited. **SIC:** 5621—Women's Clothing Stores.

★ 63480 ★ Lane Bryant
1459 Eastlake Sq.
Tampa, FL 33610
(813)626-0869
Ultimate Parent: Limited. **SIC:** 5651—Family Clothing Stores.

★ 63481 ★ Lens Crafters
2022 Tampa Bay Ctr. Mall
Tampa, FL 33607
(813)875-8474
Ultimate Parent: United States Shoe. **SIC:** 5999—Miscellaneous Retail Stores Nec.

★ 63482 ★ Lerner Shop
3302 Tampa Bay Ctr. 207
Tampa, FL 33607
(813)870-3593
Ultimate Parent: Limited. **SIC:** 5651—Family Clothing Stores.

★ 63483 ★ Lerner Shop
2361 E. Lake Ave.
Tampa, FL 33610
(813)621-3300
Ultimate Parent: Limited. **SIC:** 5651—Family Clothing Stores.

★ 63484 ★ Liberty Business Credit Cor
4350 W. Cypress St. 820
Tampa, FL 33607
(813)874-6079
Ultimate Parent: Inland Steel Industries. **SIC:** 6159—Miscellaneous Business Credit Institutions.

★ 63485 ★ Liberty Mutual Insurance Co.
5426 Bay Ctr. Dr.
Tampa, FL 33609
(813)286-0910
Ultimate Parent: Liberty Mutual Group. **SIC:** 6411—Insurance Agents, Brokers & Service.

★ 63486 ★ The Limited
3302 W. Tampa Bay Blvd.
Tampa, FL 33607
(813)877-6490
Ultimate Parent: Limited. **SIC:** 5651—Family Clothing Stores.

★ 63487 ★ The Limited
711 S. Dakota Ave.
Tampa, FL 33606
(813)251-6393
Ultimate Parent: Limited. **SIC:** 5621—Women's Clothing Stores.

★ 63488 ★ The Limited
129 Westshore Plz.
Tampa, FL 33609
(813)286-8527
Ultimate Parent: Limited. **SIC:** 5651—Family Clothing Stores.

★ 63489 ★ The Limited Express
125 Westshore Plz.
Tampa, FL 33609
(813)287-0024
Ultimate Parent: Limited. **SIC:** 5621—Women's Clothing Stores.

★ 63490 ★ Linens N Things
15064 N. Dale Mabry Hwy.
Tampa, FL 33618
Ultimate Parent: Melville. **SIC:** 5719—Miscellaneous Home Furnishings Stores; 5719—Miscellaneous Home Furnishings Stores.

★ 63491 ★ Marathon Petroleum Co.
425 S. 20th St.
Tampa, FL 33605
(813)248-6268
Ultimate Parent: USX Corp. **SIC:** 5172—Petroleum Products Nec.

★ 63492 ★ Marshalls Department Store
3661 W. Waters Ave.
Tampa, FL 33614
(813)931-1822
Ultimate Parent: Melville. **SIC:** 5651—Family Clothing Stores.

★ 63493 ★ Mary Kay Cosm
7404 Harney Rd.
Tampa, FL 33637
(813)985-4613
Ultimate Parent: Mary Kay Cosmetics. **SIC:** 5999—Miscellaneous Retail Stores Nec.

★ 63494 ★ Mary Kay Cosmetics
5419 Britwell Ct.
Tampa, FL 33624
(813)968-3001
Ultimate Parent: Mary Kay Cosmetics. **SIC:** 5999—Miscellaneous Retail Stores Nec.

★ 63495 ★ Massachusetts Mutual Life Insurance
2502 N. Rocky Point Dr.
Tampa, FL 33607
(813)882-9554
Ultimate Parent: Massasucetts Mutual Life.

★ 63496 ★ McDonalds
4333 W. Hillsborough Ave.
Tampa, FL 33614
(813)886-4311
Ultimate Parent: McDonald's. **SIC:** 5812—Eating Places.

★ 63497 ★ McDonalds Restaurants
1905 N. Dale Mabry Hwy.
Tampa, FL 33607
(813)876-1118
Ultimate Parent: McDonald's. **SIC:** 5812—Eating Places.

★ 63498 ★ McDonalds Restaurants
7909 W. Hillsborough Ave.
Tampa, FL 33615
(813)884-0229
Ultimate Parent: McDonald's. **SIC:** 5812—Eating Places.

★ 63499 ★ McDonalds Restaurants
2205 E. Fletcher Ave.
Tampa, FL 33612
(813)971-4775
Ultimate Parent: McDonald's. **SIC:** 5812—Eating Places.

★ 63500 ★ McDonalds Restaurants
920 E. Fowler Ave.
Tampa, FL 33612
(813)971-8922
Ultimate Parent: McDonald's. **SIC:** 5812—Eating Places.

★ 63501 ★ Mcduff Appliance & Electron
2228 University Sq.
Tampa, FL 33612
(813)977-6981
Ultimate Parent: Tandy Corp. **SIC:** 5719—Miscellaneous Home Furnishings Stores.

★ 63502 ★ Mellon Fin Services Corp.
10640 N. 56th St.
Tampa, FL 33617
(813)985-6733
Ultimate Parent: Mellon Bank Corp. **SIC:** 6141—Personal Credit Institutions.

★ 63503 ★ Memorial Hospital of Tampa
2901 Swann Ave.
Tampa, FL 33609
(813)877-0441
Officer: Keith Henthorne, Executive Director. **Ultimate Parent:** American Medical Holdings. **SIC:** 8062—General Medical & Surgical Hospitals.

★ 63504 ★ Mobil Mart
2928 E. Fowler Ave.
Tampa, FL 33612
(813)972-3706
Ultimate Parent: Mobil. **SIC:** 5541—Gasoline Service Stations.

★ 63505 ★ National Rx Services Inc. (Tampa)
8408 Benjamin Rd.
Tampa, FL 33634
(813)886-0705 **Fax:** (813)882-3869
Officer: Robert Landi, Vice President & General Manager. **Ultimate Parent:** Medco Containment Services.

★ 63506 ★ New England Mutl Life Insur
1805 N. Westshore Blvd.
Tampa, FL 33607
(813)872-0362
Ultimate Parent: New England Mutual Life. **SIC:** 6371—Pension, Health & Welfare Funds.

★ 63507 ★ New England Mutual Life Insurance
5510 W. La Salle St.
Tampa, FL 33607
(813)289-1835
Ultimate Parent: New England Mutual Life. **SIC:** 6371—Pension, Health & Welfare Funds; 6411—Insurance Agents, Brokers & Service.

SIC: 6411—Insurance Agents, Brokers & Service.

★ 63508 ★ New York Life
Southeastern Agencies
7650 W. Courtney, Ste. 300
Cambell, Causeway
Tampa, FL 33607
(813)281-0100 **Fax:** (813)281-0110
Officer: Richard Fox, General Manager.
Ultimate Parent: New York Life.

★ 63509 ★ New York Life Tampa Group Sales Office
Eastern Group Marketing Zone
3030 N. Rocky Point Dr. W., Ste. 250
Tampa, FL 33607
(813)286-8711 **Fax:** (813)289-6089
Officer: Michael Robertson, Group Manager. **Ultimate Parent:** New York Life.

★ 63510 ★ New York life Tampa General Office
Southeastern Agencies
PO Box 22968
Tampa, FL 33622
(813)281-0100 **Fax:** (813)281-0110
Officer: Richard Fox, General Manager.
Ultimate Parent: New York Life.

★ 63511 ★ Northwest Airlines Inc.
5729 Hoover Blvd.
Tampa, FL 33634
(813)883-3200
Ultimate Parent: NWA. **SIC:** 4512—Air Transportation—Scheduled.

★ 63512 ★ Norwest Mortgage Inc.
1715 N. Westshore Blvd.
Tampa, FL 33607
(813)877-3627
Ultimate Parent: Norwest Corp. **SIC:** 6162—Mortgage Bankers & Correspondents.

★ 63513 ★ O'Donnell-Usen USA
5024 Uceta Rd.
Tampa, FL 33619
(813)241-1500
Company Type: Division. **Location Type:** Plant. **Officer:** Tom Lavan, Vice President & General Manager. **Ultimate Parent:** Conagra.

★ 63514 ★ Otis Elevator Co.
1212 W. Cass St.
Tampa, FL 33606
(813)251-1841
Ultimate Parent: United Technologies. **SIC:** 3534—Elevators & Moving Stairways; 5084—Industrial Machinery & Equipment.

★ 63515 ★ Outboard Marine Corp.
Four Winds Yacht Div.
5109 Cone Rd.
Tampa, FL 33610
Company Type: Division. **Ultimate Parent:** Outboard Marine. **SIC:** 3732—Boat Building & Repairing.

★ 63516 ★ Pepsi-Cola Bottling Co.
Tampa
11315 N. 30th St.
Tampa, FL 33612
Company Type: Division. **Ultimate Parent:** Pepsico. **SIC:** 2086—Bottled & Canned Soft Drinks.

★ 63517 ★ Pepsi-Cola Co.
5555 N. 50th St.
Tampa, FL 33610
(813)622-7584
Ultimate Parent: Pepsico. **SIC:** 2086—Bottled & Canned Soft Drinks.

★ 63518 ★ Petite Sophisticate
3302 W. Tampa Bay Blvd.
Tampa, FL 33607
(813)875-8040
Ultimate Parent: United States Shoe. **SIC:** 5621—Women's Clothing Stores.

★ 63519 ★ Pitney Bowes
5404 Cypress Ctr. Dr.
Tampa, FL 33609
(813)289-9431
Officer: Larry Kessler, Manager. **Ultimate Parent:** Pitney Bowes. **SIC:** 3663—Radio & T.V. Communications Equipment.

★ 63520 ★ Pizza Hut
7023 W. Hillsborough Ave.
Tampa, FL 33634
(813)886-0204
Ultimate Parent: Pepsico. SIC: 5812—
Eating Places.

★ 63521 ★ Pizza Hut
4511 W. Gandy Blvd.
Tampa, FL 33611
(813)839-8368
Ultimate Parent: Pepsico. SIC: 5812—
Eating Places.

★ 63522 ★ Pizza Hut
3611 W. Hillsborough Ave.
Tampa, FL 33614
(813)874-2969
Ultimate Parent: Pepsico. SIC: 5812—
Eating Places.

★ 63523 ★ Pizza Hut
8546 N. Dale Mabry Hwy.
Tampa, FL 33614
(813)932-3667
Ultimate Parent: Pepsico. SIC: 5812—
Eating Places.

★ 63524 ★ Pizza Hut
8426 N. Florida Ave.
Tampa, FL 33604
(813)935-0512
Ultimate Parent: Pepsico. SIC: 5812—
Eating Places.

★ 63525 ★ Pizza Hut
8600 N. 56th St.
Tampa, FL 33617
(813)988-0008
Ultimate Parent: Pepsico. SIC: 5812—
Eating Places.

★ 63526 ★ Pizza Hut
716 N. Dale Mabry Hwy.
Tampa, FL 33609
(813)870-3312
Ultimate Parent: Pepsico. SIC: 5812—
Eating Places.

★ 63527 ★ Pizza Hut
1202 E. Fowler Ave.
Tampa, FL 33612
(813)971-4424
Ultimate Parent: Pepsico. SIC: 5812—
Eating Places.

★ 63528 ★ Pizza Hut
3405 E. Hillsborough Ave.
Tampa, FL 33610
(813)238-1212
Ultimate Parent: Pepsico. SIC: 5812—
Eating Places.

★ 63529 ★ Pizza Hut
4001 E. Busch Blvd.
Tampa, FL 33617
(813)985-2297
Ultimate Parent: Pepsico. SIC: 5812—
Eating Places.

★ 63530 ★ Pizza Hut
902 W. Busch Blvd.
Tampa, FL 33612
(813)932-4448
Ultimate Parent: Pepsico. SIC: 5812—
Eating Places.

★ 63531 ★ Pizza Hut
3010 W. Gandy Blvd.
Tampa, FL 33611
(813)837-8051
Ultimate Parent: Pepsico. SIC: 5812—
Eating Places.

★ 63532 ★ Pizza Hut
1500 S. Church Ave.
Tampa, FL 33629
(813)251-0761
Ultimate Parent: Pepsico. SIC: 5812—
Eating Places.

★ 63533 ★ Pizza Hut
2304 E. Bearss Ave.
Tampa, FL 33613
(813)971-4430
Ultimate Parent: Pepsico. SIC: 5812—
Eating Places.

★ 63534 ★ Pizza Hut
7512 Paula Dr.
Tampa, FL 33615
(813)884-1972
Ultimate Parent: Pepsico. SIC: 5812—
Eating Places.

★ 63535 ★ Pizza Hut
2501 N. 50th St.
Tampa, FL 33619
(813)248-3425
Ultimate Parent: Pepsico. SIC: 5812—
Eating Places.

★ 63536 ★ Pizza Hut Region
Training
6323 Benjamin Rd.
Tampa, FL 33634
(813)888-5200
Ultimate Parent: Pepsico. SIC: 5812—
Eating Places; 8299—Schools &
Educational Services Nec.

★ 63537 ★ PNC Trust Co. of
Florida, NA
One Tampa City Ctr., Ste. 2400
Tampa, FL 33602-5814
(813)273-0030 Fax: (813)223-2110
Location Type: Headquarters. Officer:
Gifford H. Hampton III, President & CEO.
Ultimate Parent: PNC Bank Corp. SIC:
6021—National Commercial Banks.

★ 63538 ★ Publix Super Market
13178 N. Dale Mabry Hwy.
Tampa, FL 33618
(813)962-6812
Ultimate Parent: Publix Super Markets.
SIC: 5411—Grocery Stores.

★ 63539 ★ Publix Super Market
16041 Tampa Palms Blvd. W
Tampa, FL 33647
(813)971-3702
Ultimate Parent: Publix Super Markets.
SIC: 5411—Grocery Stores.

★ 63540 ★ Publix Super Market
11502 N. 53rd St.
Tampa, FL 33617
(813)988-1980
Ultimate Parent: Publix Super Markets.
SIC: 5411—Grocery Stores.

★ 63541 ★ Publix Super Market
11782 State Rd. 574
Tampa, FL 33610
(813)684-6029
Ultimate Parent: Publix Super Markets.
SIC: 5411—Grocery Stores.

★ 63542 ★ Publix Super Market
10019 W. Hillsborough Ave.
Tampa, FL 33615
(813)886-9300
Ultimate Parent: Publix Super Markets.
SIC: 5411—Grocery Stores.

★ 63543 ★ Publix Super Market
Rural Route 4
Tampa, FL 33626
(813)961-5832
Ultimate Parent: Publix Super Markets.
SIC: 5411—Grocery Stores.

★ 63544 ★ Publix Super Market
6001 N. Nebraska Ave.
Tampa, FL 33604
(813)236-1331
Ultimate Parent: Publix Super Markets.
SIC: 5411—Grocery Stores.

★ 63545 ★ Publix Super Market
3615 W. Gandy Blvd.
Tampa, FL 33611
(813)831-2691
Ultimate Parent: Publix Super Markets.
SIC: 5411—Grocery Stores.

★ 63546 ★ Publix Super Market
2724 Hillsboro Plz.
Tampa, FL 33602
(813)877-5859
Ultimate Parent: Publix Super Markets.
SIC: 5411—Grocery Stores.

★ 63547 ★ Publix Super Market
1313 S. Dale Mabry Hwy.
Tampa, FL 33629
(813)251-8681
Ultimate Parent: Publix Super Markets.
SIC: 5411—Grocery Stores.

★ 63548 ★ Publix Super Market
2724 W. Hillsborough Ave.
Tampa, FL 33614
(813)877-5859
Ultimate Parent: Publix Super Markets.
SIC: 5411—Grocery Stores.

★ 63549 ★ Publix Super Markets
2724 W. Hillsborough Ave.
Tampa, FL 33614
(813)877-5859
Ultimate Parent: Publix Super Markets.
SIC: 5411—Grocery Stores.

★ 63550 ★ Publix Super Markets
1313 S. Dale Mabry Hwy.
Tampa, FL 33629
(813)251-8681
Ultimate Parent: Publix Super Markets.
SIC: 5411—Grocery Stores.

★ 63551 ★ Publix Super Markets
Inc.
3615 W. Gandy Blvd.
Tampa, FL 33611
(813)831-2691
Ultimate Parent: Publix Super Markets.
SIC: 5411—Grocery Stores.

★ 63552 ★ Publix Super Markets
Inc.
2724 Hillsboro Plz.
Tampa, FL 33602
(813)877-5859
Ultimate Parent: Publix Super Markets.
SIC: 5411—Grocery Stores.

★ 63553 ★ Publix Super Markets
Inc.
6001 N. Nebraska Ave.
Tampa, FL 33604
(813)236-1331
Ultimate Parent: Publix Super Markets.
SIC: 5411—Grocery Stores.

★ 63554 ★ Pulte Home Corp.
5907 Breckenridge Pky.
Tampa, FL 33610
(813)623-1561
Ultimate Parent: Pulte. SIC: 1521—
Single-Family Housing Construction.

★ 63555 ★ Pulte Home Corp.
502 S. 82nd St.
Tampa, FL 33619
(813)623-3953
Ultimate Parent: Pulte. SIC: 1521—
Single-Family Housing Construction.

★ 63556 ★ Pulte Home Corp.
11204 Ridge Dale Rd. N
Tampa, FL 33617
(813)985-2277
Ultimate Parent: Pulte. SIC: 1521—
Single-Family Housing Construction.

★ 63557 ★ Pulte Home Corp.
River Run
Tampa, FL 33617
(813)985-4027
Ultimate Parent: Pulte. SIC: 1521—
Single-Family Housing Construction.

★ 63558 ★ Radio Shack
241 Westshore Plz.
Tampa, FL 33609
(813)286-0365
Company Type: Division. Ultimate Parent:
Tandy Corp. SIC: 5731—Radio, Television
& Electronics Stores.

★ 63559 ★ Radio Shack
730 W. Martin Luther King Blvd.
Tampa, FL 33603
(813)681-6127
Company Type: Division. Ultimate Parent:
Tandy Corp. SIC: 5719—Miscellaneous
Home Furnishings Stores.

★ 63560 ★ Radio Shack
3302 W. Tampa Bay Blvd.
Tampa, FL 33607
(813)876-3657
Company Type: Division. Ultimate Parent:
Tandy Corp. SIC: 5731—Radio, Television
& Electronics Stores.

★ 63561 ★ Radio Shack
4029 W. Kennedy Blvd.
Tampa, FL 33609
(813)289-9735
Company Type: Division. Ultimate Parent:
Tandy Corp. SIC: 5731—Radio, Television
& Electronics Stores.

★ 63562 ★ Radio Shack
4555 W. Kennedy Blvd.
Tampa, FL 33609
Company Type: Division. Ultimate Parent:
Tandy Corp. SIC: 5734—Computer &
Software Stores.

★ 63563 ★ Radio Shack
2263 University Sq.
Tampa, FL 33612
(813)971-1517
Company Type: Division. Ultimate Parent:
Tandy Corp. SIC: 5731—Radio, Television
& Electronics Stores.

★ 63564 ★ Radio Shack
3302 W. Buffalo Ave. 1060
Tampa, FL 33607
(813)877-7775
Company Type: Division. Ultimate Parent:
Tandy Corp. SIC: 5719—Miscellaneous
Home Furnishings Stores.

★ 63565 ★ Radio Shack
2027 N. Tampa St.
Tampa, FL 33602
(813)876-3657
Company Type: Division. Ultimate Parent:
Tandy Corp. SIC: 5065—Electronic Parts &
Equipment Nec.

★ 63566 ★ Radio Shack
2204 S. Dale Mabry Hwy.
Tampa, FL 33629
(813)251-2191
Company Type: Division. Ultimate Parent:
Tandy Corp. SIC: 5731—Radio, Television
& Electronics Stores.

★ 63567 ★ Radio Shack
1288 Eastlake Sq.
Tampa, FL 33610
(813)621-2976
Company Type: Division. Ultimate Parent:
Tandy Corp. SIC: 5065—Electronic Parts &
Equipment Nec.

★ 63568 ★ Radio Shack
15023 N. Florida Ave.
Tampa, FL 33613
(813)961-8478
Company Type: Division. Ultimate Parent:
Tandy Corp. SIC: 5719—Miscellaneous
Home Furnishings Stores.

★ 63569 ★ Radio Shack
1825 E. Fowler Ave.
Tampa, FL 33612
(813)971-1130
Company Type: Division. Ultimate Parent:
Tandy Corp. SIC: 5065—Electronic Parts &
Equipment Nec.

★ 63570 ★ Radio Shack
2213 E. Hillsborough Ave.
Tampa, FL 33610
(813)239-3434
Company Type: Division. Ultimate Parent:
Tandy Corp. SIC: 5065—Electronic Parts &
Equipment Nec; 5731—Radio, Television &
Electronics Stores.

★ 63571 ★ Radio Shack
3850 Britton Plz.
Tampa, FL 33611
(813)839-2074
Company Type: Division. Ultimate Parent:
Tandy Corp. SIC: 5719—Miscellaneous
Home Furnishings Stores; 5731—Radio,
Television & Electronics Stores.

★ 63572 ★ Radio Shack
4027 W. Kennedy Blvd.
Tampa, FL 33609
(813)879-1532
Company Type: Division. Ultimate Parent:
Tandy Corp. SIC: 5065—Electronic Parts &
Equipment Nec.

★ 63573 ★ Radio Shack
4555 W. Kennedy Blvd.
Tampa, FL 33609
Company Type: Division. Ultimate Parent:
Tandy Corp. SIC: 7373—Computer
Integrated Systems Design.

★ 63574 ★ Radio Shack
4555 W. Kennedy Blvd.
Tampa, FL 33609
Company Type: Division. Ultimate Parent:
Tandy Corp. SIC: 7379—Computer Related
Services Nec.

★ 63575 ★ Recovery Services
International
1300 N. Westshore Blvd.
Tampa, FL 33607
(813)872-0540
Ultimate Parent: Cigna Corp. SIC: 6411—
Insurance Agents, Brokers & Service.

★ **63576** ★ **Reynolds Metal Co.**
10420 Malcolm Mckinley Dr.
Tampa, FL 33612-6409
Ultimate Parent: Reynolds Metals Co. **SIC:**
3411—Metal Cans.

★ **63577** ★ **Reynolds Metals Co. Tampa Can Plant**
10420 Malcolm Mckinley Dr.
Tampa, FL 33612-6409
Ultimate Parent: Reynolds Metals Co. **SIC:**
3411—Metal Cans.

★ **63578** ★ **Rite Aid**
2217 University Square Mall
Tampa, FL 33612
Ultimate Parent: Rite Aid. **SIC:** 5912—Drug
Stores & Proprietary Stores.

★ **63579** ★ **Rite Aid Discount Pharmacy**
3806 S. Manhattan Ave.
Tampa, FL 33611
(813)837-1986
Ultimate Parent: Rite Aid. **SIC:** 5912—Drug
Stores & Proprietary Stores.

★ **63580** ★ **Rite Aid Pharm**
8420 Sheldon Rd.
Tampa, FL 33615
Ultimate Parent: Rite Aid. **SIC:** 5912—Drug
Stores & Proprietary Stores.

★ **63581** ★ **Rite Aid Pharmacy**
8827 N. Florida Ave.
Tampa, FL 33604
(813)935-8321
Ultimate Parent: Rite Aid. **SIC:** 5912—Drug
Stores & Proprietary Stores.

★ **63582** ★ **Ryder Truck Rental**
5901 N. Nebraska Ave.
Tampa, FL 33604
(813)238-4220
Ultimate Parent: Ryder System. **SIC:**
7513—Truck Rental & Leasing Without
Drivers.

★ **63583** ★ **Ryder Truck Rental**
2524 E. Busch Blvd.
Tampa, FL 33612
(813)933-4469
Ultimate Parent: Ryder System. **SIC:**
7513—Truck Rental & Leasing Without
Drivers.

★ **63584** ★ **Ryder Truck Rental**
6701 N. Dale Mabry Hwy.
Tampa, FL 33614
(813)872-9961
Ultimate Parent: Ryder System. **SIC:**
7513—Truck Rental & Leasing Without
Drivers.

★ **63585** ★ **Ryder Truck Rental**
7749 Adamo Dr.
Tampa, FL 33619
(813)623-1304
Ultimate Parent: Ryder System. **SIC:**
7513—Truck Rental & Leasing Without
Drivers.

★ **63586** ★ **Ryder Truck Rental**
401 E. Bearss Ave.
Tampa, FL 33613
(813)962-6424
Ultimate Parent: Ryder System. **SIC:**
7513—Truck Rental & Leasing Without
Drivers.

★ **63587** ★ **Seagram Sons Inc/ Joseph E**
5430 Bay Path
Tampa, FL 33615
(813)879-2029
Ultimate Parent: J.E. Seagram & Sons, Inc.
SIC: 5085—Industrial Supplies.

★ **63588** ★ **Service Merchandise**
1251 E. Fowler Ave.
Tampa, FL 33612
(813)977-3900
Ultimate Parent: Service Merchandise Co.,
Inc. **SIC:** 5944—Jewelry Stores.

★ **63589** ★ **Service Merchandise**
5701 Eastlake Sq.
Tampa, FL 33610
(813)623-2861
Ultimate Parent: Service Merchandise Co.,
Inc. **SIC:** 5961—Catalog & Mail-Order
Houses.

★ **63590** ★ **Shell Oil Co.**
Commerce St.
Tampa, FL 33612
(813)831-1121
Ultimate Parent: Shell Oil Co. **SIC:** 2911—
Petroleum Refining.

★ **63591** ★ **Shell Oil Co.**
1805 N. Westshore Blvd.
Tampa, FL 33607
(813)877-5741
Ultimate Parent: Shell Oil Co. **SIC:** 5172—
Petroleum Products Nec.

★ **63592** ★ **Shell Service Food Mart**
3650 S. Dale Mabry Hwy.
Tampa, FL 33629
(813)831-9652
Ultimate Parent: Shell Oil Co. **SIC:** 5411—
Grocery Stores.

★ **63593** ★ **Shell Station**
6812 N. 56th St.
Tampa, FL 33610
(813)888-7152
Ultimate Parent: Shell Oil Co. **SIC:** 5541—
Gasoline Service Stations.

★ **63594** ★ **Sico Inc.**
Rural Route 4
Tampa, FL 33626
(813)962-0440
Ultimate Parent: American Life. **SIC:**
1541—Industrial Buildings & Warehouses.

★ **63595** ★ **Sico Inc.**
Florida Ave. N
Tampa, FL 33613
(813)962-0440
Ultimate Parent: American Life. **SIC:**
6531—Real Estate Agents & Managers.

★ **63596** ★ **Sico Inc.**
15810 Lake Magdalene Blvd.
Tampa, FL 33613
(813)963-6783
Ultimate Parent: American Life. **SIC:**
1541—Industrial Buildings & Warehouses.

★ **63597** ★ **Signet Investment Corp.**
5521 W. Cypress St.
Tampa, FL 33607
(813)289-1776
Ultimate Parent: Signet Banking Corp. **SIC:**
6531—Real Estate Agents & Managers.

★ **63598** ★ **Singleton Seafood Co.**
5024 Uceta Rd.
PO Box 2819
Tampa, FL 33619
(813)241-1501 **Fax:** (813)248-6030
Company Type: Division. **Location Type:**
Plant. **Officer:** Jesse Gonzalez. **Ultimate
Parent:** Conagra.

★ **63599** ★ **Sloan Paper Co.**
9866 Currie Davis Dr.
Tampa, FL 33619-2651
(813)621-0707
Officer: Mike Branden. **Ultimate Parent:**
Alco Standard Corp. **SIC:** 5113—Industrial
& Personal Service Paper; 2732—Book
Printing.

★ **63600** ★ **Smalley Transportation Co.**
4224 Henderson Blvd.
PO Box 31708
Tampa, FL 33631-3708
(813)254-0442 **Fax:** (813)254-5601
Officer: Jim Crisp, President. **Ultimate
Parent:** Yellow Corp.

★ **63601** ★ **Specialty Products**
6507 N. 54th St.
Tampa, FL 33610-1907
(813)621-5371
Officer: John Stephens. **Ultimate Parent:**
Avery Dennison Corp. **SIC:** 1742—
Plastering, Drywall & Insulation; 5033—
Roofing, Siding & Insulation; 5039—
Construction Materials Nec.

★ **63602** ★ **Standard Register Co.**
5131 Tampa West Blvd.
Tampa, FL 33634
(813)886-5511
Officer: Lawrence McConnell, Plant
Manager. **Ultimate Parent:** Standard
Register. **SIC:** 2672—Coated & Laminated
Paper Nec; 2759—Commercial Printing
Nec.

★ **63603** ★ **State Mutual of America**
1211 N. Westshore Blvd.
Tampa, FL 33607
(813)289-9280
Ultimate Parent: State Mututal of America.
SIC: 6411—Insurance Agents, Brokers &
Service.

★ **63604** ★ **Stop & Shop**
280519 PO Box
Tampa, FL 33682
Ultimate Parent: Stop & Shop.

★ **63605** ★ **Sun Refining & Marketing Co.**
425 S. 20th St.
Tampa, FL 33605
(813)248-1807
Ultimate Parent: Sun. **SIC:** 5172—
Petroleum Products Nec.

★ **63606** ★ **Syscon Corp.**
4302 Henderson Blvd.
Tampa, FL 33629
(813)254-8922
Ultimate Parent: Harnischfeger Industries.
SIC: 7373—Computer Integrated Systems
Design.

★ **63607** ★ **Taco Bell**
7325 W. Waters Ave.
Tampa, FL 33634
(813)882-0448
Ultimate Parent: Pepsico. **SIC:** 5812—
Eating Places.

★ **63608** ★ **Taco Bell**
3302 W. Buffalo Ave.
Tampa, FL 33607
(813)870-3758
Ultimate Parent: Pepsico. **SIC:** 5812—
Eating Places.

★ **63609** ★ **Taco Bell**
2031 Skipper Rd.
Tampa, FL 33613
(813)971-8743
Ultimate Parent: Pepsico. **SIC:** 5812—
Eating Places.

★ **63610** ★ **Taco Bell**
18 Trand Ct
Tampa, FL 33629
(813)870-3758
Ultimate Parent: Pepsico. **SIC:** 5812—
Eating Places.

★ **63611** ★ **Tampa Coca-Cola Bottling Co.**
9102 Sabal Industrial Blvd.
Tampa, FL 33619
Ultimate Parent: Coca-Cola Enterprises.
SIC: 2086—Bottled & Canned Soft Drinks.

★ **63612** ★ **Texaco Food Mart**
4150 W. Hillsborough Ave.
Tampa, FL 33614
(813)873-9108
Ultimate Parent: Texaco. **SIC:** 5411—
Grocery Stores.

★ **63613** ★ **Texaco Food Mart**
8339 W. Waters Ave.
Tampa, FL 33615
(813)884-9920
Ultimate Parent: Texaco. **SIC:** 5411—
Grocery Stores; 5541—Gasoline Service
Stations.

★ **63614** ★ **Texaco Food Mart**
6825 N. Habana Ave.
Tampa, FL 33614
(813)935-9038
Ultimate Parent: Texaco. **SIC:** 5411—
Grocery Stores.

★ **63615** ★ **Texaco Food Mart**
3102 S. Macdill Ave.
Tampa, FL 33629
(813)837-2037
Ultimate Parent: Texaco. **SIC:** 5411—
Grocery Stores.

★ **63616** ★ **Texaco Food Mart & Gas Stat**
2911 E. Fowler Ave.
Tampa, FL 33612
(813)972-8865
Ultimate Parent: Texaco. **SIC:** 5541—
Gasoline Service Stations.

★ **63617** ★ **Texaco Foods**
3602 W. Gandy Blvd.
Tampa, FL 33611
(813)839-9037
Ultimate Parent: Texaco. **SIC:** 5541—
Gasoline Service Stations.

★ **63618** ★ **Texaco Inc.**
2911 E. Fowler Ave.
Tampa, FL 33612
(813)977-5741
Ultimate Parent: Texaco. **SIC:** 5411—
Grocery Stores.

★ **63619** ★ **Texaco No 208**
2720 W. Buffalo Ave.
Tampa, FL 33607
(813)879-9420
Ultimate Parent: Texaco. **SIC:** 5411—
Grocery Stores.

★ **63620** ★ **Texaco Refining & Marketing**
519 N. 19th St.
Tampa, FL 33605
(813)248-3121
Ultimate Parent: Texaco. **SIC:** 5172—
Petroleum Products Nec; 5172—Petroleum
Products Nec.

★ **63621** ★ **Tg Lee Foods Inc.**
4219 E. 19th Ave.
Tampa, FL 33605
(813)621-7805
Ultimate Parent: Dean Foods. **SIC:** 5451—
Dairy Products Stores.

★ **63622** ★ **This End Up**
3302 W. Tampa Bay Blvd.
Tampa, FL 33607
(813)874-2110
Ultimate Parent: Melville. **SIC:** 5712—
Furniture Stores.

★ **63623** ★ **Tj Maxx**
7555 W. Hillsborough Ave.
Tampa, FL 33615
(813)885-1800
Ultimate Parent: TJX. **SIC:** 5651—Family
Clothing Stores.

★ **63624** ★ **Torrington Co. the**
5420 Bay Ctr. Dr.
Tampa, FL 33609
(813)286-7494
Ultimate Parent: Ingersoll-Rand. **SIC:**
3562—Ball & Roller Bearings.

★ **63625** ★ **Town & Country Medical Center**
6001 Webb Rd.
Tampa, FL 33615
(813)885-6666
Ultimate Parent: American Medical
Holdings. **SIC:** 8062—General Medical &
Surgical Hospitals.

★ **63626** ★ **Toys R US**
1235 E. Fowler Ave.
Tampa, FL 33612
(813)971-0091
Ultimate Parent: Toys "R" US. **SIC:** 5641—
Children's & Infants' Wear Stores; 5945—
Hobby, Toy & Game Shops.

★ **63627** ★ **Trailways Bus Systems**
525 E. Madison St.
Tampa, FL 33602
(813)229-2078
Ultimate Parent: Greyhound Lines Inc. **SIC:**
4212—Local Trucking Without Storage.

★ **63628** ★ **Trailways Bus Terminal**
1525 E. Madison
Tampa, FL 33602
(813)229-1831
Ultimate Parent: Greyhound Lines Inc. **SIC:**
4111—Local & Suburban Transit.

★ **63629** ★ **Trans World Airlines Inc.**
Intl Airport
Tampa, FL 33622
(813)883-3236
Ultimate Parent: Trans World Airlines. **SIC:**
4512—Air Transportation—Scheduled.

★ 63630 ★　Trans World Airlines,
Inc.
Tampa International Airport St.
Tampa, FL 33607
(813)276-3240
Ultimate Parent: Trans World Airlines. **SIC:**
4512—Air Transportation—Scheduled.

★ 63631 ★　Transamerica
Occidental Life Insurance
9743 W. Hillsborough Ave.
Tampa, FL 33615
(813)872-2658
Ultimate Parent: Transamerica Occidental
Life Insurance. **SIC:** 6411—Insurance
Agents, Brokers & Service.

★ 63632 ★　U S Design
2715 N. 58th St.
Tampa, FL 33619
(813)621-2011
Ultimate Parent: Maxtor. **SIC:** 7311—
Advertising Agencies.

★ 63633 ★　Unijax Inc.
2614 E. Henry Ave.
Tampa, FL 33610-4438
(813)236-5781
Officer: Drew Perkins. **Ultimate Parent:**
Alco Standard Corp. **SIC:** 5111—Printing &
Writing Paper.

★ 63634 ★　Union Oil Co. of
California
1623 Port Ave.
Tampa, FL 33605
(813)248-1961
Ultimate Parent: Unocal Corp. **SIC:** 5172—
Petroleum Products Nec.

★ 63635 ★　Unisys Corp.
3825 Henderson Blvd.
Tampa, FL 33629
(813)289-9422
Ultimate Parent: Unisys Corp. **SIC:** 5112—
Stationery & Office Supplies.

★ 63636 ★　Unisys Corp.
2434 W. Prospect Rd.
Tampa, FL 33629
(813)286-6232
Ultimate Parent: Unisys Corp.

★ 63637 ★　Unisys Corp.
1511 N. Westshore Blvd. 400
Tampa, FL 33607
(813)286-6200
Ultimate Parent: Unisys Corp. **SIC:** 7372—
Prepackaged Software; 7373—Computer
Integrated Systems Design.

★ 63638 ★　United Brake Systems
Inc.
3112 3rd Ave.
Tampa, FL 33605
(813)248-4515
Ultimate Parent: Echlin. **SIC:** 3714—Motor
Vehicle Parts & Accessories.

★ 63639 ★　United Parcel Service
5100 Acline Dr. E
Tampa, FL 33619
(813)251-6341
Ultimate Parent: United Parcel Service of
America. **SIC:** 4215—Courier Services
Except by Air.

★ 63640 ★　United Technologies
Auto
5100 W. Waters Ave.
Tampa, FL 33634
(813)885-4785
Officer: Mike Aday, Manager. **Ultimate
Parent:** United Technologies. **SIC:** 3679—
Electronic Components Nec.

★ 63641 ★　United Technologies
Automotive
5100 W. Waters Ave.
Tampa, FL 33634
Ultimate Parent: United Technologies. **SIC:**
3679—Electronic Components Nec.

★ 63642 ★　Valspar Corp.
6110 Gunn Hwy.
Tampa, FL 33624
Ultimate Parent: Valspar Corp. **SIC:**
2851—Paints & Allied Products.

★ 63643 ★　Valspar Corp. Fed
6110 Gunn Hwy.
Tampa, FL 33624
Ultimate Parent: Valspar Corp. **SIC:**
2851—Paints & Allied Products.

★ 63644 ★　Verex Assurance Inc.
5201 W. Kennedy Blvd.
Tampa, FL 33609
(813)872-5628
Ultimate Parent: Dial Corp. **SIC:** 6159—
Miscellaneous Business Credit Institutions.

★ 63645 ★　Victoria's Secret
2132 E. Fowler Ave. 210
Tampa, FL 33612
(813)972-5982
Ultimate Parent: Limited. **SIC:** 5699—
Miscellaneous Apparel & Accessory Stores.

★ 63646 ★　Victoria's Secret
1608 W. Snow Cir.
Tampa, FL 33606
(813)254-6229
Ultimate Parent: Limited. **SIC:** 5651—
Family Clothing Stores.

★ 63647 ★　Wal Mart
11720 State Rd. 574
Tampa, FL 33610
(813)681-6654
Ultimate Parent: Wal-Mart Stores, Inc. **SIC:**
5311—Department Stores.

★ 63648 ★　Waldenbooks
Westshore
Tampa, FL 33609
(813)876-8096
Ultimate Parent: K-Mart. **SIC:** 5942—Book
Stores.

★ 63649 ★　Waldenbooks
345 Westshore Plz.
Tampa, FL 33609
(813)286-8096
Ultimate Parent: K-Mart. **SIC:** 5942—Book
Stores.

★ 63650 ★　Waldenbooks
3302 W. Buffalo Ave.
Tampa, FL 33607
(813)879-3284
Ultimate Parent: K-Mart. **SIC:** 5942—Book
Stores.

★ 63651 ★　Walgreen Drug Stores
102 W. Fletcher Ave.
Tampa, FL 33612
(813)933-7808
Ultimate Parent: Walgreen Co. **SIC:**
5912—Drug Stores & Proprietary Stores;
7384—Photofinishing Laboratories.

★ 63652 ★　Walgreen Drug Stores
3806 Britton Plz.
Tampa, FL 33611
(813)839-8345
Ultimate Parent: Walgreen Co. **SIC:**
5912—Drug Stores & Proprietary Stores.

★ 63653 ★　Walgreen Drug Stores
9219 N. 56th St.
Tampa, FL 33617
(813)985-8517
Ultimate Parent: Walgreen Co. **SIC:**
5912—Drug Stores & Proprietary Stores.

★ 63654 ★　Walgreen Drug Stores
3914 W. Hillsborough Ave.
Tampa, FL 33614
(813)879-3491
Ultimate Parent: Walgreen Co. **SIC:**
5912—Drug Stores & Proprietary Stores;
7384—Photofinishing Laboratories.

★ 63655 ★　Walgreen Drug Stores
225 Westshore Plz.
Tampa, FL 33609
(813)287-8108
Ultimate Parent: Walgreen Co. **SIC:**
5912—Drug Stores & Proprietary Stores;
5921—Liquor Stores.

★ 63656 ★　Walgreen Drug Stores
Temple
Tampa, FL 33612
(813)621-5334
Ultimate Parent: Walgreen Co. **SIC:**
5912—Drug Stores & Proprietary Stores.

★ 63657 ★　Walgreen Drug Stores
2199 W. Busch Blvd.
Tampa, FL 33612
Ultimate Parent: Walgreen Co. **SIC:**
5912—Drug Stores & Proprietary Stores.

★ 63658 ★　Walgreen Drug Stores
11778 State Rd. 574
Tampa, FL 33610
(813)689-3818
Ultimate Parent: Walgreen Co. **SIC:**
5912—Drug Stores & Proprietary Stores.

★ 63659 ★　Jim Walter Corp.
1 Metro Ctr.
4010 Boy Scout Blvd.
Tampa, FL 33607
(813)873-4190 **Fax:** (813)873-4430
Officer: Dennis M Rass, CEO. **Ultimate
Parent:** Walter Industries, Inc. **Employee
Count:** 3000. **Sales:** 609 M.

★ 63660 ★　Walter Industries, Inc.
1500 N. Dale Mabry Hwy.
Tampa, FL 33607
(813)871-4811 **Fax:** (813)871-4430
Company Type: Headquarters. **Officer:** G.
Robert Durham, CEO. **Employee Count:**
7500. **Sales:** 1291.3 M. **Fortune 500:**
Largest U.S. Industrial Corporations:
Ranking 306.

★ 63661 ★　Warren Petroleum Co.
5105 W. Tyson Ave.
Tampa, FL 33611
(813)831-1711
Ultimate Parent: Chevron Corp. **SIC:**
5172—Petroleum Products Nec.

★ 63662 ★　Warren Petroleum Co.
14499 N. Dale Mabry Hwy.
Tampa, FL 33618
(813)960-1500
Ultimate Parent: Chevron Corp. **SIC:**
2911—Petroleum Refining.

★ 63663 ★　World Book
Childcraft
6005 Soaring Ave.
Tampa, FL 33617-9302
(813)980-0664
Ultimate Parent: Berkshire Hathaway. **SIC:**
5963—Direct Selling Establishments.

★ 63664 ★　Xomox Corp.
5100 W. Kennedy Blvd.
Tampa, FL 33609
(813)876-3565
Ultimate Parent: Emerson Electric Co. Inc.
SIC: 5085—Industrial Supplies; 5999—
Miscellaneous Retail Stores Nec.

Tarpon

★ 63665 ★　Fortune Bank, ASB
905 Martin Luther King Jr. Dr., Ste. 100
Tarpon, FL
(813)934-5786
Location Type: Branch office. **Ultimate
Parent:** Fortune Bancorp. **SIC:** 6021—
National Commercial Banks.

Tarpon Springs

★ 63666 ★　Barnett Bank of
Pinellas County
125 Klosterman Rd.
Tarpon Springs, FL 34689-9756
(813)939-9188
Company Type: Subsidiary. **Location
Type:** Branch office. **Officer:** D. Sheridan
Brooks, Manager. **Ultimate Parent:** Barnett
Banks. **SIC:** 6022—State Commercial
Banks.

★ 63667 ★　Barnett Bank of
Pinellas County
203 E. Tarpon Ave.
Tarpon Springs, FL 34689-4317
(813)939-9187
Company Type: Subsidiary. **Location
Type:** Branch office. **Officer:** Theo Mahinis,
Vice President. **Ultimate Parent:** Barnett
Banks. **SIC:** 6022—State Commercial
Banks.

Tavares

★ 63668 ★　Barnett Bank of Lake
County, NA
600 W. Burleigh Ave.
Tavares, FL 32778-2363
(904)589-5000
Company Type: Subsidiary. **Location
Type:** Branch office. **Officer:** Sue Crabill,
Vice President. **Ultimate Parent:** Barnett
Banks. **SIC:** 6021—National Commercial
Banks.

★ 63669 ★　First Union National
Bank of Florida
350 E. Burleigh Ave.
Tavares, FL 32778-2403
(904)343-3360
Location Type: Branch office. **Ultimate
Parent:** First Union Corp. **SIC:** 6021—
National Commercial Banks.

★ 63670 ★　First Union National
Bank of Florida
122 E. Main St.
Tavares, FL 32778-3806
(904)742-3645
Location Type: Branch office. **Ultimate
Parent:** First Union Corp. **SIC:** 6021—
National Commercial Banks.

★ 63671 ★　Rite-Aid
452 E. Burleigh Blvd.
Tavares, FL 32778
(904)343-7541
Ultimate Parent: Rite Aid. **SIC:** 5912—Drug
Stores & Proprietary Stores.

Tavernier

★ 63672 ★　Barnett Bank of the
Keys
92200 Overseas Hwy.
Tavernier, FL 33070
(305)292-3901
Company Type: Subsidiary. **Location
Type:** Branch office. **Officer:** Cyn Delee
Dalton, Manager. **Ultimate Parent:** Barnett
Banks. **SIC:** 6022—State Commercial
Banks.

Temple Ter

★ 63673 ★　Ace Hardware &
Locksmith
13108 N. 56th St.
Temple Ter, FL 33617
(813)988-3488
Ultimate Parent: Ace Hardware. **SIC:**
5251—Hardware Stores.

★ 63674 ★　McDonalds
Restaurants
6906 N. 56th St.
Temple Ter, FL 33617
(813)985-1270
Ultimate Parent: McDonald's.
SIC: 5812—Eating Places.

★ 63675 ★　Publix Super Market
8901 N. 56th St.
Temple Ter, FL 33617
(813)988-1165
Ultimate Parent: Publix Super Markets.
SIC: 5411—Grocery Stores.

Temple Terrace

★ 63676 ★　Barnett Bank of
Tampa
10904 N. 56th St.
Temple Terrace, FL 33617-3029
(813)985-9638
Company Type: Subsidiary. **Location
Type:** Branch office. **Officer:** Judi
Dunnigan, Vice President. **Ultimate Parent:**
Barnett Banks. **SIC:** 6022—State
Commercial Banks.

★ 63677 ★　Food Lion
5014 E. Busch Blvd.
Temple Terrace, FL 33617
(813)985-6311
Ultimate Parent: Food Lion.

★ 63678 ★　GTE Data Services
Inc.
PO Box 290152
Temple Terrace, FL 33687-0152
(813)978-4000
Company Type: Subsidiary. **Ultimate
Parent:** GTE. **SIC:** 7374—Data Processing
& Preparation.

★ 63679 ★　Texaco Foodmart
9201 N. 46th St.
Temple Terrace, FL 33617
(813)988-9785
Ultimate Parent: Texaco. **SIC:** 5411—
Grocery Stores.

Tequesta

★ 63680 ★   Barnett Bank of Palm Beach County
150 Tequesta Dr.
Tequesta, FL 33469-2773
(407)747-4006
Company Type: Subsidiary. **Location Type:** Branch office. **Officer:** Andrew Paccioco, Manager. **Ultimate Parent:** Barnett Banks. **SIC:** 6022—State Commercial Banks.

★ 63681 ★   Savings of America
Home Savings of America, FSB
225 US Hwy. 1
Tequesta, FL 33469-2741
(407)747-2222
Location Type: Branch office. **Officer:** Mary Ann Stanton, Manager. **Ultimate Parent:** H. F. Ahmanson. **SIC:** 6021—National Commercial Banks.

Titusville

★ 63682 ★   AmSouth Bank of Florida
905 Cheney Hwy.
Titusville, FL 32780-6902
(407)268-2022
Location Type: Branch office. **Ultimate Parent:** AmSouth Bancorp. **SIC:** 6022—State Commercial Banks.

★ 63683 ★   AmSouth Bank of Florida
2525 Garden St.
Titusville, FL 32796-3190
(407)268-2022
Location Type: Branch office. **Ultimate Parent:** AmSouth Bancorp. **SIC:** 6022—State Commercial Banks.

★ 63684 ★   Barnett Bank of Central Florida, NA
2600 Barna Ave.
Titusville, FL 32780-3460
(407)268-3337
Company Type: Subsidiary. **Location Type:** Branch office. **Officer:** Tim Myers, Area Manager. **Ultimate Parent:** Barnett Banks. **SIC:** 6021—National Commercial Banks.

★ 63685 ★   First Union National Bank of Florida
802 Cheney Hwy.
Titusville, FL 32780-6968
(407)383-3540
Location Type: Branch office. **Ultimate Parent:** First Union Corp. **SIC:** 6021—National Commercial Banks.

★ 63686 ★   First Union National Bank of Florida
219 Indian River
Titusville, FL 32796
(407)383-3500
Location Type: Branch office. **Ultimate Parent:** First Union Corp. **SIC:** 6021—National Commercial Banks.

★ 63687 ★   First Union National Bank of Florida
2475 S. Washington Ave.
Titusville, FL 32780-5015
(407)383-3551
Location Type: Branch office. **Ultimate Parent:** First Union Corp. **SIC:** 6021—National Commercial Banks.

★ 63688 ★   Great Western Bank
2700 S. Washington Ave.
Titusville, FL 32780
Ultimate Parent: Great Western Financial Corp. **SIC:** 6022—State Commercial Banks.

★ 63689 ★   Greyhound Bus Station
20 N. Washington Ave.
Titusville, FL 32796
(407)267-8760
Ultimate Parent: Greyhound Lines Inc. **SIC:** 4131—Intercity & Rural Bus Transportation; 4173—Bus Terminal & Service Facilities; 7011—Hotels & Motels.

★ 63690 ★   Grumman Technical Services Corp.
1250 Grumman Pl.
Titusville, FL 32780-7934
(407)268-7934
Company Type: Subsidiary. **Ultimate Parent:** Grumman. **SIC:** 4581—Airports, Flying Fields & Services. **Employee Count:** 2000. **Sales:** 133 M.

★ 63691 ★   Hertz Rent-A-Car
3500 Cheney Hwy.
Titusville, FL 32780
(407)267-7707
Ultimate Parent: Hertz. **SIC:** 7514—Passenger Car Rental.

★ 63692 ★   Kentucky Fried Chicken
212 Garden St.
Titusville, FL 32796
(407)267-4465
Ultimate Parent: Pepsico. **SIC:** 5812—Eating Places.

★ 63693 ★   Kentucky Fried Chicken
2850 S. Washington Ave.
Titusville, FL 32780
(407)269-7216
Ultimate Parent: Pepsico. **SIC:** 5812—Eating Places.

★ 63694 ★   Lerner Shop
2500 S. Washington Ave.
Titusville, FL 32780
(407)267-8350
Ultimate Parent: Limited. **SIC:** 5651—Family Clothing Stores.

★ 63695 ★   Lockheed Space Operations Co.
1100 Lockheed Way
Titusville, FL 32780
(407)383-2200 **Fax:** (407)867-3859
Officer: Gerald T. Oppliger, President. **Ultimate Parent:** Lockheed Corp.

★ 63696 ★   McDonnell Douglas Astronautics Co.
701 Columbia Blvd.
Titusville, FL 32780
Ultimate Parent: McDonnell Douglas. **SIC:** 3489—Ordnance & Accessories Nec; 3761—Guided Missiles & Space Vehicles.

★ 63697 ★   McDonnell Douglas Missile Systems Co.
701 Columbia Blvd.
Titusville, FL 32780
Ultimate Parent: McDonnell Douglas. **SIC:** 3489—Ordnance & Accessories Nec; 3761—Guided Missiles & Space Vehicles.

★ 63698 ★   Pizza Hut
3758 S. Washington Ave.
Titusville, FL 32780
(407)267-2800
Ultimate Parent: Pepsico. **SIC:** 5812—Eating Places.

★ 63699 ★   Publix Super Market
3265 Garden St.
Titusville, FL 32796
(407)383-0511
Ultimate Parent: Publix Super Markets. **SIC:** 5411—Grocery Stores.

★ 63700 ★   Publix Super Market
3545 S. Hopkins Ave.
Titusville, FL 32780
(407)267-7745
Ultimate Parent: Publix Super Markets. **SIC:** 5411—Grocery Stores.

★ 63701 ★   Publix Super Markets
3545 S. Hopkins Ave.
Titusville, FL 32780
(407)267-7745
Ultimate Parent: Publix Super Markets. **SIC:** 5411—Grocery Stores.

★ 63702 ★   Radio Shack
110 Miracle City Mall
Titusville, FL 32780
(407)267-6860
Company Type: Division. **Ultimate Parent:** Tandy Corp. **SIC:** 5719—Miscellaneous Home Furnishings Stores; 5734—Computer & Software Stores.

★ 63703 ★   Ryder Truck Rental
1501 S. Washington Ave.
Titusville, FL 32780
(407)269-2901
Ultimate Parent: Ryder System. **SIC:** 7513—Truck Rental & Leasing Without Drivers.

★ 63704 ★   Taco Bell
550 S. Brown Ave.
Titusville, FL 32796
(407)264-2754
Ultimate Parent: Pepsico. **SIC:** 6513—Apartment Building Operators.

★ 63705 ★   Taco Bell
1795 S. Washington Ave.
Titusville, FL 32780
(407)267-7987
Ultimate Parent: Pepsico. **SIC:** 5812—Eating Places.

★ 63706 ★   Technical Service Operating Unit
1250 Grumman Pl.
Titusville, FL 32780-7900
(407)268-8400 **Fax:** (407)268-8357
Company Type: Subsidiary. **Officer:** Fred W. Haise, President. **Ultimate Parent:** Grumman.

★ 63707 ★   Texaco Service Station
1500 Harrison St.
Titusville, FL 32780
(407)269-4360
Ultimate Parent: Texaco. **SIC:** 5541—Gasoline Service Stations.

★ 63708 ★   Waldenbooks
2500 S. Washington Ave.
Titusville, FL 32780
(407)267-7650
Ultimate Parent: K-Mart. **SIC:** 5942—Book Stores.

Treasure Island

★ 63709 ★   Barnett Bank of Pinellas County
175 Treasure Island Causeway
Treasure Island, FL 33706-4777
(813)892-1158
Company Type: Subsidiary. **Location Type:** Branch office. **Officer:** Debra Daly, Manager. **Ultimate Parent:** Barnett Banks. **SIC:** 6022—State Commercial Banks.

★ 63710 ★   First of America Bank
245 107th Ave.
Treasure Island, FL 33704
(813)367-3754
Location Type: Branch office. **Ultimate Parent:** First of America Bank Corp. **SIC:** 6021—National Commercial Banks.

Umatilla

★ 63711 ★   Barnett Bank of Lake County, NA
700 N. Central Ave.
Umatilla, FL 32784-9063
(904)589-5000
Company Type: Subsidiary. **Location Type:** Branch office. **Officer:** Mike Stephen, Assistant Vice President. **Ultimate Parent:** Barnett Banks. **SIC:** 6021—National Commercial Banks.

★ 63712 ★   Barnett Bank of Lake County, NA
481 US Hwy. 441
Umatilla, FL 32784
(904)589-5000
Company Type: Subsidiary. **Location Type:** Branch office. **Officer:** Roger Belli, Vice President. **Ultimate Parent:** Barnett Banks. **SIC:** 6021—National Commercial Banks.

Valparaiso

★ 63713 ★   Vanguard Bank & Trust Co.
23 John Sims Pky.
Valparaiso, FL 32580-1042
(904)729-5500 **Fax:** (904)729-5599
Company Type: Subsidiary. **Location Type:** Branch office. **Officer:** Roger Farrar, President & CEO. **Ultimate Parent:** Synovus Financial Corp. **SIC:** 6021—National Commercial Banks.

Valrico

★ 63714 ★   Barnett Bank of Tampa
3414 Bell Shoales Rd.
Valrico, FL 33594
(813)225-8860
Company Type: Subsidiary. **Location Type:** Branch office. **Officer:** Sandy Atwood, Assistant Vice President. **Ultimate Parent:** Barnett Banks. **SIC:** 6022—State Commercial Banks.

★ 63715 ★   Digital Equipment Corp.
1926 Sydney Rd.
Valrico, FL 33594
(813)286-6747
Ultimate Parent: Digital Equipment Corp.

★ 63716 ★   Pizza Hut
3220 Lithia Pinecrest Rd.
Valrico, FL 33594
(813)653-4396
Ultimate Parent: Pepsico. **SIC:** 5812—Eating Places.

Venice

★ 63717 ★   Barnett Bank of Southwest Florida
304 W. Venice Ave.
Venice, FL 34285-2003
(813)951-4800
Company Type: Subsidiary. **Location Type:** Branch office. **Officer:** Rob Torrington, Manager. **Ultimate Parent:** Barnett Banks. **SIC:** 6021—National Commercial Banks.

★ 63718 ★   Barnett Bank of Southwest Florida
2090 S. Tamiami Trl.
Venice, FL 34293-5047
(813)951-4800
Company Type: Subsidiary. **Location Type:** Branch office. **Officer:** Nancy Furry, Manager. **Ultimate Parent:** Barnett Banks. **SIC:** 6021—National Commercial Banks.

★ 63719 ★   Barnett Bank of Southwest Florida
1270 Jacaranda Blvd.
Venice, FL 34292
(813)951-4800
Company Type: Subsidiary. **Location Type:** Branch office. **Officer:** Mario Pezzella, Manager. **Ultimate Parent:** Barnett Banks. **SIC:** 6021—National Commercial Banks.

★ 63720 ★   Barnett Bank of Southwest Florida
1490 S. Venice By-Pass
Venice, FL 34293
(813)951-4800
Company Type: Subsidiary. **Location Type:** Branch office. **Officer:** Rusty Glendenning, Manager. **Ultimate Parent:** Barnett Banks. **SIC:** 6021—National Commercial Banks.

★ 63721 ★   Citizens Federal Bank, FSB
1673 US 41 Bypass 5
Venice, FL 34293-1663
(813)493-1578
Location Type: Branch office. **Officer:** Liz Jarvis, Manager. **Ultimate Parent:** CSF Holdings.

★ 63722 ★   First of America Bank
1729 S. Tamiami Trl.
Venice, FL 34293
(813)435-6440
Location Type: Branch office. **Ultimate Parent:** First of America Bank Corp. **SIC:** 6021—National Commercial Banks.

★ 63723 ★   First Union National Bank of Florida
1301 41 Bypass St.
Venice, FL 34292
(813)497-5534
Location Type: Branch office. **Ultimate Parent:** First Union Corp. **SIC:** 6021—National Commercial Banks.

★ 63724 ★ First Union National Bank of Florida
555 S. Tamiami Trl.
Venice, FL 34285-2927
(813)485-1541
Location Type: Branch office. Ultimate Parent: First Union Corp. SIC: 6021—National Commercial Banks.

★ 63725 ★ First Union National Bank of Florida
1301 US 41 Bypass S.
Venice, FL 34292
(813)497-6567
Location Type: Branch office. Ultimate Parent: First Union Corp. SIC: 6021—National Commercial Banks.

★ 63726 ★ Greyhound Bus Lines
344 US 41 Bypass V S.
Venice, FL 34292
(813)485-1001
Ultimate Parent: Greyhound Lines Inc. SIC: 4131—Intercity & Rural Bus Transportation.

★ 63727 ★ Matco Tools
4417 Tortoise Rd.
Venice, FL 34293
(813)497-5382
Ultimate Parent: Danaher Corp. SIC: 5099—Durable Goods Nec.

★ 63728 ★ Mobil Servicenter Venice
120 US 41 Bypass
Venice, FL 34292
(813)485-2646
Ultimate Parent: Mobil. SIC: 5541—Gasoline Service Stations.

★ 63729 ★ NBD Bank, FSB
1320 E. Venice Ave.
Venice, FL 34292-2104
(813)484-0461 Fax: (813)485-1715
Location Type: Headquarters. Officer: Robert G. Wing, Chairman, President & CEO. Ultimate Parent: NBD Bancorp. SIC: 6021—National Commercial Banks.

★ 63730 ★ Pizza Hut
395 US 41 Bypass V N
Venice, FL 34292
(813)484-0466
Ultimate Parent: Pepsico. SIC: 5812—Eating Places.

★ 63731 ★ Professional Accounting Ser
3611 Roslyn Rd.
Venice, FL 34293
(813)497-4090
Ultimate Parent: Olsten. SIC: 8721—Accounting, Auditing & Bookkeeping.

★ 63732 ★ Publix Super Market
1667 Jacaranda Plz.
Venice, FL 34293
(813)493-4110
Ultimate Parent: Publix Super Markets. SIC: 5411—Grocery Stores.

★ 63733 ★ Publix Super Markets
1667 Jacaranda Plz.
Venice, FL 34293
(813)493-4110
Ultimate Parent: Publix Super Markets. SIC: 5411—Grocery Stores.

★ 63734 ★ Radio Shack
474 Us 41 Byp V N
Venice, FL 34292
(813)485-6017
Company Type: Division. Ultimate Parent: Tandy Corp. SIC: 5731—Radio, Television & Electronics Stores.

★ 63735 ★ Rite Aid Corp.
472 Us 41 Byp N
Venice, FL 34292
(813)485-6861
Ultimate Parent: Rite Aid. SIC: 5912—Drug Stores & Proprietary Stores.

★ 63736 ★ Savings of America
Home Savings of America, FSB
1761 Tamiami Trl.
Venice, FL 34293-1642
(813)493-0989
Location Type: Branch office. Officer: Sandra Finger, Manager. Ultimate Parent: H. F. Ahmanson. SIC: 6021—National Commercial Banks.

★ 63737 ★ Texaco Service Station
1500 US 41 Bypass V S
Venice, FL 34293
(813)497-2391
Ultimate Parent: Texaco. SIC: 5541—Gasoline Service Stations.

★ 63738 ★ Walgreen Pharmacy
1643 S. Venice Blvd.
Venice, FL 34293
(813)493-3925
Ultimate Parent: Walgreen Co. SIC: 5999—Miscellaneous Retail Stores Nec.

Vero Beach

★ 63739 ★ Barnett Bank of the Treasure Coast
5780 20th St.
Vero Beach, FL 32966-4641
(407)770-3851
Company Type: Subsidiary. Location Type: Branch office. Officer: Thomas Bartolucci, Vice President. Ultimate Parent: Barnett Banks. SIC: 6022—State Commercial Banks.

★ 63740 ★ Barnett Bank of the Treasure Coast
1500 N. A1A
Vero Beach, FL 32963
(407)770-3861
Company Type: Subsidiary. Location Type: Branch office. Officer: Susan Cato Humanes, Vice President. Ultimate Parent: Barnett Banks. SIC: 6022—State Commercial Banks.

★ 63741 ★ Barnett Bank of the Treasure Coast
6300 N. A1A
Vero Beach, FL 32963-3406
(407)770-3821
Company Type: Subsidiary. Location Type: Branch office. Officer: Sue Tompkins, Vice President & Office Manager. Ultimate Parent: Barnett Banks. SIC: 6022—State Commercial Banks.

★ 63742 ★ Barnett Bank of the Treasure Coast
1450 US Hwy. No. 1
Vero Beach, FL 32960-4714
(407)770-3831
Company Type: Subsidiary. Location Type: Branch office. Officer: Dan Marciante, Assistant Vice President & Office Manager. Ultimate Parent: Barnett Banks. SIC: 6022—State Commercial Banks.

★ 63743 ★ Barnett Bank of the Treasure Coast
601 21st St.
Vero Beach, FL 32960-5494
(407)770-3801
Company Type: Subsidiary. Location Type: Branch office. Officer: Cyn Delee Dalton, Vice President. Ultimate Parent: Barnett Banks. SIC: 6022—State Commercial Banks.

★ 63744 ★ Blue Goose Growers Inc.
45 St.
Vero Beach, FL 32963
(407)567-4381
Ultimate Parent: Dole Food. SIC: 0723—Crop Preparation Services for Market.

★ 63745 ★ Citizens Federal Bank, FSB
2046 Treasure Coast Plz.
Vero Beach, FL 32960-0949
(407)569-0915
Location Type: Branch office. Ultimate Parent: CSF Holdings. SIC: 6021—National Commercial Banks.

★ 63746 ★ Coast to Coast Janitor
1745 Old Dixie Hwy.
Vero Beach, FL 32960
(407)567-2015
Ultimate Parent: Servistar Corp. SIC: 7349—Building Maintenance Services Nec.

★ 63747 ★ Coast to Coast Janitor Service
1745 Dixie Ave. SW
Vero Beach, FL 32962
(407)567-2015
Ultimate Parent: Servistar Corp. SIC: 7349—Building Maintenance Services Nec.

★ 63748 ★ Coca Cola Bottling Co.
3339 St. Lucie Blvd.
Vero Beach, FL 32960
(407)567-9915
Ultimate Parent: Coca-Cola Enterprises. SIC: 2086—Bottled & Canned Soft Drinks.

★ 63749 ★ Diebold Inc.
907 7th Ave.
Vero Beach, FL 32960
(407)567-7255
Ultimate Parent: Diebold, Inc. SIC: 7382—Security Systems Services.

★ 63750 ★ First Union National Bank of Florida
1001 20th Pl.
Vero Beach, FL 32960-6491
(407)778-6081
Location Type: Branch office. Ultimate Parent: First Union Corp. SIC: 6021—National Commercial Banks.

★ 63751 ★ First Union National Bank of Florida
2001 58th Ave.
Vero Beach, FL 32966-4620
(407)778-6174
Location Type: Branch office. Ultimate Parent: First Union Corp. SIC: 6021—National Commercial Banks.

★ 63752 ★ First Union National Bank of Florida
500 Beachland Blvd.
Vero Beach, FL 32963-1795
(407)778-6066
Location Type: Branch office. Ultimate Parent: First Union Corp. SIC: 6021—National Commercial Banks.

★ 63753 ★ First Union National Bank of Florida
8055 20th St.
Vero Beach, FL 32966-1320
(407)778-6040
Location Type: Branch office. Ultimate Parent: First Union Corp. SIC: 6021—National Commercial Banks.

★ 63754 ★ First Union National Bank of Florida
150 S. US Hwy. 1
Vero Beach, FL 32962-3605
(407)778-6112
Location Type: Branch office. Ultimate Parent: First Union Corp. SIC: 6021—National Commercial Banks.

★ 63755 ★ First Union National Bank of Florida
1780 US Hwy. 1
Vero Beach, FL 32960-6204
(407)778-1900
Location Type: Branch office. Ultimate Parent: First Union Corp. SIC: 6021—National Commercial Banks.

★ 63756 ★ First Union National Bank of Forida
395 21st St.
Vero Beach, FL 32960-5447
(407)778-6181
Location Type: Branch office. Ultimate Parent: First Union Corp. SIC: 6021—National Commercial Banks.

★ 63757 ★ Greyhound Bus Lines
905 S. Us 1
Vero Beach, FL 32962
(407)562-6588
Ultimate Parent: Greyhound Lines Inc. SIC: 4142—Bus Charter Service Except Local.

★ 63758 ★ Hercules, Inc.
7625 9th St. SW
Vero Beach, FL 32962
Ultimate Parent: Hercules. SIC: 2099—Food Preparations Nec.

★ 63759 ★ Hercules Inc.
7625 Ninth Street, SW
Vero Beach, FL 32962
Ultimate Parent: Hercules. SIC: 2099—Food Preparations Nec.

★ 63760 ★ Kroger Wesco Foods Co.
7150 20th St.
Vero Beach, FL 32966
(407)569-6488
Ultimate Parent: Kroger. SIC: 5149—Groceries & Related Products Nec.

★ 63761 ★ National City Trust Co.
3350 Hwy. A1A
Vero Beach, FL 32963
(407)231-7555
Company Type: Subsidiary. Location Type: Branch office. Ultimate Parent: National City Corp. SIC: 6021—National Commercial Banks.

★ 63762 ★ Ocean Spray Cranberries Inc.
925 74th Ave. SW
Vero Beach, FL 32968
(407)562-0800
Ultimate Parent: Ocean Spray. SIC: 0723—Crop Preparation Services for Market.

★ 63763 ★ Pappagallo
6100 1st St. SW
Vero Beach, FL 32968
(407)231-1181
Ultimate Parent: United States Shoe. SIC: 5621—Women's Clothing Stores.

★ 63764 ★ Pennzoil Prodcts Co.
3209 Dodger Rd.
Vero Beach, FL 32960
(407)562-3988
Ultimate Parent: Pennzoil. SIC: 5172—Petroleum Products Nec.

★ 63765 ★ Pennzoil Products Co.
3209 Dodger Rd.
Vero Beach, FL 32960
(407)562-3988
Ultimate Parent: Pennzoil. SIC: 5172—Petroleum Products Nec.

★ 63766 ★ Piggly Wiggly
701 21st St.
Vero Beach, FL 32960
(407)562-2224
Ultimate Parent: Bruno's. SIC: 5411—Grocery Stores.

★ 63767 ★ Pizza Hut
670 S. Us 1
Vero Beach, FL 32962
(407)462-0650
Ultimate Parent: Pepsico. SIC: 5812—Eating Places.

★ 63768 ★ PNC Trust Co. of Florida, NA
5065 N. A1A
Vero Beach, FL 32963-1288
(407)231-6910
Location Type: Branch office. Officer: Gifford H. Hampton III, President & CEO. Ultimate Parent: PNC Bank Corp. SIC: 6021—National Commercial Banks.

★ 63769 ★ Savings of America
Home Savings of America, FSB
2050 US Hwy. 1
Vero Beach, FL 32960-5483
(407)569-3700
Location Type: Branch office. Officer: Christine Day, Manager. Ultimate Parent: H. F. Ahmanson. SIC: 6021—National Commercial Banks.

★ 63770 ★ Walgreen Drug Stores
1555 Us 1
Vero Beach, FL 32960
(407)569-0505
Ultimate Parent: Walgreen Co. SIC: 5999—Miscellaneous Retail Stores Nec.

★ 63771 ★ Walgreen Drug Stores
1555 Indian Rv Shopping Plz.
Vero Beach, FL 32960
(407)562-0505
Ultimate Parent: Walgreen Co. SIC: 5912—Drug Stores & Proprietary Stores; 5921—Liquor Stores.

Village of Golf

★ 63772 ★ Walgreen Drug Stores
3663 Woolbright Rd.
Village of Golf, FL 33436
(407)734-5104
Ultimate Parent: Walgreen Co. SIC: 7389—Business Services Nec.

Vlg of Golf

★ 63773 ★ Publix Super Market
3775 Woolbright Rd.
Vlg of Golf, FL 33436
(407)734-4401
Ultimate Parent: Publix Super Markets.
SIC: 5411—Grocery Stores.

★ 63774 ★ Publix Super Markets Inc.
3775 Woolbright Rd.
Vlg of Golf, FL 33436
(407)734-4401
Ultimate Parent: Publix Super Markets.
SIC: 5411—Grocery Stores.

W Palm Beach

★ 63775 ★ Ace Hardware
4050 Us 1 S
W Palm Beach, FL 33408
(407)624-1338
Ultimate Parent: Ace Hardware. **SIC:**
5251—Hardware Stores.

★ 63776 ★ Ace Hardware & Building Sup
1657 PO Box
W Palm Beach, FL 33402
(407)872-2011
Ultimate Parent: Ace Hardware.

★ 63777 ★ Ace Hardware Store No. 540
1649 N. Military Trl
W Palm Beach, FL 33409
(407)683-2171
Ultimate Parent: Ace Hardware. **SIC:**
5251—Hardware Stores.

★ 63778 ★ Amerada Hess Corp.
1216 Northlake Blvd.
W Palm Beach, FL 33403
(407)844-6680
Ultimate Parent: Amerada Hess. **SIC:**
5541—Gasoline Service Stations.

★ 63779 ★ Bayly Martin & Fay Inc.
3300 P G a Blvd.
W Palm Beach, FL 33410
(407)622-6585
Ultimate Parent: Anheuser-Busch. **SIC:**
6411—Insurance Agents, Brokers &
Service.

★ 63780 ★ Burdines Home Cleaning Service
W Palm Bch
W Palm Beach, FL 33410
(407)655-6884
Ultimate Parent: Federated Department
Stores. **SIC:** 7217—Carpet & Upholstery
Cleaning.

★ 63781 ★ Burdines Travel Bureau
Palm Bch Mall
W Palm Beach, FL 33401
(407)684-0840
Ultimate Parent: Federated Department
Stores. **SIC:** 4729—Passenger
Transportation Arrangement Nec.

★ 63782 ★ Burdines Variety Store
1801 Palm Bch Lake Blvd.
W Palm Beach, FL 33401
(407)684-4494
Ultimate Parent: Federated Department
Stores. **SIC:** 5331—Variety Stores.

★ 63783 ★ Casual Corner
Palm Beach Mall
W Palm Beach, FL 33401
(407)683-5529
Ultimate Parent: United States Shoe. **SIC:**
5621—Women's Clothing Stores.

★ 63784 ★ Casual Corner
Palm Beach Mall
W Palm Beach, FL 33407
(407)683-5529
Ultimate Parent: United States Shoe. **SIC:**
5621—Women's Clothing Stores.

★ 63785 ★ Coast to Coast Food
6342 Forest Hill Blvd.
W Palm Beach, FL 33415
(407)968-4919
Ultimate Parent: Servistar Corp. **SIC:**
8741—Management Services.

★ 63786 ★ Delta Air Lines
240 Royal Palm Beach Blvd.
W Palm Beach, FL 33411
(407)655-5300
Ultimate Parent: Delta Air Lines, Inc. **SIC:**
4512—Air Transportation—Scheduled.

★ 63787 ★ Delta Air Lines
Palm Beach International Airport
W Palm Beach, FL 33406
(407)683-4126
Ultimate Parent: Delta Air Lines, Inc. **SIC:**
4512—Air Transportation—Scheduled.

★ 63788 ★ Delta Air Lines Inc.
Palm Bch International a
W Palm Beach, FL 33406
(407)683-4126
Ultimate Parent: Delta Air Lines, Inc. **SIC:**
4512—Air Transportation—Scheduled.

★ 63789 ★ Emery Worldwide
Palm Bch
W Palm Beach, FL 33410
(407)684-0557
Ultimate Parent: Consolidated Freightways.
SIC: 4512—Air Transportation—Scheduled.

★ 63790 ★ Exxon Co. USA
4361 Northlake Blvd.
W Palm Beach, FL 33410
(407)626-0110
Ultimate Parent: Exxon. **SIC:** 5541—
Gasoline Service Stations.

★ 63791 ★ Great Western Bank
4470 Northlake Blvd.
W Palm Beach, FL 33410
(407)626-5552
Ultimate Parent: Great Western Financial
Corp. **SIC:** 6022—State Commercial Banks.

★ 63792 ★ Hit or Miss
1937 S. Military Trl.
W Palm Beach, FL 33415
(407)684-2540
Ultimate Parent: TJX. **SIC:** 5651—Family
Clothing Stores.

★ 63793 ★ Kentucky Fried Chicken
754 Park Ave.
W Palm Beach, FL 33403
(407)848-0333
Ultimate Parent: Pepsico. **SIC:** 5812—
Eating Places.

★ 63794 ★ Kentucky Fried Chicken
3231 S. Dixie Hwy.
W Palm Beach, FL 33405
(407)832-7333
Ultimate Parent: Pepsico. **SIC:** 5812—
Eating Places.

★ 63795 ★ Mary Kay Costmetics
508 5th Ter
W Palm Beach, FL 33418
(407)627-7044
Ultimate Parent: Mary Kay Cosmetics.

★ 63796 ★ Mobil Oil Gas Station
Rural Route 2
W Palm Beach, FL 33418
(407)969-3753
Ultimate Parent: Mobil. **SIC:** 5541—
Gasoline Service Stations.

★ 63797 ★ Mutual of New York
2801 Ponce De Leon Blvd.
W Palm Beach, FL 33411
(407)832-2438
Ultimate Parent: Mutual of New York. **SIC:**
6411—Insurance Agents, Brokers &
Service.

★ 63798 ★ Owens Corning Fiberglas Cor
541 State Rd. 7 S
W Palm Beach, FL 33414
(407)833-7038
Ultimate Parent: Owens-Corning. **SIC:**
1742—Plastering, Drywall & Insulation.

★ 63799 ★ Pizza Hut
4607 N. Australian Ave.
W Palm Beach, FL 33407
(407)862-7771
Ultimate Parent: Pepsico. **SIC:** 5812—
Eating Places.

★ 63800 ★ Pizza Hut
1501 Cressant
W Palm Beach, FL 33408
(407)842-1876
Ultimate Parent: Pepsico. **SIC:** 5812—
Eating Places.

★ 63801 ★ Publix Super Market
3000 Broadway
W Palm Beach, FL 33407
(407)844-3447
Ultimate Parent: Publix Super Markets.
SIC: 5411—Grocery Stores.

★ 63802 ★ Publix Super Market
7601 S. Dixie Hwy.
W Palm Beach, FL 33405
(407)585-2888
Ultimate Parent: Publix Super Markets.
SIC: 5411—Grocery Stores.

★ 63803 ★ Publix Super Market
489 Okeechobee Blvd.
W Palm Beach, FL 33401
(407)687-0445
Ultimate Parent: Publix Super Markets.
SIC: 5411—Grocery Stores.

★ 63804 ★ Publix Super Market
11566 Us 1
W Palm Beach, FL 33408
(407)622-0804
Ultimate Parent: Publix Super Markets.
SIC: 5411—Grocery Stores.

★ 63805 ★ Publix Super Market
9900 Alternate a a 1
W Palm Beach, FL 33410
(407)624-0935
Ultimate Parent: Publlx Super Markets.
SIC: 5411—Grocery Stores.

★ 63806 ★ Publix Super Markets
7601 S. Dixie Hwy.
W Palm Beach, FL 33405
(407)585-2888
Ultimate Parent: Publix Super Markets.
SIC: 5411—Grocery Stores.

★ 63807 ★ Publix Super Markets
3000 Broadway
W Palm Beach, FL 33407
(407)844-3447
Ultimate Parent: Publix Super Markets.
SIC: 5411—Grocery Stores.

★ 63808 ★ Radio Shack
33 Palm Bch Mall
W Palm Beach, FL 33401
(407)683-1502
Company Type: Division. **Ultimate Parent:**
Tandy Corp. **SIC:** 5731—Radio, Television
& Electronics Stores.

★ 63809 ★ Radio Shack
4356 Okeechobee Blvd.
W Palm Beach, FL 33409
(407)684-1131
Company Type: Division. **Ultimate Parent:**
Tandy Corp. **SIC:** 5731—Radio, Television
& Electronics Stores.

★ 63810 ★ Radio Shack
1801 Palm Bch
W Palm Beach, FL 33411
(407)683-1502
Company Type: Division. **Ultimate Parent:**
Tandy Corp. **SIC:** 5731—Radio, Television
& Electronics Stores.

★ 63811 ★ Radio Shack
4640 Forest Hill Blvd.
W Palm Beach, FL 33415
(407)967-4791
Company Type: Division. **Ultimate Parent:**
Tandy Corp. **SIC:** 5734—Computer &
Software Stores.

★ 63812 ★ Radio Shack
400 Northlake Blvd.
W Palm Beach, FL 33408
(407)844-8069
Company Type: Division. **Ultimate Parent:**
Tandy Corp. **SIC:** 5731—Radio, Television
& Electronics Stores.

★ 63813 ★ Rite-Aid
512 Belvedere Rd.
W Palm Beach, FL 33405
(407)833-9326
Ultimate Parent: Rite Aid. **SIC:** 5912—Drug
Stores & Proprietary Stores.

★ 63814 ★ Ryder Truck Rental
Blue Heron Blvd.
W Palm Beach, FL 33404
(407)863-7439
Ultimate Parent: Ryder System. **SIC:**
7389—Business Services Nec.

★ 63815 ★ Taco Bell
3800 Northlake Blvd.
W Palm Beach, FL 33403
(407)694-8967
Ultimate Parent: Pepsico. **SIC:** 5812—
Eating Places.

★ 63816 ★ Trailways Bus System
501 S. Olive Ave.
W Palm Beach, FL 33401
(407)832-0141
Ultimate Parent: Greyhound Lines Inc. **SIC:**
4131—Intercity & Rural Bus Transportation.

★ 63817 ★ Trans World Airlines
1000 Pbia Fl
W Palm Beach, FL 33406
(407)655-3776
Ultimate Parent: Trans World Airlines. **SIC:**
4512—Air Transportation—Scheduled.

★ 63818 ★ Transamerica Occidental Life Insurance
824 Us 1
W Palm Beach, FL 33408
(407)627-3233
Ultimate Parent: Transamerica Occidental
Life Insurance. **SIC:** 6411—Insurance
Agents, Brokers & Service.

★ 63819 ★ United Parcel Service
940 W. 15th St.
W Palm Beach, FL 33404
(407)659-3166
Ultimate Parent: United Parcel Service of
America. **SIC:** 7389—Business Services
Nec.

★ 63820 ★ Waldenbooks
Palm Bch Mall
W Palm Beach, FL 33401
(407)683-2807
Ultimate Parent: K-Mart. **SIC:** 5942—Book
Stores.

★ 63821 ★ Walgreen
225 Clematis St.
W Palm Beach, FL 33401
(407)833-2427
Ultimate Parent: Walgreen Co. **SIC:**
7384—Photofinishing Laboratories.

★ 63822 ★ Walgreen Drug Stores
4050 Us 1 S
W Palm Beach, FL 33408
(407)627-8308
Ultimate Parent: Walgreen Co. **SIC:**
5912—Drug Stores & Proprietary Stores.

★ 63823 ★ Wells Fargo Guard Services
3359 Belvedere Rd.
W Palm Beach, FL 33406
(407)471-4022
Ultimate Parent: Borg Warner Automotive.
SIC: 7381—Detective & Armored Car
Services.

W Palm Beach

★ 63824 ★ Kay Bee Toy Inc.
3101 P G a Blvd.
W Palm Beach Fl, FL 33410
(407)624-1546
Ultimate Parent: Melville. **SIC:** 5945—
Hobby, Toy & Game Shops.

★ 63825 ★ First of America Bank
4696 Cresthaven Rd.
W. Palm Beach, FL 33406
(407)433-1505
Location Type: Branch office. **Ultimate
Parent:** First of America Bank Corp. **SIC:**
6021—National Commercial Banks.

★ 63826 ★ First of America Bank
2088 Haverhill Rd.
W. Palm Beach, FL 33417
(407)471-1600
Location Type: Branch office. **Ultimate
Parent:** First of America Bank Corp. **SIC:**
6021—National Commercial Banks.

Wauchula

★ 63827 ★   Cf Ind Inc.
1549 PO Box
Wauchula, FL 33873
(813)533-0528
Ultimate Parent: CF Industries.

★ 63828 ★   Mobil Mining & Minerals Co.
Hwy. 664-A
Wauchula, FL 33873
(813)773-3225
Ultimate Parent: Mobil. **SIC:** 3295—Minerals—Ground or Treated.

Webster

★ 63829 ★   First Union National Bank of Florida
210 N. Market Blvd.
Webster, FL 33597-9442
(904)793-7119
Location Type: Branch office. **Ultimate Parent:** First Union Corp. **SIC:** 6021—National Commercial Banks.

Welaka

★ 63830 ★   Barnett Bank of the St. Johns
Hwy. 309
Welaka, FL 32193
(904)596-8224
Company Type: Subsidiary. **Location Type:** Branch office. **Ultimate Parent:** Barnett Banks. **SIC:** 6022—State Commercial Banks.

Wellington

★ 63831 ★   First Union National Bank of Florida
1314 Greenview Shores Blvd.
Wellington, FL 33414
(407)838-4940
Location Type: Branch office. **Ultimate Parent:** First Union Corp. **SIC:** 6021—National Commercial Banks.

West Hollywood

★ 63832 ★   Barnett Bank of Broward County, NA
5906 Pembroke Rd.
West Hollywood, FL 33023-2342
(305)981-7501
Company Type: Subsidiary. **Location Type:** Branch office. **Officer:** Michael Marino, Manager. **Ultimate Parent:** Barnett Banks. **SIC:** 6021—National Commercial Banks.

West Melbourne

★ 63833 ★   Barnett Bank of Central Florida, NA
3003 New Haven
West Melbourne, FL 32904-3605
(407)727-3400
Company Type: Subsidiary. **Location Type:** Branch office. **Officer:** John Moran, Manager. **Ultimate Parent:** Barnett Banks. **SIC:** 6021—National Commercial Banks.

★ 63834 ★   First Union National Bank of Florida
100 W. New Haven Ave.
West Melbourne, FL 32904-4054
(407)984-7467
Location Type: Branch office. **Ultimate Parent:** First Union Corp. **SIC:** 6021—National Commercial Banks.

★ 63835 ★   First Union National Bank of Florida
1420 S. Wickham Rd.
West Melbourne, FL 32901-2447
(407)984-7440
Location Type: Branch office. **Ultimate Parent:** First Union Corp. **SIC:** 6021—National Commercial Banks.

West Miami

★ 63836 ★   First Union National Bank of Florida
950 SW 57th Ave.
West Miami, FL 33144-5084
(305)263-1037
Location Type: Branch office. **Ultimate Parent:** First Union Corp. **SIC:** 6021—National Commercial Banks.

West Palm Beach

★ 63837 ★   American Savings of FL FSB
5849 Okeechobee Blvd.
West Palm Beach, FL 33417-4352
(407)684-2040
Location Type: Branch office. **Ultimate Parent:** American Savings of Florida. **SIC:** 6035—Federal Savings Institutions; 6021—National Commercial Banks.

★ 63838 ★   American Savings of Florida, FSB
West Palm Beach, FL
Location Type: Branch office. **Ultimate Parent:** American Savings of Florida. **SIC:** 6035—Federal Savings Institutions; 6211—Security Brokers & Dealers.

★ 63839 ★   Bankers Trust Co.
505 S. Flagler Dr., 6th Fl.
West Palm Beach, FL 33401-5923
(407)833-2470
Location Type: Branch office. **Officer:** John Stewart. **Ultimate Parent:** Bankers Trust New York Corp. **SIC:** 6021—National Commercial Banks.

★ 63840 ★   Bankers Trust Co. of Florida NA
505 S. Flagler Dr., Ste. 6
West Palm Beach, FL 33401-5923
(407)833-2470
Company Type: Subsidiary. **Officer:** Mary B. Lehman, Chairman of the Board. **Ultimate Parent:** Bankers Trust New York Corp. **SIC:** 6021—National Commercial Banks. **Employee Count:** 22.

★ 63841 ★   Barnett Bank of Palm Beach County
1827 N. Military Trl.
West Palm Beach, FL 33409-4784
(407)835-6561
Company Type: Subsidiary. **Location Type:** Branch office. **Officer:** Frank Young, Manager. **Ultimate Parent:** Barnett Banks. **SIC:** 6022—State Commercial Banks.

★ 63842 ★   Barnett Bank of Palm Beach County
7320 S. Dixie Hwy.
West Palm Beach, FL 33405-4895
(407)433-2419
Company Type: Subsidiary. **Location Type:** Branch office. **Officer:** J. T. Jones, Manager. **Ultimate Parent:** Barnett Banks. **SIC:** 6022—State Commercial Banks.

★ 63843 ★   Barnett Bank of Palm Beach County
5337 N. Military Trl.
West Palm Beach, FL 33407-3048
(407)835-6575
Company Type: Subsidiary. **Location Type:** Branch office. **Officer:** Linda Mason, Manager. **Ultimate Parent:** Barnett Banks. **SIC:** 6022—State Commercial Banks.

★ 63844 ★   Barnett Bank of Palm Beach County
1974 Palm Beach Lakes Blvd.
West Palm Beach, FL 33409-3590
(407)835-6553
Company Type: Subsidiary. **Location Type:** Branch office. **Officer:** Susan Hoffer, Manager. **Ultimate Parent:** Barnett Banks. **SIC:** 6022—State Commercial Banks.

★ 63845 ★   Barnett Bank of Palm Beach County
5737 Okeechobe Blvd.
West Palm Beach, FL 33417-4396
(407)666-6616
Company Type: Subsidiary. **Location Type:** Branch office. **Officer:** Frank Young, Manager. **Ultimate Parent:** Barnett Banks. **SIC:** 6022—State Commercial Banks.

★ 63846 ★   Barnett Bank of Palm Beach County
12850 W. Forest Hill Blvd.
West Palm Beach, FL 33414-4717
(407)966-7731
Company Type: Subsidiary. **Location Type:** Branch office. **Officer:** James Springer, Manager. **Ultimate Parent:** Barnett Banks. **SIC:** 6022—State Commercial Banks.

★ 63847 ★   Barnett Bank of Palm Beach County
505 S. Flagler Dr.
West Palm Beach, FL 33401-5923
(407)835-6000 **Fax:** (407)838-2377 **Telex:** 5109537410
Company Type: Subsidiary. **Location Type:** Branch office. **Officer:** R. Michael Strickland, Chairman, President & CEO. **Ultimate Parent:** Barnett Banks. **SIC:** 6022—State Commercial Banks.

★ 63848 ★   BellSouth Mobility
1889 Palm Beach Lakes Blvd.
West Palm Beach, FL 33409-3501
(407)478-7344
Ultimate Parent: BellSouth Corp. **SIC:** 4812—Radiotelephone Communications.

★ 63849 ★   Burdines
1801 Palm Bch Lakes Blvd.
West Palm Beach, FL 33401
(407)684-4311
Ultimate Parent: Federated Department Stores. **SIC:** 5399—Miscellaneous General Merchandise Store.

★ 63850 ★   Burdines
1243 W. 25th St.
West Palm Beach, FL 33404
(407)844-9811
Ultimate Parent: Federated Department Stores.

★ 63851 ★   California Federal Bank
1201 Federal Hwy.
West Palm Beach, FL 33403
(407)694-1667
Ultimate Parent: California Federal Bank. **SIC:** 6099—Functions Related to Deposit Banking.

★ 63852 ★   Chase Home Mortgage Corp.
2300 Palm Beach Lake Blvd.
West Palm Beach, FL 33409
(407)471-3900
Ultimate Parent: Chase Manhattan Corp. **SIC:** 6141—Personal Credit Institutions.

★ 63853 ★   Courtyard by Marriott
600 Northpoint Pky.
West Palm Beach, FL 33407
(407)640-9000
Ultimate Parent: Marriott International. **SIC:** 7011—Hotels & Motels.

★ 63854 ★   Daniel Radiator Corp.
6667 White Dr.
West Palm Beach, FL 33407
Ultimate Parent: Handy & Harman. **SIC:** 3714—Motor Vehicle Parts & Accessories; 5013—Motor Vehicle Supplies & New Parts.

★ 63855 ★   Delta Air Lines
1555 Palm Beach Lakes Blvd.
West Palm Beach, FL 33401
(407)233-6210
Ultimate Parent: Delta Air Lines, Inc.

★ 63856 ★   First Union National Bank of Florida
1801 Palm Beach Lakes Blvd.
West Palm Beach, FL 33401-2009
(407)838-4900
Location Type: Branch office. **Ultimate Parent:** First Union Corp. **SIC:** 6021—National Commercial Banks.

★ 63857 ★   First Union National Bank of Florida
4900 Okeechobee Blvd.
West Palm Beach, FL 33417-4688
(407)838-5324
Location Type: Branch office. **Ultimate Parent:** First Union Corp. **SIC:** 6021—National Commercial Banks.

★ 63858 ★   First Union National Bank of Florida
4300 Forest Hill Blvd.
West Palm Beach, FL 33406-5798
(407)838-5210
Location Type: Branch office. **Ultimate Parent:** First Union Corp. **SIC:** 6021—National Commercial Banks.

★ 63859 ★   First Union National Bank of Florida
4575 Gum Club Rd.
West Palm Beach, FL 33415-2848
(407)838-5220
Location Type: Branch office. **Ultimate Parent:** First Union Corp. **SIC:** 6021—National Commercial Banks.

★ 63860 ★   First Union National Bank of Florida
2685 Forest Hill Blvd.
West Palm Beach, FL 33406-5930
(407)533-7716
Location Type: Branch office. **Ultimate Parent:** First Union Corp. **SIC:** 6021—National Commercial Banks.

★ 63861 ★   First Union National Bank of Florida
802 Southern Blvd.
West Palm Beach, FL 33405-2595
(407)838-5635
Location Type: Branch office. **Ultimate Parent:** First Union Corp. **SIC:** 6021—National Commercial Banks.

★ 63862 ★   First Union National Bank of Florida
303 Banyan Blvd.
West Palm Beach, FL 33401
(407)838-5210
Location Type: Branch office. **Ultimate Parent:** First Union Corp. **SIC:** 6021—National Commercial Banks.

★ 63863 ★   First Union National Bank of Florida
11900 Forest Hill Blvd.
West Palm Beach, FL 33413-6248
(407)838-5368
Location Type: Branch office. **Ultimate Parent:** First Union Corp. **SIC:** 6021—National Commercial Banks.

★ 63864 ★   Firstar Trust Co. of Florida, NA
515 N. Flagler Dr.
West Palm Beach, FL 33401-4321
(407)832-8200 **Fax:** (407)659-0396
Company Type: Subsidiary. **Location Type:** Branch office. **Officer:** Philip L. Dunmire, President & CEO. **Ultimate Parent:** Firstar Corp. **SIC:** 6021—National Commercial Banks.

★ 63865 ★   Florida Power & Light Co., Inc.
700 Universe Blvd.
West Palm Beach, FL 33408-2657
(407)694-4000
Company Type: Subsidiary. **Officer:** James L. Broadhead, Chairman of the Board & CEO. **Ultimate Parent:** FPL Group. **SIC:** 4911—Electric Services; 6531—Real Estate Agents & Managers. **Employee Count:** 14500. **Sales:** 5.1 M.

★ 63866 ★   FPL Group Inc.
700 Universe Blvd.
West Palm Beach, FL 33408-2657
(407)694-4000
Officer: James L. Broadhead, Vh. Bd. Pr. **Ultimate Parent:** FPL Group. **SIC:** 4911—Electric Services; 6512—Nonresidential Building Operators; 0174—Citrus Fruits; 4841—Cable & Other Pay Television Services; 8742—Management Consulting Services. **Employee Count:** 147000. **Sales:** 5.1 M.

★ 63867 ★   The Gap
1801 Palm Beach Lakes Blvd.
West Palm Beach, FL 33401
(407)684-2503
Ultimate Parent: GAP. **SIC:** 5621—Women's Clothing Stores.

★ 63868 ★   Glendale Federal Bank F S B
800 Us Hwy. 1
West Palm Beach, FL 33408
(407)694-8680
Ultimate Parent: Glendale Federal. **SIC:** 6099—Functions Related to Deposit Banking.

★ 63869 ★ **Great Western Bank**
631 Us Hwy. 1
West Palm Beach, FL 33408
(407)863-2100
Ultimate Parent: Great Western Financial
Corp. **SIC:** 6162—Mortgage Bankers &
Correspondents.

★ 63870 ★ **Great Western Bank**
2959 N. Military Trl
West Palm Beach, FL 33409
(407)478-9101
Ultimate Parent: Great Western Financial
Corp. **SIC:** 6099—Functions Related to
Deposit Banking.

★ 63871 ★ **Hertz Rent-A-Car**
2700 N. Ocean Dr.
West Palm Beach, FL 33404
(407)848-9100
Ultimate Parent: Hertz. **SIC:** 7539—
Automotive Repair Shops Nec.

★ 63872 ★ **Home Depot Inc.**
3860 Northlake Blvd.
West Palm Beach, FL 33403
(407)627-9555
Ultimate Parent: Home Depot. **SIC:** 5211—
Lumber & Other Building Materials.

★ 63873 ★ **Johnson Controls Inc.**
3866 Prospect Ave.
West Palm Beach, FL 33404
(407)881-7200
Ultimate Parent: Johnson Controls Inc.
SIC: 5063—Electrical Apparatus &
Equipment.

★ 63874 ★ **Kentucky Fried Chicken**
1581 W. Blue Heron Blvd.
West Palm Beach, FL 33404
(407)848-5219
Ultimate Parent: Pepsico. **SIC:** 5812—
Eating Places.

★ 63875 ★ **Kentucky Fried Chicken**
2563 Northlake Blvd.
West Palm Beach, FL 33403
(407)845-6115
Ultimate Parent: Pepsico. **SIC:** 5812—
Eating Places.

★ 63876 ★ **Kentucky Fried Chicken**
1258 Palm Beach Lakes Blvd.
West Palm Beach, FL 33401
(407)659-2220
Ultimate Parent: Pepsico. **SIC:** 5812—
Eating Places.

★ 63877 ★ **Kentucky Fried Chicken**
4720 Broadway
West Palm Beach, FL 33407
(407)848-6211
Ultimate Parent: Pepsico. **SIC:** 5812—
Eating Places.

★ 63878 ★ **Kentucky Fried Chicken**
980 N. Military Trl
West Palm Beach, FL 33415
(407)683-8898
Ultimate Parent: Pepsico. **SIC:** 5812—
Eating Places.

★ 63879 ★ **Lane Bryant**
53 Palm Beach Mall
West Palm Beach, FL 33401
(407)683-6255
Ultimate Parent: Limited. **SIC:** 5651—
Family Clothing Stores.

★ 63880 ★ **Lerner Shop**
80 Palm Beach Mall
West Palm Beach, FL 33401
(407)683-8830
Ultimate Parent: Limited. **SIC:** 5651—
Family Clothing Stores.

★ 63881 ★ **Macy's**
3107 P G a Blvd.
West Palm Beach, FL 33410
(407)775-8985
Ultimate Parent: R. H. Macy. **SIC:** 5311—
Department Stores.

★ 63882 ★ **Mary Kay Cosemetics**
1051 Summit Pl
West Palm Beach, FL 33415
(407)689-3294
Ultimate Parent: Mary Kay Cosmetics. **SIC:**
7699—Repair Services Nec.

★ 63883 ★ **Mary Kay Cosmetics**
295 W. Shadyside Cir.
West Palm Beach, FL 33415
(407)683-1591
Ultimate Parent: Mary Kay Cosmetics. **SIC:**
5999—Miscellaneous Retail Stores Nec.

★ 63884 ★ **McDonald's**
100 State Rd. 7 S
West Palm Beach, FL 33414
(407)795-7001
Ultimate Parent: McDonald's.

★ 63885 ★ **McDonalds Office**
2610 Old Okeechobee Rd.
West Palm Beach, FL 33409
(407)684-2626
Ultimate Parent: McDonald's.
SIC: 5812—Eating Places.

★ 63886 ★ **Mellon Financial Services Corp.**
4738 Okeechobee Blvd.
West Palm Beach, FL 33417
(407)686-8447
Ultimate Parent: Mellon Bank Corp. **SIC:**
6062—State Credit Unions; 6141—Personal
Credit Institutions.

★ 63887 ★ **Mobil Oil**
1100 Royal Palm Beach Blvd.
West Palm Beach, FL 33411
(407)790-1581
Ultimate Parent: Mobil. **SIC:** 5599—
Automotive Dealers Nec.

★ 63888 ★ **National City Trust Co.**
1401 Forum Way
Ste. 503
West Palm Beach, ГL 33401-2324
(407)697-2424 **Fax:** (407)684-4577
Company Type: Subsidiary. **Location
Type:** Branch office. **Officer:** Gary L.
Galbreath, President & CEO. **Ultimate
Parent:** National City Corp. **SIC:** 6021—
National Commercial Banks.

★ 63889 ★ **Norwest Mortgage Inc.**
1897 Palm Beach Lake Blvd.
West Palm Beach, FL 33409
(407)471-3440
Ultimate Parent: Norwest Corp. **SIC:**
6162—Mortgage Bankers &
Correspondents.

★ 63890 ★ **Pci Industries Inc.**
9845 PO Box
West Palm Beach, FL 33419
Ultimate Parent: RPM, Inc. **SIC:** 2891—
Adhesives & Sealants.

★ 63891 ★ **Pizza Hut**
435 Clematis St.
West Palm Beach, FL 33401
Ultimate Parent: Pepsico. **SIC:** 5812—
Eating Places.

★ 63892 ★ **Pizza Hut**
6591 Forest Hill Blvd.
West Palm Beach, FL 33413
(407)433-2225
Ultimate Parent: Pepsico. **SIC:** 5812—
Eating Places.

★ 63893 ★ **Pizza Hut**
160 N. Military Trl.
West Palm Beach, FL 33415
(407)684-2552
Ultimate Parent: Pepsico. **SIC:** 5812—
Eating Places.

★ 63894 ★ **Publix Super Market**
831 Village Blvd.
West Palm Beach, FL 33409
(407)478-1313
Ultimate Parent: Publix Super Markets.
SIC: 5411—Grocery Stores.

★ 63895 ★ **Publix Super Markets**
831 Village Blvd.
West Palm Beach, FL 33409
(407)478-1313
Ultimate Parent: Publix Super Markets.
SIC: 5411—Grocery Stores.

★ 63896 ★ **Rite Aid Discount Pharmacie**
512 Belvedere Rd.
West Palm Beach, FL 33405
(407)655-3526
Ultimate Parent: Rite Aid. **SIC:** 5912—Drug
Stores & Proprietary Stores.

★ 63897 ★ **Ryder Truck Rental**
2915 Northlake Blvd.
West Palm Beach, FL 33403
(407)848-7275
Ultimate Parent: Ryder System. **SIC:**
7389—Business Services Nec.

★ 63898 ★ **Ryder Truck Rental**
2677 Old Okeechobee Rd.
West Palm Beach, FL 33409
(407)683-9194
Ultimate Parent: Ryder System. **SIC:**
7389—Business Services Nec.

★ 63899 ★ **Sam's Wholesale Warehouse**
3131 PO Box
West Palm Beach, FL 33402
(407)684-0100
Ultimate Parent: Wal-Mart Stores, Inc.

★ 63900 ★ **Savings of America**
Home Savings of America, FSB
6000 Okeechobee Blvd.
West Palm Beach, FL 33417-4380
(407)478-6345
Location Type: Branch office. **Officer:**
Cheryl Burt, Manager. **Ultimate Parent:** H.
F. Ahmanson. **SIC:** 6021—National
Commercial Banks.

★ 63901 ★ **Savings of America**
Home Savings of America, FSB
4869 Okeechobee Blvd.
West Palm Beach, FL 33417-4627
(407)471-7990
Location Type: Branch office. **Officer:** Patti
Ficarra, Manager. **Ultimate Parent:** H. F.
Ahmanson. **SIC:** 6021—National
Commercial Banks.

★ 63902 ★ **Taco Bell**
4361 Okeechobee Blvd.
West Palm Beach, FL 33409
(407)471-1818
Ultimate Parent: Pepsico. **SIC:** 5812—
Eating Places.

★ 63903 ★ **Taco Bell**
4466 Forest Hill Blvd.
West Palm Beach, FL 33406
(407)439-3337
Ultimate Parent: Pepsico. **SIC:** 5812—
Eating Places.

★ 63904 ★ **Ten Minute Oil Change**
3315 S. Dixie Hwy.
West Palm Beach, FL 33405
(407)655-7374
Ultimate Parent: Pennzoil. **SIC:** 7539—
Automotive Repair Shops Nec.

★ 63905 ★ **Triarc**
777 S. Fagler Dr.
West Palm Beach, FL 33401
(407)653-4000
Company Type: Headquarters. **Officer:**
Nelson Peltz. **Employee Count:** 14100.
Sales: 1231.9 M. **Fortune 500:** Largest
U.S. Industrial Corporations: Ranking 316.

★ 63906 ★ **Victoria's Secret**
3101 PGA Blvd.
West Palm Beach, FL 33410
(407)626-5451
Ultimate Parent: Limited. **SIC:** 5699—
Miscellaneous Apparel & Accessory Stores.

★ 63907 ★ **Walgreen Drug Stores**
1801 Palm Beach Lake Blvd.
West Palm Beach, FL 33401
(407)686-7049
Ultimate Parent: Walgreen Co. **SIC:**
5812—Eating Places.

★ 63908 ★ **Walgreen Drug Stores**
7719 S. Dixie Hwy.
West Palm Beach, FL 33405
(407)582-5613
Ultimate Parent: Walgreen Co. **SIC:**
5912—Drug Stores & Proprietary Stores;
7384—Photofinishing Laboratories.

★ 63909 ★ **Walgreen Drug Stores**
20 E. 30th St.
West Palm Beach, FL 33404
(407)848-6641
Ultimate Parent: Walgreen Co. **SIC:**
5912—Drug Stores & Proprietary Stores.

★ 63910 ★ **Walgreen Drug Stores**
4704 Forest Hill Blvd.
West Palm Beach, FL 33415
(407)969-1808
Ultimate Parent: Walgreen Co. **SIC:**
7389—Business Services Nec.

★ 63911 ★ **Walgreen Drug Stores**
850 N. Military Trl.
West Palm Beach, FL 33415
(407)471-1004
Ultimate Parent: Walgreen Co. **SIC:**
7389—Business Services Nec.

White Springs

★ 63912 ★ **Occidental Chemical Corp.**
State Rd. 137
White Springs, FL 32096
Ultimate Parent: Occidental Petroleum
Corp. **SIC:** 2874—Phosphatic Fertilizers;
2819—Industrial Inorganic Chemicals Nec.

★ 63913 ★ **Occidental Chemical Corp.**
Agricultural Products
County Rd. 137
White Springs, FL 32096-0300
Company Type: Division. **Ultimate Parent:**
Occidental Petroleum Corp. **SIC:** 2874—
Phosphatic Fertilizers; 2819—Industrial
Inorganic Chemicals Nec.

Wildwood

★ 63914 ★ **Armco Advanced Materials Corp.**
Hwy. 301 N.
Wildwood, FL 34785-9699
Ultimate Parent: Armco. **SIC:** 3317—Steel
Pipe & Tubes.

★ 63915 ★ **Ferro Corp.**
900 Peebles Blvd.
Wildwood, FL 34785
Ultimate Parent: Ferro Corp. **SIC:** 2821—
Plastics Materials & Resins.

★ 63916 ★ **First Union National Bank of Florida**
406 S. Main St.
Wildwood, FL 34785-4531
(904)748-0158
Location Type: Branch office. **Ultimate
Parent:** First Union Corp. **SIC:** 6021—
National Commercial Banks.

★ 63917 ★ **Radio Shack**
206 S. Dr.
Wildwood, FL 34785
(904)748-2021
Company Type: Division. **Ultimate Parent:**
Tandy Corp. **SIC:** 5731—Radio, Television
& Electronics Stores.

Winter Garden

★ 63918 ★ **AmSouth Bank of Florida**
343 W. Hwy. 50
Winter Garden, FL 34787
(407)656-3633
Location Type: Branch office. **Ultimate
Parent:** AmSouth Bancorp. **SIC:** 6022—
State Commercial Banks.

★ 63919 ★ **Clark Equipment Co., Inc.**
1158 Elboc Way
Winter Garden, FL 34787
(407)877-7000
Ultimate Parent: Clark Equipment Co. **SIC:**
5075—Warm Air Heating & Air-Conditioning.

★ 63920 ★ **Crown Cork & Seal Co. Inc.**
Winter Garden Can Div.
851 E. Maple St.
Winter Garden, FL 34787-0369
Company Type: Division. **Ultimate Parent:**
Crown Cork & Seal. **SIC:** 3411—Metal
Cans.

★ 63921 ★ **First Union National Bank of Florida**
100 W. Plant St.
Winter Garden, FL 34787-3143
(407)877-4250
Location Type: Branch office. **Ultimate
Parent:** First Union Corp. **SIC:** 6021—
National Commercial Banks.

★ 63922 ★　**Kentucky Fried Chicken**
1049 S. Dillard St.
Winter Garden, FL 34787
(407)656-4101
Ultimate Parent: Pepsico. **SIC:** 5812—
Eating Places.

★ 63923 ★　**Radio Shack**
1003 S. Dillard St.
Winter Garden, FL 34787
(407)656-6638
Company Type: Division. **Ultimate Parent:**
Tandy Corp. **SIC:** 5731—Radio, Television
& Electronics Stores.

★ 63924 ★　**Taco Bell**
409 E. Hwy. 50
Winter Garden, FL 34787
(407)877-9188
Ultimate Parent: Pepsico. **SIC:** 5812—
Eating Places.

★ 63925 ★　**Texaco Food Mart**
705 S. Dillard St.
Winter Garden, FL 34787
(407)656-5659
Ultimate Parent: Texaco. **SIC:** 5411—
Grocery Stores.

★ 63926 ★　**Walgreen Drug Stores**
457 E. Hwy. 50
Winter Garden, FL 34787
(407)656-1144
Ultimate Parent: Walgreen Co. **SIC:**
5912—Drug Stores & Proprietary Stores.

Winter Haven

★ 63927 ★　**Albertson's, No. 4377**
1965 8th St, NE
Winter Haven, FL 33881
(813)273-4331
Ultimate Parent: Albertson's Inc. **SIC:**
5411—Grocery Stores.

★ 63928 ★　**Barnett Bank of Polk County**
901 Cypress Gardens Blvd.
Winter Haven, FL 33880-4634
(813)297-1395
Company Type: Subsidiary. **Location
Type:** Branch office. **Officer:** Douglas A.
Blouin, Vice President. **Ultimate Parent:**
Barnett Banks. **SIC:** 6022—State
Commercial Banks.

★ 63929 ★　**Barnett Bank of Polk County**
3010 Cypress Gardens
Winter Haven, FL 33884-2245
(813)324-0105
Company Type: Subsidiary. **Location
Type:** Branch office. **Officer:** Sherri
Macklin, Manager. **Ultimate Parent:** Barnett
Banks. **SIC:** 6022—State Commercial
Banks.

★ 63930 ★　**Barnett Bank of Polk County**
930 Havendale Blvd.
Winter Haven, FL 33881-1352
(813)297-1415
Company Type: Subsidiary. **Location
Type:** Branch office. **Officer:** Lisa Arcuri,
Manager. **Ultimate Parent:** Barnett Banks.
SIC: 6022—State Commercial Banks.

★ 63931 ★　**Barnett Bank of Polk County**
1099 1st St.
Winter Haven, FL 33880-3612
(813)297-1409
Company Type: Subsidiary. **Location
Type:** Branch office. **Officer:** Vince Krakav,
Personal Banking Officer. **Ultimate Parent:**
Barnett Banks. **SIC:** 6022—State
Commercial Banks.

★ 63932 ★　**Barnett Bank of Polk County**
11 5th St.
Winter Haven, FL 33880
(813)294-7711
Company Type: Subsidiary. **Location
Type:** Branch office. **Officer:** Dennis Beck,
Vice President. **Ultimate Parent:** Barnett
Banks. **SIC:** 6022—State Commercial
Banks.

★ 63933 ★　**Fantasy-Blankebaer Corp.**
1000 American Superior Blvd. PO Box 1579
Winter Haven, FL 33882
Ultimate Parent: Universal Foods Corp.
SIC: 2087—Flavoring Extracts & Syrups
Nec.

★ 63934 ★　**First Union National Bank of Florida**
1001 Havendale Blvd.
Winter Haven, FL 33881-1381
(813)291-6510
Location Type: Branch office. **Ultimate
Parent:** First Union Corp. **SIC:** 6021—
National Commercial Banks.

★ 63935 ★　**First Union National Bank of Florida**
203 Ave. A NW
Winter Haven, FL 33882
(813)294-3101
Location Type: Branch office. **Ultimate
Parent:** First Union Corp. **SIC:** 6021—
National Commercial Banks.

★ 63936 ★　**First Union National Bank of Florida**
3899 Recker Hwy.
Winter Haven, FL 33880-1910
(813)294-4151
Location Type: Branch office. **Ultimate
Parent:** First Union Corp. **SIC:** 6021—
National Commercial Banks.

★ 63937 ★　**First Union National Bank of Florida**
5720 Cypress Gardens Blvd.
Winter Haven, FL 33884-2269
(813)291-6570
Location Type: Branch office. **Ultimate
Parent:** First Union Corp. **SIC:** 6021—
National Commercial Banks.

★ 63938 ★　**First Union National Bank of Florida**
7000 State Rd. 544 E
Winter Haven, FL 33881-9531
(813)421-3487
Location Type: Branch office. **Ultimate
Parent:** First Union Corp. **SIC:** 6021—
National Commercial Banks.

★ 63939 ★　**First Union National Bank of Florida**
514 Cypress Gardens Blvd.
Winter Haven, FL 33880-4447
(813)294-3884
Location Type: Branch office. **Ultimate
Parent:** First Union Corp. **SIC:** 6021—
National Commercial Banks.

★ 63940 ★　**Florida Cypress Gardens, Inc.**
2641 S. Lake Summit Dr.
Winter Haven, FL 33884
(813)324-2111
Company Type: Subsidiary. **Officer:**
William Reynolds, Executive Vice President
& General Manager. **Ultimate Parent:**
Agway Inc. **SIC:** 7999—Amusement &
Recreation Nec.

★ 63941 ★　**Greyhound Bus Lines**
900 6th St. NW
Winter Haven, FL 33881
(813)299-4332
Ultimate Parent: Greyhound Lines Inc. **SIC:**
4212—Local Trucking Without Storage.

★ 63942 ★　**Kentucky Fried Chicken**
113 Cypress Gardens Blvd. SE
Winter Haven, FL 33880
(813)299-1990
Ultimate Parent: Pepsico. **SIC:** 5812—
Eating Places.

★ 63943 ★　**Kentucky Fried Chicken**
3105 Havendale Blvd. NW
Winter Haven, FL 33881
(813)967-9830
Ultimate Parent: Pepsico. **SIC:** 5812—
Eating Places; 5812—Eating Places.

★ 63944 ★　**Lerner Shop**
101 Winter Haven Mall
Winter Haven, FL 33880
(813)294-8037
Ultimate Parent: Limited. **SIC:** 5651—
Family Clothing Stores.

★ 63945 ★　**Mary Kay Cosmetics**
1329 N. Lake Otis Dr. SE
Winter Haven, FL 33880
(813)293-2598
Ultimate Parent: Mary Kay Cosmetics.

★ 63946 ★　**McDonalds Restaurants**
Havendale Blvd.
Winter Haven, FL 33881
(813)967-6910
Ultimate Parent: May Department Stores.
SIC: 5812—Eating Places.

★ 63947 ★　**Nekoosa Packaging**
1910 42nd St. NW
Winter Haven, FL 33881
(813)967-0641
Ultimate Parent: Georgia-Pacific. **SIC:**
2657—Folding Paperboard Boxes.

★ 63948 ★　**Pizza Hut**
997 Havendale Blvd. NW
Winter Haven, FL 33881
(813)293-4327
Ultimate Parent: Pepsico. **SIC:** 5812—
Eating Places.

★ 63949 ★　**Radio Shack**
1528 3rd St. SW
Winter Haven, FL 33880
(813)294-6908
Company Type: Division. **Ultimate Parent:**
Tandy Corp. **SIC:** 5731—Radio, Television
& Electronics Stores.

★ 63950 ★　**Radio Shack**
339 Havendale Blvd.
Winter Haven, FL 33881
(813)967-2972
Company Type: Division. **Ultimate Parent:**
Tandy Corp. **SIC:** 1521—Single-Family
Housing Construction.

★ 63951 ★　**Rollins Burdick Hunter Fla**
101 Avenue C SW
Winter Haven, FL 33880
(813)299-8221
Ultimate Parent: Aon Corp. **SIC:** 6411—
Insurance Agents, Brokers & Service.

★ 63952 ★　**Ryder Truck Rental**
1200 3rd St. SW
Winter Haven, FL 33880
(813)294-2994
Ultimate Parent: Ryder System. **SIC:**
7513—Truck Rental & Leasing Without
Drivers.

★ 63953 ★　**Taco Bell**
1799 3rd St. SW
Winter Haven, FL 33880
(813)293-7790
Ultimate Parent: Pepsico. **SIC:** 5812—
Eating Places; 6531—Real Estate Agents &
Managers.

★ 63954 ★　**Texaco Food Mart**
1701 Recker Hwy.
Winter Haven, FL 33880
(813)297-9018
Ultimate Parent: Texaco. **SIC:** 5541—
Gasoline Service Stations.

★ 63955 ★　**Waldenbooks**
50 Winter Haven Mall
Winter Haven, FL 33880
(813)294-9030
Ultimate Parent: K-Mart. **SIC:** 5942—Book
Stores.

★ 63956 ★　**Walgreen Drug Stores**
170 Winter Haven Mall
Winter Haven, FL 33880
(813)294-8877
Ultimate Parent: Walgreen Co. **SIC:**
5812—Eating Places; 5912—Drug Stores &
Proprietary Stores.

★ 63957 ★　**Walgreen Drug Stores**
1368 6th St. NW
Winter Haven, FL 33881
(813)293-2129
Ultimate Parent: Walgreen Co. **SIC:**
5912—Drug Stores & Proprietary Stores.

Winter Park

★ 63958 ★　**Albertson's**
483 N. Semoran Blvd.
Winter Park, FL 32792
(407)671-6200
Ultimate Parent: Albertson's Inc. **SIC:**
5411—Grocery Stores; 5499—
Miscellaneous Food Stores.

★ 63959 ★　**AmSouth Bank of Florida**
220 W. Fairbanks Ave.
Winter Park, FL 32789-4329
(407)740-6222
Location Type: Branch office. **Ultimate
Parent:** AmSouth Bancorp. **SIC:** 6022—
State Commercial Banks.

★ 63960 ★　**AmSouth Bank of Florida**
925 S. Orlando Ave.
Winter Park, FL 32789-4848
(407)649-1900
Location Type: Branch office. **Ultimate
Parent:** AmSouth Bancorp. **SIC:** 6022—
State Commercial Banks.

★ 63961 ★　**Banana Republic**
102 N. Park Ave.
Winter Park, FL 32789
(407)629-2339
Ultimate Parent: GAP. **SIC:** 5651—Family
Clothing Stores.

★ 63962 ★　**Barnett Bank of Central Florida, NA**
1111 S. Lakemont Ave.
Winter Park, FL 32789
Company Type: Subsidiary. **Location
Type:** Branch office. **Officer:** Nancy
Pardue, Manager. **Ultimate Parent:** Barnett
Banks. **SIC:** 6021—National Commercial
Banks.

★ 63963 ★　**Barnett Bank of Central Florida, NA**
250 Park Ave. S
PO Box 1000
Winter Park, FL 32790-1000
(407)420-2800 **Fax:** (407)420-2848
Company Type: Subsidiary. **Location
Type:** Branch office. **Officer:** Thomas H.
Yochum, President & CEO. **Ultimate
Parent:** Barnett Banks. **SIC:** 6021—National
Commercial Banks.

★ 63964 ★　**Barnett Bank of Central Florida, NA**
1500 Lee Rd.
Winter Park, FL 32789-2285
(407)646-3450
Company Type: Subsidiary. **Location
Type:** Branch office. **Officer:** David
Marcello, Area Manager. **Ultimate Parent:**
Barnett Banks. **SIC:** 6021—National
Commercial Banks.

★ 63965 ★　**Chase Home Mortgage Corp.**
1801 Lee Rd.
Winter Park, FL 32789
(407)645-5194
Ultimate Parent: Chase Manhattan Corp.
SIC: 6141—Personal Credit Institutions;
6162—Mortgage Bankers &
Correspondents.

★ 63966 ★　**Coast to Coast Assoc Inc.**
2323 Lee Rd.
Winter Park, FL 32789
(407)740-5100
Ultimate Parent: Servistar Corp. **SIC:**
8713—Surveying Services.

★ 63967 ★　**Coast to Coast Collection**
2020 W. Fairbanks Ave.
Winter Park, FL 32789
(407)629-4414
Ultimate Parent: Servistar Corp. **SIC:**
8049—Offices of Health Practitioners Nec.

★ 63968 ★　**Collective Mortgage Service**
1850 Lee Rd.
Winter Park, FL 32789
(407)628-5353
Ultimate Parent: Collective Bancorp. **SIC:**
6141—Personal Credit Institutions.

★ 63969 ★　**Continental Indus Inc.**
280 W. Canton Ave.
Winter Park, FL 32789
(407)740-0800
Ultimate Parent: Handy & Harman. **SIC:**
6531—Real Estate Agents & Managers.

★ 63970 ★ Continental Industries Inc.
280 W. Canton Ave.
Winter Park, FL 32789
(407)740-8000
Ultimate Parent: Handy & Harman. SIC: 6531—Real Estate Agents & Managers.

★ 63971 ★ Electronic Data Systems
1025 S. Semoran Blvd.
Winter Park, FL 32792
(407)678-8868
Ultimate Parent: Electronic Data Systems. SIC: 7374—Data Processing & Preparation.

★ 63972 ★ Exxon Car Wash
909 PO Box
Winter Park, FL 32790
Ultimate Parent: Exxon. SIC: 5541—Gasoline Service Stations; 7542—Car Washes.

★ 63973 ★ Exxon Corp.
1011 N. Wymore Rd.
Winter Park, FL 32789
(407)645-5517
Ultimate Parent: Exxon. SIC: 3699—Electrical Equipment & Supplies Nec.

★ 63974 ★ First Union National Bank of Florida
5600 Red Bug Lake Rd.
Winter Park, FL 32708
(407)699-0077
Location Type: Branch office. Ultimate Parent: First Union Corp. SIC: 6021—National Commercial Banks.

★ 63975 ★ First Union National Bank of Florida
275 S. New York Ave.
Winter Park, FL 32789-4203
(407)628-4800
Location Type: Branch office. Ultimate Parent: First Union Corp. SIC: 6021—National Commercial Banks.

★ 63976 ★ First Union National Bank of Florida
4010 N. Golden Rod Rd.
Winter Park, FL 32789
(407)657-3142
Location Type: Branch office. Ultimate Parent: First Union Corp. SIC: 6021—National Commercial Banks.

★ 63977 ★ First Union National Bank of Florida
2525 Aloma Ave.
Winter Park, FL 32789-3498
(407)657-3173
Location Type: Branch office. Ultimate Parent: First Union Corp. SIC: 6021—National Commercial Banks.

★ 63978 ★ First Union National Bank of Florida
631 S. Orlando Ave.
Winter Park, FL 32789
(407)539-7080
Location Type: Branch office. Ultimate Parent: First Union Corp. SIC: 6021—National Commercial Banks.

★ 63979 ★ The Gap
500 N. Orlando Ave. 1348
Winter Park, FL 32789
(407)629-1649
Ultimate Parent: GAP. SIC: 5651—Family Clothing Stores.

★ 63980 ★ Hamilton Hallmark
7079 University Blvd.
Winter Park, FL 32791
(407)657-3300
Location Type: Branch office. Ultimate Parent: Avnet. SIC: 5065—Electronic Parts & Equipment Nec.

★ 63981 ★ Hertz Rent-A-Car
370 Blue Heron Dr.
Winter Park, FL 32789
(407)644-0394
Ultimate Parent: Hertz. SIC: 7514—Passenger Car Rental.

★ 63982 ★ Jiffy Lube
2289 N. Semoran Blvd.
Winter Park, FL 32792
(407)671-6769
Ultimate Parent: Pennzoil. SIC: 7539—Automotive Repair Shops Nec.

★ 63983 ★ Kelly Assisted Living Servi
2281 Lee Rd.
Winter Park, FL 32789
(407)629-5969
Ultimate Parent: Kelly Services. SIC: 8099—Health & Allied Services Nec.

★ 63984 ★ Kentucky Fried Chicken
2233 Lee Rd.
Winter Park, FL 32789
(407)629-9291
Ultimate Parent: Pepsico. SIC: 5812—Eating Places.

★ 63985 ★ Kentucky Fried Chicken
2212 Aloma Ave.
Winter Park, FL 32792
(407)644-3260
Ultimate Parent: Pepsico. SIC: 5812—Eating Places.

★ 63986 ★ Lerner Shop
500 N. Orlando Ave. 1208
Winter Park, FL 32789
(407)628-9552
Ultimate Parent: Limited. SIC: 5621—Women's Clothing Stores.

★ 63987 ★ Mobil Self Service
100 S. Semoran Blvd.
Winter Park, FL 32792
(407)671-5419
Ultimate Parent: Mobil. SIC: 5541—Gasoline Service Stations.

★ 63988 ★ Pizza Hut
525 S. Orlando Ave.
Winter Park, FL 32789
(407)740-6850
Ultimate Parent: Pepsico. SIC: 5812—Eating Places.

★ 63989 ★ Pizza Hut
3748 Howell Branch Rd.
Winter Park, FL 32792
(407)677-7144
Ultimate Parent: Pepsico. SIC: 5812—Eating Places.

★ 63990 ★ Pizza Hut
2607 N. Semoran Blvd.
Winter Park, FL 32792
(407)678-3330
Ultimate Parent: Pepsico. SIC: 5812—Eating Places.

★ 63991 ★ Publix Super Market
Hollienna Shopping Ctr.
Winter Park, FL 32789
(407)677-3457
Ultimate Parent: Publix Super Markets. SIC: 5411—Grocery Stores.

★ 63992 ★ Radio Shack
465 S. Semoran Blvd.
Winter Park, FL 32792
(407)677-1190
Company Type: Division. Ultimate Parent: Tandy Corp. SIC: 5065—Electronic Parts & Equipment Nec.

★ 63993 ★ Radio Shack
500 N. Orlando Ave.
Winter Park, FL 32789
(407)647-8646
Company Type: Division. Ultimate Parent: Tandy Corp. SIC: 5731—Radio, Television & Electronics Stores.

★ 63994 ★ Russell Associates Inc.
144 E. Comstock Ave.
Winter Park, FL 32789
(407)628-2138
Ultimate Parent: Pall. SIC: 5088—Transportation Equipment & Supplies.

★ 63995 ★ Taco Bell
690 S. Orlando Ave.
Winter Park, FL 32789
Ultimate Parent: Pepsico. SIC: 5812—Eating Places.

★ 63996 ★ Texaco Food Mart
6999 W. B Bill Mac Gee Hwy.
Winter Park, FL 32789
(407)290-2414
Ultimate Parent: Texaco. SIC: 5411—Grocery Stores.

★ 63997 ★ Texaco Self Service Station
7373 University Blvd.
Winter Park, FL 32792
(407)657-6903
Ultimate Parent: Texaco. SIC: 5541—Gasoline Service Stations.

★ 63998 ★ Variable Annuity Life Insurance
110 University Park Dr.
Winter Park, FL 32792
(407)679-1090
Ultimate Parent: Variable Annuity Life. SIC: 6411—Insurance Agents, Brokers & Service.

★ 63999 ★ Victoria's Secret
236 N. Park Ave.
Winter Park, FL 32789
(407)740-0494
Ultimate Parent: Limited. SIC: 5651—Family Clothing Stores.

★ 64000 ★ Washington Inventory Servic
6853 W. B Bill Mac Gee Hwy.
Winter Park, FL 32789
(407)834-5094
Ultimate Parent: Huffy. SIC: 7374—Data Processing & Preparation.

Winter Springs

★ 64001 ★ Mary Kay Cosmetics
240 3rd St.
Winter Springs, FL 32708
(407)327-1295
Ultimate Parent: Mary Kay Cosmetics. SIC: 5999—Miscellaneous Retail Stores Nec.

★ 64002 ★ Mobil Oil Corp.
5885 Red Bug Lake Rd.
Winter Springs, FL 32708
(407)696-2225
Ultimate Parent: Mobil. SIC: 5541—Gasoline Service Stations.

★ 64003 ★ Pizza Hut
1335 Tuscawilla Rd.
Winter Springs, FL 32708
(407)695-6200
Ultimate Parent: Pepsico. SIC: 5812—Eating Places.

★ 64004 ★ Taco Bell
1345 Tuscawilla Rd.
Winter Springs, FL 32708
(407)695-8226
Ultimate Parent: Pepsico. SIC: 5812—Eating Places.

Yulee

★ 64005 ★ Stone Container Corp.
N. Hwy. 17
Yulee, FL 32097
(904)225-5121
Officer: Charles E. Berry, President. Ultimate Parent: Stone Container Corp. SIC: 2673—Bags—Plastics, Laminated & Coated; 2674—Bags—Uncoated Paper & Multiwall.

Zellwood

★ 64006 ★ Barnett Bank of Central Florida, NA
3116 Washington St.
Zellwood, FL 32798
(305)889-1155
Company Type: Subsidiary. Location Type: Branch office. Officer: Debi Hope, Manager. Ultimate Parent: Barnett Banks. SIC: 6021—National Commercial Banks.

★ 64007 ★ W. R. Grace & Co.
Connecticut Construction Products Div.
6445 W. Jones Ave.
Zellwood, FL 32798
Company Type: Division. Ultimate Parent: W. R. Grace. SIC: 2899—Chemical Preparations Nec.

Zephyrhills

★ 64008 ★ Barnett Bank of Pasco County
7344 Gall Blvd.
Zephyrhills, FL 33540-2504
(813)783-0830
Company Type: Subsidiary. Location

Type: Branch office. Officer: John Braumuller, Manager. Ultimate Parent: Barnett Banks. SIC: 6022—State Commercial Banks.

★ 64009 ★ Barnett Bank of Pasco County
37215 State Rd. 54 W
Zephyrhills, FL 33541
(813)783-0811
Company Type: Subsidiary. Location Type: Branch office. Officer: Kim Schuknecht, Manager. Ultimate Parent: Barnett Banks. SIC: 6022—State Commercial Banks.

★ 64010 ★ First Union National Bank of Florida
38421 5th Ave.
Zephyrhills, FL 33540
(813)783-6300
Location Type: Branch office. Ultimate Parent: First Union Corp. SIC: 6021—National Commercial Banks.

★ 64011 ★ First Union National Bank of Florida
38008 North Ave.
Zephyrhills, FL 33540
(813)783-6316
Location Type: Branch office. Ultimate Parent: First Union Corp. SIC: 6021—National Commercial Banks.

★ 64012 ★ Greyhound Bus Lines
38841 County Rd. 54 E
Zephyrhills, FL 33540
(813)782-1016
Ultimate Parent: Greyhound Lines Inc. SIC: 4131—Intercity & Rural Bus Transportation.

★ 64013 ★ Kentucky Fried Chicken
2466 W. Bay Dr.
Zephyrhills, FL 33541
(813)584-1763
Ultimate Parent: Pepsico. SIC: 5812—Eating Places.

★ 64014 ★ Kentucky Fried Chicken
5506 Gall Blvd.
Zephyrhills, FL 33541
(813)782-3502
Ultimate Parent: Pepsico. SIC: 5812—Eating Places.

★ 64015 ★ Kentucky Fried Chicken
8800 Ulmerton Rd. SW
Zephyrhills, FL 33541
(813)530-4376
Ultimate Parent: Pepsico. SIC: 5812—Eating Places.

★ 64016 ★ Kmart Discount Stores
13100 66th St. N
Zephyrhills, FL 33543
(813)530-9466
Ultimate Parent: K-Mart. SIC: 5191—Farm Supplies.

★ 64017 ★ Pizza Hut
6548 Gall Blvd.
Zephyrhills, FL 33541
(813)788-7643
Ultimate Parent: Pepsico. SIC: 5812—Eating Places.

★ 64018 ★ Pizza Hut
700 S. Missouri Ave.
Zephyrhills, FL 33540
(813)446-7923
Ultimate Parent: Pepsico. SIC: 5812—Eating Places.

★ 64019 ★ Pizza Hut
2884 E. Bay Dr.
Zephyrhills, FL 33541
(813)535-0761
Ultimate Parent: Pepsico. SIC: 5812—Eating Places.

★ 64020 ★ Publix Super Market
10801 Starkey Rd.
Zephyrhills, FL 33543
(813)393-7517
Ultimate Parent: Publix Super Markets. SIC: 5812—Eating Places.

★ **64021** ★   **Publix Super Market**
Midway Shopping Ctr.
Zephyrhills, FL 33540
(813)585-5638 (813)584-7151
Ultimate Parent: Sears Roebuck & Co.
SIC: 5531—Automobile & Home Supply
Stores. **Ultimate Parent:** Publix Super
Markets. **SIC:** 5812—Eating Places.

★ **64022** ★   **Publix Super Market**
713 Market Sq.
Zephyrhills, FL 33540
(813)782-9587
Ultimate Parent: Publix Super Markets.
SIC: 5411—Grocery Stores.

★ **64023** ★   **Publix Super Markets**
10801 Starkey Rd.
Zephyrhills, FL 33543
(813)393-7517
Ultimate Parent: Publix Super Markets.
SIC: 5812—Eating Places.

★ **64024** ★   **Publix Super Markets**
Inc.
12022 Indian Rocks Rd.
Zephyrhills, FL 33544
(813)595-2514
Ultimate Parent: Publix Super Markets.
SIC: 5812—Eating Places.

★ **64025** ★   **Radio Shack**
11630 Oakhurst Rd.
Zephyrhills, FL 33544
(813)596-6103
Company Type: Division. **Ultimate Parent:**
Tandy Corp. **SIC:** 5065—Electronic Parts &
Equipment Nec.

★ **64026** ★   **Radio Shack**
2200 E. Bay Dr.
Zephyrhills, FL 33541
(813)584-2839
Company Type: Division. **Ultimate Parent:**
Tandy Corp. **SIC:** 5731—Radio, Television
& Electronics Stores.

★ **64027** ★   **Radio Shack**
7248 Gall Blvd.
Zephyrhills, FL 33541
Company Type: Division. **Ultimate Parent:**
Tandy Corp. **SIC:** 5731—Radio, Television
& Electronics Stores.

★ **64028** ★   **Taco Bell**
2535 E. Bay Dr.
Zephyrhills, FL 33541
(813)531-8655
Ultimate Parent: Pepsico. **SIC:** 5812—
Eating Places.

★ **64029** ★   **Walgreen Drug Stores**
5417 Village Market
Zephyrhills, FL 33543
(813)973-2095
Ultimate Parent: Walgreen Co. **SIC:**
7389—Business Services Nec.

★ **64030** ★   **Walgreen Drug Stores**
715 Market Sq.
Zephyrhills, FL 33540
(813)782-9581
Ultimate Parent: Walgreen Co. **SIC:**
5912—Drug Stores & Proprietary Stores.

★ **64031** ★   **Walgreen Drug Stores**
1052 Ulmerton Rd. SW
Zephyrhills, FL 33540
(813)581-1833
Ultimate Parent: Walgreen Co. **SIC:**
5912—Drug Stores & Proprietary Stores.

★ **64032** ★   **Western Auto Supply**
Co.
950 N. Missouri Ave.
Zephyrhills, FL 33540
(813)585-5638
Ultimate Parent: Sears Roebuck & Co.
SIC: 5531—Automobile & Home Supply
Stores.

GEORGIA

401 Carswell Ave.

★ 64033 ★ **Bank South NA/Waycross Main Office**
401 Carswell Ave.
401 Carswell Ave., GA 31501
(912)287-2400
Company Type: Subsidiary. **Location Type:** Branch office. **Officer:** P. Owen Herrin Jr., President. **Ultimate Parent:** Bank South Corp. **SIC:** 6021—National Commercial Banks.

Acworth

★ 64034 ★ **Ace Hardware**
1164 Alabama Rd. NW
Acworth, GA 30102
(404)926-0957
Ultimate Parent: Ace Hardware.

★ 64035 ★ **Fleet Finance Inc. Acworth**
5399 Bells Ferry Rd. NE
Acworth, GA 30102
(404)926-4401
Ultimate Parent: Fleet Financial Group.

★ 64036 ★ **Jiffy Lube Acworth/Woodstock**
1196 Alabama Rd.
Acworth, GA 30102
(404)591-9205
Ultimate Parent: Pennzoil.

★ 64037 ★ **Kentucky Fried Chicken**
5040 Glade Rd. NW
Acworth, GA 30101
(404)974-5420
Ultimate Parent: Pepsico.

★ 64038 ★ **Kentucky Fried Chicken Regional**
1061 Alabama Rd. NW
Acworth, GA 30102
(404)926-0160
Ultimate Parent: Pepsico.

★ 64039 ★ **Kmart Stores**
5500 Bells Ferry Rd.
Acworth, GA 30102
(404)928-6318
Ultimate Parent: K-Mart.

★ 64040 ★ **Kmart Stores**
5300 Bartow Rd.
Acworth, GA 30101
(404)975-0095
Ultimate Parent: K-Mart.

★ 64041 ★ **Kmart Stores Pharmacy**
5300 Bartow Rd. NW
Acworth, GA 30101
(404)975-0098
Ultimate Parent: K-Mart.

★ 64042 ★ **Kroger Pharmacies**
1200 Alabama Rd. NW
Acworth, GA 30102
(404)924-9105
Ultimate Parent: Kroger.

★ 64043 ★ **Kroger Vot the Retail Stores**
1200 Alabama Rd.
Acworth, GA 30102
(404)924-9102
Ultimate Parent: Kroger.

★ 64044 ★ **Mary Kay Cosmetics**
Indep Sales
569 Delphinium Blvd. NW
Acworth, GA 30102
(404)926-2747
Ultimate Parent: Mary Kay Cosmetics.

★ 64045 ★ **Mary Kay Cosmetics**
Indep Sales
613 Mistflower Dr. NW
Acworth, GA 30102
(404)928-2039
Ultimate Parent: Mary Kay Cosmetics.

★ 64046 ★ **McDonald's Restaurants**
5600 Bells Ferry Rd. NW
Acworth, GA 30102
(404)928-6947
Ultimate Parent: McDonald's.

★ 64047 ★ **Pizza Hut**
1033 Alabama Rd.
Acworth, GA 30102
(404)928-9967
Ultimate Parent: Pepsico.

★ 64048 ★ **Pizza Hut**
5070 Glade Rd. NW
Acworth, GA 30101
(404)975-7444
Ultimate Parent: Pepsico.

★ 64049 ★ **Radio Shack**
5558 Bells Ferry Rd. NW
Acworth, GA 30102
(404)928-9903
Company Type: Division. **Ultimate Parent:** Tandy Corp.

★ 64050 ★ **Radio Shack**
5080 Glade Rd.
Acworth, GA 30101
(404)974-9972
Company Type: Division. **Ultimate Parent:** Tandy Corp.

★ 64051 ★ **Ryder Truck Rental**
1565 W. Alabama Rd. NW
Acworth, GA
(404)974-9749
Ultimate Parent: Ryder System.

★ 64052 ★ **Ryder Truck Rental**
4514 Cobb Pkwy NW
Acworth, GA 30101
(404)974-9059
Ultimate Parent: Ryder System.

★ 64053 ★ **Taco Bell**
5080 Glade Rd. NW
Acworth, GA 30101
(404)974-7926
Ultimate Parent: Pepsico.

★ 64054 ★ **Texaco**
3525 Cherokee Rd.
Acworth, GA 30102
(404)974-2366
Ultimate Parent: Texaco.

Adel

★ 64055 ★ **Greyhound Bus Station**
820 S. Hutchinson Ave.
Adel, GA 31620
(912)896-3292
Ultimate Parent: Greyhound Lines Inc. **SIC:** 4131—Intercity & Rural Bus Transportation.

★ 64056 ★ **Rite Aid Pharmacy**
401 N. Burwell Ave.
Adel, GA 31620
(912)896-2300
Ultimate Parent: Rite Aid. **SIC:** 5912—Drug Stores & Proprietary Stores.

★ 64057 ★ **Ryder Truck Rental**
301 S. Hutchinson Ave.
Adel, GA 31620
(912)896-4220
Ultimate Parent: Ryder System. **SIC:** 7513—Truck Rental & Leasing Without Drivers.

★ 64058 ★ **Weyerhaeuser Co.**
801 Cook St.
Adel, GA 31620
(912)896-2215
Officer: Bruce Leet, Manager. **Ultimate Parent:** Weyerhaeuser Co. **SIC:** 2493—Reconstituted Wood Products.

★ 64059 ★ **Weyerhaeuser Particleboard Mill**
801 Cook St.
Adel, GA 31620
Ultimate Parent: Weyerhaeuser Co. **SIC:** 2493—Reconstituted Wood Products.

Albany

★ 64060 ★ **Acme Business Products**
408 Sands Dr.
Albany, GA 31705
(912)228-1725
Officer: Jimmy Clifton, Manager. **Ultimate Parent:** Alco Standard Corp. **SIC:** 3663—Radio & T.V. Communications Equipment.

★ 64061 ★ **Air Products & Chemicals Inc.**
1220 Gillionville Rd.
Albany, GA 31707-3938
(912)432-0536
Officer: Tim H. Goatley, Manager. **Ultimate Parent:** Air Products & Chemicals, Inc. **SIC:** 5047—Medical & Hospital Equipment; 5084—Industrial Machinery & Equipment; 5085—Industrial Supplies; 7359—Equipment Rental & Leasing Nec; 2813—Industrial Gases.

★ 64062 ★ **Air Products & Chemicals Inc.**
1220 Gillionville Rd. PO Box 3370
Albany, GA 31708
Ultimate Parent: Air Products & Chemicals, Inc. **SIC:** 2813—Industrial Gases.

★ 64063 ★ **Air Products & Chemicals, Inc.**
205 Baldwin Dr.
Albany, GA 31707
(912)432-1247
Ultimate Parent: Air Products & Chemicals, Inc. **SIC:** 5099—Durable Goods Nec.

★ 64064 ★ **Casual Corner**
New Albany Mall
Albany, GA 31702
(912)432-1261
Ultimate Parent: United States Shoe. **SIC:** 5621—Women's Clothing Stores.

★ 64065 ★ **Cooper Tire Co.**
3300 Sylvester Rd.
Albany, GA 31703
Ultimate Parent: Cooper Tire & Rubber Co. Inc. **SIC:** 3011—Tires & Inner Tubes.

★ 64066 ★ **Diebold Inc.**
1408 W. 3rd Ave.
Albany, GA 31707
(912)432-9352
Ultimate Parent: Diebold, Inc. **SIC:** 7373—Computer Integrated Systems Design.

★ 64067 ★ **First State Bank & Trust Co.**
1522 W. 3rd Ave.
Albany, GA 31707
(912)435-8318
Ultimate Parent: Michigan National Corp. **SIC:** 6022—State Commercial Banks.

★ 64068 ★ **First State Bank & Trust Co.**
2415 Sylvester Rd.
Albany, GA 31705
(912)432-8407
Ultimate Parent: Michigan National Corp. **SIC:** 6099—Functions Related to Deposit Banking.

★ 64069 ★ **First State Bank & Trust Co.**
2616 Dawson Rd.
Albany, GA 31707
(912)432-8000
Ultimate Parent: Michigan National Corp. **SIC:** 6099—Functions Related to Deposit Banking.

★ 64070 ★ **First State Bank & Trust Co.**
1720 S. Slappey Blvd.
Albany, GA 31701
(912)432-8416
Ultimate Parent: Michigan National Corp. **SIC:** 6099—Functions Related to Deposit Banking.

★ 64071 ★ **First State Bank & Trust Co.**
333 W. Broad Ave.
Albany, GA 31701
(912)432-8063
Ultimate Parent: Michigan National Corp. **SIC:** 6099—Functions Related to Deposit Banking.

★ 64072 ★ **First Union National Bank of Georgia**
701 N. Westover Blvd.
Albany, GA 31707
(912)430-8214
Location Type: Branch office. **Ultimate Parent:** First Union Corp. **SIC:** 6021—National Commercial Banks.

★ 64073 ★ **First Union National Bank of Georgia**
241 Pine Ave.
Albany, GA 31708-6001
(912)430-8214
Location Type: Branch office. **Ultimate Parent:** First Union Corp. **SIC:** 6021—National Commercial Banks.

★ 64074 ★ **Georgia Federal Bank F S B**
241 Pine Ave.
Albany, GA 31708
(912)432-8200
Ultimate Parent: First Union Corp. **SIC:** 6022—State Commercial Banks; 6035—Federal Savings Institutions.

★ 64075 ★ **Georgia-Pacific Corp.**
405 Maxwell Dr.
Albany, GA 31701-8101
Ultimate Parent: Georgia-Pacific. **SIC:** 2653—Corrugated & Solid Fiber Boxes.

★ 64076 ★ **Johnson Controls Inc.**
3168 PO Box
Albany, GA 31706
(912)435-6111
Ultimate Parent: Johnson Controls Inc. **SIC:** 5063—Electrical Apparatus & Equipment.

★ 64077 ★ **Kentucky Fried Chicken**
912 S. Slappey Blvd.
Albany, GA 31701
(912)888-7532
Ultimate Parent: Pepsico. **SIC:** 5812—Eating Places.

★ 64078 ★ **Kmart Discount Stores**
2525 Dawson Rd.
Albany, GA 31707
(912)435-5646
Ultimate Parent: K-Mart. **SIC:** 5912—Drug Stores & Proprietary Stores.

★ 64079 ★ **Kmart Discount Stores**
1420 Radium Springs Rd.
Albany, GA 31705
(912)439-7014
Ultimate Parent: K-Mart. **SIC:** 5531—Automobile & Home Supply Stores; 5531—Automobile & Home Supply Stores.

★ 64080 ★ Kroger Food Co.
2511 Sylvester Rd.
Albany, GA 31705
(912)435-0825
Ultimate Parent: Kroger. SIC: 5499—
Miscellaneous Food Stores.

★ 64081 ★ Manpower, Inc.
121 S. Washington St.
Albany, GA 31701
(912)883-2428
Ultimate Parent: Manpower, Inc. SIC:
7363—Help Supply Services.

★ 64082 ★ Merck & Co. Inc.
Flint River Plant
3517 Radium Springs Rd.
Albany, GA 31708
Location Type: Plant. Ultimate Parent:
Merck. SIC: 2833—Medicinals & Botanicals.

★ 64083 ★ Miller Brewing Co.
405 Cordele Rd.
Albany, GA 31708
Ultimate Parent: Philip Morris. SIC: 2082—
Malt Beverages.

★ 64084 ★ Mutual of New York
112 Westfield Rd.
Albany, GA 31707
(912)436-7411
Ultimate Parent: Mutual of New York. SIC:
6411—Insurance Agents, Brokers &
Service.

★ 64085 ★ Pepsi-Cola
Distributing Co.
1011 Randolph Ave.
Albany, GA 31707
(912)436-9553
Officer: Hilton Longshore, Manager.
Ultimate Parent: Pepsico. SIC: 2086—
Bottled & Canned Soft Drinks.

★ 64086 ★ Pizza Hut
1018 N. Slappey Blvd.
Albany, GA 31701
(912)435-2737
Ultimate Parent: Pepsico. SIC: 5812—
Eating Places.

★ 64087 ★ Procter & Gamble Co.
Paper Products
US Rte. 19 S
Albany, GA 31702
Ultimate Parent: Procter & Gamble Co.
SIC: 2600—Paper & Allied Products.

★ 64088 ★ Procter & Gamble
Paper Product Co.
512 Liberty Expy. SE
Albany, GA 31705
Ultimate Parent: Procter & Gamble Co.
SIC: 2676—Sanitary Paper Products;
2621—Paper Mills.

★ 64089 ★ Radio Shack
2601 Dolphin Rd.
Albany, GA 31707
(912)883-7790
Company Type: Division. Ultimate Parent:
Tandy Corp. SIC: 5065—Electronic Parts &
Equipment Nec.

★ 64090 ★ Radio Shack
Midtown Shopping Ctr.
Albany, GA 31702
(912)883-5037
Company Type: Division. Ultimate Parent:
Tandy Corp. SIC: 5065—Electronic Parts &
Equipment Nec.

★ 64091 ★ Ryder Truck Rental
2310 N. Monroe St.
Albany, GA 31701
(912)883-5552
Ultimate Parent: Ryder System. SIC:
7513—Truck Rental & Leasing Without
Drivers.

★ 64092 ★ Security Bank & Trust
Co. of Albany
401 Pine Ave.
Albany, GA 31701-2459
(912)430-7000
Location Type: Branch office. Ultimate
Parent: Synovus Financial Corp. SIC:
6021—National Commercial Banks.

★ 64093 ★ Security Bank & Trust
Co. of Albany
2819 Old Dawson Rd.
Albany, GA 31707-1513
Location Type: Branch office. Officer:
Marion Holland, Manager. Ultimate Parent:

Synovus Financial Corp. SIC: 6021—
National Commercial Banks.

★ 64094 ★ Security Bank & Trust
Co. of Albany
PO Box 1912
Albany, GA 31703-6901
Location Type: Branch office. Ultimate
Parent: Synovus Financial Corp. SIC:
6021—National Commercial Banks.

★ 64095 ★ Security Bank & Trust
Co. of Albany
2107 E. Broad Ave.
Albany, GA 31705-2317
(912)430-7020
Location Type: Branch office. Officer:
Cecil Gamble, Manager. Ultimate Parent:
Synovus Financial Corp. SIC: 6021—
National Commercial Banks.

★ 64096 ★ Security Bank & Trust
Co. of Albany
2619 Gillionville Rd.
Albany, GA 31707-3003
(912)430-7030
Location Type: Branch office. Officer:
Debbie Ratliff, Manager. Ultimate Parent:
Synovus Financial Corp. SIC: 6021—
National Commercial Banks.

★ 64097 ★ Trust Co. Bank of
South Georgia, National Assoc.
917 Forrester Dr.
Albany, GA 31742
(912)995-4494
Ultimate Parent: Suntrust Banks. SIC:
6021—National Commercial Banks.

★ 64098 ★ Union Oil Co. of
California
1162 Gillionville Rd.
Albany, GA 31707
(912)435-5471
Ultimate Parent: Unocal Corp. SIC: 5172—
Petroleum Products Nec.

★ 64099 ★ United Parcel Service
2219 Toledo Dr.
Albany, GA 31705
(912)282-9790
Ultimate Parent: United Parcel Service of
America. SIC: 4215—Courier Services
Except by Air.

Alma

★ 64100 ★ Fleetwood Homes
Industrial Park
Alma, GA 31510
(912)632-6789
Officer: Gary Hauder, Manager. Ultimate
Parent: Fleetwood Enterprises, Inc. SIC:
2451—Mobile Homes.

★ 64101 ★ Pizza Hut
906 S. Pierce St.
Alma, GA 31510
(912)632-8629
Ultimate Parent: Pepsico. SIC: 5812—
Eating Places.

Alpharetta

★ 64102 ★ Ace Hardware
4700 Hwy. 19
Alpharetta, GA 30201
(404)475-5688
Ultimate Parent: Ace Hardware.

★ 64103 ★ Ace Hardware
27 S. Main St.
Alpharetta, GA 30201
(404)475-6531
Ultimate Parent: Ace Hardware.

★ 64104 ★ Bank South, NA
10945 State Bridge Rd.
Alpharetta, GA 30202
(404)751-3084
Company Type: Subsidiary. Location
Type: Branch office. Officer: Lisa Sayre,
Manager. Ultimate Parent: Bank South
Corp. SIC: 6021—National Commercial
Banks.

★ 64105 ★ Bank South, NA
3080 Old Alabama Rd.
Alpharetta, GA 30201-5051
(404)442-0451
Company Type: Subsidiary. Location
Type: Branch office. Officer: Michael
Proctor, Manager. Ultimate Parent: Bank

South Corp. SIC: 6021—National
Commercial Banks.

★ 64106 ★ Bank South, NA
244 S. Main St.
Alpharetta, GA 30201
(404)751-3070
Company Type: Subsidiary. Location
Type: Branch office. Officer: Shirley
Grigsby, Manager. Ultimate Parent: Bank
South Corp. SIC: 6021—National
Commercial Banks.

★ 64107 ★ Bank South, NA
3000 Old Alabama Rd.
Alpharetta, GA 30202
(404)751-3077
Company Type: Subsidiary. Location
Type: Branch office. Officer: Michael
Proctor, Manager. Ultimate Parent: Bank
South Corp. SIC: 6021—National
Commercial Banks.

★ 64108 ★ Cbs News
2875 Arborwoods Dr.
Alpharetta, GA 30202
(404)518-9883
Ultimate Parent: CBS.

★ 64109 ★ Digital Equipment
Corp.
5555 Windward Pky.
Alpharetta, GA 30201
(404)343-1175
Ultimate Parent: Digital Equipment Corp.

★ 64110 ★ First Union National
Bank of Georgia
6503 Northpoint Pky.
Alpharetta, GA 30201
(404)594-2060
Location Type: Branch office. Ultimate
Parent: First Union Corp. SIC: 6021—
National Commercial Banks.

★ 64111 ★ First Union National
Bank of Georgia
21 N. Main St.
Alpharetta, GA 30201-1695
(404)751-3050
Location Type: Branch office. Ultimate
Parent: First Union Corp. SIC: 6021—
National Commercial Banks.

★ 64112 ★ Jiffy Lube Alpharetta
2965 Holcomb Bridge Rd.
Alpharetta, GA 30202
(404)594-1988
Ultimate Parent: Pennzoil.

★ 64113 ★ Kentucky Fried
Chicken
110 S. Main St.
Alpharetta, GA 30201
(404)664-5158
Ultimate Parent: Pepsico.

★ 64114 ★ Kroger Co. the Kroge
Pharmacies
10945 State Bridge Rd.
Alpharetta, GA 30202
(404)751-3010
Ultimate Parent: Kroger.

★ 64115 ★ Kroger Co. the Retail
Stores
10945 State Bridge Rd.
Alpharetta, GA 30202
(404)751-3000
Ultimate Parent: Kroger.

★ 64116 ★ Kroger Co. the Retail
Stores
3000 Old Alabamam Rd.
Alpharetta, GA 30202
(404)751-7384
Ultimate Parent: Kroger.

★ 64117 ★ Kroger Pharmacies
3000 Old Alabama Rd.
Alpharetta, GA 30202
(404)751-7388
Ultimate Parent: Kroger.

★ 64118 ★ Louisiana Pacific
Corp.
70 Meansell Ct
Alpharetta, GA
(404)587-0723
Ultimate Parent: Louisiana-Pacific.

★ 64119 ★ Mary Kay Cosmetics
Indep Sales
115 Fairway Ridge Dr.
Alpharetta, GA 30202
(404)993-2077
Ultimate Parent: Mary Kay Cosmetics.

★ 64120 ★ McDonald's
Restaurants
10975 State Bridge Rd.
Alpharetta, GA 30202
(404)667-1113
Ultimate Parent: McDonald's.

★ 64121 ★ McDonald's
Restaurants
2950 Holcomb Bridge Rd.
Alpharetta, GA 30202
(404)998-7710
Ultimate Parent: McDonald's.

★ 64122 ★ McDonald's
Restaurants
305 S. Main St.
Alpharetta, GA 30201
(404)442-1085
Ultimate Parent: McDonald's.

★ 64123 ★ Nationsbank Honor-
Cirrus L Sta
10905 Jones Bridge Rd.
Alpharetta, GA 30202
(404)442-2470
Ultimate Parent: Nationsbank Corp.

★ 64124 ★ Nationsbank Offices
Atlanta Ar
State Bridge 10905 J
Alpharetta, GA 30202
(404)442-2470
Ultimate Parent: Nationsbank Corp.

★ 64125 ★ Norwest Mortgage
Inc.
900 Alpha Ct
Alpharetta, GA 30201
(404)664-6995
Ultimate Parent: Norwest Corp.

★ 64126 ★ Pizza Hut
10945 State Bridge Rd.
Alpharetta, GA 30202
(404)740-8686
Ultimate Parent: Pepsico.

★ 64127 ★ Pizza Hut
8514 Holcomb Bridge Rd.
Alpharetta, GA 30202
(404)993-0300
Ultimate Parent: Pepsico.

★ 64128 ★ Pizza Hut
241 S. Main St.
Alpharetta, GA 30201
(404)751-8585
Ultimate Parent: Pepsico.

★ 64129 ★ Pulte Home Corp.s
Georgi
4885 Agate Dr.
Alpharetta, GA 30202
(404)442-8033
Ultimate Parent: Pulte.

★ 64130 ★ Pulte Home Corp.
Georgia
5085 Cinnabar Dr.
Alpharetta, GA 30202
(404)664-0687
Ultimate Parent: Pulte.

★ 64131 ★ Radio Shack
2880 Holcomb Bridge Rd.
Alpharetta, GA 30202
(404)992-1067
Company Type: Division. Ultimate Parent:
Tandy Corp.

★ 64132 ★ Ryder Truck Rental
8650 Nesbit Ferry Rd.
Alpharetta, GA 30202
(404)518-0522
Ultimate Parent: Ryder System.

★ 64133 ★ Ryder Truck Rental
4830 Atlanta Hwy.
Alpharetta, GA
(404)667-9552
Ultimate Parent: Ryder System.

★ 64134 ★ Ryder Truck Rental
515 N. Main St.
Alpharetta, GA 30201
(404)751-0960
Ultimate Parent: Ryder System.

★ 64135 ★ **T J Maxx**
7631 North Point Pky.
Alpharetta, GA
(404)640-0398
Ultimate Parent: TJX.

★ 64136 ★ **Taco Bell**
106 S. Main St.
Alpharetta, GA 30201
(404)664-5107
Ultimate Parent: Pepsico.

Americus

★ 64137 ★ **Davidson Exterior Trim Textron**
Rte. 6 Box 10
Americus, GA 31709
Ultimate Parent: Textron. **SIC:** 3714—Motor Vehicle Parts & Accessories.

★ 64138 ★ **Davidson Exterior Trim Textron**
Rte. 6 Box 10, Brady Rd.
Americus, GA 31709
Ultimate Parent: Textron. **SIC:** 3714—Motor Vehicle Parts & Accessories.

★ 64139 ★ **Housing Supply Inc.**
Industrial Blvd. PO Box 1105
Americus, GA 31709
Ultimate Parent: Fleetwood Enterprises, Inc. **SIC:** 2499—Wood Products Nec.

★ 64140 ★ **Imc Fertilizer Inc.**
1611 Oak Ave.
Americus, GA 31709
Ultimate Parent: IMC Fertilizer Group. **SIC:** 2874—Phosphatic Fertilizers.

★ 64141 ★ **Kentucky Fried Chicken**
1039 E. Forsyth St.
Americus, GA 31709
(912)924-6780
Ultimate Parent: Pepsico. **SIC:** 5812—Eating Places.

★ 64142 ★ **Piggly Wiggly**
421 Cotton Ave.
Americus, GA 31709
(912)924-2432
Ultimate Parent: Bruno's. **SIC:** 7699—Repair Services Nec.

★ 64143 ★ **Pizza Hut**
1041 E. Forsyth St.
Americus, GA 31709
(912)924-1027
Ultimate Parent: Pepsico. **SIC:** 5812—Eating Places.

★ 64144 ★ **Sumter Bank & Trust Co.**
1404 E. Forsyth St.
Americus, GA 31709
Location Type: Branch office. **Ultimate Parent:** Synovus Financial Corp. **SIC:** 6021—National Commercial Banks.

★ 64145 ★ **Sumter Bank & Trust Co.**
201 E. Lamar Rd.
Box 767
Americus, GA 31709
(912)924-0301 **Fax:** (912)928-3747
Location Type: Branch office. **Ultimate Parent:** Synovus Financial Corp. **SIC:** 6021—National Commercial Banks.

★ 64146 ★ **Trailways Bus System**
510 W. Forsyth St.
Americus, GA 31709
(912)924-2738
Ultimate Parent: Greyhound Lines Inc. **SIC:** 4131—Intercity & Rural Bus Transportation.

Andersonville

★ 64147 ★ **American Cyanamid Co.**
RR 1 Box 540
Andersonville, GA 31711-9509
(912)472-7581
Officer: J. B. Phillips. **Ultimate Parent:** American Cyanamid Co. **SIC:** 3295—Minerals—Ground or Treated.

★ 64148 ★ **Mary Kay Cosmetics**
Ellavile St.
Andersonville, GA 31711
(912)472-2015
Ultimate Parent: Mary Kay Cosmetics.

Arlington

★ 64149 ★ **Citgo Food Mart**
Highland Ave.
Arlington, GA 31713
(912)725-3167
Ultimate Parent: Citgo Petroleum. **SIC:** 5411—Grocery Stores.

★ 64150 ★ **West Foods**
Hwy. 62
Arlington, GA 31713
(912)725-4742
Ultimate Parent: Dole Food. **SIC:** 5411—Grocery Stores.

Ashburn

★ 64151 ★ **Golden Peanut Co. Ashburn Plant**
PO Box 488
Ashburn, GA 31714-0488
(912)567-3311
Location Type: Plant. **Officer:** C. B. Stowers. **Ultimate Parent:** Archer Daniels Midland Co. **SIC:** 2096—Potato Chips & Similar Snacks; 5145—Confectionery.

Athens

★ 64152 ★ **ACME Business Products**
130 Conrad Dr.
Athens, GA 30601-2105
(706)353-0368
Ultimate Parent: Alco Standard Corp. **SIC:** 5999—Miscellaneous Retail Stores Nec; 5044—Office Equipment.

★ 64153 ★ **Athens First Bank & First**
124 Hancock
Athens, GA 30601-2720
(706)357-7000 **Fax:** (706)357-7079
Location Type: Branch office. **Ultimate Parent:** Synovus Financial Corp. **SIC:** 6021—National Commercial Banks.

★ 64154 ★ **Athens First Bank & Trust**
PO Box 1747
Athens, GA 30603-1747
Location Type: Branch office. **Ultimate Parent:** Synovus Financial Corp. **SIC:** 6021—National Commercial Banks.

★ 64155 ★ **Athens First Bank & Trust**
1855 Barnett Shoals Rd.
Athens, GA 30605-3010
(706)357-7030
Location Type: Branch office. **Ultimate Parent:** Synovus Financial Corp. **SIC:** 6021—National Commercial Banks.

★ 64156 ★ **Athens First Bank & Trust**
233 W. Hancock Ave.
Athens, GA 30601-2727
(706)357-7010
Location Type: Branch office. **Officer:** Ken Edwards, Manager. **Ultimate Parent:** Synovus Financial Corp. **SIC:** 6021—National Commercial Banks.

★ 64157 ★ **Athens First Bank & Trust**
310 Alps Rd.
Athens, GA 30606
(706)357-7020
Location Type: Branch office. **Officer:** Janet Slavin, Manager. **Ultimate Parent:** Synovus Financial Corp. **SIC:** 6021—National Commercial Banks.

★ 64158 ★ **Athens First Bank & Trust**
2365 Jefferson Rd.
Athens, GA 30606
(706)357-7060
Location Type: Branch office. **Ultimate Parent:** Synovus Financial Corp. **SIC:** 6021—National Commercial Banks.

★ 64159 ★ **Athens First Bank & Trust**
1871 N. Elm St.
Athens, GA 30529
(706)335-3599
Location Type: Branch office. **Officer:** Darlen Brown, Manager. **Ultimate Parent:** Synovus Financial Corp. **SIC:** 6021—National Commercial Banks.

★ 64160 ★ **Bank South**
475 E. Broad St.
Athens, GA 30601-2820
(706)354-5500
Location Type: Branch office. **Officer:** Robert H. Ridgway III. **Ultimate Parent:** Bank South Corp. **SIC:** 6021—National Commercial Banks; 6022—State Commercial Banks; 6141—Personal Credit Institutions.

★ 64161 ★ **Bank South, NA**
475 E. Broad St.
Athens, GA 30601
(706)354-5500
Company Type: Subsidiary. **Location Type:** Branch office. **Officer:** Linda Hammond, Manager. **Ultimate Parent:** Bank South Corp. **SIC:** 6021—National Commercial Banks.

★ 64162 ★ **Bank South, NA**
2234 W. Broad St.
Athens, GA 30606
(706)353-3028
Company Type: Subsidiary. **Location Type:** Branch office. **Officer:** Lisa Loudermilk, Manager. **Ultimate Parent:** Bank South Corp. **SIC:** 6021—National Commercial Banks.

★ 64163 ★ **Bank South NA/ Athens Main Office**
475 E. Broad St.
Athens, GA 30613
(706)354-5300
Company Type: Subsidiary. **Location Type:** Branch office. **Officer:** Robert H. Ridgway III, President. **Ultimate Parent:** Bank South Corp. **SIC:** 6021—National Commercial Banks.

★ 64164 ★ **Carrier Transicold**
700 Olympic Dr.
Athens, GA 30601
Ultimate Parent: United Technologies. **SIC:** 3585—Refrigeration & Heating Equipment.

★ 64165 ★ **Champion International Corp.**
600 Dairypak Rd.
Athens, GA 30603-1627
Ultimate Parent: Champion International. **SIC:** 2656—Sanitary Food Containers.

★ 64166 ★ **Eaton Corp.**
695 Indian Hill Rd.
Athens, GA 30601
(706)543-5250
Officer: Bob Wolf, Manager. **Ultimate Parent:** Eaton Corp. **SIC:** 3714—Motor Vehicle Parts & Accessories.

★ 64167 ★ **Eaton Corp.**
Supercharger Div.
695 Indian Hills Rd.
Athens, GA 30601
(706)543-5250
Company Type: Division. **Location Type:** Plant. **Ultimate Parent:** Eaton Corp. **SIC:** 3691—Storage Batteries.

★ 64168 ★ **Gold Kist Inc.**
Poultry Division
170 Omet St.
Athens, GA 30601
(404)548-5641
Company Type: Division. **Location Type:** Plant. **Ultimate Parent:** Gold Kist. **SIC:** 2013—Sausages & Other Prepared Meats.

★ 64169 ★ **Gold Kist Inc. Poultry**
170 Oneta St.
Athens, GA 30601
Ultimate Parent: Gold Kist. **SIC:** 2015—Poultry Slaughtering & Processing.

★ 64170 ★ **Louisiana Pacific Corp., OSB**
Hwy. 441
Athens, GA 30613
Ultimate Parent: Louisiana-Pacific. **SIC:** 2493—Reconstituted Wood Products.

★ 64171 ★ **Louisiana-Pacific Osb**
Hwy. 441
Athens, GA 30603
Ultimate Parent: Louisiana-Pacific. **SIC:** 2493—Reconstituted Wood Products.

★ 64172 ★ **Noramco Inc.**
1440 Olympic Dr.
Athens, GA 30601-1652
Ultimate Parent: Johnson & Johnson. **SIC:** 2833—Medicinals & Botanicals; 2869—Industrial Organic Chemicals Nec.

★ 64173 ★ **Oliver Rubber Co.**
215 Oneta St.
Athens, GA 30601
(706)546-0220
Officer: Ralph M. Snow Jr., Vice President. **Ultimate Parent:** Standard Products. **SIC:** 2296—Tire Cord & Fabrics; 3011—Tires & Inner Tubes; 3069—Fabricated Rubber Products Nec.

★ 64174 ★ **Oliver Rubber Co. Athens**
215 Oneta St.
Athens, GA 30601-1840
Ultimate Parent: Standard Products. **SIC:** 3011—Tires & Inner Tubes; 3069—Fabricated Rubber Products Nec.

★ 64175 ★ **Reliance Electric Co.**
Collins Industrial Blvd.
Athens, GA 30601
(706)549-3871
Officer: James H. Biggers, Manager. **Ultimate Parent:** Reliance Electric. **SIC:** 3621—Motors & Generators; 3625—Relays & Industrial Controls.

★ 64176 ★ **Seaboard Farms of Athens Inc.**
Feed Mill
Tallassee Rd.
Athens, GA 30603-0000
Ultimate Parent: Seaboard Corp. **SIC:** 2048—Prepared Feeds Nec.

★ 64177 ★ **Seaboard Farms of Athens Inc.**
Processing Plant
898 Barber St.
Athens, GA 30601-0000
Location Type: Plant. **Ultimate Parent:** Seaboard Corp. **SIC:** 2015—Poultry Slaughtering & Processing.

★ 64178 ★ **Westinghouse Electric Corp.**
Newton Bridge Rd.
Athens, GA 30613-5599
Ultimate Parent: Westinghouse Electric Corp. **SIC:** 3612—Transformers Except Electronic.

Atlanta

★ 64179 ★ **Fleet Finance Inc. Branch Opera**
211 Perimeter Ctr. Pky.
Atl, GA
(404)392-2400
Ultimate Parent: Fleet Financial Group.

★ 64180 ★ **Gap Stores the**
1309 Cumberland Mall NW
Atl, GA
(404)433-3263
Ultimate Parent: GAP.

★ 64181 ★ **Ryder Truck Rental**
1202 Stewart Ave.
Atl, GA
(404)752-5188
Ultimate Parent: Ryder System.

★ 64182 ★ **Southern Electric International**
Suite 400 100 Ashfor
Atl, GA
(404)261-4700
Ultimate Parent: Southern. **SIC:** 4911—Electric Services.

★ 64183 ★ **Structure**
1425 Cumberland Mall NW
Atl, GA
(404)438-7221
Ultimate Parent: Limited.

★ 64184 ★ **Texaco**
3113 Campbellton Rd. SW
Atl, GA
(404)344-8488
Ultimate Parent: Texaco.

★ 64185 ★ **Texaco**
5640 Northside Dr. NW
Atl, GA
(404)952-7270
Ultimate Parent: Texaco.

★ 64186 ★ **Ryder Truck Rental**
Atl Ga, GA
(404)634-5204
Ultimate Parent: Ryder System.

★ 64187 ★ **Aaron Rents**
3001 N. Fulton Dr., NE
Atlanta, GA 30363-0001
(404)231-0011
Officer: R. C. Loudermilk Sr., Chairman of
the Board & President. **Ultimate Parent:**
Betz Laboratories Inc. **SIC:** 7359—
Equipment Rental & Leasing Nec; 5712—
Furniture Stores; 5731—Radio, Television &
Electronics Stores; 5722—Household
Appliance Stores; 5932—Used Merchandise
Stores; 2512—Upholstered Household
Furniture. **Employee Count:** 1500. **Sales:**
144 M.

★ 64188 ★ **Abercrombie & Fitch**
3500 Phipps Plz.
Atlanta, GA 30326
(404)233-8522
Ultimate Parent: Limited.

★ 64189 ★ **ABF Freight System
Inc.**
3535 Best Friend Rd.
Atlanta, GA 30340-3515
(404)449-0005
Location Type: Branch office. **Ultimate
Parent:** Arkansas Best. **SIC:** 4212—Local
Trucking Without Storage.

★ 64190 ★ **Abitibi Price Sales
Corp.**
2580 Cumberland Pky. NW
Atlanta, GA 30339-3909
(404)333-1700
Ultimate Parent: Alco Standard Corp. **SIC:**
2621—Paper Mills.

★ 64191 ★ **Abitibi Price Sales
Corp.**
2580 Cumberland Pky. NW
Atlanta, GA 30339-3909
(404)333-1700
Ultimate Parent: Alco Standard Corp. **SIC:**
2621—Paper Mills.

★ 64192 ★ **Ace Hardware**
1279 Glenwood Ave. SE
Atlanta, GA 30316
(404)627-5757
Ultimate Parent: Ace Hardware.

★ 64193 ★ **Ace Hardware**
1248 W. Paces Ferry Rd. NW
Atlanta, GA 30327
(404)261-6000
Ultimate Parent: Ace Hardware.

★ 64194 ★ **Ace Hardware**
626 Glen Iris Dr. NE
Atlanta, GA 30308
(404)872-6651
Ultimate Parent: Ace Hardware.

★ 64195 ★ **Ace Hardware-Bates**
1709 Howell Mill Rd. NW
Atlanta, GA 30318
(404)351-4240
Ultimate Parent: Ace Hardware.

★ 64196 ★ **Ace Hardware Co.**
1709 Howell Mill Rd. NW
Atlanta, GA 30318
(404)351-4240
Ultimate Parent: Ace Hardware.

★ 64197 ★ **Ace Hardware of
Fayette**
Ga Hwy. 85 S
Atlanta, GA
(404)461-1164
Ultimate Parent: Ace Hardware.

★ 64198 ★ **Ace Hardware-Smith**
1248 W. Paces Ferry Rd. NW
Atlanta, GA 30327
(404)261-6000
Ultimate Parent: Ace Hardware.

★ 64199 ★ **Ace Hardware-
Workbench**
345 Killian Hill Rd.
Atlanta, GA
(404)923-3330
Ultimate Parent: Ace Hardware.

★ 64200 ★ **Ace Hardware-
Workbench**
2983 N. Druid Hills Rd. NE
Atlanta, GA 30329
(404)325-8000
Ultimate Parent: Ace Hardware.

★ 64201 ★ **Advance Security**
2964 Peachtree Rd. NE, Ste. 300
PO Box 52619
Atlanta, GA 30305
(404)231-1210 **Fax:** (404)231-0345
Company Type: Subsidiary. **Officer:** G.
Massimei, President. **Ultimate Parent:**
Figgie International.

★ 64202 ★ **Advance Security Inc.**
2964 Peachtree Rd. NW
Atlanta, GA 30305-2118
(404)231-1210
Company Type: Subsidiary. **Ultimate
Parent:** Figgie International. **SIC:** 7381—
Detective & Armored Car Services.

★ 64203 ★ **Agra Tech Seeds Inc.**
244 Perimeter Ctr. Pky. NE
PO Box 2210
Atlanta, GA 30301
(404)393-5000 **Fax:** (404)393-5347
Company Type: Subsidiary. **Officer:** Darrel
O. Grabow, President. **Ultimate Parent:**
Gold Kist.

★ 64204 ★ **Agra Trade Financing
Inc.**
244 Perimeter Ctr. Pky. NE
PO Box 2210
Atlanta, GA 30301
(404)393-5000 **Fax:** (404)393-5347
Company Type: Subsidiary. **Officer:**
Robert T. Bennett, President. **Ultimate
Parent:** Gold Kist.

★ 64205 ★ **Agri International Inc.**
244 Perimeter Ctr. Pky. NE
PO Box 2210
Atlanta, GA 30301
(404)393-5000 **Fax:** (404)393-5347
Company Type: Subsidiary. **Officer:**
Gaylord O. Coan, President. **Ultimate
Parent:** Gold Kist.

★ 64206 ★ **Agvestments Inc.**
244 Perimeter Ctr. Pky. NE
PO Box 2210
Atlanta, GA 30301
(404)393-5000
Company Type: Subsidiary. **Officer:** Wade
W. Johnson, President. **Ultimate Parent:**
Gold Kist.

★ 64207 ★ **AIG Aviation, Inc.**
100 Colony Sq. NE
Atlanta, GA 30361-6201
(404)249-1800
Officer: John A. Myers, President. **Ultimate
Parent:** American International Group, Inc.
SIC: 6411—Insurance Agents, Brokers &
Service. **Employee Count:** 104.

★ 64208 ★ **AIG Aviation, Inc.**
100 Colony Sq.
Atlanta, GA 30361
(404)249-1800
Officer: John A. Myers, Pres. & CEO.
Ultimate Parent: American International
Group, Inc. **SIC:** 6331—Fire, Marine &
Casualty Insurance.

★ 64209 ★ **Air Products &
Chemicals, Inc.**
990 Hammond Dr. NE
Atlanta, GA 30328-5505
(404)671-1891
Officer: Charles Bennett Sou. **Ultimate
Parent:** Air Products & Chemicals, Inc. **SIC:**
2899—Chemical Preparations Nec; 3564—
Blowers & Fans.

★ 64210 ★ **Air Products &
Chemicals Inc.**
3424 Miller Dr.
Atlanta, GA 30341-2414
(404)451-2711
Ultimate Parent: Air Products & Chemicals,
Inc. **SIC:** 5169—Chemicals & Allied
Products Nec.

★ 64211 ★ **Air Treads Inc.**
1000 Tradeport Blvd.
Atlanta, GA 30354-2924
(404)362-3600
Company Type: Subsidiary. **Officer:** J.
David Wolf, Chairman of the Board; Chief
Executive Officer. **Ultimate Parent:**
Goodyear Tire & Rubber. **SIC:** 3011—Tires
& Inner Tubes; 4581—Airports, Flying Fields
& Services; 7534—Tire Retreading & Repair
Shops. **Employee Count:** 486. **Sales:**
100000000 M.

★ 64212 ★ **Air Treads Inc.**
1000 Tradeport Blvd., Ste. 1010
Atlanta, GA 30354
(404)362-3600 **Fax:** (404)362-3684
Company Type: Subsidiary. **Officer:** J.
David Wolf, Chairman & CEO. **Ultimate
Parent:** Goodyear Tire & Rubber.

★ 64213 ★ **Alberto Culver Co.**
800 Wharton Dr. SW
Atlanta, GA 30336
(404)696-1052
Ultimate Parent: Alberto-Culver Co. Inc.

★ 64214 ★ **Alcoa Recycling
Services**
1328 Lakewood Ave.SE
Atlanta, GA 30315-2313
(404)624-1319
Location Type: Branch office. **Officer:**
Thomas B. Drew. **Ultimate Parent:**
Aluminum Co. of America–Alcoa. **SIC:**
4953—Refuse Systems.

★ 64215 ★ **Alcoa Recycling
Services**
1328 Lakewood Ave. SE
Atlanta, GA 30315-2313
(404)624-1319
Location Type: Branch office. **Officer:**
Thomas B. Drew. **Ultimate Parent:**
Aluminum Co. of America–Alcoa. **SIC:**
4953—Refuse Systems.

★ 64216 ★ **All American Gourmet
Co. Inc.**
5475 Bucknell Dr. SW
Atlanta, GA 30336
Ultimate Parent: Philip Morris. **SIC:** 2038—
Frozen Specialties Nec.

★ 64217 ★ **Allied Signal General
Aviation**
Atlanta, GA
(404)477-5376
Ultimate Parent: Allied-Signal Inc.

★ 64218 ★ **Amerada Hess Corp.**
2836 Woodwin Rd.
Atlanta, GA 30360-3122
(404)458-5588
Location Type: Branch office. **Officer:**
James a. Timms. **Ultimate Parent:**
Amerada Hess. **SIC:** 5172—Petroleum
Products Nec; 1311—Crude Petroleum &
Natural Gas.

★ 64219 ★ **American Business
Machines Inc.**
2100 Riveredge Pky. NW, No. 1200
Atlanta, GA 30328
(404)953-8300
Officer: W.J. Biggers, Chairman. **Ultimate
Parent:** Alco Standard Corp. **SIC:** 2677—
Envelopes; 2731—Book Publishing; 2732—
Book Printing.

★ 64220 ★ **American Cellular
Communications**
500 Northpark Town Ctr.
1100 Abernathy Rd., Ste. 500
Atlanta, GA 30328
(404)604-6541 **Fax:** (404)604-6545
Officer: B. F. Holcomb, President. **Ultimate
Parent:** BellSouth Corp.

★ 64221 ★ **American Cellular
Communications Corp.**
5600 Glenridge Dr., Ste. 480
Atlanta, GA 30342
(404)847-3840
Company Type: Subsidiary. **Ultimate
Parent:** BellSouth Corp.

★ 64222 ★ **American Cellular
Communications Corp.**
1100 Abernathy Rd. NE
Atlanta, GA 30328-5646
(404)604-6100
Company Type: Subsidiary. **Officer:** Ben
Holcomb, President. **Ultimate Parent:**
BellSouth Corp. **SIC:** 4812—Radiotelephone
Communications. **Employee Count:** 600.
Sales: 42 M.

★ 64223 ★ **American Cyanamid
Co.**
115 Perimeter Ctr. Pl. NE
Atlanta, GA 30346-1238
(404)668-1100
Location Type: Branch office. **Ultimate
Parent:** American Cyanamid Co. **SIC:**
5169—Chemicals & Allied Products Nec.

★ 64224 ★ **American Cyanamid
Co.**
Lederle Laboratories Division
115 Perimeter Ctr. Pl.
Atlanta, GA
(404)668-1100
Ultimate Parent: American Cyanamid Co.

★ 64225 ★ **American General
Finance**
5495 Old National Hwy., Ste. B
Atlanta, GA 30349-3252
(404)767-9392
Location Type: Branch office. **Ultimate
Parent:** American General Corp. **SIC:**
6141—Personal Credit Institutions; 6162—
Mortgage Bankers & Correspondents.

★ 64226 ★ **American General
Finance**
5725 Buford Hwy. NE Rm. 201
Atlanta, GA 30340-1232
(404)451-7001
Location Type: Branch office. **Officer:** J. B.
Woodring. **Ultimate Parent:** American
General Corp. **SIC:** 6141—Personal Credit
Institutions; 6162—Mortgage Bankers &
Correspondents.

★ 64227 ★ **American General
Finance**
5252 Roswell Rd. NE
Atlanta, GA 30342-1915
(404)252-9840
Location Type: Branch office. **Officer:**
Wayne Harrell. **Ultimate Parent:** American
General Corp. **SIC:** 6141—Personal Credit
Institutions; 6162—Mortgage Bankers &
Correspondents.

★ 64228 ★ **American General
Finance**
1936 N. Druid Hills Rd. NE
Atlanta, GA 30319-4120
(404)320-1464
Location Type: Branch office. **Ultimate
Parent:** American General Corp. **SIC:**
6141—Personal Credit Institutions; 6162—
Mortgage Bankers & Correspondents.

★ 64229 ★ **American General
Finance Inc.**
5495 Old National Hwy., Ste. B
Atlanta, GA 30349-3252
(404)767-9392
Location Type: Branch office. **Ultimate
Parent:** American General Corp. **SIC:**
6141—Personal Credit Institutions; 6162—
Mortgage Bankers & Correspondents.

★ 64230 ★ **American General
Finance Inc.**
5725 Buford Hwy. NE Rm. 201
Atlanta, GA 30340-1232
(404)451-7001
Location Type: Branch office. **Officer:** J. B.
Woodring. **Ultimate Parent:** American
General Corp. **SIC:** 6141—Personal Credit
Institutions; 6162—Mortgage Bankers &
Correspondents.

★ 64231 ★ **American General
Finance Inc.**
5252 Roswell Rd. NE
Atlanta, GA 30342-1915
(404)252-9840
Location Type: Branch office. **Officer:**
Wayne Harrell. **Ultimate Parent:** American
General Corp. **SIC:** 6141—Personal Credit
Institutions; 6162—Mortgage Bankers &
Correspondents.

★ 64232 ★ **American General
Finance Inc.**
1936 N. Druid Hills Rd. NE
Atlanta, GA 30319-4120
(404)320-1464
Location Type: Branch office. **Ultimate
Parent:** American General Corp. **SIC:**
6141—Personal Credit Institutions; 6162—
Mortgage Bankers & Correspondents.

★ 64233 ★ **American International Recover**
270 Carpenter Dr.
Atlanta, GA 30328
(404)250-7190
Ultimate Parent: American International Group, Inc.

★ 64234 ★ **APAC Holdings, Inc.**
3340 Peachtree Rd. NE, Ste. 600
Atlanta, GA 30326
(404)261-2610
Company Type: Subsidiary. **Officer:** Charles F. Potts, President. **Ultimate Parent:** Ashland Oil. **SIC:** 1611—Highway & Street Construction; 3531—Construction Machinery; 1442—Construction Sand & Gravel.

★ 64235 ★ **APAC Inc.**
3340 Peachtree Rd. NE, Ste. 600
Atlanta, GA 30326
(404)392-5300
Company Type: Subsidiary. **Officer:** Charles F. Potts, President. **Ultimate Parent:** Ashland Oil.

★ 64236 ★ **Apl Land Transport Services Inc.**
1040 Crown Pointe Pkwy NE
Atlanta, GA 30338
(404)395-8000
Ultimate Parent: American President Companies, Ltd.

★ 64237 ★ **Arrow Electronics Inc. Arrow/Ki**
4250 River Green Pkwy NW
Atlanta, GA
(404)497-1300
Ultimate Parent: Arrow Electronics.

★ 64238 ★ **AST Research Inc.**
47 Perimeter Ctr. Eas
Atlanta, GA 30346
(404)392-0011
Ultimate Parent: AST Research.

★ 64239 ★ **AST Research Inc.**
223 Perimeter Ctr. Pky. NE
Atlanta, GA 30346-1301
(404)392-0011
Location Type: Branch office. **Ultimate Parent:** AST Research.

★ 64240 ★ **AT&T**
6701 Roswell Rd. NE
Atlanta, GA 30328
(404)573-4000
Officer: Joseph Mauriello, Vice President. **Ultimate Parent:** AT&T. **SIC:** 3661—Telephone & Telegraph Apparatus.

★ 64241 ★ **Atlanta Baking Co.**
165 Bailey St. SW
PO Box 4996
Atlanta, GA 30302
(404)653-9700 **Fax:** (404)653-9780
Company Type: Subsidiary. **Officer:** Jerry Palmer, President. **Ultimate Parent:** Flowers Industries.

★ 64242 ★ **Atlanta Baking Co., Inc.**
165 Bailey St. SW
Atlanta, GA 30314-4801
(404)653-9700
Company Type: Subsidiary. **Officer:** Jerry F. Parmer, President. **Ultimate Parent:** Flowers Industries. **SIC:** 2051—Bread, Cake & Related Products; 5149—Groceries & Related Products Nec. **Employee Count:** 525. **Sales:** 60 M.

★ 64243 ★ **Atlanta Group, Inc.**
3565 Piedmont Rd., Bldg. 2
Atlanta, GA 30363
(404)261-3400
Company Type: Subsidiary. **Officer:** Michael Gough, President. **Ultimate Parent:** Alexander & Alexander Services. **SIC:** 6411—Insurance Agents, Brokers & Service.

★ 64244 ★ **Atlantic Envelope Co.**
1700 Northside Dr., NW
Atlanta, GA 30318
(404)351-5011 **Fax:** (404)355-4785
Officer: J. Randolph Zook, President. **Ultimate Parent:** National Service Industries.

★ 64245 ★ **Avery Dennison Soabar Systems**
4908 Windhaven Ct.
Atlanta, GA 30338-5106
(404)394-0310
Ultimate Parent: Avery Dennison Corp. **SIC:** 2679—Converted Paper Products Nec.

★ 64246 ★ **Avon Products**
Atlanta, GA
(404)233-0989
Ultimate Parent: Avon Products, Inc.

★ 64247 ★ **Avon Products Inc.**
Atlanta, GA
(404)289-7003
Ultimate Parent: Avon Products, Inc.

★ 64248 ★ **Avon Sales & Distribution Branch**
PO Box 4667
Atlanta, GA 30303
(404)458-5161
Officer: James Wilcox, Area Vice President. **Ultimate Parent:** Avon Products, Inc. **SIC:** 5122—Drugs, Proprietaries & Sundries.

★ 64249 ★ **Banana Republic Retail Clothing**
4400 Ashford Dunwoody Rd.
Atlanta, GA 30346
(404)393-1130
Ultimate Parent: GAP.

★ 64250 ★ **Bank South**
8331 Roswell Rd.
Atlanta, GA 30350-2810
(404)552-5770
Ultimate Parent: Bank South Corp. **SIC:** 6021—National Commercial Banks.

★ 64251 ★ **Bank South Corp.**
55 Marietta St., NW
Atlanta, GA 30303
(404)529-4521 **Fax:** (404)521-7347
Officer: Patrick L. Flinn, CEO. **Ultimate Parent:** Bank South Corp. **Employee Count:** 2937. **Sales:** 467 M.

★ 64252 ★ **Bank South Corp.**
PO Box 5092
Atlanta, GA 30302
Company Type: Headquarters. **Ultimate Parent:** Bank South Corp.

★ 64253 ★ **Bank South Corp.**
55 Marietta St.
PO Box 5092
Atlanta, GA 30302
(404)529-4000 **Fax:** (404)529-4127
Company Type: Headquarters. **Officer:** Patrick L. Flynn, Chairman, President, & CEO. **SIC:** 6712—Bank Holding Companies; 6531—Real Estate Agents & Managers; 6021—National Commercial Banks; 6162—Mortgage Bankers & Correspondents; 6411—Insurance Agents, Brokers & Service. **Employee Count:** 2900.

★ 64254 ★ **Bank South Home Equity**
3301 Buckeye Rd.
Atlanta, GA 30341
(404)452-2007
Company Type: Subsidiary. **Location Type:** Branch office. **Ultimate Parent:** Bank South Corp. **SIC:** 6162—Mortgage Bankers & Correspondents.

★ 64255 ★ **Bank South Leasing Inc.**
875 Johnson Ferry Rd.
Atlanta, GA 30342-1410
(404)257-5843
Location Type: Branch office. **Officer:** Thomas E. Lazenby. **Ultimate Parent:** Bank South Corp. **SIC:** 6159—Miscellaneous Business Credit Institutions.

★ 64256 ★ **Bank South Leasing, Inc.**
3301 Buckeye Rd.
Atlanta, GA 30341
(404)257-5873
Officer: Thomas E. Lazenby, President. **Ultimate Parent:** Bank South Corp. **SIC:** 6100—Nondepository Institutions.

★ 64257 ★ **Bank South Life Insurance Corp.**
55 Marietta St.
Atlanta, GA 30303
Company Type: Subsidiary. **Ultimate Parent:** Bank South Corp. **SIC:** 6411—Insurance Agents, Brokers & Service.

★ 64258 ★ **Bank South Mortgage Inc.**
3280 Holcomb Bridge Rd.
Atlanta, GA 30344
(404)368-3007
Ultimate Parent: Bank South Corp. **SIC:** 6162—Mortgage Bankers & Correspondents.

★ 64259 ★ **Bank South Mortgage Inc.**
5775 Glenridge Dr.
Atlanta, GA 30328
(404)257-5800
Company Type: Subsidiary. **Officer:** E. Metz Bizzell, President. **Ultimate Parent:** Bank South Corp. **SIC:** 6162—Mortgage Bankers & Correspondents. **Employee Count:** 24.

★ 64260 ★ **Bank South Mortgage Inc.**
5775 Glenridge Dr., NE
Atlanta, GA 30328
(404)257-5800
Location Type: Branch office. **Officer:** E. Metz Bizzell. **Ultimate Parent:** Bank South Corp. **SIC:** 6162—Mortgage Bankers & Correspondents; 6021—National Commercial Banks; 6141—Personal Credit Institutions.

★ 64261 ★ **Bank South NA**
1733 Washington Ave.
Atlanta, GA
(404)559-6060
Location Type: Branch office. **Officer:** Melissa Morgan. **Ultimate Parent:** Bank South Corp. **SIC:** 6021—National Commercial Banks; 6022—State Commercial Banks.

★ 64262 ★ **Bank South NA**
325 Mt. Vernon Hwy., NE
Atlanta, GA 30328
(404)847-3400
Location Type: Branch office. **Officer:** Marie Lanier. **Ultimate Parent:** Bank South Corp. **SIC:** 6021—National Commercial Banks; 6022—State Commercial Banks.

★ 64263 ★ **Bank South NA**
55 Marietta St., NW
Atlanta, GA 30303-2807
(404)529-4111
Company Type: Headquarters. **Officer:** Patrick L. Flynn. **Ultimate Parent:** Bank South Corp. **SIC:** 6021—National Commercial Banks; 6162—Mortgage Bankers & Correspondents; 6512—Nonresidential Building Operators; 6531—Real Estate Agents & Managers; 6712—Bank Holding Companies.

★ 64264 ★ **Bank South, NA**
1870 Piedmont Rd. NE
Atlanta, GA 30324-4839
(404)876-6615
Company Type: Subsidiary. **Location Type:** Branch office. **Ultimate Parent:** Bank South Corp. **SIC:** 6021—National Commercial Banks.

★ 64265 ★ **Bank South, NA**
4581 Dallas St.
Atlanta, GA 30101-5313
(404)974-4241
Company Type: Subsidiary. **Location Type:** Branch office. **Officer:** Mark Thomsen, Manager. **Ultimate Parent:** Bank South Corp. **SIC:** 6021—National Commercial Banks.

★ 64266 ★ **Bank South, NA**
260 Peachtree St.
Atlanta, GA 30303-2815
(404)681-9529
Company Type: Subsidiary. **Location Type:** Branch office. **Ultimate Parent:** Bank South Corp. **SIC:** 6021—National Commercial Banks.

★ 64267 ★ **Bank South, NA**
100 W. Paces Ferry Rd.
Atlanta, GA 30305-1399
(404)261-4886
Company Type: Subsidiary. **Location Type:** Branch office. **Ultimate Parent:** Bank South Corp. **SIC:** 6021—National Commercial Banks.

★ 64268 ★ **Bank South, NA**
1355 Peachtree St. NE
Atlanta, GA 30309-3269
(404)873-6940
Company Type: Subsidiary. **Location Type:** Branch office. **Officer:** Brent Adams, Manager. **Ultimate Parent:** Bank South Corp. **SIC:** 6021—National Commercial Banks.

★ 64269 ★ **Bank South, NA**
2 Midtown Plz.
1360 Peachtree St.
Atlanta, GA 30309
(404)873-6940
Company Type: Subsidiary. **Location Type:** Branch office. **Ultimate Parent:** Bank South Corp. **SIC:** 6021—National Commercial Banks.

★ 64270 ★ **Bank South, NA**
956 Ponce de Leon Ave.
Atlanta, GA 30306
(404)881-3568
Company Type: Subsidiary. **Location Type:** Branch office. **Officer:** Susan Lee, Manager. **Ultimate Parent:** Bank South Corp. **SIC:** 6021—National Commercial Banks.

★ 64271 ★ **Bank South, NA**
100 Cumberland Cir. NW
Atlanta, GA 30339
(404)850-5450
Company Type: Subsidiary. **Location Type:** Branch office. **Officer:** Debbie Clemmons, Manager. **Ultimate Parent:** Bank South Corp. **SIC:** 6021—National Commercial Banks.

★ 64272 ★ **Bank South, NA**
1535 Chattahoochee Ave. NW
Atlanta, GA 30318
(404)605-7000
Company Type: Subsidiary. **Location Type:** Branch office. **Officer:** Julia Hurt, Manager. **Ultimate Parent:** Bank South Corp. **SIC:** 6021—National Commercial Banks.

★ 64273 ★ **Bank South, NA**
133 Peachtree St. NE
Atlanta, GA 30303
(404)330-0755
Company Type: Subsidiary. **Location Type:** Branch office. **Officer:** Dale Dockter, Manager. **Ultimate Parent:** Bank South Corp. **SIC:** 6021—National Commercial Banks.

★ 64274 ★ **Bank South, NA**
3116 Peachtree Rd. NE
Atlanta, GA 30305
(404)262-6340
Company Type: Subsidiary. **Location Type:** Branch office. **Officer:** Mitzi Linginfelter, Manager. **Ultimate Parent:** Bank South Corp. **SIC:** 6021—National Commercial Banks.

★ 64275 ★ **Bank South, NA**
411 Flat Shoals Ave. SE
Atlanta, GA 30316
(404)330-0750
Company Type: Subsidiary. **Location Type:** Branch office. **Officer:** Diann Robinson, Manager. **Ultimate Parent:** Bank South Corp. **SIC:** 6021—National Commercial Banks.

★ 64276 ★ **Bank South, NA**
85 10th St. NE
Atlanta, GA 30309
(404)881-3564
Company Type: Subsidiary. **Location Type:** Branch office. **Officer:** Mary Sego, Manager. **Ultimate Parent:** Bank South Corp. **SIC:** 6021—National Commercial Banks.

★ 64277 ★ **Bank South, NA**
875 Selig Dr. SE
Atlanta, GA 30336
(404)699-9570
Company Type: Subsidiary. **Location Type:** Branch office. **Officer:** Brenda Dent, Manager. **Ultimate Parent:** Bank South Corp. **SIC:** 6021—National Commercial Banks.

★ 64278 ★   Bank South, NA
2223 N. Druid Hills Rd. NE
Atlanta, GA 30329
(404)248-2250
Company Type: Subsidiary. **Location Type:** Branch office. **Officer:** Alicia Boone, Manager. **Ultimate Parent:** Bank South Corp. **SIC:** 6021—National Commercial Banks.

★ 64279 ★   Bank South, NA
2292 Henderson Mill Rd. NE
Atlanta, GA 30345
(404)621-5380
Company Type: Subsidiary. **Location Type:** Branch office. **Officer:** Bette Durham, Manager. **Ultimate Parent:** Bank South Corp. **SIC:** 6021—National Commercial Banks.

★ 64280 ★   Bank South, NA
2391 Peachtree Rd. NE
Atlanta, GA 30305
(404)238-0111
Company Type: Subsidiary. **Location Type:** Branch office. **Officer:** Joan Devine, Manager. **Ultimate Parent:** Bank South Corp. **SIC:** 6021—National Commercial Banks.

★ 64281 ★   Bank South, NA
3414 Peachtree Rd. NE
Atlanta, GA 30326
(404)238-0100
Company Type: Subsidiary. **Location Type:** Branch office. **Officer:** Julia Hurt, Manager. **Ultimate Parent:** Bank South Corp. **SIC:** 6021—National Commercial Banks.

★ 64282 ★   Bank South, NA
1700 Monroe Dr.
Atlanta, GA 30324
(404)881-3574
Company Type: Subsidiary. **Location Type:** Branch office. **Officer:** Jennifer Campbell, Manager. **Ultimate Parent:** Bank South Corp. **SIC:** 6021—National Commercial Banks.

★ 64283 ★   Bank South, NA
633 Evans St. SW
Atlanta, GA 30310
(404)756-1000
Company Type: Subsidiary. **Location Type:** Branch office. **Officer:** Dave Walters, Manager. **Ultimate Parent:** Bank South Corp. **SIC:** 6021—National Commercial Banks.

★ 64284 ★   Bank South, NA
8331 Roswell Rd.
Atlanta, GA 30338
(404)552-5770
Company Type: Subsidiary. **Location Type:** Branch office. **Officer:** Natashia Bush, Manager. **Ultimate Parent:** Bank South Corp. **SIC:** 6021—National Commercial Banks.

★ 64285 ★   Bank South, NA
1715 Howell Mill Rd.
Atlanta, GA 30318
(404)605-7005
Company Type: Subsidiary. **Location Type:** Branch office. **Officer:** Lee Johnson, Manager. **Ultimate Parent:** Bank South Corp. **SIC:** 6021—National Commercial Banks.

★ 64286 ★   Bank South, NA
3300 Cobb Pky.
Atlanta, GA 30339
(404)850-6295
Company Type: Subsidiary. **Location Type:** Branch office. **Officer:** Yvonne Patterson, Manager. **Ultimate Parent:** Bank South Corp. **SIC:** 6021—National Commercial Banks.

★ 64287 ★   Bank South, NA
4920 Roswell Rd.
Atlanta, GA 30342-2636
(404)847-3408
Company Type: Subsidiary. **Location Type:** Branch office. **Officer:** Greg Towle, Manager. **Ultimate Parent:** Bank South Corp. **SIC:** 6021—National Commercial Banks.

★ 64288 ★   Bank South NA/
Buckhead
3116 Peachtree Rd., NE
Atlanta, GA 30305
(404)262-6340
Company Type: Subsidiary. **Location Type:** Branch office. **Officer:** Mitzi Linginfelter, V.P & Branch Mgr. **Ultimate Parent:** Bank South Corp. **SIC:** 6021—National Commercial Banks.

★ 64289 ★   Bank South NA/Fulton
Industrial
875 Selig Dr., SE
Atlanta, GA 30336
(404)699-9570
Company Type: Subsidiary. **Location Type:** Branch office. **Officer:** Brenda Heard, Branch Mgr. **Ultimate Parent:** Bank South Corp. **SIC:** 6021—National Commercial Banks.

★ 64290 ★   Bank South NA/Fulton
Industries
875 Selig Dr., SW
Atlanta, GA 30336-2284
(404)756-0101
Location Type: Branch office. **Officer:** Brenda Heard. **Ultimate Parent:** Bank South Corp. **SIC:** 6021—National Commercial Banks.

★ 64291 ★   Bank South NA/Lenox
3414 Peachtree Rd., NE
Atlanta, GA 30326-1113
(404)238-0100
Location Type: Branch office. **Officer:** Treicia Parker. **Ultimate Parent:** Bank South Corp. **SIC:** 6021—National Commercial Banks.

★ 64292 ★   Bank South NA/
Midtown
85 Tenth St., NE
Atlanta, GA 30309
(404)881-3564
Company Type: Subsidiary. **Location Type:** Branch office. **Officer:** Mary Sego, Mgr. **Ultimate Parent:** Bank South Corp. **SIC:** 6021—National Commercial Banks.

★ 64293 ★   Bank South NA/Sandy
Springs
325 Mt. Vernon Rd., NE
Atlanta, GA 30328
(404)847-3400
Company Type: Subsidiary. **Location Type:** Branch office. **Officer:** Kathy Darville, Manager. **Ultimate Parent:** Bank South Corp. **SIC:** 6021—National Commercial Banks.

★ 64294 ★   Bath & Body Works
Cumberland Mall
Atlanta, GA
(404)432-8611
Ultimate Parent: Limited.

★ 64295 ★   Bath & Body Works
Lenox Sq.
Atlanta, GA
(404)233-1256
Ultimate Parent: Limited.

★ 64296 ★   Bear Stearns
Companies Inc.
950 E. Paces Ferry Rd. NE
Atlanta, GA 30326
(404)842-4000
Location Type: Branch office. **Ultimate Parent:** Bear Stearns. **SIC:** 6341—Insurance & Diversified Financial Companies; 6211—Security Brokers & Dealers.

★ 64297 ★   Bear Stearns & Co.,
Inc.
950 E. Paces Ferry Rd. NE, Ste. 23
Atlanta, GA 30326-1142
(404)842-4000
Location Type: Branch office. **Officer:** Michael J. Montgoris. **Ultimate Parent:** Bear Stearns. **SIC:** 6211—Security Brokers & Dealers; 6221—Commodity Contracts Brokers & Dealers.

★ 64298 ★   Bear Stearns & Co.,
Inc. Atlanta
950 E. Paces Ferry Rd. NE
Atlanta, GA 30326
(404)842-4000
Location Type: Branch office. **Officer:** Michael J. Montgoris, Senior Managing Director. **Ultimate Parent:** Bear Stearns. **SIC:** 6211—Security Brokers & Dealers.

★ 64299 ★   Bell Atlantic Bus
Systems Svc.
22 Perimeter Ctr. East
Atlanta, GA 30346
(404)551-5600
Officer: Michael C. Yu. **Ultimate Parent:** Bell Atlantic Corp. **SIC:** 7378—Computer Maintenance & Repair.

★ 64300 ★   Bell Atlantic Tricon
400 Northridge Rd.
Atlanta, GA 30350-3312
(404)998-9884
Ultimate Parent: Bell Atlantic Corp. **SIC:** 6141—Personal Credit Institutions.

★ 64301 ★   Bell Atlantic Tricon
Lease Corp.
400 Northridge Rd.
Atlanta, GA 30350-3312
(404)998-9445
Ultimate Parent: Bell Atlantic Corp. **SIC:** 6159—Miscellaneous Business Credit Institutions.

★ 64302 ★   Bell South Advanced
Networks
1100 Johnson Ferry Rd., Ste. 900
Atlanta, GA 30342
(404)874-2900 **Fax:** (404)847-2980
Company Type: Subsidiary. **Officer:** Douglas A. Bullett, President. **Ultimate Parent:** BellSouth Corp.

★ 64303 ★   Bell South
Advertising & Publishing Corp.
59 Executive Park S.
Atlanta, GA 30329
(404)982-7000 **Fax:** (404)982-7298
Company Type: Subsidiary. **Officer:** Donald J. Perozzi, President. **Ultimate Parent:** BellSouth Corp.

★ 64304 ★   Bell South
Enterprises, Inc.
1100 Peachtree St. NE
Atlanta, GA 30309-4510
(404)249-4000
Company Type: Subsidiary. **Officer:** W. O. McCoy, President. **Ultimate Parent:** BellSouth Corp. **SIC:** 4813—Telephone Communications Except Radiotelephone; 4812—Radiotelephone Communications; 7311—Advertising Agencies; 2741—Miscellaneous Publishing. **Employee Count:** 15000. **Sales:** 2 M.

★ 64305 ★   Bell South
Information Systems Inc.
1100 Peachtree St. NE, Ste. 300
Atlanta, GA 30309-4599
(404)249-4600 **Fax:** (404)249-4771
Company Type: Subsidiary. **Officer:** Robert G. Haley, President. **Ultimate Parent:** BellSouth Corp.

★ 64306 ★   Bell South
International Inc.
1100 Peachtree St. NE, Ste. 400
Atlanta, GA 30309
(404)249-4300 **Fax:** (404)249-4880
Company Type: Subsidiary. **Officer:** Charles B. Coe, President. **Ultimate Parent:** BellSouth Corp.

★ 64307 ★   Bell South Mobile
Data Inc.
1100 Peachtree St. NE, Ste. 1014
Atlanta, GA 30309
(404)249-4300 **Fax:** (404)249-4767
Company Type: Branch. **Officer:** Michael K. Harrell, President. **Ultimate Parent:** BellSouth Corp.

★ 64308 ★   Bell South Mobility
Inc.
500 Northpark Town Ctr.
1100 Abernathy Rd.
Ste 500
Atlanta, GA 30328
(404)604-6100
Company Type: Subsidiary. **Officer:** Odie Donald, President. **Ultimate Parent:** BellSouth Corp.

★ 64309 ★   Bell South
Telecommunications
675 W. Peachtree St. NE
Atlanta, GA 30375
(404)529-8611
Company Type: Subsidiary. **Officer:** F. D. Ackerman, President & CEO. **Ultimate Parent:** BellSouth Corp.

★ 64310 ★   BellSouth Advanced
Networks, Inc.
1100 Johnson Ferry Rd., Ste. 900
Atlanta, GA 30342
(404)847-2900
Company Type: Subsidiary. **Ultimate Parent:** BellSouth Corp.

★ 64311 ★   Bellsouth Advertising
& Publishing Corp.
59 Executive Pk. Dr. S, Rm. 420
Atlanta, GA 30329
(404)982-7000
Company Type: Subsidiary. **Ultimate Parent:** BellSouth Corp.

★ 64312 ★   Bellsouth Advertising
& Publishing Corp.
59 Executive Park S
Atlanta, GA 30329-2218
(404)982-7000
Company Type: Subsidiary. **Officer:** Donald J. Perrozi, President. **Ultimate Parent:** BellSouth Corp. **SIC:** 2741—Miscellaneous Publishing. **Employee Count:** 2950. **Sales:** 223 M.

★ 64313 ★   BellSouth Advertising
& Publishing Corp.
2295 Parklake Dr. NE, Rm. 490
Atlanta, GA 30345
(404)491-1900 **Fax:** (404)982-7296
Officer: Barry Mansell, Human Resources Director. **Ultimate Parent:** BellSouth Corp. **SIC:** 2741—Miscellaneous Publishing. **Employee Count:** 9000.

★ 64314 ★   BellSouth Business
Systems, Inc.
675 W. Peachtree St. NE, Ste 4510
Atlanta, GA 30375
(404)529-5600
Company Type: Subsidiary. **Ultimate Parent:** BellSouth Corp.

★ 64315 ★   Bellsouth Cellular
Corp.
5600 Glenridge Dr., Ste. 480
Atlanta, GA 30342
(404)847-0400
Company Type: Subsidiary. **Ultimate Parent:** BellSouth Corp.

★ 64316 ★   BellSouth
Communications, Inc.
675 W. Peachtree St. NE, Ste. 4429
Atlanta, GA 30375
(404)529-8322
Company Type: Subsidiary. **Ultimate Parent:** BellSouth Corp.

★ 64317 ★   BellSouth Corp.
1155 Peachtree St. NE
Atlanta, GA 30309
(404)249-2000 **Fax:** (404)249-5599
Company Type: Headquarters. **Officer:** John L. Clendenin, Chairman of the Board & President. **SIC:** 4813—Telephone Communications Except Radiotelephone; 4812—Radiotelephone Communications; 2741—Miscellaneous Publishing; 5065—Electronic Parts & Equipment Nec; 7322—Adjustment & Collection Services; 7359—Equipment Rental & Leasing Nec; 6719—Holding Companies Nec. **Employee Count:** 95084. **Fortune Service 500:** Ranking 2.

★ 64318 ★   BellSouth Enterprises
Inc.
1100 Peachtree St.
Atlanta, GA 30309-4599
(404)249-4135
Officer: William O. McCoy, President. **Ultimate Parent:** BellSouth Corp. **SIC:** 4812—Radiotelephone Communications; 4813—Telephone Communications Except Radiotelephone; 6719—Holding Companies Nec. **Employee Count:** 12000. **Sales:** 1680 M.

★ 64319 ★   BellSouth Financial
Services Corp.
1800 Century Blvd. NE
Atlanta, GA 30345-3201
(404)329-4200
Company Type: Subsidiary. **Officer:** Anne-Maire Sparrow, President. **Ultimate Parent:** BellSouth Corp. **SIC:** 7359—Equipment Rental & Leasing Nec. **Employee Count:** 37. **Sales:** 100 M.

★ 64320 ★ BellSouth
International, Inc.
1100 Peachtree St. NE, Ste. 1024
Atlanta, GA 30342-4599
(404)249-4800
Company Type: Subsidiary. **Ultimate
Parent:** BellSouth Corp.

★ 64321 ★ BellSouth Mobility,
Inc.
5600 Glenridge Dr., Ste. 480
Atlanta, GA 30342
(404)847-3636
Company Type: Subsidiary. **Ultimate
Parent:** BellSouth Corp.

★ 64322 ★ BellSouth Mobility
Inc.
5600 Glenridge Dr.
Atlanta, GA 30342
(404)847-3600
Officer: Robert Tonsfeldt, President.
Ultimate Parent: BellSouth Corp. **SIC:**
4812—Radiotelephone Communications.
Employee Count: 1200. **Sales:** 150 M.

★ 64323 ★ BellSouth Systems
Integration, Inc.
600 Embassy Row, Ste. 300
Atlanta, GA 30328
(404)551-2551
Company Type: Subsidiary. **Ultimate
Parent:** BellSouth Corp.

★ 64324 ★ BellSouth Telecom
Inc.
675 W. Peachtree St. NE
Atlanta, GA 30308-1952
(404)529-8611
Location Type: Branch office. **Officer:** F.
Duane Ackerman. **Ultimate Parent:**
BellSouth Corp. **SIC:** 4813—Telephone
Communications Except Radiotelephone.

★ 64325 ★ BellSouth
Telecommunications Inc.
675 W. Peachtree St. NE
Atlanta, GA 30308-1952
(404)529-2526
Company Type: Subsidiary. **Officer:** F. D.
Ackerman, President & CEO. **Ultimate
Parent:** BellSouth Corp. **SIC:** 4813—
Telephone Communications Except
Radiotelephone; 2741—Miscellaneous
Publishing; 5065—Electronic Parts &
Equipment Nec. **Employee Count:** 82900.
Sales: 13 M.

★ 64326 ★ BellSouth
/telecommunictions Inc.
1155 Peachtree St., NE
Atlanta, GA 30367
(404)249-2000
Ultimate Parent: BellSouth Corp. **SIC:**
4813—Telephone Communications Except
Radiotelephone. **Employee Count:** 8500.
Sales: 12000 M.

★ 64327 ★ Beneficial Business
Brokers Inc.
3 Dunwoody Pk.
Atlanta, GA 30338-6704
(404)393-9335
Ultimate Parent: Beneficial. **SIC:** 6794—
Patent Owners & Lessors; 7389—Business
Services Nec.

★ 64328 ★ Bethlehem Steel
Corp.
1117 Perimeter Ctr. W. NE
Atlanta, GA 30338-5417
(404)394-7777
Ultimate Parent: Bethlehem Steel Corp.
SIC: 5072—Hardware.

★ 64329 ★ Blount Construction
Co. Inc.
66 Peachtree Park Dr.
Atlanta, GA 30309-1319
(404)355-8927
Company Type: Division. **Officer:** George
C. Blount, President. **Ultimate Parent:**
Blount Inc. **SIC:** 1611—Highway & Street
Construction; 2951—Asphalt Paving
Mixtures & Blocks. **Employee Count:** 60.
Sales: 10 M.

★ 64330 ★ Boeing Co. the
400 Colony Square
Atlanta, GA 30361
(404)870-9151
Ultimate Parent: Boeing.

★ 64331 ★ Boyle-Midway
Household Products Inc.
4111 Pleasantdale Rd.
Atlanta, GA 30340
Ultimate Parent: American Home Products.
SIC: 2879—Agricultural Chemicals Nec;
2842—Polishes & Sanitation Goods.

★ 64332 ★ Bristol-Myers Squibb
Co.
5625 Fulton Industrial Blvd. SW
Atlanta, GA 30336
(404)349-4000
Officer: Ed Sullo, Manager. **Ultimate
Parent:** Bristol-Myers Squibb. **SIC:** 2752—
Commercial Printing—Lithographic.

★ 64333 ★ Bristol-Myers Squibb
Co.
5625 Fulton Industrial Blvd. SW
Atlanta, GA 30336
(404)349-4000
Officer: Ed Sullo, Manager. **Ultimate
Parent:** Bristol-Myers Squibb. **SIC:** 2752—
Commercial Printing—Lithographic.

★ 64334 ★ Browning Ferris
Industries Georgia Inc.
8607 Roberts Dr.
Atlanta, GA 30350-2230
(404)640-2210
Officer: Tom Anderson. **Ultimate Parent:**
Browning-Ferris Industries. **SIC:** 4953—
Refuse Systems.

★ 64335 ★ Burlington Industries
Inc.
2000 Riveredge Pky. NW
Atlanta, GA 30328-4618
(404)955-4261
Location Type: Branch office. **Ultimate
Parent:** Burlington Industries, Equity. **SIC:**
2399—Fabricated Textile Products Nec.

★ 64336 ★ Burlington Northern
Railroad
2301 Parklake Dr. NE
Atlanta, GA 30345
(404)938-2044
Ultimate Parent: Burlington Northern.

★ 64337 ★ Burlington Northern
Railroad I
2301 Parklake Dr. NE
Atlanta, GA 30345
(404)938-4311
Ultimate Parent: Burlington Northern.

★ 64338 ★ Burlington Northern
Railroad M
2301 Parklake Dr. NE
Atlanta, GA 30345
(404)938-2118
Ultimate Parent: Burlington Northern.

★ 64339 ★ Burlington Northern
Railroad O
2301 Parklake Dr. NE
Atlanta, GA 30345
(404)938-2529
Ultimate Parent: Burlington Northern.

★ 64340 ★ Casual Corner
Southlake Mall
Atlanta, GA
(404)961-4655
Ultimate Parent: United States Shoe.

★ 64341 ★ Casual Corner
Town Ctr. at Cobb
Atlanta, GA
(404)424-8111
Ultimate Parent: United States Shoe.

★ 64342 ★ Casual Corner
Northlake Mall
Atlanta, GA 30345
(404)939-6967
Ultimate Parent: United States Shoe.

★ 64343 ★ Casual Corner
2206 Perimeter Mall NE
Atlanta, GA 30346
(404)394-3185
Ultimate Parent: United States Shoe.

★ 64344 ★ Casual Corner
Cumberland Mall
Atlanta, GA
(404)435-2685
Ultimate Parent: United States Shoe.

★ 64345 ★ Casual Corner
Lenox Sq.
Atlanta, GA 30326
(404)233-8288
Ultimate Parent: United States Shoe.

★ 64346 ★ Casual Corner District
Office
4800 Briarcliff Rd. NE
Atlanta, GA 30345
(404)621-0235
Ultimate Parent: United States Shoe.

★ 64347 ★ Cato Oil & Grease Co.
3480 Browns Mill Rd.
Atlanta, GA 30354
Ultimate Parent: Kerr-McGee. **SIC:** 2992—
Lubricating Oils & Greases.

★ 64348 ★ Centel Cellular Inc.
245 Perimeter Center Pky., Ste. 400
Atlanta, GA 30346
(404)804-3400
Company Type: Subsidiary. **Officer:**
Dennis L. Whipple, President & CEO.
Ultimate Parent: GTE. **SIC:** 4812—
Radiotelephone Communications; 5999—
Miscellaneous Retail Stores Nec. **Employee
Count:** 1144. **Sales:** 286 M.

★ 64349 ★ Centex-Hamby
Construction, Inc.
990 Hammond Dr., Ste. 500
Atlanta, GA 30328
(404)399-5678 **Fax:** (404)399-6290
Officer: Denval B. Hamby, President &
CEO. **Ultimate Parent:** Centex.

★ 64350 ★ Charles Schwab &
Co.
400 Colony Square
Atlanta, GA 30361
(404)874-0257
Ultimate Parent: Charles Schwab Corp.

★ 64351 ★ Charles Schwab &
Co. Inc.
3333 Cumberland Cir. NW
Atlanta, GA 30339
(404)988-0770
Ultimate Parent: Charles Schwab Corp.

★ 64352 ★ Charles Schwab &
Co. Inc.
1100 Abernathy Rd. NE
Atlanta, GA 30328
(404)671-9590
Ultimate Parent: Charles Schwab Corp.

★ 64353 ★ Charles Schwab &
Co. Inc.
400 Colony Square
Atlanta, GA 30361
(404)874-6695
Ultimate Parent: Charles Schwab Corp.

★ 64354 ★ Cigna Healthplan of
Georgia Inc.
1360 Peachtree St. NE, Ste. 1300
Atlanta, GA 30309
(404)881-9779
Company Type: Subsidiary. **Officer:** Terri
L. Branning, President. **Ultimate Parent:**
Cigna Corp. **SIC:** 6324—Hospital & Medical
Service Plans. **Employee Count:** 102.

★ 64355 ★ Cincinnati Insurance
Co.
Workers Compensation Div.
Atlanta, GA
(404)662-8753
Ultimate Parent: Cincinnati Financial.

★ 64356 ★ Cincinnati Insurance
Co. Casualty Cla
3500 Piedmont Rd. NE
Atlanta, GA 30305
(404)261-3938
Ultimate Parent: Cincinnati Financial.

★ 64357 ★ Circuit City
1968 Greenbriar Pky. SW
Atlanta, GA 30331
(404)349-5422
Ultimate Parent: Circuit City Stores.

★ 64358 ★ Circuit City
3400 Wooddale Dr. NE
Atlanta, GA 30326
(404)233-2060
Ultimate Parent: Circuit City Stores.

★ 64359 ★ Circuit City
Operations Center
3755 Atlanta Industrial P
Atlanta, GA 30331
(404)699-2109
Ultimate Parent: Circuit City Stores.

★ 64360 ★ Citgo Food Mart
1959 Lakewood Ave. SE
Atlanta, GA 30315
(404)624-4242
Ultimate Parent: Citgo Petroleum.

★ 64361 ★ Citgo Food Mart
2565 Bankhead Hwy. NW
Atlanta, GA 30318
(404)792-1013
Ultimate Parent: Citgo Petroleum.

★ 64362 ★ Citgo Mart
903 Peachtree St. NE
Atlanta, GA 30309
(404)881-9758
Ultimate Parent: Citgo Petroleum.

★ 64363 ★ Citgo Mart
1854 Stewart Ave. SW
Atlanta, GA 30315
(404)758-8758
Ultimate Parent: Citgo Petroleum.

★ 64364 ★ City National Bank of
Washi
56766 PO Box
Atlanta, GA 30343
Ultimate Parent: City National Corp. **SIC:**
6021—National Commercial Banks.

★ 64365 ★ Claris Corp.
1117 Perimeter Ctr. Wes
Atlanta, GA
(404)391-0116
Ultimate Parent: Apple Computer.

★ 64366 ★ Coast to Coast
Investigative S
1604 Howell Mill Rd. NW
Atlanta, GA
(404)352-3988
Ultimate Parent: Servistar Corp.

★ 64367 ★ Coca-Cola
1 Coca-Cola Plaza NW
Atlanta, GA 30313
(404)676-2121
Company Type: Headquarters. **Officer:**
Robert C. Goizuta. **Sales:** 13957 M.
Fortune 500: Largest U.S. Industrial
Corporations: Ranking 32.

★ 64368 ★ Coca-Cola Bottling
Atlanta, GA
(404)944-4340
Ultimate Parent: Coca-Cola Enterprises.

★ 64369 ★ Coca-Cola Bottling
Com Metro S
8250 Dunwoody Place
Atlanta, GA 30350
(404)998-4455
Ultimate Parent: Coca-Cola Enterprises.

★ 64370 ★ Coca-Cola Bottling
Co. the
100 Galleria Pkwy NW
Atlanta, GA 30339
(404)852-7000
Ultimate Parent: Coca-Cola Enterprises.

★ 64371 ★ Coca-Cola Bottling
Co.
Atlanta, GA
(404)819-2765
Ultimate Parent: Coca-Cola Enterprises.

★ 64372 ★ Coca-Cola Bottling
Co.
Atlanta, GA
(404)852-7300
Ultimate Parent: Coca-Cola Enterprises.

★ 64373 ★ Coca-Cola Bottling
Co. of Shreveprot Inc.
1 Coca-Cola Plz. NW
Atlanta, GA 30313-2419
(404)676-2100
Officer: James M. Stevens, Chairman.
Ultimate Parent: Coca-Cola Enterprises.
SIC: 2086—Bottled & Canned Soft Drinks;
5046—Commercial Equipment Nec; 5962—
Merchandising Machine Operators.
Employee Count: 180.

★ 64374 ★ Coca-Cola Co.
1 Coca-Cola Plz.
PO Drawer 1734
Atlanta, GA 30301
(404)676-2121 **Fax:** (404)676-6792 **Telex:**
4999186
Officer: Roberto C. Goizueta, Chairman &
CEO. **Ultimate Parent:** Coca-Cola.
Employee Count: 24970.

★ 64375 ★ Coca-Cola
Enterprises
1 Coca-Cola Plz. NW
Atlanta, GA 30313
(404)676-2100
Company Type: Headquarters. **Officer:**
Summerfield K. Johnston Jr. **Employee
Count:** 26500. **Fortune 500:** Largest U.S.
Industrial Corporations: Ranking 97.

★ 64376 ★ Coca-Cola
Enterprises Inc.
1 Coca-Cola Plz.
PO Drawer 1734
Atlanta, GA 30301
Officer: M. Douglas Ivester, Chairman.
Ultimate Parent: Coca-Cola.

★ 64377 ★ Coca-Cola Financial
Corp.
1 Coca-Cola Plz.
PO Drawer 1734
Atlanta, GA 30301
Officer: Carolyn H. Baldwin, President.
Ultimate Parent: Coca-Cola.

★ 64378 ★ Coca Cola U S a
7734 PO Box
Atlanta, GA 30357
(404)462-4546
Ultimate Parent: Coca-Cola. **SIC:** 5149—
Groceries & Related Products Nec.

★ 64379 ★ Coca-Cola USA
3791 Browns Mill Rd.
Atlanta, GA 30354-2946
Ultimate Parent: Coca-Cola. **SIC:** 2087—
Flavoring Extracts & Syrups Nec.

★ 64380 ★ Coca-Cola USA
1001 Great Southwest Pky.
Atlanta, GA 30336
Ultimate Parent: Coca-Cola. **SIC:** 2087—
Flavoring Extracts & Syrups Nec.

★ 64381 ★ Coca-Cola USA
3791 Browns Mill Road,SW
Atlanta, GA 30354
Ultimate Parent: Coca-Cola. **SIC:** 2087—
Flavoring Extracts & Syrups Nec.

★ 64382 ★ Coca-Cola USA
1 Coca-Cola Plz.
PO Drawer 1734
Atlanta, GA 30301
Officer: M. Douglas Ivester, President.
Ultimate Parent: Coca-Cola.

★ 64383 ★ Colonial Pipeline
945 E. Paces Ferry Rd.
Atlanta, GA 30326
(404)261-1470
Company Type: Headquarters. **Officer:**
Donald R. Brinkley. **Employee Count:** 715.
Fortune Service 500: Ranking 45.

★ 64384 ★ Colonial Pipeline Co.
Chat
3120 Parrott Ave. NW
Atlanta, GA 30318
(404)794-3922
Ultimate Parent: Colonial Pipeline.

★ 64385 ★ Colonial Pipeline Co.
Hart
Hartsfield International Airport
Atlanta, GA
(404)767-4175
Ultimate Parent: Colonial Pipeline.

★ 64386 ★ Colonial Pipeline Co.
Inc.
945 E. Paces Ferry Rd. NE
Atlanta, GA 30326-1125
(404)261-1470
Ultimate Parent: Colonial Pipeline. **SIC:**
4613—Refined Petroleum Pipelines.

★ 64387 ★ Colonial Pipeline Co.
Main
945 E. Paces Ferry Rd. NE
Atlanta, GA 30326
(404)841-2600
Ultimate Parent: Colonial Pipeline.

★ 64388 ★ Columbian Chemicals
Co.
1600 Parkwood Cir. NW
Atlanta, GA 30339
(404)951-5700
Ultimate Parent: Phelps Dodge.

★ 64389 ★ ConAgra Frozen
Foods
150 Interstate N. Pky. NW
Atlanta, GA 30339
(404)955-4505
Company Type: Division. **Location Type:**
Sales office. **Officer:** Mark Hammond, Vice
President of Sales, South. **Ultimate Parent:**
Conagra.

★ 64390 ★ Congress Financial
Corp.
1000 Parkwood Cir. NW
Atlanta, GA 30339
(404)956-0094
Ultimate Parent: Corestates Financial Corp.

★ 64391 ★ Consolidated Papers
Inc.
4 Executive Park East
Atlanta, GA 30329
(404)248-0909
Ultimate Parent: Consolidated Papers.

★ 64392 ★ Constar International
Inc.
5375 Drake Dr. SW
Atlanta, GA 30336-2408
(404)691-4256
Company Type: Subsidiary. **Officer:** James
B. Baker, Chairman of the Board & CEO.
Ultimate Parent: Crown Cork & Seal. **SIC:**
3089—Plastics Products Nec; 3085—
Plastics Bottles. **Employee Count:** 3600.
Sales: 680 M.

★ 64393 ★ Contel Cellular
Communications Inc.
245 Perimeter Ctr. Pky.
Atlanta, GA 30346
(404)391-8000 **Fax:** (404)391-1876
Company Type: Subsidiary. **Officer:**
Dennis L. Whipple, President & CEO.
Ultimate Parent: GTE.

★ 64394 ★ Continental Bank
950 E. Paces Ferry Rd. NE
Atlanta, GA
(404)364-3300
Ultimate Parent: Midlantic Corp.

★ 64395 ★ Courtyard by Marriott
2045 S. Park Pl NW
Atlanta, GA 30339
(404)955-3838
Ultimate Parent: Marriott International.

★ 64396 ★ Courtyard by Marriott
1236 Executive Park Dr. NE
Atlanta, GA 30329
(404)728-0708
Ultimate Parent: Marriott International.

★ 64397 ★ Courtyard by Marriott
3000 Cumberland Cir. NW
Atlanta, GA 30339
(404)952-2555
Ultimate Parent: Marriott International.

★ 64398 ★ Courtyard by Marriott
1132 Techwood Dr. NW
Atlanta, GA 30318
(404)607-1112
Ultimate Parent: Marriott International.

★ 64399 ★ Cray Research Inc.
200 Westpark Dr.
Atlanta, GA
(404)631-0909
Ultimate Parent: Cray Research, Inc.

★ 64400 ★ Crown Beverage
Packaging Inc.
650 Selig Dr.
Atlanta, GA 30336
Ultimate Parent: Crown Cork & Seal. **SIC:**
3411—Metal Cans.

★ 64401 ★ Crown Cork & Seal
Co. Inc.
125 Ottley Dr.
Atlanta, GA 30324-3924
Ultimate Parent: Crown Cork & Seal. **SIC:**
3411—Metal Cans.

★ 64402 ★ Daniel Radiator Corp.
2115 General Truman NW
Atlanta, GA 30318
Ultimate Parent: Handy & Harman. **SIC:**
3714—Motor Vehicle Parts & Accessories;
5013—Motor Vehicle Supplies & New Parts.

★ 64403 ★ Delta Air Cargo
1600 Aviation Blvd.
Atlanta, GA
(404)714-7000
Ultimate Parent: Delta Air Lines, Inc.

★ 64404 ★ Delta Air Lines
4711 Best Rd.
Atlanta, GA 30337
(404)765-5000
Ultimate Parent: Delta Air Lines, Inc.

★ 64405 ★ Delta Air Lines
Office Bldg. A-2 Hartsfield
Atlanta, GA
(404)715-2501
Ultimate Parent: Delta Air Lines, Inc.

★ 64406 ★ Delta Air Lines
Hartsfield Atlanta International
Atlanta, GA
(404)715-2600
Ultimate Parent: Delta Air Lines, Inc.

★ 64407 ★ Delta Air Lines
1201 W. Peachtree
Atlanta, GA
(404)881-2500
Ultimate Parent: Delta Air Lines, Inc.

★ 64408 ★ Delta Air Lines
159 Armour Dr. NE
Atlanta, GA 30324
(404)885-9945
Ultimate Parent: Delta Air Lines, Inc.

★ 64409 ★ Delta Air Lines
2525 Camp Creek Pky.
Atlanta, GA 30337
(404)765-5000
Ultimate Parent: Delta Air Lines, Inc.

★ 64410 ★ Delta Air Lines
1030 Delta Blvd.
Atlanta, GA 30320
(404)715-4548
Ultimate Parent: Delta Air Lines, Inc.

★ 64411 ★ Delta Air Lines Credit
Union
Atlanta, GA
(404)715-4725
Ultimate Parent: Delta Air Lines, Inc.

★ 64412 ★ Delta Air Lines, Inc.
Hartsfield Atlanta International Airport
Atlanta, GA 30320
(404)715-2600 **Fax:** (404)767-8499
Company Type: Headquarters. **Officer:**
Ronald W. Allen, President, Chairman of the
Board & CEO. **SIC:** 4512—Air
Transportation—Scheduled; 5172—
Petroleum Products Nec. **Employee Count:**
73533. **Sales:** 11 M. **Fortune Service 500:**
Ranking 4.

★ 64413 ★ Delta Air Lines, Inc.-
Air Cargo
1600 Aviation Blvd. Hartsf
Atlanta, GA
(404)714-7500
Ultimate Parent: Delta Air Lines, Inc.

★ 64414 ★ Delta Air Lines Inc.
Baggage Se
Hartsfield Atlanta I
Atlanta, GA
(404)714-7266
Ultimate Parent: Delta Air Lines, Inc.

★ 64415 ★ Delta Air Lines Inc.
City Ticke
2525 Camp Creek Parkway
Atlanta, GA 30337
(404)765-5000
Ultimate Parent: Delta Air Lines, Inc.

★ 64416 ★ Delta Air Lines Inc.
Credit Uni
Atlanta, GA
(404)715-4725
Ultimate Parent: Delta Air Lines, Inc.

★ 64417 ★ Delta Air Lines Inc.
Delta Colo
159 Armour Dr. NE
Atlanta, GA 30324
(404)885-9945
Ultimate Parent: Delta Air Lines, Inc.

★ 64418 ★ Delta Air Lines Inc.
District M
1201 W. Peachtree One Atla
Atlanta, GA
(404)881-2500
Ultimate Parent: Delta Air Lines, Inc.

★ 64419 ★ Delta Air Lines Inc.
Employment
Office Bldg. A-2 Hart
Atlanta, GA
(404)715-2501
Ultimate Parent: Delta Air Lines, Inc.

★ 64420 ★ Delta Air Lines Inc.
General of
Hartsfield Atl Inter
Atlanta, GA
(404)715-2600
Ultimate Parent: Delta Air Lines, Inc.

★ 64421 ★ Delta Air Lines, Inc.-
Passenger
Atlanta, GA
(404)714-7250
Ultimate Parent: Delta Air Lines, Inc.

★ 64422 ★ Delta Air Lines, Inc.-
Personnel
Atlanta, GA
(404)715-2521
Ultimate Parent: Delta Air Lines, Inc.

★ 64423 ★ Diebold Inc. Sales
2030 Powers Ferry Rd. NW
Atlanta, GA 30339
(404)612-5400
Ultimate Parent: Diebold, Inc.

★ 64424 ★ Dsc Communications
Corp.
115 Perimeter Ctr. Pl
Atlanta, GA 30346
(404)399-1099
Ultimate Parent: DSC Communications.

★ 64425 ★ Dun & Bradstreet
Software
3445 Peachtree Rd., NE
Atlanta, GA 30326
(404)239-2000 **Fax:** (404)239-2220 **Telex:**
549638
Company Type: Subsidiary. **Officer:** John
P. Imlay Jr., Chairman of the Board.
Ultimate Parent: Dun & Bradstreet. **SIC:**
7372—Prepackaged Software; 7371—
Computer Programming Services.
Employee Count: 2600. **Sales:** 533 M.

★ 64426 ★ Durr Medical
Corporation
3720 Zip Industrial Blvd.
Atlanta, GA
(404)767-8282
Ultimate Parent: Bergen Brunswig Corp.

★ 64427 ★ Eds
6145 Barfield Rd. NE
Atlanta, GA 30328
(404)255-4988
Ultimate Parent: Electronic Data Systems.

★ 64428 ★ Emc Corp.
1100 Johnson Ferry Rd. NE
Atlanta, GA 30342
(404)705-4750
Ultimate Parent: EMC.

★ 64429 ★ Equitable Agri-
Business Inc.
7000 Central Pky. NE, Ste. 915
Atlanta, GA 30328
(404)391-7199
Company Type: Subsidiary. **Officer:** Craig
Johns, President, CEO. **Ultimate Parent:**
Equitable Life Assurance. **SIC:** 6163—Loan
Brokers. **Employee Count:** 125.

★ 64430 ★   Equitable Real Estate Investment Management Inc.
3414 Peachtree Rd. NE
Atlanta, GA 30326-1113
(404)239-5000
Company Type: Subsidiary. **Officer:** George R. Puskar, Chairman of the Board, CEO. **Ultimate Parent:** Equitable Life Assurance. **SIC:** 6531—Real Estate Agents & Managers. **Employee Count:** 2000. **Sales:** 200 M.

★ 64431 ★   Equitable Variable Life Insurance
3414 Peachtree Rd. NE
Atlanta, GA 30326
(404)266-1200
Ultimate Parent: Equitable Variable Life.

★ 64432 ★   Exxon
635 Lindbergh Dr. NE
Atlanta, GA 30324
(404)237-9221
Ultimate Parent: Exxon.

★ 64433 ★   Exxon Car Care
2901 Peachtree Rd. NE
Atlanta, GA 30305
(404)237-4652
Ultimate Parent: Exxon.

★ 64434 ★   Exxon Car Care Center
77 E. Perimeter Dek NE
Atlanta, GA 30338
(404)393-1150
Ultimate Parent: Exxon.

★ 64435 ★   Exxon Chemical Co.
400 Interstate North Pky.
Atlanta, GA 30339
(404)955-2300
Ultimate Parent: Exxon.

★ 64436 ★   Exxon Co. USA
77 E. Perimeter Dek NE
Atlanta, GA 30338
(404)393-1150
Ultimate Parent: Exxon.

★ 64437 ★   Exxon Co. USA
1050 Crown Pointe Pky. NE
Atlanta, GA 30338
(404)698-6820
Ultimate Parent: Exxon.

★ 64438 ★   Exxon Shop
247 Moreland Ave. SE
Atlanta, GA 30316
(404)659-6758
Ultimate Parent: Exxon.

★ 64439 ★   Exxon Shop
101 Hightower Rd. NW
Atlanta, GA 30311
(404)699-0836
Ultimate Parent: Exxon.

★ 64440 ★   Fairfield Inn by Marriott
2155 Ranchwood Dr. NE
Atlanta, GA 30345
(404)491-7444
Ultimate Parent: Marriott International.

★ 64441 ★   Federal Express Corp.
Atlanta, GA
(404)559-5900
Ultimate Parent: Federal Express.

★ 64442 ★   Federal Home Loan Mortgage Corp. (Freddie Mac)- Southeast/Southwest Region
2839 Paces Ferry Rd. NW, Ste. 708
Atlanta, GA 30339
(404)438-3800
Location Type: Branch office. **Ultimate Parent:** Federal Home Loan Mortgage. **SIC:** 6111—Federal & Federally-Sponsored Credit.

★ 64443 ★   Federal Mogul Corp.
201 Wharton Cir. SW
Atlanta, GA 30336
(404)691-3622
Ultimate Parent: Federal-Mogul Corp.

★ 64444 ★   Federal National Mortgage Association
950 E. Paces Ferry Rd. NE
Atlanta, GA 30326
(404)398-6242
Ultimate Parent: Federal National Mortgage Association.

★ 64445 ★   First American Corp.
3032 B Cliff Rd. NE, Ste. 6
Atlanta, GA 30329
(404)325-1321
Officer: Doris L. Waller, Chairman of the Board. **Ultimate Parent:** First American Corp. **SIC:** 6311—Life Insurance. **Employee Count:** 7.

★ 64446 ★   First Brands Corp.
2970 Clairmont Rd. NE
Atlanta, GA 30329
(404)728-5678
Ultimate Parent: First Brands Corp.

★ 64447 ★   First Data Resources
2957 Clairmont Rd. NE
Atlanta, GA 30329
(404)728-8600
Ultimate Parent: First Data Corp.

★ 64448 ★   First Financial Management Corp.
3 Corporate Sq.
Atlanta, GA 30329
(404)321-0120
Company Type: Headquarters. **Officer:** Patrick H. Thomas. **Employee Count:** 11500. **Sales:** 1659.8 M. **Fortune Service 500:** Ranking 90.

★ 64449 ★   First Union Corp. of Georgia
999 Peachtree St., Ste. 1200
Atlanta, GA 30309
Company Type: Subsidiary. **Officer:** Robert C. McMahan, Chairman of the Board & CEO. **Ultimate Parent:** First Union Corp. **SIC:** 6712—Bank Holding Companies. **Employee Count:** 872. **Sales:** 283,932,000 M.

★ 64450 ★   First Union National Bank of Georgia
PO Box 740074
Atlanta, GA 30374
(404)827-7100 **Fax:** (404)225-4120
Company Type: Subsidiary. **Officer:** Harold R. Hansen, Chairman of the Board, CEO. **Ultimate Parent:** First Union Corp. **SIC:** 6162—Mortgage Bankers & Correspondents. **Employee Count:** 1840. **Sales:** 520,939,000 M.

★ 64451 ★   First Union National Bank of Georgia
1605 Moore Dr. NE
Atlanta, GA 30324-5003
(404)898-1700
Location Type: Branch office. **Ultimate Parent:** First Union Corp. **SIC:** 6021—National Commercial Banks.

★ 64452 ★   First Union National Bank of Georgia
3235 Peachtree Rd. NE
Atlanta, GA 30305-2432
(404)842-4620
Location Type: Branch office. **Ultimate Parent:** First Union Corp. **SIC:** 6021—National Commercial Banks.

★ 64453 ★   First Union National Bank of Georgia
3975 Peachtree Rd. NE
Atlanta, GA 30319-3374
(404)365-4600
Location Type: Branch office. **Ultimate Parent:** First Union Corp. **SIC:** 6021—National Commercial Banks.

★ 64454 ★   First Union National Bank of Georgia
241 Peachtree St. NE
Atlanta, GA 30303-1498
(404)330-7150
Location Type: Branch office. **Ultimate Parent:** First Union Corp. **SIC:** 6021—National Commercial Banks.

★ 64455 ★   First Union National Bank of Georgia
3080 Campbellton Rd. SW
Atlanta, GA 30311-5410
(404)346-5860
Location Type: Branch office. **Ultimate Parent:** First Union Corp. **SIC:** 6021—National Commercial Banks.

★ 64456 ★   First Union National Bank of Georgia
2085 Stewart Ave. SW
Atlanta, GA 30315-5926
(404)669-2230
Location Type: Branch office. **Ultimate Parent:** First Union Corp. **SIC:** 6021—National Commercial Banks.

★ 64457 ★   First Union National Bank of Georgia
6344 Roswell Rd.
Atlanta, GA 30328-3231
(404)865-5460
Location Type: Branch office. **Ultimate Parent:** First Union Corp. **SIC:** 6021—National Commercial Banks.

★ 64458 ★   First Union National Bank of Georgia
2905 Cobb Pky.
Atlanta, GA 30339
(404)916-3000
Location Type: Branch office. **Ultimate Parent:** First Union Corp. **SIC:** 6021—National Commercial Banks.

★ 64459 ★   First Union National Bank of Georgia
921 Ralph David Abernathy Blvd. SW
Atlanta, GA 30310-1891
(404)752-1800
Location Type: Branch office. **Ultimate Parent:** First Union Corp. **SIC:** 6021—National Commercial Banks.

★ 64460 ★   First Union National Bank of Georgia
4570 Ashford-Dunwoody Rd.
Atlanta, GA 30346
(404)865-2555
Location Type: Branch office. **Ultimate Parent:** First Union Corp. **SIC:** 6021—National Commercial Banks.

★ 64461 ★   First Union National Bank of Georgia
20 Marietta St.
Atlanta, GA 30303-2809
(404)330-2440
Location Type: Branch office. **Ultimate Parent:** First Union Corp. **SIC:** 6021—National Commercial Banks.

★ 64462 ★   First Union National Bank of Georgia
3680 Roswell Rd. NW & Piedmont
Atlanta, GA 30342-4416
(404)848-7120
Location Type: Branch office. **Ultimate Parent:** First Union Corp. **SIC:** 6021—National Commercial Banks.

★ 64463 ★   First Union National Bank of Georgia
3051 Akers Mill Rd. NW
Atlanta, GA 30339
(404)916-3520
Location Type: Branch office. **Ultimate Parent:** First Union Corp. **SIC:** 6021—National Commercial Banks.

★ 64464 ★   First Union National Bank of Georgia
6000 Sandy Springs Cir. NW
Atlanta, GA 30328-3864
(404)256-6940
Location Type: Branch office. **Ultimate Parent:** First Union Corp. **SIC:** 6021—National Commercial Banks.

★ 64465 ★   First Union National Bank of Georgia
8877 Roswell Rd. NE
Atlanta, GA 30350-1846
(404)993-2338
Location Type: Branch office. **Ultimate Parent:** First Union Corp. **SIC:** 6021—National Commercial Banks.

★ 64466 ★   First Union National Bank of Georgia
1544 Piedmont Ave. NE
Atlanta, GA 30324-5018
(404)870-3005
Location Type: Branch office. **Ultimate Parent:** First Union Corp. **SIC:** 6021—National Commercial Banks.

★ 64467 ★   First Union National Bank of Georgia
100 Galleria Pky.
Atlanta, GA 30339-3122
(404)852-2660
Location Type: Branch office. **Ultimate Parent:** First Union Corp. **SIC:** 6021—National Commercial Banks.

★ 64468 ★   First Union National Bank of Georgia
999 Peachtree St.
Atlanta, GA 30309-3964
(404)865-3010
Location Type: Branch office. **Ultimate Parent:** First Union Corp. **SIC:** 6021—National Commercial Banks.

★ 64469 ★   First Union National Bank of Georgia
2970 Peachtree Rd.
Atlanta, GA 30305-2110
(404)365-3870
Location Type: Branch office. **Ultimate Parent:** First Union Corp. **SIC:** 6021—National Commercial Banks.

★ 64470 ★   Fleet Finance, Inc.
211 Perimeter Pk.
Atlanta, GA 30341
(404)452-2200
Company Type: Subsidiary. **Officer:** Harold Owens, President. **Ultimate Parent:** Fleet Financial Group. **SIC:** 6141—Personal Credit Institutions. **Employee Count:** 939. **Sales:** 18449000 M.

★ 64471 ★   Fleet Finance Inc. Cumming
416 Atanta Hwy. Cumming G
Atlanta, GA
(404)688-3869
Ultimate Parent: Fleet Financial Group.

★ 64472 ★   Foot Action
Greenbriar Mall
Atlanta, GA
(404)349-0576
Ultimate Parent: Melville.

★ 64473 ★   The Gap
Town Ctr. at Cobb
Atlanta, GA
(404)426-1045
Ultimate Parent: GAP.

★ 64474 ★   The Gap
1118 Northlake Mall NE
Atlanta, GA 30345
(404)938-1365
Ultimate Parent: GAP.

★ 64475 ★   The Gap
102 Lower Alabama St. SW
Atlanta, GA 30303
(404)522-0027
Ultimate Parent: GAP.

★ 64476 ★   The Gap
5775 Peachtree Dunwoody Rd.
Atlanta, GA 30342
(404)252-0034
Ultimate Parent: GAP.

★ 64477 ★   The Gap
Perimeter Mall
Atlanta, GA
(404)394-6848
Ultimate Parent: GAP.

★ 64478 ★   The Gap
3065 Headland Dr. SW
Atlanta, GA 30311
(404)349-8600
Ultimate Parent: GAP.

★ 64479 ★   The Gap
Lenox Sq. Shopping Ctr.
Atlanta, GA
(404)233-3229
Ultimate Parent: GAP.

★ 64480 ★   The Gap
4800 Briarcliff Rd. NE
Atlanta, GA 30345
(404)938-1365
Ultimate Parent: GAP.

★ 64481 ★   The Gap
Gwinnett Place Mall
Atlanta, GA
(404)476-0117
Ultimate Parent: GAP.

★ 64482 ★   The Gap
1309 Cumberland Mall NW
Atlanta, GA
(404)433-3263
Ultimate Parent: GAP.

★ 64483 ★　　The Gap Kids
4400 Ashford Dunwoody Rd.
Atlanta, GA 30346
(404)392-9155
Ultimate Parent: GAP.

★ 64484 ★　　Gap Stores the
Perimeter Mall
Atlanta, GA
(404)394-6848
Ultimate Parent: GAP.

★ 64485 ★　　Gap Stores the
3065 Headland Dr. SW
Atlanta, GA 30311
(404)349-8600
Ultimate Parent: GAP.

★ 64486 ★　　Gap Stores the
Lenox Square Shoppin
Atlanta, GA
(404)233-3229
Ultimate Parent: GAP.

★ 64487 ★　　Gap Stores the
4800 Briarcliff Rd. NE
Atlanta, GA 30345
(404)938-1365
Ultimate Parent: GAP.

★ 64488 ★　　Gap Stores the
Gwinnett Place Mall
Atlanta, GA
(404)476-0117
Ultimate Parent: GAP.

★ 64489 ★　　Gap Stores the
Regional Office
5775 Peachtree Dunwoody R
Atlanta, GA 30342
(404)252-0034
Ultimate Parent: GAP.

★ 64490 ★　　Gap Stores the
Underground Atl
102 Lower Alabama St. SW
Atlanta, GA 30303
(404)522-0027
Ultimate Parent: GAP.

★ 64491 ★　　General American Life
Insuranc
12 Piedmont Ctr.
Atlanta, GA 30305
(404)237-0709
Ultimate Parent: General American Life.

★ 64492 ★　　General American Life
Insuranc
1050 Crown Pointe Pkwy NE
Atlanta, GA 30338
(404)512-5160
Ultimate Parent: General American Life.

★ 64493 ★　　General Instrument
Corp.
Comm/Scope Cable Division
2221 Peachtree Rd. NE
Atlanta, GA 30309
(404)814-9711
Ultimate Parent: General Instrument Corp.

★ 64494 ★　　Genesis Underwriting
Mgt Co. 7
3525 Piedmont Rd. NE
Atlanta, GA 30305
(404)365-6800
Ultimate Parent: General Re.

★ 64495 ★　　Genuine Parts
2999 Circle 75 Pky.
Atlanta, GA 30339
(404)953-1700
Company Type: Headquarters. **Officer:**
Larry L. Prince. **Fortune Service 500:**
Ranking 24.

★ 64496 ★　　Genuine Parts
Mid-South Division
2999 Circle 75 Pky.
Atlanta, GA 30339
(404)956-2216
Company Type: Subsidiary. **Ultimate
Parent:** Genuine Parts.

★ 64497 ★　　Genuine Parts
Piedmont Division
2999 Circle 75 Pky.
Atlanta, GA 30339
Fax: (404)956-2216
Company Type: Subsidiary. **Ultimate
Parent:** Genuine Parts.

★ 64498 ★　　Genuine Parts
Rayloc Div.
600 Rayloc Dr. SW
Atlanta, GA 30336
(404)691-3780
Company Type: Division. **Officer:** Joseph
White, President. **Ultimate Parent:** Genuine
Parts. **SIC:** 3714—Motor Vehicle Parts &
Accessories.

★ 64499 ★　　Genuine Parts
Southeast Division
5420 Peachtree Industrial Blvd.
Atlanta, GA 30071
(404)449-7211 **Fax:** (404)449-8817
Company Type: Subsidiary. **Ultimate
Parent:** Genuine Parts.

★ 64500 ★　　Genuine Parts Co.
2999 Circle 75 Pky.
Atlanta, GA 30339
(404)953-1700 **Fax:** (404)956-2211
Company Type: Headquarters. **Ultimate
Parent:** Genuine Parts.

★ 64501 ★　　Genuine Parts Co.
Rayloc Div.
600 Rayloc Dr. SW
Atlanta, GA 30378
Company Type: Division. **Ultimate Parent:**
Genuine Parts. **SIC:** 3714—Motor Vehicle
Parts & Accessories.

★ 64502 ★　　Genuine Parts Co.
Rayloc Div.
600 Rayloc Dr. NW
Atlanta, GA 30378
Company Type: Division. **Ultimate Parent:**
Genuine Parts. **SIC:** 3714—Motor Vehicle
Parts & Accessories.

★ 64503 ★　　Genuine Parts Co.,
Inc.
2999 Circle 75 Pky., NW
Atlanta, GA 30339-3050
(404)953-1700
Officer: Larry L. Prince, Chairman of the
Board & Chief Executive Officer. **Ultimate
Parent:** Genuine Parts. **SIC:** 5013—Motor
Vehicle Supplies & New Parts; 5084—
Industrial Machinery & Equipment; 5112—
Stationery & Office Supplies; 5021—
Furniture. **Employee Count:** 18000. **Sales:**
4000000 M.

★ 64504 ★　　Georgia Federal Bank,
FSB
20 Marietta St.
Atlanta, GA 30303
(404)330-2400
Company Type: Subsidiary. **Officer:**
William Farr III, President. **Ultimate Parent:**
First Union Corp. **SIC:** 6035—Federal
Savings Institutions.

★ 64505 ★　　Georgia Gulf
400 Perimeter Ctr. Terrace
Atlanta, GA 30346
(404)395-4500
Company Type: Headquarters. **Officer:**
Jerry R. Satrum. **Sales:** 768.9 M. **Fortune
500:** Largest U.S. Industrial Corporations:
Ranking 36.

★ 64506 ★　　Georgia Gulf Corp.
400 Perimeter Ctr. Ter., Ste. 595
Atlanta, GA 30346
(404)395-4500 **Fax:** (404)395-4529
Company Type: Headquarters. **Ultimate
Parent:** Georgia Gulf.

★ 64507 ★　　Georgia Gulf Corp.
400 Perimeter Ctr. Ter. NE
Atlanta, GA 30346
(404)395-4500
Officer: James R. Kuse, Chairman.
Ultimate Parent: Georgia Gulf. **SIC:** 2812—
Alkalies & Chlorine; 2819—Industrial
Inorganic Chemicals Nec; 2821—Plastics
Materials & Resins.

★ 64508 ★　　Georgia-Pacific
133 Peachtree St. NE
Atlanta, GA 30303
(404)652-4000
Company Type: Headquarters. **Officer:** A.
D. Correll. **Sales:** 12330 M. **Fortune 500:**
Largest U.S. Industrial Corporations:
Ranking 36.

★ 64509 ★　　GK Stores Inc.
244 Perimeter Ctr. Pky. NE
PO Box 2210
Atlanta, GA 30301
(404)393-5000 **Fax:** (404)393-5347
Company Type: Subsidiary. **Officer:**
Stanley C. Rogers, President. **Ultimate
Parent:** Gold Kist.

★ 64510 ★　　Gold Kist
244 Perimeter Ctr. Pky.
Atlanta, GA 30346
(404)393-5000
Company Type: Headquarters. **Officer:**
Harold O. Chitwood. **Employee Count:**
14000. **Sales:** 1401 M. **Fortune 500:**
Largest U.S. Industrial Corporations:
Ranking 289.

★ 64511 ★　　Gold Kist Inc.
244 Perimeter Ctr. Pky. NE
PO Box 2210
Atlanta, GA 30346-2302
(404)393-5000 **Fax:** (404)393-5347
Company Type: Headquarters. **Officer:**
W.P. Smith, Chairman of the Board.
Ultimate Parent: Gold Kist. **SIC:** 0254—
Poultry Hatcheries; 0251—Broiler, Fryer &
Roaster Chickens; 2015—Poultry
Slaughtering & Processing; 2011—Meat
Packing Plants; 5999—Miscellaneous Retail
Stores Nec; 5261—Retail Nurseries &
Garden Stores. **Employee Count:** 12500.
Sales: 130000 M.

★ 64512 ★　　Gold Kist Inc.
Poultry Division
244 Perimeter Ctr. Pky. NE
PO Box 2210
Atlanta, GA 30301
(404)393-5170
Company Type: Division. **Officer:** Kenneth
Whitmire, Vice President Poultry. **Ultimate
Parent:** Gold Kist. **SIC:** 2013—Sausages &
Other Prepared Meats.

★ 64513 ★　　Golden Peanut Co.
1100 Johnson Ferry Rd. NE
Atlanta, GA 30342-1708
(404)843-7850
Company Type: Division. **Officer:** Michael
A. Stimpert, Chief Executive Vice President.
Ultimate Parent: Archer Daniels Midland.
SIC: 5159—Farm-Product Raw
Materials Nec; 2076—Vegetable Oil Mills
Nec. **Employee Count:** 1000. **Sales:** 550
M.

★ 64514 ★　　Golden Peanuts Co.
1100 Johnson Ferry Rd.
Atlanta, GA 30342-1707
(404)843-7850
Company Type: Headquarters. **Officer:**
Larry Lemley. **Ultimate Parent:** Archer
Daniels Midland Co. **SIC:** 0139—Field
Crops Except Cash Grains Nec; 2076—
Vegetable Oil Mills Nec; 5149—Groceries &
Related Products Nec; 5159—Farm-Product
Raw Materials Nec.

★ 64515 ★　　Golden Poultry Co.
Inc.
244 Perimeter Ctr. Pky. NE
PO Box 2210
Atlanta, GA 30346-2302
(404)393-5000 **Fax:** (404)393-5347
Company Type: Subsidiary. **Officer:** E.
Carlyle Ragans, President & CEO. **Ultimate
Parent:** Gold Kist. **SIC:** 2015—Poultry
Slaughtering & Processing. **Employee
Count:** 3950. **Sales:** 336000 M.

★ 64516 ★　　Greyhound Bus Lines
District O
81 International Blvd. N
Atlanta, GA 30303
(404)584-1710
Ultimate Parent: Greyhound Lines Inc.

★ 64517 ★　　Greyhound Bus Lines
Local Info
3750 Venture Dr.
Atlanta, GA
(404)476-7659
Ultimate Parent: Greyhound Lines Inc.

★ 64518 ★　　Greyhound Bus Lines
Local Info
4232 Wendell Dr. SW
Atlanta, GA 30336
(404)691-6017
Ultimate Parent: Greyhound Lines Inc.

★ 64519 ★　　Greyhound Bus Lines
Transporta
81 International Blvd. N
Atlanta, GA 30303
(404)584-1728
Ultimate Parent: Greyhound Lines Inc.

★ 64520 ★　　Greystone Realty
Corp.
6201 Powers Ferry Rd. NW
Atlanta, GA 30339
(404)859-9803
Ultimate Parent: New York Life.

★ 64521 ★　　Groupamerica
Insurance Co.
2 Parkway Ctr.
Atlanta, GA
(404)514-0701
Ultimate Parent: Connecticut Mutual Life.

★ 64522 ★　　GTE Cellular
Communications Corp.
245 Perimeter Center Pky.
Atlanta, GA 30346
(404)391-8000
Company Type: Subsidiary. **Ultimate
Parent:** GTE. **SIC:** 4812—Radiotelephone
Communications.

★ 64523 ★　　GTE Customer
Networks, Inc.
PO Box 105339
1117 Perimeter Center West., Ste. 200
Atlanta, GA 30348
(404)698-5800 **Fax:** (404)394-5169
Company Type: Subsidiary. **Ultimate
Parent:** GTE. **SIC:** 4899—Communications
Services Nec.

★ 64524 ★　　GTE Customer
Networks Inc.
1117 Perimeter Center Pky.
Atlanta, GA 30338-5417
(404)698-5800
Company Type: Subsidiary. **Officer:** H.
David Fanning, President. **Ultimate Parent:**
GTE. **SIC:** 7629—Electrical Repair Shops
Nec; 5065—Electronic Parts & Equipment
Nec. **Employee Count:** 630. **Sales:** 78.3 M.

★ 64525 ★　　GTE Mobile
Communications Inc.
245 Perimeter Center Pky.
Atlanta, GA 30346-2304
(404)391-8000
Company Type: Subsidiary. **Officer:** Terry
S. Parker, Interim President. **Ultimate
Parent:** GTE. **SIC:** 4812—Radiotelephone
Communications; 5999—Miscellaneous
Retail Stores Nec. **Employee Count:** 677.
Sales: 47.3 (est) M.

★ 64526 ★　　GTE Mobile
Communications Inc.
245 Perimeter Ctr. Pkwy.
Atlanta, GA 30346
(404)391-8000 **Fax:** (404)391-1876
Company Type: Subsidiary. **Ultimate
Parent:** GTE. **SIC:** 6719—Holding
Companies Nec.

★ 64527 ★　　GTE Mobilenet Inc.
245 Perimeter Cnt. Pkwy.
Atlanta, GA 30346
(404)391-8000
Company Type: Subsidiary. **Ultimate
Parent:** GTE.

★ 64528 ★　　GTE Mobilnet Inc.
245 Perimeter Center Pky.
Atlanta, GA 30346-2304
(404)391-8000
Company Type: Subsidiary. **Officer:** Ron
Grawert, President. **Ultimate Parent:** GTE.
SIC: 4812—Radiotelephone
Communications. **Employee Count:** 485.
Sales: 686 M.

★ 64529 ★　　Gte Supply
2580 Cumberland Pkwy NW
Atlanta, GA 30339
(404)433-1838
Ultimate Parent: GTE.

★ 64530 ★　　GTE
**Telecommunications Products &
Services**
245 Perimeter Ctr. Pky.
Atlanta, GA 30348
(404)391-8000 **Fax:** (404)394-6788
Company Type: Subsidiary. **Officer:** Terry
S. Parker, President. **Ultimate Parent:**
GTE.

★ 64531 ★ Hertz Rent-A-Car
Hartsfield International Airport
Atlanta, GA
(404)530-2925
Ultimate Parent: Hertz.

★ 64532 ★ Hertz Rent-A-Car Car
Rental Lo
202 Courtland St. NE
Atlanta, GA 30303
(404)659-3000
Ultimate Parent: Hertz. SIC: 7514—
Passenger Car Rental.

★ 64533 ★ Hertz Rent-A-Car
Rental Locati
246 Perimeter Ctr. Pky.
Atlanta, GA 30346
(404)394-6500
Ultimate Parent: Hertz.

★ 64534 ★ Hertz Rent-A-Car
Rental Locati
3300 Lenox Rd. NE
Atlanta, GA 30326
(404)237-2660
Ultimate Parent: Hertz.

★ 64535 ★ Hertz Rent-A-Car
Rental Locati
290 Interstate Pky. NW
Atlanta, GA 30339
(404)952-7900
Ultimate Parent: Hertz.

★ 64536 ★ Hit or Miss Wms
Apparel Distri
4400 Ashford Dunwoody Rd.
Atlanta, GA 30346
(404)390-0108
Ultimate Parent: TJX.

★ 64537 ★ Hit or Miss Wms
Apparel Retail
2965 Cobb Pkwy NW
Atlanta, GA 30339
(404)951-0828
Ultimate Parent: TJX.

★ 64538 ★ Hit or Miss Wms
Apparel Retail
4400 Ashford Dunwoody Rd.
Atlanta, GA 30346
(404)395-9620
Ultimate Parent: TJX.

★ 64539 ★ Home Depot
2727 Paces Ferry Rd. NW
Atlanta, GA 30339
(404)433-8211
Company Type: Headquarters. Officer:
Bernard Marcus. Employee Count: 50600.
Fortune 500: Largest U.S. Industrial
Corporations: Ranking 15.

★ 64540 ★ Home Depot, Inc.
2727 Paces Ferry Rd.
Atlanta, GA 30339
(404)433-8211 Fax: (404)431-2707
Company Type: Headquarters. Officer:
Bernard Marcus, Chairman. Ultimate
Parent: Home Depot. Employee Count:
30000.

★ 64541 ★ Home Depot Inc. the
Stores Atla
3850 Jonesboro Rd. SE
Atlanta, GA 30354
(404)361-0420
Ultimate Parent: Home Depot.

★ 64542 ★ Household Mortgage
Services
6795 Hunters Trace Cir. NE
Atlanta, GA 30328
(404)392-9450
Ultimate Parent: Household International.

★ 64543 ★ Human Affairs
International
120 Ralph Mcgill Blvd. NE
Atlanta, GA 30308
(404)892-1968
Ultimate Parent: Aetna Life & Annuity. SIC:
9721—International Affairs.

★ 64544 ★ Human Affairs
International Inc.
1100 Johnson Ferry Rd. NE
Atlanta, GA 30342
(404)252-3132
Ultimate Parent: Aetna Life & Annuity.

★ 64545 ★ IBM Corp.
1201 W. Peachtree St.
Atlanta, GA 30367
(404)877-7161
Ultimate Parent: IBM.

★ 64546 ★ IBM Corp. Sales
4111 Northside Pkwy.
Atlanta, GA 30327
(404)238-7000
Ultimate Parent: IBM.

★ 64547 ★ IDS Financial
Services Inc.
1200 Ashwood Pky., Ste. 150
Atlanta, GA 30338-4725
(404)396-7840
Location Type: Branch office. Officer: Ron
Caruso. Ultimate Parent: American
Express Co. SIC: 6141—Personal Credit
Institutions; 6211—Security Brokers &
Dealers; 6282—Investment Advice.

★ 64548 ★ Illinois Tool Works
Devilbiss Spray Booth Div.
520 Wharton Cir.
Atlanta, GA 30336
Company Type: Subsidiary. Officer: Philip
Fondy, General Manager. Ultimate Parent:
Illinois Tool Works.

★ 64549 ★ Inacomp Computer
Centers Advan
5505 Roswell Rd. NE
Atlanta, GA 30342
(404)252-9611
Ultimate Parent: Beneficial.

★ 64550 ★ Integris
6 W. Druid Hills Dr. NE
Atlanta, GA 30329
(404)982-2270
Ultimate Parent: Honeywell.

★ 64551 ★ Intelligent Media
Ventures, Inc.
1100 Peachtree St. NE
Atlanta, GA 30309
(404)249-4340
Company Type: Subsidiary. Ultimate
Parent: BellSouth Corp.

★ 64552 ★ Interpublic Group of
Companies
615 Peachtree St. NE
Atlanta, GA
(404)874-6144
Ultimate Parent: Interpublic Group.

★ 64553 ★ Jackson National Life
Insurance Co.
1000 Circle 75 Pkwy NW
Atlanta, GA 30339
(404)956-8311
Ultimate Parent: Jackson National Life.

★ 64554 ★ Jiffy Lube
4995 Roswell Rd. NE
Atlanta, GA 30342
(404)256-3646
Ultimate Parent: Pennzoil.

★ 64555 ★ Jiffy Lube Buckhead
1742 Howell Mill Rd. NW
Atlanta, GA 30318
(404)351-6274
Ultimate Parent: Pennzoil.

★ 64556 ★ Jiffy Lube Buford
Hwy
3979 Buford Hwy. NE
Atlanta, GA 30345
(404)320-7857
Ultimate Parent: Pennzoil.

★ 64557 ★ Jiffy Lube
International
6045 Barfield Rd. NE
Atlanta, GA 30328
(404)256-1454
Ultimate Parent: Pennzoil.

★ 64558 ★ Johnson Controls Inc.
Credit of
1100 Circle 75 Pkwy NW
Atlanta, GA 30339
(404)953-1828
Ultimate Parent: Johnson Controls Inc.

★ 64559 ★ Johnson Controls Inc.
Service D
650 Wharton Dr. SW
Atlanta, GA 30336
(404)696-2593
Ultimate Parent: Johnson Controls Inc.

★ 64560 ★ Johnson Controls Inc.
Southeast
1100 Circle 75 Pkwy NW
Atlanta, GA 30339
(404)955-8633
Ultimate Parent: Johnson Controls Inc.

★ 64561 ★ Johnson Controls Inc.
Systems S
650 Wharton Dr. SW
Atlanta, GA 30336
(404)696-2590
Ultimate Parent: Johnson Controls Inc.

★ 64562 ★ Johnston Coca-Cola
Bottling Group Inc.
1 Coca-Cola Plz. NW
Atlanta, GA 30313-2419
(404)676-2100
Officer: Summerfield Johnston Jr.,
Chairman. Ultimate Parent: Coca-Cola
Enterprises. SIC: 2086—Bottled & Canned
Soft Drinks. Employee Count: 5500.

★ 64563 ★ Jostens Learning
Corp.
100 Hartsfield Centre Pk.
Atlanta, GA 30354
(404)762-0406
Ultimate Parent: Jostens.

★ 64564 ★ Kay-Bee Toy & Hobby
Shop Inc.
Market Square Mall
Atlanta, GA
(404)321-6226
Ultimate Parent: Melville.

★ 64565 ★ Kay-Bee Toy & Hobby
Shop Inc.
Town Ctr. at Cobb
Atlanta, GA
(404)425-2700
Ultimate Parent: Melville.

★ 64566 ★ Kay-Bee Toy & Hobby
Shop Inc.
1000 Cumberland Mall
Atlanta, GA 30339
(404)434-1805
Ultimate Parent: Melville.

★ 64567 ★ Kay-Bee Toy & Hobby
Shop Inc.
Gwinnett Place Mall
Atlanta, GA
(404)476-9515
Ultimate Parent: Melville.

★ 64568 ★ Kay-Bee Toy & Hobby
Shop Inc.
4400 Ashford Dunwoody Rd.
Atlanta, GA 30346
(404)396-9776
Ultimate Parent: Melville.

★ 64569 ★ Kemper Securities
Inc.
3399 Peachtree Rd. NE
Atlanta, GA 30326
(404)364-5100
Ultimate Parent: Kemper.

★ 64570 ★ Kentucky Fried
Chicken
1880 Stewart Ave. SW
Atlanta, GA 30315
(404)752-9272
Ultimate Parent: Pepsico.

★ 64571 ★ Kentucky Fried
Chicken
2625 Piedmont Rd. NE
Atlanta, GA 30324
(404)816-6342
Ultimate Parent: Pepsico.

★ 64572 ★ Kentucky Fried
Chicken
425 Ponce De Leon Ave. NE
Atlanta, GA 30308
(404)874-1400
Ultimate Parent: Pepsico.

★ 64573 ★ Kentucky Fried
Chicken
355 Moreland Ave. SE
Atlanta, GA 30316
(404)523-2541
Ultimate Parent: Pepsico.

★ 64574 ★ Kentucky Fried
Chicken
25 Peachtree St. NE
Atlanta, GA 30303
(404)577-6683
Ultimate Parent: Pepsico.

★ 64575 ★ Kentucky Fried
Chicken
1766 Howell Mill Rd. NW
Atlanta, GA 30318
(404)351-6945
Ultimate Parent: Pepsico.

★ 64576 ★ Kentucky Fried
Chicken
301 Main St. Cedartown Ga
Atlanta, GA
(404)748-8146
Ultimate Parent: Pepsico.

★ 64577 ★ Kentucky Fried
Chicken
1335 Gordon St. SW
Atlanta, GA 30310
(404)755-7100
Ultimate Parent: Pepsico.

★ 64578 ★ Kentucky Fried
Chicken
8 Hightower Rd. NW
Atlanta, GA 30311
(404)691-7455
Ultimate Parent: Pepsico.

★ 64579 ★ Kentucky Fried
Chicken
15 Georgia Ave. SE
Atlanta, GA 30312
(404)223-5028
Ultimate Parent: Pepsico.

★ 64580 ★ Kentucky Fried
Chicken
2354 Glenwood Ave. SE
Atlanta, GA 30317
(404)373-7469
Ultimate Parent: Pepsico.

★ 64581 ★ Kentucky Fried
Chicken
1437 Campbellton Rd. SW
Atlanta, GA 30311
(404)755-4313
Ultimate Parent: Pepsico.

★ 64582 ★ Kentucky Fried
Chicken
2637 Cobb Pky. NW
Atlanta, GA 30339
(404)850-0940
Ultimate Parent: Pepsico.

★ 64583 ★ Kentucky Fried
Chicken
1660 Bankhead Hwy. NW
Atlanta, GA 30318
(404)794-1605
Ultimate Parent: Pepsico.

★ 64584 ★ Kentucky Fried
Chicken
3901 Buford Hwy. NE
Atlanta, GA 30329
(404)634-8416
Ultimate Parent: Pepsico.

★ 64585 ★ Kentucky Fried
Chicken
23 Ashby St. SW
Atlanta, GA 30314
(404)753-2033
Ultimate Parent: Pepsico.

★ 64586 ★ Kentucky Fried
Chicken
3604 Bakers Ferry Rd. SW
Atlanta, GA 30331
(404)696-3186
Ultimate Parent: Pepsico.

★ 64587 ★ Kentucky Fried
Chicken
Atlanta, GA
(404)427-4291
Ultimate Parent: Pepsico.

★ 64588 ★ Kmart Stores
2581 Piedmont Rd. NE
Atlanta, GA 30324
(404)261-6900
Ultimate Parent: K-Mart.

★ 64589 ★ Kmart Stores
2975 Headland Dr. SW
Atlanta, GA 30311
(404)349-4810
Ultimate Parent: K-Mart.

★ 64590 ★ Kmart Stores
5925 Old National Hwy.
Atlanta, GA 30349
(404)996-2922
Ultimate Parent: K-Mart.

★ 64591 ★ Kmart Stores
2176 Bankhead Ave. NW
Atlanta, GA 30318
(404)799-1771
Ultimate Parent: K-Mart.

★ 64592 ★ Kmart Stores
2901 Clairmont Rd. NE
Atlanta, GA 30329
(404)634-1526
Ultimate Parent: K-Mart.

★ 64593 ★ Kmart Stores
Automotive
2975 Headland Dr. SW
Atlanta, GA 30311
(404)344-3312
Ultimate Parent: K-Mart.

★ 64594 ★ Kmart Stores
Automotive
2581 Piedmont Rd. NE
Atlanta, GA 30324
(404)261-5390
Ultimate Parent: K-Mart.

★ 64595 ★ Kmart Stores
Automotive
2901 Clairmont Rd. NE
Atlanta, GA 30329
(404)633-5212
Ultimate Parent: K-Mart.

★ 64596 ★ Kmart Stores
Pharmacy
2975 Headland Dr. SW
Atlanta, GA 30311
(404)349-1376
Ultimate Parent: K-Mart.

★ 64597 ★ Kmart Stores
Pharmacy
230 Cleveland Ave. SW
Atlanta, GA 30315
(404)767-2686
Ultimate Parent: K-Mart.

★ 64598 ★ Kroger Co. the Alt
Executive of
2175 Parklake Dr. NE
Atlanta, GA
(404)496-7493
Ultimate Parent: Kroger.

★ 64599 ★ Kroger Co. the
Altanta Executiv
2175 Parklake Dr. NE
Atlanta, GA
(404)496-7514
Ultimate Parent: Kroger.

★ 64600 ★ Kroger Co. the Atl
Executive of
2175 Parklake Dr. NE
Atlanta, GA
(404)496-7410
Ultimate Parent: Kroger.

★ 64601 ★ Kroger Co. the
Atlanta Executiv
2175 Parklake Dr. NE
Atlanta, GA
(404)496-7454
Ultimate Parent: Kroger.

★ 64602 ★ Kroger Co. the Kroger
Pharmacie
6650 Rosell Rd. NW
Atlanta, GA
(404)256-2779
Ultimate Parent: Kroger.

★ 64603 ★ Kroger Co. the
Lakewood Freezer
3300 Lakewood Ave. SW
Atlanta, GA 30310
(404)758-0636
Ultimate Parent: Kroger.

★ 64604 ★ Kroger Co. the Retail
Sotres
3855 Buford Hwy. NE
Atlanta, GA 30329
(404)633-6220
Ultimate Parent: Kroger.

★ 64605 ★ Kroger Co. the Retail
Stores
6650 Roswell Rd. NE
Atlanta, GA 30328
(404)256-3434
Ultimate Parent: Kroger.

★ 64606 ★ Kroger Co. the Retail
Stores
2685 Stewart Ave. SW
Atlanta, GA 30315
(404)761-7409
Ultimate Parent: Kroger.

★ 64607 ★ Kroger Co. the Retail
Stores
3330 Piedmont Rd. NE
Atlanta, GA 30305
(404)237-8022
Ultimate Parent: Kroger.

★ 64608 ★ Kroger Co. the Retail
Stores
725 Ponce De Leon Ave. NE
Atlanta, GA 30306
(404)875-2701
Ultimate Parent: Kroger.

★ 64609 ★ Kroger Co. the Retail
Stores
1700 Monroe Dr. NE
Atlanta, GA 30324
(404)872-0782
Ultimate Parent: Kroger.

★ 64610 ★ Kroger Co. the Retail
Stores
1455 Moreland Ave. SE
Atlanta, GA 30316
(404)622-4456
Ultimate Parent: Kroger.

★ 64611 ★ Kroger Co. the Retail
Stores
1715 Howell Mill Rd. NW
Atlanta, GA 30318
(404)355-7886
Ultimate Parent: Kroger.

★ 64612 ★ Kroger Co. the Retail
Stores
2205 Lavista Rd. NE
Atlanta, GA 30329
(404)633-8694
Ultimate Parent: Kroger.

★ 64613 ★ Kroger Co. the Retail
Stores
590 Cascade Ave. SW
Atlanta, GA 30310
(404)755-8937
Ultimate Parent: Kroger.

★ 64614 ★ Kroger Co. the Retail
Stores
3030 Headland Dr. SW
Atlanta, GA 30311
(404)344-7802
Ultimate Parent: Kroger.

★ 64615 ★ Kroger Cot the Atl
Executive O
2175 Parklake Dr. NE
Atlanta, GA
(404)762-1212
Ultimate Parent: Kroger.

★ 64616 ★ Kroger Pharamacies
3330 Piedmont Rd. NE
Atlanta, GA 30305
(404)233-9484
Ultimate Parent: Kroger.

★ 64617 ★ Kroger Pharmacies
3455 Peachtree Industrial
Atlanta, GA
(404)476-7985
Ultimate Parent: Kroger.

★ 64618 ★ Kroger Pharmacies
1700 Monroe Dr. NE
Atlanta, GA 30324
(404)872-0785
Ultimate Parent: Kroger.

★ 64619 ★ Kroger Pharmacies
1455 Moreland Ave. SE
Atlanta, GA 30316
(404)622-4496
Ultimate Parent: Kroger.

★ 64620 ★ Kroger Pharmacies
1715 Howell Mill Rd. NW
Atlanta, GA 30318
(404)355-7889
Ultimate Parent: Kroger.

★ 64621 ★ Kroger Pharmacies
2205 Lavista Rd. NE
Atlanta, GA 30329
(404)633-4201
Ultimate Parent: Kroger.

★ 64622 ★ Kroger Pharmacies
3855 Buford Hwy. NE
Atlanta, GA 30329
(404)325-5292
Ultimate Parent: Kroger.

★ 64623 ★ Kroger Pharmacies
590 Casade Rd. SW
Atlanta, GA
(404)758-4644
Ultimate Parent: Kroger.

★ 64624 ★ Kroger Vo the Atlanta
Executiv
2175 Parklake Dr. NE
Atlanta, GA
(404)496-7431
Ultimate Parent: Kroger.

★ 64625 ★ Kroger's Co. the
Retail Stores
4920 Roswell Rd. NE
Atlanta, GA 30342
(404)843-3080
Ultimate Parent: Kroger.

★ 64626 ★ Krogers Pharmacy
Kroger Co. the
4920 Roswell Rd. NE
Atlanta, GA 30342
(404)843-3225
Ultimate Parent: Kroger. SIC: 5122—
Drugs, Proprietaries & Sundries.

★ 64627 ★ Lane Bryant
Town Ctr. Mall
Atlanta, GA
(404)422-8805
Ultimate Parent: Limited.

★ 64628 ★ Lane Bryant
218 Peachtree St. NW
Atlanta, GA 30303
(404)681-3434
Ultimate Parent: Limited.

★ 64629 ★ Lane Bryant
Perimeter Mall
Atlanta, GA
(404)551-9671
Ultimate Parent: Limited.

★ 64630 ★ Lane Bryant
Greenbriar Mall
Atlanta, GA
(404)344-8840
Ultimate Parent: Limited.

★ 64631 ★ Lane Bryant
Northlake Mall
Atlanta, GA 30345
(404)934-1216
Ultimate Parent: Limited.

★ 64632 ★ Lane Bryant
1426 Cumberland Mall NW
Atlanta, GA
(404)434-1117
Ultimate Parent: Limited.

★ 64633 ★ Lanier
International Operations
2300 Parklake Dr. NE
Atlanta, GA 30345
(404)496-9500 Fax: (404)493-2388
Company Type: Subsidiary. Officer: David
J. Marini, Executive Vice President &
General Manager. Ultimate Parent: Harris.

★ 64634 ★ Lanier Worldwide Inc.
2300 Parklane Dr. NE
Atlanta, GA 30345
(404)496-9500 Fax: (404)493-2388
Company Type: Subsidiary. Officer:
Wesley E. Cantrell, President & CEO.
Ultimate Parent: Harris.

★ 64635 ★ Lasalle National Bank
5901-B Peachtree Dun
Atlanta, GA
(404)394-0600
Ultimate Parent: LaSalle National Corp.

★ 64636 ★ Leggett & Platt Inc.
Masterack Div.
905 Memorial Dr. SE
Atlanta, GA 30316
Company Type: Division. Ultimate Parent:
Leggett & Platt Inc. SIC: 2542—Partitions &
Fixtures Except Wood.

★ 64637 ★ Leggett & Platt Inc.
Masterack Div.
905 Memorial Dr. SE
Atlanta, GA 30316
Company Type: Division. Ultimate Parent:
Leggett & Platt Inc. SIC: 2542—Partitions &
Fixtures Except Wood.

★ 64638 ★ Leggett & Platt Inc.
Masterack Div.
905 Memorail Drive, SE
Atlanta, GA 30316
Ultimate Parent: Leggett & Platt Inc. SIC:
2542—Partitions & Fixtures Except Wood.

★ 64639 ★ Lehman Brothers
3414 Peachtree Rd. NE
Atlanta, GA 30326
(404)262-4800
Ultimate Parent: American Express Co.

★ 64640 ★ Lehman Brothers
200 Monarch Plaza
Atlanta, GA 30326
(404)262-4842
Ultimate Parent: American Express Co.

★ 64641 ★ Lens Crafters
128 Lenox Way NE
Atlanta, GA 30324
(404)239-0784
Ultimate Parent: United States Shoe.

★ 64642 ★ Lens Crafters
Gwinnett Pl
Atlanta, GA 30336
(404)623-9137
Ultimate Parent: United States Shoe.

★ 64643 ★ Lerner Shop
Greenbriar Mall
Atlanta, GA 30331
(404)344-1668
Ultimate Parent: Limited.

★ 64644 ★ Lerner Shop
62 Peachtree St. SW
Atlanta, GA 30303
(404)522-6728
Ultimate Parent: Limited.

★ 64645 ★ Lerner Shop
1437 Cumberland Mall NW
Atlanta, GA
(404)432-2874
Ultimate Parent: Limited.

★ 64646 ★ Lerner Shop
Northlake Mall
Atlanta, GA
(404)493-1970
Ultimate Parent: Limited.

★ 64647 ★ The Limited
3393 Peachtree Rd. NE
Atlanta, GA 30326
(404)237-8504
Ultimate Parent: Limited.

★ 64648 ★ The Limited
4400 Ashford Dunwoody Rd.
Atlanta, GA 30346
(404)399-1880
Ultimate Parent: Limited.

★ 64649 ★ The Limited
Northlake Mall
Atlanta, GA
(404)908-2332
Ultimate Parent: Limited.

★ 64650 ★ The Limited
Peachtree St. NE
Atlanta, GA 30303
(404)523-1728
Ultimate Parent: Limited.

★ 64651 ★   The Limited
Perimeter Mall
Atlanta, GA
(404)394-4780
Ultimate Parent: Limited.

★ 64652 ★   The Limited
Lenox Square
Atlanta, GA
(404)262-1626
Ultimate Parent: Limited.

★ 64653 ★   The Limited
Market Square
Atlanta, GA
(404)633-1976
Ultimate Parent: Limited.

★ 64654 ★   The Limited
Cumberland Mall
Atlanta, GA
(404)435-2201
Ultimate Parent: Limited.

★ 64655 ★   The Limited Express
1515 Northlake Mall NE No
Atlanta, GA 30345
(404)493-6803
Ultimate Parent: Limited.

★ 64656 ★   The Limited Express
Lenox Square
Atlanta, GA
(404)233-1226
Ultimate Parent: Limited.

★ 64657 ★   The Limited Express
50 Lower Alabama St. SW
Atlanta, GA 30303
(404)681-1685
Ultimate Parent: Limited.

★ 64658 ★   The Limited Express
1141 Cumberland Mall NW
Atlanta, GA
(404)438-0332
Ultimate Parent: Limited.

★ 64659 ★   The Limited Express
4400 Ashford Dunwoody Rd.
Atlanta, GA 30346
(404)399-7722
Ultimate Parent: Limited.

★ 64660 ★   The Limited Regional
Office
4400 Ashford Dunwoody Rd.
Atlanta, GA 30346
(404)396-1052
Ultimate Parent: Limited.

★ 64661 ★   Linens 'n Things
Sandy Springs
6125 Roswell Rd. NE
Atlanta, GA 30328
(404)843-1115
Ultimate Parent: Melville.

★ 64662 ★   Liz Claiborne Inc.
250 Spring St. NW
Atlanta, GA 30303
(404)880-9850
Ultimate Parent: Liz Claiborne.

★ 64663 ★   Lockheed-Latin
America
2401 Lake Park Dr., Ste. 265
Atlanta, GA 30080
(404)916-2535 **Fax:** (404)916-2588 **Telex:**
797847
Company Type: Subsidiary. **Ultimate Parent:** Lockheed Corp.

★ 64664 ★   Loral Information
Display Systems
6765 Peachtree Industrial Blvd.
Atlanta, GA 30360
(404)448-1604 **Fax:** (404)448-9163
Company Type: Division. **Ultimate Parent:**
Loral Corp. **SIC:** 3674—Semiconductors &
Related Devices.

★ 64665 ★   Lsi Logic
4 Concourse Pkwy NE
Atlanta, GA 30328
(404)395-3800
Ultimate Parent: LSI Logic Corp.

★ 64666 ★   Macy's
Snapfinger Distribution
Atlanta, GA 30335
(404)987-6100
Company Type: Branch. **Ultimate Parent:**
R. H. Macy. **SIC:** 5311—Department Stores.

★ 64667 ★   Macy's
Northlake Mall
Atlanta, GA 30345
(404)491-2985
Company Type: Branch. **Officer:** Mitzi
Wood. **Ultimate Parent:** R. H. Macy. **SIC:**
5311—Department Stores.

★ 64668 ★   Macy's
Lenox Sq.
Atlanta, GA 30326
(404)231-8985
Company Type: Branch. **Ultimate Parent:**
R. H. Macy. **SIC:** 5311—Department Stores.

★ 64669 ★   Manville Corp.
Packaging Div.
100 Cumberland Circle
Atlanta, GA 30339
(404)916-7955
Company Type: Division. **Officer:** Gary
Pichon, Executive Vice President -
Converting. **Ultimate Parent:** Manville Corp.
SIC: 2621—Paper Mills; 2671—Paper
Coated & Laminated—Packaging.

★ 64670 ★   Marriott Hotels,
Resorts Suites
6120 Peachtree
Atlanta, GA 30328
(404)668-0808
Ultimate Parent: Marriott International.

★ 64671 ★   Marriott Hotels,
Resorts Suites
246 Perimeter Ctr. Pky.
Atlanta, GA 30346
(404)394-6500
Ultimate Parent: Marriott International.

★ 64672 ★   Marriott Hotels,
Resorts Suites
35 14th St. NW
Atlanta, GA 30309
(404)876-8888
Ultimate Parent: Marriott International.

★ 64673 ★   Marriott Hotels,
Resorts Suites
3300 Lenox Rd. NE
Atlanta, GA 30326
(404)262-3344
Ultimate Parent: Marriott International.

★ 64674 ★   Marriott Hotels,
Resorts Suites
265 Peachtree Ctr. Ave.
Atlanta, GA 30303
(404)521-0000
Ultimate Parent: Marriott International.

★ 64675 ★   Marriott Management
Services
380 Interstate North Pky.
Atlanta, GA 30339
(404)859-0081
Ultimate Parent: Marriott International.

★ 64676 ★   Marshalls
East Lake Shopping C
Atlanta, GA
(404)971-2604
Ultimate Parent: Melville.

★ 64677 ★   Marshalls
Buckhead Crossing
Atlanta, GA
(404)233-3848
Ultimate Parent: Melville.

★ 64678 ★   Martin Marietta
Aggregates
Cumming St. SE
Atlanta, GA 30316
(404)887-6711
Ultimate Parent: Martin Marietta.

★ 64679 ★   Mary Kay Cosmetics
Indep Sales
67 Clifton St. SE
Atlanta, GA 30317
(404)378-0075
Ultimate Parent: Mary Kay Cosmetics.

★ 64680 ★   Mary Kay Cosmetics
Indep Sales
2010 Eldorado Dr. NE
Atlanta, GA 30345
(404)325-8670
Ultimate Parent: Mary Kay Cosmetics.

★ 64681 ★   Mary Kay Cosmetics
Indep Sales
2962 Parc Lorraine Cir.
Atlanta, GA
(404)981-0913
Ultimate Parent: Mary Kay Cosmetics.

★ 64682 ★   Mary Kay Cosmetics
Indep Sales
1073 Mill Creek Manor NE
Atlanta, GA 30319
(404)252-7780
Ultimate Parent: Mary Kay Cosmetics.

★ 64683 ★   Mary Kay Cosmetics
Indep Sales
125 Cannon Gate Cir. S
Atlanta, GA
(404)463-1926
Ultimate Parent: Mary Kay Cosmetics.

★ 64684 ★   Massachusetts Mutual
Life Insurance
1050 Crown Pointe Pky. NE
Atlanta, GA 30338
(404)804-8484
Ultimate Parent: Massasucetts Mutual Life.

★ 64685 ★   Massachusetts Mutual
Life Insurance
115 Perimeter Centers Pl.
Atlanta, GA 30346
(404)391-9300
Ultimate Parent: Massasucetts Mutual Life.

★ 64686 ★   Massachusetts Mutual
Life Insurance Co.
1100 Abernathy Rd. NE
Atlanta, GA 30328
(404)399-7773
Ultimate Parent: Massasucetts Mutual Life.

★ 64687 ★   Massachusetts Mutual
Life Insurance Co.
245 Peachtree Ctr. N
Atlanta, GA 30303
(404)658-9600
Ultimate Parent: Massasucetts Mutual Life.

★ 64688 ★   Masury-Columbia
Atlanta, GA
(404)594-2254
Ultimate Parent: IVAX.

★ 64689 ★   Matson Intermodal
Systems
465 Sawtell Ave. SE
Atlanta, GA 30315-5217
Ultimate Parent: Alexander & Baldwin Inc.
SIC: 4212—Local Trucking Without Storage.

★ 64690 ★   Maxtor Corp.
1000 Abernathy Rd. NE
Atlanta, GA 30328
(404)392-0584
Ultimate Parent: Maxtor.

★ 64691 ★   McDonald's Corp.
5901 Peachtree Dunwoody Rd.
Atlanta, GA 30328
(404)399-5067
Ultimate Parent: McDonald's.

★ 64692 ★   McDonald's Corp.
Atlanta, GA
(404)659-1071
Ultimate Parent: McDonald's.

★ 64693 ★   McDonald's
Restaurant
35 Forsyth St. SW
Atlanta, GA 30303
(404)524-8457
Ultimate Parent: McDonald's.

★ 64694 ★   McDonald's
Restaurants
4400 Ashford Dunwoody Rd.
Atlanta, GA 30346
(404)698-8865
Ultimate Parent: McDonald's.

★ 64695 ★   McDonald's
Restaurants
6049 Roswell Rd. NE
Atlanta, GA 30328
(404)252-1421
Ultimate Parent: McDonald's.

★ 64696 ★   McDonald's
Restaurants
2929 Peachtree Rd. NE
Atlanta, GA 30305
(404)365-9727
Ultimate Parent: McDonald's.

★ 64697 ★   McDonald's
Restaurants
2517 Piedmont Rd. NE
Atlanta, GA 30324
(404)262-9409
Ultimate Parent: McDonald's.

★ 64698 ★   McDonald's
Restaurants
3324 Nothside Pky. NW
Atlanta, GA
(404)262-2288
Ultimate Parent: McDonald's.

★ 64699 ★   McDonald's
Restaurants
Omni International
Atlanta, GA
(404)522-0907
Ultimate Parent: McDonald's.

★ 64700 ★   McDonald's
Restaurants
1105 Northside Dr. NW
Atlanta, GA 30318
(404)876-6766
Ultimate Parent: McDonald's.

★ 64701 ★   McDonald's
Restaurants
Northside Hospital
Atlanta, GA
(404)250-1504
Ultimate Parent: McDonald's.

★ 64702 ★   McDonald's
Restaurants
266 N. Dixie Ave. Cartersville
Atlanta, GA
(404)522-6931
Ultimate Parent: McDonald's.

★ 64703 ★   McDonald's
Restaurants
2210 N. Druid Hills Rd. NE
Atlanta, GA 30329
(404)321-5188
Ultimate Parent: McDonald's.

★ 64704 ★   McDonald's
Restaurants
912 Martin Luther King J
Atlanta, GA 30314
(404)756-9970
Ultimate Parent: McDonald's.

★ 64705 ★   McDonald's
Restaurants
3534 Martin Luther King J
Atlanta, GA 30331
(404)691-5533
Ultimate Parent: McDonald's.

★ 64706 ★   McDonald's
Restaurants
2588 Gresham Rd. SE
Atlanta, GA 30316
(404)243-1303
Ultimate Parent: McDonald's.

★ 64707 ★   McDonald's
Restaurants
Hwy. 92 & Mayberry St.
Atlanta, GA
(404)992-6117
Ultimate Parent: McDonald's.

★ 64708 ★   McDonald's
Restaurants
1824 Cheshire Bridge Rd. N
Atlanta, GA 30324
(404)872-9561
Ultimate Parent: McDonald's.

★ 64709 ★   McDonald's
Restaurants
1166 Gordon St. SW
Atlanta, GA 30310
(404)755-4489
Ultimate Parent: McDonald's.

★ 64710 ★   McDonald's
Restaurants
4010 Peachtree Rd. NE
Atlanta, GA
(404)364-0006
Ultimate Parent: McDonald's.

★ 64711 ★   McDonald's
Restaurants
35 Butler St. SE
Atlanta, GA 30303
(404)688-3255
Ultimate Parent: McDonald's.

★ 64712 ★ McDonald's
Restaurants
1260 Cumberland Mall NW
Atlanta, GA
(404)436-2598
Ultimate Parent: McDonald's.

★ 64713 ★ McDonald's
Restaurants
1994 Howell Mill Rd. NW
Atlanta, GA
(404)350-9351
Ultimate Parent: McDonald's.

★ 64714 ★ McDonald's
Restaurants
2707 Bankhead Hwy. NW
Atlanta, GA 30318
(404)799-3631
Ultimate Parent: McDonald's.

★ 64715 ★ McDonald's
Restaurants
80 Butler St. NE
Atlanta, GA 30303
(404)577-8244
Ultimate Parent: McDonald's.

★ 64716 ★ McDonald's
Restaurants Regional
5901 Peachtree Dunwoody R
Atlanta, GA 30328
(404)399-5067
Ultimate Parent: McDonald's.

★ 64717 ★ MCI Business
Services
MCI Ctr., 3 Ravinia Dr.
Atlanta, GA 30346-2102
(404)668-6000 Fax: (404)668-6475
Officer: Timothy F. Price, President.
Ultimate Parent: MCI Communications.

★ 64718 ★ Mead
Coated Board Div.
950 E. Paces Ferry Rd., Ste. 2075
Atlanta, GA 30326
(404)262-7770 Fax: (404)239-6486
Officer: P. Carter Smith, President.
Ultimate Parent: Mead.

★ 64719 ★ Mead
Packaging Div. Atlanta Plant
1105 Herndon St. NW
Atlanta, GA 30318
Company Type: Division. Location Type:
Plant. Ultimate Parent: Mead. SIC: 2679—
Converted Paper Products Nec.

★ 64720 ★ Mead
Packaging Div. Atlanta Plant
1105 Herndon Street, NW
Atlanta, GA 30318
Company Type: Division. Location Type:
Plant. Ultimate Parent: Mead. SIC: 2600—
Paper & Allied Products.

★ 64721 ★ Mead Containerboard
950 W. Marietta St., NW
Atlanta, GA 30318
(404)897-2100 Fax: (404)897-2124
Officer: Richard P. Rossetti, President.
Ultimate Parent: Mead.

★ 64722 ★ Mead Ink Products
949 Herndon St. NW
Atlanta, GA 30318
Ultimate Parent: Mead. SIC: 2393—Textile
Bags; 2893—Printing Ink; 2741—
Miscellaneous Publishing.

★ 64723 ★ Mead Packaging
1040 W. Marietta St., NW
Atlanta, GA 30318
(404)875-2711 Fax: (404)897-6383
Officer: Ian W. Millar, President. Ultimate
Parent: Mead.

★ 64724 ★ Merisel
4100 Westpark Dr. SW
Atlanta, GA 30336
(404)344-1400
Ultimate Parent: Merisel.

★ 64725 ★ Metlife Capitol Corp.
Fi
7000 Central Park Way NE
Atlanta, GA
(404)668-1009
Ultimate Parent: Metropolitan Life.

★ 64726 ★ Metromail Corp.
1100 Johnson Ferry Rd. NE
Atlanta, GA 30342
(404)252-4799
Ultimate Parent: R. R. Donnelley & Sons.

★ 64727 ★ Microsoft Corp.,
Consulting Service
Atlanta, GA
(404)392-7575
Ultimate Parent: Microsoft.

★ 64728 ★ Microsoft Corp.,
Education Service
Atlanta, GA
(404)392-7519
Ultimate Parent: Microsoft.

★ 64729 ★ Microsoft Corp., Sales
Atlanta, GA
(404)392-7400
Ultimate Parent: Microsoft.

★ 64730 ★ Midas-Internaional
Corp. Region
6151 Powers Ferry Rd. NW
Atlanta, GA 30339
(404)952-2011
Ultimate Parent: Whitman Corp.

★ 64731 ★ Mobil Oil
400 Interstate North Pky.
Atlanta, GA 30339
(404)980-4360
Ultimate Parent: Mobil.

★ 64732 ★ Monarch Industries
175 W. Wieuca Rd. NE
Atlanta, GA 30342-3254
(404)256-5969
Ultimate Parent: Avery Dennison Corp.
SIC: 7363—Help Supply Services.

★ 64733 ★ Monsanto Co.
320 Interstate N. Pky. Ste. 500
Atlanta, GA 30339-2201
(404)951-7600
Company Type: Branch. Officer: Pat
Cobb. Ultimate Parent: Monsanto. SIC:
5169—Chemicals & Allied Products Nec;
2899—Chemical Preparations Nec.

★ 64734 ★ Mrs Smith's Frozen
Foods
5601 Bucknell Dr. SW
Atlanta, GA 30336
(404)344-6065
Ultimate Parent: Kansas City South
Industries.

★ 64735 ★ Mrs. Smith's Frozen
Foods
5601 Bucknell Drive, SW
Atlanta, GA 30336
Ultimate Parent: Kellogg Co. SIC: 2053—
Frozen Bakery Products Except Bread.

★ 64736 ★ Mrs. Smith's Frozen
Foods Co.
5601 Bucknell Dr. SW
Atlanta, GA 30336
Ultimate Parent: Kellogg Co. SIC: 2053—
Frozen Bakery Products Except Bread.

★ 64737 ★ Mutual of New York/
Mony
5775-E Glenridge Dr.
Atlanta, GA
(404)256-5775
Ultimate Parent: Mutual of New York.

★ 64738 ★ Mutual of New York/
Mony Atlant
3343 Peachtree Rd. NE
Atlanta, GA 30326
(404)261-6669
Ultimate Parent: Mutual of New York.

★ 64739 ★ Mutual of New York/
Mony Region
3343 Peachtree Rd. NE
Atlanta, GA 30326
(404)262-9112
Ultimate Parent: Mutual of New York.

★ 64740 ★ Nabisco Brands Inc.
1400 Murphy Ave. SW
Atlanta, GA 30310
Ultimate Parent: RJR Nabisco Holdings.
SIC: 2052—Cookies & Crackers.

★ 64741 ★ Nabisco Foods Group
300 Galleria Pkwy NW
Atlanta, GA 30339
(404)850-3900
Ultimate Parent: Rite Aid.

★ 64742 ★ Nabisco Foods Group
300 Galleria Pkwy NW
Atlanta, GA 30339
(404)850-3900
Ultimate Parent: Rite Aid.

★ 64743 ★ Nabisco Foods Group
300 Galleria Pkwy NW
Atlanta, GA 30339
(404)850-3965
Ultimate Parent: Rite Aid.

★ 64744 ★ Nabisco Foods Group
Bakery
1400 Murphy Ave. SW
Atlanta, GA 30310
(404)756-6000
Ultimate Parent: Rite Aid.

★ 64745 ★ Nalco Chemical Co.
Water Division
5775 Glenridge Dr. NE
Atlanta, GA 30328
(404)252-3119
Ultimate Parent: Nalco Chemical Co.

★ 64746 ★ Nalco Chemical Co.
Unisolve
5775 Glenridge Dr. NE
Atlanta, GA 30328
(404)256-0210
Ultimate Parent: Nalco Chemical Co.

★ 64747 ★ Nalco Chemical Co.
Utility Chem
5775 Glenridge Dr. NE
Atlanta, GA 30328
(404)255-6461
Ultimate Parent: Nalco Chemical Co.

★ 64748 ★ National Chemsearch
1775 The Exchange NW
Atlanta, GA 30339
(404)952-1693
Ultimate Parent: NCH.

★ 64749 ★ National Linen
Service
1420 Peachtree St., NE
Atlanta, GA 30309
Fax: (404)853-6002
Officer: Gerald V. Gurbacki, President.
Ultimate Parent: National Service
Industries.

★ 64750 ★ National Service
Industries
1420 Peachtree St. NE
Atlanta, GA 30309
(404)853-1000
Company Type: Headquarters. Officer: D.
Raymond Riddle. Employee Count: 22200.
Sales: 1805 M. Fortune 500: Largest U.S.
Industrial Corporations: Ranking 241.

★ 64751 ★ National Service
Industries, Inc.
1420 Peachtree St., NE
Atlanta, GA 30309
(404)853-1000 Fax: (404)853-1001
Officer: D. Raymand Riddle, President &
CEO. Ultimate Parent: National Service
Industries. Employee Count: 22000.

★ 64752 ★ Nationsbank
222 Mitchell St. SW
Atlanta, GA 30303
(404)969-0550
Ultimate Parent: Nationsbank Corp.

★ 64753 ★ Nationsbank
Atlanta, GA
(404)607-5684
Ultimate Parent: Nationsbank Corp.

★ 64754 ★ Nationsbank
Atlanta, GA
(404)607-4940
Ultimate Parent: Nationsbank Corp.

★ 64755 ★ Nationsbank
Atlanta, GA
(404)581-3930
Ultimate Parent: Nationsbank Corp.

★ 64756 ★ Nationsbank
Atlanta, GA
(404)581-5008
Ultimate Parent: Nationsbank Corp.

★ 64757 ★ Nationsbank
Atlanta, GA
(404)491-4383
Ultimate Parent: Nationsbank Corp.

★ 64758 ★ Nationsbank
Atlanta, GA
(404)607-5662
Ultimate Parent: Nationsbank Corp.

★ 64759 ★ Nationsbank
222 Mitchell St. SW
Atlanta, GA 30303
(404)331-9905
Ultimate Parent: Nationsbank Corp.

★ 64760 ★ Nationsbank Acct
Activity Inf
South Expressway 380
Atlanta, GA 30340
(404)523-0900
Ultimate Parent: Nationsbank Corp.

★ 64761 ★ Nationsbank ATM Div.
Atlanta, GA
(404)584-0604
Ultimate Parent: Nationsbank Corp.

★ 64762 ★ Nationsbank Atm
Honor-Cirrus L
5442 Peachtree Rd.
Atlanta, GA 30341
(404)452-2270
Ultimate Parent: Nationsbank Corp.

★ 64763 ★ Nationsbank Atm
Honor-Cirrus L
2818 East Point St.
Atlanta, GA 30344
(404)765-1966
Ultimate Parent: Nationsbank Corp.

★ 64764 ★ Nationsbank Atm
Honor-Cirrus L
400 Ernest Barnest Barre
Atlanta, GA
(404)423-5177
Ultimate Parent: Nationsbank Corp.

★ 64765 ★ Nationsbank Atm
Honor-Cirrus L
4050 Buford Hwy.
Atlanta, GA 30345
(404)581-2121
Ultimate Parent: Nationsbank Corp.

★ 64766 ★ Nationsbank Atm
Honor-Cirrus L
2035 Campbellton Rd.
Atlanta, GA 30311
(404)752-0673
Ultimate Parent: Nationsbank Corp.

★ 64767 ★ Nationsbank Check
Verification
Atlanta, GA
(404)969-1305
Ultimate Parent: Nationsbank Corp.

★ 64768 ★ Nationsbank Check
Verification
Atlanta, GA
(404)969-0550
Ultimate Parent: Nationsbank Corp.

★ 64769 ★ Nationsbank
Commercial Account Information
Atlanta, GA
(404)969-1305
Ultimate Parent: Nationsbank Corp.

★ 64770 ★ Nationsbank
Corporate Customer Office
Atlanta, GA
(404)969-0348
Ultimate Parent: Nationsbank Corp.

★ 64771 ★ Nationsbank
Departments
Nationsbank Plz.
Atlanta, GA
(404)607-6100
Ultimate Parent: Nationsbank Corp.

★ 64772 ★ Nationsbank
Departments Atm in
3057 Hargrove Rd.
Atlanta, GA 30339
(404)953-5661
Ultimate Parent: Nationsbank Corp.

★ 64773 ★　Nationsbank
Departments Atm in
222 Mitchell St. SW
Atlanta, GA 30303
(404)607-2918
Ultimate Parent: Nationsbank Corp.

★ 64774 ★　Nationsbank
Departments Non-Pr
600 Ptree St.
Atlanta, GA
(404)607-5860
Ultimate Parent: Nationsbank Corp.

★ 64775 ★　Nationsbank
Departments Person
715 Peachtree St.
Atlanta, GA
(404)607-3401
Ultimate Parent: Nationsbank Corp.

★ 64776 ★　Nationsbank
Departments Privat
600 Ptree St.
Atlanta, GA
(404)607-5175
Ultimate Parent: Nationsbank Corp.

★ 64777 ★　Nationsbank
Departments Prof&E
1 Perimeter Ctr.E
Atlanta, GA 30346
(404)392-2950
Ultimate Parent: Nationsbank Corp.

★ 64778 ★　Nationsbank
Departments Prof&E
14 Piedmont Ctr.
Atlanta, GA 30305
(404)264-2840
Ultimate Parent: Nationsbank Corp.

★ 64779 ★　Nationsbank
Departments Prof&E
225 Peachtree St.
Atlanta, GA
(404)332-2703
Ultimate Parent: Nationsbank Corp.

★ 64780 ★　Nationsbank
Departments Real E
Windy Hill
Atlanta, GA
(404)953-5620
Ultimate Parent: Nationsbank Corp.

★ 64781 ★　Nationsbank
Departments Real E
Northeast Ctr.
Atlanta, GA
(404)491-4016
Ultimate Parent: Nationsbank Corp.

★ 64782 ★　Nationsbank Homnor-
Cirrus L Un
50 Upper Alabama St.
Atlanta, GA 30303
(404)581-2121
Ultimate Parent: Nationsbank Corp.

★ 64783 ★　Nationsbank Honor-
Ccirrus L Sn
2550 Odum St.
Atlanta, GA
(404)978-5980
Ultimate Parent: Nationsbank Corp.

★ 64784 ★　Nationsbank Honor-
Cirrus
1000 Southlake Mall
Atlanta, GA
(404)581-2121
Ultimate Parent: Nationsbank Corp.

★ 64785 ★　Nationsbank Honor-
Cirrus Fulto
4160 Fulton Industrial Blvd.
Atlanta, GA
(404)581-2121
Ultimate Parent: Nationsbank Corp.

★ 64786 ★　Nationsbank Honor-
Cirrus L
562 Lee St. SW
Atlanta, GA 30310
(404)752-0660
Ultimate Parent: Nationsbank Corp.

★ 64787 ★　Nationsbank Honor-
Cirrus L Hor
2800 Lawrence-Swanee Rd.
Atlanta, GA
(404)932-7140
Ultimate Parent: Nationsbank Corp.

★ 64788 ★　Nationsbank Honor-
Cirrus L How
1775 Howell Mill Rd.
Atlanta, GA 30318
(404)350-2038
Ultimate Parent: Nationsbank Corp.

★ 64789 ★　Nationsbank Honor-
Cirrus L Law
395 Grayson Hwy.
Atlanta, GA
(404)995-3165
Ultimate Parent: Nationsbank Corp.

★ 64790 ★　Nationsbank Honor-
Cirrus L Len
3393 Peachtree Rd. NE
Atlanta, GA 30326
(404)581-2121
Ultimate Parent: Nationsbank Corp.

★ 64791 ★　Nationsbank Honor-
Cirrus L Lil
494 Indian Trail Rd.
Atlanta, GA
(404)564-6760
Ultimate Parent: Nationsbank Corp.

★ 64792 ★　Nationsbank Honor-
Cirrus L Lin
2581 Piedmont Rd.
Atlanta, GA 30324
(404)264-2880
Ultimate Parent: Nationsbank Corp.

★ 64793 ★　Nationsbank Honor-
Cirrus L Lit
337 Moreland Ave.
Atlanta, GA
(404)332-2690
Ultimate Parent: Nationsbank Corp.

★ 64794 ★　Nationsbank Honor-
Cirrus L Mar
35 Broad St.
Atlanta, GA
(404)581-2009
Ultimate Parent: Nationsbank Corp.

★ 64795 ★　Nationsbank Honor-
Cirrus L Pea
2367 Ptree Rd. NE
Atlanta, GA 30305
(404)264-2860
Ultimate Parent: Nationsbank Corp.

★ 64796 ★　Nationsbank Honor-
Cirrus L Per
1 Perimeter Ctr.East
Atlanta, GA 30346
(404)392-2990
Ultimate Parent: Nationsbank Corp.

★ 64797 ★　Nationsbank Honor-
Cirrus L Pie
3565 Piedmont Rd. NE 11
Atlanta, GA
(404)264-2895
Ultimate Parent: Nationsbank Corp.

★ 64798 ★　Nationsbank Honor-
Cirrus L Pla
600 Peachtree St.
Atlanta, GA 30308
(404)607-4850
Ultimate Parent: Nationsbank Corp.

★ 64799 ★　Nationsbank Honor-
Cirrus L Pow
5640 Northside Dr.
Atlanta, GA
(404)581-2121
Ultimate Parent: Nationsbank Corp.

★ 64800 ★　Nationsbank Honor-
Cirrus L Ros
4492 Roswell Rd.
Atlanta, GA 30342
(404)256-7370
Ultimate Parent: Nationsbank Corp.

★ 64801 ★　Nationsbank Honor-
Cirrus L San
6075 Roswell Rd.
Atlanta, GA 30328
(404)256-7350
Ultimate Parent: Nationsbank Corp.

★ 64802 ★　Nationsbank Honor-
Cirrus L Smy
4567 S. Cobb Dr.
Atlanta, GA
(404)333-1690
Ultimate Parent: Nationsbank Corp.

★ 64803 ★　Nationsbank Honor-
Cirrus L Sou
1200 Morrow Industrial Blvd.
Atlanta, GA
(404)968-2000
Ultimate Parent: Nationsbank Corp.

★ 64804 ★　Nationsbank Honor-
Cirrus L Sto
5505 N. Henry Blvd.
Atlanta, GA
(404)389-2920
Ultimate Parent: Nationsbank Corp.

★ 64805 ★　Nationsbank Honor-
Cirrus L Toc
2963 N. Druid Hills Rd.
Atlanta, GA 30329
(404)329-4803
Ultimate Parent: Nationsbank Corp.

★ 64806 ★　Nationsbank Honor-
Cirrus L Twi
200 Piedmont Ave.
Atlanta, GA
(404)581-2121
Ultimate Parent: Nationsbank Corp.

★ 64807 ★　Nationsbank Honor-
Cirrus L Wes
1280 W. Paces Ferry Rd. NW
Atlanta, GA 30327
(404)264-2900
Ultimate Parent: Nationsbank Corp.

★ 64808 ★　Nationsbank Honor-
Cirrus Marke
2052 Lawrenceville Hwy.
Atlanta, GA
(404)329-4810
Ultimate Parent: Nationsbank Corp.

★ 64809 ★　Nationsbank Honor-
Cirrus Midto
715 Ptree St.
Atlanta, GA
(404)581-2121
Ultimate Parent: Nationsbank Corp.

★ 64810 ★　Nationsbank Honor-
Cirrus Mitch
206 Mitchell St.
Atlanta, GA 30303
(404)581-2464
Ultimate Parent: Nationsbank Corp.

★ 64811 ★　Nationsbank Honor-
Cirrus North
2059 Northlake Pkwy
Atlanta, GA
(404)581-2121
Ultimate Parent: Nationsbank Corp.

★ 64812 ★　Nationsbank Honor-
Cirrus Palis
1819 Ptree Rd. NE
Atlanta, GA 30309
(404)350-2029
Ultimate Parent: Nationsbank Corp.

★ 64813 ★　Nationsbank Honor-
Cirrus Peach
231 Peachtree St. NE
Atlanta, GA 30303
(404)332-2700
Ultimate Parent: Nationsbank Corp.

★ 64814 ★　Nationsbank Honor-
Cirrus Peach
500 Northlake Dr.
Atlanta, GA 30354
(404)631-3200
Ultimate Parent: Nationsbank Corp.

★ 64815 ★　Nationsbank Honor-
Cirrus Peach
3475 Peachtree Rd. NE
Atlanta, GA 30326
(404)264-2870
Ultimate Parent: Nationsbank Corp.

★ 64816 ★　Nationsbank Honor-
Cirrus Perim
4400 Ashford Dunwoody Rd.
Atlanta, GA 30346
(404)581-2121
Ultimate Parent: Nationsbank Corp.

★ 64817 ★　Nationsbank Honor-
Cirrus Power
1920 Powers Fry Rd.
Atlanta, GA 30339
(404)953-5630
Ultimate Parent: Nationsbank Corp.

★ 64818 ★　Nationsbank Honor-
Cirrus River
6656 Church St.
Atlanta, GA
(404)581-2121
Ultimate Parent: Nationsbank Corp.

★ 64819 ★　Nationsbank Honor-
Cirrus Russe
75 Spring St. SW
Atlanta, GA
(404)581-2121
Ultimate Parent: Nationsbank Corp.

★ 64820 ★　Nationsbank Honor-
Cirrus Shall
3182 Johnson Fwy Rd.
Atlanta, GA
(404)594-3466
Ultimate Parent: Nationsbank Corp.

★ 64821 ★　Nationsbank Honor-
Cirrus South
3800 Browns Mill Rd. SE
Atlanta, GA 30354
(404)765-1940
Ultimate Parent: Nationsbank Corp.

★ 64822 ★　Nationsbank Honor-
Cirrus Spelm
350 Spelman Ln. Manley Ct
Atlanta, GA
(404)581-2121
Ultimate Parent: Nationsbank Corp.

★ 64823 ★　Nationsbank Honor-
Cirrus Tenth
1088 Ptree St. NE
Atlanta, GA 30309
(404)870-3040
Ultimate Parent: Nationsbank Corp.

★ 64824 ★　Nationsbank Honor-
Cirrus Tri-C
2225 Jonesboro Rd.
Atlanta, GA 30315
(404)991-7760
Ultimate Parent: Nationsbank Corp.

★ 64825 ★　Nationsbank Honor-
Crrus Mablet
4901 Floyd Rd.
Atlanta, GA
(404)944-4090
Ultimate Parent: Nationsbank Corp.

★ 64826 ★　Nationsbank
Honorcirrus Pharr
340 Pharr Rd.
Atlanta, GA 30305
(404)264-2800
Ultimate Parent: Nationsbank Corp.

★ 64827 ★　Nationsbank Honr-
Cirrus L Shan
6737 Londonderry Way
Atlanta, GA
(404)969-3790
Ultimate Parent: Nationsbank Corp.

★ 64828 ★　Nationsbank Instant
Check Information
Atlanta, GA
(404)331-8534
Ultimate Parent: Nationsbank Corp.

★ 64829 ★　Nationsbank Instant
Check Information Div.
Atlanta, GA
(404)584-0604
Ultimate Parent: Nationsbank Corp.

★ 64830 ★　Nationsbank
International Banking Dept.
Atlanta, GA
(404)607-2204
Ultimate Parent: Nationsbank Corp.

★ 64831 ★　Nationsbank
International Banking Departments
Atlanta, GA
(404)607-5152
Ultimate Parent: Nationsbank Corp.

★ 64832 ★　Nationsbank
International Banking Departments
Atlanta, GA
(404)607-5279
Ultimate Parent: Nationsbank Corp.

★ 64833 ★ Nationsbank
Marketing Departments
Atlanta, GA
(404)607-4374
Ultimate Parent: Nationsbank Corp.

★ 64834 ★ Nationsbank Ofc
Atlana Area Co.
Conyers 1887 Ga Hwy.
Atlanta, GA
(404)523-0900
Ultimate Parent: Nationsbank Corp.

★ 64835 ★ Nationsbank Ofc
Atlanta Area
Decatur Towncenter 1
Atlanta, GA
(404)523-0900
Ultimate Parent: Nationsbank Corp.

★ 64836 ★ Nationsbank Ofc
Atlanta Area
Dunwoody 2454
Atlanta, GA 30338
(404)523-0900
Ultimate Parent: Nationsbank Corp.

★ 64837 ★ Nationsbank Ofc
Atlanta Area
Cumberland 3057 Harg
Atlanta, GA
(404)523-0900
Ultimate Parent: Nationsbank Corp.

★ 64838 ★ Nationsbank Ofc
Atlanta Area
Dunwoody 2454
Atlanta, GA 30338
(404)969-0550
Ultimate Parent: Nationsbank Corp.

★ 64839 ★ Nationsbank Ofc
Atlanta Area
Decatur Towncenter 1
Atlanta, GA
(404)969-0550
Ultimate Parent: Nationsbank Corp.

★ 64840 ★ Nationsbank Ofc
Atlanta Area
Douglasville 6559 E
Atlanta, GA
(404)969-0550
Ultimate Parent: Nationsbank Corp.

★ 64841 ★ Nationsbank Ofc
Atlanta Area
Concourse 2
Atlanta, GA
(404)392-2960
Ultimate Parent: Nationsbank Corp.

★ 64842 ★ Nationsbank Ofc
Atlanta Area
Cumberland 3057 Harg
Atlanta, GA
(404)969-0550
Ultimate Parent: Nationsbank Corp.

★ 64843 ★ Nationsbank Ofc
Atlanta Area
Dunwoody 2454
Atlanta, GA 30338
(404)392-2972
Ultimate Parent: Nationsbank Corp.

★ 64844 ★ Nationsbank Ofc
Atlanta Area
Dunwoody 2454
Atlanta, GA 30338
(404)392-2970
Ultimate Parent: Nationsbank Corp.

★ 64845 ★ Nationsbank Ofc
Atlanta Area
Decatur Towncenter 1
Atlanta, GA
(404)371-6932
Ultimate Parent: Nationsbank Corp.

★ 64846 ★ Nationsbank Ofcs
Alanta Area
Buford Mall 4394 Ga
Atlanta, GA
(404)523-0900
Ultimate Parent: Nationsbank Corp.

★ 64847 ★ Nationsbank Ofcs Atl
Acc Activ
Atlantic Ctr. 1201
Atlanta, GA
(404)523-0900
Ultimate Parent: Nationsbank Corp.

★ 64848 ★ Nationsbank Ofcs
Atla Area Acc
Ansley Mall 1674 Mon
Atlanta, GA
(404)523-0900
Ultimate Parent: Nationsbank Corp.

★ 64849 ★ Nationsbank Ofcs
Atla T Area L
Ansley Mall 1674 Mon
Atlanta, GA
(404)870-3032
Ultimate Parent: Nationsbank Corp.

★ 64850 ★ Nationsbank Ofcs
Atlanta Acc
Austell 2765 Mosley
Atlanta, GA
(404)523-0900
Ultimate Parent: Nationsbank Corp.

★ 64851 ★ Nationsbank Ofcs
Atlanta Area
Marietta Street 35 B
Atlanta, GA 30303
(404)581-2121
Ultimate Parent: Nationsbank Corp.

★ 64852 ★ Nationsbank Ofcs
Atlanta Area
2358 Cascade Ave. SW
Atlanta, GA 30311
(404)752-0668
Ultimate Parent: Nationsbank Corp.

★ 64853 ★ Nationsbank Ofcs
Atlanta Area
Chamblee Plaza 5442
Atlanta, GA
(404)969-0550
Ultimate Parent: Nationsbank Corp.

★ 64854 ★ Nationsbank Ofcs
Atlanta Area
Campbellton Road 203
Atlanta, GA
(404)969-0550
Ultimate Parent: Nationsbank Corp.

★ 64855 ★ Nationsbank Ofcs
Atlanta Area
Buford Mall 4394 Ga
Atlanta, GA
(404)969-0550
Ultimate Parent: Nationsbank Corp.

★ 64856 ★ Nationsbank Ofcs
Atlanta Area
3005 Peachtree
Atlanta, GA
(404)264-2838
Ultimate Parent: Nationsbank Corp.

★ 64857 ★ Nationsbank Ofcs
Atlanta Area
3005 Peachtree
Atlanta, GA
(404)523-0900
Ultimate Parent: Nationsbank Corp.

★ 64858 ★ Nationsbank Ofcs
Atlanta Area
Buckhead 3005 Ptree
Atlanta, GA 30305
(404)264-2800
Ultimate Parent: Nationsbank Corp.

★ 64859 ★ Nationsbank Ofcs
Atlanta Area
Austell 2765 Mosley
Atlanta, GA
(404)969-0550
Ultimate Parent: Nationsbank Corp.

★ 64860 ★ Nationsbank Ofcs
Atlanta Area
2050 Bankhead
Atlanta, GA
(404)969-0550
Ultimate Parent: Nationsbank Corp.

★ 64861 ★ Nationsbank Ofcs
Atlanta Area
Atlanta Plaza 950 E
Atlanta, GA
(404)523-0900
Ultimate Parent: Nationsbank Corp.

★ 64862 ★ Nationsbank Ofcs
Atlanta Area
Atlantic Ctr. 1201
Atlanta, GA
(404)969-0550
Ultimate Parent: Nationsbank Corp.

★ 64863 ★ Nationsbank Ofcs
Atlanta Area
Ansley Mall 1674 Mon
Atlanta, GA
(404)870-3030
Ultimate Parent: Nationsbank Corp.

★ 64864 ★ Nationsbank Ofcs
Atlanta Area
Ansley Mall 1674 Mon
Atlanta, GA
(404)969-0550
Ultimate Parent: Nationsbank Corp.

★ 64865 ★ Nationsbank Ofcs
Atlnta Area
Atlanta Plaza 950 E
Atlanta, GA
(404)969-0550
Ultimate Parent: Nationsbank Corp.

★ 64866 ★ Nationsbank Officces
Atlanta
Lindbergh Plaza 2581
Atlanta, GA
(404)264-2884
Ultimate Parent: Nationsbank Corp.

★ 64867 ★ Nationsbank Officces
Atlanta
1000 Abernathy Rd. NE
Atlanta, GA 30328
(404)392-2940
Ultimate Parent: Nationsbank Corp.

★ 64868 ★ Nationsbank Offices
Atlant
Chamblee Plaza 5442
Atlanta, GA
(404)452-2271
Ultimate Parent: Nationsbank Corp.

★ 64869 ★ Nationsbank Offices
Atlant
Lilburn 494 Indian T
Atlanta, GA
(404)969-0550
Ultimate Parent: Nationsbank Corp.

★ 64870 ★ Nationsbank Offices
Atlanta
Peachtree Ctr. 22
Atlanta, GA
(404)332-2702
Ultimate Parent: Nationsbank Corp.

★ 64871 ★ Nationsbank Offices
Atlanta
Marietta Square 121
Atlanta, GA
(404)523-0900
Ultimate Parent: Nationsbank Corp.

★ 64872 ★ Nationsbank Offices
Atlanta
West Paces Ferry 128
Atlanta, GA
(404)969-0550
Ultimate Parent: Nationsbank Corp.

★ 64873 ★ Nationsbank Offices
Atlanta
Toco Hills 2963 N. Dr.
Atlanta, GA
(404)969-0550
Ultimate Parent: Nationsbank Corp.

★ 64874 ★ Nationsbank Offices
Atlanta
West End 562 Lee St.
Atlanta, GA
(404)969-0550
Ultimate Parent: Nationsbank Corp.

★ 64875 ★ Nationsbank Offices
Atlanta
South Expressway 380
Atlanta, GA 30340
(404)765-1945
Ultimate Parent: Nationsbank Corp.

★ 64876 ★ Nationsbank Offices
Atlanta
Tenth Street 1088 Pe
Atlanta, GA
(404)870-3046
Ultimate Parent: Nationsbank Corp.

★ 64877 ★ Nationsbank Offices
Atlanta
Roswel-Wieucca 4492
Atlanta, GA
(404)523-0900
Ultimate Parent: Nationsbank Corp.

★ 64878 ★ Nationsbank Offices
Atlanta
Roswell-Wieuca 4492
Atlanta, GA
(404)256-7376
Ultimate Parent: Nationsbank Corp.

★ 64879 ★ Nationsbank Offices
Atlanta
2367 Peachtree Rd. NE
Atlanta, GA 30305
(404)264-2860
Ultimate Parent: Nationsbank Corp.

★ 64880 ★ Nationsbank Offices
Atlanta
Riverdale 6656
Atlanta, GA
(404)991-7750
Ultimate Parent: Nationsbank Corp.

★ 64881 ★ Nationsbank Offices
Atlanta
Piedmont Ctr. 3535
Atlanta, GA
(404)523-0900
Ultimate Parent: Nationsbank Corp.

★ 64882 ★ Nationsbank Offices
Atlanta
3535 Piedmont Rd. NE 11
Atlanta, GA 30305
(404)264-2895
Ultimate Parent: Nationsbank Corp.

★ 64883 ★ Nationsbank Offices
Atlanta
Perimeter Center 1
Atlanta, GA
(404)392-2998
Ultimate Parent: Nationsbank Corp.

★ 64884 ★ Nationsbank Offices
Atlanta
Perimeter Ctr. 1 P
Atlanta, GA
(404)523-0900
Ultimate Parent: Nationsbank Corp.

★ 64885 ★ Nationsbank Offices
Atlanta
5442 Peachtree Rd.
Atlanta, GA 30341
(404)452-2270
Ultimate Parent: Nationsbank Corp.

★ 64886 ★ Nationsbank Offices
Atlanta
Peachtree Ctr. 229
Atlanta, GA
(404)969-0550
Ultimate Parent: Nationsbank Corp.

★ 64887 ★ Nationsbank Offices
Atlanta
Peachtree Lenox 3475
Atlanta, GA
(404)264-2870
Ultimate Parent: Nationsbank Corp.

★ 64888 ★ Nationsbank Offices
Atlanta
Peachtree Palicsades
Atlanta, GA
(404)969-0550
Ultimate Parent: Nationsbank Corp.

★ 64889 ★ Nationsbank Offices
Atlanta
Peachtree Ctr. 229
Atlanta, GA
(404)523-0900
Ultimate Parent: Nationsbank Corp.

★ 64890 ★ Nationsbank Offices
Atlanta
Peachtree City 500 N
Atlanta, GA
(404)969-0550
Ultimate Parent: Nationsbank Corp.

★ 64891 ★ Nationsbank Offices
Atlanta
Peachtree Battle 236
Atlanta, GA
(404)969-0550
Ultimate Parent: Nationsbank Corp.

★ 64892 ★ Nationsbank Offices
Atlanta
Peachtree Ctr. 229
Atlanta, GA
(404)332-2700
Ultimate Parent: Nationsbank Corp.

★ 64893 ★ Nationsbank Offices
Atlanta
Old Gordon 3885 Old
Atlanta, GA
(404)969-0550
Ultimate Parent: Nationsbank Corp.

★ 64894 ★ Nationsbank Offices
Atlanta
Peachtree Lenox 347
Atlanta, GA
(404)523-0900
Ultimate Parent: Nationsbank Corp.

★ 64895 ★ Nationsbank Offices
Atlanta
Northpark Town Ctr.
Atlanta, GA
(404)523-0900
Ultimate Parent: Nationsbank Corp.

★ 64896 ★ Nationsbank Offices
Atlanta
Northpark Town Ctr.
Atlanta, GA
(404)969-0550
Ultimate Parent: Nationsbank Corp.

★ 64897 ★ Nationsbank Offices
Atlanta
Nationsbank Plz. 60
Atlanta, GA
(404)607-4850
Ultimate Parent: Nationsbank Corp.

★ 64898 ★ Nationsbank Offices
Atlanta
North Hills 3322
Atlanta, GA 30341
(404)523-0900
Ultimate Parent: Nationsbank Corp.

★ 64899 ★ Nationsbank Offices
Atlanta
Mitchell Street 206
Atlanta, GA 30303
(404)581-3414
Ultimate Parent: Nationsbank Corp.

★ 64900 ★ Nationsbank Offices
Atlanta
2240 N. Druid Hills Rd. NE
Atlanta, GA 30329
(404)329-4820
Ultimate Parent: Nationsbank Corp.

★ 64901 ★ Nationsbank Offices
Atlanta
Marietta Street 35 B
Atlanta, GA 30303
(404)969-0550
Ultimate Parent: Nationsbank Corp.

★ 64902 ★ Nationsbank Offices
Atlanta
Market Square 2052 L
Atlanta, GA
(404)523-0900
Ultimate Parent: Nationsbank Corp.

★ 64903 ★ Nationsbank Offices
Atlanta
Marietta Square 121
Atlanta, GA
(404)969-0550
Ultimate Parent: Nationsbank Corp.

★ 64904 ★ Nationsbank Offices
Atlanta
Marietta Street 35 B
Atlanta, GA 30303
(404)581-2009
Ultimate Parent: Nationsbank Corp.

★ 64905 ★ Nationsbank Offices
Atlanta
Little Five Points 3
Atlanta, GA
(404)969-0550
Ultimate Parent: Nationsbank Corp.

★ 64906 ★ Nationsbank Offices
Atlanta
Mableton 4901 Floyd
Atlanta, GA
(404)969-0550
Ultimate Parent: Nationsbank Corp.

★ 64907 ★ Nationsbank Offices
Atlanta
Lindbergh Plaza 2581
Atlanta, GA
(404)969-0550
Ultimate Parent: Nationsbank Corp.

★ 64908 ★ Nationsbank Offices
Atlanta
Lawrenceville 615 Hwy.
Atlanta, GA
(404)995-3151
Ultimate Parent: Nationsbank Corp.

★ 64909 ★ Nationsbank Offices
Atlanta
Lawrenceville Town C
Atlanta, GA
(404)995-3165
Ultimate Parent: Nationsbank Corp.

★ 64910 ★ Nationsbank Offices
Atlanta
Greenbriar 3011 Head
Atlanta, GA
(404)969-0550
Ultimate Parent: Nationsbank Corp.

★ 64911 ★ Nationsbank Offices
Atlanta
Howell Mill 1775 How
Atlanta, GA
(404)969-0550
Ultimate Parent: Nationsbank Corp.

★ 64912 ★ Nationsbank Offices
Atlanta
Fayetteville 219 Ba
Atlanta, GA
(404)969-0550
Ultimate Parent: Nationsbank Corp.

★ 64913 ★ Nationsbank Offices
Atlanta
Forest Park 842 Main
Atlanta, GA
(404)523-0900
Ultimate Parent: Nationsbank Corp.

★ 64914 ★ Nationsbank Offices
Atlanta
Evans Mill Road 2930
Atlanta, GA
(404)523-0900
Ultimate Parent: Nationsbank Corp.

★ 64915 ★ Nationsbank Offices
Atlanta
Executive Park 2240
Atlanta, GA
(404)969-0550
Ultimate Parent: Nationsbank Corp.

★ 64916 ★ Nationsbank Offices
Atlanta
East Point 2818 East
Atlanta, GA 30344
(404)765-1976
Ultimate Parent: Nationsbank Corp.

★ 64917 ★ Nationsbank Offices
Atlanta
Emory Village 1615 N
Atlanta, GA
(404)329-4833
Ultimate Parent: Nationsbank Corp.

★ 64918 ★ Nationsbank Offices
Atlanta
Cascade 2358 Cascade
Atlanta, GA
(404)752-0671
Ultimate Parent: Nationsbank Corp.

★ 64919 ★ Nationsbank Offices
Atlanta
3322 Chamblee Tucker Rd.
Atlanta, GA 30341
(404)452-2150
Ultimate Parent: Nationsbank Corp.

★ 64920 ★ Nationsbank Offices
Atlanta
Lakewood Christian Mall
Atlanta, GA
(404)969-0550
Ultimate Parent: Nationsbank Corp.

★ 64921 ★ Nationsbank Offices
Atlanta
1000 Abernathy Rd. NE
Atlanta, GA 30328
(404)392-2940
Ultimate Parent: Nationsbank Corp.

★ 64922 ★ Nationsbank Offices
Atlanta
Market Square 2052 L
Atlanta, GA
(404)329-4812
Ultimate Parent: Nationsbank Corp.

★ 64923 ★ Nationsbank Offices
Atlanta
1819 Peachtree Rd. NE
Atlanta, GA 30309
(404)350-2029
Ultimate Parent: Nationsbank Corp.

★ 64924 ★ Nationsbank Offices
Atlanta Area
Liburn 494 Indian Trl.
Atlanta, GA
(404)564-6764
Ultimate Parent: Nationsbank Corp.

★ 64925 ★ Nationsbank Offices
Atlanta Area
Old Gordon 3885 Old
Atlanta, GA
(404)523-0900
Ultimate Parent: Nationsbank Corp.

★ 64926 ★ Nationsbank Offices
Atlanta Area
Chamblee Plaza 5442
Atlanta, GA
(404)452-2276
Ultimate Parent: Nationsbank Corp.

★ 64927 ★ Nationsbank Offices
Atlanta Area
Mitchell Street 206
Atlanta, GA 30303
(404)523-0900
Ultimate Parent: Nationsbank Corp.

★ 64928 ★ Nationsbank Offices
Atlanta Area
Peachtree Lenox 3475
Atlanta, GA
(404)969-0550
Ultimate Parent: Nationsbank Corp.

★ 64929 ★ Nationsbank Offices
Atlanta Ar
Emory Village 1615 N
Atlanta, GA
(404)969-0550
Ultimate Parent: Nationsbank Corp.

★ 64930 ★ Nationsbank Personal
Account Informaiton
Atlanta, GA
(404)523-0900
Ultimate Parent: Nationsbank Corp.

★ 64931 ★ Nationsbank Personal
Accounts Department
Atlanta, GA
(404)491-4530
Ultimate Parent: Nationsbank Corp.

★ 64932 ★ Nationsbank Saturday
Banking O
6075 Roswell Rd.
Atlanta, GA 30328
(404)256-7350
Ultimate Parent: Nationsbank Corp.

★ 64933 ★ Nationsbank Saturday
Banking O
4567 S. Cobb Dr.
Atlanta, GA
(404)333-1690
Ultimate Parent: Nationsbank Corp.

★ 64934 ★ Nationsbank Saturday
Banking O
5199 Old National Hwy.
Atlanta, GA 30349
(404)765-1991
Ultimate Parent: Nationsbank Corp.

★ 64935 ★ Nationsbank Saturday
Banking O
3005 Peachtree Rd. NE
Atlanta, GA 30305
(404)264-2800
Ultimate Parent: Nationsbank Corp.

★ 64936 ★ Nationsbank Saturday
Banking O
842 Main St.
Atlanta, GA
(404)362-5030
Ultimate Parent: Nationsbank Corp.

★ 64937 ★ Nationsbank Saturday
Banking O
5505 N. Henry Blvd.
Atlanta, GA
(404)389-2920
Ultimate Parent: Nationsbank Corp.

★ 64938 ★ Nationsbank Saturday
Banking O
494 Indian Trl. Rd.
Atlanta, GA
(404)564-6760
Ultimate Parent: Nationsbank Corp.

★ 64939 ★ Nationsbank Saturday
Banking O
2052 Lawrenceville Hwy.
Atlanta, GA
(404)329-4810
Ultimate Parent: Nationsbank Corp.

★ 64940 ★ Nationsbank Saturday
Banking O
6656 Church St.
Atlanta, GA
(404)991-7750
Ultimate Parent: Nationsbank Corp.

★ 64941 ★ Nationsbank Saturday
Banking O
4394 Ga Hwy. 20
Atlanta, GA
(404)932-7130
Ultimate Parent: Nationsbank Corp.

★ 64942 ★ Nationsbank Saturday
Banking O
3011 Headland Dr.
Atlanta, GA 30344
(404)346-4310
Ultimate Parent: Nationsbank Corp.

★ 64943 ★ Nationsbank Saturday
Banking O
219 Banks Station
Atlanta, GA
(404)460-3510
Ultimate Parent: Nationsbank Corp.

★ 64944 ★ Nationsbank Saturday
Bk Ofcs D
8755 Roswell Rd.
Atlanta, GA 30350
(404)594-6860
Ultimate Parent: Nationsbank Corp.

★ 64945 ★ Nationsbank Savings
Account Departments
Atlanta, GA
(404)969-0550
Ultimate Parent: Nationsbank Corp.

★ 64946 ★ Nationsbank Savings
Account Departments
Atlanta, GA
(404)969-1305
Ultimate Parent: Nationsbank Corp.

★ 64947 ★ Nationsbank
Securities Departments
Atlanta, GA
(404)581-4386
Ultimate Parent: Nationsbank Corp.

★ 64948 ★ Nationsbank Security
Emergency Office
Atlanta, GA
(404)581-0888
Ultimate Parent: Nationsbank Corp.

★ 64949 ★ Nationsbank Stop
Payments Departments
Atlanta, GA
(404)969-0550
Ultimate Parent: Nationsbank Corp.

★ 64950 ★ Nationsbank Stop
Payments Departments
Atlanta, GA
(404)969-0550
Ultimate Parent: Nationsbank Corp.

★ 64951 ★ Nationsbank Student
Loan Departments
Atlanta, GA
(404)491-4171
Ultimate Parent: Nationsbank Corp.

★ 64952 ★ Nationsbank for
Those Areas No
222 Mitchell St. SW
Atlanta, GA 30303
(404)581-2121
Ultimate Parent: Nationsbank Corp.

★ 64953 ★ Nationsbank Training
Departments
Atlanta, GA
(404)607-5911
Ultimate Parent: Nationsbank Corp.

★ 64954 ★ Nationsbank Trust Div.
Atlanta, GA
(404)607-2951
Ultimate Parent: Nationsbank Corp.

★ 64955 ★ Nationsbank Trust Div.
Atlanta, GA
(404)607-3031
Ultimate Parent: Nationsbank Corp.

★ 64956 ★ Nationsbank Trust Div.
Atlanta, GA
(404)607-4803
Ultimate Parent: Nationsbank Corp.

★ 64957 ★ Nationsbank Trust Div.
Atlanta, GA
(404)607-4681
Ultimate Parent: Nationsbank Corp.

★ 64958 ★ Nationsbank Trust Div.
Atlanta, GA
(404)607-5318
Ultimate Parent: Nationsbank Corp.

★ 64959 ★ Nationsbank Trust Div.
Atlanta, GA
(404)607-4530
Ultimate Parent: Nationsbank Corp.

★ 64960 ★ Nationsbank Trust Div.
Atlanta, GA
(404)607-4535
Ultimate Parent: Nationsbank Corp.

★ 64961 ★ Nationsbank Trust Div.
Atlanta, GA
(404)607-4507
Ultimate Parent: Nationsbank Corp.

★ 64962 ★ Nationsbank Trust Div.
Atlanta, GA
(404)607-4519
Ultimate Parent: Nationsbank Corp.

★ 64963 ★ Nationsbank Trust Div.
Atlanta, GA
(404)607-2492
Ultimate Parent: Nationsbank Corp.

★ 64964 ★ Nationsbank Trust Div.
Atlanta, GA
(404)607-3107
Ultimate Parent: Nationsbank Corp.

★ 64965 ★ Nationsbank 24 Hour Departments
Atlanta, GA
(404)491-4530
Ultimate Parent: Nationsbank Corp.

★ 64966 ★ Nationsbank 24 Hour Jobline
Atlanta, GA
(404)491-4530
Ultimate Parent: Nationsbank Corp.

★ 64967 ★ Navistar International Transpo
3350 Northlake Pkwy NE
Atlanta, GA 30345
(404)934-0660
Ultimate Parent: Navistar International.

★ 64968 ★ NCR Corp.
1587 Northeast Expwy. NE
Atlanta, GA 30329
(404)321-8946
Officer: Tom Balsman, Manager. Ultimate Parent: AT&T. SIC: 2761—Manifold Business Forms.

★ 64969 ★ Ncr Corp. Atlanta Distri
5 Executive Park Dr. NE
Atlanta, GA 30329
(404)321-8800
Ultimate Parent: AT&T.

★ 64970 ★ New York Life
PO Box 4869
Atlanta, GA 30302
(404)938-0080
Officer: Steven Nelson, Assistant Vice President. Ultimate Parent: New York Life.

★ 64971 ★ New York Life Atlanta Group Claims Office
Western Group Claims Region
PO Box 105095
Atlanta, GA 30348
(800)388-4580 Fax: (404)840-9068
Ultimate Parent: New York Life.

★ 64972 ★ New York Life Atlanta Group Sales Office
Central Group Marketing Zone Office
600 Embassy Row, Ste. 490
Atlanta, GA 30328
(404)393-4688 Fax: (404)668-9213
Officer: Rick Brown, Group Manager. Ultimate Parent: New York Life.

★ 64973 ★ New York Life Greater Atlanta Office
Southeasten Agencies
400 Embassy Row, Ste. 100
Atlanta, GA 30328
(404)395-2500 Fax: (404)395-2603
Officer: John Allen, General Manager. Ultimate Parent: New York Life.

★ 64974 ★ New York Life South Atlantic Pension Region
Eastern Pension Zone
400 Embassy Row, Ste. 430
Atlanta, GA 30328-1667
(404)392-0557 Fax: (404)392-0757
Officer: Winship Story, Regional Manager. Ultimate Parent: New York Life.

★ 64975 ★ New York Life Southeastern Agencies
600 Embassy Row, Ste. 400, 4th Fl.
Atlanta, GA 30328
(404)394-1294
Officer: Richard Painter, Senior Vice President. Ultimate Parent: New York Life.

★ 64976 ★ Newell Window Furnishing
Atlanta, GA
(404)442-3271
Ultimate Parent: New York Times.

★ 64977 ★ North American Van Lines Inc.
6140 Purdue Dr. SW
Atlanta, GA 30336
(404)349-3331
Ultimate Parent: Norfolk Southern.

★ 64978 ★ North Bros. Co.
3250 Woodstock Rd., SE
Atlanta, GA 30316
(404)627-1381 Fax: (404)622-1310
Officer: Dennis Harris, President. Ultimate Parent: National Service Industries.

★ 64979 ★ Norwest Mortgage Inc.
5881 Glenridge Dr. NE 770
Atlanta, GA 30328
(404)257-1983
Ultimate Parent: Norwest Corp.

★ 64980 ★ Oglethorpe Power Corp. E
Atlanta, GA
(404)270-7939
Ultimate Parent: Oglethorpe Power.

★ 64981 ★ Oglethorpe Power Corp. Ga Elect
Atlanta, GA
(404)270-6950
Ultimate Parent: Oglethorpe Power.

★ 64982 ★ Ore-Ida Inc.
Atlanta, GA
(404)971-0075
Ultimate Parent: H.J. Heinz.

★ 64983 ★ Otis Elevator Co.
1575 Northside Dr. NW
Atlanta, GA 30318
(404)355-1991
Ultimate Parent: United Technologies.

★ 64984 ★ Otis Elevator Construction
303 Peachtree St. NE
Atlanta, GA 30308
(404)525-8336
Ultimate Parent: United Technologies.

★ 64985 ★ Owens-Brockway Glass Container Inc.
3107 Sylvan Rd.
Atlanta, GA 30354
Ultimate Parent: Owens-Illinois. SIC: 3221—Glass Containers.

★ 64986 ★ Owens-Corning Fiberglas Corp.
4795 Frederick Dr. SW
Atlanta, GA 30336
(404)691-3910
Officer: Bill Vahle, Manager. Ultimate Parent: Owens-Corning. SIC: 2952—Asphalt Felts & Coatings.

★ 64987 ★ Owens-Corning Fiberglass
Roofing Plant
4795 Frederick Dr.
Atlanta, GA 30336
Location Type: Plant. Ultimate Parent: Owens-Corning. SIC: 2952—Asphalt Felts & Coatings; 2951—Asphalt Paving Mixtures & Blocks.

★ 64988 ★ Owens-Corning Fiberglass
Trumbull Plant
4775 Frederick Dr.
Atlanta, GA 30336
Location Type: Plant. Ultimate Parent: Owens-Corning. SIC: 2952—Asphalt Felts & Coatings; 2951—Asphalt Paving Mixtures & Blocks.

★ 64989 ★ Owens-Illinois Glass Container Inc.
3107 Sylvan Rd.
Atlanta, GA 30354
Ultimate Parent: Owens-Illinois. SIC: 3221—Glass Containers.

★ 64990 ★ Owens Illinois Inc.
3490 Hamilton Blvd. SE
Atlanta, GA 30354
(404)766-9613
Officer: J P De Vries, Manager. Ultimate Parent: Owens-Illinois. SIC: 3089—Plastics Products Nec.

★ 64991 ★ Pacific Financial
950 E. Paces Ferry Rd. NE
Atlanta, GA 30326
(404)240-6996
Ultimate Parent: Pacific Mutual Life.

★ 64992 ★ Pandel Inc.
21 River Rd. Cartersville
Atlanta, GA
(404)577-2878
Ultimate Parent: Interface Inc.

★ 64993 ★ Pappagallo
4200 Paces Ferry Rd. NW
Atlanta, GA 30339
(404)333-0705
Ultimate Parent: United States Shoe.

★ 64994 ★ Pappagallo
3500 Peachtree Re NE
Atlanta, GA
(404)240-0977
Ultimate Parent: United States Shoe.

★ 64995 ★ Payless Shoesource
2841 Greenbriar Pky. SW
Atlanta, GA 30331
(404)349-6919
Ultimate Parent: May Department Stores.

★ 64996 ★ Payless Shoesource
527 Moreland Ave. SE
Atlanta, GA 30316
(404)622-5010
Ultimate Parent: May Department Stores.

★ 64997 ★ Payless Shoesource
2685 Bankhead Hwy. NW
Atlanta, GA 30318
(404)794-5277
Ultimate Parent: May Department Stores.

★ 64998 ★ Payless Shoesource
Southlake Festival
Atlanta, GA
(404)968-0170
Ultimate Parent: May Department Stores.

★ 64999 ★ Payless Shoesource
1899 Stewart Ave. SW
Atlanta, GA 30315
(404)755-4385
Ultimate Parent: May Department Stores.

★ 65000 ★ Payless Shoesource
619 Boulevard NE
Atlanta, GA 30308
(404)872-1599
Ultimate Parent: May Department Stores.

★ 65001 ★ Payless Shoesource
3024 Martin Luther King Jr.
Atlanta, GA 30311
(404)696-7779
Ultimate Parent: May Department Stores.

★ 65002 ★ Payment Services Co.
5775 Peachtree Dunwoody R
Atlanta, GA 30342
(404)250-6170
Ultimate Parent: First Financial Management Corp.

★ 65003 ★ Pennzoil Products Co.
Atlanta, GA
(404)441-1103
Ultimate Parent: Pennzoil.

★ 65004 ★ Pennzoil Products Co.
6255 Barfield Rd. NE
Atlanta, GA 30328
(404)843-2434
Ultimate Parent: Pennzoil.

★ 65005 ★ Pennzoil Products Company
6255 Barfield Rd. NE
Atlanta, GA 30328
(404)843-2434
Ultimate Parent: Pennzoil.

★ 65006 ★ Penton Publishing
3400 Peachtree Rd. NE
Atlanta, GA 30326
(404)237-5528
Ultimate Parent: Pittway.

★ 65007 ★ Pepsi-Cola Bottling Co.
1480 Chattahoochee Ave. NW
Atlanta, GA 30318
(404)355-1480
Officer: Alfred McDonald, Manager. Ultimate Parent: Pepsico. SIC: 2086—Bottled & Canned Soft Drinks.

★ 65008 ★ Perma Products
PO Box 43308
Atlanta, GA 30336-0308
(404)346-0040
Officer: Bob Schmitz. Ultimate Parent: American Brands Inc. SIC: 2653—Corrugated & Solid Fiber Boxes.

★ 65009 ★ Perma Products Inc.
4175 Boulder Ridge Dr. SW
Atlanta, GA 30336
(404)346-0040
Ultimate Parent: American Brands Inc. SIC: 2653—Corrugated & Solid Fiber Boxes.

★ 65010 ★ Personal Performance Consultants
999 Peachtree St. NE
Atlanta, GA
(404)872-3988
Ultimate Parent: Merck.

★ 65011 ★ Pet Inc.
1039 Grant St. SE
Atlanta, GA 30315
(404)622-8146
Officer: Earl Stallworth, Manager. Ultimate Parent: Pet. SIC: 2051—Bread, Cake & Related Products.

★ 65012 ★ Petite Sophisticate
1251 Northlake Mall NE
Atlanta, GA 30345
(404)934-0940
Ultimate Parent: United States Shoe.

★ 65013 ★ Petite Sophisticate
1414 Perimeter Mall NE
Atlanta, GA 30346
(404)396-3653
Ultimate Parent: United States Shoe.

★ 65014 ★   Petite Sophisticate
Gwinnett Place Mall
Atlanta, GA
(404)476-4278
Ultimate Parent: United States Shoe.

★ 65015 ★   Petite Sophisticate
76 Lenox Sq. Mall
Atlanta, GA 30326
(404)266-8494
Ultimate Parent: United States Shoe.

★ 65016 ★   Petite Sophisticate
1219 Cumberland Mall NW
Atlanta, GA 30339
(404)436-4929
Ultimate Parent: United States Shoe.

★ 65017 ★   PHH US Mortgage
990 Hammond Dr. NE
Atlanta, GA 30328
(404)396-8840
Ultimate Parent: PHH.

★ 65018 ★   Piggly Wiggly
2746 Clairmont Rd. NE
Atlanta, GA 30329
(404)634-2833
Ultimate Parent: Bruno's.

★ 65019 ★   Piggly Wiggly
230 Cleveland Ave. SW
Atlanta, GA 30315-8208
(404)767-8027
Location Type: Branch office. Officer:
David Holder. Ultimate Parent: Bruno's.
SIC: 5411—Grocery Stores.

★ 65020 ★   Pitney Bowes Credit
Corp.
1050 Crowne Pointe Pkwy N
Atlanta, GA 30338
(404)551-4500
Ultimate Parent: Pitney Bowes.

★ 65021 ★   Pizza Hut
1955 Stewart Ave. SW
Atlanta, GA 30315
(404)761-7851
Ultimate Parent: Pepsico.

★ 65022 ★   Pizza Hut
460 North Ave.
Atlanta, GA 30354
(404)876-7551
Ultimate Parent: Pepsico.

★ 65023 ★   Pizza Hut
2608 Piedmont Rd. NE
Atlanta, GA 30324
(404)239-0562
Ultimate Parent: Pepsico.

★ 65024 ★   Pizza Hut
1851 Corporate Blvd. NE
Atlanta, GA 30329
(404)633-1227
Ultimate Parent: Pepsico.

★ 65025 ★   Pizza Hut
2078 Henderson Mill Rd. NE
Atlanta, GA 30345
(404)493-3542
Ultimate Parent: Pepsico.

★ 65026 ★   Pizza Hut
614 Bankhead Hwy.
Atlanta, GA
(404)832-1166
Ultimate Parent: Pepsico.

★ 65027 ★   Pizza Hut
6303 Roswell Rd. NE
Atlanta, GA 30328
(404)843-0600
Ultimate Parent: Pepsico.

★ 65028 ★   Pizza Hut
4830 Redan Rd.
Atlanta, GA
(404)296-9800
Ultimate Parent: Pepsico.

★ 65029 ★   Pizza Hut
4381 Roswell Rd. NE
Atlanta, GA 30342
(404)257-8800
Ultimate Parent: Pepsico.

★ 65030 ★   Pizza Hut
387 Cleveland Ave. SW
Atlanta, GA 30315
(404)305-9800
Ultimate Parent: Pepsico.

★ 65031 ★   Pizza Hut
2636 Martin Luther King J
Atlanta, GA 30311
(404)691-5200
Ultimate Parent: Pepsico.

★ 65032 ★   Pizza Hut
929-C Spring St. NW
Atlanta, GA
(404)872-3400
Ultimate Parent: Pepsico.

★ 65033 ★   Pizza Hut
1955 Cambellton Rd. SW
Atlanta, GA 30311
(404)752-8200
Ultimate Parent: Pepsico.

★ 65034 ★   Pizza Hut
1203 Collier Rd. NW
Atlanta, GA 30318
(404)352-7711
Ultimate Parent: Pepsico.

★ 65035 ★   Pizza Hut
901-D S. Park St. Caro
Atlanta, GA
(404)832-9000
Ultimate Parent: Pepsico.

★ 65036 ★   Pizza Hut
3690 Campbellton Rd. SW
Atlanta, GA 30331
(404)349-1000
Ultimate Parent: Pepsico.

★ 65037 ★   Pizza Hut
Atlanta, GA
(404)662-5555
Ultimate Parent: Pepsico.

★ 65038 ★   Pizza Hut Inc.
1719 Calibre Woods Dr. NE
Atlanta, GA 30329
(404)325-3482
Ultimate Parent: Pepsico.

★ 65039 ★   Polaroid Corp.
5601 Fulton Industrial Blvd.
Atlanta, GA 30378
(404)346-1717
Ultimate Parent: Polaroid.

★ 65040 ★   Potlatch Corp.
600 Embassy Row NE
Atlanta, GA 30328
(404)391-0070
Ultimate Parent: Potlatch.

★ 65041 ★   Ppg Industries Inc.
1030 White St. SW
Atlanta, GA 30310
(404)753-1891
Ultimate Parent: PPG Industries Inc.

★ 65042 ★   Ppg Industries Inc.
1450 Chattahoochee Ave. NW
Atlanta, GA 30318
(404)352-3957
Ultimate Parent: PPG Industries Inc.

★ 65043 ★   PPG Industries Inc.
1377 Oakleigh Dr.
Atlanta, GA 30344
(404)761-7771
Officer: Vincent Sarni, President. Ultimate
Parent: PPG Industries Inc. SIC: 2851—
Paints & Allied Products.

★ 65044 ★   Provident National
Assurance
4920 Roswell Rd. NE 43
Atlanta, GA 30342
Ultimate Parent: Provident Life & Accident.
SIC: 6371—Pension, Health & Welfare
Funds; 6411—Insurance Agents, Brokers &
Service.

★ 65045 ★   Prudential Secruities
Inc,
14 Piedmont Ctr.
Atlanta, GA 30305
(404)842-9000
Ultimate Parent: Prudential of America.

★ 65046 ★   Prudential Securities
Inc.
4 Piedmont Ctr.
Atlanta, GA 30305
(404)262-5940
Ultimate Parent: Prudential of America.

★ 65047 ★   Publix Super Market
2849 Paces Ferry Rd. NW
Atlanta, GA 30339
(404)319-3679
Ultimate Parent: Publix Super Markets.

★ 65048 ★   Publix Super Markets
Atlanta D
2849 Paces Ferry Rd. NW
Atlanta, GA 30339
(404)319-3679
Ultimate Parent: Publix Super Markets.

★ 65049 ★   Pulte Home Corp.
Atlanta, GA
(404)381-3450
Ultimate Parent: Pulte.

★ 65050 ★   Quality Park Product
3350 Hamilton Blvd. SW
Atlanta, GA 30354
(404)766-9691
Officer: Jim Roney, Manager. Ultimate
Parent: Alco Standard Corp. SIC: 2677—
Envelopes; 2678—Stationery Products;
2679—Converted Paper Products Nec.

★ 65051 ★   Quality Park Product
3350 Hamilton Blvd. SW
Atlanta, GA 30354
(404)766-9691
Officer: Jim Roney, Manager. Ultimate
Parent: Alco Standard Corp. SIC: 2677—
Envelopes; 2678—Stationery Products;
2679—Converted Paper Products Nec.

★ 65052 ★   Quality Park Products
3350 Hamilton Blvd. SW
Atlanta, GA 30354
(404)766-9691
Officer: Jim Roney, Manager. Ultimate
Parent: Alco Standard Corp. SIC: 2677—
Envelopes; 2678—Stationery Products;
2679—Converted Paper Products Nec;
5112—Stationery & Office Supplies.

★ 65053 ★   Quotron Systems
1050 Crown Poine Pkwy NE
Atlanta, GA 30338
(404)391-9480
Ultimate Parent: Citicorp.

★ 65054 ★   R R Donnelley
Financial
1100 Peachtree St. NE
Atlanta, GA 30309
(404)892-9393
Ultimate Parent: R. R. Donnelley & Sons.

★ 65055 ★   R R Donnelley & Sons
Co.
1175 Peachtree St. NE
Atlanta, GA 30309
(404)874-2800
Ultimate Parent: R. R. Donnelley & Sons.

★ 65056 ★   Radio Shack
Gwinnett Place Mall
Atlanta, GA
(404)476-7379
Company Type: Division. Ultimate Parent:
Tandy Corp.

★ 65057 ★   Radio Shack
900 Circle 75 Pkwy NW
Atlanta, GA 30339
(404)850-9899
Company Type: Division. Ultimate Parent:
Tandy Corp.

★ 65058 ★   Radio Shack
Lenox Square
Atlanta, GA
(404)262-7953
Company Type: Division. Ultimate Parent:
Tandy Corp.

★ 65059 ★   Radio Shack
Toco Hills Shopping
Atlanta, GA
(404)633-1007
Company Type: Division. Ultimate Parent:
Tandy Corp.

★ 65060 ★   Radio Shack
West End Mall
Atlanta, GA
(404)752-7377
Company Type: Division. Ultimate Parent:
Tandy Corp.

★ 65061 ★   Radio Shack
5992 Roswell Rd. NW
Atlanta, GA 30328
(404)255-6718
Company Type: Division. Ultimate Parent:
Tandy Corp.

★ 65062 ★   Radio Shack
2685 Stewart Ave. SW
Atlanta, GA 30315
(404)768-5340
Company Type: Division. Ultimate Parent:
Tandy Corp.

★ 65063 ★   Radio Shack
Northlake Mall
Atlanta, GA 30345
(404)939-2614
Company Type: Division. Ultimate Parent:
Tandy Corp.

★ 65064 ★   Radio Shack
Perimeter
Atlanta, GA 30346
(404)394-3933
Company Type: Division. Ultimate Parent:
Tandy Corp.

★ 65065 ★   Radio Shack
Lindbergh Plaza
Atlanta, GA
(404)266-0748
Company Type: Division. Ultimate Parent:
Tandy Corp.

★ 65066 ★   Radio Shack
Northeast Plaza Shop
Atlanta, GA
(404)634-2364
Company Type: Division. Ultimate Parent:
Tandy Corp.

★ 65067 ★   Radio Shack
Lenox Sq.
Atlanta, GA 30324
(404)262-7949
Company Type: Division. Ultimate Parent:
Tandy Corp.

★ 65068 ★   Radio Shack
Lenox Square Mall
Atlanta, GA
(404)262-2589
Company Type: Division. Ultimate Parent:
Tandy Corp.

★ 65069 ★   Radio Shack
900 Circle 75 Pkwy NW
Atlanta, GA 30339
(404)850-9892
Company Type: Division. Ultimate Parent:
Tandy Corp.

★ 65070 ★   Radio Shack
Greenbriar Mall
Atlanta, GA
(404)349-0751
Company Type: Division. Ultimate Parent:
Tandy Corp.

★ 65071 ★   Radio Shack
900 Circle 75 Pkwy NW
Atlanta, GA 30339
(404)850-9993
Company Type: Division. Ultimate Parent:
Tandy Corp.

★ 65072 ★   Radio Shack
Avondale Mall
Atlanta, GA
(404)284-7722
Company Type: Division. Ultimate Parent:
Tandy Corp.

★ 65073 ★   Radio Shack
Ansley Mall
Atlanta, GA
(404)873-6488
Company Type: Division. Ultimate Parent:
Tandy Corp.

★ 65074 ★   Rayloc
Rebuilding Division
600 Rayloc Dr.
Atlanta, GA 30336-1633
(404)691-3780 Fax: (404)696-9107
Company Type: Subsidiary. Ultimate
Parent: Genuine Parts.

★ 65075 ★ Regional Newspaper Group
The Monarch Plz., 3414 Peachtree Rd., NE
Atlanta, GA 30326
(404)262-5656 Fax: (404)262-5649
Officer: James C. Weeks, President & COO. Ultimate Parent: New York Times.

★ 65076 ★ Reliance Insurance Co.
5660 New Northside Dr. NW
Atlanta, GA 30328
(404)933-2800
Ultimate Parent: Reliance Group Holdings.
SIC: 6411—Insurance Agents, Brokers & Service.

★ 65077 ★ Rhone-Poulenc Rorer
2295 Parklake Dr. NE
Atlanta, GA 30345
(404)493-6522
Ultimate Parent: Rhone-Poulenc Rorer.

★ 65078 ★ Richards S P Co. Ofc Supls Redi
101 Villanova Dr. SW
Atlanta, GA 30336
(404)346-1026
Ultimate Parent: Genuine Parts.

★ 65079 ★ Rite Aid Corp.
Atlanta, GA
(404)303-1679
Ultimate Parent: Rite Aid.

★ 65080 ★ Riverside Furniture
240 Peachtree St. NW
Atlanta, GA 30303
Ultimate Parent: Arkansas Best. SIC: 2599—Furniture & Fixtures Nec.

★ 65081 ★ Riverwood International Corp.
3350 Cumberland Cir., Ste. 1600
Atlanta, GA 30339
(404)644-3000 Fax: (404)644-3004
Officer: W. Thomas Stephens, Chairman of the Board. Ultimate Parent: Manville Corp.

★ 65082 ★ Riverwood International Corp.
3350 Cumberland Circle
Atlanta, GA 30339
(404)644-3000 Fax: (404)644-3004
Company Type: Subsidiary. Officer: Thomas H. Johnson, President CEO.
Ultimate Parent: Manville Corp. SIC: 2621—Paper Mills; 2631—Paperboard Mills.

★ 65083 ★ Rollins Burdick Hunter
400 Interstate No Pkwy N
Atlanta, GA 30339
(404)951-1700
Ultimate Parent: Aon Corp.

★ 65084 ★ Ryder Truck Rental
875 Washington St. SW
Atlanta, GA 30315
(404)523-2901
Ultimate Parent: Ryder System.

★ 65085 ★ Ryder Truck Rental
Virginia Ave. at Airpo
Atlanta, GA
(404)767-0428
Ultimate Parent: Ryder System.

★ 65086 ★ Ryder Truck Rental
6600 Button Gwinnett Driv
Atlanta, GA 30340
(404)449-1341
Ultimate Parent: Ryder System.

★ 65087 ★ Ryder Truck Rental
4707 Mendel Ct Fltn Indus
Atlanta, GA
(404)696-3996
Ultimate Parent: Ryder System.

★ 65088 ★ Ryder Truck Rental
Powder Springs Rd.
Atlanta, GA
(404)943-3322
Ultimate Parent: Ryder System.

★ 65089 ★ Ryder Truck Rental
Lavista at I-285
Atlanta, GA
(404)939-5200
Ultimate Parent: Ryder System.

★ 65090 ★ Ryder Truck Rental
Main St. East Point
Atlanta, GA
(404)968-8920
Ultimate Parent: Ryder System.

★ 65091 ★ Ryder Truck Rental
Highpoint/Westend
Atlanta, GA
(404)968-8920
Ultimate Parent: Ryder System.

★ 65092 ★ Ryder Truck Rental
Jonesboro Rd. at I-75
Atlanta, GA
(404)968-8920
Ultimate Parent: Ryder System.

★ 65093 ★ Ryder Truck Rental
Windy Hill & I-75
Atlanta, GA
(404)916-1661
Ultimate Parent: Ryder System.

★ 65094 ★ Ryder Truck Rental
501 W. Pike
Atlanta, GA
(404)962-6030
Ultimate Parent: Ryder System.

★ 65095 ★ Ryder Truck Rental
268 Westminster Dr. NE
Atlanta, GA 30309
(404)892-1387
Ultimate Parent: Ryder System.

★ 65096 ★ Ryder Truck Rental
South Loop&Coob Pky.
Atlanta, GA
(404)355-2544
Ultimate Parent: Ryder System.

★ 65097 ★ Ryder Truck Rental
Tara Blvd. at I-75s
Atlanta, GA
(404)478-1378
Ultimate Parent: Ryder System.

★ 65098 ★ Ryder Truck Rental
S Cobb Dr. at Austell
Atlanta, GA
(404)436-8621
Ultimate Parent: Ryder System.

★ 65099 ★ Ryder Truck Rental
South Loop 120
Atlanta, GA
(404)422-3890
Ultimate Parent: Ryder System.

★ 65100 ★ Ryder Truck Rental
Roswell Rd. at Aberna
Atlanta, GA
(404)551-9552
Ultimate Parent: Ryder System.

★ 65101 ★ Ryder Truck Rental
Roswell Rd. at Holcom
Atlanta, GA
(404)587-1146
Ultimate Parent: Ryder System.

★ 65102 ★ Ryder Truck Rental
2459 Roosevelt Hwy.
Atlanta, GA 30337
(404)766-6221
Ultimate Parent: Ryder System.

★ 65103 ★ Ryder Truck Rental
Roswell Rd. & Holcomb
Atlanta, GA
(404)587-5177
Ultimate Parent: Ryder System.

★ 65104 ★ Ryder Truck Rental
3240 Peachtree Rd. NE
Atlanta, GA 30305
(404)237-1005
Ultimate Parent: Ryder System.

★ 65105 ★ Ryder Truck Rental
Ponce De Leon at I-2
Atlanta, GA
(404)292-7246
Ultimate Parent: Ryder System.

★ 65106 ★ Ryder Truck Rental
Peachtree at Piedmont
Atlanta, GA
(404)816-7455
Ultimate Parent: Ryder System.

★ 65107 ★ Ryder Truck Rental
Peachtree
Atlanta, GA
(404)242-8403
Ultimate Parent: Ryder System.

★ 65108 ★ Ryder Truck Rental
Nesbit Ferry
Atlanta, GA
(404)518-0522
Ultimate Parent: Ryder System.

★ 65109 ★ Ryder Truck Rental
Northcrest Rd. at I-8
Atlanta, GA
(404)414-0334
Ultimate Parent: Ryder System.

★ 65110 ★ Ryder Truck Rental
Morgan Falls
Atlanta, GA
(404)913-9675
Ultimate Parent: Ryder System.

★ 65111 ★ Ryder Truck Rental
Mountain at Hwy. 78
Atlanta, GA
(404)938-9440
Ultimate Parent: Ryder System.

★ 65112 ★ Ryder Truck Rental
Marietta Square
Atlanta, GA
(404)429-8061
Ultimate Parent: Ryder System.

★ 65113 ★ Ryder Truck Rental
4797 Mendel Ct SW
Atlanta, GA 30336
(404)739-0219
Ultimate Parent: Ryder System.

★ 65114 ★ Ryder Truck Rental
I-75 & Old Dixie Hwy.
Atlanta, GA
(404)363-9744
Ultimate Parent: Ryder System.

★ 65115 ★ Ryder Truck Rental
Indian Trail at I-85
Atlanta, GA
(404)923-0247
Ultimate Parent: Ryder System.

★ 65116 ★ Ryder Truck Rental
Hwy. 400 at Holcomb B
Atlanta, GA
(404)594-8030
Ultimate Parent: Ryder System.

★ 65117 ★ Ryder Truck Rental
Hwy. 85
Atlanta, GA
(404)997-0187
Ultimate Parent: Ryder System.

★ 65118 ★ Ryder Truck Rental
Hambrick at Memorial
Atlanta, GA
(404)508-8376
Ultimate Parent: Ryder System.

★ 65119 ★ Ryder Truck Rental
Hwy. 29 & Patterson R
Atlanta, GA
(404)985-4224
Ultimate Parent: Ryder System.

★ 65120 ★ Ryder Truck Rental
Gwinnett Place Mall
Atlanta, GA
(404)476-8724
Ultimate Parent: Ryder System.

★ 65121 ★ Ryder Truck Rental
Forest Pky. at Jones
Atlanta, GA
(404)361-1094
Ultimate Parent: Ryder System.

★ 65122 ★ Ryder Truck Rental
Greenbriar Mall Area
Atlanta, GA
(404)349-8796
Ultimate Parent: Ryder System.

★ 65123 ★ Ryder Truck Rental
Covington Hwy&I-285
Atlanta, GA
(404)284-7625
Ultimate Parent: Ryder System.

★ 65124 ★ Ryder Truck Rental
Dobbins Afb Area
Atlanta, GA
(404)429-9381
Ultimate Parent: Ryder System.

★ 65125 ★ Ryder Truck Rental
4501 Circle 75 Pkwy NW
Atlanta, GA 30339
(404)951-2024
Ultimate Parent: Ryder System.

★ 65126 ★ Ryder Truck Rental
4900 Circle 75 Pkwy NW
Atlanta, GA 30339
(404)421-0041
Ultimate Parent: Ryder System.

★ 65127 ★ Ryder Truck Rental
Buford Hwy. at I-285
Atlanta, GA
(404)455-8968
Ultimate Parent: Ryder System.

★ 65128 ★ Ryder Truck Rental
Chamblee Tucker at I
Atlanta, GA
(404)458-7872
Ultimate Parent: Ryder System.

★ 65129 ★ Ryder Truck Rental
Brookhaven
Atlanta, GA
(404)457-5797
Ultimate Parent: Ryder System.

★ 65130 ★ Ryder Truck Rental
Buford Hwy.
Atlanta, GA
(404)449-1341
Ultimate Parent: Ryder System.

★ 65131 ★ Ryder Truck Rental
Beaver Ruin&I-85
Atlanta, GA
(404)564-0064
Ultimate Parent: Ryder System.

★ 65132 ★ Ryder Truck Rental
Briarcliff at Sage H
Atlanta, GA
(404)873-3823
Ultimate Parent: Ryder System.

★ 65133 ★ Ryder Truck Rental
501 Amsterdam Ave. NE
Atlanta, GA 30306
(404)607-7003
Ultimate Parent: Ryder System.

★ 65134 ★ Ryder Truck Rental
Washington Road&I-28
Atlanta, GA
(404)968-8920
Ultimate Parent: Ryder System.

★ 65135 ★ Ryder Truck Rental
37 Amlajack Rd.
Atlanta, GA
(404)251-1100
Ultimate Parent: Ryder System.

★ 65136 ★ Ryder Truck Rental
2035 Hills Ave. NW
Atlanta, GA 30318
(404)355-2530
Ultimate Parent: Ryder System.

★ 65137 ★ Sales Technologies
3399 Ptree Rd. NE
Atlanta, GA 30326
(404)841-4000
Ultimate Parent: Dun & Bradstreet.

★ 65138 ★ Sales Technologies
Lenox Bldg., Ste. 700
3399 Peachtree Rd. NE
Atlanta, GA 30376
(404)841-4000 Fax: (404)841-4115
Company Type: Subsidiary. Officer: Charles A. Johnson, Chairman. Ultimate Parent: Dun & Bradstreet. SIC: 7372—Prepackaged Software.

★ 65139 ★ Sales Technologies
3399 Peachtree Rd. NE
Atlanta, GA 30326
(404)841-4000
Company Type: Subsidiary. Officer: James R. Bensman, President & CEO. Ultimate Parent: Dun & Bradstreet. SIC: 7372—Prepackaged Software.

★ 65140 ★   Salomon Brothers Inc.
5000 Ga-Pacific Ctr.
Atlanta, GA
(404)827-7600
Ultimate Parent: Salomon, Inc.

★ 65141 ★   Schuller International Inc/Manville Fib
3300 Cumberland Cir.
Atlanta, GA 30339
(404)644-3000
Ultimate Parent: Manville Corp.

★ 65142 ★   Schuller International Inc./Manville Fib
Industrial Way Winde
Atlanta, GA
(404)867-4571
Ultimate Parent: Manville Corp.

★ 65143 ★   Schwab Charles & Co. Inc.
400 Colony Sq.
Atlanta, GA
(404)874-6695
Ultimate Parent: Charles Schwab Corp.

★ 65144 ★   Scientific-Atlanta, Inc.
1 Technology Pky. S.
Atlanta, GA 30092
(404)903-5000 Fax: (404)441-4617
Company Type: Headquarters. Officer: James W. Napier. Employee Count: 3600. Sales: 730.6 M. Fortune 500: Largest U.S. Industrial Corporations: Ranking 434.

★ 65145 ★   Seabury & Smith Inc.
133 Peachtree St. NE
Atlanta, GA 30303
(404)526-8800
Ultimate Parent: Marsh & McLennan.

★ 65146 ★   Seagate Technology
210 Interstate North Pky.
Atlanta, GA 30339
(404)952-0652
Ultimate Parent: Seagate Technology, Inc.

★ 65147 ★   Selig Chemical Ind.
840 Selig Dr. SW
Atlanta, GA 30336
Ultimate Parent: National Service Industries. SIC: 2842—Polishes & Sanitation Goods; 5100—Wholesale Trade—Nondurable Goods.

★ 65148 ★   Selig Chemical Industries
840 Selig Dr. SW
Atlanta, GA 30336
Ultimate Parent: National Service Industries. SIC: 2842—Polishes & Sanitation Goods; 4225—General Warehousing & Storage.

★ 65149 ★   Service Merchandise
2489 Cheshire Bridge Rd. N
Atlanta, GA 30324
(404)633-2911
Ultimate Parent: Service Merchandise Co., Inc.

★ 65150 ★   Service Merchandise
2750 Cobb Pkwy NW
Atlanta, GA 30339
(404)952-2661
Ultimate Parent: Service Merchandise Co., Inc.

★ 65151 ★   Service Merchandise
5930 Rowelll Rd. NW
Atlanta, GA
(404)252-7081
Ultimate Parent: Service Merchandise Co., Inc.

★ 65152 ★   Shell Food Mart
2020 Bolton Rd. NW
Atlanta, GA 30318
(404)794-3528
Ultimate Parent: Shell Oil Co.

★ 65153 ★   Shell Food Mart
3460 Cascade Rd. SW
Atlanta, GA 30311
(404)699-0918
Ultimate Parent: Shell Oil Co.

★ 65154 ★   Shell Oil Company Asphalt Sale
320 Interstate North Pky.
Atlanta, GA 30339
(404)955-4600
Ultimate Parent: Shell Oil Co.

★ 65155 ★   Shell Oil Company Eastern Dist
320 Interstate North Pky.
Atlanta, GA 30339
(404)955-4600
Ultimate Parent: Shell Oil Co.

★ 65156 ★   Shell Oil Company Jobber Sales
320 Interstate North Pkwy.
Atlanta, GA
(404)955-4600
Ultimate Parent: Shell Oil Co.

★ 65157 ★   Shell Oil Company Lubricant Sa
320 Interstate North Pky.
Atlanta, GA 30339
(404)955-4600
Ultimate Parent: Shell Oil Co.

★ 65158 ★   Smith Barney Harris Upham & Co.
3399 Peachtree Rd. NE
Atlanta, GA 30326-1120
(404)266-0090
Company Type: Branch. Officer: Michael J. Grace. Ultimate Parent: Automatic Data Processing, Inc. SIC: 6211—Security Brokers & Dealers.

★ 65159 ★   Sonoco Products Co.
2490 Old Marietta Rd. NW
Atlanta, GA 30318
(404)799-3814
Officer: Rick Turner, Manager. Ultimate Parent: Sonoco Products. SIC: 2655—Fiber Cans, Drums & Similar Products.

★ 65160 ★   Southern
64 Perimeter Ctr. E
Atlanta, GA 30346
(404)393-0650
Company Type: Headquarters. Officer: Edward L. Addison. Employee Count: 28743. Fortune Service 500: Ranking 6.

★ 65161 ★   The Southern Co.
64 Perimeter Ctr. East
Atlanta, GA 30346
(404)393-0650 Fax: (404)668-3559
Officer: Edward L. Addison, CEO. Ultimate Parent: Southern. Employee Count: 29085. Sales: 8489 M.

★ 65162 ★   Southern Copy Machines Inc.
250 Williams St. NW
Atlanta, GA 30303-1032
(404)223-0456
Ultimate Parent: Alco Standard Corp. SIC: 5999—Miscellaneous Retail Stores Nec.

★ 65163 ★   Southern Copy Machines Inc.
250 Williams St. NW
Atlanta, GA 30303-1032
(404)223-0456
Ultimate Parent: Alco Standard Corp. SIC: 5999—Miscellaneous Retail Stores Nec.

★ 65164 ★   Spartan Express Inc.
2700 Moreland Ave. SE
Atlanta, GA 30315
(404)608-1848
Ultimate Parent: Roadway Services.

★ 65165 ★   Sports Authority
3230 Northlake Pkwy NE
Atlanta, GA 30345
(404)270-1644
Ultimate Parent: K-Mart.

★ 65166 ★   Sports Authority
2963 Cobb Pkwy NW
Atlanta, GA 30339
(404)955-6662
Ultimate Parent: K-Mart.

★ 65167 ★   Standard Register Co.
5775 Peachtree Dun Rd. NE, 350E
Atlanta, GA 30342
(404)252-1550
Officer: Jim Biesccker, Manager. Ultimate Parent: Standard Register. SIC: 2761—Manifold Business Forms.

★ 65168 ★   Stanley-Bostitch Inc.
5101 Fulton Industrial Blvd.
Atlanta, GA 30336
Ultimate Parent: Stanley Works. SIC: 3559—Special Industry Machinery Nec.

★ 65169 ★   State Street Bank & Trust Co.
3414 Peachtree Rd. NE
Atlanta, GA 30326
(404)364-9500
Ultimate Parent: State St. Boston Corp.

★ 65170 ★   Stevens Graphics Inc.
713 R D Abernathy Blvd. SW
Atlanta, GA 30310
(404)753-1121
Location Type: Branch office. Officer: W. J. Davidson. Ultimate Parent: BellSouth Corp. SIC: 2759—Commercial Printing Nec; 2732—Book Printing; 2752—Commercial Printing—Lithographic; 2754—Commercial Printing—Gravure.

★ 65171 ★   Stevens Graphics, Inc.
713 Glenn St. SW
Atlanta, GA 30310
(404)753-1121
Company Type: Subsidiary. Ultimate Parent: BellSouth Corp.

★ 65172 ★   Stevens Graphics, Inc.
713 Ralph David Abernathy Blvd.
Atlanta, GA 30310
(404)753-1121
Company Type: Subsidiary. Officer: William J. Davidson, President. Ultimate Parent: BellSouth Corp. SIC: 2741—Miscellaneous Publishing; 2752—Commercial Printing—Lithographic. Employee Count: 950. Sales: 166 M.

★ 65173 ★   Stone Container Corp. Corrugate
400 Lagrange Blvd. SW
Atlanta, GA 30336
(404)344-2541
Ultimate Parent: Stone Container Corp.

★ 65174 ★   Stone Container Corp. Corrugate
1235 Chattahoochee Ave. NW
Atlanta, GA 30318
(404)355-2480
Ultimate Parent: Stone Container Corp.

★ 65175 ★   Structure
Underground
Atlanta, GA
(404)223-3555
Ultimate Parent: Limited.

★ 65176 ★   Structure
North Lake Mall
Atlanta, GA
(404)939-1477
Ultimate Parent: Limited.

★ 65177 ★   Structure
Perimeter Mall
Atlanta, GA
(404)390-0706
Ultimate Parent: Limited.

★ 65178 ★   Structure
Lenox Mall
Atlanta, GA
(404)261-6173
Ultimate Parent: Limited.

★ 65179 ★   Sun Trust Bank Inc.
25 Park Place SE
Atlanta, GA 30303
(404)588-7711 Fax: (404)827-6001
Officer: James B. Williams, CEO. Ultimate Parent: Suntrust Banks. Employee Count: 18956. Sales: 3089 M.

★ 65180 ★   Sunlink Corp.
1100 Peachtree St. NE
Ste 1100
Atlanta, GA 30309-4599
(404)249-4683 Fax: (404)982-7201
Company Type: Subsidiary. Officer: Thomas Gaither, President. Ultimate Parent: BellSouth Corp.

★ 65181 ★   Suntrust Banks
25 Park Pl. NE
Atlanta, GA 30303
(404)588-7711
Company Type: Headquarters. Officer: James B. Williams. Employee Count: 19532. Fortune Service 500: Ranking 18.

★ 65182 ★   T J Maxx
2146 Henderson Mill Rd. NE
Atlanta, GA 30345
(404)491-6076
Ultimate Parent: TJX.

★ 65183 ★   T J Maxx Real Estate Ofc
1900 The Exchange NW
Atlanta, GA 30339
(404)952-9495
Ultimate Parent: TJX.

★ 65184 ★   T J Maxx Regional Office
1900 The Exchange NW
Atlanta, GA 30339
(404)952-8435
Ultimate Parent: TJX.

★ 65185 ★   Taco Bell
3393 Peachtree Rd. NE
Atlanta, GA 30326
(404)231-0675
Ultimate Parent: Pepsico.

★ 65186 ★   Taco Bell
American Fare
Atlanta, GA
(404)938-6892
Ultimate Parent: Pepsico.

★ 65187 ★   Taco Bell
4400 Ashford Dunwoody Rd.
Atlanta, GA 30346
(404)399-7794
Ultimate Parent: Pepsico.

★ 65188 ★   Taco Bell
6560 Roswell Rd. NW
Atlanta, GA 30328
(404)255-3495
Ultimate Parent: Pepsico.

★ 65189 ★   Taco Bell
2400 N. Druid Hills Rd. NE
Atlanta, GA 30329
(404)634-9698
Ultimate Parent: Pepsico.

★ 65190 ★   Taco Bell
429 Ponce De Leon Ave. NE
Atlanta, GA 30308
(404)876-3559
Ultimate Parent: Pepsico.

★ 65191 ★   Taco Bell
1761 Howell Mill Rd. NW
Atlanta, GA 30318
(404)355-4997
Ultimate Parent: Pepsico.

★ 65192 ★   Taco Bell
545 Lee St. SW
Atlanta, GA 30310
(404)753-8518
Ultimate Parent: Pepsico.

★ 65193 ★   Taco Bell
1 Cnn Ctr.
Atlanta, GA 30335
(404)584-5132
Ultimate Parent: Pepsico.

★ 65194 ★   Taco Bell
2840 Greenbriar Pkwy SW
Atlanta, GA 30331
(404)344-5764
Ultimate Parent: Pepsico.

★ 65195 ★   Target Stores Retail Stores
235 Johnson Ferry Rd. NW
Atlanta, GA
(404)256-4600
Ultimate Parent: Dayton Hudson.

★ 65196 ★   Target Stores Retail Stores
2400 N. Druid Hills Rd. NE
Atlanta, GA 30329
(404)325-3211
Ultimate Parent: Dayton Hudson.

★ 65197 ★   TDS Healthcare Systems Corp.
200 Ashford Ctr. N
Atlanta, GA 30338
Company Type: Subsidiary. Ultimate Parent: ALLTEL Corp.

★ 65198 ★ Teachers Insurance & Annuity
5 Concourse Pkwy NE
Atlanta, GA 30328
(404)399-5200
Ultimate Parent: Teachers Insurance & Annuity.

★ 65199 ★ TechSouth, Inc.
50 Executive Pk. Dr. NE, Rm. 420
Atlanta, GA 30329
(404)982-7400
Company Type: Subsidiary. Ultimate Parent: BellSouth Corp.

★ 65200 ★ Techsouth Publishing Services
3135 Presidential Dr.
Atlanta, GA 30340-3907
(404)452-0072
Company Type: Subsidiary. Officer: Richard Donner, President. Ultimate Parent: BellSouth Corp. SIC: 2721—Periodicals. Employee Count: 300. Sales: 33 M.

★ 65201 ★ Texaco
5700 Roswell Rd. NW
Atlanta, GA 30342
(404)252-5579
Ultimate Parent: Texaco.

★ 65202 ★ Texaco
1892 Howell Mill Rd. NW
Atlanta, GA 30318
(404)352-5704
Ultimate Parent: Texaco.

★ 65203 ★ Texaco
2565 Paces Ferry Rd. NW
Atlanta, GA 30339
(404)438-7198
Ultimate Parent: Texaco.

★ 65204 ★ Texaco Express Lube
5640 Northside Dr. NW
Atlanta, GA 30328
(404)952-2577
Ultimate Parent: Texaco.

★ 65205 ★ Texaco Express Lube
2965 Buford Hwy. NE
Atlanta, GA 30329
(404)321-3671
Ultimate Parent: Texaco.

★ 65206 ★ Texaco Food Mart
2691 Bouldercrest Rd. SE
Atlanta, GA 30316
(404)244-9966
Ultimate Parent: Texaco.

★ 65207 ★ Texas Instruments Defense System
1600 Parkwood Cir. NW
Atlanta, GA 30339
(404)955-2775
Ultimate Parent: Texas Instruments.

★ 65208 ★ This End Up Furniture Co.
4400 Ashford Dunwoody Rd.
Atlanta, GA 30346
(404)901-9510
Ultimate Parent: Melville.

★ 65209 ★ Thom Mcan Shoe Store
Town Ctr.
Atlanta, GA
(404)422-5746
Ultimate Parent: Melville.

★ 65210 ★ Thom Mcan Shoe Store
Lenox Square
Atlanta, GA
(404)233-0495
Ultimate Parent: Melville.

★ 65211 ★ Thom Mcan Shoe Store
Shannon Mall
Atlanta, GA
(404)306-1813
Ultimate Parent: Melville.

★ 65212 ★ 3 Com
5 Concourse Pkwy NE
Atlanta, GA 30328
(404)395-2370
Ultimate Parent: 3 COM.

★ 65213 ★ 3M
2860 Bankers Industrial Dr.
Atlanta, GA 30360-2713
(404)447-7000
Company Type: Branch. Ultimate Parent: Minnesota Mining & Mfg. SIC: 5085—Industrial Supplies; 5169—Chemicals & Allied Products Nec.

★ 65214 ★ Thrift Drug Express Pharmacy
210 Interstate North Pky.
Atlanta, GA 30339
(404)980-6662
Ultimate Parent: J.C. Penney.

★ 65215 ★ Time Electronics
200 Galleria Pky., Ste. 1740
Atlanta, GA 30339
(404)984-0126
Location Type: Branch office. Ultimate Parent: Avnet. SIC: 5065—Electronic Parts & Equipment Nec.

★ 65216 ★ Tip-Transport International Po
1612 Moreland Ave. SE
Atlanta, GA 30316
(404)627-3526
Ultimate Parent: General Electric.

★ 65217 ★ Toys R US
2997 Cobb Pky. NW
Atlanta, GA 30339
(404)951-8052
Ultimate Parent: Toys "R" US.

★ 65218 ★ Tracy Locke Inc.
3060 Peachtree Rd. NW
Atlanta, GA 30305
(404)814-0207
Ultimate Parent: Omnicom Group.

★ 65219 ★ Trans World Airlines Inc.
Atlanta Hartsfield I
Atlanta, GA
(404)530-2626
Ultimate Parent: Trans World Airlines.

★ 65220 ★ Trans World Airlines Inc.
50 Hurt Plz. SE
Atlanta, GA 30303
(404)522-5738
Ultimate Parent: Trans World Airlines.

★ 65221 ★ Trans World Airlines Inc.
Atlanta Hartshield
Atlanta, GA
(404)530-2623
Ultimate Parent: Trans World Airlines.

★ 65222 ★ Transamerica Occidental Life Insurance
1117 Perimeter Ctr. Wes
Atlanta, GA
(404)851-9470
Ultimate Parent: Transamerica Occidental Life Insurance.

★ 65223 ★ Transamerica Premier Insurance
2309 Parklake Dr. NE
Atlanta, GA 30345
(404)939-7374
Ultimate Parent: Transamerica.

★ 65224 ★ Treadco, Inc.
987 Sampler Way
Atlanta, GA 30344-1808
(404)768-4426
Ultimate Parent: Arkansas Best. SIC: 5531—Automobile & Home Supply Stores; 7534—Tire Retreading & Repair Shops.

★ 65225 ★ Tuner Broadcasting System, Inc. (was Turner Communications Corp.)
One CNN Ctr.
Atlanta, GA 30303
(404)827-1700
Officer: R.E. Turner, Chairman. Ultimate Parent: Turner Broadcasting System, Inc. SIC: 4841—Cable & Other Pay Television Services; 4833—Television Broadcasting Stations; 6794—Patent Owners & Lessors; 7941—Sports Clubs, Managers & Promoters. Employee Count: 5239. Sales: 17698920000 M.

★ 65226 ★ Turner Broadcasting System, Inc.
1 CNN Ctr.
100 International Blvd.
Atlanta, GA 30303
(404)827-1700 Fax: (404)827-2437
Company Type: Headquarters. Officer: Robert E. Turner, CEO. Employee Count: 5317. Sales: 1921.6 M. Fortune Service 500: Ranking 82.

★ 65227 ★ Turner Home Entertainment
One Cnn Ctr.
Atlanta, GA 30335
(404)827-3066
Ultimate Parent: Turner Broadcasting System, Inc.

★ 65228 ★ Ungermann-Bass Inc.
2839 Paces Ferry Rd. NW
Atlanta, GA 30339
(404)431-0100
Ultimate Parent: Tandem.

★ 65229 ★ Unijax Inc.
1595 Marietta Blvd. NW
Atlanta, GA 30318-3642
(404)355-6460
Officer: Alan McCain. Ultimate Parent: Alco Standard Corp. SIC: 5113—Industrial & Personal Service Paper; 2621—Paper Mills; 1000—Metal Mining.

★ 65230 ★ Unisys Corp. Local Sales
4151 Ashford Dunwoody Rd.
Atlanta, GA 30319
(404)851-3000
Ultimate Parent: Unisys Corp.

★ 65231 ★ United Parcel Service
Atlanta, GA
(404)913-6000
Ultimate Parent: United Parcel Service of America.

★ 65232 ★ United Parcel Service
Atlanta, GA
(404)913-6000
Ultimate Parent: United Parcel Service of America.

★ 65233 ★ United Parcel Service
400 Perimeter Ctr.
Atlanta, GA 30346
(404)913-7737
Ultimate Parent: United Parcel Service of America.

★ 65234 ★ United Parcel Service of America
400 Perimeter Ctr.
Atlanta, GA 30346
(404)913-6000
Company Type: Headquarters. Officer: Kent C. Nelson, CEO. Employee Count: 286000. Fortune Service 500: Ranking 1.

★ 65235 ★ United Parcel Service/ UPS Customer Service
Atlanta, GA
(404)432-9494
Ultimate Parent: United Parcel Service of America.

★ 65236 ★ Unum Life Insurance
3 Ravinia Dr. NE
Atlanta, GA 30346
(404)392-3200
Ultimate Parent: Unum Life. SIC: 6411—Insurance Agents, Brokers & Service.

★ 65237 ★ US Gypsum Co.
1000 Abernathy Rd. NE
Atlanta, GA 30328
(404)396-8735
Ultimate Parent: USG Corp.

★ 65238 ★ US Gypsum Co.
1000 Abernathy Rd. NE
Atlanta, GA 30328
(404)393-0770
Ultimate Parent: USG Corp.

★ 65239 ★ Valley National Financial Service
900 Circle 75 Pkwy NW
Atlanta, GA 30339
(404)933-8370
Ultimate Parent: Banc One Corp.

★ 65240 ★ Valvoline Instant Oil Change
1604 Howell Mill Rd. NW
Atlanta, GA 30318
(404)351-5530
Ultimate Parent: Ashland Oil.

★ 65241 ★ Victoria's Secret
1370 Cumberland Mall NW
Atlanta, GA 30339
(404)435-2600
Ultimate Parent: Limited.

★ 65242 ★ Victoria's Secret
4800 Briarcliff Rd. NE
Atlanta, GA 30345
(404)939-3031
Ultimate Parent: Limited.

★ 65243 ★ Victoria's Secret
3393 Peachtree Rd. NE
Atlanta, GA 30326
(404)365-8860
Ultimate Parent: Limited.

★ 65244 ★ Victoria's Secret
Southlake Mall
Atlanta, GA
(404)961-8383
Ultimate Parent: Limited.

★ 65245 ★ Victoria's Secret
Gwinnett Place Mall
Atlanta, GA
(404)497-0755
Ultimate Parent: Limited.

★ 65246 ★ Victoria's Secret
184 Lower Alabama St. SW
Atlanta, GA 30303
(404)522-9062
Ultimate Parent: Limited.

★ 65247 ★ W. R. Grace & Co.
5210 Phillip Lee Dr.
Atlanta, GA 30336
Ultimate Parent: W. R. Grace. SIC: 2821—Plastics Materials & Resins.

★ 65248 ★ W. R. Grace & Co.
Container Products Div.
5225 Phillip Lee Dr. SW
Atlanta, GA 30336
Company Type: Division. Ultimate Parent: W. R. Grace. SIC: 2891—Adhesives & Sealants.

★ 65249 ★ W. R. Grace & Co.
Dewey & Almy Chemical Div.
5225 Phillip Lee Dr. SW
Atlanta, GA 30336
Company Type: Division. Ultimate Parent: W. R. Grace. SIC: 2891—Adhesives & Sealants.

★ 65250 ★ W. W. Grainger Inc.
Grainger Division
1721 Marietta Blvd. NW
Atlanta, GA 30318
(404)355-1984
Ultimate Parent: W. W. Grainger.

★ 65251 ★ W. W. Grainger Inc.
Grainger Division
3430 Empire Blvd. SW
Atlanta, GA 30354
(404)762-9202
Ultimate Parent: W. W. Grainger.

★ 65252 ★ Wachovia Bank Departments Bank
Atlanta, GA
(404)332-5000
Ultimate Parent: Wachovia Corp.

★ 65253 ★ Wadsworth/Alert Laboratories Inc.
Atlanta, GA
(404)664-4557
Ultimate Parent: Corning.

★ 65254 ★ Wal Mart Discount Cities
4125 Hwy. 20
Atlanta, GA
(404)271-8210
Ultimate Parent: Wal-Mart Stores, Inc.

★ 65255 ★ Wal Mart Discount Cities
1355 East-West Connector
Atlanta, GA
(404)732-8001
Ultimate Parent: Wal-Mart Stores, Inc.

★ 65256 ★   Wal Mart Discount
Cities
Georgia Hwy. 92 E
Atlanta, GA
(404)949-0252
Ultimate Parent: Wal-Mart Stores, Inc.

★ 65257 ★   Wal Mart Discount
Cities
1825 Rockbridge Road
Atlanta, GA
(404)469-8570
Ultimate Parent: Wal-Mart Stores, Inc.

★ 65258 ★   Wal Mart Discount
Cities
4700 Jonesboro Road
Atlanta, GA
(404)964-6036
Ultimate Parent: Wal-Mart Stores, Inc.

★ 65259 ★   Wal Mart Discount
Cities
2135 East Main Street
Atlanta, GA 30344
(404)979-1911
Ultimate Parent: Wal-Mart Stores, Inc.

★ 65260 ★   Wal Mart Discount
Cities
31 Mays Crossing Shopping Ctr.
Atlanta, GA
(404)389-4905
Ultimate Parent: Wal-Mart Stores, Inc.

★ 65261 ★   Wal Mart Discount
Cities
7055 Hwy. 85 South
Atlanta, GA
(404)994-0657
Ultimate Parent: Wal-Mart Stores, Inc.

★ 65262 ★   Wal Mart Discount
Cities
1580 Holcomb Bridge Road
Atlanta, GA
(404)641-0021
Ultimate Parent: Wal-Mart Stores, Inc.

★ 65263 ★   Wal Mart Discount
Cities
3100 Johnson Ferry Road
Atlanta, GA
(404)640-7225
Ultimate Parent: Wal-Mart Stores, Inc.

★ 65264 ★   Wal Mart Discount
Cities
6065 Jonesboro Road
Atlanta, GA
(404)968-0660
Ultimate Parent: Wal-Mart Stores, Inc.

★ 65265 ★   Wal Mart Discount
Cities
455 Clayton Street South
Atlanta, GA
(404)995-0102
Ultimate Parent: Wal-Mart Stores, Inc.

★ 65266 ★   Wal Mart Discount
Cities
200 Cobb Parkway South
Atlanta, GA
(404)424-0405
Ultimate Parent: Wal-Mart Stores, Inc.

★ 65267 ★   Wal Mart Discount
Cities
915 North Glynn Street
Atlanta, GA
(404)460-0726
Ultimate Parent: Wal-Mart Stores, Inc.

★ 65268 ★   Wal Mart Discount
Cities
5989 Stewart Parkway
Atlanta, GA
(404)489-7361
Ultimate Parent: Wal-Mart Stores, Inc.

★ 65269 ★   Wal Mart Discount
Cities
1630 Pleasant Hill Road
Atlanta, GA 30349
(404)925-2722
Ultimate Parent: Wal-Mart Stores, Inc.

★ 65270 ★   Wal Mart Discount
Cities
270 Dallas Market Square
Atlanta, GA
(404)443-2670
Ultimate Parent: Wal-Mart Stores, Inc.

★ 65271 ★   Wal Mart Discount
Cities Stock
31 Mays Crossing Shoppi
Atlanta, GA
(404)474-5083
Ultimate Parent: Wal-Mart Stores, Inc.

★ 65272 ★   Waldenbooks
Town Ctr. at Cobb
Atlanta, GA
(404)427-7810
Ultimate Parent: K-Mart.

★ 65273 ★   Waldenbooks
Spalding Woods Villa
Atlanta, GA
(404)448-7539
Ultimate Parent: K-Mart.

★ 65274 ★   Waldenbooks
Northlake Mall
Atlanta, GA 30345
(404)938-2441
Ultimate Parent: K-Mart.

★ 65275 ★   Waldenbooks
Perimeter Mall
Atlanta, GA 30341
(404)394-0489
Ultimate Parent: K-Mart.

★ 65276 ★   Wall Street Journal
11 Piedmont Ctr. NE
Atlanta, GA 30305
(404)233-2544
Officer: Roy Singleton, Manager. Ultimate
Parent: Dow Jones. SIC: 2711—
Newspapers.

★ 65277 ★   Wall Street Journal
11 Piedmont Ctr. NE
Atlanta, GA 30305
(404)233-9663
Ultimate Parent: Dow Jones.

★ 65278 ★   Wall Street Journal
11 Piedmont Ctr. NE
Atlanta, GA 30305
(404)233-2831
Ultimate Parent: Dow Jones.

★ 65279 ★   Wall Street Journal
11 Piedmont Ctr. NE
Atlanta, GA 30305
(404)233-2544
Ultimate Parent: Dow Jones.

★ 65280 ★   Washington Specialty
Metals
Atlanta, GA
(404)938-5306
Ultimate Parent: Lukens.

★ 65281 ★   Wells Fargo Armored
Service Corp.
6165 Barfield Rd., Ste. 200
Atlanta, GA 30328
(404)256-0540 Fax: (404)847-3144
Officer: Hugh Sawyer, President. Ultimate
Parent: Borg Warner Automotive.

★ 65282 ★   Wells Fargo Armored
Services Corp.
6165 Barfield Rd. NE
Atlanta, GA 30328-4309
(404)256-0540
Officer: Hugh Sawyer, President. Ultimate
Parent: Borg Warner Automotive. SIC:
7381—Detective & Armored Car Services.
Employee Count: 3400.

★ 65283 ★   Wells Fargo Guard
Service
1430 W. Peachtree St. NW
Atlanta, GA 30309
(404)876-4444
Ultimate Parent: Borg Warner Automotive.

★ 65284 ★   Wells Fargo Guard
Services Operations
6060 McDonough Dr.
Atlanta, GA 30315
(404)441-1054
Ultimate Parent: Borg Warner Automotive.

★ 65285 ★   Westinghouse
Electric
1299 Northside Dr. NW
Atlanta, GA 30318
(404)885-5200
Officer: Irvin Hollins, Manager. Ultimate
Parent: Westinghouse Electric Corp. SIC:
3699—Electrical Equipment & Supplies Nec.

★ 65286 ★   Westvaco Corp. Fine
Pape
2 Ravinia Dr. NE
Atlanta, GA 30346
(404)668-1074
Ultimate Parent: WestVaco Corp.

★ 65287 ★   Weyerhaeuser Co.
1270 Tacoma Dr. NW
Atlanta, GA 30318
(404)355-5971
Ultimate Parent: Weyerhaeuser Co.

★ 65288 ★   WGNX-Channel 46
News
1810 Briarcliff Rd. NE
Atlanta, GA 30329
(404)325-3015
Ultimate Parent: Tribune Co.

★ 65289 ★   Windsor Insurance
Co.
1300 Parwood Cir. NW
Atlanta, GA
(404)951-5599
Ultimate Parent: General Cable Corp.

★ 65290 ★   Wise Foods
2840 Mt. Wilkinson Pky., No. 300
Atlanta, GA 30339
(404)433-3100
Officer: Greg Sprich, Vice President.
Ultimate Parent: Borden, Inc. SIC: 2096—
Potato Chips & Similar Snacks.

★ 65291 ★   W.R. Grace & Co.
5210 Phillip Lee Dr.
Atlanta, GA 30336
Ultimate Parent: W. R. Grace. SIC: 2821—
Plastics Materials & Resins.

★ 65292 ★   W.R. Grace & Co.
Dewey & Almy Chemical Div.
5225 Philip Lee Dr. SW
Atlanta, GA 30336
Company Type: Division. Ultimate Parent:
W. R. Grace. SIC: 2891—Adhesives &
Sealants.

★ 65293 ★   Wrigley W M Jr Co.
4500 Atlanta Hwy.
Atlanta, GA
(404)525-3511
Ultimate Parent: William Wrigley Jr. Co.

★ 65294 ★   WXIA TV-11
1611 W. Peachtree St. NE
Atlanta, GA 30309
(404)892-1611
Ultimate Parent: Gannett.

★ 65295 ★   WXIA TV-11 Alive 11
Alive Data
Atlanta, GA
(404)744-1111
Ultimate Parent: Gannett.

★ 65296 ★   WXIA TV-11 Alive
News Hotline
Atlanta, GA
(404)873-9107
Ultimate Parent: Gannett.

★ 65297 ★   Wyeth-Ayerst
Laboratories Inc.
221 Armour Dr. NE
Atlanta, GA 30324
(404)607-8305
Ultimate Parent: American Home Products.

★ 65298 ★   Zenger-Miller
Associates
4170 Ashford Dunwoody Rd.
Atlanta, GA 30319
(404)843-8098
Ultimate Parent: Times Mirror Co.

★ 65299 ★   Zeno Systems of
Georgia Inc.
2080 Peachtree Industrial Ct.
Atlanta, GA 30341
(404)454-9000
Company Type: Subsidiary. Officer: James
McCarter, President. Ultimate Parent: Alco
Standard Corp. SIC: 5044—Office
Equipment; 7359—Equipment Rental &
Leasing Nec.

★ 65300 ★   Zep Manufacturing
Co.
1310 Seaboard Industrial Blvd., NW
Atlanta, GA 30318
(404)352-1680 Fax: (404)350-6268
Officer: Harry Maziar, President. Ultimate
Parent: National Service Industries.

★ 65301 ★   ZEP Manufacturing
Co.
1310 Seaboard Industrial Blvd. NW
Atlanta, GA 30318
(404)352-1680
Officer: Harry Maziar, President. Ultimate
Parent: National Service Industries. SIC:
2899—Chemical Preparations Nec; 3999—
Manufacturing Industries Nec; 2841—Soap
& Other Detergents; 2842—Polishes &
Sanitation Goods; 2843—Surface Active
Agents; 2844—Toilet Preparations.

★ 65302 ★   Zep Manufacturing
Co. Executive
1310 Seaboard Industrial
Atlanta, GA 30318
(404)352-1680
Ultimate Parent: National Service
Industries.

★ 65303 ★   Zep Mfg. Co.
1310 Seaboard Industrial Blvd. NW
Atlanta, GA 30318
Ultimate Parent: National Service
Industries. SIC: 2841—Soap & Other
Detergents; 2842—Polishes & Sanitation
Goods; 2843—Surface Active Agents;
2844—Toilet Preparations.

★ 65304 ★   Bell South Cellular
Corp.
500 Northpark Town Ctr.
1100 Abernathy Rd Ste 500
Atlantga, GA 30328
(404)604-6100
Company Type: Subsidiary. Officer: Stan
Hamm. Ultimate Parent: BellSouth Corp.

Atlantic

★ 65305 ★   Georgia-Pacific Corp.
133 Peachtree St. NE
Atlantic, GA 30303
(404)652-4000 Fax: (404)827-7010
Company Type: Headquarters. Officer: T.
Marshall Hahn Jr., Chairman. Ultimate
Parent: Georgia-Pacific. SIC: 2431—
Millwork; 2611—Pulp Mills; 2621—Paper
Mills. Employee Count: 52000.

★ 65306 ★   Lanier
Worldwide Strategic Marketing
1700 Chantilly Dr. NE
Atlantic, GA 30324
(404)496-9500
Company Type: Subsidiary. Officer: Tony
E. Amason, Vice President & General
Manager. Ultimate Parent: Harris.

Attapulgus

★ 65307 ★   Engelhard Corp.
Engelhard Rd.
Attapulgus, GA 31715
(912)465-3341
Officer: Jim Culliton, Manager. Ultimate
Parent: Engelhard Corp. SIC: 2819—
Industrial Inorganic Chemicals Nec; 3295—
Minerals—Ground or Treated.

★ 65308 ★   Engelhard Corp.
Depot Rd.
Attapulgus, GA 31715
Ultimate Parent: Engelhard Corp. SIC:
2819—Industrial Inorganic Chemicals Nec.

Auburn

★ 65309 ★   Bank South, NA
1310 Atlanta Hwy. NW
Auburn, GA 30203
(404)963-0082
Company Type: Subsidiary. Location
Type: Branch office. Officer: Raymond
Copeland, Manager. Ultimate Parent: Bank
South Corp. SIC: 6021—National
Commercial Banks.

★ 65310 ★   Martin Marietta
Aggregates
301 Parks Mill Rd.
Auburn, GA 30203
(404)963-6123
Ultimate Parent: Martin Marietta.

Augusta

★ 65311 ★ APAC
1 Apac Industrial Way
Augusta, GA 30907
(706)738-5341
Officer: Don Holley, Manager. **Ultimate Parent:** Ashland Oil. **SIC:** 2951—Asphalt Paving Mixtures & Blocks.

★ 65312 ★ Arcadian Corp.
Augusta Plant
23 Columbia Nitrogen Rd.
Augusta, GA 30903
Location Type: Plant. **Ultimate Parent:** Arcadian Corp. **SIC:** 2873—Nitrogenous Fertilizers.

★ 65313 ★ Arcadian Fertilizer LP
PO Box 1483
Augusta, GA 30903-1483
(706)849-6100
Ultimate Parent: Arcadian Corp. **SIC:** 2875—Fertilizers—Mixing Only.

★ 65314 ★ Archer Daniels Midland Co.
960 Molly Pond Rd.
Augusta, GA 30901
(706)722-8866
Officer: Roger Cauthen, Manager. **Ultimate Parent:** Archer Daniels Midland Co. **SIC:** 2075—Soybean Oil Mills; 2076—Vegetable Oil Mills Nec; 2079—Edible Fats & Oils Nec.

★ 65315 ★ Borden Inc.
914 Telfair St.
Augusta, GA 30901
(706)722-4661
Officer: Z. T. Sharron, Manager. **Ultimate Parent:** Borden, Inc. **SIC:** 2024—Ice Cream & Frozen Desserts; 2026—Fluid Milk.

★ 65316 ★ Burlington Coat Factory
1329 Augusta West Pky.
Augusta, GA 30909-6428
(706)738-2452
Location Type: Branch office. **Officer:** Norland Alston, General Manager. **Ultimate Parent:** Burlington Industries, Equity. **SIC:** 5311—Department Stores; 5999—Miscellaneous Retail Stores Nec.

★ 65317 ★ ConAgra Feed Co.
980 Molly Pond Rd.
Augusta, GA 30901
(404)722-6681 **Fax:** (404)722-4561
Officer: Clarence T. Barinowski, President. **Ultimate Parent:** Conagra.

★ 65318 ★ Cummins Military Systems
2950 Old Savannah Rd.
Augusta, GA 30916-6766
Ultimate Parent: Cummins Engine Co. **SIC:** 3711—Motor Vehicles & Car Bodies.

★ 65319 ★ Cummins Military Systems Co.
2950 Old Savannah Rd.
Augusta, GA 30916-6766
Ultimate Parent: Cummins Engine Co. **SIC:** 3711—Motor Vehicles & Car Bodies.

★ 65320 ★ Federal Paper Board Co.
Hwy. 56
Augusta, GA 30906
(706)793-8753
Officer: Robert Dansby, Manager. **Ultimate Parent:** Federal Paper Board. **SIC:** 2421—Sawmills & Planing Mills—General; 2631—Paperboard Mills.

★ 65321 ★ Federal Paper Board Co. Inc. Augusta
Hwy. 56 S.
Augusta, GA 30906
Ultimate Parent: Federal Paper Board. **SIC:** 2631—Paperboard Mills.

★ 65322 ★ Federal Paper Board Co. Inc.-Augusta Operations
Hwy. 56 South
Augusta, GA 30913-1699
Ultimate Parent: Federal Paper Board. **SIC:** 2631—Paperboard Mills.

★ 65323 ★ First Union National Bank of Georgia
3133 Washington Rd.
Augusta, GA 30907-3835
(706)868-2130
Location Type: Branch office. **Ultimate**

Parent: First Union Corp. **SIC:** 6021—National Commercial Banks.

★ 65324 ★ First Union National Bank of Georgia
2835 Washington Rd.
Augusta, GA 30909-2173
(706)667-2270
Location Type: Branch office. **Ultimate Parent:** First Union Corp. **SIC:** 6021—National Commercial Banks.

★ 65325 ★ First Union National Bank of Georgia
3602 Walton Way Ext.
Augusta, GA 30909-1833
(706)667-2285
Location Type: Branch office. **Ultimate Parent:** First Union Corp. **SIC:** 6021—National Commercial Banks.

★ 65326 ★ First Union National Bank of Georgia
1478 Walton Way
Augusta, GA 30901-2649
(706)821-6820
Location Type: Branch office. **Ultimate Parent:** First Union Corp. **SIC:** 6021—National Commercial Banks.

★ 65327 ★ First Union National Bank of Georgia
1751 Gordon Hwy.
Augusta, GA 30904-5169
(706)667-2240
Location Type: Branch office. **Ultimate Parent:** First Union Corp. **SIC:** 6021—National Commercial Banks.

★ 65328 ★ First Union National Bank of Georgia
3430 Wrightsboro Rd.
Augusta, GA 30909-2510
(706)667-2255
Location Type: Branch office. **Ultimate Parent:** First Union Corp. **SIC:** 6021—National Commercial Banks.

★ 65329 ★ First Union National Bank of Georgia
3115 Peach Orchard Rd.
Augusta, GA 30906-2403
(706)771-5900
Location Type: Branch office. **Ultimate Parent:** First Union Corp. **SIC:** 6021—National Commercial Banks.

★ 65330 ★ First Union National Bank of Georgia
699 Broad St.
Augusta, GA 30901-1456
(706)823-2500
Location Type: Branch office. **Ultimate Parent:** First Union Corp. **SIC:** 6021—National Commercial Banks.

★ 65331 ★ G. D. Searle & Co.
1750 Lovers Ln.
Augusta, GA 30901
Ultimate Parent: Monsanto. **SIC:** 2834—Pharmaceutical Preparations.

★ 65332 ★ Georgia Pacific Corp.
999 5th St.
Augusta, GA 30901
(706)724-1577
Officer: Jake Berger, Manager. **Ultimate Parent:** Georgia-Pacific. **SIC:** 3275—Gypsum Products.

★ 65333 ★ JB White & Co.
Regency Mall, Ste. 300
Augusta, GA 30904
(404)790-7070
Officer: Paul E. McLynch, President. **Ultimate Parent:** Mercantile Stores.

★ 65334 ★ Kendall Co.
1816 Marvin Griffin Rd.
Augusta, GA 30906
Ultimate Parent: Colgate-Palmolive. **SIC:** 2200—Textile Mill Products.

★ 65335 ★ Luker Inc.
514 National Ave.
Augusta, GA 30901-3840
(706)724-0244
Company Type: Subsidiary. **Officer:** S. Troy Smith, President. **Ultimate Parent:** Gold Kist. **SIC:** 3556—Food Products Machinery. **Employee Count:** 25. **Sales:** 2.8 M.

★ 65336 ★ Monsanto Co.
1610 Marvin Griffin Rd.
Augusta, GA 30906
Ultimate Parent: Monsanto. **SIC:** 2819—Industrial Inorganic Chemicals Nec; 2874—Phosphatic Fertilizers.

★ 65337 ★ Monsanto Co.
PO Box 1473
Augusta, GA 30903-1473
(706)798-4346
Company Type: Branch. **Officer:** James A. Labanosky. **Ultimate Parent:** Monsanto. **SIC:** 2819—Industrial Inorganic Chemicals Nec; 5169—Chemicals & Allied Products Nec.

★ 65338 ★ Nutrasweet Co.
1750 Lovers Ln.
Augusta, GA 30901
Ultimate Parent: Monsanto. **SIC:** 2869—Industrial Organic Chemicals Nec.

★ 65339 ★ Olin
Augusta Plant
2402 Loop Hwy. 56
Augusta, GA 30913
Location Type: Plant. **Ultimate Parent:** Olin Corp. **SIC:** 2812—Alkalies & Chlorine; 2819—Industrial Inorganic Chemicals Nec.

★ 65340 ★ Olin
Augusta Plant
2402 Loop Hwy. 56
Augusta, GA 30906
Location Type: Plant. **Ultimate Parent:** Olin Corp. **SIC:** 2812—Alkalies & Chlorine; 2819—Industrial Inorganic Chemicals Nec.

★ 65341 ★ Olin Corp.
2402 State Hwy. 56 Loop
Augusta, GA 30906
(706)798-1510
Officer: Joseph C. Rytlewski, Manager. **Ultimate Parent:** Olin Corp. **SIC:** 2812—Alkalies & Chlorine; 2819—Industrial Inorganic Chemicals Nec.

★ 65342 ★ Olin Corp.
Augusta Plant
2402 Hwy. 56 Loop
Augusta, GA 30906
Location Type: Plant. **Ultimate Parent:** Olin Corp. **SIC:** 2812—Alkalies & Chlorine; 2819—Industrial Inorganic Chemicals Nec.

★ 65343 ★ Olin Corp.
Augusta Plant
2402 Loop Hwy. 56
Augusta, GA 30913
Location Type: Plant. **Ultimate Parent:** Olin Corp. **SIC:** 2812—Alkalies & Chlorine; 2819—Industrial Inorganic Chemicals Nec.

★ 65344 ★ Pepsi-Cola Bottling Co.
501 Bobby Jones Expy.
Augusta, GA 30907
(706)860-2790
Officer: Bob Marshall, Manager. **Ultimate Parent:** Pepsico. **SIC:** 2086—Bottled & Canned Soft Drinks.

★ 65345 ★ Procter & Gamble Manuf. Co.
3464 Old Savannah Rd.
Augusta, GA 30906-9318
Ultimate Parent: Procter & Gamble Co. **SIC:** 2841—Soap & Other Detergents.

★ 65346 ★ Procter & Gamble Mfg. Co.
3464 Old Savannah Rd.
Augusta, GA 30906-9318
Ultimate Parent: Procter & Gamble Co. **SIC:** 2841—Soap & Other Detergents.

★ 65347 ★ Southern Wood Piedmont Co.
1650 Nixon Rd.
Augusta, GA 30903
Ultimate Parent: ITT Rayonier Inc. **SIC:** 2491—Wood Preserving.

★ 65348 ★ Textron Inc.
E-Z-Go Div.
1451 Marvin Griffin Rd.
Augusta, GA 30913-2699
Ultimate Parent: Textron. **SIC:** 3799—Transportation Equipment Nec.

Austell

★ 65349 ★ Bindley Western Drug
8055 Troon Cir.
Austell, GA 30001-7849
(404)739-5030
Ultimate Parent: Bindley-Western Industries, Inc. **SIC:** 5122—Drugs, Proprietaries & Sundries; 5122—Drugs, Proprietaries & Sundries.

★ 65350 ★ Bindley Western Drug Co.
Georgia
8055 Troon Cir.
Austell, GA 30001
(404)739-5030 **Fax:** (404)739-8133
Company Type: Subsidiary. **Officer:** G Sidney Anderson, Division Manager. **Ultimate Parent:** Bindley-Western Industries, Inc.

★ 65351 ★ Coca-Cola Bottling Co. the
450 Lee Industrial Blvd.
Austell, GA 30001
(404)944-4340
Ultimate Parent: Coca-Cola Enterprises.

★ 65352 ★ Colonial Pipeline Atlanta Junc
3925 Anderson Farm Rd. SW
Austell, GA 30001
(404)948-8700
Ultimate Parent: Colonial Pipeline.

★ 65353 ★ Colonial Pipeline Co. Main
3925 Anderson Farm Rd. SW
Austell, GA 30001
(404)948-8700
Ultimate Parent: Colonial Pipeline.

★ 65354 ★ Kmart Stores Automotive
3753 Austell Rd. SW
Austell, GA 30001
(404)948-5079
Ultimate Parent: K-Mart.

★ 65355 ★ Marshalls
3999 Austell Rd. SW
Austell, GA 30001
(404)948-7276
Ultimate Parent: Melville.

★ 65356 ★ Radio Shack
1355 East-West Connector
Austell, GA
(404)944-1004
Company Type: Division. **Ultimate Parent:** Tandy Corp.

★ 65357 ★ Ryder Truck Rental
Austell Rd.
Austell, GA
(404)948-4646
Ultimate Parent: Ryder System.

★ 65358 ★ Taco Bell
1642 Mulkey Rd. SW
Austell, GA 30001
(404)941-0332
Ultimate Parent: Pepsico.

★ 65359 ★ Target Stores
3751 Floyd Rd. SW
Austell, GA 30001
(404)436-3999
Ultimate Parent: Dayton Hudson.

★ 65360 ★ Tip-Transport International Po
7330 Delta Cir. SW
Austell, GA 30001
(404)944-9505
Ultimate Parent: General Electric.

Avondale Esta

★ 65361 ★ Nationsbank Ofcs Atl Area Acc
Avonsale 52 N. Avonda
Avondale Esta, GA
(404)523-0900
Ultimate Parent: Nationsbank Corp.

★ 65362 ★ Nationsbank Ofcs Atlanta Area
Avonsale 52 N. Avonda
Avondale Esta, GA
(404)297-1190
Ultimate Parent: Nationsbank Corp.

Bainbridge

★ 65363 ★ American Electric
213 Airport Rd.
Bainbridge, GA 31717-1610
Ultimate Parent: Thomas & Betts. SIC:
3699—Electrical Equipment & Supplies Nec.

★ 65364 ★ Colonial Pipeline Co.
1907 E. Shotwell St.
Bainbridge, GA 31717
(912)246-4900
Ultimate Parent: Colonial Pipeline. SIC:
4619—Pipelines Nec.

★ 65365 ★ Golden Peanut Co.
916 Dothan Rd.
Bainbridge, GA 31717-3059
(912)246-5633
Officer: Robert T. Parker. Ultimate Parent:
Archer Daniels Midland Co. SIC: 5159—
Farm-Product Raw Materials Nec.

★ 65366 ★ Golden Peanut Co.
Newton Hwy.
Bainbridge, GA 31717
(912)246-9950
Ultimate Parent: Archer Daniels Midland
Co. SIC: 5159—Farm-Product Raw
Materials Nec.

★ 65367 ★ Kentucky Fried
Chicken
1023 E. Shotwell St.
Bainbridge, GA 31717
(912)246-3696
Ultimate Parent: Pepsico. SIC: 5812—
Eating Places.

★ 65368 ★ Pepsi-Cola Bottling
Co.
112 W. Louise St.
Bainbridge, GA 31717
(912)246-3474
Officer: Sammy Gray, President. Ultimate
Parent: Pepsico. SIC: 2086—Bottled &
Canned Soft Drinks.

★ 65369 ★ Pizza Hut
1238 E. Shotwell St.
Bainbridge, GA 31717
(912)246-2607
Ultimate Parent: Pepsico. SIC: 5812—
Eating Places.

★ 65370 ★ Taco Bell
1400 E. Shotwell St.
Bainbridge, GA 31717
(912)246-3983
Ultimate Parent: Pepsico. SIC: 5812—
Eating Places.

★ 65371 ★ Texaco Food Mart
100 W. Calhoun St.
Bainbridge, GA 31717
(912)246-4550
Ultimate Parent: Texaco. SIC: 5411—
Grocery Stores; 5921—Liquor Stores.

★ 65372 ★ Thomas & Betts Corp.
213 Airport Rd.
Bainbridge, GA 31717-1610
Ultimate Parent: Thomas & Betts. SIC:
3648—Lighting Equipment Nec.

★ 65373 ★ Trailways Bus Depot
1414 Dothan Rd.
Bainbridge, GA 31717
(912)246-1491
Ultimate Parent: Greyhound Lines Inc. SIC:
4173—Bus Terminal & Service Facilities.

★ 65374 ★ Trinity Industries_Inc.
Structural Steel Plant 64
2431 Airport Rd.
Bainbridge, GA 31717
Ultimate Parent: Trinity Industries. SIC:
3441—Fabricated Structural Metal.

Baldwin

★ 65375 ★ Duck Head Apparel
Co.
Airport Rd.
Baldwin, GA 30511
(706)778-7141
Officer: Ronald Mize, Plant Manager.
Ultimate Parent: Delta Woodside
Industries. SIC: 2325—Men's/Boys'
Trousers & Slacks.

Ball Ground

★ 65376 ★ Gold Kist Inc. By-
Products Plant
Rte. 3 Box 110
Ball Ground, GA 30107
Ultimate Parent: Gold Kist. SIC: 2077—
Animal & Marine Fats & Oils.

★ 65377 ★ Tyson Foods Inc.
Rte. 3
Ball Ground, GA 30107
Ultimate Parent: Tyson Foods, Inc. SIC:
2015—Poultry Slaughtering & Processing.

★ 65378 ★ Tyson Foods Inc.
15995 E. Cherokee Dr.
Ball Ground, GA 30107
(404)479-8796
Officer: Donadl Carnes, Manager. Ultimate
Parent: Tyson Foods, Inc. SIC: 2048—
Prepared Feeds Nec.

Barnesville

★ 65379 ★ Ryder Truck Rental
129 Carleeta St.
Barnesville, GA 30204
(404)358-0167
Ultimate Parent: Ryder System. SIC:
7513—Truck Rental & Leasing Without
Drivers.

Baxley

★ 65380 ★ Longs Drugs
403 N. Main St.
Baxley, GA 31513
(912)367-2481
Ultimate Parent: Longs Drug Stores. SIC:
5912—Drug Stores & Proprietary Stores.

Baxley Georgi

★ 65381 ★ Kentucky Fried
Chicken
Rural Route 7
Baxley Georgi, GA 31513
(912)367-4600
Ultimate Parent: Pepsico. SIC: 5812—
Eating Places.

Blairsville

★ 65382 ★ Georgia Boot Inc.
Blairsville Plant
Shoe Factory Rd.
Blairsville, GA 30512
Ultimate Parent: Johnson & Johnson. SIC:
3143—Men's Footwear Except Athletic.

Blue Ridge

★ 65383 ★ Shaw Industries Inc.
Willingham Cir.
Blue Ridge, GA 30513
(706)632-3078
Officer: Larry Smith, Manager. Ultimate
Parent: Shaw Industries, Inc. SIC: 2281—
Yarn Spinning Mills.

Bogart

★ 65384 ★ Athens First Bank &
Trust
4000 Atlanta Hwy.
Bogart, GA 30622
(706)357-7121
Location Type: Branch office. Officer:
Deborah Williams, Manager. Ultimate
Parent: Synovus Financial Corp. SIC:
6021—National Commercial Banks.

★ 65385 ★ Foamex L.P.
Vahala
375 Commerce Blvd.
Bogart, GA 30622
Ultimate Parent: Foamex. SIC: 3086—
Plastics Foam Products.

★ 65386 ★ Pepsi-Cola Bottling
Co.
Hwy. 29 & 78
Bogart, GA 30622
(404)725-2900
Officer: Mike Garrison, Manager. Ultimate
Parent: Pepsico. SIC: 2086—Bottled &
Canned Soft Drinks.

Boston

★ 65387 ★ Commercial Bank
200 W. Jefferson St.
Boston, GA 31626-9778
(912)498-8500
Location Type: Branch office. Officer: L.J.
Miller, Senior Vice President. Ultimate
Parent: Synovus Financial Corp. SIC:
6021—National Commercial Banks.

Bowdon

★ 65388 ★ Commercial Bank
College St.
Bowdon, GA 30108
(404)258-5561
Ultimate Parent: First Virginia Banks Inc.
SIC: 6036—Savings Institutions Except
Federal.

★ 65389 ★ Piggly Wiggly
105 Bowdon Ctr.
Bowdon, GA 30108
(404)258-2207
Ultimate Parent: Bruno's. SIC: 5499—
Miscellaneous Food Stores.

★ 65390 ★ Radio Shack
111 W. College St.
Bowdon, GA 30108
(404)258-5261
Company Type: Division. Ultimate Parent:
Tandy Corp. SIC: 5731—Radio, Television
& Electronics Stores.

★ 65391 ★ Radio Shack
Columbus Sq.
Bowdon, GA 30108
(404)568-7200
Company Type: Division. Ultimate Parent:
Tandy Corp. SIC: 5734—Computer &
Software Stores.

★ 65392 ★ Rite Aid Discount
Pharmacy
106 Bowdon Ctr.
Bowdon, GA 30108
(404)258-3023
Ultimate Parent: Rite Aid. SIC: 5912—Drug
Stores & Proprietary Stores.

Bremen

★ 65393 ★ Burlington Klopman
Fabrics
611 Smith St. S
Bremen, GA 30110-1919
(404)537-0328
Ultimate Parent: Burlington Industries,
Equity. SIC: 5131—Piece Goods & Notions.

★ 65394 ★ First Union National
Bank of Georgia
501 Alabama Ave.
Bremen, GA 30110-2007
(706)537-2351
Location Type: Branch office. Ultimate
Parent: First Union Corp. SIC: 6021—
National Commercial Banks.

★ 65395 ★ Greyhound Bus Lines
Hwy. 27
Bremen, GA 30110
(404)537-6127
Ultimate Parent: Greyhound Lines Inc. SIC:
4131—Intercity & Rural Bus Transportation.

Broxton

★ 65396 ★ Fleetwood Homes
Ambrose Hwy.
Broxton, GA 31519
(912)359-2392
Officer: Charles E. Lott, President. Ultimate
Parent: Fleetwood Enterprises, Inc. SIC:
2451—Mobile Homes.

Brunswick

★ 65397 ★ Ace Hardware
100 Community Rd.
Brunswick, GA 31520
(912)265-5527
Ultimate Parent: Ace Hardware. SIC:
5251—Hardware Stores.

★ 65398 ★ Ace Hardware Inc.
205 Monck St.
Brunswick, GA 31520
(912)265-1321
Ultimate Parent: Ace Hardware. SIC:
5251—Hardware Stores.

★ 65399 ★ ACME Business
Products
3025 1 2 Altama Ave.
Brunswick, GA 31520-4608
(912)264-6675
Officer: Don R. Simpson. Ultimate Parent:
Alco Standard Corp. SIC: 5999—
Miscellaneous Retail Stores Nec; 5044—
Office Equipment.

★ 65400 ★ ACME Business
Products
3025 Altama Ave.
Brunswick, GA 31520-4608
(912)264-6675
Officer: Don R. Simpson. Ultimate Parent:
Alco Standard Corp. SIC: 5999—
Miscellaneous Retail Stores Nec; 5044—
Office Equipment.

★ 65401 ★ Barnett Bank of
Southeast Georgia, NA
3028 Norwich St.
Brunswick, GA 31520-4516
(912)261-4200
Company Type: Subsidiary. Location
Type: Branch office. Ultimate Parent:
Barnett Banks. SIC: 6022—State
Commercial Banks.

★ 65402 ★ Barnett Bank of
Southeast Georgia, NA
700 Gloucester St.
PO Box 1398
Brunswick, GA 31521-1398
(912)261-4200 Fax: (912)261-4358
Company Type: Subsidiary. Location
Type: Branch office. Officer: James H.
Hunt, President & CEO. Ultimate Parent:
Barnett Banks. SIC: 6021—National
Commercial Banks.

★ 65403 ★ Barnett Bank of
Southeast Georgia, NA
2914 Cypress Mill Rd.
Brunswick, GA 31520-2856
(912)261-4200
Company Type: Subsidiary. Location
Type: Branch office. Officer: Elzie A.
Jacobs, Vice President. Ultimate Parent:
Barnett Banks. SIC: 6021—National
Commercial Banks.

★ 65404 ★ Coastal Bank of
Georgia
1500 Newcastle St.
Brunswick, GA 31520-6899
(912)262-5200 Fax: (912)264-4743
Location Type: Branch office. Ultimate
Parent: Synovus Financial Corp. SIC:
6021—National Commercial Banks.

★ 65405 ★ Coastal Bank of
Georgia
4501 Altama Ave.
Brunswick, GA 31520-3038
(912)264-8622
Location Type: Branch office. Ultimate
Parent: Synovus Financial Corp. SIC:
6021—National Commercial Banks.

★ 65406 ★ Coastal Bank of
Georgia
PO Box 1024
Brunswick, GA 31521-1024
Location Type: Branch office. Ultimate
Parent: Synovus Financial Corp. SIC:
6021—National Commercial Banks.

★ 65407 ★ Creditquick Inc.
2923 Cypress Mill Rd. 2
Brunswick, GA 31520
Ultimate Parent: Barnett Banks. SIC:
6159—Miscellaneous Business Credit
Institutions.

★ 65408 ★ Food Lion
5711 Altama Ave.
Brunswick, GA 31520
(912)262-0097
Ultimate Parent: Food Lion. SIC: 5411—
Grocery Stores.

★ 65409 ★   **Georgia Pacific Corp.**
W. 9th St.
Brunswick, GA 31520
(912)265-5780
Officer: Johathon R. Miller, Manager.
Ultimate Parent: Georgia-Pacific. **SIC:**
2411—Logging; 2611—Pulp Mills; 2631—
Paperboard Mills.

★ 65410 ★   **Georgia Pacific Corp.**
Union St.
Brunswick, GA 31520
(912)265-1700
Officer: Oscar B. Covington Jr., Manager.
Ultimate Parent: Georgia-Pacific. **SIC:**
3275—Gypsum Products.

★ 65411 ★   **Georgia-Pacific Corp.
Brunswick Operations**
West 9th St. PO Box 1438
Brunswick, GA 31521
Ultimate Parent: Georgia-Pacific. **SIC:**
2611—Pulp Mills; 2631—Paperboard Mills.

★ 65412 ★   **Georgia-Pacific Corp.
Sterling Sawmill**
Grants Ferry Rd.
Brunswick, GA 31521
Ultimate Parent: Georgia-Pacific. **SIC:**
2491—Wood Preserving.

★ 65413 ★   **Greyhound Bus Lines**
1101 Gloucester St.
Brunswick, GA 31520
(912)265-2800
Ultimate Parent: Greyhound Lines Inc. **SIC:**
4111—Local & Suburban Transit.

★ 65414 ★   **Hercules Inc.
Brunswick Plant**
2801 Cook St.
Brunswick, GA 31520
Ultimate Parent: Hercules. **SIC:** 2861—
Gum & Wood Chemicals; 2869—Industrial
Organic Chemicals Nec.

★ 65415 ★   **Kentucky Fried
Chicken**
2801 Cypress Mill Rd.
Brunswick, GA 31520
(912)264-2256
Ultimate Parent: Pepsico. **SIC:** 5812—
Eating Places.

★ 65416 ★   **Kentucky Fried
Chicken**
New Jesup Hwy.
Brunswick, GA 31520
(912)267-0384
Ultimate Parent: Pepsico. **SIC:** 5812—
Eating Places.

★ 65417 ★   **Kroger Pharmacy**
4980 Altama Ave.
Brunswick, GA 31520
(912)267-0323
Ultimate Parent: Kroger. **SIC:** 5912—Drug
Stores & Proprietary Stores.

★ 65418 ★   **Lowe's**
117 Altama Connector Blvd.
Brunswick, GA 31520
(912)264-3063
Ultimate Parent: Lowe's. **SIC:** 5039—
Construction Materials Nec.

★ 65419 ★   **Mini Mart**
181 Walker Rd.
Brunswick, GA 31520
(912)264-3180
Ultimate Parent: Kroger. **SIC:** 5411—
Grocery Stores.

★ 65420 ★   **Piggly Wiggly**
4999 Altama Ave.
Brunswick, GA 31520
(912)264-5411
Ultimate Parent: Bruno's. **SIC:** 5411—
Grocery Stores.

★ 65421 ★   **Pizza Hut**
314 Glyndale Dr.
Brunswick, GA 31520
(912)267-0827
Ultimate Parent: Pepsico. **SIC:** 5812—
Eating Places.

★ 65422 ★   **Pizza Hut**
4441 Altama Ave.
Brunswick, GA 31520
(912)264-5884
Ultimate Parent: Pepsico. **SIC:** 5812—
Eating Places.

★ 65423 ★   **Radio Shack**
4529 Altama Ave.
Brunswick, GA 31520
(912)264-8562
Company Type: Division. **Ultimate Parent:**
Tandy Corp. **SIC:** 5731—Radio, Television
& Electronics Stores.

★ 65424 ★   **Radio Shack**
157 Glynn Pl
Brunswick, GA 31520
(912)267-1750
Company Type: Division. **Ultimate Parent:**
Tandy Corp. **SIC:** 5731—Radio, Television
& Electronics Stores.

★ 65425 ★   **Ryder Truck Rental**
550 Young Ln.
Brunswick, GA 31520
(912)265-0211
Ultimate Parent: Ryder System. **SIC:**
7513—Truck Rental & Leasing Without
Drivers.

★ 65426 ★   **Scm Glidco Organics
Corp.**
1 1/2 Miles East of I-95 & Us 17 N. Junction
Brunswick, GA 31525
Ultimate Parent: Hanson Industries. **SIC:**
2869—Industrial Organic Chemicals Nec.

★ 65427 ★   **Scm Glidco Organics
Corp.**
Rte. 6, Box 6010
Brunswick, GA 31520
Ultimate Parent: Hanson Industries. **SIC:**
2869—Industrial Organic Chemicals Nec.

★ 65428 ★   **Shell Co. Trust**
2900 Glynn Ave.
Brunswick, GA 31520
(912)267-6275
Ultimate Parent: Shell Oil Co. **SIC:** 6531—
Real Estate Agents & Managers.

★ 65429 ★   **Wal Mart Discount
City**
Glynn Plz.
Brunswick, GA 31520
(912)265-9600
Ultimate Parent: Wal-Mart Stores, Inc. **SIC:**
5311—Department Stores.

★ 65430 ★   **Waldenbooks**
148 Glynn Pl
Brunswick, GA 31520
(912)267-7170
Ultimate Parent: K-Mart. **SIC:** 5942—Book
Stores.

Buford

★ 65431 ★   **Ace Hardware**
4300 Hwy. 20 NE
Buford, GA 30518
(404)932-1458
Ultimate Parent: Ace Hardware.

★ 65432 ★   **Bank South, NA**
1601 Buford Hwy.
Buford, GA 30518
(404)932-7150
Company Type: Subsidiary. **Location
Type:** Branch office. **Officer:** Angie Tucker,
Manager. **Ultimate Parent:** Bank South
Corp. **SIC:** 6021—National Commercial
Banks.

★ 65433 ★   **Kentucky Fried
Chicken**
4368 Hwy. 20 NE
Buford, GA 30518
(404)945-4878
Ultimate Parent: Pepsico.

★ 65434 ★   **Kmart Stores**
1605 Buford Hwy. NE
Buford, GA 30518
(404)945-0078
Ultimate Parent: K-Mart.

★ 65435 ★   **Kmart Stores
Pharmacy**
1605 Buford Hwy.
Buford, GA 30518
(404)945-0507
Ultimate Parent: K-Mart.

★ 65436 ★   **Kroger Co. the Retail
Sotres**
1605 Bufrod Hwy. NE
Buford, GA
(404)945-3558
Ultimate Parent: Kroger.

★ 65437 ★   **Kroger Pharmacies**
1605 Buford Hwy.
Buford, GA 30518
(404)945-4077
Ultimate Parent: Kroger.

★ 65438 ★   **Mary Kay Cosmetics**
3237 Ivy Lake Ct. NE
Buford, GA 30518
(404)932-5587
Ultimate Parent: Mary Kay Cosmetics.

★ 65439 ★   **McDonald's
Restaurant**
4358 Hwy. 20
Buford, GA 30518
(404)945-7867
Ultimate Parent: McDonald's.

★ 65440 ★   **Pizza Hut**
1525 Buford Hwy. NE
Buford, GA 30518
(404)271-2300
Ultimate Parent: Pepsico.

★ 65441 ★   **PMS Consolidated**
4837 Newton Terrace
Buford, GA 30518
Ultimate Parent: M.A.Hanna. **SIC:** 3087—
Custom Compound of Purchased Resins.

★ 65442 ★   **Pms Consolidated
Fiber Service**
4837 Newton Ter
Buford, GA 30518
(404)932-0548
Ultimate Parent: M.A.Hanna.

★ 65443 ★   **Radio Shack**
4125 Hwy. 20 NE
Buford, GA 30518
(404)945-2211
Company Type: Division. **Ultimate Parent:**
Tandy Corp.

★ 65444 ★   **Ryder Truck Rental**
1426 Buford Hwy. NE
Buford, GA 30518
(404)932-8427
Ultimate Parent: Ryder System.

★ 65445 ★   **Taco Bell**
4291 Hwy. 20 NE
Buford, GA 30518
(404)932-5681
Ultimate Parent: Pepsico.

Byron

★ 65446 ★   **Citizens Bank**
Hwy. 49 & Dunbar Rd.
Byron, GA 31008-9793
(912)956-2600
Location Type: Branch office. **Ultimate
Parent:** Synovus Financial Corp. **SIC:**
6021—National Commercial Banks.

Cairo

★ 65447 ★   **Piggly Wiggly**
355 8th Ave. NE
Cairo, GA 31728
(912)377-4296
Ultimate Parent: Bruno's. **SIC:** 5411—
Grocery Stores.

★ 65448 ★   **Pizza Hut**
399 38th Blvd. NE
Cairo, GA 31728
(912)377-6444
Ultimate Parent: Pepsico. **SIC:** 5812—
Eating Places.

★ 65449 ★   **Radio Shack**
Hwy. 84 E
Cairo, GA 31728
(912)677-7120
Company Type: Division. **Ultimate Parent:**
Tandy Corp. **SIC:** 5046—Commercial
Equipment Nec.

★ 65450 ★   **W. B. Roddenbery
Co., Inc.**
17 1st Ave. NE
PO Box 60
Cairo, GA 31728
(912)377-2102 **Fax:** (912)377-5797
Company Type: Subsidiary. **Officer:** James
Greisinger, President. **Ultimate Parent:**
Dean Foods. **SIC:** 2035—Pickles, Sauces &
Salad Dressings.

★ 65451 ★   **W. B. Roddenbery
Co., Inc.**
Peanut Butter Division
4th Ave. SE
Cairo, GA 31728
Location Type: Plant. **Officer:** Jerry Cox,
Plant Manager. **Ultimate Parent:** Dean
Foods.

★ 65452 ★   **W. B. Roddenbery
Co., Inc.**
Pickle Division
4th Ave. SE
Cairo, GA 31728
Location Type: Plant. **Officer:** Tom
Schwalbe, Plant Manager. **Ultimate Parent:**
Dean Foods. **SIC:** 2035—Pickles, Sauces &
Salad Dressings.

★ 65453 ★   **W. B. Roddenbery
Co., Inc.**
Syrup Division
1st St. NW
Cairo, GA 31728
Location Type: Plant. **Officer:** Joey Martin,
Plant Manager. **Ultimate Parent:** Dean
Foods.

★ 65454 ★   **Ryder Truck Rental**
716 2d Ave. SE
Cairo, GA 31728
(912)377-5663
Ultimate Parent: Ryder System. **SIC:**
7513—Truck Rental & Leasing Without
Drivers.

★ 65455 ★   **Torrington Co.**
2525 Torrington Ave.
Cairo, GA 31728
Ultimate Parent: Ingersoll-Rand. **SIC:**
3565—Packaging Machinery.

★ 65456 ★   **Trailways Bus Station**
401 N. Broad St.
Cairo, GA 31728
(912)377-3452
Ultimate Parent: Greyhound Lines Inc. **SIC:**
4111—Local & Suburban Transit; 4173—
Bus Terminal & Service Facilities.

★ 65457 ★   **United Parcel Service**
Rural Route 1
Cairo, GA 31728
(912)377-3850
Ultimate Parent: United Parcel Service of
America. **SIC:** 4215—Courier Services
Except by Air.

★ 65458 ★   **United Parcel Service**
RR 1
Cairo, GA 31728
(912)377-3850
Ultimate Parent: United Parcel Service of
America. **SIC:** 4215—Courier Services
Except by Air.

★ 65459 ★   **Wal Mart**
305 8th Ave. NE
Cairo, GA 31728
(912)377-1394
Ultimate Parent: Wal-Mart Stores, Inc. **SIC:**
5311—Department Stores.

Calhoun

★ 65460 ★   **Bowater Inc.**
Hwy. 41 N
Calhoun, GA 30701
(706)629-8634
Ultimate Parent: Bowater. **SIC:** 2411—
Logging.

★ 65461 ★   **Burlington Industries**
313 Hickory Knoll Ln. SW
Calhoun, GA 30701-7113
(706)629-4547
Ultimate Parent: Burlington Industries,
Equity. **SIC:** 5131—Piece Goods & Notions.

★ 65462 ★   **Echota Cushion**
Hwy. 41 N
PO Box 489
Calhoun, GA 30701
Ultimate Parent: Leggett & Platt Inc. **SIC:**
2821—Plastics Materials & Resins.

★ 65463 ★   **Echota Cushion Inc.**
Hwy. 41 N.
Calhoun, GA 30701
Ultimate Parent: Leggett & Platt Inc. **SIC:**
3086—Plastics Foam Products.

★ 65464 ★ Echota Cushion Inc.
Hwy. 41 North PO Box 489
Calhoun, GA 30701
Ultimate Parent: Leggett & Platt Inc. SIC:
3086—Plastics Foam Products.

★ 65465 ★ Gold Kist Inc. Feed
Mill
Calhoun Industrial Blvd.
Calhoun, GA 30701
Ultimate Parent: Gold Kist. SIC: 2048—
Prepared Feeds Nec.

★ 65466 ★ Goodyear Tire &
Rubber Co.
1601 Hwy. 41 SW
Calhoun, GA 30701
Ultimate Parent: Goodyear Tire & Rubber.
SIC: 2821—Plastics Materials & Resins.

★ 65467 ★ Harbison-Walker
Refractories Dresser Industries Inc.
McDaniel Station Rd.
Calhoun, GA 30701
Ultimate Parent: Dresser Industries Inc.
SIC: 3297—Nonclay Refractories.

★ 65468 ★ Litton Industrial
Automation Disc Abrasives
Grinders
Rte. 6 Bellwood Rd.
Calhoun, GA 30701
Ultimate Parent: Litton Industries. SIC:
3291—Abrasive Products.

★ 65469 ★ Litton Industrial
Automation Disc Grinders &
Abrasives
Rte. 6 Bellwood Rd.
Calhoun, GA 30701
Ultimate Parent: Litton Industries. SIC:
3291—Abrasive Products.

★ 65470 ★ Litton Industrial
Automation Systems Inc. (Disc
Grinders & Abrasives)
PO Box 969
Calhoun, GA 30703-0969
(706)625-1270 Fax: (706)625-1211
Officer: Jim Hermann, President & CEo.
Ultimate Parent: Litton Industries.

★ 65471 ★ Litton Industries Disc
Grinders & Abrasives Div.
674 Richmond Rd.
PO Box 969
Calhoun, GA 30701-0969
(706)625-1270
Company Type: Division. Location Type:
Plant. Ultimate Parent: Litton Industries.

★ 65472 ★ Omc Calhoun
100 Marine Dr.
Calhoun, GA 30701
Ultimate Parent: Outboard Marine. SIC:
3519—Internal Combustion Engines Nec.

★ 65473 ★ Piggly-Wiggly
Gordon Hills Shopping Ctr.
Calhoun, GA 30701
(706)629-4831
Location Type: Branch office. Officer: Billy
Tierce. Ultimate Parent: Bruno's. SIC:
5411—Grocery Stores.

★ 65474 ★ Shaw Industries Inc.
S Industrial Blvd.
Calhoun, GA 30701
(706)629-7761
Officer: Benny Holloway, Manager.
Ultimate Parent: Shaw Industries, Inc. SIC:
2281—Yarn Spinning Mills.

★ 65475 ★ Springs Industries
Bath Fashions
175 N. Industrial Blvd.
Calhoun, GA 30701
Ultimate Parent: Springs Industries. SIC:
2273—Carpets & Rugs.

★ 65476 ★ Springs Industries,
Inc.
175 N. Industrial Blvd.
Calhoun, GA 30701
(706)629-4541
Officer: Marion Putnam, Manager. Ultimate
Parent: Springs Industries. SIC: 2273—
Carpets & Rugs.

★ 65477 ★ Terrington/Fafnir
2118 S. Hwy. 41
Calhoun, GA 30701
Ultimate Parent: Ingersoll-Rand. SIC:
3562—Ball & Roller Bearings.

Camilla

★ 65478 ★ Dixon Hardware &
Furniture Co. Inc.
33-35 W. Broad St.
Camilla, GA 31730
(912)336-8291
Officer: Ray E. Dixon, President. Ultimate
Parent: Ace Hardware. SIC: 5251—
Hardware Stores; 5712—Furniture Stores;
5722—Household Appliance Stores; 0191—
General Farms—Primarily Crop. Employee
Count: 7.

★ 65479 ★ Golden Peanut Co.
PO Box 548
Camilla, GA 31730-5048
(912)336-0785
Officer: Jum Mercer. Ultimate Parent:
Archer Daniels Midland Co. SIC: 2076—
Vegetable Oil Mills Nec; 5145—
Confectionery.

★ 65480 ★ Golden Peanut Co.
42 N. Ellis St.
Camilla, GA 31730
(912)336-0785
Officer: Jim Mercer, Manager. Ultimate
Parent: Archer Daniels Midland Co. SIC:
2076—Vegetable Oil Mills Nec.

★ 65481 ★ Piggly Wiggly
60 N. Scott St.
Camilla, GA 31730
(912)336-5518
Ultimate Parent: Bruno's. SIC: 5411—
Grocery Stores.

★ 65482 ★ Pizza Hut
61 N. Us Hwy. 19
Camilla, GA 31730
(912)336-0201
Ultimate Parent: Pepsico. SIC: 5812—
Eating Places.

★ 65483 ★ Trailways Bus Station
79 N. Harney St.
Camilla, GA 31730
(912)336-0711
Ultimate Parent: Greyhound Lines Inc. SIC:
4131—Intercity & Rural Bus Transportation.

Canton

★ 65484 ★ Pizza Hut
151 Marietta Hwy.
Canton, GA 30114
(404)479-8775
Ultimate Parent: Pepsico.

★ 65485 ★ Pizza Hut
151 Herndon Ln.
Canton, GA 30114
(404)479-8775
Ultimate Parent: Pepsico. SIC: 5812—
Eating Places.

★ 65486 ★ Ryder Truck Rental
Hwy. 140
Canton, GA 30114
(404)479-6033
Ultimate Parent: Ryder System. SIC:
7513—Truck Rental & Leasing Without
Drivers.

★ 65487 ★ Seaboard Farms of
Canton Inc.
Univeter Rd.
Canton, GA 30114
Ultimate Parent: Seaboard Corp. SIC:
2000—Food & Kindred Products.

★ 65488 ★ Seaboard Farms of
Canton Inc.
Feedmill
654 Univeter Rd. Box 907
Canton, GA 30114
Ultimate Parent: Seaboard Corp. SIC:
2015—Poultry Slaughtering & Processing.

Carrollton

★ 65489 ★ At&T Fitel Co.
201 Adamson Industrial Blvd.
Carrollton, GA 30117
Ultimate Parent: AT&T. SIC: 4813—
Telephone Communications Except
Radiotelephone.

★ 65490 ★ Citizens Bank & Trust
of West Georgia
115 College St.
Carrollton, GA 30117-3129
(404)836-6900 Fax: (404)836-6923
Location Type: Branch office. Ultimate
Parent: Synovus Financial Corp. SIC:
6021—National Commercial Banks.

★ 65491 ★ Citizens Bank & Trust
of West Georgia
810 S. Park St.
Carrollton, GA 30117-8723
(404)836-6920
Location Type: Branch office. Ultimate
Parent: Synovus Financial Corp. SIC:
6021—National Commercial Banks.

★ 65492 ★ Citizens Bank & Trust
of West Georgia
PO Box 2127
Carrollton, GA 30117-7303
Location Type: Branch office. Ultimate
Parent: Synovus Financial Corp.

★ 65493 ★ Citizens Bank & Trust
of West Georgia
609 Bankhead Ave.
Carrollton, GA 30117-1915
(404)834-9053
Location Type: Branch office. Ultimate
Parent: Synovus Financial Corp. SIC:
6021—National Commercial Banks.

★ 65494 ★ Citizens Bank & Trust
of West Georgia
US Hwy. 27 N
Carrollton, GA 30117
(404)836-6926
Location Type: Branch office. Ultimate
Parent: Synovus Financial Corp. SIC:
6021—National Commercial Banks.

★ 65495 ★ Gold Kist Inc. Poultry
616 Kings Bridge Rd.
Carrollton, GA 30117
Ultimate Parent: Gold Kist. SIC: 2015—
Poultry Slaughtering & Processing.

★ 65496 ★ Kentucky Fried
Chicken
575 Bankhead Hwy.
Carrollton, GA 30117
(404)834-5723
Ultimate Parent: Pepsico. SIC: 5812—
Eating Places.

★ 65497 ★ Pizza Hut
103 Stoney Point Cove
Carrollton, GA 30117
(404)834-6112
Ultimate Parent: Pepsico.

Cartersville

★ 65498 ★ Bi-Lo
433 E. Main St.
Cartersville, GA 30120
(404)386-6092
Ultimate Parent: Penn Traffic. SIC: 5411—
Grocery Stores.

★ 65499 ★ First Brands Corp.
101 Old Mill Rd.
Cartersville, GA 30120
(404)382-2330
Officer: J.J. Brubaker, Manager. Ultimate
Parent: Shaw Industries, Inc. SIC: 2673—
Bags—Plastics, Laminated & Coated.

★ 65500 ★ First Brands Corp.
Cartersville Ga
Cartersville, GA
(404)382-2330
Ultimate Parent: First Brands Corp.

★ 65501 ★ Gold Kist Inc. Feed
Mill
Red Comb Dr.
Cartersville, GA 30120
Ultimate Parent: Gold Kist. SIC: 2048—
Prepared Feeds Nec.

★ 65502 ★ Goodyear Cartersville
Mill
8 Goodyear Ave.
Cartersville, GA 30120
Ultimate Parent: Goodyear Tire & Rubber.
SIC: 2296—Tire Cord & Fabrics.

★ 65503 ★ Nationsbank Real
Estate Departments
Cartersville, GA
(404)386-1409
Ultimate Parent: Nationsbank Corp.

★ 65504 ★ Pandel Inc.
21 River Dr.
Cartersville, GA 30120
(706)382-1034 Fax: (706)386-3251
Company Type: Subsidiary. Officer: C.
Edward Terry, President. Ultimate Parent:
Interface Inc.

★ 65505 ★ Pizza Hut
122 Morningside Dr.
Cartersville, GA 30120
(404)382-1919
Ultimate Parent: Pepsico. SIC: 5812—
Eating Places.

★ 65506 ★ Rockland React-Rite
Inc.
PO Box 1600
Cartersville, GA 30120
(706)386-1046 Fax: (706)382-3146
Company Type: Subsidiary. Officer: C.
Edward Terry, President. Ultimate Parent:
Interface Inc.

★ 65507 ★ Rockland React-Rite
Inc.
405 Old Mill Rd.
Cartersville, GA 30120
Ultimate Parent: Interface Inc. SIC: 2869—
Industrial Organic Chemicals Nec.

★ 65508 ★ Ryder Truck Rental
S Erwin
Cartersville, GA 30120
(404)382-2393
Ultimate Parent: Ryder System. SIC:
7359—Equipment Rental & Leasing Nec.

Cedar Springs

★ 65509 ★ Georgia Pacific Corp.
Hwy. 273 W
Cedar Springs, GA 31732
(912)372-5541
Officer: Ed Pumphry, Manager. Ultimate
Parent: Georgia-Pacific. SIC: 2435—
Hardwood Veneer & Plywood; 2436—
Softwood Veneer & Plywood; 2621—Paper
Mills.

★ 65510 ★ Great Southern Paper
Hwy. 273 W.
Cedar Springs, GA 31732
Ultimate Parent: Georgia-Pacific. SIC:
2631—Paperboard Mills.

Cedartown

★ 65511 ★ Hon Co.
907 West Ave.
Cedartown, GA 30125
Ultimate Parent: Hon Industries. SIC:
2522—Office Furniture Except Wood;
5044—Office Equipment.

★ 65512 ★ Kentucky Fried
Chicken
301 N. Main St.
Cedartown, GA 30125
(404)748-8146
Ultimate Parent: Pepsico. SIC: 5812—
Eating Places.

★ 65513 ★ Transamerica
Occidental Life Insurance
248 Tuck Rd.
Cedartown, GA 30125
(404)748-1465
Ultimate Parent: Transamerica Occidental
Life Insurance. SIC: 6211—Security Brokers
& Dealers.

Centerville

★ 65514 ★ Bank South, NA
2770 Watson Blvd.
Centerville, GA 31028-1241
(912)953-3500
Company Type: Subsidiary. Location
Type: Branch office. Officer: Ray Anthoine,
Manager. Ultimate Parent: Bank South
Corp. SIC: 6021—National Commercial
Banks.

★ 65515 ★   Bank South NA/
Centerville
2770 Watson Blvd.
Centerville, GA 31028
(912)953-3506
Company Type: Subsidiary. Location
Type: Branch office. Officer: Ray Anthoine,
Mgr. Ultimate Parent: Bank South Corp.
SIC: 6021—National Commercial Banks.

Chamblee

★ 65516 ★   Ace Hardware
3541 Chamblee Tucker Rd.
Chamblee, GA 30341
(404)455-6131
Ultimate Parent: Ace Hardware.

★ 65517 ★   Ace Hardware Home
Center
3541 Chamblee Tucker Rd.
Chamblee, GA 30341
(404)455-6131
Ultimate Parent: Ace Hardware.

★ 65518 ★   Ace Hardware-
Workbench
5466 Peachtree Industrial Blvd.
Chamblee, GA
(404)458-8058
Ultimate Parent: Ace Hardware.

★ 65519 ★   Bank South, NA
4498 Chamblee Dunwoody Rd.
Chamblee, GA 30338
(404)454-0974
Company Type: Subsidiary. Location
Type: Branch office. Officer: Linda Hurand,
Manager. Ultimate Parent: Bank South
Corp. SIC: 6021—National Commercial
Banks.

★ 65520 ★   Bank South, NA
4532 Chamblee Dunwoody St.
Chamblee, GA 30338-6202
(404)458-0196
Company Type: Subsidiary. Location
Type: Branch office. Ultimate Parent: Bank
South Corp. SIC: 6021—National
Commercial Banks.

★ 65521 ★   Bank South, NA
3358 Chamblee Tucker Rd.
Chamblee, GA 30341
(404)454-0972
Company Type: Subsidiary. Location
Type: Branch office. Officer: Shay
Buchanan, Manager. Ultimate Parent: Bank
South Corp. SIC: 6021—National
Commercial Banks.

★ 65522 ★   First Data Resources
3300 Northeast Expy.
Chamblee, GA 30341
(404)458-0655
Ultimate Parent: First Data Corp.

★ 65523 ★   First Union National
Bank of Georgia
3601 Chamblee-Tucker Rd. & I-285
Chamblee, GA 30341-4480
(404)939-2933
Location Type: Branch office. Ultimate
Parent: First Union Corp. SIC: 6021—
National Commercial Banks.

★ 65524 ★   First Union National
Bank of Georgia
3312 Chamblee Tucker Rd.
Chamblee, GA 30341-2267
(404)297-2950
Location Type: Branch office. Ultimate
Parent: First Union Corp. SIC: 6021—
National Commercial Banks.

★ 65525 ★   First Union National
Bank of Georgia
5465 Peachtree Industrial Blvd.
Chamblee, GA 30341-2267
(404)936-1300
Location Type: Branch office. Ultimate
Parent: First Union Corp. SIC: 6021—
National Commercial Banks.

★ 65526 ★   Fleet Finance Inc.
Central Coll
14 Perimeter Park Blvd.
Chamblee, GA
(404)458-9373
Ultimate Parent: Fleet Financial Group.

★ 65527 ★   Fleet Finance Inc. Reo
Dept
14 Perimeter Park Dr.
Chamblee, GA 30341
(404)452-1616
Ultimate Parent: Fleet Financial Group.

★ 65528 ★   Grumman Systems
Support
14 Perimeter Park Dr.
Chamblee, GA 30341
(404)455-8828
Ultimate Parent: Grumman.

★ 65529 ★   Jiffy Lube Chamblee
5559 Peachtree Industrial Blvd.
Chamblee, GA
(404)454-6163
Ultimate Parent: Pennzoil.

★ 65530 ★   Kentucky Fried
Chicken
5030 Buford Hwy. NE
Chamblee, GA 30341
(404)451-5414
Ultimate Parent: Pepsico.

★ 65531 ★   Kentucky Fried
Chicken
2201 Savoy Dr.
Chamblee, GA 30341
(404)458-4716
Ultimate Parent: Pepsico.

★ 65532 ★   Kroger Pharmacies
3358 Chamblee Tucker Rd.
Chamblee, GA 30341
(404)452-7638
Ultimate Parent: Kroger.

★ 65533 ★   Krogers Co. the Retail
Sotres
3358 Chamblee Tucker Rd.
Chamblee, GA 30341
(404)452-7636
Ultimate Parent: Kroger.

★ 65534 ★   Marathon Petroleum
Co. Southern
1954 Airport Rd.
Chamblee, GA 30341
(404)452-8060
Ultimate Parent: USX Corp.

★ 65535 ★   Nationsbank Atm
Honor-Cirrus L
5001 Buford Hwy. NE
Chamblee, GA 30341
(404)452-2140
Ultimate Parent: Nationsbank Corp.

★ 65536 ★   Nationsbank Honor-
Cirrus North
3322 Chamblee Tucker Rd.
Chamblee, GA 30341
(404)452-2150
Ultimate Parent: Nationsbank Corp.

★ 65537 ★   Nationsbank Ofcs
Atlanta Area
Buford Hwy. 5001
Chamblee, GA
(404)969-0550
Ultimate Parent: Nationsbank Corp.

★ 65538 ★   Nationsbank Saturday
Banking O
5001 Buford Hwy. NE
Chamblee, GA 30341
(404)452-2140
Ultimate Parent: Nationsbank Corp.

★ 65539 ★   Personal Performance
Consultants
3190 NE Expy.
Chamblee, GA
(404)457-4266
Ultimate Parent: Medco Containment
Services.

★ 65540 ★   Pizza Hut
5577 Peachtree Industrial
Chamblee, GA 30341
(404)458-7271
Ultimate Parent: Pepsico.

★ 65541 ★   Radio Shack
5500 Peachtree Industrial
Chamblee, GA 30341
(404)458-1336
Company Type: Division. Ultimate Parent:
Tandy Corp.

★ 65542 ★   Ryder Truck Rental
5475 Peachtree Industrial
Chamblee, GA 30341
(404)457-4729
Ultimate Parent: Ryder System.

★ 65543 ★   Ryder Truck Rental
Chamblee Plaza
Chamblee, GA
(404)452-0923
Ultimate Parent: Ryder System.

★ 65544 ★   Table Pride Inc.
1940 Will Ross Ct
Chamblee, GA 30341
(404)455-7464
Ultimate Parent: Flowers Industries.

★ 65545 ★   Taco Bell
2081 Savoy Dr.
Chamblee, GA 30341
(404)458-4536
Ultimate Parent: Pepsico.

★ 65546 ★   Texaco
4301 North Peachtree Rd.
Chamblee, GA 30341
(404)936-8622
Ultimate Parent: Texaco.

★ 65547 ★   Texaco
2690 Shallowford Rd. NE
Chamblee, GA 30341
(404)452-7820
Ultimate Parent: Texaco.

★ 65548 ★   Texaco
3495 Chamblee Tucker Rd.
Chamblee, GA 30341
(404)458-1951
Ultimate Parent: Texaco.

★ 65549 ★   US Gypsum Co.
4859 New Peachtree Rd.
Chamblee, GA 30341
Ultimate Parent: USG Corp. SIC: 3274—
Lime.

★ 65550 ★   US Gypsum Co.
4859 New Peachtree Rd.
Chamblee, GA 30341
(404)457-4364
Location Type: Plant. Ultimate Parent:
USG Corp.

★ 65551 ★   Washington Inventory
Service
3300 NE Expy. Access
Chamblee, GA 30366
(404)986-0083
Ultimate Parent: Huffy.

★ 65552 ★   Westvaco Corp.
5625 New Peachtree Rd.
Chamblee, GA 30341
(404)458-9801
Officer: Cindy Miller, Manager. Ultimate
Parent: WestVaco Corp. SIC: 2656—
Sanitary Food Containers; 2677—
Envelopes.

★ 65553 ★   Westvaco Corp.
Envelope
5625 New Peachtree Rd.
Chamblee, GA 30341
(404)458-9801
Ultimate Parent: WestVaco Corp.

Chatsworth

★ 65554 ★   Cohutta Banking Co.
211 3rd Ave.
Chatsworth, GA 30705-2945
(706)695-9431 Fax: (706)695-8250
Location Type: Branch office. Officer:
Edward E. Lewandowski, President & CEO.
Ultimate Parent: Synovus Financial Corp.
SIC: 6021—National Commercial Banks.

★ 65555 ★   Cohutta Banking Co.
PO Box 10
Chatsworth, GA 30705-0010
Location Type: Branch office. Ultimate
Parent: Synovus Financial Corp. SIC:
6021—National Commercial Banks.

★ 65556 ★   First Union National
Bank of Georgia
106 Fort St.
Chatsworth, GA 30705
(404)695-4597
Location Type: Branch office. Ultimate
Parent: First Union Corp. SIC: 6021—
National Commercial Banks.

★ 65557 ★   Schering-Plough
Healthcare Products
Hwy. 411 & Duvall Rd.
Chatsworth, GA 30705
Ultimate Parent: Schering-Plough Corp.
SIC: 3086—Plastics Foam Products; 3086—
Plastics Foam Products; 3086—Plastics
Foam Products; 3086—Plastics Foam
Products; 3086—Plastics Foam Products;
3086—Plastics Foam Products.

★ 65558 ★   Shaw Industries Inc.
Green Rd.
Chatsworth, GA 30705
(706)695-4558
Officer: Jim Mc Allister, Manager. Ultimate
Parent: Shaw Industries, Inc. SIC: 2281—
Yarn Spinning Mills.

★ 65559 ★   Shaw Industries Inc.
109 Industrial Blvd.
Chatsworth, GA 30705
(706)695-9691
Officer: Greg Bruner, Manager. Ultimate
Parent: Shaw Industries, Inc. SIC: 2281—
Yarn Spinning Mills.

Chickamauga

★ 65560 ★   Cohutta Banking Co.
101 Wilder Rd.
Chickamauga, GA 30707-1735
(706)375-3103
Location Type: Branch office. Officer:
Carolyn Walker, Manager. Ultimate Parent:
Synovus Financial Corp. SIC: 6021—
National Commercial Banks.

Clarkston

★ 65561 ★   Avnet
Freeman Products
Parknorth Business Ctr.
715 Parknorth Blvd., Ste. 110
Clarkston, GA 30021
(404)297-9088
Company Type: Division. Ultimate Parent:
Avnet. SIC: 5099—Durable Goods Nec.

★ 65562 ★   Electronic Data
Systems
736 Park North Blvd.
Clarkston, GA 30021
(404)297-3700
Ultimate Parent: Electronic Data Systems.

★ 65563 ★   Kentucky Fried
Chicken
4540 E. Ponce De Leon Ave.
Clarkston, GA 30021
(404)270-1448
Ultimate Parent: Pepsico.

Claxton

★ 65564 ★   Ace Hardware
105 W. Main St.
Claxton, GA 30417
(912)739-4702
Ultimate Parent: Ace Hardware. SIC:
5722—Household Appliance Stores.

★ 65565 ★   Georgia Pacific Corp.
PO Box 608
Claxton, GA 30417
(912)739-4803
Officer: Rex Hill, Manager. Ultimate
Parent: Georgia-Pacific.

★ 65566 ★   Trailways Bus Station
515 W. Main St.
Claxton, GA 30417
(912)739-4919
Ultimate Parent: Greyhound Lines Inc. SIC:
4131—Intercity & Rural Bus Transportation.

Clyattville

★ 65567 ★   Packaging Corp. of
America Valdosta
Hwy. 31 S. & Papermill Rd.
Clyattville, GA 31601
Ultimate Parent: Tenneco Inc. SIC: 2631—
Paperboard Mills.

★ 65568 ★   Packaging Corp. of
America Valdosta Facility
Hwy. 31 S. & Hwy. 376
Clyattville, GA 31601
Ultimate Parent: Tenneco Inc. SIC: 2631—
Paperboard Mills.

Cobbtown

★ 65569 ★   Blue Goose Growers Inc.
Cobbtown, GA 30420
(912)684-5050
Ultimate Parent: Dole Food. **SIC:** 5148—Fresh Fruits & Vegetables.

Cochran

★ 65570 ★   Bi-Lo
1010 Dykes St. NE
Cochran, GA 31014
(912)474-4507
Ultimate Parent: Penn Traffic. **SIC:** 5411—Grocery Stores.

★ 65571 ★   National Services Ind.
Lithonia Lighting Div.
1001 West Dykes St.
Cochran, GA 31014-0272
Company Type: Division. **Ultimate Parent:** National Service Industries. **SIC:** 3646—Commercial Lighting Fixtures; 3645—Residential Lighting Fixtures.

★ 65572 ★   Nsi Inc.
Lithonia Lighting Div.
1001 W. Dykes St.
Cochran, GA 31014-0272
Company Type: Division. **Ultimate Parent:** National Service Industries. **SIC:** 3646—Commercial Lighting Fixtures; 3645—Residential Lighting Fixtures.

Codele

★ 65573 ★   Pepsi-Cola Co.
2302 9th Ave. E
Codele, GA 31015
(912)273-4468
Ultimate Parent: Pepsico. **SIC:** 2086—Bottled & Canned Soft Drinks.

College Park

★ 65574 ★   Ace Hardware
3737 Main St.
College Park, GA 30337
(404)767-8666
Ultimate Parent: Ace Hardware.

★ 65575 ★   Amerada Hess Corp.
4910 Riverdale Rd.
College Park, GA 30337
(404)991-2054
Ultimate Parent: Amerada Hess.

★ 65576 ★   Atlanta Coca-Cola Bottling Co. - College Park Plant
4755 Edison Dr.
College Park, GA 30337
Ultimate Parent: Coca-Cola Enterprises. **SIC:** 2086—Bottled & Canned Soft Drinks.

★ 65577 ★   Bank South, NA
1876 Princeton Dr.
College Park, GA 30337
(404)559-6070
Company Type: Subsidiary. **Location Type:** Branch office. **Officer:** Lee Ann Hawkins, Manager. **Ultimate Parent:** Bank South Corp. **SIC:** 6021—National Commercial Banks.

★ 65578 ★   Bank South NA/ College Park
1876 Princeton Ave.
College Park, GA 30337
(404)559-6070
Company Type: Subsidiary. **Location Type:** Branch office. **Officer:** Lee Ann Hawkins, Branch Mgr. **Ultimate Parent:** Bank South Corp. **SIC:** 6021—National Commercial Banks.

★ 65579 ★   BASF Corp.
1507 Pine Dr.
College Park, GA 30349
(404)991-3151
Ultimate Parent: BASF Corp.

★ 65580 ★   Burlington Air Express
5149 Southridge Pky.
College Park, GA 30349
(404)997-9467
Ultimate Parent: Pittston.

★ 65581 ★   Coca-Cola Bottling Com Metro S
5300 Buffington Rd.
College Park, GA 30349
(404)669-2400
Ultimate Parent: Coca-Cola Enterprises.

★ 65582 ★   Courtyard by Marriott
2050 Sullivan Rd.
College Park, GA 30337
(404)997-2220
Ultimate Parent: Marriott International.

★ 65583 ★   Fairfield Inn by Marriott
2451 Old National Pky.
College Park, GA 30349
(404)761-8371
Ultimate Parent: Marriott International.

★ 65584 ★   First National Bank of Georgia
3581 Main St.
College Park, GA 30337-2697
(404)669-2200
Location Type: Branch office. **Ultimate Parent:** First Union Corp. **SIC:** 6021—National Commercial Banks.

★ 65585 ★   Hertz Rent-A-Car Regional Travel
4751 Best Rd.
College Park, GA 30337
(404)768-3543
Ultimate Parent: Hertz.

★ 65586 ★   Kentucky Fried Chicken
5245 Old National Hwy.
College Park, GA 30349
(404)761-6972
Ultimate Parent: Pepsico.

★ 65587 ★   Kroger Co. the Retail Stores
5134 Old National Hwy.
College Park, GA 30349
(404)767-3317
Ultimate Parent: Kroger.

★ 65588 ★   Kroger Pharmacies
5134 Old National Hwy.
College Park, GA 30349
(404)767-4633
Ultimate Parent: Kroger.

★ 65589 ★   Marriott Hotels, Resorts Suites
4711 Best Rd.
College Park, GA 30337
(404)766-7900
Ultimate Parent: Marriott International.

★ 65590 ★   McDonald's Restaurants
4930 Riverdale Rd.
College Park, GA 30337
(404)996-4244
Ultimate Parent: McDonald's.

★ 65591 ★   McDonald's Restaurants
5115 Old National Hwy.
College Park, GA 30349
(404)766-0659
Ultimate Parent: McDonald's.

★ 65592 ★   Nationsbank Departments Employ
6000 Feldwood Rd.
College Park, GA 30349
(404)774-6011
Ultimate Parent: Nationsbank Corp.

★ 65593 ★   Nationsbank Departments Person
6000 Feldwood Rd.
College Park, GA 30349
(404)774-6011
Ultimate Parent: Nationsbank Corp.

★ 65594 ★   Nationsbank Honor-Cirrus South
6000 Feldwood Rd.
College Park, GA 30349
(404)581-2121
Ultimate Parent: Nationsbank Corp.

★ 65595 ★   Nationsbank Offices Atlanta
Old National Hwy.
College Park, GA
(404)969-0550
Ultimate Parent: Nationsbank Corp.

★ 65596 ★   Nationsbank Old National Hwy
5199 Old National Hwy.
College Park, GA 30349
(404)765-1991
Ultimate Parent: Nationsbank Corp.

★ 65597 ★   Payless Shoesource
5120 Old National Hwy.
College Park, GA 30349
(404)765-9052
Ultimate Parent: May Department Stores.

★ 65598 ★   Pizza Hut
5238 Old National Hwy.
College Park, GA 30349
(404)761-1121
Ultimate Parent: Pepsico.

★ 65599 ★   Pizza Hut
6085 Old National Hwy.
College Park, GA 30349
(404)907-4600
Ultimate Parent: Pepsico.

★ 65600 ★   Radio Shack
5151 Old National Hwy.
College Park, GA 30349
(404)767-6914
Company Type: Division. **Ultimate Parent:** Tandy Corp.

★ 65601 ★   Ryder Truck Rental
5620 Old National Hwy.
College Park, GA 30349
(404)768-0390
Ultimate Parent: Ryder System.

★ 65602 ★   Ryder Truck Rental
Old National Hwy.
College Park, GA
(404)907-0047
Ultimate Parent: Ryder System.

★ 65603 ★   Service Merchandise
4855a Old National
College Park, GA
(404)762-6221
Ultimate Parent: Service Merchandise Co., Inc.

★ 65604 ★   Shell Food Mart
4875 Old National Hwy.
College Park, GA 30337
(404)761-7453
Ultimate Parent: Shell Oil Co.

★ 65605 ★   Sysco Food Services of Atlanta
2225 River Dale Rd.
College Park, GA 30337
(404)765-9900
Ultimate Parent: Sysco.

★ 65606 ★   Target Stores Retail Stores Co.
5025 Old National Hwy.
College Park, GA 30349
(404)762-7711
Ultimate Parent: Dayton Hudson.

★ 65607 ★   Texaco Food Mart
2413 Roosevelt Hwy.
College Park, GA 30337
(404)766-8274
Ultimate Parent: Texaco.

★ 65608 ★   Texaco Food Shop
5110 Riverdale Rd.
College Park, GA 30349
(404)991-3001
Ultimate Parent: Texaco.

★ 65609 ★   Tombstone Pizza Corp.
4893 Riverdale Rd.
College Park, GA 30337
(404)996-3230
Ultimate Parent: Philip Morris.

★ 65610 ★   Trugreen Chemlawn
1874 Sullivan Rd.
College Park, GA 30337
(404)996-8483
Ultimate Parent: ServiceMaster Co.

★ 65611 ★   Valvoline Inc.
4680 Edison Dr.
College Park, GA 30337
(404)762-6676
Ultimate Parent: Ashland Oil.

★ 65612 ★   Xerox Computer Services
1676 Phoenix Pkwy
College Park, GA 30349
(404)996-9662
Ultimate Parent: Xerox Corp.

Colquitt

★ 65613 ★   Piggly Wiggly
Bainbridge Hwy.
Colquitt, GA 31737
(912)758-3568
Ultimate Parent: Bruno's. **SIC:** 5411—Grocery Stores.

★ 65614 ★   Security Bank & Trust Co. of Albany
104 E. Crawford St.
Colquitt, GA 31737-1321
(912)758-3461
Officer: R. W. Little Jr., Manager. **Ultimate Parent:** Synovus Financial Corp. **SIC:** 6021—National Commercial Banks.

Columbus

★ 65615 ★   AFLAC Federal Credit Union
1932 Wynnton Rd.
Columbus, GA 31999
(706)596-3591 **Fax:** (706)323-6046
Officer: J. Clark Neaves Jr., President & CEO. **Ultimate Parent:** American Family Life Assurance Co. **SIC:** 6061—Federal Credit Unions.

★ 65616 ★   AFLAC Inc.
1932 Wynnton Rd.
Columbus, GA 31999
(706)323-3431 **Fax:** (706)323-1448
Officer: Daniel P. Amos, President & CEO. **Ultimate Parent:** American Family Life Assurance Co.

★ 65617 ★   American Family Life Assurance Co.
1932 Wynnton Rd.
Columbus, GA 31999-0001
(706)323-3431
Company Type: Headquarters. **Officer:** Daniel Paul Amos, President & CEO. **SIC:** 6321—Accident & Health Insurance; 6311—Life Insurance; 4832—Radio Broadcasting Stations; 6061—Federal Credit Unions; 6324—Hospital & Medical Service Plans; 6399—Insurance Carriers Nec; 6411—Insurance Agents, Brokers & Service; 7011—Hotels & Motels; 8741—Management Services. **Employee Count:** 31363. **Sales:** 13172 M. **Fortune Service 500:** Ranking 26.

★ 65618 ★   American Family Life Assurance Co.
Broadcast Div.
1932 Wynnton Rd.
Columbus, GA 31999-0001
(706)596-5053
Company Type: Division. **Officer:** Leroy Paul, President. **Ultimate Parent:** American Family Life Assurance Co. **SIC:** 4833—Television Broadcasting Stations. **Employee Count:** 551. **Sales:** 61 M.

★ 65619 ★   American General Finance
2485 Airport Thruway
Columbus, GA 31904
(706)324-6684
Location Type: Branch office. **Officer:** Gina M. Taylor. **Ultimate Parent:** American General Corp. **SIC:** 6141—Personal Credit Institutions.

★ 65620 ★   American General Finance Inc.
3803 Macon Rd.
Columbus, GA 31907-2205
(404)372-3232
Officer: Paul Masterson. **Ultimate Parent:** American General Corp. **SIC:** 6141—Personal Credit Institutions.

★ 65621 ★   American General Finance Inc.
3803 Macon Rd.
Columbus, GA 31907-2205
(404)372-3232
Location Type: Branch office. **Officer:** Paul Masterson. **Ultimate Parent:** American General Corp. **SIC:** 6141—Personal Credit Institutions.

★ 65622 ★ **American General Finance Inc.**
2485 Airport Thrwy.
Columbus, GA 31904
(706)324-6684
Location Type: Branch office. **Officer:** Gina M. Taylor. **Ultimate Parent:** American General Corp. **SIC:** 6141—Personal Credit Institutions.

★ 65623 ★ **Colmbus Bank & Trust Co.**
3172 Macon Rd.
Columbus, GA 31906-1709
(706)649-2671
Location Type: Branch office. **Ultimate Parent:** Synovus Financial Corp. **SIC:** 6021—National Commercial Banks.

★ 65624 ★ **Columbus Bank & Trust**
1230 13th Ave.
Columbus, GA 31901-2610
(706)649-2651
Location Type: Branch office. **Ultimate Parent:** Synovus Financial Corp. **SIC:** 6021—National Commercial Banks.

★ 65625 ★ **Columbus Bank & Trust Co.**
6000 Milgen Rd.
Columbus, GA 31907
(706)649-4713
Location Type: Branch office. **Ultimate Parent:** Synovus Financial Corp. **SIC:** 6021—National Commercial Banks.

★ 65626 ★ **Columbus Bank & Trust Co.**
1901 8th Ave.
Columbus, GA 31901-1508
(706)649-4741
Location Type: Branch office. **Ultimate Parent:** Synovus Financial Corp. **SIC:** 6021—National Commercial Banks.

★ 65627 ★ **Columbus Bank & Trust Co.**
1686 Ingersol & Gaudette
Columbus, GA 31905
Location Type: Branch office. **Ultimate Parent:** Synovus Financial Corp. **SIC:** 6021—National Commercial Banks.

★ 65628 ★ **Columbus Bank & Trust Co.**
1000 4th Ave.
Columbus, GA 31901-2506
(706)649-2631
Location Type: Branch office. **Ultimate Parent:** Synovus Financial Corp. **SIC:** 6021—National Commercial Banks.

★ 65629 ★ **Columbus Bank & Trust Co.**
326 Manchester Rd.
Columbus, GA 31904
(706)649-2711
Location Type: Branch office. **Ultimate Parent:** Synovus Financial Corp. **SIC:** 6021—National Commercial Banks.

★ 65630 ★ **Columbus Bank & Trust Co.**
5736 Whitesville Rd.
Columbus, GA 31904-3045
(706)649-2721
Location Type: Branch office. **Ultimate Parent:** Synovus Financial Corp. **SIC:** 6021—National Commercial Banks.

★ 65631 ★ **Columbus Bank & Trust Co.**
3861 Miller Rd.
Columbus, GA 31904-4778
(706)649-2691
Location Type: Branch office. **Ultimate Parent:** Synovus Financial Corp. **SIC:** 6021—National Commercial Banks.

★ 65632 ★ **Columbus Bank & Trust Co.**
5431 Forest Rd.
Columbus, GA 31907
(706)649-2701
Location Type: Branch office. **Ultimate Parent:** Synovus Financial Corp. **SIC:** 6021—National Commercial Banks.

★ 65633 ★ **Columbus Bank & Trust Co.**
4034 Buena Vista
Columbus, GA 31907-3804
(706)649-2681
Ultimate Parent: Synovus Financial Corp. **SIC:** 6021—National Commercial Banks.

★ 65634 ★ **Columbus Bank & Trust Co.**
3900 2nd Ave.
Columbus, GA 31904-7423
(706)649-2641
Location Type: Branch office. **Ultimate Parent:** Synovus Financial Corp. **SIC:** 6021—National Commercial Banks.

★ 65635 ★ **Columbus Bank & Trust Co.**
2500 Weems Rd.
Columbus, GA 31909
(706)649-2708
Ultimate Parent: Synovus Financial Corp. **SIC:** 6021—National Commercial Banks.

★ 65636 ★ **Columbus Bank & Trust Co.**
1535 Benning Dr.
Columbus, GA 31903-2114
(706)649-2661
Location Type: Branch office. **Ultimate Parent:** Synovus Financial Corp. **SIC:** 6021—National Commercial Banks.

★ 65637 ★ **Columbus Bank & Trust Co.**
6739 River Rd.
Columbus, GA 31904
(706)649-5731
Ultimate Parent: Synovus Financial Corp. **SIC:** 6021—National Commercial Banks.

★ 65638 ★ **Columbus Coca-Cola Bottling Inc.**
6055 Coca-Cola Blvd.
Columbus, GA 31909-5532
(706)563-9940
Company Type: Subsidiary. **Officer:** James L. Moore Jr., Pr. **Ultimate Parent:** Coca-Cola Bottling Consol. **SIC:** 5149—Groceries & Related Products Nec. **Employee Count:** 235. **Sales:** 44.5 (est) M.

★ 65639 ★ **Columbus Towel**
1412 Front Ave.
Columbus, GA 31901
Ultimate Parent: Fieldcrest Cannon. **SIC:** 2211—Broadwoven Fabric Mills—Cotton.

★ 65640 ★ **First Union National Bank of Georgia**
1914 Thruway & Ballwood Connector
Columbus, GA 31904-4468
(706)649-3865
Location Type: Branch office. **Ultimate Parent:** First Union Corp. **SIC:** 6021—National Commercial Banks.

★ 65641 ★ **First Union National Bank of Georgia**
1969 Manchester Expy.
Columbus, GA 31904-6753
(706)649-3820
Location Type: Branch office. **Ultimate Parent:** First Union Corp. **SIC:** 6021—National Commercial Banks.

★ 65642 ★ **First Union National Bank of Georgia**
3471 Courtyard Way
Columbus, GA 31909-5379
(706)649-3850
Location Type: Branch office. **Ultimate Parent:** First Union Corp. **SIC:** 6021—National Commercial Banks.

★ 65643 ★ **First Union National Bank of Georgia**
2450 Wynton Rd.
Columbus, GA 31906-2543
(706)649-3835
Location Type: Branch office. **Ultimate Parent:** First Union Corp. **SIC:** 6021—National Commercial Banks.

★ 65644 ★ **First Union National Bank of Georgia**
3436 Victory Dr.
Columbus, GA 31903-2116
(706)685-7130
Location Type: Branch office. **Ultimate Parent:** First Union Corp. **SIC:** 6021—National Commercial Banks.

★ 65645 ★ **First Union National Bank of Georgia**
10th Ave. & 18th St.
Columbus, GA 31901
(706)649-3875
Location Type: Branch office. **Ultimate Parent:** First Union Corp. **SIC:** 6021—National Commercial Banks.

★ 65646 ★ **First Union National Bank of Georgia**
101 13th St.
Columbus, GA 31901-2101
(706)571-6500
Location Type: Branch office. **Ultimate Parent:** First Union Corp. **SIC:** 6021—National Commercial Banks.

★ 65647 ★ **Pepsi-Cola Co.**
4356 Allied Dr.
Columbus, GA 31906
(706)687-1240
Officer: David Hawkins, Manager. **Ultimate Parent:** Pepsico. **SIC:** 2086—Bottled & Canned Soft Drinks.

★ 65648 ★ **Pratt & Whitney**
8801 Macon Rd.
Columbus, GA 31908
Ultimate Parent: United Technologies. **SIC:** 3724—Aircraft Engines & Engine Parts.

★ 65649 ★ **Precision Fabrication Center**
4800 Cargo Dr.
Columbus, GA 31907
Ultimate Parent: Textron. **SIC:** 3728—Aircraft Parts & Equipment Nec.

★ 65650 ★ **Royal Crown Cola Co.**
1000 10th Ave.
Columbus, GA 31901
Ultimate Parent: Chesapeake. **SIC:** 2086—Bottled & Canned Soft Drinks.

★ 65651 ★ **Synovus Financial Corp.**
901 Front Ave., Ste. 301
Columbus, GA 31901
(706)649-2387 **Fax:** (706)649-2479
Company Type: Headquarters. **Officer:** James H. Blanchard, CEO. **Employee Count:** 4798. **Fortune Service 500:** Ranking 86.

★ 65652 ★ **Synovus Financial Corp.**
1 Arsenal Pl.
Columbus, GA 31901
(706)649-2387 **Fax:** (706)649-2342
Ultimate Parent: Synovus Financial Corp.

★ 65653 ★ **Textron Aerospace Prods.**
4800 Cargo Dr.
Columbus, GA 31907
Ultimate Parent: Textron. **SIC:** 3728—Aircraft Parts & Equipment Nec.

★ 65654 ★ **Total System Services Inc.**
1200 Sixth Ave.
Columbus, GA 31902
(706)649-2204 **Fax:** (706)649-4499
Officer: Richard W. Ussery, CEO. **Ultimate Parent:** Synovus Financial Corp. **Employee Count:** 1411. **Sales:** 152 M.

★ 65655 ★ **Unijax Inc.**
1553 Blanchard Blvd.
Columbus, GA 31901-3407
(706)327-7448
Officer: F. Adickes. **Ultimate Parent:** Alco Standard Corp. **SIC:** 5111—Printing & Writing Paper; 2621—Paper Mills; 5087—Service Establishment Equipment; 5113—Industrial & Personal Service Paper.

★ 65656 ★ **Unijax Inc.**
1553 Blanchard Blvd.
Columbus, GA 31901-3407
(706)327-7448
Officer: F. Adickes. **Ultimate Parent:** Alco Standard Corp. **SIC:** 5111—Printing & Writing Paper; 2621—Paper Mills; 5087—Service Establishment Equipment; 5113—Industrial & Personal Service Paper.

★ 65657 ★ **West Point Pepperell**
3201 1st Ave.
Columbus, GA 31904
Ultimate Parent: West Point Stevens. **SIC:** 2211—Broadwoven Fabric Mills—Cotton.

★ 65658 ★ **Worthington Cylinders Corp.**
7701 Chattsworth Rd.
Columbus, GA 31907
Ultimate Parent: Worthington Industries, Inc. **SIC:** 3499—Fabricated Metal Products Nec.

Commerce

★ 65659 ★ **ALLTEL Georgia Inc.**
103 Georgia Ave.
PO Box 439
Commerce, GA 30529
(706)335-5571 **Fax:** (706)355-3100
Ultimate Parent: ALLTEL Corp. **SIC:** 4812—Radiotelephone Communications.

★ 65660 ★ **Gold Kist Inc. Feed Mill**
Hwy. 334
Commerce, GA 30529
Ultimate Parent: Gold Kist. **SIC:** 2048—Prepared Feeds Nec.

★ 65661 ★ **J. M. Huber Corp.**
Rte. 5 Hwy. 334
Commerce, GA 30529
Ultimate Parent: J. M. Huber. **SIC:** 2493—Reconstituted Wood Products.

★ 65662 ★ **J. M. Huber Corp.**
PO Box 670
Commerce, GA 30529
Ultimate Parent: J. M. Huber. **SIC:** 2493—Reconstituted Wood Products.

Conley

★ 65663 ★ **Navistar International Transpo**
3355 Moreland Ave.
Conley, GA 30027
(404)363-2170
Ultimate Parent: Navistar International.

★ 65664 ★ **United Brake Sys. Inc.**
4140 Bonsal Rd. SE
Conley, GA 30027
Ultimate Parent: Echlin. **SIC:** 3714—Motor Vehicle Parts & Accessories.

★ 65665 ★ **United Brake Systems Inc.**
4140 Bonsal Rd.
Conley, GA 30027
(404)366-1135
Ultimate Parent: Echlin.

Conyers

★ 65666 ★ **Air Products & Chemicals Inc.**
1535 Old Covington Rd. NE
Conyers, GA 30208-5001
(404)922-5911
Location Type: Branch office. **Officer:** Eldon Perkins, Manager. **Ultimate Parent:** Air Products & Chemicals, Inc. **SIC:** 2813—Industrial Gases.

★ 65667 ★ **Bank South**
1600 Hwy. 20 NE
Conyers, GA 30207-3735
(404)929-5633
Ultimate Parent: Bank South Corp. **SIC:** 6021—National Commercial Banks.

★ 65668 ★ **Bank South**
1745 GA Hwy. 138
Conyers, GA 30208
(404)929-5635
Location Type: Branch office. **Ultimate Parent:** Bank South Corp. **SIC:** 6021—National Commercial Banks.

★ 65669 ★ **Bank South NA**
1745 Hwy. 138
Conyers, GA 30208
(404)929-5627
Location Type: Branch office. **Officer:** Carol Davis. **Ultimate Parent:** Bank South Corp. **SIC:** 6022—State Commercial Banks; 6021—National Commercial Banks; 6141—Personal Credit Institutions.

★ 65670 ★ **Bank South, NA**
1600 Georgia Hwy. 20 N
Conyers, GA 30207
(404)929-5633
Company Type: Subsidiary. **Location Type:** Branch office. **Officer:** Janet Brewer, Manager. **Ultimate Parent:** Bank South Corp. **SIC:** 6021—National Commercial Banks.

★ 65671 ★ **Bank South, NA**
2355 Salem Rd.
Conyers, GA 30208
(404)929-5627
Company Type: Subsidiary. **Location Type:** Branch office. **Officer:** Debbie Everson, Manager. **Ultimate Parent:** Bank South Corp. **SIC:** 6021—National Commercial Banks.

★ 65672 ★ **Bank South, NA**
1745 Hwy. 138
Conyers, GA 30208
(404)929-5635
Company Type: Subsidiary. **Location Type:** Branch office. **Officer:** Charley Grant, Manager. **Ultimate Parent:** Bank South Corp. **SIC:** 6021—National Commercial Banks.

★ 65673 ★ **Bank South, NA**
1088 West Ave.
Conyers, GA 30207
(404)929-5620
Company Type: Subsidiary. **Location Type:** Branch office. **Officer:** Terence Lewis, Manager. **Ultimate Parent:** Bank South Corp. **SIC:** 6021—National Commercial Banks.

★ 65674 ★ **Bank South, NA**
1540 Hwy. 138 SE
Conyers, GA 30208
(404)929-5615
Company Type: Subsidiary. **Location Type:** Branch office. **Officer:** Rebecca Koivisto, Manager. **Ultimate Parent:** Bank South Corp. **SIC:** 6021—National Commercial Banks.

★ 65675 ★ **Bank South NA Conyers**
1540 Hwy. 138 SE
Conyers, GA 30208
(404)922-9950
Company Type: Subsidiary. **Location Type:** Branch office. **Ultimate Parent:** Bank South Corp. **SIC:** 6021—National Commercial Banks.

★ 65676 ★ **Biolab Inc.**
1735 Dogwood Dr.
Conyers, GA 30207-5039
Ultimate Parent: Great Lakes Chemical. **SIC:** 2899—Chemical Preparations Nec.

★ 65677 ★ **Continental Industries Inc.**
1221 Millcrest Wk NW
Conyers, GA
(404)860-0519
Ultimate Parent: Handy & Harman.

★ 65678 ★ **DAP Inc.**
1900 Rockdale Industrial Blvd.
Conyers, GA 30207
Ultimate Parent: USG Corp. **SIC:** 2891—Adhesives & Sealants.

★ 65679 ★ **First Union National Bank of Georgia**
1440 Hwy. 138 SE & I-20
Conyers, GA 30208-1285
(404)929-5650
Location Type: Branch office. **Ultimate Parent:** First Union Corp. **SIC:** 6021—National Commercial Banks.

★ 65680 ★ **Fleet Finance Inc. Conyers**
1745 Hwy. 138
Conyers, GA
(404)483-8787
Ultimate Parent: Fleet Financial Group.

★ 65681 ★ **Foamex L.P.**
1705-A Industrial Blvd.
Conyers, GA 30207
Ultimate Parent: Foamex. **SIC:** 3086—Plastics Foam Products.

★ 65682 ★ **H. B. Fuller Co.**
1417 Parker Rd.
Conyers, GA 30207
Ultimate Parent: H. B. Fuller. **SIC:** 2851—Paints & Allied Products.

★ 65683 ★ **Jiffy Lube Conyers**
1664 Hwy. 138
Conyers, GA
(404)922-9868
Ultimate Parent: Pennzoil.

★ 65684 ★ **Kentucky Fried Chicken**
1675 Georgia Hwy. 138
Conyers, GA 30208
(404)483-1900
Ultimate Parent: Pepsico.

★ 65685 ★ **Kmart Stores**
1485 Hwy. 138 SE
Conyers, GA 30208
(404)922-7824
Ultimate Parent: K-Mart.

★ 65686 ★ **Kmart Stores Pharmacy**
1485 Hwy. 138 SE
Conyers, GA 30208
(404)922-5133
Ultimate Parent: K-Mart.

★ 65687 ★ **Kroger Co. the Retail Stores**
1745 Hwy. 138 SE
Conyers, GA 30208
(404)922-8753
Ultimate Parent: Kroger.

★ 65688 ★ **Kroger Pharmacies**
1745 Hwy. 138
Conyers, GA 30208
(404)922-0447
Ultimate Parent: Kroger.

★ 65689 ★ **Lithonia Lighting Co.**
Industrial Blvd.
PO Box A
Conyers, GA 30207
(404)922-9000 **Fax:** (404)922-1677
Officer: Jim H. McClung, President. **Ultimate Parent:** National Service Industries.

★ 65690 ★ **Mary Kay Cosmetics**
Indep Sales
2613 Harvest Dr.
Conyers, GA 30208
(404)483-6327
Ultimate Parent: Mary Kay Cosmetics.

★ 65691 ★ **Mary Kay Cosmetics**
Indep Sales
2666 Club Forest Dr. SE
Conyers, GA 30208
(404)388-7003
Ultimate Parent: Mary Kay Cosmetics.

★ 65692 ★ **McDonald's Restaurants**
1765 Hwy. 138
Conyers, GA
(404)483-7472
Ultimate Parent: McDonald's.

★ 65693 ★ **National Services Ind.**
Lithonia Lighting Div.
1335 Industrial Blvd.
Conyers, GA 30207-0087
Company Type: Division. **Ultimate Parent:** National Service Industries. **SIC:** 3646—Commercial Lighting Fixtures; 3645—Residential Lighting Fixtures.

★ 65694 ★ **Nationsbank Ofc Atlanta Area C**
Conyers 1887 Ga Hwy.
Conyers, GA
(404)922-0884
Ultimate Parent: Nationsbank Corp.

★ 65695 ★ **Nationsbank Real Estate Departments**
Conyers, GA
(404)922-2212
Ultimate Parent: Nationsbank Corp.

★ 65696 ★ **Pizza Hut**
3504 Ga Hwy. 20
Conyers, GA
(404)760-0077
Ultimate Parent: Pepsico.

★ 65697 ★ **Pizza Hut**
1237 Iris Dr. SE
Conyers, GA 30208
(404)918-6969
Ultimate Parent: Pepsico.

★ 65698 ★ **Radio Shack**
1444 Old Salem Rd.
Conyers, GA 30208
(404)483-6499
Company Type: Division. **Ultimate Parent:** Tandy Corp.

★ 65699 ★ **Raymond Engineering Inc.**
659 Bayberry Way SE
Conyers, GA 30208
(404)483-9592
Ultimate Parent: Kaman.

★ 65700 ★ **Ryder Truck Rental**
Sigman Rd. & I-20
Conyers, GA
(404)922-6643
Ultimate Parent: Ryder System.

★ 65701 ★ **Ryder Truck Rental**
1439 Old Salem Rd. SE
Conyers, GA
(404)388-9455
Ultimate Parent: Ryder System.

★ 65702 ★ **Ryder Truck Rental**
1464 Klondike Rd.
Conyers, GA 30207
(404)483-5556
Ultimate Parent: Ryder System.

★ 65703 ★ **Ryder Truck Rental**
1464 Old Klondike Rd.
Conyers, GA
(404)483-5556
Ultimate Parent: Ryder System.

★ 65704 ★ **Sealy Stearns & Foster Bedding**
1705 Rockdale Industrial Blvd.
Conyers, GA 30207
(404)483-3810
Officer: Jack Wallace, Manager. **Ultimate Parent:** Sealy. **SIC:** 2515—Mattresses & Bedsprings.

★ 65705 ★ **Taco Bell**
1537 Hwy. 138 SE
Conyers, GA 30208
(404)483-4407
Ultimate Parent: Pepsico.

★ 65706 ★ **Target Stores Retail Stores Co.**
1648 Hwy. 138
Conyers, GA 30208
(404)929-3300
Ultimate Parent: Dayton Hudson.

★ 65707 ★ **Texaco**
1437 Hwy. 138
Conyers, GA 30208
(404)922-0941
Ultimate Parent: Texaco.

★ 65708 ★ **Texaco**
1202 West Ave.
Conyers, GA 30207
(404)929-0088
Ultimate Parent: Texaco.

★ 65709 ★ **Texaco Food Mart**
7876 Old Covington Hwy.
Conyers, GA 30207
(404)483-3623
Ultimate Parent: Texaco.

Cordele

★ 65710 ★ **Exxon Distributor**
415 6th Ave. W
Cordele, GA 31015
(912)273-5282
Ultimate Parent: Exxon. **SIC:** 5172—Petroleum Products Nec.

★ 65711 ★ **Golden Peanut Co.**
PO Box 878
Cordele, GA 31015-0878
(912)273-4255
Officer: Bill Leverette. **Ultimate Parent:** Archer Daniels Midland Co. **SIC:** 2068—Salted & Roasted Nuts & Seeds.

★ 65712 ★ **Golden Peanut Co.**
801 9th St. N
Cordele, GA 31015
(912)273-4255
Officer: W. J. Leverette, Plant Manager. **Ultimate Parent:** Archer Daniels Midland Co.

★ 65713 ★ **Greyhound Bus Lines**
506 Greer St.
Cordele, GA 31015
Ultimate Parent: Greyhound Lines Inc. **SIC:** 4111—Local & Suburban Transit.

★ 65714 ★ **Piggly Wiggly**
Southgate Shopping Ctr.
Cordele, GA 31015
(912)273-3195
Ultimate Parent: Bruno's. **SIC:** 5411—Grocery Stores.

★ 65715 ★ **Piggly Wiggly**
1011 16th Ave. E
Cordele, GA 31015
(912)273-7757
Ultimate Parent: Bruno's. **SIC:** 5411—Grocery Stores.

★ 65716 ★ **Piggly Wiggly Southern**
Southgate Shop Ct
Cordele, GA 31015
(912)273-3195
Ultimate Parent: Bruno's. **SIC:** 5411—Grocery Stores.

★ 65717 ★ **Pizza Hut**
1510 16th Ave. E
Cordele, GA 31015
(912)273-1291
Ultimate Parent: Pepsico. **SIC:** 5812—Eating Places.

★ 65718 ★ **Radio Shack**
1413 16th Ave. E. G
Cordele, GA 31015
Company Type: Division. **Ultimate Parent:** Tandy Corp. **SIC:** 5065—Electronic Parts & Equipment Nec.

★ 65719 ★ **Ryder Truck Rental**
107 Cemetery
Cordele, GA 31015
(912)273-1664
Ultimate Parent: Ryder System. **SIC:** 7389—Business Services Nec.

★ 65720 ★ **Ryder Truck Rental**
Midway Rd.
Cordele, GA 31015
(912)273-6005
Ultimate Parent: Ryder System. **SIC:** 7359—Equipment Rental & Leasing Nec.

★ 65721 ★ **Wal Mart Discount Cities**
1407 16th Ave. E
Cordele, GA 31015
(912)273-9270
Ultimate Parent: Wal-Mart Stores, Inc. **SIC:** 5311—Department Stores.

Cornelia

★ 65722 ★ **Ethicon, Inc.**
70 Clarkesville Hwy.
Cornelia, GA 30531
Ultimate Parent: Johnson & Johnson. **SIC:** 3841—Surgical & Medical Instruments; 3842—Surgical Appliances & Supplies; 2841—Soap & Other Detergents; 2842—Polishes & Sanitation Goods.

Covington

★ 65723 ★ **Bard Urological**
8195 Industrial Blvd.
Covington, GA 30209
(404)784-6100 **Fax:** (404)786-4619
Company Type: Subsidiary. **Officer:** P.J. Ehret, President. **Ultimate Parent:** C. R. Bard.

★ 65724 ★ **C. R. Bard Inc.**
Bard Urological
8195 N. Industrial Blvd.
Covington, GA 30209-2695
Ultimate Parent: C. R. Bard. **SIC:** 3841—Surgical & Medical Instruments.

★ 65725 ★   **Coast to Coast**
1144 Monticello St. SW
Covington, GA 30209
(404)786-7979
Ultimate Parent: Servistar Corp. **SIC:**
5531—Automobile & Home Supply Stores.

★ 65726 ★   **C.R. Bard Inc.**
Urological Division
8195 Industrial Blvd. NE
Covington, GA 30209
(404)784-6100
Ultimate Parent: C. R. Bard.

★ 65727 ★   **H. B. Fuller Co.**
12110 Harland Dr. NE
Covington, GA 30209
Ultimate Parent: H. B. Fuller. **SIC:** 2821—
Plastics Materials & Resins.

★ 65728 ★   **H.B. Fuller Co.**
Asc Div.
12110 Harland Drive NE
Covington, GA 30209
Company Type: Division. **Ultimate Parent:**
H. B. Fuller. **SIC:** 2821—Plastics Materials
& Resins.

★ 65729 ★   **Hercules Inc.**
Alcovy Rd.
Covington, GA 30209
Ultimate Parent: Hercules. **SIC:** 2824—
Organic Fibers—Noncellulosic.

★ 65730 ★   **Kentucky Fried Chicken**
6103 Us 278 W
Covington, GA 30209
(404)786-8790
Ultimate Parent: Pepsico. **SIC:** 5812—
Eating Places.

★ 65731 ★   **Kmart Stores**
6239 Turner Lake Rd.
Covington, GA
(404)787-7877
Ultimate Parent: K-Mart.

★ 65732 ★   **Kmart Stores Pharmacy**
6239 Turner Lake Rd.
Covington, GA
(404)787-8292
Ultimate Parent: K-Mart.

★ 65733 ★   **Kmart Stores Portrait Studio**
Covington, GA
(404)787-5948
Ultimate Parent: K-Mart.

★ 65734 ★   **Kroger Co.**
3139 Us 278 E
Covington, GA 30209
(404)787-0724
Ultimate Parent: Kroger. **SIC:** 5411—
Grocery Stores.

★ 65735 ★   **Mead Corp.**
4146 Hwy. 278
Covington, GA 30209
(404)786-4616
Ultimate Parent: Mead. **SIC:** 5932—Used
Merchandise Stores.

★ 65736 ★   **Mobil Chemical**
PO Box 71
Covington, GA 30209-0071
(404)786-5372
Officer: G. Auth. **Ultimate Parent:** Mobil.
SIC: 3089—Plastics Products Nec; 3086—
Plastics Foam Products.

★ 65737 ★   **Mobil Chemical Co.**
8170 Alcovy Rd. NE
Covington, GA 30209-2560
(706)786-5372
Ultimate Parent: Mobil. **SIC:** 5162—
Plastics Materials & Basic Shapes; 3086—
Plastics Foam Products.

★ 65738 ★   **Mobil Oil Corp.**
Alvoy Rd.
Covington, GA 30209
(404)786-5372
Ultimate Parent: Mobil. **SIC:** 3089—
Plastics Products Nec.

★ 65739 ★   **Pizza Hut**
3283 Hwy. 278 NE
Covington, GA 30209
(404)786-4331
Ultimate Parent: Pepsico. **SIC:** 5812—
Eating Places.

★ 65740 ★   **Radio Shack**
3112 Us 278 E
Covington, GA 30209
(404)787-0205
Company Type: Division. **Ultimate Parent:**
Tandy Corp. **SIC:** 5731—Radio, Television
& Electronics Stores.

★ 65741 ★   **Rite Aid**
3132 Us 278 E
Covington, GA 30209
(404)787-2120
Ultimate Parent: Rite Aid. **SIC:** 5912—Drug
Stores & Proprietary Stores.

★ 65742 ★   **Valspar Corp.**
9308 Industrial Dr.
Covington, GA 30209-2619
Ultimate Parent: Valspar Corp. **SIC:**
2851—Paints & Allied Products.

★ 65743 ★   **Wal Mart**
9218 Us 278 E
Covington, GA 30209
(404)787-8030
Ultimate Parent: Wal-Mart Stores, Inc. **SIC:**
5311—Department Stores.

Cumming

★ 65744 ★   **Bank South, NA**
201 W. Main St.
Cumming, GA 30130
(706)781-3400
Company Type: Subsidiary. **Location
Type:** Branch office. **Officer:** Martin
Wellborn, Manager. **Ultimate Parent:** Bank
South Corp. **SIC:** 6021—National
Commercial Banks.

★ 65745 ★   **Bank South, NA**
537 Lakeland Plz.
Cumming, GA 30130
(706)889-0023
Company Type: Subsidiary. **Location
Type:** Branch office. **Officer:** Mike Rogers,
Manager. **Ultimate Parent:** Bank South
Corp. **SIC:** 6021—National Commercial
Banks.

★ 65746 ★   **Bank South NA/ Cumming**
201 W. Main St.
Cumming, GA 30130
(706)887-7793
Company Type: Subsidiary. **Location
Type:** Branch office. **Officer:** Martin
Welborn, President. **Ultimate Parent:** Bank
South Corp. **SIC:** 6021—National
Commercial Banks.

★ 65747 ★   **Kentucky Fried Chicken**
Atlanta Hwy.
Cumming, GA 30130
(404)887-8522
Ultimate Parent: Pepsico. **SIC:** 5812—
Eating Places.

★ 65748 ★   **Pizza Hut**
670 Atlanta Rd.
Cumming, GA 30130
(404)889-1740
Ultimate Parent: Pepsico. **SIC:** 5812—
Eating Places.

★ 65749 ★   **Russell Corp.**
330 W. Maple St.
Cumming, GA 30130
(404)889-9266
Ultimate Parent: Russell. **SIC:** 2321—
Men's/Boys' Shirts.

★ 65750 ★   **Ryder Truck Rental**
Old Buford Rd.
Cumming, GA
(404)889-1656
Ultimate Parent: Ryder System.

★ 65751 ★   **Tyson Foods Inc.**
340 W. Maple St.
Cumming, GA 30130
(404)887-2344
Officer: Mart Massey, Plant Manager.
Ultimate Parent: Tyson Foods, Inc. **SIC:**
2015—Poultry Slaughtering & Processing.

Dacula

★ 65752 ★   **Colonial Pipeline Co. Dacu**
Stanley Rd.
Dacula, GA
(404)963-3149
Ultimate Parent: Colonial Pipeline.

Dahlonega

★ 65753 ★   **Burlington Industries Inc.**
Pine Tree Way
Dahlonega, GA 30533
(706)864-3311
Officer: David D. Silcox, Manager. **Ultimate
Parent:** Burlington Industries, Equity. **SIC:**
2221—Broadwoven Fabric Mills—Manmade;
2281—Yarn Spinning Mills.

★ 65754 ★   **Burlington Industries Inc. Pine**
1000 Pine Tree Rd. SE
Dahlonega, GA 30533-1369
(706)864-3311
Officer: David Silcox. **Ultimate Parent:**
Burlington Industries, Equity. **SIC:** 2211—
Broadwoven Fabric Mills—Cotton; 5099—
Durable Goods Nec.

★ 65755 ★   **Torrington Co.**
Bearing Div.
300 Torrington Dr.
Dahlonega, GA 30533
Company Type: Division. **Ultimate Parent:**
Ingersoll-Rand. **SIC:** 3562—Ball & Roller
Bearings.

Dallas

★ 65756 ★   **Ace Hardware-Butlers**
1097 Merchants Dr.
Dallas, GA 30132
(404)445-9484
Ultimate Parent: Ace Hardware.

★ 65757 ★   **Armstrong World Industries Inc.**
351 S. Industrial Park Dr.
Dallas, GA 30132
Ultimate Parent: Armstrong World
Industries. **SIC:** 3086—Plastics Foam
Products.

★ 65758 ★   **Delta Air Lines**
1076 Atlanta Hwy.
Dallas, GA 30132
(404)443-2511
Ultimate Parent: Delta Air Lines, Inc.

★ 65759 ★   **Delta Air Lines Inc. Delta Auto**
1076 Atlanta Hwy.
Dallas, GA 30132
(404)443-2511
Ultimate Parent: Delta Air Lines, Inc.

★ 65760 ★   **Exxon Food Shop**
1541 Marietta Hwy.
Dallas, GA 30132
(404)443-1056
Ultimate Parent: Exxon.

★ 65761 ★   **Kentucky Fried Chicken**
1297 Atlanta Hwy.
Dallas, GA 30132
(404)443-2056
Ultimate Parent: Pepsico.

★ 65762 ★   **Mary Kay Cosmetics**
Indep Sales
1210 Cedarstone Dr.
Dallas, GA 30132
(404)445-6427
Ultimate Parent: Mary Kay Cosmetics.

★ 65763 ★   **McDonald's Restaurants**
Macland Rd.
Dallas, GA
(404)445-9713
Ultimate Parent: McDonald's.

★ 65764 ★   **Pizza Hut**
1925 Marietta Hwy.
Dallas, GA 30132
(404)443-8800
Ultimate Parent: Pepsico.

★ 65765 ★   **Pizza Hut**
1257 Merchamts Dr.
Dallas, GA 30132
(404)443-2122
Ultimate Parent: Pepsico.

★ 65766 ★   **Ryder Truck Rental**
331 Main St.
Dallas, GA 30132
(404)445-0620
Ultimate Parent: Ryder System.

★ 65767 ★   **Shaw Industries Inc.**
1400 N. Industrial Blvd.
Dallas, GA 30132
(404)445-6044
Officer: Ken Mc Kinney, Manager. **Ultimate
Parent:** Shaw Industries, Inc. **SIC:** 2281—
Yarn Spinning Mills.

★ 65768 ★   **Ww Henry Co.**
350 S. Industrial Park Dr.
Dallas, GA 30132
Ultimate Parent: Armstrong World
Industries. **SIC:** 2891—Adhesives &
Sealants.

Dalton

★ 65769 ★   **Allied-Signal Inc.**
2100 Fiber Park Dr.
Dalton, GA 30720
(706)226-3300
Officer: Ronald P. Roy Jr., Manager.
Ultimate Parent: Allied-Signal Inc. **SIC:**
2655—Fiber Cans, Drums & Similar
Products; 3552—Textile Machinery.

★ 65770 ★   **Allied-Signal Inc.**
2100 Fiber Park Dr.
Dalton, GA 30720-3739
(706)226-3300
Officer: Robert C. Vanhorn. **Ultimate
Parent:** Allied-Signal Inc. **SIC:** 5084—
Industrial Machinery & Equipment; 2299—
Textile Goods Nec; 2655—Fiber Cans,
Drums & Similar Products; 3552—Textile
Machinery.

★ 65771 ★   **American Emulsions Co. Inc.**
1202 Dozier St.
Dalton, GA 30721
Ultimate Parent: RPM, Inc. **SIC:** 2843—
Surface Active Agents.

★ 65772 ★   **BASF Corp.**
500 Holiday Dr.
Dalton, GA 30720
(706)226-5122
Ultimate Parent: BASF Corp. **SIC:** 2299—
Textile Goods Nec; 2655—Fiber Cans,
Drums & Similar Products; 3552—Textile
Machinery.

★ 65773 ★   **BASF Corp.**
Fibers Division
500 Holiday Ave.
Dalton, GA 30720-3703
(706)226-5122
Company Type: Division. **Location Type:**
Branch office. **Officer:** Steve Robinson.
Ultimate Parent: BASF Corp. **SIC:** 2299—
Textile Goods Nec; 2655—Fiber Cans,
Drums & Similar Products; 5084—Industrial
Machinery & Equipment; 5199—Nondurable
Goods Nec.

★ 65774 ★   **Collins & Aikman Corp.**
Floor Covering Div.
1220 Royal Dr.
Dalton, GA 30720
Company Type: Division. **Ultimate Parent:**
Collins & Aikman Group. **SIC:** 2273—
Carpets & Rugs.

★ 65775 ★   **Collins & Aikman Corp.**
Floor Covering Div.
1000 Vista Dr.
Dalton, GA 30720
Company Type: Division. **Ultimate Parent:**
Collins & Aikman Group. **SIC:** 2273—
Carpets & Rugs.

★ 65776 ★   **Color-Tech Plant**
Lakeland Rd.
Dalton, GA 30720
Ultimate Parent: Armstrong World
Industries. **SIC:** 2273—Carpets & Rugs.

★ 65777 ★ **Conagra Broiler Co.**
433 S. Hamilton St.
Dalton, GA 30720
(706)278-3212
Company Type: Division. **Location Type:**
Plant. **Officer:** Bob Bahr, Plant Manager.
Ultimate Parent: Conagra. **SIC:** 2015—
Poultry Slaughtering & Processing.

★ 65778 ★ **Conagra Poultry Co.**
433 S. Hamilton St.
Dalton, GA 30722
Ultimate Parent: Conagra. **SIC:** 0251—
Broiler, Fryer & Roaster Chickens.

★ 65779 ★ **Conagra Poultry Co.**
433 South Hamilton St.
Dalton, GA 30720
Ultimate Parent: Conagra. **SIC:** 2000—
Food & Kindred Products.

★ 65780 ★ **Dalton Plant**
1468 Prosser Dr. SE
Dalton, GA 30720
(706)277-3000
Location Type: Plant. **Ultimate Parent:**
Dow Chemical Co. USA. **SIC:** 2819—
Industrial Inorganic Chemicals Nec.
Employee Count: 70.

★ 65781 ★ **Dow Chemical Dalton Site**
1468 Prosser Dr. SE
Dalton, GA 30720
Ultimate Parent: Dow Chemical Co. USA.
SIC: 2821—Plastics Materials & Resins;
2822—Synthetic Rubber.

★ 65782 ★ **Dow Chemical Dalton Site**
1468 Prosser Drive, SE
Dalton, GA 30720
Ultimate Parent: Dow Chemical Co. USA.
SIC: 2821—Plastics Materials & Resins;
2822—Synthetic Rubber.

★ 65783 ★ **First Union National Bank of Georgia**
1237 Cleveland Rd.
Dalton, GA 30721-8675
(706)278-2020
Location Type: Branch office. **Ultimate Parent:** First Union Corp. **SIC:** 6021—
National Commercial Banks.

★ 65784 ★ **First Union National Bank of Georgia**
1300 Walnut Ave.
Dalton, GA 30720-3800
(404)278-0804
Location Type: Branch office. **Ultimate Parent:** First Union Corp. **SIC:** 6021—
National Commercial Banks.

★ 65785 ★ **First Union National Bank of Georgia**
204 W. Cuyler St.
Dalton, GA 30720-8209
(706)278-2020
Location Type: Branch office. **Ultimate Parent:** First Union Corp. **SIC:** 6021—
National Commercial Banks.

★ 65786 ★ **Marketing Services**
Industrial Blvd.
PO Box 1103
Dalton, GA 30720
(404)272-1977 **Fax:** (404)266-1680
Officer: James E. Brown, Chairman of the Board. **Ultimate Parent:** National Service Industries.

★ 65787 ★ **Rhone-Poulenc Inc. Lyndal Chemicals**
1338 Coronet Dr.
Dalton, GA 30720
Ultimate Parent: Rhone-Poulenc Rorer.
SIC: 2869—Industrial Organic Chemicals Nec.

★ 65788 ★ **Shaw Industries Inc.**
PO Drawer 2128
Dalton, GA 30722
(706)278-3812 **Fax:** (706)275-1040
Ultimate Parent: Shaw Industries, Inc.

★ 65789 ★ **Shaw Industries Inc.**
616 E. Walnut Ave.
Dalton, GA 30721
(706)278-3812
Officer: J. C. Shaw, Chairman. **Ultimate Parent:** Shaw Industries, Inc. **SIC:** 2273—
Carpets & Rugs; 3271—Concrete Block & Brick; 3272—Concrete Products Nec.

★ 65790 ★ **Shaw Industries, Inc.**
616 E. Walnut Ave.
Dalton, GA 30720
(706)278-3812
Company Type: Headquarters. **Officer:**
Robert E. Shaw. **Employee Count:** 21706.
Sales: 2320.8 M. **Fortune 500:** Largest
U.S. Industrial Corporations: Ranking 200.

★ 65791 ★ **Springs Industries, Inc.**
2208 S. Hamilton St.
Dalton, GA 30721
(706)277-7502
Officer: Dan Robertson, President.
Ultimate Parent: Springs Industries. **SIC:**
2273—Carpets & Rugs.

★ 65792 ★ **Vulcan Materials Co.**
585 Cherokee Boys Estate Rd. NE
Dalton, GA 30721
(706)259-3361
Ultimate Parent: Vulcan Materials Co. **SIC:**
3281—Cut Stone & Stone Products.

Dawson

★ 65793 ★ **Pizza Hut**
922 Forrester Dr. SE
Dawson, GA 31742
(912)995-5881
Ultimate Parent: Pepsico. **SIC:** 5812—
Eating Places.

★ 65794 ★ **Trailway Bus Terminal**
403 S. Main St.
Dawson, GA 31742
(912)995-2636
Ultimate Parent: Greyhound Lines Inc. **SIC:**
4131—Intercity & Rural Bus Transportation;
4173—Bus Terminal & Service Facilities.

Decator

★ 65795 ★ **Bio-Lab Inc./ Hydrotech Chemical Corp.**
627 E. College Ave.
Decator, GA 30030
(404)378-1753 **Fax:** (404)371-6988
Company Type: Subsidiary. **Officer:** Larry
Bloom, President. **Ultimate Parent:** Great
Lakes Chemical.

Decatur

★ 65796 ★ **Ace Hardware**
601 E. College Ave.
Decatur, GA 30030
(404)373-3335
Ultimate Parent: Ace Hardware.

★ 65797 ★ **Ace Hardware-Smith Open 7 Days**
601 E. College Ave.
Decatur, GA 30030
(404)373-3335
Ultimate Parent: Ace Hardware.

★ 65798 ★ **Bank South NA**
163 Clairmont Ave.
Decatur, GA 30033
(404)370-7324
Location Type: Branch office. **Officer:**
William Strom. **Ultimate Parent:** Bank
South Corp.

★ 65799 ★ **Bank South, NA**
2626 Rainbow Way
Decatur, GA 30034
(404)244-7343
Company Type: Subsidiary. **Location Type:** Branch office. **Officer:** Antoinette
Chapman, Manager. **Ultimate Parent:** Bank
South Corp. **SIC:** 6021—National
Commercial Banks.

★ 65800 ★ **Bank South, NA**
3479 Memorial Dr.
Decatur, GA 30032
(404)286-6668
Company Type: Subsidiary. **Location Type:** Branch office. **Officer:** Denise
Campbell, Manager. **Ultimate Parent:** Bank
South Corp. **SIC:** 6021—National
Commercial Banks.

★ 65801 ★ **Bio-Lab Inc.**
627 E. College Ave.
Decatur, GA 30030-4148
(404)378-1753
Company Type: Subsidiary. **Officer:**
Marshall Bloom, Chairman of the Board &
CEO. **Ultimate Parent:** Great Lakes

Chemical. **SIC:** 2812—Alkalies & Chlorine;
3589—Service Industry Machinery Nec.
Employee Count: 750. **Sales:** 200 M.

★ 65802 ★ **Bio-Lab, Inc.**
627 E. College Ave.
Decatur, GA 30030
(404)378-1753
Company Type: Subsidiary. **Ultimate Parent:** Great Lakes Chemical. **SIC:** 2834—
Pharmaceutical Preparations.

★ 65803 ★ **Casual Corner**
N Dekalb Mall
Decatur, GA 30033
(404)634-1592
Ultimate Parent: United States Shoe.

★ 65804 ★ **Casual Corner General Office**
2048 Lawrenceville Hwy. C
Decatur, GA 30033
(404)321-0604
Ultimate Parent: United States Shoe.

★ 65805 ★ **Circuit City**
4512 Memorial Dr.
Decatur, GA 30032
(404)299-2001
Ultimate Parent: Circuit City Stores.

★ 65806 ★ **Citgo Food Mart**
4052 Glenwood Rd.
Decatur, GA 30032
(404)289-4694
Ultimate Parent: Citgo Petroleum.

★ 65807 ★ **Citgo Food Mart**
2781 E. College Ave.
Decatur, GA 30030
(404)377-4977
Ultimate Parent: Citgo Petroleum.

★ 65808 ★ **Citgo Mart**
1050 Holcombe Rd.
Decatur, GA 30032
(404)292-9296
Ultimate Parent: Citgo Petroleum.

★ 65809 ★ **Coast to Coast Tire & Wheel**
4139 Glenwood Rd.
Decatur, GA 30032
(404)284-0332
Ultimate Parent: Servistar Corp.

★ 65810 ★ **Coca-Cola Bottling Com Metro S**
2400 Mellon Ct
Decatur, GA 30035
(404)981-4400
Ultimate Parent: Coca-Cola Enterprises.

★ 65811 ★ **Delta Air Lines**
5303 Dividend Dr.
Decatur, GA 30035
(404)593-2025
Ultimate Parent: Delta Air Lines, Inc.

★ 65812 ★ **Delta Air Lines Inc. Delta Comp**
5303 Dividend Dr.
Decatur, GA 30035
(404)593-2025
Ultimate Parent: Delta Air Lines, Inc.

★ 65813 ★ **Exxon Shop**
5400 Covington Hwy.
Decatur, GA 30035
(404)987-5737
Ultimate Parent: Exxon.

★ 65814 ★ **First Union National Bank of Georgia**
3553 Memorial Dr.
Decatur, GA 30032-2711
(404)286-3100
Location Type: Branch office. **Ultimate Parent:** First Union Corp. **SIC:** 6021—
National Commercial Banks.

★ 65815 ★ **First Union National Bank of Georgia**
2675 N. Decatur Rd.
Medical Ctr. Professional Bldg., Ste. 114
Decatur, GA 30033
(404)508-7150
Location Type: Branch office. **Ultimate Parent:** First Union Corp. **SIC:** 6021—
National Commercial Banks.

★ 65816 ★ **First Union National Bank of Georgia**
2038-J Lawrenceville Hwy.
Decatur, GA 30033-4330
(404)320-0725
Location Type: Branch office. **Ultimate Parent:** First Union Corp. **SIC:** 6021—
National Commercial Banks.

★ 65817 ★ **First Union National Bank of Georgia**
250 Ponce De Leon
Decatur, GA 30030-3406
(404)371-4242
Location Type: Branch office. **Ultimate Parent:** First Union Corp. **SIC:** 6021—
National Commercial Banks.

★ 65818 ★ **First Union National Bank of Georgia**
2942 N. Druid Hills Rd.
Decatur, GA 30033
(404)320-0734
Location Type: Branch office. **Ultimate Parent:** First Union Corp. **SIC:** 6021—
National Commercial Banks.

★ 65819 ★ **First Union National Bank Georgia**
4825 Flat Shoals Rd.
Decatur, GA 30034-5297
(404)297-2965
Location Type: Branch office. **Ultimate Parent:** First Union Corp. **SIC:** 6021—
National Commercial Banks.

★ 65820 ★ **First Union National Bank of Georgia**
2851 Candler Rd.
Decatur, GA 30034-1413
(404)865-2150
Location Type: Branch office. **Ultimate Parent:** First Union Corp. **SIC:** 6021—
National Commercial Banks.

★ 65821 ★ **Fleet Finance Inc. Decatur**
2446 Wesley Chapel Rd.
Decatur, GA 30035
(404)981-1737
Ultimate Parent: Fleet Financial Group.

★ 65822 ★ **Greyhound Bus Lines Local Info**
333 Commerce Dr.
Decatur, GA 30030
(404)373-3263
Ultimate Parent: Greyhound Lines Inc.

★ 65823 ★ **Hit or Miss Wms Apparel Region**
4570 Memorial Dr.
Decatur, GA 30032
(404)296-9618
Ultimate Parent: TJX.

★ 65824 ★ **Hit or Miss Wms Apparel Retail**
4570 Memorial Dr.
Decatur, GA 30032
(404)296-0703
Ultimate Parent: TJX.

★ 65825 ★ **Hit or Miss Wms Apparel Retail**
2845 Candler Rd.
Decatur, GA 30034
(404)241-0875
Ultimate Parent: TJX.

★ 65826 ★ **Home Depot Inc. the Stores Deca**
4380 Memorial Dr.
Decatur, GA 30032
(404)296-2334
Ultimate Parent: Home Depot.

★ 65827 ★ **International Paper Co.**
4283 Memorial Dr.
Decatur, GA 30032
(404)292-3168
Ultimate Parent: International Paper Co.

★ 65828 ★ **Jiffy Lube Decatur**
2727 Wesley Chapel Rd.
Decatur, GA 30034
(404)284-4435
Ultimate Parent: Pennzoil.

★ 65829 ★   Jiffy Lube Decatur
2207 Lawrenceville Hwy.
Decatur, GA 30033
(404)321-5796
Ultimate Parent: Pennzoil.

★ 65830 ★   Kentucky Fried
Chicken
4484 Memorial Dr.
Decatur, GA 30032
(404)294-6953
Ultimate Parent: Pepsico.

★ 65831 ★   Kentucky Fried
Chicken
2532 Wesley Chapel Rd.
Decatur, GA 30035
(404)593-2248
Ultimate Parent: Pepsico.

★ 65832 ★   Kentucky Fried
Chicken
1829 Lawrenceville Hwy.
Decatur, GA 30033
(404)325-4404
Ultimate Parent: Pepsico.

★ 65833 ★   Kentucky Fried
Chicken
3607 Memorial Dr.
Decatur, GA 30032
(404)284-4072
Ultimate Parent: Pepsico.

★ 65834 ★   Kentucky Fried
Chicken
4114 Covington Hwy.
Decatur, GA 30032
(404)289-3067
Ultimate Parent: Pepsico.

★ 65835 ★   Kentucky Fried
Chicken
3555 Flat Shoals Rd.
Decatur, GA 30034
(404)241-8120
Ultimate Parent: Pepsico.

★ 65836 ★   Kentucky Fried
Chicken
2020 Candler Rd.
Decatur, GA 30032
(404)288-2459
Ultimate Parent: Pepsico.

★ 65837 ★   Kmart Stores
2395 Wesley Chapel Rd.
Decatur, GA 30035
(404)808-0606
Ultimate Parent: K-Mart.

★ 65838 ★   Kmart Stores
Automotive
2395 Wesley Chapel Rd.
Decatur, GA 30035
(404)808-9110
Ultimate Parent: K-Mart.

★ 65839 ★   Kmart Stores
Pharmacy
2395 Wesley Chapel Rd.
Decatur, GA 30035
(404)808-7107
Ultimate Parent: K-Mart.

★ 65840 ★   Kraft General Foods
Inc.
501 Dekalb Industrial Way
Decatur, GA 30031
Ultimate Parent: Philip Morris. **SIC:** 2035—
Pickles, Sauces & Salad Dressings; 2079—
Edible Fats & Oils Nec; 2099—Food
Preparations Nec.

★ 65841 ★   Kraft Inc.
501 Dekalb Industrial Way
Decatur, GA 30031
Ultimate Parent: Philip Morris. **SIC:** 2033—
Canned Fruits & Vegetables; 2035—Pickles,
Sauces & Salad Dressings; 2079—Edible
Fats & Oils Nec; 2099—Food Preparations
Nec.

★ 65842 ★   Kroger Co. the Kroger
Pharmaci
2385 Wesley Chapel Rd.
Decatur, GA 30035
(404)987-1400
Ultimate Parent: Kroger.

★ 65843 ★   Kroger Co. the Retail
Sotes
2626 Rainbow Way
Decatur, GA 30034
(404)243-3014
Ultimate Parent: Kroger.

★ 65844 ★   Kroger Co. the Retail
Stores
2385 Wesley Chapel Rd.
Decatur, GA 30035
(404)987-0633
Ultimate Parent: Kroger.

★ 65845 ★   Kroger Co. the Retail
Stores
1709 Church St.
Decatur, GA 30033
(404)296-2888
Ultimate Parent: Kroger.

★ 65846 ★   Kroger Co. the Retail
Stores
3479 Memorial Dr.
Decatur, GA 30032
(404)286-5780
Ultimate Parent: Kroger.

★ 65847 ★   Kroger Co. the Retail
Stroes
1554 N. Decatur Rd. NE
Decatur, GA
(404)378-2822
Ultimate Parent: Kroger.

★ 65848 ★   Kroger Pharmacies
3479 Memorial Dr.
Decatur, GA 30032
(404)286-5788
Ultimate Parent: Kroger.

★ 65849 ★   Lane Bryant
S Dekalb Mall
Decatur, GA 30034
(404)243-0683
Ultimate Parent: Limited.

★ 65850 ★   Lerner Shop
10 S. Dekalb Mall
Decatur, GA 30034
(404)243-0131
Ultimate Parent: Limited.

★ 65851 ★   LFE Corp.
Traffic Control Division
4289 Memorial Dr.
Decatur, GA 30032
(404)294-6367
Ultimate Parent: Mark IV Industries.

★ 65852 ★   LFE Corp.
Traffic Control Division
4289 Memorial Dr.
Decatur, GA 30032
(404)294-6367
Ultimate Parent: Mark IV Industries.

★ 65853 ★   LFE Corp.
Traffic Control Division
4289 Memorial Dr.
Decatur, GA 30032
(404)294-6367
Ultimate Parent: Mark IV Industries.

★ 65854 ★   Macy's
Avondale Mall
Decatur, GA 30030
(404)288-3882
Ultimate Parent: R. H. Macy. **SIC:** 5311—
Department Stores.

★ 65855 ★   Marshalls
2300 Miller Rd.
Decatur, GA 30035
(404)987-1717
Ultimate Parent: Melville.

★ 65856 ★   Mary Kay Cosmetics
Indep Sales
3225 Harbor View Ct.
Decatur, GA 30034
(404)243-3398
Ultimate Parent: Mary Kay Cosmetics.

★ 65857 ★   Mary Kay Cosmetics
Indep Sales
3996 Brookside Pkwy
Decatur, GA 30034
(404)322-8541
Ultimate Parent: Mary Kay Cosmetics.

★ 65858 ★   McDonald's
Restaurants
3893 N. Druid Hills Rd.
Decatur, GA 30033
(404)248-0507
Ultimate Parent: ld's.

★ 65859 ★   McDonald's
Restaurants
2636 Wesley Chapel Rd.
Decatur, GA 30034
(404)284-5309
Ultimate Parent: McDonald's.

★ 65860 ★   McDonald's
Restaurants
3531 Flat Shoals Rd.
Decatur, GA 30034
(404)243-0390
Ultimate Parent: McDonald's.

★ 65861 ★   McDonald's
Restaurants
4034 Glenwood Rd.
Decatur, GA 30032
(404)288-5390
Ultimate Parent: McDonald's.

★ 65862 ★   McDonald's
Restaurants
1917 Candler Rd.
Decatur, GA 30032
(404)288-8997
Ultimate Parent: McDonald's.

★ 65863 ★   Nationsbank Acct
Activity Inf
South Dekalb 2850 Ca
Decatur, GA
(404)523-0900
Ultimate Parent: Nationsbank Corp.

★ 65864 ★   Nationsbank Atm
Honor-Cirrus L
3819 N. Decatur Rd.
Decatur, GA 30032
(404)297-1180
Ultimate Parent: Nationsbank Corp.

★ 65865 ★   Nationsbank Honor-
Cirrus L Sou
2850 Candler Rd.
Decatur, GA 30034
(404)244-4262
Ultimate Parent: Nationsbank Corp.

★ 65866 ★   Nationsbank Ofc
Atlanta Area a
Dekalb College 3819
Decatur, GA
(404)523-0900
Ultimate Parent: Nationsbank Corp.

★ 65867 ★   Nationsbank Ofc
Atlanta Area C
Dekalb College 3819
Decatur, GA
(404)969-0550
Ultimate Parent: Nationsbank Corp.

★ 65868 ★   Nationsbank Ofc
Atlanta Area L
Dekalb College 3819
Decatur, GA
(404)297-1182
Ultimate Parent: Nationsbank Corp.

★ 65869 ★   Nationsbank Ofc
Atlanta Area N
3819 N. Decatur Rd.
Decatur, GA 30032
(404)297-1180
Ultimate Parent: Nationsbank Corp.

★ 65870 ★   Nationsbank Ofc
Atlanta Area N
150 E. Ponce De Leon Ave.
Decatur, GA 30030
(404)371-6930
Ultimate Parent: Nationsbank Corp.

★ 65871 ★   Nationsbank Ofcs
Atlanta Area
Belvedere 1272 Colum
Decatur, GA
(404)523-0900
Ultimate Parent: Nationsbank Corp.

★ 65872 ★   Nationsbank Offices
Atlanta Ar
South Dekalb 2850 Ca
Decatur, GA
(404)969-0550
Ultimate Parent: Nationsbank Corp.

★ 65873 ★   Nationsbank Saturday
Banking O
2850 Candler Rd.
Decatur, GA 30034
(404)244-4262
Ultimate Parent: Nationsbank Corp.

★ 65874 ★   Navistar International
Transportation C
5240 Snapfinger Park Dr.
Decatur, GA 30035
(404)987-0743
Ultimate Parent: Navistar International.

★ 65875 ★   Payless Shoesource
3588 Memorial Dr.
Decatur, GA 30032
(404)286-4709
Ultimate Parent: May Department Stores.

★ 65876 ★   Payless Shoesource
2598 Candler Rd.
Decatur, GA 30034
(404)241-8829
Ultimate Parent: May Department Stores.

★ 65877 ★   Payless Shoesource
4520 Glenwood Rd.
Decatur, GA 30032
(404)284-4608
Ultimate Parent: May Department Stores.

★ 65878 ★   Payless Shoesource
2458 Wesley Chapel Rd.
Decatur, GA 30035
(404)987-7597
Ultimate Parent: May Department Stores.

★ 65879 ★   Personal Performance
Consultan
125 Clairemont Ave.
Decatur, GA 30030
(404)370-0574
Ultimate Parent: Merck.

★ 65880 ★   Personal Performance
Consultants
125 Clairemont Ave.
Decatur, GA 30030
(404)370-0574
Ultimate Parent: Medco Containment
Services.

★ 65881 ★   Piggly Wiggly
2112 Candler Rd.
Decatur, GA 30032
(404)288-4528
Ultimate Parent: Bruno's.

★ 65882 ★   Pizza Hut
2641 N. Decatur Rd.
Decatur, GA 30033
(404)373-4379
Ultimate Parent: Pepsico.

★ 65883 ★   Pizza Hut
4202 Rainbow Dr.
Decatur, GA 30034
(404)289-0238
Ultimate Parent: Pepsico.

★ 65884 ★   Pizza Hut
2581 Candler Rd.
Decatur, GA 30032
(404)241-5506
Ultimate Parent: Pepsico.

★ 65885 ★   Pizza Hut
4193-A Snapfinger Woods
Decatur, GA 30035
(404)288-9200
Ultimate Parent: Pepsico.

★ 65886 ★   Pizza Hut
1303-A Columbia Dr.
Decatur, GA
(404)288-9800
Ultimate Parent: Pepsico.

★ 65887 ★   Radio Shack
4191 Snapfinger Woods Dr.
Decatur, GA 30035
(404)288-7677
Company Type: Division. **Ultimate Parent:**
Tandy Corp.

★ 65888 ★   Radio Shack
South Dekalb Mall
Decatur, GA
(404)243-4434
Company Type: Division. **Ultimate Parent:**
Tandy Corp.

★ 65889 ★   Radio Shack
Service Merchandise
Decatur, GA
(404)292-5166
Company Type: Division. Ultimate Parent:
Tandy Corp.

★ 65890 ★   Radio Shack
Market Square at nor
Decatur, GA
(404)633-8002
Company Type: Division. Ultimate Parent:
Tandy Corp.

★ 65891 ★   Ralph Wilson Plastics Co.
2323 Park Central Blvd.
Decatur, GA 30035
(404)593-2424
Officer: Bill Clark, Manager. Ultimate
Parent: Premark International. SIC: 3083—
Laminated Plastics Plate & Sheet; 3089—
Plastics Products Nec.

★ 65892 ★   Rhone-Poulenc Rorer
3310 Colonial Pkwy
Decatur, GA 30034
(404)243-2000
Ultimate Parent: Rhone-Poulenc Rorer.

★ 65893 ★   Ryder Truck Rental
2852 N. Decatur Rd.
Decatur, GA 30033
(404)294-4587
Ultimate Parent: Ryder System.

★ 65894 ★   Ryder Truck Rental
1210 Clairmont Rd.
Decatur, GA 30030
(404)636-9365
Ultimate Parent: Ryder System.

★ 65895 ★   Service Merchandise
2595 Candler Rd.
Decatur, GA 30032
(404)243-3070
Ultimate Parent: Service Merchandise Co., Inc.

★ 65896 ★   Service Merchandise
4570 Memorial Dr.
Decatur, GA 30032
(404)296-6210
Ultimate Parent: Service Merchandise Co., Inc.

★ 65897 ★   Sullivan Graphics Inc.
5307 Snapfinger Woods Dr.
Decatur, GA 30035
(404)593-0833
Ultimate Parent: Morgan Stanley Group.

★ 65898 ★   T J Maxx
4380 Memorial Dr.
Decatur, GA 30032
(404)296-9284
Ultimate Parent: TJX.

★ 65899 ★   Taco Bell
4468 Glenwood Rd.
Decatur, GA 30032
(404)284-0970
Ultimate Parent: Pepsico.

★ 65900 ★   Taco Bell
2436 Wesley Chapel Rd.
Decatur, GA 30035
(404)593-8730
Ultimate Parent: Pepsico.

★ 65901 ★   Taco Bell
1715 Church St.
Decatur, GA 30033
(404)292-1037
Ultimate Parent: Pepsico.

★ 65902 ★   Target Stores Retail Stores
4000 Covington Hwy.
Decatur, GA 30032
(404)288-5000
Ultimate Parent: Dayton Hudson.

★ 65903 ★   Texaco
2585 Wesley Chapel Rd.
Decatur, GA 30035
(404)593-1387
Ultimate Parent: Texaco.

★ 65904 ★   Texaco
2146 Lawrenceville Hwy.
Decatur, GA 30033
(404)315-7139
Ultimate Parent: Texaco.

★ 65905 ★   Texaco
4640 Memorial Dr.
Decatur, GA 30032
(404)296-8326
Ultimate Parent: Texaco.

★ 65906 ★   Texaco Food Mart
2399 Columbia Dr.
Decatur, GA 30032
(404)289-5683
Ultimate Parent: Texaco.

★ 65907 ★   Texaco Food Shop
4124 Covington Hwy.
Decatur, GA 30032
(404)286-0084
Ultimate Parent: Texaco.

★ 65908 ★   Toys R US
2842 Whites Mill Rd.
Decatur, GA 30034
(404)243-4333
Ultimate Parent: Toys "R" US.

★ 65909 ★   Valvoline Instant Oil Change
4960 Covington Hwy.
Decatur, GA 30035
(404)288-7498
Ultimate Parent: Ashland Oil.

★ 65910 ★   Valvoline Instant Oil Change
3775 N. Druid Hills Rd.
Decatur, GA 30033
(404)633-9001
Ultimate Parent: Ashland Oil.

★ 65911 ★   Valvoline Instant Oil Change
1875 Candler Rd.
Decatur, GA 30032
(404)288-6303
Ultimate Parent: Ashland Oil.

★ 65912 ★   Wal Mart Discount Cities
2496 Wesley Chapel Rd.
Decatur, GA 30035
(404)593-3540
Ultimate Parent: Wal-Mart Stores, Inc.

Deepstep

★ 65913 ★   Engelhard Corp. Washington Co. Mine
Hwy. 24 Near Deepstep
Deepstep, GA 31082
Ultimate Parent: Engelhard Corp. SIC:
1455—Kaolin & Ball Clay.

★ 65914 ★   Engelhard Kaolin Co. Scott Mine
Hwy. 24 Near Deepstep
Deepstep, GA 31082
Ultimate Parent: Engelhard Corp. SIC:
1455—Kaolin & Ball Clay.

Deluth

★ 65915 ★   Arnet Computer
3425 Corporate Way, Ste. G
Deluth, GA 30136
(404)623-5430
Location Type: Branch office. Ultimate
Parent: Avnet. SIC: 5045—Computers,
Peripherals & Software; 7379—Computer
Related Services Nec.

Donalsonville

★ 65916 ★   Golden Peanut Co.
210 W. 1st St.
Donalsonville, GA 31745-1582
(912)524-2213
Ultimate Parent: Archer Daniels Midland
Co. SIC: 5159—Farm-Product Raw
Materials Nec.

★ 65917 ★   Piggly Wiggly
W 3rd
Donalsonville, GA 31745
(912)524-5407
Ultimate Parent: Bruno's. SIC: 5499—
Miscellaneous Food Stores.

Doraville

★ 65918 ★   Amerada Hess Corp.
3781 Northeast Expwy Acce
Doraville, GA
(404)458-3261
Ultimate Parent: Amerada Hess.

★ 65919 ★   Asgrow Seed Co.
4420 Bankers Cir.
Doraville, GA 30360
(404)448-0445
Ultimate Parent: Upjohn Co.

★ 65920 ★   Bank South, NA
6715 Peachtree Industrial Blvd.
Doraville, GA 30360
(404)368-3032
Company Type: Subsidiary. Location
Type: Branch office. Officer: Deborah
Salguero, Manager. Ultimate Parent: Bank
South Corp. SIC: 6021—National
Commercial Banks.

★ 65921 ★   BASF Corp.
3077 Oakcliff Industrial
Doraville, GA 30340
(404)451-0030
Ultimate Parent: BASF Corp.

★ 65922 ★   Citgo Petroleum Corp.
3877 Flowers Rd.
Doraville, GA 30360
(404)457-5268
Ultimate Parent: Citgo Petroleum.

★ 65923 ★   Citgo Petroleum Environmental
3896 Flowers Dr.
Doraville, GA 30360
(404)458-8322
Ultimate Parent: Citgo Petroleum.

★ 65924 ★   Colonial Pipeline Co. Dora
2794 Woodwin Rd.
Doraville, GA 30360
(404)451-3808
Ultimate Parent: Colonial Pipeline.

★ 65925 ★   Digital Equipment Corp.
4000 Dekalb Technology Pk.
Doraville, GA 30340
(404)454-0680
Ultimate Parent: Digital Equipment Corp.

★ 65926 ★   Eaton Corp.
3001 McCall Dr.
Doraville, GA 30340
(404)451-2331
Officer: Winston Statton, Manager.
Ultimate Parent: Eaton Corp. SIC: 3625—
Relays & Industrial Controls.

★ 65927 ★   Exxon Co. USA
4143 Winters Chapel Rd.
Doraville, GA 30360
(404)458-7437
Ultimate Parent: Exxon.

★ 65928 ★   First Union National Bank of Georgia
5772 Buford Hwy.
Doraville, GA 30340-1207
(404)936-1315
Location Type: Branch office. Ultimate
Parent: First Union Corp. SIC: 6021—
National Commercial Banks.

★ 65929 ★   Fleet Finance Inc. Atlanta
6317 Peachtree Industrial
Doraville, GA 30360
(404)458-0727
Ultimate Parent: Fleet Financial Group.

★ 65930 ★   Georgia Pacific Corp.
2351 Button Gwinnett Dr. NW
Doraville, GA 30340
(404)441-5050
Officer: Steve Hardin, Manager. Ultimate
Parent: Georgia-Pacific. SIC: 2431—
Millwork.

★ 65931 ★   Greyhound Bus Lines Local Info
3068 Chestnut Dr.
Doraville, GA 30340
(404)458-9169
Ultimate Parent: Greyhound Lines Inc.

★ 65932 ★   Harris Adacom
3785 Presidential Pkwy
Doraville, GA 30340
(404)454-7660
Ultimate Parent: Harris.

★ 65933 ★   Kentucky Fried Chicken
5677 Buford Hwy.
Doraville, GA 30340
(404)452-8857
Ultimate Parent: Pepsico.

★ 65934 ★   Kentucky Fried Chicken
3283 Northcrest Rd.
Doraville, GA 30340
(404)270-1455
Ultimate Parent: Pepsico.

★ 65935 ★   Kmart Stores Automotive
5597 Boford Hwy.
Doraville, GA
(404)451-5034
Ultimate Parent: K-Mart.

★ 65936 ★   Kmart Stores Pharmacy
5597 Buford Hwy.
Doraville, GA 30340
(404)455-7218
Ultimate Parent: K-Mart.

★ 65937 ★   Kroger
Bakery Division Sales Office
4035 Presidential Pkwy
Doraville, GA 30340
(404)936-8287
Ultimate Parent: Kroger.

★ 65938 ★   Kroger
Dairy Division
4035 Presidential Pkwy
Doraville, GA 30340
(404)451-6850
Ultimate Parent: Kroger.

★ 65939 ★   Kroger Co. Snack Div
4035 Presidential Pkwy
Doraville, GA 30340
(404)458-0776
Ultimate Parent: Kroger.

★ 65940 ★   Marathon Oil Co.
6293 New Peachtree Rd.
Doraville, GA 30340
(404)457-7233
Ultimate Parent: USX Corp.

★ 65941 ★   Marathon Oil Co. Doraville Terminal
6293 New Peachtree Rd.
Doraville, GA 30340
(404)457-7233
Ultimate Parent: USX Corp.

★ 65942 ★   Mary Kay Cosmetics
Indep Sales
6940 Lockridge Dr.
Doraville, GA 30360
(404)392-0808
Ultimate Parent: Mary Kay Cosmetics.

★ 65943 ★   Ncr Corp.
3980 Dekalb Technology Pk.
Doraville, GA 30340
(404)936-4100
Ultimate Parent: AT&T.

★ 65944 ★   Phillips Pipe Line Co.
4149 Winters Chapel Rd.
Doraville, GA 30360
(404)457-3026
Ultimate Parent: Phillips Petroleum.

★ 65945 ★   Pizza Hut
4957 Winters Chapel Rd.
Doraville, GA 30360
(404)901-9800
Ultimate Parent: Pepsico.

★ 65946 ★   Radio Shack
5760 Buford Hwy.
Doraville, GA 30340
(404)458-1942
Company Type: Division. Ultimate Parent:
Tandy Corp.

★ 65947 ★   Ryder Truck Rental
3590 Northeast Expwy Acce
Doraville, GA
(404)987-8916
Ultimate Parent: Ryder System.

★ 65948 ★   Ryder Truck Rental
6594 Button Gwinnett Driv
Doraville, GA 30340
(404)449-5141
Ultimate Parent: Ryder System.

★ 65949 ★   Service Merchandise
5745 Buford Hwy.
Doraville, GA 30340
(404)458-8521
Ultimate Parent: Service Merchandise Co.,
Inc.

★ 65950 ★   Shell Oil Co.
4064 Winters Chapel Rd.
Doraville, GA 30360
(404)452-1429
Ultimate Parent: Shell Oil Co.

★ 65951 ★   Sloan Paper Co.
3587 Oakcliff Rd.
Doraville, GA 30340
(404)447-9000
Company Type: Division. Ultimate Parent:
Alco Standard Corp. SIC: 5111—Printing &
Writing Paper.

★ 65952 ★   Star Manufacturing
Co.
5736 Buford Hwy.
Doraville, GA 30340
(404)458-5571
Ultimate Parent: Merrill Lynch Life.

★ 65953 ★   T J Maxx
5600 Buford Hwy.
Doraville, GA 30340
(404)451-0964
Ultimate Parent: TJX.

★ 65954 ★   Taco Bell
5164 Buford Hwy. NE
Doraville, GA 30340
(404)451-5122
Ultimate Parent: Pepsico.

★ 65955 ★   Target Stores Retail
Stores
5766 Buford Hwy. NE
Doraville, GA 30340
(404)455-8900
Ultimate Parent: Dayton Hudson.

★ 65956 ★   Texaco
5020 Winters Chapel Rd.
Doraville, GA 30360
(404)393-8466
Ultimate Parent: Texaco.

★ 65957 ★   Texaco Food Mart
6399 Peachtree Industrial
Doraville, GA 30360
(404)457-2639
Ultimate Parent: Texaco.

★ 65958 ★   Texaco Food Mart
4580 Winters Chapel Rd.
Doraville, GA 30360
(404)449-7774
Ultimate Parent: Texaco.

★ 65959 ★   Texaco Lubricants
Companies
4127 Winters Chapel Rd.
Doraville, GA 30360
(404)936-4600
Ultimate Parent: Texaco.

★ 65960 ★   Texaco Mortor Tune
Center Dora
5097 Buford Hwy. NE
Doraville, GA 30340
(404)451-6977
Ultimate Parent: Texaco.

★ 65961 ★   Texaco Sales
Terminal
4127 Winters Chapel Rd.
Doraville, GA 30360
(404)451-0181
Ultimate Parent: Texaco.

Doreville

★ 65962 ★   Bank South NA/
Peachtree Park
6715 Peachtree Industrial Blvd.
Doraville, GA 30360
(404)368-3032
Company Type: Subsidiary. Location
Type: Branch office. Officer: Deborah
Salguero, Branch Mgr. Ultimate Parent:
Bank South Corp. SIC: 6021—National
Commercial Banks.

Dougals

★ 65963 ★   Bank South NA/
Douglas
100 S. Pearl Ave.
Dougals, GA 31533
(912)384-2701
Company Type: Subsidiary. Location
Type: Branch office. Officer: Jared R.
Stevens, President. Ultimate Parent: Bank
South Corp. SIC: 6021—National
Commercial Banks.

Douglas

★ 65964 ★   Bank South-Douglas
901 W. Ward St.
Douglas, GA 31533-1918
(912)384-2701
Location Type: Branch office. Officer:
Jared R. Stevens. Ultimate Parent: Bank
South Corp. SIC: 6021—National
Commercial Banks; 6022—State
Commercial Banks; 6141—Personal Credit
Institutions.

★ 65965 ★   Bank South, NA
100 S. Pearl Ave.
Douglas, GA 31533-3863
(912)384-2701
Company Type: Subsidiary. Location
Type: Branch office. Officer: Alicia Rucker,
Manager. Ultimate Parent: Bank South
Corp. SIC: 6021—National Commercial
Banks.

★ 65966 ★   Joseph Campbell Co.
601 E. Johnson St.
PO Box 1307
Douglas, GA 31533
(912)384-7900
Company Type: Subsidiary. Officer: D. R.
DeValle, General Manager. Ultimate
Parent: Campbell Soup.

★ 65967 ★   Fleetwood Homes
Northside Industrial Park
Douglas, GA 31533
(912)384-1147
Officer: Mike Yates, Manager. Ultimate
Parent: Fleetwood Enterprises, Inc. SIC:
2451—Mobile Homes; 2452—Prefabricated
Wood Buildings.

★ 65968 ★   Golden Poultry Co.
McNeal Dr.
Douglas, GA 31533
Ultimate Parent: Gold Kist. SIC: 2000—
Food & Kindred Products.

★ 65969 ★   Golden Poultry Co.
Inc.
Mac Neal Dr.
Douglas, GA 31533
(912)384-3406
Ultimate Parent: Gold Kist. SIC: 5144—
Poultry & Poultry Products; 5499—
Miscellaneous Food Stores.

★ 65970 ★   Joseph Campbell Co.
601 E. Johnson St.
Douglas, GA 31533-1307
Ultimate Parent: Campbell Soup. SIC:
2015—Poultry Slaughtering & Processing.

★ 65971 ★   Kentucky Fried
Chicken
S Peterson Ave.
Douglas, GA 31533
(912)384-7464
Ultimate Parent: Pepsico. SIC: 5812—
Eating Places.

★ 65972 ★   Piggly Wiggly
901 W. Ward St.
Douglas, GA 31533
(912)384-5225
Ultimate Parent: Bruno's. SIC: 5411—
Grocery Stores.

★ 65973 ★   Pizza Hut
Us 441
Douglas, GA 31533
(912)384-5914
Ultimate Parent: Pepsico. SIC: 5812—
Eating Places.

★ 65974 ★   Radio Shack
903 S. Madison Ave.
Douglas, GA 31533
(912)384-0485
Company Type: Division. Ultimate Parent:
Tandy Corp. SIC: 5731—Radio, Television

& Electronics Stores; 5736—Musical
Instruments Stores.

★ 65975 ★   Ryder Truck Rental
Mcneal Dr.
Douglas, GA 31533
(912)384-7287
Ultimate Parent: Ryder System. SIC:
7389—Business Services Nec.

★ 65976 ★   Texaco Express Lube
1126 SE Bowens Mill Rd.
Douglas, GA 31533
(912)384-5823
Ultimate Parent: Texaco. SIC: 7539—
Automotive Repair Shops Nec.

★ 65977 ★   Trust Co. Bank of
Coffee County
904 S. Peterson Ave.
Douglas, GA 31533-2931
(912)383-5258
Officer: James C. Carter, Manager.
Ultimate Parent: Suntrust Banks. SIC:
6021—National Commercial Banks.

★ 65978 ★   Trust Co. Bank of
Coffee County
201 S. Peterson Ave.
Douglas, GA 31533-3837
(912)384-1820 Fax: (912)383-5210
Officer: W.L. Willis, President & CEO.
Ultimate Parent: Suntrust Banks. SIC:
6021—National Commercial Banks.

★ 65979 ★   Trust Co. Bank of
Coffee County
808 W. Ward St.
Douglas, GA 31533-3137
(912)383-5260
Officer: Carolyn Bray, Manager. Ultimate
Parent: Suntrust Banks. SIC: 6021—
National Commercial Banks.

★ 65980 ★   Wal Mart
1322 S. Peterson Ave.
Douglas, GA 31533
(912)384-9909
Ultimate Parent: Wal-Mart Stores, Inc.

★ 65981 ★   Wal Mart Warehouse
700 SW Bowens Mill Rd.
Douglas, GA 31533
(912)384-7373
Ultimate Parent: Wal-Mart Stores, Inc. SIC:
5399—Miscellaneous General Merchandise
Store.

★ 65982 ★   Westfield Homes of
Georgia
1515 Kellogg Rd.
Douglas, GA 31533
(912)384-1818
Officer: Asa Whitfield, Manager. Ultimate
Parent: Fleetwood Enterprises, Inc. SIC:
2451—Mobile Homes; 2452—Prefabricated
Wood Buildings.

Douglasville

★ 65983 ★   Ace Hardware
6530 Church St.
Douglasville, GA 30134
(404)942-7044
Ultimate Parent: Ace Hardware.

★ 65984 ★   Citgo Food Mart
2060 Fairburn Rd.
Douglasville, GA 30135
(404)949-8506
Ultimate Parent: Citgo Petroleum.

★ 65985 ★   First Union National
Bank of Georgia
9557 Hwy. 5
Douglasville, GA 30135-1511
(404)920-3700
Location Type: Branch office. Ultimate
Parent: First Union Corp. SIC: 6021—
National Commercial Banks.

★ 65986 ★   Kentucky Fried
Chicken
5620 Fairburn Rd.
Douglasville, GA 30134
(404)489-0182
Ultimate Parent: Pepsico.

★ 65987 ★   Kentucky Fried
Chicken
Market Sq.
Douglasville, GA 30135
(404)949-1440
Ultimate Parent: Pepsico.

★ 65988 ★   Kmart Stores
Pharmacy
9552 Hwy. 5
Douglasville, GA 30135
(404)949-2570
Ultimate Parent: K-Mart.

★ 65989 ★   Kroger Co. the Retail
Stores
3251 Hwy. 5
Douglasville, GA 30135
(404)920-1880
Ultimate Parent: Kroger.

★ 65990 ★   Kroger Pharmacies
3251 Hwy. 5
Douglasville, GA 30135
(404)920-1884
Ultimate Parent: Kroger.

★ 65991 ★   McDonalds
Restaurants
6072 Fairburn Rd.
Douglasville, GA 30134
(404)942-5953
Ultimate Parent: McDonald's.

★ 65992 ★   Nationsbank Honor-
Cirrus L Hig
9443 Hwy. 5
Douglasville, GA 30135
(404)920-3727
Ultimate Parent: Nationsbank Corp.

★ 65993 ★   Nationsbank Ofc
Atlanta Area N
6559 Church St.
Douglasville, GA 30134
(404)920-3722
Ultimate Parent: Nationsbank Corp.

★ 65994 ★   Nationsbank Offices
Atlanta Ar
Hwy. 5 9443
Douglasville, GA 30135
(404)920-3727
Ultimate Parent: Nationsbank Corp.

★ 65995 ★   Nationsbank Real
Estate Departments
Douglasville, GA
(404)489-2571
Ultimate Parent: Nationsbank Corp.

★ 65996 ★   Nationsbank Saturday
Banking O
9443 Hwy. 5
Douglasville, GA 30135
(404)920-3727
Ultimate Parent: Nationsbank Corp.

★ 65997 ★   Pizza Hut
9611 Hwy. 5
Douglasville, GA 30135
(404)920-5000
Ultimate Parent: Pepsico.

★ 65998 ★   Pizza Hut
5636 Fairburn Rd.
Douglasville, GA 30134
(404)920-5050
Ultimate Parent: Pepsico.

★ 65999 ★   Radio Shack
3111 Hwy. 5
Douglasville, GA 30135
(404)949-4855
Company Type: Division. Ultimate Parent:
Tandy Corp.

★ 66000 ★   Ryder Truck Rental
Bright Star Road
Douglasville, GA
(404)942-7357
Ultimate Parent: Ryder System.

★ 66001 ★   Ryder Truck Rental
8650 Club Dr.
Douglasville, GA 30134
(404)942-5881
Ultimate Parent: Ryder System.

★ 66002 ★   Taco Bell
5845 Stewart Pkwy
Douglasville, GA 30135
(404)942-8667
Ultimate Parent: Pepsico.

★ 66003 ★   Taco Bell
5611 Fairburn Rd.
Douglasville, GA 30134
(404)489-2113
Ultimate Parent: Pepsico.

★ 66004 ★   **Texaco**
5652 Fairburn Rd.
Douglasville, GA 30134
(404)949-3378
Ultimate Parent: Texaco.

★ 66005 ★   **Texaco Express Lube**
2980 Hwy. 5
Douglasville, GA 30135
(404)920-9096
Ultimate Parent: Texaco.

Dry Branch

★ 66006 ★   **Engelhard Kaolin Co. Griffin Mine**
Asbury Church Rd.
Dry Branch, GA 31020
Ultimate Parent: Engelhard Corp. **SIC:** 1455—Kaolin & Ball Clay.

★ 66007 ★   **Engelhard Kaolin Corp. Griffin Mine**
Asbury Church Rd.
Dry Branch, GA 31020
Ultimate Parent: Engelhard Corp. **SIC:** 1455—Kaolin & Ball Clay.

Dublin

★ 66008 ★   **First Union National Bank of Georgia**
105 Shamrock Dr.
Dublin, GA 31021-3018
(912)275-0380
Location Type: Branch office. **Ultimate Parent:** First Union Corp. **SIC:** 6021—National Commercial Banks.

★ 66009 ★   **Globe Life Insurance Co.**
126 W. Mary St.
Dublin, GA 31021
(912)272-1714
Ultimate Parent: Life Insurance Co. of Virginia. **SIC:** 6411—Insurance Agents, Brokers & Service.

★ 66010 ★   **Greyhound Bus Terminial**
620 E. Jackson St.
Dublin, GA 31021
(912)272-2912
Ultimate Parent: Greyhound Lines Inc. **SIC:** 4131—Intercity & Rural Bus Transportation.

★ 66011 ★   **Payless Shoesource**
1947 Macon Rd.
Dublin, GA 31021
(912)272-0300
Ultimate Parent: May Department Stores. **SIC:** 5661—Shoe Stores.

★ 66012 ★   **Piggly Wiggly**
613 Central Dr.
Dublin, GA 31021
(912)275-3650
Ultimate Parent: Bruno's. **SIC:** 5411—Grocery Stores.

★ 66013 ★   **Piggly Wiggly Southern Inc.**
613 Central Dr.
Dublin, GA 31021
(912)275-3650
Ultimate Parent: Bruno's. **SIC:** 5411—Grocery Stores.

★ 66014 ★   **Pizza Hut**
Us 80
Dublin, GA 31021
(912)272-8800
Ultimate Parent: Pepsico. **SIC:** 5812—Eating Places.

★ 66015 ★   **Radio Shack**
Westgate Shopping Ctr.
Dublin, GA 31021
(912)272-7669
Company Type: Division. **Ultimate Parent:** Tandy Corp. **SIC:** 5065—Electronic Parts & Equipment Nec.

★ 66016 ★   **Rite Aid Discount Phrmcy**
1923 Macon Rd.
Dublin, GA 31021
(912)272-0135
Ultimate Parent: Rite Aid. **SIC:** 5912—Drug Stores & Proprietary Stores.

★ 66017 ★   **Ryder Truck Rental**
Us 441 S
Dublin, GA 31021
(912)272-7755
Ultimate Parent: Ryder System. **SIC:** 7513—Truck Rental & Leasing Without Drivers.

Duluth

★ 66018 ★   **Arrow Electronics**
Commercial Systems Div.
Ste. C 3400 Corporate Way
Duluth, GA 30136
(404)623-8825
Company Type: Division. **Location Type:** Distribution center. **Officer:** Dave Miller, General Manager. **Ultimate Parent:** Arrow Electronics. **SIC:** 5045—Computers, Peripherals & Software.

★ 66019 ★   **Arrow/Kierulff Electronics**
Ste E. 4250 River Green Pkwy
Duluth, GA 30136
(404)497-1300
Company Type: Division. **Location Type:** Distribution center. **Officer:** Bernie Kenner, General Manager. **Ultimate Parent:** Arrow Electronics. **SIC:** 5065—Electronic Parts & Equipment Nec.

★ 66020 ★   **AT&T Co. Software Solutions**
3425 Corporate Way, Ste. B
Duluth, GA 30136-2579
(404)418-2000
Officer: Jess Solomon, President & Secretary. **Ultimate Parent:** AT&T. **SIC:** 7373—Computer Integrated Systems Design. **Employee Count:** 48. **Sales:** 4 M.

★ 66021 ★   **Bank South, NA**
3542 Satellite Blvd.
Duluth, GA 30136-4665
(404)497-3046
Company Type: Subsidiary. **Location Type:** Branch office. **Ultimate Parent:** Bank South Corp. **SIC:** 6021—National Commercial Banks.

★ 66022 ★   **Bank South, NA**
4245 Pleasant Hill Rd.
Duluth, GA 30136
(404)623-3442
Company Type: Subsidiary. **Location Type:** Branch office. **Ultimate Parent:** Bank South Corp. **SIC:** 6021—National Commercial Banks.

★ 66023 ★   **Bank South, NA**
2180 Pleasant Hill Rd.
Duluth, GA 30136
(404)497-3305
Company Type: Subsidiary. **Location Type:** Branch office. **Officer:** Chris Curry, Manager. **Ultimate Parent:** Bank South Corp. **SIC:** 6021—National Commercial Banks.

★ 66024 ★   **Bank South, NA**
2150 Pleasant Hill Rd.
Duluth, GA 30136
(404)497-3300
Company Type: Subsidiary. **Location Type:** Branch office. **Officer:** Kathy Gyselinck, Manager. **Ultimate Parent:** Bank South Corp. **SIC:** 6021—National Commercial Banks.

★ 66025 ★   **Bank South, NA**
3468 Hwy. 120
Duluth, GA 30136
(404)476-2211
Company Type: Subsidiary. **Location Type:** Branch office. **Officer:** Janet Sanchez, Manager. **Ultimate Parent:** Bank South Corp. **SIC:** 6021—National Commercial Banks.

★ 66026 ★   **Bank South, NA**
3455 Peachtree Industrial Blvd.
Duluth, GA 30130
(404)497-3311
Company Type: Subsidiary. **Location Type:** Branch office. **Officer:** Cheryl Delugach, Manager. **Ultimate Parent:** Bank South Corp. **SIC:** 6021—National Commercial Banks.

★ 66027 ★   **Bowater Inc.**
4235 Buford Hwy.
Duluth, GA 30136-4229
(404)476-2898
Officer: Misty Daniels. **Ultimate Parent:** Bowater. **SIC:** 5099—Durable Goods Nec; 0811—Timber Tracts.

★ 66028 ★   **Burlington Coat Factory Warehouse**
3750 Venture Dr.
Duluth, GA 30136-5002
(404)497-0033
Location Type: Branch office. **Ultimate Parent:** Burlington Industries, Equity. **SIC:** 5311—Department Stores.

★ 66029 ★   **Casual Corner**
Gwinnett Pl
Duluth, GA 30136
(404)476-7418
Ultimate Parent: United States Shoe.

★ 66030 ★   **Courtyard by Marriott**
3550 Venture Pky.
Duluth, GA 30136
(404)476-4666
Ultimate Parent: Marriott International.

★ 66031 ★   **Delta Air Lines**
3355 Breckinridge Blvd. NW
Duluth, GA 30136
(404)923-1373
Ultimate Parent: Delta Air Lines, Inc.

★ 66032 ★   **Delta Air Lines, Inc.**
3355 Breckinridge Blvd. NW
Duluth, GA 30136
(404)806-6800
Ultimate Parent: Delta Air Lines, Inc.

★ 66033 ★   **Delta Apparel**
3355 Breckenridge Blvd.
Duluth, GA 30136
(800)285-4456
Company Type: Subsidiary. **Ultimate Parent:** Delta Woodside Industries. **SIC:** 2322—Men's/Boys' Underwear & Nightwear; 2329—Men's/Boys' Clothing Nec; 2339—Women's/Misses' Outerwear Nec.

★ 66034 ★   **Fairfield Inn by Marriott**
3500 Venture Pkwy
Duluth, GA 30136
(404)623-9300
Ultimate Parent: Marriott International.

★ 66035 ★   **Ferro Corp.**
3914 Pine Needle Dr.
Duluth, GA 30136
(404)476-9293
Ultimate Parent: Ferro Corp.

★ 66036 ★   **First Union National Bank of Georgia**
3400 Satellite Blvd.
Duluth, GA 30136-4643
(404)497-4100
Location Type: Branch office. **Ultimate Parent:** First Union Corp. **SIC:** 6021—National Commercial Banks.

★ 66037 ★   **Foundation Health Pharmaceutic**
2444 Hwy. 120 NW
Duluth, GA 30136
(404)813-8355
Ultimate Parent: Foundation Health Corp.

★ 66038 ★   **Hill's Pet Nutrition Inc. Pet S**
2500 Meadowbrook Pkwy NW
Duluth, GA 30136
(404)497-9500
Ultimate Parent: Colgate-Palmolive.

★ 66039 ★   **Hit or Miss Wms Apparel Retail**
2100 Pleasant Hill Rd.
Duluth, GA 30136
(404)476-0877
Ultimate Parent: TJX.

★ 66040 ★   **Kay-Bee Toy & Hobby Shop Inc.**
2100 Pleasant Hill Rd.
Duluth, GA 30136
(404)476-7472
Ultimate Parent: Melville.

★ 66041 ★   **Kentucky Fried Chicken**
2080 Pleasant Hill Rd. NW
Duluth, GA 30136
(404)497-8344
Ultimate Parent: Pepsico.

★ 66042 ★   **Kids R US**
1960 Day Dr. NW
Duluth, GA 30136
(404)623-4208
Ultimate Parent: Toys "R" US.

★ 66043 ★   **Kids R US No. 1241**
1960 Day Dr. NW
Duluth, GA 30136
(404)623-4208
Ultimate Parent: Toys "R" US.

★ 66044 ★   **Kmart Stores**
3455 Peachtree Industrial
Duluth, GA 30136
(404)476-4299
Ultimate Parent: K-Mart.

★ 66045 ★   **Kmart Stores Pharmacy**
3455 Peachtree Industrial
Duluth, GA 30136
(404)476-4727
Ultimate Parent: K-Mart.

★ 66046 ★   **Kroger Co. the Retail Stores**
3455 Peachtree Industrial
Duluth, GA 30136
(404)476-7914
Ultimate Parent: Kroger.

★ 66047 ★   **Kroger Co. the Retail Stores**
2180 Pleasant Hill Rd. NW
Duluth, GA 30136
(404)476-3500
Ultimate Parent: Kroger.

★ 66048 ★   **Kroger Pharmacies**
2180 Pleasant Hill Rd.
Duluth, GA 30136
(404)476-3531
Ultimate Parent: Kroger.

★ 66049 ★   **Lane Bryant**
Gwinnett Pl Mall
Duluth, GA 30136
(404)476-7139
Ultimate Parent: Limited.

★ 66050 ★   **The Limited**
Pleasant Hill Rd. NW
Duluth, GA 30136
(404)476-3655
Ultimate Parent: Limited.

★ 66051 ★   **The Limited**
Gwinnett Pl
Duluth, GA 30136
(404)476-7672
Ultimate Parent: Limited.

★ 66052 ★   **The Limited Express**
2100 Pleasant Hill Rd. NW
Duluth, GA 30136
(404)476-7688
Ultimate Parent: Limited.

★ 66053 ★   **Linens N Things Duluth Store**
3675 Satellite Blvd.
Duluth, GA 30136
(404)476-9252
Ultimate Parent: Melville.

★ 66054 ★   **Macy's**
Gwinett Pl.
Duluth, GA 30136
(404)476-6985
Company Type: Branch. **Ultimate Parent:** R. H. Macy. **SIC:** 5311—Department Stores.

★ 66055 ★   **Marshalls**
3675 Satellie Blvd.
Duluth, GA
(404)497-1052
Ultimate Parent: Melville.

★ 66056 ★   **Mary Kay Cosmetics**
1963 Ashview Ct. NW
Duluth, GA 30136
(404)497-1963
Ultimate Parent: Mary Kay Cosmetics.

★ 66057 ★ **Mary Kay Cosmetics**
Indep Sales
3563 Wood Acres Blvd.
Duluth, GA 30136
(404)476-5640
Ultimate Parent: Mary Kay Cosmetics.

★ 66058 ★ **McDonald's Restaurants**
1963 Pleasant Hill Rd.
Duluth, GA 30136
(404)476-0774
Ultimate Parent: McDonald's.

★ 66059 ★ **McDonald's Restaurants**
2100 Pleasant Hill Rd.
Duluth, GA 30136
(404)476-0773
Ultimate Parent: McDonald's.

★ 66060 ★ **Melville Corp.**
2400 Pleasant Hill Rd. NW
Duluth, GA 30136
(404)476-8570
Ultimate Parent: Melville.

★ 66061 ★ **Nationsbank Honor-Cirrus L How**
3595 Peachtree Industrial
Duluth, GA 30136
(404)497-4620
Ultimate Parent: Nationsbank Corp.

★ 66062 ★ **Nationsbank Offices Atlanta Ar**
3595 Peachtree Industrial
Duluth, GA 30136
(404)497-4620
Ultimate Parent: Nationsbank Corp.

★ 66063 ★ **Nationsbank Offices Atlanta Ar**
Gwinnett Place 3552
Duluth, GA 30136
(404)523-0900
Ultimate Parent: Nationsbank Corp.

★ 66064 ★ **Nationsbank Offices Atlanta Ar**
Howell Ferry 3595 Pe
Duluth, GA 30136
(404)497-4623
Ultimate Parent: Nationsbank Corp.

★ 66065 ★ **Nationsbank Offices Atlata Are**
Howell Ferry 3595 Pe
Duluth, GA 30136
(404)523-0900
Ultimate Parent: Nationsbank Corp.

★ 66066 ★ **Payless Shoesource**
2100 Pleasant Hill Rd. NW
Duluth, GA 30136
(404)623-6702
Ultimate Parent: May Department Stores.

★ 66067 ★ **Payless Shoesource**
3675 Satellite Blvd.
Duluth, GA 30136
(404)476-4472
Ultimate Parent: May Department Stores.

★ 66068 ★ **Pizza Hut**
2070 Pleasant Hill Rd.
Duluth, GA 30136
(404)476-0637
Ultimate Parent: Pepsico.

★ 66069 ★ **Pizza Hut**
3175 Buford Hwy. NW
Duluth, GA 30136
(404)623-5800
Ultimate Parent: Pepsico.

★ 66070 ★ **Pizza Hut**
4601 Satellite Blvd.
Duluth, GA 30136
(404)246-0246
Ultimate Parent: Pepsico.

★ 66071 ★ **Prints Plus**
2100 Pleasant Hill Rd. NW
Duluth, GA 30136
(404)418-1871
Ultimate Parent: Melville.

★ 66072 ★ **Pulse Communications Inc/Subsi**
2741 Old Coach Rd. NW
Duluth, GA 30136
(404)476-4091
Ultimate Parent: Hubbell.

★ 66073 ★ **Pulte Home Corp. Georgia**
3100 Breckinridge Blvd. NW
Duluth, GA 30136
(404)381-3450
Ultimate Parent: Pulte.

★ 66074 ★ **Pulte Home Corp. Georgia**
6070 Carriage Park Way
Duluth, GA 30136
(404)623-9963
Ultimate Parent: Pulte.

★ 66075 ★ **Pulte Home Corp. Model Home**
3890 Longlake Dr. NW
Duluth, GA 30136
(404)476-7064
Ultimate Parent: Pulte.

★ 66076 ★ **Radio Shack**
Gwinnett Place Mall
Duluth, GA
(404)476-0685
Company Type: Division. **Ultimate Parent:** Tandy Corp.

★ 66077 ★ **Rockwell International Corp. Msd (Duluth)**
1800 Satellite Blvd.
Duluth, GA 30136
Ultimate Parent: Rockwell International Corp. **SIC:** 3600—Electronic & Other Electrical Equipment; 3679—Electronic Components Nec.

★ 66078 ★ **Rockwell International Msd (Duluth)**
1800 Satellite Blvd.
Duluth, GA 30136
Ultimate Parent: Rockwell International Corp. **SIC:** 3769—Space Vehicle Equipment Nec.

★ 66079 ★ **Ryder Truck Rental**
4091 Blue Ridge Industria
Duluth, GA
(404)476-4891
Ultimate Parent: Ryder System.

★ 66080 ★ **Service Merchandise**
2075 Market St.
Duluth, GA 30136
(404)476-9037
Ultimate Parent: Service Merchandise Co., Inc.

★ 66081 ★ **Sports Authority**
3450 Steve Reynolds Blvd.
Duluth, GA 30136
(404)418-9354
Ultimate Parent: K-Mart.

★ 66082 ★ **T J Maxx**
3675 Satellite Blvd.
Duluth, GA 30136
(404)497-1049
Ultimate Parent: TJX.

★ 66083 ★ **Taco Bell**
4165 Pleasant Hill Rd. NW
Duluth, GA 30136
(404)813-9978
Ultimate Parent: Pepsico.

★ 66084 ★ **Taco Bell**
2121 Pleasant Hill Rd.
Duluth, GA 30136
(404)476-8514
Ultimate Parent: Pepsico.

★ 66085 ★ **Target Stores Retail Stores**
2300 Pleasant Hill Rd. NW
Duluth, GA 30136
(404)623-3519
Ultimate Parent: Dayton Hudson.

★ 66086 ★ **Texaco**
2060 Pleasant Hill Rd. NW
Duluth, GA 30136
(404)623-8304
Ultimate Parent: Texaco.

★ 66087 ★ **Texaco**
3841 Satellite Blvd. NW
Duluth, GA 30136
(404)623-9301
Ultimate Parent: Texaco.

★ 66088 ★ **Texaco**
3495 Peachtree Industrial
Duluth, GA 30136
(404)623-6144
Ultimate Parent: Texaco.

★ 66089 ★ **Texaco Express Lube**
3975 Pleasant Hill Rd. NW
Duluth, GA 30136
(404)497-9571
Ultimate Parent: Texaco.

★ 66090 ★ **Texaco Express Lube Auto Serv**
3556 Buford Hwy. NW
Duluth, GA 30136
(404)497-0685
Ultimate Parent: Texaco.

★ 66091 ★ **Tfx Medical**
2450 Meadowbrook Pkwy NW
Duluth, GA 30136
(404)623-0816
Ultimate Parent: Teleflex.

★ 66092 ★ **Toys R US**
2131 Pleasant Hill Rd.
Duluth, GA 30136
(404)476-4646
Ultimate Parent: Toys "R" US.

★ 66093 ★ **Wal Mart Vision Center**
1630 Pleasant Hill Rd.
Duluth, GA 30136
(404)925-2722
Ultimate Parent: Wal-Mart Stores, Inc.

★ 66094 ★ **Waldenbooks**
Gwinnett Pl Mall
Duluth, GA 30136
(404)476-7341
Ultimate Parent: K-Mart.

★ 66095 ★ **Whirlpool Financial Corp.**
3675 Crestwood Pkwy NW
Duluth, GA 30136
(404)279-4649
Ultimate Parent: Whirlpool Corp.

★ 66096 ★ **Witco Corp.**
Concarb Division
3675 Crestwood Pkwy NW
Duluth, GA 30136
(404)279-8802
Ultimate Parent: Witco Corp.

Dunwoody

★ 66097 ★ **Ace Hardware**
1316 Dunwoody Village Pky.
Dunwoody, GA 30338
(404)394-6938
Ultimate Parent: Ace Hardware.

★ 66098 ★ **Ace Hardware**
2514 Mt Vernon Rd.
Dunwoody, GA 30338
(404)393-9700
Ultimate Parent: Ace Hardware.

★ 66099 ★ **Alberto Culver**
5901-B Peachtree Dun
Dunwoody, GA
(404)390-7117
Ultimate Parent: Alberto-Culver Co. Inc.

★ 66100 ★ **Bank South, NA**
135 Perimeter Ctr. W
Dunwoody, GA 30346-1223
(404)698-5240
Company Type: Subsidiary. **Location Type:** Branch office. **Officer:** Tami Buttrey, Manager. **Ultimate Parent:** Bank South Corp. **SIC:** 6021—National Commercial Banks.

★ 66101 ★ **Bank South, NA**
4545 Chamblee Dunwoody Rd.
Dunwoody, GA 30338-6210
(404)698-5255
Company Type: Subsidiary. **Location Type:** Branch office. **Officer:** Bill Walker, Manager. **Ultimate Parent:** Bank South Corp. **SIC:** 6021—National Commercial Banks.

★ 66102 ★ **Bank South, NA**
2090 Dunwoody Club Dr.
Dunwoody, GA 30338
(404)698-5262
Company Type: Subsidiary. **Location Type:** Branch office. **Officer:** Julie Kramer, Manager. **Ultimate Parent:** Bank South Corp. **SIC:** 6021—National Commercial Banks.

★ 66103 ★ **Bank South NA/ Dunwoody**
4545 Chamblee-Dunwoody Rd.
Dunwoody, GA 30338
(404)698-5255
Company Type: Subsidiary. **Location Type:** Branch office. **Officer:** Michelle Daniels, Mgr. **Ultimate Parent:** Bank South Corp. **SIC:** 6021—National Commercial Banks.

★ 66104 ★ **BNY Financial Corp.**
100 Ashford Ctr. North
Dunwoody, GA 30338
(404)698-5100
Ultimate Parent: Bank of New York Co.

★ 66105 ★ **Cisco Systems**
400 Northridge Pointe
Dunwoody, GA
(404)640-4700
Ultimate Parent: Cisco Systems Inc.

★ 66106 ★ **Compaq Computer Corp.**
400 Northridge Rd.
Dunwoody, GA 30350
(404)594-0652
Ultimate Parent: Compaq Computer.

★ 66107 ★ **Delta Air Lines**
365 Northridge Rd.
Dunwoody, GA 30350
(404)804-2268
Ultimate Parent: Delta Air Lines, Inc.

★ 66108 ★ **Delta Air Lines Inc. Delta Data**
365 Northridge Rd.
Dunwoody, GA 30350
(404)804-2268
Ultimate Parent: Delta Air Lines, Inc.

★ 66109 ★ **First Union National Bank of Georgia**
1630 Mt Vernon Rd. & Chamblee-Dunwoody Rd.
Dunwoody, GA 30338-4299
(404)399-7920
Location Type: Branch office. **Ultimate Parent:** First Union Corp. **SIC:** 6021—National Commercial Banks.

★ 66110 ★ **First United Financial Service**
8211 Dunwoody Pl
Dunwoody, GA 30350
(404)641-7290
Ultimate Parent: First Chicago Corp.

★ 66111 ★ **Hoechst Roussel Pharmaceutical**
900 Ashwood Pkwy
Dunwoody, GA 30338
(404)551-8910
Ultimate Parent: Hoechst Celanese Corp.

★ 66112 ★ **Jiffy Lube**
7505 Roswell Rd.
Dunwoody, GA 30350
(404)668-9147
Ultimate Parent: Pennzoil.

★ 66113 ★ **Jiffy Lube Dunwoody**
1343 Dunwody Village Pky.
Dunwoody, GA 30338
(404)396-2539
Ultimate Parent: Pennzoil.

★ 66114 ★ **Kroger Co. the Retail Stores**
8331 Roswell Rd.
Dunwoody, GA 30350
(404)998-3040
Ultimate Parent: Kroger.

★ 66115 ★ **Kroger Co. the Retail Stores**
4498 Chamblee Dunwoody Rd.
Dunwoody, GA 30338
(404)451-8350
Ultimate Parent: Kroger.

★ 66116 ★ **Kroger Co. the Retail Stores**
2090 Dunwoody Club Dr.
Dunwoody, GA 30350
(404)391-9035
Ultimate Parent: Kroger.

★ 66117 ★ Kroger Pharmacies
2090 Dunwoody Club Dr.
Dunwoody, GA 30350
(404)391-9792
Ultimate Parent: Kroger.

★ 66118 ★ Kroger Pharmacies
8331 Roswell Rd.
Dunwoody, GA 30350
(404)998-3043
Ultimate Parent: Kroger.

★ 66119 ★ Lapp Insulator Co.
7 Dunwoody Pk.
Dunwoody, GA 30338
(404)551-9062
Ultimate Parent: Great American
Management & Investment.

★ 66120 ★ Mary Kay Cosmetics
Indep Sales
1828 Club Forest Ct.
Dunwoody, GA 30338
(404)399-6604
Ultimate Parent: Mary Kay Cosmetics.

★ 66121 ★ McDonald's
Restaurants
2460 Jett Ferry Rd.
Dunwoody, GA 30338
(404)395-1716
Ultimate Parent: McDonald's.

★ 66122 ★ McDonald's
Restaurants
8505 Roswell Rd.
Dunwoody, GA 30350
(404)993-8513
Ultimate Parent: McDonald's.

★ 66123 ★ McDonnell Douglas
Helicopter Co.
23 Wing Mill Rd.
Dunwoody, GA 30350
(404)393-2774
Ultimate Parent: McDonnell Douglas.

★ 66124 ★ Nationsbank Ofc
Atlanta Area a
Dunwoody Place 8755
Dunwoody, GA 30350
(404)523-0900
Ultimate Parent: Nationsbank Corp.

★ 66125 ★ Nationsbank Ofc
Atlanta Area C
Dunwoody Place 8755
Dunwoody, GA 30350
(404)969-0550
Ultimate Parent: Nationsbank Corp.

★ 66126 ★ Nationsbank Ofc
Atlanta Area N
Dunwoody Place 8755
Dunwoody, GA 30350
(404)594-6860
Ultimate Parent: Nationsbank Corp.

★ 66127 ★ Norwest Mortgage
Inc.
500 Sugar Mill Rd.
Dunwoody, GA 30350
(404)998-3938
Ultimate Parent: Norwest Corp.

★ 66128 ★ Penn Mutual Life
Insurance Co.
900 Ashwood Pkwy
Dunwoody, GA 30338
(404)604-9966
Ultimate Parent: Penn Mutual Life.

★ 66129 ★ Pizza Hut
5592 Chamblee Dunwoody Rd.
Dunwoody, GA 30338
(404)393-4721
Ultimate Parent: Pepsico.

★ 66130 ★ Pizza Hut
8290 Roswell Rd.
Dunwoody, GA 30350
(404)640-4747
Ultimate Parent: Pepsico.

★ 66131 ★ Professional
Accounting Servuc
3 Dunwoody Pk.
Dunwoody, GA 30338
(404)396-6923
Ultimate Parent: Olsten.

★ 66132 ★ Pulte Home Corp.
2378 Briarleigh Way
Dunwoody, GA 30338
(404)394-3110
Ultimate Parent: Pulte.

★ 66133 ★ Quintus Corp.
2300 Peachford Rd.
Dunwoody, GA 30338
(404)455-7555
Ultimate Parent: Intergraph.

★ 66134 ★ Radio Shack
8819 Roswell Rd.
Dunwoody, GA 30350
(404)993-0907
Company Type: Division. Ultimate Parent:
Tandy Corp.

★ 66135 ★ Ryder Truck Rental
100 Ashford Ctr. North
Dunwoody, GA 30338
(404)395-1277
Ultimate Parent: Ryder System.

★ 66136 ★ Service Merchandise
8610 Roswell Rd.
Dunwoody, GA 30350
(404)587-4200
Ultimate Parent: Service Merchandise Co.,
Inc.

★ 66137 ★ Springs Industries
8601 Dunwoody Pl
Dunwoody, GA 30350
(404)642-0257
Ultimate Parent: Springs Industries.

★ 66138 ★ Texaco
5546 Chamblee Dunwoody Rd.
Dunwoody, GA 30338
(404)393-8613
Ultimate Parent: Texaco.

★ 66139 ★ Variable Annuity Life
Insurance
1100 Ashwood Pkwy
Dunwoody, GA 30338
(404)395-4700
Ultimate Parent: Variable Annuity Life. SIC:
6411—Insurance Agents, Brokers &
Service.

★ 66140 ★ Vlasic Foods Inc.
1536 Dunwoody Village Pky.
Dunwoody, GA 30338
(404)394-0794
Ultimate Parent: Campbell Soup.

East Point

★ 66141 ★ Bank South, NA
2840 E. Point St.
East Point, GA 30344-3202
(404)763-3644
Company Type: Subsidiary. Location
Type: Branch office. Ultimate Parent: Bank
South Corp. SIC: 6021—National
Commercial Banks.

★ 66142 ★ Bank South, NA
3099 Washington Ave.
East Point, GA 30344-4455
(404)762-6244
Company Type: Subsidiary. Location
Type: Branch office. Officer: Debbie
Reeves, Manager. Ultimate Parent: Bank
South Corp. SIC: 6021—National
Commercial Banks.

★ 66143 ★ Bank South NA/East
Point
1733 Washington Ave.
East Point, GA 30344
(404)559-6060
Company Type: Subsidiary. Location
Type: Branch office. Officer: Debbie
Reeves, Mgr. Ultimate Parent: Bank South
Corp. SIC: 6021—National Commercial
Banks.

★ 66144 ★ First Union National
Bank of Georgia
2791 East Point St. SW
East Point, GA 30344-3292
(404)669-2625
Location Type: Branch office. Ultimate
Parent: First Union Corp. SIC: 6021—
National Commercial Banks.

★ 66145 ★ International Paper
2323 N. Sylvan Rd.
East Point, GA 30344
Ultimate Parent: International Paper Co.
SIC: 2656—Sanitary Food Containers.

★ 66146 ★ Kentucky Fried
Chicken
1394 Virginia Ave.
East Point, GA 30344
(404)767-8158
Ultimate Parent: Pepsico.

★ 66147 ★ Kentucky Fried
Chicken
2690 Sylvan Rd.
East Point, GA 30344
(404)763-8220
Ultimate Parent: Pepsico.

★ 66148 ★ Kroger Co. the
Reclaim Center
981 Milledge St.
East Point, GA 30344
(404)762-9189
Ultimate Parent: Kroger.

★ 66149 ★ McDonald's
Restaurants
3183 Main St.
East Point, GA 30344
(404)767-8049
Ultimate Parent: McDonald's.

★ 66150 ★ McDonald's
Restaurants
1203 Virginia Ave.
East Point, GA 30344
(404)559-9659
Ultimate Parent: McDonald's.

★ 66151 ★ Nationsbank Real
Estate Departments
East Point, GA
(404)765-1957
Ultimate Parent: Nationsbank Corp.

★ 66152 ★ Pizza Hut
3126 Washington Rd.
East Point, GA 30344
(404)669-8400
Ultimate Parent: Pepsico.

★ 66153 ★ Ppg Architectural
Finishes
1377 Oakleigh Dr.
East Point, GA 30344
Ultimate Parent: PPG Industries Inc. SIC:
2851—Paints & Allied Products.

★ 66154 ★ Taco Bell
3129 Washington Rd.
East Point, GA 30344
(404)767-7908
Ultimate Parent: Pepsico.

★ 66155 ★ Texaco Food Mart
3289 Washington Rd.
East Point, GA 30344
(404)762-0936
Ultimate Parent: Texaco.

★ 66156 ★ Texaco Food Mart No
2048
2048 Stanton Rd.
East Point, GA 30344
(404)762-8985
Ultimate Parent: Texaco.

Eastman

★ 66157 ★ Greyhound Bus Lines
908 College St.
Eastman, GA 31023
(912)374-3771
Ultimate Parent: Greyhound Lines Inc. SIC:
4131—Intercity & Rural Bus Transportation.

★ 66158 ★ Kentucky Fried
Chicken
811 College St.
Eastman, GA 31023
(912)374-6276
Ultimate Parent: Pepsico. SIC: 5812—
Eating Places.

★ 66159 ★ Piggly Wiggly
5 Ave.
Eastman, GA 31023
(912)374-2281
Ultimate Parent: Bruno's. SIC: 5411—
Grocery Stores.

★ 66160 ★ Piggly Wiggly
Southern Inc.
5 Ave.
Eastman, GA 31023
(912)374-2281
Ultimate Parent: Bruno's. SIC: 5411—
Grocery Stores.

★ 66161 ★ Radio Shack
108 Main St. SE
Eastman, GA 31023
(912)374-3742
Company Type: Division. Ultimate Parent:
Tandy Corp. SIC: 5065—Electronic Parts &
Equipment Nec.

★ 66162 ★ Reynolds Metals Co.
1 Industrial Dr.
Eastman, GA 31023
(912)374-4746
Officer: James Green, Manager. Ultimate
Parent: Reynolds Metals Co. SIC: 3444—
Sheet Metal Work.

★ 66163 ★ Wal Mart Discount
Cities
1307 Oak St. NW
Eastman, GA 31023
(912)374-7782
Ultimate Parent: Wal-Mart Stores, Inc. SIC:
5311—Department Stores.

Edison

★ 66164 ★ Kaiser Aluminum &
Chemical
324 Deport St.
Edison, GA 31746
(912)835-2216
Ultimate Parent: Maxxam. SIC: 5191—
Farm Supplies.

Elberton

★ 66165 ★ Allied-Signal Inc.
Autolite-Elberton
Minerial Springs Rd. PO Box 578
Elberton, GA 30635
Ultimate Parent: Allied-Signal Inc. SIC:
3694—Engine Electrical Equipment.

★ 66166 ★ Alliedsignal
Autolite
Mineral Springs Rd, PO Box 578
Elberton, GA 30635
Ultimate Parent: Allied-Signal Inc. SIC:
3694—Engine Electrical Equipment.

Ellabell

★ 66167 ★ Georgia Pacific Corp.
State Hwy. 204 E
Ellabell, GA 31308
(912)858-2211
Officer: Michael Green, Manager. Ultimate
Parent: Georgia-Pacific. SIC: 2421—
Sawmills & Planing Mills—General.

Ellaville

★ 66168 ★ Shell Station
Ebenezer Rd.
Ellaville, GA 31806
(912)937-2903
Ultimate Parent: Shell Oil Co. SIC: 5599—
Automotive Dealers Nec.

Ellenwood

★ 66169 ★ Pizza Hut
1778 Panola Rd.
Ellenwood, GA 30049
(404)808-7500
Ultimate Parent: Pepsico.

Ellijay

★ 66170 ★ Gold Kist Inc. Poultry
75 Industrial Blvd.
Ellijay, GA 30540
Ultimate Parent: Gold Kist. SIC: 2015—
Poultry Slaughtering & Processing.

Eton

★ 66171 ★   Cohutta Banking Co.
Hwy. 411
Eton, GA 30724
(706)695-9431
Location Type: Branch office. **Officer:**
Jean Sherman, Manager. **Ultimate Parent:**
Synovus Financial Corp. **SIC:** 6021—
National Commercial Banks.

Evans

★ 66172 ★   First Union National Bank of Georgia
4321 Washington Rd.
Evans, GA 30809-9512
(706)868-4620
Location Type: Branch office. **Ultimate Parent:** First Union Corp. **SIC:** 6021—
National Commercial Banks.

Fairburn

★ 66173 ★   Citgo Food Max
490 Fairburn Rd. SW
Fairburn, GA
(404)691-2902
Ultimate Parent: Citgo Petroleum.

★ 66174 ★   Lane Bryant
Shannon Mall
Fairburn, GA 30213
(404)964-7325
Ultimate Parent: Limited.

★ 66175 ★   Lerner Shop
Shannon Mall
Fairburn, GA 30213
(404)964-4410
Ultimate Parent: Limited.

★ 66176 ★   McDonald's Restaurants
7480 Old National Hwy.
Fairburn, GA 30213
(404)907-7505
Ultimate Parent: McDonald's.

★ 66177 ★   Owens-Corning Fiberglas Corp.
7000 McLarin Rd.
Fairburn, GA 30213
Ultimate Parent: Owens-Corning. **SIC:**
3296—Mineral Wool.

★ 66178 ★   Owens-Corning Fiberglass
7000 McLarin Rd.
Fairburn, GA 30213
Ultimate Parent: Owens-Corning. **SIC:**
3296—Mineral Wool.

★ 66179 ★   Porex Technologies Corp.
500 Bohannon Rd.
Fairburn, GA 30213-2875
Ultimate Parent: Medco Containment
Services. **SIC:** 3089—Plastics Products
Nec.

★ 66180 ★   Porex Technologies Corp. of Georgia
500 Bohannon Rd.
Fairburn, GA 30213-2875
Ultimate Parent: Medco Containment
Services. **SIC:** 3089—Plastics Products
Nec.

★ 66181 ★   Ralston Purina Co.
5001 Fayetteville Rd.
Fairburn, GA 30213
Ultimate Parent: Ralston Purina. **SIC:**
2047—Dog & Cat Food.

★ 66182 ★   Ryder Truck Rental
Hihgway 138
Fairburn, GA
(404)968-8920
Ultimate Parent: Ryder System.

★ 66183 ★   Texaco
2275 Hwy. 138
Fairburn, GA 30213
(404)994-0437
Ultimate Parent: Texaco.

Fairmount

★ 66184 ★   Solem Ind.
Rte. 1 Gordon St.
Fairmount, GA 30139
Ultimate Parent: J. M. Huber. **SIC:** 2819—
Industrial Inorganic Chemicals Nec.

★ 66185 ★   Solem Industries Inc.
Rte. 1 Box 13 S. Gordon Rd.
Fairmount, GA 30139
Ultimate Parent: J. M. Huber. **SIC:** 2800—
Chemicals & Allied Products.

Fayetteville

★ 66186 ★   Ace Hardware
870 E. Lanier Ave.
Fayetteville, GA 30214
(404)461-0323
Ultimate Parent: Ace Hardware.

★ 66187 ★   Bank South, NA
3000 State Hwy. 138
Fayetteville, GA 30214
(404)460-3650
Company Type: Subsidiary. **Location Type:** Branch office. **Ultimate Parent:** Bank
South Corp. **SIC:** 6021—National
Commercial Banks.

★ 66188 ★   Bank South, NA
710 N. Glynn St.
Fayetteville, GA 30214-1144
(404)460-3634
Company Type: Subsidiary. **Location Type:** Branch office. **Officer:** Judy Morrow,
Manager. **Ultimate Parent:** Bank South
Corp. **SIC:** 6021—National Commercial
Banks.

★ 66189 ★   Bank South, NA
145 W. Lanier Ave.
Fayetteville, GA 30214-1674
(404)461-3471
Company Type: Subsidiary. **Location Type:** Branch office. **Officer:** Bonnie Irwin,
Manager. **Ultimate Parent:** Bank South
Corp. **SIC:** 6021—National Commercial
Banks.

★ 66190 ★   First Union National Bank of Georgia
655 N. Jefferson Davis Dr.
Fayetteville, GA 30214-1649
Location Type: Branch office. **Ultimate Parent:** First Union Corp. **SIC:** 6021—
National Commercial Banks.

★ 66191 ★   Kentucky Fried Chicken
242 Banks Crossing
Fayetteville, GA 30214
(404)460-0204
Ultimate Parent: Pepsico.

★ 66192 ★   Kmart Stores
240 Banks Crossing
Fayetteville, GA 30214
(404)461-0110
Ultimate Parent: K-Mart.

★ 66193 ★   Kmart Stores Pharmacy
240 Banks Crossing
Fayetteville, GA 30214
(404)461-0316
Ultimate Parent: K-Mart.

★ 66194 ★   Kroger Co. the Retail Sotres
134 Banks Crossing
Fayetteville, GA 30214
(404)461-7602
Ultimate Parent: Kroger.

★ 66195 ★   Kroger Pharmaciess
134 Banks Crossing
Fayetteville, GA 30214
(404)461-7632
Ultimate Parent: Kroger.

★ 66196 ★   Mary Kay Cosmetics
Indep Sales
151 Patricia Ln.
Fayetteville, GA 30214
(404)461-0500
Ultimate Parent: Mary Kay Cosmetics.

★ 66197 ★   Nationsbank Real Estate Departments
Fayetteville, GA
(404)460-3500
Ultimate Parent: Nationsbank Corp.

★ 66198 ★   Norwest Mortgage Inc.
350 W. Stonewall Ave.
Fayetteville, GA
(404)460-9590
Ultimate Parent: Norwest Corp.

★ 66199 ★   Payless Shoesource
164 Banks Crest
Fayetteville, GA
(404)460-0466
Ultimate Parent: May Department Stores.

★ 66200 ★   Pizza Hut
650 N. Glynn St.
Fayetteville, GA
(404)460-3030
Ultimate Parent: Pepsico.

★ 66201 ★   Radio Shack
Hudson Plaza
Fayetteville, GA 30214
(404)461-1166
Company Type: Division. **Ultimate Parent:**
Tandy Corp.

★ 66202 ★   Ryder Truck Rental
South Glynn St.
Fayetteville, GA
(404)461-2772
Ultimate Parent: Ryder System.

★ 66203 ★   Ryder Truck Rental
105 North 85 Pkwy
Fayetteville, GA 30214
(404)631-8850
Ultimate Parent: Ryder System.

★ 66204 ★   Taco Bell
246 Banks Crsg
Fayetteville, GA 30214
(404)460-8770
Ultimate Parent: Pepsico.

Fitzgerald

★ 66205 ★   Aeroquip Corp.
381 Benjamin H. Hill Dr. E
Fitzgerald, GA 31750
(912)423-9376
Officer: Tommy White, Manager. **Ultimate Parent:** Trinova Corp. **SIC:** 3083—
Laminated Plastics Plate & Sheet; 3089—
Plastics Products Nec; 3544—Special Dies,
Tools, Jigs & Fixtures.

★ 66206 ★   Bank South, NA
102 W. Roanoke Dr.
Fitzgerald, GA 31750
(912)423-4321
Company Type: Subsidiary. **Location Type:** Branch office. **Officer:** Becky Powell,
Manager. **Ultimate Parent:** Bank South
Corp. **SIC:** 6021—National Commercial
Banks.

★ 66207 ★   Bank South, NA
115 E. Pine St.
Fitzgerald, GA 31750
(912)423-4321
Company Type: Subsidiary. **Location Type:** Branch office. **Officer:** Martha Rewis,
Manager. **Ultimate Parent:** Bank South
Corp. **SIC:** 6021—National Commercial
Banks.

★ 66208 ★   Bank South NA/ Fitzgerald
103 W. Roanoke Dr.
Fitzgerald, GA 31750
(912)423-4321 **Fax:** (912)423-6656
Company Type: Subsidiary. **Location Type:** Branch office. **Officer:** Charles M.
Harper III, President. **Ultimate Parent:** Bank
South Corp. **SIC:** 6022—State Commercial
Banks.

★ 66209 ★   Fitzgerald Railcar Services
Rip Wiley Rd.
Fitzgerald, GA 31750
Ultimate Parent: IMC Fertilizer Group. **SIC:**
3743—Railroad Equipment.

★ 66210 ★   Greyhound Bus Lines
Village Shopping Ctr.
Fitzgerald, GA 31750
(912)423-3192
Ultimate Parent: Greyhound Lines Inc. **SIC:**
4111—Local & Suburban Transit.

★ 66211 ★   Piggly Wiggly
202 W. Central Ave.
Fitzgerald, GA 31750
(912)423-4926
Ultimate Parent: Bruno's. **SIC:** 5411—
Grocery Stores.

★ 66212 ★   Pizza Hut
Colony Dr.
Fitzgerald, GA 31750
(912)423-2023
Ultimate Parent: Pepsico. **SIC:** 5812—
Eating Places.

★ 66213 ★   Shaw Industries Inc.
169 Benjamin H. Hill Dr. E.
Fitzgerald, GA 31750
(912)423-8753
Officer: George Kirkpatrick, Manager.
Ultimate Parent: Shaw Industries, Inc. **SIC:**
2281—Yarn Spinning Mills.

Flowery Branch

★ 66214 ★   Avery Dennison Corp.
PO Box 547
Flowery Br, GA 30542-0547
(404)967-3371
Officer: Ron Briskie. **Ultimate Parent:**
Avery Dennison Corp. **SIC:** 3552—Textile
Machinery; 2679—Converted Paper
Products Nec; 2759—Commercial Printing
Nec.

★ 66215 ★   Avery Dennison
4350 Avery Dr.
Flowery Branch, GA 30542-2836
Ultimate Parent: Avery Dennison Corp.
SIC: 2700—Printing & Publishing.

★ 66216 ★   Avery Dennison- Avery International
Business Systems Div.
Thurman Tanner Rd.
PO Box 574
Flowery Branch, GA 30502
(706)967-3371
Company Type: Division. **Ultimate Parent:**
Avery Dennison Corp. **SIC:** 2671—Paper
Coated & Laminated—Packaging; 3569—
General Industrial Machinery Nec.

★ 66217 ★   Combustion Technologies Inc.
4515 Cantrell Rd.
Flowery Branch, GA 30542
Ultimate Parent: Cummins Engine Co. **SIC:**
3499—Fabricated Metal Products Nec;
3592—Carburetors, Pistons, Rings &
Valves; 3471—Plating & Polishing.

★ 66218 ★   Gold Kist Inc. Agri- Service Feed Mill
4634 Radford Rd.
Flowery Branch, GA 30542
Ultimate Parent: Gold Kist. **SIC:** 2043—
Cereal Breakfast Foods.

★ 66219 ★   Gold Kist Inc. Feed Mill
4634 Radford Rd.
Flowery Branch, GA 30542
Ultimate Parent: Gold Kist. **SIC:** 2048—
Prepared Feeds Nec.

★ 66220 ★   Reliance Electric Co.
4349 Avery Dr.
Flowery Branch, GA 30542
Ultimate Parent: Reliance Electric. **SIC:**
3621—Motors & Generators.

★ 66221 ★   William Wrigley Co.
4500 Old Atlanta Hwy.
Flowery Branch, GA 30542
(404)967-6181
Ultimate Parent: William Wrigley Jr. Co.
SIC: 2067—Chewing Gum.

Folkston

★ 66222 ★   Bank South NA/ Folkston
802 S. Second St.
Folkston, GA 31537
(912)496-7382
Company Type: Subsidiary. **Location Type:** Branch office. **Ultimate Parent:** Bank
South Corp. **SIC:** 6021—National
Commercial Banks.

★ 66223 ★ **Rite Aid Discount Phrmcy**
T G Y Shopping Ctr.
Folkston, GA 31537
(912)496-3362
Ultimate Parent: Rite Aid. **SIC:** 5912—Drug Stores & Proprietary Stores.

★ 66224 ★ **Union Camp Corp.**
103 Mays Blvd.
Folkston, GA 31537
(912)496-2551
Officer: Larry Howell, Manager. **Ultimate Parent:** Union Camp Corp. **SIC:** 2421—Sawmills & Planing Mills—General.

Forest Park

★ 66225 ★ **Ace Hardware Co.**
858 Main St.
Forest Park, GA 30050
(404)366-3455
Ultimate Parent: Ace Hardware.

★ 66226 ★ **Ace Hardware No. 679**
858 Main St.
Forest Park, GA 30050
(404)366-3455
Ultimate Parent: Ace Hardware.

★ 66227 ★ **Air Treads Inc.**
Atlanta Div.
14 Royal Oak Dr.
Forest Park, GA 30050
Company Type: Division. **Ultimate Parent:** Goodyear Tire & Rubber. **SIC:** 3911—Jewelry & Precious Metal.

★ 66228 ★ **Bank South, NA**
1066 Main St.
Forest Park, GA 30050
(404)362-8500
Company Type: Subsidiary. **Location Type:** Branch office. **Officer:** Sylvia Roach, Manager. **Ultimate Parent:** Bank South Corp. **SIC:** 6021—National Commercial Banks.

★ 66229 ★ **Bank South NA/Forest Park**
1066 Main St.
Forest Park, GA 30050
(404)362-8500
Company Type: Subsidiary. **Location Type:** Branch office. **Officer:** Sylvia Roach, Mgr. **Ultimate Parent:** Bank South Corp. **SIC:** 6021—National Commercial Banks.

★ 66230 ★ **Boeing Co. the**
5585 Old Dixie Rd.
Forest Park, GA 30050
(404)363-1951
Ultimate Parent: Boeing.

★ 66231 ★ **Brownell Electro Inc.**
5690 S. Field Ct., Ste. 200
Forest Park, GA 30050
(404)362-9009
Location Type: Branch office. **Ultimate Parent:** Avnet. **SIC:** 5063—Electrical Apparatus & Equipment.

★ 66232 ★ **Clorox Co.**
17 Lake Mirror Rd.
Forest Park, GA 30050
Ultimate Parent: Clorox Co. **SIC:** 2842—Polishes & Sanitation Goods; 3085—Plastics Bottles.

★ 66233 ★ **Dan-Co Bakery**
301 Monty Ind. Blvd.
Forest Park, GA 30050
(404)366-1650 **Fax:** (404)366-1828
Company Type: Subsidiary. **Officer:** Benny Christiansen, President. **Ultimate Parent:** Flowers Industries.

★ 66234 ★ **H. B. Fuller Co.**
4630 Lake Mirror Pl.
Forest Park, GA 30050
Ultimate Parent: H. B. Fuller. **SIC:** 2891—Adhesives & Sealants.

★ 66235 ★ **H.B. Fuller Co.**
4630 Lake Mirror Pl.
Forest Park, GA 30050
Ultimate Parent: H. B. Fuller. **SIC:** 2891—Adhesives & Sealants.

★ 66236 ★ **Jim Walter Homes Inc. Regional**
6080 Frontage Rd.
Forest Park, GA 30050
(404)363-6995
Ultimate Parent: Walter Industries, Inc.

★ 66237 ★ **Jim Walter Homes Inc. Sales Office**
6080 Frontage Rd.
Forest Park, GA 30050
(404)366-0299
Ultimate Parent: Walter Industries, Inc.

★ 66238 ★ **Kentucky Fried Chicken**
4845 Jonesboro Rd.
Forest Park, GA 30050
(404)363-2534
Ultimate Parent: Pepsico.

★ 66239 ★ **Kmart Stores Automotive**
6200 Frontage Rd.
Forest Park, GA 30050
(404)363-8924
Ultimate Parent: K-Mart.

★ 66240 ★ **Kmart Stores Pharmacy**
6200 Frontage Rd.
Forest Park, GA 30050
(404)361-3153
Ultimate Parent: K-Mart.

★ 66241 ★ **McDonald's Restaurants**
5021 Old Dixie Rd.
Forest Park, GA 30050
(404)366-0789
Ultimate Parent: McDonald's.

★ 66242 ★ **McDonald's Restaurants**
3907 Jonesboro Rd.
Forest Park, GA 30050
(404)363-8122
Ultimate Parent: McDonald's.

★ 66243 ★ **Merico Inc.**
273 Central Ave.
Forest Park, GA 30050
Ultimate Parent: Anheuser-Busch. **SIC:** 2045—Prepared Flour Mixes & Doughs.

★ 66244 ★ **Nationsbank Departments Nation**
531 Forest Pkwy
Forest Park, GA 30050
(404)361-5343
Ultimate Parent: Nationsbank Corp.

★ 66245 ★ **Piggly Wiggly**
4769 Jonesboro Rd.
Forest Park, GA 30050
(404)363-8932
Ultimate Parent: Bruno's.

★ 66246 ★ **Piggly Wiggly of Atlanta**
4769 Jonesboro Rd.
Forest Park, GA 30050-4318
(404)363-8932
Officer: Gene Tyler. **Ultimate Parent:** Bruno's. **SIC:** 5411—Grocery Stores.

★ 66247 ★ **Pizza Hut**
4886 Jonesboro Rd.
Forest Park, GA 30050
(404)366-0505
Ultimate Parent: Pepsico.

★ 66248 ★ **Radio Shack**
4841 Jonesboro Rd.
Forest Park, GA 30050
(404)363-4124
Company Type: Division. **Ultimate Parent:** Tandy Corp.

★ 66249 ★ **Sonoco Products Co.**
4858 Old Dixie Hwy.
Forest Park, GA 30050
(404)361-4800
Ultimate Parent: Sonoco Products. **SIC:** 2655—Fiber Cans, Drums & Similar Products; 3089—Plastics Products Nec.

★ 66250 ★ **Taco Bell**
4465 Jonesboro Rd.
Forest Park, GA 30050
(404)361-6509
Ultimate Parent: Pepsico.

★ 66251 ★ **Union Camp Corp.**
5115 Pine Tree St.
Forest Park, GA 30050
Ultimate Parent: Union Camp Corp. **SIC:** 2653—Corrugated & Solid Fiber Boxes.

★ 66252 ★ **Union Camp Corp.**
Container
5115 Pinetree St.
Forest Park, GA 30050
(404)366-9118
Ultimate Parent: Union Camp Corp.

Forsyth

★ 66253 ★ **Bank South, NA**
35 S. Lee St.
Forsyth, GA 31029-1700
(912)994-2831
Company Type: Subsidiary. **Location Type:** Branch office. **Officer:** Don Griffin, Manager. **Ultimate Parent:** Bank South Corp. **SIC:** 6021—National Commercial Banks.

★ 66254 ★ **Bank South NA/Forsyth**
35 S. Lee St.
Forsyth, GA 31029
(912)994-2831
Company Type: Subsidiary. **Location Type:** Branch office. **Officer:** W. Don Griffith, President. **Ultimate Parent:** Bank South Corp. **SIC:** 6021—National Commercial Banks.

★ 66255 ★ **Wal Mart Discount Cities**
120 N. Lee St.
Forsyth, GA 31029
(912)994-0163
Ultimate Parent: Wal-Mart Stores, Inc. **SIC:** 5311—Department Stores.

Fort Benning

★ 66256 ★ **First Union National Bank of Georgia**
109 Wold Ave.
Fort Benning, GA 30904-3066
(706)685-7000
Location Type: Branch office. **Ultimate Parent:** First Union Corp. **SIC:** 6021—National Commercial Banks.

★ 66257 ★ **First Union National Bank of Georgia**
9320 Marne Rd.
Fort Benning, GA 30905
(706)682-1135
Location Type: Branch office. **Ultimate Parent:** First Union Corp. **SIC:** 6021—National Commercial Banks.

Fort Gordon

★ 66258 ★ **First Union National Bank of Georgia**
35th St.
Fort Gordon, GA 30905
(706)771-5960
Location Type: Branch office. **Ultimate Parent:** First Union Corp. **SIC:** 6021—National Commercial Banks.

Fort Valley

★ 66259 ★ **Piggly Wiggly**
438 Vineville St.
Fort Valley, GA 31030
(912)825-5040
Ultimate Parent: Bruno's. **SIC:** 5499—Miscellaneous Food Stores.

★ 66260 ★ **Piggly Wiggly Southern Inc.**
438 Vineville St.
Fort Valley, GA 31030
(912)825-5040
Ultimate Parent: Bruno's. **SIC:** 5499—Miscellaneous Food Stores.

Fortson

★ 66261 ★ **APAC**
2930 Smith Rd.
Fortson, GA 31808
(706)322-1401
Ultimate Parent: Ashland Oil. **SIC:** 2951—Asphalt Paving Mixtures & Blocks.

★ 66262 ★ **Vulcan Materials Co.**
9205 Fortson Rd.
Fortson, GA 31808
(706)324-3617
Officer: Charles V. Munn, Manager. **Ultimate Parent:** Vulcan Materials Co. **SIC:** 3281—Cut Stone & Stone Products.

Ft. Valley

★ 66263 ★ **Citizens Bank**
302 Vineville St.
PO Box 1199
Ft. Valley, GA 31030-4112
(912)825-8611 **Fax:** (912)825-2982
Location Type: Branch office. **Officer:** Cleon E. Moore, Chairman of the Board, President & CEO. **Ultimate Parent:** Sysco. **SIC:** 6021—National Commercial Banks.

Gainesville

★ 66264 ★ **Aetna Financial Services Inc.**
911 Green St. NE
Gainesville, GA 30501
(404)534-4521
Ultimate Parent: Aetna Life. **SIC:** 6062—State Credit Unions.

★ 66265 ★ **Agri-Bio Corp.**
966 Dorsey
Gainesville, GA 30503
(404)536-0111 **Fax:** (404)535-7886
Company Type: Subsidiary. **Officer:** Dr. H.L. Easterbrooks, V.P. & Gen. Mgr. **Ultimate Parent:** American Home Products. **SIC:** 2833—Medicinals & Botanicals; 2834—Pharmaceutical Preparations.

★ 66266 ★ **BellSouth Mobility**
500 Broad St. E.
Gainesville, GA 30501-3728
(706)536-7678
Ultimate Parent: BellSouth Corp. **SIC:** 5065—Electronic Parts & Equipment Nec.

★ 66267 ★ **Bi-Lo Store No 216**
975 Dawsonville Rd.
Gainesville, GA 30501
(404)531-1122
Ultimate Parent: Penn Traffic. **SIC:** 5411—Grocery Stores.

★ 66268 ★ **Chicopee**
Hwy. 13
PO Box 2537
Gainesville, GA 30503
Ultimate Parent: Johnson & Johnson. **SIC:** 2211—Broadwoven Fabric Mills—Cotton; 3000—Rubber & Miscellaneous Plastics Products.

★ 66269 ★ **Chicopee**
Hwy. 13
PO Box 2537
Gainesville, GA 30503
Ultimate Parent: Johnson & Johnson. **SIC:** 2211—Broadwoven Fabric Mills—Cotton; 3000—Rubber & Miscellaneous Plastics Products.

★ 66270 ★ **Conagra Broiler Co.**
949 Industrial Blvd.
Gainesville, GA 30501
Ultimate Parent: Conagra. **SIC:** 2015—Poultry Slaughtering & Processing.

★ 66271 ★ **Conagra Broiler Co.**
PO Box 1810
Gainesville, GA 30503
Ultimate Parent: Conagra. **SIC:** 2015—Poultry Slaughtering & Processing.

★ 66272 ★ **Conagra Poultry Co.**
949 Industrial Blvd.
Gainesville, GA 30501
Ultimate Parent: Conagra. **SIC:** 0251—Broiler, Fryer & Roaster Chickens.

★ 66273 ★ **ESI Inc.**
1150 Aviation Blvd.
Gainesville, GA 30501-6845
(706)535-2921
Ultimate Parent: Browning-Ferris Industries. **SIC:** 5083—Farm & Garden Machinery.

★ 66274 ★ **Express**
Lakeshore Mall
Gainesville, GA 30501
(404)536-6063
Ultimate Parent: Limited. **SIC:** 5621—Women's Clothing Stores.

★ 66275 ★ Harris Calorfic Co.
2645 Murphy Blvd.
Gainesville, GA 30504
(404)536-8801 Fax: (404)535-0544
Company Type: Division. Officer: S. Peter
Allman, President & CEO. Ultimate Parent:
Lincoln Electric Co. SIC: 3548—Welding
Apparatus.

★ 66276 ★ Harris Calorific
1058 PO Box
Gainesville, GA 30503
(404)536-8801
Ultimate Parent: Lincoln Electric Co.

★ 66277 ★ Harris Calorific
2345 Murphy Blvd.
Gainesville, GA 30504
Ultimate Parent: Emerson Electric Co. Inc.
SIC: 3549—Metalworking Machinery Nec;
5084—Industrial Machinery & Equipment.

★ 66278 ★ Kentucky Fried
Chicken
Mundy Mill Rd.
Gainesville, GA 30501
(404)536-0662
Ultimate Parent: Pepsico. SIC: 5812—
Eating Places.

★ 66279 ★ Kroger Co.
275 Shallowford Rd.
Gainesville, GA 30504
(404)536-1611
Ultimate Parent: Kroger. SIC: 5499—
Miscellaneous Food Stores.

★ 66280 ★ Lane Bryant
Lakeshore Mall
Gainesville, GA 30501
(404)535-7423
Ultimate Parent: Limited. SIC: 5651—
Family Clothing Stores.

★ 66281 ★ Liberty Mutual
Insurance Companie
2875 Browns Bridge Rd.
Gainesville, GA 30504
(404)536-8761
Ultimate Parent: Liberty Mutual Group.
SIC: 6411—Insurance Agents, Brokers &
Service.

★ 66282 ★ The Limited
Lakeshore Mall
Gainesville, GA 30501
(404)532-0541
Ultimate Parent: Limited. SIC: 5651—
Family Clothing Stores.

★ 66283 ★ Lincoln Electric Co.
Harris Calorific Div.
2345 Murphy Blvd.
Gainesville, GA 30504
Company Type: Division. Ultimate Parent:
Lincoln Electric Co. SIC: 3548—Welding
Apparatus.

★ 66284 ★ Lowe's
235 Shallowford Dr.
Gainesville, GA 30504
(404)534-1821
Ultimate Parent: Lowe's. SIC: 5039—
Construction Materials Nec.

★ 66285 ★ Pappagallo
Thompson Rd.
Gainesville, GA 30506
(404)536-6595
Ultimate Parent: United States Shoe. SIC:
5621—Women's Clothing Stores.

★ 66286 ★ Pizza Hut
Mundy Mill Rd.
Gainesville, GA 30501
(404)536-3681
Ultimate Parent: Pepsico. SIC: 5812—
Eating Places.

★ 66287 ★ Pizza Hut
1501 Browns Bridge Rd.
Gainesville, GA 30501
(404)532-7401
Ultimate Parent: Pepsico. SIC: 5812—
Eating Places.

★ 66288 ★ Radio Shack
Lakeshore Mall
Gainesville, GA 30501
(404)534-7974
Company Type: Division. Ultimate Parent:
Tandy Corp. SIC: 5731—Radio, Television
& Electronics Stores.

★ 66289 ★ Radio Shack
Mundy Mill Rd.
Gainesville, GA 30504
(404)287-7922
Company Type: Division. Ultimate Parent:
Tandy Corp. SIC: 5065—Electronic Parts &
Equipment Nec.

★ 66290 ★ Ryder Truck Rental
1567 Monroe Dr.
Gainesville, GA 30507
(404)534-3678
Ultimate Parent: Ryder System. SIC:
7359—Equipment Rental & Leasing Nec;
7513—Truck Rental & Leasing Without
Drivers.

★ 66291 ★ Shell Service Station
College Sq.
Gainesville, GA 30501
(404)534-1622
Ultimate Parent: Shell Oil Co. SIC: 5541—
Gasoline Service Stations.

★ 66292 ★ Sterwin Laboratories
322 Oak St.
Gainesville, GA 30501
(404)534-7356
Ultimate Parent: Imcera Group. SIC:
8734—Testing Laboratories.

★ 66293 ★ Teledyne
Gainesville Division
1215 Palmour Dr.
Gainesville, GA 30501
Ultimate Parent: Teledyne. SIC: 3764—
Space Propulsion Units & Parts.

★ 66294 ★ Trust Co. Bank of
North Georgia
601 Tri-County Plz.
Gainesville, GA 30130-2757
(404)887-6134
Officer: Ken Shugart. Ultimate Parent:
Suntrust Banks. SIC: 6021—National
Commercial Banks.

★ 66295 ★ Trust Co. Bank of
North Georgia
1804 Brown Bridge Rd.
Gainesville, GA 30501-4726
(404)535-9600
Officer: Rachel Rigdon, Manager. Ultimate
Parent: Suntrust Banks. SIC: 6021—
National Commercial Banks.

★ 66296 ★ Trust Co. Bank of
North Georgia
605 S. Enota Dr.
Gainesville, GA 30501-2470
(404)535-9600
Officer: Tim Taylor, Manager. Ultimate
Parent: Suntrust Banks. SIC: 6021—
National Commercial Banks.

★ 66297 ★ Trust Co. Bank of
North Georgia
427 Oak St.
PO Box 1418
Gainesville, GA 30503-1418
(404)535-9600 Fax: (404)535-9644
Officer: James E. Mathis Jr., President &
CEO. Ultimate Parent: Suntrust Banks.
SIC: 6021—National Commercial Banks.

★ 66298 ★ Trust Co. Bank of
North Georgia
3626 Mundy Mill Rd.
Gainesville, GA 30501-8219
(404)535-9600
Officer: Gary Anderson, Manager. Ultimate
Parent: Suntrust Banks. SIC: 6021—
National Commercial Banks.

★ 66299 ★ Wal Mart Discount
Cty
2275 Browns Bridge Rd.
Gainesville, GA 30501
(404)535-7604
Ultimate Parent: Wal-Mart Stores, Inc. SIC:
5311—Department Stores.

Gainsville

★ 66300 ★ Pepsi-Cola Bottling
Co.
2220 Centennial Dr.
Gainesville, GA 30504
(404)534-5221
Officer: Robert Phillips, Manager. Ultimate
Parent: Pepsico. SIC: 2086—Bottled &
Canned Soft Drinks.

Garden City

★ 66301 ★ GAF Building
Materials Corp.
Brampton Rd.
Garden City, GA 31408
(912)964-1517
Company Type: Subsidiary. Officer: Mike
Ferraro, Manager. Ultimate Parent: GAF
Corp. SIC: 2431—Millwork; 2952—Asphalt
Felts & Coatings.

Georgia South

★ 66302 ★ Radio Shack
Perlis Plz.
Georgia South, GA 31709
(912)924-4890
Company Type: Division. Ultimate Parent:
Tandy Corp. SIC: 5734—Computer &
Software Stores.

Glennville

★ 66303 ★ Exxon Service Center
805 S. Main St.
Glennville, GA 30427
(912)654-2838
Ultimate Parent: Exxon. SIC: 5541—
Gasoline Service Stations.

★ 66304 ★ Rite Aid Pharmacy
Glennville Plz.
Glennville, GA 30427
(912)654-9647
Ultimate Parent: Rite Aid. SIC: 5912—Drug
Stores & Proprietary Stores.

Glenwood

★ 66305 ★ Wheeler County
Hospital
3 St.
Glenwood, GA 30428
(912)523-5113
Ultimate Parent: Columbia Healthcare
Corp. SIC: 8062—General Medical &
Surgical Hospitals.

Gordon

★ 66306 ★ Engelhard Corp.
Hwy. 18 Spur
Gordon, GA 31031
(912)946-7500
Officer: Ken W. Jackman, President.
Ultimate Parent: Engelhard Corp. SIC:
3295—Minerals—Ground or Treated.

★ 66307 ★ Engelhard Corp.
Gordon Plant
PO Box 37
Gordon, GA 31031
Ultimate Parent: Engelhard Corp. SIC:
1455—Kaolin & Ball Clay.

Gray

★ 66308 ★ Ace Hardware
Hwy. 129 Clinton St.
Gray, GA 31032
(912)986-6132
Ultimate Parent: Ace Hardware. SIC:
5251—Hardware Stores.

Griffin

★ 66309 ★ Bank South NA
433 W. Taylor St.
Griffin, GA 30223-2817
(404)227-1313
Location Type: Branch office. Officer:
William H. Cooper. Ultimate Parent: Bank
South Corp. SIC: 6021—National
Commercial Banks; 6022—State
Commercial Banks; 6141—Personal Credit
Institutions; 6162—Mortgage Bankers &
Correspondents.

★ 66310 ★ Bank South NA/Griffin
433 W. Taylor St.
Griffin, GA 30224
(706)227-1313
Company Type: Subsidiary. Location
Type: Branch office. Officer: Bill Cooper,
President. Ultimate Parent: Bank South
Corp. SIC: 6021—National Commercial
Banks.

★ 66311 ★ Borden Chemical Inc.
1201 Pine Hill Rd.
Griffin, GA 30224
Ultimate Parent: Borden, Inc. SIC: 3081—
Unsupported Plastics Film & Sheet.

★ 66312 ★ Borden Inc.
1201 S. Pine Hill Rd.
Griffin, GA 30223
(404)228-4600
Officer: Rick Penczek, Manager. Ultimate
Parent: Borden, Inc. SIC: 3089—Plastics
Products Nec.

★ 66313 ★ Borden Inc.
Packaging & Industrial Products
1201 Pine Hill Rd.
Griffin, GA 30224
Company Type: Division. Ultimate Parent:
Borden, Inc. SIC: 3081—Unsupported
Plastics Film & Sheet.

★ 66314 ★ Essex Specialty
Products
913 W. Taylor St.
Griffin, GA 30223
(404)228-3736
Ultimate Parent: Dow Chemical Co. USA.

★ 66315 ★ First Union National
Bank of Georgia
100 S. Hill St.
Griffin, GA 30223-3402
(404)229-3900
Location Type: Branch office. Ultimate
Parent: First Union Corp. SIC: 6021—
National Commercial Banks.

★ 66316 ★ First Union National
Bank of Georgia
1482 W. McIntosh Rd.
Griffin, GA 30223-1288
(404)229-3960
Location Type: Branch office. Ultimate
Parent: First Union Corp. SIC: 6021—
National Commercial Banks.

★ 66317 ★ Greyhound Bus Lines
414 E. Taylor St.
Griffin, GA 30223
(404)227-9590
Ultimate Parent: Greyhound Lines Inc. SIC:
4142—Bus Charter Service Except Local.

★ 66318 ★ Kentucky Fried
Chicken
131 E. Solomon St.
Griffin, GA 30223
(404)227-3678
Ultimate Parent: Pepsico. SIC: 5812—
Eating Places.

★ 66319 ★ Piggly Wiggly
1659 N. Griffin Sq.
Griffin, GA 30223
(404)227-1034
Ultimate Parent: Bruno's. SIC: 5411—
Grocery Stores.

★ 66320 ★ Piggly Wiggly
Southern Inc.
1659 N. Griffin Sq.
Griffin, GA 30223
(404)227-1034
Ultimate Parent: Bruno's. SIC: 5411—
Grocery Stores.

★ 66321 ★ Pizza Hut
1432 Hwy. 16 Grif
Griffin, GA
(404)228-4400
Ultimate Parent: Pepsico.

★ 66322 ★ Radio Shack
1665 N. Expy.
Griffin, GA 30223
(404)228-8333
Company Type: Division. Ultimate Parent:
Tandy Corp. SIC: 5734—Computer &
Software Stores.

★ 66323 ★ Ryder Truck Rental
371 N. Expy.
Griffin, GA 30223
(404)229-2344
Ultimate Parent: Ryder System. SIC:
7389—Business Services Nec.

★ 66324 ★   **Spalding Regional Hospital**
601 S. 8th St.
Griffin, GA 30223
(706)228-2721
Officer: Phil Shaw, Executive Director.
Ultimate Parent: American Medical Holdings. **SIC:** 8062—General Medical & Surgical Hospitals.

★ 66325 ★   **Specialty Products Co.**
121 W. Bank St.
Griffin, GA 30223-3050
(404)228-5845
Officer: J. Lewis. **Ultimate Parent:** Avery Dennison Corp. **SIC:** 5999—Miscellaneous Retail Stores Nec; 5087—Service Establishment Equipment; 5111—Printing & Writing Paper; 5169—Chemicals & Allied Products Nec.

★ 66326 ★   **Taco Bell**
1633 N. Expy.
Griffin, GA 30223
(404)229-5481
Ultimate Parent: Pepsico. **SIC:** 5812—Eating Places.

★ 66327 ★   **Union Camp Corp.**
1304 Arthur K. Bolton Pky.
Griffin, GA 30223
(404)227-4573
Officer: Kurt Strater, Manager. **Ultimate Parent:** Union Camp Corp. **SIC:** 3089—Plastics Products Nec.

Hagan

★ 66328 ★   **Georgia Pacific Corp.**
Chip N. Saw
Hagan, GA 30429
(912)739-4801
Officer: Lyle Rex Hill, Manager. **Ultimate Parent:** Georgia-Pacific. **SIC:** 2421—Sawmills & Planing Mills—General.

Hamilton

★ 66329 ★   **First Union National Bank of Georgia**
Hwy. 27
Hamilton, GA 31811
(706)628-4221
Location Type: Branch office. **Ultimate Parent:** First Union Corp. **SIC:** 6021—National Commercial Banks.

Hampton

★ 66330 ★   **First Union National Bank of Georgia**
17 E. Main St.
Hampton, GA 30228-2116
(404)946-4248
Location Type: Branch office. **Ultimate Parent:** First Union Corp. **SIC:** 6021—National Commercial Banks.

★ 66331 ★   **Georgia Pacific Corp.**
100 Georgia Pacific Way
Hampton, GA 30228
(404)946-4571
Location Type: Plant. **Officer:** Ray Galante, Plant Manager. **Ultimate Parent:** Georgia-Pacific. **SIC:** 2952—Asphalt Felts & Coatings.

Hapeville

★ 66332 ★   **Ace Hardware**
597 Central Ave.
Hapeville, GA 30354
(404)767-1554
Ultimate Parent: Ace Hardware.

★ 66333 ★   **First Union National Bank of Georgia**
590 S. Central Ave.
Hapeville, GA 30354-1648
(404)669-2610
Location Type: Branch office. **Ultimate Parent:** First Union Corp. **SIC:** 6021—National Commercial Banks.

★ 66334 ★   **Ford Motor Co., Atlanta Assembly Plant**
340 Henry Ford Ave.
Hapeville, GA 30354
Location Type: Plant. **Ultimate Parent:** Ford Motor Co. **SIC:** 3711—Motor Vehicles & Car Bodies.

★ 66335 ★   **Greyhound Bus Line Local Info**
438 S. Central Ave.
Hapeville, GA 30354
(404)767-0777
Ultimate Parent: Greyhound Lines Inc.

★ 66336 ★   **Greyhound Bus Lines Local Info**
438 Henry Ford Ii Ave.
Hapeville, GA 30354
(404)762-9581
Ultimate Parent: Greyhound Lines Inc.

★ 66337 ★   **Nationsbank Atm Honor-Cirrus L**
1031 Virginia Ave.
Hapeville, GA
(404)581-2121
Ultimate Parent: Nationsbank Corp.

★ 66338 ★   **Pizza Hut**
876 Virginia Ave.
Hapeville, GA 30354
(404)763-3481
Ultimate Parent: Pepsico.

★ 66339 ★   **Ryder Truck Rental**
Virginia Ave.
Hapeville, GA
(404)767-0428
Ultimate Parent: Ryder System.

★ 66340 ★   **Ryder Truck Rental**
951 Virginia Ave.
Hapeville, GA 30354
(404)669-0815
Ultimate Parent: Ryder System.

Hartwell

★ 66341 ★   **Athens First Bank & Trust**
405 W. Howell
Hartwell, GA 30643
(706)376-3911
Location Type: Branch office. **Officer:** Marion A. Butler, Manager. **Ultimate Parent:** Synovus Financial Corp. **SIC:** 6021—National Commercial Banks.

★ 66342 ★   **Monroe Auto Equipment Co.**
200 McIntyre Dr.
Hartwell, GA 30643
Ultimate Parent: Tenneco Inc. **SIC:** 3714—Motor Vehicle Parts & Accessories.

Hazelhurst

★ 66343 ★   **Bank of Hazelhurst**
1220 S. Tallahassee St.
Hazlehurst, GA 31539-2922
(912)375-4228
Location Type: Branch office. **Ultimate Parent:** Synovus Financial Corp. **SIC:** 6021—National Commercial Banks.

★ 66344 ★   **Bank of Hazelhurst**
PO Box 128
Hazlehurst, GA 31539-0128
Location Type: Branch office. **Ultimate Parent:** Synovus Financial Corp. **SIC:** 6021—National Commercial Banks.

★ 66345 ★   **Bank of Hazelurst**
208 S. Tallahassee
Hazlehurst, GA 31539-2732
(912)375-4228 **Fax:** (912)375-4210
Location Type: Branch office. **Officer:** Jack C. Floyd, President & CEO. **Ultimate Parent:** Synovus Financial Corp. **SIC:** 6021—National Commercial Banks.

Hazlehurst

★ 66346 ★   **Emerson Electric Co.**
Alco Controls Div.
400 E. 1st St.
Hazlehurst, GA 31539
Company Type: Division. **Ultimate Parent:** Emerson Electric Co. Inc. **SIC:** 3822—Environmental Controls.

★ 66347 ★   **Emerson Electric Co. Inc.**
Alco Controls Div.
400 E. 1st St.
Hazlehurst, GA 31539
Ultimate Parent: Emerson Electric Co. Inc. **SIC:** 3822—Environmental Controls.

★ 66348 ★   **Piggly Wiggly**
300 S. Tallahassee St.
Hazlehurst, GA 31539
(912)375-5823
Ultimate Parent: Bruno's. **SIC:** 5411—Grocery Stores.

Hinesville

★ 66349 ★   **Ace Hardware**
Hwy. 196 W
Hinesville, GA 31313
(912)368-3394
Ultimate Parent: Ace Hardware. **SIC:** 5251—Hardware Stores.

★ 66350 ★   **First Union National Bank of Georgia**
Liberty Square Shopping Ctr.
Hinesville, GA 31313-4617
(912)876-7141
Location Type: Branch office. **Ultimate Parent:** First Union Corp. **SIC:** 6021—National Commercial Banks.

★ 66351 ★   **Food Lion**
103 H General Screven Way
Hinesville, GA 31313
(912)368-4266
Ultimate Parent: Food Lion. **SIC:** 5411—Grocery Stores.

★ 66352 ★   **Food Lion Inc.**
103 H General Screven Way
Hinesville, GA 31313
(912)368-4266
Ultimate Parent: Food Lion. **SIC:** 5411—Grocery Stores.

★ 66353 ★   **Georgia Federal Bank F S B**
Liberty Sq.
Hinesville, GA 31313
(912)876-7141
Ultimate Parent: First Union Corp. **SIC:** 6099—Functions Related to Deposit Banking.

★ 66354 ★   **Greyhound Bus Lines**
Fraser Cir.
Hinesville, GA 31313
(912)368-4777
Ultimate Parent: Greyhound Lines Inc. **SIC:** 4212—Local Trucking Without Storage.

★ 66355 ★   **Piggly Wiggly**
Kmart Plz.
Hinesville, GA 31313
(912)368-2228
Ultimate Parent: Bruno's. **SIC:** 5411—Grocery Stores.

★ 66356 ★   **Pizza Hut**
730 E. Oglethorpe Hwy.
Hinesville, GA 31313
(912)876-0101
Ultimate Parent: Pepsico. **SIC:** 5812—Eating Places.

★ 66357 ★   **Ryder Truck Rental**
428 Gen Screven Way
Hinesville, GA 31313
(912)368-3535
Ultimate Parent: Ryder System. **SIC:** 5521—Used Car Dealers.

Hiram

★ 66358 ★   **Kmart Stores**
2229 Pace Parkway
Hiram, GA
(404)439-8522
Ultimate Parent: K-Mart.

★ 66359 ★   **Kmart Stores Pharmacy**
2229 Pace Parkway
Hiram, GA
(404)439-8258
Ultimate Parent: K-Mart.

★ 66360 ★   **Kroger Co. the Retail Sotres**
2205 Atlanta Hwy.
Hiram, GA 30141
(404)943-0107
Ultimate Parent: Kroger.

★ 66361 ★   **Kroger Pharmacies**
2205 Atlanta Hwy.
Hiram, GA 30141
(404)943-0451
Ultimate Parent: Kroger.

★ 66362 ★   **Radio Shack**
Paulding Commons
Hiram, GA
(404)439-5000
Company Type: Division. **Ultimate Parent:** Tandy Corp.

★ 66363 ★   **Texaco Food Mart Hiram**
1677 Atlanta Hwy.
Hiram, GA 30141
(404)445-2750
Ultimate Parent: Texaco.

Homerville

★ 66364 ★   **Rite Aid Disc Pharmacy**
607 N. Church St.
Homerville, GA 31634
(912)487-5117
Ultimate Parent: Rite Aid. **SIC:** 5912—Drug Stores & Proprietary Stores.

Jackson

★ 66365 ★   **Mary Kay Cosmetsics**
Rural Route 2
Jackson, GA 30233
(404)775-7400
Ultimate Parent: Mary Kay Cosmetics.

★ 66366 ★   **Pizza Hut**
811 E. 3rd St.
Jackson, GA 30233
(404)775-6884
Ultimate Parent: Pepsico. **SIC:** 5812—Eating Places.

Jekyll Island

★ 66367 ★   **Barnett Bank of Southeast Georgia, NA**
18 Beachview Dr.
Jekyll Island, GA 31520-0816
(912)261-4200
Company Type: Subsidiary. **Location Type:** Branch office. **Officer:** Thelma Jones, Vice President. **Ultimate Parent:** Barnett Banks. **SIC:** 6021—National Commercial Banks.

Jessup

★ 66368 ★   **Barnett Bank of Southeast Georgia, NA**
204 Cherry St.
Jessup, GA 31545
(912)427-2011
Company Type: Subsidiary. **Location Type:** Branch office. **Officer:** Dell Kieth, Vice President. **Ultimate Parent:** Barnett Banks. **SIC:** 6021—National Commercial Banks.

Jesue

★ 66369 ★   **Trust Co. Bank of Southeast Georgia, National Assoc.**
175 S. Macon St.
Jesue, GA 31545-3509
(912)427-1400
Officer: Charles A. Lyons, Manager. **Ultimate Parent:** Suntrust Banks. **SIC:** 6021—National Commercial Banks.

Jesup

★ 66370 ★   **ITT Rayonier Inc.**
Jessup Div.
Savannah Hwy. PO Box 2070
Jesup, GA 31545-0207
Company Type: Division. **Ultimate Parent:** ITT Rayonier Inc. **SIC:** 2611—Pulp Mills.

★ 66371 ★   **ITT Rayonier Inc.**
Jesup Pulp Div.
Savannah Hwy.
Jesup, GA 31545-2070
Company Type: Division. **Ultimate Parent:** ITT Rayonier Inc. **SIC:** 2611—Pulp Mills.

★ 66372 ★   **Pizza Hut**
25511 S. Hwy. 301
Jesup, GA 31545
(912)427-4231
Ultimate Parent: Pepsico. **SIC:** 5812—Eating Places.

★ 66373 ★   Ryder Truck Rental
Savannah St.
Jesup, GA 31545
(912)427-8250
Ultimate Parent: Ryder System. SIC:
7513—Truck Rental & Leasing Without
Drivers.

★ 66374 ★   Trailways Bus Station
74 Walnut Sq.
Jesup, GA 31545
(912)427-6101
Ultimate Parent: Greyhound Lines Inc. SIC:
4131—Intercity & Rural Bus Transportation.

★ 66375 ★   Zippy Mart Inc.
602 W. Cherry St.
Jesup, GA 31545
(912)427-9843
Ultimate Parent: Crown Central Petroleum
Corp. SIC: 5411—Grocery Stores.

Jonesboro

★ 66376 ★   Bank South, NA
825 Southway Dr.
Jonesboro, GA 30236-2240
(404)473-5260
Company Type: Subsidiary. Location
Type: Branch office. Officer: Tommy Dahl,
Manager. Ultimate Parent: Bank South
Corp. SIC: 6021—National Commercial
Banks.

★ 66377 ★   Bank South, NA
8059 Tara Blvd.
Jonesboro, GA 30236
(404)473-5268
Company Type: Subsidiary. Location
Type: Branch office. Officer: Stephanie
Woods, Manager. Ultimate Parent: Bank
South Corp. SIC: 6021—National
Commercial Banks.

★ 66378 ★   Fleet Finance Inc.
Jonesboro
7202 Tara Blvd.
Jonesboro, GA 30236
(404)478-8912
Ultimate Parent: Fleet Financial Group.

★ 66379 ★   Jiffy Lube Jonesboro
6581 Tara Blvd.
Jonesboro, GA 30236
(404)471-1285
Ultimate Parent: Pennzoil.

★ 66380 ★   Kawneer Co. Inc.
7468 Hwy. 54 PO Box 516
Jonesboro, GA 30236
Ultimate Parent: Cyprus Amax Minerals.
SIC: 3354—Aluminum Extruded Products.

★ 66381 ★   Kentucky Fried
Chicken
6169 S. Expy.
Jonesboro, GA 30236
(404)968-4005
Ultimate Parent: Pepsico.

★ 66382 ★   Kentucky Fried
Chicken
8687 Tara Blvd.
Jonesboro, GA 30236
(404)471-4379
Ultimate Parent: Pepsico.

★ 66383 ★   Kmart Stores
7965 Tara Blvd.
Jonesboro, GA 30236
(404)477-0521
Ultimate Parent: K-Mart.

★ 66384 ★   Kmart Stores
Pharmacy
7965 Tara Blvd.
Jonesboro, GA 30236
(404)471-3130
Ultimate Parent: K-Mart.

★ 66385 ★   Kroger Co. the Retail
Stores
8059 Tara Blvd.
Jonesboro, GA 30236
(404)478-5700
Ultimate Parent: Kroger.

★ 66386 ★   McDonald's
Restaurants
6623 Tara Blvd.
Jonesboro, GA 30236
(404)478-3283
Ultimate Parent: McDonald's.

★ 66387 ★   McDonald's
Restaurants
7894 Tara Blvd.
Jonesboro, GA 30236
(404)477-1020
Ultimate Parent: McDonald's.

★ 66388 ★   McDonald's
Restaurants
8530 Hwy. 85
Jonesboro, GA 30236
(404)477-9293
Ultimate Parent: McDonald's.

★ 66389 ★   Nalco Chemical Co.
7536 Georgia Hwy. 54
Jonesboro, GA 30236
Ultimate Parent: Nalco Chemical Co. SIC:
2899—Chemical Preparations Nec; 2843—
Surface Active Agents; 2869—Industrial
Organic Chemicals Nec; 2992—Lubricating
Oils & Greases; 5169—Chemicals & Allied
Products Nec.

★ 66390 ★   Nalco Chemical Co.
Warehouse
7536 Hwy. 54 N
Jonesboro, GA 30236
(404)478-0210
Ultimate Parent: Nalco Chemical Co.

★ 66391 ★   Nationsbank Acct
Activity Inf
South Clayton 7906 T
Jonesboro, GA
(404)523-0900
Ultimate Parent: Nationsbank Corp.

★ 66392 ★   Nationsbank Honor-
Cirrus L Sou
7906 Tara Blvd.
Jonesboro, GA 30236
(404)473-8700
Ultimate Parent: Nationsbank Corp.

★ 66393 ★   Nationsbank Offices
Atlanta Ar
South Clayton 7906 T
Jonesboro, GA
(404)969-0550
Ultimate Parent: Nationsbank Corp.

★ 66394 ★   PHH US Mortgage
Corp.
238 Stockbridge Rd.
Jonesboro, GA 30236
(404)603-2585
Ultimate Parent: PHH.

★ 66395 ★   Pizza Hut
8633 Tara Blvd.
Jonesboro, GA 30236
(404)471-4147
Ultimate Parent: Pepsico.

★ 66396 ★   Ryder Truck Rental
Hwy. 54 & Southla
Jonesboro, GA
(404)968-8920
Ultimate Parent: Ryder System.

★ 66397 ★   Ryder Truck Rental
7197 Tara Blvd.
Jonesboro, GA 30236
(404)719-9801
Ultimate Parent: Ryder System.

★ 66398 ★   Shell Food Mart
211 N. Main St.
Jonesboro, GA 30236
(404)478-8778
Ultimate Parent: Shell Oil Co.

★ 66399 ★   Shell Mini Mart
7264 Tara Blvd.
Jonesboro, GA 30236
(404)471-3357
Ultimate Parent: Shell Oil Co.

★ 66400 ★   Taco Bell
8127 Tara Blvd.
Jonesboro, GA 30236
(404)603-2380
Ultimate Parent: Pepsico.

★ 66401 ★   Taco Bell
641 Morrow Industrial Bl
Jonesboro, GA 30236
(404)961-4337
Ultimate Parent: Pepsico.

★ 66402 ★   Target Stores Retail
Stores
6525 Tara Blvd.
Jonesboro, GA 30236
(404)477-9690
Ultimate Parent: Dayton Hudson.

★ 66403 ★   Texaco
8139 Tara Blvd.
Jonesboro, GA 30236
(404)471-2687
Ultimate Parent: Texaco.

★ 66404 ★   Texaco Express Lube
& Tune
8016 Tara Blvd.
Jonesboro, GA 30236
(404)471-5634
Ultimate Parent: Texaco.

★ 66405 ★   Texaco Food Mart
6980 Tara Blvd.
Jonesboro, GA 30236
(404)478-6923
Ultimate Parent: Texaco.

★ 66406 ★   Thoroughbred
Plastics Corp.
7480 Saybrook Trl.
Jonesboro, GA 30236-2679
(404)603-8908
Ultimate Parent: Brown-Forman. SIC:
3089—Plastics Products Nec.

Kennesaw

★ 66407 ★   Bank South, NA
2710 Town Ctr. Dr.
Kennesaw, GA 30144
(404)528-8255
Company Type: Subsidiary. Location
Type: Branch office. Officer: Debbie
Altman, Manager. Ultimate Parent: Bank
South Corp. SIC: 6021—National
Commercial Banks.

★ 66408 ★   Bath & Body Works
400 Ernest W. Barrett Pky.
Kennesaw, GA 30144
(404)422-1698
Ultimate Parent: Limited.

★ 66409 ★   Beneficial Georgia
Inc.
440 Ernest W. Barrett Pky.
Kennesaw, GA 30144-4901
(404)499-8630
Ultimate Parent: Beneficial. SIC: 6141—
Personal Credit Institutions; 6162—
Mortgage Bankers & Correspondents.

★ 66410 ★   Circuit City
2801 George Busbee Pky. N
Kennesaw, GA 30144
(404)590-7444
Ultimate Parent: Circuit City Stores.

★ 66411 ★   Citgo Food Mart
3631 Cherokee St. NW
Kennesaw, GA
(404)426-6846
Ultimate Parent: Citgo Petroleum.

★ 66412 ★   Dana Corp.
Weatherhead Division
1025 Cobb International B
Kennesaw, GA 30144
(404)429-9388
Ultimate Parent: Dana Corp.

★ 66413 ★   First Union National
Bank of Georgia
2849 Dallas St.
Kennesaw, GA 30144-2785
(404)423-3340
Location Type: Branch office. Ultimate
Parent: First Union Corp. SIC: 6021—
National Commercial Banks.

★ 66414 ★   First Union National
Bank of Georgia
510 Roberts Ct. NW
Kennesaw, GA 30144
(404)429-2700
Location Type: Branch office. Ultimate
Parent: First Union Corp. SIC: 6021—
National Commercial Banks.

★ 66415 ★   Fort Howard Corp.
1201 Roberts Blvd. NW
Kennesaw, GA 30144
(404)426-5711
Ultimate Parent: Fort Howard.

★ 66416 ★   The Gap Kids
400 Ernest W. Barrett Pky.
Kennesaw, GA 30144
(404)425-6003
Ultimate Parent: GAP.

★ 66417 ★   Interface Research
Corp.
100 Chastain Center Blvd.
Ste. 165
Kennesaw, GA 30144
(404)421-9555 Fax: (404)424-1888
Company Type: Subsidiary. Officer: C.
Edward Terry, President. Ultimate Parent:
Interface Inc.

★ 66418 ★   Johnson Controls Inc.
Mid-Marke
820 Shallowford Rd. NE
Kennesaw, GA 30144
(404)516-0133
Ultimate Parent: Johnson Controls Inc.

★ 66419 ★   Kay-Bee Toy & Hobby
Shop Inc.
400 Ernest W. Barrett Pky.
Kennesaw, GA 30144
(404)426-7253
Ultimate Parent: Melville.

★ 66420 ★   Kentucky Fried
Chicken
1970 N. Cobb Pkwy
Kennesaw, GA 30144
(404)422-9716
Ultimate Parent: Pepsico.

★ 66421 ★   Kids R US
2646 George Busbee Pky. N
Kennesaw, GA 30144
(404)426-0725
Ultimate Parent: Toys "R" US.

★ 66422 ★   Kids R US No. 1240
2646 George Busbee Pkwy N
Kennesaw, GA 30144
(404)426-0725
Ultimate Parent: Toys "R" US.

★ 66423 ★   Kmart Stores
Pharmacy
1200 Barrett Pkwy NW
Kennesaw, GA 30144
(404)422-1842
Ultimate Parent: K-Mart.

★ 66424 ★   Kroger Co. the Retail
Sotres
3330 Cobb Pkwy NW
Kennesaw, GA
(404)975-8652
Ultimate Parent: Kroger.

★ 66425 ★   Kroger Pharmacies
3330 Cobb Pkwy NW
Kennesaw, GA
(404)975-8776
Ultimate Parent: Kroger.

★ 66426 ★   Lerner Shop
400 Ernest W. Barrett Pky.
Kennesaw, GA 30144
(404)427-6949
Ultimate Parent: Limited.

★ 66427 ★   The Limited Express
400 Ernest W. Barrett Pky.
Kennesaw, GA 30144
(404)427-0745
Ultimate Parent: Limited.

★ 66428 ★   Linens 'n Things
Cobb Place
800 Ernest W. Barrett Pky.
Kennesaw, GA 30144
(404)422-7242
Ultimate Parent: Melville.

★ 66429 ★   Marshalls
425 Ernest W. Barrett Pky.
Kennesaw, GA 30144
(404)424-2064
Ultimate Parent: Melville.

★ 66430 ★   Mary Kay Cosmetics
Indep Sales
2729 Elmhurst Blvd.
Kennesaw, GA 30144
(404)427-3202
Ultimate Parent: Mary Kay Cosmetics.

★ 66431 ★　McDonald's
Restaurants
305 Ernest W. Barrett Pky.
Kennesaw, GA 30144
(404)423-9141
Ultimate Parent: McDonald's.

★ 66432 ★　McDonald's
Restaurants
U.S. 41 & Hwy. 293
Kennesaw, GA
(404)427-6918
Ultimate Parent: McDonald's.

★ 66433 ★　National
Semiconductor Corp.
3182 Pine Knoll Ct NW
Kennesaw, GA 30144
(404)419-1801
Ultimate Parent: National Semiconductor
Corp.

★ 66434 ★　National
Semiconductor Corp.
4710 Misty Lake Ct NE
Kennesaw, GA 30144
(404)516-0719
Ultimate Parent: National Semiconductor
Corp.

★ 66435 ★　Nationsbank Honor-
Cirrus L Wad
4400 Wade Green Rd.
Kennesaw, GA 30144
(404)423-5194
Ultimate Parent: Nationsbank Corp.

★ 66436 ★　Nationsbank Ofc
Atlanta Area C
2597 George Busbee Pkwy
Kennesaw, GA 30144
(404)523-0900
Ultimate Parent: Nationsbank Corp.

★ 66437 ★　Nationsbank Ofcs
Atlanta Area
Bells Ferry 4300 Bel
Kennesaw, GA 30144
(404)969-0550
Ultimate Parent: Nationsbank Corp.

★ 66438 ★　Nationsbank Offices
Atlanta Ar
2597 George Busbee Pkwy
Kennesaw, GA 30144
(404)423-5177
Ultimate Parent: Nationsbank Corp.

★ 66439 ★　Nationsbank Offices
Atlanta Ar
Wade Green 4400 Wade
Kennesaw, GA 30144
(404)423-5194
Ultimate Parent: Nationsbank Corp.

★ 66440 ★　Payless Shoesource
400 Ernest W. Barrett Pky.
Kennesaw, GA 30144
(404)419-7794
Ultimate Parent: May Department Stores.

★ 66441 ★　Petite Sophisticate
Town Ctr. at Cobb
Kennesaw, GA 30144
(404)423-9188
Ultimate Parent: United States Shoe.

★ 66442 ★　Pizza Hut
2491 George Busbee Pkwy N
Kennesaw, GA 30144
(404)425-5858
Ultimate Parent: Pepsico.

★ 66443 ★　Pizza Hut
400 Ernest W. Barrett Pky.
Kennesaw, GA 30144
(404)421-0752
Ultimate Parent: Pepsico.

★ 66444 ★　Pizza Hut
3600 Shiloh Rd.
Kennesaw, GA 30144
(404)427-6900
Ultimate Parent: Pepsico.

★ 66445 ★　Radio Shack
Town Ctr. Mall
Kennesaw, GA
(404)423-1478
Company Type: Division. Ultimate Parent:
Tandy Corp.

★ 66446 ★　Radio Shack
1930-A Cobb Parkway
Kennesaw, GA
(404)419-9912
Company Type: Division. Ultimate Parent:
Tandy Corp.

★ 66447 ★　Ryder Truck Rental
2115 Cobb Pkwy NW
Kennesaw, GA
(404)425-5558
Ultimate Parent: Ryder System.

★ 66448 ★　Service Merchandise
800 W. Ernest Barrett Pky.
Kennesaw, GA 30144
(404)426-4560
Ultimate Parent: Service Merchandise Co.,
Inc.

★ 66449 ★　Sports Authority
850 Cobb Place Blvd. NW
Kennesaw, GA 30144
(404)426-1444
Ultimate Parent: K-Mart.

★ 66450 ★　Structure
400 Ernest W. Barrett Pky.
Kennesaw, GA 30144
(404)419-0162
Ultimate Parent: Limited.

★ 66451 ★　T J Maxx
425 Ernest W. Barrett Pky.
Kennesaw, GA 30144
(404)919-8530
Ultimate Parent: TJX.

★ 66452 ★　Taco Bell
400 Ernest W. Barrett Pky.
Kennesaw, GA 30144
(404)424-0007
Ultimate Parent: Pepsico.

★ 66453 ★　Taco Bell
1906 Cobb Pkwy NW
Kennesaw, GA
(404)424-8863
Ultimate Parent: Pepsico.

★ 66454 ★　Texaco
2145 Cobb Pkwy NW
Kennesaw, GA
(404)424-6242
Ultimate Parent: Texaco.

★ 66455 ★　Texaco
3300 Frey Rd.
Kennesaw, GA 30144
(404)422-0946
Ultimate Parent: Texaco.

★ 66456 ★　Texaco
465 Barrett Pkwy NW
Kennesaw, GA 30144
(404)422-7503
Ultimate Parent: Texaco.

★ 66457 ★　This End Up Inc.
400 Ernest W. Barrett Pky.
Kennesaw, GA 30144
(404)424-3342
Ultimate Parent: Melville.

★ 66458 ★　Tj Maxx District Office
Kennesaw, GA
(404)919-0941
Ultimate Parent: TJX.

★ 66459 ★　Toys R US
501 Roberts Ct NW
Kennesaw, GA 30144
(404)424-9100
Ultimate Parent: Toys "R" US.

★ 66460 ★　Tri Valley Growers
1255 Roberts Blvd. NW
Kennesaw, GA 30144
(404)429-0734
Ultimate Parent: Tri Valley Growers.

★ 66461 ★　Victoria's Secret
Town Ctr. at Cobb
Kennesaw, GA 30144
(404)427-4308
Ultimate Parent: Limited.

★ 66462 ★　Vulcan Materials Co.
1272 Duncan Rd. NW
Kennesaw, GA 30144
(404)427-2401
Officer: Freddy Wehunt, Manager. Ultimate
Parent: Vulcan Materials Co. SIC: 3281—
Cut Stone & Stone Products.

★ 66463 ★　Wal Mart Discount
Cities
4200 Wade Green Rd.
Kennesaw, GA 30144
(404)423-1211
Ultimate Parent: Wal-Mart Stores, Inc.

★ 66464 ★　Wiltel
Communications Systems
500 Chastain Ctr. Blvd.
Kennesaw, GA 30144
(404)590-3855
Ultimate Parent: Williams Companies, Inc.

Kings Bay

★ 66465 ★　Coastal Bank of
Georgia
Kings Bay Naval Submarine Base
Kings Bay, GA 31547-5000
(912)882-4848
Location Type: Branch office. Officer:
James L. Wells, Manager. Ultimate Parent:
Synovus Financial Corp. SIC: 6021—
National Commercial Banks.

Kingsland

★ 66466 ★　Barnett Bank of
Southeast Georgia, NA
21 S. Lee St.
Kingsland, GA 31548
(912)729-5611
Company Type: Subsidiary. Location
Type: Branch office. Officer: Glenda
Foddrell, Assistant Vice President. Ultimate
Parent: Barnett Banks. SIC: 6021—National
Commercial Banks.

★ 66467 ★　Citizens State Bank
64 E. King St.
Kingsland, GA 31548
(912)729-5615
Ultimate Parent: Liberty National Bancorp.
SIC: 6022—State Commercial Banks.

La Fayette

★ 66468 ★　Buster Brown Apparel
Inc.
24476 Hwy. 193 Hwy. 193 West
La Fayette, GA 30728
Ultimate Parent: Gerber Products. SIC:
2330—Women's/Misses' Outerwear.

★ 66469 ★　Cohutta Banking Co.
201 W. Patton
La Fayette, GA 30728-2244
(706)638-5400
Location Type: Branch office. Officer:
Bernard Wheeler, Senior Vice President.
Ultimate Parent: Synovus Financial Corp.
SIC: 6021—National Commercial Banks.

★ 66470 ★　Rge Corp.
1507 Broomtown Rd.
La Fayette, GA 30728-1408
Ultimate Parent: General Electric. SIC:
3631—Household Cooking Equipment.

★ 66471 ★　Roper Corp.
1507 Broomtown Rd.
La Fayette, GA 30728-3407
(706)638-5100
Location Type: Branch office. Officer: Don
Kelley, President. Ultimate Parent: General
Electric. SIC: 3631—Household Cooking
Equipment. Employee Count: 2200. Sales:
163 M.

★ 66472 ★　Shaw Industries Inc.
Broomtown Rd.
La Fayette, GA 30728
(706)638-4011
Officer: Gary Horton, Manager. Ultimate
Parent: Shaw Industries, Inc. SIC: 2281—
Yarn Spinning Mills.

La Grange

★ 66473 ★　Commerce Bank &
Trust Co. of Troup County
200 N. Greenwood St.
La Grange, GA 30240-2698
(706)880-2200 Fax: (706)880-2280
Location Type: Branch office. Officer:
Robert L. Carmichael, President & CEO.
Ultimate Parent: Synovus Financial Corp.
SIC: 6021—National Commercial Banks.

★ 66474 ★　Commercial Bank &
Trust Co. of Troup County
PO Box 250
La Grange, GA 30241-0250
Location Type: Branch office. Ultimate
Parent: Synovus Financial Corp. SIC:
6021—National Commercial Banks.

★ 66475 ★　Commercial Bank &
Trust Co. of Troup County
203-A Commerce Ave.
La Grange, GA 30240-2358
(706)880-2320
Location Type: Branch office. Officer:
Barbara T. Stephens. Ultimate Parent:
Synovus Financial Corp. SIC: 6021—
National Commercial Banks.

★ 66476 ★　Commercial Bank &
Trust Co. of Troup County
1724 West Point Rd.
La Grange, GA 30240-4040
(706)880-2300
Location Type: Branch office. Officer:
Rose Sherrer, Assistant Vice President.
Ultimate Parent: Synovus Financial Corp.
SIC: 6021—National Commercial Banks.

★ 66477 ★　Daniel Radiator Corp.
1602 Orchard Hill Rd.
La Grange, GA 30240
Ultimate Parent: Handy & Harman. SIC:
3714—Motor Vehicle Parts & Accessories;
5013—Motor Vehicle Supplies & New Parts.

★ 66478 ★　Duracell USA
1567 Lukken Industrial Dr. W
La Grange, GA 30240-5799
Ultimate Parent: Duracell International Inc.
SIC: 3692—Primary Batteries—Dry & Wet.

★ 66479 ★　Interface Flooring
Sys. Inc. Inc.
1503 Orchard Hill Rd.
La Grange, GA 30240-5709
Ultimate Parent: Interface Inc. SIC: 2273—
Carpets & Rugs.

★ 66480 ★　Interface Flooring
Systems Inc.
1503 Orchard Hill Rd.
La Grange, GA 30240-5709
Ultimate Parent: Interface Inc. SIC: 2273—
Carpets & Rugs.

★ 66481 ★　Interface Flooring
Systems Inc.
Orchard Hill Rd.
La Grange, GA 30240
Ultimate Parent: Interface Inc. SIC: 2273—
Carpets & Rugs.

★ 66482 ★　Interface Inc.
Orchard Hill Rd.
PO Box 1503
La Grange, GA 30241
(706)882-1891 Fax: (706)992-0500
Officer: Ray C. Anderson, Chairman,
President & CEO. Ultimate Parent:
Interface Inc. Employee Count: 3700.
Sales: 500 illion M.

★ 66483 ★　Kimberly-Clark
1300 Orchard Hill Rd.
La Grange, GA 30240
Ultimate Parent: Kimberly-Clark. SIC:
2297—Nonwoven Fabrics.

★ 66484 ★　Kimberly-Clark Corp.
Lagrange Mill
1300 Orchard Hill Rd.
La Grange, GA 30240-3068
Ultimate Parent: Kimberly-Clark. SIC:
2297—Nonwoven Fabrics.

★ 66485 ★　Lagrange Molded
Products Inc.
1513 Redding Dr.
La Grange, GA 30240
Ultimate Parent: Lanchaster Colony. SIC:
3089—Plastics Products Nec.

★ 66486 ★　Lagrange Molded
Products Inc.
1513 Redding Dr.
La Grange, GA 30240
Ultimate Parent: Lanchaster Colony. SIC:
3069—Fabricated Rubber Products Nec.

★ 66487 ★ Trust Co. Bank of
Columbus, N.A.
LaFayette Pky.
La Fayette, GA 30240
(706)883-3441
Ultimate Parent: Suntrust Banks. SIC:
6021—National Commercial Banks.

★ 66488 ★ Trust Co. Bank of
Columbus, N.A.
307 Church St.
La Grange, GA 30240-2796
Officer: Chavies E. Sweat, Manager.
Ultimate Parent: Suntrust Banks. SIC:
6021—National Commercial Banks.

★ 66489 ★ Turst Co. Bank of
Columbus, N.A.
Lee's Crossing
La Grange, GA 30240-6428
(706)883-3436
Ultimate Parent: Suntrust Banks. SIC:
6021—National Commercial Banks.

★ 66490 ★ Union Camp Corp.
1603 Orchard Hill Rd.
La Grange, GA 30240
Ultimate Parent: Union Camp Corp. SIC:
2673—Bags—Plastics, Laminated &
Coated.

★ 66491 ★ Vulcan Materials Co.
Vulcan Material Rd.
La Grange, GA 30240
(706)882-8872
Officer: Roger Dunlap, Manager. Ultimate
Parent: Vulcan Materials Co. SIC: 3281—
Cut Stone & Stone Products.

Lafayette

★ 66492 ★ Imperial Bondware
Hwy. 27 N
Lafayette, GA 30728
(706)638-4036
Officer: Sid Smith, Manager. Ultimate
Parent: Federal Paper Board. SIC: 2656—
Sanitary Food Containers; 3089—Plastics
Products Nec.

LaGrange

★ 66493 ★ Interface Inc.
Orchard Hill Rd.
LaGrange, GA 30240
(706)882-1891
Company Type: Headquarters. Officer:
Ray C. Anderson. Employee Count: 4424.
Sales: 625 M. Fortune 500: Largest U.S.
Industrial Corporations: Ranking 492.

★ 66494 ★ LaGrange Molded
Products, Inc.
PO Box 1707
LaGrange, GA 30241
(706)884-1711
Company Type: Subsidiary. Ultimate
Parent: Lanchaster Colony. SIC: 3069—
Fabricated Rubber Products Nec.
Employee Count: 245.

Lake City

★ 66495 ★ Bank South, NA
5402 B Jonesboro Rd.
Lake City, GA 30260
(404)366-5806
Company Type: Subsidiary. Location
Type: Branch office. Ultimate Parent: Bank
South Corp. SIC: 6021—National
Commercial Banks.

Lake Park

★ 66496 ★ Capezio Factory
Direct
105 Frontage Rd.
Lake Park, GA 31636
(912)559-4422
Ultimate Parent: United States Shoe. SIC:
5661—Shoe Stores.

★ 66497 ★ First State Bank &
Trust Co. of Valdosta
302 Hwy. 376
Lake Park, GA 31636-9763
(912)559-0341
Location Type: Branch office. Officer: Sara
Coggins, Assistant Vice President. Ultimate
Parent: Synovus Financial Corp. SIC:
6021—National Commercial Banks.

Lavonia

★ 66498 ★ Athens First Bank &
Trust
22 West Ave.
Lavonia, GA
(706)356-4016
Location Type: Branch office. Officer:
Nora Patrick, Manager. Ultimate Parent:
Synovus Financial Corp. SIC: 6021—
National Commercial Banks.

Lawrenceille

★ 66499 ★ Kmart Stores
Pharmacy
665 Hwy. 120
Lawrenceille, GA
(404)995-5424
Ultimate Parent: K-Mart.

Lawrenceville

★ 66500 ★ Ametek
Haveg Div.
Lawrenceville, GA
(404)822-9707
Company Type: Division. Ultimate Parent:
Ametek Inc.

★ 66501 ★ Bank South NA
2100 Riverside Pky.
Lawrenceville, GA 30243-5914
(404)822-5308
Location Type: Branch office. Officer:
Marjorie Martini. Ultimate Parent: Bank
South Corp. SIC: 6022—State Commercial
Banks; 6021—National Commercial Banks.

★ 66502 ★ Bank South, NA
455 Hwy. 20
Lawrenceville, GA 30245
(404)822-5305
Company Type: Subsidiary. Location
Type: Branch office. Ultimate Parent: Bank
South Corp. SIC: 6021—National
Commercial Banks.

★ 66503 ★ Bank South, NA
2080 Riverside Dr.
Lawrenceville, GA 30244
(404)995-9605
Company Type: Subsidiary. Location
Type: Branch office. Officer: Jennifer
Velleca, Manager. Ultimate Parent: Bank
South Corp. SIC: 6021—National
Commercial Banks.

★ 66504 ★ Bank South, NA
185 Gwinnett Dr.
Lawrenceville, GA 30245
(404)822-5300
Company Type: Subsidiary. Location
Type: Branch office. Officer: Phyllis
Newbern, Manager. Ultimate Parent: Bank
South Corp. SIC: 6021—National
Commercial Banks.

★ 66505 ★ Bank South, NA
River Exchange
2100 Riverside Pky.
Lawrenceville, GA 30245
(404)822-5308
Company Type: Subsidiary. Location
Type: Branch office. Officer: Vicky Sumlar,
Manager. Ultimate Parent: Bank South
Corp. SIC: 6021—National Commercial
Banks.

★ 66506 ★ BFI Waste Systems
75 Curtis Rd.
Lawrenceville, GA 30245-7311
(404)339-9393
Location Type: Branch office. Ultimate
Parent: Browning-Ferris Industries. SIC:
4953—Refuse Systems.

★ 66507 ★ Coast to Coast
Computers
593 Axton Ct SW
Lawrenceville, GA 30244
(404)978-1704
Ultimate Parent: Servistar Corp.

★ 66508 ★ Coca-Cola Bottling
Com Metro S
924 Buford Dr.
Lawrenceville, GA 30243
(404)963-8103
Ultimate Parent: Coca-Cola Enterprises.

★ 66509 ★ Datamyte Corp.
1710 Highland Oaks Way NE
Lawrenceville, GA
(404)682-8658
Ultimate Parent: Rockwell International
Corp.

★ 66510 ★ Delta Air Lines
629 Airport Rd. NE
Lawrenceville, GA 30245
(404)339-9900
Ultimate Parent: Delta Air Lines, Inc.

★ 66511 ★ Delta Air Lines Inc.
Delta Bail
629 Airport Rd. NE
Lawrenceville, GA 30245
(404)339-9900
Ultimate Parent: Delta Air Lines, Inc.

★ 66512 ★ Exxon Shop
840 Scenic Hwy. SW
Lawrenceville, GA 30245
(404)962-5333
Ultimate Parent: Exxon.

★ 66513 ★ First Union National
Bank of Georgia
3590 Club Dr.
Lawrenceville, GA 30244
(404)717-2300
Location Type: Branch office. Ultimate
Parent: First Union Corp. SIC: 6021—
National Commercial Banks.

★ 66514 ★ First Union National
Bank of Georgia
161 S. Clayton St.
Lawrenceville, GA 30245-5716
(404)963-5102
Location Type: Branch office. Ultimate
Parent: First Union Corp. SIC: 6021—
National Commercial Banks.

★ 66515 ★ Jiffy Lube
Lawrenceville
465 W. Pike St.
Lawrenceville, GA 30245
(404)963-6915
Ultimate Parent: Pennzoil.

★ 66516 ★ Kentucky Fried
Chicken
139 S. Clayton St.
Lawrenceville, GA 30245
(404)963-2922
Ultimate Parent: Pepsico.

★ 66517 ★ Kentucky Fried
Chicken
675 Hwy. 120 NW
Lawrenceville, GA
(404)822-4745
Ultimate Parent: Pepsico.

★ 66518 ★ Kmart Stores
665 Hwy. 120
Lawrenceville, GA 30245
(404)995-5213
Ultimate Parent: K-Mart.

★ 66519 ★ Kmart Stores
3625 Sweetwater Connector
Lawrenceville, GA
(404)923-9570
Ultimate Parent: K-Mart.

★ 66520 ★ Kroger Co. the Retail
Stores
455 Hwy. 20
Lawrenceville, GA 30245
(404)962-1063
Ultimate Parent: Kroger.

★ 66521 ★ Kroger Co. the Retail
Stores
2100 Riverside Pkwy NW
Lawrenceville, GA 30243
(404)962-0890
Ultimate Parent: Kroger.

★ 66522 ★ Kroger Pharmacies
455 Hwy. 20
Lawrenceville, GA 30245
(404)962-3515
Ultimate Parent: Kroger.

★ 66523 ★ Kroger Pharmacies
2100 Riverside Pkwy NW
Lawrenceville, GA 30243
(404)962-1197
Ultimate Parent: Kroger.

★ 66524 ★ Mary Kay Cosmetics
Indep Sales
1270 Silverwood Ct. NE
Lawrenceville, GA 30243
(404)963-0733
Ultimate Parent: Mary Kay Cosmetics.

★ 66525 ★ Mary Kay Cosmetics
Indep Sales
3633 Vineyard Way
Lawrenceville, GA 30244
(404)978-3131
Ultimate Parent: Mary Kay Cosmetics.

★ 66526 ★ McDonald's
Restaurants
Duluth Hwy.
Lawrenceville, GA
(404)995-9410
Ultimate Parent: McDonald's.

★ 66527 ★ McDonald's
Restaurants
865 Scenic Hwy.
Lawrenceville, GA 30245
(404)339-8343
Ultimate Parent: McDonald's.

★ 66528 ★ Nationsbank Offices
Atlanta Ar
Five Forks Oak 840 O
Lawrenceville, GA
(404)978-5990
Ultimate Parent: Nationsbank Corp.

★ 66529 ★ Nationsbank Real
Estate Departments
Lawrenceville, GA
(404)995-3160
Ultimate Parent: Nationsbank Corp.

★ 66530 ★ Pizza Hut
198 Scenic Hwy.
Lawrenceville, GA 30245
(404)962-1391
Ultimate Parent: Pepsico.

★ 66531 ★ Pizza Hut
1164 Hwy. 29
Lawrenceville, GA
(404)513-8400
Ultimate Parent: Pepsico.

★ 66532 ★ Pizza Hut
3001 River Dr.
Lawrenceville, GA 30244
(404)985-3777
Ultimate Parent: Pepsico.

★ 66533 ★ PPG Industries Inc.
1000 Northbrook Pkwy
Lawrenceville, GA
(404)962-8927
Ultimate Parent: PPG Industries Inc.

★ 66534 ★ Pulte Home Corp.
665 Rosedown Way NE
Lawrenceville, GA 30243
(404)513-7063
Ultimate Parent: Pulte.

★ 66535 ★ Pulte Home Corp.
Georgia
3170 Binghampton Ln. NW
Lawrenceville, GA 30244
(404)513-8686
Ultimate Parent: Pulte.

★ 66536 ★ Quaker State Minit
Lube Inc.
1056 Pleasant Hill Rd.
Lawrenceville, GA 30244
(404)717-7059
Ultimate Parent: Quaker State.

★ 66537 ★ Radio Shack
110 S. Clayton St.
Lawrenceville, GA 30245
(404)963-1939
Company Type: Division. Ultimate Parent:
Tandy Corp.

★ 66538 ★ Sterling Advertising
1290 Stampmill Way NW
Lawrenceville, GA 30243
(404)513-3410
Ultimate Parent: Lowe's.

★ 66539 ★ Taco Bell
685 W. Pike St. NW
Lawrenceville, GA 30245
(404)339-7541
Ultimate Parent: Pepsico.

★ 66540 ★   Taco Bell
2929 Five Forks Trickum R
Lawrenceville, GA 30244
(404)978-8458
Ultimate Parent: Pepsico.

★ 66541 ★   Texaco
664 Buford Dr.
Lawrenceville, GA 30245
(404)822-9953
Ultimate Parent: Texaco.

★ 66542 ★   Texaco Food Mart
662 Duluth Hwy.
Lawrenceville, GA 30245
(404)963-1317
Ultimate Parent: Texaco.

★ 66543 ★   Universal Instruments
Corp.
532 Cricket Hill Tr SW
Lawrenceville, GA 30244
(404)978-3200
Ultimate Parent: Dover Corp.

★ 66544 ★   Universal-Rundle
Corp.
105 S. Perry St. SW
Lawrenceville, GA 30245
(404)963-1593
Ultimate Parent: Nortek.

★ 66545 ★   Valvoline Instant Oil
Change
1350 Pleasant Hill Rd. NW
Lawrenceville, GA 30244
(404)381-1825
Ultimate Parent: Ashland Oil.

★ 66546 ★   Valvoline Instant Oil
Change
214 Scenic Hwy. SW
Lawrenceville, GA 30245
(404)963-0991
Ultimate Parent: Ashland Oil.

★ 66547 ★   Wal Mart Vision
Center
296 S. Clayton St.
Lawrenceville, GA 30245
(404)822-4268
Ultimate Parent: Wal-Mart Stores, Inc.

★ 66548 ★   Wika Instrument
Corp.
1000 Wiegand Blvd.
Lawrenceville, GA 302435868
Ultimate Parent: Alexander & Alexander
Services. **SIC:** 3823—Process Control
Instruments.

Leesburg

★ 66549 ★   Martin Marietta
Aggregates
Leesburg, GA 31763
(912)759-6435
Ultimate Parent: Martin Marietta. **SIC:**
1422—Crushed & Broken Limestone.

Leslie

★ 66550 ★   Sumter Bank & Trust
Co.
422 Bailey Ave.
Leslie, GA 31764
(912)874-4925
Location Type: Branch office. **Officer:** W.T.
Anderson Jr., Manager. **Ultimate Parent:**
Synovus Financial Corp. **SIC:** 6021—
National Commercial Banks.

Lifton

★ 66551 ★   Union Camp Corp.
Industrial Pk.
Lifton, GA 31794
(912)386-8900
Officer: Art Pryor, Manager. **Ultimate
Parent:** Union Camp Corp. **SIC:** 2673—
Bags—Plastics, Laminated & Coated;
2674—Bags—Uncoated Paper & Multiwall.

Lilburn

★ 66552 ★   Ace Hardware
5355 Five Forks Trickum R
Lilburn, GA 30247
(404)921-5938
Ultimate Parent: Ace Hardware.

★ 66553 ★   Bank South, NA
3050 Five Forks Trickum
Lilburn, GA 30247
(404)985-3445
Company Type: Subsidiary. **Location
Type:** Branch office. **Officer:** Faith Prescott,
Manager. **Ultimate Parent:** Bank South
Corp. **SIC:** 6021—National Commercial
Banks.

★ 66554 ★   Bank South, NA
4794 Hwy. 20
Lilburn, GA 30247
(404)564-5929
Company Type: Subsidiary. **Location
Type:** Branch office. **Officer:** Jeff
Zimmerman, Manager. **Ultimate Parent:**
Bank South Corp. **SIC:** 6021—National
Commercial Banks.

★ 66555 ★   Bank South, NA
4153 Hwy. 29
Lilburn, GA 30247
(404)564-5934
Company Type: Subsidiary. **Location
Type:** Branch office. **Officer:** David
Callahan, Manager. **Ultimate Parent:** Bank
South Corp. **SIC:** 6021—National
Commercial Banks.

★ 66556 ★   Citgo Food Mart
331 Rockbridge Rd. SW
Lilburn, GA 30247
(404)381-0917
Ultimate Parent: Citgo Petroleum.

★ 66557 ★   Exxon Shop
930 Indian Trail-Lilburn
Lilburn, GA
(404)923-6757
Ultimate Parent: Exxon.

★ 66558 ★   First Union National
Bank of Georgia
5505 Lawrenceville Hwy.
Lilburn, GA 30247
(404)279-3085
Location Type: Branch office. **Ultimate
Parent:** First Union Corp. **SIC:** 6021—
National Commercial Banks.

★ 66559 ★   First Union National
Bank of Georgia
4265 Hwy. 29
Lilburn, GA 30247-3427
(404)564-4100
Location Type: Branch office. **Ultimate
Parent:** First Union Corp. **SIC:** 6021—
National Commercial Banks.

★ 66560 ★   Jiffy Lube Lilburn
341 Killian Hill Rd.
Lilburn, GA
(404)279-1955
Ultimate Parent: Pennzoil.

★ 66561 ★   Kentucky Fried
Chicken
4120 Hwy. 29
Lilburn, GA 30247
(404)925-9942
Ultimate Parent: Pepsico.

★ 66562 ★   Kmart Stores
Automotive
4155 Hwy. 29
Lilburn, GA 30247
(404)923-1455
Ultimate Parent: K-Mart.

★ 66563 ★   Kmart Stores
Pharmacy
3625 Sweetwater Connection
Lilburn, GA
(404)923-9163
Ultimate Parent: K-Mart.

★ 66564 ★   Kmart Stores
Pharmacy
4155 Hwy. 29
Lilburn, GA 30247
(404)923-9100
Ultimate Parent: K-Mart.

★ 66565 ★   Kroger Co Retail
Stores
4153 Hwy. 29 NW
Lilburn, GA 30247
(404)921-5804
Ultimate Parent: Kroger.

★ 66566 ★   Kroger Co. the Retail
Stores
3050 Five Forks Trivkum Rd.
Lilburn, GA 30247
(404)978-9264
Ultimate Parent: Kroger.

★ 66567 ★   Kroger Pharmacies
4153 Hwy. 29 NW
Lilburn, GA 30247
(404)925-7921
Ultimate Parent: Kroger.

★ 66568 ★   Kroger Pharmacies
3050 Five Forks Trivkum Rd.
Lilburn, GA 30247
(404)985-3720
Ultimate Parent: Kroger.

★ 66569 ★   Land O'lakes Inc.
4683 Hwy. 29 NW
Lilburn, GA 30247
(404)925-2290
Ultimate Parent: Land O'Lakes.

★ 66570 ★   Mary Kay Cosmetics
Indep Sales
1428 Ridgewood Dr.
Lilburn, GA 30247
(404)923-2116
Ultimate Parent: Mary Kay Cosmetics.

★ 66571 ★   McDonald's
Restaurants
3015 Five Forks Trivkum Rd.
Lilburn, GA 30247
(404)979-5332
Ultimate Parent: McDonald's.

★ 66572 ★   Morton International
Arspc Polymer
1908 Joe Hewatt Rd. SW
Lilburn, GA 30247-2518
(404)972-3142
Ultimate Parent: Morton International. **SIC:**
5169—Chemicals & Allied Products Nec.

★ 66573 ★   Nationsbank
Departments Nation
4683 Hwy. 29
Lilburn, GA 30247
(404)925-8633
Ultimate Parent: Nationsbank Corp.

★ 66574 ★   Nationsbank Offices
Atlanta Ar
94 Indian Trl.
Lilburn, GA 30247
(404)523-0900
Ultimate Parent: Nationsbank Corp.

★ 66575 ★   Norwest Mortgage
Inc.
620 Hillcrest Rd. NW
Lilburn, GA 30247
(404)381-2766
Ultimate Parent: Norwest Corp.

★ 66576 ★   Pizza Hut
4271 Us Hwy. 29
Lilburn, GA
(404)717-8800
Ultimate Parent: Pepsico.

★ 66577 ★   Pizza Hut
4104 Hwy. 29
Lilburn, GA 30247
(404)381-1500
Ultimate Parent: Pepsico.

★ 66578 ★   Radio Shack
K Mart Shpng Ctr.
Lilburn, GA 30247
(404)921-9544
Company Type: Division. **Ultimate Parent:**
Tandy Corp.

★ 66579 ★   Taco Bell
4225 Hwy. 29
Lilburn, GA 30247
(404)923-7056
Ultimate Parent: Pepsico.

★ 66580 ★   Texaco
4032 Us Hwy. 78
Lilburn, GA
(404)978-2338
Ultimate Parent: Texaco.

★ 66581 ★   Texaco
5414 Five Forks Trickum R
Lilburn, GA 30247
(404)925-0649
Ultimate Parent: Texaco.

★ 66582 ★   Valvoline Instant Oil
Change
4545 Hwy. 29 NW
Lilburn, GA 30247
(404)925-2233
Ultimate Parent: Ashland Oil.

★ 66583 ★   Valvoline Instant Oil
Change
4545 Hwy. 29 NW
Lilburn, GA 30247
(404)925-2233
Ultimate Parent: Ashland Oil.

Lithia Spring

★ 66584 ★   Circuit City Service
Center
320 Thornton Rd.
Lithia Spring, GA 30057
(404)732-2800
Ultimate Parent: Circuit City Stores.

★ 66585 ★   Pizza Hut
6915 S. Sweetwater Rd.
Lithia Spring, GA 30057
(404)732-1000
Ultimate Parent: Pepsico.

★ 66586 ★   Taco Bell
987 Thornton Rd.
Lithia Spring, GA 30057
(404)739-8676
Ultimate Parent: Pepsico.

★ 66587 ★   Texaco
900 Thornton Rd.
Lithia Spring, GA 30057
(404)948-4093
Ultimate Parent: Texaco.

★ 66588 ★   Valvoline Instant Oil
Change
205 Thornton Rd.
Lithia Spring, GA 30057
(404)732-1848
Ultimate Parent: Ashland Oil.

Lithia Springs

★ 66589 ★   Exxon Shop
3042 Bankhead Hwy.
Lithia Springs, GA 30057
(404)739-4981
Ultimate Parent: Exxon.

★ 66590 ★   Reynolds & Reynolds
Co.
1650 Westfork Dr., Ste. 101
Lithia Springs, GA 30057
(404)739-0695
Officer: John Langston, Manager. **Ultimate
Parent:** Reynolds & Reynolds. **SIC:** 2761—
Manifold Business Forms.

★ 66591 ★   Vulcan Materials Co.
7620 N. County Line Rd.
Lithia Springs, GA 30057
(404)948-6424
Officer: S J Bohannon, Manager. **Ultimate
Parent:** Vulcan Materials Co. **SIC:** 3281—
Cut Stone & Stone Products.

Lithonia

★ 66592 ★   Avnet
Mechanics Choice
5054 Minola Rd.
Lithonia, GA 30058
(404)981-2300
Location Type: Branch office. **Ultimate
Parent:** Avnet. **SIC:** 5013—Motor Vehicle
Supplies & New Parts.

★ 66593 ★   Essex Group Inc.
6588 Marbut
Lithonia, GA 30058
Ultimate Parent: Morgan Stanley Group.
SIC: 3351—Copper Rolling & Drawing.

★ 66594 ★   First Union National
Bank of Georgia
6920 Main St.
Lithonia, GA 30058-4498
(404)482-3840
Location Type: Branch office. **Ultimate
Parent:** First Union Corp. **SIC:** 6021—
National Commercial Banks.

★ 66595 ★ Kentucky Fried
Chicken
2747 Evans Mill Rd.
Lithonia, GA 30058
(404)482-6523
Ultimate Parent: Pepsico.

★ 66596 ★ Ltv Steel Tubular
Products Co.
2063 Adriatic Dr.
Lithonia, GA 30058
(404)482-1213
Ultimate Parent: LTV.

★ 66597 ★ McDonald's
Restaurants
2791 Panola Rd.
Lithonia, GA 30058
(404)981-9711
Ultimate Parent: McDonald's.

★ 66598 ★ McDonald's
Restaurants
3460 Hwy. 124 SW
Lithonia, GA 30058
(404)985-6930
Ultimate Parent: McDonald's.

★ 66599 ★ Nationsbank Honor-
Cirrus L Pan
6138 Covington Hwy.
Lithonia, GA 30058
(404)593-5460
Ultimate Parent: Nationsbank Corp.

★ 66600 ★ Nationsbank Offices
Atlanta Ar
2930 Evans Mill Rd.
Lithonia, GA 30038
(404)482-0600
Ultimate Parent: Nationsbank Corp.

★ 66601 ★ Nationsbank Offices
Atlanta Ar
6138 Covington Hwy.
Lithonia, GA 30058
(404)593-5460
Ultimate Parent: Nationsbank Corp.

★ 66602 ★ Pet, Inc.
2200 Lithonia Industrial Blvd.
PO Box 957
Lithonia, GA 30058
(404)482-5082 Fax: (404)482-2534
Location Type: Plant. Officer: Gordon
Powell, Plant Manager. Ultimate Parent:
Pet. SIC: 2038—Frozen Specialties Nec.

★ 66603 ★ Pet Inc.
Grocery Operations
2200 Lithonia Industrial Blvd.
Lithonia, GA 30058-4695
Company Type: Division. Ultimate Parent:
Pet. SIC: 2038—Frozen Specialties Nec.

★ 66604 ★ Pizza Hut
452 S. Deshon Rd.
Lithonia, GA 30058
(404)498-1500
Ultimate Parent: Pepsico.

★ 66605 ★ Pizza Hut
2717 Evans Mills Rd.
Lithonia, GA
(404)484-2929
Ultimate Parent: Pepsico.

★ 66606 ★ Radio Shack
2920 Evans Mill Rd.
Lithonia, GA 30038
(404)482-6001
Company Type: Division. Ultimate Parent:
Tandy Corp.

★ 66607 ★ Ryder Truck Rental
7550 Covington Hwy.
Lithonia, GA 30058
(404)482-6908
Ultimate Parent: Ryder System.

★ 66608 ★ Ryder Truck Rental
Panola & Turner Hill
Lithonia, GA
(404)961-1639
Ultimate Parent: Ryder System.

★ 66609 ★ Stone Container Corp.
1995 Lithonia Industrial Blvd.
Lithonia, GA 30058
(404)482-1433
Officer: John Thompson, Manager.
Ultimate Parent: Stone Container Corp.
SIC: 3554—Paper Industries Machinery.

★ 66610 ★ Stone Container Corp.
Corrugate
1995 Lithonia Industrial
Lithonia, GA 30058
(404)482-1433
Ultimate Parent: Stone Container Corp.

★ 66611 ★ Texaco
2827 Evans Mill Rd.
Lithonia, GA 30058
(404)482-6930
Ultimate Parent: Texaco.

★ 66612 ★ W. R. Grace & Co.
Connecticut Construction Products Div.
6606 Marshall Blvd.
Lithonia, GA 30058
Company Type: Division. Ultimate Parent:
W. R. Grace. SIC: 2899—Chemical
Preparations Nec.

★ 66613 ★ Weyerhaeuser Paper
Co.
6792 Marbut Rd.
Lithonia, GA 30058
(404)482-8821
Officer: Thomas A. Bucher, Manager.
Ultimate Parent: Weyerhaeuser Co. SIC:
2652—Setup Paperboard Boxes.

Loganville

★ 66614 ★ Kentucky Fried
Chicken
4453 Hwy. 78
Loganville, GA 30249
(404)466-6519
Ultimate Parent: Pepsico.

★ 66615 ★ McDonald's
Restaurants
4638 Hwy. 78
Loganville, GA 30249
(404)466-2002
Ultimate Parent: McDonald's.

★ 66616 ★ National Bank of
Walton County
Hwy. 78
Loganville, GA 30249-9735
(404)466-8635
Location Type: Branch office. Officer:
Doug L. Cathey, Vice President. Ultimate
Parent: Synovus Financial Corp. SIC:
6021—National Commercial Banks.

★ 66617 ★ Pizza Hut
4630 Atlanta Hwy.
Loganville, GA
(404)466-1056
Ultimate Parent: Pepsico.

★ 66618 ★ Radio Shack
4660 Hwy. 83 SW
Loganville, GA
(404)466-0666
Company Type: Division. Ultimate Parent:
Tandy Corp.

Louisville

★ 66619 ★ First National Bank &
Trust Co.
Broad St.
Louisville, GA 30434
(912)625-2000
Ultimate Parent: Society Corp. SIC: 6099—
Functions Related to Deposit Banking.

★ 66620 ★ Piggly Wiggly
Peachtree Plz.
Louisville, GA 30434
(912)625-7933
Officer: David Brookins, Manager. Ultimate
Parent: Fleming. SIC: 3544—Special Dies,
Tools, Jigs & Fixtures.

★ 66621 ★ Piggly Wiggly
Peachtree St.
Louisville, GA 30434
(912)625-7933
Ultimate Parent: Bruno's. SIC: 5411—
Grocery Stores.

★ 66622 ★ Piggly Wiggly
Peachtree Plz.
Louisville, GA 30434
(912)625-7933
Officer: David Brookins, Manager. Ultimate
Parent: Bruno's. SIC: 3544—Special Dies,
Tools, Jigs & Fixtures.

★ 66623 ★ Piggly Wiggly
Southern Inc.
Peachtree St.
Louisville, GA 30434
(912)625-7933
Ultimate Parent: Bruno's. SIC: 5411—
Grocery Stores.

★ 66624 ★ Thermo King Corp.
Rte. 3, Box 35
Louisville, GA 30434
Location Type: Plant. Ultimate Parent:
Westinghouse Electric Corp. SIC: 3585—
Refrigeration & Heating Equipment.

★ 66625 ★ Union Camp Corp.
Hwy. 17 S
Louisville, GA 30434
(912)625-8156
Ultimate Parent: Union Camp Corp. SIC:
2411—Logging.

★ 66626 ★ Union Camp Corp.
Midville Rd.
Louisville, GA 30434
(912)625-7296
Ultimate Parent: Union Camp Corp. SIC:
2411—Logging.

★ 66627 ★ Westinghouse
Electric Corp.
Thermo King Corp.
1430 Hwy. 24 E. Box 35
Louisville, GA 30434
Ultimate Parent: Westinghouse Electric
Corp. SIC: 3585—Refrigeration & Heating
Equipment.

★ 66628 ★ Westinghouse
Electric Corp.
Thermo King Corp.
Rte. 3 Box 35
Louisville, GA 30434
Ultimate Parent: Westinghouse Electric
Corp. SIC: 3585—Refrigeration & Heating
Equipment.

Luthersville

★ 66629 ★ Bank of Coweta
24 N. Main St.
Luthersville, GA 30251
(404)927-6418
Location Type: Branch office. Officer:
Anthony L. Rosser, Assistant Vice
President. Ultimate Parent: Synovus
Financial Corp. SIC: 6021—National
Commercial Banks.

Lyerly

★ 66630 ★ Lyerly Rug Mill
Hwy. 114
Lyerly, GA 30730
Ultimate Parent: Fieldcrest Cannon. SIC:
2273—Carpets & Rugs.

★ 66631 ★ Lyerly Rug Mill
Rte. 1 Hwy. 114
Lyerly, GA 30730
Ultimate Parent: Fieldcrest Cannon. SIC:
2273—Carpets & Rugs.

Lyons

★ 66632 ★ Piggly Wiggly
116 N. State St.
Lyons, GA 30436
(912)526-8551
Ultimate Parent: Bruno's. SIC: 5411—
Grocery Stores.

Mableton

★ 66633 ★ First Union National
Bank of Georgia
5606 Mableton Pky. SE
Mableton, GA 30059-3304
(404)739-3600
Location Type: Branch office. Ultimate
Parent: First Union Corp. SIC: 6021—
National Commercial Banks.

★ 66634 ★ Kentucky Fried
Chicken
981 Bankhead Hwy. SW
Mableton, GA 30059
(404)739-5353
Ultimate Parent: Pepsico.

★ 66635 ★ Kmart Stores
5590 Mableton Pkwy
Mableton, GA 30059
(404)941-2038
Ultimate Parent: K-Mart.

★ 66636 ★ Kmart Stores
Pharmacy
5590 Mableton Pkwy
Mableton, GA 30059
(404)941-2652
Ultimate Parent: K-Mart.

★ 66637 ★ Kroger Co. the Retail
Stores
5345 Floyd Rd. SW
Mableton, GA 30059
(404)941-7757
Ultimate Parent: Kroger.

★ 66638 ★ Kroger Pharmacies
5345 Floyd Rd. SW
Mableton, GA 30059
(404)944-2800
Ultimate Parent: Kroger.

★ 66639 ★ Payless Shoesource
5590 Mableton Pky. SW
Mableton, GA 30059
(404)941-8211
Ultimate Parent: May Department Stores.

★ 66640 ★ Pizza Hut
1150 Bankhead Hwy. SW
Mableton, GA 30059
(404)739-7739
Ultimate Parent: Pepsico.

★ 66641 ★ Radio Shack
Village Shopping Ctr.
Mableton, GA
(404)941-3617
Company Type: Division. Ultimate Parent:
Tandy Corp.

★ 66642 ★ Taco Bell
737 Bankhead Hwy. SW
Mableton, GA 30059
(404)944-3194
Ultimate Parent: Pepsico.

Macon

★ 66643 ★ Acme Business
Products
1667 Eisenhower Pky.
Macon, GA 31206
(912)788-7416
Company Type: Division. Officer: E. Earl
Benson, President. Ultimate Parent: Alco
Standard Corp. SIC: 5046—Commercial
Equipment Nec.

★ 66644 ★ Alco Capital Resource
1667 Eisenhower Pky.
Macon, GA 31206
(912)788-7416
Officer: Richard P. Maier, President.
Ultimate Parent: Alco Standard Corp. SIC:
6159—Miscellaneous Business Credit
Institutions.

★ 66645 ★ Alco Capital Resource
Inc.
1738 Bass Rd.
Macon, GA 31210-1043
(912)471-2300
Company Type: Division. Officer: Richard
P. Maier, President. Ultimate Parent: Alco
Standard Corp. SIC: 6159—Miscellaneous
Business Credit Institutions. Employee
Count: 91.

★ 66646 ★ Alco Capital Resource
Inc.
1738 Bass Rd.
Macon, GA 31210-1043
(912)471-2300
Company Type: Division. Officer: Richard
P. Maier, President. Ultimate Parent: Alco
Standard Corp. SIC: 6159—Miscellaneous
Business Credit Institutions. Employee
Count: 91.

★ 66647 ★ American Family Life
Assurance
154 Broadway
Macon, GA 31201
(912)742-1446
Ultimate Parent: American Family Life
Assurance Co. SIC: 6411—Insurance
Agents, Brokers & Service.

★ 66648 ★ American General
Finance
3079 Pio Nono Ave.
Macon, GA 31206-3025
(912)781-0820
Location Type: Branch office. Officer: Jeff
Goldsmith. Ultimate Parent: American
General Corp. SIC: 6141—Personal Credit
Institutions.

★ 66649 ★ American General
Finance Inc.
3200 Riverside Dr., Ste. B200
Macon, GA 31210-2550
(912)741-1042
Location Type: Branch office. Officer:
Lance N. Grove. Ultimate Parent: American
General Corp. SIC: 6141—Personal Credit
Institutions.

★ 66650 ★ American General
Finance Inc.
3079 Pio Nono Ave.
Macon, GA 31206-3025
(912)781-0820
Location Type: Branch office. Officer: Jeff
Goldsmith. Ultimate Parent: American
General Corp. SIC: 6141—Personal Credit
Institutions.

★ 66651 ★ Archer Daniels
Midland Co.
PO Box 1603
Macon, GA 31206
(912)743-9571
Officer: John Ross. Ultimate Parent:
Archer Daniels Midland Co. SIC: 2075—
Soybean Oil Mills; 2099—Food Preparations
Nec.

★ 66652 ★ Armstrong World Ind.
Inc.
4520 Broadway
Macon, GA 31213-4288
Ultimate Parent: Armstrong World
Industries. SIC: 3296—Mineral Wool.

★ 66653 ★ Armstrong World
Industries Inc.
4520 Broadway
Macon, GA 31206
Ultimate Parent: Armstrong World
Industries. SIC: 3296—Mineral Wool.

★ 66654 ★ Bank South
220 Tom Hill Sr. Blvd.
Macon, GA 31210-1815
(912)749-9255
Location Type: Branch office. Officer:
Beverly Wilson. Ultimate Parent: Bank
South Corp. SIC: 6022—State Commercial
Banks; 6021—National Commercial Banks.

★ 66655 ★ Bank South Macon
515 Mulberry St.
Macon, GA 31201-2712
(912)749-9300
Location Type: Branch office. Officer: H.M.
Ponder Jr. Ultimate Parent: Bank South
Corp. SIC: 6036—Savings Institutions
Except Federal; 6021—National Commercial
Banks; 6091—Nondeposit Trust Facilities;
6141—Personal Credit Institutions; 6712—
Bank Holding Companies.

★ 66656 ★ Bank South Macon
Wesleyan Sta
4650 Forsyth Rd.
Macon, GA 31210-4420
(912)749-9258
Location Type: Branch office. Officer:
Jamey Harrelson. Ultimate Parent: Bank
South Corp. SIC: 6022—State Commercial
Banks; 6021—National Commercial Banks.

★ 66657 ★ Bank South NA
3920 Riverside Dr.
Macon, GA 31210-1803
Location Type: Branch office. Ultimate
Parent: Bank South Corp. SIC: 6022—State
Commercial Banks.

★ 66658 ★ Bank South, NA
614 Shurling Dr.
Macon, GA 31211-1937
(912)749-9280
Company Type: Subsidiary. Location
Type: Branch office. Officer: Janey
Harrelson, Manager. Ultimate Parent: Bank
South Corp. SIC: 6021—National
Commercial Banks.

★ 66659 ★ Bank South, NA
4650 Forsyth Rd.
Macon, GA 31210
(912)749-9258
Company Type: Subsidiary. Location
Type: Branch office. Ultimate Parent: Bank
South Corp. SIC: 6021—National
Commercial Banks.

★ 66660 ★ Bank South, NA
3318 Viveville Ave.
Macon, GA 31204-1244
(912)749-9270
Company Type: Subsidiary. Location
Type: Branch office. Officer: Delores
Nesmith, Manager. Ultimate Parent: Bank
South Corp. SIC: 6021—National
Commercial Banks.

★ 66661 ★ Bank South, NA
2930 Riverside Dr.
Macon, GA 31204-1244
(912)749-9260
Company Type: Subsidiary. Location
Type: Branch office. Officer: Ruth Lawson,
Manager. Ultimate Parent: Bank South
Corp. SIC: 6021—National Commercial
Banks.

★ 66662 ★ Bank South, NA
3714 Eisenhower Pky.
Macon, GA 31206-3668
(912)749-9290
Company Type: Subsidiary. Location
Type: Branch office. Officer: William Marsh,
Manager. Ultimate Parent: Bank South
Corp. SIC: 6021—National Commercial
Banks.

★ 66663 ★ Bank South, NA
3945 Pio Nono Ave.
Macon, GA 31206-3043
(912)749-9250
Company Type: Subsidiary. Location
Type: Branch office. Officer: Steve
Williams, Manager. Ultimate Parent: Bank
South Corp. SIC: 6021—National
Commercial Banks.

★ 66664 ★ Bank South, NA
220 Tom Hill Sr. Blvd.
Macon, GA 31210-1815
(912)749-9255
Company Type: Subsidiary. Location
Type: Branch office. Officer: Leigh
Crawford, Manager. Ultimate Parent: Bank
South Corp. SIC: 6021—National
Commercial Banks.

★ 66665 ★ Bank South, NA
770 Pine St.
Macon, GA 31201-2147
(912)749-9275
Company Type: Subsidiary. Location
Type: Branch office. Officer: Robin
Simpson, Manager. Ultimate Parent: Bank
South Corp. SIC: 6021—National
Commercial Banks.

★ 66666 ★ Bank South, NA
660 North Ave.
Macon, GA 31211-1494
(912)749-9295
Company Type: Subsidiary. Location
Type: Branch office. Officer: Gwen Hicks,
Manager. Ultimate Parent: Bank South
Corp. SIC: 6021—National Commercial
Banks.

★ 66667 ★ Bank South, NA
3670 Eisenhower Pky.
Macon, GA 31206-3661
(912)749-9285
Company Type: Subsidiary. Location
Type: Branch office. Officer: Burton
Blackmar, Manager. Ultimate Parent: Bank
South Corp. SIC: 6021—National
Commercial Banks.

★ 66668 ★ Bank South, NA
515 Mulberry St.
Macon, GA 31201-2712
(912)749-9300
Company Type: Subsidiary. Location
Type: Branch office. Officer: Chris Cliett,
Manager. Ultimate Parent: Bank South
Corp. SIC: 6021—National Commercial
Banks.

★ 66669 ★ Bank South NA/
Macon
515 Mulberry St.
Macon, GA 31201
(912)749-9300
Company Type: Subsidiary. Location

Type: Branch office. Officer: George H.
Hall, Chairman & CEO. Ultimate Parent:
Bank South Corp. SIC: 6021—National
Commercial Banks; 6712—Bank Holding
Companies. Employee Count: 300.

★ 66670 ★ Betz Laboratories
7519 NE Industrial Blvd.
Macon, GA 31206
(912)784-9492
Ultimate Parent: Betz Laboratories Inc.
SIC: 2899—Chemical Preparations Nec.

★ 66671 ★ Betz Laboratories Inc.
7525 NE Industrial Blvd.
Macon, GA 31206
Ultimate Parent: Betz Laboratories Inc.
SIC: 2899—Chemical Preparations Nec.

★ 66672 ★ Betz Laboratories Inc.
7525 NE Industrial Blvd.
Macon, GA 31206
Ultimate Parent: Betz Laboratories Inc.
SIC: 2899—Chemical Preparations Nec.

★ 66673 ★ Betz Labs
7525 NE Industrial Blvd.
Macon, GA 31206
(912)781-8882
Location Type: Branch office. Officer: Dan
Brooks. Ultimate Parent: Betz Laboratories
Inc. SIC: 2899—Chemical Preparations
Nec; 5169—Chemicals & Allied Products
Nec; 8734—Testing Laboratories.

★ 66674 ★ Boeing Georgia Inc.
7979 NE Industrial Blvd.
Macon, GA 31297
Ultimate Parent: Boeing. SIC: 3728—
Aircraft Parts & Equipment Nec.

★ 66675 ★ Borden Inc.
4700 Pio Nono Ave.
Macon, GA 31206
(912)788-5733
Officer: Ernest Smith, Manager. Ultimate
Parent: Borden, Inc. SIC: 2024—Ice Cream
& Frozen Desserts; 2026—Fluid Milk;
2033—Canned Fruits & Vegetables.

★ 66676 ★ Borden Inc.
Dairy
4700 Pio Nono Ave.
Macon, GA 31206
Company Type: Division. Ultimate Parent:
Borden, Inc. SIC: 2026—Fluid Milk.

★ 66677 ★ Borden Inc.
Dairy
4700 Pio Nono Ave.
Macon, GA 31206
Company Type: Division. Ultimate Parent:
Borden, Inc. SIC: 2026—Fluid Milk.

★ 66678 ★ Borden Inc.
Grocery & Specialty Products
4700 Pio Nono Ave.
Macon, GA 31206
Company Type: Division. Ultimate Parent:
Borden, Inc. SIC: 2026—Fluid Milk.

★ 66679 ★ Burlington Coat
Factory
2525 Pio Nono Ave.
Macon, GA 31206-3162
(912)788-4900
Location Type: Branch office. Officer:
Helen Farrell. Ultimate Parent: Burlington
Industries, Equity. SIC: 5311—Department
Stores.

★ 66680 ★ Circus World Toy
Stores Inc.
Macon
Macon, GA 31206
(912)477-7400
Ultimate Parent: Melville. SIC: 5945—
Hobby, Toy & Game Shops.

★ 66681 ★ Conagra Flour Mill
211 Lower Poplar St.
Macon, GA 31202
Ultimate Parent: Conagra. SIC: 2045—
Prepared Flour Mixes & Doughs.

★ 66682 ★ Delta Air Lines
667 Walnut St.
Macon, GA 31201
(912)743-2523
Ultimate Parent: Delta Air Lines, Inc. SIC:
4729—Passenger Transportation
Arrangement Nec.

★ 66683 ★ Delta Air Lines Inc.
667 Walnut St.
Macon, GA 31201
(912)743-2523
Ultimate Parent: Delta Air Lines, Inc. SIC:
4729—Passenger Transportation
Arrangement Nec.

★ 66684 ★ Emery Worldwide
1053 Willingham Dr.
Macon, GA 31201
(912)746-1260
Ultimate Parent: Consolidated Freightways.
SIC: 4512—Air Transportation—Scheduled.

★ 66685 ★ Exxon
3109 Hillcrest Ave.
Macon, GA 31204
(912)746-0211
Ultimate Parent: Exxon. SIC: 5599—
Automotive Dealers Nec.

★ 66686 ★ First Union National
Bank of Georgia
2069 Riverside Dr.
Macon, GA 31204-2049
(912)851-6930
Location Type: Branch office. Ultimate
Parent: First Union Corp. SIC: 6021—
National Commercial Banks.

★ 66687 ★ First Union National
Bank of Georgia
455 Walnut St.
Macon, GA 31201-3464
(912)742-6361
Location Type: Branch office. Ultimate
Parent: First Union Corp. SIC: 6021—
National Commercial Banks.

★ 66688 ★ First Union National
Bank of Georgia
3957 Vineville Ave.
Macon, GA 31210-5020
(912)471-2130
Location Type: Branch office. Ultimate
Parent: First Union Corp. SIC: 6021—
National Commercial Banks.

★ 66689 ★ First Union National
Bank of Georgia
3710 Northside Dr.
Macon, GA 31210-2408
(912)749-8070
Location Type: Branch office. Ultimate
Parent: First Union Corp. SIC: 6021—
National Commercial Banks.

★ 66690 ★ First Union National
Bank of Georgia
3535 Mercer University Dr.
Macon, GA 31204-4903
(912)471-2120
Location Type: Branch office. Ultimate
Parent: First Union Corp. SIC: 6021—
National Commercial Banks.

★ 66691 ★ Hertz Rent-A-Car
Lewis B Wilson Airport
Macon, GA 31201
(912)788-3600
Ultimate Parent: Hertz. SIC: 7514—
Passenger Car Rental.

★ 66692 ★ Jiffy Lube
3753 Pio Nono Ave.
Macon, GA 31206
(912)781-1096
Ultimate Parent: Pennzoil. SIC: 7538—
General Automotive Repair Shops.

★ 66693 ★ Jiffy Lube of East
Macon
1045 Gray Hwy.
Macon, GA 31211
(912)742-0766
Ultimate Parent: Pennzoil. SIC: 7539—
Automotive Repair Shops Nec.

★ 66694 ★ J.M. Huber Corp.
Rte. 4-Huber
Macon, GA 31298
Ultimate Parent: J. M. Huber. SIC: 2893—
Printing Ink.

★ 66695 ★ Kentucky Fried
Chicken
1019 Riverside Dr.
Macon, GA 31201
(912)743-5002
Ultimate Parent: Pepsico. SIC: 5812—
Eating Places.

★ 66696 ★ Kroger Co.
3076 Riverside Dr.
Macon, GA 31210
(912)477-6755
Ultimate Parent: Kroger. SIC: 5812—
Eating Places.

★ 66697 ★ Kroger's
660 North Ave.
Macon, GA 31211
(912)746-6300
Ultimate Parent: Kroger. SIC: 5411—
Grocery Stores.

★ 66698 ★ Macy's
14 Macon Mall
Macon, GA 31206
(912)471-3882
Ultimate Parent: R. H. Macy. SIC: 5311—
Department Stores.

★ 66699 ★ New York Life Macon
General Office
Southeastern Agencies
Box 958
Macon, GA 31202
(912)742-7341 Fax: (912)741-3814
Officer: James Edward Muse III, General
Manager. Ultimate Parent: New York Life.

★ 66700 ★ New York Life Macon
General Office
Southeastern Agencies
577 Mulberry Street
Macon, GA 31201
(912)742-7341 Fax: (912)741-3814
Officer: James Edward Muse III, General
Manager. Ultimate Parent: New York Life.

★ 66701 ★ Otis Elevator Co.
425 2nd St.
Macon, GA 31201
(912)745-8234
Ultimate Parent: United Technologies. SIC:
5084—Industrial Machinery & Equipment.

★ 66702 ★ Pepsi-Cola Bottling
Co.
4541 Houston Ave.
Macon, GA 31206
(404)253-4564
Officer: John Johnson, President. Ultimate
Parent: Pepsico. SIC: 2086—Bottled &
Canned Soft Drinks.

★ 66703 ★ Piggly Wiggly
Westgate Shopping Ctr.
Macon, GA 31206
(912)781-4525
Ultimate Parent: Bruno's. SIC: 5411—
Grocery Stores.

★ 66704 ★ Piggly Wiggly
Bloomfield Village Shopping Ctr.
Macon, GA 31206
(912)781-0628
Ultimate Parent: Bruno's. SIC: 5912—Drug
Stores & Proprietary Stores.

★ 66705 ★ Pizza Hut
3694 Mercer University Dr.
Macon, GA 31204
(912)474-9330
Ultimate Parent: Pepsico. SIC: 5812—
Eating Places.

★ 66706 ★ Principal Mutual Life
6096 PO Box
Macon, GA 31208
(912)746-1689
Ultimate Parent: Principal Mutual Life.

★ 66707 ★ Radio Shack
3884 Pio Nono Ave.
Macon, GA 31206
(912)788-7025
Company Type: Division. Ultimate Parent:
Tandy Corp. SIC: 5065—Electronic Parts &
Equipment Nec.

★ 66708 ★ Residential Services
653 2nd St.
Macon, GA 31201-2817
(912)741-8165
Officer: Cecil Baldwin. Ultimate Parent:
Browning-Ferris Industries. SIC: 8059—
Nursing & Personal Care Nec.

★ 66709 ★ Ryder Truck Rental
705 Gray Hwy.
Macon, GA 31211
(912)743-6292
Ultimate Parent: Ryder System. SIC:
7359—Equipment Rental & Leasing Nec.

★ 66710 ★ Ryder Truck Rental
91 Spring St.
Macon, GA 31201
(912)742-4297
Ultimate Parent: Ryder System. SIC:
7359—Equipment Rental & Leasing Nec.

★ 66711 ★ Ryder Truck Rental
3377 Mercer University Dr.
Macon, GA 31204
(912)743-1131
Ultimate Parent: Ryder System. SIC:
7513—Truck Rental & Leasing Without
Drivers.

★ 66712 ★ Safety Kleen Corp.
6580 Hawkinsville Rd.
Macon, GA 31206
(912)788-9398
Ultimate Parent: Safety-Kleen. SIC: 5013—
Motor Vehicle Supplies & New Parts.

★ 66713 ★ Sam's Wholesale
Club
Fulton Mill Rd.
Macon, GA 31206
(912)474-1036
Ultimate Parent: Wal-Mart Stores, Inc. SIC:
5144—Poultry & Poultry Products.

★ 66714 ★ Taco Bell
1212 Eisenhower Pky.
Macon, GA 31206
(912)788-9211
Ultimate Parent: Pepsico. SIC: 5812—
Eating Places.

★ 66715 ★ Texaco Food Mart
2765 Houston Ave.
Macon, GA 31206
(912)788-1884
Ultimate Parent: Texaco. SIC: 5541—
Gasoline Service Stations.

★ 66716 ★ Trailways Bus
Systemm
466 Broadway
Macon, GA 31201
(912)742-7320
Ultimate Parent: Greyhound Lines Inc. SIC:
4131—Intercity & Rural Bus Transportation.

★ 66717 ★ Trailways Inc.
466 Broadway
Macon, GA 31201
(912)742-7327
Ultimate Parent: Greyhound Lines Inc. SIC:
4131—Intercity & Rural Bus Transportation.

★ 66718 ★ Trane Commercial
Self-Contained Systems Business
Unit
7610 Industrial Hwy.
Macon, GA 31206
(912)781-6495
Officer: Tom Heffernan, Vice President &
General Manager. Ultimate Parent:
American Standard. SIC: 3585—
Refrigeration & Heating Equipment; 3433—
Heating Equipment Except Electric; 3564—
Blowers & Fans.

★ 66719 ★ Trust Co. Bank of
Middle Georgia, N.A.
606 Cherry St.
PO Box 4248
Macon, GA 31208-4248
(912)741-2265 Fax: (912)741-1539
Officer: J. Alan Neal, President & CEO.
Ultimate Parent: Suntrust Banks. SIC:
6021—National Commercial Banks.

★ 66720 ★ Unijax Inc.
7515 NE Industrial Blvd.
Macon, GA 31206
(912)784-9000
Officer: H. Allen Zebell. Ultimate Parent:
Alco Standard Corp. SIC: 5111—Printing &
Writing Paper; 2621—Paper Mills; 5087—
Service Establishment Equipment; 5113—
Industrial & Personal Service Paper.

★ 66721 ★ Unisys Corp.
5107 PO Box
Macon, GA 31208
Ultimate Parent: Unisys Corp. SIC: 5099—
Durable Goods Nec.

★ 66722 ★ United Parcel Service
235 South St.
Macon, GA 31206
(912)742-5686
Ultimate Parent: United Parcel Service of
America. SIC: 4215—Courier Services
Except by Air.

★ 66723 ★ Wal Mart Discount
Cities
2525 Pio Nono Ave.
Macon, GA 31206
(912)781-0866
Ultimate Parent: Wal-Mart Stores, Inc. SIC:
5399—Miscellaneous General Merchandise
Store.

★ 66724 ★ Western Auto Supply
Co.
NE Plaza Shopping Plz.
Macon, GA 31201
(912)742-6391
Ultimate Parent: Sears Roebuck & Co.
SIC: 5531—Automobile & Home Supply
Stores.

★ 66725 ★ Western Auto Supply
Co.
213 3rd St.
Macon, GA 31201
(912)742-1456
Ultimate Parent: Sears Roebuck & Co.
SIC: 5531—Automobile & Home Supply
Stores.

★ 66726 ★ World Book
Childcraft
3981 Pio Nono Ave.
Macon, GA 31206-3043
(912)788-7626
Ultimate Parent: Berkshire Hathaway. SIC:
5963—Direct Selling Establishments.

★ 66727 ★ World Book
Childcraft
883 Green Oak Ter.
Macon, GA 31210-3239
(912)477-5473
Ultimate Parent: Berkshire Hathaway. SIC:
5963—Direct Selling Establishments.

Madison

★ 66728 ★ Georgia-Pacific Corp.
Madison Plywood
4891 Mead Rd.
Madison, GA 30650
Ultimate Parent: Georgia-Pacific. SIC:
2436—Softwood Veneer & Plywood.

★ 66729 ★ Trust Co. Bank of NE
Georgia, N.A.
286 Hancock St.
Madison, GA 30650-1305
(706)342-1331
Officer: Robert E. Mason, Manager.
Ultimate Parent: Suntrust Banks. SIC:
6021—National Commercial Banks.

Marietta

★ 66730 ★ Ace Hardware
1435 Terrell Mill Rd.
Marietta, GA 30067
(404)952-2345
Ultimate Parent: Ace Hardware.

★ 66731 ★ Ace Hardware
3600 Dalls Rd. SW
Marietta, GA 30064
(404)425-1100
Ultimate Parent: Ace Hardware.

★ 66732 ★ Ace Hardware
2940 Canton Rd.
Marietta, GA 30066
(404)428-0500
Ultimate Parent: Ace Hardware.

★ 66733 ★ Ace Hardware
775 Whitlock Ave.
Marietta, GA 30064
(404)422-1646
Ultimate Parent: Ace Hardware.

★ 66734 ★ Ace Hardware
Ragsdale
2940 Canton Rd.
Marietta, GA 30066
(404)428-0500
Ultimate Parent: Ace Hardware.

★ 66735 ★ Amgen Inc.
1850 Parkway Pl SE
Marietta, GA 30067
(404)423-8080
Ultimate Parent: Amgen.

★ 66736 ★ AMP Packaging
Systems
4444 Cove Island Dr.
Marietta, GA 30067-3616
(404)971-3559
Ultimate Parent: AMP Inc. SIC: 5065—
Electronic Parts & Equipment Nec.

★ 66737 ★ Atlanta Coca-Cola
Bottling Co.
1091 Industrial Park Dr.
Marietta, GA 30337
Ultimate Parent: Coca-Cola Enterprises.
SIC: 2086—Bottled & Canned Soft Drinks.

★ 66738 ★ Atlanta Coca-Cola
Bottling Co. - Marietta Plant
1091 Industrial Park Dr.
Marietta, GA 30062
Ultimate Parent: Coca-Cola Enterprises.
SIC: 2086—Bottled & Canned Soft Drinks.

★ 66739 ★ Avery Dennison Corp.
Aigner Products Div.
Bldg. 900 Ste. 116
1395 Marietta Pkwy
Marietta, GA 30067
(904)427-7351
Company Type: Division. Ultimate Parent:
Avery Dennison Corp. SIC: 2759—
Commercial Printing Nec.

★ 66740 ★ Bank South, NA
1422 Terrell Mill Rd.
Marietta, GA 30067
(404)952-6325
Company Type: Subsidiary. Location
Type: Branch office. Ultimate Parent: Bank
South Corp. SIC: 6021—National
Commercial Banks.

★ 66741 ★ Bank South, NA
1347 Church St. Ext.
Marietta, GA 30060-7913
(404)428-0033
Company Type: Subsidiary. Location
Type: Branch office. Officer: Anne
Matthews, Manager. Ultimate Parent: Bank
South Corp. SIC: 6021—National
Commercial Banks.

★ 66742 ★ Bank South, NA
3590 Dallas Hwy. SW
Marietta, GA 30064-2750
(404)426-0704
Company Type: Subsidiary. Location
Type: Branch office. Officer: Tim Martin,
Manager. Ultimate Parent: Bank South
Corp. SIC: 6021—National Commercial
Banks.

★ 66743 ★ Bank South, NA
2475 Windy Hill Rd.
Marietta, GA 30067-8604
(404)952-1030
Company Type: Subsidiary. Location
Type: Branch office. Officer: Sherron
Sargeant, Manager. Ultimate Parent: Bank
South Corp. SIC: 6021—National
Commercial Banks.

★ 66744 ★ Bank South, NA
1899 Powers Ferry Rd., Ste. 110
Marietta, GA 30067-9402
(404)984-0470
Company Type: Subsidiary. Location
Type: Branch office. Ultimate Parent: Bank
South Corp. SIC: 6021—National
Commercial Banks.

★ 66745 ★ Bank South, NA
2786 Sandy Plains Rd. NE
Marietta, GA 30062
(404)971-4017
Company Type: Subsidiary. Location
Type: Branch office. Officer: Russell Artz,
Manager. Ultimate Parent: Bank South
Corp. SIC: 6021—National Commercial
Banks.

★ 66746 ★ Bank South, NA
1274 Johnson Ferry Rd.
Marietta, GA 30068-2799
(404)973-0818
Company Type: Subsidiary. Location
Type: Branch office. Officer: Libby Pitner,
Manager. Ultimate Parent: Bank South
Corp. SIC: 6021—National Commercial
Banks.

★ 66747 ★   Bank South, NA
140 NE Cherokee St. NE
Marietta, GA 30060-7913
(404)429-3833
Company Type: Subsidiary. Location
Type: Branch office. Officer: Joyce Self,
Manager. Ultimate Parent: Bank South
Corp. SIC: 6021—National Commercial
Banks.

★ 66748 ★   Bank South, NA
1430 Roswell Rd.
Marietta, GA 30062-3615
(404)429-2896
Company Type: Subsidiary. Location
Type: Branch office. Officer: Dianne Moss,
Manager. Ultimate Parent: Bank South
Corp. SIC: 6021—National Commercial
Banks.

★ 66749 ★   Bank South, NA
1122 Powers Ferry Rd.
Marietta, GA 30067
(404)850-6290
Company Type: Subsidiary. Location
Type: Branch office. Officer: Kevin Isgette,
Manager. Ultimate Parent: Bank South
Corp. SIC: 6021—National Commercial
Banks.

★ 66750 ★   Bank South, NA
4880 Lower Roswell Rd.
Marietta, GA 30068
(404)578-7395
Company Type: Subsidiary. Location
Type: Branch office. Officer: Kim McCraw,
Manager. Ultimate Parent: Bank South
Corp. SIC: 6021—National Commercial
Banks.

★ 66751 ★   Bank South, NA
3030 Windy Hill Rd.
Marietta, GA 30067
(404)953-7334
Company Type: Subsidiary. Location
Type: Branch office. Officer: Greg Lutz,
Manager. Ultimate Parent: Bank South
Corp. SIC: 6021—National Commercial
Banks.

★ 66752 ★   Bank South, NA
3595 Canton Rd.
Marietta, GA 30066
(404)928-8114
Company Type: Subsidiary. Location
Type: Branch office. Officer: Jennifer
Harber, Manager. Ultimate Parent: Bank
South Corp. SIC: 6021—National
Commercial Banks.

★ 66753 ★   Bank South NA
3600 Dallas Hwy.
Marietta, GA 30064-1616
(404)333-3350
Location Type: Branch office. Officer: Amy
Allen. Ultimate Parent: Bank South Corp.
SIC: 6022—State Commercial Banks;
6021—National Commercial Banks; 6141—
Personal Credit Institutions.

★ 66754 ★   Bank South NA
2667 Powder Springs Rd.
Marietta, GA 30064-4520
(404)333-3357
Location Type: Branch office. Ultimate
Parent: Bank South Corp. SIC: 6022—State
Commercial Banks; 6021—National
Commercial Banks; 6141—Personal Credit
Institutions; 6141—Personal Credit
Institutions.

★ 66755 ★   Bank South NA/
Sprayberry
2595 Sandy Plains Rd., NE
Marietta, GA 30066
(404)578-7390
Company Type: Subsidiary. Location
Type: Branch office. Officer: Chris Terelli,
Mgr. Ultimate Parent: Bank South Corp.
SIC: 6021—National Commercial Banks.

★ 66756 ★   Bank South NA/Windy
Hill
3030 Windy Hill Rd.
Marietta, GA 30067
(404)953-7334
Company Type: Subsidiary. Location
Type: Branch office. Officer: Debbie
Clemmons, Mgr. Ultimate Parent: Bank
South Corp. SIC: 6021—National
Commercial Banks.

★ 66757 ★   BASF Corp.
Engineering Plastics
3450 Sheridan Chase
Marietta, GA 30067-4336
(404)977-4417
Location Type: Branch office. Ultimate
Parent: BASF Corp. SIC: 2821—Plastics
Materials & Resins.

★ 66758 ★   Burlington Coat
Factory Warehouse
1255 Roswell Rd.
Marietta, GA 30062-3610
(404)971-2327
Location Type: Branch office. Ultimate
Parent: Burlington Industries, Equity. SIC:
5311—Department Stores; 5661—Shoe
Stores.

★ 66759 ★   Champion
International Corp/Ne
2300 Windy Ridge Pkwy SE
Marietta, GA 30067
(404)955-0123
Ultimate Parent: Champion International.
SIC: 9721—International Affairs.

★ 66760 ★   Champion
International Corp. Pr
2300 Windy Ridge Pkwy SE
Marietta, GA 30067
(404)955-0123
Ultimate Parent: Champion International.
SIC: 9721—International Affairs.

★ 66761 ★   Citgo Food Mart
1991 Marietta Blvd. NW
Marietta, GA
(404)351-9277
Ultimate Parent: Citgo Petroleum.

★ 66762 ★   Citgo Food Mart
1526 Austell Rd. SE
Marietta, GA 30060
(404)590-0636
Ultimate Parent: Citgo Petroleum.

★ 66763 ★   Citgo Food Mart
690 Cherokee St. NE
Marietta, GA 30060
(404)429-1063
Ultimate Parent: Citgo Petroleum.

★ 66764 ★   Computer Associates
Inc.
2300 Windy Ridge Pkwy SE
Marietta, GA 30067
(404)953-9276
Ultimate Parent: Computer Associates
International.

★ 66765 ★   Copier Consultants
Inc.
775 Franklin Rd.
Marietta, GA 30067-7803
(404)590-1400
Ultimate Parent: Alco Standard Corp. SIC:
5044—Office Equipment.

★ 66766 ★   Courtyard by Marriott
2455 Delk Rd. SE
Marietta, GA 30067
(404)956-1188
Ultimate Parent: Marriott International.

★ 66767 ★   Dole Fresh Fruit Co.
3258 Catkin Ct NE
Marietta, GA 30066
(404)565-8171
Ultimate Parent: Dole Food.

★ 66768 ★   Eagle Picher Industry
Inc.
2225 Smoke Stone Cir. NE
Marietta, GA 30062
(404)992-2881
Ultimate Parent: Eagle-Picher Industries
Inc.

★ 66769 ★   Exxon Co. USA
4244 Roswell Rd.
Marietta, GA 30062
(404)971-5025
Ultimate Parent: Exxon.

★ 66770 ★   First National Bank of
Georgia
827 Church St.
Marietta, GA 30060-7229
(404)423-2275
Location Type: Branch office. Ultimate
Parent: First Union Corp. SIC: 6021—
National Commercial Banks.

★ 66771 ★   First Union National
Bank of Georgia
3726 Washington Rd.
Marietta, GA 30907-2867
(706)868-4607
Location Type: Branch office. Ultimate
Parent: First Union Corp. SIC: 6021—
National Commercial Banks.

★ 66772 ★   First Union National
Bank of Georgia
761 Powder Springs Rd.
Marietta, GA 30064-3633
(404)423-4000
Location Type: Branch office. Ultimate
Parent: First Union Corp. SIC: 6021—
National Commercial Banks.

★ 66773 ★   First Union National
Bank of Georgia
3601 Sandy Plains Rd. NE
Marietta, GA 30066
(404)827-7100
Location Type: Branch office. Ultimate
Parent: First Union Corp. SIC: 6021—
National Commercial Banks.

★ 66774 ★   First Union National
Bank of Georgia
1547 Powers Ferry Rd.
Marietta, GA 30067-5413
(404)933-2710
Location Type: Branch office. Ultimate
Parent: First Union Corp. SIC: 6021—
National Commercial Banks.

★ 66775 ★   First Union National
Bank of Georgia
1329 Johnson's Ferry Rd.
Marietta, GA 30068-5405
(404)865-3190
Location Type: Branch office. Ultimate
Parent: Barnett Bank of Alachua County,
NA. SIC: 6021—National Commercial
Banks.

★ 66776 ★   First Union National
Bank of Georgia
4046 Austell Rd.
Marietta, GA 30060-5715
(404)819-3060
Location Type: Branch office. Ultimate
Parent: First Union Corp. SIC: 6021—
National Commercial Banks.

★ 66777 ★   First Union National
Bank of Georgia
2850 Canton Rd.
Marietta, GA 30066-5441
(404)423-2270
Location Type: Branch office. Ultimate
Parent: First Union Corp. SIC: 6021—
National Commercial Banks.

★ 66778 ★   First Union National
Bank of Georgia
751 Whitlock Ave.
Marietta, GA 30064
(404)423-2280
Location Type: Branch office. Ultimate
Parent: First Union Corp. SIC: 6021—
National Commercial Banks.

★ 66779 ★   First Union National
Bank of Georgia
602 Roswell St.
Marietta, GA 30060-2181
(404)865-3300
Location Type: Branch office. Ultimate
Parent: First Union Corp. SIC: 6021—
National Commercial Banks.

★ 66780 ★   The Gap
Market Sq. at Dekalb
Marietta, GA 30066
(404)634-4594
Ultimate Parent: GAP.

★ 66781 ★   Gap Stores the
Market Sq. at Dekalb
Marietta, GA 30066
(404)634-4594
Ultimate Parent: GAP.

★ 66782 ★   Georgia Federal Bank
F S B
2201 Roswell Rd.
Marietta, GA 30062
Ultimate Parent: First Union Corp. SIC:
6099—Functions Related to Deposit
Banking.

★ 66783 ★   Greyhound Bus Lines
Local Info
1250 S. Marietta Pkwy SE
Marietta, GA 30060
(404)427-1602
Ultimate Parent: Greyhound Lines Inc.

★ 66784 ★   Hertz Rent-A-Car Car
Rental Lo
1551 Cobb Pkwy SE
Marietta, GA
(404)426-4211
Ultimate Parent: Hertz.

★ 66785 ★   Hewlett Packard Co.
2000 Park Dr.
Marietta, GA 30060
(404)955-1500
Ultimate Parent: Hewlett-Packard.

★ 66786 ★   Hit or Miss Wms
Apparel Retail
2205 Roswell Rd. NE
Marietta, GA 30062
(404)565-0250
Ultimate Parent: TJX.

★ 66787 ★   Hit or Miss Wms
Apparel Retail
2550 Sandy Plains Rd. NE
Marietta, GA 30066
(404)565-8554
Ultimate Parent: TJX.

★ 66788 ★   IBM Corp.
3100 Windy Hill Rd.
Marietta, GA 30067
(404)835-3000
Ultimate Parent: IBM. SIC: 3599—
Industrial Machinery Nec.

★ 66789 ★   Jiffy Lube Marietta
686 Powder Springs St.
Marietta, GA 30064
(404)423-0115
Ultimate Parent: Pennzoil.

★ 66790 ★   Jiffy Lube Marietta
3418 Canton Rd. NE
Marietta, GA 30066
(404)424-6505
Ultimate Parent: Pennzoil.

★ 66791 ★   Jim Walter Homes
Inc.
931 N. Cobb Pkwy SE
Marietta, GA
(404)428-9533
Ultimate Parent: Walter Industries, Inc.

★ 66792 ★   Kentucky Fried
Chicken
1130 Powder Springs St. SE
Marietta, GA
(404)428-5881
Ultimate Parent: Pepsico.

★ 66793 ★   Kentucky Fried
Chicken
650 Whitlock Ave. SW
Marietta, GA 30064
(404)427-5656
Ultimate Parent: Pepsico.

★ 66794 ★   Kentucky Fried
Chicken
2540 Delk Rd.
Marietta, GA 30067
(404)980-0848
Ultimate Parent: Pepsico.

★ 66795 ★   Kentucky Fried
Chicken
690 Johnson Ferry Rd. NE
Marietta, GA 30068
(404)565-0947
Ultimate Parent: Pepsico.

★ 66796 ★   Kentucky Fried
Chicken
3012 Canton Rd. NE
Marietta, GA 30066
(404)427-6866
Ultimate Parent: Pepsico.

★ 66797 ★   Kentucky Fried
Chicken
12 Cobb Pkwy NE
Marietta, GA
(404)422-4716
Ultimate Parent: Pepsico.

★ 66798 ★ **Kentucky Fried Chicken**
3800 Austell Rd. SW
Marietta, GA 30060
(404)739-7696
Ultimate Parent: Pepsico.

★ 66799 ★ **Kmart Stores**
1140 Roswell Rd. NE
Marietta, GA 30062
(404)427-5356
Ultimate Parent: K-Mart.

★ 66800 ★ **Kmart Stores**
3605 Sandy Plains Rd.
Marietta, GA 30066
(404)977-7715
Ultimate Parent: K-Mart.

★ 66801 ★ **Kmart Stores**
4269 Roswell Rd.
Marietta, GA 30062
(404)977-2102
Ultimate Parent: K-Mart.

★ 66802 ★ **Kmart Stores Automotive**
3605 Sandy Plains Rd.
Marietta, GA 30066
(404)977-1778
Ultimate Parent: K-Mart.

★ 66803 ★ **Kmart Stores Automotive**
1140 Roswell Rd. NE
Marietta, GA 30062
(404)427-5378
Ultimate Parent: K-Mart.

★ 66804 ★ **Kmart Stores Pharmacy**
3605 Sandy Plains Rd. NE
Marietta, GA 30066
(404)977-8694
Ultimate Parent: K-Mart.

★ 66805 ★ **Kmart Stores Pharmacy**
4269 Roswell Rd.
Marietta, GA 30062
(404)977-1865
Ultimate Parent: K-Mart.

★ 66806 ★ **Kmart Stores Pharmacy**
1140 Roswll Rd. NE
Marietta, GA
(404)424-9588
Ultimate Parent: K-Mart.

★ 66807 ★ **Kroger Co. the Retail Sotrs**
2667 Powder Springs Rd. SW
Marietta, GA 30064
(404)943-0034
Ultimate Parent: Kroger.

★ 66808 ★ **Kroger Co. the Retail Stores**
2550 Sandy Plains Rd. NE
Marietta, GA 30066
(404)578-0129
Ultimate Parent: Kroger.

★ 66809 ★ **Kroger Co. the Retail Stores**
4880 Lower Roswell Rd. NE
Marietta, GA 30068
(404)971-8801
Ultimate Parent: Kroger.

★ 66810 ★ **Kroger Co. the Retail Stores**
1803 Roswell Rd. NE
Marietta, GA 30062
(404)971-6858
Ultimate Parent: Kroger.

★ 66811 ★ **Kroger Co. the Retail Stores**
3595 Canton Rd.
Marietta, GA 30066
(404)924-7930
Ultimate Parent: Kroger.

★ 66812 ★ **Kroger Co. the Retail Stores**
3600 Dallas Rd. SW
Marietta, GA 30064
(404)424-0040
Ultimate Parent: Kroger.

★ 66813 ★ **Kroger Pharmacies**
2667 Powder Springs Rd. SW
Marietta, GA 30064
(404)943-0085
Ultimate Parent: Kroger.

★ 66814 ★ **Kroger Pharmacies**
1122 Powers Feery Rd. SE
Marietta, GA
(404)955-3474
Ultimate Parent: Kroger.

★ 66815 ★ **Kroger Pharmacies**
3600 Dallas Hwy. SW
Marietta, GA 30064
(404)425-0552
Ultimate Parent: Kroger.

★ 66816 ★ **Kroger Pharmacies**
4880 Lower Roswell Rd. NE
Marietta, GA 30068
(404)971-8661
Ultimate Parent: Kroger.

★ 66817 ★ **Kroger Pharmacies Kroger Co. Th**
736 Whitlock Ave.
Marietta, GA 30064
(404)429-0152
Ultimate Parent: Kroger.

★ 66818 ★ **Kroger Pharmacies Kroger Co. Th**
1803 Roswell Rd.
Marietta, GA 30062
(404)973-5110
Ultimate Parent: Kroger.

★ 66819 ★ **The Limited**
1410 Cobb Pky. S
Marietta, GA 30062
(404)435-2201
Ultimate Parent: Limited.

★ 66820 ★ **Linens 'n Things Marietta Stor**
1440 Roswell Rd. NE
Marietta, GA 30062
(404)973-8881
Ultimate Parent: Melville.

★ 66821 ★ **Lockheed Aeronautical Systems Co.**
86 S. Cobb Dr.
Marietta, GA 30063
(404)494-4411 **Fax:** (404)494-6263
Company Type: Division. **Ultimate Parent:** Lockheed Corp. **SIC:** 3721—Aircraft.

★ 66822 ★ **Lockheed Aeronautical Systems Co.-Georgia (Afp 6)**
86 South Cobb Dr.
Marietta, GA 30063
Ultimate Parent: Lockheed Corp. **SIC:** 3271—Concrete Block & Brick.

★ 66823 ★ **Marshalls**
2211 Roswell Rd. NE
Marietta, GA 30062
(404)971-2604
Ultimate Parent: Melville.

★ 66824 ★ **Mary Kay Cosmetics**
Indep Sales
158 Wedgewood Ct.
Marietta, GA 30068
(404)971-1677
Ultimate Parent: Mary Kay Cosmetics.

★ 66825 ★ **Mary Kay Cosmetics**
Indep Sales
2931 Dara
Marietta, GA 30066
(404)565-2424
Ultimate Parent: Mary Kay Cosmetics.

★ 66826 ★ **Mary Kay Cosmetics**
Indep Sales
2075 Old Forge Way NE
Marietta, GA 30068
(404)641-1319
Ultimate Parent: Mary Kay Cosmetics.

★ 66827 ★ **Mary Kay Cosmetics**
Indep Sales
555 Bellemeade Dr. SW
Marietta, GA 30060
(404)422-6697
Ultimate Parent: Mary Kay Cosmetics.

★ 66828 ★ **Mary Kay Cosmetics**
Indep Sales
3528 Claridge Dr.
Marietta, GA 30066
(404)926-3672
Ultimate Parent: Mary Kay Cosmetics.

★ 66829 ★ **Mary Kay Cosmetics**
Indep Sales
279 E. Valoley Dr. SE
Marietta, GA
(404)971-9181
Ultimate Parent: Mary Kay Cosmetics.

★ 66830 ★ **Massachusetts Mutual Life Insurance**
2500 Windy Ridge Pky. SE
Marietta, GA 30067
(404)952-0212
Ultimate Parent: Massasucetts Mutual Life.

★ 66831 ★ **Mayfield Dairy Farms Inc.**
1971 Delk Industrial Blvd.
Marietta, GA 30067
(404)952-3292
Officer: John Raper, Manager. **Ultimate Parent:** Dean Foods. **SIC:** 2024—Ice Cream & Frozen Desserts.

★ 66832 ★ **McDonald's Restaurants**
2700 Windy Hill Rd. SE
Marietta, GA 30067
(404)955-8833
Ultimate Parent: McDonald's.

★ 66833 ★ **McDonald's Restaurants**
2782 Sandy Plains Rd. NE
Marietta, GA 30066
(404)977-2469
Ultimate Parent: McDonald's.

★ 66834 ★ **McDonald's Restaurants**
778 Whitlock Ave. SW
Marietta, GA 30064
(404)425-8768
Ultimate Parent: McDonald's.

★ 66835 ★ **McDonald's Restaurants**
1495 Roswell Rd. NE
Marietta, GA 30062
(404)973-5752
Ultimate Parent: McDonald's.

★ 66836 ★ **McDonald's Restaurants**
3101 Roswell Rd. NE
Marietta, GA 30062
(404)565-8663
Ultimate Parent: McDonald's.

★ 66837 ★ **McDonald's Restaurants**
1291 Bells Ferry Rd. NW
Marietta, GA 30066
(404)423-7255
Ultimate Parent: McDonald's.

★ 66838 ★ **McDonald's Restaurants**
1195 Powder Springs St. SW
Marietta, GA
(404)421-0722
Ultimate Parent: McDonald's.

★ 66839 ★ **McDonald's Restaurants**
1305 Powers Ferry Rd. SE
Marietta, GA 30067
(404)951-2383
Ultimate Parent: McDonald's.

★ 66840 ★ **McDonald's Restaurants**
3010 Canton Rd. NE
Marietta, GA 30066
(404)428-1982
Ultimate Parent: McDonald's.

★ 66841 ★ **Monsanto Agricultural Co.**
1515 Johnson Ferry Rd.
Marietta, GA 30062-6438
(404)565-0375
Ultimate Parent: Monsanto. **SIC:** 5169—Chemicals & Allied Products Nec.

★ 66842 ★ **Nationsbank Account Activity I**
Windy Hill 2501 Wind
Marietta, GA 30067
(404)523-0900
Ultimate Parent: Nationsbank Corp.

★ 66843 ★ **Nationsbank Acct Activity Inf**
Shallowford Falls 31
Marietta, GA
(404)523-0900
Ultimate Parent: Nationsbank Corp.

★ 66844 ★ **Nationsbank Departments Nation**
2501 Windy Hill Rd.
Marietta, GA 30067
(404)955-2570
Ultimate Parent: Nationsbank Corp.

★ 66845 ★ **Nationsbank Honor-Cirrus L Mar**
121 Haynes St.
Marietta, GA 30060
(404)423-5188
Ultimate Parent: Nationsbank Corp.

★ 66846 ★ **Nationsbank Honor-Cirrus L Par**
4851 Lower Roswell Rd.
Marietta, GA 30068
(404)578-3640
Ultimate Parent: Nationsbank Corp.

★ 66847 ★ **Nationsbank Honor-Cirrus L Pow**
2693 Powder Springs Rd.
Marietta, GA 30064
(404)439-2360
Ultimate Parent: Nationsbank Corp.

★ 66848 ★ **Nationsbank Honor-Cirrus L Spr**
2480 Sandy Plains Rd.
Marietta, GA 30066
(404)578-3650
Ultimate Parent: Nationsbank Corp.

★ 66849 ★ **Nationsbank Honor-Cirrus L Win**
2501 Windy Hill Rd.
Marietta, GA 30067
(404)953-5600
Ultimate Parent: Nationsbank Corp.

★ 66850 ★ **Nationsbank Honor-Cirrus Villa**
3596 Dallas Hwy.
Marietta, GA 30064
(404)429-5100
Ultimate Parent: Nationsbank Corp.

★ 66851 ★ **Nationsbank Ofc Atl Area Accou**
Sprayberry 2480 Sand
Marietta, GA
(404)523-0900
Ultimate Parent: Nationsbank Corp.

★ 66852 ★ **Nationsbank Ofc Atlanta Area L**
East Lake 2055 Roswe
Marietta, GA
(404)578-3334
Ultimate Parent: Nationsbank Corp.

★ 66853 ★ **Nationsbank Ofc Atlanta Area N**
East Lake 2055 Roswe
Marietta, GA
(404)578-3331
Ultimate Parent: Nationsbank Corp.

★ 66854 ★ **Nationsbank Ofcs Atlanta Area**
Cobb Parkway 1090 in
Marietta, GA
(404)969-0550
Ultimate Parent: Nationsbank Corp.

★ 66855 ★ **Nationsbank Offices Atlanta Area**
Powers Ferry 1920 Po
Marietta, GA
(404)953-5633
Ultimate Parent: Nationsbank Corp.

★ 66856 ★ **Nationsbank Offices Atlanta Ar**
Village Green 3596 D
Marietta, GA
(404)429-5100
Ultimate Parent: Nationsbank Corp.

★ 66857 ★   Nationsbank Offices
Atlanta Ar
Windy Hill 2501 Wind
Marietta, GA 30067
(404)969-0550
Ultimate Parent: Nationsbank Corp.

★ 66858 ★   Nationsbank Offices
Atlanta Ar
Shallowford Falls 31
Marietta, GA
(404)969-0550
Ultimate Parent: Nationsbank Corp.

★ 66859 ★   Nationsbank Offices
Atlanta Ar
Sprayberry 2480 Sand
Marietta, GA
(404)578-3653
Ultimate Parent: Nationsbank Corp.

★ 66860 ★   Nationsbank Offices
Atlanta Ar
Powder Springs 2693
Marietta, GA 30064
(404)439-2360
Ultimate Parent: Nationsbank Corp.

★ 66861 ★   Nationsbank Offices
Atlanta Ar
Powers Ferry 1920 Po
Marietta, GA
(404)969-0550
Ultimate Parent: Nationsbank Corp.

★ 66862 ★   Nationsbank Offices
Atlanta Ar
Parkaire 4851 Lower
Marietta, GA
(404)969-0550
Ultimate Parent: Nationsbank Corp.

★ 66863 ★   Nationsbank Offices
Atlanta Ar
Powder 2693 Powder S
Marietta, GA
(404)523-0900
Ultimate Parent: Nationsbank Corp.

★ 66864 ★   Nationsbank Offices
Atlanta Ar
4851 Lower Roswell Rd.
Marietta, GA 30068
(404)578-3640
Ultimate Parent: Nationsbank Corp.

★ 66865 ★   Nationsbank Offices
Atlanta Ar
Panola Rd. 6138 Cov
Marietta, GA
(404)523-0900
Ultimate Parent: Nationsbank Corp.

★ 66866 ★   Nationsbank Offices
Atlanta Ar
East Lake 2055 Roswe
Marietta, GA
(404)969-0550
Ultimate Parent: Nationsbank Corp.

★ 66867 ★   Nationsbank Offices
Atlanta Ar
121 Haynes St.
Marietta, GA 30060
(404)423-5188
Ultimate Parent: Nationsbank Corp.

★ 66868 ★   Nationsbank Offices
Atlanta Ar
Cobb Parkway 1090 in
Marietta, GA
(404)423-5171
Ultimate Parent: Nationsbank Corp.

★ 66869 ★   Nationsbank Real
Estate Departments
Marietta, GA
(404)953-5620
Ultimate Parent: Nationsbank Corp.

★ 66870 ★   Nationsbank Saturday
Banking O
2501 Windy Hill Rd.
Marietta, GA 30067
(404)953-5600
Ultimate Parent: Nationsbank Corp.

★ 66871 ★   Nationsbank Saturday
Banking O
4851 Lower Roswell Rd.
Marietta, GA 30068
(404)578-3640
Ultimate Parent: Nationsbank Corp.

★ 66872 ★   Payless Shoesource
200 Cobb Pky. SE
Marietta, GA
(404)426-0366
Ultimate Parent: May Department Stores.

★ 66873 ★   Pizza Hut
1315 Rowers Ferry Rd. SE
Marietta, GA
(404)955-6494
Ultimate Parent: Pepsico.

★ 66874 ★   Pizza Hut
660 Whitlock Ave. SW
Marietta, GA 30064
(404)427-4000
Ultimate Parent: Pepsico.

★ 66875 ★   Pizza Hut
1470 Roswell Rd. NE
Marietta, GA 30062
(404)509-5858
Ultimate Parent: Pepsico.

★ 66876 ★   Pizza Hut
1480 Terrell Mill Rd.
Marietta, GA 30067
(404)953-8900
Ultimate Parent: Pepsico.

★ 66877 ★   Pizza Hut
12 Jones Shaw Rd.
Marietta, GA
(404)436-7000
Ultimate Parent: Pepsico.

★ 66878 ★   Pizza Hut
4961 Lower Roswell Rd. NE
Marietta, GA 30068
(404)977-3200
Ultimate Parent: Pepsico.

★ 66879 ★   Pizza Hut
2800 Canton Rd.
Marietta, GA 30066
(404)590-7000
Ultimate Parent: Pepsico.

★ 66880 ★   Pizza Hut
2565 E. Piedmont Rd. NE
Marietta, GA 30062
(404)578-4200
Ultimate Parent: Pepsico.

★ 66881 ★   Pizza Hut
2204 Roswell Rd.
Marietta, GA 30062
(404)971-6932
Ultimate Parent: Pepsico.

★ 66882 ★   Pizza Hut
690 Sandtown Rd.
Marietta, GA 30060
(404)429-1689
Ultimate Parent: Pepsico.

★ 66883 ★   Pizza Hut
3660 Austell Rd.
Marietta, GA 30060
(404)435-4800
Ultimate Parent: Pepsico.

★ 66884 ★   Publix Super Market
3605 Sandy Plains Rd. NE
Marietta, GA 30066
(404)578-6000
Ultimate Parent: Publix Super Markets.

★ 66885 ★   Publix Super Market
1100 Johnson Ferry Rd. NE
Marietta, GA 30068
(404)509-2360
Ultimate Parent: Publix Super Markets.
SIC: 5122—Drugs, Proprietaries &
Sundries.

★ 66886 ★   Publix Super Market
1750 Powder Springs Rd. SW
Marietta, GA 30064
(404)423-4160
Ultimate Parent: Publix Super Markets.

★ 66887 ★   Publix Super Markets
3605 Sandy Plains Rd. NE
Marietta, GA 30066
(404)578-6000
Ultimate Parent: Publix Super Markets.

★ 66888 ★   Publix Super Markets
1100 Johnson Ferry Rd. NE
Marietta, GA 30068
(404)509-2350
Ultimate Parent: Publix Super Markets.

★ 66889 ★   Publix Super Markets
1100 Johnson Ferry Rd. NE
Marietta, GA 30068
(404)509-2360
Ultimate Parent: Publix Super Markets.
SIC: 5122—Drugs, Proprietaries &
Sundries.

★ 66890 ★   Publix Super Markets
1750 Powder Springs Rd. SW
Marietta, GA 30064
(404)423-4160
Ultimate Parent: Publix Super Markets.

★ 66891 ★   Publix Super Markets
1750 Powder Springs Rd. SW
Marietta, GA 30064
(404)423-4164
Ultimate Parent: Publix Super Markets.
SIC: 5122—Drugs, Proprietaries &
Sundries.

★ 66892 ★   Publix Super Markets
3605 Sandy Plains Rd. NE
Marietta, GA 30066
(404)578-6800
Ultimate Parent: Publix Super Markets.
SIC: 5122—Drugs, Proprietaries &
Sundries.

★ 66893 ★   Publix Super Markets
3605 Sandy Plains Rd. NE
Marietta, GA 30066
(404)578-6000
Ultimate Parent: Publix Super Markets.

★ 66894 ★   Publix Super Markets
1750 Powder Springs Rd. SW
Marietta, GA 30064
(404)423-4160
Ultimate Parent: Publix Super Markets.

★ 66895 ★   Publix Super Markets
3605 Sandy Plains Rd. NE
Marietta, GA 30066
(404)578-6444
Ultimate Parent: Publix Super Markets.

★ 66896 ★   Publix Super Markets
1100 Johnson Ferry Rd. NE
Marietta, GA 30068
(404)509-2350
Ultimate Parent: Publix Super Markets.

★ 66897 ★   Publix Super Markets
1750 Powder Springs Rd. SW
Marietta, GA 30064
(404)423-4170
Ultimate Parent: Publix Super Markets.

★ 66898 ★   Quantum Corp.
376 Powder Spring St. SE
Marietta, GA
(404)499-9433
Ultimate Parent: Quantum Corp.

★ 66899 ★   Radio Shack
4273 Roswell Rd.
Marietta, GA 30062
(404)971-1495
Company Type: Division. **Ultimate Parent:**
Tandy Corp.

★ 66900 ★   Radio Shack
2550 Sandy Plains Rd.
Marietta, GA 30066
(404)971-8317
Company Type: Division. **Ultimate Parent:**
Tandy Corp.

★ 66901 ★   Radio Shack
1307 Powers Ferry Rd. SE
Marietta, GA 30067
(404)955-7262
Company Type: Division. **Ultimate Parent:**
Tandy Corp.

★ 66902 ★   Radio Shack
1465 Roswell Rd.
Marietta, GA 30062
(404)973-6263
Company Type: Division. **Ultimate Parent:**
Tandy Corp.

★ 66903 ★   Radio Shack
1150 Powder Spring St. SW
Marietta, GA
(404)428-9978
Company Type: Division. **Ultimate Parent:**
Tandy Corp.

★ 66904 ★   Reliance Motion
Control Co.
2751 Saddle Ridge Lake Dr.
Marietta, GA 30062
(404)971-2669
Ultimate Parent: Reliance Electric.

★ 66905 ★   Rhone Poulenc Inc.
1525 Church St.
Marietta, GA 30060
(404)867-1250
Officer: Mike Villers, Plant Manager.
Ultimate Parent: Rhone-Poulenc Rorer.
SIC: 2819—Industrial Inorganic Chemicals
Nec; 2851—Paints & Allied Products;
2861—Gum & Wood Chemicals.

★ 66906 ★   Rhone-Poulenc
Specialty Chemicals Co.
1525 Church St. Extension
Marietta, GA 30060
Ultimate Parent: Rhone-Poulenc Rorer.
SIC: 2899—Chemical Preparations Nec;
2843—Surface Active Agents.

★ 66907 ★   Rubbermaid
Commercial Products
2862 Johnson Ferry Rd. NE
Marietta, GA 30062
(404)518-4100
Ultimate Parent: Rubbermaid.

★ 66908 ★   Ryder Truck Rental
1551 Cobb Pkwy SE
Marietta, GA
(404)429-9381
Ultimate Parent: Ryder System.

★ 66909 ★   Ryder Truck Rental
542 Wylie Rd. SE
Marietta, GA 30067
(404)422-6146
Ultimate Parent: Ryder System.

★ 66910 ★   Ryder Truck Rental
598 Powder Springs St. SE
Marietta, GA
(404)425-5847
Ultimate Parent: Ryder System.

★ 66911 ★   Ryder Truck Rental
2745 Sandy Plains Rd. NE
Marietta, GA 30066
(404)973-6189
Ultimate Parent: Ryder System.

★ 66912 ★   Ryder Truck Rental
1784 Lower Roswell Rd. NE
Marietta, GA 30068
(404)977-1062
Ultimate Parent: Ryder System.

★ 66913 ★   Ryder Truck Rental
404 Powder Springs St. SE
Marietta, GA
(404)423-1268
Ultimate Parent: Ryder System.

★ 66914 ★   Ryder Truck Rental
2511 Canton Rd. NE
Marietta, GA 30066
(404)428-5747
Ultimate Parent: Ryder System.

★ 66915 ★   Ryder Truck Rental
249 Cobb Pkwy NE
Marietta, GA
(404)590-7815
Ultimate Parent: Ryder System.

★ 66916 ★   Sigma Diagnostics
203 Sope Creek Ln. NE
Marietta, GA 30068
(404)578-0206
Ultimate Parent: Sigma-Aldrich.

★ 66917 ★   Sonoco Products Co.
1724 Sands Pl SE
Marietta, GA 30067
(404)952-0968
Ultimate Parent: Sonoco Products. **SIC:**
2653—Corrugated & Solid Fiber Boxes.

★ 66918 ★   Sonoco Semi-Bulk
Packaging
1850 Parkway Pl. 820
Marietta, GA 30067
(404)423-2500
Officer: Randy Kelley, President. **Ultimate
Parent:** Sonoco Products. **SIC:** 3089—
Plastics Products Nec; 3412—Metal Barrels,
Drums & Pails.

★ 66919 ★ Southern Ice Cream
Specialties
1058 King Industrial Dr.
Marietta, GA 30065
Ultimate Parent: Kroger.

★ 66920 ★ Springs Industries
2613 Ainsley Ct NE
Marietta, GA 30066
(404)591-8270
Ultimate Parent: Springs Industries.

★ 66921 ★ T J Maxx
1205 Johnson Ferry Rd. NE
Marietta, GA 30068
(404)565-1321
Ultimate Parent: TJX.

★ 66922 ★ T J Maxx
1901 Terrell Mill Rd.
Marietta, GA 30067
(404)955-1326
Ultimate Parent: TJX.

★ 66923 ★ Taco Bell
2971 Shallowford Rd. NE
Marietta, GA 30066
(404)578-9432
Ultimate Parent: Pepsico.

★ 66924 ★ Taco Bell
2169 Roswell Rd. NE
Marietta, GA 30062
(404)565-2051
Ultimate Parent: Pepsico.

★ 66925 ★ Taco Bell
2714 Sandy Plains Rd.
Marietta, GA 30066
(404)977-5388
Ultimate Parent: Pepsico.

★ 66926 ★ Taco Bell
4880 Lower Roswell Rd. NE
Marietta, GA 30068
(404)578-6379
Ultimate Parent: Pepsico.

★ 66927 ★ Taco Bell
1180 Powder Springs Rd. SW
Marietta, GA 30064
(404)590-7388
Ultimate Parent: Pepsico.

★ 66928 ★ Taco Bell
2835 Canton Rd. NE
Marietta, GA 30066
(404)422-0181
Ultimate Parent: Pepsico.

★ 66929 ★ Taco Bell
165 Cobb Pky. S
Marietta, GA 30062
(404)427-5565
Ultimate Parent: Pepsico.

★ 66930 ★ Taco Bell District
Office
1395 Marietta Pkwy SE
Marietta, GA 30067
(404)426-7410
Ultimate Parent: Pepsico.

★ 66931 ★ Target Stores Retail
Stores
805 Sandy Plains Rd. NE
Marietta, GA 30066
(404)428-5100
Ultimate Parent: Dayton Hudson.

★ 66932 ★ Texaco
1280 Johnson Ferry Rd. NE
Marietta, GA 30068
(404)973-6338
Ultimate Parent: Texaco.

★ 66933 ★ Texaco
680 Johnson Fwy. NE
Marietta, GA 30062
(404)971-1981
Ultimate Parent: Texaco.

★ 66934 ★ Texaco
2365 Delk Rd.
Marietta, GA 30067
(404)955-3299
Ultimate Parent: Texaco.

★ 66935 ★ Texaco
3324 Canton Rd.
Marietta, GA 30066
(404)422-7716
Ultimate Parent: Texaco.

★ 66936 ★ Texaco
2678 Windy Hill Rd.
Marietta, GA 30067
(404)952-7499
Ultimate Parent: Texaco.

★ 66937 ★ Texaco
2715 Sandy Plains Rd. NE
Marietta, GA 30066
(404)971-0021
Ultimate Parent: Texaco.

★ 66938 ★ Texaco
2375 Shallowford Rd. NE
Marietta, GA 30066
(404)591-7555
Ultimate Parent: Texaco.

★ 66939 ★ Texaco Express Lube
4696 Lower Roswell Rd. NE
Marietta, GA 30068
(404)973-5710
Ultimate Parent: Texaco.

★ 66940 ★ Texaco Express Lube
Sandy Plai
850 Sandy Plains Rd. NE
Marietta, GA 30066
(404)590-9335
Ultimate Parent: Texaco.

★ 66941 ★ Texaco Star
Convenience Store
850 Sandy Plains Rd. NE
Marietta, GA 30066
(404)427-4922
Ultimate Parent: Texaco.

★ 66942 ★ Union Camp Corp.
3653 Canton Rd. NE
Marietta, GA 30066
(404)924-8225
Ultimate Parent: Union Camp Corp.

★ 66943 ★ Union Camp Corp.
Chemical
1267 Windburn Dr. NE
Marietta, GA 30066
(404)973-1791
Ultimate Parent: Union Camp Corp.

★ 66944 ★ US Fleet Leasing
1827 Powers Ferry Rd. SE
Marietta, GA 30067
(404)952-3524
Ultimate Parent: Ford Motor Co.

★ 66945 ★ Varian Associates
Radiation Div.
2250 New Market Pky. SE
Marietta, GA 30067
(404)955-1775
Company Type: Division. Ultimate Parent:
Varian Associates, Inc.

★ 66946 ★ W. W. Grainger Inc.
Grainger Division
2255 Northwest Pky. SE
Marietta, GA 30067
(404)955-8758
Ultimate Parent: W. W. Grainger.

★ 66947 ★ Wal Mart Discount
Pharmacy
200 Cobb Pky. S
Marietta, GA 30062
(404)423-0213
Ultimate Parent: Wal-Mart Stores, Inc. SIC:
5122—Drugs, Proprietaries & Sundries.

★ 66948 ★ Wal Mart Vision
Center
3100 Johnson Ferry Rd.
Marietta, GA 30062
(404)992-5900
Ultimate Parent: Wal-Mart Stores, Inc.

★ 66949 ★ Waldenbooks
Cumberland Mall
Marietta, GA
(404)432-3288
Ultimate Parent: K-Mart.

★ 66950 ★ Waldenbooks & More
1197 Johnson Ferry Rd. NE
Marietta, GA 30068
(404)977-7091
Ultimate Parent: K-Mart.

★ 66951 ★ Washington Inventory
Service I
1827 Powers Ferry Rd.
Marietta, GA 30067
(404)955-6383
Ultimate Parent: Huffy.

★ 66952 ★ Weirton Steel Corp.
2748 Princeton Mill Ct NE
Marietta, GA 30068
(404)565-2004
Ultimate Parent: Weirton Steel Corp.

★ 66953 ★ Willamette Industries
Inc.
3901 Roswell Rd. NE
Marietta, GA 30062
(404)578-9187
Ultimate Parent: Willamette Industries, Inc.

Martinez

★ 66954 ★ First Union National
Bank of Georgia
101 S. Belair Rd.
Martinez, GA 30907-9110
(706)868-4631
Location Type: Branch office. Ultimate
Parent: First Union Corp. SIC: 6021—
National Commercial Banks.

Mc Donough

★ 66955 ★ Ecolab Inc. Mc
Donough Plant
261 Hwy. 155 S.
Mc Donough, GA 30253
Ultimate Parent: Ecolab Inc. SIC: 2841—
Soap & Other Detergents; 2842—Polishes &
Sanitation Goods.

★ 66956 ★ McDonald's
Restaurants
Hampton St.
Mc Donough, GA 30253
(404)957-2371
Ultimate Parent: McDonald's.

★ 66957 ★ Nationsbank Offices
Atlanta
Mc Donough 135 Keys F
Mc Donough, GA 30253
(404)954-4300
Ultimate Parent: Nationsbank Corp.

★ 66958 ★ Nationsbank
Saturday Banking
135 Keys Ferry St.
Mc Donough, GA 30253
(404)954-4300
Ultimate Parent: Nationsbank Corp.

★ 66959 ★ Radio Shack
49 Macon St.
Mc Donough, GA 30253
(404)957-5691
Company Type: Division. Ultimate Parent:
Tandy Corp.

Mc Intyre

★ 66960 ★ Engelhard Corp.
Mc Intyre, GA 31054
(912)946-7500
Ultimate Parent: Engelhard Corp. SIC:
1455—Kaolin & Ball Clay.

★ 66961 ★ Engelhard Corp.
Daveyville Plant
Hwy. 57
Mc Intyre, GA 31054
Ultimate Parent: Engelhard Corp. SIC:
1455—Kaolin & Ball Clay.

★ 66962 ★ Engelhard Corp.
Edgar Plant
Hwy. 57
Mc Intyre, GA 31054
Ultimate Parent: Engelhard Corp. SIC:
1455—Kaolin & Ball Clay.

★ 66963 ★ Engelhard Corp.
Klondyke Mine
Mt. Carmel Church Rd.
Mc Intyre, GA 31054
Ultimate Parent: Engelhard Corp. SIC:
1455—Kaolin & Ball Clay.

★ 66964 ★ Engelhard Corp.
Mcintyre-Edgars Plant
Hwy. 57
Mc Intyre, GA 31054
Ultimate Parent: Engelhard Corp. SIC:
1455—Kaolin & Ball Clay.

★ 66965 ★ Engelhard Corp.
Toddville Plant
Hwy. 57
Mc Intyre, GA 31054
Ultimate Parent: Engelhard Corp. SIC:
1455—Kaolin & Ball Clay.

Mc Rae

★ 66966 ★ Roper Corp. Outdoor
Power Equipment
Hwy. 23 East
Mc Rae, GA 31055
Ultimate Parent: General Electric. SIC:
3524—Lawn & Garden Equipment.

McDonough

★ 66967 ★ Baxter Healthcare
621 Macon St.
McDonough, GA 30253-3531
(404)957-1211
Officer: Bill Johnson. Ultimate Parent:
Baxter International. SIC: 2326—
Men's/Boys' Work Clothing; 8741—
Management Services.

★ 66968 ★ Kentucky Fried
Chicken
1078 Hwy. 20
Mcdonough, GA
(404)954-9304
Ultimate Parent: Pepsico.

★ 66969 ★ Pizza Hut
1104 Hwy. 20
McDonough, GA
(404)957-4827
Ultimate Parent: Pepsico.

★ 66970 ★ Taco Bell
1025 W. Hwy. 81
Mcdonough, GA
(404)914-9435
Ultimate Parent: Pepsico.

McIntyre

★ 66971 ★ Engelhard Corp.
McIntyre-Toddville Plant
Hwy. 57
McIntyre, GA 31054
Ultimate Parent: Engelhard Corp. SIC:
1455—Kaolin & Ball Clay.

McRae

★ 66972 ★ Golden Peanut Co.
512 Oil Mill Rd.
McRae, GA 31055-1169
(912)686-6541
Officer: Gerald Lann. Ultimate Parent:
Archer Daniels Midland Co. SIC: 5159—
Farm-Product Raw Materials Nec.

Meldrim

★ 66973 ★ Union Camp Corp.
Sawmill Div.
Old River Rd.
Meldrim, GA 31318
(912)748-7310
Company Type: Division. Officer: Terry
Bishop, Plant Manager. Ultimate Parent:
Union Camp Corp. SIC: 2421—Sawmills &
Planing Mills—General.

Milledgeville

★ 66974 ★ Drinnon Inc.
1 Union-Recorder Plz.
Milledgeville, GA 31061
(912)452-0567
Company Type: Division. Ultimate Parent:
Knight-Ridder. SIC: 2711—Newspapers;
2752—Commercial Printing—Lithographic.

★ 66975 ★ **First Federal S & L**
100 E. Green St.
Milledgeville, GA 31061-3410
(912)453-3411
Company Type: Headquarters. **Officer:** Al
Baggarly. **Ultimate Parent:** Bancorp Hawaii.
SIC: 6035—Federal Savings Institutions;
6021—National Commercial Banks; 6162—
Mortgage Bankers & Correspondents.

★ 66976 ★ **Grumman**
Aircraft Systems Div.
90 Hwy. 22 W.
Milledgeville, GA 31061-9699
Company Type: Division. **Ultimate Parent:**
Grumman. **SIC:** 3728—Aircraft Parts &
Equipment Nec.

★ 66977 ★ **Grumman**
Aircraft Systems Div.
Hwy. 22 W.
Milledgeville, GA 31061
Company Type: Division. **Ultimate Parent:**
Grumman. **SIC:** 3728—Aircraft Parts &
Equipment Nec.

★ 66978 ★ **Grumman Aerospace
& Electronics**
90 Hwy. 22 W.
Milledgeville, GA 31061-9699
Ultimate Parent: Grumman. **SIC:** 3728—
Aircraft Parts & Equipment Nec.

★ 66979 ★ **Hertz Rent-A-Car**
Hatcher Sq.
Milledgeville, GA 31061
(912)453-3200
Ultimate Parent: Hertz. **SIC:** 7514—
Passenger Car Rental.

★ 66980 ★ **Kentucky Fried
Chicken**
S Elbert
Milledgeville, GA 31061
(912)452-3720
Ultimate Parent: Pepsico. **SIC:** 5812—
Eating Places.

★ 66981 ★ **Piggly Wiggly**
441 N
Milledgeville, GA 31061
(912)453-3406
Ultimate Parent: Bruno's. **SIC:** 5411—
Grocery Stores.

★ 66982 ★ **Piggly Wiggly**
121 N. Wilkinson St.
Milledgeville, GA 31061
(912)452-1114
Ultimate Parent: Bruno's. **SIC:** 5411—
Grocery Stores.

★ 66983 ★ **Piggly Wiggly
Southern Inc.**
121 N. Wilkinson St.
Milledgeville, GA 31061
(912)452-1114
Ultimate Parent: Bruno's. **SIC:** 5411—
Grocery Stores.

★ 66984 ★ **Radio Shack**
2485 N. Columbia St.
Milledgeville, GA 31061
(912)453-8667
Company Type: Division. **Ultimate Parent:**
Tandy Corp. **SIC:** 5734—Computer &
Software Stores.

★ 66985 ★ **Union Recorder**
1 Union Recorder Plz.
Milledgeville, GA 31061
(912)452-0567
Ultimate Parent: Knight-Ridder. **SIC:**
7313—Radio, T.V. & Publisher
Representatives.

★ 66986 ★ **Waldenbooks**
Hatcher Sq.
Milledgeville, GA 31061
(912)452-5600
Ultimate Parent: K-Mart. **SIC:** 5942—Book
Stores.

Millendgeville

★ 66987 ★ **Shaw Industries Co.**
901 S. Wayne St.
Millendgeville, GA 31061
(912)453-3448
Officer: Eddie Middlebrooks, Manager.
Ultimate Parent: Shaw Industries, Inc. **SIC:**
2281—Yarn Spinning Mills; 2399—
Fabricated Textile Products Nec.

Monroe

★ 66988 ★ **Athens First Bank &
Trust**
202 S. Madison Ave.
Monroe, GA 30655-1612
(706)267-7564
Company Type: Subsidiary. **Location
Type:** Branch office. **Officer:** Marianne
Dietzel. **Ultimate Parent:** Sysco. **SIC:**
6021—National Commercial Banks.

★ 66989 ★ **Duck Head Apparel
Co.**
Atlanta Hwy.
Monroe, GA 30655
(404)267-2192
Officer: David Hill, Manager. **Ultimate
Parent:** Delta Woodside Industries. **SIC:**
2311—Men's/Boys' Suits & Coats; 2325—
Men's/Boys' Trousers & Slacks.

★ 66990 ★ **Duck Head Apparel
Co.**
Henson Dr.
Monroe, GA 30655
(404)267-6581
Officer: Bobby Weatherford, Manager.
Ultimate Parent: Delta Woodside
Industries. **SIC:** 2311—Men's/Boys' Suits &
Coats; 2325—Men's/Boys' Trousers &
Slacks; 2329—Men's/Boys' Clothing Nec.

★ 66991 ★ **Kentucky Fried
Chicken**
110 W. Spring St.
Monroe, GA 30655
(404)267-8933
Ultimate Parent: Pepsico. **SIC:** 5812—
Eating Places.

★ 66992 ★ **National Bank of
Walton County**
140 E. Washington St.
Monroe, GA 30655-1618
(706)267-6511 **Fax:** (706)267-3046
Location Type: Branch office. **Officer:** J.
Keith Caudell, President & CEO. **Ultimate
Parent:** Synovus Financial Corp. **SIC:**
6021—National Commercial Banks.

★ 66993 ★ **National Bank of
Walton County**
PO Box 728
Monroe, GA 30655-0728
Location Type: Branch office. **Ultimate
Parent:** Synovus Financial Corp. **SIC:**
6021—National Commercial Banks.

★ 66994 ★ **Universal Rundle
Corp.**
Vine St.
Monroe, GA 30655
(404)267-4591
Officer: Robert R. Rowlands, Vice
President. **Ultimate Parent:** Nortek. **SIC:**
3261—Vitreous Plumbing Fixtures.

★ 66995 ★ **Universal-Rundle
Corp.**
PO Box 828 Vine St.
Monroe, GA 30655
Ultimate Parent: Nortek. **SIC:** 3261—
Vitreous Plumbing Fixtures.

Montezuma

★ 66996 ★ **American Cyanamid
Co.**
Hwy. 49
Montezuma, GA 31063
(912)472-7581
Location Type: Branch office. **Ultimate
Parent:** American Cyanamid Co. **SIC:**
1499—Miscellaneous Nonmetallic Minerals.

Monticello

★ 66997 ★ **Bank South**
208 E. Green St.
Monticello, GA 31064-1010
(706)468-8801
Location Type: Branch office. **Officer:**
Thurman L. Willis Jr. **Ultimate Parent:** Bank
South Corp. **SIC:** 6021—National
Commercial Banks; 6022—State
Commercial Banks; 6141—Personal Credit
Institutions; 6162—Mortgage Bankers &
Correspondents.

★ 66998 ★ **Bank South, NA**
208 E. Green St.
Monticello, GA 31064
(706)468-8801
Company Type: Subsidiary. **Location
Type:** Branch office. **Officer:** Lynda Sue
McMichael, Manager. **Ultimate Parent:**
Bank South Corp. **SIC:** 6021—National
Commercial Banks.

★ 66999 ★ **Bank South NA/
Jasper**
208 Green St.
Monticello, GA 31064
(706)468-8801
Company Type: Subsidiary. **Location
Type:** Branch office. **Officer:** Thurman L.
Willis Jr., President. **Ultimate Parent:** Bank
South Corp. **SIC:** 6021—National
Commercial Banks.

★ 67000 ★ **Georgia-Pacific Corp.
Monticello Panelboard**
Hwy. 83 S.
Monticello, GA 31064
Ultimate Parent: Georgia-Pacific. **SIC:**
2493—Reconstituted Wood Products.

★ 67001 ★ **Georgia-Pacific Corp.
Monticello Pine Plywood**
Hwy. 83 South
Monticello, GA 31064
Ultimate Parent: Georgia-Pacific. **SIC:**
2493—Reconstituted Wood Products.

★ 67002 ★ **Georgia-Pacific Corp.
Monticello Plywood**
Hwy. 83 S.
Monticello, GA 31064
Ultimate Parent: Georgia-Pacific. **SIC:**
2436—Softwood Veneer & Plywood.

Morrow

★ 67003 ★ **Bank South, NA**
1135 Morrow Industrial Blvd.
Morrow, GA 30260
(404)968-6304
Company Type: Subsidiary. **Location
Type:** Branch office. **Officer:** Brenda
Kremple, Manager. **Ultimate Parent:** Bank
South Corp. **SIC:** 6021—National
Commercial Banks.

★ 67004 ★ **Bank South NA Lake
Harbin**
2397 Lake Harbin Rd.
Morrow, GA 30260
(404)968-6300
Company Type: Subsidiary. **Location
Type:** Branch office. **Officer:** Jane Kinney,
Branch Mgr. **Ultimate Parent:** Bank South
Corp. **SIC:** 6021—National Commercial
Banks.

★ 67005 ★ **Bristol Myers Squibb
Co.**
1700 Mount Zion Rd.
Morrow, GA 30260-3014
(404)961-0560
Ultimate Parent: Bristol-Myers Squibb. **SIC:**
5122—Drugs, Proprietaries & Sundries.

★ 67006 ★ **Circuit City**
1241 Morrow Industrial Bl
Morrow, GA 30260
(404)968-3959
Ultimate Parent: Circuit City Stores.

★ 67007 ★ **Ecco Inc.**
1324 Southern Rd.
Morrow, GA 30260
(404)961-7570
Ultimate Parent: Itel.

★ 67008 ★ **Express**
1000 Southlake Mall
Morrow, GA 30260
(404)960-9419
Ultimate Parent: Limited.

★ 67009 ★ **Fairfield Inn by
Marriott**
1599 Adamson Pkwy.
Morrow, GA
(404)961-6044
Ultimate Parent: Marriott International.

★ 67010 ★ **Foot Action USA**
1000 Southlake Mall
Morrow, GA 30260
(404)961-4699
Ultimate Parent: Melville.

★ 67011 ★ **The Gap**
Southlake Mall
Morrow, GA 30260
(404)961-4838
Ultimate Parent: GAP.

★ 67012 ★ **Gap Stores**
Southlake Mall
Morrow, GA 30260
(404)961-4838
Ultimate Parent: GAP.

★ 67013 ★ **Hit or Miss**
1120 Morrow Industrial Blvd.
Morrow, GA 30260
(404)961-4502
Ultimate Parent: TJX.

★ 67014 ★ **Jiffy Lube Lake City**
5150 Jonesboro Rd.
Morrow, GA 30260
(404)366-5395
Ultimate Parent: Pennzoil.

★ 67015 ★ **Kay-Bee Toy & Hobby
Shop Inc.**
1000 Southlake Mall
Morrow, GA 30260
(404)968-1516
Ultimate Parent: Melville.

★ 67016 ★ **Kelly Springfield Tire
Co.**
6878 Kelly Ave.
Morrow, GA 30260
(404)961-7714
Ultimate Parent: Goodyear Tire & Rubber.

★ 67017 ★ **Kelly Springfield Tire
Co. the**
1310 Citizens Pkwy
Morrow, GA 30260
(404)968-6887
Ultimate Parent: Goodyear Tire & Rubber.

★ 67018 ★ **Kentucky Fried
Chicken**
1493 Mt Zion Rd.
Morrow, GA 30260
(404)968-5621
Ultimate Parent: Pepsico.

★ 67019 ★ **Kroger Co. the Retail
Stores**
5226 Jonesboro Rd.
Morrow, GA 30260
(404)363-9360
Ultimate Parent: Kroger.

★ 67020 ★ **Kroger Pharmacies**
5226 Jonesboro Rd.
Morrow, GA 30260
(404)363-0080
Ultimate Parent: Kroger.

★ 67021 ★ **Lane Bryant**
Southlake Mall
Morrow, GA 30260
(404)968-8700
Ultimate Parent: Limited.

★ 67022 ★ **Lerner Shop**
Southlake Mall
Morrow, GA 30260
(404)961-4692
Ultimate Parent: Limited.

★ 67023 ★ **The Limited**
Southlake Mall
Morrow, GA
(404)961-4828
Ultimate Parent: Limited.

★ 67024 ★ **Linens 'n Things
Southlake/She**
1353 Morrow Industrial Blvd.
Morrow, GA 30260
(404)968-4850
Ultimate Parent: Melville.

★ 67025 ★ **Macy's**
Morrow, GA 30260
(404)961-3995
Company Type: Branch. **Ultimate Parent:**
R. H. Macy. **SIC:** 5311—Department Stores.

★ 67026 ★ **Marshalls**
1096 Morrow Industrial Blvd.
Morrow, GA 30260
(404)961-0612
Ultimate Parent: Melville.

★ 67027 ★ Mary Kay Cosemtics
Indep Sales
1631 Oxford Dr.
Morrow, GA 30260
(404)968-0390
Ultimate Parent: Mary Kay Cosmetics.

★ 67028 ★ McDonald's
Restaurants
5192 Jonesboro Rd.
Morrow, GA 30260
(404)361-0567
Ultimate Parent: McDonald's.

★ 67029 ★ Nationsbank Acct
Activity Inf
Southlake Branch 120
Morrow, GA
(404)523-0900
Ultimate Parent: Nationsbank Corp.

★ 67030 ★ Nationsbank Offices
Atlanta Ar
Southlake Branch 120
Morrow, GA
(404)968-2000
Ultimate Parent: Nationsbank Corp.

★ 67031 ★ Nutrasweet Co.
1491 Mt Zion Rd.
Morrow, GA 30260
(404)968-1632
Ultimate Parent: Monsanto.

★ 67032 ★ Payless Shoesource
Southlake Mall
Morrow, GA
(404)961-7674
Ultimate Parent: May Department Stores.

★ 67033 ★ Petite Sophisticate
2434 Southlake Mall
Morrow, GA 30260
(404)960-8969
Ultimate Parent: United States Shoe.

★ 67034 ★ Pizza Hut
6671 S. Main St.
Morrow, GA 30260
(404)961-6200
Ultimate Parent: Pepsico.

★ 67035 ★ Pizza Hut
1201 Southlake Mall
Morrow, GA 30260
(404)968-4007
Ultimate Parent: Pepsico.

★ 67036 ★ Pizza Hut
5707 Jonesboro Rd.
Morrow, GA 30260
(404)968-6644
Ultimate Parent: Pepsico.

★ 67037 ★ Price Pfister, Inc.
1161 Commerce Rd.
Morrow, GA 30260
(404)961-1600
Ultimate Parent: Black & Decker Corp.

★ 67038 ★ Radio Shack
1106 Southlake Mall
Morrow, GA 30260
(404)961-1647
Company Type: Division. Ultimate Parent:
Tandy Corp.

★ 67039 ★ Radio Shack
1106 Southlake Mall
Morrow, GA 30260
(404)961-1540
Company Type: Division. Ultimate Parent:
Tandy Corp.

★ 67040 ★ Ryder Truck Rental
5480 Jonesboro Rd.
Morrow, GA 30260
(404)361-3076
Ultimate Parent: Ryder System.

★ 67041 ★ Ryder Truck Rental
7180 Jonesboro Rd.
Morrow, GA 30260
(404)968-8920
Ultimate Parent: Ryder System.

★ 67042 ★ Ryder Truck Rental
Morrow Industrial Bl
Morrow, GA
(404)968-8920
Ultimate Parent: Ryder System.

★ 67043 ★ Service Merchandise
1400 Morrow Industrial Bl
Morrow, GA 30260
(404)961-6020
Ultimate Parent: Service Merchandise Co.,
Inc.

★ 67044 ★ Sherwin-Williams Co.
6795 S. Main St.
Morrow, GA 30260
(404)961-7780
Officer: Dilip R. Tamhane, Manager.
Ultimate Parent: Sherwin-Williams Co. SIC:
2841—Soap & Other Detergents; 2851—
Paints & Allied Products.

★ 67045 ★ Sports Authority
1360 Morrow Industrial Bl
Morrow, GA 30260
(404)968-8787
Ultimate Parent: K-Mart.

★ 67046 ★ Structure
Southlake Mall
Morrow, GA
(404)961-2851
Ultimate Parent: Limited.

★ 67047 ★ T J Maxx
1536 Southlake Pkwy
Morrow, GA 30260
(404)961-5281
Ultimate Parent: TJX.

★ 67048 ★ Taco Bell
6259 Jonesboro Rd.
Morrow, GA 30260
(404)968-4455
Ultimate Parent: Pepsico.

★ 67049 ★ Texaco
6655 Jonesboro Rd.
Morrow, GA 30260
(404)968-0516
Ultimate Parent: Texaco.

★ 67050 ★ Thrift Drug
1361 Southern Rd.
Morrow, GA 30260
(404)961-7541
Ultimate Parent: J.C. Penney.

★ 67051 ★ Toys R US
1496 Mount Zion Rd.
Morrow, GA 30260
(404)961-1331
Ultimate Parent: Toys "R" US.

★ 67052 ★ Waldenbooks
Southlake Mall
Morrow, GA
(404)961-6499
Ultimate Parent: K-Mart.

Mouetrie

★ 67053 ★ Universal Forest
Products, Inc.
Industrial Pk.
Mouetrie, GA 31768
(912)985-4009
Officer: James Ward, President. Ultimate
Parent: Universal Forest Products. SIC:
2421—Sawmills & Planing Mills—General;
2435—Hardwood Veneer & Plywood;
2439—Structural Wood Members Nec.

Moultrie

★ 67054 ★ Hertz Rent-A-Car
201 S. Main St.
Moultrie, GA 31768
(912)985-6994
Ultimate Parent: Hertz. SIC: 7514—
Passenger Car Rental.

★ 67055 ★ Kmart Store
103 Talmadge Dr.
Moultrie, GA 31768
(912)985-2120
Ultimate Parent: K-Mart. SIC: 5311—
Department Stores.

★ 67056 ★ Miller Brewing Co.
Moultrie
Thomasville Hwy. US 319 S.
Moultrie, GA 31768
Company Type: Division. Ultimate Parent:
Philip Morris. SIC: 3411—Metal Cans.

★ 67057 ★ Miller Brewing Co.
Moultrie Container Plant
Thomasville Hwy. PO Box 1299
Moultrie, GA 31768
Location Type: Plant. Ultimate Parent:
Philip Morris. SIC: 3411—Metal Cans.

★ 67058 ★ Miller Brewing Co.
Moultrie Container Plant
Hwy. 319 S.
Moultrie, GA 31768
Location Type: Plant. Ultimate Parent:
Philip Morris. SIC: 3411—Metal Cans.

★ 67059 ★ Piggly Wiggly
Sunset Plz.
Moultrie, GA 31768
(912)985-7525
Ultimate Parent: Bruno's. SIC: 5411—
Grocery Stores.

★ 67060 ★ Piggly Wiggly
912 1st Ave. SE
Moultrie, GA 31768
(912)985-5513
Ultimate Parent: Bruno's. SIC: 5411—
Grocery Stores.

★ 67061 ★ Piggly Wiggly
2 Ave. SE
Moultrie, GA 31768
(912)985-5513
Ultimate Parent: Bruno's. SIC: 5411—
Grocery Stores.

★ 67062 ★ Pizza Hut
601 1st Ave. SE
Moultrie, GA 31768
(912)985-2513
Ultimate Parent: Pepsico. SIC: 5812—
Eating Places.

★ 67063 ★ Radio Shack
Moultrie Plz.
Moultrie, GA 31768
(912)985-1877
Company Type: Division. Ultimate Parent:
Tandy Corp. SIC: 5065—Electronic Parts &
Equipment Nec.

★ 67064 ★ Ryder Truck Rental
Tifton Hwy.
Moultrie, GA 31768
(912)985-0500
Ultimate Parent: Ryder System. SIC:
7359—Equipment Rental & Leasing Nec.

★ 67065 ★ Universal Forest
Prods Inc.
Industrial
Moultrie, GA 31768
(912)985-4009
Ultimate Parent: Universal Forest Products.
SIC: 2499—Wood Products Nec.

Mreat

★ 67066 ★ Publix Super Markets
1100 Johnson Ferry Rd. NE
Mreat, GA
(404)509-2350
Ultimate Parent: Publix Super Markets.

Nahunta

★ 67067 ★ Greyhound Bus Lines
Nahunta, GA 31553
(912)462-5629
Ultimate Parent: Greyhound Lines Inc. SIC:
4131—Intercity & Rural Bus Transportation.

Nashville

★ 67068 ★ Greyhound Bus
Station
Ray City Hwy.
Nashville, GA 31639
(912)686-3105
Ultimate Parent: Greyhound Lines Inc. SIC:
4131—Intercity & Rural Bus Transportation.

★ 67069 ★ Radio Shack
Alapaha Hwy.
Nashville, GA 31639
(912)686-2867
Company Type: Division. Ultimate Parent:
Tandy Corp. SIC: 5731—Radio, Television
& Electronics Stores.

★ 67070 ★ Rite-Aid Drugs
414 E. Mcpherson Ave.
Nashville, GA 31639
(912)686-9901
Ultimate Parent: Rite Aid. SIC: 5912—Drug
Stores & Proprietary Stores.

Newman

★ 67071 ★ Bank of Coweta
3130 Hwy. 34 E
Newman, GA 30263
(404)254-7722
Location Type: Branch office. Officer: Ann
B. Hand, Vice President. Ultimate Parent:
Synovus Financial Corp. SIC: 6021—
National Commercial Banks.

★ 67072 ★ Bank of Coweta
192 Temple Ave.
Newman, GA 30263-1658
(404)253-9600
Location Type: Branch office. Officer:
Brenda B. Clark, Vice President. Ultimate
Parent: Synovus Financial Corp. SIC:
6021—National Commercial Banks.

★ 67073 ★ Bank of Coweta
36 S. Court Sq.
Newman, GA 30263-2049
(404)253-9400
Location Type: Branch office. Officer: Gail
S. Carnes, Vice President. Ultimate Parent:
Synovus Financial Corp. SIC: 6021—
National Commercial Banks.

★ 67074 ★ Bank of Coweta
48 Bullsboro
Newman, GA 30263-1461
(404)253-2651
Location Type: Branch office. Officer:
Jena G. Parks. Ultimate Parent: Synovus
Financial Corp. SIC: 6021—National
Commercial Banks.

Newnan

★ 67075 ★ Ace Hardware Store
77 Turkey Creek
Newnan, GA 30263
(404)251-0418
Ultimate Parent: Ace Hardware. SIC:
5251—Hardware Stores.

★ 67076 ★ Bank of Coweta
PO Box 1218
Newnan, GA 30264-1218
Location Type: Branch office. Ultimate
Parent: Synovus Financial Corp. SIC:
6021—National Commercial Banks.

★ 67077 ★ Bank of Coweta
110 Jefferson St.
Newnan, GA 30236-1421
(404)253-1340 Fax: (404)254-2309
Location Type: Branch office. Officer: W.
Scott Wilson, President & CEO. Ultimate
Parent: Synovus Financial Corp. SIC:
6021—National Commercial Banks.

★ 67078 ★ Bowater
Southern Div.
525 Greenville St. Ext. Rte. 8
Newnan, GA 30263-9808
(404)253-4969
Officer: James Argroves. Ultimate Parent:
Bowater. SIC: 2611—Pulp Mills; 0811—
Timber Tracts; 6519—Real Property
Lessors Nec.

★ 67079 ★ Bowater Southern
RR 8
Newnan, GA 30263
(404)253-4969
Ultimate Parent: Bowater. SIC: 6519—Real
Property Lessors Nec.

★ 67080 ★ Eckerd Corp.
Eckerd Drug Co.
36 Herring Rd.
Newnan, GA 30265
(404)253-9620
Company Type: Headquarters. Ultimate
Parent: Eckerd Corp. SIC: 5912—Drug
Stores & Proprietary Stores.

★ 67081 ★ First Union National
Bank of Georgia
30 Greenville St.
Newnan, GA 30263-2602
(706)254-6300
Location Type: Branch office. Ultimate
Parent: First Union Corp. SIC: 6021—
National Commercial Banks.

★ 67082 ★ James River Corp.
76 Sprayberry Rd.
Newnan, GA 30264
Ultimate Parent: James River Corp. of
Virginia. **SIC:** 2657—Folding Paperboard
Boxes.

★ 67083 ★ Kroger Co
64 Bullsboro Dr.
Newnan, GA 30263
(404)253-9747
Ultimate Parent: Kroger. **SIC:** 5411—
Grocery Stores.

★ 67084 ★ Pepsi-Cola Bottling
Co.
50 Christopher Ct.
Newnan, GA 30265
(404)253-4564
Officer: Barry Hayes, Manager. **Ultimate
Parent:** Pepsico. **SIC:** 2086—Bottled &
Canned Soft Drinks.

★ 67085 ★ Shaw Industries Inc.
E. Neunan Rd.
Newnan, GA 30263
(404)253-5391
Officer: Rick Daugherty, Manager. **Ultimate
Parent:** Shaw Industries, Inc. **SIC:** 2281—
Yarn Spinning Mills; 2399—Fabricated
Textile Products Nec.

★ 67086 ★ Wheelabrator Corp.
27 Amlajack Blvd.
Newnan, GA 30265
(404)251-6778
Ultimate Parent: WMX Technologies, Inc.
SIC: 5084—Industrial Machinery &
Equipment.

★ 67087 ★ William L. Bonnell Co.
Inc.
25 Bonnell St.
Newnan, GA 30263
Ultimate Parent: Ethyl. **SIC:** 3354—
Aluminum Extruded Products.

Norcross

★ 67088 ★ Ace Hardware
4624 Jimmy Carter Blvd.
Norcross, GA 30093
(404)934-0200
Ultimate Parent: Ace Hardware.

★ 67089 ★ Ace Hardware
3960 Holcomb Bridge Rd. NW
Norcross, GA 30092
(404)448-3390
Ultimate Parent: Ace Hardware.

★ 67090 ★ Advanced Micro
Devices Inc.
15 Technology Pkwy Sout
Norcross, GA
(404)449-7920
Ultimate Parent: Advanced Micro Devices
Inc.

★ 67091 ★ Allegheny Ludlum
Corp.
3300 Holcomb Bridge Rd.
Norcross, GA 30093
(404)292-1230
Officer: Doug Weiss, Manager. **Ultimate
Parent:** Allegheny Ludlum Corp. **SIC:**
3312—Blast Furnaces & Steel Mills.

★ 67092 ★ Allegheny Ludlum
Steel Corp.
3300 Holcomb Bridge Rd. NW
Norcross, GA 30092
(404)448-0130
Ultimate Parent: Allegheny Ludlum Corp.

★ 67093 ★ ALLTEL Supply Inc.
6625 The Corners Pkwy., Ste. 400
Norcross, GA 30092
(404)448-5210
Company Type: Subsidiary. **Ultimate
Parent:** ALLTEL Corp. **SIC:** 3661—
Telephone & Telegraph Apparatus; 5065—
Electronic Parts & Equipment Nec.

★ 67094 ★ Alumax
5655 Peachtree Pky.
Norcross, GA 30092
(404)246-6600
Company Type: Headquarters. **Officer:**
Allen Born, CEO. **Ultimate Parent:** Alumax
Inc. **Sales:** 2347 M. **Fortune 500:** Largest
U.S. Industrial Corporations: Ranking 196.

★ 67095 ★ Alumax Inc.
5655 Peachtree Pky.
Norcross, GA 30092
(404)246-6600 **Fax:** (404)246-6691
Company Type: Headquarters. **Officer:**
Allen Born, Chairman & CEO. **SIC:** 3334—
Primary Aluminum; 3353—Aluminum Sheet,
Plate & Foil; 3354—Aluminum Extruded
Products; 3446—Architectural Metal Work;
3442—Metal Doors, Sash & Trim; 3448—
Prefabricated Metal Buildings; 3444—Sheet
Metal Work; 6719—Holding Companies
Nec. **Employee Count:** 14142. **Sales:** 2347
M. **Fortune 500:** Largest U.S. Industrial
Corporations: Ranking 196.

★ 67096 ★ American Greetings
Corp.
5300 Oakbrook Pky.
Norcross, GA 30093-2249
(404)381-7620
Ultimate Parent: American Greetings. **SIC:**
5112—Stationery & Office Supplies.

★ 67097 ★ AT & T Network
Systems
2000 Northeast Expwy.
Norcross, GA 30071
(404)447-2000
Officer: James Carboy, Manager. **Ultimate
Parent:** AT&T. **SIC:** 3661—Telephone &
Telegraph Apparatus.

★ 67098 ★ At&T
2000 NE Expressway
Norcross, GA 30071
Ultimate Parent: AT&T. **SIC:** 3357—
Nonferrous Wiredrawing & Insulating;
2813—Industrial Gases.

★ 67099 ★ At&T Network
Systems
2000 NE Expressway
Norcross, GA 30071
Ultimate Parent: AT&T. **SIC:** 3357—
Nonferrous Wiredrawing & Insulating;
2813—Industrial Gases.

★ 67100 ★ Atlanta Casualty Co.
3169 Holcomb Ridge Rd.
Norcross, GA 30071
(404)447-8930
Officer: Robert L. Lowe, President.
Ultimate Parent: American Financial. **SIC:**
6331—Fire, Marine & Casualty Insurance.

★ 67101 ★ Bank South, NA
3280 Holcomb Bridge Rd.
Norcross, GA 30071
(404)368-3000
Company Type: Subsidiary. **Location
Type:** Branch office. **Officer:** Jack Regan,
Manager. **Ultimate Parent:** Bank South
Corp. **SIC:** 6021—National Commercial
Banks.

★ 67102 ★ Bank South, NA
5340 Peachtree Industrial Blvd.
Norcross, GA 30071
(404)368-3024
Company Type: Subsidiary. **Location
Type:** Branch office. **Officer:** Tracy Robbins
Causey, Manager. **Ultimate Parent:** Bank
South Corp. **SIC:** 6021—National
Commercial Banks.

★ 67103 ★ Bank South, NA
4995 Jimmy Carter Blvd.
Norcross, GA 30093
(404)564-5940
Company Type: Subsidiary. **Location
Type:** Branch office. **Officer:** Chris Rowell,
Manager. **Ultimate Parent:** Bank South
Corp. **SIC:** 6021—National Commercial
Banks.

★ 67104 ★ Baxter Healthcare
Corp.
6154 Atlantic Blvd.
Norcross, GA 30071-1305
(404)449-6288
Officer: Dave Wietecha. **Ultimate Parent:**
Baxter International. **SIC:** 3842—Surgical
Appliances & Supplies.

★ 67105 ★ BellSouth
Communication Systems
3100 Northwoods Pl.
Norcross, GA 30071-1563
(404)242-1311
Ultimate Parent: BellSouth Corp. **SIC:**
5999—Miscellaneous Retail Stores Nec.

★ 67106 ★ Career Image
Distribution Ctr
5850 Peachtree Industrial
Norcross, GA 30071
(404)242-9551
Ultimate Parent: United States Shoe.

★ 67107 ★ Circuit City
5495 Jimmy Carter Blvd. NW
Norcross, GA 30093
(404)662-0557
Ultimate Parent: Circuit City Stores.

★ 67108 ★ Citgo Petroleum Corp.
5255 Triangle Pky. NW
Norcross, GA 30092
(404)416-9003
Ultimate Parent: Citgo Petroleum.

★ 67109 ★ Courtyard by Marriott
3209 Holcomb Bridge Rd. NW
Norcross, GA 30092
(404)446-3777
Ultimate Parent: Marriott International.

★ 67110 ★ Data General Co.
1626 Jeurgens Ct.
Norcross, GA 30093
(404)441-1923
Company Type: Subsidiary. **Ultimate
Parent:** Data General.

★ 67111 ★ Dow Corning Corp.
Atlanta Plant
4291 Communications Dr.
Norcross, GA 30093-3000
Ultimate Parent: Dow Corning. **SIC:**
2890—Miscellaneous Chemical Products.

★ 67112 ★ Dow Corning Corp.
Norcross Plant
4291 Communications Dr.
Norcross, GA 30093
Ultimate Parent: Dow Corning. **SIC:**
2890—Miscellaneous Chemical Products;
2295—Coated Fabrics—Not Rubberized.

★ 67113 ★ Electronic Data
Systems
3000 Business Park Dr.
Norcross, GA 30071
(404)662-0508
Ultimate Parent: Electronic Data Systems.

★ 67114 ★ Exxon
1995 Indian Trail Rd.
Norcross, GA 30071
(404)446-7962
Ultimate Parent: Exxon.

★ 67115 ★ Fairfield Inn by
Marriott
6650 Bay Cir. NW
Norcross, GA 30071
(404)441-1999
Ultimate Parent: Marriott International.

★ 67116 ★ Federal Paper Board
Co. Inc.
6625 The Corners Pkwy NW
Norcross, GA 30092
(404)449-3695
Ultimate Parent: Federal Paper Board.

★ 67117 ★ First Union National
Bank of Georgia
5405 Jimmy Carter Blvd.
Norcross, GA 30093-1504
(404)242-2850
Location Type: Branch office. **Ultimate
Parent:** First Union Corp. **SIC:** 6021—
National Commercial Banks.

★ 67118 ★ First Union National
Bank of Georgia
5525 Peachtree Pky.
Norcross, GA 30092
(404)242-2840
Location Type: Branch office. **Ultimate
Parent:** First Union Corp. **SIC:** 6021—
National Commercial Banks.

★ 67119 ★ First Union National
Bank of Georgia
6155 S. Buford Hwy.
Norcross, GA 30071-2394
(404)242-2800
Location Type: Branch office. **Ultimate
Parent:** First Union Corp. **SIC:** 6021—
National Commercial Banks.

★ 67120 ★ General Electric Co.
205 Scientific Dr.
Norcross, GA 30092
(404)662-1000
Officer: Dave Sapp, Manager. **Ultimate
Parent:** General Electric. **SIC:** 2821—
Plastics Materials & Resins.

★ 67121 ★ Hamilton Hallmark
5825D Peachtree Corners E
Norcross, GA 30092
Location Type: Branch office. **Ultimate
Parent:** Avnet. **SIC:** 5065—Electronic Parts
& Equipment Nec.

★ 67122 ★ Harris Adacom
3500 Parkway Ln. NW
Norcross, GA 30092
(404)246-4640
Ultimate Parent: Harris.

★ 67123 ★ Hewlett Packard Co.
3607 Parkway Ln. NW
Norcross, GA 30092
(404)446-0359
Ultimate Parent: Hewlett-Packard.

★ 67124 ★ Hewlett-Packard Co.
Sales
3607 Parkway Ln. NW
Norcross, GA 30092
(404)448-1894
Ultimate Parent: Hewlett-Packard.

★ 67125 ★ Inland Materials
Distribution Group Inc.
4400 Peachtree Industrial Blvd.
PO Box 4725
Norcross, GA 30091-4725
(404)368-4311 **Fax:** (404)368-4305
Company Type: Subsidiary. **Officer:**
Robert J. Darnall, Chairman & CEO.
Ultimate Parent: Inland Steel Industries.

★ 67126 ★ ITW Fluid Products
4366 Shockleford Rd.
Norcross, GA 30093
(404)279-7788 **Fax:** (800)952-5823
Company Type: Subsidiary. **Officer:** Larry
Bly, General Manager. **Ultimate Parent:**
Illinois Tool Works.

★ 67127 ★ Jiffy Lube Norcross
2084 Beaver Ruin Rd.
Norcross, GA 30071
(404)662-5399
Ultimate Parent: Pennzoil.

★ 67128 ★ Jiffy Lube Norcross
4861 Jimmy Carter Blvd.
Norcross, GA 30093
(404)921-4267
Ultimate Parent: Pennzoil.

★ 67129 ★ J.M. Huber Corp.
Solem Division
4940 Peachtree Industrial
Norcross, GA 30071
(404)441-1301
Ultimate Parent: J. M. Huber.

★ 67130 ★ J.M. Tull Metals Co.
Inc.
4400 Peachtree Industrial Blvd.
Norcross, GA 30091
(404)368-4311 **Fax:** (404)368-4230
Company Type: Subsidiary. **Officer:**
Edward S. Heys, President. **Ultimate
Parent:** Inland Steel Industries.

★ 67131 ★ Kentucky Fried
Chicken
5220 Jimmy Carter Blvd.
Norcross, GA 30093
(404)448-5270
Ultimate Parent: Pepsico.

★ 67132 ★ Kentucky Fried
Chicken
4025 Holcomb Bridge Rd. NW
Norcross, GA 30092
(404)242-7186
Ultimate Parent: Pepsico.

★ 67133 ★ Kentucky Fried
Chicken Regional
3150 Holcomb Bridge Rd. NW
Norcross, GA 30071
(404)446-8330
Ultimate Parent: Pepsico.

★ 67134 ★   Kmart Stores
4975 Jimmy Carter Blvd.
Norcross, GA 30093
(404)925-0220
Ultimate Parent: K-Mart.

★ 67135 ★   Kmart Stores
Automotive
4975 Jimmy Carter Blvd.
Norcross, GA 30093
(404)925-0225
Ultimate Parent: K-Mart.

★ 67136 ★   Kmart Stores
Pharmacy
4975 Jimmy Carter Blvd.
Norcross, GA 30093
(404)925-4737
Ultimate Parent: K-Mart.

★ 67137 ★   Kroger Co. the Kroger
Pharmacie
6050 Singleton Rd. NW
Norcross, GA
(404)242-3344
Ultimate Parent: Kroger.

★ 67138 ★   Kroger Co. the Retail
Stores
6050 Peachtree Pkwy
Norcross, GA 30092
(404)449-7686
Ultimate Parent: Kroger.

★ 67139 ★   Kroger Co. the Retail
Stores
6050 Singleton Rd. NW
Norcross, GA 30093
(404)242-3340
Ultimate Parent: Kroger.

★ 67140 ★   Kroger Floral Delivery
Center
6050 Peachtree Pkwy NW
Norcross, GA 30092
(404)447-0886
Ultimate Parent: Kroger.

★ 67141 ★   Kroger Pharmacies
6050 Peachtree Pkwy
Norcross, GA 30092
(404)449-1986
Ultimate Parent: Kroger.

★ 67142 ★   Kuppenheimer
Manufacturing Co., Inc.
5555 Oakbrook Pky.
Norcross, GA 30093
(404)449-5877 **Fax:** (404)449-5877
Company Type: Subsidiary. **Officer:** Larry
Levy, President & CEO. **Ultimate Parent:**
Hartmarx.

★ 67143 ★   Land O'lakes Inc.
3091 Governors Lake Dr. NW
Norcross, GA 30071
(404)242-6449
Ultimate Parent: Land O'Lakes.

★ 67144 ★   Macmillan/MacGraw-
Hill
School Division
6510 Jimmy Carter Blvd.
Norcross, GA 30071
(404)448-7997
Ultimate Parent: McGraw-Hill.

★ 67145 ★   Marriott Hotels,
Resorts Suites
475 Technology Pky.
Norcross, GA 30092
(404)263-8558
Ultimate Parent: Marriott International.

★ 67146 ★   Maynard Electronics
6525 The Corners Pkwy NW
Norcross, GA 30092
(404)447-4613
Ultimate Parent: Conner Peripherals Inc.

★ 67147 ★   McDonald's
Restaurants
7070 Jimmy Carter Blvd. NW
Norcross, GA 30092
(404)263-0506
Ultimate Parent: McDonald's.

★ 67148 ★   McDonald's
Restaurants
6615 Mcdonough Dr.
Norcross, GA
(404)449-5359
Ultimate Parent: McDonald's.

★ 67149 ★   McDonald's
Restaurants
1650 Indian Trail-Lilburn
Norcross, GA 30093
(404)564-2161
Ultimate Parent: McDonald's.

★ 67150 ★   McDonald's
Restaurants
4135 Jimmy Carter Blvd.
Norcross, GA 30093
(404)938-1358
Ultimate Parent: McDonald's.

★ 67151 ★   McDonald's
Restaurants
5535 Buford Hwy.
Norcross, GA 30071
(404)441-7634
Ultimate Parent: McDonald's.

★ 67152 ★   Milcare
3607 Parkway Ln. NW
Norcross, GA 30092
(404)263-9672
Ultimate Parent: Herman Miller.

★ 67153 ★   Mobil Chemical Co.
6525 The Corners Pky. NW
Norcross, GA 30092
(404)446-3848
Ultimate Parent: Mobil. **SIC:** 5999—
Miscellaneous Retail Stores Nec.

★ 67154 ★   National
Semiconductor
500 Pinnacle Ct NW
Norcross, GA 30071
(404)903-1800
Ultimate Parent: National Semiconductor
Corp.

★ 67155 ★   Nationsbank Atm
Honor-Cirrus L
1470 Beaver Ruin Rd.
Norcross, GA 30093
(404)279-8980
Ultimate Parent: Nationsbank Corp.

★ 67156 ★   Nationsbank Honor-
Cirrus L Ind
5125 Oakbrook Pkwy
Norcross, GA 30093
(404)564-8300
Ultimate Parent: Nationsbank Corp.

★ 67157 ★   Nationsbank Honor-
Cirrus L Jim
5813 Jimmy Carter Blvd.
Norcross, GA 30071
(404)242-1155
Ultimate Parent: Nationsbank Corp.

★ 67158 ★   Nationsbank Ofcs
Atlanta Area
1470 Beaver Ruin
Norcross, GA 30093
(404)523-0900
Ultimate Parent: Nationsbank Corp.

★ 67159 ★   Nationsbank Offices
Atlanta Area
Jimmy Carter 5813
Norcross, GA 30071
(404)242-1155
Ultimate Parent: Nationsbank Corp.

★ 67160 ★   Nationsbank Offices
Atanta Are
Indian Trail 5125
Norcross, GA
(404)564-8303
Ultimate Parent: Nationsbank Corp.

★ 67161 ★   Nationsbank Offices
Atlanta Ar
Jimmy Carter 5813
Norcross, GA 30071
(404)523-0900
Ultimate Parent: Nationsbank Corp.

★ 67162 ★   Nationsbank Offices
Atlanta Ar
3210 Holcomb Bridge Rd.
Norcross, GA 30092
(404)242-1600
Ultimate Parent: Nationsbank Corp.

★ 67163 ★   Nationsbank Offices
Atlanta Ar
Indian Trl. 5125
Norcross, GA
(404)564-8300
Ultimate Parent: Nationsbank Corp.

★ 67164 ★   New York Life Atlanta
Group Claims Office
Western Group Claims Region
Scott Mitchell Complex
5720 Peachtree Pky., Ste. 310
Norcross, GA 30092
(800)388-4580 **Fax:** (404)840-9068
Officer: Linda Stegall, Group Claims
Director. **Ultimate Parent:** New York Life.

★ 67165 ★   North Riverside
Holding Inc.
50 Technology Pk.
Norcross, GA 30092-2906
(404)446-5556
Company Type: Subsidiary. **Officer:**
Thomas R. Barry, President. **Ultimate
Parent:** Great American Management &
Investment. **SIC:** 6799—Investors Nec;
5013—Motor Vehicle Supplies & New Parts.
Employee Count: 350. **Sales:** 25.7 (est) M.

★ 67166 ★   Pitney Bowes
600 Pinnacle Ct.
Norcross, GA 30071
(404)446-9700
Officer: Jeff Schultz, Manager. **Ultimate
Parent:** Pitney Bowes. **SIC:** 3663—Radio &
T.V. Communications Equipment.

★ 67167 ★   Pizza Hut
5528 Jimmy Carter Blvd. NW
Norcross, GA 30093
(404)246-1300
Ultimate Parent: Pepsico.

★ 67168 ★   Pizza Hut
6045 Peachtree Pkwy NW
Norcross, GA 30092
(404)263-9500
Ultimate Parent: Pepsico.

★ 67169 ★   Plus Mark
5300 Oakbrook Pkwy NW
Norcross, GA 30093
(404)564-2151
Ultimate Parent: American Greetings.

★ 67170 ★   Publix Super Market
1250 Tech Dr. NW
Norcross, GA 30093
(404)717-3150
Ultimate Parent: Publix Super Markets.
SIC: 5122—Drugs, Proprietaries &
Sundries.

★ 67171 ★   Publix Super Markets
1250 Tech Dr. NW
Norcross, GA 30093
(404)921-8521
Ultimate Parent: Publix Super Markets.

★ 67172 ★   Publix Super Markets
1250 Tech Dr. NW
Norcross, GA 30093
(404)717-3150
Ultimate Parent: Publix Super Markets.
SIC: 5122—Drugs, Proprietaries &
Sundries.

★ 67173 ★   Publix Super Markets
1250 Tech Dr. NW
Norcross, GA 30093
(404)717-3154
Ultimate Parent: Publix Super Markets.

★ 67174 ★   Radio Shack
4975 Jimmy Carter Blvd. NW
Norcross, GA 30093
(404)925-1287
Company Type: Division. **Ultimate Parent:**
Tandy Corp.

★ 67175 ★   Russell Corp.
5335 Triangle Pkwy NW
Norcross, GA 30092
(404)242-0914
Ultimate Parent: Russell.

★ 67176 ★   Ryder Truck Rental
3330 Peachtree Corners Ci
Norcross, GA 30092
(404)729-8979
Ultimate Parent: Ryder System.

★ 67177 ★   Ryder Truck Rental
5493 E. Goshen Springs Rd.
Norcross, GA
(404)717-9172
Ultimate Parent: Ryder System.

★ 67178 ★   Ryder Truck Rental
5010 Jimmy Carter Blvd. NW
Norcross, GA 30093
(404)447-9897
Ultimate Parent: Ryder System.

★ 67179 ★   Ryder Truck Rental
5374 Goshen Springs Rd.
Norcross, GA 30093
(404)923-2733
Ultimate Parent: Ryder System.

★ 67180 ★   Schuller International
Inc/Manville Fib
3300 Holcomb Bridge Rd.
Norcross, GA 30092
(404)449-3300
Ultimate Parent: Manville Corp.

★ 67181 ★   Scientific-Atla Inc.
Network Sy
4356 Communications Dr.
Norcross, GA 30093
(404)903-6001
Ultimate Parent: Scientific-Atlanta, Inc.

★ 67182 ★   Scientific-Atlanta Inc.
Nwtwork
4356 Communications Dr.
Norcross, GA 30093
(404)903-5000
Ultimate Parent: Scientific-Atlanta, Inc.

★ 67183 ★   Simmonds Precision
Products Su
5696 Peachtree Pkwy NW
Norcross, GA 30092
(404)242-2670
Ultimate Parent: Hercules.

★ 67184 ★   Southern Copy
Machines, Inc.
6971 Peachtree Industrial Blvd.
Norcross, GA 30092
(404)448-0770
Officer: William Currin, President. **Ultimate
Parent:** Alco Standard Corp.

★ 67185 ★   Southern Copy
Machines, Inc.
6971 Peachtree Industrial Blvd.
Norcross, GA 30092
(404)448-0770 **Fax:** (404)447-0716
Company Type: Division. **Officer:** William
F. Curran, President. **Ultimate Parent:** Alco
Standard Corp. **SIC:** 5044—Office
Equipment; 5046—Commercial Equipment
Nec.

★ 67186 ★   Standard Cap & Seal
Inc.
3150 Clinton Ct
Norcross, GA 30071
(404)476-9088
Ultimate Parent: Sonoco Products.

★ 67187 ★   Standard Office
Systems, Inc.
1880 Beaver Ridge Cir. NW, No. A
Norcross, GA 30071
(404)449-9106
Officer: Lowell Fox, Owner. **Ultimate
Parent:** Alco Standard Corp. **SIC:** 3663—
Radio & T.V. Communications Equipment.

★ 67188 ★   Standard Office
Systems, Inc.
1880 Beaver Ridge Circle NW, No. A
Norcross, GA 30071
(404)449-9106
Officer: Lowell Fox, Owner. **Ultimate
Parent:** Alco Standard Corp. **SIC:** 3663—
Radio & T.V. Communications Equipment.

★ 67189 ★   Stockholder Systems
Inc.
4411 E. Jones Bridge Rd. NW
Norcross, GA 30092
(404)441-3387
Ultimate Parent: Nynex.

★ 67190 ★   Superior Coffee &
Foods
6680-F Jones Mill Ct
Norcross, GA 30092
(404)446-6645
Ultimate Parent: Sara Lee Corp.

★ 67191 ★   Taco Bell
5518 Jimmy Carter Blvd. NW
Norcross, GA 30093
(404)446-7744
Ultimate Parent: Pepsico.

★ 67192 ★ **Taco Bell**
6385 Peachtree Industrial
Norcross, GA 30092
(404)448-6718
Ultimate Parent: Pepsico.

★ 67193 ★ **Taco Bell**
1720 Indian Trail Rd.
Norcross, GA 30093
(404)923-5830
Ultimate Parent: Pepsico.

★ 67194 ★ **Tec Systems**
4295 Steve Reynolds Blvd.
Norcross, GA 30093
(404)923-6393
Ultimate Parent: W. R. Grace.

★ 67195 ★ **Tektronix Inc.**
650 Engineering Dr.
Norcross, GA 30092
(404)449-4770
Ultimate Parent: Tektronix, Inc.

★ 67196 ★ **Texaco**
6367 Jimmy Carter Blvd.
Norcross, GA 30071
(404)449-1188
Ultimate Parent: Texaco.

★ 67197 ★ **Texaco**
5500 Spalding Dr.
Norcross, GA 30092
(404)263-7657
Ultimate Parent: Texaco.

★ 67198 ★ **Texaco**
4125 Jimmy Carter Blvd.
Norcross, GA 30093
(404)496-9993
Ultimate Parent: Texaco.

★ 67199 ★ **Texaco**
5476 Jimmy Carter Blvd.
Norcross, GA 30093
(404)242-8674
Ultimate Parent: Texaco.

★ 67200 ★ **Texaco**
7800 Holcomb Bridge Rd.
Norcross, GA 30092
(404)441-3597
Ultimate Parent: Texaco.

★ 67201 ★ **Texaco**
1745 Indian Trail
Norcross, GA 30093
(404)381-9973
Ultimate Parent: Texaco.

★ 67202 ★ **3M Scotchtint Window Film**
6611 Bay Cir.
Norcross, GA 30071-1211
(404)662-5000
Ultimate Parent: Minnesota Mining & Mfg.
SIC: 5169—Chemicals & Allied Products Nec.

★ 67203 ★ **Time Electronics**
4045 Wetherburn Way
Norcross, GA 30071
(404)368-0969
Location Type: Branch office. **Ultimate Parent:** Avnet. **SIC:** 5065—Electronic Parts & Equipment Nec.

★ 67204 ★ **Treadco Inc.**
6517 Warren Dr. NE
Norcross, GA 30093
(404)447-0846
Ultimate Parent: Arkansas Best.

★ 67205 ★ **Trugreen Chemlawn**
4575 S. Old Peachtree Rd.
Norcross, GA 30071
(404)448-2013
Ultimate Parent: ServiceMaster Co.

★ 67206 ★ **UST Inc.**
5300 Oakbrook Pkwy NW
Norcross, GA 30093
(404)381-6000
Ultimate Parent: UST Inc.

★ 67207 ★ **Vanguard Financial Services Inc.**
1770 Indian Trail-Liburn
Norcross, GA 30093
(404)381-4900
Ultimate Parent: Old Kent Financial Corp.

★ 67208 ★ **Varian Associates, Inc.**
3000 Northwoods Pky. NW
Norcross, GA 30071
(404)441-3408
Ultimate Parent: Varian Associates, Inc.

★ 67209 ★ **Vulcan Materials Co.**
1707 Beaver Ruin Rd.
Norcross, GA 30093
(404)923-2532
Officer: Ricky Vickery, Manager. **Ultimate Parent:** Vulcan Materials Co. **SIC:** 3281—Cut Stone & Stone Products.

★ 67210 ★ **W. W. Grainger Inc.**
Grainger Division
2105 Nancy Hanks Dr.
Norcross, GA 30071
(404)263-7150
Ultimate Parent: W. W. Grainger.

★ 67211 ★ **Walker Manufacturing Co.**
5672 Peachtree Pkwy Wn
Norcross, GA
(404)449-7014
Ultimate Parent: Tenneco Inc.

★ 67212 ★ **Wells Fargo Guard Services Administration**
6060 McDonough Dr. NW
Norcross, GA 30093
(404)441-1050
Ultimate Parent: Borg Warner Automotive.

★ 67213 ★ **York International Corp.**
1750 Corporate Dr.
Norcross, GA 30093
(404)925-0409
Officer: Jim Hyde, Manager. **Ultimate Parent:** York International Corp. **SIC:** 3585—Refrigeration & Heating Equipment.

★ 67214 ★ **Zeno Systems of Georgia Inc.**
2815 Colonnades Ct.
Norcross, GA 30071-1588
(404)446-7100
Officer: James P. McCarter, President.
Ultimate Parent: Alco Standard Corp. **SIC:** 5999—Miscellaneous Retail Stores Nec.
Employee Count: 62.

Nroc

★ 67215 ★ **Ryder Truck Rental**
Jimmy Carter Blvd&I-
Nroc, GA
(404)246-1784
Ultimate Parent: Ryder System.

Oakwood

★ 67216 ★ **Radio Shack**
College Sq.
Oakwood, GA 30566
(404)536-4772
Company Type: Division. **Ultimate Parent:** Tandy Corp. **SIC:** 5731—Radio, Television & Electronics Stores.

Oconee

★ 67217 ★ **Engelhard Corp. Gardner Plant**
Kaolin Rd.
Oconee, GA 31067
Ultimate Parent: Engelhard Corp. **SIC:** 1455—Kaolin & Ball Clay.

Oglethorpe

★ 67218 ★ **Buckeye Cellulose Corp.**
Old Stage Coach Rd.
Oglethorpe, GA 31068
Ultimate Parent: Procter & Gamble Co.
SIC: 2611—Pulp Mills.

★ 67219 ★ **Procter & Gamble Cellulose Co.**
Old Stage Coach Rd.
Oglethorpe, GA 31068
Ultimate Parent: Procter & Gamble Co.
SIC: 2611—Pulp Mills.

★ 67220 ★ **Weyerhaeuser**
Old Stagecoach Rd.
Oglethorpe, GA 31068
(912)472-2527
Officer: John B. Crowe, Manager. **Ultimate Parent:** Weyerhaeuser Co. **SIC:** 2611—Pulp Mills; 2621—Paper Mills; 2679—Converted Paper Products Nec.

★ 67221 ★ **Weyerhaeuser Co.**
Old Stagecoach Rd.
Oglethorpe, GA 31068
Ultimate Parent: Weyerhaeuser Co. **SIC:** 2611—Pulp Mills.

Palmetto

★ 67222 ★ **Bank South, NA**
509 Toombs St.
Palmetto, GA 30268-1214
(404)463-4546
Company Type: Subsidiary. **Location Type:** Branch office. **Ultimate Parent:** Bank South Corp. **SIC:** 6021—National Commercial Banks.

Peachtree

★ 67223 ★ **Ace Hardware Workbench**
2365 Peachtree Rd. NE
Peachtree, GA
(404)841-9525
Ultimate Parent: Ace Hardware.

★ 67224 ★ **Banana Republic Regional Office**
5775 Peachtree Dunwoody Rd.
Peachtree, GA
(404)252-1758
Ultimate Parent: GAP.

★ 67225 ★ **Beckman Instruments Inc.**
3353 Peachtree Rd. NE
Peachtree, GA
(404)364-3474
Ultimate Parent: Beckman Instruments.

★ 67226 ★ **Capezio**
3500 Peachtree Rd. NE
Peachtree, GA
(404)237-9423
Ultimate Parent: United States Shoe.

★ 67227 ★ **Casual Corner**
210 Ptree St. NW
Peachtree, GA
(404)588-9929
Ultimate Parent: United States Shoe.

★ 67228 ★ **Charles Schwab & Co. Inc.**
3399 Peachtree Rd. NE
Peachtree, GA
(404)231-1114
Ultimate Parent: Charles Schwab Corp.

★ 67229 ★ **Coast to Coast Inc. Collision R**
3232 Peachtree Rd. NE
Peachtree, GA
(404)239-0163
Ultimate Parent: Servistar Corp.

★ 67230 ★ **Colonial Pipeline Co. Main**
Dekalb-Peachtree Air
Peachtree, GA
(404)457-8319
Ultimate Parent: Colonial Pipeline.

★ 67231 ★ **Courtyard by Marriott**
6250 Peachtree Dunwoody R
Peachtree, GA
(404)393-1000
Ultimate Parent: Marriott International.

★ 67232 ★ **Materials Group**
Fasson Roll Materials Div.
316 Hwy. 74 S.
Peachtree, GA 30269
(404)487-7516
Company Type: Division. **Ultimate Parent:** Avery Dennison Corp. **SIC:** 2671—Paper Coated & Laminated—Packaging.

Peachtree Cit

★ 67233 ★ **Ace Hardware**
2006 W. Hwy. 54
Peachtree Cit, GA 30269
(404)487-7533
Ultimate Parent: Ace Hardware.

★ 67234 ★ **Kentucky Fried Chicken**
494 Crosstown Dr.
Peachtree Cit, GA 30269
(404)631-3786
Ultimate Parent: Pepsico.

★ 67235 ★ **Kmart Stores**
400 Crosstown Rd.
Peachtree Cit, GA 30269
(404)487-2295
Ultimate Parent: K-Mart.

★ 67236 ★ **Kmart Stores Pharmacy**
400 Crosstown Rd.
Peachtree Cit, GA 30269
(404)487-2095
Ultimate Parent: K-Mart.

★ 67237 ★ **Kroger Pharmacies**
564 Crosstown Rd.
Peachtree Cit, GA 30269
(404)487-3749
Ultimate Parent: Kroger.

★ 67238 ★ **McDonald's Restaurant**
1105 Crosstown Ct
Peachtree Cit, GA
(404)631-1463
Ultimate Parent: McDonald's.

★ 67239 ★ **McDonald's Restaurants**
709 Crossings East
Peachtree Cit, GA 30269
(404)631-0831
Ultimate Parent: McDonald's.

★ 67240 ★ **Taco Bell**
1140 Crosstown Dr.
Peachtree Cit, GA
(404)631-9193
Ultimate Parent: Pepsico.

★ 67241 ★ **Telenex Corp.**
101 Retreat Pt
Peachtree Cit, GA 30269
(404)631-4131
Ultimate Parent: General Signal.

Peachtree City

★ 67242 ★ **Avery Dennison**
Fasson Roll Div.
316 Hwy. 74 S.
Peachtree City, GA 30269-2097
Company Type: Division. **Ultimate Parent:** Avery Dennison Corp. **SIC:** 2672—Coated & Laminated Paper Nec.

★ 67243 ★ **Georgia-Pacific Resins Inc.**
411 Dividend Dr.
Peachtree City, GA 30269
Ultimate Parent: Georgia-Pacific. **SIC:** 2821—Plastics Materials & Resins.

★ 67244 ★ **Kroger Co. the Retail Stores**
564 Crosstown Dr.
Peachtree City, GA 30269
(404)487-3602
Ultimate Parent: Kroger.

★ 67245 ★ **Mini Mart 54**
314 Hwy. 54
Peachtree City, GA 30269
(404)487-5748
Ultimate Parent: Kroger.

★ 67246 ★ **Nationsbank Ofcs Atlanta Area**
Braelinn Village 496
Peachtree City, GA
(404)631-3225
Ultimate Parent: Nationsbank Corp.

★ 67247 ★ **Nationsbank Offices Atlanta Ar**
Glenloch 2338 Hwy. 54
Peachtree City, GA
(404)969-0550
Ultimate Parent: Nationsbank Corp.

★ 67248 ★ Nationsbank Saturday
Banking O
2338 Hwy. 54 E. P
Peachtree City, GA
(404)631-3216
Ultimate Parent: Nationsbank Corp.

★ 67249 ★ NCR Corp.
200 Hwy. 74 S
Peachtree City, GA 30269
(404)487-7000
Officer: Robert Bertelsbeck, Manager.
Ultimate Parent: AT&T. SIC: 2761—
Manifold Business Forms.

★ 67250 ★ Valvoline Instant Oil
Change
949 Crosstown Dr.
Peachtree City, GA 30269
(404)487-6420
Ultimate Parent: Ashland Oil.

★ 67251 ★ Nationsbank Honor-
Cirrus L Gle
666 Hwy. 54 E
Peachtree Cty, GA
(404)631-3216
Ultimate Parent: Nationsbank Corp.

★ 67252 ★ Pizza Hut
1110 Crosstown Ct
Peachtree City, GA
(404)487-4700
Ultimate Parent: Pepsico.

★ 67253 ★ Ryder Truck Rental
Downtown
Peachtrr City, GA
(404)968-8920
Ultimate Parent: Ryder System.

Pearson

★ 67254 ★ Fleetwood Homes of
Ga. Inc. No. 54
Hwy. 82
Pearson, GA 31642
Ultimate Parent: Fleetwood Enterprises,
Inc. SIC: 3711—Motor Vehicles & Car
Bodies.

★ 67255 ★ Georgia-Pacific Corp.
Pearson Sawmill
Hwy. 82
Pearson, GA 31642
Ultimate Parent: Georgia-Pacific. SIC:
2491—Wood Preserving.

★ 67256 ★ Trailways Bus Station
Pearson, GA 31642
(912)422-3957
Ultimate Parent: Greyhound Lines Inc. SIC:
4131—Intercity & Rural Bus Transportation.

Pelham

★ 67257 ★ Piggly Wiggly
Curry St.
Pelham, GA 31779
(912)294-8656
Ultimate Parent: Bruno's. SIC: 5411—
Grocery Stores.

★ 67258 ★ Trust Co. Bank of
South Georgia, N.A.
108 Hand Ave.
Pelham, GA 31779-1244
(912)294-2691
Officer: Ira J. Cook, Manager. Ultimate
Parent: Suntrust Banks. SIC: 6021—
National Commercial Banks.

Perry

★ 67259 ★ Bank South Houston
Co.
1005 Northside Dr.
Perry, GA 31069-3345
(912)987-2405
Location Type: Branch office. Officer:
Gary Bishop. Ultimate Parent: Bank South
Corp. SIC: 6021—National Commercial
Banks; 6022—State Commercial Banks;
6141—Personal Credit Institutions.

★ 67260 ★ Bank South, NA
1005 Northside Dr.
Perry, GA 31069-3345
(912)987-2405
Company Type: Subsidiary. Location
Type: Branch office. Officer: Andy Flowers,
Manager. Ultimate Parent: Bank South
Corp. SIC: 6021—National Commercial
Banks.

★ 67261 ★ Bank South NA/
Houston County
1005 Northside Dr.
Perry, GA 31069
(912)987-2405
Company Type: Subsidiary. Location
Type: Branch office. Officer: Jim
McClarnon, President. Ultimate Parent:
Bank South Corp. SIC: 6021—National
Commercial Banks.

★ 67262 ★ Briggs & Stratton
Corp.
3300 Valley Dr.
Perry, GA 31069
(912)987-3300
Ultimate Parent: Briggs & Stratton. SIC:
5013—Motor Vehicle Supplies & New Parts.

★ 67263 ★ CB&T Bank of Middle
Georgia
916 Main St.
Perry, GA 31069
(912)987-0011
Location Type: Branch office. Officer: Mike
Jackson, Manager. Ultimate Parent:
Synovus Financial Corp. SIC: 6021—
National Commercial Banks.

★ 67264 ★ Crown Beverage
Packaging
240 Hwy. 247 Spur
Perry, GA 31069
Ultimate Parent: Crown Cork & Seal. SIC:
3411—Metal Cans.

★ 67265 ★ Crown Beverage
Packaging Inc.
240 Hwy. 247 Spur
Perry, GA 31069
Ultimate Parent: Crown Cork & Seal. SIC:
3411—Metal Cans.

★ 67266 ★ Kentucky Fried
Chicken
1416 Sam Nunn Blvd.
Perry, GA 31069
(912)987-0255
Ultimate Parent: Pepsico. SIC: 5812—
Eating Places.

★ 67267 ★ Pizza Hut
1344 Sam Nunn Blvd.
Perry, GA 31069
(912)987-0359
Ultimate Parent: Pepsico. SIC: 5812—
Eating Places.

Pine Mountain

★ 67268 ★ First Union National
Bank of Georgia
102 Broad St.
Pine Mountain, GA 31822
(706)663-2221
Location Type: Branch office. Ultimate
Parent: First Union Corp. SIC: 6021—
National Commercial Banks.

Plains

★ 67269 ★ Golden Peanut Co.
103 S. Bond St.
Plains, GA 31780-9508
(912)824-7601
Ultimate Parent: Archer Daniels Midland
Co. SIC: 5159—Farm-Product Raw
Materials Nec.

Pooler

★ 67270 ★ Food Lion
13 Pooler Sq.
Pooler, GA 31322
(912)748-0943
Ultimate Parent: Food Lion. SIC: 5411—
Grocery Stores.

★ 67271 ★ Food Lion Inc.
13 Pooler Sq.
Pooler, GA 31322
(912)748-0943
Ultimate Parent: Food Lion. SIC: 5411—
Grocery Stores.

★ 67272 ★ Union Camp Corp.
Hwy. 280
Pooler, GA 31322
(912)748-6742
Ultimate Parent: Union Camp Corp. SIC:
5112—Stationery & Office Supplies.

Port Wentworth

★ 67273 ★ Arcadian Corp.
Savannah Plant
5540 Hwy. 21
Port Wentworth, GA 31407
Location Type: Plant. Ultimate Parent:
Arcadian Corp. SIC: 2873—Nitrogenous
Fertilizers.

★ 67274 ★ Arcadian Corp.
Savannah Plant
GA Hwy. 21 N.
Port Wentworth, GA 31407
Location Type: Plant. Ultimate Parent:
Arcadian Corp. SIC: 2873—Nitrogenous
Fertilizers.

★ 67275 ★ Georgia-Pacific
Resins Inc.
Crossgate Rd.
Port Wentworth, GA 31407
Ultimate Parent: Georgia-Pacific. SIC:
2821—Plastics Materials & Resins.

★ 67276 ★ Savannah Sugar
Refinery
Oxnard Dr.
Port Wentworth, GA 31407
Ultimate Parent: Savannah Foods &
Industries, Inc. SIC: 2062—Cane Sugar
Refining.

★ 67277 ★ Stone Container Corp.
1 Bonnybridge Rd.
Port Wentworth, GA 31407
Ultimate Parent: Stone Container Corp.
SIC: 2631—Paperboard Mills.

★ 67278 ★ Stone Savannah River
Pulp & Paper
1 Bonnybridge Rd.
Port Wentworth, GA 31407
Ultimate Parent: Stone Container Corp.
SIC: 2631—Paperboard Mills.

Powder Spring

★ 67279 ★ Kentucky Fried
Chicken
4023 Power Springs Rd. SW
Powder Spring, GA
(404)439-7846
Ultimate Parent: Pepsico.

★ 67280 ★ Marathon Oil Co.
3895 Anderson Farm Rd. SW
Powder Spring, GA
(404)948-8550
Ultimate Parent: USX Corp.

★ 67281 ★ Marathon Oil Co.
3895 Anderson Farm Rd. SW
Powder Spring, GA
(404)941-0440
Ultimate Parent: USX Corp.

★ 67282 ★ Marathon Oil Co.
3895 Anderson Farm Rd. SW
Powder Spring, GA
(404)948-8550
Ultimate Parent: USX Corp.

★ 67283 ★ McDonald's
Restaurants
4021 Powder Springs Rd. SW
Powder Spring, GA 30073
(404)439-6031
Ultimate Parent: McDonald's.

★ 67284 ★ Pizza Hut
3309 New Macland Rd.
Powder Spring, GA 30073
(404)943-3400
Ultimate Parent: Pepsico.

★ 67285 ★ Taco Bell
4042 Powder Springs Rd. SW
Powder Spring, GA 30073
(404)943-0759
Ultimate Parent: Pepsico.

Powder Springs

★ 67286 ★ First Union National
Bank of Georgia
4180 Marietta St. SW
Powder Springs, GA 30073-2696
(404)739-3620
Location Type: Branch office. Ultimate
Parent: First Union Corp. SIC: 6021—
National Commercial Banks.

Quitman

★ 67287 ★ Greyhound Bus
Station
108 N. Jefferson St.
Quitman, GA 31643
(912)263-4324
Ultimate Parent: Greyhound Lines Inc. SIC:
4173—Bus Terminal & Service Facilities.

★ 67288 ★ Kentucky Fried
Chicken
1304 W. Screven St.
Quitman, GA 31643
(912)263-9246
Ultimate Parent: Pepsico. SIC: 5812—
Eating Places.

★ 67289 ★ Piggly Wiggly
1306 W. Screven St.
Quitman, GA 31643
(912)263-8975
Ultimate Parent: Bruno's. SIC: 5411—
Grocery Stores; 5541—Gasoline Service
Stations.

★ 67290 ★ Pizza Hut
1204 W. Screven St.
Quitman, GA 31643
(912)263-9314
Ultimate Parent: Pepsico. SIC: 5812—
Eating Places.

★ 67291 ★ Radio Shack
901 W. Screven St.
Quitman, GA 31643
(912)263-4222
Company Type: Division. Ultimate Parent:
Tandy Corp. SIC: 5731—Radio, Television
& Electronics Stores.

★ 67292 ★ Rite-Aid Pharmacy
1306 W. Screven St.
Quitman, GA 31643
(912)263-9947
Ultimate Parent: Rite Aid. SIC: 5912—Drug
Stores & Proprietary Stores.

Rahun Gap

★ 67293 ★ Burlington Industries
Inc.
Kellys Creek Rd.
Rahun Gap, GA 30568
(706)746-5311
Officer: Frank Greenburg, President.
Ultimate Parent: Burlington Industries,
Equity. SIC: 2273—Carpets & Rugs.

Red Oak

★ 67294 ★ Vulcan Materials Co.
5414 Buffington Rd.
Red Oak, GA 30272
(404)766-5231
Officer: John T. Corn, Manager. Ultimate
Parent: Vulcan Materials Co. SIC: 3281—
Cut Stone & Stone Products.

Reynolds

★ 67295 ★ Citizens State Bank
PO Box 277
Reynolds, GA 31076
(912)847-3465
Ultimate Parent: Liberty National Bancorp.
SIC: 6099—Functions Related to Deposit
Banking.

Richmond Hill

★ 67296 ★   Food Lion
Ways Station
Richmond Hill, GA 31324
(912)756-4555
Ultimate Parent: Food Lion. SIC: 5411—
Grocery Stores.

★ 67297 ★   Hobart Corp.
Pmi Food Equipment Group
US Hwy. 17 S.
Richmond Hill, GA 31324
Company Type: Division. Ultimate Parent:
Premark International. SIC: 3556—Food
Products Machinery.

★ 67298 ★   Pmi
Food Equipment Group Hobart Corp.
US Hwy. 17 S.
Richmond Hill, GA 31324
Company Type: Division. Ultimate Parent:
Premark International. SIC: 3556—Food
Products Machinery.

Rincon

★ 67299 ★   Fort Howard Corp.
Bakerhill Rd. Rte. 1
Rincon, GA 31326
Ultimate Parent: Fort Howard. SIC: 2621—
Paper Mills.

★ 67300 ★   Fort Howard Corp.
Rte. 1 Bakerhill Rd.
Rincon, GA 31326-0828
Ultimate Parent: Fort Howard. SIC: 2621—
Paper Mills.

★ 67301 ★   Fort Howard Paper
Corp.
RR 1 Fort Howard Rd.
Rincon, GA 31326
(912)826-2111
Officer: Carson Chapman, Manager.
Ultimate Parent: Fort Howard. SIC: 2297—
Nonwoven Fabrics; 2621—Paper Mills;
2676—Sanitary Paper Products.

★ 67302 ★   Union Camp Corp.
Rincon, GA 31326
(912)826-5556
Ultimate Parent: Union Camp Corp. SIC:
7389—Business Services Nec.

Riverdale

★ 67303 ★   Ace Hardware Co.
7459 Hwy. 85
Riverdale, GA 30274
(404)996-2442
Ultimate Parent: Ace Hardware.

★ 67304 ★   Bank South
7125 Hwy. 85
Riverdale, GA 30274-2900
(404)991-5367
Ultimate Parent: Bank South Corp. SIC:
6021—National Commercial Banks.

★ 67305 ★   Bank South NA
567 Valley Hill Rd., SW
Riverdale, GA 30274
(404)991-5370
Location Type: Branch office. Officer: Joe
Acker. Ultimate Parent: Bank South Corp.
SIC: 6021—National Commercial Banks;
6022—State Commercial Banks; 6141—
Personal Credit Institutions.

★ 67306 ★   Bank South, NA
7125 Georgia Hwy. 85
Riverdale, GA 30274
(404)991-5367
Company Type: Subsidiary. Location
Type: Branch office. Officer: Kay Roberts,
Manager. Ultimate Parent: Bank South
Corp. SIC: 6021—National Commercial
Banks.

★ 67307 ★   Bank South, NA
6653 Church St.
Riverdale, GA 30274-2211
(404)997-7945
Company Type: Subsidiary. Location
Type: Branch office. Ultimate Parent: Bank
South Corp. SIC: 6021—National
Commercial Banks.

★ 67308 ★   Bank South NA/
Riverdale
567 Valley Hill Rd.
Riverdale, GA 30274
(404)991-5370
Company Type: Subsidiary. Location
Type: Branch office. Officer: Bonnie Irwin,
Branch Mgr. Ultimate Parent: Bank South
Corp. SIC: 6021—National Commercial
Banks.

★ 67309 ★   Career Image Inc.
8060 Woodlake Dr.
Riverdale, GA 30274
(404)473-4741
Ultimate Parent: United States Shoe.

★ 67310 ★   Citgo Food Mart
8425 Hwy. 85
Riverdale, GA 30274
(404)477-8797
Ultimate Parent: Citgo Petroleum.

★ 67311 ★   First Union National
Bank of Georgia
7541 Georgia Hwy. 85
Riverdale, GA 30274
(404)477-3880
Location Type: Branch office. Ultimate
Parent: First Union Corp. SIC: 6021—
National Commercial Banks.

★ 67312 ★   Jiffy Lube Riverdale
7633 Hwy. 85
Riverdale, GA 30274
(404)477-2632
Ultimate Parent: Pennzoil.

★ 67313 ★   Kentucky Fried
Chicken
6892 Hwy. 85
Riverdale, GA 30274
(404)994-1479
Ultimate Parent: Pepsico.

★ 67314 ★   Kroger Co. the Retail
Stores
7125 Hwy. 85
Riverdale, GA 30274
(404)996-2508
Ultimate Parent: Kroger.

★ 67315 ★   Mary Kay Cosmetics
Indep Sales
7307 Ferwood Dr.
Riverdale, GA
(404)997-0516
Ultimate Parent: Mary Kay Cosmetics.

★ 67316 ★   Nationsbank Honor-
Cirrus Point
8529 Hwy. 85
Riverdale, GA 30274
(404)473-8715
Ultimate Parent: Nationsbank Corp.

★ 67317 ★   Nationsbank Offices
Atlanta Ar
Tri-County Station 2
Riverdale, GA
(404)991-7760
Ultimate Parent: Nationsbank Corp.

★ 67318 ★   Nationsbank Offices
Atlanta Ar
Pointe South 8529 Hwy.
Riverdale, GA 30274
(404)473-8715
Ultimate Parent: Nationsbank Corp.

★ 67319 ★   Nationsbank Offices
Atlanta Ar
Pointe South 8529 Hwy.
Riverdale, GA 30274
(404)969-0550
Ultimate Parent: Nationsbank Corp.

★ 67320 ★   Payless Shoesource
7119 Hwy. 85
Riverdale, GA 30274
(404)996-9467
Ultimate Parent: May Department Stores.

★ 67321 ★   Pizza Hut
723 SW Hwy. 138
Riverdale, GA 30274
(404)997-1934
Ultimate Parent: Pepsico.

★ 67322 ★   Pizza Hut
8411 Hwy. 85
Riverdale, GA 30274
(404)603-6800
Ultimate Parent: Pepsico.

★ 67323 ★   Pizza Hut
7295 Hwy. 85
Riverdale, GA 30274
(404)907-9000
Ultimate Parent: Pepsico.

★ 67324 ★   Radio Shack
6602 Hwy. 85
Riverdale, GA 30274
(404)997-6464
Company Type: Division. Ultimate Parent:
Tandy Corp.

★ 67325 ★   Shell Food Mart
7530 Hwy. 85
Riverdale, GA 30274
(404)473-9512
Ultimate Parent: Shell Oil Co.

★ 67326 ★   Taco Bell
6865 Hwy. 85
Riverdale, GA 30274
(404)997-7357
Ultimate Parent: Pepsico.

★ 67327 ★   Texaco Food Mart
126 Valley Hill Rd.
Riverdale, GA 30274
(404)473-1979
Ultimate Parent: Texaco.

★ 67328 ★   Texaco Food Mart
7292 Bethsaida Dr.
Riverdale, GA 30296
(404)991-9657
Ultimate Parent: Texaco.

★ 67329 ★   Valvoline Instant Oil
Change
6941 Hwy. 85
Riverdale, GA 30274
(404)996-3652
Ultimate Parent: Ashland Oil.

★ 67330 ★   Valvoline Instant Oil
Change
6941 Hwy. 85
Riverdale, GA 30274
(404)996-3652
Ultimate Parent: Ashland Oil.

★ 67331 ★   Waldenbooks
7145 Hwy. 85 S
Riverdale, GA 30274
(404)991-3634
Ultimate Parent: K-Mart.

Rockmart

★ 67332 ★   Loral Engineered
Fabrics
Goodyear St.
Rockmart, GA 30153-0548
Ultimate Parent: Loral Corp. SIC: 3000—
Rubber & Miscellaneous Plastics Products;
3069—Fabricated Rubber Products Nec;
3728—Aircraft Parts & Equipment Nec.

★ 67333 ★   Rockland React-Rite
Inc.
327 Industrial Dr.
Rockmart, GA 30153
Ultimate Parent: Interface Inc. SIC: 2869—
Industrial Organic Chemicals Nec.

★ 67334 ★   Trust Co. Bank of NW
Georgia, N.A.
500 Elm St.
Rockmart, GA 30153-2930
(404)684-7881
Officer: W. Roger Waldrop, Manager.
Ultimate Parent: Suntrust Banks. SIC:
6021—National Commercial Banks.

Rome

★ 67335 ★   Citizens First Bank
701 Broad St.
Rome, GA 30161
(706)291-9772 Fax: (706)234-5981
Location Type: Branch office. Officer:
Roger F. Smith, President & CEO. Ultimate
Parent: Synovus Financial Corp. SIC:
6021—National Commercial Banks.

★ 67336 ★   Citizens First Bank
PO Box 1313
Rome, GA 30162-1313
Location Type: Branch office. Ultimate
Parent: Synovus Financial Corp. SIC:
6021—National Commercial Banks.

★ 67337 ★   First Union National
Bank of Georgia
1311 Dean St.
Rome, GA 30161-6433
(706)290-6171
Location Type: Branch office. Ultimate
Parent: First Union Corp. SIC: 6021—
National Commercial Banks.

★ 67338 ★   First Union National
Bank of Georgia
2 Redmond Rd.
Rome, GA 30161-1534
(706)290-6160
Location Type: Branch office. Ultimate
Parent: First Union Corp. SIC: 6021—
National Commercial Banks.

★ 67339 ★   First Union National
Bank of Georgia
501 Broad St.
Rome, GA 30161-3009
(706)290-6100
Location Type: Branch office. Ultimate
Parent: First Union Corp. SIC: 6021—
National Commercial Banks.

★ 67340 ★   First Union National
Bank of Georgia
800 Shorter Ave.
Rome, GA 30161-4134
(706)290-6180
Location Type: Branch office. Ultimate
Parent: First Union Corp. SIC: 6021—
National Commercial Banks.

★ 67341 ★   GE Co. Medium
Transformer Operation
1935 Redmond Circle
Rome, GA 30161
Ultimate Parent: General Electric. SIC:
3612—Transformers Except Electronic.

★ 67342 ★   General Electric Co.
Redmond Cir.
Rome, GA 30165
(706)291-3000
Officer: E. T. Curley, Manager. Ultimate
Parent: General Electric. SIC: 3612—
Transformers Except Electronic.

★ 67343 ★   Inland Container
Corp.
216 Mays Bridge Rd. SW
Rome, GA 30161
Ultimate Parent: Temple-Inland. SIC:
2653—Corrugated & Solid Fiber Boxes.

★ 67344 ★   Inland-Rome, Inc.
238 Mays Bridge Rd. SW
Rome, GA 30162-1551
Ultimate Parent: Temple-Inland. SIC:
2611—Pulp Mills; 2631—Paperboard Mills.

★ 67345 ★   Pepsi-Cola Co.
4900 New Calhoun Hwy. NE
Rome, GA 30161
(706)235-8844
Ultimate Parent: Pepsico. SIC: 2086—
Bottled & Canned Soft Drinks.

★ 67346 ★   Pet Bakery
101 Clark Ave.
Rome, GA 30165
(706)291-1540
Ultimate Parent: Pet. SIC: 2051—Bread,
Cake & Related Products.

★ 67347 ★   Trust Co. Bank of NW
Georgia, N.A.
500 Calhoun Ave.
Rome, GA 30161-5421
(706)291-4774
Officer: Judy Early, Manager. Ultimate
Parent: Suntrust Banks. SIC: 6021—
National Commercial Banks.

★ 67348 ★   Trust Co. Bank of NW
Georgia, N.A.
522 Shorter Ave.
Rome, GA 30165-4201
(706)291-1171
Officer: Barbara Segars, Manager.
Ultimate Parent: Suntrust Banks. SIC:
6021—National Commercial Banks.

★ 67349 ★   Trust Co. Bank of NW
Georgia, N.A.
2401 Shorter Ave.
Rome, GA 30165-1914
(706)291-2991
Officer: Joyce Minshew, Manager. Ultimate
Parent: Suntrust Banks. SIC: 6021—
National Commercial Banks.

★ 67350 ★ Trust Co. Bank of NW Georgia, N.A.
1300 Dean St.
Rome, GA 30161-6434
(706)291-9299
Officer: Alvis Trotter, Manager. Ultimate Parent: Suntrust Banks. SIC: 6021—National Commercial Banks.

★ 67351 ★ Trust Co. Bank of NW Georgia, N.A.
100 E. 2nd Ave.
Rome, GA 30161
(706)291-4421 Fax: (706)236-4383
Officer: Donald M. Keiser, President & CEO. Ultimate Parent: Suntrust Banks. SIC: 6021—National Commercial Banks.

★ 67352 ★ Trust Co. Bank of NW Georgia, N.A.
2923 Martha Berry Hwy.
Rome, GA 30161-4201
(706)291-8625
Officer: April Rickman, Manager. Ultimate Parent: Suntrust Banks. SIC: 6021—National Commercial Banks.

Rosewell

★ 67353 ★ Gate City Oil Equipment Co., Inc.
2000 Northfield Ct.
Rosewell, GA 30076-3825
(404)475-1900
Company Type: Division. Ultimate Parent: Lubrizol.

Roswell

★ 67354 ★ Ace Hardware
4651 Woodstock Rd. NE
Roswell, GA 30075
(404)587-3535
Ultimate Parent: Ace Hardware.

★ 67355 ★ Ace Hardware Inc.
597 Holcomb Bridge Rd.
Roswell, GA 30076
(404)993-0749
Ultimate Parent: Ace Hardware.

★ 67356 ★ Amdahl Federal Service Corp.
11865 Old Mountain Park Rd.
Roswell, GA 30075
(404)587-5840
Ultimate Parent: Amdahl Corp.

★ 67357 ★ American General Finance
861 Holcomb Bridge Rd.
Roswell, GA 30076-1954
(404)641-9899
Location Type: Branch office. Ultimate Parent: American General Corp. SIC: 6141—Personal Credit Institutions.

★ 67358 ★ American General Finance Inc.
861 Holcomb Bridge Rd.
Roswell, GA 30076-1954
(404)641-9899
Location Type: Branch office. Ultimate Parent: American General Corp. SIC: 6141—Personal Credit Institutions.

★ 67359 ★ Bank South NA
10779 Alpharetta Hwy.
Roswell, GA 30076-1424
(404)522-5777
Location Type: Branch office. Officer: Betsy Blaine. Ultimate Parent: Bank South Corp. SIC: 6021—National Commercial Banks; 6022—State Commercial Banks.

★ 67360 ★ Bank South NA
910 Holcomb Bridge Rd.
Roswell, GA 30076-4339
(404)552-5760
Location Type: Branch office. Officer: Hazel Fouts. Ultimate Parent: Bank South Corp. SIC: 6021—National Commercial Banks; 6022—State Commercial Banks; 6141—Personal Credit Institutions.

★ 67361 ★ Bank South, NA
4455 Shallowford Rd.
Roswell, GA 30075
(404)552-1719
Company Type: Subsidiary. Location Type: Branch office. Ultimate Parent: Bank South Corp. SIC: 6021—National Commercial Banks.

★ 67362 ★ Bank South, NA
1327 Holcomb Bridge Rd.
Roswell, GA 30076
(404)552-5772
Company Type: Subsidiary. Location Type: Branch office. Officer: Virginia Roberson, Manager. Ultimate Parent: Bank South Corp. SIC: 6021—National Commercial Banks.

★ 67363 ★ Bank South, NA
4750 Sandy Plains Rd.
Roswell, GA 30075
(404)552-5781
Company Type: Subsidiary. Location Type: Branch office. Officer: Terri Hansen, Manager. Ultimate Parent: Bank South Corp. SIC: 6021—National Commercial Banks.

★ 67364 ★ Bank South NA/Roswell
910 Holcomb Bridge Rd.
Roswell, GA 30076
(404)552-5760
Company Type: Subsidiary. Location Type: Branch office. Officer: Hazel Fouts, Branch Mgr. Ultimate Parent: Bank South Corp. SIC: 6021—National Commercial Banks.

★ 67365 ★ California Federal Bank
7385 Roswell Rd. NE
Roswell, GA
(404)393-3665
Ultimate Parent: California Federal Bank.

★ 67366 ★ Citgo Food Mart
5866 Roswell Rd.
Roswell, GA
(404)851-9338
Ultimate Parent: Citgo Petroleum.

★ 67367 ★ Courtyard by Marriott
1500 Market Blvd.
Roswell, GA 30076
(404)992-7200
Ultimate Parent: Marriott International.

★ 67368 ★ Dynapert
600 Currin Ct.
Roswell, GA 30076-3583
(404)641-9123
Ultimate Parent: Black & Decker Corp. SIC: 3569—General Industrial Machinery Nec.

★ 67369 ★ First Union National Bank of Georgia
4701 Sandy Plains
Roswell, GA 30075-1638
(404)594-2050
Location Type: Branch office. Ultimate Parent: First Union Corp. SIC: 6021—National Commercial Banks.

★ 67370 ★ First Union National Bank of Georgia
1490 Holcomb Bridge Rd.
Roswell, GA 30076-2518
(404)594-2070
Location Type: Branch office. Ultimate Parent: First Union Corp. SIC: 6021—National Commercial Banks.

★ 67371 ★ First Union National Bank of Georgia
11560 Alpharetta Hwy.
Roswell, GA 30076-3803
(404)594-2040
Location Type: Branch office. Ultimate Parent: First Union Corp. SIC: 6021—National Commercial Banks.

★ 67372 ★ First Union National Bank of Georgia
37 Magnolia St.
Roswell, GA 30075-4299
(404)594-2000
Location Type: Branch office. Ultimate Parent: First Union Corp. SIC: 6021—National Commercial Banks.

★ 67373 ★ First Union National Bank of Georgia
675 Holcomb Bridge Rd.
Roswell, GA 30076-1511
(404)594-2030
Location Type: Branch office. Ultimate Parent: First Union Corp. SIC: 6021—National Commercial Banks.

★ 67374 ★ Hit or Miss Wms Apparel Retail
1425 Market Blvd.
Roswell, GA 30076
(404)552-7984
Ultimate Parent: TJX.

★ 67375 ★ Inacomp Computer Centers
1125 North Meadow Pkwy
Roswell, GA
(404)751-0500
Ultimate Parent: Beneficial.

★ 67376 ★ Inacomp Computer Centers
1125 N. Meadow Pkwy
Roswell, GA
(404)751-9400
Ultimate Parent: Beneficial.

★ 67377 ★ Kentucky Fried Chicken
676 Holcomb Bridge Rd.
Roswell, GA 30076
(404)993-2330
Ultimate Parent: Pepsico.

★ 67378 ★ Kentucky Fried Chicken Regional
4720 Alabama Rd.
Roswell, GA 30075
(404)993-3787
Ultimate Parent: Pepsico.

★ 67379 ★ Kmart Stores
606 Holcomb Bridge Road
Roswell, GA 30076
(404)992-9525
Ultimate Parent: K-Mart.

★ 67380 ★ Kmart Stores Automotive
606 Holcomb Bridge Road
Roswell, GA 30076
(404)992-5511
Ultimate Parent: K-Mart.

★ 67381 ★ Kmart Stores Pharmacy
606 Holcomb Bridge Rd.
Roswell, GA 30076
(404)992-8388
Ultimate Parent: K-Mart.

★ 67382 ★ Kmart Stores Portrait Studio
Roswell, GA
(404)587-2896
Ultimate Parent: K-Mart.

★ 67383 ★ Kroger Co. the Kroge Pharmacies
4401 Shallowford Rd.
Roswell, GA 30075
(404)641-8024
Ultimate Parent: Kroger.

★ 67384 ★ Kroger Co. the Kroger Pharmacie
4651 Woodstock Rd.
Roswell, GA 30075
(404)552-1325
Ultimate Parent: Kroger.

★ 67385 ★ Kroger Co. the Retail Sotres
4651 Woodstock Rd.
Roswell, GA 30075
(404)552-0745
Ultimate Parent: Kroger.

★ 67386 ★ Kroger Co. the Retail Stores
10779 Alpharetta Hwy.
Roswell, GA 30076
(404)998-6281
Ultimate Parent: Kroger.

★ 67387 ★ Kroger Co. the Retail Stores
4401 Shallowford Rd.
Roswell, GA 30075
(404)641-7317
Ultimate Parent: Kroger.

★ 67388 ★ Kroger Pharmacies
10779 Alpharetta Hwy.
Roswell, GA 30076
(404)998-6284
Ultimate Parent: Kroger.

★ 67389 ★ Lehman Brothers Institutional Fund
10900 Crabapple Rd.
Roswell, GA 30075
(404)993-0047
Ultimate Parent: American Express Co.

★ 67390 ★ Linens 'n Things Kings Market
955 Market Blvd.
Roswell, GA
(404)993-4446
Ultimate Parent: Melville.

★ 67391 ★ M & I First National Leasing C
1080 Holcomb Bridge Rd.
Roswell, GA 30076
(404)552-6666
Ultimate Parent: Marshall & Ilsley Corp.

★ 67392 ★ Mary Kay Cosmetics
Indep Sales
4724 Shallowford Rd.
Roswell, GA 30075
(404)641-0315
Ultimate Parent: Mary Kay Cosmetics.

★ 67393 ★ Mary Kay Cosmetics
Indep Sales
11235 West Rd.
Roswell, GA 30075
(404)518-0788
Ultimate Parent: Mary Kay Cosmetics.

★ 67394 ★ McDonald's Restaurants
591 Holcomb Bridge Rd.
Roswell, GA 30076
(404)992-2974
Ultimate Parent: McDonald's.

★ 67395 ★ Molex-Etc Inc.
10935 Crabapple Rd.
Roswell, GA 30075-3032
(404)518-4950
Ultimate Parent: Molex. SIC: 3699—Electrical Equipment & Supplies Nec.

★ 67396 ★ Molex Inc.
9755 Dogwood Rd.
Roswell, GA 30075
(404)992-3715
Ultimate Parent: Molex.

★ 67397 ★ Morton Salt
11111 Houze Rd.
Roswell, GA 30076
(404)587-3155
Ultimate Parent: Morton International.

★ 67398 ★ Nationsbank Honor-Cirrus L Hol
1329 Holcomb Bridge Rd.
Roswell, GA 30076
(404)594-6840
Ultimate Parent: Nationsbank Corp.

★ 67399 ★ Nationsbank Honor-Cirrus L Ros
10750 Alpharetta Hwy.
Roswell, GA 30076
(404)594-3454
Ultimate Parent: Nationsbank Corp.

★ 67400 ★ Nationsbank Honor-Cirrus L Ros
610 Holcomb Bridge Rd.
Roswell, GA 30076
(404)581-2121
Ultimate Parent: Nationsbank Corp.

★ 67401 ★ Nationsbank Honor-Cirrus L San
4751 Alabama Rd.
Roswell, GA 30075
(404)594-6850
Ultimate Parent: Nationsbank Corp.

★ 67402 ★ Nationsbank Ofcs Atla Area Act
Alpharetta 11725 Alp
Roswell, GA 30076
(404)523-0900
Ultimate Parent: Nationsbank Corp.

★ 67403 ★ Nationsbank Ofcs Atla Area Alp
Alpharetta 11725 Alp
Roswell, GA 30076
(404)442-2464
Ultimate Parent: Nationsbank Corp.

★ 67404 ★   Nationsbank Ofcs
Atlaanta Area
Alpharetta 11725 Alp
Roswell, GA 30076
(404)969-0550
Ultimate Parent: Nationsbank Corp.

★ 67405 ★   Nationsbank Offices
Atlanta Area
Holcomb Bridge 1329
Roswell, GA 30076
(404)969-0550
Ultimate Parent: Nationsbank Corp.

★ 67406 ★   Nationsbank Offices
Atlanta Area
Holcomb Bridge 1329
Roswell, GA 30076
(404)594-6840
Ultimate Parent: Nationsbank Corp.

★ 67407 ★   Nationsbank Offices
Atlanta
Roswell 10750 Alphar
Roswell, GA
(404)969-0550
Ultimate Parent: Nationsbank Corp.

★ 67408 ★   Nationsbank Offices
Atlanta
Sandy Plains 4751 Al
Roswell, GA 30075
(404)594-6850
Ultimate Parent: Nationsbank Corp.

★ 67409 ★   Nationsbank Offices
Atlanta
Holcomb Bridge 1329
Roswell, GA 30076
(404)523-0900
Ultimate Parent: Nationsbank Corp.

★ 67410 ★   Nationsbank Saturday
Banking
11725 Alpharetta Hwy.
Roswell, GA 30076
(404)442-2464
Ultimate Parent: Nationsbank Corp.

★ 67411 ★   North Fulton Regional
Hospital
3000 Hospital Blvd.
Roswell, GA 30076
(404)751-2500
Officer: Fred Bailey, Executive Director.
Ultimate Parent: American Medical
Holdings. **SIC:** 8062—General Medical &
Surgical Hospitals.

★ 67412 ★   Pizza Hut
10670 Hwy. 19
Roswell, GA
(404)992-4327
Ultimate Parent: Pepsico.

★ 67413 ★   Pizza Hut
1580 Holcomb Bridge Rd.
Roswell, GA 30076
(404)993-9100
Ultimate Parent: Pepsico.

★ 67414 ★   Pizza Hut
4401 Shallowford Rd. NE
Roswell, GA 30075
(404)640-8800
Ultimate Parent: Pepsico.

★ 67415 ★   Pizza Hut
665-D Holcomb Bridge
Roswell, GA
(404)642-6600
Ultimate Parent: Pepsico.

★ 67416 ★   Pizza Hut
4674 Sandy Plains Rd. NE
Roswell, GA 30075
(404)992-9900
Ultimate Parent: Pepsico.

★ 67417 ★   Radio Shack
608 Holcomb Bridge Rd.
Roswell, GA 30076
(404)992-2013
Company Type: Division. **Ultimate Parent:**
Tandy Corp.

★ 67418 ★   Security Connecticut
Life Insu
960 Holcomb Bridge Rd.
Roswell, GA 30076
(404)993-1153
Ultimate Parent: Lincoln National Life.

★ 67419 ★   Taco Bell
715 Holcomb Bridge Rd.
Roswell, GA 30076
(404)992-1617
Ultimate Parent: Pepsico.

★ 67420 ★   Target Stores Retail
Stores
610 Holcomb Bridge Rd.
Roswell, GA 30076
(404)993-7500
Ultimate Parent: Dayton Hudson.

★ 67421 ★   Texaco
1100 Holcomb Bridge Rd.
Roswell, GA 30076
(404)992-8659
Ultimate Parent: Texaco.

★ 67422 ★   Texaco
10761 Alpharetta Hwy.
Roswell, GA 30076
(404)993-7306
Ultimate Parent: Texaco.

★ 67423 ★   Texaco
890 Atlanta St.
Roswell, GA 30075
(404)993-1213
Ultimate Parent: Texaco.

★ 67424 ★   Thermo Jarrell Ash
4274 Shipyard Trce
Roswell, GA 30075
(404)587-3726
Ultimate Parent: Thermo Electron Corp.

★ 67425 ★   Universal Data
Systems
1080 Holcomb Bridge Rd.
Roswell, GA 30076
(404)998-2715
Ultimate Parent: Motorola Inc.

★ 67426 ★   W. W. Grainger Inc.
Grainger Division
1455 Hembree Rd.
Roswell, GA 30076
(404)475-1487
Ultimate Parent: W. W. Grainger.

★ 67427 ★   Waldenbooks
Roswell Village Shopping
Roswell, GA 30076
(404)992-5770
Ultimate Parent: K-Mart.

Sandersville

★ 67428 ★   Coast to Coast Home
& Auto
116 Malone St.
Sandersville, GA 31082
(912)552-5334
Ultimate Parent: Servistar Corp. **SIC:**
5531—Automobile & Home Supply Stores;
5722—Household Appliance Stores.

★ 67429 ★   Duck Head Apparel
Co.
1006 S. Harris St.
Sandersville, GA 31082
(912)552-3965
Officer: Annie Minor, Plant Manager.
Ultimate Parent: Delta Woodside
Industries. **SIC:** 2321—Men's/Boys' Shirts;
2331—Women's/Misses' Blouses & Shirts.

★ 67430 ★   Piggly Wiggly
306 S. Harris St.
Sandersville, GA 31082
(912)552-2361
Ultimate Parent: Bruno's. **SIC:** 5411—
Grocery Stores.

★ 67431 ★   Piggly Wiggly
Southern Inc.
306 S. Harris St.
Sandersville, GA 31082
(912)552-2361
Ultimate Parent: Bruno's. **SIC:** 5411—
Grocery Stores.

★ 67432 ★   Trailways Bus
Systems
210 W. Haynes St.
Sandersville, GA 31082
(912)552-2176
Ultimate Parent: Greyhound Lines Inc. **SIC:**
4131—Intercity & Rural Bus Transportation.

Sandy Springs

★ 67433 ★   Bank South, NA
6160 Roswell Rd.
Sandy Springs, GA 30328-3909
(404)256-4700
Company Type: Subsidiary. **Location
Type:** Branch office. **Ultimate Parent:** Bank
South Corp. **SIC:** 6021—National
Commercial Banks.

★ 67434 ★   Bank South, NA
325 Mt. Vernon Rd.
Atlanta
Sandy Springs, GA 30328
(404)847-3400
Company Type: Subsidiary. **Location
Type:** Branch office. **Officer:** Treicia
Brooks, Manager. **Ultimate Parent:** Bank
South Corp. **SIC:** 6021—National
Commercial Banks.

★ 67435 ★   Csc Credit Services
5775-A Glenridge Dr.
Sandy Springs, GA
(404)252-5155
Ultimate Parent: Computer Sciences.

★ 67436 ★   Kentucky Fried
Chicken
6125 Roswell Rd. NE
Sandy Springs, GA 30328
(404)255-5167
Ultimate Parent: Pepsico.

★ 67437 ★   Kmart Stores
5925 Roswell Rd. NE
Sandy Springs, GA 30328
(404)255-7330
Ultimate Parent: K-Mart.

★ 67438 ★   Kmart Stores
Pharmacy
5925 Roswell Rd. NE
Sandy Springs, GA 30328
(404)256-5795
Ultimate Parent: K-Mart.

★ 67439 ★   Nationsbank Offices
Atlanta Ar
6075 Roswell Rd.
Sandy Springs, GA 30328
(404)969-0550
Ultimate Parent: Nationsbank Corp.

Savannah

★ 67440 ★   American Family Life
Assurance
359 Commercial Dr.
Savannah, GA 31406
(912)352-1808
Ultimate Parent: American Family Life
Assurance Co. **SIC:** 6411—Insurance
Agents, Brokers & Service.

★ 67441 ★   American General
Finance
8408 Abercorn St.
Savannah, GA 31406-3499
(912)927-7330
Location Type: Branch office. **Officer:**
Michael E. Stover. **Ultimate Parent:**
American General Corp. **SIC:** 6141—
Personal Credit Institutions.

★ 67442 ★   American General
Finance
7712 Waters Rd.
Savannah, GA 31406-3814
(912)354-7770
Location Type: Branch office. **Officer:**
Leon Parrish. **Ultimate Parent:** American
General Corp. **SIC:** 6141—Personal Credit
Institutions.

★ 67443 ★   American General
Finance Inc.
7712 Waters Rd.
Savannah, GA 31406-3814
(912)354-7770
Location Type: Branch office. **Officer:**
Leon Parrish. **Ultimate Parent:** American
General Corp. **SIC:** 6141—Personal Credit
Institutions.

★ 67444 ★   American General
Finance Inc.
8408 Abercorn St.
Savannah, GA 31406-3499
(912)927-7330
Location Type: Branch office. **Officer:**
Michael E. Stover. **Ultimate Parent:**

American General Corp. **SIC:** 6141—
Personal Credit Institutions.

★ 67445 ★   APAC
45 Telfair Pl.
Savannah, GA 31401
(912)233-0142
Officer: Lonnie R. Carroll, Manager.
Ultimate Parent: Ashland Oil. **SIC:** 2951—
Asphalt Paving Mixtures & Blocks; 3281—
Cut Stone & Stone Products.

★ 67446 ★   Arcadian Corp.
PO Box 18388
Savannah, GA 31418-0388
(912)966-5566
Ultimate Parent: Arcadian Corp. **SIC:**
2875—Fertilizers—Mixing Only.

★ 67447 ★   Bank South, NA
308 Johnny Mercer Dr.
Savannah, GA 31410
(912)897-0036
Company Type: Subsidiary. **Location
Type:** Branch office. **Officer:** Lynn Palmer,
Manager. **Ultimate Parent:** Bank South
Corp. **SIC:** 6021—National Commercial
Banks.

★ 67448 ★   Bank South, NA
1976 E. Victory Dr.
Savannah, GA 31404
(912)238-0905
Company Type: Subsidiary. **Location
Type:** Branch office. **Officer:** Linda Bowerr,
Manager. **Ultimate Parent:** Bank South
Corp. **SIC:** 6021—National Commercial
Banks.

★ 67449 ★   Bank South, NA
401 Mall Blvd.
Savannah, GA 31406-4806
(912)355-6000
Company Type: Subsidiary. **Location
Type:** Branch office. **Officer:** Susan Hailey,
Manager. **Ultimate Parent:** Bank South
Corp. **SIC:** 6021—National Commercial
Banks.

★ 67450 ★   Bank South, NA
11605 Abercorn Expy.
Savannah, GA 31419
(912)925-6515
Company Type: Subsidiary. **Location
Type:** Branch office. **Officer:** Beth Agee,
Manager. **Ultimate Parent:** Bank South
Corp. **SIC:** 6021—National Commercial
Banks.

★ 67451 ★   Bank South, NA
216 Hwy. 80
Garden City
Savannah, GA 31408
(912)964-1102
Company Type: Subsidiary. **Location
Type:** Branch office. **Officer:** Pam Parker,
Manager. **Ultimate Parent:** Bank South
Corp. **SIC:** 6021—National Commercial
Banks.

★ 67452 ★   Bank South, NA
7 E. Congress St.
Savannah, GA 31401-3341
(912)235-3800
Company Type: Subsidiary. **Location
Type:** Branch office. **Officer:** Carole Hill,
Manager. **Ultimate Parent:** Bank South
Corp. **SIC:** 6021—National Commercial
Banks.

★ 67453 ★   Bank South NA-
Savannah
11601 Abercorn Expy.
Savannah, GA 31419
(912)925-6515
Ultimate Parent: Bank South Corp. **SIC:**
6099—Functions Related to Deposit
Banking.

★ 67454 ★   Bank South NA/
Savannah Main Office
7 E. Congress St.
Savannah, GA 31401
(912)235-3800
Company Type: Subsidiary. **Location
Type:** Branch office. **Officer:** Tommy
Hester, President. **Ultimate Parent:** Bank
South Corp. **SIC:** 6021—National
Commercial Banks.

★ 67455 ★ Beatrice/Hunt-Wesson Inc. Savannah Refinery
Lathrop Ave.
Savannah, GA 31401
Ultimate Parent: Conagra. SIC: 2079—Edible Fats & Oils Nec.

★ 67456 ★ BellSouth Advertising & Publishing
1000 Business Ctr. Dr., Ste. 50
Savannah, GA 31405-1326
(912)232-2726
Officer: W. L. Saferight. Ultimate Parent: BellSouth Corp. SIC: 7313—Radio, T.V. & Publisher Representatives; 7311—Advertising Agencies.

★ 67457 ★ Burlington Coat Factory
7939 Abercom Expy.
Savannah, GA 31406-3414
(912)925-9801
Location Type: Branch office. Officer: Charles Hartman. Ultimate Parent: Burlington Industries, Equity. SIC: 5311—Department Stores; 5651—Family Clothing Stores.

★ 67458 ★ Caribbean Lumber Co.
Hutchinson Island
Savannah, GA 31498-2687
Ultimate Parent: Hercules. SIC: 2491—Wood Preserving.

★ 67459 ★ Coast to Coast Express
2345 Louisville Rd.
Savannah, GA 31401
(912)233-4855
Ultimate Parent: Servistar Corp. SIC: 4213—Trucking Except Local.

★ 67460 ★ Delta Air Lines
Savannah
Savannah, GA 31401
(912)964-1607
Ultimate Parent: Delta Air Lines, Inc. SIC: 4729—Passenger Transportation Arrangement Nec.

★ 67461 ★ Delta Air Lines
Travis Field
Savannah, GA 31401
(912)966-3410
Ultimate Parent: Delta Air Lines, Inc. SIC: 4512—Air Transportation—Scheduled.

★ 67462 ★ Delta Air Lines
De Soto Hilton
Savannah, GA 31401
(912)234-1221
Ultimate Parent: Delta Air Lines, Inc. SIC: 4724—Travel Agencies.

★ 67463 ★ Delta Air Lines Inc.
De Soto Hilton Arcad
Savannah, GA 31401
(912)234-1221
Ultimate Parent: Delta Air Lines, Inc. SIC: 4724—Travel Agencies.

★ 67464 ★ Delta Air Lines Inc.
Savannah
Savannah, GA 31401
(912)964-1607
Ultimate Parent: Delta Air Lines, Inc. SIC: 4729—Passenger Transportation Arrangement Nec.

★ 67465 ★ Delta Air Lines Inc.
Travis Field
Savannah, GA 31401
(912)966-3410
Ultimate Parent: Delta Air Lines, Inc. SIC: 4512—Air Transportation—Scheduled.

★ 67466 ★ Federal Express Corp.
280 PO Box
Savannah, GA 31402
(912)964-9261
Ultimate Parent: Federal Express. SIC: 7389—Business Services Nec.

★ 67467 ★ First Union National Bank of Georgia
14009 Abercm St.
Savannah, GA 31419-1902
(912)235-4756
Location Type: Branch office. Ultimate Parent: First Union Corp. SIC: 6021—National Commercial Banks.

★ 67468 ★ First Union National Bank of Georgia
16 Stephenson St.
Savannah, GA 31405
(912)235-4746
Location Type: Branch office. Ultimate Parent: First Union Corp. SIC: 6021—National Commercial Banks.

★ 67469 ★ First Union National Bank of Georgia
319 Johnny Mercer Blvd.
Savannah, GA 31410-2116
(912)235-4761
Location Type: Branch office. Ultimate Parent: First Union Corp. SIC: 6021—National Commercial Banks.

★ 67470 ★ First Union National Bank of Georgia
20 Bank St.
Savannah, GA 31411-2918
(912)235-4806
Location Type: Branch office. Ultimate Parent: First Union Corp. SIC: 6021—National Commercial Banks.

★ 67471 ★ First Union National Bank of Georgia
4807 Waters Ave.
Savannah, GA 31404-6221
(912)235-4726
Location Type: Branch office. Ultimate Parent: First Union Corp. SIC: 6021—National Commercial Banks.

★ 67472 ★ First Union National Bank of Georgia
2225 E. Victory Dr.
Savannah, GA 31404-3918
(912)235-4716
Location Type: Branch office. Ultimate Parent: First Union Corp. SIC: 6021—National Commercial Banks.

★ 67473 ★ First Union National Bank of Georgia
1120 Bull St.
Savannah, GA 31401-6435
(912)235-4701
Location Type: Branch office. Ultimate Parent: First Union Corp. SIC: 6021—National Commercial Banks.

★ 67474 ★ First Union National Bank of Georgia
3500 Ogeechee Rd.
Savannah, GA 31405-2906
(912)235-4711
Location Type: Branch office. Ultimate Parent: First Union Corp.

★ 67475 ★ First Union National Bank of Georgia
2 E. Bryan St.
Savannah, GA 31401-2655
(912)944-2000
Location Type: Branch office. Ultimate Parent: First Union Corp. SIC: 6021—National Commercial Banks.

★ 67476 ★ The Gap
7 Oglethorpe Mall
Savannah, GA 31406
(912)355-9446
Ultimate Parent: GAP. SIC: 5651—Family Clothing Stores.

★ 67477 ★ Georgia Federal Bank, F S B
111 Barnard St.
Savannah, GA 31401
(912)235-5500
Ultimate Parent: First Union Corp. SIC: 6022—State Commercial Banks; 6099—Functions Related to Deposit Banking.

★ 67478 ★ Georgia Federal Bank FSB
PO Box 9209
Savannah, GA 31412
(912)265-0110
Ultimate Parent: First Union Corp. SIC: 6035—Federal Savings Institutions; 6036—Savings Institutions Except Federal; 6159—Miscellaneous Business Credit Institutions.

★ 67479 ★ Georgia-Pacific Corp. Savannah Plywood
Old Louisville Rd.
Savannah, GA 31498
Ultimate Parent: Georgia-Pacific. SIC: 2435—Hardwood Veneer & Plywood.

★ 67480 ★ Great Dane Trailers Inc.
600 E. Lathrop Ave.
Savannah, GA 31402-0067
Ultimate Parent: International Controls. SIC: 3715—Truck Trailers.

★ 67481 ★ Great Dane Trailers Inc.
East Lathrop Ave.
Savannah, GA 31402-0067
Ultimate Parent: International Controls. SIC: 3715—Truck Trailers.

★ 67482 ★ Gulfstream Aerospace Corp.
PO Box 2206 M/S D-02
Savannah, GA 31402
Ultimate Parent: Chrysler Corp. SIC: 3721—Aircraft.

★ 67483 ★ Hercules Inc.
Specialty Chemicals Div.
Old Louisville Rd.
Savannah, GA 31401
Company Type: Division. Ultimate Parent: Hercules. SIC: 2821—Plastics Materials & Resins; 2869—Industrial Organic Chemicals Nec; 2899—Chemical Preparations Nec.

★ 67484 ★ Hercules Specialty Chemicals Co.
Old Louisville Rd.
Savannah, GA 31401
Ultimate Parent: Hercules. SIC: 2821—Plastics Materials & Resins; 2843—Surface Active Agents; 2869—Industrial Organic Chemicals Nec.

★ 67485 ★ Hershey Chocolate USA
11 Artley Rd.
Savannah, GA 31408
(912)748-6186
Location Type: Plant. Officer: Carol Rich, Plant Manager. Ultimate Parent: Hershey Foods. SIC: 2032—Canned Specialties.

★ 67486 ★ Hertz Rent-A-Car Corp.
Travis Field
Savannah, GA 31401
(912)964-9595
Ultimate Parent: Hertz. SIC: 7514—Passenger Car Rental.

★ 67487 ★ Hunt-Wesson Inc.
Lathrop Ave.
Savannah, GA 31402-0247
(912)233-7911
Location Type: Plant. Officer: W. M. Baczynski, Plant Manager. Ultimate Parent: Conagra.

★ 67488 ★ Hunt-Wesson Inc. Savannah Refinery
Lathrop Ave.
Savannah, GA 31401
Ultimate Parent: Conagra. SIC: 2079—Edible Fats & Oils Nec.

★ 67489 ★ IBM Corp.
400 Mall Blvd.
Savannah, GA 31406
(912)352-8915
Ultimate Parent: IBM. SIC: 7389—Business Services Nec.

★ 67490 ★ IDS Financial Services Inc.
6606 Abercorn St.
Savannah, GA 31405-5817
Location Type: Branch office. Ultimate Parent: American Express Co.

★ 67491 ★ Intermarine USA
301 North Lathrop Ave.
Savannah, GA 31401
Ultimate Parent: Hercules. SIC: 3731—Ship Building & Repairing.

★ 67492 ★ Katalistiks Inc.
1800 E. President St.
Savannah, GA 31404-3815
Ultimate Parent: Union Carbide Corp. SIC: 2819—Industrial Inorganic Chemicals Nec.

★ 67493 ★ Kmart Pharmacy
33 Montgomery St.
Savannah, GA 31404
(912)927-1448
Ultimate Parent: K-Mart. SIC: 5912—Drug Stores & Proprietary Stores.

★ 67494 ★ Kroger
107 Red Fox Dr.
Savannah, GA 31419
(912)925-0095
Ultimate Parent: Kroger. SIC: 1521—Single-Family Housing Construction.

★ 67495 ★ Kroger Sav-On
318 Mall Blvd.
Savannah, GA 31406
(912)354-7134
Ultimate Parent: Kroger. SIC: 5411—Grocery Stores.

★ 67496 ★ Kroger Sav-On Pharmacy Dept
318 Mall Blvd.
Savannah, GA 31406
(912)354-7431
Ultimate Parent: Kroger. SIC: 5912—Drug Stores & Proprietary Stores.

★ 67497 ★ Kroger Savon Food&Drug
1900 E. Victory Dr.
Savannah, GA 31404
(912)236-0750
Ultimate Parent: Kroger. SIC: 5912—Drug Stores & Proprietary Stores.

★ 67498 ★ Kroger Supermarket
4224 Augusta Rd.
Savannah, GA 31408
(912)964-8217
Ultimate Parent: Kroger. SIC: 5411—Grocery Stores.

★ 67499 ★ Manville/Schuller Inc.
1 Foundation Dr.
Savannah, GA 31498
Ultimate Parent: Manville Corp. SIC: 2952—Asphalt Felts & Coatings.

★ 67500 ★ New York Life Savannah General Office
Southeastern Agencies
6600 Abercorn St., Ste. 200
Savannah, GA 31405
(912)355-3353 Fax: (912)356-1777
Officer: Faith Cuda, General Manager. Ultimate Parent: New York Life.

★ 67501 ★ New York Life Savannah General Office
Southeastern Agencies
Box 23469
Savannah, GA 31403-3469
(912)355-3353 Fax: (912)356-1777
Officer: Faith Cuda, General Manager. Ultimate Parent: New York Life.

★ 67502 ★ Otis Elevator Co.
6 W. State St.
Savannah, GA 31401
(912)233-2269
Ultimate Parent: United Technologies. SIC: 1796—Installing Building Equipment Nec.

★ 67503 ★ Pennzoil Product Co.
9 Telfair Pl
Savannah, GA 31401
(912)236-3125
Ultimate Parent: Pennzoil. SIC: 5172—Petroleum Products Nec.

★ 67504 ★ Pennzoil Product Co.
9 Telfair Pl
Savannah, GA 31401
(912)236-3125
Ultimate Parent: Pennzoil. SIC: 5172—Petroleum Products Nec.

★ 67505 ★ Pepsi-Cola Bottling Co.
4009 Montgomery St.
Savannah, GA 31405
(912)233-9291
Officer: Bud Miller, Manager. Ultimate Parent: Pepsico. SIC: 2086—Bottled & Canned Soft Drinks.

★ 67506 ★ Piggly Wiggly
2142 E. Victory Dr.
Savannah, GA 31404
(912)234-3491
Ultimate Parent: Bruno's. SIC: 5411—Grocery Stores.

★ 67507 ★ Piggly Wiggly
Abercorn Largo
Savannah, GA 31419
(912)925-5953
Ultimate Parent: Bruno's. SIC: 5411—Grocery Stores.

★ 67508 ★   Ryder Truck Rental
2237 E. Victory Dr. A
Savannah, GA 31404
(912)236-1739
Ultimate Parent: Ryder System. SIC:
7389—Business Services Nec.

★ 67509 ★   Ryder Truck Rental
600 E. De Renne Ave.
Savannah, GA 31405
(912)358-4850
Ultimate Parent: Ryder System. SIC:
7513—Truck Rental & Leasing Without
Drivers.

★ 67510 ★   Safeco Insurance Co.
of America
6606 Abercorn St.
Savannah, GA 31405
(912)352-7307
Ultimate Parent: Safeco. SIC: 6411—
Insurance Agents, Brokers & Service.

★ 67511 ★   Sam's Wholesale
Club
3609 Ogeechee Rd.
Savannah, GA 31405
(912)238-1446
Ultimate Parent: Wal-Mart Stores, Inc. SIC:
5141—Groceries—General Line.

★ 67512 ★   Savannah Foods &
Industries, Inc.
2 E. Bryan St.
Savannah, GA 31401
(912)234-1261 Fax: (912)238-0252
Company Type: Headquarters. Officer:
William W. Sprague III. Employee Count:
2244. Sales: 1122.9 M. Fortune 500:
Largest U.S. Industrial Corporations:
Ranking 341.

★ 67513 ★   Shell Service
2320 Ogeechee Rd.
Savannah, GA 31401
(912)236-1867
Ultimate Parent: Shell Oil Co. SIC: 5947—
Gift, Novelty & Souvenir Shops; 5947—Gift,
Novelty & Souvenir Shops.

★ 67514 ★   Specialty Products &
Insulation
222 SE Lathrop Ave.
Savannah, GA 31401-2138
(912)238-8326
Ultimate Parent: Avery Dennison Corp.
SIC: 5169—Chemicals & Allied Products
Nec; 5211—Lumber & Other Building
Materials.

★ 67515 ★   Stone Container Corp.
1 Bonnybridge Rd.
Savannah, GA 31407
(912)964-1271
Officer: Jim Lewis, Manager. Ultimate
Parent: Stone Container Corp. SIC: 2621—
Paper Mills; 2631—Paperboard Mills;
2674—Bags—Uncoated Paper & Multiwall.

★ 67516 ★   T J Maxx Store
740 Abercorn St.
Savannah, GA 31401
(912)352-4550
Ultimate Parent: TJX. SIC: 5651—Family
Clothing Stores.

★ 67517 ★   Trailways Bus System
226 W. Broad St.
Savannah, GA 31401
(912)233-4104
Ultimate Parent: Greyhound Lines Inc. SIC:
4131—Intercity & Rural Bus Transportation.

★ 67518 ★   Trust Co. Bank of
Savannah, N.A.
33 Bull St.
Savannah, GA 31401-3334
(912)944-1000 Fax: (912)944-1270
Officer: W. Harry Swicord, President &
CEO. Ultimate Parent: Suntrust Banks.
SIC: 6021—National Commercial Banks.

★ 67519 ★   Trust Co. of Georgia
Bank of Savannah, N.A.
13060 Akerman Ext.
Savannah, GA 31419
(912)921-1112
Officer: Kathy A. Ford, Manager. Ultimate
Parent: Suntrust Banks. SIC: 6021—
National Commercial Banks.

★ 67520 ★   Trust Co. of Georgia
Bank of Savannah, N.A.
324 Johnny Mercer Blvd.
Savannah, GA 31410-2115
(912)944-1122
Officer: Carol L. Brown, Manager. Ultimate
Parent: Suntrust Banks. SIC: 6021—
National Commercial Banks.

★ 67521 ★   Trust Co. of Georgia
Bank of Savannah, N.A.
330 Mall Blvd.
Savannah, GA 31406-4875
(912)944-1112
Officer: Carolyn Provost, Manager.
Ultimate Parent: Suntrust Banks. SIC:
6021—National Commercial Banks.

★ 67522 ★   Trust Co. of Georgia
Bank of Savannah, N.A.
10310 Abercorn Expy.
Savannah, GA 31406-4552
(912)944-1102
Officer: Mary T. Rowse, Manager. Ultimate
Parent: Suntrust Banks. SIC: 6021—
National Commercial Banks.

★ 67523 ★   Trust Co. of Georgia
Bank of Savannah, N.A.
2815 Skidaway Rd.
Savannah, GA 31404-4411
(912)944-1052
Officer: William D. Hazlie, Manager.
Ultimate Parent: Suntrust Banks. SIC:
6021—National Commercial Banks.

★ 67524 ★   Trust Co. of Georgia
Bank of Savannah, N.A.
Bourne Ave. & Terminal
Savannah, GA 31408
(912)944-1091
Officer: Janice Stricklin, Manager. Ultimate
Parent: Suntrust Banks. SIC: 6021—
National Commercial Banks.

★ 67525 ★   Trust Co. of Georgia
Bank of Savannah, N.A.
610 E. DeRenne Ave.
Savannah, GA 31405-6714
(912)944-1032
Officer: Billy D. Reese, Manager. Ultimate
Parent: Suntrust Banks. SIC: 6021—
National Commercial Banks.

★ 67526 ★   Trust Co. of Georgia
Bank of Savannah, N.A.
702 W. Oglethorpe Ave.
Savannah, GA 31401-2308
(912)944-1072
Ultimate Parent: Suntrust Banks. SIC:
6021—National Commercial Banks.

★ 67527 ★   Trust Co. of Georgia
Bank of Savannah, N.A.
2505 Abercorn St.
Savannah, GA 31401-9132
(912)944-1062
Officer: Harrich Grtknecht, Manager.
Ultimate Parent: Suntrust Banks. SIC:
6021—National Commercial Banks.

★ 67528 ★   Trust Co. of Georgia
Bank of Savannah, N.A.
301 Mitchell Blvd.
Savannah, GA 31408
(912)944-1042
Officer: Jane T. Byrdic, Manager. Ultimate
Parent: Suntrust Banks. SIC: 6021—
National Commercial Banks.

★ 67529 ★   Unijax Inc.
216 SE Lathrop Ave.
Savannah, GA 31401-2138
(912)236-1366
Officer: William Mullen. Ultimate Parent:
Alco Standard Corp. SIC: 5084—Industrial
Machinery & Equipment; 5087—Service
Establishment Equipment; 5113—Industrial
& Personal Service Paper.

★ 67530 ★   Union Camp Corp.
W. Lathrop Ave.
Savannah, GA 31408
Ultimate Parent: Union Camp Corp. SIC:
2611—Pulp Mills; 2631—Paperboard Mills;
2821—Plastics Materials & Resins; 2653—
Corrugated & Solid Fiber Boxes; 2861—
Gum & Wood Chemicals; 2674—Bags—
Uncoated Paper & Multiwall.

★ 67531 ★   Union Camp Corp.
West Lathrop Ave. PO Box 570
Savannah, GA 31402
Ultimate Parent: Union Camp Corp. SIC:
2611—Pulp Mills; 2631—Paperboard Mills.

★ 67532 ★   Union Camp Corp.
Woodlands Div.
1201 W. Lothrop Ave.
Savannah, GA 31401
(912)238-6000
Company Type: Division. Officer: Sidney
Nutting, Vice President. Ultimate Parent:
Union Camp Corp. SIC: 2621—Paper Mills;
2631—Paperboard Mills; 2653—Corrugated
& Solid Fiber Boxes.

★ 67533 ★   Wal Mart Discount
City
Largo Plz.
Savannah, GA 31401
(912)925-6810
Ultimate Parent: Wal-Mart Stores, Inc. SIC:
5311—Department Stores.

Screven

★ 67534 ★   Ace Hardware of
Screven
70 PO Box
Screven, GA 31560
(912)579-6595
Ultimate Parent: Ace Hardware. SIC:
5251—Hardware Stores.

★ 67535 ★   Trust Co. Bank of SE
Georgia, N.A.
J.L. Tyre St.
Screven, GA 31560-9601
(912)579-2265
Officer: Juenite T. Roberson. Ultimate
Parent: Suntrust Banks. SIC: 6021—
National Commercial Banks.

Senoia

★ 67536 ★   Bank of Coweta
Hwy. 16
Senoia, GA 30276
(404)599-8400
Location Type: Branch office. Officer:
Hazel E. Thompson, Vice President.
Ultimate Parent: Synovus Financial Corp.
SIC: 6021—National Commercial Banks.

Shellman

★ 67537 ★   Lilly Research
Laboratories
Hwy. 41 S
Shellman, GA 31786
(912)679-5280
Ultimate Parent: Eli Lilly. SIC: 5169—
Chemicals & Allied Products Nec.

Smyrna

★ 67538 ★   APAC
3111 Port Cobb Dr. SE
Smyrna, GA 30080
(404)351-4430
Officer: Sam Talley, President. Ultimate
Parent: Ashland Oil. SIC: 2951—Asphalt
Paving Mixtures & Blocks.

★ 67539 ★   Apac Georgia Inc.
MacDougald Warren Div.
3130 Port Cobb Dr.
Smyrna, GA 30080
Company Type: Division. Ultimate Parent:
Ashland Oil. SIC: 2950—Asphalt Paving &
Roofing Materials.

★ 67540 ★   Avnet
Electro-Air Corp.
500 Lake Ridge Dr. SE
Smyrna, GA 30082
(404)432-1130 Fax: (404)952-0765
Ultimate Parent: Avnet.

★ 67541 ★   Bank South
3300 S. Cobb Dr.
Smyrna, GA 30080-4118
(404)850-6295
Ultimate Parent: Bank South Corp. SIC:
6021—National Commercial Banks.

★ 67542 ★   Bank South
3315-1 S. Cobb Dr.
Smyrna, GA 30080
(404)333-3384
Location Type: Branch office. Officer: Amy
Allen. Ultimate Parent: Bank South Corp.
SIC: 6021—National Commercial Banks;
6022—State Commercial Banks; 6141—
Personal Credit Institutions; 6162—
Mortgage Bankers & Correspondents.

★ 67543 ★   Bank South, NA
2475 S. Cobb Dr. SW
Smyrna, GA 30080-1870
(404)433-8922
Company Type: Subsidiary. Location
Type: Branch office. Officer: Chris Terilli,
Manager. Ultimate Parent: Bank South
Corp. SIC: 6021—National Commercial
Banks.

★ 67544 ★   Bank South, NA
3315-1 S. Cobb Dr.
Smyrna, GA 30080
(404)333-3384
Company Type: Subsidiary. Location
Type: Branch office. Officer: Susan
Rudolph, Manager. Ultimate Parent: Bank
South Corp. SIC: 6021—National
Commercial Banks.

★ 67545 ★   Bank South NA/
Smyrna
3315-1 S, Cobb Dr.
Smyrna, GA 30080
(404)333-3384
Company Type: Subsidiary. Location
Type: Branch office. Officer: Amy Allen,
Branch Mgr. Ultimate Parent: Bank South
Corp. SIC: 6021—National Commercial
Banks.

★ 67546 ★   Circuit City
1968 Cobb Pky. SE
Smyrna, GA 30080
(404)955-6866
Ultimate Parent: Circuit City Stores.

★ 67547 ★   Colonial Pipeline Co.
Smyr
2745 Spring Rd. SE
Smyrna, GA 30080
(404)436-8336
Ultimate Parent: Colonial Pipeline.

★ 67548 ★   Dewalt Industrial Tool
Co.
2550 Cobb Pky.
Smyrna, GA 30080-0869
(404)956-0869
Company Type: Branch. Ultimate Parent:
Black & Decker Corp. SIC: 5082—
Construction & Mining Machinery.

★ 67549 ★   Eds
2033 Lake Park Dr. SE
Smyrna, GA 30080
(404)435-5681
Ultimate Parent: Electronic Data Systems.

★ 67550 ★   First Union National
Bank of Georgia
3261 S. Cobb Dr.
Smyrna, GA 30080-4197
(404)438-5300
Location Type: Branch office. Ultimate
Parent: First Union Corp. SIC: 6021—
National Commercial Banks.

★ 67551 ★   Fleet Finance Inc.
Smyrna
821 Concord Rd.
Smyrna, GA
(404)435-4424
Ultimate Parent: Fleet Financial Group.

★ 67552 ★   Interlake Packaging
Corp.
5000 Highland Pkwy SE
Smyrna, GA 30082
(404)432-9222
Ultimate Parent: Interlake.

★ 67553 ★   Kentucky Fried
Chicken
4499 S. Cobb Dr.
Smyrna, GA 30080
(404)435-9862
Ultimate Parent: Pepsico.

★ 67554 ★   Kentucky Fried
Chicken
2431 S. Cobb Dr. SE
Smyrna, GA 30080
(404)436-8000
Ultimate Parent: Pepsico.

★ 67555 ★   Kmart Store
3205 S. Cobb Dr.
Smyrna, GA 30080
(404)432-0017
Ultimate Parent: K-Mart.

★ 67556 ★ **Kmart Stores Pharmacy**
3205 A South Cobb Dr.
Smyrna, GA
(404)432-0542
Ultimate Parent: K-Mart.

★ 67557 ★ **Kroger Co. the Retail Stores**
3315 S. Cobb Dr. SE
Smyrna, GA 30080
(404)433-8380
Ultimate Parent: Kroger.

★ 67558 ★ **Kroger Pharmacies Kroger Co. Th**
3315 S. Cobb Dr.
Smyrna, GA 30080
(404)433-8392
Ultimate Parent: Kroger.

★ 67559 ★ **Lerner Shop**
Cobb Ctr. Mall
Smyrna, GA
(404)436-4977
Ultimate Parent: Limited.

★ 67560 ★ **Nationsbank Acct Activity Inf**
4567 S. Cobb Dr.
Smyrna, GA 30080
(404)523-0900
Ultimate Parent: Nationsbank Corp.

★ 67561 ★ **Nationsbank Offices Atlanta Ar**
4567 S. Cobb Dr.
Smyrna, GA 30080
(404)969-0550
Ultimate Parent: Nationsbank Corp.

★ 67562 ★ **Payless Shoesource**
2432 Atlanta Rd.
Smyrna, GA 30080
(404)432-0846
Ultimate Parent: May Department Stores.

★ 67563 ★ **Pizza Hut**
2771 New Spring Rd. NW
Smyrna, GA
(404)952-8054
Ultimate Parent: Pepsico.

★ 67564 ★ **Pizza Hut**
1531 Spring Rd. SE
Smyrna, GA
(404)438-9600
Ultimate Parent: Pepsico.

★ 67565 ★ **Pizza Hut**
3815 S. Cobb Dr. SE
Smyrna, GA 30080
(404)431-5888
Ultimate Parent: Pepsico.

★ 67566 ★ **Pizza Hut**
2542 Atlanta Rd.
Smyrna, GA 30080
(404)434-7493
Ultimate Parent: Pepsico.

★ 67567 ★ **PPG Industries Inc.**
6400 Highland Pkwy SE
Smyrna, GA 30082
(404)438-1816
Ultimate Parent: PPG Industries Inc.

★ 67568 ★ **Radio Shack**
Cumberland Mall
Smyrna, GA
(404)434-3507
Company Type: Division. **Ultimate Parent:** Tandy Corp.

★ 67569 ★ **Radio Shack**
Cumberland Mall
Smyrna, GA
(404)434-1479
Company Type: Division. **Ultimate Parent:** Tandy Corp.

★ 67570 ★ **Radio Shack**
Concorde Village Shopping
Smyrna, GA
(404)435-7271
Company Type: Division. **Ultimate Parent:** Tandy Corp.

★ 67571 ★ **Richards S P Co. Ofc Supls**
6300 Highland Pky. SE
Smyrna, GA 30082
(404)436-6881
Ultimate Parent: Genuine Parts.

★ 67572 ★ **Ryder Truck Rental**
Cumberland Mall Area
Smyrna, GA
(404)333-0177
Ultimate Parent: Ryder System.

★ 67573 ★ **Ryder Truck Rental**
4757 S. Cobb Dr. SE
Smyrna, GA 30080
(404)333-0177
Ultimate Parent: Ryder System.

★ 67574 ★ **S. P. Richards Co.**
6300 Highlands Pky.
Smyrna, GA 30082
(404)434-4571 **Fax:** (404)433-3570
Company Type: Subsidiary. **Ultimate Parent:** Genuine Parts.

★ 67575 ★ **S. P. Richards Co., Inc.**
6300 Highlands Pky.
Smyrna, GA 30082-7231
(404)436-6881
Officer: Tom Gallagher, Chairman of the Board. **Ultimate Parent:** Genuine Parts. **SIC:** 5112—Stationery & Office Supplies; 5021—Furniture. **Employee Count:** 1500. **Sales:** 550000000 M.

★ 67576 ★ **Taco Bell**
5161 S. Cobb Dr. SE
Smyrna, GA 30080
(404)794-2525
Ultimate Parent: Pepsico.

★ 67577 ★ **Taco Bell**
2624 Cobb Pkwy SE
Smyrna, GA 30080
(404)988-0479
Ultimate Parent: Pepsico.

★ 67578 ★ **Taco Bell**
2721 S. Cobb Dr.
Smyrna, GA 30080
(404)432-9836
Ultimate Parent: Pepsico.

★ 67579 ★ **Target Stores District Offices**
2201 Cobb Pky. SE
Smyrna, GA 30080
(404)952-1218
Ultimate Parent: Dayton Hudson.

★ 67580 ★ **Target Stores Retail Stores**
2201 S. Cobb Pky. SE
Smyrna, GA
(404)952-2241
Ultimate Parent: Dayton Hudson.

★ 67581 ★ **Tec Systems**
1600 Wilson Way SE
Smyrna, GA 30082
(404)435-1300
Ultimate Parent: W. R. Grace.

★ 67582 ★ **Time Electronics**
500 Lake Ridge Dr. NE
Smyrna, GA 30082
(404)432-1900
Location Type: Branch office. **Ultimate Parent:** Avnet. **SIC:** 5065—Electronic Parts & Equipment Nec.

★ 67583 ★ **Valvoline Instant Oil Change**
2671 S. Cobb Dr. SE
Smyrna, GA 30080
(404)434-4225
Ultimate Parent: Ashland Oil.

★ 67584 ★ **Valvoline Instant Oil Change**
2671 S. Cobb Dr. SE
Smyrna, GA 30080
(404)434-4225
Ultimate Parent: Ashland Oil.

★ 67585 ★ **ZEP Manufacturing Co.**
3008 Olympic Industrial Dr. SE
Smyrna, GA 30080
(404)355-3120
Officer: Walter Bates, Manager. **Ultimate Parent:** National Service Industries. **SIC:** 2842—Polishes & Sanitation Goods; 3589—Service Industry Machinery Nec.

★ 67586 ★ **Zep Manufacturing Co. Atlanta S**
3008 Olympic Industrial D
Smyrna, GA 30080
(404)355-3120
Ultimate Parent: National Service Industries.

Snellville

★ 67587 ★ **Ace Hardware**
1997 Scenic Hwy.
Snellville, GA 30278
(404)972-8080
Ultimate Parent: Ace Hardware.

★ 67588 ★ **Bank South, NA**
2467 E. Main St.
Snellville, GA 30278
(404)985-3420
Company Type: Subsidiary. **Location Type:** Branch office. **Officer:** Polly Epps, Manager. **Ultimate Parent:** Bank South Corp. **SIC:** 6021—National Commercial Banks.

★ 67589 ★ **First Union National Bank of Georgia**
2333 E. Main St.
Snellville, GA 30278-3334
(404)978-3777
Location Type: Branch office. **Ultimate Parent:** First Union Corp. **SIC:** 6021—National Commercial Banks.

★ 67590 ★ **Food Lion**
2135 E. Main St. SE
Snellville, GA 30278
(404)978-8208
Ultimate Parent: Food Lion.

★ 67591 ★ **Food Lion Inc.**
2135 E. Main St. SE
Snellville, GA 30278
(404)978-8208
Ultimate Parent: Food Lion.

★ 67592 ★ **Jiffy Lube Snellville**
2564 W. Main St.
Snellville, GA 30278
(404)979-6886
Ultimate Parent: Pennzoil.

★ 67593 ★ **Kentucky Fried Chicken**
2662 W. Main St.
Snellville, GA 30278
(404)972-1935
Ultimate Parent: Pepsico.

★ 67594 ★ **Kmart Stores**
2420 Wisteria Dr.
Snellville, GA 30278
(404)972-0553
Ultimate Parent: K-Mart.

★ 67595 ★ **Kmart Stores Pharmacy**
2420 Wisteria Dr.
Snellville, GA 30278
(404)972-1592
Ultimate Parent: K-Mart.

★ 67596 ★ **Kroger Company**
1385 Ridgefield Dr.
Snellville, GA
(404)978-9971
Ultimate Parent: Kroger.

★ 67597 ★ **Kroger Co. the Retail Stores**
4002 Hwy. 78
Snellville, GA 30278
(404)979-7008
Ultimate Parent: Kroger.

★ 67598 ★ **Kroger Co. the Retail Stores**
2419 E. Main St. SW
Snellville, GA 30278
(404)979-8535
Ultimate Parent: Kroger.

★ 67599 ★ **Kroger Pharmacies**
2419 E. Main St.
Snellville, GA 30278
(404)979-8444
Ultimate Parent: Kroger.

★ 67600 ★ **Kroger Pharmacies**
4002 Hwy. 78
Snellville, GA 30278
(404)979-8772
Ultimate Parent: Kroger.

★ 67601 ★ **Linens 'n Things Snellville St**
2314 Henry Clower Blvd. SW
Snellville, GA 30278
(404)985-0808
Ultimate Parent: Melville.

★ 67602 ★ **Mary Kay Cosmetics**
Indep Sales
1365 Barnsley Wk SW
Snellville, GA 30278
(404)979-8055
Ultimate Parent: Mary Kay Cosmetics.

★ 67603 ★ **Mary Kay Cosmetics**
Indep Sales
2503 Schooner Cove
Snellville, GA 30278
(404)972-4317
Ultimate Parent: Mary Kay Cosmetics.

★ 67604 ★ **Mary Kay Cosmetics**
Indep Sales
2015 Clipper Straits
Snellville, GA 30278
(404)979-1300
Ultimate Parent: Mary Kay Cosmetics.

★ 67605 ★ **McDonald's Restaurants**
Hwy. 78
Snellville, GA
(404)972-0259
Ultimate Parent: McDonald's.

★ 67606 ★ **Mutual of New York/ Mony Atlant**
2463 Heritage Village
Snellville, GA 30278
(404)979-1301
Ultimate Parent: Mutual of New York.

★ 67607 ★ **Nationsbank Acct Activity Inf**
2550 Odum St.
Snellville, GA 30278
(404)523-0900
Ultimate Parent: Nationsbank Corp.

★ 67608 ★ **Nationsbank Offices Atlanta Ar**
2550 Odum St.
Snellville, GA 30278
(404)978-5980
Ultimate Parent: Nationsbank Corp.

★ 67609 ★ **Pizza Hut**
2296-D Henry Clower
Snellville, GA
(404)985-4300
Ultimate Parent: Pepsico.

★ 67610 ★ **Pizza Hut**
2661 W. Main St.
Snellville, GA 30278
(404)972-3424
Ultimate Parent: Pepsico.

★ 67611 ★ **Radio Shack**
2135 E. Main St. SW
Snellville, GA 30278
(404)972-6546
Company Type: Division. **Ultimate Parent:** Tandy Corp.

★ 67612 ★ **Taco Bell**
2617 W. Main St. SW
Snellville, GA 30278
(404)972-9230
Ultimate Parent: Pepsico.

★ 67613 ★ **Target Stores Retail Stores**
2140 McGee Rd.
Snellville, GA 30278
(404)979-4300
Ultimate Parent: Dayton Hudson.

★ 67614 ★ **Wal Mart Vision Center**
2135 E. Main St.
Snellville, GA 30278
(404)979-8651
Ultimate Parent: Wal-Mart Stores, Inc.

Social Circle

★ 67615 ★ **Hudson Foods Inc.**
National Egg Products Div.
351 Ronthor Rd.
Social Circle, GA 30279
Company Type: Division. **Ultimate Parent:** Hudson Foods.

Sparta

★ 67616 ★ **Duck Head Apparel Co.**
108 E. Adams St.
Sparta, GA 31087
(706)444-5287
Officer: Kermit House, Manager. **Ultimate Parent:** Delta Woodside Industries. **SIC:** 2325—Men's/Boys' Trousers & Slacks.

St Simons is

★ 67617 ★ **Cincinnati Insurance Co.**
1672 Frederica Rd.
St Simons is, GA 31522
(912)638-6111
Ultimate Parent: Cincinnati Financial. **SIC:** 6411—Insurance Agents, Brokers & Service.

★ 67618 ★ **Food Lion**
1701 Frederica Rd.
St Simons is, GA 31522
(912)638-4105
Ultimate Parent: Food Lion. **SIC:** 5411—Grocery Stores.

★ 67619 ★ **Georgia Federal Bank F S B**
1625 Frederica Rd.
St Simons is, GA 31522
(912)638-9071
Ultimate Parent: First Union Corp. **SIC:** 6159—Miscellaneous Business Credit Institutions.

★ 67620 ★ **Kentucky Fried Chicken**
1809 Frederica Rd.
St Simons is, GA 31522
(912)638-9013
Ultimate Parent: Pepsico. **SIC:** 5812—Eating Places.

St. Mary's

★ 67621 ★ **Coastal Bank of Georgia**
2601 Osborne Rd.
St. Mary's, GA 31558-2549
(912)882-3601
Location Type: Branch office. **Officer:** James L. Wells. **Ultimate Parent:** Synovus Financial Corp. **SIC:** 6021—National Commercial Banks.

St. Marys

★ 67622 ★ **Bank South NA**
2442 Osborne Rd.
St. Marys, GA 31558-2545
(912)882-4283
Location Type: Branch office. **Officer:** Gary D. Willis. **Ultimate Parent:** Bank South Corp. **SIC:** 6021—National Commercial Banks; 6022—State Commercial Banks.

★ 67623 ★ **Bank South NA/St. Mary's**
2442 Osborne Rd.
St. Marys, GA 31558
(912)882-4283
Company Type: Subsidiary. **Location Type:** Branch office. **Officer:** Gary Willis, President. **Ultimate Parent:** Bank South Corp. **SIC:** 6021—National Commercial Banks.

★ 67624 ★ **Barnett Bank of Southeast Georgia, NA**
2712 Osborne Rd.
St. Marys, GA 31558-1503
(912)673-6060
Company Type: Subsidiary. **Location Type:** Branch office. **Officer:** John Minor, Vice President. **Ultimate Parent:** Barnett Banks. **SIC:** 6021—National Commercial Banks.

★ 67625 ★ **Johnson Controls Inc.**
1468 PO Box
St. Marys, GA 31558
(912)673-8603
Ultimate Parent: Johnson Controls Inc.

St. Simons Island

★ 67626 ★ **Barnett Bank of Southeast Georgia, NA**
1811 Frederica Rd.
St. Simons Island, GA 31520-1843
(912)638-3314
Company Type: Subsidiary. **Location Type:** Branch office. **Officer:** Nick Doster, Vice President. **Ultimate Parent:** Barnett Banks. **SIC:** 6021—National Commercial Banks.

★ 67627 ★ **Coastal Bank of Georgia**
1625 Frederica Rd.
St. Simons Island, GA 31522-2511
(912)638-2531
Location Type: Branch office. **Officer:** P.B. Salter Jr., Manager. **Ultimate Parent:** Sysco. **SIC:** 6021—National Commercial Banks.

★ 67628 ★ **Coastal Bank of Georgia**
529 Beachview Dr.
St. Simons Island, GA 31522-4705
(912)638-2513
Location Type: Branch office. **Officer:** P.B. Smither Jr., Manager. **Ultimate Parent:** Synovus Financial Corp. **SIC:** 6021—National Commercial Banks.

★ 67629 ★ **Trust Co. Bank of SE Georgia, N.A.**
2203 Demere Rd.
St. Simons Island, GA 31522-1606
(912)638-3348
Officer: Judith Griffin, Manager. **Ultimate Parent:** Suntrust Banks. **SIC:** 6021—National Commercial Banks.

★ 67630 ★ **Trust Co. Bank of SE Georgia, N.A.**
701 Sea Island Rd.
St. Simons Island, GA 31522-1769
(912)638-4978
Officer: Lisa Parmelpe, Manager. **Ultimate Parent:** Suntrust Banks. **SIC:** 6021—National Commercial Banks.

Stateboro

★ 67631 ★ **Sea Island Bank**
PO Box 568
Stateboro, GA 30459-0568
Location Type: Branch office. **Ultimate Parent:** Synovus Financial Corp. **SIC:** 6021—National Commercial Banks.

Statesboro

★ 67632 ★ **American Family Life Assur**
220 N. Main St.
Statesboro, GA 30458
(912)764-3828
Ultimate Parent: American Family Life Assurance Co. **SIC:** 6411—Insurance Agents, Brokers & Service.

★ 67633 ★ **American Family Life Assurance**
220 N. Main St.
Statesboro, GA 30458
(912)764-3828
Ultimate Parent: American Family Life Assurance Co. **SIC:** 6411—Insurance Agents, Brokers & Service.

★ 67634 ★ **Emerson Electric Co.**
Brooks Instrument Div.
Hwy. 301 N.
Statesboro, GA 30458-0450
Company Type: Division. **Ultimate Parent:** Emerson Electric Co. Inc. **SIC:** 3821—Laboratory Apparatus & Furniture; 3561—Pumps & Pumping Equipment.

★ 67635 ★ **Greyhound Bus Depot**
23 N. Zetterower Ave.
Statesboro, GA 30458
(912)764-2712
Ultimate Parent: Greyhound Lines Inc. **SIC:** 4131—Intercity & Rural Bus Transportation; 4173—Bus Terminal & Service Facilities.

★ 67636 ★ **H. K. Porter/Wiss**
Old River Rd.
Statesboro, GA 30458
Ultimate Parent: Cooper Industries. **SIC:** 3421—Cutlery.

★ 67637 ★ **H.K. Porter/Wiss**
Old River Rd.
Statesboro, GA 30458
Ultimate Parent: Cooper Industries. **SIC:** 3423—Hand & Edge Tools Nec; 3421—Cutlery.

★ 67638 ★ **Kentucky Fried Chicken**
202 N. Main St.
Statesboro, GA 30458
(912)764-6197
Ultimate Parent: Pepsico. **SIC:** 5812—Eating Places.

★ 67639 ★ **Lorillard Inc.**
220 N. Main St.
Statesboro, GA 30458
(912)764-4882
Ultimate Parent: Loews. **SIC:** 2111—Cigarettes.

★ 67640 ★ **Louisiana Pacific Corp.**
Hwy. 301 S
Statesboro, GA 30458
Ultimate Parent: Louisiana-Pacific. **SIC:** 2421—Sawmills & Planing Mills—General; 2491—Wood Preserving.

★ 67641 ★ **Piggly Wiggly**
40 S. Main St.
Statesboro, GA 30458
(912)764-2900
Ultimate Parent: Bruno's. **SIC:** 5411—Grocery Stores.

★ 67642 ★ **Pizza Hut**
129 S. Main St.
Statesboro, GA 30458
(912)764-5489
Ultimate Parent: Pepsico. **SIC:** 5812—Eating Places.

★ 67643 ★ **Professional Accounting Ser**
604 Fair Rd.
Statesboro, GA 30458
(912)681-1548
Ultimate Parent: Olsten. **SIC:** 8721—Accounting, Auditing & Bookkeeping.

★ 67644 ★ **Radio Shack**
College Plz.
Statesboro, GA 30458
(912)681-1760
Company Type: Division. **Ultimate Parent:** Tandy Corp. **SIC:** 5046—Commercial Equipment Nec.

★ 67645 ★ **Rite Aid Pharmacy**
603 Northside Dr. W
Statesboro, GA 30458
(912)489-8197
Ultimate Parent: Rite Aid. **SIC:** 5912—Drug Stores & Proprietary Stores.

★ 67646 ★ **Sea Island Bank**
2 E. Main St.
Statesboro, GA 30459-4966
(912)489-8661 **Fax:** (912)489-8391
Location Type: Branch office. **Officer:** David H. Averitt, President & CEO. **Ultimate Parent:** Synovus Financial Corp. **SIC:** 6021—National Commercial Banks.

★ 67647 ★ **Sea Island Bank**
600 Fair Rd.
Statesboro, GA 30458-5477
(912)489-8661
Location Type: Branch office. **Officer:** J. Garrett Nevil, Assistant Vice President. **Ultimate Parent:** Synovus Financial Corp. **SIC:** 6021—National Commercial Banks.

★ 67648 ★ **Sea Island Bank**
Brammen St.
Statesboro, GA 30458-8053
(912)489-8661
Location Type: Branch office. **Officer:** Sue H. Hall, Vice President. **Ultimate Parent:** Synovus Financial Corp. **SIC:** 6021—National Commercial Banks.

★ 67649 ★ **Sea Island Park**
Northside Dr.
Statesboro, GA 30458-5477
(912)489-8661
Location Type: Branch office. **Officer:** Jewell Bowman, Manager. **Ultimate Parent:** Synovus Financial Corp. **SIC:** 6021—National Commercial Banks.

★ 67650 ★ **Stop & Shop**
E Northside Dr.
Statesboro, GA 30458
(912)764-4378
Ultimate Parent: Stop & Shop. **SIC:** 5411—Grocery Stores.

★ 67651 ★ **Union Camp Corp.**
Holland Industrial Pk.
Statesboro, GA 30458
(912)764-6945
Officer: Marcia Horton, Manager. **Ultimate Parent:** Union Camp Corp. **SIC:** 2653—Corrugated & Solid Fiber Boxes.

★ 67652 ★ **Wal Mart**
Statesboro Mall
Statesboro, GA 30458
(912)489-8691
Ultimate Parent: Wal-Mart Stores, Inc. **SIC:** 5311—Department Stores.

★ 67653 ★ **Western Auto Supply Co.**
208 N. Edgewood Dr.
Statesboro, GA 30458
(912)681-1149
Ultimate Parent: Sears Roebuck & Co. **SIC:** 5531—Automobile & Home Supply Stores.

Statham

★ 67654 ★ **People's Bank**
Hwy. 29
Statham, GA 30666
(404)725-5721
Ultimate Parent: People's Bank. **SIC:** 6099—Functions Related to Deposit Banking.

Sterling

★ 67655 ★ **Georgia-Pacific Corp. Sterling Sawmill**
Hwy. 99
Sterling, GA 31521
Ultimate Parent: Georgia-Pacific. **SIC:** 2491—Wood Preserving.

Stockbridge

★ 67656 ★ **Bank South, NA**
3618 Hwy. 138 SE
Stockbridge, GA 30281
(404)389-3182
Company Type: Subsidiary. **Location Type:** Branch office. **Officer:** Debbie Dickinson, Manager. **Ultimate Parent:** Bank South Corp. **SIC:** 6021—National Commercial Banks.

★ 67657 ★ **Citgo Express**
4779 N. Henry Blvd.
Stockbridge, GA 30281
(404)474-5996
Ultimate Parent: Citgo Petroleum.

★ 67658 ★ **First Union National Bank of Georgia**
113 Hwy. 138 W.
Stockbridge, GA 30281-4254
(404)460-2415
Location Type: Branch office. **Ultimate Parent:** First Union Corp. **SIC:** 6021—National Commercial Banks.

★ 67659 ★ **Kentucky Fried Chicken**
102 Hwy. 138
Stockbridge, GA
(404)474-0131
Ultimate Parent: Pepsico.

★ 67660 ★ **Kmart Stores**
3879 Hwy. 138 South East
Stockbridge, GA 30281
(404)389-4333
Ultimate Parent: K-Mart.

★ 67661 ★ **Kmart Stores Pharmacy**
3879 Hwy. 138 South East
Stockbridge, GA 30281
(404)389-3933
Ultimate Parent: K-Mart.

★ 67662 ★ **Kroger Co. the Retail Stores**
3618 Hwy. 138 SE
Stockbridge, GA 30281
(404)474-5377
Ultimate Parent: Kroger.

257

★ 67663 ★ **Kroger Pharmacies**
3618 Hwy. 138 SE
Stockbridge, GA 30281
(404)474-5309
Ultimate Parent: Kroger.

★ 67664 ★ **Nationsbank Offices Atlanta Ar**
5505 N. Henry Blvd.
Stockbridge, GA 30281
(404)969-0550
Ultimate Parent: Nationsbank Corp.

★ 67665 ★ **Pizza Hut**
79 Hwy. 138
Stockbridge, GA
(404)389-9211
Ultimate Parent: Pepsico.

★ 67666 ★ **Pizza Hut**
4491 N. Henry Blvd.
Stockbridge, GA 30281
(404)474-7788
Ultimate Parent: Pepsico.

★ 67667 ★ **Radio Shack**
May-S Point Ii
Stockbridge, GA
(404)474-9294
Company Type: Division. **Ultimate Parent:** Tandy Corp.

★ 67668 ★ **Ryder Truck Rental**
Hwy. 42
Stockbridge, GA
(404)389-4482
Ultimate Parent: Ryder System.

★ 67669 ★ **Taco Bell**
3887 Hwy. 138
Stockbridge, GA
(404)389-5422
Ultimate Parent: Pepsico.

★ 67670 ★ **Texaco Foodmart**
4475 N. Henry Blvd.
Stockbridge, GA 30281
(404)507-0221
Ultimate Parent: Texaco.

★ 67671 ★ **Vulcan Materials Co.**
152 Quarry Rd.
Stockbridge, GA 30281
(404)474-8711
Officer: Wally Brown, Manager. **Ultimate Parent:** Vulcan Materials Co. **SIC:** 3281—Cut Stone & Stone Products.

Stone Mountain

★ 67672 ★ **McDonald's Restaurants**
456 S. Stone Mountain Lit
Stone Mountai, GA 30088
(404)498-6747
Ultimate Parent: McDonald's.

★ 67673 ★ **Radio Shack**
5295 Hwy. 78
Stone Mountai, GA 30087
(404)469-1218
Company Type: Division. **Ultimate Parent:** Tandy Corp.

★ 67674 ★ **Taco Bell**
5160 Hwy. 78 SW
Stone Mountai, GA 30087
(404)978-9511
Ultimate Parent: Pepsico.

★ 67675 ★ **Taco Bell**
5201 Memorial Dr.
Stone Mountain, GA 30083
(404)296-8666
Ultimate Parent: Pepsico.

★ 67676 ★ **Texaco**
4837 Memorial Dr.
Stone Mountai, GA 30083
(404)292-5209
Ultimate Parent: Texaco.

★ 67677 ★ **Texaco**
5260 Hwy. 78 Park Pl
Stone Mountain, GA 30087
(404)498-4408
Ultimate Parent: Texaco.

★ 67678 ★ **Bank South NA**
5295 Hwy. 78
Stone Mountain, GA 30087-3414
(404)621-5394
Location Type: Branch office. **Officer:** Candy Newsome. **Ultimate Parent:** Bank South Corp. **SIC:** 6022—State Commercial Banks.

★ 67679 ★ **Bank South NA**
1232 S. Hairston Rd.
Stone Mountain, GA 30088-2715
(404)297-6803
Location Type: Branch office. **Officer:** Mackilyn Hicks. **Ultimate Parent:** Bank South Corp. **SIC:** 6022—State Commercial Banks.

★ 67680 ★ **Bank South NA**
5567 Memorial Dr., Ste. C
Stone Mountain, GA 30083-3262
(404)297-6800
Location Type: Branch office. **Officer:** Jim Payton. **Ultimate Parent:** Bank South Corp. **SIC:** 6022—State Commercial Banks.

★ 67681 ★ **Bank South, NA**
5295 Hwy. 78
Stone Mountain, GA 30087
(404)879-5090
Company Type: Subsidiary. **Location Type:** Branch office. **Officer:** Michele Harper, Manager. **Ultimate Parent:** Bank South Corp. **SIC:** 6021—National Commercial Banks.

★ 67682 ★ **Bank South, NA**
1249 Old Tucker Ln.
Stone Mountain, GA 30087
(404)564-5936
Company Type: Subsidiary. **Location Type:** Branch office. **Officer:** Scott Hudgins, Manager. **Ultimate Parent:** Bank South Corp. **SIC:** 6021—National Commercial Banks.

★ 67683 ★ **Bank South, NA**
5567-C Memorial Dr.
Stone Mountain, GA 30083
(404)297-6800
Company Type: Subsidiary. **Location Type:** Branch office. **Officer:** Shelly Mix, Manager. **Ultimate Parent:** Bank South Corp. **SIC:** 6021—National Commercial Banks.

★ 67684 ★ **Bank South, NA**
1698 Mountain Industrial Blvd.
Stone Mountain, GA 30083
(404)621-5388
Company Type: Subsidiary. **Location Type:** Branch office. **Officer:** Tim Adler, Manager. **Ultimate Parent:** Bank South Corp. **SIC:** 6021—National Commercial Banks.

★ 67685 ★ **Bank South NA/Stone Mountain**
1698 Mountain Industrial Blvd.
Stone Mountain, GA 30083
(404)621-5388
Company Type: Subsidiary. **Location Type:** Branch office. **Officer:** Tim Adler, Mgr. **Ultimate Parent:** Bank South Corp. **SIC:** 6021—National Commercial Banks.

★ 67686 ★ **BASF Corp.**
708 Mountain Oaks Pky.
Stone Mountain, GA 30087-4738
(404)498-3706
Ultimate Parent: BASF Corp. **SIC:** 2821—Plastics Materials & Resins.

★ 67687 ★ **Baxter International**
Scientific Products Division
1750 Stone Ridge Dr.
Stone Mountain, GA 30083
(404)934-4070
Ultimate Parent: Baxter International.

★ 67688 ★ **Container Corp. of America**
5853 E. Ponce De Leon
Stone Mountain, GA 30083
Ultimate Parent: Jefferson Smurfit Corp. **SIC:** 2631—Paperboard Mills; 2421—Sawmills & Planing Mills—General.

★ 67689 ★ **First Union National Bank of Georgia**
6006 Memorial Dr.
Stone Mountain, GA 30083-2852
(404)297-1150
Location Type: Branch office. **Ultimate Parent:** First Union Corp. **SIC:** 6021—National Commercial Banks.

★ 67690 ★ **First Union National Bank of Georgia**
3860 Rockridge Rd.
Stone Mountain, GA 30083-4047
(404)508-7140
Location Type: Branch office. **Ultimate Parent:** First Union Corp. **SIC:** 6021—National Commercial Banks.

★ 67691 ★ **First Union National Bank of Georgia**
6063 Memorial Dr.
Stone Mountain, GA 30083-2804
(404)879-3400
Location Type: Branch office. **Ultimate Parent:** First Union Corp. **SIC:** 6021—National Commercial Banks.

★ 67692 ★ **First Union National Bank of Georgia**
4798 Redan Rd.
Stone Mountain, GA 30088-2721
(404)865-2960
Location Type: Branch office. **Ultimate Parent:** First Union Corp. **SIC:** 6021—National Commercial Banks.

★ 67693 ★ **Jiffy Lube Stone Mountain**
1247 S. Hairston Rd.
Stone Mountain, GA 30088
(404)593-1813
Ultimate Parent: Pennzoil.

★ 67694 ★ **Kentucky Fried Chicken**
1701 Mountain Industrial Blvd.
Stone Mountain, GA 30083
(404)270-0776
Ultimate Parent: Pepsico.

★ 67695 ★ **Kentucky Fried Chicken**
7492 Waters Edge Dr.
Stone Mountain, GA 30087
Ultimate Parent: Pepsico. **SIC:** 5812—Eating Places.

★ 67696 ★ **Kentucky Fried Chicken**
5290 Hwy. 78 SW
Stone Mountain, GA 30087
(404)498-9291
Ultimate Parent: Pepsico.

★ 67697 ★ **Kentucky Fried Chicken**
5681 Memorial Dr.
Stone Mountain, GA 30083
(404)292-0302
Ultimate Parent: Pepsico.

★ 67698 ★ **Kmart Stores**
Stone Mountain, GA
(404)294-8244
Ultimate Parent: K-Mart.

★ 67699 ★ **Kmart Stores**
1701 Mountain Industrial
Stone Mountain, GA 30083
(404)938-0151
Ultimate Parent: K-Mart.

★ 67700 ★ **Kmart Stores**
5615 Memorial Dr.
Stone Mountain, GA 30083
(404)294-4330
Ultimate Parent: K-Mart.

★ 67701 ★ **Kmart Stores Automotive**
5615 Memorial Dr.
Stone Mountain, GA 30083
(404)292-7851
Ultimate Parent: K-Mart.

★ 67702 ★ **Kmart Stores Pharmacy**
1701 Mountain Industrial
Stone Mountain, GA 30083
(404)939-2946
Ultimate Parent: K-Mart.

★ 67703 ★ **Kmart Stores Pharmacy**
5615 Memorial Dr.
Stone Mountain, GA 30083
(404)296-1601
Ultimate Parent: K-Mart.

★ 67704 ★ **Kroger Co. the Kroge Pharmacies**
1232 S. Hairston Rd.
Stone Mountain, GA 30088
(404)292-5542
Ultimate Parent: Kroger.

★ 67705 ★ **Kroger Co. the Retail Stores**
1232 S. Hairston Rd.
Stone Mountain, GA 30088
(404)292-6009
Ultimate Parent: Kroger.

★ 67706 ★ **Kroger Co. the Retail Stores**
5295 Hwy. 78 SW
Stone Mountain, GA
(404)498-3939
Ultimate Parent: Kroger.

★ 67707 ★ **Kroger Co. the Retail Stores**
5567 Memorial Dr.
Stone Mountain, GA 30083
(404)296-1750
Ultimate Parent: Kroger.

★ 67708 ★ **Kroger Pharmacies**
5567 Memorial Dr.
Stone Mountain, GA 30083
(404)299-3077
Ultimate Parent: Kroger.

★ 67709 ★ **Kroger Pharmacies**
5295 Hwy. 78
Stone Mountain, GA 30087
(404)498-3976
Ultimate Parent: Kroger.

★ 67710 ★ **Linens 'n Things Stone Mountai**
5232 Memorial Dr.
Stone Mountain, GA 30083
(404)292-0070
Ultimate Parent: Melville.

★ 67711 ★ **Linens 'n Things Stone Mountai**
5370 Hwy. 78 SW
Stone Mountain, GA 30087
(404)498-9566
Ultimate Parent: Melville.

★ 67712 ★ **Marshalls**
6011 Memorial Dr.
Stone Mountain, GA 30083
(404)469-4005
Ultimate Parent: Melville.

★ 67713 ★ **Marshalls**
5370 Hwy. 78 SW
Stone Mountain, GA 30087
(404)413-0945
Ultimate Parent: Melville.

★ 67714 ★ **Mary Kay Cosmetics**
Indep Sales
890 Wakehurst Pl.
Stone Mountain, GA 30083
(404)296-5073
Ultimate Parent: Mary Kay Cosmetics.

★ 67715 ★ **Mary Kay Cosmetics**
Indep Sales
1138 Redan Way
Stone Mountain, GA 30088
(404)413-6937
Ultimate Parent: Mary Kay Cosmetics.

★ 67716 ★ **Mary Kay Cosmetics**
Indep Sales
4276 Bramwell Dr.
Stone Mountain, GA 30083
(404)294-0930
Ultimate Parent: Mary Kay Cosmetics.

★ 67717 ★ **McDonald's Restaurants**
919 N. Hairston Rd.
Stone Mountain, GA 30083
(404)292-5450
Ultimate Parent: McDonald's.

★ **67718** ★ **McDonald's Restaurants**
1198 S. Hairston Rd.
Stone Mountain, GA 30088
(404)296-0606
Ultimate Parent: McDonald's.

★ **67719** ★ **McDonald's Restaurants**
5225 Hwy. 78
Stone Mountain, GA 30087
(404)469-3305
Ultimate Parent: McDonald's.

★ **67720** ★ **McDonald's Restaurants**
5019 Memorial Dr.
Stone Mountain, GA 30083
(404)292-3819
Ultimate Parent: McDonald's.

★ **67721** ★ **Nationsbank Honor-Cirrus L Hai**
4845 Rockbridge Rd.
Stone Mountain, GA 30083
(404)581-2121
Ultimate Parent: Nationsbank Corp.

★ **67722** ★ **Nationsbank Honor-Cirrus Mount**
5330 Hwy. 78
Stone Mountain, GA 30087
(404)498-5250
Ultimate Parent: Nationsbank Corp.

★ **67723** ★ **Nationsbank Offices Atlant Are**
Hairston Rd. 4845
Stone Mountain, GA
(404)523-0900
Ultimate Parent: Nationsbank Corp.

★ **67724** ★ **Nationsbank Offices Atlanta Area**
Mountain Park 5330 H
Stone Mountain, GA
(404)969-0550
Ultimate Parent: Nationsbank Corp.

★ **67725** ★ **Nationsbank Offices Atlanta Ar**
Hairston Rd. 4845
Stone Mountain, GA
(404)297-1185
Ultimate Parent: Nationsbank Corp.

★ **67726** ★ **Nationsbank Offices Atlanta Ar**
Mountain Park 5330 H
Stone Mountain, GA 30087
(404)498-5250
Ultimate Parent: Nationsbank Corp.

★ **67727** ★ **Nationsbank Saturday Banking O**
5330 Hwy. 78
Stone Mountain, GA 30087
(404)498-5250
Ultimate Parent: Nationsbank Corp.

★ **67728** ★ **Payless Shoesource**
5615 Memorial Dr.
Stone Mountain, GA 30083
(404)292-2195
Ultimate Parent: May Department Stores.

★ **67729** ★ **Piggly Wiggly**
1179 S. Hairston Rd.
Stone Mountain, GA 30088
(404)292-1019
Ultimate Parent: Bruno's.

★ **67730** ★ **Pizza Hut**
1130 S. Hairston Rd.
Stone Mountain, GA 30088
(404)292-9292
Ultimate Parent: Pepsico.

★ **67731** ★ **Pizza Hut**
5302-B Memorial Dr.
Stone Mountain, GA
(404)501-0300
Ultimate Parent: Pepsico.

★ **67732** ★ **Pizza Hut**
1900-L Rockbridge Rd.
Stone Mountain, GA
(404)498-8200
Ultimate Parent: Pepsico.

★ **67733** ★ **Radio Shack**
5437 Memorial Dr.
Stone Mountain, GA
(404)296-0295
Company Type: Division. **Ultimate Parent:** Tandy Corp.

★ **67734** ★ **Ryder Truck Rental**
840 Hambrick Rd.
Stone Mountain, GA
(404)292-7055
Ultimate Parent: Ryder System.

★ **67735** ★ **T J Maxx**
5370 Hwy. 78 SW
Stone Mountain, GA 30087
(404)413-0800
Ultimate Parent: TJX.

★ **67736** ★ **Waldenbooks & More**
5251 Memorial Dr.
Stone Mountain, GA
(404)297-8865
Ultimate Parent: K-Mart.

Summerville

★ **67737** ★ **Georgia Rug Mill**
Lyerly St.
Summerville, GA 30747
Ultimate Parent: Fieldcrest Cannon. **SIC:** 2273—Carpets & Rugs.

Suwanee

★ **67738** ★ **Allied Plywood Corp.**
420 Sawmill Dr. NE
Suwanee, GA 30174
(404)945-0774
Ultimate Parent: Ply Gem.

★ **67739** ★ **Avon Products Inc.**
425 Horizon Dr. NE
Suwanee, GA 30174
(404)271-6600
Ultimate Parent: Avon Products, Inc.

★ **67740** ★ **Avon Products Inc.**
425 Horizon Dr. NE
Suwanee, GA 30174
(404)271-6100
Ultimate Parent: Avon Products, Inc.

★ **67741** ★ **Avon Products Inc.**
425 Horizon Dr. 4
Suwanee, GA 30174
Ultimate Parent: Avon Products, Inc. **SIC:** 5999—Miscellaneous Retail Stores Nec.

★ **67742** ★ **Bergen Brunswig Corp.**
1085 Satellite Blvd. NW
Suwanee, GA
(404)623-3193
Ultimate Parent: Bergen Brunswig Corp.

★ **67743** ★ **Delta Air Lines**
1338 Old Peachtree Rd. NW
Suwanee, GA 30174
(404)476-3797
Ultimate Parent: Delta Air Lines, Inc.

★ **67744** ★ **Delta Air Lines Inc. Delta Appr**
1338 Old Peachtree Rd. NW
Suwanee, GA 30174
(404)476-3797
Ultimate Parent: Delta Air Lines, Inc.

★ **67745** ★ **Martin Marietta Aggreghates Fo**
3561 Peachtree Pkwy
Suwanee, GA 30174
(404)577-7455
Ultimate Parent: Martin Marietta.

★ **67746** ★ **McDonald's Restaurants**
3110 Lawrenceville Suwane
Suwanee, GA
(404)932-8348
Ultimate Parent: McDonald's.

★ **67747** ★ **Nationsbank Offices Atlanta Area**
Horizons 2800 Lawren
Suwanee, GA
(404)932-7140
Ultimate Parent: Nationsbank Corp.

★ **67748** ★ **Nationsbank Offices Atlanta**
Horizons 2800 Lawren
Suwanee, GA
(404)932-7143
Ultimate Parent: Nationsbank Corp.

★ **67749** ★ **Pizza Hut**
2850 Lawrenceville Suwane
Suwanee, GA
(404)945-1300
Ultimate Parent: Pepsico.

★ **67750** ★ **Pms Consolidated Corporate Hea**
800 Satellite Blvd. NW
Suwanee, GA 30174
(404)271-6600
Ultimate Parent: M.A.Hanna.

★ **67751** ★ **Taco Bell**
50 Gwinco Blvd. NW
Suwanee, GA 30174
(404)932-0447
Ultimate Parent: Pepsico.

Swainsboro

★ **67752** ★ **Greyhound Bus Line**
520 S. Main St.
Swainsboro, GA 30401
(912)237-8613
Ultimate Parent: Greyhound Lines Inc. **SIC:** 4212—Local Trucking Without Storage.

★ **67753** ★ **Kentucky Fried Chicken**
302 S. Main St.
Swainsboro, GA 30401
(912)237-5133
Ultimate Parent: Pepsico. **SIC:** 5812—Eating Places.

★ **67754** ★ **George J. Meyer Manufacturing**
PO Box F
Swainsboro, GA 30401
(912)237-7056
Officer: Joe Hazlett, Manager. **Ultimate Parent:** Figgie International. **SIC:** 3556—Food Products Machinery; 3599—Industrial Machinery Nec.

★ **67755** ★ **Piggly Wiggly**
503 S. Main St.
Swainsboro, GA 30401-2727
(912)237-8266
Ultimate Parent: Bruno's. **SIC:** 5141—Groceries—General Line.

★ **67756** ★ **Pizza Hut**
309 S. Main St.
Swainsboro, GA 30401
(912)237-2221
Ultimate Parent: Pepsico. **SIC:** 5812—Eating Places.

★ **67757** ★ **Radio Shack**
S Main St.
Swainsboro, GA 30401
(912)237-5995
Company Type: Division. **Ultimate Parent:** Tandy Corp. **SIC:** 5731—Radio, Television & Electronics Stores.

★ **67758** ★ **Rite Aid Disc Pharmacy**
103 Pnes St. E
Swainsboro, GA 30401
(912)237-2605
Ultimate Parent: Rite Aid. **SIC:** 5912—Drug Stores & Proprietary Stores.

★ **67759** ★ **Roper Corp.**
Electric Rd.
Swainsboro, GA 30401
Ultimate Parent: General Electric. **SIC:** 3524—Lawn & Garden Equipment; 3479—Metal Coating & Allied Services; 3398—Metal Heat Treating.

★ **67760** ★ **Union Camp Corp.**
Meadowlake Pky.
Swainsboro, GA 30401
(912)237-2900
Ultimate Parent: Union Camp Corp. **SIC:** 2411—Logging.

★ **67761** ★ **Wal Mart Discount Cities**
501 S. Main St.
Swainsboro, GA 30401
(912)237-3318
Ultimate Parent: Wal-Mart Stores, Inc. **SIC:** 5311—Department Stores.

Swanee Mission

★ **67762** ★ **PMS Consolidated**
800 Satellite Blvd.
Swanee Mission, GA 30174
(404)271-6800 **Fax:** (404)271-6800
Company Type: Subsidiary. **Officer:** Joseph W. Bauer, President. **Ultimate Parent:** M.A.Hanna.

★ **67763** ★ **Weirton Steel Corp.**
2361 Shore View Ct NW
Swanee Mission, GA 30174
(404)339-3645
Ultimate Parent: Weirton Steel Corp.

Sylvania

★ **67764** ★ **BASF Corp.**
Fibers
405 Mims Rd.
Sylvania, GA 30467
Company Type: Division. **Ultimate Parent:** BASF Corp. **SIC:** 2281—Yarn Spinning Mills.

★ **67765** ★ **BASF Fibers**
405 Mims Rd.
Sylvania, GA 30467
(912)564-7185
Officer: John W. Waggoner, Manager. **Ultimate Parent:** BASF Corp. **SIC:** 2281—Yarn Spinning Mills.

★ **67766** ★ **Coca-Cola Bottling Co.**
Bessy Bridge Rd.
Sylvania, GA 30467
(912)564-2562
Ultimate Parent: Coca-Cola Enterprises. **SIC:** 2086—Bottled & Canned Soft Drinks.

★ **67767** ★ **Exxon**
301 S. Main St.
Sylvania, GA 30467
(912)863-9947
Ultimate Parent: Exxon. **SIC:** 7513—Truck Rental & Leasing Without Drivers.

★ **67768** ★ **Exxon Co. USA**
301 S
Sylvania, GA 30467
(912)863-4217
Ultimate Parent: Exxon. **SIC:** 5172—Petroleum Products Nec.

★ **67769** ★ **First Union National Bank of Georgia**
105 S. Main
Sylvania, GA 30467-2219
(912)564-7431
Location Type: Branch office. **Ultimate Parent:** First Union Corp. **SIC:** 6021—National Commercial Banks.

★ **67770** ★ **Piggly Wiggly**
101 Mims Rd.
Sylvania, GA 30467
(912)564-2407
Ultimate Parent: Bruno's. **SIC:** 5411—Grocery Stores.

★ **67771** ★ **Torrington Co.**
Friendship Rd. PO Box 1667
Sylvania, GA 30467
Ultimate Parent: Ingersoll-Rand. **SIC:** 3562—Ball & Roller Bearings.

★ **67772** ★ **Torrington Co. Inc.**
Friendship Rd.
Sylvania, GA 30467
(912)564-7151
Ultimate Parent: Ingersoll-Rand. **SIC:** 3562—Ball & Roller Bearings.

★ **67773** ★ **Warner's**
1113 S. Main St.
Sylvania, GA 30467
(912)564-7441
Officer: Ray Thompson, Plant Manager. **Ultimate Parent:** Warnaco Group. **SIC:** 2331—Women's/Misses' Blouses & Shirts; 2337—Women's/Misses' Suits & Coats; 2339—Women's/Misses' Outerwear Nec.

Sylvester

★ 67774 ★   Hunt-Wesson Inc.
101 S. Seabrook
Sylvester, GA 31791
(912)776-8814
Location Type: Plant. **Officer:** S. T. Camp,
Plant Manager. **Ultimate Parent:** Conagra.

★ 67775 ★   Piggly Wiggly
623 W. Franklin St.
Sylvester, GA 31791
(912)776-5668
Ultimate Parent: Bruno's. **SIC:** 5411—
Grocery Stores.

★ 67776 ★   Pizza Hut
Hwy. 82
Sylvester, GA 31791
(912)776-6976
Ultimate Parent: Pepsico. **SIC:** 5812—
Eating Places.

**★ 67777 ★   Trailways Bus
Systems**
112 N. Main St.
Sylvester, GA 31791
(912)776-2012
Ultimate Parent: Greyhound Lines Inc. **SIC:**
4131—Intercity & Rural Bus Transportation.

**★ 67778 ★   Trust Co. Bank of
South Georgia, N.A.**
201 N. Isabella St.
Sylvester, GA 31791-2169
(912)776-8400
Officer: Don Monk, President. **Ultimate
Parent:** Suntrust Banks. **SIC:** 6021—
National Commercial Banks.

Tallapposa

**★ 67779 ★   Citizens Bank & Trust
of West Georgia**
77 E. Atlanta St.
Tallapposa, GA 30176-1401
(706)574-2102
Location Type: Branch office. **Officer:**
David Greene, Manager. **Ultimate Parent:**
Synovus Financial Corp. **SIC:** 6021—
National Commercial Banks.

Talmo

**★ 67780 ★   Mott's Prepared
Foods**
Rte. 1 Hwy. 332
PO Box 1490
Talmo, GA 30575
(706)693-2241
Company Type: Division. **Location Type:**
Plant. **Ultimate Parent:** Conagra.

Temple

**★ 67781 ★   Citizens Bank & Trust
of West Georgia**
Sage St.
Temple, GA 30179
(404)562-3278
Location Type: Branch office. **Officer:**
Joyce Fain, Manager. **Ultimate Parent:**
Synovus Financial Corp. **SIC:** 6021—
National Commercial Banks.

Tennille

★ 67782 ★   Bank South
306 N. Main St.
Tennille, GA 31089-1121
(912)552-7317
Location Type: Branch office. **Officer:** Don
M. Thigpen. **Ultimate Parent:** Bank South
Corp. **SIC:** 6022—State Commercial Banks;
6021—National Commercial Banks; 6141—
Personal Credit Institutions; 6162—
Mortgage Bankers & Correspondents.

★ 67783 ★   Bank South, NA
206 N. Main St.
Tennille, GA 31089-1121
(912)552-7317
Company Type: Subsidiary. **Location
Type:** Branch office. **Officer:** Kay Bedgood,
Manager. **Ultimate Parent:** Bank South
Corp. **SIC:** 6021—National Commercial
Banks.

**★ 67784 ★   Bank South NA/
Tennille**
206 N. Main St.
Tennille, GA 31089
(912)552-7317
Company Type: Subsidiary. **Location
Type:** Branch office. **Officer:** Don M.
Thigpen, President. **Ultimate Parent:** Bank
South Corp. **SIC:** 6022—State Commercial
Banks.

Thomaston

**★ 67785 ★   Federal Paper Board
Co.**
600 Poplar Dr.
Thomaston, GA 30286
(706)647-6671
Location Type: Plant. **Officer:** John
DePasquale, Plant Manager. **Ultimate
Parent:** Federal Paper Board. **SIC:** 2652—
Setup Paperboard Boxes; 2657—Folding
Paperboard Boxes.

Thomasvile

★ 67786 ★   Warner Co.
2125 N. Martin Luther King Dr.
Thomasville, GA 31792
(912)226-8264
Officer: Frank Mason, Manager. **Ultimate
Parent:** WMX Technologies, Inc. **SIC:**
2341—Women's/Children's Underwear;
2342—Bras, Girdles & Allied Garments.

Thomasville

**★ 67787 ★   Baked Products
Group**
US Hwy. 19, S.
PO Box 1338
Thomasville, GA 31799-1338
(912)226-9110 **Fax:** (912)226-1318
Company Type: Subsidiary. **Officer:**
George E. Deese, President & CEO.
Ultimate Parent: Flowers Industries.

★ 67788 ★   Cake Products Group
US Hwy. 19, S.
PO Box 1338
Thomasville, GA 31799-1338
(912)226-9110 **Fax:** (912)226-1318
Company Type: Subsidiary. **Officer:** Gary
L. Harrison, President & CEO. **Ultimate
Parent:** Flowers Industries.

★ 67789 ★   Commercial Bank
101 S. Crawford St.
Thomasville, GA 31792-5502
(912)226-3535 **Fax:** (912)228-7037
Location Type: Branch office. **Officer:** Fred
D. Jefferson, President & CEO. **Ultimate
Parent:** Synovus Financial Corp. **SIC:**
6021—National Commercial Banks.

★ 67790 ★   Commercial Bank
PO Box 710
Thomasville, GA 31799-0710
Location Type: Branch office. **Ultimate
Parent:** Synovus Financial Corp. **SIC:**
6021—National Commercial Banks.

★ 67791 ★   Commercial Bank
215 E. Jefferson
Thomasville, GA 31792-5140
(912)226-3535
Location Type: Branch office. **Officer:** Jim
Chavaux, Manager. **Ultimate Parent:**
Synovus Financial Corp. **SIC:** 6021—
National Commercial Banks.

★ 67792 ★   Commercial Bank
2400 E. Pinetree Blvd.
Thomasville, GA 31792-4827
(912)226-3662
Location Type: Branch office. **Officer:** R.
M. Groover, Assistant Vice President.
Ultimate Parent: Synovus Financial Corp.
SIC: 6021—National Commercial Banks.

**★ 67793 ★   Compressor
Components Textron Inc.**
1211 Old Albany Rd.
Thomasville, GA 31792
Ultimate Parent: Textron. **SIC:** 3724—
Aircraft Engines & Engine Parts.

★ 67794 ★   Flowers Baking Co.
236 S. Madison St.
Thomasville, GA 31792
(912)226-5331
Officer: Terrell Kirkland, President.

Ultimate Parent: Flowers Industries. **SIC:**
2051—Bread, Cake & Related Products.

**★ 67795 ★   Flowers Baking Co. of
Thomasville Inc.**
236 N. Madison St.
PO Box 1219
Thomasville, GA 31799-1219
(912)226-5331 **Fax:** (912)228-0674
Company Type: Subsidiary. **Officer:** Terrell
Kirkland, President. **Ultimate Parent:**
Flowers Industries.

**★ 67796 ★   Flowers Holding Co.
of South Carolina Inc.**
US Hwy. 19
Thomasville, GA 31792-9841
(912)226-9110
Company Type: Subsidiary. **Officer:** Amos
R. McMullian, Chairman of the Board.
Ultimate Parent: Flowers Industries. **SIC:**
2051—Bread, Cake & Related Products.
Employee Count: 460. **Sales:** 34.7 M.

★ 67797 ★   Flowers Industries
200 US Hwy. 19 S
Thomasville, GA 31792
(912)226-9110
Company Type: Headquarters. **Officer:**
Amos R. McMullian. **Sales:** 962.1 M.
Fortune 500: Largest U.S. Industrial
Corporations: Ranking 371.

**★ 67798 ★   Flowers Industries,
Inc.**
Hwy. 19 S.
Thomasville, GA 31792
Ultimate Parent: Flowers Industries.

**★ 67799 ★   Flowers Industries
Inc.**
US Hwy. 19 S
PO Box 1338
Thomasville, GA 31799-1338
(912)226-9110 **Fax:** (912)226-9231
Company Type: Headquarters. **Officer:**
Amos R. McMullian. **Ultimate Parent:**
Flowers Industries. **Employee Count:** 9030.

**★ 67800 ★   Kentucky Fried
Chicken**
1604 E. Jackson St.
Thomasville, GA 31792
(912)228-0539
Ultimate Parent: Pepsico. **SIC:** 5812—
Eating Places.

**★ 67801 ★   Penn Mutual Life
Insurance Co.**
107 N. Broad St.
Thomasville, GA 31792
(912)226-2323
Ultimate Parent: Penn Mutual Life. **SIC:**
6411—Insurance Agents, Brokers &
Service.

★ 67802 ★   Pizza Hut
322 E. Jackson St.
Thomasville, GA 31792
(912)226-9166
Ultimate Parent: Pepsico. **SIC:** 5812—
Eating Places.

★ 67803 ★   Pizza Hut
2116 E. Pinetree Blvd.
Thomasville, GA 31792
(912)226-3333
Ultimate Parent: Pepsico. **SIC:** 5812—
Eating Places.

★ 67804 ★   Ryder Truck Rental
611 S. Hansell St.
Thomasville, GA 31792
(912)226-6685
Ultimate Parent: Ryder System. **SIC:**
7359—Equipment Rental & Leasing Nec.

★ 67805 ★   Ryder Truck Rental
Moultrie Rd.
Thomasville, GA 31792
(912)226-6409
Ultimate Parent: Ryder System. **SIC:**
7513—Truck Rental & Leasing Without
Drivers.

**★ 67806 ★   Timberlake Grocery
Co.**
1030 Campbell St.
Thomasville, GA 31792
(912)226-3616
Ultimate Parent: Nash Finch. **SIC:** 5141—
Groceries—General Line.

**★ 67807 ★   Trust Co. Bank of
South Georgia**
200 N. Crawford St.
Thomasville, GA 31792
(912)226-6812
Ultimate Parent: Suntrust Banks. **SIC:**
6021—National Commercial Banks; 6022—
State Commercial Banks.

**★ 67808 ★   Trust Co. Bank of
South Georgia, N.A.**
1327 Remington
Thomasville, GA 31792-4838
(912)226-6812
Ultimate Parent: Suntrust Banks. **SIC:**
6021—National Commercial Banks.

**★ 67809 ★   Trust Co. Bank of
South Georgia, N.A.**
200 N. Crawford St.
Thomasville, GA 31792-5123
(912)226-6812
Officer: Stephen H. Cheney. **Ultimate
Parent:** Suntrust Banks. **SIC:** 6021—
National Commercial Banks.

Thomson

**★ 67810 ★   Hoover Treated Wood
Prods. Inc.**
266 Wire Rd. NW
Thomson, GA 30824
Ultimate Parent: Ply Gem. **SIC:** 2491—
Wood Preserving.

**★ 67811 ★   Hoover Treated Wood
Products**
Wire Rd.
Thomson, GA 30824
Ultimate Parent: Ply Gem. **SIC:** 2491—
Wood Preserving.

**★ 67812 ★   Hoover Treated Wood
Products, Inc.**
Knox Shopping Ctr.
PO Box 746
Thomson, GA 30824
(404)595-5058 **Fax:** (404)595-1326
Officer: Jack B. Smith, Chairman. **Ultimate
Parent:** Ply Gem.

**★ 67813 ★   Temple-Inland Forest
Products Corp.**
Old Taylor Town Rd.
Thomson, GA 30824
Ultimate Parent: Temple-Inland. **SIC:**
2493—Reconstituted Wood Products.

**★ 67814 ★   Trust Co. Bank of
Aujusta, N.A.**
Rte. 3 Washington Rd.
Thomson, GA 30824-9803
(706)595-1234
Officer: Sue Walker. **Ultimate Parent:**
Suntrust Banks. **SIC:** 6021—National
Commercial Banks.

**★ 67815 ★   Trust Co. Bank of
Aujusta, N.A.**
201 Jackson St.
Thomson, GA 30824-2020
(706)595-1234
Officer: Sue Walker, Manager. **Ultimate
Parent:** Suntrust Banks. **SIC:** 6021—
National Commercial Banks.

**★ 67816 ★   United Technologies
Auto**
1884 Warenton Hwy.
Thomson, GA 30824
(706)595-5105
Officer: James Thompson, Manager.
Ultimate Parent: United Technologies. **SIC:**
3089—Plastics Products Nec.

**★ 67817 ★   United Technologies
Automotive Thomson Plant**
1884 Warrenton Hwy.
Thomson, GA 30824
Ultimate Parent: United Technologies. **SIC:**
2295—Coated Fabrics—Not Rubberized;
2297—Nonwoven Fabrics.

Tifton

★ 67818 ★   Avon Products Inc.
Hwy. 41 S
Tifton, GA 31794
(912)382-3249
Ultimate Parent: Avon Products, Inc. **SIC:**
5999—Miscellaneous Retail Stores Nec.

★ 67819 ★ **Central Soya Co. Inc.**
Union Rd. & I-75
Tifton, GA 31794
Ultimate Parent: Central Soya. **SIC:** 2048—Prepared Feeds Nec.

★ 67820 ★ **Central Soya Feed Co. Inc.**
Union St. at I-75
Tifton, GA 31794
Ultimate Parent: Central Soya. **SIC:** 2048—Prepared Feeds Nec.

★ 67821 ★ **First Community Bank of Tifton**
1002 W. 2nd St.
Tifton, GA 31794-4268
(912)387-2650
Location Type: Branch office. **Officer:** Warren H. Marchant Jr., Manager. **Ultimate Parent:** Synovus Financial Corp. **SIC:** 6021—National Commercial Banks.

★ 67822 ★ **First Community Bank of Tifton**
1810 Tift Ave.
Tifton, GA 31794-3542
(912)387-2660
Location Type: Branch office. **Officer:** Velma Fletcher, Manager. **Ultimate Parent:** Synovus Financial Corp. **SIC:** 6021—National Commercial Banks.

★ 67823 ★ **First Community Bank of Tifton**
218 Love Ave.
Tifton, GA 31794-4454
Location Type: Branch office. **Officer:** T. Howard Dorsett, President & CEO. **Ultimate Parent:** Synovus Financial Corp. **SIC:** 6021—National Commercial Banks.

★ 67824 ★ **First Community Bank of Tifton**
PO Box 8
Tifton, GA 31793-0008
Location Type: Branch office. **Ultimate Parent:** Synovus Financial Corp. **SIC:** 6021—National Commercial Banks.

★ 67825 ★ **Greyhound Bus Lines**
602 N. Central Ave.
Tifton, GA 31794
(912)382-1868
Ultimate Parent: Greyhound Lines Inc. **SIC:** 4111—Local & Suburban Transit.

★ 67826 ★ **Kaiser Aluminum & Chemical**
US 41 S.
Tifton, GA 31794
(912)382-3303
Ultimate Parent: Maxxam. **SIC:** 2833—Medicinals & Botanicals.

★ 67827 ★ **Piggly Wiggly**
205 E. 8th St.
Tifton, GA 31794
(912)382-7877
Ultimate Parent: Bruno's. **SIC:** 5812—Eating Places.

★ 67828 ★ **Radio Shack**
Town
Tifton, GA 31794
(912)382-4881
Company Type: Division. **Ultimate Parent:** Tandy Corp. **SIC:** 5046—Commercial Equipment Nec.

★ 67829 ★ **Shaw Industries Inc.**
Vernon St.
Tifton, GA 31794
(912)386-8610
Officer: Donny Robertson, Manager. **Ultimate Parent:** Shaw Industries, Inc. **SIC:** 2281—Yarn Spinning Mills.

★ 67830 ★ **Short & Paulk Supply Co. Inc.**
710 S. Main St.
Tifton, GA 31794-4824
(912)382-2314
Officer: Jordan Short IV, President. **Ultimate Parent:** Ace Hardware. **SIC:** 5251—Hardware Stores; 2439—Structural Wood Members Nec; 2431—Millwork; 7359—Equipment Rental & Leasing Nec; 5033—Roofing, Siding & Insulation. **Employee Count:** 55.

★ 67831 ★ **Tifton Aluminum Co., Inc.**
Southwell Blvd.
PO Box 88
Tifton, GA 31793-0088
(912)382-7330
Location Type: Branch office. **Officer:** Ronald W. Hawkins, President. **Ultimate Parent:** Aluminum Co. of America—Alcoa. **SIC:** 3354—Aluminum Extruded Products. **Employee Count:** 800.

★ 67832 ★ **Trust Co. Bank of South Georgia, N.A.**
200 John Howard Way
Tifton, GA 31794-4357
(912)382-4411
Ultimate Parent: Suntrust Banks. **SIC:** 6021—National Commercial Banks.

★ 67833 ★ **Trust Co. Bank of South Georgia, N.A.**
605 W. 2nd St.
Tifton, GA 31794-4257
(912)382-4411
Officer: James P. Atwater, President. **Ultimate Parent:** Suntrust Banks. **SIC:** 6021—National Commercial Banks.

Tifton Georgi

★ 67834 ★ **Union Camp Corp.**
Tifton Tft Indl Park
Tifton Georgi, GA 31794
(912)386-8900
Ultimate Parent: Union Camp Corp. **SIC:** 5113—Industrial & Personal Service Paper.

Toccoa

★ 67835 ★ **Aeroquip Corp.**
Meadowbrook Park
Toccoa, GA 30577
(706)779-3351
Officer: John Bryan, Manager. **Ultimate Parent:** Trinova Corp. **SIC:** 3728—Aircraft Parts & Equipment Nec.

★ 67836 ★ **Ferro Corp.**
Color Div.
Meadowbrook Industrial Pk.
Toccoa, GA 30577
(706)779-3341
Company Type: Division. **Officer:** J. E. Hooker, Manager. **Ultimate Parent:** Ferro Corp. **SIC:** 2816—Inorganic Pigments.

★ 67837 ★ **Reliance Comm/Tec Reliance Electric**
Meadowbrook Industrial Park
Toccoa, GA 30577
Ultimate Parent: Reliance Electric. **SIC:** 3661—Telephone & Telegraph Apparatus.

★ 67838 ★ **Shaw Industries Inc.**
181 Collier Rd.
Toccoa, GA 30577
(706)888-8466
Officer: Joe Blevins, Manager. **Ultimate Parent:** Shaw Industries, Inc. **SIC:** 2281—Yarn Spinning Mills; 2299—Textile Goods Nec.

Toomsboro

★ 67839 ★ **Engelhard Corp. Dixie Mine**
Buckhorn Lake Rd.
Toomsboro, GA 31090
Ultimate Parent: Engelhard Corp. **SIC:** 1455—Kaolin & Ball Clay.

★ 67840 ★ **Engelhard Corp. Gibraltar Mine**
Hwy. 112 Near Toomsboro
Toomsboro, GA 31090
Ultimate Parent: Engelhard Corp. **SIC:** 1455—Kaolin & Ball Clay.

Townsend

★ 67841 ★ **Union Camp Corp.**
Townsend, GA 31331
(912)832-4731
Ultimate Parent: Union Camp Corp. **SIC:** 2679—Converted Paper Products Nec.

Trenton

★ 67842 ★ **Hudson International Conductors**
US Hwy. 11 N.
Trenton, GA 30752
Ultimate Parent: Phelps Dodge. **SIC:** 3357—Nonferrous Wiredrawing & Insulating; 3351—Copper Rolling & Drawing.

★ 67843 ★ **Shaw Industries Inc.**
776 N. Main St.
Trenton, GA 30752
(706)657-6847
Officer: Clay Osborn, Manager. **Ultimate Parent:** Shaw Industries, Inc. **SIC:** 2281—Yarn Spinning Mills.

Tucker

★ 67844 ★ **Bank South NA**
3959 Lavista Rd., Ste. A
Tucker, GA 30084-5137
(404)621-5386
Location Type: Branch office. **Officer:** Lee Corvin. **Ultimate Parent:** Bank South Corp. **SIC:** 6022—State Commercial Banks.

★ 67845 ★ **Bank South, NA**
3959 La Vista Rd.
Tucker, GA 30084
(404)621-5386
Company Type: Subsidiary. **Location Type:** Branch office. **Officer:** Tracie Arnold, Manager. **Ultimate Parent:** Bank South Corp. **SIC:** 6021—National Commercial Banks.

★ 67846 ★ **Bausch & Lomb Inc.**
Oral Care Div.
5243 Royal Woods Pky.
Tucker, GA 30084
(404)934-1232
Company Type: Subsidiary. **Officer:** James N. Doyle Jr., President. **Ultimate Parent:** Bausch & Lomb Inc.

★ 67847 ★ **Beneficial Georgia Inc.**
3939 Lavista Rd.
Tucker, GA 30084-5137
(404)939-8050
Officer: Brian Williams. **Ultimate Parent:** Beneficial. **SIC:** 6141—Personal Credit Institutions; 6162—Mortgage Bankers & Correspondents.

★ 67848 ★ **Courtyard by Marriott**
4083 Lavista Rd.
Tucker, GA 30084
(404)938-1200
Ultimate Parent: Marriott International.

★ 67849 ★ **Del Monte Foods Atlanta Sales**
100 Crescent Ctr. Pky.
Tucker, GA 30084
(404)938-9779
Ultimate Parent: Del Monte Foods.

★ 67850 ★ **Del Monte Foods Midsouth Sales**
100 Crescent Centre Pkwy
Tucker, GA 30084
(404)938-9791
Ultimate Parent: Del Monte Foods.

★ 67851 ★ **Del Monte Foods Southeast Regi**
100 Crescent Centre Pkwy
Tucker, GA 30084
(404)938-0938
Ultimate Parent: Del Monte Foods.

★ 67852 ★ **Deluxe Check Printers**
5331 Royal Woods Pky.
Tucker, GA 30084
Ultimate Parent: Deluxe Corp. **SIC:** 2752—Commercial Printing—Lithographic.

★ 67853 ★ **Deluxe Check Printers Inc.**
5331 Royal Woods Pky.
Tucker, GA 30084
Ultimate Parent: Deluxe Corp. **SIC:** 2782—Blankbooks & Looseleaf Binders; 2752—Commercial Printing—Lithographic.

★ 67854 ★ **European Bakers, Ltd.**
5055 S. Royal Atlanta Dr.
Tucker, GA 30084-3019
(404)723-6180
Company Type: Subsidiary. **Officer:** Dave Gaddis, President. **Ultimate Parent:** Flowers Industries. **SIC:** 2051—Bread, Cake & Related Products. **Employee Count:** 200. **Sales:** 20000 M.

★ 67855 ★ **First Union National Bank of Georgia**
4070 Lavista Rd.
Tucker, GA 30084-5216
(404)270-3960
Location Type: Branch office. **Ultimate Parent:** First Union Corp. **SIC:** 6021—National Commercial Banks.

★ 67856 ★ **Flowers Specialty Baked Foods**
5055 S. Royal Atlanta Dr.
Tucker, GA 30084
(404)934-4800
Officer: Mike Bramlett, President. **Ultimate Parent:** Flowers Industries. **SIC:** 2051—Bread, Cake & Related Products.

★ 67857 ★ **Hormel Foods Corp.**
3367 Montreal Industrial Way v
Tucker, GA 30084
(404)908-4000
Location Type: Plant. **Officer:** Del Doe, Plant Manager. **Ultimate Parent:** Hormel Foods. **SIC:** 2032—Canned Specialties.

★ 67858 ★ **Jiffy Lube Tucker**
3367 Lawrenceville Hwy.
Tucker, GA 30084
(404)493-8614
Ultimate Parent: Pennzoil.

★ 67859 ★ **Jiffy Lube Tucker**
3194 Norcross Tucker Rd.
Tucker, GA 30084
(404)939-4937
Ultimate Parent: Pennzoil.

★ 67860 ★ **Johnson Controls Inc. Control P**
4419 Cowan Rd.
Tucker, GA 30084
(404)938-3958
Ultimate Parent: Johnson Controls Inc.

★ 67861 ★ **Kentucky Fried Chicken**
3989 Lawrenceville Hwy.
Tucker, GA 30084
(404)493-9323
Ultimate Parent: Pepsico.

★ 67862 ★ **Kids R US**
3983 Lavista Rd.
Tucker, GA 30084
(404)723-0303
Ultimate Parent: Toys "R" US.

★ 67863 ★ **Kroger Co Retail Stores**
6425 Hwy. 29
Tucker, GA 30084
(404)938-1772
Ultimate Parent: Kroger.

★ 67864 ★ **Kroger Co. the Retail Stores**
3959 Lavista Rd.
Tucker, GA 30084
(404)939-6304
Ultimate Parent: Kroger.

★ 67865 ★ **Kroger Pharmacies**
3959 Lavista Rd.
Tucker, GA 30084
(404)934-6442
Ultimate Parent: Kroger.

★ 67866 ★ **Mary Kay Cosmetics**
Indep Sales
4405 Bonaparte Dr.
Tucker, GA 30084
(404)496-0779
Ultimate Parent: Mary Kay Cosmetics.

★ 67867 ★ **Massachusetts Mutual Life Insurance**
100 Crescent Centre Pky.
Tucker, GA 30084
(404)939-1223
Ultimate Parent: Massasucetts Mutual Life.

★ 67868 ★ **Medtronic**
Neuro Div.
3469 Lawrenceville Hwy.
Tucker, GA 30084
(404)938-8887
Company Type: Division. **Ultimate Parent:** Medtronic Inc.

★ 67869 ★   Morton International
Ind Chemls
2191 Northlake Pky.
Tucker, GA 30084-4101
(404)723-0808
Ultimate Parent: Morton International. SIC:
5169—Chemicals & Allied Products Nec.

★ 67870 ★   National Vendors
2046 Weems Rd.
Tucker, GA 30084
(404)934-0810
Ultimate Parent: Crane.

★ 67871 ★   Nationsbank
Departments Nation
2059 Northlake Pkwy
Tucker, GA 30084
(404)491-4411
Ultimate Parent: Nationsbank Corp.

★ 67872 ★   Nationsbank
Departments Person
2059 Northlake Pkwy
Tucker, GA 30084
(404)491-4051
Ultimate Parent: Nationsbank Corp.

★ 67873 ★   Nationsbank Honor-
Cirrus North
4144 Lavista Rd.
Tucker, GA 30084
(404)491-5420
Ultimate Parent: Nationsbank Corp.

★ 67874 ★   Nationsbank Honor-
Cirrus Tucke
2333 Main St.
Tucker, GA 30084
(404)491-5400
Ultimate Parent: Nationsbank Corp.

★ 67875 ★   Nationsbank Offices
Atlanta Ar
Northlake 4144 Lavis
Tucker, GA
(404)523-0900
Ultimate Parent: Nationsbank Corp.

★ 67876 ★   Nationsbank Offices
Atlanta Ar
2333 Main St.
Tucker, GA 30084
(404)491-5404
Ultimate Parent: Nationsbank Corp.

★ 67877 ★   Nationsbank Offices
Attlanta a
2333 Main St.
Tucker, GA 30084
(404)491-5400
Ultimate Parent: Nationsbank Corp.

★ 67878 ★   Natkin Service Co.
Tucker, GA 30084
(404)934-5020
Ultimate Parent: American International
Group, Inc. SIC: 5075—Warm Air Heating &
Air-Conditioning.

★ 67879 ★   New York Life Atlanta
Central Service Office
1927 Lakeside Pky., Ste. 622
Tucker, GA 30084
(404)938-0080
Officer: Steven Nelson, Assistant Vice
President. Ultimate Parent: New York Life.

★ 67880 ★   Oglethorpe Power
2100 E. Exchange Pl.
Tucker, GA
(404)270-7600
Company Type: Headquarters. Officer:
T.D. Kilgore. Employee Count: 505.
Fortune Service 500: Ranking 48.

★ 67881 ★   Oglethorpe Power
Corp.
2100 E. Exchange Pl
Tucker, GA 30084
(404)270-7600
Ultimate Parent: Oglethorpe Power.

★ 67882 ★   Payless Shoesource
6425 Lawrenceville Hwy. NW
Tucker, GA 30084
(404)938-5915
Ultimate Parent: May Department Stores.

★ 67883 ★   Pizza Hut
4286 Chamblee Tucker Rd.
Tucker, GA 30084
(404)938-3000
Ultimate Parent: Pepsico.

★ 67884 ★   Pizza Hut
4421 Hugh Howell Rd.
Tucker, GA 30084
(404)938-0501
Ultimate Parent: Pepsico.

★ 67885 ★   Ppm Inc.
1875 Forge St.
Tucker, GA 30084
Ultimate Parent: Union Pacific Corp. SIC:
4500—Transportation by Air.

★ 67886 ★   Ryder Truck Rental
2660 Mountain Industrial
Tucker, GA 30084
(404)414-9217
Ultimate Parent: Ryder System.

★ 67887 ★   Service Merchandise
1990 W. Exchange Pl
Tucker, GA 30084
(404)491-7575
Ultimate Parent: Service Merchandise Co.,
Inc.

★ 67888 ★   Sherwin-Williams Co.
11 Lavista Office Park 107
Tucker, GA 30084
(404)621-6760
Officer: Dick Wilson, President. Ultimate
Parent: Sherwin-Williams Co. SIC: 2851—
Paints & Allied Products.

★ 67889 ★   Southern Heritage
Insurance Co.
100 Crescent Centre Pkwy
Tucker, GA 30084
(404)934-5057
Ultimate Parent: Geico.

★ 67890 ★   Southern Heritage
Insurance Co., Inc.
100 Crescent Ctr. Pky.
Tucker, GA 30084-7039
(404)934-5057
Company Type: Subsidiary. Officer:
Thomas W. Crawford, President. Ultimate
Parent: Geico. SIC: 6331—Fire, Marine &
Casualty Insurance. Employee Count: 45.

★ 67891 ★   Speciality Products
Group
5087 S. Royal Atlanta Blvd.
Tucker, GA 30084
(404)934-4800 Fax: (404)938-9349
Company Type: Subsidiary. Officer: Mike
Bramlett, President. Ultimate Parent:
Flowers Industries.

★ 67892 ★   Star Manufacturing
Co.
125 Royal Woods Ct. SW
Tucker, GA 30084
(404)270-2900
Ultimate Parent: Merrill Lynch Life.

★ 67893 ★   Taco Bell
4100 Lawrenceville Hwy.
Tucker, GA 30084
(404)934-4576
Ultimate Parent: Pepsico.

★ 67894 ★   Taco Bell
3967 La Vis
Tucker, GA 30084
(404)939-3829
Ultimate Parent: Pepsico.

★ 67895 ★   Target Stores Retail
Stores
6425 Lawrenceville Hwy.
Tucker, GA 30084
(404)934-9750
Ultimate Parent: Dayton Hudson.

★ 67896 ★   Texaco
4118 Lavista Rd.
Tucker, GA 30084
(404)934-2247
Ultimate Parent: Texaco.

★ 67897 ★   Texaco Express Lube
4118a La Vis
Tucker, GA 30084
(404)934-6117
Ultimate Parent: Texaco.

★ 67898 ★   Toys R US
4033 Lavista Rd.
Tucker, GA 30084
(404)938-4321
Ultimate Parent: Toys "R" US.

★ 67899 ★   Union Camp Corp.
1975 Lakeside Pky.
Tucker, GA 30084
(404)621-2200
Ultimate Parent: Union Camp Corp. SIC:
2621—Paper Mills; 2679—Converted Paper
Products Nec.

★ 67900 ★   Union Camp Corp.
1975 Lakeside Pky.
Tucker, GA 30084
(404)621-2200
Ultimate Parent: Union Camp Corp.

★ 67901 ★   Union Camp Corp.
Audit
1975 Lakeside Pky.
Tucker, GA 30084
(404)621-2200
Ultimate Parent: Union Camp Corp.

★ 67902 ★   Union Camp Corp.
Bag
1975 Lakeside Pky.
Tucker, GA 30084
(404)621-2200
Ultimate Parent: Union Camp Corp.

★ 67903 ★   Union Camp Corp.
Container
1975 Lakeside Pkwy
Tucker, GA 30084
(404)723-8280
Ultimate Parent: Union Camp Corp.

★ 67904 ★   Union Camp Corp.
Container
1975 Lakeside Pky.
Tucker, GA 30084
(404)621-2200
Ultimate Parent: Union Camp Corp.

★ 67905 ★   Union Camp Corp.
Atlanta
1975 Lakeside Pky.
Tucker, GA 30084
(404)621-2200
Ultimate Parent: Union Camp Corp.

★ 67906 ★   Union Carbide
Chemicals & Plastics
2043 Steel Dr.
Tucker, GA 30084
Ultimate Parent: Union Carbide Corp. SIC:
2821—Plastics Materials & Resins.

★ 67907 ★   Union Carbide Corp.
2043 Steel Dr.
Tucker, GA 30084
Ultimate Parent: Union Carbide Corp. SIC:
2821—Plastics Materials & Resins.

★ 67908 ★   W. W. Grainger Inc.
Grainger Division
4761 Hugh Howell Rd.
Tucker, GA 30084
(404)496-9994
Ultimate Parent: W. W. Grainger.

★ 67909 ★   Xomox Corp.
4732 N. Royal Atlanta Dr.
Tucker, GA 30084
(404)939-7760
Ultimate Parent: Emerson Electric Co. Inc.

Tunnel Hill

★ 67910 ★   Conagra Feed Mill
402 Main St.
Tunnel Hill, GA 30755
Ultimate Parent: Conagra. SIC: 2048—
Prepared Feeds Nec.

Union City

★ 67911 ★   Bank South NA
4550 Jonesboro Rd.
Union City, GA 30291-2050
(404)991-5377
Location Type: Branch office. Officer:
Belinda Cross. Ultimate Parent: Bank
South Corp. SIC: 6021—National
Commercial Banks; 6141—Personal Credit
Institutions; 6162—Mortgage Bankers &
Correspondents.

★ 67912 ★   Casual Corner
Shannon Mall
Union City, GA 30291
(404)969-0085
Ultimate Parent: United States Shoe.

★ 67913 ★   The Gap
143 Shannon Mall
Union City, GA 30291
(404)969-1141
Ultimate Parent: GAP.

★ 67914 ★   Gap Stores
Shannon Mall
Union City, GA
(404)969-1141
Ultimate Parent: GAP.

★ 67915 ★   Gap Stores
143 Shannon Mall
Union City, GA 30291
(404)969-1141
Ultimate Parent: GAP.

★ 67916 ★   Jiffy Lube Union City
4620 Jonesboro Rd.
Union City, GA 30291
(404)964-5869
Ultimate Parent: Pennzoil.

★ 67917 ★   Kay-Bee Toy & Hobby
Shop Inc.
Shannon Mall
Union City, GA 30291
(404)964-0216
Ultimate Parent: Melville.

★ 67918 ★   Kentucky Fried
Chicken
6787 Shannon Pky.
Union City, GA 30291
(404)964-5600
Ultimate Parent: Pepsico.

★ 67919 ★   Kroger Co. the Retail
Stores
4550 Jonesboro Rd.
Union City, GA 30291
(404)969-0269
Ultimate Parent: Kroger.

★ 67920 ★   Kroger Pharmacies
4450 Jonesboro Rd.
Union City, GA 30291
(404)969-0267
Ultimate Parent: Kroger.

★ 67921 ★   The Limited Express
1000 Shannon South Pk.
Union City, GA
(404)969-1466
Ultimate Parent: Limited.

★ 67922 ★   Linens 'n Things
Shannon Mall
6903 Londonderry Way
Union City, GA 30291
(404)969-8300
Ultimate Parent: Melville.

★ 67923 ★   McDonald's
Restaurants
4605 Jonesboro Rd.
Union City, GA 30291
(404)964-7674
Ultimate Parent: McDonald's.

★ 67924 ★   Nationsbank Acct
Activity Inf
Shannon Southpark 67
Union City, GA
(404)523-0900
Ultimate Parent: Nationsbank Corp.

★ 67925 ★   Nationsbank Offices
Atlanta Ar
Shannon Southpark 67
Union City, GA
(404)969-0550
Ultimate Parent: Nationsbank Corp.

★ 67926 ★   Pizza Hut
6901 Londonderry Way
Union City, GA 30291
(404)969-0612
Ultimate Parent: Pepsico.

★ 67927 ★   Radio Shack
Shannon Mall
Union City, GA
(404)969-0077
Company Type: Division. Ultimate Parent:
Tandy Corp.

★ 67928 ★   Ryder Truck Rental
Shannon Mall
Union City, GA
(404)969-8937
Ultimate Parent: Ryder System.

★ 67929 ★ **Taco Bell**
4661 Jonesboro Rd.
Union City, GA 30291
(404)306-0851
Ultimate Parent: Pepsico.

★ 67930 ★ **Taco Bell**
739 Shannon South Pk.
Union City, GA
(404)969-7126
Ultimate Parent: Pepsico.

★ 67931 ★ **Texaco**
4597 Jonesboro Rd.
Union City, GA 30291
(404)964-1799
Ultimate Parent: Texaco.

★ 67932 ★ **Toys R US**
6781 Londonderry Way
Union City, GA 30291
(404)964-5751
Ultimate Parent: Toys "R" US.

★ 67933 ★ **Universal Forest Products**
6843 Goodson Rd.
Union City, GA 30291
(404)964-2278
Ultimate Parent: Universal Forest Products.

★ 67934 ★ **Waldenbooks**
Shannon Mall
Union City, GA 30291
(404)969-0079
Ultimate Parent: K-Mart.

Union Point

★ 67935 ★ **Universal Rundle Corp.**
1 Industrial Blvd.
Union Point, GA 30669
(706)486-4133
Officer: Don N. Ellis, Manager. **Ultimate Parent:** Nortek. **SIC:** 3089—Plastics Products Nec.

★ 67936 ★ **Universal Rundle Corp.**
1 Industrial Park
Union Point, GA 30669
Ultimate Parent: Nortek. **SIC:** 3000—Rubber & Miscellaneous Plastics Products.

★ 67937 ★ **Universal-Rundle Corp.**
Fiberglass Div.
1 Industrial Park
Union Point, GA 30669
Company Type: Division. **Ultimate Parent:** Nortek. **SIC:** 3088—Plastics Plumbing Fixtures.

Valdosta

★ 67938 ★ **ACME Business Products**
1810 N. Ashley St. Ste. 10
Valdosta, GA 31602-3025
Officer: Julie Greenhaw. **Ultimate Parent:** Alco Standard Corp. **SIC:** 5044—Office Equipment; 5999—Miscellaneous Retail Stores Nec.

★ 67939 ★ **Air Products & Chemicals, Inc.**
621 W. Savannah Ave.
Valdosta, GA 31601
(912)242-3419
Ultimate Parent: Air Products & Chemicals, Inc. **SIC:** 3564—Blowers & Fans; 7692—Welding Repair.

★ 67940 ★ **American Family Life Assurance**
1601 N. Ashley St.
Valdosta, GA 31602
(912)247-1826
Ultimate Parent: American Family Life Assurance Co. **SIC:** 6411—Insurance Agents, Brokers & Service.

★ 67941 ★ **Archer Daniels Midland Co.**
Clay Rd.
Valdosta, GA 31603-1589
Ultimate Parent: Archer Daniels Midland Co. **SIC:** 2075—Soybean Oil Mills.

★ 67942 ★ **Archer Daniels Midland Co.**
PO Box 1589
Valdosta, GA 31603-1589
(912)242-0100
Officer: Kevin Burgard. **Ultimate Parent:** Archer Daniels Midland Co. **SIC:** 2075—Soybean Oil Mills.

★ 67943 ★ **Casual Corner**
1180 Valdosta Mall
Valdosta, GA 31602
(912)247-1563
Ultimate Parent: United States Shoe. **SIC:** 5651—Family Clothing Stores.

★ 67944 ★ **First Federal S & L**
411 N. Patterson St.
Valdosta, GA 31601-4605
(912)244-0164
Company Type: Headquarters. **Officer:** J. L. Newbern Jr. **Ultimate Parent:** Bancorp Hawaii. **SIC:** 6035—Federal Savings Institutions; 6141—Personal Credit Institutions.

★ 67945 ★ **First State Bank & Trust Co.**
PO Box 1248
Valdosta, GA 31603
Ultimate Parent: Michigan National Corp. **SIC:** 6022—State Commercial Banks.

★ 67946 ★ **First State Bank & Trust Co.**
George St.
Valdosta, GA 31602
(912)333-0833
Ultimate Parent: Michigan National Corp. **SIC:** 6099—Functions Related to Deposit Banking.

★ 67947 ★ **First State Bank & Trust Co.**
2815 N. Ashley St.
Valdosta, GA 31602
(912)242-5725
Ultimate Parent: Michigan National Corp.

★ 67948 ★ **First State Bank & Trust Co.**
527 N. Patterson St.
Valdosta, GA 31601
(912)242-5725
Ultimate Parent: Michigan National Corp. **SIC:** 6099—Functions Related to Deposit Banking.

★ 67949 ★ **First State Bank & Trust Co. of Valdosta**
527 N. Patterson
Valdosta, GA 31601-4607
(912)242-5725 **Fax:** (912)245-5578
Location Type: Branch office. **Officer:** J. Edward Norris, President & CEO. **Ultimate Parent:** Synovus Financial Corp. **SIC:** 6021—National Commercial Banks.

★ 67950 ★ **First State Bank & Trust Co. of Valdosta**
PO Box 1248
Valdosta, GA 31603-1248
Location Type: Branch office. **Ultimate Parent:** Synovus Financial Corp. **SIC:** 6021—National Commercial Banks.

★ 67951 ★ **First State Bank & Trust Co. of Valdosta**
1731 Norman Dr.
Valdosta, GA 31601-3575
(912)242-5725
Location Type: Branch office. **Officer:** Jeanette Cain, Vice President. **Ultimate Parent:** Synovus Financial Corp. **SIC:** 6021—National Commercial Banks.

★ 67952 ★ **First State Bank & Trust Co. of Valdosta**
1201 S. Patterson St.
Valdosta, GA 31601-6349
(912)242-5725
Location Type: Branch office. **Officer:** Gary Crumby, Manager. **Ultimate Parent:** Synovus Financial Corp. **SIC:** 6021—National Commercial Banks.

★ 67953 ★ **First State Bank & Trust Co. of Valdosta**
5293 Schrader St.
Moody AFB
Valdosta, GA 31602-3842
(912)333-0833
Location Type: Branch office. **Officer:** Nell Martin, Manager. **Ultimate Parent:** Synovus

Financial Corp. **SIC:** 6021—National Commercial Banks.

★ 67954 ★ **First State Bank & Trust Co. of Valdosta**
2815 N. Ashley
Valdosta, GA 31602-1806
(912)242-5725
Location Type: Branch office. **Officer:** Ed Hutchinson, Manager. **Ultimate Parent:** Synovus Financial Corp. **SIC:** 6021—National Commercial Banks.

★ 67955 ★ **First Union National Bank of Georgia**
3307 N. Valdosta Rd.
Valdosta, GA 31603
(912)245-5770
Location Type: Branch office. **Ultimate Parent:** First Union Corp. **SIC:** 6021—National Commercial Banks.

★ 67956 ★ **First Union National Bank of Georgia**
300 N. Patterson St.
Valdosta, GA 31601-5519
(912)245-5700
Location Type: Branch office. **Ultimate Parent:** First Union Corp. **SIC:** 6021—National Commercial Banks.

★ 67957 ★ **Food Lion**
1715 Norman Dr.
Valdosta, GA 31601
(912)244-0251
Ultimate Parent: Food Lion. **SIC:** 5411—Grocery Stores.

★ 67958 ★ **Food Lion**
302 Perimeter Rd.
Valdosta, GA 31602
(912)244-5788
Ultimate Parent: Food Lion. **SIC:** 5411—Grocery Stores.

★ 67959 ★ **Gold Kist Inc. Feed Mill**
407 Clay Rd.
Valdosta, GA 31601
Ultimate Parent: Gold Kist. **SIC:** 2048—Prepared Feeds Nec.

★ 67960 ★ **Hertz Rent-A-Car**
Municipal Airport
Valdosta, GA 31601
(912)242-7070
Ultimate Parent: Hertz. **SIC:** 7514—Passenger Car Rental.

★ 67961 ★ **Kentucky Fried Chicken**
1207 N. Ashley St.
Valdosta, GA 31601
(912)242-1120
Ultimate Parent: Pepsico. **SIC:** 5812—Eating Places.

★ 67962 ★ **Kentucky Fried Chicken**
5 Pine St.
Valdosta, GA 31601
(912)247-0666
Ultimate Parent: Pepsico. **SIC:** 5812—Eating Places.

★ 67963 ★ **Kentucky Fried Chicken**
3026 N. Ashley St.
Valdosta, GA 31602
(912)247-0666
Ultimate Parent: Pepsico. **SIC:** 5812—Eating Places.

★ 67964 ★ **Kentucky Fried Chicken**
1300 N. Saint Augustine Rd.
Valdosta, GA 31601
(912)242-2145
Ultimate Parent: Pepsico. **SIC:** 5812—Eating Places.

★ 67965 ★ **Lane Bryant**
1700 Norman Dr. 1026
Valdosta, GA 31601
(912)244-0645
Ultimate Parent: Limited. **SIC:** 5651—Family Clothing Stores.

★ 67966 ★ **Pepsi-Cola Bottling Co.**
1525 Madison Hwy.
Valdosta, GA 31601
(912)244-2833
Location Type: Plant. **Officer:** Gary Prine,

Plant Manager. **Ultimate Parent:** Pepsico. **SIC:** 2086—Bottled & Canned Soft Drinks.

★ 67967 ★ **Pizza Hut**
3024 N. Ashley St.
Valdosta, GA 31602
(912)244-9484
Ultimate Parent: Pepsico. **SIC:** 5812—Eating Places.

★ 67968 ★ **Pizza Hut**
1823 W. Hill Ave.
Valdosta, GA 31601
(912)244-5224
Ultimate Parent: Pepsico. **SIC:** 5812—Eating Places.

★ 67969 ★ **Pizza Hut**
404 E. Northside Dr.
Valdosta, GA 31602
(912)247-9094
Ultimate Parent: Pepsico. **SIC:** 5812—Eating Places.

★ 67970 ★ **Pizza Hut**
1616 N. Ashley St.
Valdosta, GA 31602
(912)244-7720
Ultimate Parent: Pepsico. **SIC:** 5812—Eating Places.

★ 67971 ★ **Radio Shack**
1700 Norman Dr. 1230
Valdosta, GA 31601
(912)247-0705
Company Type: Division. **Ultimate Parent:** Tandy Corp. **SIC:** 5719—Miscellaneous Home Furnishings Stores; 5731—Radio, Television & Electronics Stores.

★ 67972 ★ **Radio Shack**
Castle Park Shopping Cent
Valdosta, GA 31601
(912)242-2640
Company Type: Division. **Ultimate Parent:** Tandy Corp. **SIC:** 5065—Electronic Parts & Equipment Nec.

★ 67973 ★ **Radio Shack**
2107 Bemiss Rd.
Valdosta, GA 31602
(912)242-2640
Company Type: Division. **Ultimate Parent:** Tandy Corp. **SIC:** 5731—Radio, Television & Electronics Stores.

★ 67974 ★ **Ryder Truck Rental**
1618 James P Rogers Dr.
Valdosta, GA 31601
(912)247-4801
Ultimate Parent: Ryder System. **SIC:** 7359—Equipment Rental & Leasing Nec; 7513—Truck Rental & Leasing Without Drivers.

★ 67975 ★ **Transamerica Occidental Life Insurance**
Bemiss Rd.
Valdosta, GA 31602
(912)247-6262
Ultimate Parent: Transamerica Occidental Life Insurance. **SIC:** 6411—Insurance Agents, Brokers & Service.

★ 67976 ★ **Unijax Inc.**
1612 James P Rogers Dr.
Valdosta, GA 31601-6518
(912)242-8274
Officer: Marjorie Winn. **Ultimate Parent:** Alco Standard Corp. **SIC:** 5113—Industrial & Personal Service Paper; 2621—Paper Mills.

★ 67977 ★ **Unijax Inc.**
1612 James P Rogers Dr.
Valdosta, GA 31601-6518
(912)242-8274
Officer: Marjorie Winn. **Ultimate Parent:** Alco Standard Corp. **SIC:** 5113—Industrial & Personal Service Paper; 2621—Paper Mills.

★ 67978 ★ **Union Camp Corp.**
1401 E. Hill Ave.
Valdosta, GA 31601
Ultimate Parent: Union Camp Corp. **SIC:** 2821—Plastics Materials & Resins; 2861—Gum & Wood Chemicals.

★ 67979 ★   **United Parcel Service**
1626 James P Rogers Dr.
Valdosta, GA 31601
(912)245-1182
Ultimate Parent: United Parcel Service of
America. **SIC:** 4215—Courier Services
Except by Air.

★ 67980 ★   **Waldenbooks**
1700 Norman Dr. 1232
Valdosta, GA 31601
(912)247-0332
Ultimate Parent: K-Mart. **SIC:** 5942—Book
Stores.

★ 67981 ★   **Zippy Mart Inc.**
70 Park Ave.
Valdosta, GA 31601
(912)247-9857
Ultimate Parent: Crown Central Petroleum
Corp.

★ 67982 ★   **Zippy Mart Inc.**
1505 E. Northside Dr.
Valdosta, GA 31602
(912)247-9857
Ultimate Parent: Crown Central Petroleum
Corp. **SIC:** 5411—Grocery Stores.

★ 67983 ★   **Zippy Mart Inc.**
912 Blanton St.
Valdosta, GA 31601
(912)244-0353
Ultimate Parent: Crown Central Petroleum
Corp. **SIC:** 5411—Grocery Stores.

Vidalia

★ 67984 ★   **Bi-Lo Inc.**
501 E. 1st St.
Vidalia, GA 30474
(912)537-0617
Ultimate Parent: Penn Traffic. **SIC:** 5411—
Grocery Stores.

★ 67985 ★   **Challenger Electric
Equipment Co.**
2803 North St. E.
Vidalia, GA 30474
Ultimate Parent: Westinghouse Electric
Corp. **SIC:** 3613—Switchgear &
Switchboard Apparatus.

★ 67986 ★   **First Union National
Bank of Georgia**
900 E. 1st St. & Hwy. 280
Vidalia, GA 30474-2337
(912)537-2221
Location Type: Branch office. **Ultimate
Parent:** First Union Corp. **SIC:** 6021—
National Commercial Banks.

★ 67987 ★   **Kentucky Fried
Chicken**
2601 E. 1st St.
Vidalia, GA 30474
Ultimate Parent: Pepsico. **SIC:** 5812—
Eating Places.

★ 67988 ★   **Pepsi-Cola Co.**
100 Currie St.
Vidalia, GA 30474
(912)537-1772
Officer: John Heart, Manager. **Ultimate
Parent:** Pepsico. **SIC:** 2086—Bottled &
Canned Soft Drinks.

★ 67989 ★   **Piggly Wiggly**
569 PO Box
Vidalia, GA 30474
(912)781-4525
Ultimate Parent: Bruno's. **SIC:** 5411—
Grocery Stores.

★ 67990 ★   **Piggly Wiggly**
100 Brinson Rd.
Vidalia, GA 30474
(912)537-9871
Ultimate Parent: Bruno's. **SIC:** 5411—
Grocery Stores.

★ 67991 ★   **Piggly Wiggly
Southern Inc.**
100 Brinson Rd.
Vidalia, GA 30474
(912)537-9871
Ultimate Parent: Bruno's. **SIC:** 5411—
Grocery Stores.

★ 67992 ★   **Pizza Hut**
604 E. 1st St.
Vidalia, GA 30474
(912)537-8933
Ultimate Parent: Pepsico. **SIC:** 5812—
Eating Places.

★ 67993 ★   **Radio Shack**
302 Sweet Onion Plz.
Vidalia, GA 30474
(912)537-2091
Company Type: Division. **Ultimate Parent:**
Tandy Corp. **SIC:** 5731—Radio, Television
& Electronics Stores.

★ 67994 ★   **RJ Reynolds Tobacco
Co. Inc.**
106 W. 1st St.
Vidalia, GA 30474
(912)537-9970
Ultimate Parent: RJR Nabisco Holdings.
SIC: 5194—Tobacco & Tobacco Products.

★ 67995 ★   **Underwriters
Adjusting Co.**
200 Maple Dr.
Vidalia, GA 30474
(912)537-8221
Ultimate Parent: Continental. **SIC:** 6411—
Insurance Agents, Brokers & Service.

★ 67996 ★   **Union Camp Corp.**
100 Church St.
Vidalia, GA 30474
(912)537-4151
Ultimate Parent: Union Camp Corp. **SIC:**
2421—Sawmills & Planing Mills—General.

★ 67997 ★   **Wal Mart**
2305 Lyons Hwy.
Vidalia, GA 30474
(912)537-0889
Ultimate Parent: Wal-Mart Stores, Inc. **SIC:**
5311—Department Stores.

Vienna

★ 67998 ★   **Georgia-Pacific Corp.
Vienna Particleboard**
Hwy. 41 S.
Vienna, GA 31092
Ultimate Parent: Georgia-Pacific. **SIC:**
2493—Reconstituted Wood Products.

★ 67999 ★   **Georgia-Pacific
Resins Inc.**
South Seventh St.
Vienna, GA 31092
Ultimate Parent: Georgia-Pacific. **SIC:**
2821—Plastics Materials & Resins; 2869—
Industrial Organic Chemicals Nec.

★ 68000 ★   **Red Kap Ind.**
E. Pine St.
Vienna, GA 31092
(912)268-2541
Officer: James Parham, Plant Manager.
Ultimate Parent: VF Corp. **SIC:** 2325—
Men's/Boys' Trousers & Slacks.

Villa Rica

★ 68001 ★   **Ace Hardware of Villa
Rica**
Hwy. 78 Tri County Plz.
Villa Rica, GA 30180
(404)459-6123
Ultimate Parent: Ace Hardware. **SIC:**
5251—Hardware Stores.

★ 68002 ★   **Citizens Bank & Trust
of West Georgia**
Bankhead Hwy.
Villa Rica, GA 30180
(404)459-5717
Location Type: Branch office. **Officer:** H.
Bradley Lipham, Manager. **Ultimate Parent:**
Synovus Financial Corp. **SIC:** 6021—
National Commercial Banks.

Warm Springs

★ 68003 ★   **Georgia-Pacific Corp.**
Warm Springs Pine Plywood
Hwy. 18
Warm Springs, GA 31830
Company Type: Division. **Ultimate Parent:**
Georgia-Pacific. **SIC:** 2436—Softwood
Veneer & Plywood.

Warner Robbins

★ 68004 ★   **Bank South NA/
Houston-Warner Robbins**
509 N. Houston Rd.
Warner Robbins, GA 31093
(912)922-4111
Company Type: Subsidiary. **Location
Type:** Branch office. **Officer:** Joan Powers,
Mgr. **Ultimate Parent:** Bank South Corp.
SIC: 6021—National Commercial Banks.

Warner Robins

★ 68005 ★   **American Family Life
Assurance**
205 Wake Forest Dr.
Warner Robins, GA 31093
(912)929-1327
Ultimate Parent: American Family Life
Assurance Co. **SIC:** 6411—Insurance
Agents, Brokers & Service.

★ 68006 ★   **Associated Business
Products**
113 S. Oaks Ln.
Warner Robins, GA 31088-6291
(912)329-8396
Ultimate Parent: Alco Standard Corp. **SIC:**
2752—Commercial Printing—Lithographic;
2761—Manifold Business Forms.

★ 68007 ★   **Bank South, NA**
302 Russell Pky.
Warner Robins, GA 31093-6169
(912)929-8491
Company Type: Subsidiary. **Location
Type:** Branch office. **Officer:** Pam Piper,
Manager. **Ultimate Parent:** Bank South
Corp. **SIC:** 6021—National Commercial
Banks.

★ 68008 ★   **Bank South, NA**
705 N. Houston Rd.
Warner Robins, GA 31093-3050
(912)922-4111
Company Type: Subsidiary. **Location
Type:** Branch office. **Officer:** Joan Powers,
Manager. **Ultimate Parent:** Bank South
Corp. **SIC:** 6021—National Commercial
Banks.

★ 68009 ★   **Boeing Co. the**
100 Alpha Mall Park
Warner Robins, GA 31088
(912)922-9926
Ultimate Parent: Boeing. **SIC:** 4512—Air
Transportation—Scheduled.

★ 68010 ★   **CB & T Bank of
Middle Georgia**
1444 Watson Blvd.
Warner Robins, GA 31093-3434
(912)929-1004 **Fax:** (912)929-1982
Location Type: Branch office. **Officer:** R.
Gary Bishop, President & CEO. **Ultimate
Parent:** Synovus Financial Corp. **SIC:**
6021—National Commercial Banks.

★ 68011 ★   **CB & T Bank of
Middle Georgia**
PO Box 2107
Warner Robins, GA 31099-2107
Location Type: Branch office. **Ultimate
Parent:** Synovus Financial Corp. **SIC:**
6021—National Commercial Banks.

★ 68012 ★   **CB&T of Middle
Georgia**
593 Russell Pky.
Warner Robins, GA 31088-7493
(912)929-7012
Location Type: Branch office. **Ultimate
Parent:** Synovus Financial Corp. **SIC:**
6021—National Commercial Banks.

★ 68013 ★   **Coca-Cola Bottling
Co.**
44 Green St.
Warner Robins, GA 31093
(912)892-9039
Ultimate Parent: Coca-Cola Enterprises.
SIC: 2086—Bottled & Canned Soft Drinks.

★ 68014 ★   **Digital Equipment
Corporati**
205 Green St.
Warner Robins, GA 31093
(912)929-8097
Ultimate Parent: Digital Equipment Corp.
SIC: 5044—Office Equipment.

★ 68015 ★   **Digital Equipment
Corp.**
1532 Watson Blvd.
Warner Robins, GA 31093
(912)929-2598
Ultimate Parent: Digital Equipment Corp.
SIC: 5046—Commercial Equipment Nec.

★ 68016 ★   **Kroger Food Stores**
115 Richard B Russell Pky.
Warner Robins, GA 31088
(912)922-9040
Ultimate Parent: Kroger.

★ 68017 ★   **Lowe's**
815 Russell Pky.
Warner Robins, GA 31088
(912)922-4421
Ultimate Parent: Lowe's. **SIC:** 5719—
Miscellaneous Home Furnishings Stores.

★ 68018 ★   **Piggly Wiggly**
2209 Moody Rd.
Warner Robins, GA 31088
Ultimate Parent: Bruno's. **SIC:** 5411—
Grocery Stores.

★ 68019 ★   **Pizza Hut**
3827 3827 Us
Warner Robins, GA 31093
(912)922-9354
Ultimate Parent: Pepsico. **SIC:** 5812—
Eating Places.

★ 68020 ★   **Ryder Truck Rental**
703 Watson Blvd.
Warner Robins, GA 31093
(912)923-0829
Ultimate Parent: Ryder System. **SIC:**
7359—Equipment Rental & Leasing Nec.

Washington

★ 68021 ★   **Duck Head Apparel
Co.**
314 Water St.
Washington, GA 30673
(706)678-2131
Officer: Doak Dingler, Manager. **Ultimate
Parent:** Delta Woodside Industries. **SIC:**
2321—Men's/Boys' Shirts.

★ 68022 ★   **Federal Paper Board
Co.**
Industrial Park
Washington, GA 30673
(706)678-1585
Officer: John Talbert, Manager. **Ultimate
Parent:** Federal Paper Board. **SIC:** 2421—
Sawmills & Planing Mills—General.

Watkinsville

★ 68023 ★   **Athens First Bank &
Trust**
Hwy. 15
Watkinsville, GA 30677
(706)769-6663
Location Type: Branch office. **Officer:**
David Williams, Manager. **Ultimate Parent:**
Synovus Financial Corp. **SIC:** 6021—
National Commercial Banks.

★ 68024 ★   **Guardian Products**
111 Barnett Shoals Rd.
Watkinsville, GA 30677
Ultimate Parent: General Cable Corp. **SIC:**
3357—Nonferrous Wiredrawing & Insulating.

Waycross

★ 68025 ★   **Anchor Savings Bank
Loan of**
203 Pendleton St.
Waycross, GA 31501
(912)283-2540
Ultimate Parent: Anchor Bancorp. **SIC:**
6162—Mortgage Bankers &
Correspondents.

★ 68026 ★   **Bank South**
1991 Albany Ave.
Waycross, GA 31503-5901
(912)287-2410
Location Type: Branch office. **Officer:**
Velma S. Studebaker. **Ultimate Parent:**
Bank South Corp. **SIC:** 6021—National
Commercial Banks.

★ 68027 ★　Bank South
1312 Plant Ave.
Waycross, GA 31501-3537
(912)287-2430
Location Type: Branch office. Officer:
Arlene King. Ultimate Parent: Bank South
Corp. SIC: 6021—National Commercial
Banks.

★ 68028 ★　Bank South, NA
1801 Knight Ave.
Waycross, GA 31501
(912)287-2420
Company Type: Subsidiary. Location
Type: Branch office. Officer: Karen
Strickland, Manager. Ultimate Parent: Bank
South Corp. SIC: 6021—National
Commercial Banks.

★ 68029 ★　Bank South, NA
401 Carswell Ave.
Waycross, GA 31501-4763
(912)287-2400
Company Type: Subsidiary. Location
Type: Branch office. Officer: P. Owen
Herrin Jr., President. Ultimate Parent: Bank
South Corp. SIC: 6021—National
Commercial Banks.

★ 68030 ★　Bank South, NA
Albany & Augusta Aves.
Waycross, GA 31501
(912)287-2410
Company Type: Subsidiary. Location
Type: Branch office. Officer: Velma
Studebaker, Manager. Ultimate Parent:
Bank South Corp. SIC: 6021—National
Commercial Banks.

★ 68031 ★　Champion
International Corp.
PO Box 1299
Waycross, GA 31502
Ultimate Parent: Champion International.
SIC: 2436—Softwood Veneer & Plywood;
2421—Sawmills & Planing Mills—General.

★ 68032 ★　First Union National
Bank of Georgia
500 Albany Ave.
Waycross, GA 31501-4715
(912)285-5090
Location Type: Branch office. Ultimate
Parent: First Union Corp. SIC: 6021—
National Commercial Banks.

★ 68033 ★　Greyhound Bus Lines
590 PO Box
Waycross, GA 31502
(912)283-7211
Ultimate Parent: Greyhound Lines Inc. SIC:
4111—Local & Suburban Transit.

★ 68034 ★　Kentucky Fried
Chicken
139 Lee Ave.
Waycross, GA 31501
(912)283-7309
Ultimate Parent: Pepsico. SIC: 5812—
Eating Places.

★ 68035 ★　Kroger
1600 Memorial Dr.
Waycross, GA 31501
(912)283-7504
Ultimate Parent: Kroger. SIC: 5411—
Grocery Stores.

★ 68036 ★　Piggly Wiggly
Hatcher Point Mall
Waycross, GA 31501
(912)285-7530
Ultimate Parent: Bruno's. SIC: 5411—
Grocery Stores.

★ 68037 ★　Radio Shack
40 Hatcher Point Mall
Waycross, GA 31501
(912)285-1336
Company Type: Division. Ultimate Parent:
Tandy Corp. SIC: 5065—Electronic Parts &
Equipment Nec.

★ 68038 ★　Rite Aid Pharmacy
701 Riverside Dr.
Waycross, GA 31501
(912)283-7101
Ultimate Parent: Rite Aid. SIC: 5912—Drug
Stores & Proprietary Stores.

★ 68039 ★　Trailways Bus System
602 Isabella St.
Waycross, GA 31501
(912)283-4248
Ultimate Parent: Greyhound Lines Inc. SIC:
4142—Bus Charter Service Except Local.

★ 68040 ★　Trust Co. Bank of SE
Georgia, N.A.
1807 Knight Ave.
Waycross, GA 31501-8013
(912)287-4432
Officer: Rhonda Hersey, Manager. Ultimate
Parent: Suntrust Banks. SIC: 6021—
National Commercial Banks.

★ 68041 ★　Trust Co. Bank of SE
Georgia, N.A.
420 Tebeau St.
Waycross, GA 31501-3652
(912)283-1510
Officer: John S. Laws, Manager. Ultimate
Parent: Suntrust Banks. SIC: 6021—
National Commercial Banks.

★ 68042 ★　Union Camp Corp.
Valdosta Hwy.
Waycross, GA 31501
(912)283-4202
Ultimate Parent: Union Camp Corp. SIC:
2411—Logging.

★ 68043 ★　Wal Mart
7 Hatcher Point Mall
Waycross, GA 31501
(912)287-1050
Ultimate Parent: Wal-Mart Stores, Inc. SIC:
5311—Department Stores.

★ 68044 ★　Waycross Molded
Products, Inc.
PO Box 58
Waycross, GA 31502
(912)285-1234
Company Type: Subsidiary. Officer: John
B. Gerlach, President. Ultimate Parent:
Lanchaster Colony. SIC: 3069—Fabricated
Rubber Products Nec. Employee Count:
331.

★ 68045 ★　Waycross Molded
Products Inc.
2450 Industrial Blvd.
Waycross, GA 31502
Ultimate Parent: Lanchaster Colony. SIC:
3061—Mechanical Rubber Goods.

Waynesboro

★ 68046 ★　First Union National
Bank of Georgia
615 Liberty St.
Waynesboro, GA 30830-1418
(706)437-2000
Location Type: Branch office. Ultimate
Parent: First Union Corp. SIC: 6021—
National Commercial Banks.

★ 68047 ★　Sunbeam Outdoor
Products
Mills Rd.
Waynesboro, GA 30830
(706)554-2154
Officer: Hank Penner, Manager. Ultimate
Parent: Sunbeam/Oster. SIC: 2514—Metal
Household Furniture; 3441—Fabricated
Structural Metal.

West Point

★ 68048 ★　West Point Stevens
400 W. 10th St.
West Point, GA 31833
(706)645-4000 Fax: (706)645-4068
Company Type: Headquarters. Officer:
Holcombe T. Green Jr., CEO. Employee
Count: 18000. Sales: 1501 M. Fortune
500: Largest U.S. Industrial Corporations:
Ranking 278.

West Woodstock

★ 68049 ★　Texaco
1617 Hwy. 92
West Wdstk, GA
(404)926-7930
Ultimate Parent: Texaco.

Whitesburg

★ 68050 ★　Citizens Bank & Trust
of West Georgia
Main St.
Whitesburg, GA 30185
(404)832-1384
Location Type: Branch office. Officer:
Wayne Allen, Manager. Ultimate Parent:
Sysco. SIC: 6021—National Commercial
Banks.

★ 68051 ★　Stop & Shop
Whitesburg
Hwy. 16
Whitesburg, GA 30185
(404)834-6370
Ultimate Parent: Stop & Shop. SIC: 5411—
Grocery Stores.

Winder

★ 68052 ★　Alkaril Chemicals
Industrial Pky. PO Box 1010
Winder, GA 30680
Ultimate Parent: GAF Corp. SIC: 2800—
Chemicals & Allied Products; 2843—Surface
Active Agents.

★ 68053 ★　Alkaril Chemicals
Industrial Pky.
Winder, GA 30680
Ultimate Parent: GAF Corp. SIC: 2800—
Chemicals & Allied Products; 2843—Surface
Active Agents.

★ 68054 ★　Alkaril Chemicals Inc.
Industrial Pky.
Winder, GA 30680
Ultimate Parent: GAF Corp. SIC: 2800—
Chemicals & Allied Products; 2843—Surface
Active Agents.

★ 68055 ★　Bank South NA
1010 N. Broad St.
Winder, GA 30680
(706)867-4641
Location Type: Branch office. Officer:
Lynn Esco. Ultimate Parent: Bank South
Corp. SIC: 6022—State Commercial Banks;
6021—National Commercial Banks.

★ 68056 ★　Bank South, NA
600 W. Athens St.
Winder, GA 30680
(706)867-9825
Company Type: Subsidiary. Location
Type: Branch office. Officer: Kennith
Lumpkin, Manager. Ultimate Parent: Bank
South Corp. SIC: 6021—National
Commercial Banks.

★ 68057 ★　Bank South, NA
102 N. Broad St.
Winder, GA 30680
(404)867-7571
Company Type: Subsidiary. Location
Type: Branch office. Officer: Pam Hill,
Manager. Ultimate Parent: Bank South
Corp. SIC: 6021—National Commercial
Banks.

★ 68058 ★　Bank South NA/
Winder Main Office
121 N. Broad St.
Winder, GA 30680
(706)867-7571
Company Type: Subsidiary. Location
Type: Branch office. Officer: Frances
Saunders, Mgr. Ultimate Parent: Bank
South Corp. SIC: 6021—National
Commercial Banks.

★ 68059 ★　Duck Head Apparel
Co.
220 E. Athens St.
Winder, GA 30680
(404)867-3111
Officer: Phillip N. Brader, President. Ultimate
Parent: Delta Woodside
Industries. SIC: 2254—Knit Underwear
Mills; 2325—Men's/Boys' Trousers &
Slacks.

★ 68060 ★　Greyhound Bus Lines
220 E. May St.
Winder, GA 30680
(404)867-3154
Ultimate Parent: Greyhound Lines Inc. SIC:
4141—Local Bus Charter Service.

★ 68061 ★　Manville Sales Corp.
Industrial Pky.
Winder, GA 30680
Ultimate Parent: Manville Corp. SIC:
3296—Mineral Wool.

★ 68062 ★　Rhone-Poulenc Inc.
Surfactants & Specialties
Industrial Pky. PO Box 1010
Winder, GA 30680
Ultimate Parent: Rhone-Poulenc Rorer.
SIC: 2843—Surface Active Agents; 2800—
Chemicals & Allied Products; 2869—
Industrial Organic Chemicals Nec.

★ 68063 ★　Rohne Poulenc Inc.
Industrial Park Way
Winder, GA 30680
(404)867-7446
Ultimate Parent: Rhone-Poulenc Rorer.
SIC: 2843—Surface Active Agents.

★ 68064 ★　Texaco Service Staion
May
Winder, GA 30680
(404)867-6711
Ultimate Parent: Texaco. SIC: 7538—
General Automotive Repair Shops.

Woodbine

★ 68065 ★　Rhone-Poulenc Ag
Co.
Eastern End of Harriett's Bluff Rd.
Woodbine, GA 31569-0428
Ultimate Parent: Rhone-Poulenc Rorer.
SIC: 2879—Agricultural Chemicals Nec.

★ 68066 ★　Rhone-Poulenc Ag
Co. Woodbine Plant
Eastern End of Harriett's Bluff Rd.
Woodbine, GA 31569-0428
Ultimate Parent: Rhone-Poulenc Rorer.
SIC: 2879—Agricultural Chemicals Nec.

★ 68067 ★　Rhone-Poulenc Inc.
Ag Co.
Eastern End of Harriett's Bluff Rd.
Woodbine, GA 31569-0428
Ultimate Parent: Rhone-Poulenc Rorer.
SIC: 2879—Agricultural Chemicals Nec.

Woodstock

★ 68068 ★　Elographics Inc.
103 Springfield Dr.
Woodstock, GA
(404)924-4181
Ultimate Parent: Raychem Corp.

★ 68069 ★　First Union National
Bank of Georgia
526 S. Main St.
Woodstock, GA 30108
(404)924-5360
Location Type: Branch office. Ultimate
Parent: First Union Corp. SIC: 6021—
National Commercial Banks.

★ 68070 ★　Kentucky Fried
Chicken
1519 Hwy. 92
Woodstock, GA 30188
(404)591-9712
Ultimate Parent: Pepsico.

★ 68071 ★　Kmart Stores
Pharmacy
5500 Bells Ferry Rd.
Woodstock, GA
(404)928-6650
Ultimate Parent: K-Mart.

★ 68072 ★　Kroger Pharmacies
3595 Canton Rd.
Woodstock, GA
(404)924-7972
Ultimate Parent: Kroger.

★ 68073 ★　McDonald's
Restaurants
1516 Hwy. 92
Woodstock, GA 30188
(404)591-8074
Ultimate Parent: McDonald's.

★ 68074 ★　Pizza Hut
621 S. Main St.
Woodstock, GA 30188
(404)926-8057
Ultimate Parent: Pepsico.

★ 68075 ★ Taco Bell
1507 Hwy. 92
Woodstock, GA 30188
(404)926-4824 (404)924-6724
Ultimate Parent: Chesapeake. **Ultimate Parent:** Pepsico.

★ 68076 ★ Wal Mart Discount Cities
1510 Georgia Hwy. 92 W
Woodstock, GA
(404)928-9030
Ultimate Parent: Wal-Mart Stores, Inc.

★ 68077 ★ Wisconsin Tissue Mills Inc.
800 Parkway 575
Woodstock, GA 30188
(404)926-4824
Ultimate Parent: Chesapeake.

KENTUCKY

Alexandria

★ 68078 ★ Hillshire Farm & Kahn's Co.
401 Bob Huber Dr.
Alexandria, KY 41001
Ultimate Parent: Sara Lee Corp. SIC: 2011—Meat Packing Plants.

★ 68079 ★ Star Bank NA, Kentucky
7630 Alexandria Pke.
Alexandria, KY 41001-1044
(606)635-2141
Location Type: Branch office. Officer: Larry Schrieber, Manager. Ultimate Parent: Star Banc Corp. SIC: 6021—National Commercial Banks.

Allen

★ 68080 ★ Greyhound Bus Lines
Allen, KY 41601
(606)874-9070
Ultimate Parent: Greyhound Lines Inc. SIC: 4131—Intercity & Rural Bus Transportation; 4111—Local & Suburban Transit; 4142—Bus Charter Service Except Local.

★ 68081 ★ Mobil Oil Service Station
Allen, KY 41601
(606)874-9381
Ultimate Parent: Mobil. SIC: 5172—Petroleum Products Nec.

★ 68082 ★ Mobil Oil Service Station
Allen, KY 41601
(606)874-9381
Ultimate Parent: Mobil SIC: 5172—Petroleum Products Nec.

Ashland

★ 68083 ★ Air Products & Chemicals Inc.
125 Russell Rd.
Ashland, KY 411011729
Ultimate Parent: Air Products & Chemicals, Inc. SIC: 2813—Industrial Gases.

★ 68084 ★ Armco Ashland Works West Works
U.S. Rte. 23 West
Ashland, KY 41105-0191
Ultimate Parent: Armco. SIC: 3312—Blast Furnaces & Steel Mills.

★ 68085 ★ Armco Steel Co.
L.P. Coke Plant
4000 E. Winchester Ave.
Ashland, KY 41101-0191
Company Type: Division. Ultimate Parent: Armco. SIC: 3312—Blast Furnaces & Steel Mills.

★ 68086 ★ Armco Steel Co.
L.P. Grey Iron Foundry
Greenup Ave. & 23rd St.
Ashland, KY 41105-0191
Company Type: Division. Ultimate Parent: Armco. SIC: 3312—Blast Furnaces & Steel Mills.

★ 68087 ★ Armco Steel Co.
L.P. West Works
US Rte. 23 W.
Ashland, KY 41105-0102
Company Type: Division. Ultimate Parent: Armco. SIC: 3312—Blast Furnaces & Steel Mills.

★ 68088 ★ Armco Steel Co.
L.P. West Works
US Rte. 23 W.
Ashland, KY 41105-0102
Company Type: Division. Ultimate Parent: Armco. SIC: 3312—Blast Furnaces & Steel Mills.

★ 68089 ★ Armco Steel Co. LP
Rte. 23
Ashland, KY 41101
(606)329-7111
Officer: John Schell. Ultimate Parent: Armco. SIC: 3316—Cold-Finishing of Steel Shapes; 3312—Blast Furnaces & Steel Mills; 3399—Primary Metal Products Nec.

★ 68090 ★ Ashland Oil Inc.
1000 Ashland Dr.
Ashland, KY 41101
(606)329-3333
Officer: John R. Hall, Chairman. Ultimate Parent: Ashland Oil. SIC: 2821—Plastics Materials & Resins; 2865—Cyclic Crudes & Intermediates; 2911—Petroleum Refining.

★ 68091 ★ Ashland Oil, Inc.
PO Box 391
Ashland, KY 41114
(606)329-3333 Fax: (606)329-5271
Company Type: Headquarters. Officer: John R. Hall, Chairman & CEO. Ultimate Parent: Ashland Oil.

★ 68092 ★ Ashland Petroleum Co.
Catlettsburg Refinery
PO Box 391
Ashland, KY 41114
Company Type: Division. Ultimate Parent: Ashland Oil. SIC: 2911—Petroleum Refining.

★ 68093 ★ Ashland Pipe Line Co.
PO Box 391
Ashland, KY 41114
(606)329-3333
Company Type: Subsidiary. Officer: Malcolm F. Howard, President. Ultimate Parent: Ashland Oil. SIC: 4612—Crude Petroleum Pipelines. Employee Count: 349.

★ 68094 ★ Columbia Coal Gasification Corp.
336 14th St.
Ashland, KY 41101
(606)324-3171
Officer: John R. Henning, President & CEO. Ultimate Parent: Columbia Gas System.

★ 68095 ★ First American Bank
1544 Winchester Ave.
Ashland, KY 41101-7923
(606)329-6000
Company Type: Subsidiary. Officer: John H. Mays, President & CEO. Ultimate Parent: First American Corp. SIC: 6022—State Commercial Banks. Employee Count: 120.

★ 68096 ★ First Federal S & L
1640 Carter Ave.
Ashland, KY 41101-7631
(606)324-5138
Company Type: Headquarters. Officer: Paul D. Leake. Ultimate Parent: Bancorp Hawaii. SIC: 6035—Federal Savings Institutions; 6141—Personal Credit Institutions; 6162—Mortgage Bankers & Correspondents.

★ 68097 ★ Indland Towing Co.
PO Box 391
Ashland, KY 41114
(606)329-3333
Company Type: Subsidiary. Officer: Bruce Tilton, Manager-Inland/Ocean Transportation. Ultimate Parent: Ashland Oil. SIC: 4492—Towing & Tugboat Services. Sales: 5500000 M.

★ 68098 ★ Inland Gas Co. Inc.
336 14th St.
Ashland, KY 41101-7541
(606)324-3171
Company Type: Subsidiary. Officer: Logan W. Wallingford, President. Ultimate Parent: Columbia Gas System. SIC: 1311—Crude Petroleum & Natural Gas; 4922—Natural Gas Transmission. Employee Count: 6.

★ 68099 ★ McDonald's Hamburgers
Summitt
Ashland, KY 41101
(606)928-2223
Ultimate Parent: McDonald's. SIC: 5812—Eating Places.

★ 68100 ★ National City Bank, Ashland Kentucky
Russell Rd.
Ashland, KY 41101
(606)329-2900
Company Type: Subsidiary. Location Type: Branch office. Officer: Tony M. Salyer, Mgr. Ultimate Parent: National City Corp. SIC: 6021—National Commercial Banks.

★ 68101 ★ National City Bank, Ashland Kentucky
US 60
Ashland, KY 41102
(606)329-2900
Company Type: Subsidiary. Location Type: Branch office. Officer: R. Bruce VanHorn, Mgr. Ultimate Parent: National City Corp. SIC: 6021—National Commercial Banks.

★ 68102 ★ National City Bank, Ashland Kentucky
213 16th St.
Ashland, KY 41101-7658
(606)329-2900
Company Type: Subsidiary. Location Type: Branch office. Ultimate Parent: National City Corp.

★ 68103 ★ National City Bank, Ashland Kentucky
Blackburn Ave.
Ashland, KY 41101
(606)329-2900
Company Type: Subsidiary. Location Type: Branch office. Officer: Sharon Noble, Mgr. Ultimate Parent: National City Corp. SIC: 6021—National Commercial Banks.

★ 68104 ★ National City Bank, Ashland Kentucky
US 60 & State Rte. 716
Ashland, KY 41101
(606)329-2900
Company Type: Subsidiary. Location Type: Branch office. Officer: R. Bruce VanHorn, Mgr. Ultimate Parent: National City Corp. SIC: 6021—National Commercial Banks.

★ 68105 ★ National City Bank, Ashland Kentucky
1000 Carter Ave.
PO Box 1270
Ashland, KY 41105-1270
(606)329-2900 Fax: (606)325-9667
Company Type: Subsidiary. Location Type: Branch office. Officer: David E. Jones, President & CEO. Ultimate Parent: National City Corp. SIC: 6021—National Commercial Banks.

★ 68106 ★ Summit Corp.
7121 Midland Trl.
Ashland, KY 41102
(606)928-3350
Ultimate Parent: American Greetings.

★ 68107 ★ Superamerica
5555 PO Box
Ashland, KY 41105
(606)329-4016
Ultimate Parent: Ashland Oil.

★ 68108 ★ Thrift Drugs
Rural Route 23
Ashland, KY 41101
(606)325-8479
Ultimate Parent: J.C. Penney. SIC: 5912—Drug Stores & Proprietary Stores.

Bagdad

★ 68109 ★ People's Bank
PO Box 128
Bagdad, KY 40003
(502)747-8957
Ultimate Parent: People's Bank. SIC: 6022—State Commercial Banks.

Barbourville

★ 68110 ★ Tremco Inc.
Treuhaft Blvd.
Barbourville, KY 40906
Ultimate Parent: B.F. Goodrich. SIC: 2891—Adhesives & Sealants; 2821—Plastics Materials & Resins.

★ 68111 ★ Warner's Warnaco Inc.
Walker Park Rd.
Barbourville, KY 40906
(606)546-3102
Officer: Pat Miller, Manager. Ultimate Parent: Warnaco Group. SIC: 2339—Women's/Misses' Outerwear Nec.

Bardstown

★ 68112 ★ American Greetings
800 American Dr.
Bardstown, KY 40004
Ultimate Parent: American Greetings. SIC: 2771—Greeting Cards.

★ 68113 ★ American Greetings Corp.
800 American Dr.
Bardstown, KY 40004-9233
(502)348-1000
Officer: Raymond Ritcheson. Ultimate Parent: American Greetings. SIC: 2771—Greeting Cards; 5112—Stationery & Office Supplies.

★ 68114 ★ Farmers Bank & Trust Co.
RR 4
Bardstown, KY 40004
(502)348-3911
Ultimate Parent: Dauphin Deposit Corp. SIC: 6022—State Commercial Banks.

★ 68115 ★ Jim Beam Brands Co.
Nazareth Rd.
Bardstown, KY 40004
(502)348-3998
Ultimate Parent: American Brands Inc. SIC: 2085—Distilled & Blended Liquors.

★ 68116 ★ Jim Beam Brands Co.
Louisville Rd.
Bardstown, KY 40004
(502)348-2450
Ultimate Parent: American Brands Inc. SIC: 2085—Distilled & Blended Liquors.

★ 68117 ★ Owens Illinois Inc.
1051 Bloomfield Rd.
Bardstown, KY 40004
(502)348-9211
Officer: Henry McLendon, Manager. Ultimate Parent: Owens-Illinois. SIC: 3089—Plastics Products Nec.

★ 68118 ★ Owens-Illinois Labels Inc. Products Inc.
1051 Bloomfield Rd.
Bardstown, KY 40004
Ultimate Parent: Owens-Illinois. SIC: 3089—Plastics Products Nec.

★ 68119 ★ Ryder Truck Rental-Oneway
512 E. Stephen Foster Ave.
Bardstown, KY 40004
(502)348-2134
Ultimate Parent: Ryder System. SIC: 7359—Equipment Rental & Leasing Nec.

★ 68120 ★ Superamerica
717 N. 3rd St.
Bardstown, KY 40004
(502)348-1208
Ultimate Parent: Ashland Oil. SIC: 5411—
Grocery Stores; 5541—Gasoline Service
Stations.

★ 68121 ★ Trim Masters Inc.
1051 Withrow Ct.
Bardstown, KY 40004
Ultimate Parent: Johnson & Johnson. SIC:
3714—Motor Vehicle Parts & Accessories.

Beaver Dam

★ 68122 ★ Wal-Mart Stores Inc.
Us 231
Beaver Dam, KY 42320
(502)274-9608
Ultimate Parent: Wal-Mart Stores, Inc. SIC:
5311—Department Stores.

Bellevue

★ 68123 ★ Liberty National Bank
of Northern Kentucky
Landmark & Riviera Dr.
Bellevue, KY 41073
(606)261-8655
Company Type: Subsidiary. Location
Type: Branch office. Officer: Jennifer L.
Brennan, Mgr. Ultimate Parent: Liberty
National Bancorp. SIC: 6021—National
Commercial Banks.

Benton

★ 68124 ★ Blue Grass
Cooperage Co., Inc.
Slaughter Rd.
Benton, KY 42025
(502)527-7411
Officer: Eddie Kissiar. Ultimate Parent:
Brown-Forman. SIC: 2429—Special Product
Sawmills Nec; 0811—Timber Tracts.

★ 68125 ★ Mary Kay Cosmetics
RR 6
Benton, KY 42025
(502)527-7540
Ultimate Parent: Mary Kay Cosmetics. SIC:
5999—Miscellaneous Retail Stores Nec.

★ 68126 ★ Texas Gas
Transmission
RR 6
Benton, KY 42025
(502)527-3137
Ultimate Parent: Transco Energy Co. SIC:
5521—Used Car Dealers.

Berea

★ 68127 ★ Hyster Co.
PO Box 426 Menelaus Pike
Berea, KY 40403
Ultimate Parent: Nacco Industries. SIC:
5500—Automotive Dealers & Service
Stations.

★ 68128 ★ Peoples Bank & Trust
Co.
419 Chestnut St.
Berea, KY 40403
(606)986-3175
Ultimate Parent: People's Bank. SIC:
6022—State Commercial Banks.

Boston

★ 68129 ★ Jim Beam Brands Co.
Hwy. 61
Boston, KY 40107
Ultimate Parent: American Brands Inc.
SIC: 2085—Distilled & Blended Liquors;
2048—Prepared Feeds Nec.

★ 68130 ★ Jim Beam Brands Co.
1600 Lebanon Junction Rd.
Boston, KY 40107-8550
(502)833-4611
Officer: Jeff Conders. Ultimate Parent:
American Brands Inc. SIC: 2085—Distilled
& Blended Liquors.

Bowling Green

★ 68131 ★ A. O. Smith
Automotive Prods. Co.
311 Vanderbilt Dr.
Bowling Green, KY 42103
Ultimate Parent: A. O. Smith. SIC: 3089—
Plastics Products Nec.

★ 68132 ★ Bada Co.
759 Hennessy Way
Bowling Green, KY 42101
Ultimate Parent: Danaher Corp. SIC:
3399—Primary Metal Products Nec.

★ 68133 ★ Bada Co.
31 W. North Access to I-65
Bowling Green, KY 42101
Ultimate Parent: Danaher Corp. SIC:
3999—Manufacturing Industries Nec.

★ 68134 ★ Casual Corner
25 Greenwood Mall
Bowling Green, KY 42104
Ultimate Parent: United States Shoe. SIC:
5651—Family Clothing Stores.

★ 68135 ★ Colt Industries Inc.
Holley Replacement Parts Div.
2800 Griffin Dr.
Bowling Green, KY 42101-5339
Company Type: Division. Ultimate Parent:
Coltec Industries. SIC: 3714—Motor Vehicle
Parts & Accessories.

★ 68136 ★ Eaton Corp.
2901 Industrial Dr.
Bowling Green, KY 42101
(502)782-1555
Officer: Steve Kavanaugh, Manager.
Ultimate Parent: Eaton Corp. SIC: 3625—
Relays & Industrial Controls; 3699—
Electrical Equipment & Supplies Nec.

★ 68137 ★ Eaton Corp.
Power Control Div.
2901 Industrial Dr.
Bowling Green, KY 42102-9002
(502)782-1555
Company Type: Division. Location Type:
Plant. Officer: Mike Brenner, Controller.
Ultimate Parent: Eaton Corp. SIC: 3613—
Switchgear & Switchboard Apparatus;
3625—Relays & Industrial Controls; 3669—
Communications Equipment Nec; 3674—
Semiconductors & Related Devices; 3714—
Motor Vehicle Parts & Accessories; 3823—
Process Control Instruments.

★ 68138 ★ Eaton Corp. Bowling
Green Plant
2901 Industrial Dr.
Bowling Green, KY 42101-4009
Ultimate Parent: Eaton Corp. SIC: 3829—
Measuring & Controlling Devices Nec.

★ 68139 ★ First American
National Bank of Kentucky
551 E. 10th
Bowling Green, KY 42101-2229
(502)782-2790 Fax: (502)781-0080
Location Type: Branch office. Officer:
Frank St. Charles III, President, CEO &
Marketing. Ultimate Parent: First American
Corp. SIC: 6021—National Commercial
Banks.

★ 68140 ★ First American
National Bank of Kentucky
PO Box 960
Bowling Green, KY 42101-0960
Location Type: Branch office. Ultimate
Parent: First American Corp. SIC: 6021—
National Commercial Banks.

★ 68141 ★ First American
National Bank of Kentucky
2009 Scottsville Rd.
Bowling Green, KY 42104
(502)745-9400
Location Type: Branch office. Officer:
Keith Beckham, Vice President. Ultimate
Parent: First American Corp. SIC: 6021—
National Commercial Banks.

★ 68142 ★ Fruit of the Loom
General Management
1 Fruit Of The Loom Dr.
Bowling Green, KY 42102-9105
(502)781-6400 Fax: (502)782-3995
Company Type: Subsidiary. Ultimate
Parent: Fruit of the Loom.

★ 68143 ★ Greyhound Bus Lines
331 E. 8th Ave.
Bowling Green, KY 42101
(502)781-4848
Ultimate Parent: Greyhound Lines Inc. SIC:
4111—Local & Suburban Transit; 4142—
Bus Charter Service Except Local; 4131—
Intercity & Rural Bus Transportation.

★ 68144 ★ Hill's Pet Nutrition
Inc.
151 Turner Ct.
Bowling Green, KY 42101
Ultimate Parent: Colgate-Palmolive. SIC:
2047—Dog & Cat Food.

★ 68145 ★ Hills Pet Products
151 Turner Ct.
Bowling Green, KY 42101
Ultimate Parent: Colgate-Palmolive. SIC:
2047—Dog & Cat Food.

★ 68146 ★ Kroger Co.
2700 Nashville Rd.
Bowling Green, KY 42101
(502)843-9091
Ultimate Parent: Kroger. SIC: 5411—
Grocery Stores.

★ 68147 ★ Limited the
Greenwood Mall
Bowling Green, KY 42101
(502)782-3355
Ultimate Parent: Limited. SIC: 5621—
Women's Clothing Stores.

★ 68148 ★ Mini Mart Foods Inc.
3 Sprigs Plz.
Bowling Green, KY 42101
(502)842-6050
Ultimate Parent: Kroger. SIC: 5411—
Grocery Stores.

★ 68149 ★ National City Bank,
Bowling Green
924 Broadway
Bowling Green, KY 42101-2540
(502)745-9230
Company Type: Subsidiary. Location
Type: Branch office. Officer: Betty
Alexander, Mgr. Ultimate Parent: National
City Corp. SIC: 6021—National Commercial
Banks.

★ 68150 ★ National City Bank,
Bowling Green
2629 Scottsville Rd.
Bowling Green, KY 42104-4410
(502)745-9303
Company Type: Subsidiary. Location
Type: Branch office. Officer: Pat Harmon,
Mgr. Ultimate Parent: National City Corp.
SIC: 6021—National Commercial Banks.

★ 68151 ★ National City Bank,
Bowling Green
1054 Fairview Ave.
Bowling Green, KY 42103-1677
(502)745-9330
Company Type: Subsidiary. Location
Type: Branch office. Officer: Bonnie
McCormack, Mgr. Ultimate Parent: National
City Corp. SIC: 6021—National Commercial
Banks.

★ 68152 ★ National City Bank,
Bowling Green
922 State St.
PO Box 90016
Bowling Green, KY 42102-9013
(502)781-6111 Fax: (502)745-9365
Company Type: Subsidiary. Location
Type: Branch office. Officer: Robert E.
Aldridge, Chairman, President, & CEO.
Ultimate Parent: National City Corp. SIC:
6021—National Commercial Banks.

★ 68153 ★ National City Bank,
Bowling Green
2215 Russellville Rd.
Bowling Green, KY 42102-5024
(502)745-9344
Company Type: Subsidiary. Location
Type: Branch office. Officer: Lillian Moore,
Mgr. Ultimate Parent: National City Corp.
SIC: 6021—National Commercial Banks.

★ 68154 ★ Northwestern Mutual
Life, Inc.
PO Box 9727
Bowling Green, KY 42102
Ultimate Parent: Northwestern Mutual Life.
SIC: 6411—Insurance Agents, Brokers &
Service.

★ 68155 ★ Osco Drug Store
2625 Scottsville Rd.
Bowling Green, KY 42104
(502)842-8104
Ultimate Parent: American Stores. SIC:
5912—Drug Stores & Proprietary Stores.

★ 68156 ★ Osco Drug Store
95 Greenwood Mall
Bowling Green, KY 42104
(502)842-8105
Ultimate Parent: American Stores. SIC:
5912—Drug Stores & Proprietary Stores.

★ 68157 ★ Payless Shoe Source
1603 W. U S. 31 by Pass
Bowling Green, KY 42101
(502)843-1783
Ultimate Parent: May Department Stores.
SIC: 5661—Shoe Stores.

★ 68158 ★ Payless Shoe Source
46 Greenwood Mall
Bowling Green, KY 42104
(502)782-9840
Ultimate Parent: May Department Stores.
SIC: 5661—Shoe Stores.

★ 68159 ★ Pepsi Cola General
Bottlers
391 N. Graham St.
Bowling Green, KY 42101
(502)782-3720
Officer: Kevin Forney, Manager. Ultimate
Parent: Pepsico. SIC: 2086—Bottled
& Canned Soft Drinks.

★ 68160 ★ Pepsi-Cola General
Bottlers
825 Graham St.
Bowling Green, KY 42101
(502)782-3720
Ultimate Parent: Pepsico. SIC:
5149—Groceries & Related Products Nec.

★ 68161 ★ Rite Aid Discount
Pharmacy
660 Us 31w Byp
Bowling Green, KY 42101
(502)843-2740
Ultimate Parent: Rite Aid. SIC: 5912—Drug
Stores & Proprietary Stores.

★ 68162 ★ Sales, Marketing,
Manufacturing, Finance &
Administration
1 Fruit Of The Loom Dr.
Bowling Green, KY 42102-9105
(502)781-6400 Fax: (502)782-3995
Company Type: Subsidiary. Ultimate
Parent: Fruit of the Loom.

★ 68163 ★ Underwriters
Adjusting Co.
1719 Ashley Cir.
Bowling Green, KY 42104
(502)781-1336
Ultimate Parent: Continental. SIC: 6411—
Insurance Agents, Brokers & Service.

★ 68164 ★ Wal-Mart Stores Inc.
Greenwood Mall
Bowling Green, KY 42101
(502)842-1653
Ultimate Parent: Wal-Mart Stores, Inc. SIC:
5311—Department Stores.

★ 68165 ★ Weyerhaeuser Co.
Bowling Green
5150 Nashville Rd. PO Box 90026
Bowling Green, KY 42101
Ultimate Parent: Weyerhaeuser Co. SIC:
2676—Sanitary Paper Products.

Bradfordsville

★ 68166 ★ People's Bank
PO Box 6
Bradfordsville, KY 40009
(502)337-2121
Ultimate Parent: People's Bank. SIC:
6029—Commercial Banks Nec.

Brandenburg

★ 68167 ★ Farmers Deposit Bank, Inc.
Rte. 2
Brandenburg, KY 40108-9802
(502)422-4422
Company Type: Subsidiary. **Location Type:** Branch office. **Ultimate Parent:** Liberty National Bancorp. **SIC:** 6021—National Commercial Banks.

★ 68168 ★ Farmers Deposit Bank, Inc.
416 E. Broadway
Brandenburg, KY 40108-1102
(502)422-2172
Company Type: Subsidiary. **Location Type:** Branch office. **Officer:** James W. Kimbell, President. **Ultimate Parent:** Liberty National Bancorp. **SIC:** 6021—National Commercial Banks.

★ 68169 ★ Olin Corp.
2450 Olin Rd.
Brandenburg, KY 40108
(502)422-2101
Officer: Tom Thomas, Manager. **Ultimate Parent:** Olin Corp. **SIC:** 2819—Industrial Inorganic Chemicals Nec; 2869—Industrial Organic Chemicals Nec.

★ 68170 ★ Olin Corp.
Hwy. 933
Brandenburg, KY 40108
Ultimate Parent: Olin Corp. **SIC:** 2869—Industrial Organic Chemicals Nec; 2841—Soap & Other Detergents; 2843—Surface Active Agents.

Buckner

★ 68171 ★ PNC Bank Kentucky Inc.
4727 W. Hwy. 146
Buckner, KY 40010-9528
(502)222-6266
Location Type: Branch office. **Ultimate Parent:** PNC Bank Corp. **SIC:** 6021—National Commercial Banks.

Buechel

★ 68172 ★ PNC Bank Kentucky Inc.
4021 Bardstown Rd.
Buechel, KY 40218-2630
(502)581-3226
Location Type: Branch office. **Ultimate Parent:** PNC Bank Corp. **SIC:** 6021—National Commercial Banks.

Burlington

★ 68173 ★ Liberty National Bank of Northern Kentucky
1750 Wildcat Blvd.
Burlington, KY 41005
(606)525-3060
Company Type: Subsidiary. **Location Type:** Branch office. **Officer:** Phyliss Stamper, Mgr. **Ultimate Parent:** Liberty National Bancorp. **SIC:** 6021—National Commercial Banks.

Calvert City

★ 68174 ★ Air Products & Chemicals Inc.
Hwy. 95
Calvert City, KY 42029
(502)395-4181
Officer: Tom Tarwater, Manager. **Ultimate Parent:** Air Products & Chemicals, Inc. **SIC:** 3149—Footwear Except Rubber Nec.

★ 68175 ★ Air Products & Chemicals Inc.
Hwy. 95
Calvert City, KY 420290097
Ultimate Parent: Air Products & Chemicals, Inc. **SIC:** 2821—Plastics Materials & Resins; 2869—Industrial Organic Chemicals Nec.

★ 68176 ★ GAF Chemicals Corp.
Hwy. 95, PO Box 37
Calvert City, KY 42029
Ultimate Parent: GAF Corp. **SIC:** 2869—Industrial Organic Chemicals Nec; 2865—Cyclic Crudes & Intermediates; 2834—Pharmaceutical Preparations; 2843—Surface Active Agents.

★ 68177 ★ Warren Petroleum Co.
Calvert City, KY 42029
(502)395-4570
Ultimate Parent: Chevron Corp. **SIC:** 4231—Trucking Terminal Facilities.

Campbellsville

★ 68178 ★ Batesville Casket Co.
901 New Columbia Rd.
Campbellsville, KY 42718
Ultimate Parent: Hillenbrand Industries. **SIC:** 3995—Burial Caskets.

★ 68179 ★ Batesville Casket Co. Inc.
901 New Columbia Rd.
Campbellsville, KY 42718
Ultimate Parent: Hillenbrand Industries. **SIC:** 3995—Burial Caskets.

★ 68180 ★ Fruit of the Loom Inc. Union Underwear
1101 Greensburg Rd.
Campbellsville, KY 42718
Ultimate Parent: Fruit of the Loom. **SIC:** 2322—Men's/Boys' Underwear & Nightwear.

★ 68181 ★ McDonald's Hamburgers
605 E. Broadway St.
Campbellsville, KY 42718
(502)465-6658
Ultimate Parent: McDonald's. **SIC:** 5812—Eating Places.

★ 68182 ★ Parker-Kalon
395 Roberts Rd.
Campbellsville, KY 42718
Ultimate Parent: Black & Decker Corp. **SIC:** 3452—Bolts, Nuts, Rivets & Washers.

★ 68183 ★ Ryder Truck Rental-Oneway
908 Lebanon Ave.
Campbellsville, KY 42718
(502)465-7199
Ultimate Parent: Ryder System. **SIC:** 7359—Equipment Rental & Leasing Nec.

Campbellsvl

★ 68184 ★ Batesville Casket Co. Inc.
1000 S. Hwy. 55
Campbellsvl, KY 42718
(502)789-2975
Ultimate Parent: Hillenbrand Industries. **SIC:** 5087—Service Establishment Equipment.

Campbellsvlle

★ 68185 ★ Fruit of the Loom
Fruit of Loom Dr.
Campbellsvlle, KY 42718
(502)343-2501
Ultimate Parent: Fruit of the Loom. **SIC:** 2254—Knit Underwear Mills.

★ 68186 ★ Fruit of the Loom
1101 Greensburg Rd.
Campbellsvlle, KY 42718
(502)465-8121
Ultimate Parent: Fruit of the Loom. **SIC:** 2254—Knit Underwear Mills.

★ 68187 ★ Fruit of the Loom
GTE
Campbellsvlle, KY 42718
(502)465-2401
Ultimate Parent: Fruit of the Loom. **SIC:** 5399—Miscellaneous General Merchandise Store.

Campton

★ 68188 ★ Mobil Tire Service
473 PO Box
Campton, KY 41301
(606)668-6860
Ultimate Parent: Mobil. **SIC:** 4121—Taxicabs.

Carrollton

★ 68189 ★ Dow Corning Corp.
US Hwy. 42 E
Carrollton, KY 41008
Ultimate Parent: Dow Chemical Co. USA. **SIC:** 2869—Industrial Organic Chemicals Nec.

★ 68190 ★ Foster Wheeler Corp.
Us 42 E
Carrollton, KY 41008
(502)347-5376
Ultimate Parent: Fortune Bancorp. **SIC:** 8712—Architectural Services.

★ 68191 ★ Kroger Co.
US 227
Carrollton, KY 41008
(502)732-5380
Ultimate Parent: Kroger. **SIC:** 5411—Grocery Stores.

★ 68192 ★ Star Bank NA, Kentucky
416 Highland Ave.
Carrollton, KY 41008-1017
(502)732-6601
Location Type: Branch office. **Officer:** Steven P. Toomey, Regulation President. **Ultimate Parent:** Star Banc Corp. **SIC:** 6021—National Commercial Banks.

★ 68193 ★ Teledyne Packaging
9th & Hawkins Sts. PO Box 326
Carrollton, KY 41008
Ultimate Parent: Teledyne. **SIC:** 3499—Fabricated Metal Products Nec.

★ 68194 ★ Teledyne Wirz
9th & Hawkins St.
Carrollton, KY 41008
Ultimate Parent: Teledyne. **SIC:** 3499—Fabricated Metal Products Nec.

Catlettsburg

★ 68195 ★ Ashland Petroleum Co.
Catlettsburg Refinery
11621 US 23
Catlettsburg, KY 41129
Ultimate Parent: Ashland Oil. **SIC:** 2911—Petroleum Refining.

★ 68196 ★ National City Bank, Ashland Kentucky
23 & England Hill Rd.
Catlettsburg, KY 41129
(606)329-2900
Company Type: Subsidiary. **Location Type:** Branch office. **Officer:** Jennifer Gray, Mgr. **Ultimate Parent:** National City Corp. **SIC:** 6021—National Commercial Banks.

★ 68197 ★ Rite Aid Inc.
Court St.
Catlettsburg, KY 41129
(606)739-4432
Ultimate Parent: Rite Aid. **SIC:** 5912—Drug Stores & Proprietary Stores.

Cave City

★ 68198 ★ Greyhound Bus Lines
Us 31 W
Cave City, KY 42127
(502)773-2200
Ultimate Parent: Greyhound Lines Inc. **SIC:** 4131—Intercity & Rural Bus Transportation; 4111—Local & Suburban Transit; 4142—Bus Charter Service Except Local.

Cecilia

★ 68199 ★ Agrico Chemical Co.
Robinson
Cecilia, KY 42724
(502)862-3291
Ultimate Parent: Freeport-McMoran. **SIC:** 5191—Farm Supplies.

Chent

★ 68200 ★ North American Stainless
100 Main St. U.S. Hwy. 42 E.
Chent, KY 41045
(502)347-6000
Company Type: Subsidiary. **Officer:** Jose LeJeune, President. **Ultimate Parent:** Armco.

Clarkson

★ 68201 ★ Agrico Chemical Co., Inc.
Clarkson, KY 42726
(502)242-2611
Ultimate Parent: Freeport-McMoran. **SIC:** 5191—Farm Supplies.

Clay

★ 68202 ★ Agrico Chemical Co.
Hwy. 132
Clay, KY 42404
(502)664-2761
Ultimate Parent: Freeport-McMoran. **SIC:** 5261—Retail Nurseries & Garden Stores.

Clermont

★ 68203 ★ Jim Beam Brands Co.
Hwy. 245
Clermont, KY 40110-9999
Ultimate Parent: American Brands Inc. **SIC:** 2085—Distilled & Blended Liquors; 2048—Prepared Feeds Nec.

★ 68204 ★ Jim Beam Brands Co.
US Hwy. 245
Clermont, KY 40110
(502)543-2221
Officer: Berry Berish. **Ultimate Parent:** American Brands Inc. **SIC:** 2085—Distilled & Blended Liquors.

Cold Spring

★ 68205 ★ Liberty National Bank of Northern Kentucky
5035 Alexandria Pke.
Cold Spring, KY 41076-1797
(606)441-8200
Company Type: Subsidiary. **Location Type:** Branch office. **Ultimate Parent:** Liberty National Bancorp. **SIC:** 6021—National Commercial Banks.

★ 68206 ★ Star Bank NA, Kentucky
3600 Alexandria Pke.
Cold Spring, KY 41076
(606)781-7800
Location Type: Branch office. **Officer:** Jan Lindsey, Assistant Vice President. **Ultimate Parent:** Star Banc Corp. **SIC:** 6021—National Commercial Banks.

Columbia

★ 68207 ★ Greyhound Bus Lines
201 N. Fortune St.
Columbia, KY 42728
(502)384-2441
Ultimate Parent: Greyhound Lines Inc. **SIC:** 4131—Intercity & Rural Bus Transportation; 4111—Local & Suburban Transit; 4142—Bus Charter Service Except Local.

Corbin

★ 68208 ★ American Greetings Corp.
American Greetings Rd.
Corbin, KY 40701-9803
Ultimate Parent: American Greetings. **SIC:** 2771—Greeting Cards.

★ 68209 ★ NCR Corp.
Industrial Park
Corbin, KY 40701
(606)528-7930
Officer: Fred Calico, Plant Manager. **Ultimate Parent:** AT&T. **SIC:** 2759—Commercial Printing Nec.

★ 68210 ★ Pepsi-Cola Bottling Co.
1000 W. 18th St.
Corbin, KY 40701
Ultimate Parent: Pepsico. **SIC:** 2086—Bottled & Canned Soft Drinks.

★ 68211 ★ Pepsi-Cola Bottling Co.
1000 18th St.
Corbin, KY 40701
(606)528-1630
Officer: Larry Morgan, Manager. **Ultimate Parent:** Pepsico. **SIC:** 2086—Bottled & Canned Soft Drinks.

★ 68212 ★ **Piggly Wiggly Food Store**
1405 S. Main St.
Corbin, KY 40701-1930
(606)528-5490
Location Type: Branch office. **Officer:** Harold E. Onkst. **Ultimate Parent:** Bruno's. **SIC:** 5411—Grocery Stores.

★ 68213 ★ **Ryder Truck Rental-Oneway**
1001 Carter St.
Corbin, KY 40701
(606)523-0274
Ultimate Parent: Ryder System. **SIC:** 7513—Truck Rental & Leasing Without Drivers.

Covington

★ 68214 ★ **Aunt Nellie's Farm Kitchens**
227 W. Southern Ave.
Covington, KY 41015
(606)431-3470
Officer: Fred Good, Manager. **Ultimate Parent:** Dean Foods. **SIC:** 2033—Canned Fruits & Vegetables.

★ 68215 ★ **Canteen Corp.**
200 W. 4th St.
Covington, KY 41011
(606)261-5094
Ultimate Parent: Firstfed Financial Corp. **SIC:** 5812—Eating Places.

★ 68216 ★ **Cigna Individual Financial Services Co.**
1717 Dixie Hwy.
Covington, KY 41011
(606)341-0303
Ultimate Parent: Cigna Corp. **SIC:** 6211—Security Brokers & Dealers.

★ 68217 ★ **Firstfed Northern Kentucky Bancorporation**
501 Main St.
Covington, KY 41011-1329
(606)431-6480
Officer: John C. Jacobs, Chairman of the Board. **Ultimate Parent:** Firstfed Financial Corp. **SIC:** 6035—Federal Savings Institutions. **Employee Count:** 93.

★ 68218 ★ **Firstfed Northern Kentucky Bancorporation Inc.**
501 Main St.
Covington, KY 41011
(606)431-6480
Officer: William G. Cason, President. **Ultimate Parent:** Firstfed Financial Corp. **SIC:** 6712—Bank Holding Companies; 6035—Federal Savings Institutions. **Employee Count:** 95. **Sales:** 17717000 M.

★ 68219 ★ **Fitness Challenge**
2615 Anderson Rd.
Covington, KY 41017
(606)331-9415
Ultimate Parent: New York Times. **SIC:** 7991—Physical Fitness Facilities.

★ 68220 ★ **Greyhound Bus Lines**
500 Madison Ave.
Covington, KY 41011
(606)431-5200
Ultimate Parent: Greyhound Lines Inc. **SIC:** 4131—Intercity & Rural Bus Transportation; 4111—Local & Suburban Transit; 4142—Bus Charter Service Except Local.

★ 68221 ★ **Greyhound Lines Inc.**
500 Madison Ave.
Covington, KY 41011
(606)431-5200
Ultimate Parent: Greyhound Lines Inc. **SIC:** 4131—Intercity & Rural Bus Transportation; 4173—Bus Terminal & Service Facilities.

★ 68222 ★ **Hit or Miss**
48 Crestview Hill Mall
Covington, KY 41017
(606)341-0004
Ultimate Parent: TJX. **SIC:** 2339—Women's/Misses' Outerwear Nec.

★ 68223 ★ **Kentucky Post**
421 Madison Ave.
Covington, KY 41011
(606)292-2600
Ultimate Parent: E.W. Scripps Co. **SIC:** 2711—Newspapers.

★ 68224 ★ **Kentucky Post**
2829 Deerfield Dr.
Covington, KY 41017
(606)331-2660
Ultimate Parent: E.W. Scripps Co.

★ 68225 ★ **Kroger Co.**
1525 Madison Ave.
Covington, KY 41011
(606)431-5566
Ultimate Parent: Kroger. **SIC:** 5411—Grocery Stores.

★ 68226 ★ **Kroger Co.**
2156 Dixie Hwy.
Covington, KY 41017
(606)331-0080
Ultimate Parent: Kroger. **SIC:** 5411—Grocery Stores.

★ 68227 ★ **Lerner Shops**
4 Crestview Hill Mall
Covington, KY 41017
(606)341-4225
Ultimate Parent: Limited. **SIC:** 5621—Women's Clothing Stores.

★ 68228 ★ **Northwestern Mutual Life**
176 Barnwood Dr.
Covington, KY 41017
(606)341-7014
Ultimate Parent: Northwestern Mutual Life. **SIC:** 6411—Insurance Agents, Brokers & Service.

★ 68229 ★ **Payless Shoe Source**
114 Crestview Hill Mall
Covington, KY 41017
(606)341-1401
Ultimate Parent: May Department Stores. **SIC:** 5661—Shoe Stores.

★ 68230 ★ **Pepsi-Cola General Bottlers**
1320 Russell St.
Covington, KY 41011
(606)291-2141
Ultimate Parent: Pepsico. **SIC:** 2086—Bottled & Canned Soft Drinks; 5962—Merchandising Machine Operators.

★ 68231 ★ **PNC Bank Northern Kentucky, NA**
404 Madison Ave.
Covington, KY 41011-1520
(606)344-3750
Location Type: Branch office. **Officer:** Ann Weiler, Assistant Vice President. **Ultimate Parent:** PNC Bank Corp. **SIC:** 6021—National Commercial Banks.

★ 68232 ★ **Ryder Truck Rental-Oneway**
12th
Covington, KY 41011
(606)291-6141
Ultimate Parent: Ryder System. **SIC:** 7359—Equipment Rental & Leasing Nec.

★ 68233 ★ **Star Bank NA, Kentucky**
3937 Winston Ave.
Covington, KY 41015-1706
(606)292-6290
Location Type: Branch office. **Officer:** Vicki Fields, Vice President. **Ultimate Parent:** Star Banc Corp. **SIC:** 6021—National Commercial Banks.

★ 68234 ★ **Star Bank NA, Kentucky**
6th & Madison Ave.
Covington, KY 41011
(606)292-6219
Location Type: Branch office. **Officer:** Yvette Carter, Assistant Vice President. **Ultimate Parent:** Star Banc Corp. **SIC:** 6021—National Commercial Banks.

★ 68235 ★ **Star Bank NA, Kentucky**
20th St. & Madison Ave.
Covington, KY 41014
(606)292-6230
Location Type: Branch office. **Officer:** Susan Griffith, Assistant Vice President. **Ultimate Parent:** Star Banc Corp. **SIC:** 6021—National Commercial Banks.

★ 68236 ★ **Star Bank NA, Kentucky**
PO Box 589
Covington, KY 41011
Location Type: Branch office. **Ultimate Parent:** Star Banc Corp. **SIC:** 6021—National Commercial Banks.

★ 68237 ★ **Star Bank NA, Kentucky**
50 E. Rivercenter Blvd.
Covington, KY 41011
(606)292-6200 **Fax:** (606)292-8430
Location Type: Branch office. **Officer:** William C. Vermillion, President. **Ultimate Parent:** Star Banc Corp. **SIC:** 6021—National Commercial Banks.

★ 68238 ★ **Superamerica**
614 W. 4th St.
Covington, KY 41011
(606)261-7557
Ultimate Parent: Ashland Oil. **SIC:** 5541—Gasoline Service Stations.

★ 68239 ★ **Union Light Heat & Power Co.**
107 Brent Spence Sq.
Covington, KY 41011
(606)381-4100
Ultimate Parent: Cincinnati Gas & Electric Co. **SIC:** 4911—Electric Services.

★ 68240 ★ **Varian Associates Inc.**
100 Crisler Ave.
Covington, KY 41017
(606)341-6400
Ultimate Parent: Varian Associates, Inc. **SIC:** 2599—Furniture & Fixtures Nec.

Crescent Springs

★ 68241 ★ **Liberty National Bank of Northern Kentucky**
735 Buttermilk Pke.
Crescent Springs, KY 41017-1303
(606)341-6500
Company Type: Subsidiary. **Location Type:** Branch office. **Officer:** Michael G. Hill, Mgr. **Ultimate Parent:** Liberty National Bancorp. **SIC:** 6021—National Commercial Banks.

★ 68242 ★ **PNC Bank Northern Kentucky, NA**
525 Buttermilk Pke.
Crescent Springs, KY 41017-1682
(606)344-3760
Location Type: Branch office. **Ultimate Parent:** PNC Bank Corp. **SIC:** 6021—National Commercial Banks.

★ 68243 ★ **Star Bank NA, Kentucky**
609 Buttermilk Pke.
Crescent Springs, KY 41017-1301
(606)292-7700
Location Type: Branch office. **Officer:** Ben Wathen, Assistant Vice President. **Ultimate Parent:** Star Banc Corp. **SIC:** 6021—National Commercial Banks.

Crestview Hills

★ 68244 ★ **Star Bank NA, Kentucky**
2741 Turkeyfoot Rd.
Crestview Hills, KY 41017-2597
(606)292-6270
Location Type: Branch office. **Officer:** Kay Romes, Assistant Vice President. **Ultimate Parent:** Star Banc Corp. **SIC:** 6021—National Commercial Banks.

Crestwood

★ 68245 ★ **Crestwood State Bank**
6518 W. Hwy. 146
PO Box 68
Crestwood, KY 40014-0068
(502)241-9425 **Fax:** (502)241-9648
Company Type: Subsidiary. **Location Type:** Branch office. **Officer:** James E. Barber, President & CEO. **Ultimate Parent:** National City Corp. **SIC:** 6021—National Commercial Banks.

★ 68246 ★ **PNC Bank Kentucky Inc.**
6402 W. Hwy. 146
Crestwood, KY 40014-9569
(502)896-5745
Location Type: Branch office. **Officer:** Shirley Boyatt, Manager. **Ultimate Parent:** PNC Bank Corp. **SIC:** 6021—National Commercial Banks.

★ 68247 ★ **Wal-Mart Stores Inc.**
6400 Crestwood Station
Crestwood, KY 40014
(502)241-5121
Ultimate Parent: Wal-Mart Stores, Inc. **SIC:** 5311—Department Stores.

Cynthiana

★ 68248 ★ **Coast to Coast Hardware**
Harrison Sq.
Cynthiana, KY 41031
(606)234-9220
Ultimate Parent: Servistar Corp. **SIC:** 5251—Hardware Stores.

★ 68249 ★ **Minnesota Mining & Mfg. Co.**
PO Box 430
Cynthiana, KY 41031
(606)234-5671
Ultimate Parent: Minnesota Mining & Mfg. **SIC:** 2679—Converted Paper Products Nec.

★ 68250 ★ **3M Co.**
301 New Lair Rd.
Cynthiana, KY 41031
(606)234-5671
Company Type: Branch. **Officer:** Gary Whitenack. **Ultimate Parent:** Minnesota Mining & Mfg. **SIC:** 2679—Converted Paper Products Nec.

★ 68251 ★ **Wal-Mart Stores Inc.**
Us 27 S
Cynthiana, KY 41031
(606)234-3232
Ultimate Parent: Wal-Mart Stores, Inc. **SIC:** 5311—Department Stores.

Danville

★ 68252 ★ **American Greeting Corp.**
S. Lebanon Rd.
Danville, KY 40422
(606)236-7200
Officer: Rod Molson. **Ultimate Parent:** American Greetings. **SIC:** 5947—Gift, Novelty & Souvenir Shops.

★ 68253 ★ **Clark Material Handling Co.**
1450 Minor Rd.
Danville, KY 40422-9653
(606)238-5000
Officer: David Rhodus. **Ultimate Parent:** Banta Corp. **SIC:** 3537—Industrial Trucks & Tractors.

★ 68254 ★ **Dana Corp.**
Victor Products Div.
500 Techwood Dr.
Danville, KY 40422
Company Type: Division. **Ultimate Parent:** Dana Corp. **SIC:** 3053—Gaskets, Packing & Sealing Devices.

★ 68255 ★ **R.R. Donnelley & Sons Co.**
Danville Manufacturing Div.
John Hill Bailey Industrial Hwy. 34
Danville, KY 40422
Company Type: Division. **Ultimate Parent:** R. R. Donnelley & Sons. **SIC:** 2752—Commercial Printing—Lithographic.

★ 68256 ★ **R.R. Donnelley & Sons Co.**
Danville Manufacturing Div.
John Hill Bailey Industrial Park, Hwy. 34
Danville, KY 40422
Ultimate Parent: R. R. Donnelley & Sons. **SIC:** 2752—Commercial Printing—Lithographic.

★ 68257 ★   R.R. Donnelley &
Sons Co.
Kentucky E. Manufacturing Div.
John Hill Bailey Industrial Park Hwy. 34
Danville, KY 40422
Company Type: Division. **Ultimate Parent:**
R. R. Donnelley & Sons. **SIC:** 2752—
Commercial Printing—Lithographic.

★ 68258 ★   GemStone Gasket Co.
PO Box 907
Danville, KY 40422
(606)236-3960
Company Type: Subsidiary. **Officer:** Steve
Moore, Plant Manager. **Ultimate Parent:**
Dana Corp. **SIC:** 3053—Gaskets, Packing &
Sealing Devices.

★ 68259 ★   Greyhound Bus Lines
508 S. 4th St.
Danville, KY 40422
(606)236-6244
Ultimate Parent: Greyhound Lines Inc. **SIC:**
4131—Intercity & Rural Bus Transportation;
4111—Local & Suburban Transit; 4142—
Bus Charter Service Except Local.

★ 68260 ★   Mary Kay Cosmetics
Greenleaf Shopping Ctr.
Danville, KY 40422
(606)236-0070
Ultimate Parent: Mary Kay Cosmetics. **SIC:**
5999—Miscellaneous Retail Stores Nec.

★ 68261 ★   Northwestern Mutual
Life Inc.
121 E. Main St.
Danville, KY 40422
(606)236-7468
Ultimate Parent: Northwestern Mutual Life.
SIC: 6411—Insurance Agents, Brokers &
Service.

★ 68262 ★   Ryder Truck Rental-
Oneway
530 S. 4th St.
Danville, KY 40422
(606)236-6211
Ultimate Parent: Ryder System. **SIC:**
7359—Equipment Rental & Leasing Nec.

★ 68263 ★   Wal-Mart Stores Inc.
Danville Sq.
Danville, KY 40422
(606)236-9550
Ultimate Parent: Wal-Mart Stores, Inc. **SIC:**
5311—Department Stores.

★ 68264 ★   Whirlpool Corp.
947 PO Box
Danville, KY 40423
(606)236-8400
Ultimate Parent: Whirlpool Corp. **SIC:**
3639—Household Appliances Nec.

★ 68265 ★   Whirlpool Corp.
Lebanon Rd.
Danville, KY 40422
(606)236-8400
Ultimate Parent: Whirlpool Corp. **SIC:**
3599—Industrial Machinery Nec.

★ 68266 ★   Whirlpool Corp.
Danville Div.
Lebanon Rd.
Danville, KY 40422
Ultimate Parent: Whirlpool Corp. **SIC:**
3639—Household Appliances Nec; 3635—
Household Vacuum Cleaners; 3621—Motors
& Generators.

Dayton

★ 68267 ★   Liberty National Bank
of Northern Kentucky
6th & McKinney
Dayton, KY 41074
(606)261-8061
Company Type: Subsidiary. **Location
Type:** Branch office. **Officer:** Sandra Poe,
Mgr. **Ultimate Parent:** Liberty National
Bancorp. **SIC:** 6021—National Commercial
Banks.

Earlington

★ 68268 ★   People's Bank &
Trust Co.
102 E. Main St.
Earlington, KY 42410
(502)383-2231
Ultimate Parent: People's Bank. **SIC:**
6022—State Commercial Banks.

Edgewood

★ 68269 ★   Liberty National Bank
of Northern Kentucky
160 Barnwood Dr.
Edgewood, KY 41017-2501
(606)341-1616
Company Type: Subsidiary. **Location
Type:** Branch office. **Officer:** Vern
Enzweiler, Mgr. **Ultimate Parent:** Liberty
National Bancorp. **SIC:** 6021—National
Commercial Banks.

★ 68270 ★   PNC Bank Northern
Kentucky, NA
3023 Dixie Hwy.
Edgewood, KY 41017-2394
(606)341-6200
Location Type: Branch office. **Officer:**
Margaret A. Boone, Banking Officer.
Ultimate Parent: PNC Bank Corp. **SIC:**
6021—National Commercial Banks.

Edmonton

★ 68271 ★   Spd Magnet Wire Co.
909 Industrial Dr.
Edmonton, KY 42129
Ultimate Parent: Phelps Dodge. **SIC:**
3357—Nonferrous Wiredrawing & Insulating.

Elizabethtown

★ 68272 ★   Ambrake Corp.
300 Ring Rd.
Elizabethtown, KY 42701
Ultimate Parent: General Motors Corp.
SIC: 3714—Motor Vehicle Parts &
Accessories.

★ 68273 ★   Coast to Coast
Hardware
Et Own Plz.
Elizabethtown, KY 42701
(502)765-2138
Ultimate Parent: Servistar Corp. **SIC:**
5231—Paint, Glass & Wallpaper Stores.

★ 68274 ★   Coast to Coast
Investments
300 W. Dixie Ave.
Elizabethtown, KY 42701
(502)769-5416
Ultimate Parent: Servistar Corp. **SIC:**
6282—Investment Advice.

★ 68275 ★   Dow Corning Corp.
Hwy. 61
Elizabethtown, KY 42701
(502)737-6466
Ultimate Parent: Dow Chemical Co. USA.
SIC: 2891—Adhesives & Sealants.

★ 68276 ★   Dow Corning Corp.
Elizabethtown Plant
760 Hodgenville Rd.
Elizabethtown, KY 42701
Ultimate Parent: Dow Chemical Co. USA.
SIC: 2891—Adhesives & Sealants; 2822—
Synthetic Rubber.

★ 68277 ★   Electronic Data
Systems
315 Ring Rd.
Elizabethtown, KY 42701
(502)769-5100
Ultimate Parent: Electronic Data Systems.
SIC: 7389—Business Services Nec.

★ 68278 ★   EMB Corp.
1203 Hawkins Dr.
Elizabethtown, KY 42701
(502)737-1996
Officer: William C. Schaffrick, President.
Ultimate Parent: Alco Standard Corp. **SIC:**
3613—Switchgear & Switchboard
Apparatus; 3625—Relays & Industrial
Controls; 3679—Electronic Components
Nec.

★ 68279 ★   Hardin County Bank
& Trust
4079 N. Dixie Ave.
Elizabethtown, KY 42701-8825
(502)769-2212
Company Type: Subsidiary. **Location
Type:** Branch office. **Officer:** Joe Stewart,
Mgr. **Ultimate Parent:** Liberty National
Bancorp. **SIC:** 6021—National Commercial
Banks.

★ 68280 ★   J C Penney Catalog
Sales
1704 N. Dixie Hwy.
Elizabethtown, KY 42701
(502)737-7452
Ultimate Parent: J.C. Penney. **SIC:** 5311—
Department Stores.

★ 68281 ★   J C Penney Co. Inc.
1704 N. Dixie Hwy.
Elizabethtown, KY 42701
(502)765-7500
Ultimate Parent: J.C. Penney. **SIC:** 5311—
Department Stores.

★ 68282 ★   Kroger Co.
930 N. Mulberry St.
Elizabethtown, KY 42701
(502)765-5229
Ultimate Parent: Kroger. **SIC:** 5411—
Grocery Stores.

★ 68283 ★   Kroger Co.
1704 N. Dixie Hwy.
Elizabethtown, KY 42701
(502)737-1707
Ultimate Parent: Kroger. **SIC:** 5411—
Grocery Stores.

★ 68284 ★   Kroger Co.
111 Towne Dr.
Elizabethtown, KY 42701
(502)737-1737
Ultimate Parent: Kroger. **SIC:** 5411—
Grocery Stores.

★ 68285 ★   Lane Bryant
1704 N. Dixie Hwy.
Elizabethtown, KY 42701
(502)737-0680
Ultimate Parent: Limited. **SIC:** 5621—
Women's Clothing Stores.

★ 68286 ★   Liberty National Bank
& Trust Co. of Hardin County
1200 N. Dixie Ave.
PO Box 339
Elizabethtown, KY 42701
(502)737-2265 **Fax:** (502)737-5342
Company Type: Subsidiary. **Location
Type:** Branch office. **Officer:** James M.
McDonnell, President & CEO. **Ultimate
Parent:** Liberty National Bancorp. **SIC:**
6021—National Commercial Banks.

★ 68287 ★   Mary Kay Cosmetics
Bardstown Rd.
Elizabethtown, KY 42701
(502)737-2391
Ultimate Parent: Mary Kay Cosmetics. **SIC:**
5999—Miscellaneous Retail Stores Nec.

★ 68288 ★   Payless Shoe Source
31 E. Town Plz.
Elizabethtown, KY 42701
(502)351-4944
Ultimate Parent: May Department Stores.
SIC: 5661—Shoe Stores.

★ 68289 ★   Pepsi-Cola General
Bottlers
1215 Hawkins Dr.
Elizabethtown, KY 42701
(502)769-2351
Ultimate Parent: Pepsico. **SIC:** 2086—
Bottled & Canned Soft Drinks.

★ 68290 ★   PNC Bank Kentucky
Inc.
1016 N. Mulberry
Elizabethtown, KY 42701-2048
(502)769-7201
Location Type: Branch office. **Ultimate
Parent:** PNC Bank Corp. **SIC:** 6021—
National Commercial Banks.

★ 68291 ★   PNC Bank Kentucky
Inc.
227 W. Dixie Ave.
Elizabethtown, KY 42701-0648
(502)769-7200
Location Type: Branch office. **Ultimate
Parent:** PNC Bank Corp. **SIC:** 6021—
National Commercial Banks.

★ 68292 ★   PNC Bank Kentucky
Inc.
703 W. Dixie Ave.
Elizabethtown, KY 42701-1010
(502)769-7292
Location Type: Branch office. **Ultimate
Parent:** PNC Bank Corp. **SIC:** 6021—
National Commercial Banks.

★ 68293 ★   PNC Bank Kentucky
Inc.
RR 2
Elizabethtown, KY 42701-9802
(502)769-7263
Location Type: Branch office. **Ultimate
Parent:** PNC Bank Corp. **SIC:** 6021—
National Commercial Banks.

★ 68294 ★   Wal-Mart Stores Inc.
Elizabethtown Plz.
Elizabethtown, KY 42701
(502)769-5961
Ultimate Parent: Wal-Mart Stores, Inc. **SIC:**
5311—Department Stores.

Elsemere

★ 68295 ★   Star Bank NA,
Kentucky
3905 Dixie Hwy.
Elsemere, KY 41018-1811
(606)292-6220
Location Type: Branch office. **Officer:** Paul
Johnson, Assistant Vice President. **Ultimate
Parent:** Star Banc Corp. **SIC:** 6021—
National Commercial Banks.

Eminence

★ 68296 ★   Brunswick Bowling &
Billiards
Hwy. 22
Eminence, KY 40019
(502)845-5666
Officer: Joe Fowler, Manager. **Ultimate
Parent:** Brunswick Corp. **SIC:** 3949—
Sporting & Athletic Goods Nec.

★ 68297 ★   Brunswick Bowling &
Billiards
US Hwy. 22
Eminence, KY 40019
(502)845-5666
Location Type: Branch office. **Officer:** Joe
Fowler. **Ultimate Parent:** Brunswick Corp.
SIC: 3949—Sporting & Athletic Goods Nec.

Erlanger

★ 68298 ★   Liberty National Bank
of Northern Kentucky
3414 Dixie Hwy.
PO Box 18100
Erlanger, KY 41018
(606)727-7200 **Fax:** (606)727-2301
Company Type: Subsidiary. **Location
Type:** Branch office. **Officer:** Jeffrey P.
Norton, President & CEO. **Ultimate Parent:**
Liberty National Bancorp. **SIC:** 6021—
National Commercial Banks.

★ 68299 ★   Litton Industrial
Services
2640 Crescent Springs Rd.
Erlanger, KY 41017
(606)341-9544 **Fax:** (606)341-9023
Company Type: Division. **Ultimate Parent:**
Litton Industries. **SIC:** 8741—Management
Services.

Fairdale

★ 68300 ★   Davies Can Co.
8191 National Tpke.
Fairdale, KY 40118
(502)361-2344
Ultimate Parent: Crown Cork & Seal. **SIC:**
3411—Metal Cans.

Falmouth

★ 68301 ★   Star Bank NA,
Kentucky
135 W. Shelby St.
Falmouth, KY 41040-1198
(606)654-3391
Location Type: Branch office. **Ultimate
Parent:** Star Banc Corp. **SIC:** 6021—
National Commercial Banks.

★ 68302 ★   Star Bank NA,
Kentucky
US Hwy. 27 & Robbins Ave.
Falmouth, KY 41040-9507
(606)654-3301
Location Type: Branch office. **Ultimate
Parent:** Star Banc Corp. **SIC:** 6021—
National Commercial Banks.

Fern Creek

★ 68303 ★   PNC Bank Kentucky Inc.
5300 Bardstown
Fern Creek, KY 40291-1931
(502)681-4009
Location Type: Branch office. **Officer:** Nelson Simpson, Manager. **Ultimate Parent:** PNC Bank Corp. **SIC:** 6021—National Commercial Banks.

★ 68304 ★   PNC Bank Kentucky Inc.
6902 Bardstown Rd.
Fern Creek, KY 40291-1058
(502)581-2076
Location Type: Branch office. **Ultimate Parent:** PNC Bank Corp. **SIC:** 6021—National Commercial Banks.

Flaherty

★ 68305 ★   Farmers Deposit Bank, Inc.
Hwy. 144 & Rte. 3
Flaherty, KY 40175-9301
(502)828-8181
Company Type: Subsidiary. **Location Type:** Branch office. **Officer:** Paul Brumfield, Mgr. **Ultimate Parent:** Liberty National Bancorp. **SIC:** 6021—National Commercial Banks.

Flatwoods

★ 68306 ★   Coast to Coast Welding & Fa
1124 Bellefonte Rd.
Flatwoods, KY 41139
(606)836-4432
Ultimate Parent: Servistar Corp. **SIC:** 1541—Industrial Buildings & Warehouses.

Florence

★ 68307 ★   Casual Corner
1088 Florence Mall
Florence, KY 41042
(606)525-7400
Ultimate Parent: United States Shoe. **SIC:** 5651—Family Clothing Stores.

★ 68308 ★   Hoechst Celanese
Engineering Plastics Div.
8040 Dixie Hwy.
Florence, KY 41042
Company Type: Division. **Ultimate Parent:** Hoechst Celanese Corp. **SIC:** 3089—Plastics Products Nec.

★ 68309 ★   Hoechst-Celanese Corp. Specialty Prods. Facility
8040 Dixie Hwy.
Florence, KY 41042
Ultimate Parent: Hoechst Celanese Corp. **SIC:** 3089—Plastics Products Nec.

★ 68310 ★   Hoechst Celanese Eng. Plastics
8040 Dixie Hwy.
Florence, KY 41042
Ultimate Parent: Hoechst Celanese Corp. **SIC:** 3089—Plastics Products Nec.

★ 68311 ★   Johnson Controls Inc.
8040 Bluegrass Dr.
Florence, KY 41042
Ultimate Parent: Johnson & Johnson. **SIC:** 3691—Storage Batteries.

★ 68312 ★   Johnson Controls Inc.
Battery Group Inc.
8040 Blue Grass Dr.
Florence, KY 41042-2987
Ultimate Parent: Johnson & Johnson. **SIC:** 3691—Storage Batteries.

★ 68313 ★   Lane Bryant
1028 Florence Mall
Florence, KY 41042
(606)371-2125
Ultimate Parent: Limited. **SIC:** 5621—Women's Clothing Stores.

★ 68314 ★   Lerner Shops
Florence Mall
Florence, KY 41042
(606)525-6786
Ultimate Parent: Limited. **SIC:** 5621—Women's Clothing Stores.

★ 68315 ★   Liberty National Bank of Northern Kentucky
8480 Hwy. US 43
Florence, KY 41042
(606)525-3050
Company Type: Subsidiary. **Location Type:** Branch office. **Officer:** Tina Breitenstein, Mgr. **Ultimate Parent:** Liberty National Bancorp. **SIC:** 6021—National Commercial Banks.

★ 68316 ★   Liberty National Bank of Northern Kentucky
Florence Mall
Florence, KY 41042
(606)525-3050
Company Type: Subsidiary. **Location Type:** Branch office. **Officer:** Sidney Mason, Mgr. **Ultimate Parent:** Liberty National Bancorp. **SIC:** 6021—National Commercial Banks.

★ 68317 ★   Liberty National Bank of Northern Kentucky
7000 Dixie Hwy.
Florence, KY 41042-1407
(606)525-3000
Company Type: Subsidiary. **Location Type:** Branch office. **Officer:** Thomas Grefer, Mgr. **Ultimate Parent:** Liberty National Bancorp. **SIC:** 6021—National Commercial Banks.

★ 68318 ★   Liberty National Bank of Northern Kentucky
7550 Mall Rd.
Florence, KY 41042
(606)525-3030
Company Type: Subsidiary. **Location Type:** Branch office. **Officer:** Bonnie Wells, Mgr. **Ultimate Parent:** Liberty National Bancorp. **SIC:** 6021—National Commercial Banks.

★ 68319 ★   Limited the
2012 Florence Mall
Florence, KY 41042
(606)525-7500
Ultimate Parent: Limited. **SIC:** 5621—Women's Clothing Stores.

★ 68320 ★   Limited Express
2114 Florence Mall
Florence, KY 41042
(606)371-7187
Ultimate Parent: Limited. **SIC:** 5621—Women's Clothing Stores.

★ 68321 ★   Litton Industrial Automation Systems
Engineered Systems Div.
7100 Industrial Rd.
Florence, KY 41042-2906
(606)525-5700
Company Type: Division. **Officer:** Robert L. Douglas, President. **Ultimate Parent:** Litton Industries. **SIC:** 3535—Conveyors & Conveying Equipment.

★ 68322 ★   Litton Industrial Contracting
7964 Kentucky Dr., No. 12
Florence, KY 41042
(606)371-1444
Company Type: Division. **Ultimate Parent:** Litton Industries. **SIC:** 3535—Conveyors & Conveying Equipment; 8741—Management Services.

★ 68323 ★   Mackey/Gravure Systems
7435 Empire Dr.
Florence, KY 41042
Ultimate Parent: Bemis Co., Inc. **SIC:** 2796—Platemaking Services.

★ 68324 ★   Payless Shoe Source
1170 Florence Mall
Florence, KY 41042
(606)371-4113
Ultimate Parent: May Department Stores. **SIC:** 5661—Shoe Stores.

★ 68325 ★   Payless Shoe Source
6714 Dixie Hwy.
Florence, KY 41042
(606)371-8904
Ultimate Parent: May Department Stores. **SIC:** 5661—Shoe Stores.

★ 68326 ★   Payless Shoesource
6714 Dixie Hwy.
Florence, KY 41042
(606)371-8904
Ultimate Parent: May Department Stores. **SIC:** 5661—Shoe Stores.

★ 68327 ★   PMS Consolidated
7915 Foundation Dr.
Florence, KY 41042
Ultimate Parent: M.A.Hanna. **SIC:** 3087—Custom Compound of Purchased Resins.

★ 68328 ★   PNC Bank Northern Kentucky, NA
7700 Mall Rd.
Florence, KY 41042-1493
(606)525-6255
Location Type: Branch office. **Officer:** Christopher A. Niehaus, Banking Officer. **Ultimate Parent:** PNC Bank Corp. **SIC:** 6021—National Commercial Banks.

★ 68329 ★   Ryder Truck Rental
7550 Empire Dr.
Florence, KY 41042
(606)371-4040
Ultimate Parent: Ryder System. **SIC:** 7359—Equipment Rental & Leasing Nec; 7513—Truck Rental & Leasing Without Drivers.

★ 68330 ★   Ryder Truck Rental-Oneway
7200 Dixie Hwy.
Florence, KY 41042
(606)371-4022
Ultimate Parent: Ryder System. **SIC:** 7359—Equipment Rental & Leasing Nec.

★ 68331 ★   Service Merchandise Catalog
7715 Mall Rd.
Florence, KY 41042
(606)371-4920
Ultimate Parent: Service Merchandise Co., Inc. **SIC:** 5399—Miscellaneous General Merchandise Store.

★ 68332 ★   Service Merchandise Catalog Sales
7715 Mall Rd.
Florence, KY 41042
(606)371-4920
Ultimate Parent: Service Merchandise Co., Inc. **SIC:** 5399—Miscellaneous General Merchandise Store.

★ 68333 ★   Shell Oil
8104 Hwy. 42nd
Florence, KY 41042
(606)371-8499
Ultimate Parent: Shell Oil Co. **SIC:** 5541—Gasoline Service Stations.

★ 68334 ★   Shell Oil
7681 Burlington Pike
Florence, KY 41042
(606)525-0934
Ultimate Parent: Shell Oil Co. **SIC:** 5541—Gasoline Service Stations.

★ 68335 ★   A.O. Smith Corp.
P.C. Div.
8160 Holton Rd.
Florence, KY 41042
Company Type: Division. **Ultimate Parent:** A. O. Smith. **SIC:** 2899—Chemical Preparations Nec.

★ 68336 ★   A.O. Smith Corp.
Protective Coatings Div.
8160 Holton Dr.
Florence, KY 41042
Company Type: Division. **Ultimate Parent:** A. O. Smith. **SIC:** 2899—Chemical Preparations Nec.

★ 68337 ★   Star Bank NA, Kentucky
6809 Burlington Pke.
Florence, KY 41042-1616
(606)283-2402
Location Type: Branch office. **Officer:** Kevin Garrett, Vice President. **Ultimate Parent:** Star Banc Corp. **SIC:** 6021—National Commercial Banks.

★ 68338 ★   Star Bank NA, Kentucky
7990 Dixie Hwy.
Florence, KY 41042-2737
(606)371-2500
Location Type: Branch office. **Officer:** Gary Winn, Vice President. **Ultimate Parent:** Star Banc Corp. **SIC:** 6021—National Commercial Banks.

★ 68339 ★   Star Bank NA, Kentucky
8461 Hwy. 42
Florence, KY 41042-9679
(606)525-2274
Location Type: Branch office. **Officer:** Tony Vogel, Assistant Vice President. **Ultimate Parent:** Star Banc Corp. **SIC:** 6021—National Commercial Banks.

★ 68340 ★   SWECO Inc.
7120 Buffington Rd.
PO Box 1509
Florence, KY 41022-1509
(606)727-1509 **Fax:** (606)727-5106
Company Type: Subsidiary. **Ultimate Parent:** Emerson Electric Co. Inc.

★ 68341 ★   Sweco Inc.
7120 New Buffington Rd.
Florence, KY 41042-2841
(606)727-5147
Company Type: Subsidiary. **Ultimate Parent:** Emerson Electric Co. Inc. **SIC:** 3559—Special Industry Machinery Nec. **Employee Count:** 270. **Sales:** 26 M.

★ 68342 ★   Sweco Inc.
8029 U.S. Hwy. 25
Florence, KY 41042
Ultimate Parent: Emerson Electric Co. Inc. **SIC:** 3449—Miscellaneous Metal Work.

★ 68343 ★   Telesat Cable
11 Spiral Dr. 15
Florence, KY 41042
(606)283-6780
Ultimate Parent: FPL Group.

★ 68344 ★   Telesat Cable T V Inc.
11 Spiral Dr.
Florence, KY 41042
(606)283-6784
Ultimate Parent: FPL Group. **SIC:** 4841—Cable & Other Pay Television Services.

★ 68345 ★   Victoria's Secret
2106 Florence Mall
Florence, KY 41042
(606)525-8818
Ultimate Parent: Limited. **SIC:** 5621—Women's Clothing Stores.

Florene

★ 68346 ★   Star Bank NA, Kentucky
4997 Houston Rd.
Florene, KY 41042
(606)292-6150
Location Type: Branch office. **Officer:** Carol Jackson, Assistant Vice President. **Ultimate Parent:** Star Banc Corp. **SIC:** 6021—National Commercial Banks.

Fort Campbell

★ 68347 ★   Greyhound Bus Lines
Fort Campbell, KY 42223
(502)431-6358
Ultimate Parent: Greyhound Lines Inc. **SIC:** 4111—Local & Suburban Transit; 4142—Bus Charter Service Except Local; 4131—Intercity & Rural Bus Transportation.

Fort Mitchell

★ 68348 ★   PNC Bank Northern Kentucky, NA
2216 Dixie Hwy.
Fort Mitchell, KY 41017
(606)578-2312 **Fax:** (606)344-3744
Location Type: Branch office. **Officer:** Ronald P. Cooney, President & CEO. **Ultimate Parent:** PNC Bank Corp. **SIC:** 6021—National Commercial Banks.

★ 68349 ★   Star Bank NA, Kentucky
2501 Dixie Hwy.
Fort Mitchell, KY 41017-3084
(606)292-6280
Location Type: Branch office. **Officer:** Diane Dirkes, Assistant Vice President. **Ultimate Parent:** Star Banc Corp. **SIC:** 6021—National Commercial Banks.

Parent: Star Banc Corp. **SIC:** 6021—National Commercial Banks.

Fort Thomas

★ 68350 ★   Liberty National Bank of Northern Kentucky
34 N. Fort Thomas Ave.
Fort Thomas, KY 41075-1583
(606)781-3700
Company Type: Subsidiary. **Location Type:** Branch office. **Officer:** N. William White, Mgr. **Ultimate Parent:** Liberty National Bancorp. **SIC:** 6021—National Commercial Banks.

★ 68351 ★   Liberty National Bank of Northern Kentucky
11 S. Grand Ave.
Fort Thomas, KY 41075-1798
(606)441-7566
Company Type: Subsidiary. **Location Type:** Branch office. **Officer:** Patrick J. O'Donnell, Mgr. **Ultimate Parent:** Liberty National Bancorp. **SIC:** 6021—National Commercial Banks.

★ 68352 ★   PNC Bank Northern Kentucky, NA
14 S. Ft. Thomas Ave.
Fort Thomas, KY 41075-1815
(606)441-2244
Location Type: Branch office. **Officer:** Blake S. Tollefsen, Banking Officer. **Ultimate Parent:** PNC Bank Corp. **SIC:** 6021—National Commercial Banks.

★ 68353 ★   Star Bank NA, Kentucky
Highland & Fort Thomas Aves.
Fort Thomas, KY 41075
(606)441-3200
Location Type: Branch office. **Officer:** Peg Dameron, Manager. **Ultimate Parent:** Star Banc Corp. **SIC:** 6021—National Commercial Banks.

Fort Wright

★ 68354 ★   PNC Bank Northern Kentucky, NA
10 Kyles Ln.
Fort Wright, KY 41011-3737
(606)344-3711
Location Type: Branch office. **Officer:** Dianne L. Linstruth, Assistant Vice President. **Ultimate Parent:** PNC Bank Corp. **SIC:** 6021—National Commercial Banks.

★ 68355 ★   Star Bank NA, Kentucky
2001 Dixie Hwy.
Fort Wright, KY 41001
(606)292-6260
Location Type: Branch office. **Officer:** Mike Allison, Vice President. **Ultimate Parent:** Star Banc Corp. **SIC:** 6021—National Commercial Banks.

Frankfort

★ 68356 ★   Allied-Signal
Allied Automotive
U.S. 421
Frankfort, KY 40601
Ultimate Parent: Allied-Signal Inc. **SIC:** 3714—Motor Vehicle Parts & Accessories.

★ 68357 ★   Allied-Signal Automotive
2001 US Hwy. 421
Frankfort, KY 40601
(502)695-2100
Officer: Chuck Landrum, Manager. **Ultimate Parent:** Allied-Signal Inc. **SIC:** 3713—Truck & Bus Bodies.

★ 68358 ★   Allied-Signal Automotive
Bendix Heavy Vehicle Systems
2001 U.S. Rte. 421 S.
Frankfort, KY 40601
Ultimate Parent: Allied-Signal Inc. **SIC:** 3714—Motor Vehicle Parts & Accessories.

★ 68359 ★   Coast to Coast Hardware
Estates Us 127 S
Frankfort, KY 40601
(502)223-1245
Ultimate Parent: Servistar Corp. **SIC:** 5251—Hardware Stores.

★ 68360 ★   General Electric Co.
Frankfort Plant
Rte. 3 Chenault Industrial Park Rd.
Frankfort, KY 40601
Ultimate Parent: General Electric. **SIC:** 3089—Plastics Products Nec.

★ 68361 ★   Jim Beam Brands Co.
US 460 E
Frankfort, KY 40601
(502)695-3010
Officer: Peter Sobel. **Ultimate Parent:** American Brands Inc. **SIC:** 2085—Distilled & Blended Liquors.

★ 68362 ★   Jim Beam Brands Co.
Georgetown Rd.
Frankfort, KY 40601
(502)695-3010
Ultimate Parent: American Brands Inc. **SIC:** 2085—Distilled & Blended Liquors.

★ 68363 ★   Kentucky Post the
End Capitol Ave.
Frankfort, KY 40601
(502)875-3339
Ultimate Parent: E.W. Scripps Co. **SIC:** 7383—News Syndicates.

★ 68364 ★   Kroger Co.
Estates Us 127s
Frankfort, KY 40601
(502)875-4944
Ultimate Parent: Kroger. **SIC:** 5411—Grocery Stores.

★ 68365 ★   Payless Shoe Source
WS US 127 S
Frankfort, KY 40601
(502)223-3342
Ultimate Parent: May Department Stores. **SIC:** 5661—Shoe Stores.

★ 68366 ★   Payless Shoesource
US 127 S
Frankfort, KY 40601
(502)223-3342
Ultimate Parent: May Department Stores. **SIC:** 5661—Shoe Stores.

★ 68367 ★   Penney J C
Estates Us 127 S
Frankfort, KY 40601
(502)875-1034
Ultimate Parent: J.C. Penney. **SIC:** 5311—Department Stores.

★ 68368 ★   Ryder Truck Rental-Oneway
1029 Louisville Rd.
Frankfort, KY 40601
(502)223-1887
Ultimate Parent: Ryder System. **SIC:** 7513—Truck Rental & Leasing Without Drivers.

★ 68369 ★   Shell One Stop
567 E. Main St.
Frankfort, KY 40601
(502)227-4355
Ultimate Parent: Shell Oil Co. **SIC:** 5411—Grocery Stores; 5541—Gasoline Service Stations.

★ 68370 ★   Texaco Inc.
521 Barrett St.
Frankfort, KY 40601
(502)227-7764
Ultimate Parent: Texaco. **SIC:** 5172—Petroleum Products Nec.

Franklin

★ 68371 ★   First American National Bank of Kentucky
303 N. Main St.
Franklin, KY 42134-1815
(502)586-4473
Location Type: Branch office. **Officer:** Brent Grow, Vice President. **Ultimate Parent:** First American Corp. **SIC:** 6021—National Commercial Banks.

★ 68372 ★   SPX Corp.
Sealed Power Div.
Rte. 6, 709 Blackjack Rd.
Franklin, KY 42134
Company Type: Division. **Ultimate Parent:** SPX Corp. **SIC:** 3592—Carburetors, Pistons, Rings & Valves.

★ 68373 ★   Weyerhaeuser Paper Co. Inc.
Broadway Ave.
Franklin, KY 42134
(502)586-8221
Ultimate Parent: Weyerhaeuser Co. **SIC:** 5113—Industrial & Personal Service Paper.

Fulton

★ 68374 ★   City National Bank
Carr Plz. Shopping Ctr.
Fulton, KY 42041
(502)472-1501
Ultimate Parent: City National Corp. **SIC:** 6021—National Commercial Banks.

★ 68375 ★   City National Bank of Fulton
306 Lake St.
Fulton, KY 42041-1530
(502)472-3300
Officer: Kenneth E. Crews, President. **Ultimate Parent:** City National Corp. **SIC:** 6021—National Commercial Banks; 6141—Personal Credit Institutions; 6162—Mortgage Bankers & Correspondents.

★ 68376 ★   McDonald's Hamburgers
103 Us 51
Fulton, KY 42041
(502)472-0221
Ultimate Parent: McDonald's. **SIC:** 5812—Eating Places.

★ 68377 ★   Security Trust Federal S&L
101 Madison St.
Fulton, KY 42041-1601
(502)472-1062
Location Type: Branch office. **Officer:** Linda Stain, Manager. **Ultimate Parent:** Union Planters Corp. **SIC:** 6021—National Commercial Banks.

★ 68378 ★   Wal-Mart Stores Inc.
Hwy. 45 Byp
Fulton, KY 42041
(502)472-1426
Ultimate Parent: Wal-Mart Stores, Inc. **SIC:** 5331—Variety Stores.

Georgetown

★ 68379 ★   Coast to Coast Hardware
Estates Lexington Rd.
Georgetown, KY 40324
(502)863-1672
Ultimate Parent: Servistar Corp. **SIC:** 5251—Hardware Stores.

★ 68380 ★   Coast to Coast Hardware
Washington Sq.
Georgetown, KY 40324
(502)863-0296
Ultimate Parent: Servistar Corp. **SIC:** 5231—Paint, Glass & Wallpaper Stores; 5251—Hardware Stores.

★ 68381 ★   Farmers Bank & Trust Co.
200 E. Main St.
Georgetown, KY 40324
(502)863-2393
Ultimate Parent: Dauphin Deposit Corp. **SIC:** 6022—State Commercial Banks.

★ 68382 ★   J C Penney Catalog Sales
751 S. Broadway St.
Georgetown, KY 40324
(502)863-3274
Ultimate Parent: J.C. Penney. **SIC:** 5311—Department Stores.

★ 68383 ★   Johnson Controls Inc.
Lemons Mill Rd.
Georgetown, KY 40324
(502)863-4150
Ultimate Parent: Johnson Controls Inc. **SIC:** 5075—Warm Air Heating & Air-Conditioning.

★ 68384 ★   Kroger Co.
1139 Lexington Rd.
Georgetown, KY 40324
(502)863-4807
Ultimate Parent: Kroger. **SIC:** 5411—Grocery Stores.

★ 68385 ★   Marshall Field
Lexington Rd.
Georgetown, KY 40324
(502)863-6320
Ultimate Parent: Dayton Hudson. **SIC:** 4581—Airports, Flying Fields & Services.

★ 68386 ★   Ryder Truck Rental
239 Triport Rd.
Georgetown, KY 40324
(502)863-0393
Ultimate Parent: Ryder System. **SIC:** 7513—Truck Rental & Leasing Without Drivers.

★ 68387 ★   Value Added Service Corp.
PO Box 729
1125 Cherry Blossom Way
Georgetown, KY 40324
(502)868-3485
Company Type: Joint venture. **Officer:** H. P. Young, COO. **Ultimate Parent:** American President Companies, Ltd. **SIC:** 5531—Automobile & Home Supply Stores; 8741—Management Services.

Ghent

★ 68388 ★   North American Stainless
100 Main St., U.S. Hwy. 42E
Ghent, KY 41045
(502)347-6000
Company Type: Division. **Ultimate Parent:** Armco.

★ 68389 ★   North American Stainless
US 42 E.
Ghent, KY 41045-9615
Ultimate Parent: Armco. **SIC:** 3316—Cold-Finishing of Steel Shapes.

Glasgow

★ 68390 ★   Aero M Inc.
20 Aberdeen Dr.
Glasgow, KY 42141
Ultimate Parent: Cooper Industries. **SIC:** 3675—Electronic Capacitors.

★ 68391 ★   R.R. Donnelley & Sons Co.
Glasgow Manufacturing Div.
Donnelley Dr.
Glasgow, KY 42141
Company Type: Division. **Ultimate Parent:** R. R. Donnelley & Sons. **SIC:** 2752—Commercial Printing—Lithographic.

★ 68392 ★   R.R. Donnelley & Sons Co.
Kentucky W. Div.
Donnelley Dr.
Glasgow, KY 42141
Company Type: Division. **Ultimate Parent:** R. R. Donnelley & Sons. **SIC:** 2752—Commercial Printing—Lithographic.

★ 68393 ★   Eaton Corp.
1320 W. Main St.
Glasgow, KY 42141
(502)651-6711
Officer: Don Doty, Manager. **Ultimate Parent:** Eaton Corp. **SIC:** 3714—Motor Vehicle Parts & Accessories.

★ 68394 ★   Eaton Corp.
Axle & Brake Div.
Rte. 68
Glasgow, KY 42141-1199
Company Type: Division. **Ultimate Parent:** Eaton Corp. **SIC:** 3714—Motor Vehicle Parts & Accessories.

★ 68395 ★   Fitness Center
Park Ave.
Glasgow, KY 42141
(502)651-9211
Ultimate Parent: New York Times. **SIC:** 7991—Physical Fitness Facilities.

★ 68396 ★   Glasgow Foods
Roseville Rd.
Glasgow, KY 42141
(502)651-8866
Location Type: Plant. **Officer:** Mike Caren, Plant Manager. **Ultimate Parent:** Conagra.

273

★ 68397 ★ Ryder Truck Rental-Oneway
609 Columbia Ave.
Glasgow, KY 42141
(502)651-9378
Ultimate Parent: Ryder System. SIC: 7513—Truck Rental & Leasing Without Drivers.

★ 68398 ★ Wal-Mart Stores Inc.
Glasgow Sq.
Glasgow, KY 42141
(502)651-6761
Ultimate Parent: Wal-Mart Stores, Inc. SIC: 5311—Department Stores.

Glendale

★ 68399 ★ PNC Bank Kentucky Inc.
Hwy. 22
Glendale, KY 42740
(502)369-8618
Location Type: Branch office. Ultimate Parent: PNC Bank Corp. SIC: 6021—National Commercial Banks.

Gravel Switch

★ 68400 ★ People's Bank
Gravel Switch, KY 40328
(502)692-3993
Ultimate Parent: People's Bank. SIC: 6029—Commercial Banks Nec.

Grayson

★ 68401 ★ McDonald's Hamburgers
751 N. Carol Malone Blvd.
Grayson, KY 41143
(606)474-8222
Ultimate Parent: McDonald's. SIC: 5812—Eating Places.

★ 68402 ★ Rite Aid Discount Pharmacy
495 N. Carol Malone Blvd.
Grayson, KY 41143
(606)474-4470
Ultimate Parent: Rite Aid.

★ 68403 ★ Ryder Truck Rental-One Way
801 N. Carol Malone Blvd.
Grayson, KY 41143
(606)474-9371
Ultimate Parent: Ryder System. SIC: 7513—Truck Rental & Leasing Without Drivers.

Greensburg

★ 68404 ★ Peoples Bank & Trust Co.
202 N. Main St. 204
Greensburg, KY 42743
(502)932-4281
Ultimate Parent: People's Bank. SIC: 6036—Savings Institutions Except Federal.

Greenup

★ 68405 ★ Ametek Inc.
300 Harris Rd.
Greenup, KY 41144-1463
(606)836-0251
Officer: Garry Lewis. Ultimate Parent: Ametek Inc. SIC: 3081—Unsupported Plastics Film & Sheet.

Greenville

★ 68406 ★ Ryder Truck Rental-Oneway
159 S. Main St.
Greenville, KY 42345
(502)338-4711
Ultimate Parent: Ryder System. SIC: 7359—Equipment Rental & Leasing Nec.

Hanson

★ 68407 ★ Liberty National Bank of Madisonville
Main & Oak Sts.
Hanson, KY 42413
(502)824-3075
Company Type: Subsidiary. Location

Type: Branch office. Officer: Marilyn Montgomery, Mgr. Ultimate Parent: Liberty National Bancorp. SIC: 6021—National Commercial Banks.

Hardinsburg

★ 68408 ★ Wal-Mart Stores Inc.
Us Hwy. 60 E
Hardinsburg, KY 40143
(502)756-6012
Ultimate Parent: Wal-Mart Stores, Inc. SIC: 5311—Department Stores.

Harlan

★ 68409 ★ Greyhound Bus Lines
107 N. Cumberland Ave.
Harlan, KY 40831
(606)573-4251
Ultimate Parent: Greyhound Lines Inc. SIC: 4131—Intercity & Rural Bus Transportation; 4111—Local & Suburban Transit; 4142—Bus Charter Service Except Local.

Harrodsburg

★ 68410 ★ Corning, Inc.
680 E. Office St.
Harrodsburg, KY 40330
Ultimate Parent: Corning. SIC: 3229—Pressed & Blown Glass Nec.

★ 68411 ★ Eaton Corp.
Tapp Rd.
Harrodsburg, KY 40330
(606)734-7711
Ultimate Parent: Eaton Corp. SIC: 5531—Automobile & Home Supply Stores.

★ 68412 ★ Greyhound Bus Lines
227 S. Greenville St.
Harrodsburg, KY 40330
(606)734-4202
Ultimate Parent: Greyhound Lines Inc. SIC: 4131—Intercity & Rural Bus Transportation; 4111—Local & Suburban Transit; 4142—Bus Charter Service Except Local.

★ 68413 ★ Kroger Co.
844 S. Collegest
Harrodsburg, KY 40330
(606)734-0078
Ultimate Parent: Kroger. SIC: 5411—Grocery Stores.

★ 68414 ★ PNC Bank Kentucky Inc.
570 Chestnut St.
Harrodsburg, KY 40330-1822
(606)734-5181
Location Type: Branch office. Ultimate Parent: PNC Bank Corp. SIC: 6021—National Commercial Banks.

★ 68415 ★ PNC Bank Kentucky Inc.
134 S. Main St.
Harrodsburg, KY 40330-1633
(606)734-4354
Location Type: Branch office. Ultimate Parent: PNC Bank Corp. SIC: 6021—National Commercial Banks.

★ 68416 ★ Ryder Truck Rental-Oneway
131 N. College St.
Harrodsburg, KY 40330
(606)734-2808
Ultimate Parent: Ryder System. SIC: 4214—Local Trucking With Storage.

★ 68417 ★ Wal-Mart Stores Inc.
848 S. College St.
Harrodsburg, KY 40330
(606)734-5721
Ultimate Parent: Wal-Mart Stores, Inc. SIC: 5311—Department Stores.

Hartford

★ 68418 ★ Marathon Fuels Inc.
Hwy. 231
Hartford, KY 42347
(502)298-7283
Ultimate Parent: USX Corp. SIC: 5983—Fuel Oil Dealers.

Hawesville

★ 68419 ★ Willamette Industries Inc.
PO Box 130 Hwy. 1406
Hawesville, KY 42348
Ultimate Parent: Willamette Industries, Inc. SIC: 2611—Pulp Mills; 2631—Paperboard Mills.

★ 68420 ★ Willamette Industries, Inc.
PO Box 130 Hwy. 146
Hawesville, KY 42348
Ultimate Parent: Willamette Industries, Inc. SIC: 2611—Pulp Mills; 2631—Paperboard Mills.

★ 68421 ★ Willamette Industries Inc.
Skillman Btm
Hawesville, KY 42348
(502)927-6961
Ultimate Parent: Willamette Industries, Inc. SIC: 2621—Paper Mills.

Hazard

★ 68422 ★ American General Finance
Town & Country Plz.
Hazard, KY 41701
(606)436-2101
Ultimate Parent: American General Corp. SIC: 6141—Personal Credit Institutions; 6162—Mortgage Bankers & Correspondents.

★ 68423 ★ American General Finance Inc.
Town & Country Plz.
Hazard, KY 41701
(606)436-2101
Location Type: Branch office. Ultimate Parent: American General Corp. SIC: 6141—Personal Credit Institutions; 6162—Mortgage Bankers & Correspondents.

★ 68424 ★ Cyprus Mountain Coals Corp.
Hwy. 80
Hazard, KY 41701
(606)439-5871
Company Type: Subsidiary. Officer: Donald P. Brown, President. Ultimate Parent: Cyprus Amax Minerals. SIC: 1221—Bituminous Coal & Lignite—Surface; 1241—Coal Mining Services. Employee Count: 476. Sales: 154 M.

★ 68425 ★ First Federal S & L
157 Main St.
Hazard, KY 41701-1805
(606)436-3860
Company Type: Headquarters. Officer: J. C. Eversole. Ultimate Parent: Bancorp Hawaii. SIC: 6035—Federal Savings Institutions.

★ 68426 ★ Greyhound Bus Lines
612 Main St.
Hazard, KY 41701
(606)436-3631
Ultimate Parent: Greyhound Lines Inc. SIC: 4111—Local & Suburban Transit; 4131—Intercity & Rural Bus Transportation; 4142—Bus Charter Service Except Local.

★ 68427 ★ Peoples Bank & Trust Co.
405 E. Main St.
Hazard, KY 41701
(606)436-2161
Ultimate Parent: People's Bank. SIC: 6022—State Commercial Banks.

★ 68428 ★ Pepsi-Cola Bottling Co.
2000 N. Main St.
Hazard, KY 41701
(606)436-3155
Officer: Mike Harris, Manager. Ultimate Parent: Pepsico. SIC: 2086—Bottled & Canned Soft Drinks.

Hebron

★ 68429 ★ Industrial Automation Systems Group
2300 Litton Ln.
Hebron, KY 41048
(606)334-3400 Fax: (606)334-3434
Officer: Joseph E. Beebe, President,

Material Handling Div. Ultimate Parent: Litton Industries.

★ 68430 ★ Litton Industrial
Unit Handling Systems Div.
2100 Litton Ln.
PO Box 10
Hebron, KY 41048-0010
(606)334-2400
Company Type: Division. Ultimate Parent: Litton Industries. SIC: 3535—Conveyors & Conveying Equipment.

★ 68431 ★ Litton Industrial Automation Systems
Automated Systems Div.
2200 Litton Ln.
PO Box 179
Hebron, KY 41048-0179
(606)334-2600
Company Type: Division. Ultimate Parent: Litton Industries. SIC: 3577—Computer Peripheral Equipment Nec; 3535—Conveyors & Conveying Equipment.

★ 68432 ★ Litton Industrial Automation Systems Inc.
2300 Litton Industrial Automation Systems Inc.
Hebron, KY 41048
(606)334-3400 Fax: (606)334-2689 Telex: 651490
Company Type: Division. Officer: Douglas Henderson, President. Ultimate Parent: Litton Industries. SIC: 3589—Service Industry Machinery Nec.

★ 68433 ★ Litton Industrial Automation Systems (Unit Handling Systems)
2300 Litton Ln.
Hebron, KY 41048-9645
(606)586-9800 Fax: (606)334-2847
Officer: Joseph W. Beebe, President, Material Handling Div. Ultimate Parent: Litton Industries.

★ 68434 ★ Litton Industries
Integrated Systems Div.
2300 Litton Ln.
Hebron, KY 41048-9645
(606)586-9800 Telex: 651490
Company Type: Division. Ultimate Parent: Litton Industries. SIC: 3577—Computer Peripheral Equipment Nec.

★ 68435 ★ Litton Material Handling Systems
2300 Litton Ln.
Hebron, KY 41048-9645
(606)586-9800
Company Type: Division. Ultimate Parent: Litton Industries. SIC: 3559—Special Industry Machinery Nec; 3535—Conveyors & Conveying Equipment.

★ 68436 ★ Litton UHS Conveyor Systems
2300 Litton Ln.
Hebron, KY 41048-0010
(606)334-2600 Fax: (606)334-2515
Officer: Joseph E. Beebe, President. Ultimate Parent: Litton Industries.

Henderson

★ 68437 ★ Accuride Corp.
2315 Adams Ln.
Henderson, KY 42420
Ultimate Parent: Phelps Dodge. SIC: 3499—Fabricated Metal Products Nec.

★ 68438 ★ Aeroquip Corp.
232 Heilman Ave.
Henderson, KY 42420
(502)826-3914
Officer: Mike McLellen, Manager. Ultimate Parent: Trinova Corp. SIC: 3089—Plastics Products Nec; 3714—Motor Vehicle Parts & Accessories.

★ 68439 ★ Agrico Chemical Co.
Geneva Rd.
Henderson, KY 42420
(502)826-6235
Ultimate Parent: Freeport-McMoran. SIC: 2873—Nitrogenous Fertilizers.

★ 68440 ★ **Bemis Co.**
Custom Resins Div.
1421 Hwy. 136 W
Henderson, KY 42420
(502)826-7641
Company Type: Division. **Officer:** W. M. Warner, President. **Ultimate Parent:** Bemis Co., Inc. **SIC:** 2821—Plastics Materials & Resins; 3089—Plastics Products Nec.

★ 68441 ★ **Custom Resins**
1421 Hwy. 136 W.
Henderson, KY 42420
Ultimate Parent: Bemis Co., Inc. **SIC:** 2821—Plastics Materials & Resins.

★ 68442 ★ **Eaton Corp.**
1491 Eaton Dr.
Henderson, KY 42420
Ultimate Parent: Eaton Corp. **SIC:** 3714—Motor Vehicle Parts & Accessories.

★ 68443 ★ **Eaton Corp.**
Geneva Rd.
Henderson, KY 42420
(502)827-2511
Ultimate Parent: Eaton Corp. **SIC:** 5013—Motor Vehicle Supplies & New Parts.

★ 68444 ★ **Eaton Corp.**
Axel & Brake Div.
1491 Eaton Dr.
Henderson, KY 42420
(502)827-2511
Company Type: Division. **Officer:** Robert N. Anders, Manager. **Ultimate Parent:** Eaton Corp. **SIC:** 3714—Motor Vehicle Parts & Accessories.

★ 68445 ★ **Exxon Co. U S a**
Alternate Us 41 S
Henderson, KY 42420
(502)826-2719
Ultimate Parent: Exxon. **SIC:** 5172—Petroleum Products Nec.

★ 68446 ★ **Exxon Co. USA**
Alternate Us 41 S
Henderson, KY 42420
(502)826-2719
Ultimate Parent: Exxon. **SIC:** 5172—Petroleum Products Nec.

★ 68447 ★ **Farmers Bank & Trust Co.**
2011 Us 60 E
Henderson, KY 42420
(502)826-2735
Ultimate Parent: Dauphin Deposit Corp. **SIC:** 6022—State Commercial Banks.

★ 68448 ★ **Farmers Bank & Trust Co.**
Eastgate Shopping Ctr.
Henderson, KY 42420
(502)826-5948
Ultimate Parent: Dauphin Deposit Corp. **SIC:** 6022—State Commercial Banks.

★ 68449 ★ **Gamco Prods. Co.**
1105 5th St.
Henderson, KY 42420
Ultimate Parent: Masco. **SIC:** 3471—Plating & Polishing; 3364—Nonferrous Die-Castings Except Aluminum; 3544—Special Dies, Tools, Jigs & Fixtures.

★ 68450 ★ **Gamco Products Co.**
1105 5th St.
Henderson, KY 42420-2803
Ultimate Parent: Masco. **SIC:** 3471—Plating & Polishing; 3364—Nonferrous Die-Castings Except Aluminum; 3544—Special Dies, Tools, Jigs & Fixtures.

★ 68451 ★ **Greyhound Bus Lines**
100 2nd St.
Henderson, KY 42420
(502)826-4317
Ultimate Parent: Greyhound Lines Inc. **SIC:** 4111—Local & Suburban Transit; 4131—Intercity & Rural Bus Transportation; 4142—Bus Charter Service Except Local.

★ 68452 ★ **McDonald's Hamburgers**
2015 Us Hwy. 41 N
Henderson, KY 42420
(502)827-1222
Ultimate Parent: McDonald's. **SIC:** 5812—Eating Places.

★ 68453 ★ **Payless Shoe Source**
228 N. Green St.
Henderson, KY 42420
(502)826-3175
Ultimate Parent: May Department Stores. **SIC:** 5661—Shoe Stores.

★ 68454 ★ **Rite Aid Discount Pharmacy**
2003 Stapp Dr.
Henderson, KY 42420
(502)827-1897
Ultimate Parent: Rite Aid. **SIC:** 5912—Drug Stores & Proprietary Stores.

★ 68455 ★ **Ryder Truck Rental-Oneway**
2808 Hwy. 41 N
Henderson, KY 42420
(502)827-0662
Ultimate Parent: Ryder System. **SIC:** 7359—Equipment Rental & Leasing Nec.

★ 68456 ★ **Sonoco Products Co.**
3100 Ohio Dr.
Henderson, KY 42420
(502)827-5637
Officer: Richard Privette, Manager. **Ultimate Parent:** Sonoco Products. **SIC:** 3499—Fabricated Metal Products Nec.

★ 68457 ★ **Sun Refining & Marketing Co.**
Geneva Rd.
Henderson, KY 42420
(502)827-1811
Ultimate Parent: Sun. **SIC:** 5172—Petroleum Products Nec.

★ 68458 ★ **Unison Transformer Services Inc.**
5801 Riverport Rd.
Henderson, KY 42420
Ultimate Parent: Union Carbide Corp. **SIC:** 2899—Chemical Preparations Nec.

★ 68459 ★ **Unison Transformer Services, Inc.**
Henderson Recovery Center
5801 Riverport Rd.
Henderson, KY 42420
Ultimate Parent: Union Carbide Corp. **SIC:** 4953—Refuse Systems.

★ 68460 ★ **Wal-Mart Stores Inc.**
Old Orchard Shopping Cent
Henderson, KY 42420
(502)826-3200
Ultimate Parent: Wal-Mart Stores, Inc. **SIC:** 5311—Department Stores.

Hickman

★ 68461 ★ **Security Trust Federal S&L**
Hwy. 1099
Hickman, KY 42050
(502)236-3914
Location Type: Branch office. **Officer:** Teresa Craddock, Manager. **Ultimate Parent:** Union Planters Corp. **SIC:** 6021—National Commercial Banks.

Hickory

★ 68462 ★ **Seaboard Farms of KY Inc.**
U.S. Hwy. 45 N.
Hickory, KY 42051
Ultimate Parent: Seaboard Corp. **SIC:** 2015—Poultry Slaughtering & Processing.

Highland Heights

★ 68463 ★ **General Cable Consumer Products Group**
4 Tesseneer Dr.
Highland Heights, KY 41076
(606)572-8650 **Fax:** (606)572-9634
Company Type: Subsidiary. **Officer:** Gregory B. Kenny, President. **Ultimate Parent:** General Cable Corp.

★ 68464 ★ **General Cable Corp.**
4 Tesseneer Dr.
Highland Heights, KY 41076
(606)572-8000
Company Type: Headquarters. **Officer:** Ronald F. Walker. **Employee Count:** 4600. **Sales:** 859.7 M. **Fortune 500:** Largest U.S. Industrial Corporations: Ranking 392.

★ 68465 ★ **General Cable Electrical Group**
4 Tesseneer Dr.
Highland Heights, KY 41076
(606)572-8501 **Fax:** (606)572-8441
Company Type: Subsidiary. **Officer:** Eugene J. Tonkovich, President. **Ultimate Parent:** General Cable Corp.

★ 68466 ★ **General Cable Manufacturing Group**
4 Tesseneer Dr.
Highland Heights, KY 41076
(606)572-8760 **Fax:** (606)572-9036
Company Type: Subsidiary. **Officer:** Joseph S. Dixon, President. **Ultimate Parent:** General Cable Corp.

★ 68467 ★ **General Cable Telecommunications & Electronics Group**
4 Tesseneer Dr.
Highland Heights, KY 41076
(606)572-8350 **Fax:** (606)572-0138
Company Type: Subsidiary. **Officer:** Joseph M. Fimingo, President. **Ultimate Parent:** General Cable Corp.

★ 68468 ★ **PNC Bank Northern Kentucky, NA**
2650 Alexandria Pke.
Highland Heights, KY 41076-1528
(606)781-4800
Location Type: Branch office. **Officer:** Timothy E. Noe, Banking Officer. **Ultimate Parent:** PNC Bank Corp. **SIC:** 6021—National Commercial Banks.

Hodgenville

★ 68469 ★ **Mary Kay Cosmetics**
614 Campbellsville Rd.
Hodgenville, KY 42748
(502)358-9818
Ultimate Parent: Mary Kay Cosmetics. **SIC:** 1799—Special Trade Contractors Nec.

★ 68470 ★ **Mary Kay Cosmetics**
1434 Tanner Rd.
Hodgenville, KY 42748
(502)358-3281
Ultimate Parent: Mary Kay Cosmetics.

★ 68471 ★ **Rite Aid Discount Pharmacy**
Lincoln Plz.
Hodgenville, KY 42748
(502)358-3186
Ultimate Parent: Rite Aid. **SIC:** 5912—Drug Stores & Proprietary Stores.

Hopkinsville

★ 68472 ★ **American General Finance**
Skyline Shopping Ctr.
Hopkinsville, KY 42240
(502)886-5216
Location Type: Branch office. **Ultimate Parent:** American General Corp. **SIC:** 6141—Personal Credit Institutions; 6162—Mortgage Bankers & Correspondents.

★ 68473 ★ **American General Finance Inc.**
Skyline Shopping Ctr.
Hopkinsville, KY 42240
(502)886-5216
Location Type: Branch office. **Ultimate Parent:** American General Corp. **SIC:** 6141—Personal Credit Institutions; 6162—Mortgage Bankers & Correspondents.

★ 68474 ★ **Black & Decker Corp.**
PO Fastenr Division
PO Box 542
Hopkinsville, KY 42241-0542
(502)886-3951
Officer: Harvard Austrew. **Ultimate Parent:** Black & Decker Corp. **SIC:** 3452—Bolts, Nuts, Rivets & Washers.

★ 68475 ★ **Black & Decker Corp.**
Pop Fasteners
Rte. 41
Hopkinsville, KY 42241-0542
Company Type: Division. **Ultimate Parent:** Black & Decker Corp. **SIC:** 3452—Bolts, Nuts, Rivets & Washers.

★ 68476 ★ **Dana Corp.**
301 Bill Bryan Blvd.
Hopkinsville, KY 42240
Ultimate Parent: Dana Corp. **SIC:** 3714—Motor Vehicle Parts & Accessories.

★ 68477 ★ **First Federal Savings Bank**
3213 LaFayette Rd.
Hopkinsville, KY 42240-3815
(502)885-1131
Company Type: Subsidiary. **Location Type:** Branch office. **Officer:** Paula Morrow, Mgr. **Ultimate Parent:** Liberty National Bancorp. **SIC:** 6021—National Commercial Banks.

★ 68478 ★ **First Federal Savings Bank**
1101 S. Main St.
Hopkinsville, KY 42241-0958
(502)886-3341
Company Type: Subsidiary. **Location Type:** Branch office. **Officer:** Will Josh Lawrence Jr., President & CEO. **Ultimate Parent:** Liberty National Bancorp. **SIC:** 6021—National Commercial Banks.

★ 68479 ★ **Greyhound Bus Lines**
602 E. 7th St.
Hopkinsville, KY 42240
(502)885-8151
Ultimate Parent: Greyhound Lines Inc. **SIC:** 4111—Local & Suburban Transit; 4131—Intercity & Rural Bus Transportation; 4142—Bus Charter Service Except Local.

★ 68480 ★ **Kroger Co.**
Park Plz.
Hopkinsville, KY 42240
(502)885-9944
Ultimate Parent: Kroger. **SIC:** 5411—Grocery Stores.

★ 68481 ★ **Mary Kay Cosmetics**
2840 Greenville Rd.
Hopkinsville, KY 42240
(502)885-3450
Ultimate Parent: Mary Kay Cosmetics. **SIC:** 5999—Miscellaneous Retail Stores Nec.

★ 68482 ★ **Pepsi Cola General Bottlers**
2307 Canton St.
Hopkinsville, KY 42240
(502)684-8413
Officer: Michael Ricks, Manager. **Ultimate Parent:** Pepsico. **SIC:** 2086—Bottled & Canned Soft Drinks.

★ 68483 ★ **Phelps Dodge Magnet Wire Co.**
S. Nashville Rd.
Hopkinsville, KY 42240-0768
Ultimate Parent: Phelps Dodge. **SIC:** 3357—Nonferrous Wiredrawing & Insulating.

★ 68484 ★ **Phelps Dodge Magnet Wire Co.**
PO Box 768
Hopkinsville, KY 42240-0768
Ultimate Parent: Phelps Dodge. **SIC:** 3357—Nonferrous Wiredrawing & Insulating.

Hustonville

★ 68485 ★ **Peoples Bank**
Bradfordsville Rd.
Hustonville, KY 40437
(606)346-4911
Ultimate Parent: People's Bank. **SIC:** 6081—Foreign Banks—Branches & Agencies; 6141—Personal Credit Institutions.

Independence

★ 68486 ★ **Star Bank NA, Kentucky**
S-L Hwy. & McCullum Rd.
Independence, KY 41051
(606)292-6240
Location Type: Branch office. **Officer:** Joan Strouse, Assistant Vice President. **Ultimate Parent:** Star Banc Corp. **SIC:** 6021—National Commercial Banks.

Irvine

★ 68487 ★   Fitness Center
Winchester Rd.
Irvine, KY 40336
(606)723-5511
Ultimate Parent: New York Times. **SIC:**
7991—Physical Fitness Facilities.

★ 68488 ★   Stop & Shop
Hardy Shopping Ctr. S
Irvine, KY 40336
(606)723-7512
Ultimate Parent: Stop & Shop. **SIC:** 5411—
Grocery Stores.

Jackson

★ 68489 ★   Fitness Center
Jett Shopping Ctr.
Jackson, KY 41339
(606)666-5480
Ultimate Parent: New York Times. **SIC:**
7991—Physical Fitness Facilities.

Jamestown

★ 68490 ★   Fruit of the Loom Inc.
Hwy. 127 N.
Jamestown, KY 42629
Ultimate Parent: Fruit of the Loom. **SIC:**
2322—Men's/Boys' Underwear & Nightwear.

**★ 68491 ★   Union Underwear Co.
Inc.**
PO Box 170
Jamestown, KY 42629
Ultimate Parent: Fruit of the Loom. **SIC:**
2300—Apparel & Other Textile Products.

**★ 68492 ★   Union Underwear Co.
Inc.**
PO Box 170, Wilson Rd.
Jamestown, KY 42629
Ultimate Parent: Fruit of the Loom. **SIC:**
2300—Apparel & Other Textile Products.

Jeffersontown

**★ 68493 ★   Corpane Industries
Inc.**
10100 Bluegrass Pky.
Jeffersontown, KY 40299
(502)491-4433
Officer: Monty Hoppestad, President.
Ultimate Parent: Dover Corp. **SIC:** 3531—
Construction Machinery.

**★ 68494 ★   National City Bank,
Kentucky**
9510 Taylorsville Rd.
Jeffersontown, KY 40299-2791
(502)581-5175
Company Type: Subsidiary. **Location
Type:** Branch office. **Officer:** Katherine
Pleasant, Mgr. **Ultimate Parent:** National
City Corp. **SIC:** 6021—National Commercial
Banks.

**★ 68495 ★   National City Bank,
Kentucky**
1819 Plantside Dr.
Jeffersontown, KY 40299-1931
(502)581-7346
Company Type: Subsidiary. **Location
Type:** Branch office. **Officer:** Lawrence
Herring, Mgr. **Ultimate Parent:** National City
Corp. **SIC:** 6021—National Commercial
Banks.

★ 68496 ★   Pitney Bowes
1901 Embassy Sq. Blvd.
Jeffersontown, KY 40299
(502)499-8571
Officer: Sydney McFarlane, Manager.
Ultimate Parent: Pitney Bowes. **SIC:**
3554—Paper Industries Machinery.

**★ 68497 ★   PNC Bank Kentuck
Inc.**
2501 Hurtsbourne Pky.
Jeffersontown, KY 40220-4004
(502)581-4630
Location Type: Branch office. **Ultimate
Parent:** PNC Bank Corp. **SIC:** 6021—
National Commercial Banks.

**★ 68498 ★   PNC Bank Kentucky
Inc.**
9503 Taylorsville Rd.
Jeffersontown, KY 40299-2799
(502)581-2206
Location Type: Branch office. **Ultimate
Parent:** PNC Bank Corp. **SIC:** 6021—
National Commercial Banks.

★ 68499 ★   Rhone Poulenc Inc.
9800 Bluegrass Pky.
Jeffersontown, KY 40299
(502)499-4011
Ultimate Parent: Rhone-Poulenc Rorer.
SIC: 2821—Plastics Materials & Resins;
2899—Chemical Preparations Nec.

★ 68500 ★   Stone Container Corp.
2108 Production Dr.
Jeffersontown, KY 40299
(502)491-4870
Officer: Mike Cash, Plant Manager.
Ultimate Parent: Stone Container Corp.
SIC: 2657—Folding Paperboard Boxes.

Kevil

★ 68501 ★   P M C Inc.
Kevil, KY 42053
(502)462-3522
Ultimate Parent: Polaroid. **SIC:** 5169—
Chemicals & Allied Products Nec.

La Grange

★ 68502 ★   Crestwood State Bank
1800 S. Hwy. 53
La Grange, KY 40031-9535
(502)222-1448
Company Type: Subsidiary. **Location
Type:** Branch office. **Officer:** Darrell Hill,
Mgr. **Ultimate Parent:** National City Corp.
SIC: 6021—National Commercial Banks.

★ 68503 ★   Kroger Co.
2034 S. Hwy. 53
La Grange, KY 40031
Ultimate Parent: Kroger. **SIC:** 5411—
Grocery Stores.

**★ 68504 ★   PNC Bank Kentucky
Inc.**
415 S. 1st St.
La Grange, KY 40031
(502)222-9433
Location Type: Branch office. **Ultimate
Parent:** PNC Bank Corp. **SIC:** 6021—
National Commercial Banks.

Lawrenceburg

★ 68505 ★   General Cable Corp.
1381 Bypass N
Lawrenceburg, KY 40342
Ultimate Parent: General Cable Corp. **SIC:**
3351—Copper Rolling & Drawing.

★ 68506 ★   House of Seagram
1225 Bonds Mill Rd.
Lawrenceburg, KY 40342
Ultimate Parent: J.E. Seagram & Sons, Inc.
SIC: 2085—Distilled & Blended Liquors.

**★ 68507 ★   Kraft General Foods
Inc.**
Factory Ave.
Lawrenceburg, KY 40342
Ultimate Parent: Philip Morris. **SIC:** 2022—
Cheese—Natural & Processed.

**★ 68508 ★   Seagram Sons Inc.
Joseph E**
Mac Brayer Rd.
Lawrenceburg, KY 40342
(502)839-3436
Ultimate Parent: J.E. Seagram & Sons, Inc.
SIC: 2085—Distilled & Blended Liquors.

Lebanon

★ 68509 ★   Kroger Co.
Lincoln Sq.
Lebanon, KY 40033
(502)692-3591
Ultimate Parent: Kroger. **SIC:** 5411—
Grocery Stores.

**★ 68510 ★   Star Bank NA,
Kentucky**
131 W. Main St.
Lebanon, KY 40033-1236
(502)692-3181
Location Type: Branch office. **Officer:**
James Richardson, Regulation President.
Ultimate Parent: Star Banc Corp. **SIC:**
6021—National Commercial Banks.

Lebanon Junction

★ 68511 ★   People's Bank
Lebanon Junction, KY 40150
(502)833-4436
Ultimate Parent: People's Bank. **SIC:**
6029—Commercial Banks Nec.

Leitchfield

**★ 68512 ★   Coast to Coast
Hardware**
Southgate Mall
Leitchfield, KY 42754
(502)259-5794
Ultimate Parent: Servistar Corp. **SIC:**
5251—Hardware Stores.

**★ 68513 ★   Northwestern Mutual
Life Inc.**
311 N. Main St.
Leitchfield, KY 42754
(502)259-6770
Ultimate Parent: Northwestern Mutual Life.
SIC: 6411—Insurance Agents, Brokers &
Service.

**★ 68514 ★   Rite Aid Discount
Pharmacy**
S Main
Leitchfield, KY 42754
(502)259-5720
Ultimate Parent: Rite Aid. **SIC:** 5912—Drug
Stores & Proprietary Stores.

★ 68515 ★   Wal-Mart Stores Inc.
Rural Route 1
Leitchfield, KY 42754
(502)259-5622
Ultimate Parent: Wal-Mart Stores, Inc. **SIC:**
5311—Department Stores.

Lewisport

**★ 68516 ★   American Olean Tile
Co.**
PO Box 450
Lewisport, KY 42351
(502)295-3140
Company Type: Subsidiary. **Ultimate
Parent:** Armstrong World Industries. **SIC:**
3253—Ceramic Wall & Floor Tile.

**★ 68517 ★   American Olean Tile
Co.**
Melanie Ln. & Fallin Ln.
Lewisport, KY 42351-0450
Ultimate Parent: Armstrong World
Industries. **SIC:** 3253—Ceramic Wall &
Floor Tile.

Lexington

**★ 68518 ★   American General
Finance**
571 New Circle Rd. NE
Lexington, KY 40505-2771
(606)293-0504
Location Type: Branch office. **Officer:**
Greg Hall. **Ultimate Parent:** American
General Corp. **SIC:** 6141—Personal Credit
Institutions; 6162—Mortgage Bankers &
Correspondents.

**★ 68519 ★   American General
Finance Inc.**
571 New Circle Rd. NE
Lexington, KY 40505-2771
(606)293-0504
Location Type: Branch office. **Officer:**
Greg Hall. **Ultimate Parent:** American
General Corp. **SIC:** 6141—Personal Credit
Institutions; 6162—Mortgage Bankers &
Correspondents.

★ 68520 ★   American Standard
Wabco Fluid Power Div.
1953 Mercer Rd.
Lexington, KY 40511
Company Type: Division. **Ultimate Parent:**
American Standard. **SIC:** 3492—Fluid
Power Valves & Hose Fittings; 3494—

Valves & Pipe Fittings Nec; 3499—
Fabricated Metal Products Nec; 3593—Fluid
Power Cylinders & Actuators.

**★ 68521 ★   American Standard
Inc.**
Wabco Fluid Power Div.
1953 Mercer Rd.
Lexington, KY 40511
Company Type: Division. **Ultimate Parent:**
American Standard. **SIC:** 3492—Fluid
Power Valves & Hose Fittings; 3494—
Valves & Pipe Fittings Nec; 3499—
Fabricated Metal Products Nec.

**★ 68522 ★   American Tobacco
Co.**
620 S. Broadway St.
Lexington, KY 40508-3140
(606)231-0187
Ultimate Parent: American Brands Inc.
SIC: 2141—Tobacco Stemming & Redrying.

★ 68523 ★   Armco Steel Corp.
851 Corporate Dr.
Lexington, KY 40503
(606)223-5868
Ultimate Parent: Armco. **SIC:** 5051—
Metals Service Centers & Offices.

★ 68524 ★   Ashland Services Co.
3475 Dabney Dr.
Lexington, KY 40509
(606)264-7777
Company Type: Subsidiary. **Officer:**
William R. Sawran, President. **Ultimate
Parent:** Ashland Oil. **SIC:** 7359—Equipment
Rental & Leasing Nec; 7374—Data
Processing & Preparation. **Employee
Count:** 548.

★ 68525 ★   Ashland Services Co.
PO Box 14000
Lexington, KY 40512
(606)264-7777 **Fax:** (606)264-7532
Company Type: Subsidiary. **Officer:**
William W. Sawran, President. **Ultimate
Parent:** Ashland Oil.

**★ 68526 ★   Auto-Graph Computer
Designing Systems, Inc.**
651 Perimeter Dr., Ste. 100
Lexington, KY 40517
(606)269-8585 **Fax:** (606)269-9821
Officer: Chuck Cleaton. **Ultimate Parent:**
Masco.

**★ 68527 ★   Automatic Data
Processing**
870 Corporate Dr., Rm. 200
Lexington, KY 40503-5418
(606)223-1799
Company Type: Branch. **Officer:** Kevin
Blair. **Ultimate Parent:** Automatic Data
Processing, Inc. **SIC:** 7374—Data
Processing & Preparation.

★ 68528 ★   Borden Inc.
Dairy
1307 Versailles Rd.
Lexington, KY 40504
Company Type: Division. **Ultimate Parent:**
Borden, Inc. **SIC:** 2026—Fluid Milk.

★ 68529 ★   Borden Inc.
Dairy
1307 Versailles Rd.
Lexington, KY 40504
Company Type: Division. **Ultimate Parent:**
Borden, Inc. **SIC:** 2026—Fluid Milk.

**★ 68530 ★   Burlington Air
Express**
601 Bizzell Dr.
Lexington, KY 40510
(606)254-8066
Ultimate Parent: Pittston. **SIC:** 4513—Air
Courier Services.

★ 68531 ★   Carolina Freight Corp.
424 Fairman Rd.
Lexington, KY 40511
(606)231-7616
Ultimate Parent: Carolina Freight. **SIC:**
4213—Trucking Except Local.

★ 68532 ★   Casual Corner
3527 Nicholasville Rd.
Lexington, KY 40503
(606)272-6677
Ultimate Parent: United States Shoe. **SIC:**
5621—Women's Clothing Stores.

★ 68533 ★ Circuit City
2690 Nicholasville Rd.
Lexington, KY 40503
(606)278-8464
Ultimate Parent: Circuit City Stores. SIC:
5731—Radio, Television & Electronics
Stores.

★ 68534 ★ Clark Material
Handling Co.
333 W. Vice St. No. 1700
Lexington, KY 40507-1600
(606)288-1200
Location Type: Branch office. Officer:
Gary Bello. Ultimate Parent: Banta Corp.
SIC: 3537—Industrial Trucks & Tractors;
3599—Industrial Machinery Nec.

★ 68535 ★ Clark Material
Handling Co.
333 W. Vine St.
Lexington, KY 40507-1622
(606)288-1200
Company Type: Subsidiary. Officer: Gary
Bello, President. Ultimate Parent: Banta
Corp. SIC: 3715—Truck Trailers; 5084—
Industrial Machinery & Equipment.

★ 68536 ★ Clark Material
Handling Co.
172 Trade St.
Lexington, KY 40510-1017
(606)488-1700
Officer: Elwyn Gillette. Ultimate Parent:
Banta Corp. SIC: 3537—Industrial Trucks &
Tractors; 5084—Industrial Machinery &
Equipment.

★ 68537 ★ Clark Material
Handling Co.
333 W. Vine St., No. 1700
Lexington, KY 40507-1600
(606)288-1200
Location Type: Branch office. Officer:
Gary Bello, President. Ultimate Parent:
Banta Corp. SIC: 3537—Industrial Trucks &
Tractors; 3599—Industrial Machinery Nec;
3715—Truck Trailers; 5084—Industrial
Machinery & Equipment.

★ 68538 ★ Copy Corp.
804 Newtown Central
Lexington, KY 40511
(606)255-5500
Officer: Jim Kincer, President. Ultimate
Parent: Alco Standard Corp. SIC: 3663—
Radio & T.V. Communications Equipment.

★ 68539 ★ Courtyard
1003 Elmendorf Dr.
Lexington, KY 40517
(606)269-5721
Ultimate Parent: Marriott International. SIC:
5947—Gift, Novelty & Souvenir Shops.

★ 68540 ★ Crestar Mortgage
Corp.
2525 Harrodsburg Rd.
Lexington, KY 40504
(606)224-4200
Ultimate Parent: Crestar Financial Corp.
SIC: 6062—State Credit Unions.

★ 68541 ★ Delta Air Lines
Blue Grass Field
Lexington, KY 40504
(606)255-2033
Ultimate Parent: Delta Air Lines, Inc. SIC:
4513—Air Courier Services.

★ 68542 ★ Delta Air Lines
Radisson Plz.
Lexington, KY 40507
(606)252-1466
Ultimate Parent: Delta Air Lines, Inc. SIC:
4724—Travel Agencies.

★ 68543 ★ Delta Air Lines
Bluegrass Army Depot
Lexington, KY 40511
(606)255-5750
Ultimate Parent: Delta Air Lines, Inc. SIC:
4512—Air Transportation—Scheduled.

★ 68544 ★ Delta Air Lines Inc.
Bluegrass Army Depot
Lexington, KY 40511
(606)255-5750
Ultimate Parent: Delta Air Lines, Inc. SIC:
4512—Air Transportation—Scheduled.

★ 68545 ★ Delta Air Lines Inc.
Radisson Plz.
Lexington, KY 40507
(606)252-1466
Ultimate Parent: Delta Air Lines, Inc. SIC:
4724—Travel Agencies.

★ 68546 ★ Digital Equipment
Corp.
2025 Leestown Rd.
Lexington, KY 40511
(606)233-9659
Ultimate Parent: Digital Equipment Corp.
SIC: 3579—Office Machines Nec.

★ 68547 ★ E-Systems Inc.
Go-Co.
Bluegrass Army Depot, Bldg. 3
Lexington, KY 40511
(606)293-3045
Officer: Paul L. Dunn, Executive Director.
Ultimate Parent: E-Systems Inc. SIC:
3663—Radio & T.V. Communications
Equipment; 3669—Communications
Equipment Nec.

★ 68548 ★ Eastman Kodak Co.
2872 Seattle Dr. 100
Lexington, KY 40509
(606)276-3159
Ultimate Parent: Eastman Kodak.

★ 68549 ★ First Federal S & L.
833 Lane Allen Rd.
Lexington, KY 40504-3605
(606)253-2605
Ultimate Parent: Bancorp Hawaii. SIC:
6162—Mortgage Bankers &
Correspondents; 6021—National
Commercial Banks; 6035—Federal Savings
Institutions.

★ 68550 ★ First Federal S & L
701 S. Broadway St.
Lexington, KY 40508-3127
(606)253-2605
Ultimate Parent: Bancorp Hawaii. SIC:
6062—State Credit Unions; 6021—National
Commercial Banks; 6035—Federal Savings
Institutions.

★ 68551 ★ First Federal S & L
3346 Tates Creek Rd.
Lexington, KY 40502-3498
(606)253-2605
Ultimate Parent: Bancorp Hawaii. SIC:
6162—Mortgage Bankers &
Correspondents; 6021—National
Commercial Banks; 6035—Federal Savings
Institutions.

★ 68552 ★ First Recovery
PO Box 14047
Lexington, KY 40512-4047
(606)264-7389
Company Type: Division. Officer: James
Huston, President. Ultimate Parent:
Ashland Oil. SIC: 5093—Scrap & Waste
Materials.

★ 68553 ★ Fitness Pro
1987 Harrodsburg Rd.
Lexington, KY 40503
(606)276-1071
Ultimate Parent: New York Times. SIC:
7991—Physical Fitness Facilities.

★ 68554 ★ Fitness Spa for Men
197 Moore Dr.
Lexington, KY 40503
(606)276-5521
Ultimate Parent: New York Times. SIC:
7991—Physical Fitness Facilities.

★ 68555 ★ General Electric Co.
903 Russell Cave Rd.
Lexington, KY 40505
(606)254-4406
Officer: Walt Nyzio, Manager. Ultimate
Parent: General Electric. SIC: 3231—
Products of Purchased Glass.

★ 68556 ★ General Electric Co.
1801 G. E. Dr.
Lexington, KY 40503
(606)277-1161
Officer: Guy Hackman, Manager. Ultimate
Parent: General Electric. SIC: 3647—
Vehicular Lighting Equipment.

★ 68557 ★ Greyhound Bus Lines
240 N. Limestone St.
Lexington, KY 40507
(606)255-7138
Ultimate Parent: Greyhound Lines Inc. SIC:
4131—Intercity & Rural Bus Transportation;
4111—Local & Suburban Transit; 4142—
Bus Charter Service Except Local.

★ 68558 ★ Hit or Miss
2317 Nicholasville Rd.
Lexington, KY 40503
(606)277-8795
Ultimate Parent: TJX. SIC: 5651—Family
Clothing Stores.

★ 68559 ★ James River Co.
451 Harbison Rd.
Lexington, KY 40511
Ultimate Parent: James River Corp. of
Virginia. SIC: 2676—Sanitary Paper
Products; 3082—Unsupported Plastics
Profile Shapes.

★ 68560 ★ James River Corp.
Harbison Rd.
Lexington, KY 40511
Ultimate Parent: James River Corp. of
Virginia. SIC: 2600—Paper & Allied
Products.

★ 68561 ★ James River Paper
Co.
Harbison Rd.
Lexington, KY 40511
Ultimate Parent: James River Corp. of
Virginia. SIC: 2600—Paper & Allied
Products.

★ 68562 ★ Jiffy Lube Oil Change
1654 Lindy Ln.
Lexington, KY 40505
(606)233-1739
Ultimate Parent: Pennzoil. SIC: 3586—
Measuring & Dispensing Pumps.

★ 68563 ★ Jiffy Lube Oil Change
801 Lane Allen Rd.
Lexington, KY 40504
(606)277-6414
Ultimate Parent: Pennzoil. SIC: 7539—
Automotive Repair Shops Nec.

★ 68564 ★ Kentucky Glass Plant
- General Electric
903 Russell Cave Pike
Lexington, KY 40505
Ultimate Parent: General Electric. SIC:
3229—Pressed & Blown Glass Nec.

★ 68565 ★ Kroger Co.
2909 Richmond Rd.
Lexington, KY 40509
(606)266-9205
Ultimate Parent: Kroger. SIC: 5411—
Grocery Stores.

★ 68566 ★ Kroger Co.
500 New Cirnw
Lexington, KY 40511
(606)233-0439
Ultimate Parent: Kroger. SIC: 5411—
Grocery Stores.

★ 68567 ★ Kroger Co.
769 New Cirne
Lexington, KY 40505
(606)255-1807
Ultimate Parent: Kroger. SIC: 5411—
Grocery Stores.

★ 68568 ★ Kroger Co.
704 E. Euclid Ave.
Lexington, KY 40502
(606)269-6805
Ultimate Parent: Kroger. SIC: 5411—
Grocery Stores.

★ 68569 ★ Kroger Co.
99 Eastland Shopping Ctr.
Lexington, KY 40505
(606)252-3974
Ultimate Parent: Kroger. SIC: 5411—
Grocery Stores.

★ 68570 ★ Kroger Co.
1865 Alexandria Dr.
Lexington, KY 40504
(606)277-8913
Ultimate Parent: Kroger. SIC: 5411—
Grocery Stores.

★ 68571 ★ Lane Bryant
3311 Nicholasville Rd.
Lexington, KY 40503
(606)271-3470
Ultimate Parent: Limited. SIC: 5621—
Women's Clothing Stores.

★ 68572 ★ Lexington Lamp Plant
1808 G.E. Dr.
Lexington, KY 40503
Ultimate Parent: General Electric. SIC:
3641—Electric Lamps.

★ 68573 ★ Limited the
3331 Nicholasville Rd.
Lexington, KY 40503
(606)272-8686
Ultimate Parent: Limited. SIC: 5621—
Women's Clothing Stores.

★ 68574 ★ Lorillard Inc.
3130 Custer Dr.
Lexington, KY 40517
(606)272-0855
Ultimate Parent: Loews. SIC: 7311—
Advertising Agencies.

★ 68575 ★ Mac's Oil &
Chemicals, Inc.
3499 Dabney Dr.
Lexington, KY
(606)264-7000 Fax: (606)264-7381
Company Type: Subsidiary. Officer: Larry
Dettan, President. Ultimate Parent:
Ashland Oil. SIC: 2842—Polishes &
Sanitation Goods. Employee Count: 80.

★ 68576 ★ Manpower Inc. of Ce
600 Perimeter Dr.
Lexington, KY 40517
(606)268-1331
Ultimate Parent: Manpower, Inc. SIC:
7363—Help Supply Services.

★ 68577 ★ McDonald's
Hamburgers
1106 New Cir. NE
Lexington, KY 40507
(606)252-5736
Ultimate Parent: McDonald's. SIC: 5812—
Eating Places.

★ 68578 ★ Meadow Gold Dairy
1307 Versailles Rd.
Lexington, KY 40504
(606)254-3818
Officer: George Bryant, Manager. Ultimate
Parent: Borden, Inc. SIC: 2024—Ice Cream
& Frozen Desserts.

★ 68579 ★ National City Bank,
Kentucky
1808 Alexandria Dr.
Lexington, KY 40504
(606)281-5471
Company Type: Subsidiary. Location
Type: Branch office. Officer: Dorothy
Wilson, Mgr. Ultimate Parent: National City
Corp. SIC: 6021—National Commercial
Banks.

★ 68580 ★ National City Bank,
Kentucky
1650 Bryan Station Rd.
Lexington, KY 40505
(606)281-5446
Company Type: Subsidiary. Location
Type: Branch office. Officer: Bill Spaulding,
Mgr. Ultimate Parent: National City Corp.
SIC: 6021—National Commercial Banks.

★ 68581 ★ National City Bank,
Kentucky
123 Cheapside
Lexington, KY 40507-1303
(606)281-5411
Company Type: Subsidiary. Location
Type: Branch office. Officer: Janie Hillard,
Mgr. Ultimate Parent: National City Corp.
SIC: 6021—National Commercial Banks.

★ 68582 ★ National City Bank,
Kentucky
720 Euclid Ave.
Lexington, KY 40502-1791
(606)281-5405
Company Type: Subsidiary. Location
Type: Branch office. Officer: Bill Marcum,
Mgr. Ultimate Parent: National City Corp.
SIC: 6021—National Commercial Banks.

★ 68583 ★ National City Bank,
Kentucky
1718 Alexandria Dr.
Lexington, KY 40504-3144
(606)281-5425
Company Type: Subsidiary. Location
Type: Branch office. Officer: Jan Ritchey,
Mgr. Ultimate Parent: National City Corp.
SIC: 6021—National Commercial Banks.

★ 68584 ★   National City Bank,
Kentucky
3397 Nicholasville Rd.
Lexington, KY 40503-3603
(606)281-5455
Company Type: Subsidiary. **Location
Type:** Branch office. **Officer:** Cindy Logan,
Mgr. **Ultimate Parent:** National City Corp.
SIC: 6021—National Commercial Banks.

★ 68585 ★   National City Bank,
Kentucky
3001 Richmond Rd.
Lexington, KY 40509-1508
(606)281-5489
Company Type: Subsidiary. **Location
Type:** Branch office. **Officer:** Jerry Davis,
Mgr. **Ultimate Parent:** National City Corp.
SIC: 6021—National Commercial Banks.

★ 68586 ★   National City Bank,
Kentucky
2452 Harrodsburg Rd.
Lexington, KY 40503-2162
(606)281-5460
Company Type: Subsidiary. **Location
Type:** Branch office. **Officer:** Teresa Page,
Mgr. **Ultimate Parent:** National City Corp.
SIC: 6021—National Commercial Banks.

★ 68587 ★   National City Bank,
Kentucky
905 S. Limestone
Lexington, KY 40503-1022
(606)281-5430
Company Type: Subsidiary. **Location
Type:** Branch office. **Officer:** Carol
Wagoner, Mgr. **Ultimate Parent:** National
City Corp. **SIC:** 6021—National Commercial
Banks.

★ 68588 ★   National City Bank,
Kentucky
3319 Tates Creek Rd.
Lexington, KY 40502-3407
(606)281-5446
Company Type: Subsidiary. **Location
Type:** Branch office. **Ultimate Parent:**
National City Corp. **SIC:** 6021—National
Commercial Banks.

★ 68589 ★   National City Bank,
Kentucky
286 New Circle Rd.
Lexington, KY 40505-2117
(606)281-5435
Company Type: Subsidiary. **Location
Type:** Branch office. **Officer:** Gegie
Deskins, Mgr. **Ultimate Parent:** National
City Corp. **SIC:** 6021—National Commercial
Banks.

★ 68590 ★   National City Bank,
Kentucky
2500 Nicholasville Rd.
Lexington, KY 40503-3306
(606)281-5480
Company Type: Subsidiary. **Location
Type:** Branch office. **Officer:** Margaret
Athon, Mgr. **Ultimate Parent:** National City
Corp. **SIC:** 6021—National Commercial
Banks.

★ 68591 ★   National City Bank,
Kentucky
4061 Tates Creek Rd.
Lexington, KY 40517-3061
(606)281-5378
Company Type: Subsidiary. **Location
Type:** Branch office. **Officer:** Jerry Davis,
Mgr. **Ultimate Parent:** National City Corp.
SIC: 6021—National Commercial Banks.

★ 68592 ★   National City Bank,
Kentucky
2323 Woodhill Rd.
Lexington, KY 40509-1023
(606)281-5485
Company Type: Subsidiary. **Location
Type:** Branch office. **Officer:** Sarah Glenn,
Mgr. **Ultimate Parent:** National City Corp.
SIC: 6021—National Commercial Banks.

★ 68593 ★   National City Bank,
Kentucky
301 E. Main St.
Lexington, KY 40507-1533
(606)281-5100
Company Type: Subsidiary. **Location
Type:** Branch office. **Officer:** Jeff Candy,
Mgr. **Ultimate Parent:** National City Corp.
SIC: 6021—National Commercial Banks.

★ 68594 ★   New York Life
Lexington General Office
Southeastern Agencies
3201 Nicholasville Rd., Ste. 500
Lexington, KY 40503
(606)272-9500 **Fax:** (606)271-0055
Officer: Randy T. Ellington, General
Manager. **Ultimate Parent:** New York Life.

★ 68595 ★   Northwestern Mutual
Life Inc.
3166 Custer Dr. 100
Lexington, KY 40517
Ultimate Parent: Northwestern Mutual Life.
SIC: 6411—Insurance Agents, Brokers &
Service.

★ 68596 ★   Northwestern Mutual
Life Inc.
801 Corporate Dr.
Lexington, KY 40503
(606)223-4545
Ultimate Parent: Northwestern Mutual Life.
SIC: 6411—Insurance Agents, Brokers &
Service.

★ 68597 ★   Pactel Paging
2416 Regency Rd.
Lexington, KY 40503
(606)276-5217
Ultimate Parent: Pacific Telesis Group.
SIC: 4812—Radiotelephone
Communications.

★ 68598 ★   Payless Shoe Source
2065 Turfland Mall
Lexington, KY 40504
(606)277-7731
Ultimate Parent: May Department Stores.
SIC: 5661—Shoe Stores.

★ 68599 ★   Payless Shoe Source
407 New Cir. NW
Lexington, KY 40511
(606)299-0605
Ultimate Parent: May Department Stores.
SIC: 5661—Shoe Stores.

★ 68600 ★   Payless Shoesource
407 New Cir. NE
Lexington, KY 40505
(606)299-0605
Ultimate Parent: May Department Stores.
SIC: 5661—Shoe Stores.

★ 68601 ★   Pennzoil Co.
239 Southland Dr.
Lexington, KY 40503
(606)278-7012
Ultimate Parent: Pennzoil. **SIC:** 5172—
Petroleum Products Nec.

★ 68602 ★   Pepsi-Cola Bottling
Co.
554 S. Forbes Rd.
Lexington, KY 40504
(606)255-3375
Officer: T. Hardig, Vice President. **Ultimate
Parent:** Pepsico. **SIC:** 2086—Bottled &
Canned Soft Drinks.

★ 68603 ★   Pitney Bowes
210 E. Reynolds Rd.
Lexington, KY 40517
(606)273-5056
Officer: Sydney McFarlane, Manager.
Ultimate Parent: Pitney Bowes. **SIC:**
3554—Paper Industries Machinery.

★ 68604 ★   PNC Bank Kentucky
Inc.
641 Euclid
Lexington, KY 40502-1759
(606)281-0466
Location Type: Branch office. **Ultimate
Parent:** PNC Bank Corp. **SIC:** 6021—
National Commercial Banks.

★ 68605 ★   PNC Bank Kentucky
Inc.
4051 Tates Creek Rd.
Lexington, KY 40517-3061
(606)281-0485
Location Type: Branch office. **Ultimate
Parent:** PNC Bank Corp. **SIC:** 6021—
National Commercial Banks.

★ 68606 ★   PNC Bank Kentucky
Inc.
771 Corporate Dr.
Lexington, KY 40503
(606)281-0400
Location Type: Branch office. **Ultimate
Parent:** PNC Bank Corp. **SIC:** 6021—
National Commercial Banks.

★ 68607 ★   PNC Bank Kentucky
Inc.
2515 Harrodsburg Rd.
Lexington, KY 40504-3353
(606)281-0456
Location Type: Branch office. **Ultimate
Parent:** PNC Bank Corp. **SIC:** 6021—
National Commercial Banks.

★ 68608 ★   PNC Bank Kentucky
Inc.
4009 Nicholasville Rd.
Lexington, KY 40503-4487
(606)281-0475
Location Type: Branch office. **Ultimate
Parent:** PNC Bank Corp. **SIC:** 6021—
National Commercial Banks.

★ 68609 ★   PNC Bank Kentucky
Inc.
3090 Richmond Rd.
Lexington, KY 40509-1507
(606)281-0481
Location Type: Branch office. **Ultimate
Parent:** PNC Bank Corp. **SIC:** 6021—
National Commercial Banks.

★ 68610 ★   PNC Bank Kentucky
Inc.
1721 Nicholasville Rd.
Lexington, KY 40503-1428
(606)281-0471
Location Type: Branch office. **Ultimate
Parent:** PNC Bank Corp. **SIC:** 6021—
National Commercial Banks.

★ 68611 ★   PNC Bank Kentucky
Inc.
101 E. Vine St.
Lexington, KY 40512-4072
(606)281-0400
Location Type: Branch office. **Ultimate
Parent:** PNC Bank Corp. **SIC:** 6021—
National Commercial Banks.

★ 68612 ★   Procter & Gamble
Manufacturing
767 E. 3rd St.
Lexington, KY 40505
(606)254-5544
Ultimate Parent: Procter & Gamble Co.
SIC: 2841—Soap & Other Detergents.

★ 68613 ★   Residence Inn by
Marriott
1080 Newtown Rd.
Lexington, KY 40511
(606)252-7500
Ultimate Parent: Marriott International. **SIC:**
7011—Hotels & Motels.

★ 68614 ★   Rite Aid Discount
Pharmacy
Stonewall Shopping Ctr.
Lexington, KY 40503
(606)223-9202
Ultimate Parent: Rite Aid. **SIC:** 5912—Drug
Stores & Proprietary Stores.

★ 68615 ★   Rite Aid Discount
Pharmacy
3120 Pimlico Pky. 2
Lexington, KY 40517
(606)272-9072
Ultimate Parent: Rite Aid. **SIC:** 5122—
Drugs, Proprietaries & Sundries.

★ 68616 ★   Rite Aid Discount
Pharmacy
4001 Nicholasville Rd.
Lexington, KY 40503
(606)271-0088
Ultimate Parent: Rite Aid. **SIC:** 5912—Drug
Stores & Proprietary Stores.

★ 68617 ★   Rite Aid Discount
Pharmacy
100 W. Main St.
Lexington, KY 40507
(606)252-9400
Ultimate Parent: Rite Aid. **SIC:** 5912—Drug
Stores & Proprietary Stores.

★ 68618 ★   Rite Aid Discount
Pharmacy
3101 Clays Mill Rd.
Lexington, KY 40503
(606)223-9950
Ultimate Parent: Rite Aid. **SIC:** 5912—Drug
Stores & Proprietary Stores.

★ 68619 ★   Rite Aid Discount
Pharmacy
404 Southland Dr.
Lexington, KY 40503
(606)277-1197
Ultimate Parent: Rite Aid. **SIC:** 5912—Drug
Stores & Proprietary Stores.

★ 68620 ★   Rite Aid Discount
Pharmacy
1050 Chinoe Rd.
Lexington, KY 40502
(606)269-4974
Ultimate Parent: Rite Aid. **SIC:** 5912—Drug
Stores & Proprietary Stores.

★ 68621 ★   Rite Aid Discount
Pharmacy
3349 Tates Creek Rd.
Lexington, KY 40502
(606)266-0414
Ultimate Parent: Rite Aid. **SIC:** 5912—Drug
Stores & Proprietary Stores.

★ 68622 ★   Ryder Truck Rental
2011 Versailles Rd.
Lexington, KY 40504
(606)259-0784
Ultimate Parent: Ryder System. **SIC:**
7513—Truck Rental & Leasing Without
Drivers.

★ 68623 ★   Ryder Truck Rental
1018 Trotwood Dr.
Lexington, KY 40511
(606)233-7115
Ultimate Parent: Ryder System. **SIC:**
7359—Equipment Rental & Leasing Nec;
7513—Truck Rental & Leasing Without
Drivers.

★ 68624 ★   Ryder Truck Rental-
One Way
341 Southland Dr.
Lexington, KY 40503
(606)278-2739
Ultimate Parent: Ryder System. **SIC:**
7513—Truck Rental & Leasing Without
Drivers.

★ 68625 ★   Security Pacific
Financial Services, Inc.
2365 Harrodsbury Rd., Ste. A160
Lexington, KY 40504-3053
(606)223-3053
Location Type: Branch office. **Ultimate
Parent:** Bankamerica Corp. **SIC:** 6141—
Personal Credit Institutions.

★ 68626 ★   Security Pacific
Financial Services, Inc.
3735 Harrodsbury Rd.
Lexington, KY 40503-4000
Location Type: Branch office. **Ultimate
Parent:** Bankamerica Corp. **SIC:** 6141—
Personal Credit Institutions; 6162—
Mortgage Bankers & Correspondents.

★ 68627 ★   Service Merchandise
Catalog
1555 New Cir. NE
Lexington, KY 40509
(606)269-8822
Ultimate Parent: Service Merchandise Co.,
Inc. **SIC:** 5399—Miscellaneous General
Merchandise Store.

★ 68628 ★   Service Merchandise
Catalog Sales
1555 New Cir. NE
Lexington, KY 40509
(606)269-8822
Ultimate Parent: Service Merchandise Co.,
Inc. **SIC:** 5399—Miscellaneous General
Merchandise Store.

★ 68629 ★   Southern
Development Co.
310 W. Short St.
Lexington, KY 40507
(606)254-2920
Ultimate Parent: Kansas City South
Industries. **SIC:** 8712—Architectural
Services.

★ 68630 ★   Southwestern
Tobacco Co.
Angliana Ave.
Lexington, KY 40508
(606)255-2451
Officer: Robert Miller, Manager. **Ultimate
Parent:** Universal Corp. **SIC:** 2131—
Chewing & Smoking Tobacco.

★ 68631 ★   **Standard Products Co.**
510 Henry Clay Blvd.
Lexington, KY 40505
(606)252-2246
Officer: Larry Sward, Manager. **Ultimate Parent:** Standard Products. **SIC:** 3465—Automotive Stampings.

★ 68632 ★   **Super America Group, Inc.**
PO Box 14000
Lexington, KY 40512
(606)264-7777 **Fax:** (606)264-2446
Company Type: Subsidiary. **Officer:** John F. Pettus, President. **Ultimate Parent:** Ashland Oil.

★ 68633 ★   **Superamerica**
900 Winchester Rd.
Lexington, KY 40505
(606)254-4182
Ultimate Parent: Ashland Oil. **SIC:** 5541—Gasoline Service Stations.

★ 68634 ★   **Superamerica**
246 Southland Dr.
Lexington, KY 40503
(606)278-8337
Ultimate Parent: Ashland Oil. **SIC:** 5541—Gasoline Service Stations.

★ 68635 ★   **Superamerica**
2301 Versailles Rd.
Lexington, KY 40504
(606)233-9798
Ultimate Parent: Ashland Oil. **SIC:** 5411—Grocery Stores; 5541—Gasoline Service Stations.

★ 68636 ★   **Superamerica**
447 New Cir. NE
Lexington, KY 40505
(606)293-5836
Ultimate Parent: Ashland Oil. **SIC:** 5541—Gasoline Service Stations.

★ 68637 ★   **Superamerica**
2900 Richmond Rd.
Lexington, KY 40509
(606)266-4218
Ultimate Parent: Ashland Oil. **SIC:** 5541—Gasoline Service Stations.

★ 68638 ★   **Superamerica**
515 E. Euclid Ave.
Lexington, KY 40502
(606)266-6390
Ultimate Parent: Ashland Oil. **SIC:** 5541—Gasoline Service Stations.

★ 68639 ★   **SuperAmerica Group, Inc.**
3499 Dabney Dr.
Lexington, KY 40509
(606)264-7777 **Fax:** (606)264-2063
Company Type: Subsidiary. **Officer:** John F. Pettus, President. **Ultimate Parent:** Ashland Oil. **SIC:** 5541—Gasoline Service Stations; 5411—Grocery Stores. **Sales:** 2,085,000,000 M.

★ 68640 ★   **Superamerica No 5677**
1401 Leestown Rd.
Lexington, KY 40511
(606)253-4704
Ultimate Parent: Ashland Oil. **SIC:** 5541—Gasoline Service Stations.

★ 68641 ★   **Superamerica Store 5675**
819 S. Limestone St.
Lexington, KY 40508
(606)252-6994
Ultimate Parent: Ashland Oil. **SIC:** 5411—Grocery Stores.

★ 68642 ★   **Terex Corp.**
Clark Material Handling Co.
333 W. Vine
Lexington, KY 40504-1640
(606)288-1200 **Fax:** (606)288-1226
Company Type: Subsidiary. **Officer:** Ronald DeFeo, President. **Ultimate Parent:** Banta Corp. **SIC:** 3537—Industrial Trucks & Tractors.

★ 68643 ★   **Trailways Bus Lines**
2260 Elkhorn St.
Lexington, KY 40505
(606)299-5974
Ultimate Parent: Greyhound Lines Inc. **SIC:** 4131—Intercity & Rural Bus Transportation; 4111—Local & Suburban Transit; 4142—Bus Charter Service Except Local.

★ 68644 ★   **Trane Air Handling Systems Business Unit**
1500 Mercer Rd.
Lexington, KY 40511
(606)259-2500
Officer: Terry Manon, Vice President & General Manager. **Ultimate Parent:** American Standard. **SIC:** 3585—Refrigeration & Heating Equipment; 3483—Ammunition Except for Small Arms; 3564—Blowers & Fans.

★ 68645 ★   **Trane Co.**
1500 Mercer Rd.
Lexington, KY 40511
Ultimate Parent: American Standard. **SIC:** 3585—Refrigeration & Heating Equipment.

★ 68646 ★   **Trans World Airlines**
Blue Grass Field
Lexington, KY 40504
(606)231-0767
Ultimate Parent: Trans World Airlines. **SIC:** 4512—Air Transportation—Scheduled.

★ 68647 ★   **Underwriters Adjusting Co.**
860 Corporate Dr.
Lexington, KY 40503
(606)223-3038
Ultimate Parent: Continental. **SIC:** 6411—Insurance Agents, Brokers & Service.

★ 68648 ★   **United Parcel Service**
1702 Mercer Rd.
Lexington, KY 40511
(606)292-9461
Ultimate Parent: United Parcel Service of America. **SIC:** 4215—Courier Services Except by Air.

★ 68649 ★   **United Parcel Service Inc.**
1702 Mercer Rd.
Lexington, KY 40511
(606)292-9461
Ultimate Parent: United Parcel Service of America. **SIC:** 4215—Courier Services Except by Air.

★ 68650 ★   **US Fidelity & Guaranty Insurance**
128 E. Reynolds Rd.
Lexington, KY 40503
(606)273-6411
Ultimate Parent: USF&G Corp. **SIC:** 6411—Insurance Agents, Brokers & Service.

★ 68651 ★   **Valvoline Inc.**
3499 Dabney Dr.
Lexington, KY 40509
(606)264-7777 **Fax:** (606)264-7381
Company Type: Subsidiary. **Officer:** John D Barr, President. **Ultimate Parent:** Ashland Oil. **SIC:** 5172—Petroleum Products Nec. **Employee Count:** 4000. **Sales:** 900,000,000 M.

★ 68652 ★   **Valvoline Inc.**
PO Box 1400
Lexington, KY
(606)264-7777 **Fax:** (606)264-7381
Company Type: Subsidiary. **Officer:** John D. Barr, President. **Ultimate Parent:** Ashland Oil.

★ 68653 ★   **Valvoline Instant Oil Chang**
715 N. Broadway St.
Lexington, KY 40508
(606)233-4584
Ultimate Parent: Ashland Oil. **SIC:** 7539—Automotive Repair Shops Nec.

★ 68654 ★   **Valvoline Instant Oil Chang**
2940 Richmond Rd.
Lexington, KY 40509
(606)269-6683
Ultimate Parent: Ashland Oil. **SIC:** 5172—Petroleum Products Nec.

★ 68655 ★   **Valvoline Instant Oil Change, Inc.**
PO Box 14046
Lexington, KY 40512-4046
(606)264-7000 **Fax:** (606)264-7049
Company Type: Subsidiary. **Officer:** Robert Harbison, President. **Ultimate Parent:** Ashland Oil. **SIC:** 5541—Gasoline Service Stations.

★ 68656 ★   **Valvoline Oil Co.**
3499 Dabney Dr.
Lexington, KY 40509
(606)268-7000
Ultimate Parent: Ashland Oil. **SIC:** 5172—Petroleum Products Nec.

★ 68657 ★   **Vulcan Materials Co.**
Richmond Rd.
Lexington, KY 40502
(606)266-1176
Ultimate Parent: Vulcan Materials Co. **SIC:** 5039—Construction Materials Nec.

★ 68658 ★   **Wang Laboratories Inc.**
821 Corporate Dr.
Lexington, KY 40503
(606)223-7483
Ultimate Parent: Wang Laboratories, Inc. **SIC:** 5046—Commercial Equipment Nec.

★ 68659 ★   **Wesco**
1721 Fortune Ct
Lexington, KY 40509
(606)293-2647
Ultimate Parent: Westinghouse Electric Corp. **SIC:** 5063—Electrical Apparatus & Equipment.

London

★ 68660 ★   **Griffin Pie Co.**
501 E. 4th St.
London, KY 40741
(606)864-5161
Officer: Robert Kidd, President. **Ultimate Parent:** Flowers Industries. **SIC:** 2051—Bread, Cake & Related Products.

★ 68661 ★   **Griffin Pie Co. Inc.**
501 E. 4th St.
London, KY 40741-4108
(606)864-5161
Company Type: Subsidiary. **Officer:** Robert W. Kidd, President. **Ultimate Parent:** Flowers Industries. **SIC:** 2051—Bread, Cake & Related Products. **Employee Count:** 580. **Sales:** 44 M.

★ 68662 ★   **Kroger Co.**
RR 6
London, KY 40741
(606)864-4311
Ultimate Parent: Kroger. **SIC:** 5411—Grocery Stores.

★ 68663 ★   **Marathon Service Station**
711 N. Main St.
London, KY 40741
(606)864-2483
Ultimate Parent: USX Corp. **SIC:** 5541—Gasoline Service Stations.

★ 68664 ★   **Payless Shoe Source**
Rural Route 6
London, KY 40741
(606)878-8641
Ultimate Parent: May Department Stores. **SIC:** 5661—Shoe Stores.

★ 68665 ★   **Rite Aid Discount Pharmacy**
80147 S. Main St.
London, KY 40741
(606)864-9964
Ultimate Parent: Rite Aid. **SIC:** 5912—Drug Stores & Proprietary Stores.

★ 68666 ★   **Rite Aid Discount Pharmacy**
Rural Route 6
London, KY 40741
(606)864-9975
Ultimate Parent: Rite Aid. **SIC:** 5912—Drug Stores & Proprietary Stores.

★ 68667 ★   **Ryder Truck Rental**
1413 S. Main St.
London, KY 40741
(606)864-2168
Ultimate Parent: Ryder System. **SIC:** 7513—Truck Rental & Leasing Without Drivers.

★ 68668 ★   **Therm-O-Disc Inc.**
Micro Devices Div.
4550 Old Whitley Rd.
London, KY 40741-9115
Ultimate Parent: Emerson Electric Co. Inc. **SIC:** 3643—Current-Carrying Wiring Devices.

★ 68669 ★   **Trailways Bus Lines**
1 75th Ext 192
London, KY 40741
(606)864-9512
Ultimate Parent: Greyhound Lines Inc. **SIC:** 4131—Intercity & Rural Bus Transportation; 4111—Local & Suburban Transit; 4142—Bus Charter Service Except Local.

★ 68670 ★   **United Parcel Service**
State Hwy. 25 S
London, KY 40741
(606)292-9461
Ultimate Parent: United Parcel Service of America. **SIC:** 4215—Courier Services Except by Air.

★ 68671 ★   **Wal-Mart Stores Inc.**
100 Hwy. 192
London, KY 40741
(606)878-6119
Ultimate Parent: Wal-Mart Stores, Inc. **SIC:** 5399—Miscellaneous General Merchandise Store.

★ 68672 ★   **Westinghouse Electric**
250 Westinghouse Dr.
London, KY 40741
(606)878-6100
Officer: Jim Kotala, Manager. **Ultimate Parent:** Westinghouse Electric Corp. **SIC:** 3613—Switchgear & Switchboard Apparatus.

Loretto

★ 68673 ★   **Star Bank NA, Kentucky**
4695 Hwy. 52
Loretto, KY 40033
(502)865-2671
Location Type: Branch office. **Officer:** Billie Miles, Manager. **Ultimate Parent:** Star Banc Corp. **SIC:** 6021—National Commercial Banks.

Louisa

★ 68674 ★   **Rite Aid Discount Pharmacy**
Louisa Plz.
Louisa, KY 41230
(606)638-4111
Ultimate Parent: Rite Aid. **SIC:** 5912—Drug Stores & Proprietary Stores.

Louisville

★ 68675 ★   **American General Finance**
7305 Preston Hwy.
Louisville, KY 40219-2742
(502)968-0176
Officer: Mike G. Campbell. **Ultimate Parent:** American General Corp. **SIC:** 6141—Personal Credit Institutions; 6162—Mortgage Bankers & Correspondents.

★ 68676 ★   **American General Finance**
10110 Dixie Hwy.
Louisville, KY 40272-3948
(502)935-0394
Ultimate Parent: American General Corp. **SIC:** 6141—Personal Credit Institutions; 6162—Mortgage Bankers & Correspondents.

★ 68677 ★   **American General Finance**
2602 Preston Hwy.
Louisville, KY 40217-2433
(502)636-3501
Ultimate Parent: American General Corp. **SIC:** 6141—Personal Credit Institutions; 6162—Mortgage Bankers & Correspondents.

★ 68678 ★   **American General Finance**
4109 Bardstown Rd.
Louisville, KY 40218-3272
(502)495-1266
Officer: Bambi C. Jones. **Ultimate Parent:** American General Corp. **SIC:** 6141—Personal Credit Institutions; 6162—Mortgage Bankers & Correspondents.

★ 68679 ★ American General Finance
4157 Shelbyville Rd.
Louisville, KY 40207-3262
(502)897-3101
Officer: R. L. Price. Ultimate Parent: American General Corp. SIC: 6141—Personal Credit Institutions; 6162—Mortgage Bankers & Correspondents.

★ 68680 ★ American General Finance
5131 Dixie Hwy.
Louisville, KY 40216-1700
(502)447-7616
Officer: Shirley G. Greenwood. Ultimate Parent: American General Corp. SIC: 6141—Personal Credit Institutions.

★ 68681 ★ American General Finance Inc.
10110 Dixie Hwy.
Louisville, KY 40272-3948
(502)935-0394
Location Type: Branch office. Ultimate Parent: American General Corp. SIC: 6141—Personal Credit Institutions; 6162—Mortgage Bankers & Correspondents.

★ 68682 ★ American General Finance Inc.
4109 Bardstown Rd.
Louisville, KY 40218-3272
(502)495-1266
Location Type: Branch office. Officer: Bambi C. Jones. Ultimate Parent: American General Corp. SIC: 6141—Personal Credit Institutions; 6162—Mortgage Bankers & Correspondents.

★ 68683 ★ American General Finance Inc.
7305 Preston Hwy.
Louisville, KY 40219-2742
(502)968-0176
Location Type: Branch office. Officer: Mike G. Campbell. Ultimate Parent: American General Corp. SIC: 6141—Personal Credit Institutions; 6162—Mortgage Bankers & Correspondents.

★ 68684 ★ American General Finance Inc.
5131 Dixie Hwy.
Louisville, KY 40216-1700
(502)447-7616
Location Type: Branch office. Officer: Shirley G. Greenwood. Ultimate Parent: American General Corp. SIC: 6141—Personal Credit Institutions.

★ 68685 ★ American General Finance Inc.
2602 Preston Hwy.
Louisville, KY 40217-2433
(502)636-3501
Location Type: Branch office. Ultimate Parent: American General Corp. SIC: 6141—Personal Credit Institutions; 6162—Mortgage Bankers & Correspondents.

★ 68686 ★ American General Finance Inc.
4157 Shelbyville Rd.
Louisville, KY 40207-3262
(502)897-3101
Location Type: Branch office. Officer: R. L. Price. Ultimate Parent: American General Corp. SIC: 6141—Personal Credit Institutions; 6162—Mortgage Bankers & Correspondents.

★ 68687 ★ American Standard Inc.
1541 S. 7th St.
Louisville, KY 40208
Ultimate Parent: American Standard. SIC: 3321—Gray & Ductile Iron Foundries; 3431—Metal Sanitary Ware.

★ 68688 ★ American Standard Inc.
1541 South Seventh Street, PO Box 1050
Louisville, KY 40208
Ultimate Parent: American Standard. SIC: 3321—Gray & Ductile Iron Foundries; 3431—Metal Sanitary Ware.

★ 68689 ★ Amgen Inc.
Louisville Distributors
12000 Plantside Dr.
Louisville, KY 40299-6305
(502)266-2700
Ultimate Parent: Amgen. SIC: 5122—Drugs, Proprietaries & Sundries.

★ 68690 ★ Anchor Hocking Corp.
1235 Liberty Ct
Louisville, KY 40203
(502)426-2412
Ultimate Parent: Newell. SIC: 5023—Homefurnishings.

★ 68691 ★ Anixter Brothers Inc.
3600 Chamberlain Ln. 122
Louisville, KY 40241
Ultimate Parent: Itel. SIC: 5051—Metals Service Centers & Offices.

★ 68692 ★ Armour Food Co.
1200 Story Ave.
Louisville, KY 40206
Ultimate Parent: Conagra. SIC: 2011—Meat Packing Plants.

★ 68693 ★ AT&T Network Systems
4110 Eastmoor Rd.
Louisville, KY 40218
(502)459-7360
Ultimate Parent: AT&T. SIC: 5063—Electrical Apparatus & Equipment.

★ 68694 ★ Automatic Data Processing
500 S. 7th St.
Louisville, KY 40203
(502)589-1432
Ultimate Parent: Automatic Data Processing, Inc. SIC: 7374—Data Processing & Preparation.

★ 68695 ★ BASF Corp.
Coatings & Inks
2148 S. 41st St.
Louisville, KY 40211
Ultimate Parent: BASF Corp. SIC: 2893—Printing Ink.

★ 68696 ★ BASF Corp.
Coatings & Inks
2148 South 41st St.
Louisville, KY 40211
Ultimate Parent: BASF Corp. SIC: 2893—Printing Ink.

★ 68697 ★ BASF Corp.
Engineering Plastics
9600 Tamarisk Pky.
Louisville, KY 40223-2858
(502)425-6906
Location Type: Branch office. Ultimate Parent: BASF Corp. SIC: 2821—Plastics Materials & Resins.

★ 68698 ★ BASF Graphic Systems
2148 S. 41st St.
Louisville, KY 40211
(502)778-4471
Officer: Norm Myatt, Manager. Ultimate Parent: BASF Corp. SIC: 2893—Printing Ink.

★ 68699 ★ Bear Automotive Service Equipment
11400 Decimal Dr.
Louisville, KY 40299
(502)267-7771
Ultimate Parent: SPX Corp. SIC: 5531—Automobile & Home Supply Stores.

★ 68700 ★ Bell Atlantic Bus Syst Servs.
4530 Bishop Ln. Ste. 108
Louisville, KY 40218-4561
(502)473-0871
Officer: Ted Weistarth. Ultimate Parent: Bell Atlantic Corp. SIC: 4813—Telephone Communications Except Radiotelephone; 7300—Business Services; 4812—Radiotelephone Communications; 7378—Computer Maintenance & Repair; 6159—Miscellaneous Business Credit Institutions; 2741—Miscellaneous Publishing; 6719—Holding Companies Nec.

★ 68701 ★ Bell South Mobility Inc.
3503 College Dr.
Louisville, KY 40299-3610
(502)267-1433
Officer: Dean Hunt. Ultimate Parent: BellSouth Corp. SIC: 4813—Telephone Communications Except Radiotelephone.

★ 68702 ★ Berry L M & Co.
303 Hurstbourne Ln.
Louisville, KY 40222
(502)423-7401
Ultimate Parent: Bell Atlantic Corp. SIC: 2741—Miscellaneous Publishing.

★ 68703 ★ Blue Grass Cooperage Co.
402 MacLean Ave.
Louisville, KY 40213
(502)368-1626
Officer: Vernon G. Connell, Vice President. Ultimate Parent: Brown-Forman. SIC: 2449—Wood Containers Nec; 3412—Metal Barrels, Drums & Pails.

★ 68704 ★ Blue Grass Cooperage Co.
402 MacLean Ave.
Louisville, KY 40213-2550
(502)368-1626
Location Type: Branch office. Officer: Ron Ralph. Ultimate Parent: Brown-Forman. SIC: 2449—Wood Containers Nec; 5085—Industrial Supplies.

★ 68705 ★ Blue Grass Cooperage Co.
402 MacLean Ave.
Louisville, KY 40213
(502)368-1626
Officer: Vernon G. Connell, Vice President. Ultimate Parent: Brown-Forman. SIC: 2449—Wood Containers Nec; 3412—Metal Barrels, Drums & Pails.

★ 68706 ★ Bluegrass Coca-Cola Bottling Co., Inc.
1661 W. Hill St.
Louisville, KY 40210-1749
(502)775-4600
Officer: S. K. Johnston Jr., Chairman. Ultimate Parent: Coca-Cola Enterprises. SIC: 5149—Groceries & Related Products Nec. Employee Count: 430.

★ 68707 ★ Bluegrass Coca Cola Inc.
1661 W. Hill St.
Louisville, KY 40210
(502)775-4600
Ultimate Parent: Coca-Cola Enterprises. SIC: 2086—Bottled & Canned Soft Drinks.

★ 68708 ★ Borden Inc.
Chemical
6200 Camp Ground Rd.
Louisville, KY 40216
Company Type: Division. Ultimate Parent: Borden, Inc. SIC: 2869—Industrial Organic Chemicals Nec; 2821—Plastics Materials & Resins; 2891—Adhesives & Sealants.

★ 68709 ★ Borden Packaging & Industrial Products
6200 Campground Rd.
Louisville, KY 40216-2199
Ultimate Parent: Borden, Inc. SIC: 2869—Industrial Organic Chemicals Nec; 2821—Plastics Materials & Resins.

★ 68710 ★ Brown-Forman
850 Dixie Hwy.
Louisville, KY 40201
(502)585-1100
Company Type: Headquarters. Officer: Owsley Brown II. Employee Count: 6700. Sales: 1415 M. Fortune 500: Largest U.S. Industrial Corporations: Ranking 286.

★ 68711 ★ Brown-Forman Beverage Co.
PO Box 1080
Louisville, KY 40201-1080
(502)585-1100 Fax: (502)774-7833
Company Type: Subsidiary. Ultimate Parent: Brown-Forman.

★ 68712 ★ Brown-Forman Beverage Co.
PO Box 1080
Louisville, KY 40201-1080
(502)585-1100 Fax: (502)774-7833
Company Type: Subsidiary. Officer: Owsley Brown II, Chairman. Ultimate Parent: Brown-Forman.

★ 68713 ★ Brown-Forman Corp.
PO Box 1080
Louisville, KY 40201-1080
(502)585-1100 Fax: (502)774-7833
Company Type: Headquarters. Officer: Owsley Brown II, President & CEO.

Ultimate Parent: Brown-Forman. Employee Count: 6700.

★ 68714 ★ Brown Forman Corp.
850 Dixie Hwy.
Louisville, KY 40210
(502)585-1100 Fax: (502)774-7876
Officer: Owsley Brown II, CEO. Ultimate Parent: Brown-Forman. Employee Count: 6700. Sales: 1665 M.

★ 68715 ★ Brown-Forman Corp.
PO Box 1080
Louisville, KY 40201-1080
(502)585-1100
Location Type: Headquarters. Officer: Owsley Brown II. Ultimate Parent: Brown-Forman. SIC: 2084—Wines, Brandy & Brandy Spirits; 2085—Distilled & Blended Liquors; 5023—Homefurnishings; 5099—Durable Goods Nec; 5182—Wines & Distilled Beverages.

★ 68716 ★ Brown Forman Corp.
850 Dixie Hwy.
Louisville, KY 40210
(502)585-1100 Fax: (502)774-7876
Ultimate Parent: Brown-Forman.

★ 68717 ★ Brown-Forman Corp.
PO Box 1080
Louisville, KY 40201-1080
(502)585-1100 Fax: (502)774-7833
Company Type: Headquarters. Ultimate Parent: Brown-Forman.

★ 68718 ★ Brown Forman Corp.
850 Dixie Hwy.
Louisville, KY 40210-1038
(502)585-1100
Officer: W. L. Lyons Brown Jr., Chairman. Ultimate Parent: Brown-Forman. SIC: 2085—Distilled & Blended Liquors; 2084—Wines, Brandy & Brandy Spirits; 3262—Vitreous China Table & Kitchenware; 3914—Silverware & Plated Ware; 3161—Luggage; 3172—Personal Leather Goods Nec; 2392—Housefurnishings Nec. Employee Count: 6700. Sales: 1691.6 M.

★ 68719 ★ Brown Forman Corp.
850 Dixie Hwy.
Louisville, KY 40210-1038
(502)585-1100
Officer: W. L. Lyons Brown Jr., Chairman. Ultimate Parent: Brown-Forman. SIC: 2085—Distilled & Blended Liquors; 2084—Wines, Brandy & Brandy Spirits; 3262—Vitreous China Table & Kitchenware; 3914—Silverware & Plated Ware; 3161—Luggage; 3172—Personal Leather Goods Nec; 2392—Housefurnishings Nec. Employee Count: 6700. Sales: 1691.6 M.

★ 68720 ★ Brown-Forman International Ltd.
PO Box 1080
Louisville, KY 40201-1080
(502)585-1100 Fax: (502)774-7833
Company Type: Subsidiary. Ultimate Parent: Brown-Forman.

★ 68721 ★ Brown-Forman International Ltd.
PO Box 1080
Louisville, KY 40201-1080
(502)585-1100 Fax: (502)774-7833
Company Type: Subsidiary. Officer: E. Peter Rutledge, Chairman & CEO. Ultimate Parent: Brown-Forman.

★ 68722 ★ Brown-Forman Production Co.
PO Box 1080
Louisville, KY 40201-1080
(502)585-1100 Fax: (502)774-7833
Company Type: Subsidiary. Officer: James B. Chiles, Senior Vice President. Ultimate Parent: Brown-Forman.

★ 68723 ★ Brown-Forman Production Co.
PO Box 1080
Louisville, KY 40201-1080
(502)585-1100 Fax: (502)774-7833
Company Type: Subsidiary. Ultimate Parent: Brown-Forman.

★ 68724 ★ **Browning Ferris Industries**
405 N. English Station Rd.
Louisville, KY 40223-3913
(502)245-1234
Officer: Bryan B. Slade. Ultimate Parent: Browning-Ferris Industries. SIC: 4953—Refuse Systems; 4212—Local Trucking Without Storage.

★ 68725 ★ **Burlington Air Express**
6704 Grade Ln.
Louisville, KY 40213
(502)367-0151
Ultimate Parent: Pittston. SIC: 4513—Air Courier Services.

★ 68726 ★ **Capital Holding**
400 W. Market St.
Louisville, KY 40202
(502)560-2000
Company Type: Headquarters. Officer: Irving W. Bailey II. Fortune Service 500: Ranking 20.

★ 68727 ★ **Carpenter E R Co. Inc.**
429 W. Muhammad Ali Blvd.
Louisville, KY 40202
(502)568-6821
Ultimate Parent: Carpenter. SIC: 5047—Medical & Hospital Equipment.

★ 68728 ★ **Casual Corner**
45 Oxmoor Mall
Louisville, KY 40222
(502)426-2215
Ultimate Parent: United States Shoe. SIC: 5651—Family Clothing Stores.

★ 68729 ★ **Circuit City**
4805 Outer Loop
Louisville, KY 40219
(502)966-8228
Ultimate Parent: Circuit City Stores. SIC: 5065—Electronic Parts & Equipment Nec; 5731—Radio, Television & Electronics Stores.

★ 68730 ★ **Circuit City**
143 Thierman Ln.
Louisville, KY 40207
(502)893-5711
Ultimate Parent: Circuit City Stores. SIC: 5731—Radio, Television & Electronics Stores.

★ 68731 ★ **Circuit City**
5120 Dixie Hwy.
Louisville, KY 40216
(502)448-0110
Ultimate Parent: Circuit City Stores. SIC: 5722—Household Appliance Stores; 5731—Radio, Television & Electronics Stores.

★ 68732 ★ **Clark Printing Co.**
1700 S. 5th St.
Louisville, KY 40208
(502)585-3396
Ultimate Parent: Terex. SIC: 2752—Commercial Printing—Lithographic.

★ 68733 ★ **Coast to Coast Lumber Co. Inc.**
4801 Sherburn Ln.
Louisville, KY 40207
(502)895-5476
Ultimate Parent: Servistar Corp. SIC: 5031—Lumber, Plywood & Millwork.

★ 68734 ★ **Coca-Cola Bottling Co. Blue Grass**
1661 Hill St.
Louisville, KY 40210
Ultimate Parent: Coca-Cola Bottling Consol. SIC: 2086—Bottled & Canned Soft Drinks.

★ 68735 ★ **Coca-Cola Bottling Co. Bluegrass**
1661 West Hill St.
Louisville, KY 40210
Ultimate Parent: Coca-Cola Bottling Consol. SIC: 2086—Bottled & Canned Soft Drinks.

★ 68736 ★ **Columbia Healthcare Corp.**
201 W. Main St.
Louisville, KY 40202
(502)572-2000
Company Type: Headquarters. Officer: Richard L. Scott. Employee Count: 65500.

Sales: 5653.0 M. Fortune Service 500: Ranking 19.

★ 68737 ★ **Copy Corp.**
11401 Bluegrass Pky.
Louisville, KY 40299
(502)267-0000
Company Type: Division. Officer: Jim A. Kincer, President. Ultimate Parent: Alco Standard Corp. SIC: 5046—Commercial Equipment Nec.

★ 68738 ★ **Crestar Mortgage Corp.**
9100 Shelbyville Rd.
Louisville, KY 40222
(502)425-8787
Ultimate Parent: Crestar Financial Corp. SIC: 6162—Mortgage Bankers & Correspondents.

★ 68739 ★ **DataServe**
9123 Galene Dr.
Louisville, KY 40299-1523
(502)267-0522
Officer: Roger W. Yockey. Ultimate Parent: BellSouth Corp. SIC: 7378—Computer Maintenance & Repair; 7373—Computer Integrated Systems Design.

★ 68740 ★ **Dean Foods Co.**
4420 Bishop Ln.
Louisville, KY 40218
Ultimate Parent: Dean Foods. SIC: 2026—Fluid Milk.

★ 68741 ★ **Dean Milk Co.**
4420 Bishop Ln.
Louisville, KY 40218
(502)451-9111
Officer: John McCormack, Vice President. Ultimate Parent: Dean Foods. SIC: 2024—Ice Cream & Frozen Desserts; 2026—Fluid Milk.

★ 68742 ★ **Dean Witter Reynolds Inc.**
320 W. Jefferson St.
Louisville, KY 40202
(502)589-3700
Location Type: Branch office. Ultimate Parent: Dean Witter Discover. SIC: 6211—Security Brokers & Dealers.

★ 68743 ★ **Delta Air Lines**
500 S. 4th Ave.
Louisville, KY 40202
(502)589-1692
Ultimate Parent: Delta Air Lines, Inc. SIC: 4512—Air Transportation—Scheduled.

★ 68744 ★ **Delta Air Lines**
Standiford Field
Louisville, KY 40221
(502)363-3544
Ultimate Parent: Delta Air Lines, Inc. SIC: 4729—Passenger Transportation Arrangement Nec.

★ 68745 ★ **Delta Air Lines**
Airport Terminal
Louisville, KY 40213
(502)361-6806
Ultimate Parent: Delta Air Lines, Inc. SIC: 4512—Air Transportation—Scheduled.

★ 68746 ★ **Delta Air Lines**
Seelbach
Louisville, KY 40202
(502)584-6151
Ultimate Parent: Delta Air Lines, Inc. SIC: 4724—Travel Agencies.

★ 68747 ★ **Delta Air Lines Air Cargo**
4613 Standard Field Dc
Louisville, KY 40213
(502)361-6800
Ultimate Parent: Delta Air Lines, Inc. SIC: 4513—Air Courier Services.

★ 68748 ★ **Delta Air Lines Inc.**
Airport Terminal
Louisville, KY 40213
(502)361-6806
Ultimate Parent: Delta Air Lines, Inc. SIC: 4512—Air Transportation—Scheduled.

★ 68749 ★ **Delta Air Lines Inc.**
Standiford Field
Louisville, KY 40221
(502)363-3544
Ultimate Parent: Delta Air Lines, Inc. SIC: 4729—Passenger Transportation Arrangement Nec.

★ 68750 ★ **Delta Air Lines Inc.**
Seelbach
Louisville, KY 40202
(502)584-6151
Ultimate Parent: Delta Air Lines, Inc. SIC: 4724—Travel Agencies.

★ 68751 ★ **Denny's Restaurant**
4030 Dutchmans Ln.
Louisville, KY 40207
(502)896-2669
Ultimate Parent: Flagstar Co. SIC: 5812—Eating Places.

★ 68752 ★ **Denny's Restaurant**
337 Whittington Pky.
Louisville, KY 40222
(502)423-0489
Ultimate Parent: Flagstar Co. SIC: 5812—Eating Places.

★ 68753 ★ **Diebold Inc.**
11360 Bluegrass Pky.
Louisville, KY 40299
(502)267-9602
Ultimate Parent: Diebold, Inc. SIC: 5046—Commercial Equipment Nec.

★ 68754 ★ **Digital Equipment Corp.**
301 Hurstbourne Ln.
Louisville, KY 40222
(502)423-7951
Ultimate Parent: Digital Equipment Corp. SIC: 5063—Electrical Apparatus & Equipment.

★ 68755 ★ **Dover Elevator Co.**
1147 Logan St.
Louisville, KY 40204
(502)636-2552
Officer: Jim Miller, Manager. Ultimate Parent: Dover Corp. SIC: 3534—Elevators & Moving Stairways.

★ 68756 ★ **Early Times Distillers Co.**
2921 Dixie Hwy.
Louisville, KY 40216-5245
(502)776-1730
Officer: Leo Reidinger. Ultimate Parent: Brown-Forman. SIC: 2085—Distilled & Blended Liquors; 7319—Advertising Nec.

★ 68757 ★ **Eastman Kodak Co.**
101 S. 5th St.
Louisville, KY 40202
(502)587-1128
Ultimate Parent: Eastman Kodak. SIC: 5946—Camera & Photographic Supply Stores.

★ 68758 ★ **Eaton Corp.**
5427 Bardstown Rd.
Louisville, KY 40291
(502)231-1234
Ultimate Parent: Eaton Corp. SIC: 3714—Motor Vehicle Parts & Accessories.

★ 68759 ★ **Engelhard Corp.**
3400 Bank St.
Louisville, KY 40212
(502)778-7331
Officer: Jim Doyle, Manager. Ultimate Parent: Engelhard Corp. SIC: 2816—Inorganic Pigments; 2865—Cyclic Crudes & Intermediates; 2819—Industrial Inorganic Chemicals Nec; 2869—Industrial Organic Chemicals Nec; 2999—Petroleum & Coal Products Nec.

★ 68760 ★ **Engelhard Corp.**
Pigments & Additives Div.
3400 Bank St.
Louisville, KY 40212-2198
Company Type: Division. Ultimate Parent: Engelhard Corp. SIC: 2816—Inorganic Pigments; 2865—Cyclic Crudes & Intermediates; 2819—Industrial Inorganic Chemicals Nec; 2869—Industrial Organic Chemicals Nec; 2999—Petroleum & Coal Products Nec.

★ 68761 ★ **Exxon Corp.**
1101 Bardstown Rd.
Louisville, KY 40204
(502)459-7197
Ultimate Parent: Exxon. SIC: 5541—Gasoline Service Stations.

★ 68762 ★ **Federal Paper Board Co.**
3661 Collins Ln.
Louisville, KY 40245
(502)423-0381
Officer: Sherri Smith, Manager. Ultimate Parent: Federal Paper Board. SIC: 2621—Paper Mills; 2657—Folding Paperboard Boxes.

★ 68763 ★ **Fitness Factory**
3099 Breckinridge Ln.
Louisville, KY 40220
(502)456-1577
Ultimate Parent: New York Times. SIC: 7991—Physical Fitness Facilities.

★ 68764 ★ **Ford Motor Co. Kentucky Truck Plant**
3001 Chamberlain Ln.
Louisville, KY 40241
Ultimate Parent: Ford Motor Co. SIC: 3713—Truck & Bus Bodies.

★ 68765 ★ **Ford Motor Co., Louisville Assembly Plant**
Fern Valley Rd. & Grade Ln.
Louisville, KY 40213
Location Type: Plant. Ultimate Parent: Ford Motor Co. SIC: 3711—Motor Vehicles & Car Bodies.

★ 68766 ★ **Gannett Direct Marketing Services Inc.**
3400 Robards Ct.
Louisville, KY 40218
(502)454-6660 Fax: (502)456-6179
Officer: Dennis Washburn, President. Ultimate Parent: Gannett.

★ 68767 ★ **GE Appliances**
Appliance Pk.
Louisville, KY 40225
(502)452-4311 Fax: (502)452-0390
Officer: J. Richard Stonesifer, President & CEO. Ultimate Parent: General Electric.

★ 68768 ★ **General Electric Co.**
11513 Commonwealth Dr.
Louisville, KY 40299
(502)423-7710
Officer: Joseph W. Bivens, Manager. Ultimate Parent: General Electric. SIC: 3844—X-Ray Apparatus & Tubes.

★ 68769 ★ **Greyhound Bus Lines**
6403 Ulrich Ave.
Louisville, KY 40219
(502)966-3315
Ultimate Parent: Greyhound Lines Inc. SIC: 4111—Local & Suburban Transit; 4131—Intercity & Rural Bus Transportation; 4142—Bus Charter Service Except Local.

★ 68770 ★ **Harshaw Chemical Co.**
3400 Bank St.
Louisville, KY 40212
Ultimate Parent: Engelhard Corp. SIC: 2816—Inorganic Pigments; 2865—Cyclic Crudes & Intermediates; 2819—Industrial Inorganic Chemicals Nec; 2869—Industrial Organic Chemicals Nec; 2999—Petroleum & Coal Products Nec.

★ 68771 ★ **Hershey Pasta Group Louisville Kentucky Plant**
2501 S. Floyd St.
Louisville, KY 40217
Ultimate Parent: Hershey Foods. SIC: 2098—Macaroni & Spaghetti.

★ 68772 ★ **Hi-Tek Polymers Inc. Plant 2700**
1515 S. 11th St.
Louisville, KY 40210
Ultimate Parent: Rhone-Poulenc Rorer. SIC: 2821—Plastics Materials & Resins; 2851—Paints & Allied Products.

★ 68773 ★ **Hit or Miss**
Timberwood Ctr.
Louisville, KY 40223
(502)964-9299
Ultimate Parent: TJX. SIC: 5621—Women's Clothing Stores.

★ 68774 ★ **Hit or Miss**
11501 Bluegrass Pky.
Louisville, KY 40299
(502)267-4667
Ultimate Parent: TJX. SIC: 5621—Women's Clothing Stores; 5651—Family Clothing Stores.

★ 68775 ★ **Hit or Miss**
5000 Shelbyville Rd.
Louisville, KY 40207
(502)897-9040
Ultimate Parent: TJX. **SIC:** 5621—
Women's Clothing Stores.

★ 68776 ★ **House of Fragrance**
400 Louisville Galleria
Louisville, KY 40202
(502)581-1611
Ultimate Parent: Eastman Kodak. **SIC:**
5999—Miscellaneous Retail Stores Nec.

★ 68777 ★ **Humana**
500 W. Main St.
Louisville, KY 40202
(502)580-1000
Company Type: Headquarters. **Officer:**
David A. Jones. **Employee Count:** 8800.
Sales: 3137 M. **Fortune Service 500:**
Ranking 40.

★ 68778 ★ **Humana Inc.**
Humana Building
500 West Main St.
Louisville, KY 40201
(502)580-1000 **Fax:** (502)580-1046
Company Type: Headquarters. **Officer:**
David A. Jones, Chairman & CEO. **Ultimate Parent:** Humana.

★ 68779 ★ **Inacomp Computer Centers**
3120 1st National Tower
Louisville, KY 40202
(502)790-1360
Ultimate Parent: Beneficial. **SIC:** 7379—
Computer Related Services Nec.

★ 68780 ★ **Inland Container Corp.**
4201 Old Shepherdsville Rd.
Louisville, KY 40218
Ultimate Parent: Temple-Inland. **SIC:**
2653—Corrugated & Solid Fiber Boxes.

★ 68781 ★ **J. Bacon & Sons**
3600 Bardstown Rd.
Louisville, KY 40218
(502)456-4000 **Fax:** (502)456-4000
Officer: Martin S. Margulis, President.
Ultimate Parent: Mercantile Stores.

★ 68782 ★ **Jiffy Lube Oil Change**
2601 Bardstown Rd.
Louisville, KY 40205
(502)454-7736
Ultimate Parent: Pennzoil. **SIC:** 7538—
General Automotive Repair Shops.

★ 68783 ★ **Jiffy Lube Oil Change**
6508 Preston Hwy.
Louisville, KY 40219
(502)969-6911
Ultimate Parent: Pennzoil. **SIC:** 7539—
Automotive Repair Shops Nec.

★ 68784 ★ **Jiffy Lube Oil Change**
4180 Westport Rd.
Louisville, KY 40207
(502)896-2905
Ultimate Parent: Pennzoil. **SIC:** 5172—
Petroleum Products Nec.

★ 68785 ★ **Jiffy Lube Oil Change**
7106 Dixie Hwy.
Louisville, KY 40258
(502)937-1227
Ultimate Parent: Pennzoil. **SIC:** 7538—
General Automotive Repair Shops.

★ 68786 ★ **Johnson Controls Battery Group Inc.**
3200 Fern Valley Rd.
Louisville, KY 40213-3598
Ultimate Parent: Johnson & Johnson. **SIC:**
3691—Storage Batteries.

★ 68787 ★ **Johnson Controls Inc.**
1808 Cargo Ct
Louisville, KY 40299
(502)491-3794
Ultimate Parent: Johnson Controls Inc.
SIC: 5084—Industrial Machinery &
Equipment.

★ 68788 ★ **KFC**
1441 Gardiner Ln.
Louisville, KY 40213
(502)456-8300 **Fax:** (502)454-2195
Officer: John M. Cranor III, President &
CEO. **Ultimate Parent:** Pepsico.

★ 68789 ★ **Kroger Co.**
3917 Southland Ter.
Louisville, KY 40216
(502)447-2330
Ultimate Parent: Kroger. **SIC:** 5411—
Grocery Stores.

★ 68790 ★ **Kroger Co.**
219 Holiday Manor Ctr.
Louisville, KY 40222
(502)425-6960
Ultimate Parent: Kroger. **SIC:** 5411—
Grocery Stores.

★ 68791 ★ **Kroger Co.**
12501 Shelbyville Rd.
Louisville, KY 40243
(502)244-7957
Ultimate Parent: Kroger. **SIC:** 5411—
Grocery Stores.

★ 68792 ★ **Kroger Co.**
10437 Dixie Hwy.
Louisville, KY 40272
(502)937-5851
Ultimate Parent: Kroger. **SIC:** 5411—
Grocery Stores.

★ 68793 ★ **Kroger Co.**
4174 Westport Rd.
Louisville, KY 40207
(502)893-2461
Ultimate Parent: Kroger. **SIC:** 5411—
Grocery Stores.

★ 68794 ★ **Kroger Co.**
9250 Westport Rd.
Louisville, KY 40242
(502)425-0065
Ultimate Parent: Kroger. **SIC:** 5411—
Grocery Stores.

★ 68795 ★ **Kroger Co.**
Village Shopping Ctr.
Louisville, KY 40207
(502)245-0666
Ultimate Parent: Kroger. **SIC:** 5411—
Grocery Stores.

★ 68796 ★ **Kroger Co.**
3115 W. Broadway St.
Louisville, KY 40211
(502)776-1182
Ultimate Parent: Kroger. **SIC:** 5411—
Grocery Stores.

★ 68797 ★ **Kroger Co.**
4211 S. 3rd St.
Louisville, KY 40214
(502)368-3065
Ultimate Parent: Kroger. **SIC:** 5411—
Grocery Stores.

★ 68798 ★ **Kroger Co.**
Southland Ter.
Louisville, KY 40216
(502)448-0525
Ultimate Parent: Kroger. **SIC:** 5411—
Grocery Stores.

★ 68799 ★ **Kroger Co.**
5733 Preston Hwy.
Louisville, KY 40219
(502)969-0557
Ultimate Parent: Kroger. **SIC:** 5411—
Grocery Stores.

★ 68800 ★ **Kroger Co.**
924 S. 2ndst
Louisville, KY 40203
(502)589-1025
Ultimate Parent: Kroger. **SIC:** 5411—
Grocery Stores.

★ 68801 ★ **Kroger Co.**
4023 Poplar Level Rd.
Louisville, KY 40213
(502)454-3914
Ultimate Parent: Kroger. **SIC:** 5411—
Grocery Stores.

★ 68802 ★ **Kroger Co.**
3126 Portland Ave.
Louisville, KY 40212
(502)776-0551
Ultimate Parent: Kroger. **SIC:** 5411—
Grocery Stores.

★ 68803 ★ **Kroger Co.**
10170 Linn Station Rd.
Louisville, KY 40223
Ultimate Parent: Kroger. **SIC:** 5411—
Grocery Stores.

★ 68804 ★ **Kroger Co.**
5533 New Cut Rd.
Louisville, KY 40214
(502)366-2302
Ultimate Parent: Kroger. **SIC:** 5411—
Grocery Stores.

★ 68805 ★ **Kroger Co.**
J Town Village Shopping Ctr.
Louisville, KY 40299
(502)267-9772
Ultimate Parent: Kroger. **SIC:** 5411—
Grocery Stores.

★ 68806 ★ **Kroger Co.**
9812 Linn Station Rd.
Louisville, KY 40223
(502)423-0943
Ultimate Parent: Kroger. **SIC:** 5411—
Grocery Stores.

★ 68807 ★ **Kroger Co.**
2209 Hikes Ln.
Louisville, KY 40218
(502)456-6622
Ultimate Parent: Kroger. **SIC:** 5411—
Grocery Stores.

★ 68808 ★ **Kroger Co.**
Holiday Manor Shopping Ctr.
Louisville, KY 40222
(502)426-6213
Ultimate Parent: Kroger. **SIC:** 5411—
Grocery Stores.

★ 68809 ★ **Kroger Co.**
1804 Dixie Hwy.
Louisville, KY 40210
(502)778-2371
Ultimate Parent: Kroger. **SIC:** 5411—
Grocery Stores.

★ 68810 ★ **Kroger Co.**
9901 Dixie Hwy.
Louisville, KY 40272
(502)935-7300
Ultimate Parent: Kroger. **SIC:** 5411—
Grocery Stores.

★ 68811 ★ **Kroger Co.**
3039 Breckinridge Ln.
Louisville, KY 40220
(502)452-6445
Ultimate Parent: Kroger. **SIC:** 5411—
Grocery Stores.

★ 68812 ★ **Kroger Co.**
7800 Crittenden Dr.
Louisville, KY 40213
(502)363-6618
Ultimate Parent: Kroger. **SIC:** 5411—
Grocery Stores.

★ 68813 ★ **Kroger Co.**
6706 Bardstownrd
Louisville, KY 40291
(502)239-2115
Ultimate Parent: Kroger. **SIC:** 5411—
Grocery Stores.

★ 68814 ★ **Kroger Co. Deli**
4023 Poplar Level Rd.
Louisville, KY 40213
(502)452-1867
Ultimate Parent: Kroger. **SIC:** 5411—
Grocery Stores.

★ 68815 ★ **Kroger Co. Deli**
10170 Linn Stationrd
Louisville, KY 40223
Ultimate Parent: Kroger. **SIC:** 5411—
Grocery Stores.

★ 68816 ★ **Kurfees Coatings Inc.**
201 E. Market St.
Louisville, KY 40202
Ultimate Parent: Servistar Corp. **SIC:**
2851—Paints & Allied Products.

★ 68817 ★ **Lane Bryant**
400 Louisville Galleria
Louisville, KY 40202
(502)582-3701
Ultimate Parent: Limited. **SIC:** 5621—
Women's Clothing Stores.

★ 68818 ★ **Lerner Shops**
517 River City Mall
Louisville, KY 40202
(502)587-0334
Ultimate Parent: Limited. **SIC:** 5621—
Women's Clothing Stores.

★ 68819 ★ **Lerner Shops**
7900 Shelbyville Rd.
Louisville, KY 40222
(502)426-5860
Ultimate Parent: Limited. **SIC:** 5621—
Women's Clothing Stores.

★ 68820 ★ **Lerner Shops**
Dixie Manor Shopping Ctr.
Louisville, KY 40258
(502)935-4526
Ultimate Parent: Limited. **SIC:** 5621—
Women's Clothing Stores.

★ 68821 ★ **Liberty National Bak & Trust Co. Of Kentucky**
2610 W. Broadway
Louisville, KY 40211-1333
(502)566-2231
Location Type: Branch office. **Ultimate Parent:** Liberty National Bancorp.

★ 68822 ★ **Liberty National Bancorp**
416 W. Jefferson St.
Louisville, KY 40202
(502)566-2000
Company Type: Headquarters. **Officer:**
Malcolm B. Chancey Jr. **Employee Count:**
2305. **Fortune Service 500:** Ranking 91.

★ 68823 ★ **Liberty National Bancorp, Inc.**
416 W. Jefferson St.
PO Box 32500
Louisville, KY 40232-2500
(502)566-2000 **Fax:** (502)566-2016
Location Type: Branch office. **Ultimate Parent:** Liberty National Bancorp.

★ 68824 ★ **Liberty National Bank & Braodcast Co. of Kentucky**
2450 Bardstown Rd.
Louisville, KY 40205-2123
(502)566-1867
Location Type: Branch office. **Officer:**
Bethany Hendrix, Assistant to the Chief.
Ultimate Parent: Liberty National Bancorp.

★ 68825 ★ **Liberty National Bank & Broadcast Co. of Kentucky**
970 Baxter Ave.
Louisville, KY 40204-2065
(502)566-1870
Location Type: Branch office. **Officer:**
Linda Rudloff. **Ultimate Parent:** Liberty
National Bancorp.

★ 68826 ★ **Liberty National Bank & Broadcast Co. of Kentucky**
6106 Dutchmans Lane
Louisville, KY 40205-3222
(502)566-2241
Location Type: Branch office. **Officer:** Lee
Ann Pipes, Assistant Vice President.
Ultimate Parent: Liberty National Bancorp.

★ 68827 ★ **Liberty National Bank & Broadcast Co. of Kentucky**
7403 Old 3rd St. Rd.
Louisville, KY 40214-4392
(502)566-2131
Location Type: Branch office. **Officer:** Pat
Magill, Vice President. **Ultimate Parent:**
Liberty National Bancorp.

★ 68828 ★ **Liberty National Bank & Broadcast Co. of Kentucky**
1718 Bardstown Rd.
Louisville, KY 40205-1295
(502)566-2161
Location Type: Branch office. **Officer:**
Walter Brown, Assistant Vice President.
Ultimate Parent: Liberty National Bancorp.

★ 68829 ★ **Liberty National Bank & Broadcast Co. of Kentucky**
3950 Kresge Way
Louisville, KY 40207-4603
(502)566-1926
Location Type: Branch office. **Officer:**
Brenda Jervis, Vice President. **Ultimate
Parent:** Liberty National Bancorp.

★ 68830 ★ **Liberty National Bank & Broadcast Co. of Kentucky**
2206 Brownsboro Rd.
Louisville, KY 40206-2141
(502)566-2741
Location Type: Branch office. **Officer:**
Andy Parker, Assistant to the Chief.
Ultimate Parent: Liberty National Bancorp.

★ 68831 ★   Liberty National Bank
& Broadcast Co. of Kentucky
1251 S. 4th St.
Louisville, KY 40203-3003
(502)566-2261
Location Type: Branch office. Officer: Troy
Edelen, Assistant Chairman of the Board.
Ultimate Parent: Liberty National Bancorp.

★ 68832 ★   Liberty National Bank
& Broadcast Co. of Kentucky
684 4th Ave.
Louisville, KY 40202
(502)566-1906
Location Type: Branch office. Officer:
Richard P. Watts II, Vice President.
Ultimate Parent: Liberty National Bancorp.

★ 68833 ★   Liberty National Bank
& Broadcast Co. of Kentucky
212 Holiday Manor
Louisville, KY 40222-6463
(502)566-2341
Location Type: Branch office. Officer:
Jane Beth McCarty, Vice President.
Ultimate Parent: Liberty National Bancorp.

★ 68834 ★   Liberty National Bank
& Broadcast Co. of Kentucky
3063 Beckinridge Lane
Louisville, KY 40220-2101
(502)566-2401
Location Type: Branch office. Officer:
Brenda Jervis, Assistant Vice President.
Ultimate Parent: Liberty National Bancorp.

★ 68835 ★   Liberty National Bank
& Broadcast Co. of Kentucky
4427 Cane Run Rd.
Louisville, KY 40216-4501
(502)566-2361
Location Type: Branch office. Officer:
Chris Conliffe, Assitant Vice President.
Ultimate Parent: Liberty National Bancorp.

★ 68836 ★   Liberty National Bank
& Broadcast Co. of Kentucky
9600 Lion Station Rd.
Louisville, KY 40222-5746
(502)566-2122
Location Type: Branch office. Officer: Jyl
Clark, Second Vice President & Regional
Manager. Ultimate Parent: Liberty National
Bancorp.

★ 68837 ★   Liberty National Bank
& Broadcast Co. of Kentucky
Stanctiford Field
Louisville, KY 40221
(502)566-2271
Location Type: Branch office. Officer: Lee
Snyder, Assistant Cashier. Ultimate Parent:
Liberty National Bancorp.

★ 68838 ★   Liberty National Bank
& Trust Co. of Kentucky
Standiford Field
Louisville, KY 40221
(502)566-2271
Location Type: Branch office. Ultimate
Parent: Liberty National Bancorp.

★ 68839 ★   Liberty National Bank
& Trust Co. of Kentucky
3950 Kresge Way
Louisville, KY 40207-4603
(502)566-1926
Location Type: Branch office. Ultimate
Parent: Liberty National Bancorp.

★ 68840 ★   Liberty National Bank
& Trust Co. of Kentucky
7403 Old 3rd St. Rd.
Louisville, KY 40214-4392
(502)566-2131
Location Type: Branch office. Ultimate
Parent: Liberty National Bancorp.

★ 68841 ★   Liberty National Bank
& Trust Co. of Kentucky
2206 Brownsboro Rd.
Louisville, KY 40206-2141
(502)566-2741
Location Type: Branch office. Ultimate
Parent: Liberty National Bancorp.

★ 68842 ★   Liberty National Bank
& Trust Co. of Kentucky
2450 Bardstown Rd.
Louisville, KY 40205-2123
(502)566-1867
Location Type: Branch office. Ultimate
Parent: Liberty National Bancorp.

★ 68843 ★   Liberty National Bank
& Trust Co. of Kentucky
684 4th Ave.
Louisville, KY 40202
(502)566-1906
Location Type: Branch office. Ultimate
Parent: Liberty National Bancorp.

★ 68844 ★   Liberty National Bank
& Trust Co. of Kentucky
4427 Cane Run Rd.
Louisville, KY 40216-4501
(502)566-2361
Location Type: Branch office. Ultimate
Parent: Liberty National Bancorp.

★ 68845 ★   Liberty National Bank
& Trust Co. of Kentucky
1251 S. 4th St.
Louisville, KY 40203-3003
(502)566-2261
Location Type: Branch office. Ultimate
Parent: Liberty National Bancorp.

★ 68846 ★   Liberty National Bank
& Trust Co. of Kentucky
6106 Dutchmans Ln.
Louisville, KY 40205-3222
(502)566-2241
Location Type: Branch office. Ultimate
Parent: Liberty National Bancorp.

★ 68847 ★   Liberty National Bank
& Trust Co. of Kentucky
1718 Bardstown Rd.
Louisville, KY 40205-1295
Location Type: Branch office. Ultimate
Parent: Liberty National Bancorp.

★ 68848 ★   Liberty National Bank
& Trust Co. of Kentucky
970 Baxter Ave.
Louisville, KY 40204-2065
(502)566-1870
Location Type: Branch office. Ultimate
Parent: Liberty National Bancorp.

★ 68849 ★   Liberty National Bank
& Trust Co. of Kentucky
212 Holiday Manor
Louisville, KY 40222-6463
(502)566-2341
Location Type: Branch office. Ultimate
Parent: Liberty National Bancorp.

★ 68850 ★   Liberty National Bank
& Trust Co. of Kentucky
3063 Breckinridge Ln.
Louisville, KY 40220-2101
Location Type: Branch office. Ultimate
Parent: Liberty National Bancorp.

★ 68851 ★   Liberty National Bank
& Trust Co. of Kentucky
5725 Preston Hwy.
Louisville, KY 40213
(502)566-2171
Location Type: Branch office. Ultimate
Parent: Liberty National Bancorp.

★ 68852 ★   Liberty National Bank
& Trust Co. of Kentucky
9600 Linn Station Rd.
Louisville, KY 40222-5746
(502)566-2122
Location Type: Branch office. Ultimate
Parent: Liberty National Bancorp.

★ 68853 ★   Liberty National Bank
& Trust Co. of Kentucky
4038 Poplar Level Rd.
Louisville, KY 40213-1524
(502)566-2431
Location Type: Branch office. Ultimate
Parent: Liberty National Bancorp.

★ 68854 ★   Liberty National Bank
& Trust Co. of Kentucky
601 S. Floyd St.
Louisville, KY 40202-1835
(502)566-1901
Location Type: Branch office. Ultimate
Parent: Liberty National Bancorp.

★ 68855 ★   Liberty National Bank
& Trust Co. of Kentucky
1481 S. 7th St.
Louisville, KY 40208-2201
(502)566-2201
Location Type: Branch office. Ultimate
Parent: Liberty National Bancorp.

★ 68856 ★   Liberty National Bank
& Trust Co. of Kentucky
1 Riverfront Plz.
Louisville, KY 40202-2948
(502)566-1625
Location Type: Branch office. Ultimate
Parent: Liberty National Bancorp.

★ 68857 ★   Liberty National Bank
& Trust Co. of Kentucky
465 4th Ave.
Louisville, KY 40202-2501
(502)566-2101
Location Type: Branch office. Ultimate
Parent: Liberty National Bancorp.

★ 68858 ★   Liberty National Bank
& Trust Co. of Kentucky
1224 S. Shelby St.
Louisville, KY 40203-2695
(502)566-2331
Location Type: Branch office. Ultimate
Parent: Liberty National Bancorp.

★ 68859 ★   Liberty National Bank
& Trust Co. of Kentucky
2610 W. Broadway
Louisville, KY 40211-1333
(502)566-2231
Location Type: Branch office. Ultimate
Parent: Liberty National Bancorp.

★ 68860 ★   Liberty National Bank
& Trust Co. of Kentucky
4825 S. 3rd. St.
Louisville, KY 40214-2152
(502)566-2321
Location Type: Branch office. Ultimate
Parent: Liberty National Bancorp.

★ 68861 ★   Liberty National Bank
& Trust Co. of Kentucky
2300 W. Market St.
Louisville, KY 40216
Location Type: Branch office. Ultimate
Parent: Liberty National Bancorp.

★ 68862 ★   Liberty National
Bankcorp., Inc. Holding Co.
PO Box 32500
Louisville, KY 40232-2500
(502)566-2000 Fax: (502)566-2016
Officer: Malcolm B. Chauncey Jr. Ultimate
Parent: Liberty National Bancorp.

★ 68863 ★   Liberty National
Bankcorp, Inc. Holding Co.
416 W. Jefferson St.
Louisville, KY 40202
(502)566-2000 Fax: (502)566-2016
Ultimate Parent: Liberty National Bancorp.

★ 68864 ★   Liberty National
Leasing Co.
416 W. Jefferson St.
Louisville, KY 40202
(502)566-2246
Ultimate Parent: Liberty National Bancorp.
SIC: 7359—Equipment Rental & Leasing
Nec.

★ 68865 ★   The Limited
400 Louisville Galleria 255
Louisville, KY 40202
(502)581-7301
Ultimate Parent: Limited. SIC: 5621—
Women's Clothing Stores.

★ 68866 ★   Limited the
260 Jefferson Mall
Louisville, KY 40219
(502)966-2153
Ultimate Parent: Limited. SIC: 5621—
Women's Clothing Stores.

★ 68867 ★   Limited the
99 Oxmoor Mall
Louisville, KY 40222
(502)426-5911
Ultimate Parent: Limited. SIC: 5621—
Women's Clothing Stores.

★ 68868 ★   Liqui Dri Foods Inc.
12650 Westport Rd.
Louisville, KY 40245
Ultimate Parent: Quaker Oates. SIC:
2051—Bread, Cake & Related Products.

★ 68869 ★   Liqui Dri Foods Inc.
4830 Jennings Ln.
Louisville, KY 40218
(502)968-4553
Ultimate Parent: Quaker Oates. SIC:
5141—Groceries—General Line.

★ 68870 ★   Logan Guildepath
200 Cable St.
Louisville, KY 40206
(502)587-1361 Fax: (502)587-2703
Company Type: Division. Ultimate Parent:
Figgie International. SIC: 3535—Conveyors
& Conveying Equipment.

★ 68871 ★   Louisville Ladder
Corp.
1163 Algonquin Pky.
Louisville, KY 40208-1619
(502)636-2811
Company Type: Subsidiary. Officer: David
L. Pringle, President. Ultimate Parent:
Emerson Electric Co. Inc. SIC: 2499—Wood
Products Nec; 3446—Architectural Metal
Work; 3499—Fabricated Metal Products
Nec; 3089—Plastics Products Nec.
Employee Count: 400. Sales: 24 M.

★ 68872 ★   Machinery
Acceptance Corp.
1400 S. 43rd St.
Louisville, KY 40211
(502)774-4441
Ultimate Parent: Stewart & Stevenson.
SIC: 5084—Industrial Machinery &
Equipment.

★ 68873 ★   Mackay/Gravure
Systems
339 E. Bloom St.
Louisville, KY 40217
Ultimate Parent: Bemis Co., Inc. SIC:
2796—Platemaking Services.

★ 68874 ★   Manpower Inc.
462 Meidinger Tower
Louisville, KY 40202
(502)583-1674
Ultimate Parent: Manpower, Inc. SIC:
7361—Employment Agencies.

★ 68875 ★   Marathon Oil
3920 Kramers Ln.
Louisville, KY 40216
(502)447-3550
Ultimate Parent: USX Corp. SIC: 2911—
Petroleum Refining; 5172—Petroleum
Products Nec.

★ 68876 ★   Marathon Oil
2100 Gardiner Ln.
Louisville, KY 40205
(502)451-9741
Ultimate Parent: USX Corp. SIC: 5172—
Petroleum Products Nec.

★ 68877 ★   Marathon Oil Co.
2100 Gardiner Ln.
Louisville, KY 40205
(502)451-9741
Ultimate Parent: USX Corp. SIC: 5172—
Petroleum Products Nec.

★ 68878 ★   Marathon Oil Co.
3920 Kramers Ln.
Louisville, KY 40216
(502)447-3550
Ultimate Parent: USX Corp. SIC: 2911—
Petroleum Refining; 5172—Petroleum
Products Nec.

★ 68879 ★   Marathon Petroleum
58309 PO Box
Louisville, KY 40268
(502)937-0121
Ultimate Parent: USX Corp. SIC: 1611—
Highway & Street Construction; 5541—
Gasoline Service Stations.

★ 68880 ★   Marathon Service
Station
3009 7th St.
Louisville, KY 40216
(502)631-5501
Ultimate Parent: USX Corp. SIC: 5541—
Gasoline Service Stations.

★ 68881 ★   Mary Kay Cosmetics
8500 3rd St.
Louisville, KY 40272
(502)366-0136
Ultimate Parent: Mary Kay Cosmetics. SIC:
5999—Miscellaneous Retail Stores Nec.

★ 68882 ★   McDonald's
Hamburgers
10219 Linn Station Rd.
Louisville, KY 40223
(502)425-8400
Ultimate Parent: McDonald's. SIC: 5812—
Eating Places.

★ **68883** ★ **Medtronic Inc.**
303 Hurstbourne Ln.
Louisville, KY 40222
(502)423-7725
Ultimate Parent: Medtronic Inc. **SIC:**
5047—Medical & Hospital Equipment.

★ **68884** ★ **Medtronic Inc.**
Lincoln
Louisville, KY 40202
(502)583-0536
Ultimate Parent: Medtronic Inc. **SIC:**
5049—Professional Equipment Nec.

★ **68885** ★ **Minnesota Mining&Mfg Co. Inc.**
10160 Linn Station Rd.
Louisville, KY 40223
(502)426-8960
Ultimate Parent: Minnesota Mining & Mfg.
SIC: 7389—Business Services Nec.

★ **68886** ★ **Mobil Oil**
1630 W. Hill St.
Louisville, KY 40210
(502)774-4411
Ultimate Parent: MNX. **SIC:** 2851—Paints
& Allied Products.

★ **68887** ★ **Mobil Oil Corp.**
1630 W. Hill St.
Louisville, KY 40210
(502)774-4411
Ultimate Parent: Mobil. **SIC:** 2851—Paints
& Allied Products.

★ **68888** ★ **Molex Inc.**
10002 Shelbyville Rd.
Louisville, KY 40223
(502)245-8336
Ultimate Parent: Molex. **SIC:** 5044—Office
Equipment.

★ **68889** ★ **Monfort Inc.**
1200 Story Ave.
Louisville, KY 40206
Ultimate Parent: Conagra. **SIC:** 2011—
Meat Packing Plants.

★ **68890** ★ **National City Bank,
Kentucky**
7600 National Tpke.
Louisville, KY 40214-4899
(502)581-5166
Company Type: Subsidiary. **Location
Type:** Branch office. **Officer:** Kathy
Showalter, Mgr. **Ultimate Parent:** National
City Corp. **SIC:** 6021—National Commercial
Banks.

★ **68891** ★ **National City Bank,
Kentucky**
3337 Newburg Rd.
Louisville, KY 40218-2449
(502)581-5242
Company Type: Subsidiary. **Location
Type:** Branch office. **Officer:** P. Stephan
Alvey, Mgr. **Ultimate Parent:** National City
Corp. **SIC:** 6021—National Commercial
Banks.

★ **68892** ★ **National City Bank,
Kentucky**
4640 Southern Pky.
Louisville, KY 40214-1486
(502)581-4400
Company Type: Subsidiary. **Location
Type:** Branch office. **Officer:** Mary Ann
Honeycutt, Mgr. **Ultimate Parent:** National
City Corp. **SIC:** 6021—National Commercial
Banks.

★ **68893** ★ **National City Bank,
Kentucky**
211 W. Oak
Ste. 172
Louisville, KY 40203-2800
(502)581-6378
Company Type: Subsidiary. **Location
Type:** Branch office. **Officer:** James
Hayden, Mgr. **Ultimate Parent:** National
City Corp. **SIC:** 6021—National Commercial
Banks.

★ **68894** ★ **National City Bank,
Kentucky**
111 W. Washington St.
Louisville, KY 40202-1354
(502)581-7877
Company Type: Subsidiary. **Location
Type:** Branch office. **Officer:** Kim Lyons,
Mgr. **Ultimate Parent:** National City Corp.
SIC: 6021—National Commercial Banks.

★ **68895** ★ **National City Bank,
Kentucky**
455 S. 4th St.
Louisville, KY 40202-2502
(502)581-5236
Company Type: Subsidiary. **Location
Type:** Branch office. **Officer:** Cathy L.
Denison, Mgr. **Ultimate Parent:** National
City Corp. **SIC:** 6021—National Commercial
Banks.

★ **68896** ★ **National City Bank,
Kentucky**
2503 Hurstbone Pky.
Louisville, KY 40220
(502)581-6373
Company Type: Subsidiary. **Location
Type:** Branch office. **Officer:** John Collopy,
Mgr. **Ultimate Parent:** National City Corp.
SIC: 6021—National Commercial Banks.

★ **68897** ★ **National City Bank,
Kentucky**
3405 W. Broadway
Louisville, KY 40211-2823
(502)581-5390
Company Type: Subsidiary. **Location
Type:** Branch office. **Officer:** Barnetta
Cosby, Mgr. **Ultimate Parent:** National City
Corp. **SIC:** 6021—National Commercial
Banks.

★ **68898** ★ **National City Bank,
Kentucky**
3100 S. 4th St.
Louisville, KY 40214-1797
(502)581-4232
Company Type: Subsidiary. **Location
Type:** Branch office. **Officer:** David Howard,
Mgr. **Ultimate Parent:** National City Corp.
SIC: 6021—National Commercial Banks.

★ **68899** ★ **National City Bank,
Kentucky**
2601 Bank St.
Louisville, KY 40212-2019
(502)581-5220
Company Type: Subsidiary. **Location
Type:** Branch office. **Officer:** Barbara
Marsh, Mgr. **Ultimate Parent:** National City
Corp. **SIC:** 6021—National Commercial
Banks.

★ **68900** ★ **National City Bank,
Kentucky**
701 W. Jefferson
Louisville, KY 40202-2742
(502)581-4040
Company Type: Subsidiary. **Location
Type:** Branch office. **Officer:** Bertha Jones,
Mgr. **Ultimate Parent:** National City Corp.
SIC: 6021—National Commercial Banks.

★ **68901** ★ **National City Bank,
Kentucky**
234 E. Gray St.
Louisville, KY 40202-1900
(502)581-6493
Company Type: Subsidiary. **Location
Type:** Branch office. **Officer:** Skip Banister,
Mgr. **Ultimate Parent:** National City Corp.
SIC: 6021—National Commercial Banks.

★ **68902** ★ **National City Bank,
Kentucky**
9900 Linn Station Rd.
Louisville, KY 40223-3809
(502)581-7710
Company Type: Subsidiary. **Location
Type:** Branch office. **Officer:** Pat Miller,
Mgr. **Ultimate Parent:** National City Corp.
SIC: 6021—National Commercial Banks.

★ **68903** ★ **National City Bank,
Kentucky**
3800 Brownsboro Rd.
Louisville, KY 40207-1822
(502)581-6640
Company Type: Subsidiary. **Location
Type:** Branch office. **Officer:** May Baker,
Mgr. **Ultimate Parent:** National City Corp.
SIC: 6021—National Commercial Banks.

★ **68904** ★ **National City Bank,
Kentucky**
5610 S. 3rd St.
Louisville, KY 40214-2616
(502)581-4140
Company Type: Subsidiary. **Location
Type:** Branch office. **Officer:** Linda Bohr,
Mgr. **Ultimate Parent:** National City Corp.
SIC: 6021—National Commercial Banks.

★ **68905** ★ **National City Bank,
Kentucky**
11202 S. Preston St.
Louisville, KY 40229-2860
(502)581-7650
Company Type: Subsidiary. **Location
Type:** Branch office. **Officer:** Sue Manning,
Mgr. **Ultimate Parent:** National City Corp.
SIC: 6021—National Commercial Banks.

★ **68906** ★ **National City Bank,
Kentucky**
329 Whittington Pky.
Louisville, KY 40222-4986
(502)581-4300
Company Type: Subsidiary. **Location
Type:** Branch office. **Officer:** Ann
Hommrich, Mgr. **Ultimate Parent:** National
City Corp. **SIC:** 6021—National Commercial
Banks.

★ **68907** ★ **National City Bank,
Kentucky**
3965 Taylorsville Rd.
Louisville, KY 40220-1494
(502)581-4430
Company Type: Subsidiary. **Location
Type:** Branch office. **Officer:** Regina Heun,
Mgr. **Ultimate Parent:** National City Corp.
SIC: 6021—National Commercial Banks.

★ **68908** ★ **National City Bank,
Kentucky**
3350 Hikes Ln.
Louisville, KY 40220
(502)581-6415
Company Type: Subsidiary. **Location
Type:** Branch office. **Officer:** Regina Heun,
Mgr. **Ultimate Parent:** National City Corp.
SIC: 6021—National Commercial Banks.

★ **68909** ★ **National City Bank,
Kentucky**
4957 Old Brownsboro Rd.
Louisville, KY 40222-6424
(502)581-4266
Company Type: Subsidiary. **Location
Type:** Branch office. **Officer:** Thomas A.
Ford, Mgr. **Ultimate Parent:** National City
Corp. **SIC:** 6021—National Commercial
Banks.

★ **68910** ★ **National City Bank,
Kentucky**
7603 Outer Loop
Louisville, KY 40228-1728
(502)581-5200
Company Type: Subsidiary. **Location
Type:** Branch office. **Officer:** Sandy G.
Parker, Mgr. **Ultimate Parent:** National City
Corp. **SIC:** 6021—National Commercial
Banks.

★ **68911** ★ **National City Bank,
Kentucky**
1200 S. 4th St.
Louisville, KY 40203-3095
(502)581-5430
Company Type: Subsidiary. **Location
Type:** Branch office. **Officer:** James
Hayden, Mgr. **Ultimate Parent:** National
City Corp. **SIC:** 6021—National Commercial
Banks.

★ **68912** ★ **National City Bank,
Kentucky**
3010 Bardstown Rd.
Louisville, KY 40205-3007
(502)581-5446
Company Type: Subsidiary. **Location
Type:** Branch office. **Officer:** Linda S.
Schaber, Mgr. **Ultimate Parent:** National
City Corp. **SIC:** 6021—National Commercial
Banks.

★ **68913** ★ **National City Bank,
Kentucky**
801 Eastern Pky.
Louisville, KY 40217-2230
(502)581-5410
Company Type: Subsidiary. **Location
Type:** Branch office. **Officer:** Mary Ann
Coomer, Mgr. **Ultimate Parent:** National
City Corp. **SIC:** 6021—National Commercial
Banks.

★ **68914** ★ **National City Bank,
Kentucky**
601 S. 4th St.
Louisville, KY 40202-2403
(502)581-4370
Company Type: Subsidiary. **Location
Type:** Branch office. **Officer:** D.J. Sturgeon,
Mgr. **Ultimate Parent:** National City Corp.
SIC: 6021—National Commercial Banks.

★ **68915** ★ **National City Bank,
Kentucky**
4098 Dutchmans Ln.
Louisville, KY 40207-4704
(502)581-4060
Company Type: Subsidiary. **Location
Type:** Branch office. **Officer:** Karen Morris,
Mgr. **Ultimate Parent:** National City Corp.
SIC: 6021—National Commercial Banks.

★ **68916** ★ **National City Bank,
Kentucky**
535 E. Broadway
Louisville, KY 40202-1707
(502)581-4120
Company Type: Subsidiary. **Location
Type:** Branch office. **Officer:** Bob Roth,
Mgr. **Ultimate Parent:** National City Corp.
SIC: 6021—National Commercial Banks.

★ **68917** ★ **National City Bank,
Kentucky**
1301 Bardstown Rd.
Louisville, KY 40204-1319
(502)581-7560
Company Type: Subsidiary. **Location
Type:** Branch office. **Officer:** Fiona Blocker,
Mgr. **Ultimate Parent:** National City Corp.
SIC: 6021—National Commercial Banks.

★ **68918** ★ **National City Bank,
Kentucky**
2123 Bardstown Rd.
Louisville, KY 40205-1915
(502)581-5333
Company Type: Subsidiary. **Location
Type:** Branch office. **Officer:** John Durham,
Mgr. **Ultimate Parent:** National City Corp.
SIC: 6021—National Commercial Banks.

★ **68919** ★ **National City Bank,
Kentucky**
2790 Brownsboro Rd.
Louisville, KY 40206-1293
(502)581-4237
Company Type: Subsidiary. **Location
Type:** Branch office. **Officer:** Rex Minrath,
Mgr. **Ultimate Parent:** National City Corp.
SIC: 6021—National Commercial Banks.

★ **68920** ★ **National City Bank,
Kentucky**
1313 Lyndon Ln.
Louisville, KY 40222-7351
(502)581-7555
Company Type: Subsidiary. **Location
Type:** Branch office. **Officer:** Natalie White,
Mgr. **Ultimate Parent:** National City Corp.
SIC: 6021—National Commercial Banks.

★ **68921** ★ **National City Bank,
Kentucky**
3447 Breckenridge Ln.
Louisville, KY 40220-3101
(502)581-6600
Company Type: Subsidiary. **Location
Type:** Branch office. **Ultimate Parent:**
National City Corp. **SIC:** 6021—National
Commercial Banks.

★ **68922** ★ **National City Bank,
Kentucky**
200 Brookside Dr.
Louisville, KY 40223-1277
(502)581-4118
Company Type: Subsidiary. **Location
Type:** Branch office. **Officer:** Mary Jo Hays,
Mgr. **Ultimate Parent:** National City Corp.
SIC: 6021—National Commercial Banks.

★ **68923** ★ **National City Bank,
Kentucky**
3001 S. Preston St.
Louisville, KY 40217-1716
(502)581-6675
Company Type: Subsidiary. **Location
Type:** Branch office. **Officer:** Todd
Ethington, Mgr. **Ultimate Parent:** National
City Corp. **SIC:** 6021—National Commercial
Banks.

★ **68924** ★ **National City Bank,
Kentucky**
14103 Shelbyville Rd.
Louisville, KY 40245-4108
(502)581-6976
Company Type: Subsidiary. **Location
Type:** Branch office. **Officer:** Richard
Herde, Mgr. **Ultimate Parent:** National City
Corp. **SIC:** 6021—National Commercial
Banks.

★ 68925 ★ National City Bank, Kentucky
4501 Outer Loop
Louisville, KY 40219
(502)581-4344
Company Type: Subsidiary. Location Type: Branch office. Ultimate Parent: National City Corp. SIC: 6021—National Commercial Banks.

★ 68926 ★ National City Bank, Kentucky
5523 New Cut Rd.
Louisville, KY 40214-4329
(502)581-7734
Company Type: Subsidiary. Location Type: Branch office. Officer: Tom Lauer, Mgr. Ultimate Parent: National City Corp. SIC: 6021—National Commercial Banks.

★ 68927 ★ National City Bank, Kentucky
101 S. 5th St.
Louisville, KY 40202
(502)581-4200 Fax: (502)581-7909
Company Type: Subsidiary. Location Type: Branch office. Officer: Morton Boyd, Chairman & CEO. Ultimate Parent: National City Corp. SIC: 6021—National Commercial Banks.

★ 68928 ★ NCR Corp.
2120 Newburg Rd.
Louisville, KY 40205
(502)456-4500
Officer: Ben Fomby, Manager. Ultimate Parent: AT&T. SIC: 2761—Manifold Business Forms.

★ 68929 ★ New York Life Louisville General Office
Southeastern Agencies
455 S. 4th St., Ste. 1250
Louisville, KY 40202
(502)589-3640 Fax: (502)269-2330
Officer: James L. Gragg, General Manager. Ultimate Parent: New York Life.

★ 68930 ★ New York Life Louisville Group Claims Office
Western Group Claims Region
PO Box 1090
Louisville, KY 40202
(800)388-5186 Fax: (502)585-5636
Officer: Andrea Brewer, Assistant Manager. Ultimate Parent: New York Life.

★ 68931 ★ New York Life Louisville Group Claims Office
Western Group Claims Region
1st National Tower, Ste. 1910
101 S. 5th St.
Louisville, KY 40202
(800)388-5186 Fax: (502)585-5636
Officer: Andrea Brewer, Assistant Manager. Ultimate Parent: New York Life.

★ 68932 ★ Northwestern Mutual Life Inc.
100 E. Liberty St.
Louisville, KY 40202
(502)589-2044
Ultimate Parent: Northwestern Mutual Life. SIC: 6411—Insurance Agents, Brokers & Service.

★ 68933 ★ Olympic Homecare Products Co.
6804 Enterprise Dr.
Louisville, KY 40214
Ultimate Parent: PPG Industries Inc. SIC: 2851—Paints & Allied Products.

★ 68934 ★ Otis Elevator Co.
1901 Production Dr.
Louisville, KY 40299
(502)491-3636
Ultimate Parent: United Technologies. SIC: 3534—Elevators & Moving Stairways; 5084—Industrial Machinery & Equipment.

★ 68935 ★ Pappagallo
93 Oxmoor Mall
Louisville, KY 40222
(502)426-0450
Ultimate Parent: United States Shoe. SIC: 5651—Family Clothing Stores.

★ 68936 ★ Payless Shoe Source
10115 Dixie Hwy.
Louisville, KY 40272
(502)935-0266
Ultimate Parent: May Department Stores. SIC: 5661—Shoe Stores.

★ 68937 ★ Payless Shoe Source
Shelbyville Rd.
Louisville, KY 40207
(502)893-8998
Ultimate Parent: May Department Stores. SIC: 5661—Shoe Stores.

★ 68938 ★ Payless Shoe Source
3671 Bashford Manor Mall
Louisville, KY 40218
(502)454-6141
Ultimate Parent: May Department Stores. SIC: 5661—Shoe Stores.

★ 68939 ★ Payless Shoe Source
5352 Dixie Hwy.
Louisville, KY 40216
(502)447-3420
Ultimate Parent: May Department Stores. SIC: 5661—Shoe Stores.

★ 68940 ★ Payless Shoe Source
3928 7th St.
Louisville, KY 40216
(502)447-9778
Ultimate Parent: May Department Stores. SIC: 5661—Shoe Stores.

★ 68941 ★ Payless Shoe Source
521 S. 4th Ave.
Louisville, KY 40202
(502)581-0098
Ultimate Parent: May Department Stores. SIC: 5661—Shoe Stores.

★ 68942 ★ Payless Shoesource
521 S. 4th Ave.
Louisville, KY 40202
(502)581-0098
Ultimate Parent: May Department Stores. SIC: 5661—Shoe Stores.

★ 68943 ★ Peoples Bank
11998 Preston Hwy.
Louisville, KY 40229
(502)957-2196
Ultimate Parent: People's Bank. SIC: 6022—State Commercial Banks.

★ 68944 ★ People's Bank
369 W. Main St.
Louisville, KY 40202
(502)589-9064
Ultimate Parent: People's Bank. SIC: 6022—State Commercial Banks.

★ 68945 ★ Pepsi-Cola Co.
4008 Crittenden Dr.
Louisville, KY 40209
(502)368-2581
Ultimate Parent: Pepsico. SIC: 2086—Bottled & Canned Soft Drinks.

★ 68946 ★ Petite Sophisticate
12 Oxmoor Mall
Louisville, KY 40222
(502)425-5797
Ultimate Parent: United States Shoe. SIC: 5651—Family Clothing Stores.

★ 68947 ★ Philip Morris Inc.
1930 Maple St.
Louisville, KY 40210
(502)566-1234
Ultimate Parent: Philip Morris. SIC: 5993—Tobacco Stores & Stands.

★ 68948 ★ Philip Morris USA
MS Complex
1930 W. Maple St.
Louisville, KY 40201
Company Type: Division. Ultimate Parent: Philip Morris. SIC: 2111—Cigarettes.

★ 68949 ★ PNC Bank Corp.-Kentucky
PO Box 33000
Louisville, KY 40202-2823
Location Type: Branch office. Ultimate Parent: PNC Bank Corp. SIC: 6021—National Commercial Banks.

★ 68950 ★ PNC Bank Corp.-Kentucky
500 W. Jefferson
Louisville, KY 40296
(502)581-2100
Location Type: Branch office. Officer: Michael N. Harrell, President. Ultimate Parent: PNC Bank Corp. SIC: 6021—National Commercial Banks.

★ 68951 ★ PNC Bank Kentucky Inc.
2500 Lime Kiln
Louisville, KY 40222
(502)681-4340
Location Type: Branch office. Ultimate Parent: PNC Bank Corp. SIC: 6021—National Commercial Banks.

★ 68952 ★ PNC Bank Kentucky Inc.
500 W. Jefferson St.
Louisville, KY 40202-2823
(502)581-2100 Fax: (502)581-2831 Telex: 204280
Location Type: Branch office. Officer: Michael N Harreld, President. Ultimate Parent: PNC Bank Corp. SIC: 6021—National Commercial Banks.

★ 68953 ★ PNC Bank Kentucky Inc.
11530 Shelbyville rd.
Louisville, KY 40243-1308
(502)681-4000
Location Type: Branch office. Officer: Michele Crum, Manager. Ultimate Parent: PNC Bank Corp. SIC: 6021—National Commercial Banks.

★ 68954 ★ PNC Bank Kentucky Inc.
2901 Bardstown Rd.
Louisville, KY 40205-3017
(502)581-4993
Location Type: Branch office. Ultimate Parent: PNC Bank Corp. SIC: 6021—National Commercial Banks.

★ 68955 ★ PNC Bank Kentucky Inc.
Heyburn Bldg.
Louisville, KY 40202-2130
(502)581-2370
Location Type: Branch office. Ultimate Parent: PNC Bank Corp. SIC: 6021—National Commercial Banks.

★ 68956 ★ PNC Bank Kentucky Inc.
1250 Bardstown Rd.
Louisville, KY 40204-1333
(502)581-3166
Location Type: Branch office. Ultimate Parent: PNC Bank Corp. SIC: 6021—National Commercial Banks.

★ 68957 ★ PNC Bank of Kentucky Inc.
4305 Cane Run Rd.
Louisville, KY 40216-4567
(502)581-3306
Location Type: Branch office. Ultimate Parent: PNC Bank Corp. SIC: 6021—National Commercial Banks.

★ 68958 ★ PNC Bank Kentucky Inc.
1106 Lyndon Ln.
Louisville, KY 40222-4318
(502)581-3276
Location Type: Branch office. Ultimate Parent: PNC Bank Corp. SIC: 6021—National Commercial Banks.

★ 68959 ★ PNC Bank Kentucky Inc.
820 eastern Pky.
Louisville, KY 40217-2297
(502)581-2026
Location Type: Branch office. Ultimate Parent: PNC Bank Corp. SIC: 6021—National Commercial Banks.

★ 68960 ★ PNC Bank Kentucky Inc.
4169 Shelbyville Rd.
Louisville, KY 40207-3202
(502)681-4003
Location Type: Branch office. Officer: Steve Ostrader, Manager. Ultimate Parent: PNC Bank Corp. SIC: 6021—National Commercial Banks.

★ 68961 ★ PNC Bank Kentucky Inc.
2292 Bardstown Rd.
Louisville, KY 40205-1972
(502)581-3330
Location Type: Branch office. Ultimate Parent: PNC Bank Corp. SIC: 6021—National Commercial Banks.

★ 68962 ★ PNC Bank Kentucky Inc.
101 Miedinger
Louisville, KY 40202-3405
(502)581-3010
Location Type: Branch office. Ultimate Parent: PNC Bank Corp. SIC: 6021—National Commercial Banks.

★ 68963 ★ PNc Bank Kentucky Inc.
5021 S. 3rd St.
Louisville, KY 40214-2207
(502)581-2166
Location Type: Branch office. Ultimate Parent: PNC Bank Corp. SIC: 6021—National Commercial Banks.

★ 68964 ★ PNC Bank Kentucky Inc.
3910 Taylorsville
Louisville, KY 40220-1493
(502)581-2126
Location Type: Branch office. Ultimate Parent: PNC Bank Corp. SIC: 6021—National Commercial Banks.

★ 68965 ★ PNC Bank Kentucky Inc.
250 E. Liberty
Louisville, KY 40202-1530
(502)581-3126
Location Type: Branch office. Ultimate Parent: PNC Bank Corp. SIC: 6021—National Commercial Banks.

★ 68966 ★ PNC Bank Kentucky Inc.
624 S. Floyd
Louisville, KY 40202-1828
(502)581-2336
Location Type: Branch office. Ultimate Parent: PNC Bank Corp. SIC: 6021—National Commercial Banks.

★ 68967 ★ PNC Bank Kentucky Inc.
7900 Shelbyville Rd.
Louisville, KY 40222-5499
(502)581-3118
Location Type: Branch office. Ultimate Parent: PNC Bank Corp. SIC: 6021—National Commercial Banks.

★ 68968 ★ PNC Bank Kentucky Inc.
6215 Old Sheperdsville Rd.
Louisville, KY 40228-1025
(502)581-2673
Location Type: Branch office. Ultimate Parent: PNC Bank Corp. SIC: 6021—National Commercial Banks.

★ 68969 ★ PNC Bank Kentucky Inc.
9700 Linn Station Rd.
Louisville, KY 40223-3805
Location Type: Branch office. Ultimate Parent: PNC Bank Corp. SIC: 6021—National Commercial Banks.

★ 68970 ★ PNC Bank Kentucky Inc.
9220 Westport Rd.
Louisville, KY 40242-3295
(502)581-2006
Location Type: Branch office. Ultimate Parent: PNC Bank Corp. SIC: 6021—National Commercial Banks.

★ 68971 ★ PNC Bank Kentucky Inc.
5500 Preston Hwy.
Louisville, KY 40219-1302
(502)581-3336
Location Type: Branch office. Ultimate Parent: PNC Bank Corp. SIC: 6021—National Commercial Banks.

★ 68972 ★ PNC Bank Kentucky Inc.
4740 Dixie Hwy.
Louisville, KY 40216-2656
(502)581-2306
Location Type: Branch office. Ultimate Parent: PNC Bank Corp. SIC: 6021—National Commercial Banks.

★ 68973 ★ **PNC Bank Kentucky Inc.**
214 Amy Ave.
Louisville, KY 40212-2598
(502)581-2226
Location Type: Branch office. **Ultimate Parent:** PNC Bank Corp. **SIC:** 6021—National Commercial Banks.

★ 68974 ★ **PNC Bank Kentucky Inc.**
1900 S. 3rd
Louisville, KY 40208-1811
(502)581-2001
Location Type: Branch office. **Ultimate Parent:** PNC Bank Corp. **SIC:** 6021—National Commercial Banks.

★ 68975 ★ **PNC Bank Kentucky Inc.**
3439 Taylor Blvd.
Louisville, KY 40215-2646
(502)581-3320
Location Type: Branch office. **Ultimate Parent:** PNC Bank Corp. **SIC:** 6021—National Commercial Banks.

★ 68976 ★ **PNC Bank Kentucky, Inc.**
2710 W. Broadway
Louisville, KY 40211
(502)581-4637
Location Type: Branch office. **Ultimate Parent:** PNC Bank Corp. **SIC:** 6021—National Commercial Banks.

★ 68977 ★ **PNC Bank Kentucky Inc.**
3340 Newsburg Rd.
Louisville, KY 40218-2498
(502)581-3216
Location Type: Branch office. **Ultimate Parent:** PNC Bank Corp. **SIC:** 6021—National Commercial Banks.

★ 68978 ★ **PNC Bank Kentucky, Inc.**
4810 Brownsboro Rd.
Louisville, KY 40207-2392
(502)581-3326
Location Type: Branch office. **Ultimate Parent:** PNC Bank Corp. **SIC:** 6021—National Commercial Banks.

★ 68979 ★ **PNC Bank Kentucky, Inc.**
12715 Shelbyville Rd.
Louisville, KY 40243-1417
(502)581-3006
Location Type: Branch office. **Ultimate Parent:** PNC Bank Corp. **SIC:** 6021—National Commercial Banks.

★ 68980 ★ **PNCBank Kentucky Inc.**
8000 Shelbyville Rd.
Louisville, KY 40222-5418
(502)581-3060
Location Type: Branch office. **Ultimate Parent:** PNC Bank Corp. **SIC:** 6021—National Commercial Banks.

★ 68981 ★ **Ppg Architectural Finishes**
6804 Enterprise Dr.
Louisville, KY 40214
Ultimate Parent: PPG Industries Inc. **SIC:** 2851—Paints & Allied Products.

★ 68982 ★ **Protein Tech. International International**
2441 S. Floyd St.
Louisville, KY 40217
Ultimate Parent: Ralston Purina. **SIC:** 2891—Adhesives & Sealants.

★ 68983 ★ **Protein Technologies Intern.**
2441 South Floyd St.
Louisville, KY 40217
Ultimate Parent: Ralston Purina. **SIC:** 2891—Adhesives & Sealants.

★ 68984 ★ **Protein Technologies International**
2441 S. Floyd St.
Louisville, KY 40217
(502)637-4761
Ultimate Parent: Ralston Purina. **SIC:** 2075—Soybean Oil Mills.

★ 68985 ★ **Pyro Chem Inc.**
4016 Brownsboro Rd.
Louisville, KY 40207
(502)897-0476
Ultimate Parent: Borg Warner Automotive. **SIC:** 4953—Refuse Systems; 5084—Industrial Machinery & Equipment.

★ 68986 ★ **Reliance Insurance Co.**
9500 Williamsburg Plz.
Louisville, KY 40222
(502)426-8080
Ultimate Parent: Reliance Group Holdings. **SIC:** 6411—Insurance Agents, Brokers & Service.

★ 68987 ★ **Reynolds Metals Co.**
4101 Camp Ground Rd.
Louisville, KY 40211
(502)775-4284
Location Type: Plant. **Officer:** Dave Zorn, Manager. **Ultimate Parent:** Reynolds Metals Co. **SIC:** 3354—Aluminum Extruded Products.

★ 68988 ★ **Reynolds Metals Co.**
4301 Produce Rd.
Louisville, KY 40218
(502)962-4052
Location Type: Plant. **Officer:** Charles Carter, Manager. **Ultimate Parent:** Reynolds Metals Co. **SIC:** 3354—Aluminum Extruded Products.

★ 68989 ★ **Reynolds Metals Co.**
2827 Hale Ave.
Louisville, KY 40211
(502)772-3616
Officer: Charles Cox, Manager. **Ultimate Parent:** Reynolds Metals Co. **SIC:** 2671—Paper Coated & Laminated—Packaging.

★ 68990 ★ **Reynolds Metals Co. Plant 15**
4301 Produce Rd.
Louisville, KY 40218
Ultimate Parent: Reynolds Metals Co. **SIC:** 3354—Aluminum Extruded Products.

★ 68991 ★ **Reynolds Metals Co. Plant 1**
2827 Hale Ave.
Louisville, KY 40211-1260
Ultimate Parent: Reynolds Metals Co. **SIC:** 3497—Metal Foil & Leaf; 3353—Aluminum Sheet, Plate & Foil; 3469—Metal Stampings Nec; 2672—Coated & Laminated Paper Nec.

★ 68992 ★ **Reynolds Metals Co. Plant 3**
4101 Camp Ground Rd.
Louisville, KY 40211
Ultimate Parent: Reynolds Metals Co. **SIC:** 3399—Primary Metal Products Nec.

★ 68993 ★ **Reynolds Metals Co. Plant 3**
4101 Camp Ground Rd.
Louisville, KY 40211
Ultimate Parent: Reynolds Metals Co. **SIC:** 3399—Primary Metal Products Nec.

★ 68994 ★ **Reynolds & Reynolds**
10401 Linn Station Rd.
Louisville, KY 40223
(502)426-5120
Ultimate Parent: Reynolds & Reynolds. **SIC:** 5046—Commercial Equipment Nec; 5112—Stationery & Office Supplies.

★ 68995 ★ **Rhone-Poulenc Inc. Plant 2700**
1515 S. 11th St.
Louisville, KY 40210
Ultimate Parent: Rhone-Poulenc Rorer. **SIC:** 2821—Plastics Materials & Resins; 2851—Paints & Allied Products.

★ 68996 ★ **Rockwell International Corp.**
Plastics Div.
4004 Collins Ln.
Louisville, KY 40223
Company Type: Division. **Ultimate Parent:** Rockwell International Corp. **SIC:** 3714—Motor Vehicle Parts & Accessories.

★ 68997 ★ **Rockwell International Corp.**
R.I. Plastics Div. Louisville Plastics Plant
4004 Collins Ln.
Louisville, KY 40216
Company Type: Division. **Location Type:** Plant. **Ultimate Parent:** Rockwell International Corp. **SIC:** 3714—Motor Vehicle Parts & Accessories; 3800—Instruments & Related Products.

★ 68998 ★ **Rohm & Haas Inc. Kentucky**
4300 Camp Ground Rd.
Louisville, KY 40216
Ultimate Parent: Rohm & Haas. **SIC:** 2821—Plastics Materials & Resins.

★ 68999 ★ **Rohm & Haas Kentucky Inc.**
4300 Camp Ground Rd.
Louisville, KY 40216
(502)449-5200
Ultimate Parent: Rohm & Haas. **SIC:** 2819—Industrial Inorganic Chemicals Nec; 2821—Plastics Materials & Resins; 2899—Chemical Preparations Nec.

★ 69000 ★ **Safety-Kleen Corp.**
751 Grade Ln.
Louisville, KY 40213
(502)368-0322
Ultimate Parent: Safety-Kleen. **SIC:** 4953—Refuse Systems; 7542—Car Washes.

★ 69001 ★ **Seagram Joseph E & Sons**
12700 Shelbyville Rd.
Louisville, KY 40243
(502)244-2404
Ultimate Parent: J.E. Seagram & Sons, Inc. **SIC:** 8711—Engineering Services.

★ 69002 ★ **Service Merchandise**
5025 Shelbyville Rd.
Louisville, KY 40207
(502)897-9421
Ultimate Parent: Service Merchandise Co., Inc. **SIC:** 5399—Miscellaneous General Merchandise Store; 5944—Jewelry Stores.

★ 69003 ★ **Service Merchandise**
Dixie Manor Shopping Ctr.
Louisville, KY 40258
(502)935-2300
Ultimate Parent: Service Merchandise Co., Inc. **SIC:** 5399—Miscellaneous General Merchandise Store.

★ 69004 ★ **Shell Oil**
2200 Arthur St.
Louisville, KY 40217
(502)635-2132
Ultimate Parent: Shell Oil Co. **SIC:** 5541—Gasoline Service Stations.

★ 69005 ★ **Shell Oil**
1501 Fulton St.
Louisville, KY 40206
(502)589-5330
Ultimate Parent: Shell Oil Co. **SIC:** 5812—Eating Places.

★ 69006 ★ **Shell Self Service Station**
3245 W. Muhammad Ali Blvd.
Louisville, KY 40212
(502)774-1163
Ultimate Parent: Shell Oil Co. **SIC:** 5541—Gasoline Service Stations.

★ 69007 ★ **Shell Self Service Station**
2200 W. Broadway St.
Louisville, KY 40211
(502)775-8151
Ultimate Parent: Shell Oil Co. **SIC:** 5541—Gasoline Service Stations.

★ 69008 ★ **Shell Self Service Station**
4422 Dixie Hwy.
Louisville, KY 40216
(502)448-1210
Ultimate Parent: Shell Oil Co. **SIC:** 5541—Gasoline Service Stations.

★ 69009 ★ **Southern Gravure Service Inc.**
2823 S. Floyd St.
Louisville, KY 40213
Ultimate Parent: Reynolds Metals Co. **SIC:** 2796—Platemaking Services.

★ 69010 ★ **Stone Container Corp.**
8004 Ashbottom Rd.
Louisville, KY 40213
(502)361-1371
Officer: Guy Link, Manager. **Ultimate Parent:** Stone Container Corp. **SIC:** 2673—Bags—Plastics, Laminated & Coated; 2674—Bags—Uncoated Paper & Multiwall.

★ 69011 ★ **Superamerica Design & Const**
4125 Algonquin Pky.
Louisville, KY 40211
(502)772-3839
Ultimate Parent: Ashland Oil. **SIC:** 1541—Industrial Buildings & Warehouses.

★ 69012 ★ **Systems Engineering**
1033 Linn Station Rd.
Louisville, KY 40223-3816
(502)425-5601
Ultimate Parent: Ball Corp. **SIC:** 7371—Computer Programming Services.

★ 69013 ★ **Target**
4172 Westport Rd.
Louisville, KY 40207
(502)897-2576
Ultimate Parent: Dayton Hudson. **SIC:** 5311—Department Stores.

★ 69014 ★ **Target**
3629 Bashford Manor Mall
Louisville, KY 40218
(502)459-9565
Ultimate Parent: Dayton Hudson. **SIC:** 5311—Department Stores.

★ 69015 ★ **Target**
7100 Preston Hwy.
Louisville, KY 40219
(502)968-5365
Ultimate Parent: Dayton Hudson. **SIC:** 5311—Department Stores.

★ 69016 ★ **Target Stores**
3629 Bashford Manor Mall
Louisville, KY 40218
(502)459-9565
Ultimate Parent: Dayton Hudson. **SIC:** 5311—Department Stores.

★ 69017 ★ **Target Stores**
7100 Preston Hwy.
Louisville, KY 40219
(502)968-5365
Ultimate Parent: Dayton Hudson. **SIC:** 5311—Department Stores.

★ 69018 ★ **Target Stores**
4172 Westport Rd.
Louisville, KY 40207
(502)897-2576
Ultimate Parent: Dayton Hudson. **SIC:** 5311—Department Stores.

★ 69019 ★ **Texaco Inc.**
4510 Bells Ln.
Louisville, KY 40211
(502)774-8611
Ultimate Parent: Texaco. **SIC:** 5172—Petroleum Products Nec.

★ 69020 ★ **Textron Financial Corp.**
1939 Goldsmith Ln.
Louisville, KY 40218
(502)451-7402
Ultimate Parent: Textron. **SIC:** 6062—State Credit Unions.

★ 69021 ★ **Thoroughbred Plastics Corp.**
11601 Electron Dr.
Louisville, KY 40299-3861
(502)267-1234
Location Type: Branch office. **Officer:** Patrick Hendricks. **Ultimate Parent:** Brown-Forman. **SIC:** 3089—Plastics Products Nec; 3085—Plastics Bottles; 5085—Industrial Supplies; 5162—Plastics Materials & Basic Shapes.

★ 69022 ★ **Toys R US**
4900 Shelbyville Rd.
Louisville, KY 40207
(502)896-1243
Ultimate Parent: Toys "R" US. **SIC:** 5945—Hobby, Toy & Game Shops.

★ **69023** ★ **Trailways Bus Lines**
213 W. Liberty St.
Louisville, KY 40202
(502)584-5336
Ultimate Parent: Greyhound Lines Inc. **SIC:**
4131—Intercity & Rural Bus Transportation;
4111—Local & Suburban Transit; 4142—
Bus Charter Service Except Local.

★ **69024** ★ **Trans World Airlines Inc.**
Airport Terminal
Louisville, KY 40213
(502)368-2561
Ultimate Parent: Trans World Airlines. **SIC:**
4512—Air Transportation—Scheduled.

★ **69025** ★ **Transamerica Occidental Life Inc.**
10101 Linn Station Rd.
Louisville, KY 40223
(502)425-8670
Ultimate Parent: Transamerica Occidental
Life Insurance. **SIC:** 6411—Insurance
Agents, Brokers & Service.

★ **69026** ★ **United Parcel Service**
8001 Ashbottom Rd.
Louisville, KY 40213
(502)363-3511
Ultimate Parent: United Parcel Service of
America. **SIC:** 4212—Local Trucking
Without Storage; 4215—Courier Services
Except by Air.

★ **69027** ★ **United Parcel Service**
11101 Bluegrass Pky.
Louisville, KY 40299
(502)267-1007
Ultimate Parent: United Parcel Service of
America. **SIC:** 4215—Courier Services
Except by Air.

★ **69028** ★ **United Parcel Service**
200 High Rise Dr.
Louisville, KY 40213
(502)962-3101
Ultimate Parent: United Parcel Service of
America. **SIC:** 4215—Courier Services
Except by Air.

★ **69029** ★ **United Parcel Service**
201 Louisville Air Park
Louisville, KY 40213
(502)363-7304
Ultimate Parent: United Parcel Service of
America. **SIC:** 4513—Air Courier Services.

★ **69030** ★ **US Fidelity & Guaranty Insurance**
9911 Shelbyville Rd.
Louisville, KY 40223
(502)429-7000
Ultimate Parent: USF&G Corp. **SIC:**
6411—Insurance Agents, Brokers &
Service.

★ **69031** ★ **US Gypsum Co.**
400 Sherburn Ln.
Louisville, KY 40207
(502)897-2529
Ultimate Parent: USG Corp. **SIC:** 5039—
Construction Materials Nec.

★ **69032** ★ **Valspar Corp.**
1630 W. Hill St.
Louisville, KY 40210
Ultimate Parent: Valspar Corp. **SIC:**
2851—Paints & Allied Products.

★ **69033** ★ **Victoria's Secret**
54 Oxmoor Mall
Louisville, KY 40222
(502)425-6343
Ultimate Parent: Limited. **SIC:** 5621—
Women's Clothing Stores.

★ **69034** ★ **Wal-Mart Stores Inc.**
10445 Dixie Hwy.
Louisville, KY 40272
(502)935-3221
Ultimate Parent: Wal-Mart Stores, Inc. **SIC:**
5399—Miscellaneous General Merchandise
Store.

★ **69035** ★ **Wal-Mart Stores Inc.**
11308 Preston Hwy.
Louisville, KY 40229
(502)968-6800
Ultimate Parent: Wal-Mart Stores, Inc. **SIC:**
5311—Department Stores.

★ **69036** ★ **Warren Petroleum Co.**
7320 La Grange Rd.
Louisville, KY 40222
(502)426-1346
Ultimate Parent: Chevron Corp. **SIC:**
1311—Crude Petroleum & Natural Gas;
5984—Liquefied Petroleum Gas Dealers.

★ **69037** ★ **Western Auto Supply Co.**
5328 S. 3rd St.
Louisville, KY 40214
(502)448-9494
Ultimate Parent: Sears Roebuck & Co.
SIC: 5531—Automobile & Home Supply
Stores.

★ **69038** ★ **Western Auto Supply Co.**
5705 Preston Hwy.
Louisville, KY 40219
(502)969-2311
Ultimate Parent: Sears Roebuck & Co.
SIC: 5531—Automobile & Home Supply
Stores.

★ **69039** ★ **Western Auto Supply Co.**
Algonguin Shopping Ctr.
Louisville, KY 40211
(502)589-3531
Ultimate Parent: Sears Roebuck & Co.
SIC: 5531—Automobile & Home Supply
Stores.

★ **69040** ★ **Wheeling Corrugating Co. Inc.**
1424 S. 15th St.
Louisville, KY 40210
(502)634-0541
Ultimate Parent: Wheeling-Pittsburgh Steel
Corp. **SIC:** 3443—Fabricated Plate Work—
Boiler Shops; 5051—Metals Service Centers
& Offices.

★ **69041** ★ **Winmar Co. Inc.**
2301 Citizens Plz.
Louisville, KY 40202
(502)426-3000
Ultimate Parent: Safeco. **SIC:** 5311—
Department Stores.

★ **69042** ★ **Winn-Dixie Louisville Inc.**
720 Locust Ln.
Louisville, KY 40213
(502)634-4761
Ultimate Parent: Winn-Dixie Stores, Inc.
SIC: 5149—Groceries & Related Products
Nec; 5411—Grocery Stores.

★ **69043** ★ **Wisconsin Tissue Mills**
2210 Meadow Dr.
Louisville, KY 40218
(502)459-2983
Ultimate Parent: Chesapeake. **SIC:** 2621—
Paper Mills.

★ **69044** ★ **Zep Manufacturing Co.**
4602 Southern Pky.
Louisville, KY 40214
(502)363-1270
Ultimate Parent: National Service
Industries. **SIC:** 5087—Service
Establishment Equipment.

★ **69045** ★ **Vulcan Materials Co.**
4200 S. Park Rd.
Louisville., KY 40219
(502)969-9341
Ultimate Parent: Vulcan Materials Co. **SIC:**
1422—Crushed & Broken Limestone.

Madisonville

★ **69046** ★ **Agrico Chemical Co. Inc.**
Anton
Madisonville, KY 42431
(502)821-2607
Ultimate Parent: Freeport-McMoran. **SIC:**
5261—Retail Nurseries & Garden Stores.

★ **69047** ★ **Dr. Pepper Bottling Co.**
308 W. Ctr. St.
Madisonville, KY 42431
(502)821-5537
Officer: Leslie Hoover, President. **Ultimate**
Parent: Dr. Pepper/Seven-Up. **SIC:** 2086—
Bottled & Canned Soft Drinks.

★ **69048** ★ **Farmers Bank & Trust Co.**
77 N. Main St.
Madisonville, KY 42431
(502)821-5150
Ultimate Parent: Dauphin Deposit Corp.
SIC: 6022—State Commercial Banks.

★ **69049** ★ **Farmers Bank & Trust Co.**
Main
Madisonville, KY 42431
(502)825-2527
Ultimate Parent: Dauphin Deposit Corp.
SIC: 6022—State Commercial Banks.

★ **69050** ★ **Farmers Bank & Trust Co.**
Briarwood Shopping Ctr.
Madisonville, KY 42431
(502)821-8005
Ultimate Parent: Dauphin Deposit Corp.
SIC: 6022—State Commercial Banks.

★ **69051** ★ **GE Aircraft Engines**
3050 Nebo Rd.
Madisonville, KY 42431
Ultimate Parent: General Electric. **SIC:**
3724—Aircraft Engines & Engine Parts.

★ **69052** ★ **General Electric Co.**
3050 Nebo Rd.
Madisonville, KY 42431
(502)825-6400
Officer: Ted Torbeck, Manager. **Ultimate**
Parent: General Electric. **SIC:** 3728—
Aircraft Parts & Equipment Nec.

★ **69053** ★ **Goodyear Tire & Rubber Co.**
Hwy. 41 N
Madisonville, KY 42431
Ultimate Parent: Goodyear Tire & Rubber.
SIC: 3011—Tires & Inner Tubes.

★ **69054** ★ **Goodyear Tire & Rubber Co.**
Hwy. 41 N., PO Box 967
Madisonville, KY 42431-0967
Ultimate Parent: Goodyear Tire & Rubber.
SIC: 3011—Tires & Inner Tubes.

★ **69055** ★ **Greyhound Bus Lines**
Federal
Madisonville, KY 42431
(502)821-3086
Ultimate Parent: Greyhound Lines Inc. **SIC:**
4111—Local & Suburban Transit; 4131—
Intercity & Rural Bus Transportation; 4142—
Bus Charter Service Except Local.

★ **69056** ★ **GTE Kentucky Carbide**
Island Ford Rd.
Madisonville, KY 42431
Ultimate Parent: GTE. **SIC:** 3339—Primary
Nonferrous Metals Nec.

★ **69057** ★ **GTE Prods. Corp. Kentucky Carbide**
1535 Island Ford Rd.
Madisonville, KY 42431
Ultimate Parent: GTE. **SIC:** 3499—
Fabricated Metal Products Nec.

★ **69058** ★ **GTE Valenite Corp.**
U.S. 41 N.
Madisonville, KY 42431
Ultimate Parent: GTE. **SIC:** 3532—Mining
Machinery.

★ **69059** ★ **GTE Valenite Corp.**
U. S. 41 North
Madisonville, KY 42431
Ultimate Parent: GTE. **SIC:** 3532—Mining
Machinery.

★ **69060** ★ **Kroger Co.**
Briarwood Shopping Ctr.
Madisonville, KY 42431
(502)821-3241
Ultimate Parent: Kroger. **SIC:** 5411—
Grocery Stores.

★ **69061** ★ **Libert National of Madisonville**
315 S. Main St.
Madisonville, KY 42431-2559
(502)824-3076
Company Type: Subsidiary. **Location**
Type: Branch office. **Officer:** Mary Ann
Cansler, Mgr. **Ultimate Parent:** Liberty

National Bancorp. **SIC:** 6021—National
Commercial Banks.

★ **69062** ★ **Liberty National Bank of Madisonville**
Parkway Plz. Mall
Madisonville, KY 42431-2775
(502)824-3074
Company Type: Subsidiary. **Location**
Type: Branch office. **Officer:** Michelle
Johnson, Mgr. **Ultimate Parent:** Liberty
National Bancorp. **SIC:** 6021—National
Commercial Banks.

★ **69063** ★ **Liberty National Bank of Madisonville**
Chelsa Dr.
Madisonville, KY 42431
(502)824-3073
Company Type: Subsidiary. **Location**
Type: Branch office. **Officer:** Sue Jones,
Mgr. **Ultimate Parent:** Liberty National
Bancorp. **SIC:** 6021—National Commercial
Banks.

★ **69064** ★ **Liberty National Bank of Madisonville**
665 E. Ctr. St.
Madisonville, KY 42431-2141
(502)824-3071
Company Type: Subsidiary. **Location**
Type: Branch office. **Officer:** Steve
Lanham, Mgr. **Ultimate Parent:** Liberty
National Bancorp. **SIC:** 6021—National
Commercial Banks.

★ **69065** ★ **Liberty National Bank of Madisonville**
1 S. Main St.
PO Drawer B
Madisonville, KY 42431-0419
(502)821-6075
Company Type: Subsidiary. **Location**
Type: Branch office. **Officer:** Mark E. Eastin
III, Chairman, President, & CEO. **Ultimate**
Parent: Liberty National Bancorp. **SIC:**
6021—National Commercial Banks.

★ **69066** ★ **McDonald's Hamburgers**
1400 N. Main St.
Madisonville, KY 42431
(502)821-8221
Ultimate Parent: McDonald's. **SIC:** 5812—
Eating Places.

★ **69067** ★ **Peoples Bank & Trust Co.**
149 S. Main St.
Madisonville, KY 42431
(502)821-1661
Ultimate Parent: People's Bank. **SIC:**
6022—State Commercial Banks.

★ **69068** ★ **Peoples Bank & Trust Co.**
E Ctr.
Madisonville, KY 42431
(502)821-4021
Ultimate Parent: People's Bank. **SIC:**
6022—State Commercial Banks.

★ **69069** ★ **People's Bank & Trust Co.**
US 41 N
Madisonville, KY 42431
(502)821-0221
Ultimate Parent: People's Bank. **SIC:**
6022—State Commercial Banks.

★ **69070** ★ **Ryder Truck Rental-Oneway**
480 E. Ctr. St.
Madisonville, KY 42431
(502)825-3755
Ultimate Parent: Ryder System. **SIC:**
7359—Equipment Rental & Leasing Nec.

★ **69071** ★ **Speed Queen Co.**
2840 Nebo Rd.
Madisonville, KY 42431
Ultimate Parent: Raytheon Co. **SIC:**
3582—Commercial Laundry Equipment.

★ **69072** ★ **Speed Queen Co.**
Hwy. 41 a NW
Madisonville, KY 42431
Ultimate Parent: Raytheon Co. **SIC:**
3582—Commercial Laundry Equipment.

★ 69073 ★   Wal-Mart Stores Inc.
Madisonville Ctr.
Madisonville, KY 42431
(502)821-1520
Ultimate Parent: Wal-Mart Stores, Inc. SIC:
5311—Department Stores.

★ 69074 ★   York International
Corp.
1000 Island Ford Rd.
Madisonville, KY 42431
(502)821-0042
Officer: John Warren, Manager. Ultimate
Parent: York International Corp. SIC:
3561—Pumps & Pumping Equipment;
3585—Refrigeration & Heating Equipment.

Manfield

★ 69075 ★   United Technologies
Auto
3566 US Hwy. 60 E
Manfield, KY 42437
(502)389-0200
Officer: Fran Maurier, Manager. Ultimate
Parent: United Technologies. SIC: 3714—
Motor Vehicle Parts & Accessories.

Marion

★ 69076 ★   Farmers Bank & Trust
Co.
201 S. Main St.
Marion, KY 42064
(502)965-3106
Ultimate Parent: Dauphin Deposit Corp.
SIC: 6022—State Commercial Banks;
6036—Savings Institutions Except Federal.

Mayfield

★ 69077 ★   Ingersoll-Rand
Centrifugal Compressor Div.
Hwy. 45 South
Mayfield, KY 42066
Company Type: Division. Ultimate Parent:
Ingersoll-Rand. SIC: 3563—Air & Gas
Compressors.

★ 69078 ★   Ingersoll-Rand Co.
Hwy. 45 S.
Mayfield, KY 42066
Ultimate Parent: Ingersoll-Rand. SIC:
3563—Air & Gas Compressors.

★ 69079 ★   McDonald's
Hamburgers
1006 Cuba Rd.
Mayfield, KY 42066
(502)247-4780
Ultimate Parent: McDonald's. SIC: 5812—
Eating Places.

★ 69080 ★   Ryder Truck Rental-
Oneway
W Farthing
Mayfield, KY 42066
(502)247-9770
Ultimate Parent: Ryder System. SIC:
7359—Equipment Rental & Leasing Nec.

★ 69081 ★   Seaboard Farms of
KY Inc.
Macedonia Rd.
Mayfield, KY 42066
Ultimate Parent: Seaboard Corp. SIC:
2048—Prepared Feeds Nec.

★ 69082 ★   Wal-Mart Stores Inc.
Mayfield Shopping Plz.
Mayfield, KY 42066
(502)247-8073
Ultimate Parent: Wal-Mart Stores, Inc. SIC:
5311—Variety Stores.

Maysville

★ 69083 ★   Browning
Manufacturing
Main & 2nd St.
Maysville, KY 41056-0687
Company Type: Division. Ultimate Parent:
Emerson Electric Co. Inc. SIC: 3566—
Speed Changers, Drives & Gears.

★ 69084 ★   Browning Mfg. Plant 1
Main & 2nd Sts.
Maysville, KY 41056-0687
Ultimate Parent: Emerson Electric Co. Inc.
SIC: 3566—Speed Changers, Drives &
Gears.

★ 69085 ★   Browning Mfg. Plant 3
526 Clark St.
Maysville, KY 41056-0687
Ultimate Parent: Emerson Electric Co. Inc.
SIC: 3566—Speed Changers, Drives &
Gears.

★ 69086 ★   Browning Mfg. Plant 2
Forest Ave.
Maysville, KY 41056-0687
Ultimate Parent: Emerson Electric Co. Inc.
SIC: 3566—Speed Changers, Drives &
Gears.

★ 69087 ★   Coast to Coast
Hardware
Bluegrass Ctr.
Maysville, KY 41056
(606)564-4279
Ultimate Parent: Servistar Corp. SIC:
5251—Hardware Stores.

★ 69088 ★   Kroger Co.
US 68
Maysville, KY 41056
(606)564-5548
Ultimate Parent: Kroger. SIC: 5411—
Grocery Stores.

★ 69089 ★   Red Kap Ind.
321 E. 3rd St.
Maysville, KY 41056
(502)755-4803
Officer: Swayne Shelton, Manager.
Ultimate Parent: VF Corp. SIC: 2339—
Women's/Misses' Outerwear Nec.

★ 69090 ★   Security Bank & Trust
Co.
Maysville, KY 41056
(606)564-3304
Ultimate Parent: Synovus Financial Corp.
SIC: 6022—State Commercial Banks.

★ 69091 ★   Superamerica
1126 Forest Ave.
Maysville, KY 41056
(606)564-4427
Ultimate Parent: Ashland Oil. SIC: 5411—
Grocery Stores.

★ 69092 ★   Vickers
743 Arnold Ave.
Maysville, KY 41056
(606)564-9341
Officer: Cliff Fryman, Manager. Ultimate
Parent: Trinova Corp. SIC: 3621—Motors &
Generators.

Melbourne

★ 69093 ★   Agrico Chemical Co.
Hwy. 8
Melbourne, KY 41059
(606)441-5904
Ultimate Parent: Freeport-McMoran. SIC:
3861—Photographic Equipment & Supplies.

Middlesboro

★ 69094 ★   Greyhound Bus Lines
525 N. 15th St.
Middlesboro, KY 40965
(606)248-1510
Ultimate Parent: Greyhound Lines Inc. SIC:
4131—Intercity & Rural Bus Transportation;
4111—Local & Suburban Transit; 4142—
Bus Charter Service Except Local.

Middletown

★ 69095 ★   National City Bank,
Kentucky
12009 Shelbyville Rd.
Middletown, KY 40243-1042
(502)581-5296
Company Type: Subsidiary. Location
Type: Branch office. Officer: Mary Jo Hays,
Mgr. Ultimate Parent: National City Corp.
SIC: 6021—National Commercial Banks.

Monticello

★ 69096 ★   Belden Wire & Cable
Intersection Hwy. 90 Bypass & 92E
Monticello, KY 42633
Ultimate Parent: Cooper Industries. SIC:
3399—Primary Metal Products Nec; 3577—
Computer Peripheral Equipment Nec;
3644—Noncurrent-Carrying Wiring Devices.

★ 69097 ★   Belden Wire & Cable
West Hwy. 92
Monticello, KY 42633
Ultimate Parent: Cooper Industries. SIC:
3357—Nonferrous Wiredrawing & Insulating.

★ 69098 ★   Coast to Coast of
Monticell
Rural Route 5
Monticello, KY 42633
(606)348-6594
Ultimate Parent: Servistar Corp. SIC:
5621—Women's Clothing Stores.

★ 69099 ★   Cooper Industries Inc.
Belden Div.
Intersection Hwy. 90 Bypass & 92 E.
Monticello, KY 42633
Company Type: Division. Ultimate Parent:
Cooper Industries. SIC: 3577—Computer
Peripheral Equipment Nec; 3643—
Current-Carrying Wiring Devices; 3644—
Noncurrent-Carrying Wiring Devices.

★ 69100 ★   Mutual Federal S & L
Association
Town
Monticello, KY 42633
(606)348-8461
Ultimate Parent: Southern National Corp.
SIC: 6022—State Commercial Banks.

Morehead

★ 69101 ★   Greyhound Bus Lines
160 E. Main St.
Morehead, KY 40351
(606)784-5507
Ultimate Parent: Greyhound Lines Inc. SIC:
4111—Local & Suburban Transit; 4131—
Intercity & Rural Bus Transportation; 4142—
Bus Charter Service Except Local.

★ 69102 ★   People's Bank
PO Box 1030
Morehead, KY 40351
(606)784-4158
Ultimate Parent: People's Bank. SIC:
6099—Functions Related to Deposit
Banking.

★ 69103 ★   Peoples Bank of
Morehead
Rural Route 32
Morehead, KY 40351
(606)783-1521
Ultimate Parent: People's Bank. SIC:
6022—State Commercial Banks.

Morganfield

★ 69104 ★   Genuine Parts Co.
Rayloc Div.
Hwy. 60 E.
Morganfield, KY 42437
Company Type: Division. Ultimate Parent:
Genuine Parts. SIC: 3999—Manufacturing
Industries Nec.

★ 69105 ★   Rayloc
Hwy. 60 East
Morganfield, KY 42437
Ultimate Parent: Genuine Parts. SIC:
3999—Manufacturing Industries Nec.

★ 69106 ★   Rayloc
3710 US Hwy. 60 E
Morganfield, KY 42437
(502)389-2364
Officer: Charles Allen, Manager. Ultimate
Parent: Genuine Parts. SIC: 2759—
Commercial Printing Nec; 3714—Motor
Vehicle Parts & Accessories.

★ 69107 ★   Sonoco Products Co.
Hwy. 60 N
Morganfield, KY 42437
(502)389-2501
Ultimate Parent: Sonoco Products. SIC:
5943—Stationery Stores.

★ 69108 ★   Texaco Inc.
Hwy. 56 E
Morganfield, KY 42437
(502)389-3780
Ultimate Parent: Texaco. SIC: 5171—
Petroleum Bulk Stations & Terminals.

★ 69109 ★   Wal-Mart Stores Inc.
Us 60 E
Morganfield, KY 42437
(502)389-1828
Ultimate Parent: Wal-Mart Stores, Inc. SIC:
5311—Department Stores.

Morgantown

★ 69110 ★   Morgantown Plastics
Co.
825 Rochester St.
Morgantown, KY 42261
Ultimate Parent: Masco. SIC: 3088—
Plastics Plumbing Fixtures.

Mortons Gap

★ 69111 ★   Liberty National Bank
of Madisonville
108 Main St.
Mortons Gap, KY 42440
(502)824-3072
Company Type: Subsidiary. Location
Type: Branch office. Officer: Bruce Arnold,
Mgr. Ultimate Parent: Liberty National
Bancorp. SIC: 6021—National Commercial
Banks.

Mount Eden

★ 69112 ★   People's Bank
Mount Eden, KY 40046
(502)477-8417
Ultimate Parent: People's Bank. SIC:
6029—Commercial Banks Nec.

Mount Sterling

★ 69113 ★   A. O. Smith Electrical
Prods. Co.
2001 Owingsville Rd.
Mount Sterling, KY 40353
Ultimate Parent: A. O. Smith. SIC: 3621—
Motors & Generators.

★ 69114 ★   A.O. Smith Electrical
Products Co.
2001 Owingsville Rd.
Mount Sterling, KY 40353
Ultimate Parent: A. O. Smith. SIC: 3621—
Motors & Generators.

★ 69115 ★   Kitchen Aid Inc.
Levee Rd.
Mount Sterling, KY 40353
Ultimate Parent: Whirlpool Corp. SIC:
3639—Household Appliances Nec.

★ 69116 ★   Kitchenaid Inc.
Levee Rd.
Mount Sterling, KY 40353
Ultimate Parent: Whirlpool Corp. SIC:
3639—Household Appliances Nec.

Mt Sterling

★ 69117 ★   Greyhound Bus Lines
439 N. Maysville St.
Mt Sterling, KY 40353
(606)498-9496
Ultimate Parent: Greyhound Lines Inc. SIC:
4111—Local & Suburban Transit; 4142—
Bus Charter Service Except Local; 4131—
Intercity & Rural Bus Transportation.

Mt Washington

★ 69118 ★   Rite Aid Discount
Pharmacy
Hwy. 44
Mt Washington, KY 40047
(502)538-8275
Ultimate Parent: Rite Aid. SIC: 5912—Drug
Stores & Proprietary Stores.

Murray

★ 69119 ★   Briggs & Stratton
Corp.
110 Main St.
Murray, KY 42071-2147
(502)759-1680
Officer: Jennifer Vaughn. Ultimate Parent:
Briggs & Stratton. SIC: 3519—Internal
Combustion Engines Nec.

★ 69120 ★   Briggs & Stratton
Corp.
110 Main St.
Murray, KY 42071
(502)759-1680
Officer: Jack Bykowski, Manager. Ultimate
Parent: Briggs & Stratton. SIC: 3519—
Internal Combustion Engines Nec.

★ 69121 ★   **Briggs & Stratton Corp.**
110 Main St.
Murray, KY 42071
(502)759-1680
Officer: Jack Bykowski, Manager. **Ultimate Parent:** Briggs & Stratton. **SIC:** 3519—Internal Combustion Engines Nec.

★ 69122 ★   **Coast to Coast Hardware**
Central Shopping Ctr.
Murray, KY 42071
(502)753-8604
Ultimate Parent: Servistar Corp. **SIC:** 5231—Paint, Glass & Wallpaper Stores; 5261—Retail Nurseries & Garden Stores.

★ 69123 ★   **Fisher-Price**
Rte. 2 E. Penny Rd.
Murray, KY 42071
Ultimate Parent: Quaker Oats. **SIC:** 3000—Rubber & Miscellaneous Plastics Products.

★ 69124 ★   **Fisher-Price**
Rte. 2 East Penny Rd.
Murray, KY 42071
Ultimate Parent: Quaker Oats. **SIC:** 3944—Games, Toys & Children's Vehicles.

★ 69125 ★   **Fisher-Price**
Rte. 2
Murray, KY 42071
Ultimate Parent: Quaker Oats. **SIC:** 3000—Rubber & Miscellaneous Plastics Products.

★ 69126 ★   **Kroger Co.**
650 Central Ctr.
Murray, KY 42071
(502)759-4641
Ultimate Parent: Kroger. **SIC:** 5411—Grocery Stores.

★ 69127 ★   **Kroger Co.**
650 N. 12th St.
Murray, KY 42071
(502)759-4642
Ultimate Parent: Kroger. **SIC:** 5411—Grocery Stores.

★ 69128 ★   **Peoples Bank of Murray**
500 Main St.
Murray, KY 42071
(502)753-3231
Ultimate Parent: People's Bank. **SIC:** 6022—State Commercial Banks.

★ 69129 ★   **Ryan Milk Co.**
100 E. Chestnut St.
Murray, KY 42071-1175
Ultimate Parent: Dean Foods. **SIC:** 2026—Fluid Milk.

★ 69130 ★   **Ryan Milk Co.**
E. Chestnut
Murray, KY 42071
Ultimate Parent: Dean Foods. **SIC:** 2026—Fluid Milk.

★ 69131 ★   **Ryan Milk Co.**
100 Chestnut St.
Murray, KY 42071
(502)753-3012
Officer: Caroline Greenfield, Executive Director. **Ultimate Parent:** Dean Foods. **SIC:** 2026—Fluid Milk.

★ 69132 ★   **Ryan Milk Co.**
PO Box 1175
Murray, KY 42071
(502)753-3012 **Fax:** (502)753-9474
Company Type: Subsidiary. **Officer:** Dan Green, President. **Ultimate Parent:** Dean Foods.

★ 69133 ★   **Ryan Milk Co. Inc.**
100 Chestnut St.
Murray, KY 42071-2100
(502)753-3012
Company Type: Subsidiary. **Officer:** Daniel E. Green, Pr. Tr. **Ultimate Parent:** Dean Foods. **SIC:** 2026—Fluid Milk; 5143—Dairy Products Except Dried or Canned. **Employee Count:** 158. **Sales:** 27.1 M.

★ 69134 ★   **Texaco Bulk Plant**
Old Concord Rd.
Murray, KY 42071
(502)753-2321
Ultimate Parent: Texaco. **SIC:** 5172—Petroleum Products Nec.

★ 69135 ★   **Wal-Mart Stores Inc.**
Central Shopping Ctr.
Murray, KY 42071
(502)759-9995
Ultimate Parent: Wal-Mart Stores, Inc. **SIC:** 5311—Department Stores.

Newport

★ 69136 ★   **Agrico Chemical Co. Inc.**
524 Licking Pike
Newport, KY 41071
(606)581-1545
Ultimate Parent: Freeport-McMoran. **SIC:** 4226—Special Warehousing & Storage Nec.

★ 69137 ★   **Kroger Co.**
2385 Alexandria Pike
Newport, KY 41076
(606)781-2325
Ultimate Parent: Kroger. **SIC:** 5411—Grocery Stores.

★ 69138 ★   **Kroger Co.**
53 6th St.
Newport, KY 41073
(606)491-4210
Ultimate Parent: Kroger. **SIC:** 5411—Grocery Stores.

★ 69139 ★   **Payless Shoe Source**
1715 Monmouth St.
Newport, KY 41071
(606)431-5667
Ultimate Parent: May Department Stores. **SIC:** 5661—Shoe Stores.

★ 69140 ★   **PNC Bank Northern Kentucky, NA**
1 Carothers Rd.
Newport, KY 41071-2415
(606)261-3500
Location Type: Branch office. **Officer:** Paul W. Scheing, Assistant Vice President. **Ultimate Parent:** PNC Bank Corp. **SIC:** 6021—National Commercial Banks.

★ 69141 ★   **Ryder Truck Rental-Oneway**
17 Carothers Rd.
Newport, KY 41071
(606)261-1397
Ultimate Parent: Ryder System. **SIC:** 7513—Truck Rental & Leasing Without Drivers.

★ 69142 ★   **Shell Self Service Station**
136 6th Ave.
Newport, KY 41074
(606)491-0829
Ultimate Parent: Shell Oil Co. **SIC:** 5541—Gasoline Service Stations.

★ 69143 ★   **Star Bank NA, Kentucky**
39 W. 10th
Newport, KY 41071-1444
(606)261-4622
Location Type: Branch office. **Officer:** Betty Monell, Manager. **Ultimate Parent:** Star Banc Corp. **SIC:** 6021—National Commercial Banks.

★ 69144 ★   **Star Bank NA, Kentucky**
810 Monmouth St.
Newport, KY 41071-1891
(606)261-5922
Location Type: Branch office. **Officer:** James Simpson, Senior Vice President. **Ultimate Parent:** Star Banc Corp. **SIC:** 6021—National Commercial Banks.

★ 69145 ★   **Star-Kist Foods, Inc.**
1 Riverfront Pl.
Newport, KY 41071
(606)655-5700 **Fax:** (606)655-5550
Company Type: Subsidiary. **Officer:** W. R. Johnson, President & CEO. **Ultimate Parent:** H.J. Heinz. **SIC:** 2013—Sausages & Other Prepared Meats; 2091—Canned & Cured Fish & Seafoods; 2092—Fresh or Frozen Prepared Fish.

★ 69146 ★   **Superamerica**
402 E. 10th St.
Newport, KY 41071
(606)431-2664
Ultimate Parent: Ashland Oil. **SIC:** 5541—Gasoline Service Stations.

Nicholasville

★ 69147 ★   **Adcom Wire Co.**
220 Stephens Dr. PO Box 250
Nicholasville, KY 40356
Ultimate Parent: Leggett & Platt Inc. **SIC:** 3315—Steel Wire & Related Products.

★ 69148 ★   **Adcom Wire Co.**
End of Stephens Dr. PO Box 250
Nicholasville, KY 40356
Ultimate Parent: Leggett & Platt Inc. **SIC:** 3315—Steel Wire & Related Products.

★ 69149 ★   **Adcom Wire Co.**
Stephens Dr.
PO Box 250
Nicholasville, KY 40340-0250
Ultimate Parent: Leggett & Platt Inc. **SIC:** 3315—Steel Wire & Related Products.

★ 69150 ★   **Adcom Wire Co.**
Stephen's Dr., PO Box 156
Nicholasville, KY 40356
Ultimate Parent: Leggett & Platt Inc. **SIC:** 3315—Steel Wire & Related Products.

★ 69151 ★   **Adcom Wire Co.**
Stephans Drive, PO Box 156
Nicholasville, KY 40356
Ultimate Parent: Leggett & Platt Inc. **SIC:** 3315—Steel Wire & Related Products.

★ 69152 ★   **Kroger Co.**
Kimberlysq
Nicholasville, KY 40356
(606)887-1201
Ultimate Parent: Kroger. **SIC:** 5411—Grocery Stores.

★ 69153 ★   **Wal-Mart Stores Inc.**
1021 N. Main St.
Nicholasville, KY 40356
(606)885-9600
Ultimate Parent: Wal-Mart Stores, Inc. **SIC:** 5311—Department Stores.

Okolona

★ 69154 ★   **National City Bank, Kentucky**
6511 Preston Hwy.
Okolona, KY 40219
(502)581-5406
Company Type: Subsidiary. **Location Type:** Branch office. **Officer:** Teri Smith, Mgr. **Ultimate Parent:** National City Corp. **SIC:** 6021—National Commercial Banks.

★ 69155 ★   **National City Bank, Kentucky**
8500 Preston Hwy.
Okolona, KY 40219-5399
(502)581-4110
Company Type: Subsidiary. **Location Type:** Branch office. **Officer:** Linda L. Zacha, Mgr. **Ultimate Parent:** National City Corp. **SIC:** 6021—National Commercial Banks.

★ 69156 ★   **PNC Bank Kentucky, Inc.**
4257 Outer Loop
Okolona, KY 40219-3850
(502)581-2276
Location Type: Branch office. **Ultimate Parent:** PNC Bank Corp. **SIC:** 6021—National Commercial Banks.

★ 69157 ★   **PNC Bank Kentucky, Inc.**
7600 Old Shepardsville Rd.
Okolona, KY 40219-2963
(502)681-4006
Location Type: Branch office. **Officer:** Mary Matheny, Manager. **Ultimate Parent:** PNC Bank Corp. **SIC:** 6021—National Commercial Banks.

Olive Hill

★ 69158 ★   **Peoples Bank**
Us 60 E
Olive Hill, KY 41164
(606)286-4451
Ultimate Parent: People's Bank. **SIC:** 6022—State Commercial Banks.

★ 69159 ★   **Rite Aid Discount Pharmacy**
Rural Route 2
Olive Hill, KY 41164
(606)286-2929
Ultimate Parent: Rite Aid. **SIC:** 5912—Drug Stores & Proprietary Stores.

Owensboro

★ 69160 ★   **Automotive Service Equipmen**
919 Pettit Rd.
Owensboro, KY 42301
(502)685-5237
Ultimate Parent: FMC.

★ 69161 ★   **Casual Corner**
5000 Frederica St.
Owensboro, KY 42301
(502)686-7969
Ultimate Parent: United States Shoe. **SIC:** 5651—Family Clothing Stores.

★ 69162 ★   **Central Bank & Trust Co.**
425 E. 18th St.
Owensboro, KY 42303
(502)686-3570
Company Type: Subsidiary. **Location Type:** Branch office. **Officer:** Kevin Carrico, Mgr. **Ultimate Parent:** National City Corp. **SIC:** 6021—National Commercial Banks.

★ 69163 ★   **Central Bank & Trust Co.**
5000 Frederica St.
Owensboro, KY 42301
(502)686-3580
Company Type: Subsidiary. **Location Type:** Branch office. **Officer:** Marilyn Kittinger, Mgr. **Ultimate Parent:** National City Corp. **SIC:** 6021—National Commercial Banks.

★ 69164 ★   **Central Bank & Trust Co.**
3030 E. 4th St.
Owensboro, KY 42303
(502)686-3540
Company Type: Subsidiary. **Location Type:** Branch office. **Officer:** David Zachary, Mgr. **Ultimate Parent:** National City Corp. **SIC:** 6021—National Commercial Banks.

★ 69165 ★   **Central Bank & Trust Co.**
2451 Frederica St.
Owensboro, KY 42301-5437
(502)686-3550
Company Type: Subsidiary. **Location Type:** Branch office. **Officer:** Terry McEnroe, Mgr. **Ultimate Parent:** National City Corp. **SIC:** 6021—National Commercial Banks.

★ 69166 ★   **Central Bank & Trust Co.**
3001 Alvey Pk. W
Owensboro, KY 42303
(502)686-3530
Company Type: Subsidiary. **Location Type:** Branch office. **Officer:** Nancy Taylor, Mgr. **Ultimate Parent:** National City Corp. **SIC:** 6021—National Commercial Banks.

★ 69167 ★   **Central Bank & Trust Co.**
2715 W. Parrish Ave.
Owensboro, KY 42301-2685
(502)686-3560
Company Type: Subsidiary. **Location Type:** Branch office. **Officer:** Tony Jones Jr., Mgr. **Ultimate Parent:** National City Corp. **SIC:** 6021—National Commercial Banks.

★ 69168 ★   **Central Bank & Trust Co.**
100 W. 3rd St.
PO Box 826
Owensboro, KY 42302-0826
(502)686-3500
Company Type: Subsidiary. **Location Type:** Branch office. **Officer:** Larry R. Mayfield, President & CEO. **Ultimate Parent:** National City Corp. **SIC:** 6021—National Commercial Banks.

★ 69169 ★   Eastman Kodak
3000 Alvey Park Dr. W
Owensboro, KY 42303
(502)926-4944
Ultimate Parent: Eastman Kodak. SIC:
5043—Photographic Equipment & Supplies.

★ 69170 ★   General Electric Co.
3301 Old Hartford Rd.
Owensboro, KY 42303
(502)926-8500
Officer: Michael Carney, Manager. Ultimate
Parent: General Electric. SIC: 3621—
Motors & Generators.

★ 69171 ★   General Electric
Motor Plant
3301 Old Hartford Rd.
Owensboro, KY 42303
Ultimate Parent: General Electric. SIC:
3621—Motors & Generators.

★ 69172 ★   Hon Co.
931 Wing Ave.
Owensboro, KY 42301
Ultimate Parent: Hon Industries. SIC:
2521—Wood Office Furniture.

★ 69173 ★   Kroger Co.
2308 E. 4th St.
Owensboro, KY 42303
(502)926-1433
Ultimate Parent: Kroger. SIC: 5411—
Grocery Stores.

★ 69174 ★   Kroger Co.
4325 Wesleyan Park Plz.
Owensboro, KY 42301
(502)684-9411
Ultimate Parent: Kroger. SIC: 5411—
Grocery Stores.

★ 69175 ★   Kroger Co.
Audubonplz
Owensboro, KY 42301
(502)926-1607
Ultimate Parent: Kroger. SIC: 5411—
Grocery Stores.

★ 69176 ★   Kroger Co.
Commerce Plz.
Owensboro, KY 42301
(502)926-1477
Ultimate Parent: Kroger. SIC: 5411—
Grocery Stores.

★ 69177 ★   Lane Bryant
5000 Frederica St.
Owensboro, KY 42301
(502)683-2055
Ultimate Parent: Limited. SIC: 5621—
Women's Clothing Stores.

★ 69178 ★   Liberty National Bank
of Owensboro
1900 Triplett
Owensboro, KY 42301-3860
(502)926-2020
Company Type: Subsidiary. Location
Type: Branch office. Officer: Bonnie Izsak,
Mgr. Ultimate Parent: Liberty National
Bancorp. SIC: 6021—National Commercial
Banks.

★ 69179 ★   Liberty National Bank
of Owensboro
2398 Frederica St.
Owensboro, KY 42301-5131
(502)926-2020
Company Type: Subsidiary. Location
Type: Branch office. Officer: Susan Jarboe,
Mgr. Ultimate Parent: Liberty National
Bancorp. SIC: 6021—National Commercial
Banks.

★ 69180 ★   Liberty National Bank
of Owensboro
1350 Carter Rd.
Owensboro, KY 42301-2648
(502)926-2020
Company Type: Subsidiary. Location
Type: Branch office. Officer: Rhonda Wells,
Mgr. Ultimate Parent: Liberty National
Bancorp. SIC: 6021—National Commercial
Banks.

★ 69181 ★   Liberty National Bank
of Owensboro
3000 Hwy. 60 E
Owensboro, KY 42301
(502)926-2020
Company Type: Subsidiary. Location
Type: Branch office. Officer: Margaret
Potter, Mgr. Ultimate Parent: Liberty

National Bancorp. SIC: 6021—National
Commercial Banks.

★ 69182 ★   Liberty National Bank
of Owensboro
3160 Hwy. 54 E
Owensboro, KY 42303
(502)926-2020
Company Type: Subsidiary. Location
Type: Branch office. Officer: Lisa Hyland,
Mgr. Ultimate Parent: Liberty National
Bancorp. SIC: 6021—National Commercial
Banks.

★ 69183 ★   Liberty National Bank
of Owensboro
200 E. 3rd St.
PO Box 886
Owensboro, KY 42302-0886
(502)926-2020
Company Type: Subsidiary. Location
Type: Branch office. Officer: Sanford L.
Peyton, Chairman, President, & CEO.
Ultimate Parent: Liberty National Bancorp.
SIC: 6021—National Commercial Banks.

★ 69184 ★   Lowe's Home Centers
Inc.
2181 PO Box
Owensboro, KY 42302
Ultimate Parent: Lowe's. SIC: 5211—
Lumber & Other Building Materials; 5251—
Hardware Stores.

★ 69185 ★   Marathon Fuels Inc.
1960 PO Box
Owensboro, KY 42302
(502)926-3440
Ultimate Parent: USX Corp. SIC: 5172—
Petroleum Products Nec.

★ 69186 ★   Marathon Gas Station
2223 Breckenridge St.
Owensboro, KY 42303
(502)926-5040
Ultimate Parent: USX Corp. SIC: 5541—
Gasoline Service Stations.

★ 69187 ★   Northwestern Mutual
Life Inc.
3520 New Hartford Rd.
Owensboro, KY 42303
(502)926-1222
Ultimate Parent: Northwestern Mutual Life.
SIC: 6411—Insurance Agents, Brokers &
Service.

★ 69188 ★   Osco Drug Store
5000 Frederica St.
Owensboro, KY 42301
(502)684-0264
Ultimate Parent: American Stores. SIC:
5912—Drug Stores & Proprietary Stores.

★ 69189 ★   Payless Shoe Source
5000 Frederica St.
Owensboro, KY 42301
(502)683-2791
Ultimate Parent: May Department Stores.
SIC: 5661—Shoe Stores.

★ 69190 ★   Pepsi Cola General
Bottlers
3081 Kentronics Dr.
Owensboro, KY 42301
(502)684-6295
Officer: Steve O'Bryan, Manager. Ultimate
Parent: Pepsico. SIC: 2086—Bottled
& Canned Soft Drinks.

★ 69191 ★   Rite Aid Discount
Pharmacy
1300 Carter Rd.
Owensboro, KY 42301
(502)683-0223
Ultimate Parent: Rite Aid. SIC: 5912—Drug
Stores & Proprietary Stores; 7217—Carpet
& Upholstery Cleaning.

★ 69192 ★   Ryder Truck Rental-
One Way
2402 Frederica St.
Owensboro, KY 42301
(502)683-6171
Ultimate Parent: Ryder System. SIC:
7359—Equipment Rental & Leasing Nec.

★ 69193 ★   Service Merchandise
4810 Frederica St.
Owensboro, KY 42301
(502)684-1191
Ultimate Parent: Service Merchandise Co.,
Inc. SIC: 5399—Miscellaneous General
Merchandise Store.

★ 69194 ★   Southern Gas Co. Inc.
810 Princeton Pky.
Owensboro, KY 42301-6166
(502)684-0221
Officer: Lewis G. Rouse. Ultimate Parent:
Bell Atlantic Corp. SIC: 4924—Natural Gas
Distribution.

★ 69195 ★   Texaco Inc.
Pleasant Valley Rd.
Owensboro, KY 42301
(502)926-3440
Ultimate Parent: Texaco. SIC: 5172—
Petroleum Products Nec.

★ 69196 ★   W. R. Grace & Co.
5525 U.S. 60 E.
Owensboro, KY 42303
Ultimate Parent: W. R. Grace. SIC: 2821—
Plastics Materials & Resins; 2672—Coated
& Laminated Paper Nec; 3081—
Unsupported Plastics Film & Sheet; 2621—
Paper Mills.

★ 69197 ★   Wal-Mart Stores Inc.
Sherwood Plz.
Owensboro, KY 42301
(502)683-7351
Ultimate Parent: Wal-Mart Stores, Inc. SIC:
5311—Department Stores.

★ 69198 ★   Wal-Mart Stores Inc.
5031 Frederica St.
Owensboro, KY 42301
Ultimate Parent: Wal-Mart Stores, Inc. SIC:
5311—Department Stores.

★ 69199 ★   W.R. Grace & Co.
5525 U.S. 60 East
Owensboro, KY 42303
Ultimate Parent: W. R. Grace. SIC: 2672—
Coated & Laminated Paper Nec; 3081—
Unsupported Plastics Film & Sheet; 2621—
Paper Mills.

Owenton

★ 69200 ★   Peoples Bank & Trust
Co.
Main St.
Owenton, KY 40359
(502)484-3466
Ultimate Parent: People's Bank. SIC:
6022—State Commercial Banks; 6036—
Savings Institutions Except Federal.

★ 69201 ★   Peoples Bank & Trust
Co.
Rural Route 3
Owenton, KY 40359
(502)484-3849
Ultimate Parent: People's Bank. SIC:
6022—State Commercial Banks.

Paducah

★ 69202 ★   Fitness Factory the
6201 Benton Rd.
Paducah, KY 42003
(502)898-6900
Ultimate Parent: New York Times. SIC:
7991—Physical Fitness Facilities.

★ 69203 ★   H. B. Fuller Co.
5000 Charter Oak Dr.
Paducah, KY 42001
Ultimate Parent: H. B. Fuller. SIC: 2891—
Adhesives & Sealants.

★ 69204 ★   Kroger Co.
3275 Irvin Cobb Dr.
Paducah, KY 42003
(502)442-2043
Ultimate Parent: Kroger. SIC: 5411—
Grocery Stores.

★ 69205 ★   Kroger Co.
501 Lone Oak Rd.
Paducah, KY 42003
(502)443-8806
Ultimate Parent: Kroger. SIC: 5411—
Grocery Stores.

★ 69206 ★   Lerner Woman
Kentucky Oaks Mall
Paducah, KY 42001
(502)443-1313
Ultimate Parent: Limited. SIC: 5621—
Women's Clothing Stores.

★ 69207 ★   Limited Express
Kentucky Oaks Mall
Paducah, KY 42001
(502)443-0060
Ultimate Parent: Limited. SIC: 5621—
Women's Clothing Stores.

★ 69208 ★   Martin Marietta
Paducah Gaseous Diffusion Plant
Hobbs Rd. (PO Box 1410)
Paducah, KY 42001
Company Type: Division. Ultimate Parent:
Martin Marietta. SIC: 2800—Chemicals &
Allied Products.

★ 69209 ★   McDonald's
Hamburgers
2208 Lone Oak Rd.
Paducah, KY 42003
(502)554-4002
Ultimate Parent: McDonald's. SIC: 5812—
Eating Places.

★ 69210 ★   Payless Shoe Source
S Beltline Hwy.
Paducah, KY 42001
(502)443-7840
Ultimate Parent: May Department Stores.
SIC: 5661—Shoe Stores.

★ 69211 ★   Payless Shoesource
S Beltline Hwy.
Paducah, KY 42001
(502)443-7840
Ultimate Parent: May Department Stores.
SIC: 5661—Shoe Stores.

★ 69212 ★   Texaco Inc.
725 N. 5th St.
Paducah, KY 42001
(502)442-7631
Ultimate Parent: Texaco. SIC: 5172—
Petroleum Products Nec.

★ 69213 ★   United Parcel Service
3921 Benton Rd.
Paducah, KY 42003
(502)292-9461
Ultimate Parent: United Parcel Service of
America. SIC: 4215—Courier Services
Except by Air.

★ 69214 ★   Wal-Mart Stores Inc.
1927 Irvin Cobb Dr.
Paducah, KY 42003
(502)442-9113
Ultimate Parent: Wal-Mart Stores, Inc. SIC:
5331—Variety Stores.

Paint Lick

★ 69215 ★   Peoples Bank
Paint Lick, KY 40461
(606)925-2511
Ultimate Parent: People's Bank. SIC:
6022—State Commercial Banks.

Paintsville

★ 69216 ★   American Standard,
Inc.
Rte. 23 S.
Paintsville, KY 41240
Ultimate Parent: American Standard. SIC:
3432—Plumbing Fixtures Fittings & Trim.

★ 69217 ★   American Standard
Inc.
Us Rte. 23 South
Paintsville, KY 41240
Ultimate Parent: American Standard. SIC:
3432—Plumbing Fixtures Fittings & Trim.

Paris

★ 69218 ★   Coast to Coast
Hardware
4237 Lexington Rd.
Paris, KY 40361
(606)987-6630
Ultimate Parent: Servistar Corp. SIC:
5251—Hardware Stores.

★ 69219 ★   Mallinckrodt Specialty
Chemicals Co.
Hwy. 68 Bypass
Paris, KY 40362-0800
Ultimate Parent: Imcera Group. SIC:
2869—Industrial Organic Chemicals Nec;
2819—Industrial Inorganic Chemicals Nec.

★ 69220 ★   Wal-Mart Stores Inc.
2000 Paris
Paris, KY 40361
(606)987-2817
Ultimate Parent: Wal-Mart Stores, Inc. SIC:
5311—Department Stores.

Park City

★ 69221 ★   Southern States
Co-Op. Inc.
Feed Div.
U.S. 31 W. N.
Park City, KY 42160
Company Type: Division. Ultimate Parent:
Southern. SIC: 2048—Prepared Feeds Nec.

Pewee Valley

★ 69222 ★   PNC Bank Kentucky,
Inc.
7500 W. Hwy. 146
Pewee Valley, KY 40056
(502)241-8848
Location Type: Branch office. Officer:
Scott Fowler, Manager. Ultimate Parent:
PNC Bank Corp. SIC: 6021—National
Commercial Banks.

★ 69223 ★   Wal-Mart Stores Inc.
6400 Crestwood
Pewee Valley, KY 40056
(502)241-5121
Ultimate Parent: Wal-Mart Stores, Inc. SIC:
5311—Department Stores.

Pikeville

★ 69224 ★   Coal-Mac, Inc.
PO Box 3428
Pikeville, KY 41501
(606)432-0171
Company Type: Subsidiary. Officer: R.
Rex Jones, President. Ultimate Parent:
Ashland Oil. SIC: 1221—Bituminous Coal &
Lignite–Surface; 1222—Bituminous Coal–
Underground.

★ 69225 ★   Greyhound Bus Lines
206 Pike St.
Pikeville, KY 41501
(606)437-6844
Ultimate Parent: Greyhound Lines Inc. SIC:
4111—Local & Suburban Transit; 4131—
Intercity & Rural Bus Transportation; 4142—
Bus Charter Service Except Local.

★ 69226 ★   Kroger Co.
116 Weddington Plz.
Pikeville, KY 41501
(606)432-5608
Ultimate Parent: Kroger. SIC: 5411—
Grocery Stores.

Pleasure Ridge Park

★ 69227 ★   National City Bank,
Kentucky
6985 Dixie Hwy.
Pleasure Ridge Park, KY 40258-3754
(502)581-5101
Company Type: Subsidiary. Location
Type: Branch office. Officer: Susie Leach,
Mgr. Ultimate Parent: National City Corp.
SIC: 6021—National Commercial Banks.

★ 69228 ★   PNC Bank of
Kentucky, Inc.
6801 Dixie Hwy.
Pleasure Ridge Park, KY 40258-3998
(502)581-2310
Location Type: Branch office. Ultimate
Parent: PNC Bank Corp. SIC: 6021—
National Commercial Banks.

Prestonsburg

★ 69229 ★   Stop & Shop
Court
Prestonsburg, KY 41653
(606)886-8436
Ultimate Parent: Stop & Shop. SIC: 5621—
Women's Clothing Stores.

Princeton

★ 69230 ★   Farmers Bank & Trust
Co.
Us 61
Princeton, KY 42445
(502)365-5526
Ultimate Parent: Dauphin Deposit Corp.
SIC: 6022—State Commercial Banks.

★ 69231 ★   Wal-Mart Stores Inc.
Us 62
Princeton, KY 42445
(502)365-7281
Ultimate Parent: Wal-Mart Stores, Inc. SIC:
5311—Department Stores.

Prospect

★ 69232 ★   Crestwood State Bank
13206 W. US Hwy. 42
Prospect, KY 40059-9202
(502)228-1169
Company Type: Subsidiary. Location
Type: Branch office. Officer: Carol
Lambert, Mgr. Ultimate Parent: National
City Corp. SIC: 6021—National Commercial
Banks.

★ 69233 ★   National City Bank,
Kentucky
9205 US Hwy. 42
Prospect, KY 40059-9307
(502)581-6499
Company Type: Subsidiary. Location
Type: Branch office. Officer: Stan E.
Packer, Mgr. Ultimate Parent: National City
Corp. SIC: 6021—National Commercial
Banks.

★ 69234 ★   PNC Bank Kentucky,
Inc.
9519 W. Hwy. 42
Prospect, KY 40059
(502)581-4723
Location Type: Branch office. Ultimate
Parent: PNC Bank Corp. SIC: 6021—
National Commercial Banks.

Providence

★ 69235 ★   Hoov-R-Line
Donan Dr.
Providence, KY 42450
Ultimate Parent: American Brands Inc.
SIC: 3089—Plastics Products Nec.

★ 69236 ★   Twentieth Century
Companies Inc.
Hoov-R-Line
Rte. 2, Donan Dr.
Providence, KY 42450
Company Type: Division. Ultimate Parent:
American Brands Inc. SIC: 3089—Plastics
Products Nec.

Radcliff

★ 69237 ★   American General
Finance
East Town Plaza Shopping Ctr.
Radcliff, KY 40160
(502)877-6141
Ultimate Parent: American General Corp.
SIC: 6141—Personal Credit Institutions.

★ 69238 ★   American General
Finance Inc.
East Town Plaza Shopping Ctr.
Radcliff, KY 40160
(502)877-6141
Location Type: Branch office. Ultimate
Parent: American General Corp. SIC:
6141—Personal Credit Institutions.

★ 69239 ★   Hardin County Bank
& Trust
500 W. Lincoln Trl. Blvd.
PO Box 309
Radcliff, KY 40159-0309
(502)351-1123
Company Type: Subsidiary. Location
Type: Branch office. Officer: James M.
McDonnell, President & CEO. Ultimate
Parent: Liberty National Bancorp. SIC:
6021—National Commercial Banks.

★ 69240 ★   Mary Kay Cosmetic
2880 Liberty St.
Radcliff, KY 40160
(502)351-8431
Ultimate Parent: Mary Kay Cosmetics. SIC:
5999—Miscellaneous Retail Stores Nec.

★ 69241 ★   PNC Bank Kentucky,
Inc.
100 N. Dixie Blvd.
Radcliff, KY 40160-1302
(502)351-3123
Location Type: Branch office. Ultimate
Parent: PNC Bank Corp. SIC: 6021—
National Commercial Banks.

Richmond

★ 69242 ★   Greyhound Bus Lines
127 S. 3rd St.
Richmond, KY 40475
(606)623-2810
Ultimate Parent: Greyhound Lines Inc. SIC:
4111—Local & Suburban Transit; 4131—
Intercity & Rural Bus Transportation; 4142—
Bus Charter Service Except Local.

★ 69243 ★   Kroger Co.
255 E. Main St.
Richmond, KY 40475
(606)623-2850
Ultimate Parent: Kroger. SIC: 5411—
Grocery Stores.

★ 69244 ★   Kroger Food & Drug
Us 25s
Richmond, KY 40475
(606)624-1091
Ultimate Parent: Kroger. SIC: 5411—
Grocery Stores.

★ 69245 ★   Lowe's Home Centers
Inc.
Marshall Kay Dr.
Richmond, KY 40475
(606)624-2002
Ultimate Parent: Lowe's. SIC: 5251—
Hardware Stores; 5211—Lumber & Other
Building Materials.

★ 69246 ★   PNC Bank Kentucky,
Inc.
128 W. Main St.
Richmond, KY 40475-1493
(606)623-2747
Location Type: Branch office. Ultimate
Parent: PNC Bank Corp. SIC: 6021—
National Commercial Banks.

★ 69247 ★   PNC Bank Kentucky,
Inc.
860 Eastern Bypass
Richmond, KY 40475-2512
(606)623-2747
Location Type: Branch office. Ultimate
Parent: PNC Bank Corp. SIC: 6021—
National Commercial Banks.

★ 69248 ★   Ryder Truck Rental-
Oneway
Big Hill Ave.
Richmond, KY 40475
(606)623-5581
Ultimate Parent: Ryder System. SIC:
7359—Equipment Rental & Leasing Nec.

★ 69249 ★   Shell Interstate
Service Station
Eastern St.
Richmond, KY 40475
(606)623-6613
Ultimate Parent: Shell Oil Co. SIC: 5541—
Gasoline Service Stations.

★ 69250 ★   Sherwin-Williams Co.
Boggs Ln. S
Richmond, KY 40475
(606)624-1240
Officer: Robert B. Geiger, Manager.
Ultimate Parent: Sherwin-Williams Co. SIC:
3479—Metal Coating & Allied Services.

★ 69251 ★   Wal-Mart Stores Inc.
Shoppers Village
Richmond, KY 40475
(606)623-0811
Ultimate Parent: Wal-Mart Stores, Inc. SIC:
5611—Men's & Boys' Clothing Stores.

Rolling Hills

★ 69252 ★   National City Bank,
Kentucky
9240 Westport Rd.
Rolling Hills, KY 40242-3296
(502)581-5350
Company Type: Subsidiary. Location
Type: Branch office. Officer: Barbara
Smith, Mgr. Ultimate Parent: National City
Corp. SIC: 6021—National Commercial
Banks.

Russell

★ 69253 ★   Ashland Oil
1000 Ashland Dr.
Russell, KY 41169
(606)329-3333
Company Type: Headquarters. Officer:
John R. Hall. Sales: 9553.9 M. Fortune
500: Largest U.S. Industrial Corporations:
Ranking 49.

★ 69254 ★   Ashland Petroleum
Co.
Ashland Dr.
Russell, KY 41169
(606)329-3333
Company Type: Subsidiary. Officer:
Robert E. Yancey Jr., President. Ultimate
Parent: Ashland Oil. SIC: 2911—Petroleum
Refining; 5172—Petroleum Products Nec.
Sales: 4800000000 M.

★ 69255 ★   Thrift Drugs
Us 23 Hwy.
Russell, KY 41169
(606)325-8479
Ultimate Parent: J.C. Penney. SIC: 5912—
Drug Stores & Proprietary Stores.

Russell Springs

★ 69256 ★   Mutual Federal S & L
Association
2198 Lakeway
Russell Springs, KY 42642
(502)866-3134
Ultimate Parent: Southern National Corp.
SIC: 6141—Personal Credit Institutions.

Russellville

★ 69257 ★   Carpenter Co. Inc.
Greenville Rd.
Russellville, KY 42276
(502)726-9513
Ultimate Parent: Carpenter. SIC: 2822—
Synthetic Rubber.

★ 69258 ★   E. R. Carpenter Co.
Inc.
Forrest Park Dr.
Russellville, KY 42276
Ultimate Parent: Carpenter. SIC: 2392—
Housefurnishings Nec.

★ 69259 ★   E. R. Carpenter Co.
Inc.
200 Forrest Park Dr.
Russellville, KY 42276
Ultimate Parent: Carpenter. SIC: 3086—
Plastics Foam Products; 2297—Nonwoven
Fabrics; 2891—Adhesives & Sealants;
3081—Unsupported Plastics Film & Sheet.

★ 69260 ★   Emerson Electric Co.
150 Emerson Bypass Rd.
Russellville, KY 42276
Ultimate Parent: Emerson Electric Co. Inc.
SIC: 3621—Motors & Generators.

★ 69261 ★   Illinois Tool Works
Inc.
Shakeproof Div.
1500 W. 9th St.
Russellville, KY 42276
Company Type: Division. Ultimate Parent:
Illinois Tool Works. SIC: 3452—Bolts, Nuts,
Rivets & Washers.

★ 69262 ★   Rockwell International
Corp. Russellville Plant
Measurement
Hwy. 68 W
Russellville, KY 42276
Ultimate Parent: Rockwell International
Corp. SIC: 3300—Primary Metal Industries.

★ 69263 ★   **Texaco Gas Station**
501 N. Main St.
Russellville, KY 42276
(502)726-8418
Ultimate Parent: Texaco. **SIC:** 5541—
Gasoline Service Stations.

★ 69264 ★   **Red Kap Ind.**
451 Johnson St.
Russelville, KY 42276
(502)726-3142
Officer: Gary Williams, Manager. **Ultimate
Parent:** VF Corp. **SIC:** 2389—Apparel &
Accessories Nec.

Salyersville

★ 69265 ★   **Rite Aid Discount
Pharmacy**
Salyersville, KY 41465
(606)349-1044
Ultimate Parent: Rite Aid. **SIC:** 5912—Drug
Stores & Proprietary Stores.

Scottsville

★ 69266 ★   **General Electric Co.**
636 Holt Dr.
Scottsville, KY 42164
(502)237-3151
Officer: Thomas R. Ice, Manager. **Ultimate
Parent:** General Electric. **SIC:** 3621—
Motors & Generators.

★ 69267 ★   **Kirsch**
2620 Gallatin Rd.
Scottsville, KY 42164
Ultimate Parent: Cooper Industries. **SIC:**
2591—Drapery Hardware, Blinds & Shades.

★ 69268 ★   **Rite Aid Discount
Pharmacy**
31 E. South
Scottsville, KY 42164
(502)237-3738
Ultimate Parent: Rite Aid. **SIC:** 5912—Drug
Stores & Proprietary Stores.

Sebree

★ 69269 ★   **Ring Around
Products Inc.**
Hwy. 132
Sebree, KY 42455
(502)835-7574
Ultimate Parent: Occidental Petroleum
Corp. **SIC:** 5261—Retail Nurseries &
Garden Stores.

Shelbyville

★ 69270 ★   **American Emblem
Tool Co.**
1251 Harry Long Rd.
Shelbyville, KY 40065-9139
(502)633-5082
Officer: Glenn Dutton. **Ultimate Parent:**
Black & Decker Corp. **SIC:** 3425—Saw
Blades & Handsaws; 5085—Industrial
Supplies.

★ 69271 ★   **Clark Printing Co.**
405 6th St.
Shelbyville, KY 40065
(502)633-4959
Ultimate Parent: Terex. **SIC:** 2752—
Commercial Printing—Lithographic; 2759—
Commercial Printing Nec.

★ 69272 ★   **Greyhound Bus Lines**
Us 60 W
Shelbyville, KY 40065
(502)633-5399
Ultimate Parent: Greyhound Lines Inc. **SIC:**
4131—Intercity & Rural Bus Transportation;
4111—Local & Suburban Transit; 4142—
Bus Charter Service Except Local.

★ 69273 ★   **Liberty National Bank
of Shelbyville**
Midland Blvd.
Shelbyville, KY 40065
(502)663-0793
Company Type: Subsidiary. **Location
Type:** Branch office. **Ultimate Parent:**
Liberty National Bancorp. **SIC:** 6021—
National Commercial Banks.

★ 69274 ★   **Liberty National Bank
of Shelbyville**
544 Main St.
PO Box 187
Shelbyville, KY 40066-0187
(502)663-4856 **Fax:** (502)663-5740
Company Type: Subsidiary. **Location
Type:** Branch office. **Officer:** Bob Rigney,
President & CEO. **Ultimate Parent:** Liberty
National Bancorp. **SIC:** 6021—National
Commercial Banks.

★ 69275 ★   **Marathon Oil**
415 2nd St.
Shelbyville, KY 40065
(502)633-3796
Ultimate Parent: USX Corp. **SIC:** 5172—
Petroleum Products Nec.

★ 69276 ★   **Marathon Oil Co.**
415 2nd St.
Shelbyville, KY 40065
(502)633-3796
Ultimate Parent: USX Corp. **SIC:** 5172—
Petroleum Products Nec.

★ 69277 ★   **Peoples Bank**
35 Village Plz.
Shelbyville, KY 40065
(502)633-6660
Ultimate Parent: People's Bank. **SIC:**
6022—State Commercial Banks.

★ 69278 ★   **Union Camp Corp.**
9 Commerce Circle
Shelbyville, KY 40065
Ultimate Parent: Union Camp Corp. **SIC:**
2673—Bags—Plastics, Laminated &
Coated.

★ 69279 ★   **Wal-Mart Stores Inc.**
190 Midland Blvd.
Shelbyville, KY 40065
(502)633-0705
Ultimate Parent: Wal-Mart Stores, Inc. **SIC:**
5311—Department Stores.

Shepherdsville

★ 69280 ★   **ALLTEL Kentucky Inc.**
229 Lees Valley Rd.
PO Box 68
Shepherdsville, KY 40165
(502)543-2231
Ultimate Parent: ALLTEL Corp. **SIC:**
4812—Radiotelephone Communications.

★ 69281 ★   **Kroger Co.**
11330 Preston Hwy.
Shepherdsville, KY 40165
(502)955-7591
Ultimate Parent: Kroger. **SIC:** 5411—
Grocery Stores.

★ 69282 ★   **Mary Kay Cosmetics**
269 Hebron Ln.
Shepherdsville, KY 40165
(502)955-9488
Ultimate Parent: Mary Kay Cosmetics. **SIC:**
5999—Miscellaneous Retail Stores Nec.

★ 69283 ★   **Peoples Bank**
331 Buckman St.
Shepherdsville, KY 40165
(502)543-3064
Ultimate Parent: People's Bank. **SIC:**
6022—State Commercial Banks.

★ 69284 ★   **Peoples Bank**
2403 E. 4th St.
Shepherdsville, KY 40165
(502)543-2226
Ultimate Parent: People's Bank. **SIC:**
6022—State Commercial Banks.

★ 69285 ★   **Peoples Bank**
Hwy. 44 E
Shepherdsville, KY 40165
(502)543-3074
Ultimate Parent: People's Bank. **SIC:**
6022—State Commercial Banks.

Shively

★ 69286 ★   **Borden Inc.**
6200 Camp Ground Rd.
Shively, KY 40216
(502)449-6200
Officer: Mike George, Manager. **Ultimate
Parent:** Borden, Inc. **SIC:** 2891—Adhesives
& Sealants; 2899—Chemical Preparations
Nec.

★ 69287 ★   **National City Bank,
Kentucky**
4726 Dixie Hwy.
Shively, KY 40216-2656
(502)581-4416
Company Type: Subsidiary. **Location
Type:** Branch office. **Officer:** Mary Ann
Rhudy, Mgr. **Ultimate Parent:** National City
Corp. **SIC:** 6021—National Commercial
Banks.

★ 69288 ★   **National City Bank,
Kentucky**
4417 Cane Run Rd.
Shively, KY 40216-4501
(502)581-6700
Company Type: Subsidiary. **Location
Type:** Branch office. **Officer:** Sherry Stuart,
Mgr. **Ultimate Parent:** National City Corp.
SIC: 6021—National Commercial Banks.

★ 69289 ★   **National City Bank,
Kentucky**
2400 Dixie Hwy.
Shively, KY 40216-5304
(502)581-5383
Company Type: Subsidiary. **Location
Type:** Branch office. **Officer:** Norma A.
Webb, Mgr. **Ultimate Parent:** National City
Corp. **SIC:** 6021—National Commercial
Banks.

Simpsonville

★ 69290 ★   **Leggett & Platt Inc.**
211 Main St. PO Box 367
Simpsonville, KY 40067
Ultimate Parent: Leggett & Platt Inc. **SIC:**
2514—Metal Household Furniture.

Smiths Grove

★ 69291 ★   **National City Bank,
Bowling Green**
Main St.
Smiths Grove, KY 42171
(502)563-2941
Company Type: Subsidiary. **Location
Type:** Branch office. **Officer:** Kirby
Johnson, Mgr. **Ultimate Parent:** National
City Corp. **SIC:** 6021—National Commercial
Banks.

Somerset

★ 69292 ★   **Exxon Co. U S a**
Oak Hill Rd.
Somerset, KY 42501
(606)679-2948
Ultimate Parent: Exxon. **SIC:** 5172—
Petroleum Products Nec; 5172—Petroleum
Products Nec.

★ 69293 ★   **General Electric Co.**
Hwy. 27 N
Somerset, KY 42501
(606)679-7341
Officer: Chuck Tyler, Manager. **Ultimate
Parent:** General Electric. **SIC:** 3231—
Products of Purchased Glass.

★ 69294 ★   **Kroger Co.**
110 Grand Central Pl.
Somerset, KY 42501
(606)678-0202
Ultimate Parent: Kroger. **SIC:** 5411—
Grocery Stores.

★ 69295 ★   **Kroger Co.**
409 Russell Spring Hwy.
Somerset, KY 42501
(606)678-5147
Ultimate Parent: Kroger. **SIC:** 5411—
Grocery Stores.

★ 69296 ★   **Mary Kay Cosmetics**
816 W. Hwy. 80
Somerset, KY 42501
(606)678-5917
Ultimate Parent: Mary Kay Cosmetics. **SIC:**
5999—Miscellaneous Retail Stores Nec.

★ 69297 ★   **Rite Aid Discount
Pharmacy**
201 S. Hwy. 27
Somerset, KY 42501
(606)679-9934
Ultimate Parent: Rite Aid. **SIC:** 5912—Drug
Stores & Proprietary Stores.

★ 69298 ★   **Tecumseh Products
Co.**
Somerset Div.
Hwy. 1247
Somerset, KY 42501-0099
Ultimate Parent: Tecumseh Products. **SIC:**
3585—Refrigeration & Heating Equipment.

Sonora

★ 69299 ★   **PNC Bank Kentucky,
Inc.**
Main St.
Sonora, KY 42776
(502)369-7128
Location Type: Branch office. **Ultimate
Parent:** PNC Bank Corp. **SIC:** 6021—
National Commercial Banks.

Springfield

★ 69300 ★   **Armour Dairy & Food
Oils Co.**
Bardstown Rd.
Springfield, KY 40069
Ultimate Parent: Conagra. **SIC:** 2023—Dry,
Condensed & Evaporated Dairy Products.

★ 69301 ★   **Armour Food
Ingredients Co.**
Bardstown Rd.
Springfield, KY 40069
Ultimate Parent: Conagra. **SIC:** 2023—Dry,
Condensed & Evaporated Dairy Products.

St. Matthews

★ 69302 ★   **Kroger Co.**
2200 Brownsboro Rd.
St. Matthews, KY 40206
(502)897-1133
Ultimate Parent: Kroger. **SIC:** 5411—
Grocery Stores.

★ 69303 ★   **National City Bank,
Kentucky**
3922 Chenoweth Sq.
St. Matthews, KY 40207-2725
(502)581-4253
Company Type: Subsidiary. **Location
Type:** Branch office. **Ultimate Parent:**
National City Corp. **SIC:** 6021—National
Commercial Banks.

★ 69304 ★   **National City Bank,
Kentucky**
3901 Frankfort Ave.
St. Matthews, KY 40207-3157
(502)581-5454
Company Type: Subsidiary. **Location
Type:** Branch office. **Officer:** Alan Kissel,
Mgr. **Ultimate Parent:** National City Corp.
SIC: 6021—National Commercial Banks.

★ 69305 ★   **National City Bank,
Kentucky**
4304 Shelbyville Rd.
St. Matthews, KY 40207-3390
(502)581-4171
Company Type: Subsidiary. **Location
Type:** Branch office. **Officer:** Frank
Ellington, Mgr. **Ultimate Parent:** National
City Corp. **SIC:** 6021—National Commercial
Banks.

★ 69306 ★   **PNC Bank Kentucky,
Inc.**
3828 Shelbyville Rd.
St. Matthews, KY 40207-3111
(502)581-3130
Location Type: Branch office. **Ultimate
Parent:** PNC Bank Corp. **SIC:** 6021—
National Commercial Banks.

★ 69307 ★   **PNC Bank Kentucky,
Inc.**
3624 Brownsboro Rd.
St. Matthews, KY 40207-1897
(502)581-3366
Location Type: Branch office. **Ultimate
Parent:** PNC Bank Corp. **SIC:** 6021—
National Commercial Banks.

★ 69308 ★   **PNC Bank Kentucky,
Inc.**
4004 Dutchmans Ln.
St. Matthews, KY 40207-4704
(502)581-2316
Location Type: Branch office. **Ultimate
Parent:** PNC Bank Corp. **SIC:** 6021—
National Commercial Banks.

★ 69309 ★   Standard Register Co.
225 Executive Park
St. Matthews, KY 40207
(502)895-5700
Officer: Don Underwood, Manager. **Ultimate Parent:** Standard Register. **SIC:** 2761—Manifold Business Forms.

Stanford

★ 69310 ★   Peoples Bank
Hustonville
607 PO Box
Stanford, KY 40484
(606)365-3505
Ultimate Parent: People's Bank. **SIC:** 6022—State Commercial Banks.

Stone

★ 69311 ★   Leslie Coal Mining
Co.
Stone, KY 41567
(606)353-7201
Ultimate Parent: Carolina Power & Light Co. **SIC:** 5989—Fuel Dealers Nec.

Taylor Mill

★ 69312 ★   PNC Bank Northern
Kentucky, NA
5512 Taylor Mill Rd.
Taylor Mill, KY 41015-2299
(606)261-1162
Location Type: Branch office. **Officer:** Patsy A. Line, Manager. **Ultimate Parent:** PNC Bank Corp. **SIC:** 6021—National Commercial Banks.

★ 69313 ★   Star Bank NA,
Kentucky
5018 Old Taylor Mill Rd.
Taylor Mill, KY 41015
(606)292-6251
Location Type: Branch office. **Officer:** Sandy Woolum, Assistant Vice President. **Ultimate Parent:** Star Banc Corp. **SIC:** 6021—National Commercial Banks.

Taylorsville

★ 69314 ★   People's Bank
Main St.
Taylorsville, KY 40071
(502)477-2244
Ultimate Parent: People's Bank. **SIC:** 6022—State Commercial Banks.

Tompkinsville

★ 69315 ★   Belden Wire & Cable
Tompkinsville
Capp Harlan Rd.
Tompkinsville, KY 42167
Ultimate Parent: Cooper Industries. **SIC:** 3357—Nonferrous Wiredrawing & Insulating.

★ 69316 ★   Cooper Industries Inc.
Belden Div.
Capp Harlan Rd.
Tompkinsville, KY 42167
Company Type: Division. **Ultimate Parent:** Cooper Industries. **SIC:** 3357—Nonferrous Wiredrawing & Insulating.

★ 69317 ★   Peoples Bank
703 N. Main St.
Tompkinsville, KY 42167
(502)487-6158
Ultimate Parent: People's Bank. **SIC:** 6022—State Commercial Banks.

★ 69318 ★   Red Kap Ind.
PO Box 637
Tompkinsville, KY 42167
(502)487-6796
Officer: Roy White, Manager. **Ultimate Parent:** VF Corp. **SIC:** 2389—Apparel & Accessories Nec.

Union

★ 69319 ★   PNC Bank, Northern
Kentucky, NA
9990 US Hwy. 42
Union, KY 41091-9793
(606)384-3390
Location Type: Branch office. **Officer:** Mary Lou Hollbrook, Assistant Vice President. **Ultimate Parent:** PNC Bank

Corp. **SIC:** 6021—National Commercial Banks.

Upton

★ 69320 ★   PNC Bank Kentucky,
Inc.
Walnut St.
Upton, KY 42784
(502)369-7330
Location Type: Branch office. **Ultimate Parent:** PNC Bank Corp. **SIC:** 6021—National Commercial Banks.

Valley Station

★ 69321 ★   National City Bank,
Kentucky
10414 Dixie Hwy.
Valley Station, KY 40272-3954
(502)581-4257
Company Type: Subsidiary. **Location Type:** Branch office. **Officer:** Carol F. Weissrock, Mgr. **Ultimate Parent:** National City Corp. **SIC:** 6021—National Commercial Banks.

★ 69322 ★   PNC Bank Kentucky,
Inc.
10439 Dixie Hwy.
Valley Station, KY 40272-3927
(502)581-3106
Location Type: Branch office. **Ultimate Parent:** PNC Bank Corp. **SIC:** 6021—National Commercial Banks.

★ 69323 ★   PNC Bank of
Kentucky, Inc.
9804 Old 3rd St. Rd.
Valley Station, KY 40272-2802
(502)581-4720
Location Type: Branch office. **Ultimate Parent:** PNC Bank Corp. **SIC:** 6021—National Commercial Banks.

Verona

★ 69324 ★   Star Bank NA,
Kentucky
14973 Walton Verona Rd.
Verona, KY 41092
(606)485-7254
Company Type: Subsidiary. **Location Type:** Branch office. **Officer:** Joyce Vest, Vice President. **Ultimate Parent:** Star Banc Corp. **SIC:** 6021—National Commercial Banks; 6035—Federal Savings Institutions.

Versailles

★ 69325 ★   GTE Prods. Corp.
900 Tyrone Pike
Versailles, KY 40383
Ultimate Parent: GTE. **SIC:** 3641—Electric Lamps.

★ 69326 ★   GTE Prods. Corp.
Versailles Glass Plant
1000 Tyrone Rd.
Versailles, KY 40383
Ultimate Parent: GTE. **SIC:** 3229—Pressed & Blown Glass Nec.

★ 69327 ★   GTE Products Corp.
Versailles Class Plant
1000 Tyrone Rd.
Versailles, KY 40383
Ultimate Parent: GTE. **SIC:** 3229—Pressed & Blown Glass Nec.

★ 69328 ★   GTE Products Corp.,
Versailles Glass Plant
1000 Tyrone Rd.
Versailles, KY 40383
Location Type: Plant. **Ultimate Parent:** GTE. **SIC:** 3229—Pressed & Blown Glass Nec.

★ 69329 ★   McDonald's
Hamburgers
102 United Dr.
Versailles, KY 40383
(606)873-5720
Ultimate Parent: McDonald's. **SIC:** 5812—Eating Places.

★ 69330 ★   Ryder Truck Rental
Us 60
Versailles, KY 40383
(606)873-8616
Ultimate Parent: Ryder System. **SIC:** 7359—Equipment Rental & Leasing Nec.

★ 69331 ★   Southern Gas Co. Inc.
160 Morgan St.
Versailles, KY 40383-1429
(606)873-5455
Officer: Leonard K. Nave. **Ultimate Parent:** Bell Atlantic Corp. **SIC:** 4924—Natural Gas Distribution.

★ 69332 ★   Texas Instruments
Inc.
300 N. Main St.
Versailles, KY 40383
Ultimate Parent: Texas Instruments. **SIC:** 3625—Relays & Industrial Controls; 3822—Environmental Controls; 3714—Motor Vehicle Parts & Accessories; 3672—Printed Circuit Boards; 3089—Plastics Products Nec; 5074—Plumbing & Hydronic Heating Supplies.

Vine Grove

★ 69333 ★   Hardin County Bank
& Trust
536 Highland Ave.
Vine Grove, KY 40175
(502)877-6070
Company Type: Subsidiary. **Location Type:** Branch office. **Officer:** Virginia Simpson, Mgr. **Ultimate Parent:** Liberty National Bancorp. **SIC:** 6021—National Commercial Banks.

Walton

★ 69334 ★   Richwood Building
Products, Inc.
315 Shoreland Dr.
Walton, KY 41094
(606)485-7444 **Fax:** (606)485-9966
Officer: Michael Vagedes, President. **Ultimate Parent:** Ply Gem.

★ 69335 ★   Star Bank NA,
Kentucky
19 N. Main St.
Walton, KY 41094-1110
(606)485-4121
Company Type: Subsidiary. **Location Type:** Branch office. **Officer:** Richard Robinson, Vice President. **Ultimate Parent:** Star Banc Corp. **SIC:** 6021—National Commercial Banks; 6035—Federal Savings Institutions.

Wayland

★ 69336 ★   National Mines Corp.
295 PO Box
Wayland, KY 41666
(606)358-2031
Ultimate Parent: National Steel. **SIC:** 1231—Anthracite Mining.

Whitesburg

★ 69337 ★   Coast to Coast
Hardware
Parkway Plz.
Whitesburg, KY 41858
(606)633-4581
Ultimate Parent: Servistar Corp. **SIC:** 5932—Used Merchandise Stores.

Whitley City

★ 69338 ★   Exxon Co.
Whitley City, KY 42653
(606)376-2984
Ultimate Parent: Exxon. **SIC:** 5983—Fuel Oil Dealers.

★ 69339 ★   Greyhound Bus Lines
Us 27
Whitley City, KY 42653
(606)376-2790
Ultimate Parent: Greyhound Lines Inc. **SIC:** 4111—Local & Suburban Transit; 4131—Intercity & Rural Bus Transportation; 4142—Bus Charter Service Except Local.

Wickliffe

★ 69340 ★   Westvaco Corp.
Fine Papers Div.
Hwy. 51 S
Wickliffe, KY 42087
Company Type: Division. **Ultimate Parent:** WestVaco Corp. **SIC:** 2621—Paper Mills; 2611—Pulp Mills.

Williamsburg

★ 69341 ★   Trailways Bus Lines
510 Main St.
Williamsburg, KY 40769
(606)549-3383
Ultimate Parent: Greyhound Lines Inc. **SIC:** 4131—Intercity & Rural Bus Transportation; 4111—Local & Suburban Transit; 4142—Bus Charter Service Except Local.

Winchester

★ 69342 ★   Coors Biotech Inc.
400 Rolling Hills Ln.
Winchester, KY 40391
Ultimate Parent: Adolph Coors. **SIC:** 2048—Prepared Feeds Nec.

★ 69343 ★   GTE Prods. Corp.
416 E. Washington St.
Winchester, KY 40391
Ultimate Parent: GTE. **SIC:** 3641—Electric Lamps.

★ 69344 ★   GTE Products Corp.
416 E. Washington St.
Winchester, KY 40391
Ultimate Parent: GTE. **SIC:** 3641—Electric Lamps.

★ 69345 ★   Krogerco
939 Byp
Winchester, KY 40391
(606)745-4959
Ultimate Parent: Kroger. **SIC:** 5411—Grocery Stores.

★ 69346 ★   Leggett & Platt Inc.
130 Ecton Rd.
Winchester, KY 40391
Ultimate Parent: Leggett & Platt Inc. **SIC:** 2514—Metal Household Furniture; 3429—Hardware Nec.

★ 69347 ★   Leggett & Platt Inc.
101 New St.
Winchester, KY 40391
Ultimate Parent: Leggett & Platt Inc. **SIC:** 2514—Metal Household Furniture; 5021—Furniture; 3429—Hardware Nec.

★ 69348 ★   McDonald's
Hamburgers
Shoppers Village
Winchester, KY 40391
(606)744-3493
Ultimate Parent: McDonald's. **SIC:** 5812—Eating Places.

★ 69349 ★   Pepsi-Cola Bottling
Co.
214 Jackson St.
Winchester, KY 40391
(606)744-2611
Officer: John Hammond, Manager. **Ultimate Parent:** Pepsico. **SIC:** 2086—Bottled & Canned Soft Drinks.

★ 69350 ★   PNC Bank Kentucky,
Inc.
120 S. Main St.
Winchester, KY 40391-2610
(606)744-1161
Location Type: Branch office. **Ultimate Parent:** PNC Bank Corp. **SIC:** 6021—National Commercial Banks.

★ 69351 ★   PNC Bank Kentucky,
Inc.
Winchester Plz.
Winchester, KY 40391-9665
(606)744-1161
Location Type: Branch office. **Ultimate Parent:** PNC Bank Corp. **SIC:** 6021—National Commercial Banks.

★ 69352 ★   PNC Bank Kentucky,
Inc.
Boonesboro Plz.
Winchester, KY 40391
(606)744-1161
Location Type: Branch office. **Ultimate Parent:** PNC Bank Corp. **SIC:** 6021—National Commercial Banks.

★ 69353 ★   Rockwell International
5555 Rockwell Rd.
Winchester, KY 40391
Ultimate Parent: Rockwell International Corp. **SIC:** 3714—Motor Vehicle Parts & Accessories.

★ 69354 ★ Rockwell International
Corp. Winchester Facility
5555 Rockwell Rd.
Winchester, KY 40391
Company Type: Division. Ultimate Parent:
Ametek Inc. SIC: 3086—Plastics Foam
Products. Ultimate Parent: Rockwell
International Corp. SIC: 3714—Motor
Vehicle Parts & Accessories.

★ 69355 ★ Southern States
Co-Op Inc. Feed Mill
5799 Rockwell Rd.
Winchester, KY 40391
Ultimate Parent: Southern. SIC: 2048—
Prepared Feeds Nec.

★ 69356 ★ Winchester Farms
Dairy
500 Rolling Hills Ln.
Winchester, KY 40391
Ultimate Parent: Kroger. SIC: 2026—Fluid
Milk.

★ 69357 ★ Zeagen Inc.
400 Rolling Hills Ln.
Winchester, KY 40391
Ultimate Parent: Adolph Coors. SIC:
2048—Prepared Feeds Nec.

Worthington

★ 69358 ★ Ametek Microfoam
US 23
Worthington, KY 41183
(606)836-0251
Ultimate Parent: Ametek Inc. SIC: 3086—
Plastics Foam Products.

Wurtland

★ 69359 ★ Ametek Inc.
Microfoam Div. Inc.
300 Harris Rd.
Wurtland, KY 41144
Company Type: Division. Ultimate Parent:
Ametek Inc. SIC: 3086—Plastics Foam
Products.

LOUISIANA

Abbeville

★ 69360 ★ **Arco Oil & Gas Co.**
Abbeville, LA 70510
(318)893-7360
Ultimate Parent: Atlantic Richfield Co., Inc.
SIC: 1311—Crude Petroleum & Natural
Gas.

★ 69361 ★ **Arco Oil & Gas Co.**
West side
Abbeville, LA 70510
(318)893-7360
Ultimate Parent: Atlantic Richfield Co., Inc.
SIC: 1311—Crude Petroleum & Natural
Gas.

★ 69362 ★ **Pennzoil Co.**
Abbeville, LA 70510
(318)893-7379
Ultimate Parent: Pennzoil. **SIC:** 1389—Oil
& Gas Field Services Nec.

★ 69363 ★ **Wal Mart**
Hwy. 14
Abbeville, LA 70510
(318)893-6485
Ultimate Parent: Wal-Mart Stores, Inc. **SIC:**
5311—Department Stores.

Addis

★ 69364 ★ **Air Products &
Chemicals Inc.**
9555 Hwy. 1 S.
Addis, LA 70710
Ultimate Parent: Air Products & Chemicals,
Inc. **SIC:** 2813—Industrial Gases.

★ 69365 ★ **Occidental Chemical
Corp.**
Hwy. 1 at E. Sid Richardson Rd.
Addis, LA 70710
Ultimate Parent: Occidental Petroleum
Corp. **SIC:** 2821—Plastics Materials &
Resins.

★ 69366 ★ **Occidental Chemical
Corp.**
Hwy. 1 E. Sid Richardson Rd.
Addis, LA 70710
Ultimate Parent: Occidental Petroleum
Corp. **SIC:** 2821—Plastics Materials &
Resins.

Alexandria

★ 69367 ★ **Albertson's Inc.**
2265 S. MacArthur Dr.
Alexandria, LA 71301-3052
(318)487-9395
Ultimate Parent: Albertson's Inc. **SIC:**
5912—Drug Stores & Proprietary Stores;
5411—Grocery Stores.

★ 69368 ★ **Borden Inc.**
Chemical
3901 Sugar House Rd.
Alexandria, LA 71302
Company Type: Division. **Ultimate Parent:**
Borden, Inc. **SIC:** 2491—Wood Preserving.

★ 69369 ★ **Borden Inc.**
Packaging & Industrial Products
3901 Sugar House Rd.
Alexandria, LA 71302
Company Type: Division. **Ultimate Parent:**
Borden, Inc. **SIC:** 2821—Plastics Materials
& Resins.

★ 69370 ★ **Butler Paper Co.**
3223 Baldwin Ave.
Alexandria, LA 71301-3506
Location Type: Branch office. **Officer:**
Alvin Michiels. **Ultimate Parent:** Alco
Standard Corp.

★ 69371 ★ **Circus World**
3437 Masonic Dr.
Alexandria, LA 71301
(318)442-7176
Ultimate Parent: Melville. **SIC:** 5945—
Hobby, Toy & Game Shops.

★ 69372 ★ **Diebold Inc.**
1756 Elliott St.
Alexandria, LA 71301
(318)443-1027
Ultimate Parent: Diebold, Inc. **SIC:** 5046—
Commercial Equipment Nec.

★ 69373 ★ **Dolphin Construction
Co.**
4600 Lee St.
Alexandria, LA 71302
(318)448-0803
Ultimate Parent: Texas Industries. **SIC:**
1541—Industrial Buildings & Warehouses;
1611—Highway & Street Construction.

★ 69374 ★ **Dolphin Construction
Co.**
1850 Macarthur Dr.
Alexandria, LA 71301
(318)487-8320
Ultimate Parent: Texas Industries. **SIC:**
1521—Single-Family Housing Construction.

★ 69375 ★ **Express**
3437 Masonic Dr.
Alexandria, LA 71301
(318)448-9723
Ultimate Parent: Limited. **SIC:** 5651—
Family Clothing Stores.

★ 69376 ★ **Exxon Co.**
2826 Lee St.
Alexandria, LA 71301
(318)443-8788
Ultimate Parent: Exxon. **SIC:** 5172—
Petroleum Products Nec.

★ 69377 ★ **Exxon Shop**
4012 Mayflower Blvd.
Alexandria, LA 71303
Ultimate Parent: Exxon. **SIC:** 7549—
Automotive Services Nec.

★ 69378 ★ **Fleet Finance Inc.**
2011 MacArthur Dr.
Alexandria, LA 71301
(318)445-2476
Ultimate Parent: Fleet Financial Group.
SIC: 6062—State Credit Unions.

★ 69379 ★ **Foot Action**
3437 Masonic Dr.
Alexandria, LA 71301
(318)473-4459
Ultimate Parent: Melville. **SIC:** 5661—Shoe
Stores.

★ 69380 ★ **Hibernia National
Bank**
3499 Masonic Dr.
Alexandria, LA 71301
(318)487-2112
Ultimate Parent: Hibernia Corp. **SIC:**
6099—Functions Related to Deposit
Banking.

★ 69381 ★ **Hibernia National
Bank**
4007 Jackson St.
Alexandria, LA 71303
(318)443-3292
Ultimate Parent: Hibernia Corp. **SIC:**
6099—Functions Related to Deposit
Banking.

★ 69382 ★ **Hibernia National
Bank**
211 4th St.
Alexandria, LA 71301
(318)487-2116
Ultimate Parent: Hibernia Corp. **SIC:**
6021—National Commercial Banks; 6022—
State Commercial Banks.

★ 69383 ★ **Hibernia National
Bank**
1400 MacArthur Dr.
Alexandria, LA 71301
(318)487-2120
Ultimate Parent: Hibernia Corp. **SIC:**
6099—Functions Related to Deposit
Banking.

★ 69384 ★ **Hibernia National
Bank**
934 3rd St.
Alexandria, LA 71301
(318)487-2265
Ultimate Parent: Hibernia Corp. **SIC:**
6021—National Commercial Banks; 6512—
Nonresidential Building Operators.

★ 69385 ★ **Kay-Bee Toy & Hobby**
3437 Masonic Dr.
Alexandria, LA 71301
(318)487-9856
Ultimate Parent: Melville. **SIC:** 5945—
Hobby, Toy & Game Shops.

★ 69386 ★ **Kentucky Fried
Chicken**
1209 Macarthur Dr.
Alexandria, LA 71303
(318)448-1022
Ultimate Parent: Pepsico. **SIC:** 5812—
Eating Places; 7538—General Automotive
Repair Shops.

★ 69387 ★ **Kentucky Fried
Chicken**
6516 Masonic Dr.
Alexandria, LA 71301
(318)445-1406
Ultimate Parent: Pepsico. **SIC:** 5812—
Eating Places.

★ 69388 ★ **Kroger Food Store**
1400 Macarthur Dr.
Alexandria, LA 71301
(318)442-1851
Ultimate Parent: Kroger. **SIC:** 4822—
Telegraph & Other Communications; 5411—
Grocery Stores.

★ 69389 ★ **Lane Bryant**
3437 Masonic Dr.
Alexandria, LA 71301
(318)445-6858
Ultimate Parent: Limited. **SIC:** 5651—
Family Clothing Stores.

★ 69390 ★ **Lerner Shop**
3441 Masonic Dr.
Alexandria, LA 71301
(318)487-9347
Ultimate Parent: Limited. **SIC:** 5621—
Women's Clothing Stores.

★ 69391 ★ **Lerner Shop**
1804 Macarthur Dr.
Alexandria, LA 71301
(318)442-5534
Ultimate Parent: Limited. **SIC:** 5651—
Family Clothing Stores.

★ 69392 ★ **The Limited**
3437 Masonic Dr.
Alexandria, LA 71301
(318)442-9719
Ultimate Parent: Limited. **SIC:** 5651—
Family Clothing Stores.

★ 69393 ★ **Louisiana Pacific
Corp.**
2301 Mill St.
Alexandria, LA 71301
(318)448-4108
Ultimate Parent: Louisiana-Pacific. **SIC:**
5031—Lumber, Plywood & Millwork.

★ 69394 ★ **Mervyn's**
3437 Masonic Dr.
Alexandria, LA 71301
(318)442-8800
Ultimate Parent: Dayton Hudson. **SIC:**
5311—Department Stores.

★ 69395 ★ **New England Mutual
Life**
1419 Peterman Dr.
Alexandria, LA 71301
(318)445-7755
Ultimate Parent: New England Mutual Life.
SIC: 6411—Insurance Agents, Brokers &
Service.

★ 69396 ★ **Otis Elevator Co.**
1407 Murray St.
Alexandria, LA 71301
(318)442-7610
Ultimate Parent: United Technologies. **SIC:**
3534—Elevators & Moving Stairways;
5084—Industrial Machinery & Equipment.

★ 69397 ★ **Pizza Hut**
2595 N. MacArthur Dr.
Alexandria, LA 71303
(318)487-6797
Ultimate Parent: Pepsico. **SIC:** 5812—
Eating Places.

★ 69398 ★ **Pizza Hut**
3927 S. MacArthur Dr.
Alexandria, LA 71302
(318)443-4400
Ultimate Parent: Pepsico. **SIC:** 5812—
Eating Places.

★ 69399 ★ **Radio Shack**
1205 Texas Ave.
Alexandria, LA 71301
(318)443-8804
Company Type: Division. **Ultimate Parent:**
Tandy Corp. **SIC:** 5065—Electronic Parts &
Equipment Nec.

★ 69400 ★ **Radio Shack**
3437 Masonic Dr. 1310
Alexandria, LA 71301
Company Type: Division. **Ultimate Parent:**
Tandy Corp. **SIC:** 5065—Electronic Parts &
Equipment Nec.

★ 69401 ★ **Rapides Bank & Trust**
201 Johnston St.
Alexandria, LA 71301
(318)473-6904
Ultimate Parent: First Commerce Corp.
SIC: 6022—State Commercial Banks.

★ 69402 ★ **Rapides Bank & Trust
Compan**
400 Murray St.
Alexandria, LA 71301
(318)487-2431
Ultimate Parent: First Commerce Corp.
SIC: 6022—State Commercial Banks.

★ 69403 ★ **Rapides Bank & Trust
Compan**
2203 Memorial Dr.
Alexandria, LA 71301
(318)487-2490
Ultimate Parent: First Commerce Corp.
SIC: 6022—State Commercial Banks.

★ 69404 ★ **Rapides Bank & Trust
Co.**
England
Alexandria, LA 71301
(318)487-2751
Ultimate Parent: First Commerce Corp.
SIC: 6029—Commercial Banks Nec.

★ 69405 ★ **Rapides Bank & Trust
Co.**
3506 Jackson St.
Alexandria, LA 71303
(318)487-2470
Ultimate Parent: First Commerce Corp.
SIC: 6022—State Commercial Banks.

★ 69406 ★ **Rapides Bank & Trust
Co.**
1700 Bank Dr.
Alexandria, LA 71301
(318)487-2483
Ultimate Parent: First Commerce Corp.
SIC: 6022—State Commercial Banks.

★ 69407 ★   **Rapides Bank & Trust Co.**
625 Bolton Ave.
Alexandria, LA 71301
(318)487-2500
Ultimate Parent: First Commerce Corp.
SIC: 6022—State Commercial Banks.

★ 69408 ★   **Rapides Bank & Trust Co.**
3311 Lower St. 3rd
Alexandria, LA 71301
(318)487-2453
Ultimate Parent: First Commerce Corp.
SIC: 6022—State Commercial Banks.

★ 69409 ★   **Ryder Truck Rental**
5003 S. Macarthur Dr.
Alexandria, LA 71302
(318)442-3412
Ultimate Parent: Ryder System. **SIC:**
7513—Truck Rental & Leasing Without Drivers.

★ 69410 ★   **Ryder Truck Rental**
1505 England Dr.
Alexandria, LA 71303
(318)487-4674
Ultimate Parent: Ryder System. **SIC:**
7359—Equipment Rental & Leasing Nec;
7513—Truck Rental & Leasing Without Drivers.

★ 69411 ★   **Taco Bell**
3840 Alexandria Mall Dr.
Alexandria, LA 71301
(318)442-6491
Ultimate Parent: Pepsico. **SIC:** 5812—
Eating Places.

★ 69412 ★   **Trailways Bus System**
530 Jackson St.
Alexandria, LA 71301
(318)445-7183
Ultimate Parent: Greyhound Lines Inc. **SIC:**
4111—Local & Suburban Transit.

★ 69413 ★   **United Parcel Service**
3509 Mac Lee Dr.
Alexandria, LA 71302
(318)442-6693
Ultimate Parent: United Parcel Service of America. **SIC:** 4215—Courier Services Except by Air.

★ 69414 ★   **Wal Mart Discount City**
1804 MacArthur Dr.
Alexandria, LA 71301
(318)445-9000
Ultimate Parent: Wal-Mart Stores, Inc. **SIC:**
5311—Department Stores.

★ 69415 ★   **Wal Mart Portrait Studio**
2601 S. MacArthur Dr.
Alexandria, LA 71301
(318)448-3700
Ultimate Parent: Wal-Mart Stores, Inc. **SIC:**
7221—Photographic Studios—Portrait.

★ 69416 ★   **Wal Mart Tire, Battery, & Auto Ctr**
1804 MacArthur Dr.
Alexandria, LA 71301
(318)445-9533
Ultimate Parent: Wal-Mart Stores, Inc. **SIC:**
7538—General Automotive Repair Shops.

★ 69417 ★   **Waldenbooks**
Alexandria Mall
Alexandria, LA 71301
(318)443-4620
Ultimate Parent: K-Mart. **SIC:** 5942—Book Stores.

★ 69418 ★   **Zebco**
Alexandria, LA 71301
(318)445-9468
Ultimate Parent: Brunswick Corp. **SIC:**
6531—Real Estate Agents & Managers.

Amelia

★ 69419 ★   **Arco Oil & Gas Co.**
Amelia, LA 70340
(504)631-2807
Company Type: Division. **Location Type:**
Branch office. **Ultimate Parent:** Atlantic Richfield Co., Inc. **SIC:** 1311—Crude Petroleum & Natural Gas.

★ 69420 ★   **Baker Hughes Tubular Services**
Hwy. 662 North
Amelia, LA 70340
Ultimate Parent: Baker Hughes. **SIC:**
3479—Metal Coating & Allied Services.

★ 69421 ★   **Baker Hughes Tubular Services Inc.**
Hwy. 662 & Bayou L'ourse
Amelia, LA 70340
Ultimate Parent: Baker Hughes. **SIC:**
3479—Metal Coating & Allied Services.

★ 69422 ★   **Baker Hughes Vetco Services**
Hwy. 662 N.
Amelia, LA 70340
Ultimate Parent: Baker Hughes. **SIC:**
3479—Metal Coating & Allied Services.

★ 69423 ★   **Union Oil Co. of California**
Union Oil Co Rd.
Amelia, LA 70340
(504)631-2557
Ultimate Parent: Unocal Corp. **SIC:** 1311—
Crude Petroleum & Natural Gas.

Amite

★ 69424 ★   **Greyhound Bus Lines**
201 NW Central Ave.
Amite, LA 70422
(504)748-7122
Ultimate Parent: Greyhound Lines Inc. **SIC:**
4131—Intercity & Rural Bus Transportation.

Arabi

★ 69425 ★   **Fleet Finance Inc.**
7557 W. Judge Perez Dr.
Arabi, LA 70032
(504)279-4491
Ultimate Parent: Fleet Financial Group.
SIC: 6141—Personal Credit Institutions.

Arcadia

★ 69426 ★   **Conagra Broiler Co.**
Hwy. 80 W
Arcadia, LA 71001
(318)263-9561
Company Type: Division. **Location Type:**
Plant. **Officer:** Marvin Moore, Plant Supervisor. **Ultimate Parent:** Conagra.

★ 69427 ★   **Conagra Broiler Co.**
Arcadia Div.
Hwy. 80 W.
Arcadia, LA 71001-0090
Company Type: Division. **Ultimate Parent:**
Conagra. **SIC:** 2015—Poultry Slaughtering & Processing; 2077—Animal & Marine Fats & Oils.

★ 69428 ★   **Conagra Broiler Co. Arcadia Feedmill**
Hwy. 80 E.
Arcadia, LA 71001
Ultimate Parent: Conagra. **SIC:** 2048—
Prepared Feeds Nec.

★ 69429 ★   **Exxon**
Hwy. 80
Arcadia, LA 71001
(318)263-8466
Ultimate Parent: Exxon. **SIC:** 7261—
Funeral Services & Crematories.

★ 69430 ★   **Stone Container Corp.**
US Hwy. 80 W
Arcadia, LA 71001
(318)263-9503
Officer: Richard A. Moak, Manager.
Ultimate Parent: Stone Container Corp.
SIC: 2671—Paper Coated & Laminated—Packaging; 2674—Bags—Uncoated Paper & Multiwall.

★ 69431 ★   **Trailways Bus System**
118 Louisiana Ave. W
Arcadia, LA 71001
(318)255-3505
Ultimate Parent: Greyhound Lines Inc. **SIC:**
4131—Intercity & Rural Bus Transportation.

★ 69432 ★   **Warren Petroleum Co.**
Hwy. 147
Arcadia, LA 71001
(318)263-2782
Ultimate Parent: Chevron Corp. **SIC:**
5172—Petroleum Products Nec.

Arnaudville

★ 69433 ★   **Mini Mart Food Store**
Hwy. 31
Arnaudville, LA 70512
(318)754-8580
Ultimate Parent: Kroger. **SIC:** 5499—
Miscellaneous Food Stores.

Athens

★ 69434 ★   **AT&T**
Athens, LA 71003
(318)258-5055
Location Type: Branch office. **Ultimate Parent:** AT&T. **SIC:** 4813—Telephone Communications Except Radiotelephone.

Baker

★ 69435 ★   **Hibernia National Bank**
2082 Main St.
Baker, LA 70714
(504)381-2041
Ultimate Parent: Hibernia Corp. **SIC:**
6021—National Commercial Banks; 6022—
State Commercial Banks.

★ 69436 ★   **Kentucky Fried Chicken**
1940 Main St.
Baker, LA 70714
(504)774-7014
Ultimate Parent: Pepsico. **SIC:** 5812—
Eating Places.

★ 69437 ★   **Radio Shack**
2026 Main St.
Baker, LA 70714
(504)778-0515
Company Type: Division. **Ultimate Parent:**
Tandy Corp. **SIC:** 5065—Electronic Parts & Equipment Nec; 5731—Radio, Television & Electronics Stores.

★ 69438 ★   **Texaco Self Service Gas**
2002 Main St.
Baker, LA 70714
(504)774-6862
Ultimate Parent: Texaco. **SIC:** 5541—
Gasoline Service Stations.

Ball

★ 69439 ★   **Piggly Wiggly**
5916 Monroe Hwy.
Ball, LA 71405
(318)640-4651
Ultimate Parent: Bruno's. **SIC:** 5411—
Grocery Stores.

Bastrop

★ 69440 ★   **International Paper**
Liquid Packaging Div.
315 Airport Rd.
Bastrop, LA 71220
Company Type: Division. **Ultimate Parent:**
International Paper Co. **SIC:** 2656—Sanitary Food Containers.

★ 69441 ★   **International Paper Aerated Stabilization Basins**
Spyker Rd.
Bastrop, LA 71220
Ultimate Parent: International Paper Co.
SIC: 2621—Paper Mills; 2611—Pulp Mills.

★ 69442 ★   **International Paper Clarifiers & Fiber Reclaimer**
Sassafras St.
Bastrop, LA 71220
Ultimate Parent: International Paper Co.
SIC: 2621—Paper Mills; 2611—Pulp Mills.

★ 69443 ★   **International Paper Louisiana Mill**
705 Colliers Ln.
Bastrop, LA 71220
Ultimate Parent: International Paper Co.
SIC: 2621—Paper Mills; 2611—Pulp Mills.

★ 69444 ★   **International Paper Louisiana Mill**
705 Colliers Ln. PO Box 312
Bastrop, LA 71220
Ultimate Parent: International Paper Co.
SIC: 2621—Paper Mills; 2611—Pulp Mills.

★ 69445 ★   **Pizza Hut**
1608 E. Madison Ave.
Bastrop, LA 71220
(318)281-6158
Ultimate Parent: Pepsico. **SIC:** 5812—
Eating Places.

★ 69446 ★   **Radio Shack**
2053 E. Madison Ave. 6
Bastrop, LA 71220
(318)283-6218
Company Type: Division. **Ultimate Parent:**
Tandy Corp. **SIC:** 7629—Electrical Repair Shops Nec.

★ 69447 ★   **Radio Shack**
2053 E. Madison Ave. 6
Bastrop, LA 71220
(318)281-6218
Company Type: Division. **Ultimate Parent:**
Tandy Corp. **SIC:** 5065—Electronic Parts & Equipment Nec.

★ 69448 ★   **Rhone-Poulenc Basic Chemical Co.**
1502 N. Washington
Bastrop, LA 71220
Ultimate Parent: Rhone-Poulenc Rorer.
SIC: 2819—Industrial Inorganic Chemicals Nec.

★ 69449 ★   **Ryder Truck Rental**
1601 E. Madison Ave.
Bastrop, LA 71220
(318)283-2879
Ultimate Parent: Ryder System. **SIC:**
7513—Truck Rental & Leasing Without Drivers.

★ 69450 ★   **Shell Truck Stop**
Rr 1
Bastrop, LA 71220
(318)281-8945
Ultimate Parent: Shell Oil Co. **SIC:** 5812—
Eating Places.

★ 69451 ★   **Stauffer Chemical Co.**
1502 N. Washington St.
Bastrop, LA 71220
Ultimate Parent: Rhone-Poulenc Rorer.
SIC: 2819—Industrial Inorganic Chemicals Nec.

★ 69452 ★   **Wal Mart**
Hwy. 165 E
Bastrop, LA 71220
(318)281-6023
Ultimate Parent: Wal-Mart Stores, Inc. **SIC:**
5311—Department Stores.

Baton Rouge

★ 69453 ★   **Ace Hardware&Garden Center**
7460 Highland Rd.
Baton Rouge, LA 70808
(504)766-3049
Ultimate Parent: Ace Hardware. **SIC:**
5211—Lumber & Other Building Materials;
5261—Retail Nurseries & Garden Stores.

★ 69454 ★   **Airborne Freight Corp.**
7050 Exchequer Dr.
Baton Rouge, LA 70809
(504)756-8977
Ultimate Parent: Airborne Freight Corp.
SIC: 4513—Air Courier Services.

★ 69455 ★   **Airborne Freight Corp.**
1126 Executive Park Ave.
Baton Rouge, LA 70806
(504)343-4710
Ultimate Parent: Airborne Freight Corp.
SIC: 4513—Air Courier Services.

★ 69456 ★   **Albertson's**
11321 Florida Blvd.
Baton Rouge, LA 70815
(504)275-8116
Ultimate Parent: Albertson's Inc. **SIC:**
5411—Grocery Stores.

★ 69457 ★   **Allied Signal**
Corner Ontario St.
Baton Rouge, LA 70805
(504)383-5222
Ultimate Parent: Allied-Signal Inc. **SIC:**
2899—Chemical Preparations Nec.

★ 69458 ★ Allied-Signal Inc.
Lupine Ave.
Baton Rouge, LA 70805
(504)383-5222
Officer: Edward C. Calimari, Manager.
Ultimate Parent: Allied-Signal Inc. SIC:
2819—Industrial Inorganic Chemicals Nec;
2869—Industrial Organic Chemicals Nec;
2899—Chemical Preparations Nec.

★ 69459 ★ Allied-Signal, Inc.
PO Box 2830
Baton Rouge, LA 70821-2830
(504)383-5222
Officer: Ed Calamari. Ultimate Parent:
Allied-Signal Inc. SIC: 2819—Industrial
Inorganic Chemicals Nec.

★ 69460 ★ Allied-Signal Inc.
Corner of Lupine & Ontario St. Sts.
Baton Rouge, LA 70805
Ultimate Parent: Allied-Signal Inc. SIC:
2869—Industrial Organic Chemicals Nec;
2819—Industrial Inorganic Chemicals Nec.

★ 69461 ★ Allied-Signal, Inc.
12875 Scenic Hwy.
Baton Rouge, LA 70807
Ultimate Parent: Allied-Signal Inc. SIC:
2821—Plastics Materials & Resins.

★ 69462 ★ Allied-Signal Inc.
Paxon Polymer
12875 Scenic Hwy. Na
Baton Rouge, LA 70807
Ultimate Parent: Allied-Signal Inc. SIC:
2821—Plastics Materials & Resins.

★ 69463 ★ American General
Finance
2134 Oneal Ln.
Baton Rouge, LA 70816-3205
(504)756-8181
Officer: Joanne Smith. Ultimate Parent:
American General Corp. SIC: 6141—
Personal Credit Institutions; 6162—
Mortgage Bankers & Correspondents.

★ 69464 ★ American General
Finance
8345-D 2nd Florida Blvd.
Baton Rouge, LA 70806
(504)928-5633
Ultimate Parent: American General Corp.
SIC: 6141—Personal Credit Institutions.

★ 69465 ★ American General
Finance
11741 Market Place Ave., Ste. C
Baton Rouge, LA 70816-6012
(504)292-4836
Officer: Patrick R. Percy. Ultimate Parent:
American General Corp. SIC: 6141—
Personal Credit Institutions; 6162—
Mortgage Bankers & Correspondents.

★ 69466 ★ American General
Finance Inc.
11741 Market Place Ave., Ste. C
Baton Rouge, LA 70816-6012
(504)292-4836
Location Type: Branch office. Officer:
Patrick R. Percy. Ultimate Parent:
American General Corp. SIC: 6141—
Personal Credit Institutions; 6162—
Mortgage Bankers & Correspondents.

★ 69467 ★ American General
Finance Inc.
2134 O'Neal Ln.
Baton Rouge, LA 70816-3205
(504)756-8181
Location Type: Branch office. Officer:
Joanne Smith. Ultimate Parent: American
General Corp. SIC: 6141—Personal Credit
Institutions; 6162—Mortgage Bankers &
Correspondents.

★ 69468 ★ American General
Finance Inc.
8345-D 2nd Florida Blvd.
Baton Rouge, LA 70806
(504)928-5633
Location Type: Branch office. Ultimate
Parent: American General Corp. SIC:
6141—Personal Credit Institutions.

★ 69469 ★ AMR Services
9430 Jackie Cochran Dr.
Baton Rouge, LA 70807-8020
(504)357-3908
Ultimate Parent: AMR Corp. SIC: 4581—
Airports, Flying Fields & Services.

★ 69470 ★ Baton Rouge Coca-
Cola Bottling Co.
10000 Dawnadele Ave.
Baton Rouge, LA 70809-2586
Ultimate Parent: Coca-Cola Bottling
Consol. SIC: 2086—Bottled & Canned Soft
Drinks.

★ 69471 ★ Beckman Instruments
Inc.
11766 S. Harrells Ferry Rd.
Baton Rouge, LA 70816
(504)293-5960
Ultimate Parent: Beckman Instruments.
SIC: 5087—Service Establishment
Equipment.

Baton rouge

★ 69472 ★ Bellsouth mobility
2751 W. Perdue Dr.
Baton rouge, LA 70814-4443
(504)924-0909
Ultimate Parent: BellSouth Corp. SIC:
4812—Radiotelephone Communications.

Baton Rouge

★ 69473 ★ Beneficial Income Tax
Service
11457 Florida Blvd.
Baton Rouge, LA 70815
(504)273-3671
Ultimate Parent: Bemis Co., Inc. SIC:
7291—Tax Return Preparation Services.

★ 69474 ★ Borden Inc.
4743 Florida Blvd.
Baton Rouge, LA 70806
(504)926-7130
Officer: Wayne Tucker, Manager. Ultimate
Parent: Borden, Inc. SIC: 2024—Ice Cream
& Frozen Desserts; 2026—Fluid Milk.

★ 69475 ★ Borden Inc.
Dairy
4743 Flordia Blvd.
Baton Rouge, LA 70806
Company Type: Division. Ultimate Parent:
Borden, Inc. SIC: 2026—Fluid Milk.

★ 69476 ★ Borden Inc. Grocery
& Speciality Prds.
4743 Florida Blvd.
Baton Rouge, LA 70806-4032
Ultimate Parent: Borden, Inc. SIC: 2026—
Fluid Milk.

★ 69477 ★ Browning Ferris
Industries BFI
12451 Leisure Rd.
Baton Rouge, LA 70807-1412
(504)356-2478
Officer: Vaughn Meiners. Ultimate Parent:
Browning-Ferris Industries. SIC: 4953—
Refuse Systems; 7699—Repair Services
Nec.

★ 69478 ★ Butler Paper Co.
12124 Industriplex Blvd.
Baton Rouge, LA 70809-5128
Location Type: Branch office. Officer: Jim
Bostic. Ultimate Parent: Alco Standard
Corp. SIC: 5111—Printing & Writing Paper;
2621—Paper Mills; 5113—Industrial &
Personal Service Paper.

★ 69479 ★ Casual Corner
9773 Cortana Pl
Baton Rouge, LA 70815
(504)928-9594
Ultimate Parent: United States Shoe. SIC:
5651—Family Clothing Stores.

★ 69480 ★ City National Bank
9650 Airline Hwy.
Baton Rouge, LA 70815-5505
(504)928-3785
Ultimate Parent: City National Corp. SIC:
6021—National Commercial Banks.

★ 69481 ★ City National Bank
215 Staring Ln.
Baton Rouge, LA 70810-4064
(504)766-9316
Officer: Jane Robert, Manager. Ultimate
Parent: City National Corp. SIC: 6021—
National Commercial Banks.

★ 69482 ★ City National Bank
10725 Perkins Rd.
Baton Rouge, LA 70810-1610
(504)769-3890
Officer: Mitchell J. Krane, Manager.
Ultimate Parent: City National Corp. SIC:
6021—National Commercial Banks.

★ 69483 ★ City National Bank
7474 Florida Blvd.
Baton Rouge, LA 70806-4638
(504)925-5441
Officer: Shirley H. Weaver, Manager.
Ultimate Parent: City National Corp. SIC:
6021—National Commercial Banks.

★ 69484 ★ City National Bank
7515 Perkins Rd.
Baton Rouge, LA 70808-4330
(504)767-4197
Ultimate Parent: City National Corp. SIC:
6021—National Commercial Banks.

★ 69485 ★ City National Bank
5861 S. Sherwood Forest Blvd.
Baton Rouge, LA 70816
(504)292-0606
Ultimate Parent: City National Corp. SIC:
6022—State Commercial Banks.

★ 69486 ★ City National Bank
250 W. State St.
Baton Rouge, LA 70802
(504)387-1404
Ultimate Parent: City National Corp. SIC:
6099—Functions Related to Deposit
Banking.

★ 69487 ★ City National Bank
2700 Plank Rd.
Baton Rouge, LA 70805
(504)357-5904
Ultimate Parent: City National Corp. SIC:
6022—State Commercial Banks.

★ 69488 ★ City National Bank
124 Riverside Mall
Baton Rouge, LA 70801
(504)387-0916
Ultimate Parent: City National Corp. SIC:
6029—Commercial Banks Nec.

★ 69489 ★ City National Bank
Perkins Rd.
Baton Rouge, LA 70809
(504)926-3850
Ultimate Parent: City National Corp. SIC:
6022—State Commercial Banks.

★ 69490 ★ City National Bank
12627 Perkins Rd.
Baton Rouge, LA 70810
(504)769-3890
Ultimate Parent: City National Corp. SIC:
6099—Functions Related to Deposit
Banking.

★ 69491 ★ City National Bank
3012 Government St.
Baton Rouge, LA 70806
(504)387-0586
Ultimate Parent: City National Corp. SIC:
6022—State Commercial Banks.

★ 69492 ★ City National Bank
Lousiana State University Union
Baton Rouge, LA 70808
(504)387-6284
Ultimate Parent: City National Corp. SIC:
6099—Functions Related to Deposit
Banking.

★ 69493 ★ City National Bank
6465 Beechwood Dr.
Baton Rouge, LA 70805
(504)355-2584
Ultimate Parent: City National Corp. SIC:
6022—State Commercial Banks.

★ 69494 ★ City National Bank
9135 Cortana Pl.
Baton Rouge, LA 70815
(504)923-3120
Ultimate Parent: City National Corp. SIC:
6022—State Commercial Banks.

★ 69495 ★ City National Bank
2828 Monterrey Dr.
Baton Rouge, LA 70814
(504)923-0402
Location Type: Branch office. Ultimate
Parent: City National Corp. SIC: 6022—
State Commercial Banks.

★ 69496 ★ City National Bank
7474 Florida Blvd.
Baton Rouge, LA 70806
(504)925-5441
Location Type: Branch office. Ultimate
Parent: City National Corp. SIC: 6022—
State Commercial Banks.

★ 69497 ★ City National Bank
7722 Scenic Hwy.
Baton Rouge, LA 70807
(504)356-4584
Ultimate Parent: City National Corp. SIC:
6022—State Commercial Banks.

★ 69498 ★ City National Bank of
Baton
445 North Blvd.
Baton Rouge, LA 70802
(504)387-2151
Ultimate Parent: City National Corp.

★ 69499 ★ City National Bank
(Br)
1818 Sherwood Forest Blvd.
Baton Rouge, LA 70816
(504)275-8350
Ultimate Parent: City National Corp.

★ 69500 ★ Coca-Cola Botting Co.
of Bat
10000 Dawnadele Ave.
Baton Rouge, LA 70809
(504)293-2570
Ultimate Parent: Coca-Cola Enterprises.
SIC: 2086—Bottled & Canned Soft Drinks;
5149—Groceries & Related Products Nec.

★ 69501 ★ Delta Air Cargo
Baton Rouge Metropolitan Airport
Baton Rouge, LA 70807
(504)358-2130
Ultimate Parent: Delta Air Lines, Inc. SIC:
4513—Air Courier Services.

★ 69502 ★ Delta Air Lines
Baton Rouge Metropolitan Airport
Baton Rouge, LA 70807
(504)358-2105
Ultimate Parent: Delta Air Lines, Inc. SIC:
4512—Air Transportation—Scheduled.

★ 69503 ★ Delta Air Lines
Ryan Airport
Baton Rouge, LA 70807
(504)356-0117
Ultimate Parent: Delta Air Lines, Inc. SIC:
4512—Air Transportation—Scheduled;
4729—Passenger Transportation
Arrangement Nec.

★ 69504 ★ Delta Air Lines
201 Lafayette St.
Baton Rouge, LA 70801
(504)356-4361
Ultimate Parent: Delta Air Lines, Inc. SIC:
4512—Air Transportation—Scheduled.

★ 69505 ★ Delta Air Lines Inc.
Ryan Airport
Baton Rouge, LA 70807
(504)356-0117
Ultimate Parent: Delta Air Lines, Inc. SIC:
4512—Air Transportation—Scheduled;
4729—Passenger Transportation
Arrangement Nec.

★ 69506 ★ Delta Air Lines Inc.
Baton Rouge Met Airport
Baton Rouge, LA 70807
(504)358-2105
Ultimate Parent: Delta Air Lines, Inc. SIC:
4512—Air Transportation—Scheduled.

★ 69507 ★ Diebold Inc.
1723 Dallas Dr.
Baton Rouge, LA 70806
(504)924-0098
Ultimate Parent: Diebold, Inc.

★ 69508 ★ Diebold Inc.
9644 Mammoth Ave.
Baton Rouge, LA 70814
(504)926-1078
Ultimate Parent: Diebold, Inc. SIC: 5044—
Office Equipment.

★ 69509 ★ Digital Equipment
Corporati
4354 Sherwood Forest Blvd.
Baton Rouge, LA 70816
(504)292-2141
Ultimate Parent: Digital Equipment Corp.
SIC: 3571—Electronic Computers; 5046—
Commercial Equipment Nec.

★ 69510 ★   Dillard Department
Stores
Cortana
Baton Rouge, LA 70815
(504)923-1712
Ultimate Parent: Dillard Department Stores.
SIC: 5311—Department Stores.

★ 69511 ★   Emery Worldwide
20280 Highland Rd.
Baton Rouge, LA 70817
Ultimate Parent: Consolidated Freightways.
SIC: 7389—Business Services Nec; 4513—
Air Courier Services.

★ 69512 ★   Ethyl Corp.
Gulf States Rd.
Baton Rouge, LA 70821
(504)359-2445
Officer: George A. Newbill, Executive
Director. Ultimate Parent: Ethyl. SIC:
2869—Industrial Organic Chemicals Nec;
2899—Chemical Preparations Nec.

★ 69513 ★   Ethyl Corp. Chemicals
451 Florida St.
Baton Rouge, LA 70801
(504)388-8011
Officer: E. Gary Cook, President. Ultimate
Parent: Ethyl. SIC: 2869—Industrial
Organic Chemicals Nec.

★ 69514 ★   Ethyl Process
Development Center
Gulf States Rd.
Baton Rouge, LA 70805
Ultimate Parent: Ethyl. SIC: 2869—
Industrial Organic Chemicals Nec.

★ 69515 ★   Exxon
7808 Greenwell Springs Rd.
Baton Rouge, LA 70814
(504)925-9961
Ultimate Parent: Exxon. SIC: 5541—
Gasoline Service Stations.

★ 69516 ★   Exxon
14879 Tiger Bend Rd.
Baton Rouge, LA 70817
(504)293-6333
Ultimate Parent: Exxon. SIC: 5541—
Gasoline Service Stations.

★ 69517 ★   Exxon
6060 Bluebonnet Blvd.
Baton Rouge, LA 70809
(504)767-7506
Ultimate Parent: Exxon. SIC: 5541—
Gasoline Service Stations.

★ 69518 ★   Exxon
7997 Plank Rd.
Baton Rouge, LA 70811
(504)357-5661
Ultimate Parent: Exxon. SIC: 5541—
Gasoline Service Stations.

★ 69519 ★   Exxon Chemical Co.
3801 Plaza Tower Dr. 100
Baton Rouge, LA 70816
Ultimate Parent: Exxon. SIC: 2899—
Chemical Preparations Nec.

★ 69520 ★   Exxon Chemical Co.
4999 Scenic Hwy.
Baton Rouge, LA 70805
(504)359-7011
Ultimate Parent: Exxon. SIC: 2899—
Chemical Preparations Nec.

★ 69521 ★   Exxon Chemical Co.
11175 Scotland Zachary Hwy.
Baton Rouge, LA 70807
(504)778-5211
Officer: William Brackney, Manager.
Ultimate Parent: Exxon SIC: 2821—Plastics
Materials & Resins.

★ 69522 ★   Exxon Chemical Co.
12480 Scenic Hwy.
Baton Rouge, LA 70807
(504)775-8950
Officer: C. H. Dupre, Manager. Ultimate
Parent: Exxon SIC: 2821—Plastics Materials
& Resins.

★ 69523 ★   Exxon Chemical Co.
4999 Scenic Hwy.
Baton Rouge, LA 70805
(504)359-7011
Officer: William Senn, Manager. Ultimate
Parent: Exxon SIC: 2822—Synthetic
Rubber; 2869—Industrial Organic Chemicals
Nec; 2911—Petroleum Refining.

★ 69524 ★   Exxon Chemical Lab
Library
4999 Scenic Hwy.
Baton Rouge, LA 70805
(504)359-5211
Ultimate Parent: Exxon. SIC: 8231—
Libraries.

★ 69525 ★   Exxon Chemical
Plastics Library
4045 Scenic Hwy.
Baton Rouge, LA 70805
(504)359-5296
Ultimate Parent: Exxon. SIC: 8231—
Libraries.

★ 69526 ★   Exxon Co. USA
3301 Scenic Hwy.
Baton Rouge, LA 70805
(504)359-7604
Ultimate Parent: Exxon. SIC: 2911—
Petroleum Refining.

★ 69527 ★   Exxon Co. USA
4045 Scenic Hwy.
Baton Rouge, LA 70805
(504)359-7711
Ultimate Parent: Exxon. SIC: 1311—Crude
Petroleum & Natural Gas.

★ 69528 ★   Exxon Co. USA
4521 Jamestown Ave.
Baton Rouge, LA 70808
(504)927-5061
Ultimate Parent: Exxon. SIC: 3089—
Plastics Products Nec.

★ 69529 ★   Exxon Co. USA
11410 Airline Hwy.
Baton Rouge, LA 70816
(504)292-4239
Ultimate Parent: Exxon. SIC: 5541—
Gasoline Service Stations.

★ 69530 ★   Exxon Pipeline Co.
12875 Scenic Hwy.
Baton Rouge, LA 70807
(504)778-1354
Ultimate Parent: Exxon. SIC: 4619—
Pipelines Nec.

★ 69531 ★   Exxon Pipeline Co.
18440 Highland Rd.
Baton Rouge, LA 70809
(504)359-1400
Ultimate Parent: Exxon. SIC: 4612—Crude
Petroleum Pipelines; 4619—Pipelines Nec.

★ 69532 ★   Exxon Pipeline Co.
18440 Highland Rd.
Baton Rouge, LA 70809
(504)359-1400
Ultimate Parent: Exxon Pipeline. SIC:
4612—Crude Petroleum Pipelines; 4619—
Pipelines Nec.

★ 69533 ★   Exxon Pipeline Co.
12875 Scenic Hwy.
Baton Rouge, LA 70807
(504)778-1354
Ultimate Parent: Exxon Pipeline. SIC:
4619—Pipelines Nec.

★ 69534 ★   Ferro Corp.
Grant Chemical
PO Box 263
Baton Rouge, LA 70821
(504)654-6801 Fax: (504)654-3208
Company Type: Subsidiary. Officer: Ed
Wroten, General Manager. Ultimate Parent:
Ferro Corp.

★ 69535 ★   First State Bank &
Trust Co.
11659 Plank Rd.
Baton Rouge, LA 70811
(504)775-7283
Ultimate Parent: Michigan National Corp.
SIC: 6022—State Commercial Banks.

★ 69536 ★   Flowers Baking Co.
1504 Florida St.
Baton Rouge, LA 70802
(504)381-9699
Officer: Rickey Spaulding, President.
Ultimate Parent: Flowers Industries. SIC:
2051—Bread, Cake & Related Products.

★ 69537 ★   Flowers Baking Co. of
Baton Rouge
1504 Florida Blvd.
PO Box 3637
Baton Rouge, LA 70821
(504)381-9699 Fax: (504)381-9733
Company Type: Subsidiary. Officer: Rick

Spalding, President. Ultimate Parent:
Flowers Industries.

★ 69538 ★   Flowers Distributing
Co.
1504 Florida Blvd.
Baton Rouge, LA 70802
(504)231-7190
Officer: Rickey Spaulding, President.
Ultimate Parent: Flowers Industries. SIC:
2051—Bread, Cake & Related Products.

★ 69539 ★   The Gap
9251 Cortana Pl
Baton Rouge, LA 70815
(504)925-5791
Ultimate Parent: GAP. SIC: 5611—Men's &
Boys' Clothing Stores; 5651—Family
Clothing Stores.

★ 69540 ★   The Gap Kids
9479 Cortana Pl
Baton Rouge, LA 70815
(504)926-6446
Ultimate Parent: GAP. SIC: 5651—Family
Clothing Stores.

★ 69541 ★   Greyhound Bus Lines
1253 Florida St.
Baton Rouge, LA 70802
(504)383-3811
Ultimate Parent: Greyhound Lines Inc. SIC:
4111—Local & Suburban Transit; 4131—
Intercity & Rural Bus Transportation; 5812—
Eating Places.

★ 69542 ★   Gulf States Utilities
Co.
5564 Essen Ln.
Baton Rouge, LA 70809
(504)767-1802
Ultimate Parent: Gulf State Utilities Co.
SIC: 4939—Combination Utility Nec.

★ 69543 ★   Gulf States Utilities
Co.
446 North Blvd.
Baton Rouge, LA 70802
(504)767-1802
Ultimate Parent: Gulf State Utilities Co.

★ 69544 ★   Hibernia National
Bank
4646 S. Sherwood Forest Blvd.
Baton Rouge, LA 70816
(504)381-2054
Ultimate Parent: Hibernia Corp.

★ 69545 ★   Hibernia National
Bank
6041 Jones Creek Rd.
Baton Rouge, LA 70817
(504)381-2053
Ultimate Parent: Hibernia Corp. SIC:
6099—Functions Related to Deposit
Banking.

★ 69546 ★   Hibernia National
Bank
9638 Florida Blvd.
Baton Rouge, LA 70815
(504)381-2042
Ultimate Parent: Hibernia Corp. SIC:
6022—State Commercial Banks.

★ 69547 ★   Hibernia National
Bank
14424 Old Hammond Hwy.
Baton Rouge, LA 70816
Ultimate Parent: Hibernia Corp. SIC:
6022—State Commercial Banks.

★ 69548 ★   Hibernia National
Bank
6581 Siegen Ln.
Baton Rouge, LA 70809
(504)381-2048
Ultimate Parent: Hibernia Corp. SIC:
6021—National Commercial Banks; 6022—
State Commercial Banks.

★ 69549 ★   Hibernia National
Bank
9405 Greenwell Springs Rd.
Baton Rouge, LA 70814
(504)927-1473
Ultimate Parent: Hibernia Corp. SIC:
6022—State Commercial Banks; 6099—
Functions Related to Deposit Banking.

★ 69550 ★   Hibernia National
Bank
5220 Government St.
Baton Rouge, LA 70806
(504)381-2047
Ultimate Parent: Hibernia Corp. SIC:
6099—Functions Related to Deposit
Banking.

★ 69551 ★   Hibernia National
Bank
4707 Perkins Rd.
Baton Rouge, LA 70808
(504)381-2052
Ultimate Parent: Hibernia Corp. SIC:
6099—Functions Related to Deposit
Banking.

★ 69552 ★   Hibernia National
Bank
5175 Plank Rd.
Baton Rouge, LA 70805
(504)381-2044
Ultimate Parent: Hibernia Corp. SIC:
6099—Functions Related to Deposit
Banking.

★ 69553 ★   Hibernia National
Bank
3875 Florida Blvd.
Baton Rouge, LA 70806
(504)382-2046
Ultimate Parent: Hibernia Corp. SIC:
6022—State Commercial Banks.

★ 69554 ★   Hibernia National
Bank
440 Riverside Mall
Baton Rouge, LA 70802
(504)381-2470
Ultimate Parent: Hibernia Corp.

★ 69555 ★   Hibernia National
Bank Inc. B
2390 Eal Ln.
Baton Rouge, LA 70816
(504)381-2051
Ultimate Parent: Hibernia Corp. SIC:
6022—State Commercial Banks.

★ 69556 ★   Hit or Miss
9622 Airline Hwy.
Baton Rouge, LA 70815
(504)927-6227
Ultimate Parent: TJX. SIC: 5651—Family
Clothing Stores.

★ 69557 ★   Hoechst Celanese
Corp. Baton Rouge Works
11911 Scenic Hwy.
Baton Rouge, LA 70807
Ultimate Parent: Hoechst Celanese Corp.
SIC: 2869—Industrial Organic Chemicals
Nec; 2899—Chemical Preparations Nec;
2821—Plastics Materials & Resins.

★ 69558 ★   Human Affairs
International
2351 Energy Dr.
Baton Rouge, LA 70808
(504)924-2944
Ultimate Parent: Aetna Life & Annuity. SIC:
7361—Employment Agencies.

★ 69559 ★   Hunter Zep
2612 Tee Dr.
Baton Rouge, LA 70895
Ultimate Parent: National Service
Industries. SIC: 2841—Soap & Other
Detergents; 2842—Polishes & Sanitation
Goods; 2843—Surface Active Agents;
2844—Toilet Preparations.

★ 69560 ★   Inacomp Computer
Centers
11441 Industriplex Blvd.
Baton Rouge, LA 70809
(504)291-9494
Ultimate Parent: Beneficial. SIC: 7372—
Prepackaged Software.

★ 69561 ★   Jiffy Lube
5744 S. Sherwood Forest Blvd.
Baton Rouge, LA 70816
(504)292-9861
Ultimate Parent: Pennzoil. SIC: 7538—
General Automotive Repair Shops.

★ 69562 ★   Jiffy Lube
4815 Perkins Rd.
Baton Rouge, LA 70808
(504)928-1975
Ultimate Parent: Pennzoil.

★ 69563 ★   Jiffy Lube
3133 Monterrey Dr.
Baton Rouge, LA 70814
(504)923-0164
Ultimate Parent: Pennzoil. SIC: 7539—
Automotive Repair Shops Nec.

★ 69564 ★   Jiffy Lube
14523 Old Hammond Hwy.
Baton Rouge, LA 70816
(504)275-4991
Ultimate Parent: Pennzoil. SIC: 7539—
Automotive Repair Shops Nec.

★ 69565 ★   Kaiser Aluminum &
Chemical
Airline Hwy.
Baton Rouge, LA 70892
(504)356-8451
Ultimate Parent: Maxxam. SIC: 3334—
Primary Aluminum.

★ 69566 ★   Kay Bee Toys
9667 Cortana Pl
Baton Rouge, LA 70815
(504)927-5501
Ultimate Parent: Melville. SIC: 5945—
Hobby, Toy & Game Shops.

★ 69567 ★   Kentucky Fried
Chicken
2151 Sherwood Forest Blvd.
Baton Rouge, LA 70816
(504)275-0923
Ultimate Parent: Pepsico. SIC: 5812—
Eating Places.

★ 69568 ★   Kentucky Fried
Chicken
Rural Route 2
Baton Rouge, LA 70817
(504)292-7929
Ultimate Parent: Pepsico. SIC: 5812—
Eating Places.

★ 69569 ★   Kentucky Fried
Chicken
8132 Scenic Hwy.
Baton Rouge, LA 70807
(504)774-2019
Ultimate Parent: Pepsico. SIC: 5812—
Eating Places.

★ 69570 ★   Kentucky Fried
Chicken
4320 Perkins Rd.
Baton Rouge, LA 70808
(504)383-5056
Ultimate Parent: Pepsico. SIC: 5812—
Eating Places.

★ 69571 ★   Kentucky Fried
Chicken
2668 Rome Dr.
Baton Rouge, LA 70814
(504)927-5238
Ultimate Parent: Pepsico. SIC: 5812—
Eating Places.

★ 69572 ★   Kentucky Fried
Chicken
6166 Florida Blvd.
Baton Rouge, LA 70806
(504)924-2416
Ultimate Parent: Pepsico. SIC: 5812—
Eating Places.

★ 69573 ★   Kentucky Fried
Chicken
9830 Florida Blvd.
Baton Rouge, LA 70815
(504)926-8692
Ultimate Parent: Pepsico. SIC: 5812—
Eating Places.

★ 69574 ★   Kentucky Fried
Chicken
6120 Airline Hwy.
Baton Rouge, LA 70805
(504)355-7583
Ultimate Parent: Pepsico. SIC: 5812—
Eating Places.

★ 69575 ★   Lane Bryant
7305 Florida Blvd.
Baton Rouge, LA 70806
(504)923-3374
Ultimate Parent: Limited. SIC: 5651—
Family Clothing Stores.

★ 69576 ★   Lane Bryant
9379 Cortana Pl
Baton Rouge, LA 70815
(504)928-5132
Ultimate Parent: Limited. SIC: 5651—
Family Clothing Stores.

★ 69577 ★   Lens Crafters
8945 Cortana Pl
Baton Rouge, LA 70815
(504)929-7994
Ultimate Parent: United States Shoe. SIC:
5995—Optical Goods Stores.

★ 69578 ★   Lerner Shop
9487 Cortana Pl
Baton Rouge, LA 70815
(504)926-6816
Ultimate Parent: Limited. SIC: 5621—
Women's Clothing Stores; 5651—Family
Clothing Stores.

★ 69579 ★   Lerner Shop
401 Riverside Mall
Baton Rouge, LA 70802
(504)343-1350
Ultimate Parent: Limited. SIC: 5621—
Women's Clothing Stores.

★ 69580 ★   The Limited
Cortana Pl
Baton Rouge, LA 70815
(504)924-7248
Ultimate Parent: Limited. SIC: 5621—
Women's Clothing Stores.

★ 69581 ★   The Limited
7305 Florida Blvd.
Baton Rouge, LA 70806
(504)923-1076
Ultimate Parent: Limited. SIC: 5651—
Family Clothing Stores.

★ 69582 ★   The Limited
9369 Cortana Pl
Baton Rouge, LA 70815
(504)927-4541
Ultimate Parent: Limited. SIC: 5651—
Family Clothing Stores.

★ 69583 ★   Lorillard Inc.
1986 Dallas Dr.
Baton Rouge, LA 70806
(504)928-1039
Ultimate Parent: Loews. SIC: 5194—
Tobacco & Tobacco Products.

★ 69584 ★   Maison Blanche
1500 Main St.
Baton Rouge, LA 70821
(504)389-7000 Fax: (504)382-3126
Officer: Philip W. Kaiser, President.
Ultimate Parent: Mercantile Stores.

★ 69585 ★   Maison Blanche Car
Care Cen
1501 Florida St.
Baton Rouge, LA 70802
(504)389-7308
Ultimate Parent: Mercantile Stores. SIC:
5531—Automobile & Home Supply Stores.

★ 69586 ★   Maison Blanche
Optical Dept
4731 North Blvd.
Baton Rouge, LA 70806
(504)927-7147
Ultimate Parent: Mercantile Stores. SIC:
5999—Miscellaneous Retail Stores Nec.

★ 69587 ★   Mary Kay Cosmetics
7613 John Newcombe Ave.
Baton Rouge, LA 70810
(504)769-0141
Ultimate Parent: Mary Kay Cosmetics. SIC:
5999—Miscellaneous Retail Stores Nec.

★ 69588 ★   Mary Kay Cosmetics,
Sales Rep.
15677 Geraldine Dr.
Baton Rouge, LA 70819
(504)272-9291
Ultimate Parent: Mary Kay Cosmetics. SIC:
2711—Newspapers.

★ 69589 ★   Mervyn's
9389 Cortana Pl
Baton Rouge, LA 70815
(504)924-7799
Ultimate Parent: Dayton Hudson. SIC:
5311—Department Stores.

★ 69590 ★   Nalco Chemical Co.
12021 Lakeland Park Blvd.
Baton Rouge, LA 70809
(504)292-6300
Ultimate Parent: Nalco Chemical Co. SIC:
2899—Chemical Preparations Nec.

★ 69591 ★   New York Life Baton
Rouge General Office
One American Pl., Ste. 800
Baton Rouge, LA 70825
(504)387-9249 Fax: (504)925-8387
Officer: K. Paul Cox, Manager. Ultimate
Parent: New York Life.

★ 69592 ★   Otis Elevator Co.
1818 Wooddale Blvd.
Baton Rouge, LA 70806
(504)924-4310
Ultimate Parent: United Technologies. SIC:
5084—Industrial Machinery & Equipment.

★ 69593 ★   Pappagallo
5274 Corporate Blvd.
Baton Rouge, LA 70808
(504)927-7093
Ultimate Parent: United States Shoe. SIC:
5621—Women's Clothing Stores.

★ 69594 ★   Penn Mutual Life
Insurance Co.
4637 Jamestown Ave.
Baton Rouge, LA 70808
(504)928-2671
Ultimate Parent: Penn Mutual Life. SIC:
6411—Insurance Agents, Brokers &
Service.

★ 69595 ★   Pennzoil Co.
439 N. 6th St.
Baton Rouge, LA 70802
(504)272-7382
Ultimate Parent: Pennzoil. SIC: 1311—
Crude Petroleum & Natural Gas.

★ 69596 ★   Pepsi-Cola Seven-Up
Group
10222 S. Perdue Ave.
Baton Rouge, LA 70814
(504)273-2441
Officer: Mike Jones, Manager. Ultimate
Parent: Pepsico. SIC: 2086—Bottled &
Canned Soft Drinks.

★ 69597 ★   Piggly Wiggly
5151 Plank Rd.
Baton Rouge, LA 70805
(504)356-4301
Ultimate Parent: Bruno's. SIC: 5411—
Grocery Stores.

★ 69598 ★   Piggly Wiggly
9301 Burbank Dr.
Baton Rouge, LA 70820
(504)766-8075
Ultimate Parent: Bruno's. SIC: 5411—
Grocery Stores.

★ 69599 ★   Pitney Bowes
9434 Interline Ave.
Baton Rouge, LA 70809
(504)926-8405
Officer: Ed Joyce, Manager. Ultimate
Parent: Pitney Bowes. SIC: 3554—Paper
Industries Machinery.

★ 69600 ★   Pizza Hut
2628 S. Sherwood Forest Blvd.
Baton Rouge, LA 70816
(504)292-1609
Ultimate Parent: Pepsico. SIC: 5812—
Eating Places.

★ 69601 ★   Pizza Hut
4665 Perkins Rd.
Baton Rouge, LA 70808
(504)924-0324
Ultimate Parent: Pepsico. SIC: 5812—
Eating Places.

★ 69602 ★   Pizza Hut
12222 Plank Rd.
Baton Rouge, LA 70811
(504)774-1974
Ultimate Parent: Pepsico. SIC: 5812—
Eating Places.

★ 69603 ★   Pizza Hut
11670 Florida Blvd.
Baton Rouge, LA 70815
(504)272-0040
Ultimate Parent: Pepsico. SIC: 5812—
Eating Places.

★ 69604 ★   Pizza Hut
4343 Nicholson Dr.
Baton Rouge, LA 70808
(504)769-8646
Ultimate Parent: Pepsico. SIC: 5812—
Eating Places.

★ 69605 ★   Pizza Hut
4763 Airline Hwy.
Baton Rouge, LA 70805
(504)356-0751
Ultimate Parent: Pepsico. SIC: 5812—
Eating Places.

★ 69606 ★   Pizza Hut
5175 Florida Blvd.
Baton Rouge, LA 70806
(504)924-6251
Ultimate Parent: Pepsico. SIC: 5812—
Eating Places.

★ 69607 ★   Pizza Hut
Rural Route 2
Baton Rouge, LA 70817
(504)291-2561
Ultimate Parent: Pepsico. SIC: 5812—
Eating Places.

★ 69608 ★   Pizza Hut
815 Florida St.
Baton Rouge, LA 70801
(504)272-0040
Ultimate Parent: Pepsico. SIC: 6531—Real
Estate Agents & Managers.

★ 69609 ★   Pizza Hut
1183 S. Flannery Rd.
Baton Rouge, LA 70815
(504)272-4068
Ultimate Parent: Pepsico. SIC: 5812—
Eating Places.

★ 69610 ★   Premier Bancorp
451 Florida St.
Baton Rouge, LA 70801
(504)332-7000
Company Type: Headquarters. Officer: G.
Lee Griffin. Employee Count: 2740.
Fortune Service 500: Ranking 97.

★ 69611 ★   Premier Bancorp, Inc.
Holding Co.
451 Florida St.
Baton Rouge, LA 70801
(504)332-7277 Fax: (504)332-7512
Officer: G. Lee Griffin, Chairman of the
Board, President & Chief Executive Officer.
Ultimate Parent: Premier Bancorp.

★ 69612 ★   Premier Bancorp, Inc.
Holding Co.
PO Box 1511
Baton Rouge, LA 70821
Officer: G. Lee Griffin, Chairman of the
Board, President & Chief Executive Officer.
Ultimate Parent: Premier Bancorp.

★ 69613 ★   Premier Bank, NA
5900 Airline Hwy.
Baton Rouge, LA 70805-3201
(504)332-4360
Location Type: Branch office. Ultimate
Parent: Premier Bancorp.

★ 69614 ★   Premier Bank, NA
415 Florida St.
PO Box 1511
Baton Rouge, LA 70821
(504)332-4052
Ultimate Parent: Premier Bancorp.

★ 69615 ★   Premier Bank, NA
11311 Florida Blvd.
Baton Rouge, LA 70815-2402
(504)332-4261
Location Type: Branch office. Ultimate
Parent: Premier Bancorp.

★ 69616 ★   Premier Bank, NA
8578 Goodwood Blvd.
Baton Rouge, LA 70806-7910
(504)332-4523
Location Type: Branch office. Ultimate
Parent: Premier Bancorp.

★ 69617 ★   Premier Bank, NA
5700 Florida Blvd.
Baton Rouge, LA 70806-4243
(504)332-4271
Location Type: Branch office. Ultimate
Parent: Premier Bancorp.

★ 69618 ★ Premier Bank, NA
1312 O'Neal Ln.
Baton Rouge, LA 70816-1956
(504)332-4850
Location Type: Branch office. Ultimate
Parent: Premier Bancorp.

★ 69619 ★ Premier Bank, NA
5321 Corporate Blvd.
Baton Rouge, LA 70808-2569
(504)332-4571
Location Type: Branch office. Ultimate
Parent: Premier Bancorp.

★ 69620 ★ Premier Bank, NA
7979 Plank Rd.
Baton Rouge, LA 70811-3997
(504)332-4431
Location Type: Branch office. Ultimate
Parent: Premier Bancorp.

★ 69621 ★ Premier Bank, NA
5255 Highland Rd.
Baton Rouge, LA 70808
(504)332-4565
Location Type: Branch office. Ultimate
Parent: Premier Bancorp.

★ 69622 ★ Premier Bank, NA
7387 Highland Rd.
Baton Rouge, LA 70806-6610
(504)332-4474
Location Type: Branch office. Ultimate
Parent: Premier Bancorp.

★ 69623 ★ Premier Bank, NA
451 Florida St.
Baton Rouge, LA 70801
(504)332-4246
Location Type: Branch office. Ultimate
Parent: Premier Bancorp.

★ 69624 ★ Premier Bank, NA
620 Laurel St.
Baton Rouge, LA 70801
(504)332-4040
Location Type: Branch office. Ultimate
Parent: Premier Bancorp.

★ 69625 ★ Premier Bank NA
1131 Millerville Rd.
Baton Rouge, LA 70816-1956
(504)332-3075
Location Type: Branch office. Officer: Judy
Bell, Manager. Ultimate Parent: Premier
Bancorp.

★ 69626 ★ Premier Bank NA
3554 S. Sherwood Forest Blvd.
Baton Rouge, LA 70816-5213
(504)332-4411
Location Type: Branch office. Officer: Kay
Pritchard, Manager. Ultimate Parent:
Premier Bancorp.

★ 69627 ★ Premier Bank NA
8751 Siegen Lane
Baton Rouge, LA 70810-1945
(504)332-4550
Officer: Virgina Knobbe, Manager. Ultimate
Parent: Premier Bancorp.

★ 69628 ★ Premier Bank NA
6170 Jones Creek Rd.
Baton Rouge, LA 70816-3015
(504)332-4455
Location Type: Branch office. Officer:
Helen Mitchner, Manager. Ultimate Parent:
Premier Bancorp.

★ 69629 ★ Premier Bank NA
3759 Perkins Rd.
Baton Rouge, LA 70808-2950
(504)332-4481
Location Type: Branch office. Officer:
Dennis Oliver, Manager. Ultimate Parent:
Premier Bancorp.

★ 69630 ★ Premier Bank NA
3955 Plank Rd.
Baton Rouge, LA 70805-4920
(504)332-4321
Location Type: Branch office. Officer:
Shirley Moore, Manager. Ultimate Parent:
Premier Bancorp.

★ 69631 ★ Premier Bank NA
4041 Government St.
Baton Rouge, LA 70806-5862
(504)332-4574
Location Type: Branch office. Officer:
Elizabeth Foil, Manager. Ultimate Parent:
Premier Bancorp.

★ 69632 ★ Premier Bank NA
2050 N. Foster Dr.
Baton Rouge, LA 70806-1009
(504)332-4381
Location Type: Branch office. Officer: Pat
Chehardy, Manager. Ultimate Parent:
Premier Bancorp.

★ 69633 ★ Premier Bank NA
4328 Drusilla Lane
Baton Rouge, LA 70809-1866
(504)332-4571
Location Type: Branch office. Officer:
Emily Breaux, Manager. Ultimate Parent:
Premier Bancorp.

★ 69634 ★ Premier Bank NA
8796 Greenwell Springs Rd.
Baton Rouge, LA 70814-2718
(504)332-4464
Location Type: Branch office. Officer: Fern
C. Miller, Manager. Ultimate Parent:
Premier Bancorp.

★ 69635 ★ Premier Bank NA
3255 Highland Rd.
Baton Rouge, LA 70808
(504)332-4565
Location Type: Branch office. Officer:
Fheda J. Cary, Manager. Ultimate Parent:
Premier Bancorp.

★ 69636 ★ Premier Bank NA
12349 Industriplex Blvd.
Baton Rouge, LA 70809-5125
(504)332-4502
Location Type: Branch office. Officer:
Parker Wilder, Manager. Ultimate Parent:
Premier Bancorp.

★ 69637 ★ Premier Bank NA
670 Laurel St.
Baton Rouge, LA 70801
Location Type: Branch office. Ultimate
Parent: Premier Bancorp.

★ 69638 ★ Radio Shack
1925 Staring Ln.
Baton Rouge, LA 70810
(504)769-2943
Company Type: Division. Ultimate Parent:
Tandy Corp. SIC: 5065—Electronic Parts &
Equipment Nec; 5731—Radio, Television &
Electronics Stores.

★ 69639 ★ Radio Shack
3120 Government St.
Baton Rouge, LA 70806
(504)344-5648
Company Type: Division. Ultimate Parent:
Tandy Corp. SIC: 5065—Electronic Parts &
Equipment Nec; 5731—Radio, Television &
Electronics Stores.

★ 69640 ★ Radio Shack
4520 Sherwood Forest Blvd.
Baton Rouge, LA 70816
(504)292-1661
Company Type: Division. Ultimate Parent:
Tandy Corp. SIC: 5065—Electronic Parts &
Equipment Nec.

★ 69641 ★ Radio Shack
6246 Florida Blvd.
Baton Rouge, LA 70806
(504)473-9446
Company Type: Division. Ultimate Parent:
Tandy Corp. SIC: 5065—Electronic Parts &
Equipment Nec.

★ 69642 ★ Radio Shack
7163 Florida Blvd.
Baton Rouge, LA 70806
(504)924-6574
Company Type: Division. Ultimate Parent:
Tandy Corp. SIC: 5731—Radio, Television
& Electronics Stores.

★ 69643 ★ Radio Shack
9607 Cortana Pl
Baton Rouge, LA 70815
(504)925-8441
Company Type: Division. Ultimate Parent:
Tandy Corp. SIC: 5731—Radio, Television
& Electronics Stores.

★ 69644 ★ Radio Shack
3432 Drusilla Ln.
Baton Rouge, LA 70809
(504)925-9047
Company Type: Division. Ultimate Parent:
Tandy Corp. SIC: 5731—Radio, Television
& Electronics Stores.

★ 69645 ★ Radio Shack
5950 Airline Hwy.
Baton Rouge, LA 70805
(504)356-3192
Company Type: Division. Ultimate Parent:
Tandy Corp. SIC: 5065—Electronic Parts &
Equipment Nec.

★ 69646 ★ Radio Shack
3088 College Dr.
Baton Rouge, LA 70808
(504)927-4247
Company Type: Division. Ultimate Parent:
Tandy Corp. SIC: 5731—Radio, Television
& Electronics Stores.

★ 69647 ★ Record Data Inc.
5723 Superior Dr.
Baton Rouge, LA 70816
(504)292-6501
Ultimate Parent: TRW, Inc. SIC: 5046—
Commercial Equipment Nec.

★ 69648 ★ Reynolds Metals Co.
Brooklyn Dr.
Baton Rouge, LA 70807
(504)358-2700
Officer: W. Sibley Thomas, Manager.
Ultimate Parent: Reynolds Metals Co. SIC:
2999—Petroleum & Coal Products Nec.

★ 69649 ★ Rhone Poulenc Basic
Chemical
Airline Hwy.
Baton Rouge, LA 70821
(504)356-7111
Ultimate Parent: Rhone-Poulenc Rorer.
SIC: 2819—Industrial Inorganic Chemicals
Nec; 2899—Chemical Preparations Nec.

★ 69650 ★ Rhone-Poulenc Basic
Chemicals Co.
1275 Airline Hwy. & Old Mississippi River
Bridge
Baton Rouge, LA 70807
Ultimate Parent: Rhone-Poulenc Rorer.
SIC: 2819—Industrial Inorganic Chemicals
Nec; 2869—Industrial Organic Chemicals
Nec.

★ 69651 ★ Rhone-Poulenc Basic
Chemicals Co.
Airline Hwy. Mississippi Bridge
Baton Rouge, LA 70807
Ultimate Parent: Rhone-Poulenc Rorer.
SIC: 2819—Industrial Inorganic Chemicals
Nec; 2869—Industrial Organic Chemicals
Nec.

★ 69652 ★ Ryder Truck Rental
Airbase Ave.
Baton Rouge, LA 70807
(504)357-2982
Ultimate Parent: Ryder System. SIC:
5113—Industrial & Personal Service Paper.

★ 69653 ★ Ryder Truck Rental
11500 S. Harrells Ferry Rd.
Baton Rouge, LA 70816
(504)927-3770
Ultimate Parent: Ryder System. SIC:
7513—Truck Rental & Leasing Without
Drivers.

★ 69654 ★ Ryder Truck Rental
10220 Florida Blvd.
Baton Rouge, LA 70815
(504)275-7851
Ultimate Parent: Ryder System. SIC:
7389—Business Services Nec.

★ 69655 ★ Ryder Truck Rental
12850 Florida Blvd.
Baton Rouge, LA 70815
(504)928-2091
Ultimate Parent: Ryder System. SIC:
5012—Automobiles & Other Motor Vehicles.

★ 69656 ★ Ryder Truck Rental
10424 Airline Hwy.
Baton Rouge, LA 70816
(504)355-0327
Ultimate Parent: Ryder System. SIC:
5113—Industrial & Personal Service Paper;
7513—Truck Rental & Leasing Without
Drivers.

★ 69657 ★ Sabre Travel
Information Network
4000 S. Sherwood Forest Blvd.
Baton Rouge, LA 70816-4374
(504)291-9387
Ultimate Parent: AMR Corp. SIC: 4512—
Air Transportation—Scheduled.

★ 69658 ★ Schuylkill Metals
Corp.
West End of Brooklawn Dr.
Baton Rouge, LA 70874
Officer: Earl Comette. Ultimate Parent:
Arrow Electronics. SIC: 2671—Paper
Coated & Laminated—Packaging.

★ 69659 ★ Service Merchandise
9501 Cortana Pl
Baton Rouge, LA 70815
(504)923-1030
Ultimate Parent: Service Merchandise Co.,
Inc. SIC: 5094—Jewelry & Precious Stones.

★ 69660 ★ Shell Oil Service
Station
1649 Eal Ln.
Baton Rouge, LA 70815
(504)275-4783
Ultimate Parent: Shell Oil Co. SIC: 5541—
Gasoline Service Stations.

★ 69661 ★ T J Maxx
9554 Cortana Pl
Baton Rouge, LA 70815
(504)923-3051
Ultimate Parent: TJX. SIC: 5651—Family
Clothing Stores.

★ 69662 ★ Taco Bell
12275 Plank Rd.
Baton Rouge, LA 70811
(504)778-1331
Ultimate Parent: Pepsico. SIC: 5812—
Eating Places.

★ 69663 ★ Taco Bell
2698 Sherwood Forest Blvd.
Baton Rouge, LA 70816
(504)292-5513
Ultimate Parent: Pepsico. SIC: 5812—
Eating Places.

★ 69664 ★ Taco Bell
2774 Highland Rd.
Baton Rouge, LA 70802
(504)387-1699
Ultimate Parent: Pepsico. SIC: 5812—
Eating Places.

★ 69665 ★ Taco Bell
7541 Perkins Rd.
Baton Rouge, LA 70808
(504)769-0703
Ultimate Parent: Pepsico. SIC: 5812—
Eating Places.

★ 69666 ★ Taco Bell
9407 Cortana Pl
Baton Rouge, LA 70815
(504)924-3383
Ultimate Parent: Pepsico. SIC: 5812—
Eating Places.

★ 69667 ★ Taco Bell
9798 Greenwell Springs Rd.
Baton Rouge, LA 70814
(504)928-0994
Ultimate Parent: Pepsico. SIC: 5812—
Eating Places.

★ 69668 ★ Taco Bell
6888 Airline Hwy.
Baton Rouge, LA 70805
(504)357-7366
Ultimate Parent: Pepsico. SIC: 5812—
Eating Places.

★ 69669 ★ Taco Bell
9656 Airline Hwy.
Baton Rouge, LA 70815
(504)927-5266
Ultimate Parent: Pepsico. SIC: 5812—
Eating Places.

★ 69670 ★ Texaco
14880 Florida Blvd.
Baton Rouge, LA 70819
(504)273-0771
Ultimate Parent: Texaco. SIC: 7542—Car
Washes.

★ 69671 ★ Texaco
3536 Drusilla Ln.
Baton Rouge, LA 70809
(504)927-5131
Ultimate Parent: Texaco. SIC: 5411—
Grocery Stores; 5541—Gasoline Service
Stations.

★ 69672 ★   Texaco Inc.
4354 S. Sherwood Forest Blvd.
Baton Rouge, LA 70816
(504)292-1687
Ultimate Parent: Texaco. SIC: 5172—
Petroleum Products Nec.

★ 69673 ★   Texaco Self Serv
3375 Perkins Rd.
Baton Rouge, LA 70808
(504)387-5135
Ultimate Parent: Texaco. SIC: 5541—
Gasoline Service Stations.

★ 69674 ★   Texaco Self Serv
2060 Oneal Ln.
Baton Rouge, LA 70816
(504)291-0059
Ultimate Parent: Texaco. SIC: 5541—
Gasoline Service Stations.

★ 69675 ★   Texaco Self Serve
5945 Airline Hwy.
Baton Rouge, LA 70805
(504)356-7879
Ultimate Parent: Texaco. SIC: 5541—
Gasoline Service Stations.

★ 69676 ★   Texaco Self-Service
6435 Winbourne Ave.
Baton Rouge, LA 70805
(504)357-7755
Ultimate Parent: Texaco. SIC: 5541—
Gasoline Service Stations.

★ 69677 ★   Texaco Self Service
9255 Airline Hwy.
Baton Rouge, LA 70815
(504)923-2440
Ultimate Parent: Texaco. SIC: 5541—
Gasoline Service Stations.

★ 69678 ★   Underwriters
Adjusting Co.
4324 Sherwood Forest Blvd.
Baton Rouge, LA 70816
(504)291-0860
Ultimate Parent: Continental. SIC: 6411—
Insurance Agents, Brokers & Service.

★ 69679 ★   Union Texas
Petroleum
Rural Route 3
Baton Rouge, LA 70810
(504)766-6372
Ultimate Parent: Union Texas Petroleum.
SIC: 1311—Crude Petroleum & Natural
Gas.

★ 69680 ★   Union Texas
Petroleum
Ben Hur Rd.
Baton Rouge, LA 70808
(504)766-6372
Ultimate Parent: Union Texas Petroleum.
SIC: 1311—Crude Petroleum & Natural
Gas.

★ 69681 ★   Unisys Corp.
8550 United Plz.
Baton Rouge, LA 70809
(504)922-4500
Ultimate Parent: Unisys Corp. SIC: 7373—
Computer Integrated Systems Design.

★ 69682 ★   United Parcel Service
Veterans Memorial Blvd.
Baton Rouge, LA 70807
(504)222-8333
Ultimate Parent: United Parcel Service of
America. SIC: 4215—Courier Services
Except by Air.

★ 69683 ★   Wal Mart
8598 Cortana Pl
Baton Rouge, LA 70815
(504)923-3400
Ultimate Parent: Wal-Mart Stores, Inc. SIC:
5311—Department Stores.

★ 69684 ★   Wal Mart
1683 Oniel Ln.
Baton Rouge, LA 70815
(504)275-7683
Ultimate Parent: Wal-Mart Stores, Inc. SIC:
5399—Miscellaneous General Merchandise
Store.

★ 69685 ★   Waldenbooks
Cortana
Baton Rouge, LA 70815
(504)924-7665
Ultimate Parent: K-Mart. SIC: 5942—Book
Stores.

★ 69686 ★   Western Auto Supply
Co.
4767 Plank Rd.
Baton Rouge, LA 70805
(504)356-3256
Ultimate Parent: Sears Roebuck & Co.
SIC: 5531—Automobile & Home Supply
Stores.

★ 69687 ★   Western Auto Supply
Co.
3079 Government St.
Baton Rouge, LA 70806
(504)383-5654
Ultimate Parent: Sears Roebuck & Co.
SIC: 5531—Automobile & Home Supply
Stores.

★ 69688 ★   Xerox Corp.
555 Hilton Ave.
Baton Rouge, LA 70808
(504)929-6700
Officer: Jack Mann, Manager. Ultimate
Parent: Xerox Corp. SIC: 3663—Radio &
T.V. Communications Equipment.

★ 69689 ★   ZEP Manufacturing
Co.
2612 Tee Dr.
Baton Rouge, LA 70814
(504)275-5850
Officer: Harry Maziar, President. Ultimate
Parent: National Service Industries. SIC:
2899—Chemical Preparations Nec.

Belle Chasse

★ 69690 ★   Chevron Chemical
Co. Oak Point Plant
Hwy. 23 S. PO Box 70
Belle Chasse, LA 70037-0070
Ultimate Parent: Chevron Corp. SIC:
2869—Industrial Organic Chemicals Nec.

★ 69691 ★   Chevron Chemical
Co. Oak Point Plant
Hwy. 23 S.
Belle Chasse, LA 70037
Ultimate Parent: Chevron Corp. SIC:
2869—Industrial Organic Chemicals Nec.

★ 69692 ★   Chevron Chemical
Co. Oak Point Plant
Hwy. 23 South
Belle Chasse, LA 70037
Ultimate Parent: Chevron Corp. SIC:
2869—Industrial Organic Chemicals Nec.

★ 69693 ★   Power Systems Diesel
Inc.
2011 Engineers Rd.
Belle Chasse, LA 70037
(504)394-5944
Officer: Paul Baron, President. Ultimate
Parent: Sundstrand. SIC: 3519—Internal
Combustion Engines Nec; 3621—Motors &
Generators; 3625—Relays & Industrial
Controls.

★ 69694 ★   Quarles Drilling Corp.
1503 Engineer Rd.
Belle Chasse, LA 70037
(504)362-3555
Company Type: Subsidiary. Officer: D. B.
Quarles, President. Ultimate Parent: CBI
Industries, Inc. SIC: 1381—Drilling Oil &
Gas Wells.

★ 69695 ★   Solar Turbines Inc.
3012 Engineers Rd.
Belle Chasse, LA 70037
(504)392-6080
Ultimate Parent: Carter-Wallace. SIC:
7699—Repair Services Nec.

Bernice

★ 69696 ★   Piggly Wiggly
4th
Bernice, LA 71222
(318)285-9697
Ultimate Parent: Bruno's. SIC: 5411—
Grocery Stores.

Berwick

★ 69697 ★   Marathon Oil Co.
1108 River Rd.
Berwick, LA 70342
(504)385-0832
Ultimate Parent: USX Corp. SIC: 5171—
Petroleum Bulk Stations & Terminals.

★ 69698 ★   Marathon Oil Co.
1108 River Rd.
Berwick, LA 70342
(504)385-0832
Ultimate Parent: USX Corp. SIC: 5171—
Petroleum Bulk Stations & Terminals.

Blanchard

★ 69699 ★   Allied-Signal Inc.
Uop Process Div.
Old Mooringsport Rd.
Blanchard, LA 71009
(318)929-3521
Company Type: Division. Ultimate Parent:
Allied-Signal Inc. SIC: 5084—Industrial
Machinery & Equipment.

★ 69700 ★   UOP Inc.
Hwy. 538 West
Blanchard, LA 71009
Ultimate Parent: Allied-Signal Inc. SIC:
2819—Industrial Inorganic Chemicals Nec;
2869—Industrial Organic Chemicals Nec.

Bogalusa

★ 69701 ★   First State Bank &
Trust Co.
724 Avenue F
Bogalusa, LA 70427
(504)732-3633
Ultimate Parent: Michigan National Corp.
SIC: 6022—State Commercial Banks.

★ 69702 ★   Gaylord Chemical
Corp.
420 Willis Ave.
Bogalusa, LA 70427
(504)732-5013
Ultimate Parent: Gaylord Container. SIC:
2869—Industrial Organic Chemicals Nec.

★ 69703 ★   Gaylord Container
Corp.
455 Avenue S
Bogalusa, LA 70427
(504)732-8800
Officer: W. E. Kemper, Manager. Ultimate
Parent: Gaylord Container. SIC: 2653—
Corrugated & Solid Fiber Boxes.

★ 69704 ★   Gaylord Container
Corp.
401 Avenue W
Bogalusa, LA 70427
(504)732-8000
Officer: Edgar L. Mizell, Manager. Ultimate
Parent: Gaylord Container. SIC: 2621—
Paper Mills; 2631—Paperboard Mills;
2653—Corrugated & Solid Fiber Boxes.

★ 69705 ★   Mobil Oil Co.
S F Ave.
Bogalusa, LA 70427
(504)732-2728
Ultimate Parent: Mobil. SIC: 5172—
Petroleum Products Nec.

★ 69706 ★   Mutual of New York
1011 Avenue I B
Bogalusa, LA 70427
(504)732-1829
Ultimate Parent: Mutual of New York. SIC:
6411—Insurance Agents, Brokers &
Service.

★ 69707 ★   Pizza Hut
220 Cumberland St.
Bogalusa, LA 70427
(504)732-2899
Ultimate Parent: Pepsico. SIC: 5812—
Eating Places.

★ 69708 ★   Radio Shack
Pine Tree Plz.
Bogalusa, LA 70427
(504)732-9529
Company Type: Division. Ultimate Parent:
Tandy Corp. SIC: 5065—Electronic Parts &
Equipment Nec.

★ 69709 ★   Trailways Bus Station
225 Alabama Ave.
Bogalusa, LA 70427
(504)732-7331
Ultimate Parent: Greyhound Lines Inc. SIC:
4131—Intercity & Rural Bus Transportation.

★ 69710 ★   Wal Mart
300 Cumberland St.
Bogalusa, LA 70427
(504)732-5870
Ultimate Parent: Wal-Mart Stores, Inc. SIC:
5311—Department Stores.

Bossier City

★ 69711 ★   Albertson's
3121 E. Texas St.
Bossier City, LA 71111
(318)747-1466
Ultimate Parent: Albertson's Inc. SIC:
5912—Drug Stores & Proprietary Stores.

★ 69712 ★   Casual Corner
2950 E. Texas St.
Bossier City, LA 71111
(318)747-4914
Ultimate Parent: United States Shoe. SIC:
5651—Family Clothing Stores.

★ 69713 ★   Citgo Quick Mart
1340 Mark Ave.
Bossier City, LA 71112
(318)424-0973
Ultimate Parent: Citgo Petroleum. SIC:
5541—Gasoline Service Stations.

★ 69714 ★   Citgo Quick Mart
1965 Airline Dr.
Bossier City, LA 71112
(318)746-5120
Ultimate Parent: Citgo Petroleum. SIC:
5541—Gasoline Service Stations.

★ 69715 ★   The Gap
2950 E. Texas St.
Bossier City, LA 71111
(318)742-5756
Ultimate Parent: GAP. SIC: 5651—Family
Clothing Stores.

★ 69716 ★   Hibernia National
Bank
2045 Airline Dr.
Bossier City, LA 71111
(318)742-2020
Ultimate Parent: Hibernia Corp. SIC:
6141—Personal Credit Institutions.

★ 69717 ★   Hibernia National
Bank
301 Benton Rd.
Bossier City, LA 71111
(318)742-3700
Ultimate Parent: Hibernia Corp. SIC:
6022—State Commercial Banks.

★ 69718 ★   Kentucky Fried
Chicken
637 Benton Rd.
Bossier City, LA 71111
(318)742-6131
Ultimate Parent: Pepsico. SIC: 5812—
Eating Places.

★ 69719 ★   Kentucky Fried
Chicken
2250 Barksdale Blvd.
Bossier City, LA 71112
(318)742-6131
Ultimate Parent: Pepsico. SIC: 5812—
Eating Places.

★ 69720 ★   Kentucky Fried
Chicken
4100 Barksdale Blvd.
Bossier City, LA 71112
(318)747-4452
Ultimate Parent: Pepsico. SIC: 5812—
Eating Places.

★ 69721 ★   Kroger Super Market
801 Benton Rd.
Bossier City, LA 71111
(318)747-1058
Ultimate Parent: Kroger. SIC: 5411—
Grocery Stores; 5912—Drug Stores &
Proprietary Stores.

★ 69722 ★   Lane Bryant
2950 E. Texas St.
Bossier City, LA 71111
(318)742-9800
Ultimate Parent: Limited. SIC: 5651—
Family Clothing Stores.

★ 69723 ★   The Limited
2950 E. Texas St.
Bossier City, LA 71111
(318)742-0590
Ultimate Parent: Limited. **SIC:** 5651—Family Clothing Stores.

★ 69724 ★   McDonalds
Hamburgers
Industrial Dr.
Bossier City, LA 71112
(318)742-4010
Ultimate Parent: McDonald's.
SIC: 5812—Eating Places.

★ 69725 ★   Pizza Hut
2216 Benton Rd.
Bossier City, LA 71111
(318)741-8249
Ultimate Parent: Pepsico. **SIC:** 5812—Eating Places.

★ 69726 ★   Pizza Hut
1981 Airline Dr.
Bossier City, LA 71112
(318)746-6865
Ultimate Parent: Pepsico. **SIC:** 5812—Eating Places.

★ 69727 ★   Pizza Hut
3416 Barksdale Blvd.
Bossier City, LA 71112
(318)747-1037
Ultimate Parent: Pepsico. **SIC:** 5812—Eating Places.

★ 69728 ★   Radio Shack
1700 Old Minden Rd. 178
Bossier City, LA 71111
(318)636-6530
Company Type: Division. **Ultimate Parent:** Tandy Corp. **SIC:** 5065—Electronic Parts & Equipment Nec.

★ 69729 ★   Radio Shack
2950 E. Texas St.
Bossier City, LA 71111
(318)742-7470
Company Type: Division. **Ultimate Parent:** Tandy Corp. **SIC:** 5065—Electronic Parts & Equipment Nec.

★ 69730 ★   Ryder Truck Rental
2395 Airline Dr.
Bossier City, LA 71111
(318)742-2080
Ultimate Parent: Ryder System. **SIC:** 7513—Truck Rental & Leasing Without Drivers.

★ 69731 ★   Service Merchandise
2950 E. Texas St.
Bossier City, LA 71111
(318)747-4000
Ultimate Parent: Service Merchandise Co., Inc. **SIC:** 5311—Department Stores.

★ 69732 ★   Sherwin Williams
Paint Stor
2108 Airline Dr.
Bossier City, LA 71111
(318)742-7800
Ultimate Parent: Sherwin-Williams Co. **SIC:** 5231—Paint, Glass & Wallpaper Stores.

★ 69733 ★   Taco Bell
1988 Airline Dr.
Bossier City, LA 71112
(318)746-9789
Ultimate Parent: Pepsico. **SIC:** 5812—Eating Places.

★ 69734 ★   Texaco Inc.
1970 Airline Dr.
Bossier City, LA 71112
(318)742-4699
Ultimate Parent: Texaco. **SIC:** 5541—Gasoline Service Stations.

★ 69735 ★   Waldenbooks
2950 E. Texas St.
Bossier City, LA 71111
(318)742-8181
Ultimate Parent: K-Mart. **SIC:** 5942—Book Stores.

★ 69736 ★   Walgreen Drug Stores
2950 E. Texas St.
Bossier City, LA 71111
(318)746-3202
Ultimate Parent: Walgreen Co. **SIC:** 5122—Drugs, Proprietaries & Sundries.

★ 69737 ★   Western Auto Supply
Co. Inc.
25 Heart O Bossier Cent
Bossier City, LA 71111
(318)746-0806
Ultimate Parent: Sears Roebuck & Co. **SIC:** 5531—Automobile & Home Supply Stores.

Braithwaite

★ 69738 ★   Amax Metals
Recovery Inc.
3607 English Turn Rd.
Braithwaite, LA 70040
Ultimate Parent: Cyprus Amax Minerals. **SIC:** 2819—Industrial Inorganic Chemicals Nec; 6700—Holding & Other Investment Offices.

★ 69739 ★   Amax Metals
Recovery Inc.
La. Hwy. 3137
Braithwaite, LA 70040
Ultimate Parent: Cyprus Amax Minerals. **SIC:** 2819—Industrial Inorganic Chemicals Nec.

Breaux Bridge

★ 69740 ★   Ace Hardware
Rees
Breaux Bridge, LA 70517
(318)332-2541
Ultimate Parent: Ace Hardware. **SIC:** 5251—Hardware Stores.

★ 69741 ★   Union Texas
Petroleum
Anse La Butte
Breaux Bridge, LA 70517
(318)332-4188
Ultimate Parent: Union Texas Petroleum. **SIC:** 5984—Liquefied Petroleum Gas Dealers.

★ 69742 ★   Wal Mart Discount
City
Lafayette St. 32
Breaux Bridge, LA 70517
(318)332-1280
Ultimate Parent: Wal-Mart Stores, Inc. **SIC:** 5399—Miscellaneous General Merchandise Store.

Broussard

★ 69743 ★   Baker Sand Control
Lafayette Manufacturing
4440 Hwy. 90 E.
Broussard, LA 70518
Ultimate Parent: Baker Hughes. **SIC:** 3533—Oil & Gas Field Machinery.

★ 69744 ★   Baker Sand Control
Lafayette Mfg.
4440 Hwy. 90 E.
Broussard, LA 70518
Ultimate Parent: Baker Hughes. **SIC:** 3533—Oil & Gas Field Machinery.

★ 69745 ★   Union Camp Corp.
204 Southpark Rd.
Broussard, LA 70518
(318)837-9091
Ultimate Parent: Union Camp Corp. **SIC:** 5113—Industrial & Personal Service Paper.

Bunkie

★ 69746 ★   Trailways Bus System
400 SW Main St.
Bunkie, LA 71322
(318)346-7678
Ultimate Parent: Greyhound Lines Inc. **SIC:** 4131—Intercity & Rural Bus Transportation.

Buras

★ 69747 ★   Radio Shack
112 Parkview Dr.
Buras, LA 70041
(504)657-9350
Company Type: Division. **Ultimate Parent:** Tandy Corp. **SIC:** 5719—Miscellaneous Home Furnishings Stores.

Calhoun

★ 69748 ★   Coast to Coast
Express
Judes Truck Stp
Calhoun, LA 71225
(318)644-5888
Ultimate Parent: Servistar Corp. **SIC:** 4731—Freight Transportation Arrangement.

Cameron

★ 69749 ★   Marathon Oil Co.
Cameron, LA 70631
(318)775-5095
Ultimate Parent: USX Corp. **SIC:** 5172—Petroleum Products Nec.

★ 69750 ★   Marathon Oil Co.
Cameron, LA 70631
(318)775-5095
Ultimate Parent: USX Corp. **SIC:** 5172—Petroleum Products Nec.

★ 69751 ★   Mobil Bulk Plant
Cameron, LA 70631
(318)775-5546
Ultimate Parent: Mobil. **SIC:** 5941—Sporting Goods & Bicycle Shops.

★ 69752 ★   Mobil Oil Corp.
Offshore Production
Cameron, LA 70631
(318)775-3200
Company Type: Branch. **Ultimate Parent:** Mobil. **SIC:** 1311—Crude Petroleum & Natural Gas.

★ 69753 ★   Mobil Oil Exploring &
Producing
Cameron, LA 70631
(318)775-3300
Ultimate Parent: Mobil. **SIC:** 1311—Crude Petroleum & Natural Gas.

★ 69754 ★   Tesoro Petroleum
Distrib Co.
Cameron, LA 70631
(318)775-5781
Ultimate Parent: Tesoro Petroleum Corp. **SIC:** 5983—Fuel Oil Dealers.

Campti

★ 69755 ★   Willamette Industries
Inc.
Hwy. 480 N
Campti, LA 71411-0377
Ultimate Parent: Willamette Industries, Inc. **SIC:** 2611—Pulp Mills; 2631—Paperboard Mills.

Carville

★ 69756 ★   Allied-Signal Inc.
5525 Hwy. 3115
Carville, LA 70721
(504)642-8311
Location Type: Plant. **Officer:** David Cope, Plant Manager. **Ultimate Parent:** Allied-Signal Inc. **SIC:** 2819—Industrial Inorganic Chemicals Nec; 2899—Chemical Preparations Nec.

★ 69757 ★   Cos-Mar Inc.
6325 Hwy. 75
Carville, LA 70721-2303
(504)642-5454
Officer: H. P. Jack, Vice President.
Ultimate Parent: General Electric. **SIC:** 2865—Cyclic Crudes & Intermediates.
Employee Count: 200. **Sales:** 29.3 M.

★ 69758 ★   Union Lake Petroleum
Corp.
5205 Hwy. 3115
Carville, LA 70721
(504)642-2100
Officer: C.D. Porter, Manager. **Ultimate Parent:** Union Texas Petroleum. **SIC:** 2822—Synthetic Rubber; 2869—Industrial Organic Chemicals Nec.

Centerville

★ 69759 ★   Columbian Chemicals
Co.
Hwy. 317
Centerville, LA 70522
Ultimate Parent: Phelps Dodge. **SIC:** 2895—Carbon Black.

★ 69760 ★   Exxon Co. USA
Garden County
Centerville, LA 70522
(318)836-5637
Ultimate Parent: Exxon. **SIC:** 1311—Crude Petroleum & Natural Gas.

★ 69761 ★   Exxon Co. USA
Bayou Slae
Centerville, LA 70522
(318)836-9622
Ultimate Parent: Exxon. **SIC:** 1311—Crude Petroleum & Natural Gas.

★ 69762 ★   Exxon Co. USA
Duck Lake Field
Centerville, LA 70522
(318)836-5414
Ultimate Parent: Exxon. **SIC:** 1311—Crude Petroleum & Natural Gas.

★ 69763 ★   Texaco Inc.
Bayou Sale
Centerville, LA 70522
(318)836-5627
Ultimate Parent: Texaco. **SIC:** 5084—Industrial Machinery & Equipment.

Chalmette

★ 69764 ★   Jiffy Lube
110 E. Judge Perez Dr.
Chalmette, LA 70043
(504)271-5996
Ultimate Parent: Pennzoil.

★ 69765 ★   Mobil Oil Chalmette
Refinery
500 W. St. Bernard Hwy.
Chalmette, LA 70043-4821
(504)279-9481
Officer: K. L. Turkington. **Ultimate Parent:** Mobil. **SIC:** 2911—Petroleum Refining; 5172—Petroleum Products Nec.

★ 69766 ★   Mobil Oil Corp.
Chalmette Refinery
500 W. St. Bernard Hwy.
Chalmette, LA 70043
Company Type: Division. **Ultimate Parent:** Mobil. **SIC:** 2911—Petroleum Refining.

★ 69767 ★   Pizza Hut
1913 E. Judge Perez Dr.
Chalmette, LA 70043
(504)277-4375
Ultimate Parent: Pepsico. **SIC:** 5812—Eating Places.

★ 69768 ★   Taco Bell
3010 Us 90 W
Chalmette, LA 70043
(504)436-1975
Ultimate Parent: Pepsico. **SIC:** 5812—Eating Places.

★ 69769 ★   Taco Bell
8317 W. Judge Perez Dr.
Chalmette, LA 70043
(504)277-4905
Ultimate Parent: Pepsico. **SIC:** 5812—Eating Places.

★ 69770 ★   Tenneco Oil Co.
500 West St. Bernard Hwy.
Chalmette, LA 70143
Ultimate Parent: Tenneco Inc. **SIC:** 2911—Petroleum Refining.

★ 69771 ★   Texaco Selfservice
2601 Paris Rd.
Chalmette, LA 70043
(504)279-8933
Ultimate Parent: Texaco. **SIC:** 5541—Gasoline Service Stations.

★ 69772 ★   Wal Mart
8535 W. Judge Perez Dr.
Chalmette, LA 70043
(504)271-4167
Ultimate Parent: Wal-Mart Stores, Inc. **SIC:** 5311—Department Stores.

★ 69773 ★   Walgreen Drug Stores
3350 Paris Rd.
Chalmette, LA 70043
(504)277-4676
Ultimate Parent: Walgreen Co. **SIC:** 5912—Drug Stores & Proprietary Stores.

★ **69774** ★ **Wall Street Journal**
2205 Creely Dr.
Chalmette, LA 70043
(504)277-8871
Ultimate Parent: Dow Jones.

Chauvin

★ **69775** ★ **International Seafood Traders**
5557 Hwy. 56
PO Box 207
Chauvin, LA 70344
(504)594-5869
Company Type: Division. **Officer:** Andrew Blanchard, Plant Manager. **Ultimate Parent:** Conagra.

Cheneyville

★ **69776** ★ **Shell Oil Co.**
Cheneyville, LA 71325
(318)279-2369
Ultimate Parent: Shell Oil Co. **SIC:** 5171—Petroleum Bulk Stations & Terminals.

Choudrant

★ **69777** ★ **Conagra Broiler Co. Feedmill**
100 N. Depot
Choudrant, LA 71227-0100
Ultimate Parent: Conagra. **SIC:** 2048—Prepared Feeds Nec.

★ **69778** ★ **Conagra Broiler Co. Feedmill**
100 North Depot
Choudrant, LA 71227
Ultimate Parent: Conagra. **SIC:** 2048—Prepared Feeds Nec.

★ **69779** ★ **Mini Mart Food Store**
Choudrant, LA 71227
(318)768-2926
Ultimate Parent: Kroger. **SIC:** 5411—Grocery Stores.

Columbia

★ **69780** ★ **Exxon Co. USA**
Hwy. 165
Columbia, LA 71418
(318)649-7406
Ultimate Parent: Exxon. **SIC:** 5172—Petroleum Products Nec.

Convent

★ **69781** ★ **Air Products & Chemicals Inc.**
Hwy. 70
Convent, LA 70723
Ultimate Parent: Air Products & Chemicals, Inc. **SIC:** 2813—Industrial Gases.

★ **69782** ★ **Occidental Chemical Corp.**
Hwy. 3214
Convent, LA 70723-9799
Ultimate Parent: Occidental Petroleum Corp. **SIC:** 2812—Alkalies & Chlorine; 2869—Industrial Organic Chemicals Nec.

★ **69783** ★ **Occidental Chemical Corp.**
7377 Hwy. 3214
Convent, LA 70723
Ultimate Parent: Occidental Petroleum Corp. **SIC:** 2812—Alkalies & Chlorine; 2869—Industrial Organic Chemicals Nec.

★ **69784** ★ **Texaco Refining & Marketing Inc.**
Foot of Sunshine Bridge La Hwy. 44
Convent, LA 70723
Ultimate Parent: Texaco. **SIC:** 2911—Petroleum Refining; 2819—Industrial Inorganic Chemicals Nec; 4400—Water Transportation; 5171—Petroleum Bulk Stations & Terminals.

Cotton Valley

★ **69785** ★ **Kerr-Mcgee Refining Corp.**
Louisiana Hwy. 7 S.
Cotton Valley, LA 71018
Ultimate Parent: Kerr-McGee. **SIC:** 2911—Petroleum Refining.

★ **69786** ★ **Kerr-Mcgee Refining Corp.**
La 7 South
Cotton Valley, LA 71018
Ultimate Parent: Kerr-McGee. **SIC:** 2911—Petroleum Refining.

★ **69787** ★ **Kerr-Mcgee Refining Corp. Corp.**
La 7 South
Cotton Valley, LA 71018
Ultimate Parent: Kerr-McGee. **SIC:** 2911—Petroleum Refining.

★ **69788** ★ **Marathon Oil Co.**
266 Webster Parish Rd.
Cotton Valley, LA 71018
(318)832-4215
Ultimate Parent: USX Corp. **SIC:** 1321—Natural Gas Liquids.

★ **69789** ★ **Marathon Oil Co.**
Treat Spur
Cotton Valley, LA 71018
(318)832-4245
Ultimate Parent: USX Corp. **SIC:** 5172—Petroleum Products Nec.

★ **69790** ★ **Marathon Oil Co.**
266 Webster Parish Rd.
Cotton Valley, LA 71018
(318)832-4215
Ultimate Parent: USX Corp. **SIC:** 1321—Natural Gas Liquids.

★ **69791** ★ **Marathon Oil Co.**
Treat Spur
Cotton Valley, LA 71018
(318)832-4245
Ultimate Parent: USX Corp. **SIC:** 5172—Petroleum Products Nec.

Coushatta

★ **69792** ★ **Sunbeam-Oster Corp.**
2415 Red Oak Rd.
Coushatta, LA 71019
Ultimate Parent: Sunbeam/Oster. **SIC:** 3639—Household Appliances Nec.

Covington

★ **69793** ★ **First Bank**
1510 PO Box
Covington, LA 70433
(504)892-8300
Ultimate Parent: Shawmut National Corp. **SIC:** 6099—Functions Related to Deposit Banking; 6141—Personal Credit Institutions.

★ **69794** ★ **Greyhound Bus Lines**
701 E. Boston St.
Covington, LA 70433
(504)892-5319
Ultimate Parent: Greyhound Lines Inc. **SIC:** 4131—Intercity & Rural Bus Transportation.

★ **69795** ★ **Hibernia National Bank**
221 N. New Hampshire St.
Covington, LA 70433
(504)893-7780
Ultimate Parent: Hibernia Corp. **SIC:** 6021—National Commercial Banks; 6022—State Commercial Banks.

★ **69796** ★ **Liberty Mutual Insurance Co.**
1600 Us 190
Covington, LA 70433
(504)893-9930
Ultimate Parent: Liberty Mutual Group. **SIC:** 6411—Insurance Agents, Brokers & Service.

★ **69797** ★ **Pizza Hut**
Hwy. 190
Covington, LA 70433
(504)892-8220
Ultimate Parent: Pepsico. **SIC:** 5812—Eating Places.

★ **69798** ★ **Texaco Self Serve**
500 N. Hwy. 190
Covington, LA 70433
(504)893-4543
Ultimate Parent: Texaco. **SIC:** 5599—Automotive Dealers Nec.

Crowley

★ **69799** ★ **ADM Miling Co.**
W Mill St.
Crowley, LA 70526
(318)783-3372
Officer: J. Elliot Dore, President. **Ultimate Parent:** Archer Daniels Midland Co. **SIC:** 2041—Flour & Other Grain Mill Products; 2044—Rice Milling.

★ **69800** ★ **Arco Oil & Gas Co.**
Faulk Rd.
Crowley, LA 70526
(318)783-2333
Ultimate Parent: Atlantic Richfield Co., Inc. **SIC:** 1311—Crude Petroleum & Natural Gas.

★ **69801** ★ **Bellsouth Mobility**
Crowley, LA 70526
(318)783-2266
Ultimate Parent: BellSouth Corp. **SIC:** 5065—Electronic Parts & Equipment Nec.

★ **69802** ★ **Radio Shack**
332 PO Box
Crowley, LA 70527
(318)948-1402
Company Type: Division. **Ultimate Parent:** Tandy Corp. **SIC:** 5736—Musical Instruments Stores.

★ **69803** ★ **Radio Shack**
265 PO Box
Crowley, LA 70527
(318)457-7854
Company Type: Division. **Ultimate Parent:** Tandy Corp. **SIC:** 5065—Electronic Parts & Equipment Nec; 7629—Electrical Repair Shops Nec.

Crown Point

★ **69804** ★ **Aluminum Boats Inc.**
End of Rosethorne Rd.
Crown Point, LA 70072
Ultimate Parent: Trinity Industries. **SIC:** 3731—Ship Building & Repairing.

Cut Off

★ **69805** ★ **McDonalds**
1604 W. Main St.
Cut Off, LA 70345
(504)798-7702
Ultimate Parent: McDonald's. **SIC:** 5812—Eating Places.

★ **69806** ★ **Pizza Hut**
4518 W. Main St.
Cut Off, LA 70345
(504)632-5878
Ultimate Parent: Pepsico. **SIC:** 5812—Eating Places.

De Quincy

★ **69807** ★ **Mini Mart Grocery**
Hwy. 12 W
De Quincy, LA 70633
(318)786-7612
Ultimate Parent: Kroger. **SIC:** 5411—Grocery Stores.

★ **69808** ★ **Trailways Bus Depot**
Lake Charles Ave.
De Quincy, LA 70633
(318)786-2823
Ultimate Parent: Greyhound Lines Inc. **SIC:** 4131—Intercity & Rural Bus Transportation.

De Ridder

★ **69809** ★ **Boise Cascade Corp.**
Deridder Mill
U.S. 190 W.
De Ridder, LA 70634
Ultimate Parent: Boise Cascade. **SIC:** 2611—Pulp Mills; 2621—Paper Mills.

★ **69810** ★ **Boise Southern Deridder Mill**
US 190
De Ridder, LA 70634
Ultimate Parent: Boise Cascade. **SIC:** 2611—Pulp Mills; 2621—Paper Mills.

★ **69811** ★ **Boise Southern Deridder Paper Mill**
US Hwy. 190
De Ridder, LA 70634
Ultimate Parent: Boise Cascade. **SIC:** 2611—Pulp Mills; 2621—Paper Mills.

★ **69812** ★ **Greyhound Bus Station**
402 W. 1st St.
De Ridder, LA 70634
(318)462-6213
Ultimate Parent: Greyhound Lines Inc. **SIC:** 4131—Intercity & Rural Bus Transportation.

★ **69813** ★ **International Paper Co. De Ridder**
300 Post Plant Rd.
De Ridder, LA 70634
Ultimate Parent: International Paper Co. **SIC:** 2491—Wood Preserving.

★ **69814** ★ **International Paper De Ridder**
300 Post Plant Rd.
De Ridder, LA 70634-0519
Ultimate Parent: International Paper Co. **SIC:** 2491—Wood Preserving.

★ **69815** ★ **Kentucky Fried Chicken**
Mahlon
De Ridder, LA 70634
(318)463-3741
Ultimate Parent: Pepsico. **SIC:** 5812—Eating Places.

★ **69816** ★ **Piggly Wiggly**
Texas
De Ridder, LA 70634
(318)463-9064
Ultimate Parent: Bruno's. **SIC:** 5411—Grocery Stores.

★ **69817** ★ **Pizza Hut**
Us 171 N
De Ridder, LA 70634
(318)462-1529
Ultimate Parent: Pepsico. **SIC:** 5191—Farm Supplies; 5812—Eating Places.

★ **69818** ★ **Radio Shack**
602 N. Pine St.
De Ridder, LA 70634
(318)463-6493
Company Type: Division. **Ultimate Parent:** Tandy Corp. **SIC:** 3714—Motor Vehicle Parts & Accessories.

★ **69819** ★ **Trailways Bus Systems**
127 E. 1st St.
De Ridder, LA 70634
(318)463-8744
Ultimate Parent: Greyhound Lines Inc. **SIC:** 4131—Intercity & Rural Bus Transportation.

★ **69820** ★ **Wal Mart**
1101 N. Pine St.
De Ridder, LA 70634
(318)463-3400
Ultimate Parent: Wal-Mart Stores, Inc. **SIC:** 5311—Department Stores.

★ **69821** ★ **Westvaco Corp.**
Crosby Rd.
De Ridder, LA 70634
Ultimate Parent: WestVaco Corp. **SIC:** 2861—Gum & Wood Chemicals; 2821—Plastics Materials & Resins; 2869—Industrial Organic Chemicals Nec; 5169—Chemicals & Allied Products Nec.

★ **69822** ★ **Westvaco Corp.**
Chemicals
Crosby Rd. Crosby Rd.
De Ridder, LA 70634
Ultimate Parent: WestVaco Corp. **SIC:** 2861—Gum & Wood Chemicals; 2821—Plastics Materials & Resins; 2869—Industrial Organic Chemicals Nec.

Delhi

★ **69823** ★ **Brunswick Corp.**
Marine Div.
802 Illinois Ave.
Delhi, LA 71232
Company Type: Division. **Ultimate Parent:** Brunswick Corp. **SIC:** 3732—Boat Building & Repairing.

★ 69824 ★ Mercury Powerboat
802 Illinois Ave.
Delhi, LA 71232
Ultimate Parent: Brunswick Corp. SIC:
3732—Boat Building & Repairing.

★ 69825 ★ Tifton Aluminum Co.,
Inc.
100 Tifton Dr.
PO Box 188
Delhi, LA 71232-9703
(318)878-9703
Location Type: Branch office. Officer:
James H. Nichols, President. Ultimate
Parent: Aluminum Co. of America—Alcoa.
SIC: 3354—Aluminum Extruded Products;
3341—Secondary Nonferrous Metals;
3479—Metal Coating & Allied Services;
3471—Plating & Polishing.

★ 69826 ★ Trailways Bus Depot
306 W. 1st St.
Delhi, LA 71232
(318)878-3461
Ultimate Parent: Greyhound Lines Inc. SIC:
4131—Intercity & Rural Bus Transportation.

★ 69827 ★ Wilsons Department
Store
104 Elm St.
Delhi, LA 71232
(318)878-2410
Ultimate Parent: Melville. SIC: 5311—
Department Stores.

Denham Springs

★ 69828 ★ Gulf States Utilities
Co.
300 Julia St.
Denham Springs, LA 70726
(504)665-6141
Ultimate Parent: Gulf State Utilities Co.
SIC: 4911—Electric Services.

★ 69829 ★ Kentucky Fried
Chicken
641 S. Range Ave.
Denham Springs, LA 70726
(504)665-7823
Ultimate Parent: Pepsico. SIC: 5812—
Eating Places.

★ 69830 ★ Pizza Hut
815 US 190 SW
Denham Springs, LA 70726
(504)664-9754
Ultimate Parent: Pepsico. SIC: 5812—
Eating Places.

★ 69831 ★ Radio Shack
2324 S. Range Ave.
Denham Springs, LA 70726
(504)664-2226
Company Type: Division. Ultimate Parent:
Tandy Corp. SIC: 5065—Electronic Parts &
Equipment Nec.

★ 69832 ★ Ralph Wilson Plastics
Denham Springs
Hwy. 190 E. Box 967
Denham Springs, LA 70726
Company Type: Division. Ultimate Parent:
Premark International. SIC: 2891—
Adhesives & Sealants.

★ 69833 ★ Ralph Wilson Plastics
Co.
Denham Springs Adhesive
Hwy. 190 E. Box 967
Denham Springs, LA 70726
Company Type: Division. Ultimate Parent:
Premark International. SIC: 2891—
Adhesives & Sealants.

DeRidder

★ 69834 ★ Boise Cascade Corp.
Hwy. 190 W
DeRidder, LA 70634
(318)462-4300
Officer: Dave Blenke, Manager. Ultimate
Parent: Boise Cascade. SIC: 2621—Paper
Mills; 2631—Paperboard Mills.

Des Allemads

★ 69835 ★ Amerada Hess Corp.
Des Allemads, LA 70030
(504)758-7576
Ultimate Parent: Amerada Hess. SIC:
1311—Crude Petroleum & Natural Gas.

Destrehan

★ 69836 ★ ADM Milling Co.
River Rd.
Destrehan, LA 70047
(504)764-9966
Officer: Dennis Whitener, Manager.
Ultimate Parent: Archer Daniels Midland
Co. SIC: 2041—Flour & Other Grain Mill
Products.

★ 69837 ★ Archer Daniels
Midland
PO Box 457
Destrehan, LA 70047-0457
(504)764-9966
Officer: Dennis Whitener. Ultimate Parent:
Archer Daniels Midland Co. SIC: 2041—
Flour & Other Grain Mill Products; 5149—
Groceries & Related Products Nec.

★ 69838 ★ Baxter International
Baxter Hospital Supply Div.
100 Campus Dr. E
Destrehan, LA 70047-5205
(504)764-2363
Company Type: Division. Ultimate Parent:
Baxter International. SIC: 5047—Medical &
Hospital Equipment.

Dodson

★ 69839 ★ Willamette Industries,
Inc.
Dodson
U.S. Hwy. 167 North
Dodson, LA 71422
Ultimate Parent: Willamette Industries, Inc.
SIC: 2436—Softwood Veneer & Plywood.

★ 69840 ★ Willamette Industries
Inc.
Dodson
Hwy. 167 N.
Dodson, LA 71422
Ultimate Parent: Willamette Industries, Inc.
SIC: 2436—Softwood Veneer & Plywood;
2491—Wood Preserving; 2421—Sawmills &
Planing Mills—General.

Donaldsonville

★ 69841 ★ Pizza Hut
1360 Hwy. 1 S
Donaldsonville, LA 70346
(504)473-6463
Ultimate Parent: Pepsico. SIC: 5812—
Eating Places.

★ 69842 ★ Shell Oil Co.
525 RR 1
Donaldsonville, LA 70346
(504)473-7507
Ultimate Parent: Shell Oil Co. SIC: 1389—
Oil & Gas Field Services Nec.

★ 69843 ★ Shell Pipeline Corp.
Hwy. 70
Donaldsonville, LA 70346
(504)473-3984
Ultimate Parent: Shell Oil Co. SIC: 5172—
Petroleum Products Nec.

Donaldsonvl

★ 69844 ★ Ace Hardware No.
2822a
301 Railroad Ave.
Donaldsonvl, LA 70346
(504)473-3797
Ultimate Parent: Ace Hardware. SIC:
5251—Hardware Stores.

★ 69845 ★ Radio Shack
Hwy. 1
Donaldsonvl, LA 70346
(504)473-9446
Company Type: Division. Ultimate Parent:
Tandy Corp. SIC: 5731—Radio, Television
& Electronics Stores.

★ 69846 ★ Shell Pipeline Corp.
Hwy. 70
Donaldsonvl, LA 70346
(504)473-3984
Ultimate Parent: Shell Oil Co. SIC: 5172—
Petroleum Products Nec.

Eunice

★ 69847 ★ Ace Hardware
161 Jeannie St.
Eunice, LA 70535
(318)457-5353
Ultimate Parent: Ace Hardware. SIC:
5251—Hardware Stores.

★ 69848 ★ Taco Bell
2121 W. Laurel Ave.
Eunice, LA 70535
(318)457-3408
Ultimate Parent: Pepsico. SIC: 5812—
Eating Places.

★ 69849 ★ Wal Mart
1960 W. Laurel Ave.
Eunice, LA 70535
(318)457-7393
Ultimate Parent: Wal-Mart Stores, Inc. SIC:
5311—Department Stores.

Farmerville

★ 69850 ★ Coast to Coast
Service Cent
208 N. E. St.
Farmerville, LA 71241
(318)368-8542
Ultimate Parent: Servistar Corp. SIC:
5541—Gasoline Service Stations.

★ 69851 ★ Conagra Broiler Co.
Hwy. 15 N
Farmerville, LA 71241
Ultimate Parent: Conagra. SIC: 2015—
Poultry Slaughtering & Processing; 2077—
Animal & Marine Fats & Oils.

★ 69852 ★ Sigma Diagnostics
286 Rural Route 3
Farmerville, LA 71241
(318)368-9741
Ultimate Parent: Sigma-Aldrich. SIC:
5169—Chemicals & Allied Products Nec.

Ferriday

★ 69853 ★ Piggly Wiggly
114 N. 1st St.
Ferriday, LA 71334
(318)757-2454
Ultimate Parent: Bruno's. SIC: 5411—
Grocery Stores.

Florien

★ 69854 ★ Boise Cascade Corp.
PO Box 128
Florien, LA 71429
(318)256-3411
Officer: Bud Fry, Manager. Ultimate
Parent: Boise Cascade. SIC: 2421—
Sawmills & Planing Mills—General.

★ 69855 ★ Fisher Sawmill
Hwy. 171
Florien, LA 71429
Ultimate Parent: Boise Cascade. SIC:
2436—Softwood Veneer & Plywood.

★ 69856 ★ Florien Plywood Plant
Hwy. 171
Florien, LA 71429
Ultimate Parent: Boise Cascade. SIC:
2436—Softwood Veneer & Plywood.

Folsom

★ 69857 ★ Ace Hardware
Hwy. 25 N
Folsom, LA 70437
(504)796-3243
Ultimate Parent: Ace Hardware. SIC:
5251—Hardware Stores.

Franklin

★ 69858 ★ Exxon Pipeline Co.
Bayou Sale
Franklin, LA 70538
(318)836-5843
Ultimate Parent: Exxon Pipeline. SIC:
1623—Water, Sewer & Utility Lines.

★ 69859 ★ Exxon Pipeline Co.
Bayou Sale
Franklin, LA 70538
(318)836-5843
Ultimate Parent: Exxon. SIC: 1623—Water,
Sewer & Utility Lines.

★ 69860 ★ Wal Mart
Us 90
Franklin, LA 70538
(318)828-2418
Ultimate Parent: Wal-Mart Stores, Inc. SIC:
5331—Variety Stores.

Galliano

★ 69861 ★ Pizza Hut
4518 Main W
Galliano, LA 70354
(504)632-5878
Ultimate Parent: Pepsico. SIC: 5812—
Eating Places.

Garyville

★ 69862 ★ Marathon Oil Co.
Airline Hwy. & Marathon Rd.
Garyville, LA 70051
(504)535-2241
Officer: George E. Lowe, Manager.
Ultimate Parent: USX Corp. SIC: 2819—
Industrial Inorganic Chemicals Nec; 2911—
Petroleum Refining.

★ 69863 ★ Marathon Oil Co.
Louisiana Refining Div.
Hwy. 61 & Marathon Ave. PO Box Ac
Garyville, LA 70051
Company Type: Division. Ultimate Parent:
USX Corp. SIC: 2911—Petroleum Refining.

★ 69864 ★ Marathon Oil Co.
Louisiana Refinery
Hwy. 61 & Marathon Ave. PO Box Ac
Garyville, LA 70051
Ultimate Parent: USX Corp. SIC: 2911—
Petroleum Refining.

★ 69865 ★ Nalco Chemical Co.
River Rd. LA Hwy. 44
Garyville, LA 70051-0844
Ultimate Parent: Nalco Chemical Co. SIC:
2869—Industrial Organic Chemicals Nec;
2899—Chemical Preparations Nec; 2819—
Industrial Inorganic Chemicals Nec; 2843—
Surface Active Agents; 5169—Chemicals &
Allied Products Nec.

★ 69866 ★ Nalco Chemical Co.
3628 Hwy. 44 LA Hwy. 44
Garyville, LA 70051-0844
Ultimate Parent: Nalco Chemical Co. SIC:
2869—Industrial Organic Chemicals Nec;
2899—Chemical Preparations Nec; 2819—
Industrial Inorganic Chemicals Nec; 2843—
Surface Active Agents; 5169—Chemicals &
Allied Products Nec.

Geidmar

★ 69867 ★ BASF Corp.
Chemical Division
Geidmar, LA 70734
(504)473-9871
Company Type: Division. Location Type:
Branch office. Ultimate Parent: BASF Corp.
SIC: 2899—Chemical Preparations Nec.

Geismar

★ 69868 ★ Allied-Signal Inc.
PO Box 226
Geismar, LA 70734-0226
(504)642-8311
Officer: D. C. Cope. Ultimate Parent:
Allied-Signal Inc. SIC: 2813—Industrial
Gases.

★ 69869 ★ Allied-Signal, Inc.
PO Box 226
Geismar, LA 70734-0226
(504)642-8311
Officer: D. C. Cope. Ultimate Parent:
Allied-Signal Inc. SIC: 2813—Industrial
Gases.

★ 69870 ★ Allied-Signal Inc.
5525 Hwy. 3115 PO Box 226
Geismar, LA 70734-0226
Ultimate Parent: Allied-Signal Inc. SIC:
2819—Industrial Inorganic Chemicals Nec.

★ 69871 ★   Allied-Signal Inc.
Hwy. 3115 PO Box 226
Geismar, LA 70734
Location Type: Plant. Ultimate Parent:
Allied-Signal Inc. SIC: 2819—Industrial
Inorganic Chemicals Nec.

★ 69872 ★   Arcadian Corp.
PO Box 307
Geismar, LA 70734-0307
(504)642-8699
Ultimate Parent: Arcadian Corp. SIC:
2875—Fertilizers—Mixing Only.

★ 69873 ★   Arcadian Fertilizer
L.P.
Hwy. 3115 & Hwy. 30
Geismar, LA 70734-0307
Ultimate Parent: Arcadian Corp. SIC:
2873—Nitrogenous Fertilizers; 2874—
Phosphatic Fertilizers.

★ 69874 ★   BASF Corp.
River Rd.
Geismar, LA 70734-0457
Ultimate Parent: BASF Corp. SIC: 2869—
Industrial Organic Chemicals Nec; 2865—
Cyclic Crudes & Intermediates; 2819—
Industrial Inorganic Chemicals Nec.

★ 69875 ★   BASF Corp.
37269 Hwy. 30
Geismar, LA 70734
(504)673-6000
Officer: William Moran, Manager. Ultimate
Parent: BASF Corp. SIC: 2821—Plastics
Materials & Resins; 2865—Cyclic Crudes &
Intermediates; 2869—Industrial Organic
Chemicals Nec.

★ 69876 ★   BASF Corp.
8404 Hwy. 75
PO Box 457
Geismar, LA 70734
(504)387-0631
Location Type: Branch office. Ultimate
Parent: BASF Corp. SIC: 2879—
Agricultural Chemicals Nec; 2819—Industrial
Inorganic Chemicals Nec; 3089—Plastics
Products Nec; 2821—Plastics Materials &
Resins. Employee Count: 892.

★ 69877 ★   BASF Corp.
Chemical Division
PO Box 457
Geismar, LA 70734
(504)387-0631
Ultimate Parent: BASF Corp. SIC: 5199—
Nondurable Goods Nec.

★ 69878 ★   Borden
Hwy. 73
Geismar, LA 70734
(504)387-5101 Fax: (504)673-0672
Officer: Joseph M. Saggese, CEO.
Ultimate Parent: Borden, Inc. Employee
Count: 740. Sales: 433 M.

★ 69879 ★   Borden Chemicals &
Plastics
4338 Hwy. 73
Geismar, LA 70734
(504)387-5101
Officer: Joseph M. Sagese, Chairman.
Ultimate Parent: Borden, Inc. SIC: 2813—
Industrial Gases; 2873—Nitrogenous
Fertilizers; 2899—Chemical Preparations
Nec.

★ 69880 ★   Enron Corp.
River Rd. Hwy. 75
Geismar, LA 70734
(504)673-6137
Officer: Shafter King, Manager. Ultimate
Parent: Enron. SIC: 2911—Petroleum
Refining.

★ 69881 ★   Rhone Poulenc Basic
Chemical
10810 Hwy. 75
Geismar, LA 70734
(504)673-5600
Ultimate Parent: Rhone-Poulenc Rorer.
SIC: 2899—Chemical Preparations Nec.

★ 69882 ★   Rhone-Poulenc Basic
Chemicals
10810 Hwy. 75
Geismar, LA 70734
Ultimate Parent: Rhone-Poulenc Rorer.
SIC: 2819—Industrial Inorganic Chemicals
Nec.

★ 69883 ★   Shell Chemical Co.
Geismar
River Rd.
Geismar, LA 70737
Location Type: Plant. Ultimate Parent:
Shell Oil Co. SIC: 2869—Industrial Organic
Chemicals Nec; 2951—Asphalt Paving
Mixtures & Blocks.

★ 69884 ★   Shell Chemical Co.
Geismar Plant
7594 Hwy. 75
Geismar, LA 70734-3505
Location Type: Plant. Ultimate Parent:
Shell Oil Co. SIC: 2819—Industrial
Inorganic Chemicals Nec; 2869—Industrial
Organic Chemicals Nec.

★ 69885 ★   Union Texas Prods.
Corp. Geismar Ethylene Plant
La Hwy. 3115
Geismar, LA 70734
Ultimate Parent: Union Texas Petroleum.
SIC: 2869—Industrial Organic Chemicals
Nec.

★ 69886 ★   Union Texas Products
Corp. Geismar Ethylene Plant
La Hwy. 3115
Geismar, LA 70734
Ultimate Parent: Union Texas Petroleum.
SIC: 2869—Industrial Organic Chemicals
Nec.

Gibson

★ 69887 ★   Shell Oil Co.
5319 Bayou Black Dr.
Gibson, LA 70356
(504)575-3321
Ultimate Parent: Shell Oil Co. SIC: 2911—
Petroleum Refining.

★ 69888 ★   Shell Oil Co.
1 PO Box
Gibson, LA 70356
(504)575-3321
Ultimate Parent: Shell Oil Co. SIC: 2911—
Petroleum Refining.

Golden Meadow

★ 69889 ★   Shell Oil Offshore Inc.
Fourchon Rd.
Golden Meadow, LA 70357
(504)396-2671
Ultimate Parent: Shell Oil Co. SIC: 1389—
Oil & Gas Field Services Nec.

Gonzales

★ 69890 ★   Greyhound Bus
Station
1014 N. Airline Hwy.
Gonzales, LA 70737
(504)644-2090
Ultimate Parent: Greyhound Lines Inc. SIC:
4111—Local & Suburban Transit.

★ 69891 ★   Kentucky Fried
Chicken
1301 N. Airline Hwy.
Gonzales, LA 70737
(504)644-6644
Ultimate Parent: Pepsico. SIC: 5812—
Eating Places.

★ 69892 ★   Liquid Carbonic
Specialty Gas Corp.
37274 Hwy. 30
Gonzales, LA 70737
Ultimate Parent: CBI Industries, Inc. SIC:
2813—Industrial Gases.

Grambling

★ 69893 ★   Greyhound Bus Lines
201 W. College Ave.
Grambling, LA 71245
(318)247-3073
Ultimate Parent: Greyhound Lines Inc. SIC:
4131—Intercity & Rural Bus Transportation.

Gramercy

★ 69894 ★   Colonial Sugars Inc.
1230 S. 5th Ave.
Gramercy, LA 70052
Ultimate Parent: Savannah Foods &
Industries, Inc. SIC: 2062—Cane Sugar
Refining.

★ 69895 ★   Colonial Sugars Inc.
1230 5th Ave.
Gramercy, LA 70052
Ultimate Parent: Savannah Foods &
Industries, Inc. SIC: 2062—Cane Sugar
Refining.

★ 69896 ★   Colonial Sugars Inc.
129 Fifth Ave.
Gramercy, LA 70052
Ultimate Parent: Savannah Foods &
Industries, Inc. SIC: 2062—Cane Sugar
Refining.

★ 69897 ★   Colonial Sugars Inc.
1250 South Fifth Ave.
Gramercy, LA 70052
Ultimate Parent: Savannah Foods &
Industries, Inc. SIC: 2062—Cane Sugar
Refining.

★ 69898 ★   Raw Materials &
Reduction Plant
Airline Hwy., P O Box 337
Gramercy, LA 70052
(504)869-5711
Ultimate Parent: Maxxam. SIC: 3334—
Primary Aluminum.

Greensburg

★ 69899 ★   Amerchol Corp.
Hwy. 43 S.
Greensburg, LA 70441
Ultimate Parent: Union Carbide Corp. SIC:
2869—Industrial Organic Chemicals Nec.

★ 69900 ★   Cellulosic Products
Inc.
Hwy. 43 South
Greensburg, LA 70441-0847
Ultimate Parent: Union Carbide Corp. SIC:
2869—Industrial Organic Chemicals Nec.

★ 69901 ★   Washington Services
7401 PO Box
Greensburg, LA 70441
(504)222-4718
Ultimate Parent: Washington Federal S&L.
SIC: 7534—Tire Retreading & Repair
Shops.

Greenwell Spg

★ 69902 ★   Radio Shack
14395 Greenwell Springs Rd.
Greenwell Spg, LA 70739
(504)261-9468
Company Type: Division. Ultimate Parent:
Tandy Corp. SIC: 5065—Electronic Parts &
Equipment Nec; 5731—Radio, Television &
Electronics Stores.

Gretna

★ 69903 ★   Jiffy Lube
International
405 Wall Blvd.
Gretna, LA 70056
(504)394-1979
Ultimate Parent: Pennzoil.

★ 69904 ★   Lerner Shop
13 Westside Shopping Ctr.
Gretna, LA 70053
(504)367-6239
Ultimate Parent: Limited. SIC: 5621—
Women's Clothing Stores.

★ 69905 ★   Lerner Shop
197 Westbank Expy.
Gretna, LA 70053
(504)362-1721
Ultimate Parent: Limited. SIC: 5621—
Women's Clothing Stores; 5651—Family
Clothing Stores.

★ 69906 ★   The Limited
197 Westbank Expy.
Gretna, LA 70053
(504)366-0104
Ultimate Parent: Limited. SIC: 5651—
Family Clothing Stores.

★ 69907 ★   Louisiana Coca-Cola
Bottling Co. Ltd.
1000 Burmaster St.
Gretna, LA 70053
Ultimate Parent: Coca-Cola Enterprises.
SIC: 2086—Bottled & Canned Soft Drinks.

★ 69908 ★   Marshalls Department
Store
21 Westside Shopping Ctr.
Gretna, LA 70053
(504)368-3032
Ultimate Parent: Melville. SIC: 5311—
Department Stores.

★ 69909 ★   Mervyn's
197 Westbank Expy.
Gretna, LA 70053
(504)368-8834
Ultimate Parent: Dayton Hudson. SIC:
5311—Department Stores.

★ 69910 ★   New York Life New
Orleans Group Claims Office
Western Group Calims Region
Oakwood Corporation Ctr.
401 Whitney Ave., Ste. 400
Gretna, LA 70053
(800)866-5173 Fax: (504)362-6433
Officer: Lee Ann Davies, Group Claims
Director. Ultimate Parent: New York Life.

★ 69911 ★   New York Life New
Orleans Group Claims Office
Western Group Claims Region
PO Box 1249
Gretna, LA 70053
(800)866-5173 Fax: (504)362-6433
Officer: Lee Ann Davies, Group Claims
Director. Ultimate Parent: New York Life.

★ 69912 ★   Pizza Hut
1632 Lafayette St.
Gretna, LA 70053
(504)363-3333
Ultimate Parent: Pepsico. SIC: 5812—
Eating Places.

★ 69913 ★   Pizza Hut
857 Terry Pky.
Gretna, LA 70056
(504)393-9933
Ultimate Parent: Pepsico. SIC: 5812—
Eating Places.

★ 69914 ★   Radio Shack
400 Lapalco Blvd.
Gretna, LA 70056
Company Type: Division. Ultimate Parent:
Tandy Corp. SIC: 5046—Commercial
Equipment Nec.

★ 69915 ★   Radio Shack
605 Lapalco Blvd.
Gretna, LA 70056
Company Type: Division. Ultimate Parent:
Tandy Corp. SIC: 7373—Computer
Integrated Systems Design.

★ 69916 ★   Texaco Self Serv Sta
799 Behrman Hwy.
Gretna, LA 70056
(504)391-0502
Ultimate Parent: Texaco. SIC: 5541—
Gasoline Service Stations.

★ 69917 ★   United Parcel Service
524 Amelia St.
Gretna, LA 70053
(504)733-7250
Ultimate Parent: United Parcel Service of
America. SIC: 4215—Courier Services
Except by Air.

★ 69918 ★   Wal Mart
925 Behrman Hwy.
Gretna, LA 70056
(504)394-0055
Ultimate Parent: Wal-Mart Stores, Inc. SIC:
5311—Department Stores.

★ 69919 ★   Waldenbooks
197 Westbank Expy.
Gretna, LA 70053
(504)368-3802
Ultimate Parent: K-Mart. SIC: 5942—Book
Stores.

★ 69920 ★   Western Auto Sup Co.
1180 Terry Pky.
Gretna, LA 70056
(504)392-7236
Ultimate Parent: Sears Roebuck & Co.
SIC: 5531—Automobile & Home Supply
Stores.

Hackberry

★ 69921 ★ Olin Corp.
Hackberry Plant
J.C. Ellender Rd.
Hackberry, LA 70645
Location Type: Plant. **Ultimate Parent:**
Olin Corp. **SIC:** 2819—Industrial Inorganic
Chemicals Nec; 2812—Alkalies & Chlorine.

Hahnville

★ 69922 ★ Agrico Chemical Co.
Taft Plant
7760 River Rd.
Hahnville, LA 70057
Ultimate Parent: Freeport-McMoran. **SIC:**
2874—Phosphatic Fertilizers.

★ 69923 ★ Union Carbide Corp.
Linde Div.
Rte. 1, Box 5
Hahnville, LA 70057
Company Type: Division. **Ultimate Parent:**
Union Carbide Corp. **SIC:** 2813—Industrial
Gases.

★ 69924 ★ Union Carbide Corp.
Indl. Chemicals
La Hwys. 18 & 3142
Hahnville, LA 70057
Ultimate Parent: Union Carbide Corp. **SIC:**
2869—Industrial Organic Chemicals Nec.

★ 69925 ★ Union Carbide Corp.
Industrial Chemicals
La. Hwy.s 18 & 3142
Hahnville, LA 70057
Ultimate Parent: Union Carbide Corp. **SIC:**
2869—Industrial Organic Chemicals Nec.

★ 69926 ★ Witco Corp.
Hwy. 3142
Hahnville, LA 70057
(504)783-6201
Officer: Joseph Daley, President. **Ultimate**
Parent: Witco Corp. **SIC:** 2821—Plastics
Materials & Resins; 2869—Industrial
Organic Chemicals Nec; 2899—Chemical
Preparations Nec.

★ 69927 ★ Witco Corp.
Argus
River Rd. & Hwy. 3142
Hahnville, LA 70057
Ultimate Parent: Witco Corp. **SIC:** 2869—
Industrial Organic Chemicals Nec.

Haknville

★ 69928 ★ Union Carbide Corp.
River Rd.
Haknville, LA 70057
(504)468-7300
Officer: Graham Painter, Manager.
Ultimate Parent: Union Carbide Corp. **SIC:**
2819—Industrial Inorganic Chemicals Nec;
2821—Plastics Materials & Resins; 2869—
Industrial Organic Chemicals Nec.

Hammond

★ 69929 ★ Greyhound Bus Lines
1000 N. Oak St.
Hammond, LA 70401
(504)345-2257
Ultimate Parent: Greyhound Lines Inc. **SIC:**
4111—Local & Suburban Transit.

★ 69930 ★ Kentucky Fried
Chicken
223 N. Morrison Blvd.
Hammond, LA 70401
(504)345-1079
Ultimate Parent: Pepsico. **SIC:** 5812—
Eating Places.

★ 69931 ★ Lerner Shop
2000 SW Railroad Ave.
Hammond, LA 70403
(504)345-5008
Ultimate Parent: Limited. **SIC:** 5621—
Women's Clothing Stores.

★ 69932 ★ Pizza Hut Inc.
2440 W. Thomas St.
Hammond, LA 70401
(504)345-4261
Ultimate Parent: Pepsico. **SIC:** 5812—
Eating Places.

★ 69933 ★ Radio Shack
Hammond Sq.
Hammond, LA 70401
(504)345-4897
Company Type: Division. **Ultimate Parent:**
Tandy Corp. **SIC:** 5065—Electronic Parts &
Equipment Nec.

★ 69934 ★ Taco Bell
2025 W. Thomas St.
Hammond, LA 70401
(504)345-1971
Ultimate Parent: Pepsico. **SIC:** 5812—
Eating Places.

★ 69935 ★ Walgreen Drug Stores
113 N. Morrison Blvd.
Hammond, LA 70401
Ultimate Parent: Walgreen Co. **SIC:**
5912—Drug Stores & Proprietary Stores.

Harahan

★ 69936 ★ Coca-Cola USA
5330 Jefferson Hwy.
Harahan, LA 70123
Ultimate Parent: Coca-Cola. **SIC:** 2087—
Flavoring Extracts & Syrups Nec.

★ 69937 ★ Witco Corp.
Harahan
1320 Sams Ave.
Harahan, LA 70123
Ultimate Parent: Witco Corp. **SIC:** 2865—
Cyclic Crudes & Intermediates; 2869—
Industrial Organic Chemicals Nec; 2843—
Surface Active Agents.

★ 69938 ★ X-Chem Inc.
6120 Jefferson Hwy.
Harahan, LA 70123
Ultimate Parent: NCH. **SIC:** 2899—
Chemical Preparations Nec.

Harvey

★ 69939 ★ Continental Bank
2150 Westbank Expy.
Harvey, LA 70058
(504)368-6200
Ultimate Parent: Midlantic Corp. **SIC:**
6029—Commercial Banks Nec.

★ 69940 ★ Gretna Machine &
Iron Works
4640 Peters Rd.
Harvey, LA 70058
Ultimate Parent: Trinity Industries. **SIC:**
3731—Ship Building & Repairing.

★ 69941 ★ Sigma Coatings Inc.
1401 Destrehan Ave.
Harvey, LA 70058
(504)347-4321
Officer: Philippe Desberg, President.
Ultimate Parent: Fina. **SIC:** 2851—Paints &
Allied Products; 2952—Asphalt Felts &
Coatings; 3479—Metal Coating & Allied
Services.

★ 69942 ★ Stewart & Stevenson
SVC
1400 Destrehan Ave.
Harvey, LA 70058
(504)347-4326
Officer: Ralston Cole, Manager. **Ultimate**
Parent: Stewart & Stevenson. **SIC:** 3511—
Turbines & Turbine Generator Sets.

★ 69943 ★ Witco Corp.
1805 4th St.
Harvey, LA 70058
(504)366-7281
Officer: Robert Williams, Manager.
Ultimate Parent: Witco Corp. **SIC:** 2843—
Surface Active Agents; 2899—Chemical
Preparations Nec; 2911—Petroleum
Refining.

Haughton

★ 69944 ★ Union Texas
Petroleum
96 PO Box
Haughton, LA 71037
(318)949-3271
Ultimate Parent: Union Texas Petroleum.
SIC: 1321—Natural Gas Liquids.

Haynesville

★ 69945 ★ Piggly Wiggly
217 W. Main St.
Haynesville, LA 71038
(318)624-0883
Ultimate Parent: Bruno's. **SIC:** 5411—
Grocery Stores.

Hodge

★ 69946 ★ Stone Container Corp.
Mill St.
Hodge, LA 71247
(318)259-4421
Officer: Roger Stone, President. **Ultimate**
Parent: Stone Container Corp. **SIC:** 2621—
Paper Mills; 2631—Paperboard Mills;
2673—Bags—Plastics, Laminated &
Coated.

★ 69947 ★ Stone Hodge Inc.
Mill St.
Hodge, LA 71247-3700
Ultimate Parent: Stone Container Corp.
SIC: 2631—Paperboard Mills; 2600—Paper
& Allied Products.

Homer

★ 69948 ★ Piggly Wiggly
404 N. 2nd St.
Homer, LA 71040
(318)927-2353
Ultimate Parent: Bruno's. **SIC:** 5411—
Grocery Stores.

Hornbeck

★ 69949 ★ AT&T
Hornbeck, LA 71439
(318)565-4363
Location Type: Branch office. **Ultimate**
Parent: AT&T. **SIC:** 4813—Telephone
Communications Except Radiotelephone.

Houma

★ 69950 ★ Baker Performance
Chemicals
1200 Dunn St.
Houma, LA 70360
(504)879-2693
Officer: Roger Quinn, Manager. **Ultimate**
Parent: Baker Hughes. **SIC:** 2843—Surface
Active Agents; 2865—Cyclic Crudes &
Intermediates; 2879—Agricultural Chemicals
Nec.

★ 69951 ★ Exxon Co. USA
1000 Magnolia St.
Houma, LA 70360
(504)872-3111
Ultimate Parent: Exxon. **SIC:** 5172—
Petroleum Products Nec.

★ 69952 ★ Exxon Co. USA
1626 Barrow St.
Houma, LA 70360
(504)872-1224
Ultimate Parent: Exxon. **SIC:** 5172—
Petroleum Products Nec.

★ 69953 ★ First Federal S & L
1983 Prospect Blvd.
Houma, LA 70363-6047
(504)868-0577
Company Type: Branch. **Ultimate Parent:**
Bancorp Hawaii. **SIC:** 6035—Federal
Savings Institutions.

★ 69954 ★ First Federal S & L
2617 W. Park Ave.
Houma, LA 70364-1718
(504)868-4970
Officer: Betty D. Marcel. **Ultimate Parent:**
Bancorp Hawaii. **SIC:** 6035—Federal
Savings Institutions.

★ 69955 ★ Fleet Finance Inc.
1303 Grand Caillou Rd.
Houma, LA 70363
(504)868-3413
Ultimate Parent: Fleet Financial Group.
SIC: 6141—Personal Credit Institutions.

★ 69956 ★ Gemoco
202 Industrial Blvd.
Houma, LA 70360
Ultimate Parent: Sequa Corp. **SIC:** 3533—
Oil & Gas Field Machinery.

★ 69957 ★ Greyhound Bus
Terminal
200 E. Park Ave.
Houma, LA 70364
(504)873-8573
Ultimate Parent: Greyhound Lines Inc. **SIC:**
4212—Local Trucking Without Storage.

★ 69958 ★ Hertz Rent-A-Car
Houma
Houma, LA 70363
(504)868-4220
Ultimate Parent: Hertz. **SIC:** 4522—Air
Transportation—Nonscheduled.

★ 69959 ★ Kentucky Fried
Chicken
1606 W. Park Ave.
Houma, LA 70364
(504)851-6218
Ultimate Parent: Pepsico. **SIC:** 5812—
Eating Places.

★ 69960 ★ Louisiana Land &
Exploratio
800 Bayou Black Dr.
Houma, LA 70360
(504)879-1517
Ultimate Parent: Louisiana Land &
Exploration. **SIC:** 6211—Security Brokers &
Dealers.

★ 69961 ★ Millpark Drilling
Fluids Inc.
Munson Slip
Houma, LA 70360
(504)879-3525
Ultimate Parent: Baker Hughes. **SIC:**
2899—Chemical Preparations Nec; 3295—
Minerals—Ground or Treated.

★ 69962 ★ Mobil Oil
Houma Air Base
Houma, LA 70363
(504)857-7300
Ultimate Parent: Mobil. **SIC:** 1311—Crude
Petroleum & Natural Gas.

★ 69963 ★ Pennzoil Co.
Hwy. 90
Houma, LA 70364
(504)876-1760
Ultimate Parent: Pennzoil. **SIC:** 1311—
Crude Petroleum & Natural Gas.

★ 69964 ★ Pizza Hut
2404 W. Park Ave.
Houma, LA 70364
(504)876-5138
Ultimate Parent: Pepsico. **SIC:** 1799—
Special Trade Contractors Nec; 5812—
Eating Places.

★ 69965 ★ Premier Bancorp
720 E. Main St.
Houma, LA 70360
(504)876-7800
Ultimate Parent: Premier Bancorp. **SIC:**
6531—Real Estate Agents & Managers.

★ 69966 ★ Radio Shack
3038 W. Park Ave.
Houma, LA 70364
(504)876-9205
Company Type: Division. **Ultimate Parent:**
Tandy Corp. **SIC:** 5065—Electronic Parts &
Equipment Nec.

★ 69967 ★ Radio Shack
2008 Grand Caillou Rd.
Houma, LA 70363
(504)868-6039
Company Type: Division. **Ultimate Parent:**
Tandy Corp. **SIC:** 5065—Electronic Parts &
Equipment Nec.

★ 69968 ★ Radio Shack
Southland Mall
Houma, LA 70364
(504)872-9409
Company Type: Division. **Ultimate Parent:**
Tandy Corp. **SIC:** 5734—Computer &
Software Stores.

★ 69969 ★ Saia Motor Freight
Line, Inc.
104 Woodlawn Ranch Rd.
PO Box A, Station 1
Houma, LA 70363
(504)868-1030 **Fax:** (504)857-2312
Officer: Louis P. Saia Jr., Chairman.
Ultimate Parent: Yellow Corp.

★ 69970 ★   Sequa Corp.
Gemoco
202 Industrial Blvd.
Houma, LA 70363
Ultimate Parent: Sequa Corp. SIC: 3533—
Oil & Gas Field Machinery.

★ 69971 ★   Sequa Corp.
Gemoco
202 Industrial Blvd.
Houma, LA 70360
Ultimate Parent: Sequa Corp. SIC: 3533—
Oil & Gas Field Machinery.

★ 69972 ★   Texaco Inc.
3218 W. Main St.
Houma, LA 70360
(504)872-5229
Ultimate Parent: Texaco. SIC: 5172—
Petroleum Products Nec.

★ 69973 ★   Union Oil Co. of
California
1st
Houma, LA 70360
(504)876-1150
Ultimate Parent: Unocal Corp. SIC: 1382—
Oil & Gas Exploration Services.

★ 69974 ★   Wal Mart Discount
City 542
1710 W. Park Ave.
Houma, LA 70364
(504)868-9771
Ultimate Parent: Wal-Mart Stores, Inc. SIC:
5311—Department Stores.

Jefferson

★ 69975 ★   Shell Oil Co.
309 Jefferson Hwy.
Jefferson, LA 70121
(504)833-8261
Officer: Ken Lang, Manager. Ultimate
Parent: Shell Oil Co. SIC: 2911—Petroleum
Refining.

★ 69976 ★   Shell Oil Co.
Metairie Plant
309 Jefferson Hwy.
Jefferson, LA 70121
Location Type: Plant. Ultimate Parent:
Shell Oil Co. SIC: 2992—Lubricating Oils &
Greases.

Jena

★ 69977 ★   Belden Wire & Cable
Hwy. 84 East
Jena, LA 71342
Ultimate Parent: Cooper Industries.

Jennings

★ 69978 ★   Coca Cola Bottling
Co.
Roberts Ave.
Jennings, LA 70546
(318)824-2157
Ultimate Parent: Coca-Cola Enterprises.
SIC: 2086—Bottled & Canned Soft Drinks.

★ 69979 ★   Greyhound Bus Lines
147 W. Plaquemine St.
Jennings, LA 70546
(318)824-0611
Ultimate Parent: Greyhound Lines Inc. SIC:
4142—Bus Charter Service Except Local.

★ 69980 ★   Piggly Wiggly
1326 N. Cutting Ave.
Jennings, LA 70546
(318)824-4443
Ultimate Parent: Bruno's. SIC: 5411—
Grocery Stores.

★ 69981 ★   Taco Bell
3007 Elton Rd.
Jennings, LA 70546
(318)824-7045
Ultimate Parent: Pepsico. SIC: 5812—
Eating Places.

★ 69982 ★   Wal Mart Discount
Cities
1322 S. Lake Arthur Ave.
Jennings, LA 70546
(318)824-9970
Ultimate Parent: Wal-Mart Stores, Inc. SIC:
5311—Department Stores.

Jonesboro

★ 69983 ★   Kentucky Fried
Chicken
860 Pershing Hwy.
Jonesboro, LA 71251
(318)259-2412
Ultimate Parent: Pepsico. SIC: 5812—
Eating Places.

★ 69984 ★   Piggly Wiggly
310 E. Main St.
Jonesboro, LA 71251
(318)259-7232
Ultimate Parent: Bruno's. SIC: 5411—
Grocery Stores.

★ 69985 ★   Pizza Hut
810 Pershing Hwy.
Jonesboro, LA 71251
(318)259-7354
Ultimate Parent: Pepsico. SIC: 5812—
Eating Places.

Jonesville

★ 69986 ★   Piggly Wiggly
Hwy. 84 W
Jonesville, LA 71343
(318)339-7854
Ultimate Parent: Bruno's. SIC: 5411—
Grocery Stores.

★ 69987 ★   Radio Shack
615 4th St.
Jonesville, LA 71343
(318)339-6109
Company Type: Division. Ultimate Parent:
Tandy Corp. SIC: 5065—Electronic Parts &
Equipment Nec.

Joyce

★ 69988 ★   Manville Forest
Products
Joyce Facility
Hwy. 34 N
Joyce, LA 71440
Company Type: Division. Ultimate Parent:
Manville Corp. SIC: 2421—Sawmills &
Planing Mills—General; 2436—Softwood
Veneer & Plywood.

Kaplan

★ 69989 ★   Mini Mart
400 W. 1st St.
Kaplan, LA 70548
(318)643-2870
Ultimate Parent: Kroger. SIC: 5411—
Grocery Stores.

★ 69990 ★   Mobil Oil Exploring &
Producing SE
RR 1
Kaplan, LA 70548-9801
(318)643-6168
Ultimate Parent: Mobil. SIC: 4924—Natural
Gas Distribution.

★ 69991 ★   Mobil Oil Inc/E&P S
Rural Route 1
Kaplan, LA 70548
(318)643-8315
Ultimate Parent: Mobil. SIC: 1311—Crude
Petroleum & Natural Gas.

Kenner

★ 69992 ★   Advanced Medical
Systems Inc.
2001 21st St.
Kenner, LA 70062
(504)469-9977
Ultimate Parent: Standard Register.

★ 69993 ★   Big Bear
1005 Veterans Blvd.
Kenner, LA 70065
(504)464-4156
Ultimate Parent: Penn Traffic. SIC: 8732—
Commercial Nonphysical Research.

★ 69994 ★   Casual Corner
1401 W. Esplanade Ave.
Kenner, LA 70065
(504)464-1903
Ultimate Parent: United States Shoe. SIC:
5651—Family Clothing Stores.

★ 69995 ★   First Financial Bank F
S B
3701 Williams Blvd.
Kenner, LA 70065
(504)561-7422
Ultimate Parent: First Financial Corp. SIC:
6022—State Commercial Banks.

★ 69996 ★   Kay-Bee Toy & Hobby
1401 W. Esplanade Ave.
Kenner, LA 70065
(504)466-5582
Ultimate Parent: Melville. SIC: 5945—
Hobby, Toy & Game Shops.

★ 69997 ★   Lens Crafters
1401 W. Esplanade Ave.
Kenner, LA 70065
(504)465-0444
Ultimate Parent: United States Shoe. SIC:
5995—Optical Goods Stores.

★ 69998 ★   The Limited Express
1401 W. Esplanade Ave.
Kenner, LA 70065
(504)468-1814
Ultimate Parent: Limited. SIC: 5651—
Family Clothing Stores.

★ 69999 ★   Mervyn's
1401 W. Esplanade Ave.
Kenner, LA 70065
(504)464-8834
Ultimate Parent: Dayton Hudson. SIC:
5399—Miscellaneous General Merchandise
Store.

★ 70000 ★   Nalco Chemical Co.
3715 Williams Blvd.
Kenner, LA 70065
(504)443-6591
Ultimate Parent: Nalco Chemical Co. SIC:
5169—Chemicals & Allied Products Nec.

★ 70001 ★   New England Mutl
Life Insurance C
11 James St.
Kenner, LA 70062
(504)469-8476
Ultimate Parent: New England Mutual Life.
SIC: 6411—Insurance Agents, Brokers &
Service.

★ 70002 ★   Petite Sophisticate
1401 W. Esplanade Ave.
Kenner, LA 70065
(504)467-3090
Ultimate Parent: United States Shoe. SIC:
5651—Family Clothing Stores.

★ 70003 ★   Pizza Hut
2633 Williams Blvd.
Kenner, LA 70062
(504)466-7614
Ultimate Parent: Pepsico. SIC: 5812—
Eating Places.

★ 70004 ★   Pizza Hut
3800 Williams Blvd.
Kenner, LA 70065
(504)443-4627
Ultimate Parent: Pepsico. SIC: 5812—
Eating Places.

★ 70005 ★   Pizza Hut
3535 Chateau Blvd.
Kenner, LA 70065
(504)468-3842
Ultimate Parent: Pepsico. SIC: 5812—
Eating Places.

★ 70006 ★   Prints Plus
1401 W. Esplanade Ave.
Kenner, LA 70065
(504)469-8803
Ultimate Parent: Melville. SIC: 7312—
Outdoor Advertising Services.

★ 70007 ★   Publix Super Market
445 Veterans Blvd.
Kenner, LA 70065
(504)469-4010
Ultimate Parent: Publix Super Markets.
SIC: 5411—Grocery Stores.

★ 70008 ★   Radio Shack
2544 Williams Blvd.
Kenner, LA 70062
(504)466-0417
Company Type: Division. Ultimate Parent:
Tandy Corp. SIC: 5065—Electronic Parts &
Equipment Nec.

★ 70009 ★   Radio Shack
1000 W. Esplanade Ave. Bldg. 20
Kenner, LA 70065
(504)443-1056
Company Type: Division. Ultimate Parent:
Tandy Corp. SIC: 5065—Electronic Parts &
Equipment Nec; 5731—Radio, Television &
Electronics Stores.

★ 70010 ★   Radio Shack
1401 W. Esplanade Ave.
Kenner, LA 70065
(504)466-7078
Company Type: Division. Ultimate Parent:
Tandy Corp. SIC: 7373—Computer
Integrated Systems Design.

★ 70011 ★   Safety Kleen Corp.
2233 Piedmont Ave.
Kenner, LA 70062
(504)468-9401
Ultimate Parent: Safety-Kleen. SIC: 6531—
Real Estate Agents & Managers.

★ 70012 ★   Safety Kleen Corp.
1194 PO Box
Kenner, LA 70063
(504)466-5718
Ultimate Parent: Safety-Kleen. SIC: 2899—
Chemical Preparations Nec; 5013—Motor
Vehicle Supplies & New Parts.

★ 70013 ★   St. Jude Medical
Center
180 W. Esplinade
Kenner, LA 70065
(504)468-8600
Officer: Jack Julius, Executive Director.
Ultimate Parent: American Medical
Holdings. SIC: 8062—General Medical &
Surgical Hospitals.

★ 70014 ★   Shell Gas Station
3501 Williams Blvd.
Kenner, LA 70065
(504)443-2736
Ultimate Parent: Shell Oil Co. SIC: 5541—
Gasoline Service Stations.

★ 70015 ★   Sparkletts Water Sys.
Auqa Vend
601 Maria St.
Kenner, LA 70062
Ultimate Parent: McKesson. SIC: 7389—
Business Services Nec.

★ 70016 ★   Sparkletts Water
Systems Aquavend
601 Maria St.
Kenner, LA 70062
Ultimate Parent: McKesson. SIC: 7389—
Business Services Nec.

★ 70017 ★   St Jude Medical
Center
180 W. Esplanade Ave.
Kenner, LA 70065
(504)468-8600
Ultimate Parent: American Medical
Holdings. SIC: 8062—General Medical &
Surgical Hospitals.

★ 70018 ★   Taco Bell
3117 Loyola Dr.
Kenner, LA 70065
(504)469-5294
Ultimate Parent: Pepsico. SIC: 5812—
Eating Places.

★ 70019 ★   Taco Bell
2629 Williams Blvd.
Kenner, LA 70062
(504)467-7238
Ultimate Parent: Pepsico. SIC: 5812—
Eating Places.

★ 70020 ★   Taco Bell
1401 W. Esplanade Ave.
Kenner, LA 70065
(504)465-9293
Ultimate Parent: Pepsico. SIC: 5812—
Eating Places.

★ 70021 ★   Tektronix Inc.
1940 I-10 Service Rd.
Kenner, LA 70065
(504)466-4445
Ultimate Parent: Tektronix, Inc. SIC:
5049—Professional Equipment Nec.

★ 70022 ★   **Victoria's Secret**
1401 W. Esplanade Ave.
Kenner, LA 70065
(504)468-2045
Ultimate Parent: Limited. **SIC:** 5651—
Family Clothing Stores.

★ 70023 ★   **Waldenbooks**
1401 W. Esplanade Ave.
Kenner, LA 70065
(504)464-4187
Ultimate Parent: K-Mart. **SIC:** 5942—Book
Stores.

★ 70024 ★   **Walgreen**
4041 Williams Blvd.
Kenner, LA 70065
(504)443-2747
Ultimate Parent: Walgreen Co. **SIC:**
5912—Drug Stores & Proprietary Stores.

Kilbourne

★ 70025 ★   **Exxon Distributor**
Hwy. 17 S
Kilbourne, LA 71253
(318)428-2591
Ultimate Parent: Exxon. **SIC:** 5172—
Petroleum Products Nec.

Kinder

★ 70026 ★   **Trailway Bus Station**
Us 165
Kinder, LA 70648
(318)639-4339
Ultimate Parent: Greyhound Lines Inc. **SIC:**
4131—Intercity & Rural Bus Transportation;
5812—Eating Places.

★ 70027 ★   **Wal Mart Discount City**
Kinder, LA 70648
(318)738-5693
Ultimate Parent: Wal-Mart Stores, Inc. **SIC:**
5331—Variety Stores.

Krotz Springs

★ 70028 ★   **Hill Petroleum Co.**
Krotz Springs Refinery
Hwy. 105 South
Krotz Springs, LA 70750-0453
Ultimate Parent: Salomon, Inc. **SIC:**
2911—Petroleum Refining.

★ 70029 ★   **Phibro Refinery**
Krotz Springs Refinery
Hwy. 105 S.
Krotz Springs, LA 70750-0453
Ultimate Parent: Salomon, Inc. **SIC:**
2911—Petroleum Refining.

★ 70030 ★   **Phibro Refining**
Hwy. 105 S.
Krotz Springs, LA 70750
Ultimate Parent: Salomon, Inc. **SIC:**
2911—Petroleum Refining.

La Place

★ 70031 ★   **Pizza Hut**
1401 W. Airline Hwy.
La Place, LA 70068
(504)652-9566
Ultimate Parent: Pepsico. **SIC:** 5812—
Eating Places; 5812—Eating Places.

Labadieville

★ 70032 ★   **Supreme Sugar Co., Inc.**
Refinery Supreme Rd.
Labadieville, LA 70372
(504)529-5877
Ultimate Parent: Archer Daniels Midland
Co. **SIC:** 2061—Raw Cane Sugar.

★ 70033 ★   **Supreme Sugar Co. Inc.**
PO Box 68
Labadieville, LA 70372-0068
(504)526-4261
Officer: Joseph Harrison Sr. **Ultimate
Parent:** Archer Daniels Midland Co. **SIC:**
2062—Cane Sugar Refining; 2061—Raw
Cane Sugar.

★ 70034 ★   **Supreme Sugar Co. Inc.**
239 Hwy. 1011
Labadieville, LA 70372
(504)526-4261
Officer: Joseph Harrison, President.
Ultimate Parent: Archer Daniels Midland
Co. **SIC:** 2062—Cane Sugar Refining.

★ 70035 ★   **Supreme Sugar Co. Inc.**
Supreme Rd.
Labadieville, LA 70372
(504)526-4261
Ultimate Parent: Archer Daniels Midland
Co. **SIC:** 2062—Cane Sugar Refining.

Lacombe

★ 70036 ★   **Ace Hardware Lacombe**
Hwy. 190
Lacombe, LA 70445
(504)882-3520
Ultimate Parent: Ace Hardware. **SIC:**
5251—Hardware Stores.

★ 70037 ★   **Hibernia National Bank**
68 PO Box
Lacombe, LA 70445
(504)882-5342
Ultimate Parent: Hibernia Corp. **SIC:**
6099—Functions Related to Deposit
Banking.

Lafayett

★ 70038 ★   **Premier Bank, NA**
5233 Johnston St.
Lafayett, LA 70503-5170
Location Type: Branch office. **Ultimate
Parent:** Premier Bancorp.

Lafayette

★ 70039 ★   **Albertson's**
2678 Johnston St.
Lafayette, LA 70503
(318)233-2940
Ultimate Parent: Albertson's Inc. **SIC:**
5411—Grocery Stores; 5912—Drug Stores
& Proprietary Stores.

★ 70040 ★   **Amerada Hess Corp.**
412 Travis St.
Lafayette, LA 70503-2432
(318)233-4635
Location Type: Branch office. **Officer:**
John W. Meyers. **Ultimate Parent:**
Amerada Hess. **SIC:** 1311—Crude
Petroleum & Natural Gas.

★ 70041 ★   **American Family Life Assurance**
319 Audubon Blvd.
Lafayette, LA 70503
(318)232-5607
Ultimate Parent: American Family Life
Assurance Co. **SIC:** 6411—Insurance
Agents, Brokers & Service; 8082—Home
Health Care Services.

★ 70042 ★   **Arco Oil & Gas Co.**
400 E. Kaliste Saloom Rd., Ste. 30
Lafayette, LA 70508-3298
(318)264-4000
Company Type: Division. **Officer:** John B.
Cheatham. **Ultimate Parent:** Atlantic
Richfield Co., Inc. **SIC:** 1311—Crude
Petroleum & Natural Gas; 1382—Oil & Gas
Exploration Services.

★ 70043 ★   **Avon Products, Inc.**
1404 Carmel Ave.
Lafayette, LA 70501
(318)235-1595
Ultimate Parent: Avon Products, Inc. **SIC:**
5999—Miscellaneous Retail Stores Nec.

★ 70044 ★   **Borden Inc.**
1308 Bertrand Dr.
Lafayette, LA 70506
(318)232-5172
Location Type: Plant. **Officer:** Bob
Burrack, Plant Manager. **Ultimate Parent:**
Borden, Inc. **SIC:** 2026—Fluid Milk; 2033—
Canned Fruits & Vegetables; 3085—Plastics
Bottles.

★ 70045 ★   **Borden Inc.**
Dairy
1308 Bertrand Dr.
Lafayette, LA 70506
Company Type: Division. **Ultimate Parent:**
Borden, Inc. **SIC:** 2026—Fluid Milk.

★ 70046 ★   **Borden Inc.**
Dairy
1308 Bertrand Dr.
Lafayette, LA 70506
Company Type: Division. **Ultimate Parent:**
Borden, Inc. **SIC:** 2026—Fluid Milk.

★ 70047 ★   **Butler Paper Co.**
119 Boyce Dr.
Lafayette, LA 70503-3305
(318)837-3802
Location Type: Branch office. **Officer:**
Richard Lantier. **Ultimate Parent:** Alco
Standard Corp. **SIC:** 2621—Paper Mills;
5111—Printing & Writing Paper.

★ 70048 ★   **Butler Paper Co.**
119 Boyce Dr.
Lafayette, LA 70503-3305
(318)837-3802
Location Type: Branch office. **Officer:**
Richard Lantier. **Ultimate Parent:** Alco
Standard Corp. **SIC:** 2621—Paper Mills;
5111—Printing & Writing Paper.

★ 70049 ★   **Casual Corner**
5725 Johnston St.
Lafayette, LA 70503
(318)981-8174
Ultimate Parent: United States Shoe. **SIC:**
5621—Women's Clothing Stores; 5651—
Family Clothing Stores.

★ 70050 ★   **Coca Cola Bottling Co.**
1314 Eraste Landry Rd.
Lafayette, LA 70506
(318)232-8413
Ultimate Parent: Coca-Cola Enterprises.
SIC: 2086—Bottled & Canned Soft Drinks;
5046—Commercial Equipment Nec; 5149—
Groceries & Related Products Nec.

★ 70051 ★   **Digital Equipment Corp.**
2020 W. Pinhook Rd.
Lafayette, LA 70508
(318)232-5877
Ultimate Parent: Digital Equipment Corp.
SIC: 7373—Computer Integrated Systems
Design.

★ 70052 ★   **Dillards**
5725 Johnston St.
Lafayette, LA 70503
(318)261-3217
Ultimate Parent: Dillard Department Stores.
SIC: 5311—Department Stores.

★ 70053 ★   **Emery Worldwide**
122 John Glenn Dr.
Lafayette, LA 70508
(318)837-9977
Ultimate Parent: Consolidated Freightways.
SIC: 4512—Air Transportation—Scheduled.

★ 70054 ★   **Exxon**
Frontage Rd.
Lafayette, LA 70501
(318)235-9561
Ultimate Parent: Exxon. **SIC:** 5541—
Gasoline Service Stations.

★ 70055 ★   **Fleet Finance Inc.**
54027 PO Box
Lafayette, LA 70505
(318)233-4200
Ultimate Parent: Fleet Financial Group.
SIC: 6141—Personal Credit Institutions.

★ 70056 ★   **Greyhound Bus Lines**
315 Lee Ave.
Lafayette, LA 70501
(318)235-1541
Ultimate Parent: Greyhound Lines Inc. **SIC:**
4111—Local & Suburban Transit; 4131—
Intercity & Rural Bus Transportation.

★ 70057 ★   **Hertz Rent-A-Car**
200 Lafayette St.
Lafayette, LA 70501
(318)233-7010
Ultimate Parent: Hertz. **SIC:** 7514—
Passenger Car Rental.

★ 70058 ★   **Hibernia National Bank**
3720 Johnston St.
Lafayette, LA 70503
(318)235-9018
Ultimate Parent: Hibernia Corp.

★ 70059 ★   **Hibernia National Bank**
213 W. Vermilion St.
Lafayette, LA 70501
(318)235-9018
Ultimate Parent: Hibernia Corp. **SIC:**
6022—State Commercial Banks; 6512—
Nonresidential Building Operators.

★ 70060 ★   **Hibernia National Bank**
124 Heymann Blvd.
Lafayette, LA 70503
(318)268-4512
Ultimate Parent: Hibernia Corp.

★ 70061 ★   **Hit or Miss**
3607 Ambassador Caffery Pky.
Lafayette, LA 70503
(318)984-4101
Ultimate Parent: TJX. **SIC:** 5651—Family
Clothing Stores.

★ 70062 ★   **Huval Bakeries Inc.**
720 W. Simcoe St.
Lafayette, LA 70501-5744
(318)232-1611
Company Type: Subsidiary. **Officer:** Gary
Davis, President. **Ultimate Parent:** Flowers
Industries. **SIC:** 2051—Bread, Cake &
Related Products. **Employee Count:** 170.
Sales: 34 M.

★ 70063 ★   **Huval Baking Co.**
720 W. Simcoe St.
PO Box 2339
Lafayette, LA 70502
(318)232-1611 **Fax:** (318)234-5769
Company Type: Subsidiary. **Officer:** Gary
Davis, President. **Ultimate Parent:** Flowers
Industries.

★ 70064 ★   **Kay Bee Toy&Hobby Shop**
Acadiana Mall
Lafayette, LA 70503
(318)981-2749
Ultimate Parent: Melville. **SIC:** 5945—
Hobby, Toy & Game Shops.

★ 70065 ★   **Kay Bee Toy&Hobby Shop**
Northgate
Lafayette, LA 70501
(318)232-9064
Ultimate Parent: Melville. **SIC:** 5945—
Hobby, Toy & Game Shops.

★ 70066 ★   **Kentucky Fried Chicken**
107 E. University Ave.
Lafayette, LA 70503
(318)269-9427
Ultimate Parent: Pepsico. **SIC:** 5812—
Eating Places.

★ 70067 ★   **Kroger**
128 Arnould Blvd.
Lafayette, LA 70506
(318)984-6672
Ultimate Parent: Kroger. **SIC:** 5411—
Grocery Stores.

★ 70068 ★   **Lane Bryant**
5725 Johnston St.
Lafayette, LA 70503
(318)988-4473
Ultimate Parent: Limited. **SIC:** 5651—
Family Clothing Stores.

★ 70069 ★   **Lens Crafters**
5725 Johnston St.
Lafayette, LA 70503
(318)989-6515
Ultimate Parent: United States Shoe. **SIC:**
3827—Optical Instruments & Lenses.

★ 70070 ★   **Lerner Shop**
5725 Johnston St.
Lafayette, LA 70503
(318)984-8172
Ultimate Parent: Limited. **SIC:** 5651—
Family Clothing Stores.

★ 70071 ★   Lerner Shop
208 NE Frontage Rd.
Lafayette, LA 70501
(318)232-8153
Ultimate Parent: Limited. SIC: 5651—
Family Clothing Stores; 5651—Family
Clothing Stores.

★ 70072 ★   The Limited Express
5725 Johnston St.
Lafayette, LA 70503
(318)988-2201
Ultimate Parent: Limited. SIC: 5621—
Women's Clothing Stores.

★ 70073 ★   Malone & Hyde of
Lafayette
1602 Pinhook Rd.
Lafayette, LA 70508-3722
(318)236-3800
Company Type: Subsidiary. Officer: John
Keyser, President. Ultimate Parent:
Fleming. SIC: 5149—Groceries & Related
Products Nec. Sales: 280 M.

★ 70074 ★   Marshalls Department
Store
3611 Ambassador Caffery Pky.
Lafayette, LA 70503
(318)988-5025
Ultimate Parent: Melville. SIC: 5311—
Department Stores.

★ 70075 ★   Mary Kay Cosmetics
501 Camellia Blvd.
Lafayette, LA 70503
(318)988-1346
Ultimate Parent: Mary Kay Cosmetics. SIC:
5999—Miscellaneous Retail Stores Nec.

★ 70076 ★   New York Life
Lafayette General Office
Western Agencies
PO Box 53126
Lafayette, LA 70505
(318)261-9800 Fax: (318)261-9832
Officer: Guy R. Broussard III, General
Manager. Ultimate Parent: New York Life.

★ 70077 ★   New York Life
Lafayette General Office
Western Agencies
400 E. Kaliste Saloom, Ste. 301
Lafayette, LA 70508
(318)261-9800 Fax: (318)261-9832
Officer: Guy R. Broussard III, General
Manager. Ultimate Parent: New York Life.

★ 70078 ★   Oilfield Service Corp.
of Am
80627 PO Box
Lafayette, LA 70598
Ultimate Parent: Great Lakes Chemical.
SIC: 1389—Oil & Gas Field Services Nec.

★ 70079 ★   OSCA
PO Box 80627
Lafayette, LA 70508-0627
(318)837-6047
Company Type: Subsidiary. Ultimate
Parent: Great Lakes Chemical. SIC: 5169—
Chemicals & Allied Products Nec.

★ 70080 ★   Osca Inc.
156 Commission Blvd.
Lafayette, LA 70508-3516
(318)837-6047
Company Type: Subsidiary. Officer:
Robert L. Hollier, President. Ultimate
Parent: Great Lakes Chemical. SIC: 1389—
Oil & Gas Field Services Nec; 5169—
Chemicals & Allied Products Nec; 7353—
Heavy Construction Equipment Rental;
8748—Business Consulting Services Nec.
Employee Count: 450. Sales: 43.9 M.

★ 70081 ★   OSCA Inc.
156 Commission Blvd.
Lafayette, LA 70598-0627
(318)237-3854 Fax: (318)837-9647
Company Type: Subsidiary. Officer:
Robert L. Hollier, President. Ultimate
Parent: Great Lakes Chemical.

★ 70082 ★   Piggly Wiggly
208 W. Willow St.
Lafayette, LA 70501
(318)237-5199
Ultimate Parent: Bruno's. SIC: 5411—
Grocery Stores.

★ 70083 ★   Piggly Wiggly
454 Heymann Blvd.
Lafayette, LA 70503
(318)232-7550
Ultimate Parent: Bruno's. SIC: 5411—
Grocery Stores.

★ 70084 ★   Pizza Hut
1821 W. Pinhook Rd.
Lafayette, LA 70508
(318)233-4568
Ultimate Parent: Pepsico. SIC: 5812—
Eating Places.

★ 70085 ★   Pizza Hut
120 NW Frontage Rd.
Lafayette, LA 70501
(318)233-6715
Ultimate Parent: Pepsico. SIC: 5812—
Eating Places.

★ 70086 ★   Pizza Hut
109 Saint Landry St.
Lafayette, LA 70506
(318)233-3335
Ultimate Parent: Pepsico. SIC: 5812—
Eating Places.

★ 70087 ★   Pizza Hut
4021 Johnston St.
Lafayette, LA 70503
(318)984-8530
Ultimate Parent: Pepsico. SIC: 5812—
Eating Places.

★ 70088 ★   Premier Bank, NA
1911 Pinhook Rd.
Lafayette, LA 70508-3225
(318)236-7380
Location Type: Branch office. Ultimate
Parent: Premier Bancorp.

★ 70089 ★   Premier Bank, NA
200 W. Congress St.
Lafayette, LA 70501-6889
(318)236-7578
Location Type: Branch office. Ultimate
Parent: Premier Bancorp.

★ 70090 ★   Premier Bank, NA
220 E. St. Mary
Lafayette, LA 70506-2036
(318)236-7000
Location Type: Branch office. Ultimate
Parent: Premier Bancorp.

★ 70091 ★   Premier Bank, NA
3200 Johnston St.
Lafayette, LA 70503-3744
(318)236-7202
Location Type: Branch office. Ultimate
Parent: Premier Bancorp.

★ 70092 ★   Premier Bank, NA
2510 Moss St.
Lafayette, LA 70501-2130
(318)236-7518
Location Type: Branch office. Ultimate
Parent: Premier Bancorp.

★ 70093 ★   Premier Bank, NA
1927 W. University
Lafayette, LA 70506-2545
(318)236-7577
Location Type: Branch office. Ultimate
Parent: Premier Bancorp.

★ 70094 ★   Premier Bank, NA
800 Pinhook Rd.
Lafayette, LA 70503-2318
(318)236-7281
Location Type: Branch office. Ultimate
Parent: Premier Bancorp.

★ 70095 ★   Premier Bank, NA
255 Southpark
Lafayette, LA 70508-3608
Location Type: Branch office. Ultimate
Parent: Premier Bancorp.

★ 70096 ★   Premier Bank, NA
1233 Kaliste Saloom Rd.
Lafayette, LA 70508-5707
(318)236-7728
Location Type: Branch office. Ultimate
Parent: Premier Bancorp.

★ 70097 ★   Premier Bank, NA
3930 W. Congress St.
Lafayette, LA 70506-6024
(318)236-7506
Location Type: Branch office. Ultimate
Parent: Premier Bancorp.

★ 70098 ★   Radio Shack
Univ Sq.
Lafayette, LA 70506
(318)235-6177
Company Type: Division. Ultimate Parent:
Tandy Corp. SIC: 5046—Commercial
Equipment Nec.

★ 70099 ★   RJ Reynolds Tobacco
Co.
107 Row
Lafayette, LA 70508
(318)237-4237
Ultimate Parent: RJR Nabisco Holdings.
SIC: 2131—Chewing & Smoking Tobacco.

★ 70100 ★   Ryder Truck Rental
210 Eraste Landry Rd.
Lafayette, LA 70506
(318)232-6473
Ultimate Parent: Ryder System. SIC:
7359—Equipment Rental & Leasing Nec.

★ 70101 ★   Ryder Truck Rental
134 Wall St.
Lafayette, LA 70506
(318)232-6470
Ultimate Parent: Ryder System. SIC:
7359—Equipment Rental & Leasing Nec;
7513—Truck Rental & Leasing Without
Drivers.

★ 70102 ★   Ryder Truck Rental
707 N. University Ave.
Lafayette, LA 70506
(318)237-5648
Ultimate Parent: Ryder System. SIC:
7513—Truck Rental & Leasing Without
Drivers.

★ 70103 ★   Ryder Truck Rental
2016 NE Evangeline Thruway
Lafayette, LA 70501
(318)237-8749
Ultimate Parent: Ryder System. SIC:
7359—Equipment Rental & Leasing Nec.

★ 70104 ★   Ryder Truck Rental
1014 Bertrand Dr.
Lafayette, LA 70506
(318)237-9026
Ultimate Parent: Ryder System. SIC:
7513—Truck Rental & Leasing Without
Drivers.

★ 70105 ★   Ryder Truck Rental
1639 E. Pinhook Rd.
Lafayette, LA 70501
(318)237-8758
Ultimate Parent: Ryder System. SIC:
5113—Industrial & Personal Service Paper.

★ 70106 ★   Stop & Shop Bar B Q
Inc.
258 Bendel Rd.
Lafayette, LA 70503
(318)232-8871
Ultimate Parent: Stop & Shop. SIC: 6531—
Real Estate Agents & Managers.

★ 70107 ★   Taco Bell
1901 W. Pinhook Rd.
Lafayette, LA 70508
(318)232-6011
Ultimate Parent: Pepsico. SIC: 5812—
Eating Places.

★ 70108 ★   Taco Bell
1901 Pinhook Rd.
Lafayette, LA 70501
(318)232-6011
Ultimate Parent: Pepsico. SIC: 5812—
Eating Places.

★ 70109 ★   Taco Bell
2406 W. Congress St.
Lafayette, LA 70506
(318)235-7750
Ultimate Parent: Pepsico. SIC: 5812—
Eating Places.

★ 70110 ★   Taco Bell
3909 Johnston St.
Lafayette, LA 70503
(318)981-3853
Ultimate Parent: Pepsico. SIC: 5812—
Eating Places.

★ 70111 ★   Taco Bell
5611 Johnston St.
Lafayette, LA 70503
(318)981-0702
Ultimate Parent: Pepsico. SIC: 5812—
Eating Places.

★ 70112 ★   Taco Bell
240 Donlon Ave.
Lafayette, LA 70501
(318)232-9749
Ultimate Parent: Pepsico. SIC: 5812—
Eating Places.

★ 70113 ★   Taco Bell
1422 Johnston St.
Lafayette, LA 70503
(318)237-5163
Ultimate Parent: Pepsico. SIC: 5812—
Eating Places.

★ 70114 ★   Texaco Inc.
109 Stewart St.
Lafayette, LA 70501
(318)235-6417
Ultimate Parent: Texaco. SIC: 1382—Oil &
Gas Exploration Services.

★ 70115 ★   Texaco Refining &
Marketing
1700 N. University Ave.
Lafayette, LA 70507
(318)237-9349
Ultimate Parent: Texaco. SIC: 5599—
Automotive Dealers Nec.

★ 70116 ★   Texaco Self Serv
1700 N. University Ave.
Lafayette, LA 70507
(318)237-3949
Ultimate Parent: Texaco. SIC: 5541—
Gasoline Service Stations.

★ 70117 ★   Texaco Self Service
2103 Frontage Rd.
Lafayette, LA 70501
(318)234-5773
Ultimate Parent: Texaco. SIC: 5541—
Gasoline Service Stations.

★ 70118 ★   Trailways Package
Xpress
1102 N. University Ave.
Lafayette, LA 70506
(318)232-7370
Ultimate Parent: Greyhound Lines Inc. SIC:
4212—Local Trucking Without Storage.

★ 70119 ★   Underwriters
Adjusting Co.
111 Rue Jean Lafitte
Lafayette, LA 70508
(318)233-9922
Ultimate Parent: Continental. SIC: 6411—
Insurance Agents, Brokers & Service.

★ 70120 ★   Union Texas
Petroleum Corp.
16 Calco Blvd.
Lafayette, LA 70503
(318)269-4100
Ultimate Parent: Union Texas Petroleum.
SIC: 2911—Petroleum Refining; 2911—
Petroleum Refining.

★ 70121 ★   US Fidelity & Gu
111 Exchange Pl
Lafayette, LA 70503
(318)232-3783
Ultimate Parent: USF&G Corp. SIC:
6411—Insurance Agents, Brokers &
Service.

★ 70122 ★   Vista Energy Inc.
601 Guilbeau Rd.
Lafayette, LA 70506
(318)981-0843
Ultimate Parent: Scecorp. SIC: 1389—Oil
& Gas Field Services Nec.

★ 70123 ★   Wal Mart
303 NW Frontage Rd.
Lafayette, LA 70501
(318)232-0083
Ultimate Parent: Wal-Mart Stores, Inc. SIC:
5311—Department Stores.

★ 70124 ★   Wal Mart Pharmacy
303 NW Frontage Rd.
Lafayette, LA 70501
(318)232-1031
Ultimate Parent: Wal-Mart Stores, Inc. SIC:
5912—Drug Stores & Proprietary Stores.

★ 70125 ★   Walgreen Drug Stores
2811 Johnston St.
Lafayette, LA 70503
(318)232-2052
Ultimate Parent: Walgreen Co. SIC:
5812—Eating Places.

★ 70126 ★   **Walgreen Louisiana Co.**
2811 Johnston St.
Lafayette, LA 70503
(318)232-2051
Ultimate Parent: Walgreen Co. **SIC:** 5912—Drug Stores & Proprietary Stores.

Lake Charles

★ 70127 ★   **Arcadian Corp.**
I-10 West
Lake Charles, LA 70602
Ultimate Parent: Arcadian Corp. **SIC:** 2873—Nitrogenous Fertilizers.

★ 70128 ★   **Arcadian Corp.**
850 Interstate 10 W
Lake Charles, LA 70602
(318)493-8600
Ultimate Parent: Arcadian Corp. **SIC:** 2899—Chemical Preparations Nec.

★ 70129 ★   **Arcadian Corp.**
PO Box 1627
Lake Charles, LA 70602-1627
(318)439-6025
Ultimate Parent: Arcadian Corp. **SIC:** 2842—Polishes & Sanitation Goods.

★ 70130 ★   **Boeing Louisiana Inc.**
4400 Legion St.
Lake Charles, LA 70602-1397
Ultimate Parent: Boeing. **SIC:** 3728—Aircraft Parts & Equipment Nec.

★ 70131 ★   **Boeing Louisiana Inc.**
4400 Legion St. M/S E3-22
Lake Charles, LA 70602-1397
Ultimate Parent: Boeing. **SIC:** 3728—Aircraft Parts & Equipment Nec.

★ 70132 ★   **Borden Inc.**
103 W. 11th St.
Lake Charles, LA 70601
(318)494-3830
Officer: Harold LaFleur, Manager. **Ultimate Parent:** Borden, Inc. **SIC:** 2024—Ice Cream & Frozen Desserts.

★ 70133 ★   **Browning-Ferris Industries**
1-10 & Cities Service Hwy.
Lake Charles, LA 70601
(318)882-1477
Location Type: Branch office. **Ultimate Parent:** Browning-Ferris Industries. **SIC:** 4953—Refuse Systems; 1521—Single-Family Housing Construction.

★ 70134 ★   **Carboline Co.**
900 Opelousas
Lake Charles, LA 70601-2273
Ultimate Parent: RPM, Inc. **SIC:** 2851—Paints & Allied Products.

★ 70135 ★   **Citgo Petroleum Corp.**
Hwy. 108 - South of I-10
Lake Charles, LA 70602
Ultimate Parent: Southland Corp. **SIC:** 2911—Petroleum Refining.

★ 70136 ★   **Citgo Quick Mart**
4500 Nelson Rd.
Lake Charles, LA 70605
(318)474-7108
Ultimate Parent: Citgo Petroleum. **SIC:** 5411—Grocery Stores.

★ 70137 ★   **Coca Cola Bottling Co.**
2401 Hwy. 14
Lake Charles, LA 70601
(318)433-1721
Ultimate Parent: Coca-Cola Enterprises. **SIC:** 5149—Groceries & Related Products Nec.

★ 70138 ★   **Emery Worldwide**
Lake
Lake Charles, LA 70606
(318)477-7663
Ultimate Parent: Consolidated Freightways. **SIC:** 4731—Freight Transportation Arrangement.

★ 70139 ★   **Gulf States Utilities Co.**
314 Broad St.
Lake Charles, LA 70601
(318)436-4351
Ultimate Parent: Gulf State Utilities Co. **SIC:** 4911—Electric Services.

★ 70140 ★   **Hertz Rent-A-Car**
Lake Charles Airport
Lake Charles, LA 70606
(318)477-0616
Ultimate Parent: Hertz. **SIC:** 7514—Passenger Car Rental.

★ 70141 ★   **Hertz Rent-A-Car**
1004 Broad St.
Lake Charles, LA 70601
(318)439-5555
Ultimate Parent: Hertz. **SIC:** 7514—Passenger Car Rental.

★ 70142 ★   **Kay Bee Toy&Hobby Shop**
Prien Lake Mall
Lake Charles, LA 70601
(318)474-9776
Ultimate Parent: Melville. **SIC:** 5945—Hobby, Toy & Game Shops.

★ 70143 ★   **Kentucky Fried Chicken**
800 Broad St.
Lake Charles, LA 70601
(318)433-8597
Ultimate Parent: Pepsico. **SIC:** 5812—Eating Places.

★ 70144 ★   **Kroger Family Center**
600 12th St.
Lake Charles, LA 70601
(318)436-3685
Ultimate Parent: Kroger. **SIC:** 5411—Grocery Stores.

★ 70145 ★   **Kroger Pharmacy**
600 12th St.
Lake Charles, LA 70601
(318)436-2508
Ultimate Parent: Kroger. **SIC:** 5912—Drug Stores & Proprietary Stores.

★ 70146 ★   **Krogers**
3009 Hwy. 14
Lake Charles, LA 70601
(318)474-3591
Ultimate Parent: Kroger. **SIC:** 5411—Grocery Stores.

★ 70147 ★   **Krogers Pharmacy**
3009 Hwy. 14
Lake Charles, LA 70601
(318)474-9983
Ultimate Parent: Kroger. **SIC:** 5912—Drug Stores & Proprietary Stores.

★ 70148 ★   **Lerner Shop**
707 Ryan St.
Lake Charles, LA 70601
(318)436-5903
Ultimate Parent: Limited. **SIC:** 5621—Women's Clothing Stores.

★ 70149 ★   **Mini Mart**
Hwy. 171
Lake Charles, LA 70601
(318)855-9928
Ultimate Parent: Kroger. **SIC:** 5411—Grocery Stores.

★ 70150 ★   **Mobil Oil Exploring & Producing SE**
751 E. Bayou Pines Dr., Ste. B
Lake Charles, LA 70601-7196
(318)491-6600
Officer: Steve Truax Offshore. **Ultimate Parent:** Mobil. **SIC:** 1311—Crude Petroleum & Natural Gas; 1382—Oil & Gas Exploration Services.

★ 70151 ★   **Nalco Chemical Co.**
130 Jamestown St.
Lake Charles, LA 70605
(318)478-8060
Ultimate Parent: Nalco Chemical Co. **SIC:** 5169—Chemicals & Allied Products Nec.

★ 70152 ★   **Olin Corp.**
Lake Charles Plant
900 I-10 W.
Lake Charles, LA 70602-2896
Location Type: Plant. **Ultimate Parent:** Olin Corp. **SIC:** 2865—Cyclic Crudes & Intermediates; 2869—Industrial Organic Chemicals Nec; 2819—Industrial Inorganic Chemicals Nec; 2812—Alkalies & Chlorine.

★ 70153 ★   **Olin Corp.**
Lake Charles Plant
I-10 West (Exit 27)
Lake Charles, LA 70602-2896
Location Type: Plant. **Ultimate Parent:** Olin Corp. **SIC:** 2812—Alkalies & Chlorine; 2819—Industrial Inorganic Chemicals Nec; 2865—Cyclic Crudes & Intermediates; 2869—Industrial Organic Chemicals Nec; 2873—Nitrogenous Fertilizers.

★ 70154 ★   **Otis Elevator Co.**
Weber Bldg.
Lake Charles, LA 70601
(318)436-3804
Ultimate Parent: United Technologies. **SIC:** 5084—Industrial Machinery & Equipment.

★ 70155 ★   **Pepsi-Cola Bottling Co.**
4040 Gerstner Memorial Dr.
Lake Charles, LA 70605
(318)477-7205
Officer: Walter Mason, Manager. **Ultimate Parent:** Pepsico. **SIC:** 2086—Bottled & Canned Soft Drinks.

★ 70156 ★   **Pizza Hut**
3909 Ryan St.
Lake Charles, LA 70605
(318)474-2043
Ultimate Parent: Pepsico. **SIC:** 5812—Eating Places.

★ 70157 ★   **Pizza Hut**
Sam Houston Jones Pky.
Lake Charles, LA 70611
(318)855-7770
Ultimate Parent: Pepsico. **SIC:** 5812—Eating Places.

★ 70158 ★   **Pizza Hut**
2624 Hwy. 14
Lake Charles, LA 70601
(318)477-3033
Ultimate Parent: Pepsico. **SIC:** 5812—Eating Places.

★ 70159 ★   **PPG Industries Inc.**
Columbia Southern Rd.
Lake Charles, LA 70601
(318)791-4500
Officer: Thomas Brown, Manager. **Ultimate Parent:** PPG Industries Inc. **SIC:** 2812—Alkalies & Chlorine; 2819—Industrial Inorganic Chemicals Nec; 2869—Industrial Organic Chemicals Nec.

★ 70160 ★   **Premier Bank, NA**
4100 Nelson Rd.
Lake Charles, LA 70605
(318)493-3272
Location Type: Branch office. **Ultimate Parent:** Premier Bancorp.

★ 70161 ★   **Premier Bank, NA**
901 Lake Shore Dr.
Lake Charles, LA 70601
(318)493-4300
Location Type: Branch office. **Ultimate Parent:** Premier Bancorp.

★ 70162 ★   **Premier Bank, NA**
135 W. McNeese St.
Lake Charles, LA 70605-5635
(318)493-3310
Location Type: Branch office. **Ultimate Parent:** Premier Bancorp.

★ 70163 ★   **Premier Bank, NA**
1201 E. Prien Lake Rd.
Lake Charles, LA 70601-8851
(318)493-3236
Location Type: Branch office. **Ultimate Parent:** Premier Bancorp.

★ 70164 ★   **Premier Bank, NA**
1530 Broad St.
Lake Charles, LA 70601-4512
(318)493-3250
Location Type: Branch office. **Ultimate Parent:** Premier Bancorp.

★ 70165 ★   **Premier Bank, National Assoc.**
1530 Broad St.
Lake Charles, LA 70601-4512
(318)493-3250
Location Type: Branch office. **Officer:** Jennell Stevens, Manager. **Ultimate Parent:** Premier Bancorp.

★ 70166 ★   **Premier Bank, National Assoc.**
1201 E. Prien Lake Rd.
Lake Charles, LA 70601-8851
(318)493-3236
Location Type: Branch office. **Officer:** Peggy Ardoin, Manager. **Ultimate Parent:** Premier Bancorp.

★ 70167 ★   **Premier Bank, National Assoc.**
135 W. Mc Neese St.
Lake Charles, LA 70605-5635
(318)493-3310
Location Type: Branch office. **Officer:** Gordon J. David, Manager. **Ultimate Parent:** Premier Bancorp.

★ 70168 ★   **Premier Bank, National Assoc.**
4100 Nelson Rd.
Lake Charles, LA 70605
(318)493-3272
Location Type: Branch office. **Officer:** Delores Wicks, Manager. **Ultimate Parent:** Premier Bancorp.

★ 70169 ★   **Radio Shack**
520 W. Prien Lake Rd.
Lake Charles, LA 70601
(318)477-4063
Company Type: Division. **Ultimate Parent:** Tandy Corp. **SIC:** 5065—Electronic Parts & Equipment Nec; 5731—Radio, Television & Electronics Stores.

★ 70170 ★   **Radio Shack**
3221 Common St.
Lake Charles, LA 70601
(318)436-6720
Company Type: Division. **Ultimate Parent:** Tandy Corp. **SIC:** 5065—Electronic Parts & Equipment Nec.

★ 70171 ★   **Service Merchandise**
3139 Hwy. 14
Lake Charles, LA 70601
(318)478-5511
Ultimate Parent: Service Merchandise Co., Inc. **SIC:** 5399—Miscellaneous General Merchandise Store.

★ 70172 ★   **Shell Gas Park**
600 W. Prien Lake Rd.
Lake Charles, LA 70601
(318)437-8473
Ultimate Parent: Shell Oil Co. **SIC:** 5541—Gasoline Service Stations.

★ 70173 ★   **Taco Bell**
1009 N. Martin Luther King Hwy.
Lake Charles, LA 70601
(318)439-0348
Ultimate Parent: Pepsico. **SIC:** 5812—Eating Places.

★ 70174 ★   **Taco Bell**
728 E. Prien Lake Rd.
Lake Charles, LA 70601
(318)478-6181
Ultimate Parent: Pepsico. **SIC:** 5812—Eating Places.

★ 70175 ★   **Taco Bell**
2434 Hwy. 14
Lake Charles, LA 70601
(318)478-2551
Ultimate Parent: Pepsico. **SIC:** 5812—Eating Places.

★ 70176 ★   **Texaco Inc. Marketing Dept**
804 15th St.
Lake Charles, LA 70601
(318)436-1243
Ultimate Parent: Texaco. **SIC:** 5541—Gasoline Service Stations.

★ 70177 ★   **Trailways Southern Lines in**
321 Lawrence St.
Lake Charles, LA 70601
(318)433-1653
Ultimate Parent: Greyhound Lines Inc. **SIC:** 4173—Bus Terminal & Service Facilities.

★ 70178 ★   **United Parcel Service**
2404 Fruge St.
Lake Charles, LA 70601
(318)452-8880
Ultimate Parent: United Parcel Service of America. **SIC:** 4215—Courier Services Except by Air.

★ 70179 ★   **Wal Mart**
4501 Nelson Rd.
Lake Charles, LA 70605
(318)474-2786
Ultimate Parent: Wal-Mart Stores, Inc. **SIC:** 5311—Department Stores.

★ 70180 ★   Wal Mart
3415 Hwy. 14
Lake Charles, LA 70605
Ultimate Parent: Wal-Mart Stores, Inc. SIC:
5311—Department Stores.

★ 70181 ★   Wal Mart Discount
City
177 Hwy. 171 N
Lake Charles, LA 70601
(318)855-1348
Ultimate Parent: Wal-Mart Stores, Inc. SIC:
5311—Department Stores.

★ 70182 ★   Wal Mart Discount
Pharmacy
3415 Hwy. 14
Lake Charles, LA 70605
Ultimate Parent: Wal-Mart Stores, Inc. SIC:
5912—Drug Stores & Proprietary Stores.

★ 70183 ★   Wal Mart Discount
Pharmacy
Hwy. 378
Lake Charles, LA 70601
(318)855-3324
Ultimate Parent: Wal-Mart Stores, Inc. SIC:
5912—Drug Stores & Proprietary Stores.

★ 70184 ★   Waldenbooks
512 Prien Lake Mall
Lake Charles, LA 70601
(318)477-4106
Ultimate Parent: K-Mart. SIC: 5942—Book
Stores.

★ 70185 ★   Walgreen Drug Stores
300 18th St.
Lake Charles, LA 70601
Ultimate Parent: Walgreen Co. SIC:
5912—Drug Stores & Proprietary Stores.

Lake Shore Dr.

★ 70186 ★   Premier Bank,
National Assoc.
901 Lake Shore Dr.
Lake Shore Dr., LA 70601
(318)493-4300
Location Type: Branch office. Officer:
James G. Boyer, Chairman of the Board &
President. Ultimate Parent: Premier
Bancorp.

Larose

★ 70187 ★   Radio Shack
Bon Ser Shopping Ctr.
Larose, LA 70373
(504)693-8377
Company Type: Division. Ultimate Parent:
Tandy Corp. SIC: 5734—Computer &
Software Stores.

★ 70188 ★   Texaco
394 PO Box
Larose, LA 70373
(504)693-7305
Ultimate Parent: Texaco. SIC: 0919—
Miscellaneous Marine Products.

Leesville

★ 70189 ★   Coca Cola Bottling
Co.
102 E. Murphy St.
Leesville, LA 71446
(318)239-3331
Ultimate Parent: Coca-Cola Enterprises.
SIC: 2086—Bottled & Canned Soft Drinks;
5149—Groceries & Related Products Nec.

★ 70190 ★   Pizza Hut
2412 Hwy. 171 S
Leesville, LA 71446
(318)238-5201
Ultimate Parent: Pepsico. SIC: 5812—
Eating Places.

★ 70191 ★   Rapides Bank & Trust
Co.
Leesville, LA 71446
(318)537-1567
Ultimate Parent: First Commerce Corp.
SIC: 6022—State Commercial Banks.

Lillie

★ 70192 ★   Willamette Ind.
Lillie
Hwy. 5
Lillie, LA 71256-0638
Ultimate Parent: Willamette Industries, Inc.
SIC: 2400—Lumber & Wood Products.

Livingston

★ 70193 ★   Hibernia National
Bank
29963 S. Magnolia St.
Livingston, LA 70754
(504)381-2852
Ultimate Parent: Hibernia Corp. SIC:
6099—Functions Related to Deposit
Banking.

Lockport

★ 70194 ★   Amerada Hess Corp.
Hwy. 308
Lockport, LA 70374
(504)532-5058
Location Type: Branch office. Ultimate
Parent: Amerada Hess. SIC: 1311—Crude
Petroleum & Natural Gas.

★ 70195 ★   Radio Shack
700 N. Hwy. 1
Lockport, LA 70374
(504)532-3092
Company Type: Division. Ultimate Parent:
Tandy Corp. SIC: 5731—Radio, Television
& Electronics Stores.

★ 70196 ★   Trinity Industries
Halter Marine Lockport Div.
Hwy. 308
Lockport, LA 70374
Company Type: Division. Ultimate Parent:
Trinity Industries. SIC: 3731—Ship Building
& Repairing.

★ 70197 ★   Trinity Industries Inc.
Lockport Div.
Hwy. 308
Lockport, LA 70374
Company Type: Division. Ultimate Parent:
Trinity Industries. SIC: 3731—Ship Building
& Repairing.

★ 70198 ★   Valentine Paper Co.
Lockport Div.
Hwy. 308
Lockport, LA 70374
Company Type: Division. Ultimate Parent:
Trinity Industries. SIC: 2621—Paper Mills.

Logansport

★ 70199 ★   Louisiana-Pacific
Corp., Plywood
Hwy. 5 N
Logansport, LA 71049
Ultimate Parent: Louisiana-Pacific. SIC:
2436—Softwood Veneer & Plywood.

Loreauville

★ 70200 ★   Texaco Inc.
Lake Fausse Pt
Loreauville, LA 70552
(318)229-4281
Ultimate Parent: Texaco. SIC: 5172—
Petroleum Products Nec.

Louisa/Ivanhoe

★ 70201 ★   Ashland Chemical Co.
Hwy. 83
Louisa/Ivanhoe, LA 70562-9320
Ultimate Parent: Ashland Oil. SIC: 2895—
Carbon Black.

Luling

★ 70202 ★   Monsanto Co.
Luling, LA 70070
(504)785-8211
Company Type: Branch. Ultimate Parent:
Monsanto. SIC: 2899—Chemical
Preparations Nec.

★ 70203 ★   Monsanto Co.
PO Box 174
Luling, LA 70070-0174
(504)785-8211
Company Type: Branch. Officer: Tony
Corley. Ultimate Parent: Monsanto. SIC:
2819—Industrial Inorganic Chemicals Nec.

★ 70204 ★   Monsanto Co.
River Rd., LA Hwy. 18
Luling, LA 70070
Ultimate Parent: Monsanto. SIC: 2879—
Agricultural Chemicals Nec; 2834—
Pharmaceutical Preparations; 2873—
Nitrogenous Fertilizers; 2869—Industrial
Organic Chemicals Nec; 2819—Industrial
Inorganic Chemicals Nec; 2865—Cyclic
Crudes & Intermediates.

Lutcher

★ 70205 ★   Peoples Drug Store
625 Front
Lutcher, LA 70071
(504)869-5010
Ultimate Parent: Melville. SIC: 5912—Drug
Stores & Proprietary Stores.

Madisonville

★ 70206 ★   Equitable
Madisonville
Hwy. 21 PO Box Drawer E
Madisonville, LA 70447
Ultimate Parent: Trinity Industries. SIC:
3731—Ship Building & Repairing.

Mandeville

★ 70207 ★   First Bank
38 PO Box
Mandeville, LA 70448
(504)626-8511
Ultimate Parent: Shawmut National Corp.
SIC: 6099—Functions Related to Deposit
Banking.

★ 70208 ★   Hibernia National
Bank
3840 Emerald Rd.
Mandeville, LA 70448
(504)626-0247
Ultimate Parent: Hibernia Corp. SIC:
6021—National Commercial Banks; 6022—
State Commercial Banks.

★ 70209 ★   McDonalds
Hamburgers
Lasalle
Mandeville, LA 70448
(504)626-7366
Ultimate Parent: McDonald's.
SIC: 5812—Eating Places.

★ 70210 ★   Radio Shack
3310 Emerald Rd.
Mandeville, LA 70448
(504)626-9314
Company Type: Division. Ultimate Parent:
Tandy Corp. SIC: 5731—Radio, Television
& Electronics Stores.

★ 70211 ★   Walgreen Drug Store
3500 Emerald Rd.
Mandeville, LA 70448
(504)626-9794
Ultimate Parent: Walgreen Co. SIC:
5912—Drug Stores & Proprietary Stores.

Mansfield

★ 70212 ★   International Paper
Co. Mansfield Mill
Hwy. 509, PO Box 999
Mansfield, LA 71052
Ultimate Parent: International Paper Co.
SIC: 2631—Paperboard Mills.

★ 70213 ★   International Paper
Mansfield Mill
Hwy. 509
Mansfield, LA 71052
Ultimate Parent: International Paper Co.
SIC: 2631—Paperboard Mills.

★ 70214 ★   Kentucky Fried
Chicken
410 Washington Ave.
Mansfield, LA 71052
(318)872-3466
Ultimate Parent: Pepsico. SIC: 5812—
Eating Places.

★ 70215 ★   Piggly Wiggly
811 Polk St.
Mansfield, LA 71052
(318)872-4026
Ultimate Parent: Bruno's. SIC: 5411—
Grocery Stores.

★ 70216 ★   Pizza Hut
103 McEnery St.
Mansfield, LA 71052
(318)872-0892
Ultimate Parent: Pepsico. SIC: 5812—
Eating Places.

★ 70217 ★   Trailways Bus
Systems
1100 Jenkins St.
Mansfield, LA 71052
(318)872-4483
Ultimate Parent: Greyhound Lines Inc. SIC:
4131—Intercity & Rural Bus Transportation.

★ 70218 ★   Wal Mart Pharmacy
1043 S. Washington St.
Mansfield, LA 71052
(318)872-5700
Ultimate Parent: Wal-Mart Stores, Inc. SIC:
5912—Drug Stores & Proprietary Stores.

Many

★ 70219 ★   Conagra Broiler Co.
100 Mcdonald Rd.
Many, LA 71449
Ultimate Parent: Conagra. SIC: 2048—
Prepared Feeds Nec.

★ 70220 ★   Pizza Hut
330 Fisher Rd.
Many, LA 71449
(318)256-5625
Ultimate Parent: Pepsico. SIC: 5812—
Eating Places.

★ 70221 ★   Trailways Bus System
505 Church St.
Many, LA 71449
(318)256-2271
Ultimate Parent: Greyhound Lines Inc. SIC:
4131—Intercity & Rural Bus Transportation.

Marksville

★ 70222 ★   Pizza Hut
317 W. Tunica Dr.
Marksville, LA 71351
(318)253-4561
Ultimate Parent: Pepsico. SIC: 5812—
Eating Places.

★ 70223 ★   Radio Shack
290 Acton Rd.
Marksville, LA 71351
(318)253-7840
Company Type: Division. Ultimate Parent:
Tandy Corp. SIC: 7629—Electrical Repair
Shops Nec.

Marrero

★ 70224 ★   Amerada Hess Corp.
200 Douglas Rd.
Marrero, LA 70072
(504)341-9561
Ultimate Parent: Amerada Hess. SIC:
4226—Special Warehousing & Storage Nec.

★ 70225 ★   Amerada Hess Corp.
River Rd.
Marrero, LA 70072
(504)341-9561
Ultimate Parent: Amerada Hess. SIC:
4226—Special Warehousing & Storage Nec.

★ 70226 ★   Exxon Shop
2699 Barataria Blvd.
Marrero, LA 70072
(504)341-9514
Ultimate Parent: Exxon. SIC: 5541—
Gasoline Service Stations.

★ 70227 ★   The Gap
1701 Barataria Blvd.
Marrero, LA 70072
(504)341-7794
Ultimate Parent: GAP. SIC: 5651—Family
Clothing Stores.

★ 70228 ★ **Lane Bryant**
1701 Barataria Blvd.
Marrero, LA 70072
(504)348-3608
Ultimate Parent: Limited. **SIC:** 5651—
Family Clothing Stores.

★ 70229 ★ **Lerner Shop**
1701 Barataria Blvd.
Marrero, LA 70072
(504)348-3031
Ultimate Parent: Limited. **SIC:** 5651—
Family Clothing Stores.

★ 70230 ★ **The Limited**
1701 Barataria Blvd.
Marrero, LA 70072
(504)347-2095
Ultimate Parent: Limited. **SIC:** 5621—
Women's Clothing Stores; 5651—Family
Clothing Stores.

★ 70231 ★ **The Limited Express**
Belle Promenade Mall
Marrero, LA 70072
(504)340-0545
Ultimate Parent: Limited. **SIC:** 5621—
Women's Clothing Stores.

★ 70232 ★ **Pizza Hut**
5025 Lapalco Blvd.
Marrero, LA 70072
(504)340-9348
Ultimate Parent: Pepsico. **SIC:** 5812—
Eating Places.

★ 70233 ★ **Radio Shack**
1701 Barataria Blvd.
Marrero, LA 70072
(504)348-8921
Company Type: Division. **Ultimate Parent:**
Tandy Corp. **SIC:** 5065—Electronic Parts &
Equipment Nec.

★ 70234 ★ **Radio Shack**
5100 Westbank Expy.
Marrero, LA 70072
(504)340-1727
Company Type: Division. **Ultimate Parent:**
Tandy Corp. **SIC:** 5731—Radio, Television
& Electronics Stores.

★ 70235 ★ **Taco Bell**
6240 Lapalco Blvd.
Marrero, LA 70072
(504)341-5367
Ultimate Parent: Pepsico. **SIC:** 5812—
Eating Places.

★ 70236 ★ **This End Up**
1701 Barataria Blvd.
Marrero, LA 70072
(504)348-7673
Ultimate Parent: Melville. **SIC:** 5712—
Furniture Stores.

★ 70237 ★ **Waldenbooks**
Bell Promenade
Marrero, LA 70072
(504)347-0342
Ultimate Parent: K-Mart. **SIC:** 5942—Book
Stores.

★ 70238 ★ **Walgreen Drug Stores**
1999 Barataria Blvd.
Marrero, LA 70072
(504)340-2297
Ultimate Parent: Walgreen Co. **SIC:**
5912—Drug Stores & Proprietary Stores.

★ 70239 ★ **Western Auto Supply
Co.**
4513 Westbank Expy.
Marrero, LA 70072
(504)347-4541
Ultimate Parent: Sears Roebuck & Co.
SIC: 5531—Automobile & Home Supply
Stores.

Mer Rouge

★ 70240 ★ **Stop & Shop Grocery**
Mer Rouge, LA 71261
(318)647-5169
Ultimate Parent: Stop & Shop. **SIC:** 5411—
Grocery Stores.

Meraux

★ 70241 ★ **Murphy Oil USA Inc.**
Meraux Louisiana Refinery
2500 East St. Bernard Hwy.
Meraux, LA 70075
Company Type: Division. **Ultimate Parent:**
Murphy Oil. **SIC:** 2911—Petroleum Refining.

★ 70242 ★ **Murphy Oil USA Inc.**
Meraux Refinery
2500 E. Saint Bernard Hwy.
Meraux, LA 70075-0100
Company Type: Division. **Ultimate Parent:**
Murphy Oil. **SIC:** 2911—Petroleum Refining.

★ 70243 ★ **Murphy Oil USA Inc.**
Meraux Refinery
2500 East St. Bernard Hwy.
Meraux, LA 70075
Company Type: Division. **Ultimate Parent:**
Murphy Oil. **SIC:** 2900—Petroleum & Coal
Products.

★ 70244 ★ **Pizza Hut**
3132 E. Judge Perez Dr.
Meraux, LA 70075
(504)279-3847
Ultimate Parent: Pepsico. **SIC:** 5812—
Eating Places.

Metairie

★ 70245 ★ **Abbott Laboratories**
Diagnostic Div.
3850 N. Causeway Blvd., Ste. 1111
Metairie, LA 70002-1752
(504)836-7152
Company Type: Division. **Officer:** Tim
McHugh. **Ultimate Parent:** Abbott
Laboratories. **SIC:** 8734—Testing
Laboratories.

★ 70246 ★ **American General
Finance**
2121 Veterans Memorial Blvd.
Metairie, LA 70002-6397
(504)834-9950
Location Type: Branch office. **Officer:**
Steven Fraker. **Ultimate Parent:** American
General Corp. **SIC:** 6141—Personal Credit
Institutions; 6162—Mortgage Bankers &
Correspondents.

★ 70247 ★ **American General
Finance Co.**
3929 Veterans Memorial Blvd.
Metairie, LA 70002-5622
(504)885-2200
Location Type: Branch office. **Officer:**
Cindy L. Weldon. **Ultimate Parent:**
American General Corp. **SIC:** 6141—
Personal Credit Institutions; 6162—
Mortgage Bankers & Correspondents.

★ 70248 ★ **American General
Finance Inc.**
2121 Veterans Memorial Blvd.
Metairie, LA 70002-6397
(504)834-9950
Location Type: Branch office. **Officer:**
Steven Fraker. **Ultimate Parent:** American
General Corp. **SIC:** 6141—Personal Credit
Institutions; 6162—Mortgage Bankers &
Correspondents.

★ 70249 ★ **American General
Finance Inc.**
3929 Veterans Memorial Blvd.
Metairie, LA 70002-5622
(504)885-2200
Location Type: Branch office. **Officer:**
Cindy L. Weldon. **Ultimate Parent:**
American General Corp. **SIC:** 6141—
Personal Credit Institutions; 6162—
Mortgage Bankers & Correspondents.

★ 70250 ★ **Anchor Glass
Container Corp.**
3445 N. Causeway
Metairie, LA 70002
(504)837-6905
Ultimate Parent: Anchor Glass Container
Corp. **SIC:** 5039—Construction Materials
Nec.

★ 70251 ★ **Bell South
Advertising & Publishing Corp.**
3850 N. Causeway Blvd., Ste. 1230
Metairie, LA 70002-1752
(504)832-0037
Officer: Jack Landefeld. **Ultimate Parent:**
BellSouth Corp. **SIC:** 2759—Commercial
Printing Nec.

★ 70252 ★ **Bell South Co.**
3101 W. Napoleon Ave., Ste. 142
Metairie, LA 70001-2901
(504)837-6700
Officer: Bill King. **Ultimate Parent:**
BellSouth Corp. **SIC:** 4812—Radiotelephone
Communications.

★ 70253 ★ **Bellsouth Mobility**
3900 N. Causeway Blvd.
Metairie, LA 70002-1742
(504)830-1800
Ultimate Parent: BellSouth Corp. **SIC:**
4812—Radiotelephone Communications.

★ 70254 ★ **Borden Inc.**
Dairy Div.
1751 Airline Hwy.
Metairie, LA 70001
Ultimate Parent: Borden, Inc. **SIC:** 2026—
Fluid Milk.

★ 70255 ★ **Casual Corner**
3301 Veterans Blvd. N
Metairie, LA 70005
(504)833-1103
Ultimate Parent: United States Shoe. **SIC:**
5651—Family Clothing Stores.

★ 70256 ★ **Centec**
4621 W. Napoleon Ave. W
Metairie, LA 70001
(504)888-1113
Ultimate Parent: Bethlehem Steel Corp.
SIC: 8721—Accounting, Auditing &
Bookkeeping.

★ 70257 ★ **Continental Bank**
3050 Severn Ave.
Metairie, LA 70002
(504)885-1855
Ultimate Parent: Midlantic Corp. **SIC:**
6022—State Commercial Banks; 6022—
State Commercial Banks.

★ 70258 ★ **Crestar Mortgage
Corp.**
2450 Severn Ave.
Metairie, LA 70001
(504)831-8136
Ultimate Parent: Crestar Financial Corp.
SIC: 6162—Mortgage Bankers &
Correspondents.

★ 70259 ★ **Csc Credit Service**
4300 I-10 Service Rd.
Metairie, LA 70001
(504)454-0933
Ultimate Parent: Computer Sciences. **SIC:**
7389—Business Services Nec.

★ 70260 ★ **Digital Equipment
Corp.**
3850 N. Cswy
Metairie, LA 70002
(504)832-8200
Ultimate Parent: Digital Equipment Corp.
SIC: 5046—Commercial Equipment Nec;
7372—Prepackaged Software.

★ 70261 ★ **First Louisiana
Acceptance Corp.**
Security Homestead Bldg.
4900 Veteran's Blvd., Ste. 1010
Metairie, LA 70002
Company Type: Subsidiary. **Ultimate
Parent:** Bank of Boston Corp. **SIC:** 6141—
Personal Credit Institutions.

★ 70262 ★ **First Security
Mortgage Cor**
3801 N. Cswy
Metairie, LA 70002
(504)834-3703
Ultimate Parent: First Security Corp. **SIC:**
6141—Personal Credit Institutions; 6162—
Mortgage Bankers & Correspondents.

★ 70263 ★ **Fleet Finance Inc.**
6313 Airline Hwy.
Metairie, LA 70003
(504)733-1900
Ultimate Parent: Fleet Financial Group.
SIC: 1521—Single-Family Housing
Construction.

★ 70264 ★ **The Gap**
3301 Veterans Blvd. N
Metairie, LA 70005
(504)835-3807
Ultimate Parent: GAP. **SIC:** 5651—Family
Clothing Stores.

★ 70265 ★ **The Gap Kids**
3301 Veterans Blvd. N
Metairie, LA 70005
(504)837-3297
Ultimate Parent: GAP. **SIC:** 5651—Family
Clothing Stores.

★ 70266 ★ **General American Life
Insur**
3445 N. Cswy
Metairie, LA 70002
(504)834-3888
Ultimate Parent: General American Life.
SIC: 6411—Insurance Agents, Brokers &
Service.

★ 70267 ★ **Greyhound Bus Lines**
216 Labarre Dr.
Metairie, LA 70001
(504)362-2700
Ultimate Parent: Greyhound Lines Inc. **SIC:**
4111—Local & Suburban Transit.

★ 70268 ★ **Hibernia National
Bank**
4949 W. Esplanade Ave.
Metairie, LA 70006
(504)586-2481
Ultimate Parent: Hibernia Corp. **SIC:**
6022—State Commercial Banks.

★ 70269 ★ **Hibernia National
Bank**
8920 Veterans Memorial Blvd.
Metairie, LA 70003
(504)587-3397
Ultimate Parent: Hibernia Corp. **SIC:**
6099—Functions Related to Deposit
Banking.

★ 70270 ★ **Hibernia National
Bank**
2201 Veterans Blvd.
Metairie, LA 70005
(504)586-2460
Ultimate Parent: Hibernia Corp. **SIC:**
6022—State Commercial Banks.

★ 70271 ★ **Hibernia National
Bank**
2201 Veterans Memorial Blvd.
Metairie, LA 70002
(504)837-8010
Ultimate Parent: Hibernia Corp. **SIC:**
6021—National Commercial Banks; 6022—
State Commercial Banks.

★ 70272 ★ **Hibernia National
Bank**
6305 Airline Hwy.
Metairie, LA 70003
(504)886-2420
Ultimate Parent: Hibernia Corp. **SIC:**
6021—National Commercial Banks; 6022—
State Commercial Banks.

★ 70273 ★ **Hibernia National
Bank**
2200 N. Cswy
Metairie, LA 70001
(504)586-2430
Ultimate Parent: Hibernia Corp. **SIC:**
6021—National Commercial Banks; 6022—
State Commercial Banks.

★ 70274 ★ **Hit or Miss**
8944 Veterans Blvd.
Metairie, LA 70003
(504)469-9889
Ultimate Parent: TJX. **SIC:** 5651—Family
Clothing Stores.

★ 70275 ★ **Jackson National Life
Insurance**
3510 N. Causeway
Metairie, LA 70002
(504)832-1767
Ultimate Parent: Jackson National Life.
SIC: 6411—Insurance Agents, Brokers &
Service.

★ 70276 ★ **Jiffy Lube**
4545 W. Esplanade Ave.
Metairie, LA 70006
(504)455-5823
Ultimate Parent: Pennzoil. **SIC:** 7538—
General Automotive Repair Shops.

★ 70277 ★ **Jiffy Lube**
3445 N. Causeway Blvd.
Metairie, LA 70002
(504)733-8338
Ultimate Parent: Pennzoil. **SIC:** 7549—
Automotive Services Nec.

★ 70278 ★   Jiffy Lube
7212 Veterans Blvd.
Metairie, LA 70003
(504)454-1192
Ultimate Parent: Pennzoil. SIC: 5541—
Gasoline Service Stations.

★ 70279 ★   Kentucky Fried
Chicken
4524 Hessmer Ave.
Metairie, LA 70002
(504)455-1914
Ultimate Parent: Pepsico. SIC: 6531—Real
Estate Agents & Managers.

★ 70280 ★   Kentucky Fried
Chicken
4312 Veterans Memorial Blvd.
Metairie, LA 70006
(504)888-7016
Ultimate Parent: Pepsico. SIC: 5812—
Eating Places.

★ 70281 ★   Kentucky Fried
Chicken
3108 Cleary Ave.
Metairie, LA 70002
(504)887-8037
Ultimate Parent: Pepsico. SIC: 5812—
Eating Places.

★ 70282 ★   Kmart Discount
Stores
7000 Veterans Memorial Blvd.
Metairie, LA 70003
(504)885-1353
Ultimate Parent: K-Mart. SIC: 5912—Drug
Stores & Proprietary Stores.

★ 70283 ★   L M Berry & Co.
3625 N. I 10 Service Rd.
Metairie, LA 70002-7029
(504)888-8550
Officer: Jerry Cheadle. Ultimate Parent:
BellSouth Corp. SIC: 7313—Radio, T.V. &
Publisher Representatives; 7311—
Advertising Agencies.

★ 70284 ★   Lane Bryant
3301 Veterans Memorial Blvd.
Metairie, LA 70002
(504)833-3772
Ultimate Parent: Limited. SIC: 5621—
Women's Clothing Stores.

★ 70285 ★   Lerner Shop
3301 Veterans Blvd. N
Metairie, LA 70005
(504)834-4506
Ultimate Parent: Limited. SIC: 5651—
Family Clothing Stores.

★ 70286 ★   Lerner Shop
3301 Veterans Memorial Blvd.
Metairie, LA 70002
(504)834-4506
Ultimate Parent: Limited. SIC: 5621—
Women's Clothing Stores.

★ 70287 ★   Liberty Mutual
Insurance Co.
3850 N. Cswy
Metairie, LA 70002
(504)837-7000
Ultimate Parent: Liberty Mutual Group.
SIC: 6411—Insurance Agents, Brokers &
Service.

★ 70288 ★   The Limited
3301 Veterans Blvd. N
Metairie, LA 70005
(504)837-1680
Ultimate Parent: Limited. SIC: 5651—
Family Clothing Stores.

★ 70289 ★   The Limited Express
3301 Veterans Blvd. N
Metairie, LA 70005
(504)831-2590
Ultimate Parent: Limited. SIC: 5651—
Family Clothing Stores.

★ 70290 ★   Maison Blanche Co.
4500 Veterans Blvd.
Metairie, LA 70005
(504)888-7200
Ultimate Parent: Mercantile Stores. SIC:
5311—Department Stores.

★ 70291 ★   Maison Blanche
Home Improve
2813 David Dr.
Metairie, LA 70003
(504)455-3131
Ultimate Parent: Mercantile Stores. SIC:
1751—Carpentry Work.

★ 70292 ★   Mobil Oil
2701 Richland Ave.
Metairie, LA 70002
(504)887-2110
Ultimate Parent: Mobil. SIC: 2911—
Petroleum Refining.

★ 70293 ★   Mutual of New York
Financial
3850 N. Causeway Blvd.
Metairie, LA 70002
(504)837-9291
Ultimate Parent: Mutual of New York. SIC:
6211—Security Brokers & Dealers.

★ 70294 ★   Mutual Savings &
Loan Assoc
2900 Clearview Pkwy
Metairie, LA 70006-6569
(504)455-2444
Location Type: Headquarters. Officer:
Michael L. Hurley. Ultimate Parent:
Berkshire Hathaway. SIC: 6035—Federal
Savings Institutions.

★ 70295 ★   NCR Corp.
2315 N. Causeway Blvd.
Metairie, LA 70001
(504)834-3740
Officer: Marvin Robinson, Manager.
Ultimate Parent: AT&T. SIC: 2761—
Manifold Business Forms.

★ 70296 ★   Otis Elevator Co.
2000 Airline Hwy.
Metairie, LA 70001
(504)835-8452
Ultimate Parent: United Technologies. SIC:
3534—Elevators & Moving Stairways;
5084—Industrial Machinery & Equipment.

★ 70297 ★   Payless Shoesource
8847 Veterans Blvd.
Metairie, LA 70003
(504)466-3638
Ultimate Parent: May Department Stores.
SIC: 5661—Shoe Stores.

★ 70298 ★   Petite Sophisticate
3301 Veterans Blvd. N
Metairie, LA 70005
(504)837-9662
Ultimate Parent: United States Shoe. SIC:
5651—Family Clothing Stores.

★ 70299 ★   Pitney Bowes Credit
Corp.
4300 S. Service Rd. W
Metairie, LA 70001
(504)454-6147
Ultimate Parent: Pitney Bowes. SIC:
5094—Jewelry & Precious Stones.

★ 70300 ★   Pitney Bowes Credit
Corp.
3925 N. I Serv Rd.
Metairie, LA 70005
(504)454-6147
Ultimate Parent: Pitney Bowes. SIC:
7323—Credit Reporting Services.

★ 70301 ★   Pizza Hut
509 Veterans Memorial Blvd.
Metairie, LA 70005
(504)837-1591
Ultimate Parent: Pepsico. SIC: 5812—
Eating Places.

★ 70302 ★   Pizza Hut
5041 Fairfield St.
Metairie, LA 70006
(504)455-8535
Ultimate Parent: Pepsico. SIC: 5812—
Eating Places.

★ 70303 ★   Pizza Hut
3934 Veterans Blvd.
Metairie, LA 70005
(504)887-8754
Ultimate Parent: Pepsico. SIC: 5812—
Eating Places.

★ 70304 ★   Pizza Hut
810 Clearview Pky.
Metairie, LA 70001
(504)455-5416
Ultimate Parent: Pepsico. SIC: 5812—
Eating Places.

★ 70305 ★   Radio Shack
5257 Veterans Memorial Blvd.
Metairie, LA 70006
(504)367-8649
Company Type: Division. Ultimate Parent:
Tandy Corp. SIC: 5065—Electronic Parts &
Equipment Nec.

★ 70306 ★   Radio Shack
5257 Veterans Blvd.
Metairie, LA 70005
(504)885-0348
Company Type: Division. Ultimate Parent:
Tandy Corp. SIC: 5731—Radio, Television
& Electronics Stores.

★ 70307 ★   Radio Shack
3301 Veterans Blvd. N
Metairie, LA 70005
(504)837-8030
Company Type: Division. Ultimate Parent:
Tandy Corp. SIC: 5731—Radio, Television
& Electronics Stores.

★ 70308 ★   Radio Shack
Lakeside Shopping Ctr.
Metairie, LA 70002
(504)837-8030
Company Type: Division. Ultimate Parent:
Tandy Corp. SIC: 5065—Electronic Parts &
Equipment Nec; 5731—Radio, Television &
Electronics Stores.

★ 70309 ★   Radio Shack
745 Veterans Blvd.
Metairie, LA 70005
(504)833-0451
Company Type: Division. Ultimate Parent:
Tandy Corp. SIC: 5065—Electronic Parts &
Equipment Nec.

★ 70310 ★   Recovery Services
International
111 Veterans Memorial Blvd.
Metairie, LA 70005
(504)833-3737
Ultimate Parent: Cigna Corp. SIC: 6411—
Insurance Agents, Brokers & Service.

★ 70311 ★   Shell Food Mart
1381 PO Box
Metairie, LA 70004
(504)833-6447
Ultimate Parent: Shell Oil Co. SIC: 5541—
Gasoline Service Stations.

★ 70312 ★   Supreme Sugar Co.,
Inc.
111 Veterans Memorial Blvd.
Metairie, LA 70005-3028
(504)831-0901
Officer: Robert J. Conlin, President.
Ultimate Parent: Archer Daniels Midland
Co. SIC: 2061—Raw Cane Sugar.
Employee Count: 138. Sales: 90 M.

★ 70313 ★   Syscon Corp.
4621 W. Napoleon Ave.
Metairie, LA 70001
(504)889-7402
Ultimate Parent: Harnischfeger Industries.
SIC: 7372—Prepackaged Software.

★ 70314 ★   Taco Bell
4001 Veterans Memorial Blvd.
Metairie, LA 70002
(504)885-7018
Ultimate Parent: Pepsico. SIC: 5812—
Eating Places.

★ 70315 ★   Taco Bell
4300 S. I Serv Rd.
Metairie, LA 70005
(504)454-0131
Ultimate Parent: Pepsico. SIC: 5812—
Eating Places.

★ 70316 ★   Taco Bell
3840 Veterans Blvd.
Metairie, LA 70005
(504)888-4633
Ultimate Parent: Pepsico. SIC: 5812—
Eating Places.

★ 70317 ★   Texaco Mini Mart &
Serv Sta
3512 SW Esplanade Ave.
Metairie, LA 70002
(504)887-8638
Ultimate Parent: Texaco. SIC: 5411—
Grocery Stores.

★ 70318 ★   Texaco Self Serve
3450 W. Esplanade Ave. N
Metairie, LA 70002
(504)885-2173
Ultimate Parent: Texaco. SIC: 5541—
Gasoline Service Stations.

★ 70319 ★   Texaco Self Service
708 Metairie Rd.
Metairie, LA 70005
(504)834-6345
Ultimate Parent: Texaco. SIC: 5541—
Gasoline Service Stations.

★ 70320 ★   Texaco Self Service
Station
2201 Clearview Pky.
Metairie, LA 70001
(504)885-6934
Ultimate Parent: Texaco. SIC: 5541—
Gasoline Service Stations.

★ 70321 ★   This End Up
3301 Veterans Blvd. N
Metairie, LA 70005
(504)837-8750
Ultimate Parent: Melville. SIC: 5712—
Furniture Stores.

★ 70322 ★   Unisys Corp.
3501 N. Cswy
Metairie, LA 70002
(504)836-5400
Ultimate Parent: Unisys Corp. SIC: 5099—
Durable Goods Nec.

★ 70323 ★   US Fidelity & Gu
2450 Severn Ave.
Metairie, LA 70001
(504)837-9970
Ultimate Parent: USF&G Corp. SIC:
6411—Insurance Agents, Brokers &
Service.

★ 70324 ★   Variable Annuity Life
Insurance
3340 Severn Ave.
Metairie, LA 70002
(504)456-9916
Ultimate Parent: Variable Annuity Life. SIC:
6411—Insurance Agents, Brokers &
Service.

★ 70325 ★   Victoria's Secret
3301 Veterans Blvd. N
Metairie, LA 70005
(504)834-2720
Ultimate Parent: Limited. SIC: 5651—
Family Clothing Stores.

★ 70326 ★   Waldenbooks
Clearview Shopping Ctr.
Metairie, LA 70002
(504)888-1275
Ultimate Parent: K-Mart. SIC: 5942—Book
Stores.

★ 70327 ★   Walgreen
3501 Severn Ave.
Metairie, LA 70002
(504)455-1535
Ultimate Parent: Walgreen Co. SIC:
5912—Drug Stores & Proprietary Stores.

★ 70328 ★   Walgreen Drug Stores
7101 Veterans Memorial Blvd.
Metairie, LA 70003
(504)834-8281
Ultimate Parent: Walgreen Co. SIC:
5912—Drug Stores & Proprietary Stores.

★ 70329 ★   Walgreen Drug Stores
110 Veterans Memorial Blvd. 160
Metairie, LA 70005
Ultimate Parent: Walgreen Co. SIC:
5912—Drug Stores & Proprietary Stores.

★ 70330 ★   Walgreen Drug Stores
7941 Airline Hwy.
Metairie, LA 70003
(504)737-1418
Ultimate Parent: Walgreen Co. SIC:
5912—Drug Stores & Proprietary Stores.

★ 70331 ★　Walgreen Drug Stores
7101 Veterans Blvd.
Metairie, LA 70003
(504)455-1839
Ultimate Parent: Walgreen Co. SIC:
5912—Drug Stores & Proprietary Stores.

★ 70332 ★　Walgreen Drugs
1507 Metairie Rd.
Metairie, LA 70005
(504)831-9756
Ultimate Parent: Walgreen Co. SIC:
5912—Drug Stores & Proprietary Stores.

★ 70333 ★　Wells Fargo Guard
Service
2121 N. Cswy
Metairie, LA 70001
(504)831-4711
Ultimate Parent: Borg Warner Automotive.
SIC: 7381—Detective & Armored Car
Services.

★ 70334 ★　Western Geophysical
Co.
4001 Division St.
Metairie, LA 70002
(504)888 3871
Ultimate Parent: Litton Industries. SIC:
1382—Oil & Gas Exploration Services.

★ 70335 ★　Western Life
Insurance Co.
3616 S. I-10 Service Rd. W
Metairie, LA 70001
(504)837-6500
Ultimate Parent: Westcorp. SIC: 6411—
Insurance Agents, Brokers & Service.

★ 70336 ★　Whirlpool Financial
Corp.
4300 S. I-10 Service Rd. W
Metairie, LA 70001
(504)888-8118
Ultimate Parent: Whirlpool Corp. SIC:
6159—Miscellaneous Business Credit
Institutions.

Metarie

★ 70337 ★　Browning-Ferris
Industries
808 L & A Rd.
Metarie, LA 70001
(504)837-8950
Officer: Thomas Nicholson, Manager.
Ultimate Parent: Browning-Ferris
Industries. SIC: 3272—Concrete Products
Nec.

Minden

★ 70338 ★　Borden Inc.
Dairy
110 Sibley Rd.
Minden, LA 71055
Company Type: Division. Ultimate Parent:
Borden, Inc. SIC: 5143—Dairy Products
Except Dried or Canned.

★ 70339 ★　Borden Inc.
Dairy
110 Sibley Rd.
Minden, LA 71055
Company Type: Division. Ultimate Parent:
Borden, Inc. SIC: 5143—Dairy Products
Except Dried or Canned.

★ 70340 ★　Coca Cola Bottling
Co. Inc.
412 Pine St.
Minden, LA 71055
(318)377-6846
Ultimate Parent: Coca-Cola Enterprises.
SIC: 5149—Groceries & Related Products
Nec.

★ 70341 ★　Inland Container
Corp.
1000 Erwin Thompson Dr.
Minden, LA 71055
Ultimate Parent: Temple-Inland. SIC:
2653—Corrugated & Solid Fiber Boxes.

★ 70342 ★　Kentucky Fried
Chicken
604 Homer Rd.
Minden, LA 71055
(318)377-8828
Ultimate Parent: Pepsico. SIC: 5812—
Eating Places.

★ 70343 ★　Piggly Wiggly
417 PO Box
Minden, LA 71058
(318)377-6657
Ultimate Parent: Bruno's. SIC: 5411—
Grocery Stores.

★ 70344 ★　Piggly Wiggly
214 Homer Rd.
Minden, LA 71055
(318)377-5109
Ultimate Parent: Bruno's. SIC: 5411—
Grocery Stores.

★ 70345 ★　Pizza Hut
930 Homer Rd.
Minden, LA 71055
(318)371-1240
Ultimate Parent: Pepsico. SIC: 5812—
Eating Places.

★ 70346 ★　Radio Shack
1110 Homer Rd.
Minden, LA 71055
(318)377-9664
Company Type: Division. Ultimate Parent:
Tandy Corp. SIC: 5065—Electronic Parts &
Equipment Nec.

★ 70347 ★　Wal Mart Discount
Cities
424 Homer Rd.
Minden, LA 71055
(318)371-0808
Ultimate Parent: Wal-Mart Stores, Inc. SIC:
5311—Department Stores.

★ 70348 ★　Zep Manufacturing
Co.
Prairie Grove
Minden, LA 71055
(318)371-2955
Ultimate Parent: National Service
Industries. SIC: 5169—Chemicals & Allied
Products Nec.

Monroe

★ 70349 ★　Ace Hardware
4600 Jackson St.
Monroe, LA 71202
(318)322-6812
Ultimate Parent: Ace Hardware. SIC:
5251—Hardware Stores.

★ 70350 ★　Borden Inc. Dairy
2407 Grand St.
Monroe, LA 71202
Ultimate Parent: Borden, Inc. SIC: 2026—
Fluid Milk.

★ 70351 ★　Casual Corner
1388 Pecanland Rd.
Monroe, LA 71203
(318)388-3391
Ultimate Parent: United States Shoe. SIC:
5651—Family Clothing Stores.

★ 70352 ★　Circus World
1226 Pecanland Rd.
Monroe, LA 71203
(318)323-1134
Ultimate Parent: Melville. SIC: 5945—
Hobby, Toy & Game Shops.

★ 70353 ★　Fleet Finance Inc.
7190 PO Box
Monroe, LA 71211
(318)325-9681
Ultimate Parent: Fleet Financial Group.
SIC: 6062—State Credit Unions; 6141—
Personal Credit Institutions.

★ 70354 ★　Foot Action
1230 Pecanland Rd.
Monroe, LA 71203
(318)388-4325
Ultimate Parent: Melville. SIC: 5661—Shoe
Stores.

★ 70355 ★　Greyhound Bus Lines
Inc.
230 Stanley Ave.
Monroe, LA 71201
(318)323-1415
Ultimate Parent: Greyhound Lines Inc.

★ 70356 ★　Kentucky Fried
Chicken
1706 Martin Luther King J Dr.
Monroe, LA 71202
(318)325-1106
Ultimate Parent: Pepsico. SIC: 5812—
Eating Places.

★ 70357 ★　Kentucky Fried
Chicken
2006 East St.
Monroe, LA 71202
(318)322-1106
Ultimate Parent: Pepsico. SIC: 5812—
Eating Places.

★ 70358 ★　The Limited
1144 Pecanland Rd.
Monroe, LA 71203
(318)322-7155
Ultimate Parent: Limited. SIC: 5651—
Family Clothing Stores.

★ 70359 ★　The Limited Express
1408 Pecanland Rd.
Monroe, LA 71203
(318)387-3365
Ultimate Parent: Limited. SIC: 5651—
Family Clothing Stores.

★ 70360 ★　Mary Kay Cosmetics
135 Selman Dr.
Monroe, LA 71203
(318)343-3714
Ultimate Parent: Mary Kay Cosmetics. SIC:
5999—Miscellaneous Retail Stores Nec.

★ 70361 ★　Mobil Mini Market
2005 US 165 Bypass
Monroe, LA 71202
(318)325-0036
Ultimate Parent: Mobil. SIC: 5541—
Gasoline Service Stations.

★ 70362 ★　New York Life Monroe
General Office
Western Agencies
300 Washington St., 3rd Fl., Ste. 300
Monroe, LA 71201
(318)387-4771 Fax: (318)361-2461
Officer: Thomas L McConathy, General
Manager. Ultimate Parent: New York Life.

★ 70363 ★　Otis Elevator Co.
300 Oak St.
Monroe, LA 71201
(318)322-7636
Ultimate Parent: United Technologies. SIC:
5084—Industrial Machinery & Equipment.

★ 70364 ★　Ouachita Coca-Cola
Bottling Co. Inc.
1300 Hwy. 165 Bypass
Monroe, LA 71201
Ultimate Parent: Coca-Cola Bottling
Consol. SIC: 2086—Bottled & Canned Soft
Drinks.

★ 70365 ★　Pennzoil Producing
Co.
2112 Justice St.
Monroe, LA 71201
(318)387-9153
Ultimate Parent: Pennzoil. SIC: 1382—Oil
& Gas Exploration Services.

★ 70366 ★　Pepsi-Cola Seven-Up
Bottling
2301 Ruffin Dr.
Monroe, LA 71202
(318)387-7282
Officer: Mike Alexander, Manager. Ultimate
Parent: Pepsico. SIC: 2086—Bottled &
Canned Soft Drinks.

★ 70367 ★　Piggly Wiggly Central
Office
900 Winnsboro Rd.
Monroe, LA 71202
(318)387-5820
Ultimate Parent: Bruno's. SIC: 5411—
Grocery Stores.

★ 70368 ★　Piggly Wiggly Central
Office
3511 Desiard St.
Monroe, LA 71203
(318)343-5627
Ultimate Parent: Bruno's. SIC: 5411—
Grocery Stores.

★ 70369 ★　Pizza Hut
3501 Desiard St.
Monroe, LA 71203
(318)345-1222
Ultimate Parent: Pepsico. SIC: 3993—
Signs & Advertising Displays; 5812—Eating
Places.

★ 70370 ★　Premier Bank, NA
130 Desiard St.
Monroe, LA 71201-7304
(318)632-7100
Location Type: Branch office. Ultimate
Parent: Premier Bancorp.

★ 70371 ★　Premier Bank, NA
603 Jackson St.
Monroe, LA 71202-8417
(318)362-7480
Location Type: Branch office. Ultimate
Parent: Premier Bancorp.

★ 70372 ★　Premier Bank, NA
700 N. 4th St.
Monroe, LA
Location Type: Branch office. Ultimate
Parent: Premier Bancorp.

★ 70373 ★　Premier Bank, NA
111 Old Bostrop Rd.
Monroe, LA 71202-4211
(318)362-7548
Location Type: Branch office. Ultimate
Parent: Premier Bancorp.

★ 70374 ★　Premier Bank, NA
1900 N. 18th St.
Monroe, LA 71201-5709
(318)362-7420
Location Type: Branch office. Ultimate
Parent: Premier Bancorp.

★ 70375 ★　Premier Bank, NA
1200 US Hwy. 165 N.
Monroe, LA 71201-5133
(318)362-7455
Location Type: Branch office. Ultimate
Parent: Premier Bancorp.

★ 70376 ★　Radio Shack
1012 Pecanland Mall
Monroe, LA 71203
(318)387-0976
Company Type: Division. Ultimate Parent:
Tandy Corp. SIC: 7373—Computer
Integrated Systems Design.

★ 70377 ★　Stop & Shop Grocery
4900 Blanks St.
Monroe, LA 71203
(318)343-8935
Ultimate Parent: Stop & Shop. SIC: 5411—
Grocery Stores.

★ 70378 ★　Superior Life
Insurance
1604 Pine St.
Monroe, LA 71201
(318)322-3971
Ultimate Parent: Nationsbank Corp. SIC:
6411—Insurance Agents, Brokers &
Service.

★ 70379 ★　Taco Bell
900 Us 165 Byp
Monroe, LA 71203
(318)343-9797
Ultimate Parent: Pepsico. SIC: 5812—
Eating Places.

★ 70380 ★　Toys R US
1350 Pecanland Rd.
Monroe, LA 71203
(318)322-8590
Ultimate Parent: Toys "R" US. SIC: 5945—
Hobby, Toy & Game Shops.

★ 70381 ★　Trailways
Incorporated
830 Us 165 Byp
Monroe, LA 71203
(318)322-5181
Ultimate Parent: Greyhound Lines Inc. SIC:
4131—Intercity & Rural Bus Transportation.

★ 70382 ★　United Parcel Service
2600 Booth St.
Monroe, LA 71201
(318)452-8880
Ultimate Parent: United Parcel Service of
America. SIC: 4215—Courier Services
Except by Air.

★ 70383 ★　Waldenbooks
1522 Pecanland Mall
Monroe, LA 71203
(318)323-2343
Ultimate Parent: K-Mart. SIC: 5942—Book
Stores.

Montegut

★ 70384 ★   Shell Pipeline Corp.
Gibson
Montegut, LA 70377
(504)575-3550
Ultimate Parent: Shell Oil Co. **SIC:** 1311—
Crude Petroleum & Natural Gas.

★ 70385 ★   Shell Pipeline Corp.
Gibson
Montegut, LA 70377
(504)575-3550
Ultimate Parent: Shell Oil Co. **SIC:** 1311—
Crude Petroleum & Natural Gas.

★ 70386 ★   Stop & Shop Grocery
Aragon Serre Rd.
Montegut, LA 70377
(504)594-3811
Ultimate Parent: Stop & Shop.

Morgan City

★ 70387 ★   McDermott
Marine Construction Fabricators Div.
Hwy. 90
Morgan City, LA 70381
Company Type: Division. **Ultimate Parent:**
McDermott. **SIC:** 3441—Fabricated
Structural Metal.

**★ 70388 ★   Mobil Exploring &
Producing US**
1200 Youngs Rd.
Morgan City, LA 70380-2937
(504)380-9550
Officer: Steve Goff. **Ultimate Parent:** Mobil.
SIC: 1382—Oil & Gas Exploration Services.

★ 70389 ★   Mobil Oil Corp.
Youngs Rd.
Morgan City, LA 70380
(504)384-9526
Ultimate Parent: Mobil. **SIC:** 5983—Fuel
Oil Dealers.

★ 70390 ★   Pizza Hut
609 Brashear Ave.
Morgan City, LA 70380
(504)385-3661
Ultimate Parent: Pepsico. **SIC:** 5812—
Eating Places.

★ 70391 ★   Pizza Hut
1646 Hwy. 90 E
Morgan City, LA 70380
(504)384-6660
Ultimate Parent: Pepsico. **SIC:** 5812—
Eating Places.

★ 70392 ★   Radio Shack
1921 Us 90 E
Morgan City, LA 70380
(504)384-6228
Company Type: Division. **Ultimate Parent:**
Tandy Corp. **SIC:** 5399—Miscellaneous
General Merchandise Store.

★ 70393 ★   Shell Oil Co.
Hwy. 90 W
Morgan City, LA 70380.
(504)395-6116
Ultimate Parent: Shell Oil Co. **SIC:** 1311—
Crude Petroleum & Natural Gas.

★ 70394 ★   Taco Bell
2002 Us 90 E
Morgan City, LA 70380
(504)384-7398
Ultimate Parent: Pepsico. **SIC:** 5812—
Eating Places.

**★ 70395 ★   Tesoro Petroleum
Distribution Co.**
Us 90 E
Morgan City, LA 70380
(504)631-0822
Ultimate Parent: Tesoro Petroleum Corp.
SIC: 1311—Crude Petroleum & Natural
Gas.

★ 70396 ★   Texaco Inc.
Bateman Lake
Morgan City, LA 70380
(504)384-7561
Ultimate Parent: Texaco. **SIC:** 1311—
Crude Petroleum & Natural Gas.

**★ 70397 ★   Union Texas
Petroleum**
Ofc Hwy. 182 W
Morgan City, LA 70380
(504)395-4912
Ultimate Parent: Union Texas Petroleum.
SIC: 5171—Petroleum Bulk Stations &
Terminals.

★ 70398 ★   Wal Mart Auto Center
412 Saint Mary Plz.
Morgan City, LA 70380
(504)395-5387
Ultimate Parent: Wal-Mart Stores, Inc. **SIC:**
7538—General Automotive Repair Shops.

Natchitoches

★ 70399 ★   Arco Pipe Line Co.
113 Hwy. 1 S
Natchitoches, LA 71457-5039
(318)352-2701
Ultimate Parent: Atlantic Richfield Co., Inc.
SIC: 1311—Crude Petroleum & Natural
Gas.

★ 70400 ★   Conagra Broiler Co.
Hwy. 1 S. Bypass
Natchitoches, LA 71457
Ultimate Parent: Conagra. **SIC:** 2015—
Poultry Slaughtering & Processing; 2077—
Animal & Marine Fats & Oils.

**★ 70401 ★   Kentucky Fried
Chicken**
107 State Hwy. 1 S
Natchitoches, LA 71457
(318)352-5555
Ultimate Parent: Pepsico. **SIC:** 5812—
Eating Places.

**★ 70402 ★   Kentucky Fried
Chicken**
107 Hwy. 1 S
Natchitoches, LA 71457
(318)352-5557
Ultimate Parent: Pepsico. **SIC:** 6513—
Apartment Building Operators.

★ 70403 ★   Pizza Hut
117 State Hwy. 1 S
Natchitoches, LA 71457
(318)357-8559
Ultimate Parent: Pepsico. **SIC:** 5812—
Eating Places.

★ 70404 ★   Taco Bell
127 State Hwy. 1 S
Natchitoches, LA 71457
(318)352-1509
Ultimate Parent: Pepsico. **SIC:** 5812—
Eating Places.

★ 70405 ★   United Parcel Service
1358 Washington St.
Natchitoches, LA 71457
(318)222-8333
Ultimate Parent: United Parcel Service of
America. **SIC:** 4215—Courier Services
Except by Air.

**★ 70406 ★   Wal Mart Discount
City**
Cane Rv Shopping Ctr.
Natchitoches, LA 71457
(318)357-0403
Ultimate Parent: Wal-Mart Stores, Inc. **SIC:**
5311—Department Stores.

New Iberia

★ 70407 ★   Ace Hardware Co. Inc.
335 W. Saint Peter St.
New Iberia, LA 70560
(318)367-2461
Ultimate Parent: Ace Hardware. **SIC:**
5251—Hardware Stores.

★ 70408 ★   Fleet Finance Inc.
136 Ctr. St.
New Iberia, LA 70560
(318)365-3471
Ultimate Parent: Fleet Financial Group.
SIC: 6141—Personal Credit Institutions.

**★ 70409 ★   Greyhound Bus
Station**
101 Perry St.
New Iberia, LA 70560
(318)364-8571
Ultimate Parent: Greyhound Lines Inc. **SIC:**
4212—Local Trucking Without Storage.

★ 70410 ★   Kroger Pharmacy
1502 E. Main St.
New Iberia, LA 70560
(318)365-4262
Ultimate Parent: Kroger. **SIC:** 5912—Drug
Stores & Proprietary Stores.

★ 70411 ★   Kroger Snack Bar
1502 E. Main St.
New Iberia, LA 70560
(318)365-8821
Ultimate Parent: Kroger. **SIC:** 5812—
Eating Places.

★ 70412 ★   Mary Kay Cosmetics
1605 Montagne St.
New Iberia, LA 70560
(318)365-5349
Ultimate Parent: Mary Kay Cosmetics. **SIC:**
5999—Miscellaneous Retail Stores Nec.

**★ 70413 ★   Morton International
Inc.**
Morton Salt Div.
Hwy. 83 S. Weeks Island
New Iberia, LA 70560
Company Type: Division. **Ultimate Parent:**
Morton International. **SIC:** 2899—Chemical
Preparations Nec.

★ 70414 ★   Premier Bank, NA
124 E. Main St.
New Iberia, LA 70560-3725
(318)365-7221
Location Type: Branch office. **Ultimate
Parent:** Premier Bancorp.

★ 70415 ★   Premier Bank, NA
1700 Ctr. St.
New Iberia, LA 70560-6642
(318)364-1771
Location Type: Branch office. **Ultimate
Parent:** Premier Bancorp.

★ 70416 ★   Premier Bank, NA
223 N. Leurs St.
New Iberia, LA 70560-2840
(318)365-7300
Location Type: Branch office. **Ultimate
Parent:** Premier Bancorp.

**★ 70417 ★   Premier Bank,
National Assoc.**
223 N. Lewis St.
New Iberia, LA 70560-2840
(318)365-7300
Location Type: Branch office. **Officer:** Al
Viatar, Manager. **Ultimate Parent:** Premier
Bancorp.

**★ 70418 ★   Premier Bank,
National Assoc.**
124 E. Main St.
New Iberia, LA 70560-3725
(318)365-7221
Location Type: Branch office. **Officer:** J.
Hubert Dumesnil, Chairman of the Board.
Ultimate Parent: Premier Bancorp.

**★ 70419 ★   Premier Bank,
National Assoc.**
1700 Ctr. St.
New Iberia, LA 70560-6642
(318)364-1771
Location Type: Branch office. **Officer:**
Cindy O. Breaux, Manager. **Ultimate
Parent:** Premier Bancorp.

★ 70420 ★   Ryder Truck Rental
1426 Ctr. St.
New Iberia, LA 70560
(318)364-3549
Ultimate Parent: Ryder System. **SIC:**
7359—Equipment Rental & Leasing Nec.

★ 70421 ★   Texaco Inc.
1329 Jane St.
New Iberia, LA 70560
(318)365-5411
Ultimate Parent: Texaco. **SIC:** 5172—
Petroleum Products Nec.

**★ 70422 ★   Wal Mart Discount
City**
939 S. Lewis St.
New Iberia, LA 70560
(318)364-3250
Ultimate Parent: Wal-Mart Stores, Inc. **SIC:**
5311—Department Stores.

New Orleans

**★ 70423 ★   Abbott Laboratories
International Co.**
1015 Distributors Row
New Orleans, LA 70123-2209
(504)731-2613
Officer: Michael R. Holland. **Ultimate
Parent:** Abbott Laboratories. **SIC:** 2834—
Pharmaceutical Preparations.

**★ 70424 ★   Air Products &
Chemicals**
14700 Intracoastal Dr.
New Orleans, LA 70129-2301
(504)254-1590
Officer: W D Greer. **Ultimate Parent:** Air
Products & Chemicals, Inc. **SIC:** 2819—
Industrial Inorganic Chemicals Nec; 2899—
Chemical Preparations Nec; 5169—
Chemicals & Allied Products Nec.

**★ 70425 ★   Air Products &
Chemicals Inc.**
14700 Intracoastal Dr.
New Orleans, LA 70129
(504)254-1590
Officer: Bill Greer, Manager. **Ultimate
Parent:** Air Products & Chemicals, Inc. **SIC:**
2813—Industrial Gases; 2873—Nitrogenous
Fertilizers.

**★ 70426 ★   Air Products &
Chemicals Inc.**
14700 Intracoastal Dr.
New Orleans, LA 70129
Ultimate Parent: Air Products & Chemicals,
Inc. **SIC:** 2813—Industrial Gases.

★ 70427 ★   Alcoa Recycling Co.
1 Seine Ct.
New Orleans, LA 70114-6553
(504)364-6160
Ultimate Parent: Aluminum Co. of America-
-Alcoa. **SIC:** 4953—Refuse Systems.

★ 70428 ★   Alcoa Recycling Co.
1 Seine Ct.
New Orleans, LA 70114-6553
(504)364-6160
Ultimate Parent: Aluminum Co. of America-
-Alcoa. **SIC:** 4953—Refuse Systems.

**★ 70429 ★   American General
Finance**
6003 Bullard Ave., Ste. 8
New Orleans, LA 70128-2834
(504)246-2521
Location Type: Branch office. **Officer:** Joe
Cassessi. **Ultimate Parent:** American
General Corp. **SIC:** 6141—Personal Credit
Institutions; 6162—Mortgage Bankers &
Correspondents.

**★ 70430 ★   American General
Finance Inc.**
6003 Bullard Ave., Ste. 8
New Orleans, LA 70128-2834
(504)246-2521
Location Type: Branch office. **Officer:** Joe
Cassessi. **Ultimate Parent:** American
General Corp. **SIC:** 6141—Personal Credit
Institutions; 6162—Mortgage Bankers &
Correspondents.

★ 70431 ★   American Steel Corp.
3368 PO Box
New Orleans, LA 70177
(504)466-4215
Ultimate Parent: National Steel. **SIC:**
5051—Metals Service Centers & Offices.

**★ 70432 ★   AmSouth of
Louisiana, Inc.**
Energy Centre
1100 Poydras, Ste. 1430
New Orleans, LA 70163
(504)885-5152
Company Type: Subsidiary. **Officer:**
George S. Shirley, Chairman of the Board &
President. **Ultimate Parent:** AmSouth
Bancorp. **SIC:** 6021—National Commercial
Banks. **Employee Count:** 2.

★ 70433 ★   Analog Devices Inc.
7023 Read Ln.
New Orleans, LA 70127
(504)244-9616
Ultimate Parent: Analog Devices, Inc. **SIC:**
5084—Industrial Machinery & Equipment.

★ **70434** ★　**Bencharge Credit Services LA Inc.**
1200 S. Clearview Pky.
New Orleans, LA 70123-2300
(504)733-7584
Ultimate Parent: Beneficial. **SIC:** 6141—Personal Credit Institutions.

★ **70435** ★　**Bunny Bread**
5646 Lewis Rd.
PO 26368
New Orleans, LA 70126
(504)241-1206 **Fax:** (504)241-0953
Company Type: Subsidiary. **Officer:** Danny J. Brinson, President. **Ultimate Parent:** Flowers Industries.

★ **70436** ★　**Bunny Bread Co.**
5646 Lewis Rd.
New Orleans, LA 70126
(504)241-1206
Officer: Denny Brinson, President. **Ultimate Parent:** Flowers Industries. **SIC:** 2051—Bread, Cake & Related Products.

★ **70437** ★　**Butler Paper**
990 N. Corporate Dr.
New Orleans, LA 70123-3331
(504)733-8890
Location Type: Branch office. **Ultimate Parent:** Alco Standard Corp. **SIC:** 5113—Industrial & Personal Service Paper.

★ **70438** ★　**Butler Paper**
990 N. Corporate Dr.
New Orleans, LA 70123-3331
(504)733-8890
Location Type: Branch office. **Ultimate Parent:** Alco Standard Corp. **SIC:** 5113—Industrial & Personal Service Paper.

★ **70439** ★　**CNG Producing Co.**
CNG Tower, 1450 Poydras St.
New Orleans, LA 70112-6000
(504)593-7000 **Fax:** (504)593-7330
Officer: David P. Hunt, President. **Ultimate Parent:** Consolidated Natural Gas.

★ **70440** ★　**Coca-Cola Bottling Co. Louisiana Ltd.**
1050 S. Jefferson Davis Pky.
New Orleans, LA 70125
Ultimate Parent: Coca-Cola Enterprises. **SIC:** 2086—Bottled & Canned Soft Drinks.

★ **70441** ★　**Coca-Cola U S a**
5330 Jefferson Hwy.
New Orleans, LA 70123
(504)733-6932
Ultimate Parent: Coca-Cola. **SIC:** 2086—Bottled & Canned Soft Drinks.

★ **70442** ★　**Delta Air Lines**
800 Airline Hwy.
New Orleans, LA 70141
(504)464-0921
Ultimate Parent: Delta Air Lines, Inc. **SIC:** 4512—Air Transportation—Scheduled.

★ **70443** ★　**Deluxe Check Printers Inc.**
4375 Michoud Blvd.
New Orleans, LA 70129
Ultimate Parent: Deluxe Corp. **SIC:** 2782—Blankbooks & Looseleaf Binders; 2752—Commercial Printing—Lithographic.

★ **70444** ★　**El Dorado Engineering Inc.**
131 S. Robertson St.
New Orleans, LA 70112
(504)561-2734 **Fax:** (504)561-2767
Officer: Dr. Terry D. Petty, President. **Ultimate Parent:** Murphy Oil.

★ **70445** ★　**Engineering & Industrial Group**
1450 Poydras St.
New Orleans, LA 70112
Officer: William L. Higgins, Executive Vice President & Group Executive. **Ultimate Parent:** McDermott.

★ **70446** ★　**Entergy**
2255 Baronne St.
New Orleans, LA 70113
(504)529-5262
Company Type: Headquarters.

★ **70447** ★　**Entergy Corp.**
PO Box 61000
New Orleans, LA 70161
Company Type: Headquarters. **Ultimate Parent:** Entergy.

★ **70448** ★　**Entergy Services Inc.**
639 Loyola Ave.
New Orleans, LA 70113-3125
(504)529-5262
Company Type: Subsidiary. **Ultimate Parent:** Entergy. **SIC:** 8741—Management Services; 8711—Engineering Services.

★ **70449** ★　**Equitable**
Halter Div.
4325 France Rd.
New Orleans, LA 70126
Company Type: Division. **Ultimate Parent:** Trinity Industries. **SIC:** 3731—Ship Building & Repairing.

★ **70450** ★　**Exxon Car Care Center**
704 Howard Ave.
New Orleans, LA 70130
(504)528-1618
Ultimate Parent: Exxon. **SIC:** 5541—Gasoline Service Stations.

★ **70451** ★　**Exxon Chemical Co.**
4450 Gen De Gaulle Dr.
New Orleans, LA 70131
(504)561-3553
Ultimate Parent: Exxon. **SIC:** 2899—Chemical Preparations Nec.

★ **70452** ★　**First Commerce Corp.**
210 Baronne St.
New Orleans, LA 70112
(504)561-1371
Company Type: Headquarters. **Officer:** Ian Arnof. **Employee Count:** 3400. **Fortune Service 500:** Ranking 80.

★ **70453** ★　**First Financial Bank-F S B**
301 Saint Charles Ave.
New Orleans, LA 70130
(504)581-9285
Ultimate Parent: First Financial Corp. **SIC:** 6159—Miscellaneous Business Credit Institutions.

★ **70454** ★　**Fleet Finance Inc.**
4429 Chef Menteur Hwy.
New Orleans, LA 70126
(504)454-8323
Ultimate Parent: Fleet Financial Group. **SIC:** 6062—State Credit Unions.

★ **70455** ★　**Fleet Finance Inc.**
3301 S. Carrollton Ave.
New Orleans, LA 70118
(504)486-5751
Ultimate Parent: Fleet Financial Group. **SIC:** 6141—Personal Credit Institutions.

★ **70456** ★　**Fleet Finance Inc.**
1464 N. Broad St.
New Orleans, LA 70119
(504)948-6573
Ultimate Parent: Fleet Financial Group. **SIC:** 7381—Detective & Armored Car Services.

★ **70457** ★　**Fleet Finance Inc.**
2353 Saint Claude Ave.
New Orleans, LA 70117
(504)947-2147
Ultimate Parent: Fleet Financial Group. **SIC:** 6141—Personal Credit Institutions.

★ **70458** ★　**P. T. Freeport Indonesia Co.**
1615 Poydras St.
New Orleans, LA 70112-1217
(504)582-4000
Company Type: Subsidiary. **Officer:** James R. Moffett, Chairman of the Board & President. **Ultimate Parent:** Freeport-McMoran. **SIC:** 1021—Copper Ores; 1041—Gold Ores; 1044—Silver Ores. **Employee Count:** 4486. **Sales:** 714 M.

★ **70459** ★　**Freeport-McMoran**
1615 Poydras St.
New Orleans, LA 70112
(504)582-4000
Company Type: Headquarters. **Officer:** James R. Moffett. **Sales:** 1610.6 M. **Fortune 500:** Largest U.S. Industrial Corporations: Ranking 264.

★ **70460** ★　**Freeport-McMoran Copper & Gold Co.**
PO Box 61119
New Orleans, LA 70161
(504)582-4000 **Fax:** (504)582-1639
Company Type: Subsidiary. **Ultimate Parent:** Freeport-McMoran.

★ **70461** ★　**Freeport-McMoran Copper & Gold Co., Inc.**
1615 Poydras St.
New Orleans, LA 70112-1217
(504)582-4000
Company Type: Subsidiary. **Officer:** James R. Moffett, Chairman of the Board. **Ultimate Parent:** Freeport-McMoran. **SIC:** 1021—Copper Ores; 1041—Gold Ores; 3341—Secondary Nonferrous Metals. **Employee Count:** 4983. **Sales:** 714 M.

★ **70462** ★　**Freeport-McMoran Inc.**
1615 Poydras St.
New Orleans, LA 70112-1217
(504)582-4000
Officer: James R. Moffett, Chairman of the Board & CEO. **Ultimate Parent:** Freeport-McMoran. **SIC:** 1479—Chemical & Fertilizer Mining Nec; 1475—Phosphate Rock; 2874—Phosphatic Fertilizers; 1021—Copper Ores; 1041—Gold Ores. **Employee Count:** 7957. **Sales:** 1.6 M.

★ **70463** ★　**Freeport-McMoran Oil & Gas Co.**
PO Box 60004
New Orleans, LA 70160
(504)582-1722 **Fax:** (504)582-1718
Company Type: Subsidiary. **Ultimate Parent:** Freeport-McMoran.

★ **70464** ★　**Freeport-McMoran Resource Partners**
1615 Poydras St.
New Orleans, LA 70112-1217
(504)582-4000
Company Type: Subsidiary. **Officer:** Rene L. Latiolais, President & CEO. **Ultimate Parent:** Freeport-McMoran. **SIC:** 1479—Chemical & Fertilizer Mining Nec; 2874—Phosphatic Fertilizers; 1475—Phosphate Rock; 2873—Nitrogenous Fertilizers; 2819—Industrial Inorganic Chemicals Nec; 6794—Patent Owners & Lessors. **Employee Count:** 2500. **Sales:** 977 M.

★ **70465** ★　**Freeport-McMoran Resource Partners Ltd.**
PO Box 61520
New Orleans, LA 70161
(504)582-4204 **Fax:** (504)582-1611
Company Type: Subsidiary. **Ultimate Parent:** Freeport-McMoran.

★ **70466** ★　**Freeport Sulphur Co.**
PO Box 61520
New Orleans, LA 70161
(504)582-4243 **Fax:** (504)582-4339
Company Type: Subsidiary. **Ultimate Parent:** Freeport-McMoran.

★ **70467** ★　**GE Consumer Service**
629 Distributors Row
New Orleans, LA 70123
(504)733-7901
Officer: Dennis Rogers, Manager. **Ultimate Parent:** General Electric. **SIC:** 3844—X-Ray Apparatus & Tubes.

★ **70468** ★　**General Electric Co.**
1115 De Armas St.
New Orleans, LA 70114
(504)367-6528
Officer: Rick Seme, Manager. **Ultimate Parent:** General Electric. **SIC:** 3599—Industrial Machinery Nec; 3825—Instruments to Measure Electricity.

★ **70469** ★　**Great River Oil & Gas Corp.**
CNG Tower
1450 Poydras St., Ste. 1520
New Orleans, LA 70112
(504)528-9321 **Fax:** (504)528-9370
Company Type: Subsidiary. **Ultimate Parent:** Georgia Gulf.

★ **70470** ★　**Greyhound Bus Lines**
5821 Plauche St.
New Orleans, LA 70123
(504)733-6753
Ultimate Parent: Greyhound Lines Inc. **SIC:** 4111—Local & Suburban Transit.

★ **70471** ★　**Greyhound Bus Lines**
2101 Earhart Blvd.
New Orleans, LA 70113
(504)524-7571
Ultimate Parent: Greyhound Lines Inc. **SIC:** 4111—Local & Suburban Transit.

★ **70472** ★　**Hertz Rent-A-Car**
20025 PO Box
New Orleans, LA 70141
(504)586-0808
Ultimate Parent: Hertz. **SIC:** 7514—Passenger Car Rental.

★ **70473** ★　**Hertz Rent-A-Car**
800 Airline Hwy.
New Orleans, LA 70141
(504)468-3695
Ultimate Parent: Hertz. **SIC:** 7514—Passenger Car Rental.

★ **70474** ★　**Hibernia Corp.**
313 Carondelet St.
New Orleans, LA 70130
(504)586-5552
Company Type: Headquarters. **Officer:** Stephen A. Hansel. **Employee Count:** 2522. **Fortune 500:** Largest U.S. Industrial Corporations: Ranking 93.

★ **70475** ★　**Hibernia Corp. Holding Co.**
PO Box 61540
New Orleans, LA 70161
(504)586-5552 **Fax:** (504)586-2367
Officer: Robert H. Boh., Chairman of the Board. **Ultimate Parent:** Hibernia Corp.

★ **70476** ★　**Hibernia Corp. Holding Co.**
313 Carondelet St.
New Orleans, LA 70130
(504)586-5552 **Fax:** (504)586-2367
Officer: Robert H. Boh, Chairman of the Board. **Ultimate Parent:** Hibernia Corp.

★ **70477** ★　**Hibernia National Bank**
8920 Veterans Blvd.
New Orleans, LA 70003
(504)587-3397
Location Type: Branch office. **Officer:** Carmen Griffin, Manager. **Ultimate Parent:** Hibernia Corp.

★ **70478** ★　**Hibernia National Bank**
7033 Canal Blvd.
New Orleans, LA 70124-3489
(504)586-5429
Location Type: Branch office. **Ultimate Parent:** Hibernia Corp.

★ **70479** ★　**Hibernia National Bank**
1867 Bardtaria Blvd.
New Orleans, LA 70072
(504)586-2470
Location Type: Branch office. **Officer:** Liz Buras, Manager. **Ultimate Parent:** Hibernia Corp.

★ **70480** ★　**Hibernia National Bank**
4041 Williams Blvd.
New Orleans, LA 70065
Location Type: Branch office. **Officer:** Carmen Griffin, Manager. **Ultimate Parent:** Hibernia Corp.

★ **70481** ★　**Hibernia National Bank**
3300 Paris Rd.
New Orleans, LA 70043
(504)585-5070
Location Type: Branch office. **Officer:** Regina McDowell, Manager. **Ultimate Parent:** Hibernia Corp.

★ **70482** ★　**Hibernia National Bank**
2200 N. Causeway Blvd.
New Orleans, LA 70001
(504)586-2430
Location Type: Branch office. **Officer:** Loretta Savoye, Manager. **Ultimate Parent:** Hibernia Corp.

★ **70483** ★　**Hibernia National Bank**
111 Veterans Blvd.
New Orleans, LA 70005
(504)586-2440
Location Type: Branch office. **Officer:** Judith Bradley, Manager. **Ultimate Parent:** Hibernia Corp.

★ 70484 ★　Hibernia National Bank
1000 W. Esplanade Ave.
New Orleans, LA 70062
(504)585-5140
Location Type: Branch office. **Officer:** Karen Braun, Manager. **Ultimate Parent:** Hibernia Corp.

★ 70485 ★　Hibernia National Bank
500 N. Carrollton Ave.
New Orleans, LA 70119
(504)585-5150
Location Type: Branch office. **Officer:** Gay Clark, Manager. **Ultimate Parent:** Hibernia Corp.

★ 70486 ★　Hibernia National Bank
2510 Williams Blvd.
New Orleans, LA 70062
(504)586-2450
Location Type: Branch office. **Officer:** Lisa Schmidt, Manager. **Ultimate Parent:** Hibernia Corp.

★ 70487 ★　Hibernia National Bank
11001 Chef Menteur Hwy.
New Orleans, LA 70127-4286
(504)586-5307
Location Type: Branch office. **Officer:** Sue Fricke, Manager. **Ultimate Parent:** Hibernia Corp.

★ 70488 ★　Hibernia National Bank
8304 I-10 Service Rd. East
New Orleans, LA 70126-3199
(504)586-5314
Location Type: Branch office. **Officer:** Gerald Davis, Manager. **Ultimate Parent:** Hibernia Corp.

★ 70489 ★　Hibernia National Bank
2141 Caton St.
New Orleans, LA 70122-3893
(504)586-5305
Location Type: Branch office. **Officer:** Ben Picone, Manager. **Ultimate Parent:** Hibernia Corp.

★ 70490 ★　Hibernia National Bank
3800 General De Gaulle Dr.
New Orleans, LA 70114-8276
(504)586-5313
Location Type: Branch office. **Officer:** Debbie Hippensteel, Manager. **Ultimate Parent:** Hibernia Corp.

★ 70491 ★　Hibernia National Bank
4300 Magazine St.
New Orleans, LA 70115-2791
(504)586-5302
Location Type: Branch office. **Ultimate Parent:** Hibernia Corp.

★ 70492 ★　Hibernia National Bank
6307 Elysian Fields Ave.
New Orleans, LA 70122-4294
(504)586-5486
Location Type: Branch office. **Officer:** Ruth Lundsgaard, Manager. **Ultimate Parent:** Hibernia Corp.

★ 70493 ★　Hibernia National Bank
701 Poydras St.
New Orleans, LA 70139-0001
(504)586-5312
Location Type: Branch office. **Officer:** Jen Cervantes, Manager. **Ultimate Parent:** Hibernia Corp.

★ 70494 ★　Hibernia National Bank
4121 Canal St.
New Orleans, LA 70119-5995
(504)586-5679
Location Type: Branch office. **Officer:** Connie Barry, Manager. **Ultimate Parent:** Hibernia Corp.

★ 70495 ★　Hibernia National Bank
6309 S. Clairborne
New Orleans, LA 70125
(504)586-5669
Location Type: Branch office. **Officer:**

Dierda Dardis, Manager. **Ultimate Parent:** Hibernia Corp.

★ 70496 ★　Hibernia National Bank
1515 Poydras St.
New Orleans, LA 70112-3723
(504)587-2700
Location Type: Branch office. **Officer:** Jen Cervantes, Manager. **Ultimate Parent:** Hibernia Corp.

★ 70497 ★　Hibernia National Bank
3157 St. Claude Ave.
New Orleans, LA 70117-6698
(504)586-5309
Location Type: Branch office. **Officer:** Raymond Lambert, Manager. **Ultimate Parent:** Hibernia Corp.

★ 70498 ★　Hibernia National Bank
3540 St. Charlee Ave.
New Orleans, LA 70115-4691
(504)586-5304
Location Type: Branch office. **Officer:** Colleen Kuhn, Manager. **Ultimate Parent:** Hibernia Corp.

★ 70499 ★　Hibernia National Bank
6235 S. Clairborne Ave.
New Orleans, LA 70125-4198
(504)586-5465
Location Type: Branch office. **Officer:** Dierda Dardis, Manager. **Ultimate Parent:** Hibernia Corp.

★ 70500 ★　Hibernia National Bank
5400 Choupitoulas
New Orleans, LA 70115
(504)585-5287
Location Type: Branch office. **Officer:** Rosie Thomas, Manager. **Ultimate Parent:** Hibernia Corp.

★ 70501 ★　Hibernia National Bank
313 Carondelet St.
New Orleans, LA 70130
(504)586-5555
Ultimate Parent: Hibernia Corp. **SIC:** 6099—Functions Related to Deposit Banking.

★ 70502 ★　Hibernia National Bank
701 Shell Sq. 1
New Orleans, LA 70139
(504)586-5312
Ultimate Parent: Hibernia Corp. **SIC:** 6022—State Commercial Banks.

★ 70503 ★　Hibernia National Bank
4219 Elysian Fields Ave.
New Orleans, LA 70122
(504)586-5647
Ultimate Parent: Hibernia Corp. **SIC:** 6099—Functions Related to Deposit Banking.

★ 70504 ★　Hibernia National Bank
880 W. Commerce Rd.
New Orleans, LA 70123
(504)587-3460
Ultimate Parent: Hibernia Corp. **SIC:** 6099—Functions Related to Deposit Banking.

★ 70505 ★　Hibernia National Bank
144 Elk Pl
New Orleans, LA 70112
(504)586-5306
Ultimate Parent: Hibernia Corp. **SIC:** 6099—Functions Related to Deposit Banking; 6022—State Commercial Banks.

★ 70506 ★　Hit or Miss
1172 S. Clearview Pky.
New Orleans, LA 70123
(504)734-0320
Ultimate Parent: TJX. **SIC:** 5621—Women's Clothing Stores; 5651—Family Clothing Stores.

★ 70507 ★　Illinois Central Railroad C
10500 PO Box
New Orleans, LA 70181
(504)734-6900
Ultimate Parent: Illinois Central **SIC:** 4011—Railroads—Line-Haul Operating; 4119—Local Passenger Transportation Nec.

★ 70508 ★　Inexco Oil Co.
909 Poydras St., Ste. 3600
New Orleans, LA 70112
Officer: John F. Greene, President. **Ultimate Parent:** Louisiana Land & Exploration.

★ 70509 ★　Kentucky Fried Chicken
1037 N. Broad St.
New Orleans, LA 70119
(504)821-4391
Ultimate Parent: Pepsico. **SIC:** 5812—Eating Places.

★ 70510 ★　Kentucky Fried Chicken
1565 Tulane Ave.
New Orleans, LA 70112
(504)524-7791
Ultimate Parent: Pepsico. **SIC:** 5812—Eating Places.

★ 70511 ★　Kentucky Fried Chicken
4450 Chef Menteur Hwy.
New Orleans, LA 70126
(504)947-5828
Ultimate Parent: Pepsico. **SIC:** 5812—Eating Places.

★ 70512 ★　Kentucky Fried Chicken
6220 Elysian Fields Ave.
New Orleans, LA 70122
(504)282-7183
Ultimate Parent: Pepsico. **SIC:** 5812—Eating Places.

★ 70513 ★　Kmart Discount Stores
4700 Gentilly Blvd.
New Orleans, LA 70119
(504)943-2451
Ultimate Parent: K-Mart. **SIC:** 5311—Department Stores.

★ 70514 ★　LL& E Petroleum Marketing , Inc.
909 Poydras St., Ste. 3600
New Orleans, LA 70112
Officer: Joel M. Wilkinson, President. **Ultimate Parent:** Louisiana Land & Exploration.

★ 70515 ★　LL&E Gas Marketing, Inc.
909 Poydras St., Ste. 3600
New Orleans, LA 70112
Officer: C. S. Kirk, Vice President. **Ultimate Parent:** Louisiana Land & Exploration.

★ 70516 ★　Louisiana Coca-Cola Bottling Co.
1050 S. Jefferson Davis Hwy.
New Orleans, LA 70125
Ultimate Parent: Coca-Cola Enterprises. **SIC:** 2086—Bottled & Canned Soft Drinks.

★ 70517 ★　Louisiana Coca-Cola Bottling Co. Ltd.
1050 S. Jefferson Davis Pky.
New Orleans, LA 70125
Ultimate Parent: Coca-Cola Enterprises. **SIC:** 2086—Bottled & Canned Soft Drinks.

★ 70518 ★　Louisiana Land & Exploration
909 Paydras St.
New Orleans, LA 70112
(504)566-6500
Company Type: Headquarters. **Officer:** H. Leighton Steward. **Employee Count:** 846. **Sales:** 815 M. **Fortune 500:** Largest U.S. Industrial Corporations: Ranking 404.

★ 70519 ★　Louisiana Land & Exploration
South America & Far East Div.
909 Poydras St., Ste. 3600
New Orleans, LA 70112
(504)566-6317 **Fax:** (504)566-6242
Company Type: Division. **Officer:** Michael J. Marfleet, General Manager. **Ultimate Parent:** Louisiana Land & Exploration.

★ 70520 ★　Louisiana Land & Exploration Co.
909 Poydras St., Ste. 3600
New Orleans, LA 70112
(504)566-6500 **Fax:** (504)566-6874 **Telex:** 584478
Officer: H. Leighton Steward, Chairman of the Board, President & CEO. **Ultimate Parent:** Louisiana Land & Exploration. **Employee Count:** 780.

★ 70521 ★　Louisiana Power & Light Co.
317 Baronne St.
New Orleans, LA 70112
(504)595-3100
Company Type: Subsidiary. **Officer:** Jerry L. Maulden, Chairman of the Board & CEO. **Ultimate Parent:** Entergy. **SIC:** 4911—Electric Services. **Employee Count:** 2097.

★ 70522 ★　M-I Drilling Fluids Co. New Orleans
6101 France Rd.
New Orleans, LA 70186
Ultimate Parent: Halliburton. **SIC:** 3295—Minerals—Ground or Treated.

★ 70523 ★　M-I Drilling Fluids New Orleans
6101 France Rd.
New Orleans, LA 70186
Ultimate Parent: Halliburton. **SIC:** 3295—Minerals—Ground or Treated.

★ 70524 ★　Maison Blanche
Lake Forest Plz.
New Orleans, LA 70127
(504)241-8121
Ultimate Parent: Mercantile Stores. **SIC:** 7631—Watch, Clock & Jewelry Repair.

★ 70525 ★　Maison Blanche Goudchaux De
901 Canal St.
New Orleans, LA 70112
(504)522-7300
Ultimate Parent: Mercantile Stores. **SIC:** 5651—Family Clothing Stores; 5812—Eating Places.

★ 70526 ★　Marshalls Department Store
1250 S. Clearview Pky.
New Orleans, LA 70123
(504)734-1151
Ultimate Parent: Melville. **SIC:** 5311—Department Stores.

★ 70527 ★　Martin Marietta Manned Space Systems
13800 Old Gentilly Rd.
PO Box 29304
New Orleans, LA 70129
(504)257-3311 **Fax:** (504)257-2109
Officer: Thomas C. Wirth, President. **Ultimate Parent:** Martin Marietta.

★ 70528 ★　Mary Kay Cosmetics
7641 Rochon Dr.
New Orleans, LA 70128
(504)241-1084
Ultimate Parent: Mary Kay Cosmetics.

★ 70529 ★　McDermott
1450 Poydras St.
New Orleans, LA 70112
(504)587-4411
Company Type: Headquarters. **Officer:** Robert E. Hawson. **Employee Count:** 16500. **Sales:** 1970 M. **Fortune 500:** Largest U.S. Industrial Corporations: Ranking 225.

★ 70530 ★　McDermott International, Inc.
1450 Poydras St.
New Orleans, LA 70112
(504)587-5400 **Fax:** (504)587-6153
Officer: Robert E. Howson, Chairman of the Board & CEO. **Ultimate Parent:** McDermott. **Employee Count:** 28500.

★ 70531 ★　McDonalds Hamburgers
4240 Louisa St.
New Orleans, LA 70126
(504)944-1712
Ultimate Parent: McDonald's. **SIC:** 5812—Eating Places.

★ 70532 ★ **McDonalds Hamburgers**
2916 Jefferson Hwy.
New Orleans, LA 70121
(504)833-3579
Ultimate Parent: McDonald's.
SIC: 5812—Eating Places.

★ 70533 ★ **Mellon Financial Service Corp.**
1415 Corporate Blvd.
New Orleans, LA 70123
(504)561-0075
Ultimate Parent: Mellon Bank Corp. **SIC:**
6162—Mortgage Bankers &
Correspondents.

★ 70534 ★ **Mellon Financial Service Corp.**
6600 Plaza Dr.
New Orleans, LA 70127
(504)246-3011
Ultimate Parent: Mellon Bank Corp. **SIC:**
6162—Mortgage Bankers &
Correspondents.

★ 70535 ★ **Michoud Assembly Facility**
13800 Old Gentilly Rd.
New Orleans, LA 70129
Ultimate Parent: Martin Marietta. **SIC:**
3769—Space Vehicle Equipment Nec;
3499—Fabricated Metal Products Nec;
3479—Metal Coating & Allied Services;
3471—Plating & Polishing.

★ 70536 ★ **Milpark Drilling Fluids (Grinding Facility)**
5100 Jourdan Road, PO Box 26335
New Orleans, LA 70186
Ultimate Parent: Baker Hughes. **SIC:**
3295—Minerals—Ground or Treated.

★ 70537 ★ **Milpark Drilling Fluids New Orleans Barite Grndg. Fac.**
5100 Jourdan Rd. PO Box 26335
New Orleans, LA 70186
Ultimate Parent: Baker Hughes. **SIC:**
3295—Minerals—Ground or Treated.

★ 70538 ★ **Milpark Drig. Fluids (New Orleans Barite) Grinding Faci**
5100 Jourdan Rd.
New Orleans, LA 70186
Ultimate Parent: Baker Hughes. **SIC:**
3295—Minerals—Ground or Treated.

★ 70539 ★ **Murphy Exploration & Production Co.**
131 S. Robertson
New Orleans, LA 70112
(504)561-2811 **Fax:** (504)561-2836
Officer: Enoch L. Dawkins, President.
Ultimate Parent: Murphy Oil.

★ 70540 ★ **New Orleans Public Service Inc.**
317 Baronne St.
New Orleans, LA 70112-1605
(504)595-3100
Company Type: Subsidiary. **Officer:** John
J. Maulden, Chairman of the Board & CEO.
Ultimate Parent: Entergy. **SIC:** 4931—
Electric & Other Services Combined; 4924—
Natural Gas Distribution; 4911—Electric
Services. **Employee Count:** 944. **Sales:**
464879000 M.

★ 70541 ★ **New York Life Acadian Sales Office**
Western Agencies
1350 Poydras St., Ste. 1800
New Orleans, LA 70112
(504)593-1800 **Fax:** (504)593-1810
Ultimate Parent: New York Life.

★ 70542 ★ **New York Life New Orleans General Office**
Western Agencies
639 Loyola Ave.
New Orleans, LA 70113
(504)569-0500 **Fax:** (504)569-0508
Officer: Marquis Jones, General Manager.
Ultimate Parent: New York Life.

★ 70543 ★ **Northrop Inc.**
1402 S. Jefferson Pky.
New Orleans, LA 70185
(504)821-9443
Ultimate Parent: Northrop Corp. **SIC:**
6512—Nonresidential Building Operators.

★ 70544 ★ **Northrop Inc.**
1111 S. Jefferson Davis Pky.
New Orleans, LA 70125
(504)482-2128
Ultimate Parent: Northrop Corp. **SIC:**
6411—Insurance Agents, Brokers &
Service.

★ 70545 ★ **Payless Shoesource**
4308 Magazine St.
New Orleans, LA 70115
(504)895-2303
Ultimate Parent: May Department Stores.
SIC: 5661—Shoe Stores.

★ 70546 ★ **Payless Shoesource**
2800 Jefferson Hwy.
New Orleans, LA 70121
(504)832-0656
Ultimate Parent: May Department Stores.
SIC: 5661—Shoe Stores.

★ 70547 ★ **Pennzoil Co.**
4739 River Rd.
New Orleans, LA 70121
(504)733-9039
Ultimate Parent: Pennzoil. **SIC:** 5172—
Petroleum Products Nec.

★ 70548 ★ **Pizza Hut**
9721 Jefferson Hwy.
New Orleans, LA 70123
(504)737-8517
Ultimate Parent: Pepsico. **SIC:** 5812—
Eating Places.

★ 70549 ★ **Radio Shack**
1100 Poydras St. 2900
New Orleans, LA 70163
Company Type: Division. **Ultimate Parent:**
Tandy Corp. **SIC:** 4812—Radiotelephone
Communications.

★ 70550 ★ **Radio Shack**
5700 Read Blvd.
New Orleans, LA 70127
(504)246-1995
Company Type: Division. **Ultimate Parent:**
Tandy Corp. **SIC:** 5065—Electronic Parts &
Equipment Nec.

★ 70551 ★ **Radio Shack**
6041 Woodland Hwy.
New Orleans, LA 70131
(504)391-9491
Company Type: Division. **Ultimate Parent:**
Tandy Corp. **SIC:** 5063—Electrical
Apparatus & Equipment.

★ 70552 ★ **RJ Reynolds Tobacco Co. Inc.**
660 Distributors Row
New Orleans, LA 70123
(504)733-1317
Ultimate Parent: RJR Nabisco Holdings.
SIC: 5194—Tobacco & Tobacco Products.

★ 70553 ★ **Ryder Truck Rental**
2929 Earhart Blvd.
New Orleans, LA 70125
(504)525-1597
Ultimate Parent: Ryder System. **SIC:**
7359—Equipment Rental & Leasing Nec.

★ 70554 ★ **Ryder Truck Rental**
4904 Jefferson Hwy.
New Orleans, LA 70121
(504)733-2660
Ultimate Parent: Ryder System. **SIC:**
7359—Equipment Rental & Leasing Nec.

★ 70555 ★ **Shell Oil Co.**
1 Shelly Sq.
New Orleans, LA 70139
(504)588-6161
Ultimate Parent: Shell Oil Co. **SIC:** 1311—
Crude Petroleum & Natural Gas.

★ 70556 ★ **Shell Pipeline Corp.**
701 Shell Sq. 1
New Orleans, LA 70139
(504)588-4822
Ultimate Parent: Shell Oil Co. **SIC:** 4619—
Pipelines Nec.

★ 70557 ★ **Shell Pipeline Corp. (Ofc)**
701 Shell Sq. 1
New Orleans, LA 70139
(504)588-4822
Ultimate Parent: Shell Oil Co. **SIC:** 4619—
Pipelines Nec.

★ 70558 ★ **Shell Service Station**
500 N. Rampart St.
New Orleans, LA 70112
(504)522-5774
Ultimate Parent: Shell Oil Co. **SIC:** 5541—
Gasoline Service Stations.

★ 70559 ★ **Solar Turbines Inc.**
6128 Jefferson Hwy.
New Orleans, LA 70123
(504)734-8076
Ultimate Parent: Carter-Wallace. **SIC:**
5074—Plumbing & Hydronic Heating
Supplies.

★ 70560 ★ **Super Saver**
4655 Michoud Blvd.
New Orleans, LA 70129
(504)254-2244
Ultimate Parent: Wal-Mart Stores, Inc. **SIC:**
5411—Grocery Stores.

★ 70561 ★ **Superior Coffee & Foods**
3918 Gravier St.
New Orleans, LA 70119
(504)486-5976
Company Type: Division. **Location Type:**
Facility. **Ultimate Parent:** Sara Lee Corp.

★ 70562 ★ **Supreme Sugar Co.**
320 One New Orleans Shell Sq.
New Orleans, LA 70126
(504)522-4176
Officer: Robert J. Conlin, President.
Ultimate Parent: Archer Daniels Midland
Co. **SIC:** 2062—Cane Sugar Refining.

★ 70563 ★ **Supreme Sugar Co. Inc.**
3201 New Orleans Shell Sq.
New Orleans, LA 70126
(504)831-0901 **Fax:** (504)831-0909
Company Type: Subsidiary. **Officer:**
Robert J. Conlin, President. **Ultimate
Parent:** Archer Daniels Midland Co.

★ 70564 ★ **Supreme Sugar Co., Inc.**
PO Box 56009
New Orleans, LA 70156-6009
(504)831-0901
Location Type: Branch office. **Officer:**
Robert J. Conlin. **Ultimate Parent:** Archer
Daniels Midland Co. **SIC:** 2062—Cane
Sugar Refining.

★ 70565 ★ **Taco Bell**
1117 S. Clearview Pky.
New Orleans, LA 70121
(504)733-4428
Ultimate Parent: Pepsico. **SIC:** 5812—
Eating Places.

★ 70566 ★ **Tesoro Petroleum Distribution**
6100 Humphreys St.
New Orleans, LA 70123
(504)733-6700
Ultimate Parent: Tesoro Petroleum Corp.
SIC: 2911—Petroleum Refining; 5172—
Petroleum Products Nec.

★ 70567 ★ **Texaco Corporate Library**
PO Box 60252
New Orleans, LA 70160
(504)595-1287
Ultimate Parent: Texaco.

★ 70568 ★ **Texaco Gas Sta**
1700 Hickory Ave.
New Orleans, LA 70123
(504)738-3962
Ultimate Parent: Texaco. **SIC:** 5541—
Gasoline Service Stations.

★ 70569 ★ **Texaco Self-Serve**
9320 Jefferson Hwy.
New Orleans, LA 70123
(504)738-9923
Ultimate Parent: Texaco. **SIC:** 5541—
Gasoline Service Stations.

★ 70570 ★ **Texaco Self Serve**
4740 Canal St.
New Orleans, LA 70119
(504)488-5205
Ultimate Parent: Texaco. **SIC:** 5172—
Petroleum Products Nec.

★ 70571 ★ **Texaco Self Serve**
2200 Gen De Gaulle Dr.
New Orleans, LA 70114
(504)367-8173
Ultimate Parent: Texaco. **SIC:** 5541—
Gasoline Service Stations.

★ 70572 ★ **Texaco Self Service**
3054 General Degaulle Dr.
New Orleans, LA 70114
(504)361-0362
Ultimate Parent: Texaco. **SIC:** 5541—
Gasoline Service Stations.

★ 70573 ★ **Textron Marine Sys. Shipyard Ops.**
19401 Chef Menteur Hwy.
New Orleans, LA 70129
Ultimate Parent: Textron. **SIC:** 3731—Ship
Building & Repairing.

★ 70574 ★ **Textron Marine Systems/Bell Halter Inc. Shipyard**
19401 Chef Menteur Hwy.
New Orleans, LA 70129-9602
Ultimate Parent: Textron. **SIC:** 3731—Ship
Building & Repairing.

★ 70575 ★ **Textron Marine Systems Shipyard Operations**
19401 Chef Menteur Hwy.
New Orleans, LA 70129
Ultimate Parent: Textron. **SIC:** 3731—Ship
Building & Repairing.

★ 70576 ★ **Total Petroleum Inc.**
2505 David Dr.
New Orleans, LA 70119
(504)454-6064
Ultimate Parent: Total Petroleum Inc. **SIC:**
5541—Gasoline Service Stations.

★ 70577 ★ **Total Petroleum Inc.**
2505 David Dr.
New Orleans, LA 70119
(504)454-6064
Ultimate Parent: Total Petroleum Inc. **SIC:**
5541—Gasoline Service Stations.

★ 70578 ★ **Trailways Bus System**
1314 Tulane Ave.
New Orleans, LA 70112
(504)522-9701
Ultimate Parent: Greyhound Lines Inc. **SIC:**
4111—Local & Suburban Transit.

★ 70579 ★ **Trailways Southern Lines in**
1314 Tulane Ave.
New Orleans, LA 70112
(504)525-4201
Ultimate Parent: Greyhound Lines Inc. **SIC:**
4111—Local & Suburban Transit.

★ 70580 ★ **Transco Exploration Co.**
935 Gravier St.
New Orleans, LA 70112
(504)524-4784
Ultimate Parent: Transco Energy Co. **SIC:**
1382—Oil & Gas Exploration Services.

★ 70581 ★ **Trinity Industries**
Equitable Div.
4325 France Rd.
New Orleans, LA 70126
Company Type: Division. **Ultimate Parent:**
Trinity Industries. **SIC:** 3731—Ship Building
& Repairing.

★ 70582 ★ **United Parcel Service**
151 Brookhollow Esplanad
New Orleans, LA 70123
(504)733-7250
Ultimate Parent: United Parcel Service of
America. **SIC:** 4212—Local Trucking
Without Storage; 4215—Courier Services
Except by Air.

★ 70583 ★ **Valspar Corp.**
150 Plauche St.
New Orleans, LA 70123
(504)733-1110
Ultimate Parent: Valspar Corp. **SIC:**
2851—Paints & Allied Products; 3479—
Metal Coating & Allied Services; 5499—
Miscellaneous Food Stores.

★ 70584 ★ **Van Waters & Rogers Inc.**
5729 Salmen St.
New Orleans, LA 70123
(504)733-8885
Ultimate Parent: Univar Corp. **SIC:** 2879—
Agricultural Chemicals Nec.

★ 70585 ★　**Walgreen Drug Stores**
Plaza Lake Forest
New Orleans, LA 70127
(504)246-5756
Ultimate Parent: Walgreen Co. **SIC:**
5912—Drug Stores & Proprietary Stores.

★ 70586 ★　**Walgreen Drug Stores**
900 Canal St.
New Orleans, LA 70112
(504)523-3875
Ultimate Parent: Walgreen Co. **SIC:**
5912—Drug Stores & Proprietary Stores.

★ 70587 ★　**Walgreen Drug Stores**
3311 Canal St.
New Orleans, LA 70119
(504)486-7493
Ultimate Parent: Walgreen Co. **SIC:**
5912—Drug Stores & Proprietary Stores.

★ 70588 ★　**Walgreen Drug Stores**
4001 General Degaulle Dr. F
New Orleans, LA 70114
(504)366-5756
Ultimate Parent: Walgreen Co. **SIC:**
5912—Drug Stores & Proprietary Stores.

★ 70589 ★　**Wemco Inc.**
966 S. White St.
New Orleans, LA 70125
(504)822-3700
Officer: Arthur C. Pulitzer, President.
Ultimate Parent: Baker Hughes. **SIC:**
2321—Men's/Boys' Shirts; 2323—
Men's/Boys' Neckwear; 2325—Men's/Boys'
Trousers & Slacks.

★ 70590 ★　**Witco Corp.**
1320 Sams Ave.
New Orleans, LA 70123
(504)733-7777
Officer: Leo Waasdorp, Manager. **Ultimate
Parent:** Witco Corp. **SIC:** 2843—Surface
Active Agents.

★ 70591 ★　**Xerox Business
Services**
5700 Citrus Blvd., No. E
New Orleans, LA 70123
(504)733-0111
Officer: Earl Gaspard, Manager. **Ultimate
Parent:** Xerox Corp. **SIC:** 2759—
Commercial Printing Nec.

Norco

★ 70592 ★　**Shell Oil Co.**
Airline Hwy.
Norco, LA 70079
(504)764-0804
Ultimate Parent: Shell Oil Co. **SIC:** 2999—
Petroleum & Coal Products Nec.

★ 70593 ★　**Shell Oil Co.**
Norco Manufacturing Complex
1205 River Rd.
Norco, LA 70079
Ultimate Parent: Shell Oil Co. **SIC:** 2911—
Petroleum Refining; 2869—Industrial
Organic Chemicals Nec.

★ 70594 ★　**Shell Oil Co.**
Norco Manufacturing Complex
265 River Rd.
Norco, LA 70079
Ultimate Parent: Shell Oil Co. **SIC:** 2869—
Industrial Organic Chemicals Nec; 2819—
Industrial Inorganic Chemicals Nec.

★ 70595 ★　**Shell Oil Co.**
Norco Manufacturing Complex
1205 River Rd.
Norco, LA 70079
Ultimate Parent: Shell Oil Co. **SIC:** 2911—
Petroleum Refining; 2869—Industrial
Organic Chemicals Nec; 2819—Industrial
Inorganic Chemicals Nec.

★ 70596 ★　**Shell Oil Co.**
Norco Manufacturing Complex
1205 River Rd.
Norco, LA 70079
Ultimate Parent: Shell Oil Co. **SIC:** 2800—
Chemicals & Allied Products; 2819—
Industrial Inorganic Chemicals Nec; 2869—
Industrial Organic Chemicals Nec; 2911—
Petroleum Refining.

Oakdale

★ 70597 ★　**Boise Cascade Corp.**
Hwy. 165 S
Oakdale, LA 71463
(318)335-1500
Officer: Jim Amos, Manager. **Ultimate
Parent:** Boise Cascade. **SIC:** 2421—
Sawmills & Planing Mills—General; 2435—
Hardwood Veneer & Plywood; 2436—
Softwood Veneer & Plywood.

★ 70598 ★　**Oakdale Plywood
Plant**
Hwy. 165 South
Oakdale, LA 71463
Ultimate Parent: Boise Cascade. **SIC:**
2436—Softwood Veneer & Plywood.

★ 70599 ★　**Piggly Wiggly**
325 Fisher St.
Oakdale, LA 71463
(318)335-2872
Ultimate Parent: Bruno's. **SIC:** 5421—Meat
& Fish Markets.

★ 70600 ★　**Pizza Hut**
Hwy. 165
Oakdale, LA 71463
(318)335-0345
Ultimate Parent: Pepsico. **SIC:** 5812—
Eating Places.

★ 70601 ★　**Trailways Bus System**
113 N. 10th St.
Oakdale, LA 71463
(318)335-0778
Ultimate Parent: Greyhound Lines Inc. **SIC:**
4131—Intercity & Rural Bus Transportation.

Oberlin

★ 70602 ★　**Coast to Coast Home
& Auto**
725 6th Ave.
Oberlin, LA 70655
(318)639-2335
Ultimate Parent: Servistar Corp. **SIC:**
5531—Automobile & Home Supply Stores.

Opelousas

★ 70603 ★　**Trailways Bus System**
149 E. South St.
Opelousas, LA 70570
(318)942-2706
Ultimate Parent: Greyhound Lines Inc. **SIC:**
4131—Intercity & Rural Bus Transportation.

★ 70604 ★　**United Parcel Service**
N Hwy. 167
Opelousas, LA 70570
(318)452-8880
Ultimate Parent: United Parcel Service of
America. **SIC:** 4215—Courier Services
Except by Air.

★ 70605 ★　**Wal Mart Tire, Battery,
& Auto Ctr**
1432 Heather Dr.
Opelousas, LA 70570
(318)942-1499
Ultimate Parent: Wal-Mart Stores, Inc. **SIC:**
7538—General Automotive Repair Shops.

Paincourtville

★ 70606 ★　**Dow Chemical Co.
Grand Bayou Plant**
Louisiana Hwy. 70 PO Drawer N
Paincourtville, LA 70391
Ultimate Parent: Dow Chemical Co. USA.
SIC: 2869—Industrial Organic Chemicals
Nec.

★ 70607 ★　**Dow Chemical Co.
Grand Bayou Plant**
Hwy. 70
Paincourtville, LA 70391
Ultimate Parent: Dow Chemical Co. USA.
SIC: 2812—Alkalies & Chlorine.

★ 70608 ★　**Dow Chemical Grand
Bayou Plant**
La. Hwy. 70, PO Drawer N
Paincourtville, LA 70391
Ultimate Parent: Dow Chemical Co. USA.
SIC: 2869—Industrial Organic Chemicals
Nec.

Paradis

★ 70609 ★　**Texaco Inc.**
Warehouse
Paradis, LA 70080
(504)758-7508
Ultimate Parent: Texaco. **SIC:** 5172—
Petroleum Products Nec.

★ 70610 ★　**Texaco Inc.**
Paradis, LA 70080
(504)758-1394
Ultimate Parent: Texaco. **SIC:** 1382—Oil &
Gas Exploration Services.

Patterson

★ 70611 ★　**Hertz Rent-A-Car**
Hwy. 182
Patterson, LA 70392
(504)395-9506
Ultimate Parent: Hertz. **SIC:** 7622—Radio
& T.V. Repair.

★ 70612 ★　**Pizza Hut**
New Us 90 W
Patterson, LA 70392
(504)395-9234
Ultimate Parent: Pepsico. **SIC:** 5812—
Eating Places.

★ 70613 ★　**Radio Shack**
New Us 90 W
Patterson, LA 70392
(504)395-2302
Company Type: Division. **Ultimate Parent:**
Tandy Corp. **SIC:** 5065—Electronic Parts &
Equipment Nec.

Pearl River

★ 70614 ★　**Ace Hardware**
94 PO Box
Pearl River, LA 70452
(504)863-5385
Ultimate Parent: Ace Hardware. **SIC:**
5251—Hardware Stores; 9131—Executive
and Legislative Combined.

Pineville

★ 70615 ★　**Dolphin Construction
Co.**
632 Paradise Rd.
Pineville, LA 71360
(318)442-1380
Ultimate Parent: Texas Industries.

★ 70616 ★　**Hibernia National
Bank**
2730 La Hwy. 28 E
Pineville, LA 71360
(318)487-2155
Ultimate Parent: Hibernia Corp. **SIC:**
6099—Functions Related to Deposit
Banking.

★ 70617 ★　**Hibernia National
Bank**
708 Main St.
Pineville, LA 71360
(318)487-2140
Ultimate Parent: Hibernia Corp. **SIC:**
6099—Functions Related to Deposit
Banking.

★ 70618 ★　**International Paper
Co. Pineville Mill**
Williams Lake Rd.
Pineville, LA 71361-5870
Ultimate Parent: International Paper Co.
SIC: 2631—Paperboard Mills; 2621—Paper
Mills.

★ 70619 ★　**International Paper
Pineville Mill**
300 Williams Lake Rd.
Pineville, LA 71361-5870
Ultimate Parent: International Paper Co.
SIC: 2631—Paperboard Mills; 2621—Paper
Mills.

★ 70620 ★　**International Paper
Pineville Mill**
Williams Lake Rd.
Pineville, LA 71361-5870
Ultimate Parent: International Paper Co.
SIC: 2631—Paperboard Mills; 2621—Paper
Mills.

★ 70621 ★　**Kentucky Fried
Chicken**
2753 Holloway Rd.
Pineville, LA 71360
(318)445-9499
Ultimate Parent: Pepsico. **SIC:** 5812—
Eating Places.

★ 70622 ★　**Kroger Food Store**
1638 Military Hwy.
Pineville, LA 71360
(318)448-1110
Ultimate Parent: Kroger. **SIC:** 6411—
Insurance Agents, Brokers & Service.

★ 70623 ★　**Mary Kay Cosmetics**
108 Iris Cir.
Pineville, LA 71360
(318)640-0724
Ultimate Parent: Mary Kay Cosmetics. **SIC:**
5999—Miscellaneous Retail Stores Nec.

★ 70624 ★　**Pepsi-Cola Seven-Up
Bottling**
101 Cenla Dr.
Pineville, LA 71360
(318)640-8700
Officer: Moe LeBlanc, Manager. **Ultimate
Parent:** Pepsico. **SIC:** 2086—Bottled &
Canned Soft Drinks.

★ 70625 ★　**Procter & Gamble
Mfg. Co.**
3701 Monroe Hwy.
Pineville, LA 71360
Ultimate Parent: Procter & Gamble Co.
SIC: 2841—Soap & Other Detergents.

★ 70626 ★　**Procter & Gamble
Mfg. Co. Co.**
3701 Monroe Hwy.
Pineville, LA 71360
Ultimate Parent: Procter & Gamble Co.
SIC: 2841—Soap & Other Detergents.

★ 70627 ★　**Radio Shack**
Edgewood Plaza Ctr.
Pineville, LA 71360
(318)442-4574
Company Type: Division. **Ultimate Parent:**
Tandy Corp. **SIC:** 5734—Computer &
Software Stores.

★ 70628 ★　**Rapides Bank & Trust
Co.**
3099 Holloway Rd.
Pineville, LA 71360
(318)487-2600
Ultimate Parent: First Commerce Corp.
SIC: 6099—Functions Related to Deposit
Banking.

★ 70629 ★　**Rapides Bank & Trust
Co.**
725 Main St.
Pineville, LA 71360
(318)487-2460
Ultimate Parent: First Commerce Corp.
SIC: 6099—Functions Related to Deposit
Banking.

★ 70630 ★　**Rapides Bank & Trust
Co.**
2951 Holloway Rd.
Pineville, LA 71360
(318)473-6940
Ultimate Parent: First Commerce Corp.
SIC: 6022—State Commercial Banks.

★ 70631 ★　**Safety Kleen Corp.**
4200 Shreveport Hwy.
Pineville, LA 71360
(318)640-2747
Ultimate Parent: Safety-Kleen. **SIC:** 5013—
Motor Vehicle Supplies & New Parts.

★ 70632 ★　**Taco Bell**
165 Monroe St.
Pineville, LA 71360
(318)640-3480
Ultimate Parent: Pepsico. **SIC:** 5812—
Eating Places.

Plaquemine

★ 70633 ★ Dow Chemical Co.
Louisiana Division
PO Box 150
Plaquemine, LA 70764
(504)389-8000
Company Type: Division. **Officer:** R. W.
Gallant, General Manager. **Ultimate Parent:**
Dow Chemical Co. USA. **SIC:** 2821—
Plastics Materials & Resins. **Employee
Count:** 2500.

Plain Dealing

**★ 70634 ★ Coast to Coast
Engineering**
104 Walnut Ave. W
Plain Dealing, LA 71064
(318)326-4228
Ultimate Parent: Servistar Corp. **SIC:**
3645—Residential Lighting Fixtures.

**★ 70635 ★ Whispering Pines
Nursing Home**
Plain Dealing, LA 71064
(318)326-4259
Ultimate Parent: Beverly Enterprises. **SIC:**
8051—Skilled Nursing Care Facilities.

Plaquemine

**★ 70636 ★ Ashland Chemical
Inc.**
Hwy. 405 River Rd.
Plaquemine, LA 70764
(504)687-6311
Officer: David E. Drummond, Manager.
Ultimate Parent: Ashland Oil. **SIC:** 2899—
Chemical Preparations Nec.

★ 70637 ★ Dow Chemical Co.
Louisiana Div.
Hwy. 1 S. PO Box 150
Plaquemine, LA 70765-0150
Company Type: Division. **Ultimate Parent:**
Dow Chemical Co. USA. **SIC:** 2812—
Alkalies & Chlorine; 2821—Plastics
Materials & Resins; 2869—Industrial
Organic Chemicals Nec.

★ 70638 ★ Exxon Express
1703 Hwy. 1 S
Plaquemine, LA 70764
(504)687-0999
Ultimate Parent: Exxon. **SIC:** 5541—
Gasoline Service Stations.

★ 70639 ★ Georgia Gulf Corp.
26100 River Rd.
Plaquemine, LA 70764
(504)685-2500
Officer: Edward A. Schmitt, Manager.
Ultimate Parent: Georgia Gulf. **SIC:** 2812—
Alkalies & Chlorine; 2821—Plastics
Materials & Resins; 2869—Industrial
Organic Chemicals Nec.

★ 70640 ★ Georgia Gulf Corp.
Evergreen Rd.
Plaquemine, LA 70764
(504)685-1200
Officer: J.R. Satrum, Chairman. **Ultimate
Parent:** Georgia Gulf. **SIC:** 2821—Plastics
Materials & Resins.

★ 70641 ★ Piggly Wiggly
1917 Hwy. 1 S
Plaquemine, LA 70764
(504)687-0822
Ultimate Parent: Bruno's. **SIC:** 5411—
Grocery Stores.

★ 70642 ★ Pizza Hut
1605 Hwy. 1 S
Plaquemine, LA 70764
(504)687-3321
Ultimate Parent: Pepsico. **SIC:** 5812—
Eating Places.

★ 70643 ★ Texaco Dist
1400 Osage Ave.
Plaquemine, LA 70764
(504)687-7383
Ultimate Parent: Texaco.

**★ 70644 ★ Wal Mart Discount
City**
919 Belleview Dr.
Plaquemine, LA 70764
(504)687-2550
Ultimate Parent: Wal-Mart Stores, Inc. **SIC:**
5311—Department Stores.

Plaucheville

**★ 70645 ★ Mini Mart Shopping
Center**
Dupont
Plaucheville, LA 71362
(318)922-3820
Ultimate Parent: Kroger. **SIC:** 5411—
Grocery Stores.

Pollock

**★ 70646 ★ Farmland Industries
Inc. Pollock Nitrogen Plant**
Abe Hall Rd.
Pollock, LA 71467
Ultimate Parent: Farmland Industries. **SIC:**
2873—Nitrogenous Fertilizers.

Ponchatoula

★ 70647 ★ Greyhound Bus Lines
190 NE Railroad Ave.
Ponchatoula, LA 70454
(504)386-6598
Ultimate Parent: Greyhound Lines Inc. **SIC:**
4111—Local & Suburban Transit.

Port Allen

★ 70648 ★ Ryder Truck Rental
1150 Le Blanc Rd.
Port Allen, LA 70767
(504)381-9069
Ultimate Parent: Ryder System. **SIC:**
7513—Truck Rental & Leasing Without
Drivers.

★ 70649 ★ Texaco Self Serv
650 S. Alexander Ave.
Port Allen, LA 70767
(504)383-7721
Ultimate Parent: Texaco. **SIC:** 5541—
Gasoline Service Stations.

★ 70650 ★ Wal Mart
2808 Court St.
Port Allen, LA 70767
(504)336-4061
Ultimate Parent: Wal-Mart Stores, Inc. **SIC:**
5311—Department Stores.

Prairieville

★ 70651 ★ Shaw Industries Inc.
36445 Perkins Rd.
Prairieville, LA 70769
(504)344-4307
Officer: Terry Braud, Manager. **Ultimate
Parent:** Shaw Industries, Inc. **SIC:** 3498—
Fabricated Pipe & Fittings.

Raceland

★ 70652 ★ Exxon Pipeline Co.
Raceland, LA 70394
(504)537-5211
Ultimate Parent: Exxon. **SIC:** 4612—Crude
Petroleum Pipelines.

**★ 70653 ★ Exxon Pipeline Co.
Inc.**
Raceland, LA 70394
(504)537-5211
Ultimate Parent: Exxon Pipeline. **SIC:**
4612—Crude Petroleum Pipelines.

★ 70654 ★ Pizza Hut
Hwy. 1
Raceland, LA 70394
(504)537-3292
Ultimate Parent: Pepsico. **SIC:** 5812—
Eating Places.

★ 70655 ★ Raceland Sugars Inc.
Hwy. 3199 E.
Raceland, LA 70394
Ultimate Parent: Savannah Foods &
Industries, Inc. **SIC:** 2061—Raw Cane
Sugar.

Rayne

**★ 70656 ★ Greyhound Bus Lines
E**
201 E. Texas Ave.
Rayne, LA 70578
(318)334-3507
Ultimate Parent: Greyhound Lines Inc. **SIC:**
4131—Intercity & Rural Bus Transportation.

★ 70657 ★ Plastics Inc.
E Hwy. 90
Rayne, LA 70578
(318)334-9601
Ultimate Parent: Newell. **SIC:** 3089—
Plastics Products Nec.

Rayville

★ 70658 ★ Radio Shack
1207 S. Louisa St.
Rayville, LA 71269
(318)728-5267
Company Type: Division. **Ultimate Parent:**
Tandy Corp. **SIC:** 5065—Electronic Parts &
Equipment Nec.

★ 70659 ★ Trailways Inc.
212 N. Benedette St.
Rayville, LA 71269
(318)728-4125
Ultimate Parent: Greyhound Lines Inc. **SIC:**
4131—Intercity & Rural Bus Transportation;
4131—Intercity & Rural Bus Transportation.

Reserve

★ 70660 ★ Betz Laboratories Inc.
500 Rosenwald St.
Reserve, LA 70084
Ultimate Parent: Betz Laboratories Inc.
SIC: 2899—Chemical Preparations Nec.

**★ 70661 ★ Hibernia National
Bank**
River Rd.
Reserve, LA 70084
(504)536-1189
Ultimate Parent: Hibernia Corp. **SIC:**
6099—Functions Related to Deposit
Banking.

**★ 70662 ★ Illinois Central
Railroad**
Railroad Ave.
Reserve, LA 70084
(504)536-3255
Ultimate Parent: Illinois Central
SIC: 4011—Railroads Line-Haul Operating.

★ 70663 ★ Rhone-Poulenc
430 NW 19th St.
Reserve, LA 70084
Ultimate Parent: Rhone-Poulenc Rorer.
SIC: 2843—Surface Active Agents.

★ 70664 ★ Shell Chemical Co.
Reserve Plant
430 NW 19th St.
Reserve, LA 70084
Location Type: Plant. **Ultimate Parent:**
Shell Oil Co. **SIC:** 2843—Surface Active
Agents.

Ringgold

★ 70665 ★ Piggly Wiggly
Ringgold, LA 71068
(318)894-9184
Ultimate Parent: Bruno's. **SIC:** 5421—Meat
& Fish Markets.

★ 70666 ★ Wilsons
Ringgold, LA 71068
(318)894-9733
Ultimate Parent: Melville. **SIC:** 5921—
Liquor Stores.

★ 70667 ★ Wilsons
Ringgold, LA 71068
(318)894-9733
Ultimate Parent: Melville. **SIC:** 5921—
Liquor Stores.

Robeline

★ 70668 ★ Mary Kay Cosmetics
Kings Hwy.
Robeline, LA 71469
(318)472-6926
Ultimate Parent: Mary Kay Cosmetics. **SIC:**
5999—Miscellaneous Retail Stores Nec.

Ruston

**★ 70669 ★ Kentucky Fried
Chicken**
211 W. California Ave.
Ruston, LA 71270
(318)255-8867
Ultimate Parent: Pepsico. **SIC:** 5812—
Eating Places.

★ 70670 ★ Piggly Wiggly
300 N. Bonner St.
Ruston, LA 71270
(318)255-1792
Ultimate Parent: Bruno's. **SIC:** 5411—
Grocery Stores.

★ 70671 ★ Pizza Hut
1101 N. Trenton St.
Ruston, LA 71270
(318)251-0424
Ultimate Parent: Pepsico. **SIC:** 5812—
Eating Places.

★ 70672 ★ Sico Inc.
Riser Rd.
Ruston, LA 71270
(318)255-2991
Ultimate Parent: American Life. **SIC:**
1521—Single-Family Housing Construction.

★ 70673 ★ Sico Inc.
788 PO Box
Ruston, LA 71273
(318)255-2991
Ultimate Parent: American Life.

★ 70674 ★ Trailways Bus System
118 W. Louisiana Ave.
Ruston, LA 71270
(318)255-3505
Ultimate Parent: Greyhound Lines Inc.

**★ 70675 ★ Wal Mart Discount
Cities**
N Park Shopping Ctr.
Ruston, LA 71270
(318)255-7855
Ultimate Parent: Wal-Mart Stores, Inc. **SIC:**
5311—Department Stores.

**★ 70676 ★ Willamette Industries
Inc.**
Ruston
2301 Mcdonald
Ruston, LA 71270
Ultimate Parent: Willamette Industries, Inc.
SIC: 2436—Softwood Veneer & Plywood.

**★ 70677 ★ Willamette Industries
Inc.**
Ruston
East Mcdonald Ave.
Ruston, LA 71270
Ultimate Parent: Willamette Industries, Inc.
SIC: 2436—Softwood Veneer & Plywood.

Scott

★ 70678 ★ Solar Turbines Inc.
Hwy. 93
Scott, LA 70583
(318)981-7114
Ultimate Parent: Carter-Wallace. **SIC:**
3724—Aircraft Engines & Engine Parts.

Shreveport

★ 70679 ★ Ace Hardware
9830 Mansfield Rd.
Shreveport, LA 71118
(318)686-2755
Ultimate Parent: Ace Hardware. **SIC:**
5251—Hardware Stores.

**★ 70680 ★ Airborne Freight
Corp.**
Shreveport, LA 71108
(318)631-0637
Ultimate Parent: Airborne Freight Corp.
SIC: 4512—Air Transportation—Scheduled.

★ 70681 ★ Amerada Hess Corp.
425 Edwards St.
Shreveport, LA 71101
(318)425-1629
Ultimate Parent: Amerada Hess. **SIC:**
5171—Petroleum Bulk Stations & Terminals.

★ 70682 ★   American General Finance
2530 Bert Kouns Industrial Loop
Shreveport, LA 71118-3153
(318)687-1411
Officer: Kathy Guin. Ultimate Parent: American General Corp. SIC: 6141—Personal Credit Institutions; 6162—Mortgage Bankers & Correspondents.

★ 70683 ★   American General Finance Inc.
6715 Pines Rd., Ste. 107
Shreveport, LA 71129-5203
(318)688-6294
Location Type: Branch office. Officer: Dennis Beck. Ultimate Parent: American General Corp. SIC: 6141—Personal Credit Institutions; 6162—Mortgage Bankers & Correspondents.

★ 70684 ★   American General Finance Inc.
1409 E. 70th St., Ste. 123
Shreveport, LA 71105-4942
(318)797-3018
Location Type: Branch office. Officer: Robert E. Tillman. Ultimate Parent: American General Corp. SIC: 6141—Personal Credit Institutions; 6162—Mortgage Bankers & Correspondents.

★ 70685 ★   American General Finance Inc.
1020 Shreveport Barksdale Hwy.
Shreveport, LA 71105-2304
(318)869-1201
Location Type: Branch office. Officer: Bill Asseff. Ultimate Parent: American General Corp. SIC: 6141—Personal Credit Institutions; 6162—Mortgage Bankers & Correspondents.

★ 70686 ★   American General Finance Inc.
2530 Bert Kouns Industrial Loop
Shreveport, LA 71118
(318)687-1411
Location Type: Branch office. Officer: Kathy Guin. Ultimate Parent: American General Corp. SIC: 6141—Personal Credit Institutions; 6162—Mortgage Bankers & Correspondents.

★ 70687 ★   American General Finance Inc.
6715 Pines Rd., Ste. 107
Shreveport, LA 71129-5203
(318)688-6294
Location Type: Branch office. Officer: Dennis Beck. Ultimate Parent: American General Corp. SIC: 6141—Personal Credit Institutions; 6162—Mortgage Bankers & Correspondents.

★ 70688 ★   American General Finance Inc.
1020 Shreveport Barksdale Hwy.
Shreveport, LA 71105-2304
(318)869-1201
Location Type: Branch office. Officer: Bill Asseff. Ultimate Parent: American General Corp. SIC: 6141—Personal Credit Institutions; 6162—Mortgage Bankers & Correspondents.

★ 70689 ★   American General Finance Inc.
1409 E. 70th St., Ste. 123
Shreveport, LA 71105-4942
(318)797-3018
Location Type: Branch office. Officer: Robert E. Tillman. Ultimate Parent: American General Corp. SIC: 6141—Personal Credit Institutions; 6162—Mortgage Bankers & Correspondents.

★ 70690 ★   Atlas Processing Co.
3333 Midway St.
Shreveport, LA 71109
Ultimate Parent: Pennzoil. SIC: 2911—Petroleum Refining.

★ 70691 ★   Beaird Industries
601 Benton Kelly Rd.
Shreveport, LA 71106
Ultimate Parent: Trinity Industries. SIC: 3443—Fabricated Plate Work—Boiler Shops.

★ 70692 ★   Borden Milk & Ice Cream
2520 Linwood Ave.
Shreveport, LA 71103
(318)425-7411
Officer: Bobby Bartley, Manager. Ultimate Parent: Borden, Inc. SIC: 2024—Ice Cream & Frozen Desserts.

★ 70693 ★   Burlington Air Express
5150 Interstate Dr.
Shreveport, LA 71109
(318)631-5670
Ultimate Parent: Pittston. SIC: 4513—Air Courier Services.

★ 70694 ★   Business Systems Inc.
1426 Hawn Ave.
Shreveport, LA 71107-6532
(318)424-9877
Officer: Chuck Dyer. Ultimate Parent: Avery Dennison Corp. SIC: 2761—Manifold Business Forms; 5112—Stationery & Office Supplies.

★ 70695 ★   Butler Paper Co.
222 W. 63rd St.
Shreveport, LA 71106-2641
(318)869-2021
Location Type: Branch office. Officer: David S. Jones, Manager. Ultimate Parent: Alco Standard Corp. SIC: 2679—Converted Paper Products Nec; 2621—Paper Mills.

★ 70696 ★   Casual Corner
8924 Jewella Ave.
Shreveport, LA 71118
(318)687-5100
Ultimate Parent: United States Shoe. SIC: 5651—Family Clothing Stores.

★ 70697 ★   Citgo Quick Mart
762 Pierremont Rd.
Shreveport, LA 71106
(318)865-1464
Ultimate Parent: Citgo Petroleum. SIC: 5411—Grocery Stores; 5541—Gasoline Service Stations.

★ 70698 ★   Coca Cola Bottling Co.
305 Stoner Ave.
Shreveport, LA 71101
(318)222-8661
Ultimate Parent: Coca-Cola Enterprises. SIC: 5093—Scrap & Waste Materials.

★ 70699 ★   Coca-Cola Bottling Co. of Sherveport
305 Stoner Ave.
Shreveport, LA 71101
Ultimate Parent: Coca-Cola Bottling Consol. SIC: 2086—Bottled & Canned Soft Drinks.

★ 70700 ★   Commercial National Bank
Commercial National Tower, 333 Texas St.
Shreveport, LA 71130
(318)429-1000 Fax: (318)429-1130 Telex: 50-7411
Company Type: Subsidiary. Officer: Steven C. Walker, Pres & CEO. Ultimate Parent: Deposit Guaranty Corp. SIC: 6022—State Commercial Banks. Employee Count: 500.

★ 70701 ★   Commercial National Bank in Shreveport
320 Milam St.
Shreveport, LA 71101-3644
(318)429-1580
Company Type: Subsidiary. Location Type: Branch office. Officer: Shelby Ellzey, Mgr. Ultimate Parent: Deposit Guaranty Corp. SIC: 6021—National Commercial Banks.

★ 70702 ★   Commercial National Bank in Shreveport
5824 Hearne Ave.
Shreveport, LA 71108-3890
(318)862-3440
Company Type: Subsidiary. Location Type: Branch office. Officer: Randy Robinson, Mgr. Ultimate Parent: Deposit Guaranty Corp. SIC: 6021—National Commercial Banks.

★ 70703 ★   Commercial National Bank in Shreveport
1263 Market St.
Shreveport, LA 71107-6692
(318)424-4954
Company Type: Subsidiary. Location Type: Branch office. Officer: Julie W. Thompson, Mgr. Ultimate Parent: Deposit Guaranty Corp. SIC: 6021—National Commercial Banks.

★ 70704 ★   Commercial National Bank in Shreveport
6800 Pines Rd.
Shreveport, LA 71129-2514
(318)683-3950
Company Type: Subsidiary. Location Type: Branch office. Officer: Andy Taylor, Mgr. Ultimate Parent: Deposit Guaranty Corp. SIC: 6021—National Commercial Banks.

★ 70705 ★   Commercial National Bank in Shreveport
4740 Line Ave.
Shreveport, LA 71106-1528
(318)869-4674
Company Type: Subsidiary. Location Type: Branch office. Officer: Paul E. Hutcheson, Mgr. Ultimate Parent: Deposit Guaranty Corp. SIC: 6021—National Commercial Banks.

★ 70706 ★   Commercial National Bank in Shreveport
1051 Shreveport-Barksdale Hwy.
Shreveport, LA 71105-2303
(318)862-3425
Company Type: Subsidiary. Location Type: Branch office. Officer: Charlotte Edwards, Mgr. Ultimate Parent: Deposit Guaranty Corp. SIC: 6021—National Commercial Banks.

★ 70707 ★   Commercial National Bank in Shreveport
3750 Youree Dr.
Shreveport, LA 71105-2139
(318)869-4656
Company Type: Subsidiary. Location Type: Branch office. Officer: Kerry Peterson, Mgr. Ultimate Parent: Deposit Guaranty Corp. SIC: 6021—National Commercial Banks.

★ 70708 ★   Commercial National Bank in Shreveport
2709 Mackey Ln.
Shreveport, LA 71118-2521
(318)688-1101
Company Type: Subsidiary. Location Type: Branch office. Officer: Andy V. Loftus III, Mgr. Ultimate Parent: Deposit Guaranty Corp. SIC: 6021—National Commercial Banks.

★ 70709 ★   Commercial National Bank in Shreveport
8655 Millicent Way
Shreveport, LA 71115-2227
(318)862-3430
Company Type: Subsidiary. Location Type: Branch office. Officer: Connie Merritt, Mgr. Ultimate Parent: Deposit Guaranty Corp. SIC: 6021—National Commercial Banks.

★ 70710 ★   Commercial National Bank in Shreveport
1751 Line Ave.
Shreveport, LA 71101-4633
(318)221-8100
Company Type: Subsidiary. Location Type: Branch office. Ultimate Parent: Deposit Guaranty Corp. SIC: 6021—National Commercial Banks.

★ 70711 ★   Commercial National Bank in Shreveport
333 Texas St.
PO Box 21119
Shreveport, LA 71152
(318)429-1000
Company Type: Subsidiary. Location Type: Branch office. Officer: Steven C. Walker, President & CEO. Ultimate Parent: Deposit Guaranty Corp. SIC: 6021—National Commercial Banks.

★ 70712 ★   Delta Air Lines
Shreveport
Shreveport, LA 71108
(318)631-1831
Ultimate Parent: Delta Air Lines, Inc. SIC: 4512—Air Transportation—Scheduled.

★ 70713 ★   Delta Air Lines
400 Texas St.
Shreveport, LA 71101
(318)424-6311
Ultimate Parent: Delta Air Lines, Inc. SIC: 4724—Travel Agencies.

★ 70714 ★   Delta Air Lines
Petrolem Tower
Shreveport, LA 71101
(318)221-3500
Ultimate Parent: Delta Air Lines, Inc. SIC: 4724—Travel Agencies.

★ 70715 ★   Delta Air Lines Inc.
400 Texas St.
Shreveport, LA 71101
(318)424-6311
Ultimate Parent: Delta Air Lines, Inc. SIC: 4724—Travel Agencies.

★ 70716 ★   Delta Air Lines Inc.
Shreveport
Shreveport, LA 71108
(318)631-1831
Ultimate Parent: Delta Air Lines, Inc. SIC: 4512—Air Transportation—Scheduled.

★ 70717 ★   Durr-Fillauer Medical Inc.
1255 N. Hearne Ave.
Shreveport, LA 71107
(318)222-3147
Ultimate Parent: Bergen Brunswig Corp. SIC: 5122—Drugs, Proprietaries & Sundries; 5912—Drug Stores & Proprietary Stores.

★ 70718 ★   Emery Worldwide
5147 Hollywood Ave.
Shreveport, LA 71109
(318)636-1336
Ultimate Parent: Consolidated Freightways. SIC: 4512—Air Transportation—Scheduled.

★ 70719 ★   Exxon
6701 Pines Rd.
Shreveport, LA 71129
(318)686-9400
Ultimate Parent: Exxon. SIC: 5541—Gasoline Service Stations.

★ 70720 ★   Exxon Shop
9000 Mansfield Rd.
Shreveport, LA 71118
(318)688-3103
Ultimate Parent: Exxon. SIC: 5411—Grocery Stores.

★ 70721 ★   Flight Systems Inc.
1400 Airport Dr.
Shreveport, LA 71107
(318)227-0347
Ultimate Parent: B.F. Goodrich. SIC: 5088—Transportation Equipment & Supplies.

★ 70722 ★   Fruehauf Trailer Corp.
2401 Grimmett Dr.
Shreveport, LA 71107-5227
(318)425-7747
Officer: Roy Meller. Ultimate Parent: Terex Corp. SIC: 5012—Automobiles & Other Motor Vehicles; 5013—Motor Vehicle Supplies & New Parts; 5561—Recreational Vehicle Dealers; 7539—Automotive Repair Shops Nec.

★ 70723 ★   General Electric Co.
7000 W. Bert Kouns Industrial Loop
Shreveport, LA 71129
(318)687-6600
Officer: Don J. Chaisson, Manager. Ultimate Parent: General Electric. SIC: 3612—Transformers Except Electronic; 3613—Switchgear & Switchboard Apparatus.

★ 70724 ★   General Electric Co.
7000 Bert Kouns Industrial Loop
Shreveport, LA 71129
Ultimate Parent: General Electric. SIC: 3612—Transformers Except Electronic.

★ 70725 ★   Hertz Rent-A-Car
Shreveport
Shreveport, LA 71108
(318)631-6710
Ultimate Parent: Hertz. SIC: 7514—Passenger Car Rental.

★ 70726 ★ Hibernia National
Bank
6161 Greenwood Rd.
Shreveport, LA 71119
(318)674-3909
Ultimate Parent: Hibernia Corp.

★ 70727 ★ Hibernia National
Bank
3715 Greenwood Rd.
Shreveport, LA 71109
Ultimate Parent: Hibernia Corp.

★ 70728 ★ Hibernia National
Bank
9181 Mansfield Rd.
Shreveport, LA 71118
(318)674-3907
Ultimate Parent: Hibernia Corp.

★ 70729 ★ Hibernia National
Bank
1201 Shreveport Barksdale Hwy.
Shreveport, LA 71105
(318)674-3905
Ultimate Parent: Hibernia Corp. SIC:
6022—State Commercial Banks.

★ 70730 ★ Hibernia National
Bank
5750 Youree Dr.
Shreveport, LA 71105
(318)869-0914
Ultimate Parent: Hibernia Corp. SIC:
6021—National Commercial Banks; 6022—
State Commercial Banks.

★ 70731 ★ Innovative Office
Systems
1610 N. Hearne Ave.
Shreveport, LA 71107
(318)424-4466
Officer: Al Skinner, Manager. Ultimate
Parent: Alco Standard Corp. SIC: 3663—
Radio & T.V. Communications Equipment.

★ 70732 ★ International Paper
Container Div.
1212 Tolmark Rd.
Shreveport, LA 71107
Company Type: Division. Ultimate Parent:
International Paper Co. SIC: 2671—Paper
Coated & Laminated—Packaging.

★ 70733 ★ James River Corp.
210 Kansas City Ave.
Shreveport, LA 71107
Ultimate Parent: James River Corp. of
Virginia. SIC: 2600—Paper & Allied
Products.

★ 70734 ★ Johnson Controls Inc.
5100 Interstate Cir.
Shreveport, LA 71109
(318)631-9110
Ultimate Parent: Johnson Controls Inc.
SIC: 1711—Plumbing, Heating & Air-
Conditioning.

★ 70735 ★ Johnson Controls Inc.
505 W. 67th St.
Shreveport, LA 71106
(318)869-1217
Ultimate Parent: Johnson Controls Inc.
SIC: 1711—Plumbing, Heating & Air-
Conditioning.

★ 70736 ★ Kay Bee Toy&Hobby
Shop
S Park Mall
Shreveport, LA 71118
(318)688-0583
Ultimate Parent: Melville. SIC: 5945—
Hobby, Toy & Game Shops.

★ 70737 ★ Kentucky Fried
Chicken
900 Shreveport Barksdale Hwy.
Shreveport, LA 71105
(318)868-9332
Ultimate Parent: Pepsico. SIC: 5812—
Eating Places.

★ 70738 ★ Kentucky Fried
Chicken
250 N. Freestate Blvd.
Shreveport, LA 71107
(318)221-2214
Ultimate Parent: Pepsico. SIC: 5812—
Eating Places; 5812—Eating Places.

★ 70739 ★ Kentucky Fried
Chicken
1801 N. Market St.
Shreveport, LA 71107
(318)226-0942
Ultimate Parent: Pepsico. SIC: 5812—
Eating Places.

★ 70740 ★ Kentucky Fried
Chicken
1616 Hollywood Ave.
Shreveport, LA 71108
(318)636-1290
Ultimate Parent: Pepsico. SIC: 5812—
Eating Places; 5812—Eating Places.

★ 70741 ★ Kentucky Fried
Chicken
9330 Mansfield Rd.
Shreveport, LA 71118
(318)686-8175
Ultimate Parent: Pepsico. SIC: 5812—
Eating Places.

★ 70742 ★ Kentucky Fried
Chicken
4001 Hearne Ave.
Shreveport, LA 71103
(318)636-6696
Ultimate Parent: Pepsico. SIC: 5812—
Eating Places.

★ 70743 ★ Kroger Super Market
6713 Pines Rd.
Shreveport, LA 71129
(318)688-2390
Ultimate Parent: Kroger. SIC: 5411—
Grocery Stores.

★ 70744 ★ Kroger Super Market
9155 Mansfield Rd.
Shreveport, LA 71118
(318)688-2010
Ultimate Parent: Kroger. SIC: 5411—
Grocery Stores.

★ 70745 ★ Kroger Super Markets
2729 W. 70th St.
Shreveport, LA 71108
(318)687-0473
Ultimate Parent: Kroger. SIC: 5411—
Grocery Stores.

★ 70746 ★ L M Berry & Co.
6425 Youree Dr., Ste. 240
Shreveport, LA 71105-4600
(318)687-7400
Officer: Bob Vaughn. Ultimate Parent:
BellSouth Corp. SIC: 7313—Radio, T.V. &
Publisher Representatives; 2759—
Commercial Printing Nec.

★ 70747 ★ Lane Bryant
3600 Mall St. N
Shreveport, LA 71104
(318)227-1904
Ultimate Parent: Limited. SIC: 5651—
Family Clothing Stores.

★ 70748 ★ Lerner Shop
8924 Jewella Ave.
Shreveport, LA 71118
(318)687-0313
Ultimate Parent: Limited. SIC: 5699—
Miscellaneous Apparel & Accessory Stores;
5651—Family Clothing Stores.

★ 70749 ★ Libbey Glass Co.
4302 Jewella Rd.
Shreveport, LA 71109
Ultimate Parent: Owens-Illinois. SIC:
3229—Pressed & Blown Glass Nec.

★ 70750 ★ The Limited
8924 Jewella Ave.
Shreveport, LA 71118
(318)688-2910
Ultimate Parent: Limited. SIC: 5621—
Women's Clothing Stores; 5651—Family
Clothing Stores.

★ 70751 ★ Mobil Service Center
1601 N. Market St.
Shreveport, LA 71107
(318)227-8817
Ultimate Parent: Mobil. SIC: 5541—
Gasoline Service Stations.

★ 70752 ★ Nalco Chemical Co.
Inc.
2920 Knight St.
Shreveport, LA 71105
(318)865-2311
Ultimate Parent: Nalco Chemical Co. SIC:
5169—Chemicals & Allied Products Nec.

★ 70753 ★ National-Oilwell
806 N. Market St.
Shreveport, LA 71107
(318)221-5214
Ultimate Parent: Armco. SIC: 5084—
Industrial Machinery & Equipment.

★ 70754 ★ New York Life
Shreveport General Office
Western Agencies
Louisianna Bank Tower
401 Edwards St. Ste. 1700
Shreveport, LA 71101
(318)222-4143 Fax: (318)424-4748
Officer: Edward J. Simoneaux, General
Manager. Ultimate Parent: New York Life.

★ 70755 ★ Olin Corp.
Hwy. 1 S.
Shreveport, LA 71135-5098
Ultimate Parent: Olin Corp. SIC: 2819—
Industrial Inorganic Chemicals Nec.

★ 70756 ★ Olin Corp.
Shreveport Plant
10889 Hwy. 1 S.
Shreveport, LA 71115
Location Type: Plant. Ultimate Parent:
Olin Corp. SIC: 2819—Industrial Inorganic
Chemicals Nec.

★ 70757 ★ Olin Corp.
Shreveport Plant
10889 La. Hwy. 1 S.
Shreveport, LA 71135-5098
Location Type: Plant. Ultimate Parent:
Olin Corp. SIC: 2819—Industrial Inorganic
Chemicals Nec.

★ 70758 ★ Olin Corp.
Shreveport Plant
Hwy. 1 S.
Shreveport, LA 71135-5098
Location Type: Plant. Ultimate Parent:
Olin Corp.

★ 70759 ★ Owens Corning
Fiberglass Co.
2715 Mackey Ln.
Shreveport, LA 71118
(318)688-9270
Ultimate Parent: Owens-Corning. SIC:
1742—Plastering, Drywall & Insulation.

★ 70760 ★ Pennzoil Products Co.
3450 Hollywood Ave.
Shreveport, LA 71109
Ultimate Parent: Pennzoil. SIC: 2992—
Lubricating Oils & Greases.

★ 70761 ★ Pennzoil Products Co.
Shreveport Packaging Plant
3450 Hollywood Ave.
Shreveport, LA 71109
Location Type: Plant. Ultimate Parent:
Pennzoil. SIC: 2992—Lubricating Oils &
Greases.

★ 70762 ★ Pepsi-Cola Co.
1501 Corporate Dr.
Shreveport, LA 71107
(318)222-1201
Ultimate Parent: Pepsico. SIC: 2086—
Bottled & Canned Soft Drinks.

★ 70763 ★ Piggly Wiggly
8912 Linwood Ave.
Shreveport, LA 71106
(318)688-2111
Ultimate Parent: Bruno's. SIC: 5411—
Grocery Stores.

★ 70764 ★ Piggly Wiggly
5000 N. Lakeshore Dr.
Shreveport, LA 71107
(318)222-3201
Ultimate Parent: Bruno's. SIC: 5141—
Groceries—General Line.

★ 70765 ★ Pitney Bowes
6301 Westport Ave.
Shreveport, LA 71129
(318)687-9111
Officer: Jim Goad, Manager. Ultimate
Parent: Pitney Bowes. SIC: 3554—Paper
Industries Machinery; 3579—Office
Machines Nec.

★ 70766 ★ Pizza Hut
6131 Greenwood Rd.
Shreveport, LA 71119
(318)636-4000
Ultimate Parent: Pepsico. SIC: 5812—
Eating Places.

★ 70767 ★ Pizza Hut
6307 Line Ave.
Shreveport, LA 71106
(318)868-5689
Ultimate Parent: Pepsico. SIC: 5812—
Eating Places.

★ 70768 ★ Pizza Hut
641 E. Kings Hwy.
Shreveport, LA 71105
(318)861-2991
Ultimate Parent: Pepsico. SIC: 5812—
Eating Places.

★ 70769 ★ Pizza Hut
1620 E. Bert Kns Indiana Loop
Shreveport, LA 71105
(318)797-5641
Ultimate Parent: Pepsico. SIC: 5812—
Eating Places.

★ 70770 ★ Pizza Hut
3940 Greenwood Rd.
Shreveport, LA 71109
(318)631-8450
Ultimate Parent: Pepsico. SIC: 5812—
Eating Places.

★ 70771 ★ Pizza Hut
2525 Southside Dr.
Shreveport, LA 71118
(318)686-8400
Ultimate Parent: Pepsico. SIC: 5812—
Eating Places.

★ 70772 ★ Radio Shack
Eastgate Plz.
Shreveport, LA 71101
(318)797-3443
Company Type: Division. Ultimate Parent:
Tandy Corp. SIC: 5065—Electronic Parts &
Equipment Nec.

★ 70773 ★ Radio Shack
8924 Jewella Ave.
Shreveport, LA 71118
(318)687-6131
Company Type: Division. Ultimate Parent:
Tandy Corp. SIC: 5065—Electronic Parts &
Equipment Nec.

★ 70774 ★ Radio Shack
1109 Shreveport Barksdale Hwy.
Shreveport, LA 71105
(318)865-9661
Company Type: Division. Ultimate Parent:
Tandy Corp. SIC: 5065—Electronic Parts &
Equipment Nec.

★ 70775 ★ Radio Shack
1748 E. 70th St.
Shreveport, LA 71105
(318)797-3443
Company Type: Division. Ultimate Parent:
Tandy Corp. SIC: 5065—Electronic Parts &
Equipment Nec.

★ 70776 ★ Radio Shack
Gate Plz. E
Shreveport, LA 71108
(318)797-3443
Company Type: Division. Ultimate Parent:
Tandy Corp.

★ 70777 ★ Reliance Insurance
Co.
2800 Youree Dr.
Shreveport, LA 71104
(318)865-7124
Ultimate Parent: Reliance Group Holdings.
SIC: 6411—Insurance Agents, Brokers &
Service.

★ 70778 ★ Ryder Truck Rental
1553 Hollywood Ave.
Shreveport, LA 71108
(318)869-4333
Ultimate Parent: Ryder System. SIC:
7513—Truck Rental & Leasing Without
Drivers.

★ 70779 ★ Ryder Truck Rental
5819 Courtesy Ln.
Shreveport, LA 71108
(318)222-5899
Ultimate Parent: Ryder System. SIC:
7513—Truck Rental & Leasing Without
Drivers.

★ 70780 ★ Ryder Truck Rental
1900 N. Market St.
Shreveport, LA 71107
(318)425-3706
Ultimate Parent: Ryder System. SIC:
7513—Truck Rental & Leasing Without
Drivers.

★ 70781 ★ Sam's Wholesale
Club
650 Port Ave.
Shreveport, LA 71109
(318)688-4014
Ultimate Parent: Wal-Mart Stores, Inc. SIC:
5099—Durable Goods Nec.

★ 70782 ★ Service Merchandise
1750 E. 70th St.
Shreveport, LA 71105
(318)797-3251
Ultimate Parent: Service Merchandise Co.,
Inc. SIC: 5944—Jewelry Stores.

★ 70783 ★ Southland Corp.
3849 Southern Ave.
Shreveport, LA 71106
(318)868-9902
Ultimate Parent: Southland Corp. SIC:
5411—Grocery Stores.

★ 70784 ★ Southwestern Electric
Power Co.
428 Travis St.
Shreveport, LA 71102
(318)222-2141 Fax: (318)425-5108
Officer: Richard H. Bremer, President &
CEO. Ultimate Parent: Central & South
West.

★ 70785 ★ Stop & Shop
2030 Cooper Rd.
Shreveport, LA 71107
(318)222-0266
Ultimate Parent: Stop & Shop. SIC: 5421—
Meat & Fish Markets.

★ 70786 ★ Super Saver
Wholesale Club
6507 Westport Ave.
Shreveport, LA 71129
(318)688-2080
Ultimate Parent: Wal-Mart Stores, Inc. SIC:
5311—Department Stores.

★ 70787 ★ Taco Bell
1630 Barton Dr.
Shreveport, LA 71107
(318)798-2787
Ultimate Parent: Pepsico. SIC: 5812—
Eating Places.

★ 70788 ★ Taco Bell
1630 E. Bert Kns Indiana Loop
Shreveport, LA 71105
(318)798-2787
Ultimate Parent: Pepsico. SIC: 5812—
Eating Places.

★ 70789 ★ Taco Bell
645 E. Kings Hwy.
Shreveport, LA 71105
(318)865-1316
Ultimate Parent: Pepsico. SIC: 5812—
Eating Places.

★ 70790 ★ Taco Bell
3500 Jewella Ave.
Shreveport, LA 71109
(318)631-9631
Ultimate Parent: Pepsico. SIC: 5812—
Eating Places.

★ 70791 ★ Texaco Fuel Man
9706 Saint Vincent Ave.
Shreveport, LA 71106
(318)868-3706
Ultimate Parent: Texaco. SIC: 2911—
Petroleum Refining.

★ 70792 ★ Texaco Incorporated
5909 Youree Dr.
Shreveport, LA 71105
(318)865-2083
Ultimate Parent: Texaco. SIC: 5541—
Gasoline Service Stations.

★ 70793 ★ Texaco Inc.
3003 Knight St.
Shreveport, LA 71105
(318)869-3031
Ultimate Parent: Texaco. SIC: 8721—
Accounting, Auditing & Bookkeeping.

★ 70794 ★ Texaco Inc.
1710 Allen Ave.
Shreveport, LA 71103
(318)222-3385
Ultimate Parent: Texaco. SIC: 5541—
Gasoline Service Stations.

★ 70795 ★ Texaco Kwik Trip
8955 Mansfield Rd.
Shreveport, LA 71118
(318)687-1854
Ultimate Parent: Texaco. SIC: 5499—
Miscellaneous Food Stores.

★ 70796 ★ Toys R US
2706 Mackey Ln.
Shreveport, LA 71118
(318)688-1879
Ultimate Parent: Toys "R" US. SIC: 5945—
Hobby, Toy & Game Shops.

★ 70797 ★ Trailways Bus System
2227 Beckett
Shreveport, LA 71106
(318)221-4205
Ultimate Parent: Greyhound Lines Inc. SIC:
4111—Local & Suburban Transit.

★ 70798 ★ Underwriters
Adjusting Co.
180 Shreve City Park Office
Shreveport, LA 71105
(318)861-0573
Ultimate Parent: Continental. SIC: 6411—
Insurance Agents, Brokers & Service.

★ 70799 ★ United Parcel Service
1123 Joseph Ave.
Shreveport, LA 71107
(318)227-9214
Ultimate Parent: United Parcel Service of
America. SIC: 3599—Industrial Machinery
Nec; 5013—Motor Vehicle Supplies & New
Parts.

★ 70800 ★ Universal Instruments
Corp.
9595 Mansfield Rd.
Shreveport, LA 71118
(318)688-4393
Ultimate Parent: Dover Corp. SIC: 8748—
Business Consulting Services Nec.

★ 70801 ★ UOP Inc.
8725 Old Morringsport Rd.
Shreveport, LA 71107
(318)929-3521
Officer: Vernon B. Chance Jr., Executive
Director. Ultimate Parent: Allied-Signal Inc.
SIC: 2819—Industrial Inorganic Chemicals
Nec; 2869—Industrial Organic Chemicals
Nec; 2899—Chemical Preparations Nec.

★ 70802 ★ Wal Mart Discount
City
737 Shreveport
Shreveport, LA 71110
(318)869-3168
Ultimate Parent: Wal-Mart Stores, Inc. SIC:
5311—Department Stores.

★ 70803 ★ Wal Mart Discount
City
8300 Jewella Rd.
Shreveport, LA 71108
(318)688-3910
Ultimate Parent: Wal-Mart Stores, Inc. SIC:
5311—Department Stores.

★ 70804 ★ Wal Mart Discount
City
6721 Pines Rd.
Shreveport, LA 71129
(318)688-7700
Ultimate Parent: Wal-Mart Stores, Inc. SIC:
5311—Department Stores.

★ 70805 ★ Waldenbooks
3600 Mall St.
Shreveport, LA 71104
(318)226-9252
Ultimate Parent: K-Mart. SIC: 5942—Book
Stores.

★ 70806 ★ Waldenbooks
S Park Mall
Shreveport, LA 71118
(318)687-1568
Ultimate Parent: K-Mart. SIC: 5942—Book
Stores.

★ 70807 ★ Wilson Foods Corp.
2400 Kings Hwy.
Shreveport, LA 71103
(318)636-6900
Ultimate Parent: Doskocil. SIC: 2011—
Meat Packing Plants.

★ 70808 ★ Xerox Corp.
2800 Youree Dr.
Shreveport, LA 71104
(318)869-2001
Officer: Don Cooper, Manager. Ultimate
Parent: Xerox Corp. SIC: 3663—Radio &
T.V. Communications Equipment.

Simmesport

★ 70809 ★ Ball Incon Glass
Packaging
PO Box 789
Simmesport, LA 71369-0789
(318)247-8041
Officer: Wayne Causey. Ultimate Parent:
Ball Corp. SIC: 3221—Glass Containers.

★ 70810 ★ Three Rivers Timber
Co. Inc.
Simmesport, LA 71369
(318)941-2934
Ultimate Parent: Scott Paper Co. SIC:
2411—Logging.

Simsboro

★ 70811 ★ Willamette Industries
Inc.
Hwy. 335
Simsboro, LA 71275
(318)247-6923
Ultimate Parent: Willamette Industries, Inc.
SIC: 3272—Concrete Products Nec.

★ 70812 ★ Willamette Industries
Inc.
Surepine
Lincoln Parish Rd. 335
Simsboro, LA 71275
Ultimate Parent: Willamette Industries, Inc.
SIC: 2493—Reconstituted Wood Products.

★ 70813 ★ Willamette Industries,
Inc.
Surepine
Lincoln Parish Rd. 335
Simsboro, LA 71275
Ultimate Parent: Willamette Industries, Inc.
SIC: 2400—Lumber & Wood Products.

Slidell

★ 70814 ★ Ace Hardware of
Slidell Inc.
1037 Robert Blvd.
Slidell, LA 70458
(504)641-1404
Ultimate Parent: Ace Hardware. SIC:
5251—Hardware Stores.

★ 70815 ★ Albertson's
1101 Front St.
Slidell, LA 70458
(504)649-1135
Ultimate Parent: Albertson's Inc. SIC:
5912—Drug Stores & Proprietary Stores.

★ 70816 ★ Albertson's
110 US 190 W
Slidell, LA 70460
(504)649-1135
Ultimate Parent: Albertson's Inc. SIC:
5912—Drug Stores & Proprietary Stores.

★ 70817 ★ Casual Corner
150 Northshore Blvd.
Slidell, LA 70460
(504)643-4874
Ultimate Parent: United States Shoe. SIC:
5651—Family Clothing Stores.

★ 70818 ★ Exxon
1675 Gause Blvd.
Slidell, LA 70458
(504)643-0610
Ultimate Parent: Exxon. SIC: 5541—
Gasoline Service Stations; 5541—Gasoline
Service Stations.

★ 70819 ★ Exxon
350 PO Box
Slidell, LA 70459
(504)649-1128
Ultimate Parent: Exxon. SIC: 5541—
Gasoline Service Stations.

★ 70820 ★ First Bank
1049 PO Box
Slidell, LA 70459
Ultimate Parent: Shawmut National Corp.
SIC: 6022—State Commercial Banks.

★ 70821 ★ First Bank
177 Us 190 W
Slidell, LA 70460
(504)641-3422
Ultimate Parent: Shawmut National Corp.
SIC: 6022—State Commercial Banks.

★ 70822 ★ First Bank
1431 Gause Blvd.
Slidell, LA 70458
(504)646-1223
Ultimate Parent: Shawmut National Corp.
SIC: 6022—State Commercial Banks.

★ 70823 ★ First Bank
Northside Plz.
Slidell, LA 70458
(504)643-2708
Ultimate Parent: Shawmut National Corp.
SIC: 6022—State Commercial Banks.

★ 70824 ★ First Bank
2200 Front St.
Slidell, LA 70458
(504)643-2700
Ultimate Parent: Shawmut National Corp.
SIC: 6099—Functions Related to Deposit
Banking.

★ 70825 ★ The Gap
150 N. Shore Sq. N
Slidell, LA 70460
(504)649-1948
Ultimate Parent: GAP. SIC: 5651—Family
Clothing Stores.

★ 70826 ★ Gaylord Chemical
Corp.
106 Galeria Blvd.
Slidell, LA 70458
(504)641-2882
Ultimate Parent: Gaylord Container. SIC:
5169—Chemicals & Allied Products Nec.

★ 70827 ★ Hibernia National
Bank
550 Pontchartrain Dr.
Slidell, LA 70458
(504)646-6660
Ultimate Parent: Hibernia Corp.

★ 70828 ★ IDS Financial
Services Inc.
737 Robert Blvd., Ste. 2
Slidell, LA 70458-1654
(504)649-4732
Location Type: Branch office. Officer: Al
Parkin. Ultimate Parent: American Express
Co. SIC: 6282—Investment Advice; 6211—
Security Brokers & Dealers.

★ 70829 ★ Jiffy Lube
1336 Gause Blvd.
Slidell, LA 70458
(504)649-3278
Ultimate Parent: Pennzoil. SIC: 5541—
Gasoline Service Stations.

★ 70830 ★ Kentucky Fried
Chicken
302 Pontchartrain Dr.
Slidell, LA 70458
(504)641-0532
Ultimate Parent: Pepsico. SIC: 5812—
Eating Places.

★ 70831 ★ Kmart Discount Store
1311 Gause Blvd.
Slidell, LA 70458
(504)649-0042
Ultimate Parent: K-Mart. SIC: 5311—
Department Stores.

★ 70832 ★ Lane Bryant
150 Northshore Blvd.
Slidell, LA 70460
(504)646-1262
Ultimate Parent: Limited. SIC: 5651—
Family Clothing Stores.

★ 70833 ★ The Limited
150 Northshore Blvd.
Slidell, LA 70460
(504)649-7954
Ultimate Parent: Limited. SIC: 5651—
Family Clothing Stores.

★ 70834 ★   The Limited Express
150 Northshore Blvd.
Slidell, LA 70460
(504)649-7948
Ultimate Parent: Limited. SIC: 5651—
Family Clothing Stores.

★ 70835 ★   Mervyn's
150 Northshore Blvd.
Slidell, LA 70460
(504)646-0491
Ultimate Parent: Dayton Hudson. SIC:
5311—Department Stores.

★ 70836 ★   Pizza Hut
1532 Gause Blvd.
Slidell, LA 70458
(504)641-6588
Ultimate Parent: Pepsico. SIC: 5812—
Eating Places.

★ 70837 ★   Radio Shack
3293 Pontchartrain Dr.
Slidell, LA 70458
(504)641-0215
Company Type: Division. Ultimate Parent:
Tandy Corp. SIC: 5065—Electronic Parts &
Equipment Nec.

★ 70838 ★   Radio Shack
1567 Gause Blvd.
Slidell, LA 70458
(504)643-0215
Company Type: Division. Ultimate Parent:
Tandy Corp. SIC: 5065—Electronic Parts &
Equipment Nec.

★ 70839 ★   Radio Shack
150 Northshore Blvd.
Slidell, LA 70460
(504)641-0215
Company Type: Division. Ultimate Parent:
Tandy Corp. SIC: 5065—Electronic Parts &
Equipment Nec.

★ 70840 ★   Taco Bell
Us 190 W
Slidell, LA 70460
(504)646-1685
Ultimate Parent: Pepsico. SIC: 5812—
Eating Places.

★ 70841 ★   Taco Bell
1681 Gause Blvd.
Slidell, LA 70458
(504)649-2722
Ultimate Parent: Pepsico. SIC: 5812—
Eating Places.

★ 70842 ★   Taco Bell
Hwy. 190
Slidell, LA 70461
(504)646-1685
Ultimate Parent: Pepsico. SIC: 5812—
Eating Places.

★ 70843 ★   Texaco Self Service
3211 Pontchartrain Dr.
Slidell, LA 70458
(504)641-6088
Ultimate Parent: Texaco. SIC: 5541—
Gasoline Service Stations.

★ 70844 ★   Texaco Self Service
1540 Gause Blvd.
Slidell, LA 70458
(504)641-6183
Ultimate Parent: Texaco. SIC: 5541—
Gasoline Service Stations.

★ 70845 ★   Wal Mart
870 E. I 10 Service Rd.
Slidell, LA 70461
Ultimate Parent: Wal-Mart Stores, Inc. SIC:
5311—Department Stores.

★ 70846 ★   Walgreen Drug Stores
1591 Gause Blvd.
Slidell, LA 70458
(504)641-5555
Ultimate Parent: Walgreen Co. SIC:
5912—Drug Stores & Proprietary Stores.

Springhill

★ 70847 ★   Arizona Chemical Co.
Hwy. 7 at S. Springhill City Limits
Springhill, LA 71075
Ultimate Parent: International Paper Co.
SIC: 2861—Gum & Wood Chemicals.

★ 70848 ★   Arizona Chemical Co.
Hwy. 7 Minden Rd.
Springhill, LA 71075
Ultimate Parent: International Paper Co.
SIC: 2861—Gum & Wood Chemicals.

★ 70849 ★   Arizona Chemical Co.
Hwy. 7, Minden Rd.
Springhill, LA 71075
Ultimate Parent: International Paper Co.
SIC: 2861—Gum & Wood Chemicals.

★ 70850 ★   International Paper
Springhill Wood Products Plt.
2600 South Arkansas St.
Springhill, LA 71075
Ultimate Parent: International Paper Co.
SIC: 2436—Softwood Veneer & Plywood.

★ 70851 ★   Kentucky Fried
Chicken
910 S. Arkansas St.
Springhill, LA 71075
(318)539-5929
Ultimate Parent: Pepsico. SIC: 5812—
Eating Places.

★ 70852 ★   Mobil Oil Company
1802 S. Arkansas St.
Springhill, LA 71075
(318)539-2594
Ultimate Parent: Mobil. SIC: 2411—
Logging.

★ 70853 ★   Piggly Wiggly
S Main Mall
Springhill, LA 71075
(318)539-3216
Ultimate Parent: Bruno's. SIC: 5411—
Grocery Stores.

★ 70854 ★   Piggly Wiggly
S Main Mall
Springhill, LA 71075
(318)539-4506
Ultimate Parent: Bruno's. SIC: 5461—
Retail Bakeries.

★ 70855 ★   Piggly Wiggly
1120 Reynolds St.
Springhill, LA 71075
(318)539-4137
Ultimate Parent: Bruno's. SIC: 5411—
Grocery Stores.

★ 70856 ★   Pizza Hut
6 PO Box
Springhill, LA 71075
(318)539-3597
Ultimate Parent: Pepsico. SIC: 5812—
Eating Places.

★ 70857 ★   Rhone-Poulenc Basic
Chemicals Co.
Old Minden Rd.
Springhill, LA 71075
Ultimate Parent: Rhone-Poulenc Rorer.
SIC: 2819—Industrial Inorganic Chemicals
Nec.

★ 70858 ★   Tyson Foods Inc.
Plain Dealing Rd.
Springhill, LA 71075
(318)539-2536
Ultimate Parent: Tyson Foods, Inc. SIC:
5142—Packaged Frozen Foods.

St. Bernard

★ 70859 ★   Hertz Rent-A-Car
Hilton Hotel 2
St. Bernard, LA 70085
(504)525-1646
Ultimate Parent: Hertz. SIC: 7514—
Passenger Car Rental.

★ 70860 ★   Union Texas
Petroleum
Toca
St. Bernard, LA 70085
(504)682-3809
Ultimate Parent: Union Texas Petroleum.
SIC: 3519—Internal Combustion Engines
Nec.

St. Francisville

★ 70861 ★   James River Paper
Co. Inc. St. Francisville
End of Hwy. 964
St. Francisville, LA 70775
Ultimate Parent: James River Corp. of
Virginia. SIC: 2611—Pulp Mills; 2621—
Paper Mills.

St. Gabriel

★ 70862 ★   Air Products &
Chemicals
PO Box 1
St. Gabriel, LA 70776-0001
(504)642-3346
Location Type: Branch office. Officer:
Donald R. Emert. Ultimate Parent: Air
Products & Chemicals, Inc. SIC: 2819—
Industrial Inorganic Chemicals Nec.

★ 70863 ★   Air Products &
Chemicals, Inc.
3790 Hwy. 30
St. Gabriel, LA 70776
(504)642-3346
Officer: Donald R. Emert, Manager.
Ultimate Parent: Air Products & Chemicals,
Inc. SIC: 2899—Chemical Preparations
Nec; 2869—Industrial Organic Chemicals
Nec.

★ 70864 ★   Air Products &
Chemicals Inc.
3790 Hwy. 30 PO Box 1
St. Gabriel, LA 70776
Ultimate Parent: Air Products & Chemicals,
Inc. SIC: 2869—Industrial Organic
Chemicals Nec.

★ 70865 ★   Air Products &
Chemicals, Inc.
Hwy. 30
St. Gabriel, LA 70776
Ultimate Parent: Air Products & Chemicals,
Inc. SIC: 2869—Industrial Organic
Chemicals Nec.

St. James

★ 70866 ★   Chevron Chemical
Co.
9901 La Hwy. 18 Bridge
St. James, LA 70086
Ultimate Parent: Chevron Corp. SIC:
2865—Cyclic Crudes & Intermediates.

★ 70867 ★   Chevron Chemical
Co.
Hwy. 18 - 1 1/2 Mile S. Sunshine Bridge
St. James, LA 70086
Ultimate Parent: Chevron Corp. SIC:
2865—Cyclic Crudes & Intermediates.

St. Landry

★ 70868 ★   Atlantic Richfield Co.
Hwy. 617
St. Landry, LA 71367
(318)836-5454
Ultimate Parent: Atlantic Richfield Co., Inc.
SIC: 1311—Crude Petroleum & Natural
Gas.

St. Martinville

★ 70869 ★   Ace Hardware
331 S. Main St.
St. Martinville, LA 70582
(318)394-6246
Ultimate Parent: Ace Hardware. SIC:
5063—Electrical Apparatus & Equipment.

★ 70870 ★   Fruit of the Loom Inc.
Martin Mills Inc.
6261 Main Hwy.
St. Martinville, LA 70582
Ultimate Parent: Fruit of the Loom. SIC:
2329—Men's/Boys' Clothing Nec; 2253—
Knit Outerwear Mills; 2254—Knit Underwear
Mills.

★ 70871 ★   Union Underwear Co.
Hwy. 31 North
St. Martinville, LA 70582
Ultimate Parent: Fruit of the Loom. SIC:
2221—Broadwoven Fabric Mills—Manmade.

★ 70872 ★   Wal Mart Discount
City
Hwy. 31
St. Martinville, LA 70582
(318)394-5525
Ultimate Parent: Wal-Mart Stores, Inc. SIC:
5311—Department Stores.

St. Rose

★ 70873 ★   GE Medical Systems
150 James Dr. E
St. Rose, LA 70087
(504)465-9481
Officer: Grover McDaniel, Manager.
Ultimate Parent: General Electric. SIC:
3844—X-Ray Apparatus & Tubes.

★ 70874 ★   Hill Petroleum Co.
St. Rose Refinery
27009 River Rd.
St. Rose, LA 70087
Ultimate Parent: Salomon, Inc. SIC:
2911—Petroleum Refining.

★ 70875 ★   Phibro Refining
St. Rose Refinery
PO Box 603-27009 PO Box 603-27009
St. Rose, LA 70087
Ultimate Parent: Salomon, Inc. SIC:
2911—Petroleum Refining.

★ 70876 ★   Phibro Refining
St. Rose Refinery
27009 River Rd. PO Box 603-27009
St. Rose, LA 70087
Ultimate Parent: Salomon, Inc. SIC:
2992—Lubricating Oils & Greases.

★ 70877 ★   Phibro Refining Inc.
St. Rose Refinery
27009 River Rd.
St. Rose, LA 70087
Ultimate Parent: Salomon, Inc. SIC:
2911—Petroleum Refining.

★ 70878 ★   Pitney Bowes
150 James Dr. E, Ste. 160
St. Rose, LA 70087
(504)468-1305
Officer: Ed Joyce, Manager. Ultimate
Parent: Pitney Bowes. SIC: 3579—Office
Machines Nec.

Sterlington

★ 70879 ★   Coast to Coast
Sterlington, LA 71280
(318)665-2124
Ultimate Parent: Servistar Corp. SIC:
5531—Automobile & Home Supply Stores.

★ 70880 ★   Imc Fertilizer Inc.
La Hwy. 2
Sterlington, LA 71280
Ultimate Parent: IMC Fertilizer Group. SIC:
2873—Nitrogenous Fertilizers.

Sulphur

★ 70881 ★   Betz Process
Chemicals
1215 S. Post Oak Rd. 2
Sulphur, LA 70663
(318)625-2080
Ultimate Parent: Betz Laboratories Inc.
SIC: 2899—Chemical Preparations Nec.

★ 70882 ★   Citgo Petroleum Corp.
1562 PO Box
Sulphur, LA 70664
(318)491-6011
Ultimate Parent: Citgo Petroleum. SIC:
2911—Petroleum Refining.

★ 70883 ★   Citgo Quick Mart
2060 S. Ruth St.
Sulphur, LA 70663
(318)528-2797
Ultimate Parent: Citgo Petroleum. SIC:
5411—Grocery Stores.

★ 70884 ★   Greyhound Bus
Station
203 W. Napoleon St.
Sulphur, LA 70663
(318)527-6618
Ultimate Parent: Greyhound Lines Inc. SIC:
4131—Intercity & Rural Bus Transportation.

★ **70885** ★ **Kroger Store**
1551 E. Napoleon St.
Sulphur, LA 70663
(318)527-9891
Ultimate Parent: Kroger. **SIC:** 5411—
Grocery Stores.

★ **70886** ★ **Oxy Petrochemicals Inc.**
Hwy. 108 S
Sulphur, LA 70663
Ultimate Parent: Occidental Petroleum Corp. **SIC:** 2869—Industrial Organic Chemicals Nec.

★ **70887** ★ **Oxychem Petrochemicals**
Lake Charles Plant
Hwy. 108 S.
Sulphur, LA 70663
Location Type: Plant. **Ultimate Parent:** Occidental Petroleum Corp. **SIC:** 2869—Industrial Organic Chemicals Nec.

★ **70888** ★ **Pizza Hut**
2625 S. Ruth St.
Sulphur, LA 70663
(318)528-2888
Ultimate Parent: Pepsico. **SIC:** 5812—Eating Places.

★ **70889** ★ **Radio Shack**
1500 S. Arizona St.
Sulphur, LA 70663
(318)625-9630
Company Type: Division. **Ultimate Parent:** Tandy Corp. **SIC:** 5065—Electronic Parts & Equipment Nec.

★ **70890** ★ **Ryder Truck Rental**
2239 E. Napoleon St.
Sulphur, LA 70663
(318)625-9948
Ultimate Parent: Ryder System. **SIC:** 7513—Truck Rental & Leasing Without Drivers.

★ **70891** ★ **Super Saver**
1600 Maplewood Dr.
Sulphur, LA 70663
(318)625-8628
Ultimate Parent: Wal-Mart Stores, Inc. **SIC:** 5411—Grocery Stores.

★ **70892** ★ **Taco Bell**
2040 S. Ruth St.
Sulphur, LA 70663
(318)527-8812
Ultimate Parent: Pepsico. **SIC:** 5812—Eating Places.

★ **70893** ★ **W. R. Grace & Co.**
Davison Rd.
Sulphur, LA 70663
Ultimate Parent: W. R. Grace. **SIC:** 2819—Industrial Inorganic Chemicals Nec.

★ **70894** ★ **W. R. Grace & Co.**
Davison Chemical Div.
1800 Davison Rd.
Sulphur, LA 70663
Company Type: Division. **Ultimate Parent:** W. R. Grace. **SIC:** 2819—Industrial Inorganic Chemicals Nec.

★ **70895** ★ **Wal Mart Discount City**
I 10
Sulphur, LA 70663
(318)625-3494
Ultimate Parent: Wal-Mart Stores, Inc. **SIC:** 5311—Department Stores.

★ **70896** ★ **Wal Mart Pharmacy**
Hwy. 108
Sulphur, LA 70663
(318)625-7057
Ultimate Parent: Wal-Mart Stores, Inc. **SIC:** 5912—Drug Stores & Proprietary Stores.

★ **70897** ★ **W.R. Grace & Co.**
Davison Rd.
Sulphur, LA 70663
Ultimate Parent: W. R. Grace. **SIC:** 2819—Industrial Inorganic Chemicals Nec.

Taft

★ **70898** ★ **Occidental Chemical Corp.**
La Hwy. 18 & La Hwy. 3142
Taft, LA 70057-0074
Ultimate Parent: Occidental Petroleum Corp. **SIC:** 2812—Alkalies & Chlorine;

2819—Industrial Inorganic Chemicals Nec; 2873—Nitrogenous Fertilizers.

★ **70899** ★ **Occidental Chemical Corp.**
Taft Ammonia Terminal
La Hwy. 18 & La Hwy. 3142
Taft, LA 70057
Company Type: Division. **Ultimate Parent:** Occidental Petroleum Corp. **SIC:** 2812—Alkalies & Chlorine; 2819—Industrial Inorganic Chemicals Nec.

★ **70900** ★ **Shell Chemical Co.**
Taft Plant
La Hwy. 18 at La Hwy. 3142
Taft, LA 70057
Location Type: Plant. **Ultimate Parent:** Shell Oil Co. **SIC:** 2821—Plastics Materials & Resins.

★ **70901** ★ **Shell Chemical Co.**
Taft Plant
La-18 at La-3142
Taft, LA 70057
Location Type: Plant. **Ultimate Parent:** Shell Oil Co. **SIC:** 2821—Plastics Materials & Resins.

★ **70902** ★ **Union Carbide Corp., Star Plant**
Hwy. 3142-Star Plantation Rd.
Taft, LA 70057
Location Type: Plant. **Ultimate Parent:** Union Carbide Corp. **SIC:** 2821—Plastics Materials & Resins.

★ **70903** ★ **Union Caride Corp. Star Plant**
Hwy. 3142 Star Plantation Rd.
Taft, LA 70057
Ultimate Parent: Union Carbide Corp. **SIC:** 2821—Plastics Materials & Resins.

★ **70904** ★ **Witco Corp.**
Argus Chemical
River Rd. & Hwy. 3142
Taft, LA 70057-0310
Ultimate Parent: Witco Corp. **SIC:** 2869—Industrial Organic Chemicals Nec.

★ **70905** ★ **Witco Corp.**
Polymer Additives
Hwy. 3142 & River Rd.
Taft, LA 70057-0310
Ultimate Parent: Witco Corp. **SIC:** 2869—Industrial Organic Chemicals Nec.

Tallulah

★ **70906** ★ **Kentucky Fried Chicken**
201 S. Chestnut St.
Tallulah, LA 71282
(318)574-1711
Ultimate Parent: Pepsico. **SIC:** 5812—Eating Places.

★ **70907** ★ **Madison Bank & Trust Co.**
13 Crothers Dr.
Tallulah, LA 71282
(318)574-5300
Ultimate Parent: National City Corp. **SIC:** 6029—Commercial Banks Nec.

★ **70908** ★ **Piggly Wiggly**
400 E. Darrow St.
Tallulah, LA 71282
(318)574-1574
Ultimate Parent: Bruno's. **SIC:** 5499—Miscellaneous Food Stores.

★ **70909** ★ **Pizza Hut**
316 N. Chestnut St.
Tallulah, LA 71282
(318)574-3244
Ultimate Parent: Pepsico. **SIC:** 5812—Eating Places.

Taylor

★ **70910** ★ **Willamette Industries Inc.**
Ada
Taylor, LA 71080
(318)843-6216
Ultimate Parent: Willamette Industries, Inc. **SIC:** 5031—Lumber, Plywood & Millwork.

★ **70911** ★ **Willamette Industries Inc.**
Taylor
Hwy. 80 West
Taylor, LA 71080
Ultimate Parent: Willamette Industries, Inc. **SIC:** 2436—Softwood Veneer & Plywood.

Thibodaux

★ **70912** ★ **Fleet Finance Inc.**
106 Canal Blvd.
Thibodaux, LA 70301
(504)446-8873
Ultimate Parent: Fleet Financial Group. **SIC:** 6141—Personal Credit Institutions.

★ **70913** ★ **Greyhound Bus Lines**
902 Jackson St.
Thibodaux, LA 70301
(504)447-1053
Ultimate Parent: Greyhound Lines Inc. **SIC:** 4131—Intercity & Rural Bus Transportation.

★ **70914** ★ **Pizza Hut**
523 St. Mary St.
Thibodaux, LA 70301
(504)447-2435
Ultimate Parent: Pepsico. **SIC:** 5812—Eating Places.

Tioga

★ **70915** ★ **Rapides Bank & Trust Co.**
Hwy. 71
Tioga, LA 71477
(318)487-2661
Ultimate Parent: First Commerce Corp. **SIC:** 6022—State Commercial Banks.

Uncle Sam

★ **70916** ★ **Agrico Chemical Co. Uncle Sam Plant**
E. Bank River Rd. Hwy. 44
Uncle Sam, LA 70792-9999
Ultimate Parent: Freeport-McMoran. **SIC:** 2874—Phosphatic Fertilizers; 2819—Industrial Inorganic Chemicals Nec.

★ **70917** ★ **Freeport Mcmoran**
Agrico Chemical Co. Div.
E. Bank River Rd.
Uncle Sam, LA 70792
Company Type: Division. **Ultimate Parent:** Freeport-McMoran. **SIC:** 2874—Phosphatic Fertilizers; 2819—Industrial Inorganic Chemicals Nec.

Union

★ **70918** ★ **Texaco Ref. & Mktg. Inc.**
Foot of Sunshine Bridge -La 44
Union, LA 70723
Ultimate Parent: Texaco. **SIC:** 2911—Petroleum Refining; 2819—Industrial Inorganic Chemicals Nec; 4400—Water Transportation; 5171—Petroleum Bulk Stations & Terminals.

Urania

★ **70919** ★ **Louisiana Pacific Corp.**
Urania, LA 71480
(318)495-3111
Ultimate Parent: Louisiana-Pacific. **SIC:** 5031—Lumber, Plywood & Millwork.

★ **70920** ★ **Louisiana Pacific Corp., OSB**
Hwy. 165 N
Urania, LA 71480
Ultimate Parent: Louisiana-Pacific. **SIC:** 2436—Softwood Veneer & Plywood; 2493—Reconstituted Wood Products; 5031—Lumber, Plywood & Millwork.

Vencie

★ **70921** ★ **Arco Oil & Gas**
McDermott Rd.
Vencie, LA 70091
(504)534-2311
Ultimate Parent: Atlantic Richfield Co., Inc. **SIC:** 1311—Crude Petroleum & Natural Gas.

Venice

★ **70922** ★ **Arco Oil & Gas Co.**
McDermott Rd.
Venice, LA 70091
(504)534-2311
Ultimate Parent: Atlantic Richfield Co., Inc. **SIC:** 1311—Crude Petroleum & Natural Gas.

★ **70923** ★ **Marathon Oil Co.**
Tidewater Rd.
Venice, LA 70091
(504)534-7595
Ultimate Parent: USX Corp. **SIC:** 1389—Oil & Gas Field Services Nec.

★ **70924** ★ **Marathon Oil Co.**
Tidewater Rd.
Venice, LA 70091
(504)534-7595
Ultimate Parent: USX Corp. **SIC:** 1389—Oil & Gas Field Services Nec.

★ **70925** ★ **Tesoro Petroleum Distribution**
Venice, LA 70091
(504)534-7544
Ultimate Parent: Tesoro Petroleum Corp. **SIC:** 5983—Fuel Oil Dealers.

★ **70926** ★ **Texaco Inc.**
Venice, LA 70091
(504)534-7717
Ultimate Parent: Texaco. **SIC:** 1311—Crude Petroleum & Natural Gas.

Vidalia

★ **70927** ★ **Aluminum Co. of America**
Hwys. 313 & 3180
PO Box 4
Vidalia, LA 71373-0004
(318)336-9601
Location Type: Branch office. **Officer:** W.W. Carruthers, Manager. **Ultimate Parent:** Aluminum Co. of America–Alcoa. **SIC:** 2819—Industrial Inorganic Chemicals Nec.

★ **70928** ★ **Aluminum Co. of America**
Logan Sewell Dr.
Vidalia, LA 71373
(318)336-9601
Ultimate Parent: Aluminum Co. of America-Alcoa. **SIC:** 5051—Metals Service Centers & Offices.

★ **70929** ★ **Coast to Coast Home & Auto**
1641 Carter St.
Vidalia, LA 71373
(318)336-7167
Ultimate Parent: Servistar Corp. **SIC:** 5531—Automobile & Home Supply Stores.

★ **70930** ★ **Piggly Wiggly**
400 Carter St.
Vidalia, LA 71373
(318)336-5906
Ultimate Parent: Bruno's. **SIC:** 5421—Meat & Fish Markets.

★ **70931** ★ **Pizza Hut**
2000 Carter St.
Vidalia, LA 71373
(318)336-4334
Ultimate Parent: Pepsico. **SIC:** 5812—Eating Places.

Ville Platte

★ **70932** ★ **Ace Hardware**
130 E. Main St.
Ville Platte, LA 70586-4561
(318)363-4876
Location Type: Branch office. **Officer:** Wayne Vidrine. **Ultimate Parent:** Ace Hardware. **SIC:** 5999—Miscellaneous Retail Stores Nec; 5231—Paint, Glass & Wallpaper Stores; 5251—Hardware Stores.

★ **70933** ★ **Cooper Industries Inc.**
Oil Tool Div.
N. 6 Holloway Blvd.
Ville Platte, LA 70586-9778
Company Type: Division. **Ultimate Parent:** Cooper Industries. **SIC:** 3533—Oil & Gas Field Machinery.

★ 70934 ★   **Radio Shack**
909 W. Lincoln Rd.
Ville Platte, LA 70586
(318)363-6655
Company Type: Division. **Ultimate Parent:**
Tandy Corp. **SIC:** 5065—Electronic Parts &
Equipment Nec.

★ 70935 ★   **Wal Mart Discount
Store**
Hwy. 167 E
Ville Platte, LA 70586
(318)363-5623
Ultimate Parent: Wal-Mart Stores, Inc. **SIC:**
5311—Department Stores.

Vivian

★ 70936 ★   **Piggly Wiggly**
Monterey Shopping Ctr.
Vivian, LA 71082
(318)375-3671
Ultimate Parent: Bruno's. **SIC:** 5411—
Grocery Stores.

★ 70937 ★   **Pizza Hut**
921 S. Pine St.
Vivian, LA 71082
(318)375-3911
Ultimate Parent: Pepsico. **SIC:** 5812—
Eating Places.

★ 70938 ★   **Wal Mart Discount
Cities**
Hwy. 1 S
Vivian, LA 71082
(318)375-4810
Ultimate Parent: Wal-Mart Stores, Inc. **SIC:**
5311—Department Stores.

Walker

★ 70939 ★   **Walker Manufacturing
Inc.**
Cane Mkt Rd.
Walker, LA 70785
(504)665-4521
Ultimate Parent: Tenneco Inc. **SIC:** 3599—
Industrial Machinery Nec.

Weeks Island

★ 70940 ★   **Morton International
Inc.**
Hwy. 83
Weeks Island, LA 70560
Ultimate Parent: Morton International. **SIC:**
2899—Chemical Preparations Nec.

Welsh

★ 70941 ★   **AT&T**
Welsh, LA 70591
(318)734-4516
Ultimate Parent: AT&T. **SIC:** 4813—
Telephone Communications Except
Radiotelephone.

West Monroe

★ 70942 ★   **AT&T**
1511 New Nathitoches Rd.
West Monroe, LA 71292-2111
(318)387-0048
Location Type: Branch office. **Officer:**
Ronald G. Rollen. **Ultimate Parent:** AT&T.
SIC: 4813—Telephone Communications
Except Radiotelephone.

★ 70943 ★   **Butler Paper Co.**
100 Johnny Bayles Dr.
West Monroe, LA 71292-6162
(318)323-8816
Location Type: Branch office. **Officer:**
Gene Simmons. **Ultimate Parent:** Alco
Standard Corp. **SIC:** 2621—Paper Mills.

★ 70944 ★   **Coated & Laminated
Products**
Jonesboro Hwy.
West Monroe, LA 71284
(318)362-2000
Company Type: Subsidiary. **Officer:** Larry
Lewandowski, Manager-Production.
Ultimate Parent: Manville Corp.

★ 70945 ★   **Manville Corp.**
Paperboard Div.
PO Box 488
West Monroe, LA 71294
(318)362-2000 **Fax:** (318)362-2133
Company Type: Division. **Officer:** Robert
Hart, Vice President & General Manager -
Paperboard. **Ultimate Parent:** Manville
Corp. **SIC:** 2621—Paper Mills.

★ 70946 ★   **Manville Corp.**
Wood Products/Forest Resources/Energy
Resources Div.
PO Box 488
West Monroe, LA 71294
(318)362-2000 **Fax:** (318)362-2133
Company Type: Division. **Officer:** Stone
Clark, Vice President & General Manager-
Forest Prods. & Resources. **Ultimate
Parent:** Manville Corp. **SIC:** 2621—Paper
Mills.

★ 70947 ★   **Manville Forest
Products**
Plant 20
1000 Jonesboro Rd.
West Monroe, LA 71291
Location Type: Plant. **Ultimate Parent:**
Manville Corp. **SIC:** 2671—Paper Coated &
Laminated—Packaging.

★ 70948 ★   **Manville Forest
Products Corp.**
Plant 70
1070 Jonesboro Rd.
West Monroe, LA 71292
Location Type: Plant. **Ultimate Parent:**
Manville Corp. **SIC:** 2657—Folding
Paperboard Boxes.

★ 70949 ★   **Manville Forest
Products Corp.**
Plant 70
1000 Jonesboro Rd.
West Monroe, LA 71291
Location Type: Plant. **Ultimate Parent:**
Manville Corp. **SIC:** 2657—Folding
Paperboard Boxes.

★ 70950 ★   **Manville Forest
Products Corp.**
Plant 70
1000 Jonesboro Rd., Station 70
West Monroe, LA 71294-0488
Location Type: Plant. **Ultimate Parent:**
Manville Corp. **SIC:** 2657—Folding
Paperboard Boxes.

★ 70951 ★   **Manville Forest
Products Corp.**
Plant 31
1031 Jonesboro Rd.
West Monroe, LA 71292
Location Type: Plant. **Ultimate Parent:**
Manville Corp. **SIC:** 2631—Paperboard
Mills.

★ 70952 ★   **Manville Forest
Products Corp.**
Plant 31
1000 Jonesboro Rd.
West Monroe, LA 71294-0488
Location Type: Plant. **Ultimate Parent:**
Manville Corp. **SIC:** 2631—Paperboard
Mills.

★ 70953 ★   **Manville Forest
Products Corp.**
Plant 20
1000 Jonesboro Rd., Station 20
West Monroe, LA 71294-0488
Location Type: Plant. **Ultimate Parent:**
Manville Corp. **SIC:** 2631—Paperboard
Mills.

★ 70954 ★   **May Supply Co., Inc.**
707 Coleman Ave.
West Monroe, LA 71292
(318)323-1844
Ultimate Parent: WLR Foods. **SIC:** 5074—
Plumbing & Hydronic Heating Supplies.

★ 70955 ★   **Piggly Wiggly**
108 Dupont Cir.
West Monroe, LA 71291
(318)368-9736
Ultimate Parent: Bruno's. **SIC:** 5411—
Grocery Stores.

★ 70956 ★   **Piggly Wiggly
Employees Federal Credit Union**
3004 N. 7th St.
West Monroe, LA 71291
(318)323-1381
Ultimate Parent: Bruno's. **SIC:** 5411—
Grocery Stores.

★ 70957 ★   **Riverwood
International USA Inc.**
1070 Jonesboro Rd.
West Monroe, LA 71292
Ultimate Parent: Manville Corp. **SIC:**
2657—Folding Paperboard Boxes.

★ 70958 ★   **Riverwood
International USA Inc.**
1031 Jonesboro Rd.
West Monroe, LA 71294-5800
Ultimate Parent: Manville Corp. **SIC:**
2631—Paperboard Mills.

★ 70959 ★   **Riverwood
International USA Inc.**
1031 Jonesboro Rd.
West Monroe, LA 71292
Ultimate Parent: Manville Corp. **SIC:**
2631—Paperboard Mills.

★ 70960 ★   **Riverwood
International USA Inc.**
1020 Jonesboro Rd.
West Monroe, LA 71292
Ultimate Parent: Manville Corp. **SIC:**
2671—Paper Coated & Laminated—
Packaging.

★ 70961 ★   **Ryder Truck Rental**
5809 Cypress St.
West Monroe, LA 71291
(318)396-4032
Ultimate Parent: Ryder System. **SIC:**
7359—Equipment Rental & Leasing Nec.

Westlake

★ 70962 ★   **Cecos International
Inc.**
918 Willow Springs Rd.
Westlake, LA 70669
(318)527-6857
Officer: Joseph R. Whelan, Vice President.
Ultimate Parent: Browning-Ferris
Industries. **SIC:** 3589—Service Industry
Machinery Nec.

★ 70963 ★   **Conoco Inc.**
2200 Old Spanish Trl.
Westlake, LA 70669
(318)491-5211
Officer: Dave Myers, Manager. **Ultimate
Parent:** E.I. DuPont De Nemours. **SIC:**
2819—Industrial Inorganic Chemicals Nec;
2911—Petroleum Refining.

★ 70964 ★   **M-I Drilling Fluids Co.
Westlake Grinding Plant**
1/2 Mile S. of I-10 W. Bank of Calcasieu
River
Westlake, LA 70669
Ultimate Parent: Halliburton. **SIC:** 3295—
Minerals—Ground or Treated.

★ 70965 ★   **M-I Drilling Fluids,
Westlake**
West Bank Calcasieu River
Box 157
Westlake, LA 70669
Ultimate Parent: Halliburton. **SIC:** 3295—
Minerals—Ground or Treated.

★ 70966 ★   **Olin Corp.**
900 I-10 W
Westlake, LA 70669
(318)491-3000
Officer: Jaswant Gill, Manager. **Ultimate
Parent:** Olin Corp. **SIC:** 2819—Industrial
Inorganic Chemicals Nec; 2865—Cyclic
Crudes & Intermediates; 2873—Nitrogenous
Fertilizers.

★ 70967 ★   **Pizza Hut**
808 Sampson St.
Westlake, LA 70669
(318)439-5555
Ultimate Parent: Pepsico. **SIC:** 5812—
Eating Places.

Westwego

★ 70968 ★   **American Cyanamid
Co.**
10800 River Rd.
Westwego, LA 70094
(504)431-9511
Ultimate Parent: American Cyanamid Co.
SIC: 2819—Industrial Inorganic Chemicals
Nec; 2821—Plastics Materials & Resins;
2824—Organic Fibers—Noncellulosic.

★ 70969 ★   **American Cyanamid
Co.**
10800 River Rd.
Westwego, LA 70094-2099
Location Type: Plant. **Ultimate Parent:**
American Cyanamid Co. **SIC:** 2819—
Industrial Inorganic Chemicals; 2869—
Industrial Organic Chemicals Nec.

★ 70970 ★   **Fleet Finance Inc.**
30 Westbank Expy.
Westwego, LA 70094
(504)367-8833
Ultimate Parent: Fleet Financial Group.
SIC: 6141—Personal Credit Institutions.

★ 70971 ★   **Pizza Hut**
812 Westbank Expy.
Westwego, LA 70094
(504)347-8413
Ultimate Parent: Pepsico. **SIC:** 5812—
Eating Places.

★ 70972 ★   **Radio Shack**
Westwood Shopping Ctr.
Westwego, LA 70094
(504)341-4528
Company Type: Division. **Ultimate Parent:**
Tandy Corp. **SIC:** 5065—Electronic Parts &
Equipment Nec.

★ 70973 ★   **Taco Bell**
3016 Hwy. 90 W
Westwego, LA 70094
(504)436-1975
Ultimate Parent: Pepsico. **SIC:** 5812—
Eating Places; 5812—Eating Places.

★ 70974 ★   **Texaco Self Serv**
1597 Hwy. 90 W
Westwego, LA 70094
(504)436-7614
Ultimate Parent: Texaco. **SIC:** 5541—
Gasoline Service Stations.

★ 70975 ★   **Texaco Self Service**
833 Westbank Expy.
Westwego, LA 70094
(504)340-1911
Ultimate Parent: Texaco. **SIC:** 5541—
Gasoline Service Stations.

★ 70976 ★   **Western Auto Supply
Co.**
1024 Westbank Expy.
Westwego, LA 70094
(504)340-1376
Ultimate Parent: Sears Roebuck & Co.
SIC: 5531—Automobile & Home Supply
Stores.

Winnfield

★ 70977 ★   **Kentucky Fried
Chicken**
419 W. Court St.
Winnfield, LA 71483
(318)628-5555
Ultimate Parent: Pepsico. **SIC:** 5812—
Eating Places.

★ 70978 ★   **Louisiana Pacific
Corp.**
Natchitoches Hwy.
Winnfield, LA 71483
(318)628-3935
Ultimate Parent: Louisiana-Pacific. **SIC:**
5031—Lumber, Plywood & Millwork.

★ 70979 ★   **Wal Mart Discount
City**
Hwy. 167
Winnfield, LA 71483
(318)628-2194
Ultimate Parent: Wal-Mart Stores, Inc. **SIC:**
5311—Department Stores.

Winnsboro

★ 70980 ★   Coca Cola Bottling Co.
710 Carter St.
Winnsboro, LA 71295
(318)435-5407
Ultimate Parent: Coca-Cola Enterprises.
SIC: 5149—Groceries & Related Products Nec.

★ 70981 ★   Pizza Hut
Lane Hwy. 15
Winnsboro, LA 71295
(318)435-9755
Ultimate Parent: Pepsico. **SIC:** 5812—Eating Places.

Zachary

★ 70982 ★   Ferro Corp.
Grant Chemical Div.
US Hwy. 61 N. at Irene Rd.
Zachary, LA 70791
Company Type: Division. **Ultimate Parent:**
Ferro Corp. **SIC:** 2819—Industrial Inorganic
Chemicals Nec; 2869—Industrial Organic
Chemicals Nec.

★ 70983 ★   Georgia-Pacific Corp. Port Hudson
Zachary-Mt. Pleasant Rd.
Zachary, LA 70791-0340
Ultimate Parent: Georgia-Pacific. **SIC:**
2611—Pulp Mills; 2621—Paper Mills;
2679—Converted Paper Products Nec.

★ 70984 ★   Georgia-Pacific Corp. Port Hudson Operations
Zachary-Mt. Pleasant Rd.
Zachary, LA 70791
Ultimate Parent: Georgia-Pacific. **SIC:**
2611—Pulp Mills; 2621—Paper Mills.

★ 70985 ★   Georgia-Pacific Corp. Port Hudson Operations
W. Mount Pleasant Rd.
Zachary, LA 70791
Ultimate Parent: Georgia-Pacific. **SIC:**
2611—Pulp Mills; 2621—Paper Mills.

★ 70986 ★   Gulf States Utilities Co.
2215 Church St.
Zachary, LA 70791
(504)654-6861
Ultimate Parent: Gulf State Utilities Co.
SIC: 4911—Electric Services.

★ 70987 ★   Marathon Pipeline Co.
Hwy. 61
Zachary, LA 70791
(504)654-8854
Ultimate Parent: USX Corp. **SIC:** 4612—
Crude Petroleum Pipelines.

★ 70988 ★   Mary Kay Cosmetics
780 Plains Port Hudson Rd.
Zachary, LA 70791
(504)654-8424
Ultimate Parent: Mary Kay Cosmetics. **SIC:**
6531—Real Estate Agents & Managers.

★ 70989 ★   Wal Mart Discount City
5460 Main St.
Zachary, LA 70791
(504)654-8120
Ultimate Parent: Wal-Mart Stores, Inc. **SIC:**
5311—Department Stores.

Zwolle

★ 70990 ★   Willamette Industries Inc.
Zwolle
La. Hwy. 482
Zwolle, LA 71486
Ultimate Parent: Willamette Industries, Inc.
SIC: 2436—Softwood Veneer & Plywood;
2491—Wood Preserving.

MARYLAND

★ 70991 ★ Calvert Village
Professional Bldg.
Prince Frederick
MD 20678-9628
(410)535-3535
Company Type: Division. Officer: Harold J.
Kahl, Chairman of the Board & President.
Ultimate Parent: Mercantile Bankshares
Corp. SIC: 6022—State Commercial Banks.
Employee Count: 64. Sales: Na M.

Aberdeen

★ 70992 ★ County Banking &
Trust Co.
1004 Beards Hill Rd.
Aberdeen, MD 21001
(410)273-0300
Company Type: Subsidiary. Location
Type: Branch office. Officer: Darren
Basore, Manager. Ultimate Parent:
Mercantile Bankshares Corp. SIC: 6021—
National Commercial Banks.

★ 70993 ★ Rite Aid
Ames Shopping.Ctr.
Aberdeen, MD 21001
(410)939-1656
Ultimate Parent: Rite Aid. SIC: 5912—Drug
Stores & Proprietary Stores.

Accident

★ 70994 ★ Texas Eastern
Transmission Corp.
Accident, MD 21520
(301)826-8137
Ultimate Parent: Panhandle Eastern. SIC:
4932—Gas & Other Services Combined.

Accokeek

★ 70995 ★ Winchester Homes
Inc.
2008 Debra Lynn Way
Accokeek, MD 20607
(301)283-0208
Ultimate Parent: Weyerhaeuser Co.

★ 70996 ★ Winchester Homes
Inc.
1908 Catherine Fran Drive
Accokeek, MD 20607
(301)283-6580
Ultimate Parent: Weyerhaeuser Co.

Adelphi

★ 70997 ★ Kmart
8001 New Hampshire Ave.
Adelphi, MD
(301)439-3400
Ultimate Parent: K-Mart.

★ 70998 ★ Rite Aid
9139 Riggs Rd.
Adelphi, MD 20783
(301)439-3234
Ultimate Parent: Rite Aid.

★ 70999 ★ Rite Aid
2340 University Blvd.
Adelphi, MD
(301)439-2882
Ultimate Parent: Rite Aid.

Annapolis

★ 71000 ★ Alliant Techsystems
Inc.
401 Defense Hwy.
Annapolis, MD 21401-7039
(410)224-4500
Location Type: Branch office. Officer:
Nelson Zagalsky. Ultimate Parent: Alliant
Techsystems Inc. SIC: 3663—Radio & T.V.
Communications Equipment; 3825—
Instruments to Measure Electricity.

★ 71001 ★ Annapolis Banking &
Trust Co.
West St.
Annapolis, MD 21401
(410)268-8011
Company Type: Subsidiary. Location
Type: Branch office. Officer: James Tucker,
Manager. Ultimate Parent: Mercantile
Bankshares Corp. SIC: 6021—National
Commercial Banks.

★ 71002 ★ Annapolis Banking &
Trust Co.
Taylor Ave.
Annapolis, MD 21401
(410)263-8545
Company Type: Subsidiary. Location
Type: Branch office. Officer: Rona Mehl,
Manager. Ultimate Parent: Mercantile
Bankshares Corp. SIC: 6021—National
Commercial Banks.

★ 71003 ★ Annapolis Banking &
Trust Co.
Bay Ridge Ave.
Annapolis, MD 21403
(410)268-4600
Company Type: Subsidiary. Location
Type: Branch office. Officer: Deborah
Bush, Manager. Ultimate Parent:
Mercantile Bankshares Corp. SIC: 6021—
National Commercial Banks.

★ 71004 ★ Annapolis Banking &
Trust Co.
4000 River Crescent Dr.
Annapolis, MD 21401-7269
(410)266-1631
Company Type: Subsidiary. Location
Type: Branch office. Officer: Mary K.
Parkinson, Manager. Ultimate Parent:
Mercantile Bankshares Corp. SIC: 6021—
National Commercial Banks.

★ 71005 ★ Annapolis Banking &
Trust Co.
236 Main St.
PO Box 311
Annapolis, MD 21404-0311
(410)268-3366 Fax: (410)626-2146
Company Type: Subsidiary. Location
Type: Branch office. Officer: Robert E.
Henel Jr., President & CEO. Ultimate
Parent: Mercantile Bankshares Corp. SIC:
6021—National Commercial Banks.

★ 71006 ★ Annapolis Banking &
Trust Co.
116 Defense Hwy., Ste. 100
Annapolis, MD 21401
(410)224-8993
Company Type: Subsidiary. Location
Type: Branch office. Officer: Janice
Marcellas, Manager. Ultimate Parent:
Mercantile Bankshares Corp. SIC: 6021—
National Commercial Banks.

★ 71007 ★ Annapolis Banking &
Trust Co.
Church Cir.
Annapolis, MD 21401-1111
(410)268-4285
Company Type: Subsidiary. Location
Type: Branch office. Officer: Kathleen
Browne, Manager. Ultimate Parent:
Mercantile Bankshares Corp. SIC: 6021—
National Commercial Banks.

★ 71008 ★ Annapolis Banking &
Trust Co.
Main St. & Church Circle
Annapolis, MD 21404
(410)268-3366
Company Type: Division. Officer: Carl A.
Tenhoopen Jr., Chairman of the Board.
Ultimate Parent: Mercantile Bankshares
Corp. Employee Count: 123.

★ 71009 ★ Casual Corner
Annapolis Mall
Annapolis, MD 21401
(410)841-6060
Ultimate Parent: United States Shoe. SIC:
5621—Women's Clothing Stores.

★ 71010 ★ Elmco Inc.
1623 Forest Dr.
Annapolis, MD 21403
(410)263-7740
Ultimate Parent: Ecolab Inc. SIC: 7359—
Equipment Rental & Leasing Nec.

★ 71011 ★ First American Bank
Maryland
129 Main St.
Annapolis, MD 21401
(410)263-6000
Ultimate Parent: First American Corp. SIC:
6141—Personal Credit Institutions.

★ 71012 ★ First Union National
Bank of Maryland
209 Main St.
Annapolis, MD 21401-2048
(410)964-4735
Company Type: Subsidiary. Location
Type: Branch office. Ultimate Parent: First
Union Corp. SIC: 6021—National
Commercial Banks.

★ 71013 ★ First Union National
Bank of Maryland
37 Parole Plz. Shopping Ctr.
Annapolis, MD 21401-3786
(410)964-4763
Company Type: Subsidiary. Location
Type: Branch office. Ultimate Parent: First
Union Corp. SIC: 6021—National
Commercial Banks.

★ 71014 ★ International
Computer Service Inc.
125 Monticello Ave.
Annapolis, MD 21401-3432
(301)858-8400
Ultimate Parent: American International
Group, Inc. SIC: 7371—Computer
Programming Services.

★ 71015 ★ Litton Industries
C. Plath North American Div.
222 Severn Ave.
Annapolis, MD 21403-2569
(410)263-6700
Company Type: Division. Ultimate Parent:
Litton Industries. SIC: 0919—Miscellaneous
Marine Products.

★ 71016 ★ Mellon Bank (MD)
2051 West St.
Annapolis, MD 21401
(410)573-1053
Company Type: Subsidiary. Location
Type: Branch office. Officer: Greg Pearce,
Manager. Ultimate Parent: Mellon Bank
Corp. SIC: 6021—National Commercial
Banks.

★ 71017 ★ Radio Shack
108 Annapls Mall
Annapolis, MD 21401
(301)841-5442
Company Type: Division. Ultimate Parent:
Tandy Corp.

★ 71018 ★ Radio Shack
108 Annapolis Mall
Annapolis, MD 21401
(301)261-8776
Company Type: Division. Ultimate Parent:
Tandy Corp.

★ 71019 ★ Radio Shack
Div. of Tandy Corp.
108 Annapolis Mall
Annapolis, MD 21401
(301)261-8776
Company Type: Division. Ultimate Parent:
Tandy Corp.

★ 71020 ★ Rite Aid
25 Parole
Annapolis, MD 21401
(410)224-3721
Ultimate Parent: Rite Aid. SIC: 5912—Drug
Stores & Proprietary Stores.

★ 71021 ★ United Services
Automobile
1023 Spa Rd.
Annapolis, MD 21403
(410)268-0037
Ultimate Parent: USAA.

★ 71022 ★ Verex Assurance Inc.
110 Meade Dr.
Annapolis, MD 21403
(410)269-0903
Ultimate Parent: Dial Corp. SIC: 6411—
Insurance Agents, Brokers & Service.

★ 71023 ★ Western Publishing
Co.
130 Hollyday Ct
Annapolis, MD 21403
(410)224-3888
Ultimate Parent: Western Publishing
Group. SIC: 2752—Commercial Printing—
Lithographic.

★ 71024 ★ Westinghouse
Electric Corp.
Oceanic Div.
895 Oceanic Dr.
Annapolis, MD 21401
Ultimate Parent: Westinghouse Electric
Corp. SIC: 3761—Guided Missiles & Space
Vehicles.

Annapolis Jct

★ 71025 ★ Intel Corp.
10010 Jct Dr. 200
Annapolis Jct, MD 20701
(410)441-1020
Ultimate Parent: Intel Corp. SIC: 7374—
Data Processing & Preparation.

★ 71026 ★ McDonald's
Hamburgers
Rural Route 198
Annapolis Jct, MD 20701
(410)792-4034
Ultimate Parent: McDonald's.

Annopolis

★ 71027 ★ New York Life
Annapolis Sales Office
Baltimore General Office
900 Bestgate Rd., 2nd Fl.
Annapolis, MD 21401
(301)224-2543
Ultimate Parent: New York Life.

Arnold

★ 71028 ★ Electro Mechanical
Energy Corp.
1197 B & A Blvd.
Arnold, MD 21012
(410)544-8563
Officer: Ole Olesen. Ultimate Parent:
Ametek Inc. SIC: 8734—Testing
Laboratories.

Baltimore

★ 71029 ★ ABF Freight System
Inc.
3510 Washington Blvd.
Baltimore, MD 21227-1638
(410)247-1638
Ultimate Parent: Arkansas Best. SIC:
4212—Local Trucking Without Storage.

★ 71030 ★　Agrico Chemical Co.
2272 S. Clinton St.
Baltimore, MD 21224
(410)276-8100
Ultimate Parent: Freeport-McMoran. **SIC:**
5191—Farm Supplies.

★ 71031 ★　Air Products &
Chemicals Inc.
1701 E. Patapsco Ave.
Baltimore, MD 21226
(410)477-2882
Officer: Mark Reed, Manager. **Ultimate
Parent:** Air Products & Chemicals, Inc. **SIC:**
2813—Industrial Gases.

★ 71032 ★　Allied-Signal Inc.
Communications System Div.
1300 E. Joppa Rd.
Baltimore, MD 21286
(410)583-4000
Company Type: Division. **Officer:** David
Passeri, President. **Ultimate Parent:**
Allied-Signal Inc. **SIC:** 3672—Printed Circuit
Boards.

★ 71033 ★　Amdahl Corp.
250 W. Pratt St.
Baltimore, MD 21201
(410)685-0846
Ultimate Parent: Amdahl Corp. **SIC:**
5099—Durable Goods Nec.

★ 71034 ★　Amdahl Corp.
400 E. Pratt St.
Baltimore, MD 21202
(410)685-0846
Ultimate Parent: Amdahl Corp. **SIC:**
5046—Commercial Equipment Nec.

★ 71035 ★　America West Airlines
BWI Airport
Baltimore, MD 21240
(410)859-3020
Ultimate Parent: America West Airlines.
SIC: 4513—Air Courier Services.

★ 71036 ★　American Credit
Indemnity
300 St. Paul Pl.
Baltimore, MD 21202-2183
(301)554-0700
Company Type: Subsidiary. **Officer:**
Volney Taylor, Chairman. **Ultimate Parent:**
Dun & Bradstreet. **SIC:** 6351—Surety
Insurance.

★ 71037 ★　American Credit
Indemnity
100 E. Pratt St.
Baltimore, MD 21202
(410)554-0700 **Fax:** (410)554-0883
Company Type: Subsidiary. **Officer:** H.
Michael Cushinsky, President. **Ultimate
Parent:** Dun & Bradstreet. **SIC:** 6351—
Surety Insurance.

★ 71038 ★　American General
Federal Credit Union
3910 Keswick Rd.
PO Box 1228
Baltimore, MD 21203-1228
(410)339-9020 **Fax:** (410)338-2694
Officer: M. Patricia O'Haire, CEO. **Ultimate
Parent:** American General Corp. **SIC:**
6061—Federal Credit Unions.

★ 71039 ★　Appraisal Services
Inc.
3655 Old Ct
Baltimore, MD 21208
(410)484-2378
Ultimate Parent: First Financial Corp. **SIC:**
6531—Real Estate Agents & Managers.

★ 71040 ★　Armco Stainless &
Alloy Prods.
3501 E. Biddle St.
Baltimore, MD 21213-4097
(410)563-5500
Ultimate Parent: Armco. **SIC:** 3312—Blast
Furnaces & Steel Mills.

★ 71041 ★　Armco Stainless &
Alloy Products
535 Dundalk Ave.
Baltimore, MD 21224-2903
(410)563-5500
Officer: Robert Rubino. **Ultimate Parent:**
Armco. **SIC:** 3312—Blast Furnaces & Steel
Mills.

★ 71042 ★　Armco Stainless &
Alloy Products
3501 E. Biddle St.
Baltimore, MD 21213
(410)563-5500
Location Type: Plant. **Officer:** Raymond E.
Hein, President. **Ultimate Parent:** Armco.
SIC: 3312—Blast Furnaces & Steel Mills.
Employee Count: 800.

★ 71043 ★　Armco Stainless &
Alloy Products (Baltimore)
3501 E. Biddle St.
Baltimore, MD 21213
(410)563-5500
Company Type: Subsidiary. **Officer:** Harry
Moxley, General Manager. **Ultimate Parent:**
Armco.

★ 71044 ★　Arrow Electronics Inc.
4801 Benson Ave.
Baltimore, MD 21227
(410)247-5200
Ultimate Parent: Arrow Electronics. **SIC:**
5211—Lumber & Other Building Materials.

★ 71045 ★　AT&T Capital Corp.
Instr. Services
BWI Airport
Baltimore, MD 21240
(410)850-4323
Ultimate Parent: AT&T. **SIC:** 5065—
Electronic Parts & Equipment Nec.

★ 71046 ★　Bac-Pritchard, Inc.
PO Box 7322
Baltimore, MD 21227
(410)799-6200
Company Type: Division. **Ultimate Parent:**
Amsted Industries Inc. **SIC:** 3443—
Fabricated Plate Work—Boiler Shops.

★ 71047 ★　Ball Corp.
Decorating & Service Div.
901 W. Ostend St.
Baltimore, MD 21230
Company Type: Division. **Ultimate Parent:**
Ball Corp. **SIC:** 3479—Metal Coating &
Allied Services.

★ 71048 ★　Ball Metal Decorating
& Service
901 W. Ostend St.
Baltimore, MD 21230-1922
Ultimate Parent: Ball Corp. **SIC:** 3479—
Metal Coating & Allied Services.

★ 71049 ★　Ball Metal Decorating
& Services
901 W. Ostend St.
Baltimore, MD 21230-1900
(410)837-6800
Officer: Mike Kachmer. **Ultimate Parent:**
Ball Corp. **SIC:** 2752—Commercial
Printing—Lithographic; 3444—Sheet Metal
Work.

★ 71050 ★　Baltimore Gas &
Electric Co.
PO Box 1475
Baltimore, MD 21203-1475
(410)783-6920
Officer: Edward A. Crooke. **Ultimate
Parent:** Baltimore Gas & Electric Co. **SIC:**
4931—Electric & Other Services Combined;
4932—Gas & Other Services Combined.

★ 71051 ★　Baltimore Gas &
Electric Co.
Gas & Electric Bldg.
Charles Center
Baltimore, MD 21201
(410)234-5000
Location Type: Branch office. **Officer:**
Edward A. Crooke, President & COO.
Ultimate Parent: Baltimore Gas & Electric
Co. **SIC:** 4911—Electric Services; 8052—
Intermediate Care Facilities; 6552—
Subdividers & Developers Nec; 6799—
Investors Nec; 8051—Skilled Nursing Care
Facilities. **Employee Count:** 9626. **Sales:**
2.4 M.

★ 71052 ★　Baltimore Gas &
Electric Co.
PO Box 1475
Baltimore, MD 21203
(410)234-5289
Ultimate Parent: Baltimore Gas & Electric
Co.

★ 71053 ★　Baltimore Gas &
Electric Co.
2020 W. Cold Spring Ln.
Baltimore, MD 21209
(410)542-8808
Ultimate Parent: Baltimore Gas & Electric
Co.

★ 71054 ★　Baltimore Gas &
Electric Co.
Greenspring Manor
Baltimore, MD 21208
(410)358-9538
Ultimate Parent: Baltimore Gas & Electric
Co.

★ 71055 ★　Baltimore Gas &
Electric Co.
4237 Old Frederick Rd.
Baltimore, MD 21229
(410)233-4000
Ultimate Parent: Baltimore Gas & Electric
Co.

★ 71056 ★　Baltimore Gas &
Electric Co.
39 W. Lexington St.
Baltimore, MD 21201-3940
(410)234-5000
Officer: Edward Cook. **Ultimate Parent:**
Baltimore Gas & Electric Co. **SIC:** 4911—
Electric Services; 4924—Natural Gas
Distribution; 7623—Refrigeration Services
Repair; 7629—Electrical Repair Shops Nec.

★ 71057 ★　Baltimore Gas &
Electric Co.
North Beach
Baltimore, MD 21203
(410)798-5539
Location Type: Branch office. **Ultimate
Parent:** Baltimore Gas & Electric Co. **SIC:**
4924—Natural Gas Distribution.

★ 71058 ★　Baltimore Gas &
Electric Co.
Lexington & Liberty Sts.
Baltimore, MD 21203
(410)234-5000
Company Type: Headquarters. **Officer:**
Christian H. Poindexter. **Employee Count:**
9112. **Fortune Service 500:** Ranking 34.

★ 71059 ★　Baltimore Specialty
Steele Corps.
3501 E. Biddle St.
Baltimore, MD 21213-4002
(410)563-5500
Officer: R. E. Hein. **Ultimate Parent:**
Armco. **SIC:** 3312—Blast Furnaces & Steel
Mills.

★ 71060 ★　Baltimore Specialty
Steels Corp.
3501 E. Biddle St.
Baltimore, MD 21213
Ultimate Parent: Armco. **SIC:** 3312—Blast
Furnaces & Steel Mills.

★ 71061 ★　Batesville Casket Co.
Inc.
1810 Howard Ln.
Baltimore, MD 21227
(410)796-2020
Ultimate Parent: Hillenbrand Industries.
SIC: 5087—Service Establishment
Equipment.

★ 71062 ★　Bell Atlantic Bus
Systems Svc
2622 Lord Baltimore Dr.
Baltimore, MD 21244-2600
(410)298-5525
Ultimate Parent: Bell Atlantic Corp. **SIC:**
7378—Computer Maintenance & Repair.

★ 71063 ★　Beneficial Income Tax
Service
5535 Harford Rd.
Baltimore, MD 21214
(410)426-6947
Ultimate Parent: Beneficial. **SIC:** 8721—
Accounting, Auditing & Bookkeeping.

★ 71064 ★　Beneficial Maryland
Inc.
1907 E. Joppa Rd. A
Baltimore, MD 21234-2764
(410)668-4770
Ultimate Parent: Beneficial. **SIC:** 6141—
Personal Credit Institutions; 6162—
Mortgage Bankers & Correspondents.

★ 71065 ★　Bethlehem Steel
Corp.
Sparrows Point Yard
Baltimore, MD 21219
(410)388-3000
Officer: David Watson. **Ultimate Parent:**
Bethlehem Steel Corp. **SIC:** 3731—Ship
Building & Repairing; 3312—Blast Furnaces
& Steel Mills.

★ 71066 ★　Black & Decker U.S.
Inc.
701 E. Joppa Rd.
Baltimore, MD 21286-5559
(410)716-3900
Company Type: Subsidiary. **Officer:** Nolan
D. Archibald, President. **Ultimate Parent:**
Black & Decker Corp. **SIC:** 3546—
Power-Driven Handtools; 3634—Electric
Housewares & Fans. **Employee Count:**
8500. **Sales:** 718 M.

★ 71067 ★　Blazer Financial
Services
3998 PO Box
Baltimore, MD 21222
(410)288-4550
Ultimate Parent: Great Western Financial
Corp. **SIC:** 6141—Personal Credit
Institutions.

★ 71068 ★　Blazer Financial
Services
5440 Harford Rd.
Baltimore, MD 21214
(410)426-5536
Ultimate Parent: Great Western Financial
Corp. **SIC:** 6141—Personal Credit
Institutions.

★ 71069 ★　BNG, Inc.
Gas & Electric Bldg.
Baltimore, MD 21201
(410)234-5913
Company Type: Subsidiary. **Officer:**
Michael J. Chesser, President. **Ultimate
Parent:** Baltimore Gas & Electric Co. **SIC:**
4923—Gas Transmission & Distribution;
4924—Natural Gas Distribution. **Employee
Count:** 6. **Sales:** 1 M.

★ 71070 ★　BNG Inc.
Spring Garden Complex
PO Box 1475
Baltimore, MD 21203
(301)234-4546
Ultimate Parent: Baltimore Gas & Electric
Co.

★ 71071 ★　BNG, Inc.
Gas & Electric Bldg.
Baltimore, MD 21201
(410)234-5913
Company Type: Subsidiary. **Officer:**
Michael J. Chesser, President. **Ultimate
Parent:** Baltimore Gas & Electric Co. **SIC:**
4923—Gas Transmission & Distribution;
4924—Natural Gas Distribution. **Employee
Count:** 6. **Sales:** 1.1 M.

★ 71072 ★　BNG, Inc.
PO Box 1475
Spring Gardens Complex
Baltimore, MD 21203
(410)234-4546
Company Type: Subsidiary. **Officer:** J.
Thomas Wellener, President. **Ultimate
Parent:** Baltimore Gas & Electric Co. **SIC:**
4924—Natural Gas Distribution. **Sales:**
1,577,468 M.

★ 71073 ★　T. Talbott Bond
7140 Windsor Blvd.
Baltimore, MD 21207
(410)265-8600
Officer: T. Talbott Bond, President.
Ultimate Parent: Alco Standard Corp. **SIC:**
5046—Commercial Equipment Nec.

★ 71074 ★　Browning-Ferris
Industries
7521 Cemetery Ln.
Baltimore, MD 21227-6336
(410)799-0520
Officer: Allen Dockery. **Ultimate Parent:**
Browning-Ferris Industries. **SIC:** 4953—
Refuse Systems.

★ 71075 ★　Browning-Ferris
Industries
Pulaski Hwy. & 68th St.
Baltimore, MD 21237
(410)686-6161
Ultimate Parent: Browning-Ferris
Industries. **SIC:** 4953—Refuse Systems.

★ 71076 ★   Carr-Lowrey Glass Co.
2201 Kloman St.
Baltimore, MD 21230
Ultimate Parent: Newell. SIC: 3221—Glass Containers.

★ 71077 ★   Casual Corner
1 Charles Ctr.
Baltimore, MD 21201
(410)539-2929
Ultimate Parent: United States Shoe. SIC: 5699—Miscellaneous Apparel & Accessory Stores.

★ 71078 ★   Chase Bank of Maryland
10 E. Baltimore St.
Baltimore, MD 21202-1630
(410)576-0030
Company Type: Subsidiary. Officer: Lywal Salles, President & CEO. Ultimate Parent: Chase Manhattan Corp. SIC: 6022—State Commercial Banks. Employee Count: 263.

★ 71079 ★   Chemical Specialties Manufacturing Corp.
3001 E. Madison St.
Baltimore, MD 21205
Ultimate Parent: RPM, Inc. SIC: 2842—Polishes & Sanitation Goods.

★ 71080 ★   Chemspec Inc.
3001 E. Madison St.
Baltimore, MD 21205
Ultimate Parent: RPM, Inc. SIC: 2842—Polishes & Sanitation Goods.

★ 71081 ★   Chesapeake & Patomic Telephone Co. of Maryland
1 E. Pratt St.
Baltimore, MD 21202
(410)539-9900 Fax: (410)393-4799
Company Type: Subsidiary. Officer: Frederick D. D'Alessio, President & CEO. Ultimate Parent: Bell Atlantic Corp.

★ 71082 ★   The Chesapeake & Potomac Co. of Maryland
1 E. Pratt St.
Baltimore, MD 21202
(410)539-9900
Company Type: Subsidiary. Officer: Frederick D. D'Alessio, President & CEO. Ultimate Parent: Bell Atlantic Corp. SIC: 4812—Radiotelephone Communications. Employee Count: 11150. Sales: 1562000000 M.

★ 71083 ★   Chesapeake & Potomac Tel Co. MD
1 E. Pratt St.
Baltimore, MD 21202-1038
(410)393-7000
Location Type: Branch office. Officer: Frederick D. D'Aleessio. Ultimate Parent: Bell Atlantic Corp. SIC: 4813—Telephone Communications Except Radiotelephone; 4812—Radiotelephone Communications.

★ 71084 ★   Chesapeake & Potomac Telephone Co. of Maryland
1 E. Pratt St.
Baltimore, MD 21202-1038
(410)539-9900
Company Type: Subsidiary. Officer: Frederick D. D'Alessio, President & CEO. Ultimate Parent: Bell Atlantic Corp. SIC: 4813—Telephone Communications Except Radiotelephone. Employee Count: 8400. Sales: 2 M.

★ 71085 ★   Chevron USA Inc. Baltimore Asphalt Terminal
1955 Chesapeake Ave.
Baltimore, MD 21226
Ultimate Parent: Chevron Corp. SIC: 2951—Asphalt Paving Mixtures & Blocks.

★ 71086 ★   Chicago Title Insurance Co.
409 Washington Ave.
Baltimore, MD 21204-4920
(410)321-0900
Ultimate Parent: Alleghany Corp. SIC: 6541—Title Abstract Offices.

★ 71087 ★   Chicago Title Insurance Co. Maryland
110 Saint Paul St.
Baltimore, MD 21202-1748
(410)727-3700
Officer: Anthony J. Byrne. Ultimate Parent: Alleghany Corp. SIC: 6541—Title Abstract Offices.

★ 71088 ★   Citgo Service Station
220 Wise Ave.
Baltimore, MD 21222
(410)282-1977
Ultimate Parent: Citgo Petroleum. SIC: 7513—Truck Rental & Leasing Without Drivers.

★ 71089 ★   Coast to Coast
6512 Baltimore National P
Baltimore, MD 21228
(410)788-0400
Ultimate Parent: Servistar Corp. SIC: 5813—Drinking Places.

★ 71090 ★   Coca-Cola USA
1215 E. Fort Ave.
Baltimore, MD 21230-5104
Ultimate Parent: Coca-Cola. SIC: 2087—Flavoring Extracts & Syrups Nec.

★ 71091 ★   Constellation Energy
250 W. Pratt St.
Baltimore, MD 21201
(410)783-2806 Fax: (410)783-2862
Company Type: Subsidiary. Officer: Bruce M. Ambler, President & CEO. Ultimate Parent: Baltimore Gas & Electric Co.

★ 71092 ★   Constellation Energy Inc.
250 W. Pratt St.
Baltimore, MD 21201-2423
(410)783-2800
Company Type: Subsidiary. Officer: Bruce Ambler, President. Ultimate Parent: Baltimore Gas & Electric Co. SIC: 6552—Subdividers & Developers Nec. Employee Count: 75. Sales: 6 M.

★ 71093 ★   Constellation Health Service, Inc.
250 W. Pratt St.
Baltimore, MD 21201
Company Type: Subsidiary. Officer: J.W. Jeffcoat, President. Ultimate Parent: Baltimore Gas & Electric Co. SIC: 8052—Intermediate Care Facilities.

★ 71094 ★   Constellation Health Services
250 W. Pratt St.
Baltimore, MD 21201
(410)783-2876 Fax: (410)738-2862
Company Type: Subsidiary. Officer: James W. Jeffcoat, President. Ultimate Parent: Baltimore Gas & Electric Co.

★ 71095 ★   Constellation Holding Inc.
250 W. Pratt St.
Baltimore, MD 21201
(410)783-2806 Fax: (410)783-2862
Company Type: Subsidiary. Officer: Christian H Poindexter, Chairman. Ultimate Parent: Baltimore Gas & Electric Co.

★ 71096 ★   Constellation Holdings Inc.
250 W. Pratt St.
Baltimore, MD 21201
(301)783-2800
Ultimate Parent: Baltimore Gas & Electric Co.

★ 71097 ★   Constellation Holdings, Inc.
250 W. Pratt St.
Baltimore, MD 21201-2423
(410)783-2800
Company Type: Subsidiary. Officer: Bruce Ambler, President & CEO. Ultimate Parent: Baltimore Gas & Electric Co. SIC: 6531—Real Estate Agents & Managers; 6552—Subdividers & Developers Nec; 8059—Nursing & Personal Care Nec. Employee Count: 900. Sales: 111 M.

★ 71098 ★   Constellation Investments
250 W. Pratt St.
Baltimore, MD 21201
(410)783-2832 Fax: (410)783-2862
Company Type: Subsidiary. Officer: Steven D. Kesler, President. Ultimate Parent: Baltimore Gas & Electric Co.

★ 71099 ★   Constellation Investments, Inc.
250 W. Pratt St., 23rd Floor
Baltimore, MD 21201
(410)783-2800
Company Type: Subsidiary. Officer: Steven D. Kesler, President. Ultimate Parent: Baltimore Gas & Electric Co. SIC: 6799—Investors Nec. Employee Count: 4. Sales: 19,075,507 M.

★ 71100 ★   Constellation Investments, Inc.
250 W. Pratt St.
Baltimore, MD 21201-2423
(410)783-2800
Company Type: Subsidiary. Officer: Steven Kesler, President. Ultimate Parent: Baltimore Gas & Electric Co. SIC: 6719—Holding Companies Nec. Employee Count: 9. Sales: 20 M.

★ 71101 ★   Constellation Real Estate Group
250 W. Pratt St.
Baltimore, MD 21201
(410)783-2885 Fax: (410)783-2862
Company Type: Subsidiary. Officer: Randall M. Griffin, President. Ultimate Parent: Baltimore Gas & Electric Co.

★ 71102 ★   Constellation Real Estate Group, Inc.
250 W. Pratt St.
Baltimore, MD 21201-2423
(410)782-2827
Company Type: Subsidiary. Officer: Bruce Ambler, Chairman of the Board. Ultimate Parent: Baltimore Gas & Electric Co. SIC: 6552—Subdividers & Developers Nec; 6531—Real Estate Agents & Managers; 8051—Skilled Nursing Care Facilities. Employee Count: 700. Sales: 84.4 M.

★ 71103 ★   Constellation Real Estate Group, Inc.
250 W. Pratt St.
Baltimore, MD 21201-2423
(410)782-2827
Company Type: Subsidiary. Officer: Bruce Ambler, Chairman of the Board. Ultimate Parent: Baltimore Gas & Electric Co. SIC: 6552—Subdividers & Developers Nec; 6531—Real Estate Agents & Managers; 8051—Skilled Nursing Care Facilities. Employee Count: 700. Sales: 84 M.

★ 71104 ★   Continental Express
BWI Airport
Baltimore, MD 21240
(410)337-2061
Ultimate Parent: Continental Airlines.

★ 71105 ★   Crown Beverage Packaging Inc.
8801 Citation Rd.
Baltimore, MD 21221
Ultimate Parent: Crown Cork & Seal. SIC: 3411—Metal Cans.

★ 71106 ★   Crown Beverage Packaging Inc. Plant 16
3701 Duncanwood Ln.
Baltimore, MD 21213
Ultimate Parent: Crown Cork & Seal. SIC: 3411—Metal Cans.

★ 71107 ★   Crown Central Holding Corp.
1 N. Charles St.
Baltimore, MD 21201-3740
(410)539-7400
Company Type: Subsidiary. Ultimate Parent: Crown Central Petroleum Corp. SIC: 5411—Grocery Stores.

★ 71108 ★   Crown Central Petroleum Corp.
1 N. Charles St.
Baltimore, MD 21201
(410)539-7400
Company Type: Headquarters. Officer: Henry A. Rosenberg Jr. Employee Count: 2934. Sales: 1451 M. Fortune 500: Largest U.S. Industrial Corporations: Ranking 281.

★ 71109 ★   Dap Inc.
4630 North Point Blvd.
Baltimore, MD 21219
Ultimate Parent: USG Corp. SIC: 2891—Adhesives & Sealants.

★ 71110 ★   Delphax Systems
7 Mayton Ct.
Baltimore, MD 21227-3959
(410)242-4584
Ultimate Parent: Avery Dennison Corp. SIC: 5085—Industrial Supplies.

★ 71111 ★   Eastern Stainless Corp.
7700 Rolling Mill Rd.
Baltimore, MD 21224-2035
(410)522-6200
Location Type: Branch office. Officer: R. C. Rubino. Ultimate Parent: Armco. SIC: 3312—Blast Furnaces & Steel Mills.

★ 71112 ★   Emhart Corp.
701 E. Joppa Rd.
Baltimore, MD 21286-5559
(410)716-3900
Company Type: Subsidiary. Officer: Michael S. Karsner, President & Treasurer. Ultimate Parent: Black & Decker Corp. SIC: 3429—Hardware Nec; 3452—Bolts, Nuts, Rivets & Washers; 3579—Office Machines Nec; 3423—Hand & Edge Tools Nec; 3949—Sporting & Athletic Goods Nec; 3559—Special Industry Machinery Nec. Employee Count: 25000. Sales: 2 M.

★ 71113 ★   Emhart Industries Inc.
701 E. Joppa Rd.
Baltimore, MD 21286-5559
(410)716-3900
Company Type: Subsidiary. Officer: Raymond A. DeVita, President. Ultimate Parent: Black & Decker Corp. SIC: 3429—Hardware Nec; 3452—Bolts, Nuts, Rivets & Washers; 3579—Office Machines Nec; 3423—Hand & Edge Tools Nec; 3949—Sporting & Athletic Goods Nec. Employee Count: 20000. Sales: 2 M.

★ 71114 ★   Esskay
3800 E. Baltimore St.
Baltimore, MD 21224
Ultimate Parent: Smithfield Foods Inc. SIC: 2011—Meat Packing Plants.

★ 71115 ★   Exxon Co.
3801 Boston St.
Baltimore, MD 21224
(410)563-5117
Ultimate Parent: Exxon. SIC: 5171—Petroleum Bulk Stations & Terminals.

★ 71116 ★   Exxon Corp.
1501 S. Clinton St.
Baltimore, MD 21224
(410)563-5100
Ultimate Parent: Exxon. SIC: 5983—Fuel Oil Dealers.

★ 71117 ★   F Z Corp.
1 N. Charles St.
Baltimore, MD 21201-3709
(410)539-7400
Company Type: Subsidiary. Ultimate Parent: Crown Central Petroleum Corp. SIC: 5411—Grocery Stores.

★ 71118 ★   First American Bank Maryland
21 W. Fayette St.
Baltimore, MD 21201
(410)752-7900
Ultimate Parent: First American Corp. SIC: 6022—State Commercial Banks.

★ 71119 ★   First American Bank Maryland
Fleet Conkling Sts
Baltimore, MD 21224
(410)675-1500
Ultimate Parent: First American Corp. SIC: 6099—Functions Related to Deposit Banking.

★ 71120 ★   First American Bank Maryland
25 W. Chesapeake Ave.
Baltimore, MD 21204
(410)321-4200
Ultimate Parent: First American Corp. SIC: 6099—Functions Related to Deposit Banking.

★ 71121 ★   First Maryland Bancorp
25 S. Charles St.
Baltimore, MD 21201
(410)244-4000
Company Type: Headquarters. Officer: Charles W. Cole Jr. Employee Count: 4585. Fortune Service 500: Ranking 65.

★ 71122 ★ First National Bank of Maryland
16 Hammonds Ln.
Baltimore, MD 21225-3685
(410)789-8600
Company Type: Subsidiary. Location Type: Branch office. Ultimate Parent: First Maryland Bancorp. SIC: 6021—National Commercial Banks.

★ 71123 ★ First National Bank of Maryland
3470 Annapolis Rd.
Baltimore, MD 21230-3404
(410)244-4122
Company Type: Subsidiary. Location Type: Branch office. Ultimate Parent: First Maryland Bancorp. SIC: 6021—National Commercial Banks.

★ 71124 ★ First National Bank of Maryland
1536 Havenwood Rd.
Baltimore, MD 21218-1690
(410)889-5551
Company Type: Subsidiary. Location Type: Branch office. Ultimate Parent: First Maryland Bancorp. SIC: 6021—National Commercial Banks.

★ 71125 ★ First National Bank of Maryland
5910 York Rd.
Baltimore, MD 21212-3096
(410)433-3100
Company Type: Subsidiary. Location Type: Branch office. Ultimate Parent: First Maryland Bancorp. SIC: 6021—National Commercial Banks.

★ 71126 ★ First National Bank of Maryland
156 Carroll Island Dr.
Baltimore, MD 21220-2208
(410)335-4636
Company Type: Subsidiary. Location Type: Branch office. Ultimate Parent: First Maryland Bancorp. SIC: 6021—National Commercial Banks.

★ 71127 ★ First National Bank of Maryland
1710 E. Northern Pky.
Baltimore, MD 21239-2199
(410)494-7063
Company Type: Subsidiary. Location Type: Branch office. Ultimate Parent: First Maryland Bancorp. SIC: 6021—National Commercial Banks.

★ 71128 ★ First National Bank of Maryland
Howard & Madison Sts.
Baltimore, MD 21201-3478
(410)728-3300
Company Type: Subsidiary. Location Type: Branch office. Ultimate Parent: First Maryland Bancorp. SIC: 6021—National Commercial Banks.

★ 71129 ★ First National Bank of Maryland
Pulaski Hwy. & Monument St.
Baltimore, MD 21224
(410)732-8139
Company Type: Subsidiary. Location Type: Branch office. Ultimate Parent: First Maryland Bancorp. SIC: 6021—National Commercial Banks.

★ 71130 ★ First National Bank of Maryland
809 Eastern Blvd.
Baltimore, MD 21221-3505
(410)686-8822
Company Type: Subsidiary. Location Type: Branch office. Ultimate Parent: First Maryland Bancorp. SIC: 6021—National Commercial Banks.

★ 71131 ★ First National Bank of Maryland
25th St. & Kirk Ave.
Baltimore, MD 21218
(410)366-5144
Company Type: Subsidiary. Location Type: Branch office. Ultimate Parent: First Maryland Bancorp. SIC: 6021—National Commercial Banks.

★ 71132 ★ First National Bank of Maryland
Holiday & Fayette Sts.
Baltimore, MD 21202
(410)244-4182
Company Type: Subsidiary. Location Type: Branch office. Ultimate Parent: First Maryland Bancorp. SIC: 6021—National Commercial Banks.

★ 71133 ★ First National Bank of Maryland
400 E. Pratt St.
Baltimore, MD 21202-3116
(410)625-5085
Company Type: Subsidiary. Location Type: Branch office. Ultimate Parent: First Maryland Bancorp. SIC: 6021—National Commercial Banks.

★ 71134 ★ First National Bank of Maryland
5201 Roland Ave.
Baltimore, MD 21210-1997
(410)494-7073
Company Type: Subsidiary. Location Type: Branch office. Ultimate Parent: First Maryland Bancorp. SIC: 6021—National Commercial Banks.

★ 71135 ★ First National Bank of Maryland
19 E. Cross St.
Baltimore, MD 21230-4003
(410)244-4110
Company Type: Subsidiary. Location Type: Branch office. Ultimate Parent: First Maryland Bancorp. SIC: 6021—National Commercial Banks.

★ 71136 ★ First National Bank of Maryland
Gilman Hall, JHU Campus
Baltimore, MD 21218
(410)494-7058
Company Type: Subsidiary. Location Type: Branch office. Ultimate Parent: First Maryland Bancorp. SIC: 6021—National Commercial Banks.

★ 71137 ★ First National Bank of Maryland
22 E. Fayette St.
Baltimore, MD 21202-6422
(410)528-1717
Company Type: Subsidiary. Location Type: Branch office. Ultimate Parent: First Maryland Bancorp. SIC: 6021—National Commercial Banks.

★ 71138 ★ First National Bank of Maryland
Eastern & Highland Aves.
Baltimore, MD 21224
(410)732-7970
Company Type: Subsidiary. Location Type: Branch office. Ultimate Parent: First Maryland Bancorp. SIC: 6021—National Commercial Banks.

★ 71139 ★ First National Bank of Maryland
5724 Wabash Ave.
Baltimore, MD 21215-3203
(410)244-4120
Company Type: Subsidiary. Location Type: Branch office. Ultimate Parent: First Maryland Bancorp. SIC: 6021—National Commercial Banks.

★ 71140 ★ First National Bank of Maryland
100 N. Greene St.
Baltimore, MD 21201-1503
(410)962-7130
Company Type: Subsidiary. Location Type: Branch office. Ultimate Parent: First Maryland Bancorp. SIC: 6021—National Commercial Banks.

★ 71141 ★ First National Bank of Maryland
1975 E. Joppa Rd.
Baltimore, MD 21234-2790
(410)668-2222
Company Type: Subsidiary. Location Type: Branch office. Ultimate Parent: First Maryland Bancorp. SIC: 6021—National Commercial Banks.

★ 71142 ★ First National Bank of Maryland
St. Paul Pl. & Saratoga St.
Baltimore, MD 21202-2662
(410)244-4150
Company Type: Subsidiary. Location Type: Branch office. Ultimate Parent: First Maryland Bancorp. SIC: 6021—National Commercial Banks.

★ 71143 ★ First National Bank of Maryland
14 Light St.
Baltimore, MD 21202-1026
(410)244-3777
Company Type: Subsidiary. Location Type: Branch office. Ultimate Parent: First Maryland Bancorp. SIC: 6021—National Commercial Banks.

★ 71144 ★ First National Bank of Maryland
7615 Bellona Rd.
Baltimore, MD 21204-6609
(410)244-4000
Company Type: Subsidiary. Location Type: Branch office. Ultimate Parent: First Maryland Bancorp. SIC: 6021—National Commercial Banks.

★ 71145 ★ First National Bank of Maryland
8812 Waltham Woods Rd.
Baltimore, MD 21209-2230
(410)244-4000
Company Type: Subsidiary. Location Type: Branch office. Ultimate Parent: First Maryland Bancorp. SIC: 6021—National Commercial Banks.

★ 71146 ★ First National Bank of Maryland
Broadway & Eastern Aves.
Baltimore, MD 21231-1265
(410)732-8065
Company Type: Subsidiary. Location Type: Branch office. Ultimate Parent: First Maryland Bancorp. SIC: 6021—National Commercial Banks.

★ 71147 ★ First National Bank of Maryland
25 S. Charles St.
Baltimore, MD 21201
(410)244-4000 Fax: (410)244-4026
Company Type: Subsidiary. Officer: Charles W. Cole Jr., President & CEO. Ultimate Parent: First Maryland Bancorp. SIC: 6021—National Commercial Banks.

★ 71148 ★ First National Bank of Maryland
6267 Kenwood Ave.
Baltimore, MD 21237-2073
(410)866-4100
Company Type: Subsidiary. Location Type: Branch office. Ultimate Parent: First Maryland Bancorp. SIC: 6021—National Commercial Banks.

★ 71149 ★ First National Bank of Maryland
6080 Falls Rd.
Baltimore, MD 21209-2230
(410)337-0011
Company Type: Subsidiary. Location Type: Branch office. Ultimate Parent: First Maryland Bancorp. SIC: 6021—National Commercial Banks.

★ 71150 ★ First Union National Bank of Maryland
Inner Harbor, 210-212 E. Lombard St.
Baltimore, MD 21202-3122
(410)964-4790
Company Type: Subsidiary. Location Type: Branch office. Ultimate Parent: First Union Corp. SIC: 6021—National Commercial Banks.

★ 71151 ★ First Union National Bank of Maryland
Fleet & Conkling Sts.
Baltimore, MD 21224
(410)964-4756
Company Type: Subsidiary. Location Type: Branch office. Ultimate Parent: First Union Corp. SIC: 6021—National Commercial Banks.

★ 71152 ★ FMC Corp.
1701 E. Patapsco Ave.
Baltimore, MD 21226
(410)355-6400
Officer: John Sanderson, Manager. Ultimate Parent: FMC. SIC: 2869—Industrial Organic Chemicals Nec; 2879—Agricultural Chemicals Nec.

★ 71153 ★ Fmc Corp. Agricultural Chemical Group
1701 E. Patapsco Ave.
Baltimore, MD 21226
Ultimate Parent: FMC. SIC: 2869—Industrial Organic Chemicals Nec; 2879—Agricultural Chemicals Nec; 2819—Industrial Inorganic Chemicals Nec.

★ 71154 ★ FMC Corp., Baltimore Plant
1701 E. Patapsco Ave.
Baltimore, MD 21226
Location Type: Plant. Ultimate Parent: FMC. SIC: 2869—Industrial Organic Chemicals Nec; 2879—Agricultural Chemicals Nec; 2819—Industrial Inorganic Chemicals Nec.

★ 71155 ★ GAF Building Materials Corp.
1500 S. Ponca St.
Baltimore, MD 21224
(410)633-7200
Company Type: Subsidiary. Officer: Adel Fadel, Manager. Ultimate Parent: GAF Corp. SIC: 2952—Asphalt Felts & Coatings; 3296—Mineral Wool.

★ 71156 ★ The Gap
Security Sq.
Baltimore, MD 21207
(410)944-7040
Ultimate Parent: GAP. SIC: 5699—Miscellaneous Apparel & Accessory Stores.

★ 71157 ★ Gap
White
Baltimore, MD 21236
(410)256-6316
Ultimate Parent: GAP. SIC: 5699—Miscellaneous Apparel & Accessory Stores.

★ 71158 ★ Gap
5737 Westview Mall
Baltimore, MD 21228
(410)788-8660
Ultimate Parent: GAP. SIC: 5699—Miscellaneous Apparel & Accessory Stores.

★ 71159 ★ General Electric Co.
920 E. Fort Ave.
Baltimore, MD 21230
(410)332-4700
Officer: David Brumbaugh, Manager. Ultimate Parent: General Electric. SIC: 3599—Industrial Machinery Nec.

★ 71160 ★ Grace Davison
PO Box 2117
Baltimore, MD 21203
(410)659-9000
Company Type: Subsidiary. Officer: James R. Hyde, President. Ultimate Parent: W. R. Grace.

★ 71161 ★ Greyhound Bus Lines
601 N. Howard St.
Baltimore, MD 21201
(410)727-4148
Ultimate Parent: Greyhound Lines Inc. SIC: 4141—Local Bus Charter Service.

★ 71162 ★ Greyhound Bus Lines
8800 Yellow Brick Rd.
Baltimore, MD 21237
(410)391-7050
Ultimate Parent: Greyhound Lines Inc. SIC: 4111—Local & Suburban Transit.

★ 71163 ★ Greyhound Bus Lines
Howard St.
Baltimore, MD 21227
(410)752-1393
Ultimate Parent: Greyhound Lines Inc. SIC: 4111—Local & Suburban Transit.

★ 71164 ★ Halethorpe Extrusions Inc.
2000 Halethorpe Ave.
Baltimore, MD 21227
Ultimate Parent: Aluminum Co. of America--Alcoa. SIC: 3354—Aluminum Extruded Products.

★ **71165** ★ **Health Care Management Corp.**
8600 La Salle Rd.
Baltimore, MD 21204
(410)296-3282
Ultimate Parent: Columbia Gas System.
SIC: 8051—Skilled Nursing Care Facilities.

★ **71166** ★ **Hertz Rent-A-Car**
501 W. Lombard St.
Baltimore, MD 21201
(410)332-3600
Ultimate Parent: Hertz. **SIC:** 7514—
Passenger Car Rental.

★ **71167** ★ **Hit or Miss**
6600 Baltimore National P
Baltimore, MD 21228
(410)744-9667
Ultimate Parent: TJX. **SIC:** 5621—
Women's Clothing Stores.

★ **71168** ★ **Hit or Miss**
1901 E. Joppa Rd.
Baltimore, MD 21234
(410)661-9607
Ultimate Parent: TJX. **SIC:** 5621—
Women's Clothing Stores.

★ **71169** ★ **Hormel & Co/Geo**
320 Hillen Rd.
Baltimore, MD 21204
(410)828-5252
Ultimate Parent: Hormel Foods. **SIC:**
5147—Meats & Meat Products.

★ **71170** ★ **Johnson & Bloy America Inc.**
3721 Old Georgetown Rd.
Baltimore, MD 21227
Ultimate Parent: Johnson & Johnson. **SIC:**
2893—Printing Ink.

★ **71171** ★ **Johnson & Bloy Inc.**
3721 Old Georgetown Rd.
Baltimore, MD 21227
Ultimate Parent: Johnson & Johnson. **SIC:**
2893—Printing Ink.

★ **71172** ★ **Kaiser Aluminum Chem Corp.**
2000 Halethorpe Ave.
Baltimore, MD 21227
(410)242-2800
Ultimate Parent: Maxxam. **SIC:** 5051—
Metals Service Centers & Offices.

★ **71173** ★ **Kirk Steiff Co.**
800 Wyman Park Dr.
Baltimore, MD 21211
(410)338-6000
Officer: James Solomon, President.
Ultimate Parent: Brown-Forman. **SIC:**
3911—Jewelry & Precious Metal; 3914—
Silverware & Plated Ware.

★ **71174** ★ **Kirk Steiff Co.**
800 Wyman Pk. Dr.
Baltimore, MD 21211-1806
(410)338-6000
Officer: James Solomon. **Ultimate Parent:**
Brown-Forman. **SIC:** 3914—Silverware &
Plated Ware; 5944—Jewelry Stores.

★ **71175** ★ **Kirk Steiff Co.**
Kirk Steiff Division
800 Wyman Park Dr.
Baltimore, MD 21211
Ultimate Parent: Brown-Forman. **SIC:**
3914—Silverware & Plated Ware; 3471—
Plating & Polishing.

★ **71176** ★ **Lees Carry out**
1211 W. Baltimore St.
Baltimore, MD 21223
(410)727-4419
Ultimate Parent: Burlington Industries,
Equity. **SIC:** 5812—Eating Places.

★ **71177** ★ **Lees Carry out**
602 N. Collington Ave.
Baltimore, MD 21205
(410)342-4154
Ultimate Parent: Burlington Industries,
Equity. **SIC:** 5812—Eating Places.

★ **71178** ★ **Lees Carry out**
2702 Pennsylvania Ave.
Baltimore, MD 21217
(410)728-6248
Ultimate Parent: Burlington Industries,
Equity. **SIC:** 5812—Eating Places.

★ **71179** ★ **Liberty Mutual Insurance Co.**
Charles Ctr. S
Baltimore, MD 21201
(410)539-3800
Ultimate Parent: Liberty Mutual Group.
SIC: 8111—Legal Services.

★ **71180** ★ **Life Insurance Co. of Va**
8501 La Salle Rd.
Baltimore, MD 21204
(410)828-6882
Ultimate Parent: Life Insurance Co. of
Virginia. **SIC:** 6411—Insurance Agents,
Brokers & Service.

★ **71181** ★ **Loyola Capital Corp.**
1300 N. Charles St.
Baltimore, MD 21201
(410)332-7000
Company Type: Headquarters. **Officer:**
Joseph W. Mosmiller. **Employee Count:**
89000. **Fortune Service 500:** Ranking 44.

★ **71182** ★ **Macy's**
White Marsh Mall
Baltimore, MD 21236
(410)931-7000
Ultimate Parent: R. H. Macy. **SIC:** 5311—
Department Stores.

★ **71183** ★ **Martin Marietta Aero & Naval Systems**
103 Chesapeake Pk. Pl.
Baltimore, MD 21220
(410)692-1000
Officer: Dr. William F. Ballhaus, President.
Ultimate Parent: Martin Marietta.

★ **71184** ★ **Martin Marietta Aero & Naval Systems**
103 Chesapeake Park Plz.
Baltimore, MD 21220
Ultimate Parent: Martin Marietta. **SIC:**
3728—Aircraft Parts & Equipment Nec;
3769—Space Vehicle Equipment Nec.

★ **71185** ★ **Martin Marietta Corp. Librar**
1450 S. Rolling Rd.
Baltimore, MD 21227
(410)247-0700
Ultimate Parent: Martin Marietta. **SIC:**
8231—Libraries.

★ **71186** ★ **Martin Marietta Laboratories**
1450 S. Rowling Rd.
Baltimore, MD 21227-3898
(410)247-0700
Officer: Ronald H. Schack, Vice President.
Ultimate Parent: Martin Marietta.

★ **71187** ★ **Mary Kay Cosmetics**
5212 Saybrook Rd.
Baltimore, MD 21206
(410)325-3881
Ultimate Parent: Mary Kay Cosmetics. **SIC:**
5999—Miscellaneous Retail Stores Nec.

★ **71188** ★ **McDonald's Carry out**
5637 Baltimore National P
Baltimore, MD 21228
(410)744-4390
Ultimate Parent: McDonald's. **SIC:** 5812—
Eating Places.

★ **71189** ★ **McDonald's Hamburgers**
4401 Reisterstown Rd.
Baltimore, MD 21215
(410)542-0500
Ultimate Parent: McDonald's. **SIC:** 5812—
Eating Places.

★ **71190** ★ **McDonald's Hamburgers**
524 W. Franklin St.
Baltimore, MD 21201
(410)669-9362
Ultimate Parent: McDonald's. **SIC:** 5812—
Eating Places.

★ **71191** ★ **McDonald's Hamburgers**
Pulaski Hwy.
Baltimore, MD 21224
(410)342-6250
Ultimate Parent: McDonald's. **SIC:** 5812—
Eating Places.

★ **71192** ★ **McDonald's Hamburgers**
502 Reisterstown Rd.
Baltimore, MD 21208
(410)484-6261
Ultimate Parent: McDonald's. **SIC:** 5812—
Eating Places.

★ **71193** ★ **McDonald's Hamburgers**
6005 Liberty Rd.
Baltimore, MD 21207
(410)265-6143
Ultimate Parent: McDonald's. **SIC:** 5812—
Eating Places.

★ **71194** ★ **McDonald's Hamburgers**
1812 N. Charles St.
Baltimore, MD 21201
(410)685-9568
Ultimate Parent: McDonald's. **SIC:** 5812—
Eating Places.

★ **71195** ★ **McDonald's Hamburgers**
3249 Frederick Ave.
Baltimore, MD 21229
(410)945-8180
Ultimate Parent: McDonald's. **SIC:** 5812—
Eating Places.

★ **71196** ★ **McDonald's Hamburgers**
7127 Harford Rd.
Baltimore, MD 21234
(410)675-6775
Ultimate Parent: McDonald's. **SIC:** 5812—
Eating Places.

★ **71197** ★ **McDonald's Hamburgers**
1202 E. Fayette St.
Baltimore, MD 21202
(410)327-1149
Ultimate Parent: McDonald's. **SIC:** 5812—
Eating Places.

★ **71198** ★ **Mercantile Bankshares Corp.**
2 Hopkins Plz.
Baltimore, MD 21203
(410)237-5900
Company Type: Headquarters. **Officer:** H.
Furlong Baldwin. **Employee Count:** 2713.
Fortune Service 500: Ranking 87.

★ **71199** ★ **Mercantile-Safe Deposit & Trust Co.**
5910 Baltimore Natl. Pke.
Baltimore, MD 21228
(410)788-2200
Company Type: Subsidiary. **Location
Type:** Branch office. **Officer:** Ernest L.
Burden, Manager. **Ultimate Parent:**
Mercantile Bankshares Corp. **SIC:** 6021—
National Commercial Banks.

★ **71200** ★ **Mercantile-Safe Deposit & Trust Co.**
2000 Joppa Rd.
Baltimore, MD 21234-2885
(410)661-4903
Company Type: Subsidiary. **Location
Type:** Branch office. **Officer:** Ann C. Ansel,
Manager. **Ultimate Parent:** Mercantile
Bankshares Corp. **SIC:** 6021—National
Commercial Banks.

★ **71201** ★ **Mercantile-Safe Deposit & Trust Co.**
5119 Roland Ave.
Baltimore, MD 21210-2192
(410)435-6300
Company Type: Subsidiary. **Location
Type:** Branch office. **Officer:** M. Katherine
Williams, Manager. **Ultimate Parent:**
Mercantile Bankshares Corp. **SIC:** 6021—
National Commercial Banks.

★ **71202** ★ **Mercantile-Safe Deposit & Trust Co.**
Calvert & Redwood Sts.
Baltimore, MD 21218-3955
(410)962-1412
Company Type: Subsidiary. **Location
Type:** Branch office. **Officer:** Charles P.
Roe, Manager. **Ultimate Parent:** Mercantile
Bankshares Corp. **SIC:** 6021—National
Commercial Banks.

★ **71203** ★ **Mercantile-Safe Deposit & Trust Co.**
Charles & Chase Sts.
Baltimore, MD 21218-4325
(410)962-1420
Company Type: Subsidiary. **Location
Type:** Branch office. **Officer:** Carl B.
Presser, Manager. **Ultimate Parent:**
Mercantile Bankshares Corp. **SIC:** 6021—
National Commercial Banks.

★ **71204** ★ **Mercantile-Safe Deposit & Trust Co.**
1100 N. Charles St.
Baltimore, MD 21234
(410)962-1420
Company Type: Subsidiary. **Location
Type:** Branch office. **Ultimate Parent:**
Mercantile Bankshares Corp. **SIC:** 6021—
National Commercial Banks.

★ **71205** ★ **Mercantile-Safe Deposit & Trust Co.**
8230 Liberty Rd.
Baltimore, MD 21207
(410)655-7800
Company Type: Subsidiary. **Location
Type:** Branch office. **Officer:** S. Denise
Peak, Manager. **Ultimate Parent:**
Mercantile Bankshares Corp. **SIC:** 6021—
National Commercial Banks.

★ **71206** ★ **Mercantile-Safe Deposit & Trust Co.**
2 Hopkins Plz.
PO Box 1477
Baltimore, MD 21203
(410)237-5900
Company Type: Subsidiary. **Location
Type:** Branch office. **Officer:** Douglas W.
Dodge, President & COO. **Ultimate Parent:**
Mercantile Bankshares Corp. **SIC:** 6021—
National Commercial Banks.

★ **71207** ★ **Mid-Atlantic Coca-Cola Bottling Co.**
701 N. Kresson St.
Baltimore, MD 21205
Ultimate Parent: Coca-Cola Enterprises.
SIC: 2086—Bottled & Canned Soft Drinks.

★ **71208** ★ **Mid-Atlantic Coca-Cola Bottling Co. Inc.**
701 N. Kresson St.
Baltimore, MD 21205
Ultimate Parent: Coca-Cola Enterprises.
SIC: 2086—Bottled & Canned Soft Drinks.

★ **71209** ★ **Miles Inc. Pemco Products**
5601 Eastern Ave.
Baltimore, MD 21224-2791
Ultimate Parent: Miles. **SIC:** 2819—
Industrial Inorganic Chemicals Nec.

★ **71210** ★ **Mobil Oil Corp.**
3445 Fairfield Rd.
Baltimore, MD 21226
(410)355-4007
Ultimate Parent: Mobil. **SIC:** 5172—
Petroleum Products Nec.

★ **71211** ★ **Monumental Paper Co.**
2201 Eagle St.
Baltimore, MD 21223-3383
(410)945-1370
Company Type: Headquarters. **Officer:**
Soll L. Selko. **Ultimate Parent:** Alco
Standard Corp. **SIC:** 5112—Stationery &
Office Supplies; 5085—Industrial Supplies;
5111—Printing & Writing Paper.

★ **71212** ★ **Nationsbank Banking Centers**
7107 Security Blvd.
Baltimore, MD 21244
(301)385-8320
Ultimate Parent: Nationsbank Corp.

★ **71213** ★ **Northwestern Mutual Life Inc.**
16 S. Calvert St.
Baltimore, MD 21202
(410)539-0084
Ultimate Parent: Northwestern Mutual Life.
SIC: 6411—Insurance Agents, Brokers &
Service.

★ 71214 ★ **Owens Illinois Inc.**
201 Kane St.
Baltimore, MD 21224
(410)633-8282
Officer: Joseph H' La More, Manager.
Ultimate Parent: Owens-Illinois. **SIC:**
3089—Plastics Products Nec.

★ 71215 ★ **Payless Shoesource**
6548 Reisterstown Rd.
Baltimore, MD 21215
(410)358-7568
Ultimate Parent: May Department Stores.
SIC: 5661—Shoe Stores.

★ 71216 ★ **Payless Shoesource**
Hollinswood Shopping Ctr.
Baltimore, MD 21230
(410)525-2926
Ultimate Parent: May Department Stores.
SIC: 5661—Shoe Stores.

★ 71217 ★ **Payless Shoesource**
112527 Light St.
Baltimore, MD 21202
(410)752-8475
Ultimate Parent: May Department Stores.
SIC: 5661—Shoe Stores.

★ 71218 ★ **Payless Shoesource**
12 E. North Ave.
Baltimore, MD 21202
(410)332-4117
Ultimate Parent: May Department Stores.
SIC: 5661—Shoe Stores.

★ 71219 ★ **Pepsi-Cola Co.**
1650 Union Ave.
Baltimore, MD 21211-1993
Ultimate Parent: Pepsico. **SIC:** 2086—
Bottled & Canned Soft Drinks.

★ 71220 ★ **Procter & Gamble
Mfg. Co.**
1422 Nicholson St.
Baltimore, MD 21230
Ultimate Parent: Procter & Gamble Co.
SIC: 2841—Soap & Other Detergents.

★ 71221 ★ **Progressive Casualty
Insurance Co.**
7133 Rutherford Rd.
Baltimore, MD 21207
(410)265-1870
Ultimate Parent: Progressive. **SIC:** 6411—
Insurance Agents, Brokers & Service.

★ 71222 ★ **Properties Inc.**
2629 N. Charles St.
Baltimore, MD 21218
(410)889-1635
Ultimate Parent: Northeast Utilities. **SIC:**
6531—Real Estate Agents & Managers.

★ 71223 ★ **Radio Shack**
White
Baltimore, MD 21236
(410)256-2252
Company Type: Division. **Ultimate Parent:**
Tandy Corp. **SIC:** 5065—Electronic Parts &
Equipment Nec.

★ 71224 ★ **Radio Shack**
Golden Ring Mall Shopping
Baltimore, MD 21237
(410)574-1055
Company Type: Division. **Ultimate Parent:**
Tandy Corp. **SIC:** 5731—Radio, Television
& Electronics Stores.

★ 71225 ★ **Radio Shack**
2003 Mondawmin Mall
Baltimore, MD 21215
(410)523-3334
Company Type: Division. **Ultimate Parent:**
Tandy Corp. **SIC:** 5734—Computer &
Software Stores.

★ 71226 ★ **Radio Shack**
Middlesex Shopping Ctr.
Baltimore, MD 21221
(410)391-5540
Company Type: Division. **Ultimate Parent:**
Tandy Corp. **SIC:** 5065—Electronic Parts &
Equipment Nec.

★ 71227 ★ **Radio Shack**
Parkside Shopping Ctr.
Baltimore, MD 21206
(410)485-3633
Company Type: Division. **Ultimate Parent:**
Tandy Corp. **SIC:** 5734—Computer &
Software Stores.

★ 71228 ★ **Radio Shack**
Rotunda
Baltimore, MD 21211
(410)366-6607
Company Type: Division. **Ultimate Parent:**
Tandy Corp. **SIC:** 5734—Computer &
Software Stores.

★ 71229 ★ **Radio Shack**
Towson
Baltimore, MD 21204
(410)821-8918
Company Type: Division. **Ultimate Parent:**
Tandy Corp. **SIC:** 5046—Commercial
Equipment Nec.

★ 71230 ★ **Radio Shack**
217 E. Baltimore St.
Baltimore, MD 21202
(410)685-5603
Company Type: Division. **Ultimate Parent:**
Tandy Corp. **SIC:** 4812—Radiotelephone
Communications.

★ 71231 ★ **Radio Shack**
6600 Baltimore Pike
Baltimore, MD 21228
(410)788-5496
Company Type: Division. **Ultimate Parent:**
Tandy Corp. **SIC:** 5065—Electronic Parts &
Equipment Nec.

★ 71232 ★ **Radio Shack**
5741 Westview Mall
Baltimore, MD 21228
(410)788-2500
Company Type: Division. **Ultimate Parent:**
Tandy Corp. **SIC:** 5065—Electronic Parts &
Equipment Nec.

★ 71233 ★ **Radio Shack**
217 E. Baltimore St.
Baltimore, MD 21202
(410)685-5603
Company Type: Division. **Ultimate Parent:**
Tandy Corp. **SIC:** 4812—Radiotelephone
Communications.

★ 71234 ★ **Radio Shack**
6600 Baltimore Pike
Baltimore, MD 21228
(410)788-5496
Company Type: Division. **Ultimate Parent:**
Tandy Corp. **SIC:** 5065—Electronic Parts &
Equipment Nec.

★ 71235 ★ **Radio Shack**
5741 Westview Mall
Baltimore, MD 21228
(410)788-2500
Company Type: Division. **Ultimate Parent:**
Tandy Corp. **SIC:** 5065—Electronic Parts &
Equipment Nec.

★ 71236 ★ **Red Star Yeast**
2100 Van Deman St. 2100 Van Deman St.
Baltimore, MD 21224
Ultimate Parent: Universal Foods Corp.
SIC: 2099—Food Preparations Nec.

★ 71237 ★ **Red Star Yeast**
Holabird Inc. Park 2100 Van Deman St.
Baltimore, MD 21224
Ultimate Parent: Universal Foods Corp.
SIC: 2099—Food Preparations Nec.

★ 71238 ★ **Red Star Yeast &
Products**
Holabird Industrial Park 2100 Van Deman
St.
Baltimore, MD 21224
Ultimate Parent: Universal Foods Corp.
SIC: 2099—Food Preparations Nec.

★ 71239 ★ **Rhone Poulenc Inc.**
3440 Fairfield Rd.
Baltimore, MD 21226
(410)355-2600
Ultimate Parent: Rhone-Poulenc Rorer.
SIC: 2819—Industrial Inorganic Chemicals
Nec; 2834—Pharmaceutical Preparations;
2841—Soap & Other Detergents.

★ 71240 ★ **Rhone-Poulenc
Surfactants & Specialties LP**
3440 Fairfield Rd.
Baltimore, MD 21226
Ultimate Parent: Rhone-Poulenc Rorer.
SIC: 2843—Surface Active Agents; 2869—
Industrial Organic Chemicals Nec.

★ 71241 ★ **Rite Aid**
North Plaza Mall
Baltimore, MD 21239
(410)661-4121
Ultimate Parent: Rite Aid. **SIC:** 5912—Drug
Stores & Proprietary Stores.

★ 71242 ★ **Rite Aid**
6622 Security Blvd.
Baltimore, MD 21207
(410)574-8750
Ultimate Parent: Rite Aid. **SIC:** 5912—Drug
Stores & Proprietary Stores.

★ 71243 ★ **Rite Aid**
E Point Shopping Ctr.
Baltimore, MD 21224
(410)288-9651
Ultimate Parent: Rite Aid. **SIC:** 5912—Drug
Stores & Proprietary Stores.

★ 71244 ★ **Rite Aid**
Hawthorne Shopping.Ctr.
Baltimore, MD 21220
(410)687-1388
Ultimate Parent: Rite Aid. **SIC:** 5912—Drug
Stores & Proprietary Stores.

★ 71245 ★ **Rite Aid**
3431 Belair Rd.
Baltimore, MD 21213
(410)483-3124
Ultimate Parent: Rite Aid. **SIC:** 5912—Drug
Stores & Proprietary Stores.

★ 71246 ★ **Rite Aid**
Woodmoor Shpcenter
Baltimore, MD 21207
(410)265-7600
Ultimate Parent: Rite Aid. **SIC:** 5912—Drug
Stores & Proprietary Stores.

★ 71247 ★ **Rite Aid**
Hilton
Baltimore, MD 21216
(410)685-9634
Ultimate Parent: Rite Aid. **SIC:** 5912—Drug
Stores & Proprietary Stores.

★ 71248 ★ **Rite Aid**
Westsidect
Baltimore, MD 21223
(410)947-0500
Ultimate Parent: Rite Aid. **SIC:** 5912—Drug
Stores & Proprietary Stores.

★ 71249 ★ **Rite Aid**
304 W. Readst
Baltimore, MD 21201
(410)728-9600
Ultimate Parent: Rite Aid. **SIC:** 5912—Drug
Stores & Proprietary Stores.

★ 71250 ★ **Rite Aid**
Walbrookplz
Baltimore, MD 21216
(410)945-8507
Ultimate Parent: Rite Aid. **SIC:** 5912—Drug
Stores & Proprietary Stores.

★ 71251 ★ **Rite Aid**
918 W. 36thst
Baltimore, MD 21211
(410)235-9883
Ultimate Parent: Rite Aid. **SIC:** 5912—Drug
Stores & Proprietary Stores.

★ 71252 ★ **Rite Aid**
3752 W. Belvedereave
Baltimore, MD 21215
(410)664-6640
Ultimate Parent: Rite Aid. **SIC:** 5912—Drug
Stores & Proprietary Stores.

★ 71253 ★ **Rite Aid**
425 Sbroadway
Baltimore, MD 21231
(410)675-9686
Ultimate Parent: Rite Aid. **SIC:** 5912—Drug
Stores & Proprietary Stores.

★ 71254 ★ **Rite Aid**
219 S. Collinsave
Baltimore, MD 21229
(410)644-1125
Ultimate Parent: Rite Aid. **SIC:** 5912—Drug
Stores & Proprietary Stores.

★ 71255 ★ **Rite Aid**
Reisterstownsquair
Baltimore, MD 21215
(410)764-3971
Ultimate Parent: Rite Aid. **SIC:** 5912—Drug
Stores & Proprietary Stores.

★ 71256 ★ **Rite Aid**
Rotunda
Baltimore, MD 21225
(410)467-3343
Ultimate Parent: Rite Aid. **SIC:** 5912—Drug
Stores & Proprietary Stores.

★ 71257 ★ **Rite Aid**
Mondawminmall
Baltimore, MD 21215
(410)728-9148
Ultimate Parent: Rite Aid. **SIC:** 5912—Drug
Stores & Proprietary Stores.

★ 71258 ★ **Rite Aid**
NW Plaza
Baltimore, MD 21208
(410)358-9777
Ultimate Parent: Rite Aid. **SIC:** 5912—Drug
Stores & Proprietary Stores.

★ 71259 ★ **Rite Aid**
Hollinswood Shopping.Ctr.
Baltimore, MD 21230
(410)644-6654
Ultimate Parent: Rite Aid. **SIC:** 5912—Drug
Stores & Proprietary Stores.

★ 71260 ★ **Rite Aid**
Homeland Shopping.Ctr.
Baltimore, MD 21212
(410)433-5910
Ultimate Parent: Rite Aid. **SIC:** 5912—Drug
Stores & Proprietary Stores.

★ 71261 ★ **Rite Aid**
Erdmanave
Baltimore, MD 21213
(410)342-2606
Ultimate Parent: Rite Aid. **SIC:** 5912—Drug
Stores & Proprietary Stores.

★ 71262 ★ **Rite Aid**
5428 Harfordrd
Baltimore, MD 21214
(410)444-1046
Ultimate Parent: Rite Aid. **SIC:** 5912—Drug
Stores & Proprietary Stores.

★ 71263 ★ **Rite Aid**
941 E. Patapscoave
Baltimore, MD 21225
(410)355-1860
Ultimate Parent: Rite Aid. **SIC:** 5912—Drug
Stores & Proprietary Stores.

★ 71264 ★ **Rite Aid**
1401 E. Cold Springln
Baltimore, MD 21239
(410)435-9054
Ultimate Parent: Rite Aid. **SIC:** 5912—Drug
Stores & Proprietary Stores.

★ 71265 ★ **Rite Aid**
2113 E. Monumentst
Baltimore, MD 21205
(410)675-2416
Ultimate Parent: Rite Aid. **SIC:** 5912—Drug
Stores & Proprietary Stores.

★ 71266 ★ **Rite Aid**
Belvedere Shopping.Ctr.
Baltimore, MD 21239
(410)664-9611
Ultimate Parent: Rite Aid. **SIC:** 5912—Drug
Stores & Proprietary Stores.

★ 71267 ★ **Rite Aid**
1100 Lgt Crsst
Baltimore, MD 21230
(410)385-5715
Ultimate Parent: Rite Aid. **SIC:** 5912—Drug
Stores & Proprietary Stores.

★ 71268 ★ **Riteaid**
Edmondson
Baltimore, MD 21229
(410)566-2720
Ultimate Parent: Rite Aid. **SIC:** 5912—Drug
Stores & Proprietary Stores.

★ 71269 ★ **Romper Room
Enterprises Inc.**
200 E. Joppa Rd.
Baltimore, MD 21204
(410)825-4576
Ultimate Parent: Hasbro. **SIC:** 7922—
Theatrical Producers & Services.

★ 71270 ★ Ryder Truck Rental Inc.
920 S. Brunswick St.
Baltimore, MD 21223
(410)233-1200
Ultimate Parent: Ryder System. SIC: 5087—Service Establishment Equipment.

★ 71271 ★ Ryder Truck Rental Inc.
8545 Philadelphia Rd.
Baltimore, MD 21237
(410)682-2700
Ultimate Parent: Ryder System. SIC: 7513—Truck Rental & Leasing Without Drivers.

★ 71272 ★ Ryder Truck Rental Inc.
Inner Harbor Ctr.
Baltimore, MD 21202
(410)752-5809
Ultimate Parent: Ryder System. SIC: 8093—Specialty Outpatient Facilities Nec.

★ 71273 ★ Scm Chemicals
7 Saint Paul St. 1010
Baltimore, MD 21202
(410)783-1120
Ultimate Parent: Hanson Industries. SIC: 2816—Inorganic Pigments.

★ 71274 ★ SCM Chemicals Inc.
7 St. Paul St., Ste. 1010
Baltimore, MD 21202-1626
(410)783-1120
Company Type: Subsidiary. Officer: Donald V. Borst, Chairman of the Board & President. Ultimate Parent: Hanson Industries. SIC: 2816—Inorganic Pigments. Employee Count: 2600. Sales: 325 (est) M.

★ 71275 ★ Scm Glidco Organics Corp.
2701 Broening Hwy.
Baltimore, MD 21222
Ultimate Parent: Hanson Industries. SIC: 2816—Inorganic Pigments; 2819—Industrial Inorganic Chemicals Nec.

★ 71276 ★ Security Pacific Financial Services, Inc.
7004 Security Blvd.
Baltimore, MD 21244-2557
(410)944-5090
Location Type: Branch office. Ultimate Parent: Bankamerica Corp. SIC: 6141—Personal Credit Institutions.

★ 71277 ★ Shell Oil Co.
2400 Petrolia Ave.
Baltimore, MD 21226
(410)354-0404
Ultimate Parent: Shell Oil Co. SIC: 5541—Gasoline Service Stations.

★ 71278 ★ Shell Oil Co.
2400 Petrolia Ave.
Baltimore, MD 21226
(410)354-0404
Ultimate Parent: Shell Oil Co. SIC: 5541—Gasoline Service Stations.

★ 71279 ★ Sherwin-Williams Co.
2325 Hollins Ferry Rd.
Baltimore, MD 21230
(410)625-8256
Officer: Jim Kearney, Manager. Ultimate Parent: Sherwin-Williams Co. SIC: 2851—Paints & Allied Products; 2891—Adhesives & Sealants.

★ 71280 ★ Signet Bank/Maryland
176 Carroll Island Rd.
Baltimore, MD 21220-2299
(410)332-5338
Company Type: Subsidiary. Location Type: Branch office. Ultimate Parent: Signet Banking Corp. SIC: 6021—National Commercial Banks.

★ 71281 ★ Signet Bank/Maryland
1241 W. Pratt St.
Baltimore, MD 21223-2600
(410)539-2377
Company Type: Subsidiary. Location Type: Branch office. Ultimate Parent: Signet Banking Corp. SIC: 6021—National Commercial Banks.

★ 71282 ★ Signet Bank/Maryland
8807 Pulaski Hwy.
Baltimore, MD 21237-3099
(410)332-5650
Company Type: Subsidiary. Location Type: Branch office. Ultimate Parent: Signet Banking Corp. SIC: 6021—National Commercial Banks.

★ 71283 ★ Signet Bank/Maryland
5701 Reisterstown Rd.
Baltimore, MD 21215-3496
(410)332-5200
Company Type: Subsidiary. Location Type: Branch office. Ultimate Parent: Signet Banking Corp. SIC: 6021—National Commercial Banks.

★ 71284 ★ Signet Bank/Maryland
4115 Ritchie Hwy.
Baltimore, MD 21225-2758
(410)332-5206
Company Type: Subsidiary. Location Type: Branch office. Ultimate Parent: Signet Banking Corp. SIC: 6021—National Commercial Banks.

★ 71285 ★ Signet Bank/Maryland
6309 York Rd.
Baltimore, MD 21212-2686
(410)332-5214
Company Type: Subsidiary. Location Type: Branch office. Ultimate Parent: Signet Banking Corp. SIC: 6021—National Commercial Banks.

★ 71286 ★ Signet Bank/Maryland
1 N. Charles St.
Baltimore, MD 21201-3709
(410)332-5410
Company Type: Subsidiary. Location Type: Branch office. Ultimate Parent: Signet Banking Corp. SIC: 6021—National Commercial Banks.

★ 71287 ★ Signet Bank/Maryland
5234 York Rd.
Baltimore, MD 21212-4295
(410)332-5289
Company Type: Subsidiary. Location Type: Branch office. Ultimate Parent: Signet Banking Corp. SIC: 6021—National Commercial Banks.

★ 71288 ★ Signet Bank/Maryland
1039 E. Baltimore
Baltimore, MD 21202-4786
(410)332-5220
Company Type: Subsidiary. Location Type: Branch office. Ultimate Parent: Signet Banking Corp. SIC: 6021—National Commercial Banks.

★ 71289 ★ Signet Bank/Maryland
2056 Harford Rd.
Baltimore, MD 21218-6289
(410)332-5295
Company Type: Subsidiary. Location Type: Branch office. Ultimate Parent: Signet Banking Corp. SIC: 6021—National Commercial Banks.

★ 71290 ★ Signet Bank/Maryland
5439 Harford Rd.
Baltimore, MD 21214-2291
(410)332-5292
Company Type: Subsidiary. Location Type: Branch office. Ultimate Parent: Signet Banking Corp. SIC: 6021—National Commercial Banks.

★ 71291 ★ Signet Bank/Maryland
4735 Liberty Heights Ave.
Baltimore, MD 21207-7196
(410)332-5305
Company Type: Subsidiary. Location Type: Branch office. Ultimate Parent: Signet Banking Corp. SIC: 6021—National Commercial Banks.

★ 71292 ★ Signet Bank/Maryland
4820 Eastern Ave.
Baltimore, MD 21224-4499
(410)332-5300
Company Type: Subsidiary. Location Type: Branch office. Ultimate Parent: Signet Banking Corp. SIC: 6021—National Commercial Banks.

★ 71293 ★ Signet Bank/Maryland
2000 Linden Ave.
Baltimore, MD 21217-4491
(410)332-5320
Company Type: Subsidiary. Location Type: Branch office. Ultimate Parent: Signet Banking Corp. SIC: 6021—National Commercial Banks.

★ 71294 ★ Signet Bank/Maryland
2008 E. Monument St.
Baltimore, MD 21207
(410)332-5305
Company Type: Subsidiary. Location Type: Branch office. Ultimate Parent: Signet Banking Corp. SIC: 6021—National Commercial Banks.

★ 71295 ★ Signet Bank/Maryland
2337 E. Northern Pky.
Baltimore, MD 21214-1197
(410)332-5326
Company Type: Subsidiary. Location Type: Branch office. Ultimate Parent: Signet Banking Corp. SIC: 6021—National Commercial Banks.

★ 71296 ★ Signet Bank/Maryland
5040 Sinclair Ln.
Baltimore, MD 21206-5999
(410)332-5279
Company Type: Subsidiary. Location Type: Branch office. Ultimate Parent: Signet Banking Corp. SIC: 6021—National Commercial Banks.

★ 71297 ★ Signet Bank/Maryland
2439 Frederick Ave.
Baltimore, MD 21223-2897
(410)332-5259
Company Type: Subsidiary. Location Type: Branch office. Ultimate Parent: Signet Banking Corp. SIC: 6021—National Commercial Banks.

★ 71298 ★ Signet Bank/Maryland
3200 W. North Ave.
Baltimore, MD 21216-3094
(410)332-5253
Company Type: Subsidiary. Location Type: Branch office. Ultimate Parent: Signet Banking Corp. SIC: 6021—National Commercial Banks.

★ 71299 ★ Signet Bank/Maryland
2030 E. Joppa Rd.
Baltimore, MD 21234-2851
(410)332-5298
Company Type: Subsidiary. Location Type: Branch office. Ultimate Parent: Signet Banking Corp. SIC: 6021—National Commercial Banks.

★ 71300 ★ Signet Bank/Maryland
6225 N. Charles St.
Baltimore, MD 21212
(410)332-4192
Company Type: Subsidiary. Location Type: Branch office. Ultimate Parent: Signet Banking Corp. SIC: 6021—National Commercial Banks.

★ 71301 ★ Signet Bank/Maryland
300 E. Lombard St.
Baltimore, MD 21202
(410)332-5245
Company Type: Subsidiary. Location Type: Branch office. Ultimate Parent: Signet Banking Corp. SIC: 6021—National Commercial Banks.

★ 71302 ★ Signet Bank/Maryland
5121 Roland Ave.
Baltimore, MD 21210-2196
(410)332-5583
Company Type: Subsidiary. Location Type: Branch office. Ultimate Parent: Signet Banking Corp. SIC: 6021—National Commercial Banks.

★ 71303 ★ Signet Bank/Maryland
36 S. Charles St.
Baltimore, MD 21201-3020
(410)332-5666
Company Type: Subsidiary. Location Type: Branch office. Ultimate Parent: Signet Banking Corp. SIC: 6021—National Commercial Banks.

★ 71304 ★ Signet Bank/Maryland
1228 N. Charles St.
Baltimore, MD 21201-5571
(410)332-5232
Company Type: Subsidiary. Location Type: Branch office. Ultimate Parent: Signet Banking Corp. SIC: 6021—National Commercial Banks.

★ 71305 ★ Signet Bank/Maryland
7 St. Paul St.
PO Box 1077
Baltimore, MD 21203-1077
(410)332-5000 Fax: (410)783-6043
Company Type: Subsidiary. Location Type: Branch office. Officer: Kenneth H. Trout, President & CEO. Ultimate Parent: Signet Banking Corp. SIC: 6021—National Commercial Banks.

★ 71306 ★ Signet Bank/Maryland
3608 Milford Mill Rd.
Baltimore, MD 21207-3383
(410)332-5314
Company Type: Subsidiary. Location Type: Branch office. Ultimate Parent: Signet Banking Corp. SIC: 6021—National Commercial Banks.

★ 71307 ★ Signode Corp.
4505 N. Point Blvd.
Baltimore, MD 21219
Ultimate Parent: Illinois Tool Works. SIC: 3479—Metal Coating & Allied Services.

★ 71308 ★ Signode Eastern Ops.
4505 N. Point Blvd.
Baltimore, MD 21219
Ultimate Parent: Illinois Tool Works. SIC: 3479—Metal Coating & Allied Services.

★ 71309 ★ Signode Supply Corp.
4505 North Point Blvd.
Baltimore, MD 21219
Ultimate Parent: Illinois Tool Works. SIC: 3499—Fabricated Metal Products Nec.

★ 71310 ★ Southern States Co-Op. Inc.
Feed Div.
2101 E. Fort Ave.
Baltimore, MD 21230
Company Type: Division. Ultimate Parent: Southern. SIC: 2048—Prepared Feeds Nec.

★ 71311 ★ Southern States Co-Op. Inc. Inc.
Stahl Point Rd. PO Box 3469
Baltimore, MD 21226
Ultimate Parent: Southern. SIC: 2875—Fertilizers—Mixing Only.

★ 71312 ★ Southland Corp.
2020 Harford Rd.
Baltimore, MD 21218
(410)235-1150
Ultimate Parent: Southland Corp. SIC: 5143—Dairy Products Except Dried or Canned.

★ 71313 ★ Standard Federal S & L Association
678 Reisterstown Rd.
Baltimore, MD 21208
(410)486-7273
Ultimate Parent: Standard Federal Bank. SIC: 6022—State Commercial Banks.

★ 71314 ★ Stop & Shop
6 E. Preston St.
Baltimore, MD 21202
(410)752-5793
Ultimate Parent: Stop & Shop. SIC: 5411—Grocery Stores.

★ 71315 ★ Structures Inc.
2115 N. Charles St.
Baltimore, MD 21218
(410)685-3100
Ultimate Parent: Limited. SIC: 1542—Nonresidential Construction Nec.

★ 71316 ★ Union Carbide Corp.
Linde Div.
7350 Carbide Rd.
Baltimore, MD 21226
Company Type: Division. Ultimate Parent: Union Carbide Corp. SIC: 2813—Industrial Gases.

★ 71317 ★ Union Carbide Corp. Indl. Gases Inc.
7350 Carbide Rd.
Baltimore, MD 21226
Ultimate Parent: Union Carbide Corp. SIC: 2813—Industrial Gases.

★ 71318 ★ **Universal Foods Corp.**
2101 Ralls Ave.
Baltimore, MD 21222
(410)633-8000
Ultimate Parent: Universal Foods Corp.
SIC: 2041—Flour & Other Grain Mill Products.

★ 71319 ★ **US Gypsum Co.**
5500 Quarantine Rd.
Baltimore, MD 21226
(410)355-2500
Ultimate Parent: USG Corp. **SIC:** 3275—Gypsum Products.

★ 71320 ★ **USF&G Corp.**
100 Light St.
Baltimore, MD 21202
(410)547-3000 **Fax:** (410)625-5682
Company Type: Headquarters. **Officer:** Norman P. Blake Jr., CEO. **Employee Count:** 6500. **Sales:** 3249 M. **Fortune Service 500:** Ranking 20.

★ 71321 ★ **Valspar Corp.**
1401 Severn St.
Baltimore, MD 21203
Ultimate Parent: Valspar Corp. **SIC:** 2851—Paints & Allied Products.

★ 71322 ★ **Volume Services Inc.**
7134 Walnut Ave.
Baltimore, MD 21208
(410)727-0440
Ultimate Parent: Flagstar Co. **SIC:** 6512—Nonresidential Building Operators.

★ 71323 ★ **Vulcan Materials Co.**
2415 Grays Rd.
Baltimore, MD 21222-5097
Ultimate Parent: Vulcan Materials Co. **SIC:** 3341—Secondary Nonferrous Metals.

★ 71324 ★ **W. R. Grace & Co.**
Davison Chemical Div.
5500 Chemical Rd.
Baltimore, MD 21226-1698
Company Type: Division. **Ultimate Parent:** W. R. Grace. **SIC:** 2819—Industrial Inorganic Chemicals Nec.

★ 71325 ★ **Waldenbooks**
Eastpoint Mall
Baltimore, MD 21224
(410)282-1077
Ultimate Parent: K-Mart. **SIC:** 5942—Book Stores.

★ 71326 ★ **Waldenbooks**
Security Sq.
Baltimore, MD 21207
(410)944-7344
Ultimate Parent: K-Mart. **SIC:** 5942—Book Stores.

★ 71327 ★ **Western Life Insurance Co.**
6660 Security Blvd.
Baltimore, MD 21207
(410)944-8787
Ultimate Parent: Westcorp. **SIC:** 6411—Insurance Agents, Brokers & Service.

★ 71328 ★ **Wjz-Tv Television Station**
1619 Gleneagle Rd.
Baltimore, MD 21239
(410)466-0013
Ultimate Parent: Westinghouse Electric Corp. **SIC:** 5099—Durable Goods Nec.

★ 71329 ★ **Worthington Steel Co.**
8911 Kelso Dr.
Baltimore, MD 21221
Ultimate Parent: Worthington Industries, Inc. **SIC:** 3316—Cold-Finishing of Steel Shapes.

★ 71330 ★ **W.R. Grace & Co.**
Davison Chemical Div.
5500 Chemical Rd.
Baltimore, MD 21226-1698
Company Type: Division. **Ultimate Parent:** W. R. Grace. **SIC:** 2819—Industrial Inorganic Chemicals Nec.

★ 71331 ★ **Xerox Corp.**
409 Washington Ave., 2nd Fl.
Baltimore, MD 21204
(410)583-5000
Officer: Felicia Gaston, Manager. **Ultimate Parent:** Xerox Corp. **SIC:** 3663—Radio & T.V. Communications Equipment.

Balto

★ 71332 ★ **Nationsbank**
31 Light St.
Balto, MD
(301)659-2045
Ultimate Parent: Nationsbank Corp.

★ 71333 ★ **Nationsbank**
31 Light St.
Balto, MD
(301)659-2051
Ultimate Parent: Nationsbank Corp.

Bel Air

★ 71334 ★ **Baltimore Gas & Electric Co.**
Hardford Mall
Bel Air, MD 21014
(410)879-4360
Ultimate Parent: Baltimore Gas & Electric Co. **SIC:** 4911—Electric Services.

★ 71335 ★ **First Virginia Bank**
37 S. Main St.
Bel Air, MD 21014-3702
(410)838-3024
Company Type: Subsidiary. **Officer:** Cornelius F. Cronin, Chairman of the Board. **Ultimate Parent:** First Virginia Banks Inc. **SIC:** 6022—State Commercial Banks. **Employee Count:** 138.

★ 71336 ★ **Forest Hill State Bank**
130 S. Bond St.
PO Box 1307
Bel Air, MD 21014-7307
(410)838-6131 **Fax:** (410)638-2029
Company Type: Subsidiary. **Location Type:** Branch office. **Officer:** Paul E. Peak, President & CEO. **Ultimate Parent:** Mercantile Bankshares Corp. **SIC:** 6021—National Commercial Banks.

★ 71337 ★ **Forest Hill State Bank**
140 N. Main St.
Bel Air, MD 21014-8857
(410)838-3050
Company Type: Subsidiary. **Location Type:** Branch office. **Officer:** Donna M. Delamar, Manager. **Ultimate Parent:** Mercantile Bankshares Corp. **SIC:** 6021—National Commercial Banks.

★ 71338 ★ **Hecht's**
Rural Route 1
Bel Air, MD 21014
(410)838-2560
Ultimate Parent: May Department Stores. **SIC:** 5311—Department Stores.

★ 71339 ★ **Signode Corp.**
4505 North Point Blvd.
Bel Air, MD 21014
Ultimate Parent: Illinois Tool Works. **SIC:** 3499—Fabricated Metal Products Nec.

★ 71340 ★ **Thrift Drug**
Campus Hill Shopping Ctr.
Bel Air, MD 21014
(410)734-4334
Ultimate Parent: J.C. Penney. **SIC:** 5049—Professional Equipment Nec.

Belair

★ 71341 ★ **Rite Aid**
575 Baldwin Pike Rd.
Belair, MD 21014
(410)838-2700
Ultimate Parent: Rite Aid. **SIC:** 5912—Drug Stores & Proprietary Stores.

Belcamp

★ 71342 ★ **Forest Hill State Bank**
1327 Riverside Pky.
Belcamp, MD 21017
(410)272-8030
Company Type: Subsidiary. **Location Type:** Branch office. **Officer:** Bernard J. Rochowiak, Manager. **Ultimate Parent:** Mercantile Bankshares Corp. **SIC:** 6021—National Commercial Banks.

★ 71343 ★ **Johnson Controls Inc.**
1207 Belmar Dr.
Belcamp, MD 21017
Ultimate Parent: Johnson & Johnson. **SIC:** 2531—Public Building & Related Furniture.

Belotsville

★ 71344 ★ **Courtyard by Marriott Distribution**
12002 A Old Balto Pike
Belotsville, MD
(301)595-1706
Ultimate Parent: Marriott International.

★ 71345 ★ **Residence Inn Distribution Ctr.**
12002 A Old Balto Pke
Belotsville, MD
(301)595-7036
Ultimate Parent: Marriott International.

★ 71346 ★ **Rite Aid**
Chestnut Hill Shopping. Ctr.
Belotsville, MD
(301)595-5727
Ultimate Parent: Rite Aid.

Beltsville

★ 71347 ★ **Air Products & Chemicals**
4041 Powder Mill Rd., Ste. 400
Beltsville, MD 20705-3106
(301)595-5110
Officer: Joh Grossman. **Ultimate Parent:** Air Products & Chemicals, Inc. **SIC:** 5169—Chemicals & Allied Products Nec.

★ 71348 ★ **Circuit City**
11011 Balto Ave.
Beltsville, MD 20705
(301)595-2925
Ultimate Parent: Circuit City Stores.

★ 71349 ★ **Citizens National Bank**
10452 Baltimore Ave.
Beltsville, MD 20705-2321
(301)937-4520
Company Type: Subsidiary. **Location Type:** Branch office. **Officer:** Ann E. Mull, Manager. **Ultimate Parent:** Mercantile Bankshares Corp. **SIC:** 6021—National Commercial Banks.

★ 71350 ★ **Cray Research, Inc.**
4041 Powder Mill Rd.
Beltsville, MD 20705
(301)595-5100
Ultimate Parent: Cray Research, Inc.

★ 71351 ★ **EG & G**
Pressure Science Inc.
11642 Old Baltimore Pke.
Beltsville, MD 20705
(301)937-4010
Officer: Robert Barrett, President. **Ultimate Parent:** EG & G. **SIC:** 3053—Gaskets, Packing & Sealing Devices.

★ 71352 ★ **EG & G Pressure Science**
11642 Old Baltimore Pike
Beltsville, MD 20705
(301)937-4010 **Fax:** (301)937-0134
Company Type: Subsidiary. **Officer:** Robert A. Barrett, Manager. **Ultimate Parent:** EG & G.

★ 71353 ★ **Exxon Co.**
11055 Balto Blvd.
Beltsville, MD 20705
(301)937-4798
Ultimate Parent: Exxon.

★ 71354 ★ **Exxon Co.**
10405 Baltimore Ave.
Beltsville, MD 20705
(301)474-4122
Ultimate Parent: Exxon.

★ 71355 ★ **Exxon Service Station**
4040 Powder Mill Rd.
Beltsville, MD 20705
(301)572-7113
Ultimate Parent: Exxon.

★ 71356 ★ **First Union National Bank of Maryland**
6985 Muirkirk Meadows Dr.
Beltsville, MD 20705
(301)650-1095
Company Type: Subsidiary. **Location Type:** Branch office. **Ultimate Parent:** First Union Corp. **SIC:** 6021—National Commercial Banks.

★ 71357 ★ **Maryland Clay Products**
7100 Muirkirk Rd.
Beltsville, MD 20705-1386
Ultimate Parent: Borden, Inc. **SIC:** 3251—Brick & Structural Clay Tile.

★ 71358 ★ **McDonald's Hamburgers**
10531 Balto Ave.
Beltsville, MD 20705
(301)937-1387
Ultimate Parent: McDonald's.

★ 71359 ★ **Micros Seplomic Inc.**
12000 Baltimore Ave.
Beltsville, MD 20750-1291
(301)490-6699 **Fax:** (301)210-6000
Officer: A.L. Giannapoulous, CEO. **Ultimate Parent:** Westinghouse Electric Corp. **Employee Count:** 385. **Sales:** 55 M.

★ 71360 ★ **Nationsbank Banking Centers**
10630 Balto Ave.
Beltsville, MD 20705
(301)572-1710
Ultimate Parent: Nationsbank Corp.

★ 71361 ★ **Price Club**
10925 Baltimore Ave.
Beltsville, MD 20705
(301)595-3400
Ultimate Parent: Price.

★ 71362 ★ **Radio Shack**
11118 Baltimore Ave.
Beltsville, MD 20705
(301)937-8090
Company Type: Division. **Ultimate Parent:** Tandy Corp.

★ 71363 ★ **Radio Shack**
11118 Baltimore Ave.
Beltsville, MD 20705
(301)937-8090
Company Type: Division. **Ultimate Parent:** Tandy Corp.

★ 71364 ★ **Rite Aid**
10456 Baltimore Ave.
Beltsville, MD 20705
(301)937-1670
Ultimate Parent: Rite Aid. **SIC:** 5122—Drugs, Proprietaries & Sundries.

Berlin

★ 71365 ★ **Peninsula Bank**
11045 Race Track Rd.
Berlin, MD 21811
(410)208-0200
Company Type: Subsidiary. **Location Type:** Branch office. **Officer:** Sarah L. Walker, Manager. **Ultimate Parent:** Mercantile Bankshares Corp. **SIC:** 6021—National Commercial Banks.

★ 71366 ★ **Peninsula Bank**
1 S. Main St.
Berlin, MD 21811-1426
(410)641-2331
Company Type: Subsidiary. **Location Type:** Branch office. **Officer:** Roxanne D. Williams, Manager. **Ultimate Parent:** Mercantile Bankshares Corp. **SIC:** 6021—National Commercial Banks.

★ 71367 ★ **Radio Shack**
Ames Plz.
Berlin, MD 21811
(410)641-4727
Company Type: Division. **Ultimate Parent:** Tandy Corp. **SIC:** 3271—Concrete Block & Brick.

★ 71368 ★ **Rite Aid**
Old
Berlin, MD 21811
(410)641-0233
Ultimate Parent: Rite Aid. **SIC:** 5912—Drug Stores & Proprietary Stores.

Berwyn Heights

★ 71369 ★ **McDonald's Hamburgers**
6219 Greenbelt Rd.
Berwyn Heights, MD
(301)345-3117
Ultimate Parent: McDonald's.

Bethesda

★ 71370 ★ **Amanda Fielding**
7101 Democracy Blvd.
Bethesda, MD 20817
(301)365-3778
Ultimate Parent: J.C. Penney.

★ 71371 ★ **Banana Republic**
Montgmry Mall
Bethesda, MD
(301)365-5507
Ultimate Parent: GAP.

★ 71372 ★ **Banc One Mortgage Corp.**
6707 Democracy Blvd.
Bethesda, MD 20817
(301)571-0015
Location Type: Branch office. **Ultimate Parent:** Banc One Corp.

★ 71373 ★ **Banc One Mortgage Corp.**
6707 Democracy Blvd.
Bethesda, MD 20817
(301)897-3901
Ultimate Parent: Banc One Corp.

★ 71374 ★ **Banc One Mortgage Corp.**
Regional
6707 Democracy Blvd.
Bethesda, MD 20817
(301)897-3900
Ultimate Parent: Banc One Corp.

★ 71375 ★ **Casual Corner**
Democracy Blvd.
Bethesda, MD
(301)365-3400
Ultimate Parent: United States Shoe.

★ 71376 ★ **Charles Schwab & Co. Inc. Bethes**
7401 Wis Ave.
Bethesda, MD
(301)951-9155
Ultimate Parent: Charles Schwab Corp.

★ 71377 ★ **Circuit City**
10490 Auto Park Dr.
Bethesda, MD 20817
(301)469-8028
Ultimate Parent: Circuit City Stores.

★ 71378 ★ **Crestar Bank Maryland**
7500 Wisconsin Ave.
Bethesda, MD 20814-3570
(301)718-9206
Company Type: Subsidiary. **Ultimate Parent:** Crestar Financial Corp. **SIC:** 6022—State Commercial Banks.

★ 71379 ★ **Crestar Bank MD**
9000 Rockville Pke., Bldg. 10
Bethesda, MD 20892
(800)351-2435
Company Type: Subsidiary. **Location Type:** Branch office. **Officer:** John Esher, Manager. **Ultimate Parent:** Crestar Financial Corp. **SIC:** 6021—National Commercial Banks.

★ 71380 ★ **Crestar Bank MD**
10245 Old George Town Rd.
Bethesda, MD 20814-1900
(800)351-2435
Company Type: Subsidiary. **Location Type:** Branch office. **Officer:** Julie Hunko, Manager. **Ultimate Parent:** Crestar Financial Corp. **SIC:** 6021—National Commercial Banks.

★ 71381 ★ **Crestar Bank MD**
Westwood, 5450 Westband Ave.
Bethesda, MD 20816-3347
(800)451-2435
Company Type: Subsidiary. **Location Type:** Branch office. **Officer:** Eric R. Wilson, Manager. **Ultimate Parent:** Crestar Financial Corp. **SIC:** 6021—National Commercial·Banks.

★ 71382 ★ **Crestar Bank MD**
4836 Woodmont Ave.
Bethesda, MD 20814
(800)351-2435
Company Type: Subsidiary. **Location Type:** Branch office. **Officer:** Jany E. Stratigeas, Manager. **Ultimate Parent:** Crestar Financial Corp. **SIC:** 6021—National Commercial Banks.

★ 71383 ★ **Crestar Bank MD**
7500 Wisconsin Ave.
PO Box 30197
Bethesda, MD 20814
(800)451-2435 **Fax:** (301)949-2556
Company Type: Subsidiary. **Location Type:** Branch office. **Officer:** Peter F. Nostrand, President. **Ultimate Parent:** Crestar Financial Corp. **SIC:** 6021—National Commercial Banks.

★ 71384 ★ **CSC Intelicom**
6707 Democracy Blvd., Ste. 1000
Bethesda, MD 20817
(301)564-6600 **Fax:** (301)571-8399
Officer: John W. Sidgmore, President. **Ultimate Parent:** Computer Sciences.

★ 71385 ★ **Electronic Data Systems-Easter**
6430 Rockledge Dr.
Bethesda, MD 20817
(301)571-6700
Ultimate Parent: Electronic Data Systems.

★ 71386 ★ **Equity Title Service Corp.**
7200 Wisconsin Ave.
Bethesda, MD 20814
(301)951-1220
Ultimate Parent: Metropolitan Financial.

★ 71387 ★ **First Union National Bank of Maryland**
3 Bethesda Metro Plz., Ste. 8006
Bethesda, MD 20814-5329
(301)650-1128
Company Type: Subsidiary. **Location Type:** Branch office. **Ultimate Parent:** First Union Corp. **SIC:** 6021—National Commercial Banks.

★ 71388 ★ **First Union National Bank of Maryland**
7900 Wisconsin Ave.
Bethesda, MD 20814-3601
(301)650-1034
Company Type: Subsidiary. **Location Type:** Branch office. **Ultimate Parent:** First Union Corp. **SIC:** 6021—National Commercial Banks.

★ 71389 ★ **First Union National Bank of Maryland**
7220 Wisconsin Ave.
Bethesda, MD 20814-4812
(301)961-5280
Company Type: Subsidiary. **Location Type:** Branch office. **Officer:** Rob Haley, Manager. **Ultimate Parent:** First Union Corp. **SIC:** 6021—National Commercial Banks.

★ 71390 ★ **First Union National Bank of Maryland**
7101 Democracy Blvd.
Bethesda, MD 20817-1018
(301)650-1025
Company Type: Subsidiary. **Location Type:** Branch office. **Ultimate Parent:** First Union Corp. **SIC:** 6021—National Commercial Banks.

★ 71391 ★ **First Union National Bank of Maryland**
6921 Arlington Rd.
Bethesda, MD 20814-5205
(301)961-5210
Company Type: Subsidiary. **Location Type:** Branch office. **Officer:** Shahla Mokhtari, Manager. **Ultimate Parent:** First Union Corp. **SIC:** 6021—National Commercial Banks.

★ 71392 ★ **Gap Kids**
Montgmry Mall
Bethesda, MD
(301)365-5504
Ultimate Parent: GAP.

★ 71393 ★ **Gap Store Inc. Maryland Stores**
Montgomery
Bethesda, MD 20817
(301)365-4500
Ultimate Parent: GAP.

★ 71394 ★ **Gap Store Inc. Maryland Stores**
Montgomery
Bethesda, MD 20817
(301)365-4500
Ultimate Parent: GAP.

★ 71395 ★ **Hot Shoppes Cafeterias**
1 Marriott Dr. Wash Dc
Bethesda, MD
(301)380-9000
Ultimate Parent: Marriott International.

★ 71396 ★ **Lenscrafters**
Montgomery Mall
Bethesda, MD
(301)365-3682
Ultimate Parent: United States Shoe.

★ 71397 ★ **Loyola Fsb Auto Dealer Financi**
7535 Old Georgtwn Rd.
Bethesda, MD 20814
(301)913-0398
Ultimate Parent: Loyola Capital Corp.

★ 71398 ★ **Loyola Fsb Banking Centers**
7535 Old Georgetown Rd.
Bethesda, MD 20814
(301)657-1604
Ultimate Parent: Loyola Capital Corp.

★ 71399 ★ **Lsi Logic Corp.**
6903 Rockledge Dr.
Bethesda, MD 20817
(301)897-5800
Ultimate Parent: LSI Logic Corp.

★ 71400 ★ **Marriott Hotels**
6711 Democracy Blvd.
Bethesda, MD 20817
(301)897-5600
Ultimate Parent: Marriott International.

★ 71401 ★ **Marriott Hotels**
5151 Pooks Hill Rd.
Bethesda, MD 20814
(301)897-9400
Ultimate Parent: Marriott International.

★ 71402 ★ **Marriott Hotels Resorts Suites**
6711 Democracy Blvd.
Bethesda, MD 20817
(301)897-5600
Ultimate Parent: Marriott International.

★ 71403 ★ **Marriott Hotels Resorts Suites**
5151 Pooks Hill Rd.
Bethesda, MD 20814
(301)897-9400
Ultimate Parent: Marriott International.

★ 71404 ★ **Marriott Senior Living Service**
Bethesda, MD
(301)380-3775
Ultimate Parent: Marriott International.

★ 71405 ★ **Marriott Senior Living Service**
Bethesda, MD
(301)380-5728
Ultimate Parent: Marriott International.

★ 71406 ★ **Martin Marietta**
6801 Rockledge Dr.
Bethesda, MD 20817
(301)897-6000
Company Type: Headquarters. **Officer:** Norman R. Augustine. **Sales:** 9435.7 M. **Fortune 500:** Largest U.S. Industrial Corporations: Ranking 51.

★ 71407 ★ **Martin Marietta Corp.**
6801 Rockledge Dr.
Bethesda, MD 20817
(301)897-6000
Ultimate Parent: Martin Marietta.

★ 71408 ★ **Martin Marietta Corp. Ov**
6801 Rockledge Drive
Bethesda, MD 20817
(301)897-6738
Ultimate Parent: Martin Marietta.

★ 71409 ★ **Martin Marietta Information Systems**
6801 Rockledge Dr.
Bethesda, MD 20817
Officer: Gary P. Mann, Vice President. **Ultimate Parent:** Martin Marietta.

★ 71410 ★ **Mary Kay Cosmetics**
7617 Dwight Dr.
Bethesda, MD 20817
Ultimate Parent: Mary Kay Cosmetics. **SIC:** 5999—Miscellaneous Retail Stores Nec.

★ 71411 ★ **Mary Kay Cosmetics Indep Sales**
7617 Dwight Dr.
Bethesda, MD 20817
(301)365-1638
Ultimate Parent: Mary Kay Cosmetics.

★ 71412 ★ **McDonald's Hamburgers**
8901 Wisconsin Ave.
Bethesda, MD 20814
(301)951-9858
Ultimate Parent: McDonald's.

★ 71413 ★ **McDonald's Hamburgers**
Bethesda Naval Base
Bethesda, MD
(301)564-9549
Ultimate Parent: McDonald's.

★ 71414 ★ **Mellon Bank (MD)**
5229 River Rd.
Bethesda, MD 20816
(301)654-3392
Company Type: Subsidiary. **Location Type:** Branch office. **Officer:** Ed Kinsella, Manager. **Ultimate Parent:** Mellon Bank Corp. **SIC:** 6021—National Commercial Banks.

★ 71415 ★ **Mellon Bank (MD)**
10329 Old Georgetown Rd.
Bethesda, MD 20814-1912
(301)530-0808
Company Type: Subsidiary. **Location Type:** Branch office. **Officer:** Susan Lemmon, Manager. **Ultimate Parent:** Mellon Bank Corp. **SIC:** 6021—National Commercial Banks.

★ 71416 ★ **Mellon Bank (MD)**
7475 Wisconsin Ave.
Bethesda, MD 20814
(301)907-0750
Company Type: Subsidiary. **Location Type:** Branch office. **Officer:** Sandra Sampson, Manager. **Ultimate Parent:** Mellon Bank Corp. **SIC:** 6021—National Commercial Banks.

★ 71417 ★ **Metropolitan Federal Savings &**
7901 Wisconsin Ave.
Bethesda, MD 20814
(301)951-6501
Ultimate Parent: Metropolitan Financial.

★ 71418 ★ **Nationsbank**
Bethesda, MD
(301)493-2985
Ultimate Parent: Nationsbank Corp.

★ 71419 ★ **Nationsbank**
6610 Rockledge Dr.
Bethesda, MD 20817
(301)571-9696
Ultimate Parent: Nationsbank Corp.

★ 71420 ★ **Nationsbank**
6610 Rockledge Dr.
Bethesda, MD 20817
(301)493-2887
Ultimate Parent: Nationsbank Corp.

★ 71421 ★ **Nationsbank**
Bethesda, MD
(301)493-2914
Ultimate Parent: Nationsbank Corp.

★ 71422 ★ **Nationsbank**
6610 Rockledge
Bethesda, MD 20817
(301)571-9024
Ultimate Parent: Nationsbank Corp.

★ 71423 ★ **Nationsbank**
7316 Wisconsin Ave.
Bethesda, MD 20814
(301)493-7111
Ultimate Parent: Nationsbank Corp.

★ 71424 ★ **Nationsbank Banking Centers**
10400 Old Georgetown Rd.
Bethesda, MD 20814
(301)270-5000
Ultimate Parent: Nationsbank Corp.

★ 71425 ★ New York Life Insurance Co. Gnl
3 Beth Metro Ctr.
Bethesda, MD
(301)654-9180
Ultimate Parent: New York Life. SIC: 6411—Insurance Agents, Brokers & Service.

★ 71426 ★ Nordstrom
7111 Democracy Blvd.
Bethesda, MD 20817
(301)365-4111
Ultimate Parent: Nordstrom.

★ 71427 ★ North American Van Lines Agent
Bethesda, MD
(301)652-5427
Ultimate Parent: Norfolk Southern.

★ 71428 ★ Northwestern Mutual Life Inusr
6410 Rockledge Dr.
Bethesda, MD 20817
(301)897-0047
Ultimate Parent: Northwestern Mutual Life.

★ 71429 ★ Petite Sophisticate
White Fint Mall
Bethesda, MD
(301)881-4174
Ultimate Parent: United States Shoe.

★ 71430 ★ Petite Sophisticate
7107 Democracy Blvd.
Bethesda, MD 20817
(301)469-4991
Ultimate Parent: United States Shoe.

★ 71431 ★ Phoenix Home Life Mutual Inc.
4550 Montgomery Ave.
Bethesda, MD 20814
(301)656-4951
Ultimate Parent: Phoenix Home Life Mutual.

★ 71432 ★ Phoenix Home Life Mutual Insurance Co.
3 Beth Metro Ctr.
Bethesda, MD
(301)986-6900
Ultimate Parent: Phoenix Home Life Mutual. SIC: 6411—Insurance Agents, Brokers & Service.

★ 71433 ★ Potomac Valley Bank
4424 Montgomery Ave.
Bethesda, MD 20814
(301)657-1974
Company Type: Subsidiary. Location Type: Branch office. Officer: Patricia S. Oliphant, Manager. Ultimate Parent: Mercantile Bankshares Corp. SIC: 6021—National Commercial Banks.

★ 71434 ★ Prudential Securities Inc.
3 Beth Metro Ctr.
Bethesda, MD
(301)961-0100
Ultimate Parent: Prudential of America.

★ 71435 ★ Radio Shack
5456 Westbard Ave.
Bethesda, MD 20816
(301)654-0454
Company Type: Division. Ultimate Parent: Tandy Corp.

★ 71436 ★ Radio Shack
8125 Wisconsin Ave.
Bethesda, MD 20814
(301)986-8844
Company Type: Division. Ultimate Parent: Tandy Corp.

★ 71437 ★ Radio Shack
5456 Westbard Ave.
Bethesda, MD 20816
(301)654-0454
Company Type: Division. Ultimate Parent: Tandy Corp.

★ 71438 ★ Radio Shack
8125 Wisconsin Ave.
Bethesda, MD 20814
(301)986-8844
Company Type: Division. Ultimate Parent: Tandy Corp.

★ 71439 ★ Residence Inn by Marriott
7335 Wisconsin Ave.
Bethesda, MD 20814
(301)718-0200
Ultimate Parent: Marriott International.

★ 71440 ★ Rite Aid
Westwood Shopping. Ctr.
Bethesda, MD
(301)656-2477
Ultimate Parent: Rite Aid.

★ 71441 ★ Smith Barney Harris Upham & Co.
11301 Rockville Pke. N
Bethesda, MD 20814
(301)984-0869
Company Type: Branch. Ultimate Parent: Automatic Data Processing, Inc. SIC: 6211—Security Brokers & Dealers.

★ 71442 ★ Standard Federal Savings Bank
5225 River Rd.
Bethesda, MD 20816
(301)654-3392
Ultimate Parent: Standard Federal Bank.

★ 71443 ★ Structure
Montgomery Mall
Bethesda, MD
(301)469-7920
Ultimate Parent: Limited.

★ 71444 ★ Teachers Insurance & Annuity
7475 Wis Ave.
Bethesda, MD
(301)986-9161
Ultimate Parent: Teachers Insurance & Annuity.

★ 71445 ★ US Leasing Internat
3 Beth Metro Ctr.
Bethesda, MD
(301)961-1928
Ultimate Parent: Ford Motor Co.

★ 71446 ★ US Leasing International
3 Bethesda Metro Ctr.
Bethesda, MD 20814
(301)961-1926
Ultimate Parent: Ford Motor Co.

★ 71447 ★ Waldenbooks Maryland Stores
Montgomery Mall
Bethesda, MD 20817
(301)469-8810
Ultimate Parent: K-Mart.

★ 71448 ★ Wang Infomation Services Corp.
Bethesda, MD
(301)657-5000
Ultimate Parent: Wang Laboratories, Inc.

★ 71449 ★ Winchester Homes Inc.
6701 Rockledge Dr.
Bethesda, MD 20817
(301)897-0170
Ultimate Parent: Weyerhaeuser Co.

★ 71450 ★ Zenger-Miller
3 Beth Metro Ctr.
Bethesda, MD
(301)961-4898
Ultimate Parent: Times Mirror Co.

★ 71451 ★ Csc Intelicom
6707 Democracy Blvd.
Betheseda, MD 20817
(301)564-6600
Ultimate Parent: Computer Sciences.

Bladensburg

★ 71452 ★ Exxon Co.
5650 Annapolis Rd.
Bladensburg, MD 20710
(301)277-5808
Ultimate Parent: Exxon.

★ 71453 ★ Exxon Service Station
5650 Annapolis Rd.
Bladensburg, MD 20710
(301)927-0075
Ultimate Parent: Exxon.

★ 71454 ★ Mini Mart
4901 57th Ave.
Bladensburg, MD 20710
(301)277-5379
Ultimate Parent: Kroger.

★ 71455 ★ Rite Aid
4920 Annapolisrd
Bladensburg, MD 20710
(301)864-5207
Ultimate Parent: Rite Aid.

Bowie

★ 71456 ★ Allstate Life Insurance
Bowie, MD
(301)464-1023
Ultimate Parent: Allstate Life.

★ 71457 ★ Citizens National Bank
1344 Crain Hwy. S
Bowie, MD 20716-1802
(301)249-6800
Company Type: Subsidiary. Location Type: Branch office. Officer: Darla Thumann, Manager. Ultimate Parent: Mercantile Bankshares Corp. SIC: 6021—National Commercial Banks.

★ 71458 ★ Citizens National Bank
3314 Superior Ln.
Bowie, MD 20715-1965
(301)464-5570
Company Type: Subsidiary. Location Type: Branch office. Officer: T.M. Scheopner, Manager. Ultimate Parent: Mercantile Bankshares Corp. SIC: 6021—National Commercial Banks.

★ 71459 ★ Delta Business Systems
4201 Northview Dr.
Bowie, MD 20716-2604
(301)262-0550
Ultimate Parent: Alco Standard Corp. SIC: 7371—Computer Programming Services.

★ 71460 ★ Exxon Co.
15711 Annapolis Rd.
Bowie, MD 20715
(301)262-4114
Ultimate Parent: Exxon.

★ 71461 ★ First Union National Bank of Maryland
15480 Annapolis Rd.
Bowie, MD 20715-1846
(301)650-1030
Company Type: Subsidiary. Location Type: Branch office. Ultimate Parent: First Union Corp. SIC: 6021—National Commercial Banks.

★ 71462 ★ Lowe's
1010 Northest Crain Hwy.
Bowie, MD
(301)249-2600
Ultimate Parent: Lowe's.

★ 71463 ★ Loyola FSB Banking Centers Bow
15460 Annapolis Rd.
Bowie, MD 20715
(301)262-5515
Ultimate Parent: Loyola Capital Corp.

★ 71464 ★ Mary Kay Cosmetics Indep Sales
1316 Peachtree Ct
Bowie, MD 20721
(301)249-6592
Ultimate Parent: Mary Kay Cosmetics.

★ 71465 ★ McDonald's Hamburgers
15998 Annapolis Rd.
Bowie, MD 20715
(301)464-0810
Ultimate Parent: McDonald's.

★ 71466 ★ McDonald's Hamburgers
12168 Central Ave.
Bowie, MD 20721
(301)390-3768
Ultimate Parent: McDonald's.

★ 71467 ★ McDonald's Hamburgers
14300 Galiant Fox Lane
Bowie, MD 20715
(301)464-0110
Ultimate Parent: McDonald's.

★ 71468 ★ Mellon Bank (MD)
3218-A Superior Ln.
Bowie, MD 20715
(410)464-0900
Company Type: Subsidiary. Location Type: Branch office. Officer: Susan Younger, Manager. Ultimate Parent: Mellon Bank Corp. SIC: 6021—National Commercial Banks.

★ 71469 ★ Nationsbank Banking Centers
6911 Laurel Bowie Rd.
Bowie, MD 20715
(301)572-1750
Ultimate Parent: Nationsbank Corp.

★ 71470 ★ Nationsbank Banking Centers
13031 Ninth St.
Bowie, MD 20720
(301)572-1760
Ultimate Parent: Nationsbank Corp.

★ 71471 ★ Radio Shack
6846 Race Track Rd.
Bowie, MD 20715
(301)262-2591
Company Type: Division. Ultimate Parent: Tandy Corp.

★ 71472 ★ Radio Shack
6846 Race Track Rd.
Bowie, MD 20715
(301)262-2591
Company Type: Division. Ultimate Parent: Tandy Corp.

★ 71473 ★ Smithfield Packing Co. Inc.
Bowie, MD
(301)262-0336
Ultimate Parent: Smithfield Foods Inc.

★ 71474 ★ Transamerica Real Estate
2125 Baldwin Ave.
Bowie, MD 20715
(301)721-0822
Ultimate Parent: Transamerica.

Bowie

★ 71475 ★ Exxon Co.
Bowie Md, MD
(301)464-2431
Ultimate Parent: Exxon.

Briggs Chaney

★ 71476 ★ Standard Federal Savings Bank
13801 Outlet Dr.
Briggs Chaney, MD
(301)890-6900
Ultimate Parent: Standard Federal Bank.

Bryans Road

★ 71477 ★ Radio Shack
Bryans Road Shopping Ctr.
Bryans Road, MD
(301)283-3330
Company Type: Division. Ultimate Parent: Tandy Corp.

★ 71478 ★ Radio Shack
Bryans Road Shopping Ctr.
Bryans Road, MD
(301)283-3330
Company Type: Division. Ultimate Parent: Tandy Corp.

Buckeystown

★ 71479 ★ Riverside Market
Point of Rocks
Buckeystown, MD 21717
(301)874-5252
Ultimate Parent: Penn Traffic. SIC: 5411—Grocery Stores.

Burtonsville

★ 71480 ★ **Citizens National Bank**
15628 Columbia Pke.
Burtonsville, MD 20866-1630
(301)421-9595
Company Type: Subsidiary. **Location Type:** Branch office. **Officer:** Sharon Devine, Manager. **Ultimate Parent:** Mercantile Bankshares Corp. **SIC:** 6021—National Commercial Banks.

★ 71481 ★ **McDonald's Hamburgers**
15569 Old Columbia Pke
Burtonsville, MD 20866
(301)384-4630
Ultimate Parent: McDonald's.

California

★ 71482 ★ **Beneficial Mortgage Co. of MD**
San Souci Plz.
California, MD 20619
(301)863-6670
Ultimate Parent: Beneficial. **SIC:** 6141—Personal Credit Institutions; 6162—Mortgage Bankers & Correspondents.

★ 71483 ★ **Hertz Rent-A-Car**
7978 Threenotch Rd.
California, MD 20619
(301)863-6624
Ultimate Parent: Hertz. **SIC:** 7514—Passenger Car Rental.

Cambridge

★ 71484 ★ **Acme Markets**
Shoal Creek Mall
Cambridge, MD 21613
(410)228-8343
Ultimate Parent: American Stores. **SIC:** 5411—Grocery Stores.

★ 71485 ★ **Del Monte Corp.**
Woods Rd.
Cambridge, MD 21613
(410)228-2713
Ultimate Parent: Del Monte Foods. **SIC:** 2032—Canned Specialties.

★ 71486 ★ **Hertz Rent-A-Car**
206 Cedar St.
Cambridge, MD 21613
(410)228-1688
Ultimate Parent: Hertz. **SIC:** 5014—Tires & Tubes.

★ 71487 ★ **Radio Shack**
Shoal Creek Mall
Cambridge, MD 21613
(410)228-9539
Company Type: Division. **Ultimate Parent:** Tandy Corp. **SIC:** 5734—Computer & Software Stores.

★ 71488 ★ **Western Publishing Co.**
806 Woods Rd.
Cambridge, MD 21613
(410)228-4000
Officer: Allen Shepard, Manager. **Ultimate Parent:** Western Publishing Group. **SIC:** 2731—Book Publishing; 2741—Miscellaneous Publishing; 2752—Commercial Printing—Lithographic.

Camp Springs

★ 71489 ★ **Progressive Casualty Insurance Co.**
5801 Allentown Rd. 408
Camp Springs, MD
(301)899-7610
Ultimate Parent: Progressive.

★ 71490 ★ **Radio Shack**
Allentown Mall
Camp Springs, MD
(301)899-7555
Company Type: Division. **Ultimate Parent:** Tandy Corp.

Cape St Clare

★ 71491 ★ **Residence Inn by Marriott**
170 Admiral Cochrane Dr.
Cape St Clare, MD 21401
(410)573-0300
Ultimate Parent: Marriott International. **SIC:** 3599—Industrial Machinery Nec.

Cape St. Claire

★ 71492 ★ **Annapolis Banking & Trust Co.**
737 College Pky. E
Cape St. Claire, MD 21401-4999
(410)757-5353
Company Type: Subsidiary. **Location Type:** Branch office. **Officer:** Barbara R. Jones, Manager. **Ultimate Parent:** Mercantile Bankshares Corp. **SIC:** 6021—National Commercial Banks.

★ 71493 ★ **Circuit City**
160 Jennifer Rd.
Cape St. Claire, MD 21401
(410)266-0941
Ultimate Parent: Circuit City Stores. **SIC:** 5065—Electronic Parts & Equipment Nec.

★ 71494 ★ **First American Bank**
209 Main St.
Cape St. Claire, MD 21401
(410)268-6400
Ultimate Parent: First American Corp. **SIC:** 6159—Miscellaneous Business Credit Institutions; 6531—Real Estate Agents & Managers.

★ 71495 ★ **First American Bank**
37 Parole Plz.
Cape St. Claire, MD 21401
(410)224-2880
Ultimate Parent: First American Corp. **SIC:** 6159—Miscellaneous Business Credit Institutions.

★ 71496 ★ **Waldenbooks**
Annapolis Mall
Cape St. Claire, MD 21401
(410)266-6065
Ultimate Parent: K-Mart. **SIC:** 5942—Book Stores.

Capital Heigh

★ 71497 ★ **Exxon Co.**
5915 George Palmer Hwy.
Capital Heigh, MD 20743
(301)336-1504
Ultimate Parent: Exxon.

★ 71498 ★ **Radio Shack**
Div. of Tandy
6258 Central Ave.
Capital Heigh, MD 20743
(301)350-3680
Company Type: Division. **Ultimate Parent:** Tandy Corp.

Capital Heights

★ 71499 ★ **Browning-Ferris Industries**
8401 Truck Way
Capital Heights, MD 20743-3621
(301)336-1000
Location Type: Branch office. **Officer:** Bob Schwartzberg. **Ultimate Parent:** Browning-Ferris Industries. **SIC:** 3339—Primary Nonferrous Metals Nec; 4953—Refuse Systems; 5084—Industrial Machinery & Equipment.

★ 71500 ★ **Coca-Cola Enterprises**
500 Dunmore Pl
Capital Heights, MD 20743
(301)336-1100
Ultimate Parent: Coca-Cola Enterprises.

★ 71501 ★ **Coca-Cola Enterprises**
51 Ritchie Rd.
Capital Heights, MD
(301)336-3800
Ultimate Parent: Coca-Cola Enterprises.

★ 71502 ★ **McDonald's Hamburgers**
6131 Martin Luther King Jr. Blvd.
Capital Heights, MD 20743
(301)925-4563
Ultimate Parent: McDonald's.

★ 71503 ★ **Rite Aid**
5931 Martin Luther King Jr
Capital Heights, MD 20743
(301)350-1400
Ultimate Parent: Rite Aid.

Capitol Heights

★ 71504 ★ **Browning-Ferris Industries**
8401 Truck Way
Capitol Heights, MD 20743
(301)336-1000
Officer: Bob Schwartzberg, Manager. **Ultimate Parent:** Browning-Ferris Industries. **SIC:** 3589—Service Industry Machinery Nec.

Catonsville

★ 71505 ★ **Dr. Pepper/Seven-Up**
6159 Edmondson Ave.
Catonsville, MD 21228
(410)747-7777
Officer: John Imbes, President. **Ultimate Parent:** Dr. Pepper/Seven-Up. **SIC:** 2086—Bottled & Canned Soft Drinks.

Cavetown

★ 71506 ★ **Winchester Homes Inc.**
4061 Powder Mill Rd.
Cavetown, MD 21720
(301)595-0080
Ultimate Parent: Weyerhaeuser Co.

Cecilton

★ 71507 ★ **County Banking & Trust Co.**
Main St.
Cecilton, MD 21903
(410)275-8131
Company Type: Subsidiary. **Location Type:** Branch office. **Officer:** Gloria Heath, Manager. **Ultimate Parent:** Mercantile Bankshares Corp. **SIC:** 6021—National Commercial Banks.

Centers Clint

★ 71508 ★ **Nationsbank Banking Centers**
8815 Woodyard Rd.
Centers Clint, MD
(301)817-7730
Ultimate Parent: Nationsbank Corp.

Chaneyville

★ 71509 ★ **Clavert Bank & Trust Co.**
Rte. 4 & Fowler Rd.
Chaneyville, MD 20689
(410)257-2600
Company Type: Subsidiary. **Location Type:** Branch office. **Officer:** Kimberly H. Freeland, Manager. **Ultimate Parent:** Mercantile Bankshares Corp. **SIC:** 6021—National Commercial Banks.

Charlotte Hall

★ 71510 ★ **First National Bank of St. Mary's**
Rte. 5
Charlotte Hall, MD 20622
(301)475-8081
Company Type: Subsidiary. **Location Type:** Branch office. **Officer:** Cindy Morgan, Manager. **Ultimate Parent:** Mercantile Bankshares Corp. **SIC:** 6021—National Commercial Banks.

Chase

★ 71511 ★ **Radio Shack**
Carroll Island Shopping Ctr.
Chase, MD 21027
(410)335-8664
Company Type: Division. **Ultimate Parent:** Tandy Corp. **SIC:** 5065—Electronic Parts & Equipment Nec.

★ 71512 ★ **Radio Shack**
Carroll Shopping Ctr.
Chase, MD 21027
(410)335-8664
Company Type: Division. **Ultimate Parent:** Tandy Corp. **SIC:** 5065—Electronic Parts & Equipment Nec.

★ 71513 ★ **Ryder Truck Rental Inc.**
317 Bowleys Quarters Rd.
Chase, MD 21027
(410)335-5800
Ultimate Parent: Ryder System. **SIC:** 7513—Truck Rental & Leasing Without Drivers.

Chesapeake Beach

★ 71514 ★ **Calvert Bank & Trust Co.**
Rte. 261 & 21st St.
Chesapeake Beach, MD 20732
(410)257-9000
Company Type: Subsidiary. **Location Type:** Branch office. **Officer:** Amanda J. Bowen, Manager. **Ultimate Parent:** Mercantile Bankshares Corp. **SIC:** 6021—National Commercial Banks.

Chesapeake City

★ 71515 ★ **County Banking & Trust Co.**
Rte. 213
Chesapeake City, MD 21915
(410)885-5600
Company Type: Subsidiary. **Location Type:** Branch office. **Officer:** Vickie Myers, Manager. **Ultimate Parent:** Mercantile Bankshares Corp. **SIC:** 6021—National Commercial Banks.

Chester

★ 71516 ★ **Banister Shoe**
Piney Narrows Rd.
Chester, MD 21619
(410)643-7308
Ultimate Parent: United States Shoe. **SIC:** 5661—Shoe Stores.

Chestertown

★ 71517 ★ **Campbell Soup Co.**
20730 Mercnec Rd.
PO Box 29
Chestertown, MD 21620
(410)778-3131
Location Type: Plant. **Officer:** Arlen Ramsey, Plant Manager. **Ultimate Parent:** Campbell Soup.

★ 71518 ★ **Campbell Soup Co. Chestertown Plant**
27030 Morgnec Rd. PO Box 29
Chestertown, MD 21620
Ultimate Parent: Campbell Soup. **SIC:** 2035—Pickles, Sauces & Salad Dressings.

★ 71519 ★ **Campbell Soup Co. Chestertown Plant**
Rte. 291 PO Box 29
Chestertown, MD 21620
Ultimate Parent: Campbell Soup. **SIC:** 2000—Food & Kindred Products.

★ 71520 ★ **Chestertown Bank of Maryland**
Washington Ave.
Chestertown, MD 21620
(410)778-6110
Company Type: Subsidiary. **Location Type:** Branch office. **Officer:** Marion R. Myers, Manager. **Ultimate Parent:** Mercantile Bankshares Corp. **SIC:** 6021—National Commercial Banks.

★ 71521 ★ **Chestertown Bank of Maryland**
501 Campus Ave., Heron Pt.
Chestertown, MD 21620
(410)778-2224
Company Type: Subsidiary. **Location Type:** Branch office. **Officer:** Judith A. Alexander, Manager. **Ultimate Parent:** Mercantile Bankshares Corp. **SIC:** 6021—National Commercial Banks.

★ 71522 ★ **Chestertown Bank of Maryland**
211-213 High St.
Chestertown, MD 21620-1517
(410)778-2400
Company Type: Subsidiary. **Location Type:** Branch office. **Officer:** Debroah W. Layton, Manager. **Ultimate Parent:** Mercantile Bankshares Corp. **SIC:** 6021—National Commercial Banks.

★ 71523 ★ **Chestertown Bank of Maryland**
211 High St.
PO Box 60
Chestertown, MD 21620-0060
(410)778-2400
Company Type: Subsidiary. **Location Type:** Branch office. **Officer:** R. Raymond Tarrach, President & CEO. **Ultimate Parent:** Mercantile Bankshares Corp. **SIC:** 6021—National Commercial Banks.

★ 71524 ★ **Radio Shack**
Kent Plz.
Chestertown, MD 21620
(410)778-0058
Company Type: Division. **Ultimate Parent:** Tandy Corp. **SIC:** 5734—Computer & Software Stores.

★ 71525 ★ **Rite Aid**
Kent Plz.
Chestertown, MD 21620
(410)778-4000
Ultimate Parent: Rite Aid. **SIC:** 5912—Drug Stores & Proprietary Stores.

Cheverly

★ 71526 ★ **Pepsi-Cola Bottling Co.**
2611 Pepsi Pl.
Cheverly, MD 20785
(301)322-7000
Officer: Tom McLoughlin, Manager. **Ultimate Parent:** Pepsico. **SIC:** 2086—Bottled & Canned Soft Drinks.

★ 71527 ★ **Saturn Corp.**
4701 Lydell Rd.
Cheverly, MD 20781
(301)772-7000
Ultimate Parent: General Motors Corp.

Chevy Chase

★ 71528 ★ **Banana Republic**
5430 Wis Ave.
Chevy Chase, MD
(301)907-7740
Ultimate Parent: GAP.

★ 71529 ★ **First Union National Bank of Maryland**
5476 Wisconsin Ave.
Chevy Chase, MD 20815-3581
(301)650-1020
Company Type: Subsidiary. **Location Type:** Branch office. **Ultimate Parent:** First Union Corp. **SIC:** 6021—National Commercial Banks.

★ 71530 ★ **Gap the**
5430 Wis Ave.
Chevy Chase, MD
(301)907-7656
Ultimate Parent: GAP.

★ 71531 ★ **Gap Kids**
5430 Wis Ave.
Chevy Chase, MD
(301)718-0886
Ultimate Parent: GAP.

★ 71532 ★ **Hoechst-Roussel Pharmaceutical**
Chevy Chase, MD
(301)656-3347
Ultimate Parent: Hoechst Celanese Corp.

★ 71533 ★ **Nationsbank Banking Centers**
4411 S. Park Ave.
Chevy Chase, MD 20815
(301)493-7130
Ultimate Parent: Nationsbank Corp.

Chillum

★ 71534 ★ **Rite Aid**
Riggs Plaza
Chillum, MD
(301)559-1555
Ultimate Parent: Rite Aid.

★ 71535 ★ **Standard Federal Savings Bank**
3030 Queens Chapel Rd.
Chillum, MD 20782
(301)779-5770
Ultimate Parent: Standard Federal Bank.

Clarksville

★ 71536 ★ **Citizens National Bank**
12431 Clarksville Rd.
Clarksville, MD 21029-1223
(410)531-2113
Company Type: Subsidiary. **Location Type:** Branch office. **Officer:** Olga J. Sealing, Manager. **Ultimate Parent:** Mercantile Bankshares Corp. **SIC:** 6021—National Commercial Banks.

Clinton

★ 71537 ★ **First Union National Bank of Maryland**
7600 Old Branch Ave.
Clinton, MD 20735-1603
(301)650-1093
Company Type: Subsidiary. **Location Type:** Branch office. **Ultimate Parent:** First Union Corp. **SIC:** 6021—National Commercial Banks.

★ 71538 ★ **First Virginia Mortgage Co.**
7700 Old Branch Ave.
Clinton, MD 20735
(301)868-9300
Ultimate Parent: First Virginia Banks Inc.

★ 71539 ★ **Kmart**
8827 Woodyard Rd.
Clinton, MD 20735
(301)868-8600
Ultimate Parent: K-Mart.

★ 71540 ★ **Mary Kay Cosmetics Indep Sales**
3601 Applecross Way
Clinton, MD 20735
(301)292-0441
Ultimate Parent: Mary Kay Cosmetics.

★ 71541 ★ **McDonald's Hamburgers**
909 PO Box
Clinton, MD 20735
Ultimate Parent: McDonald's. **SIC:** 5812—Eating Places.

★ 71542 ★ **McDonald's Hamburgers**
8905 Stuart Ln.
Clinton, MD 20735
(301)868-7777
Ultimate Parent: McDonald's.

★ 71543 ★ **Southland Corp.**
7801 Old Branch Ave.
Clinton, MD 20735
(301)868-3772
Ultimate Parent: Southland Corp.

★ 71544 ★ **Winchester Homes Inc.**
7100 Dewdrop Way
Clinton, MD 20735
(301)856-2959
Ultimate Parent: Weyerhaeuser Co.

Cockeysville

★ 71545 ★ **Becton Dickinson Microbiology Systems**
250 Schilling Cir.
Cockeysville, MD 21030
(410)771-0100 **Fax:** (410)584-7121
Company Type: Subsidiary. **Officer:** Anthony Pasquarelli, President. **Ultimate Parent:** Becton Dickinson.

★ 71546 ★ **Casual Corner**
Hunt Valley Mall
Cockeysville, MD 21030
(410)666-7403
Ultimate Parent: United States Shoe. **SIC:** 5621—Women's Clothing Stores.

★ 71547 ★ **Exxon Co.**
Cockeysville, MD 21031
(410)785-6660
Ultimate Parent: Exxon. **SIC:** 5599—Automotive Dealers Nec.

★ 71548 ★ **First American Bank Maryland**
10283 York Rd.
Cockeysville, MD 21030
(410)666-7200
Ultimate Parent: First American Corp. **SIC:** 6022—State Commercial Banks.

★ 71549 ★ **First Union National Bank of Maryland**
10283 York Rd.
Cockeysville, MD 21030-3295
(410)964-4749
Company Type: Subsidiary. **Location Type:** Branch office. **Ultimate Parent:** First Union Corp. **SIC:** 6021—National Commercial Banks.

★ 71550 ★ **Maryland Specialty Wire Inc.**
100 Cockeysville Rd.
Cockeysville, MD 21030
(410)785-2500 **Fax:** (410)785-4835
Company Type: Subsidiary. **Officer:** Richard Nash Jr., President. **Ultimate Parent:** Handy & Harman. **SIC:** 3496—Miscellaneous Fabricated Wire Products.

★ 71551 ★ **Mccormick & Co. Inc.**
Food Service Div.
10950 Beaver Dam Rd.
Cockeysville, MD 21030
Company Type: Division. **Ultimate Parent:** McCormick & Co. Inc. **SIC:** 2033—Canned Fruits & Vegetables; 2035—Pickles, Sauces & Salad Dressings.

★ 71552 ★ **McCormick & Co. Inc.**
Hunt Valley Condiment Plant
10950 Beaver Dam Rd.
Cockeysville, MD 21030
Location Type: Plant. **Ultimate Parent:** McCormick & Co. Inc. **SIC:** 2035—Pickles, Sauces & Salad Dressings.

★ 71553 ★ **Radio Shack**
Hunt Valley Mall
Cockeysville, MD 21031
(410)666-5358
Company Type: Division. **Ultimate Parent:** Tandy Corp. **SIC:** 5046—Commercial Equipment Nec.

★ 71554 ★ **Radio Shack**
Yorktowne Plz.
Cockeysville, MD 21030
(410)666-0161
Company Type: Division. **Ultimate Parent:** Tandy Corp. **SIC:** 5065—Electronic Parts & Equipment Nec.

★ 71555 ★ **Rite Aid**
Yorktowne Shopping.Ctr.
Cockeysville, MD 21030
(410)666-2878
Ultimate Parent: Rite Aid. **SIC:** 5912—Drug Stores & Proprietary Stores.

★ 71556 ★ **Waldenbooks**
Hunt Valley Mall
Cockeysville, MD 21030
(410)771-0848
Ultimate Parent: K-Mart. **SIC:** 5942—Book Stores.

Cockeysville Hunt Valley

★ 71557 ★ **Martin Marietta Magnesia Specialities, Inc.**
Executive Pl. II
Cockeysville Hunt Valley, MD 21070
(410)527-3700
Officer: Stephen P. Zelnak Jr., President. **Ultimate Parent:** Martin Marietta.

Cockys Height Valley

★ 71558 ★ **Baltimore Gas**
11212 York Rd.
Cockys Height Valley, MD 21030
(410)625-6207
Ultimate Parent: Baltimore Gas & Electric Co. **SIC:** 7389—Business Services Nec.

Cockysville Hunt Valley

★ 71559 ★ **Standard Register Co.**
216 Schilling Cir.
Cockysville Hunt Valley, MD 21031
(410)785-2700
Officer: Frank Constantino, Manager. **Ultimate Parent:** Standard Register. **SIC:** 2759—Commercial Printing Nec.

College Park

★ 71560 ★ **Amecom**
5115 Calvert Rd.
College Park, MD 20740-3898
(301)864-5600 **Fax:** (301)864-5955
Officer: Charles B. Hoffman, President. **Ultimate Parent:** Litton Industries.

★ 71561 ★ **Exxon Co.**
8401 Baltimore Blvd.
College Park, MD 20740
(301)474-2791
Ultimate Parent: Exxon.

★ 71562 ★ **Exxon Co.**
7110 Balto Blvd.
College Park, MD 20740
(301)864-3400
Ultimate Parent: Exxon.

★ 71563 ★ **Litton Industries, Inc.**
Amercom Div.
5115 Calvert Rd.
College Park, MD 20740-3898
(301)864-5600 **Fax:** (301)864-5275
Company Type: Division. **Officer:** C.B. Hofman, President. **Ultimate Parent:** Litton Industries. **SIC:** 3661—Telephone & Telegraph Apparatus; 3663—Radio & T.V. Communications Equipment; 3812—Search & Navigation Equipment.

★ 71564 ★ **Nationsbank Banking Centers**
7370 Balto Ave.
College Park, MD 20740
(301)454-8412
Ultimate Parent: Nationsbank Corp.

★ 71565 ★ **Radio Shack**
7316 Baltimore Ave.
College Park, MD 20740
(301)779-2121
Company Type: Division. **Ultimate Parent:** Tandy Corp.

★ 71566 ★ **Rite Aid**
Hollywood Plaza Shopping. Ctr.
College Park, MD
(301)441-4582
Ultimate Parent: Rite Aid.

College Pk

★ 71567 ★ **Fuel Management Systems Inc.**
4920 Niagara Rd.
College Pk, MD
(301)220-2220
Ultimate Parent: MNX.

★ 71568 ★ **McDonald's Hamburgers**
8204 Balto Ave.
College Pk, MD
(301)474-9111
Ultimate Parent: McDonald's.

★ 71569 ★ **Sutter Corp.**
10011 Ri Ave.
College Pk, MD
(301)474-8403
Ultimate Parent: Columbia Healthcare Corp.

Collegepark

★ 71570 ★ **Rite Aid**
Ph Hollywood Plz.
Collegepark, MD 20740
(301)474-9271
Ultimate Parent: Rite Aid.

Colmar Manor

★ 71571 ★   McDonald's Hamburgers
4201 Bladensburg Rd.
Colmar Manor, MD
(301)864-3161
Ultimate Parent: McDonald's.

Columbia

★ 71572 ★   Allied-Signal Aerospace Co.
Aerospace Technology & Micro.
9140 Old Annapolis Rd.
Columbia, MD 210451998
Ultimate Parent: Allied-Signal Inc. **SIC:** 3674—Semiconductors & Related Devices.

★ 71573 ★   Allied-Signal Aerospace Co.
Technology & Microelectronics
9140 Old Annapolis Rd. Md. Rte. 108
Columbia, MD 21045
Ultimate Parent: Allied-Signal Inc. **SIC:** 3674—Semiconductors & Related Devices.

★ 71574 ★   Allied-Signal Technical Service
1 Bendix Rd.
Columbia, MD 21045-1832
(410)964-7000
Officer: H. Joseph Engle, President & Chairman of the Board. **Ultimate Parent:** Allied-Signal Inc. **SIC:** 4899—Communications Services Nec; 3764—Space Propulsion Units & Parts; 3769—Space Vehicle Equipment Nec. **Employee Count:** 7000. **Sales:** 500 M.

★ 71575 ★   Amdahl Corp.
20 Columbia Corporate C
Columbia, MD 21044
(410)992-0090
Ultimate Parent: Amdahl Corp. **SIC:** 5099—Durable Goods Nec.

★ 71576 ★   Arnet Computer
6822 Oak Hall Ln.
Columbia, MD 21045
(301)995-3571
Location Type: Branch office. **Ultimate Parent:** Avnet. **SIC:** 5045—Computers, Peripherals & Software; 7379—Computer Related Services Nec.

★ 71577 ★   Arrow/Kieulff Electronics
8300 Gurford Rd.
Columbia, MD 21046
(410)995-6002
Company Type: Division. **Location Type:** Distribution center. **Officer:** Michael Gary, General Manager. **Ultimate Parent:** Arrow Electronics. **SIC:** 5065—Electronic Parts & Equipment Nec.

★ 71578 ★   Baxter Healthcare Corp. Hospital
8851 McGraw Rd.
Columbia, MD 21045-4713
(410)290-8500
Ultimate Parent: Baxter International. **SIC:** 5047—Medical & Hospital Equipment.

★ 71579 ★   Burlington Coat Factory
Columbia Eastgate Shopping Ctr.
Columbia, MD 21045
(410)799-9802
Ultimate Parent: Burlington Industries, Equity. **SIC:** 5311—Department Stores.

★ 71580 ★   Cigna Healthplan Mid-Atlantic Inc.
9700 Patuxent Woods Dr.
Columbia, MD 21046-1526
(301)720-5800
Company Type: Subsidiary. **Officer:** Timothy P. Fitzgerald, President. **Ultimate Parent:** Cigna Corp. **SIC:** 6324—Hospital & Medical Service Plans.

★ 71581 ★   Constellation Real Estate Inc.
8815 Centre Park Dr.
Columbia, MD 21045
(410)596-1199
Ultimate Parent: Baltimore Gas & Electric Co.

★ 71582 ★   D
9050 Red Branch Rd.
Columbia, MD 21045-2176
(410)992-1760
Ultimate Parent: Bell Atlantic Corp. **SIC:** 5049—Professional Equipment Nec.

★ 71583 ★   Del Monte Corp.
3 N. Lake Frnt Bldg. N
Columbia, MD 21044
(410)992-9100
Ultimate Parent: Del Monte Foods. **SIC:** 5141—Groceries—General Line.

★ 71584 ★   Diebold Inc.
6570 Dobbin Rd.
Columbia, MD 21045
(410)997-5434
Ultimate Parent: Diebold, Inc. **SIC:** 4226—Special Warehousing & Storage Nec.

★ 71585 ★   First American Bank Maryland
8910 Route 108
Columbia, MD 21045
(410)992-0250
Ultimate Parent: First American Corp. **SIC:** 6029—Commercial Banks Nec.

★ 71586 ★   First American Bank Maryland
8088 Centre Park Dr.
Columbia, MD 21045
(410)997-5219
Ultimate Parent: First American Corp. **SIC:** 6099—Functions Related to Deposit Banking.

★ 71587 ★   First Union National Bank of Maryland
8808 Centre Pk. Dr.
Columbia, MD 21045-2126
(410)964-4720
Company Type: Subsidiary. **Location Type:** Branch office. **Ultimate Parent:** First Union Corp. **SIC:** 6021—National Commercial Banks.

★ 71588 ★   First Union National Bank of Maryland
10005 Old Columbia Rd.
Columbia, MD 21046-1702
(410)964-4727
Company Type: Subsidiary. **Location Type:** Branch office. **Ultimate Parent:** First Union Corp. **SIC:** 6021—National Commercial Banks.

★ 71589 ★   First Union National Bank of Maryland
5950 Symphony Woods Rd.
Columbia, MD 21044-3521
(410)964-4700
Company Type: Subsidiary. **Location Type:** Branch office. **Ultimate Parent:** First Union Corp. **SIC:** 6021—National Commercial Banks.

★ 71590 ★   General Electric Co.
6905 Oakland Mills Rd., No. D
Columbia, MD 21045
(410)290-9260
Officer: Cathy Morris, Manager. **Ultimate Parent:** General Electric. **SIC:** 3699—Electrical Equipment & Supplies Nec.

★ 71591 ★   General Electric Co.
9001 Snowden River Pky.
Columbia, MD 21046
Ultimate Parent: General Electric. **SIC:** 3631—Household Cooking Equipment.

★ 71592 ★   General Electric Co. Columbia Plant Operations
9001 Snowden River Pky.
Columbia, MD 21046-1799
Ultimate Parent: General Electric. **SIC:** 3631—Household Cooking Equipment.

★ 71593 ★   Hamilton Hallmark
6822 Oak Hall Ln.
Columbia, MD 21045
Location Type: Branch office. **Ultimate Parent:** Avnet. **SIC:** 5065—Electronic Parts & Equipment Nec.

★ 71594 ★   KMS Group
1 Centre Park
Columbia, MD 21045
(410)730-9092
Ultimate Parent: Baltimore Gas & Electric Co. **SIC:** 1542—Nonresidential Construction Nec.

★ 71595 ★   KMS Group, Inc.
8808 One Centre Park Dr.
Columbia, MD 21201
(410)730-9092
Company Type: Subsidiary. **Officer:** P.M. Kirk, President. **Ultimate Parent:** Baltimore Gas & Electric Co. **SIC:** 6512—Nonresidential Building Operators; 6513—Apartment Building Operators; 6514—Dwelling Operators Except Apartments.

★ 71596 ★   Mary Kay Cosmetics Inc.
9029 Flicker Pl
Columbia, MD 21045
(410)997-3156
Ultimate Parent: Mary Kay Cosmetics.

★ 71597 ★   Nationsbank Banking Centers Co.
8640 Guilford Rd.
Columbia, MD 21046
(301)381-7718
Ultimate Parent: Nationsbank Corp.

★ 71598 ★   NCR Corp.
10277 Wincopin Cir.
Columbia, MD 21044-3408
(410)997-4220
Ultimate Parent: AT&T. **SIC:** 2761—Manifold Business Forms.

★ 71599 ★   Radio Shack
Columbia
Columbia, MD 21044
(410)995-0085
Company Type: Division. **Ultimate Parent:** Tandy Corp. **SIC:** 5731—Radio, Television & Electronics Stores.

★ 71600 ★   Reliance Insurance Co.
5565 Sterrett Pl.
Columbia, MD 21044
(410)992-4511
Ultimate Parent: Reliance Group Holdings. **SIC:** 6411—Insurance Agents, Brokers & Service.

★ 71601 ★   Syscon Corp.
9841 Broken Land Pky.
Columbia, MD 21046
(410)964-8300
Ultimate Parent: Harnischfeger Industries. **SIC:** 8748—Business Consulting Services Nec.

★ 71602 ★   Texas Instruments
8815 Centre Park Dr.
Columbia, MD 21045
(301)621-4675
Ultimate Parent: Texas Instruments.

★ 71603 ★   Time Electronics
9051 Red Branch Rd.
Columbia, MD 21045
(301)964-3090
Location Type: Branch office. **Ultimate Parent:** Avnet. **SIC:** 5065—Electronic Parts & Equipment Nec.

★ 71604 ★   W. R. Grace & Co. Washington Research Center
7379 Rte. 32
Columbia, MD 21044
Ultimate Parent: W. R. Grace. **SIC:** 8731—Commercial Physical Research.

★ 71605 ★   Wells Fargo Armored Services
8940 State Rte. 108
Columbia, MD 21045
(410)964-1950
Ultimate Parent: Borg Warner Automotive. **SIC:** 2761—Manifold Business Forms.

★ 71606 ★   Wells Fargo Armored SVC
8940 State Route 108
Columbia, MD 21045
(410)964-1950
Officer: William Delauro, Manager. **Ultimate Parent:** Wells Fargo & Co. **SIC:** 2761—Manifold Business Forms.

★ 71607 ★   Willamette Industries Inc.
Amer City Building
Columbia, MD
(301)982-1922
Ultimate Parent: Willamette Industries, Inc.

★ 71608 ★   W.R. Grace
Research Division
Washington Research Ctr.
7379 Rte. 32
Columbia, MD 21044
(410)531-4000 **Fax:** (410)531-4367
Company Type: Subsidiary. **Officer:** Dr. Francois P. Van Bemoortere, President. **Ultimate Parent:** W. R. Grace.

Coral Hills

★ 71609 ★   McDonald's Hamburgers
4857 Marlboro Pike
Coral Hills, MD
(301)735-4544
Ultimate Parent: McDonald's.

★ 71610 ★   Nationsbank Banking Centers
4743 Marlboro Pike
Coral Hills, MD
(301)817-7790
Ultimate Parent: Nationsbank Corp.

Cpe St Claire

★ 71611 ★   The Gap 1410
161 Annapolis Mall 1410
Cpe St Claire, MD 21401
(410)841-5122
Ultimate Parent: GAP. **SIC:** 5699—Miscellaneous Apparel & Accessory Stores.

Crisfield

★ 71612 ★   Peninsula Bank
943 W. Main St.
Crisfield, MD 21817-1031
(410)968-0990
Company Type: Subsidiary. **Location Type:** Branch office. **Officer:** Sandra Nelson-Buttrill, Manager. **Ultimate Parent:** Mercantile Bankshares Corp. **SIC:** 6021—National Commercial Banks.

★ 71613 ★   Peninsula Bank
101 Potomac St.
Crisfield, MD 21817
(410)968-2120
Company Type: Subsidiary. **Location Type:** Branch office. **Officer:** Paul T. Ward, Manager. **Ultimate Parent:** Mercantile Bankshares Corp. **SIC:** 6021—National Commercial Banks.

Crofton

★ 71614 ★   Citizens National Bank
1298 MD Rte. 3
Crofton, MD 21114
(410)721-3100
Company Type: Subsidiary. **Location Type:** Branch office. **Officer:** Kim Hebron, Manager. **Ultimate Parent:** Mercantile Bankshares Corp. **SIC:** 6021—National Commercial Banks.

★ 71615 ★   First Union National Bank of Maryland
2001 Davidsonville Rd.
Crofton, MD 21114-1317
(410)964-4788
Company Type: Subsidiary. **Location Type:** Branch office. **Ultimate Parent:** First Union Corp. **SIC:** 6021—National Commercial Banks.

★ 71616 ★   Loyola Fsb Regional Administra
2133 Defense Hwy.
Crofton, MD 21114
(301)261-6730
Ultimate Parent: Loyola Capital Corp.

★ 71617 ★   Standard Federal S & L
1669 Crofton Ctr.
Crofton, MD 21114
(410)261-3200
Ultimate Parent: Standard Federal Bank. **SIC:** 6159—Miscellaneous Business Credit Institutions.

★ 71618 ★   Standard Federal S & L Bank
1669 Crofton Ctr.
Crofton, MD 21114
(301)261-3200
Ultimate Parent: Standard Federal Bank.

Crumpton

★ 71619 ★ **Chestertown Bank of Maryland**
Rtes. 544 & 290
Crumpton, MD 21628
(410)778-5544
Company Type: Subsidiary. **Location Type:** Branch office. **Officer:** Jacqueline Brown, Manager. **Ultimate Parent:** Mercantile Bankshares Corp. **SIC:** 6021—National Commercial Banks.

Cumberland

★ 71620 ★ **Chesapeake & Potomac Tel Co. MD**
425 Blackiston Ave.
Cumberland, MD 21502-4361
(301)724-9954
Ultimate Parent: Bell Atlantic Corp. **SIC:** 4813—Telephone Communications Except Radiotelephone.

★ 71621 ★ **Chesapeake & Potomac Tel Co. MD**
24 S. Centre St.
Cumberland, MD 21502-3018
(301)759-1800
Ultimate Parent: Bell Atlantic Corp. **SIC:** 4813—Telephone Communications Except Radiotelephone.

★ 71622 ★ **First National Bank & Trust Co.**
71 Baltimore St.
Cumberland, MD 21502
(301)777-4740
Ultimate Parent: Society Corp. **SIC:** 6022—State Commercial Banks.

★ 71623 ★ **Greyhound Bus Lines**
201 Glenn St.
Cumberland, MD 21502
(301)722-6226
Ultimate Parent: Greyhound Lines Inc. **SIC:** 4111—Local & Suburban Transit; 4131—Intercity & Rural Bus Transportation.

★ 71624 ★ **Hertz Rent-A-Car Licensee**
322 S. Centre St.
Cumberland, MD 21502
(301)722-2522
Ultimate Parent: Hertz. **SIC:** 7514—Passenger Car Rental.

★ 71625 ★ **Kelly-Springfield Tire Co.**
Willowbrook Rd.
Cumberland, MD 21502
(301)777-6000 **Fax:** (301)777-6008
Company Type: Subsidiary. **Officer:** Lee N. Fiedler, President. **Ultimate Parent:** Goodyear Tire & Rubber.

★ 71626 ★ **Kelly-Springfield Tire Co.**
Willobrook Rd.
Cumberland, MD 21502
(301)777-6000 **Fax:** (301)777-6060
Company Type: Subsidiary. **Ultimate Parent:** Goodyear Tire & Rubber.

★ 71627 ★ **Kelly Springfield Tire Co.**
Associate Brands Div.
Willowbrook Rd.
Cumberland, MD 21502
(301)777-6200
Company Type: Division. **Ultimate Parent:** Goodyear Tire & Rubber. **SIC:** 3011—Tires & Inner Tubes.

★ 71628 ★ **Kelly-Springfield Tire Co.**
Custom Brands Div.
Willowbrook Rd.
Cumberland, MD 21502
(301)777-6000
Company Type: Division. **Ultimate Parent:** Goodyear Tire & Rubber. **SIC:** 3011—Tires & Inner Tubes.

★ 71629 ★ **Kelly-Springfield Tire Co. Inc.**
12501 Willowbrook Rd.
Cumberland, MD 21502-2554
(301)777-6000
Company Type: Subsidiary. **Officer:** Lee N. Fiedler, President; Chief Executive Officer. **Ultimate Parent:** Goodyear Tire & Rubber. **SIC:** 3011—Tires & Inner Tubes;

5014—Tires & Tubes. **Employee Count:** 6874. **Sales:** 712000000 M.

★ 71630 ★ **Kelly Springfield Tire Co. T**
Willowbrook Rd.
Cumberland, MD 21502
(301)777-6000
Ultimate Parent: Goodyear Tire & Rubber. **SIC:** 3011—Tires & Inner Tubes.

★ 71631 ★ **New York Life Insurance Co.**
118 Baltimore St.
Cumberland, MD 21502
(301)722-8565
Ultimate Parent: New York Life. **SIC:** 6411—Insurance Agents, Brokers & Service.

★ 71632 ★ **Potomac Edison Co.**
700 E. 4th St.
Cumberland, MD 21502-4295
(301)722-4500
Officer: Nancy K. Neff. **Ultimate Parent:** Allegheny Power System. **SIC:** 4911—Electric Services.

★ 71633 ★ **Radio Shack**
6 PO Box
Cumberland, MD 21502
(301)729-8164
Company Type: Division. **Ultimate Parent:** Tandy Corp. **SIC:** 5731—Radio, Television & Electronics Stores.

★ 71634 ★ **Radio Shack**
Country Club Mall
Cumberland, MD 21502
(301)729-0874
Company Type: Division. **Ultimate Parent:** Tandy Corp. **SIC:** 3571—Electronic Computers.

★ 71635 ★ **Radio Shack**
6 PO Box
Cumberland, MD 21502
(301)729-8164
Company Type: Division. **Ultimate Parent:** Tandy Corp. **SIC:** 5731—Radio, Television & Electronics Stores.

★ 71636 ★ **Rite Aid**
1050 Industrial Blvd. W
Cumberland, MD 21502
(301)724-6100
Ultimate Parent: Rite Aid. **SIC:** 5912—Drug Stores & Proprietary Stores.

★ 71637 ★ **Thrift Drug**
Winchester Rd.
Cumberland, MD 21502
(301)729-2144
Ultimate Parent: J.C. Penney. **SIC:** 5049—Professional Equipment Nec; 5912—Drug Stores & Proprietary Stores.

★ 71638 ★ **Thrift Drug**
White Oaks Shopping Ctr.
Cumberland, MD 21502
(301)722-4080
Ultimate Parent: J.C. Penney. **SIC:** 5049—Professional Equipment Nec.

★ 71639 ★ **United Parcel Service**
211 Bowen St.
Cumberland, MD 21502
(301)777-1313
Ultimate Parent: United Parcel Service of America. **SIC:** 4215—Courier Services Except by Air.

Damascus

★ 71640 ★ **McDonald's Hamburgers**
26429 Ridge Rd.
Damascus, MD 20872
(301)253-4777
Ultimate Parent: McDonald's.

Darlington

★ 71641 ★ **Forest Hill State Bank**
1101 Main St.
Darlington, MD 21034-1417
(410)838-4971
Company Type: Subsidiary. **Location Type:** Branch office. **Officer:** Edna D. Reeves, Manager. **Ultimate Parent:** Mercantile Bankshares Corp. **SIC:** 6021—National Commercial Banks.

Denton

★ 71642 ★ **Peoples Bank of Maryland**
39 Denton Plz.
Denton, MD 21629
(410)479-3312
Company Type: Subsidiary. **Location Type:** Branch office. **Officer:** Carol Sparks, Mgr. **Ultimate Parent:** Mercantile Bankshares Corp. **SIC:** 6021—National Commercial Banks.

★ 71643 ★ **Peoples Bank of Maryland**
207 Market St.
PO Box 220
Denton, MD 21629-0220
(410)479-2600 **Fax:** (410)479-2610
Company Type: Subsidiary. **Location Type:** Branch office. **Officer:** Jeffrey N. Heflebower, President & CEO. **Ultimate Parent:** Mercantile Bankshares Corp. **SIC:** 6021—National Commercial Banks.

★ 71644 ★ **Thrift Drug**
920 Market St.
Denton, MD 21629
(410)479-3400
Ultimate Parent: J.C. Penney. **SIC:** 5912—Drug Stores & Proprietary Stores.

Derwood

★ 71645 ★ **Exxon Service Station**
17651 Redland Rd.
Derwood, MD 20855
(301)948-7343
Ultimate Parent: Exxon.

★ 71646 ★ **McDonald's Hamburgers**
15801 Frederick Rd.
Derwood, MD
(301)948-5470
Ultimate Parent: McDonald's.

★ 71647 ★ **Nationsbank Banking Centers**
17647 Redlnd
Derwood, MD 20855
(301)963-5322
Ultimate Parent: Nationsbank Corp.

★ 71648 ★ **Radio Shack**
7208 Munster Mill Rd.
Derwood, MD
(301)977-9672
Company Type: Division. **Ultimate Parent:** Tandy Corp.

★ 71649 ★ **Radio Shack**
7208 Muncstr Mill Rd.
Derwood, MD
(301)977-9672
Company Type: Division. **Ultimate Parent:** Tandy Corp.

Dethesda

★ 71650 ★ **New York Life Chevy Chase General Office**
Southeastern Agencies
3 Bethesda Metro Ctr., Ste. 520
Dethesda, MD 20814
(301)654-9180 **Fax:** (301)654-0733
Officer: James Edwin Adkins, General Manager. **Ultimate Parent:** New York Life.

District Heights

★ 71651 ★ **Burlington Coat Factory Warehouse**
3420 Donnell Dr.
District Heights, MD 20747-3214
(301)736-6685
Ultimate Parent: Burlington Industries, Equity. **SIC:** 5311—Department Stores.

★ 71652 ★ **Crestar Bank MD**
6224 Marlboro Pke.
District Heights, MD 20747-2899
(800)451-2435
Company Type: Subsidiary. **Location Type:** Branch office. **Officer:** Richard Howgard, Mgr. **Ultimate Parent:** Crestar Financial Corp. **SIC:** 6021—National Commercial Banks.

District Heights Forestville

★ 71653 ★ **Western Auto Supply Co.**
Pennmar Shopping Ctr.
District Heights Forestville, MD 20747
(301)736-4000
Ultimate Parent: Sears Roebuck & Co. **SIC:** 5531—Automobile & Home Supply Stores.

Dorsey

★ 71654 ★ **First National Bank of Maryland**
7257 Parkway Dr.
Dorsey, MD 21076-1306
(301)769-7878
Company Type: Subsidiary. **Location Type:** Branch office. **Officer:** Michael Bateman, Mgr. **Ultimate Parent:** First Union Corp. **SIC:** 6021—National Commercial Banks.

Dunkirk Md

★ 71655 ★ **Radio Shack**
Dunkirk Town Ctr.
Dunkirk Md, MD 20754
(410)257-9422
Company Type: Division. **Ultimate Parent:** Tandy Corp. **SIC:** 5065—Electronic Parts & Equipment Nec.

East Riverdale

★ 71656 ★ **Nationsbank Banking Centers**
5710 Riverdale Rd.
East Riverdale, MD
(301)454-8494
Ultimate Parent: Nationsbank Corp.

Easton

★ 71657 ★ **ACME Markets**
RR 33
Easton, MD 21601
(410)822-7073
Ultimate Parent: American Stores. **SIC:** 5411—Grocery Stores.

★ 71658 ★ **Black & Decker Corp.**
Power Tools Group
28712 Glebe Rd.
Easton, MD 21601
Ultimate Parent: Black & Decker Corp. **SIC:** 3546—Power-Driven Handtools.

★ 71659 ★ **Black & Decker USA**
28712 Glebe Rd.
Easton, MD 21601-7430
(410)822-6770
Officer: Jerry Whiteside. **Ultimate Parent:** Black & Decker Corp. **SIC:** 3546—Power-Driven Handtools; 3423—Hand & Edge Tools Nec.

★ 71660 ★ **Radio Shack**
Tred Avon Sq.
Easton, MD 21601
(410)822-6252
Company Type: Division. **Ultimate Parent:** Tandy Corp. **SIC:** 5065—Electronic Parts & Equipment Nec.

★ 71661 ★ **St. Michaels Bank**
104 Marlboro Rd.
Easton, MD 21601
(410)820-6080
Company Type: Subsidiary. **Location Type:** Branch office. **Officer:** Tracy Berrigan, Mgr. **Ultimate Parent:** Mercantile Bankshares Corp. **SIC:** 6021—National Commercial Banks.

★ 71662 ★ **St. Michaels Bank**
113-114 Tidewater Inn
Easton, MD 21601
(410)820-8600
Company Type: Subsidiary. **Location Type:** Branch office. **Officer:** Anne M. Ray, Mgr. **Ultimate Parent:** Mercantile Bankshares Corp. **SIC:** 6021—National Commercial Banks.

Edgewater

★ 71663 ★   Annapolis Banking &
Trust Co.
Maryland Rte. 2 & Lee Airport
Edgewater, MD 21037-9802
(410)956-4800
Company Type: Subsidiary. Location
Type: Branch office. Officer: Gordon F.
Ueberroth, Mgr. Ultimate Parent:
Mercantile Bankshares Corp. SIC: 6021—
National Commercial Banks.

Edgewood

★ 71664 ★   Ace Hardware
414 Edgewood Rd.
Edgewood, MD 21040
(410)676-9094
Ultimate Parent: Ace Hardware. SIC:
5251—Hardware Stores.

★ 71665 ★   Radio Shack
1841 Pulaski Hwy.
Edgewood, MD 21040
(410)679-4777
Company Type: Division. Ultimate Parent:
Tandy Corp. SIC: 5065—Electronic Parts &
Equipment Nec.

★ 71666 ★   Radio Shack
1841 Pulaski Hwy.
Edgewood, MD 21040
(410)679-4777
Company Type: Division. Ultimate Parent:
Tandy Corp. SIC: 5065—Electronic Parts &
Equipment Nec.

★ 71667 ★   Western Auto Supply
Co.
2715 Pulaski Hwy.
Edgewood, MD 21040-1307
(410)676-2332
Officer: Leroy M. Love Sr., Owner.
Ultimate Parent: Ace Hardware. SIC:
5531—Automobile & Home Supply Stores;
5251—Hardware Stores. Employee Count:
6.

Eldersburg

★ 71668 ★   Westminster Bank &
Trust Co. of Carroll County
2038 Liberty Rd.
Eldersburg, MD 21784-6696
(410)795-5151
Company Type: Subsidiary. Location
Type: Branch office. Officer: V. Carol
Yetman, Mgr. Ultimate Parent: Mercantile
Bankshares Corp. SIC: 6021—National
Commercial Banks.

Elkton

★ 71669 ★   Acme Markets
101 Big Elk Mall
Elkton, MD 21921
(410)398-4925
Ultimate Parent: American Stores. SIC:
5411—Grocery Stores.

★ 71670 ★   Air Products &
Chemicals, Inc.
329 W. Main St.
Elkton, MD 21921
(410)398-2190
Officer: Artis Williams, Manager. Ultimate
Parent: Air Products & Chemicals, Inc. SIC:
2821—Plastics Materials & Resins; 2891—
Adhesives & Sealants.

★ 71671 ★   County Banking &
Trust Co.
100 Big Elk Mall
Elkton, MD 21921-5913
(410)398-2400
Company Type: Subsidiary. Location
Type: Branch office. Officer: Lee Snead,
Mgr. Ultimate Parent: Mercantile
Bankshares Corp. SIC: 6021—National
Commercial Banks.

★ 71672 ★   County Banking &
Trust Co.
123 North St.
PO Box 100
Elkton, MD 21921-0001
(410)398-2600 Fax: (410)398-2600
Company Type: Subsidiary. Location
Type: Branch office. Officer: S. Dell Foxx
III, President, CEO, & CFO. Ultimate

Parent: Mercantile Bankshares Corp. SIC:
6021—National Commercial Banks.

★ 71673 ★   Radio Shack
119 Big Elk Mall
Elkton, MD 21921
(410)398-4848
Company Type: Division. Ultimate Parent:
Tandy Corp. SIC: 5065—Electronic Parts &
Equipment Nec.

★ 71674 ★   Rite Aid
103 Big Elkmall
Elkton, MD 21921
(410)398-9595
Ultimate Parent: Rite Aid. SIC: 5912—Drug
Stores & Proprietary Stores.

★ 71675 ★   Thiokol Corp.
Elkton Division
55 Thiokol Rd.
Elkton, MD 21921
Ultimate Parent: Thiokol Corp. SIC: 3764—
Space Propulsion Units & Parts.

Ellicott City

★ 71676 ★   Citgo
4 Frederick Rd.
Ellicott City, MD 21043
(410)465-8070
Ultimate Parent: Citgo Petroleum. SIC:
5541—Gasoline Service Stations.

★ 71677 ★   Citizens National
Bank
4900 C. Waterloo Rd.
Ellicott City, MD 21043-6664
(410)465-8979
Company Type: Subsidiary. Location
Type: Branch office. Officer: Richard Good,
Mgr. Ultimate Parent: Mercantile
Bankshares Corp. SIC: 6021—National
Commercial Banks.

★ 71678 ★   Mary Kay Cosmetics
4041 Larkspring Row
Ellicott City, MD 21043
(410)461-5030
Ultimate Parent: Mary Kay Cosmetics.

★ 71679 ★   Radio Shack
Chatham Mall Shopping
Ellicott City, MD 21043
(410)465-1117
Company Type: Division. Ultimate Parent:
Tandy Corp. SIC: 5065—Electronic Parts &
Equipment Nec.

★ 71680 ★   Radio Shack
Chatham Mall
Ellicott City, MD 21043
(410)465-1117
Company Type: Division. Ultimate Parent:
Tandy Corp. SIC: 5065—Electronic Parts &
Equipment Nec.

Elton

★ 71681 ★   County Banking &
Trust Co.
133 Bridge St.
Elton, MD 21921-5326
(410)398-2600
Company Type: Subsidiary. Location
Type: Branch office. Officer: Raymond
Lindsey, Mgr. Ultimate Parent: Mercantile
Bankshares Corp. SIC: 6021—National
Commercial Banks.

Federalsburg

★ 71682 ★   Overnite
Transportation Co.
469 PO Box
Federalsburg, MD 21632
(410)754-5707
Ultimate Parent: Union Pacific Corp. SIC:
4213—Trucking Except Local.

★ 71683 ★   Pet Inc.
300 Reliance Rd.
Federalsburg, MD 21632
(410)754-5000
Officer: Elon Batemand, Manager. Ultimate
Parent: Pet. SIC: 2051—Bread, Cake &
Related Products.

Ferestville

★ 71684 ★   First Union National
Bank of Maryland
7714 Marlboro Pke.
Ferestville, MD 20747
(301)650-1079
Company Type: Subsidiary. Location
Type: Branch office. Ultimate Parent: First
Union Corp. SIC: 6021—National
Commercial Banks.

Forest Heights

★ 71685 ★   Payless Shoesource
5225 Indian Head Hwy.
Forest Heights, MD
(301)567-5550
Ultimate Parent: May Department Stores.

Forest Hill

★ 71686 ★   Forest Hill State Bank
2334 Rock Spring Rd.
Forest Hill, MD 21050-1628
(410)836-5200
Company Type: Subsidiary. Location
Type: Branch office. Officer: Stephen
Hyman, Mgr. Ultimate Parent: Mercantile
Bankshares Corp. SIC: 6021—National
Commercial Banks.

Forestville

★ 71687 ★   Casual Corner
Forest Village Park
Forestville, MD
(301)568-6446
Ultimate Parent: United States Shoe.

★ 71688 ★   Gap Stores
Forest Village Park
Forestville, MD
(301)735-6344
Ultimate Parent: GAP.

★ 71689 ★   Gap Stores the
Marlyand Stores
Forest Village Park
Forestville, MD
(301)735-6344
Ultimate Parent: GAP.

★ 71690 ★   Kmart
3101 Donnell Drive
Forestville, MD 20747
(301)568-6600
Ultimate Parent: K-Mart.

★ 71691 ★   Mary Kay Cosmetics
Indep Sales
1922 Glendora Dr.
Forestville, MD 20747
(301)336-3375
Ultimate Parent: Mary Kay Cosmetics.

★ 71692 ★   McDonald's
Hamburgers
6704 Chavez Ln.
Forestville, MD 20747
(301)568-9064
Ultimate Parent: McDonald's.

★ 71693 ★   Radio Shack
Forestville Plaza
Forestville, MD
(301)735-5990
Company Type: Division. Ultimate Parent:
Tandy Corp.

★ 71694 ★   Radio Shack
Silver Hill Plaza
Forestville, MD
(301)420-5225
Company Type: Division. Ultimate Parent:
Tandy Corp.

★ 71695 ★   Radio Shack
Forest Village Park
Forestville, MD
(301)735-8222
Company Type: Division. Ultimate Parent:
Tandy Corp.

★ 71696 ★   Radio Shack
Forest Village Park
Forestville, MD
(301)735-8222
Company Type: Division. Ultimate Parent:
Tandy Corp.

★ 71697 ★   Radio Shack
Silvr Hill Plaza
Forestville, MD
(301)420-5225
Company Type: Division. Ultimate Parent:
Tandy Corp.

★ 71698 ★   Radio Shack
Forestvle Plaza
Forestville, MD
(301)735-5990
Company Type: Division. Ultimate Parent:
Tandy Corp.

★ 71699 ★   Service Merchandise
5562 Silver Hill Rd.
Forestville, MD 20747
(301)735-3094
Ultimate Parent: Service Merchandise Co.,
Inc.

★ 71700 ★   Standard Federal
Savings Bank
3443 Donnell Dr.
Forestville, MD 20747
(301)967-2210
Ultimate Parent: Standard Federal Bank.

Fork

★ 71701 ★   Greyhound Bus Lines
2204 Pulaski Hwy.
Fork, MD 21051
(410)679-1011
Ultimate Parent: Greyhound Lines Inc. SIC:
4111—Local & Suburban Transit.

Forrest Heights

★ 71702 ★   McDonald's
Hamburgers
5501 Livingston Rd.
Forrest Heights, MD
(301)839-1536
Ultimate Parent: McDonald's.

Forrest Village

★ 71703 ★   Waldenbooks
Maryland Stores
Forest Village Park
Forrest Village, MD
(301)568-6911
Ultimate Parent: K-Mart.

Forrestville

★ 71704 ★   Nationsbank Banking
Centers Fo
7520 Marlboro Pike
Forrestville, MD
(301)817-7760
Ultimate Parent: Nationsbank Corp.

Fort George G. Meade

★ 71705 ★   Citizens Naitonal
Bank
Reece Rd./McArthur Blvd.
Fort George G. Meade, MD 20755
(410)569-5300
Company Type: Subsidiary. Location
Type: Branch office. Officer: Nina E.
Hendrix, Mgr. Ultimate Parent: Mercantile
Bankshares Corp. SIC: 6021—National
Commercial Banks.

★ 71706 ★   Department of
Defense Special Process Lab
9700 Samford Rd.
Fort George G. Meade, MD 20775
Ultimate Parent: National Semiconductor
Corp. SIC: 3674—Semiconductors &
Related Devices.

Fort George Mead

★ 71707 ★   Winchester Homes
Inc.
906 Redmoor
Fort George Mead, MD 20755
(410)551-0043
Ultimate Parent: Weyerhaeuser Co.

Fort Howard

★ 71708 ★   Vulcan Materials Co.
Grays Rd.
Fort Howard, MD 21052
(410)477-2822
Ultimate Parent: Vulcan Materials Co.

★ 71709 ★   Vulcan Materials Co.
Grays Rd.
Fort Howard, MD 21052
(410)477-2822
Ultimate Parent: Vulcan Materials Co.

Fort Washingt

★ 71710 ★   Radio Shack
Livingston Square
Fort Washingt, MD
(301)248-5151
Company Type: Division. **Ultimate Parent:**
Tandy Corp.

★ 71711 ★   Radio Shack
Livngstn Square
Fort Washingt, MD
(301)248-5151
Company Type: Division. **Ultimate Parent:**
Tandy Corp.

Fort Washington

★ 71712 ★   Payless Shoesource
922 Swain Creek Rd.
Fort Washington, MD
(301)292-0912
Ultimate Parent: May Department Stores.

★ 71713 ★   Rite Aid
Fort Washington Ctr.
Fort Washington, MD
(301)292-2000
Ultimate Parent: Rite Aid.

Frederick

★ 71714 ★   BFI Waste Systems
5848 Urbana Pke.
Frederick, MD 21701-7222
(301)662-6363
Ultimate Parent: Browning-Ferris
Industries. **SIC:** 4953—Refuse Systems.

★ 71715 ★   Casual Corner
7331 Ridge Rd.
Frederick, MD 21702
(301)371-4222
Ultimate Parent: United States Shoe. **SIC:**
7231—Beauty Shops.

★ 71716 ★   Casual Corner
Francis
Frederick, MD 21701
(301)662-0001
Ultimate Parent: United States Shoe. **SIC:**
5621—Women's Clothing Stores.

★ 71717 ★   Clorox Co.
605 E. Church St.
Frederick, MD 21701
Ultimate Parent: Clorox Co. **SIC:** 2842—
Polishes & Sanitation Goods.

**★ 71718 ★   Clorox Co. Frederick
Plant**
605 E. Church St.
Frederick, MD 21701
Ultimate Parent: Clorox Co. **SIC:** 2842—
Polishes & Sanitation Goods.

**★ 71719 ★   Deer Park Spring
Water Inc.**
6836 English Muffin Way
Frederick, MD 21701
(301)733-2727
Ultimate Parent: Clark Refinfing &
Marketing. **SIC:** 5149—Groceries & Related
Products Nec.

**★ 71720 ★   Equitable Life
Insurance Co.**
Frederick Shopping Ctr.
Frederick, MD 21701
(301)662-4988
Ultimate Parent: American General Corp.
SIC: 6411—Insurance Agents, Brokers &
Service.

**★ 71721 ★   Equitable Life
Insurance Co.**
108 Frederick Shopping Ctr.
Frederick, MD 21702
(301)662-4988
Ultimate Parent: American General Corp.
SIC: 6411—Insurance Agents, Brokers &
Service.

★ 71722 ★   Exxon Auto Repair
284 Montevue Ln.
Frederick, MD 21702
(301)694-8484
Ultimate Parent: Exxon. **SIC:** 5541—
Gasoline Service Stations.

**★ 71723 ★   First American Bank
Maryland**
Festival at Frederic
Frederick, MD 21701
(301)663-5516
Ultimate Parent: First American Corp. **SIC:**
6099—Functions Related to Deposit
Banking.

**★ 71724 ★   First American Bank
Maryland**
102 Baughmans Ln.
Frederick, MD 21702
(301)663-0766
Ultimate Parent: First American Corp. **SIC:**
6099—Functions Related to Deposit
Banking.

**★ 71725 ★   First Union Naitonal
Bank of Maryland**
102 Baughman's Ln.
Frederick, MD 21701-4011
(301)663-0766
Company Type: Subsidiary. **Location
Type:** Branch office. **Ultimate Parent:** First
Union Corp. **SIC:** 6021—National
Commercial Banks.

**★ 71726 ★   First Union National
Bank of Maryland**
482 Prospect Blvd.
Frederick, MD 21701
(301)663-5516
Company Type: Subsidiary. **Location
Type:** Branch office. **Ultimate Parent:** First
Union Corp. **SIC:** 6021—National
Commercial Banks.

**★ 71727 ★   Fredericktown Bank &
Trust Co.**
470 W. Patrick St.
Frederick, MD 21701-4858
(301)695-0691
Company Type: Subsidiary. **Location
Type:** Branch office. **Officer:** David A.
Folge, Mgr. **Ultimate Parent:** Mercantile
Bankshares Corp. **SIC:** 6021—National
Commercial Banks.

**★ 71728 ★   Fredericktown Bank &
Trust Co.**
401 S. Jefferson St.
Frederick, MD 21701-6272
(301)695-0693
Company Type: Subsidiary. **Location
Type:** Branch office. **Officer:** Janet L.
Jenkins, Mgr. **Ultimate Parent:** Mercantile
Bankshares Corp. **SIC:** 6021—National
Commercial Banks.

**★ 71729 ★   Fredericktown Bank &
Trust Co.**
Professional Bldg., 198 Thomas Johnson
Dr.
Frederick, MD 21701-4317
(301)695-0695
Company Type: Subsidiary. **Location
Type:** Branch office. **Officer:** Catherine L.
Smith, Mgr. **Ultimate Parent:** Mercantile
Bankshares Corp. **SIC:** 6021—National
Commercial Banks.

**★ 71730 ★   Fredericktown Bank &
Trust Co.**
1205 W. Patrick St.
Frederick, MD 21701-3905
(301)695-0800
Company Type: Subsidiary. **Location
Type:** Branch office. **Officer:** June Z.
Gilbert, Mgr. **Ultimate Parent:** Mercantile
Bankshares Corp. **SIC:** 6021—National
Commercial Banks.

**★ 71731 ★   Fredericktown Bank &
Trust Co.**
30 N. Market St.
PO Box 510
Frederick, MD 21705-0510
(301)662-8231 **Fax:** (301)662-4172
Company Type: Subsidiary. **Location
Type:** Branch office. **Officer:** Robert E.
Gearinger, President & CEO. **Ultimate
Parent:** Mercantile Bankshares Corp. **SIC:**
6021—National Commercial Banks.

**★ 71732 ★   McDonald's
Hamburgers**
Rte. 2 & Rte. 4 Prince
Frederick, MD 21701
(301)855-9428
Ultimate Parent: McDonald's.

★ 71733 ★   Mini Mart
12439 Creagerstown Rd.
Frederick, MD 21701
(301)898-3033
Ultimate Parent: Kroger. **SIC:** 5411—
Grocery Stores.

★ 71734 ★   Nationsbank
1070 W. Patrick St.
Frederick, MD 21702
(301)698-6073
Ultimate Parent: Nationsbank Corp.

**★ 71735 ★   Nationsbank Banking
Centers**
1070 W. Patrick St.
Frederick, MD 21702
(301)698-6080
Ultimate Parent: Nationsbank Corp.

**★ 71736 ★   Nationsbank Banking
Centers**
805 W. Seventh St.
Frederick, MD 21701
(301)698-6030
Ultimate Parent: Nationsbank Corp.

**★ 71737 ★   Nationsbank Banking
Centers Ev**
5704 Buckeystown Pike
Frederick, MD 21701
(301)698-6019
Ultimate Parent: Nationsbank Corp.

**★ 71738 ★   New York Life
Insurance Co.**
409 N. Market St.
Frederick, MD 21701
(301)663-1105
Ultimate Parent: New York Life. **SIC:**
6411—Insurance Agents, Brokers &
Service.

★ 71739 ★   Potomac Edison Co.
421 E. Patrick St.
Frederick, MD 21701-5729
(301)695-5700
Officer: Alan J. Noia. **Ultimate Parent:**
Allegheny Power System. **SIC:** 4911—
Electric Services.

★ 71740 ★   Potomac Edison Co.
Frederick County
Frederick, MD 21705
(301)695-5700
Ultimate Parent: Allegheny Power System.
SIC: 4911—Electric Services.

★ 71741 ★   Radio Shack
Frederick Shoppers World
Frederick, MD 21701
(301)695-8440
Company Type: Division. **Ultimate Parent:**
Tandy Corp. **SIC:** 7373—Computer
Integrated Systems Design; 5734—
Computer & Software Stores.

★ 71742 ★   Radio Shack
47 Frederick Towne Mall
Frederick, MD 21702
(301)663-6345
Company Type: Division. **Ultimate Parent:**
Tandy Corp. **SIC:** 5065—Electronic Parts &
Equipment Nec.

★ 71743 ★   Radio Shack
4 Francis Scott Key Mill
Frederick, MD 21701
(301)694-9119
Company Type: Division. **Ultimate Parent:**
Tandy Corp. **SIC:** 5065—Electronic Parts &
Equipment Nec.

★ 71744 ★   Radio Shack
14 Frederick Ave.
Frederick, MD 21701
(301)694-9166
Company Type: Division. **Ultimate Parent:**
Tandy Corp. **SIC:** 5731—Radio, Television
& Electronics Stores.

★ 71745 ★   Radio Shack
Frederick Shopping World
Frederick, MD 21701
(301)695-8440
Company Type: Division. **Ultimate Parent:**
Tandy Corp. **SIC:** 7373—Computer
Integrated Systems Design; 5734—
Computer & Software Stores.

★ 71746 ★   Rite Aid
4 Old Camprd
Frederick, MD 21702
(301)473-9774
Ultimate Parent: Rite Aid. **SIC:** 5912—Drug
Stores & Proprietary Stores.

★ 71747 ★   Service Merchandise
Frederick Shopping World
Frederick, MD 21701
(301)694-7600
Ultimate Parent: Service Merchandise Co.,
Inc. **SIC:** 5399—Miscellaneous General
Merchandise Store.

★ 71748 ★   Solarex Corp.
630 Solarex Ct
Frederick, MD 21701
(301)698-4200
Ultimate Parent: Amoco Corp.

**★ 71749 ★   Standard Federal
Savings Bank**
6 East St.
Frederick, MD 21701
(301)694-3310
Ultimate Parent: Standard Federal Bank.
SIC: 6162—Mortgage Bankers &
Correspondents.

**★ 71750 ★   Thomas' Frozen
Foods Inc.**
7110 English Muffin Way
Frederick, MD 21701
(301)694-8100
Company Type: Division. **Location Type:**
Plant. **Officer:** Gary Willis, Plant Manager.
Ultimate Parent: CPC International. **SIC:**
2038—Frozen Specialties Nec.

★ 71751 ★   Toys R US
1308 W. Patrick St.
Frederick, MD 21702
(301)694-7278
Ultimate Parent: Toys "R" US. **SIC:** 5945—
Hobby, Toy & Game Shops.

★ 71752 ★   Waldenbooks
Fredrick Town Mall
Frederick, MD 21701
(301)663-8277
Ultimate Parent: K-Mart. **SIC:** 5942—Book
Stores.

★ 71753 ★   Waldenbooks
57 Frederick Towne Mall
Frederick, MD 21702
(301)663-8277
Ultimate Parent: K-Mart. **SIC:** 5942—Book
Stores.

Frostburg

★ 71754 ★   Fidelity Bank
300 E. Main St.
Frostburg, MD 21532-2017
(301)689-2222
Company Type: Subsidiary. **Location
Type:** Branch office. **Officer:** Jo Ann Spiker,
Mgr. **Ultimate Parent:** Mercantile
Bankshares Corp. **SIC:** 6021—National
Commercial Banks.

★ 71755 ★   Fidelity Bank
59 E. Main St.
PO Box 50
Frostburg, MD 21532-0050
(301)689-1111 **Fax:** (301)689-1114
Company Type: Subsidiary. **Location
Type:** Branch office. **Officer:** C. Joseph
Cunningham III, President & CEO. **Ultimate
Parent:** Mercantile Bankshares Corp. **SIC:**
6021—National Commercial Banks.

★ 71756 ★ **Greyhound Bus Lines**
11 W. Main St.
Frostburg, MD 21532
(301)689-6651
Ultimate Parent: Greyhound Lines Inc. **SIC:**
4131—Intercity & Rural Bus Transportation.

★ 71757 ★ **Rite Aid**
Frostburg Plz.
Frostburg, MD 21532
(301)689-3447
Ultimate Parent: Rite Aid. **SIC:** 5912—Drug
Stores & Proprietary Stores.

Fruitland

★ 71758 ★ **Crown Cork & Seal Co.**
PO Box C
Fruitland, MD 21826
Ultimate Parent: Crown Cork & Seal. **SIC:**
3410—Metal Cans & Shipping Containers.

★ 71759 ★ **Crown Cork & Seal Co. Inc.**
Rte. 13 PO Box 338
Fruitland, MD 21826
Ultimate Parent: Crown Cork & Seal. **SIC:**
3411—Metal Cans.

Gaithersburg

★ 71760 ★ **Amanda Fielding**
701 Russell Ave.
Gaithersburg, MD 20877
(301)417-0500
Ultimate Parent: J.C. Penney.

★ 71761 ★ **Arrow Electronics Inc. Arrow-Ki**
200 Perry Parkway
Gaithersburg, MD 20877
(301)670-1600
Ultimate Parent: Arrow Electronics.

★ 71762 ★ **Arrow/Kieulft Electronics**
200 Perry Pky.
Gaithersburg, MD 20877
(301)670-1600
Company Type: Division. **Location Type:**
Distribution center. **Officer:** Jim Markisohn,
Vice President & General Manager.
Ultimate Parent: Arrow Electronics. **SIC:**
5065—Electronic Parts & Equipment Nec.

★ 71763 ★ **August Max Woman**
701 Russell Ave.
Gaithersburg, MD 20877
(301)948-4627
Ultimate Parent: United States Shoe.

★ 71764 ★ **Beneficial Mortgage Co. of Maryland**
Gaithersburg Plz. Shopping Ctr.
Gaithersburg, MD 20877
(301)330-8388
Location Type: Branch office. **Ultimate
Parent:** Beneficial. **SIC:** 6141—Personal
Credit Institutions; 6162—Mortgage Bankers
& Correspondents.

★ 71765 ★ **Casual Corner**
Lakeforest Mall
Gaithersburg, MD 20879
(301)977-3100
Ultimate Parent: United States Shoe.

★ 71766 ★ **Circuit City**
602 Quince Orchard Rd.
Gaithersburg, MD 20878
(301)990-3958
Ultimate Parent: Circuit City Stores.

★ 71767 ★ **Courtyard by Marriott**
805 Russell Ave.
Gaithersburg, MD 20879
(301)670-0008
Ultimate Parent: Marriott International.

★ 71768 ★ **Crestar Bank MD**
18568 Gaithersburg-Laytonsville Rd.
Gaithersburg, MD 20879-4709
(800)451-2435
Company Type: Subsidiary. **Location
Type:** Branch office. **Officer:** Garth Culham,
Mgr. **Ultimate Parent:** Crestar Financial
Corp. **SIC:** 6021—National Commercial
Banks.

★ 71769 ★ **Crestar Bank MD**
9401 Key West Ave.
Gaithersburg, MD 20850-3335
(800)451-2435
Company Type: Subsidiary. **Location
Type:** Branch office. **Officer:** Franklin
Clemmer, Mgr. **Ultimate Parent:** Crestar
Financial Corp. **SIC:** 6021—National
Commercial Banks.

★ 71770 ★ **Electro Mechanical Design Services**
16618 Oakmont Ave.
Gaithersburg, MD 20877-4178
(301)840-5710
Officer: Pat Roney. **Ultimate Parent:**
Ametek Inc. **SIC:** 3671—Electron Tubes;
5065—Electronic Parts & Equipment Nec.

★ 71771 ★ **Electronic Data Systems Health**
200 Orchard Ridge Dr.
Gaithersburg, MD 20878
(301)990-4800
Ultimate Parent: Electronic Data Systems.

★ 71772 ★ **Exxon Co.**
Gaithersburg, MD
(301)948-2444
Ultimate Parent: Exxon.

★ 71773 ★ **Exxon Co.**
16425 Frederick Rd.
Gaithersburg, MD
(301)948-2022
Ultimate Parent: Exxon.

★ 71774 ★ **Exxon Co.**
408 N. Frederick Ave.
Gaithersburg, MD 20877
(301)926-1132
Ultimate Parent: Exxon.

★ 71775 ★ **Exxon Service Station**
19205 Watkins Mill Rd.
Gaithersburg, MD 20879
(301)869-3310
Ultimate Parent: Exxon.

★ 71776 ★ **First American Bank NA**
607 N. Frederick Ave.
Gaithersburg, MD 20879
Ultimate Parent: First American Corp. **SIC:**
6099—Functions Related to Deposit
Banking.

★ 71777 ★ **First Security Mortgage Inc.**
Gaithersburg, MD
(301)258-0437
Ultimate Parent: First Security Corp.

★ 71778 ★ **First Union National Bank of Maryland**
8019 Snouffers School Rd.
Gaithersburg, MD 20879-4735
(301)948-8230
Company Type: Subsidiary. **Location
Type:** Branch office. **Ultimate Parent:** First
Union Corp. **SIC:** 6021—National
Commercial Banks.

★ 71779 ★ **First Union National Bank of Maryland**
607 N. Frederick Ave.
Gaithersburg, MD 20877-3306
(301)650-1055
Company Type: Subsidiary. **Location
Type:** Branch office. **Ultimate Parent:** First
Union Corp. **SIC:** 6021—National
Commercial Banks.

★ 71780 ★ **First Union National Bank of Maryland**
20 Montgomery Village Ave.
Gaithersburg, MD 20879-3581
(301)961-5270
Company Type: Subsidiary. **Location
Type:** Branch office. **Officer:** Janine Gray,
Mgr. **Ultimate Parent:** First Union Corp.
SIC: 6021—National Commercial Banks.

★ 71781 ★ **The Gap Kids**
Lakefrst Mall
Gaithersburg, MD
(301)869-3838
Ultimate Parent: GAP.

★ 71782 ★ **Gap Stores Inc.**
Lakeforest
Gaithersburg, MD 20879
(301)869-2424
Ultimate Parent: GAP.

★ 71783 ★ **Gap Stores Inc. Maryland Stores**
Lakeforest
Gaithersburg, MD 20879
(301)869-2424
Ultimate Parent: GAP.

★ 71784 ★ **Halliburton Nus Corp.**
910 Clopper Rd.
Gaithersburg, MD 20878
(301)258-6000
Ultimate Parent: Halliburton.

★ 71785 ★ **Hertz Rent-A-Car**
596 N. Frederick Ave.
Gaithersburg, MD 20877
(301)948-1669
Ultimate Parent: Hertz. **SIC:** 7514—
Passenger Car Rental.

★ 71786 ★ **Hit or Miss**
Montgomery Village
Gaithersburg, MD
(301)948-5483
Ultimate Parent: TJX.

★ 71787 ★ **Home Depot**
15740 Shady Grove Rd.
Gaithersburg, MD 20877
(301)330-4900
Ultimate Parent: Home Depot.

★ 71788 ★ **Home Depot Inc.**
15740 Shady Grove Rd.
Gaithersburg, MD 20877
(301)330-4900
Ultimate Parent: Home Depot.

★ 71789 ★ **Marriott Hotels**
9751 Washingtonian Blvd.
Gaithersburg, MD 20878
(301)590-0044
Ultimate Parent: Marriott International.

★ 71790 ★ **Marriott Hotels Resorts Suites**
9751 Washingtonian Blvd.
Gaithersburg, MD 20878
(301)590-0044
Ultimate Parent: Marriott International.

★ 71791 ★ **Mary Kay Cosmetics Indep Sales**
20105 Waringwood Way
Gaithersburg, MD 20879
(301)869-6561
Ultimate Parent: Mary Kay Cosmetics.

★ 71792 ★ **Mary Kay Cosmetics Indep Sales**
18 Almaden Pl
Gaithersburg, MD 20878
(301)948-9569
Ultimate Parent: Mary Kay Cosmetics.

★ 71793 ★ **Mayflower Moving & Storage**
19020 Laytonsville Rd.
Gaithersburg, MD 20882
(301)258-0299
Ultimate Parent: Mayflower Group.

★ 71794 ★ **McDonald's Hamburgers**
83 Bureau Dr.
Gaithersburg, MD 20878
(301)948-5567
Ultimate Parent: McDonald's.

★ 71795 ★ **McDonald's Hamburgers**
18273 Flower Hill Way
Gaithersburg, MD 20879
(301)948-6432
Ultimate Parent: McDonald's.

★ 71796 ★ **McDonald's Hamburgers**
598 North Frederick Ave.
Gaithersburg, MD 20877
(301)948-3899
Ultimate Parent: McDonald's.

★ 71797 ★ **McDonald's Hamburgers**
12130 Darnsten Rd.
Gaithersburg, MD
(301)948-5207
Ultimate Parent: McDonald's.

★ 71798 ★ **Mellon Bank (MD)**
1600 Shady Grove Rd.
Gaithersburg, MD 20877
(301)921-1040
Company Type: Subsidiary. **Location

★ 71799 ★ **Mellon Bank (MD)**
19114 Montgomery Village Ave.
Gaithersburg, MD 20879-2797
(301)948-8200
Company Type: Subsidiary. **Location
Type:** Branch office. **Officer:** Lori Roop,
Mgr. **Ultimate Parent:** Mellon Bank Corp.
SIC: 6021—National Commercial Banks.

★ 71800 ★ **Nationsbank Banking Centers**
22 Summit Ave.
Gaithersburg, MD 20877
(301)963-5300
Ultimate Parent: Nationsbank Corp.

★ 71801 ★ **Nationsbank Banking Centers**
19294 Montgomery Village Ave.
Gaithersburg, MD 20879
(301)963-5344
Ultimate Parent: Nationsbank Corp.

★ 71802 ★ **Nationsbank Banking Centers**
1048 Quince Orchard Rd.
Gaithersburg, MD 20878
(301)963-5350
Ultimate Parent: Nationsbank Corp.

★ 71803 ★ **Nationsbank Banking Centers Ga**
594 N. Frederick Ave.
Gaithersburg, MD 20877
(301)963-5360
Ultimate Parent: Nationsbank Corp.

★ 71804 ★ **New York Life Insurance Co.**
Gaithersburg, MD
(301)330-1624
Ultimate Parent: New York Life.

★ 71805 ★ **New York Lifestyle Inc.**
7917 Cessna Ave.
Gaithersburg, MD 20879
(301)670-9383
Ultimate Parent: New York Life.

★ 71806 ★ **Payless Shoesource**
9659 Lost Knife Rd.
Gaithersburg, MD 20877
(301)921-4335
Ultimate Parent: May Department Stores.

★ 71807 ★ **Potomac Valley Bank**
702 Russell Ave.
Gaithersburg, MD 20877-2606
(301)963-7600 **Fax:** (301)963-7683
Company Type: Subsidiary. **Location
Type:** Branch office. **Officer:** R. Dennis
Homberg, Mgr. **Ultimate Parent:** Mercantile
Bankshares Corp. **SIC:** 6021—National
Commercial Banks.

★ 71808 ★ **Price Club of Gaithersburg**
880 Russell Ave.
Gaithersburg, MD 20879
(301)417-1500
Ultimate Parent: Price.

★ 71809 ★ **Price Club Hearing Aid Departm**
880 Russell Ave.
Gaithersburg, MD 20879
(301)417-1530
Ultimate Parent: Price.

★ 71810 ★ **Pulte Home Corp. Potomac**
444 North Fredrck Ave.
Gaithersburg, MD 20877
(301)921-8707
Ultimate Parent: Pulte.

★ 71811 ★ **Quinton Instrument Co.**
14824 Keeneland Cir.
Gaithersburg, MD 20878
(301)258-7424
Ultimate Parent: American Home Products.

★ 71812 ★ **Radio Shack**
Lakeforest
Gaithersburg, MD 20879
(301)963-0655
Company Type: Division. **Ultimate Parent:**
Tandy Corp.

Type: Branch office. **Officer:** Zachary
Koutssandreas, Mgr. **Ultimate Parent:**
Mellon Bank Corp. **SIC:** 6021—National
Commercial Banks.

★ 71813 ★ Radio Shack
Gaithersburg Sq.
Gaithersburg, MD 20877
(301)948-0060
Company Type: Division. **Ultimate Parent:** Tandy Corp.

★ 71814 ★ Radio Shack
Gaithersburg Sq.
Gaithersburg, MD 20877
(301)948-0060
Company Type: Division. **Ultimate Parent:** Tandy Corp.

★ 71815 ★ Rite Aid
Walnut Hill Shopping. Ctr.
Gaithersburg, MD
(301)869-7770
Ultimate Parent: Rite Aid.

★ 71816 ★ Standard Federal Savings Bank
Gaithersburg, MD
(301)696-4000
Location Type: Branch office. **Ultimate Parent:** Standard Federal Bank.

★ 71817 ★ Trugreen-Chemlawn
9230 Gaither Rd.
Gaithersburg, MD 20877
(301)840-8090
Ultimate Parent: ServiceMaster Co.

★ 71818 ★ Trugreen-Chemlawn Commercial D
9230 Gaither Rd.
Gaithersburg, MD 20877
(301)948-4434
Ultimate Parent: ServiceMaster Co.

★ 71819 ★ Watkins-Johnson Co.
700 Quince Orchard Rd.
Gaithersburg, MD 20878
Ultimate Parent: Johnson & Johnson. **SIC:** 3663—Radio & T.V. Communications Equipment.

★ 71820 ★ Colonial Pipeline Co.
Gaithrsbrg Md, MD
(301)948-1211
Ultimate Parent: Colonial Pipeline.

Galena

★ 71821 ★ Chestertown Bank of Maryland
Rtes. 213 & 290
Galena, MD 21635-9703
(410)649-5665
Company Type: Subsidiary. **Location Type:** Branch office. **Officer:** Connie P. Price, Mgr. **Ultimate Parent:** Mercantile Bankshares Corp. **SIC:** 6021—National Commercial Banks.

Gamber

★ 71822 ★ Westminster Bank & Trust Co.
4007 Sykesille Rd., Finksburg
Gamber, MD 21048
(410)795-2166
Company Type: Subsidiary. **Location Type:** Branch office. **Officer:** Judith A. England, Mgr. **Ultimate Parent:** Mercantile Bankshares Corp. **SIC:** 6021—National Commercial Banks.

Germantown

★ 71823 ★ Ace Hardware
19600 Fredrck Rd.
Germantown, MD 20876
(301)428-3201
Ultimate Parent: Ace Hardware.

★ 71824 ★ Amdahl Corp.
Germantown, MD
(301)972-4653
Ultimate Parent: Amdahl Corp.

★ 71825 ★ Crestar Bank MD
1206 Wisteria Dr.
Germantown, MD 20874
(800)451-2435
Company Type: Subsidiary. **Location Type:** Branch office. **Officer:** William S. Sims, Mgr. **Ultimate Parent:** Crestar Financial Corp. **SIC:** 6021—National Commercial Banks.

★ 71826 ★ Hit or Miss
13052 Middlebrook Rd.
Germantown, MD
(301)972-5227
Ultimate Parent: TJX.

★ 71827 ★ McDonald's Hamburgers
19660 Gunners Branch Rd.
Germantown, MD 20876
(301)353-0443
Ultimate Parent: McDonald's.

★ 71828 ★ Nationsbank Banking Centers Ge
19700 Darnestown Germantown Rd.
Germantown, MD 20874
(301)963-5370
Ultimate Parent: Nationsbank Corp.

★ 71829 ★ Potomac Valley Bank
12801 Wisteria Dr.
Germantown, MD 20874-5251
(301)916-0200
Company Type: Subsidiary. **Location Type:** Branch office. **Officer:** Patrick Shurney, Mgr. **Ultimate Parent:** Mercantile Bankshares Corp. **SIC:** 6021—National Commercial Banks.

★ 71830 ★ Pulte Home Corp.
3 Milestne Manor Ct
Germantown, MD 20876
(301)540-0001
Ultimate Parent: Pulte.

★ 71831 ★ Rite Aid
13065 Wisteria Dr.
Germantown, MD 20874
(301)540-1707
Ultimate Parent: Rite Aid.

★ 71832 ★ Standard Federal Savings Bank
Germantown, MD
(301)428-1700
Location Type: Branch office. **Ultimate Parent:** Standard Federal Bank.

Glen Burnie

★ 71833 ★ Baltimore Gas & Electric Co.
106 Dover Rd. NE
Glen Burnie, MD 21060
(410)787-9000
Ultimate Parent: Baltimore Gas & Electric Co.

★ 71834 ★ Baltimore Gas & Electric Co.
7317 Parkway Dr.
Glen Burnie, MD 21061
(410)859-9000
Ultimate Parent: Baltimore Gas & Electric Co.

★ 71835 ★ Baltimore Gas & Electric Co.
100 Aquahart Rd.
Glen Burnie, MD 21061
(410)761-0134
Ultimate Parent: Baltimore Gas & Electric Co. **SIC:** 5722—Household Appliance Stores.

★ 71836 ★ Burlington Coat Factory
Jumpers Mall
Glen Burnie, MD 21061
(410)787-9555
Location Type: Branch office. **Ultimate Parent:** Burlington Industries, Equity. **SIC:** 5311—Department Stores.

★ 71837 ★ Citgo
521 S. Camp Meade Rd.
Glen Burnie, MD 21061
(410)859-3204
Ultimate Parent: Citgo Petroleum. **SIC:** 5599—Automotive Dealers Nec.

★ 71838 ★ Delta Air Lines Inc.
Baltimore-Washington International Airport
Glen Burnie, MD 21061
(410)859-1200
Ultimate Parent: Delta Air Lines, Inc. **SIC:** 4512—Air Transportation—Scheduled.

★ 71839 ★ Electronic Systems Group
314 South Hammonds Ferry Rd.
Glen Burnie, MD 21061
Ultimate Parent: Westinghouse Electric Corp. **SIC:** 5065—Electronic Parts & Equipment Nec.

★ 71840 ★ Electronic Systems Group
Materials Acquistion Center
314 South Hammonds Ferry Rd.
Glen Burnie, MD 21061
Ultimate Parent: Westinghouse Electric Corp. **SIC:** 3600—Electronic & Other Electrical Equipment.

★ 71841 ★ First American Bank Maryland
7984 Crain Hwy. S
Glen Burnie, MD 21061
(410)787-6025
Ultimate Parent: First American Corp. **SIC:** 6022—State Commercial Banks.

★ 71842 ★ First Union National Bank of Maryland
7984 Crain Hwy.
Glen Burnie, MD 21061-4999
(410)964-4715
Company Type: Subsidiary. **Location Type:** Branch office. **Ultimate Parent:** First Union Corp. **SIC:** 6021—National Commercial Banks.

★ 71843 ★ Macy's
Marley Sta. Mall
Glen Burnie, MD 21061
(410)760-2100
Company Type: Branch. **Ultimate Parent:** R. H. Macy. **SIC:** 5311—Department Stores.

★ 71844 ★ Martin Marietta Ocean Systems Operations
6711 Baymeadow Dr.
Glen Burnie, MD 21060
Ultimate Parent: Martin Marietta. **SIC:** 3812—Search & Navigation Equipment.

★ 71845 ★ Material Aquisition Center
314 Hammonds Ferry Rd.
Glen Burnie, MD 21061
Ultimate Parent: Westinghouse Electric Corp. **SIC:** 5065—Electronic Parts & Equipment Nec.

★ 71846 ★ McDonald's Hamburgers
7425 Ritchie Hwy.
Glen Burnie, MD 21061
(410)760-6160
Ultimate Parent: McDonald's. **SIC:** 5812—Eating Places.

★ 71847 ★ McDonald's Hamburgers
7010 Ritchie Hwy.
Glen Burnie, MD 21061
(410)761-6060
Ultimate Parent: McDonald's. **SIC:** 1521—Single-Family Housing Construction.

★ 71848 ★ Radio Shack
Glen Burnie Mall
Glen Burnie, MD 21061
(410)761-1880
Company Type: Division. **Ultimate Parent:** Tandy Corp. **SIC:** 5046—Commercial Equipment Nec.

★ 71849 ★ Radio Shack
Glen Burnie Mall
Glen Burnie, MD 21061
(410)761-1880
Company Type: Division. **Ultimate Parent:** Tandy Corp. **SIC:** 5046—Commercial Equipment Nec.

Glenelg

★ 71850 ★ Citizens National Bank
Ten Oaks Plz., 3900 Ten Oaks Rd.
Glenelg, MD 21737
(410)531-5355
Company Type: Subsidiary. **Location Type:** Branch office. **Officer:** David Tamburrino, Mgr. **Ultimate Parent:** Mercantile Bankshares Corp. **SIC:** 6021—National Commercial Banks.

Glenn Dale

★ 71851 ★ Citgo
11002 Lanham Severn Rd.
Glenn Dale, MD 20769
(301)464-8876
Ultimate Parent: Citgo Petroleum.

Grantsville

★ 71852 ★ Rite Aid
Grantsville Shopping.Ctr.
Grantsville, MD 21536
(301)895-5315
Ultimate Parent: Rite Aid. **SIC:** 5912—Drug Stores & Proprietary Stores.

Greeblt

★ 71853 ★ Temple-Inland Mortgage Corp.
7500 Greenway Ctr. Dr.
Greeblt, MD
(301)220-0110
Ultimate Parent: Temple-Inland.

Greenbelt

★ 71854 ★ Banc One Mortgage Corp.
6411 Ivy Lane
Greenbelt, MD 20770
(301)441-8130
Ultimate Parent: Banc One Corp.

★ 71855 ★ Burlington Coat Factory
6158 Greenbelt Rd.
Greenbelt, MD 20770-1020
(301)982-2386
Ultimate Parent: Burlington Industries, Equity. **SIC:** 6512—Nonresidential Building Operators; 5712—Furniture Stores.

★ 71856 ★ Courtyard by Marriott
6301 Golden Triangle Dr.
Greenbelt, MD 20770
(301)441-3311
Ultimate Parent: Marriott International.

★ 71857 ★ Crestar Bank MD
7701 Greenbelt Rd., Ste. 110
Greenbelt, MD 20770-2037
(800)451-2435
Company Type: Subsidiary. **Location Type:** Branch office. **Officer:** Lori Pickert, Mgr. **Ultimate Parent:** Crestar Financial Corp. **SIC:** 6021—National Commercial Banks.

★ 71858 ★ Digital Equipment Corp. Landove
Sales at 6406 Ivy Ln.
Greenbelt, MD
(301)459-7900
Ultimate Parent: Digital Equipment Corp.

★ 71859 ★ Exxon Service Station
5900 Greenblelt Rd.
Greenbelt, MD 20770
(301)474-7707
Ultimate Parent: Exxon.

★ 71860 ★ First Security Mortgage
7315 Hanover Pky.
Greenbelt, MD 20770
(301)513-5000
Ultimate Parent: First Security Corp.

★ 71861 ★ First Union National Bank of Maryland
6401 Golden Triangle Dr.
Greenbelt, MD 20770-3202
(301)650-1124
Company Type: Subsidiary. **Location Type:** Branch office. **Ultimate Parent:** First Union Corp. **SIC:** 6021—National Commercial Banks.

★ 71862 ★ Gap Stores the Maryland Stores
Greenway Plaza
Greenbelt, MD
(301)345-9755
Ultimate Parent: GAP.

★ 71863 ★ Hit or Miss
Greenway Shopping Ctr.
Greenbelt, MD 20770
(301)345-7522
Ultimate Parent: TJX.

★ 71864 ★ **Huntington Mortgage Co.**
6401 Golden Triangle Dr.
Greenbelt, MD 20770
(301)982-5427
Ultimate Parent: Huntington Bancshares.

★ 71865 ★ **Kmart**
8829 Greenbelt Rd.
Greenbelt, MD 20770
(301)552-4753
Ultimate Parent: K-Mart.

★ 71866 ★ **Loyola Fsb Baning Centers**
6329 Greenbelt Rd.
Greenbelt, MD 20770
(301)345-8448
Ultimate Parent: Loyola Capital Corp.

★ 71867 ★ **Mellon Bank (MD)**
7515 Greenbelt Rd.
Greenbelt, MD 20770-3484
(301)441-8055
Company Type: Subsidiary. **Location Type:** Branch office. **Officer:** Eve Solawy, Mgr. **Ultimate Parent:** Mellon Bank Corp. **SIC:** 6021—National Commercial Banks.

★ 71868 ★ **Nationsbank**
6411 Ivy Ln.
Greenbelt, MD 20770
(301)270-7869
Ultimate Parent: Nationsbank Corp.

★ 71869 ★ **Nationsbank Banking Centers**
7595 Hanover Parkway
Greenbelt, MD 20770
(301)454-8430
Ultimate Parent: Nationsbank Corp.

★ 71870 ★ **Nationsbank Banking Centers**
8827 Greenblt Rd. Ciprno S
Greenbelt, MD
(301)454-8450
Ultimate Parent: Nationsbank Corp.

★ 71871 ★ **Nationsbank Banking Centers**
103 Century
Greenbelt, MD 20770
(301)572-1730
Ultimate Parent: Nationsbank Corp.

★ 71872 ★ **Radio Shack**
7587 Greenbelt Rd.
Greenbelt, MD 20770
(301)474-0883
Company Type: Division. **Ultimate Parent:** Tandy Corp.

★ 71873 ★ **Radio Shack**
Beltway Plaza
Greenbelt, MD
(301)474-0500
Company Type: Division. **Ultimate Parent:** Tandy Corp.

★ 71874 ★ **Radio Shack**
Beltway Plaza
Greenbelt, MD
(301)474-0500
Company Type: Division. **Ultimate Parent:** Tandy Corp.

★ 71875 ★ **Radio Shack**
7587 Greenblt Rd.
Greenbelt, MD 20770
(301)474-0883
Company Type: Division. **Ultimate Parent:** Tandy Corp.

★ 71876 ★ **Southland Corp.**
8900 Edmonston Rd.
Greenbelt, MD
(301)474-5165
Ultimate Parent: Southland Corp.

★ 71877 ★ **Sports Authority**
6250 Greenbelt Rd.
Greenbelt, MD 20770
(301)220-4120
Ultimate Parent: K-Mart.

★ 71878 ★ **Standard Federal S & L Association**
7515 Greenbelt Rd.
Greenbelt, MD 20770
(301)841-8055
Ultimate Parent: Standard Federal Bank. **SIC:** 6036—Savings Institutions Except Federal.

★ 71879 ★ **Washington Inventory Service**
8955 Edmnstn Rd.
Greenbelt, MD
(301)474-0117
Ultimate Parent: Huffy.

Greenbelt

★ 71880 ★ **Lockheed Technical Operations**
7833 Walker Dr.
Greentbelt, MD
(301)982-0012
Ultimate Parent: Lockheed Corp.

Hagerstown

★ 71881 ★ **Food Lion**
761 E. Wilson Blvd.
Hagerstown, MD 21740
(301)791-0353
Ultimate Parent: Food Lion. **SIC:** 5411—Grocery Stores.

★ 71882 ★ **Greyhound Bus Lines**
31 E. Antietam St.
Hagerstown, MD 21740
(301)739-7420
Ultimate Parent: Greyhound Lines Inc. **SIC:** 4131—Intercity & Rural Bus Transportation; 4212—Local Trucking Without Storage.

★ 71883 ★ **Hertz Rent-A-Car**
1735 Virginia Ave.
Hagerstown, MD 21740
(301)790-1840
Ultimate Parent: Hertz. **SIC:** 7514—Passenger Car Rental.

★ 71884 ★ **Mary Kay Cosmetics**
1905 Stone Valley Dr.
Hagerstown, MD 21740
(301)582-3839
Ultimate Parent: Mary Kay Cosmetics. **SIC:** 5999—Miscellaneous Retail Stores Nec.

★ 71885 ★ **NCR Corp.**
Rte 63 & Williamsport
Hagerstown, MD 21740
(301)739-5335
Ultimate Parent: AT&T. **SIC:** 7378—Computer Maintenance & Repair; 5044—Office Equipment.

★ 71886 ★ **New York Life Insurance Co.**
140 W. Washington St.
Hagerstown, MD 21740
(301)791-3399
Ultimate Parent: New York Life. **SIC:** 6411—Insurance Agents, Brokers & Service.

★ 71887 ★ **Otis Elevator Co.**
50 Summit Ave.
Hagerstown, MD 21740
(301)733-0307
Ultimate Parent: United Technologies. **SIC:** 5084—Industrial Machinery & Equipment.

★ 71888 ★ **The Potomac Edison Co.**
Downsville Pke.
Hagerstown, MD 21740
(301)790-3400
Company Type: Subsidiary. **Ultimate Parent:** Allegheny Power System. **SIC:** 4911—Electric Services.

★ 71889 ★ **Potomac Edison Co.**
209 Bower Ave.
Hagerstown, MD 21740
(301)791-5600
Ultimate Parent: Allegheny Power System. **SIC:** 4911—Electric Services.

★ 71890 ★ **Potomac Edison Co.**
14035 Downsville Pke.
Hagerstown, MD 21740-1732
(301)790-3400
Location Type: Branch office. **Officer:** Alan J. Nola, President. **Ultimate Parent:** Allegheny Power System. **SIC:** 4911—Electric Services. **Employee Count:** 1092. **Sales:** 687 M.

★ 71891 ★ **PPG Industries Inc.**
1303 Dual Hwy.
Hagerstown, MD 21740
(301)790-0680
Ultimate Parent: PPG Industries Inc. **SIC:** 5198—Paints, Varnishes & Supplies.

★ 71892 ★ **Radio Shack**
1573 Potomac Ave.
Hagerstown, MD 21740
(301)733-5268
Company Type: Division. **Ultimate Parent:** Tandy Corp. **SIC:** 5731—Radio, Television & Electronics Stores.

★ 71893 ★ **Radio Shack**
100 Tandy Dr.
Hagerstown, MD 21740
(301)739-1312
Company Type: Division. **Ultimate Parent:** Tandy Corp. **SIC:** 5065—Electronic Parts & Equipment Nec.

★ 71894 ★ **Reynolds & Reynolds Co.**
14515 Pennsylvania Ave.
Hagerstown, MD 21742
(301)790-3110
Officer: Mike McLemore, Manager. **Ultimate Parent:** Reynolds & Reynolds. **SIC:** 2761—Manifold Business Forms.

★ 71895 ★ **Rite Aid**
825 W. Hillcrest Rd.
Hagerstown, MD 21742
Ultimate Parent: Rite Aid. **SIC:** 5912—Drug Stores & Proprietary Stores.

★ 71896 ★ **Rohr Inc.**
18238 Showalter Rd.
Hagerstown, MD 21742
(301)790-9500
Ultimate Parent: Rohr. **SIC:** 3724—Aircraft Engines & Engine Parts; 3728—Aircraft Parts & Equipment Nec.

★ 71897 ★ **Rohr Industries Inc.**
Showalter Rd.
Hagerstown, MD 21740-9183
Ultimate Parent: Rohr. **SIC:** 3728—Aircraft Parts & Equipment Nec.

★ 71898 ★ **Rohr Industries Inc.**
Rural Route 6
Hagerstown, MD 21740
(301)790-9500
Ultimate Parent: Rohr. **SIC:** 3721—Aircraft.

Hampstead

★ 71899 ★ **The Black & Decker Corp.**
626 Hanover Pike
Hampstead, MD 21074-2049
(410)239-5000
Company Type: Branch. **Officer:** John Hayes. **Ultimate Parent:** Black & Decker Corp. **SIC:** 3452—Bolts, Nuts, Rivets & Washers.

★ 71900 ★ **Black & Decker Inc.**
Facilities Group
626 Hanover Pke.
Hampstead, MD 21074
Ultimate Parent: Black & Decker Corp. **SIC:** 3545—Machine Tool Accessories; 3546—Power-Driven Handtools; 3634—Electric Housewares & Fans.

Hancock

★ 71901 ★ **Fleetwood Travel Trailers Inc.**
35 South St.
Hancock, MD 21750
(301)678-5521
Officer: Frank Subasic, Manager. **Ultimate Parent:** Fleetwood Enterprises, Inc. **SIC:** 3711—Motor Vehicles & Car Bodies; 3792—Travel Trailers & Campers.

★ 71902 ★ **Fleetwood Travel Trailers of Maryland Inc. 28**
35 South St. PO Box 458
Hancock, MD 21750
Ultimate Parent: Fleetwood Enterprises, Inc. **SIC:** 3792—Travel Trailers & Campers.

★ 71903 ★ **Genuine Parts Co.**
Rayloc Div.
100 Rayloc Dr.
Hancock, MD 21750
Company Type: Division. **Ultimate Parent:** Genuine Parts. **SIC:** 3714—Motor Vehicle Parts & Accessories.

★ 71904 ★ **Genuine Parts Co.**
Rayloc Div.
100 Rayloc Dr.
Hancock, MD 21750-0167
Company Type: Division. **Ultimate Parent:** Genuine Parts. **SIC:** 3714—Motor Vehicle Parts & Accessories.

★ 71905 ★ **Radio Shack**
101 E. Main St.
Hancock, MD 21750
(301)678-6000
Company Type: Division. **Ultimate Parent:** Tandy Corp. **SIC:** 5065—Electronic Parts & Equipment Nec.

★ 71906 ★ **Radio Shack**
Div. of Tandy Corp.
101 E. Main St.
Hancock, MD 21750
(301)678-6000
Company Type: Division. **Ultimate Parent:** Tandy Corp. **SIC:** 5065—Electronic Parts & Equipment Nec.

★ 71907 ★ **Rayloc**
Rayloc Div.
100 Rayloc Dr.
Hancock, MD 21750
Company Type: Division. **Ultimate Parent:** Genuine Parts. **SIC:** 3714—Motor Vehicle Parts & Accessories.

★ 71908 ★ **Rayloc Co.**
100 Rayloc Dr.
Hancock, MD 21750
(301)678-5555
Officer: Ron Shives, Manager. **Ultimate Parent:** Genuine Parts. **SIC:** 3714—Motor Vehicle Parts & Accessories.

Hanover

★ 71909 ★ **Danaher Tool Group**
7200 Standard Dr.
Hanover, MD 21076
(410)712-0410
Officer: Phil Stake, Manager. **Ultimate Parent:** Danaher Corp. **SIC:** 3423—Hand & Edge Tools Nec.

★ 71910 ★ **Deluxe Corp.**
7480 Candlewood Rd.
Hanover, MD 21076
Ultimate Parent: Deluxe Corp. **SIC:** 2782—Blankbooks & Looseleaf Binders; 2752—Commercial Printing—Lithographic.

★ 71911 ★ **GE Medical Systems**
7455 New Ridge Rd., No. T
Hanover, MD 21076
(410)850-0910
Officer: Scott McCabe, Manager. **Ultimate Parent:** General Electric. **SIC:** 3844—X-Ray Apparatus & Tubes.

★ 71912 ★ **Nationwide Papers**
7190 Parkway Dr.
Hanover, MD 21076
(410)796-5400
Ultimate Parent: Champion International. **SIC:** 5943—Stationery Stores.

★ 71913 ★ **Pulte Home Corp.**
7223 Parkway Dr.
Hanover, MD 21076
(410)796-8950
Ultimate Parent: Pulte. **SIC:** 8742—Management Consulting Services.

Havre De Grace

★ 71914 ★ **American Cyanamid Co.**
1300 Revolution St.
Havre De Grace, MD 21078-3899
Location Type: Plant. **Ultimate Parent:** American Cyanamid Co. **SIC:** 2891—Adhesives & Sealants; 2295—Coated Fabrics—Not Rubberized; 3499—Fabricated Metal Products Nec.

★ 71915 ★   **American Cyanamid Co.**
1300 Revolution St.
Havre De Grace, MD 21078-3800
(410)939-1910
Officer: Mike Reed. **Ultimate Parent:** American Cyanamid Co. **SIC:** 2819—Industrial Inorganic Chemicals Nec; 3354—Aluminum Extruded Products; 5169—Chemicals & Allied Products Nec; 2821—Plastics Materials & Resins; 2891—Adhesives & Sealants; 3469—Metal Stampings Nec.

★ 71916 ★   **County Banking & Trust Co.**
313 N. Union Ave.
Havre De Grace, MD 21078-2898
(301)939-3000
Company Type: Subsidiary. **Location Type:** Branch office. **Ultimate Parent:** Mercantile Bankshares Corp. **SIC:** 6021—National Commercial Banks.

★ 71917 ★   **County Banking & Trust Co.**
238 N. Washington
Havre De Grace, MD 21078-2909
(410)939-3000
Company Type: Subsidiary. **Location Type:** Branch office. **Officer:** Ted Bartow, Mgr. **Ultimate Parent:** Mercantile Bankshares Corp. **SIC:** 6021—National Commercial Banks.

★ 71918 ★   **Pepsi-Cola Bottling Co.**
1328 Old Post Rd.
Havre DeGrace, MD 21078
(410)458-1136
Officer: Clark Connellee, President. **Ultimate Parent:** Pepsico. **SIC:** 2086—Bottled & Canned Soft Drinks.

Hillcrest Heights

★ 71919 ★   **Casual Corner**
Iverson Mall
Hillcrest Heights, MD
(301)423-7272
Ultimate Parent: United States Shoe.

★ 71920 ★   **Exxon Co.**
3399 Branch Ave.
Hillcrest Heights, MD
(301)894-3222
Ultimate Parent: Exxon.

Hollywood

★ 71921 ★   **First National Bank of St. Mary's**
Rte. 235 & St. John Rd.
Hollywood, MD 20636-9617
(301)475-8081
Company Type: Subsidiary. **Location Type:** Branch office. **Officer:** M.E. Goldsborough, Mgr. **Ultimate Parent:** Mercantile Bankshares Corp. **SIC:** 6021—National Commercial Banks.

★ 71922 ★   **Mary Kay Cosmetics**
561 PO Box
Hollywood, MD 20636
(301)373-5969
Ultimate Parent: Mary Kay Cosmetics.

Hughesville

★ 71923 ★   **Bank of Southern Maryland**
Rte. 5
Hughesville, MD 20637
(301)274-3121
Company Type: Subsidiary. **Location Type:** Branch office. **Officer:** William A. Roberts III, Mgr. **Ultimate Parent:** Mercantile Bankshares Corp. **SIC:** 6021—National Commercial Banks.

Hunt Valley

★ 71924 ★   **Becton Dickinson Advanced Diagnostics**
225 International Cir.
Hunt Valley, MD 21030
(410)785-6257 **Fax:** (410)785-6240
Company Type: Subsidiary. **Officer:**

Vincent A. Forlenza, President. **Ultimate Parent:** Becton Dickinson.

★ 71925 ★   **Becton Dickinson & Co.**
250 Schilling Cir.
Hunt Valley, MD 21030
(410)771-0100
Ultimate Parent: Becton Dickinson. **SIC:** 3841—Surgical & Medical Instruments. **Employee Count:** 922.

★ 71926 ★   **CSX Intermodal Inc.**
200 International Cir., Ste. 4500
Hunt Valley, MD 21031
(410)584-0100 **Fax:** (410)584-0780
Officer: M. McNeil Porter, President & CEO. **Ultimate Parent:** CSX Corp.

★ 71927 ★   **CSX Intermodal Inc.**
200 International Cir.
Hunt Valley, MD 21030-1331
(410)584-0100
Company Type: Subsidiary. **Officer:** M. McNeil Porter, President. **Ultimate Parent:** CSX Corp. **SIC:** 4499—Water Transportation Services Nec. **Employee Count:** 1599. **Sales:** 810 M.

★ 71928 ★   **McCormick**
Schilling Cir.
211 Schilling Cir.
Hunt Valley, MD 21031
(410)527-6000 **Fax:** (410)527-6267
Company Type: Division. **Officer:** Harold J. Handley, Senior Vice President. **Ultimate Parent:** McCormick & Co. Inc.

★ 71929 ★   **McCormick**
Shilling Div.
211 Schilling Cir.
Hunt Valley, MD 21031
(410)527-6000
Company Type: Division. **Ultimate Parent:** McCormick & Co. Inc.

★ 71930 ★   **McCormick & Co. Inc.**
Flavor Group
226 Schilling Cir.
Hunt Valley, MD 21031
(410)771-7500
Company Type: Division. **Officer:** Howard Kympton, Vice President & General Manager Flavor Division. **Ultimate Parent:** McCormick & Co. Inc. **SIC:** 2035—Pickles, Sauces & Salad Dressings.

★ 71931 ★   **McCormick & Co. Inc.**
Flavor Group
10850 Beaver Dam Rd.
Hunt Valley, MD 21031
(410)771-7744
Company Type: Division. **Location Type:** Plant. **Officer:** Jay Stout, Plant Manager. **Ultimate Parent:** McCormick & Co. Inc. **SIC:** 2035—Pickles, Sauces & Salad Dressings.

★ 71932 ★   **McCormick & Co. Inc.**
Food Service Div.
350 Clubhouse Ln.
Hunt Valley, MD 21031
(410)771-7077
Company Type: Division. **Location Type:** Plant. **Officer:** Gary Lindsay, Plant Manager. **Ultimate Parent:** McCormick & Co. Inc.

★ 71933 ★   **McCormick & Co. Inc.**
Food Service Div.
226 Schilling Cir.
Hunt Valley, MD 21031
(410)771-7500
Company Type: Division. **Ultimate Parent:** McCormick & Co. Inc.

★ 71934 ★   **McCormick & Co. Inc.**
Food Service Div.
226 Schilling Cir.
Hunt Valley, MD 21031
(410)771-7500 **Fax:** (410)772-7182
Company Type: Division. **Officer:** Bob Murphy, Vice President & General Manager. **Ultimate Parent:** McCormick & Co. Inc.

★ 71935 ★   **McCormick & Co. Inc.**
Shilling Div.
1100 McCormick Rd.
Hunt Valley, MD 21031
(410)771-7778
Company Type: Division. **Location Type:** Plant. **Ultimate Parent:** McCormick & Co. Inc.

★ 71936 ★   **McCormick Ingredients**
10901 Gilroy Rd.
Hunt Valley, MD 21031
(410)771-5000 **Fax:** (410)771-5148
Officer: Randall B. Jensen, Vice President. **Ultimate Parent:** McCormick & Co. Inc.

★ 71937 ★   **McCormick Ingredients Spice Mill**
10901 Gilroy Rd.
Hunt Valley, MD 21031
Ultimate Parent: McCormick & Co. Inc. **SIC:** 2099—Food Preparations Nec.

★ 71938 ★   **McCormick-Stange Flavor Div.**
226 Schilling Cir.
Hunt Valley, MD 21031
(410)771-7500 **Fax:** (410)785-4947
Officer: Gary W. Zimmerman, Vice President & General Manager. **Ultimate Parent:** McCormick & Co. Inc.

★ 71939 ★   **Noxell Corp.**
93 Beaver Ct.
Hunt Valley, MD 21030-2098
Ultimate Parent: Procter & Gamble Co. **SIC:** 2844—Toilet Preparations.

★ 71940 ★   **Noxell Corp.**
11050 York Rd.
Hunt Valley, MD 21030-2098
Ultimate Parent: Procter & Gamble Co. **SIC:** 2844—Toilet Preparations.

★ 71941 ★   **PHH**
11333 McCormick Rd.
Hunt Valley, MD 21031
(410)771-3600
Company Type: Headquarters. **Officer:** Robert D. Kunish. **Employee Count:** 4834. **Sales:** 2021 M. **Fortune 500:** Largest U.S. Industrial Corporations: Ranking 74.

★ 71942 ★   **PHH Corp.**
11333 McCormick Rd.
Hunt Valley, MD 21031-1000
(410)771-3600 **Fax:** (410)771-1123
Officer: Robert D. Kunisch, Chairman, President & CEO. **Ultimate Parent:** PHH. **Employee Count:** 4800.

★ 71943 ★   **PHH Fleet America**
307 International Cir.
Hunt Valley, MD 21030-1337
(410)771-1900 **Fax:** (410)771-3362
Officer: William F. Alder, President. **Ultimate Parent:** PHH.

★ 71944 ★   **PPG Industries**
10820 Gilroy Rd.
Hunt Valley, MD 21031
(410)666-9100
Ultimate Parent: PPG Industries Inc. **SIC:** 1793—Glass & Glazing Work.

★ 71945 ★   **Westinghouse Electric Corp.**
Integrated Logistics Support
111 Schilling Rd. Mccormick Industrial Park
Hunt Valley, MD 21203
Ultimate Parent: Westinghouse Electric Corp. **SIC:** 3699—Electrical Equipment & Supplies Nec; 3829—Measuring & Controlling Devices Nec; 3825—Instruments to Measure Electricity.

★ 71946 ★   **Westinghouse Electric Corp.**
Integrated Logistics Support
1111 Schilling Rd. (Mccormick Industrial Park)
Hunt Valley, MD 21030
Ultimate Parent: Westinghouse Electric Corp. **SIC:** 3699—Electrical Equipment & Supplies Nec; 3829—Measuring & Controlling Devices Nec; 3825—Instruments to Measure Electricity.

★ 71947 ★   **Westinghouse Electric Corp.**
Integrated Logistics Support
1111 Schilling Rd.
Hunt Valley, MD 21030
Ultimate Parent: Westinghouse Electric Corp. **SIC:** 3600—Electronic & Other Electrical Equipment.

Huntingtown

★ 71948 ★   **Structure Corp.**
1880 Oldfield Dr.
Huntingtown, MD 20639
(410)535-1889
Ultimate Parent: Limited. **SIC:** 4213—Trucking Except Local.

Hurlock

★ 71949 ★   **Conagra Broiler Co. Feed Mill**
Rte. 392 PO Box 340 Feed Mill
Hurlock, MD 21643
Ultimate Parent: Conagra. **SIC:** 2048—Prepared Feeds Nec.

★ 71950 ★   **Conagra Broiler Co. Hurlock Processing Plant**
100 Nealson St. PO Box 340
Hurlock, MD 21643
Ultimate Parent: Conagra. **SIC:** 2015—Poultry Slaughtering & Processing.

★ 71951 ★   **Crown Beverage Packaging Inc. Plant 24**
200 Nelson St. PO Box 310
Hurlock, MD 21643
Ultimate Parent: Crown Cork & Seal. **SIC:** 3411—Metal Cans.

Hyattsville

★ 71952 ★   **Air Products & Chemicals Inc.**
2900 52nd Ave.
Hyattsville, MD 20781
Ultimate Parent: Air Products & Chemicals, Inc. **SIC:** 2813—Industrial Gases.

★ 71953 ★   **August Max Woman**
Prince Georges Plaza
Hyattsville, MD
(301)559-2833
Ultimate Parent: United States Shoe.

★ 71954 ★   **Browning-Ferris Industries**
3310 Kenilworth Ave.
Hyattsville, MD 20781
(301)927-1800
Officer: Mike Shaw, Manager. **Ultimate Parent:** Browning-Ferris Industries. **SIC:** 3589—Service Industry Machinery Nec.

★ 71955 ★   **Browning-Ferris Industries Inc.**
3310 Kenilworth Ave.
Hyattsville, MD 20781-1011
(301)927-1800
Location Type: Branch office. **Officer:** Mike Shaw. **Ultimate Parent:** Browning-Ferris Industries. **SIC:** 3339—Primary Nonferrous Metals Nec; 4953—Refuse Systems.

★ 71956 ★   **Crestar Bank MD**
3600 East-West Hwy.
Hyattsville, MD 20782-2014
(800)451-2435
Company Type: Subsidiary. **Location Type:** Branch office. **Officer:** Darla M. Howard, Mgr. **Ultimate Parent:** Crestar Financial Corp. **SIC:** 6021—National Commercial Banks.

★ 71957 ★   **Exxon Service Station**
3250 Kenilworth Ave.
Hyattsville, MD 20781
(301)277-6869
Ultimate Parent: Exxon.

★ 71958 ★   **Gap Stores Inc.**
Prince Georges Plz.
Hyattsville, MD 20782
(301)559-5600
Ultimate Parent: GAP.

★ 71959 ★   **Gap Stores Inc. Maryland Stores**
Prince Georges Plz.
Hyattsville, MD 20782
(301)559-5600
Ultimate Parent: GAP.

★ 71960 ★   **Kids R US**
3500 East West Hwy.
Hyattsville, MD 20782
(301)853-2202
Ultimate Parent: Toys "R" US.

★ 71961 ★　Kmart
6411 Riggs Road
Hyattsville, MD 20783
(301)853-3102
Ultimate Parent: K-Mart.

★ 71962 ★　Lenscrafters
Landover Mall
Hyattsville, MD
(301)322-5515
Ultimate Parent: United States Shoe.

★ 71963 ★　Lenscrafters
Prince Georges Plaza
Hyattsville, MD
(301)559-1110
Ultimate Parent: United States Shoe.

★ 71964 ★　Mary Kay Cosmetics
1835 E. Univ Blvd.
Hyattsville, MD
(301)445-7929
Ultimate Parent: Mary Kay Cosmetics.

★ 71965 ★　Mary Kay Cosmetics
Indep Sales
6710 Ingrhm St.
Hyattsville, MD
(301)577-0843
Ultimate Parent: Mary Kay Cosmetics.

★ 71966 ★　McDonald's
Hamburgers
1030 Largo Ctr. Dr.
Hyattsville, MD 20785
(301)499-7241
Ultimate Parent: McDonald's.

★ 71967 ★　McDonald's
Hamburgers
2306 University Blvd. E
Hyattsville, MD 20783
(301)422-0220
Ultimate Parent: McDonald's.

★ 71968 ★　Nationsbank Banking
Centers
6505 Belcrest Rd. Prince G
Hyattsville, MD
(301)454-8470
Ultimate Parent: Nationsbank Corp.

★ 71969 ★　Nationsbank Banking
Centers
5214 Balto Ave.
Hyattsville, MD 20781
(301)270-5000
Ultimate Parent: Nationsbank Corp.

★ 71970 ★　Nationsbank Banking
Centers Hy
3413 Kenilworth Ave.
Hyattsville, MD 20781
(301)454-8440
Ultimate Parent: Nationsbank Corp.

★ 71971 ★　Nationsbank Banking
Centers La
7515 Annapolis Rd.
Hyattsville, MD 20784
(301)454-8406
Ultimate Parent: Nationsbank Corp.

★ 71972 ★　Nationsbank Banking
Centers We
5416 Queens Chapel Rd.
Hyattsville, MD 20782
(301)270-7930
Ultimate Parent: Nationsbank Corp.

★ 71973 ★　Nationsbank Banking
Cneters
6495 Nh Ave.
Hyattsville, MD
(301)270-5000
Ultimate Parent: Nationsbank Corp.

★ 71974 ★　North American Van
Lines International
4318 Kenilworth Ave.
Hyattsville, MD 20781
(301)779-2090
Ultimate Parent: Norfolk Southern.

★ 71975 ★　PPG Industries Inc.
4600 Ingraham St.
Hyattsville, MD 20781
(301)779-7455
Ultimate Parent: PPG Industries Inc.

★ 71976 ★　Pulte Home Corp.
3114 Muskogee St.
Hyattsville, MD 20783
(301)445-4726
Ultimate Parent: Pulte.

★ 71977 ★　Radio Shack
7702 Frederick Rd.
Hyattsville, MD 20784
Company Type: Division. Ultimate Parent:
Tandy Corp. SIC: 5046—Commercial
Equipment Nec.

★ 71978 ★　Radio Shack
Prince Georges Plz.
Hyattsville, MD 20782
(301)559-2266
Company Type: Division. Ultimate Parent:
Tandy Corp.

★ 71979 ★　Radio Shack
Prince Georges Plz.
Hyattsville, MD 20782
(301)559-2266
Company Type: Division. Ultimate Parent:
Tandy Corp.

Jarrettsville

★ 71980 ★　Forest Hill State Bank
3712 Norrisville Rd.
Jarrettsville, MD 21084-1419
(410)692-6185
Company Type: Subsidiary. Location
Type: Branch office. Officer: Sandra M.
Benedetto, Mgr. Ultimate Parent:
Mercantile Bankshares Corp. SIC: 6021—
National Commercial Banks.

Jessup

★ 71981 ★　Baltimore Aircoil Co.
7595 Montevideo Rd.
Jessup, MD 20794
(410)799-6200 Fax: (410)799-6416
Company Type: Subsidiary. Officer: M. J.
McKenna, President. Ultimate Parent:
Amsted Industries Inc. SIC: 3569—General
Industrial Machinery Nec.

★ 71982 ★　BFI Services Group
Jessup, MD 20794
(410)880-4828
Ultimate Parent: Browning-Ferris
Industries. SIC: 5082—Construction &
Mining Machinery.

★ 71983 ★　Citizens National
Bank
7720 Washington Blvd.
Jessup, MD 21227-6505
(410)799-5005
Company Type: Subsidiary. Location
Type: Branch office. Officer: Craig Curtin,
Mgr. Ultimate Parent: Mercantile
Bankshares Corp. SIC: 6021—National
Commercial Banks.

★ 71984 ★　Garrett-Buchanan Co.
8261 Preston Ct.
Jessup, MD 20794-9371
(410)792-8069
Officer: John McDonald, Manager. Ultimate
Parent: Alco Standard Corp. SIC: 2677—
Envelopes; 5112—Stationery & Office
Supplies; 5113—Industrial & Personal
Service Paper; 5943—Stationery Stores.

★ 71985 ★　S. P. Richards Co.
8231-C Stayton Dr.
Jessup, MD
(301)470-3214
Ultimate Parent: Genuine Parts.

★ 71986 ★　Trane Co.
8201 Stayton Dr.
Jessup, MD 20794
(410)792-8007
Ultimate Parent: American Standard. SIC:
1711—Plumbing, Heating & Air-
Conditioning.

★ 71987 ★　Westvaco Corp.
8301 Patuxent Range Rd.
Jessup, MD 20794
(410)792-9940
Ultimate Parent: WestVaco Corp. SIC:
5112—Stationery & Office Supplies.

★ 71988 ★　ZEP Manufacturing
Co.
8230 Sandy Ct., Ste. D
Jessup, MD 20794
(410)792-8261
Officer: David Andersen, Manager.
Ultimate Parent: National Service
Industries. SIC: 2842—Polishes &
Sanitation Goods.

★ 71989 ★　Zep Manufacturing
Co.
8230-D Sandy Ct
Jessup, MD
(301)565-2128
Ultimate Parent: National Service
Industries.

Joppa

★ 71990 ★　Quaker State Oil
Refining Co.
818 Pulaski Hwy.
Joppa, MD 21085
(410)676-5444
Ultimate Parent: Quaker State. SIC:
5172—Petroleum Products Nec.

Keedysville

★ 71991 ★　Chesapeake &
Potomac Tel Co. MD
95 N. Main St., Rte. 1
Keedysville, MD 21756-1342
(301)797-2200
Ultimate Parent: Bell Atlantic Corp. SIC:
4813—Telephone Communications Except
Radiotelephone.

Kensington

★ 71992 ★　Crestar Bank MD
3740 University Blvd. W
Kensington, MD 20895-2100
(800)451-2435
Company Type: Subsidiary. Location
Type: Branch office. Officer: Claudine
Celestino, Mgr. Ultimate Parent: Crestar
Financial Corp. SIC: 6021—National
Commercial Banks.

★ 71993 ★　Delta Air Lines
Kensington, MD
(301)468-2282
Ultimate Parent: Delta Air Lines, Inc.

★ 71994 ★　First Union National
Bank of Maryland
10400 Connecticut Ave.
Kensington, MD 20895-3910
(301)650-1120
Company Type: Subsidiary. Location
Type: Branch office. Ultimate Parent: First
Union Corp. SIC: 6021—National
Commercial Banks.

★ 71995 ★　First Union National
Bank of Maryland
10821 Connecticut Ave.
Kensington, MD 20895-2134
(301)961-5220
Company Type: Subsidiary. Location
Type: Branch office. Officer: Art Paholski,
Mgr. Ultimate Parent: First Union Corp.
SIC: 6021—National Commercial Banks.

★ 71996 ★　Lenscrafters
Wheaton Plaza
Kensington, MD
(301)949-3960
Ultimate Parent: United States Shoe.

★ 71997 ★　Lenscrafters
Wheaton Plaza
Kensington, MD
(301)949-0170
Ultimate Parent: United States Shoe.

★ 71998 ★　McDonald's
Hamburgers
2741 University Blvd. W
Kensington, MD 20895
(301)942-2412
Ultimate Parent: McDonald's.

★ 71999 ★　Nationsbank New
Accounts Rates Div.
Kensington, MD
(301)949-6400
Ultimate Parent: Nationsbank Corp.

★ 72000 ★　Radio Shack
White Flint Mall
Kensington, MD
(301)984-9540
Company Type: Division. Ultimate Parent:
Tandy Corp.

★ 72001 ★　Radio Shack
White Flint Mall
Kensington, MD
(301)984-9540
Company Type: Division. Ultimate Parent:
Tandy Corp.

★ 72002 ★　Structure
White Flint Mall
Kensington, MD
(301)984-9157
Ultimate Parent: Limited.

La Plata

★ 72003 ★　Bank of Southern
Maryland
Rte. 6 & US 301
La Plata, MD 20646-9631
(301)934-1000
Company Type: Subsidiary. Location
Type: Branch office. Ultimate Parent:
Mercantile Bankshares Corp. SIC: 6021—
National Commercial Banks.

★ 72004 ★　Bank of Southern
Maryland
304 Charles St.
PO Box X
La Plata, MD 20646-0660
(301)934-1000 Fax: (301)932-6470
Company Type: Subsidiary. Location
Type: Branch office. Officer: Wesley E.
Hughes Jr., President & CEO. Ultimate
Parent: Mercantile Bankshares Corp. SIC:
6021—National Commercial Banks.

★ 72005 ★　Coca-Cola
Enterprises
400 E. Chas St.
La Plata, MD
(301)934-4381
Ultimate Parent: Coca-Cola Enterprises.

★ 72006 ★　McDonald's
Hamburgers
519 N. Route 301
La Plata, MD
(301)870-3260
Ultimate Parent: McDonald's.

Landover

★ 72007 ★　Avery Dennison Label
8500 Ardmore Ardwick Rd.
Landover, MD
(301)772-0030
Ultimate Parent: Avery Dennison Corp.

★ 72008 ★　Circuit City
6231 Columbia Park Rd.
Landover, MD 20785
(301)386-4444
Ultimate Parent: Circuit City Stores.

★ 72009 ★　Circuit City
2099 Bright Seat Rd.
Landover, MD 20785
(301)386-5020
Ultimate Parent: Circuit City Stores.

★ 72010 ★　Circuit City Division
Office
1200 Mercantile Ln.
Landover, MD 20785
(301)386-6120
Ultimate Parent: Circuit City Stores.

★ 72011 ★　Courtyard by Marriott
8330 Corporate Dr.
Landover, MD 20785
(301)577-3373
Ultimate Parent: Marriott International.

★ 72012 ★　Exxon Service Station
7106 George N. Palmer Hwy.
Landover, MD
(301)322-8800
Ultimate Parent: Exxon.

★ 72013 ★　Exxon Service Station
7106 Martin Luther King J
Landover, MD 20785
(301)322-3233
Ultimate Parent: Exxon.

★ 72014 ★　Exxon Service Station
7106 George N. Palmer Hwy.
Landover, MD
(301)322-5927
Ultimate Parent: Exxon.

★ 72015 ★ First Union Naitonal
Bank of Maryland
9201 Basil Ct.
Landover, MD 20785-5310
(301)650-1097
Company Type: Subsidiary. Location
Type: Branch office. Ultimate Parent: First
Union Corp. SIC: 6021—National
Commercial Banks.

★ 72016 ★ First Union National
Bank of Maryland
7700 Landover Rd.
Landover, MD 20785-2135
(301)650-1013
Company Type: Subsidiary. Location
Type: Branch office. Ultimate Parent: First
Union Corp. SIC: 6021—National
Commercial Banks.

★ 72017 ★ Gap Stores
Landover Mall
Landover, MD
(301)341-5588
Ultimate Parent: GAP.

★ 72018 ★ Gap Stores the
Maryland Stores
Landvr Mall
Landover, MD
(301)341-5588
Ultimate Parent: GAP.

★ 72019 ★ GFS
6300 Sheriff Rd.
Landover, MD 20785
(301)618-4969
Company Type: Subsidiary. Officer:
Michael J. Bush, Vice President, Real
Estate. Ultimate Parent: Giant Food.

★ 72020 ★ Giant Food
6300 Sheriff Rd.
Landover, MD 20785
(301)341-4100
Company Type: Headquarters. Officer:
Israel Cohen. SIC: 2026—Fluid Milk.
Employee Count: 23700. Sales: 3473 M.
Fortune Service 500: Ranking 39.

★ 72021 ★ Giant Food Dairy
6300 Sheriff Rd.
Landover, MD 20785
Ultimate Parent: Giant Food. SIC: 2026—
Fluid Milk.

★ 72022 ★ Giant Food Inc.
6300 Sherriff Rd.
Landover, MD 20785
(301)341-4100
Company Type: Headquarters. Officer:
Israel Cohen, Chairman & CEO. Ultimate
Parent: Giant Food. Employee Count:
25000.

★ 72023 ★ Martin Marietta Corp.
Services Inc.
8000 Corporate Dr.
Landover, MD 20785
(301)459-3100
Ultimate Parent: Martin Marietta.

★ 72024 ★ Mary Kay Cosmetics
Indep Sales
811 Finch Dr.
Landover, MD 20785
(301)336-5862
Ultimate Parent: Mary Kay Cosmetics.

★ 72025 ★ McDonald's
Hamburgers
7708 Landover Rd.
Landover, MD 20785
(301)322-1885
Ultimate Parent: McDonald's.

★ 72026 ★ McDonald's
Hamburgers
8710 Central Ave.
Landover, MD 20785
(301)336-2787
Ultimate Parent: McDonald's.

★ 72027 ★ Mckesson Drug Co.
7721 Polk St.
Landover, MD 20785
(301)322-1100
Ultimate Parent: McKesson.

★ 72028 ★ Overnite
Transportation Co.
2400 Beaver Rd.
Landover, MD 20785
(301)773-6770
Ultimate Parent: Union Pacific Corp.

★ 72029 ★ Payless Shoesource
916 Largo Ctr. Dr.
Landover, MD 20785
(301)336-1273
Ultimate Parent: May Department Stores.

★ 72030 ★ Radio Shack
Landover Mall
Landover, MD
(301)772-0010
Company Type: Division. Ultimate Parent:
Tandy Corp.

★ 72031 ★ Radio Shack
Landover Mall Shopping
Landover, MD
(301)772-0010
Company Type: Division. Ultimate Parent:
Tandy Corp.

★ 72032 ★ Rite Aid
Dodge Park Shopping. Ctr.
Landover, MD
(301)773-2002
Ultimate Parent: Rite Aid.

★ 72033 ★ Super G Inc.
6300 Sheriff Rd.
Landover, MD 20785
(301)341-4102
Ultimate Parent: Giant Food.

★ 72034 ★ Toys R US
3636 Pennsy Dr.
Landover, MD 20785
(301)792-4502
Ultimate Parent: Toys "R" US.

★ 72035 ★ Trugreen-Chemlawn
3839 Ironwood Pl.
Landover, MD 20785
(301)386-5700
Ultimate Parent: ServiceMaster Co.

★ 72036 ★ Waldenbooks
Maryland Stores
Landover Mall
Landover, MD
(301)322-9220
Ultimate Parent: K-Mart.

★ 72037 ★ Washington Inventory
Service
7515 Annapolis Rd.
Landover, MD 20784
(301)459-0422
Ultimate Parent: Huffy.

Landover Hill

★ 72038 ★ Casual Corner
Capital Plaza
Landover Hill, MD
(301)322-1188
Ultimate Parent: United States Shoe.

★ 72039 ★ McDonald's
Hamburgers
6200 Annapolis Rd.
Landover Hill, MD 20784
(301)772-2308
Ultimate Parent: McDonald's.

Langley Park

★ 72040 ★ First Union National
Bank of Maryland
New Hampshire Ave. & University Blvd.
Langley Park, MD 20783
(301)431-0311
Company Type: Subsidiary. Location
Type: Branch office. Ultimate Parent: First
Union Corp. SIC: 6021—National
Commercial Banks.

★ 72041 ★ Mellon Bank (MD)
7911 New Hampshire Ave.
Langley Park, MD 20783-4685
(301)439-9260
Company Type: Subsidiary. Location
Type: Branch office. Officer: Debbie Keats,
Mgr. Ultimate Parent: Mellon Bank Corp.
SIC: 6021—National Commercial Banks.

★ 72042 ★ Nationsbank Banking
Centers
7950 New Hampshire Ave.
Langley Park, MD 20783
(301)270-7870
Ultimate Parent: Nationsbank Corp.

★ 72043 ★ Radio Shack
1161 University Blvd. E
Langley Park, MD 20783
(301)439-6688
Company Type: Division. Ultimate Parent:
Tandy Corp.

★ 72044 ★ Radio Shack
1161 University Blvd. E
Langley Park, MD 20783
(301)439-6688
Company Type: Division. Ultimate Parent:
Tandy Corp.

★ 72045 ★ Rite Aid
Hampshire Langley Shopping. Ctr.
Langley Park, MD
(301)439-4400
Ultimate Parent: Rite Aid.

Langley Pk

★ 72046 ★ Hit or Miss
7663 New Hampshire Ave.
Langley Pk, MD
(301)439-7385
Ultimate Parent: TJX.

★ 72047 ★ Toys R US
University & 23rd St.
Langley Pk, MD
(301)422-4080
Ultimate Parent: Toys "R" US.

Lanham

★ 72048 ★ Bell Atlantic Bus
Systems Svc.
4391 Nicole Dr.
Lanham, MD 20706-4349
(301)731-4505
Ultimate Parent: Bell Atlantic Corp. SIC:
7378—Computer Maintenance & Repair.

★ 72049 ★ Bell Atlantic Mobile
9700-E Martin Luther King Jr. H
Lanham, MD 20706-1837
(301)459-0660
Ultimate Parent: Bell Atlantic Corp. SIC:
5065—Electronic Parts & Equipment Nec;
4813—Telephone Communications Except
Radiotelephone.

★ 72050 ★ Computer Sciences
Health & Administrative Services
4601 Presidents Dr.
Lanham, MD 20706
(301)306-9100 Fax: (301)306-1359
Officer: Kenneth Van Wagner, President.
Ultimate Parent: Computer Sciences.

★ 72051 ★ Martin Marietta Corp.
Inc.
4701 Forbes Blvd.
Lanham, MD 20706
(301)306-8000
Ultimate Parent: Martin Marietta.

★ 72052 ★ Mary Kay Cosmetics
Indep Sales
6511 Dawnwood Dr.
Lanham, MD 20706
(301)552-2984
Ultimate Parent: Mary Kay Cosmetics.

★ 72053 ★ McDonald's
Hamburgers
9007 Annapolis Rd.
Lanham, MD 20706
(301)577-2505
Ultimate Parent: McDonald's.

★ 72054 ★ New York Life
Washington Group Claims Office
Eastern Group Claims
10001 Derekwood Ln., Ste. 115
Lanham, MD 20706
(800)695-4389 Fax: (301)459-0410
Officer: Stephanie Batch, Group Claims
Director. Ultimate Parent: New York Life.

★ 72055 ★ Payless Shoesource
9433 Annapolis Rd.
Lanham, MD 20706
(301)731-8013
Ultimate Parent: May Department Stores.

★ 72056 ★ Radio Shack
7702-B Frederick Ave.
Lanham, MD
(301)459-6611
Company Type: Division. Ultimate Parent:
Tandy Corp.

★ 72057 ★ Radio Shack
7702-B Fredrick Ave.
Lanham, MD
(301)459-6611
Company Type: Division. Ultimate Parent:
Tandy Corp.

★ 72058 ★ Toys R US
8201 Annapolis Rd.
Lanham, MD 20706
(301)459-6070
Ultimate Parent: Toys "R" US.

Lanham Seabro

★ 72059 ★ Paramax Systems
Corp.
10265 Aerospace Rd.
Lanham Seabro, MD 20706
(301)794-2700
Ultimate Parent: Unisys Corp.

Lanham Seabrook

★ 72060 ★ Loral AeroSys
7375 Executive Pl.
Lanham Seabrook, MD
(301)805-0300 Fax: (301)805-0517
Company Type: Division. Ultimate Parent:
Loral Corp. SIC: 8711—Engineering
Services.

★ 72061 ★ US Design Corp.
4311 Forbes Blvd.
Lanham Seabrook, MD 20706
(301)577-2880
Company Type: Subsidiary. Ultimate
Parent: Maxtor. SIC: 3572—Computer
Storage Devices. Employee Count: 32.

Largo

★ 72062 ★ Crestar Bank MD
1010 Largo Ctr. Way
Largo, MD 20785
(800)451-2435
Company Type: Subsidiary. Location
Type: Branch office. Officer: Lee Wright,
Mgr. Ultimate Parent: Crestar Financial
Corp. SIC: 6021—National Commercial
Banks.

★ 72063 ★ Rite Aid
12108 Central Ave.
Largo, MD
(301)249-0910
Ultimate Parent: Rite Aid.

Laurel

★ 72064 ★ Casual Corner
Laurel Centre
Laurel, MD 20707
(301)490-4755
Ultimate Parent: United States Shoe. SIC:
5621—Women's Clothing Stores.

★ 72065 ★ Citizens National
Bank
390 Main St.
Laurel, MD 20707-4199
(301)725-3100
Company Type: Subsidiary. Location
Type: Branch office. Officer: Janet L. Able,
Mgr. Ultimate Parent: Mercantile
Bankshares Corp. SIC: 6021—National
Commercial Banks.

★ 72066 ★ Citizens National
Bank
Laurel Shopping Ctr., 1025 Washington
Blvd.
Laurel, MD 20707-6102
(301)725-3900
Company Type: Subsidiary. Location
Type: Branch office. Officer: Judith Long,
Mgr. Ultimate Parent: Mercantile
Bankshares Corp. SIC: 6021—National
Commercial Banks.

★ 72067 ★ Citizens National
Bank
Montpelier Plz., 12613 Laurel-Bowie Rd.
Laurel, MD 20708
(301)490-6000
Company Type: Subsidiary. Location
Type: Branch office. Officer: Leslie Holland,
Mgr. Ultimate Parent: Mercantile
Bankshares Corp. SIC: 6021—National
Commercial Banks.

★ 72068 ★   Citizens National
Bank
1344 Ashton Rd.
Laurel, MD 21076-3119
(410)850-0407
Company Type: Subsidiary. Location
Type: Branch office. Officer: Merdell
Howell, Mgr. Ultimate Parent: Mercantile
Bankshares Corp. SIC: 6021—National
Commercial Banks.

★ 72069 ★   Citizens National
Banks
4th Main St.
Laurel, MD 20707
(301)725-3100
Company Type: Division. Officer: J Donald
Henyon, Chairman of the Board. Ultimate
Parent: Mercantile Bankshares Corp.
Employee Count: 187. Sales: Na M.

★ 72070 ★   Crestar Bank MD
14070 Baltimore Ave.
Laurel, MD 20707
(800)451-2435
Company Type: Subsidiary. Location
Type: Branch office. Officer: A. Cabell
Angle Jr., Mgr. Ultimate Parent: Crestar
Financial Corp. SIC: 6021—National
Commercial Banks.

★ 72071 ★   First American Bank
608 Washington Blvd. S
Laurel, MD 20707
Ultimate Parent: First American Corp. SIC:
6099—Functions Related to Deposit
Banking.

★ 72072 ★   First American Bank
NA
608 Washington Blvd. S
Laurel, MD 20707
(301)725-6800
Ultimate Parent: First American Corp. SIC:
6099—Functions Related to Deposit
Banking.

★ 72073 ★   First Union National
Bank of Maryland
11200 Scaggsville Rd.
Laurel, MD 20707-1044
(301)604-2822
Company Type: Subsidiary. Location
Type: Branch office. Ultimate Parent: First
Union Corp. SIC: 6021—National
Commercial Banks.

★ 72074 ★   First Union National
Bank of Maryland
608 Washington Blvd.
Laurel, MD 20707-4642
(301)725-6800
Company Type: Subsidiary. Location
Type: Branch office. Ultimate Parent: First
Union Corp. SIC: 6021—National
Commercial Banks.

★ 72075 ★   First Union National
Bank of Maryland
New Laurel Ctr.
Laurel, MD 20707
(301)953-1951
Company Type: Subsidiary. Location
Type: Branch office. Officer: Marsha
Maloney, Mgr. Ultimate Parent: First Union
Corp. SIC: 6021—National Commercial
Banks.

★ 72076 ★   Gap
Laurel Centre
Laurel, MD 20707
(301)490-3333
Ultimate Parent: GAP. SIC: 5713—Floor
Covering Stores.

★ 72077 ★   Hertz Rent-A-Car
2501 Fort Meade Rd.
Laurel, MD 20724
(410)776-7280
Ultimate Parent: Hertz. SIC: 7514—
Passenger Car Rental.

★ 72078 ★   J C Penney Co.
1137 Rural Route 1
Laurel, MD 20723
(410)490-1133
Ultimate Parent: J.C. Penney. SIC: 5311—
Department Stores.

★ 72079 ★   Loyola Fsb Banking
Centers Lau
13990 Balto Ave.
Laurel, MD 20707
(301)725-2900
Ultimate Parent: Loyola Capital Corp.

★ 72080 ★   McDonald's
Hamburgers
14810 Balto Blvd.
Laurel, MD 20707
(301)953-3368
Ultimate Parent: McDonald's.

★ 72081 ★   Nationsbank Banking
Centers
13600 Laurel Bowie Rd.
Laurel, MD 20708
(301)572-1740
Ultimate Parent: Nationsbank Corp.

★ 72082 ★   Nationsbank Banking
Centers
207 Bowie Rd.
Laurel, MD 20707
(301)572-1770
Ultimate Parent: Nationsbank Corp.

★ 72083 ★   Pulte Home Corp.
10231 Old Scaggsvle Rd.
Laurel, MD 20707
(301)792-0495
Ultimate Parent: Pulte. SIC: 1521—
Single-Family Housing Construction.

★ 72084 ★   Radio Shack
Laurel Shopng Ctr.
Laurel, MD
(301)953-2111
Company Type: Division. Ultimate Parent:
Tandy Corp.

★ 72085 ★   Radio Shack
Laurel Centre
Laurel, MD
(301)776-5111
Company Type: Division. Ultimate Parent:
Tandy Corp.

★ 72086 ★   Radio Shack
Laurel Shopping Ctr.
Laurel, MD
(301)953-2111
Company Type: Division. Ultimate Parent:
Tandy Corp.

★ 72087 ★   Rite Aid
Laurel Plaza
Laurel, MD
(301)776-5566
Ultimate Parent: Rite Aid.

★ 72088 ★   Rite Aid
12612 Laurel-Bowierd
Laurel, MD 20708
(301)490-5000
Ultimate Parent: Rite Aid.

★ 72089 ★   Rite Aid
Laurel Centre
Laurel, MD
(301)776-1755
Ultimate Parent: Rite Aid.

★ 72090 ★   Southland Corp.
9115-A Whiskey Botto
Laurel, MD
(301)953-0363
Company Type: Division. Ultimate Parent:
Southland Corp. SIC: 6531—Real Estate
Agents & Managers.

★ 72091 ★   Standard Federal S&L
14724 Baltimore Washington Blvd.
Laurel, MD 20707
(301)776-9790
Ultimate Parent: Standard Federal Bank.
SIC: 6022—State Commercial Banks.

★ 72092 ★   Standard Federal
Savings Bank
14724 Baltimore Ave.
Laurel, MD 20707
(301)470-2990
Ultimate Parent: Standard Federal Bank.

★ 72093 ★   Waldenbooks
Maryland Stores
Laurel Centre
Laurel, MD 20707
(301)953-3807
Ultimate Parent: K-Mart.

★ 72094 ★   Westvaco Corp.
11101 Johns Hopkins Rd.
Laurel, MD 20723
(301)953-2575
Ultimate Parent: WestVaco Corp. SIC:
8731—Commercial Physical Research.

★ 72095 ★   Westvaco Corp.
Whisky Bottom Industrial Pk.
Laurel, MD 20707
(301)792-7513
Ultimate Parent: WestVaco Corp. SIC:
5112—Stationery & Office Supplies.

★ 72096 ★   Westvaco Corp.
Research
11101 Johns Hopkins Rd.
Laurel, MD 20723
(301)497-1300
Ultimate Parent: WestVaco Corp.

★ 72097 ★   Winchester Homes
Inc.
9410 Loch Leven Ct
Laurel, MD 20723
(301)369-9111
Ultimate Parent: Weyerhaeuser Co.

Leonardtown

★ 72098 ★   Chesapeake &
Potomac Phone Co.
328 N. Washington St.
Leonardtown, MD 20650-3835
(301)475-8901
Ultimate Parent: Bell Atlantic Corp. SIC:
4813—Telephone Communications Except
Radiotelephone.

★ 72099 ★   First National Bank of
St. Mary's
Jefferson St.
Leonardtown, MD 20650
(301)475-8084
Company Type: Subsidiary. Location
Type: Branch office. Officer: Brenda K.
Webb, Mgr. Ultimate Parent: Mercantile
Bankshares Corp. SIC: 6021—National
Commercial Banks.

★ 72100 ★   First National Bank of
St. Mary's
5 E. Park St.
PO Box 655
Leonardtown, MD 20650-0655
(301)475-8081 Fax: (301)475-3331
Company Type: Subsidiary. Location
Type: Branch office. Officer: John A.
Candela, President & CEO. Ultimate
Parent: Mercantile Bankshares Corp. SIC:
6021—National Commercial Banks.

Lexington Park

★ 72101 ★   First National Bank of
St. Mary's
429 Great Mills Rd.
Lexington Park, MD 20653-1299
(301)475-8081
Company Type: Subsidiary. Location
Type: Branch office. Officer: Dorothy M.
McFadden, Mgr. Ultimate Parent:
Mercantile Bankshares Corp. SIC: 6021—
National Commercial Banks.

★ 72102 ★   First National Bank of
St. Mary's
Rte. 235 & Millstone Landing Rd.
Lexington Park, MD 20653-9501
(301)475-8081
Company Type: Subsidiary. Location
Type: Branch office. Officer: Sharon
Owens, Mgr. Ultimate Parent: Mercantile
Bankshares Corp. SIC: 6021—National
Commercial Banks.

Lexington Pk

★ 72103 ★   Radio Shack
8 Saint Marys Sq.
Lexington Pk, MD 20653
(301)863-7911
Company Type: Division. Ultimate Parent:
Tandy Corp. SIC: 5065—Electronic Parts &
Equipment Nec.

Linthicum

★ 72104 ★   Advanced Technology
Labroatories
Nursery & Winterson Roads
Linthicum, MD 21090
Ultimate Parent: Westinghouse Electric
Corp. SIC: 3674—Semiconductors &
Related Devices.

★ 72105 ★   Electronic Systems
Group
Friendship Site
Rte. 170 - Camp Meade Rd.
Linthicum, MD 21090
Ultimate Parent: Westinghouse Electric
Corp. SIC: 3679—Electronic Components
Nec.

Linthicum Heights

★ 72106 ★   Advanced Technology
Lab
Intersection of Nursery & Winterson Rd.
Linthicum Heights, MD 21090
Ultimate Parent: Westinghouse Electric
Corp. SIC: 3674—Semiconductors &
Related Devices.

★ 72107 ★   Delta Air Lines Inc.
793 Elkridge Landing Rd.
Linthicum Heights, MD 21090
(410)768-9000
Ultimate Parent: Delta Air Lines, Inc. SIC:
4724—Travel Agencies.

★ 72108 ★   Delta Air Lines Inc.
Airport Investment Bldg.
Linthicum Heights, MD 21090
(410)859-3100
Ultimate Parent: Delta Air Lines, Inc. SIC:
4724—Travel Agencies.

★ 72109 ★   Digital Equipment
Corp.
1306 Concourse Dr. 100
Linthicum Heights, MD 21090
Ultimate Parent: Digital Equipment Corp.
SIC: 5046—Commercial Equipment Nec.

★ 72110 ★   Electronic Systems
Group
Frienship Site
Rte. 170-Camp Mead
Linthicum Heights, MD 21090
Ultimate Parent: Westinghouse Electric
Corp. SIC: 3699—Electrical Equipment &
Supplies Nec; 3679—Electronic
Components Nec; 7629—Electrical Repair
Shops Nec.

★ 72111 ★   Westinghouse
Electric Corp.
Advanced Technology Laboratories
1212 Winterson Rd. & Winterson Rds.
Linthicum Heights, MD 21090
Ultimate Parent: Westinghouse Electric
Corp. SIC: 3674—Semiconductors &
Related Devices; 3679—Electronic
Components Nec; 3825—Instruments to
Measure Electricity; 3823—Process Control
Instruments.

★ 72112 ★   Westinghouse
Electric Corp.
Advanced Technology Laboratory
Intersection of Nursery & Winterson Rds.
Linthicum Heights, MD 21090
Ultimate Parent: Westinghouse Electric
Corp. SIC: 3674—Semiconductors &
Related Devices.

★ 72113 ★   Westinghouse
Electric Corp.
Electronic Systems Group
7323 Aviation Blvd. & Winterson Rd.
Linthicum Heights, MD 21090
Ultimate Parent: Westinghouse Electric
Corp. SIC: 3812—Search & Navigation
Equipment; 7629—Electrical Repair Shops
Nec.

Lothian

★ 72114 ★   Winstead Co. Inc.
Lothian, MD 20711
(410)627-3675
Ultimate Parent: Universal Corp. SIC:
5159—Farm-Product Raw Materials Nec.

Luke

★ 72115 ★   Westvaco Corp.
300 Praft St.
Luke, MD 21540
(301)359-3311
Officer: Roger Dandridge, Vice President.
Ultimate Parent: WestVaco Corp. SIC:
2754—Commercial Printing—Gravure.

★ 72116 ★   Westvaco Corp.
Fine Paper
300 Pratt St.
Luke, MD 21540-1099
Company Type: Division. **Ultimate Parent:**
WestVaco Corp. **SIC:** 2621—Paper Mills.

Lutherville

★ 72117 ★   Nationsbank Banking
Centers
1821 York Rd.
Lutherville, MD 21093
(301)252-2252
Ultimate Parent: Nationsbank Corp.

Lutherville Timonium

★ 72118 ★   Baltimore Gas &
Electric Co.
Mchenry Ralston
Lutherville Timonium, MD 21093
(410)486-4558
Ultimate Parent: Baltimore Gas & Electric
Co.

★ 72119 ★   Black & Decker US
Inc.
5 Castlewall Ct.
Lutherville Timonium, MD 21093-7002
Ultimate Parent: Black & Decker Corp.
SIC: 5072—Hardware; 3423—Hand & Edge
Tools Nec; 3546—Power-Driven Handtools.

★ 72120 ★   Radio Shack
York Ridge Plz.
Lutherville-Timnum, MD 21093
(410)561-2001
Company Type: Division. **Ultimate Parent:**
Tandy Corp. **SIC:** 5046—Commercial
Equipment Nec.

★ 72121 ★   Rite Aid
3 E. Seminary Ave.
Lutherville-Timnum, MD 21093
(410)321-7171
Ultimate Parent: Rite Aid. **SIC:** 5912—Drug
Stores & Proprietary Stores.

Mallow Heights

★ 72122 ★   Circuit City
3551 32nd Ave.
Mallow Heights, MD
(301)630-0875
Ultimate Parent: Circuit City Stores.

Manchester

★ 72123 ★   Westminster Bank &
Trust Co. of Carroll County
2965 Manchester Rd.
Manchester, MD 21102
(410)374-4885
Company Type: Subsidiary. **Location
Type:** Branch office. **Officer:** Donna L.
Healey, Mgr. **Ultimate Parent:** Mercantile
Bankshares Corp. **SIC:** 6021—National
Commercial Banks.

Marion Station

★ 72124 ★   Peninsula Bank
28388 Crisfield-Marion Rd.
Marion Station, MD 21838
(410)623-2388
Company Type: Subsidiary. **Location
Type:** Branch office. **Officer:** James R.
Byrd III, Mgr. **Ultimate Parent:** Mercantile
Bankshares Corp. **SIC:** 6021—National
Commercial Banks.

Marland Area

★ 72125 ★   Hot Shoppes
Cafeterias
Wheaton Plaza
Marland Area, MD
(301)949-7056
Ultimate Parent: Marriott International.

Marlow Height

★ 72126 ★   Standard Federal
Savings Bank
Marlow Height, MD
(301)423-4414
Location Type: Branch office. **Ultimate
Parent:** Standard Federal Bank.

Marlow Heights

★ 72127 ★   Hit or Miss
3915 Branch Ave.
Marlow Heights, MD
(301)899-6484
Ultimate Parent: TJX.

★ 72128 ★   Toys R US
4721 Auth Pl
Marlow Heights, MD
(301)423-6614
Ultimate Parent: Toys "R" US.

Maryland Area

★ 72129 ★   Hot Shoppes
Cafeterias
Prince George's Plz.
Maryland Area, MD
(301)559-7433
Ultimate Parent: Marriott International.

★ 72130 ★   Hot Shoppes
Cafeterias
Langley Park 7900 Nh
Maryland Area, MD
(301)434-0437
Ultimate Parent: Marriott International.

★ 72131 ★   Hot Shoppes
Cafeterias
Prince Georges Plaza
Maryland Area, MD
(301)559-7433
Ultimate Parent: Marriott International.

★ 72132 ★   Hot Shoppes
Cafeterias
Marlow Heights Shopping Mall
Maryland Area, MD
(301)423-6469
Ultimate Parent: Marriott International.

Maugansville

★ 72133 ★   New York Life
Insurance Co.
135 Greenfield Ave.
Maugansville, MD 21767
(301)790-3553
Ultimate Parent: New York Life. **SIC:**
6411—Insurance Agents, Brokers &
Service.

Middle Brook

★ 72134 ★   Nationsbank Banking
Centers
19704 Frederick Rd.
Middle Brook, MD
(301)963-5384
Ultimate Parent: Nationsbank Corp.

Middletown

★ 72135 ★   New York Life
Insurance
Middletown, MD 21769
(301)371-6540
Ultimate Parent: New York Life. **SIC:**
6411—Insurance Agents, Brokers &
Service.

Mitchellville

★ 72136 ★   Nationsbank Banking
Centers
10200 Lake Arbor Way
Mitchellville, MD 20721
(301)817-7810
Ultimate Parent: Nationsbank Corp.

Montgomery

★ 72137 ★   Airborne Freight
Corp.
Montgomery, MD
(301)549-3181
Ultimate Parent: Airborne Freight Corp.

★ 72138 ★   Variable Annuity Life
Insurance
7310 Riotchie Hwy.
Montgomery, MD
(301)768-2330
Ultimate Parent: Variable Annuity Life. **SIC:**
6411—Insurance Agents, Brokers &
Service.

Montgomery Co

★ 72139 ★   Casual Corner
Virginia Seven Corne
Montgomery Co, MD
(301)533-7555
Ultimate Parent: United States Shoe.

★ 72140 ★   Charles Schwab &
Co. Inc. Gaithe
555 Quince Orchard Rd.
Montgomery Co, MD
(301)216-0577
Ultimate Parent: Charles Schwab Corp.

★ 72141 ★   Diebold Inc. Nights
Sundays & H
Montgomery Co, MD
(301)696-8195
Ultimate Parent: Diebold, Inc.

★ 72142 ★   Diebold Inc. Service
Dept
Montgomery Co, MD
(301)696-8195
Ultimate Parent: Diebold, Inc.

★ 72143 ★   Lenscrafters
St Charles Towne Ctr.
Montgomery Co, MD
(301)705-8450
Ultimate Parent: United States Shoe.

★ 72144 ★   Lenscrafters
St Charles Towne Ctr.
Montgomery Co, MD
(301)705-8444
Ultimate Parent: United States Shoe.

★ 72145 ★   Owens-Corning
Fiberglass Corp.
900 17th St. NW
Montgomery Co, MD
(301)296-3296
Ultimate Parent: Owens-Corning.

★ 72146 ★   Standard Federal
Savings Bank
Montgomery Co, MD
(301)696-4000
Location Type: Branch office. **Ultimate
Parent:** Standard Federal Bank.

★ 72147 ★   Standard Federal
Savings Bank
Montgomery Co, MD
(301)696-4430
Ultimate Parent: Standard Federal Bank.

★ 72148 ★   Structure
Lake Forest Mall
Montgomery Co, MD
(301)216-9739
Ultimate Parent: Limited.

★ 72149 ★   Wall Street Journal
the News B
1025 Connecticut Ave. NW
Montgomery Co, MD
(301)862-9200
Ultimate Parent: Dow Jones.

Mount Airy

★ 72150 ★   Mary Kay Cosmetics
Indep Sales
13250 Penn Shop Rd.
Mount Airy, MD 21771
(301)831-7475
Ultimate Parent: Mary Kay Cosmetics.

Mt Rainer

★ 72151 ★   Nationsbank Banking
Centers
3716 Rhode Island Ave.
Mt Rainer, MD
(301)454-8484
Ultimate Parent: Nationsbank Corp.

New Windsor

★ 72152 ★   Shell Service Station
2605 Liberty Rd.
New Windsor, MD 21776
(410)775-0231
Ultimate Parent: Shell Oil Co. **SIC:** 7538—
General Automotive Repair Shops.

North East

★ 72153 ★   Chesapeake Wood
Treating Co.
102 Peninsula Dr.
North East, MD 21901. **SIC:** 2491—
Wood Preserving.

★ 72154 ★   County Banking &
Trust Co.
1 S. Main St.
North East, MD 21901-3999
(410)287-9600
Company Type: Subsidiary. **Location
Type:** Branch office. **Officer:** Laura Sutton,
Mgr. **Ultimate Parent:** Mercantile
Bankshares Corp. **SIC:** 6021—National
Commercial Banks.

★ 72155 ★   Eckerd Drugs
North East Mall
North East, MD 21901
(410)287-5220
Ultimate Parent: Eckerd Corp. **SIC:** 5912—
Drug Stores & Proprietary Stores.

★ 72156 ★   New York Life
Insurance Co.
116 S. Main St.
North East, MD 21901
(410)287-8844
Ultimate Parent: New York Life. **SIC:**
6411—Insurance Agents, Brokers &
Service.

Oakland

★ 72157 ★   Bausch & Lomb Inc.
State Hwy. 135
Oakland, MD 21550
(301)334-9933
Officer: Harry Sumtter, Manager. **Ultimate
Parent:** Bausch & Lomb Inc. **SIC:** 3851—
Ophthalmic Goods.

★ 72158 ★   Potomac Edison Co.
471 N. 3rd St.
Oakland, MD 21550-1113
(301)334-1000
Ultimate Parent: Allegheny Power System.
SIC: 4911—Electric Services.

★ 72159 ★   Wood Products Inc.
8th St.
Oakland, MD 21550
(301)334-9451
Officer: Max A. Messenger, President.
Ultimate Parent: Federal Paper Board.
SIC: 2861—Gum & Wood Chemicals.

Ocean City

★ 72160 ★   Hertz Rent-A-Car
Ocean
Ocean City, MD 21842
(410)289-8355
Ultimate Parent: Hertz. **SIC:** 1711—
Plumbing, Heating & Air-Conditioning.

★ 72161 ★   Mary Kay Cosmetics
Walthan
Ocean City, MD 21842
(410)289-7591
Ultimate Parent: Mary Kay Cosmetics. **SIC:**
5999—Miscellaneous Retail Stores Nec.

★ 72162 ★   McDonald's
Hamburgers
32 St.
Ocean City, MD 21842
(410)289-3436
Ultimate Parent: McDonald's. **SIC:** 8021—
Offices & Clinics of Dentists.

★ 72163 ★   Otis Elevator Co.
4206 Coastal Hwy.
Ocean City, MD 21842
(410)524-3773
Ultimate Parent: United Technologies. **SIC:**
1796—Installing Building Equipment Nec.

★ 72164 ★   **Peninsula Bank**
3409 Coastal Hwy.
Ocean City, MD 21842-3332
(410)289-3444
Company Type: Subsidiary. **Location Type:** Branch office. **Officer:** Terri L. Johnson, Mgr. **Ultimate Parent:** Mercantile Bankshares Corp. **SIC:** 6021—National Commercial Banks.

★ 72165 ★   **Peninsula Bank**
12910 Coastal Hwy.
Ocean City, MD 21842-4719
(410)250-3000
Company Type: Subsidiary. **Location Type:** Branch office. **Officer:** Tom Mears, Mgr. **Ultimate Parent:** Mercantile Bankshares Corp. **SIC:** 6021—National Commercial Banks.

Odenton

★ 72166 ★   **Citizens National Bank**
1145 Annapolis Rd.
Odenton, MD 21113-1601
(410)551-6200
Company Type: Subsidiary. **Location Type:** Branch office. **Officer:** Bettie Krietzer, Mgr. **Ultimate Parent:** Mercantile Bankshares Corp. **SIC:** 6021—National Commercial Banks.

★ 72167 ★   **International Paper Co.**
Nevamar Div.
8339 Telegraph Rd.
Odenton, MD 21113-1397
Fax: (410)672-0340
Company Type: Division. **Ultimate Parent:** International Paper Co. **SIC:** 2891—Adhesives & Sealants.

★ 72168 ★   **KMS Group at Piney Orchard**
Odenton, MD 21113
(410)672-5558
Ultimate Parent: Baltimore Gas & Electric Co. **SIC:** 6552—Subdividers & Developers Nec.

★ 72169 ★   **KMS Group at Piney Orchard**
Odenton, MD 21113
(410)672-5558
Ultimate Parent: Baltimore Gas & Electric Co. **SIC:** 6552—Subdividers & Developers Nec.

★ 72170 ★   **Radio Shack**
1554 Annapolis Rd.
Odenton, MD 21113
Company Type: Division. **Ultimate Parent:** Tandy Corp. **SIC:** 5731—Radio, Television & Electronics Stores.

★ 72171 ★   **Scientific Atlanta Inc.**
5100 Philadelphia Way
Odenton, MD 21113
(410)793-0725
Ultimate Parent: Scientific-Atlanta, Inc. **SIC:** 3663—Radio & T.V. Communications Equipment.

Olney

★ 72172 ★   **Exxon of Olney**
18000 Georgia Ave.
Olney, MD 20832
(301)774-6100
Ultimate Parent: Exxon.

★ 72173 ★   **Exxon Service Station**
18000 Georgia Ave.
Olney, MD 20832
(301)774-6100
Ultimate Parent: Exxon.

★ 72174 ★   **First Union National Bank of Maryland**
18100 Town Ctr. Rd.
Olney, MD 20832-1483
(301)774-4434
Company Type: Subsidiary. **Location Type:** Branch office. **Ultimate Parent:** First Union Corp. **SIC:** 6021—National Commercial Banks.

★ 72175 ★   **Mary Kay Cosmetics**
Indep Sales
Olney, MD
(301)774-4227
Ultimate Parent: Mary Kay Cosmetics.

★ 72176 ★   **Nationsbank Banking Centers**
3200 Sandy Rd.
Olney, MD
(301)929-4420
Ultimate Parent: Nationsbank Corp.

★ 72177 ★   **NCR Corp.**
Olney, MD 20832
(301)924-4844
Ultimate Parent: AT&T. **SIC:** 7378—Computer Maintenance & Repair.

★ 72178 ★   **Radio Shack**
Olney Village Mall
Olney, MD
(301)924-2473
Company Type: Division. **Ultimate Parent:** Tandy Corp.

★ 72179 ★   **Radio Shack**
Olney Village Mall
Olney, MD
(301)924-2473
Company Type: Division. **Ultimate Parent:** Tandy Corp.

★ 72180 ★   **Ryder Truck Rental Inc.**
500 Olney-Sandy Rd.
Olney, MD 20832
(301)774-0012
Ultimate Parent: Ryder System.

★ 72181 ★   **Standard Federal Savings Bank**
18100 Village Mart Dr.
Olney, MD 20832
(301)774-3311
Ultimate Parent: Standard Federal Bank.

Owings Mills

★ 72182 ★   **American General Finance**
10201 Reisterstown Rd.
Owings Mills, MD 21117-3605
(410)363-3710
Location Type: Branch office. **Ultimate Parent:** American General Corp. **SIC:** 6141—Personal Credit Institutions; 6162—Mortgage Bankers & Correspondents.

★ 72183 ★   **American General Finance Inc.**
10201 Reisterstown Rd.
Owings Mills, MD 21117-3605
(410)363-3710
Location Type: Branch office. **Ultimate Parent:** American General Corp. **SIC:** 6141—Personal Credit Institutions; 6162—Mortgage Bankers & Correspondents.

★ 72184 ★   **Diebold Inc.**
11447 Cron Hill Dr. J
Owings Mills, MD 21117
Ultimate Parent: Diebold, Inc. **SIC:** 5046—Commercial Equipment Nec.

★ 72185 ★   **First Union National Bank of Maryland**
25 Crossroads Dr.
Owings Mills, MD 21117-5421
(410)356-0212
Company Type: Subsidiary. **Location Type:** Branch office. **Ultimate Parent:** First Union Corp. **SIC:** 6021—National Commercial Banks.

★ 72186 ★   **Fort Howard Corp.**
10100 Reisterstown Rd.
Owings Mills, MD 21117
Ultimate Parent: Fort Howard. **SIC:** 2621—Paper Mills.

★ 72187 ★   **Fort Howard Cup Corp.**
10100 Reisterstown Rd.
Owings Mills, MD 21117-3815
Ultimate Parent: Fort Howard. **SIC:** 2051—Bread, Cake & Related Products; 2656—Sanitary Food Containers; 2676—Sanitary Paper Products; 2679—Converted Paper Products Nec; 3089—Plastics Products Nec.

★ 72188 ★   **Hit or Miss**
9940 Reisterstown Rd.
Owings Mills, MD 21117
(410)363-9891
Ultimate Parent: TJX. **SIC:** 5621—Women's Clothing Stores.

★ 72189 ★   **Macy's**
Town Ctr. Mall
Owings Mills, MD 21117
(410)363-7400
Ultimate Parent: R. H. Macy. **SIC:** 5311—Department Stores.

★ 72190 ★   **PTS Liquidation, Co.**
10461 Mill Run Cir.
Owings Mills, MD 21117
Company Type: Subsidiary. **Officer:** Joseph J. Rava, President. **Ultimate Parent:** Alexander & Alexander Services.

★ 72191 ★   **Radio Shack**
Garrison Forest Plz.
Owings Mills, MD 21117
(410)363-4313
Company Type: Division. **Ultimate Parent:** Tandy Corp. **SIC:** 5065—Electronic Parts & Equipment Nec.

Owingsmills

★ 72192 ★   **Rite Aid**
Garrison Forest Ctr.
Owingsmills, MD 21117
(410)363-0455
Ultimate Parent: Rite Aid. **SIC:** 5912—Drug Stores & Proprietary Stores.

Oxon Hill

★ 72193 ★   **Exxon Service Station**
Livingston & St. Barn
Oxon Hill, MD
(301)839-9897
Ultimate Parent: Exxon.

★ 72194 ★   **Exxon Service Station**
4453 Wheeler Rd.
Oxon Hill, MD 20745
(301)894-3340
Ultimate Parent: Exxon.

★ 72195 ★   **Exxon Service Station**
801 Southern Ave.
Oxon Hill, MD
(301)630-0880
Ultimate Parent: Exxon.

★ 72196 ★   **First Union National Bank of Maryland**
6175 Oxon Hill Rd.
Oxon Hill, MD 20745-3108
(301)839-6073
Company Type: Subsidiary. **Location Type:** Branch office. **Ultimate Parent:** First Union Corp. **SIC:** 6021—National Commercial Banks.

★ 72197 ★   **Kmart**
6163 Oxon Hill Road
Oxon Hill, MD 20745
(301)839-0550
Ultimate Parent: K-Mart.

★ 72198 ★   **McDonald's Hamburgers**
801 Southern Ave.
Oxon Hill, MD
(301)630-5811
Ultimate Parent: McDonald's.

★ 72199 ★   **McDonald's Hamburgers**
5500 St. Barnabas Rd.
Oxon Hill, MD 20745
(301)423-1776
Ultimate Parent: McDonald's.

★ 72200 ★   **McDonald's Hamburgers**
Rte. 5 Charlotte Hall
Oxon Hill, MD
(301)870-8426
Ultimate Parent: McDonald's.

★ 72201 ★   **McDonald's Hamburgers**
9596 Livingston Rd.
Oxon Hill, MD 20744
(301)248-9565
Ultimate Parent: McDonald's.

★ 72202 ★   **McDonald's Hamburgers**
6126 Oxon Hill Rd.
Oxon Hill, MD 20745
(301)839-1070
Ultimate Parent: McDonald's.

★ 72203 ★   **McDonald's Hamburgers**
7100 Allentown Rd.
Oxon Hill, MD 20744
(301)449-1998
Ultimate Parent: McDonald's.

★ 72204 ★   **Nationsbank Banking Centers**
6345 Livingston Rd.
Oxon Hill, MD 20745
(301)817-7740
Ultimate Parent: Nationsbank Corp.

★ 72205 ★   **Payless Shoesource**
6157-A Oxon Hill Rd.
Oxon Hill, MD
(301)567-9089
Ultimate Parent: May Department Stores.

★ 72206 ★   **Radio Shack**
6149 Livingston Rd.
Oxon Hill, MD 20745
(301)567-2011
Company Type: Division. **Ultimate Parent:** Tandy Corp.

★ 72207 ★   **Radio Shack**
6149 Livngstn Rd.
Oxon Hill, MD 20745
(301)567-2011
Company Type: Division. **Ultimate Parent:** Tandy Corp.

★ 72208 ★   **Rite Aid**
Oxon Hill Shopping. Ctr.
Oxon Hill, MD
(301)839-4300
Ultimate Parent: Rite Aid.

★ 72209 ★   **Standard Federal Savings Bank**
6301 Livingston Rd. a
Oxon Hill, MD 20745
(301)567-3100
Location Type: Branch office. **Ultimate Parent:** Standard Federal Bank.

★ 72210 ★   **Washington Inventory Service**
7408 Livngston Rd.
Oxon Hill, MD 20745
(301)567-3991
Ultimate Parent: Huffy.

Pasadena

★ 72211 ★   **Annapolis Banking & Trust Co.**
3201 Mountain Rd.
Pasadena, MD 21122-2056
(410)360-2252
Company Type: Subsidiary. **Location Type:** Branch office. **Officer:** Linda L. Downing, Mgr. **Ultimate Parent:** Mercantile Bankshares Corp. **SIC:** 6021—National Commercial Banks.

★ 72212 ★   **Rite Aid**
Fort Smallwood Rd.
Pasadena, MD 21122
(410)255-5361
Ultimate Parent: Rite Aid. **SIC:** 5912—Drug Stores & Proprietary Stores.

★ 72213 ★   **Winchester Homes Inc.**
7870 Red Lion Way
Pasadena, MD 21122
(410)437-3660
Ultimate Parent: Weyerhaeuser Co. **SIC:** 6531—Real Estate Agents & Managers.

Patuxent River

★ 72214 ★   **First National Bank of St. Mary's**
Cedar Point Rd.
Patuxent River, MD 20670
(301)475-8081
Company Type: Subsidiary. **Location Type:** Branch office. **Officer:** Joan M. Dean, Mgr. **Ultimate Parent:** Mercantile Bankshares Corp. **SIC:** 6021—National Commercial Banks.

Perryville

★ 72215 ★ Coastal Unilube Inc.
950 Principio Furnace Rd.
Perryville, MD 21903
Ultimate Parent: Coastal Corp. SIC:
2992—Lubricating Oils & Greases; 3085—
Plastics Bottles.

Phoenix

★ 72216 ★ Rite Aid
1 Manor Shopping.Ctr.
Phoenix, MD 21131
(410)666-9704
Ultimate Parent: Rite Aid. SIC: 5912—Drug
Stores & Proprietary Stores.

Pittsville

★ 72217 ★ Peninsula Bank
Railroad Ave.
Pittsville, MD 21850-9776
(410)835-8333
Company Type: Subsidiary. Location
Type: Branch office. Officer: Clifton B.
Thaw, Mgr. Ultimate Parent: Mercantile
Bankshares Corp. SIC: 6021—National
Commercial Banks.

Pocomoke City

★ 72218 ★ Campbell Soup Co.
Clarke Ave. PO Box 89
Pocomoke City, MD 21851-0089
Ultimate Parent: Campbell Soup. SIC:
2038—Frozen Specialties Nec.

★ 72219 ★ Chesapeake Wood
Treating
33675 Costen Rd.
Pocomoke City, MD 21851
Ultimate Parent: Chesapeake. SIC: 2491—
Wood Preserving.

★ 72220 ★ Chesapeake Wood
Treating
U.S. 13 North
Pocomoke City, MD 21851
Ultimate Parent: Chesapeake. SIC: 2491—
Wood Preserving.

★ 72221 ★ Chesapeake Wood
Treating Co.
U.S. 13 North
Pocomoke City, MD 21851
Ultimate Parent: Chesapeake. SIC: 2491—
Wood Preserving.

★ 72222 ★ McDonald's
Hamburgers
Linden Dr.
Pocomoke City, MD 21851
(410)957-2777
Ultimate Parent: McDonald's. SIC: 5812—
Eating Places.

★ 72223 ★ Peninsula Bank
600 Linden Ave.
Pocomoke City, MD 21851
(410)957-2553
Company Type: Subsidiary. Location
Type: Branch office. Officer: H. Dennis
Bodley, Mgr. Ultimate Parent: Mercantile
Bankshares Corp. SIC: 6021—National
Commercial Banks.

★ 72224 ★ Peninsula Bank
105 Market St.
Pocomoke City, MD 21851-1024
(410)957-2500
Company Type: Subsidiary. Location
Type: Branch office. Officer: Gloria G.
Pennewell, Mgr. Ultimate Parent:
Mercantile Bankshares Corp. SIC: 6021—
National Commercial Banks.

Poolesville

★ 72225 ★ McDonald's
Hamburgers
19630 Fisher Ave.
Poolesville, MD 20837
(301)349-5920
Ultimate Parent: McDonald's.

Potomac

★ 72226 ★ Crestar Bank MD
9812 Falls Rd.
Potomac, MD 20854-3976
(800)451-2435
Company Type: Subsidiary. Location
Type: Branch office. Officer: Jack Nichols,
Mgr. Ultimate Parent: Crestar Financial
Corp. SIC: 6021—National Commercial
Banks.

★ 72227 ★ Crestar Bank MD
7941 Tuckerman Ln.
Potomac, MD 20854
(301)451-2435
Company Type: Subsidiary. Location
Type: Branch office. Officer: Valerie
Manuel, Mgr. Ultimate Parent: Crestar
Financial Corp. SIC: 6021—National
Commercial Banks.

★ 72228 ★ Exxon Service Station
10127 River Rd.
Potomac, MD 20854
(301)299-9228
Ultimate Parent: Exxon.

★ 72229 ★ First Union National
Bank of Maryland
10128 River Rd.
Potomac, MD 20854
(301)299-1958
Company Type: Subsidiary. Location
Type: Branch office. Ultimate Parent: First
Union Corp. SIC: 6021—National
Commercial Banks.

★ 72230 ★ First Union National
Bank of Maryland
9812 Falls Rd.
Potomac, MD 20854-3976
(301)961-5227
Company Type: Subsidiary. Location
Type: Branch office. Officer: Michelle Karl,
Mgr. Ultimate Parent: First Union Corp.
SIC: 6021—National Commercial Banks.

★ 72231 ★ The Gap
10101 River Rd.
Potomac, MD 20854
(301)983-5020
Ultimate Parent: GAP.

★ 72232 ★ Nationsbank Banking
Centers
10000 Falls Rd.
Potomac, MD 20854
(301)493-7166
Ultimate Parent: Nationsbank Corp.

★ 72233 ★ Potomac Valley Bank
10113 River Rd.
Potomac, MD 20854-4904
(301)365-0828
Company Type: Subsidiary. Location
Type: Branch office. Officer: John Bruning,
Mgr. Ultimate Parent: Mercantile
Bankshares Corp. SIC: 6021—National
Commercial Banks.

★ 72234 ★ Radio Shack
7905 Tuckerman Ln.
Potomac, MD 20854
(301)299-9100
Company Type: Division. Ultimate Parent:
Tandy Corp.

★ 72235 ★ Radio Shack
7905 Tuckerman Ln.
Potomac, MD 20854
(301)299-9100
Company Type: Division. Ultimate Parent:
Tandy Corp.

★ 72236 ★ Rite Aid
Potomac Shopping. Ctr.
Potomac, MD
(301)299-8600
Ultimate Parent: Rite Aid.

Preston

★ 72237 ★ Preston Corp.
151 Easton Blvd.
Preston, MD 21655
(410)673-7151 Fax: (410)673-2925
Officer: George E. Powell III, Chairman.
Ultimate Parent: Yellow Corp.

★ 72238 ★ Preston Trucking Co.,
Inc.
151 Easton Blvd.
Preston, MD 21655
(410)673-7151 Fax: (410)673-2644
Officer: Leo H. Suggs, President. Ultimate
Parent: Yellow Corp.

Prince Frederick

★ 72239 ★ Calvert Bank & Trust
Co.
Rte. 4 & Dares Beach Rd.
PO Box 590
Prince Frederick, MD 20678-0590
(410)535-3535 Fax: (410)535-3504
Company Type: Subsidiary. Location
Type: Branch office. Officer: Harold J.
Kahl, Chairman, President, & CEO.
Ultimate Parent: Mercantile Bankshares
Corp. SIC: 6021—National Commercial
Banks.

★ 72240 ★ Calvert Bank & Trust
Co.
Prince Frederick Shopping Ctr.
Prince Frederick, MD 20678
(410)535-0700
Company Type: Subsidiary. Location
Type: Branch office. Officer: Gail W.
Reeder, Mgr. Ultimate Parent: Mercantile
Bankshares Corp. SIC: 6021—National
Commercial Banks.

★ 72241 ★ Radio Shack
Calvert Village Shopping Ctr.
Prince Frederick, MD 20678
(410)535-1775
Company Type: Division. Ultimate Parent:
Tandy Corp. SIC: 5731—Radio, Television
& Electronics Stores.

Princess Anne

★ 72242 ★ Peninsula Bank
30389 Mt. Vernon Rd.
Princess Anne, MD 21853
(410)651-2404
Company Type: Subsidiary. Location
Type: Branch office. Officer: Kathy M.
Johnson, Mgr. Ultimate Parent: Mercantile
Bankshares Corp. SIC: 6021—National
Commercial Banks.

★ 72243 ★ Peninsula Bank
11738 Somerset Ave.
PO Box 219
Priness Anne, MD 21853-0219
(410)651-2400 Fax: (410)651-0179
Company Type: Subsidiary. Location
Type: Branch office. Officer: Hugh W.
Mohler, President & CEO. Ultimate Parent:
Mercantile Bankshares Corp. SIC: 6021—
National Commercial Banks.

Queenstown

★ 72244 ★ Conagra
Delmarva Div.
Bloomingdale Rd.
Queenstown, MD 21658
(410)827-7423 Fax: (410)827-7559
Company Type: Division. Location Type:
Headquarters. Officer: Harold Marshall,
Plant Manager. Ultimate Parent: Conagra.

Randallstown

★ 72245 ★ Radio Shack
Randallstown Plz.
Randallstown, MD 21133
(410)922-5446
Company Type: Division. Ultimate Parent:
Tandy Corp. SIC: 5731—Radio, Television
& Electronics Stores.

★ 72246 ★ Rite Aid
Liberty Ct.
Randallstown, MD 21133
(410)922-5333
Ultimate Parent: Rite Aid. SIC: 5912—Drug
Stores & Proprietary Stores.

Reisterstown

★ 72247 ★ Radio Shack
Reisterstown Shopping Ctr.
Reisterstown, MD 21136
(410)833-9449
Company Type: Division. Ultimate Parent:
Tandy Corp. SIC: 5731—Radio, Television
& Electronics Stores.

Rising Sun

★ 72248 ★ County Banking &
Trust Co.
Main & Walnut St.
Rising Sun, MD 21911
(410)658-5571
Company Type: Subsidiary. Location
Type: Branch office. Officer: Debbie Jones,
Mgr. Ultimate Parent: Mercantile
Bankshares Corp. SIC: 6021—National
Commercial Banks.

★ 72249 ★ New York Life
Insurance
Montgomery
Rising Sun, MD 21911
(410)658-4808
Ultimate Parent: New York Life. SIC:
6411—Insurance Agents, Brokers &
Service.

Riva

★ 72250 ★ Annapolis Banking &
Trust Co.
Riva Rd. & Admiral
Riva, MD 21140
(410)224-4715
Company Type: Subsidiary. Location
Type: Branch office. Officer: Darlene
Chojnowski, Mgr. Ultimate Parent:
Mercantile Bankshares Corp. SIC: 6021—
National Commercial Banks.

Riverdale

★ 72251 ★ McDonald's
Hamburgers
6100 Balto Ave.
Riverdale, MD 20737
(301)277-7266
Ultimate Parent: McDonald's.

★ 72252 ★ McDonald's
Hamburgers
5600 Riverdale Rd.
Riverdale, MD
(301)277-6849
Ultimate Parent: McDonald's.

★ 72253 ★ Rite Aid
6818 Riverdale Rd.
Riverdale, MD 20737
(301)577-4554
Ultimate Parent: Rite Aid.

Rock Hall

★ 72254 ★ Chestertown Bank of
Maryland
Rte. 20
Rock Hall, MD 21661
(410)639-7400
Company Type: Subsidiary. Location
Type: Branch office. Officer: Patricia A.
Heinefield, Mgr. Ultimate Parent:
Mercantile Bankshares Corp. SIC: 6021—
National Commercial Banks.

Rockville

★ 72255 ★ Ahmanson Morgage
Co.
11821 Parklawn Dr., Ste. 300
Rockville, MD 20852-2539
(301)468-9117
Ultimate Parent: H. F. Ahmanson. SIC:
6162—Mortgage Bankers &
Correspondents.

★ 72256 ★ Banana Republic
Lakefrst Mall
Rockville, MD
(301)417-0061
Ultimate Parent: GAP.

★ 72257 ★   **Bell Atlantic Bus Systems Svc.**
1375 Piccard Dr. Ste. 325
Rockville, MD 20850-4311
(301)417-0010
Ultimate Parent: Bell Atlantic Corp. **SIC:** 7378—Computer Maintenance & Repair.

★ 72258 ★   **Business Systems Support Group Inc.**
1700 Rockvile Pke.
Rockville, MD 20852-1631
(301)881-1177
Ultimate Parent: Avery Dennison Corp. **SIC:** 7371—Computer Programming Services.

★ 72259 ★   **Casual Corner**
White Flint Mall
Rockville, MD 20852
(301)770-1424
Ultimate Parent: United States Shoe.

★ 72260 ★   **Circuit City**
845 Rockville Pke.
Rockville, MD
(301)424-6981
Ultimate Parent: Circuit City Stores.

★ 72261 ★   **Coca-Cola Enterprises**
75 Derwood Cir.
Rockville, MD 20850
(301)762-9160
Ultimate Parent: Coca-Cola Enterprises.

★ 72262 ★   **Continental Banking Co.**
1175 Taft St.
Rockville, MD 20850
(301)424-4901
Ultimate Parent: Midlantic Corp.

★ 72263 ★   **Courtyard by Marriott**
2500 Research Blvd.
Rockville, MD 20850
(301)670-6700
Ultimate Parent: Marriott International.

★ 72264 ★   **Crestar Bank MD**
112 Halpine Rd.
Rockville, MD 20852-1618
(800)451-2435
Company Type: Subsidiary. **Location Type:** Branch office. **Officer:** Jill C. Bremer, Mgr. **Ultimate Parent:** Crestar Financial Corp. **SIC:** 6021—National Commercial Banks.

★ 72265 ★   **Crestar Bank MD**
11921 Rockville Pke., Ste. 102
Rockville, MD 20852-2737
(800)451-2435
Company Type: Subsidiary. **Location Type:** Branch office. **Officer:** Diane Coleman-Brown, Mgr. **Ultimate Parent:** Crestar Financial Corp. **SIC:** 6021—National Commercial Banks.

★ 72266 ★   **Ctx Mortgage Co.**
12300 Twinbrk Pkwy
Rockville, MD
(301)881-0990
Ultimate Parent: Centex.

★ 72267 ★   **Delta Air Lines Inc.**
1700 Rockville Pke.
Rockville, MD 20852
(301)468-2282
Ultimate Parent: Delta Air Lines, Inc.

★ 72268 ★   **Diebold Inc. Bank Equipment**
Rockville, MD
(301)294-2280
Ultimate Parent: Diebold, Inc.

★ 72269 ★   **Diebold Inc. Commercial Sales**
Rockville, MD
(301)294-2250
Ultimate Parent: Diebold, Inc.

★ 72270 ★   **EG & G Washington Analytical Servies Center**
1396 Piccard Dr.
Rockville, MD 20850
(301)840-3000 **Fax:** (301)258-9522
Company Type: Subsidiary. **Officer:** Keith de Clercq, Manager. **Ultimate Parent:** EG & G.

★ 72271 ★   **Exxon Service Station**
200 N. Washington St.
Rockville, MD 20850
(301)762-2333
Ultimate Parent: Exxon.

★ 72272 ★   **Exxon Service Station**
700 Rockville Pike
Rockville, MD 20852
(301)762-4300
Ultimate Parent: Exxon.

★ 72273 ★   **Exxon Service Station**
12600 Twinbrook Pky.
Rockville, MD 20852
(301)881-8511
Ultimate Parent: Exxon.

★ 72274 ★   **Exxon Service Station**
510 Hungerford Dr.
Rockville, MD 20850
(301)762-9889
Ultimate Parent: Exxon.

★ 72275 ★   **First Colony Life Insurance Co.**
11820 Parklawn Dr.
Rockville, MD 20852
(301)770-2266
Ultimate Parent: First Colony Life.

★ 72276 ★   **First Union National Bank of Maryland**
11616 Rockville Pke.
Rockville, MD 20852
(301)961-5100 **Fax:** (301)986-0622
Company Type: Subsidiary. **Officer:** Joseph L. Malone, President & CEO.
Ultimate Parent: First Union Corp. **SIC:** 6021—National Commercial Banks.
Employee Count: 123.

★ 72277 ★   **First Union National Bank of Maryland**
15100 Frederick Rd.
Rockville, MD 20850-1108
(301)424-6141
Company Type: Subsidiary. **Location Type:** Branch office. **Ultimate Parent:** First Union Corp. **SIC:** 6021—National Commercial Banks.

★ 72278 ★   **First Union National Bank of Maryland**
51 Monroe St.
Rockville, MD 20850-2419
(301)251-1303
Company Type: Subsidiary. **Location Type:** Branch office. **Ultimate Parent:** First Union Corp. **SIC:** 6021—National Commercial Banks.

★ 72279 ★   **First Union National Bank of Maryland**
110 Congressional Ln.
Rockville, MD 20852-1503
(301)650-1045
Company Type: Subsidiary. **Location Type:** Branch office. **Ultimate Parent:** First Union Corp. **SIC:** 6021—National Commercial Banks.

★ 72280 ★   **First Union National Bank of Maryland**
5600 Fishers Ln.
Rockville, MD 20852-1750
(301)961-5251
Company Type: Subsidiary. **Location Type:** Branch office. **Officer:** Chinh Arima, Mgr. **Ultimate Parent:** First Union Corp. **SIC:** 6021—National Commercial Banks.

★ 72281 ★   **First Union National Bank of Maryland**
1101 Nelson St.
Rockville, MD 20850-2030
(301)961-5240
Company Type: Subsidiary. **Location Type:** Branch office. **Officer:** Hilda Iqbal, Mgr. **Ultimate Parent:** First Union Corp. **SIC:** 6021—National Commercial Banks.

★ 72282 ★   **First Union National Bank of Maryland**
12244 Rockville Pke.
Rockville, MD 20852
(800)677-3778 **Fax:** (301)986-0622
Company Type: Subsidiary. **Location Type:** Branch office. **Officer:** Glenn E. Kinard, President & CEO. **Ultimate Parent:** First Union Corp. **SIC:** 6021—National Commercial Banks.

★ 72283 ★   **Gap Stores Inc.**
Congressional
Rockville, MD 20852
(301)984-6228
Ultimate Parent: GAP.

★ 72284 ★   **Gap Stores Inc. Mayland Stores**
Congressional
Rockville, MD 20852
(301)984-6228
Ultimate Parent: GAP.

★ 72285 ★   **GE Information Services**
401 N. Washington St.
Rockville, MD 20850
Officer: Hellene S. Runtagh, President & CEO. **Ultimate Parent:** General Electric.

★ 72286 ★   **Gte Supply**
2440 Resrch Blvd.
Rockville, MD 20850
(301)948-1033
Ultimate Parent: GTE.

★ 72287 ★   **Hartford Life the**
11921 Rockvl Pike
Rockville, MD
(301)770-9090
Ultimate Parent: Hartford Life.

★ 72288 ★   **Hit or Miss**
Federal Plaza
Rockville, MD
(301)231-5120
Ultimate Parent: TJX.

★ 72289 ★   **Kids R US**
11818 Rockville Pike
Rockville, MD
(301)770-0660
Ultimate Parent: Toys "R" US.

★ 72290 ★   **Kids R US**
11818 Rockvl Pike
Rockville, MD
(301)770-0660
Ultimate Parent: Toys "R" US.

★ 72291 ★   **Lenscrafters**
Lake Forest Mall
Rockville, MD
(301)948-2691
Ultimate Parent: United States Shoe.

★ 72292 ★   **Liberty Financial Services Inc.**
1401 Rockville Pke.
Rockville, MD
(301)253-0300
Ultimate Parent: Liberty National Bancorp.

★ 72293 ★   **Loyola Fsb Bank Centers Rockvi**
2131 Veirs Mill Rd.
Rockville, MD 20851
(301)424-3377
Ultimate Parent: Loyola Capital Corp.

★ 72294 ★   **Martin Marietta Corp. Srvcs Inc.**
15850 Crabbs Branch Way
Rockville, MD 20855
(301)258-4050
Ultimate Parent: Martin Marietta.

★ 72295 ★   **Mary Kay Cosmetics Indep Sale**
17904 Hollingsworth Dr.
Rockville, MD 20855
(301)840-0618
Ultimate Parent: Mary Kay Cosmetics.

★ 72296 ★   **Mary Kay Cosmetics Indep Sales**
7717 Goodflw Way
Rockville, MD 20855
(301)948-6277
Ultimate Parent: Mary Kay Cosmetics.

★ 72297 ★   **McDonald's Hamburgers**
1390 Rockville Pke
Rockville, MD
(301)881-6811
Ultimate Parent: McDonald's.

★ 72298 ★   **Mellon Bank (MD)**
1647 Rockville Pke.
Rockville, MD 20852-1685
(301)881-6030
Company Type: Subsidiary. **Location Type:** Branch office. **Officer:** Tony McBarnette, Mgr. **Ultimate Parent:** Mellon Bank Corp. **SIC:** 6021—National Commercial Banks.

★ 72299 ★   **Mellon Bank (MD)**
1903 Research Blvd.
Rockville, MD 20850-3163
(301)217-9390
Company Type: Subsidiary. **Location Type:** Branch office. **Officer:** Jeff Stewart, Mgr. **Ultimate Parent:** Mellon Bank Corp. **SIC:** 6021—National Commercial Banks.

★ 72300 ★   **Metropolitan Federal S&L**
502 Hungerford Dr.
Rockville, MD 20850
(301)294-6860
Ultimate Parent: Metropolitan Financial.

★ 72301 ★   **Metropolitan Federal Svgs&Lan**
Rockville, MD
(301)294-6868
Ultimate Parent: Metropolitan Financial.

★ 72302 ★   **Nabanco**
6110 Exectve Blvd.
Rockville, MD 20852
(301)230-0330
Ultimate Parent: First Financial Management Corp.

★ 72303 ★   **Nationsbank Banking Centers**
255 N. Washington St.
Rockville, MD 20850
(301)251-3640
Ultimate Parent: Nationsbank Corp.

★ 72304 ★   **Nationsbank Banking Centers**
11800 Rockville Pike Montr
Rockville, MD
(301)493-7125
Ultimate Parent: Nationsbank Corp.

★ 72305 ★   **Nationsbank Banking Centers**
1601 East Gude Dr.
Rockville, MD 20850
(301)929-4477
Ultimate Parent: Nationsbank Corp.

★ 72306 ★   **Nationsbank Banking Centers**
15911 Frederick Rd. Shady Grove
Rockville, MD
(301)963-5333
Ultimate Parent: Nationsbank Corp.

★ 72307 ★   **Nationsbank Banking Centers**
9210 Corprte Blvd. Shady G
Rockville, MD
(301)963-5390
Ultimate Parent: Nationsbank Corp.

★ 72308 ★   **Nationsbank Banking Ctrs Rockv**
9210 Corprte Blvd. Shady G
Rockville, MD
(301)891-7400
Ultimate Parent: Nationsbank Corp.

★ 72309 ★   **New York Life Insurance Co.**
1130 Rockville Pike
Rockville, MD 20852
(301)770-3800
Ultimate Parent: New York Life. **SIC:** 6411—Insurance Agents, Brokers & Service.

★ 72310 ★   **New York Life Washington Group Sales Office**
Eastern Group Marketing Zone
One Central Plz.
11300 Rockville Pk, Ste. 706
Rockville, MD 20852
(301)770-3800 **Fax:** (301)468-8973
Officer: Kirk Diehl, Group Manager.
Ultimate Parent: New York Life.

★ 72311 ★   **New York Lifestyle Inc.**
1592-C Rockville Pke.
Rockville, MD
(301)881-0442
Ultimate Parent: New York Life.

★ 72312 ★   **Payless Shoesource**
12266 Rockville Pke
Rockville, MD
(301)230-9358
Ultimate Parent: May Department Stores.

Bank Corp. **SIC:** 6021—National Commercial Banks.

★ **72313** ★　**Potomac Valley Bank**
260 E. Jefferson St.
Rockville, MD 20850-2333
(301)340-8660
Company Type: Subsidiary. **Location Type:** Branch office. **Officer:** John Gilfrich, Mgr. **Ultimate Parent:** Mercantile Bankshares Corp. **SIC:** 6021—National Commercial Banks.

★ **72314** ★　**Pulte Home Corp.**
7744-A Epsln Dr.
Rockville, MD
(301)869-9500
Ultimate Parent: Pulte.

★ **72315** ★　**Radio Shack**
1600 Rockville Pk.
Rockville, MD 20852
(301)881-8323
Company Type: Division. **Ultimate Parent:** Tandy Corp.

★ **72316** ★　**Radio Shack**
1592 Rockville Pk.
Rockville, MD 20852
Company Type: Division. **Ultimate Parent:** Tandy Corp. **SIC:** 5065—Electronic Parts & Equipment Nec.

★ **72317** ★　**Radio Shack**
777 Hungerford Dr.
Rockville, MD 20850
(301)279-7557
Company Type: Division. **Ultimate Parent:** Tandy Corp.

★ **72318** ★　**Radio Shack**
777 Hungerford Dr.
Rockville, MD 20850
(301)279-7557
Company Type: Division. **Ultimate Parent:** Tandy Corp.

★ **72319** ★　**Rite Aid**
5600 Fishers Lane
Rockville, MD
(301)881-7721
Ultimate Parent: Rite Aid.

★ **72320** ★　**Rite Aid**
Loehmans Plaza
Rockville, MD
(301)881-7716
Ultimate Parent: Rite Aid.

★ **72321** ★　**Rite Aid**
Loehmansplz
Rockville, MD 20852
(301)881-1910
Ultimate Parent: Rite Aid.

★ **72322** ★　**Shell Oil Co.**
15200 Shady Grove Rd.
Rockville, MD 20850
(301)921-4132
Ultimate Parent: Shell Oil Co.

★ **72323** ★　**Shell Oil Co.**
15200 Shady Grove Rd.
Rockville, MD 20850
(301)921-4132
Ultimate Parent: Shell Oil Co.

★ **72324** ★　**Signature Travel**
1750 Rockville Pke.
Rockville, MD
(301)230-2111
Ultimate Parent: Washington Mutual Savings Bank.

★ **72325** ★　**Sports Authority**
12055 Rockville Pke
Rockville, MD
(301)231-8650
Ultimate Parent: K-Mart.

★ **72326** ★　**Standard Federal Savings Bank**
Rockville, MD
(301)921-6700
Location Type: Branch office. **Ultimate Parent:** Standard Federal Bank.

★ **72327** ★　**Temple-Inland Mortgage Corp.**
1700 Rockvl Pke
Rockville, MD
(301)770-5757
Ultimate Parent: Temple-Inland.

★ **72328** ★　**Tj Maxx**
1776 E. Jefferson St.
Rockville, MD 20852
(301)881-3857
Ultimate Parent: TJX.

★ **72329** ★　**Toys R US**
11800 Rockville Pike
Rockville, MD 20852
(301)770-3376
Ultimate Parent: Toys "R" US.

★ **72330** ★　**Waldenbooks Maryland Stores**
Lake Forest Shopping
Rockville, MD
(301)921-9248
Ultimate Parent: K-Mart.

★ **72331** ★　**Wiltel Inc.**
600 Jefferson St.
Rockville, MD 20852
(301)738-8100
Ultimate Parent: Williams Companies, Inc.

★ **72332** ★　**Winchester Homes Incorporat**
818 W. Diamond Ave.
Rockville, MD
(301)670-1010
Ultimate Parent: Weyerhaeuser Co.

Salisbury

★ **72333** ★　**Acme Markets**
Twilley Ctr.
Salisbury, MD 21801
(410)742-9384
Ultimate Parent: American Stores. **SIC:** 5411—Grocery Stores.

★ **72334** ★　**Acme Markets**
307 Civic Ave.
Salisbury, MD 21801
(410)641-9813
Ultimate Parent: American Stores. **SIC:** 5411—Grocery Stores.

★ **72335** ★　**BFI Waste Systems**
US 13 N
Salisbury, MD 21801
(410)749-1551
Ultimate Parent: Browning-Ferris Industries. **SIC:** 4953—Refuse Systems.

★ **72336** ★　**Browning-Ferris Inc.**
US 13 N
Salisbury, MD 21801
(410)835-2521
Ultimate Parent: Browning-Ferris Industries. **SIC:** 4953—Refuse Systems.

★ **72337** ★　**Campbell Soup Co.**
West Rd. & Isabella PO Box 1618
Salisbury, MD 21801
Ultimate Parent: Campbell Soup. **SIC:** 2038—Frozen Specialties Nec.

★ **72338** ★　**Campbell Soup Co.**
West Rd. PO Box 1618
Salisbury, MD 21802
Ultimate Parent: Campbell Soup. **SIC:** 2038—Frozen Specialties Nec.

★ **72339** ★　**Campbell Soup Co.**
PO Box 1618 West Rd.
Salisbury, MD 21801
Ultimate Parent: Campbell Soup. **SIC:** 2038—Frozen Specialties Nec.

★ **72340** ★　**Casual Corner**
68 Salisbury Mall
Salisbury, MD 21801
(410)546-0998
Ultimate Parent: United States Shoe. **SIC:** 5621—Women's Clothing Stores.

★ **72341** ★　**Dresser Industries Inc.**
Wayne Div.
124 W. College Ave.
Salisbury, MD 21802
Company Type: Division. **Ultimate Parent:** Dresser Industries Inc. **SIC:** 3586—Measuring & Dispensing Pumps.

★ **72342** ★　**Dresser Industries Inc.**
Wayne Division
Administrative Headquarters
124 W. College Ave.
Salisbury, MD 21801
(410)546-6600 **Fax:** (410)546-6821
Company Type: Subsidiary. **Ultimate Parent:** Dresser Industries Inc.

★ **72343** ★　**Eaton Corp.**
Heinemann Products
2300 Northwood Dr.
Salisbury, MD 21801
(410)546-9778
Officer: Tom Wenger, Manager. **Ultimate Parent:** Eaton Corp. **SIC:** 3613—Switchgear & Switchboard Apparatus.

★ **72344** ★　**Eaton Corp.**
Heinemann Products Commercial Controls Div.
2300 Northwood Dr.
Salisbury, MD 21801
(410)546-9778 **Fax:** (410)546-2116
Company Type: Division. **Location Type:** Plant. **Officer:** Steven I. Burack, Managers Business Unit. **Ultimate Parent:** Eaton Corp. **SIC:** 3613—Switchgear & Switchboard Apparatus. **Employee Count:** 435.

★ **72345** ★　**Eaton Corp. Heinemann Products**
2300 Northwood Dr.
Salisbury, MD 21801
Ultimate Parent: Eaton Corp. **SIC:** 3613—Switchgear & Switchboard Apparatus.

★ **72346** ★　**Greyhound Bus Lines**
Snow Hill Rd.
Salisbury, MD 21801
(410)749-5502
Ultimate Parent: Greyhound Lines Inc. **SIC:** 4131—Intercity & Rural Bus Transportation.

★ **72347** ★　**Hertz Rent-A-Car Licensee**
Salisbury Mall
Salisbury, MD 21801
(410)749-2235
Ultimate Parent: Hertz. **SIC:** 7514—Passenger Car Rental.

★ **72348** ★　**K & L Microwave Inc.**
408 Coles Circle
Salisbury, MD 21801-3214
(410)749-2424
Company Type: Subsidiary. **Ultimate Parent:** Dover Corp. **SIC:** 3679—Electronic Components Nec; 3825—Instruments to Measure Electricity; 3675—Electronic Capacitors.

★ **72349** ★　**McDonald's Hamburgers**
Us 13 Northbond
Salisbury, MD 21801
(410)546-5110
Ultimate Parent: McDonald's. **SIC:** 5812—Eating Places.

★ **72350** ★　**McDonald's Hamburgers**
1305 S. Salisbury Blvd.
Salisbury, MD 21801
(410)749-5888
Ultimate Parent: McDonald's. **SIC:** 5812—Eating Places.

★ **72351** ★　**Occidental Chemical**
Rte. 11, Box 37, Goodard Blvd.
Salisbury, MD 21801
Ultimate Parent: Occidental Petroleum Corp. **SIC:** 3081—Unsupported Plastics Film & Sheet; 2754—Commercial Printing—Gravure.

★ **72352** ★　**Occidental Chemical Corp.**
Rte. 11 Box 37 Goodard Pky.
Salisbury, MD 21801
Ultimate Parent: Occidental Petroleum Corp. **SIC:** 3081—Unsupported Plastics Film & Sheet; 3083—Laminated Plastics Plate & Sheet; 2754—Commercial Printing—Gravure.

★ **72353** ★　**Occidental Chemical Corp.**
Rte. 11, Box 37, Goddard Pky.
Salisbury, MD 21801
Ultimate Parent: Occidental Petroleum Corp. **SIC:** 3000—Rubber & Miscellaneous Plastics Products.

★ **72354** ★　**Peninsula Bank**
110 N. Division St.
Salisbury, MD 21801-4942
(410)543-2400
Company Type: Subsidiary. **Location Type:** Branch office. **Officer:** Thomas W. Keller, Mgr. **Ultimate Parent:** Mercantile Bankshares Corp. **SIC:** 6021—National Commercial Banks.

★ **72355** ★　**Peninsula Bank**
301 Civic Ave.
Salisbury, MD 21801
(410)546-3194
Company Type: Subsidiary. **Location Type:** Branch office. **Officer:** Susan G. Wells, Mgr. **Ultimate Parent:** Mercantile Bankshares Corp. **SIC:** 6021—National Commercial Banks.

★ **72356** ★　**Peninsula Bank**
1512 S. Salisbury Blvd.
Salisbury, MD 21801-7138
(410)543-2743
Company Type: Subsidiary. **Location Type:** Branch office. **Officer:** John J. Simson, Mgr. **Ultimate Parent:** Mercantile Bankshares Corp. **SIC:** 6021—National Commercial Banks.

★ **72357** ★　**Pepsi-Cola Bottling Co.**
330 Snow Hill Rd.
Salisbury, MD 21801
(410)546-1136
Officer: Richard Hazel, President. **Ultimate Parent:** Pepsico. **SIC:** 2086—Bottled & Canned Soft Drinks.

★ **72358** ★　**Petite Sophisticate**
Centre
Salisbury, MD 21801
(410)749-1984
Ultimate Parent: United States Shoe. **SIC:** 5699—Miscellaneous Apparel & Accessory Stores.

★ **72359** ★　**Radio Shack**
Shoppers World Shop
Salisbury, MD 21801
(410)546-9223
Company Type: Division. **Ultimate Parent:** Tandy Corp. **SIC:** 5046—Commercial Equipment Nec.

★ **72360** ★　**Radio Shack**
Shoppers World Shop
Salisbury, MD 21801
(410)546-9223
Company Type: Division. **Ultimate Parent:** Tandy Corp. **SIC:** 5046—Commercial Equipment Nec.

★ **72361** ★　**Rite Aid**
S Salisburyblvd
Salisbury, MD 21801
(410)548-3783
Ultimate Parent: Rite Aid. **SIC:** 5912—Drug Stores & Proprietary Stores.

★ **72362** ★　**Standard Register Co.**
600 Marvel Rd.
Salisbury, MD 21801
(410)546-2211
Officer: S. G. Miller, Manager. **Ultimate Parent:** Standard Register. **SIC:** 2761—Manifold Business Forms.

★ **72363** ★　**Thrift Drug**
309 Civic Ave.
Salisbury, MD 21801
(410)749-0205
Ultimate Parent: J.C. Penney. **SIC:** 5912—Drug Stores & Proprietary Stores.

★ **72364** ★　**Toys R US**
Twilley Centre
Salisbury, MD 21801
(410)742-5900
Ultimate Parent: Toys "R" US. **SIC:** 1711—Plumbing, Heating & Air-Conditioning.

★ **72365** ★　**US Marine/Bayliner**
2305 Northwood Dr.
Salisbury, MD 21801
Ultimate Parent: Brunswick Corp. **SIC:** 3732—Boat Building & Repairing.

Seabrook

★ 72366 ★ **Loral AeroSys**
7375 Executive Pl., Ste. 400
Seabrook, MD 20706
(301)805-0540 **Fax:** (301)805-0517
Officer: David L. Blanchard, President.
Ultimate Parent: Loral Corp.

★ 72367 ★ **New York Life Insurance**
9809 Good Luck Rd.
Seabrook, MD
(301)794-7082
Ultimate Parent: New York Life.

★ 72368 ★ **Rite Aid**
Eastgate Shopping. Ctr.
Seabrook, MD
(301)262-6779
Ultimate Parent: Rite Aid.

Severn

★ 72369 ★ **Ace Hardware**
574 Ritchie Hwy.
Severn, MD 21144
(410)544-0611
Ultimate Parent: Ace Hardware. **SIC:** 5719—Miscellaneous Home Furnishings Stores.

Severna Park

★ 72370 ★ **Annapolis Banking & Trust Co.**
Ritchie Hwy. & McKinsey Rd.
Severna Park, MD 21146-1100
(410)647-2120
Company Type: Subsidiary. **Location Type:** Branch office. **Officer:** Brian Bucci, Mgr. **Ultimate Parent:** Mercantile Bankshares Corp. **SIC:** 6021—National Commercial Banks.

★ 72371 ★ **Banc One Mortgage Corp.**
650 Richie Hwy.
Severna Park, MD
(301)261-2410
Ultimate Parent: Banc One Corp.

★ 72372 ★ **Citgo Service Station**
Mac Kinsey Hwy.
Severna Park, MD 21146
(410)647-2935
Ultimate Parent: Citgo Petroleum. **SIC:** 5541—Gasoline Service Stations.

★ 72373 ★ **First American Bank**
585 Ritchie Hwy.
Severna Park, MD 21146
(410)544-0028
Ultimate Parent: First American Corp. **SIC:** 6159—Miscellaneous Business Credit Institutions.

★ 72374 ★ **First Union National Bank of Maryland**
601 Ritchie Hwy.
Severna Park, MD 21146-3911
(410)544-0028
Company Type: Subsidiary. **Location Type:** Branch office. **Ultimate Parent:** First Union Corp. **SIC:** 6021—National Commercial Banks.

★ 72375 ★ **McDonald's Hamburgers**
Baltimore Annapolis Blvd.
Severna Park, MD 21146
(410)544-0595
Ultimate Parent: McDonald's. **SIC:** 5812—Eating Places.

★ 72376 ★ **North American Van Lines**
4318 Kenilworth Ave.
Severna Park, MD 21146
(410)793-0567
Ultimate Parent: Norfolk Southern. **SIC:** 4214—Local Trucking With Storage.

★ 72377 ★ **Radio Shack**
Severna Park Mall
Severna Park, MD 21146
(410)647-1617
Company Type: Division. **Ultimate Parent:** Tandy Corp. **SIC:** 5065—Electronic Parts & Equipment Nec.

★ 72378 ★ **Radio Shack**
Severna Park Mall
Severna Park, MD 21146
(410)647-1617
Company Type: Division. **Ultimate Parent:** Tandy Corp. **SIC:** 5065—Electronic Parts & Equipment Nec.

★ 72379 ★ **Winchester Homes Inc.**
8375 Jumpers Hole Rd.
Severna Park, MD 21146
(410)544-1366
Ultimate Parent: Weyerhaeuser Co. **SIC:** 1521—Single-Family Housing Construction.

Severnapark

★ 72380 ★ **Rite Aid**
553 Baltimore Annapolis Blvd.
Severnapark, MD 21146
(410)647-0451
Ultimate Parent: Rite Aid. **SIC:** 5912—Drug Stores & Proprietary Stores.

★ 72381 ★ **Rite Aid**
Severna Park Business Ctr.
Severnapark, MD 21146
(410)647-9882
Ultimate Parent: Rite Aid. **SIC:** 5912—Drug Stores & Proprietary Stores.

Silver Spring

★ 72382 ★ **Radio Shack**
15747 Columbia Pick
Sil Sprng-Clo, MD
(301)421-9168
Company Type: Division. **Ultimate Parent:** Tandy Corp.

★ 72383 ★ **AT&T Federal Systems**
8403 Colesville Rd., 16th Fl.
Silver Spring, MD 20910
(301)608-4000 **Fax:** (301)608-5521
Company Type: Subsidiary. **Officer:** Richard J. Lombardi, Vice President, Business Communications Services. **Ultimate Parent:** AT&T.

★ 72384 ★ **Bell Atlantic Mobile Systems**
12520 Prosprty Dr.
Silver Spring, MD 20904
(301)680-2570
Ultimate Parent: Bell Atlantic Corp.

★ 72385 ★ **Centech**
8405 Colesville Rd.
Silver Spring, MD
(301)585-4800
Ultimate Parent: Bethlehem Steel Corp.

★ 72386 ★ **Courtyard by Marriott**
12521 Prosperity Dr.
Silver Spring, MD 20904
(301)680-8500
Ultimate Parent: Marriott International.

★ 72387 ★ **Crestar Bank MD**
3876 International Dr.
Silver Spring, MD 20906-1548
(800)451-2435
Company Type: Subsidiary. **Location Type:** Branch office. **Officer:** Jacquie Oden-Eyler, Mgr. **Ultimate Parent:** Crestar Financial Corp. **SIC:** 6021—National Commercial Banks.

★ 72388 ★ **Crestar Bank MD**
8700 Georgia Ave.
Silver Spring, MD 20910-3606
(800)451-2435
Company Type: Subsidiary. **Location Type:** Branch office. **Officer:** Robert Tapscott, Mgr. **Ultimate Parent:** Crestar Financial Corp. **SIC:** 6021—National Commercial Banks.

★ 72389 ★ **Crestar Bank MD**
13711 Georgia Ave.
Silver Spring, MD 20906-5216
(800)451-2435
Company Type: Subsidiary. **Location Type:** Branch office. **Officer:** Victoria Contreras, Mgr. **Ultimate Parent:** Crestar Financial Corp. **SIC:** 6021—National Commercial Banks.

★ 72390 ★ **Diebold Inc.**
616 Kemp Mill Forest Dr.
Silver Spring, MD 20902
(301)680-0822
Ultimate Parent: Diebold, Inc.

★ 72391 ★ **Dow Jones & Co.**
11501 Columbia Pk.
Silver Spring, MD 20904
(301)622-2900
Officer: William Horner, Manager. **Ultimate Parent:** Dow Jones. **SIC:** 2711—Newspapers.

★ 72392 ★ **Exxon Co.**
12601 Old Columbia Pike
Silver Spring, MD 20904
(301)622-3238
Ultimate Parent: Exxon.

★ 72393 ★ **Exxon Co.**
10711 Columbia Pike
Silver Spring, MD 20901
(301)593-1036
Ultimate Parent: Exxon.

★ 72394 ★ **Exxon Service Station**
701 University Blvd.
Silver Spring, MD
(301)434-5560
Ultimate Parent: Exxon.

★ 72395 ★ **Exxon Service Station**
13420 New Hampshire Ave.
Silver Spring, MD 20904
(301)384-1100
Ultimate Parent: Exxon.

★ 72396 ★ **Exxon Service Station**
13400 Old Columbia Pike
Silver Spring, MD 20904
(301)622-0788
Ultimate Parent: Exxon.

★ 72397 ★ **Exxon Service Station**
12321 Georgia Ave.
Silver Spring, MD 20906
(301)949-1494
Ultimate Parent: Exxon.

★ 72398 ★ **Exxon Service Station**
14011 Georgia Ave.
Silver Spring, MD 20906
(301)871-6777
Ultimate Parent: Exxon.

★ 72399 ★ **First Citizens Mortgage Corp.**
Pershing Dr. & Fenton
Silver Spring, MD
(301)565-8975
Ultimate Parent: First Chicago Corp.

★ 72400 ★ **First Citizens Mortgage Corp.**
12501 Prosprty Dr.
Silver Spring, MD 20904
(301)622-9002
Ultimate Parent: First Chicago Corp.

★ 72401 ★ **First National Bank Maryland**
8701 Georgia Ave.
Silver Spring, MD 20910
Ultimate Parent: First American Corp. **SIC:** 6099—Functions Related to Deposit Banking.

★ 72402 ★ **First Union National Bank of Maryland**
8701 Georgia Ave.
Silver Spring, MD 20910-3713
(301)650-1000
Company Type: Subsidiary. **Location Type:** Branch office. **Ultimate Parent:** First Union Corp. **SIC:** 6021—National Commercial Banks.

★ 72403 ★ **First Union National Bank of Maryland**
12500 Prosperity Dr.
Silver Spring, MD 20904
(301)650-1090
Company Type: Subsidiary. **Location Type:** Branch office. **Ultimate Parent:** First Union Corp. **SIC:** 6021—National Commercial Banks.

★ 72404 ★ **First Union National Bank of Maryland**
8401 Colesville Rd.
Silver Spring, MD 20910-3312
(301)565-7000
Company Type: Subsidiary. **Location Type:** Branch office. **Ultimate Parent:** First Union Corp. **SIC:** 6021—National Commercial Banks.

★ 72405 ★ **First Union National Bank of Maryland**
8630 Georgia Ave.
Silver Spring, MD 20910-3404
(301)961-5227
Company Type: Subsidiary. **Location Type:** Branch office. **Officer:** Carol Kempf, Mgr. **Ultimate Parent:** First Union Corp. **SIC:** 6021—National Commercial Banks.

★ 72406 ★ **First Union National Bank of Maryland**
8737 Colesville Rd.
Silver Spring, MD 20910-3921
(301)588-0276
Company Type: Subsidiary. **Location Type:** Branch office. **Ultimate Parent:** First Union Corp. **SIC:** 6021—National Commercial Banks.

★ 72407 ★ **Greyhound Bus Lines**
8100 Fenton St.
Silver Spring, MD 20910
(301)588-5110
Ultimate Parent: Greyhound Lines Inc.

★ 72408 ★ **Greyhound Bus Lines**
Fare & Schedule Info
Silver Spring, MD
(301)565-2662
Ultimate Parent: Greyhound Lines Inc.

★ 72409 ★ **Hit or Miss**
8661 Colsville Rd.
Silver Spring, MD
(301)588-0353
Ultimate Parent: TJX.

★ 72410 ★ **Hit or Miss**
13834 Outlet Dr.
Silver Spring, MD 20904
(301)572-6757
Ultimate Parent: TJX.

★ 72411 ★ **Information Systems & Services Inc.**
8403 Colesville Rd., Ste. 750
Silver Spring, MD 20910
(301)588-3800 **Fax:** (301)588-3986
Ultimate Parent: Sequa Corp.

★ 72412 ★ **Kmart**
14014 Connecticut Ave.
Silver Spring, MD 20906
(301)871-6640
Ultimate Parent: K-Mart.

★ 72413 ★ **Loyola Fsb Banking Centers**
1372 Lamberton Dr.
Silver Spring, MD 20902
(301)649-5464
Ultimate Parent: Loyola Capital Corp.

★ 72414 ★ **Loyola Fsb Banking Centers Lei**
3866 International Dr.
Silver Spring, MD 20906
(301)598-7000
Ultimate Parent: Loyola Capital Corp.

★ 72415 ★ **McDonald's Hamburgers**
12312 Georgia Ave.
Silver Spring, MD
(301)929-0372
Ultimate Parent: McDonald's.

★ 72416 ★ **McDonald's Hamburgers**
2207 Bel Pre Rd.
Silver Spring, MD 20906
(301)598-8993
Ultimate Parent: McDonald's.

★ 72417 ★ **McDonald's Hamburgers**
504 E. Randolph Rd.
Silver Spring, MD 20904
(301)384-1400
Ultimate Parent: McDonald's.

★ 72418 ★ **Mellon Bank (MD)**
1330 East-West Hwy.
Silver Spring, MD 20910-3245
(301)587-5225
Company Type: Subsidiary. **Location Type:** Branch office. **Officer:** Terry Alsop, Mgr. **Ultimate Parent:** Mellon Bank Corp. **SIC:** 6021—National Commercial Banks.

Union Corp. **SIC:** 6021—National Commercial Banks.

★ 72419 ★ Mid-Atlantic Coca-Cola Bottling Co. Inc.
1710 Elton Rd.
Silver Spring, MD 20903
Ultimate Parent: Coca-Cola Enterprises.
SIC: 2086—Bottled & Canned Soft Drinks.

★ 72420 ★ Nationsbank
Silver Spring, MD
(301)270-5000
Ultimate Parent: Nationsbank Corp.

★ 72421 ★ Nationsbank Banking Centers
8788 Ga Ave.
Silver Spring, MD
(301)270-7260
Ultimate Parent: Nationsbank Corp.

★ 72422 ★ Nationsbank Banking Centers
12125 Viers Mill Rd.
Silver Spring, MD 20906
(301)929-4470
Ultimate Parent: Nationsbank Corp.

★ 72423 ★ Nationsbank Banking Centers
11429 Columbia Pike White
Silver Spring, MD
(301)929-4480
Ultimate Parent: Nationsbank Corp.

★ 72424 ★ Nationsbank Banking Centers
13810 Conn Ave.
Silver Spring, MD
(301)929-4440
Ultimate Parent: Nationsbank Corp.

★ 72425 ★ Nationsbank Banking Centers
10151 Colsville Rd. Woodmoor
Silver Spring, MD
(301)929-4433
Ultimate Parent: Nationsbank Corp.

★ 72426 ★ Nationsbank Banking Centers Si
8722 Flower Ave.
Silver Spring, MD 20901
(301)270-7030
Ultimate Parent: Nationsbank Corp.

★ 72427 ★ Nationsbank Banking Centers Si
8252 Georgia Ave.
Silver Spring, MD 20910
(301)270-7850
Ultimate Parent: Nationsbank Corp.

★ 72428 ★ Nationsbank Banking Centers Si
2101 Belpre Rd.
Silver Spring, MD 20906
(301)929-4455
Ultimate Parent: Nationsbank Corp.

★ 72429 ★ Nationsbank Cash Flow Cards
Silver Spring, MD
(301)891-7400
Ultimate Parent: Nationsbank Corp.

★ 72430 ★ Nationsbank Customer Cash Flow Cards
Silver Spring, MD
(301)270-5011
Ultimate Parent: Nationsbank Corp.

★ 72431 ★ Nationsbank Customer Service
Washington Metro Are
Silver Spring, MD
(301)891-7400
Ultimate Parent: Nationsbank Corp.

★ 72432 ★ Nationsbank Customer Service Dept.
Silver Spring, MD
(301)270-7081
Ultimate Parent: Nationsbank Corp.

★ 72433 ★ New York Life Insurance Co.
8403 Colsvle Rd.
Silver Spring, MD
(301)587-3282
Ultimate Parent: New York Life. SIC: 6411—Insurance Agents, Brokers & Service.

★ 72434 ★ Radio Shack
White Oak Shopng Ctr.
Silver Spring, MD
(301)593-4767
Company Type: Division. Ultimate Parent: Tandy Corp.

★ 72435 ★ Radio Shack
8213 Georgia Ave.
Silver Spring, MD 20910
(301)565-0055
Company Type: Division. Ultimate Parent: Tandy Corp.

★ 72436 ★ Radio Shack
White Oak Shopping Ctr.
Silver Spring, MD 20906
(301)593-5995
Company Type: Division. Ultimate Parent: Tandy Corp.

★ 72437 ★ Radio Shack
15747 Columbia Pick
Silver Spring, MD
(301)421-9168
Company Type: Division. Ultimate Parent: Tandy Corp.

★ 72438 ★ Radio Shack
White Oak Shopping Ctr.
Silver Spring, MD 20906
(301)593-5995
Company Type: Division. Ultimate Parent: Tandy Corp.

★ 72439 ★ Radio Shack
8213 Georgia Ave.
Silver Spring, MD 20910
(301)565-0055
Company Type: Division. Ultimate Parent: Tandy Corp.

★ 72440 ★ Rite Aid
8559 Georgia Ave.
Silver Spring, MD
(301)588-6788
Ultimate Parent: Rite Aid.

★ 72441 ★ Rite Aid
White Oak Shopping. Ctr.
Silver Spring, MD
(301)593-5400
Ultimate Parent: Rite Aid.

★ 72442 ★ Rite Aid
Aspen Hill Shopping. Ctr.
Silver Spring, MD
(301)871-6400
Ultimate Parent: Rite Aid.

★ 72443 ★ Ryder Truck Rental Inc.
1339 East-West Hwy.
Silver Spring, MD
(301)589-6011
Ultimate Parent: Ryder System.

★ 72444 ★ Southland Corp.
1738 Elton Rd.
Silver Spring, MD 20903
(301)445-5494
Ultimate Parent: Southland Corp.

★ 72445 ★ Transamerica Occidental Life Insurance
12501 Prosprty Dr.
Silver Spring, MD 20904
(301)680-9610
Ultimate Parent: Transamerica Occidental Life Insurance.

★ 72446 ★ Wall Street Journal the
11501 Columbia Pike
Silver Spring, MD 20904
(301)622-9612
Ultimate Parent: Dow Jones.

★ 72447 ★ Wall Street Journal the All Ot
11501 Columbia Pike
Silver Spring, MD 20904
(301)622-2900
Ultimate Parent: Dow Jones.

★ 72448 ★ Wall Street Journal the Classi
11501 Columbia Pike
Silver Spring, MD 20904
(301)622-2900
Ultimate Parent: Dow Jones.

★ 72449 ★ New York Life Silver Springs Office
Southeastern Agencies
Metro Plz. Bldg. II
8403 Colesville Rd. 6th Fl.
Silver Springs, MD
(301)587-3282 Fax: (301)587-0277
Officer: Alex Baqir, General Manager.
Ultimate Parent: New York Life.

Simpsonville

★ 72450 ★ Citizens National Bank
6761 Old Columbia
Simpsonville, MD 21150
(410)997-8055
Company Type: Subsidiary. Location Type: Branch office. Officer: J. Edward Harrison, Mgr. Ultimate Parent: Mercantile Bankshares Corp. SIC: 6021—National Commercial Banks.

Sivler Spring

★ 72451 ★ Mellon Bank (MD)
11140 New Hampshire Ave.
Sivler Spring, MD 20904-2692
(301)593-2866
Company Type: Subsidiary. Location Type: Branch office. Officer: Carolyn Bryant, Mgr. Ultimate Parent: Mellon Bank Corp. SIC: 6021—National Commercial Banks.

Snow Hill

★ 72452 ★ Holly Farms Foods, Inc.-Snow Hill Feed Mill
207 Bay St.
PO Box 227
Snow Hill, MD 21863
Ultimate Parent: Tyson Foods, Inc. SIC: 2048—Prepared Feeds Nec.

Snow Hills

★ 72453 ★ Tyson Foods Inc.
6033 Tyson Ln.
Snow Hills, MD 21863
(410)632-1166
Officer: Richard Ennis, Manager. Ultimate Parent: Tyson Foods, Inc. SIC: 2015—Poultry Slaughtering & Processing; 2048—Prepared Feeds Nec.

Solomons

★ 72454 ★ Ace Hardware
20688 Solomons Hwy.
Solomons, MD 20688
(410)326-3222
Ultimate Parent: Ace Hardware. SIC: 6531—Real Estate Agents & Managers.

★ 72455 ★ Calvert Bank & Trust Co.
Patuxent Plz.
Solomons, MD 20688
(410)326-2141
Company Type: Subsidiary. Location Type: Branch office. Officer: Sherry Reid, Mgr. Ultimate Parent: Mercantile Bankshares Corp. SIC: 6021—National Commercial Banks.

South Capital Heights

★ 72456 ★ McDonald's Hamburgers
1420 Addison Rd.
South Capital Heights, MD
(301)499-2778
Ultimate Parent: McDonald's.

South Wheaton

★ 72457 ★ National City Mortgage Co.
310 Wheaton Plaza
South Wheaton, MD
(301)949-1400
Ultimate Parent: National City Corp.

Sparks

★ 72458 ★ BD Primary Care Diagnostics
7 Loverton Cir.
Sparks, MD 21152-0370
(410)316-4000 Fax: (410)316-4066
Company Type: Subsidiary. Officer: Walter Rampata, Vice President & General Manager. Ultimate Parent: Becton Dickinson.

★ 72459 ★ Becton Dickinson Diagnostic Instrument Systems
7 Loverton Cir.
Sparks, MD 21152-0999
(410)316-4000 Fax: (410)316-4066
Company Type: Subsidiary. Officer: Edward J. Ludwig, President. Ultimate Parent: Becton Dickinson.

★ 72460 ★ McCormick & Co., Inc.
18 Loveton Cir.
PO Box 6000
Sparks, MD 21152-6000
(410)771-7301 Fax: (410)527-8289
Officer: Bailey A. Thomas, Chairman of the Board & CEO. Ultimate Parent: McCormick & Co. Inc. Employee Count: 8000.

★ 72461 ★ McCormick & Co. Inc.
18 Loveton Cir.
Sparks, MD 21152
(410)771-7301
Company Type: Headquarters. Officer: Bailey A. Thomas. Employee Count: 8600. Sales: 1557 M. Fortune 500: Largest U.S. Industrial Corporations: Ranking 270.

Sparrows Poin

★ 72462 ★ Air Products & Chemicals
Reservoir
Sparrows Poin, MD 21052
(410)477-2882
Ultimate Parent: Air Products & Chemicals, Inc.

Sparrows Point

★ 72463 ★ Bethlehem Steel Corp.
Baltimore Marine
Sparrows Point Shipyard
Sparrows Point, MD 21219
Company Type: Division. Ultimate Parent: Bethlehem Steel Corp. SIC: 3731—Ship Building & Repairing.

★ 72464 ★ Bethlehem Steel Corp.
Bethship Div.
Sparrows Point Shipyard
Sparrows Point, MD 21219-2599
Ultimate Parent: Bethlehem Steel Corp.
SIC: 3731—Ship Building & Repairing.

★ 72465 ★ Bethlehem Steel Corp.
Marine
Sparrows Point Shipyard
Sparrows Point, MD 21219
Company Type: Division. Ultimate Parent: Bethlehem Steel Corp. SIC: 3731—Ship Building & Repairing.

★ 72466 ★ Bethlehem Steel Corp.
Sparrows Point Div.
Main Office Bldg., Rte. 151
Sparrows Point, MD 21219
(410)388-3000
Company Type: Division. Officer: Duane R. Dunham, President. Ultimate Parent: Bethlehem Steel Corp. SIC: 3312—Blast Furnaces & Steel Mills; 3316—Cold-Finishing of Steel Shapes.

★ 72467 ★ Bethlehem Steel Corp.
Sparrows Point Division
5111 Northpoint Blvd.
Sparrows Point, MD 21219
(410)388-7201
Company Type: Subsidiary. Officer: Duane R. Dunham, President. Ultimate Parent: Bethlehem Steel Corp.

★ 72468 ★ **Bethlehem Steel Corp.**
Sparrows Point Plant
5111 N. Point Blvd.
Sparrows Point, MD 21219
Location Type: Plant. **Ultimate Parent:** Bethlehem Steel Corp. **SIC:** 3312—Blast Furnaces & Steel Mills; 3316— Cold-Finishing of Steel Shapes.

St Michaels

★ 72469 ★ **St Michaels Bank**
Talbot St.
St Michaels, MD 21663
(410)745-5091
Ultimate Parent: Mercantile Bankshares Corp. **SIC:** 6022—State Commercial Banks.

★ 72470 ★ **St Michaels Bank**
Rural Route 33
St Michaels, MD 21663
(410)745-5131
Ultimate Parent: Mercantile Bankshares Corp. **SIC:** 6162—Mortgage Bankers & Correspondents.

St. Charles

★ 72471 ★ **Nationsbank Banking Centers**
300 Smallwood Village Ctr.
St. Charles, MD 20602
(301)645-3330
Ultimate Parent: Nationsbank Corp.

St. Michaels

★ 72472 ★ **St. Michaels Bank**
213 Talbot St.
PO Box 70
St. Michaels, MD 21663-0070
(410)745-5091 **Fax:** (410)745-3590
Company Type: Subsidiary. **Location Type:** Branch office. **Officer:** William W. Duncan Jr., President & CEO. **Ultimate Parent:** Mercantile Bankshares Corp. **SIC:** 6021—National Commercial Banks.

★ 72473 ★ **St. Michaels Bank**
Rte. 33 & Lincoln Ave.
St. Michaels, MD 21663
(410)475-3770
Company Type: Subsidiary. **Location Type:** Branch office. **Officer:** Milly Wroten, Mgr. **Ultimate Parent:** Mercantile Bankshares Corp. **SIC:** 6021—National Commercial Banks.

Sudlersville

★ 72474 ★ **Chestertown Bank of Maryland**
Main St.
Sudlersville, MD 21668
(410)438-3181
Company Type: Subsidiary. **Location Type:** Branch office. **Officer:** Thomas F. Walls, Mgr. **Ultimate Parent:** Mercantile Bankshares Corp. **SIC:** 6021—National Commercial Banks.

Suitland

★ 72475 ★ **Exxon Co.**
4785 Allentown Rd.
Suitland, MD 20746
(301)736-1122
Ultimate Parent: Exxon.

★ 72476 ★ **Kmart**
3911 St. Barnabas Rd.
Suitland, MD 20746
(301)423-4990
Ultimate Parent: K-Mart.

★ 72477 ★ **McDonald's Hamburgers**
4777 Allentown Rd.
Suitland, MD 20746
(301)735-1641
Ultimate Parent: McDonald's.

★ 72478 ★ **McDonald's Hamburgers**
4835 Silver Hill Rd.
Suitland, MD 20746
(301)735-1683
Ultimate Parent: McDonald's.

★ 72479 ★ **Nationsbank Banking Centers**
6950 Carroll Ave.
Suitland, MD
(301)270-7095
Ultimate Parent: Nationsbank Corp.

★ 72480 ★ **Nationsbank Banking Centers**
4831 Silver Hill Rd.
Suitland, MD 20746
(301)817-7770
Ultimate Parent: Nationsbank Corp.

★ 72481 ★ **Price Club**
4501 Auth Pl
Suitland, MD 20746
(301)423-6303
Ultimate Parent: Price.

★ 72482 ★ **Rite Aid**
4705 Silver Hillrd
Suitland, MD 20746
(301)736-2900
Ultimate Parent: Rite Aid.

Sumner

★ 72483 ★ **Potomac Valley Bank**
4701 Sangamore Rd.
Sumner, MD 20816-2508
(301)229-0100
Company Type: Subsidiary. **Location Type:** Branch office. **Officer:** Harold Butler, Mgr. **Ultimate Parent:** Mercantile Bankshares Corp. **SIC:** 6021—National Commercial Banks.

Sw

★ 72484 ★ **Casual Corner**
408 L'enfant Plaza Ctr.
Sw, MD
(301)554-5240
Ultimate Parent: United States Shoe.

Sykesville

★ 72485 ★ **Radio Shack**
Carrolltown Shopping Ctr.
Sykesville, MD 21784
(410)795-7611
Company Type: Division. **Ultimate Parent:** Tandy Corp. **SIC:** 5731—Radio, Television & Electronics Stores.

★ 72486 ★ **Radio Shack**
Carrolltowne Shopping Ctr.
Sykesville, MD 21784
(410)795-7611
Company Type: Division. **Ultimate Parent:** Tandy Corp. **SIC:** 5731—Radio, Television & Electronics Stores.

★ 72487 ★ **Rite Aid**
Carrolltown Mall Pl.
Sykesville, MD 21784
(410)795-0660
Ultimate Parent: Rite Aid. **SIC:** 5912—Drug Stores & Proprietary Stores.

Takoma Park

★ 72488 ★ **Exxon Service Station**
6900 Nh Ave.
Takoma Park, MD
(301)270-6688
Ultimate Parent: Exxon.

★ 72489 ★ **McDonald's Hamburgers**
6301 New Hampshire Ave.
Takoma Park, MD
(301)270-2749
Ultimate Parent: McDonald's.

Taneytown

★ 72490 ★ **Mary Kay Cosmetics**
463 Berry Ct
Taneytown, MD 21787
(410)751-1302
Ultimate Parent: Mary Kay Cosmetics. **SIC:** 5999—Miscellaneous Retail Stores Nec.

Temple Hills

★ 72491 ★ **Exxon Service Station**
6211 Old Branch Ave.
Temple Hills, MD 20748
(301)449-8181
Ultimate Parent: Exxon.

★ 72492 ★ **Exxon Service Station**
5622 St. Barnabas Rd.
Temple Hills, MD 20745
(301)894-2611
Ultimate Parent: Exxon.

★ 72493 ★ **First Security Mortgage**
5833 Allentown Way
Temple Hills, MD 20748
(301)449-3700
Ultimate Parent: First Security Corp.

★ 72494 ★ **Nationsbank Banking Centers**
6323 Allentown Rd.
Temple Hills, MD 20748
(301)817-7780
Ultimate Parent: Nationsbank Corp.

★ 72495 ★ **Nationsbank Banking Centers**
2324 Ivrsn St.
Temple Hills, MD 20748
(301)817-7720
Ultimate Parent: Nationsbank Corp.

★ 72496 ★ **Quality Care Dialysis Center**
6357 Old Branch Ave.
Temple Hills, MD 20748
(301)449-4166
Ultimate Parent: W. R. Grace.

★ 72497 ★ **Radio Shack**
3911 Branch Ave.
Temple Hills, MD 20748
(301)423-7505
Company Type: Division. **Ultimate Parent:** Tandy Corp.

★ 72498 ★ **Rite Aid**
Marlow Heights Shopping. Ctr.
Temple Hills, MD
(301)423-3005
Ultimate Parent: Rite Aid.

★ 72499 ★ **Rite Aid**
Rosecroft Shopping. Ctr.
Temple Hills, MD
(301)630-9200
Ultimate Parent: Rite Aid.

★ 72500 ★ **Southland Corp.**
6311 Allentown Rd.
Temple Hills, MD 20748
(301)449-1012
Ultimate Parent: Southland Corp.

Tilghman

★ 72501 ★ **St. Michaels Bank**
Rte. 33 & Main St.
Tilghman, MD 21671
(410)886-2275
Company Type: Subsidiary. **Location Type:** Branch office. **Ultimate Parent:** Mercantile Bankshares Corp. **SIC:** 6021— National Commercial Banks.

Timonium

★ 72502 ★ **Filterite, Plant 1**
2033 Greenspring Dr.
Timonium, MD 21093
Ultimate Parent: Brunswick Corp. **SIC:** 3569—General Industrial Machinery Nec.

★ 72503 ★ **Filterite, Plant 2**
2120 Greenspring Dr.
Timonium, MD 21093
Ultimate Parent: Brunswick Corp. **SIC:** 3569—General Industrial Machinery Nec.

Towson

★ 72504 ★ **Allied-Signal Inc.**
Bendix Communications
1300 E. Joppa Rd.
Towson, MD 21204
Ultimate Parent: Allied-Signal Inc. **SIC:** 3669—Communications Equipment Nec.

★ 72505 ★ **Allied-Signal Inc.**
Communication Systems
1300 E. Joppa Rd.
Towson, MD 21286
Ultimate Parent: Allied-Signal Inc. **SIC:** 3669—Communications Equipment Nec.

★ 72506 ★ **Black & Decker Corp.**
701 E. Joppa Rd.
Towson, MD 21286
(410)716-3900 **Fax:** (410)716-2933
Company Type: Headquarters. **Officer:** Nolan D. Archibald, Chairman of the Board & President. **SIC:** 3546—Power-Driven Handtools; 3553—Woodworking Machinery; 3541—Machine Tools—Metal Cutting Types; 2599—Furniture & Fixtures Nec; 3634—Electric Housewares & Fans; 3635— Household Vacuum Cleaners. **Employee Count:** 37300. **Sales:** 4882 M. **Fortune 500:** Largest U.S. Industrial Corporations: Ranking 106.

★ 72507 ★ **First Union National Bank of Maryland**
25 W. Chesapeake Ave.
Towson, MD 21204-4820
(410)321-4200
Company Type: Subsidiary. **Location Type:** Branch office. **Ultimate Parent:** First Union Corp. **SIC:** 6021—National Commercial Banks.

★ 72508 ★ **Nationsbank Banking Centers**
2 W. Pa Ave.
Towson, MD 21204
(301)385-8370
Ultimate Parent: Nationsbank Corp.

★ 72509 ★ **New York Life Baltimore General Office**
Court Towers
210 W. Pennsylvania Ave., 3rd Fl.
Towson, MD 21204
(410)321-6161 **Fax:** (410)938-8229
Officer: John P. Kauserud III, Manager.
Ultimate Parent: New York Life.

★ 72510 ★ **Power Tools & Accessories**
701 E. Joppa Rd.
Towson, MD 21286
(410)716-7000 **Fax:** (410)716-7021
Company Type: Subsidiary. **Officer:** Gary T. DiCamillo, President. **Ultimate Parent:** Black & Decker Corp.

Union Bridge

★ 72511 ★ **New York Life Insurance Co.**
2535 Uniontown Rd.
Union Bridge, MD 21791
(410)775-2469
Ultimate Parent: New York Life. **SIC:** 6411—Insurance Agents, Brokers & Service.

Union Mills

★ 72512 ★ **Westminster Bank & Trust Co. of Carroll County**
3416 Littlestown Pke.
Union Mills, MD 21158-2015
(410)346-7115
Company Type: Subsidiary. **Location Type:** Branch office. **Officer:** Gloria Young, Mgr. **Ultimate Parent:** Mercantile Bankshares Corp. **SIC:** 6021—National Commercial Banks.

Upper Marlboro

★ 72513 ★ **Exxon Service Station**
8700 Pennsylvania Ave.
Upper Marlbor, MD 20772
(301)735-1173
Ultimate Parent: Exxon.

★ 72514 ★ **Butler Paper Co.**
331 Prince Georges Blvd. No. 1658
Upper Marlboro, MD 20772-7410
Location Type: Branch office. **Officer:** Tom Jacokes. **Ultimate Parent:** Alco Standard Corp. **SIC:** 5113—Industrial & Personal Service Paper.

★ 72515 ★　Butler Paper Co.
331 Prince Georges Blvd. No. 1658
Upper Marlboro, MD 20772-7410
Location Type: Branch office. **Officer:** Tom
Jacokes. **Ultimate Parent:** Alco Standard
Corp. **SIC:** 5113—Industrial & Personal
Service Paper.

★ 72516 ★　Exxon Service Station
Rte. 301
Upper Marlboro, MD
(301)627-2504
Ultimate Parent: Exxon.

★ 72517 ★　First Virginia Bank
Maryland
9420 Pennsylvania Ave.
Upper Marlboro, MD 20772-2698
(301)599-8600
Company Type: Subsidiary. **Officer:** Gilbert
R. Glordand, Chairman of the Board.
Ultimate Parent: First Virginia Banks Inc.
SIC: 6022—State Commercial Banks.

★ 72518 ★　First Virginia Bank -
Maryland
9420 Pennsylvania Ave.
Upper Marlboro, MD 20772-3617
(301)599-8600
Company Type: Subsidiary. **Officer:** Gilbert
R. Giordano, Chairman of the Board.
Ultimate Parent: First Virginia Banks Inc.
SIC: 6022—State Commercial Banks.
Employee Count: 131.

★ 72519 ★　Nationsbank Banking
Centers
10600 Campus Way
Upper Marlboro, MD 20772
(301)817-7700
Ultimate Parent: Nationsbank Corp.

★ 72520 ★　Nationsbank Banking
Centers Up
14701 Governor Oden Bowie
Upper Marlboro, MD 20772
(301)386-7753
Ultimate Parent: Nationsbank Corp.

★ 72521 ★　Rite Aid
Marlton Plaza
Upper Marlboro, MD
(301)868-0303
Ultimate Parent: Rite Aid.

★ 72522 ★　Mary Kay Cosmetics
Indep Sales
9904 Cone Ct
Upper Marlborough, MD 20772
(301)868-4918
Ultimate Parent: Mary Kay Cosmetics.

★ 72523 ★　Mary Kay Cosmetics
Indep Sales
12220 Westview Dr.
Upper Marlborough, MD 20772
(301)627-1743
Ultimate Parent: Mary Kay Cosmetics.

★ 72524 ★　Mary Kay Cosmetics
by Teresa W
14101 Kern Ct
Upper Marlborough, MD 20772
(301)952-1392
Ultimate Parent: Mary Kay Cosmetics.

★ 72525 ★　Nordstrom
839 Commerce Dr.
Upper Marlborough, MD 20772
(301)390-7800
Ultimate Parent: Nordstrom.

Vienna

★ 72526 ★　Bell Atlantic Mobile
Systems
1577 Spring Hill Rd.
Vienna, MD 21869
(410)547-1181
Ultimate Parent: Bell Atlantic Corp. **SIC:**
5065—Electronic Parts & Equipment Nec.

Waldorf

★ 72527 ★　Crestar Bank MD
4817-B Festival Way
Waldorf, MD 20601
(800)451-2435
Company Type: Subsidiary. **Location
Type:** Branch office. **Officer:** Jim Lusby,
Mgr. **Ultimate Parent:** Crestar Financial

Corp. **SIC:** 6021—National Commercial
Banks.

★ 72528 ★　First Union National
Bank of Maryland
200 Mall Cir.
Waldorf, MD 20603
(301)645-2900
Company Type: Subsidiary. **Location
Type:** Branch office. **Ultimate Parent:** First
Union Corp. **SIC:** 6021—National
Commercial Banks.

★ 72529 ★　Greyhound Bus Lines
Old Washington Hwy.
Waldorf, MD 20601
(301)645-5334
Ultimate Parent: Greyhound Lines Inc. **SIC:**
4111—Local & Suburban Transit.

★ 72530 ★　Kmart
1266 Us Hwy. 301 S
Waldorf, MD
(301)843-9844
Ultimate Parent: K-Mart.

★ 72531 ★　McDonald's
Hamburgers
180 Mall Circle Dr.
Waldorf, MD
(301)843-4995
Ultimate Parent: McDonald's.

★ 72532 ★　McDonald's
Hamburgers
Rte. 4 Box 27
Waldorf, MD 20601
(301)843-1291
Ultimate Parent: McDonald's.

★ 72533 ★　Radio Shack
Waldorf Shoppers World
Waldorf, MD 20601
(301)843-1611
Company Type: Division. **Ultimate Parent:**
Tandy Corp.

★ 72534 ★　Radio Shack
St Mary's Sq.
Waldorf, MD 20601
(301)863-5855
Company Type: Division. **Ultimate Parent:**
Tandy Corp. **SIC:** 5734—Computer &
Software Stores.

★ 72535 ★　Radio Shack
Waldorf Shoppers World
Waldorf, MD 20601
(301)843-1611
Company Type: Division. **Ultimate Parent:**
Tandy Corp.

★ 72536 ★　Radio Shack
St Mary's Sq.
Waldorf, MD 20601
(301)863-5855
Company Type: Division. **Ultimate Parent:**
Tandy Corp. **SIC:** 5734—Computer &
Software Stores.

★ 72537 ★　Radio Shack
St Chas Town Ctr.
Waldorf, MD
(301)843-5791
Company Type: Division. **Ultimate Parent:**
Tandy Corp.

★ 72538 ★　Washington Inventory
Service
278 N. Washngtn Rd.
Waldorf, MD
(301)843-0192
Ultimate Parent: Huffy.

Walkersville

★ 72539 ★　Fredericktown Bank &
Trust Co.
Rte. 194 & Glade Blvd.
Walkersville, MD 21793
(301)845-6811
Company Type: Subsidiary. **Location
Type:** Branch office. **Officer:** Susan K.
Zimmerman, Mgr. **Ultimate Parent:**
Mercantile Bankshares Corp. **SIC:** 6021—
National Commercial Banks.

Westminster

★ 72540 ★　Bell Atlantic Mobile
1203 New Windsor Rd.
Westminster, MD 21158-6704
(410)876-9356
Ultimate Parent: Bell Atlantic Corp. **SIC:**

4813—Telephone Communications Except
Radiotelephone.

★ 72541 ★　J C Penney Co.
400 N. Ctr. St.
Westminster, MD 21157
(410)848-5100
Ultimate Parent: J.C. Penney. **SIC:** 5399—
Miscellaneous General Merchandise Store.

★ 72542 ★　Radio Shack
Westminster Shopping Ctr.
Westminster, MD 21157
(410)848-4211
Company Type: Division. **Ultimate Parent:**
Tandy Corp. **SIC:** 5065—Electronic Parts &
Equipment Nec.

★ 72543 ★　Radio Shack
Div. of Tandy Corp.
Westminster Shopping Ctr.
Westminster, MD 21157
(410)848-4211
Company Type: Division. **Ultimate Parent:**
Tandy Corp. **SIC:** 5065—Electronic Parts &
Equipment Nec.

★ 72544 ★　Rite Aid
140 S. Villagec
Westminster, MD 21157
(410)848-0212
Ultimate Parent: Rite Aid. **SIC:** 5999—
Miscellaneous Retail Stores Nec.

★ 72545 ★　3M Co.
1030 Baltimore Blvd.
Westminster, MD 21157-7024
(410)848-5920
Company Type: Branch. **Officer:** Patrick
Kotten. **Ultimate Parent:** Minnesota Mining
& Mfg. **SIC:** 2752—Commercial Printing—
Lithographic; 3993—Signs & Advertising
Displays; 7312—Outdoor Advertising
Services.

★ 72546 ★　Waldenbooks
400 N. Ctr. St. 205
Westminster, MD 21157
(410)876-8440
Ultimate Parent: K-Mart. **SIC:** 5999—
Miscellaneous Retail Stores Nec.

★ 72547 ★　Westminster Bank &
Trust Co. of Carroll County
Englar Rd. & Rte. 140
Westminster, MD 21157
(410)848-1940
Company Type: Subsidiary. **Location
Type:** Branch office. **Officer:** Terry L.
Hollinger, Mgr. **Ultimate Parent:** Mercantile
Bankshares Corp. **SIC:** 6021—National
Commercial Banks.

★ 72548 ★　Westminster Bank &
Trust Co. of Carroll County
630 Baltimore Blvd.
Westminster, MD 21157-6197
(410)848-2330
Company Type: Subsidiary. **Location
Type:** Branch office. **Officer:** Leonard P.
Easton, Mgr. **Ultimate Parent:** Mercantile
Bankshares Corp. **SIC:** 6021—National
Commercial Banks.

★ 72549 ★　Westminster Bank &
Trust Co. of Carroll County
71 E. Main
PO Box 29
Westminster, MD 21158-0929
(410)848-9300 **Fax:** (410)876-7737
Company Type: Subsidiary. **Location
Type:** Branch office. **Officer:** Ferdinand A.
Ruppel Jr., President & CEO. **Ultimate
Parent:** Mercantile Bankshares Corp. **SIC:**
6021—National Commercial Banks.

Wheaton

★ 72550 ★　Capezio
Wheaton Plaza
Wheaton, MD
(301)946-7293
Ultimate Parent: United States Shoe.

★ 72551 ★　Circuit City
Wheaton Plaza
Wheaton, MD
(301)946-1580
Ultimate Parent: Circuit City Stores.

★ 72552 ★　Crestar Bank MD
Wheaton Plz. Shopping Ctr.
Wheaton, MD 20902-2538
(800)451-2435
Company Type: Subsidiary. **Location
Type:** Branch office. **Officer:** Helen Poole,
Mgr. **Ultimate Parent:** Crestar Financial
Corp. **SIC:** 6021—National Commercial
Banks.

★ 72553 ★　Exxon Service Station
11290 Veirs Mill Rd.
Wheaton, MD 20902
(301)949-9641
Ultimate Parent: Exxon.

★ 72554 ★　First Union National
Bank of Maryland
Wheaton Plz. Shopping Ctr.
Wheaton, MD 20902-2538
(301)650-1040
Company Type: Subsidiary. **Location
Type:** Branch office. **Ultimate Parent:** First
Union Corp. **SIC:** 6021—National
Commercial Banks.

★ 72555 ★　Gap Stores
Wheaton Plaza
Wheaton, MD
(301)946-4664
Ultimate Parent: GAP.

★ 72556 ★　Gap Stores the
Maryland Stores
Wheaton Plaza
Wheaton, MD
(301)946-4664
Ultimate Parent: GAP.

★ 72557 ★　Kids R US
Employment Office
10901 Georgia Ave.
Wheaton, MD
(301)949-6544
Ultimate Parent: Toys "R" US.

★ 72558 ★　Mellon Bank (MD)
13721 Georgia Ave.
Wheaton, MD 20906-5299
(301)946-1700
Company Type: Subsidiary. **Location
Type:** Branch office. **Officer:** Carol Bobick,
Mgr. **Ultimate Parent:** Mellon Bank Corp.
SIC: 6021—National Commercial Banks.

★ 72559 ★　Mellon Bank (MD)
2335 Glenallen Ave.
Wheaton, MD 20905-3572
(301)946-2607
Company Type: Subsidiary. **Location
Type:** Branch office. **Officer:** Anne Knight,
Mgr. **Ultimate Parent:** Mellon Bank Corp.
SIC: 6021—National Commercial Banks.

★ 72560 ★　Nationsbank
2601 University Blvd.
Wheaton, MD 20902
(301)650-4387
Ultimate Parent: Nationsbank Corp.

★ 72561 ★　Nationsbank Banking
Centers
2601 Univ Blvd. W
Wheaton, MD 20902
(301)495-8022
Ultimate Parent: Nationsbank Corp.

★ 72562 ★　Petite Sophisticate
Wheaton Plaza
Wheaton, MD
(301)942-4012
Ultimate Parent: United States Shoe.

★ 72563 ★　Radio Shack
11147 Viers Mill Rd.
Wheaton, MD 20902
(301)933-6640
Company Type: Division. **Ultimate Parent:**
Tandy Corp.

★ 72564 ★　Radio Shack
13846 Georgia Ave.
Wheaton, MD
(301)871-8300
Company Type: Division. **Ultimate Parent:**
Tandy Corp.

★ 72565 ★　Radio Shack
11147 Viers Mill Rd.
Wheaton, MD 20902
(301)933-6640
Company Type: Division. **Ultimate Parent:**
Tandy Corp.

★ 72566 ★　Radio Shack
13846 Ga Ave.
Wheaton, MD
(410)795-3100 (301)871-8300
Company Type: Subsidiary. **Location Type:** Branch office. **Officer:** William J. Norton, Mgr. **Ultimate Parent:** Mercantile Bankshares Corp. **SIC:** 6021—National Commercial Banks. **Company Type:** Division. **Ultimate Parent:** Tandy Corp.

★ 72567 ★　Waldenbooks
Maryland Stores
Wheaton Plaza
Wheaton, MD
(301)946-0202
Ultimate Parent: K-Mart.

Wheaton Plaza

★ 72568 ★　August Max Woman
Wheaton Plaza, MD
(301)949-1589
Ultimate Parent: United States Shoe.

White Marsh M

★ 72569 ★　J C Penney Co.
White Marsh Mall
White Marsh M, MD 21162
(410)256-3210
Ultimate Parent: J.C. Penney. **SIC:** 7231—Beauty Shops.

Whiteford

★ 72570 ★　Forest Hill State Bank
2408 Whiteford Rd,.
Whiteford, MD 21160-1219
(410)452-5266
Company Type: Subsidiary. **Location Type:** Branch office. **Officer:** Robert A. Schwalenberg, Mgr. **Ultimate Parent:** Mercantile Bankshares Corp. **SIC:** 6021—National Commercial Banks.

★ 72571 ★　Mccorquodale
Process Inc.
2737 Whiteford Rd.
Whiteford, MD 21160
Ultimate Parent: Bowater. **SIC:** 2851—Paints & Allied Products.

Williamsport

★ 72572 ★　Aeroquip Corp.
RR 2, Box 42P
Williamsport, MD 21795
(301)223-8811
Officer: Greg Shaffer, Manager. **Ultimate Parent:** Trinova Corp. **SIC:** 3089—Plastics Products Nec.

★ 72573 ★　Park Corp.
Governors Ln.
Williamsport, MD 21795
(301)223-5296
Ultimate Parent: American Stores. **SIC:** 5511—New & Used Car Dealers.

Winfield

★ 72574 ★　Westminster Bank & Trust Co. of Carroll County
1621 W. Liberty Rd., Sykesville
Winfield, MD 21784-9345
(410)875-2550
Company Type: Subsidiary. **Location Type:** Branch office. **Officer:** Jennifer A. Wright, Mgr. **Ultimate Parent:** Mercantile Bankshares Corp. **SIC:** 6021—National Commercial Banks.

Woodbine

★ 72575 ★　Westminster Bank & Trust Co. of Carroll County
15920 Old Frederick Rd.
Woodbine, MD 21797
(410)795-3100
Company Type: Subsidiary. **Location Type:** Branch office. **Officer:** William J. Norton, Mgr. **Ultimate Parent:** Mercantile Bankshares Corp. **SIC:** 6021—National Commercial Banks.

MISSISSIPPI

Aberdeen

★ 72576 ★   Illinois Central R R Co.
E Commerce
Aberdeen, MS 39730
(601)369-2501
Ultimate Parent: Illinois Central.
SIC: 4011— Railroads Line-Haul Operating.

★ 72577 ★   Lees Carpets
W Commerce
Aberdeen, MS 39730
(601)369-4143
Ultimate Parent: Burlington Industries, Equity. **SIC:** 5713—Floor Covering Stores.

★ 72578 ★   Pizza Hut
101 Hwy. 45 N
Aberdeen, MS 39730
(601)369-6085
Ultimate Parent: Pepsico. **SIC:** 5812—Eating Places.

★ 72579 ★   Super Saver
611 State Hwy. 25 W
Aberdeen, MS 39730
(601)369-7047
Ultimate Parent: Wal-Mart Stores, Inc. **SIC:** 5411—Grocery Stores.

★ 72580 ★   Texaco Distributors
N Meridian
Aberdeen, MS 39730
(601)369-2601
Ultimate Parent: Texaco. **SIC:** 5172—Petroleum Products Nec.

★ 72581 ★   Walker Manufacturing Co.
613 S. Matubba St.
Aberdeen, MS 39730
(601)369-8161
Ultimate Parent: Tenneco Inc. **SIC:** 3714—Motor Vehicle Parts & Accessories.

Ackerman

★ 72582 ★   Hackney Inc.
PO Box 330
Ackerman, MS 39735
Ultimate Parent: Trinity Industries. **SIC:** 3462—Iron & Steel Forgings.

Amory

★ 72583 ★   Black & Decker Corp.
True Temper Sports
Hwy. 25 S
Amory, MS 38821
Company Type: Division. **Ultimate Parent:** Black & Decker Corp. **SIC:** 3317—Steel Pipe & Tubes.

★ 72584 ★   Burlington Northern Railroa
101 Front St. N
Amory, MS 38821
(601)256-4184
Ultimate Parent: Burlington Northern. **SIC:** 4119—Local Passenger Transportation Nec.

★ 72585 ★   Piggly Wiggly
2 Glendale Shopping Ctr.
Amory, MS 38821
(601)256-9757
Ultimate Parent: Brune's. **SIC:** 5411—Grocery Stores.

★ 72586 ★   Red Kap Ind.
Hwy. 278 E.
Amory, MS 38821
(601)256-7181
Officer: Graham Howell, Manager. **Ultimate Parent:** VF Corp. **SIC:** 2325—Men's/Boys' Trousers & Slacks.

★ 72587 ★   Red Kap Ind.
60278 Hatley Rd.
Amory, MS 38821
(601)256-7154
Officer: Graham Howell, Manager. **Ultimate Parent:** VF Corp. **SIC:** 2325—Men's/Boys' Trousers & Slacks.

★ 72588 ★   Texaco Service Station
904 Main St. N
Amory, MS 38821
(601)256-9095
Ultimate Parent: Texaco. **SIC:** 5541—Gasoline Service Stations.

★ 72589 ★   True Temper
Sports Division
PO Box E
Amory, MS 38821-0407
(601)256-5605
Company Type: Branch. **Officer:** Charles H. Brown. **Ultimate Parent:** Black & Decker Corp. **SIC:** 3471—Plating & Polishing; 3317—Steel Pipe & Tubes; 3949—Sporting & Athletic Goods Nec.

Artesia

★ 72590 ★   United Cement Co.
State Hwy. 45
Artesia, MS 39736
Ultimate Parent: Texas Industries. **SIC:** 3241—Cement—Hydraulic.

Ashland

★ 72591 ★   Piggly Wiggly
Ashland, MS 38603
(601)224-6202
Ultimate Parent: Bruno's. **SIC:** 5411—Grocery Stores.

Baldwyn

★ 72592 ★   Red Kap Ind.
911 Hwy. 45 N
Baldwyn, MS 38824
(601)365-3361
Officer: Ken Houston, Manager. **Ultimate Parent:** VF Corp. **SIC:** 2321—Men's/Boys' Shirts; 2325—Men's/Boys' Trousers & Slacks; 2337—Women's/Misses' Suits & Coats.

Batesville

★ 72593 ★   Batesville Casket Co. Inc.
310 Crowne Rd.
Batesville, MS 38606
Ultimate Parent: Hillenbrand Industries. **SIC:** 3995—Burial Caskets.

★ 72594 ★   Crown Cork & Seal Co., Inc.
195 Crown Rd.
Batesville, MS 38606
Ultimate Parent: Crown Cork & Seal. **SIC:** 3411—Metal Cans.

★ 72595 ★   Crown Cork & Seal Co. Inc.
Hwy. 35 North
Batesville, MS 38606
Ultimate Parent: Crown Cork & Seal. **SIC:** 3411—Metal Cans.

★ 72596 ★   Crown Cork & Seal Co. Inc.
Hwy. 35 North
Batesville, MS 38606
Ultimate Parent: Crown Cork & Seal. **SIC:** 3411—Metal Cans.

★ 72597 ★   Parker Hannifin
Hwy. 6 W.
Batesville, MS 38606
Ultimate Parent: Parker Hannifin. **SIC:** 3714—Motor Vehicle Parts & Accessories.

★ 72598 ★   Parker Hannifin Corp.
Hwy. 6 W.
Batesville, MS 38606
Ultimate Parent: Parker Hannifin. **SIC:** 3714—Motor Vehicle Parts & Accessories.

★ 72599 ★   Parker Hannifin Corp. Acd
Hwy. 6 E.
Batesville, MS 38606
Ultimate Parent: Parker Hannifin. **SIC:** 3714—Motor Vehicle Parts & Accessories.

★ 72600 ★   Pepsi-Cola Seven-Up Bottling
180 Corporate Dr.
Batesville, MS 38606
(601)563-8622
Officer: Charles Wooten, Manager. **Ultimate Parent:** Pepsico. **SIC:** 2086—Bottled & Canned Soft Drinks.

★ 72601 ★   Personal Finance Co.
185 Hwy. 51 N
Batesville, MS 38606
(601)563-7617
Ultimate Parent: Minnesota Mutual Life. **SIC:** 6141—Personal Credit Institutions.

★ 72602 ★   United Parcel Service
US 51 S
Batesville, MS 38606
(601)222-8088
Ultimate Parent: United Parcel Service of America. **SIC:** 4215—Courier Services Except by Air.

★ 72603 ★   United Parcel Service
Us 51 S
Batesville, MS 38606
(601)222-8088
Ultimate Parent: United Parcel Service of America. **SIC:** 4215—Courier Services Except by Air.

Bay Springs

★ 72604 ★   Piggly Wiggly
Hwy. 15
Bay Springs, MS 39422
(601)764-2164
Ultimate Parent: Bruno's. **SIC:** 5411—Grocery Stores.

Bay St Louis

★ 72605 ★   Pizza Hut
Us 90 W
Bay St Louis, MS 39520
(601)467-3155
Ultimate Parent: Pepsico. **SIC:** 5812—Eating Places.

★ 72606 ★   Trailway Enterprises
603 Us 90 W
Bay St Louis, MS 39520
(601)467-6004
Ultimate Parent: Greyhound Lines Inc. **SIC:** 4231—Trucking Terminal Facilities.

Bay St. Louis

★ 72607 ★   General Electric Plastics Baymar
Port Bienville Industrial Park
Bay St. Louis, MS 39521-2520
Ultimate Parent: General Electric. **SIC:** 2821—Plastics Materials & Resins.

Belmont

★ 72608 ★   First American National Bank
Hwy. 25 N
Belmont, MS 38827
(601)454-9381
Ultimate Parent: First American Corp. **SIC:** 6022—State Commercial Banks.

★ 72609 ★   First American National Bank
Hwy. 25 N
Belmont, MS 38827
(601)454-9381
Ultimate Parent: First American Corp. **SIC:** 6022—State Commercial Banks.

★ 72610 ★   Piggly Wiggly
627 Hwy. 25 S
Belmont, MS 38827
(601)423-3651
Ultimate Parent: Bruno's. **SIC:** 5411—Grocery Stores.

★ 72611 ★   Underwriters Adjusting Co.
Belmont, MS 38827
(601)454-9542
Ultimate Parent: Continental. **SIC:** 6411—Insurance Agents, Brokers & Service.

Belzoni

★ 72612 ★   Greyhound Bus Lines
108 S. Hayden St.
Belzoni, MS 39038
(601)247-2150
Ultimate Parent: Greyhound Lines Inc. **SIC:** 4131—Intercity & Rural Bus Transportation.

★ 72613 ★   Kentucky Fried Chicken
Hwy. 49 W
Belzoni, MS 39038
(601)247-4434
Ultimate Parent: Pepsico. **SIC:** 5812—Eating Places.

★ 72614 ★   Longs Drug Store
110 E. Jackson St.
Belzoni, MS 39038
(601)247-1695
Ultimate Parent: Longs Drug Stores. **SIC:** 5912—Drug Stores & Proprietary Stores.

Biloxi

★ 72615 ★   Borden Inc.
152 Caillavet St.
Biloxi, MS 39530
(601)432-7856
Location Type: Plant. **Officer:** Norris Sumrall, Plant Manager. **Ultimate Parent:** Borden, Inc. **SIC:** 2024—Ice Cream & Frozen Desserts.

★ 72616 ★   Coast to Coast Seafood Inc.
542 Bayview Ave.
Biloxi, MS 39530
Ultimate Parent: Servistar Corp. **SIC:** 5146—Fish & Seafoods.

★ 72617 ★   Coast to Coast Services
2650 Beach Blvd.
Biloxi, MS 39531
(601)385-1720
Ultimate Parent: Servistar Corp. **SIC:** 7361—Employment Agencies.

★ 72618 ★   Heinz Pet Prods.
185 8th St.
Biloxi, MS 39530
Ultimate Parent: Pet. **SIC:** 2047—Dog & Cat Food.

★ 72619 ★   Heinz Pet Prods.
265 Beach Blvd.
Biloxi, MS 39530
Ultimate Parent: Pet. **SIC:** 2047—Dog & Cat Food.

★ 72620 ★   Heinz Pet Products
265 Beach Blvd.
Biloxi, MS 39530
Ultimate Parent: Pet. **SIC:** 2047—Dog & Cat Food.

★ 72621 ★ **Heinz Pet Products**
185 Eighth St.
Biloxi, MS 39530
Ultimate Parent: Pet. **SIC:** 2047—Dog &
Cat Food.

★ 72622 ★ **Hertz Rent-A-Car**
11138 E. Beach Blvd.
Biloxi, MS 39530
(601)432-1431
Ultimate Parent: Hertz. **SIC:** 7514—
Passenger Car Rental.

★ 72623 ★ **Kentucky Fried
Chicken**
10271 Diberville Blvd.
Biloxi, MS 39530
(601)392-3306
Ultimate Parent: Pepsico. **SIC:** 5812—
Eating Places.

★ 72624 ★ **Kentucky Fried
Chicken**
4060 Pass Rd.
Biloxi, MS 39531
(601)388-3119
Ultimate Parent: Pepsico. **SIC:** 5812—
Eating Places.

★ 72625 ★ **Kroger Co. the**
94013 Pass Rd.
Biloxi, MS 39531
(601)392-7823
Ultimate Parent: Kroger. **SIC:** 5411—
Grocery Stores.

★ 72626 ★ **Kroger Co. the**
490 Iberville Rd.
Biloxi, MS 39531
(601)392-0251
Ultimate Parent: Kroger. **SIC:** 5411—
Grocery Stores.

★ 72627 ★ **Kroger No 395**
10290 Diberville Blvd.
Biloxi, MS 39532
(601)392-0251
Ultimate Parent: Kroger. **SIC:** 5411—
Grocery Stores.

★ 72628 ★ **Lane Bryant**
2630 Beach Blvd.
Biloxi, MS 39531
(601)388-7098
Ultimate Parent: Limited. **SIC:** 5651—
Family Clothing Stores.

★ 72629 ★ **Lerner Shop**
Edgewater Plz.
Biloxi, MS 39531
(601)388-5831
Ultimate Parent: Limited. **SIC:** 5621—
Women's Clothing Stores.

★ 72630 ★ **The Limited**
2630 Beach Blvd.
Biloxi, MS 39531
(601)388-3110
Ultimate Parent: Limited. **SIC:** 5651—
Family Clothing Stores.

★ 72631 ★ **Piggly Wiggly**
424 Howard Ave.
Biloxi, MS 39530
(601)435-5309
Ultimate Parent: Bruno's. **SIC:** 5411—
Grocery Stores.

★ 72632 ★ **Pizza Hut**
W Beach Blvd.
Biloxi, MS 39531
(601)374-2580
Ultimate Parent: Pepsico. **SIC:** 5812—
Eating Places.

★ 72633 ★ **Pizza Hut**
541 Central Ave.
Biloxi, MS 39532
(601)392-9290
Ultimate Parent: Pepsico. **SIC:** 5812—
Eating Places.

★ 72634 ★ **Pizza Hut**
Popps Fwy.
Biloxi, MS 39531
(601)388-4839
Ultimate Parent: Pepsico. **SIC:** 5812—
Eating Places.

★ 72635 ★ **Pizza Hut**
511 Beach Blvd.
Biloxi, MS 39530
(601)374-6651
Ultimate Parent: Pepsico. **SIC:** 5812—
Eating Places.

★ 72636 ★ **Pizza Hut**
2872 Byp
Biloxi, MS 39531
(601)374-5500
Ultimate Parent: Pepsico. **SIC:** 5812—
Eating Places.

★ 72637 ★ **Pizza Hut**
1698 Pass Rd.
Biloxi, MS 39531
(601)864-1111
Ultimate Parent: Pepsico. **SIC:** 5812—
Eating Places.

★ 72638 ★ **Radio Shack**
90 Edgewater Mall
Biloxi, MS 39531
(601)388-6627
Company Type: Division. **Ultimate Parent:**
Tandy Corp. **SIC:** 5731—Radio, Television
& Electronics Stores.

★ 72639 ★ **Star-Kist Foods, Inc.**
PO Drawer 208
Biloxi, MS 39533
(601)374-1373
Company Type: Subsidiary. **Location
Type:** Facility. **Officer:** Gary Ebeling, Plant
General Manager. **Ultimate Parent:** H.J.
Heinz.

★ 72640 ★ **Taco Bell**
3208 Beach Blvd.
Biloxi, MS 39531
(601)388-2292
Ultimate Parent: Pepsico. **SIC:** 5812—
Eating Places.

★ 72641 ★ **Trailways Bus System**
W Railroad
Biloxi, MS 39530
(601)374-4200
Ultimate Parent: Greyhound Lines Inc. **SIC:**
4141—Local Bus Charter Service.

★ 72642 ★ **Western Auto Supply
C**
430 Central Ave.
Biloxi, MS 39532
(601)392-2299
Ultimate Parent: Sears Roebuck & Co.
SIC: 5087—Service Establishment
Equipment.

Booneville

★ 72643 ★ **E. R. Carpenter Co.
Inc.**
500 East Parker Dr.
Booneville, MS 38829
Ultimate Parent: Carpenter. **SIC:** 3086—
Plastics Foam Products.

★ 72644 ★ **Kentucky Fried
Chicken**
513 N. 2nd St.
Booneville, MS 38829
(601)728-4782
Ultimate Parent: Pepsico. **SIC:** 5812—
Eating Places.

★ 72645 ★ **Parker Hannifin Corp.**
200 Parker Dr.
Booneville, MS 38829
Ultimate Parent: Parker Hannifin. **SIC:**
3999—Manufacturing Industries Nec.

★ 72646 ★ **Piggly Wiggly**
103 S. 2nd St.
Booneville, MS 38829
(601)728-7138
Ultimate Parent: Bruno's. **SIC:** 5411—
Grocery Stores.

★ 72647 ★ **Pizza Hut**
429 N. 2nd St.
Booneville, MS 38829
(601)728-3034
Ultimate Parent: Pepsico. **SIC:** 5812—
Eating Places.

★ 72648 ★ **Red Kap Ind.**
200 Bridge St.
Booneville, MS 38829
(601)728-7702
Officer: Tom Collins, Manager. **Ultimate
Parent:** VF Corp. **SIC:** 2325—Men's/Boys'
Trousers & Slacks.

★ 72649 ★ **Trailways Bus System**
Hwy. 4 Bypass
Booneville, MS 38829
(601)728-5988
Ultimate Parent: Greyhound Lines Inc. **SIC:**
4131—Intercity & Rural Bus Transportation.

★ 72650 ★ **Wal Mart Discount
City**
1105 N. 2nd St.
Booneville, MS 38829
Ultimate Parent: Wal-Mart Stores, Inc. **SIC:**
5331—Variety Stores.

Brandon

★ 72651 ★ **Pizza Hut**
91 Reservoir Sq.
Brandon, MS 39042
(601)992-1183
Ultimate Parent: Pepsico. **SIC:** 5812—
Eating Places.

★ 72652 ★ **Pizza Hut**
Hwy. 80 E
Brandon, MS 39042
(601)825-4000
Ultimate Parent: Pepsico. **SIC:** 5812—
Eating Places.

Brookhaven

★ 72653 ★ **Diebold Inc.**
136 E. Chippewa St.
Brookhaven, MS 39601
(601)833-4922
Ultimate Parent: Diebold, Inc. **SIC:** 5044—
Office Equipment.

★ 72654 ★ **First Bank**
750 Brookway Blvd.
Brookhaven, MS 39601
(601)835-3143
Ultimate Parent: Shawmut National Corp.
SIC: 6099—Functions Related to Deposit
Banking.

★ 72655 ★ **Greyhound Bus Lines**
N Jackson
Brookhaven, MS 39601
(601)833-4251
Ultimate Parent: Greyhound Lines Inc. **SIC:**
4111—Local & Suburban Transit; 4131—
Intercity & Rural Bus Transportation.

★ 72656 ★ **Illinois Central
Railroad**
650 N. Railroad Ave.
Brookhaven, MS 39601
(601)833-5021
Ultimate Parent: Illinois Central
SIC: 4119— Local Passenger Transportation

★ 72657 ★ **Kentucky Fried
Chicken**
755 Brookway Blvd.
Brookhaven, MS 39601
(601)833-1033
Ultimate Parent: Pepsico. **SIC:** 5812—
Eating Places.

★ 72658 ★ **Ryder Truck Rental**
Un
Brookhaven, MS 39601
(601)833-0806
Ultimate Parent: Ryder System. **SIC:**
4214—Local Trucking With Storage.

Bruce

★ 72659 ★ **Weyerhaeuser Co.**
Railroad Ave.
Bruce, MS 38915
(601)983-7311
Officer: Bill Dansby, Manager. **Ultimate
Parent:** Weyerhaeuser Co. **SIC:** 2421—
Sawmills & Planing Mills—General.

★ 72660 ★ **Weyerhaeuser Co.**
511 Railroad St.
Bruce, MS 38915
Ultimate Parent: Weyerhaeuser Co. **SIC:**
2421—Sawmills & Planing Mills—General.

Carthage

★ 72661 ★ **Kentucky Fried
Chicken**
205 Hwy. 16 E
Carthage, MS 39051
(601)267-3661
Ultimate Parent: Pepsico. **SIC:** 5812—
Eating Places.

★ 72662 ★ **Piggly Wiggly**
301 S. Van Buren St.
Carthage, MS 39051
(601)267-9291
Ultimate Parent: Bruno's. **SIC:** 4822—
Telegraph & Other Communications.

★ 72663 ★ **Trailways Bus System**
105 Hwy. 35 S
Carthage, MS 39051
(601)267-9129
Ultimate Parent: Greyhound Lines Inc. **SIC:**
4131—Intercity & Rural Bus Transportation.

Charleston

★ 72664 ★ **Piggly Wiggly**
307 W. Main St.
Charleston, MS 38921
(601)647-5550
Ultimate Parent: Bruno's. **SIC:** 5411—
Grocery Stores.

Clarksdale

★ 72665 ★ **ADM Co.**
Lyon Blvd.
Clarksdale, MS 38614
(601)627-9241
Officer: Jack Jennings, Manager. **Ultimate
Parent:** Archer Daniels Midland Co. **SIC:**
2075—Soybean Oil Mills.

★ 72666 ★ **Air Products &
Chemicals, Inc.**
Hwy. 49 S
Clarksdale, MS 38614
(601)624-2547
Ultimate Parent: Air Products & Chemicals,
Inc. **SIC:** 3569—General Industrial
Machinery Nec.

★ 72667 ★ **Archer Daniels
Midland Co.**
PO Box 10
Clarksdale, MS 38614-0010
(601)627-9241
Officer: Jack Jennings. **Ultimate Parent:**
Archer Daniels Midland Co. **SIC:** 2075—
Soybean Oil Mills.

★ 72668 ★ **Archer Daniels
Midland Co. (Adm)**
Lyon Rd.
Clarksdale, MS 38614
Ultimate Parent: Archer Daniels Midland
Co. **SIC:** 2075—Soybean Oil Mills.

★ 72669 ★ **Cooper Tire Co.**
2205 4th St.
Clarksdale, MS 38614
Ultimate Parent: Cooper Tire & Rubber Co.
Inc. **SIC:** 3011—Tires & Inner Tubes.

★ 72670 ★ **Cooper Tire & Rubber
Co.**
2205 Fourth St.
Clarksdale, MS 38614
Ultimate Parent: Cooper Tire & Rubber Co.
Inc. **SIC:** 3011—Tires & Inner Tubes.

★ 72671 ★ **Corbin & Russwin
Architectural**
PO Box 760
Clarksdale, MS 38614-0760
(601)624-8391
Company Type: Headquarters. **Officer:**
Tom Allen. **Ultimate Parent:** Black &
Decker Corp. **SIC:** 3429—Hardware Nec.

★ 72672 ★ **Corbin & Russwin
Architectural Hardware**
Hwy. 322 PO Box 760
Clarksdale, MS 38614
Ultimate Parent: Black & Decker Corp.
SIC: 3429—Hardware Nec.

★ 72673 ★ **Delta Wire Corp.**
110 Industrial Dr.
Clarksdale, MS 38614
Ultimate Parent: Johnson & Johnson. **SIC:**
3315—Steel Wire & Related Products.

★ 72674 ★　　Exxon
1230 Leflore Ave.
Clarksdale, MS 38614
(601)624-2055
Ultimate Parent: Exxon. **SIC:** 5541—
Gasoline Service Stations.

★ 72675 ★　　IBM Corp.
Clarksdale, MS 38614
(601)627-7588
Ultimate Parent: IBM. **SIC:** 5734—
Computer & Software Stores.

★ 72676 ★　　Kentucky Fried
Chicken
Hwy. 61
Clarksdale, MS 38614
(601)627-3844
Ultimate Parent: Pepsico. **SIC:** 5812—
Eating Places.

★ 72677 ★　　Piggly Wiggly
1018 State
Clarksdale, MS 38614
(601)624-9772
Ultimate Parent: Bruno's. **SIC:** 5411—
Grocery Stores.

★ 72678 ★　　Pizza Hut
Hwy. 61 S
Clarksdale, MS 38614
(601)627-4680
Ultimate Parent: Pepsico. **SIC:** 5812—
Eating Places.

★ 72679 ★　　Pizza Hut
Clarksdale Shopping Ctr.
Clarksdale, MS 38614
(601)627-2218
Ultimate Parent: Pepsico. **SIC:** 5812—
Eating Places.

★ 72680 ★　　Shell Food Mart
435 S. State St.
Clarksdale, MS 38614
(601)624-2850
Ultimate Parent: Shell Oil Co. **SIC:** 5411—
Grocery Stores.

★ 72681 ★　　Wal Mart
836 S. State St.
Clarksdale, MS 38614
(601)627-1133
Ultimate Parent: Wal-Mart Stores, Inc. **SIC:**
5311—Department Stores.

Cleveland

★ 72682 ★　　Baxter Healthcare
Corp.
Hwy. 61 N
Cleveland, MS 38732
(601)843-9421
Officer: Jim Kessing. **Ultimate Parent:**
Baxter International. **SIC:** 2834—
Pharmaceutical Preparations; 3841—
Surgical & Medical Instruments; 5122—
Drugs, Proprietaries & Sundries; 3085—
Plastics Bottles; 3089—Plastics Products
Nec.

★ 72683 ★　　Greyhound Bus Lines
Hwy. 61 S
Cleveland, MS 38732
(601)843-5113
Ultimate Parent: Greyhound Lines Inc. **SIC:**
4111—Local & Suburban Transit.

★ 72684 ★　　Kroger Delicatessen
306 E. Sunflower Rd.
Cleveland, MS 38732
(601)846-7484
Ultimate Parent: Kroger. **SIC:** 5499—
Miscellaneous Food Stores.

Clinton

★ 72685 ★　　Kentucky Fried
Chicken
15 W. Lakeview Dr.
Clinton, MS 39056
(601)924-7232
Ultimate Parent: Pepsico. **SIC:** 5812—
Eating Places.

★ 72686 ★　　Kroger Pharmacy
Springride Shopping Ctr.
Clinton, MS 39056
(601)924-7422
Ultimate Parent: Kroger. **SIC:** 5912—Drug
Stores & Proprietary Stores.

★ 72687 ★　　Kroger 377
406 Springridge Rd.
Clinton, MS 39056
(601)924-7421
Ultimate Parent: Kroger. **SIC:** 5499—
Miscellaneous Food Stores.

★ 72688 ★　　Lowe's Home Center
240 PO Box
Clinton, MS 39060
Ultimate Parent: Lowe's. **SIC:** 5039—
Construction Materials Nec.

★ 72689 ★　　Manville Forest
Products Corp.
Industrial Park Dr.
Clinton, MS 39056
Ultimate Parent: Manville Corp. **SIC:**
2600—Paper & Allied Products.

Coffeeville

★ 72690 ★　　Piggly Wiggly of
Coffeeville
400 Oklahoma St.
Coffeeville, MS 38922
(601)675-8253
Ultimate Parent: Bruno's. **SIC:** 5411—
Grocery Stores.

Coldwater

★ 72691 ★　　Black & Decker Corp.
Pop Fastners Division
633 Woods St.
Coldwater, MS 38618-9540
(601)622-5109
Ultimate Parent: Black & Decker Corp.
SIC: 5072—Hardware.

★ 72692 ★　　Mpi Inc.
485 Industrial Dr.
Coldwater, MS 38618
Ultimate Parent: Leggett & Platt Inc. **SIC:**
3000—Rubber & Miscellaneous Plastics
Products.

Collins

★ 72693 ★　　Amerada Hess Corp.
Hwy. 588
Collins, MS 39428
Location Type: Branch office. **Ultimate
Parent:** Amerada Hess. **SIC:** 2911—
Petroleum Refining.

★ 72694 ★　　Colonial Pipeline Inc.
Old Hwy. 49 S
Collins, MS 39428
(601)765-8317
Ultimate Parent: Colonial Pipeline. **SIC:**
4612—Crude Petroleum Pipelines.

★ 72695 ★　　Exxon Co. Terminal
Hwy. 49 S
Collins, MS 39428
(601)765-8918
Ultimate Parent: Exxon. **SIC:** 5172—
Petroleum Products Nec.

★ 72696 ★　　Piggly Wiggly
1001 Holly Ave.
Collins, MS 39428
(601)765-6116
Ultimate Parent: Bruno's. **SIC:** 5421—Meat
& Fish Markets.

★ 72697 ★　　Underwriters
Adjusting Co.
Sunset Rd.
Collins, MS 39428
(601)765-4725
Ultimate Parent: Continental. **SIC:** 6411—
Insurance Agents, Brokers & Service.

Columbia

★ 72698 ★　　Exxon Co. USA
Hwy. 98 Bypass
Columbia, MS 39429
(601)736-3969
Ultimate Parent: Exxon. **SIC:** 5172—
Petroleum Products Nec.

★ 72699 ★　　Piggly Wiggly
Northgate Shopping Ctr.
Columbia, MS 39429
(601)736-5191
Ultimate Parent: Bruno's. **SIC:** 5411—
Grocery Stores.

★ 72700 ★　　Radio Shack
781 Hwy. 98
Columbia, MS 39429
(601)736-2319
Company Type: Division. **Ultimate Parent:**
Tandy Corp. **SIC:** 5719—Miscellaneous
Home Furnishings Stores.

★ 72701 ★　　Wal Mart
807 Hwy. 98
Columbia, MS 39429
(601)731-1193
Ultimate Parent: Wal-Mart Stores, Inc. **SIC:**
5311—Department Stores.

Columbus

★ 72702 ★　　APAC
462 Lake Norris Rd.
Columbus, MS 39701
(601)328-6555
Officer: Bascom A. Atkins Jr., President.
Ultimate Parent: Ashland Oil. **SIC:** 2951—
Asphalt Paving Mixtures & Blocks; 3273—
Ready-Mixed Concrete; 3295—Minerals—
Ground or Treated.

★ 72703 ★　　Beloit Manhattan
402 Yorkville Park Square
Columbus, MS 39702-9677
Ultimate Parent: Harnischfeger Industries.
SIC: 3554—Paper Industries Machinery;
3599—Industrial Machinery Nec.

★ 72704 ★　　Burlington Northern
Railroa
2 Ave. S
Columbus, MS 39701
(601)328-7001
Ultimate Parent: Burlington Northern. **SIC:**
4011—Railroads—Line-Haul Operating.

★ 72705 ★　　Casual Corner
Univ Mall
Columbus, MS 39701
(601)329-2482
Ultimate Parent: United States Shoe. **SIC:**
5621—Women's Clothing Stores.

★ 72706 ★　　Circus World Toy
Stores
Leigh
Columbus, MS 39701
(601)327-5722
Ultimate Parent: Melville. **SIC:** 5945—
Hobby, Toy & Game Shops.

★ 72707 ★　　Columbus Pulp &
Paper Complex
Carson Rd.
Columbus, MS 39703-1830
Ultimate Parent: Weyerhaeuser Co. **SIC:**
2621—Paper Mills; 2611—Pulp Mills.

★ 72708 ★　　Diversitech General
Yorkville Rd.
Columbus, MS 39702
Ultimate Parent: Gencorp. **SIC:** 2295—
Coated Fabrics—Not Rubberized.

★ 72709 ★　　Fleet Finance Inc.
207 5th Ave. S
Columbus, MS 39701
(601)328-0534
Ultimate Parent: Fleet Financial Group.
SIC: 6141—Personal Credit Institutions.

★ 72710 ★　　Gencorp Inc.
133 Yorkville Rd. W
Columbus, MS 39702
(601)327-1522
Officer: Dalton Windham, Manager.
Ultimate Parent: Gencorp. **SIC:** 2295—
Coated Fabrics—Not Rubberized; 3081—
Unsupported Plastics Film & Sheet; 3089—
Plastics Products Nec.

★ 72711 ★　　Gencorp Polymer
Prods.
133 Yorkville Rd. E.
Columbus, MS 39703
Ultimate Parent: Gencorp. **SIC:** 2295—
Coated Fabrics—Not Rubberized.

★ 72712 ★　　Gencorp Polymer
Products
Yorkville Rd.
Columbus, MS 39703
Ultimate Parent: Gencorp. **SIC:** 2295—
Coated Fabrics—Not Rubberized.

★ 72713 ★　　Hertz Rent-A-Car
Licensee
Goldn Tr Rgnl a
Columbus, MS 39701
(601)328-3293
Ultimate Parent: Hertz. **SIC:** 5932—Used
Merchandise Stores.

★ 72714 ★　　IBM Corp.
2212 5th St. N.
Columbus, MS 39701
(601)328-4011
Ultimate Parent: IBM. **SIC:** 5999—
Miscellaneous Retail Stores Nec.

★ 72715 ★　　Kentucky Fried
Chicken
2007 Hwy. 82 E
Columbus, MS 39701
(601)328-8047
Ultimate Parent: Pepsico. **SIC:** 5812—
Eating Places.

★ 72716 ★　　Kentucky Fried
Chicken
703 Hwy. 45 N
Columbus, MS 39701
(601)328-2333
Ultimate Parent: Pepsico. **SIC:** 5812—
Eating Places.

★ 72717 ★　　Kerr-Mcgee Chemical
Corp.
2300 14th Ave. & 20th St. N.
Columbus, MS 39701
Ultimate Parent: Kerr-McGee. **SIC:** 2491—
Wood Preserving.

★ 72718 ★　　McDonalds
Restaurant
1505 Hwy. 45 N
Columbus, MS 39701
(601)328-9444
Ultimate Parent: McDonald's.
SIC: 5812—Eating Places.

★ 72719 ★　　McDonalds
Restaurant
2516 Hwy. 82 E
Columbus, MS 39701
(601)328-7065
Ultimate Parent: McDonald's.
SIC: 5812—Eating Places.

★ 72720 ★　　Pepsi-Cola Bottling
Co.
1447 Industrial Park Rd.
Columbus, MS 39705
(601)328-5061
Officer: Lee Moses, Manager. **Ultimate
Parent:** Pepsico. **SIC:** 2086—Bottled &
Canned Soft Drinks.

★ 72721 ★　　Personal Finance Co.
128 5th Ave. N
Columbus, MS 39701
(601)328-5131
Ultimate Parent: Minnesota Mutual Life.
SIC: 6141—Personal Credit Institutions.

★ 72722 ★　　Pizza Hut
522 Hwy. 82 E
Columbus, MS 39701
(601)328-1222
Ultimate Parent: Pepsico. **SIC:** 5812—
Eating Places.

★ 72723 ★　　Pizza Hut
2215 Hwy. 45 N
Columbus, MS 39701
(601)327-4472
Ultimate Parent: Pepsico. **SIC:** 5812—
Eating Places.

★ 72724 ★　　Pizza Hut
1801 Hwy. 45 N
Columbus, MS 39701
Ultimate Parent: Pepsico. **SIC:** 5812—
Eating Places.

★ 72725 ★　　Radio Shack
Leigh
Columbus, MS 39701
(601)327-5824
Company Type: Division. **Ultimate Parent:**
Tandy Corp. **SIC:** 5065—Electronic Parts &
Equipment Nec.

★ 72726 ★　　Radio Shack
Gateway Shopping Ctr.
Columbus, MS 39701
(601)327-6813
Company Type: Division. **Ultimate Parent:**
Tandy Corp. **SIC:** 5731—Radio, Television
& Electronics Stores.

★ 72727 ★ **Red Kap Ind.**
826 17th Ave. S
Columbus, MS 39701
(601)327-8522
Officer: Frank Culver, Manager. **Ultimate Parent:** VF Corp. **SIC:** 2325—Men's/Boys' Trousers & Slacks; 2339—Women's/Misses' Outerwear Nec.

★ 72728 ★ **Super Saver**
2408 Main
Columbus, MS 39701
(601)328-9973
Ultimate Parent: Wal-Mart Stores, Inc. **SIC:** 5411—Grocery Stores.

★ 72729 ★ **J. L. Teel Co., Inc.**
3602 Hwy. 45 N
Columbus, MS 39701
(601)327-6665 **Fax:** (601)327-6674
Company Type: Division. **Officer:** James L. Teel, President. **Ultimate Parent:** Alco Standard Corp. **SIC:** 5044—Office Equipment; 5046—Commercial Equipment Nec.

★ 72730 ★ **Trailways Bus System**
904 Main St.
Columbus, MS 39701
(601)328-4732
Ultimate Parent: Greyhound Lines Inc. **SIC:** 4131—Intercity & Rural Bus Transportation.

★ 72731 ★ **United Technologies Auto**
401 S. McCrary Rd.
Columbus, MS 39702
(601)328-4150
Officer: David Livingston, Vice President. **Ultimate Parent:** United Technologies. **SIC:** 3621—Motors & Generators; 3714—Motor Vehicle Parts & Accessories.

★ 72732 ★ **United Technologies Electro Systems**
McCrary Rd.
PO Box 2228
Columbus, MS 39704-2228
Ultimate Parent: United Technologies. **SIC:** 3621—Motors & Generators; 3694—Engine Electrical Equipment; 3714—Motor Vehicle Parts & Accessories.

★ 72733 ★ **Weyerhaeuser Co.**
Carson Rd.
Columbus, MS 39701
(601)243-4000
Officer: Paul Jethro, President. **Ultimate Parent:** Weyerhaeuser Co. **SIC:** 2621—Paper Mills.

Corinth

★ 72734 ★ **BASF Inmont Corp.**
Sawyer Rd.
Corinth, MS 38834
(601)287-4130
Ultimate Parent: BASF Corp. **SIC:** 5084—Industrial Machinery & Equipment.

★ 72735 ★ **Caterpillar Inc.**
202 Cardinal Dr.
Corinth, MS 38834
Ultimate Parent: Caterpillar. **SIC:** 3519—Internal Combustion Engines Nec.

★ 72736 ★ **Caterpillar Remanufactured Products Group**
202 Cardinal Dr.
Corinth, MS 38834
Ultimate Parent: Caterpillar. **SIC:** 3519—Internal Combustion Engines Nec.

★ 72737 ★ **Dana Corp.**
Corinth Plant
Fulton & Golding Dr.
Corinth, MS 38834
(601)287-1481
Ultimate Parent: Dana Corp. **SIC:** 3561—Pumps & Pumping Equipment; 3569—General Industrial Machinery Nec.

★ 72738 ★ **Dana Corp.**
Mobile Fluid Products Div.
Fulton Dr.
Corinth, MS 38834
Company Type: Division. **Ultimate Parent:** Dana Corp. **SIC:** 3561—Pumps & Pumping Equipment.

★ 72739 ★ **Kentucky Fried Chicken**
1121 PO Box
Corinth, MS 38834
(601)286-9334
Ultimate Parent: Pepsico. **SIC:** 5812—Eating Places.

★ 72740 ★ **Kimberly-Clark Corp.**
Rte. 8 Kendrick Rd.
Corinth, MS 38834
Ultimate Parent: Kimberly-Clark. **SIC:** 2297—Nonwoven Fabrics.

★ 72741 ★ **Pepsi-Cola Distributing Co.**
1502 S. Johns St.
Corinth, MS 38834
(601)286-6401
Ultimate Parent: Pepsico. **SIC:** 2086—Bottled & Canned Soft Drinks.

★ 72742 ★ **Personal Finance Co.**
2040 N. Village Shopping Ctr.
Corinth, MS 38834
(601)286-8421
Ultimate Parent: Minnesota Mutual Life. **SIC:** 6141—Personal Credit Institutions.

★ 72743 ★ **Pizza Hut**
4 St.
Corinth, MS 38834
(601)286-5400
Ultimate Parent: Pepsico. **SIC:** 5812—Eating Places.

★ 72744 ★ **Pizza Hut**
1212 Hwy. 72 E
Corinth, MS 38834
(601)286-6050
Ultimate Parent: Pepsico. **SIC:** 5812—Eating Places.

★ 72745 ★ **Radio Shack**
123 Hwy. 72 E
Corinth, MS 38834
(601)287-7169
Company Type: Division. **Ultimate Parent:** Tandy Corp. **SIC:** 5065—Electronic Parts & Equipment Nec.

★ 72746 ★ **Trailway Bus Station**
204 Hwy. 72 E
Corinth, MS 38834
(601)287-1466
Ultimate Parent: Greyhound Lines Inc. **SIC:** 4131—Intercity & Rural Bus Transportation.

★ 72747 ★ **Wal Mart Discount Cities**
Southgate Plz.
Corinth, MS 38834
(601)287-3148
Ultimate Parent: Wal-Mart Stores, Inc. **SIC:** 5311—Department Stores.

Crystal Springs

★ 72748 ★ **Greyhound Bus Lines**
Hwy. 51
Crystal Springs, MS 39059
(601)892-9982
Ultimate Parent: Greyhound Lines Inc. **SIC:** 4131—Intercity & Rural Bus Transportation.

★ 72749 ★ **Kentucky Fried Chicken**
203 E. Georgetown St.
Crystal Springs, MS 39059
(601)892-2971
Ultimate Parent: Pepsico. **SIC:** 5812—Eating Places.

★ 72750 ★ **Piggly Wiggly**
200 Lee Ave.
Crystal Springs, MS 39059
(601)892-2041
Ultimate Parent: Bruno's. **SIC:** 5411—Grocery Stores.

Dennis

★ 72751 ★ **Piggly Wiggly**
505 S. 2nd
Dennis, MS 38838
(601)454-7163
Ultimate Parent: Bruno's. **SIC:** 5411—Grocery Stores.

Durant

★ 72752 ★ **Piggly Wiggly**
404 N. Jackson St.
Durant, MS 39063
(601)653-3521
Ultimate Parent: Bruno's. **SIC:** 5411—Grocery Stores.

★ 72753 ★ **Trailways Bus Systems**
113 N. Jackson St.
Durant, MS 39063
(601)653-6451
Ultimate Parent: Greyhound Lines Inc. **SIC:** 4131—Intercity & Rural Bus Transportation.

Ellisville

★ 72754 ★ **Mary Kay Cosmet Consultants**
510 Hill St.
Ellisville, MS 39437
(601)477-3948
Ultimate Parent: Mary Kay Cosmetics. **SIC:** 8721—Accounting, Auditing & Bookkeeping.

★ 72755 ★ **Pizza Hut**
110 Us 11 S
Ellisville, MS 39437
(601)477-9047
Ultimate Parent: Pepsico. **SIC:** 5812—Eating Places.

Escatawpa

★ 72756 ★ **Circus World**
1262 Singing Rv Mall
Escatawpa, MS 39552
(601)497-2296
Ultimate Parent: Melville. **SIC:** 5945—Hobby, Toy & Game Shops.

★ 72757 ★ **Lane Bryant**
1274 Singing Rv Mall
Escatawpa, MS 39552
(601)497-6463
Ultimate Parent: Limited. **SIC:** 5651—Family Clothing Stores.

★ 72758 ★ **Moss Point Marine**
7801 Trintiy Dr.
Escatawpa, MS 39552
Ultimate Parent: Trinity Industries. **SIC:** 3731—Ship Building & Repairing.

★ 72759 ★ **Radio Shack**
1134 Singing Rv Mall
Escatawpa, MS 39552
(601)497-5079
Company Type: Division. **Ultimate Parent:** Tandy Corp. **SIC:** 5731—Radio, Television & Electronics Stores.

★ 72760 ★ **Service Merchandise**
5000 Singing Rv Mall
Escatawpa, MS 39552
(601)497-5200
Ultimate Parent: Service Merchandise Co., Inc. **SIC:** 5399—Miscellaneous General Merchandise Store.

★ 72761 ★ **Trinity Industries**
Moss Point Marine Div.
3304 Roberts Rd.
Escatawpa, MS 39552
Ultimate Parent: Trinity Industries. **SIC:** 3731—Ship Building & Repairing.

★ 72762 ★ **Waldenbooks**
1250 Singing Rv Mall
Escatawpa, MS 39552
(601)497-5404
Ultimate Parent: K-Mart. **SIC:** 5942—Book Stores.

★ 72763 ★ **Walgreen Drug Stores**
1162 Singing Rv Mall
Escatawpa, MS 39552
(601)497-6400
Ultimate Parent: Walgreen Co. **SIC:** 5912—Drug Stores & Proprietary Stores.

Eupora

★ 72764 ★ **Personal Finance Co.**
214 Hwy. 9 N
Eupora, MS 39744
(601)258-8342
Ultimate Parent: Minnesota Mutual Life. **SIC:** 6141—Personal Credit Institutions.

★ 72765 ★ **Piggly Wiggly**
301 E. Roane Ave.
Eupora, MS 39744
(601)258-7382
Ultimate Parent: Bruno's. **SIC:** 5421—Meat & Fish Markets.

★ 72766 ★ **Texaco Service Station**
102 E. Roane Ave.
Eupora, MS 39744
(601)258-4651
Ultimate Parent: Texaco. **SIC:** 5541—Gasoline Service Stations.

★ 72767 ★ **Wilsons Dept Store**
128 N. Dunn St.
Eupora, MS 39744
(601)258-2301
Ultimate Parent: Melville. **SIC:** 5311—Department Stores.

Fayette

★ 72768 ★ **Fayette Enterprise Inc.**
PO Box 188
Fayette, MS 39069
(601)786-3473
Company Type: Subsidiary. **Ultimate Parent:** Armstrong World Industries. **SIC:** 2499—Wood Products Nec.

★ 72769 ★ **Fayette Enterprises, Inc.**
Industrial Park Hwy. 33
Fayette, MS 39069
(601)786-3473
Officer: Connie Kanoy, Manager. **Ultimate Parent:** Armstrong World Industries. **SIC:** 2426—Hardwood Dimension & Flooring Mills.

Flora

★ 72770 ★ **Mary Kay Cosmetics**
156 PO Box
Flora, MS 39071
(601)879-3229
Ultimate Parent: Mary Kay Cosmetics.

Florence

★ 72771 ★ **ALLTEL Mississippi Inc.**
101 Lewis St.
PO Box 7
Florence, MS 39073
(601)845-6544
Ultimate Parent: ALLTEL Corp. **SIC:** 4812—Radiotelephone Communications.

★ 72772 ★ **Shell Oil Co.**
300 Shell Oil Rd.
Florence, MS 39073
(601)845-2252
Officer: Arthur Mc Alpin, Manager. **Ultimate Parent:** Shell Oil Co. **SIC:** 2819—Industrial Inorganic Chemicals Nec.

Forest

★ 72773 ★ **Kentucky Fried Chicken**
Woodland Dr.
Forest, MS 39074
(601)469-3361
Ultimate Parent: Pepsico. **SIC:** 5812—Eating Places.

★ 72774 ★ **Pizza Hut**
836 Us 35 N
Forest, MS 39074
(601)469-1799
Ultimate Parent: Pepsico. **SIC:** 5812—Eating Places.

★ 72775 ★ **Radio Shack**
830 Us 35 N
Forest, MS 39074
(601)469-4761
Company Type: Division. **Ultimate Parent:** Tandy Corp. **SIC:** 5065—Electronic Parts & Equipment Nec.

★ 72776 ★　Sara Lee Bakery
1225 Jack Lee Dr.
Forest, MS 39074
(601)469-3096
Company Type: Division. **Location Type:**
Facility. **Officer:** Dale Gribble, Executive
Director of Operations. **Ultimate Parent:**
Sara Lee Corp.

★ 72777 ★　Sara Lee Bakery
Jack Lee Dr.
Forest, MS 39074
Ultimate Parent: Sara Lee Corp. **SIC:**
2053—Frozen Bakery Products Except
Bread.

★ 72778 ★　Trailways Bus Station
Hwy. 80 E
Forest, MS 39074
(601)469-3941
Ultimate Parent: Greyhound Lines Inc. **SIC:**
4131—Intercity & Rural Bus Transportation.

Fulton

★ 72779 ★　Piggly Wiggly
208 E. Main St.
Fulton, MS 38843
(601)862-3140
Ultimate Parent: Bruno's. **SIC:** 5411—
Grocery Stores.

★ 72780 ★　Wal Mart Discount
City
Southgate Shopping Ctr.
Fulton, MS 38843
(601)862-2143
Ultimate Parent: Wal-Mart Stores, Inc. **SIC:**
5311—Department Stores.

Gallman

★ 72781 ★　Georgia Gulf Corp.
20043 Hwy. 51
Gallman, MS 39077
(601)892-5612
Officer: L.B. Totty, Manager. **Ultimate
Parent:** Georgia Gulf. **SIC:** 2821—Plastics
Materials & Resins.

★ 72782 ★　Magnetek
19120 Hwy. 51
Gallman, MS 39077
Ultimate Parent: Magnetek Inc. **SIC:**
3357—Nonferrous Wiredrawing & Insulating.

★ 72783 ★　Magnetek Universal
Manufacturing
US Hwy. 51 S
Gallman, MS 39077
Ultimate Parent: Magnetek Inc. **SIC:**
3357—Nonferrous Wiredrawing & Insulating.

Gautier

★ 72784 ★　Exxon
2301 Hwy. 90
Gautier, MS 39553
(601)497-1746
Ultimate Parent: Exxon. **SIC:** 5541—
Gasoline Service Stations.

★ 72785 ★　Pizza Hut
Ladnier Rd.
Gautier, MS 39553
(601)497-4006
Ultimate Parent: Pepsico. **SIC:** 5812—
Eating Places.

★ 72786 ★　Shell Oil Self Service
2900 Us 90 W
Gautier, MS 39553
(601)497-4003
Ultimate Parent: Shell Oil Co. **SIC:** 5541—
Gasoline Service Stations.

★ 72787 ★　Taco Bell
2701 Jackson Sq.
Gautier, MS 39553
(601)497-6858
Ultimate Parent: Pepsico. **SIC:** 5812—
Eating Places.

Golden

★ 72788 ★　First American
National Bank
Hwy. 366
Golden, MS 38847
(601)454-3454
Ultimate Parent: First American Corp. **SIC:**

6099—Functions Related to Deposit
Banking; 6022—State Commercial Banks.

Greenville

★ 72789 ★　APAC
805 N. Harvey St.
Greenville, MS 38701
(601)378-8481
Officer: Craig Sansing, Manager. **Ultimate
Parent:** Ashland Oil. **SIC:** 2951—Asphalt
Paving Mixtures & Blocks; 3295—
Minerals—Ground or Treated.

★ 72790 ★　BASF Corp.
103 BASF Rd.
Greenville, MS 38701
(601)335-4737
Ultimate Parent: BASF Corp. **SIC:** 8731—
Commercial Physical Research.

★ 72791 ★　Browning-Ferris
Industries
Landfill Rd.
Greenville, MS 38704
(601)335-1014
Ultimate Parent: Browning-Ferris
Industries. **SIC:** 4953—Refuse Systems.

★ 72792 ★　Casual Corner
Rural Route 3
Greenville, MS 38703
(601)335-6306
Ultimate Parent: United States Shoe. **SIC:**
5651—Family Clothing Stores.

★ 72793 ★　Citgo
1686 State Hwy. 1 N
Greenville, MS 38701
(601)379-8989
Ultimate Parent: Citgo Petroleum. **SIC:**
5541—Gasoline Service Stations.

★ 72794 ★　Cooper Steel
1381 Pickett St.
Greenville, MS 38703
Ultimate Parent: Cooper Industries. **SIC:**
3312—Blast Furnaces & Steel Mills.

★ 72795 ★　Copper Steel Co.
1381 Pickett St.
Greenville, MS 38701
Ultimate Parent: Cooper Industries. **SIC:**
3312—Blast Furnaces & Steel Mills.

★ 72796 ★　Deposit Guaranty
Mortgage C
1427 S. Main St.
Greenville, MS 38701
(601)334-7496
Ultimate Parent: Deposit Guaranty Corp.
SIC: 6162—Mortgage Bankers &
Correspondents.

★ 72797 ★　Exxon
2339 Us 82 E
Greenville, MS 38701
(601)378-3931
Ultimate Parent: Exxon. **SIC:** 5541—
Gasoline Service Stations.

★ 72798 ★　Exxon
Rr 3
Greenville, MS 38703
(601)378-3928
Ultimate Parent: Exxon. **SIC:** 5541—
Gasoline Service Stations.

★ 72799 ★　Exxon Shop
711 E. Reed Rd.
Greenville, MS 38701
(601)332-4642
Ultimate Parent: Exxon. **SIC:** 5541—
Gasoline Service Stations.

★ 72800 ★　Greyhound Bus Lines
1849 Us 82 E
Greenville, MS 38701
(601)335-2633
Ultimate Parent: Greyhound Lines Inc. **SIC:**
4131—Intercity & Rural Bus Transportation;
4173—Bus Terminal & Service Facilities.

★ 72801 ★　Kay-Bee Toy & Hobby
Shop
Rural Route 3
Greenville, MS 38703
(601)378-9226
Ultimate Parent: Melville. **SIC:** 5945—
Hobby, Toy & Game Shops.

★ 72802 ★　Kay Bee Toy&Hobby
Shops
Greenville Mall
Greenville, MS 38701
(601)378-9226
Ultimate Parent: Melville. **SIC:** 5945—
Hobby, Toy & Game Shops.

★ 72803 ★　Kentucky Fried
Chicken
1911 Us 82 E
Greenville, MS 38701
(601)334-9551
Ultimate Parent: Pepsico. **SIC:** 5812—
Eating Places.

★ 72804 ★　Kentucky Fried
Chicken
1923 Hwy. 82 E
Greenville, MS 38703
(601)334-9551
Ultimate Parent: Pepsico. **SIC:** 5812—
Eating Places.

★ 72805 ★　Kentucky Fried
Chicken
608 W. Alexander St.
Greenville, MS 38701
(601)335-2421
Ultimate Parent: Pepsico. **SIC:** 5812—
Eating Places.

★ 72806 ★　Kroger
2315 Us 82 E
Greenville, MS 38701
(601)335-3387
Ultimate Parent: Kroger. **SIC:** 5411—
Grocery Stores.

★ 72807 ★　Kroger 950
2315 Hwy. 82 E
Greenville, MS 38703
(601)335-3388
Ultimate Parent: Kroger. **SIC:** 5499—
Miscellaneous Food Stores.

★ 72808 ★　Massachusetts Mutual
Life Insurance
819 Main St.
Greenville, MS 38701
(601)332-7291
Ultimate Parent: Massacuetts Mutual Life.
SIC: 6411—Insurance Agents, Brokers &
Service.

★ 72809 ★　Nicholson Saw
1825 N. Theobald St.
Greenville, MS 38701
Ultimate Parent: Cooper Industries. **SIC:**
3425—Saw Blades & Handsaws.

★ 72810 ★　Pappagallo
531 Hwy. 82 E
Greenville, MS 38701
(601)334-3969
Ultimate Parent: United States Shoe. **SIC:**
5661—Shoe Stores.

★ 72811 ★　Pepsi-Cola Bottling
Co.
718 Main St.
Greenville, MS 38701
(601)332-7563
Officer: Scott Rainwater, Manager.
Ultimate Parent: Pepsico. **SIC:** 2086—
Bottled & Canned Soft Drinks.

★ 72812 ★　Pizza Hut
1490 Us 82 E
Greenville, MS 38701
(601)332-6425
Ultimate Parent: Pepsico. **SIC:** 5812—
Eating Places.

★ 72813 ★　Pizza Hut
1409 Hwy. 82 E
Greenville, MS 38703
(601)332-6425
Ultimate Parent: Pepsico. **SIC:** 5812—
Eating Places.

★ 72814 ★　Pizza Hut
Rural Route 3
Greenville, MS 38703
(601)332-2300
Ultimate Parent: Pepsico. **SIC:** 5812—
Eating Places.

★ 72815 ★　Pizza Hut
1601 Hwy. 1 S
Greenville, MS 38701
(601)332-2300
Ultimate Parent: Pepsico. **SIC:** 5812—
Eating Places.

★ 72816 ★　Platte Chemical Co.
N. Raceway Rd.
Greenville, MS 38704
Ultimate Parent: Conagra. **SIC:** 2879—
Agricultural Chemicals Nec.

★ 72817 ★　Platte Chemical Co.
North Raceway Rd.
Greenville, MS 38704-5156
Ultimate Parent: Conagra. **SIC:** 2879—
Agricultural Chemicals Nec.

★ 72818 ★　Raytheon Service Co.
1836 Hwy. 82 E
Greenville, MS 38703
(601)335-5150
Ultimate Parent: Raytheon Co. **SIC:**
4899—Communications Services Nec.

★ 72819 ★　Reliable Electric
Products Co.
956 N. Broadway St.
Greenville, MS 38701
(601)378-3612
Officer: Jim Parkerson, Manager. **Ultimate
Parent:** Reliance Electric. **SIC:** 3644—
Noncurrent-Carrying Wiring Devices.

★ 72820 ★　Ryder Truck Rental
1570 Hwy. 1 S
Greenville, MS 38701
(601)332-9517
Ultimate Parent: Ryder System. **SIC:**
7359—Equipment Rental & Leasing Nec.

★ 72821 ★　Taco Bell
1719 Us 82 E
Greenville, MS 38701
(601)335-6562
Ultimate Parent: Pepsico. **SIC:** 5812—
Eating Places.

★ 72822 ★　Trailways Bus Station
738 Washington Ave.
Greenville, MS 38701
(601)332-0551
Ultimate Parent: Greyhound Lines Inc. **SIC:**
4131—Intercity & Rural Bus Transportation.

★ 72823 ★　Transamerica
Occidental Lif
129 State Hwy. 1 S
Greenville, MS 38701
(601)335-1883
Ultimate Parent: Transamerica Occidental
Life Insurance. **SIC:** 6411—Insurance
Agents, Brokers & Service.

★ 72824 ★　US Fidelity
606 Washington Ave.
Greenville, MS 38701
(601)355-2321
Ultimate Parent: USF&G Corp. **SIC:**
6411—Insurance Agents, Brokers &
Service.

★ 72825 ★　Vlasic Foods
Hwy. 82 West
Greenville, MS 38701
Ultimate Parent: Campbell Soup. **SIC:**
2035—Pickles, Sauces & Salad Dressings.

★ 72826 ★　Vlasic Foods Inc.
84 Vlasic Rd.
Greenville, MS 38701
Ultimate Parent: Campbell Soup. **SIC:**
2035—Pickles, Sauces & Salad Dressings.

★ 72827 ★　Vlasic Foods Inc.
Hwy. 82 West
Greenville, MS 38701
Ultimate Parent: Campbell Soup. **SIC:**
2035—Pickles, Sauces & Salad Dressings.

★ 72828 ★　Wal Mart
Rural Route 3
Greenville, MS 38703
(601)332-9801
Ultimate Parent: Wal-Mart Stores, Inc. **SIC:**
5311—Department Stores.

★ 72829 ★　Wal Mart
1746 Hwy. 1 S
Greenville, MS 38701
(601)332-9801
Ultimate Parent: Wal-Mart Stores, Inc. **SIC:**
5311—Department Stores.

★ 72830 ★　Wal Mart Discount
City
Mainstream Mall
Greenville, MS 38701
(601)378-3665
Ultimate Parent: Wal-Mart Stores, Inc. **SIC:**
5311—Department Stores.

Greenwood

★ 72831 ★   American Family Life Assrnc
307 Lamar St.
Greenwood, MS 38930
(601)453-8773
Ultimate Parent: American Family Life Assurance Co. SIC: 6411—Insurance Agents, Brokers & Service.

★ 72832 ★   American Family Life Assurance
307 Lamar St.
Greenwood, MS 38930
(601)453-8773
Ultimate Parent: American Family Life Assurance Co. SIC: 6411—Insurance Agents, Brokers & Service.

★ 72833 ★   Greyhound Bus Lines
325 Main St.
Greenwood, MS 38930
(601)453-7232
Ultimate Parent: Greyhound Lines Inc. SIC: 4111—Local & Suburban Transit.

★ 72834 ★   Hertz Rent-A-Car
916 Hwy. 82 W
Greenwood, MS 38930
(601)455-3488
Ultimate Parent: Hertz. SIC: 7514—Passenger Car Rental.

★ 72835 ★   IBM Corp.
205 Fulton St.
Greenwood, MS 38930
(601)453-1015
Ultimate Parent: IBM. SIC: 5044—Office Equipment.

★ 72836 ★   Kentucky Fried Chicken
Hwy. 82
Greenwood, MS 38930
(601)453-6771
Ultimate Parent: Pepsico. SIC: 5812—Eating Places.

★ 72837 ★   Piggly Wiggly
203 W. Park Ave.
Greenwood, MS 38930
(601)453-7873
Ultimate Parent: Bruno's. SIC: 5411—Grocery Stores.

★ 72838 ★   Piggly Wiggly
Hwy. 7
Greenwood, MS 38930
(601)455-4911
Ultimate Parent: Bruno's. SIC: 5411—Grocery Stores.

★ 72839 ★   Pizza Hut
Park Ave.
Greenwood, MS 38930
(601)455-1784
Ultimate Parent: Pepsico. SIC: 5812—Eating Places.

★ 72840 ★   Radio Shack
Highland Park Shpg C
Greenwood, MS 38930
(601)453-6241
Company Type: Division. Ultimate Parent: Tandy Corp. SIC: 5734—Computer & Software Stores.

Grenada

★ 72841 ★   Kentucky Fried Chicken
699 Sunset Dr.
Grenada, MS 38901
(601)226-4686
Ultimate Parent: Pepsico. SIC: 5812—Eating Places.

★ 72842 ★   Kroger's
Grenada Sq.
Grenada, MS 38901
(601)226-3057
Ultimate Parent: Kroger. SIC: 5411—Grocery Stores.

★ 72843 ★   Louisiana Pacific Corp.
Hwy. 51 S
Grenada, MS 38901
(601)227-1860
Ultimate Parent: Louisiana-Pacific. SIC: 0811—Timber Tracts; 2421—Sawmills & Planing Mills—General; 2491—Wood Preserving.

★ 72844 ★   Pizza Hut
Grenada Plz.
Grenada, MS 38901
(601)226-6262
Ultimate Parent: Pepsico. SIC: 5812—Eating Places.

★ 72845 ★   Radio Shack
1340 S. Commerce St.
Grenada, MS 38901
(601)226-0839
Company Type: Division. Ultimate Parent: Tandy Corp. SIC: 5065—Electronic Parts & Equipment Nec.

★ 72846 ★   Randall Textron
Hwy. 332 East
Grenada, MS 38901
Ultimate Parent: Textron. SIC: 3471—Plating & Polishing; 3465—Automotive Stampings.

★ 72847 ★   Randall Textron Inc.
Hwy. 332 E
Grenada, MS 38901
Ultimate Parent: Textron. SIC: 3471—Plating & Polishing; 3465—Automotive Stampings.

★ 72848 ★   Taco Bell
1317 Sunset Dr.
Grenada, MS 38901
(601)226-0949
Ultimate Parent: Pepsico. SIC: 5812—Eating Places.

★ 72849 ★   Trailways Bus System
48 Cherry St.
Grenada, MS 38901
(601)226-1871
Ultimate Parent: Greyhound Lines Inc. SIC: 4131—Intercity & Rural Bus Transportation.

Gulfport

★ 72850 ★   Coast to Coast Express
1528 30th Ave.
Gulfport, MS 39501
(601)868-8624
Ultimate Parent: Servistar Corp. SIC: 7389—Business Services Nec.

★ 72851 ★   Cole Engineering
2601 19th St.
Gulfport, MS 39501
(601)868-9111
Ultimate Parent: Giant Food.

★ 72852 ★   Continental Express
Regional Airport
Gulfport, MS 39501
(601)863-6280
Ultimate Parent: Continental Airlines. SIC: 4512—Air Transportation—Scheduled.

★ 72853 ★   Dr. Pepper Bottling Co.
3701 25th Ave.
Gulfport, MS 39501
(601)863-8272
Officer: E. Clifton Milner Jr., Manager. Ultimate Parent: Dr. Pepper/Seven-Up. SIC: 2086—Bottled & Canned Soft Drinks.

★ 72854 ★   Emery Worldwide
2420 28th St.
Gulfport, MS 39501
(601)868-9079
Ultimate Parent: Consolidated Freightways. SIC: 4215—Courier Services Except by Air.

★ 72855 ★   Fleet Finance Inc.
9350 Hwy. 49
Gulfport, MS 39503
(601)864-7961
Ultimate Parent: Fleet Financial Group. SIC: 6162—Mortgage Bankers & Correspondents.

★ 72856 ★   Hertz Rent-A-Car
Gulfport-Biloxi Airport
Gulfport, MS 39503
(601)863-2761
Ultimate Parent: Hertz. SIC: 7514—Passenger Car Rental.

★ 72857 ★   Hertz Rent-A-Car
Regional Airport
Gulfport, MS 39501
(601)863-2761
Ultimate Parent: Hertz. SIC: 7514—Passenger Car Rental.

★ 72858 ★   Kentucky Fried Chicken
2510 R B Meadow Blvd.
Gulfport, MS 39501
(601)864-2540
Ultimate Parent: Pepsico. SIC: 5812—Eating Places.

★ 72859 ★   Kentucky Fried Chicken
12198 Us 49
Gulfport, MS 39501
(601)832-3633
Ultimate Parent: Pepsico. SIC: 5812—Eating Places.

★ 72860 ★   Kroger Co.
11240 Us 49
Gulfport, MS 39501
(601)832-1446
Ultimate Parent: Kroger. SIC: 5411—Grocery Stores.

★ 72861 ★   Kroger's
665 E. Pass Rd.
Gulfport, MS 39507
(601)896-9216
Ultimate Parent: Kroger. SIC: 5411—Grocery Stores.

★ 72862 ★   Lerner Shop
2515 13th St.
Gulfport, MS 39501
(601)863-6233
Ultimate Parent: Limited. SIC: 5621—Women's Clothing Stores; 5651—Family Clothing Stores.

★ 72863 ★   Manpower, Inc.
2500 14th St.
Gulfport, MS 39501
(601)864-4200
Ultimate Parent: Manpower, Inc. SIC: 7363—Help Supply Services.

★ 72864 ★   People's Bank
12020 Us 49
Gulfport, MS 39503
(601)867-2268
Ultimate Parent: People's Bank. SIC: 6022—State Commercial Banks.

★ 72865 ★   Pizza Hut
3620 W. Beach Blvd.
Gulfport, MS 39501
(601)863-1560
Ultimate Parent: Pepsico. SIC: 5812—Eating Places.

★ 72866 ★   Pizza Hut
Orange Grove Shopping Ctr.
Gulfport, MS 39503
(601)832-6078
Ultimate Parent: Pepsico. SIC: 5812—Eating Places.

★ 72867 ★   Pizza Hut
801 E. Pass Rd.
Gulfport, MS 39507
(601)896-5113
Ultimate Parent: Pepsico. SIC: 5812—Eating Places.

★ 72868 ★   Pizza Hut
14297 Dedeaux Rd.
Gulfport, MS 39503
(601)831-1803
Ultimate Parent: Pepsico. SIC: 5812—Eating Places.

★ 72869 ★   Pizza Hut Inc.
10 Orange Grv Shopping Ctr.
Gulfport, MS 39501
(601)832-6078
Ultimate Parent: Pepsico. SIC: 5812—Eating Places.

★ 72870 ★   Radio Shack
Hardy Ct
Gulfport, MS 39501
(601)864-9788
Company Type: Division. Ultimate Parent: Tandy Corp. SIC: 5065—Electronic Parts & Equipment Nec.

★ 72871 ★   Radio Shack
Orange Grv Shopping Ctr.
Gulfport, MS 39503
(601)832-2428
Company Type: Division. Ultimate Parent: Tandy Corp. SIC: 5065—Electronic Parts & Equipment Nec.

★ 72872 ★   Radio Shack
21 Pass Rd.
Gulfport, MS 39507
(601)864-9788
Company Type: Division. Ultimate Parent: Tandy Corp. SIC: 5731—Radio, Television & Electronics Stores.

★ 72873 ★   Radio Shack
11312 Orange Grv Shopping Ctr.
Gulfport, MS 39501
(601)832-2428
Company Type: Division. Ultimate Parent: Tandy Corp. SIC: 5065—Electronic Parts & Equipment Nec.

★ 72874 ★   Ryder Truck Rental
11548 Dedeaux Rd.
Gulfport, MS 39503
(601)831-1066
Ultimate Parent: Ryder System. SIC: 7513—Truck Rental & Leasing Without Drivers.

★ 72875 ★   Service Merchandise
2001 E. Pass Rd.
Gulfport, MS 39507
(601)896-3030
Ultimate Parent: Service Merchandise Co., Inc. SIC: 5961—Catalog & Mail-Order Houses.

★ 72876 ★   Sterling Drug Inc.
3600 25th Ave.
Gulfport, MS 39501
(601)863-1702
Officer: Nick Foto, Manager. Ultimate Parent: Eastman Kodak. SIC: 2834—Pharmaceutical Preparations; 2844—Toilet Preparations.

★ 72877 ★   Sterling Health
3600 25th Ave.
Gulfport, MS 39501
Ultimate Parent: Eastman Kodak. SIC: 2834—Pharmaceutical Preparations.

★ 72878 ★   Taco Bell
2417 25th St.
Gulfport, MS 39501
(601)868-2653
Ultimate Parent: Pepsico. SIC: 5812—Eating Places.

★ 72879 ★   Taco Bell
1375 E. Pass Rd.
Gulfport, MS 39507
(601)897-2300
Ultimate Parent: Pepsico. SIC: 5812—Eating Places.

★ 72880 ★   Trailways
2707 13th St.
Gulfport, MS 39501
(601)863-1022
Ultimate Parent: Greyhound Lines Inc. SIC: 4173—Bus Terminal & Service Facilities.

★ 72881 ★   US Fidelity & Gu
2301 14th St.
Gulfport, MS 39501
(601)863-2710
Ultimate Parent: USF&G Corp. SIC: 6411—Insurance Agents, Brokers & Service.

★ 72882 ★   Wal Mart
9350 Us 49
Gulfport, MS 39501
(601)865-0555
Ultimate Parent: Wal-Mart Stores, Inc. SIC: 5311—Department Stores.

★ 72883 ★   Western Geophysical Co.
3413 B Ave.
Gulfport, MS 39507
(601)868-5571
Ultimate Parent: Litton Industries. SIC: 1389—Oil & Gas Field Services Nec.

Hamilton

★ 72884 ★   Kerr-Mcgee Chemical Corp.
Hwy. 45 North
Hamilton, MS 39746
Ultimate Parent: Kerr-McGee. SIC: 2816—Inorganic Pigments.

★ 72885 ★ Kerr-Mcgee Chemical Corp.
U.S. Hwy. 45 South
Hamilton, MS 39746-0180
Ultimate Parent: Kerr-McGee. SIC: 2816—Inorganic Pigments.

★ 72886 ★ Kerr-Mcgee Chemical Corp. Electrolytic Plant
U.S. Hwy. 45 S.
Hamilton, MS 39746
Ultimate Parent: Kerr-McGee. SIC: 2819—Industrial Inorganic Chemicals Nec; 3313—Electrometallurgical Products.

★ 72887 ★ Kerr-Mcgee Chemical Corp. Pigment Plant
U.S. Hwy. 45 N.
Hamilton, MS 39746
Ultimate Parent: Kerr-McGee. SIC: 2816—Inorganic Pigments.

Hattiesburg

★ 72888 ★ Bf Goodrich Co. Hattiesburg Plant
1301 W. 7th St.
Hattiesburg, MS 39401
Ultimate Parent: B.F. Goodrich. SIC: 2822—Synthetic Rubber.

★ 72889 ★ Exxon Co. USA
15 Professional Pky.
Hattiesburg, MS 39402
(601)268-6660
Ultimate Parent: Exxon. SIC: 1382—Oil & Gas Exploration Services.

★ 72890 ★ Hercules Inc.
W. 7th St.
Hattiesburg, MS 39401
Ultimate Parent: Hercules. SIC: 2861—Gum & Wood Chemicals; 2821—Plastics Materials & Resins; 2869—Industrial Organic Chemicals Nec; 2899—Chemical Preparations Nec.

★ 72891 ★ Hertz Rent-A-Car Licensee
Pine
Hattiesburg, MS 39401
(601)544-4914
Ultimate Parent: Hertz. SIC: 7514—Passenger Car Rental.

★ 72892 ★ Inland Container Corp.
2501 Inland Park
Hattiesburg, MS 39401
Ultimate Parent: Temple-Inland. SIC: 2653—Corrugated & Solid Fiber Boxes.

★ 72893 ★ Inland Container Corp. No. 24
2501 Inland Park
Hattiesburg, MS 39401
Ultimate Parent: Temple-Inland. SIC: 2653—Corrugated & Solid Fiber Boxes.

★ 72894 ★ Pepsi-Cola Co.
70 Old Rawls Springs Rd.
Hattiesburg, MS 39402
(601)268-2266
Ultimate Parent: Pepsico. SIC: 2086—Bottled & Canned Soft Drinks.

★ 72895 ★ Radio Shack
Univ
Hattiesburg, MS 39401
(601)264-5462
Company Type: Division. Ultimate Parent: Tandy Corp. SIC: 5065—Electronic Parts & Equipment Nec.

★ 72896 ★ Ryder Truck Rental
222 Us 49 S
Hattiesburg, MS 39401
(601)544-5033
Ultimate Parent: Ryder System. SIC: 7513—Truck Rental & Leasing Without Drivers.

★ 72897 ★ Ryder Truck Rental
300 Broadway Dr.
Hattiesburg, MS 39401
(601)545-7276
Ultimate Parent: Ryder System. SIC: 5113—Industrial & Personal Service Paper.

★ 72898 ★ Texaco Food Mart
2502 Hardy St.
Hattiesburg, MS 39401
(601)584-8405
Ultimate Parent: Texaco. SIC: 5411—Grocery Stores.

★ 72899 ★ Trailways Bus System
1400 W. Pine St.
Hattiesburg, MS 39401
(601)545-3530
Ultimate Parent: Greyhound Lines Inc. SIC: 4141—Local Bus Charter Service.

★ 72900 ★ Western Geophysical Co.
Rural Route 4
Hattiesburg, MS 39402
(601)264-3996
Ultimate Parent: Litton Industries. SIC: 5084—Industrial Machinery & Equipment.

Heidelberg

★ 72901 ★ Amerada Hess Corp.
Heidelberg, MS 39439
(601)787-3441
Location Type: Branch office. Ultimate Parent: Amerada Hess. SIC: 4612—Crude Petroleum Pipelines.

Hernando

★ 72902 ★ Alumax Extrusions Inc.
2785 Mccracken Rd.
Hernando, MS 38632
Ultimate Parent: Alumax Inc. SIC: 3354—Aluminum Extruded Products.

★ 72903 ★ Pyroil Performance Products
720 Vaiden Dr.
Hernando, MS 38632
(601)429-0405 Fax: (601)429-1927
Company Type: Division. Officer: Larry Detten, President. Ultimate Parent: Ashland Oil. SIC: 2911—Petroleum Refining. Employee Count: 50.

Hollandale

★ 72904 ★ Farm Fresh Catfish Co.
Opal St.
Hollandale, MS 38748
(601)827-2204
Company Type: Division. Ultimate Parent: Hormel Foods. SIC: 2000—Food & Kindred Products.

★ 72905 ★ Farm Fresh Catfish Co.
Opal St.
Hollandale, MS 38748
Ultimate Parent: Hormel Foods. SIC: 2092—Fresh or Frozen Prepared Fish.

★ 72906 ★ Farm Fresh Catfish Co.
PO Box 85
Hollandale, MS 38748
(601)827-2204 Fax: (601)827-7348
Company Type: Subsidiary. Officer: Robert W. Wells, Chairman. Ultimate Parent: Hormel Foods. SIC: 2091—Canned & Cured Fish & Seafoods; 2092—Fresh or Frozen Prepared Fish.

★ 72907 ★ Farm Fresh Catfish Co. Inc.
Hollandale Industrial Park
Hollandale, MS 38748
(601)827-2204
Ultimate Parent: Hormel Foods. SIC: 2092—Fresh or Frozen Prepared Fish.

Holly Springs

★ 72908 ★ Greyhound Bus Lines
184 N. Memphis St.
Holly Springs, MS 38635
(601)252-4339
Ultimate Parent: Greyhound Lines Inc. SIC: 5411—Grocery Stores.

★ 72909 ★ Kentucky Fried Chicken
525 Miss Hwy. 7 N
Holly Springs, MS 38635
(601)252-2351
Ultimate Parent: Pepsico. SIC: 5812—Eating Places.

★ 72910 ★ Sunbeam-Oster Household Products
Hwy. 7 N.
Holly Springs, MS 38635
Ultimate Parent: Sunbeam/Oster. SIC: 3471—Plating & Polishing.

★ 72911 ★ Sunbeam Oster Household Products
Hwy. 7 N.
Holly Springs, MS 38635
(601)252-4912
Officer: Mike Green, Plant Manager. Ultimate Parent: Sunbeam/Oster. SIC: 3634—Electric Housewares & Fans.

★ 72912 ★ Wal Mart
Hwy. 78
Holly Springs, MS 38635
(601)252-2211
Ultimate Parent: Wal-Mart Stores, Inc. SIC: 5331—Variety Stores.

Horn Lake

★ 72913 ★ Dover Elevator International Inc.
6266 Hurt Rd.
Horn Lake, MS 38637
(601)393-2110
Officer: John B. Apple, CEO. Ultimate Parent: Dover Corp. SIC: 3534—Elevators & Moving Stairways.

★ 72914 ★ Dover Elevator Systems Inc.
6266 Hurt Rd.
Horn Lake, MS 38637-2306
(601)393-2110
Company Type: Subsidiary. Ultimate Parent: Dover Corp. SIC: 3534—Elevators & Moving Stairways.

★ 72915 ★ Flavorite Labs. Inc.
5980 Hurt Rd.
Horn Lake, MS 38637
Ultimate Parent: M.A.Hanna. SIC: 2035—Pickles, Sauces & Salad Dressings; 2099—Food Preparations Nec.

Houston

★ 72916 ★ Alcoa Fujikura Ltd.
1000 Pep Dr.
Houston, MS 38851
(601)456-5323
Officer: Mike Palmer, Manager. Ultimate Parent: Aluminum Co. of America–Alcoa. SIC: 3714—Motor Vehicle Parts & Accessories.

★ 72917 ★ Alcoa Fujikura Ltd.
1000 Pep Dr.
Houston, MS 38851
(601)456-5323
Officer: Mike Palmer, Manager. Ultimate Parent: Aluminum Co. of America–Alcoa. SIC: 3714—Motor Vehicle Parts & Accessories.

★ 72918 ★ Gold Medal
Hwy. 8 W
Houston, MS 38851
(601)628-8756
Officer: Allen G. Atkinson, President. Ultimate Parent: General Mills. SIC: 2426—Hardwood Dimension & Flooring Mills; 2599—Furniture & Fixtures Nec.

★ 72919 ★ Mpi Inc.
400 Third Ave.
Houston, MS 38851
Ultimate Parent: Leggett & Platt Inc. SIC: 3000—Rubber & Miscellaneous Plastics Products.

★ 72920 ★ Piggly Wiggly
224 N. Jefferson St.
Houston, MS 38851
(601)456-3538
Ultimate Parent: Bruno's. SIC: 5411—Grocery Stores.

★ 72921 ★ Piggly Wiggly Interstate
207 S. Jackson St.
Houston, MS 38851-2624
(601)456-3731
Officer: James Larson. Ultimate Parent: Bruno's. SIC: 5411—Grocery Stores.

★ 72922 ★ Pizza Hut
Hwy. 15
Houston, MS 38851
(601)456-2001
Ultimate Parent: Pepsico. SIC: 5812—Eating Places.

★ 72923 ★ Texaco Oil Distributors
Hwy. 8 W
Houston, MS 38851
(601)456-2318
Ultimate Parent: Texaco. SIC: 5172—Petroleum Products Nec.

★ 72924 ★ Union Camp Corp.
4th Ave. North
Houston, MS 38851
Ultimate Parent: Union Camp Corp. SIC: 2653—Corrugated & Solid Fiber Boxes.

★ 72925 ★ Union Camp Corp.
4 Ave. N
Houston, MS 38851
(601)456-4251
Ultimate Parent: Union Camp Corp. SIC: 5113—Industrial & Personal Service Paper.

★ 72926 ★ Wal Mart Discount Cities
Hwy. 8 E
Houston, MS 38851
(601)456-5711
Ultimate Parent: Wal-Mart Stores, Inc. SIC: 5311—Department Stores.

Indianola

★ 72927 ★ Coast to Coast Home & Auto
1205 State Hwy. 448
Indianola, MS 38751
(601)887-3310
Ultimate Parent: Servistar Corp. SIC: 5531—Automobile & Home Supply Stores.

★ 72928 ★ Kentucky Fried Chicken
301 US 82 E
Indianola, MS 38751
(601)887-5842
Ultimate Parent: Pepsico. SIC: 5812—Eating Places.

★ 72929 ★ Piggly Wiggly
102 S. Front Ave.
Indianola, MS 38751
(601)887-1868
Ultimate Parent: Bruno's. SIC: 5411—Grocery Stores; 5431—Fruit & Vegetable Markets.

★ 72930 ★ Pizza Hut
700 US 82 E
Indianola, MS 38751
(601)887-4688
Ultimate Parent: Pepsico. SIC: 5812—Eating Places.

★ 72931 ★ Wal Mart Discount City
Hwy. 82
Indianola, MS 38751
(601)887-3320
Ultimate Parent: Wal-Mart Stores, Inc. SIC: 5311—Department Stores.

Isola

★ 72932 ★ Country Skillet Catfish Co.
PO Box 271
Isola, MS 38754
Company Type: Division. Location Type: Headquarters. Officer: Dick Stevens, President. Ultimate Parent: Conagra.

Itta Bena

★ 72933 ★ **Piggly Wiggly 255**
101 Schley St.
Itta Bena, MS 38941-2020
(601)254-7150
Ultimate Parent: Bruno's. **SIC:** 5032—
Brick, Stone & Related Materials.

Iuka

★ 72934 ★ **First American National Bank**
114 Pearl St.
Iuka, MS 38852
(601)423-3656
Ultimate Parent: First American Corp. **SIC:** 6021—National Commercial Banks; 6022—State Commercial Banks.

★ 72935 ★ **Personal Finance Co.**
119 E. Eastport St.
Iuka, MS 38852
(601)423-5491
Ultimate Parent: Minnesota Mutual Life. **SIC:** 6141—Personal Credit Institutions.

★ 72936 ★ **Vulcan Materials Co.**
Providence Rd.
Iuka, MS 38852
(601)423-5234
Officer: Alan Gulledge, Manager. **Ultimate Parent:** Vulcan Materials Co. **SIC:** 3274—Lime; 3295—Minerals—Ground or Treated.

Jackson

★ 72937 ★ **Abbott Laboratories**
7211 S. Siwell Rd.
Jackson, MS 39212-9776
(601)371-1060
Ultimate Parent: Abbott Laboratories. **SIC:** 5169—Chemicals & Allied Products Nec.

★ 72938 ★ **ABF Freight System Inc.**
4501 I 55 S
Jackson, MS 39212-5528
(601)372-0125
Location Type: Branch office. **Ultimate Parent:** Arkansas Best. **SIC:** 4212—Local Trucking Without Storage; 4213—Trucking Except Local.

★ 72939 ★ **Aetna Financial Services Inc.**
723 N. President St.
Jackson, MS 39202
(601)969-2064
Ultimate Parent: Aetna Life. **SIC:** 6411—Insurance Agents, Brokers & Service.

★ 72940 ★ **American Family Life Assurance**
5160 Galaxie Dr.
Jackson, MS 39206
(601)362-7373
Ultimate Parent: American Family Life Assurance Co. **SIC:** 6411—Insurance Agents, Brokers & Service.

★ 72941 ★ **American General Finance**
5446 Executive Pl.
Jackson, MS 39206-4197
(601)362-7751
Ultimate Parent: American General Corp. **SIC:** 6141—Personal Credit Institutions; 6162—Mortgage Bankers & Correspondents.

★ 72942 ★ **American General Finance Inc.**
720 Larson St.
Jackson, MS 39202-3436
(601)969-9332
Officer: C. E. Brown. **Ultimate Parent:** American General Corp. **SIC:** 6141—Personal Credit Institutions; 6162—Mortgage Bankers & Correspondents.

★ 72943 ★ **American General Finance Inc.**
5446 Executive Pl.
Jackson, MS 39206-4197
(601)362-7751
Location Type: Branch office. **Ultimate Parent:** American General Corp. **SIC:** 6141—Personal Credit Institutions; 6162—Mortgage Bankers & Correspondents.

★ 72944 ★ **American General Finance Inc.**
720 Larson St.
Jackson, MS 39202-3436
(601)969-9332
Location Type: Branch office. **Officer:** C. E. Brown. **Ultimate Parent:** American General Corp. **SIC:** 6141—Personal Credit Institutions; 6162—Mortgage Bankers & Correspondents.

★ 72945 ★ **APAC**
5090 S. McRaven Rd.
Jackson, MS 39204
(601)922-8000
Officer: David Barton, President. **Ultimate Parent:** Ashland Oil. **SIC:** 2951—Asphalt Paving Mixtures & Blocks; 3295—Minerals—Ground or Treated.

★ 72946 ★ **Armstrong World Industries Inc.**
1085 US Hwy. 80 W.
Jackson, MS 39204
Ultimate Parent: Armstrong World Industries. **SIC:** 3996—Hard Surface Floor Coverings Nec.

★ 72947 ★ **Armstrong World Industries Inc.**
1085 US Rte. 80 W
Jackson, MS 39204
Ultimate Parent: Armstrong World Industries. **SIC:** 3996—Hard Surface Floor Coverings Nec.

★ 72948 ★ **Armstrong World Industries Inc.**
Jackson Plant
1085 US Rte. 80 W
Jackson, MS 39204
Location Type: Plant. **Ultimate Parent:** Armstrong World Industries. **SIC:** 3996—Hard Surface Floor Coverings Nec.

★ 72949 ★ **Bell Atlantic Busn Sys Servs**
3010 Lakeland CV Ste. Q
Jackson, MS 39208-9708
(601)936-4800
Officer: Tommy Lee. **Ultimate Parent:** Bell Atlantic Corp. **SIC:** 7373—Computer Integrated Systems Design.

★ 72950 ★ **Borden Foodservice**
4350 Industrial Dr.
Jackson, MS 39209
(601)973-8800 **Fax:** (601)353-2411
Company Type: Division. **Location Type:** Plant. **Officer:** Mark Drozdowski, Operations Manager. **Ultimate Parent:** Borden, Inc.

★ 72951 ★ **Borden Inc.**
1101 Hwy. 80 W
Jackson, MS 39204
(601)948-5242
Location Type: Plant. **Officer:** Neil Hillstrom, Plant Manager. **Ultimate Parent:** Borden, Inc. **SIC:** 2023—Dry, Condensed & Evaporated Dairy Products; 2024—Ice Cream & Frozen Desserts; 2026—Fluid Milk.

★ 72952 ★ **Borden Inc.**
Dairy Division
1101 Hwy. 80 W
Jackson, MS 39204
Company Type: Division. **Ultimate Parent:** Borden, Inc. **SIC:** 2026—Fluid Milk.

★ 72953 ★ **Borden Inc. Dairy**
1101 Hwy. 80 W.
Jackson, MS 39204
Ultimate Parent: Borden, Inc. **SIC:** 2026—Fluid Milk.

★ 72954 ★ **Borden Inc. Foodservice**
4350 Industrial Dr.
Jackson, MS 39201
Ultimate Parent: Borden, Inc. **SIC:** 2033—Canned Fruits & Vegetables; 2035—Pickles, Sauces & Salad Dressings.

★ 72955 ★ **Browning-Ferris Industries**
1716 N. County Line Rd.
Jackson, MS 39213-9208
(601)982-9488
Ultimate Parent: Browning-Ferris Industries. **SIC:** 8731—Commercial Physical Research; 4953—Refuse Systems.

★ 72956 ★ **Casual Corner**
1220 Maywood Mart
Jackson, MS 39211
(601)362-0311
Ultimate Parent: United States Shoe. **SIC:** 5651—Family Clothing Stores.

★ 72957 ★ **Casual Corner**
70 Metro Center Mall
Jackson, MS 39209
(601)354-3290
Ultimate Parent: United States Shoe. **SIC:** 5651—Family Clothing Stores.

★ 72958 ★ **Casual Corner**
1200 E. County Line Rd.
Jackson, MS 39211
(601)856-3111
Ultimate Parent: United States Shoe. **SIC:** 5621—Women's Clothing Stores.

★ 72959 ★ **Challenger Electrical Equipment Corp.**
750 Boling St.
Jackson, MS 39225
Ultimate Parent: Westinghouse Electric Corp. **SIC:** 3699—Electrical Equipment & Supplies Nec.

★ 72960 ★ **Circus World Toy Store**
Metro Ctr. Mall
Jackson, MS 39201
(601)969-1378
Ultimate Parent: Melville. **SIC:** 5945—Hobby, Toy & Game Shops.

★ 72961 ★ **Circus World Toy Store**
33 Metrocenter Mall
Jackson, MS 39209
(601)969-1378
Ultimate Parent: Melville. **SIC:** 5945—Hobby, Toy & Game Shops.

★ 72962 ★ **Coast to Coast Video**
Rural Route 1
Jackson, MS 39212
(601)371-1076
Ultimate Parent: Servistar Corp. **SIC:** 7622—Radio & T.V. Repair.

★ 72963 ★ **Cutter Biological**
930 Bailey Ave.
Jackson, MS 39203
(601)354-2310
Ultimate Parent: Miles. **SIC:** 8734—Testing Laboratories.

★ 72964 ★ **Delta Air Lines**
Al C. Thompson Field
Jackson, MS 39208
(601)939-5200
Ultimate Parent: Delta Air Lines, Inc. **SIC:** 4512—Air Transportation—Scheduled.

★ 72965 ★ **Delta Air Lines**
Deposit Guaranty Plaza B
Jackson, MS 39201
(601)939-5200
Ultimate Parent: Delta Air Lines, Inc. **SIC:** 4724—Travel Agencies.

★ 72966 ★ **Delta Air Lines**
1501 Lakeland Dr.
Jackson, MS 39216
(601)939-5200
Ultimate Parent: Delta Air Lines, Inc. **SIC:** 4724—Travel Agencies; 7922—Theatrical Producers & Services.

★ 72967 ★ **Delta Air Lines Inc.**
Deposit Guar Plaza B
Jackson, MS 39201
(601)939-5200
Ultimate Parent: Delta Air Lines, Inc. **SIC:** 4724—Travel Agencies.

★ 72968 ★ **Deposit Guaranty Corp.**
219 E. Capitol st.
Jackson, MS 39205
(601)354-8211 **Fax:** (601)968-4644
Company Type: Headquarters. **Officer:** E. B. Robinson Jr., Chairman of the Board & CEO. **SIC:** 6712—Bank Holding Companies. **Employee Count:** 2575. **Fortune Service 500:** Ranking 92.

★ 72969 ★ **Deposit Guaranty Corp.**
PO Box 1200
Jackson, MS 39215-1200
Company Type: Headquarters. **Ultimate Parent:** Deposit Guaranty Corp.

★ 72970 ★ **Deposit Guaranty Investments; Inc.**
210 E. Capital St.
Jackson, MS 39205
(601)354-8497
Company Type: Subsidiary. **Officer:** John Porter, Pres. **Ultimate Parent:** Deposit Guaranty Corp. **SIC:** 6211—Security Brokers & Dealers.

★ 72971 ★ **Deposit Guaranty Mortgage C**
2372 W. Us 80 Fl
Jackson, MS 39204
(601)968-6901
Ultimate Parent: Deposit Guaranty Corp. **SIC:** 6162—Mortgage Bankers & Correspondents.

★ 72972 ★ **Deposit Guaranty Mortgage C**
1485 Livingston Ln.
Jackson, MS 39213
(601)364-5300
Ultimate Parent: Deposit Guaranty Corp. **SIC:** 6162—Mortgage Bankers & Correspondents.

★ 72973 ★ **Deposit Guaranty Mortgage Co.**
210 E. Capitol St.
Jackson, MS 39205
(601)968-6850 **Fax:** (601)968-6842
Company Type: Subsidiary. **Officer:** Alan H. Walters, President. **Ultimate Parent:** Deposit Guaranty Corp. **SIC:** 6162—Mortgage Bankers & Correspondents. **Employee Count:** 116.

★ 72974 ★ **Deposit Guaranty National Bank**
210 E. Capitol St.
Jackson, MS 39205
(601)354-8211 **Fax:** (601)354-8192
Company Type: Subsidiary. **Officer:** E. B. Robinson Jr., Chairman of the Board & CEO. **Ultimate Parent:** Deposit Guaranty Corp. **SIC:** 6021—National Commercial Banks. **Employee Count:** 2136.

★ 72975 ★ **Diablo Services Corp.**
745 N. State St.
Jackson, MS 39202
(601)354-4608
Ultimate Parent: Tosco Corp. **SIC:** 8748—Business Consulting Services Nec.

★ 72976 ★ **Diebold Inc.**
122 S. Springridge Rd.
Jackson, MS 39209
(601)922-6210
Ultimate Parent: Diebold, Inc. **SIC:** 5046—Commercial Equipment Nec.

★ 72977 ★ **Digital Equipment Corp.**
460 Briarwood Dr.
Jackson, MS 39206
(601)957-2702
Ultimate Parent: Digital Equipment Corp. **SIC:** 5046—Commercial Equipment Nec.

★ 72978 ★ **Electronic Data Systems**
317 E. Capitol St.
Jackson, MS 39201
(601)949-3115
Ultimate Parent: Electronic Data Systems. **SIC:** 7374—Data Processing & Preparation.

★ 72979 ★ **Emery Worldwide**
Allen
Jackson, MS 39205
(601)939-3544
Ultimate Parent: Consolidated Freightways. **SIC:** 4512—Air Transportation—Scheduled.

★ 72980 ★ **Engelhard Corp.**
600 E. McDowell Rd.
Jackson, MS 39204
(601)948-3966
Officer: Larry Shaffer, Manager. **Ultimate Parent:** Engelhard Corp. **SIC:** 2819—Industrial Inorganic Chemicals Nec; 2899—Chemical Preparations Nec; 3295—Minerals—Ground or Treated.

★ 72981 ★ **Entergy Operations Inc.**
1340 Echelon Pky.
Jackson, MS 39213-8210
(601)984-9000
Company Type: Subsidiary. **Ultimate Parent:** Entergy. **SIC:** 4911—Electric Services.

★ 72982 ★ Exxon Car Wash
3910 Hanging Moss Rd.
Jackson, MS 39206
(601)982-9866
Ultimate Parent: Exxon. SIC: 7542—Car
Washes.

★ 72983 ★ Exxon Co. USA
5104 Heatherton Dr.
Jackson, MS 39211
Ultimate Parent: Exxon. SIC: 1311—Crude
Petroleum & Natural Gas.

★ 72984 ★ Fleet Finance Inc.
2310 Us 80 W
Jackson, MS 39204
(601)948-4021
Ultimate Parent: Fleet Financial Group.
SIC: 6062—State Credit Unions.

★ 72985 ★ G & W Life Insurance
Co.
210 E. Capitol St.
Jackson, MS 39205
(601)354-8497
Company Type: Subsidiary. Officer: Buzz
Lowery, Mgr. Ultimate Parent: Deposit
Guaranty Corp. SIC: 6311—Life Insurance.

★ 72986 ★ The Gap
Metro Ctr. Mall
Jackson, MS 39201
(601)969-6952
Ultimate Parent: GAP. SIC: 5611—Men's &
Boys' Clothing Stores.

★ 72987 ★ Gayfers
Jackson
Jackson, MS 39213
(601)981-9400
Ultimate Parent: Mercantile Stores. SIC:
5311—Department Stores.

★ 72988 ★ Hertz Rent-A-Car
Al C Thompson Field
Jackson, MS 39208
(601)939-7600
Ultimate Parent: Hertz. SIC: 7514—
Passenger Car Rental.

★ 72989 ★ Hertz Rent-A-Car
Jackson Apts.
Jackson, MS 39203
(601)939-5312
Ultimate Parent: Hertz. SIC: 7514—
Passenger Car Rental.

★ 72990 ★ Illinois Central
Railroad
2151 N. Mill St.
Jackson, MS 39202
(601)949-1800
Ultimate Parent: Illinois Central

★ 72991 ★ Jackson Coca-Cola
Bottling Co.
1421 Hwy. 80 W
Jackson, MS 39204
Ultimate Parent: Coca-Cola Bottling
Consol.

★ 72992 ★ Jiffy Lube
54076 PO Box
Jackson, MS 39288
Ultimate Parent: Pennzoil. SIC: 7539—
Automotive Repair Shops Nec.

★ 72993 ★ Johnson Controls Inc.
696 Pearl
Jackson, MS 39208
(601)932-4111
Ultimate Parent: Johnson Controls Inc.
SIC: 1711—Plumbing, Heating & Air-
Conditioning.

★ 72994 ★ Kay Bee Toy & Hobby
Shop
112 Metrocenter Mall
Jackson, MS 39209
(601)969-0790
Ultimate Parent: Melville. SIC: 5945—
Hobby, Toy & Game Shops.

★ 72995 ★ Kay Bee Toy&Hobby
Shops
Jackson
Jackson, MS 39213
(601)366-2926
Ultimate Parent: Melville. SIC: 5945—
Hobby, Toy & Game Shops.

★ 72996 ★ Kentucky Fried
Chicken
220 W. Woodrow Wilson Ave.
Jackson, MS 39213
(601)362-7014
Ultimate Parent: Pepsico. SIC: 5812—
Eating Places.

★ 72997 ★ Kentucky Fried
Chicken
1675 Terry Rd.
Jackson, MS 39204
(601)948-4800
Ultimate Parent: Pepsico. SIC: 5812—
Eating Places.

★ 72998 ★ Kentucky Fried
Chicken
2974 Terry Rd.
Jackson, MS 39212
(601)372-8212
Ultimate Parent: Pepsico. SIC: 5812—
Eating Places.

★ 72999 ★ Kentucky Fried
Chicken
350 Meadowbrook Rd.
Jackson, MS 39206
(601)366-9641
Ultimate Parent: Pepsico. SIC: 5812—
Eating Places.

★ 73000 ★ Kentucky Fried
Chicken
2530 Robinson St.
Jackson, MS 39209
(601)355-2976
Ultimate Parent: Pepsico. SIC: 5812—
Eating Places.

★ 73001 ★ Kentucky Fried
Chicken
Hwy. 80 E
Jackson, MS 39208
(601)939-5035
Ultimate Parent: Pepsico. SIC: 5812—
Eating Places.

★ 73002 ★ Kentucky Fried
Chicken
4854 I N. 55
Jackson, MS 39211
(601)366-1698
Ultimate Parent: Pepsico. SIC: 5812—
Eating Places.

★ 73003 ★ Kentucky Fried
Chicken
3296 Hwy. 80 W
Jackson, MS 39204
(601)353-0134
Ultimate Parent: Pepsico. SIC: 5812—
Eating Places.

★ 73004 ★ Kroger Co.
3171 Robinson St.
Jackson, MS 39209
(601)922-0220
Ultimate Parent: Kroger. SIC: 5411—
Grocery Stores.

★ 73005 ★ Kroger Co.
311 W. Northside Dr.
Jackson, MS 39206
(601)366-2464
Ultimate Parent: Kroger. SIC: 5411—
Grocery Stores.

★ 73006 ★ Kroger Co.
4910 I N
Jackson, MS 39206
(601)366-1141
Ultimate Parent: Kroger. SIC: 5411—
Grocery Stores.

★ 73007 ★ Kroger Co.
2101 Raymond Rd.
Jackson, MS 39212
(601)371-0311
Ultimate Parent: Kroger. SIC: 5411—
Grocery Stores.

★ 73008 ★ Kroger Co.
E County Line Rd.
Jackson, MS 39211
(601)956-0335
Ultimate Parent: Kroger. SIC: 5912—Drug
Stores & Proprietary Stores.

★ 73009 ★ Kroger Co. No 346
2885 Terry Rd.
Jackson, MS 39212
(601)372-2768
Ultimate Parent: Kroger. SIC: 5411—
Grocery Stores.

★ 73010 ★ Kroger Grocery
5802 Us 80 E
Jackson, MS 39208
(601)825-3373
Ultimate Parent: Kroger. SIC: 5411—
Grocery Stores.

★ 73011 ★ Kroger Supermarket
201 George Wallace Dr.
Jackson, MS 39208
(601)932-2325
Ultimate Parent: Kroger. SIC: 5411—
Grocery Stores.

★ 73012 ★ Kroger Warehouse
199 Interstate Dr.
Jackson, MS 39218
(601)939-0911
Ultimate Parent: Kroger. SIC: 4225—
General Warehousing & Storage.

★ 73013 ★ Lane Bryant
Northpark Mall
Jackson, MS 39211
(601)957-3447
Ultimate Parent: Limited. SIC: 5621—
Women's Clothing Stores.

★ 73014 ★ Lane Bryant
Metro Ctr. Mall
Jackson, MS 39201
(601)969-3078
Ultimate Parent: Limited. SIC: 5621—
Women's Clothing Stores.

★ 73015 ★ Lerner Shop
Jackson
Jackson, MS 39213
(601)982-8979
Ultimate Parent: Limited. SIC: 5621—
Women's Clothing Stores.

★ 73016 ★ Lerner Shop
1169 Metrocenter
Jackson, MS 39209
(601)982-8979
Ultimate Parent: Limited. SIC: 5651—
Family Clothing Stores.

★ 73017 ★ Lerner Shop
Metro Ctr. Mall
Jackson, MS 39201
(601)354-3649
Ultimate Parent: Limited. SIC: 5621—
Women's Clothing Stores.

★ 73018 ★ The Limited
Metro Ctr. Mall
Jackson, MS 39201
(601)969-0807
Ultimate Parent: Limited. SIC: 5621—
Women's Clothing Stores.

★ 73019 ★ The Limited
46 Metrocenter Mall
Jackson, MS 39209
(601)969-0807
Ultimate Parent: Limited. SIC: 5651—
Family Clothing Stores.

★ 73020 ★ The Limited
Highland Village
Jackson, MS 39211
(601)981-4250
Ultimate Parent: Limited. SIC: 5621—
Women's Clothing Stores; 5651—Family
Clothing Stores.

★ 73021 ★ The Limited Express
1129 Metro Ctr. Mall
Jackson, MS 39201
(601)352-8220
Ultimate Parent: Limited. SIC: 5621—
Women's Clothing Stores.

★ 73022 ★ The Limited Express
9 Metrocenter Mall
Jackson, MS 39209
(601)352-8220
Ultimate Parent: Limited. SIC: 5651—
Family Clothing Stores.

★ 73023 ★ Lowe's Home Center
5210 Us 80 W
Jackson, MS 39209
(601)922-8121
Ultimate Parent: Lowe's. SIC: 5039—
Construction Materials Nec.

★ 73024 ★ Mary Kay Cosmetics
191 Ted Cir.
Jackson, MS 39218
(601)932-5505
Ultimate Parent: Mary Kay Cosmetics.

★ 73025 ★ Mississippi Power &
Light Co.
308 E. Pearl St.
Jackson, MS 39201-3408
(601)969-2311
Company Type: Subsidiary. Officer: Jerry
L. Maulden, Chairman of the Board & CEO.
Ultimate Parent: Entergy. SIC: 4911—
Electric Services. Employee Count: 1507.
Sales: 82 M.

★ 73026 ★ Northrop Corp.
5440 Highland Dr.
Jackson, MS 39206
(601)981-4122
Ultimate Parent: Northrop Corp. SIC:
3721—Aircraft.

★ 73027 ★ Otis Elevator Co.
810 Foley St.
Jackson, MS 39202
(601)948-3506
Ultimate Parent: United Technologies. SIC:
3534—Elevators & Moving Stairways;
5084—Industrial Machinery & Equipment.

★ 73028 ★ Pappagallo
1060 E. County Line Rd.
Jackson, MS 39211
(601)956-0776
Ultimate Parent: United States Shoe. SIC:
5621—Women's Clothing Stores.

★ 73029 ★ Penn Mutual Life
Insurance
248 E. Capitol St.
Jackson, MS 39201
(601)969-2966
Ultimate Parent: Penn Mutual Life. SIC:
6411—Insurance Agents, Brokers &
Service.

★ 73030 ★ Pepsi-Cola Bottling
Co.
2550 Medgar Evers Blvd.
Jackson, MS 39213
(601)982-4160
Officer: William Brown, President. Ultimate
Parent: Pepsico. SIC: 2086—Bottled &
Canned Soft Drinks.

★ 73031 ★ Pizza Hut
6500 Old Canton Rd.
Jackson, MS 39211
(601)956-2820
Ultimate Parent: Pepsico. SIC: 5812—
Eating Places.

★ 73032 ★ Pizza Hut
5571 Robinson Rd.
Jackson, MS 39204
(601)373-9374
Ultimate Parent: Pepsico. SIC: 5812—
Eating Places.

★ 73033 ★ Pizza Hut
1766 Ellis Ave.
Jackson, MS 39204
(601)373-6843
Ultimate Parent: Pepsico. SIC: 5812—
Eating Places.

★ 73034 ★ Pizza Hut
4745 I N. 55
Jackson, MS 39206
(601)362-5052
Ultimate Parent: Pepsico. SIC: 5812—
Eating Places.

★ 73035 ★ Pizza Hut
4580 Clinton Blvd.
Jackson, MS 39209
(601)922-0450
Ultimate Parent: Pepsico. SIC: 5812—
Eating Places.

★ 73036 ★ Pizza Hut
2430 Bailey Ave.
Jackson, MS 39213
(601)982-1366
Ultimate Parent: Pepsico. SIC: 5812—
Eating Places.

★ 73037 ★ Pizza Hut
1880 Lakeland Dr.
Jackson, MS 39216
(601)982-4190
Ultimate Parent: Pepsico. SIC: 5812—
Eating Places.

★ 73038 ★ Pizza Hut
3115 Terry Rd.
Jackson, MS 39212
(601)373-4939
Ultimate Parent: Pepsico. SIC: 5812—
Eating Places.

★ 73039 ★ Radio Shack
Jackson
Jackson, MS 39213
(601)981-4760
Company Type: Division. Ultimate Parent:
Tandy Corp. SIC: 5731—Radio, Television
& Electronics Stores.

★ 73040 ★ Radio Shack
Westland Plz.
Jackson, MS 39209
(601)352-5001
Company Type: Division. Ultimate Parent:
Tandy Corp. SIC: 5046—Commercial
Equipment Nec.

★ 73041 ★ Radio Shack
Metro Ctr. Mall
Jackson, MS 39201
(601)969-0850
Company Type: Division. Ultimate Parent:
Tandy Corp. SIC: 5065—Electronic Parts &
Equipment Nec.

★ 73042 ★ Radio Shack
Queens Mall W
Jackson, MS 39209
(601)922-9725
Company Type: Division. Ultimate Parent:
Tandy Corp. SIC: 5731—Radio, Television
& Electronics Stores.

★ 73043 ★ Radio Shack
Deville Plz.
Jackson, MS 39204
(601)956-5843
Company Type: Division. Ultimate Parent:
Tandy Corp. SIC: 5065—Electronic Parts &
Equipment Nec.

★ 73044 ★ Radio Shack
Jackson Apts
Jackson, MS 39203
(601)373-4120
Company Type: Division. Ultimate Parent:
Tandy Corp. SIC: 5065—Electronic Parts &
Equipment Nec.

★ 73045 ★ Radio Shack
Country
Jackson, MS 39204
(601)956-5509
Company Type: Division. Ultimate Parent:
Tandy Corp. SIC: 5065—Electronic Parts &
Equipment Nec.

★ 73046 ★ Radio Shack
4200 N. State St.
Jackson, MS 39206
(601)981-5101
Company Type: Division. Ultimate Parent:
Tandy Corp. SIC: 5731—Radio, Television
& Electronics Stores.

★ 73047 ★ Radio Shack
3554 Us 80 E
Jackson, MS 39208
(601)939-3377
Company Type: Division. Ultimate Parent:
Tandy Corp. SIC: 5065—Electronic Parts &
Equipment Nec.

★ 73048 ★ Radio Shack
6554 Old Canton Rd.
Jackson, MS 39211
(601)956-5509
Company Type: Division. Ultimate Parent:
Tandy Corp. SIC: 5731—Radio, Television
& Electronics Stores.

★ 73049 ★ Radio Shack
2640 Terry Rd.
Jackson, MS 39204
(601)372-4353
Company Type: Division. Ultimate Parent:
Tandy Corp. SIC: 5731—Radio, Television
& Electronics Stores.

★ 73050 ★ Radio Shack
45 Jackson Mall
Jackson, MS 39213
(601)366-6226
Company Type: Division. Ultimate Parent:
Tandy Corp. SIC: 5731—Radio, Television
& Electronics Stores.

★ 73051 ★ Radio Shack
36 Metrocenter Mall
Jackson, MS 39209
(601)969-0858
Company Type: Division. Ultimate Parent:
Tandy Corp. SIC: 5731—Radio, Television
& Electronics Stores.

★ 73052 ★ Radio Shack
1335 Ellis Ave.
Jackson, MS 39204
(601)353-6721
Company Type: Division. Ultimate Parent:
Tandy Corp. SIC: 5065—Electronic Parts &
Equipment Nec; 5731—Radio, Television &
Electronics Stores.

★ 73053 ★ Radio Shack
5050 I N
Jackson, MS 39206
(601)956-5843
Company Type: Division. Ultimate Parent:
Tandy Corp. SIC: 5731—Radio, Television
& Electronics Stores.

★ 73054 ★ Ryder Truck Rental
425 Hwy. 49 S
Jackson, MS 39218
(601)932-4734
Ultimate Parent: Ryder System. SIC:
5113—Industrial & Personal Service Paper.

★ 73055 ★ Ryder Truck Rental
1500 Hwy. 49 S
Jackson, MS 39208
(601)932-4385
Ultimate Parent: Ryder System. SIC:
7359—Equipment Rental & Leasing Nec.

★ 73056 ★ Ryder Truck Rental
4340 Milwaukee St.
Jackson, MS 39209
(601)948-3601
Ultimate Parent: Ryder System. SIC:
7513—Truck Rental & Leasing Without
Drivers.

★ 73057 ★ Sam's Wholesale
Club
590 Raymond Rd.
Jackson, MS 39204
(601)857-8920
Ultimate Parent: Wal-Mart Stores, Inc. SIC:
5099—Durable Goods Nec.

★ 73058 ★ Septem Energy
Resources Inc.
Echelon 1
1340 Echelon Pky.
Jackson, MS 39213
(601)984-9000
Company Type: Subsidiary. Officer: Edwin
Lupberger, Chairman of the Board. Ultimate
Parent: Entergy. SIC: 4911—Electric
Services. Sales: 723410000 M.

★ 73059 ★ Service Merchandise
4060 Metro Dr.
Jackson, MS 39209
(601)354-3200
Ultimate Parent: Service Merchandise Co.,
Inc. SIC: 5961—Catalog & Mail-Order
Houses.

★ 73060 ★ Service Merchandise
5250 I N
Jackson, MS 39206
(601)956-4814
Ultimate Parent: Service Merchandise Co.,
Inc. SIC: 5944—Jewelry Stores.

★ 73061 ★ Service Merchandise
Catalog
4060 Metro Dr.
Jackson, MS 39209
(601)354-3200
Ultimate Parent: Service Merchandise Co.,
Inc. SIC: 5961—Catalog & Mail-Order
Houses.

★ 73062 ★ Shell Mini Mart
Hwy. 49 S
Jackson, MS 39208
(601)939-7496
Ultimate Parent: Shell Oil Co. SIC: 5541—
Gasoline Service Stations.

★ 73063 ★ Shell Truck Stop
5714 Medgar Evers Blvd.
Jackson, MS 39213
(601)362-4738
Ultimate Parent: Shell Oil Co. SIC: 5411—
Grocery Stores.

★ 73064 ★ Sloan Paper Co.
300 Commerce Park Dr.
Jackson, MS 39213-7054
(601)362-9601
Officer: James Fox. Ultimate Parent: Alco
Standard Corp. SIC: 5113—Industrial &
Personal Service Paper; 5111—Printing &
Writing Paper.

★ 73065 ★ Southland Oil Co.
5170 Galaxie Dr.
Jackson, MS 39206
(601)981-4151
Officer: Roger G. McGrath, President.
Ultimate Parent: Burlington Resources.
SIC: 2911—Petroleum Refining.

★ 73066 ★ Specialty Food
Products
4240 Industrial Dr.
PO Box 10627
Jackson, MS 39209
(601)948-8570 Fax: (601)978-7179
Company Type: Division. Officer: William
E. Boyd, General Manager. Ultimate
Parent: Sara Lee Corp. SIC: 2035—Pickles,
Sauces & Salad Dressings.

★ 73067 ★ System Energy
Resources Inc.
1340 Echelon Pky.
Jackson, MS 39213-8210
(601)984-9000
Company Type: Subsidiary. Officer: Edwin
Lupberger, Chairman of the Board. Ultimate
Parent: Entergy. SIC: 4911—Electric
Services. Employee Count: 6. Sales: 723
M.

★ 73068 ★ System Energy
Resources Inc.
188 E. Capitol St.
Jackson, MS 39201
(601)960-9600
Ultimate Parent: Entergy. SIC: 8742—
Management Consulting Services.

★ 73069 ★ Taco Bell
3051 Us 80 E
Jackson, MS 39208
(601)939-0340
Ultimate Parent: Pepsico. SIC: 5812—
Eating Places.

★ 73070 ★ Taco Bell
3276 Us 80 W
Jackson, MS 39204
(601)355-2957
Ultimate Parent: Pepsico. SIC: 5812—
Eating Places.

★ 73071 ★ Taco Bell
330 E. Northside Dr.
Jackson, MS 39206
(601)981-0673
Ultimate Parent: Pepsico. SIC: 5812—
Eating Places.

★ 73072 ★ Taco Bell
2214 Metrocenter
Jackson, MS 39209
(601)355-0358
Ultimate Parent: Pepsico. SIC: 5812—
Eating Places.

★ 73073 ★ Texaco
1734 N. Mill St.
Jackson, MS 39202
(601)948-2201
Ultimate Parent: Texaco. SIC: 5541—
Gasoline Service Stations.

★ 73074 ★ Texaco Oil & Gas
3073 Terry Rd.
Jackson, MS 39212
(601)373-1730
Ultimate Parent: Texaco. SIC: 5541—
Gasoline Service Stations.

★ 73075 ★ Texaco USA
3900 Lakeland Dr. 504
Jackson, MS 39208
Ultimate Parent: Texaco. SIC: 1311—
Crude Petroleum & Natural Gas; 5172—
Petroleum Products Nec.

★ 73076 ★ Toys R US
3850 Us 80 W
Jackson, MS 39209
(601)922-0199
Ultimate Parent: Toys "R" US. SIC: 5945—
Hobby, Toy & Game Shops.

★ 73077 ★ Trane Co.
639 Monroe St.
Jackson, MS 39202
(601)353-4926
Ultimate Parent: American Standard. SIC:
5075—Warm Air Heating & Air-Conditioning.

★ 73078 ★ Twb Inc.
825 W. Northside Dr.
Jackson, MS 39206
(601)362-2274
Ultimate Parent: Worthington Industries,
Inc.

★ 73079 ★ Underwriters
Adjusting Co.
5225 Galaxie Dr.
Jackson, MS 39206
(601)981-7210
Ultimate Parent: Continental. SIC: 6411—
Insurance Agents, Brokers & Service.

★ 73080 ★ Union Oil Co. of
California
5058 N. State St.
Jackson, MS 39206
(601)366-7676
Ultimate Parent: Unocal Corp. SIC: 5172—
Petroleum Products Nec.

★ 73081 ★ Unisys Corp.
5380 I N
Jackson, MS 39206
(601)956-5004
Ultimate Parent: Unisys Corp. SIC: 7373—
Computer Integrated Systems Design.

★ 73082 ★ United Parcel Service
605 E. Mcdowell Rd.
Jackson, MS 39204
(601)948-7510
Ultimate Parent: United Parcel Service of
America. SIC: 4212—Local Trucking
Without Storage; 4215—Courier Services
Except by Air.

★ 73083 ★ US Fidelity & Gu
2 Le Fleurs Sq.
Jackson, MS 39211
(601)982-5555
Ultimate Parent: USF&G Corp. SIC:
6411—Insurance Agents, Brokers &
Service.

★ 73084 ★ Variable Annuity Life
Insurance
2310 Us 80 W
Jackson, MS 39204
(601)354-0838
Ultimate Parent: Variable Annuity Life. SIC:
6411—Insurance Agents, Brokers &
Service.

★ 73085 ★ Vickers
5353 Highland Dr.
Jackson, MS 39206
(601)981-2811
Officer: Tommy Horton, Manager. Ultimate
Parent: Trinova Corp. SIC: 3728—Aircraft
Parts & Equipment Nec.

★ 73086 ★ Vickers Inc.
5353 Highland Dr.
Jackson, MS 39206
(601)981-2811
Ultimate Parent: Trinova Corp. SIC:
3728—Aircraft Parts & Equipment Nec.

★ 73087 ★ Vickers Inc.
Aerospace Marine Defense
5353 Highland Dr.
Jackson, MS 39206-3449
Ultimate Parent: Trinova Corp. SIC:
3599—Industrial Machinery Nec; 3594—
Fluid Power Pumps & Motors; 3561—
Pumps & Pumping Equipment; 3568—
Power Transmission Equipment Nec.

★ 73088 ★ Victoria's Secret
45 Metrocenter Mall
Jackson, MS 39209
(601)355-0200
Ultimate Parent: Limited. SIC: 5651—
Family Clothing Stores.

★ 73089 ★ Wal Mart Discount
City
1775 Ellis Isle Shopping Ctr.
Jackson, MS 39204
(601)372-2898
Ultimate Parent: Wal-Mart Stores, Inc. SIC:
5311—Department Stores.

★ **73090** ★ **Wal Mart Discount City**
5800 Us 80 E
Jackson, MS 39208
(601)939-8024
Ultimate Parent: Wal-Mart Stores, Inc. **SIC:** 5399—Miscellaneous General Merchandise Store.

★ **73091** ★ **Waldenbooks**
Metro Ctr. Mall
Jackson, MS 39201
(601)969-6949
Ultimate Parent: K-Mart. **SIC:** 5942—Book Stores.

★ **73092** ★ **Waldenbooks**
20 Metrocenter Mall
Jackson, MS 39209
(601)969-6949
Ultimate Parent: K-Mart. **SIC:** 5942—Book Stores.

★ **73093** ★ **Waldenbooks**
1200 E. County Line Rd.
Jackson, MS 39211
(601)957-3763
Ultimate Parent: K-Mart. **SIC:** 5942—Book Stores.

★ **73094** ★ **Warren Petroleum Co.**
5135 Galaxie Dr.
Jackson, MS 39206
(601)362-6942
Ultimate Parent: Chevron Corp. **SIC:** 5984—Liquefied Petroleum Gas Dealers.

★ **73095** ★ **Western Auto Supply Codel**
4350 Industrial Dr.
Jackson, MS 39209
(601)352-8348
Ultimate Parent: Sears Roebuck & Co. **SIC:** 5399—Miscellaneous General Merchandise Store.

Kosciusko

★ **73096** ★ **Kentucky Fried Chicken**
109 State Hwy. 12 E
Kosciusko, MS 39090
(601)289-6602
Ultimate Parent: Pepsico. **SIC:** 5812—Eating Places.

★ **73097** ★ **Pizza Hut**
506 Hwy. 35 Bypass
Kosciusko, MS 39090
(601)289-7115
Ultimate Parent: Pepsico. **SIC:** 5812—Eating Places.

★ **73098** ★ **Wal Mart Discount City**
State Hwy. 12 W
Kosciusko, MS 39090
(601)289-3422
Ultimate Parent: Wal-Mart Stores, Inc. **SIC:** 5399—Miscellaneous General Merchandise Store.

Laurel

★ **73099** ★ **Baker Performance Chemicals**
3705 Industrial Blvd.
Laurel, MS 39440
(601)649-1955
Officer: Jerry Fenton, Manager. **Ultimate Parent:** Baker Hughes. **SIC:** 2869—Industrial Organic Chemicals Nec.

★ **73100** ★ **Exxon Co. USA**
1300 N. Meridian Ave.
Laurel, MS 39440
(601)425-2394
Ultimate Parent: Exxon. **SIC:** 5541—Gasoline Service Stations.

★ **73101** ★ **Greyhound Bus Lines**
460 N. Magnolia St.
Laurel, MS 39440
(601)426-2311
Ultimate Parent: Greyhound Lines Inc. **SIC:** 4111—Local & Suburban Transit.

★ **73102** ★ **Kroger Co.**
Hwy. 15 N
Laurel, MS 39440
(601)426-6044
Ultimate Parent: Kroger. **SIC:** 5411—Grocery Stores.

★ **73103** ★ **Lerner Shop**
17 Sawmill Sq.
Laurel, MS 39440
(601)425-5441
Ultimate Parent: Limited. **SIC:** 5651—Family Clothing Stores.

★ **73104** ★ **Masonite Corp. Bldg. Products Group**
1001 S. 4th Ave.
Laurel, MS 39440
Ultimate Parent: International Paper Co. **SIC:** 2493—Reconstituted Wood Products.

★ **73105** ★ **Masonite Corp. Hardboard Group**
S. Fourth Ave.
Laurel, MS 39440
Ultimate Parent: USG Corp. **SIC:** 2493—Reconstituted Wood Products.

★ **73106** ★ **Piggly Wiggly**
Westland Mart Shopping Ctr.
Laurel, MS 39440
(601)425-3111
Ultimate Parent: Bruno's. **SIC:** 5411—Grocery Stores.

★ **73107** ★ **Pizza Hut**
1015 Hwy. 15 N
Laurel, MS 39440
(601)649-3942
Ultimate Parent: Pepsico. **SIC:** 5812—Eating Places.

★ **73108** ★ **Tesoro Petroleum Distribution Co.**
Hwy. 11 N
Laurel, MS 39440
(601)425-4661
Ultimate Parent: Tesoro Petroleum Corp. **SIC:** 5983—Fuel Oil Dealers.

★ **73109** ★ **Trailway Bus Station**
648 Cross St.
Laurel, MS 39440
(601)428-5128
Ultimate Parent: Greyhound Lines Inc. **SIC:** 4111—Local & Suburban Transit.

Leakesville

★ **73110** ★ **Piggly Wiggly**
Leakesville, MS 39451
(601)394-2357
Ultimate Parent: Bruno's. **SIC:** 5411—Grocery Stores.

Leland

★ **73111** ★ **Greyhound Bus Lines**
404 N. Broad St.
Leland, MS 38756
(601)686-2514
Ultimate Parent: Greyhound Lines Inc. **SIC:** 4131—Intercity & Rural Bus Transportation.

★ **73112** ★ **La-Z-Boy Leland**
Rte. 2
PO Box 500
Leland, MS 38756
(601)686-4151 **Fax:** (601)686-9721
Officer: M. Wesley Simpson, Vice President. **Ultimate Parent:** La-Z-Boy Chair.

★ **73113** ★ **La-Z-Boy Leland**
Old Hwy. 61 N. Rte. 2 Box 500
Leland, MS 38756
Ultimate Parent: La-Z-Boy Chair. **SIC:** 2521—Wood Office Furniture.

Lexington

★ **73114** ★ **Fleetwood Homes**
100 Fleetwood Cir.
Lexington, MS 39095
(601)834-1005
Officer: Steve Smith, Manager. **Ultimate Parent:** Fleetwood Enterprises, Inc. **SIC:** 2451—Mobile Homes.

★ **73115** ★ **Piggly Wiggly**
Hwy. 12
Lexington, MS 39095
(601)834-3447
Ultimate Parent: Bruno's. **SIC:** 5411—Grocery Stores.

★ **73116** ★ **Texaco on the Square**
408 Court Sq.
Lexington, MS 39095
(601)834-9937
Ultimate Parent: Texaco. **SIC:** 5541—Gasoline Service Stations.

Liberty

★ **73117** ★ **First Bank**
520 PO Box
Liberty, MS 39645
(601)657-8003
Ultimate Parent: Shawmut National Corp. **SIC:** 6099—Functions Related to Deposit Banking.

Long Beach

★ **73118** ★ **Otis Elevator Co.**
109 Thompson Dr.
Long Beach, MS 39560
(601)863-5464
Ultimate Parent: United Technologies. **SIC:** 1796—Installing Building Equipment Nec; 5084—Industrial Machinery & Equipment.

Louisville

★ **73119** ★ **Georgia-Pacific Corp. Plywood Plant**
Pl Hwy. 15 S
Louisville, MS 39339
Ultimate Parent: Georgia-Pacific. **SIC:** 2436—Softwood Veneer & Plywood.

★ **73120** ★ **Georgia-Pacific Corp. Resins Plant**
Armstrong St. PO Box 309
Louisville, MS 39339
Ultimate Parent: Georgia-Pacific. **SIC:** 2821—Plastics Materials & Resins.

★ **73121** ★ **Georgia Pacific Resins Inc.**
Armstrong St. PO Box 309
Louisville, MS 39339
Ultimate Parent: Georgia-Pacific. **SIC:** 2821—Plastics Materials & Resins.

★ **73122** ★ **Georgia-Pacific Resins Inc. Resins Plant**
Armstrong St.
Louisville, MS 39339
Ultimate Parent: Georgia-Pacific. **SIC:** 2821—Plastics Materials & Resins.

★ **73123** ★ **McDonalds**
401 Church
Louisville, MS 39339
(601)773-9637
Ultimate Parent: McDonald's. **SIC:** 5812—Eating Places.

★ **73124** ★ **Piggly Wiggly**
608 N. Church Ave.
Louisville, MS 39339
(601)773-8252
Ultimate Parent: Bruno's. **SIC:** 5411—Grocery Stores.

★ **73125** ★ **TRW Seat Belt Systems**
907 W. Main St.
Louisville, MS 39339
(601)773-8712
Officer: Bob Brooks, Plant Manager. **Ultimate Parent:** TRW, Inc. **SIC:** 2399—Fabricated Textile Products Nec; 3679—Electronic Components Nec.

★ **73126** ★ **Wal Mart Discount City**
Hwy. 15 N
Louisville, MS 39339
(601)773-7823
Ultimate Parent: Wal-Mart Stores, Inc. **SIC:** 5311—Department Stores.

Lucedale

★ **73127** ★ **Coca Cola Bottling Co. Inc.**
Hwy. 98 E
Lucedale, MS 39452
(601)947-4541
Ultimate Parent: Coca-Cola Enterprises. **SIC:** 2086—Bottled & Canned Soft Drinks.

★ **73128** ★ **Piggly Wiggly**
W Main
Lucedale, MS 39452
(601)947-3811
Ultimate Parent: Bruno's. **SIC:** 5411—Grocery Stores.

★ **73129** ★ **Stop & Shop**
1005 Hwy. 63 S
Lucedale, MS 39452
(601)947-4067
Ultimate Parent: Stop & Shop. **SIC:** 5411—Grocery Stores.

Lumberton

★ **73130** ★ **Cooper Power Systems**
100 Industrial Pky.
Lumberton, MS 39455
Ultimate Parent: Cooper Industries. **SIC:** 3612—Transformers Except Electronic.

★ **73131** ★ **Mcgraw Edison**
100 Industrial Pky.
Lumberton, MS 39455
Ultimate Parent: Cooper Industries. **SIC:** 3612—Transformers Except Electronic.

★ **73132** ★ **Southland Oil Co. Lumberton**
Hwy. 11 N.
Lumberton, MS 39455
Ultimate Parent: Southland Corp. **SIC:** 2911—Petroleum Refining; 2911—Petroleum Refining.

Maben

★ **73133** ★ **Wilsons**
2nd Ave.
Maben, MS 39750
(601)263-8277
Ultimate Parent: Melville. **SIC:** 5949—Sewing, Needlework & Piece Goods.

Macon

★ **73134** ★ **California Manufacturing Co.**
PO Box 271
Macon, MS 39341-0271
(601)726-4255
Location Type: Headquarters. **Ultimate Parent:** Avon Products, Inc. **SIC:** 2329—Men's/Boys' Clothing Nec; 5137—Women's/Children's Clothing.

Madison

★ **73135** ★ **Ace Hardware**
218 Us 51 S
Madison, MS 39110
(601)856-5555
Ultimate Parent: Ace Hardware. **SIC:** 5251—Hardware Stores.

★ **73136** ★ **Mellon Financial Service Corp.**
2144 Lake Shore Dr.
Madison, MS 39110
(601)856-4496
Ultimate Parent: Mellon Bank Corp. **SIC:** 6141—Personal Credit Institutions.

★ **73137** ★ **Parker Hannifin Corp.**
147 W. Hoy Rd.
Madison, MS 39110
Ultimate Parent: Parker Hannifin. **SIC:** 3492—Fluid Power Valves & Hose Fittings.

Magee

★ **73138** ★ **Exxon Service Center**
Corner of Hwy. 49
Magee, MS 39111
(601)849-4600
Ultimate Parent: Exxon. **SIC:** 7538—General Automotive Repair Shops.

★ **73139** ★ **Wal Mart Department Store**
Hwy. 49 North by
Magee, MS 39111
(601)849-2628
Ultimate Parent: Wal-Mart Stores, Inc. **SIC:** 5311—Department Stores.

Magnolia

★ 73140 ★   **First Bank**
282 E. Bay St.
Magnolia, MS 39652
(601)783-5071
Ultimate Parent: Shawmut National Corp.
SIC: 6022—State Commercial Banks.

Marion

★ 73141 ★   **Clark Printing Co.**
5407 Lexeton
Marion, MS 39342
(601)483-6387
Ultimate Parent: Terex. **SIC:** 2752—
Commercial Printing—Lithographic.

Mathiston

★ 73142 ★   **Red Kap Ind.**
Hwy. 82
Mathiston, MS 39752
(601)263-8274
Officer: Jerry Riggan, Manager. **Ultimate
Parent:** VF Corp. **SIC:** 2325—Men's/Boys'
Trousers & Slacks.

Mc Comb

★ 73143 ★   **First Bank**
Broadway 3rd
Mc Comb, MS 39648
(601)684-2231
Ultimate Parent: Shawmut National Corp.
SIC: 6022—State Commercial Banks.

★ 73144 ★   **Illinois Central
Railroad**
South Blvd.
Mc Comb, MS 39648
(601)684-0846
Ultimate Parent: Illinois Central.
SIC: 4011—RailroadsLine-Haul Operating.

★ 73145 ★   **Kentucky Fried
Chicken**
1000 Delaware Ave.
Mc Comb, MS 39348
(601)684-4744
Ultimate Parent: Pepsico. **SIC:** 5812—
Eating Places.

★ 73146 ★   **Kentucky Fried
Chicken**
123 W. Presley Blvd.
Mc Comb, MS 39648
(601)684-6841
Ultimate Parent: Pepsico. **SIC:** 5812—
Eating Places.

★ 73147 ★   **Kroger Food Store**
Delaware
Mc Comb, MS 39648
(601)684-7867
Ultimate Parent: Kroger. **SIC:** 5411—
Grocery Stores.

★ 73148 ★   **Pizza Hut**
1116 Delaware Ave.
Mc Comb, MS 39648
(601)684-9800
Ultimate Parent: Pepsico. **SIC:** 5812—
Eating Places.

★ 73149 ★   **Radio Shack**
Edgewood Mall
Mc Comb, MS 39648
(601)684-4165
Company Type: Division. **Ultimate Parent:**
Tandy Corp. **SIC:** 5731—Radio, Television
& Electronics Stores.

★ 73150 ★   **Shell Oil Co.**
115 Nehi Cir.
Mc Comb, MS 39648
(601)249-2862
Ultimate Parent: Shell Oil Co. **SIC:** 1382—
Oil & Gas Exploration Services.

★ 73151 ★   **Thrift Drugs**
119 W. Presley Blvd.
Mc Comb, MS 39648
(601)684-3401
Ultimate Parent: J.C. Penney. **SIC:** 5912—
Drug Stores & Proprietary Stores.

★ 73152 ★   **Underwriters
Adjusting Co.**
907 Delaware Ave.
Mc Comb, MS 39648
(601)684-1371
Ultimate Parent: Continental. **SIC:** 6411—
Insurance Agents, Brokers & Service.

★ 73153 ★   **Wal Mart**
Smithdale Rd.
Mc Comb, MS 39648
(601)684-1074
Ultimate Parent: Wal-Mart Stores, Inc. **SIC:**
5311—Department Stores.

McComb

★ 73154 ★   **Amerada Hess Corp.**
Delaware Ave.
McComb, MS 39648
(601)684-2371
Location Type: Branch office. **Ultimate
Parent:** Amerada Hess. **SIC:** 4612—Crude
Petroleum Pipelines.

★ 73155 ★   **Pepsi Cola Bottling
Co.**
1096 Hwy. 98 E
McComb, MS 39648
(601)684-2281
Officer: Bill Brown, President. **Ultimate
Parent:** Pepsico. **SIC:** 2086—Bottled &
Canned Soft Drinks.

Mendenhall

★ 73156 ★   **Magnetek**
Hwy. 49 S.
Mendenhall, MS 39114
Ultimate Parent: Magnetek Inc. **SIC:**
3612—Transformers Except Electronic.

★ 73157 ★   **Magnetek Universal
Manufacturing**
Hwy. 49 S.
Mendenhall, MS 39114
Ultimate Parent: Magnetek Inc. **SIC:**
3612—Transformers Except Electronic.

Meridan

★ 73158 ★   **APAC**
4412 Interchange Rd.
Meridan, MS 39307
(601)693-5025
Officer: Murry Stewart Jr., Manager.
Ultimate Parent: Ashland Oil. **SIC:** 2951—
Asphalt Paving Mixtures & Blocks.

Meridian

★ 73159 ★   **Avery Dennison**
4100 Hwy. 45 N
Meridian, MS 39301-1203
(601)483-0611
Officer: Jerry Harrison. **Ultimate Parent:**
Avery Dennison Corp. **SIC:** 2621—Paper
Mills; 7389—Business Services Nec.

★ 73160 ★   **Borden Inc.**
3705 7th St.
Meridian, MS 39307
(601)693-5421
Officer: Russell Reed, Manager. **Ultimate
Parent:** Borden, Inc. **SIC:** 2026—Fluid Milk.

★ 73161 ★   **Citgo Petroleum Corp.**
65 Ave.
Meridian, MS 39305
(601)483-6128
Ultimate Parent: Citgo Petroleum. **SIC:**
5172—Petroleum Products Nec.

★ 73162 ★   **Deposit Guaranty
Mortgage C**
1515 14th St.
Meridian, MS 39301
(601)483-3804
Ultimate Parent: Deposit Guaranty Corp.
SIC: 6141—Personal Credit Institutions;
6162—Mortgage Bankers &
Correspondents.

★ 73163 ★   **Greyhound Bus Lines**
212 21st Ave.
Meridian, MS 39301
(601)693-1663
Ultimate Parent: Greyhound Lines Inc. **SIC:**
4111—Local & Suburban Transit.

★ 73164 ★   **Hertz Rent-A-Car
System**
1001 Hwy. 11 S
Meridian, MS 39307
(601)485-4774
Ultimate Parent: Hertz. **SIC:** 7514—
Passenger Car Rental.

★ 73165 ★   **Kentucky Fried
Chicken**
2881 Tom Bailey Dr.
Meridian, MS 39301
(601)693-4431
Ultimate Parent: Pepsico. **SIC:** 5812—
Eating Places.

★ 73166 ★   **Kentucky Fried
Chicken**
3125 8th St.
Meridian, MS 39301
(601)693-1502
Ultimate Parent: Pepsico. **SIC:** 5812—
Eating Places.

★ 73167 ★   **Kentucky Fried
Chicken**
4326 8th St.
Meridian, MS 39307
(601)693-1502
Ultimate Parent: Pepsico. **SIC:** 5812—
Eating Places.

★ 73168 ★   **Kroger Co.**
22 Ave.
Meridian, MS 39305
(601)693-3161
Ultimate Parent: Kroger. **SIC:** 5411—
Grocery Stores.

★ 73169 ★   **Lerner Shop**
Village Fair Mall
Meridian, MS 39301
(601)693-2335
Ultimate Parent: Limited. **SIC:** 5621—
Women's Clothing Stores; 5651—Family
Clothing Stores.

★ 73170 ★   **Lockheed Systems
Corp.**
Lasc-Georgia Div.
Marion-Russell Rd.
Meridian, MS 39301
Company Type: Division. **Ultimate Parent:**
Lockheed Corp. **SIC:** 3721—Aircraft.

★ 73171 ★   **Ludlow Corp.
Laminating**
5312 Water Tower Rd.
Meridian, MS 39301
(601)483-0333
Officer: Phillip Riddle, Manager. **Ultimate
Parent:** Tyco International. **SIC:** 2672—
Coated & Laminated Paper Nec.

★ 73172 ★   **Owens Corning
Fiberglass**
Hwy. 11 S
Meridian, MS 39305
(601)482-0151
Ultimate Parent: Owens-Corning. **SIC:**
2655—Fiber Cans, Drums & Similar
Products.

★ 73173 ★   **Penn Mutual Life
Insurance Co.**
Citizens Bank Bldg.
Meridian, MS 39301
(601)693-5666
Ultimate Parent: Penn Mutual Life. **SIC:**
6311—Life Insurance.

★ 73174 ★   **Pizza Hut**
4537 35th Ave.
Meridian, MS 39305
(601)483-7777
Ultimate Parent: Pepsico. **SIC:** 5812—
Eating Places.

★ 73175 ★   **Pizza Hut**
4720 8th St.
Meridian, MS 39307
Ultimate Parent: Pepsico. **SIC:** 5812—
Eating Places.

★ 73176 ★   **Pizza Hut**
2018 N. Frontage Rd.
Meridian, MS 39301
(601)485-7401
Ultimate Parent: Pepsico. **SIC:** 5812—
Eating Places.

★ 73177 ★   **Radio Shack**
College Park Shopping Ctr.
Meridian, MS 39301
(601)483-0645
Company Type: Division. **Ultimate Parent:**
Tandy Corp. **SIC:** 5065—Electronic Parts &
Equipment Nec; 5731—Radio, Television &
Electronics Stores.

★ 73178 ★   **Ryder Truck Rental**
Sellars Dr.
Meridian, MS 39301
(601)485-9527
Ultimate Parent: Ryder System. **SIC:**
5113—Industrial & Personal Service Paper;
7513—Truck Rental & Leasing Without
Drivers.

★ 73179 ★   **Taco Bell**
4821 8th St.
Meridian, MS 39307
(601)693-5396
Ultimate Parent: Pepsico. **SIC:** 5812—
Eating Places.

★ 73180 ★   **Texaco**
1802 N. Frontage Rd.
Meridian, MS 39301
(601)485-6045
Ultimate Parent: Texaco. **SIC:** 5541—
Gasoline Service Stations.

★ 73181 ★   **Texaco South Service
Center**
Rural Route 3
Meridian, MS 39301
(601)485-7372
Ultimate Parent: Texaco. **SIC:** 5541—
Gasoline Service Stations.

★ 73182 ★   **Trailways Bus System**
601 23rd Ave.
Meridian, MS 39301
(601)693-2595
Ultimate Parent: Greyhound Lines Inc. **SIC:**
4131—Intercity & Rural Bus Transportation.

★ 73183 ★   **Wal Mart**
1710 State Hwy. 19 N
Meridian, MS 39307
(601)482-0425
Ultimate Parent: Wal-Mart Stores, Inc. **SIC:**
5311—Department Stores.

★ 73184 ★   **Wal Mart**
Rural Route 6
Meridian, MS 39301
(601)485-2250
Ultimate Parent: Wal-Mart Stores, Inc. **SIC:**
5311—Department Stores.

★ 73185 ★   **Wal Mart Discount
Cities**
1524 State Hwy. 19 N
Meridian, MS 39307
(601)482-3170
Ultimate Parent: Wal-Mart Stores, Inc. **SIC:**
5912—Drug Stores & Proprietary Stores.

Monticello

★ 73186 ★   **Georgia-Pacific Corp.**
Sandifer Hwy. 5 Miles N. of Monticello
Monticello, MS 39654-0608
Ultimate Parent: Georgia-Pacific. **SIC:**
2611—Pulp Mills; 2631—Paperboard Mills;
2861—Gum & Wood Chemicals.

★ 73187 ★   **Georgia Pacific Corp.**
Sandifer Hwy. Monticello
Monticello, MS 39654-0608
Ultimate Parent: Georgia-Pacific. **SIC:**
2611—Pulp Mills; 2631—Paperboard Mills;
2861—Gum & Wood Chemicals.

★ 73188 ★   **Georgia Pacific Corp.
Monticello Mill**
Sandifer Hwy. (5 Miles North of Monticello)
Monticello, MS 39654-0608
Ultimate Parent: Georgia-Pacific. **SIC:**
2611—Pulp Mills; 2631—Paperboard Mills;
2861—Gum & Wood Chemicals.

Morton

★ 73189 ★   **Carthage Machine Co.
Southern**
711 Hwy. 80 W
Morton, MS 39117
(601)732-8986 **Fax:** (601)732-8986
Company Type: Division. **Ultimate Parent:**
CBI Industries, Inc. **SIC:** 3554—Paper
Industries Machinery.

★ 73190 ★   Piggly Wiggly
647 Hwy. 80 W
Morton, MS 39117
(601)732-8381
Ultimate Parent: Bruno's. SIC: 5411—
Grocery Stores.

Moss Point

★ 73191 ★   Halter Marine Inc.
Moss Point Div.
5801 Elder Ferry Rd.
Moss Point, MS 39562-8767
Company Type: Division. Ultimate Parent:
Trinity Industries. SIC: 3731—Ship Building
& Repairing.

★ 73192 ★   International Paper
Co. Moss Point Mill
2019 Grierson Street, PO Box P
Moss Point, MS 39563
Ultimate Parent: International Paper Co.
SIC: 2611—Pulp Mills; 2621—Paper Mills;
2631—Paperboard Mills.

★ 73193 ★   International Paper-
Moss Point Mill
2019 Grierson St.
PO Box P
Moss Point, MS 39563
Ultimate Parent: International Paper Co.
SIC: 2611—Pulp Mills; 2621—Paper Mills;
2631—Paperboard Mills; 2672—Coated &
Laminated Paper Nec.

★ 73194 ★   Kentucky Fried
Chicken
4300 Main St.
Moss Point, MS 39563
(601)475-6880
Ultimate Parent: Pepsico. SIC: 5812—
Eating Places.

★ 73195 ★   Morton International
Polmer Systems
5724 Elder Ferry Rd.
Moss Point, MS 39563-9752
Ultimate Parent: Morton International. SIC:
2869—Industrial Organic Chemicals Nec;
2821—Plastics Materials & Resins; 2822—
Synthetic Rubber.

★ 73196 ★   Trinity Industries
Halter Marine Moss Point Div.
1049 Elder Ferry Rd.
Moss Point, MS 39563
Company Type: Division. Ultimate Parent:
Trinity Industries. SIC: 3731—Ship Building
& Repairing.

Natchez

★ 73197 ★   Greyhound Bus Line
103 Lower Woodville Rd.
Natchez, MS 39120
(601)445-5291
Ultimate Parent: Greyhound Lines Inc. SIC:
4131—Intercity & Rural Bus Transportation.

★ 73198 ★   Greyhound Bus Lines
108 Seargent Prentiss Dr.
Natchez, MS 39120
(601)445-8225
Ultimate Parent: Greyhound Lines Inc. SIC:
4142—Bus Charter Service Except Local.

★ 73199 ★   International Paper
Cmpany Natchez Mill
312 Lower Woodville Rd.
PO Box 311
Natchez, MS 39120
Ultimate Parent: International Paper Co.
SIC: 2611—Pulp Mills.

★ 73200 ★   International Paper
Natchez Mill
61 Carthage Point Rd.
Natchez, MS 39120
Ultimate Parent: International Paper Co.
SIC: 2611—Pulp Mills.

★ 73201 ★   International Paper
Natchez Mill
312 Lower Woodville Rd. PO Box 311
Natchez, MS 39120
Ultimate Parent: International Paper Co.
SIC: 2611—Pulp Mills.

★ 73202 ★   Kentucky Fried
Chicken
Hwy. 61 S
Natchez, MS 39120
(601)442-0992
Ultimate Parent: Pepsico. SIC: 5812—
Eating Places.

★ 73203 ★   Mobil Oil
Explor&Produc Se
Hwy. 61 S
Natchez, MS 39120
(601)442-2563
Ultimate Parent: Mobil. SIC: 1311—Crude
Petroleum & Natural Gas.

★ 73204 ★   Mutual of New York
158 Booker St.
Natchez, MS 39120
(601)442-3531
Ultimate Parent: Mutual of New York. SIC:
6411—Insurance Agents, Brokers &
Service.

★ 73205 ★   Payless Shoesource
105 Lower Woodville Rd.
Natchez, MS 39120
(601)446-7768
Ultimate Parent: May Department Stores.
SIC: 5661—Shoe Stores.

★ 73206 ★   Piggly Wiggly
Us 61 N
Natchez, MS 39120
(601)442-3861
Ultimate Parent: Bruno's. SIC: 5411—
Grocery Stores.

★ 73207 ★   Piggly Wiggly
29 Us 61 S
Natchez, MS 39120
(601)442-7101
Ultimate Parent: Bruno's. SIC: 5411—
Grocery Stores.

★ 73208 ★   Piggly Wiggly
196 S. Seargent Prentiss Dr.
Natchez, MS 39120
(601)442-2501
Ultimate Parent: Bruno's. SIC: 5411—
Grocery Stores.

★ 73209 ★   Pizza Hut
Natchez, MS 39120
(601)445-9700
Ultimate Parent: Pepsico. SIC: 5812—
Eating Places.

★ 73210 ★   Pizza Hut
27 Us 61 S
Natchez, MS 39120
(601)446-8421
Ultimate Parent: Pepsico. SIC: 5812—
Eating Places.

★ 73211 ★   Ryder Truck Rental
100 Lower Woodville Rd.
Natchez, MS 39120
(601)445-2367
Ultimate Parent: Ryder System. SIC:
7359—Equipment Rental & Leasing Nec.

★ 73212 ★   United Parcel Service
635 Highland Blvd.
Natchez, MS 39120
(601)222-8080
Ultimate Parent: United Parcel Service of
America. SIC: 4215—Courier Services
Except by Air.

★ 73213 ★   Wal Mart Discount
Cities
Magnolia Mall
Natchez, MS 39120
(601)442-7920
Ultimate Parent: Wal-Mart Stores, Inc. SIC:
5311—Department Stores.

Nettleton

★ 73214 ★   Texaco Tire Center
Hwy. 45 S
Nettleton, MS 38858
(601)963-3733
Ultimate Parent: Texaco. SIC: 5531—
Automobile & Home Supply Stores.

New Albany

★ 73215 ★   Kentucky Fried
Chicken
610 Bankhead St. W
New Albany, MS 38652
(601)534-9697
Ultimate Parent: Pepsico. SIC: 5812—
Eating Places.

★ 73216 ★   Pizza Hut
Coltur Dr.
New Albany, MS 38652
(601)534-8100
Ultimate Parent: Pepsico. SIC: 5812—
Eating Places.

★ 73217 ★   Radio Shack
312 Main St. E
New Albany, MS 38652
(601)534-2613
Company Type: Division. Ultimate Parent:
Tandy Corp. SIC: 5731—Radio, Television
& Electronics Stores.

★ 73218 ★   Wal Mart Discunt
Cities
Hwy. 78 W
New Albany, MS 38652
(601)534-8156
Ultimate Parent: Wal-Mart Stores, Inc. SIC:
5311—Department Stores.

Newton

★ 73219 ★   La-Z-Boy S. South
33 Scanlan St.
Newton, MS 39345
Ultimate Parent: La-Z-Boy Chair. SIC:
2512—Upholstered Household Furniture.

★ 73220 ★   La-Z-Boy South
33 Scanlan
Newton, MS 39345
(601)683-3354 Fax: (601)683-6950
Officer: Earl W. Bryan, Vice President.
Ultimate Parent: La-Z-Boy Chair.

Ocean Springs

★ 73221 ★   Beneficial Mississippi
Inc.
Ocean Spring Pk. Side Sq. Shopping Ctr.
Ocean Springs, MS 39564
(601)432-8667
Ultimate Parent: Beneficial. SIC: 6141—
Personal Credit Institutions.

★ 73222 ★   Southland Corp.
921 Porter St.
Ocean Springs, MS 39564
(601)875-5060
Ultimate Parent: Southland Corp. SIC:
6531—Real Estate Agents & Managers.

★ 73223 ★   Taco Bell
14190 Hwy. 90
Ocean Springs, MS 39564
(601)872-1877
Ultimate Parent: Pepsico. SIC: 5812—
Eating Places.

Okolona

★ 73224 ★   Avon Manufacturing
Co. Inc.
PO Box 326
Okolona, MS 38860-0326
Location Type: Headquarters. Ultimate
Parent: Avon Products, Inc. SIC: 2512—
Upholstered Household Furniture; 2599—
Furniture & Fixtures Nec.

★ 73225 ★   Sav-On-Drugs of
Okolona
203 S. Church St.
Okolona, MS 38860-1608
(601)447-5400
Officer: Larry Knotts. Ultimate Parent:
American Stores. SIC: 5912—Drug Stores &
Proprietary Stores.

Olive Branch

★ 73226 ★   Continental Group
Inc.
8652 Hacks Cross Rd.
Olive Branch, MS 38654
(601)895-4330
Ultimate Parent: Continental Assurance
Co. Inc. SIC: 3089—Plastics Products Nec.

★ 73227 ★   Dana Corp.
8225 Hacks Cross Rd.
Olive Branch, MS 38654
(601)895-1011
Ultimate Parent: Dana Corp. SIC: 3714—
Motor Vehicle Parts & Accessories.

★ 73228 ★   H C Industries Inc.
8363 Cedar Ridge St.
Olive Branch, MS 38654
(601)895-8040
Officer: Jo Brown, Manager. Ultimate
Parent: Aluminum Co. of America--Alcoa.
SIC: 3089—Plastics Products Nec; 3466—
Crowns & Closures.

★ 73229 ★   H.C. Industries Inc.
Closure Systems
PO Box 429
Olive Branch, MS 38654-0429
(601)895-8040
Company Type: Division. Location Type:
Branch office. Officer: David Pritchett.
Ultimate Parent: Aluminum Co. of America-
-Alcoa. SIC: 3089—Plastics Products Nec.

★ 73230 ★   Thompson & Formby
Inc.
10136 Magnolia Dr.
Olive Branch, MS 38654
Ultimate Parent: Eastman Kodak. SIC:
2851—Paints & Allied Products.

★ 73231 ★   Thompson &
Formby's Inc.
10136 Magnolia Dr.
Olive Branch, MS 38654
(601)895-5594
Officer: Bill Stewart, President. Ultimate
Parent: Eastman Kodak. SIC: 2851—Paints
& Allied Products; 2899—Chemical
Preparations Nec; 2992—Lubricating Oils &
Greases.

★ 73232 ★   True Temper
Sports Division
8706 Deerfield Dr.
Olive Branch, MS 38618-9540
(601)895-4142
Company Type: Headquarters. Officer:
Joseph Kaferle. Ultimate Parent: Black &
Decker Corp. SIC: 3949—Sporting &
Athletic Goods Nec; 3363—Aluminum Die-
Castings; 3751—Motorcycles, Bicycles &
Parts.

★ 73233 ★   True Temper Sports
8706 Deerfield Dr.
Olive Branch, MS 38654
Ultimate Parent: Black & Decker Corp.
SIC: 3949—Sporting & Athletic Goods Nec.

★ 73234 ★   Tyler Refrigeration
Corp.
11042 Wildwood Dr.
Olive Branch, MS 38654
Ultimate Parent: American Standard. SIC:
3585—Refrigeration & Heating Equipment.

Oxford

★ 73235 ★   Emerson Electri Co.
Inc.
Emerson Motor Div.
Hwy. 7 North
Oxford, MS 38655
Ultimate Parent: Emerson Electric Co. Inc.
SIC: 3621—Motors & Generators.

★ 73236 ★   Emerson Electric Co.
Emerson Motor Div.
Rte. 7 Box 924
Oxford, MS 38655
Company Type: Division. Ultimate Parent:
Emerson Electric Co. Inc. SIC: 3621—
Motors & Generators.

★ 73237 ★   Emerson Electric Co.
Emerson Motor Div.
Hwy. 7 N.
Oxford, MS 38655
Company Type: Division. Ultimate Parent:
Emerson Electric Co. Inc. SIC: 3621—
Motors & Generators.

★ 73238 ★   Emerson Motor Co.
Hwy. 7 North
Oxford, MS 38655
Ultimate Parent: Emerson Electric Co. Inc.
SIC: 3621—Motors & Generators.

★ 73239 ★ Hertz Rent-A-Car
Licensee
Airport Rd.
Oxford, MS 38655
(601)234-4231
Ultimate Parent: Hertz. SIC: 7514—
Passenger Car Rental.

★ 73240 ★ Kentucky Fried
Chicken
Eastgate Shopping Ctr.
Oxford, MS 38655
(601)234-1230
Ultimate Parent: Pepsico. SIC: 5812—
Eating Places.

★ 73241 ★ Kroger Food Store
E Univ. Ave.
Oxford, MS 38655
(601)236-1414
Ultimate Parent: Kroger. SIC: 5411—
Grocery Stores.

★ 73242 ★ Lawn-Boy
Oxford
13 Industrial Park Dr.
Oxford, MS 38655
Company Type: Division. Ultimate Parent:
Outboard Marine. SIC: 3519—Internal
Combustion Engines Nec; 3524—Lawn &
Garden Equipment.

★ 73243 ★ Outboard Marine
Corp.
13 Industrial Park Dr.
Oxford, MS 38655
Ultimate Parent: Outboard Marine. SIC:
3519—Internal Combustion Engines Nec;
3524—Lawn & Garden Equipment.

★ 73244 ★ Pizza Hut
Hwy. 6 W
Oxford, MS 38655
(601)234-0611
Ultimate Parent: Pepsico. SIC: 5812—
Eating Places.

★ 73245 ★ Pizza Hut
1506 University Ave.
Oxford, MS 38655
(601)234-8307
Ultimate Parent: Pepsico. SIC: 5812—
Eating Places.

★ 73246 ★ Trailways Bus Station
925 Van Buren Ave.
Oxford, MS 38655
(601)234-1424
Ultimate Parent: Greyhound Lines Inc. SIC:
4131—Intercity & Rural Bus Transportation.

★ 73247 ★ Wal Mart Discount
City
Oakwood Plz.
Oxford, MS 38655
(601)234-9131
Ultimate Parent: Wal-Mart Stores, Inc. SIC:
5311—Department Stores.

★ 73248 ★ Waldenbooks
1111 Jackson Ave. W
Oxford, MS 38655
(601)236-5883
Ultimate Parent: K-Mart. SIC: 5942—Book
Stores.

★ 73249 ★ Whirlpool Corp.
Old Taylor Rd.
Oxford, MS 38655
Ultimate Parent: Whirlpool Corp. SIC:
3631—Household Cooking Equipment.

★ 73250 ★ Whirlpool Corp.
927 Whirlpool Dr.
Oxford, MS 38655
Ultimate Parent: Whirlpool Corp. SIC:
3631—Household Cooking Equipment.

Pascagoula

★ 73251 ★ Bird-Johnson Co.
3719 Industrial Rd.
Pascagoula, MS 39581
Ultimate Parent: Johnson & Johnson. SIC:
3364—Nonferrous Die-Castings Except
Aluminum.

★ 73252 ★ Chevron Products Co.
Pascagoula Refinery
Hwy. 611 S.
Pascagoula, MS 39581
Ultimate Parent: Chevron Corp. SIC:
2911—Petroleum Refining; 2869—Industrial
Organic Chemicals Nec; 2873—Nitrogenous

Fertilizers; 2911—Petroleum Refining;
2869—Industrial Organic Chemicals Nec;
2873—Nitrogenous Fertilizers.

★ 73253 ★ Chevron USA Inc.
Pascagoula Refinery
Hwy. 611 S
Pascagoula, MS 39581
Ultimate Parent: Chevron Corp. SIC:
2911—Petroleum Refining; 2869—Industrial
Organic Chemicals Nec; 2873—Nitrogenous
Fertilizers.

★ 73254 ★ Chevron USA Inc.
Pascagoula Refinery
PO Box 1300, Industrial Rd. Hwy. 611
Pascagoula, MS 39567
Ultimate Parent: Chevron Corp. SIC:
2911—Petroleum Refining; 2869—Industrial
Organic Chemicals Nec; 2873—Nitrogenous
Fertilizers.

★ 73255 ★ Circus World
Singing Rv Mall
Pascagoula, MS 39567
(601)497-2296
Ultimate Parent: Melville. SIC: 5945—
Hobby, Toy & Game Shops.

★ 73256 ★ Greyhound Bus Lines
517 Live Oak Ave.
Pascagoula, MS 39567
(601)769-5255
Ultimate Parent: Greyhound Lines Inc. SIC:
4131—Intercity & Rural Bus Transportation.

★ 73257 ★ Heinz Pet Prods.
202 Watts Ave.
Pascagoula, MS 39567
Ultimate Parent: Pet. SIC: 2047—Dog &
Cat Food.

★ 73258 ★ Heinz Pet Products
202 Watts Ave.
Pascagoula, MS 39567
Ultimate Parent: Pet. SIC: 2047—Dog &
Cat Food.

★ 73259 ★ Hertz Rent-A-Car
100 Terminal Ave.
Pascagoula, MS 39567
(601)475-5599
Ultimate Parent: Hertz. SIC: 7514—
Passenger Car Rental.

★ 73260 ★ Ingalls Shipbuilding
1000 W. River Rd.
Pascagoula, MS 39568
(601)935-1122 Fax: (601)935-1126
Officer: Gerald J. St. Pe, President.
Ultimate Parent: Litton Industries.

★ 73261 ★ Ingalls Shipbuilding
Inc.
1000 Litton Access Rd.
Pascagoula, MS 39568-0149
Ultimate Parent: Litton Industries. SIC:
3731—Ship Building & Repairing; 3441—
Fabricated Structural Metal; 3443—
Fabricated Plate Work—Boiler Shops.

★ 73262 ★ Ingalls Shipbuilding
Inc.
Litton Access Rd.
Pascagoula, MS 39568-0149
Ultimate Parent: Litton Industries. SIC:
3731—Ship Building & Repairing; 3441—
Fabricated Structural Metal; 3443—
Fabricated Plate Work—Boiler Shops.

★ 73263 ★ Lerner Shop
Singing Rv Mall
Pascagoula, MS 39567
(601)497-6428
Ultimate Parent: Limited. SIC: 5621—
Women's Clothing Stores.

★ 73264 ★ Litton
Ingalls Shipbuilding Div.
1000 W. River Rd.
PO Box 149
Pascagoula, MS 39567
(601)935-1122
Company Type: Division. Officer: Alton J.
Brann, President. Ultimate Parent: Litton
Industries. SIC: 3731—Ship Building &
Repairing.

★ 73265 ★ Marine Engineering &
Production
1000 W. River Rd.
Pascagoula, MS 39567
(601)395-1122
Company Type: Division. Ultimate Parent:
Litton Industries.

★ 73266 ★ Pizza Hut
3534 Denny Ave.
Pascagoula, MS 39581
(601)769-7300
Ultimate Parent: Pepsico. SIC: 5812—
Eating Places.

★ 73267 ★ Pizza Hut
Escatawpa Shopping Ctr.
Pascagoula, MS 39563
(601)475-7771
Ultimate Parent: Pepsico. SIC: 5812—
Eating Places.

★ 73268 ★ Pizza Hut
2828 Belair St.
Pascagoula, MS 39567
(601)762-2220
Ultimate Parent: Pepsico. SIC: 5812—
Eating Places.

★ 73269 ★ Pizza Hut
2828 Old Mobile Ave.
Pascagoula, MS 39567
(601)762-9124
Ultimate Parent: Pepsico. SIC: 5812—
Eating Places.

★ 73270 ★ Radio Shack
3221 Denny Ave.
Pascagoula, MS 39581
(601)769-6784
Company Type: Division. Ultimate Parent:
Tandy Corp. SIC: 5731—Radio, Television
& Electronics Stores.

★ 73271 ★ Ryder Truck Rental
3118 Market St.
Pascagoula, MS 39567
(601)762-0759
Ultimate Parent: Ryder System. SIC:
7513—Truck Rental & Leasing Without
Drivers.

★ 73272 ★ Taco Bell
Jackson Sq.
Pascagoula, MS 39567
(601)497-6858
Ultimate Parent: Pepsico. SIC: 5812—
Eating Places.

★ 73273 ★ Wal Mart
4253 Denny Ave.
Pascagoula, MS 39581
(601)762-9662
Ultimate Parent: Wal-Mart Stores, Inc. SIC:
5399—Miscellaneous General Merchandise
Store.

Pearl

★ 73274 ★ American Cyanamid
Co.
550 Gulf Line Rd.
Pearl, MS 39208
Ultimate Parent: American Cyanamid Co.
SIC: 2833—Medicinals & Botanicals.

★ 73275 ★ American Cyanamid
Co.
Shulton
550 Gulf Line Rd.
Pearl, MS 39208
Ultimate Parent: American Cyanamid Co.
SIC: 2833—Medicinals & Botanicals.

★ 73276 ★ Clorox Co.
550 Gulf Line Rd.
Pearl, MS 39208-3401
Ultimate Parent: Clorox Co. SIC: 2833—
Medicinals & Botanicals.

★ 73277 ★ Clorox Co. Jackson
Plant
550 Gulf Line Rd.
Pearl, MS 39208-3401
Ultimate Parent: Clorox Co. SIC: 2842—
Polishes & Sanitation Goods.

Pearlington

★ 73278 ★ GE Plastics
3531 Port & Harbor Dr.
Pearlington, MS 39572
(601)467-8210
Officer: Steve Grover, Manager. Ultimate
Parent: General Electric. SIC: 2869—
Industrial Organic Chemicals Nec.

Philadelphia

★ 73279 ★ Louisiana Pacific
Corp.
239 Gum St.
Philadelphia, MS 39350
(601)656-8540
Ultimate Parent: Louisiana-Pacific. SIC:
5211—Lumber & Other Building Materials.

★ 73280 ★ Pizza Hut
915 Holland Ave.
Philadelphia, MS 39350
(601)656-8291
Ultimate Parent: Pepsico. SIC: 5812—
Eating Places.

★ 73281 ★ Radio Shack
513 Ctr. Ave.
Philadelphia, MS 39350
(601)656-1234
Company Type: Division. Ultimate Parent:
Tandy Corp. SIC: 5731—Radio, Television
& Electronics Stores.

★ 73282 ★ US Electrical Motors
Hwy. 15 N. PO Box 608
Philadelphia, MS 39350
Ultimate Parent: Emerson Electric Co. Inc.
SIC: 3621—Motors & Generators.

★ 73283 ★ US Motors
Hwy. 15 North
Philadelphia, MS 39350
Ultimate Parent: Emerson Electric Co. Inc.
SIC: 3621—Motors & Generators.

★ 73284 ★ Wal Mart Discount
City
Louisville Rd.
Philadelphia, MS 39350
(601)656-3082
Ultimate Parent: Wal-Mart Stores, Inc. SIC:
5311—Department Stores.

★ 73285 ★ Weyerhaeuser Co.
Deweese Rd.
Philadelphia, MS 39350
(601)656-5300
Officer: Dale Brumfield, Manager. Ultimate
Parent: Weyerhaeuser Co. SIC: 2421—
Sawmills & Planing Mills—General; 2436—
Softwood Veneer & Plywood.

★ 73286 ★ Weyerhaeuser Co.
Weyerhaeuser Rd.
Philadelphia, MS 39350
Ultimate Parent: Weyerhaeuser Co. SIC:
2421—Sawmills & Planing Mills—General;
2436—Softwood Veneer & Plywood.

★ 73287 ★ Witco Corp.
931 Hwy. 19 N
Philadelphia, MS 39350
(601)656-7921
Location Type: Plant. Officer: George
Smith, Plant Manager. Ultimate Parent:
Witco Corp. SIC: 3089—Plastics Products
Nec.

★ 73288 ★ Witco Corp.
Richardson Battery Parts
931 Hwy. 19 N.
Philadelphia, MS 39350
Ultimate Parent: Witco Corp. SIC: 3089—
Plastics Products Nec.

★ 73289 ★ Witco Corp.
Richardson Battery Parts
Hwy. 19 North
Philadelphia, MS 39350
Ultimate Parent: Witco Corp. SIC: 3089—
Plastics Products Nec.

Picayune

★ 73290 ★ Arizona Chemical Co.
815 N. Beech St.
Picayune, MS 39466
Ultimate Parent: International Paper Co.
SIC: 2861—Gum & Wood Chemicals.

★ 73291 ★ Arizona Chemical Co.
815 North Beech St.
Picayune, MS 39466
Ultimate Parent: International Paper Co.
SIC: 2800—Chemicals & Allied Products.

★ 73292 ★ Greyhound Bus Lines
1611 Hwy. 11 N
Picayune, MS 39466
(601)798-3112
Ultimate Parent: Greyhound Lines Inc. SIC:
4111—Local & Suburban Transit.

★ 73293 ★   **Pizza Hut**
201 Hwy. 43 S
Picayune, MS 39466
(601)798-7683
Ultimate Parent: Pepsico. SIC: 5812—
Eating Places.

★ 73294 ★   **Radio Shack**
306 W. Canal St.
Picayune, MS 39466
(601)798-4915
Company Type: Division. Ultimate Parent:
Tandy Corp. SIC: 7622—Radio & T.V.
Repair.

★ 73295 ★   **Sylvachem Corp.**
815 N. Beech St.
Picayune, MS 39466
Ultimate Parent: International Paper Co.
SIC: 2800—Chemicals & Allied Products.

★ 73296 ★   **Wal Mart Discount
Cities**
799 Picayune Pl
Picayune, MS 39466
(601)799-1060
Ultimate Parent: Wal-Mart Stores, Inc. SIC:
5311—Department Stores.

Pickens

★ 73297 ★   **Hudson's**
524 PO Box
Pickens, MS 39146
(601)468-2057
Ultimate Parent: Dayton Hudson.

★ 73298 ★   **Super Saver**
1308 Hwy. 51 S
Pickens, MS 39146
(601)468-9148
Ultimate Parent: Wal-Mart Stores, Inc. SIC:
5411—Grocery Stores.

Pontotoc

★ 73299 ★   **E. R. Carpenter Co.
Inc.**
Pontotoc Industrial Park
Pontotoc, MS 38863
Ultimate Parent: Carpenter. SIC: 3086—
Plastics Foam Products.

★ 73300 ★   **E.R. Carpenter Co.
Inc.**
PO Box 476 Pontotoc Industrial Park
Pontotoc, MS 38863
Ultimate Parent: Carpenter. SIC: 2392—
Housefurnishings Nec.

★ 73301 ★   **Itw Paslode**
364 Stafford Blvd.
Pontotoc, MS 38863
Ultimate Parent: Illinois Tool Works. SIC:
3496—Miscellaneous Fabricated Wire
Products.

★ 73302 ★   **Kentucky Fried
Chicken**
104 Hwy. 15 N
Pontotoc, MS 38863
(601)489-2403
Ultimate Parent: Pepsico. SIC: 5812—
Eating Places.

★ 73303 ★   **Paslode Corp.**
364 Stafford Blvd.
Pontotoc, MS 38863
Ultimate Parent: Illinois Tool Works. SIC:
3452—Bolts, Nuts, Rivets & Washers.

★ 73304 ★   **Personal Finance Co.**
31 Lafayette St.
Pontotoc, MS 38863
(601)489-7261
Ultimate Parent: Minnesota Mutual Life.
SIC: 6141—Personal Credit Institutions.

Poplarville

★ 73305 ★   **Piggly Wiggly**
102 N. Dauphine St.
Poplarville, MS 39470
(601)795-8061
Ultimate Parent: Bruno's. SIC: 5411—
Grocery Stores.

Port Gibson

★ 73306 ★   **Radio Shack**
Hwy. 61 N
Port Gibson, MS 39150
(601)437-8630
Company Type: Division. Ultimate Parent:
Tandy Corp. SIC: 5731—Radio, Television
& Electronics Stores.

Prentiss

★ 73307 ★   **Piggly Wiggly**
Prentiss, MS 39474
(601)792-5280
Ultimate Parent: Bruno's. SIC: 5411—
Grocery Stores.

Purvis

★ 73308 ★   **Amerada Hess Corp.**
PO Box 425
Purvis, MS 39475
(601)794-6081
Officer: H. M. Stevens. Ultimate Parent:
Amerada Hess. SIC: 2911—Petroleum
Refining.

★ 73309 ★   **Amerada Hess Corp.**
US Hwy. 11 N.
Purvis, MS 39475
Ultimate Parent: Amerada Hess. SIC:
2911—Petroleum Refining.

★ 73310 ★   **Amerada Hess Corp.**
Purvis Refinery
Purvis, MS 39475
(601)584-8401
Location Type: Branch office. Ultimate
Parent: Amerada Hess. SIC: 2911—
Petroleum Refining.

Quitman

★ 73311 ★   **Amerada Hess Corp.**
Hwy. 511 E
Quitman, MS 39355
(601)776-2712
Ultimate Parent: Amerada Hess. SIC:
1311—Crude Petroleum & Natural Gas.

Raymond

★ 73312 ★   **Diebold Inc.**
Rural Route 2
Raymond, MS 39154
(601)922-6210
Ultimate Parent: Diebold, Inc. SIC: 7382—
Security Systems Services.

★ 73313 ★   **Radio Shack**
Northpark Mall
Raymond, MS 39154
(601)857-1838
Company Type: Division. Ultimate Parent:
Tandy Corp. SIC: 5731—Radio, Television
& Electronics Stores.

Redwood

★ 73314 ★   **International Paper
Vicksburg Mill**
Hwy. 3 N.
Redwood, MS 39156
Ultimate Parent: International Paper Co.
SIC: 2631—Paperboard Mills.

Richland

★ 73315 ★   **Weyerhaeuser Paper
Co.**
211 Carrier Blvd.
Richland, MS 39218
Ultimate Parent: Weyerhaeuser Co. SIC:
2653—Corrugated & Solid Fiber Boxes.

Rideland

★ 73316 ★   **Xerox Corp.**
805 S. Wheatley St., Ste. 600
Rideland, MS 39157
(601)956-4008
Ultimate Parent: Xerox Corp. SIC: 3663—
Radio & T.V. Communications Equipment.

Ridgeland

★ 73317 ★   **Casual Corner**
212 N. Park Mall
Ridgeland, MS 39157
(601)956-3111
Ultimate Parent: United States Shoe. SIC:
5651—Family Clothing Stores.

★ 73318 ★   **The Gap**
185 N. Park Mall
Ridgeland, MS 39157
(601)957-3728
Ultimate Parent: GAP. SIC: 5651—Family
Clothing Stores.

★ 73319 ★   **Kay Bee Toy & Hobby**
240 N. Park Mall
Ridgeland, MS 39157
(601)956-0194
Ultimate Parent: Melville. SIC: 5945—
Hobby, Toy & Game Shops.

★ 73320 ★   **Kentucky Fried
Chicken**
1068 E. County Line Rd.
Ridgeland, MS 39157
(601)956-7635
Ultimate Parent: Pepsico. SIC: 5812—
Eating Places.

★ 73321 ★   **Krogers Pharmacy**
2000 E. County Line Rd.
Ridgeland, MS 39157
(601)956-0335
Ultimate Parent: Kroger. SIC: 5912—Drug
Stores & Proprietary Stores.

★ 73322 ★   **Lane Bryant**
174 N. Park Mall
Ridgeland, MS 39157
(601)957-3447
Ultimate Parent: Limited. SIC: 5651—
Family Clothing Stores.

★ 73323 ★   **Lerner Shop**
259 N. Park Mall
Ridgeland, MS 39157
(601)956-8356
Ultimate Parent: Limited. SIC: 5651—
Family Clothing Stores.

★ 73324 ★   **The Limited**
210 N. Park Mall
Ridgeland, MS 39157
(601)956-0093
Ultimate Parent: Limited. SIC: 5651—
Family Clothing Stores.

★ 73325 ★   **The Limited Express**
173 N. Park Mall
Ridgeland, MS 39157
(601)956-5458
Ultimate Parent: Limited. SIC: 5651—
Family Clothing Stores.

★ 73326 ★   **Mobile
Communications Corp. of America**
1800 E. County Line Rd., Ste. 300
Ridgeland, MS 39157-1916
(601)977-1601
Company Type: Subsidiary. Officer: Steve
Pazian, President. Ultimate Parent:
BellSouth Corp. SIC: 4899—
Communications Services Nec; 7389—
Business Services Nec; 4812—
Radiotelephone Communications.
Employee Count: 1271. Sales: 2 M.

★ 73327 ★   **Mobilecomm of Ohio
Inc.**
1800 E. County Line Rd.
Ridgeland, MS 39157-1916
(601)977-0888
Company Type: Subsidiary. Officer: Steve
Pazian, President. Ultimate Parent:
BellSouth Corp. SIC: 4812—Radiotelephone
Communications. Sales: 2 M.

★ 73328 ★   **Radio Shack**
168 N. Park Mall
Ridgeland, MS 39157
(601)957-1838
Company Type: Division. Ultimate Parent:
Tandy Corp. SIC: 5065—Electronic Parts &
Equipment Nec.

★ 73329 ★   **Victoria's Secret**
275 N. Park Mall
Ridgeland, MS 39157
(601)957-1644
Ultimate Parent: Limited. SIC: 5651—
Family Clothing Stores.

★ 73330 ★   **Wal Mart**
815 S. Wheatley St.
Ridgeland, MS 39157
(601)956-2717
Ultimate Parent: Wal-Mart Stores, Inc. SIC:
5311—Department Stores.

★ 73331 ★   **Waldenbooks**
225 N. Park Mall
Ridgeland, MS 39157
(601)951-3763
Ultimate Parent: K-Mart. SIC: 5942—Book
Stores.

Ripley

★ 73332 ★   **Pizza Hut**
Walmart Ctr.
Ripley, MS 38663
(601)837-4578
Ultimate Parent: Pepsico. SIC: 5812—
Eating Places.

Ruleville

★ 73333 ★   **Greyhound Bus Lines**
N Ruby Ave.
Ruleville, MS 38771
(601)756-4841
Ultimate Parent: Greyhound Lines Inc. SIC:
4111—Local & Suburban Transit.

★ 73334 ★   **Piggly Wiggly**
427 PO Box
Ruleville, MS 38771
Ultimate Parent: Bruno's. SIC: 5411—
Grocery Stores.

Saltillo

★ 73335 ★   **E. R. Carpenter Co.
Inc.**
Turner Industrial Park
Saltillo, MS 38866
Ultimate Parent: Carpenter. SIC: 3086—
Plastics Foam Products.

Sandersville

★ 73336 ★   **Southland Oil Co.**
Hwy. 11 N
Sandersville, MS 39477
(601)426-3241
Officer: Jim Satcher, Manager. Ultimate
Parent: Burlington Resources. SIC: 2911—
Petroleum Refining.

★ 73337 ★   **Southland Oil Co.
Sandersville**
Hwy. 11 N
Sandersville, MS 39477
Ultimate Parent: Southland Corp. SIC:
2911—Petroleum Refining.

Sardis

★ 73338 ★   **Piggly Wiggly**
113 S. Main St.
Sardis, MS 38666
(601)487-1711
Ultimate Parent: Bruno's. SIC: 5411—
Grocery Stores.

Senatobia

★ 73339 ★   **Kentucky Fried
Chicken**
E Main
Senatobia, MS 38668
(601)562-5996
Ultimate Parent: Pepsico. SIC: 5812—
Eating Places.

★ 73340 ★   **Pizza Hut**
402 E. Main St.
Senatobia, MS 38668
(601)562-7361
Ultimate Parent: Pepsico. SIC: 5812—
Eating Places.

★ 73341 ★   **Shell Self Service**
200 E. Main St.
Senatobia, MS 38668
(601)562-8442
Ultimate Parent: Shell Oil Co. SIC: 5541—
Gasoline Service Stations.

Shaw

★ 73342 ★ **Greyhound Bus Lines**
Hwy. 61 N
Shaw, MS 38773
(601)754-3871
Ultimate Parent: Greyhound Lines Inc. **SIC:** 4131—Intercity & Rural Bus Transportation.

Shelby

★ 73343 ★ **Greyhound Bus Lines**
S Hwy. 61
Shelby, MS 38774
(601)398-7215
Ultimate Parent: Greyhound Lines Inc. **SIC:** 4131—Intercity & Rural Bus Transportation.

Shubuta

★ 73344 ★ **Sunbeam Oster**
Hwy. 45 N
Shubuta, MS 39360
(601)687-1531
Officer: Hilton Davis, Executive Director. **Ultimate Parent:** Sunbeam/Oster. **SIC:** 3596—Scales & Balances Except Laboratory.

Smithville

★ 73345 ★ **Piggly Wiggly**
Hwy. 25 S
Smithville, MS 38870
(601)651-4848
Ultimate Parent: Bruno's. **SIC:** 5411—Grocery Stores.

Southaven

★ 73346 ★ **American Electric**
8735 Hamilton Rd.
Southaven, MS 38671
Ultimate Parent: Thomas & Betts. **SIC:** 3646—Commercial Lighting Fixtures; 3449—Miscellaneous Metal Work.

★ 73347 ★ **Deposit Guaranty Mortgage C**
1633 Stateline Rd. W
Southaven, MS 38671
(601)393-8625
Ultimate Parent: Deposit Guaranty Corp. **SIC:** 6162—Mortgage Bankers & Correspondents.

★ 73348 ★ **Kentucky Fried Chicken**
975 Stateline Rd. W
Southaven, MS 38671
(601)393-7750
Ultimate Parent: Pepsico. **SIC:** 5812—Eating Places.

★ 73349 ★ **Kmart Discount Stores**
560 Stateline Rd. W
Southaven, MS 38671
(601)342-1603
Ultimate Parent: K-Mart. **SIC:** 5941—Sporting Goods & Bicycle Shops.

★ 73350 ★ **Kroger Co**
465 Stateline Rd. W
Southaven, MS 38671
(601)393-2675
Ultimate Parent: Kroger. **SIC:** 5411—Grocery Stores.

★ 73351 ★ **Kroger Pharmacy**
465 Stateline Rd. W
Southaven, MS 38671
(601)393-3426
Ultimate Parent: Kroger. **SIC:** 5912—Drug Stores & Proprietary Stores.

★ 73352 ★ **Magnetek-Century Electric**
5660 Plum Tree Dr.
Southaven, MS 38671-9818
(601)349-0883
Ultimate Parent: Magnetek Inc. **SIC:** 5063—Electrical Apparatus & Equipment.

★ 73353 ★ **Mary Kay Cosmetics**
8747 Millbranch Rd.
Southaven, MS 38671
(601)342-0285
Ultimate Parent: Mary Kay Cosmetics. **SIC:** 5999—Miscellaneous Retail Stores Nec.

★ 73354 ★ **Pizza Hut**
150 Stateline Rd. W
Southaven, MS 38671
(601)342-5500
Ultimate Parent: Pepsico. **SIC:** 5812—Eating Places.

★ 73355 ★ **Radio Shack**
1259 Stateline Rd. W
Southaven, MS 38671
(601)393-5735
Company Type: Division. **Ultimate Parent:** Tandy Corp. **SIC:** 7629—Electrical Repair Shops Nec.

★ 73356 ★ **Taco Bell**
979 Stateline Rd. W
Southaven, MS 38671
(601)393-6882
Ultimate Parent: Pepsico. **SIC:** 5541—Gasoline Service Stations; 5812—Eating Places.

★ 73357 ★ **Terex**
PO Box 923
Southaven, MS 38671-0923
(601)342-5477
Officer: Bruce F. Fiddler. **Ultimate Parent:** Terex Corp. **SIC:** 3531—Construction Machinery.

★ 73358 ★ **Terex Corp.**
PO Box 923
Southaven, MS 38671-0923
(601)342-5477
Officer: Bruce F. Fiddler. **Ultimate Parent:** Terex Corp. **SIC:** 3531—Construction Machinery.

★ 73359 ★ **Wal Mart**
385 Stateline Rd. W
Southaven, MS 38671
(601)342-2642
Ultimate Parent: Wal-Mart Stores, Inc. **SIC:** 5311—Department Stores.

★ 73360 ★ **Walgreen**
201 Stateline Rd. W
Southaven, MS 38671
(601)342-2904
Ultimate Parent: Walgreen Co. **SIC:** 5912—Drug Stores & Proprietary Stores.

Starkville

★ 73361 ★ **Borden Inc.**
200 S. Montgomery St.
Starkville, MS 39759
(601)323-4420
Officer: Travis D. Vernon, Manager. **Ultimate Parent:** Borden, Inc. **SIC:** 2023—Dry, Condensed & Evaporated Dairy Products.

★ 73362 ★ **Borden Inc.**
Grocery
200 S. Montgomery St.
Starkville, MS 39759
Company Type: Division. **Ultimate Parent:** Borden, Inc. **SIC:** 2023—Dry, Condensed & Evaporated Dairy Products.

★ 73363 ★ **Borden Inc.**
Grocery & Specialty Products
200 S. Montgomery St.
Starkville, MS 39759
Company Type: Division. **Ultimate Parent:** Borden, Inc. **SIC:** 2023—Dry, Condensed & Evaporated Dairy Products.

★ 73364 ★ **Borden Inc.**
North American Foods Div.
200 S. Montgomery St.
Starkville, MS 39759
(601)323-4420
Company Type: Division. **Location Type:** Plant. **Officer:** Travis D. Vernon, Plant Manager. **Ultimate Parent:** Borden, Inc.

★ 73365 ★ **Kentucky Fried Chicken**
Hwy. 12
Starkville, MS 39759
(601)323-1944
Ultimate Parent: Pepsico. **SIC:** 5812—Eating Places.

★ 73366 ★ **Kroger 325**
800 Louisville Rd.
Starkville, MS 39759
(601)323-8616
Ultimate Parent: Kroger. **SIC:** 5499—Miscellaneous Food Stores.

★ 73367 ★ **Personal Finance Co.**
670 PO Box
Starkville, MS 39759
(601)323-7572
Ultimate Parent: Minnesota Mutual Life. **SIC:** 6141—Personal Credit Institutions.

★ 73368 ★ **Piggly Wiggly**
1507 Hwy. 12
Starkville, MS 39759
(601)323-0892
Ultimate Parent: Bruno's. **SIC:** 5421—Meat & Fish Markets.

★ 73369 ★ **Pizza Hut**
Hwy. 12 E
Starkville, MS 39759
(601)323-6340
Ultimate Parent: Pepsico. **SIC:** 5812—Eating Places.

★ 73370 ★ **Pizza Hut**
211 College View St.
Starkville, MS 39759
(601)324-2321
Ultimate Parent: Pepsico. **SIC:** 5812—Eating Places.

★ 73371 ★ **Radio Shack**
Univ Sq.
Starkville, MS 39759
(601)323-7426
Company Type: Division. **Ultimate Parent:** Tandy Corp. **SIC:** 5065—Electronic Parts & Equipment Nec.

Stewart

★ 73372 ★ **Mini Mart Number Two**
83 Rr 1
Stewart, MS 39767
Ultimate Parent: Kroger. **SIC:** 5411—Grocery Stores.

Stonewall

★ 73373 ★ **Burlington Sportswear**
PO Box 8
Stonewall, MS 39363-0008
(601)659-7021
Location Type: Headquarters. **Officer:** Milton Breeze. **Ultimate Parent:** Burlington Industries, Equity. **SIC:** 2211—Broadwoven Fabric Mills—Cotton.

★ 73374 ★ **Burlington Sportswear**
Hwy. 513
Stonewall, MS 39363
(601)659-7021
Officer: Hunter Breeze, Manager. **Ultimate Parent:** Burlington Industries, Equity. **SIC:** 2211—Broadwoven Fabric Mills—Cotton.

Sumrall

★ 73375 ★ **Piggly Wiggly**
102 Main
Sumrall, MS 39482
(601)758-3532
Ultimate Parent: Bruno's. **SIC:** 5411—Grocery Stores.

Taylorsville

★ 73376 ★ **Georgia-Pacific Corp.**
Resins Div.
Hwy. 28 W. PO Box 556
Taylorsville, MS 39168
Company Type: Division. **Ultimate Parent:** Georgia-Pacific. **SIC:** 2821—Plastics Materials & Resins; 2869—Industrial Organic Chemicals Nec.

★ 73377 ★ **Georgia-Pacific Corp. Particleboard**
Hwy. 28 W.
Taylorsville, MS 39168
Ultimate Parent: Georgia-Pacific. **SIC:** 2493—Reconstituted Wood Products.

★ 73378 ★ **Georgia-Pacific Resins Inc. Particleboard**
Hwy. 28 W. PO Box 556
Taylorsville, MS 39168
Ultimate Parent: Georgia-Pacific. **SIC:** 2821—Plastics Materials & Resins; 2869—Industrial Organic Chemicals Nec.

★ 73379 ★ **Piggly Wiggly**
Taylorsville, MS 39168
(601)785-4640
Ultimate Parent: Bruno's. **SIC:** 5411—Grocery Stores.

Tchula

★ 73380 ★ **Greyhound Bus Lines**
101 E. Main St.
Tchula, MS 39169
(601)235-5376
Ultimate Parent: Greyhound Lines Inc. **SIC:** 5541—Gasoline Service Stations.

Tinsley

★ 73381 ★ **Pennzoil Products Co.**
Tinsley, MS 39173
(601)746-4843
Ultimate Parent: Pennzoil. **SIC:** 1311—Crude Petroleum & Natural Gas.

Tishomingo

★ 73382 ★ **Heil Co.**
Hwy. 25 N
Tishomingo, MS 38873
(601)438-7800
Officer: Les Quay, Plant Manager. **Ultimate Parent:** Dover Corp. **SIC:** 3713—Truck & Bus Bodies.

Tunica

★ 73383 ★ **Piggly Wiggly**
Hwy. 61 S
Tunica, MS 38676
(601)363-3170
Ultimate Parent: Bruno's. **SIC:** 5411—Grocery Stores.

Tupelo

★ 73384 ★ **Action Industries Inc.**
Hwy. 45 S
Tupelo, MS 38802
(601)566-7211
Company Type: Division. **Ultimate Parent:** Interco. **SIC:** 2512—Upholstered Household Furniture.

★ 73385 ★ **Air Products & Chemicals, Inc.**
821 President St.
Tupelo, MS 38801
(601)842-5138
Ultimate Parent: Air Products & Chemicals, Inc. **SIC:** 5084—Industrial Machinery & Equipment.

★ 73386 ★ **Borden Inc.**
Dairy
429 Eason Blvd.
Tupelo, MS 38801
Company Type: Division. **Ultimate Parent:** Borden, Inc. **SIC:** 2024—Ice Cream & Frozen Desserts.

★ 73387 ★ **Borden Inc.**
Dairy
429 Eason Blvd.
Tupelo, MS 38801
Company Type: Division. **Ultimate Parent:** Borden, Inc. **SIC:** 2024—Ice Cream & Frozen Desserts.

★ 73388 ★ **Borden Inc.**
Grocery & Specialty Products
429 Eason Blvd.
Tupelo, MS 38801
Company Type: Division. **Ultimate Parent:** Borden, Inc. **SIC:** 2024—Ice Cream & Frozen Desserts.

★ 73389 ★ **Borden Milk & Ice Cream**
429 Eason Blvd.
Tupelo, MS 38801
(601)842-7415
Officer: Hershell Pearce, Manager. **Ultimate Parent:** Borden, Inc. **SIC:** 2024—Ice Cream & Frozen Desserts; 2026—Fluid Milk.

★ 73390 ★   Burlington Northern
Rr
142 PO Box
Tupelo, MS 38802
(601)842-1621
Ultimate Parent: Burlington Northern. SIC:
4011—Railroads—Line-Haul Operating.

★ 73391 ★   Butler Paper
623 W. Main St.
Tupelo, MS 38801-3759
(601)842-1906
Ultimate Parent: Alco Standard Corp. SIC:
5111—Printing & Writing Paper.

★ 73392 ★   Butler Paper
623 W. Main St.
Tupelo, MS 38801-3759
(601)842-1906
Ultimate Parent: Alco Standard Corp. SIC:
5111—Printing & Writing Paper.

★ 73393 ★   Cooper Tire Co.
1689 S. Green St.
Tupelo, MS 38802
Ultimate Parent: Cooper Tire & Rubber Co.
Inc. SIC: 3011—Tires & Inner Tubes.

★ 73394 ★   Cooper Tire & Rubber
Co.
1689 S. Green St.
Tupelo, MS 38802-0170
Ultimate Parent: Cooper Tire & Rubber Co.
Inc. SIC: 3011—Tires & Inner Tubes.

★ 73395 ★   Day-Brite Lighting
Inc.
1015 S. Green St.
Tupelo, MS 38801
Ultimate Parent: Emerson Electric Co. Inc.
SIC: 3643—Current-Carrying Wiring
Devices; 3646—Commercial Lighting
Fixtures; 3648—Lighting Equipment Nec.

★ 73396 ★   Delta International
Machinery Corp.
1200 S. Gloster PO Box 1508
Tupelo, MS 38801-1508
Ultimate Parent: Pentair. SIC: 3553—
Woodworking Machinery; 3541—Machine
Tools—Metal Cutting Types.

★ 73397 ★   Delta International
Machinery Corp.
1200 S. Gloster PO Box 1508
Tupelo, MS 38801-1508
Ultimate Parent: Pentair. SIC: 3553—
Woodworking Machinery; 3541—Machine
Tools—Metal Cutting Types.

★ 73398 ★   Delta International
Machinery Corp.
1200 S. Gloster
Tupelo, MS 38802-1508
Ultimate Parent: Pentair. SIC: 3553—
Woodworking Machinery.

★ 73399 ★   Deposit Guaranty
Mortgage C
707 W. Main St.
Tupelo, MS 38801
(601)841-1112
Ultimate Parent: Deposit Guaranty Corp.
SIC: 6141—Personal Credit Institutions.

★ 73400 ★   FMC Corp.
Hwy. 45 N
Tupelo, MS 38801
(601)869-5711
Officer: Elmer Doty, Manager. Ultimate
Parent: FMC. SIC: 3535—Conveyors &
Conveying Equipment.

★ 73401 ★   FMC Corp., Tupelo
Plant
Hwy. 145, Turner Industrial Pk.
Tupelo, MS 38802-1370
Location Type: Plant. Ultimate Parent:
FMC. SIC: 3535—Conveyors & Conveying
Equipment.

★ 73402 ★   Foamex
Kihi Foamex
12 Service Dr.
Tupelo, MS 38802
Ultimate Parent: Foamex. SIC: 3086—
Plastics Foam Products.

★ 73403 ★   Foot Action 8099
1001 Barnes Crossing Rd.
Tupelo, MS 38801
(601)680-3326
Ultimate Parent: Melville. SIC: 5699—
Miscellaneous Apparel & Accessory Stores.

★ 73404 ★   Greyhound Bus Lines
201 Commerce St.
Tupelo, MS 38801
(601)842-4557
Ultimate Parent: Greyhound Lines Inc. SIC:
4111—Local & Suburban Transit.

★ 73405 ★   Hertz Rent-A-Car
632 Crossover Rd.
Tupelo, MS 38801
(601)842-9149
Ultimate Parent: Hertz. SIC: 7514—
Passenger Car Rental.

★ 73406 ★   Hertz Rent-A-Car
Licensee
Tupelo Airport
Tupelo, MS 38801
(601)844-9148
Ultimate Parent: Hertz. SIC: 7514—
Passenger Car Rental.

★ 73407 ★   Kentucky Fried
Chicken
508 N. Gloster St.
Tupelo, MS 38801
(601)842-4154
Ultimate Parent: Pepsico. SIC: 5812—
Eating Places.

★ 73408 ★   Kroger Food Store
Industrial Rd.
Tupelo, MS 38801
(601)842-4740
Ultimate Parent: Kroger. SIC: 5411—
Grocery Stores.

★ 73409 ★   L & P Foam Inc.
1118 S. Canal St.
Tupelo, MS 38801-1118
Ultimate Parent: Leggett & Platt Inc. SIC:
3069—Fabricated Rubber Products Nec.

★ 73410 ★   L&P Foam Inc.
1118 Canal St.
Tupelo, MS 38801-1118
Ultimate Parent: Leggett & Platt Inc. SIC:
3069—Fabricated Rubber Products Nec.

★ 73411 ★   Leggett & Platt Inc.
Urethane Foam Div.
1118 S. Veterans Blvd.
Tupelo, MS 38801
Company Type: Division. Ultimate Parent:
Leggett & Platt Inc. SIC: 3086—Plastics
Foam Products.

★ 73412 ★   McDonalds
1710 S. Gloster St.
Tupelo, MS 38801
(601)842-9600
Ultimate Parent: McDonald's.
SIC: 5812—Eating Places.

★ 73413 ★   Mini Mart
908 Lawndale Dr.
Tupelo, MS 38801
(601)842-4950
Ultimate Parent: Kroger.

★ 73414 ★   Olympic Prods. Co.
1116 S. Veterans Blvd.
Tupelo, MS 38802-1767
Ultimate Parent: Cone Mills. SIC: 3086—
Plastics Foam Products.

★ 73415 ★   Olympic Products Co.
1116 S. Canal St.
Tupelo, MS 38802-1767
Ultimate Parent: Cone Mills. SIC: 3089—
Plastics Products Nec.

★ 73416 ★   Pepsi-Cola Bottling
Co.
620 E. President St.
Tupelo, MS 38801
(601)841-8750
Officer: Bob Poland, President. Ultimate
Parent: Pepsico. SIC: 2086—Bottled &
Canned Soft Drinks.

★ 73417 ★   Personal Finance Co.
115 S. Gathier
Tupelo, MS 38801
(601)842-1176
Ultimate Parent: Minnesota Mutual Life.
SIC: 6141—Personal Credit Institutions.

★ 73418 ★   Pizza Hut
921 S. Gloster St.
Tupelo, MS 38801
(601)844-2158
Ultimate Parent: Pepsico. SIC: 5812—
Eating Places.

★ 73419 ★   Pizza Hut
2607 W. Main St.
Tupelo, MS 38801
(601)842-4081
Ultimate Parent: Pepsico. SIC: 5812—
Eating Places.

★ 73420 ★   Pizza Hut
603 N. Gloster St.
Tupelo, MS 38801
(601)844-6400
Ultimate Parent: Pepsico. SIC: 5812—
Eating Places.

★ 73421 ★   Radio Shack
Downtown Mall
Tupelo, MS 38801
(601)844-4705
Company Type: Division. Ultimate Parent:
Tandy Corp. SIC: 5065—Electronic Parts &
Equipment Nec.

★ 73422 ★   Radio Shack
Tupelo Mall
Tupelo, MS 38801
(601)844-7910
Company Type: Division. Ultimate Parent:
Tandy Corp. SIC: 5065—Electronic Parts &
Equipment Nec.

★ 73423 ★   Red Kap Ind.
Old Hwy. 45 N
Tupelo, MS 38801
(601)842-4733
Officer: Harry Salyer, Manager. Ultimate
Parent: VF Corp. SIC: 2325—Men's/Boys'
Trousers & Slacks.

★ 73424 ★   Ryder Truck Rental
104 Mattox St.
Tupelo, MS 38801
(601)844-1931
Ultimate Parent: Ryder System. SIC:
5113—Industrial & Personal Service Paper.

★ 73425 ★   Ryder Truck Rental
1009 Wilson St.
Tupelo, MS 38801
(601)844-0435
Ultimate Parent: Ryder System. SIC:
5113—Industrial & Personal Service Paper.

★ 73426 ★   Stanley Hardware
Wondura Products
1141 Ryder St.
Tupelo, MS 38801
Company Type: Division. Ultimate Parent:
Stanley Works. SIC:
3231—Products of Purchased Glass;
3089—Plastics Products Nec; 2499—Wood
Products Nec.

★ 73427 ★   Stone Container Corp.
1679 S. Green St.
Tupelo, MS 38801
(601)842-4940
Officer: Steve White, Manager. Ultimate
Parent: Stone Container Corp. SIC: 2653—
Corrugated & Solid Fiber Boxes.

★ 73428 ★   Walgreen
Tupelo Mall
Tupelo, MS 38801
(601)844-3500
Ultimate Parent: Walgreen Co. SIC:
5912—Drug Stores & Proprietary Stores.

Tutwiler

★ 73429 ★   ACME Frame
Products of Mississippi
PO Box 426
Tutwiler, MS 38963-0426
(601)345-8381
Company Type: Headquarters. Officer:
Doyle Pruett. Ultimate Parent: American
Greetings. SIC: 2499—Wood Products Nec;
5023—Homefurnishings.

Tylertown

★ 73430 ★   Pennzoil Producing
Co.
Dexter
Tylertown, MS 39667
(601)876-6069
Ultimate Parent: Pennzoil. SIC: 1382—Oil
& Gas Exploration Services.

★ 73431 ★   Piggly Wiggly
813 Beulah Ave.
Tylertown, MS 39667
(601)876-2624
Ultimate Parent: Bruno's. SIC: 5411—
Grocery Stores.

Union

★ 73432 ★   Piggly Wiggly
206 W. Jackson Rd.
Union, MS 39365
(601)774-5591
Ultimate Parent: Bruno's. SIC: 5411—
Grocery Stores.

Utica

★ 73433 ★   Casual Corner
212 Northpark Mall
Utica, MS 39175
(601)956-3111
Ultimate Parent: United States Shoe. SIC:
5651—Family Clothing Stores.

★ 73434 ★   The Gap
185 Northpark Mall
Utica, MS 39175
(601)957-3728
Ultimate Parent: GAP. SIC: 5651—Family
Clothing Stores.

★ 73435 ★   Kay Bee Toy & Hobby
240 Northpark Mall
Utica, MS 39175
(601)956-0194
Ultimate Parent: Melville. SIC: 5945—
Hobby, Toy & Game Shops.

★ 73436 ★   Kroger Co.
2000 E. County Line Rd.
Utica, MS 39175
(601)956-0331
Ultimate Parent: Kroger. SIC: 5411—
Grocery Stores.

★ 73437 ★   Lane Bryant
174 Northpark Mall
Utica, MS 39175
(601)957-3447
Ultimate Parent: Limited. SIC: 5651—
Family Clothing Stores.

★ 73438 ★   Lens Crafters
224 Northpark Mall
Utica, MS 39175
(601)957-6556
Ultimate Parent: United States Shoe. SIC:
5995—Optical Goods Stores.

★ 73439 ★   Lerner Shop
259 Northpark Mall
Utica, MS 39175
(601)956-8356
Ultimate Parent: Limited. SIC: 5651—
Family Clothing Stores.

★ 73440 ★   The Limited Express
173 Northpark Mall
Utica, MS 39175
(601)956-5458
Ultimate Parent: Limited. SIC: 5651—
Family Clothing Stores.

★ 73441 ★   Radio Shack
168 Northpark Mall
Utica, MS 39175
(601)957-1838
Company Type: Division. Ultimate Parent:
Tandy Corp. SIC: 5065—Electronic Parts &
Equipment Nec.

★ 73442 ★   Victoria's Secret
275 Northpark Mall
Utica, MS 39175
(601)957-1644
Ultimate Parent: Limited. SIC: 5651—
Family Clothing Stores.

★ 73443 ★   Waldenbooks
225 Northpark Mall
Utica, MS 39175
(601)957-3763
Ultimate Parent: K-Mart. SIC: 5942—Book
Stores.

Vaiden

★ 73444 ★   Piggly Wiggly
Hwy. 51
Vaiden, MS 39176
(601)464-5239
Ultimate Parent: Bruno's. SIC: 5411—
Grocery Stores.

Verona

★ 73445 ★ E. R. Carpenter Co. Inc. Tupelo
Tupelo Lee Industrial Park S.
Verona, MS 38879
Ultimate Parent: Carpenter. **SIC:** 3086—Plastics Foam Products.

★ 73446 ★ E.R. Carpenter Co., Inc.
Lee Industrial Park S
Verona, MS 38879
Ultimate Parent: Carpenter. **SIC:** 3086—Plastics Foam Products.

★ 73447 ★ Foamax Products Inc.
Lee Industrial Park S
Verona, MS 38879
Ultimate Parent: Foamex. **SIC:** 3086—Plastics Foam Products.

★ 73448 ★ Foamex LP
Kihi Foamex
Lee Industrial Pk. S. Lipford Rd.
Verona, MS 38879
Ultimate Parent: Foamex. **SIC:** 3086—Plastics Foam Products.

★ 73449 ★ Foamex LP
Kihi Foamex
Lee Industrial Park S. Lip Ford Rd.
Verona, MS 38879
Ultimate Parent: Foamex. **SIC:** 3086—Plastics Foam Products.

★ 73450 ★ Stylelander Metal Stamping Inc.
5113 Raymond Rd.
Verona, MS 38879
Ultimate Parent: Leggett & Platt Inc. **SIC:** 3460—Metal Forgings & Stampings.

★ 73451 ★ Tecumseh Products Co.
Hwy. 45 S
Verona, MS 38879
Ultimate Parent: Tecumseh Products. **SIC:** 3632—Household Refrigerators & Freezers.

Vicksburg

★ 73452 ★ Greyhound Bus Lines
1511 Walnut St.
Vicksburg, MS 39180
(601)636-1163
Ultimate Parent: Greyhound Lines Inc. **SIC:** 4111—Local & Suburban Transit.

★ 73453 ★ International Paper Co. Vicksburg Mill
PO Box 950
Vicksburg, MS 39181
Ultimate Parent: International Paper Co. **SIC:** 2631—Paperboard Mills.

★ 73454 ★ International Paper Vicksburg Mill
PO Box 950
Vicksburg, MS 39181
Ultimate Parent: International Paper Co. **SIC:** 2631—Paperboard Mills.

★ 73455 ★ Kentucky Fried Chicken
3407 Washington St.
Vicksburg, MS 39180
(601)638-2114
Ultimate Parent: Pepsico. **SIC:** 5812—Eating Places.

★ 73456 ★ Kentucky Fried Chicken
2915 Clay St.
Vicksburg, MS 39180
(601)638-3416
Ultimate Parent: Pepsico. **SIC:** 5812—Eating Places.

★ 73457 ★ Kentucky Fried Chicken
3144 Indiana Ave.
Vicksburg, MS 39180
(601)638-2115
Ultimate Parent: Pepsico. **SIC:** 5812—Eating Places.

★ 73458 ★ Lerner Shop
3110 Battlefield Mall
Vicksburg, MS 39180
(601)636-3666
Ultimate Parent: Limited. **SIC:** 5651—Family Clothing Stores.

★ 73459 ★ Mutual of New York
1 National Bank Bldg.
Vicksburg, MS 39180
(601)636-7442
Ultimate Parent: Mutual of New York. **SIC:** 6411—Insurance Agents, Brokers & Service.

★ 73460 ★ Radio Shack
Battlefield Mall
Vicksburg, MS 39180
(601)638-6032
Company Type: Division. **Ultimate Parent:** Tandy Corp. **SIC:** 5734—Computer & Software Stores.

★ 73461 ★ Ryder Truck Rental
742 Cain Ridge Rd.
Vicksburg, MS 39180
(601)638-3944
Ultimate Parent: Ryder System. **SIC:** 7359—Equipment Rental & Leasing Nec.

★ 73462 ★ Shell Self Service
Hwy. 27
Vicksburg, MS 39180
(601)636-9903
Ultimate Parent: Shell Oil Co. **SIC:** 5541—Gasoline Service Stations.

★ 73463 ★ Sigmaform Corp.
Hwy. 61 South
Vicksburg, MS 39180
Ultimate Parent: Raychem Corp. **SIC:** 3089—Plastics Products Nec.

★ 73464 ★ Waldenbooks
Battlefld Village Shopping Ctr.
Vicksburg, MS 39180
(601)638-9236
Ultimate Parent: K-Mart. **SIC:** 5942—Book Stores.

Walnut

★ 73465 ★ Dover Elevator Co.
Hwy. 15 S
Walnut, MS 38683
(601)223-4025
Officer: Johnny Abdon, Manager. **Ultimate Parent:** Dover Corp. **SIC:** 3625—Relays & Industrial Controls.

Water Valley

★ 73466 ★ Colt Industries Inc.
Holley Automotive Div.
Hwy. 32 & 7
Water Valley, MS 38965
Company Type: Division. **Ultimate Parent:** Coltec Industries. **SIC:** 3714—Motor Vehicle Parts & Accessories.

★ 73467 ★ Coltec Industries Inc.
Holley Automotive Div.
Hwy. 32 & 7
Water Valley, MS 38965
Company Type: Division. **Ultimate Parent:** Coltec Industries. **SIC:** 3714—Motor Vehicle Parts & Accessories.

★ 73468 ★ Mott's
Blue Coach
190 Lafayette St.
PO Box 708
Water Valley, MS 38965
(601)473-1771
Company Type: Division. **Location Type:** Headquarters. **Officer:** Tom Colutta, Executive Vice President. **Ultimate Parent:** Conagra.

★ 73469 ★ Mott's - Blue Coach Foods
PO Box 708
Water Valley, MS 38965
(601)473-1771 **Fax:** (601)473-3021
Officer: Jerry R. Nelson, President. **Ultimate Parent:** Conagra.

★ 73470 ★ Piggly Wiggly
Valley Shopping Ctr.
Water Valley, MS 38965
(601)473-3838
Ultimate Parent: Bruno's. **SIC:** 5411—Grocery Stores.

★ 73471 ★ Pizza Hut
907 Railroad St.
Water Valley, MS 38965
(601)473-4302
Ultimate Parent: Pepsico. **SIC:** 5812—Eating Places.

Waynesboro

★ 73472 ★ Ace Hardware&Equipment Co.
700 South St.
Waynesboro, MS 39367
(601)735-5533
Ultimate Parent: Ace Hardware. **SIC:** 5251—Hardware Stores.

★ 73473 ★ Kentucky Fried Chicken
700 Miss Dr.
Waynesboro, MS 39367
(601)735-4911
Ultimate Parent: Pepsico. **SIC:** 5812—Eating Places.

★ 73474 ★ Trailways Bus Systems
406 Court St.
Waynesboro, MS 39367
(601)735-3661
Ultimate Parent: Greyhound Lines Inc. **SIC:** 4131—Intercity & Rural Bus Transportation.

West Point

★ 73475 ★ Babcock & Wilcox Co.
PO Box 1297 E. Half Mile St.
West Point, MS 39773
Ultimate Parent: McDermott. **SIC:** 3443—Fabricated Plate Work—Boiler Shops.

★ 73476 ★ Brunswick Marine/Fisher Plant
PO Box 1256
West Point, MS 39773-1256
(601)494-1786
Location Type: Headquarters. **Officer:** Scott Sloan. **Ultimate Parent:** Brunswick Corp. **SIC:** 3732—Boat Building & Repairing.

★ 73477 ★ Bryan Foods Inc.
One Churchill Rd.
PO Box 1177
West Point, MS 39773
(601)494-8741 **Fax:** (601)495-4505
Company Type: Division. **Officer:** Roger Loeffelbein, Chairman & Pres. **Ultimate Parent:** Sara Lee Corp. **SIC:** 2013—Sausages & Other Prepared Meats.

★ 73478 ★ Bryan Foods Inc.
1 Churchill Rd.
PO Box 1177
West Point, MS 39773
(601)494-3741 **Fax:** (601)495-4505
Company Type: Division. **Location Type:** Facility. **Ultimate Parent:** Sara Lee Corp. **SIC:** 2013—Sausages & Other Prepared Meats.

★ 73479 ★ Bryan Foods Inc.
100 Churchhill Rd. PO Box 1177
West Point, MS 39773
Ultimate Parent: Sara Lee Corp. **SIC:** 2011—Meat Packing Plants.

★ 73480 ★ Fisher Marine
Hwy. 45 South
West Point, MS 39773
Ultimate Parent: Brunswick Corp. **SIC:** 3732—Boat Building & Repairing.

★ 73481 ★ Fisher Marine
Hwy. 45 South PO Box 1256
West Point, MS 39773
Ultimate Parent: Brunswick Corp. **SIC:** 3732—Boat Building & Repairing.

★ 73482 ★ Fisher Marine
Hiwaym 45 South PO Box 1256
West Point, MS 39773
Ultimate Parent: Brunswick Corp. **SIC:** 3732—Boat Building & Repairing.

★ 73483 ★ Kentucky Fried Chicken
502 Us 45 N
West Point, MS 39773
(601)494-2714
Ultimate Parent: Pepsico. **SIC:** 5812—Eating Places.

★ 73484 ★ Personal Finance Co.
132 Commerce St.
West Point, MS 39773
(601)494-7401
Ultimate Parent: Minnesota Mutual Life. **SIC:** 6141—Personal Credit Institutions; 6141—Personal Credit Institutions.

★ 73485 ★ Pizza Hut
Hwy. 45 N
West Point, MS 39773
(601)494-2404
Ultimate Parent: Pepsico. **SIC:** 5812—Eating Places.

★ 73486 ★ Sara Lee Corp.
1 Churchill Rd.
West Point, MS 39773
(601)494-3741
Company Type: Division. **Officer:** Roger Loeffelbein, President, CEO. **Ultimate Parent:** Sara Lee Corp.

★ 73487 ★ Wal Mart Discount Cities
411 W. Main St. D
West Point, MS 39773
(601)494-4508
Ultimate Parent: Wal-Mart Stores, Inc. **SIC:** 5311—Department Stores.

★ 73488 ★ West Point Casket Co.
Lone Oak Dr.
West Point, MS 39773
Ultimate Parent: West Point Stevens. **SIC:** 3995—Burial Caskets.

Wiggins

★ 73489 ★ International Paper
1633 S. First St.
Wiggins, MS 39577
Ultimate Parent: International Paper Co. **SIC:** 2491—Wood Preserving.

★ 73490 ★ International Paper
Old Hwy. 49 South
Wiggins, MS 39577
Ultimate Parent: International Paper Co. **SIC:** 2491—Wood Preserving.

★ 73491 ★ International Paper
Old Hwy. 49 South PO Box 37
Wiggins, MS 39577
Ultimate Parent: International Paper Co. **SIC:** 2491—Wood Preserving.

★ 73492 ★ Piggly Wiggly
116 S. 2nd St.
Wiggins, MS 39577
(601)928-3912
Ultimate Parent: Bruno's. **SIC:** 5411—Grocery Stores.

★ 73493 ★ Radio Shack
230 N. Magnolia Dr.
Wiggins, MS 39577
(601)928-3441
Company Type: Division. **Ultimate Parent:** Tandy Corp. **SIC:** 5045—Computers, Peripherals & Software.

Winona

★ 73494 ★ Piggly Wiggly
409 Summit St.
Winona, MS 38967
(601)283-4554
Ultimate Parent: Bruno's. **SIC:** 5411—Grocery Stores.

★ 73495 ★ Trailways Bus Depot
140 Hwy. 51 N
Winona, MS 38967
(601)283-4344
Ultimate Parent: Greyhound Lines Inc. **SIC:** 4131—Intercity & Rural Bus Transportation.

★ 73496 ★ Wal Mart
Hwy. 51 S
Winona, MS 38967
(601)283-3814
Ultimate Parent: Wal-Mart Stores, Inc. **SIC:** 5331—Variety Stores.

Woodville

★ 73497 ★ Super Saver
Woodville, MS 39669
(601)888-9948
Ultimate Parent: Wal-Mart Stores, Inc. **SIC:** 5541—Gasoline Service Stations.

Yazoo City

★ 73498 ★   **Burdines**
Hwy. 3
Yazoo City, MS 39194
(601)746-9871
Ultimate Parent: Federated Department
Stores. **SIC:** 5813—Drinking Places.

★ 73499 ★   **Burdines Body Shop**
Valley
Yazoo City, MS 39194
(601)746-6804
Ultimate Parent: Federated Department
Stores. **SIC:** 7538—General Automotive
Repair Shops.

★ 73500 ★   **Burdines Upholstery Shop**
Honeycutt Rd.
Yazoo City, MS 39194
(601)746-7055
Ultimate Parent: Federated Department
Stores. **SIC:** 7538—General Automotive
Repair Shops.

★ 73501 ★   **Exxon Oil Marketers**
675 E. 8th St.
Yazoo City, MS 39194
(601)746-2893
Ultimate Parent: Exxon. **SIC:** 5172—
Petroleum Products Nec.

★ 73502 ★   **Greyhound Bus Terminal**
Hwy. 49
Yazoo City, MS 39194
(601)746-1221
Ultimate Parent: Greyhound Lines Inc. **SIC:**
4111—Local & Suburban Transit.

★ 73503 ★   **Kentucky Fried Chicken**
1950 Hwy. 49 E
Yazoo City, MS 39194
(601)746-1232
Ultimate Parent: Pepsico. **SIC:** 8093—
Specialty Outpatient Facilities Nec.

★ 73504 ★   **McDonalds Restaurant**
Yazoo City, MS 39194
(601)746-6386
Ultimate Parent: May Department Stores.
SIC: 5812—Eating Places.

★ 73505 ★   **Pizza Hut**
Yazoo Ville Shopping Ctr.
Yazoo City, MS 39194
(601)746-7991
Ultimate Parent: Pepsico. **SIC:** 5812—
Eating Places.

★ 73506 ★   **Radio Shack**
Hwy. 49
Yazoo City, MS 39194
(601)746-8381
Company Type: Division. **Ultimate Parent:**
Tandy Corp. **SIC:** 5065—Electronic Parts &
Equipment Nec.

★ 73507 ★   **Texaco Inc.**
1805 Hwy. 49 E
Yazoo City, MS 39194
(601)746-2423
Ultimate Parent: Texaco. **SIC:** 5172—
Petroleum Products Nec.

Aberdeen

★ 73509 ★ Branch Banking & Trust Co.
Johnson St. & US Hwy. 1
Aberdeen, NC 28315
(910)692-7335
Company Type: Subsidiary. **Location Type:** Branch office. **Officer:** Mary M. Saunders, Mgr. **Ultimate Parent:** Southern National Corp. **SIC:** 6021—National Commercial Banks.

★ 73510 ★ Branch Banking & Trust Co.
205 Knight St.
Aberdeen, NC 28315-2824
(910)944-2327
Company Type: Subsidiary. **Location Type:** Branch office. **Ultimate Parent:** Southern National Corp. **SIC:** 6021—National Commercial Banks.

★ 73511 ★ Branch Banking & Trust Co.
US Hwy. 1 S, Town & Country Shopping Ctr.
Aberdeen, NC 28315-9559
(910)944-7124
Company Type: Subsidiary. **Location Type:** Branch office. **Ultimate Parent:** Southern National Corp. **SIC:** 6021—National Commercial Banks.

★ 73512 ★ Carolina Power & Light Co.
223 N. Pinehurst St.
Aberdeen, NC 28315
(919)944-2141
Ultimate Parent: Carolina Power & Light Co. **SIC:** 4911—Electric Services.

★ 73513 ★ Carolina Power & Light Co.
223 N. Pinehurst St.
Aberdeen, NC 28315
(919)944-2141
Location Type: Branch office. **Ultimate Parent:** Carolina Power & Light Co. **SIC:** 4911—Electric Services.

★ 73514 ★ Food Lion
1308 Sandhills Blvd. N
Aberdeen, NC 28315
(919)692-2700
Ultimate Parent: Food Lion. **SIC:** 5411—Grocery Stores.

★ 73515 ★ Food Lion
Us 1 N
Aberdeen, NC 28315
(919)692-7270
Ultimate Parent: Food Lion. **SIC:** 7997—Membership Sports & Recreation Clubs.

★ 73516 ★ Pizza Hut
1040 Sandhills Blvd. N
Aberdeen, NC 28315
(919)944-7669
Ultimate Parent: Pepsico. **SIC:** 5812—Eating Places.

★ 73517 ★ Radio Shack
Town
Aberdeen, NC 28315
(919)944-2600
Company Type: Division. **Ultimate Parent:** Tandy Corp. **SIC:** 5734—Computer & Software Stores.

★ 73518 ★ Radio Shack
1701 Sandhills Blvd. N. B
Aberdeen, NC 28315
Company Type: Division. **Ultimate Parent:** Tandy Corp. **SIC:** 5731—Radio, Television & Electronics Stores.

★ 73519 ★ Rite Aid Discount Pharmacy
1017 Town Country Shopping Ctr.
Aberdeen, NC 28315
(919)944-2365
Ultimate Parent: Rite Aid. **SIC:** 5912—Drug Stores & Proprietary Stores.

★ 73520 ★ Sandhill Telephone Co.
211 N. Poplar St.
PO Box 977
Aberdeen, NC 28315
(910)944-7100
Company Type: Subsidiary. **Ultimate Parent:** ALLTEL Corp. **SIC:** 4812—Radiotelephone Communications.

Advance

★ 73521 ★ First Union National Bank of North Carolina
US Hwy. 158 & NC Hwy. 801
Advance, NC 27006
(910)761-3947
Company Type: Subsidiary. **Location Type:** Branch office. **Ultimate Parent:** First Union Corp. **SIC:** 6021—National Commercial Banks.

Ahoskie

★ 73522 ★ Ace Hardware
1300 Memorial Dr. E
Ahoskie, NC 27910
(919)332-8038
Ultimate Parent: Ace Hardware. **SIC:** 5251—Hardware Stores.

★ 73523 ★ First-Citizens Bank & Trust Co.
224 W. Main St.
Ahoskie, NC 27910-3318
(919)332-5033
Location Type: Branch office. **Ultimate Parent:** First Citizens Bancshares, Inc. **SIC:** 6021—National Commercial Banks.

★ 73524 ★ First-Citizens Bank & Trust Co.
700 E. Church St.
Ahoskie, NC 27910-2904
(919)332-6191
Location Type: Branch office. **Officer:** Charles W. Hughes Jr., Vice President. **Ultimate Parent:** First Citizens Bancshares, Inc. **SIC:** 6021—National Commercial Banks.

★ 73525 ★ Ryder Truck Rental
Rural Route 3
Ahoskie, NC 27910
(919)332-3464
Ultimate Parent: Ryder System. **SIC:** 7359—Equipment Rental & Leasing Nec.

Albemarle

★ 73526 ★ Collins & Aikman Corp. Albemarle Plant
313 Bethany Church Rd.
Albemarle, NC 28001
Ultimate Parent: Collins & Aikman Group. **SIC:** 2262—Finishing Plants—Manmade.

★ 73527 ★ Collins & Aikman Corp. Albemarle Plant
313 Bethany Rd.
Albemarle, NC 28001
Ultimate Parent: Collins & Aikman Group. **SIC:** 2262—Finishing Plants—Manmade.

★ 73528 ★ First Bank
2317 Us Hwy. 52 N
Albemarle, NC 28001
(704)982-6060
Ultimate Parent: Shawmut National Corp. **SIC:** 6099—Functions Related to Deposit Banking.

★ 73529 ★ First Bank
160 W. Main St.
Albemarle, NC 28001
(704)983-6690
Ultimate Parent: Shawmut National Corp. **SIC:** 6022—State Commercial Banks.

★ 73530 ★ First Bank
1935 E. Main St.
Albemarle, NC 28001
(704)982-4949
Ultimate Parent: Shawmut National Corp. **SIC:** 6099—Functions Related to Deposit Banking.

★ 73531 ★ First Bank
120 N. 1st St.
Albemarle, NC 28001
(704)982-8734
Ultimate Parent: Shawmut National Corp. **SIC:** 6099—Functions Related to Deposit Banking.

★ 73532 ★ First-Citizens Bank & Trust Co.
1910 W. Main St.
Albemarle, NC 28001-5420
(704)983-1121
Location Type: Branch office. **Ultimate Parent:** First Citizens Bancshares, Inc. **SIC:** 6021—National Commercial Banks.

★ 73533 ★ First-Citizens Bank & Trust Co.
330 2nd St.
Albemarle, NC 28001-3904
(704)983-1121
Location Type: Branch office. **Ultimate Parent:** First Citizens Bancshares, Inc. **SIC:** 6021—National Commercial Banks.

★ 73534 ★ First Union National Bank of North Carolina
811 Hwy. 24/27 Bypass E
Albemarle, NC 28001
(704)982-9161
Company Type: Subsidiary. **Location Type:** Branch office. **Ultimate Parent:** First Union Corp. **SIC:** 6021—National Commercial Banks.

★ 73535 ★ First Union National Bank of North Carolina
500 N. 1st St.
Albemarle, NC 28001
(704)982-9161
Company Type: Subsidiary. **Location Type:** Branch office. **Ultimate Parent:** First Union Corp. **SIC:** 6021—National Commercial Banks.

★ 73536 ★ Food Lion
833 Hwy. 24 Bypass E. 27
Albemarle, NC 28001
(704)982-5817
Ultimate Parent: Food Lion. **SIC:** 5411—Grocery Stores.

★ 73537 ★ Frist-Citizens Bank & Trust CO.
352 N. 1st St.
Albemarle, NC 28001-3935
(704)983-1121
Location Type: Branch office. **Officer:** W. D. Lawhon Jr., Senior Vice President. **Ultimate Parent:** First Citizens Bancshares, Inc. **SIC:** 6021—National Commercial Banks.

★ 73538 ★ Kentucky Fried Chicken
409 S. 1st St.
Albemarle, NC 28001
(704)982-0143
Ultimate Parent: Pepsico. **SIC:** 5812—Eating Places.

★ 73539 ★ Kentucky Fried Chicken
1465 Us 52 N
Albemarle, NC 28001
(704)982-9500
Ultimate Parent: Pepsico. **SIC:** 5812—Eating Places.

★ 73540 ★ Metal Forge Co.
1600 Woodhurst Ln.
Albemarle, NC 28001
(704)983-4146
Officer: Richard Long, Manager. **Ultimate Parent:** General Signal. **SIC:** 3714—Motor Vehicle Parts & Accessories.

★ 73541 ★ Metal Forge Co.
Protective Coatings Div.
1301 Mabry Dr.
Albemarle, NC 28001
Company Type: Division. **Ultimate Parent:** General Signal. **SIC:** 3479—Metal Coating & Allied Services.

★ 73542 ★ Taco Bell
Hwy. 24 Byp E. 27
Albemarle, NC 28001
(704)982-6394
Ultimate Parent: Pepsico. **SIC:** 5812—Eating Places.

★ 73543 ★ Wachovia Bank & Trust Compa
200 E. Main St.
Albemarle, NC 28001
(704)983-4126
Ultimate Parent: Wachovia Corp. **SIC:** 6099—Functions Related to Deposit Banking.

★ 73544 ★ Wal Mart
700 Hwy. 24 Bypass 27
Albemarle, NC 28001
(704)983-6830
Ultimate Parent: Wal-Mart Stores, Inc. **SIC:** 5311—Department Stores.

Albermarle

★ 73545 ★ First Union National Bank of North Carolina
103 N. 2nd St.
Albemarle, NC 28001-4803
(704)982-9161
Company Type: Subsidiary. **Location Type:** Branch office. **Ultimate Parent:** First Union Corp. **SIC:** 6021—National Commercial Banks.

Andrews

★ 73546 ★ First Union National Bank of North Carolina
107 E. 2nd St.
Andrews, NC 28901
(704)321-4141
Company Type: Subsidiary. **Location Type:** Branch office. **Ultimate Parent:** First Union Corp. **SIC:** 6021—National Commercial Banks.

★ 73547 ★ OMC Andrews
1000 Hwy. 19 129 W
Andrews, NC 28901
(704)837-5311
Officer: Harold Smith, Manager. **Ultimate Parent:** Outboard Marine. **SIC:** 3566—Speed Changers, Drives & Gears.

★ 73548 ★   Omc-Andrews
1000 Hwy. 19-129 W.
Andrews, NC 28901
Ultimate Parent: Outboard Marine. **SIC:**
3566—Speed Changers, Drives & Gears.

★ 73549 ★   Outboard Marine
Corp.
1000 Hwy. 19-129 W
Andrews, NC 28901
Ultimate Parent: Outboard Marine. **SIC:**
3519—Internal Combustion Engines Nec.

★ 73550 ★   Wachovia Bank &
Trust Co. N
Andrews, NC 28901
(704)321-4285
Ultimate Parent: Wachovia Corp. **SIC:**
6141—Personal Credit Institutions.

Angier

★ 73551 ★   Branch Banking &
Trust Co.
203 E. Depot St.
Angier, NC 27501
(919)639-2240
Company Type: Subsidiary. **Location
Type:** Branch office. **Officer:** David A.
Speaks, Mgr. **Ultimate Parent:** Southern
National Corp. **SIC:** 6021—National
Commercial Banks.

★ 73552 ★   First-Citizens Bank &
Trust Co.
104 W. Depot St.
Angier, NC 27501
(919)639-2277
Location Type: Branch office. **Officer:**
Sherwood Blackwood, Assistant Vice
President. **Ultimate Parent:** First Citizens
Bancshares, Inc. **SIC:** 6021—National
Commercial Banks.

Apex

★ 73553 ★   Branch Banking &
Trust Co.
303 S. Salem St.
Apex, NC 27502-1826
(919)362-7531
Company Type: Subsidiary. **Location
Type:** Branch office. **Ultimate Parent:**
Southern National Corp. **SIC:** 6021—
National Commercial Banks.

★ 73554 ★   Data General Corp.
Technology Dr.
Apex, NC 27502
Ultimate Parent: Data General. **SIC:**
3500—Industrial Machinery & Equipment.

★ 73555 ★   Data General Corp.
Hwy. 55
Apex, NC 27502
(919)362-4800
Officer: Ralph Hudson, Manager. **Ultimate
Parent:** Data General. **SIC:** 3571—
Electronic Computers; 3577—Computer
Peripheral Equipment Nec; 3679—Electronic
Components Nec; 3672—Printed Circuit
Boards.

★ 73556 ★   Food Lion
Hwy. 55 S
Apex, NC 27502
(919)362-0801
Ultimate Parent: Food Lion. **SIC:** 5411—
Grocery Stores.

★ 73557 ★   Lufkin
Lufkin Rd.
Apex, NC 27502
Ultimate Parent: Cooper Industries. **SIC:**
3999—Manufacturing Industries Nec.

★ 73558 ★   Tipper Tie Inc.
2000 Lufkin Rd.
Apex, NC 27502
(919)362-8811
Officer: Charles M. Heard, President.
Ultimate Parent: Dover Corp. **SIC:** 3556—
Food Products Machinery.

★ 73559 ★   Tipper Tie Inc.
2000 Lufkin Rd.
Apex, NC 27502-7068
(919)362-8811
Company Type: Subsidiary. **Ultimate
Parent:** Dover Corp. **SIC:** 3429—Hardware
Nec.

★ 73560 ★   Wachovia Bank &
Trust Co.
101 S. Edinburgh Dr.
Apex, NC 27502
(919)481-3667
Ultimate Parent: Wachovia Corp. **SIC:**
6099—Functions Related to Deposit
Banking.

Archdale

★ 73561 ★   First Union National
Bank of North Carolina
11100 N. Main St., High Point
Archdale, NC 27263-2162
(910)887-5846
Company Type: Subsidiary. **Location
Type:** Branch office. **Ultimate Parent:** First
Union Corp. **SIC:** 6021—National
Commercial Banks.

★ 73562 ★   UNIFI, Inc.
116 Petty St.
Archdale, NC 27263
(910)431-2174
Officer: Mike Ward, Plant Manager.
Ultimate Parent: UNIFI, Inc. **SIC:** 2281—
Yarn Spinning Mills.

Arden

★ 73563 ★   Air Products &
Chemicals
5 Winners Cir.
Arden, NC 28704-3156
(704)687-0066
Ultimate Parent: Air Products & Chemicals,
Inc. **SIC:** 5085—Industrial Supplies.

★ 73564 ★   Crown Cork & Seal
Co. Inc.
90 Christ School Rd.
Arden, NC 28704
Ultimate Parent: Crown Cork & Seal. **SIC:**
3411—Metal Cans.

★ 73565 ★   Day International
95 Glenn Bridge Rd.
Arden, NC 28704
Ultimate Parent: M.A.Hanna. **SIC:** 3069—
Fabricated Rubber Products Nec.

★ 73566 ★   Day International Inc.
95 Glenn Bridge Rd.
Arden, NC 28704
Ultimate Parent: M.A.Hanna. **SIC:** 3069—
Fabricated Rubber Products Nec.

★ 73567 ★   Eaton Corp.
94 Glenn Bridge Rd. Rte. 1 Box 1A
Arden, NC 28704
Ultimate Parent: Eaton Corp. **SIC:** 3625—
Relays & Industrial Controls.

★ 73568 ★   Eaton Corp.
Logic Control Div.
Glen Bridge & Long Shools Rd.
Arden, NC 28704
(704)684-9861
Company Type: Division. **Location Type:**
Plant. **Officer:** Tom Ackerman, Manager
Bus. **Ultimate Parent:** Eaton Corp. **SIC:**
3625—Relays & Industrial Controls.

★ 73569 ★   First Union National
Bank of North Carolina
2397 Hendersonville Rd.
Arden, NC 28704-3149
(704)684-3566
Company Type: Subsidiary. **Location
Type:** Branch office. **Ultimate Parent:** First
Union Corp. **SIC:** 6021—National
Commercial Banks.

★ 73570 ★   Hertz Rent-A-Car
Asheville Airport
Arden, NC 28704
(704)684-6455
Ultimate Parent: Hertz. **SIC:** 7514—
Passenger Car Rental.

★ 73571 ★   Rite Aid Discount
Pharmacie
Us 25 Edgewood Dr.
Arden, NC 28704
(704)684-9259
Ultimate Parent: Rite Aid.

★ 73572 ★   Wachovia Bank &
Trust Co. N
Us 25
Arden, NC 28704
(704)684-6268
Ultimate Parent: Wachovia Corp. **SIC:**
6022—State Commercial Banks.

★ 73573 ★   Westinghouse
Electric
22 Heywood Rd.
Arden, NC 28704
(704)684-2381
Officer: Jerry Palmer, Manager. **Ultimate
Parent:** Westinghouse Electric Corp. **SIC:**
3625—Relays & Industrial Controls; 3699—
Electrical Equipment & Supplies Nec.

★ 73574 ★   Westinghouse
Electric Corp.
22 Heywood Rd.
Arden, NC 28704
Ultimate Parent: Westinghouse Electric
Corp. **SIC:** 3629—Electrical Industrial
Apparatus Nec.

★ 73575 ★   Westinghouse
Electric Corp.
Heywood Rd.
Arden, NC 28704
Ultimate Parent: Westinghouse Electric
Corp. **SIC:** 3629—Electrical Industrial
Apparatus Nec.

Asheboro

★ 73576 ★   AT & T Family Federal
Credit Union
1510-M E. Dixie Dr.
Asheboro, NC 27203
(910)625-6500
Location Type: Branch office. **Officer:** Bill
Warren, Manager. **Ultimate Parent:** AT&T.
SIC: 6061—Federal Credit Unions.

★ 73577 ★   Bankers Trust of
North Carolina
261 N. Fayetteville St.
Asheboro, NC 27203-5529
(919)226-2600
Location Type: Branch office. **Officer:**
Eddie Allen. **Ultimate Parent:** Bankers
Trust New York Corp. **SIC:** 6022—State
Commercial Banks; 6021—National
Commercial Banks; 6141—Personal Credit
Institutions.

★ 73578 ★   Black & Decker Corp.
1758 S. Fayetteville St.
Asheboro, NC 27203
Ultimate Parent: Black & Decker Corp.
SIC: 3634—Electric Housewares & Fans.

★ 73579 ★   Black & Decker Corp.
Household Products Group
1758 S. Fayetteville St.
Asheboro, NC 27203
Ultimate Parent: Black & Decker Corp.
SIC: 3634—Electric Housewares & Fans.

★ 73580 ★   Black & Decker
Housewares Group
1758 S. Fayetteville St.
Asheboro, NC 27203-7356
(919)626-1600
Officer: Richard Richardson. **Ultimate
Parent:** Black & Decker Corp. **SIC:** 3634—
Electric Housewares & Fans; 5722—
Household Appliance Stores.

★ 73581 ★   Burlington Industries
Inc.
1947 N. Fayetteville St.
Asheboro, NC 27203
(910)672-2111
Officer: Mike Carico, Manager. **Ultimate
Parent:** Burlington Industries, Equity. **SIC:**
2221—Broadwoven Fabric Mills—Manmade.

★ 73582 ★   Burlington Industries
Inc.
1947 N. Federal St.
Asheboro, NC 27203
(919)672-2111
Officer: Michael Carico. **Ultimate Parent:**
Burlington Industries, Equity. **SIC:** 2211—
Broadwoven Fabric Mills—Cotton.

★ 73583 ★   CPC Foodservice
PO Box 4008
Asheboro, NC 27204
(910)672-9018
Company Type: Division. **Officer:** Jack
Marcus, Plant Manager. **Ultimate Parent:**

CPC International. **SIC:** 2033—Canned
Fruits & Vegetables.

★ 73584 ★   Dixie Furniture Co.
Inc.
728 S. Fayetteville St.
Asheboro, NC 27203-6406
Ultimate Parent: Masco. **SIC:** 2511—Wood
Household Furniture.

★ 73585 ★   Eveready Battery Co.
Inc.
419 Art Bryan Dr.
Asheboro, NC 27203
Ultimate Parent: Ralston Purina. **SIC:**
3692—Primary Batteries—Dry & Wet.

★ 73586 ★   Eveready Battery Co.
Inc.
800 Albemarle Rd.
Asheboro, NC 27203
Ultimate Parent: Ralston Purina. **SIC:**
3692—Primary Batteries—Dry & Wet.

★ 73587 ★   Georgia-Pacific Corp.
Packaging Div.
200 McDowell Rd.
Asheboro, NC 27203
Company Type: Division. **Ultimate Parent:**
Georgia-Pacific. **SIC:** 2653—Corrugated &
Solid Fiber Boxes.

★ 73588 ★   Kayser-Roth Corp.
Asheboro Plant
515 W. Balfour Ave.
Asheboro, NC 27203
Ultimate Parent: Collins & Aikman Group.
SIC: 2252—Hosiery Nec.

★ 73589 ★   Kentucky Fried
Chicken
968 S. Fayetteville St.
Asheboro, NC 27203
(919)629-3229
Ultimate Parent: Pepsico. **SIC:** 5812—
Eating Places.

★ 73590 ★   Oliver Rubber Co.
408 Telephone Ave.
Asheboro, NC 27203
Ultimate Parent: Standard Products. **SIC:**
3011—Tires & Inner Tubes; 3069—
Fabricated Rubber Products Nec.

★ 73591 ★   Oliver Rubber Co.
Asheboro
408 Telephone Ave.
Asheboro, NC 27203
Ultimate Parent: Standard Products. **SIC:**
3011—Tires & Inner Tubes; 3069—
Fabricated Rubber Products Nec.

★ 73592 ★   Pizza Hut
Fayetteville St.
Asheboro, NC 27203
(919)625-5600
Ultimate Parent: Pepsico. **SIC:** 5812—
Eating Places.

★ 73593 ★   Radio Shack
Randolph Mall
Asheboro, NC 27203
(919)629-3945
Company Type: Division. **Ultimate Parent:**
Tandy Corp. **SIC:** 5065—Electronic Parts &
Equipment Nec.

★ 73594 ★   Rite Aid Discount
Pharmacie
472 E. Dixie Dr.
Asheboro, NC 27203
(919)629-9044
Ultimate Parent: Rite Aid. **SIC:** 5912—Drug
Stores & Proprietary Stores.

★ 73595 ★   Rite Aid Discount
Pharmacie
341 N. Fayetteville St.
Asheboro, NC 27203
(919)629-1455
Ultimate Parent: Rite Aid. **SIC:** 5912—Drug
Stores & Proprietary Stores.

★ 73596 ★   Ryder Truck Rental
801 E. Dixie Dr.
Asheboro, NC 27203
(919)629-1798
Ultimate Parent: Ryder System. **SIC:**
7359—Equipment Rental & Leasing Nec.

★ 73597 ★ Sara Lee Knit Products
1305 S. Fayetteville St.
Asheboro, NC 27203
Location Type: Plant. Ultimate Parent: Sara Lee Corp. SIC: 2322—Men's/Boys' Underwear & Nightwear.

★ 73598 ★ Wachovia Bank & Trust
15 S. Fayetteville St.
Asheboro, NC 27203
(919)626-1000
Ultimate Parent: Wachovia Corp. SIC: 6099—Functions Related to Deposit Banking.

★ 73599 ★ Wachovia Bank & Trust Co.
15 S. Fayetteville St.
Asheboro, NC 27203
(919)625-5165
Ultimate Parent: Wachovia Corp. SIC: 6022—State Commercial Banks.

★ 73600 ★ Wachovia Bank & Trust Co.
901 E. Dixie Dr.
Asheboro, NC 27203
(919)626-1029
Ultimate Parent: Wachovia Corp. SIC: 6099—Functions Related to Deposit Banking.

Asheville

★ 73601 ★ ACME Business Products
200 Ridgefield Ct.
Asheville, NC 28806-2254
(704)665-4080
Ultimate Parent: Alco Standard Corp. SIC: 5044—Office Equipment.

★ 73602 ★ Ball-Icon Glass Packaging
1856 Hendersonville Rd.
Asheville, NC 28803-3207
Officer: James Tucker. Ultimate Parent: Ball Corp. SIC: 3200—Stone, Clay & Glass Products.

★ 73603 ★ Ball Incon Glass Packaging
1856 Hendersonville Rd.
Asheville, NC 28803
(704)274-2255
Officer: Jim Tucker, Manager. Ultimate Parent: Ball Corp. SIC: 3221—Glass Containers.

★ 73604 ★ Ball-Incon Glass Packaging
1 NW Pack Sq.
Asheville, NC 28801
(704)258-1527
Ultimate Parent: Ball Corp. SIC: 3211—Flat Glass.

★ 73605 ★ Ball - Incon Glass Packaging Corp.
1856 Hendersonville Rd.
Asheville, NC 28803
Ultimate Parent: Ball Corp. SIC: 3221—Glass Containers.

★ 73606 ★ Bi-Lo Super Market One-Hund
801 Fairview Rd.
Asheville, NC 28803
(704)299-1508
Ultimate Parent: Penn Traffic. SIC: 5411—Grocery Stores.

★ 73607 ★ Branch Banking & Trust Co.
1 Pack Sq.
Asheville, NC 28801-3423
(704)255-8181
Company Type: Subsidiary. Location Type: Branch office. Ultimate Parent: Southern National Corp. SIC: 6021—National Commercial Banks.

★ 73608 ★ Branch Banking & Trust Co.
850 Merrimon Ave.
Asheville, NC 28804-2405
(704)255-8181
Company Type: Subsidiary. Location Type: Branch office. Officer: James A. Evans III, Mgr. Ultimate Parent: Southern National Corp. SIC: 6021—National Commercial Banks.

★ 73609 ★ Chase Packaging Corp.
3055 Sweeten Creek Rd.
Asheville, NC 28803
Ultimate Parent: Union Camp Corp. SIC: 2754—Commercial Printing—Gravure.

★ 73610 ★ Coca Cola Bottling Co.
Clayton Rd.
Asheville, NC 28801
(704)684-1273
Ultimate Parent: Coca-Cola Enterprises. SIC: 5046—Commercial Equipment Nec.

★ 73611 ★ Dr. T.C. Smith Co.
280 Hanover St.
Asheville, NC 28806-4052
(704)258-1869
Company Type: Subsidiary. Officer: Frank S. Smith III, Chairman of the Board. Ultimate Parent: Bergen Brunswig Corp. SIC: 5122—Drugs, Proprietaries & Sundries; 5047—Medical & Hospital Equipment. Employee Count: 130. Sales: 141 M.

★ 73612 ★ Exxon Co. USA
Executiv Park Bldg.
Asheville, NC 28801
(704)254-5681
Ultimate Parent: Exxon. SIC: 5172—Petroleum Products Nec.

★ 73613 ★ First-Citizens Bank & Trust Co.
Cane Creek Rd.
Asheville, NC 28703
(704)257-5820
Location Type: Branch office. Ultimate Parent: First Citizens Bancshares, Inc. SIC: 6021—National Commercial Banks.

★ 73614 ★ First-Citizens Bank & Trust Co.
975 Smoky Park Hwy.
Asheville, NC 28802
(704)257-5700
Location Type: Branch office. Ultimate Parent: First Citizens Bancshares, Inc. SIC: 6021—National Commercial Banks.

★ 73615 ★ First-Citizens Bank & Trust Co.
601 Leicester Hwy.
Asheville, NC 28802
(704)257-5700
Location Type: Branch office. Ultimate Parent: First Citizens Bancshares, Inc. SIC: 6021—National Commercial Banks.

★ 73616 ★ First-Citizens Bank & Trust Co.
800 Fairview Ave.
Asheville, NC 28802
(704)257-5700
Location Type: Branch office. Ultimate Parent: First Citizens Bancshares, Inc. SIC: 6021—National Commercial Banks.

★ 73617 ★ First-Citizens Bank & Trust Co.
625 Merrimon Ave.
Asheville, NC 28802
(704)257-5700
Location Type: Branch office. Ultimate Parent: First Citizens Bancshares, Inc. SIC: 6021—National Commercial Banks.

★ 73618 ★ First-Citizens Bank & Trust Co.
1375 W. Patton Ave.
Asheville, NC 28802
(704)257-5700
Location Type: Branch office. Ultimate Parent: First Citizens Bancshares, Inc. SIC: 6021—National Commercial Banks.

★ 73619 ★ First-Citizens Bank & Trust Co.
768 Hendersonville Ave.
Asheville, NC 28802
(704)257-5700
Location Type: Branch office. Ultimate Parent: First Citizens Bancshares, Inc. SIC: 6021—National Commercial Banks.

★ 73620 ★ First-Citizens Bank & Trust Co.
1201 Tunnel Rd.
Asheville, NC 28805-2104
(704)257-5700
Location Type: Branch office. Ultimate Parent: First Citizens Bancshares, Inc. SIC: 6021—National Commercial Banks.

★ 73621 ★ First-Citizens Bank & Trust Co.
108 Patton Ave.
Asheville, NC 28802
(704)257-5700
Location Type: Branch office. Officer: Bill N. Clark, Senior Vice President. Ultimate Parent: First Citizens Bancshares, Inc. SIC: 6021—National Commercial Banks.

★ 73622 ★ First Union National Bank of North Carolina
700 Haywood Rd.
Asheville, NC 28806-3261
(704)251-7111
Company Type: Subsidiary. Location Type: Branch office. Ultimate Parent: First Union Corp. SIC: 6021—National Commercial Banks.

★ 73623 ★ First Union National Bank of North Carolina
1 Angle St.
Asheville, NC 28803-2627
(704)251-7111
Company Type: Subsidiary. Location Type: Branch office. Ultimate Parent: First Union Corp. SIC: 6021—National Commercial Banks.

★ 73624 ★ First Union National Bank of North Carolina
771 Tunnel Rd.
Asheville, NC 28805-1918
(704)251-7111
Company Type: Subsidiary. Location Type: Branch office. Ultimate Parent: First Union Corp. SIC: 6021—National Commercial Banks.

★ 73625 ★ First Union National Bank of North Carolina
711 Merrimon Ave.
Asheville, NC 28804-2414
(704)251-7111
Company Type: Subsidiary. Location Type: Branch office. Ultimate Parent: First Union Corp. SIC: 6021—National Commercial Banks.

★ 73626 ★ First Union National Bank of North Carolina
Asheville Plz. W
Smokey Pk., Hwys. 19 & 23
Asheville, NC 28806-1167
(704)251-7111
Company Type: Subsidiary. Location Type: Branch office. Ultimate Parent: First Union Corp. SIC: 6021—National Commercial Banks.

★ 73627 ★ First Union National Bank of North Carolina
82 Palton Ave.
Asheville, NC 28801-3319
(704)251-7111
Company Type: Subsidiary. Location Type: Branch office. Ultimate Parent: First Union Corp. SIC: 6021—National Commercial Banks.

★ 73628 ★ Food Lion
55 Weaverville Rd.
Asheville, NC 28804
(704)645-3928
Ultimate Parent: Food Lion. SIC: 5411—Grocery Stores.

★ 73629 ★ Food Lion Inc. Store No. 519
55 Weaverville Rd.
Asheville, NC 28804
(704)645-3928
Ultimate Parent: Food Lion. SIC: 5411—Grocery Stores.

★ 73630 ★ Greyhound Bus Station
495 Haywood Rd.
Asheville, NC 28806
(704)253-8451
Ultimate Parent: Greyhound Lines Inc. SIC: 4724—Travel Agencies.

★ 73631 ★ Pepsi-Cola Bottling
601 Sweeten Creek Rd.
Asheville, NC 28803
(704)274-4600
Officer: Lee Teeter, President. Ultimate Parent: Pepsico. SIC: 2086—Bottled & Canned Soft Drinks; 2087—Flavoring Extracts & Syrups Nec.

★ 73632 ★ Pizza Hut
671 Merrimon Ave.
Asheville, NC 28804
(704)254-4235
Ultimate Parent: Pepsico. SIC: 5812—Eating Places.

★ 73633 ★ Pizza Hut
16008 PO Box
Asheville, NC 28816
(704)667-3500
Ultimate Parent: Pepsico. SIC: 5812—Eating Places.

★ 73634 ★ Radio Shack
Arden Plz.
Asheville, NC 28801
(704)274-5282
Company Type: Division. Ultimate Parent: Tandy Corp. SIC: 5065—Electronic Parts & Equipment Nec.

★ 73635 ★ Rite Aid Discount Pharmacie
New Leicester Hwy.
Asheville, NC 28806
(704)255-9367
Ultimate Parent: Rite Aid. SIC: 5912—Drug Stores & Proprietary Stores.

★ 73636 ★ Rite Aid Discount Pharmacie
25 Edgewood Rd.
Asheville, NC 28804
(704)684-7181
Ultimate Parent: Rite Aid. SIC: 5912—Drug Stores & Proprietary Stores.

★ 73637 ★ Ryder Truck Rental
4 Tunl Rd.
Asheville, NC 28801
(704)254-0836
Ultimate Parent: Ryder System. SIC: 7353—Heavy Construction Equipment Rental.

★ 73638 ★ Underwriters Adjusting Co.
170 Woodfin St.
Asheville, NC 28801
(704)254-2619
Ultimate Parent: Continental. SIC: 6411—Insurance Agents, Brokers & Service.

★ 73639 ★ Wachovia Bank & Trust Co.
Hwy. 25
Asheville, NC 28803
(704)255-2241
Ultimate Parent: Wachovia Corp. SIC: 6022—State Commercial Banks.

★ 73640 ★ Wachovia Bank & Trust Co.
Asheville, NC 28803
(704)255-2000
Ultimate Parent: Wachovia Corp. SIC: 6029—Commercial Banks Nec.

★ 73641 ★ Wachovia Bank & Trust Co. N
2510 PO Box
Asheville, NC 28802
Ultimate Parent: Wachovia Corp. SIC: 6099—Functions Related to Deposit Banking.

Atlantic Beach

★ 73642 ★ Ace Hardware & Marine
Peddlers Whf
Atl Beach, NC 28512
(919)726-7202
Ultimate Parent: Ace Hardware. SIC: 5941—Sporting Goods & Bicycle Shops.

★ 73643 ★ Wachovia Bank & Trust
314 Salter Path
Atlantic Beach, NC 28512
(919)240-1853
Ultimate Parent: Wachovia Corp. SIC: 6099—Functions Related to Deposit Banking.

Aulander

★ 73644 ★ Golden Peanut Co.
301 W. Pearl St.
Aulander, NC 27805
(919)345-1661
Officer: Gaylord Coan, President. **Ultimate Parent:** Archer Daniels Midland Co. **SIC:** 2064—Candy & Other Confectionery Products; 2068—Salted & Roasted Nuts & Seeds.

Aurora

★ 73645 ★ Wachovia Bank & Trust Co. N
5 St.
Aurora, NC 27806
(919)322-4161
Ultimate Parent: Wachovia Corp. **SIC:** 6022—State Commercial Banks.

Autryville

★ 73646 ★ First Citizens Bank & Trust Co.
102 Mill St.
Autryville, NC 28318
(910)525-4057
Location Type: Branch office. **Officer:** Linda K. Spell, Assistant Vice President. **Ultimate Parent:** First Citizens Bancshares, Inc. **SIC:** 6021—National Commercial Banks.

Ayden

★ 73647 ★ Branch Banking & Trust Co.
1410 W. 3rd St.
Ayden, NC 28513-2352
(919)746-3043
Company Type: Subsidiary. **Location Type:** Branch office. **Officer:** L. Gray Mathis, Mgr. **Ultimate Parent:** Southern National Corp. **SIC:** 6021—National Commercial Banks.

Badin

★ 73648 ★ Alcoa
Hwy. 740
Badin, NC 28009-8103
(704)422-3621
Location Type: Branch office. **Ultimate Parent:** Aluminum Co. of America--Alcoa. **SIC:** 3334—Primary Aluminum.

★ 73649 ★ Alcoa
Hwy. 740
Badin, NC 28009-8103
(704)422-3621
Location Type: Branch office. **Ultimate Parent:** Aluminum Co. of America--Alcoa. **SIC:** 3334—Primary Aluminum.

★ 73650 ★ Alcoa Badin Works
Hwy. 740 P.O Box 576
Badin, NC 28009
Ultimate Parent: Aluminum Co. of America--Alcoa. **SIC:** 3334—Primary Aluminum.

★ 73651 ★ Aluminum Co. of America
Albemarle Rd.
Badin, NC 28009
(704)422-3621
Ultimate Parent: Aluminum Co. of America--Alcoa. **SIC:** 3334—Primary Aluminum.

★ 73652 ★ Aluminum Co. of America Badin Works
PO Box 576
Albemarle Rd.
Badin, NC 28009
(704)422-3621
Location Type: Branch office. **Officer:** Larry Tate, Manager. **Ultimate Parent:** Aluminum Co. of America--Alcoa. **SIC:** 3334—Primary Aluminum.

★ 73653 ★ Aluminum Co. of America Badin Works
Albemarle Rd.
PO Box 576
Badin, NC 28009
(704)422-3621
Location Type: Branch office. **Officer:** Larry Tate, Manager. **Ultimate Parent:** Aluminum Co. of America--Alcoa. **SIC:** 3334—Primary Aluminum.

★ 73654 ★ Yadkin, Inc.
Hwy. 740
Badin, NC 28009
(704)422-5633
Officer: N.L. Pierson, President. **Ultimate Parent:** Aluminum Co. of America--Alcoa. **SIC:** 4911—Electric Services. **Employee Count:** 33.

Bakersville

★ 73655 ★ First Union National Bank of North Carolina
114 Mitchell Ave.
Bakersville, NC 28705
(704)688-2117
Company Type: Subsidiary. **Location Type:** Branch office. **Ultimate Parent:** First Union Corp. **SIC:** 6021—National Commercial Banks.

Balfour

★ 73656 ★ Berkeley Mills
32 Smythe Ave.
Balfour, NC 28792-8503
Ultimate Parent: Kimberly-Clark. **SIC:** 2297—Nonwoven Fabrics; 2679—Converted Paper Products Nec.

Banner Elk

★ 73657 ★ First-Citizens Bank & Trust Co.
Hwy. 54
Banner Elk, NC 28604
(704)898-5155
Location Type: Branch office. **Ultimate Parent:** First Citizens Bancshares, Inc. **SIC:** 6021—National Commercial Banks.

★ 73658 ★ First Union National Bank of North Carolina
Rte. 2, Hwy. 184
Banner Elk, NC 28604-9702
(704)262-4690
Company Type: Subsidiary. **Location Type:** Branch office. **Ultimate Parent:** First Union Corp. **SIC:** 6021—National Commercial Banks.

Banson

★ 73659 ★ First-Citizens Bank & Trust Co.
301 E. Main St.
Banson, NC 27504-1510
(919)894-8131
Location Type: Branch office. **Ultimate Parent:** First Citizens Bancshares, Inc. **SIC:** 6021—National Commercial Banks.

★ 73660 ★ First-Citizens Bank & Trust Co.
NC Hwys. 50 & 96
Banson, NC 27504-9440
(919)894-8131
Location Type: Branch office. **Ultimate Parent:** First Citizens Bancshares, Inc. **SIC:** 6021—National Commercial Banks.

Barber

★ 73661 ★ Southern States Co-Op. Inc. Barber Feed Mill
Hwy. 70 PO Box 16
Barber, NC 27008
Ultimate Parent: Southern. **SIC:** 2048—Prepared Feeds Nec.

Bayboro

★ 73662 ★ First-Citizens Bank & Trust Co.
409 Broad St.
Bayboro, NC 28571
(919)249-1462
Location Type: Branch office. **Ultimate Parent:** First Citizens Bancshares, Inc. **SIC:** 6021—National Commercial Banks.

★ 73663 ★ First-Citizens Bank & Trust Co.
Hwy. 306
Bayboro, NC 28510
(919)249-0655
Location Type: Branch office. **Ultimate Parent:** First Citizens Bancshares, Inc. **SIC:** 6021—National Commercial Banks.

★ 73664 ★ First-Citizens Bank & Trust Co.
4th & Main Sts.
Bayboro, NC 28515
(919)745-4141
Location Type: Branch office. **Officer:** E. Eugene Hooks, Senior Vice President. **Ultimate Parent:** First Citizens Bancshares, Inc. **SIC:** 6021—National Commercial Banks.

★ 73665 ★ Wachovia Bank & Trust
Hwy. 55 E
Bayboro, NC 28515
(919)745-3141
Ultimate Parent: Wachovia Corp. **SIC:** 6099—Functions Related to Deposit Banking.

Beaufort

★ 73666 ★ Branch Banking & Trust Co.
617 Front St.
Beaufort, NC 28516-2209
(919)728-4501
Company Type: Subsidiary. **Location Type:** Branch office. **Officer:** Joseph S. Johnson Jr., Mgr. **Ultimate Parent:** Southern National Corp. **SIC:** 6021—National Commercial Banks.

★ 73667 ★ First-Citizens Bank & Trust Co.
US Hwy. 70 & Hwy. 101
Beaufort, NC 28516-9520
(919)728-3171
Location Type: Branch office. **Ultimate Parent:** First Citizens Bancshares, Inc. **SIC:** 6021—National Commercial Banks.

★ 73668 ★ First-Citizens Bank & Trust Co.
Hwy. 70 E. & State Rd. 1350
Beaufort, NC 28579-9501
(919)728-3171
Location Type: Branch office. **Ultimate Parent:** First Citizens Bancshares, Inc. **SIC:** 6021—National Commercial Banks.

★ 73669 ★ First-Citizens Bank & Trust Co.
411 Front St.
Beaufort, NC 28516-2126
(919)728-3171
Location Type: Branch office. **Officer:** James T. Spencer, Vice President. **Ultimate Parent:** First Citizens Bancshares, Inc. **SIC:** 6021—National Commercial Banks.

★ 73670 ★ Wachovia Bank & Trust
Us Hwy. 70 E
Beaufort, NC 28516
(919)728-2901
Ultimate Parent: Wachovia Corp. **SIC:** 6099—Functions Related to Deposit Banking.

Belhaven

★ 73671 ★ Wachovia Bank & Trust Co. N
301 Main St.
Belhaven, NC 27810
(919)943-2131
Ultimate Parent: Wachovia Corp. **SIC:** 6022—State Commercial Banks.

Belmont

★ 73672 ★ Burlington Industries Inc.
325 Peach Orchard Rd.
Belmont, NC 28012
(704)825-9141
Officer: Don Wall, Manager. **Ultimate Parent:** Burlington Industries, Equity. **SIC:** 2399—Fabricated Textile Products Nec.

★ 73673 ★ Burlington Industries William G. Lord
Eagle Rd.
Belmont, NC 28012
(704)825-9841
Officer: Al Blaylock. **Ultimate Parent:** Burlington Industries, Equity. **SIC:** 2399—Fabricated Textile Products Nec; 2221—Broadwoven Fabric Mills—Manmade; 5714—Drapery & Upholstery Stores.

★ 73674 ★ Food Lion
526 Woodlawn Ave.
Belmont, NC 28012
(704)827-3836
Ultimate Parent: Food Lion. **SIC:** 5411—Grocery Stores.

★ 73675 ★ Wachovia Bank & Trust
518 Woodlawn Ave.
Belmont, NC 28012
(704)827-2456
Ultimate Parent: Wachovia Corp. **SIC:** 6022—State Commercial Banks.

★ 73676 ★ Wachovia Bank & Trust
Abbey Plz.
Belmont, NC 28012
(704)825-0261
Ultimate Parent: Wachovia Corp. **SIC:** 6022—State Commercial Banks.

★ 73677 ★ Wachovia Bank & Trust
32 N. Main St.
Belmont, NC 28012
(704)825-0200
Ultimate Parent: Wachovia Corp. **SIC:** 6022—State Commercial Banks.

★ 73678 ★ Wachovia Bank & Trust Co. N
Catawba St.
Belmont, NC 28012
(704)825-5176
Ultimate Parent: Wachovia Corp. **SIC:** 6022—State Commercial Banks.

★ 73679 ★ Wachovia Bank & Trust Co. N
Abbey Plz.
Belmont, NC 28012
(704)825-3767
Ultimate Parent: Wachovia Corp. **SIC:** 6022—State Commercial Banks.

Benson

★ 73680 ★ Branch Banking & Trust Co.
307 E. Main St.
Benson, NC 27504-1510
(919)894-8531
Company Type: Subsidiary. **Location Type:** Branch office. **Officer:** Trudy B. Benson-Weaver, Mgr. **Ultimate Parent:** Southern National Corp. **SIC:** 6021—National Commercial Banks.

★ 73681 ★ First-Citizens Bank & Trust Co.
NC Hwy. 50 & Hwy. 210
Benson, NC 27504-9440
(919)894-8131
Location Type: Branch office. **Ultimate Parent:** First Citizens Bancshares, Inc. **SIC:** 6021—National Commercial Banks.

★ 73682 ★ First-Citizens Bank & Trust Co.
100 W. Main St.
Benson, NC 27504-1344
(919)894-8131
Location Type: Branch office. **Officer:** John W. Wood III, Vice President. **Ultimate Parent:** First Citizens Bancshares, Inc. **SIC:** 6021—National Commercial Banks.

★ 73683 ★ Food Lion
203 S. Walton Dr.
Benson, NC 27504
(919)894-2085
Ultimate Parent: Food Lion. **SIC:** 5411—Grocery Stores.

★ 73684 ★ Food Lion Inc.
203 S. Walton Dr.
Benson, NC 27504
(919)894-2085
Ultimate Parent: Food Lion. **SIC:** 5411—Grocery Stores.

★ 73685 ★ Piggly Wiggly
S Wall
Benson, NC 27504
(919)894-2113
Ultimate Parent: Bruno's. **SIC:** 5411—Grocery Stores.

Bessemer City

★ 73686 ★ **Coca Cola Bottling Co.**
925 E. Marion St.
Bessemer City, NC 28016
(704)629-5771
Ultimate Parent: Coca-Cola Enterprises.
SIC: 2086—Bottled & Canned Soft Drinks.

★ 73687 ★ **First Union National Bank of North Carolina**
124 W. Virginia Ave.
Bessemer City, NC 28016-2373
(704)629-2294
Company Type: Subsidiary. **Location Type:** Branch office. **Ultimate Parent:** First Union Corp. **SIC:** 6021—National Commercial Banks.

★ 73688 ★ **FMC Corp.**
Lithium Div.
Hwy. 161
Bessemer City, NC 28016-0795
Company Type: Division. **Ultimate Parent:** FMC. **SIC:** 2819—Industrial Inorganic Chemicals Nec; 2869—Industrial Organic Chemicals Nec.

★ 73689 ★ **Lithium Corp. of America**
Hwy. 161
Bessemer City, NC 28016-0795
Ultimate Parent: FMC. **SIC:** 2819—Industrial Inorganic Chemicals Nec; 2869—Industrial Organic Chemicals Nec.

★ 73690 ★ **Lithium Corp. of America**
FMC Lithium Div.
Hwy. 161
Bessemer City, NC 28016-0795
Company Type: Division. **Ultimate Parent:** FMC. **SIC:** 2819—Industrial Inorganic Chemicals Nec; 2869—Industrial Organic Chemicals Nec.

Bethel

★ 73691 ★ **Wachovia Bank & Trust Co. N**
N Railroad
Bethel, NC 27812
(919)825-8851
Ultimate Parent: Wachovia Corp. **SIC:** 6022—State Commercial Banks.

Bethlehem

★ 73692 ★ **First-Citizens Bank & Trust**
Rink Dam Rd. & US Hwy. 127
Bethlehem, NC 28603
(704)495-8281
Location Type: Branch office. **Officer:** Wlater I. Garrett, Vice President. **Ultimate Parent:** First Citizens Bancshares, Inc. **SIC:** 6021—National Commercial Banks.

★ 73693 ★ **First Union National Bank of North Carolina**
Hwy. 127 & Rink Dam Rd.
Bethlehem, NC 28601-9370
(704)495-8221
Company Type: Subsidiary. **Location Type:** Branch office. **Ultimate Parent:** First Union Corp. **SIC:** 6021—National Commercial Banks.

Black Creek

★ 73694 ★ **Branch Banking & Trust Co.**
101 N. Ctr. St.
Black Creek, NC 27813
(919)399-4357
Ultimate Parent: Southern National Corp. **SIC:** 6022—State Commercial Banks.

Black Mountain

★ 73695 ★ **Cooper Industries Inc.**
Bussmann Div.
1000 Craigmont Rd.
Black Mountain, NC 28711
Company Type: Division. **Ultimate Parent:** Cooper Industries. **SIC:** 3613—Switchgear & Switchboard Apparatus.

★ 73696 ★ **Cooper Industries Inc.**
Bussmann Div.
1000 Craigmont Rd.
Black Mountain, NC 28711
Company Type: Division. **Ultimate Parent:** Cooper Industries. **SIC:** 3613—Switchgear & Switchboard Apparatus.

★ 73697 ★ **First Union National Bank of North Carolina**
200 Hwy. 9 S
Black Mountain, NC 28711-3116
(704)669-8463
Company Type: Subsidiary. **Location Type:** Branch office. **Ultimate Parent:** First Union Corp. **SIC:** 6021—National Commercial Banks.

★ 73698 ★ **Kentucky Fried Chicken**
Hwy. 9
Black Mountain, NC 28711
(704)669-5133
Ultimate Parent: Pepsico. **SIC:** 5812—Eating Places.

★ 73699 ★ **Trailways Bus Lines**
E State Rd.
Black Mountain, NC 28711
(704)669-2184
Ultimate Parent: Greyhound Lines Inc. **SIC:** 4131—Intercity & Rural Bus Transportation.

Bladenboro

★ 73700 ★ **First-Citizens Bank & Trust Co.**
100 S. Mian St.
Bladenboro, NC 28320
(704)295-3162
Location Type: Branch office. **Ultimate Parent:** First Citizens Bancshares, Inc. **SIC:** 6021—National Commercial Banks.

Blowing Rock

★ 73701 ★ **First-Citizens Bank & Trust Co.**
1154 N. Mian St.
Blowing Rock, NC 28605
(704)295-3162
Location Type: Branch office. **Ultimate Parent:** First Citizens Bancshares, Inc. **SIC:** 6021—National Commercial Banks.

★ 73702 ★ **First Union National Bank of North Carolina**
1154 N. Main St.
Blowing Rock, NC 28605
(704)262-4694
Company Type: Subsidiary. **Location Type:** Branch office. **Ultimate Parent:** First Union Corp. **SIC:** 6021—National Commercial Banks.

★ 73703 ★ **Pizza Hut**
Us 321
Blowing Rock, NC 28605
(704)295-7080
Ultimate Parent: Pepsico. **SIC:** 5812—Eating Places.

Boiling Springs

★ 73704 ★ **Branch Banking & Trust Co.**
N Main St.
Boiling Springs, NC 28017
(704)434-6123
Company Type: Subsidiary. **Location Type:** Branch office. **Officer:** Debbie Davis, Mgr. **Ultimate Parent:** Southern National Corp. **SIC:** 6021—National Commercial Banks.

Bolton

★ 73705 ★ **Federal Paper Board Co., Inc.**
338 PO Box
Bolton, NC 28423
(919)655-8701
Ultimate Parent: Federal Paper Board. **SIC:** 0811—Timber Tracts.

Bonlee

★ 73706 ★ **Golden Poultry**
Old U.S. Hwy. 421
Bonlee, NC 27312
Ultimate Parent: Gold Kist. **SIC:** 2048—Prepared Feeds Nec.

★ 73707 ★ **Golden Poultry Co.**
Old U.S. Hwy. 421 N.
Bonlee, NC 27213
Ultimate Parent: Gold Kist. **SIC:** 2048—Prepared Feeds Nec.

★ 73708 ★ **Golden Poultry Feed Mill**
Old U.S. Hwy. 421 N.
Bonlee, NC 27213
Ultimate Parent: Gold Kist. **SIC:** 2048—Prepared Feeds Nec.

Boone

★ 73709 ★ **Branch Banking & Trust Co.**
350 Blowing Rock Rd.
Boone, NC 28607-4131
(704)264-0821
Company Type: Subsidiary. **Location Type:** Branch office. **Ultimate Parent:** Southern National Corp. **SIC:** 6021—National Commercial Banks.

★ 73710 ★ **First-Citizens Bank & Trust Co.**
538 Blowing Rock Rd.
Boone, NC 28607
(704)264-7353
Location Type: Branch office. **Officer:** Mark Transou, Vice President. **Ultimate Parent:** First Citizens Bancshares, Inc. **SIC:** 6021—National Commercial Banks.

★ 73711 ★ **First Union National Bank of North Carolina**
345 Blowing Rock Rd.
Boone, NC 28607-4121
(704)262-4628
Company Type: Subsidiary. **Location Type:** Branch office. **Ultimate Parent:** First Union Corp. **SIC:** 6021—National Commercial Banks.

★ 73712 ★ **First Union National Bank of North Carolina**
210 College St., Boone Campus
Boone, NC 28608
(704)262-4628
Company Type: Subsidiary. **Location Type:** Branch office. **Ultimate Parent:** First Union Corp. **SIC:** 6021—National Commercial Banks.

★ 73713 ★ **First Union National Bank of North Carolina**
211 E. King St.
Boone, NC 28607-4043
(704)262-4628
Company Type: Subsidiary. **Location Type:** Branch office. **Ultimate Parent:** First Union Corp. **SIC:** 6021—National Commercial Banks.

★ 73714 ★ **Kentucky Fried Chicken**
335 Blowing Rock Rd.
Boone, NC 28607
(704)264-4405
Ultimate Parent: Pepsico. **SIC:** 5812—Eating Places.

★ 73715 ★ **Pizza Hut**
202 Blowing Rock Rd.
Boone, NC 28607
(704)264-2401
Ultimate Parent: Pepsico. **SIC:** 5812—Eating Places.

★ 73716 ★ **Radio Shack**
Watauga Village Shopping Cent
Boone, NC 28607
(704)264-1818
Company Type: Division. **Ultimate Parent:** Tandy Corp. **SIC:** 5065—Electronic Parts & Equipment Nec.

★ 73717 ★ **Taco Bell**
414 Blowing Rock Rd.
Boone, NC 28607
(704)264-4766
Ultimate Parent: Pepsico. **SIC:** 5812—Eating Places.

★ 73718 ★ **Thom Mcan Factory Outlet**
Boone Heights Shopping Ctr.
Boone, NC 28607
(704)264-8061
Ultimate Parent: Melville. **SIC:** 5661—Shoe Stores.

★ 73719 ★ **Trailway Laundry Inc.**
833 E. King St.
Boone, NC 28607
(704)264-8415
Ultimate Parent: Greyhound Lines Inc. **SIC:** 7212—Garment Pressing & Cleaners' Agents; 7217—Carpet & Upholstery Cleaning.

★ 73720 ★ **Waldenbooks**
Boone Mall
Boone, NC 28607
(704)264-4084
Ultimate Parent: K-Mart. **SIC:** 5942—Book Stores.

Bostic

★ 73721 ★ **First Union National Bank of North Carolina**
Main & Carson St.
Bostic, NC 28018
(704)248-4228
Company Type: Subsidiary. **Location Type:** Branch office. **Ultimate Parent:** First Union Corp. **SIC:** 6021—National Commercial Banks.

★ 73722 ★ **Wachovia Bank & Trust**
Hwy. 401 Bypass
Bostic, NC 28018
(704)433-9375
Ultimate Parent: Wachovia Corp. **SIC:** 6099—Functions Related to Deposit Banking.

Brevard

★ 73723 ★ **First-Citizens Bank & Trust Co.**
122 S. Broad St.
Brevard, NC 28712-3730
(704)884-2818
Location Type: Branch office. **Officer:** Billy R. Higgins, Vice President. **Ultimate Parent:** First Citizens Bancshares, Inc. **SIC:** 6021—National Commercial Banks.

★ 73724 ★ **First Union National Bank of North Carolina**
1011 Asheville Hwy.
Brevard, NC 28712-3005
(704)884-9101
Company Type: Subsidiary. **Location Type:** Branch office. **Ultimate Parent:** First Union Corp. **SIC:** 6021—National Commercial Banks.

★ 73725 ★ **First Union National Bank of North Carolina**
73 W. Main St.
Brevard, NC 28712-3697
(704)884-9101
Company Type: Subsidiary. **Location Type:** Branch office. **Ultimate Parent:** First Union Corp. **SIC:** 6021—National Commercial Banks.

★ 73726 ★ **Pizza Hut**
708 N. Broad St.
Brevard, NC 28712
(704)884-4041
Ultimate Parent: Pepsico. **SIC:** 5812—Eating Places.

Broadway

★ 73727 ★ **Branch Banking & Trust Co.**
117 W. Main St.
Broadway, NC 27505-9522
(919)258-3821
Company Type: Subsidiary. **Location Type:** Branch office. **Officer:** Charles T. Lyles, Mgr. **Ultimate Parent:** Southern National Corp. **SIC:** 6021—National Commercial Banks.

Browns Summit

★ **73728** ★ **Allen-Bradley Co.**
5925 Summit Ave.
Browns Summit, NC 27214
Ultimate Parent: Rockwell International
Corp. **SIC:** 3676—Electronic Resistors.

★ **73729** ★ **Procter & Gamble Manufacturing Co.**
6200 Bryan Park Rd.
Browns Summit, NC 27214
Ultimate Parent: Procter & Gamble Co.
SIC: 2844—Toilet Preparations.

★ **73730** ★ **Procter & Gamble Mfg. Co.**
6200 Bryan Park Rd.
Browns Summit, NC 27214
Ultimate Parent: Procter & Gamble Co.
SIC: 2844—Toilet Preparations.

Bryson City

★ **73731** ★ **First-Citizens Bank & Trust Co.**
51 Main St.
Bryson City, NC 28713
(704)488-3145
Location Type: Branch office. **Officer:**
David R. Cable, Vice President. **Ultimate Parent:** First Citizens Bancshares, Inc. **SIC:** 6021—National Commercial Banks.

★ **73732** ★ **Nantahala Power & Light Co.**
PO Drawer O
Bryson City, NC 28713
(704)488-2116
Company Type: Subsidiary. **Officer:** E. N. Hedgepeth Jr., Chairman of the Board & President. **Ultimate Parent:** Duke Power. **SIC:** 4911—Electric Services.

Burgaw

★ **73733** ★ **First-Citizens Bank & Trust Co.**
Rankin & Church
Burgaw, NC 28421
(910)283-5358
Location Type: Branch office. **Ultimate Parent:** First Citizens Bancshares, Inc. **SIC:** 6021—National Commercial Banks.

★ **73734** ★ **First-Citizens Bank & Trust Co.**
214 E. Fremont St.
Burgaw, NC 28425
(910)259-4042
Location Type: Branch office. **Ultimate Parent:** First Citizens Bancshares, Inc. **SIC:** 6021—National Commercial Banks.

★ **73735** ★ **First-Citizens Bank & Trust Co.**
Wilmington & Hwy. 117
Burgaw, NC 28425
(910)259-2132
Location Type: Branch office. **Ultimate Parent:** First Citizens Bancshares, Inc. **SIC:** 6021—National Commercial Banks.

★ **73736** ★ **First-Citizens Bank & Trust Co.**
100 W. Fremont St.
Burgaw, NC 28425
(910)259-2132
Location Type: Branch office. **Officer:** R. F. Humphrey II, Vice President. **Ultimate Parent:** First Citizens Bancshares, Inc. **SIC:** 6021—National Commercial Banks.

★ **73737** ★ **Rite Aid Pharmacy**
Wright Hwy. 53
Burgaw, NC 28425
(919)259-5585
Ultimate Parent: Rite Aid. **SIC:** 5912—Drug Stores & Proprietary Stores.

Burlington

★ **73738** ★ **Adhesive Technologies Corp.**
710 Koury Dr.
Burlington, NC 27215-6721
(919)229-7086 **Fax:** (919)229-7020
Officer: Larry Johnson, General Manager.
Ultimate Parent: Minnesota Mining & Mfg.

★ **73739** ★ **American General Finance**
214 W. Front St.
Burlington, NC 27215-3729
(919)228-1357
Location Type: Branch office. **Officer:** Garrette E. White. **Ultimate Parent:** American General Corp. **SIC:** 6141—Personal Credit Institutions.

★ **73740** ★ **American General Finance Inc.**
214 W. Front St.
Burlington, NC 27215-3729
(919)228-1357
Location Type: Branch office. **Officer:** Garrette E. White. **Ultimate Parent:** American General Corp. **SIC:** 6141—Personal Credit Institutions.

★ **73741** ★ **AT & T Family Federal Credit Union**
2630 Ramada Rd. I-85 Plz.
Burlington, NC 27215
(910)222-0101
Location Type: Branch office. **Officer:** Annette Milton, Manager. **Ultimate Parent:** AT&T. **SIC:** 6061—Federal Credit Unions.

★ **73742** ★ **At&T Technologies Inc.**
204 Graham-Hopedale Rd.
Burlington, NC 27215
Ultimate Parent: AT&T. **SIC:** 3661—Telephone & Telegraph Apparatus.

★ **73743** ★ **Branch Banking & Trust Co.**
2040 S. Church St.
Burlington, NC 27502
(910)228-7800
Company Type: Subsidiary. **Location Type:** Branch office. **Officer:** Karl F. Burrows, Manager. **Ultimate Parent:** Southern National Corp. **SIC:** 6021—National Commercial Banks.

★ **73744** ★ **Branch Banking & Trust Co.**
144 Huffman Mill Rd.
Burlington, NC 27215-5113
(910)227-0161
Company Type: Subsidiary. **Location Type:** Branch office. **Officer:** Thomas K. Manning, Mgr. **Ultimate Parent:** Southern National Corp. **SIC:** 6021—National Commercial Banks.

★ **73745** ★ **Burlington Coat Factory Warehouse**
1304 Plaza Dr.
Burlington, NC 27215-7165
(919)229-9862
Location Type: Branch office. **Officer:** Jan Jones. **Ultimate Parent:** Burlington Industries, Equity. **SIC:** 5311—Department Stores; 5651—Family Clothing Stores; 5661—Shoe Stores.

★ **73746** ★ **Burlington Industries Inc.**
906 N. Anthony St.
Burlington, NC 27217-6663
(919)228-2608
Officer: Bill Dix. **Ultimate Parent:** Burlington Industries, Equity. **SIC:** 2261—Finishing Plants—Cotton.

★ **73747** ★ **Burlington Industries/Pioneer Plant**
1305 Graham St.
Burlington, NC 27217-6148
(919)228-2616
Officer: Don Shepherd. **Ultimate Parent:** Burlington Industries, Equity. **SIC:** 2281—Yarn Spinning Mills.

★ **73748** ★ **Burlington Manufactures Outlet Center**
2389 Corporation Pky.
Burlington, NC 27215-6751
(919)227-2872
Ultimate Parent: Burlington Industries, Equity. **SIC:** 5311—Department Stores; 6512—Nonresidential Building Operators.

★ **73749** ★ **Burlington Outlet Mall**
2589 Eric Ln.
Burlington, NC 27215-5498
(919)228-0088
Officer: Kaye P. Morgan. **Ultimate Parent:** Burlington Industries, Equity. **SIC:** 5311—Department Stores; 6512—Nonresidential Building Operators.

★ **73750** ★ **Burlington Shoe Outlet**
930 Plantation Dr.
Burlington, NC 27215-6713
(919)227-2010
Officer: Amanda Wiles. **Ultimate Parent:** Burlington Industries, Equity. **SIC:** 5311—Department Stores; 5661—Shoe Stores.

★ **73751** ★ **Burlington Shoes**
PO Box 2097
Burlington, NC 27216-2097
Ultimate Parent: Burlington Industries, Equity. **SIC:** 5661—Shoe Stores.

★ **73752** ★ **Cluett Hosiery Annedeen Hosiery Mill**
661 Plaid St.
Burlington, NC 27216
Ultimate Parent: West Point Stevens. **SIC:** 2252—Hosiery Nec.

★ **73753** ★ **First Union National Bank of North Carolina**
Holly Hill Mall, Hwy. 70-A
Burlington, NC 27215
(910)222-6320
Company Type: Subsidiary. **Location Type:** Branch office. **Ultimate Parent:** First Union Corp. **SIC:** 6021—National Commercial Banks.

★ **73754** ★ **First Union National Bank of North Carolina**
244 W. Davis St.
Burlington, NC 27215-3719
(910)222-6320
Company Type: Subsidiary. **Location Type:** Branch office. **Ultimate Parent:** First Union Corp. **SIC:** 6021—National Commercial Banks.

★ **73755** ★ **GB Labels**
1070 S. Riverview Dr.
Burlington, NC 27217
(910)227-2703
Ultimate Parent: American Brands Inc. **SIC:** 2672—Coated & Laminated Paper Nec; 2752—Commercial Printing—Lithographic.

★ **73756** ★ **Graphic Systems**
2209 Tucker St.
Burlington, NC 27215-6738
(919)228-0188
Officer: Vernon Moore. **Ultimate Parent:** Avery Dennison Corp. **SIC:** 5943—Stationery Stores; 7336—Commercial Art & Graphic Design.

★ **73757** ★ **IBM Corp.**
1100 W. Market St.
Burlington, NC 27215
(919)226-0263
Ultimate Parent: IBM. **SIC:** 5734—Computer & Software Stores.

★ **73758** ★ **Kentucky Fried Chicken**
435 N. Church St.
Burlington, NC 27217
(919)227-2731
Ultimate Parent: Pepsico. **SIC:** 5812—Eating Places.

★ **73759** ★ **Pizza Hut**
3574 PO Box
Burlington, NC 27215
(919)227-3702
Ultimate Parent: Pepsico. **SIC:** 5812—Eating Places.

★ **73760** ★ **Radio Shack**
Cum Park Plz.
Burlington, NC 27215
(919)228-8167
Company Type: Division. **Ultimate Parent:** Tandy Corp. **SIC:** 5065—Electronic Parts & Equipment Nec.

★ **73761** ★ **Ryder Truck Rental**
778 S. Graham Hopedale Rd.
Burlington, NC 27217
(919)222-0526
Ultimate Parent: Ryder System. **SIC:** 7389—Business Services Nec.

★ **73762** ★ **3M Adhesive Technology Corp.**
710 Koury Dr.
Burlington, NC 27215-6721
(919)229-7086
Officer: Larry Johnson. **Ultimate Parent:** Minnesota Mining & Mfg. **SIC:** 2679—

Converted Paper Products Nec; 2621—Paper Mills.

★ **73763** ★ **Wachovia Bank & Tr Co. N a B**
1534 N. Church St.
Burlington, NC 27217
(919)229-3830
Ultimate Parent: Wachovia Corp. **SIC:** 6099—Functions Related to Deposit Banking.

★ **73764** ★ **Westvaco Corp.**
753 Koury Dr.
Burlington, NC 27215
(919)227-4772
Ultimate Parent: WestVaco Corp. **SIC:** 5113—Industrial & Personal Service Paper.

Burnsville

★ **73765** ★ **First-Citizens Bank & Trust Co.**
364 E. Bypass
Burnsville, NC 28714-3396
(704)682-6191
Location Type: Branch office. **Officer:** Gerald Presnell, Vice President. **Ultimate Parent:** First Citizens Bancshares, Inc. **SIC:** 6021—National Commercial Banks.

★ **73766** ★ **First Union National Bank of North Carolina**
422 E. Bypass, Hwy. 19 E
Burnsville, NC 28714-3338
(704)682-6131
Company Type: Subsidiary. **Location Type:** Branch office. **Ultimate Parent:** First Union Corp. **SIC:** 6021—National Commercial Banks.

★ **73767** ★ **First Union National Bank of North Carolina**
109 Town Sq., 1 E. Main St.
Burnsville, NC 28714-2934
(704)682-6131
Company Type: Subsidiary. **Location Type:** Branch office. **Ultimate Parent:** First Union Corp. **SIC:** 6021—National Commercial Banks.

★ **73768** ★ **OMC Burnsville**
Hwy. 19 E
Burnsville, NC 28714
(704)682-2131
Officer: Gene Jole, Plant Manager. **Ultimate Parent:** Outboard Marine. **SIC:** 3519—Internal Combustion Engines Nec.

★ **73769** ★ **Omc Burnsville**
Hwy. 19 E.
Burnsville, NC 28714
Ultimate Parent: Outboard Marine. **SIC:** 3519—Internal Combustion Engines Nec.

★ **73770** ★ **OMC, Burnsville**
PO Box 10, Hwy. 19 E
Burnsville, NC 28714
Ultimate Parent: Outboard Marine. **SIC:** 3519—Internal Combustion Engines Nec.

Butner

★ **73771** ★ **Branch Banking & Trust Co.**
Dutch Village Shopping Ctr.
Butner, NC 27509
(919)528-4944
Company Type: Subsidiary. **Location Type:** Branch office. **Ultimate Parent:** Southern National Corp. **SIC:** 6021—National Commercial Banks.

★ **73772** ★ **Branch Banking & Trust Co.**
402 Central Ave.
Butner, NC 27509-1915
(919)575-4591
Company Type: Subsidiary. **Location Type:** Branch office. **Ultimate Parent:** Southern National Corp. **SIC:** 6021—National Commercial Banks.

Camp LeJeune

★ 73773 ★ First-Citizens Bank & Trust Co.
TC Bldg. 1003
9th St.
Camp LeJeune, NC 28542
(910)353-3113
Location Type: Branch office. **Ultimate Parent:** First Citizens Bancshares, Inc. **SIC:** 6021—National Commercial Banks.

★ 73774 ★ First-Citizens Bank & Trust Co.
Rm. C120
Bldg. H-100
Camp LeJeune, NC 28452
(910)353-4125
Location Type: Branch office. **Ultimate Parent:** First Citizens Bancshares, Inc. **SIC:** 6021—National Commercial Banks.

★ 73775 ★ First-Citizens Bank & Trust Co.
Bldg. 2459, Iwo Jima Blvd.
Camp LeJeune, NC 28546-9681
(910)353-3113
Location Type: Branch office. **Ultimate Parent:** First Citizens Bancshares, Inc. **SIC:** 6021—National Commercial Banks.

★ 73776 ★ First-Citizens Bank & Trust Co.
Bldg. 87, Holcombe Blvd.
Camp LeJeune, NC 28542
(910)353-3113
Location Type: Branch office. **Officer:** Robert T. Walters, Senior Vice President. **Ultimate Parent:** First Citizens Bancshares, Inc. **SIC:** 6021—National Commercial Banks.

Canton

★ 73777 ★ Champion International Corp.
1289 PO Box
Canton, NC 28716
(704)287-4010
Ultimate Parent: Champion International. **SIC:** 0831—Forest Products.

★ 73778 ★ First-Citizens Bank & Trust Co.
37 Park St.
Canton, NC 28716-4396
(704)648-2308
Location Type: Branch office. **Officer:** Douglas J. Smith, Assistant Vice President. **Ultimate Parent:** First Citizens Bancshares, Inc. **SIC:** 6021—National Commercial Banks.

★ 73779 ★ First Union National Bank of North Carolina
101 Main St.
Canton, NC 28716-4390
(704)648-3526
Company Type: Subsidiary. **Location Type:** Branch office. **Ultimate Parent:** First Union Corp. **SIC:** 6021—National Commercial Banks.

★ 73780 ★ Kentucky Fried Chicken
79 Park St.
Canton, NC 28716
(704)648-3335
Ultimate Parent: Pepsico. **SIC:** 5812—Eating Places.

★ 73781 ★ Pizza Hut
Canton Plz.
Canton, NC 28716
(704)648-6780
Ultimate Parent: Pepsico. **SIC:** 5812—Eating Places.

Caroleen

★ 73782 ★ Burlington Industries Inc.
PO Box 158
Caroleen, NC 28019-0158
(704)657-6376
Officer: Steve Meador. **Ultimate Parent:** Burlington Industries, Equity. **SIC:** 2281—Yarn Spinning Mills; 2399—Fabricated Textile Products Nec.

Carolina Beach

★ 73783 ★ Branch Banking & Trust Co.
7 N. Lake Pk. Blvd.
Carolina Beach, NC 28428-4926
(910)458-9028
Company Type: Subsidiary. **Location Type:** Branch office. **Ultimate Parent:** Southern National Corp. **SIC:** 6021—National Commercial Banks.

Carrboro

★ 73784 ★ Kentucky Fried Chicken
319 E. Main St.
Carrboro, NC 27510
(919)929-1169
Ultimate Parent: Pepsico. **SIC:** 5812—Eating Places.

Carthage

★ 73785 ★ Branch Banking & Trust Co.
Courthouse Sq. & Dawn
Carthage, NC 28327
(910)947-2241
Company Type: Subsidiary. **Location Type:** Branch office. **Officer:** Charles W. LaRue, Mgr. **Ultimate Parent:** Southern National Corp. **SIC:** 6021—National Commercial Banks.

★ 73786 ★ Branch Banking & Trust Co.
Monroe St.
Carthage, NC 28327
(910)947-5683
Company Type: Subsidiary. **Location Type:** Branch office. **Ultimate Parent:** Southern National Corp. **SIC:** 6021—National Commercial Banks.

Cary

★ 73787 ★ Branch Banking & Trust Co.
2000 Regency Pk.
Cary, NC 27511-8506
(919)467-6100
Company Type: Subsidiary. **Location Type:** Branch office. **Ultimate Parent:** Southern National Corp. **SIC:** 6021—National Commercial Banks.

★ 73788 ★ Branch Banking & Trust Co.
Kildaire Farm Rd.
Cary, NC 27511
(919)467-0111
Company Type: Subsidiary. **Location Type:** Branch office. **Ultimate Parent:** Southern National Corp.

★ 73789 ★ Branch Banking & Trust Co.
N. Harrison Ave. & NW Maynard Rd.
Cary, NC 27511
(919)467-6100
Company Type: Subsidiary. **Location Type:** Branch office. **Officer:** B. Garrett Thompson, Mgr. **Ultimate Parent:** Southern National Corp. **SIC:** 6021—National Commercial Banks.

★ 73790 ★ Branch Banking & Trust Co.
200 E. Chatham St.
Cary, NC 27511-3492
(919)467-0111
Company Type: Subsidiary. **Location Type:** Branch office. **Officer:** Michael D. Wilson, Mgr. **Ultimate Parent:** Southern National Corp. **SIC:** 6021—National Commercial Banks.

★ 73791 ★ Branch Banking & Trust Co.
848 E. Maynard Rd.
Cary, NC 27511-4206
(919)467-2451
Company Type: Subsidiary. **Location Type:** Branch office. **Officer:** W. Bruce Lawson, Manager. **Ultimate Parent:** Southern National Corp. **SIC:** 6021—National Commercial Banks.

★ 73792 ★ Brookshore Lithographers
1135 Kildaire Farm Rd.
Cary, NC 27511-4587
(919)460-4587
Ultimate Parent: Banta Corp. **SIC:** 2752—Commercial Printing—Lithographic.

★ 73793 ★ Brookshore Lithographers Corp.
1135 Kildaire Farm Rd.
Cary, NC 27511-4587
(919)460-4587
Ultimate Parent: Banta Corp. **SIC:** 2752—Commercial Printing—Lithographic.

★ 73794 ★ Empire
Detroit Steel Div.
104 Kettlebridge Dr.
Cary, NC 27511-6346
(919)387-1810
Company Type: Division. **Ultimate Parent:** Armco. **SIC:** 3312—Blast Furnaces & Steel Mills.

★ 73795 ★ First-Citizens Bank & Trust Co.
1825 Kildaire Farms Rd.
Cary, NC 27511-6527
(919)859-3631
Location Type: Branch office. **Officer:** Ernest F. McAllister, Vice President. **Ultimate Parent:** First Citizens Bancshares, Inc. **SIC:** 6021—National Commercial Banks.

★ 73796 ★ First Union National Bank of North Carolina
1122 Kildaire Farm Rd.
Cary, NC 27511-4523
(919)881-6016
Company Type: Subsidiary. **Location Type:** Branch office. **Ultimate Parent:** First Union Corp. **SIC:** 6021—National Commercial Banks.

★ 73797 ★ First Union National Bank of North Carolina
305 Colonnade Way
Cary, NC 27511
(919)881-6016
Company Type: Subsidiary. **Location Type:** Branch office. **Ultimate Parent:** First Union Corp. **SIC:** 6021—National Commercial Banks.

★ 73798 ★ First Union National Bank of North Carolina
1201 Walnut St.
Cary, NC 27511-4216
(919)881-6016
Company Type: Subsidiary. **Location Type:** Branch office. **Ultimate Parent:** First Union Corp. **SIC:** 6021—National Commercial Banks.

★ 73799 ★ Mary Kay Cosmetics Independent
911 Reedy Creek Rd.
Cary, NC 27513
(919)467-6672
Ultimate Parent: Mary Kay Cosmetics. **SIC:** 5999—Miscellaneous Retail Stores Nec.

★ 73800 ★ Pulte Home Corp.
401 Harrison Oaks Blvd.
Cary, NC 27513
Ultimate Parent: Pulte. **SIC:** 6531—Real Estate Agents & Managers.

★ 73801 ★ Wachovia Bank & Trust
1107 Walnut St.
Cary, NC 27511
(919)755-7604
Ultimate Parent: Wachovia Corp. **SIC:** 6099—Functions Related to Deposit Banking.

Cashiers

★ 73802 ★ Wachovia Bank & Trust
Nc Hwy. 107 Us 64
Cashiers, NC 28717
(704)743-2431
Ultimate Parent: Wachovia Corp. **SIC:** 6099—Functions Related to Deposit Banking.

Castle Hayne

★ 73803 ★ Occidental Chemical Corp.
Castle Hayne Plant
Off State Rd. 1002 PO Box 368
Castle Hayne, NC 28429
Location Type: Plant. **Ultimate Parent:** Occidental Petroleum Corp. **SIC:** 2819—Industrial Inorganic Chemicals Nec.

★ 73804 ★ Occidental Chemical Corp.
Castle Hayne Plant
5408 Holly Shelter Rd.
PO Box 368
Castle Hayne, NC 28429
Location Type: Plant. **Ultimate Parent:** Occidental Petroleum Corp. **SIC:** 2819—Industrial Inorganic Chemicals Nec.

★ 73805 ★ Piggly Wiggly
Castle Hayne, NC 28429
(919)675-2144
Ultimate Parent: Bruno's. **SIC:** 5411—Grocery Stores.

Catawba

★ 73806 ★ Comm/Scope Inc.
6519 Comm/Scope Rd. PO Box 199
Catawba, NC 28609
Ultimate Parent: General Instrument Corp. **SIC:** 3496—Miscellaneous Fabricated Wire Products.

Chadbourn

★ 73807 ★ Branch Banking & Trust Co.
625 Brown St.
Chadbourn, NC 28431-1305
(910)654-5166
Company Type: Subsidiary. **Location Type:** Branch office. **Officer:** Larry G. Tew, Manager. **Ultimate Parent:** Southern National Corp. **SIC:** 6021—National Commercial Banks.

★ 73808 ★ First-Citizens Bank & Trust Co.
633 N. Brown St.
Chadbourn, NC 28431-1305
(910)654-3138
Location Type: Branch office. **Ultimate Parent:** First Citizens Bancshares, Inc. **SIC:** 6021—National Commercial Banks.

Chapel Hill

★ 73809 ★ Branch Banking & Trust Co.
143 Rosemary St.
Chapel Hill, NC 27514-3528
(919)967-7089
Company Type: Subsidiary. **Location Type:** Branch office. **Officer:** Earl W. Lye, Mgr. **Ultimate Parent:** Southern National Corp. **SIC:** 6021—National Commercial Banks.

★ 73810 ★ Branch Banking & Trust Co.
1406 E. Franklin Ave.
Chapel Hill, NC 27514-2883
(919)929-0441
Company Type: Subsidiary. **Location Type:** Branch office. **Ultimate Parent:** Southern National Corp. **SIC:** 6021—National Commercial Banks.

★ 73811 ★ First-Citizens Bank & Trust Co.
1650 E. Franklin St.
Chapel Hill, NC 27514-5819
(919)967-7031
Location Type: Branch office. **Ultimate Parent:** First Citizens Bancshares, Inc. **SIC:** 6021—National Commercial Banks.

★ 73812 ★ First-Citizens Bank & Trust Co.
134 E. Franklin St.
Chapel Hill, NC 27514-3616
(919)967-7031
Location Type: Branch office. **Officer:** Don Liles, Manager. **Ultimate Parent:** First Citizens Bancshares, Inc. **SIC:** 6021—National Commercial Banks.

★ **73813** ★ **First Union National Bank of North Carolina**
University Mall Shopping Ctr., 201 Estes Dr.
Chapel Hill, NC 27514-7001
(919)967-2263
Company Type: Subsidiary. **Location Type:** Branch office. **Ultimate Parent:** First Union Corp. **SIC:** 6021—National Commercial Banks.

★ **73814** ★ **First Union National Bank of North Carolina**
105 E. Franklin St.
Chapel Hill, NC 27514-3620
(919)967-2263
Company Type: Subsidiary. **Location Type:** Branch office. **Ultimate Parent:** First Union Corp. **SIC:** 6021—National Commercial Banks.

★ **73815** ★ **Food Lion**
1129 Weaver Dairy Rd.
Chapel Hill, NC 27514
(919)929-0458
Ultimate Parent: Food Lion. **SIC:** 5411—Grocery Stores.

★ **73816** ★ **Human Affairs International**
400 Eastowne Dr.
Chapel Hill, NC 27514
(919)968-0083
Ultimate Parent: Aetna Life & Annuity. **SIC:** 8699—Membership Organizations Nec.

★ **73817** ★ **McDonalds of Chapel Hill**
University Mall
Chapel Hill, NC 27514
(919)967-2676
Ultimate Parent: May Department Stores. **SIC:** 5812—Eating Places.

★ **73818** ★ **Pizza Hut**
109 S. Estes Dr.
Chapel Hill, NC 27514
(919)942-7713
Ultimate Parent: Pepsico. **SIC:** 5812—Eating Places.

★ **73819** ★ **Pizza Hut**
110 W. Franklin St.
Chapel Hill, NC 27516
(919)929-3605
Ultimate Parent: Pepsico. **SIC:** 5812—Eating Places.

★ **73820** ★ **Rite Aid Discount Pharmacy**
109 E. Franklin St.
Chapel Hill, NC 27514
(919)968-9249
Ultimate Parent: Rite Aid. **SIC:** 5912—Drug Stores & Proprietary Stores.

★ **73821** ★ **Taco Bell**
120 E. Franklin St.
Chapel Hill, NC 27514
(919)968-0140
Ultimate Parent: Pepsico. **SIC:** 5812—Eating Places.

★ **73822** ★ **Wachovia Bank & Trust**
165 E. Franklin St.
Chapel Hill, NC 27514
(919)929-0311
Ultimate Parent: Wachovia Corp. **SIC:** 6099—Functions Related to Deposit Banking.

★ **73823** ★ **Wachovia Bank & Trust**
101 Banks Dr.
Chapel Hill, NC 27514
(919)929-6700
Ultimate Parent: Wachovia Corp. **SIC:** 6099—Functions Related to Deposit Banking.

★ **73824** ★ **Wachovia Bank & Trust Co. N**
129 S. Estes Dr.
Chapel Hill, NC 27514
(919)967-7061
Ultimate Parent: Wachovia Corp. **SIC:** 6022—State Commercial Banks.

Charlotte

★ **73825** ★ **Pepsi-Cola Bottling Co.**
2820 South Blvd.
Charlotte, NC 28209
(704)523-6761
Officer: Dale Halton, President. **Ultimate Parent:** Pepsico. **SIC:** 2086—Bottled & Canned Soft Drinks.

★ **73826** ★ **Ace Hardware of Charlotte**
2422 Park Rd.
Charlotte, NC 28203
(704)332-2231
Ultimate Parent: Ace Hardware. **SIC:** 5251—Hardware Stores.

★ **73827** ★ **Adm Milling Co.**
Interstate Div.
620 W. 10th St.
Charlotte, NC 28202
Company Type: Division. **Ultimate Parent:** Archer Daniels Midland Co. **SIC:** 2041—Flour & Other Grain Mill Products.

★ **73828** ★ **AGR Co.**
11016 Granite St.
Charlotte, NC 28273
Ultimate Parent: RPM, Inc. **SIC:** 3069—Fabricated Rubber Products Nec.

★ **73829** ★ **Air Products & Chemicals**
11900 Goodrich Dr.
Charlotte, NC 28273-2350
(704)588-2350
Location Type: Branch office. **Officer:** John Tallman. **Ultimate Parent:** Air Products & Chemicals, Inc. **SIC:** 3564—Blowers & Fans; 3559—Special Industry Machinery Nec.

★ **73830** ★ **Allied Automotive**
Bendix
701 I-85 N
Charlotte, NC 28216
Ultimate Parent: Allied-Signal Inc. **SIC:** 3714—Motor Vehicle Parts & Accessories.

★ **73831** ★ **Allied-Signal Inc.**
Bendix Automotive
701 I-85 N.
Charlotte, NC 28216
Ultimate Parent: Allied-Signal Inc. **SIC:** 3714—Motor Vehicle Parts & Accessories.

★ **73832** ★ **Amerada Hess Corp.**
7615 Old Mount Holly Rd.
Charlotte, NC 28214
(704)399-8378
Ultimate Parent: Amerada Hess. **SIC:** 5172—Petroleum Products Nec.

★ **73833** ★ **Amerada Hess Corp.**
7615 Old Mt. Holly Rd.
Charlotte, NC 28214-1792
(704)399-8378
Location Type: Branch office. **Officer:** J. Hamilton. **Ultimate Parent:** Amerada Hess. **SIC:** 5172—Petroleum Products Nec.

★ **73834** ★ **American Cyanamid Co.**
8309 Wilkinson Blvd.
Charlotte, NC 28214-9052
(704)394-4361
Officer: Jim Treck. **Ultimate Parent:** American Cyanamid Co. **SIC:** 2821—Plastics Materials & Resins; 2843—Surface Active Agents; 2891—Adhesives & Sealants; 5169—Chemicals & Allied Products Nec; 2869—Industrial Organic Chemicals Nec.

★ **73835** ★ **American Cyanamid Co.**
8309 Wilkinson Blvd.
Charlotte, NC 28214
Ultimate Parent: American Cyanamid Co. **SIC:** 2821—Plastics Materials & Resins; 2869—Industrial Organic Chemicals Nec.

★ **73836** ★ **American Family Life Assurance**
516 Fenton Pl.
Charlotte, NC 28207
(704)376-2276
Ultimate Parent: American Family Life Assurance Co. **SIC:** 6411—Insurance Agents, Brokers & Service.

★ **73837** ★ **American General Finance**
7508 E. Independence Blvd.
Charlotte, NC 28227-9405
(704)536-3815
Officer: Dave Litz. **Ultimate Parent:** American General Corp. **SIC:** 6141—Personal Credit Institutions.

★ **73838** ★ **American General Finance Inc.**
9010 Monroe Rd.
Charlotte, NC 28270-1435
(704)847-7429
Location Type: Branch office. **Officer:** Rick Martinez. **Ultimate Parent:** American General Corp. **SIC:** 6141—Personal Credit Institutions.

★ **73839** ★ **American General Finance Inc.**
7508 E. Independence Blvd.
Charlotte, NC 28227-9405
(704)536-3815
Location Type: Branch office. **Officer:** Dave Litz. **Ultimate Parent:** American General Corp. **SIC:** 6141—Personal Credit Institutions.

★ **73840** ★ **Amicon Inc.**
4344 Wilmount Rd.
Charlotte, NC 28208-6799
(704)329-0200
Company Type: Subsidiary. **Officer:** Giovanni Peterlongo, President. **Ultimate Parent:** W. R. Grace. **SIC:** 3625—Relays & Industrial Controls. **Employee Count:** 28. **Sales:** 6000000 M.

★ **73841** ★ **AMP Inc.**
6400 Old Dowd Rd.
Charlotte, NC 28214
(704)391-4600
Location Type: Plant. **Officer:** Jim Boyce, Manager. **Ultimate Parent:** AMP Inc. **SIC:** 3678—Electronic Connectors; 3679—Electronic Components Nec.

★ **73842** ★ **AT & T Family Federal Credit Union**
Duke Power Electric Ctr. EC3N, Box 1006
Charlotte, NC 28201-1006
(704)382-1500
Location Type: Branch office. **Officer:** Suzanne Hersek, Manager. **Ultimate Parent:** AT&T. **SIC:** 6061—Federal Credit Unions.

★ **73843** ★ **AT&T Family Federal Credit Union**
Charlotte, NC
Location Type: Branch office. **Ultimate Parent:** AT&T. **SIC:** 6061—Federal Credit Unions.

★ **73844** ★ **Atchison, Topeka & Santa Fe Railway Co.**
7221 Quail Ridge Dr.
Charlotte, NC 28226
(704)541-0298
Ultimate Parent: Santa Fe Pacific Corp. **SIC:** 4011—Railroads—Line-Haul Operating.

★ **73845** ★ **Atlantic Design Co. Inc.**
5601 Wilkinson Blvd.
Charlotte, NC 28208
Ultimate Parent: Ogden. **SIC:** 3672—Printed Circuit Boards.

★ **73846** ★ **Avery Dennison**
5501 Executive Ctr. Dr., Ste. 1
Charlotte, NC 28212-8823
(704)536-5508
Officer: Gary F. Sickinger. **Ultimate Parent:** Avery Dennison Corp. **SIC:** 2752—Commercial Printing—Lithographic.

★ **73847** ★ **Avery Dennison Soabar Production Group**
7520 E. Independence Blvd.
Charlotte, NC 28227-9405
(704)568-9050
Officer: Grady Williamson. **Ultimate Parent:** Avery Dennison Corp. **SIC:** 2679—Converted Paper Products Nec.

★ **73848** ★ **Banta Corp.**
Freuhauf Div.
Fruehauf Dr.
Charlotte, NC 28210
(704)588-0150
Company Type: Affiliate. **Location Type:** Plant. **Officer:** J. E. Caywood, COO.

Ultimate Parent: Banta Corp. **SIC:** 3715—Truck Trailers. **Employee Count:** 790.

★ **73849** ★ **BASF Corp.**
4330 Chesapeake Dr.
Charlotte, NC 28216
(704)392-4313
Officer: Carl T. Poteat, Manager. **Ultimate Parent:** BASF Corp. **SIC:** 2679—Converted Paper Products Nec; 2865—Cyclic Crudes & Intermediates; 2893—Printing Ink.

★ **73850** ★ **BASF Corp.**
4330 Chesapeake Dr.
Charlotte, NC 28216
Ultimate Parent: BASF Corp. **SIC:** 2869—Industrial Organic Chemicals Nec.

★ **73851** ★ **BASF Corp.**
1701 Westinghouse Blvd.
Charlotte, NC 28241
Ultimate Parent: BASF Corp. **SIC:** 2893—Printing Ink.

★ **73852** ★ **BASF Corp.**
Chemical
4330 Chesapeake Dr.
Charlotte, NC 28216
Company Type: Division. **Ultimate Parent:** BASF Corp. **SIC:** 2869—Industrial Organic Chemicals Nec.

★ **73853** ★ **BASF Corp.**
Coatings & Inks
1701 Westinghouse Blvd.
Charlotte, NC 28273
Ultimate Parent: BASF Corp. **SIC:** 2893—Printing Ink.

★ **73854** ★ **BASF Corp.**
Coatings & Inks
1701 Westinghouse Blvd.
Charlotte, NC 28241
Ultimate Parent: BASF Corp. **SIC:** 2893—Printing Ink.

★ **73855** ★ **BASF Structural Materials Inc.**
11501 Steele Creek Rd.
Charlotte, NC 28217
Ultimate Parent: BASF Corp. **SIC:** 3600—Electronic & Other Electrical Equipment.

★ **73856** ★ **BASF Structural Materials Inc.**
13504 A South Point Blvd.
Charlotte, NC 28217
(704)588-7950
Company Type: Subsidiary. **Ultimate Parent:** BASF Corp.

★ **73857** ★ **Baxter Scientific Products**
8350 Arrowbridge Blvd.
Charlotte, NC 28273-5679
(704)525-1021
Officer: Chris Dobbins. **Ultimate Parent:** Baxter International. **SIC:** 5047—Medical & Hospital Equipment.

★ **73858** ★ **Bellsouth Advertising & Publishing**
9144 Arrow Point Blvd.
Charlotte, NC 28273-8188
(704)527-7910
Officer: Jerry Cheadle. **Ultimate Parent:** BellSouth Corp. **SIC:** 2741—Miscellaneous Publishing; 7311—Advertising Agencies.

★ **73859** ★ **BellSouth Advertising & Publishing**
4600 Park Rd., Ste. 100
PO Box 668200
Charlotte, NC 28266
(704)522-5500
Company Type: Subsidiary. **Ultimate Parent:** BellSouth Corp. **SIC:** 2741—Miscellaneous Publishing.

★ **73860** ★ **Bi-Lo**
101 Eastway Dr.
Charlotte, NC 28213
(704)595-8995
Ultimate Parent: Penn Traffic. **SIC:** 5411—Grocery Stores.

★ **73861** ★ **Bi-Lo Pharmacy**
101 Eastway Dr.
Charlotte, NC 28213
(704)597-8154
Ultimate Parent: Penn Traffic. **SIC:** 5912—Drug Stores & Proprietary Stores.

★ 73862 ★   Bindley Western Drug
Co.
North Carolina
10900A S. Commerce Blvd.
Charlotte, NC 28273
(704)588-6843 Fax: (704)588-7532
Company Type: Subsidiary. Officer:
Ronald M. Glover, Vice President & Division
Manager. Ultimate Parent: Bindley-Western
Industries, Inc.

★ 73863 ★   Black & Decker US
Distr Ctr
200 Crompton St.
Charlotte, NC 28273-6204
(704)588-0951
Company Type: Branch. Officer: Michele
Batcho. Ultimate Parent: Black & Decker
Corp. SIC: 3639—Household Appliances
Nec.

★ 73864 ★   Brad Ragan, Inc.
4404 G. Stuart Andrew Blvd.
Charlotte, NC 28217
(704)521-2100
Company Type: Subsidiary. Ultimate
Parent: Goodyear Tire & Rubber. SIC:
5531—Automobile & Home Supply Stores.

★ 73865 ★   Branch Banking &
Trust Co.
3420 Shamrock Dr.
Charlotte, NC 28215
(704)532-9793
Company Type: Subsidiary. Location
Type: Branch office. Ultimate Parent:
Southern National Corp. SIC: 6021—
National Commercial Banks.

★ 73866 ★   Branch Banking &
Trust Co.
2520 Sardis Rd.
Charlotte, NC 28227
(704)845-9155
Company Type: Subsidiary. Location
Type: Branch office. Ultimate Parent:
Southern National Corp. SIC: 6021—
National Commercial Banks.

★ 73867 ★   Branch Banking &
Trust Co.
6869 Fairview Rd.
Charlotte, NC 28210
(704)362-4300
Company Type: Subsidiary. Location
Type: Branch office. Ultimate Parent:
Southern National Corp. SIC: 6021—
National Commercial Banks.

★ 73868 ★   Branch Banking &
Trust Co.
325 Sharon Amity Rd.
Charlotte, NC 28211-3005
(704)365-3662
Company Type: Subsidiary. Location
Type: Branch office. Ultimate Parent:
Southern National Corp. SIC: 6021—
National Commercial Banks.

★ 73869 ★   Branch Banking &
Trust Co.
6234 Albemarle Rd.
Charlotte, NC 28212-2801
(704)563-9479
Company Type: Subsidiary. Location
Type: Branch office. Ultimate Parent:
Southern National Corp. SIC: 6021—
National Commercial Banks.

★ 73870 ★   Branch Banking &
Trust Co.
300 Archdale Dr.
Charlotte, NC 28217-4213
(704)529-0471
Company Type: Subsidiary. Location
Type: Branch office. Ultimate Parent:
Southern National Corp. SIC: 6021—
National Commercial Banks.

★ 73871 ★   Branch Banking &
Trust Co.
7521 Pineville Matthews Rd.
Charlotte, NC 28226-3907
(704)542-6959
Company Type: Subsidiary. Location
Type: Branch office. Ultimate Parent:
Southern National Corp. SIC: 6021—
National Commercial Banks.

★ 73872 ★   Branch Banking &
Trust Co.
111 Yorkmont
Charlotte, NC 28217-2021
(704)527-5435
Company Type: Subsidiary. Location

Type: Branch office. Ultimate Parent:
Southern National Corp. SIC: 6021—
National Commercial Banks.

★ 73873 ★   Branch Banking &
Trust Co.
8558 University City Blvd.
Charlotte, NC 28213-3580
(704)549-1761
Company Type: Subsidiary. Location
Type: Branch office. Ultimate Parent:
Southern National Corp. SIC: 6021—
National Commercial Banks.

★ 73874 ★   Branch Banking &
Trust Co.
3558 Wilkinson Blvd.
Charlotte, NC 28208-5544
(704)399-1807
Company Type: Subsidiary. Location
Type: Branch office. Ultimate Parent:
Southern National Corp. SIC: 6021—
National Commercial Banks.

★ 73875 ★   Branch Banking &
Trust Co.
200 S. College St.
Charlotte, NC 28289-0001
(704)338-5500
Company Type: Subsidiary. Location
Type: Branch office. Officer: E.F. Dehnert
Jr., Manager. Ultimate Parent: Southern
National Corp. SIC: 6021—National
Commercial Banks.

★ 73876 ★   Branch Banking &
Trust Co.
101 Queens Rd.
Charlotte, NC 28204
(704)333-8024
Ultimate Parent: Southern National Corp.

★ 73877 ★   Branch Banking &
Trust Co.
250 E. Woodlawn Rd.
Charlotte, NC 28217
(704)371-7007
Ultimate Parent: Southern National Corp.

★ 73878 ★   Branch Banking &
Trust Co.
8006 Mallard Creek Rd.
Charlotte, NC 28262
(704)596-8820
Ultimate Parent: Southern National Corp.
SIC: 6099—Functions Related to Deposit
Banking.

★ 73879 ★   Branch Banking &
Trust Co.
325 S. Sharon Amity Rd.
Charlotte, NC 28211
(704)365-3662
Ultimate Parent: Southern National Corp.
SIC: 6099—Functions Related to Deposit
Banking.

★ 73880 ★   Branch Banking &
Trust Co.
Rural Route 3
Charlotte, NC 28212
(704)545-8134
Ultimate Parent: Southern National Corp.
SIC: 6022—State Commercial Banks.

★ 73881 ★   Branch Banking &
Trust Co.
324 S. Tryon St.
Charlotte, NC 28202
(704)535-5070
Ultimate Parent: Southern National Corp.
SIC: 6022—State Commercial Banks.

★ 73882 ★   Branch Banking &
Trust Co.
4401 E. Independence Blvd.
Charlotte, NC 28205
(704)535-5070
Ultimate Parent: Southern National Corp.
SIC: 6022—State Commercial Banks.

★ 73883 ★   Branch Banking &
Trust Co.
3059 Eastway Dr.
Charlotte, NC 28205
(704)371-7010
Ultimate Parent: Southern National Corp.

★ 73884 ★   Brnach Banking &
Trust Co.
3720 Monroe Rd.
Charlotte, NC 28217-2021
(704)332-9976
Company Type: Subsidiary. Location
Type: Branch office. Ultimate Parent:

Southern National Corp. SIC: 6021—
National Commercial Banks.

★ 73885 ★   Brownell Electro Inc.
3201 Woodpark Blvd.
Charlotte, NC 28206
(704)597-1270
Location Type: Branch office. Ultimate
Parent: Avnet. SIC: 5063—Electrical
Apparatus & Equipment.

★ 73886 ★   Burlington Air
Express
Charlotte Douglass International
Charlotte, NC 28208
(704)359-8428
Ultimate Parent: Pittston. SIC: 4513—Air
Courier Services; 4513—Air Courier
Services.

★ 73887 ★   Capezio Dance Shop
3108 Monroe Rd.
Charlotte, NC 28205
(704)333-4653
Ultimate Parent: United States Shoe. SIC:
5947—Gift, Novelty & Souvenir Shops.

★ 73888 ★   Capital Finance
Group, Inc.
1 1st Union Ctr.
Charlotte, NC 28288
(704)372-9550
Company Type: Subsidiary. Officer: M.
Douglas Crisp, President. Ultimate Parent:
First Union Corp. SIC: 6159—Miscellaneous
Business Credit Institutions; 6141—Personal
Credit Institutions. Employee Count: 3.
Sales: 1,290,805 M.

★ 73889 ★   Casual Corner
5437 Eastland Mall
Charlotte, NC 28205
(704)568-8506
Ultimate Parent: United States Shoe. SIC:
5651—Family Clothing Stores.

★ 73890 ★   Casual Corner Corp.
509 Scholtz Rd.
Charlotte, NC 28217
(704)527-3414
Ultimate Parent: United States Shoe. SIC:
5621—Women's Clothing Stores.

★ 73891 ★   Central Soya Co. Inc.
Simpson
Charlotte, NC 28205
(704)372-1536
Ultimate Parent: Central Soya. SIC:
5099—Durable Goods Nec.

★ 73892 ★   Church Street Capital
Corp.
422 S. Church St.
Charlotte, NC 28242-0001
(704)382-7111
Company Type: Subsidiary. Ultimate
Parent: Duke Power.

★ 73893 ★   Circuit City
5831 South Blvd.
Charlotte, NC 28217
(704)527-7365
Ultimate Parent: Circuit City Stores. SIC:
5731—Radio, Television & Electronics
Stores.

★ 73894 ★   Circuit City
6432 E. Independence Blvd.
Charlotte, NC 28212
(704)536-9995
Ultimate Parent: Circuit City Stores. SIC:
6552—Subdividers & Developers Nec.

★ 73895 ★   Circuit City
5352 South Blvd.
Charlotte, NC 28210
(704)527-7365
Ultimate Parent: Circuit City Stores. SIC:
5731—Radio, Television & Electronics
Stores.

★ 73896 ★   Circuit City
6100 E. Independence Blvd.
Charlotte, NC 28212
(704)567-0900
Ultimate Parent: Circuit City Stores. SIC:
5722—Household Appliance Stores; 5731—
Radio, Television & Electronics Stores.

★ 73897 ★   Circus World
Eastland Mall
Charlotte, NC 28212
(704)535-4317
Ultimate Parent: Melville. SIC: 5945—
Hobby, Toy & Game Shops.

★ 73898 ★   Circus World
5647 Eastland Mall
Charlotte, NC 28205
(704)535-4317
Ultimate Parent: Melville. SIC: 5945—
Hobby, Toy & Game Shops.

★ 73899 ★   Citgo Quick Mart
6134 Plaza
Charlotte, NC 28215
(704)568-9378
Ultimate Parent: Citgo Petroleum. SIC:
5411—Grocery Stores.

★ 73900 ★   City National Bank
101 Queens Rd.
Charlotte, NC 28204
(704)376-1126
Ultimate Parent: City National Corp. SIC:
6029—Commercial Banks Nec.

★ 73901 ★   City National Bank
200 S. Tryon St.
Charlotte, NC 28202
(704)375-4441
Ultimate Parent: City National Corp. SIC:
6029—Commercial Banks Nec.

★ 73902 ★   City National Bank
3059 Eastway Dr.
Charlotte, NC 28205
(704)375-4441
Ultimate Parent: City National Corp. SIC:
6022—State Commercial Banks.

★ 73903 ★   City National Bank
6424 Fairview Rd.
Charlotte, NC 28210
(704)364-6033
Ultimate Parent: City National Corp. SIC:
6029—Commercial Banks Nec.

★ 73904 ★   Clorox Co.
800 Gesco St.
Charlotte, NC 28208
Ultimate Parent: Clorox Co. SIC: 2842—
Polishes & Sanitation Goods.

★ 73905 ★   Clorox Co. Charlotte
Plant
800 Gesco St.
Charlotte, NC 28208
Ultimate Parent: Clorox Co. SIC: 2842—
Polishes & Sanitation Goods.

★ 73906 ★   Coast to Coast
Express
8700 Red Oak Blvd.
Charlotte, NC 28217
(704)523-1040
Ultimate Parent: Servistar Corp. SIC:
4213—Trucking Except Local.

★ 73907 ★   Coastal Unilube Inc.
7201 Old Mt. Holly Rd.
Charlotte, NC 28214
Ultimate Parent: Coastal Corp. SIC:
2992—Lubricating Oils & Greases; 3085—
Plastics Bottles.

★ 73908 ★   Coca-Cola Bottling
Co. Consolidated
1900 Rexford Rd.
Charlotte, NC 28211-3440
(704)551-4400
Officer: J. Frank Harrison Jr., Chairman of
the Board. Ultimate Parent: Coca-Cola
Bottling Consol. SIC: 2086—Bottled &
Canned Soft Drinks. Employee Count:
4000. Sales: 655 M.

★ 73909 ★   Coca-Cola Bottling
Consol.
1900 Rexford Rd.
Charlotte, NC 28211
(704)551-4400
Company Type: Headquarters. Officer:
James L. Moore Jr. Employee Count:
5000. Fortune 500: Largest
U.S. Industrial Corporations: Ranking 456.

★ 73910 ★   Collins & Aiken
Holding II Corp.
8320 University Executive Pk.
Charlotte, NC 28262-3353
(704)548-2350
Officer: James R. Birle, Co-Chairman of the
Board. Ultimate Parent: Collins & Aikman
Group. SIC: 2221—Broadwoven Fabric
Mills—Manmade; 2273—Carpets & Rugs;
5211—Lumber & Other Building Materials;
2252—Hosiery Nec; 2251—Women's
Hosiery Except Socks; 3728—Aircraft Parts
& Equipment Nec. Employee Count:
29500. Sales: 2.1 M.

★ 73911 ★　Collins & Aikman
PO Box 32665
Charlotte, NC 28232
(704)547-8500 **Fax:** (704)548-2081
Officer: Thomas Hannah, President & CEO.
Ultimate Parent: Collins & Aikman Group.

★ 73912 ★　Collins Aikman Corp.
701 McCullough Dr.
Charlotte, NC 28262-3318
(704)547-8500
Company Type: Subsidiary. **Officer:**
Thomas E. Hannah, President & CEO.
Ultimate Parent: Collins & Aikman Group.
SIC: 2221—Broadwoven Fabric Mills—
Manmade; 2281—Yarn Spinning Mills;
2282—Throwing & Winding Mills; 2258—
Lace & Warp Knit Fabric Mills; 2273—
Carpets & Rugs; 2679—Converted Paper
Products Nec. **Employee Count:** 12500.
Sales: 968 M.

★ 73913 ★　Collins & Aikman
Group
8320 University Executive Park
Charlotte, NC 28262
(704)548-2350
Company Type: Headquarters. **Officer:** D.
A. Stockman. **Sales:** 2225.4 M. **Fortune
500:** Largest U.S. Industrial Corporations:
Ranking 207.

★ 73914 ★　Collins & Aikman
Group, Inc.
8320 University Executive Park, Ste. 102
Charlotte, NC 28262
(704)547-8500 **Fax:** (704)548-2145
Officer: David A. Stockman, Co-Chairman
& Co-CEO. **Ultimate Parent:** Collins &
Aikman Group. **Employee Count:** 22500.

★ 73915 ★　Collins & Aikman
Holdings Corp.
8320 University Executive Pk.
Charlotte, NC 28262-3353
(704)548-2379
Company Type: Subsidiary. **Officer:** James
R. Birle, Co-Chairman of the Board.
Ultimate Parent: Collins & Aikman Group.
SIC: 2221—Broadwoven Fabric Mills—
Manmade; 5211—Lumber & Other Building
Materials; 2252—Hosiery Nec; 2273—
Carpets & Rugs; 2679—Converted Paper
Products Nec; 3728—Aircraft Parts &
Equipment Nec. **Employee Count:** 29500.
Sales: 1.6 M.

★ 73916 ★　Color Response Inc.
3101 Stafford Dr.
Charlotte, NC 28208-9556
(704)392-1153
Ultimate Parent: Banta Corp.

★ 73917 ★　Color Response Inc.
3101 Stafford Dr.
Charlotte, NC 28208
Ultimate Parent: Banta Corp. **SIC:** 2796—
Platemaking Services.

★ 73918 ★　Con-Way Southern
Express Inc.
1338 Hundred Oak Dr.
Charlotte, NC 28217-3900
(704)523-2723
Company Type: Subsidiary. **Officer:** Tom
Smith, President. **Ultimate Parent:**
Consolidated Freightways. **SIC:** 4213—
Trucking Except Local. **Employee Count:**
1500. **Sales:** 95 M.

★ 73919 ★　Crescent Resources
Inc.
PO Box 1003
Charlotte, NC 28201
(704)373-3012 **Fax:** (704)382-1867
Company Type: Subsidiary. **Ultimate
Parent:** Duke Power.

★ 73920 ★　Crescent Resources
Inc.
400 S. Tryon St.
Charlotte, NC 28202-1915
(704)373-3012
Company Type: Subsidiary. **Officer:**
Richard C. Ranson, Chairman of the Board
& CEO. **Ultimate Parent:** Duke Power. **SIC:**
0811—Timber Tracts. **Employee Count:**
70. **Sales:** 38 M.

★ 73921 ★　Crescent Resources
Inc.
PO Box 2695
Charlotte, NC 28234
(704)373-3012
Company Type: Subsidiary. **Officer:**

Richard C. Ranson, President. **Ultimate
Parent:** Duke Power. **SIC:** 0811—Timber
Tracts. **Employee Count:** 48. **Sales:**
11354250 M.

★ 73922 ★　Dana Corp.
Spicer Universal
2833 Westport Rd.
Charlotte, NC 28208
(704)399-2533
Location Type: Plant. **Ultimate Parent:**
Dana Corp. **SIC:** 3714—Motor Vehicle Parts
& Accessories.

★ 73923 ★　Delta Air Freight
4818 Expy. Dr.
Charlotte, NC 28208
(704)398-3730
Ultimate Parent: Delta Air Lines, Inc. **SIC:**
4513—Air Courier Services.

★ 73924 ★　Delta Air Lines
Charlotte Douglas International
Charlotte, NC 28208
(704)398-3700
Ultimate Parent: Delta Air Lines, Inc. **SIC:**
4512—Air Transportation—Scheduled;
4513—Air Courier Services.

★ 73925 ★　Delta Air Lines, Inc.
Charles Douglas International
Charlotte, NC 28208
(704)398-3722
Ultimate Parent: Delta Air Lines, Inc. **SIC:**
4512—Air Transportation—Scheduled;
4513—Air Courier Services.

★ 73926 ★　Delta/Cyklop
Strapping
1440 G Westinghouse Blvd.
Charlotte, NC 28217
(704)588-7882 **Fax:** (704)588-6838
Company Type: Subsidiary. **Officer:**
George A. Sim, Vice President & General
Manager. **Ultimate Parent:** Illinois Tool
Works.

★ 73927 ★　Dexter Corp.
Mogul Div.
1201 S. Graham St.
Charlotte, NC 28203
Company Type: Division. **Ultimate Parent:**
Dexter Corp. **SIC:** 2899—Chemical
Preparations Nec.

★ 73928 ★　Dexter Water
Management Inc.
1201 S. Graham St.
Charlotte, NC 28203
(704)375-5726
Ultimate Parent: Dexter Corp. **SIC:** 5074—
Plumbing & Hydronic Heating Supplies.

★ 73929 ★　Dexter Water
Management Sys. Mogul Corp.
1201 S. Graham St.
Charlotte, NC 28203
Ultimate Parent: Dexter Corp. **SIC:** 2899—
Chemical Preparations Nec.

★ 73930 ★　Diebold Inc.
2700 Westport Rd.
Charlotte, NC 28208
(704)394-0146
Ultimate Parent: Diebold, Inc. **SIC:** 5046—
Commercial Equipment Nec; 5999—
Miscellaneous Retail Stores Nec.

★ 73931 ★　Digital Equipment
Corp.
4235 South Stream Blvd.
Charlotte, NC 28219
(704)357-5384
Ultimate Parent: Digital Equipment Corp.

★ 73932 ★　Dover Elevator Co.
3418 Vane Ct.
Charlotte, NC 28206
(704)334-5971
Officer: Julian Schreibeis, Manager.
Ultimate Parent: Dover Corp. **SIC:** 3534—
Elevators & Moving Stairways.

★ 73933 ★　Dow Jones & Co.
9140 Research Dr.
Charlotte, NC 28262
(704)547-0852
Officer: Michele Bakarich, Manager.
Ultimate Parent: Dow Jones. **SIC:** 2711—
Newspapers.

★ 73934 ★　Duke Energy Corp.
400 S. Tryon St.
Charlotte, NC 28202-1915
(704)373-7653
Company Type: Subsidiary. **Officer:** M.
Rhem Wooten Jr., President. **Ultimate
Parent:** Duke Power. **SIC:** 6799—Investors
Nec; 8711—Engineering Services.
Employee Count: 19. **Sales:** 40 M.

★ 73935 ★　Duke Engineering &
Services Inc.
PO Box 36911
Charlotte, NC 28236
Company Type: Subsidiary. **Officer:** John
F. Norris Jr., President. **Ultimate Parent:**
Duke Power. **SIC:** 8711—Engineering
Services. **Employee Count:** 100.

★ 73936 ★　Duke Engineering &
Services Inc.
PO Box 1004
Charlotte, NC 28201
(704)382-9800 **Fax:** (704)382-8389
Company Type: Subsidiary. **Ultimate
Parent:** Duke Power.

★ 73937 ★　Duke/Fluor Daniel
PO Box 1011
Charlotte, NC 28201-1011
(704)357-3271
Company Type: Joint venture. **Officer:**
Ronald F. Green, President. **Ultimate
Parent:** Duke Power. **SIC:** 8711—
Engineering Services; 1629—Heavy
Construction Nec.

★ 73938 ★　Duke Power
422 S. Church St.
Charlotte, NC 28242
(704)594-0887
Company Type: Headquarters. **Officer:**
William H. Grigg. **Employee Count:** 18274.
Fortune Service 500: Ranking 23.

★ 73939 ★　Duke Power Co.
422 S. Church St.
Charlotte, NC 28242-0001
(704)373-4011 (800)488-3853 **Fax:**
(704)373-8038
Company Type: Headquarters. **Officer:**
William S. Lee, Chairman of the Board,
President & CEO. **Ultimate Parent:** Duke
Power. **SIC:** 4911—Electric Services;
0811—Timber Tracts.

★ 73940 ★　Duke Power Co. Inc.
422 S. Church St.
Charlotte, NC 28242-0001
(704)373-4011
Officer: William S. Lee, President &
Chairman of the Board. **Ultimate Parent:**
Duke Power. **SIC:** 4911—Electric Services;
6552—Subdividers & Developers Nec;
0811—Timber Tracts; 5722—Household
Appliance Stores; 8741—Management
Services; 6799—Investors Nec. **Employee
Count:** 18200. **Sales:** 4 M.

★ 73941 ★　Eckerd Corp.
Eckerd Drug Co.
1776 Statesville
Charlotte, NC 28269
(704)371-8000
Company Type: Headquarters. **Officer:**
David Hensley, Vice President. **Ultimate
Parent:** Eckerd Corp. **SIC:** 5912—Drug
Stores & Proprietary Stores.

★ 73942 ★　Electronic Data
Systems Corp.
9014 Research Dr.
Charlotte, NC 28262
(704)549-5000
Ultimate Parent: Electronic Data Systems.
SIC: 7374—Data Processing & Preparation.

★ 73943 ★　Emery Worldwide
Browhill Cir.
Charlotte, NC 28208
(704)394-6161
Ultimate Parent: Consolidated Freightways.
SIC: 4512—Air Transportation—Scheduled.

★ 73944 ★　Evtech
9103 Forsyth Park Dr.
Charlotte, NC 28273
(704)588-2112
Officer: Everette Bond, Executive Director.
Ultimate Parent: Eastman Kodak. **SIC:**
3399—Primary Metal Products Nec; 3479—
Metal Coating & Allied Services.

★ 73945 ★　Evtech a Kodak Co.
9103 Forsyth Park Dr.
Charlotte, NC 28241
Ultimate Parent: Eastman Kodak. **SIC:**
3087—Custom Compound of Purchased
Resins.

★ 73946 ★　Exxon Co. USA
5601 Seventy Ctr. Dr.
Charlotte, NC 28217
(704)529-4204
Ultimate Parent: Exxon. **SIC:** 2911—
Petroleum Refining.

★ 73947 ★　Exxon Express
4235 Providence Rd.
Charlotte, NC 28211
(704)364-8659
Ultimate Parent: Exxon. **SIC:** 5541—
Gasoline Service Stations.

★ 73948 ★　Exxon Shop
4501 Randolph Rd.
Charlotte, NC 28211
(704)527-4427
Ultimate Parent: Exxon. **SIC:** 5411—
Grocery Stores.

★ 73949 ★　Exxon Shop
3100 N. Sharon Amity Rd.
Charlotte, NC 28205
(704)535-0543
Ultimate Parent: Exxon. **SIC:** 5411—
Grocery Stores.

★ 73950 ★　Federal Paper Board
Co. Inc.
2 S. Executive
Charlotte, NC 28202
(704)554-1200
Ultimate Parent: Federal Paper Board.
SIC: 2631—Paperboard Mills.

★ 73951 ★　Federated Metals
Corp.
3812 Lovett Rd.
Charlotte, NC 28210
(704)552-1751
Ultimate Parent: Asarco. **SIC:** 5051—
Metals Service Centers & Offices.

★ 73952 ★　First-Citizens Bank &
Trust Co.
7010 Albemarle Rd.
Charlotte, NC 28227-8123
(704)335-4000
Location Type: Branch office. **Ultimate
Parent:** First Citizens Bancshares, Inc. **SIC:**
6021—National Commercial Banks.

★ 73953 ★　First-Citizens Bank &
Trust Co.
4802 Wilmount Rd.
Charlotte, NC 28208-6328
(704)335-4000
Location Type: Branch office. **Ultimate
Parent:** First Citizens Bancshares, Inc. **SIC:**
6021—National Commercial Banks.

★ 73954 ★　First-Citizens Bank &
Trust Co.
6501 Old Dowd Rd.
Charlotte, NC 28231
(704)335-4000
Location Type: Branch office. **Ultimate
Parent:** First Citizens Bancshares, Inc. **SIC:**
6021—National Commercial Banks.

★ 73955 ★　First-Citizens Bank &
Trust Co.
3050 Eastway Dr.
Charlotte, NC 28205-5642
(704)335-4000
Location Type: Branch office. **Ultimate
Parent:** First Citizens Bancshares, Inc. **SIC:**
6021—National Commercial Banks.

★ 73956 ★　First-Citizens Bank &
Trust Co.
4327 N. Tyron St.
Charlotte, NC 28213-6918
(704)335-4000
Location Type: Branch office. **Ultimate
Parent:** First Citizens Bancshares, Inc. **SIC:**
6021—National Commercial Banks.

★ 73957 ★　First-Citizens Bank &
Trust Co.
4325 Randolph Blvd.
Charlotte, NC 28211-2323
(704)335-4000
Location Type: Branch office. **Ultimate
Parent:** First Citizens Bancshares, Inc. **SIC:**
6021—National Commercial Banks.

★ 73958 ★   First-Citizens Bank & Trust Co.
5400 South Blvd.
Charlotte, NC 28217-2709
(704)335-4000
Location Type: Branch office. Ultimate Parent: First Citizens Bancshares, Inc. SIC: 6021—National Commercial Banks.

★ 73959 ★   First-Citizens Bank & Trust Co.
2480 Wilkinson Blvd.
Charlotte, NC 28208-5639
(704)335-4000
Location Type: Branch office. Ultimate Parent: First Citizens Bancshares, Inc. SIC: 6021—National Commercial Banks.

★ 73960 ★   First-Citizens Bank & Trust Co.
2903 Freedom Dr.
Charlotte, NC 28208-3857
(704)335-4000
Location Type: Branch office. Ultimate Parent: First Citizens Bancshares, Inc. SIC: 6021—National Commercial Banks.

★ 73961 ★   First-Citizens Bank & Trust Co.
1531 Woodlawn Rd.
Charlotte, NC 28209-2235
(704)335-4000
Location Type: Branch office. Ultimate Parent: First Citizens Bancshares, Inc. SIC: 6021—National Commercial Banks.

★ 73962 ★   First-Citizens Bank & Trust Co.
209 S. Church St.
Charlotte, NC 28202-3210
(704)335-4000
Location Type: Branch office. Ultimate Parent: First Citizens Bancshares, Inc. SIC: 6021—National Commercial Banks.

★ 73963 ★   First-Citizens Bank & Trust Co.
3130 Milton Rd.
Charlotte, NC 28215-5500
(704)335-4000
Location Type: Branch office. Ultimate Parent: First Citizens Bancshares, Inc. SIC: 6021—National Commercial Banks.

★ 73964 ★   First-Citizens Bank & Trust Co.
2310 Catawba Ave.
Charlotte, NC 28103
(704)335-4115
Location Type: Branch office. Ultimate Parent: First Citizens Bancshares, Inc. SIC: 6021—National Commercial Banks.

★ 73965 ★   First-Citizens Bank & Trust Co.
7200 Matthews Mint Hill Rd.
Charlotte, NC 28227-9513
(704)545-9791
Location Type: Branch office. Ultimate Parent: First Citizens Bancshares, Inc. SIC: 6021—National Commercial Banks.

★ 73966 ★   First-Citizens Bank & Trust Co.
1300 Matthews Township Pkwy
Charlotte, NC 28105-4600
(704)845-5555
Location Type: Branch office. Ultimate Parent: First Citizens Bancshares, Inc. SIC: 6021—National Commercial Banks.

★ 73967 ★   First-Citizens Bank & Trust Co.
6709 N. Tyron St.
Charlotte, NC 28213
(704)335-4104
Location Type: Branch office. Ultimate Parent: First Citizens Bancshares, Inc. SIC: 6021—National Commercial Banks.

★ 73968 ★   First-Citizens Bank & Trust Co.
6201 Fairview Rd.
Charlotte, NC 28210-3237
(704)335-4000
Location Type: Branch office. Ultimate Parent: First Citizens Bancshares, Inc. SIC: 6021—National Commercial Banks.

★ 73969 ★   First-Citizens Bank & Trust Co.
7837 Pineville-Matthews Rd.
Charlotte, NC 28226-3911
(704)335-4000
Location Type: Branch office. Ultimate Parent: First Citizens Bancshares, Inc. SIC: 6021—National Commercial Banks.

★ 73970 ★   First-Citizens Bank & Trust Co.
5541 E. Independence Blvd.
Charlotte, NC 28212
(704)335-4000
Location Type: Branch office. Ultimate Parent: First Citizens Bancshares, Inc. SIC: 6021—National Commercial Banks.

★ 73971 ★   First-Citizens Bank & Trust Co.
3201 Freedom Dr.
Charlotte, NC 28208-2806
(704)335-4000
Location Type: Branch office. Ultimate Parent: First Citizens Bancshares, Inc. SIC: 6021—National Commercial Banks.

★ 73972 ★   First-Citizens Bank & Trust Co.
802 Providence Rd.
Charlotte, NC 28207-2228
(704)335-4000
Location Type: Branch office. Ultimate Parent: First Citizens Bancshares, Inc. SIC: 6021—National Commercial Banks.

★ 73973 ★   First-Citizens Bank & Trust Co.
5706 Central Ave.
Charlotte, NC 28212-2720
(704)335-4000
Location Type: Branch office. Ultimate Parent: First Citizens Bancshares, Inc. SIC: 6021—National Commercial Banks.

★ 73974 ★   First-Citizens Bank & Trust Co.
4517 Randolph Rd.
Charlotte, NC 28211-2953
(704)335-4000
Location Type: Branch office. Ultimate Parent: First Citizens Bancshares, Inc. SIC: 6021—National Commercial Banks.

★ 73975 ★   First-Citizens Bank & Trust Co.
128 S. Tyron St.
Charlotte, NC 28202-5001
(704)335-4000
Location Type: Branch office. Ultimate Parent: First Citizens Bancshares, Inc. SIC: 6021—National Commercial Banks.

★ 73976 ★   First Federal S & L
801 E. Morehead St.
Charlotte, NC 28202-2729
(704)335-4400
Company Type: Branch. Officer: Robert T. Waugh. Ultimate Parent: Bancorp Hawaii. SIC: 6035—Federal Savings Institutions.

★ 73977 ★   First Union Brokerage Services, Inc.
1 1st Union Ctr.
Charlotte, NC 28288
(704)374-6927
Company Type: Subsidiary. Officer: Dwight Moody, President. Ultimate Parent: First Union Corp. SIC: 6221—Commodity Contracts Brokers & Dealers. Employee Count: 272. Sales: 42,695,563 M.

★ 73978 ★   First Union Commercial Corp.
1 1st Union Ctr.
Charlotte, NC 28288
(704)374-6000
Company Type: Subsidiary. Officer: Daniel W. Mathis, President & CEO. Ultimate Parent: First Union Corp. SIC: 6153—Short-Term Business Credit; 6159—Miscellaneous Business Credit Institutions. Employee Count: 58. Sales: 75,740,378 M.

★ 73979 ★   First Union Corp.
1 1st Union Ctr., 301 S. College St.
Charlotte, NC 28288-0201
(704)374-6161 Fax: (704)374-4609
Company Type: Headquarters. Officer: Edward E. Crutchfield, Chairman of the Board & CEO. Ultimate Parent: First Union Corp. SIC: 6712—Bank Holding Companies. Employee Count: 28672. Sales: 5,648,088,000 M.

★ 73980 ★   First Union Corp.
1 1st Union Ctr.
Charlotte, NC 28288-0013
(704)374-6565
Officer: Edward E. Crutchfield, CEO. Ultimate Parent: First Union Corp. SIC: 6712—Bank Holding Companies; 6021—National Commercial Banks. Employee Count: 23459. Sales: 3509334000 M.

★ 73981 ★   First Union Corp.
301 S. Tryon St.
Charlotte, NC 28288
(704)374-6161
Company Type: Headquarters. Officer: Edward E. Crutchfield Jr. Fortune Service 500: Ranking 9.

★ 73982 ★   First Union Futures Corp.
1 1st Union Ctr.
Charlotte, NC 28288
(704)372-9550
Company Type: Subsidiary. Officer: John P. Evans, President. Ultimate Parent: First Union Corp. SIC: 6221—Commodity Contracts Brokers & Dealers. Employee Count: 23.

★ 73983 ★   First Union Home Equity Corp.
301 S. College St., 5th FL.
Charlotte, NC 28288
(704)331-6500
Company Type: Subsidiary. Officer: James E. Maynar, President. Ultimate Parent: First Union Corp. SIC: 6162—Mortgage Bankers & Correspondents. Employee Count: 491.

★ 73984 ★   First Union Mortgage Corp.
2 1st Union Ctr.
Charlotte, NC 28288
(704)374-6161
Company Type: Subsidiary. Officer: James A. Abbott, President & CEO. Ultimate Parent: First Union Corp. SIC: 6162—Mortgage Bankers & Correspondents. Employee Count: 1344.

★ 73985 ★   First Union National Bank of North Carolina
One 1st Union Ctr.
Charlotte, NC 28288
(704)374-6161
Company Type: Subsidiary. Officer: Frank H. Dunn Jr., Chairman of the Board, CEO. Ultimate Parent: First Union Corp. SIC: 6021—National Commercial Banks. Employee Count: 6690. Sales: 1,508,715,000 M.

★ 73986 ★   First Union National Bank of North Carolina
8600 Park Rd.
Charlotte, NC 28210-5805
(704)374-6161
Company Type: Subsidiary. Location Type: Branch office. Ultimate Parent: First Union Corp. SIC: 6021—National Commercial Banks.

★ 73987 ★   First Union National Bank of North Carolina
Queensgate Shopping Ctr.
2735 Ashley Rd.
Charlotte, NC 28208
(704)374-6161
Company Type: Subsidiary. Location Type: Branch office. Ultimate Parent: First Union Corp. SIC: 6021—National Commercial Banks.

★ 73988 ★   First Union National Bank of North Carolina
1616 Central Ave.
Charlotte, NC 28205-5016
(704)374-6161
Company Type: Subsidiary. Location Type: Branch office. Ultimate Parent: First Union Corp. SIC: 6021—National Commercial Banks.

★ 73989 ★   First Union National Bank of North Carolina
Park Rd. Shopping Ctr.
1625 Woodlawn Rd.
Charlotte, NC 28209-2150
(704)374-6161
Company Type: Subsidiary. Location Type: Branch office. Ultimate Parent: First Union Corp. SIC: 6021—National Commercial Banks.

★ 73990 ★   First Union National Bank of North Carolina
839 Providence Rd.
Charlotte, NC 28207-2244
(704)374-6161
Company Type: Subsidiary. Location Type: Branch office. Ultimate Parent: First Union Corp. SIC: 6021—National Commercial Banks.

★ 73991 ★   First Union National Bank of North Carolina
800 E. Sugar Creek Rd.
Charlotte, NC 28205-1320
(704)374-6161
Company Type: Subsidiary. Location Type: Branch office. Ultimate Parent: First Union Corp. SIC: 6021—National Commercial Banks.

★ 73992 ★   First Union National Bank of North Carolina
1 First Union Ctr.
301 S. College St.
Charlotte, NC 28202
(704)374-6161
Company Type: Subsidiary. Location Type: Branch office. Ultimate Parent: First Union Corp. SIC: 6021—National Commercial Banks.

★ 73993 ★   First Union National Bank of North Carolina
Independence Sq. Shopping Ctr.
6228 Idlewild Rd.
Charlotte, NC 28212-6955
(704)374-6161
Company Type: Subsidiary. Location Type: Branch office. Ultimate Parent: First Union Corp. SIC: 6021—National Commercial Banks.

★ 73994 ★   First Union National Bank of North Carolina
2803 Freedom Dr.
Charlotte, NC 28203
(704)374-6161
Company Type: Subsidiary. Location Type: Branch office. Ultimate Parent: First Union Corp. SIC: 6021—National Commercial Banks.

★ 73995 ★   First Union National Bank of North Carolina
1625 South Blvd.
Charlotte, NC 28203-4725
(704)374-6161
Company Type: Subsidiary. Location Type: Branch office. Ultimate Parent: First Union Corp. SIC: 6021—National Commercial Banks.

★ 73996 ★   First Union National Bank of North Carolina
2610 W. Sugar Creek Rd.
Charlotte, NC 28213-7365
(704)374-6161
Company Type: Subsidiary. Location Type: Branch office. Ultimate Parent: First Union Corp. SIC: 6021—National Commercial Banks.

★ 73997 ★   First Union National Bank of North Carolina
8464 Belhaven Blvd.
Charlotte, NC 28216-6103
(704)374-6161
Company Type: Subsidiary. Location Type: Branch office. Ultimate Parent: First Union Corp. SIC: 6021—National Commercial Banks.

★ 73998 ★   First Union National Bank of North Carolina
225 S. Sharon Amity Rd.
Charlotte, NC 28211-2803
(704)374-6161
Company Type: Subsidiary. Location Type: Branch office. Ultimate Parent: First Union Corp. SIC: 6021—National Commercial Banks.

★ 73999 ★   First Union National Bank of North Carolina
301 S. McDowell St.
Charlotte, NC 28204-2622
(704)374-6161
Company Type: Subsidiary. Location Type: Branch office. Ultimate Parent: First Union Corp. SIC: 6021—National Commercial Banks.

★ **74000** ★   **First Union National Bank of North Carolina**
6420 Carmel Rd.
Charlotte, NC 28211
(704)374-6161
Company Type: Subsidiary. **Location Type:** Branch office. **Ultimate Parent:** First Union Corp. **SIC:** 6021—National Commercial Banks.

★ **74001** ★   **First Union National Bank of North Carolina**
741 Westinghouse Blvd.
Charlotte, NC 28210
(704)374-6161
Company Type: Subsidiary. **Location Type:** Branch office. **Ultimate Parent:** First Union Corp. **SIC:** 6021—National Commercial Banks.

★ **74002** ★   **First Union National Bank of North Carolina**
2821 Pineville-Matthews Rd.
Charlotte, NC 28226
(704)374-6161
Company Type: Subsidiary. **Location Type:** Branch office. **Ultimate Parent:** First Union Corp. **SIC:** 6021—National Commercial Banks.

★ **74003** ★   **First Union National Bank of North Carolina**
Amity Gardens Shopping Ctr.
3800 E. Independence Blvd.
Charlotte, NC 28205
(704)374-6161
Company Type: Subsidiary. **Location Type:** Branch office. **Ultimate Parent:** First Union Corp. **SIC:** 6021—National Commercial Banks.

★ **74004** ★   **First Union National Bank of North Carolina**
9005 Albermorle Rd.
Charlotte, NC 28212
(704)374-6161
Company Type: Subsidiary. **Location Type:** Branch office. **Ultimate Parent:** First Union Corp. **SIC:** 6021—National Commercial Banks.

★ **74005** ★   **First Union National Bank of North Carolina**
6053 Wilora Lake Rd.
Charlotte, NC 28212
(704)383-5960
Company Type: Subsidiary. **Location Type:** Branch office. **Ultimate Parent:** First Union Corp. **SIC:** 6021—National Commercial Banks.

★ **74006** ★   **First Union National Bank of North Carolina**
2 First Union Plz.
301 S. Tryon St.
Charlotte, NC 28288
(704)374-6161
Company Type: Subsidiary. **Location Type:** Branch office. **Officer:** Frank H. Dunn Jr., Chairman & CEO. **Ultimate Parent:** First Union Corp. **SIC:** 6021—National Commercial Banks.

★ **74007** ★   **First Union National Bank of North Carolina**
5605-77 Ctr. Dr.
Charlotte, NC 28217
(704)374-6161
Company Type: Subsidiary. **Location Type:** Branch office. **Ultimate Parent:** First Union Corp. **SIC:** 6021—National Commercial Banks.

★ **74008** ★   **First Union National Bank of North Carolina**
8700 J.M. Keynes Dr.
Charlotte, NC 28213-8427
(704)374-6161
Company Type: Subsidiary. **Location Type:** Branch office. **Ultimate Parent:** First Union Corp. **SIC:** 6021—National Commercial Banks.

★ **74009** ★   **First Union National Bank of North Carolina**
South Park Shopping Ctr.
6501 Morrison Blvd.
Charlotte, NC 28211-3531
(704)374-6161
Company Type: Subsidiary. **Location Type:** Branch office. **Ultimate Parent:** First Union Corp. **SIC:** 6021—National Commercial Banks.

★ **74010** ★   **First Union National Bank of North Carolina**
Starmount Shopping Ctr.
6101 South Blvd.
Charlotte, NC 28210
(704)374-6161
Company Type: Subsidiary. **Location Type:** Branch office. **Ultimate Parent:** First Union Corp. **SIC:** 6021—National Commercial Banks.

★ **74011** ★   **First Union Securities Inc.**
1 1st Union Ctr.
Charlotte, NC 28288
Company Type: Subsidiary. **Officer:** John Evans, President. **Ultimate Parent:** First Union Corp. **Employee Count:** 49. **Sales:** 34,278,660 M.

★ **74012** ★   **First Union Transportation Services Inc.**
1 1st Union Ctr.
Charlotte, NC 28288
(704)374-3112
Company Type: Subsidiary. **Officer:** John Georgius, President. **Ultimate Parent:** First Union Corp. **SIC:** 4731—Freight Transportation Arrangement. **Employee Count:** 8. **Sales:** 31,422 M.

★ **74013** ★   **Firstmark Development Corp.**
6035 Florence Ave.
Charlotte, NC 28212
(704)536-1495
Ultimate Parent: First Savings Bank. **SIC:** 6531—Real Estate Agents & Managers.

★ **74014** ★   **Food Lion**
RR 9
Charlotte, NC 28216
(704)393-3754
Ultimate Parent: Food Lion. **SIC:** 5411—Grocery Stores.

★ **74015** ★   **Food Lion**
3700 E. Independence Blvd.
Charlotte, NC 28205
(704)568-8295
Ultimate Parent: Food Lion. **SIC:** 5411—Grocery Stores.

★ **74016** ★   **Food Lion**
7400 Plaza Rd.
Charlotte, NC 28215
(704)567-6143
Ultimate Parent: Food Lion. **SIC:** 5411—Grocery Stores.

★ **74017** ★   **Food Lion**
Derita Crossroads
Charlotte, NC 28269
(704)596-9455
Ultimate Parent: Food Lion. **SIC:** 5411—Grocery Stores.

★ **74018** ★   **Food Lion**
9000 J M Keynes Dr.
Charlotte, NC 28262
(704)547-1547
Ultimate Parent: Food Lion. **SIC:** 5411—Grocery Stores.

★ **74019** ★   **Food Lion**
RR 1
Charlotte, NC 28227
(704)545-8941
Ultimate Parent: Food Lion. **SIC:** 5411—Grocery Stores.

★ **74020** ★   **Food Lion**
5601 S. Blvd.
Charlotte, NC 28210
(704)525-9072
Ultimate Parent: Food Lion. **SIC:** 5411—Grocery Stores.

★ **74021** ★   **Food Lion**
9848 Monroe Rd.
Charlotte, NC 28270
(704)847-2443
Ultimate Parent: Food Lion. **SIC:** 5411—Grocery Stores.

★ **74022** ★   **Food Lion Inc.**
Derita Crossroads
Charlotte, NC 28269
(704)596-9455
Ultimate Parent: Food Lion. **SIC:** 5411—Grocery Stores.

★ **74023** ★   **Food Lion Inc.**
9000 J M Keynes Dr.
Charlotte, NC 28262
(704)547-1547
Ultimate Parent: Food Lion. **SIC:** 5411—Grocery Stores.

★ **74024** ★   **Fruehauf Trailer Corp.**
Fruehauf Dr.
Charlotte, NC 28210
(704)588-0150
Company Type: Affiliate. **Location Type:** Plant. **Officer:** J. E. Caywood, COO. **Ultimate Parent:** Terex Corp. **SIC:** 3715—Truck Trailers. **Employee Count:** 790.

★ **74025** ★   **The Gap**
Southpark Shopping
Charlotte, NC 28211
(704)364-9534
Ultimate Parent: GAP. **SIC:** 5699—Miscellaneous Apparel & Accessory Stores.

★ **74026** ★   **Gap Stores**
Southpark Shopping
Charlotte, NC 28211
(704)364-9534
Ultimate Parent: GAP. **SIC:** 5699—Miscellaneous Apparel & Accessory Stores.

★ **74027** ★   **General American Life Insurance C**
7422 Carmel Executive Par Dr.
Charlotte, NC 28226
(704)541-7272
Ultimate Parent: General American Life. **SIC:** 6411—Insurance Agents, Brokers & Service.

★ **74028** ★   **General Electric Co.**
12037 Goodrich Dr.
Charlotte, NC 28273
(704)587-1300
Officer: Al Tarkenton, Manager. **Ultimate Parent:** General Electric. **SIC:** 3599—Industrial Machinery Nec.

★ **74029** ★   **General Financial Agency, Inc.**
2 1st Union Ctr.
Charlotte, NC 28288-0201
(704)324-0201
Company Type: Subsidiary. **Officer:** William E. Selvy, President. **Ultimate Parent:** First Union Corp. **SIC:** 6321—Accident & Health Insurance; 6311—Life Insurance. **Employee Count:** 9.

★ **74030** ★   **General Polymers**
3930 Glenwood Dr.
Charlotte, NC 28208
(704)392-2121
Officer: Berry Gillion, Manager. **Ultimate Parent:** Ashland Oil. **SIC:** 2821—Plastics Materials & Resins.

★ **74031** ★   **Great Atlantic & Pacific Te**
4459 Central Ave.
Charlotte, NC 28205
(704)536-1872
Ultimate Parent: Great Atlantic & Pacific Tea. **SIC:** 5411—Grocery Stores.

★ **74032** ★   **Greyhound Bus Lines**
601 W. Trade St.
Charlotte, NC 28202
(704)372-3555
Ultimate Parent: Greyhound Lines Inc. **SIC:** 4111—Local & Suburban Transit.

★ **74033** ★   **Hertz Rent-A-Car**
Douglas
Charlotte, NC 28219
(704)394-9321
Ultimate Parent: Hertz. **SIC:** 7514—Passenger Car Rental.

★ **74034** ★   **Hertz Rent-A-Car**
6500 Fairview Rd.
Charlotte, NC 28210
(704)364-6141
Ultimate Parent: Hertz. **SIC:** 7514—Passenger Car Rental.

★ **74035** ★   **Hit or Miss**
160 S. Sharon Amity Rd.
Charlotte, NC 28211
(704)364-2524
Ultimate Parent: TJX. **SIC:** 5651—Family Clothing Stores.

★ **74036** ★   **Hit or Miss**
500 Tyvola Rd.
Charlotte, NC 28217
(704)525-6057
Ultimate Parent: TJX. **SIC:** 5651—Family Clothing Stores.

★ **74037** ★   **Hit or Miss**
3126 Milton Rd.
Charlotte, NC 28215
(704)537-8379
Ultimate Parent: TJX. **SIC:** 5651—Family Clothing Stores.

★ **74038** ★   **Hit or Miss**
401 S. Independence Blvd.
Charlotte, NC 28204
(704)374-9364
Ultimate Parent: TJX. **SIC:** 5621—Women's Clothing Stores.

★ **74039** ★   **Hit or Miss**
5620 E. Independence Blvd.
Charlotte, NC 28212
(704)535-1377
Ultimate Parent: TJX. **SIC:** 5651—Family Clothing Stores.

★ **74040** ★   **Hit or Miss**
238 Midtown Sq.
Charlotte, NC 28204
(704)373-0695
Ultimate Parent: TJX. **SIC:** 5651—Family Clothing Stores.

★ **74041** ★   **Hoechst Celanese**
Seperations Products Div.
13800 S. Lakes Dr.
Charlotte, NC 28217
Company Type: Division. **Ultimate Parent:** Hoechst Celanese Corp. **SIC:** 3089—Plastics Products Nec.

★ **74042** ★   **Hoechst-Celanese Charlotte Specialty Chemicals Group**
4331 Chesapeake Dr.
Charlotte, NC 28216
Ultimate Parent: Hoechst Celanese Corp. **SIC:** 2865—Cyclic Crudes & Intermediates; 2893—Printing Ink; 2843—Surface Active Agents.

★ **74043** ★   **Hoechst Celanese Charlotte Spg**
4331 Chesapeake Dr.
Charlotte, NC 28216
Ultimate Parent: Hoechst Celanese Corp. **SIC:** 2865—Cyclic Crudes & Intermediates; 2893—Printing Ink; 2843—Surface Active Agents.

★ **74044** ★   **Hoechst-Celanese Corp.**
Seperations Products Div.
13800 S. Lakes Dr.
Charlotte, NC 28273
Company Type: Division. **Ultimate Parent:** Hoechst Celanese Corp. **SIC:** 3081—Unsupported Plastics Film & Sheet.

★ **74045** ★   **Hoechst-Celanese Corp. Dreyfus Research Park**
2300 Archdale Dr.
Charlotte, NC 28210
Ultimate Parent: Hoechst Celanese Corp. **SIC:** 2824—Organic Fibers—Noncellulosic; 2821—Plastics Materials & Resins; 2823—Cellulosic Manmade Fibers.

★ **74046** ★   **Hoechst Celanese Dreyfus Research Park**
2300 Archdale Dr.
Charlotte, NC 28210
Ultimate Parent: Hoechst Celanese Corp. **SIC:** 2824—Organic Fibers—Noncellulosic.

★ **74047** ★   **Household Mortgage Services**
7422 Carmel Executive Par Dr.
Charlotte, NC 28226
(704)542-9466
Ultimate Parent: Household International. **SIC:** 6162—Mortgage Bankers & Correspondents.

★ **74048** ★   **Human Affairs International**
301 S. Mcdowell St.
Charlotte, NC 28204
(704)377-5324
Ultimate Parent: Aetna Life & Annuity. **SIC:** 8322—Individual & Family Services.

★ 74049 ★   Jiffy Lube
5123 Central Ave.
Charlotte, NC 28205
(704)563-8200
Ultimate Parent: Pennzoil.

★ 74050 ★   Jiffy Lube
3717 Freedom Dr.
Charlotte, NC 28208
(704)394-1017
Ultimate Parent: Pennzoil.

★ 74051 ★   Jiffy Lube of
Charlotte
6324 S. Blvd.
Charlotte, NC 28210
(704)553-7505
Ultimate Parent: Pennzoil.

★ 74052 ★   Jiffy Lube of
Charlotte
812 S. Kings Dr.
Charlotte, NC 28204
(704)372-5433
Ultimate Parent: Pennzoil.

★ 74053 ★   Kentucky Fried
Chicken
5920 Pineville Rd.
Charlotte, NC 28210
(704)552-2468
Ultimate Parent: Pepsico. SIC: 5812—
Eating Places.

★ 74054 ★   Kentucky Fried
Chicken
1600 Remount Rd.
Charlotte, NC 28208
(704)334-0268
Ultimate Parent: Pepsico. SIC: 5812—
Eating Places.

★ 74055 ★   Kentucky Fried
Chicken
2801 Freedom Dr.
Charlotte, NC 28208
(704)394-6730
Ultimate Parent: Pepsico. SIC: 5812—
Eating Places.

★ 74056 ★   Kentucky Fried
Chicken
2619 N. Sharon Amity Rd.
Charlotte, NC 28205
(704)536-2767
Ultimate Parent: Pepsico. SIC: 5812—
Eating Places.

★ 74057 ★   Kentucky Fried
Chicken
1501 E. Independence Blvd.
Charlotte, NC 28205
(704)377-7951
Ultimate Parent: Pepsico. SIC: 5812—
Eating Places.

★ 74058 ★   Kentucky Fried
Chicken
5000 E. Independence Blvd.
Charlotte, NC 28212
(704)568-3077
Ultimate Parent: Pepsico. SIC: 5812—
Eating Places.

★ 74059 ★   Kentucky Fried
Chicken
500 Archdale Dr.
Charlotte, NC 28217
(704)527-0280
Ultimate Parent: Pepsico. SIC: 5812—
Eating Places.

★ 74060 ★   Kentucky Fried
Chicken
2121 Beatties Ford Rd.
Charlotte, NC 28216
(704)398-0161
Ultimate Parent: Pepsico. SIC: 5812—
Eating Places.

★ 74061 ★   Kentucky Fried
Chicken
6424 Albemarle Rd.
Charlotte, NC 28212
(704)537-3070
Ultimate Parent: Pepsico. SIC: 5812—
Eating Places.

★ 74062 ★   Kraft General Foods
500 Dalton Ave.
Charlotte, NC 28206
Ultimate Parent: Philip Morris. SIC: 2024—
Ice Cream & Frozen Desserts.

★ 74063 ★   Kraft General Foods
Frozen Products
500 Dalton Ave.
Charlotte, NC 28206
Ultimate Parent: Philip Morris. SIC: 2024—
Ice Cream & Frozen Desserts.

★ 74064 ★   Kroger Sav on Food
2226 Park Rd.
Charlotte, NC 28203
(704)376-0337
Ultimate Parent: Kroger. SIC: 5912—Drug
Stores & Proprietary Stores.

★ 74065 ★   Kroger Sav on
Food&Drug
9101 Pinevle Matthws
Charlotte, NC 28211
(704)542-5150
Ultimate Parent: Kroger. SIC: 5411—
Grocery Stores.

★ 74066 ★   Kroger Sav-On
2301 Westinghouse Blvd.
Charlotte, NC 28273
(704)588-5779
Ultimate Parent: Kroger. SIC: 5411—
Grocery Stores.

★ 74067 ★   Kroger Sav-On
3301 Freedom Dr.
Charlotte, NC 28208
(704)399-8321
Ultimate Parent: Kroger. SIC: 5411—
Grocery Stores.

★ 74068 ★   Lane Bryant
Eastland
Charlotte, NC 28212
(704)568-1613
Ultimate Parent: Limited. SIC: 5621—
Women's Clothing Stores.

★ 74069 ★   Lane Bryant
5615 Eastland Mall
Charlotte, NC 28205
(704)568-1613
Ultimate Parent: Limited. SIC: 5651—
Family Clothing Stores.

★ 74070 ★   Lerner Shop
5455 Eastland Mall
Charlotte, NC 28205
(704)536-2707
Ultimate Parent: Limited. SIC: 5651—
Family Clothing Stores.

★ 74071 ★   Liberty Mutual
Insurance Co.
5624 Executive Ctr. Dr.
Charlotte, NC 28212
(704)535-3150
Ultimate Parent: Liberty Mutual Group.
SIC: 6411—Insurance Agents, Brokers &
Service.

★ 74072 ★   The Limited
5445 Eastland Mall
Charlotte, NC 28205
(704)568-7236
Ultimate Parent: Limited. SIC: 5651—
Family Clothing Stores.

★ 74073 ★   The Limited
Southpark Shopping
Charlotte, NC 28211
(704)365-4148
Ultimate Parent: Limited. SIC: 5621—
Women's Clothing Stores; 5651—Family
Clothing Stores.

★ 74074 ★   The Limited
Independence Ctr. 1
Charlotte, NC 28202
(704)335-0456
Ultimate Parent: Limited. SIC: 5651—
Family Clothing Stores.

★ 74075 ★   The Limited
Eastland
Charlotte, NC 28212
(704)568-7236
Ultimate Parent: Limited. SIC: 5621—
Women's Clothing Stores.

★ 74076 ★   The Limited Express
5653 Eastland Mall
Charlotte, NC 28205
(704)537-0765
Ultimate Parent: Limited. SIC: 5651—
Family Clothing Stores.

★ 74077 ★   The Limited Express
S Park Shopping Ctr.
Charlotte, NC 28211
(704)362-0420
Ultimate Parent: Limited. SIC: 5651—
Family Clothing Stores.

★ 74078 ★   Linens N Things
Charlottetown Mall
Charlotte, NC 28204
(704)333-1180
Ultimate Parent: Melville. SIC: 5719—
Miscellaneous Home Furnishings Stores.

★ 74079 ★   Martin Marietta
Aggregates
4225 Beatties Ford Rd.
Charlotte, NC 28216
(704)392-1333
Ultimate Parent: Martin Marietta. SIC:
1411—Dimension Stone.

★ 74080 ★   Martin Marietta
Aggregates
11325 Texland Blvd.
Charlotte, NC 28273
(704)588-1471
Ultimate Parent: Martin Marietta. SIC:
5032—Brick, Stone & Related Materials;
5039—Construction Materials Nec.

★ 74081 ★   Mary Kay Cosmetics
5200 N. Poplar St.
Charlotte, NC 28202
(704)335-7223
Ultimate Parent: Mary Kay Cosmetics. SIC:
5999—Miscellaneous Retail Stores Nec.

★ 74082 ★   Massachusetts Mutual
Life Insurance
212 S. Tryon St.
Charlotte, NC 28281
(704)377-4079
Ultimate Parent: Massasuchetts Mutual Life.
SIC: 6411—Insurance Agents, Brokers &
Service.

★ 74083 ★   Meridian Properties
Inc.
3222 Glen Ter
Charlotte, NC 28211
(704)365-3728
Ultimate Parent: Meridian Bancorp. SIC:
6531—Real Estate Agents & Managers.

★ 74084 ★   Metro Mobile CTS of
Charlotte, Inc.
4700 Sweden Rd.
Charlotte, NC 28217
(704)552-5185
Ultimate Parent: Bell Atlantic Corp. SIC:
4812—Radiotelephone Communications.

★ 74085 ★   Mobil Oil Corp.
502 Tom Sadler Rd.
Charlotte, NC 28214
(704)399-0424
Ultimate Parent: Mobil. SIC: 5172—
Petroleum Products Nec.

★ 74086 ★   Nalco Chemical Co.
5550 Seventy Dr. 7
Charlotte, NC 28217
(704)523-4821
Ultimate Parent: Nalco Chemical Co. SIC:
5169—Chemicals & Allied Products Nec.

★ 74087 ★   National Dairy
Products Corp.
500 Dalton Ave.
Charlotte, NC 28206
Ultimate Parent: Philip Morris. SIC: 2024—
Ice Cream & Frozen Desserts.

★ 74088 ★   Nationsbank Corp.
100 N. Tryon St.
Charlotte, NC 28255
(704)386-5000
Company Type: Headquarters. Officer:
Hugh L. McColl Jr. Employee Count:
57463. Fortune Service 500: Ranking 3.

★ 74089 ★   Nationsbank Services
Inc.
One Nationsbank Plz.
Charlotte, NC 28255
(704)386-8468
Ultimate Parent: Nationsbank Corp.

★ 74090 ★   Navistar International
Tran
6101 Idlewild Rd.
Charlotte, NC 28212
(704)535-0754
Ultimate Parent: Navistar International.

SIC: 5012—Automobiles & Other Motor
Vehicles.

★ 74091 ★   Ncr Corp.
8030 Arrowridge Blvd.
Charlotte, NC 28217
(704)527-1800
Ultimate Parent: AT&T. SIC: 5046—
Commercial Equipment Nec.

★ 74092 ★   New York Life
Charlotte General Office
Southeastern Agencies
100 N. Tryon St., Ste. 3000
Charlotte, NC 28202
(704)371-8500 Fax: (704)376-5525
Officer: Joseph B. Hogan Jr., General
Manager. Ultimate Parent: New York Life.

★ 74093 ★   New York Life
Charlotte Group Sales Office
Eastern Group Marketing Zone
4500 Cameron Valley Pky., Ste. 230
Charlotte, NC 28211
(704)364-3972 Fax: (704)365-3821
Officer: Gordon Alford, Group Manager.
Ultimate Parent: New York Life.

★ 74094 ★   Northwest Fabrics &
Crafts
PO Box 7400
Charlotte, NC 28241
(704)587-5700 Fax: (704)588-4896
Officer: Dean C. Emmans, President.
Ultimate Parent: Conagra.

★ 74095 ★   Nucor Corp.
2100 Rexford Rd.
Charlotte, NC 28211
(704)366-7000
Company Type: Headquarters. Officer: F.
Kenneth Iverson. Employee Count: 5900.
Sales: 2254 M. Fortune 500: Largest U.S.
Industrial Corporations: Ranking 205.

★ 74096 ★   Nucor Corp.
Cold Finish Div.
2100 Rexford Rd.
Charlotte, NC 28211
Company Type: Division. Officer: Ladd
Hall, General Manager (Brigham City, UT).
Ultimate Parent: Nucor Corp.

★ 74097 ★   Nucor Corp.
Steel Div.
2100 Rexford Rd.
Charlotte, NC 28211
Company Type: Division. Officer: A Jay
Bowcutt, General Manager (Plymouth, UT).
Ultimate Parent: Nucor Corp.

★ 74098 ★   Nucor Corp.
Vulcraft Div.
2100 Rexford Rd.
Charlotte, NC 28211
Company Type: Division. Officer: James
E. Campbell, General Manager (Fort Payne,
AL). Ultimate Parent: Nucor Corp.

★ 74099 ★   Nucor Corp.
Wire Div.
2100 Rexford Rd.
Charlotte, NC 28211
Company Type: Division. Officer: Ronald
Thompson, Project Manager (Lancaster
SC). Ultimate Parent: Nucor Corp.

★ 74100 ★   Owens Corning
Fiberglas Cor
5601 Ctr. Dr. 77
Charlotte, NC 28217
(704)523-3061
Ultimate Parent: Owens-Corning. SIC:
5033—Roofing, Siding & Insulation.

★ 74101 ★   Owens Corning
Fiberglass
4100 Chesapeake Dr.
Charlotte, NC 28216
(704)392-8366
Ultimate Parent: Owens-Corning. SIC:
5943—Stationery Stores; 5039—
Construction Materials Nec; 5943—
Stationery Stores.

★ 74102 ★   Painewebber Inc.
301 S. College St.
Charlotte, NC 28202
(704)343-4000
Ultimate Parent: Paine Webber Group.
SIC: 6211—Security Brokers & Dealers.

★ 74103 ★ **Paramount Parks**
8720 Red Oak Blvd., Ste. 315
Charlotte, NC 28217
(704)525-5250 **Fax:** (704)525-2960
Officer: Nelson Schwab III, Chairman &
CEO. **Ultimate Parent:** Paramount
Communications

★ 74104 ★ **Permatech**
400 W. Tremont Ave.
Charlotte, NC 28203-4948
(704)334-0065
Ultimate Parent: Aluminum Co. of America-
-Alcoa. **SIC:** 3999—Manufacturing Industries
Nec.

★ 74105 ★ **Pet Dairy**
PO Box 5187
Charlotte, NC 28225
(704)333-1121
Officer: Tony Stogner, Manager. **Ultimate
Parent:** Pet. **SIC:** 2026—Fluid Milk.

★ 74106 ★ **Pitney Bowes Credit
Corp.**
201 S. College St.
Charlotte, NC 28244
(704)332-2154
Ultimate Parent: Pitney Bowes. **SIC:**
6141—Personal Credit Institutions.

★ 74107 ★ **Pizza Hut**
3044 Eastway Dr.
Charlotte, NC 28205
Ultimate Parent: Pepsico. **SIC:** 5812—
Eating Places.

★ 74108 ★ **Pizza Hut**
3900 Wilkinson Blvd.
Charlotte, NC 28208
(704)394-8616
Ultimate Parent: Pepsico. **SIC:** 5812—
Eating Places.

★ 74109 ★ **Pizza Hut**
4119 N. Tryon St.
Charlotte, NC 28206
(704)596-5879
Ultimate Parent: Pepsico. **SIC:** 5812—
Eating Places.

★ 74110 ★ **Pizza Hut**
5516 S. Blvd.
Charlotte, NC 28210
(704)525-4371
Ultimate Parent: Pepsico. **SIC:** 5812—
Eating Places.

★ 74111 ★ **Pizza Hut**
3101 Freedom Dr.
Charlotte, NC 28208
(704)399-5989
Ultimate Parent: Pepsico. **SIC:** 5812—
Eating Places.

★ 74112 ★ **Pizza Hut**
1909 Milton Rd.
Charlotte, NC 28215
(704)535-0694
Ultimate Parent: Pepsico. **SIC:** 5812—
Eating Places.

★ 74113 ★ **Pizza Hut**
5422 E. Independence Blvd.
Charlotte, NC 28212
(704)537-8123
Ultimate Parent: Pepsico. **SIC:** 5812—
Eating Places.

★ 74114 ★ **Pizza Hut**
1307 East Blvd.
Charlotte, NC 28203
(704)376-3789
Ultimate Parent: Pepsico. **SIC:** 5812—
Eating Places.

★ 74115 ★ **Pizza Hut**
1307 E. Blvd.
Charlotte, NC 28203
(704)372-7521
Ultimate Parent: Pepsico. **SIC:** 5812—
Eating Places.

★ 74116 ★ **Pizza Hut**
3657 E. Independence Blvd.
Charlotte, NC 28205
(704)535-4440
Ultimate Parent: Pepsico. **SIC:** 5812—
Eating Places.

★ 74117 ★ **Pizza Hut**
6404 Albemarle Rd.
Charlotte, NC 28212
(704)536-3511
Ultimate Parent: Pepsico. **SIC:** 5812—
Eating Places.

★ 74118 ★ **Polymer Technology**
4751 Amity Pl
Charlotte, NC 28212
(704)535-7205
Ultimate Parent: Bausch & Lomb Inc.

★ 74119 ★ **Pony Express Courier
Corp.**
5550 77 Ctr. Dr., Ste. 320
Charlotte, NC 28210
(704)527-7121 **Fax:** (704)521-8917
Officer: Bob Moree, President. **Ultimate
Parent:** Borg Warner Automotive.

★ 74120 ★ **Pony Express Courier
Corp.**
5550 Ctr. Dr.
Charlotte, NC 28210
(704)527-7121
Officer: Bob E. Moree, President. **Ultimate
Parent:** Borg Warner Automotive. **SIC:**
4215—Courier Services Except by Air.
Employee Count: 5500.

★ 74121 ★ **Porter Cable Corp.**
4612 South Blvd.
Charlotte, NC 28209
(704)525-4410
Ultimate Parent: Pentair. **SIC:** 5072—
Hardware.

★ 74122 ★ **Precision Steel
Warehouse**
2027 Gateway Blvd.
Charlotte, NC 28208-2735
(704)394-3341
Officer: Darrel Walters. **Ultimate Parent:**
Berkshire Hathaway. **SIC:** 5051—Metals
Service Centers & Offices.

★ 74123 ★ **Qualex Inc.**
2513 Distribution St.
Charlotte, NC 28203
Officer: C. Ray Smith, Vice President.
Ultimate Parent: Eastman Kodak. **SIC:**
3861—Photographic Equipment & Supplies.

★ 74124 ★ **R R Donnelley & Sons
Co.**
212 S. Tryon St.
Charlotte, NC 28281
(704)333-0647
Ultimate Parent: R. R. Donnelley & Sons.
SIC: 2732—Book Printing.

★ 74125 ★ **Radio Shack**
Independence Shpg Ctr.
Charlotte, NC 28246
(704)536-1520
Company Type: Division. **Ultimate Parent:**
Tandy Corp. **SIC:** 5065—Electronic Parts &
Equipment Nec.

★ 74126 ★ **Radio Shack**
Tryon Mall Ctr.
Charlotte, NC 28213
(704)527-3472
Company Type: Division. **Ultimate Parent:**
Tandy Corp. **SIC:** 5065—Electronic Parts &
Equipment Nec.

★ 74127 ★ **Radio Shack**
N C Plz. N
Charlotte, NC 28202
(704)333-8435
Company Type: Division. **Ultimate Parent:**
Tandy Corp. **SIC:** 5065—Electronic Parts &
Equipment Nec.

★ 74128 ★ **Radio Shack**
Southpark Shopping
Charlotte, NC 28211
(704)366-1196
Company Type: Division. **Ultimate Parent:**
Tandy Corp. **SIC:** 5065—Electronic Parts &
Equipment Nec.

★ 74129 ★ **Radio Shack**
5401 South Blvd.
Charlotte, NC 28217
(704)527-7440
Company Type: Division. **Ultimate Parent:**
Tandy Corp. **SIC:** 5065—Electronic Parts &
Equipment Nec.

★ 74130 ★ **Radio Shack**
6827 Newell Hkry Grv 24r
Charlotte, NC 28215
(704)567-0318
Company Type: Division. **Ultimate Parent:**
Tandy Corp. **SIC:** 5731—Radio, Television
& Electronics Stores.

★ 74131 ★ **Radio Shack**
160 S. Sharon Amity Rd.
Charlotte, NC 28211
(704)364-9546
Company Type: Division. **Ultimate Parent:**
Tandy Corp. **SIC:** 5065—Electronic Parts &
Equipment Nec.

★ 74132 ★ **Radio Shack**
8524 University City Blvd.
Charlotte, NC 28213
(704)549-1626
Company Type: Division. **Ultimate Parent:**
Tandy Corp. **SIC:** 5731—Radio, Television
& Electronics Stores.

★ 74133 ★ **Radio Shack**
1 Ncnb Plz.
Charlotte, NC 28280
(704)333-8429
Company Type: Division. **Ultimate Parent:**
Tandy Corp. **SIC:** 5734—Computer &
Software Stores.

★ 74134 ★ **Radio Shack**
5401 S. Blvd.
Charlotte, NC 28210
(704)523-1258
Company Type: Division. **Ultimate Parent:**
Tandy Corp. **SIC:** 5731—Radio, Television
& Electronics Stores.

★ 74135 ★ **Radio Shack**
2 N. C B Plz. N
Charlotte, NC 28280
(704)333-8435
Company Type: Division. **Ultimate Parent:**
Tandy Corp. **SIC:** 5065—Electronic Parts &
Equipment Nec.

★ 74136 ★ **Radio Shack**
4500 N. Tryon St.
Charlotte, NC 28213
(704)596-7989
Company Type: Division. **Ultimate Parent:**
Tandy Corp. **SIC:** 5065—Electronic Parts &
Equipment Nec; 5731—Radio, Television &
Electronics Stores.

★ 74137 ★ **Radio Shack**
3046 Eastway Dr.
Charlotte, NC 28205
(704)567-2422
Company Type: Division. **Ultimate Parent:**
Tandy Corp. **SIC:** 5731—Radio, Television
& Electronics Stores.

★ 74138 ★ **Radio Shack**
3150 Freedom Dr.
Charlotte, NC 28208
(704)394-4447
Company Type: Division. **Ultimate Parent:**
Tandy Corp. **SIC:** 5065—Electronic Parts &
Equipment Nec.

★ 74139 ★ **Radio Shack**
Eastland
Charlotte, NC 28212
(704)537-4932
Company Type: Division. **Ultimate Parent:**
Tandy Corp. **SIC:** 5065—Electronic Parts &
Equipment Nec; 5734—Computer &
Software Stores.

★ 74140 ★ **Radio Shack**
5641 Eastland Mall
Charlotte, NC 28205
(704)537-4932
Company Type: Division. **Ultimate Parent:**
Tandy Corp. **SIC:** 5731—Radio, Television
& Electronics Stores.

★ 74141 ★ **Radio Shack**
3732 E. Independence Blvd.
Charlotte, NC 28205
(704)535-6320
Company Type: Division. **Ultimate Parent:**
Tandy Corp. **SIC:** 5046—Commercial
Equipment Nec.

★ 74142 ★ **Radio Shack**
5628 E. Independence Blvd.
Charlotte, NC 28212
(704)536-1520
Company Type: Division. **Ultimate Parent:**
Tandy Corp. **SIC:** 5731—Radio, Television
& Electronics Stores.

★ 74143 ★ **Record Data Inc.**
1420 E. 4th St.
Charlotte, NC 28204
(704)372-9183
Ultimate Parent: TRW, Inc. **SIC:** 6531—
Real Estate Agents & Managers.

★ 74144 ★ **Recovery Services
International**
4801 E. Independence Blvd.
Charlotte, NC 28212
(704)568-1348
Ultimate Parent: Cigna Corp. **SIC:** 6411—
Insurance Agents, Brokers & Service.

★ 74145 ★ **Reneer Films Corp.**
2700 Nevada Blvd.
Charlotte, NC 28273
(704)588-0919
Ultimate Parent: Gencorp. **SIC:** 5946—
Camera & Photographic Supply Stores.

★ 74146 ★ **Rite Aid Discount
Pharmacy**
4104 Carmel Rd.
Charlotte, NC 28226
(704)542-9012
Ultimate Parent: Rite Aid. **SIC:** 5912—Drug
Stores & Proprietary Stores.

★ 74147 ★ **Rite Aid Pharmacy**
3208 Wilkinson Blvd.
Charlotte, NC 28208
(704)393-9634
Ultimate Parent: Rite Aid. **SIC:** 5912—Drug
Stores & Proprietary Stores.

★ 74148 ★ **Rite Aid Pharmacy**
5615 Closeburn Rd.
Charlotte, NC 28210
(704)392-1352
Ultimate Parent: Rite Aid. **SIC:** 5912—Drug
Stores & Proprietary Stores.

★ 74149 ★ **Rohm & Haas**
Unocal Chemical Div.
6101 Orr Rd.
Charlotte, NC 28213
Company Type: Division. **Ultimate Parent:**
Rohm & Haas. **SIC:** 2821—Plastics
Materials & Resins.

★ 74150 ★ **Rohm & Haas**
Unocal Chemical Div.
14700 Mallard Creek Rd.
Charlotte, NC 28213
Company Type: Division. **Ultimate Parent:**
Rohm & Haas. **SIC:** 2821—Plastics
Materials & Resins.

★ 74151 ★ **Rohm & Haas**
Unocal Chemical Div.
14700 Mallard Rd.
Charlotte, NC 28262
Company Type: Division. **Ultimate Parent:**
Rohm & Haas. **SIC:** 2821—Plastics
Materials & Resins.

★ 74152 ★ **Rohm & Haas Co.**
6101 Orr Rd.
Charlotte, NC 28213
(704)596-3021
Officer: Martin Hurlich, Manager. **Ultimate
Parent:** Rohm & Haas. **SIC:** 2821—Plastics
Materials & Resins.

★ 74153 ★ **Ryder Truck Rental**
1409 W. Craighead Rd.
Charlotte, NC 28206
(704)596-9200
Ultimate Parent: Ryder System. **SIC:**
7359—Equipment Rental & Leasing Nec;
7513—Truck Rental & Leasing Without
Drivers.

★ 74154 ★ **Ryder Truck Rental**
8539 Monroe Rd.
Charlotte, NC 28212
(704)535-6008
Ultimate Parent: Ryder System. **SIC:**
7513—Truck Rental & Leasing Without
Drivers.

★ 74155 ★ **Shannon Properties**
7520 E. Independence Blvd., Ste. 240
Charlotte, NC 28227
(704)527-5006
Company Type: Subsidiary. **Ultimate
Parent:** Dana Corp. **SIC:** 6531—Real
Estate Agents & Managers.

★ 74156 ★ **Shannon Properties
Inc.**
7520 E. Independence Blvd.
Charlotte, NC 28227-9405
(704)536-5700
Company Type: Subsidiary. **Ultimate
Parent:** Dana Corp.

★ 74157 ★　**Shaw Industries Plant**
10901 Texland Blvd.
Charlotte, NC 28273
(704)588-1272
Officer: Robert Belden, Manager. **Ultimate Parent:** Shaw Industries, Inc. **SIC:** 2273—Carpets & Rugs.

★ 74158 ★　**Shell Oil**
3301 Woodpark Blvd.
Charlotte, NC 28206
(704)394-1126
Ultimate Parent: Shell Oil Co. **SIC:** 5172—Petroleum Products Nec.

★ 74159 ★　**Skinner Macaroni Co.**
2121 Thrift Rd.
Charlotte, NC 28208
(704)375-1655
Ultimate Parent: Hershey Foods. **SIC:** 5141—Groceries—General Line.

★ 74160 ★　**Snyder Production Center Consolidated**
4901 Chesapeake Dr.
Charlotte, NC 28216-2999
Ultimate Parent: Coca-Cola Bottling Consol. **SIC:** 2086—Bottled & Canned Soft Drinks.

★ 74161 ★　**Soabar Group**
Soabar Products Group
5500 N. Sharon Amity Rd.
Charlotte, NC 28215
(704)537-3223
Company Type: Division. **Ultimate Parent:** Avery Dennison Corp. **SIC:** 3555—Printing Trades Machinery.

★ 74162 ★　**Sonoco Fibre Drum Inc.**
900 Westinghouse Blvd.
Charlotte, NC 28273
(704)588-3007
Officer: Jimmy Lopez, Manager. **Ultimate Parent:** Sonoco Products. **SIC:** 2655—Fiber Cans, Drums & Similar Products; 3412—Metal Barrels, Drums & Pails.

★ 74163 ★　**Standard Register Co.**
5950 Fairview Rd.
Charlotte, NC 28210
(704)554-1411
Officer: D. P. Lawlor, Manager. **Ultimate Parent:** Standard Register. **SIC:** 2761—Manifold Business Forms.

★ 74164 ★　**Stanhome Inc.**
10203 York Rd.
Charlotte, NC 28273
(704)588-2492
Ultimate Parent: Stanhome. **SIC:** 7319—Advertising Nec.

★ 74165 ★　**T J Maxx**
4706 Pineville Rd.
Charlotte, NC 28210
(704)525-9111
Ultimate Parent: TJX. **SIC:** 5311—Department Stores.

★ 74166 ★　**Taco Bell**
5417 Eastland Mall
Charlotte, NC 28205
(704)537-0691
Ultimate Parent: Pepsico. **SIC:** 5812—Eating Places.

★ 74167 ★　**Taco Bell**
5518 S. Blvd.
Charlotte, NC 28210
(704)525-8830
Ultimate Parent: Pepsico. **SIC:** 5812—Eating Places.

★ 74168 ★　**Taco Bell**
800 S. Kings Dr.
Charlotte, NC 28204
(704)333-4625
Ultimate Parent: Pepsico. **SIC:** 5812—Eating Places.

★ 74169 ★　**Texaco Inc.**
410 Tom Sadler Rd.
Charlotte, NC 28214
(704)399-3301
Ultimate Parent: Texaco. **SIC:** 1311—Crude Petroleum & Natural Gas.

★ 74170 ★　**Texaco Station & Deli**
3215 Interstate S. 85
Charlotte, NC 28208
(704)393-0034
Ultimate Parent: Texaco. **SIC:** 5541—Gasoline Service Stations.

★ 74171 ★　**This End Up**
5517 Eastland Mall
Charlotte, NC 28205
(704)568-2295
Ultimate Parent: Melville. **SIC:** 5712—Furniture Stores.

★ 74172 ★　**This End Up Furniture Co.**
Eastland Mall
Charlotte, NC 28212
(704)568-2295
Ultimate Parent: Melville. **SIC:** 5712—Furniture Stores.

★ 74173 ★　**Time Electronics**
9800 Southern Pine Blvd.
Charlotte, NC 28273
(704)522-7600
Ultimate Parent: Avnet. **SIC:** 7389—Business Services Nec.

★ 74174 ★　**Torrington Co**
6623 Executive Cir.
Charlotte, NC 28212
(704)535-5690
Ultimate Parent: Ingersoll-Rand. **SIC:** 3562—Ball & Roller Bearings.

★ 74175 ★　**Toys R US**
6138 E. Independence Blvd.
Charlotte, NC 28212
(704)568-3102
Ultimate Parent: Toys "R" US. **SIC:** 5945—Hobby, Toy & Game Shops.

★ 74176 ★　**Trailways Inc.**
600 W. 8th St.
Charlotte, NC 28202
(704)372-0826
Ultimate Parent: Greyhound Lines Inc. **SIC:** 4131—Intercity & Rural Bus Transportation.

★ 74177 ★　**Trane/Service First**
4500 Morris Field Dr.
Charlotte, NC 28208
Ultimate Parent: American Standard. **SIC:** 3585—Refrigeration & Heating Equipment.

★ 74178 ★　**Trane/Servicefirst Service First**
4500 Morris Field Dr.
Charlotte, NC 28208
Ultimate Parent: American Standard. **SIC:** 3585—Refrigeration & Heating Equipment.

★ 74179 ★　**Trans World Airlines**
5601 Seventy Ctr. Dr.
Charlotte, NC 28217
(704)523-9029
Ultimate Parent: Trans World Airlines. **SIC:** 4512—Air Transportation—Scheduled.

★ 74180 ★　**Transamerica Occidental Life Insurance**
4822 Albemarle Rd.
Charlotte, NC 28205
(704)567-6068
Ultimate Parent: Transamerica Occidental Life Insurance. **SIC:** 6411—Insurance Agents, Brokers & Service.

★ 74181 ★　**Transamerica Occidental Life Insurance**
841 Baxter St.
Charlotte, NC 28202
(704)372-8510
Ultimate Parent: Transamerica Occidental Life Insurance. **SIC:** 6411—Insurance Agents, Brokers & Service.

★ 74182 ★　**Underwriters Adjusting Co.**
1 Woodlawn Green
Charlotte, NC 28217
(704)525-6251
Ultimate Parent: Continental. **SIC:** 6411—Insurance Agents, Brokers & Service.

★ 74183 ★　**Unijax, Inc.**
1000 N. Hoskins Rd.
Charlotte, NC 28216-3435
(704)392-9341
Officer: John F. Pfeiffer, Manager. **Ultimate Parent:** Alco Standard Corp. **SIC:** 2677—Envelopes; 5111—Printing & Writing Paper.

★ 74184 ★　**Unijax Inc.**
1000 N. Hoskins Rd.
Charlotte, NC 28216-3435
(704)392-9341
Officer: Joseph Ryan. **Ultimate Parent:** Alco Standard Corp. **SIC:** 5111—Printing & Writing Paper.

★ 74185 ★　**Union Carbide Coatings Service Corp.**
8501 Old Statesville Rd.
Charlotte, NC 28213
Ultimate Parent: Union Carbide Corp. **SIC:** 3479—Metal Coating & Allied Services.

★ 74186 ★　**Union Carbide Corp.**
8501 Old Statesville Rd.
Charlotte, NC 28213
Ultimate Parent: Union Carbide Corp. **SIC:** 3479—Metal Coating & Allied Services.

★ 74187 ★　**Union Oil Co. of California**
4801 E. Independence Blvd.
Charlotte, NC 28212
(704)536-5260
Ultimate Parent: Unocal Corp. **SIC:** 5172—Petroleum Products Nec.

★ 74188 ★　**United Brake Sys. Inc.**
453 Atando Ave.
Charlotte, NC 28206
Ultimate Parent: Echlin. **SIC:** 3714—Motor Vehicle Parts & Accessories.

★ 74189 ★　**United Brake Systems Inc.**
453 Atando Ave.
Charlotte, NC 28206
(704)333-7126
Ultimate Parent: Echlin. **SIC:** 3069—Fabricated Rubber Products Nec; 3714—Motor Vehicle Parts & Accessories.

★ 74190 ★　**United Parcel Service**
1514 N. Graham St.
Charlotte, NC 28206
(704)372-6020
Ultimate Parent: United Parcel Service of America. **SIC:** 4213—Trucking Except Local; 4215—Courier Services Except by Air.

★ 74191 ★　**Unocal Corp.**
Unocal Chemicals Div.
14700 Mallard Creek Rd.
Charlotte, NC 28213
Company Type: Division. **Ultimate Parent:** Unocal Corp. **SIC:** 2821—Plastics Materials & Resins.

★ 74192 ★　**Unocal Corp.**
Unocal Chemicals Div.
6101 Orr Rd.
Charlotte, NC 28213-6325
Company Type: Division. **Ultimate Parent:** Unocal Corp. **SIC:** 2821—Plastics Materials & Resins.

★ 74193 ★　**Van Waters & Rogers Inc.**
4901 Bellhaven Blvd.
Charlotte, NC 28216
(704)399-4255
Ultimate Parent: Univar Corp. **SIC:** 3861—Photographic Equipment & Supplies.

★ 74194 ★　**Verex Assurance Inc.**
4801 E. Independence Blvd.
Charlotte, NC 28212
(704)535-7450
Ultimate Parent: Dial Corp. **SIC:** 6411—Insurance Agents, Brokers & Service.

★ 74195 ★　**Victoria's Secret**
5603 Eastland Mall
Charlotte, NC 28205
(704)568-7200
Ultimate Parent: Limited. **SIC:** 5651—Family Clothing Stores.

★ 74196 ★　**Wachovia Bank & Trust**
400 S. Tryon St.
Charlotte, NC 28275
(704)378-5111
Ultimate Parent: Wachovia Corp. **SIC:** 6099—Functions Related to Deposit Banking.

★ 74197 ★　**Wachovia Bank & Trust**
8800 J M Keynes Dr.
Charlotte, NC 28262
(704)378-5338
Ultimate Parent: Wachovia Corp. **SIC:** 6022—State Commercial Banks.

★ 74198 ★　**Wachovia Bank & Trust Compa**
712 Tyvola Rd.
Charlotte, NC 28217
(704)378-5043
Ultimate Parent: Wachovia Corp. **SIC:** 6021—National Commercial Banks; 6022—State Commercial Banks.

★ 74199 ★　**Wachovia Bank & Trust Co.**
300 S. Sharon Amity Rd.
Charlotte, NC 28211
(704)378-5415
Ultimate Parent: Wachovia Corp. **SIC:** 6022—State Commercial Banks.

★ 74200 ★　**Wachovia Bank & Trust Co.**
400 S. Tryon St.
Charlotte, NC 28202
(704)378-5111
Ultimate Parent: Wachovia Corp. **SIC:** 6141—Personal Credit Institutions.

★ 74201 ★　**Wachovia Bank & Trust Co. N**
1500 Westinghouse Blvd.
Charlotte, NC 28273
(704)378-5154
Ultimate Parent: Wachovia Corp. **SIC:** 6022—State Commercial Banks.

★ 74202 ★　**Wachovia Bank & Trust Co. N**
6021 Westinghouse Blvd.
Charlotte, NC 28217
(704)378-5154
Ultimate Parent: Wachovia Corp. **SIC:** 6022—State Commercial Banks.

★ 74203 ★　**Wachovia Bank & Trust Co. N**
201 S. College St.
Charlotte, NC 28244
(704)378-5091
Ultimate Parent: Wachovia Corp.

★ 74204 ★　**Wachovia Bank & Trust Co. N**
2823 South Blvd.
Charlotte, NC 28209
(704)378-5332
Ultimate Parent: Wachovia Corp. **SIC:** 6022—State Commercial Banks.

★ 74205 ★　**Wachovia Bank & Trust Co. N**
6300 Conference Dr.
Charlotte, NC 28212
(704)378-5126
Ultimate Parent: Wachovia Corp. **SIC:** 6022—State Commercial Banks.

★ 74206 ★　**Wachovia Bank & Trust Co. N**
5641 Hovis Rd.
Charlotte, NC 28216
(704)378-5275
Ultimate Parent: Wachovia Corp. **SIC:** 6022—State Commercial Banks.

★ 74207 ★　**Wachovia Bank & Trust Co. N**
1211 Ashley Rd.
Charlotte, NC 28208
(704)378-5299
Ultimate Parent: Wachovia Corp. **SIC:** 6022—State Commercial Banks.

★ 74208 ★　**Wachovia Bank & Trust Co. Na**
1900 Randolph Rd.
Charlotte, NC 28207
(704)378-5027
Ultimate Parent: Wachovia Corp.

★ 74209 ★　**Wachovia Bank & Trust Co. Na**
400 S. Tryon St.
Charlotte, NC 28282
(704)378-5111
Ultimate Parent: Wachovia Corp.

★ 74210 ★　**Wachovia Bank & Trust Co. Na**
4501 Park Rd.
Charlotte, NC 28209
(704)378-5223
Ultimate Parent: Wachovia Corp. **SIC:** 6022—State Commercial Banks.

★ 74211 ★ **Wachovia Bank & Trust Co. Na**
1065 Providence Rd.
Charlotte, NC 28207
(704)378-5392
Ultimate Parent: Wachovia Corp. **SIC:** 6099—Functions Related to Deposit Banking.

★ 74212 ★ **Wachovia Bank & Trust Co. Na**
2300 N. Graham St.
Charlotte, NC 28206
(704)378-5474
Ultimate Parent: Wachovia Corp.

★ 74213 ★ **Wachovia Bank & Trust Co. Na**
4111 N. Tryon St.
Charlotte, NC 28206
(704)378-5306
Ultimate Parent: Wachovia Corp. **SIC:** 6099—Functions Related to Deposit Banking.

★ 74214 ★ **Wachovia Bank & Trust Co. Na**
801 Kenilworth Ave.
Charlotte, NC 28204
(704)378-5022
Ultimate Parent: Wachovia Corp.

★ 74215 ★ **Wachovia Bank & Trust Co. Na**
6555 Morrison Blvd.
Charlotte, NC 28211
(704)378-5444
Ultimate Parent: Wachovia Corp. **SIC:** 6099—Functions Related to Deposit Banking.

★ 74216 ★ **Wachovia Bank & Trust Co. Na**
5637 Albemarle Rd.
Charlotte, NC 28212
(704)378-5052
Ultimate Parent: Wachovia Corp. **SIC:** 6022—State Commercial Banks.

★ 74217 ★ **Wachovia Bank & Trust Co. Na**
3665 E. Independence Blvd.
Charlotte, NC 28205
(704)378-5002
Ultimate Parent: Wachovia Corp.

★ 74218 ★ **Waldenbooks**
5643 Eastland Mall
Charlotte, NC 28205
(704)568-5782
Ultimate Parent: K-Mart. **SIC:** 5942—Book Stores.

★ 74219 ★ **Waldenbooks**
107 Independence Ctr. 1
Charlotte, NC 28202
(704)376-1574
Ultimate Parent: K-Mart. **SIC:** 5942—Book Stores.

★ 74220 ★ **Waldenbooks**
Eastland
Charlotte, NC 28212
(704)568-5782
Ultimate Parent: K-Mart. **SIC:** 5942—Book Stores.

★ 74221 ★ **Waldenbooks Co.**
Freedom
Charlotte, NC 28208
(704)394-3722
Ultimate Parent: K-Mart. **SIC:** 5942—Book Stores.

★ 74222 ★ **Waldenbooks & More**
5416 S. Blvd.
Charlotte, NC 28210
(704)521-9730
Ultimate Parent: K-Mart. **SIC:** 5942—Book Stores.

★ 74223 ★ **Wall Street Journal**
9140 Research Dr.
Charlotte, NC 28262
(704)547-0900
Ultimate Parent: Dow Jones. **SIC:** 7383—News Syndicates.

★ 74224 ★ **Wellman Inc.**
5146 Parkway Plaza Blvd.
Charlotte, NC 28217
(704)357-2280
Officer: Ernie Taylor, Manager. **Ultimate Parent:** Wellman Inc.

SIC: 2399—Fabricated Textile Products Nec.

★ 74225 ★ **Wellman Inc.**
10801 Nations Ford Rd.
Charlotte, NC 28241
(704)588-0758
Officer: Bill Bazemore, Vice President. **Ultimate Parent:** Wellman Inc.
SIC: 2399—Fabricated Textile Products Nec; 2821—Plastics Materials & Resins.

★ 74226 ★ **Westinghouse Electric**
5101 Westinghouse Blvd.
Charlotte, NC 28273
(704)551-5100
Location Type: Plant. **Officer:** George Dann, Plant Manager. **Ultimate Parent:** Westinghouse Electric Corp. **SIC:** 3511—Turbines & Turbine Generator Sets; 3621—Motors & Generators.

★ 74227 ★ **Westinghouse Electric Corp.**
Turbine Generator
5101 Westinghouse Blvd.
Charlotte, NC 28273
Ultimate Parent: Westinghouse Electric Corp. **SIC:** 3511—Turbines & Turbine Generator Sets.

★ 74228 ★ **Westvaco Corp.**
4 Woodlawn Green
Charlotte, NC 28217
(704)372-9330
Ultimate Parent: WestVaco Corp. **SIC:** 2677—Envelopes.

★ 74229 ★ **Weyerhaeuser Paper Co.**
8720 Red Oak Blvd.
Charlotte, NC 28217
(704)527-4878
Ultimate Parent: Weyerhaeuser Co. **SIC:** 2621—Paper Mills.

★ 74230 ★ **Whirlpool Financial Corp.**
6401 Carmel Rd.
Charlotte, NC 28226
(704)541-7158
Ultimate Parent: Whirlpool Corp. **SIC:** 6062—State Credit Unions.

★ 74231 ★ **Zimmer Patient Care System**
5701 Executive Ctr. Dr.
Charlotte, NC 28212
(704)568-9120
Ultimate Parent: Bristol-Myers Squibb. **SIC:** 8721—Accounting, Auditing & Bookkeeping.

★ 74232 ★ **ADM Miling Co.**
620 W. 10th St.
Charlottte, NC 28202
(704)332-3165
Officer: Dennis Tucker, Manager. **Ultimate Parent:** Archer Daniels Midland Co. **SIC:** 2041—Flour & Other Grain Mill Products.

Cherokee

★ 74233 ★ **First-Citizens Bank & Trust Co.**
US Hwy. 441 N.
Cherokee, NC 28719
(704)497-2041
Location Type: Branch office. **Officer:** Jerry W. Boone, Vice President. **Ultimate Parent:** First Citizens Bancshares, Inc. **SIC:** 6021—National Commercial Banks.

★ 74234 ★ **Kentucky Fried Chicken**
Cherokee Shopping Ctr.
Cherokee, NC 28719
(704)497-9444
Ultimate Parent: Pepsico. **SIC:** 5812—Eating Places.

Cherry Point

★ 74235 ★ **First-Citizens Bank & Trust Co.**
Carteret Rd.
Cherry Point, NC 28533
(919)447-2077
Location Type: Branch office. **Ultimate**

Parent: First Citizens Bancshares, Inc. **SIC:** 6021—National Commercial Banks.

★ 74236 ★ **First-Citizens Bank & Trust Co.**
Bldg. 3918
Roosevelt Blvd.
Cherry Point, NC 28533
(919)447-2077
Location Type: Branch office. **Officer:** Michael P. Sullivan, Assistant Vice President. **Ultimate Parent:** First Citizens Bancshares, Inc. **SIC:** 6021—National Commercial Banks.

Cherryville

★ 74237 ★ **Branch Banking & Trust Co.**
100 S. Mountain St.
Cherryville, NC 28021-3421
(704)435-5491
Company Type: Subsidiary. **Location Type:** Branch office. **Officer:** J. Donald Ballard, Manager. **Ultimate Parent:** Southern National Corp. **SIC:** 6021—National Commercial Banks.

★ 74238 ★ **Brnach Banking & Trust Co.**
1001 E. Church St.
Cherryville, NC 28021-2916
(704)435-1415
Company Type: Subsidiary. **Location Type:** Branch office. **Ultimate Parent:** Southern National Corp. **SIC:** 6021—National Commercial Banks.

★ 74239 ★ **Carolina Freight**
1201 E. Church St.
Cherryville, NC 28021
(704)435-6811
Company Type: Headquarters. **Officer:** Lary R. Scott. **Fortune Service 500:** Ranking 38.

★ 74240 ★ **Carolina Freight Carriers Corp.**
Hwy. 150
Cherryville, NC 28021-3017
(704)435-6811
Company Type: Subsidiary. **Officer:** Kenneth G. Younger, ChBd. **Ultimate Parent:** Carolina Freight. **SIC:** 4213—Trucking Except Local. **Employee Count:** 7104. **Sales:** 593 M.

★ 74241 ★ **Carolina Freight Carriers Corp.**
N. Carolina Hwy. 150 E
Cherryville, NC 28021
Fax: (704)435-4919
Officer: James D. Carlton, President. **Ultimate Parent:** Carolina Freight.

★ 74242 ★ **Carolina Freight Corp.**
1201 E. Church St.
Cherryville, NC 28021-2116
(704)435-6811
Officer: Kenneth G. Younger, ChBd & CEO. **Ultimate Parent:** Carolina Freight. **SIC:** 4213—Trucking Except Local; 4212—Local Trucking Without Storage. **Employee Count:** 10516. **Sales:** 801 M.

★ 74243 ★ **Carolina Freight Corp.**
N. Carolina Hwy. 150 E
Cherryville, NC 28021
(704)435-6811 **Fax:** (704)435-8981
Ultimate Parent: Carolina Freight.
Employee Count: 11100.

★ 74244 ★ **Carrier Computer Services, Inc.**
300 Commerce Dr.
Cherryville, NC 28021
(704)435-5801 **Fax:** (704)435-5075
Officer: John W. Rudasill, President. **Ultimate Parent:** Carolina Freight.

★ 74245 ★ **Complete Leasing Concepts, Inc.**
N. Carolina Hwy. 150 E
Cherryville, NC 28021
Officer: Bob Rains, President. **Ultimate Parent:** Carolina Freight.

★ 74246 ★ **Innivative Logistics Inc.**
N. Carolina Hwy. 150 E
Cherryville, NC 28021
Officer: Phillip G. Deely, President & Treasurer. **Ultimate Parent:** Carolina Freight.

★ 74247 ★ **Kentucky Fried Chicken**
709 E. Church St.
Cherryville, NC 28021
(704)435-9090
Ultimate Parent: Pepsico. **SIC:** 5812—Eating Places.

★ 74248 ★ **Motor Carrier Insurance, Ltd.**
N. Carolina Hwy. 150 E
Cherryville, NC 28021
Officer: John L. Fraley Jr., Chairman of the Board. **Ultimate Parent:** Carolina Freight.

★ 74249 ★ **Pepsi-Cola Bottling Co.**
152 Commerce Dr.
Cherryville, NC 28021
(704)435-8801
Officer: Gene Pharr, Manager. **Ultimate Parent:** Pepsico. **SIC:** 2086—Bottled & Canned Soft Drinks.

★ 74250 ★ **Rite Aid**
302 E. Main St.
Cherryville, NC 28021
(704)435-3290
Ultimate Parent: Rite Aid. **SIC:** 5912—Drug Stores & Proprietary Stores.

China Grove

★ 74251 ★ **First Union National Bank of North Carolina**
125 N. Main St.
China Grove, NC 28023-2527
(704)857-2435
Company Type: Subsidiary. **Location Type:** Branch office. **Ultimate Parent:** First Union Corp. **SIC:** 6021—National Commercial Banks.

★ 74252 ★ **Food Lion**
503 Hwy. 29 N
China Grove, NC 28023
(704)857-6189
Ultimate Parent: Food Lion. **SIC:** 5411—Grocery Stores.

Cinton

★ 74253 ★ **First-Citizens Bank & Trust Co.**
Union School Rd.
Cinton, NC 28393
(910)592-7321
Location Type: Branch office. **Ultimate Parent:** First Citizens Bancshares, Inc. **SIC:** 6021—National Commercial Banks.

Claremont

★ 74254 ★ **Citizens Savings Bank, SSB**
107 E. Main St.
Claremont, NC 28610
(704)459-9228
Company Type: Subsidiary. **Location Type:** Branch office. **Officer:** Ginger Carpenter, Mgr. **Ultimate Parent:** Southern National Corp. **SIC:** 6021—National Commercial Banks.

★ 74255 ★ **First Union National Bank of North Carolina**
102 E. Main St.
Claremont, NC 28610
(704)459-7152
Company Type: Subsidiary. **Location Type:** Branch office. **Ultimate Parent:** First Union Corp. **SIC:** 6021—National Commercial Banks.

★ 74256 ★ **Southern Furniture Co. of Conover Inc. -Catawba Plant**
State Rd. 1722 PO Box 160
Claremont, NC 28610
Ultimate Parent: Southern. **SIC:** 2511—Wood Household Furniture.

Clayton

★ 74257 ★ **Branch Banking & Trust Co.**
315 E. Main St.
Clayton, NC 27520-2463
(919)553-6131
Company Type: Subsidiary. **Location Type:** Branch office. **Ultimate Parent:** Southern National Corp. **SIC:** 6021—National Commercial Banks.

★ 74258 ★　Champion Products
Inc.
S. Atkinson St.
Clayton, NC 27520
Ultimate Parent: Sara Lee Corp. SIC:
2389—Apparel & Accessories Nec.

★ 74259 ★　Champion Products
Inc.
Atkinson St. .
Clayton, NC 27520
Ultimate Parent: Sara Lee Corp. SIC:
2389—Apparel & Accessories Nec.

★ 74260 ★　Data General Corp.
Nc Hwy. 42-E PO Box 186
Clayton, NC 27520
Ultimate Parent: Data General. SIC:
3672—Printed Circuit Boards.

★ 74261 ★　Data General Corp.
PO Box 186, Hwy. 42E
Clayton, NC 27520
Ultimate Parent: Data General. SIC:
3679—Electronic Components Nec.

★ 74262 ★　Data General Corp.
PO Box 186 N.C. Hwy. 42-E
Clayton, NC 27520
Ultimate Parent: Data General. SIC:
3679—Electronic Components Nec.

★ 74263 ★　Data General Corp.
Hwy. 42 E
Clayton, NC 27520
(919)553-5076
Company Type: Division. Location Type:
Plant. Officer: Charles Johnson, Plant
Manager. Ultimate Parent: Data General.
SIC: 3672—Printed Circuit Boards; 3571—
Electronic Computers; 3577—Computer
Peripheral Equipment Nec; 3679—Electronic
Components Nec.

★ 74264 ★　First-Citizens Bank &
Trust Co.
302 E. Main St.
Clayton, NC 27520-2464
(919)553-7151
Location Type: Branch office. Ultimate
Parent: First Citizens Bancshares, Inc. SIC:
6021—National Commercial Banks.

★ 74265 ★　Miles Inc. Cutter
Biological
Hwy. 70 E.
Clayton, NC 27520-0507
Ultimate Parent: Miles. SIC: 2836—
Biological Products Except Diagnostic.

★ 74266 ★　Radio Shack
611 Us Hwy. 70 E
Clayton, NC 27520
(919)553-6186
Company Type: Division. Ultimate Parent:
Tandy Corp. SIC: 5719—Miscellaneous
Home Furnishings Stores.

Clemmons

★ 74267 ★　Branch Banking &
Trust Co.
2561 Lewisville-Clemmons Rd.
Clemmons, NC 27012-8709
(910)723-3604
Company Type: Subsidiary. Location
Type: Branch office. Ultimate Parent:
Southern National Corp. SIC: 6021—
National Commercial Banks.

★ 74268 ★　First-Citizens Bank &
Trust Co.
2554 Lewisville-Clemmons Rd.
Clemmons, NC 27012-8749
(910)766-4334
Location Type: Branch office. Officer:
Connie C. Perry, Manager. Ultimate
Parent: First Citizens Bancshares, Inc. SIC:
6021—National Commercial Banks.

★ 74269 ★　First Union National
Bank of North Carolina
2565 Lewisville-Clemmons Rd.
Clemmons, NC 27012-8712
(910)761-3940
Company Type: Subsidiary. Location
Type: Branch office. Ultimate Parent: First
Union Corp. SIC: 6021—National
Commercial Banks.

★ 74270 ★　Food Lion
Lewisville Clemmons Rd.
Clemmons, NC 27012
(919)766-6491
Ultimate Parent: Food Lion. SIC: 5411—
Grocery Stores.

★ 74271 ★　Pizza Hut
1340 PO Box
Clemmons, NC 27012
(919)766-0538
Ultimate Parent: Pepsico. SIC: 5812—
Eating Places.

★ 74272 ★　Varian Associates
802 Birch Ln.
Clemmons, NC 27012
(919)996-1039
Ultimate Parent: Varian Associates, Inc.
SIC: 5047—Medical & Hospital Equipment.

★ 74273 ★　Wachovia Bank &
Trust
Middlebrook Hwy. 158
Clemmons, NC 27012
(919)766-6406
Ultimate Parent: Wachovia Corp. SIC:
6099—Functions Related to Deposit
Banking.

Cliffside

★ 74274 ★　Cliffside Plant
Hwy. 221A
Cliffside, NC 28024
Ultimate Parent: Cone Mills. SIC: 2211—
Broadwoven Fabric Mills—Cotton; 2261—
Finishing Plants—Cotton.

★ 74275 ★　Cone Mills Corp.
Cliffside Plant
Main St.
Cliffside, NC 28024
Ultimate Parent: Cone Mills. SIC: 2211—
Broadwoven Fabric Mills—Cotton; 2261—
Finishing Plants—Cotton.

★ 74276 ★　First-Citizens Bank &
Trust Co.
Main St. & Hwy. 221-A
Cliffside, NC 28076
(704)657-5349
Location Type: Branch office. Ultimate
Parent: First Citizens Bancshares, Inc. SIC:
6021—National Commercial Banks.

★ 74277 ★　First-Citizens Bank &
Trust Co.
N. Main & 2nd Ave.
Cliffside, NC 28204
(704)657-5351
Location Type: Branch office. Officer:
Robert L. Hunt, Manager. Ultimate Parent:
First Citizens Bancshares, Inc. SIC: 6021—
National Commercial Banks.

Clinton

★ 74278 ★　American Family Life
Assurance
701 Beamon St.
Clinton, NC 28328
(919)592-4466
Ultimate Parent: American Family Life
Assurance Co. SIC: 6411—Insurance
Agents, Brokers & Service.

★ 74279 ★　Branch Banking &
Trust Co.
217 Lisbon St.
Clinton, NC 28328-4116
(910)592-0111
Company Type: Subsidiary. Location
Type: Branch office. Ultimate Parent:
Southern National Corp. SIC: 6021—
National Commercial Banks.

★ 74280 ★　Branch Banking &
Trust Co.
1106 Sunset Ave.
Clinton, NC 28328-3820
(910)592-1771
Company Type: Subsidiary. Location
Type: Branch office. Ultimate Parent:
Southern National Corp. SIC: 6021—
National Commercial Banks.

★ 74281 ★　Branch Banking &
Trust Co.
501 Warsaw Rd.
Clinton, NC 28328-3629
(910)592-7121
Company Type: Subsidiary. Location

Type: Branch office. Officer: Richard
DeBose, Manager. Ultimate Parent:
Southern National Corp. SIC: 6021—
National Commercial Banks.

★ 74282 ★　Carolina Power &
Light Co.
222 Wall St.
Clinton, NC 28328
(919)592-6117
Ultimate Parent: Carolina Power & Light
Co. SIC: 4911—Electric Services.

★ 74283 ★　Carolina Power &
Light Co.
222 Wall St.
Clinton, NC 28328
(919)592-6117
Ultimate Parent: Carolina Power & Light
Co. SIC: 4911—Electric Services.

★ 74284 ★　First-Citizens Bank &
Trust Co.
600 College St.
Clinton, NC 28328-3502
(910)592-4694
Location Type: Branch office. Ultimate
Parent: First Citizens Bancshares, Inc. SIC:
6021—National Commercial Banks.

★ 74285 ★　First-Citizens Bank &
Trust Co.
NC Hwy. 41
Clinton, NC 28444-9503
(910)532-4363
Location Type: Branch office. Ultimate
Parent: First Citizens Bancshares, Inc. SIC:
6021—National Commercial Banks.

★ 74286 ★　First-Citizens Bank &
Trust Co.
925 Sunset Ave.
Clinton, NC 28328-3815
(910)592-2155
Location Type: Branch office. Ultimate
Parent: First Citizens Bancshares, Inc. SIC:
6021—National Commercial Banks.

★ 74287 ★　First-Citizens Bank &
Trust Co.
302 Northeast Blvd.
Clinton, NC 28328-2424
(910)592-2155
Location Type: Branch office. Ultimate
Parent: First Citizens Bancshares, Inc. SIC:
6021—National Commercial Banks.

★ 74288 ★　First-Citizens Bank &
Trust Co.
201 E. Main St.
Clinton, NC 28328-4030
(910)592-2155
Location Type: Branch office. Officer:
Benjamin E. Woodruff, Senior Vice
President. Ultimate Parent: First Citizens
Bancshares, Inc. SIC: 6021—National
Commercial Banks.

★ 74289 ★　First Union National
Bank of North Carolina
Clinton Plz. Shopping Ctr.
357 Northeast Blvd.
Clinton, NC 28328
(910)592-7031
Company Type: Subsidiary. Location
Type: Branch office. Ultimate Parent: First
Union Corp. SIC: 6021—National
Commercial Banks.

★ 74290 ★　First Union National
Bank of North Carolina
111 Elizabeth St.
Clinton, NC 28328-4017
(910)592-7031
Company Type: Subsidiary. Location
Type: Branch office. Ultimate Parent: First
Union Corp. SIC: 6021—National
Commercial Banks.

★ 74291 ★　Food Lion
319 North Blvd.
Clinton, NC 28328
(919)592-2169
Ultimate Parent: Food Lion. SIC: 5411—
Grocery Stores.

★ 74292 ★　Kentucky Fried
Chicken
500 Raleigh Rd.
Clinton, NC 28328
(919)592-5778
Ultimate Parent: Pepsico. SIC: 5812—
Eating Places.

★ 74293 ★　Piggly Wiggly
N East Blvd.
Clinton, NC 28328
(919)592-3001
Ultimate Parent: Bruno's. SIC: 5411—
Grocery Stores.

★ 74294 ★　Piggly Wiggly
Shamrock Plz.
Clinton, NC 28328
(919)592-5385
Ultimate Parent: Bruno's. SIC: 5411—
Grocery Stores.

★ 74295 ★　Piggly Wiggly
815 College St.
Clinton, NC 28328
(919)592-6162
Ultimate Parent: Bruno's. SIC: 5411—
Grocery Stores.

★ 74296 ★　Pizza Hut
129 Southeast Blvd.
Clinton, NC 28328
(919)592-1542
Ultimate Parent: Pepsico. SIC: 5812—
Eating Places.

★ 74297 ★　Pizza Hut
1200 Sunset Ave.
Clinton, NC 28328
(919)592-9333
Ultimate Parent: Pepsico. SIC: 5812—
Eating Places.

Coats

★ 74298 ★　Branch Banking &
Trust Co.
300 N. McKinley St.
Coats, NC 27521
(910)897-7726
Company Type: Subsidiary. Location
Type: Branch office. Officer: Larry R. Byrd,
Mgr. Ultimate Parent: Southern National
Corp. SIC: 6021—National Commercial
Banks.

★ 74299 ★　First-Citizens Bank &
Trust Co.
100 N. McKinley St.
Coats, NC 27521
(910)897-7741
Location Type: Branch office. Officer:
Darrell H. Smith, Vice President. Ultimate
Parent: First Citizens Bancshares, Inc. SIC:
6021—National Commercial Banks.

Coinjock

★ 74300 ★　Exxon
Hwy. 158
Coinjock, NC 27923
(919)453-3302
Ultimate Parent: Exxon. SIC: 5411—
Grocery Stores.

Columbus

★ 74301 ★　Food Lion
231 W. Mills St.
Columbus, NC 28722
(704)894-8286
Ultimate Parent: Food Lion. SIC: 5411—
Grocery Stores.

★ 74302 ★　Food Lion Inc.
231 W. Mills St.
Columbus, NC 28722
(704)894-8286
Ultimate Parent: Food Lion. SIC: 5411—
Grocery Stores.

Concord

★ 74303 ★　Ace Hardware
298 Moore Dr. NW
Concord, NC 28025
(704)788-3721
Ultimate Parent: Ace Hardware. SIC:
7231—Beauty Shops.

★ 74304 ★　Ace Hardware of
Concord
1101 Us 29 N
Concord, NC 28025
(704)786-7100
Ultimate Parent: Ace Hardware. SIC:
5251—Hardware Stores.

★ 74305 ★   **American General Finance Inc.**
845 Church St. N, Ste. 103
Concord, NC 28025-4300
(704)786-1180
Location Type: Branch office. **Officer:** Dan Fleagle. **Ultimate Parent:** American General Corp. **SIC:** 6021—National Commercial Banks.

★ 74306 ★   **American General Finance Inc.**
845 Church St. N, Ste. 103
Concord, NC 28025-4300
(704)786-1180
Officer: Dan Fleagle. **Ultimate Parent:** American General Corp. **SIC:** 9100—Executive, Legislative & General.

★ 74307 ★   **Bi-Lo Grocery**
840 Us 29 N
Concord, NC 28025
(704)782-4822
Ultimate Parent: Penn Traffic. **SIC:** 5411—Grocery Stores.

★ 74308 ★   **Cannon Chemical Co.**
326 Mcgill Ave. NW
Concord, NC 28025
Ultimate Parent: Fieldcrest Cannon. **SIC:** 2899—Chemical Preparations Nec.

★ 74309 ★   **Cardinal Freight Carriers, Inc.**
5333 Davidson Hwy.
Concord, NC 28027
(704)786-6125 **Fax:** (704)788-6617
Officer: Ed Randolph, President & Treasurer. **Ultimate Parent:** Carolina Freight.

★ 74310 ★   **Exxon Express**
540 Lake Concord Rd. NE
Concord, NC 28025
(704)788-7220
Ultimate Parent: Exxon. **SIC:** 5411—Grocery Stores.

★ 74311 ★   **First Bank**
1484 Us 29 N
Concord, NC 28025
(704)786-7102
Ultimate Parent: Shawmut National Corp. **SIC:** 6022—State Commercial Banks.

★ 74312 ★   **First-Citizens Bank & Trust Co.**
789 Hwy. 29 N.
Concord, NC 28025-6035
(704)786-5112
Location Type: Branch office. **Ultimate Parent:** First Citizens Bancshares, Inc. **SIC:** 6021—National Commercial Banks.

★ 74313 ★   **First-Citizens Bank & Trust Co.**
18 Lake Concord Rd. NE
Concord, NC 28025-3016
(704)786-5112
Location Type: Branch office. **Officer:** Kenneth E. Yelton, Vice President. **Ultimate Parent:** First Citizens Bancshares, Inc. **SIC:** 6021—National Commercial Banks.

★ 74314 ★   **Food Lion**
730 Cabarrus Ave. W
Concord, NC 28027
(704)788-3175
Ultimate Parent: Food Lion. **SIC:** 5411—Grocery Stores.

★ 74315 ★   **Food Lion**
860 Union St. S
Concord, NC 28025
(704)782-3166
Ultimate Parent: Food Lion. **SIC:** 5411—Grocery Stores.

★ 74316 ★   **Mastercraft Fabric Corp. Concord Plant**
312 Office Dr. SW
Concord, NC 28027
Ultimate Parent: Collins & Aikman Group. **SIC:** 2262—Finishing Plants—Manmade.

★ 74317 ★   **Philip Morris USA**
Cabarrus Manufacturing Center
3231 Hwy. 29 S.
Concord, NC 28027
Company Type: Division. **Ultimate Parent:** Philip Morris. **SIC:** 2111—Cigarettes.

★ 74318 ★   **Phillip Morris USA**
Cabarrus
3321 Hwy. 29 S.
Concord, NC 28025
Company Type: Division. **Ultimate Parent:** Philip Morris. **SIC:** 2111—Cigarettes.

★ 74319 ★   **Pizza Hut**
697 Church St. N
Concord, NC 28025
(704)786-5612
Ultimate Parent: Pepsico. **SIC:** 5812—Eating Places.

★ 74320 ★   **Pizza Hut**
793 Cabarrus Ave. W
Concord, NC 28027
(704)788-7888
Ultimate Parent: Pepsico. **SIC:** 5812—Eating Places.

★ 74321 ★   **Radio Shack**
1480 Carolina Mall
Concord, NC 28025
(704)786-2316
Company Type: Division. **Ultimate Parent:** Tandy Corp. **SIC:** 5731—Radio, Television & Electronics Stores.

★ 74322 ★   **Radio Shack**
Concord Parkade Shopping
Concord, NC 28025
(704)782-7600
Company Type: Division. **Ultimate Parent:** Tandy Corp. **SIC:** 5065—Electronic Parts & Equipment Nec.

★ 74323 ★   **Taco Bell**
1489 Us 29 N
Concord, NC 28025
(704)788-9732
Ultimate Parent: Pepsico. **SIC:** 5812—Eating Places.

★ 74324 ★   **Wachovia Bank & Trust**
50 Union St. N
Concord, NC 28025
(704)788-3122
Ultimate Parent: Wachovia Corp. **SIC:** 6099—Functions Related to Deposit Banking.

★ 74325 ★   **Wachovia Bank & Trust Co.**
868 Church St. N
Concord, NC 28025
(704)782-3113
Ultimate Parent: Wachovia Corp.

★ 74326 ★   **Waldenbooks**
Carolina Mall
Concord, NC 28025
(704)786-1812
Ultimate Parent: K-Mart. **SIC:** 5942—Book Stores.

Conover

★ 74327 ★   **Broyhill Furniture Ind. Inc. Conover Plant**
409 2nd Ave.
Conover, NC 28613
Ultimate Parent: Interco. **SIC:** 2511—Wood Household Furniture.

★ 74328 ★   **Conover Inc. Southern Furniture Co. Main Pl**
1099 2nd Ave. Pl. SE
Conover, NC 28613
Ultimate Parent: Southern. **SIC:** 2512—Upholstered Household Furniture.

★ 74329 ★   **Conover Inc. Southern Furniture Co.-Plant 2**
1815 Emanuel Church Rd.
Conover, NC 28613
Ultimate Parent: Southern. **SIC:** 2512—Upholstered Household Furniture.

★ 74330 ★   **E. R. Carpenter Co. Inc.**
2009 Keisler Rd. PO Box 879
Conover, NC 28613-0879
Ultimate Parent: Carpenter. **SIC:** 3086—Plastics Foam Products.

★ 74331 ★   **E.R. Carpenter Co. Inc.**
2009 Keisler Rd. PO Box 879
Conover, NC 28613
Ultimate Parent: Carpenter. **SIC:** 3086—Plastics Foam Products.

★ 74332 ★   **Foamex**
Foamex L.P.
408 Mclin Creek Rd.
Conover, NC 28613
Ultimate Parent: Foamex. **SIC:** 3086—Plastics Foam Products.

★ 74333 ★   **Foamex L.P.**
639 4th St.
Conover, NC 28613
Ultimate Parent: Foamex. **SIC:** 3086—Plastics Foam Products.

★ 74334 ★   **Kentucky Fried Chicken**
Hwy. 64
Conover, NC 28613
(704)464-8070
Ultimate Parent: Pepsico. **SIC:** 5812—Eating Places.

★ 74335 ★   **Radio Shack**
Hwy. 64
Conover, NC 28613
(704)464-9783
Company Type: Division. **Ultimate Parent:** Tandy Corp. **SIC:** 5065—Electronic Parts & Equipment Nec.

★ 74336 ★   **Southern Furniture Co. Conover Inc.**
1099 2nd Ave. Pl. SE
Conover, NC 28613
Ultimate Parent: Southern. **SIC:** 2511—Wood Household Furniture.

★ 74337 ★   **Southern Furniture Co. of Conover Inc.**
1099 2nd Ave. Pl. South East
Conover, NC 28613
Ultimate Parent: Southern. **SIC:** 2512—Upholstered Household Furniture.

★ 74338 ★   **Spartan Express Inc.**
Hwy. 64 W
Conover, NC 28613
(704)464-5046
Ultimate Parent: Roadway Services. **SIC:** 4213—Trucking Except Local.

★ 74339 ★   **Thomasville Upholstery, Inc.**
1118 Hwy. 70A
Conover, NC 28613
(704)322-5830
Officer: Darrell Jones, Manager. **Ultimate Parent:** Armstrong World Industries. **SIC:** 2812—Alkalies & Chlorine.

Conway

★ 74340 ★   **First-Citizens Bank & Trust Co.**
201 W. Main
Conway, NC 27820-9610
(919)585-0304
Location Type: Branch office. **Officer:** Jim V. Troutman, Vice President. **Ultimate Parent:** First Citizens Bancshares, Inc. **SIC:** 6021—National Commercial Banks.

★ 74341 ★   **Georgia-Pacific Corp. Conway Hardboard**
Ampac Rd.
Conway, NC 27820
Ultimate Parent: Georgia-Pacific. **SIC:** 2493—Reconstituted Wood Products.

★ 74342 ★   **Georgia Pacific Resins Inc.**
Ampac Rd.
Conway, NC 27820
Ultimate Parent: Georgia-Pacific. **SIC:** 2821—Plastics Materials & Resins; 2869—Industrial Organic Chemicals Nec.

★ 74343 ★   **Georgia-Pacific Resins Inc. Conway Hardboard**
Ampac Rd.
Conway, NC 27820
Ultimate Parent: Georgia-Pacific. **SIC:** 2821—Plastics Materials & Resins; 2869—Industrial Organic Chemicals Nec.

Cordova

★ 74344 ★   **Burlington Industries Inc.**
Old Cherow Hwy.
Cordova, NC 28330
(910)997-5001
Officer: Dale Ormsby, Manager. **Ultimate Parent:** Burlington Industries, Equity. **SIC:** 2221—Broadwoven Fabric Mills—Manmade; 2399—Fabricated Textile Products Nec.

★ 74345 ★   **Burlington Industries Richmond Plant**
Cordova, NC 28330
(919)997-5001
Ultimate Parent: Burlington Industries, Equity. **SIC:** 2399—Fabricated Textile Products Nec.

Cornelius

★ 74346 ★   **Ace Hardware Co. Inc.**
20510 N. Main St.
Cornelius, NC 28031
(704)892-1212
Ultimate Parent: Ace Hardware. **SIC:** 5992—Florists.

★ 74347 ★   **Foamex L.P.**
Foamex Division
Hwy. 115 & Bailey Rd.
Cornelius, NC 28031
Ultimate Parent: Foamex. **SIC:** 3086—Plastics Foam Products.

★ 74348 ★   **Food Lion**
20420 Norman Xing
Cornelius, NC 28031
(704)892-4115
Ultimate Parent: Food Lion. **SIC:** 5411—Grocery Stores.

Cramerton

★ 74349 ★   **Branch Banking & Trust Co.**
109 Ctr. St.
Cramerton, NC 28032-1400
(704)824-4318
Company Type: Subsidiary. **Location Type:** Branch office. **Officer:** Joanne L. England, Mgr. **Ultimate Parent:** Southern National Corp. **SIC:** 6021—National Commercial Banks.

★ 74350 ★   **Branch Banking & Trust Co.**
Ctr. St.
Cramerton, NC 28032
(704)824-4318
Ultimate Parent: Southern National Corp. **SIC:** 6022—State Commercial Banks.

★ 74351 ★   **Burlington Industries/ Lakewood Plant**
Eastwood Dr.
Cramerton, NC 28032
(704)825-3075
Officer: Mike Lawson. **Ultimate Parent:** Burlington Industries, Equity. **SIC:** 2269—Finishing Plants Nec.

★ 74352 ★   **Food Lion**
200 Market St.
Cramerton, NC 28032
(704)824-4757
Ultimate Parent: Food Lion. **SIC:** 5411—Grocery Stores.

Creedmoor

★ 74353 ★   **Branch Banking & Trust Co.**
608 N. Main St.
Creedmoor, NC 27522
(919)528-1526
Company Type: Subsidiary. **Location Type:** Branch office. **Ultimate Parent:** Southern National Corp. **SIC:** 6021—National Commercial Banks.

★ 74354 ★   **Ivac Co.**
100 Ivac Way
Creedmoor, NC 27522
Ultimate Parent: Eli Lilly. **SIC:** 3843—Dental Equipment & Supplies.

★ 74355 ★   **Ivac Corp.**
1515 Ivac Way
Creedmoor, NC 27522
Ultimate Parent: Eli Lilly. **SIC:** 3841—Surgical & Medical Instruments.

★ 74356 ★   **Ivac Corp.**
100 Ivac Way
Creedmoor, NC 27522
Ultimate Parent: Eli Lilly. **SIC:** 3843—Dental Equipment & Supplies.

Dallas

★ 74357 ★　　Branch Banking &
Trust Co.
501 W. Trade St.
Dallas, NC 28034-1540
(704)922-7854
Company Type: Subsidiary. **Location
Type:** Branch office. **Officer:** Mark B.
Rouse, Mgr. **Ultimate Parent:** Southern
National Corp. **SIC:** 6021—National
Commercial Banks.

Davidson

★ 74358 ★　　Ingersoll Rand
Small Compressor Div.
800 B Beaty St.
Davidson, NC 28036
Company Type: Division. **Ultimate Parent:**
Ingersoll-Rand. **SIC:** 3563—Air & Gas
Compressors.

Denton

★ 74359 ★　　Burlington Industries
Bombay Rd.
Denton, NC 27239
(704)869-4511
Location Type: Branch office. **Ultimate
Parent:** Burlington Industries, Equity. **SIC:**
2399—Fabricated Textile Products Nec.

★ 74360 ★　　Burlington Industries
Inc.
Bombay Rd.
Denton, NC 27239
(704)869-4511
Officer: Maurice Atwell, Manager. **Ultimate
Parent:** Burlington Industries, Equity. **SIC:**
2257—Weft Knit Fabric Mills; 2258—Lace &
Warp Knit Fabric Mills; 2399—Fabricated
Textile Products Nec.

Denver

★ 74361 ★　　Branch Banking &
Trust Co.
Hwy. 16
Denver, NC 28037-8417
(704)483-9351
Company Type: Subsidiary. **Location
Type:** Branch office. **Officer:** Dan Gordon,
Mgr. **Ultimate Parent:** Southern National
Corp. **SIC:** 6021—National Commercial
Banks.

Dobson

★ 74362 ★　　First-Citizens Bank &
Trust Co.
217 N. Main St.
Dobson, NC 27017
(910)386-8149
Location Type: Branch office. **Officer:**
Charles L. Davis, Assistant Vice President.
Ultimate Parent: First Citizens Bancshares,
Inc. **SIC:** 6021—National Commercial
Banks.

Drexel

★ 74363 ★　　Adams-Millis Drexel
Knitting
100 Mill St.
Drexel, NC 28619
Ultimate Parent: Sara Lee Corp. **SIC:**
2252—Hosiery Nec.

★ 74364 ★　　Casual Corner
Vly Hill Mall
Drexel, NC 28619
(704)324-4841
Ultimate Parent: United States Shoe. **SIC:**
5621—Women's Clothing Stores.

★ 74365 ★　　Drexel Heritage
Furnishings Inc.
101 N. Main St.
Drexel, NC 28619
(704)433-3000 **Fax:** (704)433-3349
Officer: Daniel M. Grow. **Ultimate Parent:**
Masco.

★ 74366 ★　　Drexel Heritage
Furniture
Plant 1
101 N. Main St.
Drexel, NC 28619
Location Type: Plant. **Ultimate Parent:**
Masco. **SIC:** 2511—Wood Household
Furniture.

★ 74367 ★　　Drexel Heritage
Furniture
Plant 1
101 N. Main St.
Drexel, NC 28619
Location Type: Plant. **Ultimate Parent:**
Masco. **SIC:** 2511—Wood Household
Furniture.

Dudley

★ 74368 ★　　Georgia-Pacific Corp.
Dudley Comply
Old Mount Olive Hwy.
Dudley, NC 28333
Ultimate Parent: Georgia-Pacific. **SIC:**
2493—Reconstituted Wood Products.

Dunham

★ 74369 ★　　First-Citizens Bank &
Trust Co.
4004 Roxboro Rd.
Dunham, NC 27707
(919)383-1828
Location Type: Branch office. **Ultimate
Parent:** First Citizens Bancshares, Inc. **SIC:**
6021—National Commercial Banks.

Dunn

★ 74370 ★　　Champion Products
Inc.
200 Champion Dr.
PO Box 1745
Dunn, NC 28334
Ultimate Parent: Sara Lee Corp. **SIC:**
2389—Apparel & Accessories Nec.

★ 74371 ★　　First-Citizens Bank &
Trust Co.
1717 W. Cumberland St.
Dunn, NC 28334-4509
(910)982-4133
Location Type: Branch office. **Ultimate
Parent:** First Citizens Bancshares, Inc. **SIC:**
6021—National Commercial Banks.

★ 74372 ★　　First-Citizens Bank &
Trust Co.
901 E. Cumberland St.
Dunn, NC 28334-5115
(910)892-4133
Location Type: Branch office. **Ultimate
Parent:** First Citizens Bancshares, Inc. **SIC:**
6021—National Commercial Banks.

★ 74373 ★　　First-Citizens Bank &
Trust Co.
200 E. Broad St.
Dunn, NC 28334-4993
(910)892-4133
Location Type: Branch office. **Officer:**
Timothy M. Brown, Area Vice President.
Ultimate Parent: First Citizens Bancshares,
Inc. **SIC:** 6021—National Commercial
Banks.

★ 74374 ★　　Gwaltney of
Smithfield
Dunn, NC 28334
(919)567-2017
Ultimate Parent: Smithfield Foods Inc. **SIC:**
5154—Livestock.

★ 74375 ★　　Mac-Page Inc.
1600 South Wilson Ave.
Dunn, NC 28334
Ultimate Parent: Central Soya.

★ 74376 ★　　Piggly Wiggly
211 N. Clinton Ave.
Dunn, NC 28334
(919)892-7941
Ultimate Parent: Bruno's. **SIC:** 5411—
Grocery Stores.

★ 74377 ★　　Radio Shack
1819 Dunn Plz.
Dunn, NC 28334
(919)892-4490
Company Type: Division. **Ultimate Parent:**

Tandy Corp. **SIC:** 5731—Radio, Television
& Electronics Stores.

★ 74378 ★　　Ryder Truck Rental
Hwy. 421 W
Dunn, NC 28334
(919)892-1174
Ultimate Parent: Ryder System. **SIC:**
7359—Equipment Rental & Leasing Nec.

Durham

★ 74379 ★　　Agricultural Products
2505 Meridian Pky.
Durham, NC 27713
(919)361-5300
Company Type: Subsidiary. **Officer:** Peter
Oakley, Group Vice President. **Ultimate
Parent:** BASF Corp.

★ 74380 ★　　Air Products &
Chemicals
4822 Industry Ln.
Durham, NC 27713-1496
(919)361-2077
Location Type: Branch office. **Officer:** Ed
Nichols. **Ultimate Parent:** Air Products &
Chemicals, Inc. **SIC:** 5169—Chemicals &
Allied Products Nec.

★ 74381 ★　　Air Products &
Chemicals
South Square Shopping Ctr.
Durham, NC 27707
(919)828-4462
Ultimate Parent: Air Products & Chemicals,
Inc. **SIC:** 5169—Chemicals & Allied
Products Nec.

★ 74382 ★　　American General
Finance
2220 N. Roxboro Rd.
Durham, NC 27704-4343
(919)471-6451
Location Type: Branch office. **Officer:**
Carolyn Bridgewater. **Ultimate Parent:**
American General Corp. **SIC:** 6141—
Personal Credit Institutions.

★ 74383 ★　　American General
Finance
3117 Shanon Rd., No. C
Durham, NC 27707-3569
(919)493-6404
Officer: Rick Lever. **Ultimate Parent:**
American General Corp. **SIC:** 6141—
Personal Credit Institutions.

★ 74384 ★　　American General
Finance Inc.
3117 Shannon Rd., No. C
Durham, NC 27707-3569
(919)493-6404
Location Type: Branch office. **Officer:** Rick
Lever. **Ultimate Parent:** American General
Corp. **SIC:** 6141—Personal Credit
Institutions.

★ 74385 ★　　American General
Finance Inc.
2220 N. Roxboro Rd.
Durham, NC 27704-4343
(919)471-6451
Location Type: Branch office. **Officer:**
Carolyn Bridgewater. **Ultimate Parent:**
American General Corp. **SIC:** 6141—
Personal Credit Institutions.

★ 74386 ★　　BASF Corp.
3 Icon Ct.
Durham, NC 27703-9111
(919)598-8399
Ultimate Parent: BASF Corp. **SIC:** 2821—
Plastics Materials & Resins.

★ 74387 ★　　BFI Waste Systems
1038 Harvest Rd.
Durham, NC 27704-5218
(919)682-2417
Location Type: Branch office. **Ultimate
Parent:** Browning-Ferris Industries. **SIC:**
4953—Refuse Systems.

★ 74388 ★　　Casual Corner
Northgate Mall
Durham, NC 27704
(919)286-9876
Ultimate Parent: United States Shoe. **SIC:**
5621—Women's Clothing Stores.

★ 74389 ★　　Casual Corner Corp.
Northgate Mall Ctr.
Durham, NC 27704
(919)286-5489
Ultimate Parent: United States Shoe. **SIC:**
5621—Women's Clothing Stores.

★ 74390 ★　　Circus World Inc.
Northgate
Durham, NC 27704
(919)286-0685
Ultimate Parent: Melville. **SIC:** 5945—
Hobby, Toy & Game Shops.

★ 74391 ★　　Exxon Co. USA
1318 Broad St.
Durham, NC 27705
(919)286-0259
Ultimate Parent: Exxon. **SIC:** 2911—
Petroleum Refining.

★ 74392 ★　　Federal Paper Board
Co.
123 Franklin St.
Durham, NC 27701
(919)688-9691
Location Type: Plant. **Officer:** Wally
Vernasco, Plant Manager. **Ultimate Parent:**
Federal Paper Board. **SIC:** 2657—Folding
Paperboard Boxes.

★ 74393 ★　　Federal Paper Board
Co. Inc.
923 Franklin St.
Durham, NC 27702
Ultimate Parent: Federal Paper Board.
SIC: 2657—Folding Paperboard Boxes.

★ 74394 ★　　Federal Paper Board
Co. Inc. Plant 49
923 Franklin St.
Durham, NC 27702
Ultimate Parent: Federal Paper Board.
SIC: 2657—Folding Paperboard Boxes.

★ 74395 ★　　First-Citizens Bank &
Trust Co.
3808 Guess Rd.
Durham, NC 27705-1550
(919)383-1828
Location Type: Branch office. **Ultimate
Parent:** First Citizens Bancshares, Inc. **SIC:**
6021—National Commercial Banks.

★ 74396 ★　　First-Citizens Bank &
Trust Co.
1308 Hwy. 54 W.
Durham, NC 27707-5506
(919)383-1828
Location Type: Branch office. **Ultimate
Parent:** First Citizens Bancshares, Inc. **SIC:**
6021—National Commercial Banks.

★ 74397 ★　　First-Citizens Bank &
Trust Co.
3200 Hillsborough Rd.
Durham, NC 27707-2662
(919)383-1828
Location Type: Branch office. **Officer:**
Gary L. Holmes, Vice President. **Ultimate
Parent:** First Citizens Bancshares, Inc. **SIC:**
6021—National Commercial Banks.

★ 74398 ★　　First Federal S & L
400 W. Main St.
Durham, NC 27701-3233
(919)682-5531
Company Type: Headquarters. **Officer:**
Gus T. Godwin. **Ultimate Parent:** Bancorp
Hawaii. **SIC:** 6035—Federal Savings
Institutions; 6021—National Commercial
Banks; 6141—Personal Credit Institutions;
6162—Mortgage Bankers &
Correspondents.

★ 74399 ★　　Food Lion
2000 Chapel Hill Rd.
Durham, NC 27707
(919)489-4695
Ultimate Parent: Food Lion. **SIC:** 5411—
Grocery Stores.

★ 74400 ★　　Food Lion
4711 Hope Valley Rd.
Durham, NC 27707
(919)493-5203
Ultimate Parent: Food Lion. **SIC:** 5411—
Grocery Stores.

★ 74401 ★　　Food Lion
2400 Holloway St.
Durham, NC 27703
(919)598-1433
Ultimate Parent: Food Lion. **SIC:** 5411—
Grocery Stores.

★ 74402 ★ **General Electric Co.**
3026 W. Cornwallis Rd.
Durham, NC 27709
(919)549-3277
Officer: George Higgins, Manager. **Ultimate Parent:** General Electric. **SIC:** 3674—Semiconductors & Related Devices; 3679—Electronic Components Nec.

★ 74403 ★ **Golden Belt Manufacturing**
807 E. Main St.
Durham, NC 27701-4020
(919)682-9394
Ultimate Parent: American Brands Inc. **SIC:** 2754—Commercial Printing—Gravure; 2679—Converted Paper Products Nec.

★ 74404 ★ **Golden Belt Manufacturing Co.**
807 E. Main St.
Durham, NC 27702-2332
(919)682-2394 **Fax:** (919)688-1751
Company Type: Subsidiary. **Ultimate Parent:** American Brands Inc.

★ 74405 ★ **Golden Belt Mfg. Co.**
807 E. Main St.
Durham, NC 27701
Ultimate Parent: American Brands Inc. **SIC:** 2754—Commercial Printing—Gravure.

★ 74406 ★ **Honeywell Inc.**
Holloway & Calvin St.
Durham, NC 27701
Ultimate Parent: Honeywell. **SIC:** 3621—Motors & Generators.

★ 74407 ★ **Honeywell Inc.**
921 Holloway St.
Durham, NC 27701
Ultimate Parent: Honeywell. **SIC:** 3621—Motors & Generators.

★ 74408 ★ **Honeywell Inc. Electro Components**
921 Holloway St.
Durham, NC 27701
Ultimate Parent: Honeywell. **SIC:** 3621—Motors & Generators.

★ 74409 ★ **IBM Corp.**
4205 S. Miami Blvd.
Durham, NC 27703
(919)543-8073
Ultimate Parent: IBM.

★ 74410 ★ **Kentucky Fried Chicken**
803 9th St.
Durham, NC 27705
(919)286-7797
Ultimate Parent: Pepsico. **SIC:** 5812—Eating Places.

★ 74411 ★ **Kentucky Fried Chicken**
910 Miami Blvd.
Durham, NC 27703
(919)682-5613
Ultimate Parent: Pepsico. **SIC:** 5812—Eating Places.

★ 74412 ★ **Kmart Discount Stores**
4215 Univ Dr.
Durham, NC 27707
(919)493-2591
Ultimate Parent: K-Mart. **SIC:** 5311—Department Stores.

★ 74413 ★ **Kroger Co. the**
5331 N. Roxboro Rd.
Durham, NC 27712
(919)471-4160
Ultimate Parent: Kroger. **SIC:** 5411—Grocery Stores.

★ 74414 ★ **The Limited**
Northgate Mall
Durham, NC 27704
(919)286-5541
Ultimate Parent: Limited. **SIC:** 5621—Women's Clothing Stores.

★ 74415 ★ **The Limited Express**
1058 W. Club Blvd.
Durham, NC 27701
(919)286-1842
Ultimate Parent: Limited. **SIC:** 5621—Women's Clothing Stores.

★ 74416 ★ **Mary Kay Cosmetics, Inc.**
3822 Regent Rd.
Durham, NC 27707
(919)489-3974
Ultimate Parent: Mary Kay Cosmetics. **SIC:** 5999—Miscellaneous Retail Stores Nec.

★ 74417 ★ **McDonalds of Durham**
Northgate
Durham, NC 27704
(919)286-1247
Ultimate Parent: McDonald's. **SIC:** 5812—Eating Places.

★ 74418 ★ **McDonalds of Durham**
4717 Apex Hwy.
Durham, NC 27713
(919)544-3768
Ultimate Parent: McDonald's. **SIC:** 5812—Eating Places.

★ 74419 ★ **Moen Inc.**
807 E. Main St.
Durham, NC 27701-4020
(919)682-9394
Location Type: Branch office. **Officer:** J. J. Galiota. **Ultimate Parent:** American Brands Inc. **SIC:** 2759—Commercial Printing Nec; 2674—Bags—Uncoated Paper & Multiwall; 2754—Commercial Printing—Gravure; 3497—Metal Foil & Leaf.

★ 74420 ★ **Mutual Savings & Loan Assoc**
315 E. Chapel Hill St.
Durham, NC 27701-3313
(919)688-1308
Location Type: Headquarters. **Officer:** F. V. Allison Jr. **Ultimate Parent:** Berkshire Hathaway. **SIC:** 6035—Federal Savings Institutions; 6021—National Commercial Banks; 6141—Personal Credit Institutions; 6162—Mortgage Bankers & Correspondents.

★ 74421 ★ **Pepsi-Cola Bottling Co.**
2717 Western Byp.
Durham, NC 27705
(919)489-2311
Location Type: Plant. **Officer:** Bobby Moon, Plant Manager. **Ultimate Parent:** Pepsico. **SIC:** 2086—Bottled & Canned Soft Drinks.

★ 74422 ★ **Petite Sophisticate**
103 Northgate Shopping Ctr.
Durham, NC 27701
(919)286-7777
Ultimate Parent: United States Shoe. **SIC:** 5399—Miscellaneous General Merchandise Store.

★ 74423 ★ **Pizza Hut**
2726 Chapel Hill Blvd.
Durham, NC 27707
(919)493-1894
Ultimate Parent: Pepsico. **SIC:** 5812—Eating Places.

★ 74424 ★ **Pizza Hut**
Hwy. 5554 Rd.
Durham, NC 27703
(919)361-2728
Ultimate Parent: Pepsico. **SIC:** 5088—Transportation Equipment & Supplies.

★ 74425 ★ **Qualex Inc.**
3000 Croasdaile Dr.
Durham, NC 27705-2507
(919)383-8535
Company Type: Subsidiary. **Officer:** Richard Finkbeiner, Co President. **Ultimate Parent:** Eastman Kodak. **SIC:** 7384—Photofinishing Laboratories; 2861—Gum & Wood Chemicals; 3861—Photographic Equipment & Supplies. **Employee Count:** 8000. **Sales:** 770 M.

★ 74426 ★ **Radio Shack**
Riverview Shopping Ctr.
Durham, NC 27702
(919)477-8987
Company Type: Division. **Ultimate Parent:** Tandy Corp. **SIC:** 5065—Electronic Parts & Equipment Nec.

★ 74427 ★ **Radio Shack**
Northgate Shopping Ctr.
Durham, NC 27704
(919)286-3264
Company Type: Division. **Ultimate Parent:** Tandy Corp. **SIC:** 5065—Electronic Parts & Equipment Nec.

★ 74428 ★ **Smith Barney Harris Upham & Co.**
3101 Petty Rd.
Durham, NC 27707-7105
(919)493-5559
Company Type: Branch. **Officer:** David Pottenger. **Ultimate Parent:** Automatic Data Processing, Inc. **SIC:** 6211—Security Brokers & Dealers.

★ 74429 ★ **Southern States Co-Op. Inc. Feed Mill**
901 Mallard Ave.
Durham, NC 27702
Ultimate Parent: Southern. **SIC:** 2048—Prepared Feeds Nec.

★ 74430 ★ **This End Up**
216 Northgate Shopping Ctr.
Durham, NC 27701
(919)286-4789
Ultimate Parent: Melville. **SIC:** 5712—Furniture Stores.

★ 74431 ★ **Unicopy Corp. of North Carolina**
4101 Capitol St.
Durham, NC 27704-2153
(919)688-3048
Ultimate Parent: Alco Standard Corp. **SIC:** 5044—Office Equipment.

★ 74432 ★ **United Parcel Service**
2008 Fay St.
Durham, NC 27704
(919)682-9191
Ultimate Parent: United Parcel Service of America. **SIC:** 4212—Local Trucking Without Storage.

★ 74433 ★ **Wachovia Bank & Trust**
4709 Hope Valley Rd.
Durham, NC 27707
(919)683-5271
Ultimate Parent: Wachovia Corp. **SIC:** 6099—Functions Related to Deposit Banking.

★ 74434 ★ **Wachovia Bank & Trust**
100 Park Dr.
Durham, NC 27709
(919)549-8035
Ultimate Parent: Wachovia Corp. **SIC:** 6022—State Commercial Banks.

★ 74435 ★ **Wachovia Bank & Trust Co.**
1900 Avondale Dr.
Durham, NC 27701
(919)683-5340
Ultimate Parent: Wachovia Corp. **SIC:** 6099—Functions Related to Deposit Banking; 6141—Personal Credit Institutions.

★ 74436 ★ **Wachovia Bank & Trust Co.**
2821 Chapel Hill Blvd.
Durham, NC 27707
(919)683-5342
Ultimate Parent: Wachovia Corp. **SIC:** 6099—Functions Related to Deposit Banking.

★ 74437 ★ **Wachovia Bank & Trust Co.**
2116 Angier Ave.
Durham, NC 27703
(919)683-5323
Ultimate Parent: Wachovia Corp. **SIC:** 6099—Functions Related to Deposit Banking.

★ 74438 ★ **Wachovia Bank & Trust Co. N**
3306 State Hwy. 54
Durham, NC 27709
(919)549-8621
Ultimate Parent: Wachovia Corp. **SIC:** 6022—State Commercial Banks.

★ 74439 ★ **Wachovia Bank & Trust Co. N**
Duke Medical Ctr.
Durham, NC 27710
(919)683-5331
Ultimate Parent: Wachovia Corp. **SIC:** 6022—State Commercial Banks.

★ 74440 ★ **Wachovia Bank & Trust Co. N**
S Square Shopping
Durham, NC 27707
(919)683-5346
Ultimate Parent: Wachovia Corp. **SIC:** 6022—State Commercial Banks.

★ 74441 ★ **Wachovia Bank & Trust Co. N**
Avondale Dr.
Durham, NC 27704
(919)683-5340
Ultimate Parent: Wachovia Corp. **SIC:** 6022—State Commercial Banks.

★ 74442 ★ **Wilsons**
5021 Wake Hwy.
Durham, NC 27703
(919)848-1542
Ultimate Parent: Melville. **SIC:** 1711—Plumbing, Heating & Air-Conditioning.

E. Fayetteville

★ 74443 ★ **Food Lion**
342 N. Eastern Blvd.
E Fayetteville, NC 28301
(919)485-8886
Ultimate Parent: Food Lion. **SIC:** 5411—Grocery Stores.

★ 74444 ★ **Food Lion Inc.**
342 N. Eastern Blvd.
E Fayetteville, NC 28301
(919)485-8886
Ultimate Parent: Food Lion. **SIC:** 5411—Grocery Stores.

★ 74445 ★ **Wachovia Bank & Trust**
697 Country Club Dr.
E Fayetteville, NC 28301
(919)433-9384
Ultimate Parent: Wachovia Corp. **SIC:** 6099—Functions Related to Deposit Banking.

E Flat Rock

★ 74446 ★ **Federal Paper Board Co.**
Spartanburg Hwy.
E Flat Rock, NC 28726
(704)692-6254
Ultimate Parent: Federal Paper Board. **SIC:** 5113—Industrial & Personal Service Paper.

E Laurinburg

★ 74447 ★ **Food Lion**
1301 Us Hwy. 15 N
E Laurinburg, NC 28352
(919)277-7550
Ultimate Parent: Food Lion. **SIC:** 5411—Grocery Stores.

East Flat Rock

★ 74448 ★ **Federal Paper Board Co.**
200 Tabor Rd.
East Flat Rock, NC 28726
(704)692-6254
Officer: Edward W. Siemering, Manager. **Ultimate Parent:** Federal Paper Board. **SIC:** 2657—Folding Paperboard Boxes; 2621—Paper Mills; 2679—Converted Paper Products Nec.

Eden

★ 74449 ★ **Blanket Finishing**
Warehouse St.
Eden, NC 27288
Ultimate Parent: Fieldcrest Cannon. **SIC:** 2261—Finishing Plants—Cotton; 2262—Finishing Plants—Manmade.

★ 74450 ★ **Branch Banking & Trust Co.**
680 S. Van Buren Rd.
Eden, NC 27288-5320
(910)623-8421
Company Type: Subsidiary. **Location Type:** Branch office. **Officer:** Herman Anderson, Manager. **Ultimate Parent:** Southern National Corp. **SIC:** 6021—National Commercial Banks.

★ 74451 ★   Central Filter
354 W. Meadow Rd.
Eden, NC 27288
Location Type: Plant. Ultimate Parent:
Fieldcrest Cannon. SIC: 2297—Nonwoven
Fabrics.

★ 74452 ★   Fieldcrest Cannon
326 E. Stadium Dr.
Eden, NC 27288
(910)627-3000
Company Type: Headquarters. Officer:
James M. Fitzgibbons. Sales: 1000.1 M.
Fortune 500: Largest U.S. Industrial
Corporations: Ranking 366.

★ 74453 ★   Fieldcrest Cannon
Inc.
326 E. Stadium Dr.
Eden, NC 27288-3523
(919)627-3000
Officer: James M. Fitzgibbons, CEO. SIC:
2259—Knitting Mills Nec; 2273—Carpets &
Rugs. Employee Count: 16953. Sales:
1,217,279,000 M.

★ 74454 ★   Fieldcrest/Cannon,
Inc.
326 E. Stadium Dr.
Eden, NC 27288
(910)627-3000
Company Type: Headquarters. Officer:
James M. Fitzgibbons, Chairman of the
Board & CEO. Ultimate Parent: Fieldcrest
Cannon. SIC: 2221—Broadwoven Fabric
Mills—Manmade; 2281—Yarn Spinning
Mills; 2211—Broadwoven Fabric Mills—
Cotton. Employee Count: 17407. Sales:
1,212,400,000 M.

★ 74455 ★   Fieldcrest Cannon
Inc. Non-Woven
Riverside Dr.
Eden, NC 27288
Ultimate Parent: Fieldcrest Cannon. SIC:
2297—Nonwoven Fabrics.

★ 74456 ★   First-Citizens Bank &
Trust
231 W. Kings Hwy.
Eden, NC 27288-5009
(910)623-9724
Location Type: Branch office. Officer: C.
Grayson Whitt, Vice President. Ultimate
Parent: First Citizens Bancshares, Inc. SIC:
6021—National Commercial Banks.

★ 74457 ★   Food Lion
842 S. Van Buren Rd.
Eden, NC 27288
Ultimate Parent: Food Lion. SIC: 5411—
Grocery Stores.

★ 74458 ★   Karastan Rug Mill
712 Henry St.
Eden, NC 27288
Ultimate Parent: Fieldcrest Cannon. SIC:
2273—Carpets & Rugs.

★ 74459 ★   Kay Bee Toys
201 E. Meadow Rd.
Eden, NC 27288
(919)623-4612
Ultimate Parent: Melville. SIC: 5945—
Hobby, Toy & Game Shops.

★ 74460 ★   Kentucky Fried
Chicken
Van Buren Rd.
Eden, NC 27288
(919)623-8414
Ultimate Parent: Pepsico. SIC: 5812—
Eating Places.

★ 74461 ★   Massachusetts Mutual
Life Insurance
640 Washington St.
Eden, NC 27288
(919)623-7307
Ultimate Parent: Massasucetts Mutual Life.
SIC: 6411—Insurance Agents, Brokers &
Service.

★ 74462 ★   Miller Brewing Co.
863 E. Meadow Rd.
Eden, NC 27288
Ultimate Parent: Philip Morris. SIC: 2082—
Malt Beverages.

★ 74463 ★   Pannill Knitting Co.
N.C. Hwy. 770 E. & State Rd. 1743
Eden, NC 27288
Ultimate Parent: Sara Lee Corp. SIC:
2253—Knit Outerwear Mills.

★ 74464 ★   Pizza Hut
251 W. Kings Hwy.
Eden, NC 27288
(919)627-4414
Ultimate Parent: Pepsico. SIC: 5812—
Eating Places.

★ 74465 ★   Radio Shack
Eden Court Apts
Eden, NC 27288
(919)627-1919
Company Type: Division. Ultimate Parent:
Tandy Corp. SIC: 5065—Electronic Parts &
Equipment Nec.

★ 74466 ★   Rite Aid Discount
Pharmacie
11 S. Van Buren Rd.
Eden, NC 27288
(919)623-9006
Ultimate Parent: Rite Aid. SIC: 5912—Drug
Stores & Proprietary Stores.

★ 74467 ★   Rite Aid Discount
Pharmacy
Medowgreen Shopping
Eden, NC 27288
(919)623-8491
Ultimate Parent: Rite Aid. SIC: 5912—Drug
Stores & Proprietary Stores.

★ 74468 ★   Sara Lee Knit
Products
Dyeing & Finishing Plant
328 Gant Rd. & State Rd. 1743
Eden, NC 27288-9582
Location Type: Plant. Ultimate Parent:
Sara Lee Corp. SIC: 2253—Knit Outerwear
Mills.

★ 74469 ★   Wachovia Bank &
Trust Co. N
665 S. Van Buren Rd.
Eden, NC 27288
(919)623-9176
Ultimate Parent: Wachovia Corp. SIC:
6022—State Commercial Banks.

Edenton

★ 74470 ★   Branch Banking &
Trust Co.
322 S. Broad St.
Edenton, NC 27932-1934
(919)482-8415
Company Type: Subsidiary. Location
Type: Branch office. Ultimate Parent:
Southern National Corp. SIC: 6021—
National Commercial Banks.

★ 74471 ★   Food Lion
Edenton Manor Apts
Edenton, NC 27932
(919)482-7784
Ultimate Parent: Food Lion. SIC: 5411—
Grocery Stores.

★ 74472 ★   Pizza Hut
Edenton Villge Shopping Ctr.
Edenton, NC 27932
(919)482-3290
Ultimate Parent: Pepsico. SIC: 5812—
Eating Places.

Elizabeth City

★ 74473 ★   Pizza Hut
1209 W. Ehringhaus St.
Elizabeth Cit, NC 27909
(919)338-3964
Ultimate Parent: Pepsico. SIC: 5812—
Eating Places.

★ 74474 ★   Branch Banking &
Trust Co.
309 E. Colonial Ave.
Elizabeth City, NC 27893-3880
(919)399-4111
Company Type: Subsidiary. Location
Type: Branch office. Ultimate Parent:
Southern National Corp. SIC: 6021—
National Commercial Banks.

★ 74475 ★   Branch Banking &
Trust Co.
306 E. Colonial Ave.
Elizabeth City, NC 27909-4306
(919)335-0888
Company Type: Subsidiary. Location
Type: Branch office. Officer: Ben Ivey, Mgr.

Ultimate Parent: Southern National Corp.
SIC: 6021—National Commercial Banks.

★ 74476 ★   Chesapeake Corp.
Wood Treating
Knobbs Creek Dr.
Elizabeth City, NC 27909
Ultimate Parent: Chesapeake. SIC: 2491—
Wood Preserving.

★ 74477 ★   Chesapeake Wood
Treating Co.
Knobbs Creek Dr.
Elizabeth City, NC 27909
Ultimate Parent: Chesapeake. SIC: 2491—
Wood Preserving.

★ 74478 ★   First-Citizens Bank &
Trust Co.
310 S. Road St.
Elizabeth City, NC 27909-4760
(919)335-2943
Location Type: Branch office. Officer: Ron
Trulington, Area Vice President. Ultimate
Parent: First Citizens Bancshares, Inc. SIC:
6021—National Commercial Banks.

★ 74479 ★   First-Citizens Bank &
Trust Co.
1609 W. Ehringhaus
Elizabeth City, NC 27909-4551
(919)335-2943
Location Type: Branch office. Ultimate
Parent: First Citizens Bancshares, Inc. SIC:
6021—National Commercial Banks.

★ 74480 ★   Food Lion
1515 W. Ehringhaus St.
Elizabeth City, NC 27909
(919)338-1676
Ultimate Parent: Food Lion. SIC: 5411—
Grocery Stores.

★ 74481 ★   Kaiser Aluminum &
Chemical
215 Charles St.
Elizabeth City, NC 27909
(919)335-4690
Ultimate Parent: Maxxam. SIC: 5191—
Farm Supplies.

★ 74482 ★   Kentucky Fried
Chicken
116 S. Hughes Blvd.
Elizabeth City, NC 27909
(919)335-5050
Ultimate Parent: Pepsico. SIC: 5812—
Eating Places.

★ 74483 ★   Pepsi-Cola Bottling
Co.
900 W. Ehringhaus St.
Elizabeth City, NC 27909
(919)335-4355
Officer: Jimmy Burns, Manager. Ultimate
Parent: Pepsico. SIC: 2086—Bottled &
Canned Soft Drinks.

★ 74484 ★   Shell Service
1332 N. Rd.
Elizabeth City, NC 27909
(919)335-1148
Ultimate Parent: Shell Oil Co. SIC: 5541—
Gasoline Service Stations.

★ 74485 ★   Wachovia Bank &
Trust
400 E. Main St.
Elizabeth City, NC 27909
(919)335-0511
Ultimate Parent: Wachovia Corp. SIC:
6099—Functions Related to Deposit
Banking.

★ 74486 ★   Taco Bell
420 N. Hughes Blvd.
Elizabeth City, NC 27909
(919)338-2000
Ultimate Parent: Pepsico. SIC: 4724—
Travel Agencies.

★ 74487 ★   Radio Shack
Southgate Mall
Elizabeth Cy, NC 27909
(919)335-4909
Company Type: Division. Ultimate Parent:
Tandy Corp. SIC: 5065—Electronic Parts &
Equipment Nec.

Elizabethtown

★ 74488 ★   Danaher Controls
Hwy. 87 N
Elizabethtown, NC 28337
(910)862-2511
Officer: J. R. Thompson, Manager.
Ultimate Parent: Danaher Corp. SIC:
3824—Fluid Meters & Counting Devices.

★ 74489 ★   First-Citizens Bank &
Trust Co.
301 W. Broad St.
Elizabethtown, NC 28337-9577
(910)862-4027
Location Type: Branch office. Officer:
Carol Edwards, Manager. Ultimate Parent:
First Citizens Bancshares, Inc. SIC: 6021—
National Commercial Banks.

★ 74490 ★   Golden Peanut Co.
Elizabethtown, NC 28337
(919)862-4528
Ultimate Parent: Archer Daniels Midland
Co. SIC: 5159—Farm-Product Raw
Materials Nec.

★ 74491 ★   Radio Shack
Westgate Plz.
Elizabethtown, NC 28337
(919)862-2628
Company Type: Division. Ultimate Parent:
Tandy Corp. SIC: 5719—Miscellaneous
Home Furnishings Stores.

★ 74492 ★   Stop & Shop Food
Mart
Hwy. 701 N
Elizabethtown, NC 28337
(910)862-2366
Ultimate Parent: Stop & Shop. SIC: 5411—
Grocery Stores.

★ 74493 ★   Veeder-Root Co.
2100 W. Broad St.
Elizabethtown, NC 28337
Ultimate Parent: Danaher Corp. SIC:
3824—Fluid Meters & Counting Devices.

★ 74494 ★   West Point Pepperell
Hwy. 87 N
Elizabethtown, NC 28337
Location Type: Plant. Ultimate Parent:
West Point Stevens. SIC: 2259—Knitting
Mills Nec.

★ 74495 ★   Westpoint Pepperell
Hwy. 87 North
Elizabethtown, NC 28337
Location Type: Plant. Ultimate Parent:
West Point Stevens. SIC: 2861—Gum &
Wood Chemicals.

Elkin

★ 74496 ★   Branch Banking &
Trust Co.
290 N. Bridge
Elkin, NC 28621-3405
(910)835-5597
Company Type: Subsidiary. Location
Type: Branch office. Ultimate Parent:
Southern National Corp. SIC: 6021—
National Commercial Banks.

★ 74497 ★   McDonalds of Elkin
Elkmont Shopping Ctr.
Elkin, NC 28621
(919)835-6048
Ultimate Parent: McDonald's.
SIC: 5812—Eating Places.

★ 74498 ★   Weyerhaeuser Co.
Hwy. 268
Elkin, NC 28621
(910)835-5100
Officer: David Craft, Manager. Ultimate
Parent: Weyerhaeuser Co. SIC: 2421—
Sawmills & Planing Mills—General.

★ 74499 ★   Weyerhaeuser Co.
Rte. 3 Off Sr 1141 Gentry Ln.
Elkin, NC 28621
Ultimate Parent: Weyerhaeuser Co. SIC:
2493—Reconstituted Wood Products.

Ellenboro

★ 74500 ★ Branch Banking & Trust Co.
Hwy. 74 & Glenn St.
Ellenboro, NC 28040-9543
(704)453-7306
Company Type: Subsidiary. **Location Type:** Branch office. **Officer:** Donna Price, Mgr. **Ultimate Parent:** Southern National Corp. **SIC:** 6021—National Commercial Banks.

Elm City

★ 74501 ★ Branch Banking & Trust Co.
117 Main St.
Elm City, NC 27822-9202
(919)236-4321
Company Type: Subsidiary. **Location Type:** Branch office. **Officer:** Janice P. Jenkins, Mgr. **Ultimate Parent:** Southern National Corp. **SIC:** 6021—National Commercial Banks.

★ 74502 ★ Donnelley Directory
1000 Donnelley Dr.
Elm City, NC 27822
(919)236-4301
Ultimate Parent: R. R. Donnelley & Sons. **SIC:** 7319—Advertising Nec.

Enfield

★ 74503 ★ Branch Banking & Trust Co.
205 Whitfield St.
Enfield, NC 27823-1341
(919)445-5186
Company Type: Subsidiary. **Location Type:** Branch office. **Officer:** William A. Spiegelberg, Mgr. **Ultimate Parent:** Southern National Corp. **SIC:** 6021—National Commercial Banks.

Enka

★ 74504 ★ APAC
Smoky Mountain Hwy.
Enka, NC 28728
(704)665-1180
Officer: Otis Vaughn, President. **Ultimate Parent:** Ashland Oil. **SIC:** 2951—Asphalt Paving Mixtures & Blocks.

★ 74505 ★ BASF Corp.
Sand Hill Rd.
Enka, NC 28728
(704)667-7110
Location Type: Branch office. **Ultimate Parent:** BASF Corp. **SIC:** 3695—Magnetic & Optical Recording Media. **Employee Count:** 1200.

★ 74506 ★ BASF Corp.
Fibers
Sand Hill Rd.
Enka, NC 28728
Company Type: Division. **Ultimate Parent:** BASF Corp. **SIC:** 2824—Organic Fibers—Noncellulosic; 2821—Plastics Materials & Resins.

★ 74507 ★ Food Lion
Westridge Market Pl
Enka, NC 28728
(704)667-8785
Ultimate Parent: Food Lion. **SIC:** 5411—Grocery Stores.

★ 74508 ★ Food Lion Inc.
Westridge Market Pl
Enka, NC 28728
(704)667-8785
Ultimate Parent: Food Lion. **SIC:** 5411—Grocery Stores.

★ 74509 ★ Pizza Hut
163 Smokey Park Hw
Enka, NC 28728
(704)667-3500
Ultimate Parent: Pepsico. **SIC:** 5812—Eating Places.

Eureka

★ 74510 ★ Branch Banking & Trust Co.
Main St.
Eureka, NC 27830
(919)242-4691
Company Type: Subsidiary. **Location Type:** Branch office. **Ultimate Parent:** Southern National Corp. **SIC:** 6021—National Commercial Banks.

Fairmont

★ 74511 ★ Branch Banking & Trust Co.
104 W. Thompson St.
Fairmont, NC 28340-1632
(910)628-7711
Company Type: Subsidiary. **Location Type:** Branch office. **Officer:** Ty Leggette, Manager. **Ultimate Parent:** Southern National Corp. **SIC:** 6021—National Commercial Banks.

Faison

★ 74512 ★ Branch Banking & Trust Co.
100 S. Railroad St.
Faison, NC 28341
(910)267-2031
Company Type: Subsidiary. **Location Type:** Branch office. **Officer:** David H. Rose, Mgr. **Ultimate Parent:** Southern National Corp. **SIC:** 6021—National Commercial Banks.

★ 74513 ★ Cates Charles F. & Sons Inc.
205 Railroad St.
Faison, NC 28341
(919)267-4711
Company Type: Subsidiary. **Officer:** William Hennessee, President. **Ultimate Parent:** Dean Foods. **SIC:** 2035—Pickles, Sauces & Salad Dressings. **Employee Count:** 475. **Sales:** 68.6 M.

★ 74514 ★ Charles F. Cates & Son Inc.
221 NW Ctr. St.
PO Box 158
Faison, NC 28341
(910)267-4711 **Fax:** (910)267-1995
Company Type: Subsidiary. **Officer:** W. L. Hennessee Jr., President. **Ultimate Parent:** Dean Foods. **SIC:** 2035—Pickles, Sauces & Salad Dressings.

★ 74515 ★ Charles F. Cates & Sons
221 NW Ctr. St.
PO Box 158
Faison, NC 28341
Location Type: Plant. **Officer:** Vic Beverage, Plant Manager. **Ultimate Parent:** Dean Foods. **SIC:** 2035—Pickles, Sauces & Salad Dressings.

★ 74516 ★ Piggly Wiggly
Railroad St.
Faison, NC 28341
(919)267-5251
Ultimate Parent: Bruno's. **SIC:** 5411—Grocery Stores.

Fallston

★ 74517 ★ Branch Banking & Trust Co.
Main St.
Fallston, NC 28042
(704)538-8509
Company Type: Subsidiary. **Location Type:** Branch office. **Officer:** Pearleen Hastings, Mgr. **Ultimate Parent:** Southern National Corp. **SIC:** 6021—National Commercial Banks.

Farmville

★ 74518 ★ Branch Banking & Trust Co.
110 W. Church St.
Farmville, NC 27828-9300
(919)753-5366
Company Type: Subsidiary. **Location Type:** Branch office. **Officer:** William R. Flowers, Mgr. **Ultimate Parent:** Southern National Corp. **SIC:** 6021—National Commercial Banks.

★ 74519 ★ Branch Banking & Trust Co.
US 264
Farmville, NC 27828
(919)758-5366
Ultimate Parent: Southern National Corp. **SIC:** 6022—State Commercial Banks.

★ 74520 ★ Collins & Aikman Corp.
Specialty Fabrics Div.
Hwy. 264 Bypass
Farmville, NC 27828-0208
Company Type: Division. **Ultimate Parent:** Collins & Aikman Group. **SIC:** 2258—Lace & Warp Knit Fabric Mills.

★ 74521 ★ Pizza Hut
Hwy. 264 Bypass
Farmville, NC 27828
(919)753-2641
Ultimate Parent: Pepsico. **SIC:** 5812—Eating Places.

★ 74522 ★ Southern States Co-Op. Inc. Feed Mill
S. Fields St. Extension
Farmville, NC 27828
Ultimate Parent: Southern. **SIC:** 2048—Prepared Feeds Nec.

Fayetteville

★ 74523 ★ Westinghouse Electric
2900 Doc Bennett Rd.
Fayetville, NC 28306
(910)483-2222
Officer: Frank Carpenter, Manager. **Ultimate Parent:** Westinghouse Electric Corp. **SIC:** 3625—Relays & Industrial Controls.

★ 74524 ★ American Family Life Assurance
111 Lamon St.
Fayetteville, NC 28301
(919)323-8357
Ultimate Parent: American Family Life Assurance Co. **SIC:** 6411—Insurance Agents, Brokers & Service.

★ 74525 ★ American General Finance
201 S. McPherson Church Rd.
Fayetteville, NC 28303-4974
(919)864-8112
Officer: Kim Lund. **Ultimate Parent:** American General Corp. **SIC:** 6141—Personal Credit Institutions.

★ 74526 ★ American General Finance
2850 Village Dr., Ste. 104
Fayetteville, NC 28304-3864
(919)323-4019
Location Type: Branch office. **Officer:** Judy A. Smith. **Ultimate Parent:** American General Corp. **SIC:** 6141—Personal Credit Institutions.

★ 74527 ★ American General Finance Inc.
2850 Village Dr., Ste. 104
Fayetteville, NC 28304-3864
(919)323-4019
Location Type: Branch office. **Officer:** Judy A. Smith. **Ultimate Parent:** American General Corp. **SIC:** 6141—Personal Credit Institutions.

★ 74528 ★ American General Finance Inc.
201 S. McPherson church Rd.
Fayetteville, NC 28303-4974
(919)864-8112
Location Type: Branch office. **Officer:** Kim Lund. **Ultimate Parent:** American General Corp. **SIC:** 6141—Personal Credit Institutions.

★ 74529 ★ Beneficial Management Corp. America
214 Fairway Dr.
Fayetteville, NC 28305-5512
(919)323-9605
Officer: Edward Lega. **Ultimate Parent:** Beneficial. **SIC:** 6141—Personal Credit Institutions.

★ 74530 ★ Beneficial North Carolina Inc.
6900 Cliffdale Rd., Ste. 221
Fayetteville, NC 28314-2872
Location Type: Branch office. **Officer:** Jerry Hudgins. **Ultimate Parent:** Beneficial. **SIC:** 6141—Personal Credit Institutions; 6162—Mortgage Bankers & Correspondents.

★ 74531 ★ BFI Waste Systems
815 Cedar Creek Rd. A
Fayetteville, NC 28301-6507
(919)485-2122
Ultimate Parent: Browning-Ferris Industries. **SIC:** 4953—Refuse Systems.

★ 74532 ★ Black & Decker Corp.
Hwy. 301 S
Fayetteville, NC 28306
(919)423-3100
Company Type: Branch. **Officer:** Kent Robertson. **Ultimate Parent:** Black & Decker Corp. **SIC:** 3546—Power-Driven Handtools; 3544—Special Dies, Tools, Jigs & Fixtures.

★ 74533 ★ Black & Decker Corp.
Power Tools Group
Hwy. 301 S. PO Box 64429
Fayetteville, NC 28306
Ultimate Parent: Black & Decker Corp. **SIC:** 3546—Power-Driven Handtools.

★ 74534 ★ Black & Decker Inc.
Power Tools Group
Hwy. 301 S. PO Box 64429
Fayetteville, NC 28306
Ultimate Parent: Black & Decker Corp. **SIC:** 3546—Power-Driven Handtools.

★ 74535 ★ Borden Inc.
Chemical
1411 Industrial Dr.
Fayetteville, NC 28302
Company Type: Division. **Ultimate Parent:** Borden, Inc. **SIC:** 2819—Industrial Inorganic Chemicals Nec; 2869—Industrial Organic Chemicals Nec; 2821—Plastics Materials & Resins.

★ 74536 ★ Borden Inc.
Package & Industrial Products
1411 Industrial Dr.
Fayetteville, NC 28302
Company Type: Division. **Ultimate Parent:** Borden, Inc. **SIC:** 2819—Industrial Inorganic Chemicals Nec; 2869—Industrial Organic Chemicals Nec; 2821—Plastics Materials & Resins.

★ 74537 ★ Borden Inc.
Package & Industrial Products
1411 Industrial Dr.
Fayetteville, NC 28302
Ultimate Parent: Borden, Inc. **SIC:** 2819—Industrial Inorganic Chemicals Nec; 2869—Industrial Organic Chemicals Nec; 2821—Plastics Materials & Resins.

★ 74538 ★ Borden Packaging & Industrial Products
1411 Industrial Dr.
Fayetteville, NC 28301
(910)483-1311
Location Type: Plant. **Officer:** Bill Floyd, Plant Manager. **Ultimate Parent:** Borden, Inc. **SIC:** 2821—Plastics Materials & Resins; 2843—Surface Active Agents; 2869—Industrial Organic Chemicals Nec; 2891—Adhesives & Sealants.

★ 74539 ★ Branch Banking & Trust Co.
Westwood Shop Ctr.
Fayetteville, NC 28314
(919)864-1007
Ultimate Parent: Southern National Corp. **SIC:** 6099—Functions Related to Deposit Banking.

★ 74540 ★ Branch Banking & Trust Co.
US Hwy. 401 N
Fayetteville, NC 28311-9353
(910)483-3195
Company Type: Subsidiary. **Location Type:** Branch office. **Ultimate Parent:** Southern National Corp. **SIC:** 6021—National Commercial Banks.

★ **74541** ★ **Branch Banking & Trust Co.**
121 Hay St.
Fayetteville, NC 28301-5649
(910)483-3193
Company Type: Subsidiary. **Location Type:** Branch office. **Officer:** Albert F. Beard III, Mgr. **Ultimate Parent:** Southern National Corp. **SIC:** 6021—National Commercial Banks.

★ **74542** ★ **Branch Banking & Trust Co.**
Marganton Rd.
Fayetteville, NC 28302
(910)483-3195
Company Type: Subsidiary. **Location Type:** Branch office. **Ultimate Parent:** Southern National Corp. **SIC:** 6021—National Commercial Banks.

★ **74543** ★ **Branch Banking & Trust Co.**
1214 Marganton Rd.
Fayetteville, NC 28305-4758
(910)483-3193
Company Type: Subsidiary. **Location Type:** Branch office. **Ultimate Parent:** Southern National Corp. **SIC:** 6021—National Commercial Banks.

★ **74544** ★ **Coast to Coast Express**
210 N. Eastern Blvd.
Fayetteville, NC 28301
(919)483-3444
Ultimate Parent: Servistar Corp. **SIC:** 4213—Trucking Except Local.

★ **74545** ★ **Diebold Inc.**
2801 Ramsey St.
Fayetteville, NC 28301
(919)822-1200
Ultimate Parent: Diebold, Inc. **SIC:** 3499—Fabricated Metal Products Nec.

★ **74546** ★ **Exxon Shop**
I S. 95
Fayetteville, NC 28306
(919)323-1597
Ultimate Parent: Exxon. **SIC:** 5411—Grocery Stores.

★ **74547** ★ **First-Citizens Bank & Trust Co.**
3626 N. Main St.
Fayetteville, NC 28348-1937
(910)424-3938
Location Type: Branch office. **Ultimate Parent:** First Citizens Bancshares, Inc. **SIC:** 6021—National Commercial Banks.

★ **74548** ★ **First-Citizens Bank & Trust Co.**
306 Cross Creek Mall
Fayetteville, NC 28302
(910)483-2141
Location Type: Branch office. **Ultimate Parent:** First Citizens Bancshares, Inc. **SIC:** 6021—National Commercial Banks.

★ **74549** ★ **First-Citizens Bank & Trust Co.**
2617 Bragg Blvd.
Fayetteville, NC 28303-4143
(910)483-2141
Location Type: Branch office. **Ultimate Parent:** First Citizens Bancshares, Inc. **SIC:** 6021—National Commercial Banks.

★ **74550** ★ **First-Citizens Bank & Trust Co.**
126 Broadfoot Ave.
Fayetteville, NC 28305-5002
(910)483-2141
Location Type: Branch office. **Ultimate Parent:** First Citizens Bancshares, Inc. **SIC:** 6021—National Commercial Banks.

★ **74551** ★ **First-Citizens Bank & Trust Co.**
2498 Gillespie St.
Fayetteville, NC 28306-3023
(910)483-2141
Location Type: Branch office. **Ultimate Parent:** First Citizens Bancshares, Inc. **SIC:** 6021—National Commercial Banks.

★ **74552** ★ **First-Citizens Bank & Trust Co.**
1490 Clinton Rd.
Fayetteville, NC 28301-5324
(910)483-2141
Location Type: Branch office. **Ultimate**

Parent: First Citizens Bancshares, Inc. **SIC:** 6021—National Commercial Banks.

★ **74553** ★ **First-Citizens Bank & Trust Co.**
1701 Owen Dr.
Fayetteville, NC 28304-3418
(910)483-2141
Location Type: Branch office. **Ultimate Parent:** First Citizens Bancshares, Inc. **SIC:** 6021—National Commercial Banks.

★ **74554** ★ **First-Citizens Bank & Trust Co.**
3604 Ramsey St.
Fayetteville, NC 28311-7646
(910)483-2141
Location Type: Branch office. **Ultimate Parent:** First Citizens Bancshares, Inc. **SIC:** 6021—National Commercial Banks.

★ **74555** ★ **First-Citizens Bank & Trust Co.**
109 Green St.
Fayetteville, NC 28301-5044
(910)483-2141
Location Type: Branch office. **Officer:** Charles I. Stewart, Area Vice President. **Ultimate Parent:** First Citizens Bancshares, Inc. **SIC:** 6021—National Commercial Banks.

★ **74556** ★ **Food Lion**
4120 Raeford Rd.
Fayetteville, NC 28304
(919)323-4591
Ultimate Parent: Food Lion. **SIC:** 5411—Grocery Stores.

★ **74557** ★ **Full Circle**
54 Reilly Rd.
Fayetteville, NC 28303
(919)867-6337
Ultimate Parent: Cenex.

★ **74558** ★ **Greyhound Bus Lines**
324 Person St.
Fayetteville, NC 28301
(919)483-6107
Ultimate Parent: Greyhound Lines Inc. **SIC:** 4111—Local & Suburban Transit.

★ **74559** ★ **Hertz Rent-A-Car**
Hwy. 301 Airport Rd.
Fayetteville, NC 28306
(919)483-8808
Ultimate Parent: Hertz. **SIC:** 7514—Passenger Car Rental.

★ **74560** ★ **Hertz Rent-A-Car Licensee**
Airport Rd.
Fayetteville, NC 28306
(919)484-1451
Ultimate Parent: Hertz. **SIC:** 7514—Passenger Car Rental.

★ **74561** ★ **Kelly-Springfield Tire Co.**
6650 Ramsey St.
Fayetteville, NC 28311-9990
Ultimate Parent: Goodyear Tire & Rubber. **SIC:** 3011—Tires & Inner Tubes.

★ **74562** ★ **Kentucky Fried Chicken**
Hwy. 301
Fayetteville, NC 28306
(919)323-1744
Ultimate Parent: Pepsico. **SIC:** 5812—Eating Places.

★ **74563** ★ **Kroger Sav on**
3650 Raleigh Rd.
Fayetteville, NC 28311
(919)822-3903
Ultimate Parent: Kroger. **SIC:** 5499—Miscellaneous Food Stores.

★ **74564** ★ **Mary Kay Cosmetics**
544 Anson Dr.
Fayetteville, NC 28311
(919)488-6653
Ultimate Parent: Mary Kay Cosmetics. **SIC:** 5999—Miscellaneous Retail Stores Nec.

★ **74565** ★ **McDonalds Hamburgers**
2820 Ramsey St.
Fayetteville, NC 28301
(919)488-4773
Ultimate Parent: McDonald's. **SIC:** 5812—Eating Places.

★ **74566** ★ **McDonalds Hamburgers**
1903 Owen Dr.
Fayetteville, NC 28306
(919)485-1027
Ultimate Parent: McDonald's. **SIC:** 5812—Eating Places.

★ **74567** ★ **Monsanto Co.**
Cedar Creek Rd.
Fayetteville, NC 28301
Ultimate Parent: Monsanto. **SIC:** 2879—Agricultural Chemicals Nec.

★ **74568** ★ **Monsanto Co./ Agricultural Grp**
Cedar Creek Rd.
Fayetteville, NC 28301
(919)323-3300
Officer: H. Van Bell. **Ultimate Parent:** Monsanto. **SIC:** 2879—Agricultural Chemicals Nec; 5169—Chemicals & Allied Products Nec.

★ **74569** ★ **National Home Life Assur Co.**
111 Lamon St.
Fayetteville, NC 28301
(919)484-8116
Ultimate Parent: National Home Life. **SIC:** 6411—Insurance Agents, Brokers & Service.

★ **74570** ★ **Pepsi-Cola Seven-Up**
131 Pepsi Ln.
Fayetteville, NC 28301
(910)483-4181
Ultimate Parent: Pepsico. **SIC:** 2086—Bottled & Canned Soft Drinks.

★ **74571** ★ **Piggly Wiggly**
3016 Murchison Rd.
Fayetteville, NC 28301
(919)488-7120
Ultimate Parent: Bruno's. **SIC:** 5411—Grocery Stores.

★ **74572** ★ **Pizza Hut**
3404 Ramsey St.
Fayetteville, NC 28311
(919)822-0580
Ultimate Parent: Pepsico. **SIC:** 5812—Eating Places.

★ **74573** ★ **Qualex Inc.**
241 Tillinghast St.
Fayetteville, NC 28301
(910)483-4658
Officer: Joel Allen, Manager. **Ultimate Parent:** Eastman Kodak. **SIC:** 3861—Photographic Equipment & Supplies.

★ **74574** ★ **Radio Shack**
115 Westwood Shopping Ctr.
Fayetteville, NC 28314
(919)864-4344
Company Type: Division. **Ultimate Parent:** Tandy Corp. **SIC:** 5731—Radio, Television & Electronics Stores.

★ **74575** ★ **Radio Shack**
Westwood Shopping Ctr.
Fayetteville, NC 28302
(919)864-4344
Company Type: Division. **Ultimate Parent:** Tandy Corp. **SIC:** 5065—Electronic Parts & Equipment Nec.

★ **74576** ★ **Stevcoknit Fabrics Co.**
902 Southern Ave.
Fayetteville, NC 28306
(910)323-5350
Officer: Frank Fisher, Manager. **Ultimate Parent:** Delta Woodside Industries. **SIC:** 2257—Weft Knit Fabric Mills; 2399—Fabricated Textile Products Nec.

★ **74577** ★ **Trailways Bus Systems**
304 Gillespie St.
Fayetteville, NC 28301
(919)483-2137
Ultimate Parent: Greyhound Lines Inc. **SIC:** 4111—Local & Suburban Transit.

★ **74578** ★ **Underwriters Adjusting Co.**
711 Executive Pl
Fayetteville, NC 28305
(919)323-0015
Ultimate Parent: Continental. **SIC:** 6411—Insurance Agents, Brokers & Service.

★ **74579** ★ **Wachovia Bank Building**
225 Green St.
Fayetteville, NC 28301
(919)323-0510
Ultimate Parent: Wachovia Corp. **SIC:** 6512—Nonresidential Building Operators.

★ **74580** ★ **Wachovia Bank & Trust**
2939 Village Dr.
Fayetteville, NC 28304
(919)323-0510
Ultimate Parent: Wachovia Corp. **SIC:** 6022—State Commercial Banks.

★ **74581** ★ **Wachovia Bank & Trust Co. N**
565 Cross Creek Mall
Fayetteville, NC 28303
(919)323-0510
Ultimate Parent: Wachovia Corp. **SIC:** 6022—State Commercial Banks.

★ **74582** ★ **Wal Mart**
372 Ramsey St.
Fayetteville, NC 28301
(919)488-1800
Ultimate Parent: Wal-Mart Stores, Inc.

★ **74583** ★ **Wellman Inc.**
Cedar Creek Rd.
Fayetteville, NC 28302
(910)323-3535
Officer: Ole Sorensen, Plant Manager. **Ultimate Parent:** Wellman Inc. **SIC:** 2821—Plastics Materials & Resins.

★ **74584** ★ **Wells Manufacturing Co. Inc.**
5655 Bragg Blvd.
Fayetteville, NC 28303
(919)867-1501
Ultimate Parent: UIS. **SIC:** 2451—Mobile Homes.

★ **74585** ★ **Westinghouse Electric Corp.**
2900 Doc Bennett Rd.
Fayetteville, NC 28306
Ultimate Parent: Westinghouse Electric Corp. **SIC:** 3625—Relays & Industrial Controls.

★ **74586** ★ **Wewstern Publishing Co.**
107 Tom Starling Rd.
Fayetteville, NC 28306
(910)424-1111
Officer: Mike Adams, Executive Director. **Ultimate Parent:** Western Publishing Group. **SIC:** 3944—Games, Toys & Children's Vehicles.

★ **74587** ★ **World Book Educational Products**
200 Owen Dr.
Fayetteville, NC 28304-3414
(919)483-3131
Location Type: Branch office. **Officer:** Betty E. White. **Ultimate Parent:** Berkshire Hathaway. **SIC:** 5963—Direct Selling Establishments; 5942—Book Stores.

Fletcher

★ **74588** ★ **Branch Banking & Trust Co.**
Asheville Hwy. 25
Fletcher, NC 28732
(704)684-0478
Company Type: Subsidiary. **Location Type:** Branch office. **Officer:** Linda Waters, Mgr. **Ultimate Parent:** Southern National Corp. **SIC:** 6021—National Commercial Banks.

★ **74589** ★ **Eaton Corp.**
Cane Creek Industrial Pk.
Fletcher, NC 28732
(704)684-3501
Officer: Kent Ammerman, Manager. **Ultimate Parent:** Eaton Corp. **SIC:** 3714—Motor Vehicle Parts & Accessories.

★ **74590** ★ **Eaton Corp.**
Fluid Power Div.
Came Creek Industrial Pk.
Fletcher, NC 28732
(704)684-3501
Company Type: Division. **Location Type:** Plant. **Officer:** Janet Mann, Controller. **Ultimate Parent:** Eaton Corp. **SIC:** 3714—Motor Vehicle Parts & Accessories.

★ **74591** ★ **Emery Worldwide**
Hwy. 25
Fletcher, NC 28732
(704)684-9891
Ultimate Parent: Consolidated Freightways. **SIC:** 4512—Air Transportation—Scheduled.

★ **74592** ★ **Ralph Wilson Plastics Co.**
Cane Creek Industrial Park
Fletcher, NC 28732
Ultimate Parent: Premark International. **SIC:** 3083—Laminated Plastics Plate & Sheet.

★ **74593** ★ **Ralph Wilson Plastics Co.**
L A White Dr.
Fletcher, NC 28732
(704)684-2351
Officer: Dale Kaulfus, Manager. **Ultimate Parent:** Premark International. **SIC:** 3083—Laminated Plastics Plate & Sheet; 3089—Plastics Products Nec.

★ **74594** ★ **Taylor Environmental Instruments**
280 Crane Creek Rd.
PO Box 1349
Fletcher, NC 28732
(704)684-5178 **Fax:** (704)687-1689
Company Type: Subsidiary. **Officer:** Robert E. Fitch, President. **Ultimate Parent:** Figgie International.

Forest City

★ **74595** ★ **A. G. Industries, Inc.**
30 Pine St.
Forest City, NC 28043-4502
Ultimate Parent: American Greetings. **SIC:** 2541—Wood Partitions & Fixtures; 2541—Wood Partitions & Fixtures.

★ **74596** ★ **Aeroquip Corp.**
Daniel Rd. Daniel Rd.
Forest City, NC 28043
Ultimate Parent: Trinova Corp. **SIC:** 3052—Rubber & Plastics Hose & Belting.

★ **74597** ★ **Aeroquip Corp.**
Rte. 7, Box 96
Forest City, NC 28043
Ultimate Parent: Trinova Corp. **SIC:** 3052—Rubber & Plastics Hose & Belting.

★ **74598** ★ **Aeroquip Corp.**
Rte. 7, Box 96 (Daniel Road)
Forest City, NC 28043-9612
Ultimate Parent: Trinova Corp. **SIC:** 3052—Rubber & Plastics Hose & Belting.

★ **74599** ★ **Aeroquip Corp.**
RR 7, Box 96
Forest City, NC 28043
(704)286-4157
Officer: Brent J. Bauer, Manager. **Ultimate Parent:** Trinova Corp. **SIC:** 3494—Valves & Pipe Fittings Nec.

★ **74600** ★ **A.G. Industries, Inc.**
30 Pine St.
Forest City, NC 28043
(704)245-9871 **Fax:** (704)245-4514
Officer: Ronald D. Miller, President. **Ultimate Parent:** American Greetings.

★ **74601** ★ **Branch Banking & Trust Co.**
333 E. Main St.
Forest City, NC 28043-3127
(704)245-9827
Company Type: Subsidiary. **Location Type:** Branch office. **Officer:** J.L. Harrill, Mgr. **Ultimate Parent:** Southern National Corp. **SIC:** 6021—National Commercial Banks.

★ **74602** ★ **Branch Banking & Trust Co.**
Trinity Mall Shopping Ctr.
Forest City, NC 28043
(908)566-2323
Company Type: Subsidiary. **Location**

Type: Branch office. **Ultimate Parent:** Southern National Corp. **SIC:** 6021—National Commercial Banks.

★ **74603** ★ **Burlington Industries Inc.**
Old Caroleen Rd.
Forest city, NC 28043
(704)245-6411
Officer: Gib Bernhardt, Manager. **Ultimate Parent:** Burlington Industries, Equity. **SIC:** 2231—Broadwoven Fabric Mills—Wool; 2262—Finishing Plants—Manmade; 2281—Yarn Spinning Mills.

★ **74604** ★ **First-Citizens Bank & Trust Co.**
109 E. Main St.
Forest City, NC 28043-3125
(704)245-7266
Location Type: Branch office. **Officer:** J. Michael Cline, Area Vice President. **Ultimate Parent:** First Citizens Bancshares, Inc. **SIC:** 6021—National Commercial Banks.

★ **74605** ★ **First-Citizens Bank & Trust Co.**
Tri City Mall
Forest City, NC 28043
(704)245-7266
Location Type: Branch office. **Ultimate Parent:** First Citizens Bancshares, Inc. **SIC:** 6021—National Commercial Banks.

★ **74606** ★ **A G Industries Inc.**
30 Pine St.
Forest City, NC 28043-4517
(704)245-9871
Location Type: Branch office. **Officer:** Mel Bunch. **Ultimate Parent:** American Greetings. **SIC:** 2541—Wood Partitions & Fixtures; 2542—Partitions & Fixtures Except Wood; 5046—Commercial Equipment Nec.

★ **74607** ★ **Kentucky Fried Chicken**
Hwy. 74 Bypass
Forest City, NC 28043
(704)245-5716
Ultimate Parent: Pepsico. **SIC:** 5812—Eating Places.

★ **74608** ★ **Novacor Chemicals Inc.**
Vance St.
Forest City, NC 28043
(704)245-8721
Ultimate Parent: Baxter International. **SIC:** 5162—Plastics Materials & Basic Shapes.

★ **74609** ★ **Parker Hannifan Corp.**
Pine St.
Forest City, NC 28043
Ultimate Parent: Parker Hannifin. **SIC:** 3494—Valves & Pipe Fittings Nec.

★ **74610** ★ **Parker-Hannifin Corp.**
Pine St.
Forest City, NC 28043
Ultimate Parent: Parker Hannifin. **SIC:** 3494—Valves & Pipe Fittings Nec.

★ **74611** ★ **Sara Lee Knit Products**
1205 W. Main St.
Forest City, NC 28043
Ultimate Parent: Sara Lee Corp. **SIC:** 2253—Knit Outerwear Mills.

Fort Bragg

★ **74612** ★ **First-Citizens Bank & Trust Co.**
Bldg. 4-2843
Rm. DB6
Fort Bragg, NC 28306
(910)497-6161
Location Type: Branch office. **Ultimate Parent:** First Citizens Bancshares, Inc. **SIC:** 6021—National Commercial Banks.

★ **74613** ★ **First-Citizens Bank & Trust Co.**
Pope Shopping Ctr.
Bldg. 356
Fort Bragg, NC 28307
(910)497-6161
Location Type: Branch office. **Ultimate**

Parent: First Citizens Bancshares, Inc. **SIC:** 6021—National Commercial Banks.

★ **74614** ★ **First-Citizens Bank & Trust Co.**
Bastogne Dr., Bldg. C5437
Fort Bragg, NC 28307
(910)497-6161
Location Type: Branch office. **Ultimate Parent:** First Citizens Bancshares, Inc. **SIC:** 6021—National Commercial Banks.

★ **74615** ★ **First-Citizens Bank & Trust Co.**
2nd St. & Gruber Rd.
Fort Bragg, NC 28307
(910)497-6161
Location Type: Branch office. **Ultimate Parent:** First Citizens Bancshares, Inc. **SIC:** 6021—National Commercial Banks.

★ **74616** ★ **First-Citizens Bank & Trust Co.**
Bldg. 41571, Reilly Rd.
Fort Bragg, NC 28307
(910)497-6161
Location Type: Branch office. **Officer:** Rudy Baker, Senior Vice President. **Ultimate Parent:** First Citizens Bancshares, Inc. **SIC:** 6021—National Commercial Banks.

★ **74617** ★ **First-Citizens Bank & Trust Co.**
S. Lucas St.
Bldg. 68950
Fort Bragg, NC 28307
(910)497-6161
Location Type: Branch office. **Ultimate Parent:** First Citizens Bancshares, Inc. **SIC:** 6021—National Commercial Banks.

★ **74618** ★ **Greyhound Bus Lines**
Woodruff Jacksn
Fort Bragg, NC 28307
(919)497-8746
Ultimate Parent: Greyhound Lines Inc. **SIC:** 4131—Intercity & Rural Bus Transportation.

Fountain

★ **74619** ★ **Branch Banking & Trust Co.**
Wilson & Jefferson Sts.
Fountain, NC 27829
(919)749-2221
Company Type: Subsidiary. **Location Type:** Branch office. **Officer:** Susan S. Owens, Mgr. **Ultimate Parent:** Southern National Corp. **SIC:** 6021—National Commercial Banks.

★ **74620** ★ **Branch Banking & Trust Co.**
E Wilson
Fountain, NC 27829
(919)749-2221
Ultimate Parent: Southern National Corp. **SIC:** 6022—State Commercial Banks.

Four Oaks

★ **74621** ★ **Federal Paper Board Co.**
4 Oaks Nc
Four Oaks, NC 27524
(919)963-3781
Ultimate Parent: Federal Paper Board. **SIC:** 0811—Timber Tracts.

Franklin

★ **74622** ★ **Belden/Cooper Industries Franklin Plant**
Hwy. 441 S.
Franklin, NC 28734
Ultimate Parent: Cooper Industries. **SIC:** 3699—Electrical Equipment & Supplies Nec.

★ **74623** ★ **Belden/Copper Industries Franklin Plant**
Hwy. 441 South PO Box 1119
Franklin, NC 28734
Ultimate Parent: Cooper Industries. **SIC:** 3357—Nonferrous Wiredrawing & Insulating.

★ **74624** ★ **Bi-Lo Store**
Macon Plz.
Franklin, NC 28734
(704)369-7056
Ultimate Parent: Penn Traffic. **SIC:** 5411—Grocery Stores.

★ **74625** ★ **First-Citizens Bank & Trust Co.**
530 Westgate Rd.
Franklin, NC 28734
(704)524-8978
Location Type: Branch office. **Ultimate Parent:** First Citizens Bancshares, Inc. **SIC:** 6021—National Commercial Banks.

★ **74626** ★ **First-Citizens Bank & Trust Co.**
3 Lolita St.
Franklin, NC 28734-2944
(704)524-8978
Location Type: Branch office. **Officer:** Ron L. Deke, Vice President. **Ultimate Parent:** First Citizens Bancshares, Inc. **SIC:** 6021—National Commercial Banks.

★ **74627** ★ **Nantahala Power & Light Co.**
PO Box 260
Franklin, NC 28734
(704)524-2121 **Fax:** (704)524-2121
Company Type: Subsidiary. **Ultimate Parent:** Allmerica Property & Casualty Companies Inc.

★ **74628** ★ **Nantahala Power Light Co.**
260 PO Box
Franklin, NC 28734
(704)524-2121
Ultimate Parent: Duke Power. **SIC:** 4911—Electric Services.

★ **74629** ★ **Nantahala Power & Light Co.**
17 W. Main St.
Franklin, NC 28734-3005
(704)524-2121
Company Type: Subsidiary. **Officer:** E. N. Hedgepeth, President. **Ultimate Parent:** Duke Power. **SIC:** 4911—Electric Services. **Employee Count:** 193. **Sales:** 60 M.

Franklinton

★ **74630** ★ **Burlington Industries Fabrics Inc.**
Louisburg Rd.
Franklinton, NC 27525
(919)494-2112
Ultimate Parent: Burlington Industries, Equity. **SIC:** 2399—Fabricated Textile Products Nec.

★ **74631** ★ **First-Citizens Bank & Trust Co.**
101 N. Main St.
Franklinton, NC 27525-1314
(919)494-2106
Location Type: Branch office. **Officer:** Spencer Renfrow, Assistant Vice President. **Ultimate Parent:** First Citizens Bancshares, Inc. **SIC:** 6021—National Commercial Banks.

Fremont

★ **74632** ★ **Branch Banking & Trust Co.**
111 E. Main St.
Fremont, NC 27830
(919)242-6011
Company Type: Subsidiary. **Location Type:** Branch office. **Ultimate Parent:** Southern National Corp. **SIC:** 6021—National Commercial Banks.

★ **74633** ★ **Branch Banking & Trust Co.**
129 E. Main St.
Fremont, NC 27830
(919)242-6176
Ultimate Parent: Southern National Corp. **SIC:** 6022—State Commercial Banks.

★ **74634** ★ **Branch Banking & Trust Co.**
Hwy. 222
Fremont, NC 27830
(919)242-4691
Ultimate Parent: Southern National Corp. **SIC:** 6022—State Commercial Banks.

Fuquay Varina

★ 74635 ★   Branch Banking & Trust Co.
210 N. Main St.
Fuquay Varina, NC 27526-1936
(919)552-5634
Company Type: Subsidiary. **Location Type:** Branch office. **Ultimate Parent:** Southern National Corp. **SIC:** 6021—National Commercial Banks.

★ 74636 ★   Branch Banking & Trust Co.
111 S. Main St.
Fuquay Varina, NC 27526-2220
(919)552-2222
Company Type: Subsidiary. **Location Type:** Branch office. **Officer:** Philip M. Bray, Mgr. **Ultimate Parent:** Southern National Corp. **SIC:** 6021—National Commercial Banks.

★ 74637 ★   Fibers Business Unit
200 Dickens Rd.
Fuquay Varina, NC 27526
(919)552-5667
Company Type: Subsidiary. **Officer:** Richard S. Roberts, President. **Ultimate Parent:** Guilford Mills Inc.

★ 74638 ★   Kentucky Fried Chicken
Hwy. 401 N
Fuquay Varina, NC 27526
(919)552-8209
Ultimate Parent: Pepsico. **SIC:** 5812—Eating Places.

★ 74639 ★   Raychem Corp.
8000 Purfoy Rd.
Fuquay Varina, NC 27526
(919)552-3811
Officer: Robert S. Teich, Manager. **Ultimate Parent:** Raychem Corp. **SIC:** 3086—Plastics Foam Products; 3089—Plastics Products Nec.

★ 74640 ★   Piggly Wiggly
101 Wake Chapel Rd.
Fuquay Varina, NC 27526
(919)552-5695
Ultimate Parent: Bruno's. **SIC:** 5411—Grocery Stores.

★ 74641 ★   Raychem Corp.
8000 Purfoy Rd. Box 259-A
Fuquay-Varina, NC 27526
Ultimate Parent: Raychem Corp. **SIC:** 3699—Electrical Equipment & Supplies Nec.

★ 74642 ★   Raychem Corp.
Rte. 4
Fuquay-Varina, NC 27526-3000
Ultimate Parent: Raychem Corp. **SIC:** 3000—Rubber & Miscellaneous Plastics Products.

Gamewell

★ 74643 ★   Kincaid Furniture Co. Plant 8
Rocky Rd. Hwy. 18
Gamewell, NC 28645
Ultimate Parent: La-Z-Boy Chair. **SIC:** 2511—Wood Household Furniture.

Garland

★ 74644 ★   Piggly Wiggly
Garland, NC 28441
(919)529-4081
Ultimate Parent: Bruno's. **SIC:** 5411—Grocery Stores.

Garner

★ 74645 ★   Branch Banking & Trust Co.
301 Vandora Springs Rd.
Garner, NC 27529-3531
(919)779-6705
Company Type: Subsidiary. **Location Type:** Branch office. **Ultimate Parent:** Southern National Corp. **SIC:** 6021—National Commercial Banks.

★ 74646 ★   First-Citizens Bank & Trust Co.
120 Aversboro Rd.
Garner, NC 27529
(919)755-7262
Location Type: Branch office. **Officer:** R. Larry Kittrell, Vice President. **Ultimate Parent:** First Citizens Bancshares, Inc. **SIC:** 6021—National Commercial Banks.

★ 74647 ★   Pizza Hut
3407 S. Wilmington St.
Garner, NC 27529
(919)772-8017
Ultimate Parent: Pepsico. **SIC:** 5812—Eating Places.

★ 74648 ★   Radio Shack
311 Tryon Rd.
Garner, NC 27529
(919)772-6696
Company Type: Division. **Ultimate Parent:** Tandy Corp. **SIC:** 5731—Radio, Television & Electronics Stores.

★ 74649 ★   Unijax Inc.
1070 Waterfield Dr. E
Garner, NC 27529
(919)779-9778
Officer: Bill Thomas, Manager. **Ultimate Parent:** Alco Standard Corp. **SIC:** 2677—Envelopes.

★ 74650 ★   Western Auto Supply Co.
336 Tryon Rd.
Garner, NC 27529
(919)772-9660
Ultimate Parent: Sears Roebuck & Co. **SIC:** 5531—Automobile & Home Supply Stores.

Gary

★ 74651 ★   Borg Warner Automotive
406 Gregson Dr.
Gary, NC 27511
(919)469-2900
Ultimate Parent: Borg Warner Automotive. **SIC:** 3663—Radio & T.V. Communications Equipment; 3679—Electronic Components Nec; 3714—Motor Vehicle Parts & Accessories.

Gastonia

★ 74652 ★   AMP Inc.
3120 Northwest Blvd.
Gastonia, NC 28052
(704)867-0271
Officer: Joe Waugh, Manager. **Ultimate Parent:** AMP Inc. **SIC:** 3643—Current-Carrying Wiring Devices; 3678—Electronic Connectors.

★ 74653 ★   AMP Inc.
1260 Shannon Bradley Rd.
Gastonia, NC 28052-1076
Ultimate Parent: AMP Inc. **SIC:** 3471—Plating & Polishing; 3678—Electronic Connectors.

★ 74654 ★   AMP Inc.
1260 Shannon Bradley Rd., Bldg. 101
Gastonia, NC 28052-1076
Ultimate Parent: AMP Inc. **SIC:** 3678—Electronic Connectors; 3643—Current-Carrying Wiring Devices.

★ 74655 ★   Amp Inc. - Bldg. 101
Shannon Bradley Rd.
Gastonia, NC 28052
Ultimate Parent: AMP Inc. **SIC:** 3678—Electronic Connectors; 3643—Current-Carrying Wiring Devices.

★ 74656 ★   Avery Dennison Co.
1640 Hargrove Ave.
Gastonia, NC 28052-1569
(704)867-8311
Officer: Keith Gaskill. **Ultimate Parent:** Avery Dennison Corp. **SIC:** 2671—Paper Coated & Laminated—Packaging; 5046—Commercial Equipment Nec; 5084—Industrial Machinery & Equipment.

★ 74657 ★   Branch Banking & Trust Co.
1207 Bessemer City Rd.
Gastonia, NC 28052-1103
(704)867-1813
Company Type: Subsidiary. **Location Type:** Branch office. **Officer:** Gloria Gordon,

Mgr. **Ultimate Parent:** Southern National Corp. **SIC:** 6021—National Commercial Banks.

★ 74658 ★   Branch Banking & Trust Co.
2831 S. York Rd.
Gastonia, NC
(704)864-2656
Company Type: Subsidiary. **Location Type:** Branch office. **Officer:** Verne Deason, Mgr. **Ultimate Parent:** Southern National Corp. **SIC:** 6021—National Commercial Banks.

★ 74659 ★   Branch Banking & Trust Co.
3070 Union Rd.
Gastonia, NC 28054-6921
(704)861-0250
Company Type: Subsidiary. **Location Type:** Branch office. **Officer:** Greg Van Dyke, Mgr. **Ultimate Parent:** Southern National Corp. **SIC:** 6021—National Commercial Banks.

★ 74660 ★   Branch Banking & Trust Co.
333 Garrison Blvd.
Gastonia, NC 28052-4070
(704)867-0284
Company Type: Subsidiary. **Location Type:** Branch office. **Officer:** Mark Rouse, Mgr. **Ultimate Parent:** Southern National Corp. **SIC:** 6021—National Commercial Banks.

★ 74661 ★   Branch Banking & Trust Co.
110 W. Wilson
Gastonia, NC 28054-8519
(704)866-6500
Company Type: Subsidiary. **Location Type:** Branch office. **Officer:** John A. Corbett, Mgr. **Ultimate Parent:** Southern National Corp. **SIC:** 6021—National Commercial Banks.

★ 74662 ★   Branch Banking & Trust Co.
649 New Hope Rd.
Gastonia, NC 28054-4046
(704)864-0381
Company Type: Subsidiary. **Location Type:** Branch office. **Ultimate Parent:** Southern National Corp. **SIC:** 6021—National Commercial Banks.

★ 74663 ★   Branch Banking & Trust Co.
Hwy. 274 & Union Rd.
Gastonia, NC 28054
(704)864-0381
Company Type: Subsidiary. **Location Type:** Branch office. **Ultimate Parent:** Southern National Corp. **SIC:** 6021—National Commercial Banks.

★ 74664 ★   Branch Banking & Trust Co.
401 E. Franklin Blvd.
Gastonia, NC 28054-7152
(704)864-0381
Company Type: Subsidiary. **Location Type:** Branch office. **Officer:** John C. Houser, Manager. **Ultimate Parent:** Southern National Corp. **SIC:** 6021—National Commercial Banks.

★ 74665 ★   Branch Banking & Trust Co.
120 S. New Hope Rd.
Gastonia, NC 28054
(704)864-4551
Ultimate Parent: Southern National Corp. **SIC:** 6099—Functions Related to Deposit Banking.

★ 74666 ★   Branch Banking & Trust Co.
3333 Union Rd.
Gastonia, NC 28056
(704)824-3587
Ultimate Parent: Southern National Corp. **SIC:** 6022—State Commercial Banks.

★ 74667 ★   Branch Banking & Trust Co.
2414 W. Franklin Blvd.
Gastonia, NC 28052
(704)867-1801
Ultimate Parent: Southern National Corp. **SIC:** 6099—Functions Related to Deposit Banking.

★ 74668 ★   Burlington Industries Inc.
1910 Hunt Ave.
Gastonia, NC 28054
(704)864-5797
Officer: Billy Faulk, Manager. **Ultimate Parent:** Burlington Industries, Equity. **SIC:** 2281—Yarn Spinning Mills.

★ 74669 ★   Burlington Industries Inc.
1627 Spencer Mountain Rd.
Gastonia, NC 28054
(704)824-2581
Officer: Don Church, Manager. **Ultimate Parent:** Burlington Industries, Equity. **SIC:** 2281—Yarn Spinning Mills; 2399—Fabricated Textile Products Nec.

★ 74670 ★   Burlington Industries/ Ranlo Plant
1627 Spencer Mountain Rd.
Gastonia, NC 28054-3000
(704)824-2581
Location Type: Branch office. **Officer:** Don Church. **Ultimate Parent:** Burlington Industries, Equity. **SIC:** 2281—Yarn Spinning Mills; 2399—Fabricated Textile Products Nec.

★ 74671 ★   Casual Corner
Eastridge
Gastonia, NC 28054
(704)865-7471
Ultimate Parent: United States Shoe. **SIC:** 5621—Women's Clothing Stores.

★ 74672 ★   Coca Cola Bottling Co. Conso
620 W. Franklin Blvd.
Gastonia, NC 28052
(704)865-6236
Ultimate Parent: Coca-Cola Enterprises. **SIC:** 2086—Bottled & Canned Soft Drinks.

★ 74673 ★   Danaher Tool Group
1228 Isley Dr., Industrial Pk.
Gastonia, NC 28052
(704)866-8701
Officer: Mike Heath, Executive Director. **Ultimate Parent:** Danaher Corp. **SIC:** 3423—Hand & Edge Tools Nec; 3483—Ammunition Except for Small Arms.

★ 74674 ★   Easco Hand Tools Inc.
1228 Isley Dr.
Gastonia, NC 28053-1698
Ultimate Parent: Danaher Corp. **SIC:** 3423—Hand & Edge Tools Nec.

★ 74675 ★   Exxon Party Shoppe
3900 E. Franklin Blvd.
Gastonia, NC 28056
(704)824-2584
Ultimate Parent: Exxon. **SIC:** 5947—Gift, Novelty & Souvenir Shops.

★ 74676 ★   First-Citizens Bank & Trust Co.
1355-B E. Garrison Blvd.
Gastonia, NC 28054-5143
(704)864-5707
Location Type: Branch office. **Ultimate Parent:** First Citizens Bancshares, Inc. **SIC:** 6021—National Commercial Banks.

★ 74677 ★   First-Citizens Bank & Trust Co.
119 E. Virginia Ave.
Gastonia, NC 28016-2341
(704)629-4174
Location Type: Branch office. **Ultimate Parent:** First Citizens Bancshares, Inc. **SIC:** 6021—National Commercial Banks.

★ 74678 ★   First-Citizens Bank & Trust Co.
1502 S. York Rd.
Gastonia, NC 28052-6100
(704)865-6271
Location Type: Branch office. **Ultimate Parent:** First Citizens Bancshares, Inc. **SIC:** 6021—National Commercial Banks.

★ 74679 ★   First-Citizens Bank & Trust Co.
145 S. Marietta St.
Gastonia, NC 28052-4195
(704)865-6271
Location Type: Branch office. **Officer:** David L. Ollis, Vice President. **Ultimate Parent:** First Citizens Bancshares, Inc. **SIC:** 6021—National Commercial Banks.

★ 74680 ★ **FMC Corp.**
449 N. Cox Rd.
Gastonia, NC 28054
(704)868-5300
Officer: Paul Schroeder, President.
Ultimate Parent: FMC. **SIC:** 2819—
Industrial Inorganic Chemicals Nec; 2899—
Chemical Preparations Nec.

★ 74681 ★ **Food Lion**
3015 Union Rd.
Gastonia, NC 28056
(704)861-0567
Ultimate Parent: Food Lion. **SIC:** 5411—
Grocery Stores.

★ 74682 ★ **Greyhound Bus Lines**
127 W. Franklin Blvd.
Gastonia, NC 28052
(704)861-8523
Ultimate Parent: Greyhound Lines Inc. **SIC:**
4131—Intercity & Rural Bus Transportation.

★ 74683 ★ **Homelite**
Little Mountain Rd.
Gastonia, NC 28054
Officer: Peter Finamore. **Ultimate Parent:**
Textron. **SIC:** 3546—Power-Driven
Handtools.

★ 74684 ★ **PMS Consolidated**
1801 Bradbury Ct.
Gastonia, NC 28052
Ultimate Parent: M.A.Hanna. **SIC:** 3087—
Custom Compound of Purchased Resins.

★ 74685 ★ **Rhone-Poulenc Inc.**
Walsh Div.
207 Telegraph Dr.
Gastonia, NC 28056
Company Type: Division. **Ultimate Parent:**
Rhone-Poulenc Rorer. **SIC:** 2821—Plastics
Materials & Resins; 2899—Chemical
Preparations Nec; 2822—Synthetic Rubber.

★ 74686 ★ **Rite-Aid**
3019 Union Rd.
Gastonia, NC 28056
(704)867-9341
Ultimate Parent: Rite Aid. **SIC:** 5912—Drug
Stores & Proprietary Stores.

★ 74687 ★ **Rite Aid Disc
Pharmacies**
3019 Union Rd.
Gastonia, NC 28056
(704)867-1034
Ultimate Parent: Rite Aid. **SIC:** 5912—Drug
Stores & Proprietary Stores.

★ 74688 ★ **Ryder Truck Rental**
Wren
Gastonia, NC 28054
(704)866-7001
Ultimate Parent: Ryder System. **SIC:**
7513—Truck Rental & Leasing Without
Drivers.

★ 74689 ★ **Sara Lee Knit
Products**
1709 Industrial Pike
Gastonia, NC 28052
Location Type: Plant. **Ultimate Parent:**
Sara Lee Corp. **SIC:** 2322—Men's/Boys'
Underwear & Nightwear.

★ 74690 ★ **Uniroyal Chemical**
214 W. Ruby Ave.
Gastonia, NC 28054
(704)864-3411
Ultimate Parent: Uniroyal Chemical. **SIC:**
2899—Chemical Preparations Nec; 5169—
Chemicals & Allied Products Nec.

★ 74691 ★ **Wachovia Bank &
Trust**
110 E. Franklin Blvd.
Gastonia, NC 28052
(704)861-2500
Ultimate Parent: Wachovia Corp. **SIC:**
6099—Functions Related to Deposit
Banking.

★ 74692 ★ **Wachovia Bank &
Trust Co.**
Akers Ctr.
Gastonia, NC 28052
(704)865-6496
Ultimate Parent: Wachovia Corp. **SIC:**
6022—State Commercial Banks.

★ 74693 ★ **Westvaco Corp.**
601 N. Modena St.
Gastonia, NC 28054
(704)864-3261
Ultimate Parent: WestVaco Corp. **SIC:**
2657—Folding Paperboard Boxes.

★ 74694 ★ **Wix/Dana Corp. Allen
Plant**
2900 Northwest Blvd.
Gastonia, NC 28052
Ultimate Parent: Dana Corp. **SIC:** 3714—
Motor Vehicle Parts & Accessories.

★ 74695 ★ **Wix/Dana Corp. Dixon
Plant**
1601 S. Merietta St.
Gastonia, NC 28052
Ultimate Parent: Dana Corp. **SIC:** 3714—
Motor Vehicle Parts & Accessories.

★ 74696 ★ **Wix/Dana Corp.
(Dixow Plant)**
1601 South Marietta St.
Gastonia, NC 28052
Ultimate Parent: Dana Corp.

Gibsonville

★ 74697 ★ **Burlington Industries
Inc.**
Hwy. 87 N
Gibsonville, NC 27249
(919)584-0321
Officer: Robert Sills. **Ultimate Parent:**
Burlington Industries, Equity. **SIC:** 2399—
Fabricated Textile Products Nec.

★ 74698 ★ **First-Citizens Bank &
Trust Co.**
237 E. Main
Gibsonville, NC 27249-2440
(910)449-4011
Location Type: Branch office. **Officer:**
Leslie C. Johnston Jr., Vice President.
Ultimate Parent: First Citizens Bancshares,
Inc. **SIC:** 6021—National Commercial
Banks.

Goldsbora

★ 74699 ★ **Hevi Duty Electric**
2701 US Hwy. 117 S
Goldsboro, NC 27530
(919)734-8900
Ultimate Parent: General Signal. **SIC:**
3612—Transformers Except Electronic.

Goldsboro

★ 74700 ★ **American General
Finance**
317 N. Spence Ave.
Goldsboro, NC 27534-4346
(919)778-5850
Location Type: Branch office. **Officer:**
Cherry Brickhouse. **Ultimate Parent:**
American General Corp. **SIC:** 6141—
Personal Credit Institutions.

★ 74701 ★ **American General
Finance Inc.**
317 N. Spence Ave.
Goldsboro, NC 27534-4346
(919)778-5850
Location Type: Branch office. **Officer:**
Cherry Brickhouse. **Ultimate Parent:**
American General Corp. **SIC:** 6141—
Personal Credit Institutions.

★ 74702 ★ **Branch Banking &
Trust Co.**
2801 Cashwell
Goldsboro, NC 27532
(919)778-6700
Company Type: Subsidiary. **Location
Type:** Branch office. **Ultimate Parent:**
Southern National Corp. **SIC:** 6021—
National Commercial Banks.

★ 74703 ★ **Branch Banking &
Trust Co.**
1326 W. Graham St.
Goldsboro, NC 27530-3730
(919)735-7801
Company Type: Subsidiary. **Location
Type:** Branch office. **Officer:** J.L.
Edmundson, Mgr. **Ultimate Parent:**
Southern National Corp. **SIC:** 6021—
National Commercial Banks.

★ 74704 ★ **Branch Banking &
Trust Co.**
201 E. Ash St.
Goldsboro, NC 27530-3730
(919)751-5502
Company Type: Subsidiary. **Location
Type:** Branch office. **Ultimate Parent:**
Southern National Corp. **SIC:** 6021—
National Commercial Banks.

★ 74705 ★ **Branch Banking &
Trust Co.**
201 N. Spence Ave.
Goldsboro, NC 27534-4317
(919)734-2064
Company Type: Subsidiary. **Location
Type:** Branch office. **Ultimate Parent:**
Southern National Corp. **SIC:** 6021—
National Commercial Banks.

★ 74706 ★ **Branch Banking &
Trust Co.**
500 N. Berkeley Ave.
Goldsboro, NC 27534-3408
(919)731-7800
Company Type: Subsidiary. **Location
Type:** Branch office. **Ultimate Parent:**
Southern National Corp. **SIC:** 6021—
National Commercial Banks.

★ 74707 ★ **Branch Banking &
Trust Co.**
435 N. Berkeley Blvd.
Goldsboro, NC 27534
(919)778-0393
Ultimate Parent: Southern National Corp.
SIC: 6099—Functions Related to Deposit
Banking.

★ 74708 ★ **Branch Banking &
Trust Co.**
1907 E. Ash St.
Goldsboro, NC 27530
(919)735-7801
Ultimate Parent: Southern National Corp.
SIC: 6022—State Commercial Banks.

★ 74709 ★ **Branch Banking &
Trust Co.**
207 E. Ash St.
Goldsboro, NC 27530
(919)731-5800
Ultimate Parent: Southern National Corp.

★ 74710 ★ **Carolina Power &
Light Co.**
300 S. Ctr. St.
Goldsboro, NC 27530
(919)735-0121
Ultimate Parent: Carolina Power & Light
Co. **SIC:** 4911—Electric Services.

★ 74711 ★ **Carolina Power &
Light Co.**
300 S. Ctr. St.
Goldsboro, NC 27530
(919)735-0121
Ultimate Parent: Carolina Power & Light
Co. **SIC:** 4911—Electric Services.

★ 74712 ★ **Coca Cola Bottling
Co.**
701 S. George St.
Goldsboro, NC 27530
(919)735-2653
Ultimate Parent: Coca-Cola Enterprises.
SIC: 5149—Groceries & Related Products
Nec.

★ 74713 ★ **Cooper Industries Inc.**
Bussmann Div.
210 Dixie Trail
Goldsboro, NC 27530
Company Type: Division. **Ultimate Parent:**
Cooper Industries. **SIC:** 3613—Switchgear
& Switchboard Apparatus.

★ 74714 ★ **First-Citizens Bank &
Trust Co,**
1214 US Hwy. 117 S.
Goldsboro, NC 27530-6814
(919)734-5134
Location Type: Branch office. **Ultimate
Parent:** First Citizens Bancshares, Inc. **SIC:**
6021—National Commercial Banks.

★ 74715 ★ **First-Citizens Bank &
Trust Co.**
2301 Wyane Memorial Dr.
Goldsboro, NC 27534-1725
(919)734-5164
Location Type: Branch office. **Ultimate
Parent:** First Citizens Bancshares, Inc. **SIC:**
6021—National Commercial Banks.

★ 74716 ★ **First-Citizens Bank &
Trust Co.**
1900 N. Berkeley Blvd.
Goldsboro, NC 27534-8233
(919)734-5164
Location Type: Branch office. **Ultimate
Parent:** First Citizens Bancshares, Inc. **SIC:**
6021—National Commercial Banks.

★ 74717 ★ **First-Citizens Bank &
Trust Co.**
123 N. Ctr. St.
Goldsboro, NC 27530-3620
(919)734-5164
Location Type: Branch office. **Officer:**
James L. Meyer, Vice President. **Ultimate
Parent:** First Citizens Bancshares, Inc. **SIC:**
6021—National Commercial Banks.

★ 74718 ★ **Food Lion**
1005 N. Spence Ave.
Goldsboro, NC 27534
(919)778-0234
Ultimate Parent: Food Lion. **SIC:** 5411—
Grocery Stores.

★ 74719 ★ **Food Lion**
1308 W. Grantham St.
Goldsboro, NC 27530
(919)736-1056
Ultimate Parent: Food Lion. **SIC:** 5411—
Grocery Stores.

★ 74720 ★ **Food Lion Inc.**
1005 N. Spence Ave.
Goldsboro, NC 27534
(919)778-0234
Ultimate Parent: Food Lion. **SIC:** 5411—
Grocery Stores.

★ 74721 ★ **General Electric
Carolina Products Plant**
900 North George St.
Goldsboro, NC 27530
Ultimate Parent: General Electric. **SIC:**
3699—Electrical Equipment & Supplies Nec.

★ 74722 ★ **General Electric Co.**
900 N. George St.
Goldsboro, NC 27530
(919)731-5100
Officer: Mark Fabere, Plant Manager.
Ultimate Parent: General Electric. **SIC:**
3643—Current-Carrying Wiring Devices.

★ 74723 ★ **Hertz Rent-A-Car
Licensee**
118 W. Chestnut St.
Goldsboro, NC 27530
(919)734-5206
Ultimate Parent: Hertz. **SIC:** 7514—
Passenger Car Rental.

★ 74724 ★ **Hevi-Duty Electric Co.**
Hwy. 117 S. PO Box 268
Goldsboro, NC 27530
Ultimate Parent: General Signal. **SIC:**
3612—Transformers Except Electronic.

★ 74725 ★ **McDonalds
Hamburgers**
2402 E. Ash St.
Goldsboro, NC 27534
(919)735-5997
Ultimate Parent: McDonald's.
SIC: 5812—Eating Places.

★ 74726 ★ **Mutual of New York**
Goldsboro Tower
Goldsboro, NC 27530
(919)734-2361
Ultimate Parent: Mutual of New York. **SIC:**
6411—Insurance Agents, Brokers &
Service.

★ 74727 ★ **Mutual of New York**
Hollowell
Goldsboro, NC 27530
(919)778-0553
Ultimate Parent: Mutual of New York. **SIC:**
6411—Insurance Agents, Brokers &
Service.

★ 74728 ★ **Pepsi-Cola Bottling
Co.**
N. Park Dr.
Goldsboro, NC 27534
(919)778-8300
Officer: Sanford Korschun, President.
Ultimate Parent: Pepsico. **SIC:** 2086—
Bottled & Canned Soft Drinks.

★ **74729** ★   **Piggly Wiggly**
415 N. Berkeley Blvd.
Goldsboro, NC 27534
(919)778-7213
Ultimate Parent: Bruno's. **SIC:** 5411—
Grocery Stores.

★ **74730** ★   **Piggly Wiggly**
100 Lionel St.
Goldsboro, NC 27530
(919)731-2709
Ultimate Parent: Bruno's. **SIC:** 5411—
Grocery Stores.

★ **74731** ★   **Pizza Hut**
2518 E. Ash St.
Goldsboro, NC 27534
(919)731-2992
Ultimate Parent: Pepsico. **SIC:** 5812—
Eating Places.

★ **74732** ★   **Radio Shack**
623 N. Berkeley Blvd.
Goldsboro, NC 27534
(919)778-1897
Company Type: Division. **Ultimate Parent:**
Tandy Corp. **SIC:** 7373—Computer
Integrated Systems Design.

★ **74733** ★   **Radio Shack**
405 N. Berkeley Blvd.
Goldsboro, NC 27534
(919)778-1114
Company Type: Division. **Ultimate Parent:**
Tandy Corp. **SIC:** 5731—Radio, Television
& Electronics Stores.

★ **74734** ★   **Ryder Truck Rental**
602 Us 70 Byp E
Goldsboro, NC 27530
(919)736-4080
Ultimate Parent: Ryder System. **SIC:**
7513—Truck Rental & Leasing Without
Drivers.

★ **74735** ★   **Standard Products Co.**
308 Fedelon Trl.
Goldsboro, NC 27530
(919)735-5394
Officer: Dale Naples, Manager. **Ultimate
Parent:** Standard Products. **SIC:** 3069—
Fabricated Rubber Products Nec; 3714—
Motor Vehicle Parts & Accessories.

★ **74736** ★   **Standard Products Co.**
Goldsboro Division
308 Fedlon Trail
Goldsboro, NC 27530-9001
Ultimate Parent: Standard Products. **SIC:**
3069—Fabricated Rubber Products Nec.

★ **74737** ★   **Taylor J P Co.**
2109 N. William St.
Goldsboro, NC 27530
(919)735-1581
Ultimate Parent: Unocal Corp. **SIC:** 0132—
Tobacco.

★ **74738** ★   **Texaco Kwik Mart No 19**
600 N. Spence Ave.
Goldsboro, NC 27534
(919)778-1956
Ultimate Parent: Texaco. **SIC:** 5411—
Grocery Stores.

★ **74739** ★   **Wachovia Bank & Trust Co.**
605 N. Berkeley Blvd.
Goldsboro, NC 27534
(919)731-9307
Ultimate Parent: Wachovia Corp.

★ **74740** ★   **Wachovia Bank & Trust Co.**
1801 E. Ash St.
Goldsboro, NC 27530
(919)735-0211
Ultimate Parent: Wachovia Corp. **SIC:**
6141—Personal Credit Institutions.

★ **74741** ★   **Wachovia Bank & Trust Co. N**
605 N. Berkeley Blvd.
Goldsboro, NC 27534
(919)778-1373
Ultimate Parent: Wachovia Corp. **SIC:**
6022—State Commercial Banks.

★ **74742** ★   **Wal Mart**
1002 N. Spence Ave.
Goldsboro, NC 27534
(919)778-3324
Ultimate Parent: Wal-Mart Stores, Inc. **SIC:**
5399—Miscellaneous General Merchandise
Store.

Goldston

★ **74743** ★   **Branch Banking & Trust Co.**
E. Goldbar Ave.
Goldston, NC 27252
(919)898-2213
Company Type: Subsidiary. **Location
Type:** Branch office. **Officer:** Dale Aldham,
Mgr. **Ultimate Parent:** Southern National
Corp. **SIC:** 6021—National Commercial
Banks.

Graham

★ **74744** ★   **Ametek Inc.**
Lamb Electric Div.
704 Myrtle Dr.
Graham, NC 27253-1955
(919)229-5591
Company Type: Division. **Officer:** Jim
Liddle. **Ultimate Parent:** Ametek Inc. **SIC:**
3621—Motors & Generators; 5063—
Electrical Apparatus & Equipment.

★ **74745** ★   **Branch Banking & Trust Co.**
1013 S. Main St.
Graham, NC 27253-4105
(910)227-0161
Company Type: Subsidiary. **Location
Type:** Branch office. **Officer:** Faye Taylor,
Mgr. **Ultimate Parent:** Southern National
Corp. **SIC:** 6021—National Commercial
Banks.

★ **74746** ★   **Branch Banking & Trust Co.**
220 S. Main St.
Graham, NC 27253-3302
(910)227-0161
Company Type: Subsidiary. **Location
Type:** Branch office. **Officer:** George C.
Ritchie, Mgr. **Ultimate Parent:** Southern
National Corp. **SIC:** 6021—National
Commercial Banks.

★ **74747** ★   **Burlington Industries Inc.**
615 W. Harden St.
Graham, NC 27253-2106
(919)228-2713
Location Type: Branch office. **Officer:**
Douglas Annas. **Ultimate Parent:** Burlington
Industries, Equity. **SIC:** 2281—Yarn
Spinning Mills.

★ **74748** ★   **Food Lion**
921 S. Main St.
Graham, NC 27253
(919)228-0583
Ultimate Parent: Food Lion. **SIC:** 5411—
Grocery Stores.

★ **74749** ★   **Kayser-Roth Corp.**
714 Interstate Service Rd.
Graham, NC 27253
Ultimate Parent: Collins & Aikman Group.
SIC: 2252—Hosiery Nec.

★ **74750** ★   **Permatech Inc.**
911 E. Elm St. PO Box 759
Graham, NC 272531904
Ultimate Parent: Aluminum Co. of America-
-Alcoa. **SIC:** 3297—Nonclay Refractories.

★ **74751** ★   **Permatech Inc.**
911 E. Elm St.
Graham, NC 27253-1907
(910)578-0701
Location Type: Branch office. **Officer:**
Joseph Trettel, President. **Ultimate Parent:**
Aluminum Co. of America–Alcoa. **SIC:**
3297—Nonclay Refractories; 3479—Metal
Coating & Allied Services.

★ **74752** ★   **SCI Manufacturing**
609 Woody Dr.
Graham, NC 27253
(919)229-3420
Ultimate Parent: SCI Systems, Inc. **SIC:**
3679—Electronic Components Nec.

★ **74753** ★   **SCI Systems Inc.**
609 Woody Dr.
Graham, NC 27253
Ultimate Parent: SCI Systems, Inc. **SIC:**
3699—Electrical Equipment & Supplies Nec.

Granite Falls

★ **74754** ★   **First-Citizens Bank & Trust Co.**
Falls Ave. & Chestnut St.
Granite Falls, NC 28630
(704)396-3156
Location Type: Branch office. **Officer:**
James L. Gant Jr., Assistant Vice President.
Ultimate Parent: First Citizens Bancshares,
Inc. **SIC:** 6021—National Commercial
Banks.

★ **74755** ★   **Hammary Furniture Co. Plant 14**
175 N. Main St.
Granite Falls, NC 28630
Ultimate Parent: La-Z-Boy Chair. **SIC:**
2511—Wood Household Furniture.

Grantsboro

★ **74756** ★   **Piggly Wiggly**
Hwy. 55 306
Grantsboro, NC 28529
(919)745-3231
Ultimate Parent: Bruno's. **SIC:** 5411—
Grocery Stores.

Greensboro

★ **74757** ★   **Kayser-Roth Hosiery**
PO Box 77077
Greenboro, NC 27417
(919)852-2030 **Fax:** (919)854-4352
Officer: Robert Seelert, President & CEO.
Ultimate Parent: Collins & Aikman Group.

★ **74758** ★   **Burlington Industries Inc.**
6008 High Point Rd.
Greensbor, NC 27407
(910)454-3141
Officer: Wayne Berry, President. **Ultimate
Parent:** Burlington Industries, Equity. **SIC:**
2841—Soap & Other Detergents; 2843—
Surface Active Agents; 2899—Chemical
Preparations Nec.

★ **74759** ★   **Air Products & Chemicals Inc.**
115 Southern Oxygen Rd.
Greensboro, NC 27407
(910)299-1361
Officer: Bill Holland, Manager. **Ultimate
Parent:** Air Products & Chemicals, Inc. **SIC:**
2813—Industrial Gases; 3548—Welding
Apparatus; 5169—Chemicals & Allied
Products Nec.

★ **74760** ★   **Allen-Bradley Co.**
Hwy. 29 N. Bryan Park Exit
Greensboro, NC 27405
Ultimate Parent: Rockwell International
Corp. **SIC:** 3676—Electronic Resistors.

★ **74761** ★   **Amerada Hess Corp.**
Greensboro Airport Rd.
Greensboro, NC 27410
(919)299-1805
Ultimate Parent: Amerada Hess. **SIC:**
5172—Petroleum Products Nec.

★ **74762** ★   **Amerada Hess Corp.**
6907 W. Market St.
Greensboro, NC 27409
(919)299-1805
Ultimate Parent: Amerada Hess. **SIC:**
5172—Petroleum Products Nec.

★ **74763** ★   **American General Finance**
2605 Randleman Rd., Ste. B
Greensboro, NC 27406-5107
(919)271-6500
Location Type: Branch office. **Officer:**
Clinton W. Remsburg. **Ultimate Parent:**
American General Corp. **SIC:** 6141—
Personal Credit Institutions; 7323—Credit
Reporting Services.

★ **74764** ★   **American General Finance**
38080 High Point Rd.
Greensboro, NC 27407-4647
(919)294-1922
Location Type: Branch office. **Officer:**
Steve Smith. **Ultimate Parent:** American
General Corp. **SIC:** 6141—Personal Credit
Institutions.

★ **74765** ★   **American General Finance**
504 Summit Ave.
Greensboro, NC 27405-7740
(919)273-2561
Location Type: Branch office. **Officer:** Billy
Gene Sipe. **Ultimate Parent:** American
General Corp. **SIC:** 6141—Personal Credit
Institutions.

★ **74766** ★   **American General Finance Inc.**
38080K High Point Rd.
Greensboro, NC 27407-4647
(919)294-1922
Location Type: Branch office. **Officer:**
Steve Smith. **Ultimate Parent:** American
General Corp. **SIC:** 6141—Personal Credit
Institutions.

★ **74767** ★   **American General Finance Inc.**
504 Summit Ave.
Greensboro, NC 27405-7740
(919)273-2561
Location Type: Branch office. **Officer:** Billy
Gene Sipe. **Ultimate Parent:** American
General Corp. **SIC:** 6141—Personal Credit
Institutions.

★ **74768** ★   **American General Finance Inc.**
2605 Randleman Rd., Ste. B
Greensboro, NC 27406-5107
(919)271-6500
Location Type: Branch office. **Officer:**
Clinton W. Remsburg. **Ultimate Parent:**
American General Corp. **SIC:** 6141—
Personal Credit Institutions; 7323—Credit
Reporting Services.

★ **74769** ★   **AMP Inc.**
615 Pegg Rd.
Greensboro, NC 27409-9414
(919)665-2650
Officer: Ernie Carnes. **Ultimate Parent:**
AMP Inc. **SIC:** 5063—Electrical Apparatus &
Equipment.

★ **74770** ★   **AMP Inc.**
219 American Ave.
Greensboro, NC 27409
(910)855-2200
Officer: Bob Bruggeworty, Manager.
Ultimate Parent: AMP Inc. **SIC:** 3678—
Electronic Connectors.

★ **74771** ★   **AMP Inc.**
4833 High Point Rd.
Greensboro, NC 27407
(910)378-6700
Ultimate Parent: AMP Inc. **SIC:** 3643—
Current-Carrying Wiring Devices; 3678—
Electronic Connectors; 3679—Electronic
Components Nec.

★ **74772** ★   **AMP Inc.**
8300 Triad Dr.
Greensboro, NC 27409
(910)668-1500
Officer: David Klein, Manager. **Ultimate
Parent:** AMP Inc. **SIC:** 3643—
Current-Carrying Wiring Devices.

★ **74773** ★   **AMP Inc.**
8300 Triad Dr.
Greensboro, NC 27409-9621
Ultimate Parent: AMP Inc. **SIC:** 3471—
Plating & Polishing; 3678—Electronic
Connectors.

★ **74774** ★   **AMP Inc.**
219 American Ave.
Greensboro, NC 27409-1803
Ultimate Parent: AMP Inc. **SIC:** 3678—
Electronic Connectors.

★ **74775** ★   **Analog Devices Inc.**
7910 Triad Ctr. Dr.
Greensboro, NC 27409
Ultimate Parent: Analog Devices, Inc. **SIC:**
3674—Semiconductors & Related Devices.

★ 74776 ★   Analog Devices Inc.
Computer Laboratories
7910 Triad Ctr. Dr.
Greensboro, NC 27409-9605
Company Type: Division. Ultimate Parent:
Analog Devices, Inc. SIC: 3674—
Semiconductors & Related Devices.

★ 74777 ★   Anchor Financial
Group
3200 Northline Ave.
Greensboro, NC 27408-7606
(919)854-5525
Ultimate Parent: Anchor Bancorp. SIC:
6162—Mortgage Bankers &
Correspondents.

★ 74778 ★   AT & T Family Federal
Credit Union
2 Centerview Dr., Ste. 103
Greensboro, NC 27407
(910)855-0466
Location Type: Branch office. Officer:
Nancy Cohen, Manager. Ultimate Parent:
AT&T. SIC: 6061—Federal Credit Unions.

★ 74779 ★   AT & T Family Federal
Credit Union
PO Box 20046
Greensboro, NC 27420
(910)279-3113
Location Type: Branch office. Officer:
Barbara Singleton, Manager. Ultimate
Parent: AT&T. SIC: 6061—Federal Credit
Unions.

★ 74780 ★   AT&T
4000 Frazier Rd.
Greensboro, NC 27407-5512
(919)855-8601
Location Type: Branch office. Officer: Nell
Watkins. Ultimate Parent: AT&T. SIC:
4813—Telephone Communications Except
Radiotelephone.

★ 74781 ★   Avery Dennison Corp.
2305 Soabar Dr.
Greensboro, NC 27406
(919)275-9371
Location Type: Branch office. Ultimate
Parent: Avery Dennison Corp. SIC: 2759—
Commercial Printing Nec.

★ 74782 ★   Avery Dennison
Soabar
2305 Soabar
Greensboro, NC 27406-3632
(919)275-9371
Officer: Robert J. Harrington. Ultimate
Parent: Avery Dennison Corp. SIC: 2759—
Commercial Printing Nec; 2671—Paper
Coated & Laminated—Packaging; 2679—
Converted Paper Products Nec; 2752—
Commercial Printing—Lithographic.

★ 74783 ★   Bankers Trust of
North Carolina
2501 Battleground Ave.
Greensboro, NC 27408-4003
(919)855-2110
Officer: Cynthia Parkins. Ultimate Parent:
Bankers Trust New York Corp. SIC: 6021—
National Commercial Banks.

★ 74784 ★   Bankers Trust of
North Carolina
2302 W. Meadowview Rd., Ste. 200
Greensboro, NC 27407-3706
(919)855-2120
Ultimate Parent: Bankers Trust New York
Corp. SIC: 6021—National Commercial
Banks.

★ 74785 ★   Bankers Trust North
Carolina
2112 N. Elm St.
Greensboro, NC 27408-5112
(919)378-6166
Location Type: Branch office. Officer:
Wanda Huey. Ultimate Parent: Bankers
Trust New York Corp. SIC: 6022—State
Commercial Banks; 6021—National
Commercial Banks.

★ 74786 ★   Bankers Trust of
North Carolina
3825 High Point Rd.
Greensboro, NC 27407-4609
(919)855-2100
Location Type: Branch office. Officer:
Cynthia T. Perkins. Ultimate Parent:
Bankers Trust New York Corp. SIC: 6022—
State Commercial Banks; 6021—National
Commercial Banks.

★ 74787 ★   Bankers Trust of
North Carolina
4817 W. Market St.
Greensboro, NC 27407-1403
(919)294-2000
Officer: Thomas Reaves. Ultimate Parent:
Bankers Trust New York Corp. SIC: 6141—
Personal Credit Institutions; 6021—National
Commercial Banks.

★ 74788 ★   BASF Fibers Corp.
629 Green Valley Rd.
Greensboro, NC 27408-7721
(919)299-8775
Location Type: Branch office. Officer: B.
Cox. Ultimate Parent: BASF Corp. SIC:
5949—Sewing, Needlework & Piece Goods.

★ 74789 ★   Branch Banking &
Trust Co.
606 College Rd.
Greensboro, NC 27410-4195
(910)271-5330
Company Type: Subsidiary. Location
Type: Branch office. Ultimate Parent:
Southern National Corp. SIC: 6021—
National Commercial Banks.

★ 74790 ★   Branch Banking &
Trust Co.
2239 Martin Luther King Blvd.
Greensboro, NC 27406-3709
(910)271-5340
Company Type: Subsidiary. Location
Type: Branch office. Ultimate Parent:
Southern National Corp. SIC: 6021—
National Commercial Banks.

★ 74791 ★   Browning-Ferris
Industries
2901 Manufacturers Rd.
Greensboro, NC 27406-4605
(919)273-8281
Location Type: Branch office. Officer:
Benny Blalock. Ultimate Parent:
Browning-Ferris Industries. SIC: 5085—
Industrial Supplies; 3567—Industrial
Furnaces & Ovens; 4953—Refuse Systems;
5093—Scrap & Waste Materials.

★ 74792 ★   Burlington Coat
Factory
3022 High Point Rd.
Greensboro, NC 27403-3653
(919)854-3663
Location Type: Branch office. Officer:
Tony Blevins. Ultimate Parent: Burlington
Industries, Equity. SIC: 5311—Department
Stores; 5651—Family Clothing Stores.

★ 74793 ★   Burlington Denim
PO Box 21207
Greensboro, NC 27420
(919)379-2369 Fax: (919)379-2834
Company Type: Subsidiary. Officer:
Bernard A. Leonard, Division President.
Ultimate Parent: Burlington Industries,
Equity.

★ 74794 ★   Burlington Industries,
Equity
3339 W. Friendly Ave.
Greensboro, NC 27410
(910)379-2000
Company Type: Headquarters. Officer:
Frank S. Greenberg. Employee Count:
23660. Sales: 2058 M. Fortune 500:
Largest U.S. Industrial Corporations:
Ranking 214.

★ 74795 ★   Burlington Industries
Inc.
PO Box 21207
Greensboro, NC 27420
(919)379-2000 Fax: (919)379-4504
Company Type: Headquarters. Officer:
Frank S. Greenberg, Chairman & CEO.
Ultimate Parent: Burlington Industries,
Equity. Employee Count: 23400.

★ 74796 ★   Burlington Industries
Inc.
3330 W. Friendly Ave.
Greensboro, NC 27410-4800
(919)379-2000
Company Type: Headquarters. Officer:
Frank S. Greenberg. Ultimate Parent:
Burlington Industries, Equity. SIC: 2211—
Broadwoven Fabric Mills—Cotton; 2221—
Broadwoven Fabric Mills—Manmade;
2231—Broadwoven Fabric Mills—Wool;
2251—Women's Hosiery Except Socks;
2252—Hosiery Nec; 2253—Knit Outerwear
Mills; 2257—Weft Knit Fabric Mills; 2258—
Lace & Warp Knit Fabric Mills; 2273—

Carpets & Rugs; 2281—Yarn Spinning Mills;
2282—Throwing & Winding Mills; 2299—
Textile Goods Nec; 2391—Curtains &
Draperies; 2392—Housefurnishings Nec;
2399—Fabricated Textile Products Nec.

★ 74797 ★   Burlington Klopman
Fabrics
PO Box 21207
Greensboro, NC 27420
(919)379-2424 Fax: (919)379-2498
Company Type: Subsidiary. Officer: Gary
P. Welchman, Division President. Ultimate
Parent: Burlington Industries, Equity.

★ 74798 ★   Burlington Madison
Yark Co.
PO Box 21207
Greensboro, NC 27420
(919)379-4747 Fax: (919)379-4513
Company Type: Subsidiary. Officer: Dan
Sullivan, Division President. Ultimate
Parent: Burlington Industries, Equity.

★ 74799 ★   Circuit City
Superstore
3826 High Point Rd.
Greensboro, NC 27407
(919)852-9111
Ultimate Parent: Circuit City Stores. SIC:
5731—Radio, Television & Electronics
Stores.

★ 74800 ★   Coca Cola Bottling
Co.
6518 Airport Pky. 200
Greensboro, NC 27409
(919)665-1919
Ultimate Parent: Coca-Cola Enterprises.
SIC: 2087—Flavoring Extracts & Syrups
Nec.

★ 74801 ★   Colonial Pipeline Co.
Rural Route 9
Greensboro, NC 27409
(919)292-0426
Ultimate Parent: Colonial Pipeline. SIC:
4619—Pipelines Nec.

★ 74802 ★   Cone Mills
1201 Maple St.
Greensboro, NC 27405
(910)379-6220
Company Type: Headquarters. Officer: J.
Patrick Danahy. Employee Count: 7800.
Sales: 7692 M. Fortune 500: Largest U.S.
Industrial Corporations: Ranking 415.

★ 74803 ★   Cone Mills Corp.
1201 Maple St.
Greensboro, NC 27405-6910
(919)379-6220
Officer: J. Patrick Danahy, President &
CEO. Ultimate Parent: Cone Mills. SIC:
2211—Broadwoven Fabric Mills—Cotton;
2221—Broadwoven Fabric Mills—Manmade;
2261—Finishing Plants—Cotton; 2262—
Finishing Plants—Manmade; 3069—
Fabricated Rubber Products Nec; 2299—
Textile Goods Nec. Employee Count:
7600. Sales: 705 M.

★ 74804 ★   Cone Mills Corp.
White Oak Plant
2420 Fairview St.
Greensboro, NC 27405
Ultimate Parent: Cone Mills. SIC: 2211—
Broadwoven Fabric Mills—Cotton; 2261—
Finishing Plants—Cotton.

★ 74805 ★   Copier Consultants
7009 Albert Pick Rd.
Greensboro, NC 27409
(910)668-0500
Company Type: Division. Officer: James
C. Carlisle, Chairman of the Board.
Ultimate Parent: Alco Standard Corp. SIC:
8742—Management Consulting Services.

★ 74806 ★   Crestar Mortgage
Corp.
620 Green Valley Rd.
Greensboro, NC 27408
(919)292-6401
Ultimate Parent: Crestar Financial Corp.
SIC: 6162—Mortgage Bankers &
Correspondents.

★ 74807 ★   Delta Air Lines
6415 Airport Pky.
Greensboro, NC 27409
(919)294-2122
Ultimate Parent: Delta Air Lines, Inc. SIC:
4512—Air Transportation—Scheduled.

★ 74808 ★   Delta Air Lines
Greensboro-High Point Airport
Greensboro, NC 27410
(919)294-2122
Ultimate Parent: Delta Air Lines, Inc. SIC:
4512—Air Transportation—Scheduled;
4512—Air Transportation—Scheduled.

★ 74809 ★   Delta Air Lines Inc.
Greensboro-High Point Airport
Greensboro, NC 27410
(919)294-2122
Ultimate Parent: Delta Air Lines, Inc. SIC:
4512—Air Transportation—Scheduled;
4512—Air Transportation—Scheduled.

★ 74810 ★   Deluxe Check Printers
Inc.
116 Landmark Dr.
Greensboro, NC 27409
Ultimate Parent: Deluxe Corp. SIC: 2752—
Commercial Printing—Lithographic; 2782—
Blankbooks & Looseleaf Binders.

★ 74811 ★   Deluxe Check Printers
Inc.
116 Landmark Dr.
Greensboro, NC 27420
Ultimate Parent: Deluxe Corp. SIC: 2782—
Blankbooks & Looseleaf Binders; 2752—
Commercial Printing—Lithographic.

★ 74812 ★   Dover Elevator Co.
3001 S. Elm Eugene St.
Greensboro, NC 27406
(910)272-4563
Officer: Frank Sain, Manager. Ultimate
Parent: Dover Corp. SIC: 3534—Elevators
& Moving Stairways.

★ 74813 ★   Dow Corning Corp.
2914 Patterson St.
Greensboro, NC 27407
Ultimate Parent: Dow Chemical Co. USA.
SIC: 2890—Miscellaneous Chemical
Products.

★ 74814 ★   Emery Worldwide
Greensboro-High Point Airport
Greensboro, NC 27410
(919)299-9362
Ultimate Parent: Consolidated Freightways.
SIC: 4731—Freight Transportation
Arrangement.

★ 74815 ★   Exxon
3028 High Point Rd.
Greensboro, NC 27403
(919)854-0418
Ultimate Parent: Exxon. SIC: 5541—
Gasoline Service Stations.

★ 74816 ★   Exxon Co. USA
6907 W. Market St.
Greensboro, NC 27409
(919)723-4220
Ultimate Parent: Exxon. SIC: 2911—
Petroleum Refining.

★ 74817 ★   Fairfield Inn by
Marriott
2003 Athena Ct
Greensboro, NC 27407
(919)294-9922
Ultimate Parent: Marriott International. SIC:
7011—Hotels & Motels.

★ 74818 ★   Federal Express Corp.
7611 Boeing Dr.
Greensboro, NC 27409
(919)668-2476
Ultimate Parent: Federal Express. SIC:
4512—Air Transportation—Scheduled.

★ 74819 ★   Federal Systems
Advanced Technologies
PO Box 25000
Greensboro, NC 27420
(910)279-7000
Officer: William A. Garrett, President.
Ultimate Parent: AT&T.

★ 74820 ★   First American Corp.
4411 W. Market St.
Greensboro, NC 27407-1331
(919)852-8410
Company Type: Subsidiary. Officer: James
A. Bethel, President. Ultimate Parent: First
American Corp. SIC: 6798—Real Estate
Investment Trusts; 8741—Management
Services. Employee Count: 250. Sales: 25
M.

★ 74821 ★   First-Citizens Bank &
Trust Co.
3017 High Point Rd.
Greensboro, NC 27403-3148
(910)271-4056
Location Type: Branch office. **Ultimate
Parent:** First Citizens Bancshares, Inc. **SIC:**
6021—National Commercial Banks.

★ 74822 ★   First-Citizens Bank &
Trust Co.
2431 Battleground Ave.
Greensboro, NC 27408-4023
(910)275-8661
Location Type: Branch office. **Ultimate
Parent:** First Citizens Bancshares, Inc. **SIC:**
6021—National Commercial Banks.

★ 74823 ★   First-Citizens Bank &
Trust Co.
1803 E. Bessemer Ave.
Greensboro, NC 27405-7246
(910)275-8661
Location Type: Branch office. **Ultimate
Parent:** First Citizens Bancshares, Inc. **SIC:**
6021—National Commercial Banks.

★ 74824 ★   First-Citizens Bank &
Trust Co.
4635 W. Market St.
Greensboro, NC 27407-1231
(910)275-8661
Location Type: Branch office. **Ultimate
Parent:** First Citizens Bancshares, Inc. **SIC:**
6021—National Commercial Banks.

★ 74825 ★   First-Citizens Bank &
Trust Co.
4708 High Point Rd.
Greensboro, NC 27404-5304
(910)275-8661
Location Type: Branch office. **Ultimate
Parent:** First Citizens Bancshares, Inc. **SIC:**
6021—National Commercial Banks.

★ 74826 ★   First-Citizens Bank &
Trust Co.
2401 Randleman Rd.
Greensboro, NC 27406-4309
(910)275-8661
Location Type: Branch office. **Ultimate
Parent:** First Citizens Bancshares, Inc. **SIC:**
6021—National Commercial Banks.

★ 74827 ★   First-Citizens Bank &
Trust Co.
3101 Yanceyville St.
Greensboro, NC 27405-4041
(910)271-4047
Location Type: Branch office. **Ultimate
Parent:** First Citizens Bancshares, Inc. **SIC:**
6021—National Commercial Banks.

★ 74828 ★   First-Citizens Bank &
Trust Co.
6400 W. Market St.
Greensboro, NC 27409-1892
(910)271-4053
Location Type: Branch office. **Ultimate
Parent:** First Citizens Bancshares, Inc. **SIC:**
6021—National Commercial Banks.

★ 74829 ★   First-Citizens Bank &
Trust Co.
3200 Northline Ave.
Greensboro, NC 27408
(910)271-4059
Location Type: Branch office. **Ultimate
Parent:** First Citizens Bancshares, Inc. **SIC:**
6021—National Commercial Banks.

★ 74830 ★   First Data Corp.
414F Gallimore Dairy Rd.
Greensboro, NC 27409-9725
(919)665-3300
Ultimate Parent: American Express Co.
SIC: 7374—Data Processing & Preparation.

★ 74831 ★   Food Lion
3714 Lawndale Dr.
Greensboro, NC 27408
(919)282-0180
Ultimate Parent: Food Lion. **SIC:** 5411—
Grocery Stores.

★ 74832 ★   Food Lion
4537 Us Hwy. 220 N
Greensboro, NC 27410
(919)643-6324
Ultimate Parent: Food Lion. **SIC:** 5411—
Grocery Stores.

★ 74833 ★   Food Lion
RR 2
Greensboro, NC 27405
(919)643-6324
Ultimate Parent: Food Lion. **SIC:** 5411—
Grocery Stores.

★ 74834 ★   Food Lion
1911 S. Chapman St.
Greensboro, NC 27403
(919)294-7000
Ultimate Parent: Food Lion. **SIC:** 5411—
Grocery Stores.

★ 74835 ★   Food Lion
3228 Randleman Rd.
Greensboro, NC 27406
(919)370-9883
Ultimate Parent: Food Lion. **SIC:** 5411—
Grocery Stores.

★ 74836 ★   Food Lion
120 W. Meadowview Rd.
Greensboro, NC 27406
(919)379-7253
Ultimate Parent: Food Lion. **SIC:** 3433—
Heating Equipment Except Electric.

★ 74837 ★   Food Lion
1914 S. Chapman St.
Greensboro, NC 27403
(919)294-3753
Ultimate Parent: Food Lion. **SIC:** 5411—
Grocery Stores.

★ 74838 ★   Food Lion
2401 Randleman Rd.
Greensboro, NC 27406
(919)273-8226
Ultimate Parent: Food Lion. **SIC:** 5411—
Grocery Stores.

★ 74839 ★   Food Lion Inc.
3714 Lawndale Dr.
Greensboro, NC 27408
(919)282-0180
Ultimate Parent: Food Lion. **SIC:** 5411—
Grocery Stores.

★ 74840 ★   Fruehauf Trailer Corp.
7045 Albert Pick Rd.
Greensboro, NC 27409-9654
(919)668-2441
Ultimate Parent: Terex Corp. **SIC:** 5012—
Automobiles & Other Motor Vehicles;
4226—Special Warehousing & Storage Nec;
5013—Motor Vehicle Supplies & New Parts;
7539—Automotive Repair Shops Nec.

★ 74841 ★   Fruehauf Trailers
7045 Albert Pick Rd.
Greensboro, NC 27409-9654
(919)668-2441
Ultimate Parent: Terex Corp. **SIC:** 5012—
Automobiles & Other Motor Vehicles;
4226—Special Warehousing & Storage Nec;
5013—Motor Vehicle Supplies & New Parts;
7539—Automotive Repair Shops Nec.

★ 74842 ★   Gilbarco Inc.
7300 W. Friendly Rd.
Greensboro, NC 27420
Ultimate Parent: General Electric. **SIC:**
3586—Measuring & Dispensing Pumps.

★ 74843 ★   Gilbarco Inc.
7300 Friendly Rd.
Greensboro, NC 27420
Ultimate Parent: General Electric. **SIC:**
3586—Measuring & Dispensing Pumps.

★ 74844 ★   Guilford Mills Inc.
4925 W. Market St.
Greensboro, NC 27407-1405
(919)316-4000 Fax: (919)316-4056
Company Type: Headquarters. **Officer:**
Charles A. Hayes, President, Chairman of
the Board & CEO. **Employee Count:** 4539.
Sales: 654 M. **Fortune 500:** Largest U.S.
Industrial Corporations: Ranking 476.

★ 74845 ★   Guilford Mills Inc.
Industrial Fabrics Div.
6001 W. Market St.
Greensboro, NC 27409
Company Type: Division. **Ultimate Parent:**
Guilford Mills Inc. **SIC:** 2258—Lace & Warp
Knit Fabric Mills.

★ 74846 ★   Guilford Mills Inc. Oak
Ridge Plant
4201 W. Market St.
Greensboro, NC 27407
Ultimate Parent: Guilford Mills Inc. **SIC:**
2258—Lace & Warp Knit Fabric Mills.

★ 74847 ★   Guilford Mills Inc. Oak
Ridge Plant
4201 W. Wendover Ave.
Greensboro, NC 27407
Ultimate Parent: Guilford Mills Inc. **SIC:**
2258—Lace & Warp Knit Fabric Mills.

★ 74848 ★   Guilford Mills Inc. W.
Market St. Plant
4925 W. Market St.
Greensboro, NC 27407
Ultimate Parent: Guilford Mills Inc. **SIC:**
2258—Lace & Warp Knit Fabric Mills.

★ 74849 ★   H. B. Fuller Co.
3005 Holt's Chapel Rd.
Greensboro, NC 27401
Ultimate Parent: H. B. Fuller. **SIC:** 2891—
Adhesives & Sealants.

★ 74850 ★   Hertz Rent-A-Car
6325 Airport Pky.
Greensboro, NC 27409
(919)668-7961
Ultimate Parent: Hertz. **SIC:** 7514—
Passenger Car Rental.

★ 74851 ★   Hit or Miss
Greensboro
Greensboro, NC 27405
(919)855-9826
Ultimate Parent: TJX. **SIC:** 5621—
Women's Clothing Stores.

★ 74852 ★   Hit or Miss
801 Merritt Dr.
Greensboro, NC 27407
(919)852-2842
Ultimate Parent: TJX. **SIC:** 5651—Family
Clothing Stores.

★ 74853 ★   Inacomp Computer
Centers
7019 Albert Pick Rd.
Greensboro, NC 27409
(919)668-9301
Ultimate Parent: Beneficial. **SIC:** 7373—
Computer Integrated Systems Design.

★ 74854 ★   Intro-Europe, Inc.
408-B Gallimore, Dairy Rd.
Greensboro, NC 27409
(919)668-4005 Fax: (919)668-4839
Officer: Rudy Van Thiel. **Ultimate Parent:**
Masco.

★ 74855 ★   Jiffy Lube
4610 W. Market St.
Greensboro, NC 27407
(919)854-1800
Ultimate Parent: Pennzoil. **SIC:** 7549—
Automotive Services Nec.

★ 74856 ★   Kayser-Roth Corp.
4905 Koger Blvd.
Greensboro, NC 27407-2639
(919)852-2030
Company Type: Subsidiary. **Officer:**
Robert L. Seelert, President & CEO.
Ultimate Parent: Collins & Aikman Group.
SIC: 2252—Hosiery Nec; 2251—Women's
Hosiery Except Socks; 5651—Family
Clothing Stores; 5632—Women's Accessory
& Specialty Stores. **Employee Count:** 5500.
Sales: 400 M.

★ 74857 ★   Kelly Assisted Living
Servi
1400 Battleground Ave.
Greensboro, NC 27408
(919)370-0796
Ultimate Parent: Kelly Services. **SIC:**
8699—Membership Organizations Nec.

★ 74858 ★   Kentucky Fried
Chicken
2613 High Point Rd.
Greensboro, NC 27403
(919)292-5306
Ultimate Parent: Pepsico. **SIC:** 5812—
Eating Places.

★ 74859 ★   Kentucky Fried
Chicken
2317 Battleground Ave.
Greensboro, NC 27408
(919)288-0473
Ultimate Parent: Pepsico. **SIC:** 5812—
Eating Places.

★ 74860 ★   Kentucky Fried
Chicken
1600 E. Bessemer Ave.
Greensboro, NC 27405
(919)275-9831
Ultimate Parent: Pepsico. **SIC:** 5812—
Eating Places.

★ 74861 ★   Kroger Co. the
4653 W. Market St.
Greensboro, NC 27407
(919)852-0555
Ultimate Parent: Kroger. **SIC:** 5411—
Grocery Stores.

★ 74862 ★   Lees Carpets
PO Box 21207
Greensboro, NC 27420
(919)379-3349 Fax: (919)379-3397
Company Type: Subsidiary. **Officer:** Larry
Queen, Division President. **Ultimate Parent:**
Burlington Industries, Equity.

★ 74863 ★   Lens Crafters
329 Seasons Mall
Greensboro, NC 27407
(919)854-1204
Ultimate Parent: United States Shoe. **SIC:**
5995—Optical Goods Stores.

★ 74864 ★   Liberty Mutual
Insurance Co.
620 Green Valley Rd.
Greensboro, NC 27408
(919)299-9910
Ultimate Parent: Liberty Mutual Group.
SIC: 6411—Insurance Agents, Brokers &
Service.

★ 74865 ★   The Limited Express
3200 Northline Ave.
Greensboro, NC 27408
(919)854-0264
Ultimate Parent: Limited. **SIC:** 5651—
Family Clothing Stores.

★ 74866 ★   Logistics
Management System
4604 Schoolway Dr.
Greensboro, NC 27406
(919)294-9092
Ultimate Parent: Fieldcrest Cannon.

★ 74867 ★   Lorillard Inc.
2525 East Market St.
Greensboro, NC 27420
Ultimate Parent: Loews. **SIC:** 2111—
Cigarettes.

★ 74868 ★   Lorillard Tobacco Co.
2525 East Market St.
Greensboro, NC 27420
Ultimate Parent: Loews. **SIC:** 2111—
Cigarettes.

★ 74869 ★   Mutual Savings &
Loan Assoc
701 E. Market St.
Greensboro, NC 27401-3245
(919)273-9753
Location Type: Branch office. **Officer:**
Gloria J. Ratliff. **Ultimate Parent:** Berkshire
Hathaway. **SIC:** 6035—Federal Savings
Institutions; 6021—National Commercial
Banks; 6141—Personal Credit Institutions;
6162—Mortgage Bankers &
Correspondents.

★ 74870 ★   New York Life
Piedmont Triad General Office
Southeastern Agencies
1801 Stanley Rd., Ste. 312
Greensboro, NC 27407
(919)299-9991 Fax: (919)299-2441
Ultimate Parent: New York Life.

★ 74871 ★   Norwest Mortgage
Inc.
4125 Walker Ave.
Greensboro, NC 27407
(919)299-1415
Ultimate Parent: Norwest Corp. **SIC:**
6062—State Credit Unions.

★ 74872 ★   Olympic Prods. Co.
4100 Pleasant Garden Rd.
Greensboro, NC 27406
Ultimate Parent: Cone Mills. **SIC:** 3086—
Plastics Foam Products.

★ 74873 ★   Olympic Prods. Co.
Rebond Plant
1601 Yanceyville St.
Greensboro, NC 27405
Ultimate Parent: Cone Mills. SIC: 3086—
Plastics Foam Products.

★ 74874 ★   Olympic Rebond
Plant
1601 Yanceyville St.
Greensboro, NC 27405
Location Type: Plant. Ultimate Parent:
Cone Mills. SIC: 3089—Plastics Products
Nec.

★ 74875 ★   Penn Mutual Life
Insurance
338 N. Elm St.
Greensboro, NC 27401
(919)275-3097
Ultimate Parent: Penn Mutual Life. SIC:
6311—Life Insurance; 6411—Insurance
Agents, Brokers & Service.

★ 74876 ★   Pizza Hut
3203 Yanceyville St.
Greensboro, NC 27405
(919)621-8500
Ultimate Parent: Pepsico. SIC: 5812—
Eating Places.

★ 74877 ★   Pizza Hut
2609 High Point Rd.
Greensboro, NC 27403
(919)299-5511
Ultimate Parent: Pepsico. SIC: 5812—
Eating Places.

★ 74878 ★   Pizza Hut
2344 Randleman Rd.
Greensboro, NC 27406
(919)378-9712
Ultimate Parent: Pepsico. SIC: 5812—
Eating Places.

★ 74879 ★   Pizza Hut
2939 Battleground Ave. B
Greensboro, NC 27408
(919)545-1199
Ultimate Parent: Pepsico. SIC: 5812—
Eating Places.

★ 74880 ★   Pizza Hut
1473 E. Cone Blvd.
Greensboro, NC 27405
(919)621-5873
Ultimate Parent: Pepsico. SIC: 5812—
Eating Places.

★ 74881 ★   Pizza Hut
2505 Battleground Ave.
Greensboro, NC 27408
(919)288-3333
Ultimate Parent: Pepsico. SIC: 5812—
Eating Places.

★ 74882 ★   Radio Shack
311 S. Westgate Dr.
Greensboro, NC 27407
(919)852-8360
Company Type: Division. Ultimate Parent:
Tandy Corp. SIC: 7373—Computer
Integrated Systems Design.

★ 74883 ★   Radio Shack
926 Summit Ave.
Greensboro, NC 27405
(919)273-6134
Company Type: Division. Ultimate Parent:
Tandy Corp. SIC: 5065—Electronic Parts &
Equipment Nec.

★ 74884 ★   Radio Shack
4639 W. Market St.
Greensboro, NC 27407
(919)294-4027
Company Type: Division. Ultimate Parent:
Tandy Corp. SIC: 5065—Electronic Parts &
Equipment Nec.

★ 74885 ★   Radio Shack
704 Pembroke Rd.
Greensboro, NC 27408
(919)852-5472
Company Type: Division. Ultimate Parent:
Tandy Corp. SIC: 5731—Radio, Television
& Electronics Stores.

★ 74886 ★   Radio Shack
66112 PO Box
Greensboro, NC 27406
Company Type: Division. Ultimate Parent:
Tandy Corp. SIC: 5065—Electronic Parts &
Equipment Nec.

★ 74887 ★   Radio Shack
4623 High Pt Rd.
Greensboro, NC 27407
(919)294-3788
Company Type: Division. Ultimate Parent:
Tandy Corp. SIC: 5731—Radio, Television
& Electronics Stores.

★ 74888 ★   Radio Shack
249 Carolina Cir.
Greensboro, NC 27405
(919)621-2914
Company Type: Division. Ultimate Parent:
Tandy Corp. SIC: 5065—Electronic Parts &
Equipment Nec; 5731—Radio, Television &
Electronics Stores.

★ 74889 ★   Radio Shack
Friendly Shopping Ctr.
Greensboro, NC 27410
(919)852-5472
Company Type: Division. Ultimate Parent:
Tandy Corp.

★ 74890 ★   Radio Shack
3722 Battleground Ave.
Greensboro, NC 27410
(919)545-3115
Company Type: Division. Ultimate Parent:
Tandy Corp. SIC: 5065—Electronic Parts &
Equipment Nec.

★ 74891 ★   Rexham Corp.
2600 Phoenix Dr.
Greensboro, NC 27406
Ultimate Parent: Bowater. SIC: 2672—
Coated & Laminated Paper Nec.

★ 74892 ★   Richardson - Vick Inc.
PO Box 18647 100 Swing Rd.
Greensboro, NC 27419
Ultimate Parent: Procter & Gamble Co.
SIC: 2834—Pharmaceutical Preparations.

★ 74893 ★   Richardson - Vicks
Inc. USA
100 Swing Rd.
Greensboro, NC 27419
Ultimate Parent: Procter & Gamble Co.
SIC: 2834—Pharmaceutical Preparations.

★ 74894 ★   Rite Aid Discount
Pharmacy
Sedgefield Gardens
Greensboro, NC 27407
(919)299-6261
Ultimate Parent: Rite Aid. SIC: 5912—Drug
Stores & Proprietary Stores.

★ 74895 ★   Rite Aid Discount
Pharmacy
3111 E. Bessemer Ave.
Greensboro, NC 27405
(919)275-7657
Ultimate Parent: Rite Aid. SIC: 5912—Drug
Stores & Proprietary Stores.

★ 74896 ★   Rite Aid Discount
Pharmacy
2140 Lawndale Dr.
Greensboro, NC 27408
(919)275-3318
Ultimate Parent: Rite Aid. SIC: 5912—Drug
Stores & Proprietary Stores.

★ 74897 ★   Rite Aid Discount
Pharmacy
2929 Battleground Ave.
Greensboro, NC 27408
(919)288-9982
Ultimate Parent: Rite Aid. SIC: 5912—Drug
Stores & Proprietary Stores.

★ 74898 ★   Rite-Aid Drug
948 Walker Ave.
Greensboro, NC 27403
(919)373-9614
Ultimate Parent: Rite Aid. SIC: 5912—Drug
Stores & Proprietary Stores.

★ 74899 ★   Rite Aid Pharmacy
3102 E. Bessemer Ave.
Greensboro, NC 27405
(919)373-9641
Ultimate Parent: Rite Aid. SIC: 5912—Drug
Stores & Proprietary Stores.

★ 74900 ★   Ryder Truck Rental
2620 Battleground Ave.
Greensboro, NC 27408
(919)282-3030
Ultimate Parent: Ryder System. SIC:
7359—Equipment Rental & Leasing Nec;
7513—Truck Rental & Leasing Without
Drivers.

★ 74901 ★   Ryder Truck Rental
3200 High Point Rd.
Greensboro, NC 27407
(919)299-8981
Ultimate Parent: Ryder System. SIC:
7359—Equipment Rental & Leasing Nec;
7513—Truck Rental & Leasing Without
Drivers.

★ 74902 ★   Ryder Truck Rental
362 W. Lee St.
Greensboro, NC 27406
(919)273-0659
Ultimate Parent: Ryder System. SIC:
7359—Equipment Rental & Leasing Nec.

★ 74903 ★   Ryder Truck Rental
4701 W. Market St.
Greensboro, NC 27407
(919)299-7687
Ultimate Parent: Ryder System. SIC:
7359—Equipment Rental & Leasing Nec.

★ 74904 ★   Ryder Truck Rental
114 Landmark Dr.
Greensboro, NC 27409
(919)299-6500
Ultimate Parent: Ryder System. SIC:
7513—Truck Rental & Leasing Without
Drivers.

★ 74905 ★   Security Pacific
Financial Services
2302 W. Meadowview Rd., Ste. 105
Greensboro, NC 27407-3706
(919)855-7817
Location Type: Branch office. Ultimate
Parent: Bankamerica Corp. SIC: 6141—
Personal Credit Institutions.

★ 74906 ★   Sedgefield Specialties
6008 High Point Rd.
Greensboro, NC 27407-7009
(919)454-3141
Officer: B. Wayne Berry. Ultimate Parent:
Burlington Industries, Equity. SIC: 2899—
Chemical Preparations Nec; 2221—
Broadwoven Fabric Mills—Manmade.

★ 74907 ★   Shelby Insurance Co.
2000 Pisgah Church Rd.
Greensboro, NC 27408
(919)282-1500
Ultimate Parent: Alleghany Corp. SIC:
6411—Insurance Agents, Brokers &
Service.

★ 74908 ★   Shell Oil Co.
6811 W. Market St.
Greensboro, NC 27409
(919)299-3511
Ultimate Parent: Shell Oil Co. SIC: 5172—
Petroleum Products Nec.

★ 74909 ★   Sherwin-Williams Co.
1025 Howard St.
Greensboro, NC 27403
(910)299-9351
Officer: S. L. Chanilo, Manager. Ultimate
Parent: Sherwin-Williams Co. SIC: 2851—
Paints & Allied Products.

★ 74910 ★   Sherwin-Williams Co.
113 Stage Coach Trl.
Greensboro, NC 27409
(910)292-3000
Officer: Sam F. Biffle, Plant Manager.
Ultimate Parent: Sherwin-Williams Co. SIC:
2851—Paints & Allied Products.

★ 74911 ★   Sherwin Williams
Paint Stor
4210 High Pt Rd.
Greensboro, NC 27407
(919)292-2966
Ultimate Parent: Sherwin-Williams Co. SIC:
5231—Paint, Glass & Wallpaper Stores.

★ 74912 ★   Soabar Group
Soabar Graphics Div.
2305 Soabar Dr.
Greensboro, NC 27406
(910)275-9371
Company Type: Division. Officer: Richard
W. Stidham, Vice President & General
Manager. Ultimate Parent: Avery Dennison
Corp. SIC: 2759—Commercial Printing Nec;
2752—Commercial Printing—Lithographic.

★ 74913 ★   Southern Food Inc.
3500 Old Battleground Rd.
Greensboro, NC 27410-2420
(919)545-3800
Officer: R. Michael Nussbaum, President.
Ultimate Parent: American Stores. SIC:

5147—Meats & Meat Products; 5148—
Fresh Fruits & Vegetables; 5142—Packaged
Frozen Foods. Employee Count: 450.
Sales: 100000 M.

★ 74914 ★   Southern Group Inc.
1718 Spring Garden St.
Greensboro, NC 27403-2742
(919)272-9321
Officer: Andy Stampley. Ultimate Parent:
Beneficial. SIC: 8742—Management
Consulting Services.

★ 74915 ★   Specialty Products &
Installation
103 Creek Ridge Rd.
Greensboro, NC 27406-4424
(919)691-0008
Ultimate Parent: Avery Dennison Corp.
SIC: 5211—Lumber & Other Building
Materials.

★ 74916 ★   Taco Bell
4809 W. Market St.
Greensboro, NC 27407
(919)855-5230
Ultimate Parent: Pepsico. SIC: 5812—
Eating Places.

★ 74917 ★   Taco Bell
2300 W. Meadowview Rd.
Greensboro, NC 27407
(919)299-0170
Ultimate Parent: Pepsico. SIC: 5812—
Eating Places.

★ 74918 ★   Taco Bell
2610 Battleground Ave.
Greensboro, NC 27408
(919)288-1086
Ultimate Parent: Pepsico. SIC: 5812—
Eating Places.

★ 74919 ★   Taco Bell
1115 Summit Ave.
Greensboro, NC 27405
(919)379-9127
Ultimate Parent: Pepsico. SIC: 5812—
Eating Places.

★ 74920 ★   Texaco Food Mart
4200 High Point Rd.
Greensboro, NC 27407
(919)292-6765
Ultimate Parent: Texaco. SIC: 5411—
Grocery Stores.

★ 74921 ★   Texaco Food Mart
13873 PO Box
Greensboro, NC 27415
(919)375-4897
Ultimate Parent: Texaco. SIC: 5541—
Gasoline Service Stations.

★ 74922 ★   Texaco Inc.
Chimney Rock Rd.
Greensboro, NC 27410
(919)294-0622
Ultimate Parent: Texaco. SIC: 5171—
Petroleum Bulk Stations & Terminals.

★ 74923 ★   Texaco Service
Station
Carolina Circle Apts.
Greensboro, NC 27405
(919)621-9916
Ultimate Parent: Texaco. SIC: 5621—
Women's Clothing Stores.

★ 74924 ★   Trailways Bus
Linescarolina
312 W. Friendly Ave.
Greensboro, NC 27401
(919)273-8696
Ultimate Parent: Greyhound Lines Inc. SIC:
4131—Intercity & Rural Bus Transportation.

★ 74925 ★   TRW Inc.
7915 Industrial Village Rd.
Greensboro, NC 27409
(910)668-3342
Officer: Mike Staffelbach, Manager.
Ultimate Parent: TRW, Inc. SIC: 3714—
Motor Vehicle Parts & Accessories.

★ 74926 ★   UNIFI, Inc.
7201 W. Friendly Ave.
Greensboro, NC 27410
(910)294-4410 Fax: (910)316-5422
Company Type: Headquarters. Officer:
William T. Kretzer, CEO. Employee Count:
6500. Sales: 1332.2 M. Fortune 500:
Largest U.S. Industrial Corporations:
Ranking 299.

★ 74927 ★ United Guaranty Corp.
201 N. Elm St.
Greensboro, NC 27401
(910)373-0232
Company Type: Subsidiary. Officer: Charles Reid, President. Ultimate Parent: American International Group, Inc. SIC: 6719—Holding Companies Nec.

★ 74928 ★ United Parcel Service
3015 Thurston Ave.
Greensboro, NC 27406
(919)373-1416
Ultimate Parent: United Parcel Service of America. SIC: 4212—Local Trucking Without Storage.

★ 74929 ★ United Parcel Service
3015 Thurston Ave.
Greensboro, NC 27406
(919)373-1416
Ultimate Parent: United Parcel Service of America. SIC: 4212—Local Trucking Without Storage.

★ 74930 ★ Wachovia Bank & Trust
604 Green Valley Rd. 204
Greensboro, NC 27408
(919)373-6077
Ultimate Parent: Wachovia Corp. SIC: 6099—Functions Related to Deposit Banking.

★ 74931 ★ Wachovia Bank & Trust Co.
Golden Gate Shopping Ctr.
Greensboro, NC 27405
(919)373-6344
Ultimate Parent: Wachovia Corp. SIC: 6099—Functions Related to Deposit Banking.

★ 74932 ★ Wachovia Bank & Trust Co. N
230 N. Elm St.
Greensboro, NC 27401
(919)373-6000
Ultimate Parent: Wachovia Corp. SIC: 6022—State Commercial Banks.

★ 74933 ★ Wachovia Bank & Trust Co. N
4004 W. Wendover Ave.
Greensboro, NC 27407
(919)373-6254
Ultimate Parent: Wachovia Corp. SIC: 6099—Functions Related to Deposit Banking.

★ 74934 ★ Wachovia Bank & Trust Co. N
Friendly Shopping Ctr.
Greensboro, NC 27408
(919)373-6363
Ultimate Parent: Wachovia Corp. SIC: 6022—State Commercial Banks.

★ 74935 ★ Wachovia Bank & Trust Co. N
Golden Gate Shopping Cent
Greensboro, NC 27405
(919)373-6345
Ultimate Parent: Wachovia Corp. SIC: 6022—State Commercial Banks.

★ 74936 ★ Wachovia Bank & Trust Co. Na
1405 Sunset Dr.
Greensboro, NC 27408
(919)373-6464
Ultimate Parent: Wachovia Corp. SIC: 6099—Functions Related to Deposit Banking.

★ 74937 ★ Wachovia Bank & Trust Co. Na
5815 W. Friendly Ave.
Greensboro, NC 27410
(919)373-6444
Ultimate Parent: Wachovia Corp. SIC: 6099—Functions Related to Deposit Banking.

★ 74938 ★ Wachovia Bank & Trust Co. Na
3602 Lawndale Dr.
Greensboro, NC 27408
(919)373-6237
Ultimate Parent: Wachovia Corp.

★ 74939 ★ Wachovia Bank & Trust Co. Na
2410 Randleman Rd.
Greensboro, NC 27406
(919)373-6161
Ultimate Parent: Wachovia Corp. SIC: 6099—Functions Related to Deposit Banking.

★ 74940 ★ Wachovia Bank & Trust Co. Na
1200 E. Bessemer Ave.
Greensboro, NC 27405
(919)373-6131
Ultimate Parent: Wachovia Corp. SIC: 6099—Functions Related to Deposit Banking.

★ 74941 ★ Wachovia Bank & Trust Co. NA
600 Four Seasons Town Ctr.
Greensboro, NC 27407
(919)373-6200
Ultimate Parent: Wachovia Corp. SIC: 6022—State Commercial Banks.

★ 74942 ★ Western Digital
1 Centerview Dr.
Greensboro, NC 27407
(919)299-6733
Ultimate Parent: Western Digital. SIC: 7373—Computer Integrated Systems Design.

★ 74943 ★ Wrangler
1421 S. Elm St.
Greensboro, NC 27406
(910)373-4275
Officer: Carolyn Belo, Manager. Ultimate Parent: VF Corp. SIC: 2325—Men's/Boys' Trousers & Slacks; 2326—Men's/Boys' Work Clothing; 3999—Manufacturing Industries Nec.

★ 74944 ★ Wrangler
335 Church St.
Greensboro, NC 27401
(910)373-3400
Officer: John Schamberger, President. Ultimate Parent: VF Corp. SIC: 2253—Knit Outerwear Mills; 2311—Men's/Boys' Suits & Coats; 2321—Men's/Boys' Shirts.

Greenville

★ 74945 ★ Ace Hardware
State Rd. 1722
Greenville, NC 27834
(919)756-2100
Ultimate Parent: Ace Hardware. SIC: 1711—Plumbing, Heating & Air-Conditioning.

★ 74946 ★ Airborne Freight Corp.
Greenville, NC 27834
(919)758-0696
Ultimate Parent: Airborne Freight Corp. SIC: 4512—Air Transportation—Scheduled.

★ 74947 ★ American General Finance
205 Greenville Blvd. SW
Greenville, NC 27834-6907
(919)756-3837
Ultimate Parent: American General Corp. SIC: 6141—Personal Credit Institutions.

★ 74948 ★ American General Finance
208 E. Arlington Blvd.
Greenville, NC 27858-5014
(919)355-3666
Ultimate Parent: American General Corp. SIC: 6141—Personal Credit Institutions.

★ 74949 ★ American General Finance Inc.
208 E. Arlington Blvd.
Greenville, NC 27858-5014
(919)355-3666
Location Type: Branch office. Ultimate Parent: American General Corp. SIC: 6141—Personal Credit Institutions.

★ 74950 ★ American General Finance Inc.
205 Greenville Blvd. SW
Greenville, NC 27834-6907
(919)756-3837
Location Type: Branch office. Ultimate Parent: American General Corp. SIC: 6141—Personal Credit Institutions.

★ 74951 ★ Branch Banking & Trust Co.
Greene St.
Greenville, NC 27834
(919)752-6889
Ultimate Parent: Southern National Corp. SIC: 6022—State Commercial Banks.

★ 74952 ★ Branch Banking & Trust Co.
Stantonsburg Rd.
Greenville, NC 27834
(919)756-7950
Ultimate Parent: Southern National Corp. SIC: 6022—State Commercial Banks.

★ 74953 ★ Carolina Leaf Tobacco Co.
N Greene Ext
Greenville, NC 27834
(919)752-2144
Ultimate Parent: Dibrell Brothers. SIC: 5159—Farm-Product Raw Materials Nec.

★ 74954 ★ Circus World
Carolina Mall E
Greenville, NC 27834
(919)756-8546
Ultimate Parent: Melville. SIC: 5945—Hobby, Toy & Game Shops.

★ 74955 ★ Citgo Service Station
1025 Dickinson Ave.
Greenville, NC 27834
(919)752-5254
Ultimate Parent: Citgo Petroleum. SIC: 5541—Gasoline Service Stations.

★ 74956 ★ Diebold Inc.
510 S. Greene St.
Greenville, NC 27834
(919)758-0515
Ultimate Parent: Diebold, Inc. SIC: 5065—Electronic Parts & Equipment Nec.

★ 74957 ★ Eveready Battery Co. Inc.
100 W. Greenville Blvd.
Greenville, NC 27834
Officer: J.C. Card. Ultimate Parent: Ralston Purina. SIC: 3692—Primary Batteries—Dry & Wet; 3691—Storage Batteries.

★ 74958 ★ Exxon Co. USA
Oakmont Dr.
Greenville, NC 27834
(919)756-5366
Ultimate Parent: Exxon. SIC: 5172—Petroleum Products Nec.

★ 74959 ★ Exxon L P Gas Co.
Bethel Hwy.
Greenville, NC 27858
(919)752-4512
Ultimate Parent: Exxon. SIC: 5984—Liquefied Petroleum Gas Dealers.

★ 74960 ★ First-Citizens Bank & Trust Co.
701 S. Memorial Dr.
Greenville, NC 27834-3737
(919)756-2427
Location Type: Branch office. Ultimate Parent: First Citizens Bancshares, Inc. SIC: 6021—National Commercial Banks.

★ 74961 ★ First-Citizens Bank & Trust Co.
1615 E. Greenville Blvd.
Greenville, NC 27834-7027
(919)756-2427
Location Type: Branch office. Ultimate Parent: First Citizens Bancshares, Inc. SIC: 6021—National Commercial Banks.

★ 74962 ★ First-Citizens Bank & Trust Co.
301 Evans Mall
Greenville, NC 27858-1832
(919)756-2427
Location Type: Branch office. Ultimate Parent: First Citizens Bancshares, Inc. SIC: 6021—National Commercial Banks.

★ 74963 ★ First-Citizens Bank & Trust Co.
3109 S. Memorial Dr.
Greenville, NC 27834
(919)756-2427
Location Type: Branch office. Officer: Terry B. Taylor, Area Vice President. Ultimate Parent: First Citizens Bancshares, Inc. SIC: 6021—National Commercial Banks.

★ 74964 ★ Hertz Rent-A-Car Licensee
Airport Rd.
Greenville, NC 27834
(919)752-7518
Ultimate Parent: Hertz. SIC: 7514—Passenger Car Rental.

★ 74965 ★ Karastan Spinning
2107 Dickinson Ave.
Greenville, NC 27834
Ultimate Parent: Fieldcrest Cannon. SIC: 2273—Carpets & Rugs.

★ 74966 ★ Lerner Shop
210 Carolina Mall E
Greenville, NC 27834
(919)756-7640
Ultimate Parent: Limited. SIC: 5621—Women's Clothing Stores.

★ 74967 ★ Microage
3514 PO Box
Greenville, NC 27836
Ultimate Parent: MicroAge. SIC: 7373—Computer Integrated Systems Design.

★ 74968 ★ Ncr Corp.
101 W. 14th St. 8
Greenville, NC 27834
Ultimate Parent: AT&T. SIC: 2761—Manifold Business Forms.

★ 74969 ★ NCR Corp.
101 W. 14th St., Ste. 8
Greenville, NC 27834-4182
(919)752-2701
Ultimate Parent: AT&T. SIC: 2761—Manifold Business Forms.

★ 74970 ★ Pepsi-Cola Bottling Co.
1807 Dickinson Ave.
Greenville, NC 27834
(919)758-2113
Officer: Thomas Minges, President. Ultimate Parent: Pepsico. SIC: 2086—Bottled & Canned Soft Drinks.

★ 74971 ★ Piggly Wiggly
2105 Dickinson Ave.
Greenville, NC 27834
(919)756-2444
Ultimate Parent: Bruno's. SIC: 5411—Grocery Stores.

★ 74972 ★ Pizza Hut
305 Greenville Blvd. SW
Greenville, NC 27834
(919)756-4320
Ultimate Parent: Pepsico. SIC: 5812—Eating Places.

★ 74973 ★ Pizza Hut
2601 E. 10th St.
Greenville, NC 27858
(919)752-4445
Ultimate Parent: Pepsico. SIC: 5812—Eating Places.

★ 74974 ★ Radio Shack
Pitt Plz.
Greenville, NC 27834
(919)756-6433
Company Type: Division. Ultimate Parent: Tandy Corp. SIC: 5731—Radio, Television & Electronics Stores.

★ 74975 ★ Radio Shack
230 Carolina Mall E
Greenville, NC 27834
(919)756-8938
Company Type: Division. Ultimate Parent: Tandy Corp. SIC: 5731—Radio, Television & Electronics Stores.

★ 74976 ★ Rite Aid of North Carolina
2814 E. 10th St.
Greenville, NC 27858
(919)758-2181
Ultimate Parent: Rite Aid. SIC: 5912—Drug Stores & Proprietary Stores.

★ 74977 ★ Ryder Truck Rental
701 Greenville Blvd. SW
Greenville, NC 27834
(919)756-8045
Ultimate Parent: Ryder System. SIC: 7359—Equipment Rental & Leasing Nec.

★ 74978 ★   **Taco Bell**
319 Greenville Blvd. SW
Greenville, NC 27834
(919)756-8231
Ultimate Parent: Pepsico. **SIC:** 5812—
Eating Places.

★ 74979 ★   **Taco Bell**
659 S. Memorial Dr.
Greenville, NC 27834
(919)757-1711
Ultimate Parent: Pepsico.

★ 74980 ★   **TRW Inc.**
2100 N. Greene St.
Greenville, NC 27834
(919)758-7411
Officer: Jim Handysidet, Manager. **Ultimate Parent:** TRW, Inc. **SIC:** 3714—Motor
Vehicle Parts & Accessories.

★ 74981 ★   **TRW Inc.**
Station Plant Steering & Suspension Div.
2100 N. Greene St.
Greenville, NC 27834-9099
Company Type: Division. **Location Type:**
Plant. **Ultimate Parent:** TRW, Inc. **SIC:**
3714—Motor Vehicle Parts & Accessories.

★ 74982 ★   **Trw Inc. Station Plant**
2100 N. Greene St.
Greenville, NC 27834
Ultimate Parent: TRW, Inc. **SIC:** 3714—
Motor Vehicle Parts & Accessories.

★ 74983 ★   **Trw Inc. Staton**
2100 N. Greene St.
Greenville, NC 27834-9099
Ultimate Parent: TRW, Inc. **SIC:** 3700—
Transportation Equipment.

★ 74984 ★   **Wachovia Bank & Trust Co.**
East Carolina Conven
Greenville, NC 27834
(919)757-7111
Ultimate Parent: Wachovia Corp. **SIC:**
6099—Functions Related to Deposit
Banking.

★ 74985 ★   **Wachovia Bank & Trust Co. N**
Pitt Plz.
Greenville, NC 27834
(919)757-7121
Ultimate Parent: Wachovia Corp. **SIC:**
6022—State Commercial Banks.

★ 74986 ★   **Wachovia Bank & Trust Co. N**
Stantonsburg Rd.
Greenville, NC 27834
(919)757-7231
Ultimate Parent: Wachovia Corp. **SIC:**
6022—State Commercial Banks.

★ 74987 ★   **Wachovia Bank & Trust Co. N**
802 E. 10th St.
Greenville, NC 27858
(919)757-7251
Ultimate Parent: Wachovia Corp. **SIC:**
6022—State Commercial Banks.

★ 74988 ★   **Wachovia Bank & Trust Co. N**
1102 N. Greene St.
Greenville, NC 27834
(919)757-7311
Ultimate Parent: Wachovia Corp. **SIC:**
6022—State Commercial Banks.

★ 74989 ★   **Waldenbooks**
222 Carolina Mall E
Greenville, NC 27834
(919)756-8725
Ultimate Parent: K-Mart. **SIC:** 5942—Book
Stores.

Grifton

★ 74990 ★   **Branch Banking & Trust Co.**
118 E. Queen St.
Grifton, NC 28530
(919)524-4128
Company Type: Subsidiary. **Location Type:** Branch office. **Officer:** Sandy Michell, Mgr. **Ultimate Parent:** Southern National Corp. **SIC:** 6021—National Commercial Banks.

Gustonia

★ 74991 ★   **Wix Corp.**
PO Box 1967
Gustonia, NC 28053
(704)864-6711
Company Type: Subsidiary. **Officer:**
Richard Forde, Vice President & General
Manager. **Ultimate Parent:** Dana Corp.
SIC: 3714—Motor Vehicle Parts &
Accessories. **Employee Count:** 2500.

Halifax

★ 74992 ★   **Branch Banking & Trust Co.**
King St.
Halifax, NC 27839
(919)583-7141
Ultimate Parent: Southern National Corp.
SIC: 6022—State Commercial Banks.

★ 74993 ★   **Branch Banking & Trust Co.**
King St.
Halifax, NC 27839
(919)583-7141
Company Type: Subsidiary. **Location Type:** Branch office. **Officer:** Linda R. Holdford, mgr. **Ultimate Parent:** Southern National Corp. **SIC:** 6021—National Commercial Banks.

Hamilton

★ 74994 ★   **Wachovia Bank & Trust Co. N**
101 S. Front St.
Hamilton, NC 27840
(919)798-6971
Ultimate Parent: Wachovia Corp. **SIC:**
6022—State Commercial Banks.

★ 74995 ★   **Westpoint Pepperell**
Hwy. 125
Hamilton, NC 27840
Location Type: Plant. **Ultimate Parent:**
West Point Stevens. **SIC:** 2253—Knit
Outerwear Mills.

Hamlet

★ 74996 ★   **Bea Fasteners Inc.**
Rte. 177 S.
Hamlet, NC 28345
Ultimate Parent: Stanley Works. **SIC:**
3496—Miscellaneous Fabricated Wire
Products.

★ 74997 ★   **Branch Banking & Trust Co.**
8 Raleigh St.
Hamlet, NC 28345-2756
(910)582-0184
Company Type: Subsidiary. **Location Type:** Branch office. **Ultimate Parent:**
Southern National Corp. **SIC:** 6021—
National Commercial Banks.

★ 74998 ★   **Food Lion**
801 W. Hamlet Ave.
Hamlet, NC 28345
(919)582-6525
Ultimate Parent: Food Lion. **SIC:** 5411—
Grocery Stores.

★ 74999 ★   **Owens-Illinois Inc.**
5 County Home Rd.
Hamlet, NC 28345
Ultimate Parent: Owens-Illinois. **SIC:**
3089—Plastics Products Nec.

★ 75000 ★   **Rite Aid**
801 W. Hamlet Ave.
Hamlet, NC 28345
(919)582-5031
Ultimate Parent: Rite Aid. **SIC:** 5912—Drug
Stores & Proprietary Stores.

★ 75001 ★   **Stanley-Bostitch Inc. Hamlet Plant**
Rte. 177 S.
Hamlet, NC 28345
Ultimate Parent: Stanley Works. **SIC:**
3496—Miscellaneous Fabricated Wire
Products.

★ 75002 ★   **Trailways Bus System**
308 Hylan Ave.
Hamlet, NC 28345
(919)582-2942
Ultimate Parent: Greyhound Lines Inc. **SIC:**
4142—Bus Charter Service Except Local.

Harkers is

★ 75003 ★   **Wachovia Bank & Trust Co.**
276 PO Box
Harkers is, NC 28531
(919)728-4161
Ultimate Parent: Wachovia Corp. **SIC:**
6022—State Commercial Banks.

Harmony

★ 75004 ★   **Holly Farms Foods Inc.**
Sheffield Rd. PO Box 146
Harmony, NC 28634
Ultimate Parent: Tyson Foods, Inc. **SIC:**
0251—Broiler, Fryer & Roaster Chickens.

★ 75005 ★   **Holly Farms Foods Inc.**
Harmony Rendering
Sheffield Rd.
PO Box 146
Harmony, NC 28634
Ultimate Parent: Tyson Foods, Inc. **SIC:**
0251—Broiler, Fryer & Roaster Chickens.

★ 75006 ★   **Tyson Foods Inc.**
Sheffield Rd.
Harmony, NC 28634
(704)546-2602
Ultimate Parent: Tyson Foods, Inc. **SIC:**
2077—Animal & Marine Fats & Oils.

Havelock

★ 75007 ★   **Branch Banking & Trust Co.**
Cherry Plz. Shopping Ctr.
Hwy. 70
Havelock, NC 28532-2499
(919)447-0611
Company Type: Subsidiary. **Location Type:** Branch office. **Officer:** Robert L.
Boggs Jr., Mgr. **Ultimate Parent:** Southern
National Corp. **SIC:** 6021—National
Commercial Banks.

★ 75008 ★   **First-Citizens Bank & Trust Co.**
Jaycee St.
Havelock, NC 28532
(919)447-1171
Location Type: Branch office. **Officer:** Dale
P. Lewis, Vice President. **Ultimate Parent:**
First Citizens Bancshares, Inc. **SIC:** 6021—
National Commercial Banks.

★ 75009 ★   **Pizza Hut**
411 W. Main St.
Havelock, NC 28532
(919)447-0297
Ultimate Parent: Pepsico. **SIC:** 5812—
Eating Places.

★ 75010 ★   **Ryder Truck Rental**
560 Us Hwy. 70 W
Havelock, NC 28532
Ultimate Parent: Ryder System. **SIC:**
7359—Equipment Rental & Leasing Nec.

Haw River

★ 75011 ★   **Burlington Maid Enterprises II**
1530 E. Main St.
Haw River, NC 27258
(910)578-3104
Officer: Jim Phillips, Manager. **Ultimate Parent:** Burlington Industries, Equity. **SIC:**
2252—Hosiery Nec.

★ 75012 ★   **Cone Mills Corp. Granite Finishing Plant**
122 E. Main St.
Haw River, NC 27258
Ultimate Parent: Cone Mills. **SIC:** 2261—
Finishing Plants—Cotton; 2262—Finishing
Plants—Manmade.

★ 75013 ★   **Cone Mills Corp. Granite Plant**
Hwy. 70
Haw River, NC 27258
Ultimate Parent: Cone Mills. **SIC:** 2261—
Finishing Plants—Cotton; 2262—Finishing
Plants—Manmade.

★ 75014 ★   **Granite Plant**
Hwy. 70
Haw River, NC 27258
Ultimate Parent: Cone Mills. **SIC:** 2261—
Finishing Plants—Cotton; 2262—Finishing
Plants—Manmade.

Hayesville

★ 75015 ★   **Wachovia Bank & Trust Co.**
237 PO Box
Hayesville, NC 28904
(704)389-6341
Ultimate Parent: Wachovia Corp. **SIC:**
6141—Personal Credit Institutions.

Henderson

★ 75016 ★   **Ball-Ball-InCon Glass**
Ball-Incon
US Hwy. 1 By-Pass, Box 887
Henderson, NC 27536
(919)492-1131 **Fax:** (919)492-3531
Company Type: Subsidiary. **Location Type:** Plant. **Officer:** William A. Jones,
Plant Manager. **Ultimate Parent:** Ball Corp.
SIC: 3221—Glass Containers.

★ 75017 ★   **Ball Incon Glass Packaging**
US Hwy. 1, Bypass S
Henderson, NC 27536
(919)492-1131
Officer: Bob Sawyer, Manager. **Ultimate Parent:** Ball Corp. **SIC:** 3221—Glass
Containers.

★ 75018 ★   **Ball-Incon Glass Packaging**
US 1 Bypass S
Henderson, NC 27536
(919)492-1131
Location Type: Branch office. **Officer:** Art
Jones. **Ultimate Parent:** Ball Corp. **SIC:**
3221—Glass Containers; 5023—
Homefurnishings; 6061—Federal Credit
Unions.

★ 75019 ★   **Ball-Incon Glass Packaging**
US 1 Bypass S
Henderson, NC 27536
(919)492-1131
Location Type: Branch office. **Officer:** Art
Jones. **Ultimate Parent:** Ball Corp. **SIC:**
3221—Glass Containers; 5023—
Homefurnishings; 6061—Federal Credit
Unions.

★ 75020 ★   **Ball-Incon Glass Packaging Corp.**
US Hwy., 1 No. Bypass
Henderson, NC 27536
Ultimate Parent: Ball Corp. **SIC:** 3221—
Glass Containers.

★ 75021 ★   **Branch Banking & Trust Co.**
632 Dabney Dr.
Henderson, NC 27536-3948
(919)492-2185
Company Type: Subsidiary. **Location Type:** Branch office. **Ultimate Parent:**
Southern National Corp. **SIC:** 6021—
National Commercial Banks.

★ 75022 ★   **Branch Banking & Trust Co.**
213 N. Chestnut St.
Henderson, NC 27536-4215
(919)492-2181
Company Type: Subsidiary. **Location Type:** Branch office. **Officer:** Braxton
Poythress, Manager. **Ultimate Parent:**
Southern National Corp. **SIC:** 6021—
National Commercial Banks.

★ 75023 ★   **Exxon Co. USA**
N Norlina Rd.
Henderson, NC 27536
(919)438-5713
Ultimate Parent: Exxon. **SIC:** 4932—Gas &
Other Services Combined.

★ 75024 ★   J.P. Taylor Co.
Raleigh Rd.
Henderson, NC 27536
(919)492-1161
Officer: James Wiliams, Manager. Ultimate Parent: Universal Corp. SIC: 2141—Tobacco Stemming & Redrying.

★ 75025 ★   Pizza Hut
Vance Sq.
Henderson, NC 27536
(919)492-8713
Ultimate Parent: Pepsico. SIC: 5812—Eating Places.

★ 75026 ★   Purolator Products Co. Air Filtration Co.
U.S. Hwy. 1 Bypass S.
Henderson, NC 27536
Ultimate Parent: Pennzoil. SIC: 3546—Power-Driven Handtools.

★ 75027 ★   Radio Shack
Henderson Mall
Henderson, NC 27536
(919)492-5721
Company Type: Division. Ultimate Parent: Tandy Corp. SIC: 5065—Electronic Parts & Equipment Nec.

★ 75028 ★   Rite Aid Corp.
Rural Route 1
Henderson, NC 27536
(919)492-7511
Ultimate Parent: Rite Aid. SIC: 8748—Business Consulting Services Nec.

★ 75029 ★   Vulcan Materials Co.
RR 6
Henderson, NC 27536
(919)438-2766
Officer: B R Stevenson, Manager. Ultimate Parent: Vulcan Materials Co. SIC: 3295—Minerals—Ground or Treated.

Hendersonville

★ 75030 ★   American General Finance
128 Four Seasons Blvd.
Hendersonville, NC 28792-2878
(704)697-9965
Officer: Tracy Moncrief. Ultimate Parent: American General Corp. SIC: 6141—Personal Credit Institutions.

★ 75031 ★   American General Finance Inc.
128 Four Seasons Blvd.
Hendersonville, NC 28792-2878
(704)697-9965
Location Type: Branch office. Officer: Tracy Moncrief. Ultimate Parent: American General Corp. SIC: 6141—Personal Credit Institutions.

★ 75032 ★   Daniels Packaging Co. Inc.
3510 Asheville Hwy.
Hendersonville, NC 28739
Ultimate Parent: Banta Corp. SIC: 2600—Paper & Allied Products.

★ 75033 ★   First-Citizens Bank & Trust Co.
2309 Spartanburg Hwy.
Hendersonville, NC 28726-2326
(704)696-7710
Location Type: Branch office. Ultimate Parent: First Citizens Bancshares, Inc. SIC: 6021—National Commercial Banks.

★ 75034 ★   First-Citizens Bank & Trust Co.
1605 Four Seasons Blvd.
Hendersonville, NC 28792-2857
(704)692-9151
Location Type: Branch office. Ultimate Parent: First Citizens Bancshares, Inc. SIC: 6021—National Commercial Banks.

★ 75035 ★   First-Citizens Bank & Trust Co.
US Hwy. 25
Hendersonville, NC 28732-9501
(704)684-7147
Location Type: Branch office. Ultimate Parent: First Citizens Bancshares, Inc. SIC: 6021—National Commercial Banks.

★ 75036 ★   First-Citizens Bank & Trust Co.
1340 Asheville Hwy.
Hendersonville, NC 28739-3414
(704)692-7226
Location Type: Branch office. Ultimate Parent: First Citizens Bancshares, Inc. SIC: 6021—National Commercial Banks.

★ 75037 ★   First-Citizens Bank & Trust Co.
1004 Spartanburg Hwy.
Hendersonville, NC 28792-5823
(704)692-9151
Location Type: Branch office. Ultimate Parent: First Citizens Bancshares, Inc. SIC: 6021—National Commercial Banks.

★ 75038 ★   First-Citizens Bank & Trust Co.
First Federal Plz.
Main St. & Sixth Ave.
Hendersonville, NC 28793
(704)696-7400
Location Type: Branch office. Officer: James F. Pope, Area Vice President. Ultimate Parent: First Citizens Bancshares, Inc. SIC: 6021—National Commercial Banks.

★ 75039 ★   First-Citizens Bank & Trust Co.
1500 Gour Seasons Blvd.
Hendersonville, NC 28792-2853
(910)692-7226
Location Type: Branch office. Ultimate Parent: First Citizens Bancshares, Inc. SIC: 6021—National Commercial Banks.

★ 75040 ★   General Electric Lighting Systems
3010 Spartanburg Hwy.
Hendersonville, NC 28739
Ultimate Parent: General Electric. SIC: 3646—Commercial Lighting Fixtures; 3363—Aluminum Die-Castings.

★ 75041 ★   Greyhound Bus Lines
1019 7th Ave. E
Hendersonville, NC 28792
(704)693-3466
Ultimate Parent: Greyhound Lines Inc. SIC: 4111—Local & Suburban Transit.

★ 75042 ★   Hudson's
444 Loop Rd.
Hendersonville, NC 28792
(704)692-4092
Ultimate Parent: Dayton Hudson. SIC: 1522—Residential Construction Nec.

★ 75043 ★   New Woman Magazine
330 N. Main St.
Hendersonville, NC 28792
(704)692-3551
Ultimate Parent: K-III Communications. SIC: 2721—Periodicals.

★ 75044 ★   Vulcan Materials Co.
Clear Creek Rd.
Hendersonville, NC 28792
(704)692-0254
Officer: Wayne Queen, Manager. Ultimate Parent: Vulcan Materials Co. SIC: 3295—Minerals—Ground or Treated.

★ 75045 ★   Wachovia Bank & Trust
1703 Brevard Rd.
Hendersonville, NC 28739
(704)696-8573
Ultimate Parent: Wachovia Corp. SIC: 6099—Functions Related to Deposit Banking.

★ 75046 ★   Wachovia Bank & Trust Co. NA
201 S. Main St.
Hendersonville, NC 28792
(704)692-5777
Ultimate Parent: Wachovia Corp. SIC: 6141—Personal Credit Institutions.

★ 75047 ★   Waldenbooks
Blue Ridge Mall
Hendersonville, NC 28739
(704)692-4957
Ultimate Parent: K-Mart. SIC: 5942—Book Stores.

Hendersonvl

★ 75048 ★   Pizza Hut
1800 Four Seasons Blvd.
Hendersonvl, NC 28792
(704)693-4188
Ultimate Parent: Pepsico. SIC: 5812—Eating Places.

★ 75049 ★   Pizza Hut
633 Spartanburg Hwy.
Hendersonvl, NC 28792
(704)692-2804
Ultimate Parent: Pepsico. SIC: 5812—Eating Places.

★ 75050 ★   Rite Aid Corp.
141 Fleming St.
Hendersonvl, NC 28739
(704)693-4304
Ultimate Parent: Rite Aid. SIC: 5912—Drug Stores & Proprietary Stores.

★ 75051 ★   Wells Manufacturing Co.
305 Thompson St.
Hendersonvl, NC 28792
(704)697-2216
Ultimate Parent: UIS. SIC: 2335—Women's/Misses' Dresses.

Hickory

★ 75052 ★   ABF Freight System Inc.
Neuville Ave.
Hickory, NC 28601
(704)397-5557
Ultimate Parent: Arkansas Best. SIC: 4212—Local Trucking Without Storage.

★ 75053 ★   Ace Hardware
2310 N. Ctr. St.
Hickory, NC 28601
(704)322-3492
Ultimate Parent: Ace Hardware. SIC: 5251—Hardware Stores.

★ 75054 ★   Adams-Millis Hoisery
74 8th St. SE
Hickory, NC 28601
Location Type: Plant. Ultimate Parent: Sara Lee Corp. SIC: 2252—Hosiery Nec.

★ 75055 ★   American Family Life Assur
42 3rd St. NW
Hickory, NC 28601
(704)324-2820
Ultimate Parent: American Family Life Assurance Co. SIC: 6411—Insurance Agents, Brokers & Service.

★ 75056 ★   American Family Life Assurance
42 3rd St. NW
Hickory, NC 28601
(704)324-2820
Ultimate Parent: American Family Life Assurance Co. SIC: 6411—Insurance Agents, Brokers & Service.

★ 75057 ★   American General Finance Inc.
747 4th St. SW
Hickory, NC 28602
(704)322-4993
Location Type: Branch office. Ultimate Parent: American General Corp. SIC: 6141—Personal Credit Institutions.

★ 75058 ★   Bell Atlantic Mobile
1260 25th St. Pl. SE
Hickory, NC 28602-9657
(704)322-3339
Officer: Larry Ingle. Ultimate Parent: Bell Atlantic Corp. SIC: 4812—Radiotelephone Communications; 5065—Electronic Parts & Equipment Nec.

★ 75059 ★   Branch Banking & Trust Co.
Hwy. 127 & State Rte. 1193
Hickory, NC 28602-8204
(704)326-4850
Company Type: Subsidiary. Location Type: Branch office. Ultimate Parent: Southern National Corp. SIC: 6021—National Commercial Banks.

★ 75060 ★   Branch Banking & Trust Co.
2141 Hwy. 70 SE
Hickory, NC 28602
(704)326-4871
Company Type: Subsidiary. Location Type: Branch office. Officer: Ron Lindler, Manager. Ultimate Parent: Southern National Corp. SIC: 6021—National Commercial Banks.

★ 75061 ★   Branch Banking & Trust Co.
106 2nd St. NW
Hickory, NC 28601-6107
(704)326-4800
Company Type: Subsidiary. Location Type: Branch office. Ultimate Parent: Southern National Corp. SIC: 6021—National Commercial Banks.

★ 75062 ★   Chicago Title Insurance Co.
201 Government Ave. SW
Hickory, NC 28602-2938
(704)328-4332
Ultimate Parent: Alleghany Corp. SIC: 6361—Title Insurance.

★ 75063 ★   Citizens Savings Bank, SSB
4035 Hwy. 127 SE
Hickory, NC 28602
(704)294-1220
Company Type: Subsidiary. Location Type: Branch office. Officer: Barbara Farnsworth, Mgr. Ultimate Parent: Southern National Corp. SIC: 6021—National Commercial Banks.

★ 75064 ★   Citizens Savings Bank, SSB
1209 9th Ave. NE
Hickory, NC 28601-4107
(704)322-6441
Company Type: Subsidiary. Location Type: Branch office. Officer: Mark Weitzel, Mgr. Ultimate Parent: Southern National Corp. SIC: 6021—National Commercial Banks.

★ 75065 ★   Citizens Savings Bank, SSB
Hwy. 127, N. Rink Dam Rd.
Hickory, NC 28601-9370
(704)495-4641
Company Type: Subsidiary. Location Type: Branch office. Officer: Ron Honeycutt, Mgr. Ultimate Parent: Southern National Corp. SIC: 6021—National Commercial Banks.

★ 75066 ★   Drexel Heritage Furniture
Plant 45
40-30th St. NW
Hickory, NC 28601
Location Type: Plant. Ultimate Parent: Masco. SIC: 2512—Upholstered Household Furniture.

★ 75067 ★   E. R. Carpenter Co. Inc.
1120 Tate Blvd. PO Box 1542
Hickory, NC 28601
Ultimate Parent: Carpenter. SIC: 3086—Plastics Foam Products.

★ 75068 ★   E R Carpenter Co. Inc.
29 St. NW
Hickory, NC 28603
(704)322-6545
Ultimate Parent: Carpenter. SIC: 5192—Books, Periodicals & Newspapers.

★ 75069 ★   First-Citizens Bank & Trust Co.
1729 N. Ctr. St.
Hickory, NC 28601-1850
(704)322-5513
Location Type: Branch office. Ultimate Parent: First Citizens Bancshares, Inc. SIC: 6021—National Commercial Banks.

★ 75070 ★   First-Citizens Bank & Trust Co.
1419 1st Ave. SW
Hickory, NC 28602-2402
(704)322-5513
Location Type: Branch office. Ultimate Parent: First Citizens Bancshares, Inc. SIC: 6021—National Commercial Banks.

★ 75071 ★ First-Citizens Bank &
Trust Co.
1862 Hwy. 70 SE
Hickory, NC 28602
(704)322-5513
Location Type: Branch office. Ultimate
Parent: First Citizens Bancshares, Inc. SIC:
6021—National Commercial Banks.

★ 75072 ★ First-Citizens Bank &
Trust Co.
1251 16th St.
Hickory, NC 28601-4240
(704)322-5513
Location Type: Branch office. Ultimate
Parent: First Citizens Bancshares, Inc. SIC:
6021—National Commercial Banks.

★ 75073 ★ First-Citizens Bank &
Trust Co.
328 1st. Ave. NW
Hickory, NC 28601-6123
(704)322-5513
Location Type: Branch office. Officer:
William C. Happer, Area Vice President.
Ultimate Parent: First Citizens Bancshares,
Inc. SIC: 6021—National Commercial
Banks.

★ 75074 ★ Fryef Regional
Medical Center
420 N. Center St.
Hickory, NC 28601
(704)322-6072
Officer: Dennis Phillips, Executive Director.
Ultimate Parent: American Medical
Holdings. SIC: 8062—General Medical &
Surgical Hospitals.

★ 75075 ★ The Gap
Valley Ct SE
Hickory, NC 28602
(704)322-1116
Ultimate Parent: GAP. SIC: 5699—
Miscellaneous Apparel & Accessory Stores.

★ 75076 ★ Gap Stores the
Valley Ct SE
Hickory, NC 28602
(704)322-1116
Ultimate Parent: GAP. SIC: 5699—
Miscellaneous Apparel & Accessory Stores.

★ 75077 ★ General Electric Co.
1223 Fairgrove Church Rd.
Hickory, NC 28602
(704)462-3000
Officer: Pete Defonzo, Manager. Ultimate
Parent: General Electric. SIC: 3612—
Transformers Except Electronic.

★ 75078 ★ General Electric Co.
Transformer Bus. Dept.
1223 Fairgrove Church Rd.
Hickory, NC 28603
Ultimate Parent: General Electric. SIC:
3612—Transformers Except Electronic.

★ 75079 ★ General Electric Co.
Transformer Business Dept.
1223 Fairgrove Church Rd.
Hickory, NC 28603
Ultimate Parent: General Electric. SIC:
3612—Transformers Except Electronic.

★ 75080 ★ Hertz Rent-A-Car
Airport Terminal Bldg.
Hickory, NC 28601
(704)327-2584
Ultimate Parent: Hertz. SIC: 7514—
Passenger Car Rental.

★ 75081 ★ Hickorycraft, Inc.
State Rd. 1474
Hickory, NC 28603
(704)322-5995 Fax: (704)322-4427
Officer: J. Don Smith. Ultimate Parent:
Masco.

★ 75082 ★ IDS Financial
Services Inc.
116 3rd St. NE
Hickory, NC 28601
(704)327-0092
Location Type: Branch office. Ultimate
Parent: American Express Co. SIC: 6211—
Security Brokers & Dealers; 6282—
Investment Advice.

★ 75083 ★ Kentucky Fried
Chicken
Hwy. 64 Southwest
Hickory, NC 28601
(704)324-2960
Ultimate Parent: Pepsico. SIC: 5812—
Eating Places.

★ 75084 ★ Kentucky Fried
Chicken
2208 N. Ctr. St.
Hickory, NC 28601
(704)328-1270
Ultimate Parent: Pepsico. SIC: 5812—
Eating Places.

★ 75085 ★ Kroger Co.
1155 Us 70
Hickory, NC 28601
(704)328-5695
Ultimate Parent: Kroger. SIC: 5411—
Grocery Stores.

★ 75086 ★ Lane Bryant
1960 Hwy. 64-70 SE
Hickory, NC 28602
(704)322-5036
Ultimate Parent: Limited. SIC: 5621—
Women's Clothing Stores.

★ 75087 ★ The Limited
236 Valley Hill Mall
Hickory, NC 28602
(704)322-6174
Ultimate Parent: Limited. SIC: 5621—
Women's Clothing Stores.

★ 75088 ★ Martin Marietta
Aggregates
1989 11th Ave. SE
Hickory, NC 28602
(704)322-8386
Ultimate Parent: Martin Marietta. SIC:
1429—Crushed & Broken Stone Nec.

★ 75089 ★ North American Van
Lines Inc.
27 1st Ave. NE
Hickory, NC 28601
(704)322-4600
Ultimate Parent: Norfolk Southern. SIC:
4213—Trucking Except Local.

★ 75090 ★ Peoples Drug Stores
Inc.
Hwy. 64 E
Hickory, NC 28601
(704)322-2530
Ultimate Parent: Melville. SIC: 5912—Drug
Stores & Proprietary Stores.

★ 75091 ★ Pepsi-Cola Bottling
Co.
2640 Main Ave. NW
Hickory, NC 28601
(704)322-8090
Officer: James Teeter, President. Ultimate
Parent: Pepsico. SIC: 2086—Bottled &
Canned Soft Drinks.

★ 75092 ★ Pet Dairy
461 US Hwy. 70 SW
Hickory, NC 28602
(704)322-3730
Officer: Lee Barco, Executive Director.
Ultimate Parent: Pet. SIC: 2024—Ice
Cream & Frozen Desserts.

★ 75093 ★ Pizza Hut
216 Hwy. 64
Hickory, NC 28601
(704)327-9788
Ultimate Parent: Pepsico. SIC: 5812—
Eating Places.

★ 75094 ★ Pizza Hut
2321 N. Ctr. St.
Hickory, NC 28601
(704)322-5984
Ultimate Parent: Pepsico. SIC: 5812—
Eating Places.

★ 75095 ★ Plastic Packaging Inc.
1246 Main Ave. SE
Hickory, NC 28602
(704)328-2466
Officer: Jake Schoonderwoerd, President.
Ultimate Parent: Ball Corp. SIC: 2673—
Bags—Plastics, Laminated & Coated;
3086—Plastics Foam Products; 3089—
Plastics Products Nec.

★ 75096 ★ Radio Shack
Hickory Plz.
Hickory, NC 28601
(704)327-4850
Company Type: Division. Ultimate Parent:
Tandy Corp. SIC: 5065—Electronic Parts &
Equipment Nec.

★ 75097 ★ Radio Shack
Valley
Hickory, NC 28601
(704)328-9406
Company Type: Division. Ultimate Parent:
Tandy Corp. SIC: 5065—Electronic Parts &
Equipment Nec.

★ 75098 ★ Radio Shack
Catawba Mall
Hickory, NC 28601
(704)328-3300
Company Type: Division. Ultimate Parent:
Tandy Corp. SIC: 5065—Electronic Parts &
Equipment Nec.

★ 75099 ★ Ryder Truck Rental
Hwy. 321
Hickory, NC 28601
(704)327-9577
Ultimate Parent: Ryder System. SIC:
5541—Gasoline Service Stations.

★ 75100 ★ Siecor Corp.
800 17th St. NW
Hickory, NC 28601-3360
(704)327-5000
Officer: Jan Suwinski, Chairman of the
Board. Ultimate Parent: Corning. SIC:
3357—Nonferrous Wiredrawing & Insulating;
3661—Telephone & Telegraph Apparatus.
Employee Count: 2500. Sales: 326 M.

★ 75101 ★ T&H Service
Merchandisers, Inc.
1520 13th St., SW
PO Box 3486
Hickory, NC 28603
(704)328-5511 Fax: (704)328-3779
Officer: Joseph M. Bentler, President.
Ultimate Parent: Nash Finch.

★ 75102 ★ Thomasville
Upholstery, Inc.
2260 Highlands Ave. NE
Hickory, NC 28601
(704)327-2597
Officer: Mark Harris, Manager. Ultimate
Parent: Armstrong World Industries. SIC:
2599—Furniture & Fixtures Nec.

★ 75103 ★ Trailways Hickory
Bus Sta
303 1st Ave. SW
Hickory, NC 28602
(704)322-1030
Ultimate Parent: Greyhound Lines Inc. SIC:
4141—Local Bus Charter Service.

★ 75104 ★ Wachovia Bank &
Trust Compa
117 4th St. NW
Hickory, NC 28601
(704)322-8350
Ultimate Parent: Wachovia Corp. SIC:
6021—National Commercial Banks; 6022—
State Commercial Banks.

★ 75105 ★ Wal Mart Discount
Cities
1840 Us Hwy. 70 SE
Hickory, NC 28602
(704)327-4891
Ultimate Parent: Wal-Mart Stores, Inc. SIC:
5311—Department Stores.

★ 75106 ★ Wilsons
Rural Route 1
Hickory, NC 28602
(704)294-3667
Ultimate Parent: Melville. SIC: 4581—
Airports, Flying Fields & Services.

★ 75107 ★ Wilsons
RR 1
Hickory, NC 28602
(704)294-3667
Ultimate Parent: Melville. SIC: 4581—
Airports, Flying Fields & Services.

★ 75108 ★ Yescor Telephony
Cable Plant
State Rd. 2308
Hickory, NC 28601
Ultimate Parent: Corning. SIC: 3999—
Manufacturing Industries Nec.

High Point

★ 75109 ★ Adams-Millis
Influential
425 S. Centennial St.
High Point, NC 27260
Location Type: Plant. Ultimate Parent:
Sara Lee Corp. SIC: 2252—Hosiery Nec.

★ 75110 ★ Adams-Millis
Wrangler
501 S. Centennial St.
High Point, NC 27260
Ultimate Parent: Sara Lee Corp. SIC:
2252—Hosiery Nec.

★ 75111 ★ Adams Millis
Wranlger
501 South Centennial St.
High Point, NC 27260
Ultimate Parent: Sara Lee Corp. SIC:
2252—Hosiery Nec.

★ 75112 ★ Borden Inc.
Chemical
1717 Ward St.
High Point, NC 27261
Company Type: Division. Ultimate Parent:
Borden, Inc. SIC: 2891—Adhesives &
Sealants.

★ 75113 ★ Borden Inc.
Dairy
1900 N. Main St.
High Point, NC 27262
Company Type: Division. Ultimate Parent:
Borden, Inc. SIC: 2024—Ice Cream &
Frozen Desserts; 2026—Fluid Milk.

★ 75114 ★ Borden Inc.
Dairy
1900 N. Main St.
High Point, NC 27262
Company Type: Division. Ultimate Parent:
Borden, Inc. SIC: 2024—Ice Cream &
Frozen Desserts; 2026—Fluid Milk.

★ 75115 ★ Borden Inc.
Package & Industrial Products
1717 Ward St.
High Point, NC 27261
Company Type: Division. Ultimate Parent:
Borden, Inc. SIC: 2891—Adhesives &
Sealants.

★ 75116 ★ Borden Inc.
Packaging & Industrial Products
1717 Ward St.
High Point, NC 27261
Company Type: Division. Ultimate Parent:
Borden, Inc. SIC: 2891—Adhesives &
Sealants.

★ 75117 ★ Branch Banking &
Trust Co.
620 N. Main St.
High Point, NC 27260-5054
(910)884-5071
Company Type: Subsidiary. Location
Type: Branch office. Ultimate Parent:
Southern National Corp. SIC: 6021—
National Commercial Banks.

★ 75118 ★ Branch Banking &
Trust Co.
High Point, NC 27262
(910)885-7333
Company Type: Subsidiary. Location
Type: Branch office. Officer: Don White,
Mgr. Ultimate Parent: Southern National
Corp. SIC: 6021—National Commercial
Banks.

★ 75119 ★ Burlington House
Upholstery
312 S. Hamilton St.
High Point, NC 27260-6629
(919)889-0724
Ultimate Parent: Burlington Industries,
Equity. SIC: 5131—Piece Goods & Notions.

★ 75120 ★ Casual Corner
1761 Westchester Dr.
High Point, NC 27262
(919)841-4911
Ultimate Parent: United States Shoe. SIC:
5651—Family Clothing Stores.

★ 75121 ★ E. R. Carpenter Co.
Inc.
1021 Springfield Rd. PO Box 7071
High Point, NC 27264
Ultimate Parent: Carpenter. SIC: 3086—
Plastics Foam Products.

★ 75122 ★   E. R. Carpenter Co.
Inc.
2130 Brevard Rd. PO Box 1370
High Point, NC 27261
Ultimate Parent: Carpenter. SIC: 3086—
Plastics Foam Products.

★ 75123 ★   Ecco Inc.
2007 Fulton Pl
High Point, NC 27263
(919)841-4300
Ultimate Parent: Itel. SIC: 2599—Furniture
& Fixtures Nec; 5021—Furniture.

★ 75124 ★   Federal Paper Board
Co.
1617 Bolingbroke Rd.
High Point, NC 27265
(919)882-0948
Ultimate Parent: Federal Paper Board.
SIC: 5085—Industrial Supplies.

★ 75125 ★   First-Citizens Bank &
Trust Co.
143 Greensboro Rd.
High Point, NC 27260-3469
(910)883-3743
Location Type: Branch office. Ultimate
Parent: First Citizens Bancshares, Inc. SIC:
6021—National Commercial Banks.

★ 75126 ★   First-Citizens Bank &
Trust Co.
10800 N. Main St.
High Point, NC 27263
(910)883-3733
Location Type: Branch office. Ultimate
Parent: First Citizens Bancshares, Inc. SIC:
6021—National Commercial Banks.

★ 75127 ★   First-Citizens Bank &
Trust Co.
700 N. Main St.
High Point, NC 27262-4334
(910)833-3700
Location Type: Branch office. Ultimate
Parent: First Citizens Bancshares, Inc. SIC:
6021—National Commercial Banks.

★ 75128 ★   First-Citizens Bank &
Trust Co.
2110 Westchester Dr.
High Point, NC 27260-8025
(910)883-3743
Location Type: Branch office. Ultimate
Parent: First Citizens Bancshares, Inc. SIC:
6021—National Commercial Banks.

★ 75129 ★   First-Citizens Bank &
Trust Co.
101 Northpoint Ave.
High Point, NC 27260-3075
(910)883-3753
Location Type: Branch office. Ultimate
Parent: First Citizens Bancshares, Inc. SIC:
6021—National Commercial Banks.

★ 75130 ★   First Citizens
Mortgage
101 S. Main St.
High Point, NC 27260
(919)882-6431
Ultimate Parent: First Citizens Bancshares,
Inc. SIC: 6531—Real Estate Agents &
Managers.

★ 75131 ★   Foamex LP
2228 Shore Dr.
High Point, NC 27264
Ultimate Parent: Foamex. SIC: 3086—
Plastics Foam Products.

★ 75132 ★   Food Lion
1818 Westchester Dr.
High Point, NC 27262
(919)884-4142
Ultimate Parent: Food Lion. SIC: 5411—
Grocery Stores.

★ 75133 ★   Food Lion
1771 Westchester Dr.
High Point, NC 27262
(919)887-1416
Ultimate Parent: Food Lion. SIC: 5411—
Grocery Stores.

★ 75134 ★   Food Lion
1107 E. Lexington Ave.
High Point, NC 27262
(919)886-7872
Ultimate Parent: Food Lion. SIC: 5411—
Grocery Stores.

★ 75135 ★   Food Lion
2300 N. Main St.
High Point, NC 27262
(919)869-7154
Ultimate Parent: Food Lion. SIC: 5411—
Grocery Stores.

★ 75136 ★   Food Lion Inc.
1818 Westchester Dr.
High Point, NC 27262
(919)884-4142
Ultimate Parent: Food Lion. SIC: 5411—
Grocery Stores.

★ 75137 ★   Greyhound Bus Lines
500 S. Main St.
High Point, NC 27260
(919)884-4575
Ultimate Parent: Greyhound Lines Inc. SIC:
4142—Bus Charter Service Except Local.

★ 75138 ★   Jiffy Lube
111 Westchester Dr.
High Point, NC 27262
(919)869-7804
Ultimate Parent: Pennzoil. SIC: 7539—
Automotive Repair Shops Nec.

★ 75139 ★   Kentucky Fried
Chicken
130 W. Lexington Ave.
High Point, NC 27262
(919)883-2221
Ultimate Parent: Pepsico. SIC: 5812—
Eating Places.

★ 75140 ★   Kentucky Fried
Chicken
906 Greensboro Rd.
High Point, NC 27260
(919)884-4080
Ultimate Parent: Pepsico. SIC: 5812—
Eating Places.

★ 75141 ★   Kentucky Fried
Chicken
2718 S. Main St.
High Point, NC 27263
(919)885-8423
Ultimate Parent: Pepsico. SIC: 5812—
Eating Places.

★ 75142 ★   Kentucky Fried
Chicken
1924 English Rd.
High Point, NC 27262
(919)883-7512
Ultimate Parent: Pepsico. SIC: 5812—
Eating Places.

★ 75143 ★   Krogers
1116 Eastchester Dr.
High Point, NC 27265
(919)887-3422
Ultimate Parent: Kroger. SIC: 5411—
Grocery Stores.

★ 75144 ★   L&P Foam Inc.
2222 Surrett Dr.
High Point, NC 27263-2222
Ultimate Parent: Leggett & Platt Inc. SIC:
3069—Fabricated Rubber Products Nec.

★ 75145 ★   Leggett & Platt Foam
Inc.
2222 Surrett Dr.
High Point, NC 27263
Ultimate Parent: Leggett & Platt Inc. SIC:
3086—Plastics Foam Products.

★ 75146 ★   Leggett & Platt
Sleeper Comp-O Nents
1639 Blandwood Dr.
High Point, NC 27260
Ultimate Parent: Leggett & Platt Inc. SIC:
2514—Metal Household Furniture; 3449—
Miscellaneous Metal Work.

★ 75147 ★   Leggett & Platt
Sleeper Components
1639 Blandwood Dr.
High Point, NC 27260
Ultimate Parent: Leggett & Platt Inc. SIC:
2514—Metal Household Furniture; 3449—
Miscellaneous Metal Work.

★ 75148 ★   Lerner Shop
1717 Westchester Dr.
High Point, NC 27262
(919)883-9415
Ultimate Parent: Limited. SIC: 5651—
Family Clothing Stores.

★ 75149 ★   Lerner Shop
Westchester Shopping Ctr.
High Point, NC 27260
(919)883-9415
Ultimate Parent: Limited. SIC: 5621—
Women's Clothing Stores.

★ 75150 ★   Lineage Home
Furnishings
4000 Lineage Ct.
PO Box 11188
High Point, NC 27265
(919)454-6688 Fax: (919)888-6933
Officer: Thomas Tilley. Ultimate Parent:
Masco.

★ 75151 ★   Maitland-Smith, Ltd.
2427 Penny Rd., Ste. 101
High Point, NC 27265
(919)889-5616 Fax: (919)887-4807
Officer: Larry Milan. Ultimate Parent:
Masco.

★ 75152 ★   Manpower, Inc.
110 Scott Ave.
High Point, NC 27262
(919)869-0172
Ultimate Parent: Manpower, Inc. SIC:
7363—Help Supply Services.

★ 75153 ★   New England Mutual
Life Insurance
258 S. Main St.
High Point, NC 27260
(919)882-1816
Ultimate Parent: New England Mutual Life.
SIC: 6411—Insurance Agents, Brokers &
Service.

★ 75154 ★   Pizza Hut
804 N. Main St.
High Point, NC 27262
(919)841-6414
Ultimate Parent: Pepsico. SIC: 5812—
Eating Places.

★ 75155 ★   Pizza Hut
2749 S. Main St.
High Point, NC 27263
(919)885-0760
Ultimate Parent: Pepsico. SIC: 5812—
Eating Places.

★ 75156 ★   Prelude Co.
2215 Shore St.
High Point, NC 27263
Ultimate Parent: Cone Mills. SIC: 5714—
Drapery & Upholstery Stores.

★ 75157 ★   Radio Shack
108 E. Fairfield Rd.
High Point, NC 27263
(919)434-6489
Company Type: Division. Ultimate Parent:
Tandy Corp. SIC: 5731—Radio, Television
& Electronics Stores.

★ 75158 ★   Radio Shack
1745 Westchester Dr.
High Point, NC 27262
(919)882-3337
Company Type: Division. Ultimate Parent:
Tandy Corp. SIC: 5731—Radio, Television
& Electronics Stores.

★ 75159 ★   Record Data Inc.
175 Northpoint Ave.
High Point, NC 27262
(919)869-5248
Ultimate Parent: TRW, Inc. SIC: 7374—
Data Processing & Preparation.

★ 75160 ★   Rice Hosiery
550 W. Fairfield Rd.
High Point, NC 27263
Ultimate Parent: Sara Lee Corp. SIC:
2251—Women's Hosiery Except Socks.

★ 75161 ★   Rite Aid Discount
Pharmacie
944 N. Main St.
High Point, NC 27262
(919)882-0165
Ultimate Parent: Rite Aid. SIC: 5912—Drug
Stores & Proprietary Stores.

★ 75162 ★   Rite Aid Discount
Pharmacy
912 E. Green Dr.
High Point, NC 27260
(919)884-2261
Ultimate Parent: Rite Aid. SIC: 5912—Drug
Stores & Proprietary Stores.

★ 75163 ★   Rite Aid Drug Store
No 1219
944 N. Main St.
High Point, NC 27262
(919)882-3272
Ultimate Parent: Rite Aid. SIC: 5912—Drug
Stores & Proprietary Stores.

★ 75164 ★   Rite Aid Pharmacy
2629 N. Main St.
High Point, NC 27265
(919)869-5318
Ultimate Parent: Rite Aid. SIC: 5912—Drug
Stores & Proprietary Stores.

★ 75165 ★   Rite Aid Pharmacy No
1224
1747 Westchester Dr.
High Point, NC 27262
(919)885-0001
Ultimate Parent: Rite Aid. SIC: 5912—Drug
Stores & Proprietary Stores.

★ 75166 ★   Rite Aid Store No
1220
802 S. Main St.
High Point, NC 27260
(919)882-4123
Ultimate Parent: Rite Aid. SIC: 5912—Drug
Stores & Proprietary Stores.

★ 75167 ★   Royal Development
Co.
325 Kettering Rd.
High Point, NC 27263
Ultimate Parent: Interco. SIC: 3429—
Hardware Nec.

★ 75168 ★   Royal Development
Co.
325 Ketterin Ct. Rd.
High Point, NC 27263
Ultimate Parent: Interco. SIC: 3429—
Hardware Nec.

★ 75169 ★   Royal Development
Co.
1417 Courtesy Rd.
High Point, NC 27260
(919)889-2569
Ultimate Parent: Interco. SIC: 3469—Metal
Stampings Nec.

★ 75170 ★   Sara Lee Corp.
1823 Eastchester Dr.
High Point, NC 27265
(910)887-9200
Company Type: Division. Officer: Richard
Noll, Chairman, CEO. Ultimate Parent:
Sara Lee Corp.

★ 75171 ★   Silver Knit Industries,
Inc.
401 S. Hamilton St.
High Point, NC 27260
Ultimate Parent: Sara Lee Corp. SIC:
2252—Hosiery Nec.

★ 75172 ★   Taco Bell
2703 S. Main St.
High Point, NC 27263
(919)883-2315
Ultimate Parent: Pepsico. SIC: 5812—
Eating Places.

★ 75173 ★   3M Co.
2401 Brevard Rd.
High Point, NC 27263-1758
(919)889-7181
Company Type: Branch. Officer: Dennis B.
O'Hara. Ultimate Parent: Minnesota Mining
& Mfg. SIC: 5085—Industrial Supplies;
3291—Abrasive Products.

★ 75174 ★   Trailways Bus System
100 Lindsay St.
High Point, NC 27262
(919)882-2000
Ultimate Parent: Greyhound Lines Inc. SIC:
4131—Intercity & Rural Bus Transportation.

★ 75175 ★   United Van Lines Inc.
1100 Redding Dr.
High Point, NC 27260
(919)882-6522
Ultimate Parent: Unigroup. SIC: 4214—
Local Trucking With Storage.

★ 75176 ★   Universal Furniture
2622 Uwharrie Rd.
High Point, NC 27263
(919)861-7200 Fax: (919)431-2124
Officer: Wesley Collins. Ultimate Parent:
Masco.

★ 75177 ★   **Valspar Corp.**
1647 English Rd.
High Point, NC 27262
(910)887-4600
Officer: John Richter, Manager. **Ultimate Parent:** Valspar Corp. **SIC:** 2851—Paints & Allied Products.

★ 75178 ★   **Valspar Corp.**
1647 English Rd.
High Point, NC 27262
(919)882-6825
Ultimate Parent: Valspar Corp. **SIC:** 2851—Paints & Allied Products.

★ 75179 ★   **Wachovia Bank and Trust**
200 N. Main St.
High Point, NC 27260
(919)887-7600
Ultimate Parent: Wachovia Corp. **SIC:** 6099—Functions Related to Deposit Banking.

★ 75180 ★   **Wachovia Bank & Trust**
1912 Westchester Dr.
High Point, NC 27262
(919)885-8697
Ultimate Parent: Wachovia Corp. **SIC:** 6099—Functions Related to Deposit Banking.

★ 75181 ★   **Wachovia Bank & Trust Co. N**
10806 N. Main St.
High Point, NC 27263
(919)431-9181
Ultimate Parent: Wachovia Corp. **SIC:** 6022—State Commercial Banks.

★ 75182 ★   **Wachovia Bank & Trust Co. N**
631 PO Box
High Point, NC 27261
(919)887-7732
Ultimate Parent: Wachovia Corp. **SIC:** 6022—State Commercial Banks.

★ 75183 ★   **Wachovia Bank & Trust Co. N**
1700 N. Main St.
High Point, NC 27262
(919)882-3123
Ultimate Parent: Wachovia Corp. **SIC:** 6022—State Commercial Banks.

Highlands

★ 75184 ★   **First-Citizens Bank & Trust Co.**
NC Hwy. 106 & Spring St.
Highlands, NC 28741
(704)526-9692
Location Type: Branch office. **Officer:** Tony Potts, Vice President. **Ultimate Parent:** First Citizens Bancshares, Inc. **SIC:** 6021—National Commercial Banks.

Hildebran

★ 75185 ★   **Drexel Heritage Furnishings Inc.**
Plant 43
Hwy. 64-70
Hildebran, NC 28637
Location Type: Plant. **Ultimate Parent:** Masco. **SIC:** 2511—Wood Household Furniture.

★ 75186 ★   **Drexel Heritage Furniture**
Plant 43
Hwy. 64-70
Hildebran, NC 28637
Location Type: Plant. **Ultimate Parent:** Masco. **SIC:** 2511—Wood Household Furniture.

★ 75187 ★   **Lexington Furniture Ind.**
Plant 10
100 1st St. NW
Hildebran, NC 28637
Location Type: Plant. **Ultimate Parent:** Masco. **SIC:** 2511—Wood Household Furniture.

★ 75188 ★   **Wachovia Bank & Trust Co. N**
Henry Rv Rd.
Hildebran, NC 28637
(704)397-5591
Ultimate Parent: Wachovia Corp. **SIC:** 6022—State Commercial Banks.

Hillsborough

★ 75189 ★   **Parker Hannifin Corp.**
Cyl. Div.
Elizabeth Brady Rd.
Hillsborough, NC 27278
Company Type: Division. **Ultimate Parent:** Parker Hannifin. **SIC:** 3494—Valves & Pipe Fittings Nec.

★ 75190 ★   **Parker Hannifin Corp.**
Cylinder Div.
325 Elizabeth Brady Rd.
Hillsborough, NC 27278
Company Type: Division. **Ultimate Parent:** Parker Hannifin. **SIC:** 3494—Valves & Pipe Fittings Nec.

Holly Ridge

★ 75191 ★   **Thorn Apple Valley Inc.**
Carolina Div.
1 Bacon Pl.
Holly Ridge, NC 28445
Company Type: Division. **Ultimate Parent:** Thorn Apple Valley. **SIC:** 2013—Sausages & Other Prepared Meats.

Hope Mills

★ 75192 ★   **Branch Banking & Trust Co.**
3618 N. Main St.
Hope Mills, NC 28348-1937
(910)486-3283
Company Type: Subsidiary. **Location Type:** Branch office. **Officer:** Bob Spicer, Manager. **Ultimate Parent:** Southern National Corp. **SIC:** 6021—National Commercial Banks.

★ 75193 ★   **Food Lion**
3182 Legion Rd.
Hope Mills, NC 28348
(919)424-1173
Ultimate Parent: Food Lion. **SIC:** 5411—Grocery Stores.

★ 75194 ★   **Pizza Hut**
3501 N. Main St.
Hope Mills, NC 28348
(919)424-3860
Ultimate Parent: Pepsico. **SIC:** 5812—Eating Places.

★ 75195 ★   **Ryder Truck Rental**
3455 Black
Hope Mills, NC 28348
(919)424-7100
Ultimate Parent: Ryder System. **SIC:** 7359—Equipment Rental & Leasing Nec; 7513—Truck Rental & Leasing Without Drivers.

Hubert

★ 75196 ★   **Omc Chris-Craft Inc.**
Chris-Craft Rd.
Hubert, NC 28539
Ultimate Parent: Outboard Marine. **SIC:** 3732—Boat Building & Repairing.

★ 75197 ★   **Ome Hydra-Sports**
100 Oceanside Dr.
Hubert, NC 28539
Ultimate Parent: Outboard Marine. **SIC:** 3732—Boat Building & Repairing.

Hudson

★ 75198 ★   **Chemical Coatings Inc.**
PO Box 669
Hudson, NC 28638-0669
Ultimate Parent: RPM, Inc. **SIC:** 2851—Paints & Allied Products.

★ 75199 ★   **First-Citizens Bank & Trust Co.**
132 Fairway Shopping Ctr.
Hudson, NC 28638-2498
(704)728-1151
Location Type: Branch office. **Officer:** M. Jeffrey Roland, Assistant Vice President. **Ultimate Parent:** First Citizens Bancshares, Inc. **SIC:** 6021—National Commercial Banks.

★ 75200 ★   **Kincaid Furniture Co.**
168 Main St.
Hudson, NC 28638
(704)728-3261 **Fax:** (704)726-8223
Officer: Steven M. Kincaid, President. **Ultimate Parent:** La-Z-Boy Chair.

★ 75201 ★   **Kincaid Furniture Co.**
PO Box 605
Hudson, NC 28638
Ultimate Parent: La-Z-Boy Chair. **SIC:** 2511—Wood Household Furniture.

★ 75202 ★   **Kincaid Furniture Co. Inc. Plant 1**
Shasta Ln.
Hudson, NC 28638
Ultimate Parent: La-Z-Boy Chair. **SIC:** 2511—Wood Household Furniture.

★ 75203 ★   **Kincaid Furniture Co. Inc. Plant 1**
168 Main St.
Hudson, NC 28638
Ultimate Parent: La-Z-Boy Chair. **SIC:** 2511—Wood Household Furniture.

★ 75204 ★   **Kincaid Furniture Co. Inc. Plant 6**
Shasta Ln.
Hudson, NC 28638
Ultimate Parent: La-Z-Boy Chair. **SIC:** 2511—Wood Household Furniture.

★ 75205 ★   **Kincaid Furniture Co. Inc. Plant 6**
168 Main St.
Hudson, NC 28638
Ultimate Parent: La-Z-Boy Chair. **SIC:** 2511—Wood Household Furniture.

Huntersville

★ 75206 ★   **AT&T**
10000 Twin Trail Dr.
Huntersville, NC 28078-6810
(704)875-7300
Ultimate Parent: AT&T. **SIC:** 4813—Telephone Communications Except Radiotelephone.

★ 75207 ★   **Food Lion**
102 S. Statesville Rd.
Huntersville, NC 28078
(704)875-1651
Ultimate Parent: Food Lion. **SIC:** 5411—Grocery Stores.

Indian Trail

★ 75208 ★   **Food Lion**
4423 Old Monroe Rd.
Indian Trail, NC 28079
(704)821-9179
Ultimate Parent: Food Lion. **SIC:** 5411—Grocery Stores.

★ 75209 ★   **Food Lion Inc.**
4423 Old Monroe Rd.
Indian Trail, NC 28079
(704)821-9179
Ultimate Parent: Food Lion. **SIC:** 5411—Grocery Stores.

Jacksonville

★ 75210 ★   **First-Citizens Bank & Trust Co.**
314 Western Blvd.
Jacksonville, NC 28546-6338
(910)455-3122
Location Type: Branch office. **Ultimate Parent:** First Citizens Bancshares, Inc. **SIC:** 6021—National Commercial Banks.

★ 75211 ★   **First-Citizens Bank & Trust Co.**
1082 Henderson Dr.
Jacksonville, NC 28540-5099
(910)455-3122
Location Type: Branch office. **Ultimate**

Parent: First Citizens Bancshares, Inc. **SIC:** 6021—National Commercial Banks.

★ 75212 ★   **First-Citizens Bank & Trust Co.**
1091 Richlands Hwy.
Jacksonville, NC 28540-2914
(910)455-3122
Location Type: Branch office. **Ultimate Parent:** First Citizens Bancshares, Inc. **SIC:** 6021—National Commercial Banks.

★ 75213 ★   **First-Citizens Bank & Trust Co.**
821 New Bridge St.
Jacksonville, NC 28540-5493
(910)455-3122
Location Type: Branch office. **Officer:** George S. Haislip Jr., Area Vice President. **Ultimate Parent:** First Citizens Bancshares, Inc. **SIC:** 6021—National Commercial Banks.

★ 75214 ★   **First-Citizens Bank & Trust Co.**
2005 N. Marine Blvd.
Jacksonville, NC 28540
(910)454-3122
Location Type: Branch office. **Ultimate Parent:** First Citizens Bancshares, Inc. **SIC:** 6021—National Commercial Banks.

★ 75215 ★   **Food Lion**
26 Branchwood Shopping Ctr.
Jacksonville, NC 28540
(919)455-8566
Ultimate Parent: Food Lion. **SIC:** 5411—Grocery Stores.

★ 75216 ★   **Food Lion**
124 College Plz.
Jacksonville, NC 28546
(919)455-7880
Ultimate Parent: Food Lion. **SIC:** 5411—Grocery Stores.

★ 75217 ★   **Jiffy Lube**
435 Western Blvd.
Jacksonville, NC 28546
(919)347-9399
Ultimate Parent: Pennzoil. **SIC:** 5541—Gasoline Service Stations.

★ 75218 ★   **Kentucky Fried Chicken**
1207 N. Marine Blvd.
Jacksonville, NC 28540
(919)455-1981
Ultimate Parent: Pepsico. **SIC:** 5812—Eating Places.

★ 75219 ★   **Lane Bryant**
Jacksonville Mall
Jacksonville, NC 28540
(919)577-7515
Ultimate Parent: Limited. **SIC:** 5651—Family Clothing Stores.

★ 75220 ★   **Lane Bryant**
340 Western Blvd.
Jacksonville, NC 28546
(919)577-7515
Ultimate Parent: Limited. **SIC:** 5651—Family Clothing Stores.

★ 75221 ★   **Lerner Shop**
349 Western Blvd.
Jacksonville, NC 28546
(919)353-8747
Ultimate Parent: Limited. **SIC:** 5651—Family Clothing Stores.

★ 75222 ★   **Lerner Shop**
Jacksonville Mall
Jacksonville, NC 28540
(919)353-8747
Ultimate Parent: Limited. **SIC:** 5621—Women's Clothing Stores; 5651—Family Clothing Stores.

★ 75223 ★   **Piggly Wiggly**
2610 Northwoods Dr.
Jacksonville, NC 28540
(919)347-2056
Ultimate Parent: Bruno's. **SIC:** 5411—Grocery Stores.

★ 75224 ★   **Pizza Hut**
Brynn Marr Shopping Ctr.
Jacksonville, NC 28540
(919)353-2555
Ultimate Parent: Pepsico. **SIC:** 5812—Eating Places.

★ 75225 ★　**Pizza Hut**
1301 Gum Branch Rd.
Jacksonville, NC 28540
(919)455-8700
Ultimate Parent: Pepsico. **SIC:** 5812—
Eating Places.

★ 75226 ★　**Pizza Hut**
Brynn Marr Shopping Ctr.
Jacksonville, NC 28546
(919)353-2555
Ultimate Parent: Pepsico. **SIC:** 5812—
Eating Places.

★ 75227 ★　**Radio Shack**
351 Western Blvd.
Jacksonville, NC 28546
(919)353-9666
Company Type: Division. **Ultimate Parent:**
Tandy Corp. **SIC:** 5731—Radio, Television
& Electronics Stores.

★ 75228 ★　**Radio Shack**
Jacksonville Mall
Jacksonville, NC 28540
(919)353-9666
Company Type: Division. **Ultimate Parent:**
Tandy Corp. **SIC:** 5065—Electronic Parts &
Equipment Nec; 5731—Radio, Television &
Electronics Stores.

★ 75229 ★　**Radio Shack**
2075 N. Marine Blvd.
Jacksonville, NC 28546
(919)347-7554
Company Type: Division. **Ultimate Parent:**
Tandy Corp. **SIC:** 5065—Electronic Parts &
Equipment Nec.

★ 75230 ★　**Taco Bell**
117 Western Blvd.
Jacksonville, NC 28546
(919)353-1832
Ultimate Parent: Pepsico. **SIC:** 5812—
Eating Places.

★ 75231 ★　**Taco Bell**
102 Marine Blvd.
Jacksonville, NC 28540
(919)346-9778
Ultimate Parent: Pepsico. **SIC:** 5812—
Eating Places.

★ 75232 ★　**Wachovia Bank &
Trust Co. N**
900 Henderson Dr.
Jacksonville, NC 28540
(919)455-2061
Ultimate Parent: Wachovia Corp. **SIC:**
6099—Functions Related to Deposit
Banking.

★ 75233 ★　**Wachovia Bank &
Trust Co. N**
146 Western Blvd.
Jacksonville, NC 28546
(919)455-2061
Ultimate Parent: Wachovia Corp.

★ 75234 ★　**Wal Mart**
100 Western Blvd.
Jacksonville, NC 28546
(919)455-2358
Ultimate Parent: Wal-Mart Stores, Inc. **SIC:**
5311—Department Stores.

★ 75235 ★　**Waldenbooks**
Jacksonville Mall
Jacksonville, NC 28540
(919)353-5767
Ultimate Parent: K-Mart. **SIC:** 5942—Book
Stores.

★ 75236 ★　**Weyerhaeuser Co.**
2728 N. Marine Blvd.
Jacksonville, NC 28540
Ultimate Parent: Weyerhaeuser Co.

Jamestown

★ 75237 ★　**Branch Banking &
Trust Co.**
120 E. Main St.
Jamestown, NC 27282-9531
(910)454-3138
Company Type: Subsidiary. **Location
Type:** Branch office. **Officer:** Randy
Sherron, Mgr. **Ultimate Parent:** Southern
National Corp. **SIC:** 6021—National
Commercial Banks.

★ 75238 ★　**Flowers Baking Co.**
801 W. Main St.
Jamestown, NC 27282
(910)841-8840
Officer: Roger Tooley, President. **Ultimate
Parent:** Flowers Industries. **SIC:** 2051—
Bread, Cake & Related Products.

★ 75239 ★　**Flowers Baking Co. of
Jamestown Inc.**
PO Box 819
Jamestown, NC 27282
(919)841-8840 **Fax:** (919)841-6643
Company Type: Subsidiary. **Officer:** Roger
Tooley, President. **Ultimate Parent:** Flowers
Industries.

★ 75240 ★　**Martin Marietta
Aggregates**
RR 11
Jamestown, NC 27282
(919)299-2211
Ultimate Parent: Martin Marietta. **SIC:**
5032—Brick, Stone & Related Materials.

★ 75241 ★　**Pizza Hut**
600 College Rd.
Jamestown, NC 27282
(919)294-6298
Ultimate Parent: Pepsico. **SIC:** 5812—
Eating Places.

★ 75242 ★　**Pizza Hut**
709 W. Main St.
Jamestown, NC 27282
(919)887-3729
Ultimate Parent: Pepsico. **SIC:** 5812—
Eating Places.

★ 75243 ★　**Texaco Food Mart No
4**
201 W. Main St.
Jamestown, NC 27282
(919)884-4099
Ultimate Parent: Texaco. **SIC:** 5411—
Grocery Stores.

★ 75244 ★　**Union Camp Corp.**
103 Ragsdale Rd.
Jamestown, NC 27282
(919)887-5400
Ultimate Parent: Union Camp Corp. **SIC:**
2657—Folding Paperboard Boxes.

★ 75245 ★　**Union Camp Corp.**
Jamestown, NC 27282
(919)454-1151
Ultimate Parent: Union Camp Corp. **SIC:**
2679—Converted Paper Products Nec.

★ 75246 ★　**Wachovia Bank &
Trust Co. N**
124 E. Main St.
Jamestown, NC 27282
(919)454-3131
Ultimate Parent: Wachovia Corp. **SIC:**
6022—State Commercial Banks.

Jamesville

★ 75247 ★　**Branch Banking &
Trust Co.**
US 64
Jamesville, NC 27846
(919)792-1136
Ultimate Parent: Southern National Corp.
SIC: 6022—State Commercial Banks.

Jefferson

★ 75248 ★　**Food Lion**
Us Hwy. 221
Jefferson, NC 28640
(919)246-2992
Ultimate Parent: Food Lion. **SIC:** 5411—
Grocery Stores.

★ 75249 ★　**Food Lion Inc.**
Us Hwy. 221
Jefferson, NC 28640
(919)246-2992
Ultimate Parent: Food Lion. **SIC:** 5411—
Grocery Stores.

Jonesville

★ 75250 ★　**Food Lion**
Off Hwy. 67 Valley Rd.
Jonesville, NC 28642
(919)526-2290
Ultimate Parent: Food Lion. **SIC:** 5411—
Grocery Stores.

★ 75251 ★　**Food Lion Inc.**
Off Hwy. 67 Valley Rd.
Jonesville, NC 28642
(919)526-2290
Ultimate Parent: Food Lion. **SIC:** 5411—
Grocery Stores.

★ 75252 ★　**Pepsi-Cola Bottling
Co.**
225 Winston Rd.
Jonesville, NC 28642
(910)789-3400
Officer: Randy Walker, Manager. **Ultimate
Parent:** Pepsico. **SIC:** 2086—Bottled &
Canned Soft Drinks.

Kannapolis

★ 75253 ★　**Bi-Lo Inc.**
Seaford Ave.
Kannapolis, NC 28081
(704)933-6880
Ultimate Parent: Penn Traffic. **SIC:** 5499—
Miscellaneous Food Stores.

★ 75254 ★　**Fieldcrest Cannon,
Inc.**
PO BOX 107
Kannapolis, NC 28081
(704)933-1221
Company Type: Division. **Ultimate Parent:**
Fieldcrest Cannon. **SIC:** 2211—Broadwoven
Fabric Mills—Cotton; 2392—
Housefurnishings Nec. **Sales:**
1,212,436,000 M.

★ 75255 ★　**Fieldcrest Cannon
Inc.**
1 Lake Dr.
Kannapolis, NC 28081
Location Type: Plant. **Ultimate Parent:**
Fieldcrest Cannon. **SIC:** 2211—Broadwoven
Fabric Mills—Cotton; 2261—Finishing
Plants—Cotton; 2269—Finishing Plants
Nec.

★ 75256 ★　**Fieldcrest Cannon
Inc.**
PO Box 107
Kannapolis, NC 28082
Ultimate Parent: Fieldcrest Cannon. **SIC:**
2211—Broadwoven Fabric Mills—Cotton;
2269—Finishing Plants Nec.

★ 75257 ★　**Fieldcrest Canon Inc.**
One Lake Dr.
Kannapolis, NC 28081
Location Type: Plant. **Ultimate Parent:**
Fieldcrest Cannon. **SIC:** 2211—Broadwoven
Fabric Mills—Cotton; 2269—Finishing Plants
Nec.

★ 75258 ★　**First Bank**
601 E. C St.
Kannapolis, NC 28083
(704)938-5126
Ultimate Parent: Shawmut National Corp.
SIC: 6022—State Commercial Banks.

★ 75259 ★　**Food Lion**
Kannapolis, NC 28081
(704)933-1137
Ultimate Parent: Food Lion. **SIC:** 5411—
Grocery Stores.

★ 75260 ★　**Food Lion**
2825 N. Cannon Blvd. B
Kannapolis, NC 28083
Ultimate Parent: Food Lion. **SIC:** 5411—
Grocery Stores.

★ 75261 ★　**Food Lion**
910 S. Cannon Blvd.
Kannapolis, NC 28083
(704)932-0107
Ultimate Parent: Food Lion. **SIC:** 5411—
Grocery Stores.

★ 75262 ★　**Food Lion**
400 E. C St.
Kannapolis, NC 28083
(704)933-1137
Ultimate Parent: Food Lion. **SIC:** 5411—
Grocery Stores.

★ 75263 ★　**Food Lion**
1746 S. Cannon Blvd.
Kannapolis, NC 28083
(704)933-6800
Ultimate Parent: Food Lion. **SIC:** 5411—
Grocery Stores.

★ 75264 ★　**Kentucky Fried
Chicken**
209 N. Cannon Blvd.
Kannapolis, NC 28083
(704)933-2201
Ultimate Parent: Pepsico. **SIC:** 5812—
Eating Places.

★ 75265 ★　**Kitchen Collection
Inc.**
104 West Ave.
Kannapolis, NC 28081
(704)938-7511
Ultimate Parent: Nacco Industries. **SIC:**
5999—Miscellaneous Retail Stores Nec.

★ 75266 ★　**Pizza Hut**
901 N. Cannon Blvd.
Kannapolis, NC 28083
(704)932-4191
Ultimate Parent: Pepsico. **SIC:** 5812—
Eating Places.

★ 75267 ★　**Radio Shack**
904 S. Cannon Blvd.
Kannapolis, NC 28083
(704)938-4317
Company Type: Division. **Ultimate Parent:**
Tandy Corp. **SIC:** 5731—Radio, Television
& Electronics Stores; 5731—Radio,
Television & Electronics Stores.

★ 75268 ★　**Taco Bell**
1100 S. Cannon Blvd.
Kannapolis, NC 28083
(704)932-0703
Ultimate Parent: Pepsico. **SIC:** 5812—
Eating Places.

Kenansville

★ 75269 ★　**Automotive &
Upholstery Fabrics Business Unit**
1754 NC 903
Kenansville, NC 28349
(919)296-5200 **Fax:** (919)296-0911
Company Type: Subsidiary. **Officer:** John
A. Emrich, President. **Ultimate Parent:**
Guilford Mills Inc.

★ 75270 ★　**Guilford Mills Inc.**
Hwy. 11
Kenansville, NC 28349
(919)296-0911
Ultimate Parent: Guilford Mills Inc. **SIC:**
2211—Broadwoven Fabric Mills—Cotton.

★ 75271 ★　**Guilford Mills Inc.
Guilford E. Plant**
Rte. 11 N.
Kenansville, NC 28345
Ultimate Parent: Guilford Mills Inc. **SIC:**
2258—Lace & Warp Knit Fabric Mills.

Kenly

★ 75272 ★　**E. R. Squibb & Sons
Inc.**
Interstate 95 S. at Exit 106
Kenly, NC 27542
Ultimate Parent: Bristol-Myers Squibb. **SIC:**
2834—Pharmaceutical Preparations.

Kernersville

★ 75273 ★　**Adams-Millis Hoisery**
Hwy. 150 N.
Kernersville, NC 27284
Location Type: Plant. **Ultimate Parent:**
Sara Lee Corp. **SIC:** 2252—Hosiery Nec.

★ 75274 ★　**Adams Millis Hoisery
Corp.**
Hwy. 150 North
Kernersville, NC 27284
Location Type: Plant. **Ultimate Parent:**
Sara Lee Corp. **SIC:** 2252—Hosiery Nec.

★ 75275 ★　**Branch Banking &
Trust Co.**
131 E. Mountain St.
Kernersville, NC 27284-2938
(910)996-2951
Company Type: Subsidiary. **Location
Type:** Branch office. **Ultimate Parent:**
Southern National Corp. **SIC:** 6021—
National Commercial Banks.

★ 75276 ★ Branch Banking & Trust Co.
237 E. Mountain St.
Kernersville, NC 27284-2951
(910)996-1333
Company Type: Subsidiary. Location Type: Branch office. Officer: Robert Reed, Manager. Ultimate Parent: Southern National Corp. SIC: 6021—National Commercial Banks.

★ 75277 ★ Digital Equipment Corp.
802 Birch Ln.
Kernersville, NC 27284
(919)996-5735
Ultimate Parent: Digital Equipment Corp. SIC: 5734—Computer & Software Stores.

★ 75278 ★ First-Citizens Bank & Trust Co.
712 Hwy. 66 S.
Kernersville, NC 27284
(910)996-7244
Location Type: Branch office. Officer: J. R. Gorham, Vice President. Ultimate Parent: First Citizens Bancshares, Inc. SIC: 6021—National Commercial Banks.

★ 75279 ★ Food Lion
617 N. Main St.
Kernersville, NC 27284
(919)996-1386
Ultimate Parent: Food Lion. SIC: 5411—Grocery Stores.

★ 75280 ★ Food Lion
Hwy. 150
Kernersville, NC 27284
(919)996-2092
Ultimate Parent: Food Lion. SIC: 5411—Grocery Stores.

★ 75281 ★ Kentucky Fried Chicken
826 S. Main St.
Kernersville, NC 27284
(919)993-2249
Ultimate Parent: Pepsico. SIC: 5812—Eating Places.

★ 75282 ★ Otis Elevator Co.
1111 E. Mountain St.
Kernersville, NC 27284
(919)996-5030
Ultimate Parent: United Technologies. SIC: 5084—Industrial Machinery & Equipment.

★ 75283 ★ Pizza Hut
903 E. Bodenhamer St.
Kernersville, NC 27284
(919)996-5501
Ultimate Parent: Pepsico. SIC: 5812—Eating Places.

★ 75284 ★ Radio Shack
Kerners Village
Kernersville, NC 27284
(919)996-7804
Company Type: Division. Ultimate Parent: Tandy Corp. SIC: 5731—Radio, Television & Electronics Stores.

★ 75285 ★ Wachovia Bank & Trust Co. N
221 E. Mountain St.
Kernersville, NC 27284
(919)996-5455
Ultimate Parent: Wachovia Corp. SIC: 6022—State Commercial Banks; 6141—Personal Credit Institutions.

Kill Devil Hills

★ 75286 ★ First-Citizens Bank & Trust Co.
Seagate North Shopping Ctr.
Kill Devil Hills, NC 27948-2036
(919)441-2871
Location Type: Branch office. Officer: Jay Dixon, Assistant Vice President. Ultimate Parent: First Citizens Bancshares, Inc. SIC: 6021—National Commercial Banks.

★ 75287 ★ Kentucky Fried Chicken
Hwy. 158 Bypass
Kill Devil Hills, NC 27948
(919)441-4001
Ultimate Parent: Pepsico. SIC: 5812—Eating Places.

★ 75288 ★ Wachovia Bank & Trust
Hwy. 158 Bypass
Kill Devil Hills, NC 27948
(919)480-3600
Ultimate Parent: Wachovia Corp. SIC: 6099—Functions Related to Deposit Banking.

King

★ 75289 ★ Branch Banking & Trust Co.
601 S. Main Rd.
King, NC 27021-9501
(910)983-2516
Company Type: Subsidiary. Location Type: Branch office. Ultimate Parent: Southern National Corp. SIC: 6021—National Commercial Banks.

★ 75290 ★ McDonalds of King
King Rd.
King, NC 27021
(919)983-3546
Ultimate Parent: May Department Stores. SIC: 5812—Eating Places.

★ 75291 ★ Pizza Hut
7935 King Rd.
King, NC 27021
(919)983-9305
Ultimate Parent: Pepsico. SIC: 5812—Eating Places.

★ 75292 ★ R. J. Reynolds Tobacco Co. Tobaccoville
7855 King Rd.
King, NC 27050-9522
Ultimate Parent: RJR Nabisco Holdings. SIC: 2111—Cigarettes.

Kings Mountain

★ 75293 ★ Branch Banking & Trust Co.
410 E. King St.
Kings Mountain, NC 28086-3421
(704)739-9573
Company Type: Subsidiary. Location Type: Branch office. Officer: J. Glenn Anderson, Mgr. Ultimate Parent: Southern National Corp. SIC: 6021—National Commercial Banks.

★ 75294 ★ Branch Banking & Trust Co.
410 E. King St.
Kings Mountain, NC 28086
(704)867-1851
Ultimate Parent: Southern National Corp. SIC: 6029—Commercial Banks Nec.

★ 75295 ★ Cyprus Foote Mineral Co.
348 Holiday Inn Rd. Southbound Service Rd.
Kings Mountain, NC 28086-0689
Ultimate Parent: Cyprus Amax Minerals. SIC: 2819—Industrial Inorganic Chemicals Nec.

★ 75296 ★ Cyprus Foote Mineral Co.
Jct. I-85 & NC-161, Southbound Service Rd.
Kings Mountain, NC 28086
Ultimate Parent: Cyprus Amax Minerals. SIC: 2819—Industrial Inorganic Chemicals Nec.

★ 75297 ★ Eaton Corp.
Transmission
Hwy. 29 S
Kings Mountain, NC 28086
(704)937-7411
Officer: Jim Rennirt, Manager. Ultimate Parent: Eaton Corp. SIC: 3714—Motor Vehicle Parts & Accessories.

★ 75298 ★ Eaton Corp.
Transmission Div.
Hwy. 29, S.
Kings Mountain, NC 28086-1728
Company Type: Division. Ultimate Parent: Eaton Corp. SIC: 3714—Motor Vehicle Parts & Accessories.

★ 75299 ★ Eaton Corp.
Transmission Div.
PO Box 1728
Hwy. 29, S
Kings Mountain, NC 28086
(704)937-7411
Company Type: Division. Location Type: Plant. Officer: Chuck Frothingham, Controller. Ultimate Parent: Eaton Corp. SIC: 3714—Motor Vehicle Parts & Accessories.

★ 75300 ★ Eaton Corp.
Transmission Div. Kings Mountain
Hwy. 29 S.
Kings Mountain, NC 28086
Company Type: Division. Ultimate Parent: Eaton Corp. SIC: 3714—Motor Vehicle Parts & Accessories.

★ 75301 ★ Eaton Corp.
Transmission Div. Kings Moutain Plant
Hwy. 29 S.
Kings Mountain, NC 28086
Company Type: Division. Location Type: Plant. Ultimate Parent: Eaton Corp. SIC: 3714—Motor Vehicle Parts & Accessories.

★ 75302 ★ Exxon Short Stop
111 W. King St.
Kings Mountain, NC 28086
(704)739-1264
Ultimate Parent: Exxon. SIC: 5541—Gasoline Service Stations.

★ 75303 ★ First-Citizens Bank & Trust Co.
403 S. Battleground Ave.
Kings Mountain, NC 28086-3603
(704)739-4576
Location Type: Branch office. Officer: Eric L. Dixon, Assistant Vice President. Ultimate Parent: First Citizens Bancshares, Inc. SIC: 6021—National Commercial Banks.

★ 75304 ★ Food Lion
1320 Shelby Rd.
Kings Mountain, NC 28086
(704)739-8044
Ultimate Parent: Food Lion. SIC: 5411—Grocery Stores.

★ 75305 ★ Kentucky Fried Chicken
413 E. King St.
Kings Mountain, NC 28086
(704)739-6911
Ultimate Parent: Pepsico. SIC: 5812—Eating Places.

★ 75306 ★ Pizza Hut
Hwy. 74 W
Kings Mountain, NC 28086
(704)739-4436
Ultimate Parent: Pepsico. SIC: 5812—Eating Places.

★ 75307 ★ Reliance Electric Co.
101 Reliance Rd.
Kings Mountain, NC 28086
(704)739-0171
Officer: Thad Roberts, Manager. Ultimate Parent: Reliance Electric. SIC: 3621—Motors & Generators.

★ 75308 ★ Termacote-Welco Co. Inc.
1051 York Rd.
Kings Mountain, NC 28086-9713
(704)739-6421
Company Type: Subsidiary. Officer: William H. Roland Jr., President & Chairman of the Board. Ultimate Parent: Foster Wheeler Corp. Employee Count: 170. Sales: 38 M.

★ 75309 ★ Thermacote Welco Co.
York Rd.
Kings Mountain, NC 28086
(704)739-6421
Ultimate Parent: Foster Wheeler Corp. SIC: 5084—Industrial Machinery & Equipment.

★ 75310 ★ Union Underwear Co. Inc.
PO Box 706
Kings Mountain, NC 28086
Ultimate Parent: Fruit of the Loom. SIC: 2300—Apparel & Other Textile Products.

★ 75311 ★ US Gypsum Co.
Grover Rd.
Kings Mountain, NC 28086
(704)739-4571
Ultimate Parent: USG Corp. SIC: 3275—Gypsum Products.

Kinston

★ 75312 ★ BFI Waste Systems
Kinston, NC 28501
(919)522-2484
Ultimate Parent: Browning-Ferris Industries. SIC: 4953—Refuse Systems; 5093—Scrap & Waste Materials.

★ 75313 ★ Branch Banking & Trust Co.
1101 W. Vernon Ave.
Kinston, NC 28501-3615
(919)527-2183
Company Type: Subsidiary. Location Type: Branch office. Ultimate Parent: Southern National Corp. SIC: 6021—National Commercial Banks.

★ 75314 ★ Branch Banking & Trust Co.
612 N. Queen
Kinston, NC 28501-4340
(919)527-2183
Company Type: Subsidiary. Location Type: Branch office. Ultimate Parent: Southern National Corp. SIC: 6021—National Commercial Banks.

★ 75315 ★ Branch Banking & Trust Co.
803 N. Queen
Kinston, NC 28501-3913
(919)527-2183
Company Type: Subsidiary. Location Type: Branch office. Ultimate Parent: Southern National Corp. SIC: 6021—National Commercial Banks.

★ 75316 ★ Branch Banking & Trust Co.
Vernon Pk. Mall Shopping Ctr.
Kinston, NC 28501-3349
(919)527-2183
Company Type: Subsidiary. Location Type: Branch office. Ultimate Parent: Southern National Corp. SIC: 6021—National Commercial Banks.

★ 75317 ★ Branch Banking & Trust Co.
2409 Heritage St.
Kinston, NC 28501
(919)527-2183
Company Type: Subsidiary. Location Type: Branch office. Ultimate Parent: Southern National Corp. SIC: 6021—National Commercial Banks.

★ 75318 ★ Exxon
18 Carver Cts A
Kinston, NC 28501
(919)522-7789
Ultimate Parent: Exxon.

★ 75319 ★ First-Citizens Bank & Trust Co.
400 E. New Bern Rd.
Kinston, NC 28501-6738
(919)527-3141
Location Type: Branch office. Ultimate Parent: First Citizens Bancshares, Inc. SIC: 6021—National Commercial Banks.

★ 75320 ★ First-Citizens Bank & Trust Co.
803 Hardee St.
Kinston, NC 28501-3349
(919)527-3141
Location Type: Branch office. Ultimate Parent: First Citizens Bancshares, Inc. SIC: 6021—National Commercial Banks.

★ 75321 ★ First-Citizens Bank & Trust Co.
607 Plaza Blvd.
Kinston, NC 28501-1616
(919)527-3141
Location Type: Branch office. Ultimate Parent: First Citizens Bancshares, Inc. SIC: 6021—National Commercial Banks.

★ 75322 ★　First-Citizens Bank &
Trust Co.
800 N. Queen St.
Kinston, NC 28501-3914
(919)527-3141
Location Type: Branch office. **Officer:**
John W. Whitley, Manager. **Ultimate
Parent:** First Citizens Bancshares, Inc. **SIC:**
6021—National Commercial Banks.

★ 75323 ★　First-Citizens Bank &
Trust Co.
Hwy. 258 N
Kinston, NC 28501-8708
(919)527-3141
Location Type: Branch office. **Ultimate
Parent:** First Citizens Bancshares, Inc. **SIC:**
6021—National Commercial Banks.

★ 75324 ★　Lenox China
1800 Dobbs Farm Rd.
Kinston, NC 28501-8997
Officer: Jack Vresics. **Ultimate Parent:**
Brown-Forman.

★ 75325 ★　Lenox China Shop
1800 Dobbs Farm Rd.
Kinston, NC 28501
(919)523-5555
Location Type: Plant. **Officer:** Jack
Versics, Plant Manager. **Ultimate Parent:**
Brown-Forman. **SIC:** 3262—Vitreous China
Table & Kitchenware.

★ 75326 ★　Pepsi-Cola Bottling
Co.
2016 W. Vernon Ave.
Kinston, NC 28501
(919)522-0232
Officer: Jeff Minges, President. **Ultimate
Parent:** Pepsico. **SIC:** 2086—Bottled &
Canned Soft Drinks.

★ 75327 ★　Piggly Wiggly
Rr 8
Kinston, NC 28501
(919)523-5727
Ultimate Parent: Bruno's. **SIC:** 5411—
Grocery Stores.

★ 75328 ★　Rite Aid Discount
Pharmacie
2412 N. Herritage St.
Kinston, NC 28501
(919)522-2276
Ultimate Parent: Rite Aid. **SIC:** 5199—
Nondurable Goods Nec.

★ 75329 ★　Smithfield Packing
Co.
2602 W. Vernon Ave.
Kinston, NC 28501
(919)522-4777
Officer: John A. Oliver, Vice President.
Ultimate Parent: Smithfield Foods Inc. **SIC:**
2011—Meat Packing Plants.

★ 75330 ★　Smithfield Packing
Co. Inc.
2602 W. Vernon Ave.
Kinston, NC 28501
Ultimate Parent: Smithfield Foods Inc. **SIC:**
2011—Meat Packing Plants.

★ 75331 ★　Wal Mart
4101 W. Vernon Ave. 70
Kinston, NC 28501
(919)527-3100
Ultimate Parent: Wal-Mart Stores, Inc.

★ 75332 ★　Waldenbooks
Vernon
Kinston, NC 28501
(919)523-3372
Ultimate Parent: K-Mart. **SIC:** 5942—Book
Stores.

Kitty Hawk

★ 75333 ★　Branch Banking &
Trust Co.
US Hwy. 158 Bypass
Kitty Hawk, NC 27893-3880
(919)399-4111
Company Type: Subsidiary. **Location
Type:** Branch office. **Ultimate Parent:**
Southern National Corp. **SIC:** 6021—
National Commercial Banks.

★ 75334 ★　Branch Banking &
Trust Co.
Hwy. 158
Kitty Hawk, NC 27949-9635
(919)261-2106
Company Type: Subsidiary. **Location
Type:** Branch office. **Ultimate Parent:**
Southern National Corp. **SIC:** 6021—
National Commercial Banks.

Knightdale

★ 75335 ★　Branch Banking &
Trust Co.
Hwy. 64 & Smithfield Rd.
Knightdale, NC 27545
(919)266-6800
Company Type: Subsidiary. **Location
Type:** Branch office. **Officer:** Laura Eason,
Mgr. **Ultimate Parent:** Southern National
Corp. **SIC:** 6021—National Commercial
Banks.

★ 75336 ★　Branch Banking &
Trust Co.
Knightdale Crossing Shopping Ctr.
Knightdale, NC 27545
(919)266-6800
Company Type: Subsidiary. **Location
Type:** Branch office. **Ultimate Parent:**
Southern National Corp. **SIC:** 6021—
National Commercial Banks.

★ 75337 ★　First-Citizen Bank &
Trust Co.
1140 N. Smithfield Rd.
Knightdale, NC 27545
(919)266-7700
Location Type: Branch office. **Officer:** Rick
Lucas, Manager. **Ultimate Parent:** First
Citizens Bancshares, Inc. **SIC:** 6021—
National Commercial Banks.

La Grange

★ 75338 ★　Crouse-Hinds Joy
Molded Products
Old U.S. 70 East (Rte. 4 Box 156)
La Grange, NC 28551
Ultimate Parent: Cooper Industries. **SIC:**
3643—Current-Carrying Wiring Devices.

★ 75339 ★　Crouse-Hinds Joy
Molded Products
Old Us 70 East (Route 4, Box 156)
La Grange, NC 28551
Ultimate Parent: Cooper Industries. **SIC:**
3643—Current-Carrying Wiring Devices.

★ 75340 ★　Crouse-Hinds Molded
Products Joy Molded Products
Old U.S. 70 E. Rte. 4 Box 156
La Grange, NC 28551
Ultimate Parent: Cooper Industries. **SIC:**
3643—Current-Carrying Wiring Devices.

LaGrange

★ 75341 ★　Branch Banking &
Trust Co.
101 S. Caswell
LaGrange, NC 28551
(919)566-3175
Company Type: Subsidiary. **Location
Type:** Branch office. **Ultimate Parent:**
Southern National Corp. **SIC:** 6021—
National Commercial Banks.

Landis

★ 75342 ★　Exxon Express
315 S. Main St.
Landis, NC 28088
(704)857-7955
Ultimate Parent: Exxon. **SIC:** 5411—
Grocery Stores.

Lansing

★ 75343 ★　First-Citizens Bank &
Trust Co.
State Hwy. 194
Lansing, NC 28643-9622
(910)384-3722
Location Type: Branch office. **Officer:**
Jarrett P. Miller, Manager. **Ultimate Parent:**
First Citizens Bancshares, Inc. **SIC:** 6021—
National Commercial Banks.

Lattimore

★ 75344 ★　Ppg Industries
New House Rd.
Lattimore, NC 28089
(704)434-2261
Ultimate Parent: PPG Industries Inc. **SIC:**
5211—Lumber & Other Building Materials.

Laurel Hill

★ 75345 ★　Laurel Hill Carpet Mill
Old Wire Rd.
Laurel Hill, NC 28351
Ultimate Parent: Fieldcrest Cannon. **SIC:**
2273—Carpets & Rugs.

★ 75346 ★　Springs Industries,
Inc.
Hwy. 79
Laurel Hill, NC 28351
(910)462-3930
Officer: James Maddox, Manager. **Ultimate
Parent:** Springs Industries. **SIC:** 2211—
Broadwoven Fabric Mills—Cotton.

Laurinburg

★ 75347 ★　Abbott Laboratories
Hwy. 401 Junction 15-501
Laurinburg, NC 28352
(919)276-6210
Officer: Jack Strum. **Ultimate Parent:**
Abbott Laboratories. **SIC:** 3841—Surgical &
Medical Instruments; 5122—Drugs,
Proprietaries & Sundries; 8734—Testing
Laboratories.

★ 75348 ★　Abbott Laboratories
Hwy. 401/15-501
Laurinburg, NC 28353
Ultimate Parent: Abbott Laboratories. **SIC:**
3841—Surgical & Medical Instruments.

★ 75349 ★　Branch Banking &
Trust Co.
1700 S. Main St.
Laurinburg, NC 28352-4134
(910)277-1401
Company Type: Subsidiary. **Location
Type:** Branch office. **Ultimate Parent:**
Southern National Corp. **SIC:** 6021—
National Commercial Banks.

★ 75350 ★　Branch Banking &
Trust Co.
400 S. Main St.
Laurinburg, NC 28352-5408
(910)276-2775
Company Type: Subsidiary. **Location
Type:** Branch office. **Officer:** Lars
Anderson, Manager. **Ultimate Parent:**
Southern National Corp. **SIC:** 6021—
National Commercial Banks.

★ 75351 ★　Eaton Corp.
401 N. Byp
Laurinburg, NC 28352
(910)276-6901
Location Type: Plant. **Officer:** Dave
Bartek, Plant Manager. **Ultimate Parent:**
Eaton Corp. **SIC:** 3069—Fabricated Rubber
Products Nec; 3714—Motor Vehicle Parts &
Accessories.

★ 75352 ★　Eaton Corp.
Golf Grip Div.
Hwy. 401 N. Bypass
Laurinburg, NC 28352
Company Type: Division. **Ultimate Parent:**
Eaton Corp. **SIC:** 3069—Fabricated Rubber
Products Nec.

★ 75353 ★　Eaton Corp.
Golf Group Div.
Hwy. 401 North
Laurinburg, NC 28352
(910)276-6901 **Fax:** (910)277-3700
Company Type: Division. **Location Type:**
Plant. **Officer:** Irving S. Hill, General
Manager. **Ultimate Parent:** Eaton Corp.
SIC: 3069—Fabricated Rubber Products
Nec.

★ 75354 ★　Manville Sales Corp.
Maxton Airport Rd. PO Box 1349
Laurinburg, NC 28352
Ultimate Parent: Manville Corp. **SIC:**
3321—Gray & Ductile Iron Foundries.

★ 75355 ★　Mini Mart
201 N. Main St.
Laurinburg, NC 28352
(919)276-9286
Ultimate Parent: Kroger. **SIC:** 5411—
Grocery Stores.

★ 75356 ★　Rite Aid of N C Inc.
Plaza Shopping Ctr.
Laurinburg, NC 28352
(919)276-7305
Ultimate Parent: Rite Aid. **SIC:** 5912—Drug
Stores & Proprietary Stores.

★ 75357 ★　Ryder Truck Rental
Hwy. 15 N
Laurinburg, NC 28352
(919)276-6398
Ultimate Parent: Ryder System. **SIC:**
7359—Equipment Rental & Leasing Nec.

★ 75358 ★　Wachovia Bank &
Trust Co.
450 S. Main St.
Laurinburg, NC 28352
(919)276-1911
Ultimate Parent: Wachovia Corp. **SIC:**
6022—State Commercial Banks.

Lawndale

★ 75359 ★　Branch Banking &
Trust Co.
300 E. Main St.
Lawndale, NC 28090
(704)538-8561
Company Type: Subsidiary. **Location
Type:** Branch office. **Officer:** Dan
Honeycutt, Mgr. **Ultimate Parent:** Southern
National Corp. **SIC:** 6021—National
Commercial Banks.

★ 75360 ★　Branch Banking &
Trust Co.
Main St.
Lawndale, NC 28090
(704)538-4611
Ultimate Parent: Southern National Corp.
SIC: 6029—Commercial Banks Nec.

Lemon Springs

★ 75361 ★　Martin Marietta
Aggregates
Lemon Springs, NC 28355
(919)776-5157
Ultimate Parent: Martin Marietta. **SIC:**
3295—Minerals—Ground or Treated.

Lenior

★ 75362 ★　First-Citizens Bank &
Trust Co.
115 Blowing Rock Blvd.
Lenior, NC 28645-4401
(704)758-4441
Location Type: Branch office. **Ultimate
Parent:** First Citizens Bancshares, Inc. **SIC:**
6021—National Commercial Banks.

Lenoir

★ 75363 ★　Ace Hardware
1447 Norwood St. SW
Lenoir, NC 28645
(704)758-9408
Ultimate Parent: Ace Hardware. **SIC:**
5251—Hardware Stores.

★ 75364 ★　Allergan Medical
Optics
637 E. Nuway Cir. NE
Lenoir, NC 28645-3647
(704)758-2343
Officer: Bill Winston. **Ultimate Parent:**
Allergan Inc. **SIC:** 2833—Medicinals &
Botanicals.

★ 75365 ★　Broyhill Furniture
Ind., Inc.
Lenoir Furn. Plant
Factory Ln.
Lenoir, NC 28645
Ultimate Parent: Interco. **SIC:** 2511—Wood
Household Furniture.

★ 75366 ★　Broyhill Furniture Ind.
Inc. Complex
Miller Hill Complex
Lenoir, NC 28645
Ultimate Parent: Interco. **SIC:** 2511—Wood
Household Furniture.

★ 75367 ★ **Broyhill Furniture Ind. Inc. Harper Plant**
125 S. Prospect St.
Lenoir, NC 28645
Ultimate Parent: Interco. **SIC:** 2511—Wood Household Furniture.

★ 75368 ★ **Broyhill Furniture Ind., Inc. P**
Pacemaker Plant
Miller Hill Complex
Lenoir, NC 28645
Ultimate Parent: Interco. **SIC:** 2511—Wood Household Furniture.

★ 75369 ★ **Broyhill Furniture Ind. Inc. Wall Systems Plt.**
Miller Hill Complex
Lenoir, NC 28645
Ultimate Parent: Interco. **SIC:** 2511—Wood Household Furniture.

★ 75370 ★ **Broyhill Furniture Ind. Inc. Whitnel Plant**
Hwy. 321A
Lenoir, NC 28645
Ultimate Parent: Interco. **SIC:** 2512—Upholstered Household Furniture.

★ 75371 ★ **Broyhill Furniture Industries Inc.**
1 Broyhill Pk.
Lenoir, NC 28633
Ultimate Parent: Interco. **SIC:** 2511—Wood Household Furniture; 2512—Upholstered Household Furniture.

★ 75372 ★ **E. R. Carpenter Co. Inc.**
Virginia St.
Lenoir, NC 28645
Ultimate Parent: Carpenter. **SIC:** 3086—Plastics Foam Products.

★ 75373 ★ **E. R. Carpenter Co. Inc.**
Miller Hill Rd. PO Box 1496
Lenoir, NC 28645
Ultimate Parent: Carpenter. **SIC:** 3086—Plastics Foam Products.

★ 75374 ★ **E. R. Carpenter Co. Inc.**
1333 Virginia St. SW
Lenoir, NC 28645
Ultimate Parent: Carpenter. **SIC:** 3086—Plastics Foam Products.

★ 75375 ★ **E.R. Carpenter Co. Inc.**
Virginia St. PO Box 1496
Lenoir, NC 28645
Ultimate Parent: Carpenter. **SIC:** 3086—Plastics Foam Products.

★ 75376 ★ **E.R. Carpenter Co. Inc.**
Miller Hill Rd.
Lenoir, NC 28645-1496
Ultimate Parent: Carpenter. **SIC:** 3086—Plastics Foam Products.

★ 75377 ★ **First-Citizens Bank & Trust Co.**
308 Connelly Springs Rd.
Lenoir, NC 28645
(704)754-0535
Location Type: Branch office. **Officer:** Charles E. Dobbin, Senior Vice President. **Ultimate Parent:** First Citizens Bancshares, Inc. **SIC:** 6021—National Commercial Banks.

★ 75378 ★ **Hammary Furniture**
2464 Norwood St., SW
Lenoir, NC 28645
(704)728-3231 **Fax:** (704)728-5063
Officer: Fred A. Preddy Jr., President. **Ultimate Parent:** La-Z-Boy Chair.

★ 75379 ★ **Hammary Furniture Co. Plant 15**
2464 Norwood St.
Lenoir, NC 28645
Ultimate Parent: La-Z-Boy Chair. **SIC:** 2511—Wood Household Furniture.

★ 75380 ★ **Industrial Systems Associates Inc.**
1248 Hickory Blvd. SE
Lenoir, NC 28645-6221
(704)728-1200
Ultimate Parent: Ball Corp. **SIC:** 5085—Industrial Supplies.

★ 75381 ★ **Kentucky Fried Chicken**
428 Blowing Rock Rd.
Lenoir, NC 28645
(704)758-2400
Ultimate Parent: Pepsico. **SIC:** 5812—Eating Places.

★ 75382 ★ **Kincaid Furniture Co. Inc. Plant 8**
Hwy. 18 & Rocky Rd.
Lenoir, NC 28645
Ultimate Parent: La-Z-Boy Chair. **SIC:** 2511—Wood Household Furniture.

★ 75383 ★ **Broyhill Furniture Ind. Inc. Lenoir Furniture & Occ.1 Plts**
Virginia St.
Lenoir, NC 28645
Ultimate Parent: Interco. **SIC:** 2511—Wood Household Furniture.

★ 75384 ★ **Peoples Drug Store Inc.**
813 West Ave. NW
Lenoir, NC 28645
(704)758-4845
Ultimate Parent: Melville. **SIC:** 5912—Drug Stores & Proprietary Stores.

★ 75385 ★ **Pizza Hut**
130 Wilkesboro Blvd. SE
Lenoir, NC 28645
(704)758-0271
Ultimate Parent: Pepsico. **SIC:** 5812—Eating Places.

★ 75386 ★ **Radio Shack**
Lenoir Mall
Lenoir, NC 28645
(704)295-9233
Company Type: Division. **Ultimate Parent:** Tandy Corp. **SIC:** 5065—Electronic Parts & Equipment Nec; 5734—Computer & Software Stores.

★ 75387 ★ **Rite Aid Discount Pharmacie**
1966 Morganton Blvd. SW
Lenoir, NC 28645
(704)754-8214
Ultimate Parent: Rite Aid. **SIC:** 5912—Drug Stores & Proprietary Stores.

★ 75388 ★ **Ryder Truck Rental**
124 Harrisburg Rd.
Lenoir, NC 28645
(704)754-4503
Ultimate Parent: Ryder System. **SIC:** 7359—Equipment Rental & Leasing Nec.

★ 75389 ★ **Thomasville Furniture Ind. Inc.**
315 Elizabeth St. NW
Lenoir, NC 28645
Ultimate Parent: Armstrong World Industries. **SIC:** 2511—Wood Household Furniture.

★ 75390 ★ **Thomasville Furniture Industries Inc.**
315 Elizabeth St. NW
Lenoir, NC 28645
Ultimate Parent: Armstrong World Industries. **SIC:** 2511—Wood Household Furniture.

★ 75391 ★ **Thomasville Furniture Industries Inc.**
315 Elizabeth St. NW
Lenoir, NC 28645
Ultimate Parent: Armstrong World Industries. **SIC:** 2511—Wood Household Furniture.

★ 75392 ★ **Trailways Bus Systems**
1057 West Ave. NW
Lenoir, NC 28645
(704)754-7421
Ultimate Parent: Greyhound Lines Inc. **SIC:** 4111—Local & Suburban Transit.

★ 75393 ★ **Yale Materials Handling Corp.**
2040 Morganton Blvd. SW
Lenoir, NC 28645
Ultimate Parent: Nacco Industries. **SIC:** 3537—Industrial Trucks & Tractors.

Lewisville

★ 75394 ★ **Branch Banking & Trust Co.**
6454 Shallowford Rd.
Lewisville, NC 27023
(910)945-3795
Company Type: Subsidiary. **Location Type:** Branch office. **Ultimate Parent:** Southern National Corp. **SIC:** 6021—National Commercial Banks.

★ 75395 ★ **Kentucky Fried Chicken**
Rural Route 4
Lewisville, NC 27023
(919)766-8630
Ultimate Parent: Pepsico. **SIC:** 5812—Eating Places.

★ 75396 ★ **Taco Bell**
Rural Route 4
Lewisville, NC 27023
(919)766-0107
Ultimate Parent: Pepsico. **SIC:** 5812—Eating Places.

Lexington

★ 75397 ★ **Branch Banking & Trust Co.**
20 S. Main St.
Lexington, NC 27292-3398
(704)246-8000
Company Type: Subsidiary. **Location Type:** Branch office. **Officer:** G. Frank Cagle, Mgr. **Ultimate Parent:** Southern National Corp. **SIC:** 6021—National Commercial Banks.

★ 75398 ★ **Branch Banking & Trust Co.**
308 W. Ctr. St.
Lexington, NC 27292
(704)249-6735
Ultimate Parent: Southern National Corp. **SIC:** 6022—State Commercial Banks.

★ 75399 ★ **Dixie Furniture Co.**
411 S. Salisbury St.
Lexington, NC 27292
Ultimate Parent: Masco. **SIC:** 2511—Wood Household Furniture.

★ 75400 ★ **Dixie Furniture Co. Inc.**
Dining Room Div.
N. Church St.
Lexington, NC 27292-1008
Company Type: Division. **Ultimate Parent:** Masco. **SIC:** 2511—Wood Household Furniture.

★ 75401 ★ **Dixie Furniture Co. Inc.**
Dining Room Div.
411 S. Salisbury St.
Lexington, NC 27292-1008
Company Type: Division. **Ultimate Parent:** Masco. **SIC:** 2511—Wood Household Furniture.

★ 75402 ★ **Duracell International Inc.**
313 Us Hwy. 64 E
Lexington, NC 27292
(704)925-0500
Ultimate Parent: Duracell International Inc. **SIC:** 8731—Commercial Physical Research.

★ 75403 ★ **Duracell USA**
305 New Hwy. 64 E
Lexington, NC 27292
(704)249-9101
Officer: Don Thompson, Manager. **Ultimate Parent:** Duracell International Inc. **SIC:** 3692—Primary Batteries—Dry & Wet.

★ 75404 ★ **Food Lion**
Hwy. 52
Lexington, NC 27292
(704)246-4637
Ultimate Parent: Food Lion.

★ 75405 ★ **Kentucky Fried Chicken**
600 S. Main St.
Lexington, NC 27292
(704)246-2666
Ultimate Parent: Pepsico. **SIC:** 5812—Eating Places.

★ 75406 ★ **Kimberly-Clark Corp.**
PO Box 2016
Lexington, NC 27293
Ultimate Parent: Kimberly-Clark. **SIC:** 2297—Nonwoven Fabrics.

★ 75407 ★ **Kimberly-Clark Corp. Lexington Mill**
Corner I-85 & Clyde Fitzgerald PO Box 2016
Lexington, NC 27293-2016
Ultimate Parent: Kimberly-Clark. **SIC:** 2297—Nonwoven Fabrics.

★ 75408 ★ **Leggett & Platt Inc.**
Hwy. 8-South
Lexington, NC 27292
Ultimate Parent: Leggett & Platt Inc. **SIC:** 3499—Fabricated Metal Products Nec.

★ 75409 ★ **Leggett & Platt Inc. Cotton Grove Plant**
Hwy. 8 S.
Lexington, NC 27292
Ultimate Parent: Leggett & Platt Inc. **SIC:** 2514—Metal Household Furniture.

★ 75410 ★ **Leggett & Platt Inc. 0701**
Hwy. 8 South, PO Box 140
Lexington, NC 27202
Ultimate Parent: Leggett & Platt Inc. **SIC:** 3499—Fabricated Metal Products Nec.

★ 75411 ★ **Lexington Furniture Ind.**
Plant 8
Brown St. Extension
Lexington, NC 27292
Location Type: Plant. **Ultimate Parent:** Masco. **SIC:** 2511—Wood Household Furniture.

★ 75412 ★ **Lexington Furniture Ind.**
Plant 1
411 S. Salisbury St.
Lexington, NC 27292
Location Type: Plant. **Ultimate Parent:** Masco. **SIC:** 2511—Wood Household Furniture.

★ 75413 ★ **Lexington Furniture Ind.**
Plant 3
N. Church St.
Lexington, NC 27292
Location Type: Plant. **Ultimate Parent:** Masco. **SIC:** 2511—Wood Household Furniture.

★ 75414 ★ **Lexington Furniture Ind.**
Plant 12
Hwy. 8 S.
Lexington, NC 27292
Location Type: Plant. **Ultimate Parent:** Masco. **SIC:** 2511—Wood Household Furniture.

★ 75415 ★ **Lexington Furniture Ind.**
Plants 4 & 5
2000 Brown St.
Lexington, NC 27292
Location Type: Plant. **Ultimate Parent:** Masco. **SIC:** 2511—Wood Household Furniture.

★ 75416 ★ **Lexington Furniture Ind. Inc.**
Plant 9
Brown St. Extension
Lexington, NC 27292
Location Type: Plant. **Ultimate Parent:** Masco. **SIC:** 2511—Wood Household Furniture.

★ 75417 ★ **Lexington Furniture Ind. Inc.**
Plant 7
Brown St. Extension
Lexington, NC 27292
Location Type: Plant. **Ultimate Parent:** Masco. **SIC:** 2511—Wood Household Furniture.

★ 75418 ★ **Lexington Furniture Industries**
PO Box 1008
Lexington, NC 27293
(704)249-5300 **Fax:** (704)249-5365
Officer: J. Smith Young. **Ultimate Parent:** Masco.

★ 75419 ★　**Lexington Furniture Industries Plant**
Plant 2
Hwy. 8 S.
Lexington, NC 27292
Location Type: Plant. **Ultimate Parent:** Masco. **SIC:** 2511—Wood Household Furniture.

★ 75420 ★　**Mutual of New York**
27 E. Ctr. St.
Lexington, NC 27292
(704)249-3862
Ultimate Parent: Mutual of New York. **SIC:** 6411—Insurance Agents, Brokers & Service.

★ 75421 ★　**Pizza Hut**
410 Piedmont Dr.
Lexington, NC 27292
(704)249-4366
Ultimate Parent: Pepsico. **SIC:** 5812—Eating Places.

★ 75422 ★　**Radio Shack**
NE Hwy. 64 W
Lexington, NC 27292
(704)249-4472
Company Type: Division. **Ultimate Parent:** Tandy Corp. **SIC:** 5065—Electronic Parts & Equipment Nec.

★ 75423 ★　**Ryder Truck Rental**
806 N. Main St.
Lexington, NC 27292
(704)249-4517
Ultimate Parent: Ryder System. **SIC:** 7513—Truck Rental & Leasing Without Drivers.

★ 75424 ★　**Sealy Mattress Co.**
700 S. State St.
Lexington, NC 27292
(704)246-2357
Officer: Robert B. Byerly, Manager. **Ultimate Parent:** Sealy. **SIC:** 2515—Mattresses & Bedsprings.

★ 75425 ★　**Stone Container Corp.**
400 Albemarle St.
Lexington, NC 27292
(704)249-9966
Officer: Harold Mc Neill, Manager. **Ultimate Parent:** Stone Container Corp. **SIC:** 2652—Setup Paperboard Boxes; 2657—Folding Paperboard Boxes; 2679—Converted Paper Products Nec.

Liberty

★ 75426 ★　**Branch Banking & Trust Co.**
Raleigh & Fayetteville Sts.
Liberty, NC 27298
(910)622-4226
Company Type: Subsidiary. **Location Type:** Branch office. **Officer:** Robert Dean Wilkie, Mgr. **Ultimate Parent:** Southern National Corp. **SIC:** 6021—National Commercial Banks.

★ 75427 ★　**Burlington Industries Inc.**
1000 E. Butler Ave.
Liberty, NC 27298-2709
(919)622-3021
Location Type: Branch office. **Officer:** Tom Coley. **Ultimate Parent:** Burlington Industries, Equity. **SIC:** 2211—Broadwoven Fabric Mills—Cotton.

★ 75428 ★　**Collier-Keyworth Co.**
PO Box 1109
Liberty, NC 27298
(919)622-0120 **Fax:** (919)622-0150
Officer: David Frohnaple, President. **Ultimate Parent:** Leggett & Platt Inc.

★ 75429 ★　**Collier Keyworth Co.**
330 N. Greensboro St.
Liberty, NC 27298
Ultimate Parent: Leggett & Platt Inc. **SIC:** 3429—Hardware Nec.

Lilesville

★ 75430 ★　**Bowater Inc.**
RR 1
Lilesville, NC 28091-9801
(704)848-4814
Officer: Steve Mims. **Ultimate Parent:** Bowater. **SIC:** 2411—Logging; 2611—Pulp Mills.

Lillington

★ 75431 ★　**Branch Banking & Trust Co.**
111 W. Front St.
Lillington, NC 27546
(910)893-4151
Company Type: Subsidiary. **Location Type:** Branch office. **Officer:** Darel Hurley, Manager. **Ultimate Parent:** Southern National Corp. **SIC:** 6021—National Commercial Banks.

★ 75432 ★　**Food Lion**
Hwy. 401 S
Lillington, NC 27546
(919)893-3921
Ultimate Parent: Food Lion. **SIC:** 5411—Grocery Stores.

★ 75433 ★　**Food Lion, Inc.**
Hwy. 401 S
Lillington, NC 27546
(919)893-3921
Ultimate Parent: Food Lion. **SIC:** 5411—Grocery Stores.

★ 75434 ★　**Red Kap Ind.**
1500 S. Main St.
Lillington, NC 27546
(910)893-4121
Officer: James Brantley, Manager. **Ultimate Parent:** VF Corp. **SIC:** 2329—Men's/Boys' Clothing Nec; 2331—Women's/Misses' Blouses & Shirts.

★ 75435 ★　**Stop & Shop**
207 E. Mac Neil
Lillington, NC 27546
(919)893-5357
Ultimate Parent: Stop & Shop. **SIC:** 5411—Grocery Stores.

Lincolnton

★ 75436 ★　**Citizens Savings Bank, SSB**
1403 E. Main St.
Lincolnton, NC 28092-3901
(704)735-8287
Company Type: Subsidiary. **Location Type:** Branch office. **Officer:** Myra Stary, Mgr. **Ultimate Parent:** Southern National Corp. **SIC:** 6021—National Commercial Banks.

★ 75437 ★　**Citizens Savings Bank, SSB**
341 E. Main St.
Lincolnton, NC 28092-3334
(704)735-8252
Company Type: Subsidiary. **Location Type:** Branch office. **Officer:** Bryan Morrison, Mgr. **Ultimate Parent:** Southern National Corp. **SIC:** 6021—National Commercial Banks.

★ 75438 ★　**First-Citizens Bank & Trust Co.**
2424 E. Main St.
Lincolnton, NC 28092-4106
(704)732-0701
Location Type: Branch office. **Ultimate Parent:** First Citizens Bancshares, Inc. **SIC:** 6021—National Commercial Banks.

★ 75439 ★　**First Federal S & L**
320 E. Main St.
Lincolnton, NC 28092-3398
(704)735-0416
Company Type: Headquarters. **Officer:** C. D. Stroup III. **Ultimate Parent:** Bancorp Hawaii. **SIC:** 6035—Federal Savings Institutions; 6141—Personal Credit Institutions; 6162—Mortgage Bankers & Correspondents; 6282—Investment Advice.

★ 75440 ★　**La-Z-Boy Lincolnton**
Burris Blvd.
Lincolnton, NC 28092
(704)735-0441 **Fax:** (704)735-2806
Officer: F. Joseph Brooks, Vice President. **Ultimate Parent:** La-Z-Boy Chair.

★ 75441 ★　**Radio Shack**
Lincolnton Plaza Ctr.
Lincolnton, NC 28092
(704)735-8994
Company Type: Division. **Ultimate Parent:** Tandy Corp. **SIC:** 5065—Electronic Parts & Equipment Nec.

★ 75442 ★　**Sonoco Products Co.**
RR 4 Hoffman Rd.
Lincolnton, NC 28092
(704)735-0464
Officer: Walt Harvey, Plant Manager. **Ultimate Parent:** Sonoco Products. **SIC:** 2655—Fiber Cans, Drums & Similar Products.

★ 75443 ★　**Wal Mart Discount Cities**
Lincolnton, NC 28092
(704)732-3095
Ultimate Parent: Wal-Mart Stores, Inc. **SIC:** 5912—Drug Stores & Proprietary Stores.

Linwood

★ 75444 ★　**Dixie Furniture Co. Inc.**
Old Linwood Rd.
Linwood, NC 27299
Ultimate Parent: Masco. **SIC:** 2511—Wood Household Furniture.

★ 75445 ★　**Leggett & Platt Inc.**
Jr. Order Home Rd. PO Box 140
Linwood, NC 27299
Ultimate Parent: Leggett & Platt Inc. **SIC:** 2514—Metal Household Furniture.

★ 75446 ★　**Leggett & Platt Inc. 0700**
Junior Home Rd.
Linwood, NC 27299
Ultimate Parent: Leggett & Platt Inc. **SIC:** 3499—Fabricated Metal Products Nec.

★ 75447 ★　**Lexington Furniture Ind.**
Plant 2
Old Linwood Rd.
Linwood, NC 27299
Location Type: Plant. **Ultimate Parent:** Masco. **SIC:** 2511—Wood Household Furniture.

Littleton

★ 75448 ★　**Branch Banking & Trust Co.**
Main St.
Littleton, NC 27850
(919)586-3101
Company Type: Subsidiary. **Location Type:** Branch office. **Officer:** Robert L. Jones, Mgr. **Ultimate Parent:** Southern National Corp. **SIC:** 6021—National Commercial Banks.

★ 75449 ★　**First-Citizens Bank & Trust Co.**
111-115 E. South Main St.
Littleton, NC 27850
(919)586-4165
Location Type: Branch office. **Officer:** David T. Semler, Assistant Vice President. **Ultimate Parent:** First Citizens Bancshares, Inc. **SIC:** 6021—National Commercial Banks.

★ 75450 ★　**Radio Shack**
E S. Main St.
Littleton, NC 27850
(919)586-5832
Company Type: Division. **Ultimate Parent:** Tandy Corp. **SIC:** 5999—Miscellaneous Retail Stores Nec.

Longview

★ 75451 ★　**E. R. Carpenter Co. Inc.**
29th St. NW & Main Ave. NW, PO Box 4247
Longview, NC 28603
Ultimate Parent: Carpenter. **SIC:** 3086—Plastics Foam Products.

★ 75452 ★　**E.R. Carpenter Co. Inc.**
29th St., NW & Main Ave. NW Box 4247
Longview, NC 28603
Ultimate Parent: Carpenter. **SIC:** 3086—Plastics Foam Products.

Louisburg

★ 75453 ★　**Abbott Laboratories**
US Hwy. 401 N
Louisburg, NC 28352
(910)276-6210
Location Type: Branch office. **Officer:** Jack

Strum, Manager. **Ultimate Parent:** Abbott Laboratories. **SIC:** 3841—Surgical & Medical Instruments.

★ 75454 ★　**First-Citizens Bank & Trust Co.**
302 Franklin Plz.
Louisburg, NC 27549-2758
(919)496-3156
Location Type: Branch office. **Ultimate Parent:** First Citizens Bancshares, Inc. **SIC:** 6021—National Commercial Banks.

Lowell

★ 75455 ★　**Branch Banking & Trust Co.**
Wilkinson Blvd. & Groves St.
Lowell, NC 28098
(704)824-3541
Company Type: Subsidiary. **Location Type:** Branch office. **Officer:** Barbara Wansley, Mgr. **Ultimate Parent:** Southern National Corp. **SIC:** 6021—National Commercial Banks.

★ 75456 ★　**Exxon Party Shoppe**
Wilkinson Blvd.
Lowell, NC 28098
(704)824-2584
Ultimate Parent: Exxon. **SIC:** 5541—Gasoline Service Stations.

Lumberton

★ 75457 ★　**Abitibi-Price Building Products**
1 Abitibi-Price Ln.
Lumberton, NC 28358
Company Type: Subsidiary. **Ultimate Parent:** Alco Standard Corp.

★ 75458 ★　**Abitibi-Price Corp.**
Abitibi-Price Ln. Hwy. 72 W
Lumberton, NC 28358
(919)739-3252
Location Type: Branch office. **Officer:** Leighton McGinn. **Ultimate Parent:** Alco Standard Corp. **SIC:** 2431—Millwork.

★ 75459 ★　**Abitibi-Price Corp.**
Abitibi-Price Ln. Hwy. 72 W
Lumberton, NC 28358
(919)739-3252
Location Type: Branch office. **Officer:** Leighton McGinn. **Ultimate Parent:** Alco Standard Corp. **SIC:** 2431—Millwork.

★ 75460 ★　**Branch Banking & Trust Co.**
2700 N. Elm St.
Lumberton, NC 28358-3012
(910)671-2710
Company Type: Subsidiary. **Location Type:** Branch office. **Officer:** Susan Stanley, Manager. **Ultimate Parent:** Southern National Corp. **SIC:** 6021—National Commercial Banks.

★ 75461 ★　**Branch Banking & Trust Co.**
1775 Roberts Ave.
Lumberton, NC 28358
(910)671-2740
Company Type: Subsidiary. **Location Type:** Branch office. **Officer:** Sara Collins, Manager. **Ultimate Parent:** Southern National Corp. **SIC:** 6021—National Commercial Banks.

★ 75462 ★　**Branch Banking & Trust Co.**
5000 Fayetteville Rd.
Lumberton, NC 28358-2108
(910)671-2730
Company Type: Subsidiary. **Location Type:** Branch office. **Officer:** Debbie Branyon, Manager. **Ultimate Parent:** Southern National Corp. **SIC:** 6021—National Commercial Banks.

★ 75463 ★　**Branch Banking & Trust Co.**
500 N. Chestnut St.
Lumberton, NC 28358-5551
(910)671-2000
Company Type: Subsidiary. **Location Type:** Branch office. **Ultimate Parent:** Southern National Corp. **SIC:** 6021—National Commercial Banks.

★ 75464 ★ **Federal Paper Board Co.**
211 Red Springs Rd.
Lumberton, NC 28358
(910)739-7596
Officer: Percy Lunsford, Manager. **Ultimate Parent:** Federal Paper Board. **SIC:** 2411—Logging.

★ 75465 ★ **Food Lion**
Us 301 a
Lumberton, NC 28358
(919)739-0226
Ultimate Parent: Food Lion. **SIC:** 5411—Grocery Stores.

★ 75466 ★ **Kayser-Roth Corp.**
Sheer Hosiery Div.
3707 W. 5th St.
Lumberton, NC 28358
Company Type: Division. **Ultimate Parent:** Collins & Aikman Group. **SIC:** 2251—Women's Hosiery Except Socks.

★ 75467 ★ **Kentucky Fried Chicken**
520 W. 2nd St.
Lumberton, NC 28358
(919)738-2658
Ultimate Parent: Pepsico. **SIC:** 5812—Eating Places.

★ 75468 ★ **Kentucky Fried Chicken**
2000 N. Roberts Ave.
Lumberton, NC 28358
(919)738-7558
Ultimate Parent: Pepsico. **SIC:** 5812—Eating Places.

★ 75469 ★ **Pepsi-Cola Bottling Co.**
400 S. Chippewa St.
Lumberton, NC 28358
(910)738-6266
Officer: Carlton Hawkins, Manager. **Ultimate Parent:** Pepsico. **SIC:** 2086—Bottled & Canned Soft Drinks.

★ 75470 ★ **Piggly Wiggly**
302 N. Pine St.
Lumberton, NC 28358
(919)738-9841
Ultimate Parent: Bruno's. **SIC:** 5411—Grocery Stores.

★ 75471 ★ **Pizza Hut**
4455 Fayetteville Rd.
Lumberton, NC 28358
(919)738-8206
Ultimate Parent: Pepsico. **SIC:** 5812—Eating Places.

★ 75472 ★ **Rite Aid Discount Pharmacy**
3549 Fayetteville Rd.
Lumberton, NC 28358
(919)738-3795
Ultimate Parent: Rite Aid. **SIC:** 5912—Drug Stores & Proprietary Stores.

★ 75473 ★ **Sara Lee Hosiery**
3601 W. Fifth St.
Lumberton, NC 28358
Ultimate Parent: Sara Lee Corp. **SIC:** 2251—Women's Hosiery Except Socks.

★ 75474 ★ **Sara Lee Knit Products**
209 S. Chestnut St.
Lumberton, NC 28358
Location Type: Plant. **Ultimate Parent:** Sara Lee Corp. **SIC:** 2257—Weft Knit Fabric Mills.

★ 75475 ★ **Wachovia Bank & Trust Co. N**
2775 N. Elm St.
Lumberton, NC 28358
(919)738-6261
Ultimate Parent: Wachovia Corp. **SIC:** 6022—State Commercial Banks.

★ 75476 ★ **West Point Pepperell**
South Chestnut St. Extension
Lumberton, NC 28359
Location Type: Plant. **Ultimate Parent:** West Point Stevens. **SIC:** 2259—Knitting Mills Nec.

★ 75477 ★ **Westpoint Pepperell**
South Chestnut St. Extension
Lumberton, NC 28359
Location Type: Plant. **Ultimate Parent:** West Point Stevens. **SIC:** 2253—Knit Outerwear Mills.

Macksville

★ 75478 ★ **Branch Banking & Trust Co.**
US Hwy. 601
Macksville, NC 27028-8715
(704)634-5951
Company Type: Subsidiary. **Location Type:** Branch office. **Ultimate Parent:** Southern National Corp. **SIC:** 6021—National Commercial Banks.

Madison

★ 75479 ★ **Branch Banking & Trust Co.**
Lang St.
Madison, NC 27025
(910)427-0263
Company Type: Subsidiary. **Location Type:** Branch office. **Ultimate Parent:** Southern National Corp. **SIC:** 6021—National Commercial Banks.

★ 75480 ★ **Branch Banking & Trust Co.**
1109 N. Hwy. St.
Madison, NC 27025-1515
(910)548-9631
Company Type: Subsidiary. **Location Type:** Branch office. **Officer:** Marcus H. Warren, Manager. **Ultimate Parent:** Southern National Corp. **SIC:** 6021—National Commercial Banks.

★ 75481 ★ **First-Citizens Bank & Trust Co.**
111 S. Market St.
Madison, NC 27025-2133
(910)548-6087
Location Type: Branch office. **Officer:** Joe I. Marshall, Area Vice President. **Ultimate Parent:** First Citizens Bancshares, Inc. **SIC:** 6021—National Commercial Banks.

★ 75482 ★ **First-Citizens Bank & Trust Co.**
815 Ayersville Rd. NW
Madison, NC 27025-1537
(910)548-6087
Location Type: Branch office. **Ultimate Parent:** First Citizens Bancshares, Inc. **SIC:** 6021—National Commercial Banks.

★ 75483 ★ **Pizza Hut**
1005 Midtown Shopping Ctr.
Madison, NC 27025
(919)427-3477
Ultimate Parent: Pepsico. **SIC:** 5812—Eating Places.

★ 75484 ★ **Rite Aid Pharmacy**
510 Midtown Shopping Ctr.
Madison, NC 27025
(919)548-9953
Ultimate Parent: Rite Aid. **SIC:** 5912—Drug Stores & Proprietary Stores.

★ 75485 ★ **UNIFI**
802 S. Ayersville Rd.
Madison, NC 27025
(910)427-4051
Officer: Harry Wilkins, Plant Manager. **Ultimate Parent:** UNIFI, Inc. **SIC:** 2252—Hosiery Nec; 2282—Throwing & Winding Mills.

★ 75486 ★ **UNIFI, Inc.**
212 Piedmont St.
Madison, NC 27025
(910)427-1227
Officer: Billy Corns, Manager. **Ultimate Parent:** UNIFI, Inc. **SIC:** 2282—Throwing & Winding Mills.

Maggic Valley

★ 75487 ★ **Branch Banking & Trust Co.**
Hwy. 19
Maggic Valley, NC 28751-9721
(704)926-3801
Company Type: Subsidiary. **Location Type:** Branch office. **Officer:** Darlene Williams, Mgr. **Ultimate Parent:** Southern

National Corp. **SIC:** 6021—National Commercial Banks.

Magnalia

★ 75488 ★ **Branch Banking & Trust Co.**
104 S. Railroad St.
Magnalia, NC 28453
(910)289-2559
Company Type: Subsidiary. **Location Type:** Branch office. **Officer:** Susan Jayner, Mgr. **Ultimate Parent:** Southern National Corp. **SIC:** 6021—National Commercial Banks.

Maiden

★ 75489 ★ **Citizens Savings Bank, SSB**
1205 E. Main St.
Maiden, NC 28650-1528
(704)428-9933
Company Type: Subsidiary. **Location Type:** Branch office. **Officer:** Geneva W. Keever, Mgr. **Ultimate Parent:** Southern National Corp. **SIC:** 6021—National Commercial Banks.

★ 75490 ★ **Delta Apparel Maiden Plant**
408 S. Main Ave.
Maiden, NC 28650
Ultimate Parent: Delta Woodside Industries. **SIC:** 2257—Weft Knit Fabric Mills; 2254—Knit Underwear Mills.

★ 75491 ★ **Delta Mills Marketing**
W. Finger St. Ext.
Maiden, NC 28650
(704)426-3261
Officer: Edwin Jeffords, Manager. **Ultimate Parent:** Delta Woodside Industries. **SIC:** 2281—Yarn Spinning Mills; 2399—Fabricated Textile Products Nec.

★ 75492 ★ **Duck Head Apparel Co.**
408 S. Main Ave.
Maiden, NC 28650
(704)428-9921
Officer: Joe Hubbard, Plant Manager. **Ultimate Parent:** Delta Woodside Industries. **SIC:** 2258—Lace & Warp Knit Fabric Mills; 2399—Fabricated Textile Products Nec.

★ 75493 ★ **First-Citizens Bank & Trust Co.**
35 E. Main St.
Maiden, NC 28650-1314
(704)428-9368
Location Type: Branch office. **Officer:** Deborah R. Burgin, Assistant Vice President. **Ultimate Parent:** First Citizens Bancshares, Inc. **SIC:** 6021—National Commercial Banks.

★ 75494 ★ **Rite Aid Discount Pharmacy**
Rural Route 1
Maiden, NC 28650
(704)428-3157
Ultimate Parent: Rite Aid. **SIC:** 5912—Drug Stores & Proprietary Stores.

★ 75495 ★ **Stevcoknit Fabric Co. Maiden**
408 S. Main Ave.
Maiden, NC 28650
Ultimate Parent: Delta Woodside Industries. **SIC:** 2257—Weft Knit Fabric Mills; 2254—Knit Underwear Mills.

Marion

★ 75496 ★ **Baxter Healthcare**
Hwy. 221 N
Marion, NC 28752
(704)756-4151
Officer: Mike Gatling, Manager. **Ultimate Parent:** Baxter International. **SIC:** 2834—Pharmaceutical Preparations.

★ 75497 ★ **Baxter Healthcare Corp.**
Hwy. 221 N
Marion, NC 28752
(704)756-4151
Location Type: Branch office. **Officer:** Mike Gatling. **Ultimate Parent:** Baxter International. **SIC:** 2834—Pharmaceutical

National Corp. **SIC:** 6021—National Commercial Banks.

Preparations; 5122—Drugs, Proprietaries & Sundries; 6061—Federal Credit Unions.

★ 75498 ★ **Coca Cola Bottling Co.**
Hwy. 226 S
Marion, NC 28752
(704)652-9865
Ultimate Parent: Coca-Cola Enterprises. **SIC:** 5921—Liquor Stores.

★ 75499 ★ **Crane Resistoflex Co.**
1 Quality Way Off Hwy. 70 W.
Marion, NC 28752
Ultimate Parent: Crane. **SIC:** 3089—Plastics Products Nec.

★ 75500 ★ **Crane Resistoflex Co.**
Old Rte. 10 Off 70 West
Marion, NC 28752
Ultimate Parent: Crane. **SIC:** 3089—Plastics Products Nec.

★ 75501 ★ **Drexel Heritage Furnishings**
Plant 2
361 Blue Ridge St.
Marion, NC 28752
Location Type: Plant. **Ultimate Parent:** Masco. **SIC:** 2511—Wood Household Furniture.

★ 75502 ★ **Drexel Heritage Furnishings Inc.**
Plant 2
361 Blue Ridge St.
Marion, NC 28752
Location Type: Plant. **Ultimate Parent:** Masco. **SIC:** 2511—Wood Household Furniture.

★ 75503 ★ **Drexel Heritage Furniture**
Plant 2
361 Blue Ridge St.
Marion, NC 28752
Location Type: Plant. **Ultimate Parent:** Masco. **SIC:** 2511—Wood Household Furniture.

★ 75504 ★ **First-Citizens Bank & Trust Co.**
640 N. Main St.
Marion, NC 28752-9763
(704)652-7515
Location Type: Branch office. **Officer:** Harold G. Walker, Vice President. **Ultimate Parent:** First Citizens Bancshares, Inc. **SIC:** 6021—National Commercial Banks.

★ 75505 ★ **Midland Brake Inc.**
Hwy. 221 S
Marion, NC 28752
(704)652-9308
Officer: Mel Shuster, Manager. **Ultimate Parent:** Echlin. **SIC:** 3563—Air & Gas Compressors; 3592—Carburetors, Pistons, Rings & Valves; 3714—Motor Vehicle Parts & Accessories.

★ 75506 ★ **Pepsi-Cola Bottling Co.**
Hwy. 221 N. Woodlawn
Marion, NC 28752
(704)765-2352
Officer: Lee Sparks, Manager. **Ultimate Parent:** Pepsico. **SIC:** 2086—Bottled & Canned Soft Drinks.

★ 75507 ★ **Trailways Inc.**
441 S. Main St.
Marion, NC 28752
(704)652-4858
Ultimate Parent: Greyhound Lines Inc. **SIC:** 4131—Intercity & Rural Bus Transportation.

Mars Hill

★ 75508 ★ **Honeywell**
Micro Switch Div.
1 Hickory Dr.
Mars Hill, NC 28754-0460
Company Type: Division. **Ultimate Parent:** Honeywell. **SIC:** 3643—Current-Carrying Wiring Devices.

★ 75509 ★ **Honeywell Inc.**
Micro Switch Div.
155 Hickory Dr.
Mars Hill, NC 28754-0460
Company Type: Division. **Ultimate Parent:** Honeywell. **SIC:** 3643—Current-Carrying Wiring Devices.

★ **75510** ★ **Mini Mart**
2241 Hwy. 213
Mars Hill, NC 28754
(704)689-2624
Ultimate Parent: Kroger. **SIC:** 7538—
General Automotive Repair Shops.

★ **75511** ★ **Wachovia Bank & Trust Co.**
Cherry
Mars Hill, NC 28754
(704)689-2500
Ultimate Parent: Wachovia Corp. **SIC:**
6022—State Commercial Banks.

★ **75512** ★ **Wachovia Bank & Trust Co.**
103 Marshall
Mars Hill, NC 28754
(704)689-2121
Ultimate Parent: Wachovia Corp. **SIC:**
6022—State Commercial Banks.

Marshall

★ **75513** ★ **First-Citizens Bank & Trust Co.**
US Hwy. 25-70 Marshall Bypass
Marshall, NC 28753
(704)649-2255
Location Type: Branch office. **Officer:**
Clyde L. Hagen, Vice President. **Ultimate
Parent:** First Citizens Bancshares, Inc. **SIC:**
6021—National Commercial Banks.

Marshville

★ **75514** ★ **Food Lion**
Hwy. 74 E
Marshville, NC 28103
(704)624-5071
Ultimate Parent: Food Lion. **SIC:** 5411—
Grocery Stores.

★ **75515** ★ **Food Lion Inc. Store**
Hwy. 74 E
Marshville, NC 28103
(704)624-5071
Ultimate Parent: Food Lion. **SIC:** 5411—
Grocery Stores.

Matthews

★ **75516** ★ **ALLTEL Carolina**
131 W. Matthews St.
PO Box 428
Matthews, NC 28106-0428
(704)847-9101
Company Type: Subsidiary. **Ultimate
Parent:** ALLTEL Corp. **SIC:** 4812—
Radiotelephone Communications.

★ **75517** ★ **American General Finance**
9010 Monroe Rd.
Matthews, NC 28105
(704)847-7429
Ultimate Parent: American General Corp.
SIC: 6141—Personal Credit Institutions.

★ **75518** ★ **Bi-Lo**
11446 E. Independence Blvd.
Matthews, NC 28105
(704)847-2380
Ultimate Parent: Penn Traffic. **SIC:** 5411—
Grocery Stores.

★ **75519** ★ **Branch Banking & Trust Co.**
733 Pineville-Matthews Rd.
Plantation Estates
Matthews, NC 28105
(704)847-9155
Company Type: Subsidiary. **Location
Type:** Branch office. **Ultimate Parent:**
Southern National Corp. **SIC:** 6021—
National Commercial Banks.

★ **75520** ★ **Branch Banking & Trust Co.**
157 N. Trade St.
Matthews, NC 28105-5771
(704)847-9155
Company Type: Subsidiary. **Location
Type:** Branch office. **Officer:** Janet G.
Gass, Mgr. **Ultimate Parent:** Southern
National Corp. **SIC:** 6021—National
Commercial Banks.

★ **75521** ★ **Branch Banking & Trust Co.**
1321 Matthews Township Pky.
Matthews, NC 28105
(704)847-1177
Company Type: Subsidiary. **Location
Type:** Branch office. **Ultimate Parent:**
Southern National Corp. **SIC:** 6021—
National Commercial Banks.

★ **75522** ★ **Branch Banking & Trust Co.**
157 S. Trade St.
Matthews, NC 28105
(704)847-9155
Ultimate Parent: Southern National Corp.
SIC: 6022—State Commercial Banks.

★ **75523** ★ **Exxon**
1700 Independence Blvd.
Matthews, NC 28105
(704)847-1189
Ultimate Parent: Exxon. **SIC:** 5541—
Gasoline Service Stations.

★ **75524** ★ **Exxon**
Matthews, NC 28105
(704)821-6246
Ultimate Parent: Exxon. **SIC:** 5541—
Gasoline Service Stations.

★ **75525** ★ **Kentucky Fried Chicken**
220 S. Trade St.
Matthews, NC 28105
(704)847-8758
Ultimate Parent: Pepsico. **SIC:** 5812—
Eating Places.

★ **75526** ★ **Liberty Mutual Insurance Co.**
Rural Route 6
Matthews, NC 28105
(704)847-8406
Ultimate Parent: Liberty Mutual Group.
SIC: 6411—Insurance Agents, Brokers &
Service.

★ **75527** ★ **Pizza Hut**
11315 E. Independence Blvd.
Matthews, NC 28105
(704)847-2603
Ultimate Parent: Pepsico. **SIC:** 5812—
Eating Places.

★ **75528** ★ **Pulte Home Corp.**
2101 N. Sardis Rd.
Matthews, NC 28105
(704)847-4575
Ultimate Parent: Pulte. **SIC:** 1541—
Industrial Buildings & Warehouses.

★ **75529** ★ **Radio Shack**
11500 E. Independence Blvd.
Matthews, NC 28105
(704)847-0703
Company Type: Division. **Ultimate Parent:**
Tandy Corp. **SIC:** 5731—Radio, Television
& Electronics Stores.

★ **75530** ★ **Rexham Corp. Matthews**
700 Crestdale St.
Matthews, NC 28105-0368
Ultimate Parent: Bowater. **SIC:** 3081—
Unsupported Plastics Film & Sheet; 3083—
Laminated Plastics Plate & Sheet.

★ **75531** ★ **Rexham Inc. Industrial Div. Matthews Plant**
Industrial Division Matthews Plant
700 Crestdale Rd.
Matthews, NC 28105
Ultimate Parent: Bowater. **SIC:** 3083—
Laminated Plastics Plate & Sheet; 3081—
Unsupported Plastics Film & Sheet.

★ **75532** ★ **Wachovia Bank & Trust**
1401 Matthews Mint Hill Rd.
Matthews, NC 28105
(704)378-5548
Ultimate Parent: Wachovia Corp. **SIC:**
6022—State Commercial Banks.

Maxton

★ **75533** ★ **Ace Hardware**
508 W. Saunders St.
Maxton, NC 28364
(919)844-9145
Ultimate Parent: Ace Hardware.

★ **75534** ★ **Campbell Soup Co.**
Rte. 2 Hwy. 71 N.
Maxton, NC 28364
Ultimate Parent: Campbell Soup. **SIC:**
2032—Canned Specialties.

★ **75535** ★ **Piggly Wiggly**
Patterson
Maxton, NC 28364
(919)844-3671
Ultimate Parent: Bruno's. **SIC:** 5411—
Grocery Stores.

★ **75536** ★ **Wachovia Bank & Trust Co. N**
130 W. Central St.
Maxton, NC 28364
(919)844-5241
Ultimate Parent: Wachovia Corp. **SIC:**
6022—State Commercial Banks.

Mayodan

★ **75537** ★ **Burlington Madison Yarn Co.**
144 Turner Rd.
Mayodan, NC 27027-8252
(919)427-4091
Officer: Jim Lilly. **Ultimate Parent:**
Burlington Industries, Equity. **SIC:** 2281—
Yarn Spinning Mills; 2221—Broadwoven
Fabric Mills—Manmade; 5131—Piece
Goods & Notions.

★ **75538** ★ **Food Lion**
409 S. 2nd Ave.
Mayodan, NC 27027
(919)548-6051
Ultimate Parent: Food Lion. **SIC:** 5411—
Grocery Stores.

★ **75539** ★ **UNIFI, Inc.**
802 Ayerville Rd.
Mayodan, NC 27127
(910)427-1536
Officer: William J. Armsield IV, President.
Ultimate Parent: UNIFI, Inc. **SIC:** 2211—
Broadwoven Fabric Mills—Cotton; 2221—
Broadwoven Fabric Mills—Manmade; 2221—
2231—Broadwoven Fabric Mills—Wool.

★ **75540** ★ **Unifi Inc. Plant 1**
Ayersville Rd. PO Box 737
Mayodan, NC 27025
Ultimate Parent: UNIFI, Inc. **SIC:** 2282—
Throwing & Winding Mills.

Maysville

★ **75541** ★ **First-Citizens Bank & Trust Co.**
602 Main St.
Maysville, NC 28555
(910)743-6241
Location Type: Branch office. **Officer:**
Randolph A. Mills Jr., Vice President.
Ultimate Parent: First Citizens Bancshares,
Inc. **SIC:** 6021—National Commercial
Banks.

★ **75542** ★ **Martin Marietta Aggregates**
Belgrade Mobile Home
Maysville, NC 28555
(919)743-6471
Ultimate Parent: Martin Marietta. **SIC:**
5039—Construction Materials Nec.

Mc Leansville

★ **75543** ★ **Wachovia Bank & Trust Co. N**
5815 W. Friendly Ave.
Mc Leansville, NC 27301
(919)373-6444
Ultimate Parent: Wachovia Corp. **SIC:**
6022—State Commercial Banks.

McAdenville

★ **75544** ★ **AT & T Family Federal Credit Union**
121 Main St.
McAdenville, NC 28101
(704)824-4639
Location Type: Branch office. **Officer:**
Tammie Kane, Manager. **Ultimate Parent:**
AT&T. **SIC:** 6061—Federal Credit Unions.

★ **75545** ★ **AT&T Family Federal Credit Union**
121 Main St.
McAdenville, NC 28101
(704)824-4639
Officer: Jacqueline P. Miller. **Ultimate
Parent:** AT&T. **SIC:** 6061—Federal Credit
Unions.

McLeansville

★ **75546** ★ **AT&T**
5440 Mill Stream Rd.
McLeansville, NC 27301
(910)279-7000
Officer: Bill Garrett, President. **Ultimate
Parent:** AT&T. **SIC:** 3663—Radio & T.V.
Communications Equipment.

Mebane

★ **75547** ★ **A. O. Smith Electrical Prods. Co.**
709 A. O. Smith Rd.
Mebane, NC 27302
Ultimate Parent: A. O. Smith. **SIC:** 3621—
Motors & Generators.

★ **75548** ★ **Adams Millis Influential**
202 North Fifth St.
Mebane, NC 27302
Location Type: Plant. **Ultimate Parent:**
Sara Lee Corp. **SIC:** 2252—Hosiery Nec.

★ **75549** ★ **Adams-Millis Influential No. 2**
202 N. 5th St.
Mebane, NC 27302
Ultimate Parent: Sara Lee Corp. **SIC:**
2252—Hosiery Nec.

★ **75550** ★ **General Electric Co.**
6801 Industrial Dr.
Mebane, NC 27302
Ultimate Parent: General Electric. **SIC:**
3600—Electronic & Other Electrical
Equipment.

★ **75551** ★ **General Electric Co.**
6801 Industrial Dr.
Mebane, NC 27302
(910)563-5561
Officer: Roger Gasaway, Manager. **Ultimate
Parent:** General Electric. **SIC:**
3613—Switchgear & Switchboard
Apparatus.

★ **75552** ★ **Rite Aid Discount Phrmcy**
Byrd's Shopping Cent
Mebane, NC 27302
(919)563-9585
Ultimate Parent: Rite Aid. **SIC:** 5912—Drug
Stores & Proprietary Stores.

★ **75553** ★ **Wachovia Bank & Trust Co. N**
101 S. 5th St.
Mebane, NC 27302
(919)563-1221
Ultimate Parent: Wachovia Corp. **SIC:**
6022—State Commercial Banks.

★ **75554** ★ **Walter Kidde Portable Equipment Inc.**
1394 South Third St.
Mebane, NC 27302-9190
Ultimate Parent: Hanson Industries. **SIC:**
3999—Manufacturing Industries Nec.

Merry Hill

★ **75555** ★ **R.J. Reynolds Tobacco Co.**
Avoca Div.
State Rd. 1502 PO Box 128
Merry Hill, NC 27957-9713
Company Type: Division. **Ultimate Parent:**
RJR Nabisco Holdings. **SIC:** 2087—
Flavoring Extracts & Syrups Nec.

Micro

★ **75556** ★ **Branch Banking & Trust Co.**
32 Railroad St.
Micro, NC 27555
(919)284-3166
Company Type: Subsidiary. **Location Type:** Branch office. **Officer:** Diane Kirby, Mgr. **Ultimate Parent:** Southern National Corp. **SIC:** 6021—National Commercial Banks.

Middlesex

★ **75557** ★ **Aeroquip Corp.**
Alternate Hwy. 264
Middlesex, NC 27557
(919)235-2121
Officer: Mike Shinners, Manager. **Ultimate Parent:** Trinova Corp. **SIC:** 3494—Valves & Pipe Fittings Nec.

★ **75558** ★ **Aeroquip Corp. Middlesex Plant**
Hwy. 264 E. Alternate PO Box 369
Middlesex, NC 27557-0369
Ultimate Parent: Trinova Corp. **SIC:** 3000—Rubber & Miscellaneous Plastics Products.

Midland

★ **75559** ★ **Pepsi-Cola Bottling Co.**
5047 Hwy. 24
Midland, NC 28017
(704)888-3800
Officer: Bob Landers, Manager. **Ultimate Parent:** Pepsico. **SIC:** 2086—Bottled & Canned Soft Drinks.

Midway Park

★ **75560** ★ **Piggly Wiggly**
Lake Cole Rd.
Midway Park, NC 28544
(919)353-0022
Ultimate Parent: Bruno's. **SIC:** 5411—Grocery Stores.

Mint Hill

★ **75561** ★ **Branch Banking & Trust Co.**
11301 Lawyers Rd.
Mint Hill, NC 28227-9312
(704)545-8134
Company Type: Subsidiary. **Location Type:** Branch office. **Officer:** Ed Cottingham, Mgr. **Ultimate Parent:** Southern National Corp. **SIC:** 6021—National Commercial Banks.

Mocksville

★ **75562** ★ **Branch Banking & Trust Co.**
212 Gaither St.
Mocksville, NC 27028
(704)634-5951
Ultimate Parent: Southern National Corp. **SIC:** 6022—State Commercial Banks.

★ **75563** ★ **Greyhound Bus Lines**
716 Yadkinville Rd.
Mocksville, NC 27028
(704)634-3636
Ultimate Parent: Greyhound Lines Inc. **SIC:** 4131—Intercity & Rural Bus Transportation.

★ **75564** ★ **Ingersoll Rand**
501 Sanford Ave.
Mocksville, NC 27028
Ultimate Parent: Ingersoll-Rand. **SIC:** 3563—Air & Gas Compressors.

★ **75565** ★ **Ingersoll-Rand Co.**
Portable Compressor Div.
501 Sanford Ave. PO Box 868
Mocksville, NC 27028
Company Type: Division. **Ultimate Parent:** Ingersoll-Rand. **SIC:** 3563—Air & Gas Compressors.

★ **75566** ★ **Lexington Furniture Ind.**
Plant 11
719 Bailey St.
Mocksville, NC 27028
Location Type: Plant. **Ultimate Parent:** Masco. **SIC:** 2511—Wood Household Furniture.

Moncure

★ **75567** ★ **Allied-Signal Fiber**
Pea Ridge Rd.
Moncure, NC 27559
(910)775-2338
Officer: Johnny Forehand, Manager. **Ultimate Parent:** Allied-Signal Inc. **SIC:** 2655—Fiber Cans, Drums & Similar Products; 2824—Organic Fibers—Noncellulosic.

★ **75568** ★ **Allied-Signal Inc.**
Fibers
Pea Ridge Rd.
Moncure, NC 275590000
Ultimate Parent: Allied-Signal Inc. **SIC:** 2824—Organic Fibers—Noncellulosic; 2821—Plastics Materials & Resins.

★ **75569** ★ **Weyerhaeuser Co.**
State Rd. 1916
Moncure, NC 27559
Ultimate Parent: Weyerhaeuser Co. **SIC:** 2499—Wood Products Nec.

★ **75570** ★ **Weyerhaeuser Co.**
1916 State Rd.
Moncure, NC 27559
(910)542-2128
Officer: Lori Beyrle, Vice President. **Ultimate Parent:** Weyerhaeuser Co. **SIC:** 2493—Reconstituted Wood Products.

★ **75571** ★ **Willamette Industries, Inc.**
RR 1916
Moncure, NC 27559
(919)542-2311
Ultimate Parent: Willamette Industries, Inc. **SIC:** 0811—Timber Tracts.

★ **75572** ★ **Willamette Industries, Inc.**
Moncure
State Rd. 1916
Moncure, NC 27559
Ultimate Parent: Willamette Industries, Inc. **SIC:** 2436—Softwood Veneer & Plywood; 2421—Sawmills & Planing Mills—General.

Monroe

★ **75573** ★ **Cooper Industries Inc. Plumb Plant**
3012 Mason St.
Monroe, NC 28110
Ultimate Parent: Cooper Industries. **SIC:** 3423—Hand & Edge Tools Nec; 3462—Iron & Steel Forgings.

★ **75574** ★ **First-Citizens Bank & Trust**
111 E. Jefferson St.
Monroe, NC 28111
(704)823-7431
Location Type: Branch office. **Officer:** Roby F. Shore, Area Vice President. **Ultimate Parent:** First Citizens Bancshares, Inc. **SIC:** 6021—National Commercial Banks.

★ **75575** ★ **First-Citizens Bank & Trust Co.**
205 E. Marshall Blvd.
Monroe, NC 28103
(704)624-2143
Location Type: Branch office. **Ultimate Parent:** First Citizens Bancshares, Inc. **SIC:** 6021—National Commercial Banks.

★ **75576** ★ **First-Citizens Bank & Trust Co.**
1821 Dickerson Blvd.
Monroe, NC 28110-2759
(704)289-8546
Location Type: Branch office. **Ultimate Parent:** First Citizens Bancshares, Inc. **SIC:** 6021—National Commercial Banks.

★ **75577** ★ **Holly Farms Foods Inc.**
Monroe Plant
Secrest Ave.
Monroe, NC 28110
Location Type: Plant. **Ultimate Parent:** Tyson Foods, Inc. **SIC:** 2048—Prepared Feeds Nec.

★ **75578** ★ **Holly Farms Foods Inc. Tyson Foods Processing Plant**
PO Box 965
Monroe, NC 28111
Ultimate Parent: Tyson Foods, Inc. **SIC:** 2015—Poultry Slaughtering & Processing.

★ **75579** ★ **Holly Farms/Tyson Foods Inc. Tyson Foods Processing Plant**
233 S. Secrest Ave.
Monroe, NC 28111
Ultimate Parent: Tyson Foods, Inc. **SIC:** 2015—Poultry Slaughtering & Processing.

★ **75580** ★ **Imo Delaval Inc.**
Airport Rd. Extension
Monroe, NC 28110-0527
Ultimate Parent: Imo Industries. **SIC:** 3561—Pumps & Pumping Equipment.

★ **75581** ★ **IMO Pumps**
Airport Rd.
PO Box 5020
Monroe, NC 28111-5020
(704)289-6511 **Fax:** (704)289-9373
Company Type: Subsidiary. **Officer:** Berry Major Jr., Vice President & General Manager. **Ultimate Parent:** Imo Industries.

★ **75582** ★ **Kentucky Fried Chicken**
2021 W. Roosevelt Blvd.
Monroe, NC 28110
(704)283-5975
Ultimate Parent: Pepsico.

★ **75583** ★ **Kroger Stores**
2118 W. Roosevelt Blvd.
Monroe, NC 28110
(704)289-8502
Ultimate Parent: Kroger. **SIC:** 5499—Miscellaneous Food Stores.

★ **75584** ★ **Metropolitan Financial Corp.**
106 S. Main St.
Monroe, NC 28112
(704)283-8566
Ultimate Parent: Metropolitan Financial. **SIC:** 6141—Personal Credit Institutions.

★ **75585** ★ **Pizza Hut**
Monroe Massachusetts
Monroe, NC 28110
(704)289-1024
Ultimate Parent: Pepsico. **SIC:** 5812—Eating Places.

★ **75586** ★ **Pizza Hut**
1011 W. Roosevelt Blvd.
Monroe, NC 28110
(704)289-2588
Ultimate Parent: Pepsico. **SIC:** 5812—Eating Places.

★ **75587** ★ **Radio Shack**
Plaza Shopping Ctr.
Monroe, NC 28110
(704)283-6690
Company Type: Division. **Ultimate Parent:** Tandy Corp. **SIC:** 5065—Electronic Parts & Equipment Nec.

★ **75588** ★ **Schrader Automotive Inc.**
1609 Airport Rd.
Monroe, NC 28110-7393
(704)289-4535
Company Type: Subsidiary. **Location Type:** Branch office. **Officer:** J. Kevin Nameth, President. **Ultimate Parent:** Arvin Industries Inc. **SIC:** 3714—Motor Vehicle Parts & Accessories; 5084—Industrial Machinery & Equipment; 3429—Hardware Nec; 3823—Process Control Instruments; 3492—Fluid Power Valves & Hose Fittings. **Employee Count:** 1800. **Sales:** 100 M.

★ **75589** ★ **Schrader Automotive Inc.**
1609 Airport Rd.
Monroe, NC 28110-7393
(704)289-4535
Company Type: Subsidiary. **Officer:** J. Kevin Nameth, President. **Ultimate Parent:** Arvin Industries Inc. **SIC:** 3714—Motor Vehicle Parts & Accessories. **Employee Count:** 1800. **Sales:** 100 M.

★ **75590** ★ **Schrader Automotive Inc.**
PO Box 5036
1609 Airport Rd.
Monroe, NC 28111-5036
(704)289-4535 **Fax:** (704)289-3543
Company Type: Subsidiary. **Officer:** J. Kevin Nameth, President. **Ultimate Parent:** Arvin Industries Inc.

★ **75591** ★ **Scott Aviation**
309 W. Crowell St.
Monroe, NC 28112
(704)283-2125
Officer: Vince Lorber, Manager. **Ultimate Parent:** Figgie International. **SIC:** 3069—Fabricated Rubber Products Nec; 3444—Sheet Metal Work; 3544—Special Dies, Tools, Jigs & Fixtures.

★ **75592** ★ **Teledyne Allvac/ Vasco**
2020 Ashcraft Ave.
Monroe, NC 28110
Ultimate Parent: Teledyne. **SIC:** 3356—Nonferrous Rolling & Drawing Nec.

★ **75593** ★ **Trailways Bus Systems**
1601 W. Roosevelt Blvd.
Monroe, NC 28110
(704)283-5311
Ultimate Parent: Greyhound Lines Inc. **SIC:** 4131—Intercity & Rural Bus Transportation.

★ **75594** ★ **Tyson Foods Inc.**
233 S. Secrest Ave.
Monroe, NC 28112
(704)283-7571
Officer: Joe Moran, Manager. **Ultimate Parent:** Tyson Foods, Inc. **SIC:** 2015—Poultry Slaughtering & Processing.

★ **75595** ★ **Waldenbooks**
Monroe Mall
Monroe, NC 28110
(704)289-1003
Ultimate Parent: K-Mart. **SIC:** 5942—Book Stores.

Mooresville

★ **75596** ★ **Aeroquip Corp.**
Hwy. 115 S
Mooresville, NC 28115
(704)663-4511
Officer: Carl D. Malz, Manager. **Ultimate Parent:** Trinova Corp. **SIC:** 3089—Plastics Products Nec; 3714—Motor Vehicle Parts & Accessories.

★ **75597** ★ **Aeroquip Corp.**
Hwy. 115 S.
Mooresville, NC 28115
Ultimate Parent: Trinova Corp. **SIC:** 3089—Plastics Products Nec.

★ **75598** ★ **Aeroquip Corp.**
Sterling Div.
Hwy. 115 South
Mooresville, NC 28115
Company Type: Division. **Ultimate Parent:** Trinova Corp. **SIC:** 3089—Plastics Products Nec.

★ **75599** ★ **Burlington Industries Inc.**
476 S. Main St.
Mooresville, NC 28115
(704)664-2611
Officer: Pryor Millner, President. **Ultimate Parent:** Burlington Industries, Equity. **SIC:** 2211—Broadwoven Fabric Mills—Cotton; 2221—Broadwoven Fabric Mills—Manmade; 2262—Finishing Plants—Manmade.

★ **75600** ★ **Carisbrook**
Templon Div.
150 Bypass PO Box 480
Mooresville, NC 28115
Company Type: Division. **Ultimate Parent:** Hanson Industries. **SIC:** 2269—Finishing Plants Nec.

★ 75601 ★ Citizens Savings Bank, SSB (Formerly Citizens S&L)
320 Plz. Dr.
Mooresville, NC 28115
(704)663-6063
Company Type: Subsidiary. Location Type: Branch office. Officer: David S. Brown Jr., Mgr. Ultimate Parent: Southern National Corp. SIC: 6021—National Commercial Banks.

★ 75602 ★ Citizens Savings Bank, SSB (Formerly Citizens S&L)
149 E. Iredell Ave.
PO Box 388
Mooresville, NC 28115-0388
(704)664-3434 Fax: (704)664-4591
Company Type: Subsidiary. Location Type: Branch office. Ultimate Parent: Southern National Corp. SIC: 6021—National Commercial Banks.

★ 75603 ★ Food Lion
Plaza Dr.
Mooresville, NC 28115
(704)663-4542
Ultimate Parent: Food Lion. SIC: 5411—Grocery Stores.

★ 75604 ★ Food Lion Inc.
Plaza Dr.
Mooresville, NC 28115
(704)663-4542
Ultimate Parent: Food Lion. SIC: 5411—Grocery Stores.

★ 75605 ★ Greyhound Bus Stop
625 Plaza Dr.
Mooresville, NC 28115
(704)663-7993
Ultimate Parent: Greyhound Lines Inc. SIC: 4111—Local & Suburban Transit.

★ 75606 ★ Parker Hannifin Corp.
US Hwy. 21 N.
Mooresville, NC 28115
Ultimate Parent: Parker Hannifin. SIC: 3451—Screw Machine Products; 3471—Plating & Polishing; 3492—Fluid Power Valves & Hose Fittings.

★ 75607 ★ Pizza Hut
663 Plaza Dr.
Mooresville, NC 28115
(704)663-0653
Ultimate Parent: Pepsico. SIC: 5812—Eating Places.

★ 75608 ★ Radio Shack
Mooresville Plaza Ctr.
Mooresville, NC 28115
(704)643-6087
Company Type: Division. Ultimate Parent: Tandy Corp. SIC: 5731—Radio, Television & Electronics Stores.

★ 75609 ★ Sterling Engineered Products
Hwy. 115 S
Mooresville, NC 28115
Ultimate Parent: Trinova Corp. SIC: 3000—Rubber & Miscellaneous Plastics Products.

Morehead City

★ 75610 ★ Ace Hardware & Marine
600 Arendell St.
Morehead City, NC 28557
(919)726-6620
Ultimate Parent: Ace Hardware. SIC: 5499—Miscellaneous Food Stores.

★ 75611 ★ Branch Banking & Trust Co.
2201 Arendell St.
Morehead City, NC 28557
(919)726-0166
Company Type: Subsidiary. Location Type: Branch office. Ultimate Parent: Southern National Corp. SIC: 6021—National Commercial Banks.

★ 75612 ★ Branch Banking & Trust Co.
Pelletier Harliar Shops
Hwy. 70
Morehead City, NC 28557-9650
(919)247-2106
Company Type: Subsidiary. Location Type: Branch office. Officer: J. Frank Bullard, Mgr. Ultimate Parent: Southern

National Corp. SIC: 6021—National Commercial Banks.

★ 75613 ★ Branch Banking & Trust Co.
Morehead Plz. Shopping Ctr.
Morehead City, NC 28557
(919)726-8061
Company Type: Subsidiary. Location Type: Branch office. Ultimate Parent: Southern National Corp. SIC: 6021—National Commercial Banks.

★ 75614 ★ Carolina Power & Light Co.
3504 Bridges St.
Morehead City, NC 28557
(919)726-7031
Ultimate Parent: Carolina Power & Light Co. SIC: 4911—Electric Services.

★ 75615 ★ Carolina Power & Light Co.
3504 Bridges St.
Morehead City, NC 28557
(919)726-7031
Ultimate Parent: Carolina Power & Light Co. SIC: 4911—Electric Services.

★ 75616 ★ First-Citizens Bank & Trust Co.
Hwy. 58 & Salter Path Rd.
Morehead City, NC 28575
(919)247-3731
Location Type: Branch office. Ultimate Parent: First Citizens Bancshares, Inc. SIC: 6021—National Commercial Banks.

★ 75617 ★ First-Citizens Bank & Trust Co.
3000 Arendell St.
Morehead City, NC 28557-3319
(919)726-6122
Location Type: Branch office. Ultimate Parent: First Citizens Bancshares, Inc. SIC: 6021—National Commercial Banks.

★ 75618 ★ First-Citizens Bank & Trust Co.
101 Morehead Ave.
Morehead City, NC 28515
(919)726-6122
Location Type: Branch office. Ultimate Parent: First Citizens Bancshares, Inc. SIC: 6021—National Commercial Banks.

★ 75619 ★ First-Citizens Bank & Trust Co.
821 Arendell St.
Morehead City, NC 28557-4215
(919)726-6122
Location Type: Branch office. Officer: Bruce Caldwell, Area Vice President. Ultimate Parent: First Citizens Bancshares, Inc. SIC: 6021—National Commercial Banks.

★ 75620 ★ First-Citizens Bank & Trust Co.
4913 Arendell St.
Morehead City, NC 28557-2602
(919)726-6122
Location Type: Branch office. Ultimate Parent: First Citizens Bancshares, Inc. SIC: 6021—National Commercial Banks.

★ 75621 ★ Food Lion
Salter Path
Morehead City, NC 28557
(919)247-6823
Ultimate Parent: Food Lion. SIC: 5411—Grocery Stores.

★ 75622 ★ Kentucky Fried Chicken
3406 Arendell St.
Morehead City, NC 28557
(919)726-6033
Ultimate Parent: Pepsico. SIC: 5812—Eating Places.

★ 75623 ★ Lawn Boy
106 N. 9th St.
Morehead City, NC 28557
(919)726-3466
Ultimate Parent: Toro Co. SIC: 0783—Ornamental Shrub & Tree Services.

★ 75624 ★ Lowe's
1409 PO Box
Morehead City, NC 28557
(919)247-2223
Ultimate Parent: Lowe's. SIC: 5251—Hardware Stores.

★ 75625 ★ Mary Kay Cosmetics
112 Bonner Ave.
Morehead City, NC 28557
(919)247-5055
Ultimate Parent: Mary Kay Cosmetics. SIC: 5999—Miscellaneous Retail Stores Nec.

★ 75626 ★ Pizza Hut
Hwy. 70
Morehead City, NC 28557
(919)726-7117
Ultimate Parent: Pepsico. SIC: 5812—Eating Places.

★ 75627 ★ Radio Shack
805 Arendell St.
Morehead City, NC 28557
(919)726-7450
Company Type: Division. Ultimate Parent: Tandy Corp. SIC: 5719—Miscellaneous Home Furnishings Stores.

★ 75628 ★ Wachovia Bank & Trust Co. N
5001 Arendell St.
Morehead City, NC 28557
(919)726-8086
Ultimate Parent: Wachovia Corp. SIC: 6099—Functions Related to Deposit Banking.

Morganton

★ 75629 ★ Astro Industries Inc.
Astro Industries Division
114 Industrial Blvd.
Morganton, NC 28655
Ultimate Parent: Borden, Inc. SIC: 2821—Plastics Materials & Resins.

★ 75630 ★ BASF Corp.
Hwy. 70 West
Morganton, NC 28655
Ultimate Parent: BASF Corp. SIC: 2851—Paints & Allied Products.

★ 75631 ★ BASF Corp.
Coatings & Inks
Hwy. 70 W
Morganton, NC 28655-1297
Ultimate Parent: BASF Corp. SIC: 2893—Printing Ink; 2851—Paints & Allied Products.

★ 75632 ★ BASF Corp.
Industrial Coatings Morganton
1110 Carbon City Rd.
Morganton, NC 28655
Ultimate Parent: BASF Corp. SIC: 2851—Paints & Allied Products.

★ 75633 ★ Borden Inc.
Astro Industries Division
114 Industrial Blvd.
Morganton, NC 28655
Ultimate Parent: Borden, Inc. SIC: 2821—Plastics Materials & Resins.

★ 75634 ★ Dana Corp.
105 Wamsutta Mill Rd.
Morganton, NC 28655
(704)433-4600
Ultimate Parent: Dana Corp. SIC: 3714—Motor Vehicle Parts & Accessories.

★ 75635 ★ Drexel Heritage Furnishings
Plant 6
101 Dixon St.
Morganton, NC 28655
Location Type: Plant. Ultimate Parent: Masco. SIC: 2511—Wood Household Furniture.

★ 75636 ★ Drexel Heritage Furnishings
Plant 33
New St.
Morganton, NC 28655
Location Type: Plant. Ultimate Parent: Masco. SIC: 2511—Wood Household Furniture.

★ 75637 ★ Drexel Heritage Furnishings
Plant 3/5
Hogan St.
Morganton, NC 28655
Location Type: Plant. Ultimate Parent: Masco. SIC: 2511—Wood Household Furniture.

★ 75638 ★ Drexel Heritage Furnishings Inc.
Plant 6
300 Church St.
Morganton, NC 28655
Location Type: Plant. Ultimate Parent: Masco. SIC: 2511—Wood Household Furniture.

★ 75639 ★ Drexel Heritage Furnishings Inc.
Plant 33
New St.
Morganton, NC 28655
Location Type: Plant. Ultimate Parent: Masco. SIC: 2511—Wood Household Furniture.

★ 75640 ★ Drexel Heritage Furnishings Inc.
Plant 3/5
Hogan St.
Morganton, NC 28655
Location Type: Plant. Ultimate Parent: Masco. SIC: 2511—Wood Household Furniture.

★ 75641 ★ Drexel Heritage Furniture
Plant 6
101 Dixon St.
Morganton, NC 28655
Location Type: Plant. Ultimate Parent: Masco. SIC: 2511—Wood Household Furniture.

★ 75642 ★ Drexel Heritage Furniture
Plant 60
410 Hogan St.
Morganton, NC 28655
Location Type: Plant. Ultimate Parent: Masco. SIC: 2511—Wood Household Furniture.

★ 75643 ★ Drexel Heritage Furniture
Plant 33
210 New St.
Morganton, NC 28655
Location Type: Plant. Ultimate Parent: Masco. SIC: 2511—Wood Household Furniture.

★ 75644 ★ Drexel Heritage Furniture
Plant 315
309 Hogan St.
Morganton, NC 28655
Location Type: Plant. Ultimate Parent: Masco. SIC: 2511—Wood Household Furniture.

★ 75645 ★ E. R. Carpenter Co. Inc.
705 Jamestown Rd. PO Box 669
Morganton, NC 28655
Ultimate Parent: Carpenter. SIC: 3086—Plastics Foam Products.

★ 75646 ★ First-Citizens Bank & Trust Co.
217 N. Sterling St.
Morganton, NC 28655
(704)437-5077
Location Type: Branch office. Ultimate Parent: First Citizens Bancshares, Inc. SIC: 6021—National Commercial Banks.

★ 75647 ★ First-Citizens Bank & Trust Co.
201 E. Meeting St.
Morganton, NC 28655-3550
(704)433-6310
Location Type: Branch office. Officer: Fred J. Whlen, Area Vice President. Ultimate Parent: First Citizens Bancshares, Inc. SIC: 6021—National Commercial Banks.

★ 75648 ★ Henredon Furn. Ind. Inc.
Henredon Rd.
Morganton, NC 28655
Ultimate Parent: Masco. SIC: 2511—Wood Household Furniture.

★ 75649 ★ Henredon Furniture Ind. Inc.
400 Henredon Rd.
Morganton, NC 28680
Ultimate Parent: Masco. SIC: 2511—Wood Household Furniture.

★ 75650 ★ Henredon Furniture Industries, Inc.
Henredon Rd.
Morganton, NC 28655
(704)437-5261 Fax: (704)437-5264
Officer: Michael K. Dugan. Ultimate Parent: Masco.

★ 75651 ★ Kentucky Fried Chicken
Hwy. 18 S
Morganton, NC 28655
(704)437-9600
Ultimate Parent: Pepsico. SIC: 5812—Eating Places.

★ 75652 ★ Pizza Hut
530 W. Fleming Dr.
Morganton, NC 28655
(704)433-5390
Ultimate Parent: Pepsico. SIC: 5812—Eating Places.

★ 75653 ★ Radio Shack
124 N. Sterling St.
Morganton, NC 28655
(704)437-5744
Company Type: Division. Ultimate Parent: Tandy Corp. SIC: 5065—Electronic Parts & Equipment Nec.

★ 75654 ★ Rite Aid Discount Pahrmacie
238 W. Fleming Dr.
Morganton, NC 28655
(704)433-1372
Ultimate Parent: Rite Aid. SIC: 5912—Drug Stores & Proprietary Stores.

★ 75655 ★ Sara Lee Knit Products
Corner I-40 Jamestown Rd. Exit 100
Morganton, NC 28655
Location Type: Plant. Ultimate Parent: Sara Lee Corp. SIC: 2253—Knit Outerwear Mills.

★ 75656 ★ Trailways Bus System
Hwy. 18 S
Morganton, NC 28655
(704)437-1294
Ultimate Parent: Greyhound Lines Inc. SIC: 4111—Local & Suburban Transit.

★ 75657 ★ Wachovia Bank & Trust Co.
Flemming Dr.
Morganton, NC 28655
(704)437-3654
Ultimate Parent: Wachovia Corp. SIC: 6022—State Commercial Banks.

★ 75658 ★ Wachovia Bank & Trust Co. N
West Ofc
Morganton, NC 28655
(704)437-3697
Ultimate Parent: Wachovia Corp. SIC: 6022—State Commercial Banks.

★ 75659 ★ Wachovia Bank & Trust Co. N
101 Union
Morganton, NC 28655
(704)437-3651
Ultimate Parent: Wachovia Corp. SIC: 6141—Personal Credit Institutions.

Morgantown

★ 75660 ★ BASF Corp.
1110 Carbon City Rd.
Morganton, NC 28655
(704)584-1771
Officer: Patrick J. Dour, Plant Manager. Ultimate Parent: BASF Corp. SIC: 2851—Paints & Allied Products.

★ 75661 ★ Kentucky Fried Chicken
Hwy. 421 N
Morganton, NC 28697
(919)667-1313
Ultimate Parent: Pepsico. SIC: 5812—Eating Places.

Morrisville

★ 75662 ★ Bristol-Myers Products
9707 Chapel Hill Rd.
Morrisville, NC 27560
(919)319-7800
Officer: Allen Norris, Manager. Ultimate Parent: Bristol-Myers Squibb. SIC: 2833—Medicinals & Botanicals.

★ 75663 ★ Bristol-Myers Products
9707 Chapel Hill Rd.
Morrisville, NC 27560
(919)319-7800
Officer: Allen Norris, Manager. Ultimate Parent: Bristol-Myers Squibb. SIC: 2833—Medicinals & Botanicals; 2834—Pharmaceutical Preparations.

★ 75664 ★ Bristol Myers Products Co.
Morrisville, NC 27560
(919)467-3500
Ultimate Parent: Bristol-Myers Squibb. SIC: 5122—Drugs, Proprietaries & Sundries.

★ 75665 ★ Bristol-Myers-Squibb Co.
9707 Chapel Hill Rd.
Morrisville, NC 27560-9394
(919)467-3500
Officer: Al Onnrs. Ultimate Parent: Bristol-Myers Squibb. SIC: 2834—Pharmaceutical Preparations.

★ 75666 ★ Escod Industries
4709 Greekstone Dr.
Suite 307
Morrisville, NC 27560
(919)941-5550 Fax: (919)941-6057
Company Type: Subsidiary. Officer: James Oberlender, President. Ultimate Parent: Insilco Corp.

★ 75667 ★ Hit or Miss
Aviation Park
Morrisville, NC 27560
(919)469-3023
Ultimate Parent: TJX. SIC: 5651—Family Clothing Stores.

★ 75668 ★ Linens 'n Things
Aviation Pky.
Morrisville, NC 27560
(919)467-2907
Ultimate Parent: Melville. SIC: 5399—Miscellaneous General Merchandise Store.

★ 75669 ★ Uni-Copy Corp.
2200 Gateway Centre Blvd., Ste. 217
Morrisville, NC 27560
(919)469-1102
Officer: Chris Corpe, Manager. Ultimate Parent: Alco Standard Corp. SIC: 3663—Radio & T.V. Communications Equipment.

Morven

★ 75670 ★ Branch Banking & Trust Co.
112 E. Main St.
Morven, NC 28119
(704)694-6521
Company Type: Subsidiary. Location Type: Branch office. Officer: Julia Williams, Manager. Ultimate Parent: Southern National Corp. SIC: 6021—National Commercial Banks.

Mount Airy

★ 75671 ★ Adams-Millis Hoisery
645 W. Pine St.
Mount Airy, NC 27030
Location Type: Plant. Ultimate Parent: Sara Lee Corp. SIC: 2252—Hosiery Nec.

★ 75672 ★ Adams Millis Hosiery Corp.
645 West Pine St.
Mount Airy, NC 27030
Location Type: Plant. Ultimate Parent: Sara Lee Corp. SIC: 2252—Hosiery Nec.

★ 75673 ★ Branch Banking & Trust Co.
601 & 2151 Rockford St.
Mount Airy, NC 27030-5205
(910)786-1741
Company Type: Subsidiary. Location Type: Branch office. Ultimate Parent: Southern National Corp. SIC: 6021—National Commercial Banks.

★ 75674 ★ Branch Banking & Trust Co.
541 N. Main St.
Mount Airy, NC 27030-3721
(910)789-9526
Company Type: Subsidiary. Location Type: Branch office. Officer: P.J. Snow, Manager. Ultimate Parent: Southern National Corp. SIC: 6021—National Commercial Banks.

★ 75675 ★ Cross Creek Apparel Inc. Dyeing Finishing
510 Riverside Dr.
Mount Airy, NC 27030
Ultimate Parent: Russell. SIC: 2253—Knit Outerwear Mills.

★ 75676 ★ First-Citizens Bank & Trust Co.
502 N. Main St.
Mount Airy, NC 27030-3722
(910)789-9561
Location Type: Branch office. Officer: J. Cooper Adams, Vice President. Ultimate Parent: First Citizens Bancshares, Inc. SIC: 6021—National Commercial Banks.

★ 75677 ★ Food Lion
1130 W. Pine St.
Mount Airy, NC 27030
(919)786-4541
Ultimate Parent: Food Lion. SIC: 5411—Grocery Stores.

★ 75678 ★ Food Lion, Inc.
Hwy. 52
Mount Airy, NC 27030
(919)789-9018
Ultimate Parent: Food Lion. SIC: 5411—Grocery Stores.

★ 75679 ★ Greyhound Bus Lines
1301 Worth
Mount Airy, NC 27030
(919)786-4711
Ultimate Parent: Greyhound Lines Inc. SIC: 4111—Local & Suburban Transit.

★ 75680 ★ Kentucky Fried Chicken
52 Bypass N
Mount Airy, NC 27030
(919)789-4090
Ultimate Parent: Pepsico. SIC: 5812—Eating Places.

★ 75681 ★ Kmart Auto Accessories & Sporting Goods
100 Mayberry Mall
Mount Airy, NC 27030
(919)786-7598
Ultimate Parent: K-Mart. SIC: 5941—Sporting Goods & Bicycle Shops.

★ 75682 ★ Quality Mills Inc. Cloth Plant
Riverside Dr.
Mount Airy, NC 27030
Ultimate Parent: Russell. SIC: 2299—Textile Goods Nec; 2399—Fabricated Textile Products Nec.

★ 75683 ★ Radio Shack
Mayberry Mall
Mount Airy, NC 27030
(919)789-1700
Company Type: Division. Ultimate Parent: Tandy Corp. SIC: 5065—Electronic Parts & Equipment Nec.

★ 75684 ★ Ryder Truck Rental
1334 W. Pnes St.
Mount Airy, NC 27030
(919)786-9878
Ultimate Parent: Ryder System. SIC: 7513—Truck Rental & Leasing Without Drivers.

★ 75685 ★ United Technologies Automative Inc.
511 Hay St.
Mount Airy, NC 27030
Ultimate Parent: United Technologies. SIC: 3000—Rubber & Miscellaneous Plastics Products.

★ 75686 ★ United Technologies Automotive Inc.
511 Hay St.
Mount Airy, NC 27030
Ultimate Parent: United Technologies. SIC: 3089—Plastics Products Nec.

Mount Gilead

★ 75687 ★ Branch Banking & Trust Co.
200 N. Main St.
Mount Gilead, NC 27306
(910)439-6133
Company Type: Subsidiary. Location Type: Branch office. Officer: Benton T. Haithcock, Manager. Ultimate Parent: Southern National Corp. SIC: 6021—National Commercial Banks.

Mount Holly

★ 75688 ★ Branch Banking & Trust Co.
150 S. Main St.
Mount Holly, NC 28120
(704)827-6726
Ultimate Parent: Southern National Corp. SIC: 6022—State Commercial Banks.

★ 75689 ★ Burlington Industries Inc.
905 W. Charlotte Ave.
Mount Holly, NC 28120-1207
(704)827-2441
Officer: Jim Williams. Ultimate Parent: Burlington Industries, Equity. SIC: 2281—Yarn Spinning Mills.

★ 75690 ★ Burlington Industries Inc.
NC Hwy. 27
Mount Holly, NC 28120
(704)827-2441
Ultimate Parent: Burlington Industries, Equity. SIC: 2399—Fabricated Textile Products Nec.

★ 75691 ★ Food Lion
799 E. Charlotte Ave.
Mount Holly, NC 28120
(704)827-0588
Ultimate Parent: Food Lion. SIC: 5411—Grocery Stores.

★ 75692 ★ Hoechst Celanese Corp. Sou-Tex Works
E. Catawba Ave.
PO Box 866
Mount Holly, NC 28120
Ultimate Parent: Hoechst Celanese Corp. SIC: 2869—Industrial Organic Chemicals Nec.

★ 75693 ★ Mary Kay Cosmetics
Sales
505 Dutchman Ave.
Mount Holly, NC 28120
(704)827-6833
Ultimate Parent: Mary Kay Cosmetics. SIC: 5999—Miscellaneous Retail Stores Nec.

Mount Olive

★ 75694 ★ Burlington Industries
401 NC Hwy. 55 W
Mount Olive, NC 28365-8529
(919)658-4915
Location Type: Branch office. Officer: Wallace Horton. Ultimate Parent: Burlington Industries, Equity. SIC: 2391—Curtains & Draperies; 2221—Broadwoven Fabric Mills-Manmade; 2399—Fabricated Textile Products Nec.

★ 75695 ★ Greyhound Bus Lines
200 S. Breazeale Ave.
Mount Olive, NC 28365
(919)658-2953
Ultimate Parent: Greyhound Lines Inc. SIC: 4131—Intercity & Rural Bus Transportation.

★ 75696 ★ Number One Building Supply Inc.
Hwy. 55 W
Mount Olive, NC 28365
(919)658-6586
Officer: David Perry, President. Ultimate Parent: Ace Hardware. SIC: 5211—Lumber & Other Building Materials. Employee Count: 14.

★ 75697 ★　Wachovia Bank &
Trust Co. N
210 N. Ctr. St.
Mount Olive, NC 28365
(919)658-6516
Ultimate Parent: Wachovia Corp. SIC:
6022—State Commercial Banks.

Mt. Airy

★ 75698 ★　Pizza Hut
52 Bypass
Mt. Airy, NC 27030
(919)789-6277
Ultimate Parent: Pepsico. SIC: 5812—
Eating Places.

Mt. Holly

★ 75699 ★　Burlington Industries
Inc.
Hwy. 27
Mt. Holly, NC 28120
(704)827-2441
Officer: Jim Williams, Manager. Ultimate
Parent: Burlington Industries, Equity. SIC:
2281—Yarn Spinning Mills; 2282—Throwing
& Winding Mills; 2399—Fabricated Textile
Products Nec.

Mt. Olive

★ 75700 ★　Burlington Industries
Inc.
401 NC Hwy. 55
Mt. Olive, NC 28365
(919)658-4915
Officer: Wallace Horton, Manager. Ultimate
Parent: Burlington Industries, Equity. SIC:
2391—Curtains & Draperies; 2399—
Fabricated Textile Products Nec.

Murphy

★ 75701 ★　Emerson Electric Co.
Special Products Div.
2001 Hwy. 64 E.
Murphy, NC 28906
Company Type: Division. Ultimate Parent:
Emerson Electric Co. Inc. SIC: 3553—
Woodworking Machinery.

★ 75702 ★　Emerson Electric Co.
SPD
2001 Hwy. 64 East
Murphy, NC 28906
Ultimate Parent: Emerson Electric Co. Inc.
SIC: 3553—Woodworking Machinery.

★ 75703 ★　First-Citizens Bank &
Trust Co.
100 Hiawassee St.
Murphy, NC 28906
(704)837-7939
Location Type: Branch office. Officer:
Robert C. Roberts, Area Vice President.
Ultimate Parent: First Citizens Bancshares,
Inc. SIC: 6021—National Commercial
Banks.

★ 75704 ★　First-Citizens Bank &
Trust Co.
Rte. 1 & US Hwy. 64
Murphy, NC 28906
(704)837-7939
Location Type: Branch office. Ultimate
Parent: First Citizens Bancshares, Inc. SIC:
6021—National Commercial Banks.

★ 75705 ★　Litton Clifton
Precision South
Slow Creek Rd. Hwy. 141
PO Box 160
Murphy, NC 28906-0160
(704)837-5115
Location Type: Plant. Ultimate Parent:
Litton Industries. SIC: 6321—Accident &
Health Insurance.

★ 75706 ★　Piggly Wiggly
Valley Village Shopping Ctr.
Murphy, NC 28906
(704)837-7808
Ultimate Parent: Bruno's. SIC: 5411—
Grocery Stores.

★ 75707 ★　Pizza Hut
Andrews Rd.
Murphy, NC 28906
(704)837-7314
Ultimate Parent: Pepsico. SIC: 5812—
Eating Places.

★ 75708 ★　Radio Shack
35 W. Hwy. 64
Murphy, NC 28906
(704)837-6776
Company Type: Division. Ultimate Parent:
Tandy Corp. SIC: 5731—Radio, Television
& Electronics Stores.

★ 75709 ★　Rite Aid Discount
Pharmacie
Vly Village Shopping Ctr.
Murphy, NC 28906
(704)837-9928
Ultimate Parent: Rite Aid. SIC: 5912—Drug
Stores & Proprietary Stores.

★ 75710 ★　Trailways
119 Tennessee St.
Murphy, NC 28906
(704)837-2925
Ultimate Parent: Greyhound Lines Inc. SIC:
4131—Intercity & Rural Bus Transportation.

★ 75711 ★　Wachovia Bank &
Trust Co. N
499 PO Box
Murphy, NC 28906
(704)837-5178
Ultimate Parent: Wachovia Corp. SIC:
6022—State Commercial Banks.

N Wilkesboro

★ 75712 ★　Pizza Hut
Hwy. 18 N
N Wilkesboro, NC 28659
(919)667-5775
Ultimate Parent: Pepsico. SIC: 5812—
Eating Places.

★ 75713 ★　Radio Shack
W Park Shopping Ctr.
N Wilkesboro, NC 28659
(919)667-2584
Company Type: Division. Ultimate Parent:
Tandy Corp. SIC: 5065—Electronic Parts &
Equipment Nec.

Nags Head

★ 75714 ★　Ace Hardware
Nags Head, NC 27959
(919)441-5644
Ultimate Parent: Ace Hardware. SIC:
5083—Farm & Garden Machinery.

★ 75715 ★　Radio Shack
31 Outerbanks Mall
Nags Head, NC 27959
(919)441-2581
Company Type: Division. Ultimate Parent:
Tandy Corp. SIC: 5734—Computer &
Software Stores.

Nashville

★ 75716 ★　First-Citizens Bank &
Trust Co.
804 E. Washington St.
Nashville, NC 27856
(919)459-9121
Location Type: Branch office. Officer:
Michael T. Bryant, Vice President. Ultimate
Parent: First Citizens Bancshares, Inc. SIC:
6021—National Commercial Banks.

New Bern

★ 75717 ★　Branch Banking &
Trust Co.
1301 Glenburnie Rd.
New Bern, NC 28562-2605
(919)633-4111
Company Type: Subsidiary. Location
Type: Branch office. Ultimate Parent:
Southern National Corp. SIC: 6021—
National Commercial Banks.

★ 75718 ★　Branch Banking &
Trust Co.
375 Tyron Palace Dr.
New Bern, NC 28560-2133
(919)633-4111
Company Type: Subsidiary. Location
Type: Branch office. Ultimate Parent:
Southern National Corp. SIC: 6021—
National Commercial Banks.

★ 75719 ★　Branch Banking &
Trust Co.
201 Neuse Blvd.
New Bern, NC 28560
(919)633-4111
Company Type: Subsidiary. Location
Type: Branch office. Officer: Ricky K.
Brown, Mgr. Ultimate Parent: Southern
National Corp. SIC: 6021—National
Commercial Banks.

★ 75720 ★　Branch Banking &
Trust Co.
3503 Clarendon Blvd.
New Bern, NC 28562
(919)637-4111
Ultimate Parent: Southern National Corp.
SIC: 6022—State Commercial Banks.

★ 75721 ★　Carolina Power &
Light Co.
3402 Trent Rd.
New Bern, NC 28562
(919)633-1124
Ultimate Parent: Carolina Power & Light
Co. SIC: 4911—Electric Services.

★ 75722 ★　Federal Paperboard
Co. Inc.
3303 Clarenden Blvd.
New Bern, NC 28560
(919)638-4363
Ultimate Parent: Federal Paper Board.
SIC: 2611—Pulp Mills.

★ 75723 ★　First-Citizens Bank &
Trust Co.
3030 Clarendon Blvd.
New Bern, NC 28562-5212
(919)633-5171
Location Type: Branch office. Ultimate
Parent: First Citizens Bancshares, Inc. SIC:
6021—National Commercial Banks.

★ 75724 ★　First-Citizens Bank &
Trust Co.
305 broad St.
New Bern, NC 28560-4948
(919)633-5171
Location Type: Branch office. Officer: Alex
S. Badger, Area Vice President. Ultimate
Parent: First Citizens Bancshares, Inc. SIC:
6021—National Commercial Banks.

★ 75725 ★　First-Citizens Bank &
Trust Co.
202 Old Hwy. 70
New Bern, NC 28523
(919)633-1115
Location Type: Branch office. Ultimate
Parent: First Citizens Bancshares, Inc. SIC:
6021—National Commercial Banks.

★ 75726 ★　First-Citizens Bank &
Trust Co.
US Hwy. 70 E.
New Bern, NC 28560
(919)633-5171
Location Type: Branch office. Ultimate
Parent: First Citizens Bancshares, Inc. SIC:
6021—National Commercial Banks.

★ 75727 ★　First-Citizens Bank &
Trust Co.
B St. & US Hwy. 17
New Bern, NC 28519
(919)633-5171
Location Type: Branch office. Ultimate
Parent: First Citizens Bancshares, Inc. SIC:
6021—National Commercial Banks.

★ 75728 ★　First-Citizens Bank &
Trust Co.
606 Fort Totten Dr.
New Bern, NC 28560-4655
(919)633-5171
Location Type: Branch office. Ultimate
Parent: First Citizens Bancshares, Inc. SIC:
6021—National Commercial Banks.

★ 75729 ★　Martin Marietta
Aggregates
2326 PO Box
New Bern, NC 28561
(919)633-5036
Ultimate Parent: Martin Marietta. SIC:
5032—Brick, Stone & Related Materials.

★ 75730 ★　Moen Inc.
101 Industrial Dr.
New Bern, NC 28562
(919)638-3300
Officer: Richard Kosco, Manager. Ultimate
Parent: American Brands Inc. SIC: 3432—
Plumbing Fixtures Fittings & Trim.

★ 75731 ★　Pepsi-Cola Bottling
Co.
3706 US Hwy. 17 S
New Bern, NC 28562
(919)637-2193
Officer: Harry Moser, Manager. Ultimate
Parent: Pepsico. SIC: 2086—Bottled &
Canned Soft Drinks.

★ 75732 ★　Radio Shack
Twin Rivers Mall
New Bern, NC 28562
(919)633-3480
Company Type: Division. Ultimate Parent:
Tandy Corp. SIC: 5065—Electronic Parts &
Equipment Nec.

★ 75733 ★　Radio Shack
2305 Neuse Blvd.
New Bern, NC 28560
(919)633-3289
Company Type: Division. Ultimate Parent:
Tandy Corp. SIC: 5065—Electronic Parts &
Equipment Nec.

★ 75734 ★　Radio Shack
Twin Rivers Mall
New Bern, NC 28560
(919)633-3480
Company Type: Division. Ultimate Parent:
Tandy Corp. SIC: 5731—Radio, Television
& Electronics Stores.

★ 75735 ★　Rite Aid Discount
Pharmacie
Twin Rivers Mall
New Bern, NC 28562
(919)633-9943
Ultimate Parent: Rite Aid. SIC: 5912—Drug
Stores & Proprietary Stores.

★ 75736 ★　Rite Aid Discount
Pharmacie
1216 S. Glenburnie Rd.
New Bern, NC 28562
(919)637-4054
Ultimate Parent: Rite Aid. SIC: 5912—Drug
Stores & Proprietary Stores.

★ 75737 ★　Wachovia Bank &
Trust
401 Tryon Palace Dr.
New Bern, NC 28560
(919)638-6121
Ultimate Parent: Wachovia Corp. SIC:
6099—Functions Related to Deposit
Banking; 6141—Personal Credit Institutions.

★ 75738 ★　Wachovia Bank &
Trust Co. N
Twin Rivers Mall
New Bern, NC 28562
(919)638-4111
Ultimate Parent: Wachovia Corp. SIC:
6022—State Commercial Banks.

★ 75739 ★　Weyerhaeuser Paper
Co.
Washington Post Rd.
New Bern, NC 28560-1391
Ultimate Parent: Weyerhaeuser Co. SIC:
2611—Pulp Mills.

Newport

★ 75740 ★　First-Citizens Bank &
Trust Co.
434 Howard Blvd.
Newport, NC 28570-9515
(919)223-5161
Location Type: Branch office. Ultimate
Parent: First Citizens Bancshares, Inc. SIC:
6021—National Commercial Banks.

★ 75741 ★　First-Citizens Bank &
Trust Co.
53 Chatham St.
Newport, NC 28570-8827
(919)223-5161
Location Type: Branch office. Officer: J.
Winston Reese, Vice President. Ultimate
Parent: First Citizens Bancshares, Inc. SIC:
6021—National Commercial Banks.

Newton

★ 75742 ★　Broyhill Furniture Ind.
Inc. Newton Plant
2309 N. College St.
Newton, NC 28658
Ultimate Parent: Interco. SIC: 2511—Wood
Household Furniture.

★ 75743 ★ Citizens Savings
Bank, SSB (Formerly Citizens
Savings Bank, Inc.)
2004 N. Main Ave.
Newton, NC 28658-2812
(704)464-5446
Company Type: Subsidiary. Location
Type: Branch office. Officer: Jan Beaudin,
Mgr. Ultimate Parent: Southern National
Corp. SIC: 6021—National Commercial
Banks.

★ 75744 ★ Citizens Savings
Bank, SSB (Formerly Citizens
Savings Bank, Inc.)
12 N. Main St.
Newton, NC 28658-3203
(704)464-1661
Company Type: Subsidiary. Location
Type: Branch office. Officer: Nick Pence,
Mgr. Ultimate Parent: Southern National
Corp. SIC: 6021—National Commercial
Banks.

★ 75745 ★ Citizens Savings
Bank, SSB (Formerly Citizens
Savings Bank, Inc.)
22 S. Main Ave.
PO Box 608
Newton, NC 28658-0608
(704)464-5750 Fax: (704)464-5795
Company Type: Subsidiary. Location
Type: Branch office. Ultimate Parent:
Southern National Corp. SIC: 6021—
National Commercial Banks.

★ 75746 ★ First-Citizens Bank &
Trust Co.
102 Leonard Ave.
Newton, NC 28658
(704)465-8606
Location Type: Branch office. Ultimate
Parent: First Citizens Bancshares, Inc. SIC:
6021—National Commercial Banks.

★ 75747 ★ First-Citizens Bank &
Trust Co.
11 S. College Ave.
Newton, NC 28658-3340
(704)464-8790
Location Type: Branch office. Officer:
David L. Phillips Jr., Vice President.
Ultimate Parent: First Citizens Bancshares,
Inc. SIC: 6021—National Commercial
Banks.

★ 75748 ★ L&P Foam Inc.
East 15th St.
Newton, NC 28658
Ultimate Parent: Leggett & Platt Inc. SIC:
3069—Fabricated Rubber Products Nec.

★ 75749 ★ Leggett & Platt Inc.
E. 15th St.
Newton, NC 28658
Ultimate Parent: Leggett & Platt Inc. SIC:
3086—Plastics Foam Products.

★ 75750 ★ Meredith/Burda Corp.
St. James Church Rd.
Newton, NC 28658
Ultimate Parent: Meredith. SIC: 2754—
Commercial Printing—Gravure.

★ 75751 ★ Pizza Hut
2025 N. Westside Blvd.
Newton, NC 28658
(704)465-3170
Ultimate Parent: Pepsico. SIC: 5812—
Eating Places.

★ 75752 ★ R. R. Donnelley
Printing Co.
St. James Church Rd.
Newton, NC 28658-0289
Ultimate Parent: R. R. Donnelley & Sons.
SIC: 2754—Commercial Printing—Gravure.

★ 75753 ★ R.R. Donnelley
Printing Co.
PO Box 289
Newton, NC 28658
(704)464-8110
Company Type: Subsidiary. Ultimate
Parent: R. R. Donnelley & Sons. SIC:
2752—Commercial Printing—Lithographic;
2759—Commercial Printing Nec.

★ 75754 ★ Thomas & Howard
Co. of Hickory, Inc.
1200 Burris Rd.
PO Box 428
Newton, NC 28658
(704)464-1010
Officer: Joseph M. Bentler, President.
Ultimate Parent: Nash Finch.

★ 75755 ★ Trailways Bus System
112 E. a St.
Newton, NC 28658
(704)464-2141
Ultimate Parent: Greyhound Lines Inc. SIC:
4131—Intercity & Rural Bus Transportation.

★ 75756 ★ West Point Pepperell
Newton Knitting Mills
2621 N. Ashe Ave.
Newton, NC 28658
Ultimate Parent: West Point Stevens. SIC:
2252—Hosiery Nec.

Newton Grove

★ 75757 ★ First-Citizens Bank &
Trust Co.
Hwy. 701
Newton Grove, NC 28366
(910)594-0994
Location Type: Branch office. Officer:
Dwayne Wiseman, Vice President. Ultimate
Parent: First Citizens Bancshares, Inc. SIC:
6021—National Commercial Banks.

★ 75758 ★ Piggly Wiggly
38 PO Box
Newton Grove, NC 28366
(919)594-1717
Ultimate Parent: Bruno's.

North Wilkesboro

★ 75759 ★ Branch Banking &
Trust Co.
901 Main St.
North Wilkesboro, NC 28659-4215
(910)667-8842
Company Type: Subsidiary. Location
Type: Branch office. Officer: Steve Parker,
Manager. Ultimate Parent: Southern
National Corp. SIC: 6021—National
Commercial Banks.

★ 75760 ★ First-Citizens Bank &
Trust Co.
116 Wilkesboro Ave.
North Wilkesboro, NC 28659
(910)667-2241
Location Type: Branch office. Officer: Joe
K. Johnson, Area Vice President. Ultimate
Parent: First Citizens Bancshares, Inc. SIC:
6021—National Commercial Banks.

★ 75761 ★ First-Citizens Bank &
Trust Co.
6 Sparta Rd.
North Wilkesboro, NC 28659
(910)838-0001
Location Type: Branch office. Ultimate
Parent: First Citizens Bancshares, Inc. SIC:
6021—National Commercial Banks.

★ 75762 ★ LF Corp.
PO Box 1111
North Wilkesboro, NC 28656
Officer: Leonard G. Herring, President.
Ultimate Parent: Lowe's.

★ 75763 ★ Lowe's
Hwy. 286 E
North Wilkesboro, NC 28659
(919)651-4000
Company Type: Headquarters. Officer:
Leonard G. Herring. Employee Count:
28843. Sales: 4538 M. Fortune Service
500: Ranking 29.

★ 75764 ★ Lowe's Co., Inc.
PO Box 1111
North Wilkesboro, NC 28656
(919)651-4000 Fax: (919)651-4766 Telex:
5109225737
Officer: Leonard G. Herring, President &
CEO. Ultimate Parent: Lowe's. Employee
Count: 25000.

★ 75765 ★ Lowe's Home
Centers, Inc.
PO Box 1111
North Wilkesboro, NC 28659
Officer: Leonard G. Herring, President.
Ultimate Parent: Lowe's.

★ 75766 ★ Sterling Advertising,
Ltd.
PO Box 1111
North Wilkesboro, NC 28656
Officer: Leonard G. Herring, President.
Ultimate Parent: Lowe's.

★ 75767 ★ Vulcan Materials Co.
Hwy. 115 S
North Wilkesboro, NC 28659
(910)838-8072
Officer: Bob Church, Manager. Ultimate
Parent: Vulcan Materials Co. SIC: 3295—
Minerals—Ground or Treated.

Norwood

★ 75768 ★ Aeroquip Corp.
U.S. Hwy. 52 S.
Norwood, NC 28128
Ultimate Parent: Trinova Corp. SIC:
3052—Rubber & Plastics Hose & Belting.

★ 75769 ★ Aeroquip Corp.
680 Lanier Rd.
Norwood, NC 28128
(704)474-3111
Officer: Leonard Hartford, Plant Manager.
Ultimate Parent: Trinova Corp. SIC:
3052—Rubber & Plastics Hose & Belting.

★ 75770 ★ Aeroquip Corp.
Industrial Products Group
680 Lanier Rd.
Norwood, NC 28128
Ultimate Parent: Trinova Corp. SIC:
3052—Rubber & Plastics Hose & Belting.

Ocean Isle Beach

★ 75771 ★ Branch Banking &
Trust Co.
113 Causeway Dr.
Ocean Isle Beach, NC 28459
(910)579-7080
Company Type: Subsidiary. Location
Type: Branch office. Ultimate Parent:
Southern National Corp. SIC: 6021—
National Commercial Banks.

Old Fort

★ 75772 ★ Branch Banking &
Trust Co.
200 E. Main St.
Old Fort, NC 28762
(704)668-7691
Company Type: Subsidiary. Location
Type: Branch office. Officer: LaGretta R.
Keaton, Mgr. Ultimate Parent: Southern
National Corp. SIC: 6021—National
Commercial Banks.

★ 75773 ★ Collins & Aikman
Corp. Old Fort Plant
4 Hwy. 70 E.
Old Fort, NC 28762
Ultimate Parent: Collins & Aikman Group.
SIC: 2273—Carpets & Rugs.

Oxford

★ 75774 ★ Branch Banking &
Trust Co.
1005 College St.
Oxford, NC 27565-2506
(919)693-2689
Company Type: Subsidiary. Location
Type: Branch office. Ultimate Parent:
Southern National Corp. SIC: 6021—
National Commercial Banks.

★ 75775 ★ Branch Banking &
Trust Co.
108 College St.
Oxford, NC 27565-2910
(919)693-4141
Company Type: Subsidiary. Location
Type: Branch office. Officer: Autry Gentry,
Manager. Ultimate Parent: Southern
National Corp. SIC: 6021—National
Commercial Banks.

★ 75776 ★ Burlington Industries
Inc.
325 Lewis St.
Oxford, NC 27565
(919)693-5126
Officer: David York, Manager. Ultimate
Parent: Burlington Industries, Equity. SIC:
2281—Yarn Spinning Mills; 2399—
Fabricated Textile Products Nec.

★ 75777 ★ Burlington Industries
Inc.
Hwy. 15
Oxford, NC 27565
(919)693-5126
Location Type: Branch office. Officer:
Dave York. Ultimate Parent: Burlington
Industries, Equity. SIC: 2399—Fabricated
Textile Products Nec; 2221—Broadwoven
Fabric Mills—Manmade.

★ 75778 ★ Food Lion
Hwy. 158
Oxford, NC 27565
(919)693-1557
Ultimate Parent: Food Lion. SIC: 5411—
Grocery Stores.

★ 75779 ★ General Processors
Inc.
246 PO Box
Oxford, NC 27565
(919)693-1116
Ultimate Parent: Standard Commercial.
SIC: 5194—Tobacco & Tobacco Products;
5194—Tobacco & Tobacco Products.

★ 75780 ★ Greyhound Bus
Station
225 Hillsboro St.
Oxford, NC 27565
(919)693-4187
Ultimate Parent: Greyhound Lines Inc. SIC:
4131—Intercity & Rural Bus Transportation.

★ 75781 ★ Kentucky Fried
Chicken
Lewis St.
Oxford, NC 27565
(919)693-3424
Ultimate Parent: Pepsico. SIC: 5812—
Eating Places.

★ 75782 ★ Lenox China
Hwy. 158
Oxford, NC 27565
(919)693-9111
Officer: Stan O. Hulsey. Ultimate Parent:
Brown-Forman. SIC: 3262—Vitreous China
Table & Kitchenware; 5023—
Homefurnishings; 5719—Miscellaneous
Home Furnishings Stores.

★ 75783 ★ Lenox China
1500 Williamsboro St.
Oxford, NC 27565
Ultimate Parent: Brown-Forman. SIC:
3262—Vitreous China Table & Kitchenware.

★ 75784 ★ Lenox China Shop
1500 Williamsboro St.
Oxford, NC 27565
(919)639-9111
Officer: Stan Hulsey, Manager. Ultimate
Parent: Brown-Forman. SIC: 3269—Pottery
Products Nec.

★ 75785 ★ Lenox China Shop
1500 Williamsboro St.
Oxford, NC 27565
(919)639-9111
Officer: Stan Hulsey, Manager. Ultimate
Parent: Brown-Forman. SIC: 3269—Pottery
Products Nec.

★ 75786 ★ Peoples Drug Store
Hilltop Shopping Ctr.
Oxford, NC 27565
(919)693-1044
Ultimate Parent: Melville. SIC: 5912—Drug
Stores & Proprietary Stores.

★ 75787 ★ Rite Aid Discount
Pharmacy
107 E. Mcclanahan St.
Oxford, NC 27565
(919)693-9619
Ultimate Parent: Rite Aid. SIC: 5912—Drug
Stores & Proprietary Stores.

★ 75788 ★ RJ Reynolds Tobacco
Co.
145 Broad St.
Oxford, NC 27565
(919)693-7413
Ultimate Parent: RJR Nabisco Holdings.
SIC: 5194—Tobacco & Tobacco Products.

★ 75789 ★ Time Electronics
613 Pine Tree Rd.
Oxford, NC 27565
(919)693-5166
Location Type: Branch office. Ultimate
Parent: Avnet. SIC: 5065—Electronic Parts
& Equipment Nec.

Paw Creek

★ 75790 ★   BFI Waste Systems
Paw Creek, NC 28130
(704)786-4950
Ultimate Parent: Browning-Ferris
Industries. SIC: 4953—Refuse Systems.

★ 75791 ★   Texaco Inc.
Terminal
Paw Creek, NC 28130
(704)394-0376
Ultimate Parent: Texaco. SIC: 5172—
Petroleum Products Nec.

Pembroke

★ 75792 ★   Fleetwood Homes
Railroad St. E
Pembroke, NC 28372
(910)521-9731
Officer: Jim Holmes, Manager. Ultimate
Parent: Fleetwood Enterprises, Inc. SIC:
2451—Mobile Homes.

★ 75793 ★   Fleetwood Homes of
North Carolina Inc. No. 41
E. Railroad Ave. PO Box 818
Pembroke, NC 28372
Ultimate Parent: Fleetwood Enterprises,
Inc. SIC: 2451—Mobile Homes.

★ 75794 ★   Piggly Wiggly
W St. 3rd
Pembroke, NC 28372
(919)521-9561
Ultimate Parent: Bruno's. SIC: 5411—
Grocery Stores.

Pikeville

★ 75795 ★   Branch Banking &
Trust Co.
109 Main St.
Pikeville, NC 27863
(919)242-5129
Company Type: Subsidiary. Location
Type: Branch office. Officer: Mark M.
Shore, Mgr. Ultimate Parent: Southern
National Corp. SIC: 6021—National
Commercial Banks.

★ 75796 ★   Branch Banking &
Trust Co.
109 W. Main St.
Pikeville, NC 27863
(919)242-5129
Ultimate Parent: Southern National Corp.
SIC: 6022—State Commercial Banks.

★ 75797 ★   Piggly Wiggly
Pikeville, NC 27863
(919)242-5181
Ultimate Parent: Bruno's. SIC: 5411—
Grocery Stores.

Pilot Mountain

★ 75798 ★   Branch Banking &
Trust Co.
108 E. Main St.
Pilot Mountain, NC 27041-9501
(910)368-2259
Company Type: Subsidiary. Location
Type: Branch office. Ultimate Parent:
Southern National Corp. SIC: 6021—
National Commercial Banks.

★ 75799 ★   First-Citizens Bank &
Trust Co.
110 W. Main St.
Pilot Mountain, NC 27041
(910)368-4705
Location Type: Branch office. Officer:
Jerry V. Venable, Vice President. Ultimate
Parent: First Citizens Bancshares, Inc. SIC:
6021—National Commercial Banks.

Pinebluff

★ 75800 ★   First Bank
140 S. Walnut St.
Pinebluff, NC 28373
(919)281-3196
Ultimate Parent: Shawmut National Corp.

Pinehurst

★ 75801 ★   Branch Banking &
Trust Co.
15 Chinquapin Rd.
Pinehurst, NC 28374
(919)295-6136
Ultimate Parent: Southern National Corp.
SIC: 6022—State Commercial Banks.

★ 75802 ★   Branch Banking &
Trust Co.
110 Applecross Rd.
Pinehurst, NC 28374
(910)692-4540
Company Type: Subsidiary. Location
Type: Branch office. Ultimate Parent:
Southern National Corp. SIC: 6021—
National Commercial Banks.

★ 75803 ★   First Bank
560 Pinehurst S
Pinehurst, NC 28374
(919)295-4810
Ultimate Parent: Shawmut National Corp.

★ 75804 ★   Food Lion
2201 Beulah Hill Rd.
Pinehurst, NC 28374
(919)295-1031
Ultimate Parent: Food Lion. SIC: 5411—
Grocery Stores.

★ 75805 ★   Pappagallo
Theatre Blvd.
Pinehurst, NC 28374
(919)295-2422
Ultimate Parent: United States Shoe. SIC:
5661—Shoe Stores.

Pinetops

★ 75806 ★   Abb Power T&D Co.
Inc.
Hwy. 43 North
Pinetops, NC 27864
Ultimate Parent: Westinghouse Electric
Corp. SIC: 3612—Transformers Except
Electronic.

★ 75807 ★   Westinghouse
Electric Corp.
Hwy. 43 North
Pinetops, NC 27864
Ultimate Parent: Westinghouse Electric
Corp. SIC: 3612—Transformers Except
Electronic.

Pineville

★ 75808 ★   Bi-Lo Pharmacy
9101 Pineville Matthews Rd.
Pineville, NC 28134
(704)542-5153
Ultimate Parent: Penn Traffic. SIC: 5912—
Drug Stores & Proprietary Stores.

★ 75809 ★   Branch Banking &
Trust Co.
9000 Pineville Matthews Rd.
Pineville, NC 28134
(704)541-8004
Ultimate Parent: Southern National Corp.
SIC: 6022—State Commercial Banks.

★ 75810 ★   Dexter Corp.
Pistisols Div.
2000 Industrial Dr.
Pineville, NC 28134-0339
Company Type: Division. Officer: Mike
Vaden. Ultimate Parent: Dexter Corp. SIC:
3000—Rubber & Miscellaneous Plastics
Products.

★ 75811 ★   Dexter Corp.
Plastisols Div.
10021 Rodney St.
Pineville, NC 28134
Company Type: Division. Ultimate Parent:
Dexter Corp. SIC: 3000—Rubber &
Miscellaneous Plastics Products.

★ 75812 ★   Dexter Plastisols
Rutland Plastics Inc.
10021 Rodney St.
Pineville, NC 28134
Ultimate Parent: Dexter Corp. SIC: 3000—
Rubber & Miscellaneous Plastics Products.

★ 75813 ★   Exxon Shop
8924 Pinevill Matthews Rd.
Pineville, NC 28134
(704)543-0823
Ultimate Parent: Exxon. SIC: 5411—
Grocery Stores.

★ 75814 ★   Federal Paper Board
7421 Carmel Executive Park
Pineville, NC 28134
(704)542-9660
Ultimate Parent: Federal Paper Board.
SIC: 2621—Paper Mills.

★ 75815 ★   Food Lion
317 S. Polk St.
Pineville, NC 28134
(704)889-2411
Ultimate Parent: Food Lion. SIC: 5411—
Grocery Stores.

★ 75816 ★   Kentucky Fried
Chicken
8822 Pinevill Matthews Rd.
Pineville, NC 28134
(704)543-0431
Ultimate Parent: Pepsico. SIC: 5812—
Eating Places.

★ 75817 ★   Lapp Insulator Co.
8000 Corporate Ctr. Dr.
Pineville, NC 28134
(704)543-0102
Ultimate Parent: Great American
Management & Investment. SIC: 7389—
Business Services Nec.

★ 75818 ★   Mary Kay Cosmetics
10411 Osprey Dr.
Pineville, NC 28134
(704)542-2414
Ultimate Parent: Mary Kay Cosmetics. SIC:
5999—Miscellaneous Retail Stores Nec.

★ 75819 ★   Pizza Hut
10705 Park Rd.
Pineville, NC 28134
(704)543-4060
Ultimate Parent: Pepsico. SIC: 5812—
Eating Places.

★ 75820 ★   Pizza Hut
8800 Pineville Matthews Rd.
Pineville, NC 28134
(704)541-3331
Ultimate Parent: Pepsico. SIC: 5812—
Eating Places.

★ 75821 ★   Radio Shack
7713 Pineville Matth Rd.
Pineville, NC 28134
(704)542-9814
Company Type: Division. Ultimate Parent:
Tandy Corp. SIC: 5731—Radio, Television
& Electronics Stores.

★ 75822 ★   Rexham Corp.
1700 Industrial Dr.
Pineville, NC 28134
Ultimate Parent: Bowater. SIC: 2657—
Folding Paperboard Boxes.

★ 75823 ★   Rexham Corp.
Pineville Plant
1700 Industrial Dr.
Pineville, NC 28134
Ultimate Parent: Bowater. SIC: 2652—
Setup Paperboard Boxes.

★ 75824 ★   Rexham Packaging
10500 Industrial Dr.
Pineville, NC 28134-6522
Ultimate Parent: Bowater. SIC: 2657—
Folding Paperboard Boxes.

★ 75825 ★   Rexham Packaging
1700 Industrial Dr.
Pineville, NC 28134
Ultimate Parent: Bowater. SIC: 2657—
Folding Paperboard Boxes.

★ 75826 ★   Rutland Plastics
9635 Industrial Dr.
Pineville, NC 28134
Ultimate Parent: Dexter Corp. SIC: 3087—
Custom Compound of Purchased Resins.

★ 75827 ★   Stone Container Corp.
Corrugated Container Div.
10201 Industrial Dr.
Pineville, NC 28134
(704)889-7671
Officer: Kenneth J. Mraz, Manager.
Ultimate Parent: Stone Container Corp.

SIC: 2653—Corrugated & Solid Fiber
Boxes.

★ 75828 ★   Wachovia Bank &
Trust Co.
7624 Matthews
Pineville, NC 28134
(704)378-5233
Ultimate Parent: Wachovia Corp. SIC:
6022—State Commercial Banks.

Pink Hill

★ 75829 ★   First-Citizens Bank &
Trust Co.
108 W. Broadway St.
Pink Hill, NC 28572
(919)568-3111
Location Type: Branch office. Officer: L. E.
Ledford Jr., Vice President. Ultimate
Parent: First Citizens Bancshares, Inc. SIC:
6021—National Commercial Banks.

Pittsboro

★ 75830 ★   First-Citizens Bank &
Trust Co.
102 Hanks St.
Pittsboro, NC 27312
(919)542-3355
Location Type: Branch office. Officer: R.
C. Warfford, Vice President. Ultimate
Parent: First Citizens Bancshares, Inc. SIC:
6021—National Commercial Banks.

★ 75831 ★   Piggly Wiggly
108 W. Salsbeury
Pittsboro, NC 27312
(919)542-2800
Ultimate Parent: Bruno's.

Pleasant Garden

★ 75832 ★   Olympic Products Co.
4100 Pleasant Garden Rd.
Pleasant Garden, NC 27406
Ultimate Parent: Cone Mills. SIC: 3089—
Plastics Products Nec.

★ 75833 ★   Thomasville Furniture
Ind. Inc.
1212 Thrower Rd.
Pleasant Garden, NC 27313
Ultimate Parent: Armstrong World
Industries. SIC: 2511—Wood Household
Furniture.

Plymouth

★ 75834 ★   Branch Banking &
Trust Co.
102 W. Main St.
Plymouth, NC 27962-1326
(919)793-4181
Company Type: Subsidiary. Location
Type: Branch office. Officer: Sherry G.
Young, Mgr. Ultimate Parent: Southern
National Corp. SIC: 6021—National
Commercial Banks.

★ 75835 ★   Branch Banking &
Trust Co.
Plymouth Plz. Shopping Ctr.
Plymouth, NC 27962
(919)793-4181
Company Type: Subsidiary. Location
Type: Branch office. Ultimate Parent:
Southern National Corp. SIC: 6021—
National Commercial Banks.

★ 75836 ★   Pizza Hut
Us 64 E
Plymouth, NC 27962
(919)793-4486
Ultimate Parent: Pepsico. SIC: 5812—
Eating Places.

★ 75837 ★   Weyeerhaeuser Co.
W. Main St. Ext
Plymouth, NC 27962
(919)793-8111
Officer: Scott Jenkins, Vice President.
Ultimate Parent: Weyerhaeuser Co. SIC:
2411—Logging; 2421—Sawmills & Planing
Mills—General; 2435—Hardwood Veneer &
Plywood.

★ 75838 ★ **Weyerhaeuser Co. Plymouth Mill**
Trowbridge Rd.
Plymouth, NC 27962
Ultimate Parent: Weyerhaeuser Co. **SIC:** 2611—Pulp Mills; 2621—Paper Mills; 2631—Paperboard Mills.

★ 75839 ★ **Weyerhaeuser Forest Prods. Co.**
Main St. Ext.
Plymouth, NC 27962
Ultimate Parent: Weyerhaeuser Co. **SIC:** 2421—Sawmills & Planing Mills—General; 2436—Softwood Veneer & Plywood; 2491—Wood Preserving.

★ 75840 ★ **Weyerhaeuser Forest Products Co.**
Main St. Extension
Plymouth, NC 27962
Ultimate Parent: Weyerhaeuser Co. **SIC:** 2421—Sawmills & Planing Mills—General; 2436—Softwood Veneer & Plywood; 2491—Wood Preserving.

★ 75841 ★ **Weyerhaeuser Forest Products Co.**
Main St. Ext.
Plymouth, NC 27962
Ultimate Parent: Weyerhaeuser Co. **SIC:** 2421—Sawmills & Planing Mills—General; 2436—Softwood Veneer & Plywood; 2491—Wood Preserving.

Princeton

★ 75842 ★ **Branch Banking & Trust Co.**
100 N. Pine St.
Princeton, NC 27569
(919)936-3541
Ultimate Parent: Southern National Corp. **SIC:** 6022—State Commercial Banks.

★ 75843 ★ **Branch Banking & Trust Co.**
100 N. Pine St.
Princeton, NC 27569
(919)936-3541
Company Type: Subsidiary. **Location Type:** Branch office. **Officer:** Judy B. Talton, Mgr. **Ultimate Parent:** Southern National Corp. **SIC:** 6021—National Commercial Banks.

★ 75844 ★ **First-Citizens Bank & Trust Co.**
201 W. Old Hwy. 70
Princeton, NC 27569
(919)936-2266
Location Type: Branch office. **Officer:** Jenette B. Raper, Manager. **Ultimate Parent:** First Citizens Bancshares, Inc. **SIC:** 6021—National Commercial Banks.

Raeford

★ 75845 ★ **Branchh Banking & Trust Co.**
201 Main St.
Raeford, NC 28376-2805
(910)875-3738
Company Type: Subsidiary. **Location Type:** Branch office. **Officer:** Harry Hodges, Manager. **Ultimate Parent:** Southern National Corp. **SIC:** 6021—National Commercial Banks.

★ 75846 ★ **Burlington Menswear/ Plant 17**
Hwy. 211 W
Raeford, NC 28376
(919)875-3731
Officer: Frank Sessoms. **Ultimate Parent:** Burlington Industries, Equity. **SIC:** 2281—Yarn Spinning Mills; 2269—Finishing Plants Nec; 2399—Fabricated Textile Products Nec.

Raleigh

★ 75847 ★ **ABF Freight System Inc.**
6004 Triangle Dr.
Raleigh, NC 27613-4743
(919)781-1096
Ultimate Parent: Arkansas Best. **SIC:** 4212—Local Trucking Without Storage.

★ 75848 ★ **Ace Hardware**
5814 Glenwood Ave.
Raleigh, NC 27612-6220
(919)781-6500
Location Type: Branch office. **Officer:** Jim Phillips. **Ultimate Parent:** Ace Hardware. **SIC:** 5231—Paint, Glass & Wallpaper Stores; 5251—Hardware Stores.

★ 75849 ★ **Ace Hardware**
4009 Wake Forest Rd.
Raleigh, NC 27609
(919)878-5600
Ultimate Parent: Ace Hardware. **SIC:** 5251—Hardware Stores.

★ 75850 ★ **Ace Hardware & Home Center**
8111 Creedmoor Rd.
Raleigh, NC 27613-4389
(919)847-1200
Ultimate Parent: Ace Hardware. **SIC:** 5231—Paint, Glass & Wallpaper Stores; 5251—Hardware Stores.

★ 75851 ★ **Ace Hardware & Home Center**
4009 Wake Forest Rd.
Raleigh, NC 27609-6842
(919)878-5600
Ultimate Parent: Ace Hardware. **SIC:** 5251—Hardware Stores.

★ 75852 ★ **Ace Hardware & Home Center**
6198 Falls of Neuse Rd.
Raleigh, NC 27609-3528
(919)790-8832
Ultimate Parent: Ace Hardware. **SIC:** 5231—Paint, Glass & Wallpaper Stores; 5251—Hardware Stores.

★ 75853 ★ **Ace Hardware&Home Center Inc.**
5814 Glenwood Ave.
Raleigh, NC 27612
(919)781-6500
Ultimate Parent: Ace Hardware. **SIC:** 5251—Hardware Stores.

★ 75854 ★ **American General Finance**
3221 Avent Ferry Rd.
Raleigh, NC 27606-2720
(919)859-0648
Officer: Karen Manger. **Ultimate Parent:** American General Corp. **SIC:** 6141—Personal Credit Institutions.

★ 75855 ★ **American General Finance**
5821A Falls of Neuse Rd.
Raleigh, NC 27609-4043
(919)872-9713
Location Type: Branch office. **Officer:** Karen Lamm. **Ultimate Parent:** American General Corp. **SIC:** 6141—Personal Credit Institutions.

★ 75856 ★ **American General Finance**
4524 Capital Blvd.
Raleigh, NC 27604-4353
(919)790-7600
Location Type: Branch office. **Ultimate Parent:** American General Corp. **SIC:** 6141—Personal Credit Institutions.

★ 75857 ★ **American General Finance Inc.**
5821A Falls of Neuse Rd.
Raleigh, NC 27609-4043
(919)872-9713
Location Type: Branch office. **Officer:** Karen Lamm. **Ultimate Parent:** American General Corp. **SIC:** 6141—Personal Credit Institutions.

★ 75858 ★ **American General Finance Inc.**
4524 Capital Blvd.
Raleigh, NC 27604-4353
(919)790-7600
Location Type: Branch office. **Ultimate Parent:** American General Corp. **SIC:** 6141—Personal Credit Institutions.

★ 75859 ★ **American General Finance Inc.**
3221 Avent Ferry Rd.
Raleigh, NC 27606-2720
(919)859-0648
Location Type: Branch office. **Officer:** Karen Manger. **Ultimate Parent:** American

General Corp. **SIC:** 6141—Personal Credit Institutions.

★ 75860 ★ **Arnet Computer**
2725 Millbrook Rd., Ste. 123
Raleigh, NC 27604
(919)790-1735
Location Type: Branch office. **Ultimate Parent:** Avnet. **SIC:** 5045—Computers, Peripherals & Software; 7379—Computer Related Services Nec.

★ 75861 ★ **Arrow/Kieulft Electronics**
5240 Greers Dairy Rd.
Raleigh, NC 27604
(919)876-3132
Company Type: Division. **Location Type:** Distribution center. **Officer:** Jim McDaniel, General Manager. **Ultimate Parent:** Arrow Electronics. **SIC:** 5065—Electronic Parts & Equipment Nec.

★ 75862 ★ **BancBoston Mortgage Corp.**
4505 Falls of Neuse Rd. Ste. 100
Raleigh, NC 27609-6265
(919)876-1084
Officer: James G. Robinson. **Ultimate Parent:** Bank of Boston Corp. **SIC:** 6141—Personal Credit Institutions; 6162—Mortgage Bankers & Correspondents.

★ 75863 ★ **Bell Atlantic Bus Systems Svc**
5511 Capital Ctr. Dr.
Raleigh, NC 27606-3365
(919)851-1100
Ultimate Parent: Bell Atlantic Corp. **SIC:** 7378—Computer Maintenance & Repair.

★ 75864 ★ **Beneficial North Carolina Inc.**
6300 Creedmoor Rd.
Raleigh, NC 27612-6708
(919)676-1056
Location Type: Branch office. **Ultimate Parent:** Beneficial. **SIC:** 6141—Personal Credit Institutions; 6162—Mortgage Bankers & Correspondents.

★ 75865 ★ **BFI Waste Systems**
700 Freedom Dr.
Raleigh, NC 27610-1402
(919)231-8201
Location Type: Branch office. **Ultimate Parent:** Browning-Ferris Industries. **SIC:** 4953—Refuse Systems.

★ 75866 ★ **Branch Banking & Trust Co.**
5424 Six Forks Rd.
Raleigh, NC 27609-4494
(919)831-4000
Company Type: Subsidiary. **Location Type:** Branch office. **Ultimate Parent:** Southern National Corp. **SIC:** 6021—National Commercial Banks.

★ 75867 ★ **Branch Banking & Trust Co.**
3107 N. Capital Blvd.
Raleigh, NC 27611
(919)831-4000
Company Type: Subsidiary. **Location Type:** Branch office. **Ultimate Parent:** Southern National Corp. **SIC:** 6021—National Commercial Banks.

★ 75868 ★ **Branch Banking & Trust Co.**
8320 Creedmoor Rd.
Raleigh, NC 27613-1373
(919)831-4000
Company Type: Subsidiary. **Location Type:** Branch office. **Ultimate Parent:** Southern National Corp. **SIC:** 6021—National Commercial Banks.

★ 75869 ★ **Branch Banking & Trust Co.**
6200 Falls of the Neuse Rd.
Raleigh, NC 27609
(919)790-9895
Company Type: Subsidiary. **Location Type:** Branch office. **Officer:** Lynn Unwin, Mgr. **Ultimate Parent:** Southern National Corp. **SIC:** 6021—National Commercial Banks.

★ 75870 ★ **Branch Banking & Trust Co.**
333 Fayetteville St.
Raleigh, NC 27601-1742
(919)831-4000
Company Type: Subsidiary. **Location Type:** Branch office. **Officer:** R. Lee Youngblood, Mgr. **Ultimate Parent:** Southern National Corp. **SIC:** 6021—National Commercial Banks.

★ 75871 ★ **Branch Banking & Trust Co.**
7447 Six Forks Rd.
Raleigh, NC 27615-6164
(919)847-6512
Company Type: Subsidiary. **Location Type:** Branch office. **Ultimate Parent:** Southern National Corp. **SIC:** 6021—National Commercial Banks.

★ 75872 ★ **Branch Banking & Trust Co.**
316 W. Edenton St.
Raleigh, NC 27603-1747
(919)834-1268
Company Type: Subsidiary. **Location Type:** Branch office. **Ultimate Parent:** Southern National Corp. **SIC:** 6021—National Commercial Banks.

★ 75873 ★ **Branch Banking & Trust Co.**
3800 Lake Boone Trl.
Raleigh, NC 27607-2994
(919)781-6190
Company Type: Subsidiary. **Location Type:** Branch office. **Ultimate Parent:** Southern National Corp. **SIC:** 6021—National Commercial Banks.

★ 75874 ★ **Branch Banking & Trust Co.**
3107 North Blvd.
Raleigh, NC 27604
(919)790-2277
Location Type: Branch office. **Ultimate Parent:** Southern National Corp. **SIC:** 6099—Functions Related to Deposit Banking.

★ 75875 ★ **Branch Banking & Trust Co.**
2601 Wake Forest Rd.
Raleigh, NC 27609
(919)828-0551
Ultimate Parent: Southern National Corp. **SIC:** 6029—Commercial Banks Nec.

★ 75876 ★ **Branch Banking & Trust Co.**
2209 Century Dr.
Raleigh, NC 27612
(919)828-0551
Ultimate Parent: Southern National Corp. **SIC:** 6022—State Commercial Banks.

★ 75877 ★ **Branch Banking & Trust Co.**
1806 Hillsborough St.
Raleigh, NC 27605
(919)828-0551
Ultimate Parent: Southern National Corp. **SIC:** 6029—Commercial Banks Nec.

★ 75878 ★ **Brownell Electro Inc.**
5245 Capital Blvd.
Raleigh, NC 27604
(919)876-6525
Location Type: Branch office. **Ultimate Parent:** Avnet. **SIC:** 5063—Electrical Apparatus & Equipment.

★ 75879 ★ **Capstone**
Electronics Div.
5230 Greens Dairy Rd.
Raleigh, NC 27604
(919)954-0600
Company Type: Division. **Officer:** Tom O'Brien, General Manager. **Ultimate Parent:** Arrow Electronics. **SIC:** 5065—Electronic Parts & Equipment Nec.

★ 75880 ★ **Carolina Power & Light Co.**
411 Fayetteville St. Mall
Raleigh, NC 27601-1748
(919)546-6111 **Fax:** (919)546-7678 **Telex:** 910383760
Officer: Sherwood H. Smith Jr., Chairman of the Board & CEO. **Ultimate Parent:** Carolina Power & Light Co. **Employee Count:** 8000.

★ 75881 ★   **Carolina Power &
Light Co.**
411 Fayette St.
Raleigh, NC 27601
(919)546-6111
Company Type: Headquarters. **Officer:**
Sherwood H. Smith Jr. **Fortune Service
500:** Ranking 33.

★ 75882 ★   **Casual Corner**
Crabtree Valley Mall
Raleigh, NC 27612
(919)782-0872
Ultimate Parent: United States Shoe. **SIC:**
6512—Nonresidential Building Operators.

★ 75883 ★   **Circus World Toy
Stores Inc.**
N Hills Fash Mall
Raleigh, NC 27609
(919)787-1453
Ultimate Parent: Melville. **SIC:** 5945—
Hobby, Toy & Game Shops.

★ 75884 ★   **Coca Cola U S a
Fountain Sl**
4328 Bland Rd.
Raleigh, NC 27609
(919)876-2846
Ultimate Parent: Coca-Cola. **SIC:** 5149—
Groceries & Related Products Nec.

★ 75885 ★   **Data General Corp.**
3120 Highwoods Blvd.
Raleigh, NC 27625
(919)876-7400
Company Type: Subsidiary. **Ultimate
Parent:** Data General.

★ 75886 ★   **Diebold Inc.**
1208 Front St.
Raleigh, NC 27609
(919)821-5676
Ultimate Parent: Diebold, Inc. **SIC:** 5044—
Office Equipment.

★ 75887 ★   **Dover Elevator Co.**
6001 Chapel Hill Rd., No. 108
Raleigh, NC 27607
(919)851-8557
Officer: Gordon Perry, Plant Manager.
Ultimate Parent: Dover Corp. **SIC:** 3534—
Elevators & Moving Stairways.

★ 75888 ★   **Emery Worldwide**
Raleigh
Raleigh, NC 27611
(919)782-8345
Ultimate Parent: Consolidated Freightways.
SIC: 4512—Air Transportation—Scheduled.

★ 75889 ★   **First-Citizens Banc
Shares Inc.**
PO Box 151
Raleigh, NC 27602
Location Type: Headquarters. **Officer:**
James Hyler Jr., President. **Ultimate
Parent:** First Citizens Bancshares, Inc. **SIC:**
6021—National Commercial Banks.

★ 75890 ★   **First-Citizens Banc
Shares Inc.**
239 Fayetteville St.
Raleigh, NC 27601-1738
(919)755-7000 **Fax:** (919)755-2844
Location Type: Headquarters. **Officer:**
James Hyler Jr., President. **Ultimate
Parent:** First Citizens Bancshares, Inc. **SIC:**
6021—National Commercial Banks.

★ 75891 ★   **First Citizens
Bancshares, Inc.**
239 Fayetteville St.
Raleigh, NC 27601
(919)755-7000
Company Type: Headquarters. **Officer:**
Lewis R. Holding. **Employee Count:** 3770.
Fortune Service 500: Ranking 83.

★ 75892 ★   **First-Citizens Bank &
Trust Co.**
2100 New Bern Ave.
Raleigh, NC 27610-2431
(919)755-7245
Location Type: Branch office. **Ultimate
Parent:** First Citizens Bancshares, Inc. **SIC:**
6021—National Commercial Banks.

★ 75893 ★   **First-Citizens Bank &
Trust Co.**
2105 Cameron St.
Raleigh, NC 27605-1312
(919)755-7127
Location Type: Branch office. **Ultimate**

Parent: First Citizens Bancshares, Inc. **SIC:**
6021—National Commercial Banks.

★ 75894 ★   **First-Citizens Bank &
Trust Co.**
3231 Edwards Mill Rd.
Raleigh, NC 27602
(919)755-7000
Location Type: Branch office. **Ultimate
Parent:** First Citizens Bancshares, Inc. **SIC:**
6021—National Commercial Banks.

★ 75895 ★   **First-Citizens Bank &
Trust Co.**
615 Hillsborough St.
Raleigh, NC 27603-1797
(919)755-7252
Location Type: Branch office. **Ultimate
Parent:** First Citizens Bancshares, Inc. **SIC:**
6021—National Commercial Banks.

★ 75896 ★   **First-Citizens Bank &
Trust Co.**
6033 Glenwood Ave.
Raleigh, NC 27612
(919)755-7272
Location Type: Branch office. **Ultimate
Parent:** First Citizens Bancshares, Inc. **SIC:**
6021—National Commercial Banks.

★ 75897 ★   **First-Citizens Bank &
Trust Co.**
2321 Stonehenge Dr.
Raleigh, NC 27603-9303
(919)755-7000
Location Type: Branch office. **Ultimate
Parent:** First Citizens Bancshares, Inc. **SIC:**
6021—National Commercial Banks.

★ 75898 ★   **First-Citizens Bank &
Trust Co.**
239 Fayetteville St.
Raleigh, NC 27601
(919)755-7000 **Fax:** (919)755-7048
Location Type: Headquarters. **Officer:**
Frank Holding Jr., President. **Ultimate
Parent:** First Citizens Bancshares, Inc. **SIC:**
6021—National Commercial Banks.

★ 75899 ★   **First-Citizens Bank &
Trust Co.**
6833 Falls of the Neuse Rd.
Raleigh, NC 27602
(919)755-2663
Location Type: Branch office. **Ultimate
Parent:** First Citizens Bancshares, Inc. **SIC:**
6021—National Commercial Banks.

★ 75900 ★   **First-Citizens Bank &
Trust Co.**
4801 Capital Blvd.
Raleigh, NC 27604-4483
(919)755-7292
Location Type: Branch office. **Ultimate
Parent:** First Citizens Bancshares, Inc. **SIC:**
6021—National Commercial Banks.

★ 75901 ★   **First-Citizens Bank &
Trust Co.**
2101 Avent Ferry Rd.
Raleigh, NC 27606-2135
(919)755-7374
Location Type: Branch office. **Ultimate
Parent:** First Citizens Bancshares, Inc. **SIC:**
6021—National Commercial Banks.

★ 75902 ★   **First-Citizens Bank &
Trust Co.**
2001 Fairview Rd.
Raleigh, NC 27608-2315
(919)755-2800
Location Type: Branch office. **Ultimate
Parent:** First Citizens Bancshares, Inc. **SIC:**
6021—National Commercial Banks.

★ 75903 ★   **First-Citizens Bank &
Trust Co.**
4205 Lassiter Mill Rd.
Raleigh, NC 27609-5749
(919)755-7212
Location Type: Branch office. **Ultimate
Parent:** First Citizens Bancshares, Inc. **SIC:**
6021—National Commercial Banks.

★ 75904 ★   **First-Citizens Bank &
Trust Co.**
5001 Falls of the Neuse Rd.
Raleigh, NC 27609-5462
Location Type: Branch office. **Ultimate
Parent:** First Citizens Bancshares, Inc. **SIC:**
6021—National Commercial Banks.

★ 75905 ★   **First-Citizens Bank &
Trust Co.**
1200 Ridge Rd.
Raleigh, NC 27607-6835
(919)755-7000
Location Type: Branch office. **Ultimate
Parent:** First Citizens Bancshares, Inc. **SIC:**
6021—National Commercial Banks.

★ 75906 ★   **First-Citizens Bank &
Trust Co.**
1839 Capital Blvd.
Raleigh, NC 27604-2144
(919)755-7132
Location Type: Branch office. **Ultimate
Parent:** First Citizens Bancshares, Inc. **SIC:**
6021—National Commercial Banks.

★ 75907 ★   **Food Lion**
8825 Six Forks Rd.
Raleigh, NC 27615
(919)848-0149
Ultimate Parent: Food Lion. **SIC:** 5411—
Grocery Stores.

★ 75908 ★   **Food Lion**
Creedmoor Rd.
Raleigh, NC 27612
(919)781-0597
Ultimate Parent: Food Lion. **SIC:** 5411—
Grocery Stores.

★ 75909 ★   **Food Lion**
4317 Falls of Neuse Rd.
Raleigh, NC 27609
(919)872-5376
Ultimate Parent: Food Lion. **SIC:** 5411—
Grocery Stores.

★ 75910 ★   **Food Lion**
3257 Avent Ferry Rd.
Raleigh, NC 27606
(919)851-3584
Ultimate Parent: Food Lion. **SIC:** 5411—
Grocery Stores.

★ 75911 ★   **The Gap**
219 E. Six Forks Rd.
Raleigh, NC 27609
(919)781-5204
Ultimate Parent: GAP. **SIC:** 5699—
Miscellaneous Apparel & Accessory Stores.

★ 75912 ★   **GE Capital Mortgage
Corp.**
6601 Six Forks Rd.
Raleigh, NC 27615-6519
(919)846-4100
Company Type: Subsidiary. **Officer:**
Gregory T. Barmore, Chairman of the Board
& President. **Ultimate Parent:** General
Electric. **SIC:** 6351—Surety Insurance.
Employee Count: 2500.

★ 75913 ★   **Hamilton Hallmark**
3510 Spring Forest Rd.
Raleigh, NC 27604
(919)878-0810
Location Type: Branch office. **Ultimate
Parent:** Avnet. **SIC:** 5065—Electronic Parts
& Equipment Nec.

★ 75914 ★   **Hertz Rent-A-Car
Licensee**
Raleigh
Raleigh, NC 27611
(919)787-6112
Ultimate Parent: Hertz. **SIC:** 7514—
Passenger Car Rental.

★ 75915 ★   **Hit or Miss**
3519 Maitland Dr.
Raleigh, NC 27610
(919)833-7716
Ultimate Parent: TJX. **SIC:** 5621—
Women's Clothing Stores; 5651—Family
Clothing Stores.

★ 75916 ★   **Industrial Systems
Associates**
6213 Angus Dr.
Raleigh, NC 27613-4740
(919)781-3112
Ultimate Parent: Ball Corp. **SIC:** 5085—
Industrial Supplies.

★ 75917 ★   **International Paper
Co. Richmond Gravure**
2215 S. Wilmington St.
Raleigh, NC 27603
Ultimate Parent: International Paper Co.
SIC: 2657—Folding Paperboard Boxes.

★ 75918 ★   **International Paper
Richmond Gravure**
2215 S. Wilmington St.
Raleigh, NC 27603
Ultimate Parent: International Paper Co.
SIC: 2657—Folding Paperboard Boxes.

★ 75919 ★   **Kentucky Fried
Chicken**
2600 S. Saunders St.
Raleigh, NC 27603
(919)821-5436
Ultimate Parent: Pepsico. **SIC:** 5812—
Eating Places.

★ 75920 ★   **Kentucky Fried
Chicken**
1314 New Bern Ave.
Raleigh, NC 27610
(919)828-9301
Ultimate Parent: Pepsico. **SIC:** 5812—
Eating Places.

★ 75921 ★   **Kentucky Fried
Chicken**
1831 North Blvd.
Raleigh, NC 27604
(919)834-5438
Ultimate Parent: Pepsico. **SIC:** 5812—
Eating Places.

★ 75922 ★   **Kentucky Fried
Chicken**
3600 Hillsborough St.
Raleigh, NC 27607
(919)828-3239
Ultimate Parent: Pepsico. **SIC:** 5812—
Eating Places.

★ 75923 ★   **Kroger No 305**
Rural Route 8
Raleigh, NC 27612
(919)870-6028
Ultimate Parent: Kroger. **SIC:** 5411—
Grocery Stores.

★ 75924 ★   **Lane Bryant**
Crabtree Valley Mall
Raleigh, NC 27612
(919)787-9345
Ultimate Parent: Limited. **SIC:** 5621—
Women's Clothing Stores.

★ 75925 ★   **Liberty Mutual
Insurance Co.**
3125 Poplarwood Ct
Raleigh, NC 27604
(919)872-4700
Ultimate Parent: Liberty Mutual Group.
SIC: 6411—Insurance Agents, Brokers &
Service.

★ 75926 ★   **The Limited**
Crabtree Valley Mall
Raleigh, NC 27612
(919)781-6110
Ultimate Parent: Limited. **SIC:** 5621—
Women's Clothing Stores.

★ 75927 ★   **Martin Marietta
Aggregates**
PO Box 30013
Raleigh, NC 27622
(919)781-4550 **Fax:** (919)783-4552
Officer: Stephen P. Zelnak Jr., President.
Ultimate Parent: Martin Marietta.

★ 75928 ★   **Martin Marietta
Materials Group**
PO Box 30013
Raleigh, NC 27622
(919)781-4550 **Fax:** (919)783-4635
Officer: Stephen P. Zelnak Jr., President.
Ultimate Parent: Martin Marietta.

★ 75929 ★   **Mary Kay Cosmetics**
Grindingstone Dr.
Raleigh, NC 27604
(919)872-2434
Ultimate Parent: Mary Kay Cosmetics.

★ 75930 ★   **Mary Kay Cosmetics**
4100 Harvey Rd.
Raleigh, NC 27604
(919)876-4222
Ultimate Parent: Mary Kay Cosmetics. **SIC:**
5999—Miscellaneous Retail Stores Nec.

★ 75931 ★ New York Life Raleigh
General Office
Southeastern Agencies
4700 Six Forks Rd., Ste. 200
Raleigh, NC 27609
(919)781-3100
Officer: Edwin F. Adkins, General Manager.
Ultimate Parent: New York Life.

★ 75932 ★ New York Life Raleigh
General Office
Southeastern Agencies
PO Box 20008
Raleigh, NC 27619
(919)781-3100
Officer: Edwin F. Adkins, General Manager.
Ultimate Parent: New York Life.

★ 75933 ★ Otis Elevator Co.
Umstead
Raleigh, NC 27612
(919)781-1555
Ultimate Parent: United Technologies. SIC:
5084—Industrial Machinery & Equipment.

★ 75934 ★ Owens Corning
Fiberglas Cor
3200 Wake Forest Rd.
Raleigh, NC 27609
(919)872-0823
Ultimate Parent: Owens-Corning. SIC:
1742—Plastering, Drywall & Insulation.

★ 75935 ★ Pizza Hut
3921 Western Blvd.
Raleigh, NC 27606
(919)851-3583
Ultimate Parent: Pepsico. SIC: 5812—
Eating Places.

★ 75936 ★ Pizza Hut
5265 Six Forks Rd.
Raleigh, NC 27609
(919)782-9368
Ultimate Parent: Pepsico. SIC: 5812—
Eating Places.

★ 75937 ★ Pizza Hut
609 W. Peace St.
Raleigh, NC 27605
(919)832-2296
Ultimate Parent: Pepsico. SIC: 5812—
Eating Places.

★ 75938 ★ Pizza Hut
1037 N. West St.
Raleigh, NC 27603
(919)833-3618
Ultimate Parent: Pepsico. SIC: 5812—
Eating Places.

★ 75939 ★ Pizza Hut
3691 New Bern Ave.
Raleigh, NC 27610
(919)833-5173
Ultimate Parent: Pepsico. SIC: 5812—
Eating Places.

★ 75940 ★ Pizza Hut
Crabtree Valley Mall
Raleigh, NC 27612
(919)782-0070
Ultimate Parent: Pepsico. SIC: 5812—
Eating Places.

★ 75941 ★ Pizza Hut
N Plaza Shopping Ctr.
Raleigh, NC 27609
(919)872-7581
Ultimate Parent: Pepsico. SIC: 5812—
Eating Places.

★ 75942 ★ Radio Shack
Kings Plz.
Raleigh, NC 27604
(919)876-5965
Company Type: Division. Ultimate Parent:
Tandy Corp. SIC: 5065—Electronic Parts &
Equipment Nec.

★ 75943 ★ Radio Shack
N Hills Mall
Raleigh, NC 27609
(919)787-6586
Company Type: Division. Ultimate Parent:
Tandy Corp. SIC: 5065—Electronic Parts &
Equipment Nec.

★ 75944 ★ Radio Shack
Crabtree Valley Mall
Raleigh, NC 27612
(919)782-6028
Company Type: Division. Ultimate Parent:
Tandy Corp. SIC: 5065—Electronic Parts &
Equipment Nec.

★ 75945 ★ Radio Shack
114 Fayetteville St.
Raleigh, NC 27601
(919)832-0128
Company Type: Division. Ultimate Parent:
Tandy Corp. SIC: 5065—Electronic Parts &
Equipment Nec; 5734—Computer &
Software Stores.

★ 75946 ★ Radio Shack
N Hills Mall
Raleigh, NC 27619
(919)782-4692
Company Type: Division. Ultimate Parent:
Tandy Corp. SIC: 5731—Radio, Television
& Electronics Stores.

★ 75947 ★ Radio Shack
Hwy. 70 W
Raleigh, NC 27619
(919)781-9380
Company Type: Division. Ultimate Parent:
Tandy Corp. SIC: 5046—Commercial
Equipment Nec.

★ 75948 ★ Radio Shack
3669 New Bern Ave.
Raleigh, NC 27610
(919)821-1781
Company Type: Division. Ultimate Parent:
Tandy Corp. SIC: 5065—Electronic Parts &
Equipment Nec.

★ 75949 ★ Rite Aid Discount
Pharmacie
3253 Avent Ferry Rd.
Raleigh, NC 27606
(919)851-9815
Ultimate Parent: Rite Aid. SIC: 5912—Drug
Stores & Proprietary Stores.

★ 75950 ★ Rite Aid Discount
Pharmacie
3229 Avent Ferry Rd.
Raleigh, NC 27606
(919)851-8840
Ultimate Parent: Rite Aid. SIC: 5912—Drug
Stores & Proprietary Stores.

★ 75951 ★ Ryder Truck Rental
5609 Spring Ct
Raleigh, NC 27604
(919)872-1230
Ultimate Parent: Ryder System. SIC:
7359—Equipment Rental & Leasing Nec.

★ 75952 ★ Ryder Truck Rental
3715 Hillsborough St.
Raleigh, NC 27607
(919)833-1279
Ultimate Parent: Ryder System. SIC:
7359—Equipment Rental & Leasing Nec.

★ 75953 ★ Ryder Truck Rental
Automotive Way
Raleigh, NC 27604
(919)828-6111
Ultimate Parent: Ryder System. SIC:
7359—Equipment Rental & Leasing Nec.

★ 75954 ★ Security Pacific
Finance Corp.
6091 Capital Blvd.
Raleigh, NC 27604-2941
(919)872-4963
Location Type: Branch office. Ultimate
Parent: Bankamerica Corp. SIC: 6141—
Personal Credit Institutions; 6162—
Mortgage Bankers & Correspondents.

★ 75955 ★ Security Pacific
Housing Services, Inc.
3100 Smoketree Ct.
Raleigh, NC 27604-1057
(919)876-1003
Location Type: Branch office. Ultimate
Parent: Bankamerica Corp. SIC: 6141—
Personal Credit Institutions.

★ 75956 ★ Standard Register
Business
900 Ridgefield Dr. 230
Raleigh, NC 27609
(919)954-0733
Officer: D. F. Donovan, Manager. Ultimate
Parent: Standard Register. SIC: 2761—
Manifold Business Forms.

★ 75957 ★ T J Maxx Store
6647 Falls of Neuse Rd.
Raleigh, NC 27615
(919)847-1602
Ultimate Parent: TJX. SIC: 5311—
Department Stores.

★ 75958 ★ Taco Bell
3220 S. Wilmington St.
Raleigh, NC 27603
(919)779-1522
Ultimate Parent: Pepsico. SIC: 5812—
Eating Places.

★ 75959 ★ Taco Bell
336 E. Six Forks Rd.
Raleigh, NC 27609
(919)832-9016
Ultimate Parent: Pepsico. SIC: 5812—
Eating Places.

★ 75960 ★ Taco Bell
6404 Glenwood Ave.
Raleigh, NC 27612
(919)787-9805
Ultimate Parent: Pepsico. SIC: 5812—
Eating Places.

★ 75961 ★ Tektronix Inc.
3725 National Dr.
Raleigh, NC 27612
(919)782-5624
Ultimate Parent: Tektronix, Inc. SIC:
5049—Professional Equipment Nec.

★ 75962 ★ Texaco Food Mart
1305 Us 70 W
Raleigh, NC 27603
(919)772-5909
Ultimate Parent: Texaco. SIC: 5411—
Grocery Stores.

★ 75963 ★ This End Up
Crabtree Valley Mall
Raleigh, NC 27612
(919)781-2069
Ultimate Parent: Melville. SIC: 5712—
Furniture Stores.

★ 75964 ★ This End Up Furniture
Co.
Westgate Rd.
Raleigh, NC 27612
(919)782-5520
Ultimate Parent: Melville. SIC: 2511—
Wood Household Furniture; 2512—
Upholstered Household Furniture.

★ 75965 ★ Time Electronics
6060 B 6 Forks Rd.
Raleigh, NC 27609
(919)847-9650
Location Type: Branch office. Ultimate
Parent: Avnet. SIC: 5065—Electronic Parts
& Equipment Nec.

★ 75966 ★ Underwriters
Adjusting Co.
3900 Barrett Dr.
Raleigh, NC 27609
(919)782-3085
Ultimate Parent: Continental. SIC: 6411—
Insurance Agents, Brokers & Service.

★ 75967 ★ Uni-Copy Corp. of
North Carolina
4101 Capital Blvd., Ste. J
Raleigh, NC 27604
(919)876-1005 Fax: (919)878-9571
Company Type: Division. Officer: Louis L.
Scantland, President. Ultimate Parent: Alco
Standard Corp. SIC: 5044—Office
Equipment; 5046—Commercial Equipment
Nec.

★ 75968 ★ United Parcel Service
4101 Atlantic Ave.
Raleigh, NC 27604
(919)790-7283
Ultimate Parent: United Parcel Service of
America. SIC: 4215—Courier Services
Except by Air.

★ 75969 ★ United Parcel Service
Rural Route 4
Raleigh, NC 27606
(919)840-0421
Ultimate Parent: United Parcel Service of
America. SIC: 4212—Local Trucking
Without Storage.

★ 75970 ★ United Parcel Service
4101 Atlantic Ave.
Raleigh, NC 27604
(919)790-7283
Ultimate Parent: United Parcel Service of
America. SIC: 4215—Courier Services
Except by Air.

★ 75971 ★ United Parcel Service
RR 4
Raleigh, NC 27606
(919)840-0421
Ultimate Parent: United Parcel Service of
America. SIC: 4212—Local Trucking
Without Storage.

★ 75972 ★ Universal Instruments
Corp.
3820 Merton Dr.
Raleigh, NC 27609
(919)782-1436
Ultimate Parent: Dover Corp. SIC: 5065—
Electronic Parts & Equipment Nec.

★ 75973 ★ Wachovia Bank &
Trust
227 Fayetteville St.
Raleigh, NC 27601
(919)755-7600
Ultimate Parent: Wachovia Corp. SIC:
6099—Functions Related to Deposit
Banking.

★ 75974 ★ Wachovia Bank &
Trust Co.
1420 Hardimont Rd.
Raleigh, NC 27609
(919)755-7755
Ultimate Parent: Wachovia Corp. SIC:
6099—Functions Related to Deposit
Banking.

★ 75975 ★ Wachovia Bank &
Trust Cc.
2001 Clark Ave.
Raleigh, NC 27605
(919)755-7912
Ultimate Parent: Wachovia Corp. SIC:
6099—Functions Related to Deposit
Banking.

★ 75976 ★ Wachovia Bank &
Trust Co. N
4530 Western Blvd.
Raleigh, NC 27606
(919)755-7956
Ultimate Parent: Wachovia Corp. SIC:
6099—Functions Related to Deposit
Banking.

★ 75977 ★ Wachovia Bank &
Trust Co. N
4220 Lassiter Mill Rd.
Raleigh, NC 27609
(919)755-7623
Ultimate Parent: Wachovia Corp. SIC:
6099—Functions Related to Deposit
Banking.

★ 75978 ★ Wachovia Bank &
Trust Co. N
3200 S. Wilmington St.
Raleigh, NC 27603
(919)755-7960
Ultimate Parent: Wachovia Corp. SIC:
6022—State Commercial Banks.

★ 75979 ★ Wachovia Bank &
Trust Co. N
4315 Glenwood Ave.
Raleigh, NC 27612
(919)755-7740
Ultimate Parent: Wachovia Corp. SIC:
6022—State Commercial Banks.

★ 75980 ★ Wachovia Bank &
Trust Co. N
2600 Hillsborough St.
Raleigh, NC 27607
(919)755-7710
Ultimate Parent: Wachovia Corp. SIC:
6022—State Commercial Banks.

★ 75981 ★ Wachovia Bank &
Trust Co. N
6623 Falls of Neuse Rd.
Raleigh, NC 27615
(919)755-7857
Ultimate Parent: Wachovia Corp. SIC:
6022—State Commercial Banks.

★ 75982 ★ Waldenbooks
4261 Six Forks Rd.
Raleigh, NC 27609
(919)781-3384
Ultimate Parent: K-Mart. SIC: 5942—Book
Stores.

★ 75983 ★   Waldenbooks
Crabtree Valley Mall
Raleigh, NC 27612
(919)782-5661
Ultimate Parent: K-Mart. **SIC:** 5942—Book Stores.

★ 75984 ★   Westinghouse Electric Corp.
2728 North Blvd.
Raleigh, NC 27604
Ultimate Parent: Westinghouse Electric Corp. **SIC:** 3825—Instruments to Measure Electricity.

Raleigh Nc

★ 75985 ★   Linens N Things
Research Triangle Ma
Raleigh Nc, NC 27607
(919)467-2907
Ultimate Parent: Melville. **SIC:** 5719—Miscellaneous Home Furnishings Stores.

Ramseur

★ 75986 ★   Branch Banking & Trust Co.
Hwy. 64 & Brady St.
Ramseur, NC 27316-9344
(910)824-4171
Company Type: Subsidiary. **Location Type:** Branch office. **Officer:** Dennis L. Burke, Mgr. **Ultimate Parent:** Southern National Corp. **SIC:** 6021—National Commercial Banks.

★ 75987 ★   First-Citizens Bank & Trust Co.
149 Jordan Rd.
Ramseur, NC 27316-9405
(704)824-4191
Location Type: Branch office. **Officer:** F. M. Sherrill, Vice President. **Ultimate Parent:** First Citizens Bancshares, Inc. **SIC:** 6021—National Commercial Banks.

Randleman

★ 75988 ★   Golden Belt Manufacturing Co.
189 Commerce Pl.
Randleman, NC 27317
(910)498-7656
Ultimate Parent: American Brands Inc. **SIC:** 2752—Commercial Printing—Lithographic; 2759—Commercial Printing Nec.

★ 75989 ★   Golden Belt Mfg. Co.
105 Commerce Pl.
Randleman, NC 27317
Ultimate Parent: American Brands Inc. **SIC:** 2752—Commercial Printing—Lithographic; 2754—Commercial Printing—Gravure.

★ 75990 ★   Goodyear Tire & Rubber Co.
800 Pineview St.
Randleman, NC 27317
Ultimate Parent: Goodyear Tire & Rubber. **SIC:** 3315—Steel Wire & Related Products; 3471—Plating & Polishing.

Ranlo

★ 75991 ★   Branch Banking & Trust Co.
Hwy. 7 & Cox Rd.
Gastonia
Ranlo, NC 28052
(704)824-3587
Company Type: Subsidiary. **Location Type:** Branch office. **Officer:** Ellen B. Fleming, Mgr. **Ultimate Parent:** Southern National Corp. **SIC:** 6021—National Commercial Banks.

Red Springs

★ 75992 ★   Branch Banking & Trust Co.
710 E. 4th St.
Red Springs, NC 28377-1327
(910)843-2407
Company Type: Subsidiary. **Location Type:** Branch office. **Ultimate Parent:** Southern National Corp. **SIC:** 6021—National Commercial Banks.

★ 75993 ★   Piggly Wiggly
4 Ave.
Red Springs, NC 28377
(919)843-3145
Ultimate Parent: Bruno's. **SIC:** 5411—Grocery Stores.

Reidsville

★ 75994 ★   American Tobacco Co.
301 N. Scales St.
Reidsville, NC 27320-2906
(910)349-6261
Company Type: Subsidiary. **Officer:** Edward S. Harlow. **Ultimate Parent:** American Brands Inc. **SIC:** 2111—Cigarettes; 2121—Cigars; 5194—Tobacco & Tobacco Products.

★ 75995 ★   American Tobacco Co.
North Scales St.
Reidsville, NC 27320
Ultimate Parent: American Brands Inc. **SIC:** 2111—Cigarettes.

★ 75996 ★   Branch Banking & Trust Co.
112 S. Main St.
Reidsville, NC 27320-3812
(910)342-5791
Company Type: Subsidiary. **Location Type:** Branch office. **Ultimate Parent:** Southern National Corp. **SIC:** 6021—National Commercial Banks.

★ 75997 ★   Burlington Industries Inc.
2361 Holiday Loop Rd.
Reidsville, NC 27320-8684
(919)342-3311
Officer: Charles Sheets. **Ultimate Parent:** Burlington Industries, Equity. **SIC:** 2392—Housefurnishings Nec.

★ 75998 ★   First-Citizens Bnak & Trust Co.
228 Gilmer St.
Reidsville, NC 27320-3810
(919)349-8492
Location Type: Branch office. **Officer:** Fred Timper, Vice President. **Ultimate Parent:** First Citizens Bancshares, Inc. **SIC:** 6021—National Commercial Banks.

★ 75999 ★   Food Lion
RR 6
Reidsville, NC 27320
(919)349-5687
Ultimate Parent: Food Lion. **SIC:** 5411—Grocery Stores.

★ 76000 ★   Golden Belt Manufacturing Co.
441 N. Scales St.
Reidsville, NC 27320-2908
(919)349-3381
Officer: R. W. Smith. **Ultimate Parent:** American Brands Inc. **SIC:** 2754—Commercial Printing—Gravure; 2732—Book Printing; 2752—Commercial Printing—Lithographic; 2759—Commercial Printing Nec.

★ 76001 ★   Golden Belt Manufacturing Co.
441 North Scales St.
Reidsville, NC 27323-2126
Ultimate Parent: American Brands Inc. **SIC:** 2754—Commercial Printing—Gravure; 3497—Metal Foil & Leaf.

★ 76002 ★   Golden Belt Mfg. Co.
441 N. Scales St.
Reidsville, NC 27323
Ultimate Parent: American Brands Inc. **SIC:** 2754—Commercial Printing—Gravure; 3497—Metal Foil & Leaf.

★ 76003 ★   Greyhound Bus Lines
305 SW Market St.
Reidsville, NC 27320
(919)349-6134
Ultimate Parent: Greyhound Lines Inc. **SIC:** 4131—Intercity & Rural Bus Transportation.

★ 76004 ★   GTE
Technical Products Div.
1704 Barnes St.
Reidsville, NC 27320
Company Type: Division. **Ultimate Parent:** GTE. **SIC:** 3499—Fabricated Metal Products Nec.

★ 76005 ★   Kentucky Fried Chicken
209 W. Harrison St.
Reidsville, NC 27320
(919)349-7029
Ultimate Parent: Pepsico. **SIC:** 5812—Eating Places.

★ 76006 ★   Miller Brewing Co.
1900 Barnes St.
Reidsville, NC 27320-1170
Ultimate Parent: Philip Morris. **SIC:** 3411—Metal Cans.

★ 76007 ★   Miller Brewing Co.
Container Div.
1900 Barnes St.
Reidsville, NC 27320-1170
Company Type: Division. **Ultimate Parent:** Philip Morris. **SIC:** 3411—Metal Cans.

★ 76008 ★   Piggly Wiggly
507 N. Scales St.
Reidsville, NC 27320
(919)349-2963
Ultimate Parent: Bruno's. **SIC:** 5411—Grocery Stores.

★ 76009 ★   Pizza Hut
1406 S. Scales St.
Reidsville, NC 27320
(919)342-3304
Ultimate Parent: Pepsico. **SIC:** 5812—Eating Places.

★ 76010 ★   Radio Shack
1619 Way St.
Reidsville, NC 27320
(919)349-2947
Company Type: Division. **Ultimate Parent:** Tandy Corp. **SIC:** 5065—Electronic Parts & Equipment Nec; 5731—Radio, Television & Electronics Stores.

★ 76011 ★   Rite Aid
660 S. Scales St.
Reidsville, NC 27320
(919)349-8236
Ultimate Parent: Rite Aid. **SIC:** 5912—Drug Stores & Proprietary Stores.

★ 76012 ★   Rite Aid of North Carolina
23 Gilmer St.
Reidsville, NC 27320
(919)349-7532
Ultimate Parent: Rite Aid. **SIC:** 5912—Drug Stores & Proprietary Stores.

★ 76013 ★   Ryder Truck Rental
1085 Freeway Dr.
Reidsville, NC 27320
(919)349-5098
Ultimate Parent: Ryder System. **SIC:** 4214—Local Trucking With Storage.

★ 76014 ★   Stop & Shop
E Us 158 Hwy.
Reidsville, NC 27320
(919)342-3221
Ultimate Parent: Stop & Shop.

★ 76015 ★   UNIFI, Inc.
2920 Vance St.
Reidsville, NC 27320
(910)342-3361
Officer: Clifford James, Manager. **Ultimate Parent:** UNIFI, Inc. **SIC:** 2281—Yarn Spinning Mills; 2399—Fabricated Textile Products Nec.

★ 76016 ★   Wachovia Bank & Trust Co. Na
231 Turner Dr.
Reidsville, NC 27320
(919)342-6825
Ultimate Parent: Wachovia Corp. **SIC:** 6099—Functions Related to Deposit Banking.

★ 76017 ★   Wachovia Bank & Trust Co. Na
227 W. Morehead St.
Reidsville, NC 27320
(919)342-6800
Ultimate Parent: Wachovia Corp. **SIC:** 6022—State Commercial Banks.

Research Triangle Park

★ 76018 ★   Data General Corp.
62 Alexander Dr.
Research Triangle Park, NC 27709
Company Type: Subsidiary. **Ultimate Parent:** Data General.

★ 76019 ★   First-Citizens Bank & Trust Co.
NC Hwy. 54
Research Triangle Park, NC 27709
(919)549-8671
Location Type: Branch office. **Officer:** R. Gregory Ferrell, Vice President. **Ultimate Parent:** First Citizens Bancshares, Inc. **SIC:** 6021—National Commercial Banks.

★ 76020 ★   GE Microelectronics Center
3026 Cornwallis Rd.
Research Triangle Park, NC 27709
Ultimate Parent: General Electric. **SIC:** 3674—Semiconductors & Related Devices.

★ 76021 ★   Harris Microelectronics Center
3026 Cornwallis Rd.
Research Triangle Park, NC 27709
Ultimate Parent: Harris. **SIC:** 3674—Semiconductors & Related Devices.

★ 76022 ★   Harris Semiconductor International Center
3026 Cornwallis Rd.
Research Triangle Park, NC 27709
Ultimate Parent: Harris. **SIC:** 3674—Semiconductors & Related Devices.

★ 76023 ★   Scm Metal Products Inc.
2601 Weck Dr.
Research Triangle Park, NC 27709
Ultimate Parent: Hanson Industries. **SIC:** 3399—Primary Metal Products Nec.

Research Triangle Pk.

★ 76024 ★   Rohne Poulenc Ag Co.
2 Alexander Dr.
Research Triangle Pk., NC 27709
(919)549-2000
Ultimate Parent: Rhone-Poulenc Rorer. **SIC:** 2879—Agricultural Chemicals Nec.

Richlands

★ 76025 ★   First-Citizens Bank & Trust Co.
110 N. Richlands Blvd.
Richlands, NC 28574-9623
(910)324-4131
Location Type: Branch office. **Officer:** Terrell Evans, Vice President. **Ultimate Parent:** First Citizens Bancshares, Inc. **SIC:** 6021—National Commercial Banks.

★ 76026 ★   Hertz Rent-A-Car Licensee
Albert Ells Arp
Richlands, NC 28574
(919)324-5300
Ultimate Parent: Hertz. **SIC:** 7514—Passenger Car Rental.

★ 76027 ★   Piggly Wiggly
Hwy. 258
Richlands, NC 28574
(919)324-3333
Ultimate Parent: Bruno's. **SIC:** 5411—Grocery Stores.

Riegelwood

★ 76028 ★   Federal Paper Board Co. Inc.
John L. Riegel Rd.
Riegelwood, NC 28456
Ultimate Parent: Federal Paper Board. **SIC:** 2611—Pulp Mills; 2621—Paper Mills; 2631—Paperboard Mills.

★ 76029 ★   Federal Paper Board Co. Inc.
Armour Rd.
Riegelwood, NC 28456-0057
Ultimate Parent: Federal Paper Board. **SIC:** 2421—Sawmills & Planing Mills—General; 2491—Wood Preserving.

★ 76030 ★ Federal Paper Board
Co. Inc. Rieglewood Operations
John L. Riegel Rd.
Riegelwood, NC 28456
Ultimate Parent: Federal Paper Board.
SIC: 2600—Paper & Allied Products;
2611—Pulp Mills; 2631—Paperboard Mills.

Rieglewood

★ 76031 ★ Federal Paper Board
Co.
John L. Riegle Rd.
Rieglewood, NC 28456
(910)655-2211
Officer: L. O. Grissom, Manager. Ultimate
Parent: Federal Paper Board. SIC: 2421—
Sawmills & Planing Mills—General; 2611—
Pulp Mills; 2621—Paper Mills.

Roanoke Rapids

★ 76032 ★ Branch Banking &
Trust Co.
1104 E. 10th St.
Roanoke Rapids, NC 27870-3008
(919)537-0411
Company Type: Subsidiary. Location
Type: Branch office. Ultimate Parent:
Southern National Corp. SIC: 6021—
National Commercial Banks.

★ 76033 ★ Branch Banking &
Trust Co.
1139 Roanoke Ave.
Roanoke Rapids, NC 27870-3703
(919)537-0411
Company Type: Subsidiary. Location
Type: Branch office. Ultimate Parent:
Southern National Corp. SIC: 6021—
National Commercial Banks.

★ 76034 ★ First-Citizens Bank &
Trust Co.
1104 E. 10th St.
Roanoke Rapids, NC 27870-3008
(919)535-1155
Location Type: Branch office. Ultimate
Parent: First Citizens Bancshares, Inc. SIC:
6021—National Commercial Banks.

★ 76035 ★ First-Citizens Bank &
Trust Co.
949 Roanoke Ave.
Roanoke Rapids, NC 27870-2700
(919)537-3546
Location Type: Branch office. Officer:
Clark E. Young, Senior Vice President.
Ultimate Parent: First Citizens Bancshares,
Inc. SIC: 6021—National Commercial
Banks.

★ 76036 ★ First-Citizens Bank &
Trust Co.
1805 E. 10th St.
Roanoke Rapids, NC 27870-4925
(919)537-3546
Location Type: Branch office. Ultimate
Parent: First Citizens Bancshares, Inc. SIC:
6021—National Commercial Banks.

★ 76037 ★ Mary Kay Cosmetics
800 Virginia
Roanoke Rapids, NC 27870
(919)537-9696
Ultimate Parent: Mary Kay Cosmetics. SIC:
5999—Miscellaneous Retail Stores Nec.

★ 76038 ★ Pizza Hut
Plaza Shopping Ctr.
Roanoke Rapids, NC 27870
(919)537-0013
Ultimate Parent: Pepsico. SIC: 5812—
Eating Places.

★ 76039 ★ Trailway Bus Station
Oakland Shopping Ctr.
Roanoke Rapids, NC 27870
(919)537-2094
Ultimate Parent: Greyhound Lines Inc. SIC:
4131—Intercity & Rural Bus Transportation.

★ 76040 ★ Waldenbooks
Becker Village Mall
Roanoke Rapids, NC 27870
(919)537-8606
Ultimate Parent: K-Mart. SIC: 5942—Book
Stores.

Roanoke Rpds

★ 76041 ★ Radio Shack
Plaza Shopctr
Roanoke Rpds, NC 27870
(919)537-7817
Company Type: Division. Ultimate Parent:
Tandy Corp. SIC: 5065—Electronic Parts &
Equipment Nec.

★ 76042 ★ Radio Shack
Becker Village Mall
Roanoke Rpds, NC 27870
(919)535-2620
Company Type: Division. Ultimate Parent:
Tandy Corp. SIC: 5065—Electronic Parts &
Equipment Nec.

★ 76043 ★ Ryder Truck Rental
1818 Roanoke Ave.
Roanoke Rpds, NC 27870
(919)537-5313
Ultimate Parent: Ryder System. SIC:
7359—Equipment Rental & Leasing Nec.

★ 76044 ★ Taco Bell
1601 Weldon Rd.
Roanoke Rpds, NC 27870
(919)537-7208
Ultimate Parent: Pepsico. SIC: 5812—
Eating Places.

Roaring River

★ 76045 ★ Abitibi-Price
Building Products
PO Box 98
Roaring River, NC 28669
(910)696-2751 Fax: (910)696-3410
Company Type: Subsidiary. Location
Type: Plant. Officer: Hugh Browder, Plant
Manager. Ultimate Parent: Alco Standard
Corp. SIC: 2493—Reconstituted Wood
Products.

★ 76046 ★ Abitibi-Price Corp.
Hwy. 268
Roaring River, NC 28669
(919)696-2751
Location Type: Branch office. Officer:
John Caplinger. Ultimate Parent: Alco
Standard Corp. SIC: 2499—Wood Products
Nec; 5211—Lumber & Other Building
Materials.

★ 76047 ★ Abitibi-Price Corp.
Hwy. 268
Roaring River, NC 28669
(919)696-2751
Location Type: Branch office. Officer:
John Caplinger. Ultimate Parent: Alco
Standard Corp. SIC: 2499—Wood Products
Nec; 5211—Lumber & Other Building
Materials.

★ 76048 ★ Holly Farms Foods
Inc.
Hwy. 268 E.
Roaring River, NC 28669
Ultimate Parent: Tyson Foods, Inc. SIC:
2048—Prepared Feeds Nec.

★ 76049 ★ Holly Farms Foods
Inc.
Roaring River Mill

Roaring River, NC 28669
Ultimate Parent: Tyson Foods, Inc. SIC:
2048—Prepared Feeds Nec.

★ 76050 ★ Holly Farms/Tyson
Foods Inc. Roaring River Feed Mill
Hwy. 268 E.
Roaring River, NC 28669
Ultimate Parent: Tyson Foods, Inc. SIC:
2048—Prepared Feeds Nec.

★ 76051 ★ Roaring River Feed
Mill Holly Farms Foods/Tyson
Foods Inc.
Hwy. 268 E.
Roaring River, NC 28669
Ultimate Parent: Tyson Foods, Inc. SIC:
2048—Prepared Feeds Nec.

★ 76052 ★ Tyson Feed Mills
Hwy. 268 E.
Roaring River, NC 28669
(910)696-2741
Officer: Phil Southern, Manager. Ultimate
Parent: Tyson Foods, Inc. SIC: 2048—
Prepared Feeds Nec.

Robbinsville

★ 76053 ★ Texaco Food Mart
Robbinsville, NC 28771
(704)479-8651
Ultimate Parent: Texaco.

Robersonville

★ 76054 ★ Eagle Snacks Inc.
200 E. Third St.
Robersonville, NC 27871
Ultimate Parent: Anheuser-Busch. SIC:
2096—Potato Chips & Similar Snacks;
2068—Salted & Roasted Nuts & Seeds.

Rockingham

★ 76055 ★ Bi-Lo Store
Richmond Plz.
Rockingham, NC 28379
(919)997-3334
Ultimate Parent: Penn Traffic. SIC: 5411—
Grocery Stores.

★ 76056 ★ Branch Banking &
Trust Co.
8 Raleigh St., Richmond Plz.
Rockingham, NC 28379-4403
(910)895-9033
Company Type: Subsidiary. Location
Type: Branch office. Ultimate Parent:
Southern National Corp. SIC: 6021—
National Commercial Banks.

★ 76057 ★ Branch Banking &
Trust Co.
104 W. Washington St.
Rockingham, NC 28379-3547
(910)895-9033
Company Type: Subsidiary. Location
Type: Branch office. Officer: James R.
Blalock, Manager. Ultimate Parent:
Southern National Corp. SIC: 6021—
National Commercial Banks.

★ 76058 ★ Carolina Power &
Light Co.
Clemmons Sawmill Rd.
Rockingham, NC 28379
(919)582-0516
Ultimate Parent: Carolina Power & Light
Co. SIC: 4911—Electric Services.

★ 76059 ★ Carolina Power &
Light Co.
Clemmons Sawmll Rd.
Rockingham, NC 28379
(919)582-0516
Ultimate Parent: Carolina Power & Light
Co. SIC: 4911—Electric Services.

★ 76060 ★ First Federal S & L
Washington St.
Rockingham, NC 28379
(919)997-4516
Company Type: Branch. Officer: Robert T.
Waugh. Officer: Juanita Cox. Ultimate
Parent: Bancorp Hawaii. SIC: 6035—
Federal Savings Institutions; 6162—
Mortgage Bankers & Correspondents.

★ 76061 ★ Fruit of the Loom Inc.
Richmond Apparel
Hwy. 74 W.
Rockingham, NC 28379
Ultimate Parent: Fruit of the Loom. SIC:
2321—Men's/Boys' Shirts; 2329—
Men's/Boys' Clothing Nec.

★ 76062 ★ Greyhound Bus
System
210 E. Broad Ave.
Rockingham, NC 28379
(919)895-5197
Ultimate Parent: Greyhound Lines Inc. SIC:
4131—Intercity & Rural Bus Transportation;
4131—Intercity & Rural Bus Transportation.

★ 76063 ★ Kentucky Fried
Chicken
300 E. Broad Ave.
Rockingham, NC 28379
(919)895-9581
Ultimate Parent: Pepsico. SIC: 5812—
Eating Places.

★ 76064 ★ Klopman Burlington
Fabrics
Hwy. 1 S
Rockingham, NC 28379
(919)997-5001
Officer: Dale Ormsby. Ultimate Parent:

Burlington Industries, Equity. SIC: 2211—
Broadwoven Fabric Mills—Cotton.

★ 76065 ★ Pepsi-Cola Bottling
Co.
1402 E. Washington St.
Rockingham, NC 28379
(910)895-9085
Location Type: Plant. Officer: Andy Jones,
Plant Manager. Ultimate Parent: Pepsico.
SIC: 2086—Bottled & Canned Soft Drinks;
3221—Glass Containers.

★ 76066 ★ Pizza Hut
Tri City Shopping Ctr.
Rockingham, NC 28379
(919)997-4061
Ultimate Parent: Pepsico. SIC: 5812—
Eating Places.

★ 76067 ★ Radio Shack
Tri City Shopping Ctr.
Rockingham, NC 28379
(919)997-4343
Company Type: Division. Ultimate Parent:
Tandy Corp. SIC: 5065—Electronic Parts &
Equipment Nec; 5731—Radio, Television &
Electronics Stores.

★ 76068 ★ Rite Aide Pharmacy
1200 Rockingham Rd.
Rockingham, NC 28379
(919)895-9210
Ultimate Parent: Rite Aid. SIC: 5912—Drug
Stores & Proprietary Stores.

★ 76069 ★ Sara Lee Hosiery
9910 Rockingham Rd.
Rockingham, NC 28379
Ultimate Parent: Sara Lee Corp. SIC:
2251—Women's Hosiery Except Socks.

★ 76070 ★ Union Underwear Co.
Inc.
Post Office Box 1874 Hwy. 74 West
Rockingham, NC 28379
Ultimate Parent: Fruit of the Loom. SIC:
2300—Apparel & Other Textile Products.

Rocky Mount

★ 76071 ★ Abbott Laboratories
Hwy. 301 N. PO Box 2226
Rocky Mount, NC 278022226
Ultimate Parent: Abbott Laboratories. SIC:
2834—Pharmaceutical Preparations.

★ 76072 ★ Abbott Laboratories
PO Box 2226 Hwy. 301 N
Rocky Mount, NC 27802
Ultimate Parent: Abbott Laboratories. SIC:
2834—Pharmaceutical Preparations.

★ 76073 ★ Allied-Signal Controls
& Accessories
3475 Wesleyan Blvd. N.
Rocky Mount, NC 27804
Ultimate Parent: Allied-Signal Inc. SIC:
3724—Aircraft Engines & Engine Parts.

★ 76074 ★ Beneficial North
Carolina Inc.
1902 Stone Rose Dr.
Rocky Mount, NC 27804-2514
(919)977-0039
Location Type: Branch office. Officer: Ruth
Cairns. Ultimate Parent: Beneficial. SIC:
6141—Personal Credit Institutions; 6162—
Mortgage Bankers & Correspondents.

★ 76075 ★ BFI Recycling
Systems
Gelo Industrial Pk.
Rocky Mount, NC 27804
(919)977-1411
Location Type: Branch office. Ultimate
Parent: Browning-Ferris Industries. SIC:
4953—Refuse Systems.

★ 76076 ★ Branch Banking &
Trust Co.
127 N. Winstead
Rocky Mount, NC 27804-2236
(919)977-9788
Company Type: Subsidiary. Location
Type: Branch office. Ultimate Parent:
Southern National Corp. SIC: 6021—
National Commercial Banks.

★ 76077 ★ **Branch Banking & Trust Co.**
200 N. Church St.
Rocky Mount, NC 27804-5403
(919)977-9788
Company Type: Subsidiary. **Location Type:** Branch office. **Officer:** John Charles Thompson, Mgr. **Ultimate Parent:** Southern National Corp. **SIC:** 6021—National Commercial Banks.

★ 76078 ★ **Browning-Ferris Industries**
1119 Instrument Dr.
Rocky Mount, NC 27804-9003
(919)977-1411
Location Type: Branch office. **Officer:** Henry L. Dunton Jr. **Ultimate Parent:** Browning-Ferris Industries. **SIC:** 4952—Sewerage Systems.

★ 76079 ★ **Burlington Industries Inc.**
Hwy. 301 N. By-Pass
Rocky Mount, NC 27803
(919)972-6300
Location Type: Branch office. **Ultimate Parent:** Burlington Industries, Equity. **SIC:** 2399—Fabricated Textile Products Nec.

★ 76080 ★ **Burlington Industries Inc.**
500 Airport Rd.
Rocky Mount, NC 27804
(919)972-6302
Ultimate Parent: Burlington Industries, Equity. **SIC:** 2221—Broadwoven Fabric Mills—Manmade; 2262—Finishing Plants—Manmade; 2399—Fabricated Textile Products Nec.

★ 76081 ★ **Burlington Industries/ Sheffield Plant**
500 Airport Rd.
Rocky Mount, NC 27804-2005
(919)972-6302
Officer: B. J. Adams. **Ultimate Parent:** Burlington Industries, Equity. **SIC:** 2261—Finishing Plants—Cotton; 2221—Broadwoven Fabric Mills—Manmade; 2399—Fabricated Textile Products Nec.

★ 76082 ★ **Exxon L P Gas Store**
1601 S. Church St.
Rocky Mount, NC 27803
(919)977-1731
Ultimate Parent: Exxon. **SIC:** 4932—Gas & Other Services Combined.

★ 76083 ★ **First-Citizens Bank & Trust Co.**
3532 Sunset Ave.
Rocky Mount, NC 27804-3408
(919)443-5048
Location Type: Branch office. **Ultimate Parent:** First Citizens Bancshares, Inc. **SIC:** 6021—National Commercial Banks.

★ 76084 ★ **First-Citizens Bank & Trust Co.**
224 S. Franklin St.
Rocky Mount, NC 27804-5709
(919)446-0611
Location Type: Branch office. **Ultimate Parent:** First Citizens Bancshares, Inc. **SIC:** 6021—National Commercial Banks.

★ 76085 ★ **First-Citizens Bank & Trust Co.**
325 Nash St.
Rocky Mount, NC 27804-5402
(919)446-0611
Location Type: Branch office. **Ultimate Parent:** First Citizens Bancshares, Inc. **SIC:** 6021—National Commercial Banks.

★ 76086 ★ **First-Citizens Bank & Trust Co.**
950 Country Club Rd.
Rocky Mount, NC 27804
(919)937-8674
Location Type: Branch office. **Ultimate Parent:** First Citizens Bancshares, Inc. **SIC:** 6021—National Commercial Banks.

★ 76087 ★ **First-Citizens Bank & Trust Co.**
119 N. Church St.
Rocky Mount, NC 27804-5402
(919)977-2424
Location Type: Branch office. **Officer:** Samuel Ashworth, Area Vice President. **Ultimate Parent:** First Citizens Bancshares, Inc. **SIC:** 6021—National Commercial Banks.

★ 76088 ★ **Food Lion**
812 Harbour Dr. W
Rocky Mount, NC 27801
(919)977-3017
Ultimate Parent: Food Lion. **SIC:** 5411—Grocery Stores.

★ 76089 ★ **Food Lion**
843 N. Fairview Rd.
Rocky Mount, NC 27801
(919)977-6594
Ultimate Parent: Food Lion. **SIC:** 5411—Grocery Stores.

★ 76090 ★ **Food Lion**
1441 Hunter Hill Rd.
Rocky Mount, NC 27804
(919)443-4131
Ultimate Parent: Food Lion. **SIC:** 5411—Grocery Stores.

★ 76091 ★ **Hertz Rent-A-Car**
401 S. Church St.
Rocky Mount, NC 27804
(919)446-4912
Ultimate Parent: Hertz. **SIC:** 7514—Passenger Car Rental.

★ 76092 ★ **Hertz Rent-A-Car**
Rocky Mount-Wilson Municipal Airport
Rocky Mount, NC 27801
(919)442-3183
Ultimate Parent: Hertz. **SIC:** 7514—Passenger Car Rental.

★ 76093 ★ **Kay Bee Toy&Hobby Inc.**
Tarrytown Mall
Rocky Mount, NC 27801
(919)443-2877
Ultimate Parent: Melville. **SIC:** 5945—Hobby, Toy & Game Shops.

★ 76094 ★ **Kentucky Fried Chicken**
1120 N. Fairview Rd.
Rocky Mount, NC 27801
(919)442-3617
Ultimate Parent: Pepsico. **SIC:** 5812—Eating Places.

★ 76095 ★ **Kentucky Fried Chicken**
Hwy. 301 N
Rocky Mount, NC 27801
(919)442-7390
Ultimate Parent: Pepsico. **SIC:** 5812—Eating Places.

★ 76096 ★ **Lerner Shop**
1100 N. Wesleyan Blvd.
Rocky Mount, NC 27804
(919)972-6882
Ultimate Parent: Limited. **SIC:** 5651—Family Clothing Stores.

★ 76097 ★ **Lerner Shop**
14 Tarrytown Mall
Rocky Mount, NC 27804
(919)443-5009
Ultimate Parent: Limited. **SIC:** 5651—Family Clothing Stores.

★ 76098 ★ **Piggly Wiggly**
540 Cokey Rd.
Rocky Mount, NC 27801
(919)446-9632
Ultimate Parent: Bruno's. **SIC:** 5411—Grocery Stores.

★ 76099 ★ **Piggly Wiggly of Rocky Mount Inc.**
540 Cokey Rd.
Rocky Mount, NC 27801-5641
(919)446-9632
Officer: Larry Ingman. **Ultimate Parent:** Bruno's. **SIC:** 5411—Grocery Stores.

★ 76100 ★ **Pizza Hut**
2820 Sunset Ave.
Rocky Mount, NC 27804
(919)443-3527
Ultimate Parent: Pepsico. **SIC:** 5812—Eating Places.

★ 76101 ★ **Radio Shack**
1100 N. Wesleyan Blvd.
Rocky Mount, NC 27804
(919)972-3808
Company Type: Division. **Ultimate Parent:** Tandy Corp. **SIC:** 5731—Radio, Television & Electronics Stores.

★ 76102 ★ **Schlage Lock Co.**
3551 N. Wesleyan Blvd.
Rocky Mount, NC 27801
Ultimate Parent: Ingersoll-Rand. **SIC:** 3429—Hardware Nec.

★ 76103 ★ **Siecor Corp. Rocky Mount Plant**
2151 N. Church St.
Rocky Mount, NC 27804
Ultimate Parent: Corning. **SIC:** 3999—Manufacturing Industries Nec.

★ 76104 ★ **Stop & Shop**
1 PO Box
Rocky Mount, NC 27802
(919)443-6698
Ultimate Parent: Stop & Shop. **SIC:** 5411—Grocery Stores.

★ 76105 ★ **Taco Bell**
2644 Sunset Ave.
Rocky Mount, NC 27804
(919)443-0747
Ultimate Parent: Pepsico. **SIC:** 5812—Eating Places.

★ 76106 ★ **Trailways Bus Line**
401 NE Main St.
Rocky Mount, NC 27801
(919)442-6200
Ultimate Parent: Greyhound Lines Inc. **SIC:** 4131—Intercity & Rural Bus Transportation.

★ 76107 ★ **Trinity Industries Inc.**
1549 Vance St.
Rocky Mount, NC 27801
Ultimate Parent: Trinity Industries. **SIC:** 3443—Fabricated Plate Work—Boiler Shops.

★ 76108 ★ **United Parcel Service**
1112 Instrument Dr.
Rocky Mount, NC 27804
(919)442-7506
Ultimate Parent: United Parcel Service of America. **SIC:** 4215—Courier Services Except by Air.

★ 76109 ★ **United Van Lines Inc.**
501 NE Main St.
Rocky Mount, NC 27801
(919)442-1188
Ultimate Parent: Unigroup. **SIC:** 4231—Trucking Terminal Facilities.

★ 76110 ★ **Wachovia Bank & Trust Co. Na**
300 Sunset Ave.
Rocky Mount, NC 27804
(919)972-4200
Ultimate Parent: Wachovia Corp. **SIC:** 6022—State Commercial Banks.

★ 76111 ★ **Waldenbooks**
1100 N. Wesleyan Blvd.
Rocky Mount, NC 27804
(919)446-9297
Ultimate Parent: K-Mart. **SIC:** 5942—Book Stores.

Rocky Mountain

★ 76112 ★ **Abbott Laboratories**
Hwy. 301 N
Rocky Mountain, NC 27801
(919)977-5711
Location Type: Branch office. **Officer:** Jerry Leedy, Manager. **Ultimate Parent:** Abbott Laboratories. **SIC:** 5122—Drugs, Proprietaries & Sundries; 8734—Testing Laboratories.

★ 76113 ★ **Pepsi-Cola Bottling Co.**
2245 N. Church St.
Rocky Mountain, NC 27804
(919)446-7181
Officer: Bill Quinn, Manager. **Ultimate Parent:** Pepsico. **SIC:** 2086—Bottled & Canned Soft Drinks.

★ 76114 ★ **Standard Products Co.**
1040 Dozier Rd.
Rocky Mountain, NC 27804
Company Type: Division. **Ultimate Parent:** Standard Products. **SIC:** 3069—Fabricated Rubber Products Nec.

Roper

★ 76115 ★ **Branch Banking & Trust Co.**
Buncombe St.
Roper, NC 27970-9601
(919)793-4349
Company Type: Subsidiary. **Location Type:** Branch office. **Officer:** Gay Pavey, Mgr. **Ultimate Parent:** Southern National Corp. **SIC:** 6021—National Commercial Banks.

Roseboro

★ 76116 ★ **Branch Banking & Trust Co.**
201 E. Roseboro St.
Roseboro, NC 28382
(910)525-5141
Company Type: Subsidiary. **Location Type:** Branch office. **Ultimate Parent:** Southern National Corp. **SIC:** 6021—National Commercial Banks.

★ 76117 ★ **Piggly Wiggly**
Fayetteville Hwy.
Roseboro, NC 28382
(910)525-5531
Ultimate Parent: Bruno's. **SIC:** 5411—Grocery Stores.

Rowland

★ 76118 ★ **Branch Banking & Trust Co.**
201 E. Main St.
Rowland, NC 28383-9519
(910)422-3314
Company Type: Subsidiary. **Location Type:** Branch office. **Officer:** Jerry Owen, Manager. **Ultimate Parent:** Southern National Corp. **SIC:** 6021—National Commercial Banks.

Roxboro

★ 76119 ★ **Ace Hardware Talbert Lumber**
349 PO Box
Roxboro, NC 27573
(919)599-1135
Ultimate Parent: Ace Hardware.

★ 76120 ★ **Air Control Products**
1303 Durham Rd.
Roxboro, NC 27573
(910)599-1141 **Fax:** (910)597-6425
Company Type: Subsidiary. **Officer:** Larry Johnson, Plant Manager. **Ultimate Parent:** Eaton Corp. **SIC:** 3714—Motor Vehicle Parts & Accessories; 3559—Special Industry Machinery Nec; 3423—Hand & Edge Tools Nec; 3829—Measuring & Controlling Devices Nec; 3823—Process Control Instruments. **Employee Count:** 450. **Sales:** 40 M.

★ 76121 ★ **Branch Banking & Trust Co.**
123 S. Lamar St.
Roxboro, NC 27573-5205
(910)599-3173
Company Type: Subsidiary. **Location Type:** Branch office. **Officer:** Janice O. Dixon, Mgr. **Ultimate Parent:** Southern National Corp. **SIC:** 6021—National Commercial Banks.

★ 76122 ★ **Collins & Aikman Corp.**
Cavel Div.
1803 N. Main St.
Roxboro, NC 27573
Company Type: Division. **Ultimate Parent:** Collins & Aikman Group. **SIC:** 2259—Knitting Mills Nec; 2262—Finishing Plants—Manmade; 2295—Coated Fabrics—Not Rubberized; 2299—Textile Goods Nec.

★ 76123 ★ **Eaton Air Controls Products**
1303 Durham Rd.
Roxboro, NC 27573
(919)599-1141
Officer: Larry Johnson, Manager. **Ultimate Parent:** Eaton Corp. **SIC:** 3423—Hand & Edge Tools Nec; 3559—Special Industry Machinery Nec; 3592—Carburetors, Pistons, Rings & Valves.

★ **76124** ★ **Eaton Corp.**
1303 Durham Rd.
Roxboro, NC 27573
Ultimate Parent: Eaton Corp. **SIC:** 3714—
Motor Vehicle Parts & Accessories; 3451—
Screw Machine Products.

★ **76125** ★ **Eaton Corp.**
US 501 S
Roxboro, NC 27573
Ultimate Parent: Eaton Corp. **SIC:** 3714—
Motor Vehicle Parts & Accessories; 3451—
Screw Machine Products.

★ **76126** ★ **Exxon Co. USA**
Oxford Rd.
Roxboro, NC 27573
(919)599-6445
Ultimate Parent: Exxon. **SIC:** 5172—
Petroleum Products Nec.

★ **76127** ★ **Fleetwood Homes**
600 Lucy Garrett Rd.
Roxboro, NC 27573
(919)597-3602
Location Type: Plant. **Officer:** B. J.
Williams, Plant Manager. **Ultimate Parent:**
Fleetwood Enterprises, Inc. **SIC:** 2451—
Mobile Homes; 2452—Prefabricated Wood
Buildings.

★ **76128** ★ **Fleetwood Motor
Homes of North Carolina Inc.**
600 Lucy Garrett Road, State Rte. 1703
Roxboro, NC 27573
Ultimate Parent: Fleetwood Enterprises,
Inc. **SIC:** 2451—Mobile Homes.

★ **76129** ★ **Kentucky Fried
Chicken**
1039 N. Madison Blvd.
Roxboro, NC 27573
(919)599-2210
Ultimate Parent: Pepsico. **SIC:** 5812—
Eating Places.

★ **76130** ★ **Pepsi-Cola Bottling
Co.**
605 S. Morgan St.
Roxboro, NC 27573
(919)599-2166
Officer: B. T. Burnett, President. **Ultimate
Parent:** Pepsico. **SIC:** 2086—Bottled &
Canned Soft Drinks.

★ **76131** ★ **Pizza Hut**
315 N. Madison Blvd.
Roxboro, NC 27573
(919)599-0505
Ultimate Parent: Pepsico. **SIC:** 5812—
Eating Places.

★ **76132** ★ **Radio Shack**
300 S. Madison Blvd.
Roxboro, NC 27573
(919)599-9296
Company Type: Division. **Ultimate Parent:**
Tandy Corp. **SIC:** 7622—Radio & T.V.
Repair.

★ **76133** ★ **Ryder Truck Rental**
Old Durham Rd.
Roxboro, NC 27573
(919)599-2111
Ultimate Parent: Ryder System. **SIC:**
7513—Truck Rental & Leasing Without
Drivers.

Rural Hall

★ **76134** ★ **Pizza Hut District
Office**
6420 Old Hwy. 52
Rural Hall, NC 27045
(919)377-9106
Ultimate Parent: Pepsico. **SIC:** 5812—
Eating Places.

★ **76135** ★ **Wachovia Bank &
Trust Co.**
7780 Old Hwy. 52
Rural Hall, NC 27045
(919)969-9120
Ultimate Parent: Wachovia Corp. **SIC:**
6022—State Commercial Banks.

★ **76136** ★ **Westinghouse
Electric**
3050 Westinghouse Rd.
Rural Hall, NC 27045
(910)969-1211
Officer: Richard Deem, Manager. **Ultimate
Parent:** Westinghouse Electric Corp. **SIC:**
3511—Turbines & Turbine Generator Sets.

Rural Hill

★ **76137** ★ **First-Citizens Bank &
Trust Co.**
6005 University Pky.
Rural Hill, NC 27045
(910)969-5571
Location Type: Branch office. **Ultimate
Parent:** First Citizens Bancshares, Inc. **SIC:**
6021—National Commercial Banks.

★ **76138** ★ **First-citizens Bank &
Trust Co.**
8175 Broad St.
Rural Hill, NC 27045
(910)969-5571
Location Type: Branch office. **Officer:** C.
T. Griggs, Vice President. **Ultimate Parent:**
First Citizens Bancshares, Inc. **SIC:** 6021—
National Commercial Banks.

★ **76139** ★ **First-Citizens Bank &
Trust Co.**
1055 Hwy. 65 N.
Rural Hill, NC 27045
(910)969-5571
Location Type: Branch office. **Ultimate
Parent:** First Citizens Bancshares, Inc. **SIC:**
6021—National Commercial Banks.

Rutherford College

★ **76140** ★ **First-Citizens Bank &
Trust Co.**
Malcolm Blvd.
Rutherford College, NC 28671
(704)874-2241
Location Type: Branch office. **Ultimate
Parent:** First Citizens Bancshares, Inc. **SIC:**
6021—National Commercial Banks.

Rutherfordton

★ **76141** ★ **Branch Banking &
Trust Co.**
201 N. Main St.
Rutherfordton, NC 28139-2503
(704)287-3395
Company Type: Subsidiary. **Location
Type:** Branch office. **Officer:** Michael S.
Bohan, Manager. **Ultimate Parent:**
Southern National Corp. **SIC:** 6021—
National Commercial Banks.

★ **76142** ★ **Branck Banking &
Trust Co.**
603 N. Washington St.
Rutherfordton, NC 28139-2413
(704)286-9168
Company Type: Subsidiary. **Location
Type:** Branch office. **Ultimate Parent:**
Southern National Corp. **SIC:** 6021—
National Commercial Banks.

★ **76143** ★ **Broyhill Furniture Ind.
Inc. Rutherford Plant**
Hwy. 221 N.
Rutherfordton, NC 28139
Ultimate Parent: Interco. **SIC:** 2511—Wood
Household Furniture.

★ **76144** ★ **Kentucky Fried
Chicken**
S Cleghorn St.
Rutherfordton, NC 28139
(704)287-9243
Ultimate Parent: Pepsico. **SIC:** 5812—
Eating Places.

★ **76145** ★ **Omc Rutherfordton**
340 Charlotte Rd.
Rutherfordton, NC 28139
Ultimate Parent: Outboard Marine. **SIC:**
3519—Internal Combustion Engines Nec.

★ **76146** ★ **Outboard Marine
Corp.**
340 Charlotte Rd.
Rutherfordton, NC 28139
Ultimate Parent: Outboard Marine. **SIC:**
3519—Internal Combustion Engines Nec.

★ **76147** ★ **Torrington Co.**
Shiloh Plant
US 221 S.
Rutherfordton, NC 28139
Location Type: Plant. **Ultimate Parent:**
Ingersoll-Rand. **SIC:** 3562—Ball & Roller
Bearings.

★ **76148** ★ **Torrington Co. Shiloh
Plant**
Hwy. 221 S.
Rutherfordton, NC 28139
Ultimate Parent: Ingersoll-Rand. **SIC:**
3562—Ball & Roller Bearings.

★ **76149** ★ **Trailways Bus
Systems**
112 W. Court St.
Rutherfordton, NC 28139
(704)287-4501
Ultimate Parent: Greyhound Lines Inc. **SIC:**
4131—Intercity & Rural Bus Transportation.

★ **76150** ★ **Wal Mart Discount
Cities**
White Oak Plz.
Rutherfordton, NC 28139
(704)287-2824
Ultimate Parent: Wal-Mart Stores, Inc. **SIC:**
5912—Drug Stores & Proprietary Stores.

S Brunswick

★ **76151** ★ **Radio Shack**
865 Rural Route 3
S Brunswick, NC 28459
(919)754-4647
Company Type: Division. **Ultimate Parent:**
Tandy Corp. **SIC:** 5719—Miscellaneous
Home Furnishings Stores; 5731—Radio,
Television & Electronics Stores.

Salisbury

★ **76152** ★ **Ace Hardware of
Salisbury**
2141 Statesville Blvd.
Salisbury, NC 28144
(704)636-6060
Ultimate Parent: Ace Hardware. **SIC:**
5251—Hardware Stores.

★ **76153** ★ **Allied-Signal**
Allied Automotive
727 Bendix Dr.
Salisbury, NC 281450988
Ultimate Parent: Allied-Signal Inc. **SIC:**
3714—Motor Vehicle Parts & Accessories.

★ **76154** ★ **Allied-Signal Corp.**
116 Glendower Dr.
Salisbury, NC 28144-9428
(704)633-5281
Officer: T. R. Miller. **Ultimate Parent:**
Allied-Signal Inc. **SIC:** 5013—Motor Vehicle
Supplies & New Parts.

★ **76155** ★ **Allied-Signal Corp.**
116 Glendower Dr.
Salisbury, NC 28144-9428
(704)633-5281
Officer: T. R. Miller. **Ultimate Parent:**
Allied-Signal Inc. **SIC:** 5013—Motor Vehicle
Supplies & New Parts.

★ **76156** ★ **Collins & Aikman
Corp.**
209 Long Meadow Dr.
Salisbury, NC 28144
Ultimate Parent: Collins & Aikman Group.
SIC: 2270—Carpets & Rugs.

★ **76157** ★ **Cone Mills Corp.
Salisbury Plant**
S. Railroad St.
Salisbury, NC 28144
Ultimate Parent: Cone Mills. **SIC:** 2211—
Broadwoven Fabric Mills—Cotton; 2261—
Finishing Plants—Cotton.

★ **76158** ★ **First-Citizens Bank &
Trust Co.**
2085 Statesville Rd.
Salisbury, NC 28144-5012
(704)637-1250
Location Type: Branch office. **Officer:** N.
Andrew Storey, Assistant Vice President.
Ultimate Parent: First Citizens Bancshares,
Inc. **SIC:** 6021—National Commercial
Banks.

★ **76159** ★ **Food Lion**
118 Avalon Dr.
Salisbury, NC 28146
(704)633-7413
Ultimate Parent: Food Lion. **SIC:** 5411—
Grocery Stores.

★ **76160** ★ **Food Lion**
Hwy. 601
Salisbury, NC 28144
(704)636-7615
Ultimate Parent: Food Lion. **SIC:** 5411—
Grocery Stores.

★ **76161** ★ **Food Lion**
Harrison Rd.
Salisbury, NC 28144
(704)633-8250
Ultimate Parent: Food Lion. **SIC:** 5141—
Groceries—General Line.

★ **76162** ★ **Food Lion**
2110 Executive Dr.
Salisbury, NC 28145
(704)633-8250
Company Type: Headquarters. **Officer:**
Thomas E. Smith. **Fortune Service 500:**
Ranking 20.

★ **76163** ★ **Food Lion Inc.**
Harrison Rd.
Salisbury, NC 28144
(704)633-8250
Ultimate Parent: Food Lion. **SIC:** 5141—
Groceries—General Line.

★ **76164** ★ **Food Lion Inc.**
2110 Executive Dr.
Salisbury, NC 28144-8900
(704)633-8250
Company Type: Subsidiary. **Officer:** Tom
E. Smith, Ch. Bd. Pr. CEO. **Ultimate
Parent:** Food Lion. **SIC:** 5411—Grocery
Stores. **Employee Count:** 57721. **Sales:**
7.1 M.

★ **76165** ★ **Food Lion Inc.**
2110 Exec. Dr., PO Box 1330
Salisbury, NC 28145-1330
(704)633-8250
Officer: Tom E. Smith, Chairman. **Ultimate
Parent:** Food Lion. **SIC:** 5411—Grocery
Stores. **Employee Count:** 59721. **Sales:**
7195923000 M.

★ **76166** ★ **General Electric Co.**
1114 Old Concord Rd.
Salisbury, NC 28146
(704)637-5200
Officer: Jim Lisk, Manager. **Ultimate
Parent:** General Electric. **SIC:** 3613—
Switchgear & Switchboard Apparatus;
3699—Electrical Equipment & Supplies Nec.

★ **76167** ★ **Hoechst-Celanese
Corp. Salisbury Plant**
Hwy. 70 W.
Salisbury, NC 28144
Ultimate Parent: Hoechst Celanese Corp.
SIC: 2824—Organic Fibers—Noncellulosic;
2821—Plastics Materials & Resins.

★ **76168** ★ **Hoechst Celanese
Salisbury Plant**
Hwy. 70 West
Salisbury, NC 28144
Ultimate Parent: Hoechst Celanese Corp.
SIC: 2824—Organic Fibers—Noncellulosic.

★ **76169** ★ **North Carolina
Finishing Co.**
Hwy. 29 N
Salisbury, NC 28145-1100
Ultimate Parent: Fieldcrest Cannon. **SIC:**
2269—Finishing Plants Nec; 2261—
Finishing Plants—Cotton; 2262—Finishing
Plants—Manmade.

★ **76170** ★ **Pizza Hut**
1333 E. Innes St.
Salisbury, NC 28146
(704)637-0811
Ultimate Parent: Pepsico. **SIC:** 5812—
Eating Places.

★ **76171** ★ **Pizza Hut**
1510 W. Innes St.
Salisbury, NC 28144
(704)637-1510
Ultimate Parent: Pepsico. **SIC:** 5812—
Eating Places.

★ **76172** ★ **Process Conveyors**
1316 N. Long St.
Salisbury, NC 28144
(704)636-3041 **Fax:** (704)636-2153
Company Type: Division. **Ultimate Parent:**
Litton Industries. **SIC:** 3535—Conveyors &
Conveying Equipment.

★ 76173 ★   Reynolds Metals Co.
200 Peeler Rd.
Salisbury, NC 28147
(704)638-3202
Ultimate Parent: Reynolds Metals Co. SIC:
3411—Metal Cans.

★ 76174 ★   Reynolds Metals Co.
Peeler Rd. Rte. 7, Box 270
Salisbury, NC 28144
Ultimate Parent: Reynolds Metals Co. SIC:
3411—Metal Cans.

★ 76175 ★   Reynolds Metals Co.
Can Div.
200 Peeler Rd.
Salisbury, NC 28144-9701
Company Type: Division. Ultimate Parent:
Reynolds Metals Co. SIC: 3411—Metal
Cans.

★ 76176 ★   Reynolds Metals Co.
Salisbury Can Plant
200 Peeler Rd.
Salisbury, NC 28144
Ultimate Parent: Reynolds Metals Co. SIC:
3411—Metal Cans.

★ 76177 ★   Reynolds Metals Co.
Salisbury Can Plant
Rte. 7 Box 270 Peeler Rd.
Salisbury, NC 28144
Ultimate Parent: Reynolds Metals Co. SIC:
3411—Metal Cans.

★ 76178 ★   Ryder Truck Rental
2185 I-85 N
Salisbury, NC 28144
(704)637-7003
Ultimate Parent: Ryder System. SIC:
7359—Equipment Rental & Leasing Nec.

★ 76179 ★   Technical Fibers
Group Salisbury Plant
Hwy. 70 West
Salisbury, NC 28144
Ultimate Parent: Hoechst Celanese Corp.
SIC: 2824—Organic Fibers—Noncellulosic.

★ 76180 ★   Universal Forest
Products, Inc.
358 Woodmill Rd.
Salisbury, NC 28147
(704)855-1600
Officer: Bob Wilson, Vice President.
Ultimate Parent: Universal Forest Products.
SIC: 2431—Millwork.

★ 76181 ★   Wachovia Bank &
Trust
132 S. Main St.
Salisbury, NC 28144
(704)633-9121
Ultimate Parent: Wachovia Corp. SIC:
6141—Personal Credit Institutions.

★ 76182 ★   Wachovia Bank &
Trust Co. N
Rowan
Salisbury, NC 28144
(704)636-7891
Ultimate Parent: Wachovia Corp. SIC:
6022—State Commercial Banks.

★ 76183 ★   Wachovia Bank &
Trust Co. N
S Main St.
Salisbury, NC 28144
(704)636-8040
Ultimate Parent: Wachovia Corp. SIC:
6022—State Commercial Banks.

★ 76184 ★   Wachovia Bank &
Trust Co. N
920 PO Box
Salisbury, NC 28145
Ultimate Parent: Wachovia Corp. SIC:
6022—State Commercial Banks.

Salisbury Nc

★ 76185 ★   Food Lion
Ketner Ctr.
Salisbury Nc, NC 28144
(704)636-8861
Ultimate Parent: Food Lion. SIC: 5411—
Grocery Stores.

Sanford

★ 76186 ★   American Cyanamid
Co.
Lederle Laboratories Division
4305 Oak Park
Sanford, NC 27330
Ultimate Parent: American Cyanamid Co.
SIC: 2834—Pharmaceutical Preparations.

★ 76187 ★   Branch Banking &
Trust Co.
145 W. Main Street
Sanford, NC 27330-5919
(919)776-8411
Company Type: Subsidiary. Location
Type: Branch office. Officer: Charles L.
Bowers Jr., Mgr. Ultimate Parent: Southern
National Corp. SIC: 6021—National
Commercial Banks.

★ 76188 ★   Branch Banking &
Trust Co.
503 Carthage St.
Sanford, NC 27330-4104
(919)776-8411
Company Type: Subsidiary. Location
Type: Branch office. Ultimate Parent:
Southern National Corp. SIC: 6021—
National Commercial Banks.

★ 76189 ★   Branch Banking &
Trust Co.
1135 Spring Ln.
Sanford, NC 27330-3461
(919)775-6000
Company Type: Subsidiary. Location
Type: Branch office. Ultimate Parent:
Southern National Corp. SIC: 6021—
National Commercial Banks.

★ 76190 ★   Branch Banking &
Trust Co.
200 N. Horner Blvd.
Sanford, NC 27330-3914
(919)775-6000
Company Type: Subsidiary. Location
Type: Branch office. Officer: Doug Gay,
Manager. Ultimate Parent: Southern
National Corp. SIC: 6021—National
Commercial Banks.

★ 76191 ★   Central Carolina
Hospital
1135 Carthage St.
Sanford, NC 27330
(919)774-2100
Officer: Jim Lathren, Executive Director.
Ultimate Parent: American Medical
Holdings. SIC: 8062—General Medical &
Surgical Hospitals.

★ 76192 ★   First-Citizens Bank &
Trust Co.
206 Carthage St.
Sanford, NC 27330-4205
(919)775-3501
Location Type: Branch office. Officer:
Thomas Rouse, Vice President. Ultimate
Parent: First Citizens Bancshares, Inc. SIC:
6021—National Commercial Banks.

★ 76193 ★   Food Lion
N Horner Blvd.
Sanford, NC 27330
(919)774-4753
Ultimate Parent: Food Lion. SIC: 5411—
Grocery Stores.

★ 76194 ★   Food Lion
1931 S. Horner Blvd.
Sanford, NC 27330
(919)775-7931
Ultimate Parent: Food Lion. SIC: 5411—
Grocery Stores.

★ 76195 ★   Golden Poultry Co.
6500 Zimmerman Rd.
Sanford, NC 27330
Ultimate Parent: Gold Kist. SIC: 2015—
Poultry Slaughtering & Processing.

★ 76196 ★   Heins Telephone Co.
106 Gordon St.
Sanford, NC 27330
(919)774-8237
Company Type: Subsidiary. Ultimate
Parent: ALLTEL Corp. SIC: 4812—
Radiotelephone Communications.

★ 76197 ★   Helikon Furniture Co.
Inc.
5000 Womack Rd.
Sanford, NC 27330
Ultimate Parent: Herman Miller. SIC:
2521—Wood Office Furniture.

★ 76198 ★   Lederle-Praxis
Biologics Inc.
4300 Oak Park Rd.
Sanford, NC 27330-9550
(919)775-7100
Officer: J. Bruce Kaylos. Ultimate Parent:
American Cyanamid Co. SIC: 2834—
Pharmaceutical Preparations; 5122—Drugs,
Proprietaries & Sundries.

★ 76199 ★   Moen Inc.
2609 Cox Mill Rd.
Sanford, NC 27330-9727
(919)258-3341
Officer: Jim H. Jones, Vice President.
Ultimate Parent: American Brands Inc.
SIC: 3432—Plumbing Fixtures Fittings &
Trim.

★ 76200 ★   Pfizer Inc.
Coty Div.
1400 Broadway Rd.
Sanford, NC 27330
Company Type: Division. Ultimate Parent:
Pfizer. SIC: 2844—Toilet Preparations.

★ 76201 ★   Piggly Wiggly Corp.
404 Wicker St.
Sanford, NC 27330
(919)776-3412
Ultimate Parent: Bruno's. SIC: 5411—
Grocery Stores.

★ 76202 ★   Pizza Hut
1923 S. Horner Blvd.
Sanford, NC 27330
(919)776-8306
Ultimate Parent: Pepsico. SIC: 5812—
Eating Places.

★ 76203 ★   Rite Aid Discount
Pharmacie
500 Wicker St.
Sanford, NC 27330
(919)776-4107
Ultimate Parent: Rite Aid. SIC: 5912—Drug
Stores & Proprietary Stores.

★ 76204 ★   Rite Aid Pharmacy
2414 S. Horner Blvd.
Sanford, NC 27330
(919)774-9109
Ultimate Parent: Rite Aid. SIC: 5912—Drug
Stores & Proprietary Stores.

★ 76205 ★   Sherwin Williams
Paint Stor
2105 S. Horner Blvd.
Sanford, NC 27330
(919)774-4718
Ultimate Parent: Sherwin-Williams Co. SIC:
5231—Paint, Glass & Wallpaper Stores.

★ 76206 ★   Trailways Bus Lines
Carolin
300 S. Gulf St.
Sanford, NC 27330
(919)775-2541
Ultimate Parent: Greyhound Lines Inc. SIC:
4131—Intercity & Rural Bus Transportation.

★ 76207 ★   Tyson Mexican
Original
800 E. Main St.
Sanford, NC 27330
Ultimate Parent: Tyson Foods, Inc. SIC:
2051—Bread, Cake & Related Products.

★ 76208 ★   Wachovia Bank &
Trust Co. N
115 N. Horner Blvd.
Sanford, NC 27330
(919)774-4563
Ultimate Parent: Wachovia Corp. SIC:
6022—State Commercial Banks.

Saratoga

★ 76209 ★   Branch Banking &
Trust Co.
104 E. Main St.
Saratoga, NC 27873
(919)238-3322
Ultimate Parent: Southern National Corp.
SIC: 6022—State Commercial Banks.

Scotland Neck

★ 76210 ★   Branch Banking &
Trust Co.
1001 Main St.
Scotland Neck, NC 27874
(919)826-3121
Ultimate Parent: Southern National Corp.
SIC: 6022—State Commercial Banks.

★ 76211 ★   Carolina Wood
Preserving
East 16th St.
Scotland Neck, NC 27874
Ultimate Parent: H.J. Heinz. SIC: 2491—
Wood Preserving.

★ 76212 ★   First-Citizens Bank &
Trust Co.
117 E. 10th St.
Scotland Neck, NC 27874-1207
(919)826-3148
Location Type: Branch office. Ultimate
Parent: First Citizens Bancshares, Inc. SIC:
6021—National Commercial Banks.

★ 76213 ★   Gilbert & Bennett Mfg.
Co.
Carolina Wood Preserving Div.
E. 16th St.
Scotland Neck, NC 27874
Company Type: Division. Ultimate Parent:
H.J. Heinz. SIC: 2491—Wood Preserving.

Seaboard

★ 76214 ★   Union Camp Corp.
Seaboard, NC 27876
(919)274-6361
Ultimate Parent: Union Camp Corp. SIC:
2435—Hardwood Veneer & Plywood.

Seagrove

★ 76215 ★   Lucks, Inc.
PO Box 510
798 NC Hwy. 705
Seagrove, NC 27341
Company Type: Subsidiary. Ultimate
Parent: American Home Products. SIC:
2032—Canned Specialties; 2033—Canned
Fruits & Vegetables.

Sealevel

★ 76216 ★   Wachovia Bank &
Trust Co. N
Us
Sealevel, NC 28577
(919)225-3731
Ultimate Parent: Wachovia Corp. SIC:
6022—State Commercial Banks.

Selina

★ 76217 ★   Branch Banking &
Trust Co.
212 N. Raeford St.
Selina, NC 27576-2835
(919)965-3741
Company Type: Subsidiary. Location
Type: Branch office. Officer: Randall E.
Liverman, Mgr. Ultimate Parent: Southern
National Corp. SIC: 6021—National
Commercial Banks.

Selma

★ 76218 ★   Ace Hardware
1207 S. Pollock St.
Selma, NC 27576
(919)965-7277
Ultimate Parent: Ace Hardware. SIC:
5251—Hardware Stores.

★ 76219 ★   Carolina Power &
Light Co.
1112 S. Pollock St.
Selma, NC 27576
(919)965-6314
Ultimate Parent: Carolina Power & Light
Co. SIC: 4911—Electric Services.

★ 76220 ★   Carolina Power &
Light Co.
1112 S. Pollock St.
Selma, NC 27576
(919)965-6314
Ultimate Parent: Carolina Power & Light
Co. SIC: 4911—Electric Services.

★ **76221** ★　**Eaton Corp.**
Aerospace & Commercial Controls Div.
PO Box 57
1100 E. Preston St.
Selma, NC 27576-0057
(919)965-2341
Company Type: Division. **Location Type:**
Plant. **Officer:** R.A. Bushy, Plant Manager.
Ultimate Parent: Eaton Corp. **SIC:** 3643—
Current-Carrying Wiring Devices.

★ **76222** ★　**First-Citizens Bank &**
Trust Co.
114 N. Raeford St.
Selma, NC 27576-2833
(919)965-8141
Location Type: Branch office. **Officer:**
James C. Woodard Jr., Vice President.
Ultimate Parent: First Citizens Bancshares,
Inc. **SIC:** 6021—National Commercial
Banks.

★ **76223** ★　**Food Lion**
Smithfield Hwy.
Selma, NC 27576
(919)965-7171
Ultimate Parent: Food Lion. **SIC:** 5411—
Grocery Stores.

★ **76224** ★　**Kentucky Fried**
Chicken
US 95 S
Selma, NC 27576
(919)965-9343
Ultimate Parent: Pepsico. **SIC:** 5812—
Eating Places.

★ **76225** ★　**Lowe's**
1606 S. Pollock St.
Selma, NC 27576
(919)934-9704
Ultimate Parent: Lowe's. **SIC:** 5039—
Construction Materials Nec.

★ **76226** ★　**Piggly Wiggly**
201 N. Raiford St.
Selma, NC 27576
(919)965-6333
Ultimate Parent: Bruno's. **SIC:** 5411—
Grocery Stores.

★ **76227** ★　**Pizza Hut**
720 Ricks Rd.
Selma, NC 27576
(919)965-2446
Ultimate Parent: Pepsico. **SIC:** 5812—
Eating Places.

Shallote

★ **76228** ★　**First-Citizens Bank &**
Trust Co.
US Hwy. 17, Main St.
Shallote, NC 28459-7173
(910)754-8151
Location Type: Branch office. **Ultimate**
Parent: First Citizens Bancshares, Inc. **SIC:**
6021—National Commercial Banks.

Shallotte

★ **76229** ★　**Branch Banking &**
Trust Co.
5002 Main St.
Shallotte, NC 28459
(910)754-7080
Company Type: Subsidiary. **Location**
Type: Branch office. **Officer:** Marshall
Woodward, Manager. **Ultimate Parent:**
Southern National Corp. **SIC:** 6021—
National Commercial Banks.

Shelby

★ **76230** ★　**AFLAC**
439 Neisler St.
Shelby, NC 28152-5001
(704)484-2300
Ultimate Parent: American Family Life
Assurance Co. **SIC:** 6324—Hospital &
Medical Service Plans.

★ **76231** ★　**AT & T Family Federal**
Credit Union
1742 E. Dixon Blvd.
Shelby, NC 28150
(704)484-1959
Location Type: Branch office. **Officer:** Kim
Lastra, Manager. **Ultimate Parent:** AT&T.
SIC: 6061—Federal Credit Unions.

★ **76232** ★　**Branch Banking &**
Trust Co.
824 Dekalb St.
Shelby, NC 28150-3914
(704)482-4321
Company Type: Subsidiary. **Location**
Type: Branch office. **Ultimate Parent:**
Southern National Corp. **SIC:** 6021—
National Commercial Banks.

★ **76233** ★　**Branch Banking &**
Trust Co.
Market Place Shopping Ctr.
1774 E. Dixon Blvd.
Shelby, NC 28150
(704)482-6553
Company Type: Subsidiary. **Location**
Type: Branch office. **Ultimate Parent:**
Southern National Corp. **SIC:** 6021—
National Commercial Banks.

★ **76234** ★　**Branch Banking &**
Trust Co.
7-9 E. Marian St.
Shelby, NC 28150-4619
(704)482-4321
Company Type: Subsidiary. **Location**
Type: Branch office. **Officer:** Jack B.
Isaacs, Mgr. **Ultimate Parent:** Southern
National Corp. **SIC:** 6021—National
Commercial Banks.

★ **76235** ★　**Branch Banking &**
Trust Co.
7 E. Marion St.
Shelby, NC 28150
(704)482-4321
Ultimate Parent: Southern National Corp.
SIC: 6022—State Commercial Banks.

★ **76236** ★　**Branch Banking &**
Trust Co.
1210 E. Marion St.
Shelby, NC 28150
(704)482-6381
Ultimate Parent: Southern National Corp.
SIC: 6022—State Commercial Banks.

★ **76237** ★　**Copeland Corp.**
4401 E. Dixon Blvd.
Shelby, NC 28150
Ultimate Parent: Emerson Electric Co. Inc.
SIC: 3585—Refrigeration & Heating
Equipment.

★ **76238** ★　**First-Citizens Bank &**
Trust Co.
331 S. Lafayette St.
Shelby, NC 28150-2317
(704)482-6341
Location Type: Branch office. **Officer:** G.
L. Robinson Jr., Vice President. **Ultimate**
Parent: First Citizens Bancshares, Inc. **SIC:**
6021—National Commercial Banks.

★ **76239** ★　**Food Lion**
Hwy. 180
Shelby, NC 28150
(704)482-5301
Ultimate Parent: Food Lion. **SIC:** 5411—
Grocery Stores.

★ **76240** ★　**Hoechst Celanese**
Hwy. 198
Shelby, NC 28150
Ultimate Parent: Hoechst Celanese Corp.
SIC: 2824—Organic Fibers—Noncellulosic;
2821—Plastics Materials & Resins.

★ **76241** ★　**Hoechst-Celanese**
Corp. Shelby Plant
Hwy. 198
Shelby, NC 28150
Ultimate Parent: Hoechst Celanese Corp.
SIC: 2824—Organic Fibers—Noncellulosic;
2821—Plastics Materials & Resins.

★ **76242** ★　**Hoechst Celanese**
Shelby Plant
Hwy. 198 (Near Earl, Nc)
Shelby, NC 28150
Ultimate Parent: Hoechst Celanese Corp.
SIC: 2824—Organic Fibers—Noncellulosic;
2821—Plastics Materials & Resins.

★ **76243** ★　**Pizza Hut**
650 E. Dixon Blvd.
Shelby, NC 28152
(704)487-1123
Ultimate Parent: Pepsico. **SIC:** 5812—
Eating Places.

★ **76244** ★　**Ppg Industries Inc.**
Rte. 4
Shelby, NC 28150
Ultimate Parent: PPG Industries Inc. **SIC:**
3229—Pressed & Blown Glass Nec.

★ **76245** ★　**PPG Industries Inc.**
940 Washburn Switch Rd.
Shelby, NC 28150
(704)434-2261
Officer: Jerry Emmert, President. **Ultimate**
Parent: PPG Industries Inc. **SIC:** 3229—
Pressed & Blown Glass Nec.

★ **76246** ★　**Radio Shack**
2001 E. Dixon Blvd.
Shelby, NC 28152
(704)482-0382
Company Type: Division. **Ultimate Parent:**
Tandy Corp. **SIC:** 5046—Commercial
Equipment Nec.

★ **76247** ★　**Radio Shack**
326 W. Dixon Blvd.
Shelby, NC 28152
(704)482-8680
Company Type: Division. **Ultimate Parent:**
Tandy Corp. **SIC:** 5065—Electronic Parts &
Equipment Nec.

Siler City

★ **76248** ★　**First National Bank &**
Trust
Hwy. 64 E
Siler City, NC 27344
(919)742-4200
Ultimate Parent: Society Corp. **SIC:** 6162—
Mortgage Bankers & Correspondents.

★ **76249** ★　**Food Lion**
Siler Crossing Shoppe
Siler City, NC 27344
(919)742-2606
Ultimate Parent: Food Lion. **SIC:** 5411—
Grocery Stores.

★ **76250** ★　**Food Lion Inc.**
Siler Crossing Shopp
Siler City, NC 27344
(919)742-2606
Ultimate Parent: Food Lion. **SIC:** 5411—
Grocery Stores.

Silver City

★ **76251** ★　**Branch Banking &**
Trust Co.
501 N. Second St.
Silver City, NC 27344-1921
(919)745-2195
Company Type: Subsidiary. **Location**
Type: Branch office. **Officer:** Michael
Willett, Mgr. **Ultimate Parent:** Southern
National Corp. **SIC:** 6021—National
Commercial Banks.

Skyland

★ **76252** ★　**Radio Shack**
1796 Hendersonville Rd.
Skyland, NC 28776
(704)274-5282
Company Type: Division. **Ultimate Parent:**
Tandy Corp. **SIC:** 5731—Radio, Television
& Electronics Stores.

Smithfield

★ **76253** ★　**Automatic Blanket**
Hwy. 95 S
Walpat Rd.
Smithfield, NC 27577
Ultimate Parent: Fieldcrest Cannon. **SIC:**
2297—Nonwoven Fabrics.

★ **76254** ★　**Automatic Blanket**
Rte. 1 Hwy. 95 S. Walpat Rd.
Smithfield, NC 27577
Ultimate Parent: Fieldcrest Cannon. **SIC:**
2297—Nonwoven Fabrics.

★ **76255** ★　**Avnet**
Channel Master
Industrial Pk. Dr.
Smithfield, NC 27577
(910)934-9711 **Fax:** (910)989-2200
Officer: Sylvester Herlihy, President.
Ultimate Parent: Avnet. **SIC:** 3600—
Electronic & Other Electrical Equipment;
3679—Electronic Components Nec; 3663—

Radio & T.V. Communications Equipment.
Employee Count: 600.

★ **76256** ★　**Burlington Industries**
Inc.
514 Hwy. 301 N
Smithfield, NC 27577
(919)934-2166
Officer: Gary Lyon, Manager. **Ultimate**
Parent: Burlington Industries, Equity. **SIC:**
2281—Yarn Spinning Mills; 2399—
Fabricated Textile Products Nec.

★ **76257** ★　**Burlington Industries**
Inc.
514 Selma Rd.
Smithfield, NC 27577-4600
(919)934-2166
Officer: Darward Stallings. **Ultimate**
Parent: Burlington Industries, Equity. **SIC:**
2281—Yarn Spinning Mills; 2221—
Broadwoven Fabric Mills—Manmade;
2399—Fabricated Textile Products Nec.

★ **76258** ★　**Capezio**
Industrial Park Dr.
Smithfield, NC 27577
(919)934-0657
Ultimate Parent: United States Shoe. **SIC:**
5661—Shoe Stores.

★ **76259** ★　**Channel Master**
Industrial Park Dr.
Smithfield, NC 27577
Ultimate Parent: Avnet. **SIC:** 3679—
Electronic Components Nec.

★ **76260** ★　**Food Lion**
401 Paleigh Rd.
Smithfield, NC 27577
(919)934-9162
Ultimate Parent: Food Lion. **SIC:** 5411—
Grocery Stores.

★ **76261** ★　**Kentucky Fried**
Chicken
Us 95 S
Smithfield, NC 27577
(919)965-9343
Ultimate Parent: Pepsico. **SIC:** 5812—
Eating Places.

★ **76262** ★　**Kentucky Fried**
Chicken
Hwy. 301 St. N
Smithfield, NC 27577
(919)934-5008
Ultimate Parent: Pepsico. **SIC:** 5812—
Eating Places.

★ **76263** ★　**Lowe's**
Rural Route 3
Smithfield, NC 27577
(919)934-9704
Ultimate Parent: Lowe's. **SIC:** 5039—
Construction Materials Nec.

★ **76264** ★　**Piggly Wiggly**
826 S. 3rd St.
Smithfield, NC 27577
(919)934-4240
Ultimate Parent: Bruno's. **SIC:** 5411—
Grocery Stores.

★ **76265** ★　**Pizza Hut**
Smithfield W
Smithfield, NC 27577
(919)934-4185
Ultimate Parent: Pepsico. **SIC:** 5812—
Eating Places.

★ **76266** ★　**Pizza Hut**
Hwy. 701
Smithfield, NC 27577
(919)934-3587
Ultimate Parent: Pepsico. **SIC:** 5521—
Used Car Dealers.

★ **76267** ★　**Pizza Hut**
Pine Sq.
Smithfield, NC 27577
(919)934-5926
Ultimate Parent: Pepsico. **SIC:** 5812—
Eating Places.

★ **76268** ★　**Radio Shack**
818 Raleigh Rd.
Smithfield, NC 27577
(919)934-7685
Company Type: Division. **Ultimate Parent:**
Tandy Corp. **SIC:** 5731—Radio, Television
& Electronics Stores.

★ 76269 ★   Texaco-Food Mart
Us 95 S
Smithfield, NC 27577
(919)965-7126
Ultimate Parent: Texaco. **SIC:** 5411—
Grocery Stores.

Snow Hill

★ 76270 ★   First-Citizens Bank &
Trust Co.
201 N. Greene St.
Snow Hill, NC 28580-1496
(919)747-3313
Location Type: Branch office. **Ultimate
Parent:** First Citizens Bancshares, Inc. **SIC:**
6021—National Commercial Banks.

★ 76271 ★   First-Citizens Bank &
Trust Co.
110 N. Greene St.
Snow Hill, NC 28580-1408
(919)747-5838
Location Type: Branch office. **Officer:** T.
Danny Garner, Vice President. **Ultimate
Parent:** First Citizens Bancshares, Inc. **SIC:**
6021—National Commercial Banks.

★ 76272 ★   First-Citizens Bank &
Trust Co.
201 Main St.
Snow Hill, NC 28538
(919)747-2871
Location Type: Branch office. **Ultimate
Parent:** First Citizens Bancshares, Inc. **SIC:**
6021—National Commercial Banks.

Southern Pines

★ 76273 ★   Branch Banking &
Trust Co.
SW Broad St. & Illinois Ave.
Southern Pines, NC 28387
(910)692-7523
Company Type: Subsidiary. **Location
Type:** Branch office. **Officer:** Susan C.
Lewis, Mgr. **Ultimate Parent:** Southern
National Corp. **SIC:** 6021—National
Commercial Banks.

★ 76274 ★   Branch Banking &
Trust Co.
200 SW Broad St.
Southern Pines, NC 28387-5406
(910)692-7101
Company Type: Subsidiary. **Location
Type:** Branch office. **Officer:** Tommie L.
Jessup, Manager. **Ultimate Parent:**
Southern National Corp. **SIC:** 6021—
National Commercial Banks.

★ 76275 ★   Carolina Power &
Light Co.
390 W. Penn Ave.
Southern Pines, NC 28387
(919)692-2052
Ultimate Parent: Carolina Power & Light
Co. **SIC:** 4911—Electric Services.

★ 76276 ★   First-Citizens Bank &
Trust Co.
390 SW Broad St.
Southern Pines, NC 28387-5407
(919)692-2052
Location Type: Branch office. **Officer:** R.
Holt Boone Jr., Vice President. **Ultimate
Parent:** First Citizens Bancshares, Inc. **SIC:**
6021—National Commercial Banks.

★ 76277 ★   Food Lion
39 Pinecrest Plz.
Southern Pines, NC 28387
(919)692-2000
Ultimate Parent: Food Lion. **SIC:** 5411—
Grocery Stores.

★ 76278 ★   Wal Mart Discount
Cities
40 Pinecrest Plz.
Southern Pines, NC 28387
(919)692-4242
Ultimate Parent: Wal-Mart Stores, Inc. **SIC:**
5311—Department Stores.

Southern Pnes

★ 76279 ★   Carolina Power &
Light Co.
390 W. Penn Ave.
Southern Pnes, NC 28387
(919)692-2052
Ultimate Parent: Carolina Power & Light
Co. **SIC:** 4911—Electric Services.

★ 76280 ★   Taco Bell
Us 15-501 S
Southern Pnes, NC 28387
(919)692-5167
Ultimate Parent: Pepsico. **SIC:** 5812—
Eating Places.

Southport

★ 76281 ★   Adm
E. Moore St.
Southport, NC 28461
Ultimate Parent: Archer Daniels Midland
Co. **SIC:** 2833—Medicinals & Botanicals.

★ 76282 ★   Archer Daniels
Midland Co.
5000 E. Moore St.
Southport, NC 28461
(910)457-5011
Officer: John Kane, Manager. **Ultimate
Parent:** Archer Daniels Midland Co. **SIC:**
2869—Industrial Organic Chemicals Nec.

★ 76283 ★   Archer Daniels
Midland Co.
Moore St. Ext.
Southport, NC 28461
(919)457-5011
Officer: John M. Kane. **Ultimate Parent:**
Archer Daniels Midland Co. **SIC:** 2869—
Industrial Organic Chemicals Nec; 5169—
Chemicals & Allied Products Nec.

★ 76284 ★   First-Citizens Bank &
Trust Co.
212 Howe St.
Southport, NC 28461-3816
(910)457-6766
Location Type: Branch office. **Officer:**
Richard Faulk, Vice President. **Ultimate
Parent:** First Citizens Bancshares, Inc. **SIC:**
6021—National Commercial Banks.

★ 76285 ★   First-Citizens Bank &
Trust Co.
130 Yaupon Dr.
Southport, NC 28456-8103
(910)278-3371
Location Type: Branch office. **Ultimate
Parent:** First Citizens Bancshares, Inc. **SIC:**
6021—National Commercial Banks.

★ 76286 ★   Kentucky Fried
Chicken
Long Beach Rd.
Southport, NC 28461
(919)457-6707
Ultimate Parent: Pepsico. **SIC:** 5812—
Eating Places.

★ 76287 ★   Pfizer Inc.
E. Moore St.
Southport, NC 28461
Ultimate Parent: Pfizer. **SIC:** 2833—
Medicinals & Botanicals.

★ 76288 ★   Radio Shack
105 W. Moore St.
Southport, NC 28461
(919)457-6393
Company Type: Division. **Ultimate Parent:**
Tandy Corp. **SIC:** 5065—Electronic Parts &
Equipment Nec.

★ 76289 ★   Rite Aid Discount
Pharm
Hwy. 87 S
Southport, NC 28461
(919)457-9377
Ultimate Parent: Rite Aid. **SIC:** 5912—Drug
Stores & Proprietary Stores.

Sparta

★ 76290 ★   Branch Banking &
Trust Co.
215 S. Main St.
Sparta, NC 28675
(910)372-4326
Company Type: Subsidiary. **Location
Type:** Branch office. **Ultimate Parent:**
Southern National Corp.

★ 76291 ★   First-Citizens Bank &
Trust Co.
Hwy. 21, E. Main St.
Sparta, NC 28675
(919)372-5651
Location Type: Branch office. **Officer:**
Gary Fulbright, Vice President. **Ultimate
Parent:** First Citizens Bancshares, Inc. **SIC:**
6021—National Commercial Banks.

★ 76292 ★   Rite Aid Discount
Pharmacie
Trojan Village Shopping Ctr.
Sparta, NC 28675
(919)372-2101
Ultimate Parent: Rite Aid. **SIC:** 5912—Drug
Stores & Proprietary Stores.

Spindale

★ 76293 ★   Branch Banking &
Trust Co.
201 Main St.
Spindale, NC 28160-1573
(704)286-3649
Company Type: Subsidiary. **Location
Type:** Branch office. **Officer:** Charles A.
Cobb, Mgr. **Ultimate Parent:** Southern
National Corp. **SIC:** 6021—National
Commercial Banks.

★ 76294 ★   Trailways Bus Station
1024 E. Main St.
Spindale, NC 28160
(704)286-2492
Ultimate Parent: Greyhound Lines Inc. **SIC:**
4173—Bus Terminal & Service Facilities.

Spring Hope

★ 76295 ★   First-Citizens Bank &
Trust Co.
103 Pine St.
Spring Hope, NC 27882
(919)478-3161
Location Type: Branch office. **Officer:**
Rodney Jones, Vice President. **Ultimate
Parent:** First Citizens Bancshares, Inc. **SIC:**
6021—National Commercial Banks.

★ 76296 ★   Masonite Corp.
International Paper
State Rd. 1306
Spring Hope, NC 27882
Ultimate Parent: International Paper Co.
SIC: 2499—Wood Products Nec.

Spring Lake

★ 76297 ★   Branch Banking &
Trust Co.
218 Bragg Blvd.
Spring Lake, NC 28390-3350
(910)486-3289
Company Type: Subsidiary. **Location
Type:** Branch office. **Officer:** Debra Borror,
Manager. **Ultimate Parent:** Southern
National Corp. **SIC:** 6021—National
Commercial Banks.

★ 76298 ★   Pizza Hut
Hwy. 87 N
Spring Lake, NC 28390
(919)497-5101
Ultimate Parent: Pepsico. **SIC:** 5812—
Eating Places.

★ 76299 ★   Radio Shack
1151 N. Bragg Blvd.
Spring Lake, NC 28390
(919)497-1820
Company Type: Division. **Ultimate Parent:**
Tandy Corp. **SIC:** 5065—Electronic Parts &
Equipment Nec.

★ 76300 ★   Trailways Bus System
223 Bragg Blvd.
Spring Lake, NC 28390
(919)497-7283
Ultimate Parent: Greyhound Lines Inc. **SIC:**
4131—Intercity & Rural Bus Transportation.

Spruce Pine

★ 76301 ★   Henredon Furn. Ind.
Inc.
Altapass Rd.
Spruce Pine, NC 28777
Ultimate Parent: Masco. **SIC:** 2511—Wood
Household Furniture.

★ 76302 ★   Henredon Furniture
Ind. Inc.
Alta Pass Rd.
Spruce Pine, NC 28777
Ultimate Parent: Masco. **SIC:** 2511—Wood
Household Furniture.

★ 76303 ★   Omc Spruce Pine
1025 Greenwood Rd.
Spruce Pine, NC 28777
Ultimate Parent: Outboard Marine. **SIC:**
3365—Aluminum Foundries.

★ 76304 ★   US Gypsum Co.
Altapass Rd.
Spruce Pine, NC 28777
(704)765-9481
Ultimate Parent: USG Corp. **SIC:** 1499—
Miscellaneous Nonmetallic Minerals.

St. Pauls

★ 76305 ★   Burlington Industries
Inc.
117 E. Armfield St.
St. Pauls, NC 28384
(910)865-3101
Officer: Pete Ivey, Manager. **Ultimate
Parent:** Burlington Industries, Equity. **SIC:**
2399—Fabricated Textile Products Nec.

★ 76306 ★   Burlington Madison
Yarn Co.
102 W. Clark St.
St. Pauls, NC 28384-1712
(919)865-3101
Location Type: Branch office. **Officer:** Jack
Ward. **Ultimate Parent:** Burlington
Industries, Equity. **SIC:** 2281—Yarn
Spinning Mills; 2399—Fabricated Textile
Products Nec.

★ 76307 ★   Piggly Wiggly
5th
St. Pauls, NC 28384
(919)865-4158
Ultimate Parent: Bruno's. **SIC:** 5411—
Grocery Stores.

Stanley

★ 76308 ★   Branch Banking &
Trust Co.
101 Main St.
Stanley, NC 28164-2201
(704)263-2201
Company Type: Subsidiary. **Location
Type:** Branch office. **Officer:** Howard W.
League, Mgr. **Ultimate Parent:** Southern
National Corp. **SIC:** 6021—National
Commercial Banks.

★ 76309 ★   Branch Banking &
Trust Co.
101 N. Main St.
Stanley, NC 28164
(704)263-2201
Ultimate Parent: Southern National Corp.
SIC: 6022—State Commercial Banks.

★ 76310 ★   Citizens Savings
Bank, SSB
110 E. Dallas
Stanley, NC 28164-2051
(704)263-5433
Company Type: Subsidiary. **Location
Type:** Branch office. **Officer:** James Sowell,
Mgr. **Ultimate Parent:** Southern National
Corp. **SIC:** 6021—National Commercial
Banks.

★ 76311 ★   Rubbermaid Specialty
Products Inc.
1200 S. Hwy. 27
Stanley, NC 28164
(704)263-9155
Ultimate Parent: Rubbermaid. **SIC:** 2519—
Household Furniture Nec; 2599—Furniture
& Fixtures Nec.

Stantonsburg

★ 76312 ★   Branch Banking &
Trust Co.
123 Main St.
Stantonsburg, NC 27883
(919)238-2193
Company Type: Subsidiary. **Location
Type:** Branch office. **Officer:** Charles E.
Sauls, Mgr. **Ultimate Parent:** Southern
National Corp. **SIC:** 6021—National
Commercial Banks.

★ 76313 ★ **Branch Banking & Trust Co.**
123 S. Main St.
Stantonsburg, NC 27883
(919)238-3296
Ultimate Parent: Southern National Corp.
SIC: 6022—State Commercial Banks.

Star

★ 76314 ★ **Fruit of the Loom Hosiery**
Star Div.
Russell Dr.
Star, NC 27356
Company Type: Division. **Ultimate Parent:** Fruit of the Loom. **SIC:** 2251—Women's Hosiery Except Socks.

Statesville

★ 76315 ★ **Aeroquip Corp.**
151 Walker Rd.
Statesville, NC 28677
Ultimate Parent: Trinova Corp. **SIC:** 3714—Motor Vehicle Parts & Accessories.

★ 76316 ★ **Branch Banking & Trust Co.**
1617 E. Broad St.
Statesville, NC 28677-4303
(704)872-9531
Company Type: Subsidiary. **Location Type:** Branch office. **Ultimate Parent:** Southern National Corp. **SIC:** 6021—National Commercial Banks.

★ 76317 ★ **Branch Banking & Trust Co.**
621 Sullivan Rd.
Statesville, NC 28677-4107
(704)873-1857
Company Type: Subsidiary. **Location Type:** Branch office. **Officer:** Larry Hughes, Manager. **Ultimate Parent:** Southern National Corp. **SIC:** 6021—National Commercial Banks.

★ 76318 ★ **Branch Banking & Trust Co.**
1913 W. Front St.
Statesville, NC 28677
(704)872-0488
Ultimate Parent: Southern National Corp. **SIC:** 6022—State Commercial Banks.

★ 76319 ★ **Bristol-Myers Squibb**
Zimmer Patient Care Div.
5601 Old Mountain Rd.
Statesville, NC 28677
(704)873-1001
Company Type: Division. **Officer:** Larry Harvey, Vice President. **Ultimate Parent:** Bristol-Myers Squibb. **SIC:** 3842—Surgical Appliances & Supplies.

★ 76320 ★ **Burlington Industries Inc.**
201 Phoenix St.
Statesville, NC 28677
(704)872-0941
Officer: Bill McGuire, Manager. **Ultimate Parent:** Burlington Industries, Equity. **SIC:** 2257—Weft Knit Fabric Mills; 2399—Fabricated Textile Products Nec.

★ 76321 ★ **Clark Equipment Co.**
I-77 & I-44
Statesville, NC 28677
Ultimate Parent: Clark Equipment Co. **SIC:** 3531—Construction Machinery; 3714—Motor Vehicle Parts & Accessories.

★ 76322 ★ **Clark-Hurth Components Box 38**
I-77 & I-40 Rte. 18 PO Box 38
Statesville, NC 28677
Ultimate Parent: Clark Equipment Co. **SIC:** 3531—Construction Machinery.

★ 76323 ★ **Clark-Hurth Components Co.**
I-77 at I-40
PO Box 1272
Statesville, NC 28677
(704)873-2811 **Fax:** (704)878-5616
Officer: John J. Reynolds, President.
Ultimate Parent: Clark Equipment Co.

★ 76324 ★ **Clark-Schwebel Fiber Glass Corp.**
535 Connor St.
Statesville, NC 28677
Ultimate Parent: Springs Industries. **SIC:** 2221—Broadwoven Fabric Mills—Manmade; 2262—Finishing Plants—Manmade.

★ 76325 ★ **Coca Cola Bottling Co. Conso**
2111 W. Front St.
Statesville, NC 28677
(704)872-3634
Ultimate Parent: Coca-Cola Enterprises. **SIC:** 5149—Groceries & Related Products Nec.

★ 76326 ★ **First-Citizens Bank & Trust Co.**
1706 E. Broad St.
Statesville, NC 28677-4306
(704)878-5900
Location Type: Branch office. **Ultimate Parent:** First Citizens Bancshares, Inc. **SIC:** 6021—National Commercial Banks.

★ 76327 ★ **First-Citizens Bank & Trust Co.**
1111 W. Front St.
Statesville, NC 28677-5050
(704)878-5900
Location Type: Branch office. **Ultimate Parent:** First Citizens Bancshares, Inc. **SIC:** 6021—National Commercial Banks.

★ 76328 ★ **First-Citizens Bank & Trust Co.**
204 E. Broad St.
Statesville, NC 28677-5325
(704)878-5900
Location Type: Branch office. **Officer:** William J. Leach, Area Vice President.
Ultimate Parent: First Citizens Bancshares, Inc. **SIC:** 6021—National Commercial Banks.

★ 76329 ★ **Food Lion**
1382 Shelton Ave.
Statesville, NC 28677
(704)873-6319
Ultimate Parent: Food Lion. **SIC:** 5411—Grocery Stores.

★ 76330 ★ **International Paper**
Uniwood Div.
Hwy. 90 W.
Statesville, NC 28677
Company Type: Division. **Ultimate Parent:** International Paper Co. **SIC:** 2672—Coated & Laminated Paper Nec.

★ 76331 ★ **International Paper Co.**
Container Div.
930 Meacham Rd.
Statesville, NC 28677
Company Type: Division. **Ultimate Parent:** International Paper Co. **SIC:** 2653—Corrugated & Solid Fiber Boxes.

★ 76332 ★ **International Paper Co.**
Uniwood Div.
Hwy. 90 W.
Statesville, NC 28677-2380
Company Type: Division. **Ultimate Parent:** International Paper Co. **SIC:** 2672—Coated & Laminated Paper Nec.

★ 76333 ★ **Pizza Hut**
106 Signal Hill Dr.
Statesville, NC 28677
(704)873-1897
Ultimate Parent: Pepsico. **SIC:** 5531—Automobile & Home Supply Stores.

★ 76334 ★ **Radio Shack**
Signal Hill Mall
Statesville, NC 28677
(704)873-5311
Company Type: Division. **Ultimate Parent:** Tandy Corp. **SIC:** 5065—Electronic Parts & Equipment Nec.

★ 76335 ★ **Rite Aid Discount Pharmacie**
1216 W. Front St.
Statesville, NC 28677
(704)873-7210
Ultimate Parent: Rite Aid. **SIC:** 5912—Drug Stores & Proprietary Stores.

★ 76336 ★ **Rubbermaid Office Products Inc.**
3330 Taylorsville Rd.
Statesville, NC 28677
(704)878-9551
Ultimate Parent: Rubbermaid. **SIC:** 3089—Plastics Products Nec.

★ 76337 ★ **Ryder Truck Rental**
Hwy. 90 W
Statesville, NC 28677
(704)873-8964
Ultimate Parent: Ryder System. **SIC:** 7513—Truck Rental & Leasing Without Drivers.

★ 76338 ★ **Southern States Co-Op. Inc. Inc.**
U.S. Hwy. 70 E. Rte. 1 Box 639
Statesville, NC 28677
Ultimate Parent: Southern. **SIC:** 2875—Fertilizers—Mixing Only.

★ 76339 ★ **Thomasville Upholstery, Inc.**
820 Cochran St.
Statesville, NC 28677
(704)872-6515
Officer: Bob Walters, President. **Ultimate Parent:** Armstrong World Industries. **SIC:** 2512—Upholstered Household Furniture; 2599—Furniture & Fixtures Nec.

★ 76340 ★ **Thomasville Upholstry Inc.**
PO Box 1826
Statesville, NC 28687
(704)872-6515 **Fax:** (704)873-6112
Company Type: Subsidiary. **Officer:** Robert P. Walters. **Ultimate Parent:** Armstrong World Industries. **Employee Count:** 700. **Sales:** 50 M.

★ 76341 ★ **Wheeling Corrugating Co.**
Industrial Dr.
Statesville, NC 28677
(704)872-2471
Ultimate Parent: Wheeling-Pittsburgh Steel Corp. **SIC:** 3443—Fabricated Plate Work—Boiler Shops.

Stedman

★ 76342 ★ **First-Citizens Bank & Trust Co.**
Hwy. 24 & Hillsboro St.
Stedman, NC 28391-9733
(910)483-3895
Location Type: Branch office. **Officer:** James P. Williams, Vice President. **Ultimate Parent:** First Citizens Bancshares, Inc. **SIC:** 6021—National Commercial Banks.

Stokesdale

★ 76343 ★ **First-Citizens Bank & Trust Co.**
8500 US 158
Stokesdale, NC 27357
(910)643-6341
Location Type: Branch office. **Officer:** Jimmy L. Carter, Assistant Vice President.
Ultimate Parent: First Citizens Bancshares, Inc. **SIC:** 6021—National Commercial Banks.

Stoneville

★ 76344 ★ **UNIFI, Inc.**
770 E. Stoneville
Stoneville, NC 27048
(910)573-9806
Officer: Bill Hughes, Manager. **Ultimate Parent:** UNIFI, Inc. **SIC:** 2211—Broadwoven Fabric Mills—Cotton; 2221—Broadwoven Fabric Mills—Manmade.

Summerfield

★ 76345 ★ **Food Lion**
Us 220
Summerfield, NC 27358
(919)643-6324
Ultimate Parent: Food Lion. **SIC:** 5411—Grocery Stores.

★ 76346 ★ **Food Lion Inc.**
Us 220
Summerfield, NC 27358
(919)643-6324
Ultimate Parent: Food Lion. **SIC:** 5411—Grocery Stores.

Sunbury

★ 76347 ★ **First-Citizens Bank & Trust Co.**
Hwy. 32
Sunbury, NC 27979-9743
(919)465-8621
Location Type: Branch office. **Officer:** Charles D. Hobbs, Vice President. **Ultimate Parent:** First Citizens Bancshares, Inc. **SIC:** 6021—National Commercial Banks.

★ 76348 ★ **First-Citizens Bank & Trust Co.**
Willeyton Rd.
Sunbury, NC 27937
(919)357-1250
Location Type: Branch office. **Ultimate Parent:** First Citizens Bancshares, Inc. **SIC:** 6021—National Commercial Banks.

Swannanoa

★ 76349 ★ **Chemtronics Inc.**
180 Old Bee Tree Rd.
Swannanoa, NC 28778
Ultimate Parent: Halliburton. **SIC:** 2869—Industrial Organic Chemicals Nec; 2892—Explosives.

★ 76350 ★ **Jet Research Center Inc.**
Defense & Aerospace Div.
180 Old Bee Tree Rd.
Swannanoa, NC 28778
Company Type: Division. **Ultimate Parent:** Halliburton. **SIC:** 2892—Explosives.

★ 76351 ★ **Ryder Truck Rental**
Patton Cove Rd.
Swannanoa, NC 28778
(704)686-5289
Ultimate Parent: Ryder System. **SIC:** 4212—Local Trucking Without Storage.

Swansboro

★ 76352 ★ **First-Citizens Bank & Trust Co.**
302 Main St.
Swansboro, NC 28584
(910)326-4306
Location Type: Branch office. **Officer:** James D. Howard, Vice President. **Ultimate Parent:** First Citizens Bancshares, Inc. **SIC:** 6021—National Commercial Banks.

★ 76353 ★ **First-Citizens Bank & Trust Co.**
307 W. B. McLean Blvd.
Swansboro, NC 28584
(919)393-2021
Location Type: Branch office. **Ultimate Parent:** First Citizens Bancshares, Inc. **SIC:** 6021—National Commercial Banks.

★ 76354 ★ **Piggly Wiggly**
Hwy. 24
Swansboro, NC 28584
(919)393-2147
Ultimate Parent: Bruno's. **SIC:** 5411—Grocery Stores.

★ 76355 ★ **Piggly Wiggly**
Northwoods Shopping Ctr.
Swansboro, NC 28584
(919)347-2056
Ultimate Parent: Bruno's. **SIC:** 5411—Grocery Stores.

Sylva

★ 76356 ★ **First-Citizens Bank & Trust Co.**
5 W. Main St.
Sylva, NC 28779
(704)586-5566
Location Type: Branch office. **Officer:** Kevin L. Wells, Vice President. **Ultimate Parent:** First Citizens Bancshares, Inc. **SIC:** 6021—National Commercial Banks.

★ 76357 ★　Kentucky Fried Chicken
Asheville Rd.
Sylva, NC 28779
(704)586-6180
Ultimate Parent: Pepsico. **SIC:** 5812—Eating Places.

Tabor City

★ 76358 ★　Branch Banking & Trust Co.
8 Hickman Rd.
Tabor City, NC 28463
(910)653-2146
Company Type: Subsidiary. **Location Type:** Branch office. **Officer:** Ned Hughes, Manager. **Ultimate Parent:** Southern National Corp. **SIC:** 6021—National Commercial Banks.

Tarbara

★ 76359 ★　Branch Banking & Trust Co.
Western Blvd.
Tarbara, NC 27886
(919)823-6101
Company Type: Subsidiary. **Location Type:** Branch office. **Ultimate Parent:** Southern National Corp. **SIC:** 6021—National Commercial Banks.

★ 76360 ★　Branch Banking & Trust Co.
1717 N. Main St.
Tarbara, NC 27886-2523
(919)823-6101
Company Type: Subsidiary. **Location Type:** Branch office. **Ultimate Parent:** Southern National Corp. **SIC:** 6021—National Commercial Banks.

★ 76361 ★　Branch Banking & Trust Co.
318 Main St.
Tarbara, NC 27886-5010
(919)823-6101
Company Type: Subsidiary. **Location Type:** Branch office. **Officer:** Robert D. Farmer II, Mgr. **Ultimate Parent:** Southern National Corp. **SIC:** 6021—National Commercial Banks.

Tarboro

★ 76362 ★　Black & Decker Corp.
3301 N. Main St.
Tarboro, NC 27886-1926
(919)641-6325
Company Type: Branch. **Officer:** Wayne Kelley. **Ultimate Parent:** Black & Decker Corp. **SIC:** 3546—Power-Driven Handtools; 3549—Metalworking Machinery Nec; 5251—Hardware Stores.

★ 76363 ★　First-Citizens Bank & Trust Co.
400 Main St.
Tarboro, NC 27886-4311
(919)823-1708
Location Type: Branch office. **Officer:** Stephen H. Martin, Assistant Vice President. **Ultimate Parent:** First Citizens Bancshares, Inc. **SIC:** 6021—National Commercial Banks.

★ 76364 ★　Piggly Wiggly
2030 Main St. N
Tarboro, NC 27886
(919)823-2466
Ultimate Parent: Bruno's. **SIC:** 5411—Grocery Stores.

★ 76365 ★　Sara Lee Bakery
Hwy. 258 S.
Tarboro, NC 27886
Ultimate Parent: Sara Lee Corp. **SIC:** 2053—Frozen Bakery Products Except Bread.

Taylorsville

★ 76366 ★　Broyhill Furniture Ind. Inc. Taylorsville Plant
Hwy. 90
Taylorsville, NC 28681
Ultimate Parent: Interco. **SIC:** 2512—Upholstered Household Furniture.

★ 76367 ★　Casual Corner Beauty Shop
305 E. Main Ave.
Taylorsville, NC 28681
(704)632-4706
Ultimate Parent: United States Shoe. **SIC:** 7231—Beauty Shops.

★ 76368 ★　E. R. Carpenter Co. Inc.
Hwy. 90 E. PO Box 455
Taylorsville, NC 28681
Ultimate Parent: Carpenter. **SIC:** 3086—Plastics Foam Products.

★ 76369 ★　McDonalds Restaurant
Hwy. 90
Taylorsville, NC 28681
(704)632-2004
Ultimate Parent: May Department Stores.

★ 76370 ★　Peoples Drug Store
327 3rd St. SW
Taylorsville, NC 28681
(704)632-2271
Ultimate Parent: Melville. **SIC:** 5047—Medical & Hospital Equipment; 5912—Drug Stores & Proprietary Stores.

Thomasville

★ 76371 ★　Armstrong World Industries
Furniture Div.
Thomasville, NC 27360
(910)472-4000
Company Type: Subsidiary. **Officer:** A. Mitchell, Vice President of Marketing. **Ultimate Parent:** Armstrong World Industries. **SIC:** 2511—Wood Household Furniture.

★ 76372 ★　Branch Banking & Trust Co.
1120 Randolph St.
Thomasville, NC 27360-5750
(910)472-3599
Company Type: Subsidiary. **Location Type:** Branch office. **Ultimate Parent:** Southern National Corp. **SIC:** 6021—National Commercial Banks.

★ 76373 ★　Branch Banking & Trust Co.
100 Salem St.
Thomasville, NC 27360-3906
(910)475-8161
Company Type: Subsidiary. **Location Type:** Branch office. **Ultimate Parent:** Southern National Corp. **SIC:** 6021—National Commercial Banks.

★ 76374 ★　Branch Banking & Trust Co.
521 National Hwy.
Thomasville, NC 27360-3042
(910)475-7151
Company Type: Subsidiary. **Location Type:** Branch office. **Officer:** H. Edward Campbell, Mgr. **Ultimate Parent:** Southern National Corp. **SIC:** 6021—National Commercial Banks.

★ 76375 ★　Cone Mills
Prelude Co.
1168 PO Box
Thomasville, NC 27361
Ultimate Parent: Cone Mills. **SIC:** 2515—Mattresses & Bedsprings.

★ 76376 ★　First-Citizens Bank & Trust Co.
1035 Randolph St.
Thomasville, NC 27360-5726
(910)472-2050
Location Type: Branch office. **Officer:** Donald W. Efird, Assistant Vice President. **Ultimate Parent:** First Citizens Bancshares, Inc. **SIC:** 6021—National Commercial Banks.

★ 76377 ★　First-Citizens Bank & Trust Co.
50 Salem St.
Thomasville, NC 27360-3937
(910)475-6157
Location Type: Branch office. **Ultimate Parent:** First Citizens Bancshares, Inc. **SIC:** 6021—National Commercial Banks.

★ 76378 ★　Ingram Plywoods Inc.
718 Bassett Dr.
Thomasville, NC 27361-0947
Ultimate Parent: Hanson Industries. **SIC:** 2435—Hardwood Veneer & Plywood; 2436—Softwood Veneer & Plywood.

★ 76379 ★　Masonite Corp.
200 Mason Way
Thomasville, NC 27360
Ultimate Parent: International Paper Co. **SIC:** 2499—Wood Products Nec; 2435—Hardwood Veneer & Plywood; 2436—Softwood Veneer & Plywood.

★ 76380 ★　Mobil Mart Inc.
1 Unity St.
Thomasville, NC 27360
(919)475-6453
Ultimate Parent: Mobil. **SIC:** 5411—Grocery Stores.

★ 76381 ★　Pizza Hut
920 Randolph St.
Thomasville, NC 27360
(919)476-2169
Ultimate Parent: Pepsico. **SIC:** 5812—Eating Places.

★ 76382 ★　Prelude Co.
105 Trinity Extension
Thomasville, NC 27360
Ultimate Parent: Cone Mills. **SIC:** 3086—Plastics Foam Products.

★ 76383 ★　Rite Aid Discoutn Pharmacie
108 E. Main St.
Thomasville, NC 27360
(919)472-7413
Ultimate Parent: Rite Aid. **SIC:** 5049—Professional Equipment Nec.

★ 76384 ★　Rite Aid Discoutn Pharmacie
600 Randolph St.
Thomasville, NC 27360
(919)476-6188
Ultimate Parent: Rite Aid. **SIC:** 5912—Drug Stores & Proprietary Stores.

★ 76385 ★　Thomas Mfg. Co. Inc.
1024 Randolph St.
Thomasville, NC 27360
Ultimate Parent: Masco. **SIC:** 3471—Plating & Polishing.

★ 76386 ★　Thomasville Forest Prods.
Rte. 2 Box 1027-B
Thomasville, NC 27360
Ultimate Parent: Lowe's. **SIC:** 2491—Wood Preserving.

★ 76387 ★　Thomasville Forest Products
Clarksbury Church Rd.
Thomasville, NC 27360
Ultimate Parent: Lowe's. **SIC:** 2491—Wood Preserving.

★ 76388 ★　Thomasville Furniture Ind. Inc.
E. Guilford & Memorial Park
Thomasville, NC 27360
Ultimate Parent: Armstrong World Industries. **SIC:** 2511—Wood Household Furniture.

★ 76389 ★　Thomasville Furniture Ind. Inc.
Plant A
W. Main & Hoover Sts.
Thomasville, NC 27360
Location Type: Plant. **Ultimate Parent:** Armstrong World Industries. **SIC:** 2511—Wood Household Furniture.

★ 76390 ★　Thomasville Furniture Ind. Inc.
Plant B
Carmalt & Fisher Ferry Sts.
Thomasville, NC 27360
Location Type: Plant. **Ultimate Parent:** Armstrong World Industries. **SIC:** 2511—Wood Household Furniture.

★ 76391 ★　Thomasville Furniture Ind. Inc.
Plant C
405 E. Main St.
Thomasville, NC 27360
Location Type: Plant. **Ultimate Parent:** Armstrong World Industries. **SIC:** 2511—Wood Household Furniture.

★ 76392 ★　Thomasville Furniture Ind. Inc.
Plant D
E. Main & Trinity Sts.
Thomasville, NC 27360
Location Type: Plant. **Ultimate Parent:** Armstrong World Industries. **SIC:** 2511—Wood Household Furniture.

★ 76393 ★　Thomasville Furniture Industries Inc.
E. Guilford & Memorial Park
Thomasville, NC 27360
Ultimate Parent: Armstrong World Industries. **SIC:** 2511—Wood Household Furniture.

★ 76394 ★　Thomasville Furniture Industries Inc.
401 E. Main St.
Thomasville, NC 27360
Ultimate Parent: Armstrong World Industries. **SIC:** 2511—Wood Household Furniture.

★ 76395 ★　Thomasville Furniture Industries Inc.
W. Main & Hoover St.
Thomasville, NC 27360
Ultimate Parent: Armstrong World Industries. **SIC:** 2511—Wood Household Furniture.

★ 76396 ★　Thomasville Furniture Industries, Inc.
PO Box 339
Thomasville, NC 27361
(919)472-4000 **Fax:** (919)472-4093
Company Type: Subsidiary. **Officer:** Frederick B. Starr, President. **Ultimate Parent:** Armstrong World Industries.

★ 76397 ★　Thomasville Furniture Industries, Inc.
Plant A
W. Main & Hoover Sts.
Thomasville, NC 27360
Location Type: Plant. **Ultimate Parent:** Armstrong World Industries. **SIC:** 2511—Wood Household Furniture.

★ 76398 ★　Thomasville Furniture Industries, Inc.
Plant B
Carmalt & Fisher Ferry St.
Thomasville, NC 27360
Location Type: Plant. **Ultimate Parent:** Armstrong World Industries. **SIC:** 2511—Wood Household Furniture.

★ 76399 ★　Thomasville Furniture Industries Inc.
Plant C
401 E. Main St.
Thomasville, NC 27360
Location Type: Plant. **Ultimate Parent:** Armstrong World Industries. **SIC:** 2511—Wood Household Furniture.

★ 76400 ★　Thomasville Furniture Industries Inc.
Plant D
E. Main & Trinity Sts
Thomasville, NC 27360
Location Type: Plant. **Ultimate Parent:** Armstrong World Industries. **SIC:** 2511—Wood Household Furniture.

★ 76401 ★　Thomasville Furniture Industries Inc.
Plant E
E. Guilford & Memorial Park
Thomasville, NC 27360
Location Type: Plant. **Ultimate Parent:** Armstrong World Industries. **SIC:** 2511—Wood Household Furniture.

★ 76402 ★　Thomasville Furniture Industries Inc.
Plant L
E. Guilford & Memorial Park
Thomasville, NC 27360
Location Type: Plant. **Ultimate Parent:** Armstrong World Industries. **SIC:** 2511—Wood Household Furniture.

★ 76403 ★　Wachovia Bank & Trust Co.
668 PO Box
Thomasville, NC 27361
Ultimate Parent: Wachovia Corp. **SIC:** 6099—Functions Related to Deposit Banking.

Trent Woods

★ 76404 ★ Moen Inc.
101 INDL Dr.
Trent Woods, NC 28562
(919)638-3300
Officer: Richard Kosco. Ultimate Parent:
American Brands Inc. SIC: 3432—Plumbing
Fixtures Fittings & Trim; 5074—Plumbing &
Hydronic Heating Supplies.

Trenton

★ 76405 ★ Branch Banking &
Trust Co.
127 W. Jones St.
Trenton, NC 28585
(919)448-2201
Company Type: Subsidiary. Location
Type: Branch office. Officer: Polly Mason,
Mgr. Ultimate Parent: Southern National
Corp. SIC: 6021—National Commercial
Banks.

Trinity

★ 76406 ★ Conitron
Rte. 2 Glenola Ave.
Trinity, NC 27370
Ultimate Parent: Cone Mills. SIC: 3089—
Plastics Products Nec.

★ 76407 ★ Conitron Chemical
Chair
Rte. 2 Glenola Ave.
Trinity, NC 27370
Ultimate Parent: Cone Mills.

Troutman

★ 76408 ★ Engineered Sintered
Components Co.
250 Old Murdock Rd.
Troutman, NC 28166
(704)528-7500 Fax: (704)528-7529
Company Type: Joint venture. Ultimate
Parent: Eaton Corp. SIC: 3714—Motor
Vehicle Parts & Accessories; 3399—Primary
Metal Products Nec.

★ 76409 ★ Thomasville
Upholstery, Inc.
Old Murdock Rd.
Troutman, NC 28166
(704)528-6630
Officer: Willie Cockrell, Manager. Ultimate
Parent: Armstrong World Industries. SIC:
2426—Hardwood Dimension & Flooring
Mills; 2512—Upholstered Household
Furniture.

Troy

★ 76410 ★ First Bank
Montgomery Sq.
Troy, NC 27371
(919)576-6171
Ultimate Parent: Shawmut National Corp.
SIC: 6022—State Commercial Banks.

Tryon

★ 76411 ★ First-Citizens Bank &
Trust Co.
600 S. Trade St.
Tryon, NC 28782-3716
(704)859-9137
Location Type: Branch office. Ultimate
Parent: First Citizens Bancshares, Inc. SIC:
6021—National Commercial Banks.

Valdese

★ 76412 ★ Duracell International
Inc.
Lovelady Ln.
Valdese, NC 28690
(704)874-4111
Ultimate Parent: Duracell International Inc.
SIC: 5063—Electrical Apparatus &
Equipment.

★ 76413 ★ Rite Aid Discount
Pharmacie
Heritage Plz.
Valdese, NC 28690
(704)874-3540
Ultimate Parent: Rite Aid. SIC: 5912—Drug
Stores & Proprietary Stores.

★ 76414 ★ Western Carolina
Savings
224 Main St. E
Valdese, NC 28690
(704)874-2141
Ultimate Parent: Southern National Corp.
SIC: 6036—Savings Institutions Except
Federal; 6141—Personal Credit Institutions.

Vanceboro

★ 76415 ★ Wachovia Bank &
Trust Co. N
Main
Vanceboro, NC 28586
(919)244-0717
Ultimate Parent: Wachovia Corp. SIC:
6022—State Commercial Banks.

★ 76416 ★ Weyerhaeuser Paper
Co.
1785 Weyerhaeuser Rd.
Vanceboro, NC 28560
Ultimate Parent: Weyerhaeuser Co. SIC:
2611—Pulp Mills.

Vass

★ 76417 ★ Branch Banking &
Trust Co.
Bank St.
Vass, NC 28394
(910)245-4011
Company Type: Subsidiary. Location
Type: Branch office. Officer: Robert
Brooks, Mgr. Ultimate Parent: Southern
National Corp. SIC: 6021—National
Commercial Banks.

W Jefferson

★ 76418 ★ Kentucky Fried
Chicken
W Jefferson, NC 28694
(919)246-8871
Ultimate Parent: Pepsico. SIC: 5812—
Eating Places.

★ 76419 ★ Peoples Drug Store
Jefferson Ave.
W Jefferson, NC 28694
(919)246-9990
Ultimate Parent: Melville. SIC: 5049—
Professional Equipment Nec.

★ 76420 ★ Ryder Truck Rental
Hwy. 221
W Jefferson, NC 28694
(919)246-5407
Ultimate Parent: Ryder System. SIC:
7513—Truck Rental & Leasing Without
Drivers.

★ 76421 ★ West Jefferson Wood
Product
Locust
W Jefferson, NC 28694
(919)246-7121
Ultimate Parent: Kimball International Inc.
SIC: 2426—Hardwood Dimension &
Flooring Mills.

Wadesboro

★ 76422 ★ Branch Banking &
Trust Co.
725 E. Caswell St.
Wadesboro, NC 28170-2303
(704)694-4814
Company Type: Subsidiary. Location
Type: Branch office. Ultimate Parent:
Southern National Corp. SIC: 6021—
National Commercial Banks.

★ 76423 ★ Branch Banking &
Trust Co.
119 W. Wade St.
Wadesboro, NC 28170-2136
(704)694-6521
Company Type: Subsidiary. Location
Type: Branch office. Officer: James A.
Hardison, Manager. Ultimate Parent:
Southern National Corp. SIC: 6021—
National Commercial Banks.

★ 76424 ★ Carolina Power &
Light Co.
307 N. Green St.
Wadesboro, NC 28170
(704)694-4196
Ultimate Parent: Carolina Power & Light
Co. SIC: 4911—Electric Services.

★ 76425 ★ Carolina Power &
Light Co.
307 N. Green St.
Wadesboro, NC 28170
(704)694-4196
Ultimate Parent: Carolina Power & Light
Co. SIC: 4911—Electric Services.

★ 76426 ★ Pizza Hut
1118 Us 74 E
Wadesboro, NC 28170
(704)694-9472
Ultimate Parent: Pepsico. SIC: 5812—
Eating Places.

★ 76427 ★ Trailways Bus
Terminal Inc.
214 N. Rutherford St.
Wadesboro, NC 28170
(704)694-2315
Ultimate Parent: Greyhound Lines Inc. SIC:
4142—Bus Charter Service Except Local;
4173—Bus Terminal & Service Facilities.

Wagram

★ 76428 ★ J. P. Stevens & Co.
Bob Stevens Plant
Air Base Rd.
Wagram, NC 28396
Ultimate Parent: West Point Stevens. SIC:
2299—Textile Goods Nec.

★ 76429 ★ West Point Pepperell
Bob Stevens Facility
Air Base Rd.
Wagram, NC 28396
Ultimate Parent: West Point Stevens. SIC:
2299—Textile Goods Nec.

Wake Forest

★ 76430 ★ Burlington Industries
Inc.
9701 Capitol Blvd.
Wake Forest, NC 27587
(919)556-3161
Officer: Sandy Thompson, Plant Manager.
Ultimate Parent: Burlington Industries,
Equity. SIC: 2257—Weft Knit Fabric Mills;
2262—Finishing Plants—Manmade; 2399—
Fabricated Textile Products Nec.

★ 76431 ★ Pizza Hut
4610 North Blvd.
Wake Forest, NC 27587
(919)872-2094
Ultimate Parent: Pepsico. SIC: 5812—
Eating Places.

★ 76432 ★ Radio Shack
4554 North Blvd.
Wake Forest, NC 27587
(919)876-8775
Company Type: Division. Ultimate Parent:
Tandy Corp. SIC: 5731—Radio, Television
& Electronics Stores.

★ 76433 ★ Schrader Bellows
12415 Capital Blvd.
Wake Forest, NC 27587
Ultimate Parent: Parker Hannifin. SIC:
3494—Valves & Pipe Fittings Nec.

★ 76434 ★ Schrader-Bellows
US 1 N.
Wake Forest, NC 27587
Ultimate Parent: Parker Hannifin. SIC:
3494—Valves & Pipe Fittings Nec.

★ 76435 ★ Taco Bell
4506 North Blvd.
Wake Forest, NC 27587
(919)872-6269
Ultimate Parent: Pepsico. SIC: 5812—
Eating Places.

Wallace

★ 76436 ★ Armour Swift-Eckrich
1170 Butterball Rd.
PO Box 819
Wallace, NC 28466
(919)285-5752
Company Type: Division. Location Type:
Plant. Officer: Tim Scanlan, Plant Manager.
Ultimate Parent: Conagra.

★ 76437 ★ Branch Banking &
Trust Co.
220 E. Main St.
Wallace, NC 28466
(919)285-3131
Ultimate Parent: Southern National Corp.
SIC: 6022—State Commercial Banks.

★ 76438 ★ Branch Banking &
Trust Co.
Hwy. 117
N. Rockfish Plz.
Wallace, NC 28466-9519
(910)285-7507
Company Type: Subsidiary. Location
Type: Branch office. Ultimate Parent:
Southern National Corp. SIC: 6021—
National Commercial Banks.

★ 76439 ★ Branch Banking &
Trust Co.
N. Norwood St.
Wallace, NC 28466
(910)285-3131
Company Type: Subsidiary. Location
Type: Branch office. Ultimate Parent:
Southern National Corp. SIC: 6021—
National Commercial Banks.

★ 76440 ★ Greyhound Bus Lines
310 N. Norwood St.
Wallace, NC 28466
(919)285-2380
Ultimate Parent: Greyhound Lines Inc. SIC:
4131—Intercity & Rural Bus Transportation.

★ 76441 ★ McDonalds of Wallace
111 S. Norwood St.
Wallace, NC 28466
(919)285-5064
Ultimate Parent: May Department Stores.
SIC: 5812—Eating Places.

★ 76442 ★ Piggly Wiggly
213 N. Norwood St.
Wallace, NC 28466
(919)285-7504
Ultimate Parent: Bruno's. SIC: 5411—
Grocery Stores.

★ 76443 ★ Piggly Wiggly
123 NE Railroad St.
Wallace, NC 28466
(919)285-3910
Ultimate Parent: Bruno's. SIC: 5411—
Grocery Stores.

★ 76444 ★ Stevcoknit Fabrics
Co.
601 S. Wilmington Rd.
Wallace, NC 28466
(910)285-3111
Officer: Dennis Durham, Vice President.
Ultimate Parent: Delta Woodside
Industries. SIC: 2299—Textile Goods Nec;
2399—Fabricated Textile Products Nec.

★ 76445 ★ Stevcoknit Fabrics
Co. Carter Plant
601 Old Wilmington Rd.
Wallace, NC 28466
Location Type: Plant. Ultimate Parent:
Delta Woodside Industries. SIC: 2257—Weft
Knit Fabric Mills; 2258—Lace & Warp Knit
Fabric Mills.

Walnut Cove

★ 76446 ★ First-Citizens Bank &
Trust Co.
424 N. Main St.
Walnut Cove, NC 27502
(910)591-7127
Location Type: Branch office. Officer: Rick
C. Fry, Vice President. Ultimate Parent:
First Citizens Bancshares, Inc. SIC: 6021—
National Commercial Banks.

Warrenton

★ 76447 ★ Branch Banking &
Trust Co.
122 S. Main St.
Warrenton, NC 27589
(919)257-3267
Ultimate Parent: Southern National Corp.
SIC: 6022—State Commercial Banks.

★ 76448 ★ **First-Citizens Bank & Trust Co.**
205 N. Main St.
Warrenton, NC 27589-1823
(919)257-2421
Location Type: Branch office. **Ultimate Parent:** First Citizens Bancshares, Inc. **SIC:** 6021—National Commercial Banks.

★ 76449 ★ **Rite Aid Discount Pharmacie**
Pharmacy Hall Shopping Ctr.
Warrenton, NC 27589
(919)257-2922
Ultimate Parent: Rite Aid. **SIC:** 5912—Drug Stores & Proprietary Stores.

Warsaw

★ 76450 ★ **Branch Banking & Trust Co.**
117 E. Hill St.
Warsaw, NC 28398-1917
(910)293-7156
Company Type: Subsidiary. **Location Type:** Branch office. **Officer:** James A. Jackson, Mgr. **Ultimate Parent:** Southern National Corp. **SIC:** 6021—National Commercial Banks.

★ 76451 ★ **Greyhound Bus Lines**
105 W. Dudley St.
Warsaw, NC 28398
(919)293-4313
Ultimate Parent: Greyhound Lines Inc. **SIC:** 4131—Intercity & Rural Bus Transportation.

Washington

★ 76452 ★ **Bonny Products Inc.**
350 Page Rd.
Washington, NC 27889-8753
(919)975-6669
Location Type: Branch office. **Officer:** Bob Furer. **Ultimate Parent:** American Brands Inc. **SIC:** 3469—Metal Stampings Nec; 3089—Plastics Products Nec.

★ 76453 ★ **Bonny Products, Inc.**
350 Page Rd.
Washington, NC 27889
(919)975-6669
Company Type: Subsidiary. **Ultimate Parent:** American Brands Inc. **SIC:** 3469—Metal Stampings Nec.

★ 76454 ★ **Coca Cola Bottling Co. Inc.**
905 W. 5th St.
Washington, NC 27889
(919)946-6106
Ultimate Parent: Coca-Cola Enterprises. **SIC:** 5149—Groceries & Related Products Nec.

★ 76455 ★ **First-Citizens Bank & Trust Co.**
Pitt St.
Washington, NC 27837
(919)752-3938
Location Type: Branch office. **Ultimate Parent:** First Citizens Bancshares, Inc. **SIC:** 6021—National Commercial Banks.

★ 76456 ★ **First-Citizens Bank & Trust Co.**
1411 Carolina Ave.
Washington, NC 27889-3313
(919)946-8144
Location Type: Branch office. **Officer:** Charles W. Allgood, Vice President. **Ultimate Parent:** First Citizens Bancshares, Inc. **SIC:** 6021—National Commercial Banks.

★ 76457 ★ **Kentucky Fried Chicken**
Hwy. 17 N
Washington, NC 27889
(919)946-1250
Ultimate Parent: Pepsico. **SIC:** 5812—Eating Places.

★ 76458 ★ **Pepsi-Cola Distributing Co.**
1849 Carolina Ave.
Washington, NC 27889
(919)946-2837
Officer: Jerry Boyd, Manager. **Ultimate Parent:** Pepsico. **SIC:** 2086—Bottled & Canned Soft Drinks.

★ 76459 ★ **Radio Shack**
829 Washington Sq.
Washington, NC 27889
(919)946-2312
Company Type: Division. **Ultimate Parent:** Tandy Corp. **SIC:** 5731—Radio, Television & Electronics Stores.

★ 76460 ★ **Rite Aide Discount Pharmacy**
Washington Shopping Ctr.
Washington, NC 27889
(919)946-1818
Ultimate Parent: Rite Aid. **SIC:** 5912—Drug Stores & Proprietary Stores.

★ 76461 ★ **Ryder Truck Rental**
Hwy. 264 E
Washington, NC 27889
(919)946-8971
Ultimate Parent: Ryder System. **SIC:** 7359—Equipment Rental & Leasing Nec; 7359—Equipment Rental & Leasing Nec.

★ 76462 ★ **Wachovia Bank & Trust Co. N**
Washington Sq.
Washington, NC 27889
(919)946-7121
Ultimate Parent: Wachovia Corp. **SIC:** 6141—Personal Credit Institutions.

Waynesville

★ 76463 ★ **Dayco Prods. Inc.**
1300 Balsam Rd.
Waynesville, NC 28786
Ultimate Parent: Mark IV Industries. **SIC:** 3052—Rubber & Plastics Hose & Belting.

★ 76464 ★ **Dayco Products Inc.**
1300 Balsam Rd.
Waynesville, NC 28786
Ultimate Parent: Mark IV Industries. **SIC:** 3052—Rubber & Plastics Hose & Belting.

★ 76465 ★ **Exxon Gas N Groceries**
1400 Balsam Rd.
Waynesville, NC 28786
(704)452-4195
Ultimate Parent: Exxon. **SIC:** 5541—Gasoline Service Stations.

★ 76466 ★ **First-Citizens Bank & Trust Co.**
627 Soco Rd.
Waynesville, NC 28751
(704)452-6300
Location Type: Branch office. **Ultimate Parent:** First Citizens Bancshares, Inc. **SIC:** 6021—National Commercial Banks.

★ 76467 ★ **First-Citizens Bank & Trust Co.**
8 Main St.
Waynesville, NC 28721-9546
(704)452-6300
Location Type: Branch office. **Ultimate Parent:** First Citizens Bancshares, Inc. **SIC:** 6021—National Commercial Banks.

★ 76468 ★ **First-Citizens Bank & Trust Co.**
101 W. Main St.
Waynesville, NC 28738-2094
(704)452-0336
Location Type: Branch office. **Ultimate Parent:** First Citizens Bancshares, Inc. **SIC:** 6021—National Commercial Banks.

★ 76469 ★ **First-Citizens Bank & Trust Co.**
301 Walnut St.
Waynesville, NC 28786-3275
(704)452-0370
Location Type: Branch office. **Officer:** C. Thomas Doughton, Area Vice President. **Ultimate Parent:** First Citizens Bancshares, Inc. **SIC:** 6021—National Commercial Banks.

★ 76470 ★ **Kentucky Fried Chicken**
Russ Ave.
Waynesville, NC 28786
(704)456-6626
Ultimate Parent: Pepsico.

★ 76471 ★ **Pizza Hut**
905 Russ Ave.
Waynesville, NC 28786
(704)452-5547
Ultimate Parent: Pepsico. **SIC:** 5812—Eating Places.

★ 76472 ★ **Radio Shack**
734 Waynesville Plz.
Waynesville, NC 28786
(704)456-6082
Company Type: Division. **Ultimate Parent:** Tandy Corp. **SIC:** 5065—Electronic Parts & Equipment Nec.

★ 76473 ★ **Trailways Bus System**
118 Miller St.
Waynesville, NC 28786
(704)456-9514
Ultimate Parent: Greyhound Lines Inc. **SIC:** 4131—Intercity & Rural Bus Transportation.

★ 76474 ★ **Wachovia Bank & Trust Co. N**
260 S. Main St.
Waynesville, NC 28786
(704)452-5175
Ultimate Parent: Wachovia Corp. **SIC:** 6141—Personal Credit Institutions.

Weaverville

★ 76475 ★ **Pizza Hut**
Woodland Hill
Weaverville, NC 28787
(704)645-5005
Ultimate Parent: Pepsico. **SIC:** 5812—Eating Places.

★ 76476 ★ **Reliance Electric Co.**
70 Reems Creek Rd.
Weaverville, NC 28787
(704)645-4235
Officer: Jim V. Chlopek, Manager. **Ultimate Parent:** Reliance Electric. **SIC:** 3366—Copper Foundries; 3568—Power Transmission Equipment Nec; 3699—Electrical Equipment & Supplies Nec.

★ 76477 ★ **Reliance Electric Co. Mechanical Drives Plant**
70 Reems Creek Rd.
Weaverville, NC 28787
Ultimate Parent: Reliance Electric. **SIC:** 3568—Power Transmission Equipment Nec.

★ 76478 ★ **Reliance Electric Mechanical Drives Plant**
Reems Creek Rd.
PO Box 635
Weaverville, NC 28787
Location Type: Plant. **Ultimate Parent:** Reliance Electric. **SIC:** 3568—Power Transmission Equipment Nec.

Weldon

★ 76479 ★ **Branch Banking & Trust Co.**
301 Washington Ave.
Weldon, NC 27890
(919)536-3178
Ultimate Parent: Southern National Corp. **SIC:** 6022—State Commercial Banks.

★ 76480 ★ **First-Citizens Bank & Trust Co.**
11 E. Third St.
Weldon, NC 27890-1510
(919)536-4131
Location Type: Branch office. **Ultimate Parent:** First Citizens Bancshares, Inc. **SIC:** 6021—National Commercial Banks.

★ 76481 ★ **First-Citizens Bank & Trust Co.**
312 Washington Ave.
Weldon, NC 27890-1550
(919)536-2111
Location Type: Branch office. **Officer:** Jim Williams, Assistant Vice President. **Ultimate Parent:** First Citizens Bancshares, Inc. **SIC:** 6021—National Commercial Banks.

Wesleyan Col

★ 76482 ★ **Texaco Service Station**
1321 Westmoreland Dr.
Wesleyan Col, NC 27804
(919)446-4342
Ultimate Parent: Texaco. **SIC:** 5541—

Gasoline Service Stations; 7538—General Automotive Repair Shops.

Wesleyan College

★ 76483 ★ **Coca-Cola Bottling Co.**
442 Church St.
Wesleyan College, NC 27804
(919)446-4117
Ultimate Parent: Coca-Cola Enterprises. **SIC:** 5099—Durable Goods Nec.

West End

★ 76484 ★ **Branch Banking & Trust Co.**
Hwy. Alt 73
West End, NC 27376
(910)673-4131
Company Type: Subsidiary. **Location Type:** Branch office. **Officer:** Robert H. Dawkins, Mgr. **Ultimate Parent:** Southern National Corp. **SIC:** 6021—National Commercial Banks.

West Jefferson

★ 76485 ★ **Dr. Pepper Bottling Co.**
159 N. 3rd Ave.
West Jefferson, NC 28694
(910)426-4591
Officer: R. K. Vannoy, President. **Ultimate Parent:** Dr. Pepper/Seven-Up. **SIC:** 2086—Bottled & Canned Soft Drinks.

★ 76486 ★ **First-Citizens Bank & Trust Co.**
Hwy. 221
West Jefferson, NC 28694-9763
(910)246-2571
Location Type: Branch office. **Ultimate Parent:** First Citizens Bancshares, Inc. **SIC:** 6021—National Commercial Banks.

★ 76487 ★ **First-Citizens Bank & Trust Co.**
Jefferson Ave. & Main St.
West Jefferson, NC 28694
(910)246-2571
Location Type: Branch office. **Officer:** Richard C. Miller, Vice President. **Ultimate Parent:** First Citizens Bancshares, Inc. **SIC:** 6021—National Commercial Banks.

★ 76488 ★ **McDonalds**
Hwy. 221 Ashemont Shopping Ctr.
West Jefferson, NC 28694
(919)246-3061
Ultimate Parent: McDonald's. **SIC:** 5812—Eating Places.

★ 76489 ★ **Thomasville Furniture Ind. Inc.**
Hice Ave.
West Jefferson, NC 28694
Ultimate Parent: Armstrong World Industries. **SIC:** 2511—Wood Household Furniture.

Whitakers

★ 76490 ★ **Consolidated Diesel Co.**
U.S. Hwy. 301 S.
Whitakers, NC 27891
Ultimate Parent: Cummins Engine Co. **SIC:** 3519—Internal Combustion Engines Nec.

★ 76491 ★ **Consolidated Diesel Co.**
PO Box 670
Whitakers, NC 27891
Ultimate Parent: Cummins Engine Co. **SIC:** 3519—Internal Combustion Engines Nec.

Whiteville

★ 76492 ★ **Branch Banking & Trust Co.**
612 N. Madison St.
Whiteville, NC 28472-3310
(910)642-7021
Company Type: Subsidiary. **Location Type:** Branch office. **Ultimate Parent:** Southern National Corp. **SIC:** 6021—National Commercial Banks.

★ 76493 ★   **Branch Banking & Trust Co.**
1329 S. Madison St.
Whiteville, NC 28472-4521
(910)642-7021
Company Type: Subsidiary. **Location Type:** Branch office. **Ultimate Parent:** Southern National Corp. **SIC:** 6021—National Commercial Banks.

★ 76494 ★   **Branch Banking & Trust Co.**
700 S. Madison St.
Whiteville, NC 28472-4612
(910)642-7021
Company Type: Subsidiary. **Location Type:** Branch office. **Officer:** Alfred J. Hackney Jr., Manager. **Ultimate Parent:** Southern National Corp. **SIC:** 6021—National Commercial Banks.

★ 76495 ★   **Carolina Power & Light Co.**
1206 S. Madison St.
Whiteville, NC 28472
(919)642-3175
Ultimate Parent: Carolina Power & Light Co. **SIC:** 4911—Electric Services.

★ 76496 ★   **Carolina Power & Light Co.**
106 Washington St.
Whiteville, NC 28472
(919)642-0524
Ultimate Parent: Carolina Power & Light Co. **SIC:** 4911—Electric Services.

★ 76497 ★   **Carolina Power & Light Co.**
1206 S. Madison St.
Whiteville, NC 28472
(919)642-3175
Ultimate Parent: Carolina Power & Light Co. **SIC:** 4911—Electric Services.

★ 76498 ★   **Carolina Power & Light Co.**
106 Washington St.
Whiteville, NC 28472
(919)642-0524
Ultimate Parent: Carolina Power & Light Co. **SIC:** 4911—Electric Services.

★ 76499 ★   **First-Citizens Bank & Trust Co.**
415 S. Madison St.
Whiteville, NC 28472-4125
(910)642-7744
Location Type: Branch office. **Ultimate Parent:** First Citizens Bancshares, Inc. **SIC:** 6021—National Commercial Banks.

★ 76500 ★   **Food Lion**
1421 Tabor City Rd.
Whiteville, NC 28472
(919)642-0332
Ultimate Parent: Food Lion. **SIC:** 5411—Grocery Stores.

★ 76501 ★   **Georgia-Pacific Corp. Whiteville Plywood**
Secondary Rd. 1436
Whiteville, NC 28472
Ultimate Parent: Georgia-Pacific. **SIC:** 2436—Softwood Veneer & Plywood.

★ 76502 ★   **Kentucky Fried Chicken**
705 N. Powell Blvd.
Whiteville, NC 28472
(919)642-3054
Ultimate Parent: Pepsico. **SIC:** 5812—Eating Places.

★ 76503 ★   **Pizza Hut**
Whiteville Plz.
Whiteville, NC 28472
(919)642-6996
Ultimate Parent: Pepsico. **SIC:** 5812—Eating Places.

★ 76504 ★   **Ryder Truck Rental**
Rural Route 5
Whiteville, NC 28472
(919)642-8823
Ultimate Parent: Ryder System. **SIC:** 7513—Truck Rental & Leasing Without Drivers.

Wilkesboro

★ 76505 ★   **Branch Banking & Trust Co.**
900 River St.
Wilkesboro, NC 28697-2724
(910)667-4060
Company Type: Subsidiary. **Location Type:** Branch office. **Officer:** Stephen Parker, Manager. **Ultimate Parent:** Southern National Corp. **SIC:** 6021—National Commercial Banks.

★ 76506 ★   **First-Citizens Bank & Trust Co.**
203 W. Main St.
Wilkesboro, NC 28697-2424
(910)667-4106
Location Type: Branch office. **Ultimate Parent:** First Citizens Bancshares, Inc. **SIC:** 6021—National Commercial Banks.

★ 76507 ★   **Holly Farms Food Service Inc.**
Highland St. PO Box 88
Wilkesboro, NC 28697
Ultimate Parent: Tyson Foods, Inc. **SIC:** 0251—Broiler, Fryer & Roaster Chickens.

★ 76508 ★   **Holly Farms Foods Inc.**
River St. NC-268 W
Wilkesboro, NC 28697
Ultimate Parent: Tyson Foods, Inc. **SIC:** 2010—Meat Products.

★ 76509 ★   **Holly Farms Foods Inc.**
River Street, NC-268 W.
PO Box 88
Wilkesboro, NC 28697
Ultimate Parent: Tyson Foods, Inc. **SIC:** 0251—Broiler, Fryer & Roaster Chickens.

★ 76510 ★   **Holly Farms Foods Inc. Cooked Products Plant**
901 Wilkes St. PO Box 88
Wilkesboro, NC 28697
Ultimate Parent: Tyson Foods, Inc. **SIC:** 2015—Poultry Slaughtering & Processing.

★ 76511 ★   **Holly Farms Foods Inc. Tyson Foods Pretreatment Plant**
103 Factory St.
Wilkesboro, NC 28697
Ultimate Parent: Tyson Foods, Inc. **SIC:** 2015—Poultry Slaughtering & Processing.

★ 76512 ★   **Holly Farms/Tyson Foods Inc. Pre-Treatment Plant**
103 Factory St. PO Box 88
Wilkesboro, NC 28697
Ultimate Parent: Tyson Foods, Inc. **SIC:** 2015—Poultry Slaughtering & Processing.

★ 76513 ★   **Holly Farms/Tyson Foods Inc. Processing Plant**
103 Factory St. PO Box 88
Wilkesboro, NC 28697
Ultimate Parent: Tyson Foods, Inc. **SIC:** 2015—Poultry Slaughtering & Processing.

★ 76514 ★   **Holly Farms/Tyson Foods Inc. Tyson Foods Pretreatment Plant**
103 Factory St.
Wilkesboro, NC 28697
Ultimate Parent: Tyson Foods, Inc. **SIC:** 2015—Poultry Slaughtering & Processing.

★ 76515 ★   **Holly Farms/Tyson Foods Inc. Waste Water Treatment**
Hwy. NC-115 & Snyder St. PO Box 88
Wilkesboro, NC 28697
Ultimate Parent: Tyson Foods, Inc. **SIC:** 2015—Poultry Slaughtering & Processing.

★ 76516 ★   **IBM Corp.**
203 W. Main St.
Wilkesboro, NC 28697
(919)838-5863
Ultimate Parent: IBM. **SIC:** 5044—Office Equipment; 5734—Computer & Software Stores.

★ 76517 ★   **Pizza Hut**
1204 School St.
Wilkesboro, NC 28697
(919)667-2023
Ultimate Parent: Pepsico. **SIC:** 5812—Eating Places.

★ 76518 ★   **Ryder Truck Rental**
1200 River St.
Wilkesboro, NC 28697
(919)667-4218
Ultimate Parent: Ryder System. **SIC:** 7359—Equipment Rental & Leasing Nec.

★ 76519 ★   **Thom Mcan Manufacturing**
Spring St. & River Rd.
Wilkesboro, NC 28697-0440
Ultimate Parent: Melville. **SIC:** 3143—Men's Footwear Except Athletic.

★ 76520 ★   **Thom Mcan Mfg. Inc.**
Spring St. & River Rd.
Wilkesboro, NC 28697-0000
Ultimate Parent: Melville. **SIC:** 3143—Men's Footwear Except Athletic; 3144—Women's Footwear Except Athletic.

★ 76521 ★   **Tyson Food Service**
108 Highland St. PO Box 88
Wilkesboro, NC 28697-0088
Ultimate Parent: Tyson Foods, Inc. **SIC:** 2015—Poultry Slaughtering & Processing.

★ 76522 ★   **Tyson Foods Inc.**
Highland St. PO Box 88
Wilkesboro, NC 28697
Ultimate Parent: Tyson Foods, Inc. **SIC:** 2015—Poultry Slaughtering & Processing.

★ 76523 ★   **Tyson Foods Inc.**
Cooked Products Div.
901 Wilkes St. PO Box 88
Wilkesboro, NC 28697
Company Type: Division. **Ultimate Parent:** Tyson Foods, Inc. **SIC:** 2015—Poultry Slaughtering & Processing.

★ 76524 ★   **Waldenbooks**
Wilkes
Wilkesboro, NC 28697
(919)838-7224
Ultimate Parent: K-Mart. **SIC:** 5199—Nondurable Goods Nec.

Williamston

★ 76525 ★   **Branch Banking & Trust Co.**
908 Washington St.
Williamston, NC 27892-2652
(919)729-2175
Company Type: Subsidiary. **Location Type:** Branch office. **Ultimate Parent:** Southern National Corp. **SIC:** 6021—National Commercial Banks.

★ 76526 ★   **Branch Banking & Trust Co.**
138 W. Main St.
Williamston, NC 27892-2472
(919)792-2175
Company Type: Subsidiary. **Location Type:** Branch office. **Officer:** Thomas M. Neville, Mgr. **Ultimate Parent:** Southern National Corp. **SIC:** 6021—National Commercial Banks.

★ 76527 ★   **Branch Banking & Trust Co.**
918 Washington St.
Williamston, NC 27892
(919)792-2175
Ultimate Parent: Southern National Corp. **SIC:** 6022—State Commercial Banks.

★ 76528 ★   **First-Citizens Bank & Trust Co.**
315 W. Main St.
Williamston, NC 27892-2317
(919)792-4154
Location Type: Branch office. **Ultimate Parent:** First Citizens Bancshares, Inc. **SIC:** 6021—National Commercial Banks.

★ 76529 ★   **First-Citizens Bank & Trust Co.**
401 W. Main St.
Williamston, NC 27892-2319
(919)792-7046
Location Type: Branch office. **Officer:** F. E. Oglesby, Vice President. **Ultimate Parent:** First Citizens Bancshares, Inc. **SIC:** 6021—National Commercial Banks.

★ 76530 ★   **Massachusetts Mutual Life Insurance**
101 Country Club Dr.
Williamston, NC 27892
(919)792-1436
Ultimate Parent: Massasucetts Mutual Life.

SIC: 6411—Insurance Agents, Brokers & Service.

★ 76531 ★   **Peoples Drug Store**
415 East Blvd.
Williamston, NC 27892
(919)792-1150
Ultimate Parent: Melville. **SIC:** 5912—Drug Stores & Proprietary Stores.

★ 76532 ★   **Piggly Wiggly**
912 Washington St.
Williamston, NC 27892
(919)792-3403
Ultimate Parent: Bruno's. **SIC:** 5411—Grocery Stores.

★ 76533 ★   **Pizza Hut**
W Blvd.
Williamston, NC 27892
(919)792-1446
Ultimate Parent: Pepsico. **SIC:** 5812—Eating Places.

★ 76534 ★   **Pizza Hut**
200 West Blvd.
Williamston, NC 27892
(919)792-1036
Ultimate Parent: Pepsico. **SIC:** 5812—Eating Places.

★ 76535 ★   **Wachovia Bank & Trust Co.**
Hwy. 17 Bypass
Williamston, NC 27892
(919)792-1581
Ultimate Parent: Wachovia Corp. **SIC:** 6022—State Commercial Banks.

★ 76536 ★   **Wachovia Bank & Trust Co.**
207 W. Main St.
Williamston, NC 27892
(919)792-7061
Ultimate Parent: Wachovia Corp. **SIC:** 6022—State Commercial Banks.

Wilmington

★ 76537 ★   **Amerada Hess Corp.**
Martin St.
Wilmington, NC 28401
(919)763-5122
Ultimate Parent: Amerada Hess. **SIC:** 5172—Petroleum Products Nec.

★ 76538 ★   **Amerada Hess Corp.**
1312 S. Front St.
Wilmington, NC 28401
(919)763-5122
Ultimate Parent: Amerada Hess. **SIC:** 2911—Petroleum Refining.

★ 76539 ★   **Arcadian Corp.**
2830 Hwy. 421 N.
Wilmington, NC 28401
Ultimate Parent: Arcadian Corp. **SIC:** 2873—Nitrogenous Fertilizers.

★ 76540 ★   **Arcadian Corp.**
PO Box 630
Wilmington, NC 28402-0630
(919)343-3100
Ultimate Parent: Arcadian Corp. **SIC:** 2879—Agricultural Chemicals Nec.

★ 76541 ★   **Branch Banking & Trust Co.**
3417 Oleander Dr.
Wilmington, NC 28403-0810
(910)799-4351
Company Type: Subsidiary. **Location Type:** Branch office. **Ultimate Parent:** Southern National Corp. **SIC:** 6021—National Commercial Banks.

★ 76542 ★   **Branch Banking & Trust Co.**
301 S. College Rd.
Wilmington, NC 28403-1690
(910)791-8137
Company Type: Subsidiary. **Location Type:** Branch office. **Ultimate Parent:** Southern National Corp. **SIC:** 6021—National Commercial Banks.

★ 76543 ★　**Branch Banking & Trust Co.**
202 N. 3rd St.
Wilmington, NC 28401-4002
(910)341-3200
Company Type: Subsidiary. **Location Type:** Branch office. **Ultimate Parent:** Southern National Corp. **SIC:** 6021—National Commercial Banks.

★ 76544 ★　**Branch Banking & Trust Co.**
3212 Oleander Dr.
Wilmington, NC 28403-0800
(910)350-6715
Company Type: Subsidiary. **Location Type:** Branch office. **Ultimate Parent:** Southern National Corp. **SIC:** 6021—National Commercial Banks.

★ 76545 ★　**Branch Banking & Trust Co.**
680 S. College Rd.
Wilmington, NC 28403-3202
(910)392-6700
Company Type: Subsidiary. **Location Type:** Branch office. **Officer:** W. Lawrence Robertson, Manager. **Ultimate Parent:** Southern National Corp. **SIC:** 6021—National Commercial Banks.

★ 76546 ★　**Cape Ind.**
Hwy. 421 N. PO Box 327
Wilmington, NC 28402-0327
Ultimate Parent: Hoechst Celanese Corp. **SIC:** 2865—Cyclic Crudes & Intermediates.

★ 76547 ★　**Cape Industries**
Hwy. 421 North
Wilmington, NC 28402-0327
Ultimate Parent: Hoechst Celanese Corp. **SIC:** 2869—Industrial Organic Chemicals Nec.

★ 76548 ★　**Carolina Power & Light Co.**
5041 New Centre Dr.
Wilmington, NC 28403
(919)350-2200
Ultimate Parent: Carolina Power & Light Co. **SIC:** 4911—Electric Services.

★ 76549 ★　**Casual Corner**
3500 Oleander Dr.
Wilmington, NC 28403
(919)791-0512
Ultimate Parent: United States Shoe. **SIC:** 5651—Family Clothing Stores.

★ 76550 ★　**Corning Inc.**
310 N. College Rd.
Wilmington, NC 28405
Ultimate Parent: Corning. **SIC:** 3999—Manufacturing Industries Nec.

★ 76551 ★　**Emery Worldwide**
RR 6
Wilmington, NC 28405
(919)762-2828
Ultimate Parent: Consolidated Freightways. **SIC:** 4213—Trucking Except Local.

★ 76552 ★　**Emery Worldwide**
3926 Market St.
Wilmington, NC 28403
(919)763-2939
Ultimate Parent: Consolidated Freightways. **SIC:** 4512—Air Transportation—Scheduled.

★ 76553 ★　**Emery Worldwide**
5030 Randall Pky.
Wilmington, NC 28403
(919)791-0550
Ultimate Parent: Consolidated Freightways. **SIC:** 4512—Air Transportation—Scheduled.

★ 76554 ★　**Exxon Co. USA**
3340 River Rd.
Wilmington, NC 28412
(919)799-0144
Ultimate Parent: Exxon. **SIC:** 5172—Petroleum Products Nec.

★ 76555 ★　**Exxon Co. USA**
River Rd.
Wilmington, NC 28403
(919)799-0610
Ultimate Parent: Exxon. **SIC:** 5172—Petroleum Products Nec.

★ 76556 ★　**Federal Paper Board Co.**
2221 J. R. Kennedy Dr.
Wilmington, NC 28405
(919)763-2921
Officer: Bill Repas, Manager. **Ultimate Parent:** Federal Paper Board. **SIC:** 2621—Paper Mills; 2657—Folding Paperboard Boxes.

★ 76557 ★　**Federal Paper Board Co. Inc.**
Federal Bldg.
Wilmington, NC 28401
(919)655-2286
Ultimate Parent: Federal Paper Board. **SIC:** 2657—Folding Paperboard Boxes.

★ 76558 ★　**Federal Paper Board Co., Inc., Plant 24**
2221 J. R. Kennedy Dr.
Wilmington, NC 28405
Ultimate Parent: Federal Paper Board. **SIC:** 2657—Folding Paperboard Boxes.

★ 76559 ★　**First-Citizens Bank & Trust Co.**
2200 S. 17th St.
Wilmington, NC 28401
(910)762-0301
Location Type: Branch office. **Ultimate Parent:** First Citizens Bancshares, Inc. **SIC:** 6021—National Commercial Banks.

★ 76560 ★　**First-Citizens Bank & Trust Co.**
312 Lake Park Blvd.
Wilmington, NC 28428-4824
(910)458-4441
Location Type: Branch office. **Ultimate Parent:** First Citizens Bancshares, Inc. **SIC:** 6021—National Commercial Banks.

★ 76561 ★　**First-Citizens Bank & Trust Co.**
2702 S. College Rd.
Wilmington, NC 28412-6804
(910)762-0301
Location Type: Branch office. **Ultimate Parent:** First Citizens Bancshares, Inc. **SIC:** 6021—National Commercial Banks.

★ 76562 ★　**First-Citizens Bank & Trust Co.**
27 S. Kerr Ave.
Wilmington, NC 28403-1416
(910)762-0301
Location Type: Branch office. **Ultimate Parent:** First Citizens Bancshares, Inc. **SIC:** 6021—National Commercial Banks.

★ 76563 ★　**First-Citizens Bank & Trust Co.**
4022 Oleander Dr.
Wilmington, NC 28403-6815
(910)762-0301
Location Type: Branch office. **Ultimate Parent:** First Citizens Bancshares, Inc. **SIC:** 6021—National Commercial Banks.

★ 76564 ★　**First-Citizens Bank & Trust Co.**
1922 Eastwood Rd.
Wilmington, NC 28403-7298
(910)762-0301
Location Type: Branch office. **Ultimate Parent:** First Citizens Bancshares, Inc. **SIC:** 6021—National Commercial Banks.

★ 76565 ★　**First-Citizens Bank & Trust Co.**
8 N. Front St.
Wilmington, NC 28401-4437
(910)762-0301
Location Type: Branch office. **Officer:** James S. Bryan, Area Vice President. **Ultimate Parent:** First Citizens Bancshares, Inc. **SIC:** 6021—National Commercial Banks.

★ 76566 ★　**Firt-Citizens Bank & Trust Co.**
502 N. College Rd.
Wilmington, NC 28402
(910)762-0301
Location Type: Branch office. **Ultimate Parent:** First Citizens Bancshares, Inc. **SIC:** 6021—National Commercial Banks.

★ 76567 ★　**Food Lion**
RR 3
Wilmington, NC 28409
(919)256-3137
Ultimate Parent: Food Lion. **SIC:** 5411—Grocery Stores.

★ 76568 ★　**Food Lion**
Ogden Village Shopping Ctr.
Wilmington, NC 28405
(919)686-9083
Ultimate Parent: Food Lion. **SIC:** 5411—Grocery Stores.

★ 76569 ★　**Food Lion**
4410 Market St.
Wilmington, NC 28403
(919)762-0524
Ultimate Parent: Food Lion. **SIC:** 5411—Grocery Stores.

★ 76570 ★　**Food Lion**
3695 Hwy. 132
Wilmington, NC 28403
(919)392-4001
Ultimate Parent: Food Lion.

★ 76571 ★　**Food Lion Inc.**
Ogden Village Shpg C
Wilmington, NC 28405
(919)686-9083
Ultimate Parent: Food Lion. **SIC:** 5411—Grocery Stores.

★ 76572 ★　**General Electric Co.**
3901 Castle Hayne
Wilmington, NC 28402
(910)675-5000
Officer: Dallas Silverthorn, Manager. **Ultimate Parent:** General Electric. **SIC:** 2869—Industrial Organic Chemicals Nec; 3629—Electrical Industrial Apparatus Nec; 3728—Aircraft Parts & Equipment Nec.

★ 76573 ★　**General Electric Co.**
Castle Hayne Rd. U.S. Rte. 117 North
Wilmington, NC 28402
Ultimate Parent: General Electric. **SIC:** 2819—Industrial Inorganic Chemicals Nec; 3356—Nonferrous Rolling & Drawing Nec; 3499—Fabricated Metal Products Nec.

★ 76574 ★　**Greyhound Bus Lines**
201 Harnett St.
Wilmington, NC 28401
(919)762-6627
Ultimate Parent: Greyhound Lines Inc. **SIC:** 4212—Local Trucking Without Storage.

★ 76575 ★　**Hertz Rent-A-Car Licensee**
New Hanover Co Airport
Wilmington, NC 28405
(919)762-1010
Ultimate Parent: Hertz. **SIC:** 7514—Passenger Car Rental.

★ 76576 ★　**Jiffy Lube**
601 Shipyard Blvd.
Wilmington, NC 28412
(919)791-9368
Ultimate Parent: Pennzoil. **SIC:** 7538—General Automotive Repair Shops; 7539—Automotive Repair Shops Nec.

★ 76577 ★　**Kentucky Fried Chicken**
7037 Wrightsville Ave.
Wilmington, NC 28403
(919)256-6611
Ultimate Parent: Pepsico. **SIC:** 5812—Eating Places.

★ 76578 ★　**Kentucky Fried Chicken**
1101 S. College Rd.
Wilmington, NC 28403
(919)799-1824
Ultimate Parent: Pepsico. **SIC:** 5812—Eating Places.

★ 76579 ★　**Kentucky Fried Chicken**
4610 Market St.
Wilmington, NC 28405
(919)799-2230
Ultimate Parent: Pepsico. **SIC:** 5812—Eating Places.

★ 76580 ★　**Kentucky Fried Chicken**
1206 N. 3rd St.
Wilmington, NC 28401
(919)763-0133
Ultimate Parent: Pepsico. **SIC:** 5812—Eating Places.

★ 76581 ★　**Kentucky Fried Chicken**
2526 Carolina Beach Rd.
Wilmington, NC 28401
(919)763-5341
Ultimate Parent: Pepsico. **SIC:** 5812—Eating Places.

★ 76582 ★　**Lerner Shop**
Independence Mall
Wilmington, NC 28403
(919)799-7774
Ultimate Parent: Limited. **SIC:** 5621—Women's Clothing Stores.

★ 76583 ★　**Massachusetts Mutual Life Insurance**
3905 Oleander Dr.
Wilmington, NC 28403
(919)799-3601
Ultimate Parent: Massacuetts Mutual Life. **SIC:** 6411—Insurance Agents, Brokers & Service.

★ 76584 ★　**Otis Elevator Co.**
201 N. Front St.
Wilmington, NC 28401
(919)762-9532
Ultimate Parent: United Technologies. **SIC:** 1796—Installing Building Equipment Nec.

★ 76585 ★　**Peoples Drug Store**
Azalea Plz.
Wilmington, NC 28403
(919)392-5350
Ultimate Parent: Melville. **SIC:** 5912—Drug Stores & Proprietary Stores.

★ 76586 ★　**Pepsi-Cola Co.**
1929 Oleander Dr.
Wilmington, NC 28403
(910)763-7375
Ultimate Parent: Pepsico. **SIC:** 2086—Bottled & Canned Soft Drinks.

★ 76587 ★　**Pizza Hut**
4016 Oleander Dr.
Wilmington, NC 28403
(919)799-3650
Ultimate Parent: Pepsico. **SIC:** 5812—Eating Places.

★ 76588 ★　**Pizza Hut**
2402 S. 17th St.
Wilmington, NC 28401
(919)392-0180
Ultimate Parent: Pepsico. **SIC:** 5812—Eating Places.

★ 76589 ★　**Radio Shack**
Long Leaf Mall
Wilmington, NC 28403
(919)799-5954
Company Type: Division. **Ultimate Parent:** Tandy Corp. **SIC:** 5065—Electronic Parts & Equipment Nec.

★ 76590 ★　**Radio Shack**
Market
Wilmington, NC 28405
(919)799-2693
Company Type: Division. **Ultimate Parent:** Tandy Corp. **SIC:** 5065—Electronic Parts & Equipment Nec.

★ 76591 ★　**Radio Shack**
3500 Oleander Dr.
Wilmington, NC 28403
(919)799-8562
Company Type: Division. **Ultimate Parent:** Tandy Corp. **SIC:** 5731—Radio, Television & Electronics Stores.

★ 76592 ★　**Radio Shack**
13 S. Kerr Ave.
Wilmington, NC 28403
(919)799-2693
Company Type: Division. **Ultimate Parent:** Tandy Corp. **SIC:** 5731—Radio, Television & Electronics Stores.

★ 76593 ★　**Radio Shack**
23 Long Leaf Mall
Wilmington, NC 28401
(919)799-5954
Company Type: Division. **Ultimate Parent:** Tandy Corp. **SIC:** 5731—Radio, Television & Electronics Stores.

★ 76594 ★　**Rite Aid Center**
3500 Oleander Dr.
Wilmington, NC 28403
(919)791-9837
Ultimate Parent: Rite Aid. **SIC:** 5912—Drug Stores & Proprietary Stores.

★ 76595 ★ Southern Gravure Service Inc.
2406 N. 23rd St.
Wilmington, NC 28401
Ultimate Parent: Reynolds Metals Co. SIC: 2796—Platemaking Services.

★ 76596 ★ Super Saver
Plaza Shopping Ctr. E
Wilmington, NC 28401
(919)256-4305
Ultimate Parent: Wal-Mart Stores, Inc. SIC: 5331—Variety Stores.

★ 76597 ★ Taco Bell
630 S. College Rd.
Wilmington, NC 28403
(919)392-3123
Ultimate Parent: Pepsico. SIC: 5812—Eating Places.

★ 76598 ★ Taco Bell
4023 Market St.
Wilmington, NC 28403
(919)763-1393
Ultimate Parent: Pepsico. SIC: 5812—Eating Places.

★ 76599 ★ Texaco Food Mart
7006 Wrightsville Ave.
Wilmington, NC 28403
(919)256-9814
Ultimate Parent: Texaco. SIC: 5541—Gasoline Service Stations.

★ 76600 ★ This End Up Furniture Co.
Independence Mall
Wilmington, NC 28403
(919)395-0732
Ultimate Parent: Melville. SIC: 5712—Furniture Stores.

★ 76601 ★ Toys R US
4510 Oleander Dr.
Wilmington, NC 28403
(919)791-9067
Ultimate Parent: Toys "R" US. SIC: 5945—Hobby, Toy & Game Shops.

★ 76602 ★ Underwriters Adjusting Co.
1632 Harbour Dr.
Wilmington, NC 28401
(919)791-0740
Ultimate Parent: Continental. SIC: 6411—Insurance Agents, Brokers & Service.

★ 76603 ★ United Parcel Service
1620 N. 23rd St.
Wilmington, NC 28405
(919)662-7506
Ultimate Parent: United Parcel Service of America. SIC: 4215—Courier Services Except by Air.

★ 76604 ★ US Fidelity & Gu
1530 Harbour Dr.
Wilmington, NC 28401
(919)799-0150
Ultimate Parent: USF&G Corp. SIC: 6411—Insurance Agents, Brokers & Service.

★ 76605 ★ Wachovia Bank & Trust Co.
1701 Shipyard Blvd.
Wilmington, NC 28403
(919)251-2405
Ultimate Parent: Wachovia Corp. SIC: 6099—Functions Related to Deposit Banking.

★ 76606 ★ Wachovia Bank & Trust Co. N
1616 Dawson St.
Wilmington, NC 28401
(919)763-0118
Ultimate Parent: Wachovia Corp. SIC: 6099—Functions Related to Deposit Banking.

★ 76607 ★ Wachovia Bank & Trust Co. N
530 S. College Rd.
Wilmington, NC 28403
(919)251-2400
Ultimate Parent: Wachovia Corp. SIC: 6022—State Commercial Banks.

★ 76608 ★ Wachovia Bank & Trust Co. N
101 N. Front St.
Wilmington, NC 28401
(919)251-2300
Ultimate Parent: Wachovia Corp. SIC: 6022—State Commercial Banks; 6141—Personal Credit Institutions.

★ 76609 ★ Wachovia Bank & Trust Co. N
3512 Oleander Dr.
Wilmington, NC 28403
(919)799-1934
Ultimate Parent: Wachovia Corp. SIC: 6099—Functions Related to Deposit Banking.

★ 76610 ★ Wachovia Bank & Trust Co. N
4195 Market St.
Wilmington, NC 28403
(919)763-1693
Ultimate Parent: Wachovia Corp. SIC: 6022—State Commercial Banks.

★ 76611 ★ Wachovia Bank & Trust Co. N
404 N. 3rd St.
Wilmington, NC 28401
(919)763-1693
Ultimate Parent: Wachovia Corp. SIC: 6022—State Commercial Banks.

★ 76612 ★ Waldenbooks
4117 Oleander Dr.
Wilmington, NC 28403
(919)392-1277
Ultimate Parent: K-Mart. SIC: 5942—Book Stores.

★ 76613 ★ Western Auto Supply Co. Inc.
805 N. 3rd St.
Wilmington, NC 28401
(919)763-3357
Ultimate Parent: Sears Roebuck & Co. SIC: 5531—Automobile & Home Supply Stores.

★ 76614 ★ Wheeling Corrugating Co.
2202 Burnette Blvd.
Wilmington, NC 28401
(910)762-9691
Officer: Carl Derstine, Manager. Ultimate Parent: Wheeling-Pittsburgh Steel Corp. SIC: 3444—Sheet Metal Work.

Wilson

★ 76615 ★ American General Finance
346 W. Ward Blvd.
Wilson, NC 27893-3591
(919)291-6662
Location Type: Branch office. Officer: Pamela K. Moore. Ultimate Parent: American General Corp. SIC: 6141—Personal Credit Institutions; 6162—Mortgage Bankers & Correspondents; 6211—Security Brokers & Dealers.

★ 76616 ★ American General Finance Inc.
346 W. Ward Blvd.
Wilson, NC 27893-3591
(919)291-6662
Location Type: Branch office. Officer: Pamela K. Moore. Ultimate Parent: American General Corp. SIC: 6141—Personal Credit Institutions; 6162—Mortgage Bankers & Correspondents; 6211—Security Brokers & Dealers.

★ 76617 ★ American Tobacco Co.
Hwy. 301 S
Wilson, NC 27893
(919)243-3095
Ultimate Parent: American Brands Inc. SIC: 5159—Farm-Product Raw Materials Nec; 4221—Farm Product Warehousing & Storage.

★ 76618 ★ Arcadian Corp.
1802 S. Baldree Rd.
Wilson, NC 27893-9508
(919)237-2989
Ultimate Parent: Arcadian Corp. SIC: 2879—Agricultural Chemicals Nec.

★ 76619 ★ BB&T Financial Corp.
223 W. Nash St.
Wilson, NC 27893
(919)399-4291 Fax: (919)399-4260
Officer: John A. Allison, CEO. Ultimate Parent: Southern National Corp. Employee Count: 4437. Sales: 617 M.

★ 76620 ★ Branch Banking & Trust Co.
1001 Goldsboro St. S
Wilson, NC 27893
(919)399-4191
Location Type: Branch office. Ultimate Parent: Southern National Corp. SIC: 6022—State Commercial Banks.

★ 76621 ★ Branch Banking & Trust Co.
223 Nash St. W
Wilson, NC 27893
(919)399-4111
Ultimate Parent: Southern National Corp. SIC: 6022—State Commercial Banks.

★ 76622 ★ Branch Banking & Trust Co.
1604 Tarboro St. W
Wilson, NC 27893
(919)399-3313
Ultimate Parent: Southern National Corp. SIC: 6022—State Commercial Banks.

★ 76623 ★ Branch Banking & Trust Co.
2000 Nash St. N
Wilson, NC 27893
(919)399-4375
Ultimate Parent: Southern National Corp. SIC: 6022—State Commercial Banks.

★ 76624 ★ Branch Banking & Trust Co.
2000 N. Nash St.
Wilson, NC 27893-1756
(919)399-4530
Company Type: Subsidiary. Location Type: Branch office. Ultimate Parent: Southern National Corp. SIC: 6021—National Commercial Banks.

★ 76625 ★ Branch Banking & Trust Co.
1604 W. Tarbara St.
Wilson, NC 27893-3432
(919)399-4111
Company Type: Subsidiary. Location Type: Branch office. Ultimate Parent: Southern National Corp. SIC: 6021—National Commercial Banks.

★ 76626 ★ Branch Banking & Trust Co.
223 W. Nash St.
Wilson, NC 27894-1847
(919)399-4111
Company Type: Subsidiary. Location Type: Branch office. Ultimate Parent: Southern National Corp. SIC: 6021—National Commercial Banks.

★ 76627 ★ Branch Banking & Trust Co.
1001 S. Goldsboro St.
Wilson, NC 27893-4947
(919)399-4558
Company Type: Subsidiary. Location Type: Branch office. Officer: Wayne F. Beard, Mgr. Ultimate Parent: Southern National Corp. SIC: 6021—National Commercial Banks.

★ 76628 ★ Central Soya Co. Inc.
Wilco Blvd.
Wilson, NC 27893
(919)237-7141
Ultimate Parent: Central Soya. SIC: 5191—Farm Supplies.

★ 76629 ★ First-Citizens Bank & Trust Co.
2401 W. Nash Rd.
Wilson, NC 27893-1360
(919)237-3131
Location Type: Branch office. Ultimate Parent: First Citizens Bancshares, Inc. SIC: 6021—National Commercial Banks.

★ 76630 ★ First-Citizens Bank & Trust Co.
S. Tarboro St.
Wilson, NC 27893-3583
(919)237-3131
Location Type: Branch office. Ultimate Parent: First Citizens Bancshares, Inc. SIC: 6021—National Commercial Banks.

★ 76631 ★ First-Citizens Bank & Trust Co.
126 W. Nash St.
Wilson, NC 27894-4013
(919)237-3131
Location Type: Branch office. Officer: Steven P. Wicker, Senior Vice President. Ultimate Parent: First Citizens Bancshares, Inc. SIC: 6021—National Commercial Banks.

★ 76632 ★ Food Lion
2101 Tarboro St. SW
Wilson, NC 27893
(919)243-3748
Ultimate Parent: Food Lion. SIC: 5411—Grocery Stores.

★ 76633 ★ Food Lion
Brentwood Ctr.
Wilson, NC 27893
(919)291-9656
Ultimate Parent: Food Lion. SIC: 5411—Grocery Stores.

★ 76634 ★ Kentucky Fried Chicken
Plaza Shopping Ctr.
Wilson, NC 27893
(919)237-4107
Ultimate Parent: Pepsico. SIC: 5812—Eating Places.

★ 76635 ★ Nucor Bearing Prods.
2401 Stantonsburg Rd.
Wilson, NC 27893
Ultimate Parent: Nucor Corp. SIC: 3562—Ball & Roller Bearings.

★ 76636 ★ Nucor Bearing Products, Inc.
PO Box 370
Wilson, NC 27893
(919)237-8181 Fax: (919)237-2777
Officer: Jeffrey P. Downing, General Manager. Ultimate Parent: Nucor Corp.

★ 76637 ★ Piggly Wiggly
314 Nash St. NE
Wilson, NC 27893
(919)237-1581
Ultimate Parent: Bruno's. SIC: 5411—Grocery Stores.

★ 76638 ★ Piggly Wiggly
309 Nash St. W
Wilson, NC 27893
(919)243-3263
Ultimate Parent: Bruno's. SIC: 5411—Grocery Stores.

★ 76639 ★ Piggly Wiggly
100 Ward Blvd. SW
Wilson, NC 27893
(919)237-8772
Ultimate Parent: Bruno's. SIC: 5411—Grocery Stores.

★ 76640 ★ Pizza Hut
2000 Nash St. N
Wilson, NC 27893
(919)291-2955
Ultimate Parent: Pepsico. SIC: 5812—Eating Places.

★ 76641 ★ Radio Shack
280 Parkwood Mall
Wilson, NC 27893
(919)291-5700
Company Type: Division. Ultimate Parent: Tandy Corp. SIC: 5731—Radio, Television & Electronics Stores; 5731—Radio, Television & Electronics Stores.

★ 76642 ★ Ryder Truck Rental
Ward Blvd.
Wilson, NC 27893
(919)291-4800
Ultimate Parent: Ryder System. SIC: 7359—Equipment Rental & Leasing Nec.

★ 76643 ★ Smithfield Packing Co.
2401 Wilco Blvd.
Wilson, NC 27893
Ultimate Parent: Smithfield Foods Inc. SIC: 2011—Meat Packing Plants.

★ 76644 ★   Spartan Express Inc.
Hwy. 58 W
Wilson, NC 27893
(919)291-9610
Ultimate Parent: Roadway Services. SIC: 4213—Trucking Except Local.

★ 76645 ★   Standard Commercial
2201 Miller Rd.
Wilson, NC 27894
(919)291-5507
Company Type: Headquarters. Officer: J. Alec G. Murray. Employee Count: 2280. Sales: 1240 M. Fortune 500: Largest U.S. Industrial Corporations: Ranking 312.

★ 76646 ★   Standard Commercial Corp.
2201 Miller Rd.
Wilson, NC 27893
(919)291-5507 Fax: (919)237-1109
Officer: J. Alec G. Murray, CEO. Ultimate Parent: Standard Commercial. Employee Count: 2280. Sales: 1042 M.

★ 76647 ★   Taco Bell
1803 Tarboro St. SW
Wilson, NC 27893
(919)237-8903
Ultimate Parent: Pepsico. SIC: 5812—Eating Places.

★ 76648 ★   Texaco
116 Ward Blvd. NW
Wilson, NC 27893
(919)243-2482
Ultimate Parent: Texaco. SIC: 5541—Gasoline Service Stations.

★ 76649 ★   Tobacco Processors, Inc.
1912 Cargill Ave. S
Wilson, NC 27893
(919)237-5131
Officer: Wayne Hicks, Manager. Ultimate Parent: Universal Corp. SIC: 2141—Tobacco Stemming & Redrying.

★ 76650 ★   Trailways
307 Green St. E
Wilson, NC 27893
(919)243-3279
Ultimate Parent: Greyhound Lines Inc. SIC: 4131—Intercity & Rural Bus Transportation.

★ 76651 ★   Wachovia Bank & Trust Compa
200 Ward Blvd. N
Wilson, NC 27893
(919)399-6200
Ultimate Parent: Wachovia Corp. SIC: 6022—State Commercial Banks.

★ 76652 ★   Wachovia Bank & Trust Co.
101 Parkwood Plz.
Wilson, NC 27893
(919)399-6232
Ultimate Parent: Wachovia Corp. SIC: 6022—State Commercial Banks.

★ 76653 ★   Walter Kidde Inc.
2500 Airport Rd.
Wilson, NC 27893
Ultimate Parent: Hanson Industries. SIC: 3999—Manufacturing Industries Nec.

★ 76654 ★   Wilson Foods Corp.
907 Ward Blvd. E
Wilson, NC 27893
(919)237-3104
Ultimate Parent: Doskocil. SIC: 2011—Meat Packing Plants.

★ 76655 ★   Wrangler
Hwy. 301 N
Wilson, NC 27893
(919)237-6101
Officer: Will Thelps, Manager. Ultimate Parent: VF Corp. SIC: 2399—Fabricated Textile Products Nec.

Windsor

★ 76656 ★   First-Citizens Bank & Trust Co.
123 Granville St.
Windsor, NC 27983-1201
(919)794-9103
Location Type: Branch office. Officer: Michael K. Hoggard, Assistant Vice President. Ultimate Parent: First Citizens Bancshares, Inc. SIC: 6021—National Commercial Banks.

★ 76657 ★   Mary Kay Cosmenics
Rural Route 4
Windsor, NC 27983
(919)794-4450
Ultimate Parent: Mary Kay Cosmetics. SIC: 7231—Beauty Shops.

★ 76658 ★   Wrangler
118 County Farm Rd.
Windsor, NC 27983
(919)794-3128
Officer: Bob Brown, Manager. Ultimate Parent: VF Corp. SIC: 2339—Women's/Misses' Outerwear Nec.

Winston Salem

★ 76659 ★   Ace Hardware Store
Sherwood Shopping Ctr.
Winston Salem, NC 27104
(919)768-3886
Ultimate Parent: Ace Hardware. SIC: 2431—Millwork.

★ 76660 ★   American General Finance
5069 University Pky.
Winston Salem, NC 27106-6098
(919)767-0072
Location Type: Branch office. Officer: Allen Wease. Ultimate Parent: American General Corp. SIC: 6141—Personal Credit Institutions.

★ 76661 ★   American General Finance Inc.
4125 Peters Creek Pky.
Winston Salem, NC 27103-4636
Location Type: Branch office. Officer: Michael King. Ultimate Parent: American General Corp. SIC: 6141—Personal Credit Institutions.

★ 76662 ★   American General Finance Inc.
5069 University Pky.
Winston Salem, NC 27106-6098
(919)767-0072
Location Type: Branch office. Officer: Allen Wease. Ultimate Parent: American General Corp. SIC: 6141—Personal Credit Institutions.

★ 76663 ★   American General Finance Inc.
4125 Peters Creek Pky.
Winston Salem, NC 27103-4636
Location Type: Branch office. Officer: Michael King. Ultimate Parent: American General Corp. SIC: 6141—Personal Credit Institutions.

★ 76664 ★   BFI-Recyclery
2876 Lowery St.
Winston Salem, NC 27101-6128
(919)724-0842
Location Type: Branch office. Ultimate Parent: Browning-Ferris Industries. SIC: 4953—Refuse Systems.

★ 76665 ★   Circuit City
Parkway Shopping Ctr.
Winston Salem, NC 27103
(919)760-0560
Ultimate Parent: Circuit City Stores. SIC: 5812—Eating Places.

★ 76666 ★   Coast to Coast Hardware
4826 Country Club Rd.
Winston Salem, NC 27104
(919)768-8855
Ultimate Parent: Servistar Corp. SIC: 5211—Lumber & Other Building Materials.

★ 76667 ★   Digital Equipment Corp.
8025 N. Point Blvd.
Winston Salem, NC 27106
(919)727-0654
Ultimate Parent: Digital Equipment Corp. SIC: 5046—Commercial Equipment Nec; 7373—Computer Integrated Systems Design.

★ 76668 ★   Exxon Car Wash
140 S. Stratford Rd.
Winston Salem, NC 27104
(919)722-3479
Ultimate Parent: Exxon. SIC: 5541—Gasoline Service Stations.

★ 76669 ★   Food Lion
7760 N. Point Blvd.
Winston Salem, NC 27106
(919)725-0200
Ultimate Parent: Food Lion. SIC: 5411—Grocery Stores.

★ 76670 ★   Food Lion
703 Jonestown Rd.
Winston Salem, NC 27103
(919)765-7560
Ultimate Parent: Food Lion. SIC: 5411—Grocery Stores.

★ 76671 ★   Food Lion
1236 Waughtown St.
Winston Salem, NC 27107
(919)784-9793
Ultimate Parent: Food Lion. SIC: 5411—Grocery Stores.

★ 76672 ★   Hertz Rent-A-Car
3800 N. Liberty St.
Winston Salem, NC 27105
(919)767-0234
Ultimate Parent: Hertz. SIC: 7514—Passenger Car Rental.

★ 76673 ★   Hertz Rent-A-Car
Airport Terminal
Winston Salem, NC 27105
(919)744-0310
Ultimate Parent: Hertz. SIC: 7539—Automotive Repair Shops Nec.

★ 76674 ★   Kroger Pharmacy
1925 Silas Creek Pky.
Winston Salem, NC 27103
(919)723-2304
Ultimate Parent: Kroger. SIC: 5411—Grocery Stores.

★ 76675 ★   Mary Kay Cosmetics
5331 Dust Devil Dr.
Winston Salem, NC 27106
(919)922-3921
Ultimate Parent: Mary Kay Cosmetics. SIC: 5999—Miscellaneous Retail Stores Nec.

★ 76676 ★   McDonalds
2110 Cloverdale Ave. 3rd Fl.
Winston Salem, NC 27103
(919)722-1333
Ultimate Parent: McDonald's. SIC: 5812—Eating Places.

★ 76677 ★   National Home Life Assurancenc
1530 Martin St.
Winston Salem, NC 27103
(919)722-1641
Ultimate Parent: National Home Life. SIC: 6411—Insurance Agents, Brokers & Service.

★ 76678 ★   Owens Illinois Glass Co.
Old Hwy. 52 S
Winston Salem, NC 27108
(910)764-2900
Officer: Ted Mc Grath, Manager. Ultimate Parent: Owens-Illinois. SIC: 3221—Glass Containers.

★ 76679 ★   Pizza Hut
3040 N. Cherry St.
Winston Salem, NC 27105
(919)724-0494
Ultimate Parent: Pepsico. SIC: 5812—Eating Places.

★ 76680 ★   Radio Shack
Parkview Shopping Ctr.
Winston Salem, NC 27103
(919)725-5552
Company Type: Division. Ultimate Parent: Tandy Corp. SIC: 5065—Electronic Parts & Equipment Nec.

★ 76681 ★   Radio Shack
Hanes Mall
Winston Salem, NC 27103
(919)768-9290
Company Type: Division. Ultimate Parent: Tandy Corp. SIC: 5065—Electronic Parts & Equipment Nec.

★ 76682 ★   Radio Shack
629 Peters Creek Pky.
Winston Salem, NC 27103
(919)722-0030
Company Type: Division. Ultimate Parent: Tandy Corp. SIC: 5046—Commercial Equipment Nec.

★ 76683 ★   RJ Reynolds Tabacco Co.
2997 PO Box
Winston Salem, NC 27102
(919)741-5514
Ultimate Parent: RJR Nabisco Holdings. SIC: 7389—Business Services Nec.

★ 76684 ★   RJ Reynolds Tobacco Co. Inc.
1100 Reynolds Blvd.
Winston Salem, NC 27105
(919)773-2000
Ultimate Parent: RJR Nabisco Holdings. SIC: 5194—Tobacco & Tobacco Products.

★ 76685 ★   Smith Barney Harris Upham & Co.
101 S. Stratford Rd.
Winston Salem, NC 27104-4213
(919)725-9411
Company Type: Branch. Officer: Morrison W. Divine III. Ultimate Parent: Automatic Data Processing, Inc. SIC: 6211—Security Brokers & Dealers.

★ 76686 ★   T J Maxx Store
Sherwood Shopping Ctr.
Winston Salem, NC 27104
(919)768-0870
Ultimate Parent: TJX. SIC: 5311—Department Stores.

★ 76687 ★   This End Up Furniture Co.
514 S. Stratford Rd.
Winston Salem, NC 27103
(919)723-4133
Ultimate Parent: Melville. SIC: 5712—Furniture Stores.

★ 76688 ★   Unisys Corp.
6209 Ramada Dr.
Winston Salem, NC 27103
(919)766-8221
Ultimate Parent: Unisys Corp. SIC: 7373—Computer Integrated Systems Design.

★ 76689 ★   Universal Data Systems
3000 Bethesda Pl
Winston Salem, NC 27103
(919)760-4184
Ultimate Parent: Motorola Inc. SIC: 3579—Office Machines Nec.

★ 76690 ★   Vulcan Materials Co.
Mideast Div.
4401 Patterson Ave.
Winston Salem, NC 27105
(910)767-4600
Company Type: Division. Officer: James W. Smack, President. Ultimate Parent: Vulcan Materials Co. SIC: 3273—Ready-Mixed Concrete; 3295—Minerals-Ground or Treated.

★ 76691 ★   Wachovia Bank & Tr Co. N a B
4626 Country Club Rd.
Winston Salem, NC 27104
(919)770-6501
Ultimate Parent: Wachovia Corp. SIC: 6099—Functions Related to Deposit Banking.

★ 76692 ★   Wachovia Bank & Tr Co. N a B
418 S. Stratford Rd.
Winston Salem, NC 27103
(919)770-5281
Ultimate Parent: Wachovia Corp. SIC: 6099—Functions Related to Deposit Banking; 6022—State Commercial Banks.

★ 76693 ★   Wachovia Bank & Trust
2150 Country Club Rd. 105
Winston Salem, NC 27104
(919)770-5671
Ultimate Parent: Wachovia Corp. SIC: 6099—Functions Related to Deposit Banking.

★ 76694 ★   Wachovia Bank and Trust Com
301 N. Main St.
Winston Salem, NC 27150
(919)770-5000
Ultimate Parent: Wachovia Corp. SIC: 6021—National Commercial Banks.

★ 76695 ★ **Wachovia Bank & Trust Co. N**
3735 University Pky.
Winston Salem, NC 27106
(919)748-6300
Ultimate Parent: Wachovia Corp. **SIC:** 6022—State Commercial Banks.

★ 76696 ★ **Wachovia Bank & Trust Co. N**
Wake
Winston Salem, NC 27109
(919)748-5457
Ultimate Parent: Wachovia Corp. **SIC:** 6022—State Commercial Banks.

★ 76697 ★ **Wachovia Bank & Trust Co. N**
676 Hanes Mall
Winston Salem, NC 27103
(919)770-6825
Ultimate Parent: Wachovia Corp. **SIC:** 6022—State Commercial Banks.

★ 76698 ★ **Wachovia Bank & Trust Co. N**
701 N. Martin Luther King J Dr.
Winston Salem, NC 27101
(919)770-5221
Ultimate Parent: Wachovia Corp. **SIC:** 6099—Functions Related to Deposit Banking.

★ 76699 ★ **Wachovia Bank & Trust Co. N**
Hanes Mall
Winston Salem, NC 27103
(919)748-6285
Ultimate Parent: Wachovia Corp. **SIC:** 6022—State Commercial Banks.

★ 76700 ★ **Wachovia Bank&Trust Co. Libr**
Wachovia
Winston Salem, NC 27101
(919)748-5000
Ultimate Parent: Wachovia Corp. **SIC:** 6029—Commercial Banks Nec.

Winston-Salem

★ 76701 ★ **AMP, Inc.**
3700 Reidsville Rd.
Winston-Salem, NC 27101
(910)725-9222
Officer: Jerry Campbell, Manager. **Ultimate Parent:** AMP Inc. **SIC:** 3084—Plastics Pipe; 3544—Special Dies, Tools, Jigs & Fixtures; 3643—Current-Carrying Wiring Devices.

★ 76702 ★ **AMP Inc.**
3900 Reidsville Rd., Bldg. 67
Winston-Salem, NC 27101-2165
Ultimate Parent: AMP Inc. **SIC:** 3678—Electronic Connectors; 3643—Current-Carrying Wiring Devices.

★ 76703 ★ **Amp Inc. Building 67**
3900 Reidsville Rd.
Winston-Salem, NC 27101-2167
Ultimate Parent: AMP Inc. **SIC:** 3471—Plating & Polishing; 3678—Electronic Connectors.

★ 76704 ★ **AT & T Family Federal Credit Union**
585 Waughtown St., Ste. 2A
Winston-Salem, NC 27107
(910)725-1955
Location Type: Branch office. **Officer:** Betty Pennington, Manager. **Ultimate Parent:** AT&T. **SIC:** 6061—Federal Credit Unions.

★ 76705 ★ **AT & T Family Federal Credit Union**
500 W. 5th St.
Winston-Salem, NC 27152
(910)770-2442
Location Type: Branch office. **Officer:** Betty Pennington, Manager. **Ultimate Parent:** AT&T. **SIC:** 6061—Federal Credit Unions.

★ 76706 ★ **AT & T Family Federal Credit Union**
PO Box 26000
Winston-Salem, NC 27114-6000
(910)659-1955 **Fax:** (910)659-3540
Company Type: Subsidiary. **Officer:** Clyde O. Padgett, Chairman, President & CEO. **Ultimate Parent:** AT&T. **SIC:** 6061—Federal Credit Unions.

★ 76707 ★ **AT & T Family Federal Credit Union**
2400 Reynolds Rd.
Winston-Salem, NC 27106
(910)727-6174
Location Type: Branch office. **Officer:** Sandy Milton, Manager. **Ultimate Parent:** AT&T. **SIC:** 6061—Federal Credit Unions.

★ 76708 ★ **Banana Republic**
752 Hanes Mall
Winston-Salem, NC 27103
(919)765-5336
Ultimate Parent: GAP. **SIC:** 5651—Family Clothing Stores.

★ 76709 ★ **Black & Decker US Inc.**
3716 High Point Rd.
Winston-Salem, NC 27107-4506
(919)727-0825
Ultimate Parent: Black & Decker Corp. **SIC:** 5085—Industrial Supplies.

★ 76710 ★ **Branch Banking & Trust Co.**
36001 Waughtown St.
Winston-Salem, NC 27107-1635
(910)723-3604
Company Type: Subsidiary. **Location Type:** Branch office. **Ultimate Parent:** Southern National Corp. **SIC:** 6021—National Commercial Banks.

★ 76711 ★ **Branch Banking & Trust Co.**
2815 Reynolda Rd.
Winston-Salem, NC 27106-3110
(910)723-3604
Company Type: Subsidiary. **Location Type:** Branch office. **Ultimate Parent:** Southern National Corp. **SIC:** 6021—National Commercial Banks.

★ 76712 ★ **Branch Banking & Trust Co.**
6000 University Pky.
Winston-Salem, NC 27105-9635
(910)723-3604
Company Type: Subsidiary. **Location Type:** Branch office. **Ultimate Parent:** Southern National Corp. **SIC:** 6021—National Commercial Banks.

★ 76713 ★ **Branch Banking & Trust Co.**
230 N. Cherry St.
Winston-Salem, NC 27101-3910
(910)723-3604
Company Type: Subsidiary. **Location Type:** Branch office. **Ultimate Parent:** Southern National Corp. **SIC:** 6021—National Commercial Banks.

★ 76714 ★ **Branch Banking & Trust Co.**
121 Jonestown Rd.
Winston-Salem, NC 27101
(910)748-5283
Company Type: Subsidiary. **Location Type:** Branch office. **Ultimate Parent:** Southern National Corp. **SIC:** 6021—National Commercial Banks.

★ 76715 ★ **Branch Banking & Trust Co.**
1 Triad Pk.
Winston-Salem, NC 27101
(910)748-5247
Company Type: Subsidiary. **Location Type:** Branch office. **Ultimate Parent:** Southern National Corp. **SIC:** 6021—National Commercial Banks.

★ 76716 ★ **Branch Banking & Trust Co.**
3125 S. Maplewood Ave.
Winston-Salem, NC 27103-3903
(910)748-5225
Company Type: Subsidiary. **Location Type:** Branch office. **Ultimate Parent:** Southern National Corp. **SIC:** 6021—National Commercial Banks.

★ 76717 ★ **Branch Banking & Trust Co.**
1401 Corporation Pky.
Winston-Salem, NC 27127-3759
(910)748-5267
Company Type: Subsidiary. **Location Type:** Branch office. **Ultimate Parent:** Southern National Corp. **SIC:** 6021—National Commercial Banks.

★ 76718 ★ **Branch Banking & Trust Co.**
3410 Robin Hood Rd.
Winston-Salem, NC 27106-4702
(910)748-5232
Company Type: Subsidiary. **Location Type:** Branch office. **Ultimate Parent:** Southern National Corp. **SIC:** 6021—National Commercial Banks.

★ 76719 ★ **Branch Banking & Trust Co.**
110 S. Stratford Rd.
Winston-Salem, NC 27104-4214
(910)748-5200
Company Type: Subsidiary. **Location Type:** Branch office. **Officer:** Jim Stewart, Manager. **Ultimate Parent:** Southern National Corp. **SIC:** 6021—National Commercial Banks.

★ 76720 ★ **Chesapeak Display & Packaging Co. Inc.**
555 Aureole St.
Winston-Salem, NC 27103-3201
(919)784-0445
Officer: George Barnes, President. **Ultimate Parent:** Chesapeake. **SIC:** 2653—Corrugated & Solid Fiber Boxes.

★ 76721 ★ **Chesapeake Display & Packaging Co.**
555 Aureole St.
Winston-Salem, NC 27117
(919)784-0445 **Fax:** (919)650-7519
Officer: George F. Barnes, President. **Ultimate Parent:** Chesapeake.

★ 76722 ★ **Corn Products**
4501 Overdale Rd.
Winston-Salem, NC 27107-2939
Ultimate Parent: CPC International. **SIC:** 2046—Wet Corn Milling.

★ 76723 ★ **Corn Products Winston-Salem Plant**
4501 Overdale Rd.
Winston-Salem, NC 27107-2939
Ultimate Parent: CPC International. **SIC:** 2046—Wet Corn Milling.

★ 76724 ★ **Engineered Polymers**
1703 Vargrave
Winston-Salem, NC 27107
Ultimate Parent: Weyerhaeuser Co. **SIC:** 3999—Manufacturing Industries Nec.

★ 76725 ★ **First-Citizens Bank & Trust Co.**
1199 Hayes Forest Rd.
Winston-Salem, NC 27106
(910)725-7241
Location Type: Branch office. **Ultimate Parent:** First Citizens Bancshares, Inc. **SIC:** 6021—National Commercial Banks.

★ 76726 ★ **First-Citizens Bank & Trust Co.**
4876 Country Club Rd.
Winston-Salem, NC 27104-4504
(910)725-7241
Location Type: Branch office. **Ultimate Parent:** First Citizens Bancshares, Inc. **SIC:** 6021—National Commercial Banks.

★ 76727 ★ **First-Citizens Bank & Trust Co.**
3031 Waughton St.
Winston-Salem, NC 27107-1634
(910)725-7241
Location Type: Branch office. **Ultimate Parent:** First Citizens Bancshares, Inc. **SIC:** 6021—National Commercial Banks.

★ 76728 ★ **First-Citizens Bank & Trust Co.**
3306 Healy Rd.
Winston-Salem, NC 27103-1402
(910)768-4393
Location Type: Branch office. **Ultimate Parent:** First Citizens Bancshares, Inc. **SIC:** 6021—National Commercial Banks.

★ 76729 ★ **First-Citizens Bank & Trust Co.**
2600 Reynolds Rd.
Winston-Salem, NC 27106-3817
(910)721-0838
Location Type: Branch office. **Ultimate Parent:** First Citizens Bancshares, Inc. **SIC:** 6021—National Commercial Banks.

★ 76730 ★ **First-Citizens Bank & Trust Co.**
2000 W. 1st St.
Winston-Salem, NC 27104-4225
(910)725-7241
Location Type: Branch office. **Officer:** R. Mont Hamrick, Area Vice President. **Ultimate Parent:** First Citizens Bancshares, Inc. **SIC:** 6021—National Commercial Banks.

★ 76731 ★ **Food Lion**
3604 Reynolda Rd.
Winston-Salem, NC 27106
(919)924-6122
Ultimate Parent: Food Lion. **SIC:** 5411—Grocery Stores.

★ 76732 ★ **Hanes Co., Inc.**
PO Box 202
Winston-Salem, NC 27102
(919)777-3353 **Fax:** (919)777-3375
Officer: John B. Talbert, President. **Ultimate Parent:** Leggett & Platt Inc.

★ 76733 ★ **Imc Fertilizer Inc.**
3105 Glenn Ave. Extension
Winston-Salem, NC 27105
Ultimate Parent: IMC Fertilizer Group. **SIC:** 2875—Fertilizers—Mixing Only.

★ 76734 ★ **Johnson Controls Inc.**
Battery Div.
2701 West Mountain St. PO Box 1002
Winston-Salem, NC 27102
Company Type: Division. **Ultimate Parent:** Johnson Controls Inc. **SIC:** 3691—Storage Batteries.

★ 76735 ★ **Johnson Controls Inc. Battery Group**
Old Greensboro Rd. PO Box 1002
Winston-Salem, NC 27102
Ultimate Parent: Johnson & Johnson. **SIC:** 3961—Costume Jewelry.

★ 76736 ★ **Johnson Controls Inc. Winston-Salem Plant**
2701 West Mountain St. PO Box 1002
Winston-Salem, NC 27102
Ultimate Parent: Johnson Controls Inc. **SIC:** 3691—Storage Batteries.

★ 76737 ★ **Pepsi-Cola Bottling Co.**
Winston-Salem
3425 Myer Lee Dr.
Winston-Salem, NC 27101
Company Type: Division. **Ultimate Parent:** Pepsico. **SIC:** 2086—Bottled & Canned Soft Drinks.

★ 76738 ★ **Phoenix Packaging Inc.**
389 12th St. NW
Winston-Salem, NC 27101
(919)759-2998
Ultimate Parent: Savannah Foods & Industries, Inc. **SIC:** 4783—Packing & Crating; 5113—Industrial & Personal Service Paper.

★ 76739 ★ **R. J. Reynolds Tobacco Co. Archer 200**
300 Cunningham Ave.
Winston-Salem, NC 27107-2203
Ultimate Parent: RJR Nabisco Holdings. **SIC:** 2754—Commercial Printing—Gravure; 3334—Primary Aluminum.

★ 76740 ★ **R. J. Reynolds Tobacco Co. Downtown**
Vine St.
Winston-Salem, NC 27102-3818
Ultimate Parent: RJR Nabisco Holdings. **SIC:** 2111—Cigarettes; 3449—Miscellaneous Metal Work.

★ 76741 ★ **R. J. Reynolds Tobacco Co. - Downtown**
401 North Main St.
Winston-Salem, NC 27102-3818
Ultimate Parent: RJR Nabisco Holdings. **SIC:** 2111—Cigarettes; 3449—Miscellaneous Metal Work; 9999—Nonclassifiable Establishments.

★ 76742 ★ **R. J. Reynolds Tobacco Co. Downtown 91-1**
Patterson & 5th Sts.
Winston-Salem, NC 27102
Ultimate Parent: RJR Nabisco Holdings. **SIC:** 2111—Cigarettes.

★ 76743 ★ R. J. Reynolds
Tobacco Co. Downtown 93-7
5th & Main St.
Winston-Salem, NC 27102
(919)269-7421
Officer: Ben York. Ultimate Parent: Blount
Inc. SIC: 3553—Woodworking Machinery;
5084—Industrial Machinery & Equipment.
Ultimate Parent: RJR Nabisco Holdings.
SIC: 2111—Cigarettes.

★ 76744 ★ R. J. Reynolds
Tobacco Co. Downtown 92-2
Fifth & Chestnut St.
Winston-Salem, NC 27102
Ultimate Parent: RJR Nabisco Holdings.
SIC: 2111—Cigarettes.

★ 76745 ★ R. J. Reynolds
Tobacco Co. Downtown 92-2
5th St.
Winston-Salem, NC 27052
Ultimate Parent: RJR Nabisco Holdings.
SIC: 2111—Cigarettes.

★ 76746 ★ R. J. Reynolds
Tobacco Co. Downtown 64
5th St.
Winston-Salem, NC 27052
Ultimate Parent: RJR Nabisco Holdings.
SIC: 2111—Cigarettes.

★ 76747 ★ R. J. Reynolds
Tobacco Co. Downtown 26
Chestnut & Belews St.
Winston-Salem, NC 27102
Ultimate Parent: RJR Nabisco Holdings.
SIC: 2111—Cigarettes.

★ 76748 ★ R. J. Reynolds
Tobacco Co. Downtown 23-1
Patterson & Fifth St.
Winston-Salem, NC 27102-3818
Ultimate Parent: RJR Nabisco Holdings.
SIC: 2111—Cigarettes.

★ 76749 ★ R. J. Reynolds
Tobacco Co. Downtown 23-1
Patterson Ave.
Winston-Salem, NC 27102
Ultimate Parent: RJR Nabisco Holdings.
SIC: 2111—Cigarettes.

★ 76750 ★ R. J. Reynolds
Tobacco Co. Dt 95-1
7th & Linden St.
Winston-Salem, NC 27102
Ultimate Parent: RJR Nabisco Holdings.
SIC: 2111—Cigarettes.

★ 76751 ★ R. J. Reynolds
Tobacco Co. Dt 90-3
Vine St.
Winston-Salem, NC 27102
Ultimate Parent: RJR Nabisco Holdings.
SIC: 2111—Cigarettes.

★ 76752 ★ R. J. Reynolds
Tobacco Co. Dt 63-1
5th & Linden St.
Winston-Salem, NC 27102
Ultimate Parent: RJR Nabisco Holdings.
SIC: 2111—Cigarettes.

★ 76753 ★ R. J. Reynolds
Tobacco Co. Whitaker Park
1101 Reynolds Blvd.
Winston-Salem, NC 27102-2959
Ultimate Parent: RJR Nabisco Holdings.
SIC: 2087—Flavoring Extracts & Syrups
Nec; 2111—Cigarettes.

★ 76754 ★ R. J. Reynolds
Tobacco Co. Whitaker Park 605-1
1101 Reynolds Blvd.
Winston-Salem, NC 27102
Ultimate Parent: RJR Nabisco Holdings.
SIC: 2111—Cigarettes.

★ 76755 ★ R. J. Reynolds
Tobacco Co. Whitaker Park 641
27-30th St.
Winston-Salem, NC 27102-2959
Ultimate Parent: RJR Nabisco Holdings.
SIC: 2111—Cigarettes; 2671—Paper
Coated & Laminated—Packaging.

★ 76756 ★ R. J. Reynolds
Tobacco Co. Whitaker Park 604
220 E. Polo Rd.
Winston-Salem, NC 27102-2959
Ultimate Parent: RJR Nabisco Holdings.
SIC: 2754—Commercial Printing—Gravure.

★ 76757 ★ R. J. Reynolds
Tobacco Co. Whitaker Park 604-1
220 E. Polo Rd.
Winston-Salem, NC 27105-2959
Ultimate Parent: RJR Nabisco Holdings.
SIC: 2111—Cigarettes; 2754—Commercial
Printing—Gravure.

★ 76758 ★ R. J. Reynolds
Tobacco Co. Wp 631-1
Shorefair & 30th St.
Winston-Salem, NC 27102
Ultimate Parent: RJR Nabisco Holdings.
SIC: 2111—Cigarettes.

★ 76759 ★ R.J. Reynolds
Tobacco Co.
1101 Reynolds Blvd.
Winston-Salem, NC 27102-2959
Ultimate Parent: RJR Nabisco Holdings.
SIC: 2111—Cigarettes.

★ 76760 ★ Sara Lee Corp.
475 Corporate Square Dr.
Winston-Salem, NC 27105
(910)519-5300
Company Type: Division. Officer: Roy
Johnson, President & CEO. Ultimate
Parent: Sara Lee Corp.

★ 76761 ★ Sara Lee Corp.
5650 University Pky.
Winston-Salem, NC 27105
(910)768-9540
Company Type: Division. Officer: Kathy
Volker, President. Ultimate Parent: Sara
Lee Corp.

★ 76762 ★ Sara Lee Direct
4045 University Pky.
Winston-Salem, NC
(910)519-7126
Company Type: Division. Ultimate Parent:
Sara Lee Corp.

★ 76763 ★ Sara Lee Graphics
320 Hanes Mill Rd.
Winston-Salem, NC 27102
Ultimate Parent: Sara Lee Corp. SIC:
2752—Commercial Printing—Lithographic.

★ 76764 ★ Sara Lee Hosiery
401 Hanes Mill Rd.
Winston-Salem, NC 27105
Ultimate Parent: Sara Lee Corp. SIC:
2251—Women's Hosiery Except Socks.

★ 76765 ★ Sara Lee Hosiery
5660 University Pky.
Winston-Salem, NC 27105
(910)519-3241
Company Type: Division. Officer: John
Piazza, CEO. Ultimate Parent: Sara Lee
Corp.

★ 76766 ★ Sara Lee Intimates
3330 Healy Dr.
Winston-Salem, NC 27103
(910)519-6053
Company Type: Division. Ultimate Parent:
Sara Lee Corp.

★ 76767 ★ Sara Lee Intimates
(BALI)
3330 Healy Dr.
Winston-Salem, NC 27103
(910)519-6053
Company Type: Division. Officer: Don
Franceschini, CEO. Ultimate Parent: Sara
Lee Corp.

★ 76768 ★ Sara Lee Knit
Products
450 Hanes Mill Rd.
Winston-Salem, NC 27105
(910)519-4400
Company Type: Division. Officer: Kirk
Beaudin, President, COO. Ultimate Parent:
Sara Lee Corp.

★ 76769 ★ Sara Lee Knit
Products
700 S. Stratford Rd.
Winston-Salem, NC 27102
Location Type: Plant. Ultimate Parent:
Sara Lee Corp. SIC: 2322—Men's/Boys'
Underwear & Nightwear.

★ 76770 ★ Sara Lee Personal
Products
470 Hanes Mill Rd.
Winston-Salem, NC 27105
(910)768-9181
Company Type: Division. Officer: Jack
Ward. Ultimate Parent: Sara Lee Corp.

★ 76771 ★ Southern National
Corp.
200 W. 2nd St.
PO Box 1260
Winston-Salem, NC 27102
(910)773-7200 Fax: (910)671-2399
Company Type: Headquarters. Officer:
John A. Alison IV, CEO. Employee Count:
6986. Fortune Service 500: Ranking 66.

★ 76772 ★ Thomasville Furniture
Ind. Inc.
Plant H
1201 N. Patterson Ave.
Winston-Salem, NC 27101
Location Type: Plant. Ultimate Parent:
Armstrong World Industries. SIC: 2511—
Wood Household Furniture.

★ 76773 ★ Thomasville Furniture
Industries Inc.
1201 N. Patterson St.
Winston-Salem, NC 27101
Ultimate Parent: Armstrong World
Industries. SIC: 2511—Wood Household
Furniture.

★ 76774 ★ Thomasville Furniture
Industries Inc.
Plant H
1201 N. Patterson St.
Winston-Salem, NC 27101
Location Type: Plant. Ultimate Parent:
Armstrong World Industries. SIC: 2511—
Wood Household Furniture.

★ 76775 ★ Wachovia Corp.
301 N. Main St.
Winston-Salem, NC 27150
(910)770-5000
Company Type: Headquarters. Officer:
L.M. Baker Jr. Employee Count: 15531.
Fortune Service 500: Ranking 22.

★ 76776 ★ Wachovia Corp.
PO Box 3099
Winston-Salem, NC 27150
Location Type: Branch office. Ultimate
Parent: Wachovia Corp. SIC: 6021—
National Commercial Banks.

★ 76777 ★ Westinghouse
Electric Corp.
3050 Westinghouse Rd.
Winston-Salem, NC 27105
Ultimate Parent: Westinghouse Electric
Corp. SIC: 3511—Turbines & Turbine
Generator Sets.

Wrightsville Beach

★ 76778 ★ Pizza Hut
101 W. Salisbury St.
Wrightsville Beach, NC 28480
(919)256-3776
Ultimate Parent: Pepsico. SIC: 5812—
Eating Places.

Yadkinville

★ 76779 ★ Kentucky Fried
Chicken
I 421
Yadkinville, NC 27055
(919)679-8686
Ultimate Parent: Pepsico. SIC: 5812—
Eating Places.

★ 76780 ★ McDonalds
Hwy. 601
Yadkinville, NC 27055
(919)679-2834
Ultimate Parent: McDonald's.
SIC: 5812—Eating Places.

★ 76781 ★ Sara Lee Hosiery
Corner of Pine & Coolidge
Yadkinville, NC 27055
Ultimate Parent: Sara Lee Corp. SIC:
2251—Women's Hosiery Except Socks.

★ 76782 ★ Unifi, Inc.
Old Hwy. 421 E
Yadkinville, NC 27055
Ultimate Parent: UNIFI, Inc. SIC: 2282—
Throwing & Winding Mills; 2269—Finishing
Plants Nec.

Zebulon

★ 76783 ★ Blount Inc.
415 US Hwy. 64, Bus W
Zebulon, NC 27597-2556
(919)269-7421
Officer: Ben York. Ultimate Parent: Blount
Inc. SIC: 3553—Woodworking Machinery;
5084—Industrial Machinery & Equipment.

OKLAHOMA

Ada

★ 76784 ★ **Coast to Coast Hardware**
801 N. Broadway Ave.
Ada, OK 74820
(405)332-8038
Ultimate Parent: Servistar Corp. **SIC:** 5251—Hardware Stores.

★ 76785 ★ **Kentucky Fried Chicken**
501 N. Mississippi Ave.
Ada, OK 74820
(405)332-7544
Ultimate Parent: Pepsico. **SIC:** 5812—Eating Places.

★ 76786 ★ **Owens-Brockway Glass Container**
300 E. Fourth St.
Ada, OK 74820
Ultimate Parent: Owens-Illinois. **SIC:** 3221—Glass Containers.

★ 76787 ★ **Pizza Hut**
1230 N. Mississippi Ave.
Ada, OK 74820
(405)332-5662
Ultimate Parent: Pepsico. **SIC:** 5812—Eating Places.

★ 76788 ★ **Super Saver**
St
Ada, OK 74820
(405)332-0552
Ultimate Parent: Wal-Mart Stores, Inc. **SIC:** 5541—Gasoline Service Stations.

★ 76789 ★ **Super Saver**
N City
Ada, OK 74820
(405)332-2429
Ultimate Parent: Wal-Mart Stores, Inc. **SIC:** 5541—Gasoline Service Stations.

★ 76790 ★ **Wal Mart Discount Cities**
1300 Industrial Access Rd.
Ada, OK 74820
(405)332-9453
Ultimate Parent: Wal-Mart Stores, Inc. **SIC:** 5311—Department Stores.

★ 76791 ★ **Wal Mart Pharmacy**
1601 N. Broadway Ave.
Ada, OK 74820
(405)332-4755
Ultimate Parent: Wal-Mart Stores, Inc. **SIC:** 5912—Drug Stores & Proprietary Stores.

Alex

★ 76792 ★ **Mobil Oil Hughes Station**
Southwest City
Alex, OK 73002
(405)785-2574
Ultimate Parent: Mobil. **SIC:** 1311—Crude Petroleum & Natural Gas.

Altus

★ 76793 ★ **Coca-Cola Bottling Co.**
601 Todd Ln.
Altus, OK 73521
(405)482-7211
Ultimate Parent: Coca-Cola Enterprises. **SIC:** 2086—Bottled & Canned Soft Drinks; 5149—Groceries & Related Products Nec.

★ 76794 ★ **Mary Kay Cosmetics**
717 N. Jackson St.
Altus, OK 73521
(405)477-4154
Ultimate Parent: Mary Kay Cosmetics. **SIC:** 5999—Miscellaneous Retail Stores Nec.

★ 76795 ★ **Pizza Hut**
1201 E. Broadway St.
Altus, OK 73521
(405)477-4444
Ultimate Parent: Pepsico. **SIC:** 5812—Eating Places.

★ 76796 ★ **Ryder Truck Rental**
728 E. Broadway St.
Altus, OK 73521
(405)482-7271
Ultimate Parent: Ryder System. **SIC:** 7359—Equipment Rental & Leasing Nec; 7513—Truck Rental & Leasing Without Drivers.

★ 76797 ★ **United Parcel Service**
1811 E. Broadway St.
Altus, OK 73521
(405)522-6575
Ultimate Parent: United Parcel Service of America. **SIC:** 4215—Courier Services Except by Air.

Alva

★ 76798 ★ **Coast to Coast Hardware**
417 College Ave.
Alva, OK 73717
(405)327-3230
Ultimate Parent: Servistar Corp. **SIC:** 5251—Hardware Stores.

★ 76799 ★ **Coast to Coast Home&Auto**
527 Barnes Ave.
Alva, OK 73717
(405)327-0149
Ultimate Parent: Servistar Corp. **SIC:** 5531—Automobile & Home Supply Stores.

★ 76800 ★ **Wal Mart Discount City**
Murray Plz.
Alva, OK 73717
(405)327-4021
Ultimate Parent: Wal-Mart Stores, Inc. **SIC:** 5311—Department Stores.

Ames

★ 76801 ★ **Farmers Elevator Co., Inc.**
Main St.
Ames, OK 73718
(405)753-4212
Officer: Howard Deleplane, Manager. **Ultimate Parent:** Archer Daniels Midland Co. **SIC:** 5153—Grain & Field Beans; 5191—Farm Supplies; 5541—Gasoline Service Stations. **Employee Count:** 19. **Sales:** 4 M.

Anadarko

★ 76802 ★ **Golden Peanut Co.**
PO Box 728
Anadarko, OK 73005-0728
(405)247-3338
Officer: David Preuninger. **Ultimate Parent:** Archer Daniels Midland Co. **SIC:** 2034—Dehydrated Fruits, Vegetables & Soups.

★ 76803 ★ **Golden Peanut Co.**
215 E. Georgia Ave.
Anadarko, OK 73005-4024
(405)247-9400
Ultimate Parent: Archer Daniels Midland Co. **SIC:** 5159—Farm-Product Raw Materials Nec.

★ 76804 ★ **Golden Peanut Co.**
3rd E. Central Blvd.
Anadarko, OK 73005
(405)247-3338
Officer: David Preuninger, Manager. **Ultimate Parent:** Archer Daniels Midland Co. **SIC:** 2034—Dehydrated Fruits, Vegetables & Soups.

★ 76805 ★ **Pizza Hut**
905 S. Mission St.
Anadarko, OK 73005
(405)247-5891
Ultimate Parent: Pepsico. **SIC:** 5812—Eating Places.

Antlers

★ 76806 ★ **Red Kap Ind.**
671 N. Hwy. 271
Antlers, OK 74523
(405)298-5565
Officer: Andy Luck, Manager. **Ultimate Parent:** VF Corp. **SIC:** 2325—Men's/Boys' Trousers & Slacks.

Apache

★ 76807 ★ **First Bank of Apache**
Coblike St.
Apache, OK 73006
(405)588-3361
Officer: Tom J. Manar, Chairman of the Board & President. **Ultimate Parent:** First Bank System. **SIC:** 6022—State Commercial Banks. **Employee Count:** 17.

Ardmore

★ 76808 ★ **American National Bank**
1901 N. Commerce St.
Ardmore, OK 73401-1382
(405)226-6222
Officer: Jesse E. Cross, President. **Ultimate Parent:** First Chicago Corp. **SIC:** 6021—National Commercial Banks. **Employee Count:** 40.

★ 76809 ★ **Arco Pipe Lie Vickers Station**
E. Cameron
Ardmore, OK 73401
(405)226-4140
Ultimate Parent: Atlantic Richfield Co., Inc. **SIC:** 4612—Crude Petroleum Pipelines.

★ 76810 ★ **Arco Pipe Line Co.**
NW of City
Ardmore, OK 73401
(405)223-7883
Location Type: Branch office. **Ultimate Parent:** Atlantic Richfield Co., Inc.

★ 76811 ★ **Arco Pipe Line Co.**
Ardmore, OK 73401
(405)223-7883
Location Type: Branch office. **Ultimate Parent:** Atlantic Richfield Co., Inc.

★ 76812 ★ **Arco Pipe Line Vickers Station**
E. Cameron
Ardmore, OK 73401
(405)226-4140
Ultimate Parent: Atlantic Richfield Co., Inc. **SIC:** 4612—Crude Petroleum Pipelines.

★ 76813 ★ **Kentucky Fried Chicken**
2611 W. Broadway Blvd.
Ardmore, OK 73401
(405)226-3242
Ultimate Parent: Pepsico. **SIC:** 5812—Eating Places.

★ 76814 ★ **Kentucky Fried Chicken**
808 N. Commerce St.
Ardmore, OK 73401
(405)223-3466
Ultimate Parent: Pepsico. **SIC:** 5812—Eating Places.

★ 76815 ★ **Mini Mart**
421 12th Ave. NW
Ardmore, OK 73401
(405)223-8260
Ultimate Parent: Kroger. **SIC:** 5411—Grocery Stores.

★ 76816 ★ **Payless Shoesource**
1000 W. Broadway Blvd.
Ardmore, OK 73401
(405)223-0652
Ultimate Parent: May Department Stores. **SIC:** 5661—Shoe Stores.

★ 76817 ★ **Pizza Hut**
800 N. Commerce St.
Ardmore, OK 73401 .
(405)226-2502
Ultimate Parent: Pepsico. **SIC:** 5812—Eating Places.

★ 76818 ★ **Radio Shack**
1107 Grand Ave.
Ardmore, OK 73401
Company Type: Division. **Ultimate Parent:** Tandy Corp. **SIC:** 5065—Electronic Parts & Equipment Nec; 5731—Radio, Television & Electronics Stores.

★ 76819 ★ **Ryder Truck Rental**
I 35
Ardmore, OK 73401
(405)226-3891
Ultimate Parent: Ryder System. **SIC:** 7359—Equipment Rental & Leasing Nec.

★ 76820 ★ **Ryder Truck Rental**
29 Fielding Ct
Ardmore, OK 73401
(405)226-9210
Ultimate Parent: Ryder System. **SIC:** 7513—Truck Rental & Leasing Without Drivers.

★ 76821 ★ **Taco Bell**
1007 N. Commerce St.
Ardmore, OK 73401
(405)223-1308
Ultimate Parent: Pepsico. **SIC:** 5812—Eating Places.

★ 76822 ★ **Texaco Inc.**
Hwy. 70 W
Ardmore, OK 73401
(405)223-2531
Ultimate Parent: Texaco. **SIC:** 1311—Crude Petroleum & Natural Gas.

★ 76823 ★ **Total Petroleum Inc.**
Cameron St. NE
Ardmore, OK 73401
(405)223-0535
Ultimate Parent: Total Petroleum Inc. **SIC:** 2911—Petroleum Refining; 5172—Petroleum Products Nec.

★ 76824 ★ **Total Petroleum Inc.**
Hwy. 142 & E. Cameron Rd.
Ardmore, OK 73401
Ultimate Parent: Total Petroleum Inc. **SIC:** 2911—Petroleum Refining.

★ 76825 ★ **Total Petroleum Inc.**
Cameron St. NE
Ardmore, OK 73401
(405)223-0535
Ultimate Parent: Total Petroleum Inc. **SIC:** 2911—Petroleum Refining; 5172—Petroleum Products Nec.

★ 76826 ★ **Wal Mart Discount Cities**
601 N. Commerce St.
Ardmore, OK 73401
(405)226-2886
Ultimate Parent: Wal-Mart Stores, Inc. **SIC:** 5311—Department Stores.

Atoka

★ 76827 ★   Pizza Hut
Hwy. 69 S
Atoka, OK 74525
(405)889-6644
Ultimate Parent: Pepsico. SIC: 5812—
Eating Places.

★ 76828 ★   Wal Mart Discount
City
Hwy. 69
Atoka, OK 74525
(405)889-6676
Ultimate Parent: Wal-Mart Stores, Inc. SIC:
5311—Department Stores.

★ 76829 ★   Wal Mart Discount
Pharmacy
Hwy. 69 S
Atoka, OK 74525
(405)889-3353
Ultimate Parent: Wal-Mart Stores, Inc. SIC:
5912—Drug Stores & Proprietary Stores.

Bartlesville

★ 76830 ★   Ace Hardware
209 N. Quapaw Ave.
Bartlesville, OK 74003
(918)336-3220
Ultimate Parent: Ace Hardware.

★ 76831 ★   Casual Corner
2350 SE Washington Blvd.
Bartlesville, OK 74006
(918)335-2466
Ultimate Parent: United States Shoe. SIC:
5621—Women's Clothing Stores; 5651—
Family Clothing Stores.

★ 76832 ★   Circus World
2350 SE Washington Blvd.
Bartlesville, OK 74006
(918)335-3110
Ultimate Parent: Melville. SIC: 5945—
Hobby, Toy & Game Shops.

★ 76833 ★   IBM Corp.
Professional Big
Bartlesville, OK 74006
(918)336-7371
Ultimate Parent: IBM. SIC: 5999—
Miscellaneous Retail Stores Nec.

★ 76834 ★   Kentucky Fried
Chicken
3125 E. Frank Phillips Blvd.
Bartlesville, OK 74006
(918)333-5332
Ultimate Parent: Pepsico. SIC: 5812—
Eating Places.

★ 76835 ★   Kmart Pharmacy
501 SE Washington Blvd.
Bartlesville, OK 74006
(918)333-9140
Ultimate Parent: K-Mart. SIC: 5912—Drug
Stores & Proprietary Stores.

★ 76836 ★   Mutual of New York
2425 Nowata Pl
Bartlesville, OK 74006
(918)335-3051
Ultimate Parent: Mutual of New York. SIC:
6411—Insurance Agents, Brokers &
Service.

★ 76837 ★   Phillips Alaska
Pipeline Corp.
4th & Keeler St.
Bartlesville, OK 74004
Ultimate Parent: Phillips Petroleum.

★ 76838 ★   Phillips Natrual Gas
Co.
4th & Keeler St.
Bartlesville, OK 74004
Ultimate Parent: Phillips Petroleum.

★ 76839 ★   Phillips Petroleum
Phillips Bldg.
Bartlesville, OK 74004
(918)661-6600
Company Type: Headquarters. Officer:
C.J. Silas. Employee Count: 19400. Sales:
12309 M. Fortune 500: Largest U.S.
Industrial Corporations: Ranking 37.

★ 76840 ★   Phillips Petroleum Co.
4th & Keeler St.
Bartlesville, OK 74004
(918)661-6600 Fax: (918)661-7636 Telex:
492455
Ultimate Parent: Phillips Petroleum.

★ 76841 ★   Phillips Petroleum Co.
United Kingdom Ltd.
4th & Keeler St.
Bartlesville, OK 74004
Ultimate Parent: Phillips Petroleum.

★ 76842 ★   Phillips Pipe Line Co.
370 Adams Bldg.
Bartlesville, OK 74004
(918)661-4166 Fax: (918)662-2304
Ultimate Parent: Phillips Petroleum.

★ 76843 ★   Phillips Puerto Rico
Core Inc.
4th & Keeler St.
Bartlesville, OK 74004
Ultimate Parent: Phillips Petroleum.

★ 76844 ★   Phillips Research
Center
Pawhuska US Hwy. 60 W.
Bartlesville, OK 74004
Ultimate Parent: Phillips Petroleum. SIC:
2869—Industrial Organic Chemicals Nec;
2879—Agricultural Chemicals Nec; 3083—
Laminated Plastics Plate & Sheet; 2899—
Chemical Preparations Nec.

★ 76845 ★   Phillips Research Ctr.
Pawhuska Rd.
US Hwy. 60 W
Bartlesville, OK 74004
Ultimate Parent: Phillips Petroleum. SIC:
2869—Industrial Organic Chemicals Nec;
2879—Agricultural Chemicals Nec; 3083—
Laminated Plastics Plate & Sheet; 2087—
Flavoring Extracts & Syrups Nec; 2821—
Plastics Materials & Resins.

★ 76846 ★   Philtankers Inc.
4th & Keeler St.
Bartlesville, OK 74004
(918)661-4121 Fax: (918)661-8142
Ultimate Parent: Phillips Petroleum.

★ 76847 ★   Pizza Hut
300 S. Cherokee Ave.
Bartlesville, OK 74003
(918)337-0976
Ultimate Parent: Pepsico. SIC: 5812—
Eating Places.

★ 76848 ★   Pizza Hut
830 S. Madison Blvd.
Bartlesville, OK 74006
(918)333-7711
Ultimate Parent: Pepsico. SIC: 5812—
Eating Places.

★ 76849 ★   Radio Shack
2350 SE Washington Blvd.
Bartlesville, OK 74006
(918)335-0300
Company Type: Division. Ultimate Parent:
Tandy Corp. SIC: 5065—Electronic Parts &
Equipment Nec.

★ 76850 ★   Radio Shack
122 Washington Park Mall
Bartlesville, OK 74006
(918)335-0307
Company Type: Division. Ultimate Parent:
Tandy Corp. SIC: 5734—Computer &
Software Stores.

★ 76851 ★   Radio Shack
576 SE Washington Blvd.
Bartlesville, OK 74006
(918)333-7766
Company Type: Division. Ultimate Parent:
Tandy Corp. SIC: 5065—Electronic Parts &
Equipment Nec.

★ 76852 ★   Ryder Truck Rental
2901 E. Frank Phillips Blvd.
Bartlesville, OK 74006
(918)335-0700
Ultimate Parent: Ryder System. SIC:
7359—Equipment Rental & Leasing Nec.

★ 76853 ★   TRW Inc.
Reda Pump Div.
509 W. Hensley Boulevard
Bartlesville, OK 74003
Company Type: Division. Ultimate Parent:
TRW, Inc. SIC: 3561—Pumps & Pumping
Equipment; 3621—Motors & Generators.

★ 76854 ★   Wal Mart Discount
Pharmacy
3901 SE Adams Rd.
Bartlesville, OK 74006
(918)333-6910
Ultimate Parent: Wal-Mart Stores, Inc. SIC:
5912—Drug Stores & Proprietary Stores.

★ 76855 ★   Waldenbooks
2350 SE Washington Blvd.
Bartlesville, OK 74006
(918)335-0866
Ultimate Parent: K-Mart. SIC: 5942—Book
Stores.

Beaver

★ 76856 ★   Cabot Petroleum
Corp.
Beaver, OK 73932
(405)625-4589
Ultimate Parent: Cabot. SIC: 4932—Gas &
Other Services Combined.

★ 76857 ★   Pizza Hut
415 Douglas Ave.
Beaver, OK 73932
(405)625-4840
Ultimate Parent: Pepsico. SIC: 5812—
Eating Places.

Bethany

★ 76858 ★   Hewlett Packard Co.
6301 N. Meridian
Bethany, OK 73008
(405)721-0200
Ultimate Parent: Hewlett-Packard. SIC:
5044—Office Equipment.

★ 76859 ★   Pizza Hut
2216 N. Rockwell Ave.
Bethany, OK 73008
(405)789-8686
Ultimate Parent: Pepsico. SIC: 5812—
Eating Places.

★ 76860 ★   Radio Shack
Rockwell Plz.
Bethany, OK 73008
(405)720-9484
Company Type: Division. Ultimate Parent:
Tandy Corp.

Bixby

★ 76861 ★   Kentucky Fried
Chicken
11753 S. Memorial Dr.
Bixby, OK 74008
(918)369-5758
Ultimate Parent: Pepsico. SIC: 5812—
Eating Places.

★ 76862 ★   Pizza Hut
12102 S. Memorial Dr.
Bixby, OK 74008
(918)369-2066
Ultimate Parent: Pepsico. SIC: 5812—
Eating Places.

★ 76863 ★   Wal Mart Discount
Cities
15100 S. Memorial Dr.
Bixby, OK 74008
(918)366-4498
Ultimate Parent: Wal-Mart Stores, Inc. SIC:
5311—Department Stores.

Blackwell

★ 76864 ★   First National Bank &
Trust
102 N. Main St.
Blackwell, OK 74631
(405)363-3313
Ultimate Parent: Society Corp. SIC: 6021—
National Commercial Banks; 6022—State
Commercial Banks.

★ 76865 ★   Kentucky Fried
Chicken
510 W. Doolin Ave.
Blackwell, OK 74631
(405)363-3333
Ultimate Parent: Pepsico. SIC: 5812—
Eating Places.

★ 76866 ★   Wal Mart
1219 W. Doolin Ave.
Blackwell, OK 74631
(405)363-4111
Ultimate Parent: Wal-Mart Stores, Inc. SIC:
5311—Department Stores.

Bradley

★ 76867 ★   Marathon Oil Co.
Bradley, OK 73011
(405)462-7328
Ultimate Parent: USX Corp. SIC: 5172—
Petroleum Products Nec.

★ 76868 ★   Marathon Oil Co.
Bradley, OK 73011
(405)462-7328
Ultimate Parent: USX Corp. SIC: 5172—
Petroleum Products Nec.

Bristow

★ 76869 ★   American National
Bank
111 W. 7th Ave.
Bristow, OK 74010-2401
(918)367-3311
Company Type: Subsidiary. Officer: Tracy
Kelly, Chairman of the Board. Ultimate
Parent: First Chicago Corp. SIC: 6021—
National Commercial Banks. Employee
Count: 120.

★ 76870 ★   Kentucky Fried
Chicken
200 W. 4th Ave.
Bristow, OK 74010
(918)367-5210
Ultimate Parent: Pepsico. SIC: 5812—
Eating Places.

★ 76871 ★   Kwikset Corp.
500 Industrial Rd. S.
Bristow, OK 74010
Ultimate Parent: Black & Decker Corp.
SIC: 3429—Hardware Nec.

★ 76872 ★   Kwikset Corp.
500 Industrial Rd.
Bristow, OK 74010-9763
(918)367-5511
Company Type: Branch. Officer: Joe
Biggs. Ultimate Parent: Black & Decker
Corp. SIC: 3429—Hardware Nec; 7699—
Repair Services Nec.

★ 76873 ★   Pizza Hut
800 S. Main St.
Bristow, OK 74010
(918)367-3353
Ultimate Parent: Pepsico. SIC: 5812—
Eating Places.

★ 76874 ★   Ryder Truck Rental
202 S. Main St.
Bristow, OK 74010
(918)367-9600
Ultimate Parent: Ryder System. SIC:
7513—Truck Rental & Leasing Without
Drivers.

★ 76875 ★   Wal Mart Discount
Co.
Ok Hwy. 48
Bristow, OK 74010
(918)367-3335
Ultimate Parent: Wal-Mart Stores, Inc. SIC:
5311—Department Stores.

★ 76876 ★   Wal Mart Pharmacy
121 W. 12th Ave.
Bristow, OK 74010
(918)367-5515
Ultimate Parent: Wal-Mart Stores, Inc. SIC:
5912—Drug Stores & Proprietary Stores.

Broken Arrow

★ 76877 ★   Ace Hardware&Home
Center
Vandever Shopping Ctr.
Broken Arrow, OK 74013
(918)455-3626
Ultimate Parent: Ace Hardware. SIC:
5083—Farm & Garden Machinery.

★ **76878** ★   **Baker Oil Tools Inc.**
3000 N. Hemlock Cir.
Broken Arrow, OK 74012
(918)455-3000
Officer: Rex Wilson, Manager. **Ultimate Parent:** Baker Hughes. **SIC:** 3494—Valves & Pipe Fittings Nec.

★ **76879** ★   **Braden Carco Gearmatic**
800 E. Dallas
Broken Arrow, OK 74012
Ultimate Parent: Paccar. **SIC:** 3531—Construction Machinery.

★ **76880** ★   **Continental Industries**
91st St.
Broken Arrow, OK 74012
Ultimate Parent: Handy & Harman. **SIC:** 3498—Fabricated Pipe & Fittings.

★ **76881** ★   **Continental Industries Inc.**
Hwy. 51 E
Broken Arrow, OK 74014
(918)258-1566
Ultimate Parent: Handy & Harman. **SIC:** 3089—Plastics Products Nec.

★ **76882** ★   **Deluxe Check Printers Inc.**
1765 N. Juniper Ave.
Broken Arrow, OK 74012
Ultimate Parent: Deluxe Corp. **SIC:** 2782—Blankbooks & Looseleaf Binders; 2752—Commercial Printing—Lithographic.

★ **76883** ★   **Dresser-Rand Compression Services**
20602 E. 81st St.
Broken Arrow, OK 74014
Ultimate Parent: Dresser Industries Inc. **SIC:** 3563—Air & Gas Compressors.

★ **76884** ★   **Kentucky Fried Chicken**
1933 S. Elm Pl
Broken Arrow, OK 74012
(918)455-0044
Ultimate Parent: Pepsico. **SIC:** 5812—Eating Places.

★ **76885** ★   **Linens N Things**
3025 N. Aspen Ave.
Broken Arrow, OK 74012
(918)251-2619
Ultimate Parent: Melville. **SIC:** 5719—Miscellaneous Home Furnishings Stores.

★ **76886** ★   **Paccar**
PACCAR Winch Div.
800 E. Dallas Ave.
Broken Arrow, OK 74012
(918)251-8511 **Fax:** (918)251-6824
Company Type: Division. **Officer:** Gerald Bowden, General Manager. **Ultimate Parent:** Paccar.

★ **76887** ★   **Piggly Wiggly**
507 N. Main St.
Broken Arrow, OK 74012
(918)251-3446
Ultimate Parent: Bruno's. **SIC:** 5411—Grocery Stores.

★ **76888** ★   **Pizza Hut**
900 S. Aspen Ave.
Broken Arrow, OK 74012
(918)251-2536
Ultimate Parent: Pepsico. **SIC:** 5812—Eating Places.

★ **76889** ★   **Sonoco Products Co.**
2514 N. Hemlock
Broken Arrow, OK 74012
(918)258-5651
Ultimate Parent: Sonoco Products. **SIC:** 2675—Die-Cut Paper & Board; 2679—Converted Paper Products Nec.

★ **76890** ★   **Wal Mart Discount Cities**
2300 E. Kenosha St.
Broken Arrow, OK 74012
(918)355-2235
Ultimate Parent: Wal-Mart Stores, Inc. **SIC:** 5311—Department Stores.

★ **76891** ★   **Wal Mart Pharmacy**
Broken Arrow Plz.
Broken Arrow, OK 74012
(918)251-1520
Ultimate Parent: Wal-Mart Stores, Inc. **SIC:** 5912—Drug Stores & Proprietary Stores.

Broken Bow

★ **76892** ★   **Mary Kay Cosmetics**
107 Maple St.
Broken Bow, OK 74728
(405)584-3895
Ultimate Parent: Mary Kay Cosmetics.

★ **76893** ★   **Mary Kay Cosmetics, Inc.**
RR 1
Broken Bow, OK 74728
(405)584-2812
Ultimate Parent: Mary Kay Cosmetics. **SIC:** 5999—Miscellaneous Retail Stores Nec.

★ **76894** ★   **Piggly Wiggly**
506 S. Park Dr.
Broken Bow, OK 74728
(405)584-3434
Ultimate Parent: Bruno's. **SIC:** 5411—Grocery Stores.

★ **76895** ★   **Tyson Foods Inc.**
Hwy. 70 S
Broken Bow, OK 74727
(405)584-9191
Officer: Chris Graves, Manager. **Ultimate Parent:** Tyson Foods, Inc. **SIC:** 2015—Poultry Slaughtering & Processing.

★ **76896** ★   **Tyson Foods Inc.**
Hwy. 259 & 70 South
Broken Bow, OK 74728
Ultimate Parent: Tyson Foods, Inc. **SIC:** 2000—Food & Kindred Products.

★ **76897** ★   **Tyson Foods Inc. Broken Bow Processing**
Hwy. 70 S.
Broken Bow, OK 74728-0220
Ultimate Parent: Tyson Foods, Inc. **SIC:** 2015—Poultry Slaughtering & Processing.

★ **76898** ★   **Tyson Foods Inc. Craig Feed Mill**
Craig Rd.
Broken Bow, OK 74728-0608
Ultimate Parent: Tyson Foods, Inc. **SIC:** 2048—Prepared Feeds Nec.

★ **76899** ★   **Wal Mart Discount Pharmacy**
Hwy. 70 S
Broken Bow, OK 74728
(405)584-3324
Ultimate Parent: Wal-Mart Stores, Inc. **SIC:** 5311—Department Stores.

★ **76900** ★   **Wal Mart Pro Pharmacy**
997 PO Box
Broken Bow, OK 74728
Ultimate Parent: Wal-Mart Stores, Inc. **SIC:** 5912—Drug Stores & Proprietary Stores.

★ **76901** ★   **Weyerhaeuser Co.**
Rte. 1 Box 618
Broken Bow, OK 74728
Location Type: Plant. **Ultimate Parent:** Weyerhaeuser Co. **SIC:** 2493—Reconstituted Wood Products.

Burns Flat

★ **76902** ★   **ALLTEL Oklahoma Inc.**
Clinton Sherman Airpark, Bldg. 825
PO Box 750
Burns Flat, OK 73624
(405)562-3171
Ultimate Parent: ALLTEL Corp. **SIC:** 4812—Radiotelephone Communications.

★ **76903** ★   **Flight Systems Inc.**
Burns Flat, OK 73624
(405)562-4116
Ultimate Parent: B.F. Goodrich. **SIC:** 2892—Explosives.

Camargo

★ **76904** ★   **Halliburton Resource Mgt**
Camargo, OK 73835
(405)926-3487
Ultimate Parent: Halliburton. **SIC:** 5084—Industrial Machinery & Equipment.

Carnegie

★ **76905** ★   **Avon Products Inc.**
9 Towne E
Carnegie, OK 73015
(405)654-2149
Ultimate Parent: Avon Products, Inc. **SIC:** 5999—Miscellaneous Retail Stores Nec.

★ **76906** ★   **Pizza Hut**
Hwy. 9 E
Carnegie, OK 73015
(405)654-1213
Ultimate Parent: Pepsico. **SIC:** 5812—Eating Places.

Catoosa

★ **76907** ★   **Agrico Chemical Co.**
N City
Catoosa, OK 74015
(918)266-151,1
Ultimate Parent: Freeport-McMoran. **SIC:** 5191—Farm Supplies.

★ **76908** ★   **Allied-Signal Inc.**
Environmental Catalysts
1301 Main Pky.
Catoosa, OK 74015
Ultimate Parent: Allied-Signal Inc. **SIC:** 3714—Motor Vehicle Parts & Accessories; 2819—Industrial Inorganic Chemicals Nec.

★ **76909** ★   **Gear Products Inc.**
1111 N. 161st Ave. E
Catoosa, OK 74015
(918)234-3044
Ultimate Parent: Blount Inc. **SIC:** 5084—Industrial Machinery & Equipment.

★ **76910** ★   **Pizza Hut**
308 N. 193 Ave. E
Catoosa, OK 74015
(918)266-3361
Ultimate Parent: Pepsico. **SIC:** 5812—Eating Places.

★ **76911** ★   **Safety Kleen Corp.**
16215 E. Marshall Ct
Catoosa, OK 74015
(918)234-5185
Ultimate Parent: Safety-Kleen. **SIC:** 5013—Motor Vehicle Supplies & New Parts.

Cement

★ **76912** ★   **Mobil Oil Corp.**
300 W. 3rd
Cement, OK 73017
(405)489-3249
Ultimate Parent: Mobil. **SIC:** 1311—Crude Petroleum & Natural Gas.

Chandler

★ **76913** ★   **Burlington Northern R R Co.**
15th
Chandler, OK 74834
(405)258-1164
Ultimate Parent: Burlington Northern. **SIC:** 4011—Railroads—Line-Haul Operating.

Chattanooga

★ **76914** ★   **First Bank**
99 PO Box
Chattanooga, OK 73528
(405)597-6666
Ultimate Parent: Shawmut National Corp. **SIC:** 6099—Functions Related to Deposit Banking.

Checotah

★ **76915** ★   **Olga**
Hwy. 69 S. & 1 40
Checotah, OK 74426
(918)473-2221
Officer: Dwitt Short, Manager. **Ultimate Parent:** Warnaco Group. **SIC:** 2339—Women's/Misses' Outerwear Nec.

★ **76916** ★   **Pizza Hut**
701 S. Broadway St.
Checotah, OK 74426
(918)473-2242
Ultimate Parent: Pepsico. **SIC:** 5812—Eating Places.

★ **76917** ★   **Wal Mart**
Hwy. 266 W
Checotah, OK 74426
(918)473-2201
Ultimate Parent: Wal-Mart Stores, Inc. **SIC:** 5311—Department Stores.

Cherokee

★ **76918** ★   **Pizza Hut**
Loop Dr.
Cherokee, OK 73728
(405)596-2548
Ultimate Parent: Pepsico. **SIC:** 5812—Eating Places.

Chester

★ **76919** ★   **Union Texas Petroleum Corp.**
Chester, OK 73838
(405)764-3397
Ultimate Parent: Union Texas Petroleum. **SIC:** 4925—Gas Production & Distribution Nec.

Chickasha

★ **76920** ★   **Arvin Industries Inc.**
Gabriel Shock Absorber Plant
PO Box 988, Methrin Industrial
Chickasha, OK 73018
(405)224-8600 **Fax:** (405)224-9005
Company Type: Division. **Location Type:** Plant. **Ultimate Parent:** Arvin Industries Inc. **SIC:** 3714—Motor Vehicle Parts & Accessories.

★ **76921** ★   **Delta Faucet Co.**
Hwy. 62 W
Chickasha, OK 73018
Ultimate Parent: Masco. **SIC:** 3432—Plumbing Fixtures Fittings & Trim; 3471—Plating & Polishing.

★ **76922** ★   **Delta Faucet Co.**
Hwy. 62 W.
Chickasha, OK 73018
Ultimate Parent: Masco. **SIC:** 3432—Plumbing Fixtures Fittings & Trim.

★ **76923** ★   **Delta Faucet of Oklahoma**
2500 Hwy. 62 W.
Chickasha, OK 73018
Ultimate Parent: Masco. **SIC:** 3432—Plumbing Fixtures Fittings & Trim.

★ **76924** ★   **Farmland Industries Inc.**
913 N. 9th St.
Chickasha, OK 73018
(405)224-5850
Officer: Jerry Gibson, Manager. **Ultimate Parent:** Farmland Industries. **SIC:** 2048—Prepared Feeds Nec.

★ **76925** ★   **First National Bank & Trust**
602 W. Grand Ave.
Chickasha, OK 73018
(405)224-2200
Ultimate Parent: Society Corp. **SIC:** 6021—National Commercial Banks.

★ **76926** ★   **Grocery USA**
501 Michigan Ave.
Chickasha, OK 73018
Ultimate Parent: Pet. **SIC:** 2038—Frozen Specialties Nec.

★ **76927** ★   **Halliburton Resource Manage**
W Hwy. 62
Chickasha, OK 73018
(405)222-3042
Ultimate Parent: Halliburton. **SIC:** 5084—Industrial Machinery & Equipment.

★ **76928** ★   **Kentucky Fried Chicken**
1228 S. 4th St.
Chickasha, OK 73018
(405)224-0101
Ultimate Parent: Pepsico. **SIC:** 5812—Eating Places.

★ **76929** ★   **Maremont Corp.**
Methvin Industrial Park
Chickasha, OK 73018
Ultimate Parent: Arvin Industries Inc. **SIC:** 3714—Motor Vehicle Parts & Accessories.

★ 76930 ★ Maremount Corp.
Shock Absorber
Methrin Industrial Park
Chickasha, OK 73023
(405)224-8600
Officer: Perry Ramsey, Manager. Ultimate
Parent: Arvin Industries Inc. SIC: 3714—
Motor Vehicle Parts & Accessories.

★ 76931 ★ Mary Kay Cosmetics
1502 W. Country Club Rd.
Chickasha, OK 73018
(405)224-8300
Ultimate Parent: Mary Kay Cosmetics. SIC:
5999—Miscellaneous Retail Stores Nec.

★ 76932 ★ Mobil Oil Corp.
Southeast City
Chickasha, OK 73018
(405)224-6508
Ultimate Parent: Mobil. SIC: 1382—Oil &
Gas Exploration Services; 7389—Business
Services Nec.

★ 76933 ★ Payless Shoesource
1928 S. 4th St.
Chickasha, OK 73018
(405)224-6770
Ultimate Parent: May Department Stores.
SIC: 5661—Shoe Stores.

★ 76934 ★ Pet, Inc.
501 Michigan Ave.
PO Box 310
Chickasha, OK 73023
(405)224-3445 Fax: (405)222-3509
Location Type: Plant. Officer: David
Leibensperger, Plant Manager. Ultimate
Parent: Pet. SIC: 2038—Frozen Specialties
Nec.

★ 76935 ★ Pet Inc.
Frozen Foods Div.
502 W. Michigan Ave.
Chickasha, OK 73018
(405)224-3445
Company Type: Division. Officer: Dave
Leibensperger, Manager. Ultimate Parent:
Pet. SIC: 2037—Frozen Fruits &
Vegetables; 2038—Frozen Specialties Nec.

★ 76936 ★ Pizza Hut
2001 S. 4th St.
Chickasha, OK 73018
(405)224-3190
Ultimate Parent: Pepsico. SIC: 5812—
Eating Places.

★ 76937 ★ Ryder Truck Rental
602 W. Choctaw Ave.
Chickasha, OK 73018
(405)224-0001
Ultimate Parent: Ryder System. SIC:
7513—Truck Rental & Leasing Without
Drivers.

★ 76938 ★ Sun Refining &
Marketing Co.
State Hwy. 19
Chickasha, OK 73018
(405)224-1135
Ultimate Parent: Sun. SIC: 5171—
Petroleum Bulk Stations & Terminals.

★ 76939 ★ Wal Mart Discount
Cities
2403 Ponderosa Dr.
Chickasha, OK 73018
(405)222-0150
Ultimate Parent: Wal-Mart Stores, Inc. SIC:
5399—Miscellaneous General Merchandise
Store.

★ 76940 ★ Wal Mart Pharmacy
2403 Ponderosa Dr.
Chickasha, OK 73018
(405)224-0292
Ultimate Parent: Wal-Mart Stores, Inc. SIC:
5912—Drug Stores & Proprietary Stores.

★ 76941 ★ Wal Mart Tire/
Automotive
2403 Ponderosa Dr.
Chickasha, OK 73018
(405)224-5019
Ultimate Parent: Wal-Mart Stores, Inc. SIC:
5311—Department Stores.

Chickasha Ok

★ 76942 ★ Mobil Oil Corporation
Southeast of City
Chickasha Ok, OK 73018
(405)224-6509
Ultimate Parent: Mobil. SIC: 1382—Oil &
Gas Exploration Services.

Choctaw

★ 76943 ★ Pizza Hut
14551 NE 23rd St.
Choctaw, OK 73020
(405)390-2505
Ultimate Parent: Pepsico.

Claremore

★ 76944 ★ Allegheny Ludlum
Corp.
401 E. 30th St. N
Claremore, OK 74017
(918)341-8711
Officer: William G. Bieber, Manager.
Ultimate Parent: Allegheny Ludlum Corp.
SIC: 3312—Blast Furnaces & Steel Mills;
3498—Fabricated Pipe & Fittings.

★ 76945 ★ Allegheny Ludlum
Corp.
PO Box 948
Hwy. 66 & Lowry Rd.
Claremore, OK 74018
(918)341-8711
Location Type: Plant. Officer: Bill Bieber,
General Manager. Ultimate Parent:
Allegheny Ludlum Corp. SIC: 3312—Blast
Furnaces & Steel Mills.

★ 76946 ★ Allegheny Ludlum
Corp. Tubular
PO Box 948
Claremore, OK 74018-0948
(918)341-8711
Location Type: Branch office. Officer: W.
G. Beiber, General Manager. Ultimate Parent: Allegheny
Ludlum Corp. SIC: 3312—Blast Furnaces &
Steel Mills; 3317—Steel Pipe & Tubes.

★ 76947 ★ Baker Hughes Prod.
Tools
Centrilift
200 W. Stuart Roosa Dr.
Claremore, OK 74017
(918)341-9600 Fax: (918)342-0260
Company Type: Division. Officer: Joseph
F. Brady, President. Ultimate Parent: Baker
Hughes. SIC: 3533—Oil & Gas Field
Machinery. Employee Count: 1250. Sales:
150000000 M.

★ 76948 ★ Centrilift
200 West Stuart Roosa
Claremore, OK 74017-3095
Ultimate Parent: Baker Hughes. SIC:
3561—Pumps & Pumping Equipment.

★ 76949 ★ Centrilift
200 W. Stuart Roosa Dr.
Claremore, OK 74017-3095
Ultimate Parent: Baker Hughes. SIC:
3561—Pumps & Pumping Equipment.

★ 76950 ★ Centrilift Cable
2210 E. L. Anderson Blvd.
Claremore, OK 74017
Ultimate Parent: Baker Hughes. SIC:
3357—Nonferrous Wiredrawing & Insulating.

★ 76951 ★ Centrilift Co.
210 El Anderson Blvd.
Claremore, OK 74017
(918)341-9600
Officer: Dave Neuroth, Vice President.
Ultimate Parent: Baker Hughes. SIC:
3533—Oil & Gas Field Machinery; 3561—
Pumps & Pumping Equipment; 3566—
Speed Changers, Drives & Gears.

★ 76952 ★ Greyhound Bus Lines
614 Patti Pag Blvdw
Claremore, OK 74017
(918)341-2135
Ultimate Parent: Greyhound Lines Inc. SIC:
4131—Intercity & Rural Bus Transportation.

★ 76953 ★ McDonalds
Restaurant
1220 W. Will Rogers Blvd.
Claremore, OK 74017
(918)342-2323
Ultimate Parent: McDonald's.

★ 76954 ★ Payless Shoesource
998 Will Rogers Blvd. W.
Claremore, OK 74017
(918)342-5882
Ultimate Parent: May Department Stores.
SIC: 5661—Shoe Stores.

★ 76955 ★ Pizza Hut
802 Will Rogers Blvd. W
Claremore, OK 74017
(918)341-8881
Ultimate Parent: Pepsico. SIC: 5812—
Eating Places.

★ 76956 ★ Radio Shack
510 S. Davis Ave.
Claremore, OK 74017
(918)341-0987
Company Type: Division. Ultimate Parent:
Tandy Corp. SIC: 5731—Radio, Television
& Electronics Stores.

★ 76957 ★ Taco Bell
1211 W. Will Rogers Blvd.
Claremore, OK 74017
(918)341-3787
Ultimate Parent: Pepsico.

★ 76958 ★ Wal Mart
Prescriptions
1500 S. Lynn Riggs Blvd.
Claremore, OK 74017
Ultimate Parent: Wal-Mart Stores, Inc. SIC:
5912—Drug Stores & Proprietary Stores.

★ 76959 ★ Worthington Cylinder
Corp.
2800 N. Lynn Riggs Blvd.
Claremore, OK 74017
Ultimate Parent: Worthington Industries,
Inc. SIC: 3499—Fabricated Metal Products
Nec.

★ 76960 ★ Worthington
Cylinders Corp.
2800 N. Lynn Riggs Blvd.
Claremore, OK 74017
Ultimate Parent: Worthington Industries,
Inc. SIC: 3443—Fabricated Plate Work—
Boiler Shops.

Cleveland

★ 76961 ★ Kentucky Fried
Chicken
800 N. Broadway St.
Cleveland, OK 74020
(918)358-5558
Ultimate Parent: Pepsico. SIC: 5812—
Eating Places.

★ 76962 ★ Wal Mart Discount
City
1004 N. Broadway St.
Cleveland, OK 74020
(918)358-3553
Ultimate Parent: Wal-Mart Stores, Inc.

★ 76963 ★ Wal Mart Discount
Pharmacy
1004 N. Broadway St.
Cleveland, OK 74020
(918)358-5269
Ultimate Parent: Wal-Mart Stores, Inc. SIC:
5912—Drug Stores & Proprietary Stores.

Clinton

★ 76964 ★ Collins & Aikman
Corp.
Auto Div. Clinton Plant
Hwy. 183 S
Clinton, OK 73601
Company Type: Division. Location Type:
Plant. Ultimate Parent: Collins & Aikman
Group. SIC: 2600—Paper & Allied Products.

★ 76965 ★ Mary Kay Cosmetics
1 Pond Ridge Rd.
Clinton, OK 73601
(405)323-1787
Ultimate Parent: Mary Kay Cosmetics. SIC:
5999—Miscellaneous Retail Stores Nec.

Colbert

★ 76966 ★ Mobil Station
Colbert, OK 74733
(405)296-2608
Ultimate Parent: Mobil. SIC: 5541—
Gasoline Service Stations.

★ 76967 ★ Stop & Shop No. 1645
Colbert, OK 74733
(405)296-7845
Ultimate Parent: Stop & Shop. SIC: 5411—
Grocery Stores.

Colgate

★ 76968 ★ Wrangler
Hwy. 75 S
Colgate, OK 74538
(405)927-2361
Officer: Bob Sutton, Manager. Ultimate
Parent: VF Corp. SIC: 2325—Men's/Boys'
Trousers & Slacks.

Collinsville

★ 76969 ★ Wal Mart Discount
City
Hwy. 20
Collinsville, OK 74021
(918)371-2024
Ultimate Parent: Wal-Mart Stores, Inc. SIC:
5311—Department Stores.

★ 76970 ★ Wal Mart Discount
Pharmacy
Hwy. 20
Collinsville, OK 74021
(918)371-2515
Ultimate Parent: Wal-Mart Stores, Inc. SIC:
5311—Department Stores.

Copan

★ 76971 ★ Arco Pipe Line Co.
North of city
Copan, OK 74022
(918)532-4392
Company Type: Division. Location Type:
Branch office. Ultimate Parent: Atlantic
Richfield Co., Inc. SIC: 2911—Petroleum
Refining.

★ 76972 ★ Arco Pipe Line Co.
Copan, OK 74022
(918)532-4392
Location Type: Branch office. Ultimate
Parent: Atlantic Richfield Co., Inc. SIC:
2911—Petroleum Refining.

Cordell

★ 76973 ★ Coast to Coast Home
& Auto
105 N. Market St.
Cordell, OK 73632
(405)832-2533
Ultimate Parent: Servistar Corp. SIC:
5531—Automobile & Home Supply Stores.

Coweta

★ 76974 ★ Mini Mart
200 Country Plz.
Coweta, OK 74429
(918)486-4411
Ultimate Parent: Kroger. SIC: 5411—
Grocery Stores.

Cushing

★ 76975 ★ Arco Pipe Line Co.
S. of city
Cushing, OK 74023
(918)225-1310
Location Type: Branch office. Ultimate
Parent: Atlantic Richfield Co., Inc. SIC:
4612—Crude Petroleum Pipelines.

★ 76976 ★ Arco Pipe Line Co.
Cushing, OK 74023
(918)225-1310
Location Type: Branch office. Ultimate
Parent: Atlantic Richfield Co., Inc. SIC:
4612—Crude Petroleum Pipelines.

★ 76977 ★ Coast to Coast
2330 E. Main St.
Cushing, OK 74023
(918)225-5322
Ultimate Parent: Servistar Corp. SIC:
5251—Hardware Stores.

★ 76978 ★   Halliburton Resource Mgt
500 E. Johnson St.
Cushing, OK 74023
(918)225-1853
Ultimate Parent: Halliburton. SIC: 5084—Industrial Machinery & Equipment.

★ 76979 ★   Kentucky Fried Chicken
723 E. Main St.
Cushing, OK 74023
(918)225-0080
Ultimate Parent: Pepsico. SIC: 5812—Eating Places; 5812—Eating Places.

★ 76980 ★   McDonalds of Cushing
2230 E. Main St.
Cushing, OK 74023
(918)225-7515
Ultimate Parent: McDonald's. SIC: 5812—Eating Places.

★ 76981 ★   Pizza Hut
1108 E. Main St.
Cushing, OK 74023
(918)225-5544
Ultimate Parent: Pepsico. SIC: 5812—Eating Places.

★ 76982 ★   Ryder Truck Rental
1010 S. Little Ave.
Cushing, OK 74023
(918)225-0932
Ultimate Parent: Ryder System. SIC: 4214—Local Trucking With Storage.

★ 76983 ★   Wal Mart Pharmacy
2004 E. Main St.
Cushing, OK 74023
(918)225-6320
Ultimate Parent: Wal-Mart Stores, Inc. SIC: 5912—Drug Stores & Proprietary Stores.

Cyril

★ 76984 ★   Underwriters Adjusting Co.
Cyril, OK 73029
(405)464-3494
Ultimate Parent: Continental. SIC: 6411—Insurance Agents, Brokers & Service.

Davis

★ 76985 ★   Exxon
200 S. D St.
Davis, OK 73030
(405)369-9022
Ultimate Parent: Exxon. SIC: 5541—Gasoline Service Stations.

★ 76986 ★   Halliburton Services Davis Mfg.
Industrial Park S. of Davis
Davis, OK 73030
Ultimate Parent: Halliburton. SIC: 3533—Oil & Gas Field Machinery.

★ 76987 ★   Halliburton Services Manufacturing Facility
Industrial Park South of Davis
Davis, OK 73030
Ultimate Parent: Halliburton. SIC: 3533—Oil & Gas Field Machinery.

Del City

★ 76988 ★   Taco Bell
4700 SE 29th St.
Del City, OK 73115
Ultimate Parent: Pepsico. SIC: 5812—Eating Places.

Dewey

★ 76989 ★   Pizza Hut
317 S. Osage Ave.
Dewey, OK 74029
(918)534-1450
Ultimate Parent: Pepsico. SIC: 5812—Eating Places.

Drumright

★ 76990 ★   Texaco Inc.
S of City
Drumright, OK 74030
(918)352-2513
Ultimate Parent: Texaco. SIC: 1389—Oil & Gas Field Services Nec.

Duncan

★ 76991 ★   Halliburton Services Manufacturing
East State Hwy. 7
Duncan, OK 73536-0100
Ultimate Parent: Halliburton. SIC: 3533—Oil & Gas Field Machinery.

★ 76992 ★   Halliburton Services Manufacturing Facility
E. State Hwy. 7
Duncan, OK 73536-0100
Ultimate Parent: Halliburton. SIC: 3533—Oil & Gas Field Machinery.

★ 76993 ★   Kentucky Fried Chicken
1208 N. Hwy. 81
Duncan, OK 73533
(405)255-1134
Ultimate Parent: Pepsico. SIC: 5812—Eating Places.

★ 76994 ★   McDonalds Restaurants
2203 N. N St.
Duncan, OK 73533
(405)252-1398
Ultimate Parent: McDonald's. SIC: 5812—Eating Places.

★ 76995 ★   Nalco Chemical
2201 Briarcrest
Duncan, OK 73533
(405)252-6053
Ultimate Parent: Nalco Chemical Co. SIC: 5169—Chemicals & Allied Products Nec.

★ 76996 ★   Pizza Hut
18 N. 81st Bypass
Duncan, OK 73533
(405)255-6996
Ultimate Parent: Pepsico. SIC: 5812—Eating Places.

★ 76997 ★   Radio Shack
508 N. 81st Hwy.
Duncan, OK 73533
(405)252-4847
Company Type: Division. Ultimate Parent: Tandy Corp. SIC: 5065—Electronic Parts & Equipment Nec.

★ 76998 ★   Taco Bell
1217 N. N St.
Duncan, OK 73533
(405)252-5404
Ultimate Parent: Pepsico. SIC: 5141—Groceries—General Line.

★ 76999 ★   Wal Mart
1520 W. Plato Rd.
Duncan, OK 73533
(405)255-5455
Ultimate Parent: Wal-Mart Stores, Inc. SIC: 5311—Department Stores.

Durant

★ 77000 ★   Lone Star Gas Co.
408 PO Box
Durant, OK 74702
Ultimate Parent: Enserch. SIC: 4932—Gas & Other Services Combined.

★ 77001 ★   McDonalds Restaurant
2227 W. Main St.
Durant, OK 74701
(405)920-0126
Ultimate Parent: McDonald's. SIC: 5812—Eating Places.

★ 77002 ★   Piggly Wiggly
423 W. Evergreen St.
Durant, OK 74701
(405)924-0235
Ultimate Parent: Bruno's. SIC: 5421—Meat & Fish Markets.

★ 77003 ★   Pizza Hut
1116 W. Main St.
Durant, OK 74701
(405)924-3908
Ultimate Parent: Pepsico. SIC: 5812—Eating Places.

Edmond

★ 77004 ★   Ace Hardware&Hm Improvement
2110 Hummingbird Ln.
Edmond, OK 73034
(405)728-1573
Ultimate Parent: Ace Hardware. SIC: 5231—Paint, Glass & Wallpaper Stores.

★ 77005 ★   Jiffy Lube
130 E. 2nd St.
Edmond, OK 73034
(405)340-6802
Ultimate Parent: Pennzoil.

★ 77006 ★   Kentucky Fried Chicken
700 N. Broadway St.
Edmond, OK 73034
(405)341-1544
Ultimate Parent: Pepsico. SIC: 5812—Eating Places.

★ 77007 ★   Mary Kay Cosmetics Inc.
1012 N. Chartrand Ave.
Edmond, OK 73034
(405)359-8047
Ultimate Parent: Mary Kay Cosmetics.

★ 77008 ★   McDonalds Hamburgers
1715 E. 2nd St.
Edmond, OK 73034
(405)348-8228
Ultimate Parent: McDonald's.

★ 77009 ★   Payless Cashways Inc.
15 SW 33rd St.
Edmond, OK 73013
(405)348-2020
Ultimate Parent: Payless Cashways. SIC: 5211—Lumber & Other Building Materials.

★ 77010 ★   Payless Shoesource
414 S. Bryant Ave.
Edmond, OK 73034
(405)348-0900
Ultimate Parent: May Department Stores. SIC: 5661—Shoe Stores.

★ 77011 ★   Pizza Hut
720 S. Broadway St.
Edmond, OK 73034
(405)341-4426
Ultimate Parent: Pepsico. SIC: 5812—Eating Places.

★ 77012 ★   Pizza Hut
921 E. Danforth Rd.
Edmond, OK 73034
(405)348-8002
Ultimate Parent: Pepsico. SIC: 5812—Eating Places.

★ 77013 ★   Pizza Hut
3408 S. Blvd.
Edmond, OK 73013
(405)341-7223
Ultimate Parent: Pepsico.

★ 77014 ★   Radio Shack
1710 E. 2nd St.
Edmond, OK 73034
(405)340-0672
Company Type: Division. Ultimate Parent: Tandy Corp. SIC: 5734—Computer & Software Stores.

★ 77015 ★   Radio Shack
3406 S. Blvd.
Edmond, OK 73013
(405)348-8463
Company Type: Division. Ultimate Parent: Tandy Corp.

★ 77016 ★   Ralston Purina Co.
13700 N. Lincoln Blvd.
Edmond, OK 73013
Ultimate Parent: Ralston Purina. SIC: 2047—Dog & Cat Food.

★ 77017 ★   RJ Reynolds Tobacco
117 N. 132 W
Edmond, OK 73013
(405)755-9161
Ultimate Parent: RJR Nabisco Holdings.

★ 77018 ★   Ryder Truck Rental
201 E. 2nd St.
Edmond, OK 73034
(405)341-7975
Ultimate Parent: Ryder System. SIC: 7513—Truck Rental & Leasing Without Drivers.

★ 77019 ★   Taco Bell
2200 W. Edmond Rd.
Edmond, OK 73034
(405)359-0289
Ultimate Parent: Pepsico.

★ 77020 ★   Taco Bell
1709 E. 2nd St.
Edmond, OK 73034
(405)341-8920
Ultimate Parent: Pepsico.

★ 77021 ★   Taco Bell
801 S. Broadway St.
Edmond, OK 73034
(405)341-5902
Ultimate Parent: Pepsico. SIC: 5812—Eating Places.

★ 77022 ★   Texaco Self Service
2225 W. Edmond Rd.
Edmond, OK 73034
(405)341-3912
Ultimate Parent: Texaco. SIC: 5541—Gasoline Service Stations.

★ 77023 ★   Texaco Self Service Inc.
1308 N. Bryant Ave.
Edmond, OK 73034
(405)341-6108
Ultimate Parent: Texaco. SIC: 5541—Gasoline Service Stations.

★ 77024 ★   Texaco Self Sv
1501 S. Blvd.
Edmond, OK 73013
(405)341-5642
Ultimate Parent: Texaco.

★ 77025 ★   Texaco Self Sv
1009 E. 2nd St.
Edmond, OK 73034
(405)348-3081
Ultimate Parent: Texaco.

★ 77026 ★   Wal Mart
3200 S. Broadway St.
Edmond, OK 73013
(405)348-8005
Ultimate Parent: Wal-Mart Stores, Inc. SIC: 5311—Department Stores.

★ 77027 ★   Wal Mart Pharmacy
3200 S. Broadway St.
Edmond, OK 73013
(405)348-3677
Ultimate Parent: Wal-Mart Stores, Inc. SIC: 5499—Miscellaneous Food Stores.

★ 77028 ★   Wal Mart Tire & Battery Ctr
3200 S. Broadway St.
Edmond, OK 73013
(405)348-0420
Ultimate Parent: Wal-Mart Stores, Inc. SIC: 7538—General Automotive Repair Shops.

★ 77029 ★   Wal Mart Warehouse
3400 S. Kelly Ave.
Edmond, OK 73013
(405)478-2045
Ultimate Parent: Wal-Mart Stores, Inc.

★ 77030 ★   Wilson Foods Corp.
3500 S. Blvd.
Edmond, OK 73013
(405)340-8111
Ultimate Parent: Doskocil.

El Reno

★ 77031 ★   Greyhound Bus Lines
2506 S. Country Club Rd.
El Reno, OK 73036
(405)262-0723
Ultimate Parent: Greyhound Lines Inc. SIC: 4131—Intercity & Rural Bus Transportation.

★ 77032 ★ Kentucky Fried Chicken
I 40
El Reno, OK 73036
(405)262-6100
Ultimate Parent: Pepsico. SIC: 5812—Eating Places.

★ 77033 ★ Pizza Hut
2415 S. Country Club Rd.
El Reno, OK 73036
(405)262-1645
Ultimate Parent: Pepsico. SIC: 5812—Eating Places.

★ 77034 ★ Ryder Truck Rental
126 PO Box
El Reno, OK 73036
Ultimate Parent: Ryder System. SIC: 7513—Truck Rental & Leasing Without Drivers.

★ 77035 ★ Wal Mart Discount City
I 40
El Reno, OK 73036
(405)262-6633
Ultimate Parent: Wal-Mart Stores, Inc. SIC: 5311—Department Stores.

★ 77036 ★ Wal Mart Pharmacy
1528 SW 27th St.
El Reno, OK 73036
(405)262-6112
Ultimate Parent: Wal-Mart Stores, Inc. SIC: 5912—Drug Stores & Proprietary Stores.

Elk City

★ 77037 ★ Greyhound Bus Lines
1422 W. 3rd St.
Elk City, OK 73644
(405)225-3108
Ultimate Parent: Greyhound Lines Inc. SIC: 4111—Local & Suburban Transit; 4173—Bus Terminal & Service Facilities.

★ 77038 ★ Ryder Truck Rental
110 Meadowridge Dr.
Elk City, OK 73644
(405)225-5256
Ultimate Parent: Ryder System. SIC: 7359—Equipment Rental & Leasing Nec; 7513—Truck Rental & Leasing Without Drivers.

Elmore City

★ 77039 ★ Mobil Pipe Line Co. Sohio Plant
Elmore City, OK 73035
(405)788-2864
Ultimate Parent: Mobil. SIC: 4612—Crude Petroleum Pipelines.

★ 77040 ★ Warren Petroleum Co.
Elmore City, OK 73035
(405)788-4411
Ultimate Parent: Chevron Corp. SIC: 5984—Liquefied Petroleum Gas Dealers.

Enid

★ 77041 ★ Ace Hardware
521 S. Grand St.
Enid, OK 73701
(405)237-3205
Ultimate Parent: Ace Hardware.

★ 77042 ★ ADM Milling Co.
1301 N. 4th St.
Enid, OK 73701
(405)237-8000
Officer: Kelvin Woods, Manager. Ultimate Parent: Archer Daniels Midland Co. SIC: 2041—Flour & Other Grain Mill Products; 2048—Prepared Feeds Nec.

★ 77043 ★ Burlington Northern Railroa
PO Box 3426
Enid, OK 73702
Ultimate Parent: Burlington Northern.

★ 77044 ★ Casual Corner
4125 W. Owen K Garriott Rd.
Enid, OK 73703
(405)237-6059
Ultimate Parent: United States Shoe. SIC: 5621—Women's Clothing Stores; 5651—Family Clothing Stores.

★ 77045 ★ Circus World Toys
4125 W. Owen K Garriott Rd.
Enid, OK 73703
(405)237-4509
Ultimate Parent: Melville. SIC: 5945—Hobby, Toy & Game Shops.

★ 77046 ★ Dillards
Oakwood
Enid, OK 73701
(405)237-2984
Ultimate Parent: Dillard Department Stores. SIC: 5311—Department Stores.

★ 77047 ★ Equity Export, Oil & Gas Inc.
2300 N. 10th St.
Enid, OK 73702
(405)233-5100
Company Type: Subsidiary. Ultimate Parent: Farmland Industries.

★ 77048 ★ Farmland
Green Division
PO Box 3408
Enid, OK 73702
(405)233-5100 Fax: (405)233-9802
Company Type: Division. Officer: H. D. Cleybergn, President. Ultimate Parent: Farmland Industries. SIC: 5153—Grain & Field Beans; 4221—Farm Product Warehousing & Storage; 0111—Wheat; 0119—Cash Grains Nec.

★ 77049 ★ Farmland Industries
Grain Div.
2300 N. 10th St.
Enid, OK 73701
(405)233-5100
Company Type: Division. Officer: Pete Peterson, Manager. Ultimate Parent: Farmland Industries. SIC: 2041—Flour & Other Grain Mill Products.

★ 77050 ★ Farmland Industries Inc.
1 Mile East of Woodring Airport
Enid, OK 73701
(405)233-3900
Officer: Sidney Sanderson, Manager. Ultimate Parent: Farmland Industries. SIC: 2819—Industrial Inorganic Chemicals Nec.

★ 77051 ★ Farmland Industries Inc.
1 Mile East of Enid Woodring Municipal Airport
Enid, OK 73701-1027
Ultimate Parent: Farmland Industries. SIC: 2873—Nitrogenous Fertilizers.

★ 77052 ★ First Gibraltar Bank
2021 W. Owen
Enid, OK 73703
(405)242-4606
Location Type: Branch office. Officer: Bob Thomas, Manager. Ultimate Parent: Bankamerica Corp. SIC: 6022—State Commercial Banks; 6035—Federal Savings Institutions.

★ 77053 ★ Hackney Inc.
4th & Willow
Enid, OK 73701
Ultimate Parent: Trinity Industries. SIC: 3498—Fabricated Pipe & Fittings.

★ 77054 ★ Hertz Rent-A-Car
528 N. Grand St.
Enid, OK 73701
(405)234-1616
Ultimate Parent: Hertz.

★ 77055 ★ Kentucky Fried Chicken
3453 PO Box
Enid, OK 73702
(405)234-4433
Ultimate Parent: Pepsico. SIC: 5812—Eating Places.

★ 77056 ★ Kentucky Fried Chicken
3904 W. Owen K Garriott Rd.
Enid, OK 73703
(405)242-5271
Ultimate Parent: Pepsico. SIC: 5812—Eating Places.

★ 77057 ★ Marine Terminal Shipping Co.
2300 N. 10th St.
Enid, OK 73702
(405)233-5100
Company Type: Subsidiary. Ultimate Parent: Farmland Industries.

★ 77058 ★ Payless Shoesource
4125 W. Owen K. Garriott Rd.
Enid, OK 73703
(405)237-4075
Ultimate Parent: May Department Stores. SIC: 5661—Shoe Stores.

★ 77059 ★ Pepsi-Cola Bottling Co.
5801 E. Owen K. Garriott Rd.
Enid, OK 73701
(405)237-5909
Officer: Terry Brandon, Manager. Ultimate Parent: Pepsico. SIC: 2086—Bottled & Canned Soft Drinks.

★ 77060 ★ Pizza Hut
210 S. Van Buren St.
Enid, OK 73703
Ultimate Parent: Pepsico. SIC: 5812—Eating Places.

★ 77061 ★ Pizza Hut
313 Rosanne St.
Enid, OK 73703
(405)233-3138
Ultimate Parent: Pepsico. SIC: 5812—Eating Places.

★ 77062 ★ Pizza Hut
4125 W. Owen K Garriott Rd.
Enid, OK 73703
Ultimate Parent: Pepsico. SIC: 5812—Eating Places.

★ 77063 ★ Quality Bakery
415 N. Grand St.
Enid, OK 73701
(405)237-2001
Ultimate Parent: Lanchaster Colony. SIC: 5461—Retail Bakeries.

★ 77064 ★ Radio Shack
4125 W. Owen
Enid, OK 73701
(405)242-2888
Company Type: Division. Ultimate Parent: Tandy Corp. SIC: 5065—Electronic Parts & Equipment Nec.

★ 77065 ★ Radio Shack
4125 W. Owen K Garriott Rd.
Enid, OK 73703
(405)242-2888
Company Type: Division. Ultimate Parent: Tandy Corp. SIC: 5731—Radio, Television & Electronics Stores.

★ 77066 ★ Radio Shack
Oakwood
Enid, OK 73701
(405)237-5143
Company Type: Division. Ultimate Parent: Tandy Corp. SIC: 5065—Electronic Parts & Equipment Nec.

★ 77067 ★ Radio Shack
206 Sunset Plz.
Enid, OK 73703
(405)233-4164
Company Type: Division. Ultimate Parent: Tandy Corp. SIC: 5731—Radio, Television & Electronics Stores.

★ 77068 ★ Ryder Truck Rental
1501 N. Van Buren St.
Enid, OK 73703
(405)237-9629
Ultimate Parent: Ryder System.

★ 77069 ★ Ryder Truck Rental
3302 N. Van Buren St.
Enid, OK 73703
(405)233-1415
Ultimate Parent: Ryder System. SIC: 7513—Truck Rental & Leasing Without Drivers.

★ 77070 ★ Service Merchandise
4125 W. Owen K Garriott Rd.
Enid, OK 73703
(405)237-8464
Ultimate Parent: Service Merchandise Co., Inc. SIC: 6221—Commodity Contracts Brokers & Dealers.

★ 77071 ★ Texaco Inc.
1108 W. Chestnut
Enid, OK 73701
(405)234-1258
Ultimate Parent: Texaco. SIC: 1381—Drilling Oil & Gas Wells.

★ 77072 ★ United Parcel Service
1834 W. Chestnut Ave.
Enid, OK 73703
(405)237-3606
Ultimate Parent: United Parcel Service of America. SIC: 4215—Courier Services Except by Air.

★ 77073 ★ Wal Mart Discount City
4406 W. Owen
Enid, OK 73701
(405)237-7963
Ultimate Parent: Wal-Mart Stores, Inc. SIC: 5311—Department Stores.

Erick

★ 77074 ★ First American Bank
120 W. Broadway
Erick, OK 73645
(405)526-3332
Company Type: Subsidiary. Officer: Billy D. Hill, Chairman of the Board & President. Ultimate Parent: First American Corp. SIC: 6022—State Commercial Banks. Employee Count: 10.

Fairfax

★ 77075 ★ Texaco Mini-Mart
200 N. Main St.
Fairfax, OK 74637
(918)642-5588
Ultimate Parent: Texaco.

★ 77076 ★ Texaco Pipeln Inc.
Rural Route 1
Fairfax, OK 74637
(918)642-5004
Ultimate Parent: Texaco.

Fairview

★ 77077 ★ Coast to Coast Store
115 S. Main St.
Fairview, OK 73737
(405)227-4478
Ultimate Parent: Servistar Corp. SIC: 5731—Radio, Television & Electronics Stores.

★ 77078 ★ Mini Mart
801 S. Main St.
Fairview, OK 73737
(405)227-3752
Ultimate Parent: Kroger. SIC: 5411—Grocery Stores.

★ 77079 ★ Pizza Hut
63 PO Box
Fairview, OK 73737
Ultimate Parent: Pepsico. SIC: 5812—Eating Places.

Fort Gibson

★ 77080 ★ Coast to Coast Home
111 S. Lee
Fort Gibson, OK 74434
(918)478-3242
Ultimate Parent: Servistar Corp.

Frederick

★ 77081 ★ First National Bank & Trust
10 St. Floral Ave.
Frederick, OK 73542
(405)335-7522
Ultimate Parent: Society Corp. SIC: 6021—National Commercial Banks.

★ 77082 ★ Kentucky Fried Chicken
715 S. 10th St.
Frederick, OK 73542
(405)335-5513
Ultimate Parent: Pepsico. SIC: 5812—Eating Places.

★ 77083 ★ Kids R US
152 PO Box
Frederick, OK 73542
(405)875-2059
Ultimate Parent: Toys "R" US. SIC: 8351—Child Day Care Services.

★ 77084 ★   Pizza Hut
618 S. 10th St.
Frederick, OK 73542
(405)335-5758
Ultimate Parent: Pepsico. SIC: 5812—
Eating Places.

★ 77085 ★   Pizza Hut
618 S. Main St.
Frederick, OK 73542
(405)335-7588
Ultimate Parent: Pepsico.

★ 77086 ★   Radio Shack
103 N. Main St.
Frederick, OK 73542
(405)335-7233
Company Type: Division. Ultimate Parent:
Tandy Corp.

Glenpool

★ 77087 ★   McDonalds
Hamburgers
110 W. 141st St.
Glenpool, OK 74033
(918)322-5357
Ultimate Parent: McDonald's.

Grove

★ 77088 ★   Coast to Coast
Honey Creek Plz.
Grove, OK 74344
(918)786-4101
Ultimate Parent: Servistar Corp. SIC:
5251—Hardware Stores.

★ 77089 ★   Eagle-Picher Ind. Inc.
Hwy. 10 & Industrial Park Rd.
Grove, OK 74344
Ultimate Parent: Eagle-Picher Industries
Inc. SIC: 3691—Storage Batteries.

★ 77090 ★   Eagle-Picher
Industries
Hwy. 10 & 25 Industrial Park Pl.
Grove, OK 74344
(918)786-5641
Location Type: Plant. Officer: Larry
Cowan, Plant Manager. Ultimate Parent:
Eagle-Picher Industries Inc. SIC: 3679—
Electronic Components Nec.

★ 77091 ★   Kentucky Fried
Chicken
Lakeview Shopping Ctr.
Grove, OK 74344
(918)786-2161
Ultimate Parent: Pepsico. SIC: 5812—
Eating Places.

★ 77092 ★   Pizza Hut
501 W. 3rd
Grove, OK 74344
(918)786-6104
Ultimate Parent: Pepsico. SIC: 5812—
Eating Places.

★ 77093 ★   Ryder Truck Rental
7th
Grove, OK 74344
(918)786-3182
Ultimate Parent: Ryder System. SIC:
7359—Equipment Rental & Leasing Nec;
7513—Truck Rental & Leasing Without
Drivers.

★ 77094 ★   Wal Mart Pharmacy
Hwy. 59 S
Grove, OK 74344
(918)786-4023
Ultimate Parent: Wal-Mart Stores, Inc. SIC:
5912—Drug Stores & Proprietary Stores.

★ 77095 ★   Wal Mart Tire & Auto
Ctr
Hwy. 59 S
Grove, OK 74344
(918)786-6106
Ultimate Parent: Wal-Mart Stores, Inc. SIC:
7538—General Automotive Repair Shops.

Guthrie

★ 77096 ★   Coca Cola Bottling
Co.
314 W. Oklahoma Ave.
Guthrie, OK 73044
(405)282-2691
Ultimate Parent: Coca-Cola Enterprises.
SIC: 5149—Groceries & Related Products
Nec.

★ 77097 ★   Kentucky Fried
Chicken
112 W. Noble Ave.
Guthrie, OK 73044
(405)282-2040
Ultimate Parent: Pepsico. SIC: 5812—
Eating Places.

★ 77098 ★   Pizza Hut
1200 S. Division St.
Guthrie, OK 73044
(405)282-0242
Ultimate Parent: Pepsico. SIC: 5812—
Eating Places.

Guymon

★ 77099 ★   Ace Hardware
1900 N. Hwy. 64
Guymon, OK 73942
(405)338-0025
Ultimate Parent: Ace Hardware. SIC:
5072—Hardware.

★ 77100 ★   City National Bank &
Trust
601 N. Main St.
Guymon, OK 73942
(405)338-6561
Ultimate Parent: City National Corp. SIC:
6021—National Commercial Banks.

★ 77101 ★   Collingwood Grain
Inc.
NW Hough
Guymon, OK 73942
(405)338-3151
Ultimate Parent: Archer Daniels Midland
Co. SIC: 5153—Grain & Field Beans.

★ 77102 ★   Farr Better Feeds
Guymon Industrial Pk.
Guymon, OK 73942-1389
Ultimate Parent: W. R. Grace. SIC: 2048—
Prepared Feeds Nec.

★ 77103 ★   Kentucky Fried
Chicken
NE Hwy. 54
Guymon, OK 73942
(405)338-8197
Ultimate Parent: Pepsico. SIC: 5812—
Eating Places.

★ 77104 ★   Mobil Pipe Line Co.
907 S. May St.
Guymon, OK 73942
(405)338-6611
Ultimate Parent: Mobil. SIC: 4619—
Pipelines Nec.

★ 77105 ★   Nalco Chemical Co.
1620 N. May St.
Guymon, OK 73942
(405)338-3918
Ultimate Parent: Nalco Chemical Co. SIC:
1389—Oil & Gas Field Services Nec.

★ 77106 ★   Payless Shoesource
1920 N. Hwy. 64
Guymon, OK 73942
(405)338-3704
Ultimate Parent: May Department Stores.
SIC: 5661—Shoe Stores.

★ 77107 ★   Pizza Hut
NE Hwy. 54
Guymon, OK 73942
(405)338-3818
Ultimate Parent: Pepsico. SIC: 5812—
Eating Places.

★ 77108 ★   Pizza Hut
Hwy. 64 N
Guymon, OK 73942
(405)338-8352
Ultimate Parent: Pepsico. SIC: 5812—
Eating Places.

★ 77109 ★   Pizza Hut
410 NW 21st St.
Guymon, OK 73942
(405)323-8352
Ultimate Parent: Pepsico. SIC: 5812—
Eating Places.

★ 77110 ★   Radio Shack
1918 N. Hwy. 64
Guymon, OK 73942
(405)338-6306
Company Type: Division. Ultimate Parent:
Tandy Corp. SIC: 5731—Radio, Television
& Electronics Stores.

★ 77111 ★   Ryder Truck Rental
1220 N. Main St.
Guymon, OK 73942
(405)338-6464
Ultimate Parent: Ryder System. SIC:
7359—Equipment Rental & Leasing Nec.

★ 77112 ★   Texaco Food Mart
NE Hwy. 54
Guymon, OK 73942
(405)338-2979
Ultimate Parent: Texaco. SIC: 5411—
Grocery Stores.

★ 77113 ★   Texaco Oil Co.
1109 Skelly Dr.
Guymon, OK 73942
(405)338-6820
Ultimate Parent: Texaco. SIC: 1311—
Crude Petroleum & Natural Gas.

★ 77114 ★   Texaco Truck Stop
Hwy. 54 Northeast
Guymon, OK 73942
(405)338-2123
Ultimate Parent: Texaco. SIC: 5812—
Eating Places.

★ 77115 ★   Texaco Truck
Terminal Cafe
Hwy. 54 N
Guymon, OK 73942
(405)338-2151
Ultimate Parent: Texaco. SIC: 5812—
Eating Places.

★ 77116 ★   United Parcel Service
809 NE 12th St.
Guymon, OK 73942
(405)338-8938
Ultimate Parent: United Parcel Service of
America. SIC: 4215—Courier Services
Except by Air.

★ 77117 ★   US Fidelity & Gu
112 E. 5th St.
Guymon, OK 73942
(405)338-6509
Ultimate Parent: USF&G Corp. SIC:
6411—Insurance Agents, Brokers &
Service.

★ 77118 ★   W. R. Grace & Co.
Farr Better Feeds
Guymon Industrial Park
Guymon, OK 73942-1389
Company Type: Division. Ultimate Parent:
W. R. Grace. SIC: 2048—Prepared Feeds
Nec.

★ 77119 ★   Wal Mart Dept Store
N Hwy. 64
Guymon, OK 73942
(405)338-1312
Ultimate Parent: Wal-Mart Stores, Inc. SIC:
5311—Department Stores.

Healdton

★ 77120 ★   Mobil Pipeline Co.
Hwy. 76 N.
Healdton, OK 73438
(405)229-1710
Company Type: Branch. Ultimate Parent:
Mobil. SIC: 4612—Crude Petroleum
Pipelines.

★ 77121 ★   Total Petroleum Inc.
Northwest City
Healdton, OK 73438
(405)229-1638
Ultimate Parent: Total Petroleum Inc. SIC:
1389—Oil & Gas Field Services Nec.

★ 77122 ★   Total Petroleum Inc.
Northwest City
Healdton, OK 73438
(405)229-1638
Ultimate Parent: Total Petroleum Inc. SIC:
1389—Oil & Gas Field Services Nec.

Hennessey

★ 77123 ★   Exxon Co. USA
98 PO Box
Hennessey, OK 73742
(405)853-4374
Ultimate Parent: Exxon. SIC: 1311—Crude
Petroleum & Natural Gas.

★ 77124 ★   Pizza Hut
Hwys 51
Hennessey, OK 73742
(405)853-7868
Ultimate Parent: Pepsico. SIC: 5812—
Eating Places.

Henrietta

★ 77125 ★   Anchor Glass
Container Corp.
RR 3, Box 59
Henrietta, OK 74437
(918)652-9631
Officer: Bill Myers, Manager. Ultimate
Parent: Anchor Glass Container Corp. SIC:
3221—Glass Containers.

★ 77126 ★   McDonalds
Restaurant
500 E. Main St.
Henrietta, OK 74437
(918)652-7757
Ultimate Parent: May Department Stores.
SIC: 5812—Eating Places.

Henryetta

★ 77127 ★   Burlington Northern
Railroa
1st
Henryetta, OK 74437
(918)652-3640
Ultimate Parent: Burlington Northern. SIC:
4011—Railroads—Line-Haul Operating.

★ 77128 ★   Greyhound Bus Lines
Hwy. 75
Henryetta, OK 74437
(918)652-3190
Ultimate Parent: Greyhound Lines Inc. SIC:
4131—Intercity & Rural Bus Transportation.

★ 77129 ★   Kentucky Fried
Chicken
412 E. Main St.
Henryetta, OK 74437
(918)652-8818
Ultimate Parent: Pepsico. SIC: 5812—
Eating Places.

★ 77130 ★   Radio Shack
406 W. Main St.
Henryetta, OK 74437
(918)652-2777
Company Type: Division. Ultimate Parent:
Tandy Corp. SIC: 5999—Miscellaneous
Retail Stores Nec.

Hinton

★ 77131 ★   Coast to Coast
106 W. Main
Hinton, OK 73047
(405)542-6264
Ultimate Parent: Servistar Corp. SIC:
5231—Paint, Glass & Wallpaper Stores.

Hobart

★ 77132 ★   Ace Hardware Store
114 W. 4th St.
Hobart, OK 73651
(405)726-3622
Ultimate Parent: Ace Hardware. SIC:
5251—Hardware Stores.

★ 77133 ★   Mary Kay Cosmet
Independ Sl
215 S. Park Rd.
Hobart, OK 73651
(405)726-5514
Ultimate Parent: Mary Kay Cosmetics. SIC:
5999—Miscellaneous Retail Stores Nec.

Holdenville

★ 77134 ★   Pizza Hut
103 Rodgers Dr.
Holdenville, OK 74848
(405)379-6044
Ultimate Parent: Pepsico. SIC: 5812—
Eating Places.

★ 77135 ★   Ryder Truck Rental
500 W. Main St.
Holdenville, OK 74848
(405)379-3460
Ultimate Parent: Ryder System. SIC:
7513—Truck Rental & Leasing Without
Drivers.

★ 77136 ★ **Wal Mart Discount City**
500 Hwy. St.
Holdenville, OK 74848
(405)379-6688
Ultimate Parent: Wal-Mart Stores, Inc. **SIC:** 5311—Department Stores.

Hollis

★ 77137 ★ **First State Bank & Trust Co.**
120 W. Jones St.
Hollis, OK 73550
(405)688-3323
Ultimate Parent: Michigan National Corp.
SIC: 6022—State Commercial Banks.

★ 77138 ★ **Pizza Hut**
Hwy. 62 W
Hollis, OK 73550
(405)688-9293
Ultimate Parent: Pepsico. **SIC:** 5812—Eating Places.

Hugo

★ 77139 ★ **Pizza Hut**
1109 E. Jackson St.
Hugo, OK 74743
(405)326-7373
Ultimate Parent: Pepsico. **SIC:** 5812—Eating Places.

★ 77140 ★ **Ryder Truck Rental**
111 E. Jackson St.
Hugo, OK 74743
(405)326-2582
Ultimate Parent: Ryder System. **SIC:** 7513—Truck Rental & Leasing Without Drivers.

★ 77141 ★ **Wal Mart Pharmacy**
Us 70
Hugo, OK 74743
(405)326-7541
Ultimate Parent: Wal-Mart Stores, Inc. **SIC:** 5912—Drug Stores & Proprietary Stores.

Idabel

★ 77142 ★ **Lone Star Gas Co.**
1431 SE Washington St.
Idabel, OK 74745
(405)286-7606
Ultimate Parent: Enserch. **SIC:** 4932—Gas & Other Services Combined.

★ 77143 ★ **Piggly Wiggly**
413 S. Central Ave.
Idabel, OK 74745
(405)286-5505
Ultimate Parent: Bruno's. **SIC:** 5421—Meat & Fish Markets.

★ 77144 ★ **Piggly Wiggly**
1423 SE Washington St.
Idabel, OK 74745
(405)286-2244
Ultimate Parent: Bruno's. **SIC:** 5411—Grocery Stores.

★ 77145 ★ **Pizza Hut**
1810 SE Washington St.
Idabel, OK 74745
(405)286-6524
Ultimate Parent: Pepsico. **SIC:** 5812—Eating Places.

★ 77146 ★ **Wal Mart Discount Cities**
901 SE Washington St.
Idabel, OK 74745
(405)286-6696
Ultimate Parent: Wal-Mart Stores, Inc.

★ 77147 ★ **Wal Mart Discount Pharmacy**
901 SE Washington St.
Idabel, OK 74745
(405)286-3323
Ultimate Parent: Wal-Mart Stores, Inc. **SIC:** 5047—Medical & Hospital Equipment; 5912—Drug Stores & Proprietary Stores.

Jenks

★ 77148 ★ **Ace Hardware**
102 S. 1st St.
Jenks, OK 74037
(918)299-4409
Ultimate Parent: Ace Hardware. **SIC:** 5251—Hardware Stores.

Kingfisher

★ 77149 ★ **Ace Hardware**
123 E. Miles Ave.
Kingfisher, OK 73750
(405)375-6770
Ultimate Parent: Ace Hardware.

★ 77150 ★ **Kentucky Fried Chicken**
102 N. Main St.
Kingfisher, OK 73750
(405)375-5464
Ultimate Parent: Pepsico. **SIC:** 5812—Eating Places.

★ 77151 ★ **Pizza Hut**
S Main
Kingfisher, OK 73750
(405)375-5749
Ultimate Parent: Pepsico. **SIC:** 5812—Eating Places.

★ 77152 ★ **Radio Shack**
210 N. Main St.
Kingfisher, OK 73750
(405)375-6473
Company Type: Division. **Ultimate Parent:** Tandy Corp.

★ 77153 ★ **Wal Mart**
896 PO Box
Kingfisher, OK 73750
Ultimate Parent: Wal-Mart Stores, Inc. **SIC:** 5912—Drug Stores & Proprietary Stores.

Lawton

★ 77154 ★ **Associated Milk Producers Inc.**
5 SE Washington Ave.
Lawton, OK 73501
(405)353-0399
Ultimate Parent: Associated Milk Producers Inc. **SIC:** 5451—Dairy Products Stores.

★ 77155 ★ **Casual Corner**
Central Mall
Lawton, OK 73501
(405)355-0607
Ultimate Parent: United States Shoe. **SIC:** 5621—Women's Clothing Stores.

★ 77156 ★ **City National Bank**
4113 W. Gore Blvd.
Lawton, OK 73505
(405)357-0891
Ultimate Parent: City National Corp. **SIC:** 6022—State Commercial Banks.

★ 77157 ★ **City National Bank & Trust**
500 SW D Ave.
Lawton, OK 73501
(405)355-3580
Ultimate Parent: City National Corp. **SIC:** 6099—Functions Related to Deposit Banking.

★ 77158 ★ **Coast to Coast**
40 NW Sheridan Rd.
Lawton, OK 73505
(405)248-1113
Ultimate Parent: Servistar Corp.

★ 77159 ★ **Goodyear Tire & Rubber Co.**
1 Goodyear Blvd.
Lawton, OK 73505
Ultimate Parent: Goodyear Tire & Rubber. **SIC:** 3011—Tires & Inner Tubes.

★ 77160 ★ **Hertz Rent-A-Car**
3401 SW 11th St.
Lawton, OK 73501
(405)355-6789
Ultimate Parent: Hertz. **SIC:** 7514—Passenger Car Rental.

★ 77161 ★ **Kay Bee Toy&Hobby Shop**
Central Mall
Lawton, OK 73501
(405)248-6884
Ultimate Parent: Melville. **SIC:** 5945—Hobby, Toy & Game Shops.

★ 77162 ★ **Kentucky Fried Chicken**
2520 NW Fort Sill Blvd.
Lawton, OK 73507
(405)355-4228
Ultimate Parent: Pepsico. **SIC:** 5812—Eating Places.

★ 77163 ★ **Kentucky Fried Chicken**
4702 NW Cache Rd.
Lawton, OK 73505
(405)355-2229
Ultimate Parent: Pepsico. **SIC:** 5812—Eating Places.

★ 77164 ★ **Lane Bryant**
62 Central Mall
Lawton, OK 73501
(405)355-5301
Ultimate Parent: Limited. **SIC:** 5651—Family Clothing Stores.

★ 77165 ★ **Mary Kay Cosmetics**
110 SW 74th St.
Lawton, OK 73505
(405)536-3613
Ultimate Parent: Mary Kay Cosmetics. **SIC:** 5999—Miscellaneous Retail Stores Nec.

★ 77166 ★ **Massachusetts Mutual Life Insurance**
4824 SE Brown St.
Lawton, OK 73501
(405)355-8281
Ultimate Parent: Massasucetts Mutual Life. **SIC:** 6411—Insurance Agents, Brokers & Service.

★ 77167 ★ **Northrop Worldwide Aircraft Services, Inc. (NWASI)**
21 NW 44th St.
Lawton, OK 73505-0108
(405)353-2733 **Fax:** (405)353-0153
Officer: W.J. Shaddix, President. **Ultimate Parent:** Northrop Corp.

★ 77168 ★ **Payless Shoesource**
1414 NW 52nd St.
Lawton, OK 73505
(405)357-0620
Ultimate Parent: May Department Stores. **SIC:** 5661—Shoe Stores.

★ 77169 ★ **Payless Shoesource**
702 NW Fort Sill Blvd.
Lawton, OK 73507
(405)353-1676
Ultimate Parent: May Department Stores. **SIC:** 5661—Shoe Stores.

★ 77170 ★ **Pepsi-Cola Bottling Co.**
101 SE B Ave.
Lawton, OK 73501
(405)353-4468
Officer: Lillian Priest, Manager. **Ultimate Parent:** Pepsico. **SIC:** 2086—Bottled & Canned Soft Drinks.

★ 77171 ★ **Pizza Hut**
2122 W. Gore Blvd.
Lawton, OK 73501
(405)353-0487
Ultimate Parent: Pepsico. **SIC:** 5812—Eating Places.

★ 77172 ★ **Pizza Hut**
1502 SW Lee Blvd.
Lawton, OK 73501
(405)357-5827
Ultimate Parent: Pepsico. **SIC:** 5812—Eating Places.

★ 77173 ★ **Ryder Truck Rental**
102 E. Lee Blvd.
Lawton, OK 73501
(405)357-6122
Ultimate Parent: Ryder System.

★ 77174 ★ **Taco Bell**
2 SW Sheridan Rd.
Lawton, OK 73501
(405)353-1793
Ultimate Parent: Pepsico. **SIC:** 5812—Eating Places.

★ 77175 ★ **Taco Bell**
2425 NW Cache Rd.
Lawton, OK 73505
Ultimate Parent: Pepsico. **SIC:** 5141—Groceries—General Line; 5812—Eating Places.

★ 77176 ★ **United Parcel Service**
664 SW Bishop Rd.
Lawton, OK 73501
(405)355-5445
Ultimate Parent: United Parcel Service of America. **SIC:** 4215—Courier Services Except by Air.

Lexington

★ 77177 ★ **Wilsons**
Hwy. 77
Lexington, OK 73051
(405)527-2344
Ultimate Parent: Melville. **SIC:** 5531—Automobile & Home Supply Stores.

Lindsay

★ 77178 ★ **Arco Oil & Gas Co.**
Hwy. 19
Lindsay, OK 73052
(405)756-3119
Location Type: Branch office. **Ultimate Parent:** Arvin Industries Inc. **SIC:** 2911—Petroleum Refining.

★ 77179 ★ **Mobil Oil Corp.**
Lindsay, OK 73052
(405)756-3161
Company Type: Branch. **Ultimate Parent:** Mobil. **SIC:** 4612—Crude Petroleum Pipelines; 1311—Crude Petroleum & Natural Gas.

★ 77180 ★ **Pizza Hut**
Hwy. 19 W
Lindsay, OK 73052
(405)756-3071
Ultimate Parent: Pepsico. **SIC:** 5812—Eating Places.

Madill

★ 77181 ★ **Kentucky Fried Chicken**
502 S. 1st Ave.
Madill, OK 73446
(405)795-5782
Ultimate Parent: Pepsico. **SIC:** 5812—Eating Places.

★ 77182 ★ **Pizza Hut**
606 N. 1st St.
Madill, OK 73446
(405)795-5543
Ultimate Parent: Pepsico. **SIC:** 5812—Eating Places.

Marietta

★ 77183 ★ **Lone Star Gas Co.**
112 W. Main St.
Marietta, OK 73448
(405)276-3175
Ultimate Parent: Enserch. **SIC:** 4925—Gas Production & Distribution Nec.

★ 77184 ★ **Pizza Hut**
State 32
Marietta, OK 73448
(405)276-2297
Ultimate Parent: Pepsico. **SIC:** 5812—Eating Places.

Marlow

★ 77185 ★ **Kentucky Fried Chicken**
S Broadway Cir.
Marlow, OK 73055
(405)658-6919
Ultimate Parent: Pepsico. **SIC:** 5812—Eating Places.

★ 77186 ★ **Wal Mart Pharmacy**
1106 S. Broadway St.
Marlow, OK 73055
(405)658-5428
Ultimate Parent: Wal-Mart Stores, Inc. **SIC:** 5912—Drug Stores & Proprietary Stores.

★ 77187 ★ **Warren Petroleum Co.**
119 Hwy. 64
Marlow, OK 73055
(405)658-3110
Ultimate Parent: Chevron Corp. **SIC:** 1321—Natural Gas Liquids.

Maud

★ 77188 ★ **Citizens State Bank**
200 W. Main St.
Maud, OK 74854
(405)374-2443
Ultimate Parent: Liberty National Bancorp. **SIC:** 6022—State Commercial Banks.

Maysville

★ 77189 ★ **Arco Pipe Line**
Maysville, OK 73057
(405)867-4833
Location Type: Branch office. **Ultimate Parent:** Atlantic Richfield Co., Inc. **SIC:** 4612—Crude Petroleum Pipelines.

Mc Alester

★ 77190 ★ **First National Bank & Trust**
235 E. Choctaw Ave.
Mc Alester, OK 74501
(918)426-0211
Ultimate Parent: Society Corp. **SIC:** 6022—State Commercial Banks.

★ 77191 ★ **Greyhound Bus Lines**
419 St.
Mc Alester, OK 74501
(918)423-6600
Ultimate Parent: Greyhound Lines Inc. **SIC:** 4142—Bus Charter Service Except Local; 4212—Local Trucking Without Storage.

★ 77192 ★ **Kentucky Fried Chicken**
116 E. Choctaw Ave.
Mc Alester, OK 74501
(918)426-0790
Ultimate Parent: Pepsico. **SIC:** 5812—Eating Places.

★ 77193 ★ **Kentucky Fried Chicken**
S Hwy. 69 Bypass
Mc Alester, OK 74501
(918)423-6774
Ultimate Parent: Pepsico. **SIC:** 5812—Eating Places.

★ 77194 ★ **Kentucky Fried Chicken**
1st
Mc Alester, OK 74501
(918)423-3673
Ultimate Parent: Pepsico. **SIC:** 5812—Eating Places.

★ 77195 ★ **Kroger,Genevieve Mrs**
309 W. Jackson Ave.
Mc Alester, OK 74501
(918)423-4778
Ultimate Parent: Kroger. **SIC:** 8299—Schools & Educational Services Nec.

★ 77196 ★ **McDonalds**
1758 E. Carl Albert Pky.
Mc Alester, OK 74501
(918)423-8050
Ultimate Parent: McDonald's. **SIC:** 5812—Eating Places.

★ 77197 ★ **Pizza Hut**
201 S. Main St.
Mc Alester, OK 74501
(918)423-6941
Ultimate Parent: Pepsico. **SIC:** 5812—Eating Places.

★ 77198 ★ **Radio Shack**
1736 E. Carl Albert Pky.
Mc Alester, OK 74501
(918)423-7507
Company Type: Division. **Ultimate Parent:** Tandy Corp. **SIC:** 5065—Electronic Parts & Equipment Nec.

★ 77199 ★ **Ryder Truck Rental**
3100 S. Hwy. 69
Mc Alester, OK 74501
(918)426-1415
Ultimate Parent: Ryder System. **SIC:** 7513—Truck Rental & Leasing Without Drivers.

★ 77200 ★ **United Parcel Service**
6 Expy. Ln.
Mc Alester, OK 74501
(918)426-5094
Ultimate Parent: United Parcel Service of America. **SIC:** 4215—Courier Services Except by Air.

★ 77201 ★ **Wal Mart Discount City**
S Hwy. 69 Bypass
Mc Alester, OK 74501
(918)423-7070
Ultimate Parent: Wal-Mart Stores, Inc. **SIC:** 5311—Department Stores.

★ 77202 ★ **Wal Mart Pharmacy**
S Hwy. 69 Bypass
Mc Alester, OK 74501
(918)423-8060
Ultimate Parent: Wal-Mart Stores, Inc. **SIC:** 5912—Drug Stores & Proprietary Stores.

Miami

★ 77203 ★ **Eagle Picher Industries Inc.**
200 E. Broadway
Miami, OK 74354
(918)542-1801
Ultimate Parent: Eagle-Picher Industries Inc. **SIC:** 1011—Iron Ores.

★ 77204 ★ **Greyhound Bus Lines**
7 E. Steve Owens Blvd.
Miami, OK 74354
(918)542-2640
Ultimate Parent: Greyhound Lines Inc. **SIC:** 4111—Local & Suburban Transit; 4131—Intercity & Rural Bus Transportation.

★ 77205 ★ **Kentucky Fried Chicken**
1027 N. Main St.
Miami, OK 74354
(918)542-6805
Ultimate Parent: Pepsico. **SIC:** 5812—Eating Places.

★ 77206 ★ **Mary Kay Cosmetics**
420 S. Eastgate Blvd.
Miami, OK 74354
(918)542-4075
Ultimate Parent: Mary Kay Cosmetics. **SIC:** 5999—Miscellaneous Retail Stores Nec.

★ 77207 ★ **Payless Shoesource**
2023 N. Main St.
Miami, OK 74354
(918)542-9207
Ultimate Parent: May Department Stores. **SIC:** 5661—Shoe Stores.

★ 77208 ★ **Pizza Hut**
101 A St. NW
Miami, OK 74354
(918)540-2471
Ultimate Parent: Pepsico. **SIC:** 5812—Eating Places.

★ 77209 ★ **Pizza Hut**
1320 N. Main St.
Miami, OK 74354
(918)542-8474
Ultimate Parent: Pepsico. **SIC:** 5812—Eating Places.

★ 77210 ★ **Ryder Truck Rental**
1407 E. Steve Owens Blvd.
Miami, OK 74354
(918)542-7460
Ultimate Parent: Ryder System. **SIC:** 7359—Equipment Rental & Leasing Nec; 7359—Equipment Rental & Leasing Nec.

★ 77211 ★ **Wal Mart**
2015 N. Main St.
Miami, OK 74354
(918)542-6651
Ultimate Parent: Wal-Mart Stores, Inc. **SIC:** 5311—Department Stores.

★ 77212 ★ **Wal Mart Discount Pharmacy**
2414 N. Main St.
Miami, OK 74354
(918)542-8429
Ultimate Parent: Wal-Mart Stores, Inc. **SIC:** 5912—Drug Stores & Proprietary Stores.

Midwest City

★ 77213 ★ **Sequa Corp.**
Chromalloy
1720 National Blvd.
Midwest City, OK 73110
Ultimate Parent: Sequa Corp. **SIC:** 3724—Aircraft Engines & Engine Parts.

★ 77214 ★ **Sequa Corp.**
Chromalloy
1720 National Blvd.
Midwest City, OK 73110
Ultimate Parent: Sequa Corp. **SIC:** 3724—Aircraft Engines & Engine Parts.

Moore

★ 77215 ★ **Texaco Exprss Lube**
517 N. Telephone Rd.
Moore, OK 73160
Ultimate Parent: Texaco.

Muldrow

★ 77216 ★ **Piggly Wiggly**
803 S. Main
Muldrow, OK 74948
(918)427-9915
Ultimate Parent: Bruno's. **SIC:** 5411—Grocery Stores.

Muskogee

★ 77217 ★ **Burlington Northern Railroa**
5 E. Fondulac St.
Muskogee, OK 74403
(918)682-3891
Ultimate Parent: Burlington Northern. **SIC:** 4011—Railroads—Line-Haul Operating.

★ 77218 ★ **First National Bank & Trust**
1140 N. York St.
Muskogee, OK 74403
(918)683-7611
Ultimate Parent: Society Corp. **SIC:** 6022—State Commercial Banks.

★ 77219 ★ **Fort Howard Corp.**
4901 E. Chandler Rd.
Muskogee, OK 74403
Ultimate Parent: Fort Howard. **SIC:** 2621—Paper Mills.

★ 77220 ★ **Fort Howard Corp.**
5600 E. Chandler Rd.
Muskogee, OK 74401
Ultimate Parent: Fort Howard. **SIC:** 2621—Paper Mills.

★ 77221 ★ **Fort Howard Paper Co.**
4901 Chandler Rd.
Muskogee, OK 74401
(918)683-7671
Officer: Karl Meyers, Manager. **Ultimate Parent:** Fort Howard. **SIC:** 2297—Nonwoven Fabrics; 2621—Paper Mills.

★ 77222 ★ **Hudson Farms Inc.**
Rural Route 7
Muskogee, OK 74401
(918)683-4351
Ultimate Parent: Hudson Foods. **SIC:** 0254—Poultry Hatcheries.

★ 77223 ★ **Kentucky Fried Chicken**
222 S. 32nd St.
Muskogee, OK 74401
(918)682-0851
Ultimate Parent: Pepsico. **SIC:** 5812—Eating Places.

★ 77224 ★ **Lane Bryant**
501 N. Main St.
Muskogee, OK 74401
(918)683-4048
Ultimate Parent: Limited. **SIC:** 5651—Family Clothing Stores.

★ 77225 ★ **O-I Brockway Glass Inc.**
Plant 3
York & Shawnee Sts
Muskogee, OK 74403
Location Type: Plant. **Ultimate Parent:** Owens-Illinois. **SIC:** 3221—Glass Containers.

★ 77226 ★ **Owens-Brockway Glass Container**
York & Shawnee Sts
Muskogee, OK 74403
Ultimate Parent: Owens-Illinois. **SIC:** 3221—Glass Containers.

★ 77227 ★ **Owens-Brockway Glass Container**
2401 E. Shawnee Rd.
Muskogee, OK 74403
(918)682-6621
Ultimate Parent: Owens-Illinois. **SIC:** 3211—Flat Glass.

★ 77228 ★ **Radio Shack**
Curts Mall
Muskogee, OK 74401
(918)683-5946
Company Type: Division. **Ultimate Parent:** Tandy Corp. **SIC:** 5731—Radio, Television & Electronics Stores.

★ 77229 ★ **Taco Bell**
315 N. 32nd St.
Muskogee, OK 74401
(918)687-4366
Ultimate Parent: Pepsico. **SIC:** 5812—Eating Places.

★ 77230 ★ **Trailways Bus Systems**
305 S. 3rd St.
Muskogee, OK 74401
(918)682-1371
Ultimate Parent: Greyhound Lines Inc. **SIC:** 4111—Local & Suburban Transit; 4131—Intercity & Rural Bus Transportation.

★ 77231 ★ **United Parcel Service**
1005 W. Shawnee Ave.
Muskogee, OK 74401
(918)687-4262
Ultimate Parent: United Parcel Service of America. **SIC:** 4215—Courier Services Except by Air.

★ 77232 ★ **US Fidelity & Gu**
1805 N. York St.
Muskogee, OK 74403
(918)682-5646
Ultimate Parent: USF&G Corp. **SIC:** 6411—Insurance Agents, Brokers & Service.

★ 77233 ★ **Wal Mart Discount Cities**
2412 E. Shawnee Ave.
Muskogee, OK 74403
(918)687-0058
Ultimate Parent: Wal-Mart Stores, Inc.

★ 77234 ★ **Wal Mart Discount City**
727 S. 32nd St.
Muskogee, OK 74401
(918)683-6666
Ultimate Parent: Wal-Mart Stores, Inc. **SIC:** 5311—Department Stores.

★ 77235 ★ **Wal Mart Discount City**
2400 E. Shawnee St.
Muskogee, OK 74403
(918)683-6666
Ultimate Parent: Wal-Mart Stores, Inc. **SIC:** 5311—Department Stores.

★ 77236 ★ **Waldenbooks**
501 N. Main St.
Muskogee, OK 74401
(918)687-3112
Ultimate Parent: K-Mart. **SIC:** 5942—Book Stores.

Mustang

★ 77237 ★ **Greyhound Bus Lines**
200 E. Park Ave.
Mustang, OK 73064
(405)873-8573
Ultimate Parent: Greyhound Lines Inc. **SIC:** 4131—Intercity & Rural Bus Transportation.

★ 77238 ★ **McDonalds Hamburgers**
101 N. Trade Ctr. Ter
Mustang, OK 73064
(405)376-4414
Ultimate Parent: McDonald's.

★ 77239 ★　Radio Shack
300 N. Mustang Rd.
Mustang, OK 73064
(405)376-3342
Company Type: Division. Ultimate Parent:
Tandy Corp. SIC: 5099—Durable Goods
Nec.

★ 77240 ★　Taco Bell
331 N. Mustang Rd.
Mustang, OK 73064
(405)376-2423
Ultimate Parent: Pepsico.

★ 77241 ★　Wal Mart Discount
200 N. Mustang Rd.
Mustang, OK 73064
(405)376-4549
Ultimate Parent: Wal-Mart Stores, Inc.

Newcastle

★ 77242 ★　Northwest Industries
Inc.
1912 E. Fox Ln.
Newcastle, OK 73065-4222
(405)387-2500
Ultimate Parent: Alco Standard Corp. SIC:
3541—Machine Tools—Metal Cutting
Types.

★ 77243 ★　Wal Mart
412 NW 32nd St.
Newcastle, OK 73065
(405)387-3400
Ultimate Parent: Wal-Mart Stores, Inc.

Ninnekah

★ 77244 ★　Mobil Oil Corp.
Chitwood Gas
Rte. 1 Box 54
Ninnekah, OK 73067-9735
(405)785-2446
Officer: Floyd Orr. Ultimate Parent: Mobil.
SIC: 3312—Blast Furnaces & Steel Mills.

Noble

★ 77245 ★　Ace Hardware of
Noble
605 N. Main St.
Noble, OK 73068
(405)872-9050
Ultimate Parent: Ace Hardware. SIC:
5063—Electrical Apparatus & Equipment.

★ 77246 ★　Union Texas
Petroleum Corp.
311 Cherry
Noble, OK 73068
(405)872-7057
Ultimate Parent: Union Texas Petroleum.
SIC: 1311—Crude Petroleum & Natural
Gas.

Norman

★ 77247 ★　Casual Corner
3439 W. Main St.
Norman, OK 73072
(405)364-9931
Ultimate Parent: United States Shoe. SIC:
5621—Women's Clothing Stores.

★ 77248 ★　Circus World Toy
Stores
Sooner
Norman, OK 73069
(405)364-9260
Ultimate Parent: Melville. SIC: 5945—
Hobby, Toy & Game Shops.

★ 77249 ★　Coors Ceramics Co.
450 24th Ave. NW
Norman, OK 73069
Ultimate Parent: Adolph Coors. SIC:
3599—Industrial Machinery Nec.

★ 77250 ★　Csc Credit Svcs
121 S. Santa Fe Ave.
Norman, OK 73069
(405)329-1900
Ultimate Parent: Computer Sciences.

★ 77251 ★　Dillard Department
Stores
Sooner
Norman, OK 73069
(405)329-2600
Ultimate Parent: Dillard Department Stores.
SIC: 5311—Department Stores.

★ 77252 ★　Foot Action Inc.
Sooner
Norman, OK 73069
(405)364-5116
Ultimate Parent: Melville. SIC: 5661—Shoe
Stores.

★ 77253 ★　Gilt Edge Farms
302 S. Porter Ave.
Norman, OK 73071
(405)321-3191
Officer: Pat McColgan, Manager. Ultimate
Parent: Dean Foods. SIC: 2024—Ice
Cream & Frozen Desserts; 2026—Fluid
Milk; 2099—Food Preparations Nec.

★ 77254 ★　Gilt Edge Farms Inc.
302 S. Porter
Norman, OK 73071
Ultimate Parent: Dean Foods. SIC: 2026—
Fluid Milk.

★ 77255 ★　Greyhound Bus Lines
136 Hal Muldrow Dr.
Norman, OK 73069
(405)321-7370
Ultimate Parent: Greyhound Lines Inc. SIC:
4111—Local & Suburban Transit.

★ 77256 ★　Jiffy Lube
1203 E. Alameda St.
Norman, OK 73071
(405)321-5208
Ultimate Parent: Pennzoil.

★ 77257 ★　Kentucky Fried
Chicken
1807 W. Lindsey St.
Norman, OK 73069
(405)321-5150
Ultimate Parent: Pepsico. SIC: 5812—
Eating Places.

★ 77258 ★　Kentucky Fried
Chicken
1201 E. Alameda St.
Norman, OK 73071
(405)321-5152
Ultimate Parent: Pepsico. SIC: 5812—
Eating Places.

★ 77259 ★　Lane Bryant
3401 W. Main St.
Norman, OK 73072
(405)329-9117
Ultimate Parent: Limited.

★ 77260 ★　Lerner Shop
3235 W. Main St.
Norman, OK 73072
(405)360-1922
Ultimate Parent: Limited. SIC: 5621—
Women's Clothing Stores.

★ 77261 ★　McDonalds
Hamburgers
1150 E. Alameda St.
Norman, OK 73071
(405)321-1228
Ultimate Parent: McDonald's.

★ 77262 ★　Mutual of New York
2401 Tee Cir.
Norman, OK 73069
(405)329-3591
Ultimate Parent: Mutual of New York. SIC:
6411—Insurance Agents, Brokers &
Service.

★ 77263 ★　Osco Drug
2600 W. Robinson St.
Norman, OK 73069
(405)360-9701
Ultimate Parent: American Stores.

★ 77264 ★　Pappagallo
3413 W. Main St.
Norman, OK 73072
(405)329-0944
Ultimate Parent: United States Shoe.

★ 77265 ★　Pappagallo
Sooner
Norman, OK 73069
(405)364-3581
Ultimate Parent: United States Shoe. SIC:
5621—Women's Clothing Stores.

★ 77266 ★　Payless Cashways
1719 24th Ave. SW
Norman, OK 73072
(405)364-4104
Ultimate Parent: Payless Cashways.

★ 77267 ★　Payless Shoesource
3301 W. Main St.
Norman, OK 73072
(405)366-1414
Ultimate Parent: May Department Stores.

★ 77268 ★　Pizza Hut
105 12th Ave. SE
Norman, OK 73071
(405)364-2724
Ultimate Parent: Pepsico. SIC: 5812—
Eating Places.

★ 77269 ★　Pizza Hut
1514 W. Lindsey St.
Norman, OK 73069
(405)321-3385
Ultimate Parent: Pepsico. SIC: 5812—
Eating Places.

★ 77270 ★　Radio Shack
Sooner
Norman, OK 73069
(405)360-3372
Company Type: Division. Ultimate Parent:
Tandy Corp. SIC: 5046—Commercial
Equipment Nec.

★ 77271 ★　Radio Shack
3321 W. Main St.
Norman, OK 73072
(405)360-2513
Company Type: Division. Ultimate Parent:
Tandy Corp. SIC: 5065—Electronic Parts &
Equipment Nec.

★ 77272 ★　Radio Shack
740 W. Main St.
Norman, OK 73069
Company Type: Division. Ultimate Parent:
Tandy Corp. SIC: 5065—Electronic Parts &
Equipment Nec.

★ 77273 ★　Ryder Truck Rental
2319 W. Lindsey St.
Norman, OK 73069
(405)364-2804
Ultimate Parent: Ryder System. SIC:
7359—Equipment Rental & Leasing Nec.

★ 77274 ★　Ryder Truck Rental
1102 24th Ave. SE
Norman, OK 73071
(405)364-4081
Ultimate Parent: Ryder System. SIC:
7513—Truck Rental & Leasing Without
Drivers.

★ 77275 ★　Taco Bell
1811 W. Lindsey St.
Norman, OK 73069
(405)360-0706
Ultimate Parent: Pepsico. SIC: 5812—
Eating Places.

★ 77276 ★　Taco Bell
1024 24th Ave. NW
Norman, OK 73069
(405)364-5204
Ultimate Parent: Pepsico.

★ 77277 ★　Taco Bell
1220 E. Lindsey St.
Norman, OK 73071
(405)364-7997
Ultimate Parent: Pepsico. SIC: 5812—
Eating Places.

★ 77278 ★　Thrifty Rent a Car
Systems, Inc.
1700 Lexington St.
Norman, OK 73069
(405)360-1644
Ultimate Parent: Chrysler Corp. SIC:
7514—Passenger Car Rental.

★ 77279 ★　Wal Mart
3400 W. Main St.
Norman, OK 73072
(405)329-4849
Ultimate Parent: Wal-Mart Stores, Inc.

★ 77280 ★　Waldenbooks
Sooner
Norman, OK 73069
(405)329-9725
Ultimate Parent: K-Mart. SIC: 5942—Book
Stores.

★ 77281 ★　York Heating & Air
Conditioning
5005 N. Interstate Dr.
Norman, OK 73069
(405)364-4040
Officer: Bob Fowler, Manager. Ultimate
Parent: York International Corp. SIC:
3585—Refrigeration & Heating Equipment.

★ 77282 ★　York International
Corp.
5005 N. Interstate Dr.
Norman, OK 73069
Ultimate Parent: York International Corp.
SIC: 3585—Refrigeration & Heating
Equipment.

★ 77283 ★　York International
Corp.
5005 North Interstate Dr.
Norman, OK 73069
Ultimate Parent: York International Corp.
SIC: 3585—Refrigeration & Heating
Equipment.

Nowata

★ 77284 ★　Pizza Hut
130 S. Ash St.
Nowata, OK 74048
(918)273-1300
Ultimate Parent: Pepsico. SIC: 5812—
Eating Places.

★ 77285 ★　Wal Mart
306 S. Ash St.
Nowata, OK 74048
(918)273-3800
Ultimate Parent: Wal-Mart Stores, Inc. SIC:
5311—Department Stores.

Okarche

★ 77286 ★　Union Texas
Petroleum Corp.
Southeast City
Okarche, OK 73762
(405)263-4980
Ultimate Parent: Union Texas Petroleum.
SIC: 5171—Petroleum Bulk Stations &
Terminals.

Okeene

★ 77287 ★　Burlington Northern
Railroad
Okeene, OK 73763
(405)822-4828
Ultimate Parent: Burlington Northern. SIC:
4011—Railroads—Line-Haul Operating.

Okemah

★ 77288 ★　Wrangler
122 SE 7th St.
Okemah, OK 74859
(918)623-0456
Officer: Ron Rogers, Manager. Ultimate
Parent: VF Corp. SIC: 2325—Men's/Boys'
Trousers & Slacks.

Oklahoma

★ 77289 ★　Ryder Truck Rental
5926 Express Way
Oklahoma, OK 73122
(405)787-5643
Ultimate Parent: Ryder System. SIC:
7513—Truck Rental & Leasing Without
Drivers.

Oklahoma City

★ 77290 ★　ABF Freight System
Inc.
1117 E. Grand Blvd.
Oklahoma City, OK 73129-8406
(405)677-0571
Officer: Mike Kelleher. Ultimate Parent:
Arkansas Best. SIC: 4212—Local Trucking
Without Storage; 4213—Trucking Except
Local.

★ 77291 ★　Ace Hardware Supply
4309 SE 15th St.
Oklahoma City, OK 73115
Ultimate Parent: Ace Hardware. SIC:
5251—Hardware Stores.

★ 77292 ★　**Air Products &
Chemicals, Inc.**
1524 S. May Ave.
Oklahoma City, OK 73108
(405)232-3456
Ultimate Parent: Air Products & Chemicals,
Inc. **SIC:** 5049—Professional Equipment
Nec; 5084—Industrial Machinery &
Equipment.

★ 77293 ★　**Airborne Freight
Corp.**
7140 Air Cargo Rd.
Oklahoma City, OK 73159
(405)681-0723
Ultimate Parent: Airborne Freight Corp.
SIC: 4513—Air Courier Services.

★ 77294 ★　**Ajax-Superior
Compressor Packaging Plant**
2101 SE 18th St.
Oklahoma City, OK 73129
Ultimate Parent: Cooper Industries. **SIC:**
3533—Oil & Gas Field Machinery.

★ 77295 ★　**Albertson's
Wholesale Meats**
4248 Charter Ave.
Oklahoma City, OK 73108
(405)943-7654
Ultimate Parent: Albertson's Inc. **SIC:**
2013—Sausages & Other Prepared Meats;
5147—Meats & Meat Products.

★ 77296 ★　**American General
Finance**
5515 NW Expressway St.
Oklahoma City, OK 73132-5222
(405)720-0241
Officer: Gaylene O'Hallorn. **Ultimate
Parent:** American General Corp. **SIC:**
6141—Personal Credit Institutions; 6162—
Mortgage Bankers & Correspondents.

★ 77297 ★　**American General
Finance**
5520 E. Reno Ave.
Oklahoma City, OK 73117-8418
(405)677-8737
Location Type: Branch office. **Ultimate
Parent:** American General Corp. **SIC:**
6141—Personal Credit Institutions; 6162—
Mortgage Bankers & Correspondents.

★ 77298 ★　**American General
Finance Inc.**
5515 NW Expressway St.
Oklahoma City, OK 73132-5222
(405)720-0241
Location Type: Branch office. **Officer:**
Gaylene O'Hallorn. **Ultimate Parent:**
American General Corp. **SIC:** 6141—
Personal Credit Institutions; 6162—
Mortgage Bankers & Correspondents.

★ 77299 ★　**American General
Finance Inc.**
5520 E. Reno Ave.
Oklahoma City, OK 73117-8418
(405)677-8737
Location Type: Branch office. **Ultimate
Parent:** American General Corp. **SIC:**
6141—Personal Credit Institutions; 6162—
Mortgage Bankers & Correspondents.

★ 77300 ★　**American General Life
Insurance Co. of Oklahoma**
209 SW 89th St., Stes. A,B,& C
Oklahoma City, OK 73139
(405)634-4171
Officer: Carroll D. Shanks, President &
CEO. **Ultimate Parent:** American General
Corp. **SIC:** 6311—Life Insurance.

★ 77301 ★　**AT & T Network
Systems**
7725 W. Reno Ave.
Oklahoma City, OK 73127
(405)491-3000
Officer: Pete Gannon, Vice President.
Ultimate Parent: AT&T. **SIC:** 3571—
Electronic Computers; 3661—Telephone &
Telegraph Apparatus.

★ 77302 ★　**Avon Products Inc.**
2000 N. Classen Blvd.
Oklahoma City, OK 73106
(405)521-1481
Ultimate Parent: Avon Products, Inc. **SIC:**
5999—Miscellaneous Retail Stores Nec.

★ 77303 ★　**Baker Hughes**
Cac Div.
11040 NW 10th St.
Oklahoma City, OK 73127
Ultimate Parent: Baker Hughes. **SIC:**
3533—Oil & Gas Field Machinery; 3561—
Pumps & Pumping Equipment; 3599—
Industrial Machinery Nec.

★ 77304 ★　**Baker Hughes Inteq.**
6205 S. Sooner Rd.
Oklahoma City, OK 73135
(405)670-1311
Officer: Heinrich Daenicke, Manager.
Ultimate Parent: Baker Hughes. **SIC:**
3533—Oil & Gas Field Machinery.

★ 77305 ★　**Beneficial Mortgage
Co. of Oklahoma**
540 E. Memorial Rd.
Oklahoma City, OK 73114-2215
(405)752-0012
Officer: Chad Sampley. **Ultimate Parent:**
Beneficial. **SIC:** 6162—Mortgage Bankers &
Correspondents; 6141—Personal Credit
Institutions.

★ 77306 ★　**Beneficial Oklahoma
Inc.**
7101 NW Exwy. St.
Oklahoma City, OK 73132-1540
(405)728-2293
Officer: Lloyd D. Mathenia. **Ultimate
Parent:** Beneficial. **SIC:** 6141—Personal
Credit Institutions; 6162—Mortgage Bankers
& Correspondents.

★ 77307 ★　**Beneficial Oklahoma
Inc.**
7864 S. Western Ave.
Oklahoma City, OK 73139-2412
(405)632-6657
Officer: Al Woodruff. **Ultimate Parent:**
Beneficial. **SIC:** 6141—Personal Credit
Institutions; 6162—Mortgage Bankers &
Correspondents.

★ 77308 ★　**Bermans the Leather
Experts**
2501 W. Memorial Rd.
Oklahoma City, OK 73134
(405)752-2697
Ultimate Parent: Melville. **SIC:** 5948—
Luggage & Leather Goods Stores.

★ 77309 ★　**Borden Inc.**
2126 N. Broadway Ave.
Oklahoma City, OK 73103
(405)232-0177
Officer: Mark Nicholson, Manager. **Ultimate
Parent:** Borden, Inc. **SIC:** 2021—Creamery
Butter; 2024—Ice Cream & Frozen
Desserts; 2026—Fluid Milk.

★ 77310 ★　**Borden Inc.**
Dairy
2126 N. Broadway
Oklahoma City, OK 73103
Company Type: Division. **Ultimate Parent:**
Borden, Inc. **SIC:** 5143—Dairy Products
Except Dried or Canned; 2026—Fluid Milk;
5451—Dairy Products Stores.

★ 77311 ★　**Borden Inc.**
Dairy
2126 N. Broadway
Oklahoma City, OK 73103
Company Type: Division. **Ultimate Parent:**
Borden, Inc. **SIC:** 2026—Fluid Milk; 5451—
Dairy Products Stores; 5143—Dairy
Products Except Dried or Canned.

★ 77312 ★　**Borden Inc. Grocery
& Specialty Products**
2126 N. Broadway
Oklahoma City, OK 73103
Ultimate Parent: Borden, Inc. **SIC:** 5143—
Dairy Products Except Dried or Canned;
2026—Fluid Milk; 5451—Dairy Products
Stores.

★ 77313 ★　**Builders Square**
7700 S. Walker Ave.
Oklahoma City, OK 73139
(405)632-0057
Company Type: Subsidiary. **Ultimate
Parent:** K-Mart. **SIC:** 5251—Hardware
Stores.

★ 77314 ★　**Builders Square**
2903 NW 36th St.
Oklahoma City, OK 73112
(405)948-7991
Company Type: Subsidiary. **Ultimate**

Parent: K-Mart. **SIC:** 5211—Lumber &
Other Building Materials.

★ 77315 ★　**Burlington Coat
Factory**
3000 NW 63rd St.
Oklahoma City, OK 73116-3698
(405)848-3100
Location Type: Branch office. **Officer:**
Jacqueline Bass. **Ultimate Parent:**
Burlington Industries, Equity. **SIC:** 5311—
Department Stores; 5651—Family Clothing
Stores.

★ 77316 ★　**Career Image**
Quail
Oklahoma City, OK 73120
(405)755-9296
Ultimate Parent: United States Shoe. **SIC:**
5621—Women's Clothing Stores.

★ 77317 ★　**Career Image**
2501 W. Memorial Rd.
Oklahoma City, OK 73134
(405)755-9296
Ultimate Parent: United States Shoe. **SIC:**
5651—Family Clothing Stores.

★ 77318 ★　**Career Image**
7000 Crossroads Mall
Oklahoma City, OK 73149
(405)632-5852
Ultimate Parent: United States Shoe. **SIC:**
5651—Family Clothing Stores.

★ 77319 ★　**Casual Corner**
2514 Shepherd Mall
Oklahoma City, OK 73107
(405)946-3042
Ultimate Parent: United States Shoe. **SIC:**
5651—Family Clothing Stores.

★ 77320 ★　**Casual Corner**
2501 W. Memorial Rd.
Oklahoma City, OK 73134
(405)751-1920
Ultimate Parent: United States Shoe. **SIC:**
5651—Family Clothing Stores.

★ 77321 ★　**Casual Corner**
1951 Penn Sq.
Oklahoma City, OK 73118
(405)840-4311
Ultimate Parent: United States Shoe. **SIC:**
5621—Women's Clothing Stores.

★ 77322 ★　**Casual Corner**
Shepherd
Oklahoma City, OK 73112
(405)946-3042
Ultimate Parent: United States Shoe. **SIC:**
5621—Women's Clothing Stores.

★ 77323 ★　**Casual Corner**
Heritage
Oklahoma City, OK 73110
(405)737-8979
Ultimate Parent: United States Shoe. **SIC:**
5621—Women's Clothing Stores.

★ 77324 ★　**Casual Corner**
1901 Northwest Expy.
Oklahoma City, OK 73116
(405)840-4311
Ultimate Parent: United States Shoe. **SIC:**
2339—Women's/Misses' Outerwear Nec;
7231—Beauty Shops.

★ 77325 ★　**Casual Corner**
Crossroads Mall
Oklahoma City, OK 73149
(405)631-7468
Ultimate Parent: United States Shoe. **SIC:**
5621—Women's Clothing Stores; 5651—
Family Clothing Stores.

★ 77326 ★　**Cato Oil & Grease Co.**
915 Martin Luther King Blvd.
Oklahoma City, OK 73117
Ultimate Parent: Kerr-McGee. **SIC:** 2992—
Lubricating Oils & Greases.

★ 77327 ★　**Circus World Toy
Stores**
Heritage
Oklahoma City, OK 73110
(405)732-0997
Ultimate Parent: Melville. **SIC:** 5945—
Hobby, Toy & Game Shops.

★ 77328 ★　**Citgo**
4836 S. Pennsylvania Ave.
Oklahoma City, OK 73119
(405)686-0163
Ultimate Parent: Citgo Petroleum. **SIC:**
5541—Gasoline Service Stations.

★ 77329 ★　**Citgo**
812 SW 44th St.
Oklahoma City, OK 73109
(405)636-0660
Ultimate Parent: Citgo Petroleum. **SIC:**
5411—Grocery Stores.

★ 77330 ★　**Citgo**
7605 E. Reno Ave.
Oklahoma City, OK 73110
(405)737-8556
Ultimate Parent: Citgo Petroleum. **SIC:**
5411—Grocery Stores.

★ 77331 ★　**Citgo**
5400 N. May Ave.
Oklahoma City, OK 73112
(405)943-2778
Ultimate Parent: Citgo Petroleum. **SIC:**
5411—Grocery Stores.

★ 77332 ★　**Citgo Food Mart**
5001 S. May Ave.
Oklahoma City, OK 73119
(405)681-3976
Ultimate Parent: Citgo Petroleum. **SIC:**
5411—Grocery Stores.

★ 77333 ★　**Citgo Quick Mart**
5801 NW 50th St.
Oklahoma City, OK 73122
(405)789-6212
Ultimate Parent: Citgo Petroleum. **SIC:**
5411—Grocery Stores.

★ 77334 ★　**Citgo Quick Mart**
7917 S. Western Ave.
Oklahoma City, OK 73139
(405)631-5707
Ultimate Parent: Citgo Petroleum. **SIC:**
5411—Grocery Stores.

★ 77335 ★　**Citgo Quick Mart**
10900 N. Western Ave.
Oklahoma City, OK 73114
(405)755-1261
Ultimate Parent: Citgo Petroleum. **SIC:**
5411—Grocery Stores; 5541—Gasoline
Service Stations.

★ 77336 ★　**Clark Printing Inc.**
109 E. Madison Ave.
Oklahoma City, OK 73105
(405)528-5396
Ultimate Parent: Terex. **SIC:** 2732—Book
Printing; 2759—Commercial Printing Nec.

★ 77337 ★　**Coast to Coast Club**
5600 E. Reno Ave.
Oklahoma City, OK 73110
(405)737-8295
Ultimate Parent: Servistar Corp. **SIC:**
8641—Civic & Social Associations.

★ 77338 ★　**Columbia Gas
Dvlpmnt Corp.**
50 Penn Pl
Oklahoma City, OK 73118
(405)840-4413
Ultimate Parent: Columbia Gas System.
SIC: 4932—Gas & Other Services
Combined.

★ 77339 ★　**Cooper Industries
Flow Control Demco Plant**
845 SE 29th
Oklahoma City, OK 73143
Ultimate Parent: Cooper Industries. **SIC:**
3494—Valves & Pipe Fittings Nec; 3471—
Plating & Polishing.

★ 77340 ★　**Cooper Industries Inc.**
Oil Tool Div.
845 SE 29th
Oklahoma City, OK 73143
Company Type: Division. **Ultimate Parent:**
Cooper Industries. **SIC:** 3494—Valves &
Pipe Fittings Nec; 3471—Plating &
Polishing.

★ 77341 ★　**Dana Corp.**
4500 SE 59th St.
Oklahoma City, OK 73135
(405)672-4500
Ultimate Parent: Dana Corp. **SIC:** 3714—
Motor Vehicle Parts & Accessories.

★ 77342 ★ **Dana Corp.**
3601 S. Thomas Rd., No. B
Oklahoma City, OK 73179
(405)682-0873
Ultimate Parent: Dana Corp. **SIC:** 3714—
Motor Vehicle Parts & Accessories.

★ 77343 ★ **Delta Air Lines**
5400 NW Grand Blvd.
Oklahoma City, OK 73112
(405)947-4280
Ultimate Parent: Delta Air Lines, Inc. **SIC:**
4724—Travel Agencies.

★ 77344 ★ **Delta Air Lines**
7100 W. Rogers World Airport
Oklahoma City, OK 73159
(405)682-7108
Ultimate Parent: Delta Air Lines, Inc. **SIC:**
4512—Air Transportation—Scheduled.

★ 77345 ★ **Diebold, Inc.**
4417 SW 21st St.
Oklahoma City, OK 73108
(405)682-9671
Ultimate Parent: Diebold, Inc. **SIC:** 5999—
Miscellaneous Retail Stores Nec; 1731—
Electrical Work.

★ 77346 ★ **Digital Equipment
Corp.**
1300 S. Meridian Ave.
Oklahoma City, OK 73108
(405)949-2929
Ultimate Parent: Digital Equipment Corp.
SIC: 5046—Commercial Equipment Nec;
5065—Electronic Parts & Equipment Nec;
7532—Top & Body Repair & Paint Shops.

★ 77347 ★ **Doskocil**
2601 Northwest Expy.
Oklahoma City, OK 73112
(405)879-5500
Company Type: Headquarters. **Officer:**
John T. Hanes. **Employee Count:** 2150.
Sales: 648 M. **Fortune 500:** Largest U.S.
Industrial Corporations: Ranking 480.

★ 77348 ★ **E R Carpenter Co.**
29 N. Mccormick St.
Oklahoma City, OK 73127
(405)942-6285
Ultimate Parent: Carpenter.

★ 77349 ★ **Eastman Christensen**
6205 S. Sooner Rd.
Oklahoma City, OK 73135
Ultimate Parent: Baker Hughes. **SIC:**
3533—Oil & Gas Field Machinery.

★ 77350 ★ **Eastman Teleco**
6205 S. Sooner Rd.
Oklahoma City, OK 73135
Ultimate Parent: Baker Hughes. **SIC:**
3533—Oil & Gas Field Machinery.

★ 77351 ★ **Emery Worldwide**
7100 W. Rogers Wrld Arp
Oklahoma City, OK 73159
(405)685-3325
Ultimate Parent: Consolidated Freightways.
SIC: 4513—Air Courier Services.

★ 77352 ★ **Esp Products**
5500 SE 59th St.
Oklahoma City, OK 73135
Ultimate Parent: Paccar. **SIC:** 3561—
Pumps & Pumping Equipment.

★ 77353 ★ **Express**
2501 W. Memorial Rd.
Oklahoma City, OK 73134
(405)752-2468
Ultimate Parent: Limited. **SIC:** 5651—
Family Clothing Stores.

★ 77354 ★ **Exxon Chemical Co.**
2701 Purdue Dr.
Oklahoma City, OK 73128
(405)686-0210
Ultimate Parent: Exxon. **SIC:** 5082—
Construction & Mining Machinery.

★ 77355 ★ **Exxon Corp.**
5124 S. Eastern Ave.
Oklahoma City, OK 73129
(405)670-3673
Ultimate Parent: Exxon. **SIC:** 3571—
Electronic Computers.

★ 77356 ★ **Exxon Corp.**
2000 N. Classen Blvd. Bldg. E
Oklahoma City, OK 73106
(405)523-4300
Ultimate Parent: Exxon. **SIC:** 1311—Crude
Petroleum & Natural Gas.

★ 77357 ★ **Federal Mogul Corp.**
2520 W. Reno Ave.
Oklahoma City, OK 73107
(405)232-3477
Ultimate Parent: Federal-Mogul Corp. **SIC:**
5531—Automobile & Home Supply Stores.

★ 77358 ★ **First Fidelity Bancorp**
1400 S. Meridian Ave.
Oklahoma City, OK 73108-1710
(405)942-8811
Officer: William M. Cameron, President.
Ultimate Parent: First Fidelity Bancorp.
SIC: 6021—National Commercial Banks.
Employee Count: 147.

★ 77359 ★ **Fleming**
6301 Waterford Blvd.
Oklahoma City, OK
(405)840-7200
Location Type: Headquarters. **Officer:**
Robert E. Stauth, CEO. **Employee Count:**
23300. **Sales:** 13092 M. **Fortune Service
500:** Ranking 2.

★ 77360 ★ **Fleming Companies
Inc.**
6301 Waterford Blvd.
Oklahoma City, OK 73118-1124
(405)840-7200
Officer: E. Dean Werries, Chairman of the
Board & CEO. **Ultimate Parent:** Fleming.
SIC: 5141—Groceries—General Line;
5147—Meats & Meat Products; 5148—
Fresh Fruits & Vegetables; 5149—Groceries
& Related Products Nec; 5142—Packaged
Frozen Foods; 5143—Dairy Products
Except Dried or Canned. **Employee Count:**
22800. **Sales:** 13 M.

★ 77361 ★ **Fleming Co. Inc.**
6301 Waterford Blvd.
P.O. Box 26647
Oklahoma City, OK 73126-0647
(405)840-7200 **Fax:** (405)841-8149
Company Type: Headquarters. **Officer:** E.
Dean Werries, Chairman. **Ultimate Parent:**
Fleming. **Employee Count:** 22800. **Sales:**
Exceed12Bill. M.

★ 77362 ★ **Fleming Cos. Inc.**
6301 Waterford Blvd.
PO Box 26647
Oklahoma City, OK 73126
(405)840-7200
Officer: E. Dean Werries, Chairman.
Ultimate Parent: Fleming. **SIC:** 5141—
Groceries—General Line; 5411—Grocery
Stores; 6159—Miscellaneous Business
Credit Institutions. **Employee Count:**
22800. **Sales:** 12937884000 M.

★ 77363 ★ **Footaction USA**
7000 Crossroads Blvd.
Oklahoma City, OK 73149
(405)634-5541
Ultimate Parent: Melville.

★ 77364 ★ **The Gap**
7000 Crossroads Blvd.
Oklahoma City, OK 73149
(405)631-6686
Ultimate Parent: GAP.

★ 77365 ★ **The Gap**
Quail
Oklahoma City, OK 73120
(405)755-2405
Ultimate Parent: GAP. **SIC:** 5611—Men's &
Boys' Clothing Stores.

★ 77366 ★ **The Gap**
Crossroads Mall
Oklahoma City, OK 73149
(405)631-6686
Ultimate Parent: GAP. **SIC:** 5611—Men's &
Boys' Clothing Stores.

★ 77367 ★ **The Gap**
Penn Sq.
Oklahoma City, OK 73118
(405)848-8273
Ultimate Parent: GAP. **SIC:** 5621—
Women's Clothing Stores.

★ 77368 ★ **The Gap**
2501 W. Memorial Rd.
Oklahoma City, OK 73134
(405)755-2405
Ultimate Parent: GAP. **SIC:** 5651—Family
Clothing Stores.

★ 77369 ★ **Gap Store**
Quail
Oklahoma City, OK 73120
(405)755-2405
Ultimate Parent: GAP. **SIC:** 5611—Men's &
Boys' Clothing Stores.

★ 77370 ★ **Gap Store**
Penn Sq.
Oklahoma City, OK 73118
(405)848-8273
Ultimate Parent: GAP. **SIC:** 5621—
Women's Clothing Stores.

★ 77371 ★ **Gap Store the**
2501 W. Memorial Rd.
Oklahoma City, OK 73134
(405)755-2405
Ultimate Parent: GAP. **SIC:** 5651—Family
Clothing Stores.

★ 77372 ★ **Gap Store**
Crossroads Mall
Oklahoma City, OK 73149
(405)631-6686
Ultimate Parent: GAP. **SIC:** 5611—Men's &
Boys' Clothing Stores.

★ 77373 ★ **General Motors Corp.**
Pontiac Motor Division
5400 NW Grand Blvd.
Oklahoma City, OK 73112
(405)843-2804
Ultimate Parent: General Motors Corp.
SIC: 7389—Business Services Nec.

★ 77374 ★ **Geo. A. Hormel & Co.**
7300 SW 29th St.
Oklahoma City, OK 73179
Ultimate Parent: Hormel Foods. **SIC:**
2000—Food & Kindred Products.

★ 77375 ★ **Governair**
4841 N. Sewell
Oklahoma City, OK 73118
Ultimate Parent: Nortek. **SIC:** 3585—
Refrigeration & Heating Equipment.

★ 77376 ★ **Greyhound Bus Line**
427 W. Sheridan Ave.
Oklahoma City, OK 73102
(405)235-6425
Ultimate Parent: Greyhound Lines Inc.

★ 77377 ★ **Greyhound Bus Lines**
427 W. Sheridan Ave.
Oklahoma City, OK 73102
(405)236-3639
Ultimate Parent: Greyhound Lines Inc. **SIC:**
4111—Local & Suburban Transit.

★ 77378 ★ **Hertz Rent-A-Car**
5701 Tinker Diagonal St.
Oklahoma City, OK 73110
(405)732-0365
Ultimate Parent: Hertz. **SIC:** 7514—
Passenger Car Rental.

★ 77379 ★ **Hertz Rent-A-Car**
7100 W. Rogers Wrld Arp
Oklahoma City, OK 73159
(405)681-2341
Ultimate Parent: Hertz. **SIC:** 7514—
Passenger Car Rental.

★ 77380 ★ **Hertz Rent-A-Car**
5601 Northwest Expy.
Oklahoma City, OK 73132
(405)721-6440
Ultimate Parent: Hertz.

★ 77381 ★ **Hertz Rent-A-Car
Licensee**
Municipal Airport
Oklahoma City, OK 73101
(405)355-6789
Ultimate Parent: Hertz. **SIC:** 5521—Used
Car Dealers.

★ 77382 ★ **Hewlett-Packard Co.**
3525 NW 56th St.
Oklahoma City, OK 73112
(405)946-9499
Ultimate Parent: Hewlett-Packard. **SIC:**
3571—Electronic Computers; 7378—
Computer Maintenance & Repair.

★ 77383 ★ **Hit or Miss**
1331 W. Memorial Rd.
Oklahoma City, OK 73114
(405)752-2883
Ultimate Parent: TJX. **SIC:** 5651—Family
Clothing Stores.

★ 77384 ★ **Hit or Miss**
8476 Northwest Expy.
Oklahoma City, OK 73162
(405)728-1130
Ultimate Parent: TJX. **SIC:** 5621—
Women's Clothing Stores; 5651—Family
Clothing Stores.

★ 77385 ★ **Hit or Miss**
2600 S. Service Rd.
Oklahoma City, OK 73160
(405)799-9032
Ultimate Parent: TJX. **SIC:** 5621—
Women's Clothing Stores.

★ 77386 ★ **Hormel Foods Corp.**
73000 SW 29th St.
Oklahoma City, OK 73179
(405)745-3471
Location Type: Plant. **Officer:** Cal Jacobs,
Plant Manager. **Ultimate Parent:** Hormel
Foods. **SIC:** 2013—Sausages & Other
Prepared Meats.

★ 77387 ★ **Imprimis Technology
Inc.**
10321 West Reno Ave.
Oklahoma City, OK 73127
Ultimate Parent: Seagate Technology, Inc.
SIC: 3500—Industrial Machinery &
Equipment.

★ 77388 ★ **Intel Corp.**
6801 N. Broadway Ext
Oklahoma City, OK 73116
(405)848-8086
Ultimate Parent: Intel Corp. **SIC:** 7373—
Computer Integrated Systems Design.

★ 77389 ★ **Jiffy Lube**
4900 N. Portland Ave.
Oklahoma City, OK 73112
(405)946-0616
Ultimate Parent: Pennzoil. **SIC:** 7539—
Automotive Repair Shops Nec.

★ 77390 ★ **Jiffy Lube**
5820 Northwest Expy.
Oklahoma City, OK 73132
(405)728-2876
Ultimate Parent: Pennzoil. **SIC:** 6282—
Investment Advice.

★ 77391 ★ **Jiffy Lube**
2401 NW 39th St.
Oklahoma City, OK 73112
(405)521-0240
Ultimate Parent: Pennzoil. **SIC:** 7539—
Automotive Repair Shops Nec.

★ 77392 ★ **Jiffy Lube**
10900 N. May Ave.
Oklahoma City, OK 73120
(405)755-2378
Ultimate Parent: Pennzoil. **SIC:** 7539—
Automotive Repair Shops Nec.

★ 77393 ★ **Jiffy Lube**
2400 N. Meridian Ave.
Oklahoma City, OK 73107
(405)942-8202
Ultimate Parent: Pennzoil. **SIC:** 7539—
Automotive Repair Shops Nec.

★ 77394 ★ **Jiffy Lube**
6930 E. Reno Ave.
Oklahoma City, OK 73110
(405)737-5009
Ultimate Parent: Pennzoil. **SIC:** 7539—
Automotive Repair Shops Nec.

★ 77395 ★ **Jiffy Lube**
7315 N. May Ave.
Oklahoma City, OK 73116
(405)840-0730
Ultimate Parent: Pennzoil. **SIC:** 7539—
Automotive Repair Shops Nec.

★ 77396 ★ **Kay-Bee Toy & Hobby
Shop**
2501 W. Memorial Rd.
Oklahoma City, OK 73134
(405)751-2976
Ultimate Parent: Melville. **SIC:** 5945—
Hobby, Toy & Game Shops.

★ 77397 ★ **Kay-Bee Toy & Hobby Shop**
2623 Shepherd Mall
Oklahoma City, OK 73107
(405)943-0009
Ultimate Parent: Melville. **SIC:** 5945—Hobby, Toy & Game Shops.

★ 77398 ★ **Kentucky Fried Chicken**
1701 W. Britton Rd.
Oklahoma City, OK 73120
(405)751-3018
Ultimate Parent: Pepsico. **SIC:** 5812—Eating Places.

★ 77399 ★ **Kentucky Fried Chicken**
5008 SE 29th St.
Oklahoma City, OK 73115
(405)677-3885
Ultimate Parent: Pepsico. **SIC:** 5812—Eating Places.

★ 77400 ★ **Kentucky Fried Chicken**
2901 SW 29th St.
Oklahoma City, OK 73119
(405)685-4197
Ultimate Parent: Pepsico. **SIC:** 5812—Eating Places.

★ 77401 ★ **Kentucky Fried Chicken**
3113 S. Western Ave.
Oklahoma City, OK 73109
(405)632-2677
Ultimate Parent: Pepsico. **SIC:** 5812—Eating Places.

★ 77402 ★ **Kentucky Fried Chicken**
7517 S. Western Ave.
Oklahoma City, OK 73139
(405)636-1143
Ultimate Parent: Pepsico. **SIC:** 5812—Eating Places.

★ 77403 ★ **Kentucky Fried Chicken**
5800 S. Pennsylvania Ave.
Oklahoma City, OK 73119
(405)681-5033
Ultimate Parent: Pepsico. **SIC:** 5812—Eating Places.

★ 77404 ★ **Kentucky Fried Chicken**
5917 S. Shields Blvd.
Oklahoma City, OK 73129
(405)634-6695
Ultimate Parent: Pepsico. **SIC:** 5812—Eating Places.

★ 77405 ★ **Kentucky Fried Chicken**
4625 NW 39th Expy.
Oklahoma City, OK 73122
(405)789-5843
Ultimate Parent: Pepsico. **SIC:** 5812—Eating Places.

★ 77406 ★ **Kentucky Fried Chicken**
1420 S. Air Depot Blvd.
Oklahoma City, OK 73110
(405)732-4644
Ultimate Parent: Pepsico. **SIC:** 5812—Eating Places.

★ 77407 ★ **Kentucky Fried Chicken**
1901 NE 23rd St.
Oklahoma City, OK 73111
(405)427-7758
Ultimate Parent: Pepsico. **SIC:** 5812—Eating Places.

★ 77408 ★ **Kentucky Fried Chicken**
1312 NW 12th St.
Oklahoma City, OK 73170
(405)799-0520
Ultimate Parent: Pepsico. **SIC:** 5812—Eating Places.

★ 77409 ★ **Kentucky Fried Chicken**
5200 N. May Ave.
Oklahoma City, OK 73112
(405)947-5738
Ultimate Parent: Pepsico. **SIC:** 5812—Eating Places.

★ 77410 ★ **Kentucky Fried Chicken**
1200 N. Moore Ave.
Oklahoma City, OK 73160
(405)794-3982
Ultimate Parent: Pepsico. **SIC:** 5812—Eating Places.

★ 77411 ★ **Kentucky Fried Chicken**
3624 N. Lincoln Blvd.
Oklahoma City, OK 73105
(405)528-2043
Ultimate Parent: Pepsico. **SIC:** 5812—Eating Places.

★ 77412 ★ **Kentucky Fried Chicken**
7120 Northwest Expy.
Oklahoma City, OK 73132
(405)722-1450
Ultimate Parent: Pepsico. **SIC:** 5812—Eating Places.

★ 77413 ★ **Kentucky Fried Chicken**
2320 NW 23rd St.
Oklahoma City, OK 73107
(405)528-6061
Ultimate Parent: Pepsico. **SIC:** 5812—Eating Places.

★ 77414 ★ **Kerr-McGee**
123 Robert S. Kerr Ave.
Oklahoma City, OK 73102
(405)270-1313
Company Type: Headquarters. **Officer:** Frank A. McPherson. **Employee Count:** 5812. **Sales:** 3281 M. **Fortune 500:** Largest U.S. Industrial Corporations: Ranking 150.

★ 77415 ★ **Lane Bryant**
2412 Shepherd Mall
Oklahoma City, OK 73107
(405)947-2183
Ultimate Parent: Limited. **SIC:** 5651—Family Clothing Stores.

★ 77416 ★ **Lane Bryant**
2501 W. Memorial Rd.
Oklahoma City, OK 73134
(405)752-9168
Ultimate Parent: Limited. **SIC:** 5651—Family Clothing Stores.

★ 77417 ★ **Lane Bryant**
1901 Northwest Expy.
Oklahoma City, OK 73116
(405)842-4990
Ultimate Parent: Limited. **SIC:** 2339—Women's/Misses' Outerwear Nec.

★ 77418 ★ **Lens Crafters**
Crossroads Mall
Oklahoma City, OK 73149
(405)631-0033
Ultimate Parent: United States Shoe. **SIC:** 8042—Offices & Clinics of Optometrists.

★ 77419 ★ **Lerner Shop**
Quail
Oklahoma City, OK 73120
(405)751-6622
Ultimate Parent: Limited. **SIC:** 5621—Women's Clothing Stores.

★ 77420 ★ **Lerner Shop**
Heritage
Oklahoma City, OK 73110
(405)737-8620
Ultimate Parent: Limited. **SIC:** 5621—Women's Clothing Stores.

★ 77421 ★ **Lerner Shop**
2621 Shepherd Mall
Oklahoma City, OK 73107
(405)947-4069
Ultimate Parent: Limited. **SIC:** 5651—Family Clothing Stores.

★ 77422 ★ **Lerner Shop**
2501 W. Memorial Rd.
Oklahoma City, OK 73134
(405)751-6622
Ultimate Parent: Limited. **SIC:** 5651—Family Clothing Stores.

★ 77423 ★ **Lerner Shop**
Crossroads Mall
Oklahoma City, OK 73149
(405)632-7263
Ultimate Parent: Limited. **SIC:** 5621—Women's Clothing Stores; 5651—Family Clothing Stores.

★ 77424 ★ **The Limited**
Quail
Oklahoma City, OK 73120
(405)751-4772
Ultimate Parent: Limited. **SIC:** 5621—Women's Clothing Stores.

★ 77425 ★ **The Limited**
2501 W. Memorial Rd.
Oklahoma City, OK 73134
(405)751-4772
Ultimate Parent: Limited. **SIC:** 5651—Family Clothing Stores.

★ 77426 ★ **The Limited**
1901 Northwest Expy.
Oklahoma City, OK 73116
(405)840-9680
Ultimate Parent: Limited. **SIC:** 2339—Women's/Misses' Outerwear Nec.

★ 77427 ★ **The Limited**
2706 Shepherd Mall
Oklahoma City, OK 73107
(405)946-5383
Ultimate Parent: Limited. **SIC:** 5651—Family Clothing Stores.

★ 77428 ★ **The Limited**
Crossroads Mall
Oklahoma City, OK 73149
(405)631-0575
Ultimate Parent: Limited. **SIC:** 5651—Family Clothing Stores.

★ 77429 ★ **The Limited Express**
1901 Northwest Expy.
Oklahoma City, OK 73116
(405)840-0167
Ultimate Parent: Limited. **SIC:** 5651—Family Clothing Stores.

★ 77430 ★ **The Limited Express**
7000 Crossroads Mall
Oklahoma City, OK 73149
(405)632-4417
Ultimate Parent: Limited. **SIC:** 5949—Sewing, Needlework & Piece Goods.

★ 77431 ★ **Little Giant Pump Co.**
3810 N. Tulsa Ave.
Oklahoma City, OK 73112
(405)947-2511
Ultimate Parent: Tecumseh Products. **SIC:** 3561—Pumps & Pumping Equipment; 5084—Industrial Machinery & Equipment.

★ 77432 ★ **Louisiana Land & Exploratio**
3030 Northwest Expy. 100
Oklahoma City, OK 73112
(405)948-5900
Ultimate Parent: Louisiana Land & Exploration. **SIC:** 1311—Crude Petroleum & Natural Gas.

★ 77433 ★ **Marathon Oil Co.**
1 City Pl
Oklahoma City, OK 73102
(405)232-2384
Ultimate Parent: USX Corp. **SIC:** 1311—Crude Petroleum & Natural Gas.

★ 77434 ★ **Marathon Oil Co.**
1 City Pl
Oklahoma City, OK 73102
(405)232-2384
Ultimate Parent: USX Corp. **SIC:** 1311—Crude Petroleum & Natural Gas.

★ 77435 ★ **Mary Kay Cosmetics**
14439 N. Pennsylvania Ave.
Oklahoma City, OK 73134
(405)943-1112
Ultimate Parent: Mary Kay Cosmetics.

★ 77436 ★ **Mccaw Communicatns**
5509 N. Pennsylvania Ave.
Oklahoma City, OK 73112
Ultimate Parent: McCaw Cellular Communications.

★ 77437 ★ **McDonalds Hamburgers**
113 NW 23rd St.
Oklahoma City, OK 73103
(405)525-4115
Ultimate Parent: McDonald's.

★ 77438 ★ **McDonalds Hamburgers**
9001 S. Pennsylvania Ave.
Oklahoma City, OK 73159
(405)691-7666
Ultimate Parent: McDonald's.

★ 77439 ★ **McDonalds Hamburgers**
9000 SE 29th St.
Oklahoma City, OK 73130
(405)769-7222
Ultimate Parent: McDonald's.

★ 77440 ★ **Mckesson Drg Co.**
26288 PO Box
Oklahoma City, OK 73126
Ultimate Parent: McKesson.

★ 77441 ★ **Mead Corp**
519 N. Kentucky Ave.
Oklahoma City, OK 73106
(405)235-1391
Ultimate Parent: Mead. **SIC:** 5113—industrial & Personal Service Paper.

★ 77442 ★ **Mead Data Central**
101 American Tower 1st
Oklahoma City, OK 73102
(405)236-3448
Ultimate Parent: Mead. **SIC:** 7374—Data Processing & Preparation.

★ 77443 ★ **Metal Container Corp.**
3713 Harmon Ave.
Oklahoma City, OK 73179-8603
Officer: Robert F. Deguilio. **Ultimate Parent:** Anheuser-Busch. **SIC:** 3411—Metal Cans; 3469—Metal Stampings Nec.

★ 77444 ★ **Metal Container Corp.**
3713 Harmon
Oklahoma City, OK 73179-8603
(405)681-5425
Officer: Robert F. Deguilio. **Ultimate Parent:** Ball Corp. **SIC:** 3469—Metal Stampings Nec; 3411—Metal Cans.

★ 77445 ★ **Microage**
7510 Broadway Exte
Oklahoma City, OK 73116
(405)842-7512
Ultimate Parent: MicroAge.

★ 77446 ★ **Mid Continent Life Insurance Co.**
PO Box 60269
Oklahoma City, OK 73146
(405)524-8444
Company Type: Subsidiary. **Officer:** Riley R. Simon, President:CEO. **Ultimate Parent:** Florida Progress.

★ 77447 ★ **Mobil Oil Corp.**
4045 NW 64th St. Ste. 400
Oklahoma City, OK 73116-1693
(405)841-2400
Company Type: Branch. **Officer:** Douglas R. Hansen. **Ultimate Parent:** Mobil. **SIC:** 5171—Petroleum Bulk Stations & Terminals.

★ 77448 ★ **Mobil Oil Corp.**
1404 S. Sooner Rd.
Oklahoma City, OK 73110
(405)427-6527
Ultimate Parent: Mobil. **SIC:** 5172—Petroleum Products Nec.

★ 77449 ★ **Nalco Chemical Co.**
7915 SW 34th St.
Oklahoma City, OK 73179
(405)745-2356
Ultimate Parent: Nalco Chemical Co.

★ 77450 ★ **National Coop Refinery Association**
Mid American Tower Bldg.
Oklahoma City, OK 73102
(405)235-8694
Ultimate Parent: National Co-op Refinery Association. **SIC:** 2911—Petroleum Refining.

★ 77451 ★ **Ncr Corp.**
4111 Perimeter Ctr. Dr.
Oklahoma City, OK 73112
(405)942-4111
Ultimate Parent: AT&T.

★ 77452 ★ New York Life
Oklahoma City General Office
Western Agencies
50 Penn Pl., Ste. 1100
Oklahoma City, OK 73118
(405)841-7400 **Fax:** (405)841-7454
Officer: Daniel B. Cunningham, General
Manager. **Ultimate Parent:** New York Life.

★ 77453 ★ New York Life
Oklahoma City Group Sales
Central Group Marketing Zone Office
6525 N. Meridian, Ste. 309
Oklahoma City, OK 73116
(405)728-7177 **Fax:** (405)728-1965
Officer: Wayman E. Lee, Group Manager.
Ultimate Parent: New York Life.

★ 77454 ★ Northrop Corp.
5600 Liberty Pky.
Oklahoma City, OK 73110
(405)736-0179
Ultimate Parent: Northrop Corp.

★ 77455 ★ Norwest Mortgage
Inc.
6525 N. Meridian Ave.
Oklahoma City, OK 73116
(405)722-9478
Ultimate Parent: Norwest Corp. **SIC:**
6141—Personal Credit Institutions.

★ 77456 ★ Oilfield Service Corp.
Amer
Grand Ctr. Bldg.
Oklahoma City, OK 73112
(405)949-0865
Ultimate Parent: Great Lakes Chemical.
SIC: 1389—Oil & Gas Field Services Nec.

★ 77457 ★ Oklahoma Canning
Co.
227 N. Quapah
Oklahoma City, OK 73107
Ultimate Parent: Coca-Cola Bottling
Consol. **SIC:** 2086—Bottled & Canned Soft
Drinks.

★ 77458 ★ Oklahoma Executive
Office
2601 NW Expy. Ste. 1000
Oklahoma City, OK 73112
(405)879-5500 **Fax:** (405)840-2441
Company Type: Subsidiary. **Officer:** John
T. Hanes, Chairman President & CEO.
Ultimate Parent: Doskocil.

★ 77459 ★ Oryx Energy
26300 PO Box
Oklahoma City, OK 73126
Ultimate Parent: Oryx Energy. **SIC:** 1311—
Crude Petroleum & Natural Gas; 5093—
Scrap & Waste Materials.

★ 77460 ★ Otis Elevator Co.
1119 Cornell Pky.
Oklahoma City, OK 73108
(405)947-1401
Ultimate Parent: United Technologies. **SIC:**
3534—Elevators & Moving Stairways.

★ 77461 ★ Owens Corning
Fiberglas Cor
3033 NW 63rd Pl.
Oklahoma City, OK 73116
(405)848-6761
Ultimate Parent: Owens-Corning. **SIC:**
5039—Construction Materials Nec.

★ 77462 ★ Pappagallo
Quail
Oklahoma City, OK 73120
(405)751-7670
Ultimate Parent: United States Shoe. **SIC:**
5661—Shoe Stores.

★ 77463 ★ Pappagallo
2501 W. Memorial Rd.
Oklahoma City, OK 73134
(405)755-6682
Ultimate Parent: United States Shoe. **SIC:**
5661—Shoe Stores.

★ 77464 ★ Payless Cashways
104 N. MacArthur Blvd.
Oklahoma City, OK 73127
(405)943-2485
Ultimate Parent: Payless Cashways. **SIC:**
5039—Construction Materials Nec; 5211—
Lumber & Other Building Materials.

★ 77465 ★ Payless Cashways
Bldg Matls
7401 S. Sooner Rd.
Oklahoma City, OK 73135
(405)672-2328
Ultimate Parent: Payless Cashways. **SIC:**
5211—Lumber & Other Building Materials.

★ 77466 ★ Payless Cashways
Bldg Matls
8907 Northwest Expy.
Oklahoma City, OK 73162
(405)721-8800
Ultimate Parent: Payless Cashways. **SIC:**
5211—Lumber & Other Building Materials.

★ 77467 ★ Payless Shoesource
City of Moore Shopping Ctr.
Oklahoma City, OK 73160
(405)799-3411
Ultimate Parent: May Department Stores.
SIC: 5661—Shoe Stores.

★ 77468 ★ Payless Shoesource
2209 SW 74th St.
Oklahoma City, OK 73159
(405)682-1731
Ultimate Parent: May Department Stores.
SIC: 5661—Shoe Stores.

★ 77469 ★ Payless Shoesource
1501 SW 75th St.
Oklahoma City, OK 73159
(405)681-2212
Ultimate Parent: May Department Stores.
SIC: 5661—Shoe Stores.

★ 77470 ★ Payless Shoesource
7000 Crossroads Blvd.
Oklahoma City, OK 73149
(405)636-0264
Ultimate Parent: May Department Stores.

★ 77471 ★ Payless Shoesource
7405 S. Shields Blvd.
Oklahoma City, OK 73149
(405)634-6962
Ultimate Parent: May Department Stores.
SIC: 5661—Shoe Stores.

★ 77472 ★ Payless Shoesource
2501 W. Memorial Rd.
Oklahoma City, OK 73134
(405)755-6128
Ultimate Parent: May Department Stores.
SIC: 5661—Shoe Stores; 5139—Footwear.

★ 77473 ★ Payless Shoesource
3007 SE 44th St.
Oklahoma City, OK 73135
(405)672-8121
Ultimate Parent: May Department Stores.
SIC: 5661—Shoe Stores.

★ 77474 ★ Payless Shoesource
2642 SW 29th St.
Oklahoma City, OK 73119
(405)631-6124
Ultimate Parent: May Department Stores.
SIC: 5661—Shoe Stores.

★ 77475 ★ Payless Shoesource
5905 NW 23rd St.
Oklahoma City, OK 73127
(405)787-8588
Ultimate Parent: May Department Stores.
SIC: 5661—Shoe Stores.

★ 77476 ★ Payless Shoesource
6302 N. May Ave.
Oklahoma City, OK 73112
(405)840-1206
Ultimate Parent: May Department Stores.
SIC: 5661—Shoe Stores.

★ 77477 ★ Payless Shoesource
4530 SE 29th St.
Oklahoma City, OK 73115
(405)672-6314
Ultimate Parent: May Department Stores.

★ 77478 ★ Payless Shoesource
7015 E. Reno Ave.
Oklahoma City, OK 73110
(405)737-2118
Ultimate Parent: May Department Stores.
SIC: 5661—Shoe Stores.

★ 77479 ★ Payless Shoesource
6905 SE 29th St.
Oklahoma City, OK 73110
(405)732-6422
Ultimate Parent: May Department Stores.
SIC: 5661—Shoe Stores.

★ 77480 ★ Payless Shoesource
2500 NW 23rd St.
Oklahoma City, OK 73107
(405)948-8813
Ultimate Parent: May Department Stores.
SIC: 5661—Shoe Stores.

★ 77481 ★ Payless Shoesource
300 W. Commerce St.
Oklahoma City, OK 73109
(405)632-1785
Ultimate Parent: May Department Stores.
SIC: 5661—Shoe Stores.

★ 77482 ★ Payless Shoesource
7228 Northwest Expy.
Oklahoma City, OK 73132
(405)721-4213
Ultimate Parent: May Department Stores.
SIC: 5661—Shoe Stores.

★ 77483 ★ Pepsi-Cola Bottling
Co.
4700 N. Santa Fe Ave.
Oklahoma City, OK 73118
(405)525-9448
Officer: Fran O'Rourke, Manager. **Ultimate
Parent:** Pepsico. **SIC:** 2086—Bottled &
Canned Soft Drinks.

★ 77484 ★ Pepsico Food
Systems Inc.
400 N. Ann Arbor Ave.
Oklahoma City, OK 73127
(405)943-7957
Officer: Rick Combs, Executive Director.
Ultimate Parent: Pepsico. **SIC:** 2086—
Bottled & Canned Soft Drinks.

★ 77485 ★ Petite Sophisticate
1901 Northwest Expy.
Oklahoma City, OK 73116
(405)840-1290
Ultimate Parent: United States Shoe. **SIC:**
5651—Family Clothing Stores.

★ 77486 ★ Petite Sophisticate
Crossroads Mall
Oklahoma City, OK 73149
(405)631-9216
Ultimate Parent: United States Shoe. **SIC:**
5137—Women's/Children's Clothing.

★ 77487 ★ Petite Sophisticate
2501 W. Memorial Rd.
Oklahoma City, OK 73134
(405)752-7454
Ultimate Parent: United States Shoe. **SIC:**
5651—Family Clothing Stores.

★ 77488 ★ Pitney Bowes Credit
Corp.
5310 Harvest Hill Rd.
Oklahoma City, OK 73132
(405)239-9171
Ultimate Parent: Pitney Bowes. **SIC:**
6141—Personal Credit Institutions.

★ 77489 ★ Pizza Hut
1239 W. Britton Rd.
Oklahoma City, OK 73114
(405)848-2649
Ultimate Parent: Pepsico. **SIC:** 5812—
Eating Places.

★ 77490 ★ Pizza Hut
4436 S. Sunnylane Rd.
Oklahoma City, OK 73115
(405)672-2762
Ultimate Parent: Pepsico.

★ 77491 ★ Pizza Hut
6324 S. Western Ave.
Oklahoma City, OK 73139
(405)631-1434
Ultimate Parent: Pepsico. **SIC:** 5812—
Eating Places.

★ 77492 ★ Pizza Hut
8811 S. Pennsylvania Ave.
Oklahoma City, OK 73159
(405)681-1640
Ultimate Parent: Pepsico. **SIC:** 5812—
Eating Places.

★ 77493 ★ Pizza Hut
1475 S. Sunnylane Rd.
Oklahoma City, OK 73115
(405)677-6883
Ultimate Parent: Pepsico. **SIC:** 5812—
Eating Places.

★ 77494 ★ Pizza Hut
2216 N. Rockwell
Oklahoma City, OK 73102
(405)789-8686
Ultimate Parent: Pepsico. **SIC:** 5812—
Eating Places.

★ 77495 ★ Pizza Hut
4227 NW 23rd St.
Oklahoma City, OK 73107
(405)946-3401
Ultimate Parent: Pepsico. **SIC:** 5812—
Eating Places.

★ 77496 ★ Pizza Hut
7801 N. May Ave.
Oklahoma City, OK 73116
(405)842-4277
Ultimate Parent: Pepsico. **SIC:** 5812—
Eating Places.

★ 77497 ★ Pizza Hut
1135 N. Midwest Blvd.
Oklahoma City, OK 73110
(405)733-4131
Ultimate Parent: Pepsico. **SIC:** 5812—
Eating Places.

★ 77498 ★ Pizza Hut
2835 French Mkt Mall
Oklahoma City, OK 73116
(405)843-5155
Ultimate Parent: Pepsico. **SIC:** 5812—
Eating Places.

★ 77499 ★ Pizza Hut
3231 N. Classen Blvd.
Oklahoma City, OK 73118
(405)525-0626
Ultimate Parent: Pepsico. **SIC:** 5812—
Eating Places.

★ 77500 ★ Pizza Hut
2225 SW 59th St.
Oklahoma City, OK 73119
(405)681-4100
Ultimate Parent: Pepsico.

★ 77501 ★ Pizza Hut
2839 S. Douglas Blvd. 110
Oklahoma City, OK 73130
Ultimate Parent: Pepsico.

★ 77502 ★ Pizza Hut
4212 SE 44th St.
Oklahoma City, OK 73135
(405)672-0777
Ultimate Parent: Pepsico.

★ 77503 ★ Pizza Hut
741 NW 12th St.
Oklahoma City, OK 73160
(405)794-4400
Ultimate Parent: Pepsico.

★ 77504 ★ Pizza Hut
4433 NW 23rd St.
Oklahoma City, OK 73107
(405)946-3419
Ultimate Parent: Pepsico.

★ 77505 ★ Pizza Hut
12200 N. May Ave.
Oklahoma City, OK 73120
(405)751-8882
Ultimate Parent: Pepsico.

★ 77506 ★ Pizza Hut
6303 N. Meridian Ave.
Oklahoma City, OK 73112
(405)720-0030
Ultimate Parent: Pepsico.

★ 77507 ★ Pizza Hut
4709 N. Lincoln Blvd.
Oklahoma City, OK 73105
(405)557-0007
Ultimate Parent: Pepsico.

★ 77508 ★ Ppg Industries Inc.
4301 N. Santa Fe Ave.
Oklahoma City, OK 73118
(405)525-6501
Ultimate Parent: PPG Industries Inc.

★ 77509 ★ Quotron Systems
4111 N. Lincoln Blvd.
Oklahoma City, OK 73105
(405)528-5767
Ultimate Parent: Citicorp. **SIC:** 5046—
Commercial Equipment Nec; 7373—
Computer Integrated Systems Design.

★ 77510 ★   Radio Shack
6400 N. Western Ave.
Oklahoma City, OK 73116
Company Type: Division. Ultimate Parent:
Tandy Corp. SIC: 5065—Electronic Parts &
Equipment Nec.

★ 77511 ★   Radio Shack
2025 S. Nicklas St.
Oklahoma City, OK 73128
Company Type: Division. Ultimate Parent:
Tandy Corp. SIC: 5731—Radio, Television
& Electronics Stores.

★ 77512 ★   Radio Shack
5839 SE 59th St.
Oklahoma City, OK 73135
(405)787-3555
Company Type: Division. Ultimate Parent:
Tandy Corp. SIC: 5065—Electronic Parts &
Equipment Nec.

★ 77513 ★   Radio Shack
1817 NW 23rd St.
Oklahoma City, OK 73106
(405)787-1722
Company Type: Division. Ultimate Parent:
Tandy Corp. SIC: 5065—Electronic Parts &
Equipment Nec.

★ 77514 ★   Radio Shack
Shepherd
Oklahoma City, OK 73112
(405)947-1894
Company Type: Division. Ultimate Parent:
Tandy Corp. SIC: 5046—Commercial
Equipment Nec.

★ 77515 ★   Radio Shack
9240 N. Pennsylvania Pl
Oklahoma City, OK 73120
(405)840-3263
Company Type: Division. Ultimate Parent:
Tandy Corp. SIC: 5065—Electronic Parts &
Equipment Nec.

★ 77516 ★   Radio Shack
2110 SW 59th St.
Oklahoma City, OK 73119
(405)681-5591
Company Type: Division. Ultimate Parent:
Tandy Corp. SIC: 5065—Electronic Parts &
Equipment Nec.

★ 77517 ★   Radio Shack
Heritage
Oklahoma City, OK 73110
(405)737-0186
Company Type: Division. Ultimate Parent:
Tandy Corp. SIC: 5046—Commercial
Equipment Nec.

★ 77518 ★   Radio Shack
2501 W. Memorial Rd.
Oklahoma City, OK 73134
(405)751-1731
Company Type: Division. Ultimate Parent:
Tandy Corp. SIC: 5065—Electronic Parts &
Equipment Nec.

★ 77519 ★   Radio Shack
2414 Shepherd Mall
Oklahoma City, OK 73107
(405)947-1894
Company Type: Division. Ultimate Parent:
Tandy Corp. SIC: 5065—Electronic Parts &
Equipment Nec.

★ 77520 ★   Radio Shack
1501 SW 74th St.
Oklahoma City, OK 73159
(405)685-6888
Company Type: Division. Ultimate Parent:
Tandy Corp. SIC: 5731—Radio, Television
& Electronics Stores.

★ 77521 ★   Radio Shack
6222 SE 15th St.
Oklahoma City, OK 73110
(405)732-2511
Company Type: Division. Ultimate Parent:
Tandy Corp.

★ 77522 ★   Radio Shack
4408 SE 44th St.
Oklahoma City, OK 73135
(405)672-7280
Company Type: Division. Ultimate Parent:
Tandy Corp. SIC: 5065—Electronic Parts &
Equipment Nec.

★ 77523 ★   Radio Shack
4403 S. Western Ave.
Oklahoma City, OK 73109
(405)632-0513
Company Type: Division. Ultimate Parent:
Tandy Corp. SIC: 5731—Radio, Television
& Electronics Stores.

★ 77524 ★   Radio Shack
11725 S. Western Ave.
Oklahoma City, OK 73170
(405)691-3220
Company Type: Division. Ultimate Parent:
Tandy Corp.

★ 77525 ★   Radio Shack
13240 PO Box
Oklahoma City, OK 73113
Company Type: Division. Ultimate Parent:
Tandy Corp. SIC: 5046—Commercial
Equipment Nec.

★ 77526 ★   Radio Shack
406 S. Eastern Ave.
Oklahoma City, OK 73160
(405)799-5755
Company Type: Division. Ultimate Parent:
Tandy Corp.

★ 77527 ★   Radio Shack
1901 Northwest Expy.
Oklahoma City, OK 73116
(405)848-8468
Company Type: Division. Ultimate Parent:
Tandy Corp. SIC: 5065—Electronic Parts &
Equipment Nec.

★ 77528 ★   Radio Shack
2214 NW 23rd St.
Oklahoma City, OK 73107
(405)528-1461
Company Type: Division. Ultimate Parent:
Tandy Corp. SIC: 5731—Radio, Television
& Electronics Stores.

★ 77529 ★   Radio Shack
6300 N. Western Ave.
Oklahoma City, OK 73118
(405)843-6636
Company Type: Division. Ultimate Parent:
Tandy Corp.

★ 77530 ★   Radio Shack
6400 N. Western Ave.
Oklahoma City, OK 73116
Company Type: Division. Ultimate Parent:
Tandy Corp. SIC: 7373—Computer
Integrated Systems Design.

★ 77531 ★   Radio Shack
6300 N. Meridian Ave.
Oklahoma City, OK 73112
(405)843-8418
Company Type: Division. Ultimate Parent:
Tandy Corp.

★ 77532 ★   Radio Shack
8325 N. Rockwell Ave.
Oklahoma City, OK 73132
(405)721-3920
Company Type: Division. Ultimate Parent:
Tandy Corp. SIC: 5731—Radio, Television
& Electronics Stores.

★ 77533 ★   Radio Shack
4903 N. May Ave.
Oklahoma City, OK 73112
(405)943-8491
Company Type: Division. Ultimate Parent:
Tandy Corp. SIC: 5065—Electronic Parts &
Equipment Nec.

★ 77534 ★   Radio Shack
10904 N. May Ave.
Oklahoma City, OK 73120
(405)751-1574
Company Type: Division. Ultimate Parent:
Tandy Corp. SIC: 5065—Electronic Parts &
Equipment Nec.

★ 77535 ★   Radio Shack
7000 Crossroads Blvd.
Oklahoma City, OK 73149
(405)632-7664
Company Type: Division. Ultimate Parent:
Tandy Corp.

★ 77536 ★   Raytheon Service Co.
Tinker AFB
Oklahoma City, OK 73145
(405)733-5098
Ultimate Parent: Raytheon Co. SIC:
7699—Repair Services Nec.

★ 77537 ★   Richards Co/S P
1326 Enterprise Ave.
Oklahoma City, OK 73128
(405)949-0765
Ultimate Parent: Genuine Parts. SIC:
5112—Stationery & Office Supplies.

★ 77538 ★   Rollins Burdick &
Hunter
2248 NW 39th St.
Oklahoma City, OK 73112
(405)525-8755
Ultimate Parent: Aon Corp. SIC: 6351—
Surety Insurance; 6411—Insurance Agents,
Brokers & Service.

★ 77539 ★   Ryder Truck Rental
2026 N. Broadway St.
Oklahoma City, OK 73160
(405)794-3167
Ultimate Parent: Ryder System.

★ 77540 ★   Ryder Truck Rental
5024 N. Meridian Ave.
Oklahoma City, OK 73112
(405)942-7358
Ultimate Parent: Ryder System. SIC:
7513—Truck Rental & Leasing Without
Drivers.

★ 77541 ★   Ryder Truck Rental
1645 W. Reno Ave.
Oklahoma City, OK 73106
(405)272-0477
Ultimate Parent: Ryder System. SIC:
5113—Industrial & Personal Service Paper;
7513—Truck Rental & Leasing Without
Drivers.

★ 77542 ★   Ryder Truck Rental
2015 Industrial Blvd.
Oklahoma City, OK 73105
(405)360-0014
Ultimate Parent: Ryder System. SIC:
7513—Truck Rental & Leasing Without
Drivers.

★ 77543 ★   Ryder Truck Rental
26847 PO Box
Oklahoma City, OK 73126
Ultimate Parent: Ryder System. SIC:
7359—Equipment Rental & Leasing Nec;
7513—Truck Rental & Leasing Without
Drivers.

★ 77544 ★   Ryder Truck Rental
8316 S. Western Ave.
Oklahoma City, OK 73139
(405)636-1685
Ultimate Parent: Ryder System. SIC:
7513—Truck Rental & Leasing Without
Drivers.

★ 77545 ★   Ryder Truck Rental
Shop
5303 N. Santa Fe Ave.
Oklahoma City, OK 73118
(405)523-2167
Ultimate Parent: Ryder System. SIC:
7359—Equipment Rental & Leasing Nec;
7513—Truck Rental & Leasing Without
Drivers.

★ 77546 ★   Safety Kleen Corp.
2 NE 9th St.
Oklahoma City, OK 73104
(405)272-0521
Ultimate Parent: Safety-Kleen. SIC: 3714—
Motor Vehicle Parts & Accessories.

★ 77547 ★   Sam's Wholesale
Club
6555 SE 29th St.
Oklahoma City, OK 73110
(405)732-2698
Ultimate Parent: Wal-Mart Stores, Inc. SIC:
5199—Nondurable Goods Nec.

★ 77548 ★   Sam's Wholesale
Club
5510 SW 5th St.
Oklahoma City, OK 73128
(405)943-9810
Ultimate Parent: Wal-Mart Stores, Inc. SIC:
7997—Membership Sports & Recreation
Clubs.

★ 77549 ★   Sam's Wholesale
Club
1121 E. Memorial Rd.
Oklahoma City, OK 73131
(405)478-1880
Ultimate Parent: Wal-Mart Stores, Inc. SIC:
5399—Miscellaneous General Merchandise
Store.

★ 77550 ★   Sam's Wholesale
Liquor Store
3625 NW 23rd St.
Oklahoma City, OK 73107
(405)943-2184
Ultimate Parent: Wal-Mart Stores, Inc. SIC:
5921—Liquor Stores.

★ 77551 ★   Schwab & Co. Inc/
Charles
110 N. Robinson Ave.
Oklahoma City, OK 73102
(405)235-7500
Ultimate Parent: Charles Schwab Corp.
SIC: 6211—Security Brokers & Dealers.

★ 77552 ★   Seagate Technology
Inc.
10321 West Reno Ave.
Oklahoma City, OK 73127
Ultimate Parent: Seagate Technology, Inc.
SIC: 3500—Industrial Machinery &
Equipment.

★ 77553 ★   Security Pacific
Financial Services Inc.
7313 S. Western Ave.
Oklahoma City, OK 73139-2007
(405)728-1891
Location Type: Branch office. Officer:
Jerry Sitser. Ultimate Parent: Bankamerica
Corp. SIC: 6141—Personal Credit
Institutions; 6162—Mortgage Bankers &
Correspondents.

★ 77554 ★   Sequa Corp.
Chromalloy
6501 Interpace
Oklahoma City, OK 73135
Ultimate Parent: Sequa Corp. SIC: 3724—
Aircraft Engines & Engine Parts.

★ 77555 ★   Service Merchandise
5901 N. May Ave.
Oklahoma City, OK 73112
(405)848-2822
Ultimate Parent: Service Merchandise Co.,
Inc. SIC: 5944—Jewelry Stores.

★ 77556 ★   Service Merchandise
7301 S. Pennsylvania Ave.
Oklahoma City, OK 73159
(405)682-1451
Ultimate Parent: Service Merchandise Co.,
Inc. SIC: 5099—Durable Goods Nec;
5944—Jewelry Stores.

★ 77557 ★   Service Merchandise
5537 Northwest Expy.
Oklahoma City, OK 73132
(405)728-2211
Ultimate Parent: Service Merchandise Co.,
Inc. SIC: 5311—Department Stores.

★ 77558 ★   Southland Royalty
Co.
100 N. Broadway Ave.
Oklahoma City, OK 73102
(405)235-5515
Ultimate Parent: Burlington Resources.
SIC: 1382—Oil & Gas Exploration Services.

★ 77559 ★   Southwest Airlines
Co.
Will Rogers World
Oklahoma City, OK 73159
(405)685-4547
Ultimate Parent: Southwest Airlines. SIC:
4512—Air Transportation—Scheduled.

★ 77560 ★   Southwest Airlines
Co.
7100 W. Rogers World Airport
Oklahoma City, OK 73159
(405)685-2249
Ultimate Parent: Southwest Airlines. SIC:
4512—Air Transportation—Scheduled.

★ 77561 ★   Star Manufacturing
Co.
8600 I
Oklahoma City, OK 73135
(405)636-2010
Ultimate Parent: Merrill Lynch Life. SIC:
3449—Miscellaneous Metal Work.

★ 77562 ★   Stop & Shop
909 NW 23rd St.
Oklahoma City, OK 73106
(405)524-0344
Ultimate Parent: Stop & Shop. SIC: 5411—
Grocery Stores.

★ 77563 ★   **Sundstrand Service Corp.**
1420 Gateway Plz.
Oklahoma City, OK 73110
(405)732-0319
Ultimate Parent: Sundstrand. **SIC:** 5088—
Transportation Equipment & Supplies.

★ 77564 ★   **Super Saver Station**
4717 S. Walker Ave.
Oklahoma City, OK 73109
(405)634-7611
Ultimate Parent: Wal-Mart Stores, Inc. **SIC:**
5411—Grocery Stores.

★ 77565 ★   **Super Saver Station**
4912 NW 10th St.
Oklahoma City, OK 73127
(405)942-6287
Ultimate Parent: Wal-Mart Stores, Inc. **SIC:**
5541—Gasoline Service Stations.

★ 77566 ★   **Super Saver Station**
3900 S. Portland Ave.
Oklahoma City, OK 73119
(405)681-3984
Ultimate Parent: Wal-Mart Stores, Inc. **SIC:**
5411—Grocery Stores.

★ 77567 ★   **Super Saver Station**
403 SE 44th St.
Oklahoma City, OK 73129
(405)634-9298
Ultimate Parent: Wal-Mart Stores, Inc. **SIC:**
5411—Grocery Stores.

★ 77568 ★   **T J Maxx**
8400 Northwest Expy.
Oklahoma City, OK 73162
(405)728-0235
Ultimate Parent: TJX. **SIC:** 5311—
Department Stores; 5651—Family Clothing
Stores.

★ 77569 ★   **Taco Bell**
8390 Northwest Expy.
Oklahoma City, OK 73162
(405)720-7576
Ultimate Parent: Pepsico. **SIC:** 5812—
Eating Places.

★ 77570 ★   **Taco Bell**
10830 N. Rockwell Ave.
Oklahoma City, OK 73162
(405)721-8850
Ultimate Parent: Pepsico. **SIC:** 5812—
Eating Places.

★ 77571 ★   **Taco Bell**
17 S. Council Rd.
Oklahoma City, OK 73127
(405)789-4853
Ultimate Parent: Pepsico. **SIC:** 5812—
Eating Places.

★ 77572 ★   **Taco Bell**
2116 SW 59th St.
Oklahoma City, OK 73119
(405)685-5520
Ultimate Parent: Pepsico. **SIC:** 5812—
Eating Places.

★ 77573 ★   **Taco Bell**
4500 NW 10th St.
Oklahoma City, OK 73127
(405)943-7216
Ultimate Parent: Pepsico. **SIC:** 5812—
Eating Places.

★ 77574 ★   **Taco Bell**
6512 S. High Ave.
Oklahoma City, OK 73149
(405)634-9455
Ultimate Parent: Pepsico. **SIC:** 5812—
Eating Places.

★ 77575 ★   **Taco Bell**
4350 Will Rogers Pky.
Oklahoma City, OK 73108
(405)942-0059
Ultimate Parent: Pepsico. **SIC:** 5812—
Eating Places.

★ 77576 ★   **Taco Bell**
936 W. Sheridan Ave.
Oklahoma City, OK 73106
(405)236-3568
Ultimate Parent: Pepsico. **SIC:** 5812—
Eating Places.

★ 77577 ★   **Taco Bell**
2635 SW 29th St.
Oklahoma City, OK 73119
(405)632-8914
Ultimate Parent: Pepsico. **SIC:** 5812—
Eating Places.

★ 77578 ★   **Taco Bell**
1428 W. Britton Rd.
Oklahoma City, OK 73114
(405)842-2666
Ultimate Parent: Pepsico. **SIC:** 5812—
Eating Places.

★ 77579 ★   **Taco Bell**
5305 S. Pennsylvania Ave.
Oklahoma City, OK 73119
(405)685-0505
Ultimate Parent: Pepsico. **SIC:** 5812—
Eating Places.

★ 77580 ★   **Taco Bell**
3601 S. Western Ave.
Oklahoma City, OK 73109
(405)631-5114
Ultimate Parent: Pepsico. **SIC:** 5812—
Eating Places.

★ 77581 ★   **Taco Bell**
2913 S. Douglas Blvd.
Oklahoma City, OK 73130
(405)733-9464
Ultimate Parent: Pepsico.

★ 77582 ★   **Taco Bell**
7101 S. May Ave.
Oklahoma City, OK 73159
(405)682-1612
Ultimate Parent: Pepsico. **SIC:** 5812—
Eating Places.

★ 77583 ★   **Taco Bell**
300 S. Air Depot Blvd.
Oklahoma City, OK 73110
(405)732-1658
Ultimate Parent: Pepsico. **SIC:** 5812—
Eating Places.

★ 77584 ★   **Taco Bell**
1735 S. Broadway St.
Oklahoma City, OK 73160
(405)794-0205
Ultimate Parent: Pepsico. **SIC:** 5812—
Eating Places.

★ 77585 ★   **Taco Bell**
2858 NW 23rd St.
Oklahoma City, OK 73107
(405)943-0388
Ultimate Parent: Pepsico. **SIC:** 5812—
Eating Places.

★ 77586 ★   **Taco Bell**
4624 NW 39th Expy.
Oklahoma City, OK 73122
(405)787-0584
Ultimate Parent: Pepsico. **SIC:** 5812—
Eating Places.

★ 77587 ★   **Taco Bell**
809 NW 12th St.
Oklahoma City, OK 73160
(405)799-7622
Ultimate Parent: Pepsico. **SIC:** 5812—
Eating Places.

★ 77588 ★   **Taco Bell**
224 NW 23rd St.
Oklahoma City, OK 73103
(405)524-0018
Ultimate Parent: Pepsico. **SIC:** 5812—
Eating Places.

★ 77589 ★   **Taco Bell**
1901 Northwest Expy.
Oklahoma City, OK 73116
(405)843-0600
Ultimate Parent: Pepsico. **SIC:** 5812—
Eating Places.

★ 77590 ★   **Taco Bell**
5634 Northwest Expy.
Oklahoma City, OK 73132
(405)721-5833
Ultimate Parent: Pepsico. **SIC:** 5812—
Eating Places.

★ 77591 ★   **Taco Bell**
6808 NE 23rd St.
Oklahoma City, OK 73141
(405)789-3555
Ultimate Parent: Pepsico. **SIC:** 5812—
Eating Places.

★ 77592 ★   **Taco Bell**
9000 NE 23rd St.
Oklahoma City, OK 73141
(405)769-9174
Ultimate Parent: Pepsico.

★ 77593 ★   **Taco Bell**
10005 Lakeshore Dr.
Oklahoma City, OK 73120
(405)848-2536
Ultimate Parent: Pepsico. **SIC:** 5812—
Eating Places.

★ 77594 ★   **Tandy Electronics**
11725 S. Western Ave.
Oklahoma City, OK 73170
(405)691-3220
Ultimate Parent: Tandy Corp. **SIC:** 5065—
Electronic Parts & Equipment Nec.

★ 77595 ★   **Target Stores Inc.**
800 SW 44th St.
Oklahoma City, OK 73109
(405)631-4411
Ultimate Parent: Dayton Hudson. **SIC:**
5311—Department Stores.

★ 77596 ★   **Target Stores Inc.**
5400 N. May Ave.
Oklahoma City, OK 73112
(405)947-6761
Ultimate Parent: Dayton Hudson. **SIC:**
5311—Department Stores.

★ 77597 ★   **Tektronix Inc.**
4400 Will Rogers Pky.
Oklahoma City, OK 73108
(405)943-8127
Ultimate Parent: Tektronix, Inc. **SIC:**
5049—Professional Equipment Nec.

★ 77598 ★   **Tektronix Inc.**
800 NE 63rd St.
Oklahoma City, OK 73105
(405)848-3361
Ultimate Parent: Tektronix, Inc. **SIC:**
3825—Instruments to Measure Electricity.

★ 77599 ★   **Tenax Corp.**
6307 Waterford Blvd.
Oklahoma City, OK 73118
(405)842-9900
Ultimate Parent: Timken Co. **SIC:** 1382—
Oil & Gas Exploration Services.

★ 77600 ★   **Tesoro Petroleum Distribution Co.**
821 S. Dewey Ave.
Oklahoma City, OK 73109
(405)235-2963
Ultimate Parent: Tesoro Petroleum Corp.
SIC: 5172—Petroleum Products Nec.

★ 77601 ★   **Texaco Exprss Lube**
4701 SE 15th St.
Oklahoma City, OK 73115
(405)672-3716
Ultimate Parent: Texaco.

★ 77602 ★   **Texaco Food Mart**
10901 N. Pennsylvania Ave.
Oklahoma City, OK 73120
(405)752-2022
Ultimate Parent: Texaco. **SIC:** 5411—
Grocery Stores.

★ 77603 ★   **Texaco Food Mart & Car Wash**
600 S. Macarthur Blvd.
Oklahoma City, OK 73128
(405)947-3528
Ultimate Parent: Texaco. **SIC:** 5541—
Gasoline Service Stations.

★ 77604 ★   **Texaco Full Service**
3201 N. Classen Blvd.
Oklahoma City, OK 73118
(405)528-9144
Ultimate Parent: Texaco. **SIC:** 5541—
Gasoline Service Stations.

★ 77605 ★   **Texaco Gas Bar**
5905 Northwest Expy.
Oklahoma City, OK 73132
(405)722-6698
Ultimate Parent: Texaco. **SIC:** 5541—
Gasoline Service Stations.

★ 77606 ★   **Texaco Gas Bar**
2100 SW 74th Expy.
Oklahoma City, OK 73159
(405)685-6139
Ultimate Parent: Texaco. **SIC:** 5541—
Gasoline Service Stations.

★ 77607 ★   **Texaco Gas Bar & Food Mart**
6340 N. May Ave.
Oklahoma City, OK 73112
(405)848-3340
Ultimate Parent: Texaco. **SIC:** 5541—
Gasoline Service Stations.

★ 77608 ★   **Texaco Gas Station**
4001 N. May Ave.
Oklahoma City, OK 73112
(405)942-3244
Ultimate Parent: Texaco. **SIC:** 5541—
Gasoline Service Stations.

★ 77609 ★   **Texaco Incorporated**
4501 NW 39th Expy.
Oklahoma City, OK 73122
(405)789-2669
Ultimate Parent: Texaco. **SIC:** 5541—
Gasoline Service Stations.

★ 77610 ★   **Texaco Inc.**
501 S. Meridian Ave.
Oklahoma City, OK 73108
(405)947-2353
Ultimate Parent: Texaco. **SIC:** 5541—
Gasoline Service Stations.

★ 77611 ★   **Texaco Inc.**
10 Vickie Dr.
Oklahoma City, OK 73115
(405)672-1335
Ultimate Parent: Texaco. **SIC:** 5172—
Petroleum Products Nec.

★ 77612 ★   **Texaco Inc.**
16 NW 63rd St.
Oklahoma City, OK 73116
(405)843-9628
Ultimate Parent: Texaco. **SIC:** 5172—
Petroleum Products Nec.

★ 77613 ★   **Texaco Incorporated Service**
9400 N. May Ave.
Oklahoma City, OK 73120
(405)752-0425
Ultimate Parent: Texaco. **SIC:** 5541—
Gasoline Service Stations.

★ 77614 ★   **Texaco Self Serv**
1301 S. Janeway Ave.
Oklahoma City, OK 73160
(405)799-7636
Ultimate Parent: Texaco.

★ 77615 ★   **Texaco Self Service**
7124 Northwest Expy.
Oklahoma City, OK 73132
(405)728-3525
Ultimate Parent: Texaco. **SIC:** 5541—
Gasoline Service Stations.

★ 77616 ★   **Texaco Self Service Inc.**
600 N. Pennsylvania Ave.
Oklahoma City, OK 73107
(405)685-0027
Ultimate Parent: Texaco. **SIC:** 5541—
Gasoline Service Stations.

★ 77617 ★   **Texaco Self Service Station**
21 NW 63rd St.
Oklahoma City, OK 73116
(405)840-0303
Ultimate Parent: Texaco. **SIC:** 5541—
Gasoline Service Stations.

★ 77618 ★   **Texaco Self Service Station**
5100 N. May Ave.
Oklahoma City, OK 73112
(405)946-1677
Ultimate Parent: Texaco. **SIC:** 5541—
Gasoline Service Stations.

★ 77619 ★   **Texaco Self Sv**
1101 W. Memorial Rd.
Oklahoma City, OK 73114
(405)755-7223
Ultimate Parent: Texaco.

★ 77620 ★   **Texaco Self Sv**
4700 SE 15th St.
Oklahoma City, OK 73115
(405)677-4024
Ultimate Parent: Texaco.

★ 77621 ★   **Texaco Self Sv**
7001 SE 29th St.
Oklahoma City, OK 73110
(405)732-8091
Ultimate Parent: Texaco.

★ 77622 ★   **Texaco Self Sv**
2700 N. Broadway St.
Oklahoma City, OK 73160
(405)799-7647
Ultimate Parent: Texaco.

★ 77623 ★   **Texaco Self Sv**
6800 N. Meridian Ave.
Oklahoma City, OK 73116
(405)843-8082
Ultimate Parent: Texaco.

★ 77624 ★   **Texaco Self Sv**
7001 E. Reno Ave.
Oklahoma City, OK 73110
(405)733-8142
Ultimate Parent: Texaco.

★ 77625 ★   **Texaco Service Station**
4500 NW 23rd St.
Oklahoma City, OK 73127
(405)943-9214
Ultimate Parent: Texaco. **SIC:** 5541—
Gasoline Service Stations.

★ 77626 ★   **Texaco Service Station**
1935 E. Reno Ave.
Oklahoma City, OK 73117
(405)232-6279
Ultimate Parent: Texaco. **SIC:** 5541—
Gasoline Service Stations.

★ 77627 ★   **Texaco Station & Food Mart**
441 SW 74th St.
Oklahoma City, OK 73139
(405)632-2040
Ultimate Parent: Texaco. **SIC:** 5541—
Gasoline Service Stations.

★ 77628 ★   **Thom Mcan Shoe Str**
7000 Crossroads Blvd.
Oklahoma City, OK 73149
(405)634-5061
Ultimate Parent: Melville.

★ 77629 ★   **Total Petroleum Inc.**
515 Central Park Dr.
Oklahoma City, OK 73105
(405)525-8100
Ultimate Parent: Total Petroleum Inc. **SIC:**
5172—Petroleum Products Nec.

★ 77630 ★   **Total Petroleum Inc.**
515 Central Park Dr.
Oklahoma City, OK 73105
(405)525-8100
Ultimate Parent: Total Petroleum Inc. **SIC:**
5172—Petroleum Products Nec.

★ 77631 ★   **Toys R US**
1119 SE 66th St.
Oklahoma City, OK 73149
(405)636-1591
Ultimate Parent: Toys "R" US. **SIC:** 5641—
Children's & Infants' Wear Stores; 5945—
Hobby, Toy & Game Shops.

★ 77632 ★   **Toys R US**
2121 NW 138th St.
Oklahoma City, OK 73134
(405)755-1335
Ultimate Parent: Toys "R" US. **SIC:** 5945—
Hobby, Toy & Game Shops.

★ 77633 ★   **Toys R US**
14045 S. Pennsylvania Ave.
Oklahoma City, OK 73170
(405)755-1335
Ultimate Parent: Toys "R" US. **SIC:** 5641—
Children's & Infants' Wear Stores.

★ 77634 ★   **Trailways American Bus Line**
427 W. Sheridan Ave.
Oklahoma City, OK 73102
(405)235-6425
Ultimate Parent: Greyhound Lines Inc. **SIC:**
4131—Intercity & Rural Bus Transportation.

★ 77635 ★   **Trans World Airlines Inc.**
7100 W. Rogers Wrld Arp
Oklahoma City, OK 73159
(405)685-5506
Ultimate Parent: Trans World Airlines. **SIC:**
4512—Air Transportation—Scheduled.

★ 77636 ★   **Trico Industries Inc.**
801 SE 59th St.
Oklahoma City, OK 73129
(405)631-9751
Ultimate Parent: Paccar. **SIC:** 1311—
Crude Petroleum & Natural Gas.

★ 77637 ★   **Trico Submersible System**
5500 SE 59th St.
Oklahoma City, OK 73135
Ultimate Parent: Paccar. **SIC:** 3561—
Pumps & Pumping Equipment.

★ 77638 ★   **Turner Corp.**
6525 N. Meridian Ave.
Oklahoma City, OK 73116
(405)721-0444
Ultimate Parent: Turner Corp. **SIC:** 6531—
Real Estate Agents & Managers.

★ 77639 ★   **Underwriters Adjusting Comp**
3030 Northwest Expy.
Oklahoma City, OK 73116
(405)948-4666
Ultimate Parent: Continental. **SIC:** 6411—
Insurance Agents, Brokers & Service.

★ 77640 ★   **Union Oil Co. of California**
13439 N. Broadway Ext
Oklahoma City, OK 73114
Ultimate Parent: Unocal Corp. **SIC:** 1311—
Crude Petroleum & Natural Gas.

★ 77641 ★   **Union Oil Co. of California**
2000 N. Classen Blvd. Bldg.
Oklahoma City, OK 73106
(405)528-7601
Ultimate Parent: Unocal Corp. **SIC:** 1382—
Oil & Gas Exploration Services.

★ 77642 ★   **Union Oil Co. of California**
4005 Northwest Expy.
Oklahoma City, OK 73116
(405)848-7676
Ultimate Parent: Unocal Corp. **SIC:** 1382—
Oil & Gas Exploration Services.

★ 77643 ★   **Union Texas Petroleum Corp.**
210 Park Ave.
Oklahoma City, OK 73102
(405)236-3731
Ultimate Parent: Union Texas Petroleum.
SIC: 1311—Crude Petroleum & Natural
Gas.

★ 77644 ★   **Union Texas Petroleum Corp.**
14000 Quail Springs Pky.
Oklahoma City, OK 73134
(405)755-8500
Ultimate Parent: Union Texas Petroleum.
SIC: 1382—Oil & Gas Exploration Services.

★ 77645 ★   **United Brake Systems Inc.**
6748 Melrose Ln.
Oklahoma City, OK 73127
(405)787-0520
Ultimate Parent: Echlin. **SIC:** 7539—
Automotive Repair Shops Nec.

★ 77646 ★   **United Parcel Service**
901 S. Portland Ave.
Oklahoma City, OK 73108
(405)948-3801
Ultimate Parent: United Parcel Service of
America. **SIC:** 4215—Courier Services
Except by Air.

★ 77647 ★   **Valley National Financial Service**
57707 PO Box
Oklahoma City, OK 73157
(405)946-3111
Ultimate Parent: Banc One Corp. **SIC:**
6062—State Credit Unions.

★ 77648 ★   **Victoria's Secret**
2501 W. Memorial Rd.
Oklahoma City, OK 73134
(405)755-5583
Ultimate Parent: Limited. **SIC:** 5651—
Family Clothing Stores.

★ 77649 ★   **Victoria's Secret**
1901 Northwest Expy.
Oklahoma City, OK 73116
(405)842-3867
Ultimate Parent: Limited. **SIC:** 5651—
Family Clothing Stores.

★ 77650 ★   **Wal Mart**
7012 Northwest Expy.
Oklahoma City, OK 73132
(405)721-8428
Ultimate Parent: Wal-Mart Stores, Inc. **SIC:**
5311—Department Stores.

★ 77651 ★   **Wal Mart**
2209 SW 74th St.
Oklahoma City, OK 73159
(405)682-1301
Ultimate Parent: Wal-Mart Stores, Inc. **SIC:**
5311—Department Stores.

★ 77652 ★   **Wal Mart Automotive**
7012 Northwest Expy.
Oklahoma City, OK 73132
(405)722-1983
Ultimate Parent: Wal-Mart Stores, Inc. **SIC:**
7538—General Automotive Repair Shops.

★ 77653 ★   **Wal Mart Discount**
2208 W. Hefner Rd.
Oklahoma City, OK 73120
(405)752-1900
Ultimate Parent: Wal-Mart Stores, Inc.

★ 77654 ★   **Wal Mart Discount City**
S I 35
Oklahoma City, OK 73160
(405)799-9581
Ultimate Parent: Wal-Mart Stores, Inc. **SIC:**
5912—Drug Stores & Proprietary Stores.

★ 77655 ★   **Waldenbooks**
2501 W. Memorial Rd.
Oklahoma City, OK 73134
(405)755-4773
Ultimate Parent: K-Mart. **SIC:** 5942—Book
Stores.

★ 77656 ★   **Waldenbooks**
Quail
Oklahoma City, OK 73120
(405)755-4773
Ultimate Parent: K-Mart. **SIC:** 5942—Book
Stores.

★ 77657 ★   **Waldenbooks**
2428 Shepherd Mall
Oklahoma City, OK 73107
(405)946-8107
Ultimate Parent: K-Mart. **SIC:** 5942—Book
Stores.

★ 77658 ★   **Waldenbooks**
1901 Northwest Expy.
Oklahoma City, OK 73116
(405)843-9510
Ultimate Parent: K-Mart. **SIC:** 5942—Book
Stores.

★ 77659 ★   **Waldenbooks**
5577 Northwest Expy.
Oklahoma City, OK 73132
(405)722-8735
Ultimate Parent: K-Mart. **SIC:** 5942—Book
Stores.

★ 77660 ★   **Waldenbooks**
Crossroads Mall
Oklahoma City, OK 73149
(405)634-5811
Ultimate Parent: K-Mart. **SIC:** 5942—Book
Stores.

★ 77661 ★   **Waldenbooks**
Heritage
Oklahoma City, OK 73110
(405)733-4060
Ultimate Parent: K-Mart. **SIC:** 5942—Book
Stores.

★ 77662 ★   **Wall Street Journal the**
15001 N. Columbia Dr.
Oklahoma City, OK 73134
(405)755-0720
Ultimate Parent: Dow Jones. **SIC:** 2711—
Newspapers.

★ 77663 ★   **Watco Inc.**
9511 N. Horseshoe Rd.
Oklahoma City, OK 73162
(405)722-1502
Ultimate Parent: Eastman Kodak. **SIC:**
5141—Groceries—General Line.

★ 77664 ★   **Wilson Brands Corp.**
2801 SW 15th St.
Oklahoma City, OK 73108
Ultimate Parent: Doskocil. **SIC:** 2013—
Sausages & Other Prepared Meats.

★ 77665 ★   **Wilson Foods Corp.**
4545 N. Lincoln Blvd.
Oklahoma City, OK 73105
(405)525-4545
Ultimate Parent: Doskocil. **SIC:** 2011—
Meat Packing Plants; 5147—Meats & Meat
Products.

★ 77666 ★   **Wilson Foods Corp.**
2801 SW 15th St.
Oklahoma City, OK 73108
(405)272-8600
Ultimate Parent: Doskocil. **SIC:** 2011—
Meat Packing Plants.

★ 77667 ★   **Wilson Foods Corp.**
2601 N.W. Expressway St.
Oklahoma City, OK 73112-7208
(405)879-5500
Company Type: Subsidiary. **Ultimate
Parent:** Doskocil. **SIC:** 2011—Meat Packing
Plants.

★ 77668 ★   **Wilson Foods Corp.**
2601 NW Expy. Ste. 1000
Oklahoma City, OK 73112
(405)879-5500 **Fax:** (405)840-2447
Company Type: Subsidiary. **Officer:** John
T. Hanes, Chairman; President; & CEO.
Ultimate Parent: Doskocil.

★ 77669 ★   **Wix Dana Corp.**
Air Refiner Div. Perry Plant
6420 S. Air Depot PO Box 95209
Oklahoma City, OK 73143
Company Type: Division. **Location Type:**
Plant. **Ultimate Parent:** Dana Corp. **SIC:**
3714—Motor Vehicle Parts & Accessories.

★ 77670 ★   **Wix Dana Corp. Perry Plant**
6420 S. Air Depot
Oklahoma City, OK 73143
Ultimate Parent: Dana Corp. **SIC:** 3714—
Motor Vehicle Parts & Accessories.

★ 77671 ★   **Xerox Corp.**
100 N. Mustang Rd.
Oklahoma City, OK 73127
Ultimate Parent: Xerox Corp. **SIC:** 3579—
Office Machines Nec.

★ 77672 ★   **Xerox Corp.**
100 N. Mustang Rd.
Oklahoma City, OK 73126
(405)324-3800
Officer: Harry Hawkey, Manager. **Ultimate
Parent:** Xerox Corp. **SIC:** 3861—
Photographic Equipment & Supplies.

★ 77673 ★   **Zeno Systems**
280 S. Quadrum Dr.
Oklahoma City, OK 73108
(405)946-9555
Officer: Rick Frederick, President. **Ultimate
Parent:** Alco Standard Corp. **SIC:** 3663—
Radio & T.V. Communications Equipment.

★ 77674 ★   **Zeno Systems of Oklahoma Inc.**
312 Quadrum Dr.
Oklahoma City, OK 73108
(405)946-9555
Company Type: Subsidiary. **Officer:** Rick
Frederick, President. **Ultimate Parent:** Alco
Standard Corp. **SIC:** 5044—Office
Equipment; 7359—Equipment Rental &
Leasing Nec.

★ 77675 ★   **Zep Manufacturing Co.**
3710 Harmon
Oklahoma City, OK 73179
(405)681-1097
Ultimate Parent: National Service
Industries. **SIC:** 2899—Chemical
Preparations Nec.

Okmulgee

★ 77676 ★   **Ball Corp.**
800 S. Madison Ave.
Okmulgee, OK 74447
(918)756-2255
Ultimate Parent: Ball Corp. **SIC:** 3089—
Plastics Products Nec.

★ 77677 ★　**Ball-Icon Glass Packaging**
800 S. Madison Ave.
Okmulgee, OK 74447-4207
(918)756-5990
Officer: Fred Kickey. **Ultimate Parent:** Ball Corp. **SIC:** 3221—Glass Containers; 3211—Flat Glass; 3229—Pressed & Blown Glass Nec.

★ 77678 ★　**Ball Incon Glass Packaging**
800 S. Madison Ave.
Okmulgee, OK 74447
(918)756-2255
Officer: Fred C. Kickey, Manager. **Ultimate Parent:** Ball Corp. **SIC:** 3221—Glass Containers.

★ 77679 ★　**Ball-Incon Glass Packaging Corp.**
800 S. Madison
Okmulgee, OK 74447
Ultimate Parent: Ball Corp. **SIC:** 3221—Glass Containers.

★ 77680 ★　**Greyhound Bus Lines**
713 E. 6th St.
Okmulgee, OK 74447
(918)756-1542
Ultimate Parent: Greyhound Lines Inc. **SIC:** 4131—Intercity & Rural Bus Transportation.

★ 77681 ★　**Merck & Co. Inc.**
Kelco Div.
1200 W. 20th St.
Okmulgee, OK 74447-4272
Company Type: Division. **Ultimate Parent:** Merck. **SIC:** 2869—Industrial Organic Chemicals Nec.

★ 77682 ★　**Merck & Co. Inc.**
Kelco Div.
1200 W. 20th St.
Okmulgee, OK 74447
Company Type: Division. **Ultimate Parent:** Merck. **SIC:** 2869—Industrial Organic Chemicals Nec.

★ 77683 ★　**Pizza Hut**
407 S. Wood Dr.
Okmulgee, OK 74447
(918)756-5202
Ultimate Parent: Pepsico. **SIC:** 5812—Eating Places.

★ 77684 ★　**Radio Shack**
220 S. Muskogee Ave.
Okmulgee, OK 74447
(918)756-5124
Company Type: Division. **Ultimate Parent:** Tandy Corp. **SIC:** 5731—Radio, Television & Electronics Stores.

Owasso

★ 77685 ★　**McDonalds Hamburgers**
715 W. Kenosha
Owasso, OK 74055
(918)272-3012
Ultimate Parent: McDonald's. **SIC:** 5812—Eating Places.

★ 77686 ★　**Wal Mart Disc Cits**
8787 N. Mingo Valley Expy.
Owasso, OK 74055
(918)272-6609
Ultimate Parent: Wal-Mart Stores, Inc.

Pauls Valley

★ 77687 ★　**Arco Pipe Line Co.**
NW of City
Pauls Valley, OK 73075
(405)238-5111
Location Type: Branch office. **Ultimate Parent:** Atlantic Richfield Co., Inc. **SIC:** 4612—Crude Petroleum Pipelines.

★ 77688 ★　**Arco Pipe Line Co.**
Pauls Valley, OK 73075
(405)238-5111
Location Type: Branch office. **Ultimate Parent:** Atlantic Richfield Co., Inc. **SIC:** 4612—Crude Petroleum Pipelines.

★ 77689 ★　**Kentucky Fried Chicken**
W City
Pauls Valley, OK 73075
(405)238-3075
Ultimate Parent: Pepsico. **SIC:** 5812—Eating Places.

★ 77690 ★　**Lone Star Gas Co.**
120 N. Chickasaw St.
Pauls Valley, OK 73075
(405)238-6493
Ultimate Parent: Enserch. **SIC:** 4932—Gas & Other Services Combined.

★ 77691 ★　**Marathon Oil Co.**
E City
Pauls Valley, OK 73075
(405)238-6125
Ultimate Parent: USX Corp. **SIC:** 5171—Petroleum Bulk Stations & Terminals.

★ 77692 ★　**Marathon Oil Co.**
E City
Pauls Valley, OK 73075
(405)238-6125
Ultimate Parent: USX Corp. **SIC:** 5171—Petroleum Bulk Stations & Terminals.

★ 77693 ★　**Pizza Hut**
801 W. Grant Ave.
Pauls Valley, OK 73075
(405)238-5650
Ultimate Parent: Pepsico. **SIC:** 5812—Eating Places.

★ 77694 ★　**Union Oil Co. of California**
N City
Pauls Valley, OK 73075
(405)238-6700
Ultimate Parent: Unocal Corp. **SIC:** 1311—Crude Petroleum & Natural Gas.

Pawhuska

★ 77695 ★　**Pizza Hut**
403 E. Main St.
Pawhuska, OK 74056
(918)287-3377
Ultimate Parent: Pepsico. **SIC:** 5812—Eating Places.

★ 77696 ★　**Radio Shack**
131 E. Main St.
Pawhuska, OK 74056
(918)287-3330
Company Type: Division. **Ultimate Parent:** Tandy Corp. **SIC:** 5731—Radio, Television & Electronics Stores.

★ 77697 ★　**Texaco Distributor**
515 Lynn Ave.
Pawhuska, OK 74056
(918)287-3979
Ultimate Parent: Texaco. **SIC:** 5171—Petroleum Bulk Stations & Terminals.

★ 77698 ★　**Wal Mart Discount Cities**
1457 W. Main St.
Pawhuska, OK 74056
(918)287-2500
Ultimate Parent: Wal-Mart Stores, Inc. **SIC:** 5311—Department Stores.

Pawnee

★ 77699 ★　**Burlington Northern Railroa**
6th
Pawnee, OK 74058
(918)762-3170
Ultimate Parent: Burlington Northern. **SIC:** 4011—Railroads—Line-Haul Operating.

★ 77700 ★　**Piggly Wiggly**
657 Harrison St.
Pawnee, OK 74058
(918)762-3228
Ultimate Parent: Bruno's. **SIC:** 5411—Grocery Stores.

Perry

★ 77701 ★　**Coast to Coast Store**
1502 Fir St.
Perry, OK 73077
(405)336-5420
Ultimate Parent: Servistar Corp. **SIC:** 5251—Hardware Stores.

★ 77702 ★　**First National Bank & Trust**
Perry, OK 73077
(405)336-5562
Ultimate Parent: Society Corp. **SIC:** 6021—National Commercial Banks.

Ponca City

★ 77703 ★　**Conoco In.**
1000 S. Pine St.
Ponca City, OK 74601
(405)767-3456
Officer: Dennis R. Parker, Vice President. **Ultimate Parent:** E.I. DuPont De Nemours. **SIC:** 2911—Petroleum Refining.

★ 77704 ★　**First National Bank & Trust**
122 E. Grand Ave.
Ponca City, OK 74601
(405)762-1644
Ultimate Parent: Society Corp. **SIC:** 6141—Personal Credit Institutions.

★ 77705 ★　**Hertz Rent-A-Car**
2000 N. Waverly St.
Ponca City, OK 74601
(405)767-2590
Ultimate Parent: Hertz. **SIC:** 7514—Passenger Car Rental.

★ 77706 ★　**Hertz Rent-A-Car Licensee**
2000 N. Waverly St.
Ponca City, OK 74601
(405)762-1920
Ultimate Parent: Hertz. **SIC:** 7514—Passenger Car Rental.

★ 77707 ★　**Mary Kay Cosmetics**
525 N. 7th St.
Ponca City, OK 74601
(405)765-0973
Ultimate Parent: Mary Kay Cosmetics. **SIC:** 5999—Miscellaneous Retail Stores Nec.

★ 77708 ★　**Occidental Petroleum Corp.**
Alathon Polymers Div.
1000 S. Pine
Ponca City, OK 74602
Company Type: Division. **Ultimate Parent:** Occidental Petroleum Corp. **SIC:** 2821—Plastics Materials & Resins.

★ 77709 ★　**Occidental Petroleum Corp.**
Alathon Polymers Div. Technology Dept.
1000 S. Pine
Ponca City, OK 74602
Company Type: Division. **Ultimate Parent:** Occidental Petroleum Corp. **SIC:** 2821—Plastics Materials & Resins.

★ 77710 ★　**Payless Shoesource**
2720 N. 14th St.
Ponca City, OK 74601
(405)762-2260
Ultimate Parent: May Department Stores. **SIC:** 5661—Shoe Stores.

★ 77711 ★　**Pizza Hut**
2315 N. 14th St.
Ponca City, OK 74601
(405)762-7729
Ultimate Parent: Pepsico. **SIC:** 5812—Eating Places.

★ 77712 ★　**Ryder Truck Rental**
1405 Princeton Ave.
Ponca City, OK 74604
(405)762-6162
Ultimate Parent: Ryder System. **SIC:** 7359—Equipment Rental & Leasing Nec.

★ 77713 ★　**Taco Bell**
2400 N. 14th St.
Ponca City, OK 74601
(405)762-9592
Ultimate Parent: Pepsico.

★ 77714 ★　**Texaco Pipeline**
1328 S. 4th St.
Ponca City, OK 74601
(405)765-2245
Ultimate Parent: Texaco.

★ 77715 ★　**United Parcel Service**
1415 W. Summit Ave.
Ponca City, OK 74601
(405)765-3259
Ultimate Parent: United Parcel Service of America. **SIC:** 4212—Local Trucking Without Storage.

★ 77716 ★　**Wal Mart Discount City**
1101 E. Prospect Ave.
Ponca City, OK 74601
Ultimate Parent: Wal-Mart Stores, Inc. **SIC:** 5311—Department Stores.

★ 77717 ★　**Witco Corp.**
Concarb
1006 Burgell Rd. PO Box 551
Ponca City, OK 74602
Ultimate Parent: Witco Corp. **SIC:** 2895—Carbon Black.

★ 77718 ★　**Witco Corp.**
Concarb
PO Box 551
Ponca City, OK 74602
Ultimate Parent: Witco Corp. **SIC:** 2895—Carbon Black.

★ 77719 ★　**Witco Corp.**
Concarb
1 Mile South Hwy.177, PO Box 551
Ponca City, OK 74602-0551
Ultimate Parent: Witco Corp. **SIC:** 2895—Carbon Black.

Poteau

★ 77720 ★　**Johnson Controls Inc.**
Hwy. 59 N
Poteau, OK 74953
Ultimate Parent: Johnson & Johnson. **SIC:** 3620—Electrical Industrial Apparatus.

★ 77721 ★　**Johnson Controls Inc.**
Hwy. 271 N
Poteau, OK 74953
(918)647-2195
Ultimate Parent: Johnson Controls Inc. **SIC:** 5084—Industrial Machinery & Equipment.

★ 77722 ★　**Johnson Controls Inc. Panel Unit**
Hwy. 59 N.
Poteau, OK 74953
Ultimate Parent: Johnson & Johnson. **SIC:** 3625—Relays & Industrial Controls.

★ 77723 ★　**Mobil Oil**
Poteau, OK 74953
(918)647-8241
Ultimate Parent: Mobil. **SIC:** 4925—Gas Production & Distribution Nec.

★ 77724 ★　**Oklahoma ALLTEL Inc.**
Poteau Industrial Pk.
101 Kerr Ave., PO Box 460
Poteau, OK 74953
(918)647-8800
Company Type: Subsidiary. **Ultimate Parent:** ALLTEL Corp. **SIC:** 4812—Radiotelephone Communications.

★ 77725 ★　**Payless Shoesource**
Northgate Shopping Ctr.
Poteau, OK 74953
(918)647-3881
Ultimate Parent: May Department Stores. **SIC:** 5661—Shoe Stores.

★ 77726 ★　**Payless Shoesource No. 2191**
Northgate Shopping Ctr.
Poteau, OK 74953
(918)647-3881
Ultimate Parent: May Department Stores. **SIC:** 5661—Shoe Stores.

★ 77727 ★　**Pizza Hut**
Hwy. 271 N
Poteau, OK 74953
(918)647-3249
Ultimate Parent: Pepsico. **SIC:** 5812—Eating Places.

★ 77728 ★　**Ryder Truck Rental**
Hwy. 271 N
Poteau, OK 74953
(918)647-9224
Ultimate Parent: Ryder System. **SIC:** 5113—Industrial & Personal Service Paper.

★ 77729 ★ **Wal Mart**
Hwy. 271 N
Poteau, OK 74953
(918)647-2154
Ultimate Parent: Wal-Mart Stores, Inc. **SIC:** 5311—Department Stores; 7538—General Automotive Repair Shops.

★ 77730 ★ **Wal Mart Pharmacy**
Hwy. 271 N
Poteau, OK 74953
(918)647-2641
Ultimate Parent: Wal-Mart Stores, Inc. **SIC:** 5912—Drug Stores & Proprietary Stores.

Prague

★ 77731 ★ **Wrangler**
Hwy. 62 W
Prague, OK 74868
(405)382-3980
Officer: Jim McClure, Manager. **Ultimate Parent:** VF Corp. **SIC:** 2325—Men's/Boys' Trousers & Slacks.

Pryor

★ 77732 ★ **Air Products & Chemicals, Inc.**
S. City
Pryor, OK 74361
(918)825-4591
Ultimate Parent: Air Products & Chemicals, Inc. **SIC:** 2813—Industrial Gases.

★ 77733 ★ **Air Products & Chemicals Inc.**
Hwy. 68
Pryor, OK 74362
Ultimate Parent: Air Products & Chemicals, Inc. **SIC:** 2813—Industrial Gases.

★ 77734 ★ **Air Products & Chemicals Inc.**
69-A & Mid-America Industrial District
Pryor, OK 74361
Ultimate Parent: Air Products & Chemicals, Inc. **SIC:** 2813—Industrial Gases.

★ 77735 ★ **Air Products & Chemicals Inc.**
Hwys 69-A & 412-B
Pryor, OK 74361
(918)825-5387
Officer: Harold Wagner, Manager. **Ultimate Parent:** Air Products & Chemicals, Inc. **SIC:** 2813—Industrial Gases.

★ 77736 ★ **Air Products & Chemicals Inc.**
Hwys. 69A & 413B
Pryor, OK 74361
(918)825-4591
Officer: Roger Allison, Plant Manager. **Ultimate Parent:** Air Products & Chemicals, Inc. **SIC:** 2813—Industrial Gases.

★ 77737 ★ **A.P. Green Industries Inc.**
Corner of 69A & 69 Hwy.
Pryor, OK 74361
Ultimate Parent: USG Corp. **SIC:** 3299—Nonmetallic Mineral Products Nec.

★ 77738 ★ **Coast to Coast**
104 E. Graham Ave.
Pryor, OK 74361
(918)825-0387
Ultimate Parent: Servistar Corp. **SIC:** 5531—Automobile & Home Supply Stores.

★ 77739 ★ **Georgia-Pacific Corp.**
Hwy. 69-A
Pryor, OK 74362
Ultimate Parent: Georgia-Pacific. **SIC:** 2631—Paperboard Mills.

★ 77740 ★ **Kentucky Fried Chicken**
2 S. Mill St.
Pryor, OK 74361
(918)825-4422
Ultimate Parent: Pepsico. **SIC:** 5812—Eating Places.

★ 77741 ★ **Lone Star Industries Inc.**
Hwy. 20
Pryor, OK 74361
(918)825-1937
Officer: Garry Harris, Manager. **Ultimate Parent:** Enserch. **SIC:** 3241—Cement—Hydraulic; 3273—Ready-Mixed Concrete.

★ 77742 ★ **Pizza Hut**
1217 PO Box
Pryor, OK 74362
(918)825-4900
Ultimate Parent: Pepsico. **SIC:** 5812—Eating Places.

★ 77743 ★ **Protein Tech. International International**
Hwy. 412B Maid
Pryor, OK 74362
Ultimate Parent: Ralston Purina. **SIC:** 2075—Soybean Oil Mills.

★ 77744 ★ **Protein Technologies International**
Hunt St. M.A.I.D.
Pryor, OK 74362
Ultimate Parent: Ralston Purina. **SIC:** 2075—Soybean Oil Mills.

★ 77745 ★ **Protein Technologies International**
Hunt Street, M.A.I.D.
Pryor, OK 74362
Ultimate Parent: Ralston Purina. **SIC:** 2051—Bread, Cake & Related Products.

★ 77746 ★ **Pryor Fndy. Inc.**
Hunt St. Hunt St.
Pryor, OK 74362
Ultimate Parent: Tenneco Inc. **SIC:** 3321—Gray & Ductile Iron Foundries.

★ 77747 ★ **Pryor Foundry Inc.**
Hunt St.
Pryor, OK 74361
Ultimate Parent: Tenneco Inc. **SIC:** 3321—Gray & Ductile Iron Foundries.

★ 77748 ★ **Radio Shack**
191 S. Mill St.
Pryor, OK 74361
(918)825-5033
Company Type: Division. **Ultimate Parent:** Tandy Corp. **SIC:** 5722—Household Appliance Stores; 5731—Radio, Television & Electronics Stores.

Purcell

★ 77749 ★ **Lone Star Gas Co.**
104 W. Main St.
Purcell, OK 73080
(405)527-2131
Ultimate Parent: Enserch. **SIC:** 4932—Gas & Other Services Combined.

★ 77750 ★ **Pizza Hut**
413 S. Green Ave.
Purcell, OK 73080
(405)527-6003
Ultimate Parent: Pepsico. **SIC:** 5812—Eating Places.

★ 77751 ★ **Radio Shack**
203 W. Main St.
Purcell, OK 73080
(405)527-9714
Company Type: Division. **Ultimate Parent:** Tandy Corp. **SIC:** 5013—Motor Vehicle Supplies & New Parts.

★ 77752 ★ **Wal Mart Discount City**
N Green Ave.
Purcell, OK 73080
(405)527-5621
Ultimate Parent: Wal-Mart Stores, Inc. **SIC:** 5311—Department Stores.

Quapaw

★ 77753 ★ **Eagle-Picher Ind. Inc. Boron Dept.**
Hwy. 69a
Quapaw, OK 74363
Ultimate Parent: Eagle-Picher Industries Inc. **SIC:** 2819—Industrial Inorganic Chemicals Nec.

★ 77754 ★ **Eagle Picher Ind. Inc. Electro-Optic Materials Dept.**
737 Hwy. 69A NE PO Box 737
Quapaw, OK 74363
Ultimate Parent: Eagle-Picher Industries Inc. **SIC:** 3339—Primary Nonferrous Metals Nec; 3341—Secondary Nonferrous Metals; 2819—Industrial Inorganic Chemicals Nec.

★ 77755 ★ **Eagle Picher Ind. Inc. Electro-Optics Mat. 1**
737 Hwy. 69A NE PO Box 737
Quapaw, OK 74363
Ultimate Parent: Eagle-Picher Industries Inc. **SIC:** 3339—Primary Nonferrous Metals Nec; 3341—Secondary Nonferrous Metals; 2819—Industrial Inorganic Chemicals Nec.

★ 77756 ★ **Eagle-Picher Ind. Inc. Electro-Optics Materials Dept.**
Hwy. 69A NE
PO Box 737
Quapaw, OK 74363
Ultimate Parent: Eagle-Picher Industries Inc. **SIC:** 3339—Primary Nonferrous Metals Nec; 3341—Secondary Nonferrous Metals; 2819—Industrial Inorganic Chemicals Nec.

★ 77757 ★ **Eagle Picher Industries**
Specialty Materials Div.
PO Box 798
Quapaw, OK 74363
(918)673-2201 **Fax:** (918)673-1052
Company Type: Headquarters. **Officer:** Jeff Wilson, Chief Operating Officer. **Ultimate Parent:** Eagle-Picher Industries Inc. **SIC:** 3295—Minerals—Ground or Treated.

★ 77758 ★ **Eagle-Picher Industries Inc.**
Hwy. 69A
Quapaw, OK 74363
(918)673-2201
Officer: Don Call, Manager. **Ultimate Parent:** Eagle-Picher Industries Inc. **SIC:** 3339—Primary Nonferrous Metals Nec.

★ 77759 ★ **Eagle-Picher Industries Inc. Boron Dept.**
798 Hwy. 69A NE
Quapaw, OK 74363
Ultimate Parent: Eagle-Picher Industries Inc. **SIC:** 2819—Industrial Inorganic Chemicals Nec.

★ 77760 ★ **Eagle Picher Industries Inc. Boron Dept.**
Hwy. 69A
Quapaw, OK 74363
Ultimate Parent: Eagle-Picher Industries Inc. **SIC:** 2819—Industrial Inorganic Chemicals Nec.

★ 77761 ★ **Eagle Picher Industries Inc. Boron Dept.**
798 Hwy. 69A NE
Quapaw, OK 74363
Ultimate Parent: Eagle-Picher Industries Inc. **SIC:** 2819—Industrial Inorganic Chemicals Nec.

★ 77762 ★ **Eagle Picher Industries Inc. Boron Dept**
798 Hwy. 69A NE
Quapaw, OK 74363-0798
Ultimate Parent: Eagle-Picher Industries Inc. **SIC:** 2819—Industrial Inorganic Chemicals Nec.

★ 77763 ★ **Eagle-Picher Specialty Materials**
737 Hwy. 69 A
Quapaw, OK 74363
(918)673-1650
Officer: Dennis Thomas, Manager. **Ultimate Parent:** Eagle-Picher Industries Inc. **SIC:** 3339—Primary Nonferrous Metals Nec.

Ratliff City

★ 77764 ★ **Arco Pipeline Co.**
Ratliff City, OK 73081
(405)856-3715
Location Type: Branch office. **Ultimate Parent:** Atlantic Richfield Co., Inc. **SIC:** 4612—Crude Petroleum Pipelines.

Ringling

★ 77765 ★ **Arco Pipe Line Co.**
Ringling, OK 73456
(405)662-2335
Location Type: Branch office. **Ultimate Parent:** Atlantic Richfield Co., Inc. **SIC:** 4612—Crude Petroleum Pipelines.

★ 77766 ★ **Arco Pipe Line Co.**
E. of city
Ringling, OK 73456
(405)662-2335
Location Type: Branch office. **Ultimate Parent:** Atlantic Richfield Co., Inc. **SIC:** 4612—Crude Petroleum Pipelines.

Ripley

★ 77767 ★ **Coca Cola Bottling Co.**
309 E. Main
Ripley, OK 74062
(918)372-8316
Ultimate Parent: Coca-Cola Enterprises. **SIC:** 2086—Bottled & Canned Soft Drinks.

Sallisaw

★ 77768 ★ **Coltec**
Automotive Div.
1300 S. Opdyke
Sallisaw, OK 74955
Company Type: Division. **Ultimate Parent:** Coltec Industries. **SIC:** 3714—Motor Vehicle Parts & Accessories.

★ 77769 ★ **Kentucky Fried Chicken**
1601 E. Cherokee St.
Sallisaw, OK 74955
(918)775-9801
Ultimate Parent: Pepsico. **SIC:** 5812—Eating Places.

★ 77770 ★ **McDonalds Restaurant**
1006 S. Kerr Blvd.
Sallisaw, OK 74955
(918)775-2840
Ultimate Parent: McDonald's.

★ 77771 ★ **Mini Mart**
245 Rural Route 3
Sallisaw, OK 74955
(918)775-9512
Ultimate Parent: Kroger. **SIC:** 5411—Grocery Stores.

★ 77772 ★ **Mini Mart No 2**
I 40
Sallisaw, OK 74955
(918)775-3981
Ultimate Parent: Kroger. **SIC:** 5411—Grocery Stores.

★ 77773 ★ **Pizza Hut**
Hwy. 64 S
Sallisaw, OK 74955
(918)775-5509
Ultimate Parent: Pepsico. **SIC:** 5812—Eating Places.

★ 77774 ★ **Ryder Truck Rental**
816 E. Cherokee St.
Sallisaw, OK 74955
(918)775-7111
Ultimate Parent: Ryder System. **SIC:** 5113—Industrial & Personal Service Paper.

★ 77775 ★ **Wal Mart Automotive**
Eastgate Shopping Ctr.
Sallisaw, OK 74955
(918)775-7129
Ultimate Parent: Wal-Mart Stores, Inc. **SIC:** 5311—Department Stores.

★ 77776 ★ **Wal Mart Discount Cities**
Eastgate Shopping Ctr.
Sallisaw, OK 74955
(918)775-4492
Ultimate Parent: Wal-Mart Stores, Inc. **SIC:** 5311—Department Stores.

★ 77777 ★ **Wal Mart Pharmacy**
E City
Sallisaw, OK 74955
(918)775-4479
Ultimate Parent: Wal-Mart Stores, Inc. **SIC:** 5912—Drug Stores & Proprietary Stores.

Sand Springs

★ 77778 ★ **Baker Performance Chemicals**
9100 W. 21st St.
Sand Springs, OK 74063
(918)245-2224
Officer: Bobby Burks, Manager. **Ultimate Parent:** Baker Hughes. **SIC:** 2899—Chemical Preparations Nec.

★ 77779 ★ **Bi-Lo Food Warehouse**
3212 Magnolia Dr.
Sand Springs, OK 74063
(918)835-3555
Ultimate Parent: Penn Traffic. **SIC:** 5411—Grocery Stores.

★ 77780 ★ **Federated Metals Corp.**
200 S. Wilson St.
Sand Springs, OK 74063
(918)245-1349
Ultimate Parent: Asarco. **SIC:** 3339—Primary Nonferrous Metals Nec.

★ 77781 ★ **Kentucky Fried Chicken**
206 N. Wilson St.
Sand Springs, OK 74063
(918)245-2363
Ultimate Parent: Pepsico. **SIC:** 5812—Eating Places.

★ 77782 ★ **Payless Shoesource**
3917 State Hwy. 97 S
Sand Springs, OK 74063
(918)245-9781
Ultimate Parent: May Department Stores. **SIC:** 5661—Shoe Stores.

★ 77783 ★ **Pizza Hut**
221 E. 2nd St.
Sand Springs, OK 74063
(918)245-9621
Ultimate Parent: Pepsico. **SIC:** 5812—Eating Places.

★ 77784 ★ **Ryder Truck Rental**
117 N. Wilson St.
Sand Springs, OK 74063
(918)241-3064
Ultimate Parent: Ryder System. **SIC:** 7513—Truck Rental & Leasing Without Drivers.

★ 77785 ★ **Stone Container Corp.**
200 W. Morrow Rd.
Sand Springs, OK 74063
(918)245-1304
Officer: Doug Youngdahl, Manager.
Ultimate Parent: Stone Container Corp.
SIC: 2679—Converted Paper Products Nec.

★ 77786 ★ **Taco Bell**
1138 E. Charles Page Blvd.
Sand Springs, OK 74063
(918)241-4207
Ultimate Parent: Pepsico. **SIC:** 5812—Eating Places.

★ 77787 ★ **Wal Mart Disc Cits**
3829 S. Hwy. 97
Sand Springs, OK 74063
(918)245-0213
Ultimate Parent: Wal-Mart Stores, Inc.

Sapulpa

★ 77788 ★ **Bartlett-Collins**
620 S. Linden
Sapulpa, OK 74066
Ultimate Parent: Lanchaster Colony. **SIC:** 3321—Gray & Ductile Iron Foundries.

★ 77789 ★ **Burlington Northern Railway**
E Hobson Ave.
Sapulpa, OK 74066
(918)227-3074
Ultimate Parent: Burlington Northern. **SIC:** 4119—Local Passenger Transportation Nec.

★ 77790 ★ **Citgo Service Station**
116 Sherlyn Ln.
Sapulpa, OK 74066
(918)622-1099
Ultimate Parent: Citgo Petroleum. **SIC:** 5541—Gasoline Service Stations.

★ 77791 ★ **Indiana Glass Co.**
PO Box 1288
Sapulpa, OK 74066
(918)224-1860
Company Type: Subsidiary. **Officer:** Robert J. Staab, President. **Ultimate Parent:** Lanchaster Colony. **SIC:** 3229—Pressed & Blown Glass Nec. **Employee Count:** 605.

★ 77792 ★ **Indiana Glass Co.**
Bartlett-Collins
620 S. Linden
Sapulpa, OK 74067
Ultimate Parent: Lanchaster Colony. **SIC:** 3229—Pressed & Blown Glass Nec.

★ 77793 ★ **Indiana Glass Sapulpa**
PO Box 1288
Sapulpa, OK 74066
(918)224-1860 **Fax:** (918)227-4589
Officer: Fred Givens, Plant Manager.
Ultimate Parent: Lanchaster Colony.

★ 77794 ★ **Kentucky Fried Chicken**
501 S. Main St.
Sapulpa, OK 74066
(918)224-6186
Ultimate Parent: Pepsico. **SIC:** 5812—Eating Places.

★ 77795 ★ **Payless Shoesource**
321 S. Main St.
Sapulpa, OK 74066
(918)224-8265
Ultimate Parent: May Department Stores. **SIC:** 5661—Shoe Stores.

★ 77796 ★ **Pizza Hut**
820 E. Dewey Ave.
Sapulpa, OK 74066
(918)227-2344
Ultimate Parent: Pepsico.

★ 77797 ★ **Radio Shack**
126 W. Taft St.
Sapulpa, OK 74066
(918)446-3166
Company Type: Division. **Ultimate Parent:** Tandy Corp. **SIC:** 5065—Electronic Parts & Equipment Nec; 5112—Stationery & Office Supplies; 5731—Radio, Television & Electronics Stores.

★ 77798 ★ **Wal Mart Discount City**
132 W. Taft St.
Sapulpa, OK 74066
(918)224-8074
Ultimate Parent: Wal-Mart Stores, Inc. **SIC:** 5311—Department Stores.

★ 77799 ★ **Wal Mart Pharmacy**
132 W. Taft St.
Sapulpa, OK 74066
(918)224-2800
Ultimate Parent: Wal-Mart Stores, Inc. **SIC:** 5912—Drug Stores & Proprietary Stores.

Sayre

★ 77800 ★ **Radio Shack**
1014 N. 4th St.
Sayre, OK 73662
(405)928-3867
Company Type: Division. **Ultimate Parent:** Tandy Corp. **SIC:** 5731—Radio, Television & Electronics Stores.

★ 77801 ★ **Ryder Truck Rental**
612 N. 6th St.
Sayre, OK 73662
(405)928-5454
Ultimate Parent: Ryder System. **SIC:** 7513—Truck Rental & Leasing Without Drivers.

Seiling

★ 77802 ★ **Southland Royalty Co.**
Seiling, OK 73663
(405)922-7257
Ultimate Parent: Burlington Resources. **SIC:** 1381—Drilling Oil & Gas Wells.

★ 77803 ★ **Southland Royalty Co.**
Seiling, OK 73663
(405)922-7257
Ultimate Parent: Burlington Resources. **SIC:** 1381—Drilling Oil & Gas Wells.

Seminole

★ 77804 ★ **Oryx Energy Co. Dgn Non**
N E. of City
Seminole, OK 74818
(405)382-4643
Ultimate Parent: Oryx Energy.

★ 77805 ★ **Pizza Hut**
1715 N. Milt Phillips Ave.
Seminole, OK 74868
(405)382-1333
Ultimate Parent: Pepsico. **SIC:** 5812—Eating Places.

★ 77806 ★ **Texaco Inc.**
512 PO Box
Seminole, OK 74818
(405)382-4326
Ultimate Parent: Texaco. **SIC:** 5199—Nondurable Goods Nec.

★ 77807 ★ **Wrangler**
900 N. Harvey Rd.
Seminole, OK 74868
(405)382-3980
Officer: Glen Siler, Manager. **Ultimate Parent:** VF Corp. **SIC:** 2325—Men's/Boys' Trousers & Slacks.

Shattuck

★ 77808 ★ **Associated Milk Producers Inc.**
406 E. Oklahoma
Shattuck, OK 73858
(405)938-2543
Ultimate Parent: Associated Milk Producers Inc. **SIC:** 5143—Dairy Products Except Dried or Canned.

★ 77809 ★ **Pizza Hut**
Hwy. 283 S
Shattuck, OK 73858
(405)938-9884
Ultimate Parent: Pepsico. **SIC:** 5812—Eating Places.

★ 77810 ★ **Radio Shack**
311 S. Main
Shattuck, OK 73858
(405)938-5277
Company Type: Division. **Ultimate Parent:** Tandy Corp. **SIC:** 5065—Electronic Parts & Equipment Nec.

Shawnee

★ 77811 ★ **Arco Pipe Line Co.**
Tool House W. of City
Shawnee, OK 74801
(405)275-1939
Ultimate Parent: Atlantic Richfield Co., Inc. **SIC:** 4612—Crude Petroleum Pipelines.

★ 77812 ★ **Arco Pipe Line Co.**
Pump Station W. of City
Shawnee, OK 74801
(405)275-1642
Ultimate Parent: Atlantic Richfield Co., Inc. **SIC:** 4612—Crude Petroleum Pipelines.

★ 77813 ★ **Arco Pipe Line Co.**
Acme Rd.
Shawnee, OK 74801
(405)273-5151
Ultimate Parent: Atlantic Richfield Co., Inc. **SIC:** 2911—Petroleum Refining; 4612—Crude Petroleum Pipelines.

★ 77814 ★ **Citgo Food Mart**
737 N. Kickapoo St.
Shawnee, OK 74801
(405)275-8428
Ultimate Parent: Citgo Petroleum. **SIC:** 5411—Grocery Stores.

★ 77815 ★ **Citgo Food Mart**
2723 N. Kickapoo St.
Shawnee, OK 74801
(405)273-1380
Ultimate Parent: Citgo Petroleum. **SIC:** 5411—Grocery Stores.

★ 77816 ★ **Eaton Corp.**
Hydraulics Div.
8701 N. Harrison St.
Shawnee, OK 74801
(405)275-5500
Company Type: Division. **Officer:** Terry Vaughman, Manager. **Ultimate Parent:** Eaton Corp. **SIC:** 3569—General Industrial Machinery Nec; 3594—Fluid Power Pumps & Motors.

★ 77817 ★ **Eaton Corp.**
Hydraulics Div.
8701 N. Harrison
Shawnee, OK 74801
(405)275-5500
Company Type: Division. **Location Type:**

Plant. **Officer:** Lowell Herzberg, Controller.
Ultimate Parent: Eaton Corp.

★ 77818 ★ **Foot Action**
4901 N. Kickapoo St.
Shawnee, OK 74801
(405)273-9146
Ultimate Parent: Melville. **SIC:** 5661—Shoe Stores.

★ 77819 ★ **Foot Action for Kids**
4901 N. Kickapoo St.
Shawnee, OK 74801
(405)273-9180
Ultimate Parent: Melville. **SIC:** 5661—Shoe Stores.

★ 77820 ★ **Kay Bee Toys**
4901 N. Kickapoo St.
Shawnee, OK 74801
(405)878-0111
Ultimate Parent: Melville. **SIC:** 5945—Hobby, Toy & Game Shops.

★ 77821 ★ **Lane Bryant**
4901 N. Kickapoo St.
Shawnee, OK 74801
(405)275-0697
Ultimate Parent: Limited. **SIC:** 5311—Department Stores.

★ 77822 ★ **Mobil Chemical Co.**
555 Wolverine Rd.
Shawnee, OK 74801
(405)275-6850
Company Type: Branch. **Officer:** John Slavens. **Ultimate Parent:** Mobil. **SIC:** 3081—Unsupported Plastics Film & Sheet; 3089—Plastics Products Nec.

★ 77823 ★ **Radio Shack**
500 W. Independence St.
Shawnee, OK 74801
(405)275-1413
Company Type: Division. **Ultimate Parent:** Tandy Corp. **SIC:** 5734—Computer & Software Stores.

★ 77824 ★ **Wal Mart**
4901 N. Kickapoo St.
Shawnee, OK 74801
(405)275-1030
Ultimate Parent: Wal-Mart Stores, Inc. **SIC:** 5311—Department Stores.

Skiatook

★ 77825 ★ **Arco Pipe Line Co.**
W. of city
Skiatook, OK 74070
(918)396-1152
Location Type: Branch office. **Ultimate Parent:** Atlantic Richfield Co., Inc. **SIC:** 4612—Crude Petroleum Pipelines.

★ 77826 ★ **Arco Pipe Line Co.**
Skiatook, OK 74070
(918)396-1152
Location Type: Branch office. **Ultimate Parent:** Atlantic Richfield Co., Inc. **SIC:** 4612—Crude Petroleum Pipelines.

★ 77827 ★ **Radio Shack**
4214 W. Rogers Blvd.
Skiatook, OK 74070
(918)371-9515
Company Type: Division. **Ultimate Parent:** Tandy Corp. **SIC:** 1389—Oil & Gas Field Services Nec.

★ 77828 ★ **Wal Mart Discount Pharmacy**
566 PO Box
Skiatook, OK 74070
Ultimate Parent: Wal-Mart Stores, Inc. **SIC:** 5912—Drug Stores & Proprietary Stores.

Skiatook Ok

★ 77829 ★ **Kentucky Fried Chicken**
1250 W. Rogers Blvd.
Skiatook Ok, OK 74070
(918)396-3230
Ultimate Parent: Pepsico. **SIC:** 5812—Eating Places.

Stigler

★ 77830 ★ Exxon Co. USA
605 E. Main St.
Stigler, OK 74462
(918)967-8711
Ultimate Parent: Exxon. SIC: 1382—Oil &
Gas Exploration Services.

★ 77831 ★ Pizza Hut
513 E. Main St.
Stigler, OK 74462
(918)967-4697
Ultimate Parent: Pepsico. SIC: 5812—
Eating Places.

★ 77832 ★ Wal Mart Discount
Pharmacy
Oklahoma Hwy. 9 E
Stigler, OK 74462
(918)967-3369
Ultimate Parent: Wal-Mart Stores, Inc. SIC:
5311—Department Stores.

Stillwater

★ 77833 ★ Ace Hardware
113 W. 9th Ave.
Stillwater, OK 74074
(405)372-0526
Ultimate Parent: Ace Hardware. SIC:
5251—Hardware Stores.

★ 77834 ★ Armstrong World
Industries
Stillwater Plant
4115 N. Perkins Rd.
Stillwater, OK 74075
Ultimate Parent: Armstrong World
Industries. SIC: 3996—Hard Surface Floor
Coverings Nec.

★ 77835 ★ Brunswick Corp.
3003 N. Perkins Rd.
Stillwater, OK 74075-2218
(405)377-1200
Officer: Barry Eller. Ultimate Parent:
Brunswick Corp. SIC: 3519—Internal
Combustion Engines Nec.

★ 77836 ★ Brunswick Mercury
Marine Plant 14
3003 N. Perkins Rd.
Stillwater, OK 74074
Ultimate Parent: Brunswick Corp. SIC:
3519—Internal Combustion Engines Nec.

★ 77837 ★ Coca Cola Bottling
Co.
47 PO Box
Stillwater, OK 74076
(405)762-5614
Ultimate Parent: Coca-Cola Enterprises.
SIC: 5149—Groceries & Related Products
Nec.

★ 77838 ★ Hertz Rent-A-Car
2020 W. Airport Rd.
Stillwater, OK 74075
(405)624-1188
Ultimate Parent: Hertz. SIC: 7514—
Passenger Car Rental.

★ 77839 ★ Mercury Marine
3003 N. Perkins Rd.
Stillwater, OK 74075
(405)377-1200
Officer: Barry Eller, Manager. Ultimate
Parent: Brunswick Corp. SIC: 3519—
Internal Combustion Engines Nec.

★ 77840 ★ Mercury Marine
Mercruiser Div.
3003 N. Perkins Rd.
Stillwater, OK 74075
Company Type: Division. Ultimate Parent:
Brunswick Corp. SIC: 3519—Internal
Combustion Engines Nec.

★ 77841 ★ Mercury Marine Plant
14
3003 North Perkins Rd.
Stillwater, OK 74074
Ultimate Parent: Brunswick Corp. SIC:
3519—Internal Combustion Engines Nec.

★ 77842 ★ Payless Shoesource
715 N. Perkins Rd.
Stillwater, OK 74075
(918)372-1619
Ultimate Parent: May Department Stores.
SIC: 5661—Shoe Stores.

★ 77843 ★ Pizza Hut
807 N. Perkins Rd.
Stillwater, OK 74075
(405)624-9200
Ultimate Parent: Pepsico. SIC: 5812—
Eating Places; 5812—Eating Places.

★ 77844 ★ Pizza Hut
2000 N. Boomer Rd.
Stillwater, OK 74075
(405)372-0966
Ultimate Parent: Pepsico. SIC: 5812—
Eating Places.

★ 77845 ★ Texaco Inc.
515 S. Kelly St.
Stillwater, OK 74074
(405)372-1717
Ultimate Parent: Texaco. SIC: 5172—
Petroleum Products Nec.

★ 77846 ★ Wal Mart Discount
City
Mac Elroy
Stillwater, OK 74075
(405)624-3131
Ultimate Parent: Wal-Mart Stores, Inc. SIC:
5311—Department Stores.

Stillwell

★ 77847 ★ Convenience
Products Group
PO Box 432
Stillwell, OK 74960
(918)696-7222 Fax: (918)696-6646
Company Type: Subsidiary. Officer: Lee
Turman, President. Ultimate Parent:
Flowers Industries.

★ 77848 ★ Stillwell Foods Inc.
5 E. Walnut
PO Box 432
Stillwell, OK 74960
(918)696-7222 Fax: (918)696-6646
Company Type: Subsidiary. Officer: Lee
Turman, President. Ultimate Parent:
Flowers Industries.

★ 77849 ★ Hudson Foods Inc.
Hwy. 59 North Rte. 3 Box 489
Stilwell, OK 74960
Ultimate Parent: Hudson Foods.

★ 77850 ★ Radio Shack
Rural Route B
Stilwell, OK 74960
(918)696-2100
Company Type: Division. Ultimate Parent:
Tandy Corp. SIC: 5944—Jewelry Stores;
7384—Photofinishing Laboratories.

★ 77851 ★ Stilwell Foods Inc.
5 W. Walnut St.
PO Box 432
Stilwell, OK 74960
(918)696-7222 Fax: (918)696-6646
Officer: Paul K. Mead, President. Ultimate
Parent: Flowers Industries. SIC: 2033—
Canned Fruits & Vegetables; 2038—Frozen
Specialties Nec; 2051—Bread, Cake &
Related Products.

★ 77852 ★ Wal Mart Discount
City
Hwy. 100 W
Stilwell, OK 74960
(918)696-3141
Ultimate Parent: Wal-Mart Stores, Inc. SIC:
5311—Department Stores.

Stratford

★ 77853 ★ Arco Pipeline Co.
W. of City
Stratford, OK 74872
(405)759-3721
Ultimate Parent: Atlantic Richfield Co., Inc.
SIC: 4612—Crude Petroleum Pipelines.

★ 77854 ★ Arco Pipeline Co.
West of City
Stratford, OK 74872
(405)759-3721
Ultimate Parent: Atlantic Richfield Co., Inc.
SIC: 4612—Crude Petroleum Pipelines.

★ 77855 ★ First American Bank
110 W. Smith
Stratford, OK 74872
(405)759-2326
Officer: Chris Bolles, Chairman of the
Board. Ultimate Parent: First American
Corp. SIC: 6022—State Commercial Banks.
Employee Count: 9.

Sulphur

★ 77856 ★ Kentucky Fried
Chicken
W City
Sulphur, OK 73086
(405)622-6235
Ultimate Parent: Pepsico. SIC: 5812—
Eating Places.

★ 77857 ★ Pizza Hut
Hwy. 7 W
Sulphur, OK 73086
(405)622-2444
Ultimate Parent: Pepsico. SIC: 5812—
Eating Places.

Tahlequah

★ 77858 ★ Pizza Hut
1006 E. Downing St.
Tahlequah, OK 74464
(918)456-5272
Ultimate Parent: Pepsico. SIC: 5812—
Eating Places.

★ 77859 ★ Radio Shack
1027 S. Muskogee Ave.
Tahlequah, OK 74464
(918)456-6759
Company Type: Division. Ultimate Parent:
Tandy Corp.

★ 77860 ★ Ryder Truck Rental
1600 N. Grand
Tahlequah, OK 74464
(918)456-5539
Ultimate Parent: Ryder System.

★ 77861 ★ Trailways Inc. Bus
Station
708 E. Downing St.
Tahlequah, OK 74464
(918)456-3242
Ultimate Parent: Greyhound Lines Inc. SIC:
4131—Intercity & Rural Bus Transportation.

★ 77862 ★ Wal Mart
Cherokee Hill Shopping Ctr.
Tahlequah, OK 74464
(918)456-8804
Ultimate Parent: Wal-Mart Stores, Inc. SIC:
5946—Camera & Photographic Supply
Stores.

★ 77863 ★ Wal Mart Pharmacy
Cherokee Hill Shopping Ctr.
Tahlequah, OK 74464
(918)456-2437
Ultimate Parent: Wal-Mart Stores, Inc. SIC:
5912—Drug Stores & Proprietary Stores.

Texhoma

★ 77864 ★ Sherman County
Grain Co.
Hwy. 54 W
Texhoma, OK 73949
(405)827-7631
Location Type: Branch office. Officer:
Burnell Kraft. Ultimate Parent: Archer
Daniels Midland Co. SIC: 5153—Grain &
Field Beans; 4221—Farm Product
Warehousing & Storage.

Thackerville

★ 77865 ★ Arco Pipeline Co.
Thackerville, OK 73459
(405)276-3040
Location Type: Branch office. Ultimate
Parent: Atlantic Richfield Co., Inc. SIC:
4612—Crude Petroleum Pipelines.

Thomas

★ 77866 ★ Burlington Northern
Railroa
300 N. 1st St.
Thomas, OK 73669
(405)661-2429
Ultimate Parent: Burlington Northern. SIC:
4011—Railroads—Line-Haul Operating.

★ 77867 ★ Mobil Oil Corp.
W City
Thomas, OK 73669
(405)661-3536
Ultimate Parent: Mobil. SIC: 4925—Gas
Production & Distribution Nec.

★ 77868 ★ Mobil Oil Corp.
RR 1 Box 177
Thomas, OK 73669-9401
(405)661-3536
Company Type: Branch. Officer: Ken
Ballard. Ultimate Parent: Mobil. SIC:
2911—Petroleum Refining; 1311—Crude
Petroleum & Natural Gas; 4925—Gas
Production & Distribution Nec.

Tishomingo

★ 77869 ★ Coast to Coastsupply
211 W. Main St.
Tishomingo, OK 73460
(405)371-3125
Ultimate Parent: Servistar Corp. SIC:
5531—Automobile & Home Supply Stores.

★ 77870 ★ Pizza Hut
Hwy. 22 E
Tishomingo, OK 73460
(405)371-2325
Ultimate Parent: Pepsico. SIC: 5812—
Eating Places.

Tulsa

★ 77871 ★ Ace Hardware
4311 E. 31st St.
Tulsa, OK 74135
(918)743-3344
Ultimate Parent: Ace Hardware.

★ 77872 ★ Ace Hardware
6325 E. Tecumseh St.
Tulsa, OK 74115
(918)838-0713
Ultimate Parent: Ace Hardware.

★ 77873 ★ Agrico Chemical Co.
1 Williams Ctr.
Tulsa, OK 74172
(918)588-2000
Ultimate Parent: Freeport-McMoran. SIC:
4612—Crude Petroleum Pipelines.

★ 77874 ★ Air Products &
Chemicals, Inc.
2512 E. 71st St.
Tulsa, OK 74136
(918)492-1812
Ultimate Parent: Air Products & Chemicals,
Inc. SIC: 7299—Miscellaneous Personal
Services Nec.

★ 77875 ★ Amerada Hess Corp.
218 W. 6th St.
Tulsa, OK 74119
(918)599-4200
Ultimate Parent: Amerada Hess. SIC:
1311—Crude Petroleum & Natural Gas;
1382—Oil & Gas Exploration Services.

★ 77876 ★ American General
Finance
2166 S. Sheridan Rd.
Tulsa, OK 74129-1002
(918)834-2276
Location Type: Branch office. Officer:
Colin Magruder. Ultimate Parent: American
General Corp. SIC: 6141—Personal Credit
Institutions; 6162—Mortgage Bankers &
Correspondents.

★ 77877 ★ American General
Finance Inc.
3161 S. 129th Ave.
Tulsa, OK 74134-3249
(918)627-1130
Officer: Leeman Smith. Ultimate Parent:
American General Corp. SIC: 6141—
Personal Credit Institutions; 6162—
Mortgage Bankers & Correspondents.

★ 77878 ★ **American General Finance Inc.**
3161 S. 129th E. Ave.
Tulsa, OK 74134-3249
(918)627-1130
Location Type: Branch office. **Officer:** Leeman Smith. **Ultimate Parent:** American General Corp. **SIC:** 6141—Personal Credit Institutions; 6162—Mortgage Bankers & Correspondents.

★ 77879 ★ **APAC**
3605 N. 129th East Ave.
Tulsa, OK 74116
(918)438-2020
Officer: Mearl Pearcy, President. **Ultimate Parent:** Ashland Oil. **SIC:** 2951—Asphalt Paving Mixtures & Blocks; 3295—Minerals—Ground or Treated; 3599—Industrial Machinery Nec.

★ 77880 ★ **Arrow/Kieulft Electronics**
12111 E. 51st St.
Tulsa, OK 74146
(918)252-7537
Company Type: Division. **Location Type:** Distribution center. **Officer:** Pete Stone, Regional Vice President. **Ultimate Parent:** Arrow Electronics. **SIC:** 5065—Electronic Parts & Equipment Nec.

★ 77881 ★ **Associated Milk Producers Inc.**
6240 E. 15th St.
Tulsa, OK 74112
(918)835-6788
Ultimate Parent: Associated Milk Producers Inc. **SIC:** 5451—Dairy Products Stores.

★ 77882 ★ **Associated Milk Producers Inc.**
6240 E. 15th St.
Tulsa, OK 74112
(918)835-6931
Ultimate Parent: Associated Milk Producers Inc. **SIC:** 5143—Dairy Products Except Dried or Canned.

★ 77883 ★ **Baltimore Trust Co. Inc.**
5101 E. Pine St.
Tulsa, OK 74115-5357
(918)832-7016
Company Type: Division. **Officer:** Paula M. Chapman, President. **Ultimate Parent:** Mercantile Bankshares Corp. **SIC:** 4213—Trucking Except Local. **Employee Count:** 168. **Sales:** 11,000,000 M.

★ 77884 ★ **Bama Pies**
2745 E. 11th St.
Tulsa, OK 74104
(918)592-0778
Officer: Paula Chapman, CEO. **Ultimate Parent:** Borden, Inc. **SIC:** 2051—Bread, Cake & Related Products.

★ 77885 ★ **Banana Republic**
1776 Utica Sq.
Tulsa, OK 74114
(918)742-2068
Ultimate Parent: GAP. **SIC:** 5651—Family Clothing Stores.

★ 77886 ★ **Bergen Brunswig Drug Co.**
9401 E. 54th St.
Tulsa, OK 74145
(918)664-9990
Ultimate Parent: Bergen Brunswig Corp. **SIC:** 2834—Pharmaceutical Preparations.

★ 77887 ★ **BFI Landfill**
20500 E. 51st
Tulsa, OK 74134
(918)355-1688
Ultimate Parent: Browning-Ferris Industries. **SIC:** 4953—Refuse Systems.

★ 77888 ★ **BFI Waste Systems**
10830 E. 45th St.
Tulsa, OK 74146-3801
(918)664-8899
Ultimate Parent: Browning-Ferris Industries. **SIC:** 4953—Refuse Systems.

★ 77889 ★ **Bi-Lo Food Warehouse**
1741 S. Yale Ave.
Tulsa, OK 74112
(918)744-0036
Ultimate Parent: Penn Traffic. **SIC:** 5411—Grocery Stores.

★ 77890 ★ **Borden Inc.**
Meadow Gold Dairy
215 N. Denver Ave.
Tulsa, OK 74103
(918)587-2417
Officer: George Streetman, Manager. **Ultimate Parent:** Borden, Inc. **SIC:** 2023—Dry, Condensed & Evaporated Dairy Products; 2024—Ice Cream & Frozen Desserts; 2026—Fluid Milk.

★ 77891 ★ **Browning-Ferris Industries**
1616 N. Pittsburgh Ave.
Tulsa, OK 74115-4150
(918)834-2244
Location Type: Branch office. **Officer:** David T. Vaught. **Ultimate Parent:** Browning-Ferris Industries. **SIC:** 4953—Refuse Systems.

★ 77892 ★ **Bruno's**
Zebco Division
6101 E. Appache
Tulsa, OK 74115
(918)836-5581 **Fax:** (918)836-0154
Company Type: Subsidiary. **Officer:** James W. Dawson, President. **Ultimate Parent:** Bruno's.

★ 77893 ★ **Brunswick Corp.**
Zebco Division
835 W. 41st St.
Tulsa, OK 74107
(918)446-1461
Ultimate Parent: Brunswick Corp. **SIC:** 5091—Sporting & Recreational Goods.

★ 77894 ★ **Builders Square**
525 N. Memorial Dr.
Tulsa, OK 74115
(918)838-0345
Company Type: Subsidiary. **Ultimate Parent:** K-Mart. **SIC:** 5039—Construction Materials Nec.

★ 77895 ★ **Builders Square**
7030 S. Memorial Dr.
Tulsa, OK 74133
(918)254-0483
Company Type: Subsidiary. **Ultimate Parent:** K-Mart. **SIC:** 1521—Single-Family Housing Construction.

★ 77896 ★ **Burlington Air Express**
3148 S. 108th Ave. E
Tulsa, OK 74146
(918)665-2115
Ultimate Parent: Pittston. **SIC:** 4513—Air Courier Services.

★ 77897 ★ **Butler Paper**
5440 S. 101st E. Ave.
Tulsa, OK 74146-5731
(918)622-9166
Officer: Kent D. Sheridan. **Ultimate Parent:** Alco Standard Corp. **SIC:** 5113—Industrial & Personal Service Paper; 5111—Printing & Writing Paper.

★ 77898 ★ **Casual Corner**
4107 S. Yale Ave.
Tulsa, OK 74135
(918)622-4182
Ultimate Parent: United States Shoe. **SIC:** 5651—Family Clothing Stores.

★ 77899 ★ **Casual Corner**
14002 E. 21st St.
Tulsa, OK 74134
(918)438-1423
Ultimate Parent: United States Shoe. **SIC:** 5651—Family Clothing Stores.

★ 77900 ★ **Casual Corner**
7021 S. Memorial Dr.
Tulsa, OK 74133
(918)252-0606
Ultimate Parent: United States Shoe. **SIC:** 5651—Family Clothing Stores.

★ 77901 ★ **Cincinnati Milacron**
5742 E. 62nd Pl
Tulsa, OK 74136
(918)494-8875
Ultimate Parent: Cincinnati Milacron. **SIC:** 5084—Industrial Machinery & Equipment.

★ 77902 ★ **Circus World No 7329**
14002 E. 21st St.
Tulsa, OK 74134
(918)234-7888
Ultimate Parent: Melville. **SIC:** 5945—Hobby, Toy & Game Shops.

★ 77903 ★ **Circus World Toys**
4107 S. Yale Ave.
Tulsa, OK 74135
(918)662-5208
Ultimate Parent: Melville. **SIC:** 5945—Hobby, Toy & Game Shops.

★ 77904 ★ **Citgo Food Mart**
2474 N. Yale Ave.
Tulsa, OK 74115
(918)834-1415
Ultimate Parent: Citgo Petroleum. **SIC:** 5541—Gasoline Service Stations.

★ 77905 ★ **Citgo Petroleum**
6100 S. Yale Ave.
Tulsa, OK 74136
(918)495-4000
Company Type: Headquarters. **Officer:** Ronald E. Hall. **Sales:** 162.1 M. **Fortune 500:** Largest U.S. Industrial Corporations: Ranking 53.

★ 77906 ★ **Citgo Petroleum Corp.**
6130 S. Yale Ave.
Tulsa, OK 74136
(918)495-4000
Ultimate Parent: Citgo Petroleum. **SIC:** 5172—Petroleum Products Nec.

★ 77907 ★ **Citgo Petroleum Corp.**
6100 S. Yale Ave.
Tulsa, OK 74136-1911
(918)495-4000
Company Type: Subsidiary. **Ultimate Parent:** Citgo Petroleum. **SIC:** 2911—Petroleum Refining; 5171—Petroleum Bulk Stations & Terminals; 4612—Crude Petroleum Pipelines; 4213—Trucking Except Local.

★ 77908 ★ **Citgo Petroleum Warehouse**
11915 E. 51st St.
Tulsa, OK 74146
(918)250-4961
Ultimate Parent: Citgo Petroleum. **SIC:** 4225—General Warehousing & Storage.

★ 77909 ★ **Citgo Pipeline Co.**
6100 S. Yale Ave., 12th Fl.
Tulsa, OK 74136-1911
(918)495-4600
Company Type: Subsidiary. **Ultimate Parent:** Citgo Petroleum. **SIC:** 4612—Crude Petroleum Pipelines.

★ 77910 ★ **Citgo Quick Mart**
3106 S. Sheridan Rd.
Tulsa, OK 74145
(918)627-6933
Ultimate Parent: Citgo Petroleum. **SIC:** 5541—Gasoline Service Stations.

★ 77911 ★ **Citgo Quick Mart**
323 W. 3rd St.
Tulsa, OK 74103
(918)583-0185
Ultimate Parent: Citgo Petroleum. **SIC:** 5411—Grocery Stores.

★ 77912 ★ **Citgo Quick Mart**
3111 S. 129th Ave. E
Tulsa, OK 74134
(918)663-1300
Ultimate Parent: Citgo Petroleum. **SIC:** 5541—Gasoline Service Stations.

★ 77913 ★ **Citgo Quick Mart**
3820 S. Peoria Ave.
Tulsa, OK 74105
(918)747-9779
Ultimate Parent: Citgo Petroleum. **SIC:** 5411—Grocery Stores.

★ 77914 ★ **Citgo Quick Mart**
2660 E. 21st St.
Tulsa, OK 74114
(918)743-9776
Ultimate Parent: Citgo Petroleum. **SIC:** 5541—Gasoline Service Stations.

★ 77915 ★ **Citgo Quick Mart**
10822 E. 41st St.
Tulsa, OK 74146
(918)627-0505
Ultimate Parent: Citgo Petroleum. **SIC:** 5541—Gasoline Service Stations.

★ 77916 ★ **Citgo Quick Mart**
10900 E. 21st St.
Tulsa, OK 74129
(918)438-1922
Ultimate Parent: Citgo Petroleum.

★ 77917 ★ **Citgo Refining & Chemicals Inc.**
6100 S. Yale Ave.
Tulsa, OK 74136-1911
(918)495-4000
Company Type: Subsidiary. **Ultimate Parent:** Citgo Petroleum. **SIC:** 2911—Petroleum Refining; 5172—Petroleum Products Nec.

★ 77918 ★ **Citgo Service Station**
5102 S. Union Ave.
Tulsa, OK 74107
(918)446-2440
Ultimate Parent: Citgo Petroleum. **SIC:** 5541—Gasoline Service Stations.

★ 77919 ★ **Coca-Cola Bottling Co. of Tu**
1224 N. Lewis Ave.
Tulsa, OK 74110
(918)585-5655
Ultimate Parent: Coca-Cola Enterprises. **SIC:** 2086—Bottled & Canned Soft Drinks; 5149—Groceries & Related Products Nec.

★ 77920 ★ **Columbian Chemicals Co. Inc.**
2431 E. 61st St.
Tulsa, OK 74136
(918)744-1770
Ultimate Parent: Phelps Dodge. **SIC:** 2895—Carbon Black.

★ 77921 ★ **Comdisco Resources Inc.**
6600 S. Yale Ave.
Tulsa, OK 74136
(918)492-9164
Ultimate Parent: Comdisco. **SIC:** 1382—Oil & Gas Exploration Services.

★ 77922 ★ **Continental Industries Inc.**
4102 S. 74 East Ave.
Tulsa, OK 74145
(918)627-5210 **Fax:** (918)622-1275
Company Type: Subsidiary. **Officer:** Richard E. Cota, President. **Ultimate Parent:** Handy & Harman. **SIC:** 3399—Primary Metal Products Nec; 3498—Fabricated Pipe & Fittings.

★ 77923 ★ **Continental Industries Inc.**
4102 S. 74th Ave. E
Tulsa, OK 74145
(918)627-5210
Ultimate Parent: Handy & Harman. **SIC:** 3089—Plastics Products Nec; 3431—Metal Sanitary Ware.

★ 77924 ★ **Continental Industries Inc.**
4102 S. 74th East Ave.
Tulsa, OK 74145
Ultimate Parent: Handy & Harman. **SIC:** 3498—Fabricated Pipe & Fittings.

★ 77925 ★ **Cray Research Inc.**
5100 E. Skelly Dr.
Tulsa, OK 74135
(918)663-9394
Ultimate Parent: Cray Research, Inc. **SIC:** 5046—Commercial Equipment Nec; 7373—Computer Integrated Systems Design.

★ 77926 ★ **Delta Air Lines**
7777 Tulsa International Airport
Tulsa, OK 74115
(918)582-6500
Ultimate Parent: Delta Air Lines, Inc. **SIC:** 4512—Air Transportation—Scheduled.

★ 77927 ★ **Delta Air Lines**
5330 E. 31st St. 210
Tulsa, OK 74135
Ultimate Parent: Delta Air Lines, Inc. **SIC:** 4724—Travel Agencies.

★ 77928 ★ **Diebold Inc.**
5445 S. 99th Ave. E
Tulsa, OK 74145
(918)622-9595
Ultimate Parent: Diebold, Inc. **SIC:** 5046—Commercial Equipment Nec.

★ 77929 ★ **Digital Equipment Corp.**
4150 S. 100th Ave. E
Tulsa, OK 74146
(918)664-1330
Ultimate Parent: Digital Equipment Corp. **SIC:** 7379—Computer Related Services Nec.

★ 77930 ★ **Dillards**
6919 S. Memorial Dr.
Tulsa, OK 74133
(918)252-0211
Ultimate Parent: Dillard Department Stores.
SIC: 5311—Department Stores.

★ 77931 ★ **Dillards**
14002 E. 21st St.
Tulsa, OK 74134
(918)438-1000
Ultimate Parent: Dillard Department Stores.
SIC: 5311—Department Stores.

★ 77932 ★ **Dollar Rent-A-Car Systems Inc.**
5330 E. 31st St.
Tulsa, OK 74135-5063
(918)660-0033
Company Type: Subsidiary. **Officer:** Gary
L. Paxtor, President & CEO. **Ultimate
Parent:** Chrysler Corp. **SIC:** 6794—Patent
Owners & Lessors; 7514—Passenger Car
Rental. **Employee Count:** 100. **Sales:** 7 M.

★ 77933 ★ **Dowell Schlumberger Inc.**
6717 S. 61st West Ave.
Tulsa, OK 74131
Ultimate Parent: Dow Chemical Co. USA.
SIC: 2899—Chemical Preparations Nec.

★ 77934 ★ **Durr-Fillauer Medical Inc.**
PO Box 581090
Tulsa, OK 74158
(405)528-7581
Ultimate Parent: Bergen Brunswig Corp.
SIC: 5047—Medical & Hospital Equipment.

★ 77935 ★ **Durr-Fillauer Medical Inc.**
1140 S. Joplin Ave.
Tulsa, OK 74112
(918)836-8751
Ultimate Parent: Bergen Brunswig Corp.
SIC: 5047—Medical & Hospital Equipment.

★ 77936 ★ **EG & G Process Measurements/Chandler Eng.**
PO Box 470710
Tulsa, OK 74147-0710
(918)250-7200 **Fax:** (918)459-0334
Company Type: Subsidiary. **Officer:** Daniel
Webster, Manager. **Ultimate Parent:** EG &
G.

★ 77937 ★ **Express Ltd.**
7021 S. Memorial Dr.
Tulsa, OK 74133
(918)252-2279
Ultimate Parent: Limited.

★ 77938 ★ **Express Ltd.**
4107 S. Yale Ave.
Tulsa, OK 74135
(918)622-2442
Ultimate Parent: Limited.

★ 77939 ★ **Fabricated Products Plant**
7311 E. 41st St.
Tulsa, OK 74145
(918)627-0100
Ultimate Parent: Maxxam. **SIC:** 2819—
Industrial Inorganic Chemicals Nec.

★ 77940 ★ **First National Bank & Trust**
15 1st Pl
Tulsa, OK 74103
(918)586-1000
Ultimate Parent: Society Corp. **SIC:** 6022—
State Commercial Banks.

★ 77941 ★ **Ford Motor Co., Tulsa Glass Plant**
5555 S. 129th East Ave.
Tulsa, OK 74121
Location Type: Plant. **Ultimate Parent:**
Ford Motor Co. **SIC:** 3211—Flat Glass.

★ 77942 ★ **Fruehauf Trailer Corp.**
1890 N. 106th E. Ave.
Tulsa, OK 74116-1511
(918)836-4300
Ultimate Parent: Terex Corp. **SIC:** 5012—
Automobiles & Other Motor Vehicles;
5013—Motor Vehicle Supplies & New Parts.

★ 77943 ★ **Fruehauf Trailers**
1890 N. 106th Ave.
Tulsa, OK 74116-1511
(918)836-4300
Ultimate Parent: Terex Corp. **SIC:** 5012—

Automobiles & Other Motor Vehicles;
5013—Motor Vehicle Supplies & New Parts.

★ 77944 ★ **The Gap**
7021 S. Memorial Dr.
Tulsa, OK 74133
(918)250-9579
Ultimate Parent: GAP. **SIC:** 5651—Family
Clothing Stores.

★ 77945 ★ **The Gap**
4107 S. Yale Ave.
Tulsa, OK 74135
(918)622-4178
Ultimate Parent: GAP. **SIC:** 5651—Family
Clothing Stores.

★ 77946 ★ **The Gap**
8901 E. 71st St. 158
Tulsa, OK 74133
(918)335-0406
Ultimate Parent: GAP. **SIC:** 5651—Family
Clothing Stores.

★ 77947 ★ **Gear Products Inc.**
1111 N. 161st E. Ave.
Tulsa, OK 74116
(918)234-3044 **Fax:** (918)234-3455
Company Type: Subsidiary. **Officer:**
Bernell Jiles, President. **Ultimate Parent:**
Blount Inc.

★ 77948 ★ **General American Life Insur**
3530 E. 31st St.
Tulsa, OK 74135
(918)749-2241
Ultimate Parent: General American Life.
SIC: 6371—Pension, Health & Welfare
Funds.

★ 77949 ★ **Greyhound Bus Liwes**
317 S. Detroit Ave.
Tulsa, OK 74120
(918)582-6148
Ultimate Parent: Greyhound Lines Inc. **SIC:**
4111—Local & Suburban Transit.

★ 77950 ★ **Hamilton Hallmark**
12121 E. 51st, Ste. 102
Tulsa, OK 74146
(918)664-0444
Location Type: Branch office. **Ultimate
Parent:** Avnet. **SIC:** 5065—Electronic Parts
& Equipment Nec.

★ 77951 ★ **Hertz Rent-A-Car**
7777 Tulsa International Airport
Tulsa, OK 74115
(918)838-1999
Ultimate Parent: Hertz. **SIC:** 7514—
Passenger Car Rental.

★ 77952 ★ **Hertz Rent-A-Car**
2525 N. 76th Ave. E
Tulsa, OK 74158
(918)838-1999
Ultimate Parent: Hertz. **SIC:** 7514—
Passenger Car Rental.

★ 77953 ★ **Hertz Rent-A-Car**
4100 S. Mingo Rd.
Tulsa, OK 74146
(918)664-6402
Ultimate Parent: Hertz.

★ 77954 ★ **Hevi Duty Nelson**
4041 S. Sheridan Rd.
Tulsa, OK 74145
(918)627-5530
Ultimate Parent: General Signal. **SIC:**
3567—Industrial Furnaces & Ovens; 3613—
Switchgear & Switchboard Apparatus;
3699—Electrical Equipment & Supplies Nec.

★ 77955 ★ **Hewlett Packard Co.**
3840 E. 103rd St.
Tulsa, OK 74137
(918)665-3300
Ultimate Parent: Hewlett-Packard. **SIC:**
5734—Computer & Software Stores.

★ 77956 ★ **Hewlett-Packard Co.**
6655 S. Lewis Ave.
Tulsa, OK 74136
(918)481-6700
Ultimate Parent: Hewlett-Packard. **SIC:**
7373—Computer Integrated Systems
Design.

★ 77957 ★ **IBM Corp.**
321 S. Boston Ave.
Tulsa, OK 74103
(918)583-7777
Ultimate Parent: IBM. **SIC:** 5999—
Miscellaneous Retail Stores Nec.

★ 77958 ★ **IDS Financial Services Inc.**
4870 S. Lewis
Tulsa, OK 74105
(918)748-8191
Location Type: Branch office. **Officer:**
Janice Ward. **Ultimate Parent:** American
Express Co. **SIC:** 6211—Security Brokers &
Dealers; 6282—Investment Advice.

★ 77959 ★ **Intel Corp.**
4157 S. Harvard Ave.
Tulsa, OK 74135
(918)749-8688
Ultimate Parent: Intel Corp. **SIC:** 7374—
Data Processing & Preparation.

★ 77960 ★ **Jiffy Lube**
6610 S. Lewis Ave.
Tulsa, OK 74136
(918)492-3298
Ultimate Parent: Pennzoil. **SIC:** 7539—
Automotive Repair Shops Nec.

★ 77961 ★ **Jiffy Lube**
3301 E. Skelly Dr.
Tulsa, OK 74135
(918)747-2640
Ultimate Parent: Pennzoil. **SIC:** 5172—
Petroleum Products Nec.

★ 77962 ★ **Jiffy Lube**
5251 S. Peoria Ave.
Tulsa, OK 74105
(918)743-6351
Ultimate Parent: Pennzoil. **SIC:** 7539—
Automotive Repair Shops Nec.

★ 77963 ★ **Jiffy Lube**
3628 S. Sheridan Rd.
Tulsa, OK 74145
(918)665-6221
Ultimate Parent: Pennzoil. **SIC:** 7539—
Automotive Repair Shops Nec.

★ 77964 ★ **Jiffy Lube**
7122 S. Memorial Dr.
Tulsa, OK 74133
(918)250-9260
Ultimate Parent: Pennzoil. **SIC:** 7539—
Automotive Repair Shops Nec.

★ 77965 ★ **Jiffy Lube**
4702 S. Mingo Rd.
Tulsa, OK 74146
(918)664-9142
Ultimate Parent: Pennzoil. **SIC:** 7539—
Automotive Repair Shops Nec.

★ 77966 ★ **Jiffy Lube**
2726 S. Harvard Ave.
Tulsa, OK 74114
(918)743-4720
Ultimate Parent: Pennzoil. **SIC:** 5541—
Gasoline Service Stations; 7539—
Automotive Repair Shops Nec.

★ 77967 ★ **Jiffy Lube**
4157 S. Harvard Ave.
Tulsa, OK 74135
(918)742-7736
Ultimate Parent: Pennzoil. **SIC:** 7539—
Automotive Repair Shops Nec.

★ 77968 ★ **Jiffy Lube**
1102 S. Garnett Rd.
Tulsa, OK 74128
(918)437-3892
Ultimate Parent: Pennzoil. **SIC:** 7539—
Automotive Repair Shops Nec.

★ 77969 ★ **Johnson Controls Inc.**
822 E. 6th St.
Tulsa, OK 74120
(918)584-4120
Ultimate Parent: Johnson Controls Inc.
SIC: 7372—Prepackaged Software.

★ 77970 ★ **Kay Bee Toy & Hobby**
7021 S. Memorial Dr.
Tulsa, OK 74133
(918)250-8311
Ultimate Parent: Melville. **SIC:** 5945—
Hobby, Toy & Game Shops.

★ 77971 ★ **Kay Bee Toys**
4107 S. Yale Ave.
Tulsa, OK 74135
(918)665-3451
Ultimate Parent: Melville. **SIC:** 5945—
Hobby, Toy & Game Shops.

★ 77972 ★ **Kay Bee Toys**
14002 E. 21st St.
Tulsa, OK 74134
(918)234-6320
Ultimate Parent: Melville. **SIC:** 5945—
Hobby, Toy & Game Shops.

★ 77973 ★ **Kentucky Fried Chicken**
3120 S. Yale Ave.
Tulsa, OK 74135
(918)747-8706
Ultimate Parent: Pepsico. **SIC:** 5812—
Eating Places.

★ 77974 ★ **Kentucky Fried Chicken**
6006 S. Peoria Ave.
Tulsa, OK 74105
(918)749-3559
Ultimate Parent: Pepsico. **SIC:** 5812—
Eating Places.

★ 77975 ★ **Kentucky Fried Chicken**
4997 S. Union Ave.
Tulsa, OK 74107
(918)446-7309
Ultimate Parent: Pepsico. **SIC:** 5812—
Eating Places.

★ 77976 ★ **Kentucky Fried Chicken**
2124 S. Garnett Rd.
Tulsa, OK 74129
(918)437-6414
Ultimate Parent: Pepsico. **SIC:** 5812—
Eating Places.

★ 77977 ★ **Kentucky Fried Chicken**
7180 S. Memorial Dr.
Tulsa, OK 74133
(918)252-1476
Ultimate Parent: Pepsico. **SIC:** 5812—
Eating Places.

★ 77978 ★ **Kentucky Fried Chicken**
4707 N. Peoria Ave.
Tulsa, OK 74126
(918)425-6866
Ultimate Parent: Pepsico. **SIC:** 5812—
Eating Places.

★ 77979 ★ **Kentucky Fried Chicken**
1444 S. Denver Ave.
Tulsa, OK 74119
(918)585-9723
Ultimate Parent: Pepsico. **SIC:** 5812—
Eating Places.

★ 77980 ★ **Kentucky Fried Chicken**
7304 E. Admiral Pl
Tulsa, OK 74115
(918)835-9864
Ultimate Parent: Pepsico. **SIC:** 5812—
Eating Places.

★ 77981 ★ **Kentucky Fried Chicken**
1634 N. Lewis Ave.
Tulsa, OK 74110
(918)587-9556
Ultimate Parent: Pepsico. **SIC:** 5812—
Eating Places.

★ 77982 ★ **Kentucky Fried Chicken**
3616 E. 11th St.
Tulsa, OK 74112
(918)836-1311
Ultimate Parent: Pepsico. **SIC:** 5812—
Eating Places.

★ 77983 ★ **Kentucky Fried Chicken**
11104 E. 21st St.
Tulsa, OK 74129
(918)437-7696
Ultimate Parent: Pepsico. **SIC:** 5812—
Eating Places.

★ **77984** ★ **Kentucky Fried Chicken**
1530 E. 11th St.
Tulsa, OK 74120
(918)584-2103
Ultimate Parent: Pepsico. **SIC:** 5812—Eating Places.

★ **77985** ★ **Kids R US**
8143 E. 11th St.
Tulsa, OK 74112
(918)838-1666
Ultimate Parent: Toys "R" US. **SIC:** 8351—Child Day Care Services.

★ **77986** ★ **Kids R US**
8143 E. 11th St.
Tulsa, OK 74112
(918)838-1666
Ultimate Parent: Toys "R" US. **SIC:** 8351—Child Day Care Services.

★ **77987** ★ **Lane Bryant**
14002 E. 21st St.
Tulsa, OK 74134
(918)437-2870
Ultimate Parent: Limited. **SIC:** 5651—Family Clothing Stores.

★ **77988** ★ **Lane Bryant**
5103 S. Sheridan Rd. 400
Tulsa, OK 74145
Ultimate Parent: Limited. **SIC:** 5651—Family Clothing Stores.

★ **77989** ★ **Lens Crafters**
7021 S. Memorial Dr.
Tulsa, OK 74133
(918)250-1050
Ultimate Parent: United States Shoe.

★ **77990** ★ **Lerner Shop**
14002 E. 21st St.
Tulsa, OK 74134
(918)234-3130
Ultimate Parent: Limited. **SIC:** 5651—Family Clothing Stores.

★ **77991** ★ **Lerner Shop**
7021 S. Memorial Dr.
Tulsa, OK 74133
(918)250-0377
Ultimate Parent: Limited. **SIC:** 5651—Family Clothing Stores.

★ **77992** ★ **Lerner Shop**
4151 S. Yale Ave.
Tulsa, OK 74135
(918)627-0961
Ultimate Parent: Limited. **SIC:** 5621—Women's Clothing Stores.

★ **77993** ★ **The Limited**
238 Williams Ctr.
Tulsa, OK 74172
(918)585-3185
Ultimate Parent: Limited. **SIC:** 5611—Men's & Boys' Clothing Stores.

★ **77994** ★ **The Limited**
2016 Utica Sq.
Tulsa, OK 74114
(918)744-1840
Ultimate Parent: Limited. **SIC:** 5651—Family Clothing Stores.

★ **77995** ★ **The Limited**
7021 S. Memorial Dr.
Tulsa, OK 74133
(918)252-0424
Ultimate Parent: Limited. **SIC:** 5651—Family Clothing Stores.

★ **77996** ★ **The Limited**
4107 S. Yale Ave.
Tulsa, OK 74135
(918)622-5500
Ultimate Parent: Limited. **SIC:** 5651—Family Clothing Stores.

★ **77997** ★ **The Limited**
14002 E. 21st St.
Tulsa, OK 74134
(918)234-7535
Ultimate Parent: Limited. **SIC:** 5651—Family Clothing Stores.

★ **77998** ★ **The Limited Express**
14002 E. 21st St.
Tulsa, OK 74134
(918)234-3553
Ultimate Parent: Limited. **SIC:** 5651—Family Clothing Stores.

★ **77999** ★ **The Limited Express**
4107 S. Yale Ave.
Tulsa, OK 74135
(918)622-2442
Ultimate Parent: Limited. **SIC:** 5651—Family Clothing Stores.

★ **78000** ★ **The Limited Express**
7021 S. Memorial Dr.
Tulsa, OK 74133
(918)252-2279
Ultimate Parent: Limited. **SIC:** 5651—Family Clothing Stores.

★ **78001** ★ **Lone Star Gas Co.**
6846 S. Canton Ave.
Tulsa, OK 74136
(918)493-7027
Ultimate Parent: Enserch. **SIC:** 4925—Gas Production & Distribution Nec.

★ **78002** ★ **Lorillard Inc.**
4528 S. Sheridan Rd.
Tulsa, OK 74145
(918)662-7010
Ultimate Parent: Loews. **SIC:** 1521—Single-Family Housing Construction.

★ **78003** ★ **Lubrizol Corp.**
5200 S. Yale Ave.
Tulsa, OK 74135
(918)496-8170
Ultimate Parent: Lubrizol. **SIC:** 5199—Nondurable Goods Nec.

★ **78004** ★ **Magnetek**
6625 S. 70th E. Ave.
Tulsa, OK 74133-1853
(918)743-6213
Officer: Bill Christianson. **Ultimate Parent:** Magnetek Inc. **SIC:** 5063—Electrical Apparatus & Equipment; 3621—Motors & Generators.

★ **78005** ★ **Manpower, Inc.**
4500 S. Garnett Rd.
Tulsa, OK 74146
(918)622-8344
Ultimate Parent: Manpower, Inc. **SIC:** 7363—Help Supply Services.

★ **78006** ★ **Mapco**
1800 S. Baltimore Ave.
Tulsa, OK 74119
(918)581-1800
Company Type: Headquarters. **Officer:** James E. Barnes. **Sales:** 2715.3 M. **Fortune 500:** Largest U.S. Industrial Corporations: Ranking 173.

★ **78007** ★ **Mapco Coal Inc.**
1717 S. Boulder Ave.
Tulsa, OK 74119
(918)581-1800
Company Type: Subsidiary. **Officer:** Joseph w. Craft III, President. **Ultimate Parent:** Mapco. **SIC:** 1221—Bituminous Coal & Lignite—Surface.

★ **78008** ★ **Mapco Inc.**
PO Box 645
Tulsa, OK 74101
Company Type: Headquarters. **Ultimate Parent:** Mapco.

★ **78009** ★ **Mapco Inc.**
1800 S. Baltimore Ave.
Tulsa, OK 74119
(918)581-1800 **Fax:** (918)599-3634
Company Type: Headquarters. **Officer:** James E. Barnes, Chairman of the Board & CEO. **Ultimate Parent:** Mapco. **SIC:** 1321—Natural Gas Liquids; 1221—Bituminous Coal & Lignite—Surface; 4613—Refined Petroleum Pipelines; 2911—Petroleum Refining; 5984—Liquefied Petroleum Gas Dealers; 5172—Petroleum Products Nec; 1222—Bituminous Coal—Underground; 2875—Fertilizers—Mixing Only; 5541—Gasoline Service Stations.

★ **78010** ★ **Mapco Natural Gas Liquids Inc.**
1800 S. Baltimore Ave.
Tulsa, OK 74119
(918)581-1800
Company Type: Subsidiary. **Officer:** Robert G. Sachse, President. **Ultimate Parent:** Mapco. **SIC:** 4613—Refined Petroleum Pipelines; 4925—Gas Production & Distribution Nec; 0782—Lawn & Garden Services; 5171—Petroleum Bulk Stations & Terminals; 5984—Liquefied Petroleum Gas Dealers.

★ **78011** ★ **Mapco Petroleum Inc.**
1800 S. Baltimore Ave.
Tulsa, OK 74119
(918)581-1800
Company Type: Subsidiary. **Officer:** W. Jeffrey Hart, President. **Ultimate Parent:** Mapco. **SIC:** 2911—Petroleum Refining; 5171—Petroleum Bulk Stations & Terminals; 5541—Gasoline Service Stations.

★ **78012** ★ **Marshalls Inc.**
14002 E. 21st St.
Tulsa, OK 74134
(918)437-6556
Ultimate Parent: Melville.

★ **78013** ★ **Marshalls Incorporation**
6808 S. Memorial Dr.
Tulsa, OK 74133
(918)250-1777
Ultimate Parent: Melville. **SIC:** 5311—Department Stores.

★ **78014** ★ **Mary Kay Cosmetics**
4404 S. Gary Ave.
Tulsa, OK 74105
(918)743-1731
Ultimate Parent: Mary Kay Cosmetics.

★ **78015** ★ **Mary Kay Cosmetics**
3737 S. 124th Ave. E
Tulsa, OK 74146
(918)663-4790
Ultimate Parent: Mary Kay Cosmetics.

★ **78016** ★ **McDonalds Restaurant**
1406 E. 71st St.
Tulsa, OK 74136
(918)494-0242
Ultimate Parent: McDonald's.

★ **78017** ★ **McDonnell Douglas**
11333 E. Pine
Tulsa, OK 74115-3833
Ultimate Parent: McDonnell Douglas. **SIC:** 3721—Aircraft.

★ **78018** ★ **McDonnell Douglas**
Tulsa
2000 N. Memorial Dr.
Tulsa, OK 74115-3833
Company Type: Division. **Ultimate Parent:** McDonnell Douglas. **SIC:** 3721—Aircraft.

★ **78019** ★ **Meadow Gold Dairy Inc.**
215 N. Denver Ave.
Tulsa, OK 74101
Ultimate Parent: Borden, Inc. **SIC:** 2026—Fluid Milk.

★ **78020** ★ **Media Networks Inc.**
5545 E. Skelly Dr.
Tulsa, OK 74135
(918)663-7660
Ultimate Parent: Minnesota Mining & Mfg. **SIC:** 7313—Radio, T.V. & Publisher Representatives.

★ **78021** ★ **Meridian Securities**
4325 E. 51st St.
Tulsa, OK 74135
(918)492-1891
Ultimate Parent: Meridian Bancorp. **SIC:** 6211—Security Brokers & Dealers.

★ **78022** ★ **Mervyn's**
4103 S. Yale Ave.
Tulsa, OK 74135
(918)627-1800
Ultimate Parent: Dayton Hudson. **SIC:** 5311—Department Stores.

★ **78023** ★ **Mervyn's**
14002 E. 21st St.
Tulsa, OK 74134
(918)438-8800
Ultimate Parent: Dayton Hudson. **SIC:** 5311—Department Stores.

★ **78024** ★ **Microsource**
4305-B South Mingo
Tulsa, OK 74146
(918)664-9696
Ultimate Parent: MicroAge.

★ **78025** ★ **Mid-Continent Casualty Co.**
1646 S. Boulder
Tulsa, OK 74119
(918)587-7221
Company Type: Subsidiary. **Officer:** J.L. Pierce, President & Chief Executive Officer.

Ultimate Parent: American Financial. **SIC:** 6331—Fire, Marine & Casualty Insurance; 6399—Insurance Carriers Nec. **Employee Count:** 240. **Sales:** 81361000 M.

★ **78026** ★ **Mirex Corp.**
1919 N. Garnett Rd.
Tulsa, OK 74116
(918)438-7000
Officer: Mike Monroe, Manager. **Ultimate Parent:** Alco Standard Corp. **SIC:** 3663—Radio & T.V. Communications Equipment.

★ **78027** ★ **Molex Inc.**
8015 S. Quebec Ave.
Tulsa, OK 74136
(918)496-0302
Ultimate Parent: Molex.

★ **78028** ★ **Nalco Chemical Co. Inc.**
7030 S. Yale Ave.
Tulsa, OK 74136
(918)494-3620
Ultimate Parent: Nalco Chemical Co. **SIC:** 4941—Water Supply; 5169—Chemicals & Allied Products Nec.

★ **78029** ★ **Ncr Corp.**
3407 S. 79th Ave. E
Tulsa, OK 74145
(918)622-4551
Ultimate Parent: AT&T. **SIC:** 5046—Commercial Equipment Nec.

★ **78030** ★ **Nelson Electric**
4041 S. Sheridan
Tulsa, OK 74035
Ultimate Parent: General Signal. **SIC:** 3613—Switchgear & Switchboard Apparatus; 3470—Metal Services Nec.

★ **78031** ★ **New England Mutual Life Insurance**
8023 E. 63rd Pl
Tulsa, OK 74133
(918)250-7591
Ultimate Parent: New England Mutual Life. **SIC:** 6411—Insurance Agents, Brokers & Service.

★ **78032** ★ **New York Life Tulsa General Office**
Western Agencies
100 W. 5th St., Ste. 700
Tulsa, OK 74103
(918)587-3301 **Fax:** (918)581-8803
Officer: Marc Ham, General Manager. **Ultimate Parent:** New York Life.

★ **78033** ★ **Norris & O'Bannon**
4615 S. 49th W. Ave.
Tulsa, OK 74107
(918)446-2610
Officer: Jim Mitchel, President. **Ultimate Parent:** Dover Corp. **SIC:** 3533—Oil & Gas Field Machinery.

★ **78034** ★ **Norwest Mortgage Inc.**
7666 E. 61st St.
Tulsa, OK 74133
(918)254-6526
Ultimate Parent: Norwest Corp. **SIC:** 6162—Mortgage Bankers & Correspondents.

★ **78035** ★ **Occidental Oil & Gas Corp.**
110 W. 7th St.
Tulsa, OK 74119
(918)561-2211
Officer: David R. Martin, President, CEO & COO. **Ultimate Parent:** Occidental Petroleum Corp.

★ **78036** ★ **Ogden Project Inc.**
2122 S. Yukon Ave.
Tulsa, OK 74107
(918)583-2553
Ultimate Parent: Ogden. **SIC:** 5211—Lumber & Other Building Materials.

★ **78037** ★ **Otis Elevator Co.**
1725 S. Main St.
Tulsa, OK 74119
Ultimate Parent: United Technologies. **SIC:** 3534—Elevators & Moving Stairways; 8711—Engineering Services.

★ 78038 ★ **Owens Corning Fiberglass**
6558 E. 42nd St.
Tulsa, OK 74145
(918)627-1220
Ultimate Parent: Owens-Corning. **SIC:** 5039—Construction Materials Nec.

★ 78039 ★ **OXY USA Inc.**
110 W. 7th St.
Tulsa, OK 74119
(918)561-2211 **Fax:** (918)561-8112
Officer: James R. Niehaus, Chairman of the Board & CEO. **Ultimate Parent:** Occidental Petroleum Corp.

★ 78040 ★ **PacifiCare of Oklahoma**
7134 S. Yale St., Ste. 700
Tulsa, OK 74136
(918)496-1200 **Fax:** (918)494-7062
Officer: David Kibbe, President. **Ultimate Parent:** Pacificare Health Systems.

★ 78041 ★ **Payless Cashways**
231 S. Memorial Dr.
Tulsa, OK 74112
(918)832-7000
Ultimate Parent: Payless Cashways. **SIC:** 5039—Construction Materials Nec.

★ 78042 ★ **Payless Cashways Building M**
8160 E. 41st St.
Tulsa, OK 74145
(918)664-6142
Ultimate Parent: Payless Cashways. **SIC:** 5039—Construction Materials Nec; 5211—Lumber & Other Building Materials.

★ 78043 ★ **Payless Cashways Inc.**
5732 S. 49th Ave. W
Tulsa, OK 74107
(918)445-1156
Ultimate Parent: Payless Cashways. **SIC:** 5211—Lumber & Other Building Materials.

★ 78044 ★ **Payless Shoesource**
7134 S. Memorial Dr.
Tulsa, OK 74133
(918)252-1929
Ultimate Parent: May Department Stores. **SIC:** 5661—Shoe Stores.

★ 78045 ★ **Payless Shoesource**
4107 S. Yale Ave.
Tulsa, OK 74135
(918)664-2946
Ultimate Parent: May Department Stores.

★ 78046 ★ **Payless Shoesource**
2319 W. Edison St.
Tulsa, OK 74127
(918)584-2199
Ultimate Parent: May Department Stores. **SIC:** 5661—Shoe Stores.

★ 78047 ★ **Payless Shoesource**
7021 S. Memorial Dr.
Tulsa, OK 74133
(918)252-1058
Ultimate Parent: May Department Stores.

★ 78048 ★ **Payless Shoesource**
5620 W. Skelly Dr.
Tulsa, OK 74107
(918)446-9404
Ultimate Parent: May Department Stores. **SIC:** 5661—Shoe Stores.

★ 78049 ★ **Payless Shoesource**
5210 N. Peoria Ave.
Tulsa, OK 74126
(918)425-5258
Ultimate Parent: May Department Stores. **SIC:** 5661—Shoe Stores.

★ 78050 ★ **Payless Shoesource**
2175 S. Sheridan Rd.
Tulsa, OK 74129
(918)836-2491
Ultimate Parent: May Department Stores. **SIC:** 5661—Shoe Stores.

★ 78051 ★ **Payless Shoesource**
7301 E. Admiral Pl.
Tulsa, OK 74115
(918)835-9793
Ultimate Parent: May Department Stores. **SIC:** 5661—Shoe Stores.

★ 78052 ★ **Payless Shoesource**
14002 E. 21st St.
Tulsa, OK 74134
(918)438-7488
Ultimate Parent: May Department Stores. **SIC:** 5661—Shoe Stores.

★ 78053 ★ **Payless Shoesource**
11517 E. 31st Pl.
Tulsa, OK 74146
(918)628-0790
Ultimate Parent: May Department Stores. **SIC:** 5661—Shoe Stores.

★ 78054 ★ **Pentastar Transportation Group Inc.**
5330 E. 31st St.
Tulsa, OK 74135-5063
(918)660-7700
Company Type: Subsidiary. **Officer:** Bennett Bidwell, Chairman of the Board. **Ultimate Parent:** Chrysler Corp. **SIC:** 7514—Passenger Car Rental. **Employee Count:** 4200. **Sales:** 524 M.

★ 78055 ★ **Pepsi-Cola Bottling Co.**
510 W. Skelly Dr.
Tulsa, OK 74107
(918)496-1200 **Fax:** (918)494-7062
Ultimate Parent: Pepsico. **SIC:** 2086—Bottled & Canned Soft Drinks.

★ 78056 ★ **Perkin Elmer Corp. Inc.**
3810 E. 103rd St.
Tulsa, OK 74137
(918)664-7161
Ultimate Parent: Perkin-Elmer. **SIC:** 5046—Commercial Equipment Nec.

★ 78057 ★ **Pitney Bowes**
3158 S. 108th E. Ave., Ste. 255
Tulsa, OK 74146
(918)663-0050
Ultimate Parent: Pitney Bowes. **SIC:** 3663—Radio & T.V. Communications Equipment.

★ 78058 ★ **Pizza Hut**
1924 S. Utica Ave.
Tulsa, OK 74104
(918)749-5041
Ultimate Parent: Pepsico. **SIC:** 5812—Eating Places.

★ 78059 ★ **Pizza Hut**
1907 S. Harvard Ave.
Tulsa, OK 74112
(918)743-7999
Ultimate Parent: Pepsico.

★ 78060 ★ **Pizza Hut**
5111 S. Harvard Ave.
Tulsa, OK 74135
(918)742-7046
Ultimate Parent: Pepsico. **SIC:** 5812—Eating Places.

★ 78061 ★ **Pizza Hut**
7404 E. Admiral Pl
Tulsa, OK 74115
(918)836-8171
Ultimate Parent: Pepsico. **SIC:** 5812—Eating Places.

★ 78062 ★ **Pizza Hut**
2313 E. 71st St.
Tulsa, OK 74136
(918)494-0219
Ultimate Parent: Pepsico. **SIC:** 5812—Eating Places.

★ 78063 ★ **Pizza Hut**
5555 E. 71st St. 8300
Tulsa, OK 74136
(918)446-8110
Ultimate Parent: Pepsico. **SIC:** 5812—Eating Places.

★ 78064 ★ **Pizza Hut**
11118 E. 21st St.
Tulsa, OK 74129
(918)437-7560
Ultimate Parent: Pepsico. **SIC:** 5812—Eating Places.

★ 78065 ★ **Pizza Hut**
9747 E. 31st St.
Tulsa, OK 74146
(918)628-1395
Ultimate Parent: Pepsico. **SIC:** 5812—Eating Places.

★ 78066 ★ **Pizza Hut**
7994 S. Sheridan Rd.
Tulsa, OK 74133
(918)496-2929
Ultimate Parent: Pepsico.

★ 78067 ★ **Pizza Hut**
4840 S. Memorial Dr.
Tulsa, OK 74145
(918)664-2233
Ultimate Parent: Pepsico. **SIC:** 5812—Eating Places.

★ 78068 ★ **Pizza Hut**
1502 S. Peoria Ave.
Tulsa, OK 74120
(918)584-6049
Ultimate Parent: Pepsico. **SIC:** 5812—Eating Places.

★ 78069 ★ **Pizza Hut District Office**
2121 S. Columbia Ave.
Tulsa, OK 74114
(918)744-0015
Ultimate Parent: Pepsico. **SIC:** 5812—Eating Places.

★ 78070 ★ **Public Service Co. of Oklahoma**
212 E. 6th St.
Tulsa, OK 74119
(918)599-2000 **Fax:** (918)599-2881
Officer: Robert L. Zemanek, President & CEO. **Ultimate Parent:** Central & South West.

★ 78071 ★ **Quarles Drilling & Exploration, Inc.**
7633 E. 63rd Pl., Ste. 500
Tulsa, OK 74103
(918)250-0515
Company Type: Division. **Officer:** D. B. Quarles, President. **Ultimate Parent:** CBI Industries, Inc. **SIC:** 1381—Drilling Oil & Gas Wells. **Employee Count:** 100.

★ 78072 ★ **Radio Shack**
5333 S. Mingo Rd.
Tulsa, OK 74146
(918)627-3303
Company Type: Division. **Ultimate Parent:** Tandy Corp. **SIC:** 7378—Computer Maintenance & Repair.

★ 78073 ★ **Radio Shack**
4528 S. Sheridan Rd.
Tulsa, OK 74145
(918)628-1876
Company Type: Division. **Ultimate Parent:** Tandy Corp. **SIC:** 5731—Radio, Television & Electronics Stores.

★ 78074 ★ **Radio Shack**
7021 S. Memorial Dr.
Tulsa, OK 74133
(918)252-7925
Company Type: Division. **Ultimate Parent:** Tandy Corp. **SIC:** 5065—Electronic Parts & Equipment Nec.

★ 78075 ★ **Radio Shack**
7810 E. Admiral Pl
Tulsa, OK 74115
(918)832-1642
Company Type: Division. **Ultimate Parent:** Tandy Corp. **SIC:** 5065—Electronic Parts & Equipment Nec.

★ 78076 ★ **Radio Shack**
1 Williams Ctr.
Tulsa, OK 74101
(918)592-0852
Company Type: Division. **Ultimate Parent:** Tandy Corp. **SIC:** 5731—Radio, Television & Electronics Stores.

★ 78077 ★ **Radio Shack**
4107 S. Yale Ave.
Tulsa, OK 74135
(918)664-0986
Company Type: Division. **Ultimate Parent:** Tandy Corp. **SIC:** 5731—Radio, Television & Electronics Stores.

★ 78078 ★ **Radio Shack**
5630 W. Skelly Dr.
Tulsa, OK 74107
(918)446-3646
Company Type: Division. **Ultimate Parent:** Tandy Corp. **SIC:** 5065—Electronic Parts & Equipment Nec; 5731—Radio, Television & Electronics Stores.

★ 78079 ★ **Radio Shack**
4528 S. Sheridan Rd. 223
Tulsa, OK 74145
Company Type: Division. **Ultimate Parent:** Tandy Corp. **SIC:** 5065—Electronic Parts & Equipment Nec.

★ 78080 ★ **Radio Shack**
5014 S. Sheridan Rd.
Tulsa, OK 74145
(918)627-3620
Company Type: Division. **Ultimate Parent:** Tandy Corp. **SIC:** 5065—Electronic Parts & Equipment Nec; 5731—Radio, Television & Electronics Stores.

★ 78081 ★ **Radio Shack**
15 S. Sheridan Rd.
Tulsa, OK 74112
(918)836-3718
Company Type: Division. **Ultimate Parent:** Tandy Corp. **SIC:** 5065—Electronic Parts & Equipment Nec.

★ 78082 ★ **Radio Shack**
3059 S. Sheridan Rd.
Tulsa, OK 74129
(918)664-6454
Company Type: Division. **Ultimate Parent:** Tandy Corp. **SIC:** 5065—Electronic Parts & Equipment Nec.

★ 78083 ★ **Radio Shack**
2605 S. Memorial Dr.
Tulsa, OK 74129
(918)663-7179
Company Type: Division. **Ultimate Parent:** Tandy Corp. **SIC:** 5065—Electronic Parts & Equipment Nec; 5731—Radio, Television & Electronics Stores.

★ 78084 ★ **Radio Shack**
4965 S. Peoria Ave.
Tulsa, OK 74105
(918)743-4802
Company Type: Division. **Ultimate Parent:** Tandy Corp. **SIC:** 5065—Electronic Parts & Equipment Nec.

★ 78085 ★ **Radio Shack**
2730 S. Harvard Ave.
Tulsa, OK 74114
(918)742-5553
Company Type: Division. **Ultimate Parent:** Tandy Corp. **SIC:** 5065—Electronic Parts & Equipment Nec.

★ 78086 ★ **Radio Shack**
6950 S. Lewis Ave.
Tulsa, OK 74136
(918)744-0270
Company Type: Division. **Ultimate Parent:** Tandy Corp. **SIC:** 5065—Electronic Parts & Equipment Nec; 5731—Radio, Television & Electronics Stores.

★ 78087 ★ **Radio Shack**
6104 E. 71st St.
Tulsa, OK 74136
(918)494-7014
Company Type: Division. **Ultimate Parent:** Tandy Corp. **SIC:** 5063—Electrical Apparatus & Equipment.

★ 78088 ★ **Radio Shack**
10105 E. Admiral Pl
Tulsa, OK 74116
(918)834-6147
Company Type: Division. **Ultimate Parent:** Tandy Corp.

★ 78089 ★ **Radio Shack**
7218 E. 41st St.
Tulsa, OK 74145
(918)663-2190
Company Type: Division. **Ultimate Parent:** Tandy Corp. **SIC:** 5046—Commercial Equipment Nec.

★ 78090 ★ **Radio Shack**
3318 E. 51st St.
Tulsa, OK 74135
(918)749-3849
Company Type: Division. **Ultimate Parent:** Tandy Corp. **SIC:** 5731—Radio, Television & Electronics Stores.

★ 78091 ★ **Radio Shack**
7 E. 2nd St.
Tulsa, OK 74103
(918)592-0852
Company Type: Division. **Ultimate Parent:** Tandy Corp. **SIC:** 5065—Electronic Parts & Equipment Nec.

★ **78092** ★ **Radio Shack**
11613 E. 31st St.
Tulsa, OK 74146
(918)663-1933
Company Type: Division. **Ultimate Parent:** Tandy Corp. **SIC:** 5065—Electronic Parts & Equipment Nec.

★ **78093** ★ **Radio Shack**
14002 E. 21st St.
Tulsa, OK 74134
(918)437-3911
Company Type: Division. **Ultimate Parent:** Tandy Corp. **SIC:** 5731—Radio, Television & Electronics Stores.

★ **78094** ★ **Rockwell International**
2000 N. Memorial Dr.
Tulsa, OK 74115
Ultimate Parent: Rockwell International Corp. **SIC:** 3728—Aircraft Parts & Equipment Nec; 3769—Space Vehicle Equipment Nec.

★ **78095** ★ **Ryder Truck Rental**
5116 S. Sheridan Rd.
Tulsa, OK 74145
(918)665-3035
Ultimate Parent: Ryder System. **SIC:** 7513—Truck Rental & Leasing Without Drivers.

★ **78096** ★ **Ryder Truck Rental**
1823 W. 51st St.
Tulsa, OK 74107
(918)446-1495
Ultimate Parent: Ryder System. **SIC:** 7519—Utility Trailer Rental.

★ **78097** ★ **Ryder Truck Rental**
3232 E. Admiral Pl
Tulsa, OK 74110
(918)587-2501
Ultimate Parent: Ryder System. **SIC:** 7359—Equipment Rental & Leasing Nec.

★ **78098** ★ **Ryder Truck Rental**
6041 S. Peoria Ave.
Tulsa, OK 74105
(918)743-7799
Ultimate Parent: Ryder System. **SIC:** 7513—Truck Rental & Leasing Without Drivers.

★ **78099** ★ **Ryder Truck Rental**
4999 S. Union Ave.
Tulsa, OK 74107
(918)446-4207
Ultimate Parent: Ryder System. **SIC:** 7513—Truck Rental & Leasing Without Drivers.

★ **78100** ★ **Ryder Truck Rental**
7630 E. 42nd Pl
Tulsa, OK 74145
(918)665-3717
Ultimate Parent: Ryder System. **SIC:** 5113—Industrial & Personal Service Paper; 7513—Truck Rental & Leasing Without Drivers.

★ **78101** ★ **Ryder Truck Rental**
10525 E. Pine St.
Tulsa, OK 74116
(918)836-0391
Ultimate Parent: Ryder System. **SIC:** 7359—Equipment Rental & Leasing Nec; 7513—Truck Rental & Leasing Without Drivers.

★ **78102** ★ **Ryder Truck Rental**
5681 S. Mingo Rd.
Tulsa, OK 74146
(918)254-6210
Ultimate Parent: Ryder System.

★ **78103** ★ **Sam's Wholesale Club**
4400 S. Sheridan Rd.
Tulsa, OK 74145
(918)627-1441
Ultimate Parent: Wal-Mart Stores, Inc. **SIC:** 5099—Durable Goods Nec.

★ **78104** ★ **Schwab Charles & Co. Inc.**
1 Williams Ctr.
Tulsa, OK 74101
(918)585-3122
Ultimate Parent: Charles Schwab Corp. **SIC:** 6211—Security Brokers & Dealers.

★ **78105** ★ **Scoot-Rice Co. Inc.**
5100 E. Skelly Dr., Ste. 700
Tulsa, OK 74135-6500
(918)628-1400
Company Type: Subsidiary. **Officer:** Ray G. Jones, President. **Ultimate Parent:** Hanson Industries. **SIC:** 5021—Furniture; 5943—Stationery Stores; 5112—Stationery & Office Supplies. **Employee Count:** 360. **Sales:** 67 M.

★ **78106** ★ **Security Pacific Financial Services Inc.**
8023 E. 63rd Pl.
Tulsa, OK 74133-1209
(918)250-3550
Officer: Kevin Highland. **Ultimate Parent:** Bankamerica Corp. **SIC:** 6141—Personal Credit Institutions; 6162—Mortgage Bankers & Correspondents.

★ **78107** ★ **Seiscor Tech. Inc.**
5311 S. 122nd East Ave.
Tulsa, OK 74145
Ultimate Parent: Raytheon Co. **SIC:** 3661—Telephone & Telegraph Apparatus.

★ **78108** ★ **Sekin Transport International**
1835 N. 106th Ave. E
Tulsa, OK 74116
(918)836-6597
Ultimate Parent: Harsco. **SIC:** 4731—Freight Transportation Arrangement.

★ **78109** ★ **Service Merchandise**
1750 S. Sheridan Rd.
Tulsa, OK 74112
(918)836-7692
Ultimate Parent: Service Merchandise Co., Inc. **SIC:** 5399—Miscellaneous General Merchandise Store; 5944—Jewelry Stores.

★ **78110** ★ **Service Merchandise**
14002 E. 21st St.
Tulsa, OK 74134
(918)438-2300
Ultimate Parent: Service Merchandise Co., Inc. **SIC:** 5311—Department Stores.

★ **78111** ★ **Seven-Up Royal Crown Cola**
3248 N. Sheridan Rd.
Tulsa, OK 74115
(918)835-6906
Officer: Leo Frankel, President. **Ultimate Parent:** Dr. Pepper/Seven-Up. **SIC:** 2086—Bottled & Canned Soft Drinks.

★ **78112** ★ **Shell Oil Co.**
6502 S. Yale Ave.
Tulsa, OK 74136
(918)496-4000
Officer: D. D. Dunlap, Vice President. **Ultimate Parent:** Shell Oil. **SIC:** 2911—Petroleum Refining.

★ **78113** ★ **Snappy Car Rental Inc.**
5330 E. 31st St.
Tulsa, OK 74135-5063
(918)660-7700
Company Type: Subsidiary. **Officer:** Richard Titterud, President. **Ultimate Parent:** Chrysler Corp. **SIC:** 7514—Passenger Car Rental. **Employee Count:** 1150. **Sales:** 86 M.

★ **78114** ★ **Southwest Airlines Co.**
7777 Tulsa International Airport
Tulsa, OK 74115
(918)836-0750
Ultimate Parent: Southwest Airlines. **SIC:** 4512—Air Transportation—Scheduled.

★ **78115** ★ **Southwestern Bell Yellow Pages**
10159 E. 11th St.
Tulsa, OK 74128
(918)835-8600
Ultimate Parent: Southwestern Bell. **SIC:** 7313—Radio, T.V. & Publisher Representatives.

★ **78116** ★ **Sun Microsystems Inc.**
3015 E. Skelly Dr.
Tulsa, OK 74105
(918)742-4470
Ultimate Parent: Sun Microsystems Inc. **SIC:** 7373—Computer Integrated Systems Design.

★ **78117** ★ **Sun Refining & Marketing**
907 S. Detroit Ave.
Tulsa, OK 74120
(918)586-6711
Officer: Joseph C. Swift, President. **Ultimate Parent:** Sun. **SIC:** 2911—Petroleum Refining.

★ **78118** ★ **Sun Refining & Marketing Co.**
2039 PO Box
Tulsa, OK 74102
Ultimate Parent: Sun. **SIC:** 2911—Petroleum Refining.

★ **78119** ★ **Sun Refining & Marketing Co.**
907 S. Detroit Ave.
Tulsa, OK 74120
(918)586-7321
Ultimate Parent: Sun. **SIC:** 2911—Petroleum Refining.

★ **78120** ★ **Super Saver Station**
12502 E. 21st St.
Tulsa, OK 74129
(918)438-2525
Ultimate Parent: Wal-Mart Stores, Inc. **SIC:** 5251—Hardware Stores.

★ **78121** ★ **T J Maxx Store**
8228 E. 61st St.
Tulsa, OK 74133
(918)250-1993
Ultimate Parent: TJX. **SIC:** 5651—Family Clothing Stores.

★ **78122** ★ **Taco Bell**
3118 E. 11th St.
Tulsa, OK 74104
Ultimate Parent: Pepsico. **SIC:** 5812—Eating Places.

★ **78123** ★ **Taco Bell**
2157 S. Sheridan Rd.
Tulsa, OK 74129
(918)838-8724
Ultimate Parent: Pepsico. **SIC:** 5812—Eating Places.

★ **78124** ★ **Taco Bell**
7021 S. Memorial Dr.
Tulsa, OK 74133
(918)254-5467
Ultimate Parent: Pepsico.

★ **78125** ★ **Taco Bell**
4909 S. Peoria Ave.
Tulsa, OK 74105
(918)742-0090
Ultimate Parent: Pepsico. **SIC:** 5812—Eating Places.

★ **78126** ★ **Taco Bell**
7810 E. Admiral Pl
Tulsa, OK 74115
(918)835-4802
Ultimate Parent: Pepsico. **SIC:** 5812—Eating Places.

★ **78127** ★ **Taco Bell**
1738 S. Garnett Rd.
Tulsa, OK 74128
(918)437-8525
Ultimate Parent: Pepsico. **SIC:** 5812—Eating Places.

★ **78128** ★ **Taco Bell**
4703 E. 51st St.
Tulsa, OK 74135
(918)481-5238
Ultimate Parent: Pepsico.

★ **78129** ★ **Taco Bell**
8109 E. 74th Pl
Tulsa, OK 74133
(918)254-6652
Ultimate Parent: Pepsico.

★ **78130** ★ **Tandy**
7218 E. 41st St.
Tulsa, OK 74145
(918)663-2190
Ultimate Parent: Tandy Corp.

★ **78131** ★ **Tandy Consumer Products Ser**
11513 E. 58th St.
Tulsa, OK 74146
(918)252-3519
Ultimate Parent: Tandy Corp. **SIC:** 5731—Radio, Television & Electronics Stores.

★ **78132** ★ **Target Stores**
7178 S. Memorial Dr.
Tulsa, OK 74133
(918)252-1621
Ultimate Parent: Dayton Hudson. **SIC:** 5311—Department Stores.

★ **78133** ★ **Target Stores**
1701 S. Yale Ave.
Tulsa, OK 74112
(918)744-1701
Company Type: Subsidiary. **Ultimate Parent:** Dauphin Deposit Corp. **SIC:** 5311—Department Stores.

★ **78134** ★ **Teradata**
10810 E. 45th St.
Tulsa, OK 74146-3801
(918)660-0900
Ultimate Parent: AT&T. **SIC:** 5045—Computers, Peripherals & Software.

★ **78135** ★ **Terex Corp.**
5400 S. 49th West Ave.
Tulsa, OK 74107
(918)446-5581 **Fax:** (918)446-0621
Company Type: Subsidiary. **Officer:** Rob Giebel, President. **Ultimate Parent:** Terex Corp. **SIC:** 3532—Mining Machinery.

★ **78136** ★ **Terex Corp.**
Terex Unit Rig
5400 S. 49th West Ave.
Tulsa, OK 74107
(918)446-5581 **Fax:** (918)446-0621
Company Type: Subsidiary. **Officer:** Rob Giebel, President. **Ultimate Parent:** Terex Corp. **SIC:** 3532—Mining Machinery.

★ **78137** ★ **Texaco**
5736 E. 41st St.
Tulsa, OK 74135
(918)665-1236
Ultimate Parent: Texaco. **SIC:** 5541—Gasoline Service Stations.

★ **78138** ★ **Texaco**
3204 W. 45th St.
Tulsa, OK 74107
(918)446-0274
Ultimate Parent: Texaco. **SIC:** 5541—Gasoline Service Stations.

★ **78139** ★ **Texaco**
6506 E. 101st St.
Tulsa, OK 74133
(918)299-1625
Ultimate Parent: Texaco. **SIC:** 5541—Gasoline Service Stations.

★ **78140** ★ **Texaco**
2030 E. 21st St.
Tulsa, OK 74114
(918)742-6812
Ultimate Parent: Texaco. **SIC:** 5541—Gasoline Service Stations.

★ **78141** ★ **Texaco Food Mart**
6051 S. Garnett Rd.
Tulsa, OK 74146
(918)250-8897
Ultimate Parent: Texaco.

★ **78142** ★ **Texaco Food Mart**
3025 S. Memorial Dr.
Tulsa, OK 74129
(918)622-8310
Ultimate Parent: Texaco. **SIC:** 5541—Gasoline Service Stations.

★ **78143** ★ **Texaco-Food Mart**
3105 S. Garnett Rd.
Tulsa, OK 74146
(918)663-7691
Ultimate Parent: Texaco. **SIC:** 5411—Grocery Stores.

★ **78144** ★ **Texaco Food Mart 160**
2109 S. Sheridan Rd.
Tulsa, OK 74129
(918)834-9709
Ultimate Parent: Texaco. **SIC:** 5411—Grocery Stores; 5541—Gasoline Service Stations.

★ **78145** ★ **Texaco Gass Barr**
7102 S. Memorial Dr.
Tulsa, OK 74133
(918)252-0966
Ultimate Parent: Texaco. **SIC:** 5541—Gasoline Service Stations.

★ 78146 ★   Texaco Incorporated
9101 S. Memorial Dr.
Tulsa, OK 74133
(918)250-8977
Ultimate Parent: Texaco. SIC: 5541—
Gasoline Service Stations.

★ 78147 ★   Texaco Inc.
104 S. Utica Ave.
Tulsa, OK 74104
(918)582-1723
Ultimate Parent: Texaco. SIC: 5541—
Gasoline Service Stations.

★ 78148 ★   Texaco Inc.
1307 W. 35th St.
Tulsa, OK 74107
(918)446-6121
Ultimate Parent: Texaco. SIC: 5172—
Petroleum Products Nec.

★ 78149 ★   Texaco Inc.
2424 E. 21st St.
Tulsa, OK 74114
(918)743-5311
Ultimate Parent: Texaco. SIC: 1382—Oil &
Gas Exploration Services.

★ 78150 ★   Texaco Inc.
8108 S. Harvard Ave.
Tulsa, OK 74137
(918)481-0313
Ultimate Parent: Texaco. SIC: 5541—
Gasoline Service Stations.

★ 78151 ★   Texaco Inc. (Ofc)
7063 E. 38th St.
Tulsa, OK 74145
(918)560-6098
Ultimate Parent: Texaco. SIC: 5172—
Petroleum Products Nec.

★ 78152 ★   Texaco Mart
1603 S. Peoria Ave.
Tulsa, OK 74120
(918)582-9303
Ultimate Parent: Texaco. SIC: 5411—
Grocery Stores.

★ 78153 ★   Texaco Mini Mart
9601 E. 21st St.
Tulsa, OK 74129
(918)664-4628
Ultimate Parent: Texaco. SIC: 5541—
Gasoline Service Stations.

★ 78154 ★   Texaco Self Serv Sta
6060 S. Yale Ave.
Tulsa, OK 74135
(918)493-6193
Ultimate Parent: Texaco. SIC: 5541—
Gasoline Service Stations.

★ 78155 ★   Texaco Self Service
Center
4970 S. Harvard Ave.
Tulsa, OK 74135
(918)749-4281
Ultimate Parent: Texaco. SIC: 5541—
Gasoline Service Stations.

★ 78156 ★   Texaco Self Service
Station
1437 S. Boulder Ave.
Tulsa, OK 74119
(918)481-0334
Ultimate Parent: Texaco. SIC: 5541—
Gasoline Service Stations.

★ 78157 ★   Texaco Self Service
Station
12909 E. 21st St.
Tulsa, OK 74134
(918)437-0343
Ultimate Parent: Texaco. SIC: 5541—
Gasoline Service Stations.

★ 78158 ★   Texaco Service
Station
1506 S. Main St.
Tulsa, OK 74119
(918)583-6462
Ultimate Parent: Texaco. SIC: 5541—
Gasoline Service Stations.

★ 78159 ★   Texaco Service
Station
1747 S. Memorial Dr.
Tulsa, OK 74112
(918)663-3485
Ultimate Parent: Texaco. SIC: 5541—
Gasoline Service Stations.

★ 78160 ★   Texaco Service
Station
5 N. Yale Ave.
Tulsa, OK 74115
(918)838-8697
Ultimate Parent: Texaco. SIC: 5541—
Gasoline Service Stations.

★ 78161 ★   Texaco Service
Station
5419 S. Harvard Ave.
Tulsa, OK 74135
(918)743-8767
Ultimate Parent: Texaco. SIC: 5541—
Gasoline Service Stations.

★ 78162 ★   Texaco Service
Station
9606 E. 71st St.
Tulsa, OK 74133
(918)254-9012
Ultimate Parent: Texaco. SIC: 5541—
Gasoline Service Stations.

★ 78163 ★   Texaco Service
Station
4548 N. Peoria Ave.
Tulsa, OK 74106
(918)425-1948
Ultimate Parent: Texaco. SIC: 5541—
Gasoline Service Stations.

★ 78164 ★   Texaco Service
Station No 2
5048 S. Sheridan Rd.
Tulsa, OK 74145
(918)664-9931
Ultimate Parent: Texaco. SIC: 5541—
Gasoline Service Stations.

★ 78165 ★   Thomas & Betts Co.
9932 E. 58th St.
Tulsa, OK 74146
Ultimate Parent: Thomas & Betts. SIC:
3643—Current-Carrying Wiring Devices;
3644—Noncurrent-Carrying Wiring Devices.

★ 78166 ★   Thomas & Betts Corp.
9932 E. 58th St. S.
Tulsa, OK 74146
Ultimate Parent: Thomas & Betts. SIC:
3643—Current-Carrying Wiring Devices;
3644—Noncurrent-Carrying Wiring Devices.

★ 78167 ★   Thrifty Rent-A-Car
System Inc.
5330 E. 31st St., Ste. 100
Tulsa, OK 74135-5063
(918)665-3930
Company Type: Subsidiary. Officer: James
R. Philion, Chairman of the Board. Ultimate
Parent: Chrysler Corp. SIC: 6794—Patent
Owners & Lessors; 7515—Passenger Car
Leasing; 7514—Passenger Car Rental;
7513—Truck Rental & Leasing Without
Drivers. Employee Count: 859. Sales: 180
M.

★ 78168 ★   Thrifty Rent a Car
Systems, Inc.
4600 S. Garnett Rd.
Tulsa, OK 74146
(918)665-3930
Ultimate Parent: Chrysler Corp. SIC:
7514—Passenger Car Rental.

★ 78169 ★   Thrifty Rent a Car
Systems, Inc.
3302 E. 51st St.
Tulsa, OK 74135
(918)496-2224
Ultimate Parent: Chrysler Corp. SIC:
7514—Passenger Car Rental.

★ 78170 ★   Thrifty Rent a Car
Systems, Inc.
4867 S. Sheridan Rd.
Tulsa, OK 74145
(918)664-8844
Ultimate Parent: Chrysler Corp. SIC:
7514—Passenger Car Rental.

★ 78171 ★   Torrington Co
9717 E. 42nd St.
Tulsa, OK 74146
(918)627-6133
Ultimate Parent: Ingersoll-Rand. SIC:
5085—Industrial Supplies.

★ 78172 ★   Total Petroleum Inc.
11331 E. 20th St.
Tulsa, OK 74128
(918)438-1896
Ultimate Parent: Total Petroleum Inc. SIC:
5541—Gasoline Service Stations.

★ 78173 ★   Total Petroleum Inc.
8196 E. 46th St.
Tulsa, OK 74145
(918)627-5577
Ultimate Parent: Total Petroleum Inc.

★ 78174 ★   Total Petroleum Inc.
11331 E. 20th St.
Tulsa, OK 74128
(918)438-1896
Ultimate Parent: Total Petroleum Inc. SIC:
5541—Gasoline Service Stations.

★ 78175 ★   Total Petroleum Inc.
8196 E. 46th St.
Tulsa, OK 74145
(918)627-5577
Ultimate Parent: Total Petroleum Inc.

★ 78176 ★   Toys R US
6910 S. Memorial Dr.
Tulsa, OK 74133
(918)252-2997
Ultimate Parent: Toys "R" US. SIC: 5941—
Sporting Goods & Bicycle Shops; 5945—
Hobby, Toy & Game Shops.

★ 78177 ★   Trailways Bus
Systems
319 S. Detroit Ave.
Tulsa, OK 74120
(918)584-3713
Ultimate Parent: Greyhound Lines Inc. SIC:
4111—Local & Suburban Transit.

★ 78178 ★   Trane Co.
5411 S. 125th East Ave. 303
Tulsa, OK 74146
(918)835-8481
Ultimate Parent: American Standard. SIC:
7623—Refrigeration Services Repair.

★ 78179 ★   Trans World Airlines
7777 Tulsa International Airport
Tulsa, OK 74115
(918)838-5122
Ultimate Parent: Trans World Airlines. SIC:
4512—Air Transportation—Scheduled.

★ 78180 ★   Trans World Airlines
4608 S. Garnett Rd.
Tulsa, OK 74146
(918)664-6911
Ultimate Parent: Trans World Airlines. SIC:
4512—Air Transportation—Scheduled.

★ 78181 ★   Transamerica
Occidental Life Insurance
15 W. 6th St.
Tulsa, OK 74119
(918)582-4942
Ultimate Parent: Transamerica Occidental
Life Insurance. SIC: 6411—Insurance
Agents, Brokers & Service.

★ 78182 ★   Transok, Inc.
2 W. 6th St.
Tulsa, OK 74119
(918)583-1121 Fax: (918)561-9341
Officer: F. Joseph Becraft, President &
CEO. Ultimate Parent: Central & South
West.

★ 78183 ★   U S Design
1444 S. Boston Ave.
Tulsa, OK 74119
(918)592-3329
Ultimate Parent: Maxtor. SIC: 1541—
Industrial Buildings & Warehouses.

★ 78184 ★   Underwriters
Adjusting Co.
9920 E. 42nd St.
Tulsa, OK 74146
(918)626-6480
Ultimate Parent: Continental. SIC: 6411—
Insurance Agents, Brokers & Service.

★ 78185 ★   United Parcel Service
5805 S. 118th Ave. E
Tulsa, OK 74146
(918)584-4404
Ultimate Parent: United Parcel Service of
America. SIC: 4215—Courier Services
Except by Air.

★ 78186 ★   United Parcel Service
5805 S. 118th Ave. E
Tulsa, OK 74146
(918)584-4404
Ultimate Parent: United Parcel Service of
America. SIC: 4215—Courier Services
Except by Air.

★ 78187 ★   US Fidelity & Gu
3840 S. East Ave. 103-D
Tulsa, OK 74129
(918)664-8010
Ultimate Parent: USF&G Corp. SIC:
6411—Insurance Agents, Brokers &
Service.

★ 78188 ★   Victoria's Secret
7021 S. Memorial Dr.
Tulsa, OK 74133
(918)250-1034
Ultimate Parent: Limited. SIC: 5651—
Family Clothing Stores.

★ 78189 ★   Wal Mart
9797 E. Admiral Pl
Tulsa, OK 74116
(918)835-9177
Ultimate Parent: Wal-Mart Stores, Inc. SIC:
7384—Photofinishing Laboratories.

★ 78190 ★   Wal Mart
7777 E. 42nd Pl
Tulsa, OK 74145
(918)622-0500
Ultimate Parent: Wal-Mart Stores, Inc. SIC:
5311—Department Stores.

★ 78191 ★   Wal Mart Auto Center
9797 E. Admiral Pl
Tulsa, OK 74116
(918)838-3286
Ultimate Parent: Wal-Mart Stores, Inc. SIC:
5531—Automobile & Home Supply Stores;
7538—General Automotive Repair Shops.

★ 78192 ★   Wal Mart Cities
8739 S. Memorial Dr.
Tulsa, OK 74133
(918)254-5900
Ultimate Parent: Wal-Mart Stores, Inc.

★ 78193 ★   Wal Mart Disc Cits
7777 E. 42nd Pl
Tulsa, OK 74145
(918)622-0539
Ultimate Parent: Wal-Mart Stores, Inc.

★ 78194 ★   Wal Mart Discount
City
9797 E. Admiral Pl
Tulsa, OK 74116
(918)838-1245
Ultimate Parent: Wal-Mart Stores, Inc. SIC:
5311—Department Stores.

★ 78195 ★   Wal Mart Discount
Store
1439 E. 71st St.
Tulsa, OK 74136
(918)496-0262
Ultimate Parent: Wal-Mart Stores, Inc. SIC:
5311—Department Stores.

★ 78196 ★   Wal Mart Insurance
Agency
2250 E. 49th St.
Tulsa, OK 74105
(918)742-1584
Ultimate Parent: Wal-Mart Stores, Inc. SIC:
6411—Insurance Agents, Brokers &
Service.

★ 78197 ★   Wal Mart Pharmacy
9797 E. Admiral Pl
Tulsa, OK 74116
(918)838-2937
Ultimate Parent: Wal-Mart Stores, Inc. SIC:
5912—Drug Stores & Proprietary Stores.

★ 78198 ★   Wal Mart Pharmacy
7777 E. 42nd Pl
Tulsa, OK 74145
(918)622-5711
Ultimate Parent: Wal-Mart Stores, Inc. SIC:
5912—Drug Stores & Proprietary Stores.

★ 78199 ★   Waldenbooks
4107 S. Yale Ave.
Tulsa, OK 74135
(918)663-7244
Ultimate Parent: K-Mart. SIC: 5942—Book
Stores.

★ 78200 ★   Waldenbooks
Southland Shopping Ctr.
Tulsa, OK 74135
(918)664-4899
Ultimate Parent: K-Mart. SIC: 5942—Book
Stores.

★ 78201 ★   Waldenbooks
11142 E. 31st St.
Tulsa, OK 74146
(918)627-0465
Ultimate Parent: K-Mart. SIC: 5942—Book
Stores.

★ 78202 ★   Waldenbooks
7021 S. Memorial Dr.
Tulsa, OK 74133
(918)250-0771
Ultimate Parent: K-Mart. SIC: 5942—Book
Stores.

★ 78203 ★   Waldenbooks
14002 E. 21st St.
Tulsa, OK 74134
(918)437-7850
Ultimate Parent: K-Mart. SIC: 5942—Book
Stores.

★ 78204 ★   Walgreen
4187 S. Yale Ave.
Tulsa, OK 74135
(918)627-9545
Ultimate Parent: Walgreen Co. SIC:
5946—Camera & Photographic Supply
Stores.

★ 78205 ★   Walgreen Drug Stores
4187 S. Yale Ave.
Tulsa, OK 74135
(918)627-9547
Ultimate Parent: Walgreen Co. SIC:
5812—Eating Places.

★ 78206 ★   Warren Petroleum Co.
1350 S. Boulder Ave.
Tulsa, OK 74119
(918)560-4000
Ultimate Parent: Chevron Corp. SIC:
5984—Liquefied Petroleum Gas Dealers.

★ 78207 ★   Wells Fargo Guard
Service
9920 E. 42nd St.
Tulsa, OK 74146
(918)622-1171
Ultimate Parent: Borg Warner Automotive.
SIC: 7381—Detective & Armored Car
Services.

★ 78208 ★   Wells Fargo Guard
Servs
4528 S. Sheridan Rd.
Tulsa, OK 74145
(918)622-1171
Ultimate Parent: Borg Warner Automotive.
SIC: 7381—Detective & Armored Car
Services.

★ 78209 ★   Willamette Industries
Inc.
3015 E. Skelly Dr.
Tulsa, OK 74105
(918)743-8988
Ultimate Parent: Willamette Industries, Inc.
SIC: 7373—Computer Integrated Systems
Design.

★ 78210 ★   Williams Brothers
Engineeri
6600 S. Yale Ave.
Tulsa, OK 74136
(918)496-5020
Ultimate Parent: Fluor. SIC: 8711—
Engineering Services.

★ 78211 ★   Williams Companies,
Inc.
1 Williams Ctr.
Tulsa, OK 74172
(918)588-2000 Fax: (918)588-2296
Company Type: Headquarters. Officer:
Keith E. Bailey. Employee Count: 7189.
Sales: 2438.2 M. Fortune Service 500:
Ranking 61.

★ 78212 ★   Xerox Corp.
4200 E. Skelly Dr., Ste. 350
Tulsa, OK 74135
(918)481-2600
Officer: Shelly Barnett, Manager. Ultimate
Parent: Xerox Corp. SIC: 3663—Radio &
T.V. Communications Equipment.

★ 78213 ★   Zebco Corp-A
Brunswick Co.
6101 E. Apache St.
Tulsa, OK 74115
(918)836-5581
Ultimate Parent: Brunswick Corp. SIC:
3949—Sporting & Athletic Goods Nec.

★ 78214 ★   Zebco Corp.
PO Box 270
Tulsa, OK 74101-0270
(918)836-5581
Location Type: Branch office. Officer: J.
W. Dawson. Ultimate Parent: Brunswick
Corp. SIC: 3949—Sporting & Athletic Goods
Nec; 6061—Federal Credit Unions.

★ 78215 ★   Zebco Corp.
6101 E. Apache St.
Tulsa, OK 74115
(918)836-5581
Officer: Jim W. Dawson, President.
Ultimate Parent: Brunswick Corp. SIC:
3949—Sporting & Athletic Goods Nec.

★ 78216 ★   Zebco Corp.
835 W. 41st St.
Tulsa, OK 74107
(918)446-1461
Officer: Bob McIntosh, Manager. Ultimate
Parent: Brunswick Corp. SIC: 3949—
Sporting & Athletic Goods Nec.

★ 78217 ★   Zep Manufacturing
Co.
1412 S. Harvard Ave.
Tulsa, OK 74112
(918)744-0373
Ultimate Parent: National Service
Industries. SIC: 1799—Special Trade
Contractors Nec.

Tulso

★ 78218 ★   American General
Finance Inc.
2166 S. Sheridan Rd.
Tulso, OK 74129-1002
(918)834-2276
Location Type: Branch office. Officer:
Colin Magruder. Ultimate Parent: American
General Corp. SIC: 6141—Personal Credit
Institutions; 6162—Mortgage Bankers &
Correspondents.

Valliant

★ 78219 ★   Burlington Northern
Railroad
Valliant, OK 74764
(405)933-4264
Ultimate Parent: Burlington Northern. SIC:
4011—Railroads—Line-Haul Operating.

★ 78220 ★   Weyerhaeuser Paper
Co.
Hwy. 70 W.
Valliant, OK 74764
Ultimate Parent: Weyerhaeuser Co. SIC:
2631—Paperboard Mills.

★ 78221 ★   Weyerhaeuser Paper
Co.
Hwy. 70 W
Valliant, OK 74764
Officer: Mike Citty, Manager. Ultimate
Parent: Weyerhaeuser Co. SIC: 2621—
Paper Mills; 2631—Paperboard Mills.

Vinita

★ 78222 ★   Coast to Coast Total
Hdwe
126 S. Scraper St.
Vinita, OK 74301
(918)256-5144
Ultimate Parent: Servistar Corp. SIC:
5251—Hardware Stores.

★ 78223 ★   Dana Corp.
Weatherhead Div.
110 N. Dana Ave.
Vinita, OK 74301
Company Type: Division. Ultimate Parent:
Dana Corp. SIC: 3432—Plumbing Fixtures
Fittings & Trim; 3494—Valves & Pipe
Fittings Nec; 3429—Hardware Nec.

★ 78224 ★   Heinz Bakery
Products
Box 125
Vinita, OK 74301
(918)256-8696
Company Type: Division. Location Type:
Plant. Officer: Tom Kennon, Plant Manager.
Ultimate Parent: H.J. Heinz. SIC: 2038—
Frozen Specialties Nec.

★ 78225 ★   Kentucky Fried
Chicken
434 S. Wilson St.
Vinita, OK 74301
(918)256-3780
Ultimate Parent: Pepsico. SIC: 5812—
Eating Places.

★ 78226 ★   Pizza Hut
426 S. Wilson St.
Vinita, OK 74301
(918)256-6311
Ultimate Parent: Pepsico. SIC: 5812—
Eating Places.

★ 78227 ★   Radio Shack
143 S. Wilson St.
Vinita, OK 74301
(918)256-2605
Company Type: Division. Ultimate Parent:
Tandy Corp. SIC: 5731—Radio, Television
& Electronics Stores.

★ 78228 ★   Ryder Truck Rental
621 N. Brewer St.
Vinita, OK 74301
(918)256-2884
Ultimate Parent: Ryder System. SIC:
7359—Equipment Rental & Leasing Nec.

★ 78229 ★   Wal Mart
Hwy. 66 S
Vinita, OK 74301
(918)256-7505
Ultimate Parent: Wal-Mart Stores, Inc. SIC:
6512—Nonresidential Building Operators.

★ 78230 ★   Wal Mart Discount
Cities
Hwy. 66 S
Vinita, OK 74301
(918)256-6435
Ultimate Parent: Wal-Mart Stores, Inc. SIC:
5912—Drug Stores & Proprietary Stores.

Wagoner

★ 78231 ★   Pizza Hut
107 S. Dewey Ave.
Wagoner, OK 74467
(918)485-2853
Ultimate Parent: Pepsico. SIC: 5812—
Eating Places.

★ 78232 ★   Radio Shack
700 W. Cherokee St.
Wagoner, OK 74467
(918)485-3081
Company Type: Division. Ultimate Parent:
Tandy Corp.

★ 78233 ★   Trailways Bus
Systems
1205 W. Cherokee St.
Wagoner, OK 74467
(918)485-9951
Ultimate Parent: Greyhound Lines Inc. SIC:
4131—Intercity & Rural Bus Transportation.

★ 78234 ★   Wal Mart Discount
Cities
Hwy. 51 W
Wagoner, OK 74467
(918)485-5558
Ultimate Parent: Wal-Mart Stores, Inc. SIC:
5311—Department Stores.

★ 78235 ★   Wal Mart
Prescriptions
Westwood Shopping Ctr.
Wagoner, OK 74467
(918)485-5567
Ultimate Parent: Wal-Mart Stores, Inc. SIC:
5912—Drug Stores & Proprietary Stores.

Walters

★ 78236 ★   Kids R US
224 W. Colorado St.
Walters, OK 73572
(405)875-2059
Ultimate Parent: Toys "R" US. SIC: 8351—
Child Day Care Services.

Watonga

★ 78237 ★   Kentucky Fried
Chicken
Hwy. 33 W
Watonga, OK 73772
(405)623-8511
Ultimate Parent: Pepsico. SIC: 5812—
Eating Places.

Watts

★ 78238 ★   Ryder Truck Rental
Hwy. 33 W
Watts, OK 74964
(918)422-5126
Ultimate Parent: Ryder System. SIC:
7359—Equipment Rental & Leasing Nec.

Weatherford

★ 78239 ★   City National Bank of
Weath
115 N. Custer St.
Weatherford, OK 73096
(405)774-2265
Ultimate Parent: City National Corp. SIC:
6021—National Commercial Banks.

★ 78240 ★   Coast to Coast Store
310 N. Washington St.
Weatherford, OK 73096
(405)772-1321
Ultimate Parent: Servistar Corp. SIC:
5261—Retail Nurseries & Garden Stores.

★ 78241 ★   Greyhound Bus Lines
124 S. Broadway St.
Weatherford, OK 73096
(405)772-2837
Ultimate Parent: Greyhound Lines Inc. SIC:
4111—Local & Suburban Transit.

★ 78242 ★   Kentucky Fried
Chicken
206 N. Washington St.
Weatherford, OK 73096
(405)772-5323
Ultimate Parent: Pepsico. SIC: 5812—
Eating Places.

★ 78243 ★   Pizza Hut
309 N. Washington St.
Weatherford, OK 73096
(405)772-2650
Ultimate Parent: Pepsico. SIC: 5812—
Eating Places.

★ 78244 ★   Wal Mart Discount
City
Us Hwy. 66 Main St.
Weatherford, OK 73096
(405)772-1408
Ultimate Parent: Wal-Mart Stores, Inc. SIC:
5311—Department Stores.

★ 78245 ★   Wal Mart Pharmacy
800 E. Main St.
Weatherford, OK 73096
(405)772-2712
Ultimate Parent: Wal-Mart Stores, Inc. SIC:
5912—Drug Stores & Proprietary Stores.

Westville

★ 78246 ★   Hudson Foods Inc.
Feedmill
Hwy. 59 Hwy. 59 N.
Westville, OK 74965
Ultimate Parent: Hudson Foods. SIC:
2048—Prepared Feeds Nec.

Wewoka

★ 78247 ★   Mini Mart
14th
Wewoka, OK 74884
(405)257-5885
Ultimate Parent: Kroger. SIC: 5411—
Grocery Stores.

★ 78248 ★   Pizza Hut
525 S. Mekusukey Ave.
Wewoka, OK 74884
(405)257-6371
Ultimate Parent: Pepsico. SIC: 5812—
Eating Places.

Wheatland

★ 78249 ★   BFI-Oklahoma Landfill
7600 SW 15th
Wheatland, OK 73097
(405)745-3091
Ultimate Parent: Browning-Ferris
Industries. SIC: 4953—Refuse Systems.

★ 78250 ★ **BFI Recycling Systems**
4625 S. Rockwell
Wheatland, OK 73097
(405)354-5269 (405)745-2941
Ultimate Parent: Wal-Mart Stores, Inc. **SIC:** 5311—Department Stores. **Location Type:** Branch office. **Ultimate Parent:** Browning-Ferris Industries. **SIC:** 4953—Refuse Systems.

★ 78251 ★ **Safety Kleen Corp.**
Gen Del
Wheatland, OK 73097
(405)232-1849
Ultimate Parent: Safety-Kleen. **SIC:** 3291—Abrasive Products.

Wilburton

★ 78252 ★ **Kentucky Fried Chicken**
413 W. Main St.
Wilburton, OK 74578
(918)465-3432
Ultimate Parent: Pepsico. **SIC:** 5812—Eating Places.

★ 78253 ★ **Pizza Hut**
Hwy. 2 N
Wilburton, OK 74578
(918)465-2386
Ultimate Parent: Pepsico. **SIC:** 5812—Eating Places.

Woodward

★ 78254 ★ **Ace Hardware**
4231 Oklahoma Ave.
Woodward, OK 73801
(405)256-5041
Ultimate Parent: Ace Hardware. **SIC:** 5211—Lumber & Other Building Materials; 5251—Hardware Stores.

★ 78255 ★ **American National Bank**
2105 Oklahoma Ave.
Woodward, OK 73801-4527
(405)254-2265
Company Type: Subsidiary. **Officer:** R. E. Atkins, Chairman of the Board. **Ultimate Parent:** First Chicago Corp. **SIC:** 6021—National Commercial Banks. **Employee Count:** 13.

★ 78256 ★ **Arco Oil & Gas Co.**
5815 Oklahoma Ave.
Woodward, OK 73801-9006
(405)256-3369
Officer: Roger L. Russell. **Ultimate Parent:** Atlantic Richfield Co., Inc. **SIC:** 1311—Crude Petroleum & Natural Gas.

★ 78257 ★ **Atlantic Richfield**
5815 Oklahoma Ave.
Woodward, OK 73801-9006
Officer: Pete Edlund. **Ultimate Parent:** Atlantic Richfield Co., Inc. **SIC:** 3569—General Industrial Machinery Nec.

★ 78258 ★ **Atlantic Richfield Co.**
5815 Oklahoma Ave.
Woodward, OK 73801-9006
Officer: Pete Edlund. **Ultimate Parent:** Atlantic Richfield Co., Inc. **SIC:** 3569—General Industrial Machinery Nec.

★ 78259 ★ **Beneficial Income Tax Service**
1424 Main St.
Woodward, OK 73801
(405)256-6451
Ultimate Parent: Bemis Co., Inc. **SIC:** 6141—Personal Credit Institutions.

★ 78260 ★ **Kentucky Fried Chicken**
2411 Oklahoma Ave.
Woodward, OK 73801
(405)256-5181
Ultimate Parent: Pepsico. **SIC:** 5812—Eating Places.

★ 78261 ★ **Mary Kay Cosmetics**
1002 Webster Ave.
Woodward, OK 73801
(405)256-5906
Ultimate Parent: Mary Kay Cosmetics. **SIC:** 5999—Miscellaneous Retail Stores Nec.

★ 78262 ★ **National-Oilwell**
600 Airpark Rd.
Woodward, OK 73801
Ultimate Parent: Armco. **SIC:** 3541—Machine Tools—Metal Cutting Types.

★ 78263 ★ **Payless Shoesource**
2808 8th St.
Woodward, OK 73801
(405)256-3607
Ultimate Parent: May Department Stores. **SIC:** 5661—Shoe Stores.

★ 78264 ★ **Pizza Hut**
1201 Oklahoma Ave.
Woodward, OK 73801
(405)256-6944
Ultimate Parent: Pepsico. **SIC:** 5812—Eating Places.

★ 78265 ★ **Radio Shack**
816 Main St.
Woodward, OK 73801
(405)256-3537
Company Type: Division. **Ultimate Parent:** Tandy Corp. **SIC:** 5719—Miscellaneous Home Furnishings Stores; 5731—Radio, Television & Electronics Stores.

★ 78266 ★ **Ryder Truck Rental**
S City
Woodward, OK 73801
(405)256-4232
Ultimate Parent: Ryder System. **SIC:** 5113—Industrial & Personal Service Paper.

★ 78267 ★ **Southland Royalty Co.**
5005 Western Ave.
Woodward, OK 73801
(405)256-8112
Ultimate Parent: Burlington Resources. **SIC:** 4925—Gas Production & Distribution Nec.

★ 78268 ★ **Trico Industries Inc.**
4300 Western Ave.
Woodward, OK 73801
(405)256-3688
Ultimate Parent: Paccar. **SIC:** 1382—Oil & Gas Exploration Services.

★ 78269 ★ **Wal Mart Discount Cities**
Downs Ave.
Woodward, OK 73801
(405)254-3331
Ultimate Parent: Wal-Mart Stores, Inc. **SIC:** 5331—Variety Stores.

★ 78270 ★ **Western Geophysical Co.**
1414 46th St.
Woodward, OK 73801
(405)254-3540
Ultimate Parent: Litton Industries. **SIC:** 1382—Oil & Gas Exploration Services.

Wright City

★ 78271 ★ **Weyerhaeuser Co.**
Hc 74
PO Box 100
Wright City, OK 74766
Ultimate Parent: Weyerhaeuser Co. **SIC:** 2436—Softwood Veneer & Plywood; 2421—Sawmills & Planing Mills—General; 2426—Hardwood Dimension & Flooring Mills.

Wynnewood

★ 78272 ★ **Kerr-Mcgee Refining Corp.**
906 S. Powell
Wynnewood, OK 73098-0305
Ultimate Parent: Kerr-McGee. **SIC:** 2911—Petroleum Refining.

★ 78273 ★ **Kerr Mcgee Refining Corp.**
906 South Powell
Wynnewood, OK 73098
Ultimate Parent: Kerr-McGee. **SIC:** 2911—Petroleum Refining.

★ 78274 ★ **Specialty Products**
Rte. 2, Box 109
Wynnewood, OK 73098-9648
(405)665-4308
Officer: C. E. Gorrell. **Ultimate Parent:** Avery Dennison Corp. **SIC:** 3089—Plastics Products Nec; 5211—Lumber & Other Building Materials.

Yale

★ 78275 ★ **Coast to Coast**
215 W. Chicago Ave.
Yale, OK 74085
(918)387-2222
Ultimate Parent: Servistar Corp. **SIC:** 5531—Automobile & Home Supply Stores.

Yukon

★ 78276 ★ **Kentucky Fried Chicken**
Hwy. 92nd
Yukon, OK 73099
(405)354-4686
Ultimate Parent: Pepsico. **SIC:** 5812—Eating Places.

★ 78277 ★ **McDonalds Hamburgers**
31 W. Main St.
Yukon, OK 73099
(405)354-1285
Ultimate Parent: McDonald's.

★ 78278 ★ **Pizza Hut**
420 E. Main St.
Yukon, OK 73099
(405)354-6665
Ultimate Parent: Pepsico. **SIC:** 5812—Eating Places.

★ 78279 ★ **Pizza Hut**
12142 W. Reno Ave.
Yukon, OK 73099
(405)324-7722
Ultimate Parent: Pepsico.

★ 78280 ★ **Radio Shack**
300 Elm Ave.
Yukon, OK 73099
(405)354-4024
Company Type: Division. **Ultimate Parent:** Tandy Corp. **SIC:** 5065—Electronic Parts & Equipment Nec.

★ 78281 ★ **Shell Oil Co.**
106 S. 3rd St.
Yukon, OK 73099
(405)354-8828
Ultimate Parent: Shell Oil Co. **SIC:** 1382—Oil & Gas Exploration Services.

★ 78282 ★ **Taco Bell**
975 S. Cornwell Dr.
Yukon, OK 73099
(405)350-1334
Ultimate Parent: Pepsico.

★ 78283 ★ **Total Petroleum Inc.**
10920 NW 10th St.
Yukon, OK 73099
(405)324-0600
Ultimate Parent: Total Petroleum Inc.

★ 78284 ★ **Total Petroleum Inc.**
10920 NW 10th St.
Yukon, OK 73099
(405)324-0600
Ultimate Parent: Total Petroleum Inc.

★ 78285 ★ **Wal Mart**
1105 S. 11th St.
Yukon, OK 73099
(405)350-1383
Ultimate Parent: Wal-Mart Stores, Inc.

★ 78286 ★ **Wal Mart Discount Cities**
Us 92
Yukon, OK 73099
(405)354-5269
Ultimate Parent: Wal-Mart Stores, Inc. **SIC:** 5311—Department Stores.

PUERTO RICO

Adjuntas

★ 78287 ★   Banco Popular de Puerto Rico
19-21 San Joaquin St.
Adjuntas, PR 00601
(809)829-2120
Company Type: Subsidiary. **Location Type:** Branch office. **Ultimate Parent:** Banponce Corp. **SIC:** 6022—State Commercial Banks.

Aguada

★ 78288 ★   Banco Popular de Puerto Rico
227 Paz St.
Aguada, PR 00602
(809)868-2500
Company Type: Subsidiary. **Location Type:** Branch office. **Ultimate Parent:** Banponce Corp. **SIC:** 6022—State Commercial Banks.

★ 78289 ★   Granger Associates of Puerto Rico Inc.
Aguada West Industrial Park, Bldg. 1
Aguada, PR 00602-0580
Ultimate Parent: DSC Communications. **SIC:** 3679—Electronic Components Nec.

Aguadilla

★ 78290 ★   Avon-Mirabella Inc.
Montana Industrial Park Lot 26 & 27
Aguadilla, PR 00605-3918
Ultimate Parent: Avon Products, Inc. **SIC:** 3961—Costume Jewelry; 3471—Plating & Polishing; 3911—Jewelry & Precious Metal.

★ 78291 ★   Banco Popular de Puerto Rico
Ins Rd. 2, Km. 129.3, Bo Victoria
Aguadilla, PR 00603
(809)891-9500
Company Type: Subsidiary. **Location Type:** Branch office. **Ultimate Parent:** Banponce Corp. **SIC:** 6022—State Commercial Banks.

★ 78292 ★   Banco Popular de Puerto Rico
Plaza Ferran Shopping Ctr.
Aguadilla, PR 00603
(809)891-4222
Company Type: Subsidiary. **Location Type:** Branch office. **Ultimate Parent:** Banponce Corp. **SIC:** 6022—State Commercial Banks.

★ 78293 ★   Banco Popular de Puerto Rico
717, Punta Borinquen
Ramey AFB
Aguadilla, PR 00604
(809)891-2737
Company Type: Subsidiary. **Location Type:** Branch office. **Ultimate Parent:** Banponce Corp. **SIC:** 6022—State Commercial Banks.

★ 78294 ★   Hewlett-Packard Co.
State Rd. 110 Km. 5.1 Aguacate Ward
Aguadilla, PR 00603
Ultimate Parent: Hewlett-Packard. **SIC:** 3500—Industrial Machinery & Equipment.

★ 78295 ★   Hewlett-Packard Oki Printed Circuits
State Rd. 110 Km 5.1 Aguacate Ward
Aguadilla, PR 00605
Ultimate Parent: Hewlett-Packard. **SIC:** 3571—Electronic Computers.

Aguas Buenas

★ 78296 ★   Banco Popular de Puerto Rico
20 Muoz Rivera St.
Aguas Buenas, PR 00703
(809)732-3591
Company Type: Subsidiary. **Location Type:** Branch office. **Ultimate Parent:** Banponce Corp. **SIC:** 6022—State Commercial Banks.

★ 78297 ★   Westinghouse Corp. of Puerto Rico
Breakers Div.
Rd. 174 Km 22.5 Call Box 146
Aguas Buenas, PR 00703
Ultimate Parent: Westinghouse Electric Corp. **SIC:** 3629—Electrical Industrial Apparatus Nec.

★ 78298 ★   Westinghouse De Pr Inc.
Breakers
Rd. 174 Km 22.5 Call Box 146
Aguas Buenas, PR 00703
Ultimate Parent: Westinghouse Electric Corp. **SIC:** 3629—Electrical Industrial Apparatus Nec.

★ 78299 ★   Westinghouse Electric Corp.
Breakers
Rte. 174 Km 22.5
Aguas Buenas, PR 00703
Ultimate Parent: Westinghouse Electric Corp. **SIC:** 3629—Electrical Industrial Apparatus Nec.

★ 78300 ★   Westinghouse Electric Corp.
Breakers
Rte. 174 Km 22.5
Aguas Buenas, PR 00703
Ultimate Parent: Westinghouse Electric Corp. **SIC:** 3629—Electrical Industrial Apparatus Nec.

★ 78301 ★   Westinghouse Puerto Rico Inc.
Breakers Div.
Rd. 174 Km 22.5 Call Box 146
Aguas Buenas, PR 00703
Ultimate Parent: Westinghouse Electric Corp. **SIC:** 3629—Electrical Industrial Apparatus Nec.

Aibonito

★ 78302 ★   Banco Popular de Puerto Rico
55 Degetau
Aibonito, PR 00705
(809)735-6191
Company Type: Subsidiary. **Location Type:** Branch office. **Ultimate Parent:** Banponce Corp. **SIC:** 6022—State Commercial Banks.

★ 78303 ★   Bryloc Inc.
Bo. Llanos Industrial Park Rd. 725
Aibonito, PR 00705
Ultimate Parent: Westinghouse Electric Corp. **SIC:** 3643—Current-Carrying Wiring Devices.

★ 78304 ★   Bryloc Inc.
Bo. Llanos Llanos Industrial Park Rd. 725 Km 0.4
Aibonito, PR 00705
Ultimate Parent: Westinghouse Electric Corp. **SIC:** 3643—Current-Carrying Wiring Devices.

Anasco

★ 78305 ★   Allergan Medical Optics
PO Box 1408 G.PO Box 1408
Anasco, PR 006101408
Ultimate Parent: Allergan Inc. **SIC:** 3851—Ophthalmic Goods.

★ 78306 ★   Caribe General Electric Products Inc.
Carr. 402 Km 1.4-1.5, Bo. Las Marias
Anasco PR 00610
Ultimate Parent: General Electric. **SIC:** 3613—Switchgear & Switchboard Apparatus.

★ 78307 ★   Caribe General Electric Products Inc.
Carr. 402. Km 1.4 - 1.5. Bo. Las Marias
Anasco PR 00610
Ultimate Parent: General Electric. **SIC:** 3613—Switchgear & Switchboard Apparatus.

Arecibo

★ 78308 ★   Banco Popular de Puerto Rico
Gonzalo Marn St., Cnr Hostos 107
Arecibo, PR 00612
(809)878-8500
Company Type: Subsidiary. **Location Type:** Branch office. **Ultimate Parent:** Banponce Corp. **SIC:** 6022—State Commercial Banks.

★ 78309 ★   Banco Popular de Puerto Rico
Plaza del Atlntico
Ins Rd. 2, Km. 80.4 San Daniel
Arecibo, PR 00612
(809)879-2703
Company Type: Subsidiary. **Location Type:** Branch office. **Ultimate Parent:** Banponce Corp. **SIC:** 6022—State Commercial Banks.

★ 78310 ★   Banco Popular de Puerto Rico
Jos De Diego & Oliver St. 354
Arecibo, PR 00612
(809)878-3434
Company Type: Subsidiary. **Location Type:** Branch office. **Ultimate Parent:** Banponce Corp. **SIC:** 6022—State Commercial Banks.

★ 78311 ★   Banco Popular de Puerto Rico
614 San Luis & Rotarios Ave.
Arecibo, PR 00612
(809)878-4949
Company Type: Subsidiary. **Location Type:** Branch office. **Ultimate Parent:** Banponce Corp. **SIC:** 6022—State Commercial Banks.

★ 78312 ★   Caribe G.E. Products Inc. Arecibo Plant
Zeno Gandia Industrial Park Rd. 129, Km. 41.0
Arecibo, PR 00613-2500
Ultimate Parent: General Electric. **SIC:** 3643—Current-Carrying Wiring Devices; 2843—Surface Active Agents; 3471—Plating & Polishing.

★ 78313 ★   Kayser-Roth Corp.
Rd. 129 Km. 40.7 Zeno Gandia Industrial Park
Arecibo, PR 00613
Ultimate Parent: Collins & Aikman Group. **SIC:** 2251—Women's Hosiery Except Socks.

★ 78314 ★   Westinghouse De Puerto Rico
Thermo King De Puerto Rico
Zeno Gandia Industrial Area B St.
Arecibo, PR 00612
Company Type: Division. **Ultimate Parent:** Westinghouse Electric Corp. **SIC:** 3585—Refrigeration & Heating Equipment.

★ 78315 ★   Westinghouse De Puerto Rico Inc.
Thermo King Div.
Zeno Gandia Industrial Area B St.
Arecibo, PR 00612
Ultimate Parent: Westinghouse Electric Corp. **SIC:** 3585—Refrigeration & Heating Equipment.

★ 78316 ★   Westinghouse Electric Corp.
Thermo King De Puerto Rico
B St. Zeno Gandia Industrial Area
Arecibo, PR 00612
Ultimate Parent: Westinghouse Electric Corp. **SIC:** 3585—Refrigeration & Heating Equipment.

Arroyo

★ 78317 ★   Banco Popular de Puerto Rico
Rd. 753 & Rd. 3
Arroyo, PR 00714
(809)839-3060
Company Type: Subsidiary. **Location Type:** Branch office. **Ultimate Parent:** Banponce Corp. **SIC:** 6022—State Commercial Banks.

★ 78318 ★   Caribe General Electric Products Inc.
State Rd. No. 3, Km. 130.2
Arroyo, PR 00714
Ultimate Parent: General Electric. **SIC:** 3625—Relays & Industrial Controls.

Barceloneta

★ 78319 ★   Abbott Chemical Inc.
State Rd. 2 Km. 58.0
Barceloneta, PR 00617
Ultimate Parent: Abbott Laboratories. **SIC:** 2833—Medicinals & Botanicals; 3841—Surgical & Medical Instruments; 2834—Pharmaceutical Preparations.

★ 78320 ★   Abbott Chemicals Inc.
Rd. 2 Km 58.0
Barceloneta, PR 00617
Ultimate Parent: Abbott Laboratories. **SIC:** 2833—Medicinals & Botanicals; 3841—Surgical & Medical Instruments; 2834—Pharmaceutical Preparations.

★ 78321 ★   Abbott Chemicals Inc.
Rd. No. 2, Km. 58.0 Cruce Davila
Barceloneta, PR 00617
Ultimate Parent: Abbott Laboratories. **SIC:** 2833—Medicinals & Botanicals; 3841—Surgical & Medical Instruments; 2834—Pharmaceutical Preparations.

★ 78322 ★   A.H. Robins Manufacturing Co.
State Rd. 2 60, 3
Barceloneta, PR 00617
(809)846-3750 **Fax:** (809)846-2580
Company Type: Subsidiary. **Officer:** David E. Smallwood, V.P. & Gen. Mgr. **Ultimate Parent:** American Home Products. **SIC:** 2834—Pharmaceutical Preparations.

★ 78323 ★   Banco Popular de Puerto Rico
Ins Rd. 2, Km. 57.9, Cruce Davila
Barceloneta, PR 00617
(809)846-6500
Company Type: Subsidiary. **Location Type:** Branch office. **Ultimate Parent:** Banponce Corp. **SIC:** 6022—State Commercial Banks.

★ 78324 ★ **Banco Popular de Puerto Rico**
No. 32 Georgetti & Union Sts.
Barceloneta, PR 00617
(809)846-3100
Company Type: Subsidiary. **Location Type:** Branch office. **Ultimate Parent:** Banponce Corp. **SIC:** 6022—State Commercial Banks.

★ 78325 ★ **Bristol-Myers Barceloneta Inc.**
State Rd. 2 Km 56.4
Barceloneta, PR 00617
Ultimate Parent: Bristol-Myers Squibb. **SIC:** 2834—Pharmaceutical Preparations.

★ 78326 ★ **Casere Foods Inc.**
P.R. Rd. 2 Km. 58.2
Barceloneta, PR 00617
Ultimate Parent: Campbell Soup. **SIC:** 2033—Canned Fruits & Vegetables.

★ 78327 ★ **General Instrument Corp. Puerto Rico**
9 Tomas Davila St.
Barceloneta, PR 00617
Ultimate Parent: General Instrument Corp. **SIC:** 3600—Electronic & Other Electrical Equipment.

★ 78328 ★ **Merck Sharp & Dohme Quimica De P.R.**
State Rd. 2 Km. 56.4
Barceloneta, PR 00617
Ultimate Parent: Merck. **SIC:** 2833—Medicinals & Botanicals; 2834—Pharmaceutical Preparations; 2899—Chemical Preparations Nec.

★ 78329 ★ **Merck Sharp & Dohme Quimica De Puerto Rico**
State Rd. 2, Km. 56.4, Bo. Trinidad
Barceloneta, PR 00617
Ultimate Parent: Merck. **SIC:** 2833—Medicinals & Botanicals; 2834—Pharmaceutical Preparations; 2899—Chemical Preparations Nec.

★ 78330 ★ **Pfizer Pharmaceuticals Inc.**
Hwy. No. 2 Km. 58.8
Barceloneta, PR 00617
Ultimate Parent: Pfizer. **SIC:** 2833—Medicinals & Botanicals.

★ 78331 ★ **Sterling Pharmaceuticals Inc.**
Rd. 140 Km. 64.4
Barceloneta, PR 00617
Ultimate Parent: Eastman Kodak. **SIC:** 2834—Pharmaceutical Preparations.

★ 78332 ★ **Upjohn Co.**
Hwy. No. 2 - Km 60.0
Barceloneta, PR 00617-1307
Ultimate Parent: Upjohn Co. **SIC:** 2834—Pharmaceutical Preparations.

★ 78333 ★ **Upjohn Manufacturing Co.**
Hwy. No. 2-Km 60.0
Barceloneta, PR 00617-1307
Ultimate Parent: Upjohn Co. **SIC:** 2834—Pharmaceutical Preparations.

★ 78334 ★ **Upjohn Mfg. Co.**
Hwy. No. 2 Km 60.0
Barceloneta, PR 00617-1307
Ultimate Parent: Upjohn Co. **SIC:** 2834—Pharmaceutical Preparations.

Barranquitas

★ 78335 ★ **Banco Popular de Puerto Rico**
Barcelo St.
Barranquitas, PR 00794
(809)857-2175
Company Type: Subsidiary. **Location Type:** Branch office. **Ultimate Parent:** Banponce Corp. **SIC:** 6022—State Commercial Banks.

Bayamon

★ 78336 ★ **H. B. Fuller Co.**
Calle C, No. 26
Bayamon, PR 00619
Ultimate Parent: H. B. Fuller. **SIC:** 2891—Adhesives & Sealants.

★ 78337 ★ **H. B. Fuller Co.**
Calle C No. 26 Luchetti Industrial Park
Bayamon, PR 00961
Ultimate Parent: H. B. Fuller. **SIC:** 2891—Adhesives & Sealants.

★ 78338 ★ **H. B. Fuller Co.**
Calle C No. 26
Bayamon, PR 00959
Ultimate Parent: H. B. Fuller. **SIC:** 2891—Adhesives & Sealants.

★ 78339 ★ **Mantecados Nevada**
Rd. 174 Km. 2-3 Urb. Ind. Minillas
Bayamon, PR 00627-8030
Ultimate Parent: Borden, Inc. **SIC:** 2024—Ice Cream & Frozen Desserts.

★ 78340 ★ **Seven-Up Bottling Co.**
Rd. 177 K 8.3 Minillas Industrial Park
Bayamon, PR 00961
Ultimate Parent: Dr. Pepper/Seven-Up. **SIC:** 2086—Bottled & Canned Soft Drinks.

★ 78341 ★ **Seven Up Bottling Co. Inc.**
Rd. 177 K 8.3 Minillas Ind Park
Bayamon, PR 00612
Ultimate Parent: Dr. Pepper/Seven-Up. **SIC:** 2086—Bottled & Canned Soft Drinks.

★ 78342 ★ **Ucar Resinas Caribe Inc.**
Luchetti Indl. Park Lot 38
Bayamon, PR 00959
Ultimate Parent: Union Carbide Corp. **SIC:** 2821—Plastics Materials & Resins.

★ 78343 ★ **Union Carbide Carbibe, Inc.**
Luchetti Industrial Park Lot 38
Bayamon, PR 00958
Ultimate Parent: Union Carbide Corp. **SIC:** 2821—Plastics Materials & Resins.

★ 78344 ★ **Union Carbide Corp. Caribe Emulsion Plant**
Luchetti Industrial Park Lot 38 B. St.
Bayamon, PR 00961
Ultimate Parent: Union Carbide Corp.

Cabo Rojo

★ 78345 ★ **Banco Popular de Puerto Rico**
102 Carbonell St. & Bo Miradero Rd. 311
Cabo Rojo, PR 00623
(809)851-5800
Company Type: Subsidiary. **Location Type:** Branch office. **Ultimate Parent:** Banponce Corp. **SIC:** 6022—State Commercial Banks.

★ 78346 ★ **Banco Popular de Puerto Rico**
18 Rius Rivera St.
Cabo Rojo, PR 00623
(809)851-1300
Company Type: Subsidiary. **Location Type:** Branch office. **Ultimate Parent:** Banponce Corp. **SIC:** 6022—State Commercial Banks.

★ 78347 ★ **Westinghouse Electric Corp.**
Cabo Rojo
Rd. 103
Cabo Rojo, PR 00623
Ultimate Parent: Westinghouse Electric Corp. **SIC:** 3629—Electrical Industrial Apparatus Nec.

Caguas

★ 78348 ★ **Arbrook Manufacturing Corp.**
State Rd. 156, Kilometers 58.8
Caguas, PR 00725
Ultimate Parent: Johnson & Johnson. **SIC:** 2834—Pharmaceutical Preparations.

★ 78349 ★ **Arbrook Mfg. Corp.**
State Rd. 156 Km. 58.8
Caguas, PR 00725
Ultimate Parent: Johnson & Johnson. **SIC:** 2834—Pharmaceutical Preparations.

★ 78350 ★ **Banco Popular de Puerto Rico**
14 Amapola St., Cnr Orquidea st. Urb Condado Viejo
Caguas, PR 00725
(809)746-4000
Company Type: Subsidiary. **Location Type:** Branch office. **Ultimate Parent:** Banponce Corp. **SIC:** 6022—State Commercial Banks.

★ 78351 ★ **Banco Popular de Puerto Rico**
Federico Degatau & Gautier Benitez St. San Alfonso
Caguas, PR 00725
(809)743-6626
Company Type: Subsidiary. **Location Type:** Branch office. **Ultimate Parent:** Banponce Corp. **SIC:** 6022—State Commercial Banks.

★ 78352 ★ **Banco Popular de Puerto Rico**
Plaza Del Carmen Mall
Caguas, PR 00725
(809)744-9301
Company Type: Subsidiary. **Location Type:** Branch office. **Ultimate Parent:** Banponce Corp. **SIC:** 6022—State Commercial Banks.

★ 78353 ★ **Banco Popular de Puerto Rico**
Caguas Mall
Rafael Cordero Ave., Int Rd. 30
Caguas, PR 00725
(809)746-5959
Company Type: Subsidiary. **Location Type:** Branch office. **Ultimate Parent:** Banponce Corp. **SIC:** 6022—State Commercial Banks.

★ 78354 ★ **Banco Popular de Puerto Rico**
18 Muoz Rivera St. & Ruiz Belvis
Caguas, PR 00725
(809)746-1951
Company Type: Subsidiary. **Location Type:** Branch office. **Ultimate Parent:** Banponce Corp. **SIC:** 6022—State Commercial Banks.

★ 78355 ★ **Banco Popular de Puerto Rico**
Villa Blanca Shopping Ctr.
Caguas, PR 00725
(809)746-0931
Company Type: Subsidiary. **Location Type:** Branch office. **Ultimate Parent:** Banponce Corp. **SIC:** 6022—State Commercial Banks.

★ 78356 ★ **Clorox Co. of Puerto Rico**
Rd. 1 Km 27.1 Ramal 798, Bo., Rio Canas
Caguas, PR 00725
Ultimate Parent: Clorox Co. **SIC:** 2842—Polishes & Sanitation Goods; 3085—Plastics Bottles.

★ 78357 ★ **Clorox Co. of Puerto Rico**
Carr 798 Km 0.9 Sector La Changa, Bo, Rio Canas
Caguas, PR 00725-9998
Ultimate Parent: Clorox Co. **SIC:** 2842—Polishes & Sanitation Goods; 3085—Plastics Bottles.

★ 78358 ★ **Searle & Co.**
State Rd. 189 Km. 2.2 Sta. Juana Ward
Caguas, PR 00725
Ultimate Parent: Monsanto. **SIC:** 2834—Pharmaceutical Preparations.

★ 78359 ★ **Searle & Co.**
State Rd. 189, Km 2.2, Santa Juana Ward
Caguas, PR 00725
Ultimate Parent: Monsanto. **SIC:** 2834—Pharmaceutical Preparations; 2860—Industrial Organic Chemicals.

Camuy

★ 78360 ★ **Banco Popular de Puerto Rico**
50 Muoz Rivera St.
Camuy, PR 00627
(809)898-4950
Company Type: Subsidiary. **Location Type:** Branch office. **Ultimate Parent:** Banponce Corp. **SIC:** 6022—State Commercial Banks.

★ 78361 ★ **Pan-Am Shoe Co. Inc.**
Pr Rd. 119 Km 3.0 PO Box 509
Camuy, PR 00627-0509
Ultimate Parent: Dexter Corp. **SIC:** 3143—Men's Footwear Except Athletic.

★ 78362 ★ **Pan Am Shoe Co. Inc.**
Pr Rd. 119, Km. 3.0
Camuy, PR 00627
Ultimate Parent: Dexter Corp. **SIC:** 3143—Men's Footwear Except Athletic.

Canovanas

★ 78363 ★ **Banco Popular de Puerto Rico**
Autonomia & Muoz Rivera Sts.
Canovanas, PR 00729
(809)876-2030
Company Type: Subsidiary. **Location Type:** Branch office. **Ultimate Parent:** Banponce Corp. **SIC:** 6022—State Commercial Banks.

★ 78364 ★ **Challenger Caribbean Corp.**
Rd. 874 Km 1.1 Bo. Torrecilla Alta
Canovanas, PR 00729
Ultimate Parent: Westinghouse Electric Corp. **SIC:** 3613—Switchgear & Switchboard Apparatus; 3629—Electrical Industrial Apparatus Nec; 3699—Electrical Equipment & Supplies Nec.

Caparra Heights

★ 78365 ★ **Arrow/Kieulff Electronics**
Caparra Heights, PR 00922
(809)788-5420
Company Type: Division. **Location Type:** Distribution center. **Ultimate Parent:** Arrow Electronics. **SIC:** 5065—Electronic Parts & Equipment Nec.

Carolina

★ 78366 ★ **Banco Popular de Puerto Rico**
4 Ignacio Arzuaga St.
Carolina, PR 00985
(809)769-1010
Company Type: Subsidiary. **Location Type:** Branch office. **Ultimate Parent:** Banponce Corp. **SIC:** 6022—State Commercial Banks.

★ 78367 ★ **Banco Popular de Puerto Rico**
Plaza Carolina Shopping Ctr.
Carolina, PR 00985
(809)752-8585
Company Type: Subsidiary. **Location Type:** Branch office. **Ultimate Parent:** Banponce Corp. **SIC:** 6022—State Commercial Banks.

★ 78368 ★ **Banco Popular de Puerto Rico**
Campo Rico Ave. & Loiza Hwy.
Carolina, PR 00982
(809)769-8125
Company Type: Subsidiary. **Location Type:** Branch office. **Ultimate Parent:** Banponce Corp. **SIC:** 6022—State Commercial Banks.

★ 78369 ★ **Banco Popular de Puerto Rico**
Pueblo Shopping Ctr.
65 Infantry Ave.
Carolina, PR 00985
(809)750-2440
Company Type: Subsidiary. **Location Type:** Branch office. **Ultimate Parent:** Banponce Corp. **SIC:** 6022—State Commercial Banks.

★ 78370 ★ **Banco Popular de Puerto Rico**
LMM Airport Bldg.
Isla Verde
Carolina, PR 00979
(809)791-0325
Company Type: Subsidiary. **Location Type:** Branch office. **Ultimate Parent:** Banponce Corp. **SIC:** 6022—State Commercial Banks.

★ 78371 ★ **Banco Popular de Puerto Rico**
Carolina Shopping Ctr.
Fragoso Ave.
Carolina, PR 00985
(809)752-6363
Company Type: Subsidiary. **Location Type:** Branch office. **Ultimate Parent:** Banponce Corp. **SIC:** 6022—State Commercial Banks.

★ 78372 ★ **Chace Precision Materials Group**
Carreta 190 Kilometer 15
Carolina, PR 00986
Ultimate Parent: GTE. **SIC:** 3499—Fabricated Metal Products Nec.

★ 78373 ★ **Crown Cork De P.R. Inc.**
Km. 12.6 Pr-3 P.R. Industrial Park
Carolina, PR 00985
Ultimate Parent: Crown Cork & Seal. **SIC:** 3411—Metal Cans.

★ 78374 ★ **Crown Cork De Puerto Rico Inc.**
Km 12.6 Pr-3 Pr Industrial Park
Carolina, PR 00985
Ultimate Parent: Crown Cork & Seal. **SIC:** 3411—Metal Cans.

★ 78375 ★ **Crown Cork De Puerto Rico, Inc.**
PO Box 817
Carolina, PR 00986
Ultimate Parent: Crown Cork & Seal. **SIC:** 3411—Metal Cans.

★ 78376 ★ **Eli Lilly Ind. Inc.**
65th Infantry Ave. Km. 12.6
Carolina, PR 00985
Ultimate Parent: Eli Lilly. **SIC:** 2834—Pharmaceutical Preparations.

★ 78377 ★ **Eli Lilly Industries, Inc.**
65th Infantry Ave., Km. 12.6
Carolina, PR 00985
Ultimate Parent: Eli Lilly. **SIC:** 2834—Pharmaceutical Preparations.

★ 78378 ★ **Lederle Parentelas Lederle Piperacillin Inc.**
Km 9.7 65th Infantry Ave.
Carolina, PR 00985
Ultimate Parent: American Cyanamid Co. **SIC:** 2834—Pharmaceutical Preparations.

★ 78379 ★ **Lederle Parenterals Inc.-Lederle Piperacillin Inc.**
Km 9.7 65th Infantry Ave.
Carolina, PR 00986-4904
Ultimate Parent: American Cyanamid Co. **SIC:** 2834—Pharmaceutical Preparations.

★ 78380 ★ **Lederle Parenterals & Lederle Piperacillin Inc.**
Km 9.7 65th Infantry Ave.
Carolina, PR 00985
Ultimate Parent: American Cyanamid Co. **SIC:** 2834—Pharmaceutical Preparations.

Cayey

★ 78381 ★ **Banco Popular de Puerto Rico**
50 Barbosa St. & Nuez Romeu St.
Cayey, PR 00738
(809)738-2828
Company Type: Subsidiary. **Location Type:** Branch office. **Ultimate Parent:** Banponce Corp. **SIC:** 6022—State Commercial Banks.

★ 78382 ★ **Banco Popular de Puerto Rico**
Nuez Romeu & Corchado
Cayey, PR 00736
(809)738-3002
Company Type: Subsidiary. **Location Type:** Branch office. **Ultimate Parent:** Banponce Corp. **SIC:** 6022—State Commercial Banks.

★ 78383 ★ **Becton Dickinson, Diagnostics Inc.**
Lot No. 6 Vicks Dr.
Cayey, PR 00736
Ultimate Parent: Becton Dickinson. **SIC:** 2835—Diagnostic Substances.

★ 78384 ★ **Becton Dickinson Diagnostics Inc.**
Lot No. 6 Vicks Dr.
Cayey, PR 00736
Ultimate Parent: Becton Dickinson. **SIC:** 2835—Diagnostic Substances.

★ 78385 ★ **Olay Co. Inc.**
Rd. 735 Km. 2.3 Rio Llano Ward
Cayey, PR 00736
Ultimate Parent: Procter & Gamble Co. **SIC:** 2834—Pharmaceutical Preparations.

★ 78386 ★ **Olay Co. Inc.**
Rd. 735 Km. 2.3
Cayey, PR 00736
Ultimate Parent: Procter & Gamble Co. **SIC:** 2834—Pharmaceutical Preparations.

★ 78387 ★ **Olay Co., Inc.**
Rd. 735, Km 2.3
Cayey, PR 00736
Ultimate Parent: Procter & Gamble Co. **SIC:** 2834—Pharmaceutical Preparations.

Ceiba

★ 78388 ★ **Banco Popular de Puerto Rico**
51 Lauro Piero Ave.
Ceiba, PR 00735
(809)885-2830
Company Type: Subsidiary. **Location Type:** Branch office. **Ultimate Parent:** Banponce Corp. **SIC:** 6022—State Commercial Banks.

Ciales

★ 78389 ★ **Banco Popular de Puerto Rico**
46-A Palmer St.
Ciales, PR 00638
(809)871-3100
Company Type: Subsidiary. **Location Type:** Branch office. **Ultimate Parent:** Banponce Corp. **SIC:** 6021—National Commercial Banks.

★ 78390 ★ **Precision Microblenders Inc.**
Calle Betances 2
Ciales, PR 00638-0786
Ultimate Parent: Central Soya. **SIC:** 2048—Prepared Feeds Nec.

★ 78391 ★ **Westinghouse De P.R. Inc.**
Thermo King Caribbean
Rd. 6685 Km. 11.2
Ciales, PR 00638
Ultimate Parent: Westinghouse Electric Corp. **SIC:** 3585—Refrigeration & Heating Equipment.

★ 78392 ★ **Westinghouse De Puerto Rico Inc.**
Thermo King Carribbean
Rd. 6685 Km. 11.2
Ciales, PR 00638
Ultimate Parent: Westinghouse Electric Corp. **SIC:** 3585—Refrigeration & Heating Equipment.

★ 78393 ★ **Westinghouse Electric Corp.**
Thermo King Carribean
Rd. 6685 Km. 11.2
Ciales, PR 00638
Ultimate Parent: Westinghouse Electric Corp. **SIC:** 3585—Refrigeration & Heating Equipment.

Cidra

★ 78394 ★ **Banco Popular de Puerto Rico**
61 Barcelo & Jamie Bonet Sts.
Cidra, PR 00739
(809)739-8431
Company Type: Subsidiary. **Location Type:** Branch office. **Ultimate Parent:** Banponce Corp. **SIC:** 6022—State Commercial Banks.

★ 78395 ★ **Caribbean Refrescos Inc.**
Rd. 172 Km 13.4
Cidra, PR 00739
Ultimate Parent: Coca-Cola. **SIC:** 2087—Flavoring Extracts & Syrups Nec.

★ 78396 ★ **Caribbean Refrescos Inc.**
State Rd. No. 172, Km 13.6
Montellano Ward
Cidra, PR 00739
Ultimate Parent: Coca-Cola. **SIC:** 2087—Flavoring Extracts & Syrups Nec.

★ 78397 ★ **Concentrate Mfg. Co. Inc.**
Lot 11-12 Cidra Industrial Park
Cidra, PR 00739-1558
Ultimate Parent: Pepsico.

★ 78398 ★ **Pepsi Cola Manufacturing Co. Inc.**
Cidra Industrial Park
Cidra, PR 00739
Ultimate Parent: Pepsico. **SIC:** 2087—Flavoring Extracts & Syrups Nec.

★ 78399 ★ **Pepsi-Cola Mfg. Co. Inc.**
Lot 11.12 Cidra Industrial Park
Cidra, PR 00739
Ultimate Parent: Pepsico. **SIC:** 2087—Flavoring Extracts & Syrups Nec.

★ 78400 ★ **Schering-Plough Inc.**
El Jibaro Incustrial
Rte. 173 Km 1.1 El Jibaro Industrial Park
Cidra, PR 00739-1980
Ultimate Parent: Schering-Plough Corp. **SIC:** 3851—Ophthalmic Goods.

Coamo

★ 78401 ★ **Banco Popular de Puerto Rico**
7 Mario Braschi St.
Coamo, PR 00769
(809)825-1135
Company Type: Subsidiary. **Location Type:** Branch office. **Ultimate Parent:** Banponce Corp. **SIC:** 6022—State Commercial Banks.

★ 78402 ★ **Westinghouse Controls**
Rd. No 14 Km 32.0
Coamo, PR 00769
Ultimate Parent: Westinghouse Electric Corp. **SIC:** 3612—Transformers Except Electronic.

★ 78403 ★ **Westinghouse Controls Inc.**
Rd. 14 Km 32.0
Coamo, PR 00769
Ultimate Parent: Westinghouse Electric Corp. **SIC:** 3612—Transformers Except Electronic.

★ 78404 ★ **Westinghouse Controls Inc.**
Rd. No. 14 Km 32.0
Coamo, PR 00769
Ultimate Parent: Westinghouse Electric Corp. **SIC:** 3612—Transformers Except Electronic.

Comerio

★ 78405 ★ **Banco Popular de Puerto Rico**
57 Georgetti St.
Comerio, PR 00782
(809)875-2860
Company Type: Subsidiary. **Location Type:** Branch office. **Ultimate Parent:** Banponce Corp. **SIC:** 6022—State Commercial Banks.

Corozal

★ 78406 ★ **Banco Popular de Puerto Rico**
Gandara & Cervantes 1 St.
Corozal, PR 00783
(809)859-2636
Company Type: Subsidiary. **Location Type:** Branch office. **Ultimate Parent:** Banponce Corp. **SIC:** 6022—State Commercial Banks.

Dorado

★ 78407 ★ **Banco Popular de Puerto Rico**
Government Ctr. Bldg.
33 Mendez Vigo St.
Dorado, PR 00646
(809)796-2010
Company Type: Subsidiary. **Location Type:** Branch office. **Ultimate Parent:** Banponce Corp. **SIC:** 6022—State Commercial Banks.

★ 78408 ★ **Ecolab Inc.**
Lots 16, 18, 19 Dorado Industrial Park
Dorado, PR 00646
Ultimate Parent: Ecolab Inc. **SIC:** 2841—Soap & Other Detergents.

★ 78409 ★ **Ecolab Manufacturing Inc.**
Lots 16,18,19 Dorado Industrial Park
Dorado, PR 00646
Ultimate Parent: Ecolab Inc. **SIC:** 2841—Soap & Other Detergents.

★ 78410 ★ **Emerson Puerto Rico Inc.**
Hwy. 693 Km. 7.3
PO Box 437
Dorado, PR 00646
Ultimate Parent: Emerson Electric Co. Inc. **SIC:** 3822—Environmental Controls.

★ 78411 ★ **Mcneil Pharmaceutical Co.**
Rd. 698 Km. O.8
Dorado, PR 00646-0710
Ultimate Parent: Johnson & Johnson. **SIC:** 2834—Pharmaceutical Preparations.

★ 78412 ★ **Mcneil Pharmaceutical Co.**
698 Km. 0.8
Dorado, PR 00646
Ultimate Parent: Johnson & Johnson. **SIC:** 2834—Pharmaceutical Preparations.

Fajardo

★ 78413 ★ **Banco Popular de Puerto Rico**
Garrido Morales Ave. & Ins Rd. 3
Fajardo, PR 00738
(809)863-0101
Company Type: Subsidiary. **Location Type:** Branch office. **Ultimate Parent:** Banponce Corp. **SIC:** 6022—State Commercial Banks.

★ 78414 ★ **Stanric Inc. Pto. Real Industrial Park**
Rd. 195 Km. 1.5 Puerto Real Industrial Park
Fajardo, PR 00738
Ultimate Parent: Standard Products. **SIC:** 3714—Motor Vehicle Parts & Accessories.

★ 78415 ★ **Stanric Inc. Pto. Real Industrial Park**
Rd. 195 Km. 1.5
Fajardo, PR 00740
Ultimate Parent: Standard Products. **SIC:** 3694—Engine Electrical Equipment.

Florida

★ 78416 ★ **Banco Popular de Puerto Rico**
225 Muoz Rivera St.
Florida, PR 00650
(809)822-2404
Company Type: Subsidiary. **Location Type:** Branch office. **Ultimate Parent:** Banponce Corp. **SIC:** 6022—State Commercial Banks.

Guanica

★ 78417 ★ **Ochoa Fertilizer Co., Inc.**
Rd. No. 333, Km. 1.9
Guanica, PR 00653-0032
Ultimate Parent: W. R. Grace. **SIC:** 2875—Fertilizers—Mixing Only.

Guayama

★ 78418 ★ Ayerst-Wyeth Pharmaceuticals Inc.
State Rd., No. 3
Km. 142.1 Jobos Ward
Guayama, PR 00784
Ultimate Parent: American Home Products.
SIC: 2834—Pharmaceutical Preparations.

★ 78419 ★ Ayerst-Wyeth Pharmaceuticals Inc.
State Rd. 3 Km. 142.1 Jobos Ward
Guayama, PR 00784
Ultimate Parent: American Home Products.
SIC: 2834—Pharmaceutical Preparations.

★ 78420 ★ Ayerst-Wyeth Pharmaceuticals, Inc.
PO Box 208
Guayama, PR 00785
(809)864-4141
Company Type: Subsidiary. Officer: Gonzala D. Mendez, V.P. & Gen. Mgr.
Ultimate Parent: American Home Products.
SIC: 2834—Pharmaceutical Preparations.

★ 78421 ★ Ayerst Wyeth Pharmaceuticals Whitehall Laboratories
Rd. 3 Km. 141.3
Guayama, PR 00784
Ultimate Parent: American Home Products.
SIC: 2834—Pharmaceutical Preparations.

★ 78422 ★ Banco Popular de Puerto Rico
61 Calimano Norte
Guayama, PR 00674
(809)864-0714
Company Type: Subsidiary. Location Type: Branch office. Ultimate Parent: Banponce Corp. SIC: 6022—State Commercial Banks.

★ 78423 ★ Banco Popular de Puerto Rico
Plaza Guayama Mall
Interstate Rd. 3, Los Veteranos Ave.
Guayama, PR 00784
(809)864-0303
Company Type: Subsidiary. Location Type: Branch office. Ultimate Parent: Banponce Corp. SIC: 6022—State Commercial Banks.

★ 78424 ★ Latas De Aluminio Reynolds Inc. Reynolds Metals Co.
State Rd. 3 Km 140.8
Guayama, PR 00784
Officer: Roberto Perez. Ultimate Parent: Reynolds Metals Co. SIC: 3411—Metal Cans.

★ 78425 ★ Philips P. R. Core Inc.
Durand/Learned Plant
Rd. 710 Km. 1 Hm. 3
Guayama, PR 00970
Location Type: Plant. Ultimate Parent: Phillips Petroleum. SIC: 2911—Petroleum Refining; 2800—Chemicals & Allied Products.

★ 78426 ★ Philips P.R. Core Inc.
Durand/Learned Plant
Philips Rd. 710 Km 1 Hm. 3
Guayama, PR 00970
Location Type: Plant. Ultimate Parent: Phillips Petroleum. SIC: 2911—Petroleum Refining.

★ 78427 ★ Phillips P. R. Core Inc. Phillips Paraxylene Inc.
Rd. 710 Km. 1.3 Las Mareas Ward
Guayama, PR 00784
Ultimate Parent: Phillips Petroleum. SIC: 2911—Petroleum Refining.

★ 78428 ★ Phillips P.R. Core Inc. Phillips Paraxylene Inc.
Rd. 710 Km. 1 Hm. 3 Las Mareas Ward
Guayama, PR 00784
Ultimate Parent: Phillips Petroleum. SIC: 2911—Petroleum Refining.

★ 78429 ★ Phillips P.R. Core/P.P. Inc.
Duran/Learned Plant
Rd. 710 Km. 1 Hm. 3
Guayama, PR 00784
Location Type: Plant. Ultimate Parent: Phillips Petroleum. SIC: 2911—Petroleum Refining; 2800—Chemicals & Allied Products.

Guayanilla

★ 78430 ★ Air Products
State Rd. 127 Km. 12.7
Guayanilla, PR 00656
Ultimate Parent: Air Products & Chemicals, Inc. SIC: 2813—Industrial Gases.

★ 78431 ★ Air Products of Puerto Rico
State Rd. 127, Kilometer 12.7
Guayanilla, PR 00656
Ultimate Parent: Air Products & Chemicals, Inc. SIC: 2813—Industrial Gases.

★ 78432 ★ Banco Popular de Puerto Rico
38-40 Muoz Rivera St.
Guayanilla, PR 00656
(809)835-3330
Company Type: Subsidiary. Location Type: Branch office. Ultimate Parent: Banponce Corp. SIC: 6022—State Commercial Banks.

★ 78433 ★ Texaco Industries Inc.
Bo. Penocillo Guayanilla Terminal Pier
Guayanilla, PR 00656
Ultimate Parent: Texaco. SIC: 2992—Lubricating Oils & Greases.

Guaynabo

★ 78434 ★ Banco Popular de Puerto Rico
Ramirez De Arellano Ave.
Guaynabo, PR 00966
(809)781-6230
Company Type: Subsidiary. Location Type: Branch office. Ultimate Parent: Banponce Corp. SIC: 6022—State Commercial Banks.

★ 78435 ★ Banco Popular de Puerto Rico
Santa Maria Shopping Ctr.
Guaynabo, PR 00969
(809)720-8761
Company Type: Subsidiary. Location Type: Branch office. Ultimate Parent: Banponce Corp. SIC: 6022—State Commercial Banks.

★ 78436 ★ Banco Popular de Puerto Rico
San Patricio Ave. & Ortegon St.
Guaynabo, PR 00968
(809)792-2960
Company Type: Subsidiary. Location Type: Branch office. Ultimate Parent: Banponce Corp. SIC: 6022—State Commercial Banks.

★ 78437 ★ Banco Popular de Puerto Rico
Los Jardines Shopping Ctr.
20 Rd., Hm. 5
Guaynabo, PR 00969
(809)720-8771
Company Type: Subsidiary. Location Type: Branch office. Ultimate Parent: Banponce Corp. SIC: 6022—State Commercial Banks.

★ 78438 ★ Banco Popular de Puerto Rico
Los Canos Ave. & Rd. 28 Zona Portuaria
Guaynabo, PR 00965
(809)792-8131
Company Type: Subsidiary. Location Type: Branch office. Ultimate Parent: Banponce Corp. SIC: 6022—State Commercial Banks.

★ 78439 ★ Banco Popular de Puerto Rico
South Health Clinic, Bldg. 501
Guaynabo, PR 00968
(809)783-8048
Company Type: Subsidiary. Location Type: Branch office. Ultimate Parent: Banponce Corp. SIC: 6022—State Commercial Banks.

★ 78440 ★ Banco Popular de Puerto Rico
Altamira Shopping Ctr.
Guaynabo, PR 00966
(809)793-7398
Company Type: Subsidiary. Location Type: Branch office. Ultimate Parent: Banponce Corp. SIC: 6022—State Commercial Banks.

Gurabo

★ 78441 ★ Banco Popular de Puerto Rico
118 Andres Aruz Rivera St., Bo Rincon
Gurabo, PR 00778
(809)737-4591
Company Type: Subsidiary. Location Type: Branch office. Ultimate Parent: Banponce Corp. SIC: 6022—State Commercial Banks.

★ 78442 ★ Johnson & Johnson Dental Care Co. (PR), Inc.
933 Rd. Km .01
Gurabo, PR 00778-9630
Ultimate Parent: Johnson & Johnson. SIC: 3999—Manufacturing Industries Nec.

★ 78443 ★ Johnson & Johnson Medical Co. Pr Inc.
933 Rd. Km. 01
Gurabo, PR 00778
Ultimate Parent: Johnson & Johnson. SIC: 3999—Manufacturing Industries Nec.

★ 78444 ★ Omb Pharmaceutical Partners
State Rd. 933 Km 0.1, Mamey Ward
Gurabo, PR 00778
Ultimate Parent: Johnson & Johnson. SIC: 2834—Pharmaceutical Preparations.

Hatillo

★ 78445 ★ Banco Popular de Puerto Rico
128 Franklin D. Roosevelt Ave.
Hatillo, PR 00659
(809)898-4760
Company Type: Subsidiary. Location Type: Branch office. Ultimate Parent: Banponce Corp. SIC: 6022—State Commercial Banks.

★ 78446 ★ Central Soya Del Norte Inc.
Calle La Militar 461 Carrizalez Word
Hatillo, PR 00659
Ultimate Parent: Central Soya. SIC: 2048—Prepared Feeds Nec.

★ 78447 ★ Central Soya Del Norte Inc.
Rd. 2 Km 80.0 Carrizales Ward
Hatillo, PR 00659
Ultimate Parent: Central Soya. SIC: 2048—Prepared Feeds Nec.

Hato Rey

★ 78448 ★ Banco Popular de Puerto Rico
526 Ponce de Len Ave., Cnr Guayama St.
Hato Rey, PR 00917
(809)753-0195
Company Type: Subsidiary. Location Type: Branch office. Ultimate Parent: Banponce Corp. SIC: 6022—State Commercial Banks.

★ 78449 ★ Banco Popular de Puerto Rico
Monte Mall Shopping Ctr.
Hato Rey, PR 00918
(809)767-3494
Company Type: Subsidiary. Location Type: Branch office. Ultimate Parent: Banponce Corp. SIC: 6022—State Commercial Banks.

★ 78450 ★ Banco Popular de Puerto Rico
68 Barbosa Ave. & Mayaguez St.
Hato Rey, PR 00917
(809)766-2020
Company Type: Subsidiary. Location Type: Branch office. Ultimate Parent: Banponce Corp. SIC: 6022—State Commercial Banks.

★ 78451 ★ Banco Popular de Puerto Rico
Expreso Popular, Lobby Popular Ctr.
209 Ponce de Len Ave.
Hato Rey, PR 00919
(809)765-9800
Company Type: Subsidiary. Location Type: Branch office. Ultimate Parent: Banponce Corp. SIC: 6022—State Commercial Banks.

★ 78452 ★ Banco Popular de Puerto Rico
268 Muoz Rivera Stop 30
Hato Rey, PR 00918
(809)754-8757
Company Type: Subsidiary. Location Type: Branch office. Ultimate Parent: Banponce Corp. SIC: 6022—State Commercial Banks.

★ 78453 ★ Banco Popular de Puerto Rico
Popular Ctr. Bldg.
209 Ponce de Len Ave.
Hato Rey, PR 00919
(809)765-9800
Company Type: Subsidiary. Location Type: Branch office. Ultimate Parent: Banponce Corp. SIC: 6022—State Commercial Banks.

★ 78454 ★ Data General Puerto Rico Inc.
Royal Bank Bldg., Ste. 255
Ponce de Leon Ave. 255
Hato Rey, PR 00919
(809)753-9364
Company Type: Subsidiary. Ultimate Parent: Data General. SIC: 3571—Electronic Computers; 3572—Computer Storage Devices; 3577—Computer Peripheral Equipment Nec.

★ 78455 ★ First Brands Puerto Rico
268 Ponce De Leon Ave., Ste. 1103
Hato Rey, PR 00918
(809)763-0222 Fax: (809)763-0752
Officer: Jose R. Rodriguez, COO. Ultimate Parent: First Brands Corp. SIC: 2673—Bags—Plastics, Laminated & Coated.

★ 78456 ★ Island Healthcare Inc.
Royal Bank Ctr.
Avenida Ponce De Leon 255, Ste. 1600
Hato Rey, PR 00902-3547
(809)250-7231 (800)462-9231 Fax: (809)250-0380
Company Type: Subsidiary. Ultimate Parent: Baxter International. SIC: 6324—Hospital & Medical Service Plans.

Hato Tejas

★ 78457 ★ Ecolab Manufacturing Inc.
Centro Industrial Corujo Carr No.2 Km 15.2
Hato Tejas, PR 00619
Ultimate Parent: Ecolab Inc.

Hormigueros

★ 78458 ★ Banco Popular de Puerto Rico
12 Mateo Fajardo Cardona St.
Hormigueros, PR 00660
(809)849-5050
Company Type: Subsidiary. Location Type: Branch office. Ultimate Parent: Banponce Corp. SIC: 6022—State Commercial Banks.

★ 78459 ★ Emerson Electric Co.
Terminal Products Div.
State Rd. No. 2 Km. 163.3
Hormigueros, PR 00660-0262
Company Type: Division. Ultimate Parent: Emerson Electric Co. Inc. SIC: 3643—Current-Carrying Wiring Devices.

Humacao

★ 78460 ★ Banco Popular de Puerto Rico
Humacao Shopping Ctr.
Font Martelo Ave.
Humacao, PR 00791
(809)852-0101
Company Type: Subsidiary. Location Type: Branch office. Ultimate Parent: Banponce Corp. SIC: 6022—State Commercial Banks.

★ 78461 ★ Caribe General Electric Products Inc. Humacao P.R.
St. Rd. 3 Km 82.0
Humacao, PR 00791
Ultimate Parent: General Electric. SIC: 3643—Current-Carrying Wiring Devices; 3914—Silverware & Plated Ware.

★ **78462** ★　**Med Rel, Inc.**
Rd. 909, Km. 0.4, Barrio Mariana
Humacao, PR 00792
Ultimate Parent: Medtronic Inc. **SIC:**
3845—Electromedical Equipment; 3841—
Surgical & Medical Instruments.

★ **78463** ★　**Squibb Mfg. Inc.**
State Rd. 3 Km. 77.5
Humacao, PR 00792
Ultimate Parent: Bristol-Myers Squibb. **SIC:**
2834—Pharmaceutical Preparations.

Isabela

★ **78464** ★　**Banco Popular de Puerto Rico**
13 Aguadilla Ave. & Jess T. Piero
Isabela, PR 00662
(809)872-2945
Company Type: Subsidiary. **Location
Type:** Branch office. **Ultimate Parent:**
Banponce Corp. **SIC:** 6022—State
Commercial Banks.

Jayuya

★ **78465** ★　**Banco Popular de Puerto Rico**
84 Guillermo Esteves St.
Jayuya, PR 00664
(809)828-3350
Company Type: Subsidiary. **Location
Type:** Branch office. **Ultimate Parent:**
Banponce Corp. **SIC:** 6022—State
Commercial Banks.

★ **78466** ★　**Baxter Healthcare Corp. of Puerto Rico**
St. Rd. 144 Km. 20.6
Jayuya, PR 00664
Ultimate Parent: Baxter International. **SIC:**
2834—Pharmaceutical Preparations; 3841—
Surgical & Medical Instruments.

Juana Diaz

★ **78467** ★　**Banco Popular de Puerto Rico**
90 Comercio St.
Juana Diaz, PR 00795
(809)837-2290
Company Type: Subsidiary. **Location
Type:** Branch office. **Ultimate Parent:**
Banponce Corp. **SIC:** 6022—State
Commercial Banks.

★ **78468** ★　**Productos Circuitos De P.R.**
Km. 66.7 Rd. 149
Juana Diaz, PR 00795
Ultimate Parent: Westinghouse Electric
Corp. **SIC:** 3672—Printed Circuit Boards.

★ **78469** ★　**Westinghouse De Puerto Rico**
Productos Circuitos De Puerto Rico
Hwy. 149 Km 66.7
Juana Diaz, PR 00795-1415
Ultimate Parent: Westinghouse Electric
Corp. **SIC:** 3672—Printed Circuit Boards.

★ **78470** ★　**Westinghouse de Puerto Rico**
Productos Circuitos De Puerto Rico
Km 66.7 - Rd. 149
Juana Diaz, PR 00795
Ultimate Parent: Westinghouse Electric
Corp. **SIC:** 3672—Printed Circuit Boards.

Juncos

★ **78471** ★　**Amgen Manufacturing, Inc.**
Kilometer 24.6
State Rd. 31
Juncos, PR 00777-4060
(809)734-2000 **Fax:** (809)734-3049
Company Type: Subsidiary. **Ultimate
Parent:** Amgen.

★ **78472** ★　**Timeplex Caribe Ltd.**
Rd. 189 Km. 12.4
Juncos, PR 00777-1539
Ultimate Parent: Unisys Corp. **SIC:** 3669—
Communications Equipment Nec.

★ **78473** ★　**Timeplex Caribe Ltd.**
PO Box 1539
Juncos, PR 00777
Ultimate Parent: Unisys Corp. **SIC:** 3669—
Communications Equipment Nec.

Lares

★ **78474** ★　**Banco Popular de Puerto Rico**
12 Vilella St.
Lares, PR 00669
(809)897-2575
Company Type: Subsidiary. **Location
Type:** Branch office. **Ultimate Parent:**
Banponce Corp. **SIC:** 6022—State
Commercial Banks.

Las Marias

★ **78475** ★　**Banco Popular de Puerto Rico**
Comercio St. & Rd. 119
Las Marias, PR 00670
(809)827-3615
Company Type: Subsidiary. **Location
Type:** Branch office. **Ultimate Parent:**
Banponce Corp. **SIC:** 6022—State
Commercial Banks.

Las Piedras

★ **78476** ★　**Bard Cardiopulmonary Inc.**
Pridco Ind. Park S. Lot 5
Las Piedras, PR 00771
Ultimate Parent: C. R. Bard. **SIC:** 3841—
Surgical & Medical Instruments.

★ **78477** ★　**Bard Cardiopulmonary Inc.**
Pridco Industrial Pk. S, Lot No. 5
Las Piedras, PR 00771-2001
Ultimate Parent: C. R. Bard. **SIC:** 3841—
Surgical & Medical Instruments.

★ **78478** ★　**Bard Cardiopulmonary Inc.**
Pridco Ind. Park South Lot 5
Las Piedras, PR 00771
Ultimate Parent: C. R. Bard. **SIC:** 3841—
Surgical & Medical Instruments.

★ **78479** ★　**Intel Puerto Rico Inc.**
PO Box 125
Las Piedras, PR 00671
Ultimate Parent: Intel Corp.

★ **78480** ★　**Johnson & Johnson Consumer Products Inc.**
Rd. 183 Km. 19.7
Las Piedras, PR 00771
Ultimate Parent: Johnson & Johnson. **SIC:**
3842—Surgical Appliances & Supplies.

★ **78481** ★　**Johnson & Johnson Orthopaedics Products Inc.**
Rd. 183 Km. 19.7
Las Piedras, PR 00771
Ultimate Parent: Johnson & Johnson. **SIC:**
3842—Surgical Appliances & Supplies.

★ **78482** ★　**Key Pharmaceuticals Puerto Rico Inc.**
Pridco Industrial Park, State Rd. 183
Las Piedras, PR 00771
Ultimate Parent: Schering-Plough Corp.
SIC: 2834—Pharmaceutical Preparations.

★ **78483** ★　**Life Savers Inc.**
Hwy. 30, Km. 21.2
PO Box 128
Las Piedras, PR 00771
Ultimate Parent: RJR Nabisco Holdings.
SIC: 2000—Food & Kindred Products.

★ **78484** ★　**Life Savers Mfg. Inc.**
Rd. 30 Km 21.2 (PO Box 128)
Las Piedras, PR 00771
Ultimate Parent: RJR Nabisco Holdings.
SIC: 2067—Chewing Gum.

★ **78485** ★　**Pamcor, Inc.**
Carr 183 KM 183
Las Piedras, PR 00771
(809)733-8196
Company Type: Affiliate. **Officer:** Marco
Pardo, President. **Ultimate Parent:** AMP
Inc. **SIC:** 3643—Current-Carrying Wiring
Devices; 3678—Electronic Connectors;
3679—Electronic Components Nec.

★ **78486** ★　**Pamcor Inc. Las Piedras Plant**
Pr Rd. 181, Km. 18.3
Las Piedras, PR 00671
Location Type: Plant. **Ultimate Parent:**
AMP Inc. **SIC:** 3643—Current-Carrying

Wiring Devices; 3471—Plating & Polishing;
3678—Electronic Connectors.

★ **78487** ★　**Schering-Plough Prodsucts Inc.**
Key Pharmaceuticals
Pridco Indl. Park State Rd. 183
Las Piedras, PR 00771
Ultimate Parent: Schering-Plough Corp.
SIC: 2834—Pharmaceutical Preparations.

★ **78488** ★　**Schering-Plough Products Inc.**
Key Pharmaceuticals
Pridco Industrial Park State Rd. 183
Las Piedras, PR 00771
Ultimate Parent: Schering-Plough Corp.
SIC: 2834—Pharmaceutical Preparations.

Luquillo

★ **78489** ★　**Banco Popular de Puerto Rico**
193 Ins. Rd. Cnr Playa Azul
Luquillo, PR 00773
(809)889-2610
Company Type: Subsidiary. **Location
Type:** Branch office. **Ultimate Parent:**
Banponce Corp. **SIC:** 6022—State
Commercial Banks.

★ **78490** ★　**Gibson Electric of Pr. Inc. Cce Plant No. 2**
Roads 992 & A, Km 0.3, Lot 7 Luquillo
Industrial Park
Luquillo, PR 00773
Ultimate Parent: GTE. **SIC:** 3313—
Electrometallurgical Products.

★ **78491** ★　**Syltron Inc. Lighting Products**
Rd. 992 Km. 0.5 Lot 15
Luquillo, PR 00673
Ultimate Parent: GTE. **SIC:** 3643—
Current-Carrying Wiring Devices.

Manati

★ **78492** ★　**Banco Popular de Puerto Rico**
Villa Mara Shopping Ctr.
Manati, PR 00674
(809)854-2030
Company Type: Subsidiary. **Location
Type:** Branch office. **Ultimate Parent:**
Banponce Corp. **SIC:** 6022—State
Commercial Banks.

★ **78493** ★　**Caribe General Electric Products Inc.**
State Hwy. No. 2 Km. 47.5
Manati, PR 00674
Ultimate Parent: General Electric. **SIC:**
3625—Relays & Industrial Controls.

★ **78494** ★　**Cyanamid Agricultural De Puerto Rico Inc.**
P.R. Rd. 2 Km. 47.2
Manati, PR 00674
Ultimate Parent: American Cyanamid Co.
SIC: 2834—Pharmaceutical Preparations;
2869—Industrial Organic Chemicals Nec.

★ **78495** ★　**Cyanamid Agricultural De Puerto Rico, Inc.**
P.R. Rd. 2 Km. 47.2
Manati, PR 00674
Ultimate Parent: American Cyanamid Co.
SIC: 2834—Pharmaceutical Preparations;
2869—Industrial Organic Chemicals Nec.

★ **78496** ★　**Cyanamid Agricultural De Puerto Rico Inc.**
Pr Rd. 2 Km 47.3
Manati, PR 00674
Ultimate Parent: American Cyanamid Co.
SIC: 2834—Pharmaceutical Preparations;
2869—Industrial Organic Chemicals Nec.

★ **78497** ★　**Cynamid Agricultural De Puerto Rico Inc.**
Pr Rd. 2 Km. 47.3
Manati, PR 00674
Ultimate Parent: American Cyanamid Co.
SIC: 2834—Pharmaceutical Preparations;
2879—Agricultural Chemicals Nec.

★ **78498** ★　**Davis & Geck, Inc.**
State Rd. No. 2, Km 47.2
Manati, PR 00674
Ultimate Parent: American Cyanamid Co.
SIC: 3842—Surgical Appliances & Supplies;
2842—Polishes & Sanitation Goods.

★ **78499** ★　**Eaton Laboratories, Inc.**
Hwy. No. 2, Km. 45.7
Manati, PR 00674
Ultimate Parent: Eaton Corp. **SIC:** 2834—
Pharmaceutical Preparations.

★ **78500** ★　**Ortho Biologics, Inc.**
Rd. NO. 2, Km. 45.6, Campo Alegre Ward
Manati, PR 00674-0463
Ultimate Parent: Johnson & Johnson. **SIC:**
2834—Pharmaceutical Preparations; 2836—
Biological Products Except Diagnostic.

★ **78501** ★　**Ortho Pharmaceuticals Inc.**
Rd. 2 Km 45.6 Campo Alegre Ward
Manati, PR 00674-0463
Ultimate Parent: Johnson & Johnson. **SIC:**
2834—Pharmaceutical Preparations.

★ **78502** ★　**Proctor & Gamble Pharmaceuticals Pr Inc.**
Hwy. 2 Km. 45.7
Manati, PR 00674
Ultimate Parent: Procter & Gamble Co.
SIC: 2834—Pharmaceutical Preparations.

★ **78503** ★　**Schering Industrial Development Corp.**
Rd. 686 Km. 0.5 Bo. Coto Norte
Manati, PR 00674
Ultimate Parent: Schering-Plough Corp.
SIC: 2833—Medicinals & Botanicals.

★ **78504** ★　**Schering-Plough Products Inc.**
Development
Rte. 686 Km. 0.5 Bo. Coto Norte
Manati, PR 00674
Ultimate Parent: Schering-Plough Corp.
SIC: 2833—Medicinals & Botanicals.

Maricao

★ **78505** ★　**Banco Popular de Puerto Rico**
De Diego & Baldorioty St.
Maricao, PR 00606
(809)838-3740
Company Type: Subsidiary. **Location
Type:** Branch office. **Ultimate Parent:**
Banponce Corp. **SIC:** 6022—State
Commercial Banks.

Mayaguez

★ **78506** ★　**Banco Popular de Puerto Rico**
Comercio & Aduana Sts.
Mayaguez, PR 00680
(809)834-0549
Company Type: Subsidiary. **Location
Type:** Branch office. **Ultimate Parent:**
Banponce Corp. **SIC:** 6022—State
Commercial Banks.

★ **78507** ★　**Banco Popular de Puerto Rico**
Mayaguez Mall Shopping Ctr.
Mayaguez Mall Sur
Mayaguez, PR 00680
(809)834-2929
Company Type: Subsidiary. **Location
Type:** Branch office. **Ultimate Parent:**
Banponce Corp. **SIC:** 6022—State
Commercial Banks.

★ **78508** ★　**Banco Popular de Puerto Rico**
Mendez Vigo & Basora Sts.
Mayaguez, PR 00680
(809)832-0476
Company Type: Subsidiary. **Location
Type:** Branch office. **Ultimate Parent:**
Banponce Corp. **SIC:** 6022—State
Commercial Banks.

★ **78509** ★　**Banco Popular de Puerto Rico**
Vista Verde Shopping Ctr.
Mayaguez, PR 00680
(809)834-8282
Company Type: Subsidiary. **Location
Type:** Branch office. **Ultimate Parent:**
Banponce Corp. **SIC:** 6022—State
Commercial Banks.

★ 78510 ★ **Banco Popular de Puerto Rico**
Post St.
Mayaguez, PR 00680
(809)834-7000
Company Type: Subsidiary. **Location Type:** Branch office. **Ultimate Parent:** Banponce Corp. **SIC:** 6022—State Commercial Banks.

★ 78511 ★ **Eli Lilly Ind. Inc.**
State Rd. 2 Km. 146.7
Mayaguez, PR 00680
Ultimate Parent: Eli Lilly. **SIC:** 2833—Medicinals & Botanicals; 2834—Pharmaceutical Preparations.

★ 78512 ★ **Eli Lilly Industries, Inc.**
State Rd. No.2, Km 146.7
Mayaguez, PR 00680
Ultimate Parent: Eli Lilly. **SIC:** 2833—Medicinals & Botanicals; 2834—Pharmaceutical Preparations.

★ 78513 ★ **Star Kist Caribe Inc.**
Rd. 341 Km 5.8
Mayaguez, PR 00680
Ultimate Parent: H.J. Heinz. **SIC:** 2047—Dog & Cat Food; 2048—Prepared Feeds Nec; 2091—Canned & Cured Fish & Seafoods.

★ 78514 ★ **Star Kist Caribe Inc.**
Carr. 341 Km. 5.8
Mayaguez, PR 00680
Ultimate Parent: H.J. Heinz. **SIC:** 2047—Dog & Cat Food; 2048—Prepared Feeds Nec; 2091—Canned & Cured Fish & Seafoods.

★ 78515 ★ **Westinghouse Abb**
Guanajibo Ind Park D St.
Mayaguez, PR 00680
Ultimate Parent: Westinghouse Electric Corp. **SIC:** 3613—Switchgear & Switchboard Apparatus.

★ 78516 ★ **Westinghouse Productos**
D St. Guanajibo Ind. Park
Mayaguez, PR 00680
Ultimate Parent: Westinghouse Electric Corp. **SIC:** 3613—Switchgear & Switchboard Apparatus.

★ 78517 ★ **Westinghouse de Puerto Rico**
Productos Westinghouse
D-Street Guanajibo Industrial Park
Mayaguez, PR 00680
Ultimate Parent: Westinghouse Electric Corp. **SIC:** 3613—Switchgear & Switchboard Apparatus.

Mayaquez

★ 78518 ★ **Star-Kist Caribe Inc.**
PO Box 3690
Mayaguez, PR 00681
(809)834-2424
Company Type: Subsidiary. **Officer:** Maurice Callaghan, General Manager. **Ultimate Parent:** H.J. Heinz. **SIC:** 2091—Canned & Cured Fish & Seafoods; 2092—Fresh or Frozen Prepared Fish.

Mercedita

★ 78519 ★ **Western Digital Caribe Inc.**
Turpeaux Ind. Park 1 a
Mercedita, PR 00715-0176
Ultimate Parent: Western Digital. **SIC:** 3999—Manufacturing Industries Nec.

Moca

★ 78520 ★ **Banco Popular de Puerto Rico**
8 Jos Calatzan La Salle St.
Moca, PR 00676
(809)877-2880
Company Type: Subsidiary. **Location Type:** Branch office. **Ultimate Parent:** Banponce Corp. **SIC:** 6022—State Commercial Banks.

Morovis

★ 78521 ★ **Banco Popular de Puerto Rico**
49 Corozal Ave.
Morovis, PR 00667
(809)862-2160
Company Type: Subsidiary. **Location Type:** Branch office. **Ultimate Parent:** Banponce Corp. **SIC:** 6022—State Commercial Banks.

Naranjito

★ 78522 ★ **Banco Popular de Puerto Rico**
5 Ignacio Morales St.
Naranjito, PR 00719
(809)869-2900
Company Type: Subsidiary. **Location Type:** Branch office. **Ultimate Parent:** Banponce Corp. **SIC:** 6022—State Commercial Banks.

Orocovis

★ 78523 ★ **Banco Popular de Puerto Rico**
11 4th of July St.
Rd. to Coamo 1
Orocovis, PR 00720
(809)867-2425
Company Type: Subsidiary. **Location Type:** Branch office. **Ultimate Parent:** Banponce Corp. **SIC:** 6022—State Commercial Banks.

Palmer

★ 78524 ★ **Caribe General Electric Products Inc.**
Rd. 191 Km-0. Hm-5
Palmer, PR 00721
Ultimate Parent: General Electric. **SIC:** 3643—Current-Carrying Wiring Devices.

Patillas

★ 78525 ★ **Banco Popular de Puerto Rico**
318 Muoz Rivera & Iglesia Sts.
Patillas, PR 00723
(809)839-2130
Company Type: Subsidiary. **Location Type:** Branch office. **Ultimate Parent:** Banponce Corp. **SIC:** 6022—State Commercial Banks.

Penuelas

★ 78526 ★ **Banco Popular de Puerto Rico**
318 Muoz Rivera St.
Penuelas, PR 00624
(809)836-1530
Company Type: Subsidiary. **Location Type:** Branch office. **Ultimate Parent:** Banponce Corp. **SIC:** 6022—State Commercial Banks.

Playa Ponce

★ 78527 ★ **National Packing Co.**
Ave. Stgo. De Los Caballeros Num. 1
Playa Ponce, PR 00731
Ultimate Parent: Ralston Purina. **SIC:** 2091—Canned & Cured Fish & Seafoods.

Ponce

★ 78528 ★ **Banco Popular de Puerto Rico**
Hostos Ave. & Marina St.
Ponce, PR 00731
(809)840-6800
Company Type: Subsidiary. **Location Type:** Branch office. **Ultimate Parent:** Banponce Corp. **SIC:** 6022—State Commercial Banks.

★ 78529 ★ **Banco Popular de Puerto Rico**
Ins. Rd. 1, Km. 124.3
Los Caobos
Ponce, PR 00731
(809)844-6040
Company Type: Subsidiary. **Location Type:** Branch office. **Ultimate Parent:**

Banponce Corp. **SIC:** 6022—State Commercial Banks.

★ 78530 ★ **Banco Popular de Puerto Rico**
Hostos Ave. & Padre Noel St.
Ponce, PR 00731
(809)842-6302
Company Type: Subsidiary. **Location Type:** Branch office. **Ultimate Parent:** Banponce Corp. **SIC:** 6022—State Commercial Banks.

★ 78531 ★ **Banco Popular de Puerto Rico**
182 Villa & Guayanilla Sts.
Ponce, PR 00731
(809)842-2240
Company Type: Subsidiary. **Location Type:** Branch office. **Ultimate Parent:** Banponce Corp. **SIC:** 6022—State Commercial Banks.

★ 78532 ★ **Banco Popular de Puerto Rico**
La Rambla Shopping Ctr.
Ponce, PR 00731
(809)843-5030
Company Type: Subsidiary. **Location Type:** Branch office. **Ultimate Parent:** Banponce Corp. **SIC:** 6022—State Commercial Banks.

★ 78533 ★ **Banco Popular de Puerto Rico**
Centro del Sur Shopping Ctr.
Buena Vista
Ponce, PR 00731
(809)840-3636
Company Type: Subsidiary. **Location Type:** Branch office. **Ultimate Parent:** Banponce Corp. **SIC:** 6022—State Commercial Banks.

★ 78534 ★ **Banco Popular de Puerto Rico**
Ponce Mall
Interstate Rd. No. 2
Ponce, PR 00731
(809)844-7200
Company Type: Subsidiary. **Location Type:** Branch office. **Ultimate Parent:** Banponce Corp. **SIC:** 6022—State Commercial Banks.

★ 78535 ★ **Echlin Ponce Inc.**
El Tuque Industrial Park B St.
Ponce, PR 00731
Ultimate Parent: Echlin. **SIC:** 3714—Motor Vehicle Parts & Accessories; 3694—Engine Electrical Equipment.

★ 78536 ★ **Hanes Menswear Inc.**
84 Hostos Ave.
Ponce, PR 00732
Ultimate Parent: Sara Lee Corp. **SIC:** 2254—Knit Underwear Mills; 2257—Weft Knit Fabric Mills.

★ 78537 ★ **Sara Lee Knit Products**
Hanes Menswear
Ave. Hostos 84
Ponce, PR 00731-0000
Ultimate Parent: Sara Lee Corp. **SIC:** 2322—Men's/Boys' Underwear & Nightwear.

Puerto Real

★ 78538 ★ **Stanric Inc.**
Rd. 195 Km 1.5 Puerto Real Station
Puerto Real, PR 00740
Ultimate Parent: Standard Products. **SIC:** 3694—Engine Electrical Equipment.

Puerto Rico

★ 78539 ★ **Banco Popular de Puerto Rico**
Mercedes Moreno Ctr. Cnr Muoz Rivera St.
Puerto Rico, PR 00603
(809)891-2085
Company Type: Subsidiary. **Location Type:** Branch office. **Ultimate Parent:** Banponce Corp. **SIC:** 6022—State Commercial Banks.

Quebradillas

★ 78540 ★ **Banco Popular de Puerto Rico**
Calle Honarir Hernandez 108
Quebradillas, PR 00678
(809)895-2545
Company Type: Subsidiary. **Location Type:** Branch office. **Ultimate Parent:** Banponce Corp. **SIC:** 6022—State Commercial Banks.

Rincon

★ 78541 ★ **Banco Popular de Puerto Rico**
2 Comercio St., Cnr Muoz Rivera
Rincon, PR 00677
(809)823-2260
Company Type: Subsidiary. **Location Type:** Branch office. **Ultimate Parent:** Banponce Corp. **SIC:** 6022—State Commercial Banks.

★ 78542 ★ **Carter P. D. Inc.**
Rte. 115, Km. 12.9
Rincon, PR 00677
Ultimate Parent: Carter-Wallace. **SIC:** 2844—Toilet Preparations.

Rio Grande

★ 78543 ★ **Banco Popular de Puerto Rico**
2 Juan Gonzlez St.
Rio Grande, PR 00745
(809)887-2570
Company Type: Subsidiary. **Location Type:** Branch office. **Ultimate Parent:** Banponce Corp. **SIC:** 6022—State Commercial Banks.

Rio Piedras

★ 78544 ★ **Pamcor Inc.**
No. 677 Ave. De Diego
Rio Piedras, PR 00924
Ultimate Parent: AMP Inc. **SIC:** 3471—Plating & Polishing; 3678—Electronic Connectors; 3643—Current-Carrying Wiring Devices; 3679—Electronic Components Nec.

Salinas

★ 78545 ★ **Banco Popular de Puerto Rico**
Muoz Rivera St.
Salinas, PR 00751
(809)824-2777
Company Type: Subsidiary. **Location Type:** Branch office. **Ultimate Parent:** Banponce Corp. **SIC:** 6022—State Commercial Banks.

San Antonio

★ 78546 ★ **Digital Equipment Corp.**
PR Rd. 110 Km 5.8
San Antonio, PR 00952
Ultimate Parent: Digital Equipment Corp. **SIC:** 3672—Printed Circuit Boards.

San German

★ 78547 ★ **Banco Popular de Puerto Rico**
Carro & Dr. Veve
San German, PR 00683
(809)892-1234
Company Type: Subsidiary. **Location Type:** Branch office. **Ultimate Parent:** Banponce Corp. **SIC:** 6022—State Commercial Banks.

★ 78548 ★ **Caribe GE Products Inc.**
Industrial Park
San German, PR 00753
Ultimate Parent: General Electric. **SIC:** 3613—Switchgear & Switchboard Apparatus.

★ 78549 ★ **Caribe G.E. Products Inc.**
El Retiro Industrial Park
San German, PR 00683-0186
Ultimate Parent: General Electric. **SIC:** 3643—Current-Carrying Wiring Devices; 3613—Switchgear & Switchboard Apparatus.

★ 78550 ★ **Digital Equipment Corp.**
PR Rd. 362, Km. 1.0
San German, PR 00953
Ultimate Parent: Digital Equipment Corp. **SIC:** 3672—Printed Circuit Boards; 3679—Electronic Components Nec.

San Juan

★ 78551 ★ **Avon Retail Group**
Avon Products, Inc.
Puerto Rico Branch G.PO Box 3774
San Juan, PR 00936
(809)743-2004
Officer: Juan Carlos Martinez, General Manager. **Ultimate Parent:** Avon Products, Inc. **SIC:** 5122—Drugs, Proprietaries & Sundries.

★ 78552 ★ **Banco Popular de Puerto Rico**
No. 1 Insular Rd., Km. 16.2
San Juan, PR 00926
(809)763-7449
Company Type: Subsidiary. **Location Type:** Branch office. **Ultimate Parent:** Banponce Corp. **SIC:** 6021—National Commercial Banks.

★ 78553 ★ **Banco Popular de Puerto Rico**
Cupey Ctr.
Rd. 176, Km. 1.2
San Juan, PR 00928
(809)751-0832
Company Type: Subsidiary. **Location Type:** Branch office. **Ultimate Parent:** Banponce Corp. **SIC:** 6022—State Commercial Banks.

★ 78554 ★ **Banco Popular de Puerto Rico**
Reparto Metropolitano Shopping Ctr.
San Juan, PR 00921
(809)758-8500
Company Type: Subsidiary. **Location Type:** Branch office. **Ultimate Parent:** Banponce Corp. **SIC:** 6022—State Commercial Banks.

★ 78555 ★ **Banco Popular de Puerto Rico**
Janer Bldg.
Universidad De Puerto Rico
San Juan, PR 00931
(809)751-0238
Company Type: Subsidiary. **Location Type:** Branch office. **Ultimate Parent:** Banponce Corp. **SIC:** 6022—State Commercial Banks.

★ 78556 ★ **Banco Popular de Puerto Rico**
Plaza Del Mercado
155 De Diego Ave.
San Juan, PR 00925
(809)765-9050
Company Type: Subsidiary. **Location Type:** Branch office. **Ultimate Parent:** Banponce Corp. **SIC:** 6022—State Commercial Banks.

★ 78557 ★ **Banco Popular de Puerto Rico**
Los Flamboyanes Shopping Ctr.
65 Infantry Ave.
San Juan, PR 00924
(809)763-3838
Company Type: Subsidiary. **Location Type:** Branch office. **Ultimate Parent:** Banponce Corp. **SIC:** 6022—State Commercial Banks.

★ 78558 ★ **Banco Popular de Puerto Rico**
1 Ins Rd., 1575 Alda St., Urb Caribe
San Juan, PR 00926
(809)767-0909
Company Type: Subsidiary. **Location Type:** Branch office. **Ultimate Parent:** Banponce Corp. **SIC:** 6022—State Commercial Banks.

★ 78559 ★ **Banco Popular de Puerto Rico**
El Senorcal Shopping Ctr.
Winston Churchill Ave.
San Juan, PR 00925
(809)751-4515
Company Type: Subsidiary. **Location Type:** Branch office. **Ultimate Parent:** Banponce Corp. **SIC:** 6022—State Commercial Banks.

★ 78560 ★ **Banco Popular de Puerto Rico**
Muoz Rivera 1125
San Juan, PR 00925
(809)767-1150
Company Type: Subsidiary. **Location Type:** Branch office. **Ultimate Parent:** Banponce Corp. **SIC:** 6022—State Commercial Banks.

★ 78561 ★ **Banco Popular de Puerto Rico**
De Diego Ave. Urb San Francisco
San Juan, PR 00926
(809)763-0588
Company Type: Subsidiary. **Location Type:** Branch office. **Ultimate Parent:** Banponce Corp. **SIC:** 6021—National Commercial Banks.

★ 78562 ★ **Banco Popular de Puerto Rico**
65 Infantry Ave.
San Juan, PR 00925
(809)766-2900
Company Type: Subsidiary. **Location Type:** Branch office. **Ultimate Parent:** Banponce Corp. **SIC:** 6022—State Commercial Banks.

★ 78563 ★ **Banco Popular de Puerto Rico**
1101 Ponce de Leon Ave., Corner Paseo De Diego
San Juan, PR 00925
(809)766-1540
Company Type: Subsidiary. **Location Type:** Branch office. **Ultimate Parent:** Banponce Corp. **SIC:** 6022—State Commercial Banks.

★ 78564 ★ **Banco Popular de Puerto Rico**
Glorieta Bldg.
Bo. Monacillos
San Juan, PR 00921
(809)753-8989
Company Type: Subsidiary. **Location Type:** Branch office. **Ultimate Parent:** Banponce Corp. **SIC:** 6022—State Commercial Banks.

★ 78565 ★ **Banco Popular de Puerto Rico**
301 Roosevelt & De Diego Aves.
San Juan, PR 00920
(809)781-7220
Company Type: Subsidiary. **Location Type:** Branch office. **Ultimate Parent:** Banponce Corp. **SIC:** 6022—State Commercial Banks.

★ 78566 ★ **Banco Popular de Puerto Rico**
Caparra Ter.
1648 Jesus T. Pinero Ave.
San Juan, PR 00920
(809)781-3037
Company Type: Subsidiary. **Location Type:** Branch office. **Ultimate Parent:** Banponce Corp. **SIC:** 6022—State Commercial Banks.

★ 78567 ★ **Banco Popular de Puerto Rico**
Baldorioty de Castro Ave. & 6 St.
San Juan, PR 00979
(809)726-5600
Company Type: Subsidiary. **Location Type:** Branch office. **Ultimate Parent:** Banponce Corp. **SIC:** 6022—State Commercial Banks.

★ 78568 ★ **Banco Popular de Puerto Rico**
No. 37 Insular Rd.
Los Gobernadores Ave.
San Juan, PR 00979
(809)791-5328
Company Type: Subsidiary. **Location Type:** Branch office. **Ultimate Parent:** Banponce Corp. **SIC:** 6022—State Commercial Banks.

★ 78569 ★ **Banco Popular de Puerto Rico**
Km. 3.5 Peparto Bechara
Marginal Kennedy Ave.
San Juan, PR 00920
(809)781-0750
Company Type: Subsidiary. **Location Type:** Branch office. **Ultimate Parent:** Banponce Corp. **SIC:** 6021—National Commercial Banks.

★ 78570 ★ **Banco Popular de Puerto Rico**
Caparra Shopping Ctr.
Franklin D. Roosevelt Ave.
San Juan, PR 00968
(809)782-0090
Company Type: Subsidiary. **Location Type:** Branch office. **Ultimate Parent:** Banponce Corp. **SIC:** 6022—State Commercial Banks.

★ 78571 ★ **Banco Popular de Puerto Rico**
206 Tetuan & San Justo Sts.
San Juan, PR 00901
(809)725-2636
Company Type: Subsidiary. **Location Type:** Branch office. **Ultimate Parent:** Banponce Corp. **SIC:** 6022—State Commercial Banks.

★ 78572 ★ **Banco Popular de Puerto Rico**
Old San Juan Bldg., No. 206
Lobby Recinto Sur St.
San Juan, PR 00901
(809)723-5354
Company Type: Subsidiary. **Location Type:** Branch office. **Ultimate Parent:** Banponce Corp. **SIC:** 6022—State Commercial Banks.

★ 78573 ★ **Banco Popular de Puerto Rico**
209 Munoz Rivera Ave.
GPO Box 2708
San Juan, PR 00936-2708
(809)765-9800 **Fax:** (809)759-7803 **Telex:** BANCPOPPDWU 3450033
Company Type: Subsidiary. **Location Type:** Branch office. **Officer:** Richard L. Carrion, Chairman, President & CEO. **Ultimate Parent:** Banponce Corp. **SIC:** 6022—State Commercial Banks.

★ 78574 ★ **Banco Popular de Puerto Rico**
301 Ponce de Leon Ave.
San Juan, PR 00901
(809)723-0158
Company Type: Subsidiary. **Location Type:** Branch office. **Ultimate Parent:** Banponce Corp. **SIC:** 6022—State Commercial Banks.

★ 78575 ★ **Banponce Corp.**
209 Ponce de Leon Ave.
San Juan, PR 00936
(809)765-9800
Company Type: Headquarters. **Officer:** Richard L. Carrion. **Fortune Service 500:** Ranking 55.

★ 78576 ★ **Best Foods Caribbean Inc.**
GPO Box 364303
San Juan, PR 00936-4303
(809)724-6969 **Fax:** (809)724-7050
Company Type: Division. **Officer:** Luis Robles, President. **Ultimate Parent:** CPC International. **SIC:** 2033—Canned Fruits & Vegetables; 2035—Pickles, Sauces & Salad Dressings.

★ 78577 ★ **Coco Lopez Manufacturing**
PO Box 364265
San Juan, PR 00936-4265
Company Type: Subsidiary. **Ultimate Parent:** Borden, Inc.

★ 78578 ★ **Executive Airlines**
PO Box 38082, Airport Station
San Juan, PR 00937-0082
(809)253-6401
Company Type: Subsidiary. **Officer:** Thomas Del Valle, President. **Ultimate Parent:** AMR Corp.

★ 78579 ★ **Productos Borden Can Division**
GPO Box 4265
San Juan, PR 00936
Company Type: Subsidiary. **Ultimate Parent:** Borden, Inc.

★ 78580 ★ **Villafane**
Fernandez Juncos Station
PO Box 19387
San Juan, PR 00910
Company Type: Subsidiary. **Ultimate Parent:** Federal-Mogul Corp.

San Lorenzo

★ 78581 ★ **Banco Popular de Puerto Rico**
7 Colon St.
San Lorenzo, PR 00754
(809)736-8454
Company Type: Subsidiary. **Location Type:** Branch office. **Ultimate Parent:** Banponce Corp. **SIC:** 6022—State Commercial Banks.

San Sebastian

★ 78582 ★ **Avon Lomalinda Inc.**
Ricardo Serrano Martinez 96 Ave.
San Sebastian, PR 00685-0153
Ultimate Parent: Avon Products, Inc. **SIC:** 3471—Plating & Polishing; 3911—Jewelry & Precious Metal; 3961—Costume Jewelry.

★ 78583 ★ **Avon Lomalinda, Inc.**
Guatemala Industrial Pk. Rd., 446 Km. 9
San Sebastian, PR 00685-0153
Ultimate Parent: Avon Products, Inc. **SIC:** 3961—Costume Jewelry.

★ 78584 ★ **Avon Lomalinda Inc.**
96 Ricardo Serrano Martinez Ave.
San Sebastian, PR 00685
Ultimate Parent: Avon Products, Inc. **SIC:** 3961—Costume Jewelry.

★ 78585 ★ **Banco Popular de Puerto Rico**
3 Jos Menedez Cardona St.
San Sebastian, PR 00685
(809)896-1615
Company Type: Subsidiary. **Location Type:** Branch office. **Ultimate Parent:** Banponce Corp. **SIC:** 6022—State Commercial Banks.

Santa Isabel

★ 78586 ★ **Allergan Optical Inc.**
Santa Isabel Industrial Park
Santa Isabel, PR 00757
Ultimate Parent: Allergan Inc. **SIC:** 3851—Ophthalmic Goods.

★ 78587 ★ **Banco Popular de Puerto Rico**
36 Muoz Rivera St.
Santa Isabel, PR 00757
(809)845-5000
Company Type: Subsidiary. **Location Type:** Branch office. **Ultimate Parent:** Banponce Corp. **SIC:** 6022—State Commercial Banks.

★ 78588 ★ **Westinghouse Electric Corp.**
Productos Electronic
Reparto Industriale La Playa
Santa Isabel, PR 00757
Ultimate Parent: Westinghouse Electric Corp. **SIC:** 3672—Printed Circuit Boards; 3621—Motors & Generators; 3677—Electronic Coils & Transformers.

★ 78589 ★ **Westinghouse Electric Corp.**
Productos Electronicos
Calle Munoz Rivera 112
Santa Isabel, PR 00757
Ultimate Parent: Westinghouse Electric Corp. **SIC:** 3629—Electrical Industrial Apparatus Nec.

★ 78590 ★ **Westinghouse de Puerto Rico**
Productos Electronicos Industriales
Calle Munoz Rivera 112
Santa Isabel, PR 00757
Ultimate Parent: Westinghouse Electric Corp. **SIC:** 3699—Electrical Equipment & Supplies Nec.

★ 78591 ★ **Westinghouse de Pureto Rico**
Productos Electronicos Industriales
Calle Munoz Rivera 112
Santa Isabel, PR 00757
Ultimate Parent: Westinghouse Electric Corp. **SIC:** 3600—Electronic & Other Electrical Equipment.

Santurce

★ 78592 ★ **Banco Popular de Puerto Rico**
Stop 26, 1900 Ponce de Len Ave.
Santurce, PR 00909
(809)727-8110
Company Type: Subsidiary. **Location Type:** Branch office. **Ultimate Parent:** Banponce Corp. **SIC:** 6022—State Commercial Banks.

★ 78593 ★ **Banco Popular de Puerto Rico**
Stop 22, 1500 Ponce de Len Ave.
Santurce, PR 00909
(809)725-5109
Company Type: Subsidiary. **Location Type:** Branch office. **Ultimate Parent:** Banponce Corp. **SIC:** 6022—State Commercial Banks.

★ 78594 ★ **Banco Popular de Puerto Rico**
Isla Grande Government Ctr. 39W, 9 Bldg.
Santurce, PR 00907
(809)725-4303
Company Type: Subsidiary. **Location Type:** Branch office. **Ultimate Parent:** Banponce Corp. **SIC:** 6022—State Commercial Banks.

★ 78595 ★ **Banco Popular de Puerto Rico**
1060 Ashford Ave. Condado
Santurce, PR 00907
(809)725-4197
Company Type: Subsidiary. **Location Type:** Branch office. **Ultimate Parent:** Banponce Corp. **SIC:** 6022—State Commercial Banks.

★ 78596 ★ **Banco Popular de Puerto Rico**
Loiza & Jefferson Sts.
Santurce, PR 00911
(809)721-5557
Company Type: Subsidiary. **Location Type:** Branch office. **Ultimate Parent:** Banponce Corp. **SIC:** 6022—State Commercial Banks.

★ 78597 ★ **Banco Popular de Puerto Rico**
Km. 3.5 Repto Bechura
Marginal
Kennedy Ave. Ins Rd. 2
Santurce, PR 00920-2998
(809)781-0750
Company Type: Subsidiary. **Location Type:** Branch office. **Ultimate Parent:** Banponce Corp. **SIC:** 6022—State Commercial Banks.

★ 78598 ★ **Banco Popular de Puerto Rico**
701 Ponce de Len Ave.
Miramar
Santurce, PR 00907
(809)723-8078
Company Type: Subsidiary. **Location Type:** Branch office. **Ultimate Parent:** Banponce Corp. **SIC:** 6022—State Commercial Banks.

★ 78599 ★ **Banco Popular de Puerto Rico**
Minillas Government Ctr., North Bldg.
Santurce, PR 00940
(809)727-7600
Company Type: Subsidiary. **Location Type:** Branch office. **Ultimate Parent:** Banponce Corp. **SIC:** 6022—State Commercial Banks.

★ 78600 ★ **Banco Popular de Puerto Rico**
Stop 15, 952 Fdez Juncos Ave.
Santurce, PR 00907
(809)722-0140
Company Type: Subsidiary. **Location Type:** Branch office. **Ultimate Parent:** Banponce Corp. **SIC:** 6022—State Commercial Banks.

★ 78601 ★ **Banco Popular de Puerto Rico**
2250 Borinquen Ave., Bo. Obrero
Santurce, PR 00915
(809)726-1045
Company Type: Subsidiary. **Location Type:** Branch office. **Ultimate Parent:** Banponce Corp. **SIC:** 6022—State Commercial Banks.

★ 78602 ★ **Banco Popular de Puerto Rico**
Roberto H. Todd Ave. & Aldea St.
Santurce, PR 00908
(809)721-1400
Company Type: Subsidiary. **Location Type:** Branch office. **Ultimate Parent:** Banponce Corp. **SIC:** 6022—State Commercial Banks.

St. Just

★ 78603 ★ **Signal Caribe Inc.**
Rd. 848 Km. 1.6
St. Just, PR 00978-0099
Ultimate Parent: Insilco Corp.

Toa Alta

★ 78604 ★ **Banco Popular de Puerto Rico**
23 Muoz Rivera St.
Toa Alta, PR 00953
(809)870-2050
Company Type: Subsidiary. **Location Type:** Branch office. **Ultimate Parent:** Banponce Corp. **SIC:** 6022—State Commercial Banks.

★ 78605 ★ **Bayamon Can Co.**
Rd. 866 Int 865 Bo. Candelaria Arenas
Toa Alta, PR 00953
Ultimate Parent: Borden, Inc. **SIC:** 3411—Metal Cans.

★ 78606 ★ **Bayamon Can Co.**
Rd. 866 - Int. 865 Candelaria Arenas
Toa Alta, PR 00949
Ultimate Parent: Borden, Inc. **SIC:** 3411—Metal Cans.

Toa Baja

★ 78607 ★ **Banco Popular de Puerto Rico**
Los Dominicos Shopping Ctr. & Rosa De Tejas St.
Toa Baja, PR 00965
(809)794-1084
Company Type: Subsidiary. **Location Type:** Branch office. **Ultimate Parent:** Banponce Corp. **SIC:** 6022—State Commercial Banks.

★ 78608 ★ **Borden Inc.**
Carr. 866 Int. 865 Km. 12.1
Bo. Candelaria Arenas
Toa Baja, PR 00949
Location Type: Branch office. **Ultimate Parent:** Borden, Inc.

★ 78609 ★ **Holsum Bakers of Puerto Rico**
State Rd. 2 Km 20.1 Candelaria Ward
Toa Baja, PR 00949
Ultimate Parent: Seaboard Corp. **SIC:** 2052—Cookies & Crackers.

★ 78610 ★ **Industrias La Famosa**
Rd. 866 & 865
Toa Baja, PR 00949
Ultimate Parent: Borden, Inc. **SIC:** 2086—Bottled & Canned Soft Drinks.

★ 78611 ★ **Industrias La Famosa**
Rd. 866 Int. 865 Bo. Candelaria Arenas
Toa Baja, PR 00949
Ultimate Parent: Borden, Inc. **SIC:** 2033—Canned Fruits & Vegetables.

★ 78612 ★ **Westinghouse Corp. of Puerto Rico**
Interruptores Div.
Rd. 854 Km. 3.5
Toa Baja, PR 00949
Company Type: Division. **Ultimate Parent:** Westinghouse Electric Corp. **SIC:** 3613—Switchgear & Switchboard Apparatus.

★ 78613 ★ **Westinghouse De Pr, Inc.**
Interruptores Div.
Rd. 854 Km 4.3
Toa Baja, PR 00949
Company Type: Division. **Ultimate Parent:** Westinghouse Electric Corp. **SIC:** 3613—Switchgear & Switchboard Apparatus; 3471—Plating & Polishing.

★ 78614 ★ **Westinghouse De Puerto Rico**
Interruptores
Rd. 854-Km 4.3
Toa Baja, PR 00949
Ultimate Parent: Westinghouse Electric Corp. **SIC:** 3613—Switchgear & Switchboard Apparatus.

Trujillo Alto

★ 78615 ★ **Banco Popular de Puerto Rico**
3 Muoz Rivera St.
Trujillo Alto, PR 00976
(809)761-5353
Company Type: Subsidiary. **Location Type:** Branch office. **Ultimate Parent:** Banponce Corp. **SIC:** 6022—State Commercial Banks.

★ 78616 ★ **Banco Popular de Puerto Rico**
Trujillo Alto Shopping Ctr.
Trujillo Alto, PR 00976
(809)755-1920
Company Type: Subsidiary. **Location Type:** Branch office. **Ultimate Parent:** Banponce Corp. **SIC:** 6022—State Commercial Banks.

Utuado

★ 78617 ★ **Banco Popular de Puerto Rico**
59 Dr. Cueto St.
Utuado, PR 00641
(809)894-2700
Company Type: Subsidiary. **Location Type:** Branch office. **Ultimate Parent:** Banponce Corp. **SIC:** 6022—State Commercial Banks.

Vega Alta

★ 78618 ★ **Banco Popular de Puerto Rico**
Plaza Caribe Mall
Ins Rd.
Vega Alta, PR 00692
(809)883-2360
Company Type: Subsidiary. **Location Type:** Branch office. **Ultimate Parent:** Banponce Corp. **SIC:** 6022—State Commercial Banks.

★ 78619 ★ **Harman Automotive Puerto Rico Inc.**
Rd. 2 Km. 30.7
Vega Alta, PR 00692
Ultimate Parent: Harvard Industries. **SIC:** 3714—Motor Vehicle Parts & Accessories.

★ 78620 ★ **Harman Automotive Puerto Rico Inc.**
Hwy. 2, Km. 30.7
Vega Alta, PR 00692
Ultimate Parent: Harvard Industries. **SIC:** 3231—Products of Purchased Glass.

★ 78621 ★ **Harman Automotive of Puerto Rico, Inc.**
Hwy. 2, Km. 30.7
Vega Alta, PR 00692
Ultimate Parent: Harvard Industries. **SIC:** 3231—Products of Purchased Glass.

★ 78622 ★ **Inland Container Corp.**
Rd. 690 Km. 1-7 North
Vega Alta, PR 00692
Ultimate Parent: Temple-Inland. **SIC:** 2653—Corrugated & Solid Fiber Boxes.

★ 78623 ★ **Owens Illinois De Puerto Rico**
Plant 138
Km 1.1 Rd. 690 Bo. Sabana Hoyos
Vega Alta, PR 00692
Location Type: Plant. **Ultimate Parent:** Owens-Illinois. **SIC:** 3221—Glass Containers.

Vega Baja

★ 78624 ★ **Banco Popular de Puerto Rico**
Vega Baja Shopping Ctr.
Vega Baja, PR 00693
(809)858-2290
Company Type: Subsidiary. **Location Type:** Branch office. **Ultimate Parent:** Banponce Corp. **SIC:** 6022—State Commercial Banks.

★ 78625 ★ **Banco Popular de Puerto Rico**
X-Tra at Vega Baja Shopping Plaza
No. 2 Rd. International 155
Vega Baja, PR 00693
(809)858-6540
Company Type: Subsidiary. **Location Type:** Branch office. **Ultimate Parent:** Banponce Corp. **SIC:** 6022—State Commercial Banks.

★ 78626 ★ **Motorola De Puerto Rico**
Rd. 686 Km. 17
Vega Baja, PR 00693
Ultimate Parent: Motorola Inc. **SIC:** 3600—Electronic & Other Electrical Equipment; 3691—Storage Batteries.

★ 78627 ★ **Motorola P.R. Operations**
Rd. 686 Km. 17.0
Vega Baja, PR 00693
Ultimate Parent: Motorola Inc. **SIC:** 3663—Radio & T.V. Communications Equipment; 3692—Primary Batteries—Dry & Wet.

★ 78628 ★ **Raychem Corp.**
Rd. 686 Km. 1.0
Vega Baja, PR 00693
Ultimate Parent: Raychem Corp. **SIC:** 3679—Electronic Components Nec; 3678—Electronic Connectors.

★ 78629 ★ **Raychem Industries**
Rd. 686 Km 1.0
Vega Baja, PR 00693-1337
Ultimate Parent: Raychem Corp. **SIC:** 3089—Plastics Products Nec.

★ 78630 ★ **Thomas & Betts Caribe Inc.**
Electrical Products Division
Cabo Caribe Industrial Park Lotes 32-34
Vega Baja, PR 00693
Ultimate Parent: Thomas & Betts. **SIC:** 3643—Current-Carrying Wiring Devices.

★ 78631 ★ **Thomas & Betts Caribe Plant I**
Cabo Caribe Industrial Ctr.
Vega Baja, PR 00694
Ultimate Parent: Thomas & Betts. **SIC:** 3643—Current-Carrying Wiring Devices; 3644—Noncurrent-Carrying Wiring Devices.

Vieques

★ 78632 ★ **Banco Popular de Puerto Rico**
115 Muoz Rivera St.
Vieques, PR 00765
(809)741-2071
Company Type: Subsidiary. **Location Type:** Branch office. **Ultimate Parent:** Banponce Corp. **SIC:** 6022—State Commercial Banks.

Villalba

★ 78633 ★ **Banco Popular de Puerto Rico**
69 Muoz Rivera St.
Villalba, PR 00765
(809)847-4050
Company Type: Subsidiary. **Location Type:** Branch office. **Ultimate Parent:** Banponce Corp. **SIC:** 6022—State Commercial Banks.

★ 78634 ★ **Medtronic Inc. Puerto Rico**
Rd. 149 Km 56.3
Villalba, PR 00766
Ultimate Parent: Medtronic Inc. **SIC:** 3841—Surgical & Medical Instruments.

★ 78635 ★   **Medtronic Pr Inc.**
Rd. 149 Km. 56.3 Call Box 6001
Villalba, PR 00766
(809)856-1072
Company Type: Subsidiary. **Location
Type:** Branch office. **Ultimate Parent:**
Banponce Corp. **SIC:** 6022—State
Commercial Banks. **Ultimate Parent:**
Medtronic Inc. **SIC:** 3845—Electromedical
Equipment.

★ 78636 ★   **Medtronic Puerto
Rico Inc.**
Carretera 149 Km 56.3
Villalba, PR 00766
Ultimate Parent: Medtronic Inc. **SIC:**
3841—Surgical & Medical Instruments.

★ 78637 ★   **Westinghouse De
Puerto Rico**
Computer & Instrumentation
Urb. La Vega Km 1.1
Villalba, PR 00766
Ultimate Parent: Westinghouse Electric
Corp. **SIC:** 3672—Printed Circuit Boards;
3823—Process Control Instruments.

Yabucoa

★ 78638 ★   **Banco Popular de
Puerto Rico**
46 Cristobal Colon St.
Yabucoa, PR 00767
(809)893-2620
Company Type: Subsidiary. **Location**

Type: Branch office. **Ultimate Parent:**
Banponce Corp. **SIC:** 6022—State
Commercial Banks.

Yauco

★ 78639 ★   **Banco Popular de
Puerto Rico**
Betances St. 25 Mattei Lluveras
Yauco, PR 00698
(809)856-1285
Company Type: Subsidiary. **Location
Type:** Branch office. **Ultimate Parent:**
Banponce Corp. **SIC:** 6022—State
Commercial Banks.

★ 78640 ★   **Banco Popular de
Puerto Rico**
July 25 St., Int. 128 Torres Navel Bldg.
Yauco, PR 00698
(809)856-1072
Company Type: Subsidiary. **Location
Type:** Branch office. **Ultimate Parent:**
Banponce Corp. **SIC:** 6022—State
Commercial Banks.

SOUTH CAROLINA

★ 78641 ★ Anchor Bank
7901 N. Kings Hwy.
SC 29572-3056
(803)449-3056
Location Type: Branch office. Officer:
Rebecca C. Hinds, Assistant Vice President.
Ultimate Parent: Anchor Bancorp. SIC:
6022—State Commercial Banks.

Abbeville

★ 78642 ★ Kentucky Fried
Chicken
Hwy. 72 W
Abbeville, SC 29620
(803)459-9821
Ultimate Parent: Pepsico. SIC: 5812—
Eating Places.

★ 78643 ★ Plexco
State Hwy. 32
Abbeville, SC 29620
Ultimate Parent: Amsted Industries Inc.
SIC: 3000—Rubber & Miscellaneous
Plastics Products.

Aiken

★ 78644 ★ Automatic Switch Co.
Hwy. 1 N.
PO Box 689
Aiken, SC 29801
Ultimate Parent: Emerson Electric Co. Inc.
SIC: 3491—Industrial Valves; 3492—Fluid
Power Valves & Hose Fittings.

★ 78645 ★ Bowater Inc.
Hwy. 302
Aiken, SC 29802
(803)648-0714
Ultimate Parent: Bowater. SIC: 0811—
Timber Tracts.

★ 78646 ★ FMC Corp.
15 Windham Blvd.
Aiken, SC 29801
(803)649-6211
Officer: Richard Fent, Manager. Ultimate
Parent: FMC. SIC: 3599—Industrial
Machinery Nec.

★ 78647 ★ Fmc Corp. Aiken
Plant
15 Windham Blvd.
Aiken, SC 29801
Ultimate Parent: FMC. SIC: 3795—Tanks
& Tank Components.

★ 78648 ★ Food Lion
1761 Whiskey Rd.
Aiken, SC 29803
(803)648-4203
Ultimate Parent: Food Lion. SIC: 5411—
Grocery Stores.

★ 78649 ★ Gorham Bronze
45 Windham Blvd.
Aiken, SC 29801
Ultimate Parent: Textron. SIC: 3300—
Primary Metal Industries.

★ 78650 ★ Greyhound Bus
Station
347 Barnwell Ave. W
Aiken, SC 29801
(803)648-6894
Ultimate Parent: Greyhound Lines Inc. SIC:
4111—Local & Suburban Transit.

★ 78651 ★ Kentucky Fried
Chicken
144 Whiskey Rd.
Aiken, SC 29801
(803)648-5700
Ultimate Parent: Pepsico. SIC: 5812—
Eating Places.

★ 78652 ★ Kentucky Fried
Chicken
1406 Richland Ave. W
Aiken, SC 29801
(803)648-0231
Ultimate Parent: Pepsico. SIC: 5812—
Eating Places.

★ 78653 ★ Owens-Corning
Fiberglas Corp.
Wagener Rd.
Aiken, SC 29801
(803)648-8351
Officer: Max Weber, Chairman. Ultimate
Parent: Owens-Corning. SIC: 2399—
Fabricated Textile Products Nec; 3229—
Pressed & Blown Glass Nec.

★ 78654 ★ Owens-Corning
Fiberglas Corp.
Hwy. 302
Aiken, SC 29801
Ultimate Parent: Owens-Corning. SIC:
3229—Pressed & Blown Glass Nec.

★ 78655 ★ Piggly Wiggly
522 York St. NE
Aiken, SC 29801
(803)649-4521
Ultimate Parent: Bruno's. SIC: 5411—
Grocery Stores.

★ 78656 ★ Radio Shack
1540 Kalmia Plz.
Aiken, SC 29801
(803)648-5805
Company Type: Division. Ultimate Parent:
Tandy Corp. SIC: 5065—Electronic Parts &
Equipment Nec.

★ 78657 ★ Ryder Truck Rental
424 Rutland Dr.
Aiken, SC 29801
(803)648-4557
Ultimate Parent: Ryder System. SIC:
7359—Equipment Rental & Leasing Nec.

★ 78658 ★ Trailways Bus Station
237 Barnwell Ave.
Aiken, SC 29801
(803)649-5483
Ultimate Parent: Greyhound Lines Inc. SIC:
4131—Intercity & Rural Bus Transportation.

★ 78659 ★ Wal Mart
Heritage Sq.
Aiken, SC 29801
(803)648-7845
Ultimate Parent: Wal-Mart Stores, Inc. SIC:
5311—Department Stores.

Allendale

★ 78660 ★ Zippy Mart Inc.
Hwy. 301
Allendale, SC 29810
(803)584-9257
Ultimate Parent: Crown Central Petroleum
Corp. SIC: 5411—Grocery Stores.

Anderson

★ 78661 ★ ACME Business
Products
800 N. Main St.
Anderson, SC 29621-5525
(803)224-8166
Ultimate Parent: Alco Standard Corp. SIC:
5044—Office Equipment.

★ 78662 ★ Avon Products Inc.
102 W. Greenville St.
Anderson, SC 29625
(803)226-3263
Ultimate Parent: Avon Products, Inc. SIC:
8111—Legal Services.

★ 78663 ★ BASF Corp.
Fibers
Master's Blvd. & Hwy. 29
Anderson, SC 29624-3025
Company Type: Division. Ultimate Parent:
BASF Corp. SIC: 2824—Organic Fibers—
Noncellulosic.

★ 78664 ★ BASF Corp.
Fibers Division
PO Box 3025
Anderson, SC 29624-0025
(803)260-7000
Company Type: Division. Location Type:
Branch office. Officer: Dan Gissendanner.
Ultimate Parent: BASF Corp. SIC: 2824—
Organic Fibers—Noncellulosic; 2399—
Fabricated Textile Products Nec; 2655—
Fiber Cans, Drums & Similar Products;
6061—Federal Credit Unions.

★ 78665 ★ BASF Corp.
Fibers' & Products
Masters Blvd. & Hwy. 29
Anderson, SC 29624-3025
Ultimate Parent: BASF Corp. SIC: 2824—
Organic Fibers—Noncellulosic.

★ 78666 ★ BASF Fibers
441 Masters Blvd.
Anderson, SC 29624
(803)260-7000
Officer: Dan Gissendanner, Manager.
Ultimate Parent: BASF Corp. SIC: 2399—
Fabricated Textile Products Nec; 2655—
Fiber Cans, Drums & Similar Products.

★ 78667 ★ Bi-Lo Inc.
700 E. Shockley Ferry Rd.
Anderson, SC 29624
(803)225-3345
Ultimate Parent: Penn Traffic. SIC: 5411—
Grocery Stores.

★ 78668 ★ Black & Decker Corp.
True Temper Sports
Rte. 6 Starr Hwy.
Anderson, SC 29624
Ultimate Parent: Black & Decker Corp.
SIC: 3423—Hand & Edge Tools Nec.

★ 78669 ★ Branch Banking &
Trust Co.
1510 N. Main St.
Anderson, SC 29621-4735
(803)231-2813
Company Type: Subsidiary. Location
Type: Branch office. Officer: Richard A.
Shirley, Manager. Ultimate Parent:
Southern National Corp. SIC: 6021—
National Commercial Banks.

★ 78670 ★ Branch Banking &
Trust Co.
2200 E. River St.
Anderson, SC 29621-6832
(803)224-9880
Company Type: Subsidiary. Location
Type: Branch office. Officer: Jerry Peeler,
Manager. Ultimate Parent: Southern
National Corp. SIC: 6021—National
Commercial Banks.

★ 78671 ★ Citgo Mini Mart
1000 US 28 Bypass
Anderson, SC 29624
(803)224-7353
Ultimate Parent: Citgo Petroleum. SIC:
5411—Grocery Stores.

★ 78672 ★ Clark-Schwebel Fiber
Glass Corp.
2200 S. Murray Ave.
Anderson, SC 29622
Ultimate Parent: Springs Industries. SIC:
2221—Broadwoven Fabric Mills—Manmade;
2262—Finishing Plants—Manmade.

★ 78673 ★ Clark-Schwebel
Fiberglas Corp.
2200 South Murray Ave.
Anderson, SC 29624
Ultimate Parent: Springs Industries.

★ 78674 ★ Clark-Schwebel
Fiberglass Corp.
2200 S. Murray Ave.
Anderson, SC 29624
Ultimate Parent: Springs Industries. SIC:
2221—Broadwoven Fabric Mills—Manmade;
2262—Finishing Plants—Manmade.

★ 78675 ★ First Union National
Bank of South Carolina
908 N. Main St.
Anderson, SC 29622-5527
(803)231-5900
Location Type: Branch office. Ultimate
Parent: First Union Corp. SIC: 6021—
National Commercial Banks.

★ 78676 ★ Greyhound Bus Lines
316 Concord Ave.
Anderson, SC 29621
(803)226-2605
Ultimate Parent: Greyhound Lines Inc. SIC:
4131—Intercity & Rural Bus Transportation.

★ 78677 ★ Jiffy Lube
1404 N. Main St.
Anderson, SC 29621
(803)226-2499
Ultimate Parent: Pennzoil. SIC: 5172—
Petroleum Products Nec; 7539—Automotive
Repair Shops Nec.

★ 78678 ★ Kentucky Fried
Chicken
3325 N. Main St.
Anderson, SC 29621
(803)261-3335
Ultimate Parent: Pepsico. SIC: 5812—
Eating Places.

★ 78679 ★ Lane Bryant
Anderson Mall
Anderson, SC 29625
(803)231-6201
Ultimate Parent: Limited. SIC: 5651—
Family Clothing Stores.

★ 78680 ★ Lerner Shop
Anderson Mall
Anderson, SC 29625
(803)225-3227
Ultimate Parent: Limited. SIC: 5651—
Family Clothing Stores.

★ 78681 ★ Otis Elevator Co.
804 E. Orr St.
Anderson, SC 29621
(803)226-4778
Ultimate Parent: United Technologies. SIC:
3534—Elevators & Moving Stairways;
5084—Industrial Machinery & Equipment.

★ 78682 ★ Owens-Corning
Fiberglas Corp.
Hwy. 815
Anderson, SC 29622
(803)296-4000
Officer: Max Weber, Chairman. Ultimate
Parent: Owens-Corning. SIC: 2821—
Plastics Materials & Resins; 3229—Pressed
& Blown Glass Nec.

★ 78683 ★ Owens Corning
Fiberglass
Hwy. 81 S.
Anderson, SC 29622
Ultimate Parent: Owens-Corning. SIC:
3229—Pressed & Blown Glass Nec; 2821—
Plastics Materials & Resins.

★ 78684 ★ Owens-Corning
Fiberglass Corp.
Hwy. 81 S
Anderson, SC 29622
Ultimate Parent: Owens-Corning. SIC:
3229—Pressed & Blown Glass Nec; 2821—
Plastics Materials & Resins.

★ 78685 ★ **Pepsi-Cola Bottling Co.**
PO Box 5036
Anderson, SC 29623
(803)224-7906
Ultimate Parent: Pepsico. **SIC:** 2086—Bottled & Canned Soft Drinks.

★ 78686 ★ **Pizza Hut**
3318 N. Main St.
Anderson, SC 29621
(803)225-0436
Ultimate Parent: Pepsico. **SIC:** 5812—Eating Places.

★ 78687 ★ **Radio Shack**
302 Pearman Dairy Rd.
Anderson, SC 29625
(803)226-0423
Company Type: Division. **Ultimate Parent:** Tandy Corp. **SIC:** 5731—Radio, Television & Electronics Stores.

★ 78688 ★ **Radio Shack**
Anderson Mall
Anderson, SC 29625
(803)226-0200
Company Type: Division. **Ultimate Parent:** Tandy Corp. **SIC:** 5731—Radio, Television & Electronics Stores.

★ 78689 ★ **Radio Shack**
Lakeside Sq.
Anderson, SC 29624
(803)226-0423
Company Type: Division. **Ultimate Parent:** Tandy Corp. **SIC:** 5065—Electronic Parts & Equipment Nec.

★ 78690 ★ **Radio Shack**
Anderson
Anderson, SC 29621
(803)226-0200
Company Type: Division. **Ultimate Parent:** Tandy Corp. **SIC:** 5065—Electronic Parts & Equipment Nec.

★ 78691 ★ **Rite Aid Discount Pharmacie**
Lakeside Shopping Ctr.
Anderson, SC 29624
(803)224-9820
Ultimate Parent: Rite Aid. **SIC:** 5912—Drug Stores & Proprietary Stores.

★ 78692 ★ **Ryder Truck Rental**
109 Ryder Ln.
Anderson, SC 29625
(803)225-4171
Ultimate Parent: Ryder System. **SIC:** 7359—Equipment Rental & Leasing Nec; 7513—Truck Rental & Leasing Without Drivers.

★ 78693 ★ **Springs Industries, Inc.**
435 E. Shockley Ferry Rd.
Anderson, SC 29624
(803)226-3490
Officer: Butler Nanney, Manager. **Ultimate Parent:** Springs Industries. **SIC:** 2211—Broadwoven Fabric Mills—Cotton; 2399—Fabricated Textile Products Nec.

★ 78694 ★ **United Parcel Service**
Rural Route 2
Anderson, SC 29625
(803)222-8333
Ultimate Parent: United Parcel Service of America. **SIC:** 4215—Courier Services Except by Air.

★ 78695 ★ **United Parcel Service**
RR 2
Anderson, SC 29625
(803)222-8333
Ultimate Parent: United Parcel Service of America. **SIC:** 4215—Courier Services Except by Air.

★ 78696 ★ **Woodside Mills Inc.**
2115 S. McDuffie St.
Anderson, SC 29624
(803)224-0251
Officer: John Woodson, Manager. **Ultimate Parent:** Delta Woodside Industries. **SIC:** 2221—Broadwoven Fabric Mills—Manmade; 2399—Fabricated Textile Products Nec.

★ 78697 ★ **Woodside Mills Inc. Haynsworth Plant**
2115 S. McDuffie St.
Anderson, SC 29624
Ultimate Parent: Delta Woodside Industries. **SIC:** 2221—Broadwoven Fabric Mills—Manmade.

Andrews

★ 78698 ★ **Business Systems**
Andrews, SC 29510
(803)221-7010
Ultimate Parent: Avery Dennison Corp. **SIC:** 7371—Computer Programming Services.

★ 78699 ★ **Piggly Wiggly**
15 W. Ashland St.
Andrews, SC 29510
(803)264-5251
Ultimate Parent: Bruno's. **SIC:** 5411—Grocery Stores.

Ballentine

★ 78700 ★ **Food Lion**
Ballentine Ctr.
Ballentine, SC 29002
(803)749-1600
Ultimate Parent: Food Lion. **SIC:** 5411—Grocery Stores.

Barnwell

★ 78701 ★ **Food Lion**
Barnwell Plz.
Barnwell, SC 29812
(803)259-5220
Ultimate Parent: Food Lion. **SIC:** 5411—Grocery Stores.

★ 78702 ★ **Piggly Wiggly**
Marlboro Ave.
Barnwell, SC 29812
(803)259-1117
Ultimate Parent: Bruno's. **SIC:** 5411—Grocery Stores.

Batesburg

★ 78703 ★ **Kentucky Fried Chicken**
E Columbia Ave.
Batesburg, SC 29006
(803)532-4725
Ultimate Parent: Pepsico. **SIC:** 5812—Eating Places.

★ 78704 ★ **Pizza Hut**
402 W. Columbia Ave.
Batesburg, SC 29006
(803)532-8123
Ultimate Parent: Pepsico. **SIC:** 5812—Eating Places.

Bath

★ 78705 ★ **Avon Products Inc.**
201 West Dr.
Bath, SC 29816
(803)593-9839
Ultimate Parent: Avon Products, Inc. **SIC:** 5999—Miscellaneous Retail Stores Nec.

Beaufort

★ 78706 ★ **Bi-Lo Super Market**
Jean Ribaut Sq.
Beaufort, SC 29902
(803)524-2771
Ultimate Parent: Penn Traffic. **SIC:** 5411—Grocery Stores.

★ 78707 ★ **First Union National Bank of South Carolina**
921 Bay St.
Beaufort, SC 29901-5567
(803)522-8088
Location Type: Branch office. **Ultimate Parent:** First Union Corp. **SIC:** 6021—National Commercial Banks.

★ 78708 ★ **Food Lion**
Salem Rd.
Beaufort, SC 29902
(803)525-6905
Ultimate Parent: Food Lion. **SIC:** 5411—Grocery Stores.

★ 78709 ★ **Greyhound Bus Station**
1307 Boundary St.
Beaufort, SC 29902
(803)524-4646
Ultimate Parent: Greyhound Lines Inc. **SIC:** 4111—Local & Suburban Transit; 4173—Bus Terminal & Service Facilities.

★ 78710 ★ **Kentucky Fried Chicken**
1013 S. Ribaut Rd.
Beaufort, SC 29902
(803)524-3805
Ultimate Parent: Pepsico. **SIC:** 5812—Eating Places.

★ 78711 ★ **Kentucky Fried Chicken**
3007 Boundary St.
Beaufort, SC 29902
(803)524-3805
Ultimate Parent: Pepsico. **SIC:** 5812—Eating Places.

★ 78712 ★ **Pennzoil**
State Hwy. 170
Beaufort, SC 29902
(803)525-6551
Ultimate Parent: Pennzoil. **SIC:** 7538—General Automotive Repair Shops.

★ 78713 ★ **Piggly Wiggly**
Jean Ribaut Rd.
Beaufort, SC 29902
(803)524-2750
Ultimate Parent: Bruno's. **SIC:** 5411—Grocery Stores.

★ 78714 ★ **Piggly Wiggly**
913 Port Republic St.
Beaufort, SC 29902
(803)524-2932
Ultimate Parent: Bruno's. **SIC:** 7359—Equipment Rental & Leasing Nec.

★ 78715 ★ **Piggly Wiggly**
880 PO Box
Beaufort, SC 29901
(803)524-2932
Ultimate Parent: Bruno's. **SIC:** 5411—Grocery Stores.

★ 78716 ★ **Pizza Hut**
1091 S. Ribaut Rd.
Beaufort, SC 29902
(803)524-6149
Ultimate Parent: Pepsico. **SIC:** 5812—Eating Places.

★ 78717 ★ **Pizza Hut**
3009 Boundary St.
Beaufort, SC 29902
(803)524-7948
Ultimate Parent: Pepsico. **SIC:** 5812—Eating Places.

★ 78718 ★ **Ryder Truck Rental**
3062 Boundary St.
Beaufort, SC 29902
(803)524-9052
Ultimate Parent: Ryder System. **SIC:** 7513—Truck Rental & Leasing Without Drivers.

★ 78719 ★ **Taco Bell**
State Hwy. 170
Beaufort, SC 29902
(803)524-4191
Ultimate Parent: Pepsico. **SIC:** 5812—Eating Places.

★ 78720 ★ **Zippy Mart Inc.**
Us 21
Beaufort, SC 29902
(803)524-4756
Ultimate Parent: Crown Central Petroleum Corp. **SIC:** 5411—Grocery Stores.

Beech Island

★ 78721 ★ **Kimberly-Clark Corp. Beech Island Mill**
Old Jackson Hwy.
Beech Island, SC 29842
Ultimate Parent: Kimberly-Clark. **SIC:** 2621—Paper Mills.

Belton

★ 78722 ★ **Amerada Hess Corp.**
Williamston Rd.
Belton, SC 29627
(803)338-5812
Ultimate Parent: Amerada Hess. **SIC:** 5983—Fuel Oil Dealers.

★ 78723 ★ **Branch Banking & Trust Co.**
723 Anderson St.
Belton, SC 29627-2101
(803)338-7727
Company Type: Subsidiary. **Location Type:** Branch office. **Officer:** Billy Joe Hall, Manager. **Ultimate Parent:** Southern National Corp. **SIC:** 6021—National Commercial Banks.

★ 78724 ★ **Branch Banking & Trust Co.**
123 O'Neal St.
Belton, SC 29627-1430
(803)338-6161
Company Type: Subsidiary. **Location Type:** Branch office. **Officer:** Mitchell Cole, Manager. **Ultimate Parent:** Southern National Corp. **SIC:** 6021—National Commercial Banks.

Bennettsville

★ 78725 ★ **Essex Group Inc.**
620 Gibson Hwy.
Bennettsville, SC 29512
Ultimate Parent: Morgan Stanley Group. **SIC:** 3643—Current-Carrying Wiring Devices; 3357—Nonferrous Wiredrawing & Insulating.

★ 78726 ★ **First Union National Bank of South Carolina**
311 E. Main St.
Bennettsville, SC 29512-3109
(803)479-8366
Ultimate Parent: First Union Corp. **SIC:** 6021—National Commercial Banks.

★ 78727 ★ **Food Lion**
202 N. US 15 Bypass
Bennettsville, SC 29512
(803)479-4155
Ultimate Parent: Food Lion. **SIC:** 5411—Grocery Stores.

★ 78728 ★ **Kentucky Fried Chicken**
US 401 Bypass W
Bennettsville, SC 29512
(803)479-8015
Ultimate Parent: Pepsico. **SIC:** 5812—Eating Places.

★ 78729 ★ **Pepsi-Cola Bottling Co.**
127 Cottingham Blvd. N
Bennettsville, SC 29512
(803)479-2816
Officer: H. E. Avent, President. **Ultimate Parent:** Pepsico. **SIC:** 2086—Bottled & Canned Soft Drinks.

★ 78730 ★ **Pizza Hut**
US 15 N. Bypass
Bennettsville, SC 29512
(803)479-8281
Ultimate Parent: Pepsico. **SIC:** 5812—Eating Places.

★ 78731 ★ **Sara Lee Hosiery**
Hwy. 115 & 401 Bypass
Bennettsville, SC 29512
Ultimate Parent: Sara Lee Corp. **SIC:** 2251—Women's Hosiery Except Socks.

★ 78732 ★ **Sara Lee Hosiery**
Rte. 15/401 Bypass
Bennettsville, SC 29512
Ultimate Parent: Sara Lee Corp. **SIC:** 2251—Women's Hosiery Except Socks.

★ 78733 ★ **United Technologies Auto**
630 Gibson Hwy.
Bennettsville, SC 29512
(803)479-6214
Officer: Greg Clark, Plant Manager. **Ultimate Parent:** United Technologies. **SIC:** 3496—Miscellaneous Fabricated Wire Products.

★ 78734 ★   **Willamette Industries Inc.**
Hwy. 912
Bennettsville, SC 29512
Ultimate Parent: Willamette Industries, Inc.
SIC: 2493—Reconstituted Wood Products.

Bethune

★ 78735 ★   **Colgate-Palmolive Co.**
500 Chestnut St.
Bethune, SC 29009
Ultimate Parent: Colgate-Palmolive. **SIC:** 2841—Soap & Other Detergents.

★ 78736 ★   **Fibertec Co.**
500 Chestnut St.
Bethune, SC 29009
Ultimate Parent: International Paper Co.
SIC: 2297—Nonwoven Fabrics; 2269—Finishing Plants Nec.

★ 78737 ★   **Veratec**
500 Chestnut St. PO Box 579
Bethune, SC 29009
Ultimate Parent: International Paper Co.
SIC: 2297—Nonwoven Fabrics; 2269—Finishing Plants Nec; 2259—Knitting Mills Nec.

Bishopville

★ 78738 ★   **Burlington Industries**
PO Box 523
Bishopville, SC 29010-0523
(803)484-5436
Location Type: Headquarters. **Officer:** Bob Reisch. **Ultimate Parent:** Burlington Industries, Equity. **SIC:** 2299—Textile Goods Nec.

★ 78739 ★   **Burlington Industries Inc.**
E. Church Ext.
Bishopville, SC 29010
(803)484-5436
Officer: Bob Reisch, Manager. **Ultimate Parent:** Burlington Industries, Equity. **SIC:** 2299—Textile Goods Nec.

★ 78740 ★   **Carolina Power & Light Co.**
121 N. Main St.
Bishopville, SC 29010
(803)484-5302
Ultimate Parent: Carolina Power & Light Co. **SIC:** 4911—Electric Services.

★ 78741 ★   **Carolina Power & Light Co.**
121 N. Main St.
Bishopville, SC 29010
(803)484-5302
Ultimate Parent: Carolina Power & Light Co. **SIC:** 4911—Electric Services.

★ 78742 ★   **Food Lion**
517 S. Main St.
Bishopville, SC 29010
(803)484-9477
Ultimate Parent: Food Lion. **SIC:** 5411—Grocery Stores.

★ 78743 ★   **Greyhound Bus Station**
251 N. Main St.
Bishopville, SC 29010
(803)484-5902
Ultimate Parent: Greyhound Lines Inc. **SIC:** 4131—Intercity & Rural Bus Transportation.

★ 78744 ★   **Piggly Wiggly**
110 S. Main St.
Bishopville, SC 29010
(803)484-6315
Ultimate Parent: Bruno's. **SIC:** 5411—Grocery Stores.

★ 78745 ★   **Pizza Hut**
331 S. Main St.
Bishopville, SC 29010
(803)484-5515
Ultimate Parent: Pepsico. **SIC:** 5812—Eating Places.

Blacksburg

★ 78746 ★   **First Union National Bank of South Carolina**
203 W. Cherokee St.
Blacksburg, SC 29702-1503
(803)839-6331
Ultimate Parent: First Union Corp. **SIC:** 6021—National Commercial Banks.

★ 78747 ★   **Vulcan Materials Co.**
239 Mill Creek Rd.
Blacksburg, SC 29702
(803)936-7902
Officer: Jim Neason, Vice President.
Ultimate Parent: Vulcan Materials Co. **SIC:** 3274—Lime; 3295—Minerals—Ground or Treated.

Blythewood

★ 78748 ★   **Bowater Inc.**
Carolina Div. Woodlands
Blythewood, SC 29016
(803)754-2922
Officer: William E. Raines. **Ultimate Parent:** Bowater. **SIC:** 2611—Pulp Mills.

★ 78749 ★   **Orchard Decorative Prods.**
1 Jenkins Bros. Rd.
Blythewood, SC 29016
Ultimate Parent: Borden, Inc. **SIC:** 2500—Furniture & Fixtures.

★ 78750 ★   **Orchard Decorative Products**
1 Jenkins Brothers Rd.
Blythewood, SC 29016
(803)754-4810
Officer: John Sullivan, Executive Director.
Ultimate Parent: Borden, Inc. **SIC:** 2679—Converted Paper Products Nec.

Bucksport

★ 78751 ★   **Food Lion**
1408 Mill Pond Rd.
Bucksport, SC 29527
(803)248-3115
Ultimate Parent: Food Lion. **SIC:** 5411—Grocery Stores.

★ 78752 ★   **Kentucky Fried Chicken**
411 Hwy. 501
Bucksport, SC 29527
(803)248-9416
Ultimate Parent: Pepsico. **SIC:** 5812—Eating Places.

Burton

★ 78753 ★   **Pepsi-Cola South Bottling Co.**
Hwy. 20
Burton, SC 29902
(803)521-1424
Officer: John Adorante, Manager. **Ultimate Parent:** Pepsico. **SIC:** 2086—Bottled & Canned Soft Drinks.

Calhoun Falls

★ 78754 ★   **Fieldcrest Cannon Inc.**
Carpet & Rug
Hwy. 81 PO Box 454
Calhoun Falls, SC 29628
Company Type: Division. **Ultimate Parent:** Fieldcrest Cannon. **SIC:** 2281—Yarn Spinning Mills; 2282—Throwing & Winding Mills.

★ 78755 ★   **Karastan**
Hwy. 81 (PO Box 454)
Calhoun Falls, SC 29628
Location Type: Plant. **Ultimate Parent:** Fieldcrest Cannon. **SIC:** 2281—Yarn Spinning Mills.

★ 78756 ★   **Karastan Bigelow**
Hwy. 81 PO Box 454
Calhoun Falls, SC 29628
Location Type: Plant. **Ultimate Parent:** Fieldcrest Cannon. **SIC:** 2281—Yarn Spinning Mills; 2282—Throwing & Winding Mills.

★ 78757 ★   **Karastan-Bigolon**
PO Box 454
Calhoun Falls, SC 29628
Location Type: Plant. **Ultimate Parent:** Fieldcrest Cannon. **SIC:** 2281—Yarn Spinning Mills.

Camden

★ 78758 ★   **Branch Banking & Trust Co.**
501 Rutledge St.
Camden, SC 29020-4311
(803)425-1610
Company Type: Subsidiary. **Location Type:** Branch office. **Ultimate Parent:** Southern National Corp. **SIC:** 6021—National Commercial Banks.

★ 78759 ★   **Food Lion**
2529 Broad St.
Camden, SC 29020
(803)432-2478
Ultimate Parent: Food Lion. **SIC:** 5411—Grocery Stores.

★ 78760 ★   **Kentucky Fried Chicken**
137 Dekalb St.
Camden, SC 29020
(803)432-3651
Ultimate Parent: Pepsico. **SIC:** 5812—Eating Places.

★ 78761 ★   **Piggly Wiggly**
5 Dekalb St.
Camden, SC 29020
(803)432-7011
Ultimate Parent: Bruno's. **SIC:** 5411—Grocery Stores.

★ 78762 ★   **Ryder Truck Rental**
1002 Dekalb St.
Camden, SC 29020
(803)432-2449
Ultimate Parent: Ryder System. **SIC:** 7359—Equipment Rental & Leasing Nec.

★ 78763 ★   **Wal Mart**
1671 Springdale Dr.
Camden, SC 29020
(803)425-5746
Ultimate Parent: Wal-Mart Stores, Inc. **SIC:** 5311—Department Stores.

Carlisle

★ 78764 ★   **Carlisle Finishing Plant**
Hwy. 121/72
Carlisle, SC 29031
Ultimate Parent: Cone Mills. **SIC:** 2261—Finishing Plants—Cotton; 2262—Finishing Plants—Manmade.

★ 78765 ★   **Carlisle Finishing Plant Carlisle Finishing Plant**
Hwy. 121/72
Carlisle, SC 29031
Ultimate Parent: Cone Mills. **SIC:** 2261—Finishing Plants—Cotton; 2262—Finishing Plants—Manmade.

★ 78766 ★   **Hoechst Celanese**
Rte. 1 Box 78
Carlisle, SC 29031
Ultimate Parent: Hoechst Celanese Corp. **SIC:** 2819—Industrial Inorganic Chemicals Nec.

★ 78767 ★   **Virginia Chemicals Co.**
Rte. 1, Box 78
Carlisle, SC 29031
Ultimate Parent: Hoechst Celanese Corp. **SIC:** 2819—Industrial Inorganic Chemicals Nec.

Catawba

★ 78768 ★   **Bowater**
Carolina Div.
5300 Cureton Ferry Rd.
Catawba, SC 29704
(803)329-6654
Ultimate Parent: Bowater. **SIC:** 2411—Logging; 2611—Pulp Mills; 2621—Paper Mills.

★ 78769 ★   **Bowater Carolina Co.**
5300 Cureton Ferry Rd.
Catawba, SC 29704
Ultimate Parent: Bowater. **SIC:** 2611—Pulp Mills; 2621—Paper Mills.

★ 78770 ★   **Bowater Inc.**
Carolina Div.
PO Box 7
Catawba, SC 29704
(803)329-6600 Fax: (803)329-2501
Company Type: Subsidiary. **Officer:** E. F. Walker, President. **Ultimate Parent:** Bowater.

★ 78771 ★   **Bowater Inc.**
Carolina Div.
PO Box 7
Catawba, SC 29704-0007
(803)329-6600
Company Type: Headquarters. **Officer:** Elvin F. Walker. **Ultimate Parent:** Bowater. **SIC:** 2621—Paper Mills; 5099—Durable Goods Nec; 6061—Federal Credit Unions.

★ 78772 ★   **Bowater Inc.**
Carolina Division
5300 Cureton Ferry Rd.
Catawba, SC 29704
Ultimate Parent: Bowater. **SIC:** 2611—Pulp Mills; 2621—Paper Mills.

★ 78773 ★   **Georgia-Pacific Corp. Catawba Hardboard**
5260 Cureton Rd.
Catawba, SC 29704
Ultimate Parent: Georgia-Pacific. **SIC:** 2493—Reconstituted Wood Products.

★ 78774 ★   **Georgia Pacific Corp. Catawba Hardboard**
5260 Cureton Ferry Rd.
Catawba, SC 29704-0066
Ultimate Parent: Georgia-Pacific. **SIC:** 2493—Reconstituted Wood Products.

Cayce

★ 78775 ★   **First Union National Bank of South Carolina**
1100 Knox Abbott Dr.
Cayce, SC 29033-3324
(803)251-4449
Ultimate Parent: First Union Corp. **SIC:** 6021—National Commercial Banks.

★ 78776 ★   **Hit or Miss**
300 Outlet Pt Blvd. 31
Cayce, SC 29033
(803)772-8397
Ultimate Parent: TJX. **SIC:** 5651—Family Clothing Stores.

★ 78777 ★   **Jiffy Lube**
1139 Knox Abbott Dr.
Cayce, SC 29033
(803)794-3333
Ultimate Parent: Pennzoil. **SIC:** 7538—General Automotive Repair Shops; 7539—Automotive Repair Shops Nec.

★ 78778 ★   **Pizza Hut**
1300 Knox Abbott Dr.
Cayce, SC 29033
(803)796-3240
Ultimate Parent: Pepsico. **SIC:** 5812—Eating Places.

★ 78779 ★   **Ryder Truck Rental**
906 Knox Abbott Dr.
Cayce, SC 29033
(803)796-4336
Ultimate Parent: Ryder System. **SIC:** 4214—Local Trucking With Storage.

★ 78780 ★   **Taco Bell**
1400 Knox Abbott Dr.
Cayce, SC 29033
(803)794-8444
Ultimate Parent: Pepsico. **SIC:** 5812—Eating Places.

Central

★ 78781 ★   **BASF Corp.**
Hwy. 93
Central, SC 29630
(803)639-6311
Officer: John Rich, Manager. **Ultimate Parent:** BASF Corp. **SIC:** 2282—Throwing & Winding Mills; 2399—Fabricated Textile Products Nec; 2899—Chemical Preparations Nec.

★ 78782 ★ BASF Corp.
Fibers
Hwy. 93
Central, SC 29630
Company Type: Division. **Location Type:** Plant. **Ultimate Parent:** BASF Corp. **SIC:** 2821—Plastics Materials & Resins; 2824—Organic Fibers—Noncellulosic.

★ 78783 ★ BASF Corp.
Fibers
Hwy. 93
Central, SC 29630
Company Type: Division. **Location Type:** Plant. **Ultimate Parent:** BASF Corp. **SIC:** 2821—Plastics Materials & Resins; 2824—Organic Fibers—Noncellulosic.

★ 78784 ★ BASF Corp.-Clemson Plant
PO Box 488
Central, SC 29630-0488
(803)639-6311
Location Type: Plant. **Officer:** John T. Rich. **Ultimate Parent:** BASF Corp. **SIC:** 2822—Synthetic Rubber; 2282—Throwing & Winding Mills; 2399—Fabricated Textile Products Nec; 5169—Chemicals & Allied Products Nec; 5199—Nondurable Goods Nec.

Chapin

★ 78785 ★ First Union National Bank of South Carolian
168 Columbia Ave.
Chapin, SC 29036
(803)345-2231
Ultimate Parent: First Union Corp. **SIC:** 6021—National Commercial Banks.

Charleston

★ 78786 ★ Albright & Wilson Americas Inc.
2151 King St. Extension
Charleston, SC 29415
Ultimate Parent: Tenneco Inc. **SIC:** 2869—Industrial Organic Chemicals Nec; 2819—Industrial Inorganic Chemicals Nec; 2821—Plastics Materials & Resins.

★ 78787 ★ Albright & Wilson Americas Inc.- Charleston Plant
2151 King St. Extension
Charleston, SC 29415
Ultimate Parent: Tenneco Inc. **SIC:** 2869—Industrial Organic Chemicals Nec; 2819—Industrial Inorganic Chemicals Nec; 2821—Plastics Materials & Resins.

★ 78788 ★ Amerada Hess Corp.
5150 Virginia Ave.
Charleston, SC 29406
(803)554-1581
Ultimate Parent: Amerada Hess. **SIC:** 5172—Petroleum Products Nec.

★ 78789 ★ Avon Products Inc.
205 King St.
Charleston, SC 29401
(803)577-7220
Ultimate Parent: Avon Products, Inc. **SIC:** 5999—Miscellaneous Retail Stores Nec.

★ 78790 ★ Banana Republic
124 Market St.
Charleston, SC 29401
(803)722-6681
Ultimate Parent: GAP. **SIC:** 5621—Women's Clothing Stores.

★ 78791 ★ Branch Banking & Trust Co.
1 Broad St.
Charleston, SC 29402
(803)937-5200
Company Type: Subsidiary. **Location Type:** Branch office. **Ultimate Parent:** Southern National Corp. **SIC:** 6021—National Commercial Banks.

★ 78792 ★ Branch Banking & Trust Co.
1112 Savannah Hwy.
Charleston, SC 29407-7854
(803)745-4125
Company Type: Subsidiary. **Location Type:** Branch office. **Ultimate Parent:** Southern National Corp. **SIC:** 6021—National Commercial Banks.

★ 78793 ★ Branch Banking & Trust Co.
1503 Old Towne Rd.
Charleston, SC 29407-6007
(803)720-5170
Company Type: Subsidiary. **Location Type:** Branch office. **Officer:** Peggy McDaniel, Manager. **Ultimate Parent:** Southern National Corp. **SIC:** 6021—National Commercial Banks.

★ 78794 ★ Branch Banking & Trust Co.
151 Meeting St.
Charleston, SC 29401-2207
(803)720-5100
Company Type: Subsidiary. **Location Type:** Branch office. **Officer:** W.B. Chisolm Leonard, Manager. **Ultimate Parent:** Southern National Corp. **SIC:** 6021—National Commercial Banks.

★ 78795 ★ Casual Corner
Citadel Mall
Charleston, SC 29407
(803)766-6512
Ultimate Parent: United States Shoe. **SIC:** 5621—Women's Clothing Stores.

★ 78796 ★ Casual Corner
Northwoods
Charleston, SC 29405
(803)797-2020
Ultimate Parent: United States Shoe. **SIC:** 5621—Women's Clothing Stores.

★ 78797 ★ Circuit City
5128 Rivers Ave.
Charleston, SC 29418
(803)744-3359
Ultimate Parent: Circuit City Stores. **SIC:** 5731—Radio, Television & Electronics Stores.

★ 78798 ★ Cummins Engine Co. Inc.
4500 Leeds Ave.
Charleston, SC 29405
Ultimate Parent: Cummins Engine Co. **SIC:** 3592—Carburetors, Pistons, Rings & Valves; 3519—Internal Combustion Engines Nec; 3714—Motor Vehicle Parts & Accessories.

★ 78799 ★ Cummins Engine Co. Inc.
2301 Leeds Ave. Suite 201
Charleston, SC 29405
Ultimate Parent: Cummins Engine Co. **SIC:** 3592—Carburetors, Pistons, Rings & Valves; 3519—Internal Combustion Engines Nec; 3714—Motor Vehicle Parts & Accessories.

★ 78800 ★ Cummins Engine Co. Inc.
2301 Leeds Ave.
Charleston, SC 29405
Ultimate Parent: Cummins Engine Co. **SIC:** 3592—Carburetors, Pistons, Rings & Valves.

★ 78801 ★ Delta Air Cargo
340 Air Cargo Ln.
Charleston, SC 29418
(803)767-7300
Ultimate Parent: Delta Air Lines, Inc. **SIC:** 4513—Air Courier Services.

★ 78802 ★ Delta Air Lines
143 King St.
Charleston, SC 29401
(803)577-3230
Ultimate Parent: Delta Air Lines, Inc. **SIC:** 4724—Travel Agencies.

★ 78803 ★ Delta Air Lines
Municipal Airport
Charleston, SC 29411
(803)747-8281
Ultimate Parent: Delta Air Lines, Inc. **SIC:** 4729—Passenger Transportation Arrangement Nec.

★ 78804 ★ Delta Air Lines
Charleston International Airport
Charleston, SC 29418
(803)577-3230
Ultimate Parent: Delta Air Lines, Inc. **SIC:** 4512—Air Transportation—Scheduled.

★ 78805 ★ Delta Air Lines Inc.
143 King St.
Charleston, SC 29401
(803)577-3230
Ultimate Parent: Delta Air Lines, Inc. **SIC:** 4724—Travel Agencies.

★ 78806 ★ Delta Air Lines Inc.
Charleston International Airport
Charleston, SC 29418
(803)577-3230
Ultimate Parent: Delta Air Lines, Inc. **SIC:** 4512—Air Transportation—Scheduled.

★ 78807 ★ Digital Equipment Corp.
4975 La Cross Rd.
Charleston, SC 29418
(803)554-8512
Ultimate Parent: Digital Equipment Corp. **SIC:** 7373—Computer Integrated Systems Design.

★ 78808 ★ Emery Worldwide
Charleston International Airport
Charleston, SC 29411
(803)747-5787
Ultimate Parent: Consolidated Freightways. **SIC:** 4512—Air Transportation—Scheduled.

★ 78809 ★ Essick Mayco
296 Eagle Rd.
Charleston, SC 29411
(803)797-5300 **Fax:** (803)553-7036
Company Type: Subsidiary. **Officer:** William J. Kriss, President. **Ultimate Parent:** Figgie International.

★ 78810 ★ Express
2060 Sam Rittenberg Blvd.
Charleston, SC 29407
(803)766-8288
Ultimate Parent: Limited. **SIC:** 5651—Family Clothing Stores.

★ 78811 ★ Exxon Shop
3700 Rivers Ave.
Charleston, SC 29405
(803)747-2849
Ultimate Parent: Exxon. **SIC:** 7539—Automotive Repair Shops Nec.

★ 78812 ★ Exxon Shop
4881 Rivers Ave.
Charleston, SC 29418
(803)747-7369
Ultimate Parent: Exxon. **SIC:** 5411—Grocery Stores.

★ 78813 ★ First Union National Bank of South Carolina
1776 Ashley River Rd.
Charleston, SC 29407
(803)724-1000
Location Type: Branch office. **Ultimate Parent:** First Union Corp. **SIC:** 6021—National Commercial Banks.

★ 78814 ★ First Union National Bank of South Carolina
177 Meeting St.
Charleston, SC 29401
(803)727-1120
Ultimate Parent: First Union Corp. **SIC:** 6021—National Commercial Banks.

★ 78815 ★ Food Lion
1119 Wappoo Rd.
Charleston, SC 29407
(803)556-3556
Ultimate Parent: Food Lion. **SIC:** 5411—Grocery Stores.

★ 78816 ★ Food Lion
7550 Dorchester Rd.
Charleston, SC 29418
(803)767-2952
Ultimate Parent: Food Lion. **SIC:** 5411—Grocery Stores.

★ 78817 ★ The Gap
Northwoods
Charleston, SC 29405
(803)572-1541
Ultimate Parent: GAP. **SIC:** 5611—Men's & Boys' Clothing Stores.

★ 78818 ★ The Gap
203 Meeting St.
Charleston, SC 29401
(803)577-2498
Ultimate Parent: GAP. **SIC:** 5651—Family Clothing Stores.

★ 78819 ★ Harley Davidson Motorcycles
4405 Dorchester Rd.
Charleston, SC 29405
(803)554-1847
Ultimate Parent: Harley-Davidson. **SIC:** 5571—Motorcycle Dealers.

★ 78820 ★ Hertz Rent-A-Car
3450 Rental Car Ln.
Charleston, SC 29418
(803)767-7043
Ultimate Parent: Hertz. **SIC:** 7514—Passenger Car Rental.

★ 78821 ★ Jiffy Lube
7601 Rivers Ave.
Charleston, SC 29418
(803)553-0196
Ultimate Parent: Pennzoil.

★ 78822 ★ Jiffy Lube
1971 Sam Rittenberg Blvd.
Charleston, SC 29407
(803)556-7732
Ultimate Parent: Pennzoil. **SIC:** 5172—Petroleum Products Nec; 7530—Automotive Repair Shops; 7538—General Automotive Repair Shops; 7539—Automotive Repair Shops Nec.

★ 78823 ★ Kay Bee Toys
120 Northwoods Mall
Charleston, SC 29418
(803)797-5092
Ultimate Parent: Melville. **SIC:** 5945—Hobby, Toy & Game Shops.

★ 78824 ★ Kelly Assisted Living Servi
1 Poston Rd.
Charleston, SC 29407
(803)556-1191
Ultimate Parent: Kelly Services. **SIC:** 8082—Home Health Care Services.

★ 78825 ★ Kentucky Fried Chicken
221 Spring St.
Charleston, SC 29403
(803)722-3781
Ultimate Parent: Pepsico. **SIC:** 5812—Eating Places.

★ 78826 ★ Kentucky Fried Chicken
5890 Rivers Ave.
Charleston, SC 29418
(803)554-1734
Ultimate Parent: Pepsico. **SIC:** 5812—Eating Places.

★ 78827 ★ Kentucky Fried Chicken
1729 Sam Rittenberg Blvd.
Charleston, SC 29407
(803)766-5773
Ultimate Parent: Pepsico. **SIC:** 5812—Eating Places.

★ 78828 ★ Kentucky Fried Chicken
483 Meeting St.
Charleston, SC 29403
(803)723-1281
Ultimate Parent: Pepsico. **SIC:** 5812—Eating Places.

★ 78829 ★ Kentucky Fried Chicken
3703 Rivers Ave.
Charleston, SC 29405
(803)747-1757
Ultimate Parent: Pepsico. **SIC:** 5812—Eating Places.

★ 78830 ★ Kentucky Fried Chicken
5237 Dorchester Rd.
Charleston, SC 29418
(803)552-0566
Ultimate Parent: Pepsico. **SIC:** 5812—Eating Places.

★ 78831 ★ Kentucky Fried Chicken
345 Folly Rd.
Charleston, SC 29412
(803)795-5211
Ultimate Parent: Pepsico. **SIC:** 5812—Eating Places.

★ 78832 ★ Lens Crafters
2060 Sam Rittenberg Blvd.
Charleston, SC 29407
(803)766-8333
Ultimate Parent: United States Shoe. SIC: 5995—Optical Goods Stores.

★ 78833 ★ Lerner Shop
Northwoods
Charleston, SC 29405
(803)797-2730
Ultimate Parent: Limited. SIC: 5621—Women's Clothing Stores.

★ 78834 ★ Lerner Shop
456 Citadel Mall
Charleston, SC 29407
(803)571-7499
Ultimate Parent: Limited. SIC: 5651—Family Clothing Stores.

★ 78835 ★ Liberty Mutual Insurance Co.
310 Meeting St.
Charleston, SC 29401
(803)556-8215
Ultimate Parent: Liberty Mutual Group. SIC: 6411—Insurance Agents, Brokers & Service.

★ 78836 ★ The Limited
2060 Sam Rittenberg Blvd.
Charleston, SC 29407
(803)571-5369
Ultimate Parent: Limited. SIC: 5651—Family Clothing Stores.

★ 78837 ★ The Limited
99 Northwoods Mall
Charleston, SC 29418
(803)797-8117
Ultimate Parent: Limited. SIC: 5651—Family Clothing Stores.

★ 78838 ★ The Limited
128 S. Market St.
Charleston, SC 29401
(803)723-4799
Ultimate Parent: Limited. SIC: 5651—Family Clothing Stores.

★ 78839 ★ The Limited Express
82 Northwoods Mall
Charleston, SC 29418
(803)797-7225
Ultimate Parent: Limited. SIC: 5651—Family Clothing Stores.

★ 78840 ★ Lockheed Aeronautical Sys. Co. Charleston Adhesive Bond Plan
4280 Pace St.
Charleston, SC 29405
Ultimate Parent: Lockheed Corp. SIC: 3271—Concrete Block & Brick.

★ 78841 ★ Lockheed Aeronautical Systems Co.
428 Pl. St.
Charleston, SC 29405
Ultimate Parent: Lockheed Corp. SIC: 3271—Concrete Block & Brick.

★ 78842 ★ Lockheed Aeronautical Systems Co.-Charleston
Pace St.
Charleston, SC 29405
Ultimate Parent: Lockheed Corp. SIC: 3271—Concrete Block & Brick.

★ 78843 ★ Marathon Petroleum Co.
5165 Virginia Ave.
Charleston, SC 29406
(803)554-5440
Ultimate Parent: USX Corp. SIC: 2911—Petroleum Refining; 5172—Petroleum Products Nec.

★ 78844 ★ Marshalls
7800 Rivers Ave.
Charleston, SC 29418
(803)764-3125
Ultimate Parent: Melville. SIC: 5311—Department Stores; 5651—Family Clothing Stores.

★ 78845 ★ Mary Kay Cosmetics
1231 Forestwood Dr.
Charleston, SC 29407
(803)572-3738
Ultimate Parent: Mary Kay Cosmetics.

★ 78846 ★ New York Life Charleston General Office
Southeastern Agencies
PO Box 20305
Charleston, SC 29413
(803)720-1900 Fax: (803)720-1919
Officer: Stephen T. Adkins, General Manager. Ultimate Parent: New York Life.

★ 78847 ★ New York Life Charleston General Office
Southeastern Agencies
200 Meeting St., Ste. 306
Charleston, SC 29401
(803)720-1900 Fax: (803)720-1919
Officer: Stephen T. Adkins, General Manager. Ultimate Parent: New York Life.

★ 78848 ★ Norwest Mortgage Inc.
2175 Ashley Phosphat Rd.
Charleston, SC 29418
(803)569-3000
Ultimate Parent: Norwest Corp. SIC: 6162—Mortgage Bankers & Correspondents.

★ 78849 ★ Payless Shoesource
6185 Rivers Ave.
Charleston, SC 29418
(803)572-5497
Ultimate Parent: May Department Stores. SIC: 5661—Shoe Stores.

★ 78850 ★ Payless Shoesource
3601 Rivers Ave.
Charleston, SC 29405
(803)747-3438
Ultimate Parent: May Department Stores. SIC: 5661—Shoe Stores.

★ 78851 ★ Petite Sophisticate
53 Northwoods Mall
Charleston, SC 29418
(803)572-3612
Ultimate Parent: United States Shoe. SIC: 5651—Family Clothing Stores.

★ 78852 ★ Piggly Wiggly
14 Sumar St.
Charleston, SC 29407
(803)571-3140
Ultimate Parent: Bruno's. SIC: 5912—Drug Stores & Proprietary Stores.

★ 78853 ★ Piggly Wiggly
1270 Yeamans Hall Rd.
Charleston, SC 29406
(803)747-6373
Ultimate Parent: Bruno's. SIC: 5411—Grocery Stores.

★ 78854 ★ Piggly Wiggly
4310 Rivers Ave.
Charleston, SC 29405
(803)554-7450
Ultimate Parent: Bruno's. SIC: 5411—Grocery Stores.

★ 78855 ★ Piggly Wiggly
1015 King St.
Charleston, SC 29403
(803)723-5226
Ultimate Parent: Bruno's. SIC: 5411—Grocery Stores.

★ 78856 ★ Piggly Wiggly
1739 Maybank Hwy.
Charleston, SC 29412
(803)795-9091
Ultimate Parent: Bruno's. SIC: 5411—Grocery Stores.

★ 78857 ★ Piggly Wiggly
5060 Dorchester Rd.
Charleston, SC 29418
(803)552-9421
Ultimate Parent: Bruno's. SIC: 5411—Grocery Stores.

★ 78858 ★ Piggly Wiggly
1807 Savannah Hwy.
Charleston, SC 29407
(803)766-5825
Ultimate Parent: Bruno's. SIC: 5411—Grocery Stores.

★ 78859 ★ Piggly Wiggly
1268 Cornwallis Dr.
Charleston, SC 29412
(803)762-0118
Ultimate Parent: Bruno's. SIC: 5411—Grocery Stores.

★ 78860 ★ Piggly Wiggly
630 Skylark Dr.
Charleston, SC 29407
(803)556-7522
Ultimate Parent: Bruno's. SIC: 5411—Grocery Stores.

★ 78861 ★ Piggly Wiggly
74 Folly Rd.
Charleston, SC 29407
(803)571-1522
Ultimate Parent: Bruno's. SIC: 5411—Grocery Stores.

★ 78862 ★ Piggly Wiggly
8780 Rivers Ave.
Charleston, SC 29418
(803)764-3039
Ultimate Parent: Bruno's. SIC: 5411—Grocery Stores.

★ 78863 ★ Piggly Wiggly
5101 Ashley Phosphate Rd.
Charleston, SC 29418
(803)552-3353
Ultimate Parent: Bruno's. SIC: 5411—Grocery Stores.

★ 78864 ★ Pizza Hut
6072 Rivers Ave.
Charleston, SC 29418
(803)744-7108
Ultimate Parent: Pepsico. SIC: 5812—Eating Places.

★ 78865 ★ Pizza Hut
1733 Sam Rittenberg Blvd.
Charleston, SC 29407
(803)556-6281
Ultimate Parent: Pepsico. SIC: 5812—Eating Places.

★ 78866 ★ Pizza Hut
5101 Ashley Phosphate Rd.
Charleston, SC 29418
(803)767-3100
Ultimate Parent: Pepsico. SIC: 5812—Eating Places.

★ 78867 ★ Pizza Hut
890 Folly Rd.
Charleston, SC 29412
(803)795-7460
Ultimate Parent: Pepsico. SIC: 5812—Eating Places.

★ 78868 ★ Pizza Hut
915 Folly Rd.
Charleston, SC 29412
(803)795-2244
Ultimate Parent: Pepsico. SIC: 5812—Eating Places.

★ 78869 ★ Pizza Hut
2571 Ashley River Rd.
Charleston, SC 29414
(803)763-3600
Ultimate Parent: Pepsico. SIC: 5812—Eating Places.

★ 78870 ★ Pizza Hut
1300 Savannah Hwy.
Charleston, SC 29407
(803)763-2700
Ultimate Parent: Pepsico. SIC: 5812—Eating Places.

★ 78871 ★ Radio Shack
3191 Ashley Phosphate Rd.
Charleston, SC 29418
(803)552-8910
Company Type: Division. Ultimate Parent: Tandy Corp. SIC: 7319—Advertising Nec.

★ 78872 ★ Radio Shack
Charlestowne Sq.
Charleston, SC 29405
(803)554-5265
Company Type: Division. Ultimate Parent: Tandy Corp. SIC: 5065—Electronic Parts & Equipment Nec.

★ 78873 ★ Radio Shack
Citadel Mall Ctr.
Charleston, SC 29407
(803)556-8462
Company Type: Division. Ultimate Parent: Tandy Corp. SIC: 5065—Electronic Parts & Equipment Nec.

★ 78874 ★ Radio Shack
Ashley Plz.
Charleston, SC 29407
(803)556-2501
Company Type: Division. Ultimate Parent:

Tandy Corp. SIC: 5046—Commercial Equipment Nec.

★ 78875 ★ Radio Shack
5900 Rivers Ave.
Charleston, SC 29418
(803)744-8203
Company Type: Division. Ultimate Parent: Tandy Corp. SIC: 5731—Radio, Television & Electronics Stores.

★ 78876 ★ Radio Shack
1720 Sam Rittnbrg Blvd. 10
Charleston, SC 29407
(803)556-6171
Company Type: Division. Ultimate Parent: Tandy Corp. SIC: 5731—Radio, Television & Electronics Stores.

★ 78877 ★ Radio Shack
2401 Mall Dr.
Charleston, SC 29418
(803)554-5265
Company Type: Division. Ultimate Parent: Tandy Corp. SIC: 5731—Radio, Television & Electronics Stores.

★ 78878 ★ Radio Shack
73 Northwoods Mall
Charleston, SC 29418
(803)553-9669
Company Type: Division. Ultimate Parent: Tandy Corp. SIC: 5731—Radio, Television & Electronics Stores.

★ 78879 ★ Radio Shack
88 Folly Rd.
Charleston, SC 29407
(803)763-3116
Company Type: Division. Ultimate Parent: Tandy Corp. SIC: 5731—Radio, Television & Electronics Stores.

★ 78880 ★ Rite Aid
72 Folly Rd.
Charleston, SC 29407
(803)763-9836
Ultimate Parent: Rite Aid. SIC: 5912—Drug Stores & Proprietary Stores.

★ 78881 ★ Rite Aid Discount Pharmacie
915 Folly Rd.
Charleston, SC 29412
(803)795-1818
Ultimate Parent: Rite Aid. SIC: 5912—Drug Stores & Proprietary Stores.

★ 78882 ★ Rite Aid Discount Pharmacy
975 Savannah Hwy.
Charleston, SC 29407
(803)556-9917
Ultimate Parent: Rite Aid. SIC: 5912—Drug Stores & Proprietary Stores.

★ 78883 ★ Rite Aid Discount Pharmacy
1268 Yeamans Hall Rd.
Charleston, SC 29406
(803)745-9389
Ultimate Parent: Rite Aid. SIC: 5912—Drug Stores & Proprietary Stores.

★ 78884 ★ Rite Aid Discount Pharmacy
1964 Ashley River Rd.
Charleston, SC 29407
(803)766-1797
Ultimate Parent: Rite Aid. SIC: 5912—Drug Stores & Proprietary Stores.

★ 78885 ★ Rite Aid Discount Pharmacy
4318 Rivers Ave.
Charleston, SC 29405
(803)745-9390
Ultimate Parent: Rite Aid. SIC: 5912—Drug Stores & Proprietary Stores.

★ 78886 ★ Rite Aid Drugs
983 Harbor View Rd.
Charleston, SC 29412
(803)795-9833
Ultimate Parent: Rite Aid. SIC: 5912—Drug Stores & Proprietary Stores.

★ 78887 ★ Ryder Truck Rental
897 Folly Rd.
Charleston, SC 29412
(803)795-5201
Ultimate Parent: Ryder System. SIC: 4214—Local Trucking With Storage.

★ 78888 ★ **Sam's Wholesale Club**
6185 Rivers Ave.
Charleston, SC 29418
(803)572-1961
Ultimate Parent: Wal-Mart Stores, Inc. **SIC:** 5099—Durable Goods Nec; 7997—Membership Sports & Recreation Clubs.

★ 78889 ★ **Service Merchandise**
7400 Rivers Ave.
Charleston, SC 29418
(803)572-2665
Ultimate Parent: Service Merchandise Co., Inc. **SIC:** 5311—Department Stores.

★ 78890 ★ **Shell Oil**
4900 Virginia Ave.
Charleston, SC 29406
(803)744-4251
Ultimate Parent: Shell Oil Co. **SIC:** 5171—Petroleum Bulk Stations & Terminals.

★ 78891 ★ **Spartan Express Inc.**
3145 Pacific St.
Charleston, SC 29418
(803)554-6565
Ultimate Parent: Roadway Services. **SIC:** 7389—Business Services Nec.

★ 78892 ★ **SSI Medical Services Inc.**
4349 Corporate Rd.
Charleston, SC 29405
(803)747-8002 **Fax:** (803)747-4020
Company Type: Subsidiary. **Officer:** Walter M. Rosebrough Jr., President & CEO.
Ultimate Parent: Hillenbrand Industries.

★ 78893 ★ **Summit Corporate Center**
2430 Mall Dr.
Charleston, SC 29406-6546
(803)723-2801
Ultimate Parent: American Greetings. **SIC:** 6512—Nonresidential Building Operators.

★ 78894 ★ **SYTECH Corp.**
2301 Leeds Ave.
Charleston, SC 29405
(803)745-1642
Ultimate Parent: Cummins Engine Co.

★ 78895 ★ **T J Maxx**
7800 Rivers Ave.
Charleston, SC 29418
(803)764-1693
Ultimate Parent: TJX. **SIC:** 5311—Department Stores.

★ 78896 ★ **T J Maxx**
1812 Sam Rittenberg Blvd.
Charleston, SC 29407
(803)763-6652
Ultimate Parent: TJX. **SIC:** 5311—Department Stores.

★ 78897 ★ **Taco Bell**
916 Savannah Hwy.
Charleston, SC 29407
(803)571-0690
Ultimate Parent: Pepsico. **SIC:** 5812—Eating Places.

★ 78898 ★ **Taco Bell**
220 Spring St.
Charleston, SC 29403
(803)722-0659
Ultimate Parent: Pepsico. **SIC:** 5812—Eating Places.

★ 78899 ★ **Taco Bell**
1871 Hwy. 7
Charleston, SC 29407
(803)571-6121
Ultimate Parent: Pepsico. **SIC:** 5812—Eating Places.

★ 78900 ★ **Taco Bell**
88 Northwoods Mall
Charleston, SC 29418
(803)553-1111
Ultimate Parent: Pepsico. **SIC:** 5812—Eating Places.

★ 78901 ★ **Taco Bell**
5647 Dorchester Rd.
Charleston, SC 29418
(803)552-7287
Ultimate Parent: Pepsico. **SIC:** 5812—Eating Places.

★ 78902 ★ **Tandy Computer Center**
1836 Ashley River Rd.
Charleston, SC 29407
(803)766-3055
Ultimate Parent: Tandy Corp. **SIC:** 7373—Computer Integrated Systems Design.

★ 78903 ★ **Texaco Inc.**
4950 Virginia Ave.
Charleston, SC 29406
(803)747-5262
Ultimate Parent: Texaco. **SIC:** 5172—Petroleum Products Nec.

★ 78904 ★ **Textone Inc.**
1770 Hock Ave.
Charleston, SC 29405
Ultimate Parent: Nortek. **SIC:** 2499—Wood Products Nec.

★ 78905 ★ **Trailways Bus System**
1939 Reynolds Ave.
Charleston, SC 29405
(803)744-6676
Ultimate Parent: Greyhound Lines Inc. **SIC:** 4131—Intercity & Rural Bus Transportation.

★ 78906 ★ **Trailways Bus Systems**
100 Calhoun St.
Charleston, SC 29401
(803)723-8649
Ultimate Parent: Greyhound Lines Inc. **SIC:** 4131—Intercity & Rural Bus Transportation.

★ 78907 ★ **United Parcel Service**
4230 Daley Ave.
Charleston, SC 29418
(803)723-7905
Ultimate Parent: United Parcel Service of America. **SIC:** 7389—Business Services Nec.

★ 78908 ★ **US Fidelity**
2154 N. Ctr. St.
Charleston, SC 29418
(803)569-0635
Ultimate Parent: USF&G Corp. **SIC:** 6411—Insurance Agents, Brokers & Service.

★ 78909 ★ **Victoria's Secret**
132 S. Market St.
Charleston, SC 29401
(803)723-0332
Ultimate Parent: Limited. **SIC:** 5651—Family Clothing Stores.

★ 78910 ★ **Waldenbooks**
2060 Sam Rittenberg Blvd.
Charleston, SC 29407
(803)766-5879
Ultimate Parent: K-Mart. **SIC:** 5942—Book Stores.

★ 78911 ★ **Waldenbooks**
2401 Mall Dr.
Charleston, SC 29418
(803)744-5808
Ultimate Parent: K-Mart. **SIC:** 5942—Book Stores.

★ 78912 ★ **Waldenbooks**
80 Northwoods Mall
Charleston, SC 29418
(803)797-3558
Ultimate Parent: K-Mart. **SIC:** 5942—Book Stores.

★ 78913 ★ **Waldenbooks**
Charlestowne Sq.
Charleston, SC 29405
(803)744-5808
Ultimate Parent: K-Mart. **SIC:** 5942—Book Stores.

★ 78914 ★ **Westvaco Corp. Library**
Virginia Ave.
Charleston, SC 29406
(803)744-8231
Ultimate Parent: WestVaco Corp. **SIC:** 7311—Advertising Agencies.

★ 78915 ★ **Wetterau Inc.**
2001 Mabelene Rd.
Charleston, SC 29418
(803)797-6700
Ultimate Parent: Supervalu. **SIC:** 5141—Groceries—General Line; 6411—Insurance Agents, Brokers & Service.

★ 78916 ★ **Woodtek/Textone Inc.**
1770 Hock Ave.
Charleston, SC 29405
Ultimate Parent: Nortek. **SIC:** 2499—Wood Products Nec.

★ 78917 ★ **Xerox Corp.**
4130 Faber Pl. Dr.
Charleston, SC 29405
(803)554-5500
Officer: Dave Dunlap, Manager. **Ultimate Parent:** Xerox Corp. **SIC:** 3663—Radio & T.V. Communications Equipment.

Cheraw

★ 78918 ★ **Cheraw Dyeing & Finishing Plant**
Jersey & West Greene St.
Cheraw, SC 29520
Ultimate Parent: Cone Mills. **SIC:** 2261—Finishing Plants—Cotton; 2262—Finishing Plants—Manmade.

★ 78919 ★ **Cooper Industries Inc. Weller Wire Wrap Plant**
State Rd.
Cheraw, SC 29520
Ultimate Parent: Texas Industries. **SIC:** 3423—Hand & Edge Tools Nec; 3546—Power-Driven Handtools; 3549—Metalworking Machinery Nec.

★ 78920 ★ **Cooper Industries Weller/Wire Wrap Plt**
State Rd.
Cheraw, SC 29520
Ultimate Parent: Cooper Industries. **SIC:** 3423—Hand & Edge Tools Nec; 3546—Power-Driven Handtools; 3549—Metalworking Machinery Nec.

★ 78921 ★ **Crown Cork & Seal Co. Inc.**
100 Evans Row
Cheraw, SC 29520
Ultimate Parent: Crown Cork & Seal. **SIC:** 3411—Metal Cans.

★ 78922 ★ **First Federal S & L**
515 Market St.
Cheraw, SC 29520-2638
(803)537-7656
Company Type: Headquarters. **Officer:** Herbert W. Watts. **Ultimate Parent:** Bancorp Hawaii. **SIC:** 6035—Federal Savings Institutions; 6162—Mortgage Bankers & Correspondents.

★ 78923 ★ **Greyhound Bus Lines**
249 2nd St.
Cheraw, SC 29520
(803)537-7582
Ultimate Parent: Greyhound Lines Inc. **SIC:** 4131—Intercity & Rural Bus Transportation.

★ 78924 ★ **Stanley Tools**
100 Stanley Rd.
Cheraw, SC 29520
Ultimate Parent: Stanley Works. **SIC:** 3423—Hand & Edge Tools Nec; 3462—Iron & Steel Forgings; 3471—Plating & Polishing.

★ 78925 ★ **Stanley Works**
100 Stanley Rd.
Cheraw, SC 29520
(803)537-9311
Officer: H.G. Allen, Manager. **Ultimate Parent:** Stanley Works. **SIC:** 3423—Hand & Edge Tools Nec.

★ 78926 ★ **Stanley Works**
Stanley Tools Division
100 Stanley Rd.
Cheraw, SC 29520
Ultimate Parent: Stanley Works. **SIC:** 3423—Hand & Edge Tools Nec; 3471—Plating & Polishing; 3398—Metal Heat Treating; 3087—Custom Compound of Purchased Resins; 3089—Plastics Products Nec.

★ 78927 ★ **Wal Mart**
801 Chesterfield Hwy.
Cheraw, SC 29520
(803)537-6381
Ultimate Parent: Wal-Mart Stores, Inc. **SIC:** 5311—Department Stores.

★ 78928 ★ **Wal Mart**
Cheraw Sq.
Cheraw, SC 29520
(803)537-7872
Ultimate Parent: Wal-Mart Stores, Inc. **SIC:** 5311—Department Stores.

Chesnee

★ 78929 ★ **Bi-Lo Food Stores**
Hwy. 221
Chesnee, SC 29323
(803)461-3141
Ultimate Parent: Penn Traffic. **SIC:** 5411—Grocery Stores.

★ 78930 ★ **Mary Kay Cosmetics**
140 Margate Cir.
Chesnee, SC 29323
(803)461-7551
Ultimate Parent: Mary Kay Cosmetics. **SIC:** 5999—Miscellaneous Retail Stores Nec.

Chester

★ 78931 ★ **Borden Inc.**
198 Saluda St.
Chester, SC 29706
(803)377-1121
Officer: Don Feltz, Manager. **Ultimate Parent:** Borden, Inc. **SIC:** 2023—Dry, Condensed & Evaporated Dairy Products.

★ 78932 ★ **Borden Inc.**
North American Foods Div.
198 Saluda St.
Chester, SC 29706
(803)377-1121
Company Type: Division. **Location Type:** Plant. **Officer:** Donald Feltz, Plant Manager. **Ultimate Parent:** Borden, Inc.

★ 78933 ★ **Branch Banking & Trust Co.**
115 Saluda St.
Chester, SC 29706-1580
(803)377-8151
Company Type: Subsidiary. **Location Type:** Branch office. **Ultimate Parent:** Southern National Corp. **SIC:** 6021—National Commercial Banks.

★ 78934 ★ **First Union National Bank of South Carolina**
Chester Mall, Hwy. 72 Bypass
Chester, SC 29706-2131
(803)385-2181
Location Type: Branch office. **Ultimate Parent:** First Union Corp. **SIC:** 6021—National Commercial Banks.

★ 78935 ★ **First Union National Bank of South Carolina**
126 Gadsden St.
Chester, SC 29706-2016
(803)385-2181
Location Type: Branch office. **Ultimate Parent:** First Union Corp. **SIC:** 6021—National Commercial Banks.

★ 78936 ★ **Food Lion**
Saluda Sq.
Chester, SC 29706
(803)377-7127
Ultimate Parent: Food Lion. **SIC:** 5411—Grocery Stores.

★ 78937 ★ **GAF Building Materials Corp.**
190 Orrs Rd.
Chester, SC 29706
(803)377-7171
Company Type: Subsidiary. **Officer:** John Toms, Manager. **Ultimate Parent:** GAF Corp. **SIC:** 3231—Products of Purchased Glass; 3229—Pressed & Blown Glass Nec.

★ 78938 ★ **Gaf Corp.**
190 Orrs Rd.
Chester, SC 29706
(803)377-7171
Ultimate Parent: GAF Corp. **SIC:** 3231—Products of Purchased Glass.

★ 78939 ★ **National Steel Corp.**
Richburg Hwy. 9
Chester, SC 29706
(803)789-5115
Ultimate Parent: National Intergroup. **SIC:** 5051—Metals Service Centers & Offices.

★ 78940 ★ **Pizza Hut**
J a Cochran By-Pass
Chester, SC 29706
(803)581-8288
Ultimate Parent: Pepsico. **SIC:** 5812—
Eating Places.

★ 78941 ★ **Ryder Truck Rental**
Richburg Hwy. 9
Chester, SC 29706
(803)789-6135
Ultimate Parent: Ryder System. **SIC:**
7513—Truck Rental & Leasing Without
Drivers.

★ 78942 ★ **Sequa Chemicals**
State Hwy. 72 Byp
Chester, SC 29706
(803)385-5181
Ultimate Parent: Sequa Corp. **SIC:** 2899—
Chemical Preparations Nec.

★ 78943 ★ **Sequa Chemicals Inc.**
1 Sequa Dr.
Chester, SC 29706-0070
Ultimate Parent: Sequa Corp. **SIC:** 2819—
Industrial Inorganic Chemicals Nec; 2821—
Plastics Materials & Resins; 2841—Soap &
Other Detergents; 2843—Surface Active
Agents; 2869—Industrial Organic Chemicals
Nec; 2899—Chemical Preparations Nec.

★ 78944 ★ **Springs Industries, Inc.**
Lancaster Rd.
Chester, SC 29706
(803)377-9200
Officer: Walter Y. Elisha, President.
Ultimate Parent: Springs Industries. **SIC:**
2211—Broadwoven Fabric Mills—Cotton;
2221—Broadwoven Fabric Mills—Manmade;
2399—Fabricated Textile Products Nec.

★ 78945 ★ **Springs Industries, Inc. Eureka**
Faluda St.
Chester, SC 29706
(803)385-4701
Officer: Bryant Sanders, Manager. **Ultimate
Parent:** Springs Industries. **SIC:** 2399—
Fabricated Textile Products Nec.

★ 78946 ★ **Willamette Industries Inc.**
Lancaster Hwy. 9
Chester, SC 29706
(803)581-7164
Ultimate Parent: Willamette Industries, Inc.
SIC: 0811—Timber Tracts.

★ 78947 ★ **Willamette Industries, Inc.**
Chester
Hwy. 9 East
Chester, SC 29706
Ultimate Parent: Willamette Industries, Inc.
SIC: 2436—Softwood Veneer & Plywood;
2421—Sawmills & Planing Mills—General.

Clemson

★ 78948 ★ **Branch Banking & Trust Co.**
1070 Tiger Blvd., Hwy. 123
Clemson, SC 29631-1422
(803)654-5574
Company Type: Subsidiary. **Location
Type:** Branch office. **Ultimate Parent:**
Southern National Corp. **SIC:** 6021—
National Commercial Banks.

★ 78949 ★ **Branch Banking & Trust Co.**
389 College Ave.
Clemson, SC 29631-1472
(803)654-5574
Company Type: Subsidiary. **Location
Type:** Branch office. **Ultimate Parent:**
Southern National Corp. **SIC:** 6021—
National Commercial Banks.

★ 78950 ★ **J. P. Stevens & Co.**
Cherry Rd.
Clemson, SC 29631
Location Type: Plant. **Ultimate Parent:**
West Point Stevens. **SIC:** 2261—Finishing
Plants—Cotton.

★ 78951 ★ **Jacobs Chuck Manufacturing Co.**
1 Jacobs Rd. PO Box 592
Clemson, SC 29633-0592
Ultimate Parent: Danaher Corp. **SIC:**
3541—Machine Tools—Metal Cutting
Types.

★ 78952 ★ **Jacobs Chuck Manufacturing Co.**
Seneca Hwy.
Clemson, SC 29633
Ultimate Parent: Danaher Corp. **SIC:**
3541—Machine Tools—Metal Cutting
Types.

★ 78953 ★ **Jacobs Chuck Mfg. Co.**
1 Jacobs Rd. PO Box 592
Clemson, SC 29631
Ultimate Parent: Danaher Corp. **SIC:**
3541—Machine Tools—Metal Cutting
Types.

★ 78954 ★ **Jacobs Man**
Jacobs Chuck Manufacturing
1 Jacobs Rd.
PO Box 592
Clemson, SC 29631
(803)654-5926
Company Type: Subsidiary. **Officer:**
Dennis D. Claramont, President. **Ultimate
Parent:** Danaher Corp. **SIC:** 3545—
Machine Tool Accessories.

★ 78955 ★ **Kentucky Fried Chicken**
Hwy. 123 Bypass
Clemson, SC 29631
(803)654-1598
Ultimate Parent: Pepsico. **SIC:** 5812—
Eating Places.

★ 78956 ★ **Pizza Hut**
123 Bypass
Clemson, SC 29631
(803)654-8646
Ultimate Parent: Pepsico. **SIC:** 5812—
Eating Places.

Clinton

★ 78957 ★ **Avery Dennison**
PO Box 270
Clinton, SC 29325-0270
(803)833-0062
Officer: Al Green. **Ultimate Parent:** Avery
Dennison Corp. **SIC:** 2759—Commercial
Printing Nec; 5999—Miscellaneous Retail
Stores Nec.

★ 78958 ★ **Avery Dennison**
Hwy. 76 E
Clinton, SC 29325
Ultimate Parent: Avery Dennison Corp.
SIC: 2754—Commercial Printing—Gravure.

★ 78959 ★ **Avery Dennison Corp.**
Security Printing Div.
Hwy. 76 E.
Clinton, SC 29325
Company Type: Division. **Ultimate Parent:**
Avery Dennison Corp. **SIC:** 2754—
Commercial Printing—Gravure.

★ 78960 ★ **Kentucky Fried Chicken**
S Broad
Clinton, SC 29325
(803)833-0524
Ultimate Parent: Pepsico. **SIC:** 5812—
Eating Places.

★ 78961 ★ **Pizza Hut**
Hwy. 56 S
Clinton, SC 29325
(803)833-5800
Ultimate Parent: Pepsico. **SIC:** 5812—
Eating Places.

★ 78962 ★ **Radio Shack**
Copeland Plz.
Clinton, SC 29325
(803)833-5861
Company Type: Division. **Ultimate Parent:**
Tandy Corp. **SIC:** 5065—Electronic Parts &
Equipment Nec; 5731—Radio, Television &
Electronics Stores.

★ 78963 ★ **Torrington Co.**
Old Laurens Rd.
Clinton, SC 29325
Ultimate Parent: Ingersoll-Rand. **SIC:**
3499—Fabricated Metal Products Nec;
3562—Ball & Roller Bearings.

Clover

★ 78964 ★ **First Union National Bank of South Carolina**
203 Bethel St.
Clover, SC 29710-1101
(803)222-4571
Location Type: Branch office. **Ultimate
Parent:** First Union Corp. **SIC:** 6021—
National Commercial Banks.

Columbia

★ 78965 ★ **Air Products & Chemicals, Inc.**
951 True St.
Columbia, SC 29209
(803)783-4640
Ultimate Parent: Air Products & Chemicals,
Inc. **SIC:** 2899—Chemical Preparations
Nec; 5084—Industrial Machinery &
Equipment.

★ 78966 ★ **Allied-Signal Inc.**
Fibers
4402 Saint Andrews Rd.
Columbia, SC 29210
Ultimate Parent: Allied-Signal Inc. **SIC:**
2821—Plastics Materials & Resins; 2824—
Organic Fibers—Noncellulosic.

★ 78967 ★ **Allied-Signal Inc.**
Fibers
4402 St. Andrews Rd.
Columbia, SC 29210
Location Type: Plant. **Ultimate Parent:**
Allied-Signal Inc. **SIC:** 2821—Plastics
Materials & Resins; 2824—Organic Fibers—
Noncellulosic.

★ 78968 ★ **AMBAC International**
1 Diesel Dr. I-77 & Killian Rd.
Columbia, SC 292020085
Ultimate Parent: AMBAC Inc. **SIC:** 3511—
Turbines & Turbine Generator Sets.

★ 78969 ★ **AMBAC International Corp.**
1 Diesel Dr.
I-77 & Killian Rd.
Columbia, SC 29223
Ultimate Parent: AMBAC Inc. **SIC:** 3519—
Internal Combustion Engines Nec.

★ 78970 ★ **AMBAC International Corp.**
PO Box 85
Columbia, SC 29202-0085
(803)735-1400
Location Type: Branch office. **Ultimate
Parent:** AMBAC Inc. **SIC:** 3511—Turbines
& Turbine Generator Sets; 3599—Industrial
Machinery Nec.

★ 78971 ★ **American General Finance Inc.**
2230 Decker Blvd., No. D
Columbia, SC 29206-3503
(803)736-4785
Location Type: Branch office. **Officer:**
Charlie Sides. **Ultimate Parent:** American
General Corp. **SIC:** 6141—Personal Credit
Institutions.

★ 78972 ★ **American General Finance Inc.**
2230 Decker Blvd., No. D
Columbia, SC 29206-3503
(803)736-4785
Officer: Charlie Sides. **Ultimate Parent:**
American General Corp. **SIC:** 6141—
Personal Credit Institutions.

★ 78973 ★ **Atlantic Soft Drink Co. Inc.**
6925 N. Main St.
Columbia, SC 29203-0261
Ultimate Parent: Pepsico. **SIC:** 2086—
Bottled & Canned Soft Drinks.

★ 78974 ★ **Bank South NA**
240 Stoneridge Dr.
Columbia, SC 29210-8010
(803)779-6636
Ultimate Parent: Bank South Corp. **SIC:**
6141—Personal Credit Institutions; 6021—
National Commercial Banks.

★ 78975 ★ **Beneficial Finance Co.**
1531 Broad River Rd.
Columbia, SC 29210-7301
(803)798-6050
Location Type: Branch office. **Officer:** Tom
Gowitzka. **Ultimate Parent:** Beneficial. **SIC:**
6141—Personal Credit Institutions; 6162—
Mortgage Bankers & Correspondents.

★ 78976 ★ **Bethlehem Steel Corp.**
7909 Parklane Rd.
Columbia, SC 29223-5666
(803)741-1951
Ultimate Parent: Bethlehem Steel Corp.
SIC: 3312—Blast Furnaces & Steel Mills.

★ 78977 ★ **Bi-Lo Inc. No 196**
7315 Garners Ferry Rd.
Columbia, SC 29209
(803)783-5425
Ultimate Parent: Penn Traffic. **SIC:** 5411—
Grocery Stores.

★ 78978 ★ **Branch Banking & Trust Co.**
1350 Browning Rd.
Columbia, SC 29201
(803)255-5590
Company Type: Subsidiary. **Location
Type:** Branch office. **Ultimate Parent:**
Southern National Corp. **SIC:** 6021—
National Commercial Banks.

★ 78979 ★ **Branch Banking & Trust Co.**
1633 Broad River Rd.
Columbia, SC 29210-7307
(803)251-3140
Company Type: Subsidiary. **Location
Type:** Branch office. **Ultimate Parent:**
Southern National Corp. **SIC:** 6021—
National Commercial Banks.

★ 78980 ★ **Branch Banking & Trust Co.**
7001 Parklane Rd.
Columbia, SC 29223-7631
(803)251-3155
Company Type: Subsidiary. **Location
Type:** Branch office. **Ultimate Parent:**
Southern National Corp. **SIC:** 6021—
National Commercial Banks.

★ 78981 ★ **Branch Banking & Trust Co.**
3403 Forest Dr., Kroger Store 012
Columbia, SC 29204-4028
(803)251-3167
Company Type: Subsidiary. **Location
Type:** Branch office. **Ultimate Parent:**
Southern National Corp. **SIC:** 6021—
National Commercial Banks.

★ 78982 ★ **Branch Banking & Trust Co.**
7315 Garners Ferry Rd., Bi-Lo Store
Columbia, SC 29209-2110
(803)251-3172
Company Type: Subsidiary. **Location
Type:** Branch office. **Ultimate Parent:**
Southern National Corp. **SIC:** 6021—
National Commercial Banks.

★ 78983 ★ **Branch Banking & Trust Co.**
1201 Main St.
Columbia, SC 29201-3200
(803)251-3192
Company Type: Subsidiary. **Location
Type:** Branch office. **Ultimate Parent:**
Southern National Corp. **SIC:** 6021—
National Commercial Banks.

★ 78984 ★ **Branch Banking & Trust Co.**
2001 Assembly St., Ste. 204
Columbia, SC 29201-2153
(803)251-3100
Company Type: Subsidiary. **Location
Type:** Branch office. **Ultimate Parent:**
Southern National Corp. **SIC:** 6021—
National Commercial Banks.

★ 78985 ★   **Branch Banking & Trust Co.**
595 St. Andrews Rd.
Columbia, SC 29210-4599
(803)251-3150
Company Type: Subsidiary. **Location Type:** Branch office. **Ultimate Parent:** Southern National Corp. **SIC:** 6021—National Commercial Banks.

★ 78986 ★   **Branch Banking & Trust Co.**
7327 St. Andrews Rd.
Columbia, SC 29063
(803)748-7196
Company Type: Subsidiary. **Location Type:** Branch office. **Officer:** Mary Plexico, Manager. **Ultimate Parent:** Southern National Corp. **SIC:** 6021—National Commercial Banks.

★ 78987 ★   **Branch Banking & Trust Co.**
7000 Garners Ferry Rd.
Columbia, SC 29209-1002
(803)748-7190
Company Type: Subsidiary. **Location Type:** Branch office. **Officer:** Dennis Roberts, Manager. **Ultimate Parent:** Southern National Corp. **SIC:** 6021—National Commercial Banks.

★ 78988 ★   **Branch Banking & Trust Co.**
8921 Two Notch Rd.
Columbia, SC 29223-6367
(803)748-7135
Company Type: Subsidiary. **Location Type:** Branch office. **Officer:** Cynthia Van Neck, Manager. **Ultimate Parent:** Southern National Corp. **SIC:** 6021—National Commercial Banks.

★ 78989 ★   **Branch Banking & Trust Co.**
1340 Bull St.
Columbia, SC 29201
(803)254-1600
Ultimate Parent: Southern National Corp. **SIC:** 6099—Functions Related to Deposit Banking.

★ 78990 ★   **Brownell Electro Inc.**
1401 St. Andrews Rd.
Columbia, SC 29210
(803)772-6111
Location Type: Branch office. **Ultimate Parent:** Avnet. **SIC:** 5063—Electrical Apparatus & Equipment.

★ 78991 ★   **Browning Ferris Industries South Atl**
4425 Bluff Rd.
Columbia, SC 29209-4509
(803)776-8900
Location Type: Branch office. **Officer:** Neil Clark. **Ultimate Parent:** Browning-Ferris Industries. **SIC:** 4212—Local Trucking Without Storage; 4953—Refuse Systems.

★ 78992 ★   **Burlington Coat Factory**
1310 Bush River Rd.
Columbia, SC 29210-6832
(803)798-7885
Ultimate Parent: Burlington Industries, Equity. **SIC:** 5311—Department Stores; 5661—Shoe Stores.

★ 78993 ★   **Carolina Eastman Co.**
Hwy. 21 S
Columbia, SC 29202
(803)794-9200
Officer: John D. Beckler, President. **Ultimate Parent:** Eastman Kodak. **SIC:** 2821—Plastics Materials & Resins; 2824—Organic Fibers—Noncellulosic; 2869—Industrial Organic Chemicals Nec.

★ 78994 ★   **Carolina Eastman Co.**
Intersection I-26 & Hwy. 21 N. PO Box 1782
Columbia, SC 29169
Ultimate Parent: Eastman Kodak. **SIC:** 2821—Plastics Materials & Resins; 2865—Cyclic Crudes & Intermediates.

★ 78995 ★   **Carolina Eastman Co.**
US Hwy. 21 & 176
PO Box 1782
Columbia, SC 29202
Ultimate Parent: Eastman Kodak. **SIC:** 2821—Plastics Materials & Resins; 2865—Cyclic Crudes & Intermediates; 2824—Organic Fibers—Noncellulosic.

★ 78996 ★   **Casual Corner**
Woodhill Mall
Columbia, SC 29209
(803)776-1185
Ultimate Parent: United States Shoe.

★ 78997 ★   **Casual Corner**
5 Dutch Sq.
Columbia, SC 29210
(803)798-6879
Ultimate Parent: United States Shoe. **SIC:** 5651—Family Clothing Stores; 5992—Florists.

★ 78998 ★   **Casual Corner**
1041 Richland St.
Columbia, SC 29201
(803)782-1228
Ultimate Parent: United States Shoe. **SIC:** 5651—Family Clothing Stores.

★ 78999 ★   **Casual Corner**
636 Cola Mall Shopping
Columbia, SC 29206
(803)788-7633
Ultimate Parent: United States Shoe. **SIC:** 5651—Family Clothing Stores.

★ 79000 ★   **Casual Corner**
Columbia
Columbia, SC 29204
(803)788-7633
Ultimate Parent: United States Shoe. **SIC:** 5621—Women's Clothing Stores.

★ 79001 ★   **Cincinnati Insurance Co.**
1300 Pickens St.
Columbia, SC 29201
(803)779-0018
Ultimate Parent: Cincinnati Financial. **SIC:** 6411—Insurance Agents, Brokers & Service.

★ 79002 ★   **Circuit City**
6833 Notch Rd.
Columbia, SC 29223
(803)736-2540
Ultimate Parent: Circuit City Stores. **SIC:** 5731—Radio, Television & Electronics Stores.

★ 79003 ★   **Citgo Oil Service Co.**
2405 Two Notch Rd.
Columbia, SC 29204
(803)254-6833
Ultimate Parent: Citgo Petroleum. **SIC:** 5541—Gasoline Service Stations.

★ 79004 ★   **Citgo Quick Mart**
3402 Main St.
Columbia, SC 29203
(803)256-1088
Ultimate Parent: Citgo Petroleum. **SIC:** 5411—Grocery Stores.

★ 79005 ★   **Citgo Quick Mart**
2731 Colonial Dr.
Columbia, SC 29203
(803)256-1045
Ultimate Parent: Citgo Petroleum. **SIC:** 5411—Grocery Stores.

★ 79006 ★   **Citgo Quick Mart**
3800 Devine St.
Columbia, SC 29205
(803)256-1042
Ultimate Parent: Citgo Petroleum. **SIC:** 5411—Grocery Stores.

★ 79007 ★   **Columbia Mall**
7201 Two Notch Rd.
Columbia, SC 29223
(803)788-4678
Ultimate Parent: R. H. Macy. **SIC:** 6512—Nonresidential Building Operators.

★ 79008 ★   **Delta Air Lines**
1201 Main St.
Columbia, SC 29201
(803)771-6620
Ultimate Parent: Delta Air Lines, Inc. **SIC:** 4512—Air Transportation—Scheduled; 4724—Travel Agencies.

★ 79009 ★   **Delta Air Lines, Inc.**
1201 Main St.
Columbia, SC 29201
(803)779-4300
Ultimate Parent: Delta Air Lines, Inc. **SIC:** 4789—Transportation Services Nec; 4729—Passenger Transportation Arrangement Nec.

★ 79010 ★   **Express**
220 Cola Mall
Columbia, SC 29206
(803)788-1817
Ultimate Parent: Limited. **SIC:** 5651—Family Clothing Stores.

★ 79011 ★   **Exxon**
8200 Two Notch Rd.
Columbia, SC 29223
(803)788-8255
Ultimate Parent: Exxon. **SIC:** 5541—Gasoline Service Stations.

★ 79012 ★   **First Union National Bank of South Carolina**
4233 Devine St.
Columbia, SC 29205-2007
Location Type: Branch office. **Ultimate Parent:** First Union Corp. **SIC:** 6021—National Commercial Banks.

★ 79013 ★   **First Union National Bank of South Carolina**
832 Bush River Rd.
Columbia, SC 29210-7515
Location Type: Branch office. **Ultimate Parent:** First Union Corp. **SIC:** 6021—National Commercial Banks.

★ 79014 ★   **First Union National Bank of South Carolina**
2200 Beltline Blvd.
Columbia, SC 29204-3907
Location Type: Branch office. **Ultimate Parent:** First Union Corp. **SIC:** 6021—National Commercial Banks.

★ 79015 ★   **First Union National Bank of South Carolina**
Columbia Ctr., 331 Harbison Blvd.
Columbia, SC 29210-4427
Location Type: Branch office. **Ultimate Parent:** First Union Corp. **SIC:** 6021—National Commercial Banks.

★ 79016 ★   **First Union National Bank of South Carolina**
9007 2 Notch Rd.
Columbia, SC 29223-7621
Location Type: Branch office. **Ultimate Parent:** First Union Corp. **SIC:** 6021—National Commercial Banks.

★ 79017 ★   **First Union National Bank of South Carolina**
1441 Main St.
Columbia, SC 29201-2805
(803)251-4400
Location Type: Branch office. **Ultimate Parent:** First Union Corp. **SIC:** 6021—National Commercial Banks.

★ 79018 ★   **Fleet Finance Inc.**
7101 Parklane Rd.
Columbia, SC 29223
(803)788-4037
Ultimate Parent: Fleet Financial Group. **SIC:** 6141—Personal Credit Institutions.

★ 79019 ★   **Fleet Mortgage Group Inc.**
1333 Main St., Ste. 700
Columbia, SC 29201-3201
(803)253-7900
Company Type: Subsidiary. **Officer:** Andrew D. Woodward Jr., Chairman of the Board & President. **Ultimate Parent:** Fleet Financial Group. **SIC:** 6162—Mortgage Bankers & Correspondents; 6719—Holding Companies Nec. **Employee Count:** 4340. **Sales:** 510 M.

★ 79020 ★   **Food Lion**
543 Saint Andrews Rd.
Columbia, SC 29210
(803)731-9225
Ultimate Parent: Food Lion. **SIC:** 5411—Grocery Stores.

★ 79021 ★   **Food Lion**
9578 Two Notch Rd.
Columbia, SC 29223
(803)788-9641
Ultimate Parent: Food Lion. **SIC:** 5411—Grocery Stores.

★ 79022 ★   **Food Lion**
1000 Harden St.
Columbia, SC 29205
(803)799-0635
Ultimate Parent: Food Lion. **SIC:** 5411—Grocery Stores.

★ 79023 ★   **Food Lion**
RR 2
Columbia, SC 29212
(803)772-0256
Ultimate Parent: Food Lion. **SIC:** 5411—Grocery Stores.

★ 79024 ★   **Food Lion**
5118 Fairfield Rd.
Columbia, SC 29203
(803)754-5141
Ultimate Parent: Food Lion. **SIC:** 5411—Grocery Stores.

★ 79025 ★   **Food Lion**
5910 Garners Ferry Rd.
Columbia, SC 29209
(803)783-3990
Ultimate Parent: Food Lion. **SIC:** 5411—Grocery Stores.

★ 79026 ★   **Food Lion**
2312 Decker Blvd.
Columbia, SC 29206
(803)788-8211
Ultimate Parent: Food Lion. **SIC:** 5411—Grocery Stores.

★ 79027 ★   **GE Consumer Service**
7499 Parklane Rd.
Columbia, SC 29223
(803)699-5125
Officer: Bob Tennell, Manager. **Ultimate Parent:** General Electric. **SIC:** 3699—Electrical Equipment & Supplies Nec.

★ 79028 ★   **General American Life Insur**
7715 Claudia Dr.
Columbia, SC 29223
(803)736-3406
Ultimate Parent: General American Life. **SIC:** 6411—Insurance Agents, Brokers & Service.

★ 79029 ★   **Hewlett-Packard Co.**
1 Harbison Way
Columbia, SC 29212
(803)732-0400
Ultimate Parent: Hewlett-Packard. **SIC:** 5049—Professional Equipment Nec; 5065—Electronic Parts & Equipment Nec.

★ 79030 ★   **Hit or Miss**
300 Outlet Pointe Blvd.
Columbia, SC 29210
(803)772-9878
Ultimate Parent: TJX. **SIC:** 5621—Women's Clothing Stores.

★ 79031 ★   **Jiffy Lube**
212099 PO Box
Columbia, SC 29221
Ultimate Parent: Pennzoil. **SIC:** 7538—General Automotive Repair Shops; 7539—Automotive Repair Shops Nec.

★ 79032 ★   **Jiffy Lube**
201 Executive Ctr. Dr.
Columbia, SC 29210
(803)772-2750
Ultimate Parent: Pennzoil. **SIC:** 7539—Automotive Repair Shops Nec.

★ 79033 ★   **Jiffy Lube**
7300 Parklane Rd.
Columbia, SC 29223
(803)736-3635
Ultimate Parent: Pennzoil. **SIC:** 7539—Automotive Repair Shops Nec.

★ 79034 ★   **Jiffy Lube**
2901 Broad River Rd.
Columbia, SC 29210
(803)798-9000
Ultimate Parent: Pennzoil. **SIC:** 7538—General Automotive Repair Shops; 7539—Automotive Repair Shops Nec.

★ 79035 ★   **Jiffy Lube**
4414 Devine St.
Columbia, SC 29205
(803)782-9999
Ultimate Parent: Pennzoil. **SIC:** 7538—General Automotive Repair Shops; 7539—Automotive Repair Shops Nec.

★ 79036 ★   **Johnson Controls Inc.**
14 Woodcross Dr.
Columbia, SC 29212
(803)781-7642
Ultimate Parent: Johnson Controls Inc. **SIC:** 3599—Industrial Machinery Nec; 7623—Refrigeration Services Repair.

★ 79037 ★ **Kentucky Fried Chicken**
10125 Notch Rd.
Columbia, SC 29223
(803)788-2372
Ultimate Parent: Pepsico. **SIC:** 5812—
Eating Places.

★ 79038 ★ **Kentucky Fried Chicken**
7351 Garners Ferry Rd.
Columbia, SC 29209
(803)783-1219
Ultimate Parent: Pepsico. **SIC:** 5812—
Eating Places.

★ 79039 ★ **Kentucky Fried Chicken**
3507 Main St.
Columbia, SC 29203
(803)252-2257
Ultimate Parent: Pepsico. **SIC:** 5812—
Eating Places.

★ 79040 ★ **Kentucky Fried Chicken**
839 Bush River Rd.
Columbia, SC 29210
(803)772-4330
Ultimate Parent: Pepsico. **SIC:** 5812—
Eating Places.

★ 79041 ★ **Kroger Sav on Food&Drugs**
Eastmont Sq.
Columbia, SC 29209
(803)783-4189
Ultimate Parent: Kroger. **SIC:** 5992—
Florists.

★ 79042 ★ **Lane Bryant**
Columbia Mall
Columbia, SC 29223
(803)736-6729
Ultimate Parent: Limited. **SIC:** 5621—
Women's Clothing Stores.

★ 79043 ★ **Lane Bryant**
320 Cola Mall Shopping
Columbia, SC 29206
(803)736-6729
Ultimate Parent: Limited. **SIC:** 5651—
Family Clothing Stores.

★ 79044 ★ **Lens Crafters**
82 Dutch Sq.
Columbia, SC 29210
(803)772-3314
Ultimate Parent: United States Shoe. **SIC:**
3827—Optical Instruments & Lenses;
5995—Optical Goods Stores.

★ 79045 ★ **Lerner Shop**
1517 Main St.
Columbia, SC 29201
(803)765-0920
Ultimate Parent: Limited. **SIC:** 5621—
Women's Clothing Stores.

★ 79046 ★ **Liberty Mutual Insurance Co.**
220 Executive Ctr. Dr.
Columbia, SC 29210
(803)731-0830
Ultimate Parent: Liberty Mutual Group.
SIC: 6411—Insurance Agents, Brokers &
Service.

★ 79047 ★ **The Limited**
420 Cola Mall Shopping
Columbia, SC 29206
(803)788-9260
Ultimate Parent: Limited. **SIC:** 5651—
Family Clothing Stores.

★ 79048 ★ **The Limited**
7201 Notch Rd.
Columbia, SC 29223
(803)788-9260
Ultimate Parent: Limited. **SIC:** 5621—
Women's Clothing Stores.

★ 79049 ★ **The Limited Express**
Columbia Mall
Columbia, SC 29223
(803)788-1817
Ultimate Parent: Limited.

★ 79050 ★ **Lowe's**
23727 PO Box
Columbia, SC 29224
Ultimate Parent: Lowe's. **SIC:** 5039—
Construction Materials Nec.

★ 79051 ★ **Mary Kay Cosmetics**
104 Tennyson St.
Columbia, SC 29223
(803)796-7290
Ultimate Parent: Mary Kay Cosmetics. **SIC:**
5999—Miscellaneous Retail Stores Nec.

★ 79052 ★ **Mary Kay Cosmetics**
1727 Stillwater Dr.
Columbia, SC 29212
(803)781-7751
Ultimate Parent: Mary Kay Cosmetics. **SIC:**
7231—Beauty Shops.

★ 79053 ★ **Mary Kay Cosmetics**
7828 Folly Ct.
Columbia, SC 29209
(803)783-3691
Ultimate Parent: Mary Kay Cosmetics. **SIC:**
5999—Miscellaneous Retail Stores Nec.

★ 79054 ★ **Mary Kay Cosmetics**
7245 St. Andrews Rd.
Columbia, SC 29212
(803)781-8937
Ultimate Parent: Mary Kay Cosmetics. **SIC:**
5999—Miscellaneous Retail Stores Nec.

★ 79055 ★ **Mini Mart**
5950 Percival Rd.
Columbia, SC 29206
(803)787-6331
Ultimate Parent: Kroger. **SIC:** 5411—
Grocery Stores.

★ 79056 ★ **New York Life Columbia General Office**
Southeastern Agencies
1441 Main St., Rm. 700
Columbia, SC 29201
(803)799-5396 **Fax:** (803)256-4501
Officer: Wayne G. Damron, General
Manager. **Ultimate Parent:** New York Life.

★ 79057 ★ **New York Life Columbia General Office**
Southeastern Agencies
PO Box 12517
Columbia, SC 29211
(803)799-5396 **Fax:** (803)256-4501
Officer: Wayne G. Damron, General
Manager. **Ultimate Parent:** New York Life.

★ 79058 ★ **Otis Elevator Co.**
1713 Taylor St.
Columbia, SC 29201
(803)771-0140
Ultimate Parent: United Technologies. **SIC:**
1796—Installing Building Equipment Nec;
5084—Industrial Machinery & Equipment.

★ 79059 ★ **Palmetto Prods. Inc.**
1720 Pineview Dr.
Columbia, SC 29290
Ultimate Parent: Owens-Corning. **SIC:**
3229—Pressed & Blown Glass Nec.

★ 79060 ★ **Pepsi-Cola Co.**
6925 N. Main St.
Columbia, SC 29203
Officer: Michael Keels. **Ultimate Parent:**
Pepsico. **SIC:** 2086—Bottled & Canned Soft
Drinks.

★ 79061 ★ **Petite Sophisticate**
756 Cola Mall Shopping
Columbia, SC 29206
(803)788-2250
Ultimate Parent: United States Shoe. **SIC:**
5651—Family Clothing Stores.

★ 79062 ★ **Piggly Wiggly**
State Farmers Mkt
Columbia, SC 29201
(803)771-7400
Ultimate Parent: Bruno's. **SIC:** 5148—
Fresh Fruits & Vegetables.

★ 79063 ★ **Piggly Wiggly**
2001 Rosewood Dr.
Columbia, SC 29205
(803)799-1448
Ultimate Parent: Bruno's. **SIC:** 5411—
Grocery Stores.

★ 79064 ★ **Piggly Wiggly**
7325 Two Notch Rd.
Columbia, SC 29223
(803)788-2890
Ultimate Parent: Bruno's. **SIC:** 5411—
Grocery Stores.

★ 79065 ★ **Piggly Wiggly**
Trenholm Plz.
Columbia, SC 29204
(803)782-7179
Ultimate Parent: Bruno's. **SIC:** 5411—
Grocery Stores.

★ 79066 ★ **Piggly Wiggly**
9940 Two Notch Rd.
Columbia, SC 29223
(803)736-9174
Ultimate Parent: Bruno's. **SIC:** 5411—
Grocery Stores.

★ 79067 ★ **Piggly Wiggly**
7412 Garners Ferry Rd.
Columbia, SC 29209
(803)776-4830
Ultimate Parent: Bruno's. **SIC:** 5411—
Grocery Stores.

★ 79068 ★ **Piggly Wiggly**
69 Running Fox Rd.
Columbia, SC 29223
(803)779-2017
Ultimate Parent: Bruno's. **SIC:** 5411—
Grocery Stores.

★ 79069 ★ **Piggly Wiggly**
Cedar Ter.
Columbia, SC 29210
(803)776-4830
Ultimate Parent: Bruno's. **SIC:** 5411—
Grocery Stores.

★ 79070 ★ **Pizza Hut**
108 Winmet Dr.
Columbia, SC 29203
(803)754-3464
Ultimate Parent: Pepsico. **SIC:** 7532—Top
& Body Repair & Paint Shops.

★ 79071 ★ **Pizza Hut**
621 Saint Andrews Rd.
Columbia, SC 29210
(803)798-2036
Ultimate Parent: Pepsico. **SIC:** 5812—
Eating Places.

★ 79072 ★ **Pizza Hut**
2811 Two Notch Rd.
Columbia, SC 29204
(803)254-2893
Ultimate Parent: Pepsico. **SIC:** 5812—
Eating Places.

★ 79073 ★ **Pizza Hut**
7385 Garners Ferry Rd.
Columbia, SC 29209
(803)776-8011
Ultimate Parent: Pepsico. **SIC:** 5812—
Eating Places.

★ 79074 ★ **Pizza Hut**
614 Ott Rd.
Columbia, SC 29205
(803)256-1662
Ultimate Parent: Pepsico. **SIC:** 5812—
Eating Places.

★ 79075 ★ **Pizza Hut**
3108 Broad River Rd.
Columbia, SC 29210
(803)798-8144
Ultimate Parent: Pepsico. **SIC:** 5812—
Eating Places.

★ 79076 ★ **Pizza Hut**
5421 1st Dr.
Columbia, SC 29206
(803)787-4008
Ultimate Parent: Pepsico. **SIC:** 5812—
Eating Places.

★ 79077 ★ **Provident Financial Corp.**
101 Greystone
Columbia, SC 29226-0001
(803)765-3261
Company Type: Subsidiary. **Location
Type:** Headquarters. **Officer:** Ralph Taylor.
Ultimate Parent: American General Corp.
SIC: 6021—National Commercial Banks;
6141—Personal Credit Institutions; 6162—
Mortgage Bankers & Correspondents;
6712—Bank Holding Companies; 6719—
Holding Companies Nec.

★ 79078 ★ **Provident Financial Corp.**
1401 Main St.
Columbia, SC 29226
(803)765-3261
Officer: Ralph Taylor, Director, Operations.

Ultimate Parent: American General Corp.
SIC: 6141—Personal Credit Institutions.

★ 79079 ★ **Radio Shack**
4840 Forest Dr.
Columbia, SC 29206
(803)782-2163
Company Type: Division. **Ultimate Parent:**
Tandy Corp. **SIC:** 5731—Radio, Television
& Electronics Stores.

★ 79080 ★ **Radio Shack**
7509 Garners Ferry Rd.
Columbia, SC 29209
(803)776-0228
Company Type: Division. **Ultimate Parent:**
Tandy Corp. **SIC:** 5731—Radio, Television
& Electronics Stores.

★ 79081 ★ **Radio Shack**
48 Dutch Sq.
Columbia, SC 29210
(803)772-8157
Company Type: Division. **Ultimate Parent:**
Tandy Corp. **SIC:** 5731—Radio, Television
& Electronics Stores.

★ 79082 ★ **Radio Shack**
6319 Main St.
Columbia, SC 29203
(803)754-8348
Company Type: Division. **Ultimate Parent:**
Tandy Corp. **SIC:** 5065—Electronic Parts &
Equipment Nec.

★ 79083 ★ **Radio Shack**
7 Oaks Shopping Ctr.
Columbia, SC 29210
(803)798-3633
Company Type: Division. **Ultimate Parent:**
Tandy Corp. **SIC:** 5065—Electronic Parts &
Equipment Nec.

★ 79084 ★ **Radio Shack**
Columbia
Columbia, SC 29204
(803)788-7972
Company Type: Division. **Ultimate Parent:**
Tandy Corp. **SIC:** 5065—Electronic Parts &
Equipment Nec.

★ 79085 ★ **Rite Aid Discount Pharmacie**
Landmark Sq.
Columbia, SC 29209
(803)776-9905
Ultimate Parent: Rite Aid. **SIC:** 5912—Drug
Stores & Proprietary Stores.

★ 79086 ★ **Rite Aid Discount Pharmacie**
1441 Main St.
Columbia, SC 29201
(803)779-9404
Ultimate Parent: Rite Aid. **SIC:** 5912—Drug
Stores & Proprietary Stores.

★ 79087 ★ **Rite Aid Discount Pharmacie**
Dentsville Sq.
Columbia, SC 29204
(803)788-9705
Ultimate Parent: Rite Aid. **SIC:** 5912—Drug
Stores & Proprietary Stores.

★ 79088 ★ **Rite Aid Discount Pharmacy**
2806 Rosewood Dr.
Columbia, SC 29205
(803)771-9183
Ultimate Parent: Rite Aid. **SIC:** 5912—Drug
Stores & Proprietary Stores.

★ 79089 ★ **Rite Aid Discount Pharmacy**
10130 Two Notch Rd.
Columbia, SC 29223
(803)788-1659
Ultimate Parent: Rite Aid. **SIC:** 5912—Drug
Stores & Proprietary Stores.

★ 79090 ★ **Rite Aid Discount Phrmcy**
Richardson Plz.
Columbia, SC 29210
(803)798-9821
Ultimate Parent: Rite Aid. **SIC:** 5912—Drug
Stores & Proprietary Stores.

★ 79091 ★ **Rite Aid Discount Phrmcy**
N Pt Shopping Ctr.
Columbia, SC 29206
(803)788-9724
Ultimate Parent: Rite Aid. **SIC:** 5912—Drug Stores & Proprietary Stores.

★ 79092 ★ **Rite Aid Drug Store**
Trenholm Plz.
Columbia, SC 29206
(803)787-8192
Ultimate Parent: Rite Aid.

★ 79093 ★ **Ryder Truck Rental**
2246 Two Notch Rd.
Columbia, SC 29204
(803)256-8217
Ultimate Parent: Ryder System. **SIC:** 4214—Local Trucking With Storage; 7513—Truck Rental & Leasing Without Drivers.

★ 79094 ★ **Ryder Truck Rental**
945 Idlewild Blvd.
Columbia, SC 29201
(803)779-7504
Ultimate Parent: Ryder System. **SIC:** 7513—Truck Rental & Leasing Without Drivers.

★ 79095 ★ **Sentry Drugs**
23685 PO Box
Columbia, SC 29224
(803)786-1555
Ultimate Parent: Fleetwood Enterprises, Inc. **SIC:** 5912—Drug Stores & Proprietary Stores.

★ 79096 ★ **Standard Federal Savings Bank**
4840 Forest Dr. 27
Columbia, SC 29206
(803)765-4510
Ultimate Parent: Standard Federal Bank. **SIC:** 6099—Functions Related to Deposit Banking.

★ 79097 ★ **Standard Federal Savings Bank**
Rural Route 2
Columbia, SC 29212
(803)765-4500
Ultimate Parent: Standard Federal Bank. **SIC:** 6035—Federal Savings Institutions.

★ 79098 ★ **Star Market**
3314 Main St.
Columbia, SC 29203
(803)799-7024
Ultimate Parent: American Stores. **SIC:** 5411—Grocery Stores.

★ 79099 ★ **Sun Microsystems Inc.**
1517 Gregg St.
Columbia, SC 29201
(803)252-3872
Ultimate Parent: Sun Microsystems Inc. **SIC:** 7378—Computer Maintenance & Repair.

★ 79100 ★ **Sunbird Boat Co.**
2348 Shop Rd.
Columbia, SC 29201
(803)799-1125
Officer: David Fagerquist, President. **Ultimate Parent:** Outboard Marine. **SIC:** 3732—Boat Building & Repairing.

★ 79101 ★ **Sunbird Boat Co. Inc.**
2348 Shop Rd.
Columbia, SC 29201
Ultimate Parent: Outboard Marine. **SIC:** 3732—Boat Building & Repairing.

★ 79102 ★ **Sunbird Boat Co. Inc.**
1501 Shop Rd.
Columbia, SC 29201
Ultimate Parent: Outboard Marine. **SIC:** 3732—Boat Building & Repairing.

★ 79103 ★ **Taco Bell**
4716 Devine St.
Columbia, SC 29209
(803)782-9915
Ultimate Parent: Pepsico. **SIC:** 5812—Eating Places.

★ 79104 ★ **Taco Bell**
9802 Two Notch Rd.
Columbia, SC 29223
(803)788-8979
Ultimate Parent: Pepsico. **SIC:** 5812—Eating Places.

★ 79105 ★ **Taco Bell**
1927 Broad River Rd.
Columbia, SC 29210
(803)798-8397
Ultimate Parent: Pepsico. **SIC:** 5812—Eating Places.

★ 79106 ★ **Taco Bell**
2632 Decker Blvd.
Columbia, SC 29206
(803)736-0876
Ultimate Parent: Pepsico. **SIC:** 5812—Eating Places.

★ 79107 ★ **This End Up Furniture Co.**
738 Cola Mall Shopping
Columbia, SC 29206
(803)736-0124
Ultimate Parent: Melville. **SIC:** 5712—Furniture Stores.

★ 79108 ★ **This End Up Furniture Co.**
Columbia
Columbia, SC 29204
(803)736-0124
Ultimate Parent: Melville. **SIC:** 2511—Wood Household Furniture.

★ 79109 ★ **Title Insurance Co. Minnesot**
Barringer Bldg.
Columbia, SC 29201
(803)799-9495
Ultimate Parent: Old Republic International. **SIC:** 6411—Insurance Agents, Brokers & Service.

★ 79110 ★ **Trailways Bus Terminal**
2015 Gervais St.
Columbia, SC 29204
(803)799-9200
Ultimate Parent: Greyhound Lines Inc. **SIC:** 4173—Bus Terminal & Service Facilities.

★ 79111 ★ **Transamerica Occidental Life Insurance**
2003 Lincoln St.
Columbia, SC 29201
(803)799-4420
Ultimate Parent: Transamerica Occidental Life Insurance. **SIC:** 6411—Insurance Agents, Brokers & Service.

★ 79112 ★ **Unijax Inc.**
845 Rosewood Dr.
Columbia, SC 29201
(803)799-1190
Officer: Pete Wood, Manager. **Ultimate Parent:** Alco Standard Corp. **SIC:** 3842—Surgical Appliances & Supplies.

★ 79113 ★ **Unijax Inc.**
845 Rosewood Dr.
Columbia, SC 29201
(803)799-1190
Officer: Pete Wood, Manager. **Ultimate Parent:** Alco Standard Corp. **SIC:** 3842—Surgical Appliances & Supplies.

★ 79114 ★ **Union Oil Co. of Cal**
3608 Carriage House Rd.
Columbia, SC 29206
(803)787-4260
Ultimate Parent: Unocal Corp. **SIC:** 5172—Petroleum Products Nec.

★ 79115 ★ **United Brake Sys. Inc.**
1280 Bluff Rd.
Columbia, SC 29201
Ultimate Parent: Echlin. **SIC:** 3714—Motor Vehicle Parts & Accessories.

★ 79116 ★ **United Brake Systems Inc.**
1238 Bluff Rd.
Columbia, SC 29201
(803)765-1446
Ultimate Parent: Echlin. **SIC:** 7539—Automotive Repair Shops Nec.

★ 79117 ★ **US Fidelity**
220 Stoneridge Dr.
Columbia, SC 29210
(803)799-9989
Ultimate Parent: USF&G Corp. **SIC:** 6411—Insurance Agents, Brokers & Service.

★ 79118 ★ **Variable Annuity Life Insurance C**
2727 Allen Pky.
Columbia, SC 29203
(803)526-5251
Ultimate Parent: American General Corp. **SIC:** 6311—Life Insurance.

★ 79119 ★ **Variable Annuity Life Insurance Co.**
2727 Allen Pky.
Columbia, SC 29203
(803)526-5251
Ultimate Parent: American General Corp. **SIC:** 6311—Life Insurance.

★ 79120 ★ **Victoria's Secret**
616 Cola Mall Shopping
Columbia, SC 29206
(803)736-0907
Ultimate Parent: Limited. **SIC:** 5651—Family Clothing Stores.

★ 79121 ★ **Wal Mart Inc.**
7501 Garners Fwy.
Columbia, SC 29209
(803)783-1277
Ultimate Parent: Wal-Mart Stores, Inc. **SIC:** 5311—Department Stores.

★ 79122 ★ **Waldenbooks**
Columbia
Columbia, SC 29204
(803)788-6963
Ultimate Parent: K-Mart. **SIC:** 5942—Book Stores.

★ 79123 ★ **Westinghouse**
Nuclear Fuel Div.
5801 Bluff Rd.
Columbia, SC 29205
Ultimate Parent: Westinghouse Electric Corp. **SIC:** 3829—Measuring & Controlling Devices Nec.

★ 79124 ★ **Westinghouse Commercial**
Nuclear Fuel
PO Drawer R
Columbia, SC 29250
Ultimate Parent: Westinghouse Electric Corp. **SIC:** 2819—Industrial Inorganic Chemicals Nec.

★ 79125 ★ **Westinghouse Commercial**
Nuclear Fuel
PO Box Drawer R
Columbia, SC 29250
Ultimate Parent: Westinghouse Electric Corp. **SIC:** 2819—Industrial Inorganic Chemicals Nec.

★ 79126 ★ **Westinghouse Electric**
5801 Bluff Rd.
Columbia, SC 29250
(803)776-2610
Officer: Ron Koga, Manager. **Ultimate Parent:** Westinghouse Electric Corp. **SIC:** 2819—Industrial Inorganic Chemicals Nec; 3559—Special Industry Machinery Nec; 3823—Process Control Instruments.

★ 79127 ★ **Whirlpool Corp.**
PO Box 11989 10700 Farrow Rd.
Columbia, SC 29211
Ultimate Parent: Whirlpool Corp. **SIC:** 3089—Plastics Products Nec.

★ 79128 ★ **Xerox Corp.**
1301 Gervais St., Ste. 800
Columbia, SC 29201
(803)256-6213
Officer: Dave Dunlap, Manager. **Ultimate Parent:** Xerox Corp. **SIC:** 3663—Radio & T.V. Communications Equipment.

★ 79129 ★ **Kentucky Fried Chicken**
3100 Notch St.
Columbia Sc, SC 29204
(803)252-1519
Ultimate Parent: Pepsico. **SIC:** 5812—Eating Places.

Conway

★ 79130 ★ **Allied Signal**
440 Allied Dr.
Conway, SC 29526
(803)349-6800
Ultimate Parent: Allied-Signal Inc. **SIC:** 3462—Iron & Steel Forgings.

★ 79131 ★ **Anchor Bank**
1500 3rd Ave.
Conway, SC 29576-5014
(803)248-6293
Location Type: Branch office. **Officer:** James F. Lewis, Vice President. **Ultimate Parent:** Anchor Bancorp. **SIC:** 6022—State Commercial Banks.

★ 79132 ★ **Burlington Handbag Factory Str.**
1408 Hwy. 501 Business
Conway, SC 29526-2700
(803)236-5505
Ultimate Parent: Burlington Industries, Equity. **SIC:** 5311—Department Stores.

★ 79133 ★ **Pepsi-Cola Bottling Co.**
2380 Hwy. 501 W
Conway, SC 29526
(803)448-5553
Ultimate Parent: Pepsico. **SIC:** 2086—Bottled & Canned Soft Drinks.

★ 79134 ★ **Piggly Wiggly**
1511 4th Ave.
Conway, SC 29526
(803)248-9112
Ultimate Parent: Bruno's. **SIC:** 5411—Grocery Stores.

★ 79135 ★ **Pizza Hut**
700 Hwy. 501
Conway, SC 29526
(803)248-7366
Ultimate Parent: Pepsico. **SIC:** 5812—Eating Places.

★ 79136 ★ **Pizza Hut**
700 Church St.
Conway, SC 29526
(803)248-5235
Ultimate Parent: Pepsico. **SIC:** 5812—Eating Places.

★ 79137 ★ **Radio Shack**
Coastal Mall
Conway, SC 29526
(803)248-5942
Company Type: Division. **Ultimate Parent:** Tandy Corp. **SIC:** 5731—Radio, Television & Electronics Stores.

★ 79138 ★ **Vitramon**
1520 4th Ave.
Conway, SC 29526
(803)248-6699
Ultimate Parent: Thomas & Betts.

★ 79139 ★ **Wal Mart**
1 Bay Village Shopping Ctr.
Conway, SC 29526
(803)365-0303
Ultimate Parent: Wal-Mart Stores, Inc. **SIC:** 5311—Department Stores.

★ 79140 ★ **Wilsons**
16 Bay Village Shopping Ctr.
Conway, SC 29526
(803)365-1991
Ultimate Parent: Melville. **SIC:** 5411—Grocery Stores.

Cowpens

★ 79141 ★ **Rite Aid Discount Pharmacy**
Hwy. 110
Cowpens, SC 29330
(803)463-4986
Ultimate Parent: Rite Aid. **SIC:** 5912—Drug Stores & Proprietary Stores.

Darlington

★ 79142 ★ **APAC**
805 Mineral Springs Rd.
Darlington, SC 29540
(803)393-2837
Officer: Dave Kilpatrick, President. **Ultimate Parent:** Ashland Oil. **SIC:** 2951—Asphalt Paving Mixtures & Blocks.

★ 79143 ★ Bi-Lo No 63
400 Lamar Rd. A
Darlington, SC 29532
(803)393-7331
Ultimate Parent: Penn Traffic. SIC: 5411—
Grocery Stores.

★ 79144 ★ Carolina Power &
Light Co.
141 Cashua St.
Darlington, SC 29532
(803)393-3511
Ultimate Parent: Carolina Power & Light
Co. SIC: 4911—Electric Services.

★ 79145 ★ Carolina Power &
Light Co.
141 Cashua St.
Darlington, SC 29532
(803)393-3511
Ultimate Parent: Carolina Power & Light
Co. SIC: 4911—Electric Services.

★ 79146 ★ First Federal S & L
266 Cashua St.
Darlington, SC 29532-2804
(803)393-4051
Company Type: Headquarters. Officer: J.
Ronald Ward. Ultimate Parent: Bancorp
Hawaii. SIC: 6035—Federal Savings
Institutions; 6021—National Commercial
Banks; 6141—Personal Credit Institutions;
6162—Mortgage Bankers &
Correspondents.

★ 79147 ★ Food Lion
500 Pearl St. A
Darlington, SC 29532
(803)395-1356
Ultimate Parent: Food Lion. SIC: 5411—
Grocery Stores.

★ 79148 ★ James River Corp.
Dixie Products
126 Avenue A
Darlington, SC 29532
Company Type: Division. Ultimate Parent:
James River Corp. of Virginia. SIC: 2650—
Paperboard Containers & Boxes.

★ 79149 ★ James River Dixie
Products
126 Ave. A
Darlington, SC 29532
Company Type: Division. Ultimate Parent:
James River Corp. of Virginia. SIC: 2600—
Paper & Allied Products.

★ 79150 ★ James River Paper
Co. Inc. Dixie Products
126 a Ave.
Darlington, SC 29532
Ultimate Parent: James River Corp. of
Virginia. SIC: 2656—Sanitary Food
Containers.

★ 79151 ★ James River Paper
Products Inc.
126 Avenue A
Darlington, SC 29532
Ultimate Parent: James River Corp. of
Virginia. SIC: 2650—Paperboard Containers
& Boxes.

★ 79152 ★ James River Paper
Products Inc.
126 Ave. A
Darlington, SC 29532
Ultimate Parent: James River Corp. of
Virginia. SIC: 2600—Paper & Allied
Products.

★ 79153 ★ Kentucky Fried
Chicken
S Main
Darlington, SC 29532
(803)393-6231
Ultimate Parent: Pepsico. SIC: 5812—
Eating Places.

★ 79154 ★ Nucor Steel
Hwy. 52 PO Box 525
Darlington, SC 29532
Ultimate Parent: Nucor Corp. SIC: 3312—
Blast Furnaces & Steel Mills.

★ 79155 ★ Piggly Wiggly
503 Pearl St.
Darlington, SC 29532
(803)393-4310
Ultimate Parent: Bruno's. SIC: 5411—
Grocery Stores.

★ 79156 ★ Pizza Hut
1384 S. Main St.
Darlington, SC 29532
(803)393-5201
Ultimate Parent: Pepsico. SIC: 6531—Real
Estate Agents & Managers.

★ 79157 ★ Rite Aid Pharm
Prescription
Darlington Plz.
Darlington, SC 29532
(803)393-4626
Ultimate Parent: Rite Aid. SIC: 5912—Drug
Stores & Proprietary Stores.

Darlington Sc

★ 79158 ★ Nucor Corp.
Dovesville Hwy.
Darlington Sc, SC 29532
(803)393-5841
Ultimate Parent: Nucor Corp. SIC: 3312—
Blast Furnaces & Steel Mills.

Dillon

★ 79159 ★ Dana Corp.
State Rd. 17
Dillon, SC 29536
(803)774-5623
Ultimate Parent: Dana Corp. SIC: 3599—
Industrial Machinery Nec.

★ 79160 ★ Dana Corp. Wix Corp.
State Rd. 17 & Hwy. 9
Dillon, SC 29536
Ultimate Parent: Dana Corp.

★ 79161 ★ Kentucky Fried
Chicken
Hwy. 301 N
Dillon, SC 29536
(803)774-5402
Ultimate Parent: Pepsico. SIC: 5812—
Eating Places.

★ 79162 ★ Mini Mart
602 W. Main St.
Dillon, SC 29536
(803)774-6220
Ultimate Parent: Kroger. SIC: 5411—
Grocery Stores.

★ 79163 ★ Pizza Hut
2nd Ave.
Dillon, SC 29536
(803)774-8206
Ultimate Parent: Pepsico. SIC: 5812—
Eating Places.

★ 79164 ★ Pizza Hut
2 Ave.
Dillon, SC 29536
(803)774-7971
Ultimate Parent: Pepsico. SIC: 5812—
Eating Places.

★ 79165 ★ Radio Shack
211 W. Main St.
Dillon, SC 29536
(803)774-6903
Company Type: Division. Ultimate Parent:
Tandy Corp. SIC: 5065—Electronic Parts &
Equipment Nec.

★ 79166 ★ Wal Mart
Dillon Plz.
Dillon, SC 29536
(803)774-5101
Ultimate Parent: Wal-Mart Stores, Inc. SIC:
5311—Department Stores.

Donalds

★ 79167 ★ Commercial Bank
Main St.
Donalds, SC 29638
(803)379-2146
Ultimate Parent: First Virginia Banks Inc.
SIC: 6022—State Commercial Banks.

Duncan

★ 79168 ★ Allied-Signal Inc.
Autolite
120 Ridgeview Ctr. Dr.
Duncan, SC 29334
Ultimate Parent: Allied-Signal Inc. SIC:
3694—Engine Electrical Equipment.

★ 79169 ★ Allied-Signal Inc.
Filter & Sparkplug Group
120 Ridgeview Circle Dr.
Duncan, SC 29304
Ultimate Parent: Allied-Signal Inc. SIC:
3694—Engine Electrical Equipment.

★ 79170 ★ Allied-Signal Inc.
Filters & Spark Plug
120 Ridgeview Circle Dr.
Duncan, SC 29334
Ultimate Parent: Allied-Signal Inc. SIC:
3694—Engine Electrical Equipment.

★ 79171 ★ Cryovac North
America
PO Box 464
Duncan, SC 29334
(803)433-2000 Fax: (803)433-2689
Company Type: Subsidiary. Officer:
William B. Sturgis, President. Ultimate
Parent: W. R. Grace.

★ 79172 ★ Hayssen
Manufacturing Co.
225 Spartangreen Blvd.
Duncan, SC 29334
(803)439-1141
Officer: David Thompson, Manager.
Ultimate Parent: Bemis Co., Inc. SIC:
3559—Special Industry Machinery Nec.

★ 79173 ★ Owens-Corning
Fiberglass Corp.
196 Ridgeview Circle
Duncan, SC 29334
Ultimate Parent: Owens-Corning. SIC:
3559—Special Industry Machinery Nec.

★ 79174 ★ Rite Aid Corp.
Duncan Park Shopping Cent
Duncan, SC 29334
(803)583-2785
Ultimate Parent: Rite Aid. SIC: 5912—Drug
Stores & Proprietary Stores.

★ 79175 ★ W. R. Grace & Co.
Connecticut Cryovac Div.
100 Rogers Bridge Rd.
Duncan, SC 29334
Company Type: Division. Ultimate Parent:
W. R. Grace. SIC: 3500—Industrial
Machinery & Equipment; 3700—
Transportation Equipment.

Easley

★ 79176 ★ Anchor Swan Inc.
Hwy. 93 & 109 Gillespie Rd. PO Box 2489
Easley, SC 29640
Ultimate Parent: Mark IV Industries. SIC:
3714—Motor Vehicle Parts & Accessories.

★ 79177 ★ Anchor Swan Inc.
Hwy. 93
PO Box2489
Easley, SC 29641
Ultimate Parent: Harvard Industries. SIC:
3714—Motor Vehicle Parts & Accessories;
3451—Screw Machine Products.

★ 79178 ★ Branch Banking &
Trust Co.
6016 Calhoun Memorial Pky.
Easley, SC 29640
(803)255-7743
Company Type: Subsidiary. Location
Type: Branch office. Ultimate Parent:
Southern National Corp. SIC: 6021—
National Commercial Banks.

★ 79179 ★ First Union National
Bank of South Carolina
Hwy. 123 Bypass & 5820 Calhoun Memorial
Hwy.
Easley, SC 29641
(803)859-3838
Location Type: Branch office. Ultimate
Parent: First Union Corp. SIC: 6021—
National Commercial Banks.

★ 79180 ★ Food Lion
1311 Bypass 123
Easley, SC 29640
(803)855-0021
Ultimate Parent: Food Lion. SIC: 5411—
Grocery Stores.

★ 79181 ★ Harvard Industries
Inc.
Anchor Swan
Hwy. 93
Easley, SC 29644
Company Type: Division. Ultimate Parent:
Harvard Industries. SIC: 3451—Screw
Machine Products.

Eastover

★ 79182 ★ Union Camp Corp.
Rte. 601
Eastover, SC 29044
Ultimate Parent: Union Camp Corp. SIC:
2621—Paper Mills.

★ 79183 ★ Union Camp Corp.
Hwy. 601
Eastover, SC 29044
(803)353-7700
Officer: Mark T. E. Watkins, Manager.
Ultimate Parent: Union Camp Corp. SIC:
2621—Paper Mills.

Edgefield

★ 79184 ★ Champion
International Corp.
Buncombe St.
Edgefield, SC 29824
(803)637-3204
Ultimate Parent: Champion International.
SIC: 2679—Converted Paper Products Nec.

★ 79185 ★ Stevcoknit Fabrics
Co.
450 Rabbit Trl.
Edgefield, SC 29824
(803)637-2005
Officer: John Nicholson, Manager. Ultimate
Parent: Delta Woodside Industries. SIC:
2281—Yarn Spinning Mills; 2399—
Fabricated Textile Products Nec.

★ 79186 ★ Tranter Inc.
Mitchell Rd.
Edgefield, SC 29824
(803)637-3166
Officer: William Brossmann, Manager.
Ultimate Parent: Dover Corp. SIC: 3433—
Heating Equipment Except Electric.

Edgemoor

★ 79187 ★ Food Lion
Brave Village Shopping Ctr.
Edgemoor, SC 29712
(803)650-1699
Ultimate Parent: Food Lion. SIC: 5411—
Grocery Stores.

Edisto Island

★ 79188 ★ Exxon Co. USA
2001 Myrtle St.
Edisto Island, SC 29438
Ultimate Parent: Exxon. SIC: 5172—
Petroleum Products Nec.

Elgin

★ 79189 ★ Hardwicke Chemical
Co.
2114 Larry Jeffers Rd.
Elgin, SC 29045
Ultimate Parent: Ethyl. SIC: 2869—
Industrial Organic Chemicals Nec.

Elloree

★ 79190 ★ Food Lion
Elloree, SC 29047
(803)897-2146
Ultimate Parent: Food Lion. SIC: 5411—
Grocery Stores.

Eutawville

★ 79191 ★ Chesapeake Wood
Treating
Hwy. 453
Eutawville, SC 29048
Ultimate Parent: Chesapeake. SIC: 2491—
Wood Preserving.

Florence

★ 79192 ★   Ace Hardware
1520 Meadows Farm Rd.
Florence, SC 29505
(803)665-1591
Ultimate Parent: Ace Hardware. **SIC:** 5251—Hardware Stores.

★ 79193 ★   Branch Banking & Trust Co.
605 S. Irby St.
Florence, SC 29501
(803)664-2351
Company Type: Subsidiary. **Location Type:** Branch office. **Officer:** Randy McDonald, Manager. **Ultimate Parent:** Southern National Corp. **SIC:** 6021—National Commercial Banks.

★ 79194 ★   Branch Banking & Trust Co.
1831 W. Evans St.
Florence, SC 29501-3333
(803)664-1010
Company Type: Subsidiary. **Location Type:** Branch office. **Officer:** Ashby Lowrimore, Manager. **Ultimate Parent:** Southern National Corp. **SIC:** 6021—National Commercial Banks.

★ 79195 ★   Caloric Corp.
1500 Range Way
Florence, SC 29501
Ultimate Parent: Raytheon Co. **SIC:** 3631—Household Cooking Equipment.

★ 79196 ★   Casual Corner
Magnolia Mall
Florence, SC 29506
(803)669-1275
Ultimate Parent: United States Shoe. **SIC:** 5621—Women's Clothing Stores.

★ 79197 ★   Circus World Toys
Magnolia
Florence, SC 29501
(803)669-2200
Ultimate Parent: Melville. **SIC:** 5945—Hobby, Toy & Game Shops.

★ 79198 ★   Exxon Co.
1035 Peninsula Dr.
Florence, SC 29501
(803)665-2376
Ultimate Parent: Exxon. **SIC:** 5172—Petroleum Products Nec.

★ 79199 ★   Fairfield Inn by Marriott
140 Dunbarton Dr.
Florence, SC 29501
(803)669-1666
Ultimate Parent: Marriott International. **SIC:** 7011—Hotels & Motels.

★ 79200 ★   First Union National Bank of South Carolina
1940 W. Hoffmeyer Rd.
Florence, SC 29501-4012
Location Type: Branch office. **Ultimate Parent:** First Union Corp. **SIC:** 6021—National Commercial Banks.

★ 79201 ★   First Union National Bank of South Carolina
291 W. Cheves St.
Florence, SC 29501-4403
(803)664-2900
Location Type: Branch office. **Ultimate Parent:** First Union Corp. **SIC:** 6021—National Commercial Banks.

★ 79202 ★   First Union National Bank of South Carolina
151 S. Irby St.
Florence, SC 29501
Location Type: Branch office. **Ultimate Parent:** First Union Corp. **SIC:** 6021—National Commercial Banks.

★ 79203 ★   Food Lion
2600 S. Irby St.
Florence, SC 29505
(803)678-9555
Ultimate Parent: Food Lion. **SIC:** 5411—Grocery Stores.

★ 79204 ★   Food Lion
2011 Hoffmeyer Rd.
Florence, SC 29501
(803)669-2086
Ultimate Parent: Food Lion. **SIC:** 5411—Grocery Stores.

★ 79205 ★   Food Lion
350 N. Cashua Dr.
Florence, SC 29501
(803)661-0964
Ultimate Parent: Food Lion. **SIC:** 5411—Grocery Stores.

★ 79206 ★   Greyhound Bus Lines
611 S. Irby St.
Florence, SC 29501
(803)662-8407
Ultimate Parent: Greyhound Lines Inc. **SIC:** 4111—Local & Suburban Transit.

★ 79207 ★   Hertz Rent-A-Car Licensee
600 N. Coit St.
Florence, SC 29501
Ultimate Parent: Hertz. **SIC:** 7514—Passenger Car Rental.

★ 79208 ★   IBM Corp.
Oaks Trail Park
Florence, SC 29506
(803)671-4700
Ultimate Parent: IBM.

★ 79209 ★   Kentucky Fried Chicken
2000 W. Evans St.
Florence, SC 29501
(803)662-8222
Ultimate Parent: Pepsico. **SIC:** 5812—Eating Places.

★ 79210 ★   Kentucky Fried Chicken
Darlington Hwy.
Florence, SC 29501
(803)665-7553
Ultimate Parent: Pepsico. **SIC:** 5812—Eating Places.

★ 79211 ★   Kentucky Fried Chicken
516 E. Palmetto St.
Florence, SC 29506
(803)662-6161
Ultimate Parent: Pepsico. **SIC:** 5812—Eating Places.

★ 79212 ★   La-Z-Boy East
901 N. Douglas
Florence, SC 29501
(803)669-2431 **Fax:** (803)664-0988
Officer: Ernest F. Mather, Vice President. **Ultimate Parent:** La-Z-Boy Chair.

★ 79213 ★   La-Z-Boy East
901 North Douglas St.
Florence, SC 29501
Ultimate Parent: La-Z-Boy Chair. **SIC:** 2512—Upholstered Household Furniture.

★ 79214 ★   La-Z-Boy East
901 N. Douglas St.
Florence, SC 29501
Ultimate Parent: La-Z-Boy Chair. **SIC:** 2512—Upholstered Household Furniture.

★ 79215 ★   Lens Crafters
2701 David H Mcleod Blvd.
Florence, SC 29501
(803)664-2000
Ultimate Parent: United States Shoe. **SIC:** 5999—Miscellaneous Retail Stores Nec.

★ 79216 ★   Lerner Shop
Magnolia
Florence, SC 29501
(803)667-4575
Ultimate Parent: Limited. **SIC:** 5621—Women's Clothing Stores.

★ 79217 ★   Mary Kay Costmetics
502 Holly Cir.
Florence, SC 29501
(803)665-4009
Ultimate Parent: Mary Kay Cosmetics. **SIC:** 5999—Miscellaneous Retail Stores Nec.

★ 79218 ★   Piggly Wiggly
1110 E. Palmetto St.
Florence, SC 29506
(803)669-5705
Ultimate Parent: Bruno's. **SIC:** 5411—Grocery Stores.

★ 79219 ★   Pizza Hut
2015 W. Evans St.
Florence, SC 29501
(803)665-7812
Ultimate Parent: Pepsico. **SIC:** 5812—Eating Places.

★ 79220 ★   Pizza Hut
Magnolia
Florence, SC 29501
(803)669-8650
Ultimate Parent: Pepsico. **SIC:** 5812—Eating Places.

★ 79221 ★   Pizza Hut
961 S. Irby St.
Florence, SC 29501
(803)665-8856
Ultimate Parent: Pepsico. **SIC:** 5812—Eating Places.

★ 79222 ★   Radio Shack
1520 S. Irby St.
Florence, SC 29505
(803)665-5628
Company Type: Division. **Ultimate Parent:** Tandy Corp. **SIC:** 5065—Electronic Parts & Equipment Nec.

★ 79223 ★   Ryder Truck Rental
2122 Jody Rd.
Florence, SC 29501
(803)669-1914
Ultimate Parent: Ryder System. **SIC:** 7359—Equipment Rental & Leasing Nec.

★ 79224 ★   Ryder Truck Rental
1301 2nd Loop
Florence, SC 29505
(803)665-8706
Ultimate Parent: Ryder System. **SIC:** 7359—Equipment Rental & Leasing Nec.

★ 79225 ★   Sara Lee Hosiery
1901 Irby St.
Florence, SC 29501
Ultimate Parent: Sara Lee Corp. **SIC:** 2251—Women's Hosiery Except Socks.

★ 79226 ★   Spartan Express Inc.
T V Rd.
Florence, SC 29501
(803)665-1441
Ultimate Parent: Roadway Services. **SIC:** 4213—Trucking Except Local.

★ 79227 ★   Stone Container Corp.
Old Georgetown Hwy.
Florence, SC 29502-4000
Ultimate Parent: Stone Container Corp. **SIC:** 2621—Paper Mills; 2631—Paperboard Mills.

★ 79228 ★   Stone Container Corp.
Containerboard & Paper Division
Old Georgetown Hwy.
Florence, SC 29501
Ultimate Parent: Stone Container Corp. **SIC:** 2621—Paper Mills; 2631—Paperboard Mills.

Fort Lawn

★ 79229 ★   Springs Industires Inc.
111 PO Box
Fort Lawn, SC 29714
(803)286-2952
Ultimate Parent: Springs Industries. **SIC:** 2221—Broadwoven Fabric Mills—Manmade.

★ 79230 ★   Springs Industries, Inc.
Hwy. 9
Fort Lawn, SC 29714
(803)286-2957
Officer: Bill Hood, Manager. **Ultimate Parent:** Springs Industries. **SIC:** 2211—Broadwoven Fabric Mills—Cotton; 2221—Broadwoven Fabric Mills—Manmade; 2391—Curtains & Draperies.

Fort Mill

★ 79231 ★   Ace Hardware & Building Sup
818 Tom Hall St.
Fort Mill, SC 29715
(803)547-7006
Ultimate Parent: Ace Hardware. **SIC:** 5251—Hardware Stores.

★ 79232 ★   Food Lion
Fort Mill Sq.
Fort Mill, SC 29715
(803)547-2945
Ultimate Parent: Food Lion. **SIC:** 5411—Grocery Stores.

★ 79233 ★   GE Medical Systems
3440 Lakemont Blvd.
Fort Mill, SC 29715
(803)548-5548
Officer: Chris Caver, Manager. **Ultimate Parent:** General Electric. **SIC:** 3844—X-Ray Apparatus & Tubes.

★ 79234 ★   Innovative Logistics Inc.
377 Carowinds Blvd.
Fort Mill, SC 29715-7854
(803)548-6493
Company Type: Subsidiary. **Officer:** Philip G. Deely, President. **Ultimate Parent:** Carolina Freight. **SIC:** 4731—Freight Transportation Arrangement; 8748—Business Consulting Services Nec. **Employee Count:** 25. **Sales:** 30 M.

★ 79235 ★   Kentucky Fried Chicken
Carowinds Blvd.
Fort Mill, SC 29715
(803)548-4943
Ultimate Parent: Pepsico. **SIC:** 5812—Eating Places.

★ 79236 ★   Sea Ray Boats Inc.
23 Abaco Ln.
Fort Mill, SC 29714
Ultimate Parent: Brunswick Corp. **SIC:** 3732—Boat Building & Repairing.

★ 79237 ★   Springs Industries
205 N. White St.
PO Box 70
Fort Mill, SC 29715
(803)547-1500
Company Type: Headquarters. **Officer:** Walter V Elisha. **Employee Count:** 20500. **Sales:** 2023 M. **Fortune 500:** Largest U.S. Industrial Corporations: Ranking 220.

★ 79238 ★   Springs Industries, Inc.
205 N. White St.
Fort Mill, SC 29715
(803)547-1500
Officer: Walter Y. Elisha, Chairman. **Ultimate Parent:** Springs Industries. **SIC:** 2211—Broadwoven Fabric Mills—Cotton; 2221—Broadwoven Fabric Mills—Manmade; 2231—Broadwoven Fabric Mills—Wool.

Fountain Inn

★ 79239 ★   Cincinnati Milacron
Milacron Dr.
Fountain Inn, SC 29644
(803)862-5581
Ultimate Parent: Cincinnati Milacron. **SIC:** 3545—Machine Tool Accessories.

★ 79240 ★   Cincinnati Milacron
Fountain Inn Div.
Milacron Dr.
Fountain Inn, SC 29644
Company Type: Division. **Ultimate Parent:** Cincinnati Milacron. **SIC:** 3541—Machine Tools—Metal Cutting Types.

★ 79241 ★   Cincinnati Milacron
Fountain Inn Div.
Milacron Dr.
Fountain Inn, SC 29644-1477
Company Type: Division. **Ultimate Parent:** Cincinnati Milacron. **SIC:** 3541—Machine Tools—Metal Cutting Types.

★ 79242 ★   Cincinnati Milacron-Heald Corp.
Fountain Inn Div.
Milacron Dr.
Fountain Inn, SC 29644
Company Type: Division. **Ultimate Parent:** Cincinnati Milacron. **SIC:** 3541—Machine Tools—Metal Cutting Types.

★ 79243 ★   Cincinnati Milacron Inc.
Fountain Inn Div.
110 Milacron Dr.
Fountain Inn, SC 29644
Company Type: Division. **Ultimate Parent:** Cincinnati Milacron. **SIC:** 3541—Machine Tools—Metal Cutting Types.

★ 79244 ★   Exxon Enterprises
Us 276
Fountain Inn, SC 29644
(803)862-5501
Ultimate Parent: Exxon. **SIC:** 8734—Testing Laboratories.

★ 79245 ★ **First Union National Bank of South Carolina**
100 S. Weston St.
Fountain Inn, SC 29644-1940
(803)862-3513
Location Type: Branch office. **Ultimate Parent:** First Union Corp. **SIC:** 6021—National Commercial Banks.

★ 79246 ★ **Flowers Baking Co.**
1405 S. Main St.
Fountain Inn, SC 29644
(803)862-4492
Officer: Herman D. Small, President.
Ultimate Parent: Flowers Industries. **SIC:** 2038—Frozen Specialties Nec; 2051—Bread, Cake & Related Products.

★ 79247 ★ **Flowers Baking Co. of Fountain Inn Inc.**
PO box 428
Fountain Inn, SC 29644
(803)862-4492 **Fax:** (803)862-2871
Company Type: Subsidiary. **Officer:** Herman D. Small, President. **Ultimate Parent:** Flowers Industries.

★ 79248 ★ **Piggly Wiggly**
S Main St.
Fountain Inn, SC 29644
(803)862-2736
Ultimate Parent: Bruno's. **SIC:** 5411—Grocery Stores.

★ 79249 ★ **Sonoco Products Co.**
102 Valley View Rd.
Fountain Inn, SC 29644
(803)862-4407
Officer: J.M. McGee, Plant Manager.
Ultimate Parent: Sonoco Products. **SIC:** 2655—Fiber Cans, Drums & Similar Products.

★ 79250 ★ **Van Dorn Co.**
Hwy. 276
Fountain Inn, SC 29644
(803)862-5521
Ultimate Parent: Crown Cork & Seal. **SIC:** 3411—Metal Cans.

★ 79251 ★ **Woodside Mills Inc.**
710 N. Woods Dr.
Fountain Inn, SC 29644
(803)967-7111
Officer: Mack Chapman, Manager. **Ultimate Parent:** Delta Woodside Industries. **SIC:** 2211—Broadwoven Fabric Mills—Cotton; 2399—Fabricated Textile Products Nec.

★ 79252 ★ **Woodside Mills Inc. Beattie Plant**
700 N. Woods Dr.
Fountain Inn, SC 29644
Ultimate Parent: Delta Woodside Industries. **SIC:** 2211—Broadwoven Fabric Mills—Cotton; 2221—Broadwoven Fabric Mills—Manmade.

★ 79253 ★ **Woodside Mills Inc. Beattie Plant**
Interstate 385
Fountain Inn, SC 29644
Ultimate Parent: Delta Woodside Industries. **SIC:** 2211—Broadwoven Fabric Mills—Cotton; 2221—Broadwoven Fabric Mills—Manmade.

★ 79254 ★ **Woodside Mills Inc. Furman Plant**
710 N. Woods Dr.
Fountain Inn, SC 29644
Ultimate Parent: Delta Woodside Industries. **SIC:** 2221—Broadwoven Fabric Mills—Manmade.

★ 79255 ★ **Woodside Mills Inc. Furman Plant**
Interstate 385
Fountain Inn, SC 29644
Ultimate Parent: Delta Woodside Industries. **SIC:** 2211—Broadwoven Fabric Mills—Cotton.

Ft. Mill

★ 79256 ★ **First Union National Bank of South Carolina**
403 Tom Hall St.
Ft. Mill, SC 29715-1740
(803)547-5551
Location Type: Branch office. **Ultimate Parent:** First Union Corp. **SIC:** 6021—National Commercial Banks.

Gaffney

★ 79257 ★ **Cellwood Products**
100 Cellwood Pl.
Gaffney, SC 29340
Ultimate Parent: Aluminum Co. of America-Alcoa. **SIC:** 3089—Plastics Products Nec.

★ 79258 ★ **Citgo Mini Mart**
301 Hampshire Dr.
Gaffney, SC 29340
(803)489-1379
Ultimate Parent: Citgo Petroleum. **SIC:** 5411—Grocery Stores.

★ 79259 ★ **First Union National Bank of South Carolina**
311 S. Limestone St.
Gaffney, SC 29340-3015
(803)787-8900
Location Type: Branch office. **Ultimate Parent:** First Union Corp. **SIC:** 6021—National Commercial Banks.

★ 79260 ★ **Kentucky Fried Chicken**
126 S. Granard St.
Gaffney, SC 29340
(803)489-7011
Ultimate Parent: Pepsico. **SIC:** 5812—Eating Places.

★ 79261 ★ **Oshkosh Truck Corp.**
Chassis Div.
552 Hyatt St.
Gaffney, SC 29341
Company Type: Division. **Ultimate Parent:** Oshkosh Truck. **SIC:** 3711—Motor Vehicles & Car Bodies.

★ 79262 ★ **Pizza Hut**
1701 W. Floyd Baker Blvd.
Gaffney, SC 29340
(803)487-4767
Ultimate Parent: Pepsico. **SIC:** 5812—Eating Places.

★ 79263 ★ **Rite Aid Discount Pharmacie**
Cherokee Shopping Ctr.
Gaffney, SC 29340
(803)489-8757
Ultimate Parent: Rite Aid.

★ 79264 ★ **Spring City Knitting Co.**
859 Victory Trail Rd.
Gaffney, SC 29340
Ultimate Parent: Sara Lee Corp. **SIC:** 2254—Knit Underwear Mills; 2253—Knit Outerwear Mills; 2269—Finishing Plants Nec.

★ 79265 ★ **Springs Industries, Inc.**
1206 Cherokee Ave.
Gaffney, SC 29340
(803)489-2513
Officer: James Barrett, Manager. **Ultimate Parent:** Springs Industries. **SIC:** 2221—Broadwoven Fabric Mills—Manmade; 2399—Fabricated Textile Products Nec.

★ 79266 ★ **Thomas & Betts Corp.**
427 Hyatt St.
Gaffney, SC 29341
Ultimate Parent: Thomas & Betts. **SIC:** 3471—Plating & Polishing.

★ 79267 ★ **Union/Butterfield Straight Line**
Beltline Rd.
Gaffney, SC 29340
Company Type: Division. **Ultimate Parent:** Litton Industries. **SIC:** 3545—Machine Tool Accessories.

★ 79268 ★ **Wal Mart**
1538 W. Floyd Baker Blvd.
Gaffney, SC 29340
(803)487-3769
Ultimate Parent: Wal-Mart Stores, Inc. **SIC:** 5399—Miscellaneous General Merchandise Store.

★ 79269 ★ **Wal Mart**
Cherokee Plz.
Gaffney, SC 29340
(803)489-1171
Ultimate Parent: Wal-Mart Stores, Inc. **SIC:** 5311—Department Stores.

Georgetown

★ 79270 ★ **Ace Hardware**
2404 Highmarket St.
Georgetown, SC 29440
(803)546-1025
Ultimate Parent: Ace Hardware. **SIC:** 5251—Hardware Stores.

★ 79271 ★ **Anchor Bank**
1187 N. Fraser St.
Georgetown, SC 29442
(803)527-9856
Location Type: Branch office. **Officer:** Daniel F. Sisu, Assistant Vice President. **Ultimate Parent:** Anchor Bancorp. **SIC:** 6022—State Commercial Banks.

★ 79272 ★ **Coast to Coast**
1043 N. Fraser St.
Georgetown, SC 29440
(803)527-8412
Ultimate Parent: Servistar Corp. **SIC:** 5251—Hardware Stores.

★ 79273 ★ **Coca-Cola Bottling Co.**
Shannon Industrial P
Georgetown, SC 29440
(803)546-4040
Ultimate Parent: Coca-Cola Enterprises. **SIC:** 5149—Groceries & Related Products Nec.

★ 79274 ★ **International Paper Co.**
Container Div.
PO Box 1420
Georgetown, SC 29442
(803)527-1381
Company Type: Division. **Ultimate Parent:** International Paper Co. **SIC:** 2653—Corrugated & Solid Fiber Boxes.

★ 79275 ★ **International Paper Georgetown Mill**
700 S. Kaminski St.
Georgetown, SC 29440
Ultimate Parent: International Paper Co. **SIC:** 2611—Pulp Mills; 2621—Paper Mills.

★ 79276 ★ **International Paper Georgetown Mill**
Kaminski St.
Georgetown, SC 29442
Ultimate Parent: International Paper Co. **SIC:** 2611—Pulp Mills; 2621—Paper Mills.

★ 79277 ★ **Kentucky Fried Chicken**
Church
Georgetown, SC 29440
(803)546-6037
Ultimate Parent: Pepsico. **SIC:** 5812—Eating Places.

Goose Creek

★ 79278 ★ **Branch Banking & Trust Co.**
144 St. James Ave.
Goose Creek, SC 29445-2924
(803)745-4107
Company Type: Subsidiary. **Location Type:** Branch office. **Ultimate Parent:** Southern National Corp. **SIC:** 6021—National Commercial Banks.

★ 79279 ★ **Figgie Packaging Systems**
300 Eagle Dr.
Goose Creek, SC 29445
(803)572-6640
Officer: Marcq Kaufmann, President. **Ultimate Parent:** Figgie International. **SIC:** 3559—Special Industry Machinery Nec; 3565—Packaging Machinery; 3569—General Industrial Machinery Nec.

★ 79280 ★ **Food Lion**
301 Crowfield Blvd.
Goose Creek, SC 29445
(803)572-0381
Ultimate Parent: Food Lion. **SIC:** 5411—Grocery Stores.

★ 79281 ★ **Food Lion Inc.**
301 Crowfield Blvd.
Goose Creek, SC 29445
(803)572-0381
Ultimate Parent: Food Lion. **SIC:** 5411—Grocery Stores.

★ 79282 ★ **General Dynamics Corp.**
2040 Bushy Pk. Rd.
Goose Creek, SC 29445
(803)863-3151
Officer: Richard Gregory, Manager. **Ultimate Parent:** General Dynamics. **SIC:** 3441—Fabricated Structural Metal; 3731—Ship Building & Repairing.

★ 79283 ★ **Haarmann & Reimer Corp.**
1636 Bushy Park Rd.
Goose Creek, SC 29445-1667
Ultimate Parent: Miles. **SIC:** 2869—Industrial Organic Chemicals Nec.

★ 79284 ★ **Kentucky Fried Chicken**
Goose Creek Blvd.
Goose Creek, SC 29445
(803)553-4441
Ultimate Parent: Pepsico. **SIC:** 5812—Eating Places.

★ 79285 ★ **Geo. J. Meyer Manufacturing**
300 Eagle Rd.
Goose Creek, SC 29445
(803)572-6640
Location Type: Branch office. **Ultimate Parent:** Figgie International. **SIC:** 3559—Special Industry Machinery Nec; 3569—General Industrial Machinery Nec; 3565—Packaging Machinery. **Employee Count:** 1700.

★ 79286 ★ **Piggly Wiggly**
Brandywine Blvd.
Goose Creek, SC 29445
(803)572-1421
Ultimate Parent: Bruno's. **SIC:** 5411—Grocery Stores.

★ 79287 ★ **Rite Aid of so Carolina Inc.**
Berkeley Sq.
Goose Creek, SC 29445
(803)553-3881
Ultimate Parent: Rite Aid. **SIC:** 5912—Drug Stores & Proprietary Stores.

Gray Court

★ 79288 ★ **Union Camp Corp.**
Gray Court, SC 29645
(803)876-2051
Ultimate Parent: Union Camp Corp. **SIC:** 2411—Logging.

Great Falls

★ 79289 ★ **Piggly Wiggly**
326 Dearborn St.
Great Falls, SC 29055
(803)482-2560
Ultimate Parent: Bruno's. **SIC:** 5411—Grocery Stores.

Greenville

★ 79290 ★ **Acme Business Product**
1075 Thousand Oaks Blvd.
Greenville, SC 29607
(803)297-3560
Company Type: Subsidiary. **Officer:** Clark King, President. **Ultimate Parent:** Alco Standard Corp. **SIC:** 3663—Radio & T.V. Communications Equipment.

★ 79291 ★ **Air Products & Chemicals**
101 Mountain Ridge Dr.
Greenville, SC 29609
(803)268-4085
Ultimate Parent: Air Products & Chemicals, Inc. **SIC:** 3567—Industrial Furnaces & Ovens.

★ 79292 ★ **Allied Color Ind.**
184 Commerce Dr.
Greenville, SC 29615
Ultimate Parent: M.A.Hanna. **SIC:** 3087—Custom Compound of Purchased Resins.

★ 79293 ★   Amerada Hess Corp.
No. 40242
300 Rutherford St.
Greenville, SC 29609
(803)242-6216
Ultimate Parent: Amerada Hess. **SIC:**
5541—Gasoline Service Stations.

★ 79294 ★   AMP AKZO Corp.
Carolina
200 Fairforest Way
Greenville, SC 29607-4609
(803)297-4100
Location Type: Branch office. **Officer:**
James J. McNamara. **Ultimate Parent:**
AMP Inc. **SIC:** 3679—Electronic
Components Nec.

★ 79295 ★   AMP-Azco Carolina
Circuits
200 Fairforest Way
Greenville, SC 29607
(803)297-4100
Officer: Jay McNamara, Manager. **Ultimate
Parent:** AMP Inc. **SIC:** 3679—Electronic
Components Nec.

★ 79296 ★   Avon Products Inc.
517 Buncombe St.
Greenville, SC 29601
(803)282-0100
Ultimate Parent: Avon Products, Inc. **SIC:**
8041—Offices & Clinics of Chiropractors.

★ 79297 ★   Bausch & Lomb Inc.
8507 Pelham Rd.
Greenville, SC 29615
(803)297-5500
Officer: Gregory W. Nielsen, Manager.
Ultimate Parent: Bausch & Lomb Inc. **SIC:**
2834—Pharmaceutical Preparations.

★ 79298 ★   Bausch & Lomb Inc.
130 Commerce Dr.
Greenville, SC 29615
(803)288-2225
Officer: Bob Hribernik, Manager. **Ultimate
Parent:** Bausch & Lomb Inc. **SIC:** 2834—
Pharmaceutical Preparations.

★ 79299 ★   Bell Atlantic Business
Systems
734B Wade Hampton Blvd.
Greenville, SC 29609-4940
(803)242-2953
Officer: Dennis Dunn. **Ultimate Parent:**
Bell Atlantic Corp. **SIC:** 5065—Electronic
Parts & Equipment Nec.

★ 79300 ★   Bell Atlantic Metro
Mobile
469 Congaree Rd.
Greenville, SC 29607-2709
(803)234-7954
Location Type: Branch office. **Officer:** Jack
Platting. **Ultimate Parent:** Bell Atlantic
Corp. **SIC:** 4812—Radiotelephone
Communications; 5065—Electronic Parts &
Equipment Nec; 5999—Miscellaneous Retail
Stores Nec.

★ 79301 ★   Beneficial
Management Corp.
1010C Woods Crossings Rd.
Greenville, SC 29607-3548
(803)288-2799
Officer: James Turner. **Ultimate Parent:**
Beneficial. **SIC:** 8732—Commercial
Nonphysical Research.

★ 79302 ★   Bi-Lo Inc.
Devonshire Rd.
Greenville, SC 29607
(803)234-1600
Ultimate Parent: Penn Traffic. **SIC:** 5411—
Grocery Stores.

★ 79303 ★   Bi-Lo Inc.
1800 Augusta St.
Greenville, SC 29605
(803)271-9744
Ultimate Parent: Penn Traffic. **SIC:** 5411—
Grocery Stores.

★ 79304 ★   Bi-Lo No One Ninety-
Five
2435 E. North St.
Greenville, SC 29615
(803)292-2209
Ultimate Parent: Penn Traffic. **SIC:** 5411—
Grocery Stores.

★ 79305 ★   Borden Inc.
Dairy
711 W. Washington St.
Greenville, SC 29601
Company Type: Division. **Ultimate Parent:**
Borden, Inc. **SIC:** 5143—Dairy Products
Except Dried or Canned; 2024—Ice Cream
& Frozen Desserts.

★ 79306 ★   Borden Inc.
Dairy
711 W. Washington St.
Greenville, SC 29601
Company Type: Division. **Ultimate Parent:**
Borden, Inc. **SIC:** 5143—Dairy Products
Except Dried or Canned; 2024—Ice Cream
& Frozen Desserts.

★ 79307 ★   Bowater
55 E. Camperdown Way
Greenville, SC 29602
(803)271-7733
Company Type: Headquarters. **Officer:**
Anthony P. Gammie. **Employee Count:**
6600. **Sales:** 13537 M. **Fortune 500:**
Largest U.S. Industrial Corporations:
Ranking 296.

★ 79308 ★   Bowater
Data Processing Division
1200 Woodruff Rd., Ste. A3
Greenville, SC 29607-5732
(803)234-9726
Officer: Michael L. Galloway. **Ultimate
Parent:** Bowater. **SIC:** 2621—Paper Mills.

★ 79309 ★   Bowater Inc.
55 E. Camperdown Way
PO Box 1028
Greenville, SC 29602
(803)271-7733 **Fax:** (803)282-9482
Company Type: Headquarters. **Officer:**
Anthony P. Gammie, Chairman & CEO.
Ultimate Parent: Bowater. **Employee
Count:** 7000.

★ 79310 ★   Bowater Inc.
PO Box 1028
Greenville, SC 29602-1028
(803)271-7733
Company Type: Headquarters. **Officer:** A.
P. Gammie. **Ultimate Parent:** Bowater. **SIC:**
2621—Paper Mills; 2421—Sawmills &
Planing Mills—General; 2611—Pulp Mills;
2672—Coated & Laminated Paper Nec;
2761—Manifold Business Forms.

★ 79311 ★   Bowater Inc.
55 E. Camperdown Way
Greenville, SC 29602
(803)271-7733
Officer: Anthony P. Gammie, CEO.
Ultimate Parent: Bowater. **Employee
Count:** 6900. **Sales:** 1354 M.

★ 79312 ★   Branch Banking &
Trust Co.
1001 Congaree Rd. Extension
Greenville, SC 29602
(803)458-2000
Company Type: Subsidiary. **Location
Type:** Branch office. **Ultimate Parent:**
Southern National Corp. **SIC:** 6021—
National Commercial Banks.

★ 79313 ★   Branch Banking &
Trust Co.
2304 W. Parker Rd.
Greenville, SC 29611-2123
(803)458-2286
Company Type: Subsidiary. **Location
Type:** Branch office. **Ultimate Parent:**
Southern National Corp. **SIC:** 6021—
National Commercial Banks.

★ 79314 ★   Branch Banking &
Trust Co.
130 W. Antrim Dr.
Greenville, SC 29607-2506
(803)458-2404
Company Type: Subsidiary. **Location
Type:** Branch office. **Ultimate Parent:**
Southern National Corp. **SIC:** 6021—
National Commercial Banks.

★ 79315 ★   Branch Banking &
Trust Co.
2204 Augusta Rd.
Greenville, SC 29605-1743
(803)255-7720
Company Type: Subsidiary. **Location
Type:** Branch office. **Ultimate Parent:**
Southern National Corp. **SIC:** 6021—
National Commercial Banks.

★ 79316 ★   Branch Banking &
Trust Co.
701 Haywood Rd.
Greenville, SC 29607-2721
(803)255-7738
Company Type: Subsidiary. **Location
Type:** Branch office. **Ultimate Parent:**
Southern National Corp. **SIC:** 6021—
National Commercial Banks.

★ 79317 ★   Branch Banking &
Trust Co.
1533 Wade Hampton Blvd.
Greenville, SC 29609-5047
(803)255-7701
Company Type: Subsidiary. **Location
Type:** Branch office. **Ultimate Parent:**
Southern National Corp. **SIC:** 6021—
National Commercial Banks.

★ 79318 ★   Branch Banking &
Trust Co.
1315 S. Pleasantburg Dr., Bi-Lo Store
Greenville, SC 29605
(803)255-7719
Company Type: Subsidiary. **Location
Type:** Branch office. **Ultimate Parent:**
Southern National Corp. **SIC:** 6021—
National Commercial Banks.

★ 79319 ★   Branch Banking &
Trust Co.
301 College St.
Greenville, SC 29601-2034
(803)458-2000
Company Type: Subsidiary. **Location
Type:** Branch office. **Ultimate Parent:**
Southern National Corp. **SIC:** 6021—
National Commercial Banks.

★ 79320 ★   Branch Banking &
Trust Co.
2000 Woodruff Rd.
Greenville, SC 29607
(803)458-2528
Company Type: Subsidiary. **Location
Type:** Branch office. **Ultimate Parent:**
Southern National Corp. **SIC:** 6021—
National Commercial Banks.

★ 79321 ★   Branch Banking &
Trust Co.
531 Mills Ave.
Greenville, SC 29605
(803)255-3400
Ultimate Parent: Southern National Corp.
SIC: 6022—State Commercial Banks.

★ 79322 ★   Burlington Cotton Co.
1533 Buncombe St.
Greenville, SC 29609-5246
(803)235-1694
Officer: James R. King. **Ultimate Parent:**
Burlington Industries, Equity. **SIC:** 5159—
Farm-Product Raw Materials Nec.

★ 79323 ★   Cacique
700 Haywood Rd.
Greenville, SC 29607
(803)288-4745
Ultimate Parent: Limited. **SIC:** 5651—
Family Clothing Stores; 5651—Family
Clothing Stores.

★ 79324 ★   Carisbrook Yarns
Franklin Div.
McGarity St.
Greenville, SC 29602
Company Type: Division. **Ultimate Parent:**
Hanson Industries. **SIC:** 2269—Finishing
Plants Nec.

★ 79325 ★   Casual Corner
Haywood Mall
Greenville, SC 29607
(803)288-4834
Ultimate Parent: United States Shoe. **SIC:**
5621—Women's Clothing Stores; 5651—
Family Clothing Stores.

★ 79326 ★   Casual Corner
225 S. Pleasantburg Dr.
Greenville, SC 29607
(803)242-5634
Ultimate Parent: United States Shoe. **SIC:**
5651—Family Clothing Stores.

★ 79327 ★   Champion
International Corp.
37 Villa Rd.
Greenville, SC 29615
(803)271-8404
Ultimate Parent: Champion International.
SIC: 5099—Durable Goods Nec.

★ 79328 ★   Circuit City
20 Haywood Rd.
Greenville, SC 29607
(803)288-1094
Ultimate Parent: Circuit City Stores. **SIC:**
5065—Electronic Parts & Equipment Nec.

★ 79329 ★   Coast to Coast
Express
Hwy. I
Greenville, SC 29605
(803)233-4247
Ultimate Parent: Servistar Corp. **SIC:**
4213—Trucking Except Local.

★ 79330 ★   Computer Associates
Inc.
1015 Lowndes Hill Rd.
Greenville, SC 29607
(803)235-5238
Ultimate Parent: Computer Associates
International. **SIC:** 7377—Computer Rental
& Leasing.

★ 79331 ★   Computer Associates
Inc.
750 Executive Ctr. Dr.
Greenville, SC 29615
(803)288-6978
Ultimate Parent: Computer Associates
International. **SIC:** 7373—Computer
Integrated Systems Design.

★ 79332 ★   Courtyard by Marriott
70 E. Orchard Park Dr.
Greenville, SC 29615
(803)234-0300
Ultimate Parent: Marriott International. **SIC:**
5812—Eating Places; 7011—Hotels &
Motels.

★ 79333 ★   Crown Metro
Aerospace
315 Echelon Rd.
Greenville, SC 29605
(803)277-1870
Officer: Carlos Rhys, President. **Ultimate
Parent:** Dexter Corp. **SIC:** 2851—Paints &
Allied Products.

★ 79334 ★   Dana Corp.
Mobile Fluid
250 Garlington Rd.
Greenville, SC 29615
(803)234-0444
Ultimate Parent: Dana Corp. **SIC:** 3511—
Turbines & Turbine Generator Sets; 3714—
Motor Vehicle Parts & Accessories.

★ 79335 ★   Dana Corp.
Mobile Fluid Products
500 Garlington Rd.
Greenville, SC 29615
(803)234-4600
Company Type: Division. **Ultimate Parent:**
Dana Corp. **SIC:** 3569—General Industrial
Machinery Nec.

★ 79336 ★   Dana Corp.
Mobile Fluid Products Division
PO Box 25000
Greenville, SC 29616
(803)234-4600 **Fax:** (803)234-4644
Company Type: Subsidiary. **Officer:** Bill
Hennessy, General Manager. **Ultimate
Parent:** Dana Corp. **SIC:** 3569—General
Industrial Machinery Nec; 3599—Industrial
Machinery Nec.

★ 79337 ★   Day International
Textiles Products
PO Box 2065
Greenville, SC 29602
(803)877-0981 **Fax:** (803)879-4173
Company Type: Subsidiary. **Officer:**
Dennis Wolters, President. **Ultimate Parent:**
M.A.Hanna.

★ 79338 ★   Delta Air Cargo
Greenville-Spartanburg Junction
Greenville, SC 29607
(803)877-6900
Ultimate Parent: Delta Air Lines, Inc. **SIC:**
4513—Air Courier Services.

★ 79339 ★   Delta Air Lines
220 N. Main St.
Greenville, SC 29601
(803)232-1504
Ultimate Parent: Delta Air Lines, Inc. **SIC:**
4512—Air Transportation—Scheduled.

★ 79340 ★ **Delta Air Lines Inc.**
220 N. Main St.
Greenville, SC 29601
(803)232-1504
Ultimate Parent: Delta Air Lines, Inc. **SIC:** 4512—Air Transportation—Scheduled.

★ 79341 ★ **Delta Woodside Industries**
233 N. Main St.
Greenville, SC 29601
(803)232-8301
Company Type: Headquarters. **Officer:** E. Erwin Maddrey II. **Employee Count:** 8500. **Sales:** 686 M. **Fortune 500:** Largest U.S. Industrial Corporations: Ranking 457.

★ 79342 ★ **Delta Woodside Industries Inc.**
233 N. Main St., No. 200
Greenville, SC 29601
(803)232-8301
Officer: E. Erwin Maddrey II, CEO. **Ultimate Parent:** Delta Woodside Industries. **SIC:** 2211—Broadwoven Fabric Mills—Cotton; 2221—Broadwoven Fabric Mills—Manmade; 2231—Broadwoven Fabric Mills—Wool.

★ 79343 ★ **Dexter Crown Metro Aerospace**
315 Echelon Rd. Donaldson Industrial Park
Greenville, SC 29605
Ultimate Parent: Dexter Corp. **SIC:** 2851—Paints & Allied Products.

★ 79344 ★ **Digital Equipment Corp.**
200 Fairforest Way
Greenville, SC 29607
Ultimate Parent: Digital Equipment Corp. **SIC:** 3672—Printed Circuit Boards.

★ 79345 ★ **Digital Equipment Corp.**
30 Patewood Dr.
Greenville, SC 29615
(803)288-8270
Ultimate Parent: Digital Equipment Corp. **SIC:** 7389—Business Services Nec.

★ 79346 ★ **Duck Head Outlet Stores**
233 N. Main St.
Greenville, SC 29601
(803)271-9250
Company Type: Division. **Ultimate Parent:** Delta Woodside Industries. **SIC:** 5311—Department Stores.

★ 79347 ★ **Exxon**
2760 Laurens Rd.
Greenville, SC 29607
(803)297-5319
Ultimate Parent: Exxon. **SIC:** 5541—Gasoline Service Stations.

★ 79348 ★ **Fairfield Inn by Marriott**
60 Roper Mountain Rd.
Greenville, SC 29607
(803)297-9996
Ultimate Parent: Marriott International. **SIC:** 7011—Hotels & Motels.

★ 79349 ★ **First Savings Bank**
301 College St.
Greenville, SC 29601
(803)458-2000
Company Type: Headquarters. **Officer:** Luther C. Boliek. **Employee Count:** 1130. **Fortune Service 500:** Ranking 48.

★ 79350 ★ **First Union National Bank of South Carolina**
2400 Wade Hampton Blvd.
Greenville, SC 29615-1146
Location Type: Branch office. **Ultimate Parent:** First Union Corp. **SIC:** 6021—National Commercial Banks.

★ 79351 ★ **First Union National Bank of South Carolina**
1301 W. Pendleton St.
Greenville, SC 29611-4833
Location Type: Branch office. **Ultimate Parent:** First Union Corp. **SIC:** 6021—National Commercial Banks.

★ 79352 ★ **First Union National Bank of South Carolina**
3622 Pelham Rd.
Greenville, SC 29615-5001
Ultimate Parent: First Union Corp. **SIC:** 6021—National Commercial Banks.

★ 79353 ★ **First Union National Bank of South Carolina**
1925 Augusta Rd.
Greenville, SC 29605-1344
Location Type: Branch office. **Ultimate Parent:** First Union Corp. **SIC:** 6021—National Commercial Banks.

★ 79354 ★ **First Union National Bank of South Carolina**
652 Haywood Rd.
Greenville, SC 29607-2737
Location Type: Branch office. **Ultimate Parent:** First Union Corp. **SIC:** 6021—National Commercial Banks.

★ 79355 ★ **First Union National Bank of South Carolina**
265 S. Pleasantburg Dr.
Greenville, SC 29607-2521
Location Type: Branch office. **Ultimate Parent:** First Union Corp. **SIC:** 6021—National Commercial Banks.

★ 79356 ★ **First Union National Bank of South Carolina**
Westowne Shopping Ctr.
1 Farrs Bridge Rd.
Greenville, SC 29611-2240
(803)255-8000
Location Type: Branch office. **Ultimate Parent:** First Union Corp. **SIC:** 6021—National Commercial Banks.

★ 79357 ★ **First Union National Bank of South Carolina**
901 Grove Rd.
Greenville, SC 29605-4211
Location Type: Branch office. **Ultimate Parent:** First Union Corp. **SIC:** 6021—National Commercial Banks.

★ 79358 ★ **First Union National Bank of South Carolina**
PO Box 1329
Greenville, SC 29602-1329
Location Type: Headquarters. **Ultimate Parent:** First Union Corp. **SIC:** 6021—National Commercial Banks.

★ 79359 ★ **First Union National Bank of South Carolina**
1st Union Tower, 1 Shelter Centre
Greenville, SC 29601-2127
(803)255-8000 **Fax:** (803)255-8246 **Telex:** 570330
Location Type: Branch office. **Ultimate Parent:** First Union Corp. **SIC:** 6021—National Commercial Banks.

★ 79360 ★ **First Union National Bank of South Carolina**
1 Shelter Pl., PO Box 1329
Greenville, SC 29601
(803)255-8000
Company Type: Subsidiary. **Officer:** Sidney B. Tate, Chairman of the Board, President & CEO. **Ultimate Parent:** First Union Corp. **SIC:** 6021—National Commercial Banks. **Employee Count:** 655. **Sales:** 125,588,000 M.

★ 79361 ★ **General Electric Co.**
300 Garlington Rd.
Greenville, SC 29615
(803)675-2000
Officer: K. E. Bruning, Manager. **Ultimate Parent:** General Electric. **SIC:** 3511—Turbines & Turbine Generator Sets.

★ 79362 ★ **Gerber Childrenswear Inc.**
531 S. Main St.
Greenville, SC 29601
(803)235-1615 **Fax:** (803)232-3335
Company Type: Subsidiary. **Officer:** Harland E. Hodges, President. **Ultimate Parent:** Gerber Products.

★ 79363 ★ **Grace Logistics Services**
Patewood Plz.
30 Patewood Dr., Ste. 270
Greenville, SC 29615
(803)281-2600 **Fax:** (803)281-2743
Company Type: Subsidiary. **Officer:** Patrick P. Grace, President. **Ultimate Parent:** W. R. Grace.

★ 79364 ★ **Grace Logistics Services Inc.**
Patewood Plaza, Ste. 270
Greenville, SC 29615-3530
(803)281-2600
Company Type: Subsidiary. **Officer:** P. P.

Grace, President. **Ultimate Parent:** W. R. Grace. **SIC:** 4213—Trucking Except Local. **Employee Count:** 327. **Sales:** 33.7000000 M.

★ 79365 ★ **Greyhound Bus Co.**
100 W. Mcbee Ave.
Greenville, SC 29601
(803)235-4060
Ultimate Parent: Greyhound Lines Inc. **SIC:** 4173—Bus Terminal & Service Facilities.

★ 79366 ★ **Greyhound Bus Lines**
121 N. Richardson St.
Greenville, SC 29601
(803)233-6328
Ultimate Parent: Greyhound Lines Inc. **SIC:** 4131—Intercity & Rural Bus Transportation.

★ 79367 ★ **Health Care Investment Analysts Inc.**
201 Brookfield Pky., Ste. 130
Greenville, SC 29607-5744
(803)288-5819
Ultimate Parent: AMBAC Inc. **SIC:** 8742—Management Consulting Services.

★ 79368 ★ **Hit or Miss**
Haywood Mall
Greenville, SC 29607
(803)297-8495
Ultimate Parent: TJX. **SIC:** 5621—Women's Clothing Stores; 5651—Family Clothing Stores.

★ 79369 ★ **Hoechst-Celanese Corp. Greenville Plant**
I-85 & Woodruff Rd.
Greenville, SC 29606
Ultimate Parent: Hoechst Celanese Corp. **SIC:** 2824—Organic Fibers—Noncellulosic.

★ 79370 ★ **Jiffy Lube**
301 Mauldin Rd.
Greenville, SC 29605
(803)299-0382
Ultimate Parent: Pennzoil.

★ 79371 ★ **Jiffy Lube**
880 S. Pleasantburg Dr.
Greenville, SC 29607
(803)271-3967
Ultimate Parent: Pennzoil. **SIC:** 6531—Real Estate Agents & Managers; 7530—Automotive Repair Shops.

★ 79372 ★ **Jiffy Lube**
2 Farrs Bridge Rd.
Greenville, SC 29611
(803)246-9327
Ultimate Parent: Pennzoil. **SIC:** 7538—General Automotive Repair Shops.

★ 79373 ★ **Jim Walter Homes Inc.**
104 Bruce Rd.
Greenville, SC 29605
(803)299-0564
Ultimate Parent: Walter Industries, Inc. **SIC:** 1521—Single-Family Housing Construction.

★ 79374 ★ **Johnson Controls, Inc.**
5818 PO Box
Greenville, SC 29606
(803)242-4230
Ultimate Parent: Johnson Controls Inc. **SIC:** 3599—Industrial Machinery Nec.

★ 79375 ★ **JPS Textile Group**
555 N. Pleasantburg Dr.
Greenville, SC 29607
(803)239-3900
Company Type: Headquarters. **Officer:** Steven M. Friedman. **Employee Count:** 8000. **Sales:** 886 M. **Fortune 500:** Largest U.S. Industrial Corporations: Ranking 387.

★ 79376 ★ **Karastan Bigelow**
Whitehorse Rd. & I-85
Greenville, SC 29605
Location Type: Plant. **Ultimate Parent:** Fieldcrest Cannon. **SIC:** 2273—Carpets & Rugs.

★ 79377 ★ **Kay-Bee Toy & Hobby Shop**
25 Greenville Mall
Greenville, SC 29607
(803)288-2531
Ultimate Parent: Melville. **SIC:** 5945—Hobby, Toy & Game Shops.

★ 79378 ★ **Kay Bee Toy & Hobby Shop**
Haywood Mall
Greenville, SC 29607
(803)297-3710
Ultimate Parent: Melville. **SIC:** 5945—Hobby, Toy & Game Shops.

★ 79379 ★ **Kay Bee Toy&Hobby Shop**
Greenville Mall
Greenville, SC 29602
(803)288-2531
Ultimate Parent: Melville. **SIC:** 5945—Hobby, Toy & Game Shops.

★ 79380 ★ **Kentucky Fried Chicken**
White Horse Rd.
Greenville, SC 29605
(803)246-7971
Ultimate Parent: Pepsico. **SIC:** 5812—Eating Places.

★ 79381 ★ **Kentucky Fried Chicken**
700 Cedar Ln.
Greenville, SC 29611
(803)271-1122
Ultimate Parent: Pepsico. **SIC:** 5812—Eating Places.

★ 79382 ★ **Kentucky Fried Chicken**
1547 Laurens Rd.
Greenville, SC 29607
(803)233-6680
Ultimate Parent: Pepsico. **SIC:** 5812—Eating Places.

★ 79383 ★ **Kentucky Fried Chicken**
1111 Augusta Rd.
Greenville, SC 29605
(803)242-0658
Ultimate Parent: Pepsico. **SIC:** 5812—Eating Places.

★ 79384 ★ **Lens Crafters**
Haywood Mall
Greenville, SC 29607
(803)234-7200
Ultimate Parent: United States Shoe. **SIC:** 5995—Optical Goods Stores.

★ 79385 ★ **Lerner Shop**
Haywood Mall
Greenville, SC 29607
(803)288-0693
Ultimate Parent: Limited. **SIC:** 5621—Women's Clothing Stores; 5651—Family Clothing Stores.

★ 79386 ★ **Lerner Shop**
Greenville Mall
Greenville, SC 29602
(803)288-0523
Ultimate Parent: Limited. **SIC:** 5621—Women's Clothing Stores.

★ 79387 ★ **The Limited**
62 Greenville Mall
Greenville, SC 29607
(803)297-0101
Ultimate Parent: Limited. **SIC:** 5651—Family Clothing Stores.

★ 79388 ★ **The Limited**
225 S. Pleasantburg Dr.
Greenville, SC 29607
(803)232-3664
Ultimate Parent: Limited. **SIC:** 5621—Women's Clothing Stores.

★ 79389 ★ **The Limited Express**
Haywood Mall
Greenville, SC 29607
(803)234-0305
Ultimate Parent: Limited. **SIC:** 5651—Family Clothing Stores.

★ 79390 ★ **Lockheed Aeromod Center, Inc.**
1044 Terminal Rd.
Greenville, SC 29605
(803)299-3350 **Fax:** (803)299-3225
Company Type: Subsidiary. **Ultimate Parent:** Lockheed Corp. **SIC:** 4581—Airports, Flying Fields & Services.

★ 79391 ★ **Lockheed Aeromod Centers Inc.**
244 Terminal Rd.
Greenville, SC 29605
Ultimate Parent: Lockheed Corp. **SIC:** 3721—Aircraft.

★ 79392 ★ **Lowe's**
3550 Rutherford Rd.
Greenville, SC 29609
(803)292-2644
Ultimate Parent: Lowe's. **SIC:** 5039—Construction Materials Nec.

★ 79393 ★ **Mary Kay Cosmetics**
18 Thornwood Ln.
Greenville, SC 29605
(803)297-3831
Ultimate Parent: Mary Kay Cosmetics. **SIC:** 5999—Miscellaneous Retail Stores Nec.

★ 79394 ★ **Metro Mobile CTS of Greenville, Inc.**
469 Congaree Rd.
Greenville, SC 29607
(803)234-7954
Ultimate Parent: Bell Atlantic Corp. **SIC:** 4812—Radiotelephone Communications.

★ 79395 ★ **Modern Office Machines Inc.**
400 Haywood Rd.
Greenville, SC 29607
(803)281-5400
Company Type: Division. **Officer:** Tecumseh Hooper Jr., President. **Ultimate Parent:** Alco Standard Corp. **SIC:** 5044—Office Equipment; 5045—Computers, Peripherals & Software; 7377—Computer Rental & Leasing; 7378—Computer Maintenance & Repair. **Employee Count:** 300.

★ 79396 ★ **Modern Office Machines Inc.**
400 Haywood Rd.
Greenville, SC 29607-4303
(803)281-5400
Officer: Tecumseh Hooper Jr., President. **Ultimate Parent:** Alco Standard Corp. **SIC:** 5044—Office Equipment; 5045—Computers, Peripherals & Software; 7377—Computer Rental & Leasing; 7359—Equipment Rental & Leasing Nec; 7699—Repair Services Nec; 5112—Stationery & Office Supplies. **Employee Count:** 300.

★ 79397 ★ **Monroe Industries Inc.**
Odom Cir.
Greenville, SC 29611
(803)233-1255
Officer: Richard E. Linville, President & Treasurer. **Ultimate Parent:** Collins & Aikman Group. **SIC:** 2261—Finishing Plants—Cotton; 2262—Finishing Plants—Manmade. **Employee Count:** 200. **Sales:** 12 M.

★ 79398 ★ **Morton International Specialty**
PO Box 3089
Greenville, SC 29602-3089
(803)292-5700
Company Type: Headquarters. **Officer:** R. P. Ellis. **Ultimate Parent:** Morton International. **SIC:** 2891—Adhesives & Sealants; 2819—Industrial Inorganic Chemicals Nec; 2821—Plastics Materials & Resins.

★ 79399 ★ **New England Mutual Life Insurance**
518 E. North St.
Greenville, SC 29601
(803)232-1568
Ultimate Parent: New England Mutual Life. **SIC:** 6411—Insurance Agents, Brokers & Service.

★ 79400 ★ **New York Life Greenville General Office**
Southeastern Agenices
550 First Union Bank Tower, 55 Beattie Pl.
Greenville, SC 29601
(803)242-5041 **Fax:** (803)242-5272
Officer: William H. Holt, General Manager. **Ultimate Parent:** New York Life.

★ 79401 ★ **Pepsi-Cola Bottling Co.**
751 State Park Rd.
Greenville, SC 29609
(803)242-6041
Ultimate Parent: Pepsico. **SIC:** 2086—Bottled & Canned Soft Drinks.

★ 79402 ★ **Pet Inc.**
Pet Dairy Group
85 Frontage Rd.
Greenville, SC 29611
(803)288-8550
Officer: Riley Cordell, Manager. **Ultimate Parent:** Pet. **SIC:** 2024—Ice Cream & Frozen Desserts.

★ 79403 ★ **Pizza Hut**
3015 White Horse Rd.
Greenville, SC 29611
(803)269-0394
Ultimate Parent: Pepsico. **SIC:** 5812—Eating Places.

★ 79404 ★ **Pizza Hut**
2660 Poinsett Hwy.
Greenville, SC 29609
(803)232-9715
Ultimate Parent: Pepsico. **SIC:** 5812—Eating Places.

★ 79405 ★ **Pizza Hut**
349 S. Pleasantburg Dr.
Greenville, SC 29607
(803)271-2090
Ultimate Parent: Pepsico. **SIC:** 5812—Eating Places.

★ 79406 ★ **Pizza Hut**
517 Cedar Ln.
Greenville, SC 29611
(803)246-8460
Ultimate Parent: Pepsico. **SIC:** 5812—Eating Places.

★ 79407 ★ **Pizza Hut**
755 N. Pleasantburg Dr.
Greenville, SC 29607
(803)232-5633
Ultimate Parent: Pepsico. **SIC:** 5812—Eating Places.

★ 79408 ★ **Principal Mutual Life Insurance Co.**
Greenville, SC 29604
(803)269-9701
Ultimate Parent: Principal Mutual Life. **SIC:** 6371—Pension, Health & Welfare Funds.

★ 79409 ★ **Procter & Gamble Mfg. Co.**
1700 Perimeter Rd. Donaldson Ctr.
Greenville, SC 29605-5287
Ultimate Parent: Procter & Gamble Co. **SIC:** 2834—Pharmaceutical Preparations.

★ 79410 ★ **Procter & Gamble Mfg. Co.**
2600 Perimeter Rd. Donaldson Ctr.
Greenville, SC 29605-5287
Ultimate Parent: Procter & Gamble Co. **SIC:** 2834—Pharmaceutical Preparations.

★ 79411 ★ **PYA Monarch Inc.**
80 International Dr.
Suite 200
Greenville, SC 29615
(803)676-8600
Company Type: Division. **Location Type:** Facility. **Ultimate Parent:** Sara Lee Corp. **SIC:** 2033—Canned Fruits & Vegetables.

★ 79412 ★ **Radio Shack**
355 Woodruff Rd.
Greenville, SC 29607
(803)297-1768
Company Type: Division. **Ultimate Parent:** Tandy Corp. **SIC:** 7378—Computer Maintenance & Repair.

★ 79413 ★ **Radio Shack**
225 S. Pleasantburg Dr.
Greenville, SC 29607
(803)242-0982
Company Type: Division. **Ultimate Parent:** Tandy Corp. **SIC:** 5065—Electronic Parts & Equipment Nec.

★ 79414 ★ **Radio Shack**
6119 White Horse Rd.
Greenville, SC 29611
(803)269-9774
Company Type: Division. **Ultimate Parent:** Tandy Corp. **SIC:** 7841—Video Tape Rental.

★ 79415 ★ **Radio Shack**
2447 Laurens Rd.
Greenville, SC 29607
(803)288-9494
Company Type: Division. **Ultimate Parent:** Tandy Corp. **SIC:** 5731—Radio, Television & Electronics Stores.

★ 79416 ★ **Radio Shack**
N Hills Shopping Ctr.
Greenville, SC 29604
(803)292-1835
Company Type: Division. **Ultimate Parent:** Tandy Corp. **SIC:** 5046—Commercial Equipment Nec.

★ 79417 ★ **Radio Shack**
1818 Augusta St.
Greenville, SC 29605
(803)233-4877
Company Type: Division. **Ultimate Parent:** Tandy Corp. **SIC:** 5731—Radio, Television & Electronics Stores.

★ 79418 ★ **Radio Shack**
Haywood Mall
Greenville, SC 29607
(803)288-8641
Company Type: Division. **Ultimate Parent:** Tandy Corp. **SIC:** 5731—Radio, Television & Electronics Stores.

★ 79419 ★ **Reliance Electric Co.**
5024 Pelham Rd.
Greenville, SC 29615
(803)288-9050
Officer: Bob McLeod, Manager. **Ultimate Parent:** Reliance Electric. **SIC:** 3566—Speed Changers, Drives & Gears.

★ 79420 ★ **Reliance Electric Co. Gear Products Plant**
5024 Pelham Rd.
Greenville, SC 29606
Ultimate Parent: Reliance Electric. **SIC:** 3566—Speed Changers, Drives & Gears.

★ 79421 ★ **Rite Aid Discount Center**
Haywood Mall
Greenville, SC 29607
(803)297-9379
Ultimate Parent: Rite Aid. **SIC:** 5912—Drug Stores & Proprietary Stores.

★ 79422 ★ **Rite Aid Discount Pharmacie**
N Hills Shopping Ctr.
Greenville, SC 29604
(803)268-0712
Ultimate Parent: Rite Aid. **SIC:** 5912—Drug Stores & Proprietary Stores.

★ 79423 ★ **Rite Aid Discount Pharmacie**
7 Farrs Bridge Rd.
Greenville, SC 29611
(803)246-7465
Ultimate Parent: Rite Aid. **SIC:** 5912—Drug Stores & Proprietary Stores.

★ 79424 ★ **Rite Aid Discount Pharmacie**
Greenville Mall
Greenville, SC 29602
(803)297-9318
Ultimate Parent: Rite Aid. **SIC:** 5912—Drug Stores & Proprietary Stores.

★ 79425 ★ **Rite Aid Discount Pharmacie**
2600 Anderson Rd.
Greenville, SC 29611
(803)269-3156
Ultimate Parent: Rite Aid. **SIC:** 5912—Drug Stores & Proprietary Stores.

★ 79426 ★ **Rite Aid Drug Store**
7 Farrs Bridge Rd.
Greenville, SC 29611
(803)246-9802
Ultimate Parent: Rite Aid. **SIC:** 5912—Drug Stores & Proprietary Stores.

★ 79427 ★ **Rite Aid Drugs**
17 Greenville Mall
Greenville, SC 29607
(803)297-9318
Ultimate Parent: Rite Aid. **SIC:** 5912—Drug Stores & Proprietary Stores.

★ 79428 ★ **Rite-Aid Drugs**
2600 Anderson Rd.
Greenville, SC 29611
(803)269-9966
Ultimate Parent: Rite Aid. **SIC:** 5912—Drug Stores & Proprietary Stores.

★ 79429 ★ **Rite Aid Pharmacy**
7 Farrs Bridge Rd.
Greenville, SC 29611
(803)246-9924
Ultimate Parent: Rite Aid. **SIC:** 5912—Drug Stores & Proprietary Stores.

★ 79430 ★ **RJ Reynolds Tobacco Co.**
1305 Laurens Rd.
Greenville, SC 29607
(803)235-0469
Ultimate Parent: RJR Nabisco Holdings. **SIC:** 5194—Tobacco & Tobacco Products.

★ 79431 ★ **Ryder Truck Rental**
Harris Rd.
Greenville, SC 29611
(803)299-0400
Ultimate Parent: Ryder System. **SIC:** 7359—Equipment Rental & Leasing Nec.

★ 79432 ★ **Sam's Wholesale Club**
2519 Laurens Rd.
Greenville, SC 29607
(803)297-3041
Ultimate Parent: Wal-Mart Stores, Inc. **SIC:** 5141—Groceries—General Line.

★ 79433 ★ **Sara Lee Bakery**
1916 Piedmont Hwy.
Greenville, SC 29605
(803)299-0604
Company Type: Division. **Location Type:** Facility. **Officer:** Bruce Holland, Production Manager. **Ultimate Parent:** Sara Lee Corp.

★ 79434 ★ **Sara Lee Corp.**
80 International Dr.
Greenville, SC 29602
(803)676-8600
Company Type: Division. **Officer:** James Carlson, CEO. **Ultimate Parent:** Sara Lee Corp.

★ 79435 ★ **Security Pacific Housing**
15 S. Main St.
Greenville, SC 29601
(803)235-8802
Ultimate Parent: Bankamerica Corp. **SIC:** 7359—Equipment Rental & Leasing Nec.

★ 79436 ★ **Sonoco Products Co.**
195 Commerce Dr.
Greenville, SC 29615
(803)297-3684
Officer: William Kuehne, Manager. **Ultimate Parent:** Sonoco Products. **SIC:** 3089—Plastics Products Nec.

★ 79437 ★ **Systems & Services**
1075 Thousand Oaks Blvd.
Greenville, SC 29607
(803)297-3560
Company Type: Division. **Officer:** Mark White, President. **Ultimate Parent:** Alco Standard Corp. **SIC:** 7359—Equipment Rental & Leasing Nec; 5046—Commercial Equipment Nec.

★ 79438 ★ **Texaco Self Service No 4**
1000 Buncombe St.
Greenville, SC 29609
(803)235-5314
Ultimate Parent: Texaco. **SIC:** 5541—Gasoline Service Stations.

★ 79439 ★ **Texaco Station**
433 N. Pleasantburg Dr.
Greenville, SC 29607
(803)232-1205
Ultimate Parent: Texaco. **SIC:** 5541—Gasoline Service Stations.

★ 79440 ★ **3M Co.**
Tape Manufacturing Div.
PO Box 5517
Greenville, SC 29606-5517
(803)277-8270
Company Type: Headquarters. **Officer:** Louis C. Sagedy. **Ultimate Parent:** Minnesota Mining & Mfg. **SIC:** 2821—Plastics Materials & Resins; 2672—Coated & Laminated Paper Nec; 3081—Unsupported Plastics Film & Sheet.

★ 79441 ★ **Trailways Bus System**
505 E. Stone Ave.
Greenville, SC 29601
(803)271-0995
Ultimate Parent: Greyhound Lines Inc. **SIC:** 4131—Intercity & Rural Bus Transportation.

★ 79442 ★ **Underwriters Adjusting Co.**
Koger Executive Ctr.
Greenville, SC 29615
(803)224-9523
Ultimate Parent: Continental. **SIC:** 6411—Insurance Agents, Brokers & Service.

★ 79443 ★ **Victoria's Secret**
Haywood Mall
Greenville, SC 29607
(803)288-3375
Ultimate Parent: Limited. **SIC:** 5651—Family Clothing Stores.

★ 79444 ★ **Wal Mart**
2429 Laurens Rd.
Greenville, SC 29607
(803)297-3031
Ultimate Parent: Wal-Mart Stores, Inc. **SIC:** 5399—Miscellaneous General Merchandise Store.

★ 79445 ★ **Wal Mart**
6119 White Horse Rd.
Greenville, SC 29611
(803)295-3181
Ultimate Parent: Wal-Mart Stores, Inc. **SIC:** 5311—Department Stores.

★ 79446 ★ **Wal Mart Discount City**
Westowne Shopping Ctr.
Greenville, SC 29609
(803)246-5665
Ultimate Parent: Wal-Mart Stores, Inc. **SIC:** 5311—Department Stores.

★ 79447 ★ **Waldenbooks**
Greenville Mall
Greenville, SC 29602
(803)288-1828
Ultimate Parent: K-Mart. **SIC:** 5942—Book Stores.

★ 79448 ★ **Waldenbooks**
Haywood Mall
Greenville, SC 29607
(803)297-1025
Ultimate Parent: K-Mart. **SIC:** 5942—Book Stores.

★ 79449 ★ **Wrangler**
110 Old Piedmont Hwy.
Greenville, SC 29611
(803)269-4531
Ultimate Parent: VF Corp.

★ 79450 ★ **Xerox Corp.**
555 N. Pleasantburg Dr.
Greenville, SC 29607
(803)242-4702
Officer: Betty Duckworth, Manager.
Ultimate Parent: Xerox Corp. **SIC:** 3663—Radio & T.V. Communications Equipment.

Greenwood

★ 79451 ★ **Ace Hardware Co. Inc.**
210 Pressley St.
Greenwood, SC 29646
(803)223-6363
Ultimate Parent: Ace Hardware. **SIC:** 5251—Hardware Stores.

★ 79452 ★ **Casual Corner**
Crosscreek Mall
Greenwood, SC 29646
(803)223-7974
Ultimate Parent: United States Shoe. **SIC:** 5621—Women's Clothing Stores.

★ 79453 ★ **Circus World Toy Stores**
Crosscreek Mall
Greenwood, SC 29646
(803)223-5611
Ultimate Parent: Melville. **SIC:** 5945—Hobby, Toy & Game Shops.

★ 79454 ★ **Cooper Power Systems**
1520 Emerald Rd.
Greenwood, SC 29646
Ultimate Parent: Cooper Industries. **SIC:** 3699—Electrical Equipment & Supplies Nec.

★ 79455 ★ **Kaiser Aluminum & Chemical Corp.**
Greenwood Forge
1508 Hwy. 246 S.
Greenwood, SC 29646
Company Type: Division. **Ultimate Parent:** Maxxam. **SIC:** 3463—Nonferrous Forgings.

★ 79456 ★ **Kentucky Fried Chicken**
1364 S. Main St.
Greenwood, SC 29646
(803)229-2011
Ultimate Parent: Pepsico. **SIC:** 5812—Eating Places.

★ 79457 ★ **Kentucky Fried Chicken**
Hwy. 72 Bypass
Greenwood, SC 29646
(803)229-2421
Ultimate Parent: Pepsico. **SIC:** 5812—Eating Places.

★ 79458 ★ **Monsanto Car Employees Cr**
PO Box 1133
Greenwood, SC 29648-1133
(803)223-2720
Company Type: Headquarters. **Officer:** William H. Love Jr. **Ultimate Parent:** Monsanto. **SIC:** 6061—Federal Credit Unions.

★ 79459 ★ **Monsanto Chemical Group-Fibers**
PO Box 1057
Greenwood, SC 29648-1057
(803)942-4200
Company Type: Headquarters. **Officer:** C. J. Rogers. **Ultimate Parent:** Monsanto. **SIC:** 2821—Plastics Materials & Resins.

★ 79460 ★ **Monsanto Co.**
Hwy. 246
Greenwood, SC 29648-0000
Ultimate Parent: Monsanto. **SIC:** 2824—Organic Fibers-Noncellulosic.

★ 79461 ★ **Piggly Wiggly**
S Main
Greenwood, SC 29646
(803)229-1181
Ultimate Parent: Bruno's. **SIC:** 5411—Grocery Stores.

★ 79462 ★ **Pizza Hut**
415 Montague Ave.
Greenwood, SC 29649
(803)223-8441
Ultimate Parent: Pepsico. **SIC:** 5812—Eating Places.

★ 79463 ★ **Pizza Hut**
Hwy. 72 Bypass
Greenwood, SC 29646
(803)223-9739
Ultimate Parent: Pepsico. **SIC:** 5812—Eating Places.

★ 79464 ★ **Radio Shack**
Crosscreek Mall
Greenwood, SC 29646
(803)229-2458
Company Type: Division. **Ultimate Parent:** Tandy Corp. **SIC:** 5065—Electronic Parts & Equipment Nec.

★ 79465 ★ **Waldenbooks**
Crosscreek Mall
Greenwood, SC 29646
(803)229-6162
Ultimate Parent: K-Mart. **SIC:** 5942—Book Stores.

★ 79466 ★ **Westinghouse Electric**
2210 Hwy. 72, Ste. 221 E
Greenwood, SC 29649
(803)229-3006
Officer: Dick Lang, Manager. **Ultimate Parent:** Westinghouse Electric Corp. **SIC:** 3612—Transformers Except Electronic; 3613—Switchgear & Switchboard Apparatus.

★ 79467 ★ **Westinghouse Electric Corp.**
2210 Laurens Rd.
Greenwood, SC 29646
Ultimate Parent: Westinghouse Electric Corp. **SIC:** 3613—Switchgear & Switchboard Apparatus.

Greer

★ 79468 ★ **Airborne Freight Corp.**
14 South Hwy.
Greer, SC 29651
(803)232-2763
Ultimate Parent: Airborne Freight Corp. **SIC:** 4512—Air Transportation—Scheduled.

★ 79469 ★ **Ball Corp.**
Unimark Plastics Division
1303 Batesville Rd.
Greer, SC 29650
Ultimate Parent: Ball Corp. **SIC:** 3089—Plastics Products Nec.

★ 79470 ★ **Branch Banking & Trust Co.**
107 Church St.
Greer, SC 29651-2551
(803)879-7151
Company Type: Subsidiary. **Location Type:** Branch office. **Ultimate Parent:** Southern National Corp. **SIC:** 6021—National Commercial Banks.

★ 79471 ★ **Branch Banking & Trust Co.**
1200 W. Wade Hampton Blvd.
Greer, SC 29650
(803)877-0715
Ultimate Parent: Southern National Corp. **SIC:** 6099—Functions Related to Deposit Banking.

★ 79472 ★ **Delta Air Lines**
Greenville-Spartanburg Junction
Greer, SC 29651
(803)877-6611
Ultimate Parent: Delta Air Lines, Inc. **SIC:** 4512—Air Transportation—Scheduled.

★ 79473 ★ **Emery Worldwide**
Greenville-Spartanburg Junction
Greer, SC 29651
(803)585-8266
Ultimate Parent: Consolidated Freightways. **SIC:** 4513—Air Courier Services.

★ 79474 ★ **Food Lion**
1318 W. Wade Hampton Blvd.
Greer, SC 29650
(803)877-8469
Ultimate Parent: Food Lion. **SIC:** 5411—Grocery Stores.

★ 79475 ★ **Hoechst-Celanese Corp.**
Hood Rd. PO Box 1400
Greer, SC 29651-1400
Ultimate Parent: Hoechst Celanese Corp. **SIC:** 2821—Plastics Materials & Resins.

★ 79476 ★ **Hoechst Celanese Corp.**
Hood Rd.
PO Box 1400
Greer, SC 29651
Ultimate Parent: Hoechst Celanese Corp. **SIC:** 2821—Plastics Materials & Resins.

★ 79477 ★ **Homelite**
Buncombe Rd.
Greer, SC 29651
Ultimate Parent: Textron. **SIC:** 3546—Power-Driven Handtools.

★ 79478 ★ **Homelite**
Homelite Division
106 S. Buncombe Rd.
Greer, SC 29651
Ultimate Parent: Textron. **SIC:** 3546—Power-Driven Handtools.

★ 79479 ★ **Kentucky Fried Chicken**
1329 W. Wade Hampton Blvd.
Greer, SC 29650
(803)848-1801
Ultimate Parent: Pepsico. **SIC:** 5812—Eating Places.

★ 79480 ★ **Massachusetts Mutual Life Insurance**
104 Inwood Ct.
Greer, SC 29650
(803)242-5551
Ultimate Parent: Massasucetts Mutual Life. **SIC:** 6411—Insurance Agents, Brokers & Service.

★ 79481 ★ **Rite Aid Discount Pharmacie**
510 N. Main St.
Greer, SC 29650
(803)877-9292
Ultimate Parent: Rite Aid. **SIC:** 5912—Drug Stores & Proprietary Stores.

★ 79482 ★ **Stevcoknit Fabrics Co.**
99 Bobo St.
Greer, SC 29650
(803)879-6705
Officer: Robert W. Humphreys, President. **Ultimate Parent:** Delta Woodside Industries. **SIC:** 2299—Textile Goods Nec.

★ 79483 ★ **Taco Bell**
1301 W. Wade Hampton Blvd.
Greer, SC 29650
(803)879-8487
Ultimate Parent: Pepsico. **SIC:** 5812—Eating Places.

★ 79484 ★ **Textron Inc.**
Homelite Division
Buncombe Rd.
Greer, SC 29651
Ultimate Parent: Textron. **SIC:** 3546—Power-Driven Handtools.

★ 79485 ★ **Textron Lycoming**
400 S. Buncombe Rd.
Greer, SC 29652-1404
Ultimate Parent: Textron. **SIC:** 3724—Aircraft Engines & Engine Parts; 3519—Internal Combustion Engines Nec.

★ 79486 ★ **Textron Lycoming**
400 South Buncombe Rd.
Greer, SC 29651
Ultimate Parent: Textron. **SIC:** 3724—Aircraft Engines & Engine Parts; 3519—Internal Combustion Engines Nec.

★ 79487 ★ **Textron Lycoming Greer Plant**
400 South Buncombe Rd.
Greer, SC 29651
Ultimate Parent: Textron. **SIC:** 3724—Aircraft Engines & Engine Parts; 3519—Internal Combustion Engines Nec.

★ 79488 ★ **Textron Lycoming Turbine Services Plant**
85 Beeco Rd.
Greer, SC 29651
Location Type: Plant. **Ultimate Parent:** Textron. **SIC:** 3724—Aircraft Engines & Engine Parts.

★ 79489 ★ **Textron Lycoming Turbine Services Plant**
87 Beeco Rd.
Greer, SC 29651
Location Type: Plant. **Ultimate Parent:** Textron. **SIC:** 3724—Aircraft Engines & Engine Parts.

★ 79490 ★ **Textron Turbine Services**
85 Beeco Rd.
Greer, SC 29650
Ultimate Parent: Textron. **SIC:** 3724—Aircraft Engines & Engine Parts.

★ 79491 ★ **Unimark Plastics**
PO Box 2750
Greer, SC 29652-2750
(803)879-8100
Company Type: Headquarters. **Officer:** Charles Worth. **Ultimate Parent:** Ball Corp. **SIC:** 3089—Plastics Products Nec.

Hampton

★ 79492 ★ **Georgia-Pacific Resins Inc.**
609 Nix St. PO Box 258
Hampton, SC 29924
Ultimate Parent: Georgia-Pacific. **SIC:** 2869—Industrial Organic Chemicals Nec.

★ 79493 ★ **Piggly Wiggly**
802 Elm St. E
Hampton, SC 29924
(803)943-2556
Ultimate Parent: Bruno's. **SIC:** 5411—Grocery Stores.

★ 79494 ★ Westinghouse
Electric Corp.
304 N. Hoover St. 304 Hoover St.
Hampton, SC 29924
Ultimate Parent: Westinghouse Electric
Corp. SIC: 3000—Rubber & Miscellaneous
Plastics Products.

★ 79495 ★ Westinghouse
Electric Corp.
304 Hoover St.
PO Box 248
Hampton, SC 29924
Ultimate Parent: Westinghouse Electric
Corp.

Hardeeville

★ 79496 ★ McDonalds
Restaurant
Hwy. 17 195
Hardeeville, SC 29927
(803)784-2885
Ultimate Parent: McDonald's.
SIC: 5812—Eating Places.

Hartsville

★ 79497 ★ First Union National
Bank of South Carolina
208 W. Home Ave.
Hartsville, SC 29550-4126
(803)332-1121
Location Type: Branch office. Ultimate
Parent: First Union Corp. SIC: 6021—
National Commercial Banks.

★ 79498 ★ Imc Fertilizer Inc.
Society Ave.
Hartsville, SC 29550
Ultimate Parent: IMC Fertilizer Group. SIC:
2874—Phosphatic Fertilizers.

★ 79499 ★ Piggly Wiggly
842 S. 5th St.
Hartsville, SC 29550
(803)332-8241
Ultimate Parent: Bruno's. SIC: 5411—
Grocery Stores.

★ 79500 ★ Pizza Hut
130 S. 5th St.
Hartsville, SC 29550
(803)332-4118
Ultimate Parent: Pepsico. SIC: 5812—
Eating Places.

★ 79501 ★ Radio Shack
151 Byp
Hartsville, SC 29550
(803)332-7687
Company Type: Division. Ultimate Parent:
Tandy Corp. SIC: 4899—Communications
Services Nec.

★ 79502 ★ Sara Lee Hosiery
Hwy. 151 Bypass
Hartsville, SC 29550
Ultimate Parent: Sara Lee Corp. SIC:
2251—Women's Hosiery Except Socks.

★ 79503 ★ Sonoco Products
N. 2nd St.
Hartsville, SC 29550
(803)383-7000
Company Type: Headquarters. Officer:
Charles W. Coker. Employee Count:
17000. Sales: 1947 M. Fortune 500:
Largest U.S. Industrial Corporations:
Ranking 228.

★ 79504 ★ Sonoco Products Co.
N. 2nd St.
Hartsville, SC 29550-0160
(803)383-7000 Fax: (803)383-7731
Officer: Charles W. Coker, CEO. Ultimate
Parent: Sonoco Products. Employee
Count: 15780. Sales: 1947 M.

★ 79505 ★ Sonoco Products Co.
N. 2nd St.
Hartsville, SC 29550
(803)383-7000
Officer: Charles W. Coker, Chairman.
Ultimate Parent: Sonoco Products. SIC:
2426—Hardwood Dimension & Flooring
Mills; 2429—Special Product Sawmills Nec;
2499—Wood Products Nec.

★ 79506 ★ Sonoco Products Co.
Hartsville
North Second St.
Hartsville, SC 29550
Ultimate Parent: Sonoco Products. SIC:
2631—Paperboard Mills; 2655—Fiber Cans,
Drums & Similar Products.

Hilton Head Island

★ 79507 ★ Radio Shack
Heritage Plz.
Hiltn Head is, SC 29928
(803)785-9630
Company Type: Division. Ultimate Parent:
Tandy Corp. SIC: 5731—Radio, Television
& Electronics Stores.

★ 79508 ★ Kentucky Fried
Chicken
Hwy. 278
Hilton Head, SC 29928
(803)785-2373
Ultimate Parent: Pepsico. SIC: 5812—
Eating Places.

★ 79509 ★ Press
130 Mathews Dr.
Hilton Head, SC 29926-3638
(803)681-8560
Officer: Frank J. Bostick. Ultimate Parent:
Banta Corp. SIC: 2752—Commercial
Printing—Lithographic.

★ 79510 ★ Airborne Freight
Corp.
50 Palmetto Bay Rd.
Hilton Head isLand, SC 29928
(803)842-5557
Ultimate Parent: Airborne Freight Corp.
SIC: 4512—Air Transportation—Scheduled.

★ 79511 ★ Anchor Bank
Pope Ave. & New Orleans Rd.
Hilton Head Island, SC 29928
(803)785-4848
Location Type: Branch office. Officer:
Donnie Jo Walden, Banking Officer.
Ultimate Parent: Anchor Bancorp. SIC:
6022—State Commercial Banks.

★ 79512 ★ Anchor Bank
2 Northridge Dr.
Hilton Head Island, SC 29926
(803)785-4848
Location Type: Branch office. Officer: Pat
Ferguson, Banking Officer. Ultimate
Parent: Anchor Bancorp. SIC: 6022—State
Commercial Banks.

★ 79513 ★ Exxon
Forest Beach Shopping Ctr.
Hilton Head Island, SC 29928
(803)785-2750
Ultimate Parent: Exxon. SIC: 5531—
Automobile & Home Supply Stores.

★ 79514 ★ First Union National
Bank of South Carolina
401 William Hilton Pky.
Hilton Head Island, SC 29926
Location Type: Branch office. Ultimate
Parent: First Union Corp. SIC: 6021—
National Commercial Banks.

★ 79515 ★ First Union National
Bank of South Carolina
200 Main St.
Hilton Head Island, SC 29926
Location Type: Branch office. Ultimate
Parent: First Union Corp. SIC: 6021—
National Commercial Banks.

★ 79516 ★ First Union National
Bank of South Carolina
2 Pope Ave.
Hilton Head Island, SC 29938-3304
(803)842-4200
Location Type: Branch office. Ultimate
Parent: First Union Corp. SIC: 6021—
National Commercial Banks.

★ 79517 ★ Hertz Rent-A-Car
6 Graves Rd.
Hilton Head Island, SC 29928
(803)785-3567
Ultimate Parent: Hertz. SIC: 7514—
Passenger Car Rental.

★ 79518 ★ The Limited
Mall at Shelter Cove
Hilton Head Island, SC 29928
(803)785-4216
Ultimate Parent: Limited. SIC: 7514—
Passenger Car Rental.

★ 79519 ★ Pappagallo
3 Heritage Plz.
Hilton Head Island, SC 29928
(803)785-7111
Ultimate Parent: United States Shoe. SIC:
2791—Typesetting.

★ 79520 ★ Pizza Hut
Hwy. 278
Hilton Head Island, SC 29928
(803)785-2230
Ultimate Parent: Pepsico. SIC: 5812—
Eating Places.

★ 79521 ★ Pizza Hut
Palmetto Bay
Hilton Head Island, SC 29928
(803)785-6321
Ultimate Parent: Pepsico. SIC: 5812—
Eating Places.

Holly Hill

★ 79522 ★ Georgia-Pacific Corp.
Holly Hill Fiberboard
Hwy. 453
Holly Hill, SC 29059
Ultimate Parent: Georgia-Pacific. SIC:
2493—Reconstituted Wood Products.

★ 79523 ★ Piggly Wiggly
96 PO Box
Holly Hill, SC 29059
(803)496-3315
Ultimate Parent: Bruno's. SIC: 5411—
Grocery Stores.

Hollywood

★ 79524 ★ First Union National
Bank of South Carolian
6213 US Hwy. 162
Hollywood, SC 29449-5709
(803)727-1000
Location Type: Branch office. Ultimate
Parent: First Union Corp. SIC: 6021—
National Commercial Banks.

★ 79525 ★ Piggly Wiggly
Hollywood, SC 29449
(803)889-2267
Ultimate Parent: Bruno's. SIC: 5411—
Grocery Stores.

Honea Path

★ 79526 ★ Becton Dickinson &
Co.
308 Church St.
Honea Path, SC 29654
Ultimate Parent: Becton Dickinson. SIC:
3069—Fabricated Rubber Products Nec.

★ 79527 ★ Bi-Lo Store
406 E. Greer St.
Honea Path, SC 29654
(803)369-6806
Ultimate Parent: Penn Traffic. SIC: 5411—
Grocery Stores.

★ 79528 ★ Branch Banking &
Trust Co.
21 W. Greer St.
Honea Path, SC 29654-1526
(803)369-0555
Company Type: Subsidiary. Location
Type: Branch office. Officer: J. Terry
Cooley, Manager. Ultimate Parent:
Southern National Corp. SIC: 6021—
National Commercial Banks.

★ 79529 ★ Macy's Hair Design
402 Carolina Ave.
Honea Path, SC 29654-1609
(803)369-1182
Officer: Macy Butler. Ultimate Parent: R.
H. Macy. SIC: 7231—Beauty Shops.

★ 79530 ★ Springs Industrial
Products
Chiquola Ave.
Honea Path, SC
(803)369-7311
Officer: Dwayne Burt, President. Ultimate
Parent: Springs Industries. SIC: 2211—
Broadwoven Fabric Mills—Cotton; 2399—
Fabricated Textile Products Nec.

★ 79531 ★ Torrington Co.
Brick Mill Rd.
Honea Path, SC 29654
Ultimate Parent: Ingersoll-Rand. SIC:
3451—Screw Machine Products; 3714—
Motor Vehicle Parts & Accessories.

★ 79532 ★ Torrington Co. Inc
Hwy. 76
Honea Path, SC 29654
(803)369-7395
Ultimate Parent: Ingersoll-Rand. SIC:
3562—Ball & Roller Bearings.

Inman

★ 79533 ★ Bi-Lo Store
Inman Plz.
Inman, SC 29349
(803)472-2993
Ultimate Parent: Penn Traffic. SIC: 5411—
Grocery Stores.

★ 79534 ★ Hudson International
Conductors
Campton Rd.
Inman, SC 29349
Ultimate Parent: Phelps Dodge. SIC:
3351—Copper Rolling & Drawing.

★ 79535 ★ Pizza Hut
12 Lyman Rd.
Inman, SC 29349
(803)472-6677
Ultimate Parent: Pepsico. SIC: 5812—
Eating Places.

★ 79536 ★ Southern Wood
Piedmont Co.
281 Creosote Rd.
Inman, SC 29349
Ultimate Parent: ITT Rayonier Inc. SIC:
2491—Wood Preserving.

Irmo

★ 79537 ★ Branch Banking &
Trust Co.
7467 Woodrow St.
Irmo, SC 29063
(803)251-3177
Company Type: Subsidiary. Location
Type: Branch office. Ultimate Parent:
Southern National Corp. SIC: 6021—
National Commercial Banks.

★ 79538 ★ Kentucky Fried
Chicken
7467 Saint Andrews Rd.
Irmo, SC 29063
(803)732-1433
Ultimate Parent: Pepsico. SIC: 5812—
Eating Places.

★ 79539 ★ Kroger Sav on Food
and Drug
7467 Woodrow St.
Irmo, SC 29063
(803)732-0423
Ultimate Parent: Kroger. SIC: 5411—
Grocery Stores.

★ 79540 ★ Rite-Aid Pharmacy
7585 Irmo Village Plz.
Irmo, SC 29063
(803)781-4100
Ultimate Parent: Rite Aid. SIC: 5912—Drug
Stores & Proprietary Stores.

Isle of Palms

★ 79541 ★ First Union National
Bank of South Carolina
1401 Palm Blvd.
Isle of Palms, SC 29451-2234
(803)727-1000
Location Type: Branch office. Ultimate
Parent: First Union Corp. SIC: 6021—
National Commercial Banks.

James Island

★ 79542 ★ First Union National Bank of South Carolina
327 Folly Rd.
James Island, SC 29412-2548
(803)724-1000
Location Type: Branch office. Ultimate Parent: First Union Corp. SIC: 6021—National Commercial Banks.

Johns Island

★ 79543 ★ Branch Banking & Trust Co.
1900 Seabrook Island Rd.
Johns Island, SC 29455
(803)768-9244
Company Type: Subsidiary. Location Type: Branch office. Officer: Cyndy Silver, Manager. Ultimate Parent: Southern National Corp. SIC: 6021—National Commercial Banks.

★ 79544 ★ Food Lion
Hwy. 17 S
Johns Island, SC 29455
(803)744-8890
Ultimate Parent: Food Lion. SIC: 5411—Grocery Stores.

Johnston

★ 79545 ★ Federal Paper Board Co.
Hwy. 121 Fruit Hill Rd.
Johnston, SC 29832
(803)275-4669
Officer: R. L. Hare, Manager. Ultimate Parent: Federal Paper Board. SIC: 2411—Logging.

★ 79546 ★ Piggly Wiggly
503 Calhoun St.
Johnston, SC 29832
(803)275-3509
Ultimate Parent: Bruno's. SIC: 5411—Grocery Stores.

Kershaw

★ 79547 ★ Archer Daniels Midland Co.
427 N. Hampton St.
Kershaw, SC 29067-1139
(803)475-3751
Officer: Frank Sherman, Manager. Ultimate Parent: Archer Daniels Midland Co. SIC: 2075—Soybean Oil Mills; 2041—Flour & Other Grain Mill Products.

★ 79548 ★ Springs Industries, Inc.
212 E. 2nd St.
Kershaw, SC 29067
(803)475-0111
Officer: Jimmy D. Collins, Manager. Ultimate Parent: Springs Industries. SIC: 2399—Fabricated Textile Products Nec.

Kinards

★ 79549 ★ Mary Kay Cos
81 PO Box
Kinards, SC 29355
(803)276-1960
Ultimate Parent: Mary Kay Cosmetics.

Kingstree

★ 79550 ★ Baxter Healthcare
Hwy. 52 N
Kingstree, SC 29556
(803)382-2315
Officer: Jerry Turner, Manager. Ultimate Parent: Baxter International. SIC: 3842—Surgical Appliances & Supplies.

★ 79551 ★ Baxter Healthcare Corp.
PO Box 510
Kingstree, SC 29556-0510
(803)382-2315
Officer: Jerry D. Turner. Ultimate Parent: Baxter International. SIC: 3842—Surgical Appliances & Supplies.

★ 79552 ★ Baxter Healthcare Corp.
Hwy. 52 N
Kingstree, SC 29556
Ultimate Parent: Baxter International. SIC: 3069—Fabricated Rubber Products Nec; 3841—Surgical & Medical Instruments.

★ 79553 ★ Colonial Rubber Works Inc.
Eastland Ave. Ext. PO Box 640
Kingstree, SC 29556
Ultimate Parent: M.A.Hanna. SIC: 3050—Hose & Belting & Gaskets & Packing.

★ 79554 ★ Food Lion
522 E. Main St.
Kingstree, SC 29556
(803)354-5561
Ultimate Parent: Food Lion. SIC: 5411—Grocery Stores.

★ 79555 ★ Food Lion Inc.
522 E. Main St.
Kingstree, SC 29556
(803)354-5561
Ultimate Parent: Food Lion. SIC: 5411—Grocery Stores.

★ 79556 ★ Greyhound Bus Lines
215 S. Longstreet St.
Kingstree, SC 29556
(803)354-9491
Ultimate Parent: Greyhound Lines Inc. SIC: 4131—Intercity & Rural Bus Transportation.

★ 79557 ★ Pepsi-Cola Bottling Co.
718 E. Main St.
Kingstree, SC 29556
(803)354-7264
Officer: George Avent, Manager. Ultimate Parent: Pepsico. SIC: 2086—Bottled & Canned Soft Drinks.

★ 79558 ★ Piggly Wiggly
206 E. Main St.
Kingstree, SC 29556
(803)354-9631
Ultimate Parent: Bruno's. SIC: 5411—Grocery Stores.

★ 79559 ★ Ryder Truck Rental
619 N. Longstreet St.
Kingstree, SC 29556
(803)354-9060
Ultimate Parent: Ryder System. SIC: 7513—Truck Rental & Leasing Without Drivers.

Lake City

★ 79560 ★ Coleman Co.
Hwy. 341 E
Lake City, SC 29560
(803)394-8893
Officer: Howard Peterson, Manager. Ultimate Parent: Fleetwood Enterprises, Inc. SIC: 3792—Travel Trailers & Campers; 3999—Manufacturing Industries Nec.

★ 79561 ★ Greyhound Bus Lines
186 Ronnie Mc Neil Blvd.
Lake City, SC 29560
(803)394-5936
Ultimate Parent: Greyhound Lines Inc.

★ 79562 ★ Greyhound Bus Lines
232 S. Ron Mcnair Blvd.
Lake City, SC 29560
(803)394-2441
Ultimate Parent: Greyhound Lines Inc. SIC: 4131—Intercity & Rural Bus Transportation.

★ 79563 ★ Piggly Wiggly
Lake City Plz.
Lake City, SC 29560
(803)394-8516
Ultimate Parent: Bruno's. SIC: 5411—Grocery Stores.

★ 79564 ★ Pizza Hut
125 N. Blvd.
Lake City, SC 29560
(803)394-2716
Ultimate Parent: Pepsico. SIC: 5812—Eating Places.

★ 79565 ★ Wal Mart
Lake City Plz.
Lake City, SC 29560
(803)394-3588
Ultimate Parent: Wal-Mart Stores, Inc. SIC: 5311—Department Stores.

Lancaster

★ 79566 ★ Aeroquip Corp.
200 Aviation Blvd.
Lancaster, SC 29720
Ultimate Parent: Trinova Corp. SIC: 3451—Screw Machine Products; 3728—Aircraft Parts & Equipment Nec.

★ 79567 ★ Bowaters Carolina Federal Credit Union
PO Box 1049
Lancaster, SC 29721-1049
(803)285-2001
Location Type: Branch office. Officer: James Mize. Ultimate Parent: Bowater. SIC: 6061—Federal Credit Unions.

★ 79568 ★ Branch Banking & Trust Co.
100 Hwy. 200 N
Lancaster, SC 29720
(803)285-7936
Company Type: Subsidiary. Location Type: Branch office. Ultimate Parent: Southern National Corp. SIC: 6021—National Commercial Banks.

★ 79569 ★ Branch Banking & Trust Co.
115 W. Arch St.
Lancaster, SC 29720-2461
(803)283-9936
Company Type: Subsidiary. Location Type: Branch office. Ultimate Parent: Southern National Corp. SIC: 6021—National Commercial Banks.

★ 79570 ★ Coca Cola Bottling Co.
Hwy. 521 Byp.
Lancaster, SC 29720
(803)283-3884
Ultimate Parent: Coca-Cola Enterprises. SIC: 5149—Groceries & Related Products Nec.

★ 79571 ★ Duracell USA
1551 Hwy. 8 Bypass
Lancaster, SC 29720
(803)285-8401
Officer: Ed Dickerson, Manager. Ultimate Parent: Duracell International Inc. SIC: 3692—Primary Batteries—Dry & Wet.

★ 79572 ★ Kentucky Fried Chicken
629 State Hwy. 9-521 Bypass E
Lancaster, SC 29720
(803)285-1656
Ultimate Parent: Pepsico. SIC: 5812—Eating Places.

★ 79573 ★ Rexham Corp. Lancaster Plant
Hwy. 9 Bypass
Lancaster, SC 29720
Ultimate Parent: Bowater. SIC: 3081—Unsupported Plastics Film & Sheet; 3083—Laminated Plastics Plate & Sheet.

★ 79574 ★ Rexham Inc. Lancaster Plant
Hwy. 9 Bypass
Lancaster, SC 29720
Ultimate Parent: Bowater. SIC: 3083—Laminated Plastics Plate & Sheet; 3081—Unsupported Plastics Film & Sheet.

★ 79575 ★ Seco Electronic
Rte. 4, Hwy. 29
PO Box 697
Lancaster, SC 29720
(803)286-6927
Company Type: Subsidiary. Officer: Ron Wenzel, President. Ultimate Parent: Dana Corp. SIC: 3568—Power Transmission Equipment Nec.

★ 79576 ★ Springs Industries
111 PO Box
Lancaster, SC 29720
(803)286-2514
Ultimate Parent: Springs Industries. SIC: 2752—Commercial Printing—Lithographic.

★ 79577 ★ Springs Industries Grace Finishing
PO Box 111 Grace Ave.
Lancaster, SC 29720
Ultimate Parent: Springs Industries. SIC: 2262—Finishing Plants—Manmade.

★ 79578 ★ Springs Industries Inc.
111 PO Box
Lancaster, SC 29721
(803)265-5347
Ultimate Parent: Springs Industries. SIC: 5949—Sewing, Needlework & Piece Goods; 7213—Linen Supply.

★ 79579 ★ Springs Industries Marketing Materials
119 Grace Ave.
Lancaster, SC 29720
(803)286-2514
Officer: Wayne Tull, Manager. Ultimate Parent: Springs Industries. SIC: 2752—Commercial Printing—Lithographic.

★ 79580 ★ Texaco Express Lube
1221 State Hwy. 9 Byp W
Lancaster, SC 29720
(803)285-5598
Ultimate Parent: Texaco.

★ 79581 ★ Thomas & Betts Lancaster
Hwy. 521 S. Hwy. 521
Lancaster, SC 29720
Ultimate Parent: Thomas & Betts. SIC: 3441—Fabricated Structural Metal; 3479—Metal Coating & Allied Services.

★ 79582 ★ Wal Mart
1204 State Hwy. 9 Bypass W
Lancaster, SC 29720
(803)286-5445
Ultimate Parent: Wal-Mart Stores, Inc. SIC: 5311—Department Stores.

Landrum

★ 79583 ★ Fieldcrest Cannon Inc.
Landrum Mills
Landrum Mills Rd.
Landrum, SC 29356
Ultimate Parent: Fieldcrest Cannon. SIC: 2273—Carpets & Rugs.

Langley

★ 79584 ★ Air Products & Chemicals Inc.
403 Carline Rd.
Langley, SC 29834
Ultimate Parent: Air Products & Chemicals, Inc. SIC: 2821—Plastics Materials & Resins.

★ 79585 ★ Air Products & Chemicals, Inc.
PO Box 38
Langley, SC 29834-0038
(803)593-4461
Officer: Alvin R. Wiley. Ultimate Parent: Air Products & Chemicals, Inc. SIC: 2821—Plastics Materials & Resins; 2891—Adhesives & Sealants.

Laurens

★ 79586 ★ Ball-Ball InCon Glass
Ball-Incon
1 Catherine St.
Laurens, SC 29360
(803)984-2541 Fax: (803)984-5222
Company Type: Subsidiary. Location Type: Plant. Officer: Harold F. Jones, Personnel Manager. Ultimate Parent: Ball Corp. SIC: 3221—Glass Containers.

★ 79587 ★ Ball-Incon Glass Packaging Corp.
1 Catherine St.
Laurens, SC 29360
Ultimate Parent: Ball Corp. SIC: 3221—Glass Containers.

★ 79588 ★ Ceramx Corp.
Hwy. 14
Laurens, SC 29630-9136
(803)682-3215
Company Type: Subsidiary. Officer: Peter S. Eichler, President. Ultimate Parent: Great American Management & Investment. SIC: 3299—Nonmetallic Mineral Products Nec; 3479—Metal Coating & Allied Services. Employee Count: 370. Sales: 23 M.

★ 79589 ★ Coca Cola Bot Co.
Laurens
Us Hwy. 76
Laurens, SC 29360
(803)984-4111
Ultimate Parent: Coca-Cola Enterprises.
SIC: 2086—Bottled & Canned Soft Drinks.

★ 79590 ★ First Union National
Bank of South Carolina
206 Hillcrest Dr.
Laurens, SC 29360
(803)984-2531
Location Type: Branch office. **Ultimate
Parent:** First Union Corp. **SIC:** 6021—
National Commercial Banks.

★ 79591 ★ Food Lion
320 Hillcrest Dr.
Laurens, SC 29360
(803)984-4502
Ultimate Parent: Food Lion. **SIC:** 5411—
Grocery Stores.

★ 79592 ★ Food Lion Inc.
320 Hillcrest Dr.
Laurens, SC 29360
(803)984-4502
Ultimate Parent: Food Lion. **SIC:** 5411—
Grocery Stores.

★ 79593 ★ General Electric
Ceramics Inc.
PO Box 89, Hwy. 14
Laurens, SC 29360-0089
Ultimate Parent: General Electric. **SIC:**
3264—Porcelain Electrical Supplies.

★ 79594 ★ North Arkansas
Wholesale Co.
2000 PO Box
Laurens, SC 29360
(803)682-1511
Ultimate Parent: Wal-Mart Stores, Inc.

★ 79595 ★ North Arkansas
Wholesale Co.
2000 PO Box
Laurens, SC 29360
(803)682-1511
Ultimate Parent: Wal-Mart Stores, Inc.

★ 79596 ★ Pizza Hut
304 N. Harper St.
Laurens, SC 29360
(803)984-4589
Ultimate Parent: Pepsico. **SIC:** 5812—
Eating Places.

★ 79597 ★ Rite Aid Discount
Phar
Us Hwy. 76
Laurens, SC 29360
(803)984-4579
Ultimate Parent: Rite Aid. **SIC:** 5912—Drug
Stores & Proprietary Stores.

★ 79598 ★ Sight & Sound
Lavonne Shopping Ctr.
Laurens, SC 29360
(803)984-4214
Ultimate Parent: Western Publishing
Group. **SIC:** 7311—Advertising Agencies.

Leeds

★ 79599 ★ Hoechst-Celanese
Corp. Leeds Plant
Leeds Rd. State Rd. 25
Leeds, SC 29031
Ultimate Parent: Hoechst Celanese Corp.
SIC: 2819—Industrial Inorganic Chemicals
Nec.

Lexington

★ 79600 ★ ALLTEL South
Carolina Inc.
106 N. Church St.
PO Box 1048
Lexington, SC 29071
(803)957-2610
Ultimate Parent: ALLTEL Corp. **SIC:**
4812—Radiotelephone Communications.

★ 79601 ★ Bi-Lo Inc.
421 Columbia Ave.
Lexington, SC 29072
(803)359-7775
Ultimate Parent: Penn Traffic. **SIC:** 5411—
Grocery Stores.

★ 79602 ★ Branch Banking &
Trust Co.
605 W. Main St., Kroger Store
Lexington, SC 29072
(803)251-3182
Company Type: Subsidiary. **Location
Type:** Branch office. **Ultimate Parent:**
Southern National Corp. **SIC:** 6021—
National Commercial Banks.

★ 79603 ★ Branch Banking &
Trust Co.
216 E. Main St.
Lexington, SC 29072-3546
(803)251-3160
Company Type: Subsidiary. **Location
Type:** Branch office. **Ultimate Parent:**
Southern National Corp. **SIC:** 6021—
National Commercial Banks.

★ 79604 ★ Giant Food World
Cola Ave.
Lexington, SC 29072
(803)359-4230
Ultimate Parent: Giant Food. **SIC:** 5411—
Grocery Stores.

★ 79605 ★ Kentucky Fried
Chicken
Hwy. 378
Lexington, SC 29072
(803)359-3018
Ultimate Parent: Pepsico. **SIC:** 5812—
Eating Places.

★ 79606 ★ Pizza Hut
514 Columbia Ave.
Lexington, SC 29072
(803)359-2071
Ultimate Parent: Pepsico. **SIC:** 5812—
Eating Places.

★ 79607 ★ Pizza Hut
760 W. Main St.
Lexington, SC 29072
(803)359-1900
Ultimate Parent: Pepsico. **SIC:** 5942—
Book Stores.

★ 79608 ★ Safety Kleen Corp.
Us 1 S
Lexington, SC 29072
(803)356-1250
Ultimate Parent: Safety-Kleen. **SIC:** 2842—
Polishes & Sanitation Goods.

★ 79609 ★ Wal Mart
918 N. Lake Dr.
Lexington, SC 29072
(803)957-4481
Ultimate Parent: Wal-Mart Stores, Inc. **SIC:**
5311—Department Stores.

Liberty

★ 79610 ★ Cooper Industries Inc.
Champion Aviation Products Div.
1230 Old Norris Rd.
Liberty, SC 29657-0686
Company Type: Division. **Ultimate Parent:**
Cooper Industries. **SIC:** 3694—Engine
Electrical Equipment.

★ 79611 ★ Cooper Industries Inc.
Champion Aviation Products Div.
Old Norris Rd.
Liberty, SC 29657
Company Type: Division. **Ultimate Parent:**
Cooper Industries. **SIC:** 3694—Engine
Electrical Equipment.

★ 79612 ★ Vulcan Materials Co.
705 Quarry Rd.
Liberty, SC 29657
(803)843-6335
Officer: Jim Neason, President. **Ultimate
Parent:** Vulcan Materials Co. **SIC:** 3295—
Minerals—Ground or Treated.

Little River

★ 79613 ★ Anchor Bank
Hwy. 17 & Baldwin Ave.
Little River, SC 29566
(803)249-7993
Location Type: Branch office. **Officer:** T.
W. Hill, Vice President. **Ultimate Parent:**
Anchor Bancorp. **SIC:** 6022—State
Commercial Banks.

★ 79614 ★ Branch Banking &
Trust Co.
Hwy. 17 N
Little River, SC 29566
(803)249-5424
Company Type: Subsidiary. **Location
Type:** Branch office. **Officer:** Brad Dawson,
Manager. **Ultimate Parent:** Southern
National Corp. **SIC:** 6021—National
Commercial Banks.

Loris

★ 79615 ★ Branch Banking &
Trust Co.
4207 Main St.
Loris, SC 29569-2611
(803)756-4091
Company Type: Subsidiary. **Location
Type:** Branch office. **Officer:** J. Joe Cox Jr.,
Manager. **Ultimate Parent:** Southern
National Corp. **SIC:** 6021—National
Commercial Banks.

★ 79616 ★ Piggly Wiggly
4307 Broad St.
Loris, SC 29569
(803)357-4556
Ultimate Parent: Bruno's. **SIC:** 5421—Meat
& Fish Markets.

Lugoff

★ 79617 ★ Dana Corp.
Spicer Systems Assembly Div.
1235 Commerce Dr.
Lugoff, SC 29078
Company Type: Division. **Ultimate Parent:**
Dana Corp. **SIC:** 3714—Motor Vehicle Parts
& Accessories.

★ 79618 ★ Exxon
Rr 1
Lugoff, SC 29078
(803)438-3384
Ultimate Parent: Exxon. **SIC:** 5541—
Gasoline Service Stations.

★ 79619 ★ First Union National
Bank of South Carolina
830 US Hwy. 1 S
Lugoff, SC 29078
(803)438-1511
Location Type: Branch office. **Ultimate
Parent:** First Union Corp. **SIC:** 6021—
National Commercial Banks.

★ 79620 ★ Food Lion
RR 1
Lugoff, SC 29078
(803)438-6040
Ultimate Parent: Food Lion. **SIC:** 5411—
Grocery Stores.

★ 79621 ★ Kentucky Fried
Chicken
Hwy. 1
Lugoff, SC 29078
(803)438-1113
Ultimate Parent: Pepsico. **SIC:** 5812—
Eating Places.

★ 79622 ★ Piggly Wiggly
Wateree Plz.
Lugoff, SC 29078
(803)438-3781
Ultimate Parent: Bruno's. **SIC:** 5411—
Grocery Stores.

Lyman

★ 79623 ★ Branch Banking &
Trust Co.
100 Inman Rd.
Lyman, SC 29365-1446
(803)879-7151
Company Type: Subsidiary. **Location
Type:** Branch office. **Ultimate Parent:**
Southern National Corp. **SIC:** 6021—
National Commercial Banks.

★ 79624 ★ Citgo Service Station
Spartanburg Hwy.
Lyman, SC 29365
(803)439-9905
Ultimate Parent: Citgo Petroleum. **SIC:**
5541—Gasoline Service Stations.

★ 79625 ★ Hertz Rent-A-Car
Greenville
Lyman, SC 29365
(803)439-4451
Ultimate Parent: Hertz. **SIC:** 7514—
Passenger Car Rental.

★ 79626 ★ Rite Aid Discount
Pharmacie
204 Spartanburg Hwy.
Lyman, SC 29365
(803)439-3754
Ultimate Parent: Rite Aid. **SIC:** 5912—Drug
Stores & Proprietary Stores.

★ 79627 ★ Springs Industries,
Inc.
Pacific St.
Lyman, SC 29365
(803)433-4494
Officer: Harold Cassidy, Manager. **Ultimate
Parent:** Springs Industries. **SIC:** 2211—
Broadwoven Fabric Mills—Cotton; 2221—
Broadwoven Fabric Mills—Manmade;
2261—Finishing Plants—Cotton.

★ 79628 ★ Springs Industries
Lyman Filter Plant
Pacific St.
Lyman, SC 29365
Ultimate Parent: Springs Industries. **SIC:**
2262—Finishing Plants—Manmade.

Manning

★ 79629 ★ Bi-Lo
601 S. Mill St.
Manning, SC 29102
(803)435-8011
Ultimate Parent: Penn Traffic. **SIC:** 5411—
Grocery Stores.

★ 79630 ★ Federal Mogul Corp.
Manning
Manning, SC 29102
(803)478-2382
Ultimate Parent: Federal-Mogul Corp. **SIC:**
3052—Rubber & Plastics Hose & Belting.

★ 79631 ★ First Union National
Bank of South Carolina
41 Mill St.
Manning, SC 29102-3215
(803)435-8815
Location Type: Branch office. **Ultimate
Parent:** First Union Corp. **SIC:** 6021—
National Commercial Banks.

★ 79632 ★ Food Lion
465 W. Boyce St.
Manning, SC 29102
(803)435-4475
Ultimate Parent: Food Lion. **SIC:** 5411—
Grocery Stores.

★ 79633 ★ Food Lion Inc.
465 W. Boyce St.
Manning, SC 29102
(803)435-4475
Ultimate Parent: Food Lion. **SIC:** 5411—
Grocery Stores.

★ 79634 ★ Kentucky Fried
Chicken
301
Manning, SC 29102
(803)854-2137
Ultimate Parent: Pepsico. **SIC:** 5812—
Eating Places.

★ 79635 ★ Piggly Wiggly
36 Sunset Dr.
Manning, SC 29102
(803)435-2118
Ultimate Parent: Bruno's. **SIC:** 5411—
Grocery Stores.

★ 79636 ★ Trailways Bus Station
Sunset Dr.
Manning, SC 29102
(803)435-4672
Ultimate Parent: Greyhound Lines Inc. **SIC:**
4131—Intercity & Rural Bus Transportation.

Marion

★ 79637 ★ Arvin Industries Inc.
AVM Div.
PO Box 729
Highway 76 E
Marion, SC 29571
(803)464-7823 **Fax:** (803)464-2362
Company Type: Division. **Offcer:** Bruce C. Walters, Vice President & General Manager. **Ultimate Parent:** Arvin Industries Inc.

★ 79638 ★ AVM Inc.
PO Box 729
Marion, SC 29571
(803)464-7823 **Fax:** (803)464-2362
Company Type: Division. **Ultimate Parent:** Arvin Industries Inc. **SIC:** 3714—Motor Vehicle Parts & Accessories.

★ 79639 ★ Avm Inc.
Hwy. 76 E.
Marion, SC 29571
Ultimate Parent: Arvin Industries Inc. **SIC:** 3499—Fabricated Metal Products Nec.

★ 79640 ★ Food Lion
1113 E. Godbold St.
Marion, SC 29571
(803)423-7700
Ultimate Parent: Food Lion. **SIC:** 5411—Grocery Stores.

★ 79641 ★ Pizza Hut
512 S. Main St.
Marion, SC 29571
(803)423-1272
Ultimate Parent: Pepsico. **SIC:** 5812—Eating Places.

★ 79642 ★ Rite Aid Discount Pharmacie
Francis Marion Plz.
Marion, SC 29571
(803)423-1103
Ultimate Parent: Rite Aid. **SIC:** 5912—Drug Stores & Proprietary Stores.

★ 79643 ★ Rite Aid Pharmacy
1450 Latta Hwy. C
Marion, SC 29571
(803)423-9301
Ultimate Parent: Rite Aid. **SIC:** 5912—Drug Stores & Proprietary Stores.

★ 79644 ★ Sara Lee Hosiery
Hwy. 576
Marion, SC 29571
Ultimate Parent: Sara Lee Corp. **SIC:** 2251—Women's Hosiery Except Socks.

★ 79645 ★ Wellman Inc.
Hwy. 41 & 501 Byp
Marion, SC 29571
(803)423-3600
Officer: Dick Broomall, Manager. **Ultimate Parent:** Wellman Inc. **SIC:** 2399—Fabricated Textile Products Nec.

Mauldin

★ 79646 ★ Branch Banking & Trust Co.
110 Main St.
Mauldin, SC 29662-2510
(803)255-7710
Company Type: Subsidiary. **Location Type:** Branch office. **Ultimate Parent:** Southern National Corp. **SIC:** 6021—National Commercial Banks.

★ 79647 ★ Dow Consumer Products Inc.
Hwy. 417
Mauldin, SC 29602
Ultimate Parent: Dow Chemical Co. USA. **SIC:** 2841—Soap & Other Detergents.

★ 79648 ★ Dowbrands
Sc Hwy. 417
Mauldin, SC 29662
Ultimate Parent: Dow Chemical Co. USA. **SIC:** 2842—Polishes & Sanitation Goods.

★ 79649 ★ Dowbrands Inc.
Hwy. 417
Mauldin, SC 29662
Ultimate Parent: Dow Chemical Co. USA. **SIC:** 2841—Soap & Other Detergents.

★ 79650 ★ Dowbrands Lp
Sc Hwy. 417
Mauldin, SC 29662
Ultimate Parent: Dow Chemical Co. USA. **SIC:** 2841—Soap & Other Detergents.

★ 79651 ★ National Cabinet Lock
200 Old Mill Rd.
Mauldin, SC 29662
Ultimate Parent: Valhi Inc. **SIC:** 3429—Hardware Nec.

★ 79652 ★ Pizza Hut
496 N. Main St.
Mauldin, SC 29662
(803)288-1600
Ultimate Parent: Pepsico. **SIC:** 5812—Eating Places.

★ 79653 ★ Radio Shack
Watley Sq.
Mauldin, SC 29662
(803)288-9980
Company Type: Division. **Ultimate Parent:** Tandy Corp. **SIC:** 5065—Electronic Parts & Equipment Nec.

Mc Bee

★ 79654 ★ A. O. Smith Water Prods. Co.
U.S. Hwy. 1 N.
Mc Bee, SC 29101
Ultimate Parent: A. O. Smith. **SIC:** 3639—Household Appliances Nec.

★ 79655 ★ A. O. Smith Water Products Co.
U.S. Hwy. 1 N.
Mc Bee, SC 29101
Ultimate Parent: A. O. Smith. **SIC:** 3639—Household Appliances Nec.

★ 79656 ★ A. O. Smith Water Products Co.
Us Hwy. 1 North
Mc Bee, SC 29101
Ultimate Parent: A. O. Smith. **SIC:** 3639—Household Appliances Nec.

★ 79657 ★ A.O. Smith Water Products Co.
U. S. Hwy. 1, North
Mc Bee, SC 29101
Ultimate Parent: A. O. Smith. **SIC:** 3639—Household Appliances Nec.

Moncks Corner

★ 79658 ★ Bard C R Inc.
Santee Cir.
Moncks Corner, SC 29461
(803)761-8300
Ultimate Parent: C. R. Bard. **SIC:** 2599—Furniture & Fixtures Nec; 5047—Medical & Hospital Equipment.

★ 79659 ★ C. R. Bard Inc.
428 Power House Rd.
Moncks Corner, SC 29461
Ultimate Parent: C. R. Bard. **SIC:** 3841—Surgical & Medical Instruments.

★ 79660 ★ C. R. Bard Inc.
Rte. 5 Santee Circle
Moncks Corner, SC 29461
Ultimate Parent: C. R. Bard. **SIC:** 3841—Surgical & Medical Instruments.

★ 79661 ★ C.R. Bard Inc.
Powerhouse Rd.
Moncks Corner, SC 29461
Ultimate Parent: C. R. Bard. **SIC:** 3841—Surgical & Medical Instruments.

★ 79662 ★ Kentucky Fried Chicken
N Hwy. 52
Moncks Corner, SC 29461
(803)747-2123
Ultimate Parent: Pepsico. **SIC:** 5812—Eating Places.

★ 79663 ★ Kentucky Fried Chicken
Us 52 N
Moncks Corner, SC 29461
(803)761-8682
Ultimate Parent: Pepsico. **SIC:** 5812—Eating Places.

★ 79664 ★ Kmart Store Auto Service
Hwy. 52
Moncks Corner, SC 29461
(803)761-8297
Ultimate Parent: K-Mart. **SIC:** 5311—Department Stores.

★ 79665 ★ Rite Aid Discount Pharmacy
1 Piggly Wiggly Sq.
Moncks Corner, SC 29461
(803)761-5353
Ultimate Parent: Rite Aid. **SIC:** 5912—Drug Stores & Proprietary Stores.

★ 79666 ★ Ryder Truck Rental
Hwy. 52 N
Moncks Corner, SC 29461
(803)761-6211
Ultimate Parent: Ryder System. **SIC:** 7513—Truck Rental & Leasing Without Drivers.

Moore

★ 79667 ★ Monsanto Co.
7601 Hwy. 221 S.
Moore, SC 29369
Ultimate Parent: Monsanto. **SIC:** 3674—Semiconductors & Related Devices.

★ 79668 ★ Monsanto Co.
Hwy. 221
Moore, SC 29369
Ultimate Parent: Monsanto. **SIC:** 3674—Semiconductors & Related Devices.

Mount Pleasant

★ 79669 ★ Branch Banking & Trust Co.
885 Johnnie Dodds Blvd.
Mount Pleasant, SC 29464
(803)745-4120
Company Type: Subsidiary. **Location Type:** Branch office. **Ultimate Parent:** Southern National Corp. **SIC:** 6021—National Commercial Banks.

★ 79670 ★ Branch Banking & Trust Co.
1021 Anna Knapp Blvd.
Mount Pleasant, SC 29464
(803)720-5124
Company Type: Subsidiary. **Location Type:** Branch office. **Officer:** Tad Little, Manager. **Ultimate Parent:** Southern National Corp. **SIC:** 6021—National Commercial Banks.

★ 79671 ★ East Cooper Community Hospital
1200 Johnny Dodd Blvd.
Mount Pleasant, SC 29464
(803)881-0100
Ultimate Parent: American Medical Holdings. **SIC:** 8062—General Medical & Surgical Hospitals.

Mt Pleasant

★ 79672 ★ Bi-Lo
923 Houston M Northcutt Blvd.
Mt Pleasant, SC 29464
(803)881-3454
Ultimate Parent: Penn Traffic. **SIC:** 5411—Grocery Stores.

★ 79673 ★ Fleet Finance Inc.
Patriots Plz.
Mt Pleasant, SC 29464
(803)881-8822
Ultimate Parent: Fleet Financial Group. **SIC:** 6159—Miscellaneous Business Credit Institutions.

★ 79674 ★ Jiffy Lube
1074 Hwy. 17 Bypass
Mt Pleasant, SC 29464
(803)881-0348
Ultimate Parent: Pennzoil. **SIC:** 5172—Petroleum Products Nec.

★ 79675 ★ Nalco Chemical Co.
389 Hwy. 17 Byp
Mt Pleasant, SC 29464
(803)881-0010
Ultimate Parent: Nalco Chemical Co. **SIC:** 2611—Pulp Mills.

★ 79676 ★ Nalco Chemical Co.
389 Us 17 Byp
Mt Pleasant, SC 29464
(803)884-1446
Ultimate Parent: Nalco Chemical Co. **SIC:** 2611—Pulp Mills.

★ 79677 ★ Piggly Wiggly
Sea Shopping Ctr.
Mt Pleasant, SC 29464
(803)884-4489
Ultimate Parent: Bruno's. **SIC:** 5411—Grocery Stores.

★ 79678 ★ Pizza Hut
E Cooper Plz.
Mt Pleasant, SC 29464
(803)884-9500
Ultimate Parent: Pepsico. **SIC:** 5812—Eating Places.

★ 79679 ★ Radio Shack
629 Us 17 B P Mtp
Mt Pleasant, SC 29464
(803)884-2411
Company Type: Division. **Ultimate Parent:** Tandy Corp. **SIC:** 5731—Radio, Television & Electronics Stores.

★ 79680 ★ Rite Aid Discount Pharmacie
Moultrie Shopping Ctr.
Mt Pleasant, SC 29464
(803)884-9191
Ultimate Parent: Rite Aid. **SIC:** 5912—Drug Stores & Proprietary Stores.

★ 79681 ★ Rite-Aid Pharmacy
612 Coleman Blvd.
Mt Pleasant, SC 29464
(803)884-4163
Ultimate Parent: Rite Aid. **SIC:** 5912—Drug Stores & Proprietary Stores.

★ 79682 ★ Taco Bell
821 Coleman Blvd.
Mt Pleasant, SC 29464
(803)884-9968
Ultimate Parent: Pepsico. **SIC:** 5812—Eating Places.

★ 79683 ★ First Union National Bank of South Carolina
516 Coleman Blvd.
Mt. Pleasant, SC 29464-4328
(803)881-7800
Location Type: Branch office. **Ultimate Parent:** First Union Corp. **SIC:** 6021—National Commercial Banks.

★ 79684 ★ First Union National Bank of South Carolina
1501 US 17 N. Bypass
Mt. Pleasant, SC 29464
(803)727-1000
Location Type: Branch office. **Ultimate Parent:** First Union Corp. **SIC:** 6021—National Commercial Banks.

★ 79685 ★ Food Lion
1113 US 17 Bypass
Mt. Pleasant, SC 29464
(803)884-5043
Ultimate Parent: Food Lion. **SIC:** 5411—Grocery Stores.

★ 79686 ★ Piggly Wiggly
661 Hwy. 17 Bypass
Mt. Pleasant, SC 29464
(803)884-5118
Ultimate Parent: Bruno's. **SIC:** 5411—Grocery Stores.

Murrells Inlet

★ 79687 ★ Anchor Bank
3205 S. Hwy. 17
Murrells Inlet, SC 29576
(803)651-6669
Location Type: Branch office. **Officer:** Kay Benton, Vice President. **Ultimate Parent:** Anchor Bancorp. **SIC:** 6022—State Commercial Banks.

★ 79688 ★ Anchor Bank
Hwy. 17 Bus
Murrells Inlet, SC 29576
(803)651-6669
Ultimate Parent: Anchor Bancorp. **SIC:** 6021—National Commercial Banks.

Myrtle Beach

★ **79689** ★ **Anchor Bank**
7901 N. Kings Hwy.
Myrtle Beach, SC 29572-3056
(803)449-6314
Officer: Julien Springs. **Ultimate Parent:** Anchor Bancorp. **SIC:** 6021—National Commercial Banks.

★ **79690** ★ **Anchor Bank**
1205 S. Kings Hwy.
Myrtle Beach, SC 29577-4504
(803)626-9685
Location Type: Branch office. **Officer:** William F. Bellamy, Vice President. **Ultimate Parent:** Anchor Bancorp. **SIC:** 6022—State Commercial Banks.

★ **79691** ★ **Anchor Bank**
2002 Oak St.
PO Box 2428
Myrtle Beach, SC 29578-2428
(803)946-3169
Officer: Stephen L. Chryst, President & CEO. **Ultimate Parent:** Anchor Bancorp. **SIC:** 6022—State Commercial Banks.

★ **79692** ★ **Anchor Bank, Inc.**
300 Hwy. 17 N
Myrtle Beach, SC 29575-6031
(803)238-5691
Officer: William G. Thomas Jr. **Ultimate Parent:** Anchor Bancorp. **SIC:** 6021—National Commercial Banks.

★ **79693** ★ **Branch Banking & Trust Co.**
601 21st Ave. N
Myrtle Beach, SC 29577
(803)626-0030
Company Type: Subsidiary. **Location Type:** Branch office. **Officer:** Ron Paige, Manager. **Ultimate Parent:** Southern National Corp. **SIC:** 6021—National Commercial Banks.

★ **79694** ★ **Business Systems Engineering**
Myrtle Beach, SC 29572
(803)272-2835
Ultimate Parent: Avery Dennison Corp. **SIC:** 7371—Computer Programming Services.

★ **79695** ★ **Circus World Toys**
US 17 Bypass
Myrtle Beach, SC 29577
(803)651-0014
Ultimate Parent: Melville. **SIC:** 5945—Hobby, Toy & Game Shops.

★ **79696** ★ **Coastal Corp.**
3002 N. Ocean Blvd.
Myrtle Beach, SC 29577-3046
(803)448-4541
Officer: Steven C. Chapman, President. **Ultimate Parent:** Coastal Corp. **SIC:** 6512—Nonresidential Building Operators. **Employee Count:** 3. **Sales:** 1 M.

★ **79697** ★ **Coastal Corp.**
3002 N. Ocean Blvd.
Myrtle Beach, SC 29577-3046
(803)448-4541
Officer: Steven C. Chapman, President. **Ultimate Parent:** Coastal Corp. **SIC:** 6512—Nonresidential Building Operators. **Employee Count:** 3. **Sales:** 1000 M.

★ **79698** ★ **First Union National Bank of South Carolina**
2110 Oak St.
Myrtle Beach, SC 29577
(803)448-2688
Location Type: Branch office. **Ultimate Parent:** First Union Corp. **SIC:** 6021—National Commercial Banks.

★ **79699** ★ **Food Lion**
6103 N. Kings Hwy.
Myrtle Beach, SC 29577
(803)449-9681
Ultimate Parent: Food Lion. **SIC:** 5411—Grocery Stores.

★ **79700** ★ **Hertz Rent-A-Car Lcns**
Myrtle Ln.
Myrtle Beach, SC 29572
(803)448-3191
Ultimate Parent: Hertz. **SIC:** 7539—Automotive Repair Shops Nec.

★ **79701** ★ **Kentucky Fried Chicken**
400 S. Kings Hwy.
Myrtle Beach, SC 29577
(803)626-9786
Ultimate Parent: Pepsico. **SIC:** 5812—Eating Places.

★ **79702** ★ **Kentucky Fried Chicken**
505 Us 17 N
Myrtle Beach, SC 29575
(803)293-5710
Ultimate Parent: Pepsico. **SIC:** 5812—Eating Places.

★ **79703** ★ **Kroger Sav-On**
9600 Us 17 a N
Myrtle Beach, SC 29577
(803)449-9671
Ultimate Parent: Kroger. **SIC:** 5411—Grocery Stores.

★ **79704** ★ **Kroger Sav-On Food & Drugs**
5900 Us 17 S
Myrtle Beach, SC 29577
(803)238-1423
Ultimate Parent: Kroger. **SIC:** 5411—Grocery Stores.

★ **79705** ★ **Lane Bryant**
10177 N. Kings Hwy.
Myrtle Beach, SC 29572
(803)272-4000
Ultimate Parent: Limited. **SIC:** 5651—Family Clothing Stores.

★ **79706** ★ **Mutual of New York**
710 21st Ave. N
Myrtle Beach, SC 29577
(803)626-5560
Ultimate Parent: Mutual of New York. **SIC:** 6411—Insurance Agents, Brokers & Service.

★ **79707** ★ **Piggly Wiggly**
Rr 5
Myrtle Beach, SC 29577
(803)293-7755
Ultimate Parent: Bruno's. **SIC:** 5421—Meat & Fish Markets.

★ **79708** ★ **Piggly Wiggly**
1100 Pine Dr.
Myrtle Beach, SC 29577
(803)448-3537
Ultimate Parent: Bruno's. **SIC:** 5411—Grocery Stores.

★ **79709** ★ **Pizza Hut**
3001 N. Kings Hwy. 2
Myrtle Beach, SC 29577
(803)448-3445
Ultimate Parent: Pepsico. **SIC:** 5812—Eating Places.

★ **79710** ★ **Radio Shack**
2500 N. Kings Hwy.
Myrtle Beach, SC 29577
(803)448-4717
Company Type: Division. **Ultimate Parent:** Tandy Corp. **SIC:** 5065—Electronic Parts & Equipment Nec.

★ **79711** ★ **Radio Shack**
10177 N. Kings Hwy.
Myrtle Beach, SC 29572
(803)272-4101
Company Type: Division. **Ultimate Parent:** Tandy Corp. **SIC:** 5731—Radio, Television & Electronics Stores.

★ **79712** ★ **Radio Shack**
Us Hwy. 17 by Pass
Myrtle Beach, SC 29577
(803)651-7098
Company Type: Division. **Ultimate Parent:** Tandy Corp. **SIC:** 5719—Miscellaneous Home Furnishings Stores.

★ **79713** ★ **Ryder Truck Rental**
2114 Hwy. 501
Myrtle Beach, SC 29577
(803)448-3696
Ultimate Parent: Ryder System. **SIC:** 7513—Truck Rental & Leasing Without Drivers.

★ **79714** ★ **Taco Bell**
10177 N. Kings Hwy.
Myrtle Beach, SC 29572
(803)272-1213
Ultimate Parent: Pepsico. **SIC:** 5812—Eating Places.

★ **79715** ★ **Taco Bell**
1012 Us 17 N
Myrtle Beach, SC 29575
(803)238-3546
Ultimate Parent: Pepsico. **SIC:** 5812—Eating Places.

★ **79716** ★ **Wal Mart**
7601 N. Kings Hwy.
Myrtle Beach, SC 29572
(803)449-9828
Ultimate Parent: Wal-Mart Stores, Inc.

★ **79717** ★ **Waldenbooks**
10177 N. Kings Hwy.
Myrtle Beach, SC 29572
(803)272-8137
Ultimate Parent: K-Mart. **SIC:** 5942—Book Stores.

★ **79718** ★ **Waldenbooks**
20 Myrtle Sq.
Myrtle Beach, SC 29575
(803)448-4534
Ultimate Parent: K-Mart. **SIC:** 5942—Book Stores.

N Myrtle Beach

★ **79719** ★ **Emery Worldwide**
N Myrtle Beach, SC 29582
(803)272-7032
Ultimate Parent: Consolidated Freightways. **SIC:** 4512—Air Transportation—Scheduled.

★ **79720** ★ **Piggly Wiggly**
1619 Hwy. 17 S
N Myrtle Beach, SC 29582
(803)272-6320
Ultimate Parent: Bruno's. **SIC:** 5411—Grocery Stores.

N. Charleston

★ **79721** ★ **Texaco Ref. & Mktg. Inc.**
4950 Virginia Ave.
N. Charleston, SC 29406
Ultimate Parent: Texaco. **SIC:** 2992—Lubricating Oils & Greases.

Newberry

★ **79722** ★ **Branch Banking & Trust Co.**
1117 Boyce St.
Newberry, SC 29108-2703
(803)276-5660
Company Type: Subsidiary. **Location Type:** Branch office. **Ultimate Parent:** Southern National Corp. **SIC:** 6021—National Commercial Banks.

★ **79723** ★ **Branch Banking & Trust Co.**
1804 Wilson Rd.
Newberry, SC 29108-2922
(803)276-8490
Company Type: Subsidiary. **Location Type:** Branch office. **Ultimate Parent:** Southern National Corp. **SIC:** 6021—National Commercial Banks.

★ **79724** ★ **Champion International Corp.**
1515 Kendall Rd.
Newberry, SC 29108
(803)276-7282
Ultimate Parent: Champion International. **SIC:** 0831—Forest Products.

★ **79725** ★ **Federal Paper Board Co.**
3287 College St.
Newberry, SC 29108
(803)276-4311
Officer: Mac Brown, Manager. **Ultimate Parent:** Federal Paper Board. **SIC:** 2421—Sawmills & Planing Mills—General; 2499—Wood Products Nec.

★ **79726** ★ **Federal Paper Board Co. Inc.**
3287 College St.
Newberry, SC 29108
(803)276-4311
Ultimate Parent: Federal Paper Board. **SIC:** 5211—Lumber & Other Building Materials; 5211—Lumber & Other Building Materials.

★ **79727** ★ **Louis Rich Co.**
Louis Rich Dr.
Newberry, SC 29108
Ultimate Parent: Philip Morris. **SIC:** 2015—Poultry Slaughtering & Processing.

★ **79728** ★ **Wal Mart**
1910 Wilson Rd.
Newberry, SC 29108
(803)276-4411
Ultimate Parent: Wal-Mart Stores, Inc. **SIC:** 5311—Department Stores.

★ **79729** ★ **Wal Mart**
Newberry Shopping Ctr.
Newberry, SC 29108
(803)276-6020
Ultimate Parent: Wal-Mart Stores, Inc. **SIC:** 5311—Department Stores.

Ninety Six

★ **79730** ★ **Rite Aid Discount Phrmcy**
N Cambridge
Ninety Six, SC 29666
(803)543-9931
Ultimate Parent: Rite Aid. **SIC:** 5912—Drug Stores & Proprietary Stores.

North Augusta

★ **79731** ★ **Bi-Lo**
109 Edgefield Rd.
North Augusta, SC 29841
(803)279-1190
Ultimate Parent: Penn Traffic. **SIC:** 5411—Grocery Stores.

★ **79732** ★ **Food Lion**
1743 Georgia Ave.
North Augusta, SC 29841
(803)278-2721
Ultimate Parent: Food Lion. **SIC:** 5411—Grocery Stores.

★ **79733** ★ **Kentucky Fried Chicken**
433 E. Martintown Rd.
North Augusta, SC 29841
(803)279-4580
Ultimate Parent: Pepsico. **SIC:** 5812—Eating Places.

★ **79734** ★ **Kroger Co**
1125 Knox Ave.
North Augusta, SC 29841
(803)279-3375
Ultimate Parent: Kroger. **SIC:** 5411—Grocery Stores.

★ **79735** ★ **Kroger Food Store**
406 E. Martintown Rd.
North Augusta, SC 29841
(803)278-4363
Ultimate Parent: Kroger. **SIC:** 5411—Grocery Stores.

★ **79736** ★ **Piggly Wiggly**
211 Edgefield Rd.
North Augusta, SC 29841
(803)278-3722
Ultimate Parent: Bruno's. **SIC:** 5411—Grocery Stores.

★ **79737** ★ **Pizza Hut**
616 E. Martintown Rd.
North Augusta, SC 29841
(803)278-1856
Ultimate Parent: Pepsico. **SIC:** 5812—Eating Places.

★ **79738** ★ **Pizza Hut**
1812 Georgia Ave.
North Augusta, SC 29841
(803)278-4313
Ultimate Parent: Pepsico. **SIC:** 5812—Eating Places.

★ **79739** ★ **Radio Shack**
207 Edgefield Rd.
North Augusta, SC 29841
(803)278-1670
Company Type: Division. **Ultimate Parent:** Tandy Corp. **SIC:** 7373—Computer Integrated Systems Design.

★ **79740** ★ **Texaco Food Mart**
226 Georgia Ave.
North Augusta, SC 29841
(803)278-5106
Ultimate Parent: Texaco. **SIC:** 5411—Grocery Stores.

★ 79741 ★   Trailer Train Co.
Hamburg Di
1 Hamburg Rd.
North Augusta, SC 29841
(803)279-1922
Ultimate Parent: Conrail, Inc. SIC: 5088—
Transportation Equipment & Supplies.

★ 79742 ★   World Book, Inc.
802 E. Martintown Rd.
North Augusta, SC 29841
(803)279-2042
Ultimate Parent: Berkshire Hathaway. SIC:
5942—Book Stores.

North Charleston

★ 79743 ★   ABF Freight System
Inc.
4151 Azalea Dr.
North Charleston, SC 29405-7405
(803)554-6071
Location Type: Branch office. Officer:
Vernon Ward. Ultimate Parent: Arkansas
Best. SIC: 4212—Local Trucking Without
Storage; 4213—Trucking Except Local.

★ 79744 ★   Ball Corp.
1258 Remount Rd.
North Charleston, SC 29406
(803)554-1596
Ultimate Parent: Ball Corp. SIC: 6062—
State Credit Unions; 1742—Plastering,
Drywall & Insulation.

★ 79745 ★   Branch Banking &
Trust Co.
5010 Dorchester Rd. & Montague Rd.
North Charleston, SC 29418-5603
(803)745-4115
Company Type: Subsidiary. Location
Type: Branch office. Ultimate Parent:
Southern National Corp. SIC: 6021—
National Commercial Banks.

★ 79746 ★   Branch Banking &
Trust Co.
4975 LaCross Rd., Ste. 110
North Charleston, SC 29418-6524
(803)745-4100
Company Type: Subsidiary. Location
Type: Branch office. Ultimate Parent:
Southern National Corp. SIC: 6021—
National Commercial Banks.

★ 79747 ★   Branch Banking &
Trust Co.
2150 Northwoods Blvd., Unit A-1000
North Charleston, SC 29418-4021
(803)745-4135
Company Type: Subsidiary. Location
Type: Branch office. Ultimate Parent:
Southern National Corp. SIC: 6021—
National Commercial Banks.

★ 79748 ★   Branch Banking &
Trust Co.
5950 Rivers Ave.
North Charleston, SC 29418-6017
(803)720-5190
Company Type: Subsidiary. Location
Type: Branch office. Officer: Gene Goode,
Manager. Ultimate Parent: Southern
National Corp. SIC: 6021—National
Commercial Banks.

★ 79749 ★   First Union National
Bank of South Carolina
7804 Rivers Ave.
North Charleston, SC 29418
(803)727-1000
Location Type: Branch office. Ultimate
Parent: First Union Corp. SIC: 6021—
National Commercial Banks.

★ 79750 ★   Texaco Lubricants
Co.
4950 Virginia Ave.
North Charleston, SC 29406
Ultimate Parent: Texaco. SIC: 2992—
Lubricating Oils & Greases.

★ 79751 ★   Texaco Ref. & Mktg.
Ing
4950 Virginia Ave.
North Charleston, SC 29406
Ultimate Parent: Texaco. SIC: 2992—
Lubricating Oils & Greases.

★ 79752 ★   Texaco Refining &
Marketing
Texaco Lubricants Division
4950 Virginia Ave.
North Charleston, SC 29406-5226
Ultimate Parent: Texaco. SIC: 2992—
Lubricating Oils & Greases.

★ 79753 ★   Westvaco Corp.
Charleston Chemical
5600 Virginia Ave.
North Charleston, SC 29406
Location Type: Plant. Ultimate Parent:
WestVaco Corp. SIC: 2861—Gum & Wood
Chemicals.

★ 79754 ★   Westvaco Corp.
Chemical Div.
Virginia Ave.
North Charleston, SC 29406
(803)740-2300
Company Type: Division. Officer: William
Major, Manager. Ultimate Parent:
WestVaco Corp. SIC: 2899—Chemical
Preparations Nec.

★ 79755 ★   WestVaco Corp.
Kraft Div.
5600 Virginia Ave.
North Charleston, SC 29406
(803)745-3000
Company Type: Division. Officer: Brantley
Thomas Jr., Manager. Ultimate Parent:
WestVaco Corp. SIC: 2621—Paper Mills;
2631—Paperboard Mills; 2821—Plastics
Materials & Resins.

★ 79756 ★   Westvaco Corp.
Kraft Div.
5600 Virginia Ave.
North Charleston, SC 29406
(803)745-3000
Company Type: Division. Ultimate Parent:
WestVaco Corp. SIC: 2611—Pulp Mills;
2621—Paper Mills; 2631—Paperboard Mills.

★ 79757 ★   Westvaco Corp.
Polychemicals
5600 Virginia Ave.
North Charleston, SC 29406
Ultimate Parent: WestVaco Corp. SIC:
2861—Gum & Wood Chemicals.

★ 79758 ★   Westvaco Corp.
Polychemicals
5600 Virginia Ave.
North Charleston, SC 29406
Ultimate Parent: WestVaco Corp. SIC:
2861—Gum & Wood Chemicals.

★ 79759 ★   Woodtek/Textone
1770 Hock Ave.
North Charleston, SC 29405
Ultimate Parent: Nortek. SIC: 2499—Wood
Products Nec.

North Myrtle Beach

★ 79760 ★   Anchor Bank
1201 Sea Mountain Hwy.
North Myrtle Beach, SC 29582-2213
(803)249-8484
Location Type: Branch office. Officer:
Wayne Wicker, Assistant Vice President.
Ultimate Parent: Anchor Bancorp. SIC:
6022—State Commercial Banks.

★ 79761 ★   Branch Banking &
Trust Co.
601 Hwy. 17 S
North Myrtle Beach, SC 29582-3337
(803)272-1380
Company Type: Subsidiary. Location
Type: Branch office. Ultimate Parent:
Southern National Corp. SIC: 6021—
National Commercial Banks.

★ 79762 ★   Kentucky Fried
Chicken
4100 Hwy. 17 S
North Myrtle Beach, SC 29582
(803)272-6325
Ultimate Parent: Pepsico. SIC: 5812—
Eating Places.

★ 79763 ★   Mary Kay Cosmetics
298 25th Ave. N
North Myrtle Beach, SC 29582
(803)249-5151
Ultimate Parent: Mary Kay Cosmetics.

★ 79764 ★   Sparkletts Water Sys.
Aqua Vend
2908 Airport Rd.
North Myrtle Beach, SC 29582
Ultimate Parent: McKesson. SIC: 7389—
Business Services Nec.

★ 79765 ★   Sparkletts Water
Systems Aquavend
2908 Airport Blvd.
North Myrtle Beach, SC 29582
Ultimate Parent: McKesson. SIC: 7389—
Business Services Nec.

Orangeburg

★ 79766 ★   Allied-Signal
Aerospace Co.
3737 Industrial Blvd.
Orangeburg, SC 29115
(803)533-1500
Officer: Keith Guthrie, Manager. Ultimate
Parent: Allied-Signal Inc. SIC: 3663—Radio
& T.V. Communications Equipment; 3669—
Communications Equipment Nec.

★ 79767 ★   Allied-Signal Inc.
Bendix Electric Power
3737 Industrial Blvd.
Orangeburg, SC 29116
Ultimate Parent: Allied-Signal Inc. SIC:
3699—Electrical Equipment & Supplies Nec.

★ 79768 ★   Branch Banking &
Trust
500 Bennett Ave.
Orangeburg, SC 29115-4296
(803)534-5143
Company Type: Subsidiary. Location
Type: Branch office. Ultimate Parent:
Southern National Corp. SIC: 6021—
National Commercial Banks.

★ 79769 ★   Branch Banking &
Trust Co.
520 Russell St. SE
Orangeburg, SC 29115-6048
(803)534-3311
Company Type: Subsidiary. Location
Type: Branch office. Ultimate Parent:
Southern National Corp. SIC: 6021—
National Commercial Banks.

★ 79770 ★   Central Soya Feed
Co. Inc.
1090 J.C. Calhoun Dr.
Orangeburg, SC 29115
Ultimate Parent: Central Soya. SIC:
2048—Prepared Feeds Nec.

★ 79771 ★   Ethyl Corp.
Cannon Bridge Rd.
Orangeburg, SC 29115
(803)534-5781
Officer: Tommy Simpson, Manager.
Ultimate Parent: Ethyl. SIC: 2869—
Industrial Organic Chemicals Nec; 2834—
Pharmaceutical Preparations.

★ 79772 ★   First Union National
Bank of South Carolina
K-Mart Shopping Ctr.
2090 Columbia Rd. NE
Orangeburg, SC 29115
Location Type: Branch office. Ultimate
Parent: First Union Corp. SIC: 6021—
National Commercial Banks.

★ 79773 ★   First Union National
Bank of South Carolina
100 Russell St. NW
Orangeburg, SC 29115-5989
(803)533-4400
Location Type: Branch office. Ultimate
Parent: First Union Corp. SIC: 6021—
National Commercial Banks.

★ 79774 ★   Food Lion
I Chestnut St.
Orangeburg, SC 29115
(803)531-3159
Ultimate Parent: Food Lion. SIC: 5411—
Grocery Stores.

★ 79775 ★   Kentucky Fried
Chicken
1590 Chestnut St. NE
Orangeburg, SC 29115
(803)534-9889
Ultimate Parent: Pepsico. SIC: 5812—
Eating Places.

★ 79776 ★   Piggly Wiggly
645 Russell St. NE
Orangeburg, SC 29115
(803)534-7708
Ultimate Parent: Bruno's. SIC: 5411—
Grocery Stores.

★ 79777 ★   Radio Shack
2 Prince of Orange M
Orangeburg, SC 29115
(803)531-1905
Company Type: Division. Ultimate Parent:
Tandy Corp. SIC: 5063—Electrical
Apparatus & Equipment.

★ 79778 ★   Stone Container Corp.
1 Mixon Mill Rd.
Orangeburg, SC 29115
(803)534-4420
Officer: Tommy Bedenbaugh, Manager.
Ultimate Parent: Stone Container Corp.
SIC: 2421—Sawmills & Planing Mills—
General; 2499—Wood Products Nec;
2611—Pulp Mills.

★ 79779 ★   Wal Mart
30 Prince of Orange Mall
Orangeburg, SC 29115
(803)539-4164
Ultimate Parent: Wal-Mart Stores, Inc. SIC:
5311—Department Stores.

Pacolet

★ 79780 ★   Pacolet Industrial
Supply Co.
Old Quarry Rd.
Pacolet, SC 29372
(803)474-2201
Ultimate Parent: Vulcan Materials Co. SIC:
3519—Internal Combustion Engines Nec.

★ 79781 ★   Vulcan Materials Co.
130 Vulcan Rd.
Pacolet, SC 29372
(803)474-2231
Officer: James E. Neason, President.
Ultimate Parent: Vulcan Materials Co. SIC:
3295—Minerals—Ground or Treated.

★ 79782 ★   Vulcan Materials Co.
390 Vulcan Rd.
Pacolet, SC 29372
(803)474-3191
Officer: H. O. Kirby, Manager. Ultimate
Parent: Vulcan Materials Co. SIC: 3281—
Cut Stone & Stone Products.

Pageland

★ 79783 ★   Challenger Electrical
Equipment Corp.
Hwy. 151 South, PO Box 38
Pageland, SC 29728
Ultimate Parent: Westinghouse Electric
Corp. SIC: 3643—Current-Carrying Wiring
Devices.

★ 79784 ★   Challenger Electrical
Equipment Inc.
Hwy. 151 Business S.
Pageland, SC 29728
Ultimate Parent: Westinghouse Electric
Corp. SIC: 3643—Current-Carrying Wiring
Devices.

Pamplico

★ 79785 ★   Delta Mills Marketing
1828 Old River Dr.
Pamplico, SC 29583
(803)493-2114
Officer: William a. Prosser, Manager.
Ultimate Parent: Delta Woodside
Industries. SIC: 2399—Fabricated Textile
Products Nec.

Pelzer

★ 79786 ★   Bi-Lo Incorporation
Hwy. 20
Pelzer, SC 29669
(803)947-6851
Ultimate Parent: Penn Traffic. SIC: 5411—
Grocery Stores.

Pendleton

★ 79787 ★   Allied-Signal
Laminate Systems
Micarta
500 Westinghouse Dr.
Pendleton, SC 29670
Ultimate Parent: Allied-Signal Inc. SIC:
3679—Electronic Components Nec.

★ 79788 ★   Westinghouse
Electric Corp.
Copper Laminates
116 Westingouse Dr.
Pendleton, SC 29670
Ultimate Parent: Westinghouse Electric
Corp. SIC: 3629—Electrical Industrial
Apparatus Nec.

★ 79789 ★   Westinghouse
Electric Corp.
Micarta Div.
116 Westinghouse Dr.
Pendleton, SC 29670
Company Type: Division. Ultimate Parent:
Westinghouse Electric Corp. SIC: 3000—
Rubber & Miscellaneous Plastics Products.

Pickens

★ 79790 ★   Magnetek/Century
Electric
211 Pendleton St.
Pickens, SC 29671-2458
(803)878-6560
Ultimate Parent: Magnetek Inc. SIC:
5063—Electrical Apparatus & Equipment.

★ 79791 ★   McDonalds
Hampton St.
Pickens, SC 29671
(803)878-4325
Ultimate Parent: McDonald's.
SIC: 5812—Eating Places.

Piedmont

★ 79792 ★   Air Products &
Chemicals, Inc.
409 Old Pelzer Rd.
Piedmont, SC 29673-8878
(803)845-3158
Location Type: Branch office. Officer:
Steven A. Pekarsky. Ultimate Parent: Air
Products & Chemicals, Inc. SIC: 2821—
Plastics Materials & Resins; 2843—Surface
Active Agents.

★ 79793 ★   Branch Banking &
Trust Co.
Hwy. 86, Piedmont Ctr.
Piedmont, SC 29673
(803)845-6987
Company Type: Subsidiary. Location
Type: Branch office. Officer: Larry A.
Dellinger, Manager. Ultimate Parent:
Southern National Corp. SIC: 6021—
National Commercial Banks.

★ 79794 ★   Delta Mills Marketing
750 Estes Dr.
Piedmont, SC 29673
(803)845-3341
Officer: David Sloan, Manager. Ultimate
Parent: Delta Woodside Industries. SIC:
2211—Broadwoven Fabric Mills—Cotton;
2399—Fabricated Textile Products Nec.

★ 79795 ★   Delta Woodside Estes
Plant
750 Estes Rd.
Piedmont, SC 29673
Ultimate Parent: Delta Woodside
Industries. SIC: 2211—Broadwoven Fabric
Mills—Cotton.

★ 79796 ★   Radio Shack
Anderson St.
Piedmont, SC 29673
(803)845-5264
Company Type: Division. Ultimate Parent:
Tandy Corp. SIC: 5734—Computer &
Software Stores.

★ 79797 ★   Rite Aid Discount
Pharmacy
Hwy. 86
Piedmont, SC 29673
(803)845-6931
Ultimate Parent: Rite Aid. SIC: 5912—Drug
Stores & Proprietary Stores.

★ 79798 ★   Vulcan Materials Co.
202 Brown Rd.
Piedmont, SC 29673
(803)277-1250
Officer: Jim Neason, President. Ultimate
Parent: Vulcan Materials Co. SIC: 3295—
Minerals—Ground or Treated.

Pontiac

★ 79799 ★   Sabre Textron
I-20 & State Rd. 53
Pontiac, SC 29045-4000
Ultimate Parent: Textron. SIC: 3425—Saw
Blades & Handsaws.

Prosperity

★ 79800 ★   Federal Paper Board
Co.
Hwy. 773
Prosperity, SC 29127
(803)364-7100
Ultimate Parent: Federal Paper Board.
SIC: 2679—Converted Paper Products Nec.

★ 79801 ★   Federal Paper Board
Co.
Hwy. 773
Prosperity, SC 29127
(803)364-7100
Officer: John Richardson, Manager.
Ultimate Parent: Federal Paper Board.
SIC: 2611—Pulp Mills.

★ 79802 ★   First Union National
Bank of South Carolina
147 Main St.
Prosperity, SC 29127
(803)364-3800
Location Type: Branch office. Ultimate
Parent: First Union Corp. SIC: 6021—
National Commercial Banks.

★ 79803 ★   Georgia-Pacific Corp.
Prosperity Pine Plywood
Hwy. 26
Prosperity, SC 29127
Ultimate Parent: Georgia-Pacific. SIC:
2436—Softwood Veneer & Plywood.

★ 79804 ★   Georgia-Pacific Corp.
Prosperity Plywood
Hwy. 26
Prosperity, SC 29127
Ultimate Parent: Georgia-Pacific. SIC:
2436—Softwood Veneer & Plywood.

★ 79805 ★   Kayser-Roth Corp.
Hwy. 76
Prosperity, SC 29127
Ultimate Parent: Collins & Aikman Group.
SIC: 2251—Women's Hosiery Except
Socks.

★ 79806 ★   Piggly Wiggly
128 Broad St.
Prosperity, SC 29127
(803)364-2307
Ultimate Parent: Bruno's. SIC: 5411—
Grocery Stores.

Ravenel

★ 79807 ★   Westvaco Corp.
Research
Old Jacksonboro Rd.
Ravenel, SC 29470
(803)889-3774
Location Type: Plant. Officer: Dave
Gerwig, Plant Manager. Ultimate Parent:
WestVaco Corp. SIC: 2611—Pulp Mills;
2679—Converted Paper Products Nec.

Richburg

★ 79808 ★   Teledyne Allvac/
Vasco
Hwy. 9
Richburg, SC 29729
Ultimate Parent: Teledyne. SIC: 3356—
Nonferrous Rolling & Drawing Nec; 3312—
Blast Furnaces & Steel Mills.

Ridgeland

★ 79809 ★   Piggly Wiggly
113 N. Jacob Smart Blvd.
Ridgeland, SC 29936
(803)726-8626
Ultimate Parent: Bruno's. SIC: 5411—
Grocery Stores.

Rock Hill

★ 79810 ★   Ace Hardware at
Newport
4800 Old York Rd.
Rock Hill, SC 29732
(803)324-2230
Ultimate Parent: Ace Hardware. SIC:
5191—Farm Supplies.

★ 79811 ★   BASF Structural
Materials
800 Celriver Rd.
Rock Hill, SC 29730
(803)329-4191
Officer: Bob Murphy, Manager. Ultimate
Parent: BASF Corp. SIC: 2655—Fiber
Cans, Drums & Similar Products; 2869—
Industrial Organic Chemicals Nec.

★ 79812 ★   BASF Structural
Materials Inc.
800 Celriver Rd.
Rock Hill, SC 29730-7420
(803)329-8000
Officer: James H. Pepper. Ultimate
Parent: BASF Corp. SIC: 3624—Carbon &
Graphite Products.

★ 79813 ★   BASF Structural
Materials Inc.
Celion Carbon Fibers
800 Celriver Rd.
Rock Hill, SC 29730
Ultimate Parent: BASF Corp. SIC: 2824—
Organic Fibers—Noncellulosic.

★ 79814 ★   BFI Waste Systems
1667 Trimnal Ln.
Rock Hill, SC 29730-8968
(803)329-3475
Location Type: Branch office. Ultimate
Parent: Browning-Ferris Industries. SIC:
4953—Refuse Systems.

★ 79815 ★   Bi-Lo Supermarket No
225
2375 N. Cherry Rd.
Rock Hill, SC 29732
(803)366-8127
Ultimate Parent: Penn Traffic. SIC: 5411—
Grocery Stores.

★ 79816 ★   Branch Banking &
Trust Co.
245 S. Herlong Ave.
Rock Hill, SC 29732
(803)366-7109
Company Type: Subsidiary. Location
Type: Branch office. Ultimate Parent:
Southern National Corp. SIC: 6021—
National Commercial Banks.

★ 79817 ★   Branch Banking &
Trust Co.
2374 N. Cherry Rd.
Rock Hill, SC 29732-2165
(803)366-3193
Company Type: Subsidiary. Location
Type: Branch office. Ultimate Parent:
Southern National Corp. SIC: 6021—
National Commercial Banks.

★ 79818 ★   Coast to Coast
Fort Mill Sq.
Rock Hill, SC 29730
(803)548-2230
Ultimate Parent: Servistar Corp. SIC:
5251—Hardware Stores.

★ 79819 ★   Exxon Car Wash
1001 W. Oakland Ave.
Rock Hill, SC 29732
(803)328-2031
Ultimate Parent: Exxon. SIC: 7542—Car
Washes.

★ 79820 ★   First Union National
Bank of South Carolina
119 Herlong Ave.
Rock Hill, SC 29732-1918
(803)366-4660
Location Type: Branch office. Ultimate
Parent: First Union Corp. SIC: 6021—
National Commercial Banks.

★ 79821 ★   First Union National
Bank of South Carolina
2043 Cherry Rd.
Rock Hill, SC 29730-2626
(803)328-6181
Location Type: Branch office. Ultimate
Parent: First Union Corp. SIC: 6021—
National Commercial Banks.

★ 79822 ★   First Union National
Bank of South Carolina
802 Cherry Rd.
Rock Hill, SC 29730-3124
(803)327-7767
Location Type: Branch office. Ultimate
Parent: First Union Corp. SIC: 6021—
National Commercial Banks.

★ 79823 ★   First Union National
Bank of South Carolina
315 E. Main St.
Rock Hill, SC 29730-5318
(803)328-6181
Location Type: Branch office. Ultimate
Parent: First Union Corp. SIC: 6021—
National Commercial Banks.

★ 79824 ★   Food Lion
2538 W. Main St.
Rock Hill, SC 29732
(803)327-2770
Ultimate Parent: Food Lion. SIC: 5411—
Grocery Stores.

★ 79825 ★   Food Lion
2685 Calanese Rd.
Rock Hill, SC 29730
(803)366-8125
Ultimate Parent: Food Lion. SIC: 5411—
Grocery Stores.

★ 79826 ★   Food Lion
1260 E. Main St.
Rock Hill, SC 29730
(803)324-7504
Ultimate Parent: Food Lion. SIC: 5411—
Grocery Stores.

★ 79827 ★   Greyhound Bus Lines
1821 Hwy. 21 S
Rock Hill, SC 29730
(803)327-9388
Ultimate Parent: Greyhound Lines Inc. SIC:
4111—Local & Suburban Transit; 4131—
Intercity & Rural Bus Transportation.

★ 79828 ★   Hoechst Celanese
Celriver Plant
2850 Cherry Rd.
Rock Hill, SC 29730
Ultimate Parent: Hoechst Celanese Corp.
SIC: 2823—Cellulosic Manmade Fibers.

★ 79829 ★   Hoechst-Celanese
Corp. Celriver Plant
2850 Cherry Rd.
Rock Hill, SC 29730
Ultimate Parent: Hoechst Celanese Corp.
SIC: 2823—Cellulosic Manmade Fibers;
2869—Industrial Organic Chemicals Nec;
2824—Organic Fibers—Noncellulosic.

★ 79830 ★   Ivax Industries Inc.
Textile Products
1880 Langston St. Industrial Park
Rock Hill, SC 29730
Ultimate Parent: IVAX. SIC: 2869—
Industrial Organic Chemicals Nec; 2843—
Surface Active Agents; 2841—Soap & Other
Detergents.

★ 79831 ★   Ivax Industries Inc.
Textile Products
1880 Langston St. R. H. Industrial Park
Rock Hill, SC 29730
Ultimate Parent: IVAX. SIC: 2869—
Industrial Organic Chemicals Nec.

★ 79832 ★   Ivax Industry Inc.
Textile Products
1880 Langston St. Industrial Park
Rock Hill, SC 29731
Ultimate Parent: IVAX. SIC: 2869—
Industrial Organic Chemicals Nec; 2834—
Pharmaceutical Preparations; 2841—Soap
& Other Detergents.

★ 79833 ★   Kentucky Fried
Chicken
21 Bypass
Rock Hill, SC 29730
(803)366-6467
Ultimate Parent: Pepsico. SIC: 5812—
Eating Places.

★ 79834 ★ Kentucky Fried Chicken
1667 Ebenezer Rd.
Rock Hill, SC 29732
(803)329-0882
Ultimate Parent: Pepsico. SIC: 5812—Eating Places.

★ 79835 ★ Miles Inc.
Organic Products Div.
730 N. Anderson Rd.
Rock Hill, SC 29730
Company Type: Division. Ultimate Parent: Miles. SIC: 2865—Cyclic Crudes & Intermediates.

★ 79836 ★ Piedmont Medical Center
222 S. Herlong Ave.
Rock Hill, SC 29732
(803)329-1234
Officer: Paul Walker, Executive Director. Ultimate Parent: American Medical Holdings. SIC: 8062—General Medical & Surgical Hospitals.

★ 79837 ★ Pizza Hut
1158 N. Cherry Rd.
Rock Hill, SC 29732
(803)366-1078
Ultimate Parent: Pepsico. SIC: 5812—Eating Places.

★ 79838 ★ Radio Shack
2188 N. Cherry Rd.
Rock Hill, SC 29732
(803)366-5904
Company Type: Division. Ultimate Parent: Tandy Corp. SIC: 5065—Electronic Parts & Equipment Nec; 5731—Radio, Television & Electronics Stores.

★ 79839 ★ Rhone-Poulenc Inc.
911 E. White St.
Rock Hill, SC 29730
Ultimate Parent: Rhone-Poulenc Rorer. SIC: 2869—Industrial Organic Chemicals Nec.

★ 79840 ★ Rite Aid Discount Pharmacy
784 E. Heckle Blvd.
Rock Hill, SC 29730
(803)324-5273
Ultimate Parent: Rite Aid. SIC: 5912—Drug Stores & Proprietary Stores.

★ 79841 ★ Rock Hill Printing & Finishing
420 W. White St.
Rock Hill, SC 29731
Ultimate Parent: Springs Industries. SIC: 2269—Finishing Plants Nec.

★ 79842 ★ Taco Bell
2540 N. Cherry Rd.
Rock Hill, SC 29732
(803)366-1883
Ultimate Parent: Pepsico. SIC: 5812—Eating Places.

★ 79843 ★ Wal Mart Discount City
York Plz.
Rock Hill, SC 29730
(803)366-9465
Ultimate Parent: Wal-Mart Stores, Inc. SIC: 5311—Department Stores.

Russellville

★ 79844 ★ Georgia- Pacific Corp. Russellville Particleboard
Old Dyke Rd.
Russellville, SC 29476
Ultimate Parent: Georgia-Pacific. SIC: 2493—Reconstituted Wood Products.

★ 79845 ★ Georgia Pacific Corp. Russellville Pine Plywood
Hwy. 35
Russellville, SC 29476
Ultimate Parent: Georgia-Pacific. SIC: 2436—Softwood Veneer & Plywood.

★ 79846 ★ Georgia-Pacific Corp. Russellville Plywood
Hwy. 35
Russellville, SC 29476
Ultimate Parent: Georgia-Pacific. SIC: 2436—Softwood Veneer & Plywood.

★ 79847 ★ Georgia-Pacific Resins Inc.
Old Commissary Rd. PO Box 147
Russellville, SC 29476
Ultimate Parent: Georgia-Pacific. SIC: 2821—Plastics Materials & Resins; 2869—Industrial Organic Chemicals Nec.

★ 79848 ★ Georgia-Pacific Resins Inc.
PO Box 147 Old Commissary Rd.
Russellville, SC 29476
Ultimate Parent: Georgia-Pacific. SIC: 2821—Plastics Materials & Resins; 2869—Industrial Organic Chemicals Nec.

Saluda

★ 79849 ★ Ace Hardware & Farm Supply
102 Travis Ave.
Saluda, SC 29138
(803)445-3472
Ultimate Parent: Ace Hardware. SIC: 5251—Hardware Stores.

★ 79850 ★ Peoples Drug Store
301 W. Butler Ave.
Saluda, SC 29138
(803)445-7313
Ultimate Parent: Melville. SIC: 5912—Drug Stores & Proprietary Stores.

★ 79851 ★ Piggly Wiggly
210 S. Jefferson St.
Saluda, SC 29138
(803)445-2955
Ultimate Parent: Bruno's. SIC: 5411—Grocery Stores.

Santee

★ 79852 ★ Food Lion
Us 301
Santee, SC 29142
(803)854-2274
Ultimate Parent: Food Lion. SIC: 5411—Grocery Stores.

★ 79853 ★ Kentucky Fried Chicken
Hwy. 6
Santee, SC 29142
(803)854-2376
Ultimate Parent: Pepsico. SIC: 5812—Eating Places.

Sellers

★ 79854 ★ International Paper Masonite Plant
Hwy. 301 S.
Sellers, SC 29592
Location Type: Plant. Ultimate Parent: International Paper Co. SIC: 2600—Paper & Allied Products.

★ 79855 ★ Masonite Corp.
Marion Plant
Hwy. 301 S
Sellers, SC 29592
Ultimate Parent: International Paper Co.

Seneca

★ 79856 ★ Engelhard Corp.
554 Mormon Church Rd.
Seneca, SC 29678
Ultimate Parent: Engelhard Corp. SIC: 3341—Secondary Nonferrous Metals; 2819—Industrial Inorganic Chemicals Nec.

★ 79857 ★ Engelhard Corp.
554 Engelhard Dr.
Seneca, SC 29678
(803)882-9841
Officer: Ruel Cheatham, Manager. Ultimate Parent: Engelhard Corp. SIC: 2819—Industrial Inorganic Chemicals Nec.

★ 79858 ★ Engelhard Corp.
Catalysts & Chemicals Div.
554 Engelhard Dr.
Seneca, SC 29678
Company Type: Division. Ultimate Parent: Engelhard Corp. SIC: 3341—Secondary Nonferrous Metals; 2819—Industrial Inorganic Chemicals Nec.

★ 79859 ★ GTE Valenite
Rte. 6 Box 336 Wells Hwy.
Seneca, SC 29678
Ultimate Parent: GTE. SIC: 3541—Machine Tools—Metal Cutting Types.

★ 79860 ★ GTE Valenite Corp. Plant 4
Rte. 6 Wells Hwy.
Seneca, SC 29678
Ultimate Parent: GTE. SIC: 3541—Machine Tools—Metal Cutting Types.

★ 79861 ★ J. P. Stevens & Co. Inc. Seneca Plant
1300 E. S. 6th St.
Seneca, SC 29678
Ultimate Parent: West Point Stevens. SIC: 2211—Broadwoven Fabric Mills—Cotton.

★ 79862 ★ McDonalds of Seneca
Hwy. 123
Seneca, SC 29678
(803)882-0444
Ultimate Parent: McDonald's. SIC: 5812—Eating Places.

★ 79863 ★ Radio Shack
Apple Dr.
Seneca, SC 29678
(803)882-1292
Company Type: Division. Ultimate Parent: Tandy Corp. SIC: 5734—Computer & Software Stores.

★ 79864 ★ True Temper
Sports Division
PO Box 1619
Seneca, SC 29679-1619
(803)882-5947
Company Type: Headquarters. Officer: Ray Harris. Ultimate Parent: Black & Decker Corp. SIC: 3949—Sporting & Athletic Goods Nec.

★ 79865 ★ True Temper Sports
150 True Temper Dr.
Seneca, SC 29678
Company Type: Division. Ultimate Parent: Black & Decker Corp. SIC: 3471—Plating & Polishing; 3499—Fabricated Metal Products Nec.

★ 79866 ★ True Temper Sports
Wells Hwy. 488
Seneca, SC 29678
Ultimate Parent: Black & Decker Corp. SIC: 3471—Plating & Polishing; 3317—Steel Pipe & Tubes; 3499—Fabricated Metal Products Nec.

Silverstreet

★ 79867 ★ Champion Forest Products
Hwy. 34 E.
Silverstreet, SC 29145
Ultimate Parent: Champion International. SIC: 2436—Softwood Veneer & Plywood.

Simpsonville

★ 79868 ★ Rite Aid Discount Pharmacy
Plains St.
Simpsonville, SC 29681
(803)963-8142
Ultimate Parent: Rite Aid. SIC: 5912—Drug Stores & Proprietary Stores.

★ 79869 ★ Ryder Truck Rental
Main
Simpsonville, SC 29681
(803)963-3402
Ultimate Parent: Ryder System. SIC: 7513—Truck Rental & Leasing Without Drivers.

★ 79870 ★ W. R. Grace & Co.
Cryovac Div.
803 N. Maple St.
Simpsonville, SC 29681
Company Type: Division. Ultimate Parent: W. R. Grace & Co. SIC: 3089—Plastics Products Nec.

★ 79871 ★ W.R. Grace & Co.
Cryovac Div.
803 N. Maple St.
Simpsonville, SC 29681
Company Type: Division. Ultimate Parent: W. R. Grace. SIC: 3089—Plastics Products Nec.

Socastee

★ 79872 ★ Branch Banking & Trust Co.
5011 Socastee Blvd.
Socastee, SC 29575-7339
(803)650-7750
Company Type: Subsidiary. Location Type: Branch office. Officer: Elizabeth Barnett, Manager. Ultimate Parent: Southern National Corp. SIC: 6021—National Commercial Banks.

Spartanburg

★ 79873 ★ Ace Hardware
8098 PO Box
Spartanburg, SC 29305
Ultimate Parent: Ace Hardware. SIC: 5251—Hardware Stores.

★ 79874 ★ Alcoa Fujikura Ltd.
Telecommunications
150 Ridgeview Ctr. Hwy. 290
Spartanburg, SC 29334
Ultimate Parent: Aluminum Co. of America-Alcoa. SIC: 3644—Noncurrent-Carrying Wiring Devices; 3643—Current-Carrying Wiring Devices.

★ 79875 ★ American Family Life Assurance
10 Metro Dr.
Spartanburg, SC 29303
(803)585-1166
Ultimate Parent: American Family Life Assurance Co. SIC: 6411—Insurance Agents, Brokers & Service.

★ 79876 ★ BASF Corp.
3455 Southport Rd.
Spartanburg, SC 29302
Ultimate Parent: BASF Corp. SIC: 2843—Surface Active Agents; 2899—Chemical Preparations Nec.

★ 79877 ★ BASF Corp.
Chemicals
3455 Southport Rd.
Spartanburg, SC 29302
Company Type: Division. Ultimate Parent: BASF Corp. SIC: 2843—Surface Active Agents; 2899—Chemical Preparations Nec.

★ 79878 ★ BASF Corp.
Chemicals Division
PO Box 2108
Spartanburg, SC 29304-2108
(803)585-3411
Company Type: Division. Location Type: Branch office. Officer: C. R. Hope. Ultimate Parent: BASF Corp. SIC: 2833—Medicinals & Botanicals; 2843—Surface Active Agents.

★ 79879 ★ Bi-Lo No 265
100 N. Town Dr.
Spartanburg, SC 29303
(803)583-1351
Ultimate Parent: Penn Traffic. SIC: 5411—Grocery Stores.

★ 79880 ★ Big Bear
610 S. Church St.
Spartanburg, SC 29301
(803)583-5607
Ultimate Parent: Penn Traffic. SIC: 5411—Grocery Stores.

★ 79881 ★ Borden Snacks Inc.
15 Ash St.
Spartanburg, SC 29303
(803)585-9011
Officer: Dennis Olexa, President. Ultimate Parent: Borden, Inc. SIC: 2099—Food Preparations Nec.

★ 79882 ★ Branch Banking & Trust Co.
1500 W. O Ezell Blvd.
Spartanburg, SC 29301
(803)574-6100
Ultimate Parent: Southern National Corp. SIC: 6022—State Commercial Banks.

★ 79883 ★ Branch Banking & Trust Co.
1461 E. Main St.
Spartanburg, SC 29302-2234
(803)582-7577
Company Type: Subsidiary. Location Type: Branch office. Ultimate Parent: Southern National Corp. SIC: 6021—National Commercial Banks.

★ 79884 ★   Branch Banking &
Trust Co.
468 E. Main St.
Spartanburg, SC 29302-1926
(803)582-7577
Company Type: Subsidiary. **Location
Type:** Branch office. **Ultimate Parent:**
Southern National Corp. **SIC:** 6021—
National Commercial Banks.

★ 79885 ★   Canteen Corp.
203 E. Main St.
Spartanburg, SC 29319
(803)597-8000
Location Type: Branch office. **Officer:**
Jerome J. Richardson, President. **Ultimate
Parent:** Flagstar Co.

★ 79886 ★   Casual Corner
1901 E. Main St.
Spartanburg, SC 29302
(803)583-8317
Ultimate Parent: United States Shoe. **SIC:**
5651—Family Clothing Stores.

★ 79887 ★   Citgo Mini Mart
118 Cedar Springs Rd.
Spartanburg, SC 29302
(803)583-5184
Ultimate Parent: Citgo Petroleum. **SIC:**
5541—Gasoline Service Stations.

★ 79888 ★   Citgo Mini Mart
1245 Asheville Hwy.
Spartanburg, SC 29303
(803)583-7071
Ultimate Parent: Citgo Petroleum. **SIC:**
5411—Grocery Stores.

★ 79889 ★   Crown Cork & Seal
Co. Inc.
930 Beaumont Ave.
Spartanburg, SC 29301
Ultimate Parent: Crown Cork & Seal. **SIC:**
3411—Metal Cans.

★ 79890 ★   Denny's, Inc.
203 E. Main St.
Spartanburg, SC 29319
(803)597-8000
Company Type: Subsidiary. **Officer:**
Jerome Richardson, Chairman of the Board
& CEO. **Ultimate Parent:** Flagstar Co. **SIC:**
5812—Eating Places.

★ 79891 ★   Denny's Inc.
203 E. Main St.
Spartanburg, SC 29319
Company Type: Subsidiary. **Officer:**
Jerome J. Richardson, President. **Ultimate
Parent:** Flagstar Co.

★ 79892 ★   Exxon Co. USA
1783 Union St.
Spartanburg, SC 29302
(803)583-4558
Ultimate Parent: Exxon. **SIC:** 5172—
Petroleum Products Nec.

★ 79893 ★   First Union National
Bank of South Carolina
1490 1/2 Wm. Ezell Blvd.
Spartanburg, SC 29301-1553
(803)596-4600
Location Type: Branch office. **Ultimate
Parent:** First Union Corp. **SIC:** 6021—
National Commercial Banks.

★ 79894 ★   First Union National
Bank of South Carolina
736 E. Main St.
Spartanburg, SC 29304-1651
(803)596-4600
Location Type: Branch office. **Ultimate
Parent:** First Union Corp. **SIC:** 6021—
National Commercial Banks.

★ 79895 ★   Flagstar Companies
203 E. Main St.
Spartanburg, SC 29319-0001
(803)597-8000
Company Type: Headquarters. **Officer:**
Paul Tierney Jr., Chairman of the Board.
Ultimate Parent: Flagstar Co. **SIC:** 6719—
Holding Companies Nec; 5812—Eating
Places.

★ 79896 ★   Flagstar Companies
Inc.
203 E. Main St.
Spartanburg, SC 29319-9722
(803)597-8000 **Fax:** (803)597-8999
Company Type: Headquarters. **Officer:**
Jerome J. Richardson, Chairman &

President & CEO. **Ultimate Parent:** Flagstar
Co. **Employee Count:** 120000.

★ 79897 ★   Flagstar Co.
203 E. Main St.
Spartanburg, SC 29319
(803)597-8000
Company Type: Headquarters. **Officer:**
Jerome J. Richardson. **Fortune Service
500:** Ranking 33.

★ 79898 ★   Flagstar Corp.
203 E. Main St.
Spartanburg, SC 29319
(803)597-8000
Company Type: Subsidiary. **Officer:** Paul
Tierney Jr., Chairman of the Board.
Ultimate Parent: Flagstar Co. **SIC:** 5812—
Eating Places.

★ 79899 ★   Flagstar Corp.
Canteen Corp.
203 E. Main St.
Spartanburg, SC 29319
(803)597-8000
Company Type: Subsidiary. **Officer:**
Jerome Richardson, President. **Ultimate
Parent:** Flagstar Co. **SIC:** 5812—Eating
Places.

★ 79900 ★   Flagstar Corp.
Recreation Services Group
203 E. Main St.
Spartanburg, SC 29319-0001
(803)597-8000
Company Type: Subsidiary. **Officer:**
Jerome Richardson, President. **Ultimate
Parent:** Flagstar Co. **SIC:** 5812—Eating
Places; 7997—Membership Sports &
Recreation Clubs.

★ 79901 ★   Flagstar Corp.
Spartan Food Systems Div.
203 E. Main St.
Spartanburg, SC 29301
(803)597-8006
Company Type: Division. **Officer:** Jerome
Richardson, Chairman of the Board & CEO.
Ultimate Parent: Flagstar Co. **SIC:** 5812—
Eating Places.

★ 79902 ★   Flagstar Corp.
TW Recreational Services Inc.
203 E. Main St.
Spartanburg, SC 29319
(803)597-8000
Company Type: Subsidiary. **Officer:**
Donald Schaefer, President. **Ultimate
Parent:** Flagstar Co. **SIC:** 7999—
Amusement & Recreation Nec.

★ 79903 ★   Flagstar Corp.
Volume Services
203 E. Main St.
Spartanburg, SC 29319-0001
(803)597-8000
Company Type: Subsidiary. **Officer:** Larry
Hatch, President. **Ultimate Parent:** Flagstar
Co. **SIC:** 5812—Eating Places.

★ 79904 ★   Flowers Baking Co.
7001 Ashville Hwy.
Spartanburg, SC 29303
(803)578-7440
Officer: C. Dan Hartley, President. **Ultimate
Parent:** Flowers Industries. **SIC:** 2051—
Bread, Cake & Related Products.

★ 79905 ★   Flowers Baking Co. of
S.C., Inc.
I-85 & Hearon Cir.
Spartanburg, SC 29305
Ultimate Parent: Flowers Industries. **SIC:**
2051—Bread, Cake & Related Products.

★ 79906 ★   Flowers Baking Co. of
South Carolina Inc.
PO Box 4367
Spartanburg, SC 29305-4367
(803)578-7440 **Fax:** (803)578-0193
Company Type: Subsidiary. **Officer:** Dan
Hartley, Vice President/General Manager.
Ultimate Parent: Flowers Industries.

★ 79907 ★   Gaf Chemical Corp.
Sims Chapel Rd.
Spartanburg, SC 29301
Ultimate Parent: GAF Corp. **SIC:** 2843—
Surface Active Agents.

★ 79908 ★   Gaf Chemicals Corp.
Sims Chapel Rd.
Spartanburg, SC 29301
Ultimate Parent: GAF Corp. **SIC:** 2843—
Surface Active Agents.

★ 79909 ★   Goodyear Tire &
Rubber Co.
1095 Simuel Rd.
Spartanburg, SC 29301
Ultimate Parent: Goodyear Tire & Rubber.
SIC: 3011—Tires & Inner Tubes.

★ 79910 ★   Greyhound Bus Lines
250 E. Saint John St.
Spartanburg, SC 29302
(803)583-4024
Ultimate Parent: Greyhound Lines Inc. **SIC:**
4111—Local & Suburban Transit; 4142—
Bus Charter Service Except Local.

★ 79911 ★   Greyhound Bus Lines
212 E. Daniel Morgan Ave.
Spartanburg, SC 29302
(803)583-3669
Ultimate Parent: Greyhound Lines Inc. **SIC:**
4173—Bus Terminal & Service Facilities.

★ 79912 ★   Hertz Rent-A-Car
Greenville St. Spartanburg Junction
Spartanburg, SC 29301
(803)877-4261
Ultimate Parent: Hertz. **SIC:** 7514—
Passenger Car Rental.

★ 79913 ★   Hoechst Celanese
Corp.
I-85 at Rd. 57
Spartanburg, SC 29304-5887
Ultimate Parent: Hoechst Celanese Corp.
SIC: 2824—Organic Fibers—Noncellulosic;
2821—Plastics Materials & Resins; 2297—
Nonwoven Fabrics.

★ 79914 ★   Hoechst-Celanese
Corp. Spartanburg
1551 Sha Ln.
Spartanburg, SC 29302
Ultimate Parent: Hoechst Celanese Corp.
SIC: 2824—Organic Fibers—Noncellulosic;
2821—Plastics Materials & Resins; 2297—
Nonwoven Fabrics.

★ 79915 ★   Hoechst Celanese
Corp. Spartanburg Plant
I-85 at Rd. 57
Spartanburg, SC 29304
Ultimate Parent: Hoechst Celanese Corp.
SIC: 2824—Organic Fibers—Noncellulosic;
2821—Plastics Materials & Resins; 2297—
Nonwoven Fabrics.

★ 79916 ★   Kentucky Fried
Chicken
393 Whitney Rd.
Spartanburg, SC 29303
(803)585-3377
Ultimate Parent: Pepsico. **SIC:** 5812—
Eating Places.

★ 79917 ★   Kentucky Fried
Chicken
1459 W. O Ezell Blvd.
Spartanburg, SC 29301
(803)574-7722
Ultimate Parent: Pepsico. **SIC:** 5812—
Eating Places.

★ 79918 ★   Long Mile Rubber Co.
1095 Simuel Rd.
Spartanburg, SC 29301
Ultimate Parent: Goodyear Tire & Rubber.
SIC: 3011—Tires & Inner Tubes.

★ 79919 ★   Massachusetts Mutual
Life Insurance
340 S. Pine St.
Spartanburg, SC 29302
(803)582-7575
Ultimate Parent: Massasucetts Mutual Life.
SIC: 6411—Insurance Agents, Brokers &
Service.

★ 79920 ★   Mini Mart
Country Club Rd.
Spartanburg, SC 29302
(803)573-5464
Ultimate Parent: Kroger. **SIC:** 5411—
Grocery Stores.

★ 79921 ★   Otis Elevator Co.
Schuyler Ofc
Spartanburg, SC 29301
(803)585-5386
Ultimate Parent: United Technologies. **SIC:**
5084—Industrial Machinery & Equipment.

★ 79922 ★   Penn Mutual Life
Insurance
841 E. Main St.
Spartanburg, SC 29302
(803)582-4597
Ultimate Parent: Penn Mutual Life. **SIC:**
6311—Life Insurance.

★ 79923 ★   Phillips Fibers Corp.
Spartanburg Plant
11 Front St.
Spartanburg, SC 29301
Location Type: Plant. **Ultimate Parent:**
Phillips Petroleum. **SIC:** 2824—Organic
Fibers—Noncellulosic.

★ 79924 ★   Piggly Wiggly
Rr 6
Spartanburg, SC 29303
(803)582-2322
Ultimate Parent: Bruno's. **SIC:** 5411—
Grocery Stores.

★ 79925 ★   Pizza Hut
102 Garner Rd.
Spartanburg, SC 29303
(803)582-8026
Ultimate Parent: Pepsico. **SIC:** 5812—
Eating Places.

★ 79926 ★   Pizza Hut
1527 Asheville Hwy.
Spartanburg, SC 29303
(803)583-9994
Ultimate Parent: Pepsico. **SIC:** 5812—
Eating Places.

★ 79927 ★   Ppg Industries Inc.
1447 E. Main St.
Spartanburg, SC 29302
(803)582-3095
Ultimate Parent: PPG Industries Inc. **SIC:**
5084—Industrial Machinery & Equipment.

★ 79928 ★   Ppg Printing Inks
Rte. 11 Box 41
Spartanburg, SC 29302
Ultimate Parent: PPG Industries Inc. **SIC:**
2893—Printing Ink.

★ 79929 ★   Quincy Family Steak
House
203 E. Main St.
Spartanburg, SC 29301
(803)597-8000
Company Type: Subsidiary. **Officer:**
Jerome Richardson, President. **Ultimate
Parent:** Flagstar Co. **SIC:** 5812—Eating
Places.

★ 79930 ★   R. R. Donnelley &
Sons Co.
Jones Rd. at Rte. 57 R.R. 1 Box 400A
Spartanburg, SC 29302
Ultimate Parent: R. R. Donnelley & Sons.
SIC: 2754—Commercial Printing—Gravure.

★ 79931 ★   R. R. Donnelley &
Sons Co. Lakeside Press
300 Jones Rd. Box 400A
Spartanburg, SC 29302
Ultimate Parent: R. R. Donnelley & Sons.
SIC: 2754—Commercial Printing—Gravure.

★ 79932 ★   Radio Shack
218 Cedar Springs Rd.
Spartanburg, SC 29302
(803)591-0195
Company Type: Division. **Ultimate Parent:**
Tandy Corp. **SIC:** 5063—Electrical
Apparatus & Equipment.

★ 79933 ★   Radio Shack
1901 E. Main St.
Spartanburg, SC 29302
(803)583-4282
Company Type: Division. **Ultimate Parent:**
Tandy Corp. **SIC:** 5731—Radio, Television
& Electronics Stores.

★ 79934 ★   Radio Shack
404 Mccravy Dr.
Spartanburg, SC 29303
(803)585-0545
Company Type: Division. **Ultimate Parent:**
Tandy Corp. **SIC:** 5065—Electronic Parts &
Equipment Nec; 5731—Radio, Television &
Electronics Stores.

★ 79935 ★ **Radio Shack**
1855 E. Main St.
Spartanburg, SC 29302
(803)585-0070
Company Type: Division. **Ultimate Parent:** Tandy Corp. **SIC:** 5065—Electronic Parts & Equipment Nec.

★ 79936 ★ **Rexham Inc.**
Industrial Division Spartanburg Plant
5670 Blackstock Rd.
Spartanburg, SC 29303
Ultimate Parent: Bowater. **SIC:** 3083—Laminated Plastics Plate & Sheet; 3081—Unsupported Plastics Film & Sheet.

★ 79937 ★ **Rhone-Poulenc Inc. Surfactants & Specialties**
399 Sims Chapel Rd.
Spartanburg, SC 29301
Ultimate Parent: Rhone-Poulenc Rorer. **SIC:** 2843—Surface Active Agents.

★ 79938 ★ **Rhone Poulenc Surfactants**
399 Sims Chapel Rd.
Spartanburg, SC 29306
(803)585-8393
Officer: Thomas Dover, Plant Manager. **Ultimate Parent:** Rhone-Poulenc Rorer. **SIC:** 2899—Chemical Preparations Nec.

★ 79939 ★ **Rite Aid Corp.**
397 W. Main St.
Spartanburg, SC 29301
(803)582-4509
Ultimate Parent: Rite Aid. **SIC:** 5912—Drug Stores & Proprietary Stores.

★ 79940 ★ **Rite Aid Corp.**
554 S. Church St.
Spartanburg, SC 29301
(803)582-7673
Ultimate Parent: Rite Aid. **SIC:** 5912—Drug Stores & Proprietary Stores.

★ 79941 ★ **Rite Aid Discount Pharmacie**
397 W. Main St.
Spartanburg, SC 29301
(803)582-9154
Ultimate Parent: Rite Aid. **SIC:** 5912—Drug Stores & Proprietary Stores.

★ 79942 ★ **Rite Aid Discount Pharmacy**
8004 Greenville Hwy.
Spartanburg, SC 29301
(803)576-9893
Ultimate Parent: Rite Aid. **SIC:** 5912—Drug Stores & Proprietary Stores.

★ 79943 ★ **Rite Aid Drug**
1312 Union St.
Spartanburg, SC 29302
(803)582-9157
Ultimate Parent: Rite Aid. **SIC:** 5912—Drug Stores & Proprietary Stores.

★ 79944 ★ **Rite Aid Drug Store No 4**
554 S. Church St.
Spartanburg, SC 29301
(803)582-9156
Ultimate Parent: Rite Aid. **SIC:** 5912—Drug Stores & Proprietary Stores.

★ 79945 ★ **Rite Aid No 1045**
172 S. Pine St.
Spartanburg, SC 29302
(803)582-9424
Ultimate Parent: Rite Aid. **SIC:** 5912—Drug Stores & Proprietary Stores.

★ 79946 ★ **Rite Aid No 1110**
100 N. Town Dr.
Spartanburg, SC 29303
(803)582-9326
Ultimate Parent: Rite Aid. **SIC:** 5912—Drug Stores & Proprietary Stores.

★ 79947 ★ **Rite Aide**
1600 Reidville Rd.
Spartanburg, SC 29301
(803)571-9995
Ultimate Parent: Rite Aid. **SIC:** 5912—Drug Stores & Proprietary Stores.

★ 79948 ★ **R.R. Donnelley & Sons Co.**
Jones Rd. at Rte. 57, R.R. 1, Box 400A
Spartanburg, SC 29302
Ultimate Parent: R. R. Donnelley & Sons. **SIC:** 2754—Commercial Printing—Gravure.

★ 79949 ★ **Ryder Truck Rental**
5604 PO Box
Spartanburg, SC 29304
(803)583-9397
Ultimate Parent: Ryder System. **SIC:** 7513—Truck Rental & Leasing Without Drivers.

★ 79950 ★ **Ryder Truck Rental**
958 E. Main St.
Spartanburg, SC 29302
(803)583-7476
Ultimate Parent: Ryder System. **SIC:** 7513—Truck Rental & Leasing Without Drivers.

★ 79951 ★ **Southern Wood Piedmont Co.**
Creosote Rd.
Spartanburg, SC 29304
Ultimate Parent: ITT Rayonier Inc. **SIC:** 2491—Wood Preserving.

★ 79952 ★ **Spartan Food Systems Inc.**
203 E.Main St.
Spartanburg, SC 29319
(803)587-8000
Company Type: Subsidiary. **Officer:** Jerome J. Richardson. **Ultimate Parent:** Flagstar Co.

★ 79953 ★ **Standard Products Co.**
100 Quality Way
Spartanburg, SC 29303
(803)578-3164
Officer: Jake Perry, Manager. **Ultimate Parent:** Standard Products. **SIC:** 3089—Plastics Products Nec.

★ 79954 ★ **T J Maxx**
1420 W. O Ezell Blvd.
Spartanburg, SC 29301
(803)587-6020
Ultimate Parent: TJX. **SIC:** 5651—Family Clothing Stores.

★ 79955 ★ **Taco Bell**
158 Westgate Mall Dr.
Spartanburg, SC 29301
(803)576-5511
Ultimate Parent: Pepsico. **SIC:** 5812—Eating Places.

★ 79956 ★ **Taco Bell**
407 Garner Rd.
Spartanburg, SC 29303
(803)585-0475
Ultimate Parent: Pepsico. **SIC:** 5812—Eating Places.

★ 79957 ★ **Texaco Inc.**
110 Camp Croft Industrial Park
Spartanburg, SC 29303
(803)583-5424
Ultimate Parent: Texaco. **SIC:** 5172—Petroleum Products Nec.

★ 79958 ★ **Texaco Self-Way**
401 Whitney Rd.
Spartanburg, SC 29303
(803)582-1575
Ultimate Parent: Texaco. **SIC:** 5541—Gasoline Service Stations.

★ 79959 ★ **Toys R US**
660 Spartan Blvd.
Spartanburg, SC 29301
(803)574-1187
Ultimate Parent: Toys "R" US. **SIC:** 5945—Hobby, Toy & Game Shops.

★ 79960 ★ **Union Camp Corp.**
345 Cedar Springs Ave.
Spartanburg, SC 29302
Ultimate Parent: Union Camp Corp. **SIC:** 2674—Bags—Uncoated Paper & Multiwall.

★ 79961 ★ **Union Camp Corp.**
Cedar Springs Rd.
Spartanburg, SC 29304
Ultimate Parent: Union Camp Corp. **SIC:** 2600—Paper & Allied Products.

★ 79962 ★ **Union Camp Corp.**
Bag
118 Camp Croft Inds Park
Spartanburg, SC 29303
(803)585-3431
Ultimate Parent: Union Camp Corp. **SIC:** 2674—Bags—Uncoated Paper & Multiwall.

★ 79963 ★ **United Parcel Service**
Rural Route 7
Spartanburg, SC 29303
Ultimate Parent: United Parcel Service of America. **SIC:** 4215—Courier Services Except by Air.

★ 79964 ★ **United Parcel Services**
Rural Route 7
Spartanburg, SC 29303
(803)583-8228
Ultimate Parent: United Parcel Service of America. **SIC:** 4215—Courier Services Except by Air.

★ 79965 ★ **Wal Mart**
2081 E. Main St.
Spartanburg, SC 29302
(803)585-6211
Ultimate Parent: Wal-Mart Stores, Inc. **SIC:** 5311—Department Stores.

★ 79966 ★ **Wal Mart**
7600 Greenville Hwy.
Spartanburg, SC 29301
(803)574-6452
Ultimate Parent: Wal-Mart Stores, Inc. **SIC:** 5331—Variety Stores.

★ 79967 ★ **Waldenbooks**
1901 E. Main St.
Spartanburg, SC 29302
(803)583-9720
Ultimate Parent: K-Mart. **SIC:** 5942—Book Stores.

★ 79968 ★ **Western Auto Supply Co.**
404 McCravy Dr.
Spartanburg, SC 29303
(803)585-0201
Ultimate Parent: Sears Roebuck & Co. **SIC:** 5531—Automobile & Home Supply Stores.

Spartenburg

★ 79969 ★ **Union Camp Corp.**
Hwy. 29 at I-85
Spartanburg, SC 29304
(803)439-3022
Officer: Pete Watson, Manager. **Ultimate Parent:** Union Camp Corp. **SIC:** 2653—Corrugated & Solid Fiber Boxes.

St Matthews

★ 79970 ★ **Piggly Wiggly**
Harry C Raysor Dr.
St Matthews, SC 29135
(803)874-1212
Ultimate Parent: Bruno's. **SIC:** 5411—Grocery Stores.

St Stephen

★ 79971 ★ **Greyhound Bus Lines**
Hwy. 52
St Stephen, SC 29479
(803)567-3470
Ultimate Parent: Greyhound Lines Inc. **SIC:** 4131—Intercity & Rural Bus Transportation.

St. George

★ 79972 ★ **Food Lion**
Hwy. 78
St. George, SC 29477
(803)563-2311
Ultimate Parent: Food Lion. **SIC:** 5411—Grocery Stores.

★ 79973 ★ **Piggly Wiggly**
Memorial Blvd.
St. George, SC 29477
(803)563-4554
Ultimate Parent: Bruno's. **SIC:** 5411—Grocery Stores.

St. Matthews

★ 79974 ★ **Branch Banking & Trust Co.**
101 N. Railroad Ave.
St. Matthews, SC 29135-1232
(803)655-5900
Company Type: Subsidiary. **Location Type:** Branch office. **Ultimate Parent:**

Southern National Corp. **SIC:** 6021—National Commercial Banks.

★ 79975 ★ **United Technologies Auto**
Belleville Rd.
St. Matthews, SC 29135
(803)874-1711
Officer: Sid Caruthers, Manager. **Ultimate Parent:** United Technologies. **SIC:** 3599—Industrial Machinery Nec.

St. Stephen

★ 79976 ★ **Reliable Electric**
315 Ravenel Rd.
St. Stephen, SC 29479
Ultimate Parent: Reliance Electric. **SIC:** 3661—Telephone & Telegraph Apparatus.

★ 79977 ★ **Reliable Electric Co.**
315 Ravenel St.
St. Stephen, SC 29479
(803)567-3162
Officer: John Walter, Manager. **Ultimate Parent:** Reliance Electric. **SIC:** 3661—Telephone & Telegraph Apparatus.

Summerton

★ 79978 ★ **Federal Mogul**
Hwy. 301 N
Summerton, SC 29148
(803)478-2382
Officer: William F. Burdick, Manager. **Ultimate Parent:** Federal-Mogul Corp. **SIC:** 3053—Gaskets, Packing & Sealing Devices.

★ 79979 ★ **Federal Mogul Corp.**
385 PO Box
Summerton, SC 29148
(803)478-2382
Ultimate Parent: Federal-Mogul Corp. **SIC:** 3299—Nonmetallic Mineral Products Nec.

★ 79980 ★ **Zippy Mart Inc.**
S Church
Summerton, SC 29148
(803)485-4525
Ultimate Parent: Crown Central Petroleum Corp. **SIC:** 5411—Grocery Stores.

Summerville

★ 79981 ★ **BFI Recycling Systems**
237 Farmington Dr.
Summerville, SC 29483-5353
(803)875-4900
Ultimate Parent: Browning-Ferris Industries. **SIC:** 5085—Industrial Supplies; 4953—Refuse Systems.

★ 79982 ★ **Branch Banking & Trust Co.**
10105 Dorchester & Trolley Rds.
Summerville, SC 29485
(803)745-4114
Company Type: Subsidiary. **Location Type:** Branch office. **Ultimate Parent:** Southern National Corp. **SIC:** 6021—National Commercial Banks.

★ 79983 ★ **Exxon Corp.**
Hwy. 78 W
Summerville, SC 29483
(803)873-5800
Ultimate Parent: Exxon. **SIC:** 2819—Industrial Inorganic Chemicals Nec.

★ 79984 ★ **First Union National Bank of South Carolina**
805 Bacon's Bridge Rd.
Summerville, SC 29485
(803)871-8850
Location Type: Branch office. **Ultimate Parent:** First Union Corp. **SIC:** 6021—National Commercial Banks.

★ 79985 ★ **Food Lion**
1230 W. Dorchester Rd.
Summerville, SC 29483
(803)875-4360
Ultimate Parent: Food Lion. **SIC:** 5411—Grocery Stores.

★ 79986 ★ **Greyhound Bus Lines**
248 N. Main St.
Summerville, SC 29483
(803)873-4781
Ultimate Parent: Greyhound Lines Inc. **SIC:** 4111—Local & Suburban Transit.

★ 79987 ★   Kentucky Fried Chicken
Main Plz.
Summerville, SC 29483
(803)871-0170
Ultimate Parent: Pepsico. SIC: 5812—Eating Places.

★ 79988 ★   Kroger Co. Inc.
147 Cantering Hills Ln.
Summerville, SC 29483
(803)554-0916
Ultimate Parent: Kroger. SIC: 5411—Grocery Stores.

★ 79989 ★   Kroger Sav-On
147 Cantering Hills Ln.
Summerville, SC 29483
(803)544-0916
Ultimate Parent: Kroger. SIC: 5411—Grocery Stores.

★ 79990 ★   Pepsi-Cola Co.
2723 W. 5th North St.
Summerville, SC 29483
(803)875-3151
Location Type: Plant. Officer: Rodney Jacobs, Manager. Ultimate Parent: Pepsico. SIC: 2086—Bottled & Canned Soft Drinks.

★ 79991 ★   Piggly Wiggly
100 W. Richardson Ave.
Summerville, SC 29483
(803)873-0461
Ultimate Parent: Bruno's. SIC: 5411—Grocery Stores.

★ 79992 ★   Pizza Hut
700 N. Main St.
Summerville, SC 29483
(803)871-0209
Ultimate Parent: Pepsico. SIC: 5812—Eating Places.

★ 79993 ★   Ryder Truck Rental
208 N. Main St.
Summerville, SC 29483
(803)871-2043
Ultimate Parent: Ryder System. SIC: 4214—Local Trucking With Storage.

★ 79994 ★   Wal Mart
Summerville Plz.
Summerville, SC 29483
(803)873-8111
Ultimate Parent: Wal-Mart Stores, Inc. SIC: 5311—Department Stores.

★ 79995 ★   Westvaco Corp.
180 Westvaco Rd.
Summerville, SC 29483
(803)871-5000
Officer: William Baughman, Manager. Ultimate Parent: WestVaco Corp. SIC: 2411—Logging.

★ 79996 ★   Westvaco Corp.
Hwy. 17
Summerville, SC 29483
(803)871-5000
Ultimate Parent: WestVaco Corp. SIC: 2411—Logging.

★ 79997 ★   Westvaco Lumber
309 N. Maple St.
Summerville, SC 29483
Location Type: Plant. Officer: M. E. Hundley, Plant Manager. Ultimate Parent: WestVaco Corp.

Sumpter

★ 79998 ★   Carolina Golden Products Co.
2050 Hwy. 15 S
Sumpter, SC 29150
(803)481-8555
Company Type: Subsidiary. Officer: Donald W. Mabe, President. Ultimate Parent: Gold Kist. SIC: 2015—Poultry Slaughtering & Processing; 2077—Animal & Marine Fats & Oils.

Sumter

★ 79999 ★   Allied-Signal Automotive
Corporate Way
Sumter, SC 29151
(803)481-9330
Officer: M. J. Kepner, Manager. Ultimate Parent: Allied-Signal Inc. SIC: 3714—Motor Vehicle Parts & Accessories.

★ 80000 ★   Allied-Signal Automotive
Corporate Way
Sumter, SC 29151
(803)481-9330
Officer: M. J. Kepner, Manager. Ultimate Parent: Allied-Signal Inc. SIC: 3714—Motor Vehicle Parts & Accessories.

★ 80001 ★   Allied-Signal Inc.
Bendix Automotive Systems
Corporate Way Sumter Industrial Park
Sumter, SC 29154
Ultimate Parent: Allied-Signal Inc. SIC: 3714—Motor Vehicle Parts & Accessories.

★ 80002 ★   Allied-Signal Inc.
Bendix Automotive Systems
Corporate Way Sumter Industrial Park
Sumter, SC 29154
Ultimate Parent: Allied-Signal Inc. SIC: 3714—Motor Vehicle Parts & Accessories.

★ 80003 ★   Allied-Signal Inc.
Braking Systems
North American, Sumter Plant Corp. Way Cr.
Sumter, SC 291502488
Ultimate Parent: Allied-Signal Inc. SIC: 3714—Motor Vehicle Parts & Accessories.

★ 80004 ★   Becton Dickinson & Co.
Vacutainer Systems
1 Airport Rd.
Sumter, SC 29150
Ultimate Parent: Becton Dickinson. SIC: 3841—Surgical & Medical Instruments.

★ 80005 ★   Becton Dickinson Systems
1 Airport Rd.
Sumter, SC 29151
Ultimate Parent: Becton Dickinson. SIC: 3841—Surgical & Medical Instruments.

★ 80006 ★   Becton Dickinson Vacutainer Systems
Airport Rd.
Sumter, SC 29151
Ultimate Parent: Becton Dickinson. SIC: 3841—Surgical & Medical Instruments.

★ 80007 ★   Bi-Lo
1300 Broad St.
Sumter, SC 29150
(803)469-7040
Ultimate Parent: Penn Traffic. SIC: 5411—Grocery Stores.

★ 80008 ★   Branch Banking & Trust Co.
1099 Broad St.
Sumter, SC 29150-2504
(803)775-9323
Company Type: Subsidiary. Location Type: Branch office. Ultimate Parent: Southern National Corp. SIC: 6021—National Commercial Banks.

★ 80009 ★   Branch Banking & Trust Co.
498 N. Guignard Dr.
Sumter, SC 29150-4058
(803)775-9323
Company Type: Subsidiary. Location Type: Branch office. Ultimate Parent: Southern National Corp. SIC: 6021—National Commercial Banks.

★ 80010 ★   Branch Banking & Trust Co.
216 N. Main St.
Sumter, SC 29150-4959
(803)775-9323
Company Type: Subsidiary. Location Type: Branch office. Ultimate Parent: Southern National Corp. SIC: 6021—National Commercial Banks.

★ 80011 ★   Campbell Soup Co.
2050 Hwy. 15 S
Sumter, SC 29150
Ultimate Parent: Campbell Soup. SIC: 2038—Frozen Specialties Nec.

★ 80012 ★   Campbell Soup Co. (Sumter Plant)
2050 Hwy. 15 South
Sumter, SC 29150
Ultimate Parent: Campbell Soup. SIC: 2038—Frozen Specialties Nec.

★ 80013 ★   Carolina Coca-Cola Bottling Co.
712 E. Liberty St.
Sumter, SC 29150-8535
Ultimate Parent: Coca-Cola Bottling Consol. SIC: 2000—Food & Kindred Products.

★ 80014 ★   Carolina Golden Products Feed Mill
Stark Ferry Rd.
Sumter, SC 29150-1001
Ultimate Parent: Gold Kist. SIC: 2048—Prepared Feeds Nec.

★ 80015 ★   Casual Corner
Jessamine Mall
Sumter, SC 29150
(803)775-9248
Ultimate Parent: United States Shoe. SIC: 5621—Women's Clothing Stores.

★ 80016 ★   Circus World Toy Store
Jessamine Mall
Sumter, SC 29150
(803)775-9647
Ultimate Parent: Melville. SIC: 5945—Hobby, Toy & Game Shops.

★ 80017 ★   Crescent/Xcelite
43-486 Co. Rd.
Sumter, SC 29154
Ultimate Parent: Cooper Industries. SIC: 3423—Hand & Edge Tools Nec.

★ 80018 ★   Crescent/Xcelite
43-486 County Rd.
Sumter, SC 29154
Ultimate Parent: Cooper Industries. SIC: 3423—Hand & Edge Tools Nec.

★ 80019 ★   First Union National Bank of South Carolina
201 N. Washington St.
Sumter, SC 29150-4204
(803)775-1225
Location Type: Branch office. Ultimate Parent: First Union Corp. SIC: 6021—National Commercial Banks.

★ 80020 ★   Greyhound Bus Lines
230 E. Hampton Ave.
Sumter, SC 29150
(803)773-8113
Ultimate Parent: Greyhound Lines Inc. SIC: 4131—Intercity & Rural Bus Transportation.

★ 80021 ★   Hertz Rent-A-Car
402 Broad St.
Sumter, SC 29150
(803)775-6088
Ultimate Parent: Hertz. SIC: 7514—Passenger Car Rental.

★ 80022 ★   Kroger Pharmacy
873 Broad St.
Sumter, SC 29150
(803)775-0115
Ultimate Parent: Kroger. SIC: 5912—Drug Stores & Proprietary Stores.

★ 80023 ★   Kroger Savon Food&Drugs
873 Broad St.
Sumter, SC 29150
(803)775-9341
Ultimate Parent: Kroger. SIC: 5411—Grocery Stores.

★ 80024 ★   Lerner Shop
10 Jessamine Mall
Sumter, SC 29150
(803)775-8262
Ultimate Parent: Limited. SIC: 5621—Women's Clothing Stores.

★ 80025 ★   McDonald's
101 N. Lafayette Dr.
Sumter, SC 29150
(803)773-8515
Ultimate Parent: McDonald's. SIC: 5812—Eating Places.

★ 80026 ★   Pappagallo
540 Bultman Dr.
Sumter, SC 29150
(803)775-0211
Ultimate Parent: United States Shoe. SIC: 5661—Shoe Stores.

★ 80027 ★   Piggly Wiggly
674 W. Liberty St.
Sumter, SC 29150
(803)775-1312
Ultimate Parent: Bruno's. SIC: 5141—Groceries—General Line.

★ 80028 ★   Pizza Hut
1120 Broad St.
Sumter, SC 29150
(803)773-5496
Ultimate Parent: Pepsico. SIC: 5812—Eating Places.

★ 80029 ★   Pizza Hut
Hwy. 441
Sumter, SC 29150
(803)499-3385
Ultimate Parent: Pepsico. SIC: 5812—Eating Places.

★ 80030 ★   Rite-Aid Pharmacy
5 Alice Dr.
Sumter, SC 29150
(803)773-3368
Ultimate Parent: Rite Aid. SIC: 5912—Drug Stores & Proprietary Stores; 5912—Drug Stores & Proprietary Stores.

★ 80031 ★   Service Merchandise
Jessamine Mall
Sumter, SC 29150
(803)778-2411
Ultimate Parent: Service Merchandise Co., Inc. SIC: 5944—Jewelry Stores.

★ 80032 ★   Taco Bell
1112 Broad St.
Sumter, SC 29150
(803)775-2984
Ultimate Parent: Pepsico. SIC: 5812—Eating Places.

★ 80033 ★   Westinghouse Electric
11 Corporate Cir.
Sumter, SC 29154
(803)481-3131
Officer: Glen Hesselbart, Manager. Ultimate Parent: Westinghouse Electric Corp. SIC: 3625—Relays & Industrial Controls; 3699—Electrical Equipment & Supplies Nec.

★ 80034 ★   Westinghouse Electric Corp.
11 Corporate Cir.
Sumter, SC 29150
Ultimate Parent: Westinghouse Electric Corp. SIC: 3612—Transformers Except Electronic.

Taylors

★ 80035 ★   Bi-Lo Inc.
Brushy Creek Rd.
Taylors, SC 29687
(803)268-7259
Ultimate Parent: Penn Traffic. SIC: 5411—Grocery Stores.

★ 80036 ★   Branch Banking & Trust Co.
3255 Wade Hampton Blvd.
Taylors, SC 29687-2803
(803)255-7733
Company Type: Subsidiary. Location Type: Branch office. Ultimate Parent: Southern National Corp. SIC: 6021—National Commercial Banks.

★ 80037 ★   Kentucky Fried Chicken
2818 Wade Hampton Blvd.
Taylors, SC 29687
(803)268-2100
Ultimate Parent: Pepsico. SIC: 5812—Eating Places.

★ 80038 ★   Mary Kay Cosmetics
2 Idonia Dr.
Taylors, SC 29687
(803)244-3426
Ultimate Parent: Mary Kay Cosmetics. SIC: 5999—Miscellaneous Retail Stores Nec.

★ 80039 ★   Pizza Hut
3317 Wade Hampton Blvd.
Taylors, SC 29687
(803)268-7961
Ultimate Parent: Pepsico. SIC: 5812—Eating Places.

★ 80040 ★ **Wal Mart**
3027 Wade Hampton Blvd.
Taylors, SC 29687
(803)292-8155
Ultimate Parent: Wal-Mart Stores, Inc. **SIC:** 5311—Department Stores.

Travelers Rest

★ 80041 ★ **Air Products & Chemicals Inc.**
1004 Geer Hwy.
Travelers Rest, SC 29690-9761
(803)834-5122
Company Type: Headquarters. **Officer:** Mike Gibbons. **Ultimate Parent:** Air Products & Chemicals, Inc. **SIC:** 2869—Industrial Organic Chemicals Nec.

★ 80042 ★ **Air Products & Chemicals Inc.**
U.S. Hwy. 276
Travelers Rest, SC 29690
Ultimate Parent: Air Products & Chemicals, Inc. **SIC:** 2869—Industrial Organic Chemicals Nec.

★ 80043 ★ **Exxon**
Geer Hwy.
Travelers Rest, SC 29690
(803)836-8934
Ultimate Parent: Exxon. **SIC:** 3569—General Industrial Machinery Nec.

★ 80044 ★ **First Union National Bank of South Carolina**
No. 5 Hawkins Rd.
Travelers Rest, SC 29690
(803)834-7215
Location Type: Branch office. **Ultimate Parent:** First Union Corp. **SIC:** 6021—National Commercial Banks.

★ 80045 ★ **Rite Aid Discount Pharmacie**
206 State Park Rd.
Travelers Rst, SC 29690
(803)834-9720
Ultimate Parent: Rite Aid. **SIC:** 5912—Drug Stores & Proprietary Stores.

Trenton

★ 80046 ★ **Shaw Industries Inc.**
Hwy. 19 & 25
Trenton, SC 29847
(803)275-3211
Officer: Dennis Cooper, Manager. **Ultimate Parent:** Shaw Industries, Inc. **SIC:** 2273—Carpets & Rugs; 2281—Yarn Spinning Mills.

Union

★ 80047 ★ **Citgo Mini Mart**
63 Duncan Bypass Park
Union, SC 29379
(803)427-4512
Ultimate Parent: Citgo Petroleum. **SIC:** 5541—Gasoline Service Stations.

★ 80048 ★ **Kentucky Fried Chicken**
Hwy. 176
Union, SC 29379
(803)427-3100
Ultimate Parent: Pepsico. **SIC:** 5812—Eating Places.

★ 80049 ★ **Torrington Co.**
Industrial Blvd.
Union, SC 29379
(803)427-0321
Ultimate Parent: Ingersoll-Rand. **SIC:** 3562—Ball & Roller Bearings.

★ 80050 ★ **Torrington Co. Tyger River**
Union Industrial Park State Rd. 194
Union, SC 29379
Ultimate Parent: Ingersoll-Rand. **SIC:** 3562—Ball & Roller Bearings.

★ 80051 ★ **Torrington Co. Tyger River Plant**
408 Industrial Park Rd.
Union, SC 29379
Ultimate Parent: Ingersoll-Rand. **SIC:** 3562—Ball & Roller Bearings.

★ 80052 ★ **Torrington Co. Tyger River Plant**
Industrial Park Rd. State Rd. 194
Union, SC 29379
Ultimate Parent: Ingersoll-Rand. **SIC:** 3562—Ball & Roller Bearings.

★ 80053 ★ **Torrington Co. Tyger River Plant**
Industrial Park State Rd. 194
Union, SC 29379
Location Type: Plant. **Ultimate Parent:** Ingersoll-Rand. **SIC:** 3562—Ball & Roller Bearings.

★ 80054 ★ **Trailways Bus Systems**
N Mountain St.
Union, SC 29379
(803)427-6707
Ultimate Parent: Greyhound Lines Inc. **SIC:** 4131—Intercity & Rural Bus Transportation.

★ 80055 ★ **Wal Mart**
Union Sq.
Union, SC 29379
(803)427-5609
Ultimate Parent: Wal-Mart Stores, Inc. **SIC:** 5311—Department Stores.

★ 80056 ★ **Wal Mart Discount City**
W Town Plz.
Union, SC 29379
(803)429-0598
Ultimate Parent: Wal-Mart Stores, Inc. **SIC:** 5311—Department Stores.

Walhalla

★ 80057 ★ **First Union National Bank of South Carolina**
3819 Blue Ridge Blvd.
Walhalla, SC 29691
(803)638-9652
Location Type: Branch office. **Ultimate Parent:** First Union Corp. **SIC:** 6021—National Commercial Banks.

★ 80058 ★ **Torrington Co.**
Torrington Rd. PO Box 100
Walhalla, SC 29691
Ultimate Parent: Ingersoll-Rand. **SIC:** 3562—Ball & Roller Bearings.

Wallace

★ 80059 ★ **Delta Mills Marketing**
4222 Delta Plant Rd.
Wallace, SC 29596
(803)537-7811
Officer: Roger Fisher, Manager. **Ultimate Parent:** Delta Woodside Industries. **SIC:** 2261—Finishing Plants—Cotton; 2262—Finishing Plants—Manmade.

★ 80060 ★ **Delta Mills Marketing Co.**
4351 Brickyard Rd.
Wallace, SC 29596
Ultimate Parent: Delta Woodside Industries. **SIC:** 2269—Finishing Plants Nec.

★ 80061 ★ **Delta Mills Marketing Co., Delta No. 3**
Hwys. 1 & 9 N
Wallace, SC 29596
Ultimate Parent: Delta Woodside Industries. **SIC:** 2269—Finishing Plants Nec.

★ 80062 ★ **Delta Mills Marketing Co. Delta Plant No. 2**
Hwy.s 1 & 9 North
Wallace, SC 29596
Ultimate Parent: Delta Woodside Industries. **SIC:** 2269—Finishing Plants Nec.

★ 80063 ★ **Delta Mills Marketing Delta Plant No. 2**
Hwys. 1 & 9 N.
Wallace, SC 29596
Ultimate Parent: Delta Woodside Industries. **SIC:** 2269—Finishing Plants Nec.

★ 80064 ★ **J. L. Anderson Co. Inc.**
Palmetto Brick Co.
Old Bennettsville Hwy.
Wallace, SC 29596
Ultimate Parent: J&L Specialty Steel. **SIC:** 3251—Brick & Structural Clay Tile.

★ 80065 ★ **Ryder Truck Rental**
Rural Route 1e
Wallace, SC 29596
(803)537-5742
Ultimate Parent: Ryder System. **SIC:** 4214—Local Trucking With Storage.

Walterboro

★ 80066 ★ **Branch Banking & Trust Co.**
104 N. Ivanhoe Dr.
Walterboro, SC 29488-3713
(803)549-1806
Company Type: Subsidiary. **Location Type:** Branch office. **Ultimate Parent:** Southern National Corp. **SIC:** 6021—National Commercial Banks.

★ 80067 ★ **Coca Cola Bottling Co.**
1211 N. Jefferies Blvd.
Walterboro, SC 29488
(803)549-5921
Ultimate Parent: Coca-Cola Enterprises. **SIC:** 2086—Bottled & Canned Soft Drinks.

★ 80068 ★ **Dayco Prods. Inc.**
Recold Rd., Colleton County Industrial Area
Walterboro, SC 29488
Ultimate Parent: Mark IV Industries. **SIC:** 3052—Rubber & Plastics Hose & Belting.

★ 80069 ★ **Dayco Products Inc.**
PO Box 1128 Recold Rd.
Walterboro, SC 29488
Ultimate Parent: Mark IV Industries. **SIC:** 3000—Rubber & Miscellaneous Plastics Products.

★ 80070 ★ **Fleet Finance Inc.**
107 Wichman St.
Walterboro, SC 29488
(803)549-5516
Ultimate Parent: Fleet Financial Group. **SIC:** 6141—Personal Credit Institutions.

★ 80071 ★ **Greyhound Bus Lines**
113 Elizabeth St.
Walterboro, SC 29488
(803)549-5031
Ultimate Parent: Greyhound Lines Inc. **SIC:** 4111—Local & Suburban Transit.

★ 80072 ★ **Kentucky Fried Chicken**
339 Jefferies Blvd.
Walterboro, SC 29488
(803)549-7613
Ultimate Parent: Pepsico. **SIC:** 5812—Eating Places.

★ 80073 ★ **Kentucky Fried Chicken**
I 95
Walterboro, SC 29488
(803)538-5887
Ultimate Parent: Pepsico. **SIC:** 5812—Eating Places.

★ 80074 ★ **N W Ball & Roller**
700 Industrial Rd.
Walterboro, SC 29488
Ultimate Parent: Ball Corp. **SIC:** 3562—Ball & Roller Bearings.

★ 80075 ★ **Nn Ball & Roller Inc.**
700 Industrial Rd.
Walterboro, SC 29488
Ultimate Parent: Ball Corp. **SIC:** 3562—Ball & Roller Bearings.

★ 80076 ★ **Piggly Wiggly**
251 Bells Hwy. A
Walterboro, SC 29488
Ultimate Parent: Bruno's. **SIC:** 5411—Grocery Stores.

★ 80077 ★ **Rite Aid Discount Pharmacie**
Ivanhoe Shopping Ctr.
Walterboro, SC 29488
(803)549-5817
Ultimate Parent: Rite Aid. **SIC:** 5912—Drug Stores & Proprietary Stores.

★ 80078 ★ **Wal Mart**
109 Beachwood Rd.
Walterboro, SC 29488
(803)549-5214
Ultimate Parent: Wal-Mart Stores, Inc. **SIC:** 7692—Welding Repair.

★ 80079 ★ **Westvaco Corp.**
Bells Hwy.
Walterboro, SC 29488
(803)538-5939
Ultimate Parent: WestVaco Corp. **SIC:** 2411—Logging.

★ 80080 ★ **Wheelabrator Corp.**
150 Recold Rd.
Walterboro, SC 29488
(803)538-2711
Officer: Ralph Cadman, Manager. **Ultimate Parent:** WMX Technologies, Inc. **SIC:** 3322—Malleable Iron Foundries; 3325—Steel Foundries Nec.

★ 80081 ★ **Zippy Mart Inc. No. 883**
Jefferies Blvd.
Walterboro, SC 29488
(803)549-5732
Ultimate Parent: Crown Central Petroleum Corp. **SIC:** 5411—Grocery Stores.

Wellford

★ 80082 ★ **Union Camp Corp.**
Hwy. US 29 I-85
Wellford, SC 29385
Ultimate Parent: Union Camp Corp. **SIC:** 2653—Corrugated & Solid Fiber Boxes.

West Columbia

★ 80083 ★ **Ace Hardware**
3914 Platt Springs Rd.
West Columbia, SC 29170
(803)957-4991
Ultimate Parent: Ace Hardware. **SIC:** 5251—Hardware Stores.

★ 80084 ★ **Baxter Physical Therapy Center**
160 Medical Cir.
West Columbia, SC 29169-3656
(803)739-4670
Officer: Ronald Vandommelen. **Ultimate Parent:** Baxter International. **SIC:** 8011—Offices & Clinics of Medical Doctors; 8049—Offices of Health Practitioners Nec.

★ 80085 ★ **Branch Banking & Trust Co.**
701 12th St.
West Columbia, SC 29169
(803)251-3130
Company Type: Subsidiary. **Location Type:** Branch office. **Ultimate Parent:** Southern National Corp. **SIC:** 6021—National Commercial Banks.

★ 80086 ★ **Branch Banking & Trust Co.**
2322 Augusta Rd., Kroger Store 982
West Columbia, SC 29169-4542
(803)251-3175
Company Type: Subsidiary. **Location Type:** Branch office. **Ultimate Parent:** Southern National Corp.

★ 80087 ★ **Branch Banking & Trust Co.**
109 N. 12th St.
West Columbia, SC 29169-6412
(803)748-7180
Company Type: Subsidiary. **Location Type:** Branch office. **Officer:** Melinda Dufford, Manager. **Ultimate Parent:** Southern National Corp. **SIC:** 6021—National Commercial Banks.

★ 80088 ★ **Delta Air Lines**
Columbia
West Columbia, SC 29169
(803)794-6002
Ultimate Parent: Delta Air Lines, Inc. **SIC:** 4512—Air Transportation—Scheduled.

★ 80089 ★ **Delta Air Lines Inc.**
Columbia
West Columbia, SC 29169
(803)794-6002
Ultimate Parent: Delta Air Lines, Inc. **SIC:** 4512—Air Transportation—Scheduled.

★ 80090 ★ **Durr-Fillauer Medical Inc.**
2413 Leaphart Rd.
West Columbia, SC 29169
(803)791-5900
Ultimate Parent: Bergen Brunswig Corp. **SIC:** 5047—Medical & Hospital Equipment; 5049—Professional Equipment Nec.

521

★ 80091 ★   **Emery Worldwide**
Columbia
West Columbia, SC 29169
(803)794-0960
Ultimate Parent: Rockwell International
Corp. **SIC:** 3714—Motor Vehicle Parts &
Accessories. **SIC:** Consolidated
Freightways. **SIC:** 4512—Air
Transportation—Scheduled.

★ 80092 ★   **Federal Express Corp.**
150 Queen Pky.
West Columbia, SC 29169
Ultimate Parent: Federal Express. **SIC:**
4215—Courier Services Except by Air;
4513—Air Courier Services.

★ 80093 ★   **Food Lion**
3975 Platt Springs Rd.
West Columbia, SC 29170
(803)755-9277
Ultimate Parent: Food Lion. **SIC:** 5411—
Grocery Stores.

★ 80094 ★   **Food Lion**
1618 Airport Blvd.
West Columbia, SC 29169
(803)791-4333
Ultimate Parent: Food Lion. **SIC:** 5411—
Grocery Stores.

★ 80095 ★   **Kentucky Fried
Chicken**
1245 Boston Ave.
West Columbia, SC 29170
(803)796-9028
Ultimate Parent: Pepsico. **SIC:** 5812—
Eating Places.

★ 80096 ★   **Kentucky Fried
Chicken**
2711 Emanuel Church Rd.
West Columbia, SC 29170
(803)356-4601
Ultimate Parent: Pepsico. **SIC:** 5812—
Eating Places.

★ 80097 ★   **Kroger Sav on
Food&Drugs**
2322 Augusta Hwy.
West Columbia, SC 29169
(803)796-3885
Ultimate Parent: Kroger. **SIC:** 5411—
Grocery Stores.

★ 80098 ★   **Martin Marietta
Aggregates**
4003 PO Box
West Columbia, SC 29171
(803)796-8320
Ultimate Parent: Martin Marietta. **SIC:**
1411—Dimension Stone.

★ 80099 ★   **Pepsi-Cola Co.**
West Columbia Plant
1964 Old Dunbar Rd.
West Columbia, SC 29172
Location Type: Plant. **Ultimate Parent:**
Pepsico. **SIC:** 2086—Bottled & Canned Soft
Drinks.

★ 80100 ★   **Piggly Wiggly**
2023 Platt Springs Rd.
West Columbia, SC 29169
(803)796-2545
Ultimate Parent: Bruno's. **SIC:** 5411—
Grocery Stores.

★ 80101 ★   **Piggly Wiggly**
2702 Emanuel Church Rd.
West Columbia, SC 29170
(803)359-2534
Ultimate Parent: Bruno's. **SIC:** 5411—
Grocery Stores.

★ 80102 ★   **Piggly Wiggly**
1916 Augusta Hwy.
West Columbia, SC 29169
(803)794-4935
Ultimate Parent: Bruno's. **SIC:** 5411—
Grocery Stores.

★ 80103 ★   **Pitney Bowes**
176 McSwain Dr.
West Columbia, SC 29169
(803)796-4841
Officer: Charles Edwards, Vice President.
Ultimate Parent: Pitney Bowes. **SIC:**
3554—Paper Industries Machinery.

★ 80104 ★   **Pizza Hut**
2725 Sunset Blvd.
West Columbia, SC 29169
(803)791-8877
Ultimate Parent: Pepsico. **SIC:** 5812—
Eating Places.

★ 80105 ★   **Radio Shack**
471 Capitol Sq.
West Columbia, SC 29169
(803)791-0223
Company Type: Division. **Ultimate Parent:**
Tandy Corp. **SIC:** 5065—Electronic Parts &
Equipment Nec.

★ 80106 ★   **Radio Shack**
Lexington Dr.
West Columbia, SC 29170
(803)791-3777
Company Type: Division. **Ultimate Parent:**
Tandy Corp. **SIC:** 5621—Women's Clothing
Stores.

★ 80107 ★   **Rite Aid Pharmacy**
2704 Emanuel Church Rd.
West Columbia, SC 29170
(803)359-8925
Ultimate Parent: Rite Aid. **SIC:** 5912—Drug
Stores & Proprietary Stores.

★ 80108 ★   **Standard Federal
Savings Bank**
615 Knox Abbott Dr.
West Columbia, SC 29033
(803)733-6700
Ultimate Parent: Standard Federal Bank.
SIC: 6035—Federal Savings Institutions.

★ 80109 ★   **Standard Federal
Savings Bank**
2830 Sunset Blvd.
West Columbia, SC 29169
(803)733-6710
Ultimate Parent: Standard Federal Bank.
SIC: 6035—Federal Savings Institutions.

★ 80110 ★   **United Parcel Service**
1782 Old Dunbar Rd.
West Columbia, SC 29172
(803)772-0325
Ultimate Parent: United Parcel Service of
America. **SIC:** 4215—Courier Services
Except by Air.

★ 80111 ★   **Wal Mart**
2307 Augusta Hwy.
West Columbia, SC 29169
(803)796-9144
Ultimate Parent: Wal-Mart Stores, Inc. **SIC:**
5311—Department Stores.

★ 80112 ★   **Zippy Mart Inc.**
1108 Augusta St.
West Columbia, SC 29169
(803)796-7150
Ultimate Parent: Crown Central Petroleum
Corp. **SIC:** 5411—Grocery Stores.

Westminister

★ 80113 ★   **Eaton Corp., U.S.
Engine Valve Corp.**
PO Box 277
Intersections 123 & 111
Westminister, SC 29693
(803)647-2061
Location Type: Plant. **Officer:** John
Brashvis, Controller. **Ultimate Parent:**
Eaton Corp. **SIC:** 5013—Motor Vehicle
Supplies & New Parts.

★ 80114 ★   **U.S. Engine Valve
Corp.**
PO Box 277
Westminister, SC 29693
(803)647-2061 **Fax:** (803)647-2649
Company Type: Joint venture. **Ultimate
Parent:** Eaton Corp.

Westminster

★ 80115 ★   **Cast Products Co.
Inc.**
Oakway Rd.
Westminster, SC 29693
(803)647-9122
Ultimate Parent: Harvard Industries. **SIC:**
3321—Gray & Ductile Iron Foundries.

★ 80116 ★   **GTE Valenite**
Rte. 3 Box 189 Hwy. 11
Westminster, SC 29693
Ultimate Parent: GTE. **SIC:** 3541—
Machine Tools—Metal Cutting Types.

★ 80117 ★   **GTE Valenite**
Rte. 5 Hwy. 11
Westminster, SC 29693
Ultimate Parent: GTE. **SIC:** 3541—
Machine Tools—Metal Cutting Types.

★ 80118 ★   **GTE Valenite Corp.
Plant 3**
Hwy. 11
Westminster, SC 29693
Ultimate Parent: GTE. **SIC:** 3541—
Machine Tools—Metal Cutting Types.

★ 80119 ★   **US Engine Valve Co.**
7039 S. Hwy. 11
Westminster, SC 29693
Ultimate Parent: Eaton Corp. **SIC:** 3592—
Carburetors, Pistons, Rings & Valves.

★ 80120 ★   **US Engine Valve Co.**
Hwy. 11 at 123
Westminster, SC 29693
Ultimate Parent: Eaton Corp. **SIC:** 3592—
Carburetors, Pistons, Rings & Valves.

White Oak

★ 80121 ★   **Bowater Inc.**
White Oak, SC 29176
(803)635-4244
Ultimate Parent: Bowater. **SIC:** 2611—Pulp
Mills.

Williamston

★ 80122 ★   **Branch Banking &
Trust Co.**
1 Greenville Dr.
Williamston, SC 29697-1507
(803)847-4511
Company Type: Subsidiary. **Location
Type:** Branch office. **Officer:** Terry D.
Nation, Manager. **Ultimate Parent:**
Southern National Corp. **SIC:** 6021—
National Commercial Banks.

★ 80123 ★   **First Union National
Bank of South Carolina**
113 E. Main St.
Williamston, SC 29697-1926
(803)847-4501
Location Type: Branch office. **Ultimate
Parent:** First Union Corp. **SIC:** 6021—
National Commercial Banks.

★ 80124 ★   **Rite Aid Discount
Pharmacie**
4646 Hawks Way
Williamston, SC 29697
(803)847-9029
Ultimate Parent: Rite Aid. **SIC:** 5912—Drug
Stores & Proprietary Stores.

Williston

★ 80125 ★   **Dayco Prods. Inc.**
108 West St.
Williston, SC 29853
Ultimate Parent: Mark IV Industries. **SIC:**
3052—Rubber & Plastics Hose & Belting.

★ 80126 ★   **Dayco Products Inc.**
108 West St.
Williston, SC 29853
Ultimate Parent: Mark IV Industries. **SIC:**
3052—Rubber & Plastics Hose & Belting.

★ 80127 ★   **Dixie-Narco**
Industrial Rd.
Williston, SC 29853
(803)266-7423 **Fax:** (803)266-3677
Officer: Robert W. Downing, President.
Ultimate Parent: Maytag.

★ 80128 ★   **Dixie-Narco Inc.**
Dixie-Narco Blvd. PO Box 68
Williston, SC 29853
Ultimate Parent: Maytag. **SIC:** 3581—
Automatic Vending Machines.

★ 80129 ★   **Dixie-Narco Inc.**
Industrial Blvd. PO Box 68
Williston, SC 29853
Ultimate Parent: Maytag. **SIC:** 3632—
Household Refrigerators & Freezers.

★ 80130 ★   **Maytag Corp.**
Admiral Co. Div.
Industrial Blvd.
Williston, SC 29853
Company Type: Division. **Ultimate Parent:**
Maytag. **SIC:** 3632—Household
Refrigerators & Freezers.

Winnsboro

★ 80131 ★   **First Union National
Bank of South Carolina**
111 S. Congress St.
Winnsboro, SC 29180-1103
(803)635-4617
Location Type: Branch office. **Ultimate
Parent:** First Union Corp. **SIC:** 6021—
National Commercial Banks.

★ 80132 ★   **Kentucky Fried
Chicken**
Hwy. 321 Bypass
Winnsboro, SC 29180
(803)635-9652
Ultimate Parent: Pepsico. **SIC:** 5812—
Eating Places.

★ 80133 ★   **Standard Products
Co.**
Hwy. 34 S.
Winnsboro, SC 29180
(803)635-5541
Officer: Jim Reid, Chairman. **Ultimate
Parent:** Standard Products. **SIC:** 3089—
Plastics Products Nec; 3999—Manufacturing
Industries Nec.

★ 80134 ★   **Trailways Bus
Terminal&Gril**
N Congress
Winnsboro, SC 29180
(803)635-4334
Ultimate Parent: Greyhound Lines Inc. **SIC:**
4111—Local & Suburban Transit.

★ 80135 ★   **Westvaco Corp.**
Hwy. 34 S
Winnsboro, SC 29180
(803)635-4604
Ultimate Parent: WestVaco Corp. **SIC:**
2411—Logging.

Woodruff

★ 80136 ★   **Pizza Hut**
Cross Anchor Rd.
Woodruff, SC 29388
(803)476-3621
Ultimate Parent: Pepsico. **SIC:** 5812—
Eating Places.

★ 80137 ★   **Rite Aid Disc Pharm**
341 N. Main St.
Woodruff, SC 29388
(803)476-3500
Ultimate Parent: Rite Aid. **SIC:** 5912—Drug
Stores & Proprietary Stores.

York

★ 80138 ★   **Champion
Laboratories Inc.**
200 Ratchford Rd.
York, SC 29745
(803)684-3205
Officer: Henry Jumper, Manager. **Ultimate
Parent:** UIS. **SIC:** 3599—Industrial
Machinery Nec.

★ 80139 ★   **First Union National
Bank of South Carolina**
12 N. Congress St.
York, SC 29745-1529
(803)684-9209
Location Type: Branch office. **Ultimate
Parent:** First Union Corp. **SIC:** 6021—
National Commercial Banks.

★ 80140 ★   **Rockwell International**
U.S. 321 Chester Hwy.
York, SC 29745
Ultimate Parent: Rockwell International
Corp. **SIC:** 3714—Motor Vehicle Parts &
Accessories.

TENNESSEE

Adamsville

★ 80141 ★ **Aqua Glass Corp.**
Industrial Pk.
Adamsville, TN 38310
(901)632-0911 **Fax:** (901)632-4232
Officer: Harry A. Boosey. **Ultimate Parent:**
Masco.

★ 80142 ★ **Aqua Glass Corp.**
Main Plant
Industrial Park
Adamsville, TN 38310
Location Type: Plant. **Ultimate Parent:**
Masco. **SIC:** 3296—Mineral Wool.

★ 80143 ★ **Magnetek Century Electric**
PO Box 333
Adamsville, TN 38310-0333
(901)632-4800
Officer: Randy Puckett. **Ultimate Parent:**
Magnetek Inc. **SIC:** 3621—Motors &
Generators.

Afton

★ 80144 ★ **Plus Mark, Inc.**
11 E. Bypass American Rd.
Afton, TN 37616
(615)639-7878 **Fax:** (615)636-2065
Officer: Erwin Weiss, President. **Ultimate Parent:** American Greetings.

★ 80145 ★ **Plus Mark Inc.**
Hwy. 11 E. By-Pass
Afton, TN 37616
Ultimate Parent: American Greetings. **SIC:**
2771—Greeting Cards; 2893—Printing Ink.

Alamo

★ 80146 ★ **People's Bank**
PO Box 10
Alamo, TN 38001
(901)696-5566
Ultimate Parent: People's Bank. **SIC:**
6099—Functions Related to Deposit
Banking.

★ 80147 ★ **Westinghouse Electric Corp.**
Rte. 1
Alamo, TN 38001
Ultimate Parent: Westinghouse Electric
Corp. **SIC:** 3612—Transformers Except
Electronic.

Alcoa

★ 80148 ★ **Alcoa**
PO Box 9158 PO Box 9158
Alcoa, TN 37701
Ultimate Parent: Aluminum Co. of America-
-Alcoa. **SIC:** 3334—Primary Aluminum.

★ 80149 ★ **Alcoa Tennessee Operations**
Hall Rd. PO Box 9158
Alcoa, TN 37701
Ultimate Parent: Aluminum Co. of America-
-Alcoa. **SIC:** 3334—Primary Aluminum;
3353—Aluminum Sheet, Plate & Foil;
3355—Aluminum Rolling & Drawing Nec.

★ 80150 ★ **Aluminum Co. of America**
300 S. Hall Rd.
PO Box 9128
Alcoa, TN 37701-9128
(615)977-2011
Location Type: Branch office. **Officer:** Don
Simonic, Manager. **Ultimate Parent:**
Aluminum Co. of America—Alcoa. **SIC:**
3334—Primary Aluminum; 3341—
Secondary Nonferrous Metals.

★ 80151 ★ **First American National Bank**
216 S. Calderwood St.
Alcoa, TN 37701-2106
(615)981-3500
Location Type: Branch office. **Ultimate Parent:** First American Corp. **SIC:** 6021—
National Commercial Banks.

★ 80152 ★ **First American National Bank**
2784 Airport Hwy.
Alcoa, TN 37701-3115
(615)981-3460
Location Type: Branch office. **Ultimate Parent:** First American Corp. **SIC:** 6021—
National Commercial Banks.

★ 80153 ★ **First FSB of Maryville**
3051 Airport Hwy.
Alcoa, TN 37701-3120
(615)983-1221
Location Type: Branch office. **Ultimate Parent:** Union Planters Corp. **SIC:** 6021—
National Commercial Banks.

★ 80154 ★ **First Tennessee Bank NA**
2807 Airport Hwy.
Alcoa, TN 37701-3116
(615)977-5111
Location Type: Branch office. **Ultimate Parent:** First Tennessee National Corp.
SIC: 6021—National Commercial Banks.

★ 80155 ★ **First Tennessee Bank NA**
112 S. Hall Rd.
Alcoa, TN 37701-2640
(615)977-5130
Location Type: Branch office. **Ultimate Parent:** First Tennessee National Corp.
SIC: 6021—National Commercial Banks.

★ 80156 ★ **Magnetek National Elec Coil**
73 Hall Rd.
Alcoa, TN 37701
(615)983-5550
Ultimate Parent: Magnetek Inc. **SIC:**
7694—Armature Rewinding Shops.

★ 80157 ★ **Wal-Mart Stores Inc.**
144 S. Hall Rd.
Alcoa, TN 37701
(615)983-7500
Ultimate Parent: Wal-Mart Stores, Inc. **SIC:**
5331—Variety Stores.

Alexandria

★ 80158 ★ **DeKalb Country Bank & Trust Co.**
Main St.
Alexandria, TN 37012
(615)529-2164
Location Type: Branch office. **Ultimate Parent:** Union Planters Corp. **SIC:** 6021—
National Commercial Banks.

★ 80159 ★ **DeKalb Country Bank Trust Co.**
PO Box 337
Alexandria, TN 37012-0337
Location Type: Branch office. **Ultimate Parent:** Union Planters Corp. **SIC:** 6021—
National Commercial Banks.

★ 80160 ★ **Dekalb County Bank & Trust Co.**
Public Sq.
Alexandria, TN 37012
(615)529-2163 **Fax:** (615)529-2300
Location Type: Branch office. **Ultimate Parent:** Union Planters Corp. **SIC:** 6021—
National Commercial Banks.

Algood

★ 80161 ★ **Citizens Bank**
167 W. Main St.
Algood, TN 38501
(615)526-2181
Location Type: Branch office. **Ultimate Parent:** Union Planters Corp. **SIC:** 6021—
National Commercial Banks.

Antioch

★ 80162 ★ **American General Finance**
5372 Mount View Rd.
Antioch, TN 37013-2307
(615)731-2206
Ultimate Parent: American General Corp.
SIC: 6141—Personal Credit Institutions;
6162—Mortgage Bankers &
Correspondents.

★ 80163 ★ **American General Finance Inc.**
5372 Mount View Rd.
Antioch, TN 37013-2307
(615)731-2206
Location Type: Branch office. **Ultimate Parent:** American General Corp. **SIC:**
6141—Personal Credit Institutions; 6162—
Mortgage Bankers & Correspondents.

★ 80164 ★ **AmSouth Bank of Tennessee**
5323 Mount View Rd.
Antioch, TN 37013
(615)731-9915
Location Type: Branch office. **Ultimate Parent:** AmSouth Bancorp. **SIC:** 6022—
State Commercial Banks; 6162—Mortgage
Bankers & Correspondents.

★ 80165 ★ **Burlington Coat Factory Warehouse**
5320 Hickory Hollow Pky.
Antioch, TN 37013-3128
(615)731-0470
Ultimate Parent: Burlington Industries,
Equity. **SIC:** 5311—Department Stores;
5661—Shoe Stores.

★ 80166 ★ **Casual Corner**
5252 Hickory Hollow Pky.
Antioch, TN 37013
(615)832-8397
Ultimate Parent: United States Shoe. **SIC:**
5621—Women's Clothing Stores; 5651—
Family Clothing Stores.

★ 80167 ★ **Eckerd Drugs**
5361 Mountainview Rd.
Antioch, TN 37013
(615)262-5744
Ultimate Parent: Eckerd Corp. **SIC:** 5912—
Drug Stores & Proprietary Stores.

★ 80168 ★ **First American National Bank**
5236 Hickory Hollow Pky.
Antioch, TN 37013
(615)736-6130
Location Type: Branch office. **Ultimate Parent:** First American Corp. **SIC:** 6021—
National Commercial Banks.

★ 80169 ★ **First Tennessee Bank NA**
5388 Hickory Hollow Pky.
Antioch, TN 37013
(615)734-6135
Location Type: Branch office. **Ultimate Parent:** First Tennessee National Corp.
SIC: 6021—National Commercial Banks.

★ 80170 ★ **Jiffy Lube Oil Change**
520 Bell Rd.
Antioch, TN 37013
(615)366-6664
Ultimate Parent: Pennzoil. **SIC:** 7539—
Automotive Repair Shops Nec.

★ 80171 ★ **Lane Bryant**
5252 Hickory Hollow Pky.
Antioch, TN 37013
(615)832-5029
Ultimate Parent: Limited. **SIC:** 5621—
Women's Clothing Stores.

★ 80172 ★ **Limited Express**
5252 Hickory Hollow Pky.
Antioch, TN 37013
(615)833-6878
Ultimate Parent: Limited. **SIC:** 5621—
Women's Clothing Stores.

★ 80173 ★ **Penney J C**
5252 Hickory Hollow Pky.
Antioch, TN 37013
(615)331-6180
Ultimate Parent: J.C. Penney. **SIC:** 5311—
Department Stores.

★ 80174 ★ **Shell Food Mart**
500 Collins Park Dr.
Antioch, TN 37013
(615)731-3517
Ultimate Parent: Shell Oil Co. **SIC:** 5411—
Grocery Stores.

★ 80175 ★ **Student Loan Marketing Association**
301 S. Perimeter Park Dr.
Antioch, TN 37013
(615)781-4248
Ultimate Parent: Student Loan Marketing
Association. **SIC:** 6062—State Credit
Unions.

★ 80176 ★ **Target**
5330 Cane Ridge Rd.
Antioch, TN 37013
(615)834-6340
Ultimate Parent: Dayton Hudson. **SIC:**
5311—Department Stores.

★ 80177 ★ **Target Stores**
5330 Cane Ridge Rd.
Antioch, TN 37013
(615)834-6340
Ultimate Parent: Dayton Hudson. **SIC:**
5311—Department Stores.

★ 80178 ★ **Union Planters National Bank**
925 Bell Rd.
Antioch, TN 37013-3191
(615)731-5812
Location Type: Branch office. **Ultimate Parent:** Union Planters Corp. **SIC:** 6021—
National Commercial Banks.

★ 80179 ★ **Weirton Steel Corp.**
3716 Folkstone Dr.
Antioch, TN 37013
(615)361-1893
Ultimate Parent: Weirton Steel Corp. **SIC:**
3312—Blast Furnaces & Steel Mills.

Arlington

★ 80180 ★ **Dow Corning Corp.**
5677 Airline Rd.
Arlington, TN 38002
(901)867-9971
Ultimate Parent: Corning. **SIC:** 5999—
Miscellaneous Retail Stores Nec.

★ 80181 ★ **Dow Corning Dow Corning Wright**
5677 Airline Rd.
Arlington, TN 38002
(901)867-9971
Company Type: Subsidiary. **Ultimate Parent:** Dow Corning.

★ 80182 ★ **Dow Corning Wright**
5677 Airline Rd.
Arlington, TN 38002
Ultimate Parent: Dow Chemical Co. USA.
SIC: 3842—Surgical Appliances & Supplies.

★ 80183 ★   **Peoples Bank**
11915 Us 70
Arlington, TN 38002
(901)867-2658
Ultimate Parent: People's Bank. **SIC:** 6022—State Commercial Banks.

Ashland City

★ 80184 ★   **First Union National Bank of Tennessee**
311 N. Main St.
Ashland City, TN 37015-1317
(615)792-5185
Location Type: Branch office. **Ultimate Parent:** First Union Corp. **SIC:** 6021—National Commercial Banks.

Athens

★ 80185 ★   **American Electric**
260 Dennis St.
Athens, TN 37303
Ultimate Parent: Thomas & Betts. **SIC:** 3644—Noncurrent-Carrying Wiring Devices; 3494—Valves & Pipe Fittings Nec.

★ 80186 ★   **Davidson Interior Trim Textron**
2110 Charles Redfern Dr.
Athens, TN 37303
Ultimate Parent: Textron. **SIC:** 3000—Rubber & Miscellaneous Plastics Products.

★ 80187 ★   **Dover Corp.**
Heil Bulk Trailer Div.
1125 Congress Pky. NE
Athens, TN 37303
(615)745-5830
Officer: Tom Pikciunas, Plant Manager. **Ultimate Parent:** Dover Corp. **SIC:** 3713—Truck & Bus Bodies; 3715—Truck Trailers; 3731—Ship Building & Repairing.

★ 80188 ★   **Fitness Center**
1313 Decatur Pike
Athens, TN 37303
(615)745-6240
Ultimate Parent: New York Times. **SIC:** 7299—Miscellaneous Personal Services Nec.

★ 80189 ★   **Heil Co.**
Northridge Industrial Park
Athens, TN 37303
(615)745-5830
Ultimate Parent: Dow Chemical Co. USA. **SIC:** 3443—Fabricated Plate Work—Boiler Shops.

★ 80190 ★   **Mayfield Dairy Farms Inc.**
813 E. Madison Ave.
Athens, TN 37303-0310
Ultimate Parent: Dean Foods. **SIC:** 2026—Fluid Milk; 2024—Ice Cream & Frozen Desserts.

★ 80191 ★   **Mayfield Dairy Farms Inc.**
806 E. Madison Ave.
Athens, TN 37303-3858
(615)745-2151
Company Type: Subsidiary. **Officer:** William D. Fischer, President. **Ultimate Parent:** Dean Foods. **SIC:** 2026—Fluid Milk; 2024—Ice Cream & Frozen Desserts. **Employee Count:** 850. **Sales:** 191 M.

★ 80192 ★   **Mini Mart**
2432 Congress Pky. NW
Athens, TN 37303
(615)745-3150
Ultimate Parent: Kroger. **SIC:** 5411—Grocery Stores.

★ 80193 ★   **Payless Shoe Source**
1635 Decatur Pike
Athens, TN 37303
(615)745-0810
Ultimate Parent: May Department Stores. **SIC:** 5661—Shoe Stores.

★ 80194 ★   **Payless Shoesource**
1635 Decatur Pike
Athens, TN 37303
(615)745-0810
Ultimate Parent: May Department Stores. **SIC:** 5661—Shoe Stores.

★ 80195 ★   **Thomas & Betts Corp.**
260 Dennis St.
Athens, TN 37303
Ultimate Parent: Thomas & Betts. **SIC:** 3644—Noncurrent-Carrying Wiring Devices; 3644—Noncurrent-Carrying Wiring Devices.

★ 80196 ★   **Wal-Mart Stores Inc.**
917 Decatur Pike
Athens, TN 37303
(615)744-7810
Ultimate Parent: Wal-Mart Stores, Inc. **SIC:** 5311—Department Stores.

Auburn Town

★ 80197 ★   **Bank of Commerce**
Main St.
Auburn Town, TN 37016
(615)464-4101
Location Type: Branch office. **Ultimate Parent:** Union Planters Corp. **SIC:** 6021—National Commercial Banks.

Bartlett

★ 80198 ★   **First Tennessee Bank NA**
6891 Summer Ave.
Bartlett, TN 38133-3811
(901)385-3029
Location Type: Branch office. **Ultimate Parent:** First Tennessee National Corp. **SIC:** 6021—National Commercial Banks.

★ 80199 ★   **Union Planters National Bank**
7790 Hwy. 64
Bartlett, TN 38133
(901)385-4025
Location Type: Branch office. **Ultimate Parent:** Union Planters Corp. **SIC:** 6021—National Commercial Banks.

★ 80200 ★   **Union Planters National Bank**
6250 Stage Rd.
Bartlett, TN 38134-3728
(901)385-4000
Location Type: Branch office. **Ultimate Parent:** Union Planters Corp. **SIC:** 6021—National Commercial Banks.

Baxter

★ 80201 ★   **Citizens Bank**
140 Main St.
Baxter, TN 38544-9245
(615)526-2181
Location Type: Branch office. **Ultimate Parent:** Union Planters Corp. **SIC:** 6021—National Commercial Banks.

Benton

★ 80202 ★   **Peoples Bank of Polk County**
Hwy. 411
Benton, TN 37307
(615)338-2836
Ultimate Parent: People's Bank. **SIC:** 6141—Personal Credit Institutions.

Big Rock

★ 80203 ★   **First American National Bank**
Hwys. 79 & 120
Big Rock, TN 37023-9772
(615)232-6004
Location Type: Branch office. **Ultimate Parent:** First American Corp. **SIC:** 6021—National Commercial Banks.

Blountville

★ 80204 ★   **First Tennessee Bank NA**
State Hwy. 37 & Central Ave.
Blountville, TN 37617-9224
(615)323-4176
Location Type: Branch office. **Ultimate Parent:** First Tennessee National Corp. **SIC:** 6021—National Commercial Banks.

★ 80205 ★   **Tri-City Bank & Trust Co.**
PO Box 277
Blountville, TN 37617-0277
(615)323-3161
Company Type: Subsidiary. **Officer:** Ralph Harr, Chairman of the Board. **Ultimate Parent:** First Virginia Banks Inc. **SIC:** 6022—State Commercial Banks. **Employee Count:** 120.

★ 80206 ★   **Tri City Bank & Trust Co.**
Main St.
Blountville, TN 37617
(615)323-3161
Ultimate Parent: First Virginia Banks Inc. **SIC:** 6022—State Commercial Banks.

★ 80207 ★   **Tri City Bank & Trust Co.**
277 PO Box
Blountville, TN 37617
(615)247-5191
Ultimate Parent: First Virginia Banks Inc. **SIC:** 6022—State Commercial Banks.

★ 80208 ★   **Tri-City & Trust Co.**
3416 Hwy. 126
PO Box 277
Blountville, TN 37617-0277
(615)323-3161
Company Type: Subsidiary. **Officer:** Ralph P. Harr, Chairman of the Board. **Ultimate Parent:** First Virginia Banks Inc. **SIC:** 6022—State Commercial Banks.

Bolivar

★ 80209 ★   **Wal-Mart Stores Inc.**
Hwy. 64 E
Bolivar, TN 38008
(901)658-7794
Ultimate Parent: Wal-Mart Stores, Inc. **SIC:** 5311—Department Stores.

Brainerd

★ 80210 ★   **AmSouth Bank of Tennessee**
5515 Brainerd Rd.
Brainerd, TN 37402
(615)894-1058
Location Type: Branch office. **Ultimate Parent:** AmSouth Bancorp. **SIC:** 6022—State Commercial Banks; 6162—Mortgage Bankers & Correspondents.

Brentwood

★ 80211 ★   **Alcoa Conductor Products Co.**
105 Westpark Dr., No. 150
Brentwood, TN 37027-5010
(615)370-4300
Location Type: Branch office. **Officer:** Jeff J. Underwood, President. **Ultimate Parent:** Aluminum Co. of America–Alcoa. **SIC:** 3643—Current-Carrying Wiring Devices.

★ 80212 ★   **Alcoa Conductor Products Co.**
105 Westpark Dr., No. 150
Brentwood, TN 37027-5010
(615)370-4300
Location Type: Branch office. **Officer:** Jeff J. Underwood, President. **Ultimate Parent:** Aluminum Co. of America–Alcoa. **SIC:** 3643—Current-Carrying Wiring Devices.

★ 80213 ★   **Alcoa Fujikura Ltd.**
105 Westpark Dr., Ste. 200
Brentwood, TN 37027-5010
(615)370-2100
Officer: Robert H. Barton, President. **Ultimate Parent:** Aluminum Co. of America-Alcoa. **SIC:** 3694—Engine Electrical Equipment; 3357—Nonferrous Wiredrawing & Insulating; 3315—Steel Wire & Related Products; 3714—Motor Vehicle Parts & Accessories. **Employee Count:** 9500.

★ 80214 ★   **Alcoa Fujikura Ltd.**
105 Westpark Dr., Ste. 200
Brentwood, TN 37027-5010
(615)370-2100
Officer: Robert H. Barton, President. **Ultimate Parent:** Aluminum Co. of America-Alcoa. **SIC:** 3694—Engine Electrical Equipment; 3357—Nonferrous Wiredrawing & Insulating; 3315—Steel Wire & Related Products; 3714—Motor Vehicle Parts & Accessories. **Employee Count:** 9500.

★ 80215 ★   **Armco Steel Inc.**
5214 Maryland Way
Brentwood, TN 37027-5034
(615)373-2772
Ultimate Parent: Armco. **SIC:** 3312—Blast Furnaces & Steel Mills.

★ 80216 ★   **Arvin Industries Inc.**
Gabriel Ride Control Products Div.
100 Westwood Pl. Ste. 300
Brentwood, TN 37027
(615)221-7433 **Fax:** (615)221-7185
Company Type: Division. **Location Type:** Plant. **Officer:** E. Leon Viars, President. **Ultimate Parent:** Arvin Industries Inc. **SIC:** 3714—Motor Vehicle Parts & Accessories.

★ 80217 ★   **Arvin Industries Inc.**
Gabriel Ride Control Products Div.
100 Westwood Pl.
Brentwood, TN 37027-5015
(615)221-7433 **Fax:** (615)221-7186
Company Type: Division. **Officer:** E. Leon Viars, President. **Ultimate Parent:** Arvin Industries Inc.

★ 80218 ★   **Bethlehem Steel Corp.**
101 Westpark Dr.
Brentwood, TN 37027-5031
(615)373-0045
Ultimate Parent: Bethlehem Steel Corp. **SIC:** 3312—Blast Furnaces & Steel Mills.

★ 80219 ★   **Boston Industrial Products**
PO Box 1708
Brentwood, TN 37024-1708
(615)377-6700 **Fax:** (615)377-1005
Company Type: Subsidiary. **Officer:** Charlie Kaake, Vice President & General Manager. **Ultimate Parent:** Dana Corp.

★ 80220 ★   **Boston Industrial Products**
1621 Vaden Blvd.
Brentwood, TN 37027
(615)377-6700
Ultimate Parent: Dana Corp. **SIC:** 3052—Rubber & Plastics Hose & Belting; 3053—Gaskets, Packing & Sealing Devices.

★ 80221 ★   **Caterpillar Inc.**
750 Old Hickory Blvd. Bld 2851
Brentwood, TN 37027
(615)373-1870
Ultimate Parent: Caterpillar. **SIC:** 5082—Construction & Mining Machinery.

★ 80222 ★   **Crestar Food Products, Inc.**
750 Old Hickory Blvd., Ste. 250
Brentwood, TN 37027
(615)377-4400 **Fax:** (615)377-4451
Company Type: Subsidiary. **Officer:** Don Kerr, President & CEO. **Ultimate Parent:** H.J. Heinz.

★ 80223 ★   **Crestar Food Products Inc.**
750 Old Hickory Blvd.
Brentwood, TN 37027-4509
(615)377-4400
Company Type: Division. **Officer:** Thane A. Pressman, President & CEO. **Ultimate Parent:** H.J. Heinz. **SIC:** 2041—Flour & Other Grain Mill Products; 5149—Groceries & Related Products Nec.

★ 80224 ★   **Dana Corp.**
Boston Industrial Products Division
PO Box 1708
Brentwood, TN 37024-1708
(615)377-6700 **Fax:** (615)377-1005
Company Type: Division. **Officer:** Charles Kaake, Vice President & General Manager. **Ultimate Parent:** Dana Corp. **SIC:** 3052—Rubber & Plastics Hose & Belting.

★ 80225 ★   **First American National Bank**
329 Franklin Rd.
Brentwood, TN 37027-5213
(615)748-2596
Location Type: Branch office. **Ultimate Parent:** First American Corp. **SIC:** 6021—National Commercial Banks.

★ 80226 ★ First American
National Bank
5054 Thoroughbred Ln.
Brentwood, TN 37027-4225
(615)748-2520
Location Type: Branch office. Ultimate
Parent: First American Corp. SIC: 6021—
National Commercial Banks.

★ 80227 ★ First Tennessee Bank
NA
3 Maryland Farms, Ste. 328
Brentwood, TN 37027
(615)790-5101
Location Type: Branch office. Ultimate
Parent: First Tennessee National Corp.
SIC: 6021—National Commercial Banks.

★ 80228 ★ First Tennessee Bank
NA
202 Franklin Rd.
Brentwood, TN 37027-5209
(615)790-5106
Location Type: Branch office. Ultimate
Parent: First Tennessee National Corp.
SIC: 6021—National Commercial Banks.

★ 80229 ★ First Union National
Bank of Tennessee
7029 Church St. E
Brentwood, TN 37027-5225
(615)373-8208
Location Type: Branch office. Ultimate
Parent: First Union Corp. SIC: 6021—
National Commercial Banks.

★ 80230 ★ Gabriel Ride Control
Products Inc.
100 Westwood Pl.
Brentwood, TN 37027-5044
(615)221-7433
Company Type: Subsidiary. Officer: Leon
Viars, President. Ultimate Parent: Arvin
Industries Inc. SIC: 3714—Motor Vehicle
Parts & Accessories. Employee Count:
1500. Sales: 350 M.

★ 80231 ★ Maremont Corp.
100 Westwood Pl.
Brentwood, TN 37027-5044
(615)221-7165
Company Type: Subsidiary. Officer: Byron
O. Pond, COO. Ultimate Parent: Arvin
Industries Inc. SIC: 5013—Motor Vehicle
Supplies & New Parts. Employee Count:
2000. Sales: 255 M.

★ 80232 ★ NCR Corp.
209 Powell Pl.
Brentwood, TN 37027-7522
(615)370-2200
Location Type: Branch office. Officer:
David Armillei. Ultimate Parent: AT&T. SIC:
2761—Manifold Business Forms; 3578—
Calculating & Accounting Equipment.

★ 80233 ★ Service Merchandise
7100 Service Merchandise Dr.
Brentwood, TN 37027
(615)660-3310
Ultimate Parent: Service Merchandise Co.,
Inc. SIC: 5399—Miscellaneous General
Merchandise Store.

★ 80234 ★ Service Merchandise
1600 Vaden Blvd.
Brentwood, TN 37027
(615)366-3451
Ultimate Parent: Service Merchandise Co.,
Inc. SIC: 5331—Variety Stores; 5399—
Miscellaneous General Merchandise Store.

★ 80235 ★ Service Merchandise
Co., Inc.
7100 Service Merchandise Dr.
Brentwood, TN 37027
(615)660-6000
Company Type: Headquarters. Officer:
Raymond Zimmerman. Employee Count:
22879. Sales: 3814.6 M. Fortune Service
500: Ranking 34.

★ 80236 ★ Southtrust Mortgage
750 Old Hickory Blvd.
Brentwood, TN 37027
(615)377-1025
Ultimate Parent: Southtrust Corp. SIC:
6162—Mortgage Bankers &
Correspondents.

★ 80237 ★ Union Planters
National Bank
4930 Thoroughbred Rd.
Brentwood, TN 37027-4226
(615)726-4281
Location Type: Branch office. Ultimate
Parent: Union Planters Corp. SIC: 6021—
National Commercial Banks.

Bristol

★ 80238 ★ Blazer Financial
Services
2010 W. State St.
Bristol, TN 37620
(615)764-4161
Ultimate Parent: Great Western Financial
Corp. SIC: 6062—State Credit Unions;
6141—Personal Credit Institutions.

★ 80239 ★ Eckerd Drugs
1107 Bluff City Hwy.
Bristol, TN 37620
(615)643-3106
Ultimate Parent: Eckerd Corp. SIC: 5912—
Drug Stores & Proprietary Stores.

★ 80240 ★ First American
National Bank
1410 Volunteer Pky.
Bristol, TN 37620-6052
(615)652-8524
Location Type: Branch office. Ultimate
Parent: First American Corp. SIC: 6021—
National Commercial Banks.

★ 80241 ★ First American
National Bank
840 State St.
Bristol, TN 37620-2559
(615)652-8500
Location Type: Branch office. Ultimate
Parent: First American Corp. SIC: 6021—
National Commercial Banks.

★ 80242 ★ First American
National Bank
1954 W. State St.
Bristol, TN 37620
(615)652-8525
Location Type: Branch office. Ultimate
Parent: First American Corp. SIC: 6021—
National Commercial Banks.

★ 80243 ★ First American Trust
Co., NA
840 State St.
Bristol, TN 37620
(615)229-0283
Location Type: Branch office. Ultimate
Parent: First American Corp. SIC: 6021—
National Commercial Banks.

★ 80244 ★ First Tennessee Bank
NA
1155 Volunteer Pky.
Bristol, TN 37620-4619
(615)968-7244
Location Type: Branch office. Ultimate
Parent: First Tennessee National Corp.
SIC: 6021—National Commercial Banks.

★ 80245 ★ First Tennessee Bank
NA
800 State St.
Bristol, TN 37620-2559
Fax: (615)968-2961
Location Type: Branch office. Ultimate
Parent: First Tennessee National Corp.
SIC: 6021—National Commercial Banks.

★ 80246 ★ Food Lion Inc. Store
340 Bluff City Hwy.
Bristol, TN 37620
(615)764-4188
Ultimate Parent: Food Lion. SIC: 5411—
Grocery Stores.

★ 80247 ★ Food Lion Inc. Store
1141 Volunteer Pky.
Bristol, TN 37620
(615)764-4189
Ultimate Parent: Food Lion. SIC: 5411—
Grocery Stores.

★ 80248 ★ Giant Food Market
Inc.
2000 W. State St.
Bristol, TN 37620
(615)764-3174
Ultimate Parent: Giant Food. SIC: 5411—
Grocery Stores.

★ 80249 ★ Greyhound Bus Lines
827 Shelby St.
Bristol, TN 37620
(615)764-6162
Ultimate Parent: Greyhound Lines Inc. SIC:
4131—Intercity & Rural Bus Transportation;
4111—Local & Suburban Transit; 4142—
Bus Charter Service Except Local.

★ 80250 ★ Kroger Co.
1346 Volunteer Pky.
Bristol, TN 37620
(615)968-5177
Ultimate Parent: Kroger. SIC: 5411—
Grocery Stores.

★ 80251 ★ Life Insurance Co. of
Virgin
1135 Volunteer Pky.
Bristol, TN 37620
(615)968-2167
Ultimate Parent: Life Insurance Co. of
Virginia. SIC: 6411—Insurance Agents,
Brokers & Service.

★ 80252 ★ Raytheon Co.
100 Vance Tank Rd.
Bristol, TN 37620
(615)652-5000
Officer: Joe Mazza, Plant Manager.
Ultimate Parent: Raytheon Co. SIC:
3761—Guided Missiles & Space Vehicles.

★ 80253 ★ Raytheon Co. Nwirp
Bristol
100 Vance Tank Rd.
Bristol, TN 37620-5698
Ultimate Parent: Raytheon Co. SIC:
3769—Space Vehicle Equipment Nec.

★ 80254 ★ Rite Aid Discount
Pharmacy
416 State St.
Bristol, TN 37620
(615)968-9965
Ultimate Parent: Rite Aid. SIC: 5912—Drug
Stores & Proprietary Stores.

★ 80255 ★ Trailways Bus Lines
2410 W. State St.
Bristol, TN 37620
(615)764-4197
Ultimate Parent: Greyhound Lines Inc. SIC:
4131—Intercity & Rural Bus Transportation;
4111—Local & Suburban Transit; 4142—
Bus Charter Service Except Local.

★ 80256 ★ Tramco Inc.
206 Delaware Ave.
Bristol, TN 37620
(615)968-4584
Ultimate Parent: B.F. Goodrich. SIC:
7694—Armature Rewinding Shops.

★ 80257 ★ Transamerica
Occidental Life Insurance
630 Locust St.
Bristol, TN 37620
(615)764-6827
Ultimate Parent: Transamerica Occidental
Life Insurance. SIC: 6411—Insurance
Agents, Brokers & Service.

Brownsville

★ 80258 ★ Greyhound Bus Lines
19 N. Russell Ave.
Brownsville, TN 38012
(901)772-2702
Ultimate Parent: Greyhound Lines Inc. SIC:
4131—Intercity & Rural Bus Transportation;
4111—Local & Suburban Transit; 4142—
Bus Charter Service Except Local.

★ 80259 ★ Kroger Co.
Bradford Sq.
Brownsville, TN 38012
(901)772-4552
Ultimate Parent: Kroger. SIC: 5411—
Grocery Stores.

★ 80260 ★ People's Bank
PO Box 726
Brownsville, TN 38012
(901)772-2919
Ultimate Parent: People's Bank. SIC:
6099—Functions Related to Deposit
Banking.

★ 80261 ★ Wal-Mart Stores Inc.
Bradford Shopping Ctr.
Brownsville, TN 38012
(901)772-4691
Ultimate Parent: Wal-Mart Stores, Inc. SIC:
5311—Department Stores.

Bruceton

★ 80262 ★ Mary Kay Cosmetics
S Carroll St.
Bruceton, TN 38317
(901)586-2270
Ultimate Parent: Mary Kay Cosmetics. SIC:
5999—Miscellaneous Retail Stores Nec.

Bulls Gap

★ 80263 ★ First Union National
Bank of Tennessee
105 N. Main St.
Bulls Gap, TN 37711-9556
(615)235-5146
Location Type: Branch office. Ultimate
Parent: First Union Corp. SIC: 6021—
National Commercial Banks.

Byrdstown

★ 80264 ★ Blue Grass
Cooperage Co.
PO Box 328
Byrdstown, TN 38549-0328
(615)864-3332
Officer: Daniel Rich. Ultimate Parent:
Brown-Forman. SIC: 2429—Special Product
Sawmills Nec.

★ 80265 ★ Pickett County Bank
& Trust Co.
PO Box 39
Byrdstown, TN 38549-0039
Location Type: Branch office. Ultimate
Parent: Union Planters Corp. SIC: 6021—
National Commercial Banks.

★ 80266 ★ Pickett County Bank
& Trust Co.
W. Main St.
Byrdstown, TN 38549
(615)864-3134 Fax: (615)864-3723
Location Type: Branch office. Ultimate
Parent: Union Planters Corp. SIC: 6021—
National Commercial Banks.

Calhoun

★ 80267 ★ Bowater Inc.
Southern Div.
Hwy. 11
Calhoun, TN 37309
(615)336-2211 Fax: (615)336-7150
Company Type: Subsidiary. Officer: J. A.
Breaux, President. Ultimate Parent:
Bowater.

★ 80268 ★ Bowater Inc.
Southern Div.
US Hwy. 11
Calhoun, TN 37309
(615)336-2211
Location Type: Branch office. Officer: J. A.
Breaux. Ultimate Parent: Bowater. SIC:
2621—Paper Mills.

★ 80269 ★ Bowater Inc.
Southern Div.
5020 Hwy. 11 S
Calhoun, TN 37309
(615)336-2211
Ultimate Parent: Bowater. SIC: 2411—
Logging; 2621—Paper Mills.

★ 80270 ★ Bowater Inc.
Southern Division
5020 Hwy. 11 S.
Calhoun, TN 37309
Ultimate Parent: Bowater. SIC: 2611—Pulp
Mills; 2621—Paper Mills.

★ 80271 ★ Bowater Inc.
Southern Division
Rte. 11
Calhoun, TN 37309
Ultimate Parent: Bowater. SIC: 2611—Pulp
Mills; 2621—Paper Mills.

★ 80272 ★ **Bowater Southern Paper Co.**
Rte. 11
Calhoun, TN 37309
Ultimate Parent: Bowater. **SIC:** 2611—Pulp
Mills; 2621—Paper Mills.

★ 80273 ★ **Bowater Southern Paper Co.**
Southern Division
Rte. 11
Calhoun, TN 37309
Ultimate Parent: Bowater. **SIC:** 2611—Pulp
Mills; 2621—Paper Mills.

★ 80274 ★ **Calhun Newsprint Co.**
Hwy. 11
Calhoun, TN 37309
(615)336-2211 **Fax:** (615)336-7150
Company Type: Subsidiary. **Officer:** D. E.
McIntyre, President. **Ultimate Parent:**
Bowater.

Camden

★ 80275 ★ **Specialty Products International**
Hwy. 70
Camden, TN 38320
(901)584-2831
Officer: M.C. Pattel. **Ultimate Parent:**
Avery Dennison Corp. **SIC:** 5099—Durable
Goods Nec.

★ 80276 ★ **Wal-Mart Stores Inc.**
Benton Ctr.
Camden, TN 38320
(901)584-6371
Ultimate Parent: Wal-Mart Stores, Inc. **SIC:**
5311—Department Stores.

★ 80277 ★ **Westvaco Corp.**
328 Rural Route 1
Camden, TN 38320
(901)584-6278
Ultimate Parent: WestVaco Corp. **SIC:**
1429—Crushed & Broken Stone Nec.

Carthage

★ 80278 ★ **Wal-Mart Stores Inc.**
Hwy. 25
Carthage, TN 37030
(615)735-2049
Ultimate Parent: Wal-Mart Stores, Inc. **SIC:**
5311—Department Stores.

★ 80279 ★ **William L. Bonnell Co., Inc.**
Hwy. 53 1.8 Miles N. of I-40
Carthage, TN 37030
Ultimate Parent: Ethyl. **SIC:** 3354—
Aluminum Extruded Products.

Caryville

★ 80280 ★ **Powell Valley Foods Co.**
Elkins Rd.
Caryville, TN 37714
Ultimate Parent: Philip Morris. **SIC:** 2013—
Sausages & Other Prepared Meats.

Celina

★ 80281 ★ **DeKalb Country Bank & Trust Co.**
Main & Dow Sts.
Celina, TN 38551
(615)243-3124
Location Type: Branch office. **Ultimate
Parent:** Union Planters Corp. **SIC:** 6021—
National Commercial Banks.

★ 80282 ★ **Hevi Duty Electric**
Hwy. 53 N
Celina, TN 38551
(615)243-3113
Ultimate Parent: General Signal. **SIC:**
3677—Electronic Coils & Transformers;
3699—Electrical Equipment & Supplies Nec.

★ 80283 ★ **Hevi-Duty Electric**
Hwy. 53 N
Celina, TN 38551
Ultimate Parent: General Signal. **SIC:**
3612—Transformers Except Electronic.

★ 80284 ★ **Hevi-Duty Electric Co.**
Hwy. 53 N.
Celina, TN 38551
Ultimate Parent: General Signal. **SIC:**
3612—Transformers Except Electronic.

★ 80285 ★ **Rite Aid Discount Pharmacy**
W Public Sq.
Celina, TN 38551
(615)243-2673
Ultimate Parent: Rite Aid. **SIC:** 5912—Drug
Stores & Proprietary Stores.

Centerville

★ 80286 ★ **Coast to Coast Home & Aut**
207 E. Public Sq.
Centerville, TN 37033
(615)729-2173
Ultimate Parent: Servistar Corp. **SIC:**
5599—Automotive Dealers Nec.

★ 80287 ★ **Giant Food Market Inc.**
Hwy. 100
Centerville, TN 37033
(615)729-4660
Ultimate Parent: Giant Food. **SIC:** 5411—
Grocery Stores.

Charleston

★ 80288 ★ **First American National Bank**
Hwy. 11
Charleston, TN 37310-9705
(615)339-4657
Location Type: Branch office. **Ultimate
Parent:** First American Corp. **SIC:** 6021—
National Commercial Banks.

★ 80289 ★ **Olin Chemicals Group**
Lower River Rd.
Charleston, TN 37310
(615)336-4000
Officer: John McIntosh, Manager. **Ultimate
Parent:** Olin Corp. **SIC:** 2812—Alkalies &
Chlorine; 2819—Industrial Inorganic
Chemicals Nec; 2899—Chemical
Preparations Nec.

★ 80290 ★ **Olin Corp.**
Charleston Facility
Lower River Rd.
Charleston, TN 37310
Location Type: Facility. **Ultimate Parent:**
Olin Corp. **SIC:** 2812—Alkalies & Chlorine;
2819—Industrial Inorganic Chemicals Nec.

Chatanooga

★ 80291 ★ **ADM Milling Co.**
PO Box 1259
Chatanooga, TN 37401-1259
(615)756-0503
Officer: Jeff Dillon. **Ultimate Parent:** Archer
Daniels Midland Co. **SIC:** 2048—Prepared
Feeds Nec; 2041—Flour & Other Grain Mill
Products; 4212—Local Trucking Without
Storage.

Chattanooga

★ 80292 ★ **ABF Freight System Inc.**
3090 S. Orchard Knob Ave.
Chattanooga, TN 37407-1416
(615)622-4571
Location Type: Branch office. **Ultimate
Parent:** Arkansas Best. **SIC:** 4212—Local
Trucking Without Storage.

★ 80293 ★ **American General Finance**
5783 Brainerd Rd.
Chattanooga, TN 37411-4011
(615)892-6720
Ultimate Parent: American General Corp.
SIC: 6141—Personal Credit Institutions;
6162—Mortgage Bankers &
Correspondents.

★ 80294 ★ **American General Finance**
3829 Ringgold Rd.
Chattanooga, TN 37412-1639
(615)624-2655
Ultimate Parent: American General Corp.
SIC: 6141—Personal Credit Institutions;

6162—Mortgage Bankers &
Correspondents.

★ 80295 ★ **American General Finance Inc.**
3829 Ringgold Rd.
Chattanooga, TN 37412-1639
(615)624-2655
Location Type: Branch office. **Ultimate
Parent:** American General Corp. **SIC:**
6141—Personal Credit Institutions; 6162—
Mortgage Bankers & Correspondents.

★ 80296 ★ **American General Finance Inc.**
5783 Brainerd Rd.
Chattanooga, TN 37411-4011
(615)892-6720
Location Type: Branch office. **Ultimate
Parent:** American General Corp. **SIC:**
6141—Personal Credit Institutions; 6162—
Mortgage Bankers & Correspondents.

★ 80297 ★ **AMR Co.**
100 Cherokee Blvd.
Chattanooga, TN 37405-3878
(615)266-3743
Ultimate Parent: AMR Corp. **SIC:** 5084—
Industrial Machinery & Equipment; 1761—
Roofing, Siding & Sheet Metal Work;
1791—Structural Steel Erection.

★ 80298 ★ **AmSouth Bank of Tennessee**
1 Union Sq.
Chattanooga, TN
(615)756-6163
Location Type: Branch office. **Ultimate
Parent:** AmSouth Bancorp. **SIC:** 6022—
State Commercial Banks; 6162—Mortgage
Bankers & Correspondents.

★ 80299 ★ **AmSouth Bank of Tennessee**
5022 Rossville Blvd.
Chattanooga, TN
(615)867-3737
Location Type: Branch office. **Ultimate
Parent:** AmSouth Bancorp. **SIC:** 6022—
State Commercial Banks; 6162—Mortgage
Bankers & Correspondents.

★ 80300 ★ **AmSouth Bank of Tennessee**
Plaza Shopping Ctr.
Chattanooga, TN
(615)886-5080
Location Type: Branch office. **Ultimate
Parent:** AmSouth Bancorp. **SIC:** 6022—
State Commercial Banks; 6162—Mortgage
Bankers & Correspondents.

★ 80301 ★ **AmSouth Bank of Tennessee**
6903 Lee Hwy.
Chattanooga, TN
(615)894-1487
Location Type: Branch office. **Ultimate
Parent:** AmSouth Bancorp. **SIC:** 6022—
State Commercial Banks; 6162—Mortgage
Bankers & Correspondents.

★ 80302 ★ **AmSouth Bank of Tennessee**
3303 Cummings Hwy.
Chattanooga, TN
(615)821-1578
Location Type: Branch office. **Ultimate
Parent:** AmSouth Bancorp. **SIC:** 6022—
State Commercial Banks; 6162—Mortgage
Bankers & Correspondents.

★ 80303 ★ **AmSouth Bank of Tennessee**
3894 Hixson Pke.
Chattanooga, TN
(615)877-1121
Location Type: Branch office. **Ultimate
Parent:** AmSouth Bancorp. **SIC:** 6022—
State Commercial Banks; 6162—Mortgage
Bankers & Correspondents.

★ 80304 ★ **AmSouth Bank of Tennessee**
4757 Hwy. 58
Chattanooga, TN
(615)894-6214
Location Type: Branch office. **Ultimate
Parent:** AmSouth Bancorp. **SIC:** 6022—
State Commercial Banks; 6162—Mortgage
Bankers & Correspondents.

★ 80305 ★ **AmSouth Bank of Tennessee**
4334 Ringgold Rd.
Chattanooga, TN
(615)624-4601
Location Type: Branch office. **Ultimate
Parent:** AmSouth Bancorp. **SIC:** 6022—
State Commercial Banks; 6162—Mortgage
Bankers & Correspondents.

★ 80306 ★ **AmSouth Bank of Tennessee**
1206 Market St.
Chattanooga, TN
(615)756-8626
Location Type: Branch office. **Ultimate
Parent:** AmSouth Bancorp. **SIC:** 6022—
State Commercial Banks; 6162—Mortgage
Bankers & Correspondents.

★ 80307 ★ **AmSouth Bank of Tennessee**
8535 Hixson Pke.
Chattanooga, TN 37402
(615)842-0503
Location Type: Branch office. **Ultimate
Parent:** AmSouth Bancorp. **SIC:** 6022—
State Commercial Banks; 6162—Mortgage
Bankers & Correspondents.

★ 80308 ★ **AmSouth Bank of Tennessee**
601 Market Ctr.
Chattanooga, TN 37402
(615)756-4600
Officer: W. Charles Mayer III, President &
CEO. **Ultimate Parent:** AmSouth Bancorp.
SIC: 6022—State Commercial Banks;
6162—Mortgage Bankers &
Correspondents.

★ 80309 ★ **AmSouth Bank of Tennessee**
1206 Market
Chattanooga, TN 37402
(615)756-8626
Ultimate Parent: AmSouth Bancorp.

★ 80310 ★ **AmSouth Bank of Tennessee**
6903 Lee Hwy.
Chattanooga, TN 37421
(615)894-1487
Ultimate Parent: AmSouth Bancorp.

★ 80311 ★ **AmSouth Bank of Tennessee**
4757 Hwy. 58
Chattanooga, TN 37416
(615)894-6214
Ultimate Parent: AmSouth Bancorp.

★ 80312 ★ **AmSouth Bank of Tennessee**
3303 Cummings Hwy.
Chattanooga, TN 37419
(615)821-1578
Ultimate Parent: AmSouth Bancorp.

★ 80313 ★ **AmSouth Bank of Tennessee**
4334 Ringgold Rd.
Chattanooga, TN 37412
(615)624-4601
Ultimate Parent: AmSouth Bancorp.

★ 80314 ★ **AmSouth Bank of Tennessee**
3894 Hixson Pike
Chattanooga, TN 37415
(615)877-1121
Ultimate Parent: AmSouth Bancorp.

★ 80315 ★ **AmSouth Bank of Tennessee**
5022 Rossville Blvd.
Chattanooga, TN 37407
(615)867-3737
Ultimate Parent: AmSouth Bancorp.

★ 80316 ★ **AmSouth Bank of Tennessee**
5515 Brainerd Rd.
Chattanooga, TN 37411
(615)894-1058
Ultimate Parent: AmSouth Bancorp.

★ 80317 ★ **AmSouth Bank of Tennessee**
1210 Taft Hwy.
Chattanooga, TN
(615)886-5080
Ultimate Parent: AmSouth Bancorp.

★ 80318 ★ **AmSouth Bank of Tennessee**
601 Market
Chattanooga, TN 37402
(615)752-1572
Ultimate Parent: AmSouth Bancorp.

★ 80319 ★ **AmSouth Bank of Tennessee**
Chattanooga, TN
(615)634-4000
Ultimate Parent: AmSouth Bancorp.

★ 80320 ★ **AmSouth Bank of Tennessee-Customer Service**
Chattanooga, TN
(615)752-1595
Ultimate Parent: AmSouth Bancorp.

★ 80321 ★ **AmSouth Bank of Tennessee Dept.**
Chattanooga, TN
(615)752-1603
Ultimate Parent: AmSouth Bancorp.

★ 80322 ★ **Anchor Glass Container**
400 W. 45th
Chattanooga, TN 37410
(615)821-6551
Ultimate Parent: Anchor Glass Container Corp.

★ 80323 ★ **Anchor Glass Container Corp.**
400 W. 45th St.
Chattanooga, TN 37410
(615)821-6551
Ultimate Parent: Anchor Glass Container Corp. **SIC:** 3229—Pressed & Blown Glass Nec.

★ 80324 ★ **Archer Daniels Midland Co.**
1200 Judd Rd.
Chattanooga, TN 37406-4711
(615)629-5495
Ultimate Parent: Archer Daniels Midland Co. **SIC:** 5046—Commercial Equipment Nec.

★ 80325 ★ **BASF Corp.**
2120 Polymer Dr.
Chattanooga, TN 37421
Ultimate Parent: BASF Corp. **SIC:** 2821—Plastics Materials & Resins; 2822—Synthetic Rubber.

★ 80326 ★ **BASF Corp.**
2200 Polymer Dr.
Chattanooga, TN 37421
Ultimate Parent: BASF Corp. **SIC:** 2822—Synthetic Rubber.

★ 80327 ★ **BASF Corp.**
3805 Amnicola Hwy.
Chattanooga, TN 37406
(615)493-2700
Location Type: Branch office. **Officer:** Joe Breunig, Manager. **Ultimate Parent:** BASF Corp. **SIC:** 3069—Fabricated Rubber Products Nec.

★ 80328 ★ **BASF Corp.**
2200 W. Polymer Dr.
Chattanooga, TN 37421
(615)855-2300
Officer: Joe Breunig, Manager. **Ultimate Parent:** BASF Corp. **SIC:** 3069—Fabricated Rubber Products Nec.

★ 80329 ★ **BASF Corp.**
Chemicals
3805 Amnicola Hwy.
Chattanooga, TN 37406
Company Type: Division. **Ultimate Parent:** BASF Corp. **SIC:** 2822—Synthetic Rubber.

★ 80330 ★ **BASF Federal Credit Union**
2225 W. Polymer Dr.
Chattanooga, TN 37421-2210
(615)892-2938
Officer: Debra Powell. **Ultimate Parent:** BASF Corp. **SIC:** 6061—Federal Credit Unions.

★ 80331 ★ **Bed & Bath Home Fashions**
3507-C Battlefield P
Chattanooga, TN
(615)861-7017
Ultimate Parent: Fieldcrest Cannon.

★ 80332 ★ **Blazer Financial Services Inc.**
108 Northgate Commercial
Chattanooga, TN 37415
(615)870-5555
Ultimate Parent: Great Western Financial Corp.

★ 80333 ★ **Browning-Ferris Industries**
1018 E. 38th St.
Chattanooga, TN 37407-2436
(615)867-4650
Location Type: Branch office. **Officer:** Bradley E. Duke. **Ultimate Parent:** Browning-Ferris Industries. **SIC:** 4953—Refuse Systems.

★ 80334 ★ **Burlington Air Express**
5910 Pinehurst Ave.
Chattanooga, TN 37421
(615)899-6354
Ultimate Parent: Pittston.

★ 80335 ★ **Burlington Madison Yarn Co.**
Maclellan Building
Chattanooga, TN 37402
(615)265-2316
Ultimate Parent: Burlington Industries, Equity.

★ 80336 ★ **Buster Brown Apparel Inc.**
2001 Wheeler Ave.
Chattanooga, TN 37406
Ultimate Parent: Gerber Products. **SIC:** 2330—Women's/Misses' Outerwear.

★ 80337 ★ **Casual Corner**
2100 Hamilton Place Blvd.
Chattanooga, TN 37421
(615)892-5117
Ultimate Parent: United States Shoe.

★ 80338 ★ **Central Soya Co. Inc.**
1200 Judd Rd.
Chattanooga, TN 37406
Ultimate Parent: Central Soya. **SIC:** 2075—Soybean Oil Mills; 2048—Prepared Feeds Nec.

★ 80339 ★ **Circuit City**
6401 Lee Hwy.
Chattanooga, TN 37421
(615)894-0409
Ultimate Parent: Circuit City Stores.

★ 80340 ★ **Colonial Pipeline Co.**
817 Pineville Rd.
Chattanooga, TN 37405
(615)266-3287
Ultimate Parent: Colonial Pipeline.

★ 80341 ★ **Colonial Pipeline Co.**
Scruggs Rd.
Chattanooga, TN
(615)891-9622
Ultimate Parent: Colonial Pipeline.

★ 80342 ★ **Colonial Pipeline Co.**
4231 Jersey Pke
Chattanooga, TN 37416
(615)892-6122
Ultimate Parent: Colonial Pipeline.

★ 80343 ★ **Coors Electronic Package Co.**
511 Manufacturers Rd.
Chattanooga, TN 37405
Ultimate Parent: Adolph Coors. **SIC:** 3264—Porcelain Electrical Supplies.

★ 80344 ★ **Courtyard by Marriott**
2210 Bams Rd.
Chattanooga, TN 37421
(615)499-4400
Ultimate Parent: Marriott International. **SIC:** 7011—Hotels & Motels.

★ 80345 ★ **Courtyard by Marriott Chattano**
2210 Bams Rd.
Chattanooga, TN 37421
(615)499-4400
Ultimate Parent: Marriott International.

★ 80346 ★ **Dean Witter Reynolds Inc.**
717 Broad
Chattanooga, TN
(615)752-4700
Location Type: Branch office. **Ultimate Parent:** Dean Witter Discover.

★ 80347 ★ **Delta Air Lines**
Chattanooga, TN
(615)855-2210
Ultimate Parent: Delta Air Lines, Inc.

★ 80348 ★ **Delta Air Lines**
125 W. Martin Luther King
Chattanooga, TN
(615)265-1485
Ultimate Parent: Delta Air Lines, Inc.

★ 80349 ★ **Delta Air Lines**
Chattanooga, TN
(615)855-2210
Ultimate Parent: Delta Air Lines, Inc.

★ 80350 ★ **Delta Air Lines Inc.**
125 W. Martin Luther King
Chattanooga, TN
(615)265-1485
Ultimate Parent: Delta Air Lines, Inc.

★ 80351 ★ **Delta Air Lines Inc. Baggage Se**
Chattanooga, TN
(615)855-2210
Ultimate Parent: Delta Air Lines, Inc.

★ 80352 ★ **Delta Air Lines Inc. District M**
125 W. Martin Luther King
Chattanooga, TN
(615)265-1485
Ultimate Parent: Delta Air Lines, Inc.

★ 80353 ★ **Delta Airlines Air Cargo**
Lovell Field
Chattanooga, TN
(615)855-2208
Ultimate Parent: Delta Air Lines, Inc.

★ 80354 ★ **Denny's Restaurant**
7641 Lee Hwy.
Chattanooga, TN 37421
(615)899-3399
Ultimate Parent: Flagstar Co.

★ 80355 ★ **Durr Medical Corp.**
2710 Amnicola Hwy.
Chattanooga, TN 37406
(615)624-9944
Officer: William H. Tittle III, Vice President. **Ultimate Parent:** Bergen Brunswig Corp. **SIC:** 3841—Surgical & Medical Instruments; 3842—Surgical Appliances & Supplies.

★ 80356 ★ **Durr Medical Inc.**
2710 Amnicola Hwy.
Chattanooga, TN 37406
(615)624-9944
Ultimate Parent: Bergen Brunswig Corp.

★ 80357 ★ **Durr Medical Inc.**
2710 Amnicola Hwy.
Chattanooga, TN 37406
(615)624-9944
Ultimate Parent: Bergen Brunswig Corp.

★ 80358 ★ **Eaton Corp.**
651 4th
Chattanooga, TN
(615)634-3239
Ultimate Parent: Eaton Corp.

★ 80359 ★ **Eckerd Drugs**
2010 McCallie Ave.
Chattanooga, TN 37404
(615)622-2545
Ultimate Parent: Eckerd Corp. **SIC:** 5912—Drug Stores & Proprietary Stores.

★ 80360 ★ **Eckerd Drugs**
4752 Hwy. 58
Chattanooga, TN 37416
(615)894-3445
Ultimate Parent: Eckerd Corp. **SIC:** 5912—Drug Stores & Proprietary Stores.

★ 80361 ★ **Eckerd Drugs**
710 Market
Chattanooga, TN 37402
(615)671-1227
Ultimate Parent: Eckerd Corp. **SIC:** 5912—Drug Stores & Proprietary Stores.

★ 80362 ★ **Eckerd Drugs**
3401 Broad St.
Chattanooga, TN 37409
(615)267-5088
Ultimate Parent: Eckerd Corp. **SIC:** 5912—Drug Stores & Proprietary Stores.

★ 80363 ★ **Eckerd Drugs**
Highland Plz.
Chattanooga, TN 37411
(615)877-5693
Ultimate Parent: Eckerd Corp.

★ 80364 ★ **Eckerd Drugs**
4038 Dayton Blvd.
Chattanooga, TN 37415
(615)877-2431
Ultimate Parent: Eckerd Corp. **SIC:** 5912—Drug Stores & Proprietary Stores.

★ 80365 ★ **Eckerd Drugs**
Brainerd Village Shopping Ctr.
Chattanooga, TN 37411
(615)855-0306
Ultimate Parent: Eckerd Corp. **SIC:** 5912—Drug Stores & Proprietary Stores.

★ 80366 ★ **Eckerd Drugs**
3532 Brainerd Rd.
Chattanooga, TN 37411
(615)297-7323
Ultimate Parent: Eckerd Corp. **SIC:** 5912—Drug Stores & Proprietary Stores.

★ 80367 ★ **Emery Worldwide ACF Co.**
5904 Pinehurst Avenue
Chattanooga, TN 37421
(615)855-1567
Ultimate Parent: Consolidated Freightways.

★ 80368 ★ **Express**
2100 Hamilton Place Blvd.
Chattanooga, TN 37421
(615)894-8750
Ultimate Parent: Limited. **SIC:** 5621—Women's Clothing Stores.

★ 80369 ★ **Exxon Co. U S a**
Bonny Oaks Dr.
Chattanooga, TN
(615)894-3610
Ultimate Parent: Exxon.

★ 80370 ★ **Exxon Co. U S a**
Bonny Oaks Dr.
Chattanooga, TN
(615)894-3610
Ultimate Parent: Exxon.

★ 80371 ★ **Fairfield Inn by Marriott**
2350 Shallowford Village
Chattanooga, TN 37421
(615)499-3800
Ultimate Parent: Marriott International. **SIC:** 7011—Hotels & Motels.

★ 80372 ★ **First American National Bank**
6238 Lee Hwy.
Chattanooga, TN 37421-6512
(615)755-6075
Location Type: Branch office. **Ultimate Parent:** First American Corp. **SIC:** 6021—National Commercial Banks.

★ 80373 ★ **First American National Bank**
725 Broad St.
Chattanooga, TN 37402-1805
(615)755-6000
Location Type: Branch office. **Ultimate Parent:** First American Corp. **SIC:** 6021—National Commercial Banks.

★ 80374 ★ **First American Trust Co., NA**
725 Broad St.
Chattanooga, TN 37401
(615)755-6039
Location Type: Branch office. **Ultimate Parent:** First American Corp. **SIC:** 6021—National Commercial Banks.

★ 80375 ★ **First Colony Life Insurance Co.**
837 Fortwood St.
Chattanooga, TN 37403
(615)267-9729
Ultimate Parent: Ethyl. **SIC:** 6411—Insurance Agents, Brokers & Service.

★ 80376 ★ **First Tennessee Bank NA**
1315 Taft Hwy.
Chattanooga, TN 37377
(615)757-4135
Location Type: Branch office. **Ultimate Parent:** First Tennessee National Corp. **SIC:** 6021—National Commercial Banks.

★ 80377 ★ First Tennessee Bank
NA
1501 English Ave.
Chattanooga, TN 37407
(615)757-4450
Location Type: Branch office. Ultimate
Parent: First Tennessee National Corp.
SIC: 6021—National Commercial Banks.

★ 80378 ★ First Tennessee Bank
NA
5414 Hixson Pke.
Chattanooga, TN 37415
(615)757-4041
Location Type: Branch office. Ultimate
Parent: First Tennessee National Corp.
SIC: 6021—National Commercial Banks.

★ 80379 ★ First Tennessee Bank
NA
3932 Dayton Blvd.
Chattanooga, TN 37415
(615)757-4213
Location Type: Branch office. Ultimate
Parent: First Tennessee National Corp.
SIC: 6021—National Commercial Banks.

★ 80380 ★ First Tennessee Bank
NA
5401 Ringgold
Chattanooga, TN 37421
(615)757-4044
Location Type: Branch office. Ultimate
Parent: First Tennessee National Corp.
SIC: 6021—National Commercial Banks.

★ 80381 ★ First Tennessee Bank
NA
1001 Airport Rd.
Chattanooga, TN 37421-2270
(615)757-4236
Location Type: Branch office. Ultimate
Parent: First Tennessee National Corp.
SIC: 6021—National Commercial Banks.

★ 80382 ★ First Tennessee Bank
NA
7820 E. Brainerd Rd.
Chattanooga, TN 37421-3298
(615)757-4223
Location Type: Branch office. Ultimate
Parent: First Tennessee National Corp.
SIC: 6021—National Commercial Banks.

★ 80383 ★ First Tennessee Bank
NA
3602 Brainerd Rd.
Chattanooga, TN 37411-3631
(615)757-4348
Location Type: Branch office. Ultimate
Parent: First Tennessee National Corp.
SIC: 6021—National Commercial Banks.

★ 80384 ★ First Tennessee Bank
NA
5526 Brainerd Rd.
Chattanooga, TN 37411-5338
(615)757-4218
Location Type: Branch office. Ultimate
Parent: First Tennessee National Corp.
SIC: 6021—National Commercial Banks.

★ 80385 ★ First Tennessee Bank
NA
1 Cherokee Blvd.
Chattanooga, TN 37405-3804
(615)757-4226
Location Type: Branch office. Ultimate
Parent: First Tennessee National Corp.
SIC: 6021—National Commercial Banks.

★ 80386 ★ First Tennessee Bank
NA
979 E. 3rd
Chattanooga, TN 37403-2136
(615)757-4427
Location Type: Branch office. Ultimate
Parent: First Tennessee National Corp.
SIC: 6021—National Commercial Banks.

★ 80387 ★ First Tennessee Bank
NA
3503 S. Broad
Chattanooga, TN 37409-1027
(615)757-4232
Location Type: Branch office. Ultimate
Parent: First Tennessee National Corp.
SIC: 6021—National Commercial Banks.

★ 80388 ★ First Tennessee Bank
NA
4430 Hwy. 58 N
Chattanooga, TN 37416-3099
(615)757-4260
Location Type: Branch office. Ultimate
Parent: First Tennessee National Corp.
SIC: 6021—National Commercial Banks.

★ 80389 ★ First Tennessee Bank
NA
2001 E. 23rd.
Chattanooga, TN 37404-5898
(615)757-4473
Location Type: Branch office. Ultimate
Parent: First Tennessee National Corp.
SIC: 6021—National Commercial Banks.

★ 80390 ★ First Tennessee Bank
NA
12 Northgate Pk.
Chattanooga, TN 37415-6902
(615)757-4292
Location Type: Branch office. Ultimate
Parent: First Tennessee National Corp.
SIC: 6021—National Commercial Banks.

★ 80391 ★ First Tennessee Bank
NA
2221 Hamilton Pl. Blvd.
Chattanooga, TN 37421-6005
(615)757-4292
Location Type: Branch office. Ultimate
Parent: First Tennessee National Corp.
SIC: 6021—National Commercial Banks.

★ 80392 ★ First Tennessee Bank
NA
701 Market St.
Chattanooga, TN 37402-4804
(615)757-4011
Location Type: Branch office. Ultimate
Parent: First Tennessee National Corp.
SIC: 6021—National Commercial Banks.

★ 80393 ★ Fitness Demands
1384 Gunbarrel Rd.
Chattanooga, TN 37421
(615)894-3319
Ultimate Parent: New York Times.

★ 80394 ★ Fitness Systems Inc.
of Chattan
3509 Ringgold Rd. East Rid
Chattanooga, TN 37412
(615)624-2622
Ultimate Parent: New York Times.

★ 80395 ★ Fitness Works
6080 Shallowford Rd.
Chattanooga, TN 37421
(615)855-4818
Ultimate Parent: New York Times.

★ 80396 ★ Food Lion Inc. Store
4707 Dayton Blvd.
Chattanooga, TN 37415
(615)870-3555
Ultimate Parent: Food Lion.

★ 80397 ★ Food Lion Inc. Store
3201 Wilcox Blvd.
Chattanooga, TN 37411
(615)698-6736
Ultimate Parent: Food Lion.

★ 80398 ★ Food Lion Inc. Store
4850 Hwy. 58
Chattanooga, TN 37416
(615)855-8291
Ultimate Parent: Food Lion.

★ 80399 ★ Food Lion Inc. Store
3971 Hixson Pke
Chattanooga, TN 37415
(615)877-0788
Ultimate Parent: Food Lion.

★ 80400 ★ Food Lion Inc. Store
816 Mountain Creek Rd.
Chattanooga, TN 37405
(615)877-8785
Ultimate Parent: Food Lion.

★ 80401 ★ Food Lion Inc. Store
4340 Ringgold Rd.
Chattanooga, TN 37412
(615)629-0556
Ultimate Parent: Food Lion.

★ 80402 ★ Food Lion Inc. Store
321 Browns Ferry Rd.
Chattanooga, TN 37419
(615)821-6061
Ultimate Parent: Food Lion.

★ 80403 ★ Food Lion Inc. Store
851
3201 Wilcox Blvd.
Chattanooga, TN 37411
(615)698-6736
Ultimate Parent: Food Lion.

★ 80404 ★ Food Lion Inc. Store
846
3971 Hixson Pke
Chattanooga, TN 37415
(615)877-0788
Ultimate Parent: Food Lion.

★ 80405 ★ Food Lion Inc. Store
661
4850 Hwy. 58
Chattanooga, TN 37416
(615)855-8291
Ultimate Parent: Food Lion.

★ 80406 ★ Food Lion Inc. Store
630
816 Mountain Creek Rd.
Chattanooga, TN 37405
(615)877-8785
Ultimate Parent: Food Lion.

★ 80407 ★ Food Lion Inc. Store
634
4340 Ringgold Rd.
Chattanooga, TN 37412
(615)629-0556
Ultimate Parent: Food Lion.

★ 80408 ★ Food Lion Inc. Store
629
321 Browns Ferry Rd.
Chattanooga, TN 37419
(615)821-6061
Ultimate Parent: Food Lion.

★ 80409 ★ Gap Kids
2100 Hamilton Place Blvd.
Chattanooga, TN 37421
(615)855-4470
Ultimate Parent: GAP.

★ 80410 ★ General Electric
Ceramics Inc.
511 Manufacturers Rd.
Chattanooga, TN 37405
Ultimate Parent: General Electric. SIC:
3264—Porcelain Electrical Supplies.

★ 80411 ★ Gold Kist Inc.
457 Dobson Ave.
Chattanooga, TN
(615)622-5182
Ultimate Parent: Gold Kist.

★ 80412 ★ Greyhound Bus Lines
515 Chestnut
Chattanooga, TN 37402
(615)265-8891
Ultimate Parent: Greyhound Lines Inc. SIC:
4131—Intercity & Rural Bus Transportation;
4111—Local & Suburban Transit; 4142—
Bus Charter Service Except Local.

★ 80413 ★ Halliburton Nus
Enviromental C
1110 Market
Chattanooga, TN 37402
(615)267-7156
Ultimate Parent: Halliburton.

★ 80414 ★ Heil Co
Uptain Bldg.
Chattanooga, TN 37411
(615)899-9100
Ultimate Parent: Dow Chemical Co. USA.

★ 80415 ★ Heil Co.
Uptain Bldg., No. 200
Chattanooga, TN 37411
(615)899-9100
Officer: Joe Heil Jr., Chairman. Ultimate
Parent: Dover Corp. SIC: 3585—
Refrigeration & Heating Equipment; 3713—
Truck & Bus Bodies; 3714—Motor Vehicle
Parts & Accessories.

★ 80416 ★ Jefferson Smurfit
Corp.
2101 Rossville Ave.
Chattanooga, TN 37408
(615)265-8244
Ultimate Parent: Jefferson Smurfit Corp.

★ 80417 ★ Kids R US
1308 E. 23rd
Chattanooga, TN 37404
(615)629-1090
Ultimate Parent: Toys "R" US.

★ 80418 ★ Lane Bryant
2100 Hamilton Place Blvd.
Chattanooga, TN 37421
(615)899-8945
Ultimate Parent: Limited. SIC: 5621—
Women's Clothing Stores.

★ 80419 ★ Lerner the
Hamilton Place
Chattanooga, TN
(615)894-9061
Ultimate Parent: Limited. SIC: 5621—
Women's Clothing Stores.

★ 80420 ★ Lerner Shops
208 Northgate Mall
Chattanooga, TN 37415
(615)875-8341
Ultimate Parent: Limited. SIC: 5621—
Women's Clothing Stores.

★ 80421 ★ Limited the
Hamilton Place
Chattanooga, TN
(615)894-8409
Ultimate Parent: Limited. SIC: 5621—
Women's Clothing Stores.

★ 80422 ★ Marriott Hotels
Resorts Suites
2 Carter Plaza
Chattanooga, TN 37402
(615)756-0002
Ultimate Parent: Marriott International. SIC:
7011—Hotels & Motels.

★ 80423 ★ Mary Kay Cosmetics
Independent
110 Pine Forest Ln.
Chattanooga, TN 37415
(615)870-1110
Ultimate Parent: Mary Kay Cosmetics.

★ 80424 ★ Mary Kay Cosmetics
Independent
6941 River Run Dr.
Chattanooga, TN 37416
(615)344-6323
Ultimate Parent: Mary Kay Cosmetics.

★ 80425 ★ Mary Kay Cosmetics
Independent
3007 15th Ave.
Chattanooga, TN 37407
(615)624-0195
Ultimate Parent: Mary Kay Cosmetics.

★ 80426 ★ McDonald's
Hamburgers
7020 Shallowford Rd.
Chattanooga, TN 37421
(615)899-3630
Ultimate Parent: McDonald's. SIC: 5812—
Eating Places.

★ 80427 ★ McDonald's
Hamburgers
6401 Ringgold Rd.
Chattanooga, TN 37412
(615)894-7911
Ultimate Parent: McDonald's. SIC: 5812—
Eating Places.

★ 80428 ★ McDonald's
Hamburgers
4502 Rossville Blvd.
Chattanooga, TN 37407
(615)867-2345
Ultimate Parent: McDonald's. SIC: 5812—
Eating Places.

★ 80429 ★ McDonald's
Hamburgers
6002 Lee Hwy.
Chattanooga, TN 37421
(615)892-1976
Ultimate Parent: McDonald's. SIC: 5812—
Eating Places.

★ 80430 ★ McDonald's
Hamburgers
813 Market
Chattanooga, TN 37402
(615)756-4927
Ultimate Parent: McDonald's. SIC: 5812—
Eating Places.

★ 80431 ★ McDonald's
Hamburgers
5440 Hwy. 153
Chattanooga, TN
(615)877-0263
Ultimate Parent: McDonald's. SIC: 5812—
Eating Places.

★ 80432 ★   McDonald's
Hamburgers
4123 Hixson Pke
Chattanooga, TN 37415
(615)875-5045
Ultimate Parent: McDonald's. SIC: 5812—
Eating Places.

★ 80433 ★   McDonald's
Hamburgers
2105 24th Street Pl
Chattanooga, TN 37407
(615)622-8318
Ultimate Parent: McDonald's. SIC: 5812—
Eating Places.

★ 80434 ★   McDonald's
Hamburgers
4608 Hwy. 58
Chattanooga, TN 37416
(615)894-9619
Ultimate Parent: McDonald's. SIC: 5812—
Eating Places.

★ 80435 ★   Merastar Insurance
Co.
537 Market
Chattanooga, TN 37402
(615)266-2886
Ultimate Parent: Geico.

★ 80436 ★   Merastar Insurance
Co.
537 Market St., Ste. 301
Chattanooga, TN 37402-1225
(615)755-7400
Officer: Al Kaltman, President & CEO.
Ultimate Parent: Geico. SIC: 6331—Fire,
Marine & Casualty Insurance. Employee
Count: 103.

★ 80437 ★   Merastar Insurance
Co. Insurance
537 Market
Chattanooga, TN 37402
(615)755-7400
Ultimate Parent: Geico.

★ 80438 ★   Mueller Co. & ORG
Chattanooga Plant
1401 Mueller Ave.
Chattanooga, TN 37406
(615)698-8811
Officer: Dale E. Day, Manager. Ultimate
Parent: Tyco International. SIC: 3491—
Industrial Valves; 3494—Valves & Pipe
Fittings Nec.

★ 80439 ★   Nationsbank Banking
Centers Ch
4710 Rossville Blvd.
Chattanooga, TN 37407
(615)867-4883
Ultimate Parent: Nationsbank Corp.

★ 80440 ★   Nationsbank Banking
Centers Ch
3620 Tennessee Ave.
Chattanooga, TN 37409
(615)265-0171
Ultimate Parent: Nationsbank Corp.

★ 80441 ★   Nationsbank Banking
Centers Ch
6 Northgate Park
Chattanooga, TN 37415
(615)870-3511
Ultimate Parent: Nationsbank Corp.

★ 80442 ★   Nationsbank Banking
Centers Ch
4409 Oakwood Dr.
Chattanooga, TN 37416
(615)894-4603
Ultimate Parent: Nationsbank Corp.

★ 80443 ★   Nationsbank Banking
Centers Ch
633 Chestnut
Chattanooga, TN 37450
(615)752-8111
Ultimate Parent: Nationsbank Corp.

★ 80444 ★   Nationsbank Banking
Centers Ch
6951 Lee Hwy.
Chattanooga, TN 37421
(615)892-9026
Ultimate Parent: Nationsbank Corp.

★ 80445 ★   Nationsbank Banking
Centers Ch
5506 Brainerd Rd.
Chattanooga, TN 37411
(615)894-4004
Ultimate Parent: Nationsbank Corp.

★ 80446 ★   Nationsbank
Commercial Departments
Chattanooga, TN
(615)755-0681
Ultimate Parent: Nationsbank Corp.

★ 80447 ★   Nationsbank
Community Departments
Chattanooga, TN
(615)755-0675
Ultimate Parent: Nationsbank Corp.

★ 80448 ★   Nationsbank
Consumer Departments
Chattanooga, TN
(615)752-8144
Ultimate Parent: Nationsbank Corp.

★ 80449 ★   Nationsbank
Departments Commer
633 Chestnut
Chattanooga, TN 37450
(615)755-3408
Ultimate Parent: Nationsbank Corp.

★ 80450 ★   Nationsbank
Executive Departments
Chattanooga, TN
(615)752-8107
Ultimate Parent: Nationsbank Corp.

★ 80451 ★   Nationsbank
Mortgage Departments
Chattanooga, TN
(615)752-8160
Ultimate Parent: Nationsbank Corp.

★ 80452 ★   Nationsbank Personal
Accounts Departments
Chattanooga, TN
(615)755-3410
Ultimate Parent: Nationsbank Corp.

★ 80453 ★   Nationsbank
Professional Accounts
Departments
Chattanooga, TN
(615)752-8115
Ultimate Parent: Nationsbank Corp.

★ 80454 ★   Nationsbank Sough
Pittsburg Wh
Hwy. 28
Chattanooga, TN
(615)658-5121
Ultimate Parent: Nationsbank Corp.

★ 80455 ★   Nationsbank South
Pittsburg Ja
111 E. Main
Chattanooga, TN 37408
(615)942-3466
Ultimate Parent: Nationsbank Corp.

★ 80456 ★   New York Life
Chattanooga
Knoxville General Office
1110 Market St., Ste. 503
Chattanooga, TN 37402
(615)756-8044
Ultimate Parent: New York Life.

★ 80457 ★   Nutri Basics Co.
3801 N. Hawthorne St.
Chattanooga, TN 37406
Ultimate Parent: Conagra. SIC: 2048—
Prepared Feeds Nec.

★ 80458 ★   Otis Elevator Co.
1502 Mccallie Ave.
Chattanooga, TN 37404
(615)622-1203
Ultimate Parent: United Technologies.

★ 80459 ★   Payless Shoe Source
Hamilton Place Mall
Chattanooga, TN
(615)892-8635
Ultimate Parent: May Department Stores.
SIC: 5661—Shoe Stores.

★ 80460 ★   Payless Shoe Source
Northate Mall
Chattanooga, TN
(615)870-9107
Ultimate Parent: May Department Stores.
SIC: 5661—Shoe Stores.

★ 80461 ★   Payless Shoe Source
5600 Brainerd Rd.
Chattanooga, TN 37411
(615)899-5443
Ultimate Parent: May Department Stores.
SIC: 5661—Shoe Stores.

★ 80462 ★   Payless Shoe Source
2115 E. 3rd
Chattanooga, TN 37404
(615)624-0388
Ultimate Parent: May Department Stores.
SIC: 5661—Shoe Stores.

★ 80463 ★   Payless Shoe Source
3704 Rossville Blvd.
Chattanooga, TN 37407
(615)867-3678
Ultimate Parent: May Department Stores.
SIC: 5661—Shoe Stores.

★ 80464 ★   Payless Shoesource
2115 E. 3rd
Chattanooga, TN 37404
(615)624-0388
Ultimate Parent: May Department Stores.

★ 80465 ★   Payless Shoesource
5600 Brainerd Rd.
Chattanooga, TN 37411
(615)899-5443
Ultimate Parent: May Department Stores.

★ 80466 ★   Payless Shoesource
Northate Mall
Chattanooga, TN
(615)870-9107
Ultimate Parent: May Department Stores.

★ 80467 ★   Payless Shoesource
Hamilton Place Mall
Chattanooga, TN
(615)892-8635
Ultimate Parent: May Department Stores.

★ 80468 ★   Penn Mutual Life
Insurance
23 N. Market
Chattanooga, TN 37405
(615)756-7834
Ultimate Parent: Penn Mutual Life.

★ 80469 ★   Pennzoil Products Co.
Chattanooga, TN
(615)894-8655
Ultimate Parent: Pennzoil.

★ 80470 ★   Pepsi-Cola Co.
3609 Amnicola Hwy.
Chattanooga, TN 37406
(615)629-6233
Officer: Ennis McPeak, Manager. Ultimate
Parent: Pepsico. SIC: 2086—Bottled &
Canned Soft Drinks.

★ 80471 ★   Petite Sophisticate
4900 Hixson Pke
Chattanooga, TN
(615)870-9968
Ultimate Parent: United States Shoe.

★ 80472 ★   Provident Life &
Accident
1 Fountain Sq.
Chattanooga, TN 37402
(615)755-1011
Company Type: Headquarters. Officer: J.
Harold Chandler. Employee Count: 4782.
Fortune Service 500: Ranking 33.

★ 80473 ★   Provident National
Assurance
1 Fountain Ave.
Chattanooga, TN 37402
Ultimate Parent: Provident Life & Accident.
SIC: 6371—Pension, Health & Welfare
Funds.

★ 80474 ★   Provident National
Assurance Co.
2115 Stein Dr.
Chattanooga, TN 37421
(615)894-0002
Ultimate Parent: Provident Life & Accident.

★ 80475 ★   Provident National
Assurance Co.
Fountain Square
Chattanooga, TN
(615)755-1901
Ultimate Parent: Provident Life & Accident.

★ 80476 ★   Putnam Investments
8012 Dancing Fern Tr
Chattanooga, TN 37421
(615)894-5212
Ultimate Parent: Marsh & McLennan.

★ 80477 ★   Reynolds & Reynolds
5916 Quintus Loop Rd.
Chattanooga, TN
(615)899-0855
Ultimate Parent: Reynolds & Reynolds.

★ 80478 ★   Roper Corp.
100 Manufacturers Rd.
Chattanooga, TN 37405
(615)752-1234
Officer: Harold Cooksey, Manager.
Ultimate Parent: General Electric. SIC:
3631—Household Cooking Equipment.

★ 80479 ★   Ryder Truck Rental &
Leasing
1823 Rossville Ave.
Chattanooga, TN 37408
(615)265-7474
Ultimate Parent: Ryder System.

★ 80480 ★   Ryder Truck Rental-
One Way
1823 Rossville Ave.
Chattanooga, TN 37408
(615)266-4205
Ultimate Parent: Ryder System.

★ 80481 ★   Ryder Truck Rental-
One Way
6613 Lee Hwy.
Chattanooga, TN 37421
(615)894-6635
Ultimate Parent: Ryder System.

★ 80482 ★   Ryder Truck Rental-
One Way
5705 Ringgold Rd.
Chattanooga, TN 37412
(615)899-5845
Ultimate Parent: Ryder System.

★ 80483 ★   Ryder Truck Rental-
One Way
9416 Apison Pke
Chattanooga, TN
(615)396-3600
Ultimate Parent: Ryder System.

★ 80484 ★   Ryder Truck Rental-
One Way
600 Commercial Ln.
Chattanooga, TN 37405
(615)870-4240
Ultimate Parent: Ryder System.

★ 80485 ★   Ryder Truck Rental-
One Way
2604 Amnicola Hwy.
Chattanooga, TN 37406
(615)698-2696
Ultimate Parent: Ryder System.

★ 80486 ★   Seaboard Farms of
Chattanooga Inc.
950 Wauhatchie Pike
Chattanooga, TN 37419
Ultimate Parent: Seaboard Corp. SIC:
2048—Prepared Feeds Nec.

★ 80487 ★   Seaboard Farms of
Chattanooga Inc.
414 W. 16th St.
Chattanooga, TN 37408
Ultimate Parent: Seaboard Corp. SIC:
2015—Poultry Slaughtering & Processing.

★ 80488 ★   Seaboard Farms of
Chattanooga Inc.
Processing Plant
414 W. 16th St.
Chattanooga, TN 37401
Company Type: Division. Ultimate Parent:
Seaboard Corp. SIC: 2015—Poultry
Slaughtering & Processing.

★ 80489 ★   Service Merchandise
2200 Hamilton Place Blvd.
Chattanooga, TN 37421
(615)899-0021
Ultimate Parent: Service Merchandise Co.,
Inc.

★ 80490 ★   Service Merchandise
30 Northgate Pk.
Chattanooga, TN 37415
(615)877-0223
Ultimate Parent: Service Merchandise Co.,
Inc.

★ 80491 ★ **Shell Oil**
4858 Hwy. 58
Chattanooga, TN 37416
Ultimate Parent: Shell Oil Co. **SIC:** 5172—
Petroleum Products Nec.

★ 80492 ★ **Sonoco Products Co.**
1900 Daisy
Chattanooga, TN 37406
(615)698-6985
Ultimate Parent: Sonoco Products.

★ 80493 ★ **Sonoco Products Co.**
1900 Daisy St.
Chattanooga, TN 37406
(615)698-6985
Officer: J.A. Horne, Manager. **Ultimate Parent:** Sonoco Products. **SIC:** 2655—Fiber
Cans, Drums & Similar Products.

★ 80494 ★ **Southern Wood Piedmont Co.**
400 E. 33rd St.
Chattanooga, TN 37401
Ultimate Parent: ITT Rayonier Inc. **SIC:**
2491—Wood Preserving.

★ 80495 ★ **Spartan Express Inc.**
2230 Polymer Dr.
Chattanooga, TN 37421
(615)899-7391
Ultimate Parent: Roadway Services.

★ 80496 ★ **Target**
5615 Lee Hwy.
Chattanooga, TN 37421
(615)899-5001
Ultimate Parent: Dayton Hudson.

★ 80497 ★ **Target**
18 Northgate Pk.
Chattanooga, TN 37415
(615)875-3100
Ultimate Parent: Dayton Hudson.

★ 80498 ★ **Target Stores**
5615 Lee Hwy.
Chattanooga, TN 37421
(615)899-5001
Ultimate Parent: Dayton Hudson.

★ 80499 ★ **Target Stores**
18 Northgate Pk.
Chattanooga, TN 37415
(615)875-3100
Ultimate Parent: Dayton Hudson.

★ 80500 ★ **Terex Corp.**
Bucyrus Construction Products
5959 Shallowford Rd.
Chattanooga, TN 37421
(615)894-9411 **Fax:** (615)894-9449
Company Type: Subsidiary. **Ultimate Parent:** Terex Corp.

★ 80501 ★ **Terex Corp.**
Koehring Cranes & Excavators
5959 Shallowford Rd.
Chattanooga, TN 37421
(615)899-6362 **Fax:** (615)899-9819
Company Type: Division. **Ultimate Parent:**
Terex Corp. **SIC:** 3531—Construction
Machinery.

★ 80502 ★ **Terex Corp. Koehring Cranes & Excavators**
Koehring Cranes
5959 Shallowford Rd.
Chattanooga, TN 37421
(615)899-6362 **Fax:** (615)899-9819
Company Type: Division. **Ultimate Parent:**
Terex Corp. **SIC:** 3531—Construction
Machinery.

★ 80503 ★ **Texaco Express Lube**
5907 Lee Hwy.
Chattanooga, TN 37421
(615)899-1188
Ultimate Parent: Texaco.

★ 80504 ★ **Texaco Refining & Marketing**
710 Manufacturers Rd.
Chattanooga, TN 37405
(615)267-8653
Ultimate Parent: Texaco.

★ 80505 ★ **Toys R US**
2200 Hamilton Place Blvd.
Chattanooga, TN 37421
(615)892-6555
Ultimate Parent: Toys "R" US.

★ 80506 ★ **Trugreen-Chemlawn**
3903-B Volunteer Dr.
Chattanooga, TN
(615)899-9689
Ultimate Parent: ServiceMaster Co.

★ 80507 ★ **Unifi Inc.**
James Bldg.
Chattanooga, TN
(615)266-8381
Ultimate Parent: UNIFI, Inc.

★ 80508 ★ **Union Pacific Railroad Co.**
Chattanooga, TN
(615)842-4516
Ultimate Parent: Union Pacific Corp.

★ 80509 ★ **Union Planers National Bank**
5736 Brainerd Rd.
Chattanooga, TN 37411-4037
(615)634-2203
Location Type: Branch office. **Ultimate Parent:** Union Planters Corp. **SIC:** 6021—
National Commercial Banks.

★ 80510 ★ **Union Planters National Bank**
5312 Ringgold Rd.
Chattanooga, TN 37412-3196
(615)634-2210
Location Type: Branch office. **Ultimate Parent:** Union Planters Corp. **SIC:** 6021—
National Commercial Banks.

★ 80511 ★ **Union Planters National Bank**
4th & Broad St.
Chattanooga, TN 37402
(615)634-2200
Location Type: Branch office. **Ultimate Parent:** Union Planters Corp. **SIC:** 6021—
National Commercial Banks.

★ 80512 ★ **Union Planters National Bank**
1 Northgate Office Pk.
Chattanooga, TN 37415-6938
(615)634-2204
Location Type: Branch office. **Ultimate Parent:** Union Planters Corp. **SIC:** 6021—
National Commercial Banks.

★ 80513 ★ **Union Planters National Bank**
1 Central Plz.
Chattanooga, TN 37401-2214
(615)634-2200
Location Type: Branch office. **Ultimate Parent:** Union Planters Corp. **SIC:** 6021—
National Commercial Banks.

★ 80514 ★ **US Fidelity & Guaranty Insurance**
Eastgate Park Ofc
Chattanooga, TN 37411
(615)894-5153
Ultimate Parent: USF&G Corp.

★ 80515 ★ **US Pipe & Foundry Co.**
1000 W. 19th St.
Chattanooga, TN 37408
Ultimate Parent: Walter Industries, Inc.
SIC: 3321—Gray & Ductile Iron Foundries.

★ 80516 ★ **US Pipe & Foundry Co. Chattanooga Valve & Fittings**
2501-2701 Chestnut St.
Chattanooga, TN 37401
Ultimate Parent: Walter Industries, Inc.
SIC: 3321—Gray & Ductile Iron Foundries.

★ 80517 ★ **Valvoline Instant Oil Change**
2200 Hamilton Place Blvd.
Chattanooga, TN 37421
(615)499-0065
Ultimate Parent: Ashland Oil.

★ 80518 ★ **Valvoline Instant Oil Change**
1750 Dayton Blvd. Red Bank
Chattanooga, TN
(615)265-6994
Ultimate Parent: Ashland Oil.

★ 80519 ★ **Valvoline Instant Oil Change**
4332 Hwy. 58
Chattanooga, TN 37416
(615)892-6342
Ultimate Parent: Ashland Oil.

★ 80520 ★ **Vulcan Materials Co.**
537 Market St. 203
Chattanooga, TN 37402
(615)266-4872
Officer: James M. Addams, Vice President.
Ultimate Parent: Vulcan Materials Co. **SIC:**
2951—Asphalt Paving Mixtures & Blocks;
3273—Ready-Mixed Concrete; 3295—
Minerals—Ground or Treated.

★ 80521 ★ **Vulcan Materials Co.**
4700 Shallowford Rd.
Chattanooga, TN
(615)892-4546
Ultimate Parent: Vulcan Materials Co.

★ 80522 ★ **Vulcan Materials Co.**
Chattanooga, TN
(615)266-4872
Ultimate Parent: Vulcan Materials Co.

★ 80523 ★ **Vulcan Materials Co.**
3960 Cromwell Rd.
Chattanooga, TN 37421
(615)892-4146
Ultimate Parent: Vulcan Materials Co.

★ 80524 ★ **W. R. Grace & Co.**
Davison Chemical Div.
4000 N. Hawthorne St.
Chattanooga, TN 37406
Company Type: Division. **Ultimate Parent:**
W. R. Grace. **SIC:** 2819—Industrial
Inorganic Chemicals Nec.

★ 80525 ★ **Wal-Mart Stores Inc.**
2020 Gunbarrel Road
Chattanooga, TN 37421
(615)899-7021
Ultimate Parent: Wal-Mart Stores, Inc.

★ 80526 ★ **Wal-Mart Stores Inc.**
5450 Hwy. 153
Chattanooga, TN
(615)870-3267
Ultimate Parent: Wal-Mart Stores, Inc.

★ 80527 ★ **Westvaco Corp.**
Container
2345 Blue Springs Rd. SW
Chattanooga, TN
(615)472-3323
Ultimate Parent: WestVaco Corp.

★ 80528 ★ **Xerox Corp.**
404 Uptain Bldg., Ste. 44
Chattanooga, TN 37411
(615)894-2842
Officer: Bob Scholl, Manager. **Ultimate Parent:** Xerox Corp. **SIC:** 3663—Radio &
T.V. Communications Equipment.

Church Hill

★ 80529 ★ **Coast to Coast Hardware**
Mt Carmel Shopping Ctr.
Church Hill, TN 37642
(615)357-6611
Ultimate Parent: Servistar Corp. **SIC:**
5941—Sporting Goods & Bicycle Shops.

★ 80530 ★ **First Union National Bank of Tennessee**
134 E. Main Blvd.
Church Hill, TN 37642-9455
(615)357-6111
Location Type: Branch office. **Ultimate Parent:** First Union Corp. **SIC:** 6021—
National Commercial Banks.

★ 80531 ★ **Kingston-Warren Corp.**
309 Press Rd.
Church Hill, TN 37642
Ultimate Parent: Harvard Industries. **SIC:**
3069—Fabricated Rubber Products Nec.

★ 80532 ★ **Kingston-Warren Corp.**
11 Kingsport Press Rd.
Church Hill, TN 37642
Ultimate Parent: Harvard Industries. **SIC:**
3069—Fabricated Rubber Products Nec.

Clarksville

★ 80533 ★ **Allied-Signal Inc.**
Bendix Automotive Systems
780 Arcata Blvd.
Clarksville, TN 37040
Ultimate Parent: Allied-Signal Inc. **SIC:**
3714—Motor Vehicle Parts & Accessories.

★ 80534 ★ **American Standard**
Trance Co. Div.
Hwy. 79 N. Guthrie Hwy.
Clarksville, TN 37041
Company Type: Division. **Ultimate Parent:**
American Standard. **SIC:** 3585—
Refrigeration & Heating Equipment.

★ 80535 ★ **American Standard**
Trane Co.
Guthrie Hwy.
Clarksville, TN 37041-1008
Company Type: Division. **Ultimate Parent:**
American Standard. **SIC:** 3585—
Refrigeration & Heating Equipment.

★ 80536 ★ **American Standard Inc.**
Trane Co. Div.
Hwy. 79 N. Guthrie Hwy.
Clarksville, TN 37041
Company Type: Division. **Ultimate Parent:**
American Standard. **SIC:** 3585—
Refrigeration & Heating Equipment.

★ 80537 ★ **Blazer Financial Services**
1598 Fort Campbell Blvd.
Clarksville, TN 37042
(615)648-8841
Ultimate Parent: Great Western Financial
Corp. **SIC:** 6141—Personal Credit
Institutions.

★ 80538 ★ **Casual Corner**
3801 Guthrie Rd.
Clarksville, TN 37043
(615)647-7054
Ultimate Parent: United States Shoe. **SIC:**
5699—Miscellaneous Apparel & Accessory
Stores.

★ 80539 ★ **First American Natioanl Bank**
649 Providence Rd.
Clarksville, TN 37042
(615)553-5274
Location Type: Branch office. **Ultimate Parent:** First American Corp. **SIC:** 6021—
National Commercial Banks.

★ 80540 ★ **First American National Bank**
Trade Winds South Schopping Ctr.
Clarksville, TN 37043
(615)553-5277
Location Type: Branch office. **Ultimate Parent:** First American Corp. **SIC:** 6021—
National Commercial Banks.

★ 80541 ★ **First American National Bank**
1485 Madison St.
Clarksville, TN 37043
(615)553-5209
Location Type: Branch office. **Ultimate Parent:** First American Corp. **SIC:** 6021—
National Commercial Banks.

★ 80542 ★ **First American National Bank**
128 N. 2nd St.
Clarksville, TN 37040-3432
(615)553-5200
Location Type: Branch office. **Ultimate Parent:** First American Corp.

★ 80543 ★ **First American National Bank**
1001 S. Riverside Dr.
Clarksville, TN 37040
(615)553-5283
Location Type: Branch office. **Ultimate Parent:** First American Corp. **SIC:** 6021—
National Commercial Banks.

★ 80544 ★ **First American Trust Co., NA**
128 N. 2nd St.
Clarksville, TN 37041
(615)553-5217
Location Type: Branch office. **Ultimate Parent:** First American Corp. **SIC:** 6021—
National Commercial Banks.

★ 80545 ★ **First Union National Bank of Tennessee**
1598 Ft. Campbell Blvd.
Clarksville, TN 37042-3545
(615)552-8698
Location Type: Branch office. **Ultimate Parent:** First Union Corp. **SIC:** 6021—
National Commercial Banks.

★ 80546 ★   **First Union National Bank of Tennessee**
1780 Madison St.
Clarksville, TN 37043-4965
(615)552-8693
Location Type: Branch office. **Ultimate Parent:** First Union Corp. **SIC:** 6021—National Commercial Banks.

★ 80547 ★   **First Union National Bank of Tennessee**
2644 Guthrie Hwy.
Clarksville, TN 37040-5836
(615)552-8686
Location Type: Branch office. **Ultimate Parent:** First Union Corp. **SIC:** 6021—National Commercial Banks.

★ 80548 ★   **First Union National Bank of Tennessee**
3301 Ft. Campbell Blvd., Hwy. 41-A
Clarksville, TN 37042-5601
(615)552-8685
Location Type: Branch office. **Ultimate Parent:** First Union Corp. **SIC:** 6021—National Commercial Banks.

★ 80549 ★   **First Union National Bank of Tennessee**
1 Public Sq.
Clarksville, TN 37040-3461
(615)552-5300
Location Type: Branch office. **Ultimate Parent:** First Union Corp. **SIC:** 6021—National Commercial Banks.

★ 80550 ★   **Frist American National Bank**
Old Trenton Rd. & Hwy. 79 N
Clarksville, TN 37040
(615)553-5228
Location Type: Branch office. **Ultimate Parent:** First American Corp. **SIC:** 6021—National Commercial Banks.

★ 80551 ★   **Greyhound Bus Lines**
11 Jefferson St.
Clarksville, TN 37040
(615)647-3336
Ultimate Parent: Greyhound Lines Inc. **SIC:** 4111—Local & Suburban Transit; 4131—Intercity & Rural Bus Transportation; 4142—Bus Charter Service Except Local.

★ 80552 ★   **J C Penney Co. Inc.**
2801 Guthrie Hwy.
Clarksville, TN 37040
(615)553-0030
Ultimate Parent: J.C. Penney. **SIC:** 5311—Department Stores.

★ 80553 ★   **Kroger Co.**
1489 Madison St.
Clarksville, TN 37040
(615)553-0254
Ultimate Parent: Kroger. **SIC:** 5411—Grocery Stores.

★ 80554 ★   **Lane Bryant**
2801 Guthrie Hwy.
Clarksville, TN 37040
(615)645-1286
Ultimate Parent: Limited. **SIC:** 5621—Women's Clothing Stores.

★ 80555 ★   **Lerner Shops**
Governor Sq.
Clarksville, TN 37040
(615)648-4516
Ultimate Parent: Limited. **SIC:** 5621—Women's Clothing Stores.

★ 80556 ★   **Lerner Woman**
2801 Guthrie Hwy.
Clarksville, TN 37040
(615)645-1287
Ultimate Parent: Limited. **SIC:** 5621—Women's Clothing Stores.

★ 80557 ★   **McDonald's Hamburgers**
1921 Madison St.
Clarksville, TN 37043
(615)552-3388
Ultimate Parent: McDonald's. **SIC:** 5812—Eating Places.

★ 80558 ★   **Trane Co.**
PO Box 1008
Clarksville, TN 37040
(615)648-6471
Officer: David R. Farris, Group Vice President. **Ultimate Parent:** American Standard.

★ 80559 ★   **Trans Unitary Products Group Commercial**
2701 Wilma Rudolph Blvd.
Clarksville, TN 37040
(615)645-6471 **Fax:** (615)648-5939
Ultimate Parent: American Standard. **SIC:** 3585—Refrigeration & Heating Equipment.

★ 80560 ★   **Uscar Carbon Co. Inc.**
Hwy. 79 N. at Hampton Station Rd.
Clarksville, TN 37040-0309
Ultimate Parent: Union Carbide Corp. **SIC:** 3624—Carbon & Graphite Products.

★ 80561 ★   **Wal-Mart Stores Inc.**
2840 Guthrie Hwy.
Clarksville, TN 37040
(615)552-0021
Ultimate Parent: Wal-Mart Stores, Inc. **SIC:** 5311—Department Stores.

★ 80562 ★   **Wal-Mart Stores Inc.**
Clarksville Sq.
Clarksville, TN 37040
(615)645-6461
Ultimate Parent: Wal-Mart Stores, Inc. **SIC:** 5311—Department Stores.

Cleveland

★ 80563 ★   **ADM Milling Co.**
430 Central Ave. NE
Cleveland, TN 37311
(615)476-7551
Officer: Phyllis Bayne, Manager. **Ultimate Parent:** Archer Daniels Midland Co. **SIC:** 2041—Flour & Other Grain Mill Products; 2046—Wet Corn Milling.

★ 80564 ★   **Allied-Signal Automotive**
3000 20th St. NE
Cleveland, TN 37312
(615)472-7151
Officer: Noe Gayton, Manager. **Ultimate Parent:** Allied-Signal Inc. **SIC:** 3292—Asbestos Products.

★ 80565 ★   **Allied-Signal Inc.**
Bendix Friction Materials
20th St. POBox 2610
Cleveland, TN 37311
Ultimate Parent: Allied-Signal Inc. **SIC:** 3292—Asbestos Products.

★ 80566 ★   **American General Finance**
2538 Keith St. NW
Cleveland, TN 37312-3738
(615)478-3039
Ultimate Parent: American General Corp. **SIC:** 6141—Personal Credit Institutions; 6162—Mortgage Bankers & Correspondents.

★ 80567 ★   **American General Finance Inc.**
2538 Keith St. NW
Cleveland, TN 37312-3738
(615)478-3039
Location Type: Branch office. **Ultimate Parent:** American General Corp. **SIC:** 6141—Personal Credit Institutions; 6162—Mortgage Bankers & Correspondents.

★ 80568 ★   **AmSouth Bank of Tennessee**
1701 Keith St.
Cleveland, TN 37311-4385
(615)479-4385
Location Type: Branch office. **Officer:** David Fair, Manager. **Ultimate Parent:** AmSouth Bancorp. **SIC:** 6022—State Commercial Banks; 6162—Mortgage Bankers & Correspondents.

★ 80569 ★   **BFI Waste Systems**
6th St. & Hill St.
Cleveland, TN 37311
(615)476-2293
Ultimate Parent: Browning-Ferris Industries. **SIC:** 4953—Refuse Systems.

★ 80570 ★   **BFI Waste Systems**
Hill St.
Cleveland, TN 37311
(615)476-2293
Officer: Roy Lewis, Manager. **Ultimate Parent:** Browning-Ferris Industries. **SIC:** 3589—Service Industry Machinery Nec.

★ 80571 ★   **Blazer Financial Services**
2441 Keith St. NW
Cleveland, TN 37311
(615)472-4503
Ultimate Parent: Great Western Financial Corp. **SIC:** 6141—Personal Credit Institutions.

★ 80572 ★   **Carpenter Co. Inc.**
2695 Lupton Ln.
Cleveland, TN 37311
(615)479-5449
Ultimate Parent: Carpenter. **SIC:** 2822—Synthetic Rubber.

★ 80573 ★   **Coca-Cola Bottling Co. Johnston**
Hwy. 64 Bypass & Ref. Ln.
Cleveland, TN 37311
Ultimate Parent: Coca-Cola Bottling Consol. **SIC:** 2086—Bottled & Canned Soft Drinks.

★ 80574 ★   **Duracell USA**
Mouse Creek Rd.
Cleveland, TN 37311
Ultimate Parent: Duracell International Inc. **SIC:** 3692—Primary Batteries—Dry & Wet.

★ 80575 ★   **Duracell USA**
501 Mouse Creek Rd., NW
Cleveland, TN 37312
(615)476-7503
Officer: Neiv Caldwell, Manager. **Ultimate Parent:** Duracell International Inc. **SIC:** 3691—Storage Batteries.

★ 80576 ★   **E. R. Carpenter Co. Inc.**
Appalachan Industrial Park
Lupton Ln.
Box 2695
Cleveland, TN 37311
Ultimate Parent: Carpenter. **SIC:** 3086—Plastics Foam Products.

★ 80577 ★   **Eaton Corp.**
Old Tasso Rd. NE
Cleveland, TN 37311
(615)472-3305
Ultimate Parent: Eaton Corp. **SIC:** 3625—Relays & Industrial Controls.

★ 80578 ★   **Eaton Corp.**
3990 Old Tasso Rd. NE
Cleveland, TN 37312
(615)472-3305
Officer: Ronald Clough, Manager. **Ultimate Parent:** Eaton Corp. **SIC:** 3613—Switchgear & Switchboard Apparatus.

★ 80579 ★   **Eaton Corp.**
Power Distribution Div.
3990 Old Tasso Rd., NE
Cleveland, TN 37311
(615)472-3305
Company Type: Division. **Location Type:** Plant. **Officer:** Russell Hobbs, Controller. **Ultimate Parent:** Eaton Corp. **SIC:** 3577—Computer Peripheral Equipment Nec; 3613—Switchgear & Switchboard Apparatus.

★ 80580 ★   **Eckerd Drugs**
820 Keith St.
Cleveland, TN 37311
(615)472-4509
Ultimate Parent: Eckerd Corp. **SIC:** 5912—Drug Stores & Proprietary Stores.

★ 80581 ★   **E.R. Carpenter Co. Inc.**
Lupton Lane, Appalachan Ind. Park, PO Box 2695
Cleveland, TN 37311
Ultimate Parent: Carpenter. **SIC:** 2392—Housefurnishings Nec.

★ 80582 ★   **Exxon Co. U S a**
1440 Frederick St. NW
Cleveland, TN 37311
(615)472-3289
Ultimate Parent: Exxon. **SIC:** 5983—Fuel Oil Dealers.

★ 80583 ★   **First American National Bank**
Village Shopping Ctr.
Cleveland, TN 37311-5844
(615)339-4670
Location Type: Branch office. **Ultimate Parent:** Firstfed Financial Corp. **SIC:** 6021—National Commercial Banks.

★ 80584 ★   **First American National Bank**
910 25th St. NW
Cleveland, TN 37311-3614
(615)339-4667
Location Type: Branch office. **Ultimate Parent:** First American Corp. **SIC:** 6021—National Commercial Banks.

★ 80585 ★   **First American National Bank**
20 Ocoee NE
Cleveland, TN 37311-5064
(615)339-4600
Location Type: Branch office. **Ultimate Parent:** First American Corp. **SIC:** 6021—National Commercial Banks.

★ 80586 ★   **Fitness Factory**
1800 Harrison Pike W
Cleveland, TN 37311
(615)479-8696
Ultimate Parent: New York Times. **SIC:** 7299—Miscellaneous Personal Services Nec.

★ 80587 ★   **Greyhound Bus Lines**
2465 Guthrie Ave. NW
Cleveland, TN 37311
(615)472-1816
Ultimate Parent: Greyhound Lines Inc. **SIC:** 4111—Local & Suburban Transit; 4131—Intercity & Rural Bus Transportation; 4142—Bus Charter Service Except Local.

★ 80588 ★   **J C Penney Co. Inc.**
Cleveland Mall
Cleveland, TN 37312
(615)472-2193
Ultimate Parent: J.C. Penney. **SIC:** 5311—Department Stores.

★ 80589 ★   **Johnston Coca-Cola Bottling Co.**
Hwy. 64 Bypass Ln.
Cleveland, TN 37311
Ultimate Parent: Coca-Cola Enterprises. **SIC:** 2086—Bottled & Canned Soft Drinks.

★ 80590 ★   **Magic Chef**
Hardwick Enamel Plant
1545 Euclid Ave. SE
Cleveland, TN 37311
Location Type: Plant. **Ultimate Parent:** Maytag. **SIC:** 3631—Household Cooking Equipment.

★ 80591 ★   **Magic Chef**
Plant 1
740 King Edward Ave.
Cleveland, TN 37311
Location Type: Plant. **Ultimate Parent:** Maytag. **SIC:** 3631—Household Cooking Equipment.

★ 80592 ★   **Magic Chef Co.**
740 King Edward Ave.
Cleveland, TN 37311
(615)472-3371 **Fax:** (615)478-4594
Officer: Donald M. Lorton, President, Diversified Products. **Ultimate Parent:** Maytag.

★ 80593 ★   **Maytag Corp.**
Magic Chef Div.
740 King Edward Ave.
Cleveland, TN 37311
Company Type: Division. **Ultimate Parent:** Maytag. **SIC:** 3631—Household Cooking Equipment.

★ 80594 ★   **McDonald's Hamburgers**
Cleveland, TN 37320
(615)478-5661
Ultimate Parent: McDonald's. **SIC:** 5812—Eating Places.

★ 80595 ★   **Mutual of New York**
805 20th St. NW
Cleveland, TN 37311
(615)479-3054
Ultimate Parent: Mutual of New York. **SIC:** 6411—Insurance Agents, Brokers & Service.

★ 80596 ★   **Rite Aid Discount Pharmacy**
2300 Red Food Dr. SE
Cleveland, TN 37323
(615)478-3850
Ultimate Parent: Rite Aid. **SIC:** 5912—Drug Stores & Proprietary Stores.

★ 80597 ★ Rite Aid Discount
Pharmacy
2737 Keith NW
Cleveland, TN 37311
(615)476-9270
Ultimate Parent: Rite Aid. SIC: 5912—Drug
Stores & Proprietary Stores.

★ 80598 ★ Rubbermaid
Commercial Proudcts
2000 Overhead Bridge Rd.
Cleveland, TN 37311
(615)476-4544
Officer: Frank McNeely, Manager. Ultimate
Parent: Rubbermaid. SIC: 2392—
Housefurnishings Nec.

★ 80599 ★ Ryder Truck Rental-
Oneway
S Lee Hwy.
Cleveland, TN 37311
(615)472-5701
Ultimate Parent: Ryder System. SIC:
5084—Industrial Machinery & Equipment.

★ 80600 ★ Schering-Plough
Healthcare Products
4207 Michigan Ave. Rd. NE
Cleveland, TN 37312
Ultimate Parent: Schering-Plough Corp.
SIC: 2844—Toilet Preparations; 2834—
Pharmaceutical Preparations; 2841—Soap
& Other Detergents; 3069—Fabricated
Rubber Products Nec; 3842—Surgical
Appliances & Supplies; 3999—
Manufacturing Industries Nec.

★ 80601 ★ Scholl Inc.
4207 Michigan Ave. Rd. NE
Cleveland, TN 37312
Ultimate Parent: Schering-Plough Corp.
SIC: 3842—Surgical Appliances & Supplies.

★ 80602 ★ Shell Super Service
170 Broad St. SW
Cleveland, TN 37311
(615)472-0723
Ultimate Parent: Shell Oil Co. SIC: 5541—
Gasoline Service Stations.

★ 80603 ★ Trailways Greyhound
Bus Lines
1422 25th St. NW
Cleveland, TN 37311
(615)472-5512
Ultimate Parent: Greyhound Lines Inc. SIC:
4131—Intercity & Rural Bus Transportation;
4111—Local & Suburban Transit; 4142—
Bus Charter Service Except Local.

★ 80604 ★ Wal-Mart Stores Inc.
25 Northwest
Cleveland, TN 37311
(615)479-5457
Ultimate Parent: Wal-Mart Stores, Inc. SIC:
5311—Department Stores.

★ 80605 ★ Westvaco
Folding Box Div.
Old Tasso Rd.
Cleveland, TN 37311
Company Type: Division. Ultimate Parent:
WestVaco Corp. SIC: 2754—Commercial
Printing—Gravure.

★ 80606 ★ Westvaco Corp.
Old Tasso Rd. NE
Cleveland, TN 37311
(615)479-9783
Ultimate Parent: WestVaco Corp. SIC:
5113—Industrial & Personal Service Paper.

★ 80607 ★ Westvaco Corp.
Blue Spring Rd.
Cleveland, TN 37311
(615)472-3323
Ultimate Parent: WestVaco Corp. SIC:
5113—Industrial & Personal Service Paper.

★ 80608 ★ Westvaco Corp.
4100 Old Tasso Rd. NE
Cleveland, TN 37312
(615)479-9783
Officer: Horace Coffey, Manager. Ultimate
Parent: WestVaco Corp. SIC: 2652—Setup
Paperboard Boxes; 2657—Folding
Paperboard Boxes.

★ 80609 ★ Westvaco Corp.
Folding Carton
4100 Old Tasso Rd. NE
Cleveland, TN 37312
Company Type: Division. Ultimate Parent:
WestVaco Corp. SIC: 2754—Commercial
Printing—Gravure.

Clifton

★ 80610 ★ People's Bank
155 Main St.
Clifton, TN 38425
(615)676-3311
Ultimate Parent: People's Bank. SIC:
6022—State Commercial Banks; 6081—
Foreign Banks—Branches & Agencies.

Clinton

★ 80611 ★ D. H. Compounding
Co.
PO Box 70
Clinton, TN 37717
(615)457-1200 Fax: (615)463-3109
Company Type: Subsidiary. Officer: R. W.
Ball, President. Ultimate Parent:
M.A.Hanna.

★ 80612 ★ First American Trust
Co., NA
505 S. Gay St.
Clinton, TN 37902
(615)521-5184
Location Type: Branch office. Ultimate
Parent: First American Corp. SIC: 6021—
National Commercial Banks.

★ 80613 ★ Rite Aid Discount
Pharmacy
505 Main St. S
Clinton, TN 37716
(615)457-2833
Ultimate Parent: Rite Aid. SIC: 5912—Drug
Stores & Proprietary Stores.

★ 80614 ★ Security Trust FS &
LA
Hwy. 25
Clinton, TN 37716-9510
(615)457-0245
Location Type: Branch office. Ultimate
Parent: Union Planters Corp. SIC: 6021—
National Commercial Banks.

★ 80615 ★ Union Planters
National Bank
351 Market
Clinton, TN 37716
(615)481-2720
Location Type: Branch office. Ultimate
Parent: Union Planters Corp. SIC: 6021—
National Commercial Banks.

College Grove

★ 80616 ★ First Union National
Bank of Tennessee
8780 Horton Hwy.
College Grove, TN 37046
(615)368-7121
Location Type: Branch office. Ultimate
Parent: First Union Corp. SIC: 6021—
National Commercial Banks.

Collierville

★ 80617 ★ Carrier Corp.
97 S. Byhalia Rd.
Collierville, TN 38017
Ultimate Parent: United Technologies. SIC:
3499—Fabricated Metal Products Nec;
3585—Refrigeration & Heating Equipment.

★ 80618 ★ Exxon Car Care
Center
796 W. Poplar Ave.
Collierville, TN 38017
(901)853-1220
Ultimate Parent: Exxon. SIC: 5541—
Gasoline Service Stations.

★ 80619 ★ Kroger Co.
240 New Byhaliard
Collierville, TN 38017
(901)853-1330
Ultimate Parent: Kroger. SIC: 5411—
Grocery Stores.

★ 80620 ★ Peoples Bank
595 W. Poplar Ave.
Collierville, TN 38017
(901)853-4666
Ultimate Parent: People's Bank. SIC:
6022—State Commercial Banks.

★ 80621 ★ Peoples Bank
108 W. Mulberry St.
Collierville, TN 38017
(901)853-4781
Ultimate Parent: People's Bank. SIC:
6022—State Commercial Banks.

★ 80622 ★ Stone Container Corp.
550 E. South St.
Collierville, TN 38017
(901)853-2800
Officer: Garland Johns, Manager. Ultimate
Parent: Stone Container Corp. SIC: 2653—
Corrugated & Solid Fiber Boxes.

★ 80623 ★ Texaco Service
Station
398 New Byhalia Rd.
Collierville, TN 38017
(901)853-5977
Ultimate Parent: Texaco. SIC: 5541—
Gasoline Service Stations.

★ 80624 ★ Wal-Mart Stores Inc.
560 W. Poplar Ave.
Collierville, TN 38017
Ultimate Parent: Wal-Mart Stores, Inc. SIC:
5311—Department Stores.

Columbia

★ 80625 ★ Blazer Financial
Services
1517 Hatcher Ln.
Columbia, TN 38401
(615)381-5520
Ultimate Parent: Great Western Financial
Corp. SIC: 6141—Personal Credit
Institutions.

★ 80626 ★ Exxon District Office
PO Box 37
Columbia, TN 38402
(615)388-1316
Ultimate Parent: Exxon.

★ 80627 ★ First Federal S & L
610 N. Garden St.
Columbia, TN 38401-3222
(615)388-0423
Company Type: Headquarters. Officer: J.
D. Oakes. Ultimate Parent: Bancorp
Hawaii. SIC: 6035—Federal Savings
Institutions; 6021—National Commercial
Banks; 6141—Personal Credit Institutions;
6162—Mortgage Bankers &
Correspondents.

★ 80628 ★ General Electric Co.
981 Industrial Park Rd.
Columbia, TN 38401
(615)381-2340
Officer: Ken Riddle, Manager. Ultimate
Parent: General Electric. SIC: 3563—Air &
Gas Compressors; 3585—Refrigeration &
Heating Equipment.

★ 80629 ★ General Electric Co.
Rte. 4, Industrial Park
Columbia, TN 38401
Ultimate Parent: General Electric. SIC:
3563—Air & Gas Compressors; 3585—
Refrigeration & Heating Equipment.

★ 80630 ★ Giant Food Inc.
Maury County Shopping Ctr.
Columbia, TN 38401
(615)388-5296
Ultimate Parent: Giant Food. SIC: 5411—
Grocery Stores.

★ 80631 ★ Greyhound Bus Lines
800 Beckett St.
Columbia, TN 38401
(615)388-6933
Ultimate Parent: Greyhound Lines Inc. SIC:
4111—Local & Suburban Transit; 4131—
Intercity & Rural Bus Transportation; 4142—
Bus Charter Service Except Local.

★ 80632 ★ Monsanto Co.
Monsanto Rd.
Columbia, TN 38401
(615)380-9300
Company Type: Branch. Officer: Bill
Perdue. Ultimate Parent: Monsanto. SIC:
2819—Industrial Inorganic Chemicals Nec;
2899—Chemical Preparations Nec.

★ 80633 ★ Monsanto Co.
Williamsport Pike
Columbia, TN 38401
Ultimate Parent: Monsanto. SIC: 2819—
Industrial Inorganic Chemicals Nec.

★ 80634 ★ Occidental Chemical
Corp.
Box 591 Santa Fe Pike
Columbia, TN 38401
Ultimate Parent: Occidental Petroleum
Corp. SIC: 2819—Industrial Inorganic
Chemicals Nec.

★ 80635 ★ Occidental Chemical
Corp.
Santa Fe Pike
Columbia, TN 38401
Ultimate Parent: Occidental Petroleum
Corp. SIC: 2819—Industrial Inorganic
Chemicals Nec.

★ 80636 ★ Occidental Chemical
Corp.
Box 591 Santa Santa Fe Pike
Columbia, TN 38401
Ultimate Parent: Occidental Petroleum
Corp. SIC: 2819—Industrial Inorganic
Chemicals Nec.

★ 80637 ★ Payless Shoe Source
800 S. James Campbell Blvd.
Columbia, TN 38401
(615)381-7124
Ultimate Parent: May Department Stores.
SIC: 5661—Shoe Stores.

★ 80638 ★ Rite Aid Discount
Pharmacy
119 Nashville Hwy.
Columbia, TN 38401
Ultimate Parent: Rite Aid. SIC: 5912—Drug
Stores & Proprietary Stores.

★ 80639 ★ Ryder Truck Rental-
One Way
105 Nashville Hwy.
Columbia, TN 38401
(615)381-0128
Ultimate Parent: Ryder System. SIC:
7359—Equipment Rental & Leasing Nec.

★ 80640 ★ Ucar Carbon Co. Inc.
Santa Fe Pike
Columbia, TN 38401
Ultimate Parent: Union Carbide Corp. SIC:
3624—Carbon & Graphite Products.

Concord Farragut

★ 80641 ★ Mayfield Dairy Farms
Inc.
9725 Truckers Ln.
Concord Farragut, TN 37922
(615)693-0851
Officer: Joe Qualls, Manager. Ultimate
Parent: Dean Foods. SIC: 2024—Ice
Cream & Frozen Desserts.

Cookevile

★ 80642 ★ Microfoam Inc.
1480 Gould Dr.
Cookevile, TN 38501-4152
(615)432-4042
Ultimate Parent: Ametek Inc. SIC: 5046—
Commercial Equipment Nec.

Cookeville

★ 80643 ★ Carolina Freight Corp.
Old Sparta Hwy.
Cookeville, TN 38501
(615)528-8882
Ultimate Parent: Carolina Freight. SIC:
4212—Local Trucking Without Storage.

★ 80644 ★ Citizens Bank
155 S. Jefferson Ave.
Towne Plz.
Cookeville, TN 38501
Location Type: Branch office. Ultimate
Parent: Union Planters Corp. SIC: 6021—
National Commercial Banks.

★ 80645 ★ Citizens Bank
PO Box 70
Cookeville, TN 38503-0070
Location Type: Headquarters. Ultimate
Parent: Union Planters Corp. SIC: 6021—
National Commercial Banks.

★ 80646 ★ Citizens Bank
10 W. Broad
Cookeville, TN 38501-2574
(615)526-2181 Fax: (615)526-4368
Location Type: Headquarters. Ultimate
Parent: Union Planters Corp. SIC: 6021—
National Commercial Banks.

★ 80647 ★ Diebold Inc.
493 E. Broad St.
Cookeville, TN 38501
(615)526-7644
Ultimate Parent: Diebold, Inc. SIC: 5063—
Electrical Apparatus & Equipment.

★ 80648 ★ E. R. Carpenter Co.
Inc.
101 Locust Ln.
Cookeville, TN 38502
Ultimate Parent: Carpenter. SIC: 3086—
Plastics Foam Products.

★ 80649 ★ E. R. Carpenter Co.
Inc.
1824 Brown Mill Rd.
Cookeville, TN 38502
Ultimate Parent: Carpenter. SIC: 3086—
Plastics Foam Products.

★ 80650 ★ Exxon Corp.
42 W. Spring St.
Cookeville, TN 38501
(615)528-1505
Ultimate Parent: Exxon. SIC: 1479—
Chemical & Fertilizer Mining Nec.

★ 80651 ★ First American
National Bank
Interstate & Willow
Cookeville, TN 38501
Location Type: Branch office. Ultimate
Parent: First American Corp. SIC: 6021—
National Commercial Banks.

★ 80652 ★ First American
National Bank
790 S. Jefferson
Cookeville, TN 38501-4030
Location Type: Branch office. Ultimate
Parent: First American Corp. SIC: 6021—
National Commercial Banks.

★ 80653 ★ First American
National Bank
990 N. Washington
Cookeville, TN 38501-2666
Location Type: Branch office. Ultimate
Parent: First American Corp. SIC: 6021—
National Commercial Banks.

★ 80654 ★ First Tennessee Bank
NA
10th St. & Washington Ave.
Cookeville, TN 38503
Location Type: Branch office. Ultimate
Parent: First Tennessee National Corp.
SIC: 6021—National Commercial Banks.

★ 80655 ★ First Tennessee Bank
NA
345 S. Jefferson Ave.
Cookeville, TN 38501-3456
(615)528-2561
Location Type: Branch office. Ultimate
Parent: First Tennessee National Corp.
SIC: 6021—National Commercial Banks.

★ 80656 ★ First Tennessee Bank
NA
305 Willow &Spring Sts.
Cookeville, TN 38503
Location Type: Branch office. Ultimate
Parent: First Tennessee National Corp.
SIC: 6021—National Commercial Banks.

★ 80657 ★ Fleetguard Inc.
1200 Fleetguard Rd.
Cookeville, TN 38501
Ultimate Parent: Cummins Engine Co. SIC:
3714—Motor Vehicle Parts & Accessories.

★ 80658 ★ Foamex LP
621 Maxwell St.
Cookeville, TN 38501
Ultimate Parent: Foamex. SIC: 3086—
Plastics Foam Products.

★ 80659 ★ Gold Medal Inc.
465 Universal Dr.
Cookeville, TN 38501
(615)432-4175
Officer: Mike Johnson, Manager. Ultimate
Parent: General Mills. SIC: 2392—
Housefurnishings Nec; 2396—Automotive &
Apparel Trimmings; 2599—Furniture &
Fixtures Nec.

★ 80660 ★ Kroger Co.
S. Jefferson
Cookeville, TN 38501
(615)526-4575
Ultimate Parent: Kroger. SIC: 5411—
Grocery Stores.

★ 80661 ★ McDonald's
Hamburgers
1001 S. Jefferson Ave.
Cookeville, TN 38501
(615)528-1010
Ultimate Parent: McDonald's. SIC: 5812—
Eating Places.

★ 80662 ★ Peoples Bank & Trust
105 N. Washington Ave.
Cookeville, TN 38501
(615)528-3211
Ultimate Parent: People's Bank. SIC:
6099—Functions Related to Deposit
Banking.

★ 80663 ★ Pepsi-Cola Co.
237 W. Spring St.
Cookeville, TN 38501
(615)528-8469
Ultimate Parent: Pepsico. SIC: 2086—
Bottled & Canned Soft Drinks.

★ 80664 ★ Porelon Inc.
1480 Gould Dr.
Cookeville, TN 38501
Ultimate Parent: Johnson & Johnson. SIC:
3000—Rubber & Miscellaneous Plastics
Products.

★ 80665 ★ Red Kap Ind.
580 S. Jefferson Ave.
Cookeville, TN 38501
(615)528-1551
Officer: Blanchard Tubb, Manager.
Ultimate Parent: VF Corp. SIC: 2326—
Men's/Boys' Work Clothing.

★ 80666 ★ Ryder Truck Rental
E 20th
Cookeville, TN 38501
(615)526-1716
Ultimate Parent: Ryder System. SIC:
7513—Truck Rental & Leasing Without
Drivers.

★ 80667 ★ Teledyne Still-Man
1011 Volunteer Dr.
Cookeville, TN 38501-0789
Ultimate Parent: Teledyne. SIC: 3631—
Household Cooking Equipment.

★ 80668 ★ Trailways Bus Lines
241 Palk Dr.
Cookeville, TN 38501
(615)526-4455
Ultimate Parent: Greyhound Lines Inc. SIC:
4131—Intercity & Rural Bus Transportation;
4111—Local & Suburban Transit; 4142—
Bus Charter Service Except Local.

★ 80669 ★ Underwriters
Adjusting Co.
112 S. Dixie Ave.
Cookeville, TN 38501
(615)526-7113
Ultimate Parent: Continental. SIC: 6411—
Insurance Agents, Brokers & Service.

★ 80670 ★ Wal-Mart Stores Inc.
768 S. Jefferson Ave.
Cookeville, TN 38501
Ultimate Parent: Wal-Mart Stores, Inc. SIC:
5311—Department Stores.

Cooksville

★ 80671 ★ First American
National Bank
105 S. Willow Ave.
Cooksville, TN 38501-3138
(615)528-7561
Location Type: Branch office. Ultimate
Parent: First American Corp. SIC: 6021—
National Commercial Banks.

Cookville

★ 80672 ★ Citizens Bank
900 E. 10th St.
Cookville, TN 38501-1906
Location Type: Branch office. Ultimate
Parent: Union Planters Corp. SIC: 6021—
National Commercial Banks.

Cordova

★ 80673 ★ Aristar Inc.
8001 Centerview Pky.
Cordova, TN 38018-4228
(901)757-7500
Company Type: Subsidiary. Officer:
Michael M. Pappas, President. Ultimate

Parent: Great Western Financial Corp. SIC:
6141—Personal Credit Institutions; 6153—
Short-Term Business Credit; 6351—Surety
Insurance.

★ 80674 ★ Blazer Financial
Services Inc.
8001 Centerview Pky.
Cordova, TN 38018-4228
(901)757-7500
Company Type: Subsidiary. Officer: Mike
M. Pappas, President. Ultimate Parent:
Great Western Financial Corp. SIC: 6141—
Personal Credit Institutions. Employee
Count: 1605.

★ 80675 ★ First Tennessee Bank
NA
8000 Trinity Rd.
Cordova, TN 38018
(901)753-3079
Location Type: Branch office. Ultimate
Parent: First Tennessee National Corp.
SIC: 6021—National Commercial Banks.

★ 80676 ★ First Tennessee Bank
NA
1750 N. Germantown Pky.
Cordova, TN 38018
(901)756-3921
Location Type: Branch office. Ultimate
Parent: First Tennessee National Corp.
SIC: 6021—National Commercial Banks.

★ 80677 ★ Sara Lee Corp.
8000 Centerview Pky., Ste. 400
Cordova, TN 38018
(901)753-1600
Company Type: Division. Officer: Jerry
Laner, President. Ultimate Parent: Sara
Lee Corp.

★ 80678 ★ Sara Lee Meats
8000 Centerview Pky., Ste. 300
Cordova, TN 38018
(901)756-4051
Company Type: Division. Officer: George
Bryan, President. Ultimate Parent: Sara
Lee Corp.

★ 80679 ★ Union Planters
National Bank
8040 Walnut Run Rd.
Cordova, TN 38018-8563
(901)756-2640
Location Type: Branch office. Ultimate
Parent: Union Planters Corp. SIC: 6021—
National Commercial Banks.

Cosby

★ 80680 ★ First Union National
Bank of Tennessee
4381 Cosby Hwy.
Cosby, TN 37722
(615)487-2600
Location Type: Branch office. Ultimate
Parent: First Union Corp. SIC: 6021—
National Commercial Banks.

Counce

★ 80681 ★ Packaging Corp. of
America
Tennessee River Pulp Division
Hwy. 57 PO Box 33
Counce, TN 38326
Ultimate Parent: Tenneco Inc. SIC: 2611—
Pulp Mills; 2621—Paper Mills.

★ 80682 ★ Tennessee River Pulp
& Paper Co.
Packaging Division
Hwy. 57
Counce, TN 38326
Ultimate Parent: Tenneco Inc. SIC: 2611—
Pulp Mills.

Covington

★ 80683 ★ Coast to Coast
Star Shopping Ctr. 106
Covington, TN 38019
(901)476-8296
Ultimate Parent: Servistar Corp. SIC:
5251—Hardware Stores.

★ 80684 ★ Delfield Co.
1 Delfield Dr.
Covington, TN 38019
Ultimate Parent: Alco Standard Corp. SIC:
3585—Refrigeration & Heating Equipment.

★ 80685 ★ Itw Paslode
1211 Hope St.
Covington, TN 38019-0707
Ultimate Parent: Illinois Tool Works. SIC:
3315—Steel Wire & Related Products.

★ 80686 ★ Kroger Co.
951 US Hwy. 51 N
Covington, TN 38019
(901)476-1798
Ultimate Parent: Kroger. SIC: 5411—
Grocery Stores.

★ 80687 ★ Wal-Mart Stores Inc.
Hwy. 51 N
Covington, TN 38019
(901)476-4492
Ultimate Parent: Wal-Mart Stores, Inc. SIC:
5331—Variety Stores.

★ 80688 ★ Wal-Mart Stores Inc.
Hwy. 51 N
Covington, TN 38019
(901)476-3800
Ultimate Parent: Wal-Mart Stores, Inc. SIC:
5311—Department Stores.

Crossville

★ 80689 ★ Aristokraft Inc.
PO Box 2539
Crossville, TN 38557-2539
(615)456-1802
Officer: Ronald Meehan. Ultimate Parent:
American Brands Inc. SIC: 2426—
Hardwood Dimension & Flooring Mills.

★ 80690 ★ Avery Dennison
PO Box 547
Crossville, TN 38557-0547
(615)484-6131
Officer: Keith Talbot. Ultimate Parent:
Avery Dennison Corp. SIC: 3953—Marking
Devices; 2891—Adhesives & Sealants;
3951—Pens & Mechanical Pencils.

★ 80691 ★ Dennison Stationery
Prods. Co. Inc.
2110 W. Ave. N.
Crossville, TN 38555-6007
Ultimate Parent: Avery Dennison Corp.
SIC: 3951—Pens & Mechanical Pencils;
3953—Marking Devices; 2891—Adhesives
& Sealants.

★ 80692 ★ Dennison Stationery
Products Co., Inc.
2110 West Ave. N
Crossville, TN 38557
Ultimate Parent: Avery Dennison Corp.
SIC: 3951—Pens & Mechanical Pencils;
3953—Marking Devices; 2891—Adhesives
& Sealants.

★ 80693 ★ Exxon Co. U S a
Hamby Ln.
Crossville, TN 38555
(615)484-5021
Ultimate Parent: Exxon. SIC: 5983—Fuel
Oil Dealers.

★ 80694 ★ Exxon Zippy Mart
Elmore Rd.
Crossville, TN 38555
(615)484-6143
Ultimate Parent: Exxon. SIC: 5541—
Gasoline Service Stations.

★ 80695 ★ First American
National Bank
585 Sparta
Crossville, TN 38555-4253
(615)484-3523
Location Type: Branch office. Ultimate
Parent: First American Corp. SIC: 6021—
National Commercial Banks.

★ 80696 ★ First American
National Bank
201 Elmore Rd.
Crossville, TN 38555-4010
(615)484-2521
Location Type: Branch office. Ultimate
Parent: First American Corp. SIC: 6021—
National Commercial Banks.

★ 80697 ★ First National Bank
Elmore Rd.
Crossville, TN 38555
Location Type: Branch office. Ultimate
Parent: Union Planters Corp. SIC: 6021—
National Commercial Banks.

★ 80698 ★ First National Bank
215 N. Main St.
Crossville, TN 38555-4508
Location Type: Branch office. Ultimate
Parent: Union Planters Corp. SIC: 6021—
National Commercial Banks.

★ 80699 ★ First National Bank
PO Drawer 429
Crossville, TN 38557-0429
Location Type: Headquarters. Ultimate
Parent: Union Planters Corp. SIC: 6021—
National Commercial Banks.

★ 80700 ★ First National Bank
812 N. Main St.
Crossville, TN 38555-4292
(615)484-6121 Fax: (615)484-8855
Location Type: Headquarters. Ultimate
Parent: Union Planters Corp. SIC: 6021—
National Commercial Banks.

★ 80701 ★ Flowers Baking Co. of
Chatanooga Inc.
1601 N. Main St.
Crossville, TN 38555-4028
(615)484-6101
Company Type: Subsidiary. Officer: Larry
Ebert, President. Ultimate Parent: Flowers
Industries. SIC: 2051—Bread, Cake &
Related Products. Employee Count: 400.
Sales: 33 M.

★ 80702 ★ Flowers Snack of
Tennessee Inc.
1601 N. Main St.
Crossville, TN 38555
(615)484-6101
Officer: Larry Ebert, President. Ultimate
Parent: Flowers Industries. SIC: 2051—
Bread, Cake & Related Products.

★ 80703 ★ Flowers Snack of
Tennessee Inc.
PO Box 495
Crossville, TN 38555
(615)484-6101 Fax: (615)484-3657
Company Type: Subsidiary. Officer: Larry
W. Ebert, President. Ultimate Parent:
Flowers Industries.

★ 80704 ★ Peoples Bank
Crossville
Hwy. 127 N
Crossville, TN 38555
(615)484-2521
Ultimate Parent: People's Bank. SIC:
6022—State Commercial Banks.

★ 80705 ★ Ryder Truck Rental
1128 West Ave. N
Crossville, TN 38555
(615)484-3411
Ultimate Parent: Ryder System. SIC:
7359—Equipment Rental & Leasing Nec.

★ 80706 ★ Trailways Bus Lines
312 Stanley St.
Crossville, TN 38555
(615)484-5461
Ultimate Parent: Greyhound Lines Inc. SIC:
4131—Intercity & Rural Bus Transportation;
4111—Local & Suburban Transit; 4142—
Bus Charter Service Except Local.

Cumberland

★ 80707 ★ Cumberland City
Bank
Main St.
Cumberland, TN 37050
(615)827-2900 Fax: (615)827-2343
Location Type: Branch office. Ultimate
Parent: Union Planters Corp. SIC: 6021—
National Commercial Banks.

Cumberland City

★ 80708 ★ Cumberland City
Bank
PO Box 6
Cumberland City, TN 37050-0006
Location Type: Branch office. Ultimate
Parent: Union Planters Corp. SIC: 6021—
National Commercial Banks.

Cumberland Gap

★ 80709 ★ Shell Super Stop
US 25 St. E
Cumberland Gap, TN 37724
(615)869-4821
Ultimate Parent: Shell Oil Co. SIC: 5411—
Grocery Stores.

Dandridge

★ 80710 ★ First Tennessee Bank
NA
1030 S. Hwy. 92
Dandridge, TN 37725
(615)397-9471
Location Type: Branch office. Ultimate
Parent: First Tennessee National Corp.
SIC: 6021—National Commercial Banks.

★ 80711 ★ First Union National
Bank of Tennessee
3901 Hwys. 411 & 92
Dandridge, TN 37725-9804
(615)397-2265
Ultimate Parent: First Union Corp. SIC:
6021—National Commercial Banks.

★ 80712 ★ First Union National
Bank of Tennessee
858 Hwy. 92
Dandridge, TN 37725-8901
(615)397-2265
Location Type: Branch office. Ultimate
Parent: First Union Corp. SIC: 6021—
National Commercial Banks.

★ 80713 ★ Heekin Can Inc.
3218 Chestnut Hill Rd.
Dandridge, TN 37725-7223
(615)623-7544
Officer: Ron Ryan. Ultimate Parent: Ball
Corp. SIC: 3411—Metal Cans.

★ 80714 ★ US Marine/Bayliner
831 Epco Dr.
Dandridge, TN 37725
Ultimate Parent: Brunswick Corp. SIC:
3732—Boat Building & Repairing.

Dayton

★ 80715 ★ AmSouth Bank of
Tennessee
401 N. Market St.
Dayton, TN 37321
(615)775-1522
Ultimate Parent: AmSouth Bancorp.

★ 80716 ★ AmSouth Bank of
Tennessee
401 N. Market St.
Dayton, TN 37321-1282
(615)775-1522
Location Type: Branch office. Officer:
Randy Wells, Manager. Ultimate Parent:
AmSouth Bancorp. SIC: 6022—State
Commercial Banks; 6162—Mortgage
Bankers & Correspondents.

★ 80717 ★ Eckerd Drugs
Richland Park Shopping Ctr.
Dayton, TN 37321
(615)775-3500
Ultimate Parent: Eckerd Corp. SIC: 5912—
Drug Stores & Proprietary Stores.

★ 80718 ★ First American
National Bank
3rd Ave. & N. Market St.
Dayton, TN 37321
(615)775-6837
Location Type: Branch office. Ultimate
Parent: First American Corp. SIC: 6021—
National Commercial Banks.

★ 80719 ★ Kayser-Roth Corp.
220 Broadway St.
Dayton, TN 37321
Ultimate Parent: Collins & Aikman Group.
SIC: 2251—Women's Hosiery Except
Socks.

★ 80720 ★ Kayser-Roth Corp.
708 N. Broadway St.
Dayton, TN 37321
Ultimate Parent: Collins & Aikman Group.
SIC: 2251—Women's Hosiery Except
Socks.

★ 80721 ★ La-Z-Boy Tennessee
500 Walnut Grove Rd.
Dayton, TN 37321
Ultimate Parent: La-Z-Boy Chair. SIC:
2512—Upholstered Household Furniture.

★ 80722 ★ La-Z-Boy Tennessee
PO Box 457
Dayton, TN 37321
(615)775-3900 Fax: (615)775-6760
Officer: David R. Brown, General Manager.
Ultimate Parent: La-Z-Boy Chair.

★ 80723 ★ United Technologies
Automotive Engineered Systems Div.
Rte. 5 Box 5009 Black Oak Ridge Rd.
Dayton, TN 37321
Company Type: Division. Ultimate Parent:
United Technologies. SIC: 3089—Plastics
Products Nec.

★ 80724 ★ Wabco Co.
Black Oak Ridge Rd.
Dayton, TN 37321
(615)775-9676
Ultimate Parent: American Standard. SIC:
3555—Printing Trades Machinery.

★ 80725 ★ Wal-Mart Stores Inc.
Hwy. 27 S
Dayton, TN 37321
(615)775-4448
Ultimate Parent: Wal-Mart Stores, Inc. SIC:
5311—Department Stores.

Decatur

★ 80726 ★ Delta Apparel
Jones St.
Decatur, TN 37322
(615)334-5726
Officer: Esther Sims, Manager. Ultimate
Parent: Delta Woodside Industries. SIC:
2321—Men's/Boys' Shirts; 2329—
Men's/Boys' Clothing Nec; 2399—
Fabricated Textile Products Nec.

★ 80727 ★ Shaw Industries Inc.
Hwy. 58 S
Decatur, TN 37322
(615)334-5752
Officer: Robert Shaw, President. Ultimate
Parent: Shaw Industries, Inc. SIC: 2269—
Finishing Plants Nec; 2281—Yarn Spinning
Mills.

Dechard

★ 80728 ★ First Union National
Bank of Tennessee
State Hwy. 50 & US Hwy. 41A
Dechard, TN 37324-9448
(615)967-5511
Location Type: Branch office. Ultimate
Parent: First Union Corp. SIC: 6021—
National Commercial Banks.

Decherd

★ 80729 ★ Tyson Foods Inc.
Alto Rd.
Decherd, TN 37324
(615)967-7881
Ultimate Parent: Tyson Foods, Inc. SIC:
0254—Poultry Hatcheries.

Delano

★ 80730 ★ Mary Kay Cosmetics
Bowater Rd.
Delano, TN 37325
(615)263-1438
Ultimate Parent: Mary Kay Cosmetics. SIC:
5999—Miscellaneous Retail Stores Nec.

Dickson

★ 80731 ★ Dickson Coca Cola
Bottling
101 Cowan Rd.
Dickson, TN 37055
(615)446-8008
Ultimate Parent: Coca-Cola Bottling
Consol. SIC: 5149—Groceries & Related
Products Nec.

★ 80732 ★ First Union Nationa
Bank of Tennessee
Hwy. 46 S. & Pomona Rd.
Dickson, TN 37055-9025
(615)446-5151
Location Type: Branch office. Ultimate
Parent: First Union Corp. SIC: 6021—
National Commercial Banks.

★ 80733 ★ First Union National
Bank of Tennessee
719 E. College St.
Dickson, TN 37055-2031
(615)446-5151
Location Type: Branch office. Ultimate
Parent: First Union Corp. SIC: 6021—
National Commercial Banks.

★ 80734 ★ Payless Shoe Source
Hwy. 46
Dickson, TN 37055
(615)446-0275
Ultimate Parent: May Department Stores.
SIC: 5661—Shoe Stores.

★ 80735 ★ Payless Shoesource
Hwy. 46
Dickson, TN 37055
(615)446-0275
Ultimate Parent: May Department Stores.
SIC: 5661—Shoe Stores.

★ 80736 ★ Red Kap Ind.
212 Hwy. 46
Dickson, TN 37055
(615)446-9071
Officer: Brad Curtis, Manager. Ultimate
Parent: VF Corp. SIC: 2321—Men's/Boys'
Shirts; 2325—Men's/Boys' Trousers &
Slacks; 2326—Men's/Boys' Work Clothing.

★ 80737 ★ Union Planters
National Bank
116 Mathis Dr.
Dickson, TN 37055-2047
(615)726-4247
Location Type: Branch office. Ultimate
Parent: Union Planters Corp. SIC: 6021—
National Commercial Banks.

Donelson

★ 80738 ★ First American
National Bank
301 Donelson Pke.
Donelson, TN 37214-3524
(615)748-2988
Location Type: Branch office. Ultimate
Parent: First American Corp. SIC: 6021—
National Commercial Banks.

Dover

★ 80739 ★ First American
National Bank
Donelson Pky. & Cedar St.
Dover, TN 37058
(615)232-5702
Location Type: Branch office. Ultimate
Parent: First American Corp. SIC: 6021—
National Commercial Banks.

Dowelltown

★ 80740 ★ DeKalb County Bank
& Trust Co.
US Hwy. 70
Dowelltown, TN 37059-9708
(615)536-5394
Location Type: Branch office. Ultimate
Parent: Union Planters Corp. SIC: 6021—
National Commercial Banks.

Dresden

★ 80741 ★ People's Bank
North Side Sq.
Dresden, TN 38225
(901)364-3193
Ultimate Parent: People's Bank. SIC:
6022—State Commercial Banks.

Dyer

★ 80742 ★ Citgo Gas & Grill
572 N. Main St.
Dyer, TN 38330
(901)692-3658
Ultimate Parent: Citgo Petroleum. SIC:
5541—Gasoline Service Stations.

Dyersburg

★ 80743 ★ **Clorox Co. Dyersburg Plant**
2450 Clorox Rd.
Dyersburg, TN 38024
Ultimate Parent: Clorox Co. **SIC:** 2841—Soap & Other Detergents.

★ 80744 ★ **Colonial Rubber Works Inc.**
150 South Connell Ave.
Dyersburg, TN 38024
Ultimate Parent: M.A.Hanna. **SIC:** 3050—Hose & Belting & Gaskets & Packing.

★ 80745 ★ **Colonial Rubber Works Inc.**
150 S. Connell Ave.
Dyersburg, TN 38024
(901)285-4353 **Fax:** (901)285-9154
Company Type: Subsidiary. **Officer:** O. D. Emery, President. **Ultimate Parent:** M.A.Hanna. **SIC:** 3050—Hose & Belting & Gaskets & Packing.

★ 80746 ★ **Dr. Pepper Pepsi-Cola Bottling**
2918 US Hwy. 51 S
Dyersburg, TN 38024
(901)285-3671
Officer: William Burks, President. **Ultimate Parent:** Dr. Pepper/Seven-Up. **SIC:** 2086—Bottled & Canned Soft Drinks.

★ 80747 ★ **First Tennessee Bank NA**
602 Hwy. 51, Bypass N
Dyersburg, TN 38024-9420
(901)286-1500
Location Type: Branch office. **Ultimate Parent:** First Tennessee National Corp. **SIC:** 6021—National Commercial Banks.

★ 80748 ★ **First Tennessee Bank NA**
205 N. Main St.
Dyersburg, TN 38024-4626
(901)286-1500
Location Type: Branch office. **Ultimate Parent:** First Tennessee National Corp. **SIC:** 6021—National Commercial Banks.

★ 80749 ★ **Forcum-Lannom Associates Inc.**
PO Box 768
Dyersburg, TN 38025
(901)285-6503 **Fax:** (901)285-6720
Officer: L.D. Pennington, Chairman of the Board. **Ultimate Parent:** Centex.

★ 80750 ★ **Forcum Lannon Associates**
768 PO Box
Dyersburg, TN 38025
(901)285-6503
Ultimate Parent: Centex. **SIC:** 8999—Services Nec.

★ 80751 ★ **Gold Kist Inc.**
Bean Mill Rd.
Dyersburg, TN 38024
(901)285-1531
Ultimate Parent: Gold Kist. **SIC:** 5153—Grain & Field Beans.

★ 80752 ★ **Greyhound Bus Lines**
1000 Forrest St.
Dyersburg, TN 38024
(901)285-5421
Ultimate Parent: Greyhound Lines Inc. **SIC:** 4111—Local & Suburban Transit; 4131—Intercity & Rural Bus Transportation; 4142—Bus Charter Service Except Local.

★ 80753 ★ **J C Penney Co. Inc.**
204 W. Court St.
Dyersburg, TN 38024
(901)285-6320
Ultimate Parent: J.C. Penney. **SIC:** 5311—Department Stores.

★ 80754 ★ **Merchants State Bank**
1801 Hwy. 51 Bypass N
Dyersburg, TN 38024
(901)287-7700
Location Type: Branch office. **Ultimate Parent:** Union Planters Corp. **SIC:** 6021—National Commercial Banks.

★ 80755 ★ **Mini Mart**
700 Harrell Ave.
Dyersburg, TN 38024
(901)285-0197
Ultimate Parent: Kroger. **SIC:** 5411—Grocery Stores.

★ 80756 ★ **Payless Shoe Source**
Lake Rd.
Dyersburg, TN 38024
(901)286-0226
Ultimate Parent: May Department Stores. **SIC:** 5661—Shoe Stores.

★ 80757 ★ **Payless Shoesource**
Lake Rd.
Dyersburg, TN 38024
(901)286-0226
Ultimate Parent: May Department Stores. **SIC:** 5661—Shoe Stores.

★ 80758 ★ **Save Trust Federal Savings Bank**
580 Hwy. Bypass E
Dyersburg, TN 38024
(901)286-4105
Location Type: Branch office. **Ultimate Parent:** Union Planters Corp. **SIC:** 6021—National Commercial Banks.

★ 80759 ★ **Save Trust Federal Savings Bank**
PO Box 708
Dyersburg, TN 38025-0708
Location Type: Headquarters. **Ultimate Parent:** Union Planters Corp. **SIC:** 6021—National Commercial Banks.

★ 80760 ★ **Save Trust Federal Savings Bank**
425 W. Court St.
Dyersburg, TN 38024-4616
(901)285-3016 **Fax:** (901)286-6495
Location Type: Headquarters. **Ultimate Parent:** Union Planters Corp. **SIC:** 6021—National Commercial Banks.

★ 80761 ★ **Texaco Food Mart**
1400 Hwy. 51 Byp S
Dyersburg, TN 38024
(901)286-5002
Ultimate Parent: Texaco. **SIC:** 5411—Grocery Stores.

★ 80762 ★ **United Parcel Service**
Samaria Bnd Rd.
Dyersburg, TN 38024
(901)342-8357
Ultimate Parent: United Parcel Service of America. **SIC:** 4215—Courier Services Except by Air.

★ 80763 ★ **Wal-Mart Stores Inc.**
2650 Lake Rd.
Dyersburg, TN 38024
(901)286-5190
Ultimate Parent: Wal-Mart Stores, Inc. **SIC:** 5311—Department Stores.

★ 80764 ★ **Wal-Mart Stores Inc.**
Dyersburg Sq.
Dyersburg, TN 38024
(901)285-9358
Ultimate Parent: Wal-Mart Stores, Inc. **SIC:** 5311—Department Stores.

Eagleville

★ 80765 ★ **Union Planters National Bank**
259 N. Main St.
Eagleville, TN 37060
(615)274-6285
Location Type: Branch office. **Ultimate Parent:** Union Planters Corp. **SIC:** 6021—National Commercial Banks.

East Ridge

★ 80766 ★ **Valvoline Instant Oil Change**
4202 Ringgold Rd.
East Ridge, TN 37412
(615)622-4336
Ultimate Parent: Ashland Oil.

Elgin

★ 80767 ★ **Bowater Inc.**
South Div.
Hwy. 52
Elgin, TN 37732
(615)627-2175
Ultimate Parent: Bowater. **SIC:** 2611—Pulp Mills.

Elizabethton

★ 80768 ★ **Great Lakes Research Corp.**
Research Blvd.
Elizabethton, TN 37643
Ultimate Parent: Great Lakes Chemical. **SIC:** 3295—Minerals—Ground or Treated; 2911—Petroleum Refining.

★ 80769 ★ **Snap On Tools Corp.**
State Line Rd.
Elizabethton, TN 37643
(615)543-5771
Officer: Tom Langwell, Manager. **Ultimate Parent:** Snap-on Tools. **SIC:** 3423—Hand & Edge Tools Nec.

★ 80770 ★ **Snap-On Tools Corp.**
State Line Rd.
Elizabethton, TN 37643
Ultimate Parent: Snap-on Tools. **SIC:** 3471—Plating & Polishing; 3545—Machine Tool Accessories; 5013—Motor Vehicle Supplies & New Parts; 5800—Eating & Drinking Places.

★ 80771 ★ **Trailways Bus Lines**
400 E
Elizabethton, TN 37643
(615)542-2831
Ultimate Parent: Greyhound Lines Inc. **SIC:** 4131—Intercity & Rural Bus Transportation; 4111—Local & Suburban Transit; 4142—Bus Charter Service Except Local.

Erin

★ 80772 ★ **Erin Bank & Trust Co.**
Main & Spring
Erin, TN 37061
(615)289-4224 **Fax:** (615)289-4229
Location Type: Headquarters. **Ultimate Parent:** Union Planters Corp. **SIC:** 6021—National Commercial Banks.

★ 80773 ★ **Erin Bank & Trust Co.**
PO Box 267
Erin, TN 37061-0267
Location Type: Headquarters. **Ultimate Parent:** Union Planters Corp. **SIC:** 6021—National Commercial Banks.

★ 80774 ★ **ITW Southern Gage Co.**
40 Midway Dr.
PO Box 509
Erin, TN 37061
(615)289-4242 **Fax:** (800)242-7142
Company Type: Subsidiary. **Officer:** Jim Osberg, General Manager. **Ultimate Parent:** Illinois Tool Works.

Erwin

★ 80775 ★ **First Tennessee Bank NA**
210 Gay St.
Erwin, TN 37650-1230
Location Type: Branch office. **Ultimate Parent:** First Tennessee National Corp. **SIC:** 6021—National Commercial Banks.

★ 80776 ★ **Red Kap Ind.**
600 Carolina Ave.
Erwin, TN 37650
(615)743-6148
Officer: David Ray, Plant Manager. **Ultimate Parent:** VF Corp. **SIC:** 2325—Men's/Boys' Trousers & Slacks; 2326—Men's/Boys' Work Clothing.

Estill Springs

★ 80777 ★ **Tyson Feed Mill**
234 Tyson Dr.
Estill Springs, TN 37330
Ultimate Parent: Tyson Foods, Inc. **SIC:** 2048—Prepared Feeds Nec.

Etowah

★ 80778 ★ **Bowater, Inc.**
105 County Rd. 875
Etowah, TN 37331
(615)263-2255
Ultimate Parent: Bowater. **SIC:** 2411—Logging.

★ 80779 ★ **J. M. Huber Corp.**
Cambria Rd. PO Box P
Etowah, TN 37331
Ultimate Parent: J. M. Huber. **SIC:** 2819—Industrial Inorganic Chemicals Nec.

★ 80780 ★ **Manville Corp.**
Hwy. 411 N. PO Box 309
Etowah, TN 37331-0309
Ultimate Parent: Manville Corp. **SIC:** 3229—Pressed & Blown Glass Nec.

★ 80781 ★ **Manville Corp.**
Hwy. 411 N. PO Box 309
Etowah, TN 37331
Ultimate Parent: Manville Corp. **SIC:** 2297—Nonwoven Fabrics.

★ 80782 ★ **Manville Sales Corp.**
Hwy. 411 N.
Etowah, TN 37331
Ultimate Parent: Manville Corp. **SIC:** 2297—Nonwoven Fabrics.

★ 80783 ★ **Schuller International Inc.**
US Hwy. 411 N.
Etowah, TN 37331-0309
Ultimate Parent: Manville Corp. **SIC:** 3229—Pressed & Blown Glass Nec.

Fairfield Glade

★ 80784 ★ **First National Bank**
Stonehenge Dr.
Fairfield Glade, TN 38555
(615)484-6121
Location Type: Branch office. **Ultimate Parent:** Union Planters Corp. **SIC:** 6021—National Commercial Banks.

Fairview

★ 80785 ★ **Berkshire Hathaway**
France
726 Fairview Blvd. W
Fairview, TN 37062-9011
(615)799-0551
Location Type: Branch office. **Officer:** William P. Melley. **Ultimate Parent:** Berkshire Hathaway. **SIC:** 3612—Transformers Except Electronic; 3625—Relays & Industrial Controls; 3677—Electronic Coils & Transformers; 3699—Electrical Equipment & Supplies Nec; 5063—Electrical Apparatus & Equipment.

★ 80786 ★ **Berkshire Hathaway**
Franee
726 Fairview Blvd.
Fairview, TN 37062
(615)799-0551
Company Type: Division. **Officer:** W. P. Melley, President. **Ultimate Parent:** Berkshire Hathaway. **SIC:** 3612—Transformers Except Electronic.

★ 80787 ★ **Pest Elimination Service**
PO Box 287
Fairview, TN 37062
(615)799-0987
Ultimate Parent: Ecolab Inc. **SIC:** 5261—Retail Nurseries & Garden Stores; 7342—Disinfecting & Pest Control Services.

Fall Branch

★ 80788 ★ **First Tennessee Bank NA**
Hwy. 93
Fall Branch, TN 37656-9401
(615)461-1276
Location Type: Branch office. **Ultimate Parent:** First Tennessee National Corp. **SIC:** 6021—National Commercial Banks.

Fayetteville

★ 80789 ★ Amana Refrigeration Inc.
1810 Wilson Pky.
Fayetteville, TN 37334
Ultimate Parent: Raytheon Co. **SIC:** 3585—Refrigeration & Heating Equipment.

★ 80790 ★ AmSouth Bank of Tennessee
310 W. College St.
Fayetteville, TN 37334-2912
(615)433-4537
Location Type: Branch office. **Officer:** Ancil Silvey, Manager. **Ultimate Parent:** AmSouth Bancorp. **SIC:** 6022—State Commercial Banks; 6162—Mortgage Bankers & Correspondents.

★ 80791 ★ AmSouth Bank of Tennessee
310 College St. W
Fayetteville, TN 37334
(615)433-4537
Ultimate Parent: AmSouth Bancorp.

★ 80792 ★ Eagle Snacks Inc.
One Eagle Dr.
Fayetteville, TN 37334
Ultimate Parent: Anheuser-Busch. **SIC:** 2096—Potato Chips & Similar Snacks.

★ 80793 ★ First Union National Bank of Tennessee
2702 Huntsville Hwy.
Fayetteville, TN 37334
Location Type: Branch office. **Ultimate Parent:** First Union Corp. **SIC:** 6021—National Commercial Banks.

★ 80794 ★ First Union National Bank of Tennessee
River Oak Shopping Ctr.
1398 Huntsville Hwy.
Fayetteville, TN 37334-3617
Location Type: Branch office. **Ultimate Parent:** First Union Corp. **SIC:** 6021—National Commercial Banks.

★ 80795 ★ First Union National Bank of Tennessee
220 E. College St.
Fayetteville, TN 37334-3046
(615)433-6141
Location Type: Branch office. **Ultimate Parent:** First Union Corp. **SIC:** 6021—National Commercial Banks.

★ 80796 ★ Greyhound Bus Lines
304 Main Ave. S
Fayetteville, TN 37334
(615)433-1272
Ultimate Parent: Greyhound Lines Inc. **SIC:** 4131—Intercity & Rural Bus Transportation; 4111—Local & Suburban Transit; 4142—Bus Charter Service Except Local.

★ 80797 ★ Kraft USA
Fayetteville
200 Eufala St.
Fayetteville, TN 37334
Company Type: Division. **Ultimate Parent:** Philip Morris. **SIC:** 2022—Cheese—Natural & Processed.

★ 80798 ★ Peoples Bank Elk Valley
Huntsville Hwy.
Fayetteville, TN 37334
(615)433-7051
Ultimate Parent: People's Bank. **SIC:** 6022—State Commercial Banks.

★ 80799 ★ Trailways Bus Lines
500 Main Ave. S
Fayetteville, TN 37334
(615)433-5414
Ultimate Parent: Greyhound Lines Inc. **SIC:** 4131—Intercity & Rural Bus Transportation; 4111—Local & Suburban Transit; 4142—Bus Charter Service Except Local.

Fort Oglethorpe

★ 80800 ★ Food Lion Inc.
904 Cloud Springs Rd.
Fort Oglethorpe, TN
(615)866-7381
Ultimate Parent: Food Lion.

★ 80801 ★ McDonald's Hamburgers
329 Lafayette Rd.
Fort Oglethorpe, TN
(615)866-9581
Ultimate Parent: McDonald's. **SIC:** 5812—Eating Places.

★ 80802 ★ Payless Shoe Source
101 Battlefield Pkwy
Fort Oglethorpe, TN
(615)866-8137
Ultimate Parent: May Department Stores. **SIC:** 5661—Shoe Stores.

★ 80803 ★ Payless Shoesource
101 Battlefield Pkwy
Fort Oglethorpe, TN
(615)866-8137
Ultimate Parent: May Department Stores.

★ 80804 ★ Wal-Mart Stores Inc.
1002 Battle Pky.
Fort Oglethorpe, TN
(615)861-5090
Ultimate Parent: Wal-Mart Stores, Inc.

Fort Oglthorpe

★ 80805 ★ Food Lion Inc. Store
Cloud Springs Rd.
Fort Oglthorpe, TN
(615)866-7381
Ultimate Parent: Food Lion.

Franklin

★ 80806 ★ Aeroquip Corp.
309 Eddy Ln. PO Box 665
Franklin, TN 37064
Ultimate Parent: Trinova Corp. **SIC:** 3083—Laminated Plastics Plate & Sheet.

★ 80807 ★ Aeroquip Corp.
Diversified Products Div.
309 Eddy Ln. PO Box 665
Franklin, TN 37064
Company Type: Division. **Ultimate Parent:** Trinova Corp. **SIC:** 3083—Laminated Plastics Plate & Sheet.

★ 80808 ★ Bellsouth Mobility
1745 Galleria Blvd.
Franklin, TN 37064-1612
(615)771-7888
Ultimate Parent: BellSouth Corp. **SIC:** 4813—Telephone Communications Except Radiotelephone.

★ 80809 ★ Black & Decker Co.
116 Alpha Dr.
Franklin, TN 37064-3902
(615)790-0550
Company Type: Branch. **Officer:** John Deemy. **Ultimate Parent:** Allergan Inc. **SIC:** 3546—Power-Driven Handtools.

★ 80810 ★ Castner-Knott Dry Goods Co.
1790 Galleria Blvd.
Franklin, TN 37064
(615)771-2100 **Fax:** (615)771-2100
Officer: Thomas Groh, President. **Ultimate Parent:** Mercantile Stores.

★ 80811 ★ First American National Bank
300 Public Sq.
Franklin, TN 37064
(615)748-2927
Location Type: Branch office. **Ultimate Parent:** First American Corp. **SIC:** 6021—National Commercial Banks.

★ 80812 ★ First American National Bank
1206 Murfreesboro Rd.
Franklin, TN 37064-1303
(615)790-1126
Location Type: Branch office. **Ultimate Parent:** First American Corp. **SIC:** 6021—National Commercial Banks.

★ 80813 ★ First Tennessee Bank NA
7082 Baker's Bridge
Franklin, TN 37064-2708
(615)790-5103
Location Type: Branch office. **Ultimate Parent:** First Tennessee National Corp. **SIC:** 6021—National Commercial Banks.

★ 80814 ★ First Tennessee Bank NA
1214 Murfreesboro rd.
Franklin, TN 37064-1300
(615)790-5105
Location Type: Branch office. **Ultimate Parent:** First Tennessee National Corp. **SIC:** 6021—National Commercial Banks.

★ 80815 ★ First Tennessee Bank NA
2200 Hillsboro Rd.
Franklin, TN 37064-6218
(615)790-5104
Location Type: Branch office. **Ultimate Parent:** First Tennessee National Corp. **SIC:** 6021—National Commercial Banks.

★ 80816 ★ First Tennessee Bank NA
236 Public Sq.
Franklin, TN 37064
(615)790-5100
Location Type: Branch office. **Ultimate Parent:** First Tennessee National Corp. **SIC:** 6021—National Commercial Banks.

★ 80817 ★ First Union National Bank of Tennessee
198 E. Main St.
Franklin, TN 37064-2516
(615)794-4526
Location Type: Branch office. **Ultimate Parent:** First Union Corp. **SIC:** 6021—National Commercial Banks.

★ 80818 ★ First Union National Bank of Tennessee
1004 Murfreesboro Rd.
Hwy. 96 E. Sugar Tree Ln.
Franklin, TN 37064-3005
(615)794-4526
Location Type: Branch office. **Ultimate Parent:** First Union Corp. **SIC:** 6021—National Commercial Banks.

★ 80819 ★ Georgia Boot Inc. Franklin Plant
214 N. Margin St.
Franklin, TN 37064
Ultimate Parent: Johnson & Johnson. **SIC:** 3143—Men's Footwear Except Athletic.

★ 80820 ★ Kroger Co.
Indiana Sq.
Franklin, TN 37064
(615)790-1010
Ultimate Parent: Kroger. **SIC:** 5411—Grocery Stores.

★ 80821 ★ Payless Shoe Source
1113 Murfreesboro Rd.
Franklin, TN 37064
(615)794-7107
Ultimate Parent: May Department Stores. **SIC:** 5661—Shoe Stores.

★ 80822 ★ Ryder Truck Rental
Jamison Bldg.
Franklin, TN 37064
(615)790-2919
Ultimate Parent: Ryder System. **SIC:** 7513—Truck Rental & Leasing Without Drivers.

★ 80823 ★ Skylark Inc.
2176 Hillsboro Rd. 120327
Franklin, TN 37064
(615)791-9830
Ultimate Parent: Scott Paper Co.

★ 80824 ★ Sterling Eng. Prods. Inc.
309 Eddy Ln. PO Box 665
Franklin, TN 37065-0665
Ultimate Parent: Trinova Corp. **SIC:** 3089—Plastics Products Nec.

★ 80825 ★ Union Planters National Bank
101 E. Main St.
Franklin, TN 37064-2515
(615)794-1532
Location Type: Branch office. **Ultimate Parent:** Union Planters Corp. **SIC:** 6021—National Commercial Banks.

★ 80826 ★ Vulcan Materials Co.
Carters Creek Pike.
Franklin, TN 37064
(615)794-3586
Ultimate Parent: Vulcan Materials Co. **SIC:** 5039—Construction Materials Nec.

★ 80827 ★ Vulcan Materials Midsouth
1701 Downs Blvd.
Franklin, TN 37064
(615)794-3586
Officer: Larry Cloyd, Manager. **Ultimate Parent:** Vulcan Materials Co. **SIC:** 3274—Lime.

★ 80828 ★ Wal-Mart Stores Inc.
Hwy. 96
Franklin, TN 37064
(615)790-3904
Ultimate Parent: Wal-Mart Stores, Inc. **SIC:** 5311—Department Stores.

★ 80829 ★ Wal-Mart Stores Inc.
1113 Murfreesboro Rd.
Franklin, TN 37064
(615)791-5525
Ultimate Parent: Wal-Mart Stores, Inc. **SIC:** 5912—Drug Stores & Proprietary Stores.

★ 80830 ★ Wal-Mart Stores Inc.
Williamson Shopping Ctr.
Franklin, TN 37064
(615)791-5520
Ultimate Parent: Wal-Mart Stores, Inc. **SIC:** 5311—Department Stores.

Gainesboro

★ 80831 ★ Aeroquip Corp.
955 Industrial Park Dr.
Gainesboro, TN 38562
Ultimate Parent: Trinova Corp. **SIC:** 3451—Screw Machine Products.

★ 80832 ★ Aeroquip Corp.
Hwy. 53 N
Gainesboro, TN 38562
Ultimate Parent: Trinova Corp. **SIC:** 3451—Screw Machine Products.

★ 80833 ★ Aeroquip Corp.
1107 N. Grundy Quarles Hwy.
Gainesboro, TN 38562
(615)268-0286
Officer: Roger Price, Manager. **Ultimate Parent:** Trinova Corp. **SIC:** 3429—Hardware Nec.

★ 80834 ★ Aeroquip Corp.
Industrial Products Div.
955 Industrial Park Dr.
Gainesboro, TN 38562
Company Type: Division. **Ultimate Parent:** Trinova Corp. **SIC:** 3451—Screw Machine Products; 3498—Fabricated Pipe & Fittings.

Gallatin

★ 80835 ★ Allied-Signal Brake Systems
375 Belvedere Dr. N
Gallatin, TN 37066
(615)451-3665
Ultimate Parent: Allied-Signal Inc. **SIC:** 3714—Motor Vehicle Parts & Accessories.

★ 80836 ★ Allied-Signal Inc.
Braking Systems Bendix Automotive
375 Belvedere Dr. N
Gallatin, TN 37066
Ultimate Parent: Allied-Signal Inc. **SIC:** 3714—Motor Vehicle Parts & Accessories.

★ 80837 ★ AmSouth Bank of Tennessee
150 W. Main St.
Gallatin, TN 37066-3251
(615)452-5098
Location Type: Branch office. **Officer:** Patricia M. Reid, Manager. **Ultimate Parent:** AmSouth Bancorp. **SIC:** 6022—State Commercial Banks; 6162—Mortgage Bankers & Correspondents.

★ 80838 ★ Blazer Financial Services
335 Nashville Pike
Gallatin, TN 37066
(615)452-5031
Ultimate Parent: Great Western Financial Corp. **SIC:** 6062—State Credit Unions.

★ 80839 ★ Donnelley Printing Co.
801 Steam Plant Rd.
Gallatin, TN 37066
Ultimate Parent: R. R. Donnelley & Sons. **SIC:** 2754—Commercial Printing—Gravure.

★ 80840 ★ R.R. Donnelley &
Sons Co.
Gallatin Manufacturing Div.
801 Steam Plant Rd.
Gallatin, TN 37066
Company Type: Division. Ultimate Parent:
R. R. Donnelley & Sons. SIC: 2754—
Commercial Printing—Gravure.

★ 80841 ★ Eaton Corp.
Axle & Brake Div.
701 S. Westland
Gallatin, TN 37066
Company Type: Division. Ultimate Parent:
Eaton Corp. SIC: 3429—Hardware Nec.

★ 80842 ★ EBM Inc.
450 Nashville Pike
Gallatin, TN 37066-7102
(615)230-7722
Ultimate Parent: Alco Standard Corp. SIC:
5044—Office Equipment.

★ 80843 ★ First American Nation
Bank
285 E. Main St.
Gallatin, TN 37066-2908
(615)452-4025
Location Type: Branch office. Ultimate
Parent: First American Corp. SIC: 6021—
National Commercial Banks.

★ 80844 ★ First American
National Bank
101 Belvedere Dr.
Gallatin, TN 37066
(615)452-5063
Location Type: Branch office. Ultimate
Parent: First American Corp. SIC: 6021—
National Commercial Banks.

★ 80845 ★ First Tennessee Bank
NA
668 Nashville Pke.
Gallatin, TN 37066-3124
(615)452-1464
Location Type: Branch office. Ultimate
Parent: First Tennessee National Corp.
SIC: 6021—National Commercial Banks.

★ 80846 ★ First Tennessee Bank
NA
128 W. Broadway
Gallatin, TN 37066-2718
(615)452-1462
Location Type: Branch office. Ultimate
Parent: First Tennessee National Corp.
SIC: 6021—National Commercial Banks.

★ 80847 ★ First Union National
Bank of Tennessee
600 W. Main St., Nashville Pke.
Gallatin, TN 37066-3124
(615)452-3228
Location Type: Branch office. Ultimate
Parent: First Union Corp. SIC: 6021—
National Commercial Banks.

★ 80848 ★ Kroger Co.
Nashville Pke.
Gallatin, TN 37066
(615)451-2802
Ultimate Parent: Kroger. SIC: 5411—
Grocery Stores.

★ 80849 ★ Kroger Co.
845 Nashville Pke.
Gallatin, TN 37066
(615)451-2803
Ultimate Parent: Kroger. SIC: 5411—
Grocery Stores.

★ 80850 ★ R. R. Donnelley &
Sons Co.
801 Steam Plant Rd.
Gallatin, TN 37066
Ultimate Parent: R. R. Donnelley & Sons.
SIC: 2754—Commercial Printing—Gravure.

★ 80851 ★ Trailways Bus Lines
340 W. Main St.
Gallatin, TN 37066
(615)452-0921
Ultimate Parent: Greyhound Lines Inc. SIC:
4131—Intercity & Rural Bus Transportation;
4111—Local & Suburban Transit; 4142—
Bus Charter Service Except Local.

★ 80852 ★ Union Planters
National Bank
617 Nashville Pke.
Gallatin, TN 37066-3102
(615)726-4362
Location Type: Branch office. Ultimate

Parent: Union Planters Corp. SIC: 6021—
National Commercial Banks.

★ 80853 ★ Wal-Mart Stores Inc.
696 Nashville Pike
Gallatin, TN 37066
(615)452-8452
Ultimate Parent: Wal-Mart Stores, Inc. SIC:
5311—Department Stores.

★ 80854 ★ Wal-Mart Stores Inc.
Hwy. 109 S
Gallatin, TN 37066
(615)452-9881
Ultimate Parent: Wal-Mart Stores, Inc. SIC:
5411—Grocery Stores.

Germantown

★ 80855 ★ Douglas/Quikut
8555 Cordes Circle
Germantown, TN 38138
(901)758-1421 Fax: (901)757-1537
Company Type: Division. Officer: Nathan
Howard, General Manager. Ultimate
Parent: Berkshire Hathaway. SIC: 2841—
Soap & Other Detergents; 3635—Household
Vacuum Cleaners; 3991—Brooms &
Brushes; 5072—Hardware; 3949—Sporting
& Athletic Goods Nec. Employee Count:
250. Sales: 30,000,000 M.

★ 80856 ★ First American
National Bank
7878 Farmington Ave.
Germantown, TN 38138-2904
(901)762-5940
Location Type: Branch office. Ultimate
Parent: First American Corp. SIC: 6021—
National Commercial Banks.

★ 80857 ★ Union Planters
National Bank
7708 Poplar Ave.
Germantown, TN 38138-3903
(901)756-2649
Location Type: Branch office. Ultimate
Parent: Union Planters Corp. SIC: 6021—
National Commercial Banks.

★ 80858 ★ Union Planters
National Bank
7540 North St.
Germantown, TN 38138-3875
(901)756-2646
Location Type: Branch office. Ultimate
Parent: Union Planters Corp. SIC: 6021—
National Commercial Banks.

Gibson

★ 80859 ★ Underwriters
Adjusting Co.
Graball Rd.
Gibson, TN 38338
(901)787-6522
Ultimate Parent: Continental. SIC: 6411—
Insurance Agents, Brokers & Service.

Gleason

★ 80860 ★ Cyprus Mines Corp.
Old Hwy. 22
Gleason, TN 38229
(901)648-5596
Ultimate Parent: Cyprus Amax Minerals.
SIC: 1455—Kaolin & Ball Clay.

Goodlettsville

★ 80861 ★ Circuit City
801 2nd Mile Pky.
Goodlettsville, TN 37072
(615)859-1806
Ultimate Parent: Circuit City Stores. SIC:
5065—Electronic Parts & Equipment Nec;
5731—Radio, Television & Electronics
Stores.

★ 80862 ★ First American
National Bank
Rivergate Mall
Goodlettsville, TN 37072-2406
(615)748-2706
Location Type: Branch office. Ultimate
Parent: First American Corp. SIC: 6021—
National Commercial Banks.

★ 80863 ★ First Union National
Bank of Tennessee
Goodlettsville.Plz.
612 Dickerson Rd.
Goodlettsville, TN 37072-1301
(615)859-7791
Location Type: Branch office. Ultimate
Parent: First Union Corp. SIC: 6021—
National Commercial Banks.

★ 80864 ★ Hit or Miss
900 Conference Dr.
Goodlettsville, TN 37072
(615)859-9842
Ultimate Parent: TJX. SIC: 5632—
Women's Accessory & Specialty Stores;
5651—Family Clothing Stores.

★ 80865 ★ Industrial Systems
120 N. Main St.
Goodlettsville, TN 37072-1555
(615)859-1597
Ultimate Parent: Ball Corp. SIC: 5084—
Industrial Machinery & Equipment.

★ 80866 ★ Lane Bryant
1000 2nd Mile Pky.
Goodlettsville, TN 37072
(615)859-6503
Ultimate Parent: Limited. SIC: 5621—
Women's Clothing Stores.

★ 80867 ★ Lerner Woman
1000 2nd Mile Pky.
Goodlettsville, TN 37072
(615)851-1355
Ultimate Parent: Limited. SIC: 5621—
Women's Clothing Stores.

★ 80868 ★ Limited Express
1000 2nd Mile Pky.
Goodlettsville, TN 37072
(615)859-6230
Ultimate Parent: Limited. SIC: 5621—
Women's Clothing Stores.

★ 80869 ★ Mapco Petroleum Inc.
515 2nd Mile Pky.
Goodlettsville, TN 37072
(615)859-3897
Ultimate Parent: Mapco. SIC: 5541—
Gasoline Service Stations.

★ 80870 ★ Oscar Mayer Foods
Corp.
201 Cartwright St.
Goodlettsville, TN 37072-1451
Ultimate Parent: Philip Morris. SIC: 2013—
Sausages & Other Prepared Meats.

★ 80871 ★ Service Merchandise
1000 2nd Mile Pky.
Goodlettsville, TN 37072
(615)851-6041
Ultimate Parent: Service Merchandise Co.,
Inc. SIC: 5944—Jewelry Stores.

★ 80872 ★ Union Planters
National Bank
2 Mile Pky.
Goodlettsville, TN 37072-2399
(615)726-4271
Location Type: Branch office. Ultimate
Parent: Union Planters Corp. SIC: 6021—
National Commercial Banks.

Gordonsville

★ 80873 ★ Dana Corp.
1 Spicer Dr.
Gordonsville, TN 38563
(615)683-8201
Ultimate Parent: Dana Corp. SIC: 3714—
Motor Vehicle Parts & Accessories.

Gray

★ 80874 ★ First Tennessee Bank
NA
Rte. 16, Suncrest Dr.
Gray, TN 37066
(615)461-1280
Location Type: Branch office. Ultimate
Parent: First Tennessee National Corp.
SIC: 6021—National Commercial Banks.

Greenback

★ 80875 ★ Gold Kist Inc.
Jena
Greenback, TN 37742
(615)856-2256
Ultimate Parent: Gold Kist. SIC: 5153—
Grain & Field Beans.

★ 80876 ★ Greenback Industries
Inc.
16621 Hwy. 411 S
Greenback, TN 37742
(615)856-3021 Fax: (615)856-3083
Company Type: Subsidiary. Officer: Alva
Moore, Vice President & General Manager.
Ultimate Parent: Handy & Harman.

★ 80877 ★ Greenback Industries,
Inc.
6621 Hwy. 411 S
Greenback, TN 37742
Ultimate Parent: Handy & Harman. SIC:
3399—Primary Metal Products Nec.

★ 80878 ★ Greenback Industries,
Inc.
Box 63, Hwy. 41
Greenback, TN 37742
Ultimate Parent: Handy & Harman. SIC:
3399—Primary Metal Products Nec.

★ 80879 ★ Greenback Industries
Inc.
Box 63, Rte. 411
Greenback, TN 37742
Ultimate Parent: Handy & Harman. SIC:
3399—Primary Metal Products Nec.

★ 80880 ★ Union Planters
National Bank
6705 Morganton Rd.
Greenback, TN 37742
(615)856-3018
Location Type: Branch office. Ultimate
Parent: Union Planters Corp. SIC: 6021—
National Commercial Banks.

Greenbrier

★ 80881 ★ First Union National
Bank of Tennessee
2550 Hwy. 41 S
College & Broad Sts.
Greenbrier, TN 37073
(615)643-4515
Location Type: Branch office. Ultimate
Parent: First Union Corp. SIC: 6021—
National Commercial Banks.

Greeneville

★ 80882 ★ Ball Corp.
Zinc Products Div.
Ball Rd. PO Box 1890
Greeneville, TN 37744-1890
Company Type: Division. Ultimate Parent:
Ball Corp. SIC: 3341—Secondary
Nonferrous Metals; 3356—Nonferrous
Rolling & Drawing Nec; 3471—Plating &
Polishing.

★ 80883 ★ Ball Corp.
Zinc Products Div.
Ball Rd.
Greeneville, TN 37744-1890
Company Type: Division. Ultimate Parent:
Ball Corp. SIC: 3341—Secondary
Nonferrous Metals; 3356—Nonferrous
Rolling & Drawing Nec; 3471—Plating &
Polishing.

★ 80884 ★ Coast to Coast Total
Hdwe
E Gate Shopping Ctr.
Greeneville, TN 37743
(615)639-0771
Ultimate Parent: Servistar Corp. SIC:
5251—Hardware Stores.

★ 80885 ★ GE Co. Component
Products Operation
1787 Chardon Rd.
Greeneville, TN 37743
Ultimate Parent: General Electric. SIC:
3612—Transformers Except Electronic.

★ 80886 ★   **Giant Food Market Inc.**
11 E. Byp
Greeneville, TN 37743
(615)639-8175
Ultimate Parent: Giant Food. SIC: 5411—Grocery Stores.

★ 80887 ★   **Pet, Inc.**
1112 W. Irish St.
Greeneville, TN 37743
(615)638-3171 Fax: (615)638-2164
Location Type: Plant. Ultimate Parent: Pet. SIC: 2023—Dry, Condensed & Evaporated Dairy Products; 2033—Canned Fruits & Vegetables.

★ 80888 ★   **Security Trust Bypass**
1436 11-E Bypass
Greeneville, TN 37743
(615)639-0221
Location Type: Branch office. Ultimate Parent: Union Planters Corp. SIC: 6021—National Commercial Banks.

★ 80889 ★   **Texaco Distributor**
Irish
Greeneville, TN 37743
(615)638-3361
Ultimate Parent: Texaco. SIC: 5172—Petroleum Products Nec.

★ 80890 ★   **TRW Inc.**
Commercial Steering Div.
Snapp Ferry Rd.
Greeneville, TN 37744-1790
Company Type: Division. Ultimate Parent: TRW, Inc. SIC: 3714—Motor Vehicle Parts & Accessories.

★ 80891 ★   **TRW Inc.**
Ross Gear Div.
Snapp Ferry Rd.
Greeneville, TN 37744-1790
Company Type: Division. Ultimate Parent: TRW, Inc. SIC: 3714—Motor Vehicle Parts & Accessories.

★ 80892 ★   **Wal-Mart Stores Inc.**
Greeneville Plz.
Greeneville, TN 37743
(615)639-8181
Ultimate Parent: Wal-Mart Stores, Inc. SIC: 5311—Department Stores.

Greenfield

★ 80893 ★   **Parker Hannifin Corp.**
Copper Products Div.
100 Parker Dr.
Greenfield, TN 38230
Company Type: Division. Ultimate Parent: Parker Hannifin. SIC: 3469—Metal Stampings Nec.

★ 80894 ★   **Stop & Shop**
Hwy. 45 E
Greenfield, TN 38230
(901)235-2529
Ultimate Parent: Stop & Shop. SIC: 5411—Grocery Stores.

Greenville

★ 80895 ★   **First Tenneseee Bank NA**
206 N. Main St.
Greenville, TN 37743-3898
(615)639-8141
Location Type: Branch office. Ultimate Parent: First Tennessee National Corp. SIC: 6021—National Commercial Banks.

★ 80896 ★   **First Tennessee Bank NA**
1634 Tusculum Blvd.
Greenville, TN 37743
Location Type: Branch office. Ultimate Parent: First Tennessee National Corp. SIC: 6021—National Commercial Banks.

★ 80897 ★   **Plus Mark, Inc.**
PO Box 549
Greenville, TN 37724
Ultimate Parent: American Greetings. SIC: 2771—Greeting Cards; 2893—Printing Ink.

Harriman

★ 80898 ★   **Bank of Roane County**
PO Box 266
Harriman, TN 37748-0266
Location Type: Headquarters. Ultimate Parent: Union Planters Corp. SIC: 6021—National Commercial Banks.

★ 80899 ★   **Bowater Woodlands**
Pulpwood Yard E. Clinton
Harriman, TN 37748
(615)882-0875
Ultimate Parent: Bowater. SIC: 5099—Durable Goods Nec; 0811—Timber Tracts.

★ 80900 ★   **Exxon Tiger Oil Co.**
929 Carter St.
Harriman, TN 37748
(615)882-8788
Ultimate Parent: Exxon. SIC: 5541—Gasoline Service Stations.

★ 80901 ★   **Frist American National Bank**
311 Runtan
Harriman, TN 37763
(615)673-5764
Location Type: Branch office. Ultimate Parent: First American Corp. SIC: 6021—National Commercial Banks.

★ 80902 ★   **Red Kap Ind.**
Hwy. 27
Harriman, TN 37748
(615)882-0755
Officer: David Shaffer, Manager. Ultimate Parent: VF Corp. SIC: 2325—Men's/Boys' Trousers & Slacks; 2326—Men's/Boys' Work Clothing.

★ 80903 ★   **Wal-Mart Stores Inc.**
Roane County Shopping Ctr.
Harriman, TN 37748
(615)882-6531
Ultimate Parent: Wal-Mart Stores, Inc. SIC: 5311—Department Stores.

Harrimen

★ 80904 ★   **Bank of Roane County**
200 Roane St.
Harrimen, TN 37748-2023
(615)882-1121 Fax: (615)882-3471
Location Type: Headquarters. Ultimate Parent: Union Planters Corp. SIC: 6021—National Commercial Banks.

Hartsville

★ 80905 ★   **Texas Boot Co.**
Western Ave.
Hartsville, TN 37074
(615)444-5440
Ultimate Parent: United States Shoe. SIC: 5661—Shoe Stores.

Helenwood

★ 80906 ★   **Mini Mart**
RR 2
Helenwood, TN 37755
(615)569-9507
Ultimate Parent: Kroger. SIC: 5411—Grocery Stores.

Henderson

★ 80907 ★   **Grinnell Corp.**
2010 Old Jackson Rd.
Henderson, TN 38340
(901)989-3551
Officer: Wilson Jones, President. Ultimate Parent: Tyco International. SIC: 3494—Valves & Pipe Fittings Nec; 3495—Wire Springs; 3498—Fabricated Pipe & Fittings.

★ 80908 ★   **Ryder Truck Rental-One Way**
245 N. Church St.
Henderson, TN 38340
(901)989-3778
Ultimate Parent: Ryder System.

★ 80909 ★   **Sonoco Products Co.**
Magic Valley Industrial Park
Henderson, TN 38340
(901)989-7124
Ultimate Parent: Sonoco Products. SIC: 5085—Industrial Supplies.

Hendersonville

★ 80910 ★   **AmSouth Bank of Tennessee**
109-A Walton Ferry Rd.
Hendersonville, TN 37075-3659
(615)824-1331
Location Type: Branch office. Officer: Rita Wilingham, Manager. Ultimate Parent: AmSouth Bancorp. SIC: 6022—State Commercial Banks; 6162—Mortgage Bankers & Correspondents.

★ 80911 ★   **Eckerd Drug Co.**
Township Sq.
Hendersonville, TN 37075
(615)822-3850
Ultimate Parent: Eckerd Corp. SIC: 5912—Drug Stores & Proprietary Stores.

★ 80912 ★   **Eckerd Drugs**
Township Sq.
Hendersonville, TN 37075
(615)822-3850
Ultimate Parent: Eckerd Corp. SIC: 5912—Drug Stores & Proprietary Stores.

★ 80913 ★   **First American National Bank**
249 E. Main St.
Hendersonville, TN 37075-2544
(615)264-1501
Location Type: Branch office. Ultimate Parent: First American Corp. SIC: 6021—National Commercial Banks.

★ 80914 ★   **First Tennessee Bank NA**
429 W. Main St.
Hendersonville, TN 37073-3310
(615)822-4900
Location Type: Branch office. Ultimate Parent: First Tennessee National Corp. SIC: 6021—National Commercial Banks.

★ 80915 ★   **First Union National Bank of Tennessee**
303 New Shackle Island Rd.
Hendersonville, TN 37075-2370
(615)822-5340
Location Type: Branch office. Ultimate Parent: First Union Corp. SIC: 6021—National Commercial Banks.

★ 80916 ★   **First Union National Bank of Tennessee**
169 E. Main St.
Hendersonville, TN 37075-2519
(615)824-7012
Location Type: Branch office. Ultimate Parent: First Union Corp. SIC: 6021—National Commercial Banks.

★ 80917 ★   **General Electric Co.**
250 East Main St.
Hendersonville, TN 37075
Ultimate Parent: General Electric. SIC: 3621—Motors & Generators.

★ 80918 ★   **ITW Dynatec**
31 Volunteer Dr.
Hendersonville, TN 37075
(615)824-3634 Fax: (615)822-6839
Company Type: Subsidiary. Officer: Valeri Lapinski, General Manager. Ultimate Parent: Illinois Tool Works.

★ 80919 ★   **Kroger Co.**
170 E. Main St.
Hendersonville, TN 37075
(615)822-6155
Ultimate Parent: Kroger. SIC: 5411—Grocery Stores.

★ 80920 ★   **Union Planters National Bank**
175 E. Main St.
Hendersonville, TN 37075-2565
(615)822-4195
Location Type: Branch office. Ultimate Parent: Union Planters Corp. SIC: 6021—National Commercial Banks.

Henning

★ 80921 ★   **People's Bank**
Main St.
Henning, TN 38041
(901)738-5001
Ultimate Parent: People's Bank. SIC: 6099—Functions Related to Deposit Banking.

Hermitage

★ 80922 ★   **American General Finance**
McKendree Towers
Hermitage, TN 37076
(615)889-0050
Officer: Jodi Caruthers. Ultimate Parent: American General Corp. SIC: 6141—Personal Credit Institutions; 6162—Mortgage Bankers & Correspondents.

★ 80923 ★   **American General Finance Inc.**
McKendree Towers
Hermitage, TN 37076
(615)889-0050
Location Type: Branch office. Officer: Jodi Caruthers. Ultimate Parent: American General Corp. SIC: 6141—Personal Credit Institutions; 6162—Mortgage Bankers & Correspondents.

★ 80924 ★   **Eckerd Drug Co.**
Hermitage Plz.
Hermitage, TN 37076
(615)889-2176
Ultimate Parent: Eckerd Corp. SIC: 5912—Drug Stores & Proprietary Stores.

★ 80925 ★   **Eckerd Drugs**
Hermitage Plz.
Hermitage, TN 37076
(615)889-2176
Ultimate Parent: Eckerd Corp. SIC: 5912—Drug Stores & Proprietary Stores.

★ 80926 ★   **First American National Bank**
4444 Lebanon Rd.
Hermitage, TN 37076-1398
(615)748-2780
Location Type: Branch office. Ultimate Parent: First American Corp. SIC: 6021—National Commercial Banks.

★ 80927 ★   **Wal-Mart Stores Inc.**
4101 Lebanon Rd.
Hermitage, TN 37076
(615)883-0201
Ultimate Parent: Wal-Mart Stores, Inc. SIC: 5311—Department Stores.

Hixson

★ 80928 ★   **American General Finance**
5035 Hixson Pke.
Hixson, TN 37343-3950
(615)875-0175
Ultimate Parent: American General Corp. SIC: 6141—Personal Credit Institutions; 6162—Mortgage Bankers & Correspondents.

★ 80929 ★   **American General Finance Inc.**
5035 Hixson Pike
Hixson, TN 37343-3950
(615)875-0175
Location Type: Branch office. Ultimate Parent: American General Corp. SIC: 6141—Personal Credit Institutions; 6162—Mortgage Bankers & Correspondents.

★ 80930 ★   **AmSouth Bank of Tennessee**
8535 Hixson Pike
Hixson, TN 37343
(615)842-0503
Ultimate Parent: AmSouth Bancorp.

★ 80931 ★   **Bowater Inc.**
5731 Hwy. 153
Hixson, TN 37343
(615)875-9073
Ultimate Parent: Bowater.

★ 80932 ★   **Casual Corner**
207 Northgate Mall
Hixson, TN
(615)877-6440
Ultimate Parent: United States Shoe.

★ 80933 ★   **Flowers Thrift & Distribution**
2001 Hamill Rd.
Hixson, TN 37343
(615)877-5034
Officer: John Hawkins, Manager. Ultimate Parent: Flowers Industries. SIC: 2051—Bread, Cake & Related Products.

★ **80934** ★   **Food Lion Inc. Store**
6210 Hixson Pke
Hixson, TN 37343
(615)843-1138
Ultimate Parent: Food Lion.

★ **80935** ★   **Macy's Close-Out**
5450 Hwy. 153
Hixson, TN 37343-3791
(615)875-2345
Ultimate Parent: R. H. Macy. **SIC:** 5311—
Department Stores.

★ **80936** ★   **Ryder Truck Rental-One Way**
Hixson, TN
(615)870-1881
Ultimate Parent: Ryder System.

★ **80937** ★   **Valvoline Instant Oil Change**
5104 Hwy. 153
Hixson, TN 37343
(615)870-8364
Ultimate Parent: Ashland Oil.

★ **80938** ★   **Wal-Mart Stores Inc.**
5450 Hwy. 153
Hixson, TN 37343
(615)875-4027
Ultimate Parent: Wal-Mart Stores, Inc.

Hohenwald

★ **80939** ★   **Boston Industrial Products**
Swan Ave.
Hohenwald, TN 38462
(615)796-3272
Ultimate Parent: Dana Corp. **SIC:** 3052—
Rubber & Plastics Hose & Belting; 3082—
Unsupported Plastics Profile Shapes;
3089—Plastics Products Nec.

★ **80940** ★   **Boston Industrial Products**
609 Swan Ave.
Hohenwald, TN 38462-9646
Ultimate Parent: Dana Corp. **SIC:** 3052—
Rubber & Plastics Hose & Belting.

★ **80941** ★   **Boston Industrial Products**
Swan Ave. at Dana Dr.
Hohenwald, TN 38462
Ultimate Parent: Dana Corp. **SIC:** 3052—
Rubber & Plastics Hose & Belting.

★ **80942** ★   **Dana Corp.**
Boston Industrial Products Div.
Swan Ave. at Dana Dr.
Hohenwald, TN 38462
Company Type: Division. **Ultimate Parent:**
Dana Corp. **SIC:** 3052—Rubber & Plastics
Hose & Belting.

★ **80943** ★   **First Citizens Bank of Hohenwald**
554 E. Main
Hohenwald, TN 38462
Location Type: Branch office. **Ultimate
Parent:** Union Planters Corp. **SIC:** 6021—
National Commercial Banks.

★ **80944** ★   **First Citizens Bank of Hohenwald**
401 W. Main St.
Hohenwald, TN 38462-1317
Location Type: Branch office. **Ultimate
Parent:** Union Planters Corp. **SIC:** 6021—
National Commercial Banks.

★ **80945** ★   **First Citizens Bank of Hohenwald**
PO Box 819
Hohenwald, TN 38462-0819
Location Type: Branch office. **Ultimate
Parent:** Union Planters Corp. **SIC:** 6021—
National Commercial Banks.

★ **80946** ★   **First Citizens Bank of Hohenwald**
10 E. Main St.
Hohenwald, TN 38462-1420
(615)796-4951
Location Type: Branch office. **Ultimate
Parent:** Union Planters Corp. **SIC:** 6021—
National Commercial Banks.

★ **80947** ★   **Wal-Mart Stores Inc.**
Hwy. 99
Hohenwald, TN 38462
(615)796-3282
Ultimate Parent: Wal-Mart Stores, Inc. **SIC:**
5311—Department Stores.

Honenwald

★ **80948** ★   **Blue Grass Cooperage Co., Inc.**
Hwy. 412
Honenwald, TN 38462
(615)796-2137
Ultimate Parent: Brown-Forman. **SIC:**
2411—Logging.

Humboldt

★ **80949** ★   **Copeland Electric Corp.**
957 W. Mullins St.
Humboldt, TN 38343-1709
(901)784-3611
Company Type: Subsidiary. **Officer:** Paul
Hatford, Vice President. **Ultimate Parent:**
Emerson Electric Co. Inc. **SIC:** 3621—
Motors & Generators. **Employee Count:**
500. **Sales:** 56 M.

★ **80950** ★   **Eaton Corp.**
899 Eaton Dr.
Humboldt, TN 38343
(901)784-1100
Location Type: Plant. **Officer:** Bob
Jackson, Plant Manager. **Ultimate Parent:**
Eaton Corp. **SIC:** 3714—Motor Vehicle
Parts & Accessories.

★ **80951** ★   **Eaton Corp.**
Axle & Brake Div.
1491 Eaton Dr.
Humboldt, TN 38343
(901)784-1100
Company Type: Division. **Location Type:**
Plant. **Officer:** Robert W. Scott, Plant
Manager. **Ultimate Parent:** Eaton Corp.
SIC: 3714—Motor Vehicle Parts &
Accessories.

★ **80952** ★   **Emerson Motor Co.**
957 W. Mullins St.
Humboldt, TN 38343
Ultimate Parent: Emerson Electric Co. Inc.
SIC: 3621—Motors & Generators.

★ **80953** ★   **J. Hungerford Smith Co.**
1500 N. Central Ave.
Humboldt, TN 38343
(901)784-3461
Location Type: Plant. **Officer:** M. A.
Chapin, Plant Manager. **Ultimate Parent:**
Conagra.

★ **80954** ★   **Merchants State Bank**
2706 E. End Dr.
Humboldt, TN 38343-2206
(901)784-2612
Location Type: Branch office. **Ultimate
Parent:** Union Planters Corp. **SIC:** 6021—
National Commercial Banks.

★ **80955** ★   **Merchants State Bank**
2110 Central
Humboldt, TN 38343-9201
(901)784-2050
Location Type: Branch office. **Ultimate
Parent:** Union Planters Corp. **SIC:** 6021—
National Commercial Banks.

★ **80956** ★   **Merchants State Bank**
801 N. 22nd Ave.
Humboldt, TN 38343
(901)784-1721
Location Type: Branch office. **Ultimate
Parent:** Union Planters Corp. **SIC:** 6021—
National Commercial Banks.

★ **80957** ★   **Merchants State Bank**
1214 Main St.
Humboldt, TN 38343-3326
(901)784-1122 **Fax:** (901)784-5092
Location Type: Headquarters. **Ultimate
Parent:** Union Planters Corp. **SIC:** 6021—
National Commercial Banks.

★ **80958** ★   **Merchants State Bank**
8 Madison Rd.
Humboldt, TN 38343
(901)784-0082
Location Type: Branch office. **Ultimate
Parent:** Union Planters Corp. **SIC:** 6021—
National Commercial Banks.

★ **80959** ★   **People's Bank**
1500 E. Main St.
Humboldt, TN 38343
(901)784-1161
Ultimate Parent: People's Bank. **SIC:**
6022—State Commercial Banks.

Huntingdon

★ **80960** ★   **Gold Kist Inc.**
Nashville Hwy.
Huntingdon, TN 38344
(901)986-5043
Ultimate Parent: Gold Kist. **SIC:** 4221—
Farm Product Warehousing & Storage.

Huntsville

★ **80961** ★   **Fruehauf Trailer Corp.**
Rte. 63
PO Box 200
Huntsville, TN 37756
(615)663-3434
Officer: Tim McKowen. **Ultimate Parent:**
Terex Corp. **SIC:** 3715—Truck Trailers.

Jackson

★ **80962** ★   **Allied-Signal Automotive**
1094 Bendix Dr.
Jackson, TN 38301
(901)423-1300
Officer: Ruth Heavner, Manager. **Ultimate
Parent:** Allied-Signal Inc. **SIC:** 3714—Motor
Vehicle Parts & Accessories.

★ **80963** ★   **Allied-Signal Automotive**
1094 Bendix Dr.
Jackson, TN 38301
(901)423-1300
Officer: Ruth Heavner, Manager. **Ultimate
Parent:** Allied-Signal Inc. **SIC:** 3714—Motor
Vehicle Parts & Accessories.

★ **80964** ★   **American Olean Tile Co.**
96 American Dr.
Jackson, TN 38301
Ultimate Parent: Armstrong World
Industries. **SIC:** 3253—Ceramic Wall &
Floor Tile.

★ **80965** ★   **Blazer Financial Services**
72 Federal St.
Jackson, TN 38305
(901)668-0413
Ultimate Parent: Great Western Financial
Corp. **SIC:** 6141—Personal Credit
Institutions.

★ **80966** ★   **Casual Corner**
Old Hickory Mall
Jackson, TN 38305
(901)668-3422
Ultimate Parent: United States Shoe. **SIC:**
5621—Women's Clothing Stores.

★ **80967** ★   **Coca-Cola Bottling Co. of Jackson Inc.**
457 Riverside Dr.
Jackson, TN 38301
Ultimate Parent: Coca-Cola Bottling
Consol. **SIC:** 2085—Distilled & Blended
Liquors.

★ **80968** ★   **Dean Witter Reynolds Inc.**
1804 Hwy. 45 Byp.
Jackson, TN 38305
(901)668-9570
Ultimate Parent: Dean Witter Discover.
SIC: 6211—Security Brokers & Dealers.

★ **80969** ★   **Diebold Inc.**
525 E. Main St.
Jackson, TN 38301
(901)427-2329
Ultimate Parent: Diebold, Inc. **SIC:** 5044—
Office Equipment.

★ **80970** ★   **Exxon Co. U S a Marketing**
18 Devonshire Sq.
Jackson, TN 38305
(901)668-7141
Ultimate Parent: Exxon. **SIC:** 5172—
Petroleum Products Nec.

★ **80971** ★   **First American National Bank**
1666 S. Highland Ave.
Jackson, TN 38301-7719
(901)422-9862
Location Type: Branch office. **Ultimate
Parent:** First American Corp. **SIC:** 6021—
National Commercial Banks.

★ **80972** ★   **First American National Bank**
246 W. Main St.
Jackson, TN 38301-6129
(901)422-9866
Location Type: Branch office. **Ultimate
Parent:** First American Corp. **SIC:** 6021—
National Commercial Banks.

★ **80973** ★   **First American National Bank**
1993 N. Highland Ave.
Jackson, TN 38305-4918
(901)422-9850
Location Type: Branch office. **Ultimate
Parent:** First American Corp. **SIC:** 6021—
National Commercial Banks.

★ **80974** ★   **First American National Bank**
101 E. Main St.
Jackson, TN 38301-6207
(901)422-9700
Location Type: Branch office. **Ultimate
Parent:** First American Corp. **SIC:** 6021—
National Commercial Banks.

★ **80975** ★   **First American National Bank**
Main St. & Highland Ave.
Jackson, TN 38301
(901)422-9017
Location Type: Branch office. **Ultimate
Parent:** First American Corp. **SIC:** 6021—
National Commercial Banks.

★ **80976** ★   **First American Trust Co., NA**
Main & Highland Ave.
Jackson, TN 38301
(901)422-9745
Location Type: Branch office. **Ultimate
Parent:** First American Corp. **SIC:** 6021—
National Commercial Banks.

★ **80977** ★   **First Security Mortgage**
7 Security Dr.
Jackson, TN 38305
(901)668-6566
Ultimate Parent: First Savings Bank. **SIC:**
6159—Miscellaneous Business Credit
Institutions.

★ **80978** ★   **First Tennessee Bank NA**
1291 S. Highland Ave.
Jackson, TN 38301-7370
Location Type: Branch office. **Ultimate
Parent:** First Tennessee National Corp.
SIC: 6021—National Commercial Banks.

★ **80979** ★   **First Tennessee Bank NA**
325 Oil Well Rd.
Jackson, TN 38301-6355
Location Type: Branch office. **Ultimate
Parent:** First Tennessee National Corp.
SIC: 6021—National Commercial Banks.

★ **80980** ★   **First Tennessee Bank NA**
620 Old Hickory Blvd.
Jackson, TN 38305-2917
Location Type: Branch office. **Ultimate
Parent:** First Tennessee National Corp.
SIC: 6021—National Commercial Banks.

★ **80981** ★   **First Tennessee Bank NA**
2066 N. Highland Ave.
Jackson, TN 38305-4919
Location Type: Branch office. **Ultimate
Parent:** First Tennessee National Corp.
SIC: 6021—National Commercial Banks.

★ **80982** ★   **First Tennessee Bank NA**
110 W. Baltimore St.
Jackson, TN 38301-6135
(901)424-5555
Location Type: Branch office. **Ultimate
Parent:** First Tennessee National Corp.
SIC: 6021—National Commercial Banks.

★ 80983 ★ First Tennessee Bank NA
180 E. Chester St.
Jackson, TN 38301-6337
Location Type: Branch office. Ultimate Parent: First Tennessee National Corp. SIC: 6021—National Commercial Banks.

★ 80984 ★ Frist American National Bank
768 W. Forest Ave.
Jackson, TN 38301-3932
(901)422-9855
Location Type: Branch office. Ultimate Parent: First American Corp. SIC: 6021—National Commercial Banks.

★ 80985 ★ Gold Kist Inc.
161 Ragland Rd.
Jackson, TN 38305
(901)668-2817
Ultimate Parent: Gold Kist. SIC: 5153—Grain & Field Beans.

★ 80986 ★ James River Corp.
727 Angline Ln.
Jackson, TN 38301
Ultimate Parent: James River Corp. of Virginia. SIC: 2671—Paper Coated & Laminated—Packaging.

★ 80987 ★ James River Paper Co. Inc.
727 Anglin Ln.
Jackson, TN 38301
Ultimate Parent: James River Corp. of Virginia. SIC: 2671—Paper Coated & Laminated—Packaging.

★ 80988 ★ Kroger Co.
Hwy. 45 S
Jackson, TN 38301
(901)427-1559
Ultimate Parent: Kroger. SIC: 5411—Grocery Stores.

★ 80989 ★ Kroger Co.
756 Old Hickory Blvd.
Jackson, TN 38305
(901)668-8831
Ultimate Parent: Kroger. SIC: 5411—Grocery Stores.

★ 80990 ★ McDonald's Hamburgers
1915 N. Highland Ave.
Jackson, TN 38305
(901)424-3692
Ultimate Parent: McDonald's. SIC: 5812—Eating Places.

★ 80991 ★ NCR Corp.
13 Weatherford Sq.
Jackson, TN 38305-2202
(901)664-3887
Ultimate Parent: AT&T. SIC: 2761—Manifold Business Forms.

★ 80992 ★ Northern Natural Gas Co.
385 Airways Blvd.
Jackson, TN 38301
(901)423-3390
Ultimate Parent: Enron. SIC: 5064—Electrical Appliances—Television & Radio.

★ 80993 ★ Payless Shoe Source
Oak Hill Shopping Ctr.
Jackson, TN 38305
(901)668-8299
Ultimate Parent: May Department Stores. SIC: 5661—Shoe Stores.

★ 80994 ★ Pepsi-Cola Bottling Co.
923 Campbell St.
Jackson, TN 38301
(901)427-8526
Officer: Ed Wright, Manager. Ultimate Parent: Pepsico. SIC: 2086—Bottled & Canned Soft Drinks.

★ 80995 ★ Porter-Cable Corp.
Hwy. 45 N. Bypass
Jackson, TN 38305
Ultimate Parent: Pentair. SIC: 3546—Power-Driven Handtools.

★ 80996 ★ Porter-Cable Corp.
Hwy. 45 N. Bypass
Jackson, TN 38302
Ultimate Parent: Pentair. SIC: 3546—Power-Driven Handtools.

★ 80997 ★ Procter & Gamble Mfg. Co.
1306 Hwy. 70 Bypass
Jackson, TN 38301
Ultimate Parent: Procter & Gamble Co. SIC: 2099—Food Preparations Nec; 2079—Edible Fats & Oils Nec; 2045—Prepared Flour Mixes & Doughs; 2052—Cookies & Crackers; 2087—Flavoring Extracts & Syrups Nec.

★ 80998 ★ Quaker Oats Co.
96 Quaker Oats Dr.
Jackson, TN 38301
Ultimate Parent: Quaker Oates. SIC: 2038—Frozen Specialties Nec.

★ 80999 ★ Quaker Oats Co.
96 Quaker Oats Dr.
Jackson, TN 38301
Ultimate Parent: Quaker Oates. SIC: 2000—Food & Kindred Products.

★ 81000 ★ Ryder Truck Rental
2690 Bells Hwy.
Jackson, TN 38305
(901)664-0031
Ultimate Parent: Ryder System. SIC: 7389—Business Services Nec.

★ 81001 ★ Ryder Truck Rental & Leasing
709 Whitehall St.
Jackson, TN 38301
(901)424-7212
Ultimate Parent: Ryder System. SIC: 7513—Truck Rental & Leasing Without Drivers.

★ 81002 ★ Sonoco Products Co.
71 Wisteria St.
Jackson, TN 38301
(901)424-3740
Officer: Bruce Brooks, Manager. Ultimate Parent: Sonoco Products. SIC: 2655—Fiber Cans, Drums & Similar Products; 3411—Metal Cans.

★ 81003 ★ Trailways Bus Lines
77 Carriage House Dr.
Jackson, TN 38305
(901)668-8703
Ultimate Parent: Greyhound Lines Inc. SIC: 4131—Intercity & Rural Bus Transportation; 4111—Local & Suburban Transit; 4142—Bus Charter Service Except Local.

★ 81004 ★ Union Planters National Bank
2634 N. Highland
Jackson, TN 38305-1845
(901)668-6977
Location Type: Branch office. Ultimate Parent: Union Planters Corp. SIC: 6021—National Commercial Banks.

★ 81005 ★ Union Planters National Bank
3310 N. Pky. E.
Jackson, TN 38301
(901)422-9517
Location Type: Branch office. Ultimate Parent: Union Planters Corp. SIC: 6021—National Commercial Banks.

★ 81006 ★ Union Planters National Bank
111 W. Main St.
Jackson, TN 38302-2647
Location Type: Branch office. Ultimate Parent: Union Planters Corp. SIC: 6021—National Commercial Banks.

★ 81007 ★ Union Planters National Bank
1956 N. Highland Ave.
Jackson, TN 38301-4509
(901)422-9531
Location Type: Branch office. Ultimate Parent: Union Planters Corp. SIC: 6021—National Commercial Banks.

★ 81008 ★ Union Planters National Bank
135 Carriage House Dr.
Jackson, TN 38305-3902
(901)425-3516
Location Type: Branch office. Ultimate Parent: Union Planters Corp. SIC: 6021—National Commercial Banks.

★ 81009 ★ Union Planters National Bank
1426 N. Highland Ave.
Jackson, TN 38301-3404
(901)422-9511
Location Type: Branch office. Ultimate Parent: Union Planters Corp. SIC: 6021—National Commercial Banks.

★ 81010 ★ Union Planters National Bank
1581 S. Highland Ave.
Jackson, TN 38301-7718
(901)422-9551
Location Type: Branch office. Ultimate Parent: Union Planters Corp. SIC: 6021—National Commercial Banks.

★ 81011 ★ Union Planters National Bank
385 N. Pky.
Jackson, TN 38305-2872
(901)422-9545
Location Type: Branch office. Ultimate Parent: Union Planters Corp. SIC: 6021—National Commercial Banks.

★ 81012 ★ Union Planters National Bank
11 Murray Guard Dr.
Jackson, TN 38305-3610
(901)422-9560
Location Type: Branch office. Ultimate Parent: Union Planters Corp. SIC: 6021—National Commercial Banks.

★ 81013 ★ Union Planters National Bank
118 N. Liberty
Jackson, TN 38302-0189
(901)422-9600
Location Type: Branch office. Ultimate Parent: Union Planters Corp. SIC: 6021—National Commercial Banks.

★ 81014 ★ Valspar Corp. Jackson
95 Quaker Oats Dr.
Jackson, TN 38301
Ultimate Parent: Valspar Corp. SIC: 2851—Paints & Allied Products.

★ 81015 ★ Vulcan Materials Co.
1944 Hwy. 45 Bypass
Jackson, TN 38305
(901)668-7357
Ultimate Parent: Vulcan Materials Co. SIC: 5039—Construction Materials Nec.

★ 81016 ★ Wal-Mart Stores Inc.
Bemis Sq.
Jackson, TN 38301
(901)422-1614
Ultimate Parent: Wal-Mart Stores, Inc. SIC: 5331—Variety Stores.

★ 81017 ★ Wal-Mart Stores Inc.
57 Carriage House Dr.
Jackson, TN 38305
(901)668-6080
Ultimate Parent: Wal-Mart Stores, Inc. SIC: 5311—Department Stores.

★ 81018 ★ Western Geophysical Co.
2000 N. Highland Ave.
Jackson, TN 38305
(901)668-3590
Ultimate Parent: Litton Industries. SIC: 5999—Miscellaneous Retail Stores Nec; 8999—Services Nec.

Jamestown

★ 81019 ★ Union Bank
N Main Church
Jamestown, TN 38556
(615)879-8111
Ultimate Parent: Union Bank. SIC: 6099—Functions Related to Deposit Banking.

Jefferson City

★ 81020 ★ Asarco Inc.
420 E. Broadway Blvd.
Jefferson City, TN 37760-2903
(615)475-2644
Ultimate Parent: Asarco. SIC: 1499—Miscellaneous Nonmetallic Minerals.

★ 81021 ★ First American National Bank
601 E. Broadway
Jefferson City, TN 37760-2899
(615)475-3861
Location Type: Branch office. Ultimate Parent: First American Corp. SIC: 6021—National Commercial Banks.

★ 81022 ★ First Union National Bank of Tennessee
149 E. Broadway
Jefferson City, TN 37770
(615)475-9040
Location Type: Branch office. Ultimate Parent: First Union Corp. SIC: 6021—National Commercial Banks.

Jellico

★ 81023 ★ Duck Head Apparel Co.
Industrial Park Rd.
Jellico, TN 37762
(615)784-9431
Officer: Judy Leach, Manager. Ultimate Parent: Delta Woodside Industries. SIC: 2321—Men's/Boys' Shirts; 2325—Men's/Boys' Trousers & Slacks.

★ 81024 ★ Union Bank
Jellico, TN 37762
(615)784-9446
Ultimate Parent: Union Bank. SIC: 6022—State Commercial Banks.

Johnson City

★ 81025 ★ Blazer Financial Services
216 Mountcastle Dr.
Johnson City, TN 37601
(615)928-2104
Ultimate Parent: Great Western Financial Corp. SIC: 6141—Personal Credit Institutions.

★ 81026 ★ Burlington Industries Inc.
2203 McKinley Rd.
Johnson City, TN 37604
(615)926-8107
Officer: Dwight Barnes, Manager. Ultimate Parent: Burlington Industries, Equity. SIC: 2221—Broadwoven Fabric Mills—Manmade; 2399—Fabricated Textile Products Nec.

★ 81027 ★ Coast to Coast Hardware
344 Suncrest Dr.
Johnson City, TN 37615
(615)477-4110
Ultimate Parent: Servistar Corp. SIC: 5211—Lumber & Other Building Materials.

★ 81028 ★ Eckerd Drugs
Food City Plz.
Johnson City, TN 37601
(615)928-6134
Ultimate Parent: Eckerd Corp. SIC: 5912—Drug Stores & Proprietary Stores.

★ 81029 ★ First American National Bank
E. Watauga & Broadway
Johnson City, TN 37601-3502
(615)282-7655
Location Type: Branch office. Ultimate Parent: First American Corp. SIC: 6021—National Commercial Banks.

★ 81030 ★ First American National Bank
W. State of Franklin Rd.
Johnson City, TN 37604
(615)282-7664
Location Type: Branch office. Ultimate Parent: First American Corp. SIC: 6021—National Commercial Banks.

★ 81031 ★ First American National Bank
208 Sunset Dr.
Johnson City, TN 37604-2521
(615)282-7600
Location Type: Branch office. Ultimate Parent: First American Corp. SIC: 6021—National Commercial Banks.

★ 81032 ★ First American Trust
Co., NA
208 Sunset Dr.
Johnson City, TN 37601
(615)282-1711
Location Type: Branch office. Ultimate
Parent: First American Corp. SIC: 6021—
National Commercial Banks.

★ 81033 ★ First Tennessee Bank
NA
2710 S. Roan St.
Johnson City, TN 37601-7588
(615)926-1151
Location Type: Branch office. Ultimate
Parent: First Tennessee National Corp.
SIC: 6021—National Commercial Banks.

★ 81034 ★ First Tennessee Bank
NA
1500 State of Franklin St.
Johnson City, TN 37604
(615)461-1200
Location Type: Branch office. Ultimate
Parent: First Tennessee National Corp.
SIC: 6021—National Commercial Banks.

★ 81035 ★ First Tennessee Bank
NA
2112 N. Roan St.
Johnson City, TN 37601-2519
(615)282-6311
Location Type: Branch office. Ultimate
Parent: First Tennessee National Corp.
SIC: 6021—National Commercial Banks.

★ 81036 ★ First Tennessee Bank
NA
1919 N. Roane St.
Johnson City, TN 37601-3115
(615)461-1200
Location Type: Branch office. Ultimate
Parent: First Tennessee National Corp.
SIC: 6021—National Commercial Banks.

★ 81037 ★ Flour City
Architectural
915 Riverview Dr.
Johnson City, TN 37601-3804
(615)928-2724
Officer: Brian Smith. Ultimate Parent:
Armco. SIC: 1721—Painting & Paper
Hanging; 2522—Office Furniture Except
Wood; 3355—Aluminum Rolling & Drawing
Nec; 3469—Metal Stampings Nec; 5099—
Durable Goods Nec.

★ 81038 ★ Flour City
Architectural Metals
915 Riverview Dr.
Johnson City, TN 37601
Ultimate Parent: Armco. SIC: 3446—
Architectural Metal Work.

★ 81039 ★ Food Lion Inc.
Creekmore Dr.
Johnson City, TN 37601
(615)282-1110
Ultimate Parent: Food Lion. SIC: 5411—
Grocery Stores.

★ 81040 ★ Food Lion Inc.
South Side Plz.
Johnson City, TN 37601
(615)928-8255
Ultimate Parent: Food Lion. SIC: 5411—
Grocery Stores.

★ 81041 ★ Food Lion Inc. Store
Creekmore Dr.
Johnson City, TN 37601
(615)282-1110
Ultimate Parent: Food Lion. SIC: 5411—
Grocery Stores.

★ 81042 ★ Food Lion Inc. Store
South Side Plz.
Johnson City, TN 37601
(615)928-8255
Ultimate Parent: Food Lion. SIC: 5411—
Grocery Stores.

★ 81043 ★ General Mills Inc.
500 W. Walnut St.
Johnson City, TN 37604
(615)928-3137
Officer: Dale Garrett, Manager. Ultimate
Parent: General Mills. SIC: 2041—Flour &
Other Grain Mill Products.

★ 81044 ★ Giant Food Market
Inc.
420 W. Walnut St.
Johnson City, TN 37604
(615)926-8167
Ultimate Parent: Giant Food. SIC: 5411—
Grocery Stores.

★ 81045 ★ Giant Food Market
Inc.
1725 W. Market St.
Johnson City, TN 37604
(615)926-2131
Ultimate Parent: Giant Food. SIC: 5411—
Grocery Stores.

★ 81046 ★ Gordon Inc.
815 Love St.
Johnson City, TN 37604
(615)928-2191
Officer: C. O. Gordon Jr., President.
Ultimate Parent: Armstrong World
Industries. SIC: 2511—Wood Household
Furniture; 2599—Furniture & Fixtures Nec.

★ 81047 ★ Gordon's Inc.
815 Love St.
Johnson City, TN 37601
(615)928-2191
Company Type: Subsidiary. Officer:
Charles O. Gordon, Chairman of the Board.
Ultimate Parent: Armstrong World
Industries. SIC: 2511—Wood Household
Furniture; 2514—Metal Household Furniture.

★ 81048 ★ Invest Financial
Corporatio
Homestead Ln.
Johnson City, TN 37604
(615)282-2476
Ultimate Parent: Kemper. SIC: 6211—
Security Brokers & Dealers.

★ 81049 ★ Kroger Co.
1919 S. Roan St.
Johnson City, TN 37601
(615)926-6429
Ultimate Parent: Kroger. SIC: 5411—
Grocery Stores.

★ 81050 ★ Lerner Shops
Miracle Mall Shopping
Johnson City, TN 37601
(615)282-4912
Ultimate Parent: Limited. SIC: 5621—
Women's Clothing Stores.

★ 81051 ★ Northwestern Mutual
Life
Life
Johnson City, TN 37601
(615)282-6103
Ultimate Parent: Northwestern Mutual Life.
SIC: 6411—Insurance Agents, Brokers &
Service.

★ 81052 ★ Penn Mutual Life
Insurance Co.
711 E. Watauga Ave.
Johnson City, TN 37601
(615)929-1036
Ultimate Parent: Penn Mutual Life. SIC:
6411—Insurance Agents, Brokers &
Service.

★ 81053 ★ Pepsi South
905 E. Lakeview Dr.
Johnson City, TN 37601
(615)928-9211
Officer: Eldo Janutolo, Manager. Ultimate
Parent: Pepsico. SIC: 2086—Bottled &
Canned Soft Drinks.

★ 81054 ★ Press Inc.
PO Box 1717
Johnson City, TN 37605-1717
(615)929-3111
Company Type: Headquarters. Officer:
Tim P. Jones. Ultimate Parent: Banta Corp.
SIC: 2711—Newspapers; 2752—
Commercial Printing—Lithographic; 7383—
News Syndicates.

★ 81055 ★ Ryder Truck Rental-
Oneway
704 Rolling Hills Dr.
Johnson City, TN 37604
(615)928-1417
Ultimate Parent: Ryder System. SIC:
7359—Equipment Rental & Leasing Nec.

★ 81056 ★ Snap-On Tools
2416 Watauga Rd.
Johnson City, TN 37601
Ultimate Parent: Snap-on Tools. SIC:
3423—Hand & Edge Tools Nec.

★ 81057 ★ Snap On Tools Corp.
2416 Watauga Rd.
Johnson City, TN 37601
(615)929-1193
Officer: John Bannas, Manager. Ultimate
Parent: Snap-on Tools. SIC: 3423—Hand &
Edge Tools Nec.

★ 81058 ★ Teledyne System
Professional Office Bldg.
Johnson City, TN 37601
(615)282-4678
Ultimate Parent: Teledyne.

★ 81059 ★ Texas Instruments
Inc.
Erwin Hwy.
Johnson City, TN 37601
(615)461-2000
Ultimate Parent: Texas Instruments. SIC:
3674—Semiconductors & Related Devices.

★ 81060 ★ Texas Instruments
Inc.
3000 Bill Garland Rd.
Johnson City, TN 37601
Ultimate Parent: Texas Instruments. SIC:
3823—Process Control Instruments.

★ 81061 ★ Wal-Mart Stores Inc.
2612 N. Roan St.
Johnson City, TN 37601
(615)282-9073
Ultimate Parent: Wal-Mart Stores, Inc. SIC:
5311—Department Stores.

Johonson City

★ 81062 ★ Eckerd Drugs
Sunset Shopping Ctr.
Johonson City, TN 37601
(615)282-5913
Ultimate Parent: Eckerd Corp. SIC: 5912—
Drug Stores & Proprietary Stores.

Jonesborough

★ 81063 ★ Aerojet Heavy Metals
Co.
Old Hwy. 11 E
Jonesborough, TN 37659
(615)753-1200
Officer: Curtis Burnette, President. Ultimate
Parent: Gencorp. SIC: 3483—Ammunition
Except for Small Arms; 3489—Ordnance &
Accessories Nec.

★ 81064 ★ Burton Rubber
Processing Inc.
Hwy. 34
Jonesborough, TN 37659
Ultimate Parent: M.A.Hanna. SIC: 3069—
Fabricated Rubber Products Nec.

★ 81065 ★ First American
National BaAnk
11 E. Bypass
Jonesborough, TN 37659
(615)282-7650
Location Type: Branch office. Ultimate
Parent: First American Corp. SIC: 6021—
National Commercial Banks.

★ 81066 ★ First Tennessee Bank
NA
11 E. Bypass
Jonesborough, TN 37659
(615)461-1278
Location Type: Branch office. Ultimate
Parent: First Tennessee National Corp.
SIC: 6021—National Commercial Banks.

★ 81067 ★ Gencorp Aerojet
Old Hwy. 115 P O Box 399
Jonesborough, TN 37659
Ultimate Parent: Gencorp. SIC: 3369—
Nonferrous Foundries Nec.

Kelso

★ 81068 ★ Peoples Bank Elk
Valley
68 PO Box
Kelso, TN 37348
(615)433-1347
Ultimate Parent: People's Bank. SIC:
6022—State Commercial Banks.

Kingsport

★ 81069 ★ Air Products &
Chemicals Inc.
2000 Moreland Dr.
Kingsport, TN 37660
Ultimate Parent: Air Products & Chemicals,
Inc. SIC: 2813—Industrial Gases.

★ 81070 ★ Air Products &
Chemicals, Inc.
425 Moreland Dr.
Kingsport, TN 37660-5469
(615)246-1168
Ultimate Parent: Air Products & Chemicals,
Inc. SIC: 5047—Medical & Hospital
Equipment; 2813—Industrial Gases.

★ 81071 ★ Air Products &
Chemicals Inc.
PO Box 178
Kingsport, TN 37662-0178
(615)247-7193
Officer: Steve Warner. Ultimate Parent: Air
Products & Chemicals, Inc. SIC: 2813—
Industrial Gases.

★ 81072 ★ Air Products &
Chemicals, Inc.
440 W. Industry Dr.
Kingsport, TN 37660
(615)247-7193
Officer: W. D. Holland, Manager. Ultimate
Parent: Air Products & Chemicals, Inc. SIC:
2813—Industrial Gases.

★ 81073 ★ Burlington Coat
Factory
1116 E. Stone Dr.
Kingsport, TN 37660-3377
(615)246-9751
Ultimate Parent: Burlington Industries,
Equity. SIC: 5311—Department Stores.

★ 81074 ★ Eastman Chemical
Co.
PO Box 511
Kingsport, TN 37662
(615)229-2000
Company Type: Subsidiary. Ultimate
Parent: Eastman Kodak.

★ 81075 ★ Eastman Chemical
Co.
201 S. Wilcox Dr.
Kingsport, TN 37660
(615)229-2000
Officer: Earnest W. Deavenport Jr.,
President. Ultimate Parent: Eastman
Kodak. SIC: 2821—Plastics Materials &
Resins; 2822—Synthetic Rubber; 2823—
Cellulosic Manmade Fibers.

★ 81076 ★ Eastman Kodak Co.
Tennessee Div.
Eastman Rd.
Kingsport, TN 37662
Company Type: Division. Ultimate Parent:
Eastman Kodak. SIC: 2869—Industrial
Organic Chemicals Nec; 2865—Cyclic
Crudes & Intermediates; 2823—Cellulosic
Manmade Fibers; 2821—Plastics Materials
& Resins.

★ 81077 ★ Eastman Kodak Co.
Tennessee Eastman Div.
Eastman Rd.
Kingsport, TN 37662
Company Type: Division. Ultimate Parent:
Eastman Kodak. SIC: 2869—Industrial
Organic Chemicals Nec; 2865—Cyclic
Crudes & Intermediates; 2823—Cellulosic
Manmade Fibers; 2821—Plastics Materials
& Resins.

★ 81078 ★ Eckerd Drugs
Parkway Plz.
Kingsport, TN 37660
(615)246-4432
Ultimate Parent: Eckerd Corp. SIC: 5912—
Drug Stores & Proprietary Stores.

★ 81079 ★ Eckerd Drugs
Fort Henry Mall
Kingsport, TN 37664
(615)246-4610
Ultimate Parent: Eckerd Corp. SIC: 5912—
Drug Stores & Proprietary Stores.

★ 81080 ★ Eckerd Drugs
4320 W. Stone
Kingsport, TN 37660
(615)247-3176
Ultimate Parent: Eckerd Corp. SIC: 5912—
Drug Stores & Proprietary Stores.

★ 81081 ★ **Eckerd Drugs**
Kingsport Mall
Kingsport, TN 37660
(615)247-4116
Ultimate Parent: Eckerd Corp. **SIC:** 5912—Drug Stores & Proprietary Stores.

★ 81082 ★ **Exxon Co.**
1114 W. Sullivan St.
Kingsport, TN 37660
(615)245-5280
Ultimate Parent: Exxon. **SIC:** 7231—Beauty Shops.

★ 81083 ★ **Exxon Co. U S a**
710 E. Sullivan St.
Kingsport, TN 37660
(615)246-3241
Ultimate Parent: Exxon. **SIC:** 5172—Petroleum Products Nec.

★ 81084 ★ **First American Natioanl Bank**
415 Broad St.
Kingsport, TN 37660-4207
(615)229-0100
Location Type: Branch office. **Ultimate Parent:** First American Corp. **SIC:** 6021—National Commercial Banks.

★ 81085 ★ **First American National Bank**
4214 Fort Henry Dr.
Kingsport, TN 37663-2228
(615)292-0380
Location Type: Branch office. **Ultimate Parent:** First American Corp. **SIC:** 6021—National Commercial Banks.

★ 81086 ★ **First American National Bank**
105 W. Stone Dr.
Kingsport, TN 37660-3256
(615)229-0388
Location Type: Branch office. **Ultimate Parent:** First American Corp. **SIC:** 6021—National Commercial Banks.

★ 81087 ★ **First American National Bank**
1797 Fort Henry Dr.
Kingsport, TN 37664-3226
(615)229-0297
Location Type: Branch office. **Ultimate Parent:** First American Corp. **SIC:** 6021—National Commercial Banks.

★ 81088 ★ **First American National Bank**
1221 Lynn Garden Dr.
Kingsport, TN 37665-1601
(615)229-0243
Location Type: Branch office. **Ultimate Parent:** First American Corp. **SIC:** 6021—National Commercial Banks.

★ 81089 ★ **First American Trust Co., NA**
415 Broad St.
Kingsport, TN 37660
(615)229-0283
Location Type: Branch office. **Ultimate Parent:** First American Corp. **SIC:** 6021—National Commercial Banks.

★ 81090 ★ **First Tennessee Bank NA**
2400 Memorial Blvd.
Kingsport, TN 37664-3343
(615)247-1141
Location Type: Branch office. **Ultimate Parent:** First Tennessee National Corp. **SIC:** 6021—National Commercial Banks.

★ 81091 ★ **First Tennessee Bank NA**
4301 Ft. Henry Dr.
Kingsport, TN 37663-2229
(615)239-3965
Location Type: Branch office. **Ultimate Parent:** First Tennessee National Corp. **SIC:** 6021—National Commercial Banks.

★ 81092 ★ **First Tennessee Bank NA**
1101 Eastman Rd.
Kingsport, TN 37664-3144
(615)378-7025
Location Type: Branch office. **Ultimate Parent:** First Tennessee National Corp. **SIC:** 6021—National Commercial Banks.

★ 81093 ★ **First Tennessee Bank NA**
235 E. Ctr. St.
Kingsport, TN 37660-4303
(615)378-7000
Location Type: Branch office. **Ultimate Parent:** First Tennessee National Corp. **SIC:** 6021—National Commercial Banks.

★ 81094 ★ **First Union National Bank of Tennessee**
901 University Blvd.
Kingsport, TN 37660
(615)246-4900
Location Type: Branch office. **Ultimate Parent:** First Union Corp. **SIC:** 6021—National Commercial Banks.

★ 81095 ★ **First Union National Bank of Tennessee**
101 E. Main St.
Kingsport, TN 37662
(615)245-2265
Location Type: Branch office. **Ultimate Parent:** First Union Corp. **SIC:** 6021—National Commercial Banks.

★ 81096 ★ **Food Lion Inc.**
5440 W. Stone Dr.
Kingsport, TN 37660
(615)246-8296
Ultimate Parent: Food Lion. **SIC:** 5411—Grocery Stores.

★ 81097 ★ **Food Lion Inc.**
Southland Shopping Ctr.
Kingsport, TN 37664
(615)247-5151
Ultimate Parent: Food Lion. **SIC:** 5411—Grocery Stores.

★ 81098 ★ **Food Lion Inc.**
Kings
Kingsport, TN 37660
(615)245-4174
Ultimate Parent: Food Lion. **SIC:** 5411—Grocery Stores.

★ 81099 ★ **Food Lion Inc.**
W Stone Dr.
Kingsport, TN 37660
(615)246-5283
Ultimate Parent: Food Lion. **SIC:** 5411—Grocery Stores.

★ 81100 ★ **Food Lion Inc. Store**
5440 W. Stone Dr.
Kingsport, TN 37660
(615)246-8296
Ultimate Parent: Food Lion. **SIC:** 5411—Grocery Stores.

★ 81101 ★ **Food Lion Inc. Store**
Kings
Kingsport, TN 37660
(615)245-4174
Ultimate Parent: Food Lion. **SIC:** 5411—Grocery Stores.

★ 81102 ★ **Food Lion Inc. Store**
Southland Shopping Ctr.
Kingsport, TN 37664
(615)247-5151
Ultimate Parent: Food Lion. **SIC:** 5411—Grocery Stores.

★ 81103 ★ **Giant Food Market Inc.**
2461 Sherwood Rd.
Kingsport, TN 37664
(615)246-9114
Ultimate Parent: Giant Food. **SIC:** 5411—Grocery Stores.

★ 81104 ★ **Giant Food Market Inc.**
Colonial Heights
Kingsport, TN 37663
(615)239-9436
Ultimate Parent: Giant Food. **SIC:** 5411—Grocery Stores.

★ 81105 ★ **Giant Food Market Inc.**
3700 PO Box
Kingsport, TN 37664
(615)247-9161
Ultimate Parent: Giant Food. **SIC:** 6512—Nonresidential Building Operators.

★ 81106 ★ **Greyhound Bus Lines**
1504 Bridgewater Dr.
Kingsport, TN 37660
(615)247-1611
Ultimate Parent: Greyhound Lines Inc. **SIC:**

4111—Local & Suburban Transit; 4131—Intercity & Rural Bus Transportation; 4142—Bus Charter Service Except Local.

★ 81107 ★ **Jiffy Lube Oil Change**
1786 Fort Henry Dr.
Kingsport, TN 37664
(615)245-3967
Ultimate Parent: Pennzoil. **SIC:** 7538—General Automotive Repair Shops.

★ 81108 ★ **Johnson Controls Inc.**
509 W. Riverport Rd.
Kingsport, TN 37660
(615)245-5491
Ultimate Parent: Johnson Controls Inc. **SIC:** 5084—Industrial Machinery & Equipment.

★ 81109 ★ **Kroger Co.**
E. Stone Dr.
Kingsport, TN 37660
(615)246-7440
Ultimate Parent: Kroger. **SIC:** 5411—Grocery Stores.

★ 81110 ★ **Lerner Shops**
Fort Henry Shopping
Kingsport, TN 37664
(615)246-4680
Ultimate Parent: Limited. **SIC:** 5621—Women's Clothing Stores.

★ 81111 ★ **McDonald's Hamburgers**
4300 W. Stone Dr.
Kingsport, TN 37660
(615)246-7911
Ultimate Parent: McDonald's. **SIC:** 5812—Eating Places.

★ 81112 ★ **Mead Corp.**
Kingsport Mill
100 Clinchfield St.
Kingsport, TN 37660
Company Type: Division. **Ultimate Parent:** Mead. **SIC:** 2621—Paper Mills; 2611—Pulp Mills.

★ 81113 ★ **Mead Paper**
PO Box 1964 W. Market St.
Kingsport, TN 37662
Ultimate Parent: Mead. **SIC:** 2621—Paper Mills; 2611—Pulp Mills.

★ 81114 ★ **Otis Elevator Co.**
320 E. Sullivan St.
Kingsport, TN 37660
(615)245-3193
Ultimate Parent: United Technologies. **SIC:** 5084—Industrial Machinery & Equipment.

★ 81115 ★ **Performance Plastics Business Unit**
137 Regional Park Dr.
Kingsport, TN 37664
Ultimate Parent: Eastman Kodak. **SIC:** 2821—Plastics Materials & Resins.

★ 81116 ★ **Rite Aid Discount Pharmacy**
1205 N. Eastman Rd.
Kingsport, TN 37664
(615)246-5836
Ultimate Parent: Rite Aid. **SIC:** 5912—Drug Stores & Proprietary Stores.

★ 81117 ★ **Rite Aid Discount Pharmacy**
5440 W. Stone Dr.
Kingsport, TN 37660
(615)246-6191
Ultimate Parent: Rite Aid. **SIC:** 5521—Used Car Dealers.

★ 81118 ★ **Service Merchandise**
1001 N. Eastman Rd.
Kingsport, TN 37664
(615)246-3377
Ultimate Parent: Service Merchandise Co., Inc. **SIC:** 5944—Jewelry Stores.

★ 81119 ★ **Trailways Bus Lines**
311 Cherokee St.
Kingsport, TN 37660
(615)246-1108
Ultimate Parent: Greyhound Lines Inc. **SIC:** 4131—Intercity & Rural Bus Transportation; 4111—Local & Suburban Transit; 4142—Bus Charter Service Except Local.

★ 81120 ★ **Tri City Bank & Trust Co.**
1772 Fort Henry Dr.
Kingsport, TN 37664
(615)247-5191
Ultimate Parent: First Virginia Banks Inc. **SIC:** 6022—State Commercial Banks.

★ 81121 ★ **Vulcan Materials Co.**
Deneen Ln.
Kingsport, TN 37660
(615)246-9141
Ultimate Parent: Vulcan Materials Co. **SIC:** 5039—Construction Materials Nec.

★ 81122 ★ **Wal-Mart Stores Inc.**
Sherwood Rd.
Kingsport, TN 37664
(615)245-3151
Ultimate Parent: Wal-Mart Stores, Inc. **SIC:** 5311—Department Stores.

★ 81123 ★ **Wal-Mart Stores Inc.**
W Stone Dr.
Kingsport, TN 37660
(615)246-4676
Ultimate Parent: Wal-Mart Stores, Inc. **SIC:** 5311—Department Stores.

Kingston

★ 81124 ★ **Bank of Roane County**
320 N. Kentucky St.
Kingston, TN 37763
(615)376-3434
Location Type: Branch office. **Ultimate Parent:** Union Planters Corp. **SIC:** 6021—National Commercial Banks.

★ 81125 ★ **Bowater Inc.**
930 W. Race St.
Kingston, TN 37763
(615)376-6185
Ultimate Parent: Bowater. **SIC:** 2411—Logging.

★ 81126 ★ **Bowater Woodlands**
930 W. Race St.
Kingston, TN 37763-2122
(615)376-6185
Ultimate Parent: Bowater. **SIC:** 5099—Durable Goods Nec; 0811—Timber Tracts.

★ 81127 ★ **First American National Bank**
113 E. Race St.
Kingston, TN 37763
(615)673-5768
Location Type: Branch office. **Ultimate Parent:** First American Corp. **SIC:** 6021—National Commercial Banks.

★ 81128 ★ **Security Trust FS & LA**
508 N. Kentucky St.
Kingston, TN 37763-2629
(615)376-4546
Location Type: Branch office. **Ultimate Parent:** Union Planters Corp. **SIC:** 6021—National Commercial Banks.

Knoxville

★ 81129 ★ **ABF Freight System Inc.**
2828 Texas Ave.
Knoxville, TN 37921-6021
(615)522-9041
Ultimate Parent: Arkansas Best. **SIC:** 4212—Local Trucking Without Storage.

★ 81130 ★ **Air Products & Chemicals Inc.**
3500 Workman Rd., Ste. A
Knoxville, TN 37921-5949
(615)584-6111
Location Type: Branch office. **Ultimate Parent:** Air Products & Chemicals, Inc. **SIC:** 5169—Chemicals & Allied Products Nec.

★ 81131 ★ **Alcoa Recycling Center**
600 N. Gay St.
Knoxville, TN 37917-7424
(615)971-1907
Ultimate Parent: Aluminum Co. of America--Alcoa. **SIC:** 4953—Refuse Systems.

★ 81132 ★ **Alcoa Recycling Center**
600 N. Gay St.
Knoxville, TN 37917-7424
(615)971-1907
Ultimate Parent: Aluminum Co. of America--Alcoa. **SIC:** 4953—Refuse Systems.

★ 81133 ★ **Allied-Signal Inc.**
Saftey Restraints Systems
1601 Midpark Rd.
Knoxville, TN 37921
Ultimate Parent: Allied-Signal Inc. **SIC:** 3714—Motor Vehicle Parts & Accessories.

★ 81134 ★ **Allied-Signal Safety Restraint**
1601 Midpark Dr.
Knoxville, TN 37921
(615)584-9141
Officer: Ransome Rauton, Manager.
Ultimate Parent: Allied-Signal Inc. **SIC:** 2399—Fabricated Textile Products Nec; 3429—Hardware Nec.

★ 81135 ★ **American General Finance**
427 W. Clinch Ave.
Knoxville, TN 37902-2124
(615)525-6111
Location Type: Branch office. **Ultimate Parent:** American General Corp. **SIC:** 6141—Personal Credit Institutions; 6162—Mortgage Bankers & Correspondents.

★ 81136 ★ **American General Finance**
9220 Kingston Pke.
Knoxville, TN 37922-2378
(615)693-2866
Ultimate Parent: American General Corp. **SIC:** 6141—Personal Credit Institutions; 6162—Mortgage Bankers & Correspondents.

★ 81137 ★ **American General Finance Inc.**
427 W. Clinch Ave.
Knoxville, TN 37902-2124
(615)525-6111
Location Type: Branch office. **Ultimate Parent:** American General Corp. **SIC:** 6141—Personal Credit Institutions; 6162—Mortgage Bankers & Correspondents.

★ 81138 ★ **American General Finance Inc.**
9220 Kingston Pike
Knoxville, TN 37922-2378
(615)693-2866
Location Type: Branch office. **Ultimate Parent:** American General Corp. **SIC:** 6141—Personal Credit Institutions; 6162—Mortgage Bankers & Correspondents.

★ 81139 ★ **American Limestone Co. Inc.**
2209 Blount Ave. SW
Knoxville, TN 37920-1956
(615)573-4501
Company Type: Subsidiary. **Officer:** W. Hoyl Gill, President. **Ultimate Parent:** Asarco. **SIC:** 1422—Crushed & Broken Limestone. **Employee Count:** 264. **Sales:** 34 M.

★ 81140 ★ **AMR Corp.**
2611 E. Magnolia Ave.
Knoxville, TN 37914-5317
(615)523-4691
Ultimate Parent: AMR Corp. **SIC:** 5049—Professional Equipment Nec.

★ 81141 ★ **Amsted Industries Inc.**
Plexco Div.
10420 Lexington Dr. PO Box 23530
Knoxville, TN 37933
Company Type: Division. **Ultimate Parent:** Amsted Industries Inc. **SIC:** 3082—Unsupported Plastics Profile Shapes.

★ 81142 ★ **APAC**
1301 Spring Hill Rd.
Knoxville, TN 37914
(615)637-1770
Officer: Hazen Hines, President. **Ultimate Parent:** Ashland Oil. **SIC:** 2951—Asphalt Paving Mixtures & Blocks.

★ 81143 ★ **Asarco Inc.**
2640 N. Broadway St.
Knoxville, TN 37917
(615)525-9536
Ultimate Parent: Asarco. **SIC:** 1031—Lead & Zinc Ores.

★ 81144 ★ **Banister Outlet Store**
601 W. Baxter Ave.
Knoxville, TN 37921
(615)525-0115
Ultimate Parent: United States Shoe. **SIC:** 5661—Shoe Stores.

★ 81145 ★ **Batesville Casket Co. Inc.**
6155 Industrial Heights Dr.
Knoxville, TN 37909
(615)588-8561
Ultimate Parent: Hillenbrand Industries. **SIC:** 5087—Service Establishment Equipment.

★ 81146 ★ **Brownell Electro Inc.**
207 Ctr. Park Dr.
Knoxville, TN 37922
(615)966-3441
Location Type: Branch office. **Ultimate Parent:** Avnet. **SIC:** 5063—Electrical Apparatus & Equipment.

★ 81147 ★ **Browning-Ferris Industries**
2400 Chipman St.
Knoxville, TN 37917-6115
(615)522-8161
Location Type: Branch office. **Ultimate Parent:** Browning-Ferris Industries. **SIC:** 4953—Refuse Systems.

★ 81148 ★ **Bruno's**
Sea Ray Division
2600 Sea Ray Blvd.
Knoxville, TN 37914
(615)522-4181 **Fax:** (615)525-4828
Company Type: Subsidiary. **Officer:** William J. Barrington, President. **Ultimate Parent:** Bruno's.

★ 81149 ★ **Brunswick Sea Ray Div.**
2600 Sea Ray Dr.
Knoxville, TN 37914
(615)522-4181
Officer: William J. Barrington, President. **Ultimate Parent:** Brunswick Corp. **SIC:** 3732—Boat Building & Repairing.

★ 81150 ★ **Butler Paper**
2734 Middlebrook Pke.
Knoxville, TN 37921-5602
(615)637-3232
Officer: Im Johnson. **Ultimate Parent:** Alco Standard Corp. **SIC:** 5113—Industrial & Personal Service Paper.

★ 81151 ★ **Butler Paper**
2734 Middlebrook Pke.
Knoxville, TN 37921-5602
(615)637-3232
Officer: Im Johnson. **Ultimate Parent:** Alco Standard Corp. **SIC:** 5113—Industrial & Personal Service Paper.

★ 81152 ★ **Carrier Corp.**
5301 National Dr.
Knoxville, TN 37914
Officer: Robert Kilduffe. **Ultimate Parent:** United Technologies. **SIC:** 3564—Blowers & Fans.

★ 81153 ★ **Casual Corner**
W Town Shopping Ctr.
Knoxville, TN 37919
(615)693-2080
Ultimate Parent: United States Shoe. **SIC:** 5621—Women's Clothing Stores.

★ 81154 ★ **Chevron Chemical Co.**
Plexco Div.
10420 Lexington Dr. 10420 Lexington Dr.
Knoxville, TN 37922
Company Type: Division. **Ultimate Parent:** Chevron Corp. **SIC:** 3084—Plastics Pipe.

★ 81155 ★ **Circuit City**
7807 Kingston Pke
Knoxville, TN 37919
(615)694-0100
Ultimate Parent: Circuit City Stores. **SIC:** 5731—Radio, Television & Electronics Stores.

★ 81156 ★ **Citgo Petroleum**
2409 Knott Rd.
Knoxville, TN 37921
(615)588-3555
Ultimate Parent: Citgo Petroleum. **SIC:** 5172—Petroleum Products Nec.

★ 81157 ★ **Citgo Petroleum Corp.**
2409 Knott Rd.
Knoxville, TN 37921
(615)588-3555
Ultimate Parent: Citgo Petroleum. **SIC:** 5172—Petroleum Products Nec.

★ 81158 ★ **Communications Inc.**
7433 Jessilee Dr.
Knoxville, TN 37938
(615)922-6486
Ultimate Parent: Avnet.

★ 81159 ★ **ConAgra Fertilizer Co.**
PO Box 59070
Knoxville, TN 37450-9070
(615)539-5400 **Fax:** (615)539-5501
Officer: Michael T. Lapsys, President.
Ultimate Parent: Conagra.

★ 81160 ★ **Dana Corp.**
Spicer Transmission
5428 N. National Dr.
Knoxville, TN 37914
(615)637-7294
Company Type: Division. **Ultimate Parent:** Dana Corp. **SIC:** 3714—Motor Vehicle Parts & Accessories.

★ 81161 ★ **Delta Air Lines**
1st
Knoxville, TN 37902
(615)690-9696
Ultimate Parent: Delta Air Lines, Inc. **SIC:** 4724—Travel Agencies.

★ 81162 ★ **Delta Air Lines Inc.**
1st
Knoxville, TN 37902
(615)690-9696
Ultimate Parent: Delta Air Lines, Inc. **SIC:** 4724—Travel Agencies.

★ 81163 ★ **Diebold Inc.**
10629 Lexington Dr.
Knoxville, TN 37932
(615)966-8746
Ultimate Parent: Diebold, Inc. **SIC:** 5044—Office Equipment.

★ 81164 ★ **Digital Equipment Corp.**
9041 Executive Park Dr.
Knoxville, TN 37923
(615)690-1521
Ultimate Parent: Digital Equipment Corp. **SIC:** 5045—Computers, Peripherals & Software.

★ 81165 ★ **Dover Elevator Co.**
400 Erin Dr.
Knoxville, TN 37919
(615)588-8517
Officer: Shawn Johnson, Manager.
Ultimate Parent: Dover Corp. **SIC:** 3534—Elevators & Moving Stairways.

★ 81166 ★ **Eckerd Drugs**
5705 Oak Ridge Hwy.
Knoxville, TN 37921
(615)588-6531
Ultimate Parent: Eckerd Corp. **SIC:** 5912—Drug Stores & Proprietary Stores.

★ 81167 ★ **Eckerd Drugs**
East Town Mall
Knoxville, TN 37919
(615)544-0040
Ultimate Parent: Eckerd Corp. **SIC:** 5912—Drug Stores & Proprietary Stores.

★ 81168 ★ **Electro Mechanical Corp.**
1228 Halifax Rd.
Knoxville, TN 37922-1433
(615)691-7505
Ultimate Parent: Ametek Inc. **SIC:** 5082—Construction & Mining Machinery.

★ 81169 ★ **First American Natioanl Bank**
220 Blout Ave.
Knoxville, TN 37920-1638
(615)521-5275
Location Type: Branch office. **Ultimate Parent:** First American Corp. **SIC:** 6021—National Commercial Banks.

★ 81170 ★ **First American National Bank**
8921 Kingston Pk.
Knoxville, TN 37923-5009
(615)673-5756
Location Type: Branch office. **Ultimate Parent:** First American Corp. **SIC:** 6021—National Commercial Banks.

★ 81171 ★ **First American National Bank**
815 S. Gay St.
Knoxville, TN 37902-1504
(615)521-5700
Location Type: Branch office. **Ultimate Parent:** First American Corp. **SIC:** 6021—National Commercial Banks.

★ 81172 ★ **First American National Bank**
6100 Kingston Pike
Knoxville, TN 37919-4019
(615)521-5300
Location Type: Branch office. **Ultimate Parent:** First American Corp. **SIC:** 6021—National Commercial Banks.

★ 81173 ★ **First American National Bank**
4422 Western Ave.
Knoxville, TN 37921-4307
(615)521-5947
Location Type: Branch office. **Ultimate Parent:** First American Corp. **SIC:** 6021—National Commercial Banks.

★ 81174 ★ **First American National Bank**
345 Dale Ave.
Knoxville, TN 37921-6719
(615)521-5295
Location Type: Branch office. **Ultimate Parent:** First American Corp. **SIC:** 6021—National Commercial Banks.

★ 81175 ★ **First American National Bank**
707 N. Broadway
Knoxville, TN 37901
(615)521-5305
Location Type: Branch office. **Ultimate Parent:** First American Corp. **SIC:** 6021—National Commercial Banks.

★ 81176 ★ **First American National Bank**
9206 Park West Blvd.
Knoxville, TN 37923-4401
(615)521-5310
Location Type: Branch office. **Ultimate Parent:** First American Corp. **SIC:** 6021—National Commercial Banks.

★ 81177 ★ **First American National Bank**
1503 Magnolia Ave.
Knoxville, TN 37917-7894
(615)521-5325
Location Type: Branch office. **Ultimate Parent:** First American Corp. **SIC:** 6021—National Commercial Banks.

★ 81178 ★ **First American National Bank**
11543 Kingston Pke.
Knoxville, TN 37922-3918
(615)521-5920
Location Type: Branch office. **Ultimate Parent:** First American Corp. **SIC:** 6021—National Commercial Banks.

★ 81179 ★ **First American National Bank**
2901 Essary Rd.
Knoxville, TN 37918-2404
(615)521-5315
Location Type: Branch office. **Ultimate Parent:** First American Corp. **SIC:** 6021—National Commercial Banks.

★ 81180 ★ **First American National Bank**
1185 Keowee Ave.
Knoxville, TN 37919-6703
(615)521-5903
Location Type: Branch office. **Ultimate Parent:** First American Corp. **SIC:** 6021—National Commercial Banks.

★ 81181 ★ First American
National Bank
7821 Kingston Pke.
Knoxville, TN 37919-5593
(615)521-5280
Location Type: Branch office. Ultimate
Parent: First American Corp. SIC: 6021—
National Commercial Banks.

★ 81182 ★ First American
National Bank
505 S. Gay St.
Knoxville, TN 37902-1504
(615)521-5100
Location Type: Branch office. Ultimate
Parent: First American Corp. SIC: 6021—
National Commercial Banks.

★ 81183 ★ First American
National Bank
7320 Chapman Hwy.
Knoxville, TN 37920-6612
(615)521-5900
Location Type: Branch office. Ultimate
Parent: First American Corp. SIC: 6021—
National Commercial Banks.

★ 81184 ★ First Mutual
Investments
155 Sherway Rd.
Knoxville, TN 37922-2224
(615)531-9895
Ultimate Parent: Bank of Boston Corp.
SIC: 6141—Personal Credit Institutions.

★ 81185 ★ First Tennessee Bank
NA
9133 Oak Ridge Hwy.
Knoxville, TN 37830
(615)971-2390
Location Type: Branch office. Ultimate
Parent: First Tennessee National Corp.
SIC: 6021—National Commercial Banks.

★ 81186 ★ First Tennessee Bank
NA
601 Market St.
Knoxville, TN 37902-2292
(615)971-2440
Location Type: Branch office. Ultimate
Parent: First Tennessee National Corp.
SIC: 6021—National Commercial Banks.

★ 81187 ★ First Tennessee Bank
NA
9607 Kingston Pke.
Knoxville, TN 37923
(615)971-2475
Location Type: Branch office. Ultimate
Parent: First Tennessee National Corp.
SIC: 6021—National Commercial Banks.

★ 81188 ★ First Tennessee Bank
NA
11200 Kingston Pke.
Knoxville, TN 37922-2808
(615)971-2100
Location Type: Branch office. Ultimate
Parent: First Tennessee National Corp.
SIC: 6021—National Commercial Banks.

★ 81189 ★ First Tennessee Bank
NA
7741 Ashville Hwy.
Knoxville, TN 37914
(615)971-2446
Location Type: Branch office. Ultimate
Parent: First Tennessee National Corp.
SIC: 6021—National Commercial Banks.

★ 81190 ★ First Tennessee Bank
NA
4805 Kingston Pke.
Knoxville, TN 37919-5185
(615)971-2442
Location Type: Branch office. Ultimate
Parent: Commercial Federal Bank, FSB.
SIC: 6021—National Commercial Banks.

★ 81191 ★ First Tennessee Bank
NA
800 S. Gay St.
Knoxville, TN 37929-9702
(615)971-2114
Location Type: Branch office. Ultimate
Parent: First Tennessee National Corp.
SIC: 6021—National Commercial Banks.

★ 81192 ★ First Tennessee Bank
NA
2900 N. Broadway
Knoxville, TN 37917-3234
(615)971-2454
Location Type: Branch office. Ultimate

Parent: First Tennessee National Corp.
SIC: 6021—National Commercial Banks.

★ 81193 ★ First Tennessee Bank
NA
911 Executive
Knoxville, TN 37923
(615)971-2443
Location Type: Branch office. Ultimate
Parent: First Tennessee National Corp.
SIC: 6021—National Commercial Banks.

★ 81194 ★ First Tennessee Bank
NA
505 17th St.
Knoxville, TN 37916
(615)971-2456
Location Type: Branch office. Ultimate
Parent: First Tennessee National Corp.
SIC: 6021—National Commercial Banks.

★ 81195 ★ First Tennessee Bank
NA
4216 Ashville Hwy.
Knoxville, TN 37914
(615)971-2451
Location Type: Branch office. Ultimate
Parent: First Tennessee National Corp.
SIC: 6021—National Commercial Banks.

★ 81196 ★ First Tennessee Bank
NA
7508 Kingston Pke.
Knoxville, TN 37919-5663
(615)971-2461
Location Type: Branch office. Ultimate
Parent: First Tennessee National Corp.
SIC: 6021—National Commercial Banks.

★ 81197 ★ First Tennessee Bank
NA
5200 Clinton Hwy.
Knoxville, TN 37912-3896
(615)971-2445
Location Type: Branch office. Ultimate
Parent: First Tennessee National Corp.
SIC: 6021—National Commercial Banks.

★ 81198 ★ First Tennessee Bank
NA
7213 Chapman Hwy.
Knoxville, TN 37920-6609
(615)971-2456
Location Type: Branch office. Ultimate
Parent: First Tennessee National Corp.
SIC: 6021—National Commercial Banks.

★ 81199 ★ First Tennessee Bank
NA
4315 Kingston Pke.
Knoxville, TN 37919-5224
(615)971-2377
Location Type: Branch office. Ultimate
Parent: First Tennessee National Corp.
SIC: 6021—National Commercial Banks.

★ 81200 ★ First Tennessee Bank
NA
502 Merchants Rd.
Knoxville, TN 37912-3803
(615)971-2144
Location Type: Branch office. Ultimate
Parent: First Tennessee National Corp.
SIC: 6021—National Commercial Banks.

★ 81201 ★ First Tennessee Bank
NA
4416 B B Chapman Hwy.
Knoxville, TN 37920-4357
(615)971-2417
Location Type: Branch office. Ultimate
Parent: First Tennessee National Corp.
SIC: 6021—National Commercial Banks.

★ 81202 ★ First Tennessee Bank
NA
3900 Western Ave.
Knoxville, TN 37921-4451
(615)971-2388
Location Type: Branch office. Ultimate
Parent: First Tennessee National Corp.
SIC: 6021—National Commercial Banks.

★ 81203 ★ First Tennessee Bank
NA
1830 W. Cumberland
Knoxville, TN 37916-3010
(615)971-2424
Location Type: Branch office. Ultimate
Parent: First Tennessee National Corp.
SIC: 6021—National Commercial Banks.

★ 81204 ★ First Tennessee Bank
NA
121 Kirkwood
Knoxville, TN 37914-4022
(615)971-2372
Location Type: Branch office. Ultimate
Parent: First Tennessee National Corp.
SIC: 6021—National Commercial Banks.

★ 81205 ★ First Tennessee Bank
NA
2929 Alcoa Hwy.
Knoxville, TN 37920-4789
(615)971-2393
Location Type: Branch office. Ultimate
Parent: First Tennessee National Corp.
SIC: 6021—National Commercial Banks.

★ 81206 ★ First Tennessee Bank
NA
1815 Downtown West Blvd.
Knoxville, TN 37919-5479
(615)971-2402
Location Type: Branch office. Ultimate
Parent: First Tennessee National Corp.
SIC: 6021—National Commercial Banks.

★ 81207 ★ First Tennessee Bank
NA
324 Cedar Bluff Rd.
Knoxville, TN 37923-4539
(615)971-2411
Location Type: Branch office. Ultimate
Parent: First Tennessee National Corp.
SIC: 6021—National Commercial Banks.

★ 81208 ★ First Tennessee Bank
NA
5225 Broadway NE
Knoxville, TN 37918-2386
(615)971-2288
Location Type: Branch office. Ultimate
Parent: First Tennessee National Corp.
SIC: 6021—National Commercial Banks.

★ 81209 ★ First Tennessee Bank
NA
6801 Maynardville Hwy.
Knoxville, TN 37918-5310
(615)971-2122
Location Type: Branch office. Ultimate
Parent: First Tennessee National Corp.
SIC: 6021—National Commercial Banks.

★ 81210 ★ First Tennessee Bank
NA
2121 Emory Rd.
Knoxville, TN 37938-4514
(615)971-2299
Location Type: Branch office. Ultimate
Parent: First Tennessee National Corp.
SIC: 6021—National Commercial Banks.

★ 81211 ★ First Tennessee Bank
NA
501 Broadway
Knoxville, TN 37917-4762
(615)971-2383
Location Type: Branch office. Ultimate
Parent: First Tennessee National Corp.
SIC: 6021—National Commercial Banks.

★ 81212 ★ Fitness Connection
8913 Farne Island Blvd.
Knoxville, TN 37923
Ultimate Parent: New York Times. SIC:
7299—Miscellaneous Personal Services
Nec.

★ 81213 ★ Giant Food Market
Inc.
5718 Asheville Hwy.
Knoxville, TN 37924
(615)546-6922
Ultimate Parent: Giant Food. SIC: 5411—
Grocery Stores.

★ 81214 ★ Giant Food Market
Inc.
7428 Kingston Pike
Knoxville, TN 37919
(615)584-3922
Ultimate Parent: Giant Food. SIC: 5411—
Grocery Stores.

★ 81215 ★ Greyhound Bus Lines
10001 Kingston Pike
Knoxville, TN 37922
(615)691-6036
Ultimate Parent: Greyhound Lines Inc. SIC:
4111—Local & Suburban Transit; 4131—
Intercity & Rural Bus Transportation; 4142—
Bus Charter Service Except Local.

★ 81216 ★ Greyhound Bus Lines
100 E. Magnolia Ave.
Knoxville, TN 37917
(615)525-9483
Ultimate Parent: Greyhound Lines Inc. SIC:
4111—Local & Suburban Transit; 4131—
Intercity & Rural Bus Transportation; 4142—
Bus Charter Service Except Local.

★ 81217 ★ Home Products Co.
2001 E. Magnolia Ave.
Knoxville, TN 37917
(615)524-1558
Ultimate Parent: First Brands Corp. SIC:
5722—Household Appliance Stores.

★ 81218 ★ Johnson Controls Inc.
6101 Industrial Heights Dr.
Knoxville, TN 37909
(615)691-2214
Ultimate Parent: Johnson Controls Inc.
SIC: 5063—Electrical Apparatus &
Equipment.

★ 81219 ★ Kroger Co.
11240 Kingstonpike
Knoxville, TN 37922
(615)966-3975
Ultimate Parent: Kroger. SIC: 5411—
Grocery Stores.

★ 81220 ★ Kroger Co.
5425 Clinton Hwy.
Knoxville, TN 37912
(615)688-3562
Ultimate Parent: Kroger. SIC: 5411—
Grocery Stores.

★ 81221 ★ Kroger Co.
Oak Ridge Hwy.
Knoxville, TN 37921
(615)525-9538
Ultimate Parent: Kroger. SIC: 5411—
Grocery Stores.

★ 81222 ★ Kroger Co.
4505 Asheville Hwy.
Knoxville, TN 37914
(615)546-4728
Ultimate Parent: Kroger. SIC: 5411—
Grocery Stores.

★ 81223 ★ Kroger Co.
7224 Chapman Hwy.
Knoxville, TN 37920
(615)579-5301
Ultimate Parent: Kroger. SIC: 5411—
Grocery Stores.

★ 81224 ★ Lerner Shops
W Town Shopping
Knoxville, TN 37919
(615)690-6525
Ultimate Parent: Limited. SIC: 5621—
Women's Clothing Stores.

★ 81225 ★ Lerner Shops
403 S. Gay St.
Knoxville, TN 37902
(615)546-1654
Ultimate Parent: Limited. SIC: 5621—
Women's Clothing Stores.

★ 81226 ★ Limited
3025 E. Towne Mall Rd.
Knoxville, TN 37924
(615)525-3666
Ultimate Parent: Limited. SIC: 5621—
Women's Clothing Stores.

★ 81227 ★ Longs Drug Store
4604 Kingston Pike
Knoxville, TN 37919
(615)588-9218
Ultimate Parent: Longs Drug Stores. SIC:
5912—Drug Stores & Proprietary Stores.

★ 81228 ★ Martin Marietta
Magnesia
1539 Coleman Rd.
Knoxville, TN 37909
(615)584-5141
Ultimate Parent: Martin Marietta. SIC:
5169—Chemicals & Allied Products Nec.

★ 81229 ★ Mary Kay Cosmetics
8312 Richland Colony Rd.
Knoxville, TN 37923
(615)690-8443
Ultimate Parent: Mary Kay Cosmetics. SIC:
5999—Miscellaneous Retail Stores Nec.

★ 81230 ★   Merritt-Holland Co.
200 Liberty St.
Knoxville, TN 37919
Ultimate Parent: Union Carbide Corp. **SIC:**
2813—Industrial Gases.

★ 81231 ★   New York Life
Knoxville General Office
Southeasten Agnecies
Two Ctr. Square
625 Gay St., 4th Fl.
Knoxville, TN 37902
(615)523-0741 **Fax:** (615)637-7353
Officer: James D. Mason. **Ultimate Parent:**
New York Life.

★ 81232 ★   Otis Elevator Co.
810 State St.
Knoxville, TN 37902
(615)525-0282
Ultimate Parent: United Technologies. **SIC:**
5084—Industrial Machinery & Equipment.

★ 81233 ★   Payless Shoe Source
Clinton Hwy.
Knoxville, TN 37912
(615)687-8191
Ultimate Parent: May Department Stores.
SIC: 5661—Shoe Stores.

★ 81234 ★   Payless Shoe Source
7220 Chapman Hwy.
Knoxville, TN 37920
(615)573-5252
Ultimate Parent: May Department Stores.
SIC: 5661—Shoe Stores.

★ 81235 ★   Payless Shoesource
Clinton Hwy.
Knoxville, TN 37912
(615)687-8191
Ultimate Parent: May Department Stores.
SIC: 5661—Shoe Stores.

★ 81236 ★   Penn Mutual Life
Insurance
1111 Northshore Dr. NW
Knoxville, TN 37919
(615)584-0174
Ultimate Parent: Penn Mutual Life. **SIC:**
6311—Life Insurance.

★ 81237 ★   Pepsi-Cola
Knoxville
2708 Federal Rd.
Knoxville, TN 37919
Company Type: Division. **Ultimate Parent:**
Pepsico. **SIC:** 2086—Bottled & Canned Soft
Drinks.

★ 81238 ★   Pepsi-Cola Bottling
Co.
2708 Federal Rd.
Knoxville, TN 37914
(615)524-0337
Officer: Jim McCune, Manager. **Ultimate
Parent:** Pepsico. **SIC:** 2086—Bottled &
Canned Soft Drinks.

★ 81239 ★   Pepsi-Cola Bottling
Co.
Knoxville
2708 Federal Rd.
Knoxville, TN 37914
Company Type: Division. **Ultimate Parent:**
Pepsico. **SIC:** 2086—Bottled & Canned Soft
Drinks.

★ 81240 ★   Plexco
10420 Lexington Dr.
Knoxville, TN 37922
Ultimate Parent: Amsted Industries Inc.
SIC: 3000—Rubber & Miscellaneous
Plastics Products.

★ 81241 ★   PPG Industries Inc.
3900 Middlebrook Pike
Knoxville, TN 37921
(615)525-2222
Ultimate Parent: PPG Industries Inc. **SIC:**
3479—Metal Coating & Allied Services.

★ 81242 ★   PPG Industries Inc.
1722 Louisville Dr.
Knoxville, TN 37921
(615)558-9066
Officer: J. Wayne Frazier, Manager.
Ultimate Parent: PPG Industries Inc. **SIC:**
3231—Products of Purchased Glass;
3442—Metal Doors, Sash & Trim.

★ 81243 ★   Roddy Coca-Cola
Bottling Co. Inc.
2200 Leslie Ave. PO Box 50338
Knoxville, TN 37921
Ultimate Parent: Coca-Cola Enterprises.
SIC: 2086—Bottled & Canned Soft Drinks.

★ 81244 ★   Rohm & Haas Inc.
Tennessee
730 Dale Ave.
Knoxville, TN 37921-6726
Ultimate Parent: Rohm & Haas. **SIC:**
2821—Plastics Materials & Resins; 2843—
Surface Active Agents; 2869—Industrial
Organic Chemicals Nec.

★ 81245 ★   Rohm & Haas
Tennessee Inc.
730 Dale Ave.
Knoxville, TN 37921
(615)521-8200
Ultimate Parent: Rohm & Haas. **SIC:**
2821—Plastics Materials & Resins; 3081—
Unsupported Plastics Film & Sheet; 3083—
Laminated Plastics Plate & Sheet.

★ 81246 ★   Sea Ray Boats Inc.
2601 Sea Ray Blvd.
Knoxville, TN 37914
Ultimate Parent: Brunswick Corp. **SIC:**
3732—Boat Building & Repairing.

★ 81247 ★   Sea Ray Boats Inc.
2600 Sea Ray Dr.
Knoxville, TN 37914
(615)522-4181
Ultimate Parent: Brunswick Corp. **SIC:**
3732—Boat Building & Repairing.

★ 81248 ★   Sea Ray Boats Inc.
Riverview
5502 Island River Dr.
Knoxville, TN 37914
Ultimate Parent: Brunswick Corp. **SIC:**
3732—Boat Building & Repairing.

★ 81249 ★   Security Trust FS &
LA
7100 Kingston Pke.
Knoxville, TN 37919-5707
(615)584-2191
Location Type: Branch office. **Ultimate
Parent:** Union Planters Corp. **SIC:** 6021—
National Commercial Banks.

★ 81250 ★   Security Trust FS &
LA
7005 Maynardville Hwy.
Knoxville, TN 37918-5737
(615)922-2106 **Fax:** (615)922-5979
Location Type: Branch office. **Ultimate
Parent:** Union Planters Corp. **SIC:** 6021—
National Commercial Banks.

★ 81251 ★   Service Merchandise
8425 Kingston Pike
Knoxville, TN 37919
(615)690-2113
Ultimate Parent: Service Merchandise Co.,
Inc. **SIC:** 5944—Jewelry Stores.

★ 81252 ★   Shannon Industries
Inc.
6220 Enterprise Dr.
Knoxville, TN 37909
(615)558-0525
Ultimate Parent: Dana Corp. **SIC:** 3479—
Metal Coating & Allied Services.

★ 81253 ★   Sloan Paper Co.
1307 Karnes Ave.
Knoxville, TN 37917-2627
(615)688-8600
Officer: Steve McMillan. **Ultimate Parent:**
Alco Standard Corp. **SIC:** 5113—Industrial
& Personal Service Paper.

★ 81254 ★   Spartan Express Inc.
2320 Century St.
Knoxville, TN 37921
(615)524-4786
Ultimate Parent: Roadway Services. **SIC:**
4213—Trucking Except Local.

★ 81255 ★   Target
8040 Ray Mears Blvd.
Knoxville, TN 37919
(615)693-2203
Ultimate Parent: Dayton Hudson. **SIC:**
5311—Department Stores.

★ 81256 ★   Target Stores
8040 Ray Mears Blvd.
Knoxville, TN 37919
(615)693-2203
Ultimate Parent: Dayton Hudson. **SIC:**
5311—Department Stores.

★ 81257 ★   Tektronix Inc.
9041 Executive Park Dr.
Knoxville, TN 37923
(615)690-6422
Ultimate Parent: Tektronix, Inc.

★ 81258 ★   Texaco Inc.
701 Langford Ave.
Knoxville, TN 37920
(615)573-8051
Ultimate Parent: Texaco. **SIC:** 5172—
Petroleum Products Nec.

★ 81259 ★   Third National
Mortgage Co.
412 Executive Tower Dr.
Knoxville, TN 37923
(615)691-3300
Ultimate Parent: Suntrust Banks. **SIC:**
6141—Personal Credit Institutions.

★ 81260 ★   Toys R US
8009 Kingston Pike
Knoxville, TN 37919
(615)690-1632
Ultimate Parent: Toys "R" US. **SIC:** 5641—
Children's & Infants' Wear Stores.

★ 81261 ★   Trailways Bus Lines
2011 Davenport Rd.
Knoxville, TN 37920
(615)573-1961
Ultimate Parent: Greyhound Lines Inc. **SIC:**
4131—Intercity & Rural Bus Transportation;
4111—Local & Suburban Transit; 4142—
Bus Charter Service Except Local.

★ 81262 ★   TRW Inc.
Transportation Electronics Div.
5008 N. National Dr.
Knoxville, TN 37914
Company Type: Division. **Ultimate Parent:**
TRW, Inc. **SIC:** 3625—Relays & Industrial
Controls.

★ 81263 ★   TRW Inc.
Transportation Electronics Div.
5008 N. National Dr.
Knoxville, TN 37914
Company Type: Division. **Ultimate Parent:**
TRW, Inc. **SIC:** 3625—Relays & Industrial
Controls.

★ 81264 ★   Trw Inc. Carr
Knoxville
5008 N. National Dr.
Knoxville, TN 37914
Ultimate Parent: TRW, Inc. **SIC:** 3625—
Relays & Industrial Controls.

★ 81265 ★   Underwriters
Adjusting Co.
9041 Executive Park Dr.
Knoxville, TN 37923
(615)693-6461
Ultimate Parent: Continental. **SIC:** 6411—
Insurance Agents, Brokers & Service.

★ 81266 ★   Union Oil Co.
4436 Royalview Rd.
Knoxville, TN 37921
(615)637-0671
Ultimate Parent: Unocal Corp. **SIC:** 5172—
Petroleum Products Nec.

★ 81267 ★   Union Planters
National Bank
302 N. Peters Rd.
Knoxville, TN 37923
(615)531-4862
Location Type: Branch office. **Ultimate
Parent:** Union Planters Corp. **SIC:** 6021—
National Commercial Banks.

★ 81268 ★   Union Planters
National Bank
5511 Clinton Hwy.
Knoxville, TN 37912-3489
(615)694-5515
Location Type: Branch office. **Ultimate
Parent:** Union Planters Corp. **SIC:** 6021—
National Commercial Banks.

★ 81269 ★   Union Planters
National Bank
8517 Kingston Pke.
Knoxville, TN 37919-5381
(615)693-7000
Location Type: Branch office. **Ultimate
Parent:** Union Planters Corp. **SIC:** 6021—
National Commercial Banks.

★ 81270 ★   Union Planters
National Bank
4600 Kingston Pke.
Knoxville, TN 37919-5230
(615)558-3592
Location Type: Branch office. **Ultimate
Parent:** Union Planters Corp. **SIC:** 6021—
National Commercial Banks.

★ 81271 ★   Union Planters
National Bank
5221 Broadway NE
Knoxville, TN 37918-2389
(615)694-5511
Location Type: Branch office. **Ultimate
Parent:** Union Planters Corp. **SIC:** 6021—
National Commercial Banks.

★ 81272 ★   Union Planters
National Bank
900 S. Gay St.
Knoxville, TN 37902-1810
(615)549-2239
Location Type: Branch office. **Ultimate
Parent:** Union Planters Corp. **SIC:** 6021—
National Commercial Banks.

★ 81273 ★   Wang Laboratories
Inc.
2 Colony Park
Knoxville, TN 37909
(615)588-1308
Ultimate Parent: Wang Laboratories, Inc.
SIC: 5046—Commercial Equipment Nec.

★ 81274 ★   Western Auto Supply
Co. Inc.
4114 Chapman Hwy.
Knoxville, TN 37920
(615)573-7934
Ultimate Parent: Sears Roebuck & Co.
SIC: 5531—Automobile & Home Supply
Stores.

★ 81275 ★   Whitle
Communications LP
333 Main Ave.
Knoxville, TN 37902
(615)595-5300 **Fax:** (615)595-5898
Officer: Chris Whittle, CEO. **Ultimate
Parent:** Time Warner, Inc. **Employee
Count:** 1089. **Sales:** 200 M.

★ 81276 ★   Whittle
Communications
333 Main
Knoxville, TN 37919
(615)595-5436
Ultimate Parent: Time Warner, Inc.

★ 81277 ★   Xerox Corp.
320 N. Cedar Bluff Rd.
Knoxville, TN 37923
(615)690-4071
Officer: Jack Waters, Manager. **Ultimate
Parent:** Xerox Corp. **SIC:** 3663—Radio &
T.V. Communications Equipment.

★ 81278 ★   Vulcan Materials Co.
3001 Alcoa Hwy.
Knoxville., TN 37920
(615)577-2511
Ultimate Parent: Vulcan Materials Co. **SIC:**
1429—Crushed & Broken Stone Nec.

★ 81279 ★   Vulcan Materials Co.
405 W. Oldham Ave.
Knoxville., TN 37917
(615)546-3800
Ultimate Parent: Vulcan Materials Co. **SIC:**
5211—Lumber & Other Building Materials.

Kodak

★ 81280 ★   Heil Co.
Dumplin Valley Rd.
Kodak, TN 37764
(615)933-4111
Ultimate Parent: Dow Chemical Co. USA.
SIC: 5013—Motor Vehicle Supplies & New
Parts.

La Vergne

★ 81281 ★ Canteen Corp.
1415 Heil Quaker Blvd.
La Vergne, TN 37086
Ultimate Parent: Firstfed Financial Corp.
SIC: 5812—Eating Places; 5962—
Merchandising Machine Operators.

★ 81282 ★ Hennessey Industries
Hennessy/Coats Div.
1601 J.P. Hennessy Dr.
La Vergne, TN 37086
(615)641-7533
Company Type: Subsidiary. Officer: Louis
Alvarez, President. Ultimate Parent:
Danaher Corp. SIC: 3559—Special Industry
Machinery Nec.

★ 81283 ★ Hennessy Industries,
Inc.
Coast Operations
1601 J.P. Hennessy Dr.
La Vergne, TN 37086-3524
(615)641-7533 (800)688-6359 Fax:
(615)793-5104
Company Type: Subsidiary. Officer: Bob
Tennison, President. Ultimate Parent:
Danaher Corp. SIC: 3714—Motor Vehicle
Parts & Accessories. Sales: 100000000 M.

★ 81284 ★ Teledyne Firth
Sterling
1 Teledyne Pl. Interchange City Industrial
Park
La Vergne, TN 37086
Ultimate Parent: Teledyne. SIC: 3545—
Machine Tool Accessories.

★ 81285 ★ Whirlpool Corp.
1714 Heil Quaker Blvd.
La Vergne, TN 37086
Ultimate Parent: Whirlpool Corp. SIC:
3585—Refrigeration & Heating Equipment;
3632—Household Refrigerators & Freezers;
3639—Household Appliances Nec.

Lafayette

★ 81286 ★ American Greetings
Corp.
PO Box 315
Lafayette, TN 37083-0315
(615)666-4607
Officer: John Spencer. Ultimate Parent:
American Greetings. SIC: 2677—Envelopes;
2678—Stationery Products; 5112—
Stationery & Office Supplies.

LaVergne

★ 81287 ★ First Tennessee Bank
NA
5211 Murfreesboro Rd.
LaVergne, TN 37086-2715
(615)793-6821
Location Type: Branch office. Ultimate
Parent: First Tennessee National Corp.
SIC: 6021—National Commercial Banks.

Lawrenceburg

★ 81288 ★ Coors Packaging Co.
2006 Liberty Ave.
Lawrenceburg, TN 38464
Ultimate Parent: Adolph Coors. SIC:
2657—Folding Paperboard Boxes.

★ 81289 ★ Graphic Packaging
Corp.
2006 Liberty Ave.
Lawrenceburg, TN 38464
Ultimate Parent: Adolph Coors. SIC:
2657—Folding Paperboard Boxes.

★ 81290 ★ Kroger Co.
1700 N. Locust Ave.
Lawrenceburg, TN 38464
(615)766-0029
Ultimate Parent: Kroger. SIC: 5411—
Grocery Stores.

★ 81291 ★ McDonald's
Hamburgers
1216 N. Locust Ave.
Lawrenceburg, TN 38464
(615)762-2454
Ultimate Parent: McDonald's. SIC: 5812—
Eating Places.

★ 81292 ★ Ucar Carbon Co. Inc.
Hwy. 43 South
Lawrenceburg, TN 38464
Ultimate Parent: Union Carbide Corp. SIC:
3624—Carbon & Graphite Products.

★ 81293 ★ Union Carbide Corp.
Hwy. 43, South
Lawrenceburg, TN 38464
Ultimate Parent: Union Carbide Corp. SIC:
3624—Carbon & Graphite Products.

★ 81294 ★ Wal-Mart Stores Inc.
2024 N. Locust Ave.
Lawrenceburg, TN 38464
(615)762-0015
Ultimate Parent: Wal-Mart Stores, Inc. SIC:
5331—Variety Stores.

Lebanon

★ 81295 ★ First American
National Bank
1102 W. Main St.
Lebanon, TN 37087-3268
(615)449-4400
Location Type: Branch office. Ultimate
Parent: First American Corp. SIC: 6021—
National Commercial Banks.

★ 81296 ★ First American
National Bank
1418B W. Main St.
Lebanon, TN 37087-3161
(615)449-5115
Location Type: Branch office. Ultimate
Parent: First American Corp. SIC: 6021—
National Commercial Banks.

★ 81297 ★ First Tennessee Bank
NA
E. Main St.
Lebanon, TN 37087-3113
(615)237-3391
Location Type: Branch office. Ultimate
Parent: First Tennessee National Corp.
SIC: 6021—National Commercial Banks.

★ 81298 ★ First Tennessee Bank
NA
249 W. Main St.
Lebanon, TN 37087-2732
(615)444-2743
Location Type: Branch office. Ultimate
Parent: First Tennessee National Corp.
SIC: 6021—National Commercial Banks.

★ 81299 ★ First Tennessee Bank
NA
1445 1/2 W. Main St.
Lebanon, TN 37087-3113
(615)449-3932
Location Type: Branch office. Ultimate
Parent: First Tennessee National Corp.
SIC: 6021—National Commercial Banks.

★ 81300 ★ Hartman Luggage Co.
Hartman Dr.
Lebanon, TN 37087
(615)444-5000
Officer: Dorothy Penix, President. Ultimate
Parent: Brown-Forman. SIC: 3161—
Luggage; 3172—Personal Leather Goods
Nec.

★ 81301 ★ Hartmann Luggage
Co.
PO Box 550
Lebanon, TN 37088-0550
(615)444-5000
Location Type: Branch office. Officer:
Dorothy Penix. Ultimate Parent:
Brown-Forman. SIC: 3172—Personal
Leather Goods Nec; 3161—Luggage.

★ 81302 ★ Kroger Co.
W. Main
Lebanon, TN 37087
(615)444-2124
Ultimate Parent: Kroger. SIC: 5411—
Grocery Stores.

★ 81303 ★ Lebanon Bank
249 W. Main St.
Lebanon, TN 37087
(615)444-2743
Ultimate Parent: First Tennessee National
Corp. SIC: 6022—State Commercial Banks.

★ 81304 ★ Lebanon Bank
Western Plz.
Lebanon, TN 37087
(615)444-8313
Ultimate Parent: First Tennessee National
Corp. SIC: 6022—State Commercial Banks.

★ 81305 ★ Lebanon Bank
127 Public Sq.
Lebanon, TN 37087
(615)444-0760
Ultimate Parent: First Tennessee National
Corp. SIC: 6022—State Commercial Banks.

★ 81306 ★ Payless Shoe Source
1445 Hwy. 109 N
Lebanon, TN 37087
(615)444-1773
Ultimate Parent: May Department Stores.
SIC: 5661—Shoe Stores.

★ 81307 ★ People's Bank
240 W. Main St.
Lebanon, TN 37087
(615)444-6305
Ultimate Parent: People's Bank. SIC:
6022—State Commercial Banks.

★ 81308 ★ Ryder Truck Rental-
One Way
1430 W. Main St.
Lebanon, TN 37087
(615)449-0226
Ultimate Parent: Ryder System. SIC:
7359—Equipment Rental & Leasing Nec.

★ 81309 ★ Texas Boot Co.
Forest Ave.
Lebanon, TN 37087
(615)444-5440
Ultimate Parent: United States Shoe. SIC:
5661—Shoe Stores.

★ 81310 ★ Trailways Bus Lines
Lebann Terminal 54
Lebanon, TN 37087
(615)444-2300
Ultimate Parent: Greyhound Lines Inc. SIC:
4111—Local & Suburban Transit; 4131—
Intercity & Rural Bus Transportation; 4142—
Bus Charter Service Except Local.

★ 81311 ★ TRW Commercial
Steering
1103 W. Baddour Pky.
Lebanon, TN 37087
(615)444-6110
Officer: Ken Caldwell, Manager. Ultimate
Parent: TRW, Inc. SIC: 3714—Motor
Vehicle Parts & Accessories.

★ 81312 ★ TRW Inc.
Commercial Steering Div.
1103 Baddour Pky.
Lebanon, TN 37087
Company Type: Division. Ultimate Parent:
TRW, Inc. SIC: 3714—Motor Vehicle Parts
& Accessories.

★ 81313 ★ TRW Inc.
Ross Gear Inc.
1103 Baddour Pky.
Lebanon, TN 37088-0250
Company Type: Division. Ultimate Parent:
TRW, Inc. SIC: 3714—Motor Vehicle Parts
& Accessories.

★ 81314 ★ Union Planters
National Bank
1436 W. Main St.
Lebanon, TN 37087-3114
(615)726-4321
Location Type: Branch office. Ultimate
Parent: Union Planters Corp. SIC: 6021—
National Commercial Banks.

★ 81315 ★ Union Planters
National Bank
214 N. Cumberland
Lebanon, TN 37087-2719
(615)726-4320
Location Type: Branch office. Ultimate
Parent: Union Planters Corp. SIC: 6021—
National Commercial Banks.

★ 81316 ★ Wal-Mart Stores Inc.
E Main Office Buildi
Lebanon, TN 37087
(615)444-4160
Ultimate Parent: Wal-Mart Stores, Inc. SIC:
5311—Department Stores.

★ 81317 ★ Wal-Mart Stores Inc.
W. Main
Lebanon, TN 37087
(615)449-0611
Ultimate Parent: Wal-Mart Stores, Inc. SIC:
5122—Drugs, Proprietaries & Sundries.

Lenoir City

★ 81318 ★ Armstar
307 Industrial Park Blvd.
Lenoir City, TN 37771
Ultimate Parent: Armstrong World
Industries. SIC: 3299—Nonmetallic Mineral
Products Nec.

★ 81319 ★ Armstar
307 Industrial Blvd.
Lenoir City, TN 37771
Ultimate Parent: Armstrong World
Industries. SIC: 3299—Nonmetallic Mineral
Products Nec.

★ 81320 ★ Camp Hosiery Inc.
213 Grand St.
PO Box 370
Lenoir City, TN 37771
Ultimate Parent: Fruit of the Loom. SIC:
2252—Hosiery Nec.

★ 81321 ★ First American
National Bank
805 E. Broadway
Lenoir City, TN 37771-3014
(615)981-3640
Location Type: Branch office. Ultimate
Parent: First American Corp. SIC: 6021—
National Commercial Banks.

★ 81322 ★ Quazite
2911 Industrial Pk. Blvd.
Lenoir City, TN 37771
Ultimate Parent: Shell Oil Co. SIC: 3089—
Plastics Products Nec.

★ 81323 ★ Quazite
300 Industrial Pk. Blvd.
Lenoir City, TN 37771
Ultimate Parent: Shell Oil Co. SIC: 3089—
Plastics Products Nec.

★ 81324 ★ Trailways Bus Lines
A St.
Lenoir City, TN 37771
(615)986-5393
Ultimate Parent: Greyhound Lines Inc. SIC:
4131—Intercity & Rural Bus Transportation;
4111—Local & Suburban Transit; 4142—
Bus Charter Service Except Local.

★ 81325 ★ Wal-Mart Stores Inc.
Hwy. 95
Lenoir City, TN 37771
(615)986-6502
Ultimate Parent: Wal-Mart Stores, Inc. SIC:
5311—Department Stores.

Lewisburg

★ 81326 ★ Kroger Co.
629 2nd Aven
Lewisburg, TN 37091
(615)359-4849
Ultimate Parent: Kroger. SIC: 5411—
Grocery Stores.

★ 81327 ★ Peoples & Union
Bank
2nd Ave. S
Lewisburg, TN 37091
Location Type: Branch office. Ultimate
Parent: First Tennessee National Corp.
SIC: 6021—National Commercial Banks.

★ 81328 ★ Peoples & Union
Bank
PO Box 2277
Lewisburg, TN 37091-1277
Location Type: Headquarters. Ultimate
Parent: First Tennessee National Corp.
SIC: 6021—National Commercial Banks.

★ 81329 ★ Peoples & Union
Bank
111 W. Commerce St.
Lewisburg, TN 37091-3343
(615)359-6222
Location Type: Branch office. Ultimate
Parent: First Tennessee National Corp.
SIC: 6021—National Commercial Banks.

★ 81330 ★   **Peoples & Union Bank**
260 N. Ellington Pky.
Lewisburg, TN 37091-2835
(615)359-6222
Location Type: Headquarters. **Ultimate Parent:** First Tennessee National Corp. **SIC:** 6021—National Commercial Banks.

★ 81331 ★   **Teledyne Lewisburg**
1425 Higgs Rd.
Lewisburg, TN 37091-0326
Ultimate Parent: Teledyne. **SIC:** 3571—Electronic Computers; 3679—Electronic Components Nec; 3699—Electrical Equipment & Supplies Nec.

★ 81332 ★   **Teledyne Monarch Rubber Lewisburg**
1701 Childress Rd.
Lewisburg, TN 37091
Ultimate Parent: Teledyne. **SIC:** 3069—Fabricated Rubber Products Nec.

★ 81333 ★   **Trailways Bus Lines**
147 E. Commerce St.
Lewisburg, TN 37091
(615)359-2258
Ultimate Parent: Greyhound Lines Inc. **SIC:** 4131—Intercity & Rural Bus Transportation; 4111—Local & Suburban Transit; 4142—Bus Charter Service Except Local.

Lexington

★ 81334 ★   **Anchor Swan Inc.**
Anchor Swan Div.
1921 N. Broad St.
Lexington, TN 38351
Company Type: Division. **Ultimate Parent:** Mark IV Industries. **SIC:** 3052—Rubber & Plastics Hose & Belting.

★ 81335 ★   **Coltec Industries**
Delavan Commercial Products
20 Delavan Dr.
Lexington, TN 38351
(901)968-8152 **Fax:** (901)968-5085
Officer: Mark H. Bartel, President. **Ultimate Parent:** Coltec Industries.

★ 81336 ★   **Daniel Radiator Corp.**
517 W. Church St.
Lexington, TN 38351
Ultimate Parent: Handy & Harman. **SIC:** 3714—Motor Vehicle Parts & Accessories; 5013—Motor Vehicle Supplies & New Parts.

★ 81337 ★   **Harvard Industries**
Anchor Swan
1900 N. Broad St.
Lexington, TN 38351
Company Type: Division. **Ultimate Parent:** Harvard Industries. **SIC:** 3052—Rubber & Plastics Hose & Belting.

★ 81338 ★   **Johnson Controls Inc.**
659 Natchez Trace Dr.
Lexington, TN 38351
Ultimate Parent: Johnson Controls Inc. **SIC:** 3465—Automotive Stampings; 3471—Plating & Polishing; 3499—Fabricated Metal Products Nec.

★ 81339 ★   **Lexington Tube Co.**
517 W. Church St.
Lexington, TN 38351
Ultimate Parent: Handy & Harman. **SIC:** 3714—Motor Vehicle Parts & Accessories; 5013—Motor Vehicle Supplies & New Parts.

★ 81340 ★   **Magnetek/Century Electric**
659 Natchez Trace Dr. N.
Lexington, TN 38351-4125
(901)968-4274
Officer: Ted Thiele. **Ultimate Parent:** Magnetek Inc. **SIC:** 3621—Motors & Generators.

★ 81341 ★   **Magnetek Century Electric Inc.**
659 Natchez Trace Dr.
Lexington, TN 38351
Ultimate Parent: Magnetek Inc. **SIC:** 3621—Motors & Generators.

★ 81342 ★   **Omc Lexington**
200 Robert Wallace Dr.
Lexington, TN 38351-0200
Ultimate Parent: Outboard Marine. **SIC:** 3519—Internal Combustion Engines Nec.

★ 81343 ★   **Omc Lexington**
Robert Wallace Dr.
Lexington, TN 38351
Ultimate Parent: Outboard Marine. **SIC:** 3519—Internal Combustion Engines Nec.

★ 81344 ★   **United Technologies**
Automotive Engineered Systems Div.
228 Rush St.
Lexington, TN 38351
Company Type: Division. **Ultimate Parent:** United Technologies. **SIC:** 3451—Screw Machine Products.

★ 81345 ★   **United Technologies Automotive Inc.**
40 Rush St.
Lexington, TN 38351
Ultimate Parent: United Technologies. **SIC:** 3451—Screw Machine Products.

Linden

★ 81346 ★   **Johnson Controls Inc.**
Squirrel Hollow Dr.
Linden, TN 37096
Ultimate Parent: Johnson & Johnson. **SIC:** 3465—Automotive Stampings; 3471—Plating & Polishing; 3714—Motor Vehicle Parts & Accessories.

Livingston

★ 81347 ★   **Aeroquip Corp.**
Industrial Park
Livingston, TN 38570
(615)823-7381
Officer: William Sweitzer, Manager. **Ultimate Parent:** Trinova Corp. **SIC:** 3089—Plastics Products Nec; 3714—Motor Vehicle Parts & Accessories.

★ 81348 ★   **American Savings Bank**
808 W. Main St.
Livingston, TN 38570-1722
(615)823-5648
Officer: Mike Qualls, Chairmard of the Board & President. **Ultimate Parent:** CSF Holdings. **SIC:** 6036—Savings Institutions Except Federal. **Employee Count:** 12.

★ 81349 ★   **Fayette Tubular Products Inc.**
H C 85
Livingston, TN 38570
(615)823-1284
Officer: Danny Kirby, Manager. **Ultimate Parent:** Danaher Corp. **SIC:** 3714—Motor Vehicle Parts & Accessories.

Loudon

★ 81350 ★   **Arvin Industries Inc.**
Maremount Exhaust Products Div.
2400 Industrial Park Blvd.
Loudon, TN 37774
(615)458-7400 **Fax:** (615)458-7415
Company Type: Division. **Officer:** Larry Van Epps, President. **Ultimate Parent:** Arvin Industries Inc.

★ 81351 ★   **Arvin Industries Inc.**
Maremount Exhaust Systems Product Div.
2400 Industrial Park Blvd.
Loudon, TN 37774
(615)458-7400 **Fax:** (615)458-7414
Company Type: Division. **Officer:** Larry Van Epps, President. **Ultimate Parent:** Arvin Industries Inc. **SIC:** 3714—Motor Vehicle Parts & Accessories; 5013—Motor Vehicle Supplies & New Parts.

★ 81352 ★   **Liquid Carbonic Carbon Dioxide Corp.**
139 Blair Bend Dr.
Loudon, TN 37774
Ultimate Parent: CBI Industries, Inc. **SIC:** 2813—Industrial Gases.

★ 81353 ★   **Maremont Corp.**
Loudon Industrial Park
Loudon, TN 37774
Ultimate Parent: Arvin Industries Inc.

★ 81354 ★   **Maremont Exhaust Products, Inc.**
2400 Industrial Park Blvd.
Loudon, TN 37774-1049
(615)458-7400
Location Type: Headquarters. **Officer:** James W. Thomas. **Ultimate Parent:** Arvin Industries Inc. **SIC:** 8734—Testing

Laboratories; 3495—Wire Springs; 3593—Fluid Power Cylinders & Actuators; 3714—Motor Vehicle Parts & Accessories; 4212—Local Trucking Without Storage; 5013—Motor Vehicle Supplies & New Parts.

★ 81355 ★   **Maremont Exhaust System**
2400 Industrial Park
Loudon, TN 37774
(615)458-4681
Company Type: Division. **Location Type:** Plant. **Ultimate Parent:** Arvin Industries Inc. **SIC:** 3714—Motor Vehicle Parts & Accessories.

★ 81356 ★   **Maremont Exhaust Systems**
Loudon Industrial Park
Loudon, TN 37774
Ultimate Parent: Arvin Industries Inc. **SIC:** 3714—Motor Vehicle Parts & Accessories.

★ 81357 ★   **Rite Aid Discount Pharmacy**
Loudon Plz.
Loudon, TN 37774
(615)458-6241
Ultimate Parent: Rite Aid. **SIC:** 5912—Drug Stores & Proprietary Stores.

Lowland

★ 81358 ★   **BASF Corp.**
Hwy. 160
Lowland, TN 37778
Ultimate Parent: BASF Corp. **SIC:** 2821—Plastics Materials & Resins; 2823—Cellulosic Manmade Fibers; 2824—Organic Fibers—Noncellulosic.

★ 81359 ★   **BASF Corp.**
Fibers
Hwy. 160
Lowland, TN 37778-0301
Company Type: Division. **Ultimate Parent:** BASF Corp. **SIC:** 2821—Plastics Materials & Resins; 2823—Cellulosic Manmade Fibers; 2824—Organic Fibers—Noncellulosic.

★ 81360 ★   **BASF Corp.**
Fibers
Hwy. 160
Lowland, TN 37778
Company Type: Division. **Ultimate Parent:** BASF Corp. **SIC:** 2821—Plastics Materials & Resins.

★ 81361 ★   **BASF Corp.**
Fibers Division
Lowland, TN 37779
(615)586-3110
Company Type: Division. **Location Type:** Branch office. **Ultimate Parent:** BASF Corp. **SIC:** 5199—Nondurable Goods Nec.

★ 81362 ★   **BASF Corp.**
Fibers Division
wy. 160
Lowland, TN 37778
(615)586-3110
Company Type: Division. **Officer:** Phil C. Greeson. **Ultimate Parent:** BASF Corp. **SIC:** 2824—Organic Fibers—Noncellulosic; 2281—Yarn Spinning Mills.

★ 81363 ★   **BASF Fibers**
Hwy. 160
Lowland, TN 37778
(615)586-3110
Officer: Thil Greeson, Manager. **Ultimate Parent:** BASF Corp. **SIC:** 2281—Yarn Spinning Mills; 2824—Organic Fibers—Noncellulosic.

Lyles

★ 81364 ★   **Coast to Coast Home & Auto**
207 E. Public Sq.
Lyles, TN 37098
(615)729-2173
Ultimate Parent: Servistar Corp. **SIC:** 5531—Automobile & Home Supply Stores.

Lynchburg

★ 81365 ★   **Jack Daniel Distillery**
Hwy. 55 PO Box 199
Lynchburg, TN 37352
Ultimate Parent: Brown-Forman. **SIC:** 2085—Distilled & Blended Liquors.

★ 81366 ★   **Jack Daniel Distillery**
PO Box 199
Lynchburg, TN 37352-0199
(615)759-4221
Officer: Don Kelley. **Ultimate Parent:** Brown-Forman. **SIC:** 2085—Distilled & Blended Liquors.

★ 81367 ★   **Jack Daniel Distillery**
Rte. 1 & Hwy. 55
Lynchburg, TN 37352
(615)759-4221
Officer: Lem Motlow, Owner. **Ultimate Parent:** Brown-Forman. **SIC:** 2085—Distilled & Blended Liquors.

★ 81368 ★   **Jack Daniel Distillery Lem Motlow Prop.**
Hwy. 50 PO Box 199
Lynchburg, TN 37352
Ultimate Parent: Brown-Forman. **SIC:** 2085—Distilled & Blended Liquors.

★ 81369 ★   **Jack Daniel Distillery Lem Motlow Prop. Inc.**
Hwy. 55
Lynchburg, TN 37352
Ultimate Parent: Brown-Forman. **SIC:** 2085—Distilled & Blended Liquors.

Madison

★ 81370 ★   **American General Finance**
121 Gallatin Rd. N
Madison, TN 37115-3701
(615)865-2485
Officer: Wanda Atkins. **Ultimate Parent:** American General Corp. **SIC:** 6141—Personal Credit Institutions; 6162—Mortgage Bankers & Correspondents.

★ 81371 ★   **American General Finance Inc.**
121 Gallatin Rd. N
Madison, TN 37115-3701
(615)865-2485
Location Type: Branch office. **Officer:** Wanda Atkins. **Ultimate Parent:** American General Corp. **SIC:** 6141—Personal Credit Institutions; 6162—Mortgage Bankers & Correspondents.

★ 81372 ★   **Dean Witter Reynolds Inc.**
1210 Gallatin Rd.
Madison, TN 37115
(615)865-1520
Location Type: Branch office. **Ultimate Parent:** Dean Witter Discover. **SIC:** 6211—Security Brokers & Dealers.

★ 81373 ★   **Eckerd Drugs**
Windlands Ctr.
Madison, TN 37115
(615)832-5191
Ultimate Parent: Eckerd Corp. **SIC:** 5912—Drug Stores & Proprietary Stores.

★ 81374 ★   **Eckerd Drugs**
1219 Gallatin Rd.
Madison, TN 37115
(615)865-8158
Ultimate Parent: Eckerd Corp. **SIC:** 5912—Drug Stores & Proprietary Stores.

★ 81375 ★   **First American National Bank**
500 Gallatin Rd.
Madison, TN 37115-3708
(615)748-2716
Location Type: Branch office. **Ultimate Parent:** First American Corp. **SIC:** 6021—National Commercial Banks.

★ 81376 ★   **First Tennesse Bank NA**
1515 N. Gallatin Rd.
Madison, TN 37115
(615)734-6125
Location Type: Branch office. **Ultimate Parent:** First Tennessee National Corp. **SIC:** 6021—National Commercial Banks.

★ 81377 ★   **Home Depot**
1584 Gallatin Rd. N
Madison, TN 37115
(615)865-9600
Ultimate Parent: Home Depot. **SIC:** 5039—Construction Materials Nec.

★ 81378 ★ **Kroger Co.**
200 Gallatin Rd.
Madison, TN 37115
(615)865-7956
Ultimate Parent: Kroger. **SIC:** 5411—
Grocery Stores.

★ 81379 ★ **Peterbilt Motors Co.**
430 Myatt Dr.
Madison, TN 37115
Ultimate Parent: Paccar. **SIC:** 3711—Motor
Vehicles & Car Bodies; 3713—Truck & Bus
Bodies.

★ 81380 ★ **Service Merchandise**
2130 Gallatin Rd. N
Madison, TN 37115
(615)851-6041
Ultimate Parent: Service Merchandise Co.,
Inc. **SIC:** 5399—Miscellaneous General
Merchandise Store.

★ 81381 ★ **Transamerica
Occidental Life Insurance**
233 PO Box
Madison, TN 37116
(615)865-8117
Ultimate Parent: Transamerica Occidental
Life Insurance. **SIC:** 6411—Insurance
Agents, Brokers & Service.

★ 81382 ★ **Union Planters
National Bank**
1009 Gallatin Rd.
Madison, TN 37115-4680
(615)726-4203
Location Type: Branch office. **Ultimate
Parent:** Union Planters Corp. **SIC:** 6021—
National Commercial Banks.

★ 81383 ★ **Union Planters
National Bank**
601 Gallatin Pke. N.
Madison, TN 37115-2808
(615)868-2265
Location Type: Branch office. **Ultimate
Parent:** Union Planters Corp. **SIC:** 6021—
National Commercial Banks.

★ 81384 ★ **Valvoline Oil Change**
1837 Gallatin Rd. N
Madison, TN 37115
(615)851-0315
Ultimate Parent: Ashland Oil.

Madisonville

★ 81385 ★ **Bank of Madisonville**
205 Warren St.
Madisonville, TN 37354-0547
(615)442-4511 **Fax:** (615)442-6645
Company Type: Subsidiary. **Officer:** Alfred
Mason, Chairman of the Board. **Ultimate
Parent:** First Virginia Banks Inc. **SIC:**
6022—State Commercial Banks.

★ 81386 ★ **Bank of Madisonville**
205 Warren St.
Madisonville, TN 37354-1049
(615)442-4511
Company Type: Subsidiary. **Officer:** Dr.
Houston Lowry, Chairman of the Board.
Ultimate Parent: First Virginia Banks Inc.
SIC: 6022—State Commercial Banks.
Employee Count: 55.

★ 81387 ★ **Ryder Truck Rental**
428 Hwy. 68
Madisonville, TN 37354
(615)442-5539
Ultimate Parent: Ryder System. **SIC:**
7389—Business Services Nec.

★ 81388 ★ **Sea Ray Boats Inc.
Cherokee Cove**
200 Sea Ray Circle
Madisonville, TN 37354
Ultimate Parent: Brunswick Corp. **SIC:**
3732—Boat Building & Repairing.

★ 81389 ★ **Wal-Mart Stores Inc.**
801 Hwy. 411 Byp P
Madisonville, TN 37354
(615)442-5237
Ultimate Parent: Wal-Mart Stores, Inc. **SIC:**
5311—Department Stores.

Manchester

★ 81390 ★ **Batesville Casket Co.**
PO Box 94 Monogard Rd.
Manchester, TN 37355
Ultimate Parent: Hillenbrand Industries.
SIC: 3995—Burial Caskets.

★ 81391 ★ **Batesville Casket Co.
Inc.**
PO Box 94 Monogard Rd.
Manchester, TN 37355
Ultimate Parent: Hillenbrand Industries.
SIC: 3995—Burial Caskets.

★ 81392 ★ **Greyhound Bus Lines**
600 Hillsboro Blvd.
Manchester, TN 37355
(615)728-9703
Ultimate Parent: Greyhound Lines Inc. **SIC:**
4111—Local & Suburban Transit; 4131—
Intercity & Rural Bus Transportation; 4142—
Bus Charter Service Except Local.

★ 81393 ★ **McDonald's
Hamburgers**
Hwy. 41
Manchester, TN 37355
(615)728-0726
Ultimate Parent: McDonald's. **SIC:** 5812—
Eating Places.

★ 81394 ★ **Payless Shoe Source**
1802 N. Jackson
Manchester, TN 37355
(615)455-1303
Ultimate Parent: May Department Stores.
SIC: 5661—Shoe Stores.

★ 81395 ★ **Wal-Mart Stores Inc.**
Hwy. 41 S
Manchester, TN 37355
(615)728-6000
Ultimate Parent: Wal-Mart Stores, Inc. **SIC:**
5311—Department Stores.

Martin

★ 81396 ★ **Associated Milk
Producers Inc.**
Oklahoma
Martin, TN 38237
(901)587-2094
Ultimate Parent: Associated Milk Producers
Inc. **SIC:** 8734—Testing Laboratories.

★ 81397 ★ **Merchants State Bank**
115 Main St.
Martin, TN 38237-2444
(901)587-9569
Location Type: Branch office. **Ultimate
Parent:** Union Planters Corp. **SIC:** 6021—
National Commercial Banks.

★ 81398 ★ **Trailways Bus Lines**
Sharon Hwy.
Martin, TN 38237
(901)587-9004
Ultimate Parent: Greyhound Lines Inc. **SIC:**
4131—Intercity & Rural Bus Transportation;
4111—Local & Suburban Transit; 4142—
Bus Charter Service Except Local.

★ 81399 ★ **Underwriters
Adjusting Co.**
101 Todd St.
Martin, TN 38237
(901)587-5641
Ultimate Parent: Continental. **SIC:** 6411—
Insurance Agents, Brokers & Service.

★ 81400 ★ **Wal-Mart Stores Inc.**
Fulton Hwy.
Martin, TN 38237
(901)587-3871
Ultimate Parent: Wal-Mart Stores, Inc. **SIC:**
5311—Department Stores.

Maryville

★ 81401 ★ **Asarco Inc.**
101 E. Harper Ave.
Maryville, TN 37801-4036
(615)977-8027
Company Type: Branch. **Ultimate Parent:**
Asarco. **SIC:** 1499—Miscellaneous
Nonmetallic Minerals.

★ 81402 ★ **Eckerd Drugs**
100 Foothills Mall
Maryville, TN 37801
(615)983-3300
Ultimate Parent: Eckerd Corp. **SIC:** 5912—
Drug Stores & Proprietary Stores.

★ 81403 ★ **Emery Worldwide**
Knoxville Metro Airport
Maryville, TN 37801
(615)970-2675
Ultimate Parent: Consolidated Freightways.
SIC: 4512—Air Transportation—Scheduled.

★ 81404 ★ **First American
National Bank**
2214 Smoky Mountain Hwy.
Maryville, TN 37801-5341
(615)981-3516
Location Type: Branch office. **Ultimate
Parent:** First American Corp. **SIC:** 6021—
National Commercial Banks.

★ 81405 ★ **First American
National Bank**
1810 W. Broadway
Maryville, TN 37801
(615)981-3650
Location Type: Branch office. **Ultimate
Parent:** First American Corp. **SIC:** 6021—
National Commercial Banks.

★ 81406 ★ **First American
National Bank**
200 E. Broadway
Maryville, TN 37802
(615)981-3612
Location Type: Branch office. **Ultimate
Parent:** First American Corp. **SIC:** 6021—
National Commercial Banks.

★ 81407 ★ **First American
National Bank**
1957 E. Broadway
Maryville, TN 37801-2974
(615)981-3470
Location Type: Branch office. **Ultimate
Parent:** First American Corp. **SIC:** 6021—
National Commercial Banks.

★ 81408 ★ **First Federal Savings
Bank of Maryville**
1614 W. Broadway Ave.
Maryville, TN 37801-5652
(615)977-4140
Location Type: Branch office. **Ultimate
Parent:** Union Planters Corp. **SIC:** 6021—
National Commercial Banks.

★ 81409 ★ **First Federal Savings
Bank of Maryville**
333 E. Broadway Ave.
Maryville, TN 37801-2418
(615)983-3710 **Fax:** (615)681-6877
Location Type: Branch office. **Ultimate
Parent:** Union Planters Corp. **SIC:** 6021—
National Commercial Banks.

★ 81410 ★ **First Tennessee Bank
NA**
1766 W. Lamar Alexander Pky.
Maryville, TN 37801-5340
(615)977-5180
Location Type: Branch office. **Ultimate
Parent:** First Tennessee National Corp.
SIC: 6021—National Commercial Banks.

★ 81411 ★ **First Tennessee Bank
NA**
2217 E. Lamar Alexander Pky.
Maryville, TN 37801-5340
(615)977-5141
Location Type: Branch office. **Ultimate
Parent:** First Tennessee National Corp.
SIC: 6021—National Commercial Banks.

★ 81412 ★ **First Tennessee Bank
NA**
205 Cusick St.
Maryville, TN 37801-4938
(615)977-5161
Location Type: Branch office. **Ultimate
Parent:** First Tennessee National Corp.
SIC: 6021—National Commercial Banks.

★ 81413 ★ **First Tennessee Bank
NA**
1520 W. Broadway
Maryville, TN 37801-5650
(615)977-5121
Location Type: Branch office. **Ultimate
Parent:** First Tennessee National Corp.
SIC: 6021—National Commercial Banks.

★ 81414 ★ **First Tennessee Bank
NA**
101 W. Broadway
Maryville, TN 37801-4787
(615)977-5100
Location Type: Branch office. **Ultimate
Parent:** First Tennessee National Corp.
SIC: 6021—National Commercial Banks.

★ 81415 ★ **First Tennessee Bank
NA**
E. Lincoln Rd. & Broadway
Maryville, TN 37801-3034
(615)977-5500
Location Type: Branch office. **Ultimate
Parent:** First Tennessee National Corp.
SIC: 6021—National Commercial Banks.

★ 81416 ★ **Giant Food Market
Inc.**
Midland Shopping Ctr.
Maryville, TN 37801
(615)984-0411
Ultimate Parent: Giant Food. **SIC:** 5411—
Grocery Stores.

★ 81417 ★ **Lerner Shops**
Foothills Mall
Maryville, TN 37801
(615)984-7279
Ultimate Parent: Limited. **SIC:** 5621—
Women's Clothing Stores.

★ 81418 ★ **Payless Shoe Source**
Midland Shopping Ctr.
Maryville, TN 37801
(615)984-1720
Ultimate Parent: May Department Stores.
SIC: 5661—Shoe Stores.

★ 81419 ★ **Payless Shoe Source**
158 Foothills Mall Dr. 16
Maryville, TN 37801
(615)745-0810
Ultimate Parent: May Department Stores.
SIC: 5661—Shoe Stores.

★ 81420 ★ **Payless Shoesource**
158 Foothills Mall Dr. 16
Maryville, TN 37801
(615)745-0810
Ultimate Parent: May Department Stores.
SIC: 5661—Shoe Stores.

★ 81421 ★ **Payless Shoesource**
Midland Shopping Ctr.
Maryville, TN 37801
(615)984-1720
Ultimate Parent: May Department Stores.
SIC: 5661—Shoe Stores.

★ 81422 ★ **Quincy Family
Steakhouse**
Hwy. 129
Maryville, TN 37801
(615)983-2473
Ultimate Parent: Flagstar Co. **SIC:** 5812—
Eating Places.

★ 81423 ★ **Rubbermaid Office
Products Inc.**
1427 William Blount Dr.
Maryville, TN 37801-8249
Ultimate Parent: Rubbermaid. **SIC:** 3089—
Plastics Products Nec.

★ 81424 ★ **Union Electric Co.**
2530 Old Eagleton Rd.
Maryville, TN 37801
(615)984-1117
Ultimate Parent: Union Electric Co. **SIC:**
1731—Electrical Work.

★ 81425 ★ **Union Electric Co.**
644 Eagleton Rd.
Maryville, TN 37804
Ultimate Parent: Union Electric Co. **SIC:**
1731—Electrical Work.

★ 81426 ★ **Union Planters
National Bank**
201 S. Washington St.
Maryville, TN 37801-4000
(615)981-1403
Location Type: Branch office. **Ultimate
Parent:** Union Planters Corp. **SIC:** 6021—
National Commercial Banks.

★ 81427 ★ **Union Planters
National Bank**
137 Foothills Mall
Maryville, TN 37801-2315
(615)981-1402
Location Type: Branch office. **Ultimate
Parent:** Union Planters Corp. **SIC:** 6021—
National Commercial Banks.

★ 81428 ★ **Vulcan Materials Co.**
1965 S. Court St.
Maryville, TN 37801
(615)983-0163
Officer: Ken Ward, Manager. **Ultimate
Parent:** Vulcan Materials Co. **SIC:** 3281—
Cut Stone & Stone Products.

Maryville.

★ 81429 ★   Vulcan Materials Co.
Duncan Pike.
Maryville., TN 37801
(615)983-0163
Ultimate Parent: Vulcan Materials Co. SIC:
5039—Construction Materials Nec.

Mascot

★ 81430 ★   Asarco Inc.
Mascot, TN 37806
(615)933-4118
Ultimate Parent: Asarco. SIC: 1422—
Crushed & Broken Limestone.

Mc Kenzie

★ 81431 ★   Coast to Coast
Hardware
Mac Kenzie Shopping Plz.
Mc Kenzie, TN 38201
(901)352-2511
Ultimate Parent: Servistar Corp. SIC:
5251—Hardware Stores.

★ 81432 ★   Rite Aid Discount
Pharmacy
Mac Kenzie Shopping Plz.
Mc Kenzie, TN 38201
(901)352-9916
Ultimate Parent: Rite Aid. SIC: 5912—Drug
Stores & Proprietary Stores.

★ 81433 ★   Rite Aid Discount
Pharmacy
Hwy. 79
Mc Kenzie, TN 38201
(901)352-7744
Ultimate Parent: Rite Aid. SIC: 5912—Drug
Stores & Proprietary Stores.

Mc Minnville

★ 81434 ★   Exxon Stanton Oil Co.
725 Morrison St.
Mc Minnville, TN 37110
(615)473-2292
Ultimate Parent: Exxon. SIC: 5172—
Petroleum Products Nec.

★ 81435 ★   Greyhound Bus Lines
308 N. Spring St.
Mc Minnville, TN 37110
(615)473-2361
Ultimate Parent: Greyhound Lines Inc. SIC:
4131—Intercity & Rural Bus Transportation;
4111—Local & Suburban Transit; 4142—
Bus Charter Service Except Local.

★ 81436 ★   Magnetek Century
Electric
204 Red Rd.
Mc Minnville, TN 37110
Ultimate Parent: Magnetek Inc. SIC:
3621—Motors & Generators.

★ 81437 ★   Magnetek Century
Electric Inc.
204 Red Rd.
Mc Minnville, TN 37110
Ultimate Parent: Magnetek Inc. SIC:
3621—Motors & Generators.

★ 81438 ★   Oster Specialty
Prods.
Rte. 9 Box 541 Cadillac Ln.
Mc Minnville, TN 37110
Ultimate Parent: Sunbeam/Oster. SIC:
3634—Electric Housewares & Fans.

★ 81439 ★   Wal-Mart Stores Inc.
300 Mac Minnville Plz.
Mc Minnville, TN 37110
(615)473-4455
Ultimate Parent: Wal-Mart Stores, Inc. SIC:
5311—Department Stores.

★ 81440 ★   Wal-Mart Stores Inc.
Plaza Shopping Ctr.
Mc Minnville, TN 37110
(615)473-4451
Ultimate Parent: Wal-Mart Stores, Inc. SIC:
5912—Drug Stores & Proprietary Stores.

McMinnville

★ 81441 ★   APAC
Hwy. 56 S.
McMinnville, TN 37110
(615)473-3133
Officer: W.J. Tramel, Manager. Ultimate
Parent: Ashland Oil. SIC: 2951—Asphalt
Paving Mixtures & Blocks.

★ 81442 ★   First American
National Bank
313 W. Main St.
McMinnville, TN 37110-2519
(615)473-5524
Location Type: Branch office. Ultimate
Parent: First American Corp. SIC: 6021—
National Commercial Banks.

★ 81443 ★   First American
National Bank
171 New Smithville Hwy.
McMinnville, TN 37110-1644
(615)473-6641
Location Type: Branch office. Ultimate
Parent: First American Corp. SIC: 6021—
National Commercial Banks.

Memphis

★ 81444 ★   Abbott Laboratories
6750 Poplar Ave., Ste. 414
Memphis, TN 38138-7416
(901)753-5882
Officer: Tom Chavez. Ultimate Parent:
Abbott Laboratories. SIC: 8734—Testing
Laboratories.

★ 81445 ★   Aetna Life & Annuity
Co.
1355 Lynnfield Rd.
Memphis, TN 38119
(901)682-0023
Ultimate Parent: Aetna Life & Annuity. SIC:
6411—Insurance Agents, Brokers &
Service.

★ 81446 ★   Air Products &
Chemicals Inc.
326 E. Bodley St.
Memphis, TN 38106
Ultimate Parent: Air Products & Chemicals,
Inc. SIC: 2813—Industrial Gases.

★ 81447 ★   Air Products &
Chemicals Inc.
2541 Harbor
Memphis, TN 38106-1444
(901)947-1141
Location Type: Branch office. Officer:
Harold Wagner. Ultimate Parent: Air
Products & Chemicals, Inc. SIC: 3599—
Industrial Machinery Nec; 5047—Medical &
Hospital Equipment; 5084—Industrial
Machinery & Equipment; 5085—Industrial
Supplies; 5169—Chemicals & Allied
Products Nec.

★ 81448 ★   American Cyanamid
Co.
6645 Stage Rd., Se. 101
Memphis, TN 38134-3828
(901)388-9156
Officer: Jim Gibbs. Ultimate Parent:
American Cyanamid Co. SIC: 5169—
Chemicals & Allied Products Nec.

★ 81449 ★   American Cyanamid
Co.
65 Germantown Ct.
Memphis, TN 38125
(901)755-4000
Ultimate Parent: American Cyanamid Co.
SIC: 5169—Chemicals & Allied Products
Nec.

★ 81450 ★   American General
Finance
4297 Stage Rd.
Memphis, TN 38128-5706
(901)382-0390
Officer: Tammi R. Turman. Ultimate
Parent: American General Corp. SIC:
6141—Personal Credit Institutions; 6162—
Mortgage Bankers & Correspondents.

★ 81451 ★   American General
Finance
2861 Poplar Ave.
Memphis, TN 38111-2023
(901)327-6084
Location Type: Branch office. Officer:
Susan Clements. Ultimate Parent:
American General Corp. SIC: 6141—
Personal Credit Institutions; 6162—
Mortgage Bankers & Correspondents.

★ 81452 ★   American General
Finance
4095 American Way
Memphis, TN 38118-8302
(901)367-2966
Location Type: Branch office. Officer:
Gary Deason. Ultimate Parent: American
General Corp. SIC: 6141—Personal Credit
Institutions; 6162—Mortgage Bankers &
Correspondents.

★ 81453 ★   American General
Finance Inc.
5266 Summer Ave.
Memphis, TN 38122-4417
(901)683-8833
Location Type: Branch office. Officer: Jo
Anne Miller. Ultimate Parent: American
General Corp. SIC: 6141—Personal Credit
Institutions; 6162—Mortgage Bankers &
Correspondents.

★ 81454 ★   American General
Finance Inc.
5266 Summer Ave.
Memphis, TN 38122-4417
(901)683-8833
Location Type: Branch office. Officer: Jo
Anne Miller. Ultimate Parent: American
General Corp. SIC: 6141—Personal Credit
Institutions; 6162—Mortgage Bankers &
Correspondents.

★ 81455 ★   American General
Finance Inc.
4297 Stage Rd.
Memphis, TN 38128-5706
(901)382-0390
Location Type: Branch office. Officer:
Tammi R. Turman. Ultimate Parent:
American General Corp. SIC: 6141—
Personal Credit Institutions; 6162—
Mortgage Bankers & Correspondents.

★ 81456 ★   American General
Finance Inc.
2861 Poplar Ave.
Memphis, TN 38111-2023
(901)327-6084
Location Type: Branch office. Officer:
Susan Clements. Ultimate Parent:
American General Corp. SIC: 6141—
Personal Credit Institutions; 6162—
Mortgage Bankers & Correspondents.

★ 81457 ★   American General
Finance Inc.
4095 American Way
Memphis, TN 38118-8302
(901)367-2966
Location Type: Branch office. Officer:
Gary Deason. Ultimate Parent: American
General Corp. SIC: 6141—Personal Credit
Institutions; 6162—Mortgage Bankers &
Correspondents.

★ 81458 ★   Anchor Hocking Corp.
3637 Park Ave.
Memphis, TN 38111
(901)324-8484
Ultimate Parent: Newell. SIC: 5719—
Miscellaneous Home Furnishings Stores.

★ 81459 ★   APAC
1311 N. Mud Island Rd.
Memphis, TN
(901)523-2464
Officer: Nicholas Haynes, President.
Ultimate Parent: Ashland Oil. SIC: 2951—
Asphalt Paving Mixtures & Blocks.

★ 81460 ★   Arcadian Corp.
5790 Millington Rd.
Memphis, TN 38127
(901)357-3300
Officer: Hugh Haraway. Ultimate Parent:
Arcadian Corp. SIC: 6061—Federal Credit
Unions; 5169—Chemicals & Allied Products
Nec.

★ 81461 ★   Arcadian Corp.
6750 Poplar Ave., Ste. 600
Memphis, TN 38138-7419
(901)758-5200
Company Type: Headquarters. Officer: K.
James Cameaux. SIC: 2873—Nitrogenous
Fertilizers; 2874—Phosphatic Fertilizers;
2869—Industrial Organic Chemicals Nec;
6799—Investors Nec.

★ 81462 ★   Arcadian Corp.
6750 Poplar Ave. 600
Memphis, TN 38138
(901)334-1804
Ultimate Parent: Arcadian Corp. SIC:
5169—Chemicals & Allied Products Nec.

★ 81463 ★   Arcadian Corp.
5790 Old Millington Rd. PO Box 27147
Memphis, TN 38127
Ultimate Parent: Arcadian Corp. SIC:
2873—Nitrogenous Fertilizers; 2813—
Industrial Gases.

★ 81464 ★   Arcadian Fertilizer, LP
6750 Poplar Ave., Ste. 600
Memphis, TN 38138-7419
(901)758-5200
Location Type: Branch office. Ultimate
Parent: Arcadian Corp. SIC: 2873—
Nitrogenous Fertilizers; 2874—Phosphatic
Fertilizers; 2869—Industrial Organic
Chemicals Nec.

★ 81465 ★   Arcadian Partners
Ltd. Partnership
6750 Poplar Ave., Ste. 600
Memphis, TN 38138-7419
(901)758-5200
Ultimate Parent: Arcadian Corp. SIC:
2873—Nitrogenous Fertilizers; 2874—
Phosphatic Fertilizers; 2869—Industrial
Organic Chemicals Nec.

★ 81466 ★   Banana Republic
7615 W. Farmington Blvd.
Memphis, TN 38138
(901)765-1658
Ultimate Parent: GAP. SIC: 5651—Family
Clothing Stores.

★ 81467 ★   Banister Shoes
3536 Canada Rd.
Memphis, TN 38134
(901)386-0063
Ultimate Parent: United States Shoe. SIC:
5661—Shoe Stores.

★ 81468 ★   Banister Shoes
5100 Park Ave.
Memphis, TN 38117
(901)767-5666
Ultimate Parent: United States Shoe. SIC:
5661—Shoe Stores.

★ 81469 ★   BASF Corp.
Urethanes
3766 Hawks Hollow Cv.
Memphis, TN 38135-9486
(901)386-0004
Ultimate Parent: BASF Corp. SIC: 5169—
Chemicals & Allied Products Nec.

★ 81470 ★   Baxter Hospital
Supply
1721 Corporate Ave.
Memphis, TN 38132-1702
(901)396-5555
Ultimate Parent: Baxter International. SIC:
5047—Medical & Hospital Equipment.

★ 81471 ★   Bell Atlantic Business
Systems Services
2750 Colony Park Dr.
Memphis, TN 38118-2079
(901)366-1021
Company Type: Subsidiary. Location
Type: Branch office. Ultimate Parent: Bell
Atlantic Corp. SIC: 7378—Computer
Maintenance & Repair.

★ 81472 ★   Bemis Co.
1975 Latham St.
Memphis, TN 38106
(901)775-2530
Officer: Richard Scoble, Manager. Ultimate
Parent: Bemis Co., Inc. SIC: 2673—Bags—
Plastics, Laminated & Coated; 2674—
Bags—Uncoated Paper & Multiwall.

★ 81473 ★   BFI-Memphis
Recyclery Inc.
1245 Morehead St.
Memphis, TN 38107-1116
(901)525-0276
Ultimate Parent: Browning-Ferris
Industries. SIC: 4953—Refuse Systems.

★ 81474 ★   BFI Waste Systems
540 Rivergate Dr.
Memphis, TN 38109-2431
(901)948-1355
Ultimate Parent: Browning-Ferris
Industries. SIC: 4953—Refuse Systems.

★ 81475 ★ **BFI Waste Systems**
3840 Homewood Rd.
Memphis, TN 38118
(901)794-3800
Officer: Mark Brantley, Manager. **Ultimate Parent:** Browning-Ferris Industries. **SIC:** 3589—Service Industry Machinery Nec.

★ 81476 ★ **Blazer Financial Services**
181254 PO Box
Memphis, TN 38181
(901)942-1501
Ultimate Parent: Great Western Financial Corp. **SIC:** 6141—Personal Credit Institutions.

★ 81477 ★ **Blazer Financial Services**
5344 Flowering Peach Dr.
Memphis, TN 38115
(901)363-7530
Ultimate Parent: Great Western Financial Corp. **SIC:** 6062—State Credit Unions; 6141—Personal Credit Institutions.

★ 81478 ★ **Blazer Financial Services**
672 Waring Rd.
Memphis, TN 38122
(901)683-4576
Ultimate Parent: Great Western Financial Corp. **SIC:** 6141—Personal Credit Institutions.

★ 81479 ★ **Block Drug Co.**
2149 Harbor Ave.
Memphis, TN 38106
(901)948-3372
Ultimate Parent: Block Drug Co., Inc. **SIC:** 2844—Toilet Preparations.

★ 81480 ★ **Block Drug Co. Inc.**
2149 Harbor Ave.
Memphis, TN 38113
Ultimate Parent: Block Drug Co., Inc. **SIC:** 2834—Pharmaceutical Preparations; 2844—Toilet Preparations.

★ 81481 ★ **Block Drug Co. Inc.**
2070 Channel St.
Memphis, TN 38113
Ultimate Parent: Block Drug Co., Inc. **SIC:** 2834—Pharmaceutical Preparations.

★ 81482 ★ **Block Drug Co., Inc.**
PO Box 13167
Memphis, TN 38113-0167
(901)948-3372
Officer: Charles F. Craig. **Ultimate Parent:** Block Drug Co., Inc. **SIC:** 2844—Toilet Preparations.

★ 81483 ★ **Boatmen's Bank of Tennessee**
6060 Poplar St.
Memphis, TN 38119
(901)529-5900
Company Type: Subsidiary. **Officer:** Charles B. Dudley III, Chairman of the Board & CEO. **Ultimate Parent:** Boatmen's Bancshares. **SIC:** 6022—State Commercial Banks. **Employee Count:** 350.

★ 81484 ★ **Broadcasting Group**
803 Channel 3 Dr.
Memphis, TN 38103
(901)577-0100 **Fax:** (901)577-0198
Officer: C. Frank Roberts, President. **Ultimate Parent:** New York Times.

★ 81485 ★ **Brownell Electro Inc.**
4670 Shelby Dr., Ste. 101
Memphis, TN 38118
(901)795-8483
Location Type: Branch office. **Ultimate Parent:** Avnet. **SIC:** 5063—Electrical Apparatus & Equipment.

★ 81486 ★ **Buring Foods**
1837 Harbor Ave.
Memphis, TN 38113
Ultimate Parent: Sara Lee Corp. **SIC:** 2013—Sausages & Other Prepared Meats.

★ 81487 ★ **Burlington Air Express**
3180 Carrier St.
Memphis, TN 38116
(901)346-0206
Ultimate Parent: Pittston. **SIC:** 4513—Air Courier Services.

★ 81488 ★ **Burlington Coat Factory**
4075 Elvis Presley Blvd.
Memphis, TN 38116-5871
(901)396-2628
Officer: Donald Mitchell. **Ultimate Parent:** Burlington Industries, Equity. **SIC:** 5311—Department Stores; 5651—Family Clothing Stores; 5661—Shoe Stores.

★ 81489 ★ **Butler Paper**
4155 Getwell Rd.
Memphis, TN 38118-6904
(901)363-0363
Ultimate Parent: Alco Standard Corp. **SIC:** 5111—Printing & Writing Paper.

★ 81490 ★ **Butler Paper**
4155 Getwell Rd.
Memphis, TN 38118-6904
(901)363-0363
Ultimate Parent: Alco Standard Corp. **SIC:** 5111—Printing & Writing Paper.

★ 81491 ★ **Cardiac Pacemakers Inc.**
8 N. 3rd St.
Memphis, TN 38103
(901)527-0089
Ultimate Parent: Eli Lilly. **SIC:** 5047—Medical & Hospital Equipment.

★ 81492 ★ **Casual Corner**
Kirby
Memphis, TN 38138
(901)754-2370
Ultimate Parent: United States Shoe. **SIC:** 5621—Women's Clothing Stores.

★ 81493 ★ **Casual Corner**
Hickory Ridge Mall
Memphis, TN 38111
(901)365-1548
Ultimate Parent: United States Shoe. **SIC:** 5621—Women's Clothing Stores.

★ 81494 ★ **Casual Corner**
6044 Hickory Ridge Mall
Memphis, TN 38115
(901)365-1548
Ultimate Parent: United States Shoe. **SIC:** 5651—Family Clothing Stores.

★ 81495 ★ **Chicago Title Insurance Co. Memphis**
61 Adams Ave.
Memphis, TN 38103-1709
(901)525-0303
Location Type: Branch office. **Officer:** Harvey A. Mitchell. **Ultimate Parent:** Alleghany Corp. **SIC:** 6361—Title Insurance; 6541—Title Abstract Offices.

★ 81496 ★ **Coca-Cola Bottling Co. of Memphis**
499 S. Hollywood St.
Memphis, TN 38111
Ultimate Parent: Coca-Cola Enterprises. **SIC:** 2086—Bottled & Canned Soft Drinks.

★ 81497 ★ **Coca-Cola Bottling Co. of Memphis Tennessee Inc.**
499 S. Hollywood St.
Memphis, TN 38111-1521
(901)454-8700
Officer: Ray George, President. **Ultimate Parent:** Coca-Cola Enterprises. **SIC:** 2086—Bottled & Canned Soft Drinks; 5962—Merchandising Machine Operators; 5812—Eating Places. **Employee Count:** 550.

★ 81498 ★ **Courtyard**
1780 Nonconnah Blvd.
Memphis, TN 38132
(901)396-3000
Ultimate Parent: Marriott International. **SIC:** 7011—Hotels & Motels.

★ 81499 ★ **Courtyards**
3357 Winchester Rd.
Memphis, TN 38118
(901)332-4365
Ultimate Parent: Marriott International. **SIC:** 6513—Apartment Building Operators.

★ 81500 ★ **Creative Expressions**
4370 Germantown Rd.
Memphis, TN 38141
(901)756-4341
Ultimate Parent: James River Corp. of Virginia. **SIC:** 5199—Nondurable Goods Nec.

★ 81501 ★ **Dean Foods Co.**
2040 Madison Ave.
Memphis, TN 38104
Ultimate Parent: Dean Foods. **SIC:** 2026—Fluid Milk.

★ 81502 ★ **Dean Witter Reynolds Inc.**
1200 Southland Mall
Memphis, TN 38116
(901)345-2201
Location Type: Branch office. **Ultimate Parent:** Dean Witter Discover. **SIC:** 6221—Commodity Contracts Brokers & Dealers.

★ 81503 ★ **Dean Witter Reynolds Inc.**
5860 Hyatt Ridgeway Pky.
Memphis, TN 38120
(901)766-6100
Location Type: Branch office. **Ultimate Parent:** Dean Witter Discover. **SIC:** 6211—Security Brokers & Dealers.

★ 81504 ★ **Dean Witter Reynolds Inc.**
4570 Poplar Ave.
Memphis, TN 38117
(901)683-5277
Location Type: Branch office. **Ultimate Parent:** Dean Witter Discover. **SIC:** 6221—Commodity Contracts Brokers & Dealers.

★ 81505 ★ **Dean Witter Reynolds Inc.**
6120 Hickory Ridge Mall
Memphis, TN 38115
(901)794-4492
Location Type: Branch office. **Ultimate Parent:** Dean Witter Discover. **SIC:** 6221—Commodity Contracts Brokers & Dealers.

★ 81506 ★ **Delta Air Lines**
Memphis International Airport
Memphis, TN 38116
(901)345-6050
Ultimate Parent: Delta Air Lines, Inc. **SIC:** 4512—Air Transportation—Scheduled.

★ 81507 ★ **Delta Air Lines**
939 Ridge Lake Blvd.
Memphis, TN 38120
(901)345-6020
Ultimate Parent: Delta Air Lines, Inc. **SIC:** 7922—Theatrical Producers & Services.

★ 81508 ★ **Deluxe Check Printers**
3815 Outland
Memphis, TN 38118
Ultimate Parent: Deluxe Corp. **SIC:** 2782—Blankbooks & Looseleaf Binders; 2752—Commercial Printing—Lithographic.

★ 81509 ★ **Deluxe Check Printers Inc.**
3815 Outland Rd.
Memphis, TN 38118
Ultimate Parent: Deluxe Corp. **SIC:** 2782—Blankbooks & Looseleaf Binders; 2752—Commercial Printing—Lithographic.

★ 81510 ★ **Dial Corp.**
1554 N. Thomas St.
Memphis, TN 38107
Ultimate Parent: Dial Corp. **SIC:** 2841—Soap & Other Detergents; 2844—Toilet Preparations.

★ 81511 ★ **Diebold Inc.**
5425 E. Raines Rd. 10
Memphis, TN 38115
(901)332-2724
Ultimate Parent: Diebold, Inc. **SIC:** 7381—Detective & Armored Car Services.

★ 81512 ★ **Diesel Recon Co.**
2680 Pershing Ave.
Memphis, TN 38112
Ultimate Parent: Cummins Engine Co. **SIC:** 3519—Internal Combustion Engines Nec.

★ 81513 ★ **Dover Elevator International Inc.**
6750 Poplar Ave. Ste. 419
Memphis, TN 38138-7416
(901)342-4300
Company Type: Subsidiary. **Ultimate Parent:** Dover Corp. **SIC:** 3534—Elevators & Moving Stairways; 1796—Installing Building Equipment Nec; 7699—Repair Services Nec.

★ 81514 ★ **Durr-Fillauer Medical Inc.**
7 N. Bellevue Blvd.
Memphis, TN 38104
(901)722-9119
Ultimate Parent: Bergen Brunswig Corp. **SIC:** 3842—Surgical Appliances & Supplies.

★ 81515 ★ **Eastman Kodak Co.**
2225 Union Ave.
Memphis, TN 38104
(901)278-5801
Ultimate Parent: Eastman Kodak. **SIC:** 5946—Camera & Photographic Supply Stores.

★ 81516 ★ **Eastman Kodak Co.**
44 N. Rembert St.
Memphis, TN 38104
(901)278-5804
Ultimate Parent: Eastman Kodak. **SIC:** 5946—Camera & Photographic Supply Stores.

★ 81517 ★ **Eaton Corp.**
774 Adams Ave.
Memphis, TN 38105
(901)526-2776
Ultimate Parent: Eaton Corp. **SIC:** 5085—Industrial Supplies.

★ 81518 ★ **Emery Worldwide**
Memphs International Arp
Memphis, TN 38130
(901)345-6010
Ultimate Parent: Consolidated Freightways. **SIC:** 4731—Freight Transportation Arrangement.

★ 81519 ★ **Enenco Inc.**
3018 Bell Ave.
Memphis, TN 38108-3415
Ultimate Parent: Witco Corp. **SIC:** 2843—Surface Active Agents.

★ 81520 ★ **Exxon Car Care Center**
6401 Poplar Ave. 500
Memphis, TN 38119
(901)767-9071
Ultimate Parent: Exxon. **SIC:** 5531—Automobile & Home Supply Stores.

★ 81521 ★ **Exxon Car Care Center**
2462 Central Ave.
Memphis, TN 38104
(901)324-5570
Ultimate Parent: Exxon. **SIC:** 7538—General Automotive Repair Shops.

★ 81522 ★ **Exxon Co. U S a**
454 Wisconsin Ave.
Memphis, TN 38106
(901)942-4634
Ultimate Parent: Exxon. **SIC:** 5172—Petroleum Products Nec.

★ 81523 ★ **Exxon Co. U S A**
454 Wisconsin Ave.
Memphis, TN 38106
(901)942-4634
Ultimate Parent: Exxon. **SIC:** 5172—Petroleum Products Nec.

★ 81524 ★ **Exxon Self Service Station**
3201 Millbranch Rd.
Memphis, TN 38116
(901)345-6518
Ultimate Parent: Exxon. **SIC:** 5541—Gasoline Service Stations.

★ 81525 ★ **Exxon Self Service Station**
5078 Stage Rd.
Memphis, TN 38128
(901)774-3312
Ultimate Parent: Exxon. **SIC:** 5411—Grocery Stores.

★ 81526 ★ **Exxon Self Service Station**
6019 Mount Moriah Rd.
Memphis, TN 38115
(901)362-9123
Ultimate Parent: Exxon. **SIC:** 5541—Gasoline Service Stations.

★ 81527 ★   Exxon Self Service
Station
3599 Hickory Hill Rd.
Memphis, TN 38115
(901)362-1738
Ultimate Parent: Exxon. SIC: 5411—
Grocery Stores.

★ 81528 ★   Exxon Service Center
4880 Summer Ave.
Memphis, TN 38122
(901)682-5822
Ultimate Parent: Exxon. SIC: 5541—
Gasoline Service Stations.

★ 81529 ★   Exxon Service Station
1300 S. Germantown Rd.
Memphis, TN 38138
(901)755-3722
Ultimate Parent: Exxon. SIC: 5541—
Gasoline Service Stations.

★ 81530 ★   Federal Express
2005 Corporate Ave.
Memphis, TN 38132
(901)369-3600
Company Type: Headquarters. Officer:
Frederick W. Smith. Fortune Service 500:
Ranking 7.

★ 81531 ★   Federal Express
Aviation Services Inc.
PO Box 727
Memphis, TN 38194
(901)369-3600
Company Type: Subsidiary. Ultimate
Parent: Federal Express. SIC: 4513—Air
Courier Services.

★ 81532 ★   Federal Express
Aviation Services Inc.
POB 727
Memphis, TN 38194
(901)369-3600 Fax: (901)332-3923
Company Type: Subsidiary. Officer: James
R. Parker, President & CEO. Ultimate
Parent: Federal Express.

★ 81533 ★   Federal Express Corp.
POB 727
Memphis, TN 38194
(901)369-3600 Fax: (901)332-3923
Company Type: Headquarters. Officer:
Frederick W. Smith, Chairman, President, &
CEO. Ultimate Parent: Federal Express.
Employee Count: 94000.

★ 81534 ★   Federal Express Corp.
PO Box 727
Memphis, TN 38132
Company Type: Headquarters. Ultimate
Parent: Federal Express.

★ 81535 ★   Federal Express Corp.
2005 Corporate Plz.
Memphis, TN 38132-1702
(901)369-3600 (800)238-5355 Fax:
(901)395-4928
Company Type: Headquarters. Officer:
Frederick W. Smith, Chairman of the Board,
President & CEO. Ultimate Parent: Federal
Express. SIC: 4513—Air Courier Services;
4512—Air Transportation—Scheduled;
3000—Rubber & Miscellaneous Plastics
Products. Employee Count: 93000. Sales:
7.5 M.

★ 81536 ★   Federal Express
Europlex Inc.
PO Box 727
Memphis, TN 38194
(901)369-3600
Company Type: Subsidiary. Ultimate
Parent: Federal Express. SIC: 4513—Air
Courier Services.

★ 81537 ★   Federal Express
International Inc.
PO Box 727
Memphis, TN 38194
(901)369-3600
Company Type: Subsidiary. Ultimate
Parent: Federal Express. SIC: 4513—Air
Courier Services.

★ 81538 ★   Federal Express
International Inc.
2005 Corporate Ave.
Memphis, TN 38132-1702
(901)369-3600
Company Type: Subsidiary. Officer:
Thomas R. Oliver, Chairman & President.
Ultimate Parent: Federal Express. SIC:
4513—Air Courier Services. Employee
Count: 7500. Sales: 382 M.

★ 81539 ★   Federal Express
International Inc.
POB 727
Memphis, TN 38194
(901)369-3600 Fax: (901)369-3923
Company Type: Subsidiary. Officer:
Joseph C. McCarty III, Senior Vice
President. Ultimate Parent: Federal
Express.

★ 81540 ★   Federal Express
Leasing Corp.
POB 727
Memphis, TN 38194
(901)369-3600 Fax: (901)332-3923
Company Type: Subsidiary. Officer: Alan
B. Graf Jr., President & CEO. Ultimate
Parent: Federal Express.

★ 81541 ★   Federal Express
Leasing Corp.
PO Box 727
Memphis, TN 38194
(901)369-3600
Company Type: Subsidiary. Ultimate
Parent: Federal Express.

★ 81542 ★   Federal Express
Logistics Inc.
PO Box 727
Memphis, TN 38194
(901)369-3600
Company Type: Subsidiary. Officer: John
Wallington, Director of Human Resources.
Ultimate Parent: Federal Express.

★ 81543 ★   Federal Express
Logistics Inc.
POB 727
Memphis, TN 38194
(901)369-3600 Fax: (901)332-3923
Company Type: Subsidiary. Officer: A.
Doyle Cloud, President. Ultimate Parent:
Federal Express.

★ 81544 ★   Federal Express
Redevelopment Corp.
POB 727
Memphis, TN 38194
(901)369-3600 Fax: (901)332-3923
Company Type: Subsidiary. Officer:
Kenneth R. Masterson, President. Ultimate
Parent: Federal Express.

★ 81545 ★   Federal Express
Redevelopment Corp.
PO Box 727
Memphis, TN 38194
(901)369-3600
Company Type: Subsidiary. Ultimate
Parent: Federal Express. SIC: 4513—Air
Courier Services.

★ 81546 ★   FedEx Aeronautics
Corp.
POB 727
Memphis, TN 38194
(901)369-3600 Fax: (901)332-3923
Company Type: Subsidiary. Officer: T.
Allan McArtor, President. Ultimate Parent:
Federal Express.

★ 81547 ★   Fedex Customs
Brokerage Corp.
PO Box 727
Memphis, TN 38194
(901)369-3600
Company Type: Subsidiary. Ultimate
Parent: Federal Express. SIC: 4513—Air
Courier Services; 4000—Railroad
Transportation.

★ 81548 ★   Fedex International
Transmission Corp.
PO Box 727
Memphis, TN 38194
(901)369-3600
Company Type: Subsidiary. Ultimate
Parent: Federal Express. SIC: 4513—Air
Courier Services.

★ 81549 ★   FedEx International
Transmission Corp.
POB 727
Memphis, TN 38194
(901)369-3600 Fax: (901)332-3923
Company Type: Subsidiary. Officer:
Dennis H. Jones, President. Ultimate
Parent: Federal Express.

★ 81550 ★   First American
National Bank
4485 Poplar Ave.
Memphis, TN 38117-3717
(901)762-5955
Location Type: Branch office. Ultimate
Parent: First American Corp. SIC: 6021—
National Commercial Banks.

★ 81551 ★   First American
National Bank
4894 Poplar Ave.
Memphis, TN 38117-5194
(901)762-5602
Location Type: Branch office. Ultimate
Parent: First American Corp. SIC: 6021—
National Commercial Banks.

★ 81552 ★   First American
National Bank
3140 S. Menden Hall Rd.
Memphis, TN 38115-2828
(901)762-5930
Location Type: Branch office. Ultimate
Parent: First American Corp. SIC: 6021—
National Commercial Banks.

★ 81553 ★   First American
National Bank
4632 Millbranch
Memphis, TN 38116-7404
(901)684-4470
Location Type: Branch office. Ultimate
Parent: First American Corp. SIC: 6021—
National Commercial Banks.

★ 81554 ★   First American
National Bank
5969 Winchester Rd.
Memphis, TN 38115-8801
(901)762-5945
Location Type: Branch office. Ultimate
Parent: First American Corp. SIC: 6021—
National Commercial Banks.

★ 81555 ★   First American
National Bank
5679 Quince Rd.
Memphis, TN 38119-7017
(901)762-5980
Location Type: Branch office. Ultimate
Parent: First American Corp. SIC: 6021—
National Commercial Banks.

★ 81556 ★   First American
National Bank
4080 Getwell Rd.
Memphis, TN 38118-6017
(901)762-5920
Location Type: Branch office. Ultimate
Parent: First American Corp. SIC: 6021—
National Commercial Banks.

★ 81557 ★   First American
National Bank
5100 Poplar Ave.
Memphis, TN 38137-0101
(901)762-5925
Location Type: Branch office. Ultimate
Parent: First American Corp. SIC: 6021—
National Commercial Banks.

★ 81558 ★   First American
National Bank
2595 James Rd.
Memphis, TN 38127-8819
(901)684-3270
Location Type: Branch office. Ultimate
Parent: First American Corp. SIC: 6021—
National Commercial Banks.

★ 81559 ★   First American
National Bank
1415 Union Ave.
Memphis, TN 38104-3626
(901)762-5970
Location Type: Branch office. Ultimate
Parent: First American Corp. SIC: 6021—
National Commercial Banks.

★ 81560 ★   First American
National Bank
3471 Elvis Presley Blvd.
Memphis, TN 38116-4331
(901)762-5975
Location Type: Branch office. Ultimate
Parent: First American Corp. SIC: 6021—
National Commercial Banks.

★ 81561 ★   First American
National Bank
6165 Poplar Ave.
Memphis, TN 38119-4714
(901)762-5960
Location Type: Branch office. Ultimate
Parent: First American Corp. SIC: 6021—
National Commercial Banks.

★ 81562 ★   First American
National Bank
44 N. 2nd St.
Memphis, TN 38103-2220
(901)684-3232
Location Type: Branch office. Ultimate
Parent: First American Corp. SIC: 6021—
National Commercial Banks.

★ 81563 ★   First American
National Bank
5090 Stage Rd.
Memphis, TN 38128-5004
(901)762-5965
Location Type: Branch office. Ultimate
Parent: First American Corp. SIC: 6021—
National Commercial Banks.

★ 81564 ★   First American Trust
Co., NA
4894 Poplar
Memphis, TN 38117
(901)684-3265
Location Type: Branch office. Ultimate
Parent: First American Corp. SIC: 6021—
National Commercial Banks.

★ 81565 ★   First Choice Co.
615 Chelsea Ave.
Memphis, TN 38107-2538
(901)525-4498
Ultimate Parent: Bindley-Western
Industries, Inc. SIC: 5014—Tires & Tubes;
5014—Tires & Tubes.

★ 81566 ★   First Tennessee Bank
NA
3885 S. Perkins
Memphis, TN 38118
(901)523-4444
Location Type: Branch office. Ultimate
Parent: First Tennessee National Corp.
SIC: 6021—National Commercial Banks.

★ 81567 ★   First Tennessee Bank
NA
8024 Hwy. 64
Memphis, TN 38133
(901)385-3045
Location Type: Branch office. Ultimate
Parent: First Tennessee National Corp.
SIC: 6021—National Commercial Banks.

★ 81568 ★   First Tennessee Bank
NA
3150 Village Shops Dr.
Memphis, TN 38138
(901)756-3930
Location Type: Branch office. Ultimate
Parent: First Tennessee National Corp.
SIC: 6021—National Commercial Banks.

★ 81569 ★   First Tennessee Bank
NA
6100 Quince
Memphis, TN 38119
(901)684-3988
Location Type: Branch office. Ultimate
Parent: First Tennessee National Corp.
SIC: 6021—National Commercial Banks.

★ 81570 ★   First Tennessee Bank
NA
579 Goodman Rd.
Memphis, TN 38111
(901)523-4444
Location Type: Branch office. Ultimate
Parent: First Tennessee National Corp.
SIC: 6021—National Commercial Banks.

★ 81571 ★   First Tennessee Bank
NA
3545 Austin Peay Hwy.
Memphis, TN 38128
(901)385-3021
Location Type: Branch office. Ultimate
Parent: First Tennessee National Corp.
SIC: 6021—National Commercial Banks.

★ 81572 ★ First Tennessee Bank
NA
1980 Germantown Rd. S
Memphis, TN 38138
(901)753-3085
Location Type: Branch office. **Ultimate**
Parent: First Tennessee National Corp.
SIC: 6021—National Commercial Banks.

★ 81573 ★ First Tennessee Bank
NA
2284 Lamar Ave.
Memphis, TN 38114-6608
(901)320-3150
Location Type: Branch office. **Ultimate**
Parent: First Tennessee National Corp.
SIC: 6021—National Commercial Banks.

★ 81574 ★ First Tennessee Bank
NA
3225 Austin Peay Hwy.
Memphis, TN 38128
(901)385-3000
Location Type: Branch office. **Ultimate**
Parent: First Tennessee National Corp.
SIC: 6021—National Commercial Banks.

★ 81575 ★ First Tennessee Bank
NA
5931 Stage Rd.
Memphis, TN 38134-4521
(901)385-3012
Location Type: Branch office. **Ultimate**
Parent: First Tennessee National Corp.
SIC: 6021—National Commercial Banks.

★ 81576 ★ First Tennessee Bank
NA
6060 Quince Rd.
Memphis, TN 38119-7271
(901)684-3978
Location Type: Branch office. **Ultimate**
Parent: First Tennessee National Corp.
SIC: 6021—National Commercial Banks.

★ 81577 ★ First Tennessee Bank
NA
604 W. Poplar Ave.
Memphis, TN 38017-2540
(901)853-3250
Location Type: Branch office. **Ultimate**
Parent: First Tennessee National Corp.
SIC: 6021—National Commercial Banks.

★ 81578 ★ First Tennessee Bank
NA
4330 Summer Ave.
Memphis, TN 38122-4089
(901)684-3973
Location Type: Branch office. **Ultimate**
Parent: First Tennessee National Corp.
SIC: 6021—National Commercial Banks.

★ 81579 ★ First Tennessee Bank
NA
4990 Poplar Ave.
Memphis, TN 38117-7603
(901)684-3943
Location Type: Branch office. **Ultimate**
Parent: First Tennessee National Corp.
SIC: 6021—National Commercial Banks.

★ 81580 ★ First Tennessee Bank
NA
1338 Union Ave.
Memphis, TN 38104-3509
(901)722-3659
Location Type: Branch office. **Ultimate**
Parent: First Tennessee National Corp.
SIC: 6021—National Commercial Banks.

★ 81581 ★ First Tennessee Bank
NA
3129 S. Menden Hall Rd.
Memphis, TN 38115-2827
(901)366-3764
Location Type: Branch office. **Ultimate**
Parent: First Tennessee National Corp.
SIC: 6021—National Commercial Banks.

★ 81582 ★ First Tennessee Bank
NA
3430 Summer Ave.
Memphis, TN 38122-3610
(901)320-3138
Location Type: Branch office. **Ultimate**
Parent: First Tennessee National Corp.
SIC: 6021—National Commercial Banks.

★ 81583 ★ First Tennessee Bank
NA
7640 Poplar Ave.
Memphis, TN 38138-3930
(901)753-3057
Location Type: Branch office. **Ultimate**
Parent: First Tennessee National Corp.
SIC: 6021—National Commercial Banks.

★ 81584 ★ First Tennessee Bank
NA
2664 N. Hollywood
Memphis, TN 38127-8804
(901)357-3390
Location Type: Branch office. **Ultimate**
Parent: First Tennessee National Corp.
SIC: 6021—National Commercial Banks.

★ 81585 ★ First Tennessee Bank
NA
3770 Lamar Ave.
Memphis, TN 38118-3705
(901)366-3757
Location Type: Branch office. **Ultimate**
Parent: First Tennessee National Corp.
SIC: 6021—National Commercial Banks.

★ 81586 ★ First Tennessee Bank
NA
4655 Poplar Ave.
Memphis, TN 38117-4431
(901)684-3957
Location Type: Branch office. **Ultimate**
Parent: First Tennessee National Corp.
SIC: 6021—National Commercial Banks.

★ 81587 ★ First Tennessee Bank
NA
1845 Kirby Pky.
Memphis, TN 38138-0626
(901)753-3069
Location Type: Branch office. **Ultimate**
Parent: First Tennessee National Corp.
SIC: 6021—National Commercial Banks.

★ 81588 ★ First Tennessee Bank
NA
910 Madison Ave.
Memphis, TN 38103-3403
(901)543-3230
Location Type: Branch office. **Ultimate**
Parent: First Tennessee National Corp.
SIC: 6021—National Commercial Banks.

★ 81589 ★ First Tennessee Bank
NA
4230 Elvis Presley Blvd.
Memphis, TN 38116-6434
(901)348-3616
Location Type: Branch office. **Ultimate**
Parent: First Tennessee National Corp.
SIC: 6021—National Commercial Banks.

★ 81590 ★ First Tennessee Bank
NA
3500 Elvis Presley Blvd.
Memphis, TN 38116-4332
(901)348-3610
Location Type: Branch office. **Ultimate**
Parent: First Tennessee National Corp.
SIC: 6021—National Commercial Banks.

★ 81591 ★ First Tennessee Bank
NA
5052 Navy Rd.
Memphis, TN 38053-2199
(901)872-3356
Location Type: Branch office. **Ultimate**
Parent: First Tennessee National Corp.
SIC: 6021—National Commercial Banks.

★ 81592 ★ First Tennessee Bank
NA
315 Poplar Ave.
Memphis, TN 38103-1907
(901)543-3220
Location Type: Branch office. **Ultimate**
Parent: First Tennessee National Corp.
SIC: 6021—National Commercial Banks.

★ 81593 ★ First Tennessee Bank
NA
3180 S. Perkins Rd.
Memphis, TN 38118-4353
(901)366-3748
Location Type: Branch office. **Ultimate**
Parent: First Tennessee National Corp.
SIC: 6021—National Commercial Banks.

★ 81594 ★ First Tennessee Bank
NA
1200 S. 3rd St.
Memphis, TN 38106-2774
(901)947-3188
Location Type: Branch office. **Ultimate**
Parent: First Tennessee National Corp.
SIC: 6021—National Commercial Banks.

★ 81595 ★ First Tennessee Bank
NA
3400 Poplar Ave.
Memphis, TN 38111-4653
(901)320-3130
Location Type: Branch office. **Ultimate**
Parent: First Tennessee National Corp.
SIC: 6021—National Commercial Banks.

★ 81596 ★ First Tennessee Bank
NA
3391 N. Watkins
Memphis, TN 38127-5589
(901)357-3383
Location Type: Branch office. **Ultimate**
Parent: First Tennessee National Corp.
SIC: 6021—National Commercial Banks.

★ 81597 ★ First Tennessee Bank
NA
1277 E. Shelby Dr.
Memphis, TN 38116-7123
(901)348-3622
Location Type: Branch office. **Ultimate**
Parent: First Tennessee National Corp.
SIC: 6021—National Commercial Banks.

★ 81598 ★ First Tennessee Bank
NA
888 White Station Rd.
Memphis, TN 38117-5766
(901)684-3981
Location Type: Branch office. **Ultimate**
Parent: First Tennessee National Corp.
SIC: 6021—National Commercial Banks.

★ 81599 ★ First Tennessee Bank
NA
2015 Brooks Rd. E
Memphis, TN 38116-2401
(901)348-3600
Location Type: Branch office. **Ultimate**
Parent: First Tennessee National Corp.
SIC: 6021—National Commercial Banks.

★ 81600 ★ First Tennessee Bank
NA
6616 Winchester Rd.
Memphis, TN 38115-4336
(901)366-3740
Location Type: Branch office. **Ultimate**
Parent: First Tennessee National Corp.
SIC: 6021—National Commercial Banks.

★ 81601 ★ First Tennessee Bank
NA
6595 Kirby Ctr. Cove
Memphis, TN 38115-4313
(901)366-3730
Location Type: Branch office. **Ultimate**
Parent: First Tennessee National Corp.
SIC: 6021—National Commercial Banks.

★ 81602 ★ First Tennessee Bank
NA
PO Box 84
Memphis, TN 38101-0084
Location Type: Branch office. **Ultimate**
Parent: First Tennessee National Corp.
SIC: 6021—National Commercial Banks.

★ 81603 ★ First Tennessee Bank
NA
1620 Madison Ave.
Memphis, TN 38104
(901)722-3872
Location Type: Branch office. **Ultimate**
Parent: First Tennessee National Corp.
SIC: 6021—National Commercial Banks.

★ 81604 ★ First Tennessee Bank
NA
165 Madison Ave.
Memphis, TN 38103-2723
(901)523-4444 **Fax:** (901)523-4266 **Telex:**
5-3800
Location Type: Branch office. **Ultimate**
Parent: First Tennessee National Corp.
SIC: 6021—National Commercial Banks.

★ 81605 ★ First Tennessee
National Corp.
PO Box 84
Memphis, TN 38101-0084
Location Type: Branch office. **Ultimate**
Parent: First Tennessee National Corp.
SIC: 6021—National Commercial Banks.

★ 81606 ★ First Tennessee
National Corp.
165 Madison Ave.
Memphis, TN 38103
(901)523-4444
Company Type: Headquarters. **Officer:**
Ronald A. Terry. **Employee Count:** 5653.
Fortune Service 500: Ranking 64.

★ 81607 ★ Fitness Equipment
5014 Poplar Ave.
Memphis, TN 38117
(901)761-9222
Ultimate Parent: New York Times.

★ 81608 ★ Fruehauf Trailer Corp.
2862 Winchester Pke.
Memphis, TN 38118
(901)345-1160
Company Type: Affiliate. **Location Type:**
Plant. **Officer:** J. J. Phillips, COO. **Ultimate**
Parent: Terex Corp. **SIC:** 3715—Truck
Trailers. **Employee Count:** 330.

★ 81609 ★ Fruehauf Trailer Corp.
2862 Winchester Pke.
Memphis, TN 38118
(901)345-1160
Company Type: Affiliate. **Location Type:**
Plant. **Officer:** J. J. Phillips, COO. **Ultimate**
Parent: Terex Corp. **SIC:** 3715—Truck
Trailers. **Employee Count:** 330.

★ 81610 ★ GE Lighting
1356 Riverside Blvd.
Memphis, TN 38109
(901)775-5200
Officer: Bill Hoelzle, Manager. **Ultimate**
Parent: General Electric. **SIC:** 3641—
Electric Lamps.

★ 81611 ★ General Electric
Memphis Lamp Plant
1356 S. Riverside
Memphis, TN 38109
Ultimate Parent: General Electric. **SIC:**
3641—Electric Lamps.

★ 81612 ★ Genuine Parts Co.
Rayloc Div.
2860 Horn Lake Rd.
Memphis, TN 38109
Company Type: Division. **Ultimate Parent:**
Genuine Parts. **SIC:** 3714—Motor Vehicle
Parts & Accessories.

★ 81613 ★ Genuine Parts Co.
Rayloc Div.
2860 Horn Lake Rd.
Memphis, TN 38109
Company Type: Division. **Ultimate Parent:**
Genuine Parts. **SIC:** 3714—Motor Vehicle
Parts & Accessories.

★ 81614 ★ Giant Food Deli
1817 S. 3rd St.
Memphis, TN 38109
(901)774-1344
Ultimate Parent: Giant Food. **SIC:** 5461—
Retail Bakeries.

★ 81615 ★ Giant Food Deli
3040 Austin Peay Hwy.
Memphis, TN 38128
(901)382-1628
Ultimate Parent: Giant Food. **SIC:** 5812—
Eating Places.

★ 81616 ★ Giant Food Market
Inc. Bakery & Deli
5252 Winchester Rd.
Memphis, TN 38118
(901)362-8256
Ultimate Parent: Giant Food. **SIC:** 5461—
Retail Bakeries.

★ 81617 ★ Graphic Systems Inc.
5125 Elmore Rd.
Memphis, TN 38134-5656
(901)372-3762
Officer: Dennis Kopcial. **Ultimate Parent:**
Avery Dennison Corp. **SIC:** 5112—
Stationery & Office Supplies; 2732—Book
Printing.

★ 81618 ★   Great Dane Trailers
Tennessee Inc.
1095 Harbor Ave.
Memphis, TN 38113-1601
Ultimate Parent: International Controls.
SIC: 3715—Truck Trailers.

★ 81619 ★   Greyhound Bus Lines
1559 Sycamore View Rd.
Memphis, TN 38134
(901)388-2135
Ultimate Parent: Greyhound Lines Inc. SIC:
4131—Intercity & Rural Bus Transportation;
4111—Local & Suburban Transit; 4142—
Bus Charter Service Except Local.

★ 81620 ★   Greyhound Bus Lines
2805 Winchester Rd.
Memphis, TN 38118
(901)794-0756
Ultimate Parent: Greyhound Lines Inc. SIC:
4131—Intercity & Rural Bus Transportation;
4111—Local & Suburban Transit; 4142—
Bus Charter Service Except Local.

★ 81621 ★   Greyhound Bus Lines
527 N. Main St.
Memphis, TN 38105
(901)523-1058
Ultimate Parent: Greyhound Lines Inc. SIC:
4111—Local & Suburban Transit; 4131—
Intercity & Rural Bus Transportation; 4142—
Bus Charter Service Except Local.

★ 81622 ★   Greyhound Bus Lines
203 Union Ave.
Memphis, TN 38103
(901)523-1111
Ultimate Parent: Greyhound Lines Inc. SIC:
4111—Local & Suburban Transit; 4131—
Intercity & Rural Bus Transportation; 4142—
Bus Charter Service Except Local.

★ 81623 ★   Greyhound Bus Lines
3152 Bellbrook Dr.
Memphis, TN 38116
(901)332-0717
Ultimate Parent: Greyhound Lines Inc. SIC:
4111—Local & Suburban Transit; 4131—
Intercity & Rural Bus Transportation; 4142—
Bus Charter Service Except Local.

★ 81624 ★   Greyhound Lines Inc.
1559 Sycamore View Rd.
Memphis, TN 38134
(901)388-2135
Ultimate Parent: Greyhound Lines Inc. SIC:
4131—Intercity & Rural Bus Transportation.

★ 81625 ★   H. B. Fuller Co.
802 Royal Ave.
Memphis, TN 38107
Ultimate Parent: H. B. Fuller. SIC: 2891—
Adhesives & Sealants.

★ 81626 ★   H.B. Fuller Co.
802 Royal Ave.
Memphis, TN 38107
Ultimate Parent: H. B. Fuller. SIC: 2891—
Adhesives & Sealants.

★ 81627 ★   Hit or Miss
3691 Hickory Hill Rd.
Memphis, TN 38115
(901)363-4174
Ultimate Parent: TJX. SIC: 5651—Family
Clothing Stores.

★ 81628 ★   Hunt-Wesson, Inc.
1351 Williams St.
Memphis, TN 38101-1759
(901)726-6929
Location Type: Plant. Officer: Ray Carroll,
Plant Manager. Ultimate Parent: Conagra.
SIC: 2079—Edible Fats & Oils Nec.

★ 81629 ★   IDS Financial
Services Inc.
5100 Poplar Ave.
Memphis, TN 38137-0111
(901)767-3661
Location Type: Branch office. Ultimate
Parent: American Express Co. SIC: 6211—
Security Brokers & Dealers; 6282—
Investment Advice.

★ 81630 ★   International Paper
Co.
Nevamar Div.
1278 Orgill Ave.
Memphis, TN 38106
Company Type: Division. Ultimate Parent:
International Paper Co. SIC: 3083—
Laminated Plastics Plate & Sheet.

★ 81631 ★   Johnson Controls Inc.
2602 Faxon Ave.
Memphis, TN 38112
(901)458-8261
Ultimate Parent: Johnson Controls Inc.
SIC: 8711—Engineering Services.

★ 81632 ★   Johnson Products
Co.
531 N. Front St.
Memphis, TN 38105
(901)525-7497
Ultimate Parent: IVAX. SIC: 5199—
Nondurable Goods Nec.

★ 81633 ★   Jostens Inc.
4429 Delp St.
Memphis, TN 38118
(901)365-3092
Ultimate Parent: Jostens. SIC: 3911—
Jewelry & Precious Metal.

★ 81634 ★   Kraft General Foods
Inc.
Frozen Dairy Group
175 Walnut
Memphis, TN 38103
Company Type: Division. Ultimate Parent:
Philip Morris. SIC: 2024—Ice Cream &
Frozen Desserts.

★ 81635 ★   Kroger Co.
2130 Exeterrd
Memphis, TN 38138
(901)754-7787
Ultimate Parent: Kroger. SIC: 5411—
Grocery Stores.

★ 81636 ★   Kroger Co.
4770 Germantown Rd.
Memphis, TN 38141
(901)756-7291
Ultimate Parent: Kroger. SIC: 5411—
Grocery Stores.

★ 81637 ★   Kroger Co.
6532 Winchester Rd.
Memphis, TN 38115
(901)795-5166
Ultimate Parent: Kroger. SIC: 5411—
Grocery Stores.

★ 81638 ★   Kroger Co.
2680 Frayser Blvd.
Memphis, TN 38127
(901)353-2604
Ultimate Parent: Kroger. SIC: 5411—
Grocery Stores.

★ 81639 ★   Kroger Co.
3226 Hwy. 51 N
Memphis, TN 38127
(901)357-2006
Ultimate Parent: Kroger. SIC: 5411—
Grocery Stores.

★ 81640 ★   Kroger Co.
2015 Exeterrd
Memphis, TN 38138
(901)755-5368
Ultimate Parent: Kroger. SIC: 5411—
Grocery Stores.

★ 81641 ★   Kroger Co.
800 Ridge Lake Blvd.
Memphis, TN 38120
(901)765-4100
Ultimate Parent: Kroger. SIC: 5411—
Grocery Stores.

★ 81642 ★   Layne & Bowler Inc.
1993 Chelsea Ave.
Memphis, TN 38108
(901)725-6300
Ultimate Parent: General Signal. SIC:
3496—Miscellaneous Fabricated Wire
Products; 3561—Pumps & Pumping
Equipment.

★ 81643 ★   Layne Bryant
4442 Memphis Mall
Memphis, TN 38103
(901)365-0018
Ultimate Parent: Limited. SIC: 5621—
Women's Clothing Stores.

★ 81644 ★   Leader Financial
Corp.
158 Madison Ave.
Memphis, TN 38103
(901)578-2000
Company Type: Headquarters. Officer:
Edgar H. Bailey. Employee Count: 738.
Fortune Service 500: Ranking 50.

★ 81645 ★   Lerner Shops
Hickory Ridge Mall
Memphis, TN 38111
(901)362-9789
Ultimate Parent: Limited. SIC: 5621—
Women's Clothing Stores.

★ 81646 ★   Lerner Shops
1279 Southland Mall
Memphis, TN 38116
(901)526-6906
Ultimate Parent: Limited. SIC: 5621—
Women's Clothing Stores.

★ 81647 ★   Lerner Shops
6093 Hickory Ridge Mall
Memphis, TN 38115
(901)362-9789
Ultimate Parent: Limited. SIC: 5621—
Women's Clothing Stores.

★ 81648 ★   Lerner Woman
6112 Hickory Ridge Mall
Memphis, TN 38115
(901)366-0034
Ultimate Parent: Limited. SIC: 5621—
Women's Clothing Stores.

★ 81649 ★   Limited the
6081 Hickory Ridge Mall
Memphis, TN 38115
(901)795-2110
Ultimate Parent: Limited. SIC: 5621—
Women's Clothing Stores.

★ 81650 ★   Limited the
7605 W. Farmington Blvd.
Memphis, TN 38138
(901)757-5001
Ultimate Parent: Limited. SIC: 5621—
Women's Clothing Stores.

★ 81651 ★   Limited Express the
6028 Hickory Ridge Mall
Memphis, TN 38115
(901)365-4478
Ultimate Parent: Limited. SIC: 5621—
Women's Clothing Stores.

★ 81652 ★   Malone & Hyde Inc.
1991 Corporate Ave.
Memphis, TN 38132
(901)395-8032 Fax: (901)325-4356
Company Type: Subsidiary. Officer:
Robert F. Harris, President. Ultimate
Parent: Fleming.

★ 81653 ★   Manville Forest
Products Corp.
Packaging
3400 Chelsea Ave.
Memphis, TN 38108
Company Type: Division. Ultimate Parent:
Manville Corp. SIC: 2600—Paper & Allied
Products; 2752—Commercial Printing—
Lithographic.

★ 81654 ★   Mapco Petroleum
Tennessee Refinary
PO Box 2930
Memphis, TN 38103-2930
(901)774-3100
Company Type: Division. Ultimate Parent:
Mapco. SIC: 2911—Petroleum Refining.

★ 81655 ★   Mapco Petroleum Inc.
543 W. Mallory Ave.
Memphis, TN 38109
Ultimate Parent: Mapco. SIC: 2911—
Petroleum Refining.

★ 81656 ★   Mary Kay Cosmetics
7554 Willey Rd.
Memphis, TN 38138
(901)754-9630
Ultimate Parent: Mary Kay Cosmetics. SIC:
5999—Miscellaneous Retail Stores Nec.

★ 81657 ★   Minnesota
Mining&Mfg Co. Inc.
3109 Directors Row
Memphis, TN 38131
(901)345-7505
Ultimate Parent: Minnesota Mining & Mfg.
SIC: 5044—Office Equipment.

★ 81658 ★   New York Life
Memphis General Office
Southeastern Agencies
Crescent Ctr.
6075 Poplar Ave., Ste. 200
Memphis, TN 38119
(901)761-1810 Fax: (901)762-4746
Officer: Eugene Cazedessus III, General
Manager. Ultimate Parent: New York Life.

★ 81659 ★   Newell Home
Hardware Co.
4533 Old Lamar Ave.
Memphis, TN 38118-7035
(901)365-1537 Fax: (901)366-3616
Officer: A. John Horn, President. Ultimate
Parent: Newell.

★ 81660 ★   Nike Inc.
8400 Winchester Rd.
Memphis, TN 38125
(901)755-6453
Ultimate Parent: Nike. SIC: 3949—Sporting
& Athletic Goods Nec.

★ 81661 ★   Northwestern Mutual
Life Inc.
2020 Exeter Rd.
Memphis, TN 38138
(901)755-1001
Ultimate Parent: Northwestern Mutual Life.
SIC: 6411—Insurance Agents, Brokers &
Service.

★ 81662 ★   Owens-Corning
Fiberglas Corp.
704 Corrine Ave.
Memphis, TN 38107
(901)525-4556
Officer: Dave Moelter, Manager. Ultimate
Parent: Owens-Corning. SIC: 3089—
Plastics Products Nec; 3296—Mineral Wool.

★ 81663 ★   Payless Shoe Source
3625 Hickory Hill Rd.
Memphis, TN 38115
(901)794-2152
Ultimate Parent: May Department Stores.
SIC: 5661—Shoe Stores.

★ 81664 ★   Peoples Bank
Shelby Ctr.
Memphis, TN 38127
(901)386-3131
Ultimate Parent: People's Bank. SIC:
6022—State Commercial Banks.

★ 81665 ★   Peoples Bank
6767 Us 70
Memphis, TN 38134
(901)386-3131
Ultimate Parent: People's Bank. SIC:
6022—State Commercial Banks.

★ 81666 ★   Piggly Wiggly Corp.
1991 Corporate Ave.
Memphis, TN 38132-1702
(901)395-8215
Company Type: Subsidiary. Officer:
Lawrence L. Crane Jr., President. Ultimate
Parent: Fleming. SIC: 6794—Patent
Owners & Lessors. Employee Count: 33.
Sales: 3 M.

★ 81667 ★   Piggly Wiggly
Memphis Inc.
888 S. White Station Rd.
Memphis, TN 38117-5703
(901)682-3617
Location Type: Branch office. Officer:
Michael G. Baker. Ultimate Parent:
Bruno's. SIC: 5411—Grocery Stores.

★ 81668 ★   Pitney Bowes
3885 S. Perkins Rd.
Memphis, TN 38118
(901)795-6500
Officer: Richard Chandler, Manager.
Ultimate Parent: Pitney Bowes. SIC:
3554—Paper Industries Machinery.

★ 81669 ★   Plough Inc.
3030 Jackson Ave.
Memphis, TN 38151
Ultimate Parent: Schering-Plough Corp.
SIC: 2834—Pharmaceutical Preparations;
2844—Toilet Preparations.

★ 81670 ★   Plough Inc.
3030 Jackson Ave. (PO Box 377)
Memphis, TN 38151
Ultimate Parent: Schering-Plough Corp.
SIC: 2834—Pharmaceutical Preparations;
2844—Toilet Preparations.

★ 81671 ★   Plough Inc.
Printing Plant
1248 Warford Ave.
Memphis, TN 38151
Location Type: Plant. Ultimate Parent:
Schering-Plough Corp. SIC: 2752—
Commercial Printing—Lithographic.

553

★ 81672 ★ Plough Printing Plant
1248 Warford Ave.
Memphis, TN 38151
Ultimate Parent: Schering-Plough Corp.
SIC: 2752—Commercial Printing—
Lithographic.

**★ 81673 ★ Procter & Gamble
Cellulose Co. Memphis Plant**
2899 Jackson Ave.
Memphis, TN 38108
Ultimate Parent: Procter & Gamble Co.
SIC: 2611—Pulp Mills.

**★ 81674 ★ Protein Tech.
International International**
4272 S. Mendenhall
Memphis, TN 38141
Ultimate Parent: Ralston Purina. **SIC:**
2075—Soybean Oil Mills.

**★ 81675 ★ Protein Technologies
International**
4272 S. Mendenhall Rd.
Memphis, TN 38115
Ultimate Parent: Ralston Purina. **SIC:**
2075—Soybean Oil Mills.

★ 81676 ★ Qo Chemicals Inc.
3324 Chelsea Ave.
Memphis, TN 38108
Ultimate Parent: Great Lakes Chemical.
SIC: 2869—Industrial Organic Chemicals
Nec.

★ 81677 ★ Qualex Inc.
3872 Delp St.
Memphis, TN 38118
(901)367-1787
Officer: Clarence Heist, Manager. **Ultimate
Parent:** Eastman Kodak. **SIC:** 2759—
Commercial Printing Nec.

**★ 81678 ★ Rexham Corp.
Memphis Plant**
2000 Latham St.
Memphis, TN 38109
Ultimate Parent: Bowater. **SIC:** 2671—
Paper Coated & Laminated—Packaging;
2600—Paper & Allied Products.

**★ 81679 ★ Reynolds & Reynolds
Co.**
3041 Getwell Rd.
Memphis, TN 38118
(901)365-0540
Ultimate Parent: Reynolds & Reynolds.
SIC: 2761—Manifold Business Forms.

★ 81680 ★ Ryder Truck Rental
540 Weakley Ave.
Memphis, TN 38107
(901)527-6258
Ultimate Parent: Ryder System. **SIC:**
7513—Truck Rental & Leasing Without
Drivers.

★ 81681 ★ Ryder Truck Rental
507 E. Brook Rd.
Memphis, TN 38116
(901)398-7670
Ultimate Parent: Ryder System. **SIC:**
7513—Truck Rental & Leasing Without
Drivers.

★ 81682 ★ Ryder Truck Rental
1135 Riverside Blvd.
Memphis, TN 38106
(901)365-1000
Ultimate Parent: Ryder System. **SIC:**
7513—Truck Rental & Leasing Without
Drivers.

**★ 81683 ★ Ryder Truck Rental &
Leasing**
1520 Texas St.
Memphis, TN 38106
(901)947-3411
Ultimate Parent: Ryder System. **SIC:**
7513—Truck Rental & Leasing Without
Drivers.

**★ 81684 ★ Ryder Truck Rental-
One Way**
5665 Quince Rd.
Memphis, TN 38119
(901)683-0524
Ultimate Parent: Ryder System. **SIC:**
7513—Truck Rental & Leasing Without
Drivers.

**★ 81685 ★ Ryder Truck Rental-
One Way**
1361 E. Shelby Dr.
Memphis, TN 38116
(901)345-6503
Ultimate Parent: Ryder System. **SIC:**
7513—Truck Rental & Leasing Without
Drivers.

**★ 81686 ★ Ryder Truck Rental-
One Way**
Midtown
Memphis, TN 38104
(901)725-9729
Ultimate Parent: Ryder System. **SIC:**
7513—Truck Rental & Leasing Without
Drivers.

**★ 81687 ★ Ryder Truck Rental-
One Way**
3rd
Memphis, TN 38109
(901)332-0879
Ultimate Parent: Ryder System. **SIC:**
7513—Truck Rental & Leasing Without
Drivers.

**★ 81688 ★ Ryder Truck Rental-
One Way**
2031 E. Brook Rd.
Memphis, TN 38116
(901)345-6489
Ultimate Parent: Ryder System. **SIC:**
7513—Truck Rental & Leasing Without
Drivers.

★ 81689 ★ Sara Lee Corp.
1837 Harbor Ave.
Memphis, TN 38113
(901)942-3221
Company Type: Division. **Officer:** Douglas
Esson, CEO. **Ultimate Parent:** Sara Lee
Corp.

**★ 81690 ★ Schering-Plough
Healthcare Products Inc.**
3030 Jackson Ave.
Memphis, TN 38151
Ultimate Parent: Schering-Plough Corp.
SIC: 2834—Pharmaceutical Preparations.

★ 81691 ★ Sealy Mattress Co.
4120 Air Trans Rd.
Memphis, TN 38118
(901)795-6460
Officer: Russell Haas, Vice President.
Ultimate Parent: Sealy. **SIC:** 2392—
Housefurnishings Nec; 2515—Mattresses &
Bedsprings.

★ 81692 ★ Service Merchandise
6120 Winchester Rd.
Memphis, TN 38115
(901)365-8667
Ultimate Parent: Service Merchandise Co.,
Inc. **SIC:** 5961—Catalog & Mail-Order
Houses.

★ 81693 ★ Shell Chemical Co.
5830 Mount Moriah Rd.
Memphis, TN 38115
(901)795-6642
Ultimate Parent: Shell Oil Co. **SIC:** 5172—
Petroleum Products Nec.

★ 81694 ★ Sonoco Products Co.
2755 Harbor Ave.
Memphis, TN 38106
(901)774-6321
Officer: Keith Lustig, Manager. **Ultimate
Parent:** Sonoco Products. **SIC:** 2299—
Textile Goods Nec; 3221—Glass
Containers.

★ 81695 ★ Sonoco Products Co.
1440 Ragan St.
Memphis, TN 38106
(901)942-2492
Officer: William Rasch, Manager. **Ultimate
Parent:** Sonoco Products. **SIC:** 2655—Fiber
Cans, Drums & Similar Products.

★ 81696 ★ Southern Co.
300 E. Georgia Ave.
Memphis, TN 38126
(901)527-2531
Ultimate Parent: Southern. **SIC:** 3552—
Textile Machinery; 3569—General Industrial
Machinery Nec.

**★ 81697 ★ Southern Cotton Oil
Co.**
2782 Chelsea Ave.
Memphis, TN 38108
Ultimate Parent: Archer Daniels Midland
Co. **SIC:** 2074—Cottonseed Oil Mills.

**★ 81698 ★ Southern Cotton Oil
Co.**
PO Box 80367
Memphis, TN 38108-0367
(901)452-3151
Officer: Tim Taylor. **Ultimate Parent:**
Archer Daniels Midland Co. **SIC:** 2074—
Cottonseed Oil Mills; 2211—Broadwoven
Fabric Mills—Cotton; 5159—Farm-Product
Raw Materials Nec.

**★ 81699 ★ Southern Cotton Oil
Co. Inc.**
2782 Chelsea Ave.
Memphis, TN 38108
(901)452-3151
Ultimate Parent: Archer Daniels Midland
Co. **SIC:** 2074—Cottonseed Oil Mills;
2075—Soybean Oil Mills; 2211—
Broadwoven Fabric Mills—Cotton.

★ 81700 ★ Summitt Insulators Pc
2775 Channel Ave.
Memphis, TN 38113-0000
Ultimate Parent: Thomas & Betts. **SIC:**
3000—Rubber & Miscellaneous Plastics
Products.

★ 81701 ★ Target
1251 Wesley Dr.
Memphis, TN 38116
(901)332-2270
Ultimate Parent: Dayton Hudson. **SIC:**
5311—Department Stores.

★ 81702 ★ Target
5119 Summer Ave.
Memphis, TN 38122
(901)683-6200
Ultimate Parent: Dayton Hudson. **SIC:**
5311—Department Stores.

★ 81703 ★ Target Stores
5119 Summer Ave.
Memphis, TN 38122
(901)683-6200
Ultimate Parent: Dayton Hudson. **SIC:**
5311—Department Stores.

★ 81704 ★ Target Stores
1251 Wesley Dr.
Memphis, TN 38116
(901)332-2270
Ultimate Parent: Dayton Hudson. **SIC:**
5311—Department Stores.

★ 81705 ★ Texaco
5930 Winchester Rd.
Memphis, TN 38115
(901)795-6924
Ultimate Parent: Texaco. **SIC:** 5541—
Gasoline Service Stations.

★ 81706 ★ Texaco Inc.
3358 N. Watkins St.
Memphis, TN 38127
(901)358-8903
Ultimate Parent: Texaco. **SIC:** 5411—
Grocery Stores.

**★ 81707 ★ Texas Instruments
Inc.**
6584 Poplar Ave.
Memphis, TN 38138
(901)761-1990
Location Type: Branch office. **Ultimate
Parent:** Texas Instruments. **SIC:** 3571—
Electronic Computers; 5084—Industrial
Machinery & Equipment.

★ 81708 ★ Thomas & Betts
1555 Lynnfield Rd.
Memphis, TN 38119
(901)682-7766 **Fax:** (901)685-1988
Company Type: Headquarters. **Officer:** T.
Kevin Dunnigan, CEO. **Employee Count:**
8000. **Sales:** 1075.9 M. **Fortune 500:**
Largest U.S. Industrial Corporations:
Ranking 351.

**★ 81709 ★ Thompson & Formby
Inc.**
825 Crossover Ln.
Memphis, TN 38117-4934
(901)685-7555
Company Type: Subsidiary. **Officer:** Bill D.
Stewart, President. **Ultimate Parent:**
Eastman Kodak. **SIC:** 2899—Chemical

Preparations Nec; 2851—Paints & Allied
Products. **Employee Count:** 350. **Sales:**
175 M.

**★ 81710 ★ Thompson &
Formby's Inc.**
825 Crossover Ln.
Memphis, TN 38117
(901)685-7555
Officer: William Stewart, President.
Ultimate Parent: Eastman Kodak.

★ 81711 ★ Tosco Corp.
6380 Briergate Dr.
Memphis, TN 38134
(901)377-6336
Ultimate Parent: Tosco Corp. **SIC:** 5172—
Petroleum Products Nec.

★ 81712 ★ Total Petroleum Inc.
6073 Mount Moriah Rd.
Memphis, TN 38115
(901)365-0460
Ultimate Parent: Total Petroleum Inc. **SIC:**
1311—Crude Petroleum & Natural Gas.

★ 81713 ★ Total Service Station
6073 Mount Moriah Rd.
Memphis, TN 38115
(901)365-0460
Ultimate Parent: Total Petroleum Inc. **SIC:**
1311—Crude Petroleum & Natural Gas.

★ 81714 ★ Trailways Bus Lines
235 Union Ave.
Memphis, TN 38103
(901)523-0200
Ultimate Parent: Greyhound Lines Inc. **SIC:**
4131—Intercity & Rural Bus Transportation;
4111—Local & Suburban Transit; 4142—
Bus Charter Service Except Local.

★ 81715 ★ Trailways Bus Lines
3243 Winchester Rd.
Memphis, TN 38118
(901)365-0149
Ultimate Parent: Greyhound Lines Inc. **SIC:**
4111—Local & Suburban Transit; 4142—
Bus Charter Service Except Local; 4131—
Intercity & Rural Bus Transportation.

★ 81716 ★ Trans State Line Inc.
1917 E. Brooks Rd.
Memphis, TN 38116-3601
(901)332-7555
Officer: William Brown. **Ultimate Parent:**
Arkansas Best. **SIC:** 4212—Local Trucking
Without Storage; 7513—Truck Rental &
Leasing Without Drivers.

★ 81717 ★ Trans World Airlines
Memphs International Arp
Memphis, TN 38116
(901)345-3743
Ultimate Parent: Trans World Airlines. **SIC:**
4512—Air Transportation—Scheduled.

**★ 81718 ★ Trans World Airlines
Inc.**
Memphs International Arp
Memphis, TN 38130
(901)345-3746
Ultimate Parent: Trans World Airlines. **SIC:**
4729—Passenger Transportation
Arrangement Nec.

★ 81719 ★ True Temper
Sports Division
871 Ridgeway Loop Rd., Ste. 210
Memphis, TN 38120-4008
(901)767-9411
Company Type: Branch. **Officer:** Ed Van
Dyke. **Ultimate Parent:** Black & Decker
Corp. **SIC:** 3949—Sporting & Athletic Goods
Nec; 2499—Wood Products Nec; 3499—
Fabricated Metal Products Nec.

★ 81720 ★ Union Planters Corp.
7130 Goodlett Farms Pky.
Memphis, TN 38018
(901)383-6000
Company Type: Headquarters. **Officer:**
Benjamin W. Rowlins Jr. **Employee Count:**
3003. **Sales:** 483 M. **Fortune Service 500:**
Ranking 82.

**★ 81721 ★ Union Planters
National Bank**
4643 Germantown Rd., Extended
Memphis, TN 38141
(901)367-4125
Location Type: Branch office. **Ultimate
Parent:** Union Planters Corp. **SIC:** 6021—
National Commercial Banks.

★ 81722 ★   Union Planters
National Bank
6743 Winchester Rd.
Memphis, TN 38115
(901)367-4130
Location Type: Branch office. Ultimate
Parent: Union Planters Corp. SIC: 6021—
National Commercial Banks.

★ 81723 ★   Union Planters
National Bank
4790 Poplar Ave.
Memphis, TN 38117-5149
(901)762-7866
Location Type: Branch office. Ultimate
Parent: Union Planters Corp. SIC: 6021—
National Commercial Banks.

★ 81724 ★   Union Planters
National Bank
4134 Elvis Presley Blvd.
Memphis, TN 38116-5878
(901)345-4360
Location Type: Branch office. Ultimate
Parent: Union Planters Corp. SIC: 6021—
National Commercial Banks.

★ 81725 ★   Union Planters
National Bank
1190 E. Shelby Dr.
Memphis, TN 38116-7124
(901)345-4369
Location Type: Branch office. Ultimate
Parent: Union Planters Corp. SIC: 6021—
National Commercial Banks.

★ 81726 ★   Union Planters
National Bank
2053 Union Ave.
Memphis, TN 38104-4034
(901)722-7057
Location Type: Branch office. Ultimate
Parent: Union Planters Corp. SIC: 6021—
National Commercial Banks.

★ 81727 ★   Union Planters
National Bank
5050 Poplar Ave.
Memphis, TN 38157-3002
(901)762-7853
Location Type: Branch office. Ultimate
Parent: Union Planters Corp. SIC: 6021—
National Commercial Banks.

★ 81728 ★   Union Planters
National Bank
4362 Summer Ave.
Memphis, TN 38122-4088
(901)762-7842
Location Type: Branch office. Ultimate
Parent: Union Planters Corp. SIC: 6021—
National Commercial Banks.

★ 81729 ★   Union Planters
National Bank
1889 S. 3rd St.
Memphis, TN 38109-7713
(901)775-8401
Location Type: Branch office. Ultimate
Parent: Union Planters Corp. SIC: 6021—
National Commercial Banks.

★ 81730 ★   Union Planters
National Bank
50 N. Front St.
Memphis, TN 38103-2126
(901)523-6909
Location Type: Branch office. Ultimate
Parent: Union Planters Corp. SIC: 6021—
National Commercial Banks.

★ 81731 ★   Union Planters
National Bank
1170 Park Pl. Ctr.
Memphis, TN 38119-5209
(901)962-7834
Location Type: Branch office. Ultimate
Parent: Union Planters Corp. SIC: 6021—
National Commercial Banks.

★ 81732 ★   Union Planters
National Bank
3535 Austin Peay Hwy.
Memphis, TN 38128-3717
(901)385-4014
Location Type: Branch office. Ultimate
Parent: Union Planters Corp. SIC: 6021—
National Commercial Banks.

★ 81733 ★   Union Planters
National Bank
5150 American Way
Memphis, TN 38115-1573
(901)367-4119
Location Type: Branch office. Ultimate
Parent: Union Planters Corp. SIC: 6021—
National Commercial Banks.

★ 81734 ★   Union Planters
National Bank
2155 Covington Pke.
Memphis, TN 38128-6994
(901)385-4021
Location Type: Branch office. Ultimate
Parent: Union Planters Corp. SIC: 6021—
National Commercial Banks.

★ 81735 ★   Union Planters
National Bank
981 Madison Ave.
Memphis, TN 38104-2100
(901)522-2851
Location Type: Branch office. Ultimate
Parent: Union Planters Corp. SIC: 6021—
National Commercial Banks.

★ 81736 ★   Union Planters
National Bank
3751 Lamar Ave.
Memphis, TN 38118-3706
(901)367-4107
Location Type: Branch office. Ultimate
Parent: Union Planters Corp. SIC: 6021—
National Commercial Banks.

★ 81737 ★   Union Planters
National Bank
2188 Frayser Blvd.
Memphis, TN 38127-5700
(901)353-8500
Location Type: Branch office. Ultimate
Parent: Union Planters Corp. SIC: 6021—
National Commercial Banks.

★ 81738 ★   Union Planters
National Bank
3485 Plaza Ave.
Memphis, TN 38111-4613
(901)325-4050
Location Type: Branch office. Ultimate
Parent: Union Planters Corp. SIC: 6021—
National Commercial Banks.

★ 81739 ★   Union Planters
National Bank
5138 Park Ave.
Memphis, TN 38117-5709
(901)762-7823
Location Type: Branch office. Ultimate
Parent: Union Planters Corp. SIC: 6021—
National Commercial Banks.

★ 81740 ★   Union Planters
National Bank
3580 S. Menden Hall Rd.
Memphis, TN 38118-4512
(901)367-4100
Location Type: Branch office. Ultimate
Parent: Union Planters Corp. SIC: 6021—
National Commercial Banks.

★ 81741 ★   Union Planters
National Bank
270 N. Cleveland St.
Memphis, TN 38104-7100
(901)722-7050
Location Type: Branch office. Ultimate
Parent: Union Planters Corp. SIC: 6021—
National Commercial Banks.

★ 81742 ★   Union Planters
National Bank
4615 Quince
Memphis, TN 38117-6546
(901)962-7873
Location Type: Branch office. Ultimate
Parent: Union Planters Corp. SIC: 6021—
National Commercial Banks.

★ 81743 ★   Union Planters
National Bank
4805 American Way
Memphis, TN 38118-2412
(901)367-4112
Location Type: Branch office. Ultimate
Parent: Union Planters Corp. SIC: 6021—
National Commercial Banks.

★ 81744 ★   Union Planters
National Bank
2269 Democrat Rd.
Memphis, TN 38132-1800
(901)345-4379
Location Type: Branch office. Ultimate
Parent: Union Planters Corp. SIC: 6021—
National Commercial Banks.

★ 81745 ★   Union Planters
National Bank
3245 Poplar Ave.
Memphis, TN 38111-3603
(901)325-4060
Location Type: Branch office. Ultimate
Parent: Union Planters Corp. SIC: 6021—
National Commercial Banks.

★ 81746 ★   Union Planters
National Bank
4451 Mall of Memphis
Memphis, TN 38118
(901)383-6000
Location Type: Branch office. Ultimate
Parent: Union Planters Corp. SIC: 6021—
National Commercial Banks.

★ 81747 ★   Union Planters
National Bank
PO Box 387
Memphis, TN 38147
Location Type: Headquarters. Ultimate
Parent: Union Planters Corp. SIC: 6021—
National Commercial Banks.

★ 81748 ★   Union Planters
National Bank
6200 Poplar
Memphis, TN 38103
(901)383-6000 Telex: 6828015
Location Type: Headquarters. Ultimate
Parent: Union Planters Corp. SIC: 6021—
National Commercial Banks.

★ 81749 ★   Union Planters
National Bank
4362 Summer Ave.
Memphis, TN 38122-4088
(901)762-7842
Location Type: Branch office. Ultimate
Parent: Union Planters Corp. SIC: 6021—
National Commercial Banks.

★ 81750 ★   Victoria's Secret
7605 W. Farmington Blvd.
Memphis, TN 38138
(901)757-5009
Ultimate Parent: Limited. SIC: 5621—
Women's Clothing Stores.

★ 81751 ★   Victoria's Secret
6068 Hickory Ridge Mall
Memphis, TN 38115
(901)363-2101
Ultimate Parent: Limited. SIC: 5621—
Women's Clothing Stores.

★ 81752 ★   Wagner Brake
Subsidiary
790 S. 4th St.
Memphis, TN 38126
Ultimate Parent: Cooper Industries. SIC:
3714—Motor Vehicle Parts & Accessories.

★ 81753 ★   Wagner Electric Corp.
790 S. 4th St.
Memphis, TN 38126
Ultimate Parent: Cooper Industries. SIC:
3714—Motor Vehicle Parts & Accessories.

★ 81754 ★   Wal-Mart Stores Inc.
6990 E. Shelby Dr.
Memphis, TN 38125
(901)757-1442
Ultimate Parent: Wal-Mart Stores, Inc. SIC:
5311—Department Stores.

★ 81755 ★   Wall Street Journal
100 N. Main St.
Memphis, TN 38103
(901)527-3564
Ultimate Parent: Dow Jones. SIC: 2711—
Newspapers.

★ 81756 ★   Wesson/Peter Pan
Foods Co.
1351 Williams Ave.
Memphis, TN 38104
Ultimate Parent: Conagra. SIC: 2079—
Edible Fats & Oils Nec.

★ 81757 ★   Western Union
International
825 Crossover Ln.
Memphis, TN 38117
(901)767-0769
Ultimate Parent: MCI Communications.
SIC: 7389—Business Services Nec.

★ 81758 ★   Weyerhaeuser Co.
3875 Air Park St.
Memphis, TN 38118
(901)363-5693
Officer: Ken Taylor, Manager. Ultimate
Parent: Weyerhaeuser Co. SIC: 2431—
Millwork.

★ 81759 ★   Weyerhaeuser Paper
Co.
1170 N. Manasses St.
Memphis, TN 38107
(901)525-5511
Officer: David Duke, Manager. Ultimate
Parent: Weyerhaeuser Co. SIC: 2652—
Setup Paperboard Boxes.

★ 81760 ★   Witco Corp.
Humko Chemical
1231 Pope St.
Memphis, TN 38108
Ultimate Parent: Witco Corp. SIC: 2869—
Industrial Organic Chemicals Nec; 2899—
Chemical Preparations Nec; 2841—Soap &
Other Detergents; 2099—Food Preparations
Nec; 2843—Surface Active Agents.

★ 81761 ★   Witco Corp.
Humko Chemical
1231 Pope St.
Memphis, TN 38108
Ultimate Parent: Witco Corp. SIC: 2869—
Industrial Organic Chemicals Nec; 2899—
Chemical Preparations Nec; 2841—Soap &
Other Detergents.

★ 81762 ★   Witco Corp.
Humko Chemical Div.
1231 Pope St.
Memphis, TN 38108
(901)320-5800
Company Type: Division. Officer: Harry
Nicholson, Manager. Ultimate Parent:
Witco Corp. SIC: 2869—Industrial Organic
Chemicals Nec.

★ 81763 ★   Witco Corp.
Humko Chemical Div.
755 Crossover Ln.
Memphis, TN 38117
(901)684-7000
Company Type: Division. Officer: E.
Charles Leonard, Manager. Ultimate
Parent: Witco Corp. SIC: 2819—Industrial
Inorganic Chemicals Nec; 2899—Chemical
Preparations Nec.

Middleton

★ 81764 ★   Dover Elevator Co.
100 Dover
Middleton, TN 38052
(901)376-8444
Officer: Eddie Carr, Manager. Ultimate
Parent: Dover Corp. SIC: 3534—Elevators
& Moving Stairways.

Milan

★ 81765 ★   A. O. Smith
Automotive Prods. Co.
52 A.O. Smith Rd.
Milan, TN 38358
Ultimate Parent: A. O. Smith. SIC: 3700—
Transportation Equipment.

★ 81766 ★   A.O. Smith
Automotive Products Co.
Telecom Dr.
Milan, TN 38358-0529
Ultimate Parent: A. O. Smith. SIC: 3714—
Motor Vehicle Parts & Accessories.

★ 81767 ★   First American
National Bank
450 S. Main St.
Milan, TN 38358-2704
(901)686-2900
Location Type: Branch office. Ultimate
Parent: First American Corp. SIC: 6021—
National Commercial Banks.

★ 81768 ★   **Foamex LP**
2050 Kefauver Rd.
Milan, TN 38358
Ultimate Parent: Foamex. **SIC:** 3086—
Plastics Foam Products.

★ 81769 ★   **Greyhound Bus Lines**
Van Hook Rd.
Milan, TN 38358
(901)686-1331
Ultimate Parent: Greyhound Lines Inc. **SIC:**
4111—Local & Suburban Transit; 4131—
Intercity & Rural Bus Transportation; 4142—
Bus Charter Service Except Local.

★ 81770 ★   **Martin Marietta**
Milan Army Ammunition Plant
Hwy. 104
Milan, TN 38358-5000
Location Type: Plant. **Ultimate Parent:**
Martin Marietta. **SIC:** 3483—Ammunition
Except for Small Arms.

★ 81771 ★   **Rite Aid Discount
Pharmacy**
Milan Plz.
Milan, TN 38358
(901)686-9321
Ultimate Parent: Rite Aid. **SIC:** 5912—Drug
Stores & Proprietary Stores.

★ 81772 ★   **Union Planters
National Bank**
2072 1st St.
Milan, TN 38358-3027
(901)686-1527
Location Type: Branch office. **Ultimate
Parent:** Union Planters Corp. **SIC:** 6021—
National Commercial Banks.

★ 81773 ★   **Union Planters
National Bank**
6066 S. 1st St.
Milan, TN 38358-9428
(901)686-7488
Location Type: Branch office. **Ultimate
Parent:** Union Planters Corp. **SIC:** 6021—
National Commercial Banks.

Millington

★ 81774 ★   **Arcadian Fertilizer LP**
5790 Old Millington Rd.
PO Box 27147
Millington, TN 38053-8306
(901)357-2311
Officer: R. P. Cloutier. **Ultimate Parent:**
Arcadian Corp. **SIC:** 2813—Industrial
Gases; 2873—Nitrogenous Fertilizers.

★ 81775 ★   **BFI Waste Systems**
7111 Old Millington Rd.
Millington, TN 38053-6211
(901)872-7200
Ultimate Parent: Browning-Ferris
Industries. **SIC:** 4953—Refuse Systems.

★ 81776 ★   **Greyhound Bus Lines**
7855 Hwy. 51 N
Millington, TN 38053
(901)872-9316
Ultimate Parent: Greyhound Lines Inc. **SIC:**
4131—Intercity & Rural Bus Transportation;
4111—Local & Suburban Transit; 4142—
Bus Charter Service Except Local.

★ 81777 ★   **Kroger Co.**
8039 US Hwy. 51 N
Millington, TN 38053
(901)872-6741
Ultimate Parent: Kroger. **SIC:** 5411—
Grocery Stores.

★ 81778 ★   **Payless Shoe Source**
8043 Hwy. 51 N
Millington, TN 38053
(901)872-7999
Ultimate Parent: May Department Stores.
SIC: 5661—Shoe Stores.

★ 81779 ★   **Wal-Mart Stores Inc.**
8235 Us 51 N
Millington, TN 38053
(901)872-6606
Ultimate Parent: Wal-Mart Stores, Inc. **SIC:**
5311—Department Stores.

Mohawk

★ 81780 ★   **Bed & Bath Etc**
Rural Route 1
Mohawk, TN 37810
(615)581-6869
Ultimate Parent: Fieldcrest Cannon. **SIC:**
5719—Miscellaneous Home Furnishings
Stores.

Monteagle

★ 81781 ★   **First National Bank**
14 College St.
Monteagle, TN 37356
(615)924-2261
Location Type: Branch office. **Ultimate
Parent:** Union Planters Corp. **SIC:** 6021—
National Commercial Banks.

Monterey

★ 81782 ★   **Citizens Bank**
210 E. Commercial Ave.
Monterey, TN 38574
(615)839-2265
Location Type: Branch office. **Ultimate
Parent:** Union Planters Corp. **SIC:** 6021—
National Commercial Banks.

Morrison

★ 81783 ★   **Carrier Corp.**
Morrison Rd.
Morrison, TN 37357
Ultimate Parent: United Technologies. **SIC:**
3585—Refrigeration & Heating Equipment.

Morristown

★ 81784 ★   **Bank of East
Tennessee**
143 E. Main St.
Morristown, TN 37814
Location Type: Branch office. **Ultimate
Parent:** Union Planters Corp. **SIC:** 6021—
National Commercial Banks.

★ 81785 ★   **Bank of East
Tennessee**
2550 E. Morris Blvd.
Morristown, TN 37814
Location Type: Branch office. **Ultimate
Parent:** Union Planters Corp. **SIC:** 6021—
National Commercial Banks.

★ 81786 ★   **Bank of East
Tennessee**
1960 W. Morris Blvd.
Morristown, TN 37814-3766
Location Type: Branch office. **Ultimate
Parent:** Union Planters Corp. **SIC:** 6021—
National Commercial Banks.

★ 81787 ★   **Bank of East
Tennessee**
2400 E. Andrew Johnson Hwy.
Morristown, TN 37814-5504
(615)587-7100
Location Type: Branch office. **Ultimate
Parent:** Union Planters Corp. **SIC:** 6021—
National Commercial Banks.

★ 81788 ★   **Bank of East
Tennessee**
201 W. Morris Blvd.
Morristown, TN 37816-1217
(615)587-7100 **Fax:** (615)587-7126
Location Type: Headquarters. **Ultimate
Parent:** Union Planters Corp. **SIC:** 6021—
National Commercial Banks.

★ 81789 ★   **Camvac International**
5705 Commerce Blvd.
Morristown, TN 37814
Ultimate Parent: Bowater. **SIC:** 2672—
Coated & Laminated Paper Nec.

★ 81790 ★   **Camvac International
Inc.**
5705 Commerce Blvd.
Morristown, TN 37814
Ultimate Parent: Bowater. **SIC:** 2672—
Coated & Laminated Paper Nec.

★ 81791 ★   **Camvac International
Inc.**
5705 Commerce Blvd.
Morristown, TN 37814
Ultimate Parent: Bowater. **SIC:** 2600—
Paper & Allied Products.

★ 81792 ★   **E. R. Carpenter Co.
Inc.**
5306 E. Tennessee Blvd.
Morristown, TN 37815
Ultimate Parent: Carpenter. **SIC:** 3086—
Plastics Foam Products.

★ 81793 ★   **E.R. Carpenter Co.
Inc.**
5306 East. Tn Blvd.
Morristown, TN 37815
Ultimate Parent: Carpenter. **SIC:** 3086—
Plastics Foam Products.

★ 81794 ★   **First Tennessee Bank
NA**
1730 W. Andrew Johnson Hwy.
Morristown, TN 37814-3737
(615)587-3700
Location Type: Branch office. **Ultimate
Parent:** First Tennessee National Corp.
SIC: 6021—National Commercial Banks.

★ 81795 ★   **First Tennessee Bank
NA**
3500 W. Andrew Johnson Hwy.
Morristown, TN 37814-3639
Location Type: Branch office. **Ultimate
Parent:** First Tennessee National Corp.
SIC: 6021—National Commercial Banks.

★ 81796 ★   **First Tennessee Bank
NA**
2301 E. Andrew Johnson Hwy.
Morristown, TN 37814-5501
Location Type: Branch office. **Ultimate
Parent:** First Tennessee National Corp.
SIC: 6021—National Commercial Banks.

★ 81797 ★   **First Tennessee Bank
NA**
1112 W. 1st St. N
Morristown, TN 37814-4554
(615)586-8021
Location Type: Branch office. **Ultimate
Parent:** First Tennessee National Corp.
SIC: 6021—National Commercial Banks.

★ 81798 ★   **Flowers Baking Co.**
1725 W. 1st N. St.
Morristown, TN 37814
(615)587-3834
Officer: F. Ray Sexton, President. **Ultimate
Parent:** Flowers Industries. **SIC:** 2051—
Bread, Cake & Related Products.

★ 81799 ★   **Flowers Baking Co.
Morristown Inc.**
1725 W. First North St.
Morristown, TN 37814
(615)586-2471 **Fax:** (615)586-3728
Company Type: Subsidiary. **Officer:** Ray
Sexton, President. **Ultimate Parent:**
Flowers Industries.

★ 81800 ★   **Foamex LP**
1806 Gluck Rd.
Morristown, TN 37816
Location Type: Plant. **Ultimate Parent:**
Foamex. **SIC:** 3086—Plastics Foam
Products.

★ 81801 ★   **Foamex L.P. Plant 1**
328 Hamblen Ave.
Morristown, TN 37814
Ultimate Parent: Foamex. **SIC:** 3086—
Plastics Foam Products.

★ 81802 ★   **Foamex L.P. Plant 3**
1 Laminite Dr.
Morristown, TN 37816
Ultimate Parent: Foamex. **SIC:** 3086—
Plastics Foam Products.

★ 81803 ★   **GE Electrial
Distribution & Control**
5320 East Morris Blvd.
Morristown, TN 37816-1919
Ultimate Parent: General Electric. **SIC:**
3613—Switchgear & Switchboard
Apparatus.

★ 81804 ★   **GE Electrical
Distribution & Control**
5320 East Morris Blvd.
Morristown, TN 37816-1919
Ultimate Parent: General Electric. **SIC:**
3613—Switchgear & Switchboard
Apparatus.

★ 81805 ★   **General Electric Co.**
5320 E. Morris Blvd.
Morristown, TN 37813
(615)581-0307
Officer: Mary Cox, Manager. **Ultimate
Parent:** General Electric. **SIC:** 3613—
Switchgear & Switchboard Apparatus;
3644—Noncurrent-Carrying Wiring Devices;
3699—Electrical Equipment & Supplies Nec.

★ 81806 ★   **NCR Corp.**
5512 E. Tennessee Blvd.
Morristown, TN 37813-1141
(615)581-1620
Location Type: Branch office. **Officer:**
Vennon Fields. **Ultimate Parent:** AT&T.
SIC: 2679—Converted Paper Products Nec;
3571—Electronic Computers; 3577—
Computer Peripheral Equipment Nec;
5112—Stationery & Office Supplies.

★ 81807 ★   **Rockwell International
Corp.**
One Rockwell Dr.
Morristown, TN 37813
Ultimate Parent: Rockwell International
Corp. **SIC:** 3714—Motor Vehicle Parts &
Accessories.

★ 81808 ★   **Ryder Truck Rental &
Leasing**
S Economy Rd.
Morristown, TN 37814
(615)581-5480
Ultimate Parent: Ryder System. **SIC:**
5511—New & Used Car Dealers.

★ 81809 ★   **Security Trust FS &
LA**
435 W. 1st North St.
Morristown, TN 37814-4640
(615)581-6210
Location Type: Branch office. **Ultimate
Parent:** Union Planters Corp. **SIC:** 6021—
National Commercial Banks.

★ 81810 ★   **Sterling Engineered
Products**
325 Desoto Ave.
Morristown, TN 37816-1973
Ultimate Parent: Trinova Corp. **SIC:**
3083—Laminated Plastics Plate & Sheet.

★ 81811 ★   **Stop & Shop**
2320 W. a Johnson Hwy.
Morristown, TN 37814
(615)586-0057
Ultimate Parent: Stop & Shop. **SIC:** 5411—
Grocery Stores.

★ 81812 ★   **Swift Independent
Packing Co.**
328 Industrial Ave.
Morristown, TN 37813
(615)581-3950
Ultimate Parent: Conagra. **SIC:** 5147—
Meats & Meat Products.

★ 81813 ★   **Trailways Bus Lines**
300 W. 1st St. N
Morristown, TN 37814
(615)586-3841
Ultimate Parent: Greyhound Lines Inc. **SIC:**
4131—Intercity & Rural Bus Transportation;
4111—Local & Suburban Transit; 4142—
Bus Charter Service Except Local.

★ 81814 ★   **Union Camp Corp.**
Hwy. 25 E
Morristown, TN 37814
Ultimate Parent: Union Camp Corp. **SIC:**
2653—Corrugated & Solid Fiber Boxes.

★ 81815 ★   **Universal Bedroom
Furniture Ltd.**
5649 E. Morris Blvd.
Morristown, TN 37814
Ultimate Parent: Masco. **SIC:** 2511—Wood
Household Furniture.

★ 81816 ★   **Vulcan Materials Co.**
Lowland Rd.
Morristown, TN 37814
(615)586-0992
Ultimate Parent: Vulcan Materials Co. **SIC:**
5039—Construction Materials Nec.

★ 81817 ★   **W. R. Grace & Co.**
5700 Commerce Blvd.
Morristown, TN 37814
Ultimate Parent: W. R. Grace. **SIC:** 3069—
Fabricated Rubber Products Nec.

★ 81818 ★   **Wal-Mart Stores Inc.**
Downtown Shopping Ctr.
Morristown, TN 37814
(615)581-3500
Ultimate Parent: Wal-Mart Stores, Inc. **SIC:**
5311—Department Stores.

★ 81819 ★   **W.R. Grace & Co.**
5700 Coomerce Blvd.
Morristown, TN 37814
Ultimate Parent: W. R. Grace. **SIC:** 3069—
Fabricated Rubber Products Nec.

Mosheim

★ 81820 ★ First Tennessee Bank NA
Main St.
Mosheim, TN 37818-9601
(615)422-4111
Ultimate Parent: First Tennessee National Corp. **SIC:** 6021—National Commercial Banks.

Mount Juliet

★ 81821 ★ Coast to Coast Hardware
1249 Mt Juliet
Mount Juliet, TN 37122
(615)754-4575
Ultimate Parent: Servistar Corp.

★ 81822 ★ First American National Bank
2425 N. Mount Juliet Rd.
Mount Juliet, TN 37122-3046
(615)736-6769
Location Type: Branch office. **Ultimate Parent:** First American Corp. **SIC:** 6021—National Commercial Banks.

★ 81823 ★ Lebanon Bank
496 PO Box
Mount Juliet, TN 37122
(615)758-5891
Ultimate Parent: First Tennessee National Corp. **SIC:** 6099—Functions Related to Deposit Banking; 6029—Commercial Banks Nec.

Mount Pleasant

★ 81824 ★ Rhone-Poulenc Ag Co.
786 Arrow Lake Rd.
Mount Pleasant, TN 38474
Ultimate Parent: Rhone-Poulenc Rorer. **SIC:** 2879—Agricultural Chemicals Nec.

★ 81825 ★ Rhone-Poulenc Ag Co.
PO Box 352
Mount Pleasant, TN 38474
Ultimate Parent: Rhone-Poulenc Rorer. **SIC:** 2879—Agricultural Chemicals Nec.

★ 81826 ★ Rhone-Poulenc Basic Chemicals Co.
Mt. Joy Rd.
Mount Pleasant, TN 38474
Ultimate Parent: Rhone-Poulenc Rorer. **SIC:** 2819—Industrial Inorganic Chemicals Nec.

★ 81827 ★ Rhone-Poulenc Inc. Ag Co.
Arrow Mines Rd.
Mount Pleasant, TN 38474
Ultimate Parent: Rhone-Poulenc Rorer. **SIC:** 2879—Agricultural Chemicals Nec.

★ 81828 ★ Stauffer Chemical Co. Furnace Plant
Mt. Joy Rd. PO Box 472
Mount Pleasant, TN 38474
Ultimate Parent: Rhone-Poulenc Rorer. **SIC:** 2819—Industrial Inorganic Chemicals Nec.

Mt. Juliet

★ 81829 ★ First Tennessee Bank NA
420 Mt. Juliet Rd.
Mt. Juliet, TN 37122
(615)758-5891
Location Type: Branch office. **Ultimate Parent:** First Tennessee National Corp. **SIC:** 6021—National Commercial Banks.

★ 81830 ★ Union Planters National Bank
Clearview Plz.
1395 N. Mt. Juliet Rd.
Mt. Juliet, TN 37122
(615)726-4322
Location Type: Branch office. **Ultimate Parent:** Union Planters Corp. **SIC:** 6021—National Commercial Banks.

Mt. Minnville

★ 81831 ★ Dr. Pepper Bottling Co.
217 Mount View St.
Mt. Minnville, TN 37110
(615)473-2108
Officer: Douglas Milner, Plant Manager. **Ultimate Parent:** Dr. Pepper/Seven-Up. **SIC:** 2086—Bottled & Canned Soft Drinks.

Mt. Pleasant

★ 81832 ★ ITW Shippers Paper Products/Airbags
1203 N. Main St.
Mt. Pleasant, TN 38474
(615)379-7731 **Fax:** (615)379-7735
Company Type: Subsidiary. **Officer:** Tom Keenan, General Manager. **Ultimate Parent:** Illinois Tool Works.

★ 81833 ★ Rhone Poulenc Basic Chemical
8000 Mt. Joy Rd.
Mt. Pleasant, TN 38474
(615)379-3251
Ultimate Parent: Rhone-Poulenc Rorer. **SIC:** 2819—Industrial Inorganic Chemicals Nec; 2899—Chemical Preparations Nec.

★ 81834 ★ Rhone Poulenc Inc.
786 Arrow Lake Rd.
Mt. Pleasant, TN 38474
(615)379-3208
Ultimate Parent: Rhone-Poulenc Rorer. **SIC:** 2879—Agricultural Chemicals Nec; 2899—Chemical Preparations Nec.

Murfreesboro

★ 81835 ★ Barfield Mfg Co. Inc.
N Barfield Rd.
Murfreesboro, TN 37130
(615)893-4977
Ultimate Parent: Masco. **SIC:** 3699—Electrical Equipment & Supplies Nec.

★ 81836 ★ Blazer Financial Services
1630 S. Church St.
Murfreesboro, TN 37130
(615)896-0497
Ultimate Parent: Great Western Financial Corp. **SIC:** 6062—State Credit Unions; 6141—Personal Credit Institutions.

★ 81837 ★ Brunswick Fishing Boat Div.
6776 Old Nashville Hwy.
Murfreesboro, TN 37129
(615)890-1593
Officer: Dan Horner, President. **Ultimate Parent:** Brunswick Corp. **SIC:** 3732—Boat Building & Repairing; 3799—Transportation Equipment Nec.

★ 81838 ★ Brunswick Marine
6776 Old Nashville Hwy.
Murfreesboro, TN 37129-8400
(615)890-1593
Officer: Dan Horner. **Ultimate Parent:** Brunswick Corp. **SIC:** 3732—Boat Building & Repairing; 3799—Transportation Equipment Nec.

★ 81839 ★ Eckerd Drugs
Smyrna Sq.
Murfreesboro, TN 37130
(615)459-5750
Ultimate Parent: Eckerd Corp. **SIC:** 5921—Liquor Stores.

★ 81840 ★ Emerson Electric Co.
Chromalox Div.
600 Ridgely Rd.
Murfreesboro, TN 37130
Company Type: Division. **Ultimate Parent:** Emerson Electric Co. Inc. **SIC:** 3699—Electrical Equipment & Supplies Nec.

★ 81841 ★ Emerson Electric Co.
Wiegand Industrial Div.
600 Ridgely Rd.
Murfreesboro, TN 37130
Company Type: Division. **Ultimate Parent:** Emerson Electric Co. Inc. **SIC:** 3699—Electrical Equipment & Supplies Nec.

★ 81842 ★ First American National Bank
319 N. Maple
Murfreesboro, TN 37130-3614
(615)849-3000
Location Type: Branch office. **Ultimate Parent:** First American Corp. **SIC:** 6021—National Commercial Banks.

★ 81843 ★ First Tennessee Bank NA
722 S. Tennessee Blvd.
Murfreesboro, TN 37130-5139
Location Type: Branch office. **Ultimate Parent:** First Tennessee National Corp. **SIC:** 6021—National Commercial Banks.

★ 81844 ★ First Tennessee Bank NA
205 NW Broad St.
Murfreesboro, TN 37130-3511
Location Type: Branch office. **Ultimate Parent:** First Tennessee National Corp. **SIC:** 6021—National Commercial Banks.

★ 81845 ★ First Tennessee Bank NA
305 W. Northfield
Murfreesboro, TN 37130-3762
(615)893-7210
Location Type: Branch office. **Ultimate Parent:** First Tennessee National Corp. **SIC:** 6021—National Commercial Banks.

★ 81846 ★ First Union National Bank of Tennessee
802 NW Broad St.
Murfreesboro, TN 37129
(615)895-9091
Location Type: Branch office. **Ultimate Parent:** First Union Corp. **SIC:** 6021—National Commercial Banks.

★ 81847 ★ Food Lion Inc. Store
1114 Mercury Blvd.
Murfreesboro, TN 37130
(615)898-0020
Ultimate Parent: Food Lion. **SIC:** 5411—Grocery Stores.

★ 81848 ★ General Electric Co.
2150 NW Broad St.
Murfreesboro, TN 37129
(615)893-2900
Officer: Mike Koelzer, Plant Manager. **Ultimate Parent:** General Electric. **SIC:** 3621—Motors & Generators.

★ 81849 ★ Giant Food Market Inc.
Memorial
Murfreesboro, TN 37130
(615)890-9020
Ultimate Parent: Giant Food. **SIC:** 5411—Grocery Stores.

★ 81850 ★ Greyhound Bus Lines
529 S. Maney Ave.
Murfreesboro, TN 37130
(615)893-5531
Ultimate Parent: Greyhound Lines Inc. **SIC:** 4111—Local & Suburban Transit; 4131—Intercity & Rural Bus Transportation; 4142—Bus Charter Service Except Local.

★ 81851 ★ Heritage Farms Dairy
1100 New Salem Hwy.
Murfreesboro, TN 37129
Ultimate Parent: Kroger. **SIC:** 2026—Fluid Milk.

★ 81852 ★ Hit or Miss
328 River Rock Blvd.
Murfreesboro, TN 37129
(615)893-0318
Ultimate Parent: TJX. **SIC:** 5651—Family Clothing Stores; 5651—Family Clothing Stores.

★ 81853 ★ Javelin Boats
880 Butler Rd.
Murfreesboro, TN 37130
Ultimate Parent: Outboard Marine. **SIC:** 3732—Boat Building & Repairing.

★ 81854 ★ Kroger Co.
1200 NW Broadst
Murfreesboro, TN 37129
(615)890-0880
Ultimate Parent: Kroger. **SIC:** 5411—Grocery Stores.

★ 81855 ★ Kroger Co.
End S. Tennessee Blvd.
Murfreesboro, TN 37130
(615)893-0184
Ultimate Parent: Kroger. **SIC:** 5411—Grocery Stores.

★ 81856 ★ Kroger Co.
W. Northfield Blvd.
Murfreesboro, TN 37129
(615)890-9873
Ultimate Parent: Kroger. **SIC:** 5411—Grocery Stores.

★ 81857 ★ Marine Group
Old Nashville Hwy. PO Box 720
Murfreesboro, TN 37133-0720
Ultimate Parent: Brunswick Corp. **SIC:** 3732—Boat Building & Repairing.

★ 81858 ★ Marine Group Inc.
Old Nashville Hwy. PO Box 720
Murfreesboro, TN 37130
Ultimate Parent: Brunswick Corp. **SIC:** 3732—Boat Building & Repairing.

★ 81859 ★ Marine Group Inc.
Old Nashville Hwy., PO Box 720
Murfreesboro, TN 37133-0720
Ultimate Parent: Brunswick Corp. **SIC:** 3732—Boat Building & Repairing.

★ 81860 ★ Omc
Fishing Boat Group Engineering
803 Park Ave.
Murfreesboro, TN 37130
Company Type: Division. **Ultimate Parent:** Outboard Marine. **SIC:** 3732—Boat Building & Repairing.

★ 81861 ★ Omc
Fishing Boat Group Inc.
880 Butler Rd.
Murfreesboro, TN 37130
Ultimate Parent: Outboard Marine. **SIC:** 3732—Boat Building & Repairing.

★ 81862 ★ Payless Shoe Source
Estates Stones Rv Plz.
Murfreesboro, TN 37130
(615)890-6320
Ultimate Parent: May Department Stores. **SIC:** 5661—Shoe Stores.

★ 81863 ★ Payless Shoesource
Estates Stones Rv Plz.
Murfreesboro, TN 37130
(615)890-6320
Ultimate Parent: May Department Stores. **SIC:** 5661—Shoe Stores.

★ 81864 ★ Penney J C
800 NW Broad St.
Murfreesboro, TN 37129
(615)890-5400
Ultimate Parent: J.C. Penney. **SIC:** 5399—Miscellaneous General Merchandise Store.

★ 81865 ★ Ryder Truck Rental
2114 N. Thompson Ln.
Murfreesboro, TN 37129
(615)783-9598
Ultimate Parent: Ryder System. **SIC:** 7513—Truck Rental & Leasing Without Drivers.

★ 81866 ★ Ryder Truck Rental & Leasing
2115 N. Thompson Ln.
Murfreesboro, TN 37129
(615)893-9951
Ultimate Parent: Ryder System. **SIC:** 7513—Truck Rental & Leasing Without Drivers.

★ 81867 ★ Ryder Truck Rental-One Way
1006 N. Tennessee Blvd.
Murfreesboro, TN 37130
(615)893-9440
Ultimate Parent: Ryder System. **SIC:** 7513—Truck Rental & Leasing Without Drivers.

★ 81868 ★ Standard Register Co.
325 Butler Dr.
Murfreesboro, TN 37130
(615)890-2151
Officer: K. D. Counts, Manager. **Ultimate Parent:** Standard Register. **SIC:** 2761—Manifold Business Forms.

★ 81869 ★ Union Planters
National Bank
615 Memorial Blvd.
Murfreesboro, TN 37130-2729
(615)890-3110
Location Type: Branch office. **Ultimate Parent:** Union Planters Corp. **SIC:** 6021—National Commercial Banks.

★ 81870 ★ Union Planters
National Bank
1861 Memorial Blvd.
Murfreesboro, TN 37129-1522
(615)896-0111
Location Type: Branch office. **Ultimate Parent:** Union Planters Corp. **SIC:** 6021—National Commercial Banks.

★ 81871 ★ Union Planters
National Bank
706 S. Church St.
Murfreesboro, TN 37130-4926
(615)895-3055
Location Type: Branch office. **Ultimate Parent:** Union Planters Corp. **SIC:** 6021—National Commercial Banks.

★ 81872 ★ Van Waters & Rogers
Inc.
912 Dashiel St.
Murfreesboro, TN 37129
(615)893-1449
Ultimate Parent: Univar Corp. **SIC:** 5199—Nondurable Goods Nec.

★ 81873 ★ Wal-Mart Stores Inc.
Memorial Blvd.
Murfreesboro, TN 37130
(615)895-5273
Ultimate Parent: Wal-Mart Stores, Inc. **SIC:** 5311—Department Stores.

★ 81874 ★ Warner's Distribution
Center
1207 Park Ave.
Murfreesboro, TN 37129
(615)896-1233
Officer: Peggy McPeak, Manager. **Ultimate Parent:** Warnaco Group. **SIC:** 2339—Women's/Misses' Outerwear Nec.

★ 81875 ★ Eckerd Drugs
1664 Memorial Blvd.
Murfressboro, TN 37129
(615)895-3724
Ultimate Parent: Eckerd Corp. **SIC:** 5912—Drug Stores & Proprietary Stores.

Nashville

★ 81876 ★ ABF Freight System
Inc.
1301 Foster Ave.
Nashville, TN 37210-4436
(615)255-5574
Location Type: Branch office. **Officer:** David Evans. **Ultimate Parent:** Arkansas Best. **SIC:** 4212—Local Trucking Without Storage; 4213—Trucking Except Local.

★ 81877 ★ ABF Freight System
Inc.
PO Box 100972
Nashville, TN 37224-0972
Location Type: Branch office. **Ultimate Parent:** Arkansas Best. **SIC:** 4212—Local Trucking Without Storage.

★ 81878 ★ AGC Life Insurance
Co.
American General Ctr.
Nashville, TN 37250-0002
(615)749-1000
Location Type: Branch office. **Officer:** James R. Tuerff, President & CEO. **Ultimate Parent:** American General Corp. **SIC:** 6311—Life Insurance. **Employee Count:** 9814.

★ 81879 ★ AGC Life Insurance
Co.
American General Ctr.
Nashville, TN 37250
(615)749-1000
Officer: James R. Tuerff, President. **Ultimate Parent:** American General Corp. **SIC:** 6311—Life Insurance.

★ 81880 ★ AGC Life Insurance
Co.
American General Ctr.
Nashville, TN 37250-0002
(615)749-1000
Officer: James R. Tuerff, President & CEO. **Ultimate Parent:** American General Corp. **SIC:** 6311—Life Insurance. **Employee Count:** 9814.

★ 81881 ★ Air Products &
Chemicals Inc.
95 White Bridge Rd.
Nashville, TN 37205-1427
(615)352-1285
Ultimate Parent: Air Products & Chemicals, Inc. **SIC:** 5169—Chemicals & Allied Products Nec.

★ 81882 ★ American General
Federal Credit Union
American General Ctr.
311 7th Ave. N
Nashville, TN 37250
(615)749-2087
Location Type: Branch office. **Officer:** Glinda Adkins, Manager. **Ultimate Parent:** American General Corp. **SIC:** 6061—Federal Credit Unions.

★ 81883 ★ American General
Finance
2708 Nolensville Rd.
Nashville, TN 37211-2219
(615)254-5631
Location Type: Branch office. **Officer:** Sue Vaughn. **Ultimate Parent:** American General Corp. **SIC:** 6141—Personal Credit Institutions; 6162—Mortgage Bankers & Correspondents.

★ 81884 ★ American General
Finance
Dolenson Plz.
Nashville, TN 37214
(615)889-7706
Officer: Sheri L. McKinney. **Ultimate Parent:** American General Corp. **SIC:** 6141—Personal Credit Institutions; 6162—Mortgage Bankers & Correspondents.

★ 81885 ★ American General
Finance Inc.
Dolenson Plz.
Nashville, TN 37214
(615)889-7706
Location Type: Branch office. **Officer:** Sheri L. McKinney. **Ultimate Parent:** American General Corp. **SIC:** 6141—Personal Credit Institutions; 6162—Mortgage Bankers & Correspondents.

★ 81886 ★ American General
Finance Inc.
2708 Nolensville Rd.
Nashville, TN 37211-2219
(615)254-5631
Location Type: Branch office. **Officer:** Sue Vaughn. **Ultimate Parent:** American General Corp. **SIC:** 6141—Personal Credit Institutions; 6162—Mortgage Bankers & Correspondents.

★ 81887 ★ American General Life
& Accedent Insurance Co.
American General Ctr.-Nashville
Nashville, TN 37250
(615)749-1000 **Fax:** (615)749-1400
Officer: Carroll D. Shanks, Vice Chairman. **Ultimate Parent:** American General Corp. **SIC:** 6331—Fire, Marine & Casualty Insurance; 6311—Life Insurance; 6321—Accident & Health Insurance; 6552—Subdividers & Developers Nec. **Employee Count:** 2003.

★ 81888 ★ American General Life
& Accident Insurance Co.
American General Ctr.
311 7th Ave. N
Nashville, TN 37250
(615)749-1000
Company Type: Subsidiary. **Officer:** James S. D'Agostino Jr., President & CEO. **Ultimate Parent:** American General Corp.

★ 81889 ★ American General
Property Insurance Co.
American General Ctr.
Nashville, TN 37250
(615)749-1000
Officer: James R. Tuerff, President. **Ultimate Parent:** American General Corp. **SIC:** 6411—Insurance Agents, Brokers & Service.

★ 81890 ★ American General
Property Insurance Co.
310 8th Ave. N
Nashville, TN 37250-0002
(615)749-1000
Officer: James R. Tuerff, President & CEO. **Ultimate Parent:** American General Corp. **SIC:** 6331—Fire, Marine & Casualty Insurance. **Employee Count:** 1.

★ 81891 ★ American General
Property Insurance Co.
310 8th Ave. N
Nashville, TN 37250-0002
(615)749-1000
Location Type: Branch office. **Officer:** James R. Tuerff, President & CEO. **Ultimate Parent:** American General Corp. **SIC:** 6331—Fire, Marine & Casualty Insurance. **Employee Count:** 1.

★ 81892 ★ AmSouth Bank of
Tennessee
2021 Richard Jones Rd.
Nashville, TN 37215-2860
(615)298-9977
Officer: William Boyd Smith, Chairman of the Board & President. **Ultimate Parent:** AmSouth Bancorp. **SIC:** 6036—Savings Institutions Except Federal. **Employee Count:** 25.

★ 81893 ★ AmSouth Bank of
Tennessee
333 Union St.
Nashville, TN 37201
(615)291-5285
Location Type: Branch office. **Ultimate Parent:** AmSouth Bancorp. **SIC:** 6022—State Commercial Banks; 6162—Mortgage Bankers & Correspondents.

★ 81894 ★ AmSouth Bank of
Tennessee
2207 Crestmoor Rd.
Nashville, TN 37215
(615)269-7249
Location Type: Branch office. **Officer:** Carolyn Trickey, Manager. **Ultimate Parent:** AmSouth Bancorp. **SIC:** 6022—State Commercial Banks; 6162—Mortgage Bankers & Correspondents.

★ 81895 ★ Apple Computer Inc.
555 Marriott Dr.
Nashville, TN 37210
(615)889-6281
Ultimate Parent: Apple Computer. **SIC:** 7373—Computer Integrated Systems Design.

★ 81896 ★ Apple Computers Inc.
545 Marriott Dr.
Nashville, TN 37210
(615)391-2000
Ultimate Parent: Apple Computer. **SIC:** 7372—Prepackaged Software.

★ 81897 ★ Armco
Bowman Metal Deck Div. Cyclops
165 Belle Forest Cir.
Nashville, TN 37221-2103
(615)662-2881
Company Type: Division. **Ultimate Parent:** Armco. **SIC:** 5051—Metals Service Centers & Offices.

★ 81898 ★ AT&T Easylink
Services
579 Huntington Pky.
Nashville, TN 37211-5961
(615)832-3112
Ultimate Parent: AT&T. **SIC:** 4899—Communications Services Nec.

★ 81899 ★ Beck/Arnley
Worldparts Corp.
1020 Space Pk. S
Nashville, TN 37211-3132
(615)834-8080
Company Type: Subsidiary. **Officer:** Randolph C. St. John, President. **Ultimate Parent:** Echlin. **SIC:** 5013—Motor Vehicle Supplies & New Parts; 3714—Motor Vehicle Parts & Accessories; 3465—Automotive Stampings. **Employee Count:** 600. **Sales:** 76 M.

★ 81900 ★ Bellsouth Mobility
2525 Perimeter Place Dr.
Nashville, TN 37214-3574
(615)872-0086
Ultimate Parent: BellSouth Corp. **SIC:** 5065—Electronic Parts & Equipment Nec.

★ 81901 ★ Bellsouth Mobility
15 Century Blvd.
Nashville, TN 37214
(615)871-2000
Ultimate Parent: BellSouth Corp. **SIC:** 7629—Electrical Repair Shops Nec.

★ 81902 ★ Beneficial Tennessee
Inc.
3802 Nolensville Rd.
Nashville, TN 37211-3402
(615)832-7090
Officer: Kelli May. **Ultimate Parent:** Beneficial. **SIC:** 6141—Personal Credit Institutions; 6162—Mortgage Bankers & Correspondents.

★ 81903 ★ Berry L M & Co.
719 Thompson Ln.
Nashville, TN 37204
(615)383-7870
Ultimate Parent: BellSouth Corp. **SIC:** 7311—Advertising Agencies.

★ 81904 ★ BFI Waste Systems
700 Murfreesboro Rd.
Nashville, TN 37210-4522
(615)244-6250
Location Type: Branch office. **Officer:** Tom Harrington. **Ultimate Parent:** Browning-Ferris Industries. **SIC:** 5084—Industrial Machinery & Equipment; 4953—Refuse Systems; 5093—Scrap & Waste Materials.

★ 81905 ★ Borden Inc.
Dairy
1710 Church St.
Nashville, TN 37203
Company Type: Division. **Ultimate Parent:** Borden, Inc. **SIC:** 2026—Fluid Milk.

★ 81906 ★ Borden Inc.
Dairy
1710 Church St.
Nashville, TN 37203
Company Type: Division. **Ultimate Parent:** Borden, Inc. **SIC:** 2026—Fluid Milk.

★ 81907 ★ Borden Inc. Diary
1710 Church St.
Nashville, TN 37203
Ultimate Parent: Borden, Inc. **SIC:** 2024—Ice Cream & Frozen Desserts.

★ 81908 ★ Borden Inc. Grocery
& Specialty Prds.
1710 Church St.
Nashville, TN 37203
Ultimate Parent: Borden, Inc. **SIC:** 2024—Ice Cream & Frozen Desserts.

★ 81909 ★ Borden Inc. Grocery
& Specialty Products
1710 Church St.
Nashville, TN 37203
Ultimate Parent: Borden, Inc. **SIC:** 2024—Ice Cream & Frozen Desserts.

★ 81910 ★ Brownell Electro Inc.
1837 Air Line Dr.
Nashville, TN 37210
(615)885-1302
Location Type: Branch office. **Ultimate Parent:** Avnet. **SIC:** 5063—Electrical Apparatus & Equipment.

★ 81911 ★ Burlington Air
Express
Briley Pky.
Nashville, TN 37217
(615)361-0590
Ultimate Parent: Pittston. **SIC:** 4513—Air Courier Services.

★ 81912 ★ Burlington Coat
Factory Warehouse
719 Thompson LA Mall 56
Nashville, TN 37204-3624
(615)385-9455
Officer: Glenn Stirsman. **Ultimate Parent:** Burlington Industries, Equity. **SIC:** 5311—Department Stores; 5651—Family Clothing Stores; 5661—Shoe Stores.

★ 81913 ★ Casual Corner
Bell Meadow Theater B
Nashville, TN 37205
(615)383-2434
Ultimate Parent: United States Shoe. **SIC:** 5621—Women's Clothing Stores.

★ 81914 ★ Casual Corner
719 Thompson Ln.
Nashville, TN 37204
(615)383-0567
Ultimate Parent: United States Shoe. SIC:
5651—Family Clothing Stores.

★ 81915 ★ Casual Corner
Green Hill Village Mall
Nashville, TN 37215
(615)298-1187
Ultimate Parent: United States Shoe. SIC:
5621—Women's Clothing Stores; 5651—
Family Clothing Stores; 6531—Real Estate
Agents & Managers.

★ 81916 ★ Casual Corner
Hickory Hollow
Nashville, TN 37221
(615)832-8397
Ultimate Parent: United States Shoe. SIC:
5621—Women's Clothing Stores.

★ 81917 ★ Caterpillar Financial
Servies Corp.
3322 W. End Ave.
Nashville, TN 37203-0986
(615)386-5800
Officer: James S. Beard, President.
Ultimate Parent: Caterpillar.

★ 81918 ★ Caterpillar Insurance
Co. Ltd.
3322 W. End Ave.
Nashville, TN 37203-0986
(615)386-5700
Officer: Linda Hall, President. Ultimate
Parent: Caterpillar.

★ 81919 ★ Centex Rodgers
Construction Co.
2620 Elm Hill Pike, St.400
Nashville, TN 37214
(615)889-4400 Fax: (615)885-6149
Officer: Edward A. Whitley, President &
CEO. Ultimate Parent: Centex.

★ 81920 ★ Charles Schwab Co.
Inc.
500 Church St. 1st Fl.
Nashville, TN 37219
(615)242-6551
Ultimate Parent: Charles Schwab Corp.
SIC: 7389—Business Services Nec.

★ 81921 ★ Circuit City
737 S. Park Dr.
Nashville, TN 37211
(615)781-2300
Ultimate Parent: Circuit City Stores. SIC:
5065—Electronic Parts & Equipment Nec.

★ 81922 ★ Circuit City
5710 Charlotte Ave.
Nashville, TN 37209
(615)356-6862
Ultimate Parent: Circuit City Stores. SIC:
5065—Electronic Parts & Equipment Nec;
5731—Radio, Television & Electronics
Stores.

★ 81923 ★ Circuit City
5333 Hickory Hollow Ln.
Nashville, TN 37221
(615)731-5125
Ultimate Parent: Circuit City Stores. SIC:
5722—Household Appliance Stores; 5731—
Radio, Television & Electronics Stores.

★ 81924 ★ Coca-Cola Bottling
Co. of Nashville
407 Craighead St.
Nashville, TN 37204
Ultimate Parent: Coca-Cola Bottling
Consol. SIC: 2086—Bottled & Canned Soft
Drinks.

★ 81925 ★ Coca-Cola Bottling
Co. Of Nashville Inc.
407 Craighead St.
Nashville, TN 37204-2333
(615)383-6230
Company Type: Subsidiary. Officer: Craig
Akins, Pr. Ultimate Parent: Coca-Cola
Bottling Consol. SIC: 2086—Bottled &
Canned Soft Drinks. Employee Count: 359.
Sales: 53.7 (est) M.

★ 81926 ★ Colonial Pipeline Co.
End Ave. N
Nashville, TN 37209
(615)297-0787
Ultimate Parent: Colonial Pipeline. SIC:
4619—Pipelines Nec.

★ 81927 ★ Crestar Mortgage
Corp.
51 Century Blvd.
Nashville, TN 37214
(615)871-4009
Ultimate Parent: Crestar Financial Corp.
SIC: 6162—Mortgage Bankers &
Correspondents.

★ 81928 ★ Dean Witter Reynolds
Inc.
Vanderbilt
Nashville, TN 37212
(615)321-3974
Location Type: Branch office. Ultimate
Parent: Dean Witter Discover. SIC: 6211—
Security Brokers & Dealers.

★ 81929 ★ Delta Air Lines
Metropolitan Airport
Nashville, TN 37217
(615)367-3220
Ultimate Parent: Delta Air Lines, Inc. SIC:
4512—Air Transportation—Scheduled.

★ 81930 ★ Delta Air Lines Inc.
Metropolitan
Nashville, TN 37217
(615)367-3220
Ultimate Parent: Delta Air Lines, Inc. SIC:
4512—Air Transportation—Scheduled.

★ 81931 ★ Denny's Restaurant
345 Harding Pl
Nashville, TN 37211
(615)832-4307
Ultimate Parent: Flagstar Co. SIC: 5812—
Eating Places.

★ 81932 ★ Denny's Restaurant
839 Briley Pky.
Nashville, TN 37217
(615)361-6649
Ultimate Parent: Flagstar Co. SIC: 5812—
Eating Places.

★ 81933 ★ Diebold Inc.
2525 Perimeter Pl 116
Nashville, TN 37214
(615)883-9020
Ultimate Parent: Diebold, Inc. SIC: 3931—
Musical Instruments; 5046—Commercial
Equipment Nec.

★ 81934 ★ Digital Equipment
Corp.
565 Marriott Dr.
Nashville, TN 37210
(615)871-7300
Ultimate Parent: Digital Equipment Corp.
SIC: 5046—Commercial Equipment Nec;
7373—Computer Integrated Systems
Design; 7378—Computer Maintenance &
Repair.

★ 81935 ★ Digital Equipment
Corp.
287 Plus Park Blvd.
Nashville, TN 37217
(615)361-5404
Ultimate Parent: Digital Equipment Corp.
SIC: 5046—Commercial Equipment Nec.

★ 81936 ★ Dixie Wire Co.
5901 California Ave.
Nashville, TN 37209
Ultimate Parent: Aluminum Co. of America-
-Alcoa. SIC: 3357—Nonferrous Wiredrawing
& Insulating.

★ 81937 ★ Dixie Wire Co.
63rd & Morrow Ave.
Nashville, TN 37209
Ultimate Parent: Aluminum Co. of America-
-Alcoa. SIC: 3357—Nonferrous Wiredrawing
& Insulating.

★ 81938 ★ Eastman Kodak Co.
44 Vantage Way
Nashville, TN 37228
(615)256-1985
Ultimate Parent: Eastman Kodak. SIC:
5044—Office Equipment; 5046—
Commercial Equipment Nec.

★ 81939 ★ Eaton Corp.
404 N. B a Dr.
Nashville, TN 37214
(615)366-0100
Ultimate Parent: Eaton Corp. SIC: 5065—
Electronic Parts & Equipment Nec.

★ 81940 ★ Eaton Corp.
3401 West End Ave.
Nashville, TN 37203
(615)298-9300
Ultimate Parent: Eaton Corp.

★ 81941 ★ Eaton Corp.
2014 Broadway
Nashville, TN 37203
(615)321-0032
Ultimate Parent: Eaton Corp. SIC: 5084—
Industrial Machinery & Equipment.

★ 81942 ★ EBM, Inc.
1625 Broadway
Nashville, TN 37203-3197
(615)256-2122 Fax: (615)242-6186
Company Type: Division. Officer: Ronald
A. Kemp, President. Ultimate Parent: Alco
Standard Corp. SIC: 5044—Office
Equipment; 5046—Commercial Equipment
Nec.

★ 81943 ★ Eckerd Drugs
Donelson Plz.
Nashville, TN 37214
(615)883-8511
Ultimate Parent: Eckerd Corp. SIC: 5912—
Drug Stores & Proprietary Stores.

★ 81944 ★ Eckerd Drugs
2400 Franklin Rd.
Nashville, TN 37204
(615)297-2275
Ultimate Parent: Eckerd Corp. SIC: 5912—
Drug Stores & Proprietary Stores.

★ 81945 ★ Eckerd Drugs
Dickerson
Nashville, TN 37207
(615)625-5744
Ultimate Parent: Eckerd Corp. SIC: 5912—
Drug Stores & Proprietary Stores.

★ 81946 ★ Eckerd Drugs
6698 Charoltte Ave.
Nashville, TN 37209
Ultimate Parent: Eckerd Corp. SIC: 5912—
Drug Stores & Proprietary Stores.

★ 81947 ★ Eckerd Drugs
3725 Clarksville Hwy.
Nashville, TN 37218
(615)255-0457
Ultimate Parent: Eckerd Corp. SIC: 5912—
Drug Stores & Proprietary Stores.

★ 81948 ★ Eckerd Drugs
21 White Bridge Rd.
Nashville, TN 37205
(615)356-2184
Ultimate Parent: Eckerd Corp. SIC: 5912—
Drug Stores & Proprietary Stores.

★ 81949 ★ Eckerd Drugs
Smith Springs Plz.
Nashville, TN 37217
(615)610-0182
Ultimate Parent: Eckerd Corp. SIC: 5912—
Drug Stores & Proprietary Stores.

★ 81950 ★ Eckerd Drugs
2416 W. End Ave.
Nashville, TN 37203
(615)321-4505
Ultimate Parent: Eckerd Corp. SIC: 5912—
Drug Stores & Proprietary Stores.

★ 81951 ★ Eckerd Drugs
Hillwood
Nashville, TN 37205
(615)356-1180
Ultimate Parent: Eckerd Corp. SIC: 5912—
Drug Stores & Proprietary Stores.

★ 81952 ★ Eckerd Drugs
5131 Nolensville Rd.
Nashville, TN 37211
(615)834-7505
Ultimate Parent: Eckerd Corp. SIC: 5912—
Drug Stores & Proprietary Stores.

★ 81953 ★ Equicor Inc.
1801 W. End Ave., Ste. 3
Nashville, TN 37203-2526
(615)320-7608
Company Type: Subsidiary. Officer:
Lawrence P. English, Ch. Bd. Ultimate
Parent: Cigna Corp. SIC: 8748—Business
Consulting Services Nec. Employee Count:
6000. Sales: 377 M.

★ 81954 ★ Equitable Life
Insurance Co.
American General Ctr.
Nashville, TN 37250
(615)749-2600
Officer: Carroll D. Shambs, President &
CEO. Ultimate Parent: American General
Corp. SIC: 6311—Life Insurance. Employee
Count: 119.

★ 81955 ★ Exxon Car Care
Centers
1101 Broadway
Nashville, TN 37203
(615)254-1988
Ultimate Parent: Exxon. SIC: 7538—
General Automotive Repair Shops.

★ 81956 ★ Exxon Car Care
Centers
227 Shelby Ave.
Nashville, TN 37213
(615)242-1706
Ultimate Parent: Exxon. SIC: 5411—
Grocery Stores.

★ 81957 ★ Exxon Car Care
Centers
1201 Briley Pky.
Nashville, TN 37217
(615)361-0900
Ultimate Parent: Exxon. SIC: 7538—
General Automotive Repair Shops.

★ 81958 ★ Exxon Car Wash
815 Gallatin Rd.
Nashville, TN 37206
(615)868-5301
Ultimate Parent: Exxon. SIC: 7542—Car
Washes.

★ 81959 ★ Exxon Co. U S a
293 Plus Park Blvd.
Nashville, TN 37217
(615)366-2202
Ultimate Parent: Exxon. SIC: 5172—
Petroleum Products Nec.

★ 81960 ★ Exxon Co. U S A
293 Plus Park Blvd.
Nashville, TN 37217
(615)366-2200
Ultimate Parent: Exxon. SIC: 5172—
Petroleum Products Nec.

★ 81961 ★ Exxon Co. U S a
Service Center
3400 W. End Ave.
Nashville, TN 37203
(615)297-6555
Ultimate Parent: Exxon. SIC: 5541—
Gasoline Service Stations.

★ 81962 ★ Ferro Corp.
Coating Div.
20 Culvert St.
Nashville, TN 37210
(615)259-2430
Company Type: Division. Officer: Tom
Sheldon, Manager. Ultimate Parent: Ferro
Corp. SIC: 2851—Paints & Allied Products;
2865—Cyclic Crudes & Intermediates;
2899—Chemical Preparations Nec.

★ 81963 ★ First American Corp.
1st American Ctr.
Nashville, TN 37237
(615)748-2100
Location Type: Branch office. Officer:
Denny C. Bottorff, President & CEO.
Ultimate Parent: First American Corp. SIC:
6021—National Commercial Banks.

★ 81964 ★ First American Corp.
First American Ctr.
Nashville, TN 37237
(615)748-2000
Company Type: Headquarters. Officer:
Dennis C. Bottorff. Employee Count: 3138.
Fortune Service 500: Ranking 77.

★ 81965 ★ First American
National Bank
2511 Nolensville Rd.
Nashville, TN 37211
(615)748-2266
Location Type: Branch office. Ultimate
Parent: First American Corp. SIC: 6021—
National Commercial Banks.

★ 81966 ★   First American
National Bank
965 Woodland St.
Nashville, TN 37206
(615)748-2383
Location Type: Branch office. Ultimate
Parent: First American Corp. SIC: 6021—
National Commercial Banks.

★ 81967 ★   First American
National Bank
5100 Charlotte Ave.
Nashville, TN 37209
(615)743-2393
Location Type: Branch office. Ultimate
Parent: First American Corp. SIC: 6021—
National Commercial Banks.

★ 81968 ★   First American
National Bank
100 Oaks Shopping Ctr.
Nashville, TN 37204
(615)748-2141
Location Type: Branch office. Ultimate
Parent: First American Corp. SIC: 6021—
National Commercial Banks.

★ 81969 ★   First American
National Bank
831 Murfreesboro Rd.
Nashville, TN 37217
(615)748-2846
Location Type: Branch office. Ultimate
Parent: First American Corp. SIC: 6021—
National Commercial Banks.

★ 81970 ★   First American
National Bank
1200 8th Ave. N
Nashville, TN 37208
(615)748-2326
Location Type: Branch office. Ultimate
Parent: First American Corp. SIC: 6021—
National Commercial Banks.

★ 81971 ★   First American
National Bank
2341 Murfreesboro
Nashville, TN 37217
(615)736-6621
Location Type: Branch office. Ultimate
Parent: First American Corp. SIC: 6021—
National Commercial Banks.

★ 81972 ★   First American
National Bank
3904 Gallatin Rd.
Nashville, TN 37216
(615)748-2772
Location Type: Branch office. Ultimate
Parent: First American Corp. SIC: 6021—
National Commercial Banks.

★ 81973 ★   First American
National Bank
1604 21st Ave. S
Nashville, TN 37212
(615)748-2401
Location Type: Branch office. Ultimate
Parent: First American Corp. SIC: 6021—
National Commercial Banks.

★ 81974 ★   First American
National Bank
5707 Nolensville Rd.
Nashville, TN 37211
(615)748-2883
Location Type: Branch office. Ultimate
Parent: First American Corp. SIC: 6021—
National Commercial Banks.

★ 81975 ★   First American
National Bank
4056 Nolensville Rd.
Nashville, TN 37211
(615)748-2478
Location Type: Branch office. Ultimate
Parent: First American Corp. SIC: 6021—
National Commercial Banks.

★ 81976 ★   First American
National Bank
3821 Green Hills Village
Nashville, TN 37215
(615)748-2488
Location Type: Branch office. Ultimate
Parent: First American Corp. SIC: 6021—
National Commercial Banks.

★ 81977 ★   First American
National Bank
123 8th Ave. S
Nashville, TN 37203
(615)748-2431
Location Type: Branch office. Ultimate
Parent: First American Corp. SIC: 6021—
National Commercial Banks.

★ 81978 ★   First American
National Bank
2409 Lebanon Rd.
Nashville, TN 37214
(615)748-2471
Location Type: Branch office. Ultimate
Parent: First American Corp. SIC: 6021—
National Commercial Banks.

★ 81979 ★   First American
National Bank
3021 West End Ave.
Nashville, TN 37203-1358
(615)748-2321
Location Type: Branch office. Ultimate
Parent: First American Corp. SIC: 6021—
National Commercial Banks.

★ 81980 ★   First American
National Bank
3608 Hwy. 70 S. Bellevue Ctr.
Nashville, TN 37221
(615)736-6150
Location Type: Branch office. Ultimate
Parent: First American Corp. SIC: 6021—
National Commercial Banks.

★ 81981 ★   First American
National Bank
3701 Clarksville Hwy.
Nashville, TN 37218-2201
(615)748-2842
Location Type: Branch office. Ultimate
Parent: First American Corp. SIC: 6021—
National Commercial Banks.

★ 81982 ★   First American
National Bank
2111 Abbott Martin Rd.
Nashville, TN 37215
(615)748-2514
Location Type: Branch office. Ultimate
Parent: First American Corp. SIC: 6021—
National Commercial Banks.

★ 81983 ★   First American
National Bank
4315 Harding Rd.
Nashville, TN 37205
(615)748-2287
Location Type: Branch office. Ultimate
Parent: First American Corp. SIC: 6021—
National Commercial Banks.

★ 81984 ★   First American
National Bank
1st American Ctr.
Nashville, TN 37237
(615)748-2000 Fax: (615)748-6088 Telex:
462-1020
Location Type: Branch office. Ultimate
Parent: First American Corp. SIC: 6021—
National Commercial Banks.

★ 81985 ★   First American
National Bank
PO Box 1351
Nashville, TN 37237
Location Type: Branch office. Ultimate
Parent: First American Corp. SIC: 6021—
National Commercial Banks.

★ 81986 ★   First American Trust
Co., NA
400 1st American Ctr.
Nashville, TN 37237
(615)748-2350 Fax: (615)748-2675
Location Type: Branch office. Ultimate
Parent: First American Corp. SIC: 6021—
National Commercial Banks.

★ 81987 ★   First American Trust
Co. NA
1st American Ctr., 4th Fl.
Nashville, TN 37237
(615)748-1403
Company Type: Subsidiary. Officer: David
K. Wilson, Chairman of the Board. Ultimate
Parent: First American Corp. SIC: 6021—
National Commercial Banks.

★ 81988 ★   First Tennessee Bank
NA
719 Thompson Ln.
Nashville, TN 37202
Location Type: Branch office. Ultimate
Parent: First Tennessee National Corp.
SIC: 6021—National Commercial Banks.

★ 81989 ★   First Tennessee Bank
NA
5544 Old Hickory Blvd.
Nashville, TN 37218-3504
(615)734-6130
Location Type: Branch office. Ultimate
Parent: First Tennessee National Corp.
SIC: 6021—National Commercial Banks.

★ 81990 ★   First Tennessee Bank
NA
47014 Hillsboro Rd.
Nashville, TN 37215-2721
(615)734-6255
Location Type: Branch office. Ultimate
Parent: First Tennessee National Corp.
SIC: 6021—National Commercial Banks.

★ 81991 ★   First Tennessee Bank
NA
511 Union St.
Nashville, TN 37219-1733
(615)734-6000
Location Type: Branch office. Ultimate
Parent: First Tennessee National Corp.
SIC: 6021—National Commercial Banks.

★ 81992 ★   First Tennessee Bank
NA
8160 Sawyer Brown Rd.
Nashville, TN 37221
(615)734-6110
Location Type: Branch office. Ultimate
Parent: First Tennessee National Corp.
SIC: 6021—National Commercial Banks.

★ 81993 ★   First Union National
Bank of Tennessee
1125 Murfreesboro Rd.
Nashville, TN 37217-2281
Location Type: Branch office. SIC: 6021—
National Commercial Banks.

★ 81994 ★   First Union National
Bank of Tennessee
4045 Nolensville Rd.
Nashville, TN 37211-4591
Location Type: Branch office. Ultimate
Parent: First Union Corp. SIC: 6021—
National Commercial Banks.

★ 81995 ★   First Union National
Bank of Tennessee
3865 Lebanon Rd.
Nashville, TN 37076-2090
Location Type: Branch office. Ultimate
Parent: First Union Corp. SIC: 6021—
National Commercial Banks.

★ 81996 ★   First Union National
Bank of Tennessee
3940 Gallatin Rd.
Nashville, TN 37216-2437
Location Type: Branch office. Ultimate
Parent: First Union Corp. SIC: 6021—
National Commercial Banks.

★ 81997 ★   First Union National
Bank of Tennessee
2121 Abbott Martin Rd.
Nashville, TN 37215-2615
Location Type: Branch office. Ultimate
Parent: First Union Corp. SIC: 6021—
National Commercial Banks.

★ 81998 ★   First Union National
Bank of Tennessee
747 Fesslers Ln.
Nashville, TN 37210-4315
Location Type: Branch office. Ultimate
Parent: First Union Corp. SIC: 6021—
National Commercial Banks.

★ 81999 ★   First Union National
Bank of Tennessee
2020 Church St.
Nashville, TN 37203-2005
Location Type: Branch office. Ultimate
Parent: First Union Corp. SIC: 6021—
National Commercial Banks.

★ 82000 ★   First Union National
Bank of Tennessee
2419 Lebanon Rd.
Nashville, TN 37214-2412
Location Type: Branch office. Ultimate
Parent: First Union Corp. SIC: 6021—
National Commercial Banks.

★ 82001 ★   First Union National
Bank of Tennessee
1711 Broadway
Nashville, TN 37203-2709
Location Type: Branch office. Ultimate
Parent: First Union Corp. SIC: 6021—
National Commercial Banks.

★ 82002 ★   First Union National
Bank of Tennessee
5711 Charlotte Ave.
Nashville, TN 37209-3290
Location Type: Branch office. Ultimate
Parent: First Union Corp. SIC: 6021—
National Commercial Banks.

★ 82003 ★   First Union National
Bank of Tennessee
Dominion Tower
150 4th Ave. N.
Nashville, TN 37219-2419
(615)251-9259
Location Type: Branch office. Ultimate
Parent: First Union Corp. SIC: 6021—
National Commercial Banks.

★ 82004 ★   First Union National
Bank of Tennessee
5312 Harding Rd.
Nashville, TN 37205-2888
Location Type: Branch office. Ultimate
Parent: First Union Corp. SIC: 6021—
National Commercial Banks.

★ 82005 ★   First Union National
Bank of Tennessee
PO Box 3377
Nashville, TN 37219-0377
Location Type: Branch office. Ultimate
Parent: First Union Corp. SIC: 6021—
National Commercial Banks.

★ 82006 ★   First Union National
Bank of Tennessee
333 Union St.
Nashville, TN 37201-1413
(615)271-1500 Fax: (615)271-1559
Location Type: Branch office. Ultimate
Parent: First Union Corp. SIC: 6021—
National Commercial Banks.

★ 82007 ★   First Union National
Bank of Tennessee
150 4th Ave. N
Nashville, TN 37219
(615)251-9200 Fax: (615)251-9266
Company Type: Subsidiary. Officer:
George L. Yowell, President & CEO.
Ultimate Parent: First Union Corp. SIC:
6022—State Commercial Banks.

★ 82008 ★   Flagship Airlines
2 International Plz., Ste. 900
Nashville, TN 37210
(615)399-6319
Company Type: Subsidiary. Officer: John
Hayes, President. Ultimate Parent: AMR
Corp.

★ 82009 ★   Flagship Airlines
2 International Plz.
Nashville, TN 37217-2011
(615)399-6600
Officer: John A. Hayes, President & CEO.
Ultimate Parent: AMR Corp. SIC: 4522—
Air Transportation—Nonscheduled.
Employee Count: 3800. Sales: 377 M.

★ 82010 ★   Fleet Finance Inc.
404 N. B a Dr.
Nashville, TN 37214
(615)367-0441
Ultimate Parent: Fleet Financial Group.
SIC: 6162—Mortgage Bankers &
Correspondents.

★ 82011 ★   Fleetguard Inc.
402 BNA Dr., Ste. 500
Nashville, TN 37217-2518
(615)367-0040
Company Type: Subsidiary. Officer: Kiran
M. Patel, President. Ultimate Parent:
Cummins Engine Co. SIC: 3569—General
Industrial Machinery Nec. Employee Count:
2100. Sales: 214 M.

★ 82012 ★   **Ford Motor Co.**
Centennial Blvd.
Nashville, TN 37209
Ultimate Parent: Ford Motor Co. **SIC:**
3211—Flat Glass.

★ 82013 ★   **Ford Motor Co.**
Nashville Glass
7200 Centennial Blvd.
Nashville, TN 37209
Ultimate Parent: Ford Motor Co. **SIC:**
3211—Flat Glass.

★ 82014 ★   **Fruehauf Inc.**
650 Murfreesboro Rd.
Nashville, TN 37210-3520
(615)256-9988
Location Type: Branch office. **Officer:**
Dave A. Dahlroos. **Ultimate Parent:** Terex
Corp. **SIC:** 5012—Automobiles & Other
Motor Vehicles; 3792—Travel Trailers &
Campers; 5013—Motor Vehicle Supplies &
New Parts.

★ 82015 ★   **GAF Building**
Materials Corp.
950 Fiber Glass Rd.
Nashville, TN 37210
(615)256-8899
Company Type: Subsidiary. **Location**
Type: Plant. **Officer:** Gary Moody, Plant
Manager. **Ultimate Parent:** GAF Corp. **SIC:**
3229—Pressed & Blown Glass Nec; 3296—
Mineral Wool.

★ 82016 ★   **Gannett**
Telemarketing
3343 Perimeter Hill Dr.
Nashville, TN 37211
(615)333-1093
Ultimate Parent: Gannett. **SIC:** 7389—
Business Services Nec.

★ 82017 ★   **Greyhound Bus Lines**
200 8th Ave. S
Nashville, TN 37203
(615)255-1691
Ultimate Parent: Greyhound Lines Inc. **SIC:**
4111—Local & Suburban Transit; 4131—
Intercity & Rural Bus Transportation; 4142—
Bus Charter Service Except Local.

★ 82018 ★   **Greyhound Bus Lines**
933 Richards Rd.
Nashville, TN 37215
(615)331-6259
Ultimate Parent: Greyhound Lines Inc. **SIC:**
4131—Intercity & Rural Bus Transportation;
4111—Local & Suburban Transit; 4142—
Bus Charter Service Except Local.

★ 82019 ★   **Greyhound Lines Inc.**
200 8th Ave. S
Nashville, TN 37203
(615)255-1691
Ultimate Parent: Greyhound Lines Inc. **SIC:**
4111—Local & Suburban Transit; 4173—
Bus Terminal & Service Facilities.

★ 82020 ★   **Gulf Life Insurance**
Co.
American General Ctr.
Nashville, TN 37250-0002
(615)749-1000
Officer: James R. Tuerff, President & CEO.
Ultimate Parent: American General Corp.
SIC: 6311—Life Insurance. **Employee**
Count: 1200.

★ 82021 ★   **Gulf Life Insurance**
Co.
American General Ctr.
Nashville, TN 37250-0002
(615)749-1000
Location Type: Branch office. **Officer:**
James R. Tuerff, President & CEO.
Ultimate Parent: American General Corp.
SIC: 6311—Life Insurance. **Employee**
Count: 1200.

★ 82022 ★   **Health Trust**
4525 Harding Rd.
Nashville, TN 37205
(615)383-4444
Company Type: Headquarters. **Officer:** R.
Clayton McWorter. **Employee Count:**
33000. **Fortune 500:** Largest U.S. Industrial
Corporations: Ranking 62.

★ 82023 ★   **Healthtrust, Inc.**
4525 Harding Rd.
Nashville, TN 37205
(615)383-4444 **Fax:** (615)298-6377
Company Type: Headquarters. **Officer:** R.
Clayton McWhorter, Chairman, President &

CEO. **Ultimate Parent:** Health Trust. **SIC:**
8741—Management Services. **Employee**
Count: 23000.

★ 82024 ★   **Hit or Miss**
100 Oaks Regal Mall
Nashville, TN 37204
(615)383-9904
Ultimate Parent: TJX. **SIC:** 5632—
Women's Accessory & Specialty Stores.

★ 82025 ★   **Hospital Corp. of**
America
1 Park Plz.
Nashville, TN 37203
(615)327-9551
Company Type: Headquarters. **Officer:**
Thomas F. Frist Jr. **Employee Count:**
65500. **Sales:** 5122 M. **Fortune Service**
500: Ranking 20.

★ 82026 ★   **Hudsons**
3216 Gallatin Rd.
Nashville, TN 37216
(615)262-5966
Ultimate Parent: Dayton Hudson. **SIC:**
5813—Drinking Places.

★ 82027 ★   **Hydra-Sports Inc.**
100 Oceanside Dr.
Nashville, TN 37204
Ultimate Parent: Outboard Marine. **SIC:**
3732—Boat Building & Repairing.

★ 82028 ★   **IDS Financial**
Services Inc.
1415 Murfreesboro Pke.
Nashville, TN 37217-2829
(615)366-4947
Location Type: Branch office. **Ultimate**
Parent: American Express Co. **SIC:** 6211—
Security Brokers & Dealers; 6282—
Investment Advice.

★ 82029 ★   **Ikg Industries**
1033 Herman St.
Nashville, TN 37208
(615)254-1915
Ultimate Parent: Harris.

★ 82030 ★   **Inacomp Computer**
Centers
330 Franklin St.
Nashville, TN 37201
(615)373-5667
Ultimate Parent: Beneficial. **SIC:** 7372—
Prepackaged Software.

★ 82031 ★   **Industrial Systems**
Inc.
2501 White Ave.
Nashville, TN 37204-2727
(615)383-0612
Officer: Bill Wood. **Ultimate Parent:** Ball
Corp. **SIC:** 3569—General Industrial
Machinery Nec.

★ 82032 ★   **Intereal Co.**
National Life Ctr.
Nashville, TN 37250
(615)749-1931
Ultimate Parent: American General Corp.
SIC: 6512—Nonresidential Building
Operators.

★ 82033 ★   **Intergraph Corp.**
5211 Linbar Dr.
Nashville, TN 37211
(615)831-5100
Ultimate Parent: Intergraph. **SIC:** 7373—
Computer Integrated Systems Design.

★ 82034 ★   **Intergraph Corp.**
475 Metroplex Dr.
Nashville, TN 37211
(615)331-2683
Ultimate Parent: Intergraph. **SIC:** 7372—
Prepackaged Software.

★ 82035 ★   **Intergraph Corp.**
2200 21st Ave. S
Nashville, TN 37212
(615)298-1380
Ultimate Parent: Intergraph. **SIC:** 7379—
Computer Related Services Nec.

★ 82036 ★   **Interstate Fire**
Insurance Co.
American General Ctr.
Nashville, TN 37250
(615)749-1610
Officer: James R. Tuerff, President.
Ultimate Parent: American General Corp.
SIC: 6331—Fire, Marine & Casualty
Insurance.

★ 82037 ★   **J C Penney Insurance**
475 Metroplex Dr.
Nashville, TN 37211
(615)781-4300
Ultimate Parent: J.C. Penney. **SIC:** 5311—
Department Stores.

★ 82038 ★   **Jack Daniel Distillery**
119 21st Ave. S., 10th Fl.
Nashville, TN 37203
(615)320-5477
Officer: Albert L. Zimlich Jr., President.
Ultimate Parent: Brown-Forman. **SIC:**
2085—Distilled & Blended Liquors.

★ 82039 ★   **Kroger Co.**
2615 Murfreesboro Rd.
Nashville, TN 37217
(615)367-2194
Ultimate Parent: Kroger. **SIC:** 5411—
Grocery Stores.

★ 82040 ★   **Kroger Co.**
3820 Nolensville Rd.
Nashville, TN 37211
(615)832-0709
Ultimate Parent: Kroger. **SIC:** 5411—
Grocery Stores.

★ 82041 ★   **Kroger Co.**
7104 Hwy. 70s
Nashville, TN 37221
(615)353-0710
Ultimate Parent: Kroger. **SIC:** 5411—
Grocery Stores.

★ 82042 ★   **Kroger Co.**
143 McGavock Pke.
Nashville, TN 37214
(615)889-0105
Ultimate Parent: Kroger. **SIC:** 5411—
Grocery Stores.

★ 82043 ★   **Kroger Co.**
2618 Elm Hillpike
Nashville, TN 37214
(615)871-2525
Ultimate Parent: Kroger. **SIC:** 5411—
Grocery Stores.

★ 82044 ★   **Kroger Co.**
3410 Gallatin Rd.
Nashville, TN 37216
(615)227-5053
Ultimate Parent: Kroger. **SIC:** 5411—
Grocery Stores.

★ 82045 ★   **Kroger Co.**
Belle Meade Plz.
Nashville, TN 37205
(615)269-5649
Ultimate Parent: Kroger. **SIC:** 5411—
Grocery Stores.

★ 82046 ★   **Kroger Co.**
5861 Charlotte Ave.
Nashville, TN 37209
(615)352-5352
Ultimate Parent: Kroger. **SIC:** 5411—
Grocery Stores.

★ 82047 ★   **Kroger Co.**
5771 Nolensville Rd.
Nashville, TN 37211
(615)834-8666
Ultimate Parent: Kroger. **SIC:** 5411—
Grocery Stores.

★ 82048 ★   **Kroger Co.**
301 Thompson Ln.
Nashville, TN 37211
(615)361-1771
Ultimate Parent: Kroger. **SIC:** 5411—
Grocery Stores.

★ 82049 ★   **Kroger Co.**
2131 Abbott Martin Rd.
Nashville, TN 37215
(615)297-7531
Ultimate Parent: Kroger. **SIC:** 5411—
Grocery Stores.

★ 82050 ★   **Kroger Co.**
3046 Dickersonrd
Nashville, TN 37207
(615)226-2110
Ultimate Parent: Kroger. **SIC:** 5411—
Grocery Stores.

★ 82051 ★   **Kroger Co.**
1700 Elm Hillpike
Nashville, TN 37210
(615)367-5400
Ultimate Parent: Kroger. **SIC:** 5411—
Grocery Stores.

★ 82052 ★   **Lerner Shops**
Hickory Hollow
Nashville, TN 37221
(615)331-3253
Ultimate Parent: Limited. **SIC:** 5621—
Women's Clothing Stores.

★ 82053 ★   **Lerner Shops**
702 Church St. 123
Nashville, TN 37203
(615)242-3814
Ultimate Parent: Limited. **SIC:** 5621—
Women's Clothing Stores.

★ 82054 ★   **Life & Casvality**
Insurance Co. of Tennessee
American General Ctr.-Nashville
Nashville, TN 37250
(615)749-1000
Officer: Carroll D. Shanks, President &
CEO. **Ultimate Parent:** American General
Corp. **SIC:** 6311—Life Insurance.

★ 82055 ★   **Limited**
Hickory Hollow
Nashville, TN 37221
(615)833-3900
Ultimate Parent: Limited. **SIC:** 5621—
Women's Clothing Stores.

★ 82056 ★   **Limited**
2286 Metrocenter Blvd.
Nashville, TN 37228
(615)255-7208
Ultimate Parent: Limited. **SIC:** 5621—
Women's Clothing Stores.

★ 82057 ★   **Limited the**
Green Hill Mall N
Nashville, TN 37215
(615)292-1210
Ultimate Parent: Limited. **SIC:** 5621—
Women's Clothing Stores.

★ 82058 ★   **Limited Express**
702 Church St. 125
Nashville, TN 37203
(615)242-8964
Ultimate Parent: Limited. **SIC:** 5621—
Women's Clothing Stores.

★ 82059 ★   **Marathon Oil**
2920 Old Hydes Ferry Rd.
Nashville, TN 37218
(615)244-3670
Ultimate Parent: USX Corp. **SIC:** 5541—
Gasoline Service Stations.

★ 82060 ★   **Marathon Oil Co.**
2920 Old Hydes Ferry Rd.
Nashville, TN 37218
(615)244-3670
Ultimate Parent: USX Corp. **SIC:** 5541—
Gasoline Service Stations.

★ 82061 ★   **McDonald's**
Hamburgers
7010 Hwy. 70 S
Nashville, TN 37221
(615)352-1529
Ultimate Parent: McDonald's. **SIC:** 5812—
Eating Places.

★ 82062 ★   **Meadow Gold Dairy**
1710 Church St.
Nashville, TN 37203
(615)329-4351
Officer: Cordell Dowlen, Manager. **Ultimate**
Parent: Borden, Inc. **SIC:** 2024—Ice Cream
& Frozen Desserts.

★ 82063 ★   **Mid Continent Life**
Insuranc
1451 Elm Hill Pike
Nashville, TN 37210
(615)360-8930
Ultimate Parent: Florida Progress. **SIC:**
6411—Insurance Agents, Brokers &
Service.

★ 82064 ★   **Mobilecomm of**
Nashville Inc.
545 Mainstream Dr., Ste. 100
Nashville, TN 37228-1201
(615)244-2337
Company Type: Subsidiary. **Officer:** Steve
Pazian, President. **Ultimate Parent:**
BellSouth Corp. **SIC:** 4812—Radiotelephone
Communications. **Employee Count:** 50.
Sales: 3 M.

★ 82065 ★ **Murphy Oil Corp.**
3767 Nolensville Rd.
Nashville, TN 37211
(615)833-4820
Ultimate Parent: Murphy Oil. **SIC:** 5172—Petroleum Products Nec.

★ 82066 ★ **Murphy Oil Corp.**
1609 63rd Ave. N
Nashville, TN 37209
(615)292-2679
Ultimate Parent: Murphy Oil. **SIC:** 5172—Petroleum Products Nec.

★ 82067 ★ **Nadco Inc.**
1525 Elm Hill Pike
Nashville, TN 37210
(615)367-9422
Ultimate Parent: Wal-Mart Stores, Inc. **SIC:** 5087—Service Establishment Equipment.

★ 82068 ★ **Nashville Foam**
911 Cherokee Ave.
Nashville, TN 37207
Ultimate Parent: Leggett & Platt Inc. **SIC:** 3086—Plastics Foam Products.

★ 82069 ★ **New York Life Nashville General Office**
Southeastern Agencies
PO Box 3413
Nashville, TN 37219
(615)252-6060 **Fax:** (615)252-6062
Officer: Jerry D. Coats, General Manager.
Ultimate Parent: New York Life.

★ 82070 ★ **New York Life Nashville General Office**
Southeastern Agencies
One Nashville Place
150 4th Ave., N., Ste. 1610
Nashville, TN 37219
(615)252-6060 **Fax:** (615)252-6062
Officer: Jerry D. Coats, General Manager.
Ultimate Parent: New York Life.

★ 82071 ★ **Northwestern Mutual Life Inc.**
162 4th Ave. N
Nashville, TN 37219
(615)742-8700
Ultimate Parent: Northwestern Mutual Life. **SIC:** 6411—Insurance Agents, Brokers & Service.

★ 82072 ★ **Occupational Health Service**
1940 Elm Hill Pike
Nashville, TN 37210
(615)889-8999
Ultimate Parent: Foundation Health Corp. **SIC:** 7374—Data Processing & Preparation.

★ 82073 ★ **Omc**
Fishing Boat Group Inc.
100 Oceanside Dr.
Nashville, TN 37204
Company Type: Division. **Ultimate Parent:** Outboard Marine. **SIC:** 3732—Boat Building & Repairing.

★ 82074 ★ **Otis Elevator Co.**
901 Charlotte Ave.
Nashville, TN 37203
(615)254-3496
Ultimate Parent: United Technologies. **SIC:** 1796—Installing Building Equipment Nec; 5084—Industrial Machinery & Equipment.

★ 82075 ★ **Payless Shoe Source**
301 Gallatin Rd.
Nashville, TN 37206
(615)262-1949
Ultimate Parent: May Department Stores. **SIC:** 5661—Shoe Stores.

★ 82076 ★ **Payless Shoe Source**
2604 Lebanon Rd.
Nashville, TN 37214
(615)883-3017
Ultimate Parent: May Department Stores. **SIC:** 5661—Shoe Stores.

★ 82077 ★ **Payless Shoe Source**
1119 12th Ave. S
Nashville, TN 37203
(615)255-4123
Ultimate Parent: May Department Stores. **SIC:** 5661—Shoe Stores.

★ 82078 ★ **Payless Shoe Source**
5615 Charlotte Ave.
Nashville, TN 37209
(615)352-3142
Ultimate Parent: May Department Stores. **SIC:** 5661—Shoe Stores.

★ 82079 ★ **Penn Mutual Life Insurance Co.**
1808 W. End Ave.
Nashville, TN 37203
(615)327-1990
Ultimate Parent: Penn Mutual Life. **SIC:** 6411—Insurance Agents, Brokers & Service.

★ 82080 ★ **Pennzoil Lube Stop**
50240 PO Box
Nashville, TN 37205
(615)333-0227
Ultimate Parent: Pennzoil. **SIC:** 5172—Petroleum Products Nec.

★ 82081 ★ **Pepsi-Cola Bottling Co.**
715 Thompson Ln.
Nashville, TN 37204
(615)890-5700
Officer: Alvin Beaman, Owner. **Ultimate Parent:** Pepsico. **SIC:** 2086—Bottled & Canned Soft Drinks.

★ 82082 ★ **Piggly Wiggly**
534 Donelson Pke.
Nashville, TN 37214-3729
(615)889-0815
Officer: Dennis Osborne. **Ultimate Parent:** Bruno's. **SIC:** 5411—Grocery Stores.

★ 82083 ★ **Pitney Bowes**
220 Venture Cir.
Nashville, TN 37228
(615)242-2424
Officer: Jack Nicholson, Manager. **Ultimate Parent:** Pitney Bowes. **SIC:** 3554—Paper Industries Machinery.

★ 82084 ★ **PPG Industries Inc.**
880 Murfreesboro Rd.
Nashville, TN 37217
(615)361-6908
Ultimate Parent: PPG Industries Inc. **SIC:** 1793—Glass & Glazing Work.

★ 82085 ★ **Quincy Family Steakhouse**
Old Lebanon Rd.
Nashville, TN 37214
(615)883-2657
Ultimate Parent: Flagstar Co. **SIC:** 5812—Eating Places.

★ 82086 ★ **Reliance Insurance Co.**
2 Vantage Way
Nashville, TN 37228
(615)244-7684
Ultimate Parent: Reliance Group Holdings. **SIC:** 6411—Insurance Agents, Brokers & Service.

★ 82087 ★ **Reliance Insurance Co.**
3322 W. End Ave.
Nashville, TN 37203
(615)298-9900
Ultimate Parent: Reliance Group Holdings. **SIC:** 6411—Insurance Agents, Brokers & Service.

★ 82088 ★ **Residence Inn by Marriott**
2300 Elm Hill Pike
Nashville, TN 37210
(615)889-7600
Ultimate Parent: Marriott International. **SIC:** 7011—Hotels & Motels.

★ 82089 ★ **Rhone Poulenc Basic Chemical**
4600 Centennial Blvd.
Nashville, TN 37209
(615)269-3415
Officer: James Raines, Manager. **Ultimate Parent:** Rhone-Poulenc Rorer. **SIC:** 2869—Industrial Organic Chemicals Nec; 2899—Chemical Preparations Nec.

★ 82090 ★ **Rhone-Poulenc Basic Chemicals Co.**
4600 Centennial Blvd.
Nashville, TN 37209
Ultimate Parent: Rhone-Poulenc Rorer. **SIC:** 2819—Industrial Inorganic Chemicals Nec.

★ 82091 ★ **Rudys Farm Co.**
107 Music City Circle
Suite 203
Nashville, TN 37214
(615)889-2391
Company Type: Division. **Officer:** John Birch, Vice President. **Ultimate Parent:** Sara Lee Corp. **SIC:** 2000—Food & Kindred Products.

★ 82092 ★ **Russell Corp.**
Wilson
Nashville, TN 37215
(615)297-8596
Ultimate Parent: Russell. **SIC:** 5131—Piece Goods & Notions.

★ 82093 ★ **Ryder Truck Rental**
3009 Dickerson Rd.
Nashville, TN 37207
(615)227-8550
Ultimate Parent: Ryder System. **SIC:** 7513—Truck Rental & Leasing Without Drivers.

★ 82094 ★ **Ryder Truck Rental & Leasing**
91 Fesslers Ln.
Nashville, TN 37210
(615)244-7494
Ultimate Parent: Ryder System. **SIC:** 7359—Equipment Rental & Leasing Nec.

★ 82095 ★ **Service Merchandise**
305 Broadway
Nashville, TN 37201
(615)242-2403
Ultimate Parent: Service Merchandise Co., Inc. **SIC:** 5311—Department Stores; 5961—Catalog & Mail-Order Houses.

★ 82096 ★ **Service Merchandise**
245 Great Cir.
Nashville, TN 37228
(615)254-2667
Ultimate Parent: Service Merchandise Co., Inc. **SIC:** 5399—Miscellaneous General Merchandise Store.

★ 82097 ★ **Service Merchandise**
4225 Nolensville Rd.
Nashville, TN 37211
(615)833-9206
Ultimate Parent: Service Merchandise Co., Inc. **SIC:** 5199—Nondurable Goods Nec.

★ 82098 ★ **Southern Companies**
2712 Landers Ave.
Nashville, TN 37211
(615)244-3012
Ultimate Parent: Southern. **SIC:** 4783—Packing & Crating; 7373—Computer Integrated Systems Design.

★ 82099 ★ **Southern Post**
715 5th Ave. S
Nashville, TN 37203
(615)254-7031
Ultimate Parent: Commercial Federal Corp. **SIC:** 7331—Direct Mail Advertising Services.

★ 82100 ★ **Southern States Asphalt Co.**
930 Youngs Ln.
Nashville, TN 37207
Ultimate Parent: Ashland Oil. **SIC:** 2951—Asphalt Paving Mixtures & Blocks.

★ 82101 ★ **Steiner Liff Textile Produc**
400 Davidson St.
Nashville, TN 37213
(615)252-2600
Ultimate Parent: Leggett & Platt Inc. **SIC:** 2221—Broadwoven Fabric Mills—Manmade; 2741—Miscellaneous Publishing.

★ 82102 ★ **Steiner Liff Textile Products Co.**
400 Davidson St.
Nashville, TN 37213
(615)734-1600 **Fax:** (615)256-1331
Officer: Bob Pease, President. **Ultimate Parent:** Leggett & Platt Inc.

★ 82103 ★ **Stone Container Corp.**
700 Cowan St.
Nashville, TN 37207
(615)256-8965
Officer: Artie W. Schlanker, Manager. **Ultimate Parent:** Stone Container Corp. **SIC:** 2653—Corrugated & Solid Fiber Boxes.

★ 82104 ★ **Studio W**
1229 17th Ave. S
Nashville, TN 37212
(615)321-4487
Ultimate Parent: Mitchell Energy & Devel. **SIC:** 2741—Miscellaneous Publishing.

★ 82105 ★ **Swift Independent Packing Co.**
723 Cowan St.
Nashville, TN 37207
(615)256-1668
Ultimate Parent: Conagra. **SIC:** 2011—Meat Packing Plants.

★ 82106 ★ **Texaco Inc. Sales Office**
6100 John a Merritt Blvd.
Nashville, TN 37209
(615)350-7077
Ultimate Parent: Texaco. **SIC:** 1311—Crude Petroleum & Natural Gas.

★ 82107 ★ **Textron Aerostructures**
1431 Vultee Blvd.
Nashville, TN 37217
Ultimate Parent: Textron. **SIC:** 3728—Aircraft Parts & Equipment Nec; 3769—Space Vehicle Equipment Nec.

★ 82108 ★ **Textron Aerostructures**
Vultee Blvd.
Nashville, TN 37203
Ultimate Parent: Textron. **SIC:** 3728—Aircraft Parts & Equipment Nec; 3769—Space Vehicle Equipment Nec.

★ 82109 ★ **Textron Aerostructures Inc.**
1431 Vultee Blvd.
Nashville, TN 37217
Ultimate Parent: Textron. **SIC:** 3728—Aircraft Parts & Equipment Nec; 3769—Space Vehicle Equipment Nec.

★ 82110 ★ **Third National Mortgage Co.**
444 James Robertson Pky.
Nashville, TN 37219
(615)748-4088
Ultimate Parent: Suntrust Banks. **SIC:** 6162—Mortgage Bankers & Correspondents.

★ 82111 ★ **3M National Advertising Co.**
1431 Poplar Ln.
Nashville, TN 37210-4519
(615)256-4400
Officer: Dan Purcell. **Ultimate Parent:** Minnesota Mining & Mfg. **SIC:** 7312—Outdoor Advertising Services.

★ 82112 ★ **Ticor Title Insurance**
315 Deadrick
Nashville, TN 37242
(615)259-2290
Ultimate Parent: Alleghany Corp. **SIC:** 6361—Title Insurance.

★ 82113 ★ **Tosco Corp.**
90 Van Buren St.
Nashville, TN 37208
(615)255-6309
Ultimate Parent: Tosco Corp. **SIC:** 5172—Petroleum Products Nec.

★ 82114 ★ **Trailways Bus Lines**
711 5th Ave. S
Nashville, TN 37203
(615)242-6373
Ultimate Parent: Greyhound Lines Inc. **SIC:** 4111—Local & Suburban Transit; 4131—Intercity & Rural Bus Transportation; 4142—Bus Charter Service Except Local.

★ 82115 ★ **Transamerica Occidental Life Inc.**
1161 Murfreesboro Rd.
Nashville, TN 37217
(615)361-0040
Ultimate Parent: Transamerica Occidental Life Insurance. **SIC:** 6411—Insurance Agents, Brokers & Service.

★ 82116 ★ **Tri-W Corp.**
121708 PO Box
Nashville, TN 37212
Ultimate Parent: Kellwood. **SIC:** 6531—Real Estate Agents & Managers.

★ 82117 ★ Underwriters Adjusting Co.
309 Plus Park Blvd.
Nashville, TN 37217
(615)366-4590
Ultimate Parent: Continental. SIC: 6411—Insurance Agents, Brokers & Service.

★ 82118 ★ Union Oil Co.
310 Philfre Ct
Nashville, TN 37217
(615)366-4910
Ultimate Parent: Unocal Corp. SIC: 4226—Special Warehousing & Storage Nec.

★ 82119 ★ Union Planters National Bank
2618 Old Lebanon
Nashville, TN 37214-2470
(615)726-4243
Location Type: Branch office. Ultimate Parent: Union Planters Corp. SIC: 6021—National Commercial Banks.

★ 82120 ★ Union Planters National Bank
4035 Nolensville Rd.
Nashville, TN 37211-4593
(615)726-4202
Location Type: Branch office. Ultimate Parent: Union Planters Corp. SIC: 6021—National Commercial Banks.

★ 82121 ★ Union Planters National Bank
5101 Harding Rd.
Nashville, TN 37205-2802
(615)726-4319
Location Type: Branch office. Ultimate Parent: Union Planters Corp. SIC: 6021—National Commercial Banks.

★ 82122 ★ Union Planters National Bank
3001 Nolensville Rd.
Nashville, TN 37211-2394
(615)726-4242
Location Type: Branch office. Ultimate Parent: Union Planters Corp. SIC: 6021—National Commercial Banks.

★ 82123 ★ Union Planters National Bank
5200 Charlotte Ave.
Nashville, TN 37209-3321
(615)726-4201
Location Type: Branch office. Ultimate Parent: Union Planters Corp. SIC: 6021—National Commercial Banks.

★ 82124 ★ Union Planters National Bank
4241 Harding Rd.
Nashville, TN 37205-2003
(615)292-1382
Location Type: Branch office. Ultimate Parent: Union Planters Corp. SIC: 6021—National Commercial Banks.

★ 82125 ★ Union Planters National Bank
401 Union St.
Nashville, TN 37219-1788
(615)244-0571
Location Type: Branch office. Ultimate Parent: Union Planters Corp. SIC: 6021—National Commercial Banks.

★ 82126 ★ Union Planters National Bank
2019 Richard Jones Rd.
Nashville, TN 37215-2858
(615)385-2210
Location Type: Branch office. Ultimate Parent: Union Planters Corp. SIC: 6021—National Commercial Banks.

★ 82127 ★ Union Planters National Bank
3939 Gallatin Rd.
Nashville, TN 37216-2432
(615)226-3222
Location Type: Branch office. Ultimate Parent: Union Planters Corp. SIC: 6021—National Commercial Banks.

★ 82128 ★ Union Planters National Bank
2930 W. End Ave.
Nashville, TN 37203-1316
(615)327-3808
Location Type: Branch office. Ultimate Parent: Union Planters Corp. SIC: 6021—National Commercial Banks.

★ 82129 ★ United Brake Sys. Inc.
419 Spence Ln.
Nashville, TN 37210
Ultimate Parent: Echlin. SIC: 3714—Motor Vehicle Parts & Accessories.

★ 82130 ★ United Parcel Service
3205 Whites Creek Pike
Nashville, TN 37207
(615)876-5277
Ultimate Parent: United Parcel Service of America. SIC: 4213—Trucking Except Local.

★ 82131 ★ Unum Life Insurance Co.
1 Commerce Pl
Nashville, TN 37219
(615)242-2153
Ultimate Parent: Unum Life. SIC: 6411—Insurance Agents, Brokers & Service.

★ 82132 ★ US Fidelity & Guaranty Insurance
3200 W. End Ave.
Nashville, TN 37203
(615)385-3200
Ultimate Parent: USF&G Corp. SIC: 6411—Insurance Agents, Brokers & Service.

★ 82133 ★ US Gypsum Co.
1102 Kermit Dr.
Nashville, TN 37217
(615)361-8419
Ultimate Parent: USG Corp. SIC: 3272—Concrete Products Nec; 5039—Construction Materials Nec.

★ 82134 ★ Valvoline Instant Oil Chang
2537 Lebanon Rd.
Nashville, TN 37214
(615)889-3809
Ultimate Parent: Ashland Oil.

★ 82135 ★ Victoria's Secret
702 Church St. 109
Nashville, TN 37203
(615)244-6573
Ultimate Parent: Limited. SIC: 5621—Women's Clothing Stores.

★ 82136 ★ Vulcan Materials Co.
611 Franklin Limestone Rd.
Nashville, TN 37217
(615)832-1120
Officer: Mike Clark, Vice President. Ultimate Parent: Vulcan Materials Co. SIC: 3679—Electronic Components Nec.

★ 82137 ★ Wal-Mart Stores Inc.
5520 Nolensville Rd.
Nashville, TN 37211
(615)331-2111
Ultimate Parent: Wal-Mart Stores, Inc. SIC: 5912—Drug Stores & Proprietary Stores.

★ 82138 ★ Wal-Mart Stores Inc.
6670 Charlotte Ave.
Nashville, TN 37209
(615)352-0100
Ultimate Parent: Wal-Mart Stores, Inc. SIC: 5311—Department Stores.

★ 82139 ★ Wal-Mart Stores Inc.
1789 Gallatin Rd.
Nashville, TN 37206
(615)868-5100
Ultimate Parent: Wal-Mart Stores, Inc. SIC: 5311—Department Stores.

★ 82140 ★ Wang Laboratories, Inc.
545 Marriott Dr.
Nashville, TN 37210
(615)888-3887
Ultimate Parent: Wang Laboratories, Inc. SIC: 5046—Commercial Equipment Nec; 7373—Computer Integrated Systems Design.

★ 82141 ★ Wang Laboratories Inc.
220 Great Cir.
Nashville, TN 37228
(615)244-9014
Ultimate Parent: Wang Laboratories, Inc. SIC: 5046—Commercial Equipment Nec.

★ 82142 ★ West Side Hospital
2221 Murphy Ave.
Nashville, TN 37203
(615)329-6000
Ultimate Parent: Hospital Corp. of America.

★ 82143 ★ West Side Hospital
2208 Patterson St.
Nashville, TN 37203
(615)329-6131
Ultimate Parent: Hospital Corp. of America. SIC: 8062—General Medical & Surgical Hospitals.

★ 82144 ★ Western Life Insurance Co.
210 25th Ave. N
Nashville, TN 37203
(615)329-4787
Ultimate Parent: Westcorp. SIC: 6411—Insurance Agents, Brokers & Service.

★ 82145 ★ Wrangler
1204 Murfreesboro Rd.
Nashville, TN 37217
(615)361-4440
Ultimate Parent: VF Corp. SIC: 5812—Eating Places.

★ 82146 ★ Xerox Corp.
3322 W. End Ave.
Nashville, TN 37203
(615)386-5200
Officer: Joe Salkin, Manager. Ultimate Parent: Xerox Corp. SIC: 3663—Radio & T.V. Communications Equipment.

★ 82147 ★ Vulcan Materials Co.
1161 Murfreesboro Rd.
Nashville., TN 37217
(615)361-8550
Ultimate Parent: Vulcan Materials Co. SIC: 5039—Construction Materials Nec.

★ 82148 ★ Vulcan Materials Co.
Central Pike.
Nashville., TN 37214
(615)883-2371
Ultimate Parent: Vulcan Materials Co. SIC: 1429—Crushed & Broken Stone Nec.

★ 82149 ★ Vulcan Materials Co.
611 Franklin Limestone Rd.
Nashville., TN 37217
(615)832-7503
Ultimate Parent: Vulcan Materials Co. SIC: 5039—Construction Materials Nec.

New Johnsonville

★ 82150 ★ Cyprus Foote Mineral Co.
Long St. & Foote Rd.
New Johnsonville, TN 37134
Ultimate Parent: Cyprus Amax Minerals. SIC: 2869—Industrial Organic Chemicals Nec.

★ 82151 ★ First American National Bank
Hwy. 70
New Johnsonville, TN 37134-9702
(615)535-2188
Location Type: Branch office. Ultimate Parent: First American Corp. SIC: 6021—National Commercial Banks.

New Market

★ 82152 ★ Asarco Inc.
1170 Reed Bull Rd.
New Market, TN 37820-4120
(615)475-2039
Ultimate Parent: Asarco. SIC: 1499—Miscellaneous Nonmetallic Minerals.

★ 82153 ★ Asarco Inc.
1977 W. Hwy. 11 E
New Market, TN 37820-3917
(615)933-5354
Ultimate Parent: Asarco. SIC: 1499—Miscellaneous Nonmetallic Minerals.

New Providence

★ 82154 ★ First American National Bank
649 Providence Blvd.
New Providence, TN 37042-4367
(615)552-7564
Location. Type: Branch office. Ultimate Parent: First American Corp. SIC: 6021—National Commercial Banks.

Newbern

★ 82155 ★ Boston Industrial Products
Hwy. 77 E
Newbern, TN 38059
(901)627-2531
Ultimate Parent: Dana Corp. SIC: 3069—Fabricated Rubber Products Nec.

★ 82156 ★ Rudys Farm Co.
Biffle Rd.
Newbern, TN 38059
Company Type: Division. Location Type: Facility. Ultimate Parent: Sara Lee Corp. SIC: 2000—Food & Kindred Products.

★ 82157 ★ Sara Lee Sausage Newbern Facility
2000 Biffle Rd.
Newbern, TN 38059
Ultimate Parent: Sara Lee Corp. SIC: 2011—Meat Packing Plants; 2013—Sausages & Other Prepared Meats.

★ 82158 ★ Save Trust Federal Savings Bank
105 Monroe Ave.
Newbern, TN 38059-1214
(901)627-2586
Location Type: Branch office. Ultimate Parent: Union Planters Corp. SIC: 6021—National Commercial Banks.

★ 82159 ★ Wrangler
402 S. Grayson St.
Newbern, TN 38059
(901)627-3223
Ultimate Parent: VF Corp. SIC: 2325—Men's/Boys' Trousers & Slacks; 2329—Men's/Boys' Clothing Nec; 2339—Women's/Misses' Outerwear Nec.

Newport

★ 82160 ★ Emerson Electric Co.
Morristown Hwy.
Newport, TN 37821
(615)623-2386
Ultimate Parent: Emerson Electric Co. Inc. SIC: 3585—Refrigeration & Heating Equipment.

★ 82161 ★ First Union National Bank of Tennessee
1512 Cosby Rd.
Newport, TN 37821-3428
Location Type: Branch office. Ultimate Parent: First Union Corp. SIC: 6021—National Commercial Banks.

★ 82162 ★ First Union National Bank of Tennessee
451 W. Broadway
Newport, TN 37821
Location Type: Branch office. Ultimate Parent: First Union Corp. SIC: 6021—National Commercial Banks.

★ 82163 ★ First Union National Bank of Tennessee
302 E. Main St.
Newport, TN 37821-3129
(615)623-2347
Location Type: Branch office. Ultimate Parent: First Union Corp. SIC: 6021—National Commercial Banks.

★ 82164 ★ Gli Inc.
365 Chemwood Dr.
Newport, TN 37821
Ultimate Parent: Great Lakes Chemical. SIC: 2899—Chemical Preparations Nec.

★ 82165 ★ Gli Inc.
Rte. 7 Box 25A Rankin Rd.
Newport, TN 37821
Ultimate Parent: Great Lakes Chemical. SIC: 2899—Chemical Preparations Nec.

★ 82166 ★ Great Lakes Chemical Corp.
380 Chemwood Dr.
Newport, TN 37821
Ultimate Parent: Great Lakes Chemical. SIC: 2869—Industrial Organic Chemicals Nec; 2879—Agricultural Chemicals Nec; 2819—Industrial Inorganic Chemicals Nec.

Niota, Tennessee

★ 82167 ★   Great Lakes Chemical Corp.
Rte. 7, Box 27, Rankin Rd.
Newport, TN 37821
Ultimate Parent: Great Lakes Chemical. **SIC:** 2869—Industrial Organic Chemicals Nec; 2879—Agricultural Chemicals Nec; 2819—Industrial Inorganic Chemicals Nec.

★ 82168 ★   Greyhound Bus Lines
700 Cosby Rd.
Newport, TN 37821
(615)623-1360
Ultimate Parent: Greyhound Lines Inc. **SIC:** 4131—Intercity & Rural Bus Transportation; 4111—Local & Suburban Transit; 4142—Bus Charter Service Except Local.

★ 82169 ★   Heekin Can Inc.
Hwy. 411
Newport, TN 37821
(615)623-7544
Officer: Ron Ryan, Manager. **Ultimate Parent:** Ball Corp. **SIC:** 2992—Lubricating Oils & Greases; 3411—Metal Cans.

★ 82170 ★   Quaker Oats Co.
540 E. Broadway
Newport, TN 37821
Ultimate Parent: Quaker Oates. **SIC:** 2033—Canned Fruits & Vegetables.

★ 82171 ★   Sonoco Products Co.
Rankin Rd. Rte. 7
Newport, TN 37821
Ultimate Parent: Sonoco Products. **SIC:** 2631—Paperboard Mills; 2655—Fiber Cans, Drums & Similar Products.

★ 82172 ★   Sonoco Products Co.
766 Industrial Rd.
Newport, TN 37821
(615)623-8611
Officer: R. L. Gibson, Manager. **Ultimate Parent:** Sonoco Products. **SIC:** 2631—Paperboard Mills.

★ 82173 ★   Sonoco Products Co.
Rankin Rd.
Newport, TN 37821
(615)623-8611
Ultimate Parent: Sonoco Products. **SIC:** 5943—Stationery Stores.

★ 82174 ★   Wal-Mart Stores Inc.
Westgate Shopping Ctr.
Newport, TN 37821
(615)623-8656
Ultimate Parent: Wal-Mart Stores, Inc. **SIC:** 5311—Department Stores.

★ 82175 ★   Wood Products Co.
880 E. Hwy. 25 70
Newport, TN 37821
(615)623-3003
Officer: Charles Rhyme, President. **Ultimate Parent:** Federal Paper Board. **SIC:** 2426—Hardwood Dimension & Flooring Mills.

Niota

★ 82176 ★   E. R. Carpenter Co. Inc.
Johnson Street, PO Box 129
Niota, TN 37826
Ultimate Parent: Carpenter. **SIC:** 2392—Housefurnishings Nec.

Nolensville

★ 82177 ★   First Tennessee Bank NA
7291 Nolensville Rd.
Nolensville, TN 37135
(615)776-2122
Location Type: Branch office. **Ultimate Parent:** First Tennessee National Corp. **SIC:** 6021—National Commercial Banks.

Norene

★ 82178 ★   People's Bank
Norene, TN 37136
(615)286-2291
Ultimate Parent: People's Bank. **SIC:** 6099—Functions Related to Deposit Banking.

Norris

★ 82179 ★   Frist American National Bank
40 W.Norris Rd.
Norris, TN 37828
(615)521-5937
Location Type: Branch office. **Ultimate Parent:** First American Corp. **SIC:** 6021—National Commercial Banks.

Oak Ridge

★ 82180 ★   Boeing
Aerospace & Electronics
767 Boeing Rd.
Oak Ridge, TN 37830-7999
Ultimate Parent: Boeing. **SIC:** 3728—Aircraft Parts & Equipment Nec.

★ 82181 ★   Boeing Defense & Space Group
767 Boeing Rd.
Oak Ridge, TN 37830
Ultimate Parent: Boeing. **SIC:** 3728—Aircraft Parts & Equipment Nec.

★ 82182 ★   Boeing Tennessee Inc.
767 Boeing Rd.
Oak Ridge, TN 37830-7999
Ultimate Parent: Boeing. **SIC:** 3728—Aircraft Parts & Equipment Nec.

★ 82183 ★   Browning-Ferris Industries
400 Warehouse Rd.
Oak Ridge, TN 37830-7238
(615)482-3656
Location Type: Branch office. **Ultimate Parent:** Browning-Ferris Industries. **SIC:** 4953—Refuse Systems.

★ 82184 ★   Citgo Service Station
1001 Oak Ridge Tpke.
Oak Ridge, TN 37830
(615)483-5458
Ultimate Parent: Citgo Petroleum. **SIC:** 5541—Gasoline Service Stations.

★ 82185 ★   Eckerd Drugs
Kings Ctr.
Oak Ridge, TN 37830
(615)487-7000
Ultimate Parent: Eckerd Corp. **SIC:** 5912—Drug Stores & Proprietary Stores.

★ 82186 ★   EG & G Instruments
801 S. Illinois Ave.
Oak Ridge, TN 37830
(615)483-2121
Officer: Mike Dunn, Manager. **Ultimate Parent:** EG & G. **SIC:** 3829—Measuring & Controlling Devices Nec; 3826—Analytical Instruments.

★ 82187 ★   EG & G Instruments/ Ortec
100 Midland Rd.
Oak Ridge, TN 37831-0895
(615)482-4411 **Fax:** (615)483-0396
Company Type: Subsidiary. **Officer:** Dave Taylor, Manager. **Ultimate Parent:** EG & G.

★ 82188 ★   EG & G Nuclear Instruments
801 S. Illinois Ave.
Oak Ridge, TN 37831-2011
Fax: (615)483-2279
Company Type: Subsidiary. **Officer:** Dave Taylor, Manager. **Ultimate Parent:** EG & G.

★ 82189 ★   Eg & G Ortec
100 Midland Ln.
Oak Ridge, TN 37830
Ultimate Parent: EG & G. **SIC:** 3826—Analytical Instruments.

★ 82190 ★   Elographics Inc.
1976 Oak Ridge Tpke.
Oak Ridge, TN 37830
(615)482-4038
Ultimate Parent: Raychem Corp. **SIC:** 3825—Instruments to Measure Electricity.

★ 82191 ★   Elographics Inc.
105 Randolph Rd.
Oak Ridge, TN 37830
(615)482-4100
Ultimate Parent: Raychem Corp. **SIC:** 5049—Professional Equipment Nec.

★ 82192 ★   First American National Bank
45 New York Ave.
Oak Ridge, TN 37830-6410
(615)521-5940
Location Type: Branch office. **Ultimate Parent:** First American Corp. **SIC:** 6021—National Commercial Banks.

★ 82193 ★   Greyhound Bus Lines
1608 Oak Ridge Tpke.
Oak Ridge, TN 37830
(615)483-6246
Ultimate Parent: Greyhound Lines Inc. **SIC:** 4142—Bus Charter Service Except Local; 4111—Local & Suburban Transit; 4131—Intercity & Rural Bus Transportation.

★ 82194 ★   Martin Marietta
Oak Ridge Y-12 Plant Dept. of Energy
Bear Creek Rd.
Oak Ridge, TN 37831
Company Type: Division. **Ultimate Parent:** Martin Marietta. **SIC:** 3499—Fabricated Metal Products Nec.

★ 82195 ★   Martin Marietta
US Doe Oak Ridge Y-12 Paint
Bear Creek Rd.
Oak Ridge, TN 37831
Location Type: Plant. **Ultimate Parent:** Martin Marietta. **SIC:** 3499—Fabricated Metal Products Nec.

★ 82196 ★   Martin Marietta
US Doe Y-12 Plant
Bear Creek Rd. PO Box 2001
Oak Ridge, TN 37831
Company Type: Division. **Ultimate Parent:** Martin Marietta. **SIC:** 3499—Fabricated Metal Products Nec; 2819—Industrial Inorganic Chemicals Nec; 3356—Nonferrous Rolling & Drawing Nec; 3369—Nonferrous Foundries Nec; 3483—Ammunition Except for Small Arms.

★ 82197 ★   Martin Marietta Energy Systems, Inc.
PO Box 2009
Oak Ridge, TN 37831
(615)576-5663 **Fax:** (615)624-3742
Officer: Clyde C. Hopkins, President. **Ultimate Parent:** Martin Marietta.

★ 82198 ★   Security Trust FS & LA
961 Oak Ridge Tpke.
Oak Ridge, TN 37830-8830
(615)483-5685
Location Type: Branch office. **Ultimate Parent:** Union Planters Corp. **SIC:** 6021—National Commercial Banks.

★ 82199 ★   Union Planters National Bank
231 Broadway, Jackson Sq.
Oak Ridge, TN 37831
(615)481-2703
Location Type: Branch office. **Ultimate Parent:** Union Planters Corp. **SIC:** 6021—National Commercial Banks.

★ 82200 ★   Union Planters National Bank
1298 Oak Ridge Tpke.
Oak Ridge, TN 37830
(615)481-2727
Location Type: Branch office. **Ultimate Parent:** Union Planters Corp. **SIC:** 6021—National Commercial Banks; 6021—National Commercial Banks.

★ 82201 ★   US Doe Oak Ridge National Laboratory
PO Box 2008
Oak Ridge, TN 37831
Ultimate Parent: Martin Marietta. **SIC:** 7300—Business Services.

★ 82202 ★   Western Auto Supply Co.
201 Wilson St.
Oak Ridge, TN 37830
(615)483-5648
Ultimate Parent: Sears Roebuck & Co. **SIC:** 5531—Automobile & Home Supply Stores.

Oakridge

★ 82203 ★   Kroger Co.
380 S. Illinois Ave.
Oakridge, TN 37830
Ultimate Parent: Kroger. **SIC:** 5411—Grocery Stores.

Old Hickory

★ 82204 ★   First American National Bank
1100 Donelson Ave.
Old Hickory, TN 37138-3113
(615)748-2711
Location Type: Branch office. **Ultimate Parent:** First American Corp. **SIC:** 6021—National Commercial Banks.

★ 82205 ★   Omc Fishing Boat Group Inc.
931 Industrial Rd.
Old Hickory, TN 37138
Ultimate Parent: Outboard Marine. **SIC:** 3732—Boat Building & Repairing.

★ 82206 ★   Omc-Stratos Boats Inc.
931 Industrial Blvd.
Old Hickory, TN 37138
Ultimate Parent: Outboard Marine. **SIC:** 3732—Boat Building & Repairing.

★ 82207 ★   Stratos Boats Inc.
931 Industrial Dr.
Old Hickory, TN 37138
Ultimate Parent: Outboard Marine. **SIC:** 3732—Boat Building & Repairing.

Oliver Springs

★ 82208 ★   Bank of Roane County
227 W. Tri-County Blvd.
Oliver Springs, TN 37840
(615)435-1777
Location Type: Branch office. **Ultimate Parent:** Union Planters Corp. **SIC:** 6021—National Commercial Banks.

★ 82209 ★   Citizens Bank & Trust
Hwy. 62
Oliver Springs, TN 37840-9514
(615)435-7284
Location Type: Branch office. **Ultimate Parent:** Union Planters Corp. **SIC:** 6021—National Commercial Banks.

★ 82210 ★   First American National Bank
849 Tri-County Blvd.
Oliver Springs, TN 37840-1003
(615)521-2295
Location Type: Branch office. **Ultimate Parent:** First American Corp. **SIC:** 6021—National Commercial Banks.

★ 82211 ★   People's Bank
PO Box 480
Oliver Springs, TN 37840
(615)435-7284
Ultimate Parent: People's Bank. **SIC:** 6141—Personal Credit Institutions.

★ 82212 ★   Rite Aid Discount Pharmacy
Tri County Shopping Ctr.
Oliver Springs, TN 37840
(615)435-7724
Ultimate Parent: Rite Aid. **SIC:** 5912—Drug Stores & Proprietary Stores.

Oneida

★ 82213 ★   Tibbals Flooring Co.
Oneida Industrial Ln.
Oneida, TN 37841
Ultimate Parent: Premark International. **SIC:** 2426—Hardwood Dimension & Flooring Mills.

★ 82214 ★   Tibbals Flooring Co.
East Plant
300 S. Main St.
Oneida, TN 37841
Location Type: Plant. **Ultimate Parent:** Premark International. **SIC:** 2426—Hardwood Dimension & Flooring Mills.

★ 82215 ★ **Tibbals Flooring Co.**
West Plant
300 S. Main St.
Oneida, TN 37841
Location Type: Plant. **Ultimate Parent:**
Premark International. **SIC:** 2421—Sawmills
& Planing Mills—General.

Paris

★ 82216 ★ **Emerson Electric Co.**
1600 Industrial Park Rd.
Paris, TN 38242
(901)642-1120
Ultimate Parent: Emerson Electric Co. Inc.
SIC: 3699—Electrical Equipment & Supplies
Nec.

★ 82217 ★ **Emerson Electric Co.**
Special Products Div.
1600 Industrial Park Rd.
Paris, TN 38242
Company Type: Division. **Ultimate Parent:**
Emerson Electric Co. Inc. **SIC:** 3553—
Woodworking Machinery.

★ 82218 ★ **Emerson Electric Co.**
Special Products Div.
1600 Industrial Park Rd.
Paris, TN 38242
Company Type: Division. **Ultimate Parent:**
Emerson Electric Co. Inc. **SIC:** 3553—
Woodworking Machinery.

★ 82219 ★ **First American National Bank**
1064 Mineral Wells Ave.
Paris, TN 38242-4904
(901)642-1310
Location Type: Branch office. **Ultimate Parent:** First American Corp. **SIC:** 6021—
National Commercial Banks.

★ 82220 ★ **First American National Bank**
101 W. Wood St.
Paris, TN 38242-9998
(901)642-8000
Location Type: Branch office. **Ultimate Parent:** First American Corp. **SIC:** 6021—
National Commercial Banks.

★ 82221 ★ **Kroger Co.**
1053 Mineral Wells St.
Paris, TN 38242
(901)644-1075
Ultimate Parent: Kroger. **SIC:** 5411—
Grocery Stores.

★ 82222 ★ **Midland Brake Inc.**
1505 Reynoldsburg Rd.
Paris, TN 38242
(901)642-4215
Officer: Joe Rainey, Manager. **Ultimate Parent:** Echlin. **SIC:** 3531—Construction
Machinery.

★ 82223 ★ **Security Bank & Trust Co.**
210 W. Washington St.
Paris, TN 38242
(901)642-6644
Ultimate Parent: Synovus Financial Corp.
SIC: 6022—State Commercial Banks.

Parrottsville

★ 82224 ★ **First Union National Bank of Tennessee**
2101 Hwy. 321
Parrottsville, TN 37843
(615)623-2171
Location Type: Branch office. **Ultimate Parent:** First Union Corp. **SIC:** 6021—
National Commercial Banks.

Parsons

★ 82225 ★ **Shannon Group**
803 S. Florida Ave.
Parsons, TN 38363
(901)847-6361
Ultimate Parent: Dana Corp. **SIC:** 3585—
Refrigeration & Heating Equipment; 3632—
Household Refrigerators & Freezers.

★ 82226 ★ **Vulcan Materials Co.**
Hwy. 69
Parsons, TN 38363
(901)847-3211
Ultimate Parent: Vulcan Materials Co. **SIC:**
5039—Construction Materials Nec.

Petersburg

★ 82227 ★ **Peoples Bank**
98 PO Box
Petersburg, TN 37144
(615)659-9994
Ultimate Parent: People's Bank. **SIC:**
6029—Commercial Banks Nec.

Pikeville

★ 82228 ★ **Johnson Controls Inc.**
Ferro Rd.
Pikeville, TN 37367
Ultimate Parent: Johnson & Johnson. **SIC:**
3465—Automotive Stampings; 3471—
Plating & Polishing; 3499—Fabricated Metal
Products Nec.

★ 82229 ★ **Johnson Controls Inc.**
1 Ferro Rd.
Pikeville, TN 37367
Ultimate Parent: Johnson & Johnson. **SIC:**
3465—Automotive Stampings; 3471—
Plating & Polishing; 3499—Fabricated Metal
Products Nec.

Piney Flats

★ 82230 ★ **Tri City Bank & Trust Co.**
Us 11 E
Piney Flats, TN 37686
(615)968-4146
Ultimate Parent: First Virginia Banks Inc.
SIC: 6022—State Commercial Banks.

Pleasant View

★ 82231 ★ **American Limestone Co. Inc.**
3025 Joe Dowlen Rd.
Pleasant View, TN 37146-9046
(615)746-5744
Ultimate Parent: Asarco. **SIC:** 1422—
Crushed & Broken Limestone.

★ 82232 ★ **First Union National Bank of Tennessee**
2640 Church St., Hwy. 48
Pleasant View, TN 37146-8184
(615)749-5061
Location Type: Branch office. **Ultimate Parent:** First Union Corp. **SIC:** 6021—
National Commercial Banks.

Portland

★ 82233 ★ **Challenger Electrical Equipment Corp.**
200 Challenger Dr.
Portland, TN 37148
Ultimate Parent: Westinghouse Electric
Corp. **SIC:** 3644—Noncurrent-Carrying
Wiring Devices.

★ 82234 ★ **First Union National Bank of Tennessee**
107 N. Broadway
Portland, TN 37148-1113
(615)325-2097
Location Type: Branch office. **Ultimate Parent:** First Union Corp. **SIC:** 6021—
National Commercial Banks.

★ 82235 ★ **Sunbeam Outdoor Products**
321 Victor Reiter Pky.
Portland, TN 37148
(615)325-9283
Officer: Gilbert Ranburger, Manager. **Ultimate Parent:** Sunbeam/Oster. **SIC:**
2514—Metal Household Furniture; 2519—
Household Furniture Nec; 2599—Furniture
& Fixtures Nec.

Powell

★ 82236 ★ **ALLTEL Tennessee Inc.**
2104 Emory Rd.
PO Box 620
Powell, TN 37849
(615)938-2211
Ultimate Parent: ALLTEL Corp. **SIC:**
4812—Radiotelephone Communications.

★ 82237 ★ **Coast to Coast Total Hdwe**
Powell Shopping Ctr.
Powell, TN 37849
(615)938-3000
Ultimate Parent: Servistar Corp. **SIC:**
5231—Paint, Glass & Wallpaper Stores.

Pulaski

★ 82238 ★ **Arvin Industires Inc.**
Gabriel Ride Control Div.
Bennett Dr.
Pulaski, TN 38478
(615)363-6561
Company Type: Division. **Officer:** Ted
Swanson, Vice President. **Ultimate Parent:**
Arvin Industries Inc. **SIC:** 3714—Motor
Vehicle Parts & Accessories.

★ 82239 ★ **Arvin Industries**
Gabriel Div.
PO Box 617
Bennett Dr.
Pulaski, TN 38478
(615)363-6561 **Fax:** (615)363-6561
Company Type: Division. **Ultimate Parent:**
Arvin Industries. **SIC:** 3714—Motor
Vehicle Parts & Accessories.

★ 82240 ★ **Avex Electronics Inc.**
302 Eighth St.
Pulaski, TN 38478
Ultimate Parent: J. M. Huber. **SIC:** 3571—
Electronic Computers.

★ 82241 ★ **Exxon Tiger Shop**
Pulaski, TN 38478
(615)363-8468
Ultimate Parent: Exxon. **SIC:** 5541—
Gasoline Service Stations.

★ 82242 ★ **Greyhound Bus Lines**
303 S. 1st St.
Pulaski, TN 38478
(615)363-1416
Ultimate Parent: Greyhound Lines Inc. **SIC:**
4111—Local & Suburban Transit; 4131—
Intercity & Rural Bus Transportation; 4142—
Bus Charter Service Except Local.

★ 82243 ★ **Johnson Controls Inc.**
1890 Mines Rd.
Pulaski, TN 38478
Ultimate Parent: Johnson & Johnson. **SIC:**
2531—Public Building & Related Furniture.

★ 82244 ★ **Maremont Corp.**
Bennett Dr.
Pulaski, TN 38478-0617
Ultimate Parent: Arvin Industries Inc. **SIC:**
3400—Fabricated Metal Products; 3451—
Screw Machine Products; 3471—Plating &
Polishing.

★ 82245 ★ **Maremont Corp.**
Pulaski Plant
Bennett Dr.
Pulaski, TN 38478-0617
Location Type: Plant. **Ultimate Parent:**
Arvin Industries Inc. **SIC:** 3400—Fabricated
Metal Products; 3451—Screw Machine
Products; 3471—Plating & Polishing.

Pulsaski

★ 82246 ★ **Arvin Industries Inc.**
Gabriel Ride Control Div.
Bennett Dr.
Pulsaski, TN 38478
(615)363-6561
Company Type: Division. **Ultimate Parent:**
Arvin Industries Inc. **SIC:** 3714—Motor
Vehicle Parts & Accessories.

★ 82247 ★ **Arvin Industries Inc.**
Gabriel Ride Control Div.
Bennett Dr.
Pulsaski, TN 38478
(615)363-6561
Company Type: Division. **Ultimate Parent:**
Arvin Industries Inc. **SIC:** 3714—Motor
Vehicle Parts & Accessories.

Ridgely

★ 82248 ★ **Peoples Bank**
107 N. Main St.
Ridgely, TN 38080
(901)264-5942
Ultimate Parent: People's Bank. **SIC:**
6022—State Commercial Banks; 6029—
Commercial Banks Nec.

Ripley

★ 82249 ★ **Farmers Union Bank**
282 1/2 Washington St.
Ripley, TN 38063-1526
(901)635-0271
Location Type: Branch office. **Ultimate Parent:** Union Planters Corp. **SIC:** 6021—
National Commercial Banks.

★ 82250 ★ **Farmers Union Bank**
345 Cleveland St.
Ripley, TN 38063
(901)635-9670
Location Type: Branch office. **Ultimate Parent:** Union Planters Corp. **SIC:** 6021—
National Commercial Banks.

★ 82251 ★ **Farmers Union Bank**
PO Box 230
Ripley, TN 38063-0230
Location Type: Headquarters. **Ultimate Parent:** Union Planters Corp. **SIC:** 6021—
National Commercial Banks.

★ 82252 ★ **Farmers Union Bank**
139-41 N. Main
Ripley, TN 38063
(901)635-2451 **Fax:** (901)635-9083
Location Type: Headquarters. **Ultimate Parent:** Union Planters Corp. **SIC:** 6021—
National Commercial Banks.

★ 82253 ★ **Greyhound Bus Lines**
199 S. Washington St.
Ripley, TN 38063
(901)635-0241
Ultimate Parent: Greyhound Lines Inc. **SIC:**
4131—Intercity & Rural Bus Transportation;
4111—Local & Suburban Transit; 4142—
Bus Charter Service Except Local.

★ 82254 ★ **Harvard Industries**
Diecast Div.
174 Viar Rd.
Ripley, TN 38063
Ultimate Parent: Harvard Industries. **SIC:**
3363—Aluminum Die-Castings; 3369—
Nonferrous Foundries Nec.

★ 82255 ★ **Harvard Industries**
Diecasting
174 Viar Rd.
Ripley, TN 38063
Ultimate Parent: Harvard Industries. **SIC:**
3369—Nonferrous Foundries Nec.

★ 82256 ★ **Harvard Industries Inc.**
Diecasting
174 Viar Rd.
Ripley, TN 38063
Company Type: Division. **Ultimate Parent:**
Harvard Industries. **SIC:** 3363—Aluminum
Die-Castings; 3369—Nonferrous Foundries
Nec.

★ 82257 ★ **Hayes Albion Corp.**
Diecasting
174 Viar Rd.
Ripley, TN 38063
Company Type: Division. **Ultimate Parent:**
Harvard Industries. **SIC:** 3363—Aluminum
Die-Castings; 3364—Nonferrous Die-
Castings Except Aluminum.

★ 82258 ★ **Magnetek Ripley Co.**
S. Industrial Park
Ripley, TN 38063
Ultimate Parent: Magnetek Inc. **SIC:**
3621—Motors & Generators.

★ 82259 ★ **Magnetek Universal Electric**
PO Box 569
Ripley, TN 38063-0569
(901)635-2421
Officer: Charles H. Albertson. **Ultimate Parent:** Magnetek Inc. **SIC:** 3621—Motors
& Generators.

★ 82260 ★ **Magnetek Universal Electric Co.**
S. Industrial Park
Ripley, TN 38063
Ultimate Parent: Magnetek Inc. **SIC:**
3621—Motors & Generators.

★ 82261 ★ **Magnetek Universal Electric Co.**
S. Industrial Park
Ripley, TN 38063
Ultimate Parent: Magnetek Inc. **SIC:**
3621—Motors & Generators.

★ 82262 ★ **Maremont Corp.**
Hwy. 51 North Industrial Park
Ripley, TN 38063
Ultimate Parent: Arvin Industries Inc. **SIC:** 3714—Motor Vehicle Parts & Accessories.

★ 82263 ★ **Merchants State Bank**
292 S. Washington St.
Ripley, TN 38063
(901)635-9311
Location Type: Branch office. **Ultimate Parent:** Union Planters Corp. **SIC:** 6021—National Commercial Banks.

★ 82264 ★ **Ripley Graphics**
1236 American Way
Ripley, TN 38063
(901)635-3000
Officer: Mark Conti, Manager. **Ultimate Parent:** American Greetings. **SIC:** 2752—Commercial Printing—Lithographic.

★ 82265 ★ **Stop & Shop**
Hwy. 51 N
Ripley, TN 38063
(901)635-3533
Ultimate Parent: Stop & Shop. **SIC:** 5411—Grocery Stores.

★ 82266 ★ **Wang Laboratories Inc.**
3434 E. Mentzer St.
Ripley, TN 38063
(901)635-7217
Ultimate Parent: Wang Laboratories, Inc. **SIC:** 5013—Motor Vehicle Supplies & New Parts.

Rockwood

★ 82267 ★ **Bank of Roane County**
104 S. Gateway County
Rockwood, TN 37854
(615)354-1172
Location Type: Branch office. **Ultimate Parent:** Union Planters Corp. **SIC:** 6021—National Commercial Banks.

★ 82268 ★ **First American National Bank**
240 W. Rockwood St.
Rockwood, TN 37852-2242
(615)354-1551
Location Type: Branch office. **Ultimate Parent:** First American Corp. **SIC:** 6021—National Commercial Banks.

★ 82269 ★ **Kayser-Roth Corp.**
425 N. Gateway Ave.
Rockwood, TN 37854
Ultimate Parent: Collins & Aikman Group. **SIC:** 2252—Hosiery Nec.

Rogersville

★ 82270 ★ **Assured Castings Corp.**
300 Industrial Park Dr.
Rogersville, TN 37857
Ultimate Parent: Leggett & Platt Inc. **SIC:** 3300—Primary Metal Industries.

★ 82271 ★ **Avery Dennison Ipc**
530 W. Main St.
Rogersville, TN 37857
Ultimate Parent: Avery Dennison Corp. **SIC:** 2754—Commercial Printing—Gravure.

★ 82272 ★ **BFI Waste Systems**
Austin Mill Rd.
Rogersville, TN 37857
(615)272-2535
Ultimate Parent: Browning-Ferris Industries. **SIC:** 5084—Industrial Machinery & Equipment; 4953—Refuse Systems.

★ 82273 ★ **Dennison Transoceanic Corp.**
530 W. Main St.
Rogersville, TN 37857
(615)272-7644
Company Type: Subsidiary. **Officer:** Karl Geiger, President. **Ultimate Parent:** Avery Dennison Corp. **SIC:** 2500—Furniture & Fixtures.

★ 82274 ★ **First Tennessee Bank NA**
Rte. 66, Bulls Gap Hwy.
Rogersville, TN 37857
(615)272-7611
Location Type: Branch office. **Ultimate**

Parent: First Tennessee National Corp. **SIC:** 6021—National Commercial Banks.

★ 82275 ★ **First Union National Bank of Tennessee**
Hwy. 66 Plz.
Rogersville, TN 37857-9062
Location Type: Branch office. **Ultimate Parent:** First Union Corp. **SIC:** 6021—National Commercial Banks.

★ 82276 ★ **First Union National Bank of Tennessee**
107 E. Main St.
Rogersville, TN 37857-3347
(615)272-7622
Location Type: Branch office. **Ultimate Parent:** First Union Corp. **SIC:** 6021—National Commercial Banks.

★ 82277 ★ **First Union National Bank of Tennessee**
Kyle & Church Sts.
Rogersville, TN 37857
Location Type: Branch office. **Ultimate Parent:** First Union Corp. **SIC:** 6021—National Commercial Banks.

★ 82278 ★ **Ipc Avery Dennison**
530 W. Main St.
Rogersville, TN 37857
Ultimate Parent: Avery Dennison Corp. **SIC:** 2754—Commercial Printing—Gravure.

★ 82279 ★ **Reliance Electric Co.**
Reliance Rd. at West Main
Rogersville, TN 37857
Ultimate Parent: Reliance Electric. **SIC:** 3568—Power Transmission Equipment Nec.

★ 82280 ★ **Reliance Electric Co.**
Reliance Rd. At W. Main St.
Rogersville, TN 37857
(615)272-2686
Officer: Terry Singleton, Manager. **Ultimate Parent:** Reliance Electric. **SIC:** 3562—Ball & Roller Bearings; 3568—Power Transmission Equipment Nec.

★ 82281 ★ **Reliance Electric Co. Co.**
Reliance Rd. & W. Main St.
Rogersville, TN 37857
Ultimate Parent: Reliance Electric. **SIC:** 3568—Power Transmission Equipment Nec.

★ 82282 ★ **TRW Inc.**
2101 W. Main St.
Rogersville, TN 37857-0000
Ultimate Parent: TRW, Inc. **SIC:** 3714—Motor Vehicle Parts & Accessories.

★ 82283 ★ **Ryder Truck Rental**
Rural Route 4
Rogersville T, TN 37857
(615)272-5897
Ultimate Parent: Ryder System. **SIC:** 7389—Business Services Nec.

★ 82284 ★ **Vulcan Materials Co.**
Shepards Chapel Rd.
Rogersville., TN 37857
(615)272-7466
Ultimate Parent: Vulcan Materials Co. **SIC:** 5039—Construction Materials Nec.

Rossville

★ 82285 ★ **Mrs. Smith's Frozen Foods Co.**
80 Morrison Rd.
PO Box 309
Rossville, TN 38066
Ultimate Parent: Kellogg Co. **SIC:** 2053—Frozen Bakery Products Except Bread.

Rutherford

★ 82286 ★ **Merchants State Bank**
Main St.
Rutherford, TN 38369
(901)665-6193
Location Type: Branch office. **Ultimate Parent:** Union Planters Corp. **SIC:** 6021—National Commercial Banks.

S Pittsburg

★ 82287 ★ **Salem Carpet Mills Inc.**
E 11th
S Pittsburg, TN 37380
(615)837-8651
Ultimate Parent: Shaw Industries, Inc. **SIC:** 5199—Nondurable Goods Nec.

★ 82288 ★ **Vulcan Materials Co.**
Hwy. 41
S. Pittsburg, TN 37380
(615)837-7833
Ultimate Parent: Vulcan Materials Co. **SIC:** 1429—Crushed & Broken Stone Nec.

★ 82289 ★ **Vulcan Materials Co.**
Marion Quarry Sq.
S. Pittsburg, TN 37380
(615)837-8621
Ultimate Parent: Vulcan Materials Co. **SIC:** 3274—Lime.

Savannah

★ 82290 ★ **Wal-Mart Stores Inc.**
S. Pickwick St.
Savannah, TN 38372
(901)925-6222
Ultimate Parent: Wal-Mart Stores, Inc. **SIC:** 5311—Department Stores.

Selmer

★ 82291 ★ **General Electric Co.**
4th St.
Selmer, TN 38375
(901)645-6121
Officer: Fred Morrison, Manager. **Ultimate Parent:** General Electric. **SIC:** 3612—Transformers Except Electronic; 3643—Current-Carrying Wiring Devices.

★ 82292 ★ **General Electric Co.**
South Fourth St.
Selmer, TN 38375
Ultimate Parent: General Electric. **SIC:** 3613—Switchgear & Switchboard Apparatus.

★ 82293 ★ **General Electric Co.**
S. Fourth St.
Selmer, TN 38375-0389
Ultimate Parent: General Electric. **SIC:** 3613—Switchgear & Switchboard Apparatus.

★ 82294 ★ **Rite Aid Discount Pharmacy**
Hwy. 45 S
Selmer, TN 38375
(901)645-4423
Ultimate Parent: Rite Aid. **SIC:** 5912—Drug Stores & Proprietary Stores.

Sevierville

★ 82295 ★ **Harman Automotive Inc.**
415 Robert Henderson Rd.
Sevierville, TN 37864
Ultimate Parent: Harvard Industries.

★ 82296 ★ **Kroger Co.**
201 Forks of River Pky.
Sevierville, TN 37862
(615)428-1544
Ultimate Parent: Kroger. **SIC:** 5411—Grocery Stores.

★ 82297 ★ **Shell Super Stop**
Hwy. 66
Sevierville, TN 37862
(615)453-1257
Ultimate Parent: Shell Oil Co. **SIC:** 5411—Grocery Stores.

★ 82298 ★ **TRW Inc.**
Fuji Valve Div.
128 River Bend Dr.
Sevierville, TN 37862
Company Type: Division. **Ultimate Parent:** TRW, Inc. **SIC:** 3592—Carburetors, Pistons, Rings & Valves.

★ 82299 ★ **Vulcan Materials Co.**
Gatlinburg Hwy.
Sevierville., TN 37862
(615)453-7104
Ultimate Parent: Vulcan Materials Co. **SIC:** 1429—Crushed & Broken Stone Nec.

Seymour

★ 82300 ★ **First American National Bank**
10225 Chapman Hwy.
Seymour, TN 37865-9506
Location Type: Branch office. **Ultimate Parent:** First American Corp. **SIC:** 6021—National Commercial Banks.

Shelbyville

★ 82301 ★ **Eaton Corp.**
111 Eaton Dr.
Shelbyville, TN 37160
(615)684-8820
Officer: Bill Dixon, Manager. **Ultimate Parent:** Eaton Corp. **SIC:** 3714—Motor Vehicle Parts & Accessories.

★ 82302 ★ **Eaton Corp.**
Transmission Div.
111 Eaton Dr.
Shelbyville, TN 37160
(615)684-8870
Company Type: Division. **Location Type:** Plant. **Officer:** Bill Dixon, Plant Manager. **Ultimate Parent:** Eaton Corp. **SIC:** 3714—Motor Vehicle Parts & Accessories.

★ 82303 ★ **Eckerd Drugs**
610 Madison St.
Shelbyville, TN 37160
(615)684-0280
Ultimate Parent: Eckerd Corp. **SIC:** 5912—Drug Stores & Proprietary Stores.

★ 82304 ★ **First American National Bank**
Spring & Holland Sts.
Shelbyville, TN 37160
(615)684-5513
Location Type: Branch office. **Ultimate Parent:** First American Corp. **SIC:** 6021—National Commercial Banks.

★ 82305 ★ **First American National Bank**
Madison St.
Shelbyville, TN 37160
Location Type: Branch office. **Ultimate Parent:** First American Corp. **SIC:** 6021—National Commercial Banks.

★ 82306 ★ **First American National Bank**
Big Springs Shopping Ctr.
Shelbyville, TN 37160
Location Type: Branch office. **Ultimate Parent:** First American Corp. **SIC:** 6021—National Commercial Banks.

★ 82307 ★ **First National Bank**
Holland St.
Shelbyville, TN 37160
Location Type: Branch office. **Ultimate Parent:** Union Planters Corp. **SIC:** 6021—National Commercial Banks.

★ 82308 ★ **First National Bank**
1401 Madison St.
Shelbyville, TN 37160-3629
Location Type: Branch office. **Ultimate Parent:** Union Planters Corp. **SIC:** 6021—National Commercial Banks.

★ 82309 ★ **First National Bank**
101 Elm St.
Shelbyville, TN 37160-2811
Location Type: Branch office. **Ultimate Parent:** Union Planters Corp. **SIC:** 6021—National Commercial Banks.

★ 82310 ★ **First National Bank**
111 N. Spring St.
Shelbyville, TN 37160
(615)684-7511 **Fax:** (615)684-8256
Location Type: Headquarters. **Ultimate Parent:** Union Planters Corp. **SIC:** 6021—National Commercial Banks.

★ 82311 ★   First Union National
Bank of Tennessee
602 N. Main St.
Shelbyville, TN 37160-3211
Location Type: Branch office. Ultimate
Parent: First Union Corp. SIC: 6021—
National Commercial Banks.

★ 82312 ★   First Union National
Bank of Tennessee
756 Madison St.
Shelbyville, TN 37160-3519
Location Type: Branch office. Ultimate
Parent: First Union Corp. SIC: 6021—
National Commercial Banks.

★ 82313 ★   First Union National
Bank of Tennessee
100 North Side Sq.
Shelbyville, TN 37160
(615)684-8000
Location Type: Branch office. Ultimate
Parent: First Union Corp. SIC: 6021—
National Commercial Banks.

★ 82314 ★   Frist National Bank
PO Box 500
Shelbyville, TN 37160-0500
Location Type: Headquarters. Ultimate
Parent: Union Planters Corp. SIC: 6021—
National Commercial Banks.

★ 82315 ★   Jostens Inc.
Nashville Hwy.
Shelbyville, TN 37160
(615)684-5290
Ultimate Parent: Jostens. SIC: 2796—
Platemaking Services.

★ 82316 ★   Krogers
1115 Madison St.
Shelbyville, TN 37160
(615)684-5142
Ultimate Parent: Kroger. SIC: 5411—
Grocery Stores.

★ 82317 ★   Stanley Tools
1200 Stanley Blvd.
Shelbyville, TN 37160
(615)684-6980
Officer: Frank Robinson, Manager.
Ultimate Parent: Stanley Works. SIC:
3423—Hand & Edge Tools Nec.

★ 82318 ★   Trailways Bus Lines
822 N. Main St.
Shelbyville, TN 37160
(615)684-6207
Ultimate Parent: Greyhound Lines Inc. SIC:
4111—Local & Suburban Transit; 4131—
Intercity & Rural Bus Transportation; 4142—
Bus Charter Service Except Local.

★ 82319 ★   Tyson Foods
W. Jackson St.
Shelbyville, TN 37160
Ultimate Parent: Tyson Foods, Inc. SIC:
2000—Food & Kindred Products.

★ 82320 ★   Tyson Foods Inc.
W. Jackson St.
Shelbyville, TN 37160
Ultimate Parent: Tyson Foods, Inc. SIC:
2015—Poultry Slaughtering & Processing;
2047—Dog & Cat Food.

★ 82321 ★   Tyson Foods Inc.
W. Jackson St. PO Box 8
Shelbyville, TN 37160
Ultimate Parent: Tyson Foods, Inc. SIC:
2000—Food & Kindred Products; 2047—
Dog & Cat Food.

★ 82322 ★   Tyson Foods Inc.
901 W. Jackson St.
Shelbyville, TN 37160
(615)684-8180
Officer: Truley Ponder, Manager. Ultimate
Parent: Tyson Foods, Inc. SIC: 2015—
Poultry Slaughtering & Processing.

Signal Mounta

★ 82323 ★   Scientific-Atlanta
1912 Hollister Rd.
Signal Mounta, TN 37377
(615)886-1913
Ultimate Parent: Scientific-Atlanta, Inc.

Smithville

★ 82324 ★   DeKalb County Bank
& Trust Co.
Broad & Short Mount
Smithville, TN 37166
(615)597-7884
Location Type: Branch office. Ultimate
Parent: Union Planters Corp. SIC: 6021—
National Commercial Banks.

★ 82325 ★   Rite Aid Discount
Pharmacy
Town Country Plz.
Smithville, TN 37166
(615)597-4200
Ultimate Parent: Rite Aid. SIC: 5912—Drug
Stores & Proprietary Stores.

Smyrna

★ 82326 ★   First American
National Bank
301 S. Lowry
Smyrna, TN 37167-2550
(615)355-0058
Location Type: Branch office. Ultimate
Parent: First American Corp. SIC: 6021—
National Commercial Banks.

★ 82327 ★   Kroger Co.
Murfreesboro Rd.
Smyrna, TN 37167
(615)459-7142
Ultimate Parent: Kroger. SIC: 5411—
Grocery Stores.

★ 82328 ★   Rite Aid Discount
Pharmacy
Country Village Shop
Smyrna, TN 37167
(615)459-0502
Ultimate Parent: Rite Aid. SIC: 5912—Drug
Stores & Proprietary Stores.

★ 82329 ★   Union Planters
National Bank
505 Nolan Dr.
Smyrna, TN 37167-5922
(615)355-0386
Location Type: Branch office. Ultimate
Parent: Union Planters Corp. SIC: 6021—
National Commercial Banks.

★ 82330 ★   Wal-Mart Stores Inc.
Old Nashville Hwy.
Smyrna, TN 37167
(615)459-0020
Ultimate Parent: Wal-Mart Stores, Inc. SIC:
5311—Department Stores.

Soddy Daisy

★ 82331 ★   Wal-Mart Stores Inc.
10049 Dayton Pike
Soddy Daisy, TN 37379
(615)332-2412
Ultimate Parent: Wal-Mart Stores, Inc.

★ 82332 ★   Wal-Mart Stores Inc.
249 PO Box
Soddy Daisy, TN 37379
Ultimate Parent: Wal-Mart Stores, Inc. SIC:
5311—Department Stores.

★ 82333 ★   Bowater Inc.
Soddy-Daisy, TN
(615)332-2476
Ultimate Parent: Bowater.

Somerville

★ 82334 ★   First State Bank of
Fayette County
16880 Hwy.
Somerville, TN 38068
(901)465-3635 Fax: (901)465-9297
Location Type: Branch office. Ultimate
Parent: Union Planters Corp. SIC: 6021—
National Commercial Banks.

★ 82335 ★   First State Bank of
Fayette County
PO Box 338
Somerville, TN 38068-0338
Location Type: Branch office. Ultimate
Parent: Union Planters Corp. SIC: 6021—
National Commercial Banks.

★ 82336 ★   Gold Kist Inc.
125 E. Latta Ln.
Somerville, TN 38068
(901)465-2864
Ultimate Parent: Gold Kist. SIC: 5153—
Grain & Field Beans.

South Pittsbu

★ 82337 ★   AmSouth Bank of
Tennessee
402 N. Cedar Ave.
South Pittsbu, TN 37380
(615)837-8645
Ultimate Parent: AmSouth Bancorp.

South Pittsburg

★ 82338 ★   AmSouth Bank of
Tennessee
402 Cedar Ave.
South Pittsburg, TN 37380-1308
(615)837-8645
Location Type: Branch office. Officer: Ron
Lowery, Manager. Ultimate Parent:
AmSouth Bancorp. SIC: 6022—State
Commercial Banks; 6162—Mortgage
Bankers & Correspondents.

★ 82339 ★   Nationsbank South
Pittsburg
406 Cedar Ave.
South Pittsburg, TN 37380
(615)837-7131
Ultimate Parent: Nationsbank Corp.

★ 82340 ★   Shaw Industries Inc.
E. 11th St.
South Pittsburg, TN 37380
(615)837-8651
Officer: Don Bratton, Manager. Ultimate
Parent: Shaw Industries, Inc. SIC: 2281—
Yarn Spinning Mills.

Sparta

★ 82341 ★   First Union National
Bank of Tennessee
6 Liberty Sq.
Sparta, TN 38583
Location Type: Branch office. Ultimate
Parent: First Union Corp. SIC: 6021—
National Commercial Banks.

★ 82342 ★   First Union National
Bank of Tennessee
445 W. Bockman Way
Sparta, TN 38583
Location Type: Branch office. Ultimate
Parent: First Union Corp. SIC: 6021—
National Commercial Banks.

★ 82343 ★   GE Co. Plastics
510 Iris Dr.
Sparta, TN 38583
Ultimate Parent: General Electric. SIC:
2821—Plastics Materials & Resins.

★ 82344 ★   Kroger Co.
W Bockmanway
Sparta, TN 38583
(615)836-3673
Ultimate Parent: Kroger. SIC: 5411—
Grocery Stores.

★ 82345 ★   Mallory Controls
Churchill Dr.
Sparta, TN 38583
Ultimate Parent: Black & Decker Corp.
SIC: 3822—Environmental Controls.

★ 82346 ★   Mallory Controls
Turntable Rd.
Sparta, TN 38583
Ultimate Parent: Emerson Electric Co. Inc.
SIC: 3822—Environmental Controls.

★ 82347 ★   Red Kap Ind.
RR 4
Sparta, TN 38583
(615)738-5217
Officer: Bert Adler, Manager. Ultimate
Parent: VF Corp. SIC: 2325—Men's/Boys'
Trousers & Slacks; 2326—Men's/Boys'
Work Clothing.

★ 82348 ★   White County
Industries Inc.
205 W. Bockman Way
Sparta, TN 38583
(615)836-3283
Ultimate Parent: Collins & Aikman Group.
SIC: 2321—Men's/Boys' Shirts.

Spring City

★ 82349 ★   Bowater Inc.
Southern Div.
New Lake Rd.
Spring City, TN 37381
(615)365-6815
Ultimate Parent: Bowater. SIC: 5099—
Durable Goods Nec.

★ 82350 ★   First American
National Bank
Railroad & Picadilly Sts.
Spring City, TN 37381
(615)755-6850
Location Type: Branch office. Ultimate
Parent: First American Corp. SIC: 6021—
National Commercial Banks.

Springfield

★ 82351 ★   Alstrip Inc.
197 Evergreen Dr.
Springfield, TN 37172
(615)382-1391
Company Type: Subsidiary. Officer:
Thomas J. Whittaker, President. Ultimate
Parent: Allegheny Ludlum Corp.

★ 82352 ★   Alstrip South
197 Evergreen Dr.
Springfield, TN 37172
Company Type: Division. Ultimate Parent:
Allegheny Ludlum Corp. SIC: 5051—Metals
Service Centers & Offices.

★ 82353 ★   American Limestone
Co.
4275 Hwy. 431 N
Springfield, TN 37172
(615)384-3524
Officer: Bob Sells, Manager. Ultimate
Parent: Asarco. SIC: 3274—Lime.

★ 82354 ★   American Limestone
Co. Inc.
PO Box 40
Springfield, TN 37172-0040
(615)384-4528
Officer: Hoyl Gill. Ultimate Parent: Asarco.
SIC: 3274—Lime; 1422—Crushed & Broken
Limestone; 1429—Crushed & Broken Stone
Nec; 3273—Ready-Mixed Concrete; 5039—
Construction Materials Nec; 5211—Lumber
& Other Building Materials.

★ 82355 ★   Delight Prods. Co.
1200 Industrial Dr.
Springfield, TN 37172
Ultimate Parent: Kroger. SIC: 2047—Dog
& Cat Food.

★ 82356 ★   First Union National
Bank of Tennessee
2125 Memorial Blvd.
Springfield, TN 37172-3936
(615)384-3541
Location Type: Branch office. Ultimate
Parent: First Union Corp. SIC: 6021—
National Commercial Banks.

★ 82357 ★   First Union National
Bank of Tennessee
402 Main St.
Springfield, TN 37172-2409
(615)384-3541
Location Type: Branch office. Ultimate
Parent: First Union Corp. SIC: 6021—
National Commercial Banks.

★ 82358 ★   Gold Kist Inc.
Hwy. 41 S
Springfield, TN 37172
(615)384-4575
Ultimate Parent: Gold Kist. SIC: 5153—
Grain & Field Beans.

★ 82359 ★   Greyhound Bus Lines
820 S. Main St.
Springfield, TN 37172
(615)384-5813
Ultimate Parent: Greyhound Lines Inc. SIC:
4111—Local & Suburban Transit; 4131—
Intercity & Rural Bus Transportation; 4142—
Bus Charter Service Except Local.

★ 82360 ★   Wal-Mart Stores Inc.
431 S
Springfield, TN 37172
(615)384-9561
Ultimate Parent: Wal-Mart Stores, Inc. SIC:
5311—Department Stores.

St. Bethlehem

★ 82361 ★ **First Union National Bank of Tennessee**
2700 Wilma Rudolph Blvd., Hwy. 79 N
St. Bethlehem, TN 37155
(615)552-8686
Location Type: Branch office. **Ultimate Parent:** First Union Corp. **SIC:** 6021—National Commercial Banks.

Straw Plains

★ 82362 ★ **Asarco Inc.**
PO Box 460
Straw Plains, TN 37871-0460
(615)933-3451
Company Type: Branch. **Officer:** Jim Bailes. **Ultimate Parent:** Asarco. **SIC:** 1031—Lead & Zinc Ores.

Strawberry Plains

★ 82363 ★ **Mary Kay Cosmetics**
Zachary Town Rd.
Strawberry Plains, TN 37871
(615)933-3330
Ultimate Parent: Mary Kay Cosmetics. **SIC:** 5999—Miscellaneous Retail Stores Nec.

Sunbright

★ 82364 ★ **Citizens Bank & Trust Co.**
Deer Lodge Rd.
Sunbright, TN 37872-9403
(615)628-2101
Location Type: Branch office. **Ultimate Parent:** Union Planters Corp. **SIC:** 6021—National Commercial Banks.

★ 82365 ★ **Peoples Bank & Trust Co.**
Sunbright, TN 37872
(615)628-2101
Ultimate Parent: People's Bank. **SIC:** 6141—Personal Credit Institutions.

Sweetwater

★ 82366 ★ **AT&T**
1179 Hwy. 68
Sweetwater, TN 37874-5162
(615)337-9920
Ultimate Parent: AT&T. **SIC:** 4813—Telephone Communications Except Radiotelephone.

Talbott

★ 82367 ★ **Bank of East Tennessee**
6000 W. Andrew Johnson Hwy.
Talbott, TN 37877
(615)587-7100
Location Type: Branch office. **Ultimate Parent:** Union Planters Corp. **SIC:** 6021—National Commercial Banks.

Tellico Plains

★ 82368 ★ **Delta Apparel**
Hwy. 68 & Rte. 4
Tellico Plains, TN 37385
(615)253-2171
Officer: Polly Graves, Manager. **Ultimate Parent:** Delta Woodside Industries. **SIC:** 2253—Knit Outerwear Mills; 2322—Men's/Boys' Underwear & Nightwear.

Tennessee Ridge

★ 82369 ★ **Cumberland City Bank**
Hwy. 147
Tennessee Ridge, TN 37178
(615)721-3308
Location Type: Branch office. **Ultimate Parent:** Union Planters Corp. **SIC:** 6021—National Commercial Banks.

Tiptonville

★ 82370 ★ **Georgia Gulf Corp.**
Hwy. 21 W.
Tiptonville, TN 38079
(901)253-7711
Officer: J.R. Greer, Manager. **Ultimate Parent:** Georgia Gulf. **SIC:** 2821—Plastics Materials & Resins; 2899—Chemical Preparations Nec.

Townsend

★ 82371 ★ **Union Planters National Bank**
7723 E. Lamar Alexander Pky.
Townsend, TN 37882
(615)981-1402
Location Type: Branch office. **Ultimate Parent:** Union Planters National Bank. **SIC:** 6021—National Commercial Banks.

Tracy City

★ 82372 ★ **First National Bank**
Depot St.
Tracy City, TN
(615)592-2741
Location Type: Branch office. **Ultimate Parent:** Union Planters Corp. **SIC:** 6021—National Commercial Banks.

Trenton

★ 82373 ★ **Bank of Trenton & Trust Co.**
115 High St.
Trenton, TN 38382-1724
(901)855-2121 **Fax:** (901)855-2324
Location Type: Headquarters. **Ultimate Parent:** Union Planters Corp. **SIC:** 6021—National Commercial Banks.

★ 82374 ★ **Bank of Trenton & Trust Co.**
PO Box 87
Trenton, TN 38382-0087
Location Type: Headquarters. **Ultimate Parent:** Union Planters Corp. **SIC:** 6021—National Commercial Banks.

Troy

★ 82375 ★ **Wrangler**
701 S. Mary Jane St.
Troy, TN 38260
(901)536-4722
Officer: Bill Vinson, Manager. **Ultimate Parent:** VF Corp. **SIC:** 2325—Men's/Boys' Trousers & Slacks; 2339—Women's/Misses' Outerwear Nec; 2369—Girls'/Children's Outerwear Nec.

Tullahoma

★ 82376 ★ **Arnold Engineering Development Center Operations**
Arnold Air Force Station
Tullahoma, TN 37389
(615)455-2611
Company Type: Subsidiary. **Officer:** J.W. Davis, Vice President & Director. **Ultimate Parent:** Arvin Industries Inc.

★ 82377 ★ **Arvin Industries Inc.**
Service Contracts Div.
110 A Mitchell Blvd.
Tullahoma, TN 37388
(615)455-4759
Company Type: Division. **Officer:** King D. Bird, Senior Vice President & General Manager. **Ultimate Parent:** Arvin Industries Inc.

★ 82378 ★ **Greyhound Bus Lines**
211 W. Carroll St.
Tullahoma, TN 37388
(615)455-3197
Ultimate Parent: Greyhound Lines Inc. **SIC:** 4111—Local & Suburban Transit; 4131—Intercity & Rural Bus Transportation; 4142—Bus Charter Service Except Local.

★ 82379 ★ **Ryder Truck Rental-Oneway**
400 N. Jackson St.
Tullahoma, TN 37388
(615)455-7509
Ultimate Parent: Ryder System. **SIC:** 7359—Equipment Rental & Leasing Nec.

Unicol

★ 82380 ★ **First Tennessee Bank NA**
US Hwy. 19-23 West
Unicol, TN 37692-9665
(615)743-4121
Location Type: Branch office. **Ultimate Parent:** First Tennessee National Corp. **SIC:** 6021—National Commercial Banks.

Union City

★ 82381 ★ **Agrico Chemical Co.**
206 S. 4th St.
Union City, TN 38261
(901)885-0327
Ultimate Parent: Freeport-McMoran. **SIC:** 1422—Crushed & Broken Limestone.

★ 82382 ★ **Goodyear Tire & Rubber Co.**
Mt Zion Rd.
Union City, TN 38261
Ultimate Parent: Goodyear Tire & Rubber. **SIC:** 3011—Tires & Inner Tubes.

★ 82383 ★ **Goodyear Tire & Rubber Co. Union City Plant**
Mt Zion Rd.
Union City, TN 38261
Ultimate Parent: Goodyear Tire & Rubber. **SIC:** 3011—Tires & Inner Tubes.

★ 82384 ★ **Greyhound Bus Lines**
421 W. Reelfoot Ave.
Union City, TN 38261
(901)885-3871
Ultimate Parent: Greyhound Lines Inc. **SIC:** 4111—Local & Suburban Transit; 4131—Intercity & Rural Bus Transportation; 4142—Bus Charter Service Except Local.

★ 82385 ★ **Kroger Co.**
1430 S. 1st St.
Union City, TN 38261
(901)885-7111
Ultimate Parent: Kroger. **SIC:** 5411—Grocery Stores.

★ 82386 ★ **McDonald's Hamburgers**
1108 Marshall St.
Union City, TN 38261
(901)885-2352
Ultimate Parent: McDonald's. **SIC:** 5812—Eating Places.

★ 82387 ★ **Merchants State Bank**
703 Reelfoot Ave.
Union City, TN 38261
(901)885-6369
Location Type: Branch office. **Ultimate Parent:** Union Planters Corp. **SIC:** 6021—National Commercial Banks.

★ 82388 ★ **Merchants State Bank**
115 Washington Ave.
Union City, TN 38261
(901)885-5451
Location Type: Branch office. **Ultimate Parent:** Union Planters Corp. **SIC:** 6021—National Commercial Banks.

★ 82389 ★ **Ryder Truck Rental**
431 W. Reelfoot Ave.
Union City, TN 38261
(901)885-7438
Ultimate Parent: Ryder System. **SIC:** 7513—Truck Rental & Leasing Without Drivers.

★ 82390 ★ **Seven-Up Bottling Co.**
1915 E. Reelfoot Ave.
Union City, TN 38261
(901)885-5141
Officer: Newell Graham, CEO. **Ultimate Parent:** Dr. Pepper/Seven-Up. **SIC:** 2086—Bottled & Canned Soft Drinks.

Vanleer

★ 82391 ★ **People's Bank**
Vanleer, TN 37181
(615)763-2235
Ultimate Parent: People's Bank. **SIC:** 6022—State Commercial Banks.

Vonore

★ 82392 ★ **Avecor Inc.**
Niles Ferry Industrial Park
Vonore, TN 37885
Ultimate Parent: M.A.Hanna. **SIC:** 3087—Custom Compound of Purchased Resins.

★ 82393 ★ **Avecor Inc.**
PO Box 278
Vonore, TN 37885
(615)884-6625 **Fax:** (615)884-6176
Company Type: Subsidiary. **Officer:** Leonard J. Klarich, President & CEO. **Ultimate Parent:** M.A.Hanna.

★ 82394 ★ **Avecor Inc.**
Avecor Dr.
Niles Ferry Industrial Park
Vonore, TN 37885
(615)884-6625
Company Type: Subsidiary. **Officer:** Leonard Klarich, President. **Ultimate Parent:** M.A.Hanna. **SIC:** 2865—Cyclic Crudes & Intermediates. **Employee Count:** 220. **Sales:** 43.6 (est) M.

★ 82395 ★ **National Seating Co.**
200 National Dr.
Vonore, TN 37885
Ultimate Parent: Sequa Corp. **SIC:** 2531—Public Building & Related Furniture.

★ 82396 ★ **Sea Ray Boats Inc.**
100 Sea Ray Cir. Tellico Lake W.
Vonore, TN 37885
Ultimate Parent: Brunswick Corp. **SIC:** 3732—Boat Building & Repairing.

★ 82397 ★ **Trw Inc. Koyo Steering Sys. Co.**
55 Excellence Way
Vonore, TN 37885
Ultimate Parent: TRW, Inc. **SIC:** 3714—Motor Vehicle Parts & Accessories.

Vonove

★ 82398 ★ **TRW Koyo Steering System**
55 Excellence Way
Vonove, TN 37885
(615)884-9200
Officer: Arvind Korde, President. **Ultimate Parent:** TRW, Inc. **SIC:** 3714—Motor Vehicle Parts & Accessories.

Wartburg

★ 82399 ★ **Citizens Bank & Trust Co.**
Eliza St.
Wartburg, TN 37887-9524
(615)346-6211 **Fax:** (615)346-7892
Location Type: Headquarters. **Ultimate Parent:** Union Planters Corp. **SIC:** 6021—National Commercial Banks.

★ 82400 ★ **Citizens Bank & Trust Co.**
PO Box 328
Wartburg, TN 37887-0328
Location Type: Headquarters. **Ultimate Parent:** Union Planters Corp. **SIC:** 6021—National Commercial Banks.

★ 82401 ★ **Peoples Bank & Trust Co.**
388 PO Box
Wartburg, TN 37887
(615)346-6266
Ultimate Parent: People's Bank. **SIC:** 8999—Services Nec.

★ 82402 ★ **Red Kap Ind.**
Redcap Rd.
Wartburg, TN 37887
(615)346-6234
Officer: Phil Marsom, Manager. **Ultimate Parent:** VF Corp. **SIC:** 2325—Men's/Boys' Trousers & Slacks; 2326—Men's/Boys' Work Clothing.

Watauga

★ 82403 ★　American Limestone
Co. Inc.
PO Box 158
Watauga, TN 37694-0158
(615)926-0111
Officer: Mike Freeman. Ultimate Parent:
Asarco. SIC: 1422—Crushed & Broken
Limestone; 1442—Construction Sand &
Gravel.

Waverly

★ 82404 ★　First American
National Bank
303 W. MAin St.
Waverly, TN 37185-1509
(615)296-1739
Location Type: Branch office. Ultimate
Parent: First American Corp. SIC: 6021—
National Commercial Banks.

★ 82405 ★　First American
National Bank
122 W. Main St.
Waverly, TN 37185-1509
(615)296-4264
Location Type: Branch office. Ultimate
Parent: First American Corp. SIC: 6021—
National Commercial Banks.

★ 82406 ★　Vulcan Materials Co.
Gorman
Waverly, TN 37185
(615)296-2443
Ultimate Parent: Vulcan Materials Co. SIC:
5039—Construction Materials Nec.

Waynesboro

★ 82407 ★　People's Bank
PO Box 718
Waynesboro, TN 38485
(615)722-3608
Ultimate Parent: People's Bank. SIC:
6029—Commercial Banks Nec.

Westmoreland

★ 82408 ★　First Union National
Bank of Tennessee
Hwys. 52 & 31 E
Westmoreland, TN 37186-9223
(615)644-2242
Location Type: Branch office. Ultimate
Parent: First Union Corp. SIC: 6021—
National Commercial Banks.

★ 82409 ★　Fleetwood Homes
4011 Fleetwood Dr.
Westmoreland, TN 37186
(615)644-2220
Officer: John Burke, Manager. Ultimate
Parent: Fleetwood Enterprises, Inc. SIC:
2451—Mobile Homes.

★ 82410 ★　Fleetwood Homes of
Tennessee Inc. No. 27
Fleetwood Dr. at Hawkins St.
Westmoreland, TN 37186
Ultimate Parent: Fleetwood Enterprises,
Inc. SIC: 3711—Motor Vehicles & Car
Bodies.

★ 82411 ★　Fleetwood Homes of
Tennessee Inc. 27
4011 Fleetwood Dr. PO Box 597
Westmoreland, TN 37186
Ultimate Parent: Fleetwood Enterprises,
Inc. SIC: 2451—Mobile Homes.

★ 82412 ★　Fleetwood Homes of
Tennessee Inc. 26
1720 Pleasant Grove Rd. PO Box 559
Westmoreland, TN 37186
Ultimate Parent: Fleetwood Enterprises,
Inc. SIC: 2451—Mobile Homes.

★ 82413 ★　Fleetwood Motor
Homes of Tennessee Inc.
Fleetwood Dr. T Hawkins St., PO Box 597
Westmoreland, TN 37186
Ultimate Parent: Fleetwood Enterprises,
Inc. SIC: 2451—Mobile Homes.

White Creek

★ 82414 ★　First Tennessee Bank
NA
4410 White Creek Pke.
White Creek, TN 37189-9127
(615)734-6266
Location Type: Branch office. Ultimate

Parent: First Tennessee National Corp.
SIC: 6021—National Commercial Banks.

★ 82415 ★　Red Kap Ind.
554 Hickory Hills Blvd.
White Creek, TN 37189
(615)876-2671
Officer: Tommy Davis, Manager. Ultimate
Parent: VF Corp. SIC: 3999—
Manufacturing Industries Nec.

White Pine

★ 82416 ★　First Tennessee Bank
NA
201 Walnut St.
White Pine, TN 37890
(615)674-2558
Location Type: Branch office. Ultimate
Parent: First Tennessee National Corp.
SIC: 6021—National Commercial Banks.

★ 82417 ★　First Union National
Bank of Tennessee
1715 E. Main St.
White Pine, TN 37890
(615)674-2501
Ultimate Parent: First Union Corp. SIC:
6021—National Commercial Banks.

Whitehouse

★ 82418 ★　First Union National
Bank of Tennessee
414 Hwy. 31 W
Whitehouse, TN 37188
(615)672-4364
Location Type: Branch office. Ultimate
Parent: First Union Corp. SIC: 6021—
National Commercial Banks.

Winchester

★ 82419 ★　First Union National
Bank of Tennessee
116 S. College St.
Winchester, TN 37398-1518
(615)967-2780
Location Type: Branch office. Ultimate
Parent: First Union Corp. SIC: 6021—
National Commercial Banks.

★ 82420 ★　Greyhound Bus Lines
109 41st Byp
Winchester, TN 37398
(615)967-0569
Ultimate Parent: Greyhound Lines Inc. SIC:
4111—Local & Suburban Transit; 4131—
Intercity & Rural Bus Transportation; 4142—
Bus Charter Service Except Local.

★ 82421 ★　Shaw Industries Inc.
4130 Cowan Hwy.
Winchester, TN 37398
(615)967-7446
Officer: Lee Shortridge, Manager. Ultimate
Parent: Shaw Industries, Inc. SIC: 2273—
Carpets & Rugs.

Woodbury

★ 82422 ★　Bank of Commerce
200 Public Sq.
Woodbury, TN 37190-1194
(615)563-5091 Fax: (615)563-5101
Location Type: Headquarters. Ultimate
Parent: Union Planters Corp. SIC: 6021—
National Commercial Banks.

★ 82423 ★　Bank of Commerce
Hwy. 70 & Adams St.
Woodbury, TN 37190-9714
(615)563-5071
Location Type: Branch office. Ultimate
Parent: Union Planters Corp. SIC: 6021—
National Commercial Banks.

★ 82424 ★　First American
National Bank
Main & McCrary Sts.
Woodbury, TN 37190-1224
(615)563-2221
Location Type: Branch office. Ultimate
Parent: First American Corp. SIC: 6021—
National Commercial Banks.

Yorkville

★ 82425 ★　Merchants State Bank
3 Nebo - Yorkville Rd.
Yorkville, TN 38389
(901)643-6333
Location Type: Branch office. Ultimate
Parent: Union Planters Corp. SIC: 6021—
National Commercial Banks.

TEXAS

★ 82426 ★ **GTE Information Services**
Dallas Fort Worth Airport
TX 75261-9810
(214)453-7000 **Fax:** (214)450-7573
Company Type: Subsidiary. **Officer:**
Thomas F. Lysaught, President. **Ultimate Parent:** GTE.

Abilene

★ 82427 ★ **BFI Regional Landfill**
FM 3034
Abilene, TX 79604
(915)672-7613
Ultimate Parent: Browning-Ferris
Industries. **SIC:** 4953—Refuse Systems.

★ 82428 ★ **Butler Paper Co.**
3301 N. 3rd St.
Abilene, TX 79603-7044
(915)672-4446
Ultimate Parent: Alco Standard Corp. **SIC:**
5113—Industrial & Personal Service Paper.

★ 82429 ★ **Career Image**
4310 Mall of Abilene N
Abilene, TX 79606
(915)692-5331
Ultimate Parent: United States Shoe. **SIC:**
5651—Family Clothing Stores.

★ 82430 ★ **Career Image**
Mall of Abilene
Abilene, TX 79605
(915)692-5331
Ultimate Parent: United States Shoe. **SIC:**
5621—Women's Clothing Stores.

★ 82431 ★ **Casual Corner**
4310 Mall of Abilene N
Abilene, TX 79606
(915)695-1511
Ultimate Parent: United States Shoe. **SIC:**
5651—Family Clothing Stores.

★ 82432 ★ **Circus World**
4310 Mall of Abilene N
Abilene, TX 79606
(915)698-0314
Ultimate Parent: Melville. **SIC:** 5945—
Hobby, Toy & Game Shops.

★ 82433 ★ **Crown Cork & Seal Co. Inc.**
1900 Clack St.
Abilene, TX 79603
Ultimate Parent: Crown Cork & Seal. **SIC:**
3411—Metal Cans.

★ 82434 ★ **Diebold Inc.**
120 Sycamore St.
Abilene, TX 79602
(915)672-6320
Ultimate Parent: Diebold, Inc. **SIC:** 5044—
Office Equipment.

★ 82435 ★ **Emery Worldwide**
4102 Wilshire Ct
Abilene, TX 79603
(915)672-8146
Ultimate Parent: Consolidated Freightways.
SIC: 4512—Air Transportation—Scheduled.

★ 82436 ★ **Foot Action**
4310 Mall of Abilene N
Abilene, TX 79606
(915)698-9298
Ultimate Parent: Melville. **SIC:** 5661—Shoe
Stores.

★ 82437 ★ **General Dynamics Corp. Abilene Facility**
300 Wall St.
Abilene, TX 79603
Ultimate Parent: General Dynamics. **SIC:**
3728—Aircraft Parts & Equipment Nec.

★ 82438 ★ **Greyhound Bus Line**
535 Cedar St.
Abilene, TX 79601
(915)677-8127
Ultimate Parent: Greyhound Lines Inc.

★ 82439 ★ **Hertz Rent-A-Car**
Abilne Manor Airport
Abilene, TX 79604
(915)673-6774
Ultimate Parent: Hertz. **SIC:** 7514—
Passenger Car Rental.

★ 82440 ★ **Kay Bee Toy & Hobby Shop**
4310 Mall of Abilene N
Abilene, TX 79606
(915)695-9521
Ultimate Parent: Melville. **SIC:** 5945—
Hobby, Toy & Game Shops.

★ 82441 ★ **Lane Bryant**
4310 Mall of Abilene N
Abilene, TX 79606
(915)698-6209
Ultimate Parent: Limited. **SIC:** 5651—
Family Clothing Stores.

★ 82442 ★ **Lerner Shop**
Westgate Mall Ctr.
Abilene, TX 79605
(915)692-6452
Ultimate Parent: Limited. **SIC:** 5621—
Women's Clothing Stores.

★ 82443 ★ **Lerner Shop**
4310 Mall of Abilene N
Abilene, TX 79606
(915)695-2485
Ultimate Parent: Limited. **SIC:** 5651—
Family Clothing Stores.

★ 82444 ★ **The Limited**
4310 Mall of Abilene N
Abilene, TX 79606
(915)695-2470
Ultimate Parent: Limited. **SIC:** 5651—
Family Clothing Stores.

★ 82445 ★ **The Limited**
4310 Buffalo Gap Rd.
Abilene, TX 79606
(915)695-2470
Ultimate Parent: Limited.

★ 82446 ★ **Lockheed Abilene Facility**
300 Wall St.
Abilene, TX 79603
Ultimate Parent: Lockheed Corp. **SIC:**
3728—Aircraft Parts & Equipment Nec.

★ 82447 ★ **Lone Star Gas Co.**
155 Hickory St.
Abilene, TX 79601
(915)677-3082
Ultimate Parent: Enserch. **SIC:** 4939—
Combination Utility Nec.

★ 82448 ★ **McDonalds Hamburgers**
3600 N. 1st St.
Abilene, TX 79603
(915)673-6564
Ultimate Parent: McDonald's.
SIC: 5812—Eating Places.

★ 82449 ★ **Mcduff Electronics**
4310 Buffalo Gap Rd.
Abilene, TX 79606
(915)692-0696
Ultimate Parent: Tandy Corp.

★ 82450 ★ **Piggly Wiggly**
1273 Butternut St.
Abilene, TX 79602
(915)677-5225
Ultimate Parent: Bruno's. **SIC:** 5411—
Grocery Stores.

★ 82451 ★ **Piggly Wiggly**
738 S. Leggett Dr.
Abilene, TX 79605
(915)692-7166
Ultimate Parent: Bruno's. **SIC:** 5411—
Grocery Stores.

★ 82452 ★ **Pizza Hut Area Office**
302 N. Willis St.
Abilene, TX 79603
(915)672-3639
Ultimate Parent: Pepsico. **SIC:** 5812—
Eating Places.

★ 82453 ★ **Radio Shack**
4310 Mall of Abilene N
Abilene, TX 79606
(915)695-2914
Company Type: Division. **Ultimate Parent:**
Tandy Corp. **SIC:** 5731—Radio, Television
& Electronics Stores.

★ 82454 ★ **Ryder Truck Rental**
6226 PO Box
Abilene, TX 79608
(915)695-3690
Ultimate Parent: Ryder System. **SIC:**
7359—Equipment Rental & Leasing Nec.

★ 82455 ★ **Ryder Truck Rental**
3981 S. 1st St.
Abilene, TX 79605
(915)673-6900
Ultimate Parent: Ryder System. **SIC:**
7359—Equipment Rental & Leasing Nec.

★ 82456 ★ **Ryder Truck Rental**
820 Hwy. 80 E
Abilene, TX 79601
(915)673-7081
Ultimate Parent: Ryder System. **SIC:**
7359—Equipment Rental & Leasing Nec.

★ 82457 ★ **Shell Oil Marketing**
101 Locust St.
Abilene, TX 79602
(915)673-4613
Ultimate Parent: Shell Oil Co.

★ 82458 ★ **Southwest Coca Cola**
1849 Albany Hwy.
Abilene, TX 79601
Ultimate Parent: Coca-Cola Bottling
Consol. **SIC:** 2086—Bottled & Canned Soft
Drinks.

★ 82459 ★ **Target Stores**
3710 Ridgemont Dr.
Abilene, TX 79606
(915)695-3001
Ultimate Parent: Dayton Hudson. **SIC:**
5311—Department Stores.

★ 82460 ★ **Texaco Inc.**
325 S. 13th St.
Abilene, TX 79602
(915)672-5416
Ultimate Parent: Texaco.

★ 82461 ★ **Texaco Incorporated Sales**
325 S. 13th St.
Abilene, TX 79602
(915)672-8485
Ultimate Parent: Texaco. **SIC:** 5171—
Petroleum Bulk Stations & Terminals.

★ 82462 ★ **Texaco Station**
1901 S. 1st St.
Abilene, TX 79602
(915)673-0080
Ultimate Parent: Texaco. **SIC:** 5541—
Gasoline Service Stations.

★ 82463 ★ **Texas Instruments Inc.**
4002 Loop 322
Abilene, TX 79602
Ultimate Parent: Texas Instruments. **SIC:**
3679—Electronic Components Nec; 3600—
Electronic & Other Electrical Equipment.

★ 82464 ★ **Trailways Bus Station**
427 Walnut St.
Abilene, TX 79601
(915)673-6176
Ultimate Parent: Greyhound Lines Inc. **SIC:**
4131—Intercity & Rural Bus Transportation;
4173—Bus Terminal & Service Facilities.

★ 82465 ★ **Trailways Bus Systems**
3501 Curry Ln.
Abilene, TX 79606
(915)673-6705
Ultimate Parent: Greyhound Lines Inc.

★ 82466 ★ **Waldenbooks**
4310 Mall of Abilene N
Abilene, TX 79606
(915)692-0985
Ultimate Parent: K-Mart. **SIC:** 5942—Book
Stores.

★ 82467 ★ **West Texas Utilities Co.**
301 Cypress St.
Abilene, TX 79601
(915)674-7000 **Fax:** (915)674-7611
Officer: Glenn Files, President & CEO.
Ultimate Parent: Central & South West.

★ 82468 ★ **West Texas Utilities Co.**
1054 N. 3rd St.
Abilene, TX 79601
(915)674-7440
Ultimate Parent: Central & South West.
SIC: 5722—Household Appliance Stores.

★ 82469 ★ **World Book**
Childcraft
4033 Avondale St.
Abilene, TX 79605-3801
(915)673-8931
Officer: Maurine Mallon. **Ultimate Parent:**
Berkshire Hathaway. **SIC:** 5963—Direct
Selling Establishments; 5942—Book Stores.

Addison

★ 82470 ★ **Arnet Computer**
4004 Beltline Rd., Ste. 200
Addison, TX 75244
(214)308-8166
Location Type: Branch office. **Ultimate Parent:** Avnet. **SIC:** 5045—Computers,
Peripherals & Software; 7379—Computer
Related Services Nec.

★ 82471 ★ **Comerica Bank-Texas**
5006 Verde Valley
Addison, TX 75240-7521
(214)969-6600
Company Type: Subsidiary. **Location Type:** Branch office. **Ultimate Parent:**
Comerica Bank. **SIC:** 6021—National
Commercial Banks.

★ 82472 ★ **Exxon Car Care Center**
Gen Del
Addison, TX 75001
(214)270-2426
Ultimate Parent: Exxon. **SIC:** 7538—
General Automotive Repair Shops.

★ 82473 ★ **Greyhound Bus Lines**
3704 Realty
Addison, TX 75001
(214)484-8144
Ultimate Parent: Greyhound Lines Inc. **SIC:**
4111—Local & Suburban Transit.

★ 82474 ★ **Mobil Research Devlpmnt Cor**
13777 Midway Rd.
Addison, TX 75001
(214)851-8111
Ultimate Parent: Mobil. **SIC:** 5172—
Petroleum Products Nec.

Alamo

★ 82475 ★ Arco Oil & Gas Co.
Alamo, TX 78516
(210)787-3021
Company Type: Division. Location Type:
Branch office. Ultimate Parent: Atlantic
Richfield Co., Inc. SIC: 4924—Natural Gas
Distribution.

★ 82476 ★ Coast to Coast Yellow
Pages
620 Ferguson W
Alamo, TX 78516
(512)781-6913
Ultimate Parent: Servistar Corp.

★ 82477 ★ Jostens Learning
Corp.
Hwy. 83 W
Alamo, TX 78516
(512)783-9333
Ultimate Parent: Jostens.

★ 82478 ★ Radio Shack
El Centro Mall
Alamo, TX 78516
(512)787-2880
Company Type: Division. Ultimate Parent:
Tandy Corp. SIC: 5734—Computer &
Software Stores.

★ 82479 ★ Rio Grande Valley
Gas Co.
506 Polk Ave. W
Alamo, TX 78516
(512)787-2871
Ultimate Parent: Valero Energy Corp.

★ 82480 ★ Thom Mcan Shoe
Store
500 N. Jackson
Alamo, TX 78516
(512)787-9010
Ultimate Parent: Melville. SIC: 5661—Shoe
Stores.

Alba

★ 82481 ★ Mitchell Energy Corp.
Alba, TX 75410
(903)765-2625
Ultimate Parent: Mitchell Energy & Devel.
SIC: 1311—Crude Petroleum & Natural
Gas.

Albany

★ 82482 ★ Warren Petroleum
Corp.
Throckmorton Hwy.
Albany, TX 76430
(915)762-2434
Ultimate Parent: Chevron Corp. SIC:
5171—Petroleum Bulk Stations & Terminals.

Alice

★ 82483 ★ Hertz Rent-A-Car
Licensee
Alice International Airport
Alice, TX 78332
(512)664-2951
Ultimate Parent: Hertz. SIC: 7514—
Passenger Car Rental.

★ 82484 ★ Kroger Family Center
1720 E. Main St.
Alice, TX 78332
(512)664-2671
Ultimate Parent: Kroger. SIC: 5411—
Grocery Stores.

★ 82485 ★ Kroger Pharmacy
1720 E. Main St.
Alice, TX 78332
(512)664-2675
Ultimate Parent: Kroger. SIC: 5912—Drug
Stores & Proprietary Stores.

★ 82486 ★ Mobil Pipeline Co.
Tec Techn
Old Magnolia Camp
Alice, TX 78332
(512)664-0779
Ultimate Parent: Mobil. SIC: 4612—Crude
Petroleum Pipelines.

★ 82487 ★ Radio Shack
1203 E. Main St.
Alice, TX 78332
(512)664-1521
Company Type: Division. Ultimate Parent:
Tandy Corp. SIC: 5065—Electronic Parts &
Equipment Nec.

★ 82488 ★ Trailways Bus System
1st
Alice, TX 78332
(512)664-2601
Ultimate Parent: Greyhound Lines Inc. SIC:
4111—Local & Suburban Transit.

Alief

★ 82489 ★ Browning-Ferris
Industries
9718 Gaines Rd.
Alief, TX 77411
(713)933-9332
Ultimate Parent: Browning-Ferris
Industries. SIC: 4953—Refuse Systems.

★ 82490 ★ Kentucky Fried
Chicken
10712 W. Bellfort
Alief, TX 77411
(713)498-4301
Ultimate Parent: Pepsico. SIC: 5812—
Eating Places.

★ 82491 ★ Kroger Food Stores
9402 Hwy. 6
Alief, TX 77411
(713)495-1375
Ultimate Parent: Kroger. SIC: 5411—
Grocery Stores.

★ 82492 ★ McDonalds
Restaurant
10638 W. Bellfort
Alief, TX 77411
(713)498-8910
Ultimate Parent: McDonald's.
SIC: 5812—Eating Places.

★ 82493 ★ Radio Shack
10810 W. Bellfort
Alief, TX 77411
(713)498-1890
Company Type: Division. Ultimate Parent:
Tandy Corp. SIC: 3699—Electrical
Equipment & Supplies Nec.

★ 82494 ★ Taco Bell
11405 Bellaire Blvd.
Alief, TX 77411
(713)498-7132
Ultimate Parent: Pepsico. SIC: 5812—
Eating Places.

Allen

★ 82495 ★ Kentucky Fried
Chicken
200 N. Greenville Ave.
Allen, TX 75002
(214)727-5336
Ultimate Parent: Pepsico. SIC: 5812—
Eating Places.

★ 82496 ★ Ryder Truck Rental
105 S. Ash Dr.
Allen, TX 75002
(214)727-1711
Ultimate Parent: Ryder System.

★ 82497 ★ Taco Bell
208 N. Greenville Ave.
Allen, TX 75002
(214)727-8226
Ultimate Parent: Pepsico. SIC: 5812—
Eating Places.

★ 82498 ★ Wal Mart
Hwy. 5
Allen, TX 75002
(214)727-5731
Ultimate Parent: Wal-Mart Stores, Inc. SIC:
5912—Drug Stores & Proprietary Stores.

Alpine

★ 82499 ★ Coast to Coast Auto
103 W. Holland Ave.
Alpine, TX 79830
(915)837-2697
Ultimate Parent: Servistar Corp. SIC:
5531—Automobile & Home Supply Stores.

★ 82500 ★ Pizza Hut
Hwy. 90 E
Alpine, TX 79830
(915)837-5501
Ultimate Parent: Pepsico. SIC: 5812—
Eating Places.

★ 82501 ★ Ryder Truck Rental
E Hwy. 90
Alpine, TX 79830
(915)837-7001
Ultimate Parent: Ryder System. SIC:
7359—Equipment Rental & Leasing Nec.

★ 82502 ★ Trailways Bus
302 E. Holland Ave.
Alpine, TX 79830
(915)837-7211
Ultimate Parent: Greyhound Lines Inc. SIC:
4131—Intercity & Rural Bus Transportation.

Altair

★ 82503 ★ Mobil Oil Co.
Altair
Altair, TX 77412
(409)234-2846
Ultimate Parent: Mobil.

★ 82504 ★ Mobil Oil Corp. Eagle
Lake P
Chesterville
Altair, TX 77412
(409)234-2731
Ultimate Parent: Mobil.

Alvin

★ 82505 ★ Cain Chemical Inc.
Chocolate Bayou Plant
FM Rd. 2917
Alvin, TX 77512
Location Type: Plant. Ultimate Parent:
Occidental Petroleum Corp. SIC: 2869—
Industrial Organic Chemicals Nec.

★ 82506 ★ Kentucky Fried
Chicken
1623 S. Gordon St.
Alvin, TX 77511
(713)585-2292
Ultimate Parent: Pepsico. SIC: 5812—
Eating Places.

★ 82507 ★ Kroger Co.
2625 Loop 35
Alvin, TX 77511
(713)331-8258
Ultimate Parent: Kroger. SIC: 5411—
Grocery Stores.

★ 82508 ★ Mobil Oil Corp.
Chocolate Bypass
Alvin, TX 77511
(713)393-1815
Ultimate Parent: Mobil. SIC: 5171—
Petroleum Bulk Stations & Terminals.

★ 82509 ★ Monsanto Co.
Fm 2917
Alvin, TX 77511
Ultimate Parent: Monsanto. SIC: 2869—
Industrial Organic Chemicals Nec; 2819—
Industrial Inorganic Chemicals Nec; 2841—
Soap & Other Detergents; 2879—
Agricultural Chemicals Nec.

★ 82510 ★ Occidental Chemical
Corp.
Fm Rd. 2917
Alvin, TX 77512
Ultimate Parent: Occidental Petroleum
Corp. SIC: 2869—Industrial Organic
Chemicals Nec.

★ 82511 ★ Oshkosh Truck Corp.
Hwy. 6 W
Alvin, TX 77511
(713)331-7648
Ultimate Parent: Oshkosh Truck. SIC:
5531—Automobile & Home Supply Stores.

★ 82512 ★ Oxychem
Petrochemicals Inc.
Fm Rd. 2917
Alvin, TX 77512
Ultimate Parent: Occidental Petroleum
Corp. SIC: 2869—Industrial Organic
Chemicals Nec.

★ 82513 ★ Payless Shoesource
1701 Loop 35
Alvin, TX 77511
(713)585-4549
Ultimate Parent: May Department Stores.
SIC: 5661—Shoe Stores.

★ 82514 ★ Pizza Hut
1215 S. Gordon St.
Alvin, TX 77511
(713)331-6009
Ultimate Parent: Pepsico. SIC: 5812—
Eating Places; 5812—Eating Places.

★ 82515 ★ Radio Shack
1801 S. Gordon St.
Alvin, TX 77511
(713)331-0941
Company Type: Division. Ultimate Parent:
Tandy Corp.

★ 82516 ★ Ryder Truck Rental
614 S. Gordon St.
Alvin, TX 77511
(713)331-6772
Ultimate Parent: Ryder System.

★ 82517 ★ Wal Mart Discount
Cities
1701 Fairway Dr.
Alvin, TX 77511
(713)585-2825
Ultimate Parent: Wal-Mart Stores, Inc. SIC:
5311—Department Stores.

★ 82518 ★ Wal Mart Tire &
Battery Ctr
1701 Fairway Dr.
Alvin, TX 77511
(713)585-6876
Ultimate Parent: Wal-Mart Stores, Inc. SIC:
7538—General Automotive Repair Shops.

★ 82519 ★ Western Atlas
Manufacturing (Alvin)
1001 Loop 35 Bypass
Alvin, TX 77511
(713)331-6451 Fax: (713)585-6358
Officer: Paul Morgan, President. Ultimate
Parent: Litton Industries.

Amarillo

★ 82520 ★ Asarco Inc.
PO Box 30200
Amarillo, TX 79120-0200
(806)383-2201
Officer: Bill McClean. Ultimate Parent:
Asarco. SIC: 3331—Primary Copper.

★ 82521 ★ Asarco Inc.
Amarillo Copper Refinery
Hwy. 136 8 Miles NE of Amarillo
Amarillo, TX 79120-0200
Company Type: Division. Ultimate Parent:
Asarco. SIC: 3331—Primary Copper.

★ 82522 ★ Asarco Inc.
Amarillo Plant
Hwy. 136 8 Miles NE of Amarillo
Amarillo, TX 79120-0200
Location Type: Plant. Ultimate Parent:
Asarco. SIC: 3331—Primary Copper.

★ 82523 ★ Asarco Inc.
Amarillo Plant
Hwy. 136, 8 NE of Amarillo
Amarillo, TX 79120-0200
Location Type: Plant. Ultimate Parent:
Asarco. SIC: 3300—Primary Metal
Industries.

★ 82524 ★ Atchison, Topeka &
Santa Fe Railway Co.
900 Santa Fe Bldg.
Amarillo, TX 79101
(806)379-3263
Ultimate Parent: Santa Fe Pacific Corp.
SIC: 4119—Local Passenger Transportation
Nec; 4011—Railroads—Line-Haul
Operating.

★ 82525 ★ Bell Helicopter
Textron Inc.
Ave. B & 5th St.
Amarillo, TX 79120
Ultimate Parent: Textron. SIC: 3720—
Aircraft & Parts.

★ 82526 ★   Borden Inc.
4945 Canyon Dr.
Amarillo, TX 79110
(806)353-2142
Officer: Dennis Tatsch, Manager. Ultimate
Parent: Borden, Inc. SIC: 2024—Ice Cream
& Frozen Desserts; 2026—Fluid Milk;
2086—Bottled & Canned Soft Drinks.

★ 82527 ★   Borden Inc.
Dairy
609 S. Grant
Amarillo, TX 79101
Company Type: Division. Ultimate Parent:
Borden, Inc. SIC: 2024—Ice Cream &
Frozen Desserts.

★ 82528 ★   Borden Inc.
Dairy
4945 Canyon Dr.
Amarillo, TX 79110
Company Type: Division. Ultimate Parent:
Borden, Inc. SIC: 2026—Fluid Milk.

★ 82529 ★   Borden Inc.
Dairy
4945 Canyon Dr.
Amarillo, TX 79110
Company Type: Division. Ultimate Parent:
Borden, Inc. SIC: 2026—Fluid Milk.

★ 82530 ★   Borden Inc.
Dairy
609 S. Grant
Amarillo, TX 79101
Company Type: Division. Ultimate Parent:
Borden, Inc. SIC: 2024—Ice Cream &
Frozen Desserts.

★ 82531 ★   Browning Ferris
Industries
4831 E. 25th Ave.
Amarillo, TX 79103-6413
(806)376-5755
Officer: Rich Wyn. Ultimate Parent:
Browning-Ferris Industries. SIC: 4953—
Refuse Systems.

★ 82532 ★   Burlington Northern
Railroa
1000 NE 3rd Ave.
Amarillo, TX 79107
(806)372-7787
Ultimate Parent: Burlington Northern. SIC:
4011—Railroads—Line-Haul Operating.

★ 82533 ★   Burlington Northern
Railroad
200 N. Arthur St.
Amarillo, TX 79107-5438
(806)374-0528
Location Type: Branch office. Ultimate
Parent: Burlington Northern. SIC: 4741—
Rental of Railroad Cars; 4011—Railroads—
Line-Haul Operating.

★ 82534 ★   Butler Paper Co.
1616 S. Kentucky St., Ste. B100
Amarillo, TX 79102-2238
(806)358-9012
Officer: Fred McMan. Ultimate Parent:
Alco Standard Corp. SIC: 5113—Industrial
& Personal Service Paper; 5111—Printing &
Writing Paper; 7377—Computer Rental &
Leasing.

★ 82535 ★   Butler Paper Co.
1616 S. Kentucky St., Ste. B100
Amarillo, TX 79102-2238
(806)358-9012
Officer: Fred McMan. Ultimate Parent:
Alco Standard Corp. SIC: 5113—Industrial
& Personal Service Paper; 5111—Printing &
Writing Paper; 7377—Computer Rental &
Leasing.

★ 82536 ★   Carpenter Paper Co.
8201 W. Amarillo Blvd.
Amarillo, TX 79106-1515
(806)358-7473
Officer: Robert Baumgardner. Ultimate
Parent: Alco Standard Corp. SIC: 5111—
Printing & Writing Paper; 2621—Paper Mills;
5113—Industrial & Personal Service Paper.

★ 82537 ★   Carpenter Paper Co.
8201 W. Amarillo Blvd.
Amarillo, TX 79106-1515
(806)358-7473
Officer: Robert Baumgardner. Ultimate
Parent: Alco Standard Corp. SIC: 5111—
Printing & Writing Paper; 2621—Paper Mills;
5113—Industrial & Personal Service Paper.

★ 82538 ★   Casual Corner
7701 Westgate Mall N
Amarillo, TX 79160
(806)358-3226
Ultimate Parent: United States Shoe. SIC:
5651—Family Clothing Stores.

★ 82539 ★   City National Bank
724 S. Polk St.
Amarillo, TX 79101
(806)374-2450
Ultimate Parent: City National Corp. SIC:
6021—National Commercial Banks; 6022—
State Commercial Banks.

★ 82540 ★   Coca-Cola Botlg Co.
701 S. Lincoln St.
Amarillo, TX 79101
(806)376-5421
Ultimate Parent: Coca-Cola Enterprises.

★ 82541 ★   Coca Cola Bottling
Co.
800 S. Johnson St.
Amarillo, TX 79101
(806)373-4222
Ultimate Parent: Coca-Cola Enterprises.
SIC: 2086—Bottled & Canned Soft Drinks.

★ 82542 ★   Crouse-Hinds
1901 Farmers Ave.
Amarillo, TX 79118
Ultimate Parent: Cooper Industries. SIC:
3699—Electrical Equipment & Supplies Nec.

★ 82543 ★   Crouse-Hinds Cooper
Industries Inc.
1901 Farmers Ave.
Amarillo, TX 79118-9701
Ultimate Parent: Cooper Industries. SIC:
3699—Electrical Equipment & Supplies Nec.

★ 82544 ★   Electronic Data
Systems
5601 W. I Hwy. 40th
Amarillo, TX 79106
(806)358-0347
Ultimate Parent: Electronic Data Systems.
SIC: 7374—Data Processing & Preparation.

★ 82545 ★   Farmland Industries
Lube Oil Blend Plant
6300 South Washington
Amarillo, TX 79105
Ultimate Parent: Farmland Industries. SIC:
2992—Lubricating Oils & Greases.

★ 82546 ★   Federal Express Corp.
5131 Canyon Dr.
Amarillo, TX 79110
(806)352-7801
Ultimate Parent: Federal Express. SIC:
4513—Air Courier Services.

★ 82547 ★   Flavorland Beef
110 Beefco Rd.
Amarillo, TX 79104
Ultimate Parent: Conagra. SIC: 2011—
Meat Packing Plants.

★ 82548 ★   Foot Action
7701 Westgate Mall N
Amarillo, TX 79160
(806)359-6068
Ultimate Parent: Melville. SIC: 5661—Shoe
Stores.

★ 82549 ★   Greyhound Bus Lines
816 S. Taylor St.
Amarillo, TX 79101
(806)376-9701
Ultimate Parent: Greyhound Lines Inc. SIC:
4131—Intercity & Rural Bus Transportation.

★ 82550 ★   Greyhound Bus Lins
700 S. Tyler St.
Amarillo, TX 79101
(806)374-5371
Ultimate Parent: Greyhound Lines Inc.

★ 82551 ★   Hit or Miss
7701 Westgate Mall N
Amarillo, TX 79160
(806)353-5816
Ultimate Parent: TJX. SIC: 5651—Family
Clothing Stores.

★ 82552 ★   Hit or Miss
7701 W. I Hwy. 40th
Amarillo, TX 79160
(806)358-9118
Ultimate Parent: TJX. SIC: 5621—
Women's Clothing Stores.

★ 82553 ★   Hudson's
2819 Civic Cir.
Amarillo, TX 79109
(806)355-6505
Ultimate Parent: Dayton Hudson. SIC:
8661—Religious Organizations.

★ 82554 ★   IBP Inc.
Farm Rd. 1912 & Hwy. 66 E
Amarillo, TX 79187
Ultimate Parent: IBP, Inc. SIC: 2011—Meat
Packing Plants; 2077—Animal & Marine
Fats & Oils.

★ 82555 ★   Kay Bee Toy Store
7701 Westgate Mall N
Amarillo, TX 79160
(806)352-5430
Ultimate Parent: Melville. SIC: 5945—
Hobby, Toy & Game Shops.

★ 82556 ★   Kay Bee Toy&Hobby
Shop Etal
Westgate
Amarillo, TX 79101
(806)352-5430
Ultimate Parent: Melville. SIC: 5945—
Hobby, Toy & Game Shops.

★ 82557 ★   Kentucky Fried
Chicken
2821 S. Western St.
Amarillo, TX 79109
(806)352-1612
Ultimate Parent: Pepsico. SIC: 5812—
Eating Places.

★ 82558 ★   Kentucky Fried
Chicken
1511 S. Nelson St.
Amarillo, TX 79104
(806)373-0501
Ultimate Parent: Pepsico. SIC: 5812—
Eating Places.

★ 82559 ★   Lane Bryant
Westgate
Amarillo, TX 79101
(806)352-4311
Ultimate Parent: Limited. SIC: 5621—
Women's Clothing Stores.

★ 82560 ★   Lane Bryant
7701 Westgate Mall N
Amarillo, TX 79160
(806)352-4311
Ultimate Parent: Limited. SIC: 5651—
Family Clothing Stores.

★ 82561 ★   Lerner Shop
7701 Westgate Mall N
Amarillo, TX 79160
(806)352-1511
Ultimate Parent: Limited. SIC: 5651—
Family Clothing Stores.

★ 82562 ★   Lerner Shop
9 Sunset Ctr.
Amarillo, TX 79102
(806)355-0131
Ultimate Parent: Limited. SIC: 5621—
Women's Clothing Stores.

★ 82563 ★   The Limited
7701 Westgate Mall N
Amarillo, TX 79160
(806)358-2996
Ultimate Parent: Limited. SIC: 5651—
Family Clothing Stores.

★ 82564 ★   The Limited
7701 W. I Hwy. 40th
Amarillo, TX 79160
(806)358-2996
Ultimate Parent: Limited.

★ 82565 ★   Maison Blanche
2740 Westhaven Village
Amarillo, TX 79109
(806)353-3523
Ultimate Parent: Mercantile Stores. SIC:
5812—Eating Places.

★ 82566 ★   Manpower, Inc. of
Amarillo
1102 W. I Hwy. 40th
Amarillo, TX 79102
(806)373-2853
Ultimate Parent: Manpower, Inc. SIC:
7363—Help Supply Services.

★ 82567 ★   Mary Kay Cosmtcs
3429 Wayne St.
Amarillo, TX 79109
(806)352-8439
Ultimate Parent: Mary Kay Cosmetics.

★ 82568 ★   Mervyn's
7701 Westgate Mall N
Amarillo, TX 79160
(806)358-2443
Ultimate Parent: Dayton Hudson. SIC:
5311—Department Stores.

★ 82569 ★   Mini Mart
14000 Canyon Dr.
Amarillo, TX 79119
(806)622-2820
Ultimate Parent: Kroger. SIC: 5541—
Gasoline Service Stations.

★ 82570 ★   Otis Elevator Co.
1416 W. 8th Ave.
Amarillo, TX 79101
(806)372-5886
Ultimate Parent: United Technologies. SIC:
3534—Elevators & Moving Stairways.

★ 82571 ★   Owens-Corning
Fiberglas Corp.
1701 Hollywood Rd.
Amarillo, TX 79110
(806)622-1582
Officer: Norm Avinger, Manager. Ultimate
Parent: Owens-Corning. SIC: 3089—
Plastics Products Nec; 3229—Pressed &
Blown Glass Nec.

★ 82572 ★   Owens-Corning
Fiberglass
1701 Hollywood Rd. PO Box 8000
Amarillo, TX 79110-8000
Ultimate Parent: Owens-Corning. SIC:
3229—Pressed & Blown Glass Nec.

★ 82573 ★   Payless Shoesource
7701 Westgate Mall N
Amarillo, TX 79160
(806)358-1558
Ultimate Parent: May Department Stores.
SIC: 5661—Shoe Stores.

★ 82574 ★   Payless Shoesource
1820 S. Western St.
Amarillo, TX 79106
(806)359-9121
Ultimate Parent: May Department Stores.
SIC: 5661—Shoe Stores.

★ 82575 ★   Pizza Hut
1500 E. Amarillo Blvd.
Amarillo, TX 79107
(806)373-9364
Ultimate Parent: Pepsico.

★ 82576 ★   Pizza Hut
5807 W. 45th Ave.
Amarillo, TX 79109
(806)359-5600
Ultimate Parent: Pepsico. SIC: 5812—
Eating Places.

★ 82577 ★   Radio Shack
7701 Westgate Mall N
Amarillo, TX 79160
(806)358-8614
Company Type: Division. Ultimate Parent:
Tandy Corp. SIC: 5731—Radio, Television
& Electronics Stores.

★ 82578 ★   Ryder Truck Rental
4308 S. Washington St.
Amarillo, TX 79110
(806)359-6006
Ultimate Parent: Ryder System. SIC:
7359—Equipment Rental & Leasing Nec.

★ 82579 ★   Southwest Airlines
Co.
Amarillo Ter
Amarillo, TX 79111
(806)335-1175
Ultimate Parent: Southwest Airlines. SIC:
4512—Air Transportation—Scheduled.

★ 82580 ★   Southwest Coca-Cola
Bottling Co.
701 S. Lincoln
Amarillo, TX 79105
Ultimate Parent: Coca-Cola Bottling
Consol. SIC: 2086—Bottled & Canned Soft
Drinks.

★ 82581 ★ **Southwestern Bell Yellow Pages**
3505 Olsen Blvd.
Amarillo, TX 79109
(806)358-9213
Ultimate Parent: Southwestern Bell. **SIC:** 2741—Miscellaneous Publishing.

★ 82582 ★ **Sparkletts Drinking Water**
112 S. Fannin St.
Amarillo, TX 79106
(806)373-5172
Ultimate Parent: McKesson. **SIC:** 5149—Groceries & Related Products Nec.

★ 82583 ★ **Texaco Inc.**
201 S. Grand St.
Amarillo, TX 79104
(806)372-3279
Ultimate Parent: Texaco. **SIC:** 2911—Petroleum Refining.

★ 82584 ★ **Texaco Vlg Svc Ctr**
3401 S. Georgia St.
Amarillo, TX 79109
(806)355-4222
Ultimate Parent: Texaco.

★ 82585 ★ **Texaco-Wstrn Sq Fd**
4500 S. Western St.
Amarillo, TX 79109
(806)353-6381
Ultimate Parent: Texaco.

★ 82586 ★ **Trailways**
700 S. Tyler St.
Amarillo, TX 79101
(806)372-8087
Ultimate Parent: Greyhound Lines Inc.

★ 82587 ★ **Tuco, Inc.**
500 S. Taylor
Amarillo, TX 78101
(713)371-7341
Company Type: Subsidiary. **Officer:** John G. L. Cabot, President. **Ultimate Parent:** Cabot. **SIC:** 5052—Coal, Other Minerals & Ores.

★ 82588 ★ **Van Waters & Rogers Inc.**
6819 Cloud Crest Dr.
Amarillo, TX 79124
(806)358-2696
Ultimate Parent: Univar Corp. **SIC:** 3861—Photographic Equipment & Supplies.

★ 82589 ★ **Waldenbooks**
Westgate
Amarillo, TX 79101
(806)358-2500
Ultimate Parent: K-Mart. **SIC:** 5942—Book Stores.

★ 82590 ★ **Weyerhaeuser Paper Co.**
4715 NE 24th Ave.
Amarillo, TX 79107
(806)381-0121
Officer: Jimmy Brown, Manager. **Ultimate Parent:** Weyerhaeuser Co. **SIC:** 2653—Corrugated & Solid Fiber Boxes.

Anahuac

★ 82591 ★ **BFI-Gulf West Landfill**
Jenkins Rd. Chambers County
Anahuac, TX 77514
(409)267-6666
Ultimate Parent: Browning-Ferris Industries. **SIC:** 4953—Refuse Systems.

★ 82592 ★ **Exxon Co. USA**
3 Kingwood Pl
Anahuac, TX 77514
(409)267-3784
Ultimate Parent: Exxon. **SIC:** 1521—Single-Family Housing Construction.

Andrews

★ 82593 ★ **Arco Oil & Gas Co.**
401 NW Mustang Dr.
Andrews, TX 79714
(915)524-1900
Company Type: Division. **Ultimate Parent:** Atlantic Richfield Co., Inc. **SIC:** 1311—Crude Petroleum & Natural Gas.

★ 82594 ★ **Coast to Coast**
104 N. Main St.
Andrews, TX 79714
Ultimate Parent: Servistar Corp. **SIC:** 5531—Automobile & Home Supply Stores.

★ 82595 ★ **Exxon Chemical Co.**
1500 N. Main St.
Andrews, TX 79714
(915)523-3295
Ultimate Parent: Exxon. **SIC:** 5199—Nondurable Goods Nec.

★ 82596 ★ **Exxon Co. USA**
Fullerton Office
Andrews, TX 79714
(915)596-4211
Ultimate Parent: Exxon. **SIC:** 1389—Oil & Gas Field Services Nec.

★ 82597 ★ **Exxon Co. USA**
Means Field
Andrews, TX 79714
(915)523-6691
Ultimate Parent: Exxon. **SIC:** 1389—Oil & Gas Field Services Nec.

★ 82598 ★ **Kentucky Fried Chicken**
Seminole Hwy.
Andrews, TX 79714
(915)523-5900
Ultimate Parent: Pepsico. **SIC:** 5812—Eating Places.

★ 82599 ★ **Mobil Pipe Line**
Odessa Hwy.
Andrews, TX 79714
(915)523-2082
Company Type: Branch. **Officer:** D. E. Day. **Ultimate Parent:** Mobil. **SIC:** 1311—Crude Petroleum & Natural Gas.

★ 82600 ★ **Mobil Producing TX & New Mex**
Big Spring Hwy.
Andrews, TX 79714
(915)524-1800
Ultimate Parent: Mobil. **SIC:** 1311—Crude Petroleum & Natural Gas.

★ 82601 ★ **Oryx Energy Co.**
300 SE Mustang Dr.
Andrews, TX 79714
(915)524-9011
Ultimate Parent: Oryx Energy.

★ 82602 ★ **Pizza Hut**
1100 N. Main St.
Andrews, TX 79714
(915)523-9835
Ultimate Parent: Pepsico. **SIC:** 5812—Eating Places.

★ 82603 ★ **Ryder Truck Rental**
111 E. Northeast Ave.
Andrews, TX 79714
(915)524-4909
Ultimate Parent: Ryder System. **SIC:** 7513—Truck Rental & Leasing Without Drivers.

★ 82604 ★ **Texaco Fd Mart 1**
101 N. Main St.
Andrews, TX 79714
(915)524-7902
Ultimate Parent: Texaco.

★ 82605 ★ **Texaco Inc.**
209 W. 12th N
Andrews, TX 79714
(915)523-3393
Ultimate Parent: Texaco.

★ 82606 ★ **Trico Industries Inc.**
910 S. Main St.
Andrews, TX 79714
(915)523-5050
Ultimate Parent: Paccar. **SIC:** 5084—Industrial Machinery & Equipment.

★ 82607 ★ **Union Oil Co. of California**
707 SW E. Ave.
Andrews, TX 79714
(915)523-7304
Ultimate Parent: Unocal Corp. **SIC:** 1311—Crude Petroleum & Natural Gas.

Angleton

★ 82608 ★ **Ace Hardware&Hm Imprvmt Center**
1224 E. Mulberry St.
Angleton, TX 77515
(409)849-6433
Ultimate Parent: Ace Hardware. **SIC:** 5251—Hardware Stores.

★ 82609 ★ **Coca Cola Bottling Co.**
1401 E. Cedar St.
Angleton, TX 77515
(409)849-8082
Ultimate Parent: Coca-Cola Enterprises. **SIC:** 5149—Groceries & Related Products Nec.

★ 82610 ★ **Mallinckrodt Medical Inc. Interventional Products Plant**
1111 S. Velasco
Angleton, TX 77515
Ultimate Parent: Imcera Group. **SIC:** 3841—Surgical & Medical Instruments.

★ 82611 ★ **Payless Shoesource**
1826 N. Velasco St.
Angleton, TX 77515
(409)849-3108
Ultimate Parent: May Department Stores. **SIC:** 5661—Shoe Stores.

★ 82612 ★ **Pizza Hut**
911 E. Mulberry St.
Angleton, TX 77515
(409)849-4372
Ultimate Parent: Pepsico. **SIC:** 5812—Eating Places.

★ 82613 ★ **Taco Bell**
1205 E. Mulberry St.
Angleton, TX 77515
(409)849-9692
Ultimate Parent: Pepsico. **SIC:** 5812—Eating Places.

★ 82614 ★ **Texaco**
1010 E. Mulberry St.
Angleton, TX 77515
(409)849-3861
Ultimate Parent: Texaco. **SIC:** 5541—Gasoline Service Stations.

★ 82615 ★ **Wal Mart Discount City**
1524 E. Mulberry St.
Angleton, TX 77515
(409)849-2341
Ultimate Parent: Wal-Mart Stores, Inc. **SIC:** 5311—Department Stores.

Anson

★ 82616 ★ **Mobil Oil Co.**
S Hwy. 277
Anson, TX 79501
(915)823-3331
Ultimate Parent: Mobil. **SIC:** 5172—Petroleum Products Nec.

Anthony

★ 82617 ★ **Mountain Pass Canning**
1200 S. Main St.
Anthony, TX 79912
Ultimate Parent: Pet. **SIC:** 2032—Canned Specialties.

★ 82618 ★ **Mountain Pass Canning Co.**
1200 Main St.
PO Box 220
Anthony, TX
(915)886-3951 **Fax:** (915)886-2705
Location Type: Plant. **Officer:** James Ferguson, Plant Manager. **Ultimate Parent:** Pet. **SIC:** 2033—Canned Fruits & Vegetables; 2035—Pickles, Sauces & Salad Dressings.

★ 82619 ★ **Old El Paso Foods**
Mountain Pass Canning
1200 S. Main St.
Anthony, TX 79821
Company Type: Division. **Ultimate Parent:** Pet. **SIC:** 2032—Canned Specialties.

★ 82620 ★ **Pet Inc. Mountain Pass Canning**
1200 S. Main St.
Anthony, TX 79821
Ultimate Parent: Pet. **SIC:** 2032—Canned Specialties.

Anton

★ 82621 ★ **Citizens State Bank**
214 N. Main
Anton, TX 79313
(806)997-4351
Ultimate Parent: Liberty National Bancorp. **SIC:** 6022—State Commercial Banks.

Aransas Pass

★ 82622 ★ **Ace Hardware**
524 S. Commercial St.
Aransas Pass, TX 78336
(512)758-7527
Ultimate Parent: Ace Hardware.

★ 82623 ★ **Ashland Chemical Co.**
Carbon Black Div.
Hwy. 35 N.
Aransas Pass, TX 78336-1860
Company Type: Division. **Ultimate Parent:** Ashland Oil. **SIC:** 2895—Carbon Black.

★ 82624 ★ **Pizza Hut**
1119 W. Wheeler Ave.
Aransas Pass, TX 78336
(512)758-2813
Ultimate Parent: Pepsico. **SIC:** 5812—Eating Places.

★ 82625 ★ **Texaco Inc.**
Allen Blvd.
Aransas Pass, TX 78336
(512)758-0260
Ultimate Parent: Texaco. **SIC:** 5171—Petroleum Bulk Stations & Terminals.

★ 82626 ★ **Texaco Inc. Warhse**
839 W. Wheeler Ave.
Aransas Pass, TX 78336
(512)758-2874
Ultimate Parent: Texaco.

Archer City

★ 82627 ★ **Lone Star Gas Co.**
206 E. Walnut
Archer City, TX 76351
(817)574-4214
Ultimate Parent: Enserch. **SIC:** 4932—Gas & Other Services Combined.

Arlington

★ 82628 ★ **Ace Hardware**
2633 S. Cooper St.
Arlington, TX 76015
(817)277-1411
Ultimate Parent: Ace Hardware.

★ 82629 ★ **Ace Hardware**
922 E. Park Row
Arlington, TX 76010
(817)548-9292
Ultimate Parent: Ace Hardware.

★ 82630 ★ **Ace Hardware Corp.**
2257 Commerce Dr.
Arlington, TX 76011
(817)649-5118
Ultimate Parent: Ace Hardware. **SIC:** 5072—Hardware; 5251—Hardware Stores.

★ 82631 ★ **Albertson's Food & Drug**
2121 N. Collins St.
Arlington, TX 76011
(817)548-1414
Ultimate Parent: Albertson's Inc. **SIC:** 5411—Grocery Stores.

★ 82632 ★ **Allied Signal Aerospace**
2225 E. Randolph Mill Rd.
Arlington, TX 76011
(817)640-5403
Ultimate Parent: Allied-Signal Inc. **SIC:** 3761—Guided Missiles & Space Vehicles.

★ 82633 ★　Associated Milk Producers Inc.
1600 Lamar Blvd. E
Arlington, TX 76011
(817)461-2674
Ultimate Parent: Associated Milk Producers Inc. SIC: 5451—Dairy Products Stores.

★ 82634 ★　Associated Milk Producers Inc.
400 N. East St.
Arlington, TX 76011
(817)261-5141
Ultimate Parent: Associated Milk Producers Inc. SIC: 0751—Livestock Services; 5143—Dairy Products Except Dried or Canned.

★ 82635 ★　Avery International Specialty Tape
4025 Woodland Park Blvd.
Arlington, TX 76013-4314
(817)265-2266
Ultimate Parent: Avery Dennison Corp. SIC: 5113—Industrial & Personal Service Paper.

★ 82636 ★　Bermans the Leather Experts
6 Flags Mall
Arlington, TX 76010
(817)640-9909
Ultimate Parent: Melville. SIC: 5699—Miscellaneous Apparel & Accessory Stores.

★ 82637 ★　Beverly Enterprises
600 Six Flags Dr., Ste. 226
Arlington, TX 76011-6328
(817)640-2393
Ultimate Parent: Beverly Enterprises. SIC: 8059—Nursing & Personal Care Nec; 8051—Skilled Nursing Care Facilities.

★ 82638 ★　Bristol Myers
2261 Brookhollow Plz. Dr.
Arlington, TX 76006-7417
(817)640-9662
Ultimate Parent: Bristol-Myers Squibb. SIC: 2834—Pharmaceutical Preparations.

★ 82639 ★　Casual Corner
419 Six Flags Dr.
Arlington, TX 76011
(817)640-1856
Ultimate Parent: United States Shoe. SIC: 5621—Women's Clothing Stores; 5651—Family Clothing Stores.

★ 82640 ★　Champion International Corp.
3715 Avenue E
Arlington, TX 76011
(817)640-1139
Ultimate Parent: Champion International. SIC: 5112—Stationery & Office Supplies.

★ 82641 ★　Circuit City
4625 S. Cooper St.
Arlington, TX 76017
(817)472-5071
Ultimate Parent: Circuit City Stores. SIC: 5719—Miscellaneous Home Furnishings Stores.

★ 82642 ★　Comerica Bank-Texas
4200 S. Cooper St.
Arlington, TX 76015
(817)784-3400
Company Type: Subsidiary. Location Type: Branch office. Ultimate Parent: Comerica Bank. SIC: 6021—National Commercial Banks.

★ 82643 ★　Comerica Bank-Texas
707 E. Lamar Blvd.
Arlington, TX 76011
(817)588-3500
Company Type: Subsidiary. Location Type: Branch office. Ultimate Parent: Comerica Bank. SIC: 6021—National Commercial Banks.

★ 82644 ★　Crown Cork & Seal Co. Inc.
315 Great SW Pkwy.
Arlington, TX 76011
Ultimate Parent: Crown Cork & Seal. SIC: 2499—Wood Products Nec.

★ 82645 ★　Dexter Corp.
Mogul Div.
609 112th St.
Arlington, TX 76011
Company Type: Division. Ultimate Parent: Dexter Corp. SIC: 2899—Chemical Preparations Nec.

★ 82646 ★　Dexter Water Management Systems
609 112th St.
Arlington, TX 76011
Ultimate Parent: Dexter Corp. SIC: 2899—Chemical Preparations Nec.

★ 82647 ★　Express Ltd.
411 Six Flags Dr.
Arlington, TX 76011
(817)633-2768
Ultimate Parent: Limited. SIC: 5621—Women's Clothing Stores.

★ 82648 ★　Exxon Car Care Center
2524 E. Park Row
Arlington, TX 76010
(817)277-7235
Ultimate Parent: Exxon. SIC: 7538—General Automotive Repair Shops.

★ 82649 ★　Exxon Car Care Center
1606 W. Randol Mill Rd.
Arlington, TX 76012
(817)265-2496
Ultimate Parent: Exxon. SIC: 5411—Grocery Stores.

★ 82650 ★　Exxon Shop
1900 E. Pioneer Pky.
Arlington, TX 76010
(817)275-0151
Ultimate Parent: Exxon. SIC: 5541—Gasoline Service Stations.

★ 82651 ★　Exxon Shop
6004 S. Cooper St.
Arlington, TX 76017
(817)784-1881
Ultimate Parent: Exxon. SIC: 5599—Automotive Dealers Nec.

★ 82652 ★　Ferro Corp.
601 N. Great Southwest Pky.
Arlington, TX 76011
Ultimate Parent: Ferro Corp. SIC: 2816—Inorganic Pigments.

★ 82653 ★　Ferro Corp.
601 North Great Southwest Pkwy.
Arlington, TX 76011
Ultimate Parent: Ferro Corp. SIC: 2816—Inorganic Pigments.

★ 82654 ★　Ferro Corp.
601 N. Great Pky. SW
Arlington, TX 76010
(817)640-5628
Ultimate Parent: Ferro Corp. SIC: 3479—Metal Coating & Allied Services.

★ 82655 ★　Ferro Corp.
4908 Thorncliffe Dr.
Arlington, TX 76016
(817)261-3615
Ultimate Parent: Ferro Corp. SIC: 2851—Paints & Allied Products.

★ 82656 ★　Fireside Books
1201 W. Arbrook Blvd.
Arlington, TX 76015
(817)467-4848
Ultimate Parent: Paramount Comunications.

★ 82657 ★　Foot Action
3811 S. Cooper St.
Arlington, TX 76015
(817)467-6474
Ultimate Parent: Melville.

★ 82658 ★　The Gap
418 Six Flags Dr.
Arlington, TX 76011
(817)649-8860
Ultimate Parent: GAP. SIC: 5611—Men's & Boys' Clothing Stores.

★ 82659 ★　Globe Life Insurance Co.
1201 N. Watson Rd.
Arlington, TX 76006
(817)640-9214
Ultimate Parent: Life Insurance Co. of Virginia.

★ 82660 ★　Greyhound Bus Station
2849 Galleria Dr.
Arlington, TX 76011
(817)640-5530
Ultimate Parent: Greyhound Lines Inc. SIC:

4142—Bus Charter Service Except Local; 4173—Bus Terminal & Service Facilities.

★ 82661 ★　Henry Co. Inc/W W
1101 Avenue G
Arlington, TX 76011
(817)640-8958
Ultimate Parent: Armstrong World Industries. SIC: 5085—Industrial Supplies.

★ 82662 ★　Hit or Miss
1124 S. Bowen Rd.
Arlington, TX 76013
(817)860-4005
Ultimate Parent: TJX. SIC: 5651—Family Clothing Stores.

★ 82663 ★　Hit or Miss
3701 S. Cooper St.
Arlington, TX 76015
(817)465-0359
Ultimate Parent: TJX. SIC: 5651—Family Clothing Stores.

★ 82664 ★　ITW Electronic Component Packaging
3400 Ave. E.
Arlington, TX 76071
(817)649-5777 Fax: (817)633-2549
Company Type: Subsidiary. Officer: Glen Huff, President. Ultimate Parent: Illinois Tool Works.

★ 82665 ★　ITW Meritex
3301 E. Randolph Mill Rd.
Arlington, TX 76011
(817)649-5777 Fax: (817)640-1021
Company Type: Subsidiary. Officer: Glenn Gray, General Manager. Ultimate Parent: Illinois Tool Works.

★ 82666 ★　Jiffy Lube
3624 S. Cooper St.
Arlington, TX 76015
(817)468-1535
Ultimate Parent: Pennzoil. SIC: 7539—Automotive Repair Shops Nec.

★ 82667 ★　Jiffy Lube
2309 W. Pioneer Pky.
Arlington, TX 76013
(817)861-4775
Ultimate Parent: Pennzoil. SIC: 7539—Automotive Repair Shops Nec.

★ 82668 ★　Jiffy Lube
619 N. Collins St.
Arlington, TX 76011
(817)861-4734
Ultimate Parent: Pennzoil. SIC: 7539—Automotive Repair Shops Nec.

★ 82669 ★　Johnson & Johnson Medical Inc.
2500 Arbrook Blvd.
Arlington, TX 76014
Ultimate Parent: Johnson & Johnson. SIC: 3069—Fabricated Rubber Products Nec.

★ 82670 ★　Kay-Bee Toy & Hobby
3811 S. Cooper St.
Arlington, TX 76015
(817)784-8222
Ultimate Parent: Melville. SIC: 5945—Hobby, Toy & Game Shops.

★ 82671 ★　Kentucky Fried Chicken
3755 S. Cooper St.
Arlington, TX 76015
(817)468-4366
Ultimate Parent: Pepsico. SIC: 5812—Eating Places.

★ 82672 ★　Kentucky Fried Chicken
607 W. Park Row
Arlington, TX 76010
(817)860-3058
Ultimate Parent: Pepsico. SIC: 5812—Eating Places.

★ 82673 ★　Kentucky Fried Chicken
808 N. Collins St.
Arlington, TX 76011
(817)461-7043
Ultimate Parent: Pepsico. SIC: 5812—Eating Places.

★ 82674 ★　Kmart
2540 E. Pioneer Pky.
Arlington, TX 76010
Ultimate Parent: K-Mart.

★ 82675 ★　Kroger Food & Drug
2475 Ascension Blvd.
Arlington, TX 76006
(817)468-3307
Ultimate Parent: Kroger. SIC: 5411—Grocery Stores.

★ 82676 ★　Kroger Food & Drug Store
5701 W. Pleasant Ridge Rd.
Arlington, TX 76016
(817)483-0666
Ultimate Parent: Kroger. SIC: 5411—Grocery Stores.

★ 82677 ★　Kroger Food Store
715 Lamar Blvd. W
Arlington, TX 76012
(817)261-8224
Ultimate Parent: Kroger. SIC: 5411—Grocery Stores.

★ 82678 ★　Kroger Food Store
2215 S. Cooper St.
Arlington, TX 76013
(817)277-1174
Ultimate Parent: Kroger. SIC: 5411—Grocery Stores.

★ 82679 ★　Kroger Food&Drug Stores
2215 S. Cooper St.
Arlington, TX 76013
(817)460-5661
Ultimate Parent: Kroger. SIC: 5912—Drug Stores & Proprietary Stores.

★ 82680 ★　Kroger Phrmcy
2580 E. Arkansas Ln.
Arlington, TX 76014
(817)861-2779
Ultimate Parent: Kroger.

★ 82681 ★　Kroger Phrmcy
5701 W. Pleasant Ridge Rd.
Arlington, TX 76016
(817)483-0354
Ultimate Parent: Kroger.

★ 82682 ★　Kroger Phrmcy
2475 Ascension Blvd.
Arlington, TX 76006
(817)275-2901
Ultimate Parent: Kroger.

★ 82683 ★　Lane Bryant
3811 S. Cooper St.
Arlington, TX 76015
(817)784-1326
Ultimate Parent: Limited. SIC: 5651—Family Clothing Stores.

★ 82684 ★　Lane Bryant
425 Six Flags Dr.
Arlington, TX 76011
(817)649-0837
Ultimate Parent: Limited. SIC: 5651—Family Clothing Stores.

★ 82685 ★　Lane Bryant
Parks at Arlington
Arlington, TX 76013
(817)784-1326
Ultimate Parent: Limited. SIC: 5621—Women's Clothing Stores.

★ 82686 ★　Lens Crafters Regional Office
3811 S. Cooper St.
Arlington, TX 76015
(817)468-7512
Ultimate Parent: United States Shoe.

★ 82687 ★　Lerner Shop
525 Duncan Perry Rd.
Arlington, TX 76011
(817)640-8884
Ultimate Parent: Limited. SIC: 5621—Women's Clothing Stores.

★ 82688 ★　Lerner Shop
3811 S. Cooper St.
Arlington, TX 76015
(817)465-2225
Ultimate Parent: Limited.

★ 82689 ★　Lerner Shop
424 Six Flags Dr.
Arlington, TX 76011
(817)649-2038
Ultimate Parent: Limited. SIC: 5651—Family Clothing Stores.

★ 82690 ★ The Limited
110 Flags Mall
Arlington, TX 76011
(817)649-1880
Ultimate Parent: Limited. SIC: 5651—
Family Clothing Stores.

★ 82691 ★ The Limited
3811 S. Cooper St.
Arlington, TX 76015
(817)468-0440
Ultimate Parent: Limited. SIC: 5651—
Family Clothing Stores.

★ 82692 ★ The Limited Express
3811 S. Cooper St.
Arlington, TX 76015
(817)465-2335
Ultimate Parent: Limited. SIC: 5651—
Family Clothing Stores.

★ 82693 ★ Lockheed Support
Systems, Inc.
1600 E. Pioneer Pkwy., Ste. 440
Arlington, TX 76010
(817)261-0295 Fax: (817)861-2855
Company Type: Division. Ultimate Parent:
Lockheed Corp. SIC: 4581—Airports, Flying
Fields & Services.

★ 82694 ★ Lockheed Support
Systems, Inc.
1600 E. Pioneer Pky., Ste. 440
Arlington, TX 76010
(817)261-0295 Fax: (817)548-5649
Officer: Robert E. Tokerud, President.
Ultimate Parent: Lockheed Corp.

★ 82695 ★ Lockheed Support
Systems Inc.
1600 E. Pioneer Pky.
Arlington, TX 76010
(817)261-0295
Ultimate Parent: Lockheed Corp. SIC:
4581—Airports, Flying Fields & Services.

★ 82696 ★ Lone Star Gas Co.
106 Stadium Dr.
Arlington, TX 76010
(817)274-4179
Ultimate Parent: Enserch. SIC: 4925—Gas
Production & Distribution Nec.

★ 82697 ★ Lone Star Gas Co.
800 E. Border St.
Arlington, TX 76010
(817)265-9361
Ultimate Parent: Enserch. SIC: 4939—
Combination Utility Nec; 5992—Florists.

★ 82698 ★ Mary Kay Cosmetics
4513 Ridgecrest Dr.
Arlington, TX 76017
(817)467-2130
Ultimate Parent: Mary Kay Cosmetics.

★ 82699 ★ Mary Kay Cosmetics
5220 Boyd Trl.
Arlington, TX 76017
(817)461-2980
Ultimate Parent: Mary Kay Cosmetics. SIC:
5999—Miscellaneous Retail Stores Nec.

★ 82700 ★ McDonalds
Restaurant
5700 Forest Bend Dr.
Arlington, TX 76017
(817)561-5037
Ultimate Parent: McDonald's.

★ 82701 ★ McDonalds
Restaurant
2422 W. Pioneer Pky.
Arlington, TX 76013
(817)261-3748
Ultimate Parent: McDonald's.

★ 82702 ★ Mcneil
Pharmaceutical
3129 Pinewood Dr.
Arlington, TX 76010
(817)640-0871
Ultimate Parent: Johnson & Johnson. SIC:
1711—Plumbing, Heating & Air-
Conditioning.

★ 82703 ★ Mobil Center Self
Service
3004 Quail Ln.
Arlington, TX 76016
(817)277-7324
Ultimate Parent: Mobil. SIC: 5541—
Gasoline Service Stations.

★ 82704 ★ Mobil Mart
2590 E. Arkansas Ln.
Arlington, TX 76014
(817)265-0282
Ultimate Parent: Mobil. SIC: 5541—
Gasoline Service Stations.

★ 82705 ★ Mobil Oil Corp.
4645 Matlock Rd.
Arlington, TX 76018
(817)467-9866
Ultimate Parent: Mobil. SIC: 5541—
Gasoline Service Stations.

★ 82706 ★ Mobil Oil Service
Station
3800 S. Cooper St.
Arlington, TX 76015
(817)467-2630
Ultimate Parent: Mobil. SIC: 5541—
Gasoline Service Stations.

★ 82707 ★ Mobil Self Service
305 Stonecreek Dr.
Arlington, TX 76014
(817)265-8069
Ultimate Parent: Mobil. SIC: 5541—
Gasoline Service Stations.

★ 82708 ★ Mobil Self Service
4121 S. Collins St.
Arlington, TX 76014
(817)465-7859
Ultimate Parent: Mobil. SIC: 5541—
Gasoline Service Stations.

★ 82709 ★ Mobil Service Station
800 W. Pioneer Pky.
Arlington, TX 76013
(817)261-9280
Ultimate Parent: Mobil. SIC: 5541—
Gasoline Service Stations.

★ 82710 ★ National
Semiconductor Corp.
1111 W. Bardin Rd.
Arlington, TX 76017
Ultimate Parent: National Semiconductor
Corp. SIC: 3674—Semiconductors &
Related Devices.

★ 82711 ★ Nationwide Life
Insurance C
2715 Avenue E
Arlington, TX 76011
(817)461-6664
Ultimate Parent: Nationwide Life. SIC:
6411—Insurance Agents, Brokers &
Service.

★ 82712 ★ Ncr Corp.
3000 Ave. F E.
Arlington, TX 76011
Ultimate Parent: AT&T. SIC: 2761—
Manifold Business Forms.

★ 82713 ★ Packaging Corp. of
America
1001 113th St.
Arlington, TX 76011
Ultimate Parent: Tenneco Inc. SIC: 2653—
Corrugated & Solid Fiber Boxes.

★ 82714 ★ Patrick Media Group
3700 E. Randolph Mill Rd.
Arlington, TX 76011
(817)640-4550
Officer: Mike Tobey, Manager. Ultimate
Parent: General Electric. SIC: 2542—
Partitions & Fixtures Except Wood; 3993—
Signs & Advertising Displays.

★ 82715 ★ Payless Shoesource
2131 S. Collins St.
Arlington, TX 76010
(817)861-2530
Ultimate Parent: May Department Stores.
SIC: 5661—Shoe Stores.

★ 82716 ★ Payless Shoesource
2911 E. Division St.
Arlington, TX 76011
(817)633-8407
Ultimate Parent: May Department Stores.

★ 82717 ★ Pennzoil Products Co.
900 N. Great Southwest Pky. 116
Arlington, TX 76011
Ultimate Parent: Pennzoil.

★ 82718 ★ Pennzoil Products Co.
900 N. Great Southwest Pky. 116
Arlington, TX 76011
Ultimate Parent: Pennzoil.

★ 82719 ★ Pepsi-Cola
Manufacturing
1000 113th St.
Arlington, TX 76011
Ultimate Parent: Pepsico. SIC: 2087—
Flavoring Extracts & Syrups Nec.

★ 82720 ★ Pepsico Inc.
1000 113th St.
Arlington, TX 76011
Ultimate Parent: Pepsico. SIC: 2087—
Flavoring Extracts & Syrups Nec.

★ 82721 ★ Petite Sophisticate
401 Six Flags Dr.
Arlington, TX 76011
(817)640-1682
Ultimate Parent: United States Shoe. SIC:
5651—Family Clothing Stores.

★ 82722 ★ Petite Sophisticate
3811 S. Cooper St.
Arlington, TX 76015
(817)784-8522
Ultimate Parent: United States Shoe. SIC:
5651—Family Clothing Stores.

★ 82723 ★ Pizza Hut
4444 W. Green Oaks Blvd.
Arlington, TX 76016
(817)483-7277
Ultimate Parent: Pepsico. SIC: 5812—
Eating Places.

★ 82724 ★ Pizza Hut
1030 W. Arkansas Ln.
Arlington, TX 76013
(817)860-6500
Ultimate Parent: Pepsico.

★ 82725 ★ Pizza Hut
2307 W. Green Oaks Blvd.
Arlington, TX 76016
(817)496-0100
Ultimate Parent: Pepsico.

★ 82726 ★ Pizza Hut
5975 S. Cooper St.
Arlington, TX 76017
(817)465-3100
Ultimate Parent: Pepsico.

★ 82727 ★ Pizza Hut
3400 S. Watson Rd.
Arlington, TX 76014
(817)465-0606
Ultimate Parent: Pepsico.

★ 82728 ★ Pizza Hut
1200 N. Fielder Rd.
Arlington, TX 76012
(817)460-2421
Ultimate Parent: Pepsico. SIC: 5812—
Eating Places.

★ 82729 ★ Pizza Hut
3779 S. Cooper St.
Arlington, TX 76015
(817)468-5777
Ultimate Parent: Pepsico. SIC: 5812—
Eating Places.

★ 82730 ★ Pizza Hut
1904 E. Pioneer Pky.
Arlington, TX 76010
(817)460-7002
Ultimate Parent: Pepsico. SIC: 5812—
Eating Places.

★ 82731 ★ Pizza Hut
1106 N. Collins St.
Arlington, TX 76011
(817)460-2122
Ultimate Parent: Pepsico. SIC: 5812—
Eating Places.

★ 82732 ★ Racquet Club
Wimbledon
5000 Racquet Club Dr.
Arlington, TX 76017
(817)465-5584
Ultimate Parent: Hartmarx. SIC: 7997—
Membership Sports & Recreation Clubs.

★ 82733 ★ Radio Shack
3811 S. Cooper St.
Arlington, TX 76015
(817)468-4463
Company Type: Division. Ultimate Parent:
Tandy Corp. SIC: 5065—Electronic Parts &
Equipment Nec.

★ 82734 ★ Radio Shack
311 SW Plaza
Arlington, TX 76016
(817)483-5785
Company Type: Division. Ultimate Parent:
Tandy Corp. SIC: 5065—Electronic Parts &
Equipment Nec.

★ 82735 ★ Radio Shack
1130 N. Fielder Rd.
Arlington, TX 76012
(817)274-7431
Company Type: Division. Ultimate Parent:
Tandy Corp. SIC: 5065—Electronic Parts &
Equipment Nec.

★ 82736 ★ Radio Shack
2247 S. Cooper St.
Arlington, TX 76013
(817)274-2160
Company Type: Division. Ultimate Parent:
Tandy Corp. SIC: 5065—Electronic Parts &
Equipment Nec; 5731—Radio, Television &
Electronics Stores.

★ 82737 ★ Radio Shack
430 Lamar Blvd. E
Arlington, TX 76011
(817)860-0069
Company Type: Division. Ultimate Parent:
Tandy Corp. SIC: 5731—Radio, Television
& Electronics Stores.

★ 82738 ★ Radio Shack
1108 N. Collins St.
Arlington, TX 76011
(817)460-7184
Company Type: Division. Ultimate Parent:
Tandy Corp. SIC: 5065—Electronic Parts &
Equipment Nec.

★ 82739 ★ Radio Shack
Forum
Arlington, TX 76010
(817)649-2518
Company Type: Division. Ultimate Parent:
Tandy Corp. SIC: 5065—Electronic Parts &
Equipment Nec.

★ 82740 ★ Radio Shack
397 Six Flags Dr.
Arlington, TX 76011
(817)649-8765
Company Type: Division. Ultimate Parent:
Tandy Corp. SIC: 5065—Electronic Parts &
Equipment Nec.

★ 82741 ★ Radio Shack
2500 E. Randol Mill Rd.
Arlington, TX 76011
(817)640-6079
Company Type: Division. Ultimate Parent:
Tandy Corp. SIC: 7373—Computer
Integrated Systems Design.

★ 82742 ★ Radio Shack
3006 E. Pioneer Pky.
Arlington, TX 76010
(817)649-3371
Company Type: Division. Ultimate Parent:
Tandy Corp. SIC: 5731—Radio, Television
& Electronics Stores.

★ 82743 ★ Ryder Truck Rental
3518 S. Cooper St.
Arlington, TX 76015
(817)472-5128
Ultimate Parent: Ryder System. SIC:
7513—Truck Rental & Leasing Without
Drivers.

★ 82744 ★ Ryder Truck Rental
2020 W. Pioneer Pky.
Arlington, TX 76013
(817)277-9961
Ultimate Parent: Ryder System. SIC:
7513—Truck Rental & Leasing Without
Drivers.

★ 82745 ★ Ryder Truck Rental
1004 W. Division St.
Arlington, TX 76012
(817)274-6078
Ultimate Parent: Ryder System.

★ 82746 ★ Ryder Truck Rental
2005 W. Pioneer Pky.
Arlington, TX 76013
(817)860-1332
Ultimate Parent: Ryder System.

★ 82747 ★ **Ryder Truck Rental**
3216 E. Pioneer Pky.
Arlington, TX 76010
(817)649-3276
Ultimate Parent: Ryder System.

★ 82748 ★ **A Schulman Inc.**
1907 Mill Run Dr.
Arlington, TX 76006
(817)265-8000
Ultimate Parent: A. Schulman, Inc.

★ 82749 ★ **Service Merchandise**
2950 E. Pioneer Pky.
Arlington, TX 76010
(817)649-0434
Ultimate Parent: Service Merchandise Co., Inc. **SIC:** 5961—Catalog & Mail-Order Houses.

★ 82750 ★ **Shell Food Mart**
4311 S. Bowen Rd.
Arlington, TX 76016
(817)467-2037
Ultimate Parent: Shell Oil Co. **SIC:** 5411—Grocery Stores.

★ 82751 ★ **Smith Corona Corp.**
3001 E. Randol Mill Rd.
Arlington, TX 76011
(817)649-5379
Ultimate Parent: Hanson Industries. **SIC:** 5044—Office Equipment.

★ 82752 ★ **Sonoco Products Co.**
2008 Exchange Dr.
Arlington, TX 76011
(817)461-5611
Officer: Lew Johnson, Manager. **Ultimate Parent:** Sonoco Products. **SIC:** 2655—Fiber Cans, Drums & Similar Products.

★ 82753 ★ **Surgikos**
2500 Arbrook Blvd.
Arlington, TX 76014
Ultimate Parent: Johnson & Johnson. **SIC:** 3842—Surgical Appliances & Supplies.

★ 82754 ★ **T J Maxx**
4225 S. Cooper St.
Arlington, TX 76015
(817)472-5080
Ultimate Parent: TJX.

★ 82755 ★ **Taco Bell**
1320 S. Cooper St.
Arlington, TX 76013
(817)277-8042
Ultimate Parent: Pepsico. **SIC:** 5812—Eating Places.

★ 82756 ★ **Taco Bell**
Parks at Arlington
Arlington, TX 76013
(817)468-8940
Ultimate Parent: Pepsico. **SIC:** 5812—Eating Places.

★ 82757 ★ **Taco Bell**
105 S. Bowen Rd.
Arlington, TX 76012
(817)277-1601
Ultimate Parent: Pepsico. **SIC:** 5812—Eating Places.

★ 82758 ★ **Taco Bell**
3311 E. Division St.
Arlington, TX 76011
(817)633-2253
Ultimate Parent: Pepsico. **SIC:** 5812—Eating Places.

★ 82759 ★ **Taco Bell**
5745 Interstate W. 20
Arlington, TX 76017
(817)478-1468
Ultimate Parent: Pepsico. **SIC:** 5812—Eating Places.

★ 82760 ★ **Taco Bell**
900 E. Arkansas Ln.
Arlington, TX 76014
(817)460-1954
Ultimate Parent: Pepsico. **SIC:** 5812—Eating Places.

★ 82761 ★ **Tandy Brands Accessories Inc.**
690 E. Lamar Blvd. 200
Arlington, TX 76011
(817)548-0090
Officer: Clayton E. Niles, Chairman. **Ultimate Parent:** Tandy Corp. **SIC:** 3111—Leather Tanning & Finishing; 3161—

Luggage; 3171—Women's Handbags & Purses.

★ 82762 ★ **Tandy Corp.**
3811 S. Cooper St.
Arlington, TX 76015
(817)468-4411
Ultimate Parent: Tandy Corp.

★ 82763 ★ **Tandy Sign Co.**
1908 Peyco Dr. S
Arlington, TX 76017
(817)467-4451
Officer: Wayne Davidson, Manager. **Ultimate Parent:** Tandy Corp. **SIC:** 3679—Electronic Components Nec; 3829—Measuring & Controlling Devices Nec; 3993—Signs & Advertising Displays.

★ 82764 ★ **Tandy Signs**
1908 Peyco Dr. S
Arlington, TX 76017
(817)467-4451
Ultimate Parent: Tandy Corp. **SIC:** 1721—Painting & Paper Hanging; 3993—Signs & Advertising Displays.

★ 82765 ★ **Texaco Express Lub**
2105 Brown Blvd.
Arlington, TX 76006
(817)640-1715
Ultimate Parent: Texaco.

★ 82766 ★ **Texaco Food Mart**
2095 S. Hwy. 360
Arlington, TX 76010
(817)649-7107
Ultimate Parent: Texaco.

★ 82767 ★ **Texaco Food Mart**
900 N. Watson Rd.
Arlington, TX 76011
(817)640-1934
Ultimate Parent: Texaco.

★ 82768 ★ **Texaco Food Mart**
1500 S. Cooper St.
Arlington, TX 76013
(817)261-2166
Ultimate Parent: Texaco. **SIC:** 5541—Gasoline Service Stations.

★ 82769 ★ **Texaco Food Mart**
901 E. Park Row
Arlington, TX 76010
(817)461-7901
Ultimate Parent: Texaco. **SIC:** 5599—Automotive Dealers Nec.

★ 82770 ★ **Texaco Foodmart**
4500 S. Bowen Rd.
Arlington, TX 76017
(817)468-5613
Ultimate Parent: Texaco. **SIC:** 5541—Gasoline Service Stations.

★ 82771 ★ **Toys R US**
4111 S. Cooper St.
Arlington, TX 76015
(817)784-0843
Ultimate Parent: Toys "R" US.

★ 82772 ★ **Underwriters Adjusting Co.**
601 Ryan Plz.
Arlington, TX 76011
(817)277-7767
Ultimate Parent: Continental. **SIC:** 6411—Insurance Agents, Brokers & Service.

★ 82773 ★ **Union Pacific Resources Co.**
1 United Tower
Arlington, TX 76012
(817)654-9148
Ultimate Parent: Union Pacific Corp.

★ 82774 ★ **Unit Distribution of Texas**
2007 Exchange Dr.
Arlington, TX 76011
(817)261-1051
Ultimate Parent: GATX Corp. **SIC:** 4225—General Warehousing & Storage.

★ 82775 ★ **United Parcel Service**
379 Exchange Dr.
Arlington, TX 76011
(817)277-3422
Ultimate Parent: United Parcel Service of America. **SIC:** 4215—Courier Services Except by Air.

★ 82776 ★ **US Shoe Corp.**
3811 S. Cooper St.
Arlington, TX 76015
(817)468-3577
Ultimate Parent: United States Shoe. **SIC:** 5651—Family Clothing Stores.

★ 82777 ★ **Victoria's Secret**
406 Six Flags Dr.
Arlington, TX 76011
(817)633-1850
Ultimate Parent: Limited. **SIC:** 5651—Family Clothing Stores.

★ 82778 ★ **Victoria's Secret**
3811 S. Cooper St.
Arlington, TX 76015
(817)465-0505
Ultimate Parent: Limited. **SIC:** 5651—Family Clothing Stores.

★ 82779 ★ **W. W. Henry Co.**
1101 Ave. G
Arlington, TX 76011
Ultimate Parent: Armstrong World Industries. **SIC:** 2891—Adhesives & Sealants.

★ 82780 ★ **Waldenbooks**
402 Six Flags Dr.
Arlington, TX 76011
(817)640-3142
Ultimate Parent: K-Mart. **SIC:** 5942—Book Stores.

★ 82781 ★ **Waldenbooks**
Parks at Arlington
Arlington, TX 76013
(817)784-0124
Ultimate Parent: K-Mart. **SIC:** 5942—Book Stores.

★ 82782 ★ **Waldenbooks**
3811 S. Cooper St.
Arlington, TX 76015
(817)784-0124
Ultimate Parent: K-Mart. **SIC:** 5942—Book Stores.

★ 82783 ★ **Waldenbooks**
6 Flags Mall
Arlington, TX 76010
(817)640-3142
Ultimate Parent: K-Mart. **SIC:** 5942—Book Stores.

★ 82784 ★ **Radio Shack**
1337 W. Wheeler Ave.
Arlington Tex, TX 76119
(512)758-5026
Company Type: Division. **Ultimate Parent:** Tandy Corp.

Aspermont

★ 82785 ★ **Piggly Wiggly**
Aspermont, TX 79502
(817)989-2242
Ultimate Parent: Bruno's. **SIC:** 5411—Grocery Stores.

Athens

★ 82786 ★ **Athens Brick Co.**
Athens Brick Rd.
Athens, TX 75751
Ultimate Parent: Texas Industries. **SIC:** 3251—Brick & Structural Clay Tile.

★ 82787 ★ **Four Winns of Texas**
4 Winn Way
Athens, TX 75751
Ultimate Parent: Outboard Marine. **SIC:** 3732—Boat Building & Repairing.

★ 82788 ★ **Four Winns of Texas Inc.**
1450 Flat Creek Rd.
Athens, TX 75751
Ultimate Parent: Outboard Marine. **SIC:** 3732—Boat Building & Repairing.

★ 82789 ★ **Kentucky Fried Chicken**
612 W. Corsicana St.
Athens, TX 75751
(214)675-1900
Ultimate Parent: Pepsico. **SIC:** 5812—Eating Places.

★ 82790 ★ **Lone Star Gas Co.**
309 E. Corsicana St.
Athens, TX 75751
(214)675-5141
Ultimate Parent: Enserch. **SIC:** 4932—Gas & Other Services Combined; 4939—Combination Utility Nec.

★ 82791 ★ **Lone Star Gas Co.**
S Palestine St.
Athens, TX 75751
(214)675-5625
Ultimate Parent: Enserch. **SIC:** 4939—Combination Utility Nec.

★ 82792 ★ **McDonalds Restaurant**
1105 E. Tyler St.
Athens, TX 75751
(903)677-3115
Ultimate Parent: McDonald's.

★ 82793 ★ **Payless Shoesource**
1107 E. Tyler St.
Athens, TX 75751
(903)677-1199
Ultimate Parent: May Department Stores.

★ 82794 ★ **Wal Mart**
1111 E. Tyler St.
Athens, TX 75751
(214)677-1090
Ultimate Parent: Wal-Mart Stores, Inc. **SIC:** 5311—Department Stores.

Atlanta

★ 82795 ★ **Exxon Co. USA Wholesale**
S Williams
Atlanta, TX 75551
(214)796-3321
Ultimate Parent: Exxon. **SIC:** 5172—Petroleum Products Nec.

★ 82796 ★ **Kentucky Fried Chicken**
Hwy. 59 Loop
Atlanta, TX 75551
(214)796-2412
Ultimate Parent: Pepsico. **SIC:** 5812—Eating Places.

★ 82797 ★ **Radio Shack**
124 E. Main St.
Atlanta, TX 75551
(214)796-5111
Company Type: Division. **Ultimate Parent:** Tandy Corp. **SIC:** 5731—Radio, Television & Electronics Stores.

★ 82798 ★ **Wal Mart Discount City**
Us 59 N
Atlanta, TX 75551
(214)796-7916
Ultimate Parent: Wal-Mart Stores, Inc. **SIC:** 5311—Department Stores.

Austin

★ 82799 ★ **Abbott Laboratories**
3900 Howard Ln.
Austin, TX 78728-6515
(512)225-2000
Officer: Darly Faulkner, Manager. **Ultimate Parent:** Abbott Laboratories. **SIC:** 3841—Surgical & Medical Instruments; 5122—Drugs, Proprietaries & Sundries; 2834—Pharmaceutical Preparations.

★ 82800 ★ **Ace Hardware**
12800 N. Lamar Blvd.
Austin, TX 78753
(512)251-4944
Ultimate Parent: Ace Hardware. **SIC:** 5251—Hardware Stores.

★ 82801 ★ **Ace Hardware**
8652 Spicewood Spring Rd.
Austin, TX 78759
(512)258-3929
Ultimate Parent: Ace Hardware. **SIC:** 5251—Hardware Stores.

★ 82802 ★ **Advanced Micro Devices**
6300 Bridge Point Pky.
Austin, TX 78730-5008
(512)346-7830
Ultimate Parent: Advanced Micro Devices Inc. **SIC:** 5065—Electronic Parts & Equipment Nec; 3679—Electronic Components Nec.

★ 82803 ★ **Advanced Micro Devices**
5900 E. Ben White Blvd.
Austin, TX 78741
(512)385-8542
Officer: H. Donald Nelson. **Ultimate Parent:** Advanced Micro Devices Inc. **SIC:** 5065—Electronic Parts & Equipment Nec; 3679—Electronic Components Nec; 3674—Semiconductors & Related Devices; 3571—Electronic Computers; 3672—Printed Circuit Boards.

★ 82804 ★ **Advanced Micro Devices Inc.**
5204 E. Ben White Blvd.
Austin, TX 78741
(512)385-8542
Ultimate Parent: Advanced Micro Devices Inc. **SIC:** 3672—Printed Circuit Boards; 3674—Semiconductors & Related Devices; 3679—Electronic Components Nec.

★ 82805 ★ **Air Products & Chemicals Inc.**
5341 Industrial Oaks Blvd.
Austin, TX 78735
(512)892-7772
Officer: J. A. Gilman, Manager. **Ultimate Parent:** Air Products & Chemicals, Inc. **SIC:** 2813—Industrial Gases; 3829—Measuring & Controlling Devices Nec.

★ 82806 ★ **Albertson's**
2000 S. I H 35
Austin, TX 78704-4434
(512)388-4025
Ultimate Parent: Albertson's Inc. **SIC:** 5411—Grocery Stores.

★ 82807 ★ **Albertson's**
12860 Research Blvd.
Austin, TX 78750-3222
(512)250-1266
Location Type: Branch office. **Officer:** Jerry Holt. **Ultimate Parent:** Albertson's Inc. **SIC:** 5411—Grocery Stores.

★ 82808 ★ **Albertson's**
1819 S. Pleasant Valley Rd.
Austin, TX 78741-3114
(512)389-0200
Location Type: Branch office. **Officer:** Pat Butler. **Ultimate Parent:** Albertson's Inc. **SIC:** 6411—Insurance Agents, Brokers & Service; 5411—Grocery Stores.

★ 82809 ★ **Albertson's**
8716 Research Blvd.
Austin, TX 78758-6498
(512)458-9233
Location Type: Branch office. **Officer:** David Seeker. **Ultimate Parent:** Albertson's Inc. **SIC:** 5411—Grocery Stores.

★ 82810 ★ **Albertson's, No. 4245**
1807 Slaughter Ln. W
Austin, TX 78748
(512)280-5174
Ultimate Parent: Albertson's Inc. **SIC:** 5411—Grocery Stores.

★ 82811 ★ **Albertson's Supermarket**
1820 W. Stassney Ln.
Austin, TX 78745-3621
(512)443-4165
Officer: Keith Jones. **Ultimate Parent:** Albertson's Inc. **SIC:** 5411—Grocery Stores.

★ 82812 ★ **America West**
3600 Manor Rd.
Austin, TX 78723
(512)479-8870
Ultimate Parent: America West Airlines. **SIC:** 4512—Air Transportation—Scheduled.

★ 82813 ★ **America West Airlines**
Baggage Claim
Austin, TX 78722
(512)479-8707
Location Type: Branch office. **Ultimate Parent:** America West Airlines. **SIC:** 4512—Air Transportation—Scheduled.

★ 82814 ★ **American Credit Services**
1714 Fortview Rd.
Austin, TX 78704
(512)440-0848
Ultimate Parent: Rochester Community Savings Bank. **SIC:** 7323—Credit Reporting Services.

★ 82815 ★ **Ametek-Houston Instrument**
8500 Cameron Rd.
Austin, TX 78753
(512)835-0900
Ultimate Parent: Ametek Inc. **SIC:** 5065—Electronic Parts & Equipment Nec.

★ 82816 ★ **Ametek Inc.**
Houston Instrument Div.
8500 Cameron Rd.
Austin, TX 78753-5399
Company Type: Division. **Ultimate Parent:** Ametek Inc. **SIC:** 3500—Industrial Machinery & Equipment.

★ 82817 ★ **Ametek Inc.**
Houston Instruments Div.
8500 Cameron Rd.
Austin, TX 78753-3599
Company Type: Division. **Ultimate Parent:** Ametek Inc. **SIC:** 3500—Industrial Machinery & Equipment.

★ 82818 ★ **Apple Computer**
2420 Ridgepoint Dr.
Austin, TX 78754-5288
Officer: Thomas J. Patterson. **Ultimate Parent:** Apple Computer. **SIC:** 7373—Computer Integrated Systems Design.

★ 82819 ★ **AT & T**
8911 Capital Texas Hwy., Ste. 1200
Austin, TX 78759
(512)343-3000
Officer: Lareda Belk, Manager. **Ultimate Parent:** AT&T. **SIC:** 3679—Electronic Components Nec.

★ 82820 ★ **Austin Coca-Cola Bottling Co. Austin Bottling**
9600 Burnett Rd.
Austin, TX 78758
Ultimate Parent: Coca-Cola Enterprises. **SIC:** 2086—Bottled & Canned Soft Drinks.

★ 82821 ★ **Baker Hughes Prod. Tools**
Tremetrics, Inc.
2215 Grand Ave. Pkwy
Austin, TX 78728-3812
(512)251-1400
Company Type: Division. **Ultimate Parent:** Baker Hughes.

★ 82822 ★ **Banana Republic**
10000 Research Blvd.
Austin, TX 78759
(512)346-0688
Ultimate Parent: GAP. **SIC:** 5651—Family Clothing Stores.

★ 82823 ★ **Banana Republic**
6001 Airport Blvd.
Austin, TX 78752
(512)459-2187
Ultimate Parent: GAP. **SIC:** 5651—Family Clothing Stores.

★ 82824 ★ **Bell Atlantic Business Systems Services**
9050 N. Capital of Texas Hwy.
Austin, TX 78759-7206
(512)346-6491
Ultimate Parent: Bell Atlantic Corp. **SIC:** 7378—Computer Maintenance & Repair.

★ 82825 ★ **Beneficial Texas Inc.**
5427 N. Interregional Hwy.
Austin, TX 78723
(512)452-0167
Ultimate Parent: Beneficial. **SIC:** 6062—State Credit Unions.

★ 82826 ★ **B.F. Goodrich Aerospace**
Component Overhaul and Repair Inc.
817 Dessau Rd.
Austin, TX 78753
(512)251-3441
Company Type: Subsidiary. **Officer:** Bruce E. Alspach, President. **Ultimate Parent:** B.F. Goodrich. **SIC:** 7629—Electrical Repair Shops Nec; 7622—Radio & T.V. Repair. **Employee Count:** 250. **Sales:** 29.7000000 M.

★ 82827 ★ **Black & Decker**
7523 Windrush Dr.
Austin, TX 78729-7471
(512)258-9961
Ultimate Parent: Black & Decker Corp. **SIC:** 3679—Electronic Components Nec.

★ 82828 ★ **Borden Inc.**
Dairy
71 Strandtman Cove
Austin, TX 78702
Company Type: Division. **Ultimate Parent:** Borden, Inc. **SIC:** 2026—Fluid Milk.

★ 82829 ★ **Borden Inc.**
Dairy
600 E. 1st St.
Austin, TX 78701
Company Type: Division. **Ultimate Parent:** Borden, Inc. **SIC:** 2026—Fluid Milk.

★ 82830 ★ **Borden Inc. Grocery & Speciality**
71 Strandtman Cove
Austin, TX 78702
Ultimate Parent: Borden, Inc. **SIC:** 2026—Fluid Milk.

★ 82831 ★ **Borden Superior Dairies Inc.**
71 Strandtman Cove
Austin, TX 78702
(512)385-2100
Location Type: Plant. **Officer:** Kermit Strackdein, Plant Manager. **Ultimate Parent:** Borden, Inc. **SIC:** 2024—Ice Cream & Frozen Desserts.

★ 82832 ★ **Builders Square**
5501 Airport Blvd.
Austin, TX 78751
(512)467-1731
Company Type: Subsidiary. **Ultimate Parent:** K-Mart. **SIC:** 5251—Hardware Stores.

★ 82833 ★ **Burlington Air Express**
1807 W. Braker Ln.
Austin, TX 78758
(512)339-9855
Ultimate Parent: Pittston. **SIC:** 4513—Air Courier Services.

★ 82834 ★ **Butler Paper Co.**
210 E. St. Elmo Rd.
Austin, TX 78745-1218
(512)442-6746
Location Type: Branch office. **Officer:** Arlon A. Bindseil. **Ultimate Parent:** Alco Standard Corp. **SIC:** 5113—Industrial & Personal Service Paper; 5111—Printing & Writing Paper.

★ 82835 ★ **Career Image**
6001 Airport Blvd.
Austin, TX 78752
(512)459-0791
Ultimate Parent: United States Shoe. **SIC:** 5651—Family Clothing Stores.

★ 82836 ★ **Casual Corner**
2525 W. Anderson Ln.
Austin, TX 78757
(512)459-0122
Ultimate Parent: United States Shoe. **SIC:** 5651—Family Clothing Stores.

★ 82837 ★ **Casual Corner**
2901 S. Capital of Texas Hwy.
Austin, TX 78746
(512)327-0089
Ultimate Parent: United States Shoe. **SIC:** 5621—Women's Clothing Stores; 5651—Family Clothing Stores.

★ 82838 ★ **Centex Materials, Inc.**
PO Box 2252
Austin, TX 78768
(512)327-3652 **Fax:** (512)328-6536
Officer: James E. Bailey, President. **Ultimate Parent:** Centex.

★ 82839 ★ **Coast to Coast**
3202 W. Anderson Ln.
Austin, TX 78757
(512)451-7775
Ultimate Parent: Servistar Corp.

★ 82840 ★ **Coca Cola Bottling Austin**
9600 Burnet Rd.
Austin, TX 78758
Ultimate Parent: Coca-Cola Enterprises. **SIC:** 2086—Bottled & Canned Soft Drinks.

★ 82841 ★ **Comerica Bank-Texas**
2315 W. Anderson Lane
Austin, TX 78752-1926
(512)458-3101
Company Type: Subsidiary. **Location Type:** Branch office. **Ultimate Parent:** Comerica Bank. **SIC:** 6021—National Commercial Banks.

★ 82842 ★ **Comerica Bank-Texas**
2414 Exposition Blvd.
Austin, TX 78703-2265
(512)472-8181
Company Type: Subsidiary. **Location Type:** Branch office. **Ultimate Parent:** Comerica Bank. **SIC:** 6021—National Commercial Banks.

★ 82843 ★ **Comerica Bank-Texas**
114 W. 7th St.
Austin, TX 78701-3005
(512)477-8181
Company Type: Subsidiary. **Location Type:** Branch office. **Ultimate Parent:** Comerica Bank. **SIC:** 6021—National Commercial Banks.

★ 82844 ★ **Comerica Bank-Texas**
13915 Burnet Rd.
Austin, TX 78728
(512)244-2265
Company Type: Subsidiary. **Location Type:** Branch office. **Ultimate Parent:** Comerica Bank. **SIC:** 6021—National Commercial Banks.

★ 82845 ★ **Computer Assocs**
3001 Bee Caves Rd.
Austin, TX 78746
(512)328-5400
Ultimate Parent: Computer Associates International.

★ 82846 ★ **Dell Computer**
9505 Arboretum Blvd.
Austin, TX 78759
(512)338-4400
Company Type: Headquarters. **Officer:** Michael S. Dell. **Employee Count:** 4650. **Sales:** 2014 M. **Fortune 500:** Largest U.S. Industrial Corporations: Ranking 222.

★ 82847 ★ **Dell Computer Corp.**
9505 Arboretum Blvd.
Austin, TX 78759-7299
(512)338-4400 (800)289-3355 **Fax:** (512)343-3653
Company Type: Headquarters. **Officer:** Michael S. Dell, Chairman of the Board & CEO. **Ultimate Parent:** Dell Computer. **SIC:** 3575—Computer Terminals; 5961—Catalog & Mail-Order Houses; 5045—Computers, Peripherals & Software; 3571—Electronic Computers. **Employee Count:** 3200. **Sales:** 2,013,924,000 M.

★ 82848 ★ **Dell Computer USA Corp.**
9505 Arboretum Blvd.
Austin, TX 78759-7260
(512)338-4400
Company Type: Subsidiary. **Officer:** Joel J. Kocher. **Ultimate Parent:** Dell Computer. **SIC:** 5045—Computers, Peripherals & Software. **Employee Count:** 118. **Sales:** 25.6 (est) M.

★ 82849 ★ **Dell Direct Sales L.P.**
9505 Arboretum Blvd.
Austin, TX 78759
Company Type: Subsidiary. **Officer:** Rob Howe, Group Vice President. **Ultimate Parent:** Dell Computer.

★ 82850 ★ **Dell International Inc.**
9505 Arboretum Blvd.
Austin, TX 78759
Company Type: Subsidiary. **Officer:** Michael S. Dell, CEO. **Ultimate Parent:** Dell Computer.

★ 82851 ★ **Dell Marketing Corp.**
9505 Arboretum Blvd.
Austin, TX 78759-7299
(512)338-4400
Company Type: Subsidiary. **Ultimate Parent:** Dell Computer. **SIC:** 5045—Computers, Peripherals & Software.

★ 82852 ★   **Dell Marketing Corp.**
9505 Aboretum Blvd.
Austin, TX 78759-7299
(512)338-4400
Company Type: Subsidiary. **Ultimate Parent:** Dell Computer. **SIC:** 5045—Computers, Peripherals & Software.

★ 82853 ★   **Dell Marketing LP**
9505 Arboretum Blvd.
Austin, TX 78759
Company Type: Subsidiary. **Officer:** Roy Harold Souine, Vice President. **Ultimate Parent:** Dell Computer.

★ 82854 ★   **Dell Products LP.**
9505 Arboretum Blvd.
Austin, TX 78759
Company Type: Subsidiary. **Officer:** Eric Harselem, Senior Vice President. **Ultimate Parent:** Dell Computer.

★ 82855 ★   **Dell U S A**
9505 Arboretum Blvd.
Austin, TX 78759
Company Type: Subsidiary. **Officer:** Joel J. Kocher, President. **Ultimate Parent:** Dell Computer.

★ 82856 ★   **Delta Air Lines**
Municipal Airport
Austin, TX 78723
(512)478-4786
Ultimate Parent: Delta Air Lines, Inc. **SIC:** 4512—Air Transportation—Scheduled.

★ 82857 ★   **Diebold Inc.**
8403 Cross Park Dr.
Austin, TX 78754
(512)837-8514
Ultimate Parent: Diebold, Inc.

★ 82858 ★   **Diebold Inc.**
8900 Shoal Creek Blvd.
Austin, TX 78758
(512)451-6796
Ultimate Parent: Diebold, Inc.

★ 82859 ★   **Dillard Department Stores**
Hancock Shopping Ctr.
Austin, TX 78751
(512)452-0311
Ultimate Parent: Dillard Department Stores. **SIC:** 5311—Department Stores.

★ 82860 ★   **Eagle Signal Controls**
8004 Cameron Rd.
Austin, TX 78753
Company Type: Subsidiary. **Ultimate Parent:** Danaher Corp.

★ 82861 ★   **Eaton Corp.**
Ion Beam Systems Div.
2433 Rutland Dr.
Austin, TX 78758
(512)837-7600
Company Type: Division. **Location Type:** Plant. **Officer:** Rick Landwehr, Controller. **Ultimate Parent:** Eaton Corp. **SIC:** 3844—X-Ray Apparatus & Tubes.

★ 82862 ★   **Eaton Corp.**
Semiconductor Equipment
2433 Rutland Dr.
Austin, TX 78758
(512)837-7600
Officer: Al Noonan, Manager. **Ultimate Parent:** Eaton Corp. **SIC:** 3674—Semiconductors & Related Devices.

★ 82863 ★   **Emery Worldwide**
6013 Techni Ctr. Dr. B
Austin, TX 78721
Ultimate Parent: Consolidated Freightways. **SIC:** 4731—Freight Transportation Arrangement.

★ 82864 ★   **Exxon**
6707 Cameron Rd.
Austin, TX 78752
(512)451-3091
Ultimate Parent: Exxon. **SIC:** 5541—Gasoline Service Stations.

★ 82865 ★   **Exxon Co.**
500 S. Lamar Blvd.
Austin, TX 78704
(512)447-2781
Ultimate Parent: Exxon. **SIC:** 5541—Gasoline Service Stations.

★ 82866 ★   **Exxon Co. USA**
5400 Balcones Dr.
Austin, TX 78731
(512)452-5422
Ultimate Parent: Exxon.

★ 82867 ★   **Exxon Co. USA**
6721 S. Congress Ave.
Austin, TX 78745
(512)441-5959
Ultimate Parent: Exxon.

★ 82868 ★   **Exxon Co. USA**
3505 Wells Branch Pky.
Austin, TX 78728
(512)388-7013
Ultimate Parent: Exxon.

★ 82869 ★   **Exxon Co. USA**
7844 Burnet Rd.
Austin, TX 78757
(512)454-5674
Ultimate Parent: Exxon.

★ 82870 ★   **Exxon Co. USA**
2616 W. Braker Ln.
Austin, TX 78758
(512)837-9920
Ultimate Parent: Exxon.

★ 82871 ★   **Exxon Co. USA**
9061 Research Blvd.
Austin, TX 78758
(512)837-4094
Ultimate Parent: Exxon. **SIC:** 5411—Grocery Stores.

★ 82872 ★   **Exxon Co. USA**
11267 Springdale Rd.
Austin, TX 78754
(512)926-4311
Ultimate Parent: Exxon. **SIC:** 5541—Gasoline Service Stations.

★ 82873 ★   **Exxon Co. USA Wholesale**
1127 Springdale Rd.
Austin, TX 78721
(512)926-2942
Ultimate Parent: Exxon. **SIC:** 5541—Gasoline Service Stations.

★ 82874 ★   **Exxon Shop**
2512 E. Riverside Dr.
Austin, TX 78741
(512)444-6226
Ultimate Parent: Exxon. **SIC:** 5541—Gasoline Service Stations.

★ 82875 ★   **Exxon Shop**
9909 Manchaca Rd.
Austin, TX 78748
(512)282-9478
Ultimate Parent: Exxon. **SIC:** 5541—Gasoline Service Stations.

★ 82876 ★   **Farm & Home Savings Associa**
1400 Lavaca St.
Austin, TX 78701
(512)478-9692
Ultimate Parent: Farm & Home Financial Corp. **SIC:** 6035—Federal Savings Institutions.

★ 82877 ★   **Foot Action**
6001 Airport Blvd. 227
Austin, TX 78752
(512)458-6255
Ultimate Parent: Melville. **SIC:** 5661—Shoe Stores.

★ 82878 ★   **Foot Action**
2901 S. Capital of Texas Hwy.
Austin, TX 78746
(512)327-4025
Ultimate Parent: Melville. **SIC:** 5661—Shoe Stores.

★ 82879 ★   **Foot Action No 8023**
2222 Guadalupe St.
Austin, TX 78705
(512)472-1841
Ultimate Parent: Melville. **SIC:** 5661—Shoe Stores.

★ 82880 ★   **The Gap**
2354 Guadalupe St.
Austin, TX 78705
(512)482-0355
Ultimate Parent: GAP. **SIC:** 5651—Family Clothing Stores.

★ 82881 ★   **The Gap**
2525 W. Anderson Ln.
Austin, TX 78757
(512)451-9286
Ultimate Parent: GAP. **SIC:** 5651—Family Clothing Stores.

★ 82882 ★   **General American Life Insurance Co.**
Austin National Bank
Austin, TX 78701
(512)472-8404
Ultimate Parent: General American Life. **SIC:** 6411—Insurance Agents, Brokers & Service.

★ 82883 ★   **Giant Food Mart**
8700 N. Lamar Blvd.
Austin, TX 78753
(512)836-9191
Ultimate Parent: Giant Food.

★ 82884 ★   **Greyhound Bus Lines**
401 Congress Ave.
Austin, TX 78701
(512)472-5423
Ultimate Parent: Greyhound Lines Inc. **SIC:** 4212—Local Trucking Without Storage.

★ 82885 ★   **Gulf States Utilities Co.**
1005 Congress Ave.
Austin, TX 78701
(512)476-6163
Ultimate Parent: Gulf State Utilities Co. **SIC:** 4911—Electric Services.

★ 82886 ★   **Hertz Rent-A-Car**
3737 Airport Blvd.
Austin, TX 78722
(512)478-9321
Ultimate Parent: Hertz. **SIC:** 7514—Passenger Car Rental.

★ 82887 ★   **Hertz Rent-A-Car**
3600 Manor Rd.
Austin, TX 78723
(512)478-9321
Ultimate Parent: Hertz. **SIC:** 7514—Passenger Car Rental.

★ 82888 ★   **Hewlett Packard Co.**
11002 Metric Blvd.
Austin, TX 78758
(512)835-6771
Ultimate Parent: Hewlett-Packard. **SIC:** 5049—Professional Equipment Nec.

★ 82889 ★   **Hit or Miss**
2901 S. Capital of Texas Hwy.
Austin, TX 78746
(512)327-5391
Ultimate Parent: TJX. **SIC:** 5621—Women's Clothing Stores; 5651—Family Clothing Stores.

★ 82890 ★   **Hit or Miss**
801 Congress Ave.
Austin, TX 78701
(512)479-6754
Ultimate Parent: TJX. **SIC:** 5044—Office Equipment.

★ 82891 ★   **Hit or Miss**
10710 Research Blvd.
Austin, TX 78759
(512)346-3331
Ultimate Parent: TJX.

★ 82892 ★   **Hit or Miss**
3300 Bee Caves Rd.
Austin, TX 78746
(512)328-9363
Ultimate Parent: TJX. **SIC:** 5651—Family Clothing Stores.

★ 82893 ★   **HMO National Network**
9171 Capital of Texas Hwy. N
Austin, TX 78759
(512)502-5100 **Fax:** (512)502-5101
Officer: Barbara Lapwing, Manager, Sales & Marketing. **Ultimate Parent:** Pacificare Health Systems.

★ 82894 ★   **Intel Corp.**
8911 N. Capital of Texas Hwy.
Austin, TX 78759
(512)454-3628
Ultimate Parent: Intel Corp. **SIC:** 7389—Business Services Nec.

★ 82895 ★   **Jiffy Lube**
12621 Research Blvd.
Austin, TX 78759
(512)250-1515
Ultimate Parent: Pennzoil. **SIC:** 7539—Automotive Repair Shops Nec.

★ 82896 ★   **Jiffy Lube**
3809 Guadalupe St.
Austin, TX 78751
(512)451-3708
Ultimate Parent: Pennzoil. **SIC:** 6531—Real Estate Agents & Managers; 7530—Automotive Repair Shops; 7539—Automotive Repair Shops Nec.

★ 82897 ★   **Jiffy Lube**
1649 Ohlen Rd.
Austin, TX 78758
(512)832-8384
Ultimate Parent: Pennzoil.

★ 82898 ★   **Johnson Controls Inc.**
4109 Todd Ln.
Austin, TX 78744
(512)441-7460
Ultimate Parent: Johnson Controls Inc. **SIC:** 5075—Warm Air Heating & Air-Conditioning; 5084—Industrial Machinery & Equipment.

★ 82899 ★   **Kay Bee Toy&Hobby Shop**
Barton Creek Sq.
Austin, TX 78746
(512)327-6073
Ultimate Parent: Melville. **SIC:** 5945—Hobby, Toy & Game Shops.

★ 82900 ★   **Kentucky Fried Chicken**
6116 W. Hwy. 290
Austin, TX 78735
(512)892-0940
Ultimate Parent: Pepsico. **SIC:** 5812—Eating Places.

★ 82901 ★   **Kentucky Fried Chicken**
3914 N. Lamar Blvd.
Austin, TX 78756
(512)454-3224
Ultimate Parent: Pepsico. **SIC:** 5812—Eating Places.

★ 82902 ★   **Kentucky Fried Chicken**
1815 W. Ben White Blvd.
Austin, TX 78704
(512)441-4061
Ultimate Parent: Pepsico. **SIC:** 5812—Eating Places.

★ 82903 ★   **Kentucky Fried Chicken**
825 E. William Cannon Dr.
Austin, TX 78745
(512)445-0896
Ultimate Parent: Pepsico. **SIC:** 5812—Eating Places.

★ 82904 ★   **Kentucky Fried Chicken**
7206 Ed Bluestein Blvd.
Austin, TX 78723
(512)926-9491
Ultimate Parent: Pepsico. **SIC:** 5812—Eating Places.

★ 82905 ★   **Kentucky Fried Chicken**
1210 Barton Springs Rd.
Austin, TX 78704
(512)476-4821
Ultimate Parent: Pepsico. **SIC:** 5812—Eating Places.

★ 82906 ★   **Kentucky Fried Chicken**
6824 Burnet Rd.
Austin, TX 78757
(512)452-2743
Ultimate Parent: Pepsico. **SIC:** 5812—Eating Places.

★ 82907 ★   **Kentucky Fried Chicken**
12633 Research Blvd.
Austin, TX 78759
(512)258-2886
Ultimate Parent: Pepsico. **SIC:** 5812—Eating Places.

★ 82908 ★ **Kentucky Fried Chicken**
5111 Airport Blvd.
Austin, TX 78751
(512)452-0012
Ultimate Parent: Pepsico. **SIC:** 5812—Eating Places.

★ 82909 ★ **Kentucky Fried Chicken**
9209 N. Lamar Blvd.
Austin, TX 78753
(512)836-9067
Ultimate Parent: Pepsico. **SIC:** 5812—Eating Places.

★ 82910 ★ **Kentucky Fried Chicken**
6818 W. Gate Blvd.
Austin, TX 78745
Ultimate Parent: Pepsico. **SIC:** 5812—Eating Places.

★ 82911 ★ **Kerox Business Services**
1321 Rutherford Ln.
Austin, TX 78753
(512)834-4900
Officer: John Oldham, Manager. **Ultimate Parent:** Xerox Corp. **SIC:** 2752—Commercial Printing—Lithographic.

★ 82912 ★ **Kids R US**
5616 Convict Ln.
Austin, TX 78745
(512)892-3322
Ultimate Parent: Toys "R" US. **SIC:** 8351—Child Day Care Services.

★ 82913 ★ **Kids R US**
2515 Enfield Rd.
Austin, TX 78703
(512)477-7178
Ultimate Parent: Toys "R" US. **SIC:** 8351—Child Day Care Services.

★ 82914 ★ **Kids R US**
5616 Convict Ln.
Austin, TX 78745
(512)892-3322
Ultimate Parent: Toys "R" US. **SIC:** 8351—Child Day Care Services.

★ 82915 ★ **Kmart Discount Stores**
13729 Research Blvd.
Austin, TX 78750
(512)331-1365
Ultimate Parent: K-Mart.

★ 82916 ★ **Lane Bryant**
2525 W. Anderson Ln.
Austin, TX 78757
(512)452-0230
Ultimate Parent: Limited. **SIC:** 5651—Family Clothing Stores.

★ 82917 ★ **Lane Bryant**
2901 S. Capital of Texas Hwy.
Austin, TX 78746
(512)327-4671
Ultimate Parent: Limited. **SIC:** 5621—Women's Clothing Stores; 5651—Family Clothing Stores.

★ 82918 ★ **Lens Crafters**
6001 Airport Blvd.
Austin, TX 78752
(512)450-1234
Ultimate Parent: United States Shoe. **SIC:** 5995—Optical Goods Stores; 8042—Offices & Clinics of Optometrists.

★ 82919 ★ **Lens Crafters**
10000 Research Blvd.
Austin, TX 78759
(512)343-9111
Ultimate Parent: United States Shoe.

★ 82920 ★ **Lerner Shop**
2901 S. Capital of Texas Hwy.
Austin, TX 78746
(512)327-2979
Ultimate Parent: Limited. **SIC:** 5611—Men's & Boys' Clothing Stores; 5651—Family Clothing Stores.

★ 82921 ★ **Lerner Shop**
6001 Airport Blvd.
Austin, TX 78752
(512)453-6047
Ultimate Parent: Limited. **SIC:** 5651—Family Clothing Stores.

★ 82922 ★ **Lerner Shop**
700 Congress Ave.
Austin, TX 78701
(512)477-7685
Ultimate Parent: Limited. **SIC:** 5399—Miscellaneous General Merchandise Store.

★ 82923 ★ **Liberty Mutual Insurance Co.**
Twin Tower Big
Austin, TX 78723
(512)458-2521
Ultimate Parent: Liberty Mutual Group. **SIC:** 6411—Insurance Agents, Brokers & Service.

★ 82924 ★ **Liberty Mutual Insurance Gr**
6705 W. Hwy. 290
Austin, TX 78735
(512)892-0727
Ultimate Parent: Liberty Mutual Group. **SIC:** 6411—Insurance Agents, Brokers & Service.

★ 82925 ★ **The Limited**
Barton Creek Sq.
Austin, TX 78746
(512)327-3962
Ultimate Parent: Limited. **SIC:** 5621—Women's Clothing Stores.

★ 82926 ★ **The Limited**
2525 W. Anderson Ln.
Austin, TX 78757
(512)451-5243
Ultimate Parent: Limited. **SIC:** 5621—Women's Clothing Stores; 5651—Family Clothing Stores.

★ 82927 ★ **The Limited**
6001 Airport Blvd.
Austin, TX 78752
(512)452-0227
Ultimate Parent: Limited. **SIC:** 5651—Family Clothing Stores.

★ 82928 ★ **The Limited Express**
2901 S. Capital of Texas Hwy.
Austin, TX 78746
(512)328-0662
Ultimate Parent: Limited. **SIC:** 5651—Family Clothing Stores.

★ 82929 ★ **Litton Industries**
Advanced Circuit Design Div.
1114 Lost Creek Blvd., Ste. 130
Austin, TX 78746-6318
(512)327-1088 **Fax:** (512)329-0404
Company Type: Division. **Ultimate Parent:** Litton Industries. **SIC:** 3679—Electronic Components Nec.

★ 82930 ★ **Lockheed Corp.**
Austin Div.
PO Box 17100
Austin, TX 78760
(512)386-0000
Company Type: Division. **Ultimate Parent:** Lockheed Corp. **SIC:** 3728—Aircraft Parts & Equipment Nec; 9661—Space Research & Technology; 1629—Heavy Construction Nec.

★ 82931 ★ **Lockheed Missiles & Space Co.**
Austin Div.
6800 Burleson Rd.
Austin, TX 78744-1016
Company Type: Division. **Ultimate Parent:** Lockheed Corp. **SIC:** 3761—Guided Missiles & Space Vehicles.

★ 82932 ★ **Mary Kay Cosmetics**
10804 Pickfair Dr.
Austin, TX 78750
(512)335-5464
Ultimate Parent: Mary Kay Cosmetics.

★ 82933 ★ **Mary Kay Cosmetics**
8014 Tantara Ct.
Austin, TX 78729
(512)258-3820
Ultimate Parent: Mary Kay Cosmetics. **SIC:** 8322—Individual & Family Services.

★ 82934 ★ **Mary Kay Cosmetics**
7225 Scenic Brook Dr.
Austin, TX 78736
(512)288-0971
Ultimate Parent: Mary Kay Cosmetics. **SIC:** 5999—Miscellaneous Retail Stores Nec.

★ 82935 ★ **Mary Kay Cosmetics Director**
2003 Barton Hills Dr.
Austin, TX 78704
(512)445-0066
Ultimate Parent: Mary Kay Cosmetics. **SIC:** 5999—Miscellaneous Retail Stores Nec; 7231—Beauty Shops.

★ 82936 ★ **Maxtor Corp.**
9020 Capital Texas Hwy.
Austin, TX 78746
(512)345-2742
Ultimate Parent: Maxtor. **SIC:** 7373—Computer Integrated Systems Design.

★ 82937 ★ **Mead Data Central**
919 Congress Ave.
Austin, TX 78701
(512)476-8144
Ultimate Parent: Mead. **SIC:** 7374—Data Processing & Preparation.

★ 82938 ★ **Mercantile Mortgage Corp.**
1033 La Posada Dr.
Austin, TX 78752
(512)458-1386
Ultimate Parent: Mercantile Bankshares Corp. **SIC:** 6162—Mortgage Bankers & Correspondents.

★ 82939 ★ **Mobil Mart**
717 E. 7th St.
Austin, TX 78701
(512)474-7808
Ultimate Parent: Mobil. **SIC:** 5541—Gasoline Service Stations.

★ 82940 ★ **Mobil Mart**
7114 N. Interregional Hwy.
Austin, TX 78752
(512)453-1759
Ultimate Parent: Mobil. **SIC:** 5541—Gasoline Service Stations.

★ 82941 ★ **Mobil Mart Service Station**
1919 S. Pleasant Valley Rd.
Austin, TX 78741
(512)389-1320
Ultimate Parent: Mobil. **SIC:** 5541—Gasoline Service Stations.

★ 82942 ★ **Mobil Oil Corp.**
1111 Springdale Rd.
Austin, TX 78721-1945
(512)926-8177
Officer: B. D. Bomba. **Ultimate Parent:** Mobil. **SIC:** 5172—Petroleum Products Nec; 5171—Petroleum Bulk Stations & Terminals.

★ 82943 ★ **Mobil Service**
1121 Rutland Dr.
Austin, TX 78758
(512)835-6977
Ultimate Parent: Mobil. **SIC:** 7699—Repair Services Nec.

★ 82944 ★ **Mobilecomm of Austin Inc.**
505 E. Huntland Dr., Ste. 160
Austin, TX 78752-3714
(512)454-4558
Company Type: Subsidiary. **Officer:** Steve Pazian, President. **Ultimate Parent:** BellSouth Corp. **SIC:** 5999—Miscellaneous Retail Stores Nec; 7359—Equipment Rental & Leasing Nec. **Employee Count:** 20. **Sales:** 750 M.

★ 82945 ★ **Molex Inc.**
3933 Steck Ave.
Austin, TX 78759
(512)453-1398
Ultimate Parent: Molex. **SIC:** 3699—Electrical Equipment & Supplies Nec.

★ 82946 ★ **National Semiconductor Corp.**
2201 Donley Dr.
Austin, TX 78758
(512)339-3085
Ultimate Parent: National Semiconductor Corp. **SIC:** 7373—Computer Integrated Systems Design.

★ 82947 ★ **New York Life Austin General Office**
1250 Capital of Texas Hwy.
Bldg. 3, Ste. 400
Austin, TX 78746
(512)329-4200 **Fax:** (512)329-4258
Officer: James B. Moore, Manager.
Ultimate Parent: New York Life.

★ 82948 ★ **Norwest Mortgage Inc.**
8800 Business Park Dr.
Austin, TX 78759
(512)346-8940
Ultimate Parent: Norwest Corp. **SIC:** 6159—Miscellaneous Business Credit Institutions; 6141—Personal Credit Institutions.

★ 82949 ★ **Otis Elevator Co.**
300 Colorado St.
Austin, TX 78701
(512)478-7917
Ultimate Parent: United Technologies. **SIC:** 1796—Installing Building Equipment Nec.

★ 82950 ★ **Otis Elevator Co.**
11500 Metric Blvd.
Austin, TX 78758
(512)339-9731
Ultimate Parent: United Technologies.

★ 82951 ★ **Pappagallo**
6001 Airport Blvd.
Austin, TX 78752
(512)458-8985
Ultimate Parent: United States Shoe. **SIC:** 5651—Family Clothing Stores.

★ 82952 ★ **Payless Shoesource**
1900 W. Ben White Blvd.
Austin, TX 78704
(512)442-6652
Ultimate Parent: May Department Stores. **SIC:** 5661—Shoe Stores.

★ 82953 ★ **Payless Shoesource**
5309 Airport Blvd.
Austin, TX 78751
(512)459-8003
Ultimate Parent: May Department Stores. **SIC:** 5661—Shoe Stores.

★ 82954 ★ **Payless Shoesource**
1110 N. IH 35
Austin, TX 78701
(512)255-0589
Ultimate Parent: May Department Stores. **SIC:** 5632—Women's Accessory & Specialty Stores.

★ 82955 ★ **Pepsi-Cola Bottling Co.**
9010 Wall St.
Austin, TX 78754
(512)832-9173
Officer: Steve Vittorini, Manager. **Ultimate Parent:** Pepsico. **SIC:** 2086—Bottled & Canned Soft Drinks.

★ 82956 ★ **Petite Sophisticate**
2901 S. Capital of Texas Hwy.
Austin, TX 78746
(512)327-5675
Ultimate Parent: United States Shoe. **SIC:** 5651—Family Clothing Stores.

★ 82957 ★ **Petite Sophisticate**
6001 Airport Blvd.
Austin, TX 78752
(512)323-2901
Ultimate Parent: United States Shoe. **SIC:** 5651—Family Clothing Stores.

★ 82958 ★ **Pitney Bowes**
2324 Ridgepoint Dr.
Austin, TX 78754
(512)928-8913
Officer: Roger Williams, Manager. **Ultimate Parent:** Pitney Bowes. **SIC:** 3663—Radio & T.V. Communications Equipment.

★ 82959 ★ **Pizza Hut**
320 W. William Cannon Dr.
Austin, TX 78745
(512)462-1166
Ultimate Parent: Pepsico. **SIC:** 5812—Eating Places.

★ 82960 ★ **Pizza Hut**
1807 Slaughter Ln. W
Austin, TX 78748
(512)282-4243
Ultimate Parent: Pepsico. **SIC:** 5812—Eating Places.

★ 82961 ★ **Pizza Hut**
1902 W. Ben White Blvd.
Austin, TX 78704
(512)444-6004
Ultimate Parent: Pepsico. **SIC:** 5812—Eating Places.

★ 82962 ★   Pizza Hut
1934 Rutland Dr.
Austin, TX 78758
(512)339-8781
Ultimate Parent: Pepsico. SIC: 5812—
Eating Places.

★ 82963 ★   Pizza Hut
2211 S. I H 35 100
Austin, TX 78741
Ultimate Parent: Pepsico. SIC: 5812—
Eating Places.

★ 82964 ★   Pizza Hut
8500 N. Lamar Blvd.
Austin, TX 78753
(512)836-2230
Ultimate Parent: Pepsico. SIC: 5812—
Eating Places.

★ 82965 ★   Pizza Hut
8776 Research Blvd.
Austin, TX 78758
(512)444-4444
Ultimate Parent: Pepsico.

★ 82966 ★   Pizza Hut
3435 Bee Caves Rd.
Austin, TX 78746
(512)328-3886
Ultimate Parent: Pepsico. SIC: 5812—
Eating Places.

★ 82967 ★   Pizza Hut
717 E. Ben White Blvd.
Austin, TX 78704
(512)447-7109
Ultimate Parent: Pepsico. SIC: 5812—
Eating Places.

★ 82968 ★   Pizza Hut
1144 Airport Blvd.
Austin, TX 78702
(512)929-7344
Ultimate Parent: Pepsico. SIC: 5812—
Eating Places.

★ 82969 ★   Pizza Hut
1811 Guadalupe St.
Austin, TX 78701
(512)320-8454
Ultimate Parent: Pepsico.

★ 82970 ★   Pizza Hut
12636 Research Blvd.
Austin, TX 78759
(512)335-5666
Ultimate Parent: Pepsico. SIC: 5812—
Eating Places.

★ 82971 ★   Pizza Hut
8213 Brodie Ln.
Austin, TX 78745
(512)280-5454
Ultimate Parent: Pepsico. SIC: 4215—
Courier Services Except by Air.

★ 82972 ★   Pizza Hut
1425 E. Rundberg Ln.
Austin, TX 78753
(512)837-9555
Ultimate Parent: Pepsico. SIC: 5812—
Eating Places.

★ 82973 ★   Pizza Hut
13215 Research Blvd.
Austin, TX 78750
(512)258-6739
Ultimate Parent: Pepsico. SIC: 5812—
Eating Places.

★ 82974 ★   Principal Mutual Life
Insurance Co.
3755 S. Capital of Texas Hwy.
Austin, TX 78704
(512)499-0941
Ultimate Parent: Principal Mutual Life. SIC:
6411—Insurance Agents, Brokers &
Service.

★ 82975 ★   Radio Shack
216 W. Martin L King Jr Blvd.
Austin, TX 78701
(512)477-4764
Company Type: Division. Ultimate Parent:
Tandy Corp. SIC: 5065—Electronic Parts &
Equipment Nec.

★ 82976 ★   Radio Shack
131 W. Oltorf St.
Austin, TX 78704
(512)444-3230
Company Type: Division. Ultimate Parent:
Tandy Corp. SIC: 5065—Electronic Parts &
Equipment Nec.

★ 82977 ★   Radio Shack
1501 W. Ben White Blvd.
Austin, TX 78704
(512)462-9977
Company Type: Division. Ultimate Parent:
Tandy Corp.

★ 82978 ★   Radio Shack
4521 W. Gate Blvd.
Austin, TX 78745
(512)892-1162
Company Type: Division. Ultimate Parent:
Tandy Corp. SIC: 5046—Commercial
Equipment Nec; 5065—Electronic Parts &
Equipment Nec.

★ 82979 ★   Radio Shack
8660 Spicewood Spring Rd.
Austin, TX 78759
(512)258-6944
Company Type: Division. Ultimate Parent:
Tandy Corp. SIC: 5065—Electronic Parts &
Equipment Nec.

★ 82980 ★   Radio Shack
2438 W. Anderson Ln. C7
Austin, TX 78757
(512)454-0994
Company Type: Division. Ultimate Parent:
Tandy Corp. SIC: 5731—Radio, Television
& Electronics Stores.

★ 82981 ★   Radio Shack
2901 S. Capital of Texas Hwy.
Austin, TX 78746
(512)327-6911
Company Type: Division. Ultimate Parent:
Tandy Corp. SIC: 5065—Electronic Parts &
Equipment Nec.

★ 82982 ★   Radio Shack
2239 S. Lamar Blvd.
Austin, TX 78704
(512)444-7300
Company Type: Division. Ultimate Parent:
Tandy Corp. SIC: 5065—Electronic Parts &
Equipment Nec.

★ 82983 ★   Radio Shack
9308 N. Lamar Blvd.
Austin, TX 78753
(512)835-4490
Company Type: Division. Ultimate Parent:
Tandy Corp. SIC: 5065—Electronic Parts &
Equipment Nec.

★ 82984 ★   Radio Shack
13776 Research Blvd.
Austin, TX 78750
(512)258-6009
Company Type: Division. Ultimate Parent:
Tandy Corp. SIC: 5065—Electronic Parts &
Equipment Nec.

★ 82985 ★   Radio Shack
1000 E. 41st St.
Austin, TX 78751
(512)454-3090
Company Type: Division. Ultimate Parent:
Tandy Corp. SIC: 5065—Electronic Parts &
Equipment Nec.

★ 82986 ★   Radio Shack
5742 Manchaca Rd.
Austin, TX 78745
Company Type: Division. Ultimate Parent:
Tandy Corp. SIC: 5065—Electronic Parts &
Equipment Nec.

★ 82987 ★   Radio Shack
6001 Airport Blvd.
Austin, TX 78752
(512)452-0686
Company Type: Division. Ultimate Parent:
Tandy Corp. SIC: 5065—Electronic Parts &
Equipment Nec; 5731—Radio, Television &
Electronics Stores.

★ 82988 ★   Radio Shack
5802 Burnet Rd.
Austin, TX 78756
(512)451-2570
Company Type: Division. Ultimate Parent:
Tandy Corp. SIC: 5731—Radio, Television
& Electronics Stores.

★ 82989 ★   Radio Shack
Southwood
Austin, TX 78704
(512)447-0371
Company Type: Division. Ultimate Parent:
Tandy Corp. SIC: 5046—Commercial
Equipment Nec.

★ 82990 ★   Radio Shack
2901 S. Capital of Texas Hwy.
Austin, TX 78746
(512)459-4238
Company Type: Division. Ultimate Parent:
Tandy Corp. SIC: 7373—Computer
Integrated Systems Design.

★ 82991 ★   Radio Shack
7112 Ed Bluestein Blvd.
Austin, TX 78723
(512)926-0501
Company Type: Division. Ultimate Parent:
Tandy Corp. SIC: 7373—Computer
Integrated Systems Design.

★ 82992 ★   Richards S P Co.
10212 Metric Blvd.
Austin, TX 78758
(512)837-8931
Ultimate Parent: Genuine Parts. SIC:
5044—Office Equipment.

★ 82993 ★   Ryder Truck Rental
1700 W. Koenig Ln.
Austin, TX 78756
(512)323-0611
Ultimate Parent: Ryder System.

★ 82994 ★   Ryder Truck Rental
4600 S. Congress Ave.
Austin, TX 78745
(512)462-2606
Ultimate Parent: Ryder System.

★ 82995 ★   Ryder Truck Rental
2425 W. Ben White Blvd.
Austin, TX 78704
(512)445-0506
Ultimate Parent: Ryder System.

★ 82996 ★   Ryder Truck Rental
12611 Research Blvd.
Austin, TX 78759
(512)462-6841
Ultimate Parent: Ryder System. SIC:
7359—Equipment Rental & Leasing Nec;
7513—Truck Rental & Leasing Without
Drivers.

★ 82997 ★   Ryder Truck Rental
2715 Hancock Dr.
Austin, TX 78731
(512)453-1029
Ultimate Parent: Ryder System. SIC:
7359—Equipment Rental & Leasing Nec.

★ 82998 ★   Ryder Truck Rental
8305 N. Lamar Blvd.
Austin, TX 78753
(512)836-7184
Ultimate Parent: Ryder System. SIC:
7359—Equipment Rental & Leasing Nec;
7513—Truck Rental & Leasing Without
Drivers.

★ 82999 ★   Ryder Truck Rental
9205 Research Blvd.
Austin, TX 78758
(512)835-9379
Ultimate Parent: Ryder System. SIC:
7539—Automotive Repair Shops Nec.

★ 83000 ★   Sam's Wholesale
Club
10601 N. Lamar Blvd.
Austin, TX 78753
(512)832-1155
Ultimate Parent: Wal-Mart Stores, Inc. SIC:
5141—Groceries—General Line.

★ 83001 ★   Seven-Up-RC-Big Red
Bottling
3411 Hidalgo St.
Austin, TX 78702
(512)385-4477
Officer: Tony Sanchez, Manager. Ultimate
Parent: Dr. Pepper/Seven-Up. SIC: 2086—
Bottled & Canned Soft Drinks.

★ 83002 ★   Shell Pipeline Corp.
4208 Terry O Ln.
Austin, TX 78745
(512)442-3142
Ultimate Parent: Shell Oil Co.

★ 83003 ★   Southland Corp.
8920 Business Park Dr.
Austin, TX 78759
(512)346-2262
Ultimate Parent: Southland Corp. SIC:
5141—Groceries—General Line.

★ 83004 ★   Southwest Airlines
Co.
3600 Manor Rd.
Austin, TX 78723
(512)476-6353
Ultimate Parent: Southwest Airlines. SIC:
4512—Air Transportation—Scheduled.

★ 83005 ★   Southwestern Bell
Yellow Pages
8716 N. Missouri Pacific Expy.
Austin, TX 78731
(512)343-5800
Ultimate Parent: Southwestern Bell. SIC:
2741—Miscellaneous Publishing.

★ 83006 ★   State Mutual of
America
314 E. Highland Mall Blvd.
Austin, TX 78752
(512)459-0018
Ultimate Parent: State Mututal of America.
SIC: 6411—Insurance Agents, Brokers &
Service.

★ 83007 ★   Stewart & Stevenson
Services
615 W. Yager Ln.
Austin, TX 78753
(512)836-2227
Ultimate Parent: Stewart & Stevenson.
SIC: 1711—Plumbing, Heating & Air-
Conditioning.

★ 83008 ★   Sun Microsystems
Inc.
9300 Jollyville Rd.
Austin, TX 78759
(512)343-0293
Ultimate Parent: Sun Microsystems Inc.
SIC: 7373—Computer Integrated Systems
Design.

★ 83009 ★   Sysco Food Services
Inc.
6600 Burleson Rd.
Austin, TX 78744
(512)385-8800
Ultimate Parent: Sysco. SIC: 5023—
Homefurnishings.

★ 83010 ★   T J Maxx Clothes
Store
9828 Great Hills Trl.
Austin, TX 78759
Ultimate Parent: TJX. SIC: 5651—Family
Clothing Stores.

★ 83011 ★   Taco Bell
1925 Airport Blvd.
Austin, TX 78722
(512)469-0225
Ultimate Parent: Pepsico. SIC: 2099—
Food Preparations Nec; 6531—Real Estate
Agents & Managers.

★ 83012 ★   Taco Bell
3501 Wells Branch Pky.
Austin, TX 78728
(512)388-3164
Ultimate Parent: Pepsico.

★ 83013 ★   Taco Bell
502 William Cannon
Austin, TX 78745
(512)447-7854
Ultimate Parent: Pepsico. SIC: 5812—
Eating Places.

★ 83014 ★   Taco Bell
1702 W. Ben White Blvd.
Austin, TX 78704
(512)444-9126
Ultimate Parent: Pepsico. SIC: 5812—
Eating Places.

★ 83015 ★   Taco Bell
1905 W. Loop
Austin, TX 78758
(512)327-4654
Ultimate Parent: Pepsico. SIC: 5812—
Eating Places.

★ 83016 ★   Taco Bell
327 S. Lamar Blvd.
Austin, TX 78704
(512)469-0444
Ultimate Parent: Pepsico. SIC: 5812—
Eating Places.

★ 83017 ★ Taco Bell
1503 W. 35th St.
Austin, TX 78703
(512)459-0693
Ultimate Parent: Pepsico. SIC: 5812—
Eating Places.

★ 83018 ★ Taco Bell
2802 Guadalupe St.
Austin, TX 78705
(512)477-2048
Ultimate Parent: Pepsico. SIC: 5812—
Eating Places.

★ 83019 ★ Taco Bell
13774 Research Blvd.
Austin, TX 78750
(512)258-7309
Ultimate Parent: Pepsico. SIC: 5812—
Eating Places.

★ 83020 ★ Taco Bell
201 E. Oltorf St.
Austin, TX 78704
(512)442-5395
Ultimate Parent: Pepsico. SIC: 5812—
Eating Places.

★ 83021 ★ Taco Bell
2320 E. Riverside Dr.
Austin, TX 78741
(512)441-8821
Ultimate Parent: Pepsico. SIC: 5812—
Eating Places.

★ 83022 ★ Taco Bell
3201 Bee Caves Rd. 180
Austin, TX 78746
Ultimate Parent: Pepsico. SIC: 5812—
Eating Places.

★ 83023 ★ Taco Bell
7015 Burnet Rd.
Austin, TX 78757
(512)453-6731
Ultimate Parent: Pepsico. SIC: 5812—
Eating Places.

★ 83024 ★ Tandem Computers
Inc.
14231 Tandem Blvd.
Austin, TX 78728
(512)244-8000
Officer: Neal Waddington, Manager.
Ultimate Parent: Tandem. SIC: 3571—
Electronic Computers; 3575—Computer
Terminals.

★ 83025 ★ Texaco
424 S. Lamar Blvd.
Austin, TX 78704
(512)482-0517
Ultimate Parent: Texaco.

★ 83026 ★ Texaco
616 W. William Cannon Dr.
Austin, TX 78745
(512)441-3366
Ultimate Parent: Texaco. SIC: 5541—
Gasoline Service Stations.

★ 83027 ★ Texaco Chemical Co.
7114 N. Lamar Blvd.
Austin, TX 78752
Ultimate Parent: Texaco. SIC: 2869—
Industrial Organic Chemicals Nec.

★ 83028 ★ Texaco Food Mart
13296 Research Blvd.
Austin, TX 78750
(512)331-6122
Ultimate Parent: Texaco. SIC: 5541—
Gasoline Service Stations.

★ 83029 ★ Texaco Food Mart
11300 N. Interregional Hwy.
Austin, TX 78753
(512)339-0669
Ultimate Parent: Texaco. SIC: 5541—
Gasoline Service Stations.

★ 83030 ★ Texaco Nw Hills
3635 N. Hills Dr.
Austin, TX 78731
(512)345-8172
Ultimate Parent: Texaco.

★ 83031 ★ Texaco One Stop
8747 Research Blvd.
Austin, TX 78758
(512)339-1814
Ultimate Parent: Texaco. SIC: 5541—
Gasoline Service Stations.

★ 83032 ★ Texaco 1 Stop
2241 W. 35th St.
Austin, TX 78703
(512)447-7676
Ultimate Parent: Texaco. SIC: 5541—
Gasoline Service Stations.

★ 83033 ★ Texaco Refining
7510 N. Missouri Pacific Expy.
Austin, TX 78731
(512)338-0702
Ultimate Parent: Texaco.

★ 83034 ★ Texaco Self Serve
9920 W. Hwy. 290
Austin, TX 78736
(512)288-5528
Ultimate Parent: Texaco.

★ 83035 ★ Texaco Self Serve
5210 Manor Rd.
Austin, TX 78723
(512)926-1084
Ultimate Parent: Texaco.

★ 83036 ★ Texaco Self Serve
3828 W. 35th St.
Austin, TX 78703
(512)458-6625
Ultimate Parent: Texaco. SIC: 5541—
Gasoline Service Stations.

★ 83037 ★ Texaco Self Serve
1601 E. Saint Elmo Rd.
Austin, TX 78744
(512)441-8832
Ultimate Parent: Texaco.

★ 83038 ★ Texaco Self Serve
3828 I N
Austin, TX 78751
(512)458-6625
Ultimate Parent: Texaco. SIC: 5541—
Gasoline Service Stations.

★ 83039 ★ Texaco Self Service
4545 S. Lamar Blvd.
Austin, TX 78745
(512)892-2686
Ultimate Parent: Texaco. SIC: 5541—
Gasoline Service Stations.

★ 83040 ★ Texaco Service
11833 Manchaca Rd.
Austin, TX 78748
(512)280-0685
Ultimate Parent: Texaco.

★ 83041 ★ Texaco Shoppers
Mart
800 E. William Cannon Dr.
Austin, TX 78745
(512)441-2829
Ultimate Parent: Texaco. SIC: 5541—
Gasoline Service Stations.

★ 83042 ★ Texaco Shoppers
Mart No 10
2250 E. Ben White Blvd.
Austin, TX 78741
(512)443-4414
Ultimate Parent: Texaco. SIC: 5541—
Gasoline Service Stations.

★ 83043 ★ Texas Copy Systems,
Inc.
3019 Alvin DeVane Bldg. 4, Ste. 400
Austin, TX 78741-7418
(512)385-5100 Fax: (512)385-2646
Company Type: Division. Officer: Daniel
G. Boylan, President. Ultimate Parent: Alco
Standard Corp. SIC: 5044—Office
Equipment; 5046—Commercial Equipment
Nec.

★ 83044 ★ Texas Instruments
Inc.
12501 Research Blvd.
Austin, TX 78759
Ultimate Parent: Texas Instruments. SIC:
3500—Industrial Machinery & Equipment;
3672—Printed Circuit Boards.

★ 83045 ★ Texas Trust Savings
Bank, FSB
8240 Mopac N
Building 2, Ste. 180
Austin, TX 78759
(512)343-6000 Fax: (512)346-0703
Officer: David W. Quinn, Chairman of the
Board & CEO. Ultimate Parent: Centex.

★ 83046 ★ 3M Co.
Telecom Markets Div.
PO Box 2963
Austin, TX 78768-2963
(512)984-3400
Company Type: Branch. Officer: Roger H.
D. Lacey. Ultimate Parent: Minnesota
Mining & Mfg. SIC: 3643—Current-Carrying
Wiring Devices; 2672—Coated & Laminated
Paper Nec; 2821—Plastics Materials &
Resins; 2899—Chemical Preparations Nec;
3089—Plastics Products Nec; 3644—
Noncurrent-Carrying Wiring Devices; 3661—
Telephone & Telegraph Apparatus; 3678—
Electronic Connectors; 3679—Electronic
Components Nec.

★ 83047 ★ Time Electronics
9300 Jollyville Rd.
Austin, TX 78759
(512)346-7346
Location Type: Branch office. Ultimate
Parent: Avnet. SIC: 5065—Electronic Parts
& Equipment Nec.

★ 83048 ★ Time Electronics
1826 Kramer Ln.
Austin, TX 78758
(512)339-3051
Ultimate Parent: Avnet.

★ 83049 ★ Toys R US
4025 S. Capital Texas Hwy.
Austin, TX 78735
(512)441-7216
Ultimate Parent: Toys "R" US. SIC: 5641—
Children's & Infants' Wear Stores.

★ 83050 ★ Toys R US
5451 N. Interregional Hwy. B
Austin, TX 78723
(512)450-1807
Ultimate Parent: Toys "R" US. SIC: 5945—
Hobby, Toy & Game Shops.

★ 83051 ★ Toys R US
4025 S. Capital of Texas Hwy.
Austin, TX 78704
(512)441-7216
Ultimate Parent: Toys "R" US. SIC: 5945—
Hobby, Toy & Game Shops.

★ 83052 ★ United Parcel Service
3206 Industrial Ter
Austin, TX 78759
(512)478-5606
Ultimate Parent: United Parcel Service of
America. SIC: 4215—Courier Services
Except by Air.

★ 83053 ★ Wal Mart
12250 Research Blvd.
Austin, TX 78759
(512)331-9924
Ultimate Parent: Wal-Mart Stores, Inc. SIC:
5311—Department Stores.

★ 83054 ★ Wal Mart Disc City
6700 Middle Fiskville Rd.
Austin, TX 78752
(512)458-8244
Ultimate Parent: Wal-Mart Stores, Inc.

★ 83055 ★ Waldenbooks
2901 S. Capital of Texas Hwy.
Austin, TX 78746
(512)327-1668
Ultimate Parent: K-Mart. SIC: 5942—Book
Stores.

★ 83056 ★ Waldenbooks & More
9722 Great Hills Trl.
Austin, TX 78759
(512)346-9481
Ultimate Parent: K-Mart.

★ 83057 ★ Walgreen
13450 Research Blvd.
Austin, TX 78750
(512)258-9151
Ultimate Parent: Walgreen Co. SIC:
5122—Drugs, Proprietaries & Sundries.

★ 83058 ★ Walgreen
3005 S. Lamar Blvd.
Austin, TX 78704
(512)443-5663
Ultimate Parent: Walgreen Co. SIC:
5122—Drugs, Proprietaries & Sundries.

★ 83059 ★ Walgreen Drug Stores
2100 W. William Cannon Dr.
Austin, TX 78745
(512)462-3223
Ultimate Parent: Walgreen Co.

★ 83060 ★ Walgreen Drug Stores
111 W. Anderson Ln.
Austin, TX 78752
(512)459-2295
Ultimate Parent: Walgreen Co. SIC:
5912—Drug Stores & Proprietary Stores.

★ 83061 ★ Walgreen Drug Stores
Barton Creek Sq.
Austin, TX 78746
(512)327-7220
Ultimate Parent: Walgreen Co. SIC:
5912—Drug Stores & Proprietary Stores.

★ 83062 ★ Walgreen Drug Stores
414 W. Stassney Ln.
Austin, TX 78745
(512)441-4343
Ultimate Parent: Walgreen Co. SIC:
5912—Drug Stores & Proprietary Stores.

★ 83063 ★ Walgreen Drug Stores
5429 N. Interregional Hwy.
Austin, TX 78723
(512)452-9451
Ultimate Parent: Walgreen Co. SIC:
5912—Drug Stores & Proprietary Stores.

★ 83064 ★ Walgreen Drug Stores
113 W. Oltorf St.
Austin, TX 78704
(512)444-2747
Ultimate Parent: Walgreen Co. SIC:
5912—Drug Stores & Proprietary Stores.

★ 83065 ★ Walgreen Drug Stores
12407 N. Missouri Pacific Expy.
Austin, TX 78758
(512)835-8093
Ultimate Parent: Walgreen Co.

★ 83066 ★ Washington Inventory
Servic
1106 Clayton Ln.
Austin, TX 78723
(512)458-3132
Ultimate Parent: Huffy. SIC: 8721—
Accounting, Auditing & Bookkeeping.

★ 83067 ★ Washington Inventory
Service
8711 Burnet Rd.
Austin, TX 78758
(512)458-3132
Ultimate Parent: Huffy. SIC: 8721—
Accounting, Auditing & Bookkeeping.

★ 83068 ★ Washington Post
Newspaper
Littlefield Bldg.
Austin, TX 78701
(512)473-2291
Ultimate Parent: Washington Post. SIC:
2711—Newspapers.

★ 83069 ★ Western Auto Supply
Co.
137 W. Oltorf St.
Austin, TX 78704
(512)442-7851
Ultimate Parent: Sears Roebuck & Co.
SIC: 5531—Automobile & Home Supply
Stores.

★ 83070 ★ Western Auto Supply
Co.
9316 N. Lamar Blvd.
Austin, TX 78753
(512)837-9991
Ultimate Parent: Sears Roebuck & Co.
SIC: 5531—Automobile & Home Supply
Stores.

★ 83071 ★ Western Digital Corp.
9442 Capitol of Texas Hwy.
Austin, TX 78746
(512)343-8544
Ultimate Parent: Western Digital. SIC:
7629—Electrical Repair Shops Nec.

★ 83072 ★ Xerox Business
Services
1321 Rutherford Ln.
Austin, TX 78753
(512)834-4900
Officer: John Oldham, Manager. Ultimate
Parent: Xerox Corp. SIC: 2752—
Commercial Printing—Lithographic.

★ 83073 ★   **Xerox Corp.**
6836 Austin Ctr. Blvd.
Austin, TX 78731
(512)343-5600
Officer: Denise Evers, Manager. **Ultimate Parent:** Xerox Corp. **SIC:** 3663—Radio & T.V. Communications Equipment.

★ 83074 ★   **Zenger-Miller & Associates**
Huntland
Austin, TX 78752
(512)453-2954
Ultimate Parent: Times Mirror Co. **SIC:** 8742—Management Consulting Services.

★ 83075 ★   **Zep Manufacturing Co.**
8105 Ripplewood Dr.
Austin, TX 78758
(512)453-7929
Ultimate Parent: National Service Industries. **SIC:** 2842—Polishes & Sanitation Goods.

★ 83076 ★   **Kentucky Fried Chicken**
8240 N. Missouri Pacifc Expy.
Austin Texas, TX 78731
(512)346-7250
Ultimate Parent: Pepsico. **SIC:** 5812—Eating Places.

Austria

★ 83077 ★   **Hamilton Hallmark**
1826-F Kramer Ln.
Austria, TX 78758
(512)837-8911
Location Type: Branch office. **Ultimate Parent:** Avnet. **SIC:** 5065—Electronic Parts & Equipment Nec.

Avinger

★ 83078 ★   **Mobil Oil Corp.**
Hwy. 155
Avinger, TX 75630
(903)562-1176
Company Type: Branch. **Ultimate Parent:** Mobil. **SIC:** 1311—Crude Petroleum & Natural Gas.

Azle

★ 83079 ★   **Lika Southwest**
200 Commerce St.
Azle, TX 76020
Ultimate Parent: Tandy Corp. **SIC:** 3672—Printed Circuit Boards.

★ 83080 ★   **McDonalds Restaurant**
597 Northwest Pky.
Azle, TX 76020
(817)444-1696
Ultimate Parent: McDonald's.
SIC: 5812—Eating Places.

★ 83081 ★   **Radio Shack**
Park Plz.
Azle, TX 76020
(817)444-1145
Company Type: Division. **Ultimate Parent:** Tandy Corp. **SIC:** 5065—Electronic Parts & Equipment Nec.

★ 83082 ★   **Tandy**
922 PO Box
Azle, TX 76020
(817)444-2571
Ultimate Parent: Tandy Corp. **SIC:** 3679—Electronic Components Nec.

★ 83083 ★   **Tandy Electronics**
200 Commerce St.
Azle, TX 76020
(817)444-2571
Officer: Robert M. McClure, President. **Ultimate Parent:** Tandy Corp. **SIC:** 3672—Printed Circuit Boards.

Bacliff

★ 83084 ★   **Southern Pacific Railroad**
Hwy. 146
Bacliff, TX 77518
(713)339-2032
Ultimate Parent: Southern Pacific Rail. **SIC:** 4011—Railroads—Line-Haul Operating.

Balch Springs

★ 83085 ★   **Comerica Bank-Texas**
4030 Pioneer Rd.
Balch Springs, TX 75180-3013
(214)557-0900
Company Type: Subsidiary. **Location Type:** Branch office. **Ultimate Parent:** Comerica Bank. **SIC:** 6021—National Commercial Banks.

Ballinger

★ 83086 ★   **Lone Star Gas Co.**
PO Box 579
Ballinger, TX 76821
(915)365-2592
Ultimate Parent: Enserch.

★ 83087 ★   **Lone Star Gas Co.**
Ballinger, TX 76821
(915)365-3311
Ultimate Parent: Enserch.

★ 83088 ★   **Lone Star Gas Co.**
Ave
Ballinger, TX 76821
(915)365-2116
Ultimate Parent: Enserch.

★ 83089 ★   **Piggly Wiggly**
108 7th
Ballinger, TX 76821
(915)365-3313
Ultimate Parent: Bruno's. **SIC:** 5411—Grocery Stores; 5421—Meat & Fish Markets.

★ 83090 ★   **Ryder Truck Rental**
Hwy. 67 S
Ballinger, TX 76821
(915)365-5878
Ultimate Parent: Ryder System.

★ 83091 ★   **Shell Oil Co.**
509 Park Ave.
Ballinger, TX 76821
(915)365-3211
Ultimate Parent: Shell Oil Co. **SIC:** 5984—Liquefied Petroleum Gas Dealers.

★ 83092 ★   **Texaco Inc.**
13th
Ballinger, TX 76821
(915)365-2231
Ultimate Parent: Texaco. **SIC:** 5172—Petroleum Products Nec.

★ 83093 ★   **Wal Mart**
Ballinger, TX 76821
(915)365-5731
Ultimate Parent: Wal-Mart Stores, Inc.

Bandera

★ 83094 ★   **Mobil Diesel Service**
Hwy. 173
Bandera, TX 78003
(512)796-4858
Ultimate Parent: Mobil. **SIC:** 7699—Repair Services Nec.

Bastrop

★ 83095 ★   **Exxon**
105 Hwy. 71
Bastrop, TX 78602
(512)321-2330
Ultimate Parent: Exxon.

★ 83096 ★   **McDonalds Restaurant**
496 Hwy. 71
Bastrop, TX 78602
(512)321-1591
Ultimate Parent: McDonald's.

★ 83097 ★   **Ryder Truck Rental**
Hwy. 71 W
Bastrop, TX 78602
(512)321-2217
Ultimate Parent: Ryder System. **SIC:** 7359—Equipment Rental & Leasing Nec.

Bay City

★ 83098 ★   **First State Bank & Trust Co.**
1916 7th St.
Bay City, TX 77414-5191
(409)245-5781
Location Type: Branch office. **Ultimate Parent:** Michigan National Corp. **SIC:** 6021—National Commercial Banks.

★ 83099 ★   **Hoechst-Celanese Chemical Group Inc.**
Fm 3057 PO Box 509
Bay City, TX 77404-0509
Ultimate Parent: Hoechst Celanese Corp. **SIC:** 2869—Industrial Organic Chemicals Nec.

★ 83100 ★   **Hoechst Celanese Chemical Group Inc.**
PO Box 509, Fm 3057 Bay City Plant
Bay City, TX 77414
Ultimate Parent: Hoechst Celanese Corp. **SIC:** 2869—Industrial Organic Chemicals Nec.

★ 83101 ★   **Kentucky Fried Chicken**
3716 7th St.
Bay City, TX 77414
(409)244-8444
Ultimate Parent: Pepsico. **SIC:** 5812—Eating Places.

★ 83102 ★   **Marathon Oil Co.**
Wharton Hwy.
Bay City, TX 77414
(409)245-9186
Ultimate Parent: USX Corp. **SIC:** 1311—Crude Petroleum & Natural Gas.

★ 83103 ★   **Marathon Oil Co.**
Wharton Hwy.
Bay City, TX 77414
(409)245-9186
Ultimate Parent: USX Corp. **SIC:** 1311—Crude Petroleum & Natural Gas.

★ 83104 ★   **Pepsi-Cola South**
1800 Marguerite St.
Bay City, TX 77414
(409)245-5777
Ultimate Parent: Pepsico. **SIC:** 5199—Nondurable Goods Nec.

★ 83105 ★   **Trailways Inc.**
2005 Avenue F
Bay City, TX 77414
(409)245-2062
Ultimate Parent: Greyhound Lines Inc. **SIC:** 4131—Intercity & Rural Bus Transportation.

Baytown

★ 83106 ★   **Air Products & Chemicals, Inc.**
8524 W. Bay Rd.
Baytown, TX 77520
(713)383-3435
Ultimate Parent: Air Products & Chemicals, Inc. **SIC:** 3999—Manufacturing Industries Nec.

★ 83107 ★   **Allenbrook Healthcare Center**
4109 Allenbrook Dr.
Baytown, TX 77521-3299
(713)422-3546
Officer: Don Baker. **Ultimate Parent:** Beverly Enterprises. **SIC:** 8059—Nursing & Personal Care Nec.

★ 83108 ★   **Casual Corner**
1408 San Jacinto Mall
Baytown, TX 77521
(713)421-5853
Ultimate Parent: United States Shoe. **SIC:** 5651—Family Clothing Stores.

★ 83109 ★   **Chevron Chemical Co.**
9500 Interstate 10 E
Baytown, TX 77521
Ultimate Parent: Chevron Corp. **SIC:** 2869—Industrial Organic Chemicals Nec;

2821—Plastics Materials & Resins; 2895—Carbon Black.

★ 83110 ★   **Circus World**
1764 San Jacinto Mall
Baytown, TX 77521
Ultimate Parent: Melville.

★ 83111 ★   **Exxon**
6203 Decker Dr.
Baytown, TX 77520
(713)424-1041
Ultimate Parent: Exxon. **SIC:** 5541—Gasoline Service Stations.

★ 83112 ★   **Exxon Chemical Americas**
13330 Hatcherville Rd.
Baytown, TX 77521
(713)428-9400
Officer: Robert L. Tusch, Manager. **Ultimate Parent:** Exxon. **SIC:** 2821—Plastics Materials & Resins; 3089—Plastics Products Nec.

★ 83113 ★   **Exxon Chemical Co.**
3525 Decker Dr.
Baytown, TX 77520
(713)428-6161
Location Type: Plant. **Officer:** Doug Walker, Plant Manager. **Ultimate Parent:** Exxon. **SIC:** 2911—Petroleum Refining.

★ 83114 ★   **Exxon Chemical Co.**
5000 Bayway Dr.
Baytown, TX 77520
(713)425-1000
Officer: Ray Floyd, Manager. **Ultimate Parent:** Exxon. **SIC:** 2821—Plastics Materials & Resins; 2822—Synthetic Rubber; 2869—Industrial Organic Chemicals Nec.

★ 83115 ★   **Exxon Chemical Co.**
4500 Bayway Dr.
Baytown, TX 77520
(713)425-5036
Ultimate Parent: Exxon.

★ 83116 ★   **Exxon Chemical Plant**
4004 PO Box
Baytown, TX 77520
(713)425-1000
Ultimate Parent: Exxon. **SIC:** 2821—Plastics Materials & Resins.

★ 83117 ★   **Exxon Co. Refinery Library**
2800 Decker Dr.
Baytown, TX 77520
(713)427-5711
Ultimate Parent: Exxon. **SIC:** 8231—Libraries.

★ 83118 ★   **Exxon Co. USA**
Pt Barrow
Baytown, TX 77520
(713)573-1532
Ultimate Parent: Exxon. **SIC:** 1311—Crude Petroleum & Natural Gas.

★ 83119 ★   **Exxon Co. USA**
Goose Creek Oil Fiel
Baytown, TX 77521
(713)422-3425
Ultimate Parent: Exxon. **SIC:** 1311—Crude Petroleum & Natural Gas.

★ 83120 ★   **Exxon Co. USA**
2800 Decker Dr.
Baytown, TX 77520
(713)425-3300
Officer: Ben Markham, Manager. **Ultimate Parent:** Exxon. **SIC:** 2819—Industrial Inorganic Chemicals Nec; 2911—Petroleum Refining; 2992—Lubricating Oils & Greases.

★ 83121 ★   **Exxon Corp.**
13330 Hatcherville Rd.
Baytown, TX 77521
(713)428-9400
Ultimate Parent: Exxon. **SIC:** 3861—Photographic Equipment & Supplies.

★ 83122 ★   **Exxon Corp.**
4001 Garth Rd.
Baytown, TX 77521
(713)427-5721
Ultimate Parent: Exxon. **SIC:** 2911—Petroleum Refining.

★ 83123 ★   **Foot Action**
1142 San Jacinto Mall
Baytown, TX 77521
(713)421-4574
Ultimate Parent: Melville. **SIC:** 5699—
Miscellaneous Apparel & Accessory Stores.

★ 83124 ★   **The Gap**
1740 San Jacinto Mall
Baytown, TX 77521
(713)420-3586
Ultimate Parent: GAP. **SIC:** 5621—
Women's Clothing Stores.

★ 83125 ★   **Hertz Rent-A-Car**
2007 N. Main St.
Baytown, TX 77520
(713)420-1645
Ultimate Parent: Hertz. **SIC:** 7514—
Passenger Car Rental.

★ 83126 ★   **J. M. Huber Corp.
Baytown Carbon Plant**
9300 Needlepoint Rd.
Baytown, TX 77521
Ultimate Parent: J. M. Huber. **SIC:** 2895—
Carbon Black.

★ 83127 ★   **J.M. Huber Baytown
Carbon Plant**
9300 Needlepoint Rd.
Baytown, TX 77521
Ultimate Parent: J. M. Huber. **SIC:** 2895—
Carbon Black.

★ 83128 ★   **J.M. Huber Carbon
Plant**
9300 Needlepoint Rd.
Baytown, TX 77521
Ultimate Parent: J. M. Huber. **SIC:** 2895—
Carbon Black.

★ 83129 ★   **Kay Bee Toy Shop**
1764 San Jacinto Mall
Baytown, TX 77521
(713)428-7686
Ultimate Parent: Melville. **SIC:** 5945—
Hobby, Toy & Game Shops.

★ 83130 ★   **Kentucky Fried
Chicken**
2206 N. Alexander Dr.
Baytown, TX 77520
(713)427-5201
Ultimate Parent: Pepsico. **SIC:** 5812—
Eating Places.

★ 83131 ★   **Lerner Shop**
1086 San Jacinto Mall
Baytown, TX 77521
(713)422-4601
Ultimate Parent: Limited. **SIC:** 5621—
Women's Clothing Stores.

★ 83132 ★   **Pizza Hut**
1301 Garth Rd.
Baytown, TX 77520
(713)427-6313
Ultimate Parent: Pepsico. **SIC:** 5812—
Eating Places.

★ 83133 ★   **Radio Shack**
1052 San Jacinto Mall
Baytown, TX 77521
(713)420-3515
Company Type: Division. **Ultimate Parent:**
Tandy Corp. **SIC:** 5731—Radio, Television
& Electronics Stores.

★ 83134 ★   **Radio Shack**
4112 Decker Dr.
Baytown, TX 77520
(713)424-1341
Company Type: Division. **Ultimate Parent:**
Tandy Corp. **SIC:** 5065—Electronic Parts &
Equipment Nec.

★ 83135 ★   **Radio Shack**
706 N. Alexander Dr.
Baytown, TX 77520
(713)427-6169
Company Type: Division. **Ultimate Parent:**
Tandy Corp. **SIC:** 5065—Electronic Parts &
Equipment Nec.

★ 83136 ★   **Rhone Poulenc Basic
Chemical**
3439 Park St.
Baytown, TX 77520
(713)427-7413
Officer: Brett Jacks, Manager. **Ultimate
Parent:** Rhone-Poulenc Rorer. **SIC:** 2819—
Industrial Inorganic Chemicals Nec.

★ 83137 ★   **Rhone-Poulenc Basic
Chemicals Co.**
3439 Park St.
Baytown, TX 77520
Ultimate Parent: Rhone-Poulenc Rorer.
SIC: 2819—Industrial Inorganic Chemicals
Nec.

★ 83138 ★   **Ryder Truck Rental**
2101 Market St.
Baytown, TX 77520
(713)428-2042
Ultimate Parent: Ryder System. **SIC:**
7513—Truck Rental & Leasing Without
Drivers.

★ 83139 ★   **Taco Bell**
1117 N. Alexander Dr.
Baytown, TX 77520
(713)422-2932
Ultimate Parent: Pepsico. **SIC:** 5812—
Eating Places.

★ 83140 ★   **Taco Bell**
1925 Garth Rd.
Baytown, TX 77520
(713)427-2461
Ultimate Parent: Pepsico. **SIC:** 5812—
Eating Places.

★ 83141 ★   **Waldenbooks**
San Jacinto Mall
Baytown, TX 77521
(713)422-5902
Ultimate Parent: K-Mart. **SIC:** 5942—Book
Stores.

Beasley

★ 83142 ★   **Hudson Products
Corp.**
Hwy. 59 & Grunwald Rd.
Beasley, TX 77417
Ultimate Parent: McDermott. **SIC:** 3443—
Fabricated Plate Work—Boiler Shops.

Beaumont

★ 83143 ★   **Betz Laboratories Inc.**
10650 Hwy. 90 W.
Beaumont, TX 77713
Ultimate Parent: Betz Laboratories Inc.
SIC: 2899—Chemical Preparations Nec.

★ 83144 ★   **Betz Laboratories Inc.**
10650 Hwy. 90 W
Beaumont, TX 77713
(409)866-4778
Location Type: Branch office. **Officer:** Jack
McAughan. **Ultimate Parent:** Betz
Laboratories Inc. **SIC:** 2819—Industrial
Inorganic Chemicals Nec; 2899—Chemical
Preparations Nec.

★ 83145 ★   **Betz Process
Chemicals Inc.**
1690 N. Major Dr., 101
Beaumont, TX 77713-8510
(409)832-0251
Officer: Victor Lovett. **Ultimate Parent:**
Betz Laboratories Inc. **SIC:** 2899—Chemical
Preparations Nec.

★ 83146 ★   **Betz Process
Chemicals Inc.**
2360 Calder St.
Beaumont, TX 77702
(409)832-0251
Ultimate Parent: Betz Laboratories Inc.
SIC: 3861—Photographic Equipment &
Supplies.

★ 83147 ★   **Betz Process
Chemicals, Inc.**
2345 I E
Beaumont, TX 77701
(409)832-0251
Ultimate Parent: Betz Laboratories Inc.
SIC: 2899—Chemical Preparations Nec.

★ 83148 ★   **Casual Corner**
Parkdale Mall
Beaumont, TX 77706
(409)898-2725
Ultimate Parent: United States Shoe. **SIC:**
5621—Women's Clothing Stores; 5651—
Family Clothing Stores.

★ 83149 ★   **Dow Jones & Co.**
5355 W. Cardinal Dr.
Beaumont, TX 77705
(409)842-3107
Officer: Paul Cousineau, Manager.

Ultimate Parent: Dow Jones. **SIC:** 2711—
Newspapers; 2721—Periodicals; 2752—
Commercial Printing—Lithographic.

★ 83150 ★   **Ecco Inc.**
1159 Park Meadow Dr.
Beaumont, TX 77706
Ultimate Parent: Itel.

★ 83151 ★   **Exxon Co. USA**
3160 Fannin St.
Beaumont, TX 77701
(409)838-6369
Ultimate Parent: Exxon. **SIC:** 5171—
Petroleum Bulk Stations & Terminals.

★ 83152 ★   **The Gap**
6155 Eastex Fwy.
Beaumont, TX 77706
(409)899-5622
Ultimate Parent: GAP.

★ 83153 ★   **The Gap**
6155 Parkdale Mall
Beaumont, TX 77706
(409)899-5622
Ultimate Parent: GAP. **SIC:** 5651—Family
Clothing Stores.

★ 83154 ★   **Goodyear Tire &
Rubber Co.**
I-10 at Smith Rd.
Beaumont, TX 77705
Ultimate Parent: Goodyear Tire & Rubber.
SIC: 2822—Synthetic Rubber; 2821—
Plastics Materials & Resins; 2869—
Industrial Organic Chemicals Nec.

★ 83155 ★   **Goodyear Tire &
Rubber Co. Beaumont Chemical
Plant**
Interstate 10 & Smith Rd.
Beaumont, TX 77705
Ultimate Parent: Goodyear Tire & Rubber.
SIC: 2822—Synthetic Rubber; 2821—
Plastics Materials & Resins; 2869—
Industrial Organic Chemicals Nec.

★ 83156 ★   **Greyhound Bus Lines**
650 Magnolia St.
Beaumont, TX 77701
(409)832-2559
Ultimate Parent: Greyhound Lines Inc. **SIC:**
4212—Local Trucking Without Storage.

★ 83157 ★   **Gulf State Utilities Co.**
350 Pine St.
Beaumont, TX 77701
(409)838-6631
Company Type: Headquarters. **Officer:**
Joseph L. Donnelly. **Employee Count:**
4765. **Fortune Service 500:** Ranking 35.

★ 83158 ★   **Gulf States Utilities
Co.**
Helbig Rd.
Beaumont, TX 77708
(409)892-1421
Ultimate Parent: Gulf State Utilities Co.

★ 83159 ★   **Gulf States Utilities
Co. Inc.**
350 Pine St.
Beaumont, TX 77701-2437
(409)838-6631
Officer: Joseph L Donnelly, President,
Chairman of the Board & CEO. **Ultimate
Parent:** Gulf State Utilities Co. **Employee
Count:** 4841. **Sales:** 2 M.

★ 83160 ★   **Hit or Miss**
5880 Eastex Fwy.
Beaumont, TX 77708
(409)892-0105
Ultimate Parent: TJX. **SIC:** 5621—
Women's Clothing Stores; 5651—Family
Clothing Stores.

★ 83161 ★   **IBM Corp.**
2825 N. 10th St.
Beaumont, TX 77703
(409)899-8300
Ultimate Parent: IBM. **SIC:** 5046—
Commercial Equipment Nec.

★ 83162 ★   **Kay Bee Toys**
6155 Eastex Fwy.
Beaumont, TX 77706
(409)892-0606
Ultimate Parent: Melville. **SIC:** 5999—
Miscellaneous Retail Stores Nec.

★ 83163 ★   **Kay Bee Toys &
Hobby**
6155 Parkdale Mall
Beaumont, TX 77706
(409)899-5900
Ultimate Parent: Melville. **SIC:** 5945—
Hobby, Toy & Game Shops.

★ 83164 ★   **Kentucky Fried
Chicken**
3970 E. Lucas Dr.
Beaumont, TX 77708
(409)892-1756
Ultimate Parent: Pepsico. **SIC:** 5812—
Eating Places.

★ 83165 ★   **Kentucky Fried
Chicken**
6750 Calder St.
Beaumont, TX 77706
(409)866-4321
Ultimate Parent: Pepsico. **SIC:** 5812—
Eating Places.

★ 83166 ★   **Kentucky Fried
Chicken**
3297 College St.
Beaumont, TX 77701
(409)833-4888
Ultimate Parent: Pepsico. **SIC:** 5812—
Eating Places.

★ 83167 ★   **Kmart Discount
Stores**
5845 Eastex Fwy.
Beaumont, TX 77706
(409)899-3690
Ultimate Parent: K-Mart.

★ 83168 ★   **Lane Bryant**
6155 Parkdale Mall
Beaumont, TX 77706
(409)899-5819
Ultimate Parent: Limited. **SIC:** 5651—
Family Clothing Stores.

★ 83169 ★   **Lerner Shop**
126 Gateway St.
Beaumont, TX 77701
(409)838-6042
Ultimate Parent: Limited. **SIC:** 5311—
Department Stores.

★ 83170 ★   **Lerner Shop**
6155 Parkdale Mall
Beaumont, TX 77706
(409)898-3926
Ultimate Parent: Limited. **SIC:** 5621—
Women's Clothing Stores; 5651—Family
Clothing Stores.

★ 83171 ★   **Liberty Mutual
Insurance Co.**
2570 Sweetgum Ln.
Beaumont, TX 77703
(409)899-1461
Ultimate Parent: Liberty Mutual Group.
SIC: 6411—Insurance Agents, Brokers &
Service.

★ 83172 ★   **The Limited**
6155 Parkdale Mall
Beaumont, TX 77706
(409)899-5624
Ultimate Parent: Limited. **SIC:** 5651—
Family Clothing Stores.

★ 83173 ★   **The Limited Express**
6155 Parkdale Mall
Beaumont, TX 77706
(409)898-8602
Ultimate Parent: Limited. **SIC:** 5651—
Family Clothing Stores.

★ 83174 ★   **Manpower, Inc.**
1255 Broadway St.
Beaumont, TX 77701
(409)835-0241
Ultimate Parent: Manpower, Inc. **SIC:**
7363—Help Supply Services.

★ 83175 ★   **Mary Kay Cosmetics**
7525 Chelsea Pl.
Beaumont, TX 77706
(409)866-5600
Ultimate Parent: Mary Kay Cosmetics. **SIC:**
6531—Real Estate Agents & Managers.

★ 83176 ★   **May Supply Co.**
5395 College St.
Beaumont, TX 77707
(409)842-3431
Ultimate Parent: WLR Foods. **SIC:** 1711—
Plumbing, Heating & Air-Conditioning;
5075—Warm Air Heating & Air-Conditioning.

★ 83177 ★ Mobil Chemical
Petroleum Div.
3868 PO Box
Beaumont, TX 77704
(409)838-6532
Ultimate Parent: Mobil. SIC: 2911—
Petroleum Refining.

★ 83178 ★ Mobil Chemical Co.
PO Box 3868
Beaumont, TX 77704-3868
(409)838-6532
Company Type: Branch. Officer: J. M.
Rieker. Ultimate Parent: Mobil. SIC:
2869—Industrial Organic Chemicals Nec.

★ 83179 ★ Mobil Chemical Co.
Olefins/Aromatics Plant
Gulf States County Rd.
Beaumont, TX 77704
Location Type: Plant. Ultimate Parent:
Mobil. SIC: 2869—Industrial Organic
Chemicals Nec.

★ 83180 ★ Mobil Chemical Co.
Bcsp
Gulf States County Rd.
Beaumont, TX 77704
Ultimate Parent: Mobil. SIC: 2869—
Industrial Organic Chemicals Nec; 2819—
Industrial Inorganic Chemicals Nec; 2821—
Plastics Materials & Resins; 2992—
Lubricating Oils & Greases.

★ 83181 ★ Mobil Oil
Beaumont Refinery
E. End of Burt St.
Beaumont, TX 77701
Company Type: Division. Ultimate Parent:
Mobil. SIC: 2911—Petroleum Refining.

★ 83182 ★ Mobil Oil Corp.
PO Box 3311
Beaumont, TX 77704-3311
(409)833-9411
Officer: B. H. Blackmon. Ultimate Parent:
Mobil. SIC: 2911—Petroleum Refining;
2992—Lubricating Oils & Greases.

★ 83183 ★ Mobil Oil Corp.
S Beaumont
Beaumont, TX 77708
(409)833-9411
Ultimate Parent: Mobil. SIC: 2911—
Petroleum Refining.

★ 83184 ★ Mobil Oil Federal
Credit Un
2250 Groves St.
Beaumont, TX 77701
(409)838-2691
Ultimate Parent: Mobil. SIC: 6099—
Functions Related to Deposit Banking.

★ 83185 ★ Mobil Oil Refining Div
3311 PO Box
Beaumont, TX 77704
(409)833-9411
Ultimate Parent: Mobil. SIC: 2911—
Petroleum Refining.

★ 83186 ★ Mobil Pipe Line
1311 E. Florida Ave.
Beaumont, TX 77705
(409)835-5222
Ultimate Parent: Mobil.

★ 83187 ★ Mobil Pipe Line Co.
87 Interstate N. 10
Beaumont, TX 77707
(409)835-7047
Ultimate Parent: Mobil. SIC: 4619—
Pipelines Nec.

★ 83188 ★ Mobil Pipe Line Co.
87 Interstate 10 N. Ste. 125
Beaumont, TX 77707-2542
(409)835-7047
Officer: Francis L. Johns. Ultimate Parent:
Mobil. SIC: 4619—Pipelines Nec.

★ 83189 ★ Neches River
Treatment Corp.
Lower Neches Valley Authority
Gulf States Rd.
Beaumont, TX 77705
Company Type: Division. Ultimate Parent:
Mobil. SIC: 2911—Petroleum Refining;
2869—Industrial Organic Chemicals Nec.

★ 83190 ★ New York Life
Beaumont Sales Office
Houston General Office
550 Fannin St., Ste. 1330
Beaumont, TX 77701
(409)838-6405
Officer: Sterling Arceneaux, Sales
Manager. Ultimate Parent: New York Life.

★ 83191 ★ Olin Chemicals Group
1400 Olin Rd.
Beaumont, TX 77705
(409)835-6641
Officer: Dave Maneman, Manager.
Ultimate Parent: Olin Corp. SIC: 2819—
Industrial Inorganic Chemicals Nec; 2899—
Chemical Preparations Nec.

★ 83192 ★ Olin Corp.
1400 Olin Rd.
Beaumont, TX 77705
Ultimate Parent: Olin Corp. SIC: 2819—
Industrial Inorganic Chemicals Nec; 2873—
Nitrogenous Fertilizers.

★ 83193 ★ Olin Corp.
Beaumont Plant
1400 Olin Rd.
Beaumont, TX 77705
Location Type: Plant. Ultimate Parent:
Olin Corp. SIC: 2819—Industrial Inorganic
Chemicals Nec; 2873—Nitrogenous
Fertilizers.

★ 83194 ★ P D Glycol
Gulf States Rd.
Beaumont, TX 77704
Ultimate Parent: Occidental Petroleum
Corp. SIC: 2869—Industrial Organic
Chemicals Nec.

★ 83195 ★ Pd Glycol
Gulf States Rd.
Beaumont, TX 77704
Ultimate Parent: Occidental Petroleum
Corp. SIC: 2869—Industrial Organic
Chemicals Nec.

★ 83196 ★ Pennzoil Co.
2650 Calder St.
Beaumont, TX 77702
(409)838-5145
Ultimate Parent: Pennzoil. SIC: 5171—
Petroleum Bulk Stations & Terminals.

★ 83197 ★ Pepsi-Cola Bottling
Co.
2750 W. Cardinal Dr.
Beaumont, TX 77705
(409)842-2111
Officer: David Waddell, Manager. Ultimate
Parent: Pepsico. SIC: 2086—Bottled &
Canned Soft Drinks.

★ 83198 ★ Petite Sophisticate
6155 Parkdale Mall
Beaumont, TX 77706
(409)898-2544
Ultimate Parent: United States Shoe. SIC:
5651—Family Clothing Stores.

★ 83199 ★ Piggly Wiggly
3295 College St.
Beaumont, TX 77701
(409)832-2857
Ultimate Parent: Bruno's. SIC: 5411—
Grocery Stores.

★ 83200 ★ Pizza Hut
175 Dowlen Rd.
Beaumont, TX 77706
(409)860-1955
Ultimate Parent: Pepsico. SIC: 5812—
Eating Places.

★ 83201 ★ Pizza Hut
5655 Eastex Fwy.
Beaumont, TX 77706
(409)898-0274
Ultimate Parent: Pepsico. SIC: 5812—
Eating Places.

★ 83202 ★ Pizza Hut
Parkway Plz.
Beaumont, TX 77701
(409)898-0274
Ultimate Parent: Pepsico. SIC: 5812—
Eating Places.

★ 83203 ★ Pizza Hut
3820 College St.
Beaumont, TX 77701
(409)832-8608
Ultimate Parent: Pepsico. SIC: 5812—
Eating Places.

★ 83204 ★ Ppg Industries Inc.
Gulf States Rd.
Beaumont, TX 77701
(409)838-4521
Ultimate Parent: PPG Industries Inc. SIC:
2819—Industrial Inorganic Chemicals Nec.

★ 83205 ★ Radio Shack
6155 Parkdale Mall
Beaumont, TX 77706
(409)898-0320
Company Type: Division. Ultimate Parent:
Tandy Corp. SIC: 5065—Electronic Parts &
Equipment Nec.

★ 83206 ★ Radio Shack
5050 College St.
Beaumont, TX 77707
(409)842-2424
Company Type: Division. Ultimate Parent:
Tandy Corp. SIC: 5065—Electronic Parts &
Equipment Nec; 5112—Stationery & Office
Supplies.

★ 83207 ★ Radio Shack
130 Gateway St.
Beaumont, TX 77701
Company Type: Division. Ultimate Parent:
Tandy Corp. SIC: 5065—Electronic Parts &
Equipment Nec.

★ 83208 ★ Radio Shack
4785 Concord Rd.
Beaumont, TX 77703
(409)892-0692
Company Type: Division. Ultimate Parent:
Tandy Corp. SIC: 5731—Radio, Television
& Electronics Stores.

★ 83209 ★ Radio Shack
5050 College St.
Beaumont, TX 77707
Company Type: Division. Ultimate Parent:
Tandy Corp. SIC: 5065—Electronic Parts &
Equipment Nec.

★ 83210 ★ Ryder Truck Rental
7425 Westpark Dr.
Beaumont, TX 77706
(409)842-0366
Ultimate Parent: Ryder System. SIC:
7513—Truck Rental & Leasing Without
Drivers.

★ 83211 ★ Sam's Wholesale
Club
1615 Interstate S. 10
Beaumont, TX 77701
(409)842-5071
Ultimate Parent: Wal-Mart Stores, Inc.

★ 83212 ★ Savings of America,
FSB
6150 Eastex Fwy.
Beaumont, TX 77708-4499
(409)898-2127
Company Type: Division. Location Type:
Branch office. Ultimate Parent: H. F.
Ahmanson. SIC: 6021—National
Commercial Banks.

★ 83213 ★ Service Merchandise
4450 Dowlen Rd.
Beaumont, TX 77706
(409)898-4000
Ultimate Parent: Service Merchandise Co.,
Inc. SIC: 5944—Jewelry Stores.

★ 83214 ★ Standard Register Co.
85 Interstate 10 N
Beaumont, TX 77707
(713)961-0200
Officer: Mike Kondelis, Manager. Ultimate
Parent: Standard Register. SIC: 2759—
Commercial Printing Nec; 2761—Manifold
Business Forms.

★ 83215 ★ Taco Bell
597 S. 11th St.
Beaumont, TX 77701
(409)835-4402
Ultimate Parent: Pepsico. SIC: 5812—
Eating Places.

★ 83216 ★ Taco Bell
6155 Parkdale Mall
Beaumont, TX 77706
(409)892-6314
Ultimate Parent: Pepsico. SIC: 5812—
Eating Places.

★ 83217 ★ Taco Bell
6475 Phelan Blvd.
Beaumont, TX 77706
(409)866-3025
Ultimate Parent: Pepsico. SIC: 5812—
Eating Places.

★ 83218 ★ Taco Bell
4325 E. Lucas Dr.
Beaumont, TX 77708
(409)892-1587
Ultimate Parent: Pepsico. SIC: 5812—
Eating Places.

★ 83219 ★ Tandy Corp. Del
4235 Calder Ave.
Beaumont, TX 77706
(409)892-4589
Ultimate Parent: Tandy Corp. SIC: 5199—
Nondurable Goods Nec.

★ 83220 ★ Texaco Food Mart
3850 Interstate S. 10
Beaumont, TX 77705
(409)842-1414
Ultimate Parent: Texaco.

★ 83221 ★ Texaco Food Mart
7395 Hwy. 105
Beaumont, TX 77713
(409)892-6821
Ultimate Parent: Texaco.

★ 83222 ★ Texaco Food Mart
1195 Interstate S. 10
Beaumont, TX 77701
(409)835-0452
Ultimate Parent: Texaco.

★ 83223 ★ Texaco Food Mart No
2
190 N. Major Dr.
Beaumont, TX 77707
(409)866-0488
Ultimate Parent: Texaco. SIC: 5411—
Grocery Stores.

★ 83224 ★ Texaco Service
Station
12034 PO Box
Beaumont, TX 77726
(409)838-5351
Ultimate Parent: Texaco. SIC: 5541—
Gasoline Service Stations.

★ 83225 ★ Texaco Station
1755 E. Cardinal Dr.
Beaumont, TX 77705
(409)833-2101
Ultimate Parent: Texaco. SIC: 5541—
Gasoline Service Stations.

★ 83226 ★ Toys R US
5910 Eastex Fwy.
Beaumont, TX 77708
(409)898-8586
Ultimate Parent: Toys "R" US. SIC: 5641—
Children's & Infants' Wear Stores; 5945—
Hobby, Toy & Game Shops.

★ 83227 ★ Trailways Bus
Systems
1076 Calder St.
Beaumont, TX 77701
(409)835-4523
Ultimate Parent: Greyhound Lines Inc. SIC:
4131—Intercity & Rural Bus Transportation.

★ 83228 ★ Unisys Corp.
85 Interstate N. 10
Beaumont, TX 77707
(409)833-9604
Ultimate Parent: Unisys Corp. SIC: 8711—
Engineering Services.

★ 83229 ★ United Parcel Service
3755 Washington Blvd.
Beaumont, TX 77705
(409)842-5879
Ultimate Parent: United Parcel Service of
America. SIC: 4215—Courier Services
Except by Air.

★ 83230 ★ Valspar Corp.
1700 Deucette St.
Beaumont, TX 77701
(409)832-5528
Officer: Bill Cease, Manager. Ultimate
Parent: Valspar Corp. SIC: 2851—Paints &
Allied Products.

★ 83231 ★ **Valspar Corp.**
Beaumont
1700 Doucette St.
Beaumont, TX 77701
Ultimate Parent: Valspar Corp. **SIC:**
2851—Paints & Allied Products.

★ 83232 ★ **Volunteer State Life**
Insurance Co.
2670 Laurel St.
Beaumont, TX 77702
(409)832-6501
Ultimate Parent: Chubb. **SIC:** 6411—
Insurance Agents, Brokers & Service.

★ 83233 ★ **Wal Mart Discount**
City
3955 Eastex Fwy.
Beaumont, TX 77706
(409)899-3618
Ultimate Parent: Wal-Mart Stores, Inc. **SIC:**
5399—Miscellaneous General Merchandise
Store.

★ 83234 ★ **Waldenbooks**
Parkdale Mall
Beaumont, TX 77706
(409)898-1673
Ultimate Parent: K-Mart. **SIC:** 5942—Book
Stores.

★ 83235 ★ **Walgreen Drug Stores**
229 Dowlen Rd.
Beaumont, TX 77706
(409)860-4411
Ultimate Parent: Walgreen Co. **SIC:**
5912—Drug Stores & Proprietary Stores.

★ 83236 ★ **Walgreen Drug Stores**
6155 Parkdale Mall
Beaumont, TX 77706
(409)898-2727
Ultimate Parent: Walgreen Co. **SIC:**
5912—Drug Stores & Proprietary Stores.

★ 83237 ★ **Washington Inventory**
Service
2490 I E
Beaumont, TX 77701
(409)892-8969
Ultimate Parent: Huffy. **SIC:** 8721—
Accounting, Auditing & Bookkeeping.

Bedford

★ 83238 ★ **Ace Hardware**
736 E. Pipeline Rd.
Bedford, TX 76021
(817)282-0752
Ultimate Parent: Ace Hardware. **SIC:**
5251—Hardware Stores.

★ 83239 ★ **Albertson's**
1300 Airport Fwy.
Bedford, TX 76022
(817)354-0622
Ultimate Parent: Albertson's Inc. **SIC:**
5411—Grocery Stores.

★ 83240 ★ **Coast to Coast**
Hardware
2816 Central Dr.
Bedford, TX 76021
(817)283-8826
Ultimate Parent: Servistar Corp. **SIC:**
5251—Hardware Stores.

★ 83241 ★ **Farm & Home**
Savings Association
2901 Brown Trl
Bedford, TX 76021
(817)281-7211
Ultimate Parent: Farm & Home Financial
Corp. **SIC:** 6036—Savings Institutions
Except Federal.

★ 83242 ★ **Jiffy Lube**
300 E. Pipeline Rd.
Bedford, TX 76021
(817)282-8453
Ultimate Parent: Pennzoil. **SIC:** 7539—
Automotive Repair Shops Nec.

★ 83243 ★ **Kroger Food&Drug**
Stores
2109 Harwood Rd.
Bedford, TX 76021
Ultimate Parent: Kroger. **SIC:** 5912—Drug
Stores & Proprietary Stores.

★ 83244 ★ **Lone Star Gas Co.**
404 Racquet Club Dr.
Bedford, TX 76022
(817)282-6702
Ultimate Parent: Enserch. **SIC:** 4939—
Combination Utility Nec.

★ 83245 ★ **McDonalds**
Restaurant
2100 Central Park Blvd.
Bedford, TX 76022
(817)354-5863
Ultimate Parent: McDonald's.

★ 83246 ★ **Mobil Oil Corp.**
3354 Harwood Rd.
Bedford, TX 76021
(817)354-0448
Ultimate Parent: Mobil. **SIC:** 2911—
Petroleum Refining.

★ 83247 ★ **Pulte Home Corp.**
Quail Hollo
6705 Wooddale Dr.
Bedford, TX 76021
(214)471-2163
Ultimate Parent: Pulte.

★ 83248 ★ **R-Tec Systems**
2100 Reliance Pky. PO Box 919
Bedford, TX 76021
Ultimate Parent: Reliance Electric. **SIC:**
3661—Telephone & Telegraph Apparatus.

★ 83249 ★ **Radio Shack**
2852 Central Dr.
Bedford, TX 76021
(817)283-2613
Company Type: Division. **Ultimate Parent:**
Tandy Corp. **SIC:** 5065—Electronic Parts &
Equipment Nec; 5731—Radio, Television &
Electronics Stores.

★ 83250 ★ **Radio Shack**
1320 Airport Fwy.
Bedford, TX 76022
(817)283-2551
Company Type: Division. **Ultimate Parent:**
Tandy Corp. **SIC:** 5065—Electronic Parts &
Equipment Nec.

★ 83251 ★ **Ryder Truck Rental**
2025 Pipeline Rd. E
Bedford, TX 76022
(817)545-9725
Ultimate Parent: Ryder System.

★ 83252 ★ **Taco Bell**
2716 Brown Trl
Bedford, TX 76021
(817)282-6870
Ultimate Parent: Pepsico. **SIC:** 5812—
Eating Places.

★ 83253 ★ **Taco Bell**
2500 Hwy. 121
Bedford, TX 76021
(817)685-9495
Ultimate Parent: Pepsico.

★ 83254 ★ **Taco Bell**
1501 Brown Trl
Bedford, TX 76022
(817)282-8043
Ultimate Parent: Pepsico. **SIC:** 5812—
Eating Places.

★ 83255 ★ **Texaco Food Mart**
1019 N. Industrial Blvd.
Bedford, TX 76021
(817)545-1640
Ultimate Parent: Texaco.

★ 83256 ★ **Texaco Service Inc.**
1840 Norwood Dr.
Bedford, TX 76022
(817)282-0972
Ultimate Parent: Texaco. **SIC:** 5599—
Automotive Dealers Nec.

Beeville

★ 83257 ★ **Exxon Co. USA**
1720 E. Houston St.
Beeville, TX 78102
(512)358-8602
Ultimate Parent: Exxon.

★ 83258 ★ **Kentucky Fried**
Chicken
200 E. Houston St.
Beeville, TX 78102
(512)358-7222
Ultimate Parent: Pepsico. **SIC:** 5812—
Eating Places.

★ 83259 ★ **Pizza Hut**
1103 N. Washington St.
Beeville, TX 78102
(512)358-2970
Ultimate Parent: Pepsico. **SIC:** 5812—
Eating Places.

★ 83260 ★ **Radio Shack**
610 E. Houston St.
Beeville, TX 78102
(512)358-2442
Company Type: Division. **Ultimate Parent:**
Tandy Corp.

★ 83261 ★ **Ryder Truck Rental**
703 N. Washington St.
Beeville, TX 78102
(512)358-2062
Ultimate Parent: Ryder System. **SIC:**
7513—Truck Rental & Leasing Without
Drivers.

★ 83262 ★ **Wal Mart Discount**
City
Us 181
Beeville, TX 78102
(512)358-4764
Ultimate Parent: Wal-Mart Stores, Inc. **SIC:**
5311—Department Stores.

★ 83263 ★ **Western Geophysical**
Co. Amer
711 S. Washington St.
Beeville, TX 78102
(512)358-8671
Ultimate Parent: Litton Industries. **SIC:**
1382—Oil & Gas Exploration Services.

Bellaire

★ 83264 ★ **Exxon**
5102 Bellaire Blvd.
Bellaire, TX 77401
(713)668-8362
Ultimate Parent: Exxon. **SIC:** 5541—
Gasoline Service Stations.

★ 83265 ★ **La Gloria Oil & Gas**
Co. Inc.
4747 Bellaire Blvd.
Bellaire, TX 77401-4515
(713)660-4500
Company Type: Subsidiary. **Ultimate**
Parent: Crown Central Petroleum Corp.
SIC: 2911—Petroleum Refining; 4612—
Crude Petroleum Pipelines; 1382—Oil &
Gas Exploration Services; 1311—Crude
Petroleum & Natural Gas.

★ 83266 ★ **Radio Shack**
4809 Bissonnet St.
Bellaire, TX 77401
(713)667-5190
Company Type: Division. **Ultimate Parent:**
Tandy Corp. **SIC:** 5046—Commercial
Equipment Nec.

★ 83267 ★ **Texaco Inc.**
4800 Fournace Pl 600
Bellaire, TX 77401
(713)432-6200
Ultimate Parent: Texaco. **SIC:** 6099—
Functions Related to Deposit Banking.

★ 83268 ★ **Texaco/Philadelphia**
2000 PO Box
Bellaire, TX 77402
(713)432-2445
Ultimate Parent: Texaco. **SIC:** 5599—
Automotive Dealers Nec.

★ 83269 ★ **Texaco Refining &**
Marketing
4800 Fournace
Bellaire, TX 77401
(713)432-2268
Ultimate Parent: Texaco. **SIC:** 7389—
Business Services Nec.

★ 83270 ★ **Texaco USA Inc.**
4800 Fournace Pl
Bellaire, TX 77401
(713)666-2532
Ultimate Parent: Texaco. **SIC:** 5541—
Gasoline Service Stations.

★ 83271 ★ **Texaco USA Inc. Adiv**
4800 Fournace Pl
Bellaire, TX 77401
(713)666-2532
Ultimate Parent: Texaco. **SIC:** 5541—
Gasoline Service Stations.

★ 83272 ★ **US Gypsum Co.**
1201 Mayo Shell
Bellaire, TX 77401
(713)672-8261
Ultimate Parent: USG Corp. **SIC:** 3272—
Concrete Products Nec.

★ 83273 ★ **Walgreen Drug Stores**
5002 Bellaire Blvd.
Bellaire, TX 77401
Ultimate Parent: Walgreen Co.

★ 83274 ★ **Wall Street Journal**
6330 W. Loop S
Bellaire, TX 77401
(713)664-8606
Ultimate Parent: Dow Jones. **SIC:** 2711—
Newspapers.

Bellville

★ 83275 ★ **Tesco Industries Inc.**
1038 E. Hacienda St.
Bellville, TX 77418
(409)865-3176
Officer: Abner E. Jackson, President.
Ultimate Parent: Dover Corp. **SIC:** 2521—
Wood Office Furniture; 2531—Public
Building & Related Furniture; 2541—Wood
Partitions & Fixtures.

Belton

★ 83276 ★ **Kentucky Fried**
Chicken
812 E. Central Ave.
Belton, TX 76513
(817)939-6574
Ultimate Parent: Pepsico. **SIC:** 5812—
Eating Places.

★ 83277 ★ **Lone Star Gas Co.**
312 E. Central Ave.
Belton, TX 76513
(817)939-2432
Ultimate Parent: Enserch. **SIC:** 4925—Gas
Production & Distribution Nec.

★ 83278 ★ **McDonalds**
Restaurant
1601 E. 6th Ave.
Belton, TX 76513
(817)939-7807
Ultimate Parent: McDonald's.

★ 83279 ★ **Pizza Hut**
Neil
Belton, TX 76513
(817)939-2191
Ultimate Parent: Pepsico. **SIC:** 5812—
Eating Places.

★ 83280 ★ **Wal Mart Discount**
2180 N. Main St.
Belton, TX 76513
(817)939-0962
Ultimate Parent: Wal-Mart Stores, Inc.

Benavides

★ 83281 ★ **Texaco Inc.**
Benavides, TX 78341
(512)256-3441
Ultimate Parent: Texaco. **SIC:** 5172—
Petroleum Products Nec.

Big Lake

★ 83282 ★ **Exxon Pipeline Co.**
Kemper Station
Big Lake, TX 76932
(915)884-2085
Ultimate Parent: Exxon.

★ 83283 ★ **Exxon Pipeline Co.**
Kemper Station
Big Lake, TX 76932
(915)884-2085
Ultimate Parent: Exxon Pipeline.

Big Spring

★ 83284 ★   Exxon
310 E. 4th St.
Big Spring, TX 79720
(915)263-7741
Ultimate Parent: Exxon. **SIC:** 5541—
Gasoline Service Stations.

★ 83285 ★   Exxon Chemical Co.
Gatesville Rd.
Big Spring, TX 79720
(915)263-4102
Ultimate Parent: Exxon. **SIC:** 2899—
Chemical Preparations Nec.

★ 83286 ★   Greyhound Bus
311 E. 3rd St.
Big Spring, TX 79720
(915)263-1331
Ultimate Parent: Greyhound Lines Inc. **SIC:**
4131—Intercity & Rural Bus Transportation.

★ 83287 ★   Greyhound Bus Lines
315 Runnels St.
Big Spring, TX 79720
(915)267-2331
Ultimate Parent: Greyhound Lines Inc. **SIC:**
4142—Bus Charter Service Except Local.

★ 83288 ★   IBM Corp.
208 Owens St.
Big Spring, TX 79720
(915)263-1990
Ultimate Parent: IBM.

★ 83289 ★   Marathon Oil Co.
1982 Delta Olds
Big Spring, TX 79720
(915)267-4477
Ultimate Parent: USX Corp.

★ 83290 ★   Mary Kay Cosmet Independent
1411 E. 18th St.
Big Spring, TX 79720
(915)267-5845
Ultimate Parent: Mary Kay Cosmetics. **SIC:**
5999—Miscellaneous Retail Stores Nec.

★ 83291 ★   Oryx Energy Co.
112 HC 63
Big Spring, TX 79720
Ultimate Parent: Oryx Energy.

★ 83292 ★   Pizza Hut
2601 Hwy. 87 S
Big Spring, TX 79720
(915)267-4153
Ultimate Parent: Pepsico. **SIC:** 5812—
Eating Places.

★ 83293 ★   Radio Shack
1801 Fm M Rd. E
Big Spring, TX 79720
(915)263-1368
Company Type: Division. **Ultimate Parent:**
Tandy Corp. **SIC:** 5065—Electronic Parts &
Equipment Nec.

★ 83294 ★   Ryder Truck Rental
3400 E. I 20
Big Spring, TX 79720
(915)263-4727
Ultimate Parent: Ryder System. **SIC:**
7359—Equipment Rental & Leasing Nec.

★ 83295 ★   Ryder Truck Rental
Industrial Park
Big Spring, TX 79720
(915)267-7145
Ultimate Parent: Ryder System. **SIC:**
7513—Truck Rental & Leasing Without
Drivers.

★ 83296 ★   Trico Industries Inc.
3406 E. Fm 700 Rd.
Big Spring, TX 79720
(915)267-7172
Ultimate Parent: Paccar. **SIC:** 5084—
Industrial Machinery & Equipment.

★ 83297 ★   UCIG Inc.
Linde Div.
200 Arnett Rd.
Big Spring, TX 79720
Company Type: Division. **Ultimate Parent:**
Union Carbide Corp. **SIC:** 2813—Industrial
Gases.

★ 83298 ★   Union Carbide Corp.
Linde Div.
200 Arnett Rd.
Big Spring, TX 79720
Company Type: Division. **Ultimate Parent:**
Union Carbide Corp. **SIC:** 2813—Industrial
Gases.

Big Springs

★ 83299 ★   Fina Oil & Chemical Co.
200 Refinery Rd.
Big Springs, TX 79720
(915)263-7661
Officer: Ronald Haddock, Chairman.
Ultimate Parent: Fina. **SIC:** 2911—
Petroleum Refining.

Bishop

★ 83300 ★   Celanese Engineering Resins Inc.
1 Mi. S. of Bishop Tx U.S. Hwy. 77 Bus.
Bishop, TX 78343
Ultimate Parent: Hoechst Celanese Corp.
SIC: 2869—Industrial Organic Chemicals
Nec; 2821—Plastics Materials & Resins.

★ 83301 ★   Celanese Engineering Resins Inc.
Resins Div.
1 Mile S. of Bishop on US Hwy. 77 Bus.
Bishop, TX 78343
Company Type: Division. **Ultimate Parent:**
Hoechst Celanese Corp. **SIC:** 2869—
Industrial Organic Chemicals Nec; 2821—
Plastics Materials & Resins.

★ 83302 ★   Hoechst Celanese Corp.
Hwy. 77 & County Rd. 4 PO Box 69
Bishop, TX 78343
Ultimate Parent: Hoechst Celanese Corp.
SIC: 2819—Industrial Inorganic Chemicals
Nec.

★ 83303 ★   Hoechst Celanese Corp. Virginia Chemicals Co.
Hwy. 77 & Country Rd. 4 PO Box 69
Bishop, TX 78343
Ultimate Parent: Hoechst Celanese Corp.
SIC: 2819—Industrial Inorganic Chemicals
Nec.

★ 83304 ★   Hoechst Celanese Specialty Chemicals Group
Hwy. 77 & County Rd. 4 PO Box 69
Bishop, TX 78343
Ultimate Parent: Hoechst Celanese Corp.
SIC: 2819—Industrial Inorganic Chemicals
Nec.

★ 83305 ★   Stratton Field Office
Stratton Field Office
Bishop, TX 78343
(512)584-3521
Officer: M.D. Reagan, Manager. **Ultimate
Parent:** Union Pacific Corp. **SIC:** 2911—
Petroleum Refining.

Boerne

★ 83306 ★   Radio Shack
266 N. Main St.
Boerne, TX 78006
(512)249-3516
Company Type: Division. **Ultimate Parent:**
Tandy Corp.

Bogata

★ 83307 ★   Texaco Inc.
Bogata, TX 75417
(214)632-4497
Ultimate Parent: Texaco. **SIC:** 5541—
Gasoline Service Stations.

Bon Wier

★ 83308 ★   Kirby Forest Ind. Inc. Bon Wier Plywood
Hwy. 363 E.
Bon Wier, TX 75928
Ultimate Parent: Louisiana-Pacific. **SIC:**
2436—Softwood Veneer & Plywood; 2436—
Softwood Veneer & Plywood.

★ 83309 ★   Kirby Forest Industries Plywood
Hwy. 363 E.
Bon Wier, TX 75928
Ultimate Parent: Louisiana-Pacific. **SIC:**
2436—Softwood Veneer & Plywood.

★ 83310 ★   Louisiana Pacific Corp.
Rte. 1
Bon Wier, TX 75928
Ultimate Parent: Louisiana-Pacific. **SIC:**
2436—Softwood Veneer & Plywood; 2421—
Sawmills & Planing Mills—General.

★ 83311 ★   Louisiana-Pacific Corp. Kirby Forest Industries
Rte. 1
Bon Wier, TX 75928
Ultimate Parent: Louisiana-Pacific. **SIC:**
2436—Softwood Veneer & Plywood; 2421—
Sawmills & Planing Mills—General.

Bonham

★ 83312 ★   General Cable Corp.
800 E. 2nd St.
Bonham, TX 75418
Ultimate Parent: General Cable Corp. **SIC:**
3357—Nonferrous Wiredrawing & Insulating.

★ 83313 ★   Piggly Wiggly
920 N. Ctr. St.
Bonham, TX 75418
(214)583-2344
Ultimate Parent: Bruno's. **SIC:** 5411—
Grocery Stores.

★ 83314 ★   Wal Mart Discount Cities
N Ctr. St.
Bonham, TX 75418
(214)583-9591
Ultimate Parent: Wal-Mart Stores, Inc. **SIC:**
5311—Department Stores.

★ 83315 ★   Wal Mart Pharmacy
Hwy. 78 N
Bonham, TX 75418
(214)583-5564
Ultimate Parent: Wal-Mart Stores, Inc. **SIC:**
5049—Professional Equipment Nec.

Borger

★ 83316 ★   Coast to Coast
601 S. Main St.
Borger, TX 79007
(806)274-4101
Ultimate Parent: Servistar Corp. **SIC:**
5531—Automobile & Home Supply Stores.

★ 83317 ★   J. M. Huber Corp. Borger Carbon Plant
Hwy. 136 & F.M. 1559
Borger, TX 79007
Ultimate Parent: J. M. Huber. **SIC:** 2895—
Carbon Black.

★ 83318 ★   J.M. Huber Borger Carbon Plant
Hwy. 136 & F.M. 1559
Borger, TX 79007-2831
Location Type: Plant. **Ultimate Parent:** J.
M. Huber. **SIC:** 2895—Carbon Black.

★ 83319 ★   Kentucky Fried Chicken
Fritch Hwy.
Borger, TX 79007
(806)273-5011
Ultimate Parent: Pepsico. **SIC:** 5812—
Eating Places.

★ 83320 ★   Payless Shoesource
222 Borger Shopping Plz.
Borger, TX 79007
(806)274-6842
Ultimate Parent: May Department Stores.
SIC: 5661—Shoe Stores.

★ 83321 ★   Phillips 66 Co.
State Hwy., Spur 119 N
Borger, TX 79008-0271
Ultimate Parent: Phillips Petroleum. **SIC:**
2911—Petroleum Refining; 2819—Industrial
Inorganic Chemicals Nec; 2869—Industrial
Organic Chemicals Nec; 2821—Plastics
Materials & Resins.

★ 83322 ★   Phillips 66 Co.
Philtex/Ryton Complex
2 Miles NE of Borger on State Spur 119
Borger, TX 79008
Company Type: Division. **Ultimate Parent:**
Phillips Petroleum. **SIC:** 2869—Industrial
Organic Chemicals Nec; 2821—Plastics
Materials & Resins.

★ 83323 ★   Pizza Hut
704 E. 3rd
Borger, TX 79007
(806)274-4189
Ultimate Parent: Pepsico. **SIC:** 5812—
Eating Places.

★ 83324 ★   Pizza Hut
1002 N. Cedar St.
Borger, TX 79007
(806)274-2681
Ultimate Parent: Pepsico. **SIC:** 9111—
Executive Offices.

★ 83325 ★   Ryder Truck Rental
700 W. Wilson St.
Borger, TX 79007
(806)274-5491
Ultimate Parent: Ryder System. **SIC:**
7513—Truck Rental & Leasing Without
Drivers.

Bowie

★ 83326 ★   Pizza Hut
404 E. Wise St.
Bowie, TX 76230
(817)872-2149
Ultimate Parent: Pepsico. **SIC:** 5812—
Eating Places.

★ 83327 ★   Radio Shack
507 Pelham St.
Bowie, TX 76230
(817)872-5381
Company Type: Division. **Ultimate Parent:**
Tandy Corp. **SIC:** 5731—Radio, Television
& Electronics Stores.

★ 83328 ★   Trailways Bus System
511 W. Wise St.
Bowie, TX 76230
(817)872-4351
Ultimate Parent: Greyhound Lines Inc. **SIC:**
4131—Intercity & Rural Bus Transportation.

Brady

★ 83329 ★   Kentucky Fried Chicken
1602 S. Bridge St.
Brady, TX 76825
(915)597-1932
Ultimate Parent: Pepsico. **SIC:** 5812—
Eating Places.

★ 83330 ★   Pizza Hut
1208 S. Bridge St.
Brady, TX 76825
(915)597-1738
Ultimate Parent: Pepsico. **SIC:** 5812—
Eating Places.

★ 83331 ★   Radio Shack
301 S. Bridge St.
Brady, TX 76825
(915)597-0003
Company Type: Division. **Ultimate Parent:**
Tandy Corp. **SIC:** 5731—Radio, Television
& Electronics Stores.

★ 83332 ★   Ryder Truck Rental
Hwy. 87 S
Brady, TX 76825
(915)597-3076
Ultimate Parent: Ryder System. **SIC:**
7359—Equipment Rental & Leasing Nec.

Brazoria

★ 83333 ★   Phillips 66 Co.
Clemens Terminal
Country Rd. 314
Brazoria, TX 77480-0866
Company Type: Division. **Ultimate Parent:**
Phillips Petroleum. **SIC:** 2911—Petroleum
Refining.

Brenham

★ 83334 ★ Charter Co.
1805 W. Main St.
Brenham, TX 77833
(409)836-4120
Ultimate Parent: American Financial. SIC:
1761—Roofing, Siding & Sheet Metal Work.

★ 83335 ★ Charter Co.
103 W. Alamo St.
Brenham, TX 77833
(409)836-1587
Ultimate Parent: American Financial. SIC:
5211—Lumber & Other Building Materials.

★ 83336 ★ Kentucky Fried
Chicken
2303 S. Day St.
Brenham, TX 77833
(409)836-0292
Ultimate Parent: Pepsico. SIC: 5812—
Eating Places.

★ 83337 ★ McDonalds
Restaurant
4 Corners Shopping Ctr.
Brenham, TX 77833
(409)836-7797
Ultimate Parent: McDonald's.
SIC: 5812—Eating Places.

★ 83338 ★ Payless Shoesource
2206 S. Market St.
Brenham, TX 77833
(409)836-6397
Ultimate Parent: May Department Stores.
SIC: 5661—Shoe Stores.

★ 83339 ★ Pizza Hut
701 W. Alamo St.
Brenham, TX 77833
(409)836-4261
Ultimate Parent: Pepsico. SIC: 5812—
Eating Places.

★ 83340 ★ Radio Shack
2208 S. Market St.
Brenham, TX 77833
(409)836-4005
Company Type: Division. Ultimate Parent:
Tandy Corp. SIC: 5731—Radio, Television
& Electronics Stores.

★ 83341 ★ Ryder Truck Rental
1705 S. Horton St.
Brenham, TX 77833
(409)836-4461
Ultimate Parent: Ryder System. SIC:
7359—Equipment Rental & Leasing Nec.

★ 83342 ★ Sealy Mattress Co.
Hwy. 290
Brenham, TX 77833
(409)836-6644
Officer: Herman Borchardt, Manager.
Ultimate Parent: Sealy. SIC: 2515—
Mattresses & Bedsprings.

★ 83343 ★ Stearns & Foster Co.
593 PO Box
Brenham, TX 77834
(512)927-4214
Ultimate Parent: Sealy. SIC: 2515—
Mattresses & Bedsprings.

★ 83344 ★ Texas Fibers
1200 Rink St.
Brenham, TX 77833
Ultimate Parent: Leggett & Platt Inc. SIC:
3086—Plastics Foam Products.

Bridge City

★ 83345 ★ Mobil Mart 1
1745 Texas Ave.
Bridge City, TX 77611
(409)735-9477
Ultimate Parent: Mobil.

★ 83346 ★ Pizza Hut
2100 Texas Ave.
Bridge City, TX 77611
(409)735-8557
Ultimate Parent: Pepsico. SIC: 5812—
Eating Places.

Bronte

★ 83347 ★ Exxon Co. USA
Humble Rd.
Bronte, TX 76933
(915)473-5421
Ultimate Parent: Exxon.

★ 83348 ★ Union Texas
Petroleum
209 Railroad NE
Bronte, TX 76933
(915)473-5161
Ultimate Parent: Union Texas Petroleum.

Brookshire

★ 83349 ★ McDonalds
I-10
Brookshire, TX 77423
(713)392-8555
Ultimate Parent: McDonald's.
SIC: 5812—Eating Places.

Brownfield

★ 83350 ★ Amerada Hess Corp.
PO Box 311
Brownfield, TX 79316
(806)755-2231
Officer: Tommy Hord, Manager. Ultimate
Parent: Amerada Hess. SIC: 2911—
Petroleum Refining.

★ 83351 ★ Coca Cola Bottling
Co. Whse
310 N. 6th St.
Brownfield, TX 79316
(806)637-2191
Ultimate Parent: Coca-Cola Enterprises.
SIC: 5921—Liquor Stores.

★ 83352 ★ Kentucky Fried
Chicken
405 S. 1st St.
Brownfield, TX 79316
(806)637-3158
Ultimate Parent: Pepsico. SIC: 5812—
Eating Places.

★ 83353 ★ Pizza Hut
301 Lubbock Rd.
Brownfield, TX 79316
(806)637-3983
Ultimate Parent: Pepsico. SIC: 5812—
Eating Places.

Brownsville

★ 83354 ★ Brownsville Medical
Center
1040 W. Jefferson St.
Brownsville, TX 78521
(210)544-1400
Ultimate Parent: American Medical
Holdings. SIC: 8062—General Medical &
Surgical Hospitals.

★ 83355 ★ Eagle Bus Mfg. Inc.
2045 Les Mauldin Blvd.
Brownsville, TX 78521
Ultimate Parent: Greyhound Lines Inc. SIC:
3711—Motor Vehicles & Car Bodies;
3713—Truck & Bus Bodies.

★ 83356 ★ Eaton Corp.
Condura
1910 Billy Mitchell Blvd.
Brownsville, TX 78521
(210)548-9780
Officer: Oscar Gonzalez, Manager.
Ultimate Parent: Eaton Corp. SIC: 3679—
Electronic Components Nec; 3999—
Manufacturing Industries Nec.

★ 83357 ★ Exxon Food Store
5195 N. Expy.
Brownsville, TX 78520
(512)350-4515
Ultimate Parent: Exxon.

★ 83358 ★ Foot Action
2330 N. Expy.
Brownsville, TX 78521
(512)541-4123
Ultimate Parent: Melville. SIC: 5661—Shoe
Stores.

★ 83359 ★ General Instrument
Corp.
9694 Coffeeport Rd.
Brownsville, TX 78521
(210)541-0600
Officer: Jack Hammar, President. Ultimate
Parent: General Instrument Corp. SIC:
3661—Telephone & Telegraph Apparatus.

★ 83360 ★ Kentucky Fried
Chicken
615 Central Blvd.
Brownsville, TX 78520
(512)546-8354
Ultimate Parent: Pepsico. SIC: 5812—
Eating Places.

★ 83361 ★ Kentucky Fried
Chicken
3025 Boca Chica Blvd.
Brownsville, TX 78521
(512)541-7311
Ultimate Parent: Pepsico. SIC: 5812—
Eating Places.

★ 83362 ★ Kmart Discount
Stores
325 Mexico Blvd.
Brownsville, TX 78520
(512)546-0328
Ultimate Parent: K-Mart.

★ 83363 ★ Kroger Co.
814 N. Expy.
Brownsville, TX 78521
(512)546-5531
Ultimate Parent: Kroger. SIC: 5311—
Department Stores.

★ 83364 ★ Lane Bryant
301 Mexico Blvd.
Brownsville, TX 78520
(512)541-6644
Ultimate Parent: Limited.

★ 83365 ★ Lerner Shop
Sunrise
Brownsville, TX 78521
(512)541-7149
Ultimate Parent: Limited. SIC: 5621—
Women's Clothing Stores.

★ 83366 ★ Lerner Shop
Amigoland Mall
Brownsville, TX 78520
(512)541-1301
Ultimate Parent: Limited. SIC: 5621—
Women's Clothing Stores.

★ 83367 ★ M-I Drilling Fluids,
Brownsville
South Side Re., Port of Brownsville
South Side Rd.
Brownsville, TX 78520
Ultimate Parent: Halliburton. SIC: 3295—
Minerals—Ground or Treated.

★ 83368 ★ M-I Drilling Fluids,
Brownsville
Port of Brownsville
South Side Rd.
Brownsville, TX 78520
Ultimate Parent: Halliburton. SIC: 3295—
Minerals—Ground or Treated.

★ 83369 ★ M-I Drilling Fluids Co.
Brownsville
South Side Rd. Port of Brownsville
Brownsville, TX 78520
Ultimate Parent: Halliburton. SIC: 3295—
Minerals—Ground or Treated.

★ 83370 ★ Magnetek Hesgon
3525 International Blvd.
Brownsville, TX 78521-3229
(210)542-5491
Officer: Armando Arista. Ultimate Parent:
Magnetek Inc. SIC: 2241—Narrow Fabric
Mills.

★ 83371 ★ Magnetek National
Electric Coil, Inc.
3330 E. 14th St.
Brownsville, TX 78521
Ultimate Parent: Magnetek Inc. SIC:
3621—Motors & Generators; 3612—
Transformers Except Electronic.

★ 83372 ★ Payless Shoesource
1064 Mexico Blvd.
Brownsville, TX 78520
(512)541-0325
Ultimate Parent: May Department Stores.
SIC: 5661—Shoe Stores.

★ 83373 ★ Pizza Hut
1179 Farm Rd. 802
Brownsville, TX 78520
(512)544-7733
Ultimate Parent: Pepsico. SIC: 5812—
Eating Places.

★ 83374 ★ Pizza Hut
245 Security Dr.
Brownsville, TX 78520
(512)541-6393
Ultimate Parent: Pepsico. SIC: 5812—
Eating Places.

★ 83375 ★ Pizza Hut
2333 Boca Chica Blvd.
Brownsville, TX 78521
(512)544-7711
Ultimate Parent: Pepsico. SIC: 5812—
Eating Places.

★ 83376 ★ Pizza Hut
1830 Central Blvd.
Brownsville, TX 78520
(512)546-8272
Ultimate Parent: Pepsico. SIC: 5812—
Eating Places.

★ 83377 ★ Radio Shack
1639 Price Rd.
Brownsville, TX 78521
(512)544-6800
Company Type: Division. Ultimate Parent:
Tandy Corp.

★ 83378 ★ Radio Shack
Sunrise
Brownsville, TX 78521
(512)546-3387
Company Type: Division. Ultimate Parent:
Tandy Corp. SIC: 5065—Electronic Parts &
Equipment Nec.

★ 83379 ★ Radio Shack
301 Mexico Blvd.
Brownsville, TX 78520
(512)546-8285
Company Type: Division. Ultimate Parent:
Tandy Corp.

★ 83380 ★ Radio Shack
1639 Price Rd.
Brownsville, TX 78521
(512)546-6156
Company Type: Division. Ultimate Parent:
Tandy Corp. SIC: 5065—Electronic Parts &
Equipment Nec.

★ 83381 ★ Ryder Truck Rental
2524 Boca Chica Blvd.
Brownsville, TX 78521
Ultimate Parent: Ryder System. SIC:
7359—Equipment Rental & Leasing Nec.

★ 83382 ★ Trailways Bus System
1134 E. St.
Brownsville, TX 78520
(512)546-7171
Ultimate Parent: Greyhound Lines Inc. SIC:
4111—Local & Suburban Transit.

★ 83383 ★ Wal Mart Discount
City
2721 Boca Chica Blvd.
Brownsville, TX 78521
(512)544-0394
Ultimate Parent: Wal-Mart Stores, Inc.

★ 83384 ★ Waldenbooks
Sunrise
Brownsville, TX 78521
(512)542-4923
Ultimate Parent: K-Mart. SIC: 5942—Book
Stores.

★ 83385 ★ Walgreen Drug Stores
Amigoland Mall
Brownsville, TX 78520
(512)546-3701
Ultimate Parent: Walgreen Co. SIC:
5912—Drug Stores & Proprietary Stores.

Brownwood

★ 83386 ★ Liberty Mutual
Insurance Co.
345 PO Box
Brownwood, TX 76804
(915)646-4383
Ultimate Parent: Liberty Mutual Group.
SIC: 6411—Insurance Agents, Brokers &
Service.

★ 83387 ★　**Pizza Hut**
507 W. Commerce St.
Brownwood, TX 76801
(915)646-2602
Ultimate Parent: Pepsico. **SIC:** 5812—
Eating Places.

★ 83388 ★　**Radio Shack**
Heartland Mall
Brownwood, TX 76801
(915)646-6123
Company Type: Division. **Ultimate Parent:**
Tandy Corp. **SIC:** 5065—Electronic Parts &
Equipment Nec.

★ 83389 ★　**Taco Bell**
300 W. Commerce St.
Brownwood, TX 76801
(915)643-1466
Ultimate Parent: Pepsico. **SIC:** 5812—
Eating Places.

★ 83390 ★　**3M Co.**
PO Box 1669
Brownwood, TX 76804-1669
(915)646-3551
Company Type: Branch. **Officer:** Barry
Melchior. **Ultimate Parent:** Minnesota
Mining & Mfg. **SIC:** 2672—Coated &
Laminated Paper Nec.

★ 83391 ★　**Vulcan Materials Co.**
377 S. Brady Hwy.
Brownwood, TX 76801
(915)646-8526
Officer: Mike Harris, Manager. **Ultimate
Parent:** Business Systems of Westch. **SIC:**
2951—Asphalt Paving Mixtures & Blocks;
3281—Cut Stone & Stone Products; 3295—
Minerals—Ground or Treated.

Bryan

★ 83392 ★　**Arco Pipeline**
1720 Groesbeck St.
Bryan, TX 77803-4416
(409)779-7231
Location Type: Branch office. **Ultimate
Parent:** Atlantic Richfield Co., Inc. **SIC:**
4612—Crude Petroleum Pipelines.

★ 83393 ★　**Citgo Petroleum Corp.**
1714 Finfeather Rd.
Bryan, TX 77801
(409)823-8911
Ultimate Parent: Citgo Petroleum. **SIC:**
5172—Petroleum Products Nec.

★ 83394 ★　**Coca Cola Bottling
Co.**
200 E. 23rd St.
Bryan, TX 77803
(409)779-7677
Ultimate Parent: Coca-Cola Enterprises.
SIC: 5143—Dairy Products Except Dried or
Canned.

★ 83395 ★　**First American Bank**
1111 Briarcrest Dr.
Bryan, TX 77802-2530
(409)268-7575
Company Type: Subsidiary. **Officer:** Don
A. Adam, Chairman. **Ultimate Parent:** First
American Corp. **SIC:** 6022—State
Commercial Banks. **Employee Count:** 160.

★ 83396 ★　**Greyhound Bus Lines**
405 E. 29th St.
Bryan, TX 77803
(409)779-8071
Ultimate Parent: Greyhound Lines Inc. **SIC:**
4131—Intercity & Rural Bus Transportation;
4212—Local Trucking Without Storage.

★ 83397 ★　**Lone Star Gas Co.**
201 S. Brewer St.
Bryan, TX 77802
(409)775-8406
Ultimate Parent: Enserch. **SIC:** 4939—
Combination Utility Nec.

★ 83398 ★　**Mobil Gas Station No
7**
2100 S. College Ave.
Bryan, TX 77801
(409)778-1570
Ultimate Parent: Mobil. **SIC:** 5541—
Gasoline Service Stations.

★ 83399 ★　**OMC Industries Inc.**
1 W. Bronze Ln.
Bryan, TX 77807
(409)779-1400
Officer: Ben Hardeman, President.

★ 83400 ★　**Pepsi-Cola Co.**
1801 Shiloh Ave.
Bryan, TX 77803
(409)779-6324
Officer: Tod Weingand, Manager. **Ultimate
Parent:** Pepsico. **SIC:** 2086—Bottled &
Canned Soft Drinks.

★ 83401 ★　**Piggly Wiggly**
200 E. 24th St.
Bryan, TX 77803
(409)822-2341
Ultimate Parent: Bruno's. **SIC:** 5411—
Grocery Stores.

★ 83402 ★　**Pizza Hut**
4340 Carter Creek Pky.
Bryan, TX 77802
(409)846-7714
Ultimate Parent: Pepsico. **SIC:** 5812—
Eating Places.

★ 83403 ★　**Pizza Hut**
3000 Briarcrest Dr.
Bryan, TX 77802
(409)776-0061
Ultimate Parent: Pepsico. **SIC:** 5812—
Eating Places.

★ 83404 ★　**Pizza Hut**
4207 Wellborn Rd.
Bryan, TX 77801
(409)693-9393
Ultimate Parent: Pepsico. **SIC:** 5812—
Eating Places.

★ 83405 ★　**Pizza Hut**
2610 S. Texas Ave.
Bryan, TX 77802
(409)779-5422
Ultimate Parent: Pepsico. **SIC:** 5812—
Eating Places.

★ 83406 ★　**Radio Shack**
1125 E. Villa Maria Rd.
Bryan, TX 77802
(409)846-7384
Company Type: Division. **Ultimate Parent:**
Tandy Corp. **SIC:** 5065—Electronic Parts &
Equipment Nec; 5731—Radio, Television &
Electronics Stores.

★ 83407 ★　**Radio Shack**
1125 E. Villa Maria Rd.
Bryan, TX 77802
(409)764-8171
Company Type: Division. **Ultimate Parent:**
Tandy Corp. **SIC:** 5065—Electronic Parts &
Equipment Nec.

★ 83408 ★　**Ryder Truck Rental**
632 W. Carson St.
Bryan, TX 77801
(409)779-5582
Ultimate Parent: Ryder System. **SIC:**
7359—Equipment Rental & Leasing Nec;
7513—Truck Rental & Leasing Without
Drivers.

★ 83409 ★　**Taco Bell**
3901 S. Texas Ave.
Bryan, TX 77802
(409)846-5880
Ultimate Parent: Pepsico. **SIC:** 5812—
Eating Places.

★ 83410 ★　**United Parcel Service**
2301 Fountain Ave.
Bryan, TX 77801
(409)779-9667
Ultimate Parent: United Parcel Service of
America. **SIC:** 4215—Courier Services
Except by Air.

★ 83411 ★　**Wal Mart Discount
City**
Texas Ave.
Bryan, TX 77803
(409)779-1904
Ultimate Parent: Wal-Mart Stores, Inc. **SIC:**
5311—Department Stores.

Ultimate Parent: Outboard Marine. **SIC:**
3325—Steel Foundries Nec; 3365—
Aluminum Foundries; 3366—Copper
Foundries.

Buda

★ 83412 ★　**Texas-Lehigh Cement
Co.**
PO Box 610
Buda, TX 78610
(512)477-2607 **Fax:** (512)295-3102
Officer: Gerald J. Essl, President. **Ultimate
Parent:** Centex.

Buffalo

★ 83413 ★　**Citizens State Bank**
Hwy. 79 Humprey St.
Buffalo, TX 75831
(214)322-4256
Ultimate Parent: Liberty National Bancorp.
SIC: 6022—State Commercial Banks.

Buna

★ 83414 ★　**Ace Hardware**
101 Main St.
Buna, TX 77612
(409)994-3587
Ultimate Parent: Ace Hardware. **SIC:**
7389—Business Services Nec.

Burkburnett

★ 83415 ★　**Kentucky Fried
Chicken**
612 Sheppard Rd.
Burkburnett, TX 76354
(817)569-2432
Ultimate Parent: Pepsico. **SIC:** 5812—
Eating Places.

★ 83416 ★　**Las Palmas Mexican
Restaurant**
724 Magnolia St.
Burkburnett, TX 76354
(817)569-2942
Ultimate Parent: Pet. **SIC:** 5812—Eating
Places.

★ 83417 ★　**Pizza Hut**
900 W. Kramer Rd.
Burkburnett, TX 76354
(817)569-3315
Ultimate Parent: Pepsico.

★ 83418 ★　**Ryder Truck Rental**
216 N. Oklahoma Cut Off
Burkburnett, TX 76354
(817)569-1891
Ultimate Parent: Ryder System.

★ 83419 ★　**Wal Mart Discount
City**
100 Expy. Access Rd.
Burkburnett, TX 76354
(817)569-2248
Ultimate Parent: Wal-Mart Stores, Inc. **SIC:**
5311—Department Stores.

★ 83420 ★　**Wal Mart Pharmacy**
100 S. Red River Expy.
Burkburnett, TX 76354
(817)569-3308
Ultimate Parent: Wal-Mart Stores, Inc.

Burleson

★ 83421 ★　**Kentucky Fried
Chicken**
600 SW Wilshire Blvd.
Burleson, TX 76028
(817)295-5002
Ultimate Parent: Pepsico. **SIC:** 5812—
Eating Places.

★ 83422 ★　**Kmart**
877 NE Alsbury Blvd.
Burleson, TX 76028
(817)447-8010
Ultimate Parent: K-Mart.

★ 83423 ★　**Pizza Hut**
230 NE Wilshire Blvd.
Burleson, TX 76028
(817)295-1261
Ultimate Parent: Pepsico. **SIC:** 5812—
Eating Places.

★ 83424 ★　**Radio Shack**
Burleson Plz.
Burleson, TX 76028
(817)295-0451
Company Type: Division. **Ultimate Parent:**
Tandy Corp. **SIC:** 5065—Electronic Parts &
Equipment Nec.

★ 83425 ★　**Ryder Truck Rental**
314 NE Wilshire Blvd.
Burleson, TX 76028
(817)447-2676
Ultimate Parent: Ryder System.

★ 83426 ★　**Taco Bell**
316 SW Wilshire Blvd.
Burleson, TX 76028
(817)295-6381
Ultimate Parent: Pepsico. **SIC:** 5812—
Eating Places.

★ 83427 ★　**Wal Mart Discount
City**
602 SW Wilshire Blvd.
Burleson, TX 76028
(817)295-1109
Ultimate Parent: Wal-Mart Stores, Inc. **SIC:**
5311—Department Stores.

Burnet

★ 83428 ★　**Pizza Hut**
701 Buchanan Dr.
Burnet, TX 78611
(512)756-6918
Ultimate Parent: Pepsico. **SIC:** 5812—
Eating Places.

★ 83429 ★　**Texaco Service Sta/
Wardens**
Hwy. 29
Burnet, TX 78611
(512)756-8218
Ultimate Parent: Texaco. **SIC:** 5014—Tires
& Tubes.

Cactus

★ 83430 ★　**Monfort Beef Dumas
Plant Fka-Sipco-D-B-A**
Schroeder Industrial Park 14 Miles N. of
Dumas
Cactus, TX 79013
Ultimate Parent: Conagra. **SIC:** 2011—
Meat Packing Plants.

Caldwell

★ 83431 ★　**AT&T**
RR 3
Caldwell, TX 77836-9803
(806)384-2201
Location Type: Branch office. **Ultimate
Parent:** AT&T. **SIC:** 4813—Telephone
Communications Except Radiotelephone.

★ 83432 ★　**Texaco Distributor**
Hwy. 21 W
Caldwell, TX 77836
(409)567-4482
Ultimate Parent: Texaco. **SIC:** 5171—
Petroleum Bulk Stations & Terminals.

Calvert

★ 83433 ★　**Lone Star Gas Co.**
Calvert, TX 77837
(409)364-2834
Ultimate Parent: Enserch. **SIC:** 4925—Gas
Production & Distribution Nec.

Camden

★ 83434 ★　**Champion
International Corp.**
PO Box 200
Camden, TX 75934
Ultimate Parent: Champion International.
SIC: 2436—Softwood Veneer & Plywood.

★ 83435 ★　**Champion
International Corp.**
Farm Rd. 62
PO Box 200
Camden, TX 75934
Ultimate Parent: Champion International.
SIC: 2436—Softwood Veneer & Plywood.

Cameron

★ 83436 ★　**Lone Star Gas Co.**
118 N. Houston Ave.
Cameron, TX 76520
(817)697-6668
Ultimate Parent: Enserch. **SIC:** 4925—Gas
Production & Distribution Nec.

★ 83437 ★ Mobil Oil Co.
Products
401 N. Travis Ave.
Cameron, TX 76520
(817)697-6472
Ultimate Parent: Mobil. SIC: 5171—
Petroleum Bulk Stations & Terminals.

★ 83438 ★ Ryder Truck Rental
1900 N. Crockett
Cameron, TX 76520
(817)697-4838
Ultimate Parent: Ryder System. SIC:
7513—Truck Rental & Leasing Without
Drivers.

★ 83439 ★ Texaco Inc.
Warehouse
208 S. Crockett Ave.
Cameron, TX 76520
(817)697-6679
Ultimate Parent: Texaco. SIC: 5171—
Petroleum Bulk Stations & Terminals.

★ 83440 ★ Webster Spring Co.
Inc.
1107 W. Industrial Blvd.
Cameron, TX 76520
(817)697-6548
Ultimate Parent: Leggett & Platt Inc. SIC:
3493—Steel Springs Except Wire.

Canadian

★ 83441 ★ Pizza Hut
322 2nd
Canadian, TX 79014
(806)323-5122
Ultimate Parent: Pepsico. SIC: 5812—
Eating Places.

Canyon

★ 83442 ★ Exxon
311 23rd St.
Canyon, TX 79015
(806)655-2228
Ultimate Parent: Exxon. SIC: 5541—
Gasoline Service Stations.

★ 83443 ★ Kentucky Fried
Chicken
102 23rd St.
Canyon, TX 79015
(806)655-1221
Ultimate Parent: Pepsico. SIC: 5812—
Eating Places.

★ 83444 ★ Radio Shack
2200 4th Ave.
Canyon, TX 79015
(806)655-9705
Company Type: Division. Ultimate Parent:
Tandy Corp. SIC: 5065—Electronic Parts &
Equipment Nec.

★ 83445 ★ Wal Mart Discount
Cities
2309 N. 3rd Ave.
Canyon, TX 79015
(806)655-1175
Ultimate Parent: Wal-Mart Stores, Inc.

Carrizo Springs

★ 83446 ★ Pizza Hut
201 Pena St.
Carrizo Springs, TX 78834
(512)876-9870
Ultimate Parent: Pepsico. SIC: 5812—
Eating Places.

Carrollton

★ 83447 ★ American Greetings
Corp.
2855 Trinity Sq. Dr.
Carrollton, TX 75006-2347
(214)416-1224
Ultimate Parent: American Greetings. SIC:
5112—Stationery & Office Supplies.

★ 83448 ★ Arrow Industries
2625 Beltline Rd., E
Carrollton, TX 75006
(214)416-6500
Officer: Steve Rosenberg, President.
Ultimate Parent: Conagra.

★ 83449 ★ Arrow/Kierulff
Electronics
3220 Comandor Dr.
Carrollton, TX 75006
(214)380-6464
Company Type: Division. Location Type:
Distribution center. Officer: Pete Stone,
Regional Vice President. Ultimate Parent:
Arrow Electronics. SIC: 5065—Electronic
Parts & Equipment Nec.

★ 83450 ★ Avery Dennison
Fasson Roll Div.
2025 McKenzie, Ste. 100
Carrollton, TX 75006-6863
(214)484-3230
Company Type: Division. Officer: D. L.
Beaver. Ultimate Parent: Avery Dennison
Corp. SIC: 5113—Industrial & Personal
Service Paper.

★ 83451 ★ Avery Dennison
Fasson Roll Div.
2025 McKenzie, Ste. 100
Carrollton, TX 75006-6863
(214)484-3230
Company Type: Division. Officer: D. L.
Beaver. Ultimate Parent: Avery Dennison
Corp. SIC: 5113—Industrial & Personal
Service Paper.

★ 83452 ★ BASF Corp.
1216 Trend Dr.
Carrollton, TX 75006
Ultimate Parent: BASF Corp. SIC: 2821—
Plastics Materials & Resins.

★ 83453 ★ Beneficial Texas Inc.
Carrollton Park Shopping Ctr.
Carrollton, TX 75006
(214)245-1592
Ultimate Parent: Beneficial. SIC: 6141—
Personal Credit Institutions.

★ 83454 ★ Beneficial Texas Inc.
514 Carrollton Park Ctr.
Carrollton, TX 75006
(214)416-8888
Ultimate Parent: Beneficial. SIC: 6159—
Miscellaneous Business Credit Institutions.

★ 83455 ★ Bergen Brunswig
Drug Co.
1843 Monetary Ln.
Carrollton, TX 75006
(214)242-2999
Ultimate Parent: Bergen Brunswig Corp.
SIC: 5122—Drugs, Proprietaries &
Sundries.

★ 83456 ★ Capstone
Electronics Div.
3220 Comandor Dr.
Carrollton, TX 75006
(214)380-9049
Company Type: Division. Officer: Steve
Mikunda, Managing Director. Ultimate
Parent: Arrow Electronics. SIC: 5065—
Electronic Parts & Equipment Nec.

★ 83457 ★ Carlton Cards
2855 Trinity Sq. Dr.
Carrollton, TX 75006-2347
(214)418-0711
Ultimate Parent: American Greetings. SIC:
5112—Stationery & Office Supplies.

★ 83458 ★ City National Bank
2630 Dewborn Rd.
Carrollton, TX 75006
(214)416-1836
Ultimate Parent: City National Corp. SIC:
6099—Functions Related to Deposit
Banking.

★ 83459 ★ City National Bank
Carrollton
2630 Denton Rd.
Carrollton, TX 75006
(214)418-1982
Ultimate Parent: City National Corp. SIC:
6021—National Commercial Banks.

★ 83460 ★ Comerica Bank-Texas
2625 N. Josey Lane
Carrollton, TX 75007-5532
(214)446-5100
Company Type: Subsidiary. Location
Type: Branch office. Ultimate Parent:
Comerica Bank. SIC: 6021—National
Commercial Banks.

★ 83461 ★ Compass Bank-Dallas
3640 Josey Ln.
Carrollton, TX 75007-3151
(214)681-5500
Company Type: Subsidiary. Location
Type: Branch office. Ultimate Parent:
Compass Bancshares. SIC: 6021—National
Commercial Banks.

★ 83462 ★ Compass Bank-Dallas
2630 Old Denton Rd.
Carrollton, TX 75007-5102
(214)418-1982
Ultimate Parent: Compass Bancshares.
SIC: 6021—National Commercial Banks.

★ 83463 ★ Compass Bank-Dallas
2908 Trinity Mills Rd.
Carrollton, TX 75006-2318
(214)418-1982
Company Type: Subsidiary. Location
Type: Branch office. Ultimate Parent:
Compass Bancshares. SIC: 6021—National
Commercial Banks.

★ 83464 ★ Core Laboratories
1875 Monetary Dr.
Carrollton, TX 75006
(214)446-2673 Fax: (214)717-4671
Officer: Joseph Saltamatia, President.
Ultimate Parent: Litton Industries.

★ 83465 ★ Exxon Service Center
3070 N. Josey Ln.
Carrollton, TX 75007
(214)492-9434
Ultimate Parent: Exxon. SIC: 5541—
Gasoline Service Stations.

★ 83466 ★ Fox Meyer Corp.
1220 Senlac Dr.
Carrollton, TX 75006
Officer: Thomas L. Anderson, President &
CEO. Ultimate Parent: National Intergroup.

★ 83467 ★ Greyhound Bus Lnes
1017 Elm
Carrollton, TX 75006
(214)242-3133
Ultimate Parent: Greyhound Lines Inc.

★ 83468 ★ Hibernia National
Bank
2625 N. Josey Ln.
Carrollton, TX 75007
(214)446-5100
Ultimate Parent: Hibernia Corp. SIC:
6099—Functions Related to Deposit
Banking.

★ 83469 ★ Hit or Miss
2710 N. Josey Ln.
Carrollton, TX 75007
(214)446-3363
Ultimate Parent: TJX.

★ 83470 ★ Home Depot Inc.
1441 E. Trinity Mills Rd.
Carrollton, TX 75006
(214)446-1300
Ultimate Parent: Home Depot. SIC: 5211—
Lumber & Other Building Materials.

★ 83471 ★ Inland Container
Corp.
2605 Belt Line Rd.
Carrollton, TX 75006
Ultimate Parent: Temple-Inland. SIC:
2653—Corrugated & Solid Fiber Boxes.

★ 83472 ★ International Paper
Container Div.
1655 S. I-35 E.
Carrollton, TX 75006
Company Type: Division. Ultimate Parent:
International Paper Co. SIC: 2653—
Corrugated & Solid Fiber Boxes.

★ 83473 ★ Jiffy Lube
1610 Marsh Ln.
Carrollton, TX 75006
(214)418-0063
Ultimate Parent: Pennzoil. SIC: 7539—
Automotive Repair Shops Nec.

★ 83474 ★ Jiffy Lube
2625 Midway Rd.
Carrollton, TX 75006
(214)380-2868
Ultimate Parent: Pennzoil. SIC: 7539—
Automotive Repair Shops Nec.

★ 83475 ★ Jiffy Lube
2502 E. Belt Line Rd.
Carrollton, TX 75006
(214)418-1151
Ultimate Parent: Pennzoil. SIC: 7539—
Automotive Repair Shops Nec.

★ 83476 ★ Johnson Controls Inc.
45 PO Box
Carrollton, TX 75006
(214)242-6523
Ultimate Parent: Johnson Controls Inc.
SIC: 1711—Plumbing, Heating & Air-
Conditioning.

★ 83477 ★ Kelly-Sprngfld Tr
1810 Kelly Blvd.
Carrollton, TX 75006
(214)418-9240
Ultimate Parent: Goodyear Tire & Rubber.

★ 83478 ★ Kit Chemicals Inc.
1200 W. Jackson Rd.
Carrollton, TX 75006
Ultimate Parent: Union Carbide Corp. SIC:
3861—Photographic Equipment & Supplies.

★ 83479 ★ Kroger Pharmacies
3044 Old Denton Rd.
Carrollton, TX 75007
(214)242-2603
Ultimate Parent: Kroger.

★ 83480 ★ Kti Chemicals Inc.
1200 W. Jackson Rd.
Carrollton, TX 75006
Ultimate Parent: Union Carbide Corp. SIC:
3861—Photographic Equipment & Supplies.

★ 83481 ★ Lone Star Gas Co.
533 Carrollton Park Cent
Carrollton, TX 75006
(214)242-4231
Ultimate Parent: Enserch. SIC: 4925—Gas
Production & Distribution Nec.

★ 83482 ★ Marshalls
2660 N. Josey Ln.
Carrollton, TX 75007
(214)446-2115
Ultimate Parent: Melville.

★ 83483 ★ Mary Kay Cosmtcs
2402 Canterbury Dr.
Carrollton, TX 75006
(214)242-3494
Ultimate Parent: Mary Kay Cosmetics.

★ 83484 ★ McDonalds
1943 N. I 35
Carrollton, TX 75006
(214)242-1472
Ultimate Parent: McDonald's.
SIC: 5812—Eating Places.

★ 83485 ★ McDonalds
Restaurant
2707 E. Belt Line Rd.
Carrollton, TX 75006
(214)416-7634
Ultimate Parent: McDonald's.

★ 83486 ★ McDonalds
Restaurant
2151 N. Josey Ln.
Carrollton, TX 75006
(214)245-2924
Ultimate Parent: McDonald's.

★ 83487 ★ Mobil Oil Corp.
2525 Rosemeade Pky.
Carrollton, TX 75007
(214)306-3177
Ultimate Parent: Mobil. SIC: 5599—
Automotive Dealers Nec.

★ 83488 ★ Mobil Oil Corp.
2775 E. Trinity Mills Rd.
Carrollton, TX 75006
(214)416-8694
Ultimate Parent: Mobil.

★ 83489 ★ Mobil Oil Corp.
3655 N. Josey Ln.
Carrollton, TX 75007
(214)492-7811
Ultimate Parent: Mobil.

★ 83490 ★ Mobil Self Serve
1010 W. Trinity Mills Rd.
Carrollton, TX 75006
(214)323-0589
Ultimate Parent: Mobil.

★ 83491 ★   Mobil Self Serve
4210 N. Josey Ln.
Carrollton, TX 75010
(214)492-6968
Ultimate Parent: Mobil.

★ 83492 ★   National Intergroup
1220 Seniac Dr.
Carrollton, TX 75006
(214)446-4800
Company Type: Headquarters. Officer: A.
J. Butler. Employee Count: 3300. Sales:
4852 M. Fortune Service 500: Ranking 22.

★ 83493 ★   National Intergroup,
Inc.
1220 Senlac Dr.
Carrollton, TX 75006
(214)446-4800 Fax: (214)446-4499 Telex:
211946
Officer: Abbey J. Butler, Co-Chairman of
the Board & Co-CEO. Ultimate Parent:
National Intergroup. Employee Count:
2350.

★ 83494 ★   Otis Engineering
Corp.
1000 W. Crosby Rd.
Carrollton, TX 75006
Ultimate Parent: Halliburton. SIC: 3533—
Oil & Gas Field Machinery.

★ 83495 ★   Otis Engineering
Corp.
2601 Beltline Rd.
Carrollton, TX 75006
Ultimate Parent: Halliburton. SIC: 3533—
Oil & Gas Field Machinery.

★ 83496 ★   Payless Shoesource
2630 N. Josey Ln.
Carrollton, TX 75007
(214)245-4270
Ultimate Parent: May Department Stores.
SIC: 5661—Shoe Stores.

★ 83497 ★   Payless Shoesource
651 Carrollton Pk. Ctr.
Carrollton, TX 75006
(214)245-5235
Ultimate Parent: May Department Stores.
SIC: 5661—Shoe Stores.

★ 83498 ★   Pizza Hut
2020 Belt Line Rd.
Carrollton, TX 75006
(214)446-1803
Ultimate Parent: Pepsico. SIC: 5812—
Eating Places.

★ 83499 ★   Pizza Hut
3065 N. Josey Ln.
Carrollton, TX 75007
(214)394-4410
Ultimate Parent: Pepsico.

★ 83500 ★   Pulte Home Corp.
1226 Normandy Dr.
Carrollton, TX 75006
(214)446-0318
Ultimate Parent: Pulte.

★ 83501 ★   Radio Shack
314 Furen Creek Village S
Carrollton, TX 75007
(214)245-0948
Company Type: Division. Ultimate Parent:
Tandy Corp. SIC: 5731—Radio, Television
& Electronics Store.

★ 83502 ★   Radio Shack
671 Carrollton Park Cent
Carrollton, TX 75006
(214)416-2889
Company Type: Division. Ultimate Parent:
Tandy Corp. SIC: 5734—Computer &
Software Stores.

★ 83503 ★   Radio Shack
Frankford
Carrollton, TX 75007
(214)492-3159
Company Type: Division. Ultimate Parent:
Tandy Corp. SIC: 5065—Electronic Parts &
Equipment Nec.

★ 83504 ★   Rooftop Systems Inc.
1811 Trinity Valley Dr.
Carrollton, TX 75006
(214)247-7447
Officer: Phil Rutledge, President. Ultimate
Parent: Dayton Hudson. SIC: 3585—
Refrigeration & Heating Equipment.

★ 83505 ★   Shipley Co.
1620 Rafe St.
Carrollton, TX 75006
(214)446-1900
Ultimate Parent: Rohm & Haas.

★ 83506 ★   Stanfast Inc.
1430 Bradley Ln.
Carrollton, TX 75007
(214)245-7366
Officer: Doug Brown, Manager. Ultimate
Parent: Standard Register. SIC: 2761—
Manifold Business Forms.

★ 83507 ★   T J Maxx Store
2540 Old Denton Rd.
Carrollton, TX 75006
(214)446-3004
Ultimate Parent: TJX. SIC: 5311—
Department Stores.

★ 83508 ★   Taco Bell
2002 I H E
Carrollton, TX 75006
(214)323-1512
Ultimate Parent: Pepsico. SIC: 5812—
Eating Places.

★ 83509 ★   Texaco
1900 N. Stemmons Fwy.
Carrollton, TX 75006
(214)245-1550
Ultimate Parent: Texaco. SIC: 5411—
Grocery Stores.

★ 83510 ★   Texaco Express Lub
2412 E. Trinity Mills Rd.
Carrollton, TX 75006
(214)416-1153
Ultimate Parent: Texaco.

★ 83511 ★   Wal Mart Discount
1025 W. Trinity Mills Rd.
Carrollton, TX 75006
(214)245-0111
Ultimate Parent: Wal-Mart Stores, Inc.

★ 83512 ★   Waldenbooks & More
Trinity Mills Apts
Carrollton, TX 75006
(214)248-0902
Ultimate Parent: K-Mart. SIC: 5942—Book
Stores.

★ 83513 ★   Weyerhaeuser Paper
2015 Country Club Dr.
Carrollton, TX 75006
(214)418-1703
Ultimate Parent: Weyerhaeuser Co. SIC:
5099—Durable Goods Nec.

★ 83514 ★   Zeno Systems Inc.
1330 Capital Pky.
Carrollton, TX 75006-3647
(214)323-8000
Ultimate Parent: Alco Standard Corp. SIC:
5044—Office Equipment.

Carthage

★ 83515 ★   Eckerd Drug Co.
415 NW Loop
Carthage, TX 75633
(214)693-2611
Ultimate Parent: Eckerd Corp. SIC: 5912—
Drug Stores & Proprietary Stores.

★ 83516 ★   Exxon Co.
1410 S. Shelby St.
Carthage, TX 75633
(214)693-6211
Ultimate Parent: Exxon. SIC: 4939—
Combination Utility Nec.

★ 83517 ★   First State Bank &
Trust Co.
110 W. Panola St.
Carthage, TX 75633
(214)693-6606
Ultimate Parent: Michigan National Corp.
SIC: 6022—State Commercial Banks.

★ 83518 ★   Greyhound Bus
Station
400 N. Adams St.
Carthage, TX 75633
(214)693-2665
Ultimate Parent: Greyhound Lines Inc. SIC:
4173—Bus Terminal & Service Facilities.

★ 83519 ★   Louisiana Pacific
Corp.
Hwy. 149 N
Carthage, TX 75633
(214)693-3861
Ultimate Parent: Louisiana-Pacific. SIC:
5031—Lumber, Plywood & Millwork.

★ 83520 ★   Pennzoil Co.
1001 S. Shelby St.
Carthage, TX 75633
(214)693-7196
Ultimate Parent: Pennzoil. SIC: 2911—
Petroleum Refining.

★ 83521 ★   Pizza Hut
1100 W. Panola St.
Carthage, TX 75633
(214)693-4331
Ultimate Parent: Pepsico. SIC: 5812—
Eating Places.

★ 83522 ★   Trailways Bus Inc.
320 E. Sabine St.
Carthage, TX 75633
(214)693-3229
Ultimate Parent: Greyhound Lines Inc. SIC:
4142—Bus Charter Service Except Local.

★ 83523 ★   Tyson Foods Inc.
800 E. Loop 59
Carthage, TX 75633-0648
Ultimate Parent: Tyson Foods, Inc. SIC:
2000—Food & Kindred Products.

★ 83524 ★   Tyson Foods Inc.
Hwy. 59 Byp.
Carthage, TX 75633
(903)693-7101
Officer: Bill Bruene, Manager. Ultimate
Parent: Tyson Foods, Inc. SIC: 2015—
Poultry Slaughtering & Processing.

★ 83525 ★   Tyson Foods Inc.
Processing Plant
800 E. Loop 59
Carthage, TX 75633-0648
Ultimate Parent: Tyson Foods, Inc. SIC:
2015—Poultry Slaughtering & Processing.

★ 83526 ★   Wal Mart
423 NW Loop
Carthage, TX 75633
(214)693-8881
Ultimate Parent: Wal-Mart Stores, Inc. SIC:
5311—Department Stores.

Cedar Hill

★ 83527 ★   Exxon
271 S. Hwy. 67
Cedar Hill, TX 75104
(214)291-1038
Ultimate Parent: Exxon. SIC: 5541—
Gasoline Service Stations.

★ 83528 ★   Kmart Discount
Stores
229 N. F M Rd. 1382
Cedar Hill, TX 75104
(214)291-0187
Ultimate Parent: K-Mart. SIC: 5399—
Miscellaneous General Merchandise Store.

★ 83529 ★   Kroger Food Stores
235 E. Fm 1382
Cedar Hill, TX 75104
(214)291-0224
Ultimate Parent: Kroger. SIC: 5912—Drug
Stores & Proprietary Stores.

★ 83530 ★   Ryder Truck Rental
691 S. Hwy. 67
Cedar Hill, TX 75104
(214)291-9291
Ultimate Parent: Ryder System. SIC:
7513—Truck Rental & Leasing Without
Drivers.

★ 83531 ★   Ryder Truck Rental
320 S. Clark Rd.
Cedar Hill, TX 75104
(214)291-1719
Ultimate Parent: Ryder System. SIC:
7389—Business Services Nec.

Cedar Park

★ 83532 ★   Exxon Co. USA
1000 N. Bell Blvd.
Cedar Park, TX 78613
(512)331-1816
Ultimate Parent: Exxon.

★ 83533 ★   McDonalds
Restaurant
1103 N. Bell Blvd.
Cedar Park, TX 78613
(512)259-5770
Ultimate Parent: McDonald's.

★ 83534 ★   Pizza Hut
1105 N. Bell Blvd.
Cedar Park, TX 78613
(512)259-4444
Ultimate Parent: Pepsico.

Celeste

★ 83535 ★   First Bank
7 PO Box
Celeste, TX 75423
(903)568-4211
Ultimate Parent: Shawmut National Corp.
SIC: 6099—Functions Related to Deposit
Banking.

Center

★ 83536 ★   Holly Farms Foods
Inc.
Center Texas Plant
1019 Shelbyville St.
PO Box 789
Center, TX 75935
Location Type: Plant. Ultimate Parent:
Tyson Foods, Inc. SIC: 0251—Broiler, Fryer
& Roaster Chickens.

★ 83537 ★   Holly Farms of Texas
Inc.
Center Texas Plant
1019 Shelbyville St.
PO Box 789
Center, TX 75935
Location Type: Plant. Ultimate Parent:
Tyson Foods, Inc. SIC: 0251—Broiler, Fryer
& Roaster Chickens.

★ 83538 ★   Holly Farms/Tyson
Foods Inc. Processing Plant
1019 Shelbyville St.
Center, TX 75935
Ultimate Parent: Tyson Foods, Inc. SIC:
2015—Poultry Slaughtering & Processing.

★ 83539 ★   Mobil Pipeline Co.
Shelbyville Hwy.
Center, TX 75935
(409)598-7895
Company Type: Branch. Ultimate Parent:
Mobil. SIC: 4612—Crude Petroleum
Pipelines.

★ 83540 ★   Pizza Hut
1007 N. Hwy. 96
Center, TX 75935
(409)598-6303
Ultimate Parent: Pepsico. SIC: 5812—
Eating Places.

★ 83541 ★   Stop & Shop Grocery
New San Augustn Hwy.
Center, TX 75935
(409)598-5592
Ultimate Parent: Stop & Shop. SIC: 5411—
Grocery Stores.

★ 83542 ★   Trailways Bus Depot
Southview Cir.
Center, TX 75935
(409)598-5480
Ultimate Parent: Greyhound Lines Inc. SIC:
4131—Intercity & Rural Bus Transportation.

★ 83543 ★   Tyson & ORG Holly
Farms Inc.
1019 Shelbyville St.
Center, TX 75935
(409)598-2723
Officer: Jack Gardner, Manager. Ultimate
Parent: Tyson Foods, Inc. SIC: 2015—
Poultry Slaughtering & Processing; 2048—
Prepared Feeds Nec.

★ 83544 ★   Wal Mart
City Hwy. 96
Center, TX 75935
(409)598-6131
Ultimate Parent: Wal-Mart Stores, Inc. SIC:
5311—Department Stores.

Channelview

★ 83545 ★   Arco
16930 Wallisville Rd.
Channelview, TX 77530
(713)452-5129
Ultimate Parent: Atlantic Richfield Co., Inc.
SIC: 4612—Crude Petroleum Pipelines.

★ 83546 ★   Arco Chemical Co.
2502 Sheldon Rd.
Channelview, TX 77530
Ultimate Parent: Atlantic Richfield Co., Inc.
SIC: 2865—Cyclic Crudes & Intermediates;
2869—Industrial Organic Chemicals Nec.

★ 83547 ★   Arco Chemical Co.
PO Box 30
Channelview, TX 77530-0030
(713)860-4000
Officer: Charles Bonney. Ultimate Parent:
Atlantic Richfield Co., Inc. SIC: 2869—
Industrial Organic Chemicals Nec; 5169—
Chemicals & Allied Products Nec.

★ 83548 ★   Chevron Chemical
Co.
1515 S. Sheldon Rd.
Channelview, TX 77530
Ultimate Parent: Chevron Corp. SIC:
3087—Custom Compound of Purchased
Resins.

★ 83549 ★   Kentucky Fried
Chicken
415 Sheldon Rd.
Channelview, TX 77530
(713)452-6149
Ultimate Parent: Pepsico. SIC: 5812—
Eating Places.

★ 83550 ★   Lyondell
Petrochemical Co.
8280 Sheldon Rd.
Channelview, TX 77530
Ultimate Parent: Atlantic Richfield Co., Inc.
SIC: 2869—Industrial Organic Chemicals
Nec; 2821—Plastics Materials & Resins.

★ 83551 ★   McDonalds
Restaurant
406 Sheldon Rd.
Channelview, TX 77530
(713)452-0785
Ultimate Parent: McDonald's.
SIC: 5812—Eating Places.

★ 83552 ★   Pizza Hut
412 Sheldon Rd.
Channelview, TX 77530
(713)452-5738
Ultimate Parent: Pepsico. SIC: 5812—
Eating Places.

★ 83553 ★   Precoat Metals
16402 Jacintoport Blvd.
Channelview, TX 77015
Ultimate Parent: Sequa Corp. SIC: 3479—
Metal Coating & Allied Services.

★ 83554 ★   Radio Shack
431 Sheldon Rd.
Channelview, TX 77530
(713)452-7573
Company Type: Division. Ultimate Parent:
Tandy Corp. SIC: 3699—Electrical
Equipment & Supplies Nec.

★ 83555 ★   Ryder Truck Rental
715 Sheldon Rd.
Channelview, TX 77530
(713)452-4409
Ultimate Parent: Ryder System. SIC:
7359—Equipment Rental & Leasing Nec.

★ 83556 ★   Taco Bell
475 Sheldon Rd.
Channelview, TX 77530
(713)452-3874
Ultimate Parent: Pepsico. SIC: 5812—
Eating Places.

Cheek

★ 83557 ★   Goodyear Tire &
Rubber Co.
Interstate 10 at Smith Rd.
Cheek, TX 77720-6003
Ultimate Parent: Goodyear Tire & Rubber.
SIC: 2822—Synthetic Rubber; 2821—
Plastics Materials & Resins; 2869—
Industrial Organic Chemicals Nec.

Childress

★ 83558 ★   Kentucky Fried
Chicken
1910 NW Ave. F
Childress, TX 79201
(817)937-3921
Ultimate Parent: Pepsico. SIC: 5812—
Eating Places.

★ 83559 ★   Pizza Hut
1209 Avenue F NW
Childress, TX 79201
(817)937-3623
Ultimate Parent: Pepsico. SIC: 5812—
Eating Places.

★ 83560 ★   Ryder Truck Rental
506 19th St. NW
Childress, TX 79201
(817)937-8711
Ultimate Parent: Ryder System. SIC:
7359—Equipment Rental & Leasing Nec.

★ 83561 ★   Ryder Truck Rental
Hwy. 287 W
Childress, TX 79201
(817)937-8435
Ultimate Parent: Ryder System. SIC:
7513—Truck Rental & Leasing Without
Drivers.

★ 83562 ★   Trailways Bus System
101 Main
Childress, TX 79201
(817)937-2551
Ultimate Parent: Greyhound Lines Inc. SIC:
4131—Intercity & Rural Bus Transportation.

★ 83563 ★   West Texas Utilities
Co.
300 Commerce St.
Childress, TX 79201
(817)937-2581
Ultimate Parent: Central & South West.
SIC: 5722—Household Appliance Stores.

Cisco

★ 83564 ★   Greyhound Bus Lines
708 E. 8th St.
Cisco, TX 76437
(817)442-1480
Ultimate Parent: Greyhound Lines Inc. SIC:
4111—Local & Suburban Transit.

★ 83565 ★   Lone Star Gas Co.
Texas Inc.
713 Avenue D
Cisco, TX 76437
(817)442-1588
Ultimate Parent: Enserch. SIC: 4932—Gas
& Other Services Combined.

★ 83566 ★   Trailways Bus System
708 E. 8th St.
Cisco, TX 76437
(817)442-2660
Ultimate Parent: Greyhound Lines Inc. SIC:
4131—Intercity & Rural Bus Transportation.

Clarendon

★ 83567 ★   Burlington Northern
Rail Rd
Clarendon, TX 79226
(806)874-3266
Ultimate Parent: Burlington Northern. SIC:
4011—Railroads—Line-Haul Operating.

Clarksville

★ 83568 ★   Lone Star Gas Co.
1700 W. Main St.
Clarksville, TX 75426
(903)427-2986
Ultimate Parent: Enserch. SIC: 4925—Gas
Production & Distribution Nec.

★ 83569 ★   Piggly Wiggly
707 W. Main St.
Clarksville, TX 75426
(214)427-3046
Ultimate Parent: Bruno's. SIC: 5411—
Grocery Stores.

★ 83570 ★   Piggly-Wiggly OFC
College Ave.
Clarksville, TX 75426
(903)427-2276
Officer: J. D. Jamison. Ultimate Parent:
Bruno's. SIC: 5411—Grocery Stores.

★ 83571 ★   Pizza Hut
2000 W. Main St.
Clarksville, TX 75426
(214)427-5276
Ultimate Parent: Pepsico. SIC: 5812—
Eating Places.

★ 83572 ★   Red Kap
Industrial Park Addition
Clarksville, TX 75426
(903)427-3888
Officer: Andy Luck, Manager. Ultimate
Parent: VF Corp. SIC: 2325—Men's/Boys'
Trousers & Slacks; 2329—Men's/Boys'
Clothing Nec.

★ 83573 ★   Ryder Truck Rental
Paris Hwy.
Clarksville, TX 75426
(214)427-3906
Ultimate Parent: Ryder System. SIC:
7513—Truck Rental & Leasing Without
Drivers.

Cleburne

★ 83574 ★   Atchison, Topeka &
Santa Fe Railway Co.
600 Gresham St.
Cleburne, TX 76031
(817)645-4561
Ultimate Parent: Santa Fe Pacific Corp.
SIC: 4011—Railroads—Line-Haul
Operating.

★ 83575 ★   Kentucky Fried
Chicken
1510 W. Henderson St.
Cleburne, TX 76031
(817)645-0701
Ultimate Parent: Pepsico. SIC: 5812—
Eating Places.

★ 83576 ★   Manville Sales Corp.
200 W. Industrial Blvd.
Cleburne, TX 76031
Ultimate Parent: Manville Corp. SIC:
3296—Mineral Wool.

★ 83577 ★   McDonalds
Restaurant
736 N. Main St.
Cleburne, TX 76031
(817)641-7911
Ultimate Parent: McDonald's.
SIC: 5812—Eating Places.

★ 83578 ★   Parker Hannifin
Hose Products Div.
2501 N. Main St.
Cleburne, TX 76031
Company Type: Division. Ultimate Parent:
Parker Hannifin. SIC: 3471—Plating &
Polishing.

★ 83579 ★   Parker Hannifin Corp.
Hose Products Div.
2501 N. Main St.
Cleburne, TX 76031
Company Type: Division. Ultimate Parent:
Parker Hannifin. SIC: 3471—Plating &
Polishing; 3492—Fluid Power Valves &
Hose Fittings.

★ 83580 ★   Payless Shoesource
1607 W. Henderson St.
Cleburne, TX 76031
(817)641-4225
Ultimate Parent: May Department Stores.

★ 83581 ★   Piggly Wiggly
1322 N. Main St.
Cleburne, TX 76031
(817)645-8431
Ultimate Parent: Bruno's. SIC: 5421—Meat
& Fish Markets.

★ 83582 ★   Pizza Hut
502 W. Henderson St.
Cleburne, TX 76031
(817)641-9047
Ultimate Parent: Pepsico. SIC: 5812—
Eating Places.

★ 83583 ★   Rubbermaid
Commercial Prods. Inc.
400 Commerce St.
Cleburne, TX 76031
Ultimate Parent: Rubbermaid. SIC: 3089—
Plastics Products Nec.

★ 83584 ★   Rubbermaid
Commercial Products
400 Commerce Blvd.
Cleburne, TX 76031
(817)641-4444
Ultimate Parent: Rubbermaid. SIC: 3089—
Plastics Products Nec.

★ 83585 ★   Rubbermaid
Commercial Products Inc.
400 Commerce St.
Cleburne, TX 76031
Ultimate Parent: Rubbermaid. SIC: 3089—
Plastics Products Nec.

★ 83586 ★   Ryder Truck Rental
1820 N. Main St.
Cleburne, TX 76031
(817)641-7362
Ultimate Parent: Ryder System.

★ 83587 ★   Ryder Truck Rental
1411 N. Main St.
Cleburne, TX 76031
(817)641-3862
Ultimate Parent: Ryder System. SIC:
7359—Equipment Rental & Leasing Nec.

★ 83588 ★   Schuller International
Inc.
200 W. Industrial Blvd.
Cleburne, TX 76031
Ultimate Parent: Manville Corp. SIC:
3296—Mineral Wool.

★ 83589 ★   Taco Bell
621 W. Henderson St.
Cleburne, TX 76031
(817)641-8282
Ultimate Parent: Pepsico. SIC: 5812—
Eating Places.

★ 83590 ★   Taco Bell
801 N. Main St.
Cleburne, TX 76031
(817)641-0802
Ultimate Parent: Pepsico.

Cleveland

★ 83591 ★   Comerica Bank-Texas
1408 E. Houston
Cleveland, TX 77327-4795
(713)592-8795
Company Type: Subsidiary. Location
Type: Branch office. Ultimate Parent:
Comerica Bank. SIC: 6021—National
Commercial Banks.

★ 83592 ★   Kentucky Fried
Chicken
Hwy. 59 N
Cleveland, TX 77327
(713)592-7905
Ultimate Parent: Pepsico. SIC: 5812—
Eating Places.

★ 83593 ★   Kirby Forest
Industries Plywood
Hwy. 787 E.
Cleveland, TX 77327
Ultimate Parent: Louisiana-Pacific. SIC:
2436—Softwood Veneer & Plywood.

★ 83594 ★   Louisiana Pacific
Corp.
Hwy. 59 S
Cleveland, TX 77327
(713)592-1429
Ultimate Parent: Louisiana-Pacific. SIC:
5031—Lumber, Plywood & Millwork.

Clifton

★ 83595 ★   Lone Star Gas Co.
110 N. Ave.
Clifton, TX 76634
(817)675-8680
Ultimate Parent: Enserch. SIC: 4932—Gas
& Other Services Combined.

Clute

★ 83596 ★   Casual Corner
100 Brazoswood Dr.
Clute, TX 77531
(409)297-7241
Ultimate Parent: United States Shoe. SIC:
5651—Family Clothing Stores.

★ 83597 ★   Circus World
100 Brazosport Blvd. N
Clute, TX 77531
(409)297-1361
Ultimate Parent: Melville. SIC: 5945—
Hobby, Toy & Game Shops.

★ 83598 ★   Foot Action
100 Brazosport Blvd. N
Clute, TX 77531
(409)297-6025
Ultimate Parent: Melville. SIC: 5661—Shoe
Stores.

★ 83599 ★   Jiffy Lube
100 Brazoswood Dr.
Clute, TX 77531
(409)297-3078
Ultimate Parent: Pennzoil.

★ 83600 ★   Lerner Shop
100 Brazosport Blvd. N
Clute, TX 77531
(409)297-2311
Ultimate Parent: Limited. SIC: 5651—
Family Clothing Stores.

★ 83601 ★   The Limited
100 Brazosport Blvd. N
Clute, TX 77531
(409)297-0129
Ultimate Parent: Limited. SIC: 5651—
Family Clothing Stores.

★ 83602 ★   Service Merchandise
100 Brazosport Blvd. N
Clute, TX 77531
(409)297-8051
Ultimate Parent: Service Merchandise Co.,
Inc. SIC: 5311—Department Stores.

★ 83603 ★   Wal Mart
120 W. Hwy. 332
Clute, TX 77531
(409)297-9752
Ultimate Parent: Wal-Mart Stores, Inc. SIC:
5311—Department Stores.

★ 83604 ★   Waldenbooks
100 Brazosport Blvd. N
Clute, TX 77531
(409)297-8412
Ultimate Parent: K-Mart. SIC: 5942—Book
Stores.

★ 83605 ★   Walgreen Drugs
103 Dixie Dr.
Clute, TX 77531
(409)265-2517
Ultimate Parent: Walgreen Co. SIC:
5912—Drug Stores & Proprietary Stores.

Coleman

★ 83606 ★   Lone Star Gas Co.
116 S. Concho St.
Coleman, TX 76834
(915)625-2114
Ultimate Parent: Enserch. SIC: 4932—Gas
& Other Services Combined.

★ 83607 ★   Pizza Hut
1601 N. Neches St.
Coleman, TX 76834
(915)625-3122
Ultimate Parent: Pepsico. SIC: 5812—
Eating Places.

College Sta

★ 83608 ★   Digital Equipment
Corp.
412 Tarrow St.
College Sta, TX 77840
(409)775-0166
Ultimate Parent: Digital Equipment Corp.
SIC: 5063—Electrical Apparatus &
Equipment.

★ 83609 ★   Hertz Rent-A-Car
Licensee
302 Jersey St.
College Sta, TX 77840
(409)696-1381
Ultimate Parent: Hertz. SIC: 7514—
Passenger Car Rental.

★ 83610 ★   Kroger Family Center
2412 S. Texas Ave.
College Sta, TX 77840
(409)693-9974
Ultimate Parent: Kroger. SIC: 5411—
Grocery Stores; 5921—Liquor Stores.

★ 83611 ★   Radio Shack
2414 S. Texas Ave.
College Sta, TX 77840
(409)764-8171
Company Type: Division. Ultimate Parent:
Tandy Corp. SIC: 5046—Commercial
Equipment Nec.

★ 83612 ★   Radio Shack
1500 Harvey Rd.
College Sta, TX 77840
(409)764-0050
Company Type: Division. Ultimate Parent:
Tandy Corp. SIC: 5065—Electronic Parts &
Equipment Nec.

★ 83613 ★   Radio Shack
1673 S. Texas Ave.
College Sta, TX 77840
(409)693-1444
Company Type: Division. Ultimate Parent:
Tandy Corp. SIC: 5065—Electronic Parts &
Equipment Nec; 5731—Radio, Television &
Electronics Stores.

★ 83614 ★   Southland Corp.
1403 Hwy. 30
College Sta, TX 77840
(409)693-9537
Ultimate Parent: Southland Corp. SIC:
5411—Grocery Stores.

★ 83615 ★   Western Auto Supply
Co.
204 Harvey Rd.
College Sta, TX 77840
(409)823-1265
Ultimate Parent: Sears Roebuck & Co.
SIC: 5013—Motor Vehicle Supplies & New
Parts.

College Station

★ 83616 ★   Casual Corner
1500 Harvey Rd.
College Station, TX 77840
(409)764-0452
Ultimate Parent: United States Shoe. SIC:
5651—Family Clothing Stores.

★ 83617 ★   Greyhound Bus
Station
1369 PO Box
College Station, TX 77841
Ultimate Parent: Greyhound Lines Inc. SIC:
4173—Bus Terminal & Service Facilities;
4212—Local Trucking Without Storage.

★ 83618 ★   Hertz Rent-A-Car
W Fm M Rd.
College Station, TX 77840
(409)546-8337
Ultimate Parent: Hertz. SIC: 7514—
Passenger Car Rental.

★ 83619 ★   Hit or Miss
1500 Harvey Rd.
College Station, TX 77840
(409)764-3076
Ultimate Parent: TJX. SIC: 5651—Family
Clothing Stores.

★ 83620 ★   Hit or Miss
Post Oak Mall
College Station, TX 77840
(409)693-9007
Ultimate Parent: TJX. SIC: 5621—
Women's Clothing Stores.

★ 83621 ★   Piggly Wiggly
2700 S. Texas Ave.
College Station, TX 77840
(409)693-2163
Ultimate Parent: Bruno's. SIC: 5411—
Grocery Stores.

★ 83622 ★   Pizza Hut
102 University Dr. E
College Station, TX 77840
(409)696-2512
Ultimate Parent: Pepsico. SIC: 5812—
Eating Places.

★ 83623 ★   Service Merchandise
1500 Harvey Rd.
College Station, TX 77840
(409)764-0022
Ultimate Parent: Service Merchandise Co.,
Inc. SIC: 5944—Jewelry Stores.

★ 83624 ★   Texaco Gas Station
3700 S. Texas Ave.
College Station, TX 77845
(409)693-1175
Ultimate Parent: Texaco. SIC: 5541—
Gasoline Service Stations.

★ 83625 ★   Texas Copy Systems
3104 Texas Ave. S
College Station, TX 77845
(409)693-9986
Officer: Steve Vaughan, Manager. Ultimate
Parent: Alco Standard Corp. SIC: 3663—
Radio & T.V. Communications Equipment.

★ 83626 ★   Westinghouse
Electric
7807 E. Bypass
College Station, TX 77845
(409)764-2200
Officer: Larry Teverbaugh, Manager.
Ultimate Parent: Westinghouse Electric
Corp. SIC: 3663—Radio & T.V.
Communications Equipment; 3679—
Electronic Components Nec.

★ 83627 ★   Westinghouse
Electric Corp.
Electronic Assembly
7807 East Bypass
College Station, TX 77840
Location Type: Plant. Ultimate Parent:
Westinghouse Electric Corp. SIC: 3679—
Electronic Components Nec; 3699—
Electrical Equipment & Supplies Nec.

★ 83628 ★   Westinghouse
Electric Corp.
Electronic Assembly Plant
7807 E. Bypass
College Station, TX 77845
Location Type: Plant. Ultimate Parent:
Westinghouse Electric Corp. SIC: 3672—
Printed Circuit Boards; 3812—Search &
Navigation Equipment.

Colleyville

★ 83629 ★   Mary Kay Cosmetics
4002 Pembrooke Pky. W
Colleyville, TX 76034
(817)540-4030
Ultimate Parent: Mary Kay Cosmetics. SIC:
5999—Miscellaneous Retail Stores Nec.

★ 83630 ★   Payless Cashways
3901 Colleyville Blvd.
Colleyville, TX 76034
(817)498-5125
Ultimate Parent: Payless Cashways.

★ 83631 ★   Taco Bell
5003 Colleyville Blvd.
Colleyville, TX 76034
(817)581-6895
Ultimate Parent: Pepsico.

Collinsville

★ 83632 ★   Circus World
Heartland Mall
Collinsville, TX 76233
(214)643-3411
Ultimate Parent: Melville. SIC: 5945—
Hobby, Toy & Game Shops.

★ 83633 ★   Coca Cola Bottling
Co.
1308 Ctr. Ave.
Collinsville, TX 76233
(214)646-7022
Ultimate Parent: Coca-Cola Enterprises.
SIC: 2086—Bottled & Canned Soft Drinks.

★ 83634 ★   Kroger Food Store
302 N. Main
Collinsville, TX 76233
(214)646-7546
Ultimate Parent: Kroger. SIC: 5411—
Grocery Stores.

★ 83635 ★   Lone Star Gas Co.
605 Fisk
Collinsville, TX 76233
(214)646-1551
Ultimate Parent: Enserch. SIC: 4925—Gas
Production & Distribution Nec.

★ 83636 ★   Union Texas
Petroleum Corp.
201 Adams
Collinsville, TX 76233
(214)643-3121
Ultimate Parent: Union Texas Petroleum.
SIC: 5172—Petroleum Products Nec.

★ 83637 ★   Walgreen Drug Stores
Heartland Mall
Collinsville, TX 76233
(214)646-7536
Ultimate Parent: Walgreen Co. SIC:
5912—Drug Stores & Proprietary Stores.

Colorado City

★ 83638 ★   Marshalls
96 Rural Route 3
Colorado City, TX 79512
(915)728-3001
Ultimate Parent: Melville. SIC: 5399—
Miscellaneous General Merchandise Store.

★ 83639 ★   Pizza Hut
2215 Hickory St.
Colorado City, TX 79512
(915)728-3331
Ultimate Parent: Pepsico. SIC: 5812—
Eating Places.

★ 83640 ★   Radio Shack
241 E. 2nd St.
Colorado City, TX 79512
(915)728-3494
Company Type: Division. Ultimate Parent:
Tandy Corp. SIC: 5731—Radio, Television
& Electronics Stores.

★ 83641 ★   Trailways Bus System
604 W. Hwy. 80
Colorado City, TX 79512
(915)728-3617
Ultimate Parent: Greyhound Lines Inc. SIC:
4131—Intercity & Rural Bus Transportation.

Comanche

★ 83642 ★   Lone Star Gas Co.
108 N. Austin St.
Comanche, TX 76442
(915)356-2100
Ultimate Parent: Enserch. SIC: 4932—Gas
& Other Services Combined.

Comfort

★ 83643 ★   Mini Mart 6
1029 Hwy. 27
Comfort, TX 78013
(512)995-3991
Ultimate Parent: Kroger. SIC: 5411—
Grocery Stores.

Commerce

★ 83644 ★   Sherwood Medical
Co.
400 Maple St.
Commerce, TX 75428-3604
Ultimate Parent: American Home Products.
SIC: 3841—Surgical & Medical Instruments.

★ 83645 ★   US Fidelity
105 King Plz.
Commerce, TX 75428
(214)886-6324
Ultimate Parent: USF&G Corp. SIC:
6411—Insurance Agents, Brokers &
Service.

Como

★ 83646 ★   Amerada Hess Corp.
531 Rural Route 1
Como, TX 75431
(903)629-3205
Ultimate Parent: Amerada Hess. SIC:
5172—Petroleum Products Nec.

Congview

★ 83647 ★　Fleetwood Travel
Trailers Inc.
810 Prowler Dr.
Congview, TX 75604
(903)759-9451
Officer: Terry Ainslie, Manager. Ultimate
Parent: Fleetwood Enterprises, Inc. SIC:
3711—Motor Vehicles & Car Bodies;
3792—Travel Trailers & Campers.

Conroe

★ 83648 ★　Albertson's, No. 4250
220 Loop W. 336
Conroe, TX 77301
(409)756-5533
Ultimate Parent: Albertson's Inc. SIC:
5411—Grocery Stores.

★ 83649 ★　Atchison, Topeka &
Santa Fe Railway Co.
102 N. 2nd St.
Conroe, TX 77301
(409)756-3050
Ultimate Parent: Santa Fe Pacific Corp.
SIC: 4011—Railroads—Line-Haul
Operating.

★ 83650 ★　Ball Corp. Ball Metal
Container
Metal Beverage Container Group
1000 N. FM 3083
Conroe, TX 77303-3579
Company Type: Division. Officer: Glenard
K. Honeycutt, Personnel Manager. Ultimate
Parent: Ball Corp.

★ 83651 ★　Ball Pack Prd. Grp.
Conroe Plant
1000 North Fm 3083
Conroe, TX 77303
Ultimate Parent: Ball Corp. SIC: 3411—
Metal Cans.

★ 83652 ★　Ball Packaging
Products Group Metal Container
Operations
1000 N. Fm 3083
Conroe, TX 77303
Ultimate Parent: Ball Corp. SIC: 3411—
Metal Cans.

★ 83653 ★　Borden Inc. Grocery
& Speciality Products
900 E. Semands St.
Conroe, TX 77301
Ultimate Parent: Borden, Inc. SIC: 2026—
Fluid Milk.

★ 83654 ★　Coca Cola Bottling
Co.
N Frazier St.
Conroe, TX 77302
(409)756-5380
Ultimate Parent: Coca-Cola Enterprises.
SIC: 2086—Bottled & Canned Soft Drinks.

★ 83655 ★　Crown Cork & Seal
Co., Inc.
2501 N. Frazier St.
Conroe, TX 77303-1750
Ultimate Parent: Crown Cork & Seal. SIC:
3411—Metal Cans.

★ 83656 ★　Crown of Texas
Hospice
100 Interstate 45 N
Conroe, TX 77301-2701
(409)788-7707
Ultimate Parent: Beverly Enterprises. SIC:
8059—Nursing & Personal Care Nec.

★ 83657 ★　Drilling Specialties
Co.
Alamo Plant
Jefferson Chemical Rd.
Conroe, TX 77303
Location Type: Plant. Ultimate Parent:
Phillips Petroleum. SIC: 2899—Chemical
Preparations Nec.

★ 83658 ★　Eckerd Corp.
Eckerd Drug Co.
7061 Interstate 45 S.
Conroe, TX 77307
(713)273-1141
Company Type: Headquarters. Officer:
Ernie Zest, Vice President. Ultimate
Parent: Eckerd Corp. SIC: 5912—Drug
Stores & Proprietary Stores.

★ 83659 ★　Exxon Co. USA
1275 Rr 4
Conroe, TX 77302
(409)231-2261
Ultimate Parent: Exxon. SIC: 1311—Crude
Petroleum & Natural Gas.

★ 83660 ★　Exxon Shop
800 W. Loop 336
Conroe, TX 77301
(409)760-4066
Ultimate Parent: Exxon.

★ 83661 ★　Exxon Shop
1300 W. Davis St.
Conroe, TX 77304
(409)760-1117
Ultimate Parent: Exxon.

★ 83662 ★　Gulf States Utilities
Co.
3000 N. Frazier St.
Conroe, TX 77303
(409)756-1161
Ultimate Parent: Gulf State Utilities Co.
SIC: 4911—Electric Services.

★ 83663 ★　Kentucky Fried
Chicken
403 E. Davis St.
Conroe, TX 77301
(409)756-7201
Ultimate Parent: Pepsico. SIC: 5812—
Eating Places.

★ 83664 ★　Kentucky Fried
Chicken
1424 Loop
Conroe, TX 77302
(409)760-3999
Ultimate Parent: Pepsico. SIC: 5812—
Eating Places.

★ 83665 ★　Kmart Discount
Stores
230 Scott St.
Conroe, TX 77301
(409)539-3336
Ultimate Parent: K-Mart.

★ 83666 ★　Kroger Pharmacy
1217 Loop W. 336
Conroe, TX 77301
(409)756-4343
Ultimate Parent: Kroger. SIC: 5912—Drug
Stores & Proprietary Stores.

★ 83667 ★　Louisiana-Pacific
Southern Div.
PO Box 3107
Conroe, TX 77305
(409)756-0541 Fax: (409)760-5999
Company Type: Division. Officer: Ronald
L. Paul, General Manager. Ultimate Parent:
Louisiana-Pacific.

★ 83668 ★　Meadowland
Creamery
900 E. Semands St. PO Box 2448
Conroe, TX 77301
Ultimate Parent: Kroger. SIC: 2026—Fluid
Milk.

★ 83669 ★　Mini Mart
3503 N. Frazier St.
Conroe, TX 77303
(409)760-1833
Ultimate Parent: Kroger. SIC: 5411—
Grocery Stores.

★ 83670 ★　Morton Salt
515 N. Main St.
Conroe, TX 77301
(409)539-2565
Ultimate Parent: Morton International. SIC:
2899—Chemical Preparations Nec.

★ 83671 ★　O/C Tanks Corp.
Jefferson Chemical Rd.
Conroe, TX 77301
Ultimate Parent: Owens-Corning. SIC:
3089—Plastics Products Nec.

★ 83672 ★　Owens Corning
Jefferson Chemical Rd.
Conroe, TX 77301
(409)756-7731
Officer: Bill Felts, Manager. Ultimate
Parent: Owens-Corning. SIC: 3089—
Plastics Products Nec; 3296—Mineral Wool;
3499—Fabricated Metal Products Nec.

★ 83673 ★　Owens Corning
Fiberglas
Jefferson Chemical Rd.
Conroe, TX 77301
Ultimate Parent: Owens-Corning. SIC:
3000—Rubber & Miscellaneous Plastics
Products.

★ 83674 ★　Owens-Corning
Fiberglas Corp.
Jefferson Chemical Rd.
Conroe, TX 77301
Ultimate Parent: Owens-Corning. SIC:
3000—Rubber & Miscellaneous Plastics
Products.

★ 83675 ★　Owens Corning
Fiberglass
Jefferson Chemical Rd.
Conroe, TX 77303
(409)756-7731
Ultimate Parent: Owens-Corning. SIC:
3052—Rubber & Plastics Hose & Belting.

★ 83676 ★　Pepsi-Cola
South North America
222 Loop 336 E.
Conroe, TX 77301
Company Type: Division. Ultimate Parent:
Pepsico. SIC: 2086—Bottled & Canned Soft
Drinks.

★ 83677 ★　Pepsi-Cola Co.
222 Loop 336 E
Conroe, TX 77301
(409)756-6606
Officer: Don Myerse, Manager. Ultimate
Parent: Pepsico. SIC: 2086—Bottled &
Canned Soft Drinks.

★ 83678 ★　Piggly Wiggly
1908 N. Frazier St.
Conroe, TX 77301
(409)539-1917
Ultimate Parent: Bruno's. SIC: 5411—
Grocery Stores.

★ 83679 ★　Pizza Hut
206 S. C Loop
Conroe, TX 77301
(409)756-7373
Ultimate Parent: Pepsico. SIC: 8742—
Management Consulting Services.

★ 83680 ★　Pizza Hut
1610 N. Frazier St.
Conroe, TX 77301
(409)756-1818
Ultimate Parent: Pepsico. SIC: 5812—
Eating Places.

★ 83681 ★　Pizza Hut
202 Avenue a
Conroe, TX 77301
(409)539-4040
Ultimate Parent: Pepsico. SIC: 6531—Real
Estate Agents & Managers.

★ 83682 ★　Radio Shack
1418 Loop W. 336
Conroe, TX 77304
(409)756-6935
Company Type: Division. Ultimate Parent:
Tandy Corp.

★ 83683 ★　Radio Shack
2017 N. Frazier St.
Conroe, TX 77301
(409)756-3422
Company Type: Division. Ultimate Parent:
Tandy Corp. SIC: 5065—Electronic Parts &
Equipment Nec.

★ 83684 ★　Ryder Truck Rental
2309 N. Frazier St.
Conroe, TX 77303
(409)539-4445
Ultimate Parent: Ryder System.

★ 83685 ★　Taco Bell
1123 N. Frazier St.
Conroe, TX 77301
(409)539-2345
Ultimate Parent: Pepsico. SIC: 5812—
Eating Places.

★ 83686 ★　Texaco Chemical Co.
Jefferson Chemical Rd.
Conroe, TX 77301
Ultimate Parent: Texaco. SIC: 2869—
Industrial Organic Chemicals Nec.

★ 83687 ★　Wal Mart
1420 Loop W. 336
Conroe, TX 77304
(409)760-2500
Ultimate Parent: Wal-Mart Stores, Inc. SIC:
5311—Department Stores.

★ 83688 ★　Wal Mart
1420 Loop
Conroe, TX 77302
(409)760-2500
Ultimate Parent: Wal-Mart Stores, Inc. SIC:
5311—Department Stores.

★ 83689 ★　Wal Mart Discount
Cities
Montgomery Plz.
Conroe, TX 77301
(409)760-2500
Ultimate Parent: Wal-Mart Stores, Inc. SIC:
5311—Department Stores.

Coppell

★ 83690 ★　Comerica Bank-Texas
200 S. Denton Tap
Coppell, TX 75019-3205
(214)393-1123
Company Type: Subsidiary. Location
Type: Branch office. Ultimate Parent:
Comerica Bank. SIC: 6021—National
Commercial Banks.

Copperas Cove

★ 83691 ★　Ace Hardware
102 S. 1st St.
Copperas Cove, TX 76522
(817)547-2131
Ultimate Parent: Ace Hardware.

★ 83692 ★　Kentucky Fried
Chicken
Hwy. D
Copperas Cove, TX 76522
(817)547-5454
Ultimate Parent: Pepsico. SIC: 5812—
Eating Places.

★ 83693 ★　Lone Star Gas Co.
205 E. Ave. E
Copperas Cove, TX 76522
(817)547-6391
Ultimate Parent: Enserch. SIC: 4932—Gas
& Other Services Combined.

★ 83694 ★　Mary Kay Cos Ind
Sales Dir
Rural Route 1
Copperas Cove, TX 76522
(817)547-1575
Ultimate Parent: Mary Kay Cosmetics. SIC:
5999—Miscellaneous Retail Stores Nec.

★ 83695 ★　Piggly Wiggly
408 Cove Ter.
Copperas Cove, TX 76522
(817)547-7300
Ultimate Parent: Bruno's. SIC: 5411—
Grocery Stores.

★ 83696 ★　Pizza Hut
106 E. Hwy. 190
Copperas Cove, TX 76522
(817)547-9696
Ultimate Parent: Pepsico. SIC: 5812—
Eating Places.

Corpis Christi

★ 83697 ★　Burlington Coat
Factory Warehouse
Sunrise Mall
Corpis Christi, TX 78412
(512)993-0235
Ultimate Parent: Burlington Industries,
Equity. SIC: 5311—Department Stores.

Corpus Christi

★ 83698 ★　Amerada Hess Corp.
1802 Poth Ln.
Corpus Christi, TX 78407
(512)884-4831
Ultimate Parent: Amerada Hess. SIC:
4226—Special Warehousing & Storage Nec.

★ 83699 ★   **American National Bank**
100 American Bank Plaza
Corpus Christi, TX 78475
(512)883-8800
Officer: George S. Hawn, Chairman of the Board. **Ultimate Parent:** First Chicago Corp. **SIC:** 6021—National Commercial Banks. **Employee Count:** 85.

★ 83700 ★   **Arco Pipeline Co.**
4560 Tibble Ln.
Corpus Christi, TX 78407-1806
(512)884-5725
Ultimate Parent: Atlantic Richfield Co., Inc. **SIC:** 4612—Crude Petroleum Pipelines.

★ 83701 ★   **Asarco Inc.**
5500 Up River Rd.
Corpus Christi, TX 78407
(512)289-0300
Officer: John Likarish, Manager. **Ultimate Parent:** Asarco. **SIC:** 3339—Primary Nonferrous Metals Nec; 3341—Secondary Nonferrous Metals.

★ 83702 ★   **Avon Products Inc.**
205 S. Carancahua St.
Corpus Christi, TX 78401
(512)884-2325
Ultimate Parent: Avon Products, Inc. **SIC:** 5999—Miscellaneous Retail Stores Nec.

★ 83703 ★   **Borden Inc.**
4930 Ayers St.
Corpus Christi, TX 78415
(512)854-5353
Officer: Dan Page, Manager. **Ultimate Parent:** Borden, Inc. **SIC:** 2023—Dry, Condensed & Evaporated Dairy Products; 2026—Fluid Milk; 2086—Bottled & Canned Soft Drinks.

★ 83704 ★   **Borden Inc.**
Dairy
4930 Ayers St.
Corpus Christi, TX 78415
Company Type: Division. **Ultimate Parent:** Borden, Inc. **SIC:** 2026—Fluid Milk.

★ 83705 ★   **Borden Inc.**
Grocery & Specialty Products
4930 Ayers St.
Corpus Christi, TX 78415
Company Type: Division. **Ultimate Parent:** Borden, Inc. **SIC:** 2026—Fluid Milk.

★ 83706 ★   **Cain Chemical Inc.**
Corpus Christi Plant
1501 McKinzie Rd.
Corpus Christi, TX 78410
Location Type: Plant. **Ultimate Parent:** Occidental Petroleum Corp. **SIC:** 2869—Industrial Organic Chemicals Nec.

★ 83707 ★   **Ccpc Chemical Inc.**
1501 McKinzie Rd. PO Box 10940
Corpus Christi, TX 78410-0940
Ultimate Parent: Occidental Petroleum Corp. **SIC:** 2869—Industrial Organic Chemicals Nec.

★ 83708 ★   **Central Power & Light Co.**
539 N. Carancahua St.
Corpus Christi, TX 78401
(512)881-5300 **Fax:** (512)882-2712
Officer: Robert R. Carey, President & CEO. **Ultimate Parent:** Central & South West.

★ 83709 ★   **Champlin Refining Co.**
1801 Nueces Bay Blvd.
Corpus Christi, TX 78408
Ultimate Parent: Union Pacific Corp. **SIC:** 2000—Food & Kindred Products.

★ 83710 ★   **Champlin Refining Co.**
7350 I-37
Corpus Christi, TX 78409
Ultimate Parent: Union Pacific Corp. **SIC:** 2911—Petroleum Refining.

★ 83711 ★   **Coastal Refining & Marketing Inc.**
1300 Cantwell Ln.
Corpus Christi, TX 78403-0521
Ultimate Parent: Coastal Corp. **SIC:** 2911—Petroleum Refining.

★ 83712 ★   **Coastal States Crude Gathering Co.**
502 Navigation
Corpus Christi, TX 78403
(512)887-3959 **Fax:** (512)887-3952
Officer: Dan J. Hill, Chairman & CEO.
Ultimate Parent: Coastal Corp.

★ 83713 ★   **Digital Equipment Corp.**
5262 S. Staples St.
Corpus Christi, TX 78411
(512)993-3740
Ultimate Parent: Digital Equipment Corp. **SIC:** 5046—Commercial Equipment Nec.

★ 83714 ★   **Exxon**
5175 I
Corpus Christi, TX 78408
(512)884-7812
Ultimate Parent: Exxon. **SIC:** 5541—Gasoline Service Stations.

★ 83715 ★   **Exxon Co. USA**
1541 S. Padre Island Dr.
Corpus Christi, TX 78416
(512)853-1132
Ultimate Parent: Exxon.

★ 83716 ★   **Exxon Co. USA**
1700 Nueces Bay Blvd.
Corpus Christi, TX 78407
(512)887-0510
Ultimate Parent: Exxon.

★ 83717 ★   **Farm & Home Savings Association**
2566 PO Box
Corpus Christi, TX 78403
(512)883-6525
Ultimate Parent: Farm & Home Financial Corp. **SIC:** 6035—Federal Savings Institutions.

★ 83718 ★   **The Gap**
5858 S. Padre Island Dr.
Corpus Christi, TX 78412
(512)991-2826
Ultimate Parent: GAP.

★ 83719 ★   **Greyhound Bus Lines**
819 S. Broadway St.
Corpus Christi, TX 78401
(512)884-9474
Ultimate Parent: Greyhound Lines Inc. **SIC:** 4111—Local & Suburban Transit.

★ 83720 ★   **Hertz Rent-A-Car**
International
Corpus Christi, TX 78401
(512)289-0777
Ultimate Parent: Hertz. **SIC:** 7514—Passenger Car Rental.

★ 83721 ★   **Hertz Rent-A-Car**
5070 PO Box
Corpus Christi, TX 78465
(512)881-9371
Ultimate Parent: Hertz. **SIC:** 7514—Passenger Car Rental.

★ 83722 ★   **Hoechst Celanese Corp. Corpus Christi Technical Ctr.**
1901 Clarkwood Rd.
Corpus Christi, TX 78469-9077
Ultimate Parent: Hoechst Celanese Corp. **SIC:** 2869—Industrial Organic Chemicals Nec.

★ 83723 ★   **Hoechst-Celanese Corp. Technical Center**
1901 Clarkwood Rd.
Corpus Christi, TX 78409
Ultimate Parent: Hoechst Celanese Corp. **SIC:** 2869—Industrial Organic Chemicals Nec.

★ 83724 ★   **ITT Life Insurance Corp.**
1800 S. Staples St.
Corpus Christi, TX 78404
(512)882-6464
Ultimate Parent: ITT. **SIC:** 6411—Insurance Agents, Brokers & Service.

★ 83725 ★   **Kentucky Fried Chicken**
4153 S. Staples St.
Corpus Christi, TX 78411
(512)852-6031
Ultimate Parent: Pepsico. **SIC:** 5812—Eating Places.

★ 83726 ★   **Kmart**
4717 S. Padre Island Dr.
Corpus Christi, TX 78411
(512)854-3004
Ultimate Parent: K-Mart.

★ 83727 ★   **Kmart**
4101 US Hwy. 77
Corpus Christi, TX 78410
(512)241-7485
Ultimate Parent: K-Mart.

★ 83728 ★   **Kmart Pharmacy**
4717 S. Padre Island Dr.
Corpus Christi, TX 78411
(512)854-4864
Ultimate Parent: K-Mart. **SIC:** 5912—Drug Stores & Proprietary Stores.

★ 83729 ★   **Kroger Family Centers**
5625 S. Padre Island Dr.
Corpus Christi, TX 78412
(512)991-1751
Ultimate Parent: Kroger. **SIC:** 5411—Grocery Stores.

★ 83730 ★   **Kroger Family Cntrs**
3500 Leopard St.
Corpus Christi, TX 78408
(512)884-4881
Ultimate Parent: Kroger. **SIC:** 5411—Grocery Stores.

★ 83731 ★   **McDonalds Restaurant**
2242 Joyce Dr.
Corpus Christi, TX 78417
(512)857-7197
Ultimate Parent: McDonald's.

★ 83732 ★   **McDonalds Restaurants**
4401 S. Staples St.
Corpus Christi, TX 78411
(512)992-7883
Ultimate Parent: McDonald's. **SIC:** 5812—Eating Places.

★ 83733 ★   **Milpark Drilling Fluids Corpus Christi Barite Grinding**
324 Manning Rd.
Corpus Christi, TX 78410
Ultimate Parent: Baker Hughes. **SIC:** 3295—Minerals—Ground or Treated.

★ 83734 ★   **Milpark Drilling Fluids (Grinding Facility)**
324 Manning Rd.
Corpus Christi, TX 78410
Ultimate Parent: Baker Hughes. **SIC:** 3295—Minerals—Ground or Treated.

★ 83735 ★   **Milpark Drlg. Fluids (Corpus Christi Barite Grinding Facility)**
324 Manning Rd.
Corpus Christi, TX 78410
Ultimate Parent: Baker Hughes. **SIC:** 3295—Minerals—Ground or Treated.

★ 83736 ★   **Mobil Oil Corp.**
2505 N. Port Ave.
Corpus Christi, TX 78401
(512)883-4385
Ultimate Parent: Mobil. **SIC:** 5172—Petroleum Products Nec.

★ 83737 ★   **Mobil Oil Corp. Field Office**
Chapman Ranch Rd.
Corpus Christi, TX 78401
(512)852-4192
Ultimate Parent: Mobil.

★ 83738 ★   **Mobil Pipe Line Co.**
4535 Ayers St.
Corpus Christi, TX 78415-1401
(512)855-3798
Ultimate Parent: Mobil. **SIC:** 5074—Plumbing & Hydronic Heating Supplies.

★ 83739 ★   **Mobil Pipe Line Co.**
2505 N. Port Ave.
Corpus Christi, TX 78401-1218
(512)850-1668
Company Type: Branch. **Officer:** C. N. Shuler. **Ultimate Parent:** Mobil. **SIC:** 4612—Crude Petroleum Pipelines; 4619—Pipelines Nec.

★ 83740 ★   **Nalco Chemical**
6000 S. Staples St.
Corpus Christi, TX 78413
(512)992-4193
Ultimate Parent: Nalco Chemical Co.

★ 83741 ★   **Nalco Chemical Co.**
4639 Corona St.
Corpus Christi, TX 78411
(512)854-3238
Ultimate Parent: Nalco Chemical Co. **SIC:** 3861—Photographic Equipment & Supplies.

★ 83742 ★   **New York Life Corpus Christi General Office**
Western Agencies
5350 S. Staples, Ste. 420
Corpus Christi, TX 78411
(512)994-1000 **Fax:** (512)991-0534
Officer: Clifford O. Silva Jr., General Manager. **Ultimate Parent:** New York Life.

★ 83743 ★   **Norwest Mortgage Inc.**
5440 Everhart Rd.
Corpus Christi, TX 78411
(512)993-5550
Ultimate Parent: Norwest Corp. **SIC:** 6141—Personal Credit Institutions.

★ 83744 ★   **Oxy Petrochemical Inc.**
Corpus Christi Plant
1501 McKinzie Rd.
Corpus Christi, TX 78410
Location Type: Plant. **Ultimate Parent:** Occidental Petroleum Corp. **SIC:** 2869—Industrial Organic Chemicals Nec.

★ 83745 ★   **Oxy Petrochemicals**
Chorpus Christi Plant
1501 McKinzie Rd.
Corpus Christi, TX 78410
Location Type: Plant. **Ultimate Parent:** Occidental Petroleum Corp. **SIC:** 2869—Industrial Organic Chemicals Nec.

★ 83746 ★   **Pennzoil Explor&Prod Co.**
Corpus Christi Natio
Corpus Christi, TX 78401
(512)883-5771
Ultimate Parent: Pennzoil. **SIC:** 1311—Crude Petroleum & Natural Gas.

★ 83747 ★   **Pepsi Cola Bottling Co.**
1401 S. Padre Island Dr.
Corpus Christi, TX 78416
(512)853-0123
Officer: Karl Koch, Owner. **Ultimate Parent:** Pepsico. **SIC:** 2086—Bottled & Canned Soft Drinks.

★ 83748 ★   **Pizza Hut**
10702 Leopard St.
Corpus Christi, TX 78410
(512)241-5628
Ultimate Parent: Pepsico. **SIC:** 5812—Eating Places.

★ 83749 ★   **Service Merchandise**
4938 S. Staples St.
Corpus Christi, TX 78411
(512)993-2950
Ultimate Parent: Service Merchandise Co., Inc. **SIC:** 5999—Miscellaneous Retail Stores Nec.

★ 83750 ★   **Shell Oil Co.**
1st City Bank Tower
Corpus Christi, TX 78477
(512)882-1263
Ultimate Parent: Shell Oil Co. **SIC:** 5171—Petroleum Bulk Stations & Terminals.

★ 83751 ★   **Shell Oil Co.**
615 N. Upper Broadway St.
Corpus Christi, TX 78477
(512)882-6081
Ultimate Parent: Shell Oil Co. **SIC:** 5171—Petroleum Bulk Stations & Terminals.

★ 83752 ★   **Southwestern Refining Co. Inc.**
1700 Nueces Bay Blvd.
Corpus Christi, TX 78408
Ultimate Parent: Kerr-McGee. **SIC:** 2911—Petroleum Refining.

★ 83753 ★ Southwestern
Refining Co. Inc. Inc.
1700 Nueces Bay Blvd.
Corpus Christi, TX 78407
Ultimate Parent: Kerr-McGee. SIC: 2911—
Petroleum Refining.

★ 83754 ★ Sun Refining &
Marketing
4901 Gemini St.
Corpus Christi, TX 78405
(512)289-6708
Ultimate Parent: Sun. SIC: 5171—
Petroleum Bulk Stations & Terminals.

★ 83755 ★ Texaco
2201 Gollihar Rd.
Corpus Christi, TX 78415
(512)851-8037
Ultimate Parent: Texaco. SIC: 5541—
Gasoline Service Stations.

★ 83756 ★ Texaco
4747 S. Padre Island Dr.
Corpus Christi, TX 78411
(512)851-1985
Ultimate Parent: Texaco. SIC: 5541—
Gasoline Service Stations.

★ 83757 ★ Texaco
30 S. Country Club Pl.
Corpus Christi, TX 78408
(512)888-9240
Ultimate Parent: Texaco. SIC: 5541—
Gasoline Service Stations.

★ 83758 ★ Texaco
10401 S. Padre Island Dr.
Corpus Christi, TX 78418
(512)937-6113
Ultimate Parent: Texaco. SIC: 5541—
Gasoline Service Stations.

★ 83759 ★ Texaco
5333 Everhart Rd.
Corpus Christi, TX 78411
(512)855-4431
Ultimate Parent: Texaco. SIC: 5172—
Petroleum Products Nec.

★ 83760 ★ Texaco Inc.
E Hwy.
Corpus Christi, TX 78402
(512)883-3262
Ultimate Parent: Texaco. SIC: 5171—
Petroleum Bulk Stations & Terminals.

★ 83761 ★ Texas Tank Ship
Agency Inc.
811 N. Carancahua St.
Corpus Christi, TX 78474
(512)887-3872
Ultimate Parent: Coastal Corp. SIC:
4724—Travel Agencies.

★ 83762 ★ Trailways Food
Services Inc.
702 N. Chaparral St.
Corpus Christi, TX 78401
(512)882-5723
Ultimate Parent: Greyhound Lines Inc. SIC:
5812—Eating Places.

★ 83763 ★ Valero Refining Co.
5900 Up River Rd.
Corpus Christi, TX 78407-9370
Ultimate Parent: Valero Energy Corp. SIC:
2911—Petroleum Refining.

★ 83764 ★ Wal Mart Discount
Cities
11330 Leopard St.
Corpus Christi, TX 78410
(512)241-5315
Ultimate Parent: Wal-Mart Stores, Inc. SIC:
5311—Department Stores.

★ 83765 ★ Wal Mart Discount
City
4833 S. Padre Island Dr.
Corpus Christi, TX 78411
(512)994-9010
Ultimate Parent: Wal-Mart Stores, Inc.

★ 83766 ★ Walgreen Drug Stores
4951 Ayers St.
Corpus Christi, TX 78415
(512)854-1081
Ultimate Parent: Walgreen Co. SIC:
5912—Drug Stores & Proprietary Stores.

★ 83767 ★ Coast to Coast Bldg
Maint
3113 Ocean Dr.
Corpus Chrsti, TX 78404
(512)883-1599
Ultimate Parent: Servistar Corp. SIC:
4953—Refuse Systems.

★ 83768 ★ Otis Elevator Co.
4410 Dillon Ln.
Corpus Chrsti, TX 78415
(512)854-6847
Ultimate Parent: United Technologies. SIC:
3534—Elevators & Moving Stairways.

★ 83769 ★ Radio Shack
2713 Tumbleweed Dr.
Corpus Chrsti, TX 78410
(512)854-2871
Company Type: Division. Ultimate Parent:
Tandy Corp. SIC: 5065—Electronic Parts &
Equipment Nec.

★ 83770 ★ Ryder Truck Rental
6100 S. Staples St.
Corpus Chrsti, TX 78413
(512)993-6569
Ultimate Parent: Ryder System. SIC:
7513—Truck Rental & Leasing Without
Drivers.

★ 83771 ★ Ryder Truck Rental
9202 PO Box
Corpus Chrsti, TX 78469
(512)883-5479
Ultimate Parent: Ryder System. SIC:
7359—Equipment Rental & Leasing Nec;
7513—Truck Rental & Leasing Without
Drivers.

★ 83772 ★ Ryder Truck Rental
5556 S. Padre Island Dr.
Corpus Chrsti, TX 78411
(512)993-5355
Ultimate Parent: Ryder System. SIC:
7359—Equipment Rental & Leasing Nec.

★ 83773 ★ Taco Bell
2744 S. Staples St.
Corpus Chrsti, TX 78404
(512)992-7291
Ultimate Parent: Pepsico. SIC: 5812—
Eating Places.

★ 83774 ★ Transamerica
Occidental Life Insurance
505 S. Water St.
Corpus Chrsti, TX 78401
(512)884-1934
Ultimate Parent: Transamerica Occidental
Life Insurance. SIC: 8742—Management
Consulting Services.

Corrigan

★ 83775 ★ Champion
International Corp.
Plant Rd.
PO Box 100-S
Corrigan, TX 75939
Ultimate Parent: Champion International.
SIC: 2436—Softwood Veneer & Plywood.

★ 83776 ★ Louisiana Pacific
Corp., OSB
Hwy. 59
Corrigan, TX 75939
Ultimate Parent: Louisiana-Pacific. SIC:
2493—Reconstituted Wood Products.

Corsicana

★ 83777 ★ Anchor Glass
Container Corp. (02) Plant
1901 S. Hwy. 287
Corsicana, TX 75110
Ultimate Parent: Anchor Glass Container
Corp. SIC: 3221—Glass Containers.

★ 83778 ★ City National Bank
1465 W. 2nd Ave.
Corsicana, TX 75110
(214)872-8333
Ultimate Parent: City National Corp. SIC:
6022—State Commercial Banks.

★ 83779 ★ Jetco Chemicals
East Hwy. 31
Corsicana, TX 75110
Ultimate Parent: Procter & Gamble Co.
SIC: 2869—Industrial Organic Chemicals
Nec.

★ 83780 ★ Kay Bee Toys
3500 W. Hwy. 31 B5
Corsicana, TX 75110
(903)872-6261
Ultimate Parent: Melville. SIC: 5945—
Hobby, Toy & Game Shops.

★ 83781 ★ Kentucky Fried
Chicken
901 W. 7th Ave.
Corsicana, TX 75110
(214)874-1670
Ultimate Parent: Pepsico. SIC: 5812—
Eating Places.

★ 83782 ★ Liberty Mutual
Insurance Co.
101 N. Beaton St.
Corsicana, TX 75110
(214)874-7461
Ultimate Parent: Liberty Mutual Group.
SIC: 6411—Insurance Agents, Brokers &
Service.

★ 83783 ★ Lone Star Gas Co.
6023 PO Box
Corsicana, TX 75151
Ultimate Parent: Enserch. SIC: 4925—Gas
Production & Distribution Nec.

★ 83784 ★ Mobil Oil Co.
S St. 15th
Corsicana, TX 75110
(214)874-3551
Ultimate Parent: Mobil. SIC: 5172—
Petroleum Products Nec.

★ 83785 ★ Mobil Pipe Line Co.
S St. 15th
Corsicana, TX 75110
(214)874-5628
Ultimate Parent: Mobil. SIC: 4619—
Pipelines Nec.

★ 83786 ★ Payless Shoesource
2029 W. 7th Ave.
Corsicana, TX 75110
(903)872-6851
Ultimate Parent: May Department Stores.
SIC: 5661—Shoe Stores.

★ 83787 ★ Pizza Hut
2409 W. 7th Ave.
Corsicana, TX 75110
(214)872-3201
Ultimate Parent: Pepsico. SIC: 5812—
Eating Places.

★ 83788 ★ Plexco
431 E. Hwy. 31
Corsicana, TX 75110
Ultimate Parent: Amsted Industries Inc.
SIC: 3000—Rubber & Miscellaneous
Plastics Products.

★ 83789 ★ Radio Shack
1803 W. 7th Ave.
Corsicana, TX 75110
(214)872-2626
Company Type: Division. Ultimate Parent:
Tandy Corp. SIC: 5065—Electronic Parts &
Equipment Nec.

★ 83790 ★ Ryder Truck Rental
S Hwy. 75
Corsicana, TX 75110
(903)872-6603
Ultimate Parent: Ryder System. SIC:
7513—Truck Rental & Leasing Without
Drivers.

★ 83791 ★ Shell Food Mart
2809 N. Beaton St.
Corsicana, TX 75110
(214)872-0509
Ultimate Parent: Shell Oil Co. SIC: 5411—
Grocery Stores.

★ 83792 ★ Shell Food Mart
1626 W. 7th Ave.
Corsicana, TX 75110
(214)874-8578
Ultimate Parent: Shell Oil Co. SIC: 5541—
Gasoline Service Stations.

★ 83793 ★ Texas Utilities Fuel
Co.
122 W. Mall Dr.
Corsicana, TX 75110
(214)874-7862
Ultimate Parent: Texas Utilities. SIC:
4923—Gas Transmission & Distribution.

★ 83794 ★ Trailways Bus System
2050 E. Hwy. 31
Corsicana, TX 75110
(214)874-4791
Ultimate Parent: Greyhound Lines Inc. SIC:
4111—Local & Suburban Transit.

★ 83795 ★ Trailways &
Greyhounds Bus
1217 S. 7th St.
Corsicana, TX 75110
(214)872-8300
Ultimate Parent: Greyhound Lines Inc. SIC:
4131—Intercity & Rural Bus Transportation.

★ 83796 ★ Wal Mart
3500 W. Hwy. 31
Corsicana, TX 75110
(903)872 6691
Ultimate Parent: Wal-Mart Stores, Inc. SIC:
5311—Department Stores.

★ 83797 ★ Waldenbooks
3500 W. Hwy. 31
Corsicana, TX 75110
(214)874-2851
Ultimate Parent: K-Mart. SIC: 5942—Book
Stores.

★ 83798 ★ Wolf Brand Products
Inc.
416 S. Main St.
Corsicana, TX 75110
(214)330-8681
Ultimate Parent: Quaker Oates. SIC:
2032—Canned Specialties.

Cost

★ 83799 ★ Marathon Oil Co.
207 PO Box
Cost, TX 78614
(512)437-5248
Ultimate Parent: USX Corp.

Cotulla

★ 83800 ★ Greyhound Bus Lines
302 S. Main St.
Cotulla, TX 78014
(512)879-2865
Ultimate Parent: Greyhound Lines Inc. SIC:
4131—Intercity & Rural Bus Transportation.

Crane

★ 83801 ★ Exxon Co. USA
Sandhills Crane
Crane, TX 79731
(915)558-7430
Ultimate Parent: Exxon.

Crockett

★ 83802 ★ Trailways Bus
Systems
Hwy. 7 W
Crockett, TX 75835
(409)544-2661
Ultimate Parent: Greyhound Lines Inc. SIC:
4131—Intercity & Rural Bus Transportation.

★ 83803 ★ Wal Mart
Loop E. 304
Crockett, TX 75835
(409)544-5661
Ultimate Parent: Wal-Mart Stores, Inc. SIC:
5912—Drug Stores & Proprietary Stores.

★ 83804 ★ Wal Mart Discount
City
Loop E. 304
Crockett, TX 75835
(409)544-5121
Ultimate Parent: Wal-Mart Stores, Inc. SIC:
5331—Variety Stores.

Crosby

★ 83805 ★ **Compass Bank**
14700 Fm 2100 Rd.
Crosby, TX 77532
(713)328-5561
Ultimate Parent: Compass Bancshares.
SIC: 6159—Miscellaneous Business Credit
Institutions.

★ 83806 ★ **Pizza Hut**
13902 Fm 2100 Rd.
Crosby, TX 77532
(713)328-2501
Ultimate Parent: Pepsico. **SIC:** 5812—
Eating Places.

★ 83807 ★ **Radio Shack**
Kroger Ctr.
Crosby, TX 77532
(713)328-4929
Company Type: Division. **Ultimate Parent:**
Tandy Corp. **SIC:** 5065—Electronic Parts &
Equipment Nec.

Crosbyton

★ 83808 ★ **Mini Mart**
810 W. Main St.
Crosbyton, TX 79322
(806)675-2510
Ultimate Parent: Kroger. **SIC:** 5411—
Grocery Stores.

★ 83809 ★ **Mobil Oil Co.**
537 S. Keith St.
Crosbyton, TX 79322
(806)675-2886
Ultimate Parent: Mobil. **SIC:** 5171—
Petroleum Bulk Stations & Terminals.

Crosley

★ 83810 ★ **Compass Bank-
Houston**
14700 FM 2100
Crosley, TX 77532-6143
(713)867-6100
Company Type: Subsidiary. **Location
Type:** Branch office. **Ultimate Parent:**
Compass Bancshares. **SIC:** 6021—National
Commercial Banks.

Cross Plains

★ 83811 ★ **Citizens State Bank**
805 N. Main
Cross Plains, TX 76443
(817)725-6141
Ultimate Parent: Liberty National Bancorp.
SIC: 6022—State Commercial Banks.

Crowell

★ 83812 ★ **Exxon Co. USA**
Crowell, TX 79227
(817)655-3391
Ultimate Parent: Exxon. **SIC:** 5171—
Petroleum Bulk Stations & Terminals.

Crowley

★ 83813 ★ **Ace Hardware**
Hwy. 1902
Crowley, TX 76036
(817)297-1051
Ultimate Parent: Ace Hardware. **SIC:**
5251—Hardware Stores.

★ 83814 ★ **Ryder Truck Rental**
1625 N. Crowley Rd.
Crowley, TX 76036
(817)297-9262
Ultimate Parent: Ryder System.

Crp Christi

★ 83815 ★ **Taco Bell**
3710 Leopard St.
Crp Christi, TX 78408
(512)881-9152
Ultimate Parent: Pepsico. **SIC:** 5812—
Eating Places.

★ 83816 ★ **Unisys Corp.**
801 N. Shoreline Blvd.
Crp Christi, TX 78401
(512)884-4885
Ultimate Parent: Unisys Corp.

Crystal City

★ 83817 ★ **Del Monte Corp.**
FM Rd., 393 Uvalde Hwy.
Crystal City, TX 78839
(210)374-3451
Officer: James R. Fullman, Manager.
Ultimate Parent: Del Monte Foods. **SIC:**
2033—Canned Fruits & Vegetables.

★ 83818 ★ **Del Monte Foods**
Plant No. 250
393 Farm Rd.
Crystal City, TX 78839
(512)374-3451
Location Type: Plant. **Ultimate Parent:** Del
Monte Foods. **SIC:** 2033—Canned Fruits &
Vegetables.

★ 83819 ★ **Del Monte Foods
Plants**
Farm Rd. 393
Crystal City, TX 78839
Ultimate Parent: RJR Nabisco Holdings.
SIC: 3411—Metal Cans.

★ 83820 ★ **Del Monte Foods
Plants 250 & 255**
Farm Rd. 393
Crystal City, TX 78839
Ultimate Parent: Del Monte Foods. **SIC:**
2033—Canned Fruits & Vegetables.

★ 83821 ★ **Pizza Hut**
Hwy. 83
Crystal City, TX 78839
(512)374-2247
Ultimate Parent: Pepsico. **SIC:** 5812—
Eating Places.

★ 83822 ★ **Del Monte Foods USA
Plant 255**
Farm Rd. 393
Crystal City, TX 78839
Ultimate Parent: RJR Nabisco Holdings.
SIC: 3411—Metal Cans.

Cuero

★ 83823 ★ **Coca Cola Bottling
Co.**
306 Main St.
Cuero, TX 77954
(512)275-6891
Ultimate Parent: Coca-Cola Enterprises.
SIC: 2086—Bottled & Canned Soft Drinks.

★ 83824 ★ **Pizza Hut**
1010 N. Esplanade St.
Cuero, TX 77954
(512)275-3111
Ultimate Parent: Pepsico. **SIC:** 5812—
Eating Places.

★ 83825 ★ **Radio Shack**
515 N. Esplanade St.
Cuero, TX 77954
(512)275-3412
Company Type: Division. **Ultimate Parent:**
Tandy Corp. **SIC:** 5731—Radio, Television
& Electronics Stores.

★ 83826 ★ **Wal Mart Discount
City**
Hwy. 87
Cuero, TX 77954
(512)275-5796
Ultimate Parent: Wal-Mart Stores, Inc. **SIC:**
5311—Department Stores; 7011—Hotels &
Motels; 7538—General Automotive Repair
Shops.

Cushing

★ 83827 ★ **Exxon**
204 PO Box
Cushing, TX 75760
(409)326-4324
Ultimate Parent: Exxon. **SIC:** 5531—
Automobile & Home Supply Stores.

Cypress

★ 83828 ★ **Pulte Home Corp.**
17171 Park Rd.
Cypress, TX 77429
(713)373-0657
Ultimate Parent: Pulte.

★ 83829 ★ **Radio Shack**
11139 Huffmeister Rd.
Cypress, TX 77429
(713)955-5383
Company Type: Division. **Ultimate Parent:**
Tandy Corp.

Dalas

★ 83830 ★ **Electronic Data
Systems Corp.**
7171 Forest Ln.
Dalas, TX 75230
(214)661-6000 **Fax:** (214)661-6043
Officer: Lester M. Alberthal Jr., Chairman,
President & CEO. **Ultimate Parent:** General
Motors Corp.

Dalhart

★ 83831 ★ **Citizens State Bank
Dalhart**
323 Denver Ave.
Dalhart, TX 79022
(806)249-6421
Ultimate Parent: Liberty National Bancorp.
SIC: 6022—State Commercial Banks.

★ 83832 ★ **Greyhound Bus Lines**
219 Denrock Ave.
Dalhart, TX 79022
(806)249-5518
Ultimate Parent: Greyhound Lines Inc. **SIC:**
4131—Intercity & Rural Bus Transportation.

★ 83833 ★ **Kentucky Fried
Chicken**
Hwy. 87 S
Dalhart, TX 79022
(806)249-2138
Ultimate Parent: Pepsico. **SIC:** 5812—
Eating Places.

★ 83834 ★ **Pizza Hut**
301 S. Hwy. 87
Dalhart, TX 79022
(806)249-5462
Ultimate Parent: Pepsico. **SIC:** 5812—
Eating Places.

★ 83835 ★ **Radio Shack**
Apache Shopping Ctr.
Dalhart, TX 79022
(806)249-5859
Company Type: Division. **Ultimate Parent:**
Tandy Corp. **SIC:** 5065—Electronic Parts &
Equipment Nec.

★ 83836 ★ **Ryder Truck Rental**
624 Denver Ave.
Dalhart, TX 79022
(806)249-4304
Ultimate Parent: Ryder System. **SIC:**
7359—Equipment Rental & Leasing Nec.

Dallas

★ 83837 ★ **Advanced Image
Systems Inc.**
2331 W. Northwest Hwy.
Dallas, TX 75220
(214)956-7086
Company Type: Subsidiary. **Officer:** James
A. Hitchocx, President. **Ultimate Parent:**
Alco Standard Corp. **SIC:** 5044—Office
Equipment; 7359—Equipment Rental &
Leasing Nec.

★ 83838 ★ **Advanced Micro
Devices**
14775 Preston Rd.
Dallas, TX 75240-7859
(214)934-9099
Ultimate Parent: Advanced Micro Devices
Inc. **SIC:** 5065—Electronic Parts &
Equipment Nec; 7371—Computer
Programming Services.

★ 83839 ★ **Airborne Freight
Corp.**
Dallas Fort Worth Airport
Dallas, TX 75261
(214)574-5900
Ultimate Parent: Airborne Freight Corp.
SIC: 4513—Air Courier Services.

★ 83840 ★ **Allied Plywood Corp.**
7125 Harry Hines Blvd.
Dallas, TX 75235
(214)630-1404
Ultimate Parent: Ply Gem.

★ 83841 ★ **Allied Plywood Corp.**
2533 Royal Ln.
Dallas, TX 75229
(214)243-6737
Ultimate Parent: Ply Gem. **SIC:** 5039—
Construction Materials Nec.

★ 83842 ★ **Allstate Life
Insurance Co.**
1 Lincoln Ctr.
Dallas, TX 75201
(214)233-4545
Ultimate Parent: Allstate Life. **SIC:** 6411—
Insurance Agents, Brokers & Service.

★ 83843 ★ **Allstate Life
Insurance Co.**
5400 LBJ Fwy.
Dallas, TX 75240
(214)770-2220
Ultimate Parent: Allstate Life. **SIC:** 6411—
Insurance Agents, Brokers & Service.

★ 83844 ★ **ALLTEL Distribution
Inc.**
10730 Composite Dr.
Dallas, TX 75220-1277
(214)350-3701
Company Type: Subsidiary. **Ultimate
Parent:** ALLTEL Corp. **SIC:** 5063—
Electrical Apparatus & Equipment; 5065—
Electronic Parts & Equipment Nec.

★ 83845 ★ **American Cyanamid
Co.**
7611 John W. Carpenter Fwy.
Dallas, TX 75247-4820
(214)631-2130
Officer: Jerry Elizondo. **Ultimate Parent:**
American Cyanamid Co. **SIC:** 5122—Drugs,
Proprietaries & Sundries.

★ 83846 ★ **American General
Group Insurance Co.**
3988 N. Central Expwy.
Dallas, TX 75204
(214)841-1000
Officer: Howard L. Korn, President & CEO.
Ultimate Parent: American General Corp.
SIC: 6311—Life Insurance; 6321—Accident
& Health Insurance. **Employee Count:** 893.

★ 83847 ★ **American Limestone
Co. Inc.**
2811 McKinney Ave.
Dallas, TX 75204-2530
(214)720-7150
Officer: Robert Ray. **Ultimate Parent:**
Asarco. **SIC:** 1422—Crushed & Broken
Limestone.

★ 83848 ★ **American Medical
Holdings**
14001 Dallas Pky.
Dallas, TX 75240
(214)789-2200
Company Type: Headquarters. **Officer:**
Robert W. O'Leary. **Fortune Service 500:**
Ranking 65.

★ 83849 ★ **American Medical
Holdings, Inc.**
PO Box 25651
Dallas, TX 75221
Company Type: Headquarters. **Ultimate
Parent:** American Medical Holdings.

★ 83850 ★ **American Medical
Holdings, Inc.**
8201 Preston Rd., Ste. 300
Dallas, TX 75225-5651
(214)360-6300 **Fax:** (214)360-6368
Company Type: Headquarters. **Officer:**
Robert W. O'Leary, Chairman of the Board
& CEO. **Ultimate Parent:** American Medical
Holdings. **SIC:** 8062—General Medical &
Surgical Hospitals; 8063—Psychiatric
Hospitals; 8069—Specialty Hospitals Except
Psychiatric; 6719—Holding Companies Nec.
Employee Count: 2900. **Sales:**
223791200d0 M.

★ 83851 ★ **Ameritrust Texas NA**
1201 Elm St., Ste. 3000
Dallas, TX 75270-2123
(214)712-3400
Company Type: Subsidiary. **Officer:**
Eugene E. Weber, Chairman of the Board &
CEO. **Ultimate Parent:** Chemical Banking
Corp. **SIC:** 6091—Nondeposit Trust
Facilities.

★ 83852 ★   **Ametek Inc.**
Westchester Plastics Div.
Carter Towers
Dallas, TX 75208
(214)946-1952
Company Type: Division. **Ultimate Parent:**
Ametek Inc. **SIC:** 2821—Plastics Materials
& Resins.

★ 83853 ★   **Ametek-U S Gauge**
11500 N. Stemmons Fwy.
Dallas, TX 75229
(214)243-7938
Ultimate Parent: Ametek Inc. **SIC:** 3824—
Fluid Meters & Counting Devices.

★ 83854 ★   **AMR Investment**
Services, Inc.
PO Box 619003
Dallas, TX 75261-9003
(817)967-3509 **Fax:** (817)967-0768
Company Type: Subsidiary. **Officer:**
William F. Quinn, President. **Ultimate**
Parent: AMR Corp.

★ 83855 ★   **APAC**
2121 Irving Blvd.
Dallas, TX 75207
(214)741-3531
Officer: Steve Robertson, President.
Ultimate Parent: Ashland Oil. **SIC:** 3951—
Pens & Mechanical Pencils.

★ 83856 ★   **Apple Computers Inc.**
12770 Merit Dr.
Dallas, TX 75251-1212
(214)770-5800
Officer: Ron L. Seifert. **Ultimate Parent:**
Apple Computer. **SIC:** 5045—Computers,
Peripherals & Software; 7373—Computer
Integrated Systems Design.

★ 83857 ★   **Arco Oil & Gas Co.**
1601 Bryan St.
Dallas, TX 75201-3402
(214)880-2500
Location Type: Branch office. **Officer:** M.
E. Wiley. **Ultimate Parent:** Atlantic Richfield
Co., Inc. **SIC:** 1311—Crude Petroleum &
Natural Gas; 1321—Natural Gas Liquids;
4924—Natural Gas Distribution; 4925—Gas
Production & Distribution Nec; 4961—Steam
& Air-Conditioning Supply; 5172—Petroleum
Products Nec; 6061—Federal Credit Unions;
6512—Nonresidential Building Operators.

★ 83858 ★   **Armco Steel Co. LP**
9910 Wood Forest Dr.
Dallas, TX 75243-4920
(214)497-9600
Ultimate Parent: Armco. **SIC:** 3312—Blast
Furnaces & Steel Mills.

★ 83859 ★   **Ashland Chemical Co.**
8201 S. Central Expy.
Dallas, TX 75239
Ultimate Parent: Ashland Oil. **SIC:** 2819—
Industrial Inorganic Chemicals Nec.

★ 83860 ★   **Ashland Chemical E**
& Lp
8201 S. Central Expy.
Dallas, TX 75216
Ultimate Parent: Ashland Oil. **SIC:** 2819—
Industrial Inorganic Chemicals Nec.

★ 83861 ★   **Associates Corp. of**
North America
PO Box 660237
Dallas, TX 75266
(214)514-4000
Officer: Reece A. Overcash Jr., Chairman
& CEO. **Ultimate Parent:** Ford Motor Co.

★ 83862 ★   **Associates First**
Capital Corp.
PO Box 660237
Dallas, TX 75266
Officer: Reece A. Overcash Jr., Chairman.
Ultimate Parent: Ford Motor Co.

★ 83863 ★   **AT & T Employees**
Credit Union
8818 Garland Rd.
Dallas, TX 75218-3994
(214)320-8875
Company Type: Subsidiary. **Officer:** T. P.
Barton, President. **Ultimate Parent:** AT&T.
SIC: 6062—State Credit Unions.

★ 83864 ★   **AT&T Commercial**
Finance
5220 Spring Valley Rd.
Dallas, TX 75240-3099
(214)385-0277
Ultimate Parent: AT&T. **SIC:** 6159—
Miscellaneous Business Credit Institutions.

★ 83865 ★   **Aviall**
3412 Putnam
Dallas, TX 75235
Ultimate Parent: Ryder System. **SIC:**
3728—Aircraft Parts & Equipment Nec.

★ 83866 ★   **Aviall**
6114 Forest Park
Dallas, TX 75235
Ultimate Parent: Ryder System. **SIC:**
3728—Aircraft Parts & Equipment Nec.

★ 83867 ★   **Aviall Forest Park**
Facility
6114 Forest Park
Dallas, TX 75235
Ultimate Parent: Ryder System. **SIC:**
3728—Aircraft Parts & Equipment Nec.

★ 83868 ★   **Avnet*Hamilton**
Hallmark
11333 Pagemill Rd.
Dallas, TX 75243
(214)343-5000
Officer: Joseph Semmer, President.
Ultimate Parent: Avnet. **SIC:** 5045—
Computers, Peripherals & Software; 5065—
Electronic Parts & Equipment Nec. **Sales:**
500,000,000 M.

★ 83869 ★   **Banana Republic**
438 Northpark Ctr.
Dallas, TX 75225
(214)739-8577
Ultimate Parent: GAP. **SIC:** 5651—Family
Clothing Stores.

★ 83870 ★   **Bank of Boston Corp.**
700 N. Peal St. Ste., 1840
Dallas, TX 75201-2845
(214)754-7071
Officer: Thomas M. Mercer. **Ultimate**
Parent: Bank of Boston Corp. **SIC:** 6141—
Personal Credit Institutions; 6021—National
Commercial Banks; 6159—Miscellaneous
Business Credit Institutions.

★ 83871 ★   **Bank of Tokyo**
2001 Ross Ave.
Dallas, TX 75201-2911
(214)954-1200
Ultimate Parent: Bank of Tokyo Trust. **SIC:**
6021—National Commercial Banks.

★ 83872 ★   **Bear Stearns**
Companies Inc.
1601 Elm St.
Dallas, TX 75201-4775
(214)754-8300
Location Type: Branch office. **Ultimate**
Parent: Bear Stearns. **SIC:** 6341—
Insurance & Diversified Financial
Companies; 6211—Security Brokers &
Dealers.

★ 83873 ★   **Bear, Stearns & Co.,**
Inc. Dallas
1601 Elm St.
Dallas, TX 75201
(214)754-8300
Location Type: Branch office. **Officer:** Hilel
A. Feinberg, Senior Managing Director.
Ultimate Parent: Bear Stearns. **SIC:**
6211—Security Brokers & Dealers.

★ 83874 ★   **Bear Stearns Secured**
Investors Inc.
1601 Elm St.
Dallas, TX 75201-7254
(214)754-8300
Ultimate Parent: Bear Stearns. **SIC:**
6159—Miscellaneous Business Credit
Institutions.

★ 83875 ★   **Bell Atlantic Corp.**
13800 Hutton Dr.
Dallas, TX 75234-9007
Location Type: Branch office. **Officer:**
Gene Neitzley. **Ultimate Parent:** Bell
Atlantic Corp. **SIC:** 7378—Computer
Maintenance & Repair; 4813—Telephone
Communications Except Radiotelephone.

★ 83876 ★   **Bell Atlantic Systems**
Lease International
14643 Dallas Pky.
Dallas, TX 75240-8800
(214)233-1818
Ultimate Parent: Bell Atlantic Corp. **SIC:**
5045—Computers, Peripherals & Software.

★ 83877 ★   **Beneficial Texas Inc.**
4041 W. Wheatland Rd.
Dallas, TX 75237-4060
(214)296-7031
Location Type: Branch office. **Ultimate**
Parent: Beneficial. **SIC:** 6141—Personal
Credit Institutions.

★ 83878 ★   **Beneficial Texas Inc.**
4452 Beltway Dr.
Dallas, TX 75244-2705
(214)490-3539
Officer: Darrlel Bender. **Ultimate Parent:**
Beneficial. **SIC:** 6141—Personal Credit
Institutions.

★ 83879 ★   **Bethlehem Steel**
Corp.
1501 Lyndon B. Johnson Fwy.
Dallas, TX 75234-6029
(214)247-5696
Ultimate Parent: Bethlehem Steel Corp.
SIC: 5051—Metals Service Centers &
Offices.

★ 83880 ★   **Betts Baking Co.**
6211 Lemmon Ave.
Dallas, TX 75209
(214)358-9211
Company Type: Subsidiary. **Officer:** Gene
Miller, COO. **Ultimate Parent:**
Anheuser-Busch. **SIC:** 2051—Bread, Cake
& Related Products.

★ 83881 ★   **Bindley Western Drug**
Co.
4217 Mint Way
Dallas, TX 75237-1688
(214)339-3744
Location Type: Branch office. **Officer:**
David M. Homeier, Executive. **Ultimate**
Parent: Bindley-Western Industries, Inc.
SIC: 5122—Drugs, Proprietaries &
Sundries; 5122—Drugs, Proprietaries &
Sundries.

★ 83882 ★   **Bindley Western Drug**
Co.
Dallas, Texas
4217 Mint Way
Dallas, TX 75237
(214)339-3744 **Fax:** (214)337-9407
Company Type: Subsidiary. **Officer:** David
M. Homeier, Vice President & Division
Manager. **Ultimate Parent:** Bindley-Western
Industries, Inc.

★ 83883 ★   **Boeing Co. Inc**
1111 W. Mockingbird Ln.
Dallas, TX 75247
(214)630-6908
Ultimate Parent: Boeing. **SIC:** 3535—
Conveyors & Conveying Equipment.

★ 83884 ★   **Borden Inc.**
5327 S. Lamar St.
Dallas, TX 75215
(214)565-0332
Officer: Carl Todd, Manager. **Ultimate**
Parent: Borden, Inc. **SIC:** 2022—Cheese—
Natural & Processed; 2026—Fluid Milk.

★ 83885 ★   **Borden Inc.**
Dairy
5327 S. Lamar St.
Dallas, TX 75215
Ultimate Parent: Borden, Inc. **SIC:** 2026—
Fluid Milk.

★ 83886 ★   **Borden Inc.**
Snacks & International Products
6333 Denton Dr.
Dallas, TX 75235
Company Type: Division. **Ultimate Parent:**
Borden, Inc. **SIC:** 2099—Food Preparations
Nec.

★ 83887 ★   **Borden Inc.**
Southwest Snacks
6333 Denton Dr.
Dallas, TX 75235
Company Type: Division. **Ultimate Parent:**
Borden, Inc. **SIC:** 2099—Food Preparations
Nec.

★ 83888 ★   **Borden Inc. Grocery**
& Speciality Prds.
5327 S. Lamar St.
Dallas, TX 75215
Ultimate Parent: Borden, Inc. **SIC:** 2026—
Fluid Milk.

★ 83889 ★   **Burlington Coat**
Factory Warehouse
3107 W. Camp Wisdom Rd.
Dallas, TX 75237-2603
(214)337-2660
Location Type: Branch office. **Ultimate**
Parent: Burlington Industries, Equity. **SIC:**
5137—Women's/Children's Clothing.

★ 83890 ★   **Burlington House**
Fabrics
2050 N. Stemmons Fwy.
Dallas, TX 75258-3100
(214)744-2300
Ultimate Parent: Burlington Industries,
Equity. **SIC:** 5131—Piece Goods & Notions.

★ 83891 ★   **Burlington Industries**
Inc.
5310 Harvest Hill Rd., Ste. 172
Dallas, TX 75230-5805
(214)934-8901
Location Type: Branch office. **Officer:**
James Frankenfield. **Ultimate Parent:**
Burlington Industries, Equity. **SIC:** 5131—
Piece Goods & Notions; 7389—Business
Services Nec.

★ 83892 ★   **Campbell Taggart Inc.**
6211 Lemmon Ave.
Dallas, TX 75209
(214)358-9211 **Fax:** (214)358-7728
Company Type: Subsidiary. **Officer:** Barry
H. Beracha, Chairman & CEO. **Ultimate**
Parent: Anheuser-Busch.

★ 83893 ★   **Capezio**
2300 Apparel Mart
Dallas, TX 75258
(214)638-7664
Ultimate Parent: United States Shoe. **SIC:**
7389—Business Services Nec.

★ 83894 ★   **Career Image**
Galleria
Dallas, TX 75243
(214)934-3231
Ultimate Parent: United States Shoe. **SIC:**
5621—Women's Clothing Stores.

★ 83895 ★   **Career Image**
13350 Dallas Pky.
Dallas, TX 75240
(214)934-3231
Ultimate Parent: United States Shoe. **SIC:**
5651—Family Clothing Stores.

★ 83896 ★   **Casual Corner**
5301 Belt Line Rd.
Dallas, TX 75240
(214)363-1178
Ultimate Parent: United States Shoe. **SIC:**
5621—Women's Clothing Stores; 5651—
Family Clothing Stores.

★ 83897 ★   **Casual Corner**
3662 W. Camp Wisdom Rd.
Dallas, TX 75237
(214)296-2956
Ultimate Parent: United States Shoe. **SIC:**
5651—Family Clothing Stores.

★ 83898 ★   **Casual Corner 095**
1511 Elm St.
Dallas, TX 75201
(214)747-9121
Ultimate Parent: United States Shoe. **SIC:**
5699—Miscellaneous Apparel & Accessory
Stores.

★ 83899 ★   **Centex**
3333 Lee Pky.
Dallas, TX 75219
(214)559-6500
Company Type: Headquarters. **Officer:**
Laurence E. Hirsch. **Fortune Service 500:**
Ranking 57.

★ 83900 ★   **Centex Bateson**
Construction Co., Inc.
10150 Monroe Dr.
PO Box 299009
Dallas, TX 75229-9009
(214)357-1891 **Fax:** (214)902-6391
Officer: Joe R. Walker, Chairman of the
Board , President & CEO. **Ultimate Parent:**
Centex.

★ 83901 ★　Centex Cement
Enterprises, Inc.
3333 Lee Pky.
PO Box 19000
Dallas, TX 75219
Officer: O.G. Dagnan, President & CEO.
Ultimate Parent: Centex.

★ 83902 ★　Centex Construction
Group Inc.
3333 Lee Pky.
PO Box 19000
Dallas, TX 75219
Fax: (214)526-4645
Officer: William J. Gillilan III, Chairman of
the Board & CEO. Ultimate Parent: Centex.

★ 83903 ★　Centex Corp.
3333 Lee Pky.
PO Box 19000
Dallas, TX 75219
(214)559-6500 Fax: (214)552-7568
Officer: Laurence E. Hirsch, Chairman of
the Board & CEO. Ultimate Parent: Centex.
Employee Count: 6500.

★ 83904 ★　Centex Real Estate
Corp./Centex Homes
3333 Lee Pky.
PO Box 1900
Dallas, TX 75219
Fax: (214)522-7625
Officer: William J. Gillilan III, Chairman of
the Board. Ultimate Parent: Centex.

★ 83905 ★　Centex Title & Escrow
Operations
3333 Lee Pky.
PO Box 19000
Dallas, TX 75219
Officer: Karren P. Bates, President.
Ultimate Parent: Centex.

★ 83906 ★　Central & South West
1616 Woodall Rodgers Fwy.
Dallas, TX 75202
(214)777-1000
Company Type: Headquarters. Officer: E.
R. Brooks. Fortune Service 500: Ranking
28.

★ 83907 ★　Central & South West
Services, Inc.
1616 Woodall Rogers Fwy.
Dallas, TX 75202
(214)777-1111
Officer: E. R. Brooks, Chairman &
President. Ultimate Parent: Central &
South West.

★ 83908 ★　Champion
International Corp.
5420 LBJ Fwy.
Dallas, TX 75240
(214)661-8505
Ultimate Parent: Champion International.
SIC: 2621—Paper Mills.

★ 83909 ★　Charles Schwab&Co
Inc.
1 Lincoln Ctr.
Dallas, TX 75201
(214)385-1561
Ultimate Parent: Charles Schwab Corp.
SIC: 6211—Security Brokers & Dealers.

★ 83910 ★　Chex Systems
12005 Ford Rd.
Dallas, TX 75234
(214)247-5100
Ultimate Parent: Deluxe Corp.

★ 83911 ★　Circle T Foods Co.
Inc.
4560 Leston Dr.
Dallas, TX 75247
Ultimate Parent: Sara Lee Corp. SIC:
2013—Sausages & Other Prepared Meats.

★ 83912 ★　Circus World
725 Northpark Ctr.
Dallas, TX 75225
(214)361-5122
Ultimate Parent: Melville. SIC: 5945—
Hobby, Toy & Game Shops.

★ 83913 ★　Circus World
5301 Belt Line Rd.
Dallas, TX 75240
(214)386-5732
Ultimate Parent: Melville. SIC: 5945—
Hobby, Toy & Game Shops.

★ 83914 ★　Circus World Toy
Stores Inc.
2034 Red Bird Mall
Dallas, TX 75237
(214)296-1081
Ultimate Parent: Melville. SIC: 5945—
Hobby, Toy & Game Shops.

★ 83915 ★　Cisco Systems Inc.
17304 Preston Rd.
Dallas, TX 75252
(214)733-6890
Ultimate Parent: Cisco Systems Inc.

★ 83916 ★　City National Bank of
Carrollton
2908 E. Trinity Mills Rd.
Dallas, TX 75252
(214)418-1982
Ultimate Parent: City National Corp. SIC:
6021—National Commercial Banks.

★ 83917 ★　Coast to Coast
Adjusters
1009 E. Jefferson Blvd.
Dallas, TX 75203
(214)946-1553
Ultimate Parent: Servistar Corp. SIC:
6411—Insurance Agents, Brokers &
Service.

★ 83918 ★　Coast to Coast Corp.
1421 W. Mockingbird Ln.
Dallas, TX 75247
(214)630-2070
Ultimate Parent: Servistar Corp. SIC:
6411—Insurance Agents, Brokers &
Service.

★ 83919 ★　Coast to Coast Exc
1707 Ashland St.
Dallas, TX 75201
(214)720-9118
Ultimate Parent: Servistar Corp.

★ 83920 ★　Coca-Cola Bottling
Co. of North Texas
8161 Moberly Ln.
Dallas, TX 75227
Ultimate Parent: Coca-Cola Enterprises.
SIC: 2086—Bottled & Canned Soft Drinks.

★ 83921 ★　Coca-Cola Bottling
Co. of North Texas
6011 Lemmon Ave. PO Box 2008
Dallas, TX 75221
Ultimate Parent: Coca-Cola Enterprises.
SIC: 2086—Bottled & Canned Soft Drinks.

★ 83922 ★　Coca Cola U S a
6445 Lemmon Ave.
Dallas, TX 75209
(214)357-4504
Ultimate Parent: Coca-Cola. SIC: 2086—
Bottled & Canned Soft Drinks.

★ 83923 ★　Coca Cola U S A
4801 Spring Valley Rd.
Dallas, TX 75244
(214)991-8820
Location Type: Branch office. Ultimate
Parent: Coca-Cola. SIC: 2086—Bottled &
Canned Soft Drinks.

★ 83924 ★　Coca-Cola USA
6445 Lemmon Ave.
Dallas, TX 75209
Ultimate Parent: Coca-Cola. SIC: 2087—
Flavoring Extracts & Syrups Nec.

★ 83925 ★　Colonial Baking Co.
6211 Lemmon Ave.
Dallas, TX 75209
(214)358-9211
Company Type: Subsidiary. Officer: C. B.
Lane, President. Ultimate Parent:
Anheuser-Busch. SIC: 2051—Bread, Cake
& Related Products.

★ 83926 ★　Comerica Bank-Texas
5944 Luther Lane
Dallas, TX 75225
(214)691-3131
Company Type: Subsidiary. Location
Type: Branch office. Ultimate Parent:
Comerica Bank. SIC: 6021—National
Commercial Banks.

★ 83927 ★　Comerica Bank-Texas
1909 Woodall Rogers Fwy.
PO Box 650282
Dallas, TX 75265-0282
(214)841-1400 Fax: (214)841-4450
Company Type: Subsidiary. Location
Type: Branch office. Ultimate Parent:

Comerica Bank. SIC: 6021—National
Commercial Banks.

★ 83928 ★　Comerica Bank-Texas
9533 Losa Dr.
Dallas, TX 75218-3526
(214)324-3535
Company Type: Subsidiary. Location
Type: Branch office. Ultimate Parent:
Comerica Bank. SIC: 6021—National
Commercial Banks.

★ 83929 ★　Comerica Bank-Texas
2964 LBJ Fwy.
Dallas, TX 75234-7603
(214)828-5841
Company Type: Subsidiary. Location
Type: Branch office. Officer: Don Johnston,
Manager. Ultimate Parent: Comerica Bank.
SIC: 6021—National Commercial Banks.

★ 83930 ★　Comerica Bank-Texas
6260 E. Mockingbird Lane
Dallas, TX 75214-2699
(214)828-5900
Company Type: Subsidiary. Location
Type: Branch office. Officer: Steve
Graham, Manager. Ultimate Parent:
Comerica Bank. SIC: 6021—National
Commercial Banks.

★ 83931 ★　Comerica Bank-Texas
5200 Forest Lane
Dallas, TX 75244-8099
(214)841-8831
Company Type: Subsidiary. Location
Type: Branch office. Ultimate Parent:
Comerica Bank. SIC: 6021—National
Commercial Banks.

★ 83932 ★　Comerica Bank-Texas
6510 Abrams Rd.
Dallas, TX 75234-7218
(214)818-2382
Company Type: Subsidiary. Location
Type: Branch office. Ultimate Parent:
Comerica Bank. SIC: 6021—National
Commercial Banks.

★ 83933 ★　Comerica Bank-Texas
753 W. Illinois Ave.
Dallas, TX 75224-1862
(214)841-5894
Company Type: Subsidiary. Location
Type: Branch office. Officer: Carl Shields,
Manager. Ultimate Parent: Comerica Bank.
SIC: 6021—National Commercial Banks.

★ 83934 ★　Comerica Bank-Texas
1300 North Park Ctr.
Dallas, TX 75225-2221
(214)890-5100
Company Type: Subsidiary. Location
Type: Branch office. Ultimate Parent:
Comerica Bank. SIC: 6021—National
Commercial Banks.

★ 83935 ★　Comerica Bank-Texas
10110 Shareview Rd.
Dallas, TX 75238-4414
(214)553-3800
Company Type: Subsidiary. Location
Type: Branch office. Ultimate Parent:
Comerica Bank. SIC: 6021—National
Commercial Banks.

★ 83936 ★　Comerica Bank-Texas
Thanksgiving Tower
1601 Elm St.
Dallas, TX 75201
(214)969-6111
Company Type: Subsidiary. Location
Type: Branch office. Ultimate Parent:
Comerica Bank. SIC: 6021—National
Commercial Banks.

★ 83937 ★　Comerica Bank-Texas
6310 Lemmon Ave.
Dallas, TX 75209-5729
(214)350-1221
Company Type: Subsidiary. Location
Type: Branch office. Ultimate Parent:
Comerica Bank. SIC: 6021—National
Commercial Banks.

★ 83938 ★　Comerica Bank-Texas
11155 Garland Rd.
Dallas, TX 75214
(214)841-1560
Company Type: Subsidiary. Location
Type: Branch office. Officer: Samuel Perry,
Manager. Ultimate Parent: Comerica Bank.
SIC: 6021—National Commercial Banks.

★ 83939 ★　Comerica Bank-Texas
2311 Abrams & Galiad
Dallas, TX 75214
(214)841-1524
Company Type: Subsidiary. Location
Type: Branch office. Officer: John
Emminger, Manager. Ultimate Parent:
Comerica Bank. SIC: 6021—National
Commercial Banks.

★ 83940 ★　Comerica Bank-Texas
8828 Stemmons Fwy.
Dallas, TX 75247-3720
(214)841-1333
Company Type: Subsidiary. Location
Type: Branch office. Ultimate Parent:
Comerica Bank. SIC: 6021—National
Commercial Banks.

★ 83941 ★　Comerica Bank-Texas
4131 N. Central Expy.
Dallas, TX 75204-3141
(214)841-1341
Company Type: Subsidiary. Location
Type: Branch office. Officer: Michon
Fulcham, Manager. Ultimate Parent:
Comerica Bank. SIC: 6021—National
Commercial Banks.

★ 83942 ★　Comerica Bank-Texas
5201 E. R.L. Thorton Fwy.
Dallas, TX 75223-2201
(214)841-1512
Company Type: Subsidiary. Location
Type: Branch office. Officer: Mike Bennett,
Manager. Ultimate Parent: Comerica Bank.
SIC: 6021—National Commercial Banks.

★ 83943 ★　Comerica Bank-Texas
6820 LBJ Fwy.
Dallas, TX 75240-6515
(214)841-1564
Company Type: Subsidiary. Location
Type: Branch office. Ultimate Parent:
Comerica Bank. SIC: 6021—National
Commercial Banks.

★ 83944 ★　Commercial Metals
7800 Stemmons Fwy.
Dallas, TX 75247
(214)715-7000
Company Type: Headquarters. Officer:
Frank Schmieder, CEO. Fortune Service
500: Ranking 93.

★ 83945 ★　Commercial Metals
7800 Stemmons Fwy.
Dallas, TX 75247
(214)689-4300
Company Type: Headquarters. Officer:
Stanley A. Rabin. Fortune Service 500:
Ranking 93.

★ 83946 ★　Compaq Computer
Corp.
5956 Sherry La Uite
Dallas, TX 75225
(214)739-8200
Ultimate Parent: Compaq Computer. SIC:
7372—Prepackaged Software.

★ 83947 ★　Compass Bank
650561 PO Box
Dallas, TX 75265
Ultimate Parent: Compass Bancshares.
SIC: 6022—State Commercial Banks.

★ 83948 ★　Compass Bank-Dallas
6071 Sherry Ln.
Dallas, TX 75225-6402
(214)369-6500
Company Type: Subsidiary. Location
Type: Branch office. Ultimate Parent:
Compass Bancshares. SIC: 6021—National
Commercial Banks.

★ 83949 ★　Compass Bank-Dallas
7777 Forest Ln., Ste. C-130
Dallas, TX 75230-2512
(214)788-6600
Company Type: Subsidiary. Location
Type: Branch office. Ultimate Parent:
Compass Bancshares. SIC: 6021—National
Commercial Banks.

★ 83950 ★　Compass Bank-Dallas
10210 N. Central Expy.
Dallas, TX 75231-3427
(214)369-6200
Company Type: Subsidiary. Location
Type: Branch office. Ultimate Parent:
Compass Bancshares. SIC: 6021—National
Commercial Banks.

★ 83951 ★ **Compass Bank-Dallas**
4201 Oak Lawn Ave.
Dallas, TX 75219-2313
(214)528-9770
Company Type: Subsidiary. **Location Type:** Branch office. **Ultimate Parent:** Compass Bancshares. **SIC:** 6021—National Commercial Banks.

★ 83952 ★ **Compass Bank-Dallas**
9090 Skillman St.
Dallas, TX 75243-8262
(214)343-0008
Company Type: Subsidiary. **Location Type:** Branch office. **Officer:** Steve Mack, Manager. **Ultimate Parent:** Compass Bancshares. **SIC:** 6021—National Commercial Banks.

★ 83953 ★ **Compass Bank-Dallas**
17950 Preston Rd., Ste. 100
Dallas, TX 75252-5793
(214)380-9516
Company Type: Subsidiary. **Location Type:** Branch office. **Ultimate Parent:** Compass Bancshares. **SIC:** 6021—National Commercial Banks.

★ 83954 ★ **Compass Bank-Dallas**
8080 N. Central Expy.
Dallas, TX 75226
(214)705-4200
Company Type: Subsidiary. **Location Type:** Branch office. **Ultimate Parent:** Compass Bancshares. **SIC:** 6021—National Commercial Banks.

★ 83955 ★ **Compass Bank-Dallas**
14755 Preston Rd.
Dallas, TX 75240-7859
(214)991-2900
Company Type: Subsidiary. **Location Type:** Branch office. **Officer:** Craig Bevil, Manager. **Ultimate Parent:** Compass Bancshares. **SIC:** 6021—National Commercial Banks.

★ 83956 ★ **Computer Associates**
2997 LBJ Fwy.
Dallas, TX 75234
(214)247-7061
Ultimate Parent: Computer Associates International. **SIC:** 5046—Commercial Equipment Nec.

★ 83957 ★ **Congress Financial Corp.**
1 Main Pl
Dallas, TX 75226
(214)761-9044
Ultimate Parent: Corestates Financial Corp. **SIC:** 6159—Miscellaneous Business Credit Institutions.

★ 83958 ★ **Cooper Tire&Rubber**
151 Regal Row
Dallas, TX 75247
(214)688-0311
Ultimate Parent: Cooper Tire & Rubber Co. Inc.

★ 83959 ★ **Cray Research Inc.**
5005 LBJ Fwy.
Dallas, TX 75244
(214)450-9530
Ultimate Parent: Cray Research, Inc.

★ 83960 ★ **CSC Logic Inc.**
9330 Lyndon B. Johnson Fwy.
Dallas, TX 75243-3436
(214)238-1898
Company Type: Subsidiary. **Officer:** Winston R. Kimzey, Pr. **Ultimate Parent:** Computer Sciences. **SIC:** 7374—Data Processing & Preparation. **Employee Count:** 310. **Sales:** 23 M.

★ 83961 ★ **CSC Logic, Inc.**
9330 L.B.J. Fwy., Ste. 500
Dallas, TX 75243
(214)238-1898 **Fax:** (214)680-3532
Officer: Winston R. Kimzey, President. **Ultimate Parent:** Computer Sciences.

★ 83962 ★ **CSW Credit, Inc.**
1616 Woodall Rogers Fwy.
Dallas, TX 75202
Fax: (214)777-1223
Officer: Glenn D. Rosilier, President. **Ultimate Parent:** Central & South West.

★ 83963 ★ **CSW Energy, Inc.**
1616 Woodall Rogers Fwy.
Dallas, TX 75202
Fax: (214)777-1223
Officer: E.R. Brooks, Chairman of the Board. **Ultimate Parent:** Central & South West.

★ 83964 ★ **CSW Leasing, Inc.**
1616 Woodall Rogers Fwy.
Dallas, TX 75202
(214)777-1111 **Fax:** (214)922-1700
Officer: E.R. Brooks, Chairman of the Board. **Ultimate Parent:** Central & South West.

★ 83965 ★ **CTX Mortgage Co.**
3333 Lee Pky.
PO Box 19000
Dallas, TX 75219
Fax: (817)834-2918
Officer: Carl N. Hearne, President. **Ultimate Parent:** Centex.

★ 83966 ★ **D Magazine**
3988 N. Central Expy., Ste. 1200
Dallas, TX 75204
(214)827-5000
Ultimate Parent: American Express Co. **SIC:** 2721—Periodicals.

★ 83967 ★ **Dap Inc.**
13555 Jupiter Rd.
Dallas, TX 75238
Ultimate Parent: USG Corp. **SIC:** 3800—Instruments & Related Products.

★ 83968 ★ **Davenport Data Processors, Inc.**
12850 Spurling Rd., 2nd Fl.
Dallas, TX 75230
(214)696-2701 **Fax:** (214)392-9817
Company Type: Subsidiary. **Officer:** Michael B. Weiner, Vice President-Sales-Texas. **Ultimate Parent:** Bankamerica Corp. **SIC:** 7374—Data Processing & Preparation. **Employee Count:** 30.

★ 83969 ★ **Decorp**
2533 Royal Ln.
Dallas, TX 75229
(214)243-5100
Ultimate Parent: Kellwood. **SIC:** 5651—Family Clothing Stores.

★ 83970 ★ **Dell Computer Corp.**
9600 Royal Ln.
Dallas, TX 75243
(214)343-0668
Ultimate Parent: Dell Computer.

★ 83971 ★ **Delta Air Lines**
Dallas Fort Worth Airport
Dallas, TX 75261
(214)574-2255
Ultimate Parent: Delta Air Lines, Inc. **SIC:** 4512—Air Transportation—Scheduled; 6512—Nonresidential Building Operators.

★ 83972 ★ **Delta Air Lines**
1401 Elm St.
Dallas, TX 75202
(214)630-3200
Ultimate Parent: Delta Air Lines, Inc. **SIC:** 4512—Air Transportation—Scheduled; 4724—Travel Agencies.

★ 83973 ★ **Delta Air Lines Inc.**
1401 Elm St. 201
Dallas, TX 75202
(214)630-3200
Ultimate Parent: Delta Air Lines, Inc. **SIC:** 4512—Air Transportation—Scheduled; 4724—Travel Agencies.

★ 83974 ★ **Delta Air Lines Marketing Office**
8700 N. Stemmons Fwy.
Dallas, TX 75247
(214)920-3232
Ultimate Parent: Delta Air Lines, Inc. **SIC:** 4512—Air Transportation—Scheduled.

★ 83975 ★ **Deluxe Check Printers Inc.**
9125 Viscount Row
Dallas, TX 75247-5477
Ultimate Parent: Deluxe Corp. **SIC:** 2782—Blankbooks & Looseleaf Binders; 2752—Commercial Printing—Lithographic.

★ 83976 ★ **Deluxe Check Printers Inc.**
9125 Viscount Row
Dallas, TX 75247
Ultimate Parent: Deluxe Corp. **SIC:** 2782—Blankbooks & Looseleaf Binders; 2752—Commercial Printing—Lithographic.

★ 83977 ★ **Diebold Inc.**
1830 Royal Ln.
Dallas, TX 75229
(214)241-1144
Ultimate Parent: Diebold, Inc. **SIC:** 5046—Commercial Equipment Nec.

★ 83978 ★ **Dr. Pepper/Seven-Up Inc.**
8144 Walnut Hill Ln.
Dallas, TX 75231
(214)360-7000
Location Type: Headquarters. **Officer:** John R. Albers. **SIC:** 2087—Flavoring Extracts & Syrups Nec. **Employee Count:** 952. **Sales:** 707 M. **Fortune 500:** Largest U.S. Industrial Corporations: Ranking 443.

★ 83979 ★ **Dr. Pepper/7-Up Companies Inc.**
8144 Walnut Hill Ln.
Dallas, TX 75231-4327
(214)360-7000
Officer: John R. Albers, Ch. Bd. Dr. **Ultimate Parent:** Dr. Pepper/Seven-Up. **SIC:** 2087—Flavoring Extracts & Syrups Nec. **Employee Count:** 930. **Sales:** 658 M.

★ 83980 ★ **Dr. Pepper/7-Up Corp.**
8144 Walnut Hill Ln.
Dallas, TX 75231-4327
(214)360-7000
Company Type: Subsidiary. **Officer:** John R. Albers, Ch. Bd. CEO. **Ultimate Parent:** Dr. Pepper/Seven-Up. **SIC:** 2087—Flavoring Extracts & Syrups Nec. **Employee Count:** 930. **Sales:** 658 M.

★ 83981 ★ **Dolphin Construction**
2474 Manana Dr.
Dallas, TX 75220
(214)353-9105
Ultimate Parent: Texas Industries. **SIC:** 1731—Electrical Work.

★ 83982 ★ **Dow Jones & Co.**
1233 Regal Row
Dallas, TX 75247
(214)631-7250
Officer: Peter Kann, Publisher. **Ultimate Parent:** Dow Jones. **SIC:** 2711—Newspapers.

★ 83983 ★ **Dresser Industries Inc.**
PO Box 718
Dallas, TX 75221
(214)740-6000 **Fax:** (214)740-6584
Company Type: Headquarters. **Ultimate Parent:** Dresser Industries Inc. **Employee Count:** 27400. **Sales:** 4000000000 M.

★ 83984 ★ **Dresser Industries Inc.**
2001 Ross Ave.
Dallas, TX 75201
(214)740-6000
Company Type: Headquarters. **Officer:** John J. Murphy. **Sales:** 4216 M. **Fortune 500:** Largest U.S. Industrial Corporations: Ranking 122.

★ 83985 ★ **Dresser Industries Inc.**
Guiberson Div.
1000 Forest Ave.
Dallas, TX 75215
Company Type: Division. **Ultimate Parent:** Dresser Industries Inc. **SIC:** 3069—Fabricated Rubber Products Nec; 3499—Fabricated Metal Products Nec; 3533—Oil & Gas Field Machinery.

★ 83986 ★ **Dresser Industries Inc.**
Security Division
3400 W. Illinois Ave.
Dallas, TX 75211
(214)333-3211 **Fax:** (214)330-2579
Company Type: Subsidiary. **Ultimate Parent:** Dresser Industries Inc.

★ 83987 ★ **Durr-Fillauer Medical Inc.**
11281 Indian Trl.
Dallas, TX 75229
(214)243-1551
Ultimate Parent: Bergen Brunswig Corp. **SIC:** 5047—Medical & Hospital Equipment.

★ 83988 ★ **E R Carpenter Co.**
4443 Bronze Way
Dallas, TX 75236
(214)263-5350
Ultimate Parent: Carpenter.

★ 83989 ★ **E. R. Carpenter Co. Inc.**
4443 Bronze Way
Dallas, TX 75236
Ultimate Parent: Carpenter. **SIC:** 3086—Plastics Foam Products.

★ 83990 ★ **E Systems Inc.**
PO Box 660248
Dallas, TX 75266-0248
(214)661-1000
Officer: E. Gene Keiffer, CEO. **Ultimate Parent:** E-Systems Inc. **SIC:** 3812—Search & Navigation Equipment; 3663—Radio & T.V. Communications Equipment; 4581—Airports, Flying Fields & Services; 3721—Aircraft. **Employee Count:** 18600. **Sales:** 2094913000 M.

★ 83991 ★ **E-Systems Inc.**
6250 LBJ Fwy.
Dallas, TX 75266
(214)661-1010 **Fax:** (214)661-8508
Company Type: Headquarters. **Officer:** E. Gene Keiffer, Chairman & CEO. **Ultimate Parent:** E-Systems Inc. **Employee Count:** 16950.

★ 83992 ★ **E-Systems Inc.**
6250 Lyndon B. Johnson Fwy.
Dallas, TX 75240
(214)661-1000
Company Type: Headquarters. **Officer:** E. Gene Keiffer, Chairman of the Board & CEO. **SIC:** 3571—Electronic Computers; 3661—Telephone & Telegraph Apparatus; 3663—Radio & T.V. Communications Equipment; 3812—Search & Navigation Equipment; 7373—Computer Integrated Systems Design; 3575—Computer Terminals; 4581—Airports, Flying Fields & Services. **Employee Count:** 16703. **Sales:** 2097 M. **Fortune 500:** Largest U.S. Industrial Corporations: Ranking 213.

★ 83993 ★ **E-Systems Inc.**
Garland Division
POB 660023
Dallas, TX 75266-0023
(214)272-0515 **Fax:** (214)272-8144
Company Type: Subsidiary. **Officer:** Marshall D. Williamson, Vice President/General Manager. **Ultimate Parent:** E-Systems Inc.

★ 83994 ★ **E-Systems Medical Electronics Inc.**
POB 660023
Dallas, TX 75266-0023
(214)272-0515 **Fax:** (214)272-5533
Company Type: Subsidiary. **Officer:** Peter A. Marino Jr., Senior Vice President. **Ultimate Parent:** E-Systems Inc.

★ 83995 ★ **Eagle Crest Foods, Inc.**
1925 Valley View Ln.
Dallas, TX 75234
(214)241-2181
Company Type: Subsidiary. **Officer:** Richard Witherspoon, President. **Ultimate Parent:** Anheuser-Busch. **SIC:** 2038—Frozen Specialties Nec. **Employee Count:** 300.

★ 83996 ★ **Eagle Crest Inc.**
1925 Valley View Ln.
Dallas, TX 75234
Ultimate Parent: Anheuser-Busch. **SIC:** 2038—Frozen Specialties Nec.

★ 83997 ★ **Eagle Snacks Inc.**
8115 Preston Rd., Ste. 300
Dallas, TX 75225
(214)265-5100 **Fax:** (214)265-5168
Company Type: Subsidiary. **Officer:** Barry H. Beracha, Chairman & CEO. **Ultimate Parent:** Anheuser-Busch.

★ 83998 ★   Eckerd Drug Co.
4311 Live Oak St.
Dallas, TX 75204
(214)827-9240
Ultimate Parent: Eckerd Corp. SIC: 5912—
Drug Stores & Proprietary Stores.

★ 83999 ★   Eckerd Drug Co.
2461 Gus Thomasson Rd.
Dallas, TX 75228
Ultimate Parent: Eckerd Corp. SIC: 5912—
Drug Stores & Proprietary Stores.

★ 84000 ★   Eckerd Drug Co. No.
848
3616 Forest Ln.
Dallas, TX 75234
(214)358-3397
Ultimate Parent: Eckerd Corp. SIC: 5912—
Drug Stores & Proprietary Stores.

★ 84001 ★   Eckerd Drug Co. No.
827
5848 Abrams Rd.
Dallas, TX 75214
(214)368-4636
Ultimate Parent: Eckerd Corp. SIC: 5912—
Drug Stores & Proprietary Stores.

★ 84002 ★   Eckerd Drug Co. No.
21
1536 S. Buckner Blvd.
Dallas, TX 75217
(214)391-2151
Ultimate Parent: Eckerd Corp. SIC: 5912—
Drug Stores & Proprietary Stores.

★ 84003 ★   EG & G Science
Support Corp.
SSC Laboratory
2550 Beckleymeade Ave.
Dallas, TX 75237-3946
(214)708-5010 Fax: (214)708-1930
Company Type: Subsidiary. Officer: Jack
Story, Director. Ultimate Parent: EG & G.

★ 84004 ★   Electronic Data
Systems
13510 Floyd Rd.
Dallas, TX 75243
(214)934-5095
Ultimate Parent: Electronic Data Systems.
SIC: 7539—Automotive Repair Shops Nec.

★ 84005 ★   Electronic Data
Systems Corp.
9250 Amberton Pky.
Dallas, TX 75243
(214)952-8600
Ultimate Parent: Electronic Data Systems.

★ 84006 ★   Ellesse USA Inc.
2300 Stemmons
Dallas, TX 75258
(214)631-0755
Ultimate Parent: Reebok International. SIC:
5136—Men's/Boys' Clothing.

★ 84007 ★   Emery Worldwide
Dallas Fort Worth Ar
Dallas, TX 75261
(214)453-0641
Ultimate Parent: Consolidated Freightways.
SIC: 4513—Air Courier Services; 7389—
Business Services Nec.

★ 84008 ★   Energy Service Co.
Inc.
1445 Ross Ave., Ste. 2700
Dallas, TX 75202-2792
(214)922-1500 Fax: (214)855-0080
Officer: Carl F. Thorn. Ultimate Parent:
Scecorp. Employee Count: 890. Sales:
246 M.

★ 84009 ★   Enserch
300 S. St. Paul St.
Dallas, TX 75201
(214)651-8700
Company Type: Headquarters. Officer:
David W. Biegler. Employee Count: 5600.
Sales: 3150 M. Fortune Service 500:
Ranking 39.

★ 84010 ★   Enserch Corp.
Enserch Ctr.
300 S. St. Paul St.
Dallas, TX 75201-5598
(214)651-8700
Officer: W. C. McCord, CEO. Ultimate
Parent: Enserch. SIC: 4923—Gas
Transmission & Distribution; 8711—
Engineering Services; 1311—Crude
Petroleum & Natural Gas; 1321—Natural
Gas Liquids; 1629—Heavy Construction

Nec. Employee Count: 10400. Sales:
2825500000 M.

★ 84011 ★   Enserch Corp.
300 South St. & Paul St.
Dallas, TX 75201-5598
(214)651-8700 Fax: (214)573-3848 Telex:
732502
Company Type: Headquarters. Officer:
William C. McCord, Chairman of the Board.
Ultimate Parent: Enserch. SIC: 1311—
Crude Petroleum & Natural Gas; 4923—Gas
Transmission & Distribution; 1542—
Nonresidential Construction Nec; 8711—
Engineering Services; 1321—Natural Gas
Liquids; 1629—Heavy Construction Nec;
8748—Business Consulting Services Nec.
Employee Count: 11000. Sales: 2834 M.

★ 84012 ★   Enserch Corp.
PO Box 999
Dallas, TX 75221-0999
Company Type: Headquarters. Ultimate
Parent: Enserch.

★ 84013 ★   Enserch Exlporation
Partners Ltd.
1817 Wood St.
Dallas, TX 75201-5605
(214)748-1110
Officer: David W. Biegler, CEO. Ultimate
Parent: Enserch. SIC: 1382—Oil & Gas
Exploration Services; 1311—Crude
Petroleum & Natural Gas. Employee
Count: 450. Sales: 165 M.

★ 84014 ★   Enserch Exploration
Inc.
1817 Wood St.
Dallas, TX 75201-5605
(214)748-1110
Company Type: Subsidiary. Officer: David
W. Biegler, Chairman of the Board & CEO.
Ultimate Parent: Enserch. SIC: 8741—
Management Services. Employee Count:
450. Sales: 16 M.

★ 84015 ★   Epsilon/Southwest
13628 Beta Dr.
Dallas, TX 75234
(214)392-2717
Company Type: Division. Ultimate Parent:
American Express Co. SIC: 7372—
Prepackaged Software.

★ 84016 ★   E.R. Carpenter Co.
Inc.
4443 Bronze Way
Dallas, TX 75236
Ultimate Parent: Carpenter. SIC: 2392—
Housefurnishings Nec.

★ 84017 ★   Exxon
11700 Plano Rd.
Dallas, TX 75243
(214)341-4768
Ultimate Parent: Exxon. SIC: 5541—
Gasoline Service Stations.

★ 84018 ★   Exxon
5707 Marvin D. Love Fwy.
Dallas, TX 75232
(214)339-4138
Ultimate Parent: Exxon. SIC: 5541—
Gasoline Service Stations.

★ 84019 ★   Exxon
300 S. Marsalis Ave.
Dallas, TX 75203
(214)943-4893
Ultimate Parent: Exxon. SIC: 5541—
Gasoline Service Stations.

★ 84020 ★   Exxon
3301 W. Davis St.
Dallas, TX 75211
(214)337-9939
Ultimate Parent: Exxon. SIC: 5541—
Gasoline Service Stations.

★ 84021 ★   Exxon
2828 N. Central Expy.
Dallas, TX 75204
(214)824-3418
Ultimate Parent: Exxon. SIC: 5541—
Gasoline Service Stations.

★ 84022 ★   Exxon
7700 N. Central Expy.
Dallas, TX 75206
(214)368-4569
Ultimate Parent: Exxon. SIC: 5541—
Gasoline Service Stations.

★ 84023 ★   Exxon
12330 Greenville Ave.
Dallas, TX 75243
(214)235-4674
Ultimate Parent: Exxon. SIC: 5411—
Grocery Stores; 5541—Gasoline Service
Stations.

★ 84024 ★   Exxon
4205 LBJ Fwy.
Dallas, TX 75244
(214)239-7751
Ultimate Parent: Exxon. SIC: 7538—
General Automotive Repair Shops.

★ 84025 ★   Exxon
7100 S. R L Thornton Fwy.
Dallas, TX 75232
(214)224-4580
Ultimate Parent: Exxon. SIC: 5541—
Gasoline Service Stations.

★ 84026 ★   Exxon
5707 M D Love Fwy.
Dallas, TX 75232
(214)331-8403
Ultimate Parent: Exxon. SIC: 5541—
Gasoline Service Stations.

★ 84027 ★   Exxon
9998 Marsh Ln.
Dallas, TX 75220
(214)352-9088
Ultimate Parent: Exxon. SIC: 5541—
Gasoline Service Stations.

★ 84028 ★   Exxon
3202 S. Lancaster Rd.
Dallas, TX 75216
(214)374-2162
Ultimate Parent: Exxon. SIC: 5541—
Gasoline Service Stations.

★ 84029 ★   Exxon
1885 John Rd. W
Dallas, TX 75228
(214)321-0890
Ultimate Parent: Exxon. SIC: 5411—
Grocery Stores; 5541—Gasoline Service
Stations.

★ 84030 ★   Exxon
8210 S. Hampton Rd.
Dallas, TX 75232
(214)224-5234
Ultimate Parent: Exxon. SIC: 5541—
Gasoline Service Stations.

★ 84031 ★   Exxon
15050 Preston Rd.
Dallas, TX 75240
(214)233-5201
Ultimate Parent: Exxon. SIC: 5541—
Gasoline Service Stations.

★ 84032 ★   Exxon
7110 S. Cockrell Hill Rd.
Dallas, TX 75236
(214)296-2470
Ultimate Parent: Exxon. SIC: 5541—
Gasoline Service Stations.

★ 84033 ★   Exxon
8302 Abrams Rd.
Dallas, TX 75243
(214)349-2169
Ultimate Parent: Exxon. SIC: 5541—
Gasoline Service Stations.

★ 84034 ★   Exxon
3803 S. Polk St.
Dallas, TX 75224
(214)371-2919
Ultimate Parent: Exxon. SIC: 5541—
Gasoline Service Stations.

★ 84035 ★   Exxon
4191 Belt Line Rd.
Dallas, TX 75244
(214)385-1804
Ultimate Parent: Exxon. SIC: 5541—
Gasoline Service Stations.

★ 84036 ★   Exxon
2316 Oak Lawn Ave.
Dallas, TX 75219
(214)521-3312
Ultimate Parent: Exxon. SIC: 5541—
Gasoline Service Stations.

★ 84037 ★   Exxon Car Care
Center
15707 Hillcrest Rd.
Dallas, TX 75248
(214)233-7034
Ultimate Parent: Exxon.

★ 84038 ★   Exxon Car Care
Center
12969 Preston Rd.
Dallas, TX 75230
(214)239-7291
Ultimate Parent: Exxon. SIC: 7538—
General Automotive Repair Shops.

★ 84039 ★   Exxon Car Care
Center
2242 S. Zang Blvd.
Dallas, TX 75224
(214)943-4431
Ultimate Parent: Exxon. SIC: 7538—
General Automotive Repair Shops.

★ 84040 ★   Exxon Car Care
Center
3082 Forest Ln.
Dallas, TX 75234
(214)241-2285
Ultimate Parent: Exxon. SIC: 5541—
Gasoline Service Stations.

★ 84041 ★   Exxon Car Care
Center
3927 Oak Lawn Ave.
Dallas, TX 75219
(214)522-3020
Ultimate Parent: Exxon. SIC: 7538—
General Automotive Repair Shops.

★ 84042 ★   Exxon Car Care
Center
10305 Ferguson Rd.
Dallas, TX 75228
(214)328-9845
Ultimate Parent: Exxon. SIC: 5541—
Gasoline Service Stations; 7538—General
Automotive Repair Shops.

★ 84043 ★   Exxon Car Care
Center
7303 W. John Carpenter Fwy.
Dallas, TX 75247
(214)631-3083
Ultimate Parent: Exxon. SIC: 5541—
Gasoline Service Stations.

★ 84044 ★   Exxon Car Care
Center
8201 E. R L Thornton Fwy.
Dallas, TX 75228
(214)328-8465
Ultimate Parent: Exxon. SIC: 5541—
Gasoline Service Stations; 7538—General
Automotive Repair Shops.

★ 84045 ★   Exxon Car Care
Center
5748 Live Oak St.
Dallas, TX 75206
(214)823-1351
Ultimate Parent: Exxon. SIC: 5541—
Gasoline Service Stations.

★ 84046 ★   Exxon Car Care
Center
3082 1st Ln.
Dallas, TX 75234
(214)241-3101
Ultimate Parent: Exxon. SIC: 5541—
Gasoline Service Stations; 7538—General
Automotive Repair Shops.

★ 84047 ★   Exxon Car Care
Center
10140 E. Northwest Hwy.
Dallas, TX 75238
(214)341-3606
Ultimate Parent: Exxon. SIC: 5541—
Gasoline Service Stations; 7538—General
Automotive Repair Shops.

★ 84048 ★   Exxon Car Wash
435 W. Illinois Ave.
Dallas, TX 75224
(214)942-7651
Ultimate Parent: Exxon. SIC: 5541—
Gasoline Service Stations; 7542—Car
Washes.

★ 84049 ★ Exxon Chemical Co.
100 N. Central Expy.
Dallas, TX 75201
(214)690-8086
Ultimate Parent: Exxon. SIC: 3089—
Plastics Products Nec.

★ 84050 ★ Exxon Co. USA
19059 Marsh Ln.
Dallas, TX 75287
(214)307-0036
Ultimate Parent: Exxon.

★ 84051 ★ Exxon Pipeline Co.
2720 Brookfield Ave.
Dallas, TX 75235
(214)357-9741
Ultimate Parent: Exxon. SIC: 4619—
Pipelines Nec.

★ 84052 ★ Exxon Pipeline Co.
2720 Brookfield Ave.
Dallas, TX 75235
(214)357-9741
Ultimate Parent: Exxon Pipeline. SIC:
4619—Pipelines Nec.

★ 84053 ★ Exxon Shop
1607 Inwood Rd.
Dallas, TX 75247
(214)263-2280
Ultimate Parent: Exxon.

★ 84054 ★ Exxon Shop
18181 Midway Rd.
Dallas, TX 75287
(214)306-9125
Ultimate Parent: Exxon.

★ 84055 ★ Exxon Shop
2052 Fort Worth Ave.
Dallas, TX 75208
(214)263-0261
Ultimate Parent: Exxon.

★ 84056 ★ Exxon Shop
2052 Fort Worth Ave.
Dallas, TX 75208
(214)942-1947
Ultimate Parent: Exxon. SIC: 5541—
Gasoline Service Stations.

★ 84057 ★ Exxon Shop
11748 Central Expy. N
Dallas, TX 75243
(214)340-9585
Ultimate Parent: Exxon.

★ 84058 ★ Exxon Shop
14106 Dallas Pky.
Dallas, TX 75240
(214)960-9986
Ultimate Parent: Exxon.

★ 84059 ★ Exxon Shop
7650 Campbell Rd.
Dallas, TX 75248
(214)248-8032
Ultimate Parent: Exxon.

★ 84060 ★ Farm & Home
Savings Association
1900 Pacific Ave.
Dallas, TX 75201
(214)748-8771
Ultimate Parent: Farm & Home Financial
Corp. SIC: 6036—Savings Institutions
Except Federal.

★ 84061 ★ Federal Express Corp.
7336 Aviation Pl
Dallas, TX 75235
(214)358-5271
Ultimate Parent: Federal Express. SIC:
4512—Air Transportation—Scheduled.

★ 84062 ★ Federal Home Loan
Mortgage
12222 Merit Dr.
Dallas, TX 75251
(214)387-0600
Ultimate Parent: Federal Home Loan
Mortgage. SIC: 6162—Mortgage Bankers &
Correspondents.

★ 84063 ★ Fina
8350 N. Central Expy.
Dallas, TX 75206
(214)750-2400
Company Type: Headquarters. Officer:
Ron W. Haddock. Sales: 3416.2 M.
Fortune 500: Largest U.S. Industrial
Corporations: Ranking 145.

★ 84064 ★ Fina Inc.
Fina Plz.
Dallas, TX 75206
(214)750-2400
Officer: Paul D. Meek, Chairman. Ultimate
Parent: Fina. SIC: 2911—Petroleum
Refining; 5541—Gasoline Service Stations;
4610—Pipelines Except Natural Gas;
2821—Plastics Materials & Resins; 1311—
Crude Petroleum & Natural Gas; 2851—
Paints & Allied Products. Employee Count:
3369. Sales: 3397523000 M.

★ 84065 ★ Fina Inc.
8350 N. Central Expy.
Dallas, TX 75206-1602
(214)750-2400
Company Type: Subsidiary. Officer: Paul
D. Meek, Chairman of the Board. Ultimate
Parent: Fina. SIC: 2911—Petroleum
Refining; 4612—Crude Petroleum Pipelines;
4412—Deep Sea Foreign Transportation of
Freight; 5172—Petroleum Products Nec;
5541—Gasoline Service Stations; 2895—
Carbon Black; 2821—Plastics Materials &
Resins; 3089—Plastics Products Nec.
Employee Count: 3665. Sales: 3.3 M.

★ 84066 ★ Fina Oil & Chemical
Co.
8350 N. Central Expy.
Dallas, TX 75206-1602
(214)750-2400
Company Type: Subsidiary. Officer: Paul
D. Meek, Chairman of the Board. Ultimate
Parent: Fina. SIC: 2911—Petroleum
Refining; 4612—Crude Petroleum Pipelines;
5172—Petroleum Products Nec; 5541—
Gasoline Service Stations; 1311—Crude
Petroleum & Natural Gas; 2821—Plastics
Materials & Resins. Employee Count:
3300. Sales: 1.9 M.

★ 84067 ★ Fina Oil & Chemical
Co.
Fina Plz.
8350 N. Central Expy.
Dallas, TX 75206
(214)750-2400 Fax: (214)750-2891
Company Type: Subsidiary. Officer: Paul
D. Meek, Chairman. Ultimate Parent: Fina.

★ 84068 ★ First Data Corp.
1950 N. Stemmons Fwy.
Dallas, TX 75207-3109
(214)746-4722
Ultimate Parent: American Express Co.
SIC: 5045—Computers, Peripherals &
Software.

★ 84069 ★ Fischbach & Moore
International Corp.
2525 Walnut Hill Ln.
Dallas, TX 75229-5681
(214)484-4586
Officer: Daniel K. Mazany, President &
CEO. Ultimate Parent: American
International Group, Inc. SIC: 1731—
Electrical Work; 1711—Plumbing, Heating &
Air-Conditioning. Employee Count: 14.
Sales: 20 M.

★ 84070 ★ Fischbach & Moore
International Group
2525 Walnut Hill Ln.
Dallas, TX 75229-5610
(214)484-4586
Location Type: Branch office. Officer:
Daniel K. Mazany. Ultimate Parent:
American International Group, Inc. SIC:
1542—Nonresidential Construction Nec;
1541—Industrial Buildings & Warehouses;
1711—Plumbing, Heating & Air-
Conditioning; 1731—Electrical Work; 3679—
Electronic Components Nec.

★ 84071 ★ Fleming Foods Of
Texas Inc. (Southern Reg)
15110 Dallas Pkwy
Ste. 500
Dallas, TX 75248
(214)450-9600 Fax: (214)450-9675
Company Type: Subsidiary. Officer: James
E. Stuard, Executive Vice President.
Ultimate Parent: Fleming.

★ 84072 ★ Fleming Foods of
Texas Inc.
15110 Dallas Pky. Ste. 500
Dallas, TX 75248-4666
(214)450-9600
Company Type: Subsidiary. Officer: James
E. Stuard, President. Ultimate Parent:
Fleming. SIC: 5141—Groceries—General

Line. Employee Count: 2000. Sales: 726
M.

★ 84073 ★ Foot Action
3940 Pipestone Dr.
Dallas, TX 75212
(214)634-7755 Fax: (214)637-5104
Officer: Ralph T. Parks, President. Ultimate
Parent: Melville.

★ 84074 ★ Foot Action U S a
3940 Pipestone Rd.
Dallas, TX 75212
(214)634-0040
Ultimate Parent: Melville. SIC: 5661—Shoe
Stores.

★ 84075 ★ Foot Action U S a
1160 Valley View Ctr.
Dallas, TX 75240
(214)386-5271
Ultimate Parent: Melville. SIC: 5661—Shoe
Stores.

★ 84076 ★ Footaction U S a
3662 W. Camp Wisdom Rd.
Dallas, TX 75237
(214)709-0780
Ultimate Parent: Melville. SIC: 5661—Shoe
Stores.

★ 84077 ★ Friction, Inc.
5108 S. Cockvell Hill Rd.
Dallas, TX 75236
(214)337-9925
Officer: Martin Brown, Manager. Ultimate
Parent: Echlin. SIC: 3714—Motor Vehicle
Parts & Accessories.

★ 84078 ★ Friction, Inc.
5108 Cockrell Hill Rd.
Dallas, TX 75211
Ultimate Parent: Echlin. SIC: 3714—Motor
Vehicle Parts & Accessories.

★ 84079 ★ GAF Building
Materials Corp.
2600 Singleton Blvd.
Dallas, TX 75212
(214)637-1060
Company Type: Subsidiary. Location
Type: Plant. Officer: Greg Cherry, Plant
Manager. Ultimate Parent: GAF Corp. SIC:
2952—Asphalt Felts & Coatings.

★ 84080 ★ The Gap
13350 Dallas Pky.
Dallas, TX 75240
(214)991-3454
Ultimate Parent: GAP.

★ 84081 ★ The Gap
738 N. Park C
Dallas, TX 75201
(214)369-5498
Ultimate Parent: GAP.

★ 84082 ★ The Gap
226 Casa Linda Plz.
Dallas, TX 75218
(214)327-0618
Ultimate Parent: GAP.

★ 84083 ★ The Gap
4980 Belt Line Rd.
Dallas, TX 75240
(214)460-6864
Ultimate Parent: GAP. SIC: 5651—Family
Clothing Stores.

★ 84084 ★ The Gap
5301 Belt Line Rd.
Dallas, TX 75240
(214)991-6455
Ultimate Parent: GAP. SIC: 5611—Men's &
Boys' Clothing Stores; 5651—Family
Clothing Stores.

★ 84085 ★ The Gap Kids
211 Northpark Ctr.
Dallas, TX 75225
(214)692-5134
Ultimate Parent: GAP. SIC: 5651—Family
Clothing Stores.

★ 84086 ★ General American Life
Insurance
2515 McKinney Ave.
Dallas, TX 75201
(214)855-0525
Ultimate Parent: General American Life.
SIC: 6411—Insurance Agents, Brokers &
Service.

★ 84087 ★ General American Life
Insurance C
8300 Douglas Ave.
Dallas, TX 75225
(214)361-8344
Ultimate Parent: General American Life.
SIC: 6411—Insurance Agents, Brokers &
Service.

★ 84088 ★ General American Life
Insurance C
5307 E. Mockingbird Ln.
Dallas, TX 75206
(214)821-1851
Ultimate Parent: General American Life.
SIC: 6411—Insurance Agents, Brokers &
Service.

★ 84089 ★ General Electric Co.
5430 Lyndon B. Johnson Fwy.
Dallas, TX 75240
(214)458-1112
Officer: Katherine Hamilton, Manager.
Ultimate Parent: General Electric. SIC:
2821—Plastics Materials & Resins; 3081—
Unsupported Plastics Film & Sheet.

★ 84090 ★ General Electric Co.
3202 Manor Way
Dallas, TX 75235
(214)902-6600
Ultimate Parent: General Electric. SIC:
3541—Machine Tools—Metal Cutting
Types; 3599—Industrial Machinery Nec;
3699—Electrical Equipment & Supplies Nec.

★ 84091 ★ General Electric Co.
11221 Pagemill Rd.
Dallas, TX 75243
(214)343-5500
Officer: Ed Plant, Manager. Ultimate
Parent: General Electric. SIC: 3825—
Instruments to Measure Electricity.

★ 84092 ★ Genuine Parts
Southwest Division
2221 W. Mockingbird Ln.
Dallas, TX 75235
(214)357-3900 Fax: (214)357-3598
Company Type: Subsidiary. Ultimate
Parent: Genuine Parts.

★ 84093 ★ Glitsch International
Inc.
4900 Singleton Blvd.
Dallas, TX 75212-3395
(214)631-3841
Company Type: Subsidiary. Officer: John
L. VanBuren, President. Ultimate Parent:
Foster Wheeler Corp. SIC: 3443—
Fabricated Plate Work—Boiler Shops.
Sales: 121 M.

★ 84094 ★ Grace Energy Corp.
13455 Noel Rd., Ste. 1500
Dallas, TX 75240-6634
(214)770-0200
Company Type: Subsidiary. Officer: J. P.
Grace, Chairman of the Board & Chief
Executive Officer. Ultimate Parent: W. R.
Grace. SIC: 1381—Drilling Oil & Gas Wells;
1389—Oil & Gas Field Services Nec;
7353—Heavy Construction Equipment
Rental; 3533—Oil & Gas Field Machinery;
5082—Construction & Mining Machinery;
1200—Coal Mining. Employee Count:
3899. Sales: 499000000 M.

★ 84095 ★ Great Western
Trucking Co. Inc.
5701 W. Kiest Blvd.
Dallas, TX 75236
(214)333-9768 Fax: (214)330-2090
Company Type: Subsidiary. Officer:
William D. Tadlock, President. Ultimate
Parent: J. B. Hunt Transport.

★ 84096 ★ Greyhound Bus Lines
1100 S. Lamar St.
Dallas, TX 75215
(214)565-1670
Ultimate Parent: Greyhound Lines Inc. SIC:
4131—Intercity & Rural Bus Transportation.

★ 84097 ★ Greyhound Bus Lines
7111 W. Carpenter J
Dallas, TX 75247
(214)634-1980
Ultimate Parent: Greyhound Lines Inc. SIC:
4111—Local & Suburban Transit.

★ 84098 ★   Greyhound Bus Lines
Commerce
Dallas, TX 75202
(214)747-8859
Ultimate Parent: Greyhound Lines Inc. SIC:
4212—Local Trucking Without Storage.

★ 84099 ★   Greyhound Bus Lines
11461 Harry Hines Blvd.
Dallas, TX 75229
(214)241-1957
Ultimate Parent: Greyhound Lines Inc. SIC:
4111—Local & Suburban Transit; 4131—
Intercity & Rural Bus Transportation.

★ 84100 ★   Greyhound Lines Inc.
15110 N. Dallas Pky., Ste. 400
Dallas, TX 75248-4665
(214)715-7000
Company Type: Headquarters. Officer:
Frank J. Schmieder, Chairman of the Board. Officer: Charles A.
Lynch, Chairman of the Board. SIC: 4111—
Local & Suburban Transit; 4215—Courier
Services Except by Air; 4142—Bus Charter
Service Except Local.

★ 84101 ★   GTE Directories Corp.
GTE Pl. at W. Airfield Dr.
Dallas, TX 75206
(214)453-7000
Company Type: Subsidiary. Officer:
Thomas F. Lysaught, President. Ultimate
Parent: GTE. SIC: 2741—Miscellaneous
Publishing. Employee Count: 46739.

★ 84102 ★   GTE Directories Sales
Corp.
GTE Pl. at W. Airfield Dr.
Dallas, TX 75206
(214)453-7000
Company Type: Subsidiary. Officer:
Sandra G. Parker, Secretary. Ultimate
Parent: GTE. SIC: 8742—Management
Consulting Services. Employee Count:
1936. Sales: 106 (est) M.

★ 84103 ★   GTE Directories
Service Corp.
GTE Pl. at W. Airfield Dr.
Dallas, TX 75206
(214)453-7000
Company Type: Subsidiary. Officer:
Thomas F. Lysaught, President. Ultimate
Parent: GTE. SIC: 2741—Miscellaneous
Publishing. Employee Count: 922. Sales:
69.5 (est) M.

★ 84104 ★   GTE Information
Services
W. Airfield Dr.
Dallas, TX 75261
(214)453-7000
Company Type: Subsidiary. Officer:
Thomas F. Lysaught, President. Ultimate
Parent: GTE. SIC: 7375—Information
Retrieval Services. Employee Count: 7000.
Sales: 497 (est) M.

★ 84105 ★   GTE Information
Services Inc.
2200 W. Airfield Dr.
Dallas, TX 75261
(214)453-7000 Fax: (214)453-7573
Company Type: Subsidiary. Ultimate
Parent: GTE. SIC: 2741—Miscellaneous
Publishing.

★ 84106 ★   GTE National
Marketing Services Inc.
GTE Pl. at W. Airfield Dr.
Dallas, TX 75261
(214)453-7000
Company Type: Subsidiary. Officer:
Sandra G. Parker, Secretary. Ultimate
Parent: GTE. SIC: 7311—Advertising
Agencies. Employee Count: 115. Sales:
42.5 (est) M.

★ 84107 ★   Guiberson AVA
4949 Joseph Hardin Dr.
PO Box 210700
Dallas, TX 75221
(214)331-3313 Fax: (214)331-9479
Company Type: Subsidiary. Ultimate
Parent: Dresser Industries Inc.

★ 84108 ★   Halliburton
500 N. Akard St.
Dallas, TX 75201
(214)978-2600
Company Type: Headquarters. Officer:
Thomas H. Cruikshank. Employee Count:
64700. Sales: 6351 M. Fortune Service
500: Ranking 17.

★ 84109 ★   Halliburton Co.
3600 Lincoln Plaza
500 N. Akard St.
Dallas, TX 75201-3391
(214)978-2600 Fax: (214)978-2611
Company Type: Headquarters. Officer:
Thomas H. Cruikshank, Chairman & CEO.
Ultimate Parent: Halliburton. Employee
Count: 69200.

★ 84110 ★   Halliburton Co. Inc.
500 N. Akard St., Ste. 3600
Dallas, TX 75201-3328
(214)978-2600
Ultimate Parent: Halliburton. SIC: 1629—
Heavy Construction Nec; 1611—Highway &
Street Construction; 1622—Bridge, Tunnel &
Elevated Highway; 8711—Engineering
Services; 1389—Oil & Gas Field Services
Nec; 6331—Fire, Marine & Casualty
Insurance.

★ 84111 ★   Halliburton Holdings
Inc.
500 N. Akard St., Ste. 3600
Dallas, TX 75201-3328
(214)978-2600
Company Type: Subsidiary. Ultimate
Parent: Halliburton. SIC: 1629—Heavy
Construction Nec; 1611—Highway & Street
Construction; 1622—Bridge, Tunnel &
Elevated Highway; 8711—Engineering
Services; 1389—Oil & Gas Field Services
Nec.

★ 84112 ★   Halliburton Resource
Manage
1525 Elm St.
Dallas, TX 75201
(214)954-6100
Ultimate Parent: Halliburton. SIC: 3563—
Air & Gas Compressors.

★ 84113 ★   Hamilton Hallmark
4004 Beltine Rd., Ste. 200
Dallas, TX 75244
(214)308-8111
Location Type: Branch office. Ultimate
Parent: Avnet. SIC: 5065—Electronic Parts
& Equipment Nec.

★ 84114 ★   Herby's Foods
6211 Lemmon Ave.
Dallas, TX 75209
(214)358-9211
Company Type: Subsidiary. Officer: Tim
McClearin, President. Ultimate Parent:
Anheuser-Busch. SIC: 2099—Food
Preparations Nec.

★ 84115 ★   Hertz Rent-A-Car
13350 Dallas Pky.
Dallas, TX 75240
(214)734-9494
Ultimate Parent: Hertz. SIC: 5812—Eating
Places; 7359—Equipment Rental & Leasing
Nec; 7514—Passenger Car Rental.

★ 84116 ★   Hertz Rent-A-Car
International Pky.
Dallas, TX 75261
(214)621-0837
Ultimate Parent: Hertz. SIC: 7514—
Passenger Car Rental.

★ 84117 ★   Hertz Rent-A-Car
8008 Cedar Springs Rd.
Dallas, TX 75235
(214)350-7071
Ultimate Parent: Hertz. SIC: 7514—
Passenger Car Rental.

★ 84118 ★   Hertz Rent-A-Car
Dallas Fort Worth Ar
Dallas, TX 75261
(214)453-0370
Ultimate Parent: Hertz. SIC: 7514—
Passenger Car Rental; 7514—Passenger
Car Rental.

★ 84119 ★   Hertz Rent-A-Car
2101 N. Stemmons Fwy.
Dallas, TX 75207
(214)744-2195
Ultimate Parent: Hertz. SIC: 7514—
Passenger Car Rental.

★ 84120 ★   Hertz Rent-A-Car
2201 N. Stemmons Fwy.
Dallas, TX 75207
(214)744-2349
Ultimate Parent: Hertz.

★ 84121 ★   Hertz Rent-A-Car
1200 Ross Ave. No. 101
Dallas, TX 75202
(214)742-6814
Ultimate Parent: Hertz. SIC: 7514—
Passenger Car Rental.

★ 84122 ★   Hertz Rent-A-Car
Love
Dallas, TX 75207
(214)350-7071
Ultimate Parent: Hertz. SIC: 7514—
Passenger Car Rental.

★ 84123 ★   Hibernia National
Bank
10501 N. Central Expy.
Dallas, TX 75231
(214)969-6610
Ultimate Parent: Hibernia Corp. SIC:
6099—Functions Related to Deposit
Banking.

★ 84124 ★   Hit or Miss
11333 E. Northwest Hwy.
Dallas, TX 75238
(214)340-2302
Ultimate Parent: TJX. SIC: 5651—Family
Clothing Stores.

★ 84125 ★   Hit or Miss
5411 W. Lovers Ln.
Dallas, TX 75209
(214)357-1380
Ultimate Parent: TJX.

★ 84126 ★   Hit or Miss
7529 Campbell Rd.
Dallas, TX 75248
(214)380-6639
Ultimate Parent: TJX. SIC: 5621—
Women's Clothing Stores; 5651—Family
Clothing Stores.

★ 84127 ★   Hit or Miss
13350 Dallas Pky.
Dallas, TX 75240
(214)233-3639
Ultimate Parent: TJX. SIC: 5621—
Women's Clothing Stores; 5651—Family
Clothing Stores.

★ 84128 ★   Hit or Miss
6780 Abrams Rd.
Dallas, TX 75231
(214)343-6623
Ultimate Parent: TJX.

★ 84129 ★   Holly Corp.
100 Crescent Ct., Ste. 1600
Dallas, TX 75201-6927
(214)871-3555 Fax: (214)871-3566
Company Type: Headquarters. Officer:
Lamar Norsworthy, Chairman, President &
CEO. Ultimate Parent: Holly Corp.
Employee Count: 511. Sales: 600000000
M.

★ 84130 ★   Holly Corp.
100 Cresent Ct.
Dallas, TX 75201
(214)871-3555
Company Type: Headquarters. Officer:
Lamar Norsworthy. Employee Count: 505.
Sales: 629.9 M. Fortune 500: Largest U.S.
Industrial Corporations: Ranking 489.

★ 84131 ★   Horchow Mail Order
Inc.
13800 Diplomat Dr.
Dallas, TX 75234
(214)888-9700 Fax: (214)888-9797
Company Type: Subsidiary. Officer: Bernie
Feiwus, President & CEO. Ultimate Parent:
Harcourt General.

★ 84132 ★   Hudson's
2222 Ross Ave.
Dallas, TX 75201
(214)720-2216
Ultimate Parent: Dayton Hudson.

★ 84133 ★   Innovative Office
Systems, Inc.
14875 Landmark Blvd.
Dallas, TX 75240-6712
(214)788-0800
Location Type: Branch office. Officer:
Harry Farnham. Ultimate Parent: Alco
Standard Corp. SIC: 5044—
Office Equipment; 7359—Equipment Rental
& Leasing Nec; 7389—Business Services
Nec; 5943—Stationery Stores; 5999—
Miscellaneous Retail Stores Nec. Employee
Count: 350.

★ 84134 ★   Innovative Office
Systems Inc.
14875 Landmark Ste. 400
Dallas, TX 75240-6756
(214)788-0800
Location Type: Branch office. Officer:
Harry Farnham. Ultimate Parent: Alco
Standard Corp. SIC: 5044—Office
Equipment; 5943—Stationery Stores;
5999—Miscellaneous Retail Stores Nec;
7389—Business Services Nec.

★ 84135 ★   Intel Corp.
12300 Ford Rd.
Dallas, TX 75234
(214)241-8087
Ultimate Parent: Intel Corp. SIC: 3699—
Electrical Equipment & Supplies Nec.

★ 84136 ★   Jackson National Life
Insurance C
12801 N. Central Expy.
Dallas, TX 75243
(214)991-9193
Ultimate Parent: Jackson National Life.
SIC: 6411—Insurance Agents, Brokers &
Service.

★ 84137 ★   Jamieson Film Co.
10425 Olympic Dr.
Dallas, TX 75220
(214)350-1283
Officer: Gary Fuller, President. Ultimate
Parent: Eastman Kodak. SIC: 3861—
Photographic Equipment & Supplies.

★ 84138 ★   J.C. Penney Business
Services, Inc.
5001 Spring Valley Rd., Ste. 650W
Dallas, TX 75244
(214)960-5100 Fax: (214)960-5275
Officer: Bernie Curran, President. Ultimate
Parent: J.C. Penney.

★ 84139 ★   J.C. Penney Co., Inc.
PO Box 10001
Dallas, TX 75301-0001
(214)431-1000 Fax: (214)591-2808
Officer: William R. Howell, Chairman &
CEO. Ultimate Parent: J.C. Penney.
Employee Count: 198000.

★ 84140 ★   JCP Realty, Inc.
PO Box 2405
Dallas, TX 75221
(214)387-6191 Fax: (214)387-7091
Officer: Jack Garvey, General Manager.
Ultimate Parent: J.C. Penney.

★ 84141 ★   Jiffy Lube
2645 S. Buckner Blvd.
Dallas, TX 75227
(214)381-2169
Ultimate Parent: Pennzoil. SIC: 7539—
Automotive Repair Shops Nec.

★ 84142 ★   Jiffy Lube
3111 W. Northwest Hwy.
Dallas, TX 75220
(214)351-3740
Ultimate Parent: Pennzoil. SIC: 7539—
Automotive Repair Shops Nec.

★ 84143 ★   Jiffy Lube
9707 Plano Rd.
Dallas, TX 75238
(214)349-3510
Ultimate Parent: Pennzoil. SIC: 7539—
Automotive Repair Shops Nec.

★ 84144 ★   Jiffy Lube
5757 Samuell Blvd.
Dallas, TX 75228
(214)381-8273
Ultimate Parent: Pennzoil.

★ 84145 ★   Jiffy Lube
3223 Fort Worth Ave.
Dallas, TX 75211
(214)330-7917
Ultimate Parent: Pennzoil. SIC: 7532—Top
& Body Repair & Paint Shops; 7539—
Automotive Repair Shops Nec.

★ 84146 ★   Jiffy Lube
4004 Lemmon Ave.
Dallas, TX 75219
(214)520-2868
Ultimate Parent: Pennzoil. SIC: 7539—
Automotive Repair Shops Nec.

★ 84147 ★   Jiffy Lube
9080 Forest Ln.
Dallas, TX 75243
(214)340-4017
Ultimate Parent: Pennzoil.

★ 84148 ★   Jiffy Lube
9809 Forest Ln.
Dallas, TX 75243
(214)669-8615
Ultimate Parent: Pennzoil.

★ 84149 ★   Jiffy Lube
9721 Audelia Rd.
Dallas, TX 75238
(214)349-0743
Ultimate Parent: Pennzoil. SIC: 7542—Car
Washes.

★ 84150 ★   Jiffy Lube
5720 E. Mockingbird Ln.
Dallas, TX 75206
(214)828-1243
Ultimate Parent: Pennzoil. SIC: 7539—
Automotive Repair Shops Nec.

★ 84151 ★   Jiffy Lube
2001 Abrams Rd.
Dallas, TX 75214
(214)821-9302
Ultimate Parent: Pennzoil. SIC: 7539—
Automotive Repair Shops Nec.

★ 84152 ★   Jiffy Lube U S a
10404 Garland Rd.
Dallas, TX 75218
(214)327-6669
Ultimate Parent: Pennzoil. SIC: 7539—
Automotive Repair Shops Nec.

★ 84153 ★   Joslins Inc.
2300 Stemmons
Dallas, TX 75258
(214)637-3075
Ultimate Parent: Mercantile Stores. SIC:
5091—Sporting & Recreational Goods.

★ 84154 ★   Kay Bee Toy&Hobby
Shop
1062 Valley View Ctr.
Dallas, TX 75240
(214)788-0349
Ultimate Parent: Melville. SIC: 5945—
Hobby, Toy & Game Shops.

★ 84155 ★   Kentucky Fried
Chicken
106 W. Illinois Ave.
Dallas, TX 75224
(214)941-1673
Ultimate Parent: Pepsico. SIC: 5812—
Eating Places.

★ 84156 ★   Kentucky Fried
Chicken
3415 W. Camp Wisdom Rd.
Dallas, TX 75237
(214)296-0509
Ultimate Parent: Pepsico. SIC: 5812—
Eating Places.

★ 84157 ★   Kentucky Fried
Chicken
2415 W. Davis St.
Dallas, TX 75211
(214)942-5011
Ultimate Parent: Pepsico. SIC: 5812—
Eating Places.

★ 84158 ★   Kentucky Fried
Chicken
3806 S. Polk St.
Dallas, TX 75224
(214)375-5188
Ultimate Parent: Pepsico. SIC: 5812—
Eating Places.

★ 84159 ★   Kentucky Fried
Chicken
301 W. Camp Wisdom Rd.
Dallas, TX 75232
(214)264-3018
Ultimate Parent: Pepsico. SIC: 5812—
Eating Places.

★ 84160 ★   Kentucky Fried
Chicken
2939 S. Ervay St.
Dallas, TX 75215
(214)421-4479
Ultimate Parent: Pepsico. SIC: 5812—
Eating Places.

★ 84161 ★   Kentucky Fried
Chicken
3414 S. Lancaster Rd.
Dallas, TX 75216
(214)371-3381
Ultimate Parent: Pepsico. SIC: 5812—
Eating Places.

★ 84162 ★   Kentucky Fried
Chicken
1200 Main St.
Dallas, TX 75202
(214)745-1344
Ultimate Parent: Pepsico. SIC: 5812—
Eating Places.

★ 84163 ★   Kentucky Fried
Chicken
1801 S. Buckner Blvd.
Dallas, TX 75217
(214)391-5771
Ultimate Parent: Pepsico. SIC: 5812—
Eating Places.

★ 84164 ★   Kentucky Fried
Chicken
4416 Live Oak St.
Dallas, TX 75204
(214)823-4333
Ultimate Parent: Pepsico. SIC: 5812—
Eating Places.

★ 84165 ★   Kentucky Fried
Chicken
3400 Lombardy Ln.
Dallas, TX 75220
(214)350-4404
Ultimate Parent: Pepsico. SIC: 5812—
Eating Places.

★ 84166 ★   Kentucky Fried
Chicken
7742 Forest Ln.
Dallas, TX 75230
(214)368-0504
Ultimate Parent: Pepsico. SIC: 5812—
Eating Places.

★ 84167 ★   Kentucky Fried
Chicken
4303 Lemmon Ave.
Dallas, TX 75219
(214)522-1690
Ultimate Parent: Pepsico. SIC: 5812—
Eating Places.

★ 84168 ★   Kentucky Fried
Chicken
6520 E. Northwest Hwy.
Dallas, TX 75231
(214)369-5800
Ultimate Parent: Pepsico. SIC: 5812—
Eating Places.

★ 84169 ★   Kentucky Fried
Chicken
3633 Forest Ln.
Dallas, TX 75234
(214)241-4120
Ultimate Parent: Pepsico. SIC: 5812—
Eating Places.

★ 84170 ★   Kentucky Fried
Chicken
7975 Belt Line Rd.
Dallas, TX 75240
(214)239-0723
Ultimate Parent: Pepsico. SIC: 5812—
Eating Places.

★ 84171 ★   Kids R US
9500 Central Expy. N
Dallas, TX 75231
(214)373-1383
Ultimate Parent: Toys "R" US.

★ 84172 ★   Kids R US
9500 Central Exprsswy N
Dallas, TX 75231
(214)373-1383
Ultimate Parent: Toys "R" US.

★ 84173 ★   Kilpatrick's Bakeries,
Inc.
6211 Lemmon Ave.
Dallas, TX 75209
(214)358-9211
Company Type: Subsidiary. Officer:
Kenneth Moreland, President. Ultimate
Parent: Anheuser-Busch. SIC: 2051—
Bread, Cake & Related Products.

★ 84174 ★   Kmart
712 S. Walton Walker Blvd.
Dallas, TX 75211
(214)330-9103
Ultimate Parent: K-Mart.

★ 84175 ★   Kmart Discount
Stores
9334 E. R L Thornton Fwy.
Dallas, TX 75228
(214)328-4367
Ultimate Parent: K-Mart.

★ 84176 ★   Kmart Discount
Stores
10740 Garland Rd.
Dallas, TX 75218
(214)324-3876
Ultimate Parent: K-Mart.

★ 84177 ★   Kroger Food Store
3616 Forest Ln.
Dallas, TX 75234
(214)358-5366
Ultimate Parent: Kroger. SIC: 5411—
Grocery Stores.

★ 84178 ★   Kroger Food Store No
464
2524 W. Ledbetter Dr.
Dallas, TX 75233
(214)333-3542
Ultimate Parent: Kroger. SIC: 5411—
Grocery Stores.

★ 84179 ★   Kroger Food Stores
2019 N. Masters Dr.
Dallas, TX 75217
(214)288-9313
Ultimate Parent: Kroger.

★ 84180 ★   Kroger Food Stores
2550 Gus Thomasson Rd.
Dallas, TX 75228
(214)321-3537
Ultimate Parent: Kroger.

★ 84181 ★   Kroger Food Stores
1800 N. Henderson Ave.
Dallas, TX 75206
(214)826-0571
Ultimate Parent: Kroger.

★ 84182 ★   Kroger Food Stores
3616 Forest Ln.
Dallas, TX 75234
(214)358-5368
Ultimate Parent: Kroger.

★ 84183 ★   Kroger Food&Drug
Stores
3035 N. Buckner Blvd.
Dallas, TX 75228
(214)324-3683
Ultimate Parent: Kroger. SIC: 5912—Drug
Stores & Proprietary Stores.

★ 84184 ★   Kroger Food&Drug
Stores
752 Wynnewood Village
Dallas, TX 75224
(214)942-3191
Ultimate Parent: Kroger. SIC: 5912—Drug
Stores & Proprietary Stores.

★ 84185 ★   Kroger Food&Drug
Stores
2524 Ledbetter
Dallas, TX 75232
(214)330-0321
Ultimate Parent: Kroger. SIC: 5411—
Grocery Stores.

★ 84186 ★   Kroger Store No 632
7205 Skillman St.
Dallas, TX 75231
(214)349-2300
Ultimate Parent: Kroger. SIC: 5411—
Grocery Stores.

★ 84187 ★   Kroger Stores
1800 N. Henderson Ave.
Dallas, TX 75206
(214)826-8470
Ultimate Parent: Kroger. SIC: 5411—
Grocery Stores.

★ 84188 ★   Kroger Stores No 421
1610 S. Westmoreland Rd.
Dallas, TX 75211
(214)330-0366
Ultimate Parent: Kroger. SIC: 5411—
Grocery Stores.

★ 84189 ★   Kroger Supermarket
17194 Preston Rd.
Dallas, TX 75248
(214)931-5794
Ultimate Parent: Kroger. SIC: 5411—
Grocery Stores.

★ 84190 ★   Kroger Warehouse
5110 Woodall St.
Dallas, TX 75247
(214)634-0652
Ultimate Parent: Kroger.

★ 84191 ★   Lafarge Corp.
3333 Fort Worth Ave.
Dallas, TX 75211
(214)337-8961
Ultimate Parent: Lafarge.

★ 84192 ★   Lane Bryant
1020 Valley View Ctr.
Dallas, TX 75240
(214)386-8800
Ultimate Parent: Limited. SIC: 5621—
Women's Clothing Stores; 5651—Family
Clothing Stores.

★ 84193 ★   Lane Bryant
3662 W. Camp Wisdom Rd.
Dallas, TX 75237
(214)296-1848
Ultimate Parent: Limited. SIC: 5651—
Family Clothing Stores.

★ 84194 ★   Lane Bryant
5301 Belt Line Rd.
Dallas, TX 75240
(214)490-4170
Ultimate Parent: Limited.

★ 84195 ★   Lane Bryant
1516 Elm St.
Dallas, TX 75201
(214)744-4433
Ultimate Parent: Limited. SIC: 5621—
Women's Clothing Stores; 5651—Family
Clothing Stores.

★ 84196 ★   Lees Carpets
2050 N. Stemmons Fwy.
Dallas, TX 75207
(214)748-8979
Ultimate Parent: Burlington Industries,
Equity. SIC: 5023—Homefurnishings.

★ 84197 ★   Lens Crafters
3662 W. Camp Wisdom Rd.
Dallas, TX 75237
(214)780-8989
Ultimate Parent: United States Shoe. SIC:
5995—Optical Goods Stores.

★ 84198 ★   Lens Crafters
5301 Belt Line Rd.
Dallas, TX 75240
(214)991-9940
Ultimate Parent: United States Shoe.

★ 84199 ★   Lerner Shop
3662 W. Camp Wisdom Rd.
Dallas, TX 75237
(214)296-3666
Ultimate Parent: Limited. SIC: 5651—
Family Clothing Stores.

★ 84200 ★   Liberty Mutual Insur
Co.
2530 Walnut Hill Ln.
Dallas, TX 75229
(214)350-7611
Ultimate Parent: Liberty Mutual Group.
SIC: 6411—Insurance Agents, Brokers &
Service.

★ 84201 ★   The Limited
1056 Valley View Ctr.
Dallas, TX 75240
(214)661-1328
Ultimate Parent: Limited. SIC: 5621—
Women's Clothing Stores; 5651—Family
Clothing Stores.

★ 84202 ★   The Limited
3662 W. Camp Wisdom Rd.
Dallas, TX 75237
(214)296-1876
Ultimate Parent: Limited. SIC: 5651—
Family Clothing Stores.

★ 84203 ★   The Limited
1020 Northpark Ctr.
Dallas, TX 75225
(214)361-6276
Ultimate Parent: Limited. SIC: 5621—
Women's Clothing Stores; 5651—Family
Clothing Stores.

★ 84204 ★   The Limited
14651 Dallas Pky.
Dallas, TX 75240
(214)960-2818
Ultimate Parent: Limited. SIC: 5621—
Women's Clothing Stores.

★ 84205 ★   The Limited
1030 N. Park C
Dallas, TX 75204
(214)361-6278
Ultimate Parent: Limited.

★ 84206 ★   The Limited
5301 Belt Line Rd.
Dallas, TX 75240
(214)980-1001
Ultimate Parent: Limited.

★ 84207 ★   The Limited
13350 Dallas Pky.
Dallas, TX 75240
(214)233-9125
Ultimate Parent: Limited.

★ 84208 ★   The Limited Express
13350 Dallas Pky.
Dallas, TX 75240
(214)239-9024
Ultimate Parent: Limited. SIC: 5621—
Women's Clothing Stores; 5651—Family
Clothing Stores.

★ 84209 ★   The Limited Express
620 Northpark Ctr.
Dallas, TX 75225
(214)373-7523
Ultimate Parent: Limited. SIC: 5621—
Women's Clothing Stores.

★ 84210 ★   Lone Star Gas Co.
2601 Logan St.
Dallas, TX 75215
(214)426-7911
Ultimate Parent: Enserch. SIC: 4939—
Combination Utility Nec.

★ 84211 ★   Long Mile Rubber Co.
6820 Forest Park Rd.
Dallas, TX 75235
Ultimate Parent: Standard Products. SIC:
3011—Tires & Inner Tubes; 3069—
Fabricated Rubber Products Nec.

★ 84212 ★   Loral Vought Stytems
PO Box 650003
Dallas, TX 75265
(214)603-9247 Fax: (214)603-0444
Officer: Jay A. Musselman, President.
Ultimate Parent: Loral Corp.

★ 84213 ★   Ltv Aerospace &
Defense Co.
9314 West Jefferson
Dallas, TX 75265-5907
Ultimate Parent: LTV. SIC: 3721—Aircraft.

★ 84214 ★   Magic Chef
923 Slocum St.
Dallas, TX 75207
(214)742-6801
Ultimate Parent: Maytag. SIC: 5064—
Electrical Appliances—Television & Radio.

★ 84215 ★   Manor Baking Co.
6211 Lemmon Ave.
Dallas, TX 75209
(214)358-9211
Company Type: Subsidiary. Officer: Leon
Medlock, President & COO. Ultimate
Parent: Anheuser-Busch. SIC: 2051—
Bread, Cake & Related Products.

★ 84216 ★   Manpower, Inc.
5787 S. Hampton Rd.
Dallas, TX 75232
(214)339-2253
Ultimate Parent: Manpower, Inc. SIC:
7361—Employment Agencies.

★ 84217 ★   Mary Kay Cosmetics
878 Stemmons Freeway
Dallas, TX 75247
(214)630-8787
Officer: John P. Rochon, CEO.

★ 84218 ★   Mary Kay Cosmetics
14651 Dallas Pky.
Dallas, TX 75240
(214)239-4211
Ultimate Parent: Mary Kay Cosmetics. SIC:
5999—Miscellaneous Retail Stores Nec.

★ 84219 ★   Mary Kay Cosmetics
2213 Connector Dr.
Dallas, TX 75220
(214)956-9800
Ultimate Parent: Mary Kay Cosmetics.

★ 84220 ★   Mary Kay Cosmetics
4081 Altoona Dr.
Dallas, TX 75233
(214)339-4334
Ultimate Parent: Mary Kay Cosmetics. SIC:
5999—Miscellaneous Retail Stores Nec.

★ 84221 ★   Mary Kay Cosmetics,
Inc.
8787 N. Stemmons Fwy.
Dallas, TX 75247
(214)630-8787
Ultimate Parent: Mary Kay Cosmetics. SIC:
5122—Drugs, Proprietaries & Sundries;
5999—Miscellaneous Retail Stores Nec.

★ 84222 ★   Mary Kay Cosmetics
Inc.
1330 Regal Row
Dallas, TX 75247
(214)638-6750
Ultimate Parent: Mary Kay Cosmetics. SIC:
5122—Drugs, Proprietaries & Sundries;
5999—Miscellaneous Retail Stores Nec.

★ 84223 ★   Massachusetts Mutual
Life Insurance
5001 LBJ Fwy.
Dallas, TX 75244
(214)233-1886
Ultimate Parent: Massasucetts Mutual Life.
SIC: 6411—Insurance Agents, Brokers &
Service.

★ 84224 ★   Materials Technology
Co.
9224 King Arthur Dr.
Dallas, TX 75247
Ultimate Parent: Air Products & Chemicals,
Inc. SIC: 3624—Carbon & Graphite
Products.

★ 84225 ★   Materials Technology
Corp.
9224 King Arthur Dr.
Dallas, TX 75247
Ultimate Parent: Air Products & Chemicals,
Inc. SIC: 3624—Carbon & Graphite
Products.

★ 84226 ★   Maxus Corporate Co.
717 N. Harwood St.
Dallas, TX 75201
Officer: Mark Gentry, President. Ultimate
Parent: Maxus Energy.

★ 84227 ★   Maxus Energy
717 N. Harwood St.
Dallas, TX 75201
(214)953-2000
Company Type: Headquarters. Officer:
Charles L. Blackburn. Sales: 786.7 M.
Fortune 500: Largest U.S. Industrial
Corporations: Ranking 411.

★ 84228 ★   Maxus Energy Corp.
717 N. Harwood St.
Dallas, TX 75201
(214)953-2145
Ultimate Parent: Maxus Energy. SIC:
8721—Accounting, Auditing & Bookkeeping.

★ 84229 ★   Maxus Exploration
Co.
717 N. Harwood St.
Dallas, TX 75201
Officer: Steven G. Crowell, President.
Ultimate Parent: Maxus Energy.

★ 84230 ★   Maxus International
Energy Co.
717 N. Harwood St.
Dallas, TX 75201
Ultimate Parent: Maxus Energy.

★ 84231 ★   McCormick & Co. Inc.
Tac Cleaning Products Group
2643 Brenner
Dallas, TX 75220
Company Type: Division. Ultimate Parent:
McCormick & Co. Inc. SIC: 2899—Chemical
Preparations Nec.

★ 84232 ★   McDonalds
8055 S. Loop 12
Dallas, TX 75217
(214)391-4133
Ultimate Parent: McDonald's.

★ 84233 ★   McDonalds
8333 S. Lancaster Rd.
Dallas, TX 75241
(214)224-4600
Ultimate Parent: McDonald's.

★ 84234 ★   McDonalds
5960 Greenville Ave.
Dallas, TX 75206
(214)369-6256
Ultimate Parent: McDonald's.
SIC: 5812—Eating Places.

★ 84235 ★   McDonalds
17606 Midway Rd.
Dallas, TX 75287
(214)733-4494
Ultimate Parent: McDonald's.

★ 84236 ★   McDonalds
10226 Garland Rd.
Dallas, TX 75218
(214)320-1990
Ultimate Parent: McDonald's.

★ 84237 ★   Meridian Express Co.
2 Lincoln Ctr.
Dallas, TX 75201
(214)980-0884
Ultimate Parent: James River Corp. of
Virginia. SIC: 4213—Trucking Except Local.

★ 84238 ★   Mobil Alaska Pipeline
Co.
1201 Elm St.
Dallas, TX 75270-2016
(214)658-2111
Company Type: Branch. Officer: Jerry C.
Durbin. Ultimate Parent: Mobil. SIC:
4612—Crude Petroleum Pipelines; 1311—
Crude Petroleum & Natural Gas; 4613—
Refined Petroleum Pipelines; 4619—
Pipelines Nec; 6061—Federal Credit
Unions.

★ 84239 ★   Mobil Chemical
Company
2730 N. Stemmons Fwy.
Dallas, TX 75207
(214)637-2230
Ultimate Parent: Mobil. SIC: 5169—
Chemicals & Allied Products Nec.

★ 84240 ★   Mobil Cheml-Films
Div
14755 Preston Rd.
Dallas, TX 75240
(214)991-9904
Ultimate Parent: Mobil. SIC: 5199—
Nondurable Goods Nec.

★ 84241 ★   Mobil & Comm
2940 Valley View Ln.
Dallas, TX 75234-4929
(214)243-4616
Ultimate Parent: Mobil. SIC: 4812—
Radiotelephone Communications; 5065—
Electronic Parts & Equipment Nec.

★ 84242 ★   Mobil Exploration &
Producing, U.S.
PO Box 650232
Dallas, TX 75265-0232
(214)951-2809 Fax: (214)951-2205
Officer: R. W. White, President. Ultimate
Parent: Mobil.

★ 84243 ★   Mobil
Exploration&Prod Serv
13777 Midway Rd.
Dallas, TX 75244
(214)851-8111
Ultimate Parent: Mobil. SIC: 5172—
Petroleum Products Nec.

★ 84244 ★   Mobil Mart
12920 Preston Rd.
Dallas, TX 75230
(214)233-7546
Ultimate Parent: Mobil. SIC: 5541—
Gasoline Service Stations.

★ 84245 ★   Mobil Mart
PO Box 845
Dallas, TX 75221
Ultimate Parent: Mobil.

★ 84246 ★   Mobil Oil Corporation
4423 Live Oak St.
Dallas, TX 75204
(214)827-3550
Ultimate Parent: Mobil. SIC: 5541—
Gasoline Service Stations.

★ 84247 ★   Mobil Oil Corp.
9351 LBJ Fwy.
Dallas, TX 75243
(214)235-7439
Ultimate Parent: Mobil. SIC: 2911—
Petroleum Refining.

★ 84248 ★   Mobil Oil Corp.
1201 Elm St.
Dallas, TX 75270
(214)670-0613
Ultimate Parent: Mobil. SIC: 1311—Crude
Petroleum & Natural Gas; 2911—Petroleum
Refining.

★ 84249 ★   Mobil Oil Exploration
& Pro
3000 Pegasus Park Dr.
Dallas, TX 75247
(214)951-2245
Ultimate Parent: Mobil. SIC: 1382—Oil &
Gas Exploration Services.

★ 84250 ★   Mobil Oil L B J
Midway
4210 LBJ Fwy.
Dallas, TX 75244
(214)788-4770
Ultimate Parent: Mobil. SIC: 5541—
Gasoline Service Stations.

★ 84251 ★   Mobil Oil 12jna
15114 Preston Rd.
Dallas, TX 75248
(214)788-2862
Ultimate Parent: Mobil.

★ 84252 ★   Mobil Self Serv
5400 Preston Rd.
Dallas, TX 75205
(214)521-0127
Ultimate Parent: Mobil.

★ 84253 ★   Mobil Self-Service
6500 E. Northwest Hwy.
Dallas, TX 75231
(214)363-0331
Ultimate Parent: Mobil. SIC: 5541—
Gasoline Service Stations.

★ 84254 ★   Mobil Selv Serv
17561 Dallas Pky.
Dallas, TX 75287
(214)250-6366
Ultimate Parent: Mobil.

★ 84255 ★   Mobil Service Station
9790 Walnut St.
Dallas, TX 75243
(214)231-5160
Ultimate Parent: Mobil. SIC: 5541—
Gasoline Service Stations.

★ 84256 ★   Mobil Station
3800 Hatcher St.
Dallas, TX 75210
(214)428-9412
Ultimate Parent: Mobil. SIC: 5541—
Gasoline Service Stations.

★ 84257 ★   Mobil Station
8421 Preston Rd.
Dallas, TX 75225
(214)363-6928
Ultimate Parent: Mobil. SIC: 5541—
Gasoline Service Stations.

★ 84258 ★   Monarch Industries
Inc. (Br)
1212 Dolton St.
Dallas, TX 75207
(214)630-4021
Ultimate Parent: Avery Dennison Corp.
SIC: 3561—Pumps & Pumping Equipment;
5084—Industrial Machinery & Equipment.

★ 84259 ★   National Projects Inc.
8111 LBJ Fwy.
Dallas, TX 75251
(214)231-8990
Ultimate Parent: Morrison Knudsen. SIC:
1541—Industrial Buildings & Warehouses.

★ 84260 ★ NCR Corp.
17304 Preston Rd.
Dallas, TX 75252-5613
(214)733-3594
Ultimate Parent: AT&T. SIC: 3679—
Electronic Components Nec.

★ 84261 ★ New York Life Dalla
Service Center
2 Energy Square
4849 Greenville Ave., Ste. 440
Dallas, TX 75206
(214)369-5085
Officer: Tish Hill, Administrative Assistant.
Ultimate Parent: New York Life.

★ 84262 ★ New York Life Dallas
General Office
Western Agencies
12201 Merit Dr., Ste. 1000
Dallas, TX 75251
(214)387-2929 Fax: (214)702-9462
Officer: Ernestine S. Beauchamp, General
Manager. Ultimate Parent: New York Life.

★ 84263 ★ New York Life Dallas
Group Claims Office
Western Group Claims Region
7502 Greenville Rd., Ste. 600
Dallas, TX 75231
(800)955-9409 Fax: (214)696-8318
Officer: Robert Bycott, Group Claims
Director. Ultimate Parent: New York Life.

★ 84264 ★ New York Life Dallas
Group Claims Office
Western Groups Claims Office
PO Box 660239
Dallas, TX 75266
(800)955-9409 Fax: (214)696-8318
Officer: Robert Bycott, Group Claims
Director. Ultimate Parent: New York Life.

★ 84265 ★ New York Life Dallas
Group Sales Office
Western Group Marketing Zone Office
12221 Merit Dr., Ste. 640
Dallas, TX 75251
(214)770-4418 Fax: (214)770-4417
Officer: Dee Givens, Group Manager.
Ultimate Parent: New York Life.

★ 84266 ★ New York Life Dallas
Service Center
PO Box 539
Dallas, TX 75221
(214)369-5085
Officer: Tish Hill, Administrative Assistant.
Ultimate Parent: New York Life.

★ 84267 ★ New York Life South
Cenntral Pension Region
Central Pension Zone
Prestonwood Tower
5151 Belt Line Rd., Ste. 347
Dallas, TX 75240
(214)934-2540 Fax: (214)980-2582
Officer: Ben Gunnarson, Regional
Manager. Ultimate Parent: New York Life.

★ 84268 ★ New York Life Westen
Group Claims Region
PO Box 660239
Dallas, TX 75266-0239
(214)692-1255 Fax: (214)696-8318
Officer: Richard Bryant, Field Administrator.
Ultimate Parent: New York Life.

★ 84269 ★ New York Life
Western Agencies
Rolm Tower
15303 Dallas Pky., Ste. 1210 1B-24
Dallas, TX 75248
(214)701-3333
Officer: Michael Reeves, Senior Vice
President. Ultimate Parent: New York Life.

★ 84270 ★ New York Life
Western Group Claims Region
7502 Greenville Ave., Ste. 495
Dallas, TX 75231
(214)693-1255 Fax: (214)696-8318
Officer: Richard A. Bryant, Field
Administration. Ultimate Parent: New York
Life.

★ 84271 ★ Northern Trust Bank
of Texas, NA
5540 Preston Rd.
Dallas, TX 75222-4165
(214)979-1160
Location Type: Branch office. Ultimate
Parent: Northern Trust Corp. SIC: 6021—
National Commercial Banks.

★ 84272 ★ Northern Trust Bank
of Texas, NA
PO Box 222230
Dallas, TX 75222-2230
Location Type: Headquarters. Ultimate
Parent: Northern Trust Corp. SIC: 6021—
National Commercial Banks.

★ 84273 ★ Northern Trust Bank
of Texas, NA
2020 Ross Ave.
Dallas, TX 75201-2964
(214)979-1160 Fax: (214)953-1447
Location Type: Branch office. Ultimate
Parent: Northern Trust Corp. SIC: 6021—
National Commercial Banks.

★ 84274 ★ Northwest Airlines
Inc.
World Trade Ctr.
Dallas, TX 75258
(214)748-0233
Ultimate Parent: NWA. SIC: 4512—Air
Transportation—Scheduled.

★ 84275 ★ Norwest Mortgage
Inc.
5787 S. Hampton Rd.
Dallas, TX 75232
(214)339-8391
Ultimate Parent: Norwest Corp. SIC:
6162—Mortgage Bankers &
Correspondents.

★ 84276 ★ Oak Farms Dairy
1114 N. Lancaster
Dallas, TX 75203
Ultimate Parent: Southland Corp.

★ 84277 ★ Occidental Chemical
Corp.
PO Box 809050
Dallas, TX 75244
Officer: Ray R. Irani, Chairman of the
Board, President, CEO & COO. Ultimate
Parent: Occidental Petroleum Corp.

★ 84278 ★ Occidental Chemical
Corp.
1100 Lenway St.
Dallas, TX 75215
Ultimate Parent: Occidental Petroleum
Corp. SIC: 2819—Industrial Inorganic
Chemicals Nec.

★ 84279 ★ Occidental Chemical
Corp.
8800 S. Central Expy.
Dallas, TX 75239
Ultimate Parent: Occidental Petroleum
Corp. SIC: 2874—Phosphatic Fertilizers.

★ 84280 ★ Oliver Rubber Co.
6820 Forest Park Rd.
Dallas, TX 75235
Ultimate Parent: Standard Products. SIC:
3061—Mechanical Rubber Goods; 3069—
Fabricated Rubber Products Nec; 3011—
Tires & Inner Tubes.

★ 84281 ★ 1 P Forest Resources
Co.
6600 LBJ Fwy.
Dallas, TX 75240
(214)934-6000
Company Type: Subsidiary. Officer:
Edward J. Kobacker, President. Ultimate
Parent: International Paper Co.

★ 84282 ★ Oryx Energy
18325 Waterview Pky.
Dallas, TX 75252
(214)470-1276
Ultimate Parent: Oryx Energy.

★ 84283 ★ Oryx Energy
13155 Noel Rd.
Dallas, TX 75240
(214)715-4000
Company Type: Headquarters. Officer:
Robert P. Hauptfuhrer. Employee Count:
1500. Sales: 1080 M. Fortune 500: Largest
U.S. Industrial Corporations: Ranking 347.

★ 84284 ★ Oryx Energy Co.
13155 Noel Rd.
Dallas, TX 75240-5067
(214)715-4000 Fax: (214)715-3311 Telex:
150240
Officer: Robert P. Haupfuhrer, Chairman &
CEO. Ultimate Parent: Oryx Energy.
Employee Count: 1600.

★ 84285 ★ Otis Elevator Co.
14288 Gillis Rd.
Dallas, TX 75244
(214)385-3043
Ultimate Parent: United Technologies.

★ 84286 ★ Otis Elevator Co.
1931 Market Ctr. Blvd. 127
Dallas, TX 75207
Ultimate Parent: United Technologies. SIC:
1796—Installing Building Equipment Nec;
3534—Elevators & Moving Stairways.

★ 84287 ★ Otis Elevator Co.
12801 N. Central Expy. 1730
Dallas, TX 75243
Ultimate Parent: United Technologies. SIC:
1796—Installing Building Equipment Nec;
3534—Elevators & Moving Stairways.

★ 84288 ★ Owens Illinois Inc.
4034 Mint Way
Dallas, TX 75237
(214)339-5211
Officer: R. J. Ratzman, Manager. Ultimate
Parent: Owens-Illinois. SIC: 3085—Plastics
Bottles; 3089—Plastics Products Nec.

★ 84289 ★ PacTel Paging
12221 Merit Dr., Rm. 800
Dallas, TX 75251
(214)458-5202 Fax: (214)788-4763
Officer: Charlie E. Jackson, President &
CEO. Ultimate Parent: Pacific Telesis
Group.

★ 84290 ★ Pappagallo
2430 Promenade
Dallas, TX 75238
(214)235-5560
Ultimate Parent: United States Shoe. SIC:
5621—Women's Clothing Stores.

★ 84291 ★ Pappagallo
638 Northpark Ctr.
Dallas, TX 75225
(214)750-0110
Ultimate Parent: United States Shoe. SIC:
5651—Family Clothing Stores.

★ 84292 ★ Payless Cashways
Bldg Matrl
1639 S. Buckner Blvd.
Dallas, TX 75217
(214)398-8333
Ultimate Parent: Payless Cashways. SIC:
5211—Lumber & Other Building Materials.

★ 84293 ★ Payless Shoesource
4333 Gannon Ln.
Dallas, TX 75237
(214)780-0980
Ultimate Parent: May Department Stores.

★ 84294 ★ Payless Shoesource
2907 N. Hampton Rd.
Dallas, TX 75212
(214)631-6144
Ultimate Parent: May Department Stores.
SIC: 5661—Shoe Stores.

★ 84295 ★ Penn Mutual Life
Insurance
8700 King George Dr.
Dallas, TX 75235
(214)638-5950
Ultimate Parent: Penn Mutual Life. SIC:
6371—Pension, Health & Welfare Funds.

★ 84296 ★ Penn Mutual Life
Insurance Co.
12900 Preston Rd.
Dallas, TX 75230
(214)661-0101
Ultimate Parent: Penn Mutual Life. SIC:
6411—Insurance Agents, Brokers &
Service.

★ 84297 ★ Penn Mutual Life
Insurance Co.
5550 LBJ Fwy.
Dallas, TX 75240
(214)387-4612
Ultimate Parent: Penn Mutual Life. SIC:
6411—Insurance Agents, Brokers &
Service.

★ 84298 ★ Pepsi-Cola South
12377 Merit Dr.
Dallas, TX 75251
(214)404-7000
Ultimate Parent: Pepsico. SIC: 2086—
Bottled & Canned Soft Drinks.

★ 84299 ★ PepsiCo Food
Systems Worldwide
2 Galleria Tower, 13455 Noel Rd., Ste.
2100
Dallas, TX 75204
(914)253-3866 Fax: (914)338-7280
Officer: Robert C. Hunter, President.
Ultimate Parent: Pepsico.

★ 84300 ★ Personal Finance Co.
Inc.
3229 Dawes Dr.
Dallas, TX 75211
(214)330-7153
Ultimate Parent: Minnesota Mutual Life.
SIC: 6159—Miscellaneous Business Credit
Institutions.

★ 84301 ★ Personal Sportswear
2300 Stemmons
Dallas, TX 75207
(214)634-2902
Ultimate Parent: Leslie Fay. SIC: 5136—
Men's/Boys' Clothing; 5137—
Women's/Children's Clothing.

★ 84302 ★ Petite Sophisticate
13350 Dallas Pky.
Dallas, TX 75240
(214)239-6063
Ultimate Parent: United States Shoe. SIC:
5621—Women's Clothing Stores; 5651—
Family Clothing Stores.

★ 84303 ★ Petite Sophisticate
3662 W. Camp Wisdom Rd.
Dallas, TX 75237
(214)709-8767
Ultimate Parent: United States Shoe. SIC:
5651—Family Clothing Stores.

★ 84304 ★ PG&E Resources Co.
5950 Berkshire Ln., Ste. 600
Dallas, TX 75225
(214)750-3800 Fax: (214)750-3883
Officer: Joseph T. Williams, President &
CEO. Ultimate Parent: Pacific Gas &
Electric.

★ 84305 ★ Phoenix Packaging
2708 Satsuma Dr.
Dallas, TX 75229
(214)620-2630
Ultimate Parent: Savannah Foods &
Industries, Inc.

★ 84306 ★ Pilgrim's Pride Corp.
2411 Ferris
Dallas, TX 75226
Ultimate Parent: Pilgrim's Pride Corp. SIC:
2000—Food & Kindred Products.

★ 84307 ★ Pilgrim's Pride Corp.
Dallas Processing
2411 Ferris
Dallas, TX 75226
Company Type: Division. Ultimate Parent:
Pilgrim's Pride Corp. SIC: 2015—Poultry
Slaughtering & Processing.

★ 84308 ★ Pitney Bowes
Management Services
501 N. Stemmons Fwy.
Dallas, TX 75207
(214)747-5445
Officer: Mark Davey, Manager. Ultimate
Parent: Pitney Bowes. SIC: 2759—
Commercial Printing Nec.

★ 84309 ★ Pizza Hut
8186 Spring Valley Rd.
Dallas, TX 75240
(214)231-9051
Ultimate Parent: Pepsico. SIC: 5812—
Eating Places.

★ 84310 ★ Pizza Hut
407 W. Illinois Ave.
Dallas, TX 75224
(214)941-6550
Ultimate Parent: Pepsico. SIC: 5812—
Eating Places.

★ 84311 ★ Pizza Hut
5859 Samuell Blvd.
Dallas, TX 75228
(214)388-4441
Ultimate Parent: Pepsico.

★ 84312 ★ Pizza Hut
80 Spring Creek Village
Dallas, TX 75248
(214)404-1116
Ultimate Parent: Pepsico.

★ 84313 ★   **Pizza Hut**
4208 Live Oak St.
Dallas, TX 75204
(214)827-9310
Ultimate Parent: Pepsico. **SIC:** 5812—
Eating Places.

★ 84314 ★   **Pizza Hut**
14152 Marsh Ln.
Dallas, TX 75234
(214)243-3443
Ultimate Parent: Pepsico.

★ 84315 ★   **Pizza Hut**
3233 Fort Worth Ave.
Dallas, TX 75211
(214)339-2158
Ultimate Parent: Pepsico. **SIC:** 5812—
Eating Places.

★ 84316 ★   **Pizza Hut**
6409 Hillcrest Ave.
Dallas, TX 75205
(214)520-1515
Ultimate Parent: Pepsico.

★ 84317 ★   **Pizza Hut**
3612 Forest Ln.
Dallas, TX 75234
(214)357-6363
Ultimate Parent: Pepsico.

★ 84318 ★   **Pizza Hut**
9363 Forest Ln.
Dallas, TX 75243
(214)235-0843
Ultimate Parent: Pepsico. **SIC:** 5812—
Eating Places.

★ 84319 ★   **Pizza Hut**
9721 Audelia Rd.
Dallas, TX 75238
(214)348-7662
Ultimate Parent: Pepsico. **SIC:** 5812—
Eating Places.

★ 84320 ★   **Pizza Hut**
6632 E. Northwest Hwy.
Dallas, TX 75231
(214)369-6885
Ultimate Parent: Pepsico. **SIC:** 5812—
Eating Places.

★ 84321 ★   **Portion Pac, Inc.**
11461 Hillguard
Dallas, TX 75243
(214)349-6125
Company Type: Subsidiary. **Location
Type:** Plant. **Ultimate Parent:** H.J. Heinz.
SIC: 2035—Pickles, Sauces & Salad
Dressings.

★ 84322 ★   **Potlatch Corp. Dairy**
7616 LBJ Fwy.
Dallas, TX 75251
(214)239-5329
Ultimate Parent: Potlatch. **SIC:** 5143—
Dairy Products Except Dried or Canned.

★ 84323 ★   **Premier Beverage Co.**
8144 Walnut Hill Ln.
Dallas, TX 75231
(214)360-7000
Officer: Michael S. McGrath, Vice
President. **Ultimate Parent:** Dr. Pepper/
Seven-Up. **SIC:** 2086—Bottled & Canned
Soft Drinks; 2087—Flavoring Extracts &
Syrups Nec; 2099—Food Preparations Nec.

★ 84324 ★   **Prints Plus**
13350 Dallas Pky.
Dallas, TX 75240
(214)661-0893
Ultimate Parent: Melville. **SIC:** 8412—
Museums & Art Galleries.

★ 84325 ★   **Procter & Gamble
Mfg. Co.**
1301 Mcdonald St.
Dallas, TX 75215
Ultimate Parent: Procter & Gamble Co.
SIC: 2841—Soap & Other Detergents.

★ 84326 ★   **Quaker Oats Co.**
2822 Glenfield St.
Dallas, TX 75233
Ultimate Parent: Quaker Oats. **SIC:**
2032—Canned Specialties.

★ 84327 ★   **Quaker State
Minituelube**
3407 W. Camp Wisdom Rd.
Dallas, TX 75237
(214)298-9972
Ultimate Parent: Quaker State. **SIC:**
7539—Automotive Repair Shops Nec.

★ 84328 ★   **Radio Shack**
729 Wynnewood Village
Dallas, TX 75224
(214)948-3201
Company Type: Division. **Ultimate Parent:**
Tandy Corp. **SIC:** 5065—Electronic Parts &
Equipment Nec; 5731—Radio, Television &
Electronics Stores.

★ 84329 ★   **Radio Shack**
320 S. Central Expy.
Dallas, TX 75201
(214)238-5065
Company Type: Division. **Ultimate Parent:**
Tandy Corp. **SIC:** 5046—Commercial
Equipment Nec.

★ 84330 ★   **Radio Shack**
5525 W. Lovers Ln.
Dallas, TX 75209
(214)358-3892
Company Type: Division. **Ultimate Parent:**
Tandy Corp. **SIC:** 5065—Electronic Parts &
Equipment Nec.

★ 84331 ★   **Radio Shack**
302 Preston Valley Shopping Cent
Dallas, TX 75240
(214)233-4802
Company Type: Division. **Ultimate Parent:**
Tandy Corp. **SIC:** 5065—Electronic Parts &
Equipment Nec.

★ 84332 ★   **Radio Shack**
Prestonwood Town Ctr.
Dallas, TX 75240
(214)239-0991
Company Type: Division. **Ultimate Parent:**
Tandy Corp. **SIC:** 5065—Electronic Parts &
Equipment Nec.

★ 84333 ★   **Radio Shack**
13933 N. Central Expy.
Dallas, TX 75243
(214)238-7913
Company Type: Division. **Ultimate Parent:**
Tandy Corp. **SIC:** 5065—Electronic Parts &
Equipment Nec.

★ 84334 ★   **Radio Shack**
10800 Preston Rd.
Dallas, TX 75230
(214)369-8616
Company Type: Division. **Ultimate Parent:**
Tandy Corp. **SIC:** 5065—Electronic Parts &
Equipment Nec; 5731—Radio, Television &
Electronics Stores.

★ 84335 ★   **Radio Shack**
3045 N. Buckner Blvd.
Dallas, TX 75228
(214)328-0676
Company Type: Division. **Ultimate Parent:**
Tandy Corp. **SIC:** 5065—Electronic Parts &
Equipment Nec; 5731—Radio, Television &
Electronics Stores.

★ 84336 ★   **Radio Shack**
12001 N. Central Expy.
Dallas, TX 75243
(214)392-0521
Company Type: Division. **Ultimate Parent:**
Tandy Corp. **SIC:** 5065—Electronic Parts &
Equipment Nec.

★ 84337 ★   **Radio Shack**
138 Marsh Ln.
Dallas, TX 75229
(214)357-7419
Company Type: Division. **Ultimate Parent:**
Tandy Corp.

★ 84338 ★   **Radio Shack**
1152 N. Buckner Blvd.
Dallas, TX 75218
(214)328-2522
Company Type: Division. **Ultimate Parent:**
Tandy Corp. **SIC:** 5065—Electronic Parts &
Equipment Nec.

★ 84339 ★   **Radio Shack**
4402 Lemmon Ave.
Dallas, TX 75219
(214)526-1741
Company Type: Division. **Ultimate Parent:**
Tandy Corp. **SIC:** 5065—Electronic Parts &

Equipment Nec; 5731—Radio, Television &
Electronics Stores.

★ 84340 ★   **Radio Shack**
3629 M D Love Fwy.
Dallas, TX 75224
(214)376-2355
Company Type: Division. **Ultimate Parent:**
Tandy Corp. **SIC:** 5065—Electronic Parts &
Equipment Nec.

★ 84341 ★   **Radio Shack**
6402 Gaston Ave.
Dallas, TX 75214
(214)824-1093
Company Type: Division. **Ultimate Parent:**
Tandy Corp. **SIC:** 5065—Electronic Parts &
Equipment Nec.

★ 84342 ★   **Radio Shack**
13000 Josey Ln.
Dallas, TX 75234
(214)241-5863
Company Type: Division. **Ultimate Parent:**
Tandy Corp. **SIC:** 5065—Electronic Parts &
Equipment Nec.

★ 84343 ★   **Radio Shack**
3552 Forest Ln.
Dallas, TX 75234
(214)350-4822
Company Type: Division. **Ultimate Parent:**
Tandy Corp. **SIC:** 5065—Electronic Parts &
Equipment Nec.

★ 84344 ★   **Radio Shack**
10520 Garland Rd.
Dallas, TX 75218
(214)328-4785
Company Type: Division. **Ultimate Parent:**
Tandy Corp.

★ 84345 ★   **Radio Shack**
13350 Dallas Pky.
Dallas, TX 75240
(214)934-2918
Company Type: Division. **Ultimate Parent:**
Tandy Corp. **SIC:** 5065—Electronic Parts &
Equipment Nec; 5731—Radio, Television &
Electronics Stores.

★ 84346 ★   **Radio Shack**
5618 E. Mockingbird Ln.
Dallas, TX 75206
(214)826-0180
Company Type: Division. **Ultimate Parent:**
Tandy Corp. **SIC:** 5065—Electronic Parts &
Equipment Nec.

★ 84347 ★   **Radio Shack**
1530 S. Buckner Blvd.
Dallas, TX 75217
(214)391-5578
Company Type: Division. **Ultimate Parent:**
Tandy Corp. **SIC:** 5065—Electronic Parts &
Equipment Nec.

★ 84348 ★   **Radio Shack**
138 Marsh Ln.
Dallas, TX 75229
(214)357-9821
Company Type: Division. **Ultimate Parent:**
Tandy Corp. **SIC:** 5731—Radio, Television
& Electronics Stores.

★ 84349 ★   **Rainbo Baking Co.**
6211 Lemmon Ave.
Dallas, TX 75209
(214)358-9211
Company Type: Subsidiary. **Officer:** Leon
Medlock, President & COO. **Ultimate
Parent:** Anheuser-Busch. **SIC:** 2051—
Bread, Cake & Related Products.

★ 84350 ★   **Ralph Wilson Plastics
Co.**
4051 La Reunion Pky. 140
Dallas, TX 75212
(214)634-2310
Officer: Tim Atkinson, Manager. **Ultimate
Parent:** Premark International. **SIC:** 2541—
Wood Partitions & Fixtures.

★ 84351 ★   **Recovery Servies
International**
1341 W. Mockingbird Ln.
Dallas, TX 75247
(214)631-4961
Ultimate Parent: Cigna Corp. **SIC:** 6411—
Insurance Agents, Brokers & Service.

★ 84352 ★   **Red Arrow Freight
Lines, Inc.**
4444 Irving Blvd.
Dallas, TX 75356-9570
(214)631-5490 **Fax:** (214)637-3208
Officer: Brett Coleman, President. **Ultimate
Parent:** Carolina Freight.

★ 84353 ★   **Red Star Yeast**
2306 Motor St.
Dallas, TX 75235
Ultimate Parent: Universal Foods Corp.
SIC: 2099—Food Preparations Nec.

★ 84354 ★   **Red Star Yeast**
2306 Amelia St.
Dallas, TX 75235
Ultimate Parent: Universal Foods Corp.
SIC: 2099—Food Preparations Nec.

★ 84355 ★   **Reliance Insurance
Co.**
Mayflower
Dallas, TX 75208
(214)263-3061
Ultimate Parent: Reliance Group Holdings.
SIC: 6411—Insurance Agents, Brokers &
Service.

★ 84356 ★   **Reneer Films Corp.**
13601 Preston Rd.
Dallas, TX 75240
(214)233-4612
Ultimate Parent: Gencorp. **SIC:** 2821—
Plastics Materials & Resins.

★ 84357 ★   **Rollins Burdick
Hunter Agcy**
14901 Quorum Dr.
Dallas, TX 75240
(214)960-2552
Ultimate Parent: Aon Corp. **SIC:** 6411—
Insurance Agents, Brokers & Service.

★ 84358 ★   **Ryder Truck Rental**
15301 Dallas Pky.
Dallas, TX 75248
(214)788-4215
Ultimate Parent: Ryder System. **SIC:**
7514—Passenger Car Rental.

★ 84359 ★   **Ryder Truck Rental**
6464 E. Northwest Hwy.
Dallas, TX 75231
(214)369-3794
Ultimate Parent: Ryder System. **SIC:**
7359—Equipment Rental & Leasing Nec.

★ 84360 ★   **Ryder Truck Rental**
6516 N. Central Expy.
Dallas, TX 75206
(214)369-4242
Ultimate Parent: Ryder System. **SIC:**
7513—Truck Rental & Leasing Without
Drivers.

★ 84361 ★   **Ryder Truck Rental**
8528 C F Hawn Fwy.
Dallas, TX 75217
(214)398-9084
Ultimate Parent: Ryder System. **SIC:**
7513—Truck Rental & Leasing Without
Drivers.

★ 84362 ★   **Ryder Truck Rental**
3500 Belt Line Rd.
Dallas, TX 75234
(214)243-5161
Ultimate Parent: Ryder System. **SIC:**
7359—Equipment Rental & Leasing Nec.

★ 84363 ★   **Ryder Truck Rental**
11359 Reeder Rd.
Dallas, TX 75229
(214)241-8570
Ultimate Parent: Ryder System. **SIC:**
7513—Truck Rental & Leasing Without
Drivers.

★ 84364 ★   **Ryder Truck Rental**
3717 S. Buckner Blvd.
Dallas, TX 75227
(214)388-3704
Ultimate Parent: Ryder System. **SIC:**
7359—Equipment Rental & Leasing Nec.

★ 84365 ★   **Ryder Truck Rental**
3915 Samuell Blvd.
Dallas, TX 75228
(214)381-9505
Ultimate Parent: Ryder System. **SIC:**
7389—Business Services Nec.

★ 84366 ★　Ryder Truck Rental
561089 PO Box
Dallas, TX 75356
(214)330-4661
Ultimate Parent: Ryder System. SIC:
7513—Truck Rental & Leasing Without
Drivers.

★ 84367 ★　Ryder Truck Rental
173304 Preston Rd.
Dallas, TX 75240
(214)380-0228
Ultimate Parent: Ryder System. SIC:
7513—Truck Rental & Leasing Without
Drivers.

★ 84368 ★　Ryder Truck Rental
11310 Harry Hines Blvd.
Dallas, TX 75229
(214)243-0508
Ultimate Parent: Ryder System.

★ 84369 ★　Ryder Truck Rental
3023 Herbert St.
Dallas, TX 75212
(214)748-5587
Ultimate Parent: Ryder System. SIC:
7513—Truck Rental & Leasing Without
Drivers.

★ 84370 ★　Ryder Truck Rental
9745 Harry Hines Blvd.
Dallas, TX 75220
(214)357-4960
Ultimate Parent: Ryder System.

★ 84371 ★　Ryder Truck Rental
3200 Halifax St.
Dallas, TX 75247
(214)634-1049
Ultimate Parent: Ryder System. SIC:
7359—Equipment Rental & Leasing Nec;
7514—Passenger Car Rental.

★ 84372 ★　Safeco Insurance Co.
of America
2701 N. Central Expy.
Dallas, TX 75204
(214)263-3581
Ultimate Parent: Safeco. SIC: 6411—
Insurance Agents, Brokers & Service.

★ 84373 ★　Safeco Insurance Co.
of America
Frito Lay Bldg.
Dallas, TX 75235
(214)357-6247
Ultimate Parent: Safeco. SIC: 6411—
Insurance Agents, Brokers & Service.

★ 84374 ★　Sam's Wholesale
Club
1959 W. Northwest Hwy.
Dallas, TX 75220
(214)556-0831
Ultimate Parent: Wal-Mart Stores, Inc. SIC:
5099—Durable Goods Nec.

★ 84375 ★　Sara Lee Corp.
4639 Irving Blvd., Ste. 304
Dallas, TX 75247
(214)630-1500
Company Type: Division. Officer: Michael
Kenter, President. Ultimate Parent: Sara
Lee Corp.

★ 84376 ★　Savings of America,
FSB
9625 Audelia Rd.
Dallas, TX 75238
(214)341-3550
Company Type: Division. Location Type:
Branch office. Ultimate Parent: H. F.
Ahmanson. SIC: 6021—National
Commercial Banks.

★ 84377 ★　Savings of America,
FSB
3550 Forest Ln.
Dallas, TX 75234-7920
(214)357-0227
Company Type: Division. Location Type:
Branch office. Ultimate Parent: H. F.
Ahmanson. SIC: 6021—National
Commercial Banks.

★ 84378 ★　Savings of America,
FSB
6060 E. Mockingbird Ln.
Dallas, TX 75206-5428
(214)826-7000
Company Type: Division. Location Type:
Branch office. Ultimate Parent: H. F.
Ahmanson. SIC: 6021—National
Commercial Banks.

★ 84379 ★　Savings of America,
FSB
10721 Preston Rd.
Dallas, TX 75230-3849
(214)750-0033
Company Type: Division. Location Type:
Branch office. Ultimate Parent: H. F.
Ahmanson. SIC: 6021—National
Commercial Banks.

★ 84380 ★　Sekin Transport
International
PO Box 655464
Dallas, TX 75265
(214)456-0730 Fax: (214)456-8550
Company Type: Subsidiary. Officer: Kim
Wertheimer, Vice President of Planning &
Development & Regional Manager. Ultimate
Parent: Harper Group, Inc.

★ 84381 ★　Shell Co.
8720 Spring Valley Rd.
Dallas, TX 75240
(214)231-3394
Ultimate Parent: Shell Oil Co. SIC: 7542—
Car Washes.

★ 84382 ★　Shell Co.
17602 Midway Rd.
Dallas, TX 75287
(214)248-7645
Ultimate Parent: Shell Oil Co.

★ 84383 ★　Shell Co.
17088 Preston Rd.
Dallas, TX 75248
(214)931-7238
Ultimate Parent: Shell Oil Co. SIC: 5541—
Gasoline Service Stations.

★ 84384 ★　Shell Service Station
4232 Lemmon Ave.
Dallas, TX 75219
(214)521-7952
Ultimate Parent: Shell Oil Co. SIC: 5541—
Gasoline Service Stations.

★ 84385 ★　Shell Service Station
1301 Empire Central
Dallas, TX 75247
Ultimate Parent: Shell Oil Co. SIC: 5541—
Gasoline Service Stations.

★ 84386 ★　Silicon Graphics Inc.
12750 Merit Dr.
Dallas, TX 75251
(214)788-4122
Ultimate Parent: Silicon Graphics. SIC:
7336—Commercial Art & Graphic Design.

★ 84387 ★　Smith Barney Harris
Upham & Co.
13355 Noel Rd.
Dallas, TX 75240-6601
(214)960-1980
Officer: Barney Smith. Ultimate Parent:
Automatic Data Processing, Inc. SIC:
6211—Security Brokers & Dealers.

★ 84388 ★　Southland
5855 Maple Ave.
Dallas, TX 75235
(214)350-7881
Ultimate Parent: Southland Corp.

★ 84389 ★　Southland Corp.
4901 Cole Ave.
Dallas, TX 75205
(214)841-6642
Ultimate Parent: Southland Corp. SIC:
5411—Grocery Stores.

★ 84390 ★　Southland Corp.
12200 Park Central Dr.
Dallas, TX 75251
(214)980-8055
Ultimate Parent: Southland Corp. SIC:
5411—Grocery Stores.

★ 84391 ★　Southland Corp.
2818 Merrell Rd.
Dallas, TX 75229
(214)358-2441
Ultimate Parent: Southland Corp. SIC:
5141—Groceries—General Line.

★ 84392 ★　Southland Corp.
2711 N. Haskell Ave.
Dallas, TX 75204
(214)828-7011
Company Type: Headquarters. Officer:
Clark J. Matthews II. Employee Count:
32406. Sales: 6744 M. Fortune Service
500: Ranking 25.

★ 84393 ★　The Southland Corp.
2711 N. Haskell Ave.
Dallas, TX 75204-2906
(214)828-7011 Fax: (214)822-7848
Officer: Clark J. Matthew II, CEO. Ultimate
Parent: Southland Corp. Employee Count:
42616. Sales: 6814 M.

★ 84394 ★　Southwest Airlines
PO Box 36611
Dallas, TX 75235-1611
(214)904-4000 Fax: (214)904-4200
Officer: Herbert D. Kelleher, CEO. Ultimate
Parent: Southwest Airlines. Employee
Count: 1139. Sales: 2297 M.

★ 84395 ★　Southwest Airlines
2702 Love Field Dr.
Dallas, TX 75235
(214)904-4000
Company Type: Headquarters. Officer:
Herbert D. Kelleher. Employee Count:
15175. Fortune Service 500: Ranking 22.

★ 84396 ★　Sparkletts Drinking
Water Corp.
1801 S. Good-Latimer Expressway
Dallas, TX 75226
Ultimate Parent: McKesson. SIC: 2086—
Bottled & Canned Soft Drinks.

★ 84397 ★　Springs Industries
Inc.
13455 Noel Rd.
Dallas, TX 75240
(214)701-9291
Ultimate Parent: Springs Industries.

★ 84398 ★　Standard Fire
Insurance Co.
1700 S. 29th Ct
Dallas, TX 75252
(214)942-6000
Ultimate Parent: Aetna Life & Casualty.
SIC: 8712—Architectural Services.

★ 84399 ★　Star Marketing Co.
7110 Holly Hill Dr.
Dallas, TX 75231
(214)696-1223
Ultimate Parent: American Stores. SIC:
5099—Durable Goods Nec.

★ 84400 ★　State Fair Foods Inc.
4560 Leston
PO Box 561223
Dallas, TX 75356
Company Type: Division. Location Type:
Plant. Officer: Helen Gomez, Plant
Superintendent. Ultimate Parent: Sara Lee
Corp.

★ 84401 ★　State Fair Foods Inc.
4639 Irvine Blvd.
Ste. 304, PO Box 561223
Dallas, TX 75356
(214)630-1500
Company Type: Division. Officer: Michael
L. Kenter, President. Ultimate Parent: Sara
Lee Corp.

★ 84402 ★　Stewart & Stevenson
SVC
3919 Irving Blvd.
Dallas, TX 75247
(214)631-5370
Officer: Bob O'Neal, President. Ultimate
Parent: Stewart & Stevenson. SIC: 3511—
Turbines & Turbine Generator Sets.

★ 84403 ★　Sullivan Graphics
14320 Midway Rd.
Dallas, TX 75244
(214)233-4046
Ultimate Parent: Morgan Stanley Group.

★ 84404 ★　Sun Microsystems
Inc.
14785 Reston Rd.
Dallas, TX 75240
(214)788-1951
Ultimate Parent: Sun Microsystems Inc.
SIC: 5046—Commercial Equipment Nec.

★ 84405 ★　T J Maxx
500 Park Forest Ctr.
Dallas, TX 75234
(214)241-4288
Ultimate Parent: TJX.

★ 84406 ★　T J Maxx Regional
Office
3003 LBJ Fwy.
Dallas, TX 75234
(214)484-2101
Ultimate Parent: TJX. SIC: 5651—Family
Clothing Stores.

★ 84407 ★　T X T Mortgage Co.
3710 Rawlins St.
PO Box 199000
Dallas, TX 75219
(214)559-9886
Officer: Ross T. Anderson, President.
Ultimate Parent: Centex.

★ 84408 ★　Taco Bell
2332 W. Ledbetter Dr.
Dallas, TX 75224
(214)339-9640
Ultimate Parent: Pepsico. SIC: 5812—
Eating Places.

★ 84409 ★　Taco Bell
2575 Walnut Hill Ln.
Dallas, TX 75229
(214)351-3481
Ultimate Parent: Pepsico. SIC: 5812—
Eating Places.

★ 84410 ★　Taco Bell
1939 S. Buckner Blvd.
Dallas, TX 75217
(214)398-5568
Ultimate Parent: Pepsico. SIC: 5812—
Eating Places.

★ 84411 ★　Taco Bell
3423 W. Camp Wisdom Rd.
Dallas, TX 75237
(214)296-7612
Ultimate Parent: Pepsico. SIC: 5812—
Eating Places.

★ 84412 ★　Taco Bell
9820 Kingsley Rd.
Dallas, TX 75238
(214)349-1139
Ultimate Parent: Pepsico. SIC: 5812—
Eating Places.

★ 84413 ★　Taco Bell
5575 N. Jim Miller Rd.
Dallas, TX 75228
(214)381-9776
Ultimate Parent: Pepsico.

★ 84414 ★　Taco Bell
3127 Inwood Rd.
Dallas, TX 75235
(214)350-2897
Ultimate Parent: Pepsico. SIC: 5812—
Eating Places.

★ 84415 ★　Taco Bell
14520 Josey Ln.
Dallas, TX 75234
(214)241-9829
Ultimate Parent: Pepsico. SIC: 5812—
Eating Places.

★ 84416 ★　Taco Bell
3223 Fort Worth Ave.
Dallas, TX 75211
(214)339-3074
Ultimate Parent: Pepsico. SIC: 5812—
Eating Places.

★ 84417 ★　Taco Bell
10325 Garland Rd.
Dallas, TX 75218
(214)328-1155
Ultimate Parent: Pepsico. SIC: 5812—
Eating Places.

★ 84418 ★　Taco Bell
3617 Forest Ln.
Dallas, TX 75234
(214)241-6518
Ultimate Parent: Pepsico. SIC: 5812—
Eating Places.

★ 84419 ★　Taco Bell
9441 Forest Ln.
Dallas, TX 75243
(214)690-9413
Ultimate Parent: Pepsico.

★ 84420 ★　Taco Bell
5502 E. Mockingbird Ln.
Dallas, TX 75206
(214)821-5751
Ultimate Parent: Pepsico. SIC: 5812—
Eating Places.

★ 84421 ★   **Tandy**
1530 S. Buckner Blvd.
Dallas, TX 75217
(214)391-5578
Ultimate Parent: Tandy Corp.

★ 84422 ★   **Target Stores**
4343 Gannon Ln.
Dallas, TX 75237
(214)709-0031
Ultimate Parent: Dayton Hudson. **SIC:**
5311—Department Stores.

★ 84423 ★   **Taylor Publishing Co.**
1550 W. Mockingbird Ln.
Dallas, TX 75235
(214)637-2800 **Fax:** (214)819-8131
Company Type: Subsidiary. **Officer:** Frank
Preiski, President. **Ultimate Parent:** Insilco
Corp.

★ 84424 ★   **Terex Corp.**
12118 Ridgefair Pl.
Dallas, TX 75234
(214)631-5967
Ultimate Parent: Terex Corp. **SIC:** 5082—
Construction & Mining Machinery; 5084—
Industrial Machinery & Equipment.

★ 84425 ★   **Texaco Food Mart**
6869 Frankford Rd.
Dallas, TX 75252
(214)596-2799
Ultimate Parent: Texaco.

★ 84426 ★   **Texaco Food Mart**
13010 Preston Rd.
Dallas, TX 75240
(214)233-9920
Ultimate Parent: Texaco.

★ 84427 ★   **Texaco Food Mart**
5602 E. Lovers Ln.
Dallas, TX 75206
(214)696-6113
Ultimate Parent: Texaco.

★ 84428 ★   **Texaco Gas Station
South**
Dallas Fort Worth Ar
Dallas, TX 75261
(214)574-5280
Ultimate Parent: Texaco. **SIC:** 5541—
Gasoline Service Stations.

★ 84429 ★   **Texaco Gasoline
Station**
3900 N. Hampton Rd.
Dallas, TX 75212
(214)744-2040
Ultimate Parent: Texaco. **SIC:** 5541—
Gasoline Service Stations.

★ 84430 ★   **Texaco Inc.**
3900 Singleton Blvd.
Dallas, TX 75212
(214)631-6193
Ultimate Parent: Texaco. **SIC:** 5172—
Petroleum Products Nec.

★ 84431 ★   **Texaco Northpk Svc**
1600 N. Park C
Dallas, TX 75204
(214)368-1388
Ultimate Parent: Texaco.

★ 84432 ★   **Texaco Refining &
Marketing**
3021 Bachman Dr.
Dallas, TX 75220
(214)350-4716
Ultimate Parent: Texaco. **SIC:** 5541—
Gasoline Service Stations.

★ 84433 ★   **Texaco Self Serv**
4275 W. Northwest Hwy.
Dallas, TX 75220
(214)352-2300
Ultimate Parent: Texaco. **SIC:** 5541—
Gasoline Service Stations.

★ 84434 ★   **Texaco Self Serv**
13010 Preston Rd.
Dallas, TX 75240
(214)233-2414
Ultimate Parent: Texaco. **SIC:** 5541—
Gasoline Service Stations.

★ 84435 ★   **Texaco Self Serv**
8207 S. Hampton Rd.
Dallas, TX 75232
(214)298-8838
Ultimate Parent: Texaco. **SIC:** 5541—
Gasoline Service Stations.

★ 84436 ★   **Texaco Self Service**
820 S. Central Expy.
Dallas, TX 75201
(214)690-0914
Ultimate Parent: Texaco. **SIC:** 5541—
Gasoline Service Stations.

★ 84437 ★   **Texaco Serv Statn**
8200 E. R L Thornton Fwy.
Dallas, TX 75228
(214)327-0294
Ultimate Parent: Texaco.

★ 84438 ★   **Texaco Service
Station**
2285 W. Northwest Hwy.
Dallas, TX 75220
(214)352-3037
Ultimate Parent: Texaco. **SIC:** 5541—
Gasoline Service Stations.

★ 84439 ★   **Texaco Service
Station**
424 S. R L Thornton Fwy.
Dallas, TX 75203
(214)942-5771
Ultimate Parent: Texaco. **SIC:** 5541—
Gasoline Service Stations.

★ 84440 ★   **Texaco Slf-Srv Ctr**
7205 Ferguson Rd.
Dallas, TX 75228
(214)327-0003
Ultimate Parent: Texaco.

★ 84441 ★   **Texaco Slf-Sv Ctr**
2923 N. Fitzhugh Ave.
Dallas, TX 75204
(214)827-8580
Ultimate Parent: Texaco.

★ 84442 ★   **Texas Boot Company**
2300 Apparel Mart
Dallas, TX 75258
(214)631-3215
Ultimate Parent: United States Shoe. **SIC:**
7389—Business Services Nec.

★ 84443 ★   **Texas Commerce
Bank NA**
2200 Ross Ave.
Dallas, TX 75201-2708
(214)922-2300
Company Type: Subsidiary. **Officer:** John
L. Adams, Chairman of the Board & CEO.
Ultimate Parent: Chemical Banking Corp.
SIC: 6021—National Commercial Banks.
Employee Count: 1695.

★ 84444 ★   **Texas Industries**
7610 Stemmons Fwy.
Dallas, TX 75247
(214)647-6700 **Fax:** (214)647-3878
Company Type: Headquarters. **Officer:**
Robert D. Rogers, CEO. **Employee Count:**
2700. **Sales:** 614 M. **Fortune 500:** Largest
U.S. Industrial Corporations: Ranking 500.

★ 84445 ★   **Texas Instruments**
13500 N. Central Expy.
Dallas, TX 75265-5474
(214)995-2011 **Fax:** (214)995-3340
Company Type: Headquarters. **Officer:**
Jerry R. Junkins, CEO. **Employee Count:**
59048. **Sales:** 8523 M. **Fortune 500:**
Largest U.S. Industrial Corporations:
Ranking 58.

★ 84446 ★   **Texas Instruments
Inc.**
8505 Forest Ln.
Dallas, TX 75243
Ultimate Parent: Texas Instruments. **SIC:**
3674—Semiconductors & Related Devices.

★ 84447 ★   **Texas Instruments
Inc.**
13500 N. Central Expressway M/S 480
Dallas, TX 75243
Ultimate Parent: Texas Instruments. **SIC:**
3674—Semiconductors & Related Devices;
3672—Printed Circuit Boards.

★ 84448 ★   **Texas Instruments
Inc.**
13500 North Central Expressway
Dallas, TX 75243
Ultimate Parent: Texas Instruments. **SIC:**
3674—Semiconductors & Related Devices;
3600—Electronic & Other Electrical
Equipment.

★ 84449 ★   **Texas Utilities**
2001 Bryan Tower
Dallas, TX 75201
(214)812-4600
Company Type: Headquarters. **Officer:**
Jerry S. Farrington. **Employee Count:**
10859. **Fortune Service 500:** Ranking 11.

★ 84450 ★   **Texas Utilities Co.**
2001 Bryan Tower
Dallas, TX 75201
(214)812-4600 **Fax:** (214)812-4079
Officer: Jerry Farrington, CEO. **Ultimate
Parent:** Texas Utilities. **Employee Count:**
10687. **Sales:** 5435 M.

★ 84451 ★   **3M**
2121 Santa Anna Ave.
Dallas, TX 75228-8100
(214)324-8100
Company Type: Branch. **Officer:** R. A.
Anderson. **Ultimate Parent:** Minnesota
Mining & Mfg. **SIC:** 5113—Industrial &
Personal Service Paper; 2672—Coated &
Laminated Paper Nec; 5085—Industrial
Supplies.

★ 84452 ★   **Title Insurance Co. of
Minn**
7557 Rambler Rd.
Dallas, TX 75231
(214)691-7586
Ultimate Parent: Old Republic International.
SIC: 6541—Title Abstract Offices.

★ 84453 ★   **Total Petroleum Inc.**
10026 Monroe Dr.
Dallas, TX 75229
(214)358-5838
Ultimate Parent: Total Petroleum Inc. **SIC:**
5171—Petroleum Bulk Stations & Terminals;
5172—Petroleum Products Nec.

★ 84454 ★   **Total Petroleum Inc.**
10026 Monroe Dr.
Dallas, TX 75229
(214)358-5838
Ultimate Parent: Total Petroleum Inc. **SIC:**
5171—Petroleum Bulk Stations & Terminals;
5172—Petroleum Products Nec.

★ 84455 ★   **Toys R US**
9500 Central Expy. N
Dallas, TX 75231
(214)363-3192
Ultimate Parent: Toys "R" US.

★ 84456 ★   **Tracy-Locke, A DDB
Needham Agency**
200 Crescent Ct.
Dallas, TX 75201
(214)969-9000 **Fax:** (214)855-2032
Officer: Mike Rawlings. **Ultimate Parent:**
Omnicom Group.

★ 84457 ★   **Trailways Bus System**
905 Slocum St.
Dallas, TX 75207
(214)655-7960
Ultimate Parent: Greyhound Lines Inc. **SIC:**
4111—Local & Suburban Transit.

★ 84458 ★   **Trailways Bus System**
315 Continental Ave.
Dallas, TX 75207
(214)655-7711
Ultimate Parent: Greyhound Lines Inc.

★ 84459 ★   **Trailways Bus System**
3710 Realty Rd.
Dallas, TX 75244
(214)247-3231
Ultimate Parent: Greyhound Lines Inc. **SIC:**
4131—Intercity & Rural Bus Transportation.

★ 84460 ★   **Trailways Bus System
Inc.**
1500 Jackson St.
Dallas, TX 75201
(214)655-7711
Ultimate Parent: Greyhound Lines Inc. **SIC:**
4131—Intercity & Rural Bus Transportation.

★ 84461 ★   **Trailways Bus
Terminal of D**
1500 Jackson St.
Dallas, TX 75201
(214)655-7000
Ultimate Parent: Greyhound Lines Inc. **SIC:**
4173—Bus Terminal & Service Facilities.

★ 84462 ★   **Trailways Commuter
Transit**
315 Continental Ave.
Dallas, TX 75207
(214)655-7023
Ultimate Parent: Greyhound Lines Inc. **SIC:**
4131—Intercity & Rural Bus Transportation.

★ 84463 ★   **Transamerica
Occidental Life Insurance**
4835 Lbj Fwy.
Dallas, TX 75244
(214)387-0290
Ultimate Parent: Transamerica Occidental
Life Insurance. **SIC:** 6411—Insurance
Agents, Brokers & Service.

★ 84464 ★   **Transport Insurance
Co.**
4100 Harry Hines Blvd.
Dallas, TX 75219
(214)526-3876 **Fax:** (214)520-4697
Company Type: Subsidiary. **Officer:** Gene
S. Yerant, Chairman of the Board &
President. **Ultimate Parent:** American
Financial. **SIC:** 6331—Fire, Marine &
Casualty Insurance. **Employee Count:** 125.
Sales: 2809000 M.

★ 84465 ★   **Travelers Lloyds
Insurance**
8140 Walnut Hill Ln.
Dallas, TX 75231
(214)750-4153
Ultimate Parent: Travelers Inc. **SIC:**
6331—Fire, Marine & Casualty Insurance.

★ 84466 ★   **Trinity Industries**
2525 Stemmons Fwy.
Dallas, TX 75207
(214)631-4420
Company Type: Headquarters. **Officer:** W.
Ray Wallace. **Employee Count:** 12600.
Sales: 1540 M. **Fortune 500:** Largest U.S.
Industrial Corporations: Ranking 273.

★ 84467 ★   **Tylor Publishing Co.**
1550 W. Mockingbird Ln.
Dallas, TX 75235
Ultimate Parent: Insilco Corp. **SIC:** 2732—
Book Printing.

★ 84468 ★   **Underwriters
Adjusting Co.**
9560 Skillman St.
Dallas, TX 75243
(214)341-0481
Ultimate Parent: Continental. **SIC:** 6411—
Insurance Agents, Brokers & Service.

★ 84469 ★   **Union Carbide Corp.**
Linde Div.
1001 Forest Ave.
Dallas, TX 75215
Company Type: Division. **Ultimate Parent:**
Union Carbide Corp. **SIC:** 2813—Industrial
Gases.

★ 84470 ★   **United Brake Systems
Inc.**
5025 Sharp St.
Dallas, TX 75247
(214)630-7900
Ultimate Parent: Echlin. **SIC:** 5013—Motor
Vehicle Supplies & New Parts; 5531—
Automobile & Home Supply Stores.

★ 84471 ★   **United Parcel Service**
4101 Mcewen Rd. 600
Dallas, TX 75244
(214)353-1269
Ultimate Parent: United Parcel Service of
America. **SIC:** 4215—Courier Services
Except by Air.

★ 84472 ★   **United Parcel Service**
Dallas-Fort Worth
Dallas, TX 75261
(214)574-2911
Ultimate Parent: United Parcel Service of
America. **SIC:** 4215—Courier Services
Except by Air.

★ 84473 ★   **United Parcel Service**
10155 Monroe Dr.
Dallas, TX 75229
(214)350-3341
Ultimate Parent: United Parcel Service of
America. **SIC:** 4212—Local Trucking
Without Storage; 4215—Courier Services
Except by Air.

★ 84474 ★   **Unitron Inc.**
10925 Miller Rd.
Dallas, TX 75238-1350
(214)340-8600
Ultimate Parent: Dana Corp. **SIC:** 3999—
Manufacturing Industries Nec; 3629—
Electrical Industrial Apparatus Nec; 3562—
Ball & Roller Bearings.

★ 84475 ★   **Universal Foods
Corp.**
100 N. Central Expy.
Dallas, TX 75201
(214)238-5237
Ultimate Parent: Universal Foods Corp.
SIC: 5499—Miscellaneous Food Stores.

★ 84476 ★   **Universal Foods
Corp.**
11414 Chairman Dr.
Dallas, TX 75243
(214)349-8777
Ultimate Parent: Universal Foods Corp.
SIC: 5113—Industrial & Personal Service
Paper.

★ 84477 ★   **Unum Life**
5151 Belt Line Rd. 956
Dallas, TX 75240
(214)241-0773
Ultimate Parent: Unum Life.

★ 84478 ★   **US Fidelity**
13355 Galleria Tower 1
Dallas, TX 75240
(214)851-1800
Ultimate Parent: USF&G Corp. **SIC:**
6411—Insurance Agents, Brokers &
Service.

★ 84479 ★   **US Gypsum Co.**
100 Texas Am Bank Bldg.
Dallas, TX 75235
(214)357-6271
Ultimate Parent: USG Corp. **SIC:** 5039—
Construction Materials Nec.

★ 84480 ★   **US Gypsum Co.**
255 Regal Row
Dallas, TX 75247
Ultimate Parent: USG Corp. **SIC:** 3296—
Mineral Wool.

★ 84481 ★   **US Navy Naval
Weapons Industrial Reserve Plant**
9314 W. Jefferson St.
Dallas, TX 75211
Ultimate Parent: LTV. **SIC:** 3721—Aircraft.

★ 84482 ★   **UTL Corp.**
1508 W. Mockingbird Ln.
Dallas, TX 75235
Ultimate Parent: Boeing. **SIC:** 3812—
Search & Navigation Equipment.

★ 84483 ★   **Valhi Inc.**
5430 LBJ Fwy., Ste. 1700
Dallas, TX 75240
(214)233-1700 **Fax:** (214)385-0586
Company Type: Headquarters. **Officer:**
Harold C. Simmons, CEO. **Employee
Count:** 7500. **Sales:** 781.7 M. **Fortune 500:**
Largest U.S. Industrial Corporations:
Ranking 413.

★ 84484 ★   **Valhi, Inc.**
3 Lincoln Ctr.
Dallas, TX 75240
(214)233-1700
Officer: Harold C. Simmons, Chairman of
the Board. **Ultimate Parent:** Valhi Inc. **SIC:**
2061—Raw Cane Sugar; 2062—Cane
Sugar Refining; 2063—Beet Sugar.

★ 84485 ★   **Variable Annuity Life
Insurance**
2655 Villa Creek Dr.
Dallas, TX 75234
(214)263-0893
Ultimate Parent: American General Corp.
SIC: 6411—Insurance Agents, Brokers &
Service.

★ 84486 ★   **Variable Annuity Life
Insurance Co.**
2655 Villa Creek Dr.
Dallas, TX 75234
(214)263-0893
Ultimate Parent: American General Corp.
SIC: 6411—Insurance Agents, Brokers &
Service.

★ 84487 ★   **Varo Inc.**
11477 Pagemill
Dallas, TX 75243
Ultimate Parent: Imo Industries. **SIC:**
3671—Electron Tubes.

★ 84488 ★   **Victoria's Secret**
522 N. Park C
Dallas, TX 75201
(214)987-9034
Ultimate Parent: Limited.

★ 84489 ★   **Victoria's Secret**
2156 Valley View Ctr.
Dallas, TX 75240
(214)490-3440
Ultimate Parent: Limited. **SIC:** 5651—
Family Clothing Stores.

★ 84490 ★   **Victoria's Secret**
5301 Belt Line Rd.
Dallas, TX 75240
(214)991-0797
Ultimate Parent: Limited. **SIC:** 5651—
Family Clothing Stores.

★ 84491 ★   **Waldenbooks**
1 City Ctr. Bldg.
Dallas, TX 75201
(214)969-0923
Ultimate Parent: K-Mart. **SIC:** 5999—
Miscellaneous Retail Stores Nec.

★ 84492 ★   **Waldenbooks**
Red Bird Mall
Dallas, TX 75237
(214)296-2712
Ultimate Parent: K-Mart. **SIC:** 5942—Book
Stores.

★ 84493 ★   **Wang Information
Services**
2030 Main St.
Dallas, TX 75201
(214)745-1823
Ultimate Parent: Wang Laboratories, Inc.

★ 84494 ★   **Westvaco Corp.**
2355 N. Stemmons Fwy.
Dallas, TX 75207
(214)638-4370
Ultimate Parent: WestVaco Corp. **SIC:**
2621—Paper Mills.

★ 84495 ★   **Westvaco Corp.**
10700 Harry Hines Blvd.
Dallas, TX 75220
(214)352-9791
Officer: A. R. Brown, Manager. **Ultimate
Parent:** WestVaco Corp. **SIC:** 2656—
Sanitary Food Containers; 2677—
Envelopes.

★ 84496 ★   **Westvaco Corp.**
Envelope
10700 Harry Hines Blvd.
Dallas, TX 75220
Ultimate Parent: WestVaco Corp. **SIC:**
2677—Envelopes.

★ 84497 ★   **Wilsonart**
Dallas, TX 75247
(800)344-2339
Ultimate Parent: Premark International.
SIC: 3089—Plastics Products Nec.

★ 84498 ★   **Wolf Brand Products
Inc.**
2929 Carlisle St.
Dallas, TX 75204
(214)871-7530
Ultimate Parent: Quaker Oats. **SIC:**
2099—Food Preparations Nec; 5141—
Groceries—General Line.

★ 84499 ★   **Wormald U S Inc.**
15806 Midway Rd.
Dallas, TX 75244
(214)239-9874
Ultimate Parent: Tyco International. **SIC:**
7389—Business Services Nec.

★ 84500 ★   **Microsource**
5025 Arapaho, Suite
Dallas,, TX 75248
(214)702-8500
Ultimate Parent: MicroAge.

Dallas-Fort Worth

★ 84501 ★   **AA Decision
Technologies Inc.**
PO Box 619616
Dallas-Fort Worth Airport
Dallas-Fort Worth, TX 75261-9616
(817)967-1468
Company Type: Subsidiary. **Officer:**
Thomas M. Cook, President. **Ultimate
Parent:** AMR Corp.

★ 84502 ★   **AMR Corp.**
AA Carco Div.
PO Box 619616
Dallas-Fort Worth Airport
Dallas-Fort Worth, TX 75261-9616
(817)963-1234 **Fax:** (817)963-2523
Company Type: Division. **Officer:** William
R. Boesch, President. **Ultimate Parent:**
AMR Corp.

★ 84503 ★   **AMR Corp.**
SABRE Computer Services
PO Box 619616
Dallas-Fort Worth Airport
Dallas-Fort Worth, TX 75261-9616
(817)963-1234 **Fax:** (817)963-2523
Company Type: Subsidiary. **Officer:** Terrell
B. Jones. **Ultimate Parent:** AMR Corp.

★ 84504 ★   **AMR Information
Services**
PO Box 619616
Dallas-Fort Worth Airport
Dallas-Fort Worth, TX 75261-9616
(817)967-3003
Company Type: Subsidiary. **Officer:** C.
Joseph Atteridge, President & CEO.
Ultimate Parent: AMR Corp.

★ 84505 ★   **AMR Investment
Services**
PO Box 619616
Dallas-Fort Worth Airport
Dallas-Fort Worth, TX 75261-9616
(817)967-1525
Company Type: Subsidiary. **Officer:**
William F. Quinn, President. **Ultimate
Parent:** AMR Corp.

★ 84506 ★   **AMR Training &
Consulting Group**
PO Box 619616
Dallas-Fort Worth Airport
Dallas-Fort Worth, TX 75261-9616
(817)963-1234 **Fax:** (817)963-2523
Company Type: Subsidiary. **Officer:** Peter
A. Pappas, President. **Ultimate Parent:**
AMR Corp.

★ 84507 ★   **SABRE Development
Services**
PO Box 619616
Dallas-Fort Worth Airport
Dallas-Fort Worth, TX 75261-9616
(817)963-1234 **Fax:** (817)963-2523
Company Type: Subsidiary. **Officer:** Bruce
D. Parker, President. **Ultimate Parent:** AMR
Corp.

★ 84508 ★   **SABRE Technology
Group**
PO Box 619616
Dallas-Fort Worth Airport
Dallas-Fort Worth, TX 75261-9616
(817)963-1234 **Fax:** (817)963-2523
Company Type: Subsidiary. **Officer:**
Kathleen M. Misunas, President & CEO.
Ultimate Parent: AMR Corp.

★ 84509 ★   **SABRE Travel
Information Network**
PO Box 619616
Dallas-Fort Worth Airport
Dallas-Fort Worth, TX 75261-9616
(817)963-1234 **Fax:** (817)963-2523
Company Type: Subsidiary. **Officer:** Jeff
Katz, President. **Ultimate Parent:** AMR
Corp.

★ 84510 ★   **Tele Service
Resources**
PO Box 619160 MD 1306 CPXI
Dallas-Fort Worth, TX 75261-9160
(817)355-8200 **Fax:** (817)354-8144
Company Type: Subsidiary. **Officer:** Keith
Woodcox, President. **Ultimate Parent:** AMR
Corp.

Dallas-Fort Worth Airport

★ 84511 ★   **AA Decision
Technologies**
Mail Drop 4462
PO Box 619616
Dallas-Fort Worth Airport, TX 75261-9616
(817)963-1234
Company Type: Subsidiary. **Ultimate
Parent:** AMR Corp.

★ 84512 ★   **AMR Corp.**
PO Box 619616
Dallas-Fort Worth Airport, TX 75261-9616
Company Type: Headquarters. **Ultimate
Parent:** AMR Corp.

★ 84513 ★   **AMR Information
Services**
4200 Amon Carter Blvd.
Mail Drop 1350
PO Box 619515
Dallas-Fort Worth Airport, TX 76155
(817)963-3055 **Fax:** (817)963-4240
Company Type: Subsidiary. **Officer:** C.J.
Atteridge, President & CEO. **Ultimate
Parent:** AMR Corp. **SIC:** 7374—Data
Processing & Preparation.

★ 84514 ★   **AMR Services Corp.**
PO Box 619616
Dallas-Fort Worth Airport, TX 75261
(817)355-1234
Company Type: Subsidiary. **Officer:**
Thomas M. Metzler, President. **Ultimate
Parent:** AMR Corp. **SIC:** 4581—Airports,
Flying Fields & Services. **Sales:** 25,900,000
M.

★ 84515 ★   **Metroflight Inc.**
PO Box 612626
Dallas-Fort Worth Airport, TX 75261
(214)929-5117 **Fax:** (214)929-5024
Company Type: Subsidiary. **Officer:** Brian
K. Miller, President. **Ultimate Parent:** AMR
Corp. **Employee Count:** 950.

★ 84516 ★   **AMR Consulting**
PO Box 619616
Dallas-Forth Worth Airport, TX 75261-9616
(817)963-1234
Company Type: Subsidiary. **Ultimate
Parent:** AMR Corp.

Danevang

★ 84517 ★   **Texaco Inc.
Production Dept**
Pierce Ln.
Danevang, TX 77432
(409)543-4391
Ultimate Parent: Texaco.

Darrouzett

★ 84518 ★   **Equity Country Inc.**
PO Box 325
Darrouzett, TX
(806)624-2311
Company Type: Subsidiary. **Ultimate
Parent:** Farmland Industries.

Dayton

★ 84519 ★   **Baker Performance
Chemicals**
Hwy. 90
Dayton, TX 77535
(409)258-5568
Officer: Robert Stearns, Manager. **Ultimate
Parent:** Baker Hughes. **SIC:** 2819—
Industrial Inorganic Chemicals Nec.

★ 84520 ★   **Baker Performance
Chemicals Inc.**
US Hwy. 90, 5 Miles West of Dayton
Dayton, TX 77535
Ultimate Parent: Baker Hughes. **SIC:**
2899—Chemical Preparations Nec.

★ 84521 ★   **Gulf States Utilities
Co.**
212 Bryan St.
Dayton, TX 77535
(409)258-2631
Ultimate Parent: Gulf State Utilities Co.
SIC: 4911—Electric Services.

★ 84522 ★　Mobil Oil Corp.
504 W. Hwy. 90
Dayton, TX 77535
(409)336-3332
Ultimate Parent: Mobil. SIC: 1382—Oil & Gas Exploration Services.

★ 84523 ★　Mobil Pipeline Stations
FM 1409
Dayton, TX 77535
(409)258-3685
Ultimate Parent: Mobil. SIC: 4612—Crude Petroleum Pipelines.

★ 84524 ★　Radio Shack
2211 Main N
Dayton, TX 77535
(409)336-8727
Company Type: Division. Ultimate Parent: Tandy Corp.

★ 84525 ★　Texaco Service Center
51 Rural Route 2
Dayton, TX 77535
(409)336-3122
Ultimate Parent: Texaco. SIC: 7538—General Automotive Repair Shops.

De Kalb

★ 84526 ★　Piggly Wiggly
150 NE Runnells
De Kalb, TX 75559
(214)667-2271
Ultimate Parent: Bruno's. SIC: 5411—Grocery Stores.

★ 84527 ★　Texaco Inc.
407 NW Front St.
De Kalb, TX 75559
(214)667-2861
Ultimate Parent: Texaco. SIC: 5171—Petroleum Bulk Stations & Terminals.

De Leon

★ 84528 ★　Golden Peanut Co.
PO Box 266
De Leon, TX 76444-0226
(817)893-2059
Officer: Milton Smith. Ultimate Parent: Archer Daniels Midland Co. SIC: 2068—Salted & Roasted Nuts & Seeds.

★ 84529 ★　Golden Peanut Processing Plant
Rte. 2
De Leon, TX 76444-9802
(817)893-2034
Location Type: Plant. Officer: Howard Valentine. Ultimate Parent: Archer Daniels Midland Co. SIC: 2096—Potato Chips & Similar Snacks.

De Soto

★ 84530 ★　Albertson's Inc.
901 N. Polk St.
De Soto, TX 75115-4013
(214)224-3544
Ultimate Parent: Albertson's Inc. SIC: 5411—Grocery Stores.

★ 84531 ★　Avery International
1404 Thistlewood Dr.
De Soto, TX 75115-7736
(214)283-9176
Ultimate Parent: Avery Dennison Corp. SIC: 5111—Printing & Writing Paper.

★ 84532 ★　Comerica Bank-Texas
911 N. Hampton Rd.
De Soto, TX 75115-3956
(214)223-1234
Company Type: Subsidiary. Location Type: Branch office. Ultimate Parent: Comerica Bank. SIC: 6021—National Commercial Banks.

★ 84533 ★　Exxon
447 E. Hwy. 67
De Soto, TX 75115
(214)780-1877
Ultimate Parent: Exxon.

★ 84534 ★　Kmart Discount Stores
845 N. Beckley Rd.
De Soto, TX 75115
(214)223-1070
Ultimate Parent: K-Mart.

★ 84535 ★　Kmart Discount Stores
845 N. Beckley Rd.
De Soto, TX 75115
(214)223-1780
Ultimate Parent: K-Mart. SIC: 5531—Automobile & Home Supply Stores.

★ 84536 ★　Pizza Hut
205 E. Pleasant Run Rd.
De Soto, TX 75115
(214)224-3558
Ultimate Parent: Pepsico. SIC: 5812—Eating Places.

★ 84537 ★　Radio Shack
1001 N. Beckley Rd.
De Soto, TX 75115
(214)227-6151
Company Type: Division. Ultimate Parent: Tandy Corp. SIC: 5065—Electronic Parts & Equipment Nec.

★ 84538 ★　Solar Turbines Inc.
215 Centre Park Blvd.
De Soto, TX 75115
Ultimate Parent: Caterpillar. SIC: 3511—Turbines & Turbine Generator Sets; 7699—Repair Services Nec.

★ 84539 ★　Taco Bell
702 N. Hampton Rd.
De Soto, TX 75115
(214)223-0069
Ultimate Parent: Pepsico.

★ 84540 ★　Zep Manufacturing Co.
525 Centre Park Blvd.
De Soto, TX 75115
(214)228-3388
Ultimate Parent: National Service Industries. SIC: 5099—Durable Goods Nec.

★ 84541 ★　ZEP Manufacturing Co.
525 E. Centre Park Blvd.
De Soto, TX 75115
(214)228-3388
Officer: Brian Shelby, Manager. Ultimate Parent: National Service Industries. SIC: 2842—Polishes & Sanitation Goods.

★ 84542 ★　Zep Mfg. Co.
525 Centre Park Blvd.
De Soto, TX 75115
Ultimate Parent: National Service Industries. SIC: 2841—Soap & Other Detergents; 2842—Polishes & Sanitation Goods; 2843—Surface Active Agents; 2844—Toilet Preparations.

Decatur

★ 84543 ★　Pizza Hut
Wise County Shopping Ctr.
Decatur, TX 76234
(817)627-3161
Ultimate Parent: Pepsico. SIC: 5812—Eating Places.

★ 84544 ★　Radio Shack
Corner Hwy. 287 5
Decatur, TX 76234
(817)627-5931
Company Type: Division. Ultimate Parent: Tandy Corp. SIC: 5731—Radio, Television & Electronics Stores.

★ 84545 ★　Wal Mart Pharmacy
Hwy. 287
Decatur, TX 76234
(817)627-3038
Ultimate Parent: Wal-Mart Stores, Inc. SIC: 5912—Drug Stores & Proprietary Stores.

Deer Park

★ 84546 ★　Air Products & Chemicals Inc.
10202 Strang Rd.
Deer Park, TX 77356
(713)479-5901
Officer: David Fritz, Manager. Ultimate Parent: Air Products & Chemicals, Inc. SIC: 2813—Industrial Gases.

★ 84547 ★　Bf Goodrich Co.
Geon Vinyl Div. Deer Park Plant
1105 Tidal Rd.
Deer Park, TX 77536-0900
Company Type: Division. Location Type: Plant. Ultimate Parent: B.F. Goodrich. SIC: 2821—Plastics Materials & Resins.

★ 84548 ★　Citgo Quick Mart
8300 Spencer Hwy.
Deer Park, TX 77536
(713)479-4048
Ultimate Parent: Citgo Petroleum. SIC: 5541—Gasoline Service Stations.

★ 84549 ★　Ethyl Corp. Pao Facility
1515 Miller Cut-Off Rd.
Deer Park, TX 77536-1900
Ultimate Parent: Ethyl. SIC: 2869—Industrial Organic Chemicals Nec.

★ 84550 ★　Fina Technology Inc.
PO Box 1200
Deer Park, TX 77536
(713)884-0500 Fax: (713)884-0623
Officer: Michael Daumerie, Director.
Ultimate Parent: Fina.

★ 84551 ★　Jiffy Lube
3417 Ctr. St.
Deer Park, TX 77536
(713)479-2653
Ultimate Parent: Pennzoil.

★ 84552 ★　Lockwood National Bank of Houston
1500 Ctr. St.
Deer Park, TX 77536
(713)479-8989
Location Type: Branch office. Ultimate Parent: Michigan National Corp. SIC: 6021—National Commercial Banks.

★ 84553 ★　Lubrizol Corp. the
41 Tidal Rd.
Deer Park, TX 77536
(713)479-2851
Ultimate Parent: Lubrizol. SIC: 3861—Photographic Equipment & Supplies.

★ 84554 ★　Lubrizol Corp. Deer Park Plant
41 Tidal Rd.
Deer Park, TX 77536-0158
Ultimate Parent: Lubrizol. SIC: 2869—Industrial Organic Chemicals Nec.

★ 84555 ★　Lubrizol Petroleum Chemicals Co.-Deer Park Plant
41 Tidal Rd.
Deer Park, TX 77536-0158
Ultimate Parent: Lubrizol. SIC: 2869—Industrial Organic Chemicals Nec.

★ 84556 ★　McDonalds of Deer Park
7437 Spencer Hwy.
Deer Park, TX 77536
(713)479-6048
Ultimate Parent: McDonald's. SIC: 5812—Eating Places.

★ 84557 ★　Occidental Chemical Corp.
1000 Tidal Rd. PO Box 500
Deer Park, TX 77536-0500
Ultimate Parent: Occidental Petroleum Corp. SIC: 2812—Alkalies & Chlorine; 2869—Industrial Organic Chemicals Nec.

★ 84558 ★　Occidental Chemical Corp.
Deer Park
1000 Tidal Rd.
Deer Park, TX 77536
Company Type: Division. Ultimate Parent: Occidental Petroleum Corp. SIC: 2812—Alkalies & Chlorine; 2869—Industrial Organic Chemicals Nec.

★ 84559 ★　Occidental Chemical Corp.
Vcm Plant
1000 Tidal Rd. PO Box 500
Deer Park, TX 77536-0500
Location Type: Plant. Ultimate Parent: Occidental Petroleum Corp. SIC: 2869—Industrial Organic Chemicals Nec.

★ 84560 ★　Praxair Inc.
622 Tidal Rd.
Deer Park, TX 77536-0250
Ultimate Parent: Praxair. SIC: 2813—Industrial Gases.

★ 84561 ★　Radio Shack
3424 Ctr. St.
Deer Park, TX 77536
(713)479-6657
Company Type: Division. Ultimate Parent: Tandy Corp. SIC: 5065—Electronic Parts & Equipment Nec.

★ 84562 ★　Radio Shack
9633 Spencer Hwy.
Deer Park, TX 77536
(713)476-9714
Company Type: Division. Ultimate Parent: Tandy Corp. SIC: 5065—Electronic Parts & Equipment Nec.

★ 84563 ★　Rohm &. Haas Inc. Texas
6600 LaPorte Freeway (Hwy. 225)
Deer Park, TX 77536
Ultimate Parent: Rohm & Haas. SIC: 2869—Industrial Organic Chemicals Nec.

★ 84564 ★　Rohm & Haas Inc. Texas
6600 LaPorte Freeway (Hwy. 225)
Deer Park, TX 77536
Ultimate Parent: Rohm & Haas. SIC: 2869—Industrial Organic Chemicals Nec.

★ 84565 ★　Rohm & Haas of Texas Inc.
6600 LaPorte Hwy.
Deer Park, TX 77536
Ultimate Parent: Rohm & Haas. SIC: 2869—Industrial Organic Chemicals Nec.

★ 84566 ★　Savings of America, FSB
3605 Ctr. St.
Deer Park, TX 77536-6101
(713)479-2351
Company Type: Division. Location Type: Branch office. Ultimate Parent: H. F. Ahmanson. SIC: 6021—National Commercial Banks.

★ 84567 ★　Shell Oil Co.
5900 Hwy. 225 E.
Deer Park, TX 77536
(713)246-4371
Officer: Steve Reeves, Manager. Ultimate Parent: Shell Oil Co. SIC: 2819—Industrial Inorganic Chemicals Nec; 2821—Plastics Materials & Resins; 2911—Petroleum Refining.

★ 84568 ★　Shell Oil Co.
Deer Park Manufacturing Complex
5900 Hwy. 225
Deer Park, TX 77536
Ultimate Parent: Shell Oil Co. SIC: 2911—Petroleum Refining; 2869—Industrial Organic Chemicals Nec; 2865—Cyclic Crudes & Intermediates; 2821—Plastics Materials & Resins.

★ 84569 ★　Shell Oil Co.
Deer Park Manufacturing Complex
Hwy. 225
Deer Park, TX 77536
Ultimate Parent: Shell Oil Co. SIC: 2911—Petroleum Refining; 2869—Industrial Organic Chemicals Nec; 2899—Chemical Preparations Nec.

★ 84570 ★　Shell Oil Co. Library
1 Shell Pl
Deer Park, TX 77536
(713)476-4371
Ultimate Parent: Shell Oil Co. SIC: 2911—Petroleum Refining.

★ 84571 ★　Taco Bell
3421 Ctr. St.
Deer Park, TX 77536
(713)479-1611
Ultimate Parent: Pepsico.

★ 84572 ★　Union Carbide Corp. Industrial Gases
622 Tidal Rd.
Deer Park, TX 77536-0250
Ultimate Parent: Union Carbide Corp. SIC: 2813—Industrial Gases.

★ 84573 ★　Union Carbide Industrial Gases Inc.
622 Tidal Rd.
Deer Park, TX 77536-0250
Ultimate Parent: Union Carbide Corp. SIC: 2813—Industrial Gases.

★ 84574 ★　W. R. Grace & Co.
Deer Park Facility
739 Battleground Rd.
Deer Park, TX 77536
Location Type: Facility. Ultimate Parent: W. R. Grace. SIC: 2869—Industrial Organic Chemicals Nec.

★ 84575 ★ Walgreen Drug Stores
1809 Ctr. St.
Deer Park, TX 77536
(713)479-8014
Ultimate Parent: Walgreen Co. SIC:
7384—Photofinishing Laboratories.

★ 84576 ★ W.R. Grace & Co.
-Deer Park
739 Battleground Rd.
Deer Park, TX 77536
Ultimate Parent: W. R. Grace. SIC: 2869—
Industrial Organic Chemicals Nec.

★ 84577 ★ W.R. Grace & Co.
Deer Park Facility
739 Battleground Rd.
Deer Park, TX 77536
Ultimate Parent: W. R. Grace. SIC: 2869—
Industrial Organic Chemicals Nec.

Del Rio

★ 84578 ★ Ace Hardware of Del
Rio Inc.
1401 Avenue F
Del Rio, TX 78840
(512)775-7446
Ultimate Parent: Ace Hardware. SIC:
5731—Radio, Television & Electronics
Stores.

★ 84579 ★ Circus World
2205 Avenue F
Del Rio, TX 78840
(512)775-1126
Ultimate Parent: Melville. SIC: 5945—
Hobby, Toy & Game Shops.

★ 84580 ★ Kentucky Fried
Chicken
1201 Avenue F
Del Rio, TX 78840
(512)775-9745
Ultimate Parent: Pepsico. SIC: 5812—
Eating Places.

★ 84581 ★ Mobil Oil Co.
102 Texas St.
Del Rio, TX 78840
(512)775-3332
Ultimate Parent: Mobil. SIC: 5171—
Petroleum Bulk Stations & Terminals.

★ 84582 ★ Pizza Hut
703 E. Gibbs St.
Del Rio, TX 78840
(512)774-5631
Ultimate Parent: Pepsico. SIC: 5812—
Eating Places.

★ 84583 ★ Pizza Hut
2114 Avenue F
Del Rio, TX 78840
(512)774-5576
Ultimate Parent: Pepsico. SIC: 5812—
Eating Places.

★ 84584 ★ Pizza Hut
Hwy. 90 W
Del Rio, TX 78840
(512)775-7405
Ultimate Parent: Pepsico. SIC: 5812—
Eating Places.

★ 84585 ★ Radio Shack
2205 Avenue F
Del Rio, TX 78840
(512)774-4649
Company Type: Division. Ultimate Parent:
Tandy Corp. SIC: 5065—Electronic Parts &
Equipment Nec.

★ 84586 ★ Taco Bell
1810 Avenue F
Del Rio, TX 78840
(512)775-5156
Ultimate Parent: Pepsico. SIC: 5812—
Eating Places.

★ 84587 ★ Ten Minute Oil
Change
1911 Avenue F
Del Rio, TX 78840
(512)775-9858
Ultimate Parent: Pennzoil. SIC: 5172—
Petroleum Products Nec; 5251—Hardware
Stores.

★ 84588 ★ Texaco Express Lube
2112 Avenue F
Del Rio, TX 78840
(512)774-1988
Ultimate Parent: Texaco. SIC: 3586—
Measuring & Dispensing Pumps.

★ 84589 ★ Trailways Bus System
608 E. Gibbs St.
Del Rio, TX 78840
(512)774-3212
Ultimate Parent: Greyhound Lines Inc. SIC:
4131—Intercity & Rural Bus Transportation.

DeLeon

★ 84590 ★ Golden Peanut Co.
301 La Salle
DeLeon, TX 76444
(817)893-2071
Officer: John Lochridge, Vice President.
Ultimate Parent: Archer Daniels Midland
Co. SIC: 2048—Prepared Feeds Nec;
2064—Candy & Other Confectionery
Products; 2068—Salted & Roasted Nuts &
Seeds.

★ 84591 ★ Golden Peanut Co.
Common Rte. 2 FM 1496
DeLeon, TX 76444
(817)893-2034
Officer: John Shell, Manager. Ultimate
Parent: Archer Daniels Midland Co. SIC:
2064—Candy & Other Confectionery
Products; 2096—Potato Chips & Similar
Snacks.

Denison

★ 84592 ★ Alcoa Building
Products
1601 Commerce Blvd.
Denison, TX 75020
Ultimate Parent: Aluminum Co. of America-
-Alcoa. SIC: 3089—Plastics Products Nec.

★ 84593 ★ Bi-Lo Wholesl Inc.
117 S. Houston Ave.
Denison, TX 75020
(903)465-5354
Ultimate Parent: Penn Traffic.

★ 84594 ★ Fleischmans Co.
2700 Texoma Dr.
Denison, TX 75020
(903)465-8901
Company Type: Division. Location Type:
Facility. Officer: Renta Lopez, Plant
Manager. Ultimate Parent: RJR Nabisco
Holdings.

★ 84595 ★ Greyhound Bus Line
1002 W. Morton St.
Denison, TX 75020
Ultimate Parent: Greyhound Lines Inc.

★ 84596 ★ Greyhound Bus Lines
1002 W. Morton St.
Denison, TX 75020
Ultimate Parent: Greyhound Lines Inc. SIC:
4111—Local & Suburban Transit; 4131—
Intercity & Rural Bus Transportation.

★ 84597 ★ Kaiser Aluminum &
Chemical
4300 S. Hwy. 75
Denison, TX 75020
(214)839-5566
Ultimate Parent: Maxxam. SIC: 3399—
Primary Metal Products Nec.

★ 84598 ★ Kentucky Fried
Chicken
401 N. Austin Ave.
Denison, TX 75020
(214)465-1577
Ultimate Parent: Pepsico. SIC: 5812—
Eating Places.

★ 84599 ★ Kroger Food Store
815 W. Crawford St.
Denison, TX 75020
(214)465-8053
Ultimate Parent: Kroger. SIC: 4822—
Telegraph & Other Communications; 5411—
Grocery Stores.

★ 84600 ★ Kwikset Corp.
2600 N. Hwy. 75A
Denison, TX 75020-9042
(903)463-1313
Officer: Stan Dunford. Ultimate Parent:
Black & Decker Corp. SIC: 3429—Hardware

Nec; 3499—Fabricated Metal Products Nec;
5072—Hardware.

★ 84601 ★ Kwikset Corp.
2600 N. Hwy. 75
Denison, TX 75020
Ultimate Parent: Black & Decker Corp.
SIC: 3429—Hardware Nec.

★ 84602 ★ McDonalds
Restaurant
600 N. Hwy. 75
Denison, TX 75020
(903)465-5075
Ultimate Parent: McDonald's.

★ 84603 ★ Pactel Paging
101 E. Main St. 160
Denison, TX 75020
Ultimate Parent: Pacific Telesis Group.

★ 84604 ★ Pizza Hut
1101 W. Main St.
Denison, TX 75020
(214)465-6115
Ultimate Parent: Pepsico. SIC: 5812—
Eating Places.

★ 84605 ★ Pizza Hut
129 W. Heron St.
Denison, TX 75020
(214)463-4807
Ultimate Parent: Pepsico. SIC: 5812—
Eating Places.

★ 84606 ★ Radio Shack
2411 S. Austin Ave.
Denison, TX 75020
(214)463-7532
Company Type: Division. Ultimate Parent:
Tandy Corp. SIC: 5065—Electronic Parts &
Equipment Nec.

★ 84607 ★ Ryder Truck Rental
500 S. Armstrong Ave.
Denison, TX 75020
(214)463-7593
Ultimate Parent: Ryder System. SIC:
7359—Equipment Rental & Leasing Nec.

★ 84608 ★ Ryder Truck Rental
1327 W. Morton St.
Denison, TX 75020
(903)465-3667
Ultimate Parent: Ryder System.

★ 84609 ★ Sonoco Products Co.
3406 Texoma Dr.
Denison, TX 75020
(903)465-8500
Officer: Nancy Roberts, Manager. Ultimate
Parent: Sonoco Products. SIC: 2655—Fiber
Cans, Drums & Similar Products.

★ 84610 ★ Taco Bell
900 S. Austin Ave.
Denison, TX 75020
(903)463-5140
Ultimate Parent: Pepsico.

★ 84611 ★ Wal Mart
2415 S. Austin Ave.
Denison, TX 75020
(214)465-3020
Ultimate Parent: Wal-Mart Stores, Inc. SIC:
5311—Department Stores.

★ 84612 ★ Wal Mart Discount
2415 S. Austin Ave.
Denison, TX 75020
(903)465-3020
Ultimate Parent: Wal-Mart Stores, Inc.

★ 84613 ★ Wal Mart Pharmacy
2415 S. Austin Ave.
Denison, TX 75020
(903)465-8035
Ultimate Parent: Wal-Mart Stores, Inc.

Denton

★ 84614 ★ Ace Hardware
618 W. University Dr.
Denton, TX 76201
(817)566-1666
Ultimate Parent: Ace Hardware. SIC:
5251—Hardware Stores.

★ 84615 ★ Casual Corner
Golden
Denton, TX 76201
(817)566-6116
Ultimate Parent: United States Shoe. SIC:
5621—Women's Clothing Stores.

★ 84616 ★ Eagle-Picher
Industries Inc.
Molding Orthane Div.
1500 I-35 W.
Denton, TX 76207
Company Type: Division. Ultimate Parent:
Eagle-Picher Industries Inc. SIC: 3069—
Fabricated Rubber Products Nec.

★ 84617 ★ Kroger Co
401 N. Elm St.
Denton, TX 76201
(817)383-2619
Ultimate Parent: Kroger. SIC: 5411—
Grocery Stores.

★ 84618 ★ Lane Bryant
Golden Triangle Mall
Denton, TX 76205
(817)382-2630
Ultimate Parent: Limited. SIC: 5651—
Family Clothing Stores.

★ 84619 ★ Lerner Shop
Golden
Denton, TX 76201
(817)566-3408
Ultimate Parent: Limited. SIC: 5621—
Women's Clothing Stores.

★ 84620 ★ Lone Star Gas Co.
106 N. Bradshaw St.
Denton, TX 76205
Ultimate Parent: Enserch. SIC: 1711—
Plumbing, Heating & Air-Conditioning;
4939—Combination Utility Nec.

★ 84621 ★ Manpower, Inc.
2220 San Jacinto Blvd.
Denton, TX 76205
(817)566-6220
Ultimate Parent: Manpower, Inc. SIC:
7363—Help Supply Services.

★ 84622 ★ Mobil Mart No 3
1105 E. University Dr.
Denton, TX 76201
(817)566-3124
Ultimate Parent: Mobil. SIC: 5541—
Gasoline Service Stations.

★ 84623 ★ Mobil Mart No 2
515 I E
Denton, TX 76205
(817)383-1117
Ultimate Parent: Mobil. SIC: 5541—
Gasoline Service Stations.

★ 84624 ★ Ohio Rubber Co.
Orthane Div.
1500 I-35 West
Denton, TX 76207
Company Type: Division. Ultimate Parent:
Eagle-Picher Industries Inc. SIC: 3069—
Fabricated Rubber Products Nec.

★ 84625 ★ Osco Drug
2321 W. University Dr.
Denton, TX 76201
(817)383-1698
Ultimate Parent: American Stores.

★ 84626 ★ Peterbilt Motors Co.
3200 Airport Rd.
Denton, TX 76205
Ultimate Parent: Paccar. SIC: 3711—Motor
Vehicles & Car Bodies; 3711—Motor
Vehicles & Car Bodies.

★ 84627 ★ Piggly Wiggly
2267 PO Box
Denton, TX 76202
(817)382-8804
Ultimate Parent: Bruno's. SIC: 5411—
Grocery Stores.

★ 84628 ★ Piggly Wiggly
1204 W. University Dr., Rm. 320
Denton, TX 76201-1771
(817)387-4313
Location Type: Branch office. Officer:
Harold F. Osborne. Ultimate Parent:
Bruno's. SIC: 5411—Grocery Stores.

★ 84629 ★ Pizza Hut
1502 W. Hickory St.
Denton, TX 76201
(817)383-9347
Ultimate Parent: Pepsico. SIC: 5812—
Eating Places.

★ 84630 ★　Pizza Hut
227 W. University Dr.
Denton, TX 76201
(817)565-9778
Ultimate Parent: Pepsico.

★ 84631 ★　Radio Shack
8 PO Box
Denton, TX 76202
(817)383-2631
Company Type: Division. Ultimate Parent:
Tandy Corp. SIC: 5065—Electronic Parts &
Equipment Nec.

★ 84632 ★　Radio Shack
415 W. University Dr.
Denton, TX 76201
(817)381-0117
Company Type: Division. Ultimate Parent:
Tandy Corp.

★ 84633 ★　Radio Shack
Golden Triangle Mall
Denton, TX 76205
(817)565-2700
Company Type: Division. Ultimate Parent:
Tandy Corp. SIC: 5065—Electronic Parts &
Equipment Nec.

★ 84634 ★　Radio Shack
Denton Ctr.
Denton, TX 76201
(817)383-2631
Company Type: Division. Ultimate Parent:
Tandy Corp. SIC: 4812—Radiotelephone
Communications.

★ 84635 ★　Radio Shack
Golden
Denton, TX 76201
(817)566-6310
Company Type: Division. Ultimate Parent:
Tandy Corp. SIC: 5731—Radio, Television
& Electronics Stores.

★ 84636 ★　Safety Kleen Corp.
Cooper Creek Rd.
Denton, TX 76201
(817)383-2611
Ultimate Parent: Safety-Kleen. SIC: 5172—
Petroleum Products Nec.

★ 84637 ★　Sally Beauty Co., Inc.
PO Box 490
Denton, TX 76202
(817)898-7500 Fax: (817)898-7775
Company Type: Subsidiary. Ultimate
Parent: Alberto-Culver Co. Inc. SIC: 5087—
Service Establishment Equipment.

★ 84638 ★　Texaco Exprss Lube
2104 Sadau Ct
Denton, TX 76205
(817)383-4225
Ultimate Parent: Texaco.

★ 84639 ★　Texaco Food Mart
1223 McCormick St.
Denton, TX 76201
(817)383-1800
Ultimate Parent: Texaco.

★ 84640 ★　Texaco Food Mart
1823 N. Elm St.
Denton, TX 76201
(817)565-1955
Ultimate Parent: Texaco. SIC: 5411—
Grocery Stores.

★ 84641 ★　Trailways Bus System
201 S. Elm St.
Denton, TX 76201
(817)387-3802
Ultimate Parent: Greyhound Lines Inc. SIC:
4111—Local & Suburban Transit.

★ 84642 ★　Trinity Industries Inc.
615 E. Sycamore
Denton, TX 76201
Ultimate Parent: Trinity Industries. SIC:
3443—Fabricated Plate Work—Boiler
Shops.

★ 84643 ★　Twin Lakes Hospital
2026 W. University Dr.
Denton, TX 76201
(817)383-4660
Ultimate Parent: National Medical
Enterprises. SIC: 8062—General Medical &
Surgical Hospitals.

★ 84644 ★　United Parcel Service
1709 Shady Oaks Dr.
Denton, TX 76205
(817)565-9150
Ultimate Parent: United Parcel Service of
America. SIC: 4215—Courier Services
Except by Air.

★ 84645 ★　Wal Mart Discount
Cities
2221 S. Loop 288
Denton, TX 76205
(817)565-1895
Ultimate Parent: Wal-Mart Stores, Inc. SIC:
5311—Department Stores; 5912—Drug
Stores & Proprietary Stores.

Denver City

★ 84646 ★　Arco Oil & Gas Co.
Plains Hwy.
Denver City, TX 79323
(806)592-4900
Location Type: Branch office. Ultimate
Parent: Atlantic Richfield Co., Inc. SIC:
1311—Crude Petroleum & Natural Gas.

★ 84647 ★　Pizza Hut
220 W. Broadway St.
Denver City, TX 79323
(806)592-3778
Ultimate Parent: Pepsico. SIC: 5812—
Eating Places.

★ 84648 ★　Shell Pipeline Corp.
Denver City, TX 79323
(806)592-2442
Ultimate Parent: Shell Oil Co. SIC: 1382—
Oil & Gas Exploration Services.

★ 84649 ★　Shell Pipeline Corp.
Denver City, TX 79323
(806)592-2442
Ultimate Parent: Shell Oil Co. SIC: 1382—
Oil & Gas Exploration Services.

Devine

★ 84650 ★　Xetron Corp.
Us 81
Devine, TX 78016
(512)663-3241
Ultimate Parent: Westinghouse Electric
Corp. SIC: 8748—Business Consulting
Services Nec.

DFW Airport

★ 84651 ★　AMR Eagle Inc.
PO Box 619616
Dallas-Fort Worth Airport
DFW Airport, TX 75261-9616
(817)967-1295
Company Type: Subsidiary. Officer:
Robert E. Martens, President. Ultimate
Parent: AMR Corp.

Diboll

★ 84652 ★　Borden Inc.
Chemical
100 W. Borden Dr.
Diboll, TX 75941
Company Type: Division. Ultimate Parent:
Borden, Inc. SIC: 2821—Plastics Materials
& Resins; 2869—Industrial Organic
Chemicals Nec; 2842—Polishes &
Sanitation Goods.

★ 84653 ★　Borden Inc.
Packaging & Industrial Prods.
100 W. Borden Dr.
Diboll, TX 75941-1299
Ultimate Parent: Borden, Inc. SIC: 2821—
Plastics Materials & Resins; 2869—
Industrial Organic Chemicals Nec; 2842—
Polishes & Sanitation Goods.

★ 84654 ★　Borden Packaging &
Industrial Products
100 W. Borden Dr.
Diboll, TX 75941
(409)829-5566
Location Type: Plant. Officer: Gary
Roberts, Plant Manager. Ultimate Parent:
Borden, Inc. SIC: 2821—Plastics Materials
& Resins; 2869—Industrial Organic
Chemicals Nec; 2891—Adhesives &
Sealants.

★ 84655 ★　Diboll Particleboard
Plant
Borden Dr.
Diboll, TX 75941
Ultimate Parent: Temple-Inland. SIC:
2493—Reconstituted Wood Products.

★ 84656 ★　Diboll Particleboard
Plant
700 Borden Dr.
Diboll, TX 75941
Ultimate Parent: Temple-Inland. SIC:
2493—Reconstituted Wood Products.

★ 84657 ★　Pineland
Fm 2426 1 Benning St.
Diboll, TX 75941
Ultimate Parent: Temple-Inland. SIC:
2300—Apparel & Other Textile Products.

★ 84658 ★　Temple-Inland
303 S. Temple Dr.
Diboll, TX 75941
(409)829-5511
Company Type: Headquarters. Officer:
Clifford J. Grum. Employee Count: 15000.
Sales: 2736 M. Fortune 500: Largest U.S.
Industrial Corporations: Ranking 171.

★ 84659 ★　Temple-Inland Forest
Production Co.
303 S. Temple Dr.
Diboll, TX 75941
(409)829-5511
Ultimate Parent: Temple-Inland. SIC:
2653—Corrugated & Solid Fiber Boxes.

★ 84660 ★　Temple-Inland Forest
Products Corp. Fiber Products
600 A. St.
Diboll, TX 75941
Ultimate Parent: Temple-Inland. SIC:
2900—Petroleum & Coal Products.

★ 84661 ★　Temple Inland Forest
Products Corp. Rigid Form
101 W. Borden Dr.
Diboll, TX 75941
Ultimate Parent: Temple-Inland. SIC:
3999—Manufacturing Industries Nec.

★ 84662 ★　Temple Inland Inc.
Drawer N
Diboll, TX 75941
(409)829-1313 Fax: (409)829-1366
Officer: Clifford J. Grum, CEO. Ultimate
Parent: Temple-Inland. Employee Count:
15000. Sales: 2736 M.

Dickinson

★ 84663 ★　Citizens State Bank
2401 Termini St.
Dickinson, TX 77539
(713)337-3565
Ultimate Parent: Liberty National Bancorp.
SIC: 6022—State Commercial Banks.

★ 84664 ★　Exxon Co. USA
Dickinson, TX 77539
(713)337-2610
Ultimate Parent: Exxon.

★ 84665 ★　Greyhound Bus Lins
2826 Main St.
Dickinson, TX 77539
(713)534-2065
Ultimate Parent: Greyhound Lines Inc.

★ 84666 ★　McDonalds
3706 Gulf Fwy.
Dickinson, TX 77539
(713)337-3390
Ultimate Parent: McDonald's.

★ 84667 ★　Pennzoil Products Co.
Dickinson
4401 Park Ave.
Dickinson, TX 77539
Company Type: Division. Ultimate Parent:
Pennzoil. SIC: 2992—Lubricating Oils &
Greases.

★ 84668 ★　Pennzoil Products Co.
Dickinson Plant (Penreco)
4401 Park Ave.
Dickinson, TX 77539
Location Type: Plant. Ultimate Parent:
Pennzoil. SIC: 2999—Petroleum & Coal
Products Nec.

★ 84669 ★　Penreco Dickinson
Pennzoil Products Co.
4401 Park Ave.
Dickinson, TX 77539
Ultimate Parent: Pennzoil. SIC: 2999—
Petroleum & Coal Products Nec.

★ 84670 ★　Pizza Hut
3486 Gulf Fwy.
Dickinson, TX 77539
(713)337-1212
Ultimate Parent: Pepsico. SIC: 5812—
Eating Places.

★ 84671 ★　Radio Shack
3335 Gulf Fwy.
Dickinson, TX 77539
(713)337-2984
Company Type: Division. Ultimate Parent:
Tandy Corp. SIC: 5065—Electronic Parts &
Equipment Nec.

★ 84672 ★　Taco Bell
104 Fm 517 Rd. W
Dickinson, TX 77539
(713)337-5189
Ultimate Parent: Pepsico. SIC: 5812—
Eating Places.

★ 84673 ★　Wal Mart Discount
Cities
3420 I Hwy. 45th
Dickinson, TX 77539
(713)337-4062
Ultimate Parent: Wal-Mart Stores, Inc.

Dimmitt

★ 84674 ★　Pizza Hut
206 S. Broadway St.
Dimmitt, TX 79027
(806)647-4233
Ultimate Parent: Pepsico. SIC: 5812—
Eating Places.

Dllas

★ 84675 ★　Savings of America,
FSB
5220 W. Lovers Ln.
Dllas, TX 75209
(214)904-1760
Company Type: Division. Location Type:
Branch office. Ultimate Parent: H. F.
Ahmanson. SIC: 6021—National
Commercial Banks.

Donna

★ 84676 ★　Citizens State Bank
132 S. Main St.
Donna, TX 78537
(512)464-3367
Ultimate Parent: Liberty National Bancorp.
SIC: 6022—State Commercial Banks.

★ 84677 ★　Pizza Hut
1309 Us Hwy. 83
Donna, TX 78537
(512)464-7855
Ultimate Parent: Pepsico.

★ 84678 ★　Pizza Hut
1309 E. Hwy. 83
Donna, TX 78537
(512)464-3384
Ultimate Parent: Pepsico. SIC: 5812—
Eating Places.

★ 84679 ★　Rio Grande Valley
Gas Co.
630 Broadway N
Donna, TX 78537
(512)262-1695
Ultimate Parent: Valero Energy Corp.

★ 84680 ★　Trailways Bus System
135 S. 8th St.
Donna, TX 78537
(512)464-2102
Ultimate Parent: Greyhound Lines Inc. SIC:
4131—Intercity & Rural Bus Transportation.

Douglassville

★ 84681 ★ Shell Oil Co.
FM 2065
Douglassville, TX 75560
(903)835-3752
Officer: Charles Cranfill, Manager. Ultimate Parent: Shell Oil Co. SIC: 2819—Industrial Inorganic Chemicals Nec; 2911—Petroleum Refining.

Dripping Springs

★ 84682 ★ Radio Shack
Ranch Rd.
Dripping Springs, TX 78620
(512)858-4735
Company Type: Division. Ultimate Parent: Tandy Corp. SIC: 5735—Record & Prerecorded Tape Stores.

Dumas

★ 84683 ★ Amax Potash Corp.
5 Miles N. of Dumas Texas PO Box 1178
Dumas, TX 79029
Ultimate Parent: Cyprus Amax Minerals. SIC: 2819—Industrial Inorganic Chemicals Nec.

★ 84684 ★ Amax Potash Corp.
5 Miles N. of Dumas (Box 1178)
Dumas, TX 79029
Ultimate Parent: Cyprus Amax Minerals. SIC: 2819—Industrial Inorganic Chemicals Nec.

★ 84685 ★ Amax Potash Corp.
5 Mi. N. of Dumas, Texas (PO Box 1178)
Dumas, TX 790291178
Ultimate Parent: Cyprus Amax Minerals. SIC: 2819—Industrial Inorganic Chemicals Nec.

★ 84686 ★ American Family Life Assurance
425 E. 1st St.
Dumas, TX 79029
(806)935-2809
Ultimate Parent: American Family Life Assurance Co. SIC: 6411—Insurance Agents, Brokers & Service.

★ 84687 ★ Exxon Distributor
124 Twichell Ave.
Dumas, TX 79029
(806)935-2897
Ultimate Parent: Exxon.

★ 84688 ★ Greyhound Bus Lines
419 Dumas Ave.
Dumas, TX 79029
(806)935-7303
Ultimate Parent: Greyhound Lines Inc. SIC: 8211—Elementary & Secondary Schools.

★ 84689 ★ Pizza Hut
1515 Dumas Ave.
Dumas, TX 79029
(806)935-6111
Ultimate Parent: Pepsico. SIC: 5812—Eating Places.

★ 84690 ★ Radio Shack
100 Cedar Ave.
Dumas, TX 79029
(806)935-2165
Company Type: Division. Ultimate Parent: Tandy Corp.

★ 84691 ★ Ryder Truck Rental
501 S. Dumas Ave.
Dumas, TX 79029
(806)935-4396
Ultimate Parent: Ryder System.

★ 84692 ★ Wal Mart
1400 Dumas Ave.
Dumas, TX 79029
(806)935-9075
Ultimate Parent: Wal-Mart Stores, Inc. SIC: 5399—Miscellaneous General Merchandise Store.

Duncanville

★ 84693 ★ Avon Products Inc.
115 E. Camp Wisdom Rd.
Duncanville, TX 75116
(214)780-1662
Ultimate Parent: Avon Products, Inc.

★ 84694 ★ Casual Corner
1023 Red Bird Mall
Duncanville, TX 75116
(214)296-2956
Ultimate Parent: United States Shoe. SIC: 5621—Women's Clothing Stores.

★ 84695 ★ Jiffy Lube
570 W. Wheatland Rd.
Duncanville, TX 75116
(214)298-2970
Ultimate Parent: Pennzoil.

★ 84696 ★ Kroger Food Stores
303 E. Camp Wisdom Rd.
Duncanville, TX 75116
(214)298-6255
Ultimate Parent: Kroger.

★ 84697 ★ Kroger Food&Drug Stores
303 E. Camp Wisdom Rd.
Duncanville, TX 75116
(214)398-9962
Ultimate Parent: Kroger. SIC: 5411—Grocery Stores.

★ 84698 ★ Kroger Stores
303 W. Camp Wisdom Rd.
Duncanville, TX 75116
(214)298-9962
Ultimate Parent: Kroger. SIC: 5411—Grocery Stores.

★ 84699 ★ Lerner Shop
1005 Red Bird Mall
Duncanville, TX 75116
(214)296-3666
Ultimate Parent: Limited. SIC: 5621—Women's Clothing Stores.

★ 84700 ★ Lone Star Gas Co.
322 S. Main St.
Duncanville, TX 75116
(214)298-3769
Ultimate Parent: Enserch. SIC: 4932—Gas & Other Services Combined.

★ 84701 ★ Norwest Mortgage Inc.
515 N. Cedar Ridge Dr.
Duncanville, TX 75116
(214)709-9985
Ultimate Parent: Norwest Corp. SIC: 6159—Miscellaneous Business Credit Institutions.

★ 84702 ★ Perma Products Co.
1346 N. Main St.
Duncanville, TX 75166-2312
(214)298-4225
Officer: Andy Patterson. Ultimate Parent: American Brands Inc. SIC: 2652—Setup Paperboard Boxes; 2653—Corrugated & Solid Fiber Boxes; 5943—Stationery Stores.

★ 84703 ★ Perma Products Co., Inc.
1346 N. Main St.
Duncanville, TX 75116
(214)298-4225
Ultimate Parent: American Brands Inc. SIC: 5046—Commercial Equipment Nec.

★ 84704 ★ Perma Products Co., Inc.
816 Mercury Ave.
Duncanville, TX 75137
(214)298-4225
Ultimate Parent: American Brands Inc. SIC: 5046—Commercial Equipment Nec.

★ 84705 ★ Perma Products Inc.
1346 N. Main St.
Duncanville, TX 75116
(214)298-4225
Ultimate Parent: American Brands Inc. SIC: 2653—Corrugated & Solid Fiber Boxes; 2782—Blankbooks & Looseleaf Binders.

★ 84706 ★ Pizza Hut
103 E. Camp Wisdom Rd.
Duncanville, TX 75116
(214)296-1737
Ultimate Parent: Pepsico. SIC: 5812—Eating Places.

★ 84707 ★ Quantum
622 Truman Ct.
Duncanville, TX 75137
(817)338-1124
Ultimate Parent: Quantum Corp.

★ 84708 ★ Radio Shack
700 S. Cockrell Hill Rd.
Duncanville, TX 75137
(214)298-7432
Company Type: Division. Ultimate Parent: Tandy Corp. SIC: 5734—Computer & Software Stores.

★ 84709 ★ Radio Shack
430 E. Wheatland Rd.
Duncanville, TX 75116
(214)298-7432
Company Type: Division. Ultimate Parent: Tandy Corp. SIC: 5065—Electronic Parts & Equipment Nec.

★ 84710 ★ Ryder Truck Rental
1006 S. Main St.
Duncanville, TX 75137
(214)296-1567
Ultimate Parent: Ryder System. SIC: 7359—Equipment Rental & Leasing Nec.

★ 84711 ★ Taco Bell
323 S. Cedar Ridge Dr.
Duncanville, TX 75116
(214)298-6268
Ultimate Parent: Pepsico. SIC: 5812—Eating Places.

★ 84712 ★ Taco Bell
423 E. Camp Wisdom Rd.
Duncanville, TX 75116
(214)298-6693
Ultimate Parent: Pepsico. SIC: 5812—Eating Places.

Dunn

★ 84713 ★ Exxon Co. USA
Knapp Texas
Dunn, TX 79516
(915)573-5953
Ultimate Parent: Exxon.

Eagle Pass

★ 84714 ★ Circus World Toys
455 S. Bibb Ave.
Eagle Pass, TX 78852
(512)773-1849
Ultimate Parent: Melville. SIC: 5945—Hobby, Toy & Game Shops.

★ 84715 ★ Exxon Products
Ferry
Eagle Pass, TX 78852
(512)773-2361
Ultimate Parent: Exxon. SIC: 5172—Petroleum Products Nec.

★ 84716 ★ Foot Action No 8025
455 S. Bibb Ave.
Eagle Pass, TX 78852
(512)773-9355
Ultimate Parent: Melville. SIC: 5661—Shoe Stores.

★ 84717 ★ Kentucky Fried Chicken
2427 E. Main St.
Eagle Pass, TX 78852
(512)773-6627
Ultimate Parent: Pepsico. SIC: 5812—Eating Places.

★ 84718 ★ Lerner Shop
Las Aguillas Mall
Eagle Pass, TX 78852
(512)773-4499
Ultimate Parent: Limited. SIC: 5621—Women's Clothing Stores.

★ 84719 ★ Mobil Oil Corp.
San Antonio Hwy.
Eagle Pass, TX 78852
(512)773-3122
Ultimate Parent: Mobil. SIC: 5172—Petroleum Products Nec.

★ 84720 ★ Pizza Hut
455 S. Bibb Ave.
Eagle Pass, TX 78852
(512)773-7733
Ultimate Parent: Pepsico. SIC: 5812—Eating Places.

★ 84721 ★ Pizza Hut
2425 E. Main St.
Eagle Pass, TX 78852
(512)773-5371
Ultimate Parent: Pepsico. SIC: 5812—Eating Places.

★ 84722 ★ Ryder Truck Rental
Loop S. 431
Eagle Pass, TX 78852
(512)773-0130
Ultimate Parent: Ryder System. SIC: 7359—Equipment Rental & Leasing Nec.

★ 84723 ★ Wal Mart Discount City
Fm 375
Eagle Pass, TX 78852
(512)773-9403
Ultimate Parent: Wal-Mart Stores, Inc. SIC: 5311—Department Stores.

Earth

★ 84724 ★ Citizens State Bank
20 PO Box
Earth, TX 79031
(806)257-3451
Ultimate Parent: Liberty National Bancorp. SIC: 6141—Personal Credit Institutions.

East Bernard

★ 84725 ★ Ring Around Prdts Inc.
20205 Fm Rd. 1164
East Bernard, TX 77435
(409)335-7561
Ultimate Parent: Occidental Petroleum Corp. SIC: 2044—Rice Milling.

East Houston

★ 84726 ★ Witco Corp.
Kendall-Amalie
4411 Eastpark Dr.
East Houston, TX 77028
Ultimate Parent: Witco Corp. SIC: 2200—Textile Mill Products.

Eastland

★ 84727 ★ Exxon Distributor
204 N. Rosswood St.
Eastland, TX 76448
(817)629-1551
Ultimate Parent: Exxon. SIC: 5172—Petroleum Products Nec.

★ 84728 ★ Greyhound Bus Lines
1004 W. Main St.
Eastland, TX 76448
(817)629-1272
Ultimate Parent: Greyhound Lines Inc. SIC: 4131—Intercity & Rural Bus Transportation.

★ 84729 ★ Lone Star Gas Co.
308 7th S
Eastland, TX 76448
(817)629-1280
Ultimate Parent: Enserch.

★ 84730 ★ Trailways Bus System
1004 W. Main St.
Eastland, TX 76448
(817)629-1044
Ultimate Parent: Greyhound Lines Inc. SIC: 4142—Bus Charter Service Except Local.

Edinburg

★ 84731 ★ Arco Oil & Gas Co.
N. Hwy. 281
Edinburg, TX 78539
(210)383-2032
Location Type: Branch office. Ultimate Parent: Atlantic Richfield Co., Inc. SIC: 4924—Natural Gas Distribution.

★ 84732 ★ First State Bank & Trust Co.
100 E. Cano St.
Edinburg, TX 78539
(512)383-0101
Ultimate Parent: Michigan National Corp. SIC: 6022—State Commercial Banks.

★ 84733 ★ International Paper
1501 N. Closner
Edinburg, TX 78539
Ultimate Parent: International Paper Co. SIC: 2653—Corrugated & Solid Fiber Boxes.

★ 84734 ★ **Kentucky Fried Chicken**
322 S. Closner Blvd.
Edinburg, TX 78539
(512)383-7342
Ultimate Parent: Pepsico. **SIC:** 5812—Eating Places.

★ 84735 ★ **Pizza Hut**
1524 W. University Dr.
Edinburg, TX 78539
(512)381-9144
Ultimate Parent: Pepsico. **SIC:** 5812—Eating Places.

★ 84736 ★ **Pizza Hut**
1802 Closner
Edinburg, TX 78539
(512)381-0991
Ultimate Parent: Pepsico. **SIC:** 5812—Eating Places.

★ 84737 ★ **Shell Oil Co.**
Farm Rd. 490
Edinburg, TX 78539
(512)687-4671
Ultimate Parent: Shell Oil Co. **SIC:** 1311—Crude Petroleum & Natural Gas.

★ 84738 ★ **Texaco Inc. Prod Dept**
919 N. 10th Ave.
Edinburg, TX 78539
(512)383-5151
Ultimate Parent: Texaco. **SIC:** 1311—Crude Petroleum & Natural Gas.

★ 84739 ★ **Texaco Service Station**
501 N. Closner Blvd.
Edinburg, TX 78539
(512)383-1882
Ultimate Parent: Texaco. **SIC:** 5541—Gasoline Service Stations.

★ 84740 ★ **Texaco Service Stations**
615 S. Closner Blvd.
Edinburg, TX 78539
(512)383-1831
Ultimate Parent: Texaco. **SIC:** 5541—Gasoline Service Stations.

★ 84741 ★ **Trailways Bus System**
1005 E. University Dr.
Edinburg, TX 78539
(512)381-8054
Ultimate Parent: Greyhound Lines Inc. **SIC:** 4111—Local & Suburban Transit.

★ 84742 ★ **Wal Mart Disc**
2412 S. Us Hwy. 281
Edinburg, TX 78539
(512)381-0924
Ultimate Parent: Wal-Mart Stores, Inc.

Edna

★ 84743 ★ **Citizens State Bank-Edna of**
701 N. Wells St.
Edna, TX 77957
(512)782-7118
Ultimate Parent: Liberty National Bancorp. **SIC:** 6099—Functions Related to Deposit Banking.

★ 84744 ★ **Mutual of New York**
201 N. Wells St.
Edna, TX 77957
(512)782-7171
Ultimate Parent: Mutual of New York. **SIC:** 6411—Insurance Agents, Brokers & Service.

El Campo

★ 84745 ★ **Coca Cola Bottling Co.**
1001 W. Jackson St.
El Campo, TX 77437
(409)543-2522
Ultimate Parent: Coca-Cola Enterprises. **SIC:** 5149—Groceries & Related Products Nec.

★ 84746 ★ **El Campo Aluminum Co.**
Rte. 3,903 Gladys St.
El Campo, TX 77437
Ultimate Parent: Reynolds Metals Co. **SIC:** 3354—Aluminum Extruded Products.

★ 84747 ★ **El Campo Aluminum Co.**
703 Gladys St.
El Campo, TX 77437
Ultimate Parent: Reynolds Metals Co. **SIC:** 3354—Aluminum Extruded Products.

★ 84748 ★ **First Bank**
1611 N. Mechanic St.
El Campo, TX 77437
(409)543-9400
Ultimate Parent: Shawmut National Corp.

★ 84749 ★ **Pizza Hut**
202 N. Mechanic St.
El Campo, TX 77437
(409)543-4242
Ultimate Parent: Pepsico. **SIC:** 5812—Eating Places.

★ 84750 ★ **Tesoro Petroleum Distribution Co.**
703 Spruce St.
El Campo, TX 77437
(409)543-2715
Ultimate Parent: Tesoro Petroleum Corp. **SIC:** 5172—Petroleum Products Nec.

★ 84751 ★ **Trailways Bus System**
220 Main St.
El Campo, TX 77437
(409)543-3333
Ultimate Parent: Greyhound Lines Inc. **SIC:** 4131—Intercity & Rural Bus Transportation.

★ 84752 ★ **Wal Mart Discount City**
Hwy. 71
El Campo, TX 77437
(409)543-7286
Ultimate Parent: Wal-Mart Stores, Inc. **SIC:** 5311—Department Stores.

★ 84753 ★ **Wal Mart Tire & Battery Ctr**
1504 N. Mechanic St.
El Campo, TX 77437
(409)543-3759
Ultimate Parent: Wal-Mart Stores, Inc. **SIC:** 7538—General Automotive Repair Shops.

El Paso

★ 84754 ★ **A. O. Smith Water Prods. Co.**
401 Frederick Rd.
El Paso, TX 79905
Ultimate Parent: A. O. Smith. **SIC:** 3499—Fabricated Metal Products Nec; 3589—Service Industry Machinery Nec.

★ 84755 ★ **Allen-Bradley Co.**
1414 Allen-Bradley Dr.
El Paso, TX 79936
Ultimate Parent: Rockwell International Corp. **SIC:** 3676—Electronic Resistors; 3624—Carbon & Graphite Products; 3679—Electronic Components Nec.

★ 84756 ★ **American General Finance**
1840 N. Lee Trevino Dr., Ste. 407
El Paso, TX 79936-4119
(915)566-9492
Location Type: Branch office. **Officer:** Eva Sotelo. **Ultimate Parent:** American General Corp. **SIC:** 6141—Personal Credit Institutions.

★ 84757 ★ **American General Finance Inc.**
1840 N. Lee Trevino Dr., Ste. 407
El Paso, TX 79936-4119
(915)566-9492
Location Type: Branch office. **Officer:** Eva Sotelo. **Ultimate Parent:** American General Corp. **SIC:** 6141—Personal Credit Institutions.

★ 84758 ★ **Armour Swift-Eckrich**
300 N. Concepcion
PO Box 10718
El Paso, TX 79997
(915)779-3072
Company Type: Division. **Location Type:** Plant. **Officer:** Greg Brakke, General Manager. **Ultimate Parent:** Conagra.

★ 84759 ★ **Asarco Inc.**
2301 W. Paisano Dr.
El Paso, TX 79922-1622
(915)541-1800
Company Type: Branch. **Officer:** Billy R.

Sloss. **Ultimate Parent:** Asarco. **SIC:** 3339—Primary Nonferrous Metals Nec.

★ 84760 ★ **Asarco Inc.**
El Paso
2301 W. Paisano
El Paso, TX 79922-1622
Company Type: Division. **Ultimate Parent:** Asarco. **SIC:** 3331—Primary Copper.

★ 84761 ★ **Asarco Inc.**
El Paso
PO Box 1111
El Paso, TX 79999
Company Type: Division. **Ultimate Parent:** Asarco. **SIC:** 3331—Primary Copper.

★ 84762 ★ **Atchison, Topeka & Santa Fe Railway Co.**
4150 Pinnacle St.
El Paso, TX 79902
(915)533-8421
Ultimate Parent: Santa Fe Pacific Corp. **SIC:** 4119—Local Passenger Transportation Nec.

★ 84763 ★ **Atchison, Topeka & Santa Fe Railway Co.**
805 S. Santa Fe St.
El Paso, TX 79901
(915)534-2364
Ultimate Parent: Santa Fe Pacific Corp.

★ 84764 ★ **Avon Products Inc.**
1505 Wyoming Ave.
El Paso, TX 79902
(915)533-1822
Ultimate Parent: Avon Products, Inc. **SIC:** 5999—Miscellaneous Retail Stores Nec.

★ 84765 ★ **Baxter Healthcare Corp.**
1 Butterfield Trl. Blvd.
El Paso, TX 79906-4901
(915)779-3681
Location Type: Branch office. **Officer:** Tony Oniel. **Ultimate Parent:** Baxter International. **SIC:** 2399—Fabricated Textile Products Nec; 5047—Medical & Hospital Equipment.

★ 84766 ★ **Bell Atlantic Business Services**
4105 Rio Bravo St., Ste. 180
El Paso, TX 79902-1011
(915)533-3804
Officer: Ernesto Zapien III. **Ultimate Parent:** Bell Atlantic Corp. **SIC:** 7378—Computer Maintenance & Repair; 5112—Stationery & Office Supplies; 8742—Management Consulting Services.

★ 84767 ★ **Bell Atlantic Mobile**
423 Executive Ctr. Blvd.
El Paso, TX 79902-1003
(915)532-5559
Location Type: Branch office. **Officer:** Ron Pullen. **Ultimate Parent:** Bell Atlantic Corp. **SIC:** 4812—Radiotelephone Communications; 4813—Telephone Communications Except Radiotelephone; 5999—Miscellaneous Retail Stores Nec.

★ 84768 ★ **Beneficial Texas Inc.**
1030 N. Zaragoza Rd.
El Paso, TX 79907-1823
(915)860-8086
Ultimate Parent: Beneficial. **SIC:** 6141—Personal Credit Institutions.

★ 84769 ★ **Beneficial Texas, Inc.**
5557 Alameda Ave.
El Paso, TX 79905-2915
(915)779-1999
Location Type: Branch office. **Officer:** Adolfo H. Gameros. **Ultimate Parent:** Beneficial. **SIC:** 6141—Personal Credit Institutions.

★ 84770 ★ **Boeing Co. the**
7500 Viscount Blvd.
El Paso, TX 79925
(915)775-2538
Ultimate Parent: Boeing. **SIC:** 8731—Commercial Physical Research.

★ 84771 ★ **Borden Inc.**
6982 Alameda Ave.
El Paso, TX 79915
(915)772-2751
Officer: Jesus Salabar, Manager. **Ultimate Parent:** Borden, Inc. **SIC:** 2024—Ice Cream & Frozen Desserts; 2026—Fluid Milk; 2086—Bottled & Canned Soft Drinks.

★ 84772 ★ **Borden Inc.**
Dairy
6982 Alameda Ave.
El Paso, TX 79915-3438
Company Type: Division. **Ultimate Parent:** Borden, Inc. **SIC:** 5143—Dairy Products Except Dried or Canned.

★ 84773 ★ **Borden Inc.**
Dairy
6982 Alameda Ave.
El Paso, TX 79915-3438
Company Type: Division. **Ultimate Parent:** Borden, Inc. **SIC:** 5143—Dairy Products Except Dried or Canned.

★ 84774 ★ **Borden Inc.**
Grocery & Specialty Products
6982 Alameda Ave.
El Paso, TX 79915-3438
Company Type: Division. **Ultimate Parent:** Borden, Inc. **SIC:** 5143—Dairy Products Except Dried or Canned.

★ 84775 ★ **Builders Square**
9521 Viscount Blvd.
El Paso, TX 79925
(915)598-9193
Company Type: Subsidiary. **Ultimate Parent:** K-Mart. **SIC:** 5039—Construction Materials Nec.

★ 84776 ★ **Burlington Air Express**
6501 Convair Rd.
El Paso, TX 79925
(915)779-2623
Ultimate Parent: Pittston. **SIC:** 4513—Air Courier Services.

★ 84777 ★ **Burlington Coat Factory Warehouse**
1323 N. Lee Trevino Dr.
El Paso, TX 79936-6416
(915)591-0333
Ultimate Parent: Burlington Industries, Equity. **SIC:** 5311—Department Stores.

★ 84778 ★ **Butler Paper Co.**
3845 Durazno Ave.
El Paso, TX 79905-1303
(915)532-6905
Location Type: Branch office. **Officer:** George J. Minellono. **Ultimate Parent:** Alco Standard Corp. **SIC:** 5113—Industrial & Personal Service Paper.

★ 84779 ★ **Casual Corner**
8401 Cielo Vis
El Paso, TX 79925
(915)779-6383
Ultimate Parent: United States Shoe. **SIC:** 5651—Family Clothing Stores.

★ 84780 ★ **Chevron Corp. El Paso Asphalt Refinery**
6550 Gateway E.
El Paso, TX 79905
Ultimate Parent: Chevron Corp. **SIC:** 2951—Asphalt Paving Mixtures & Blocks.

★ 84781 ★ **Chevron USA Inc.**
El Paso Refinery
6501 Trowbridge Dr.
El Paso, TX 79905
Ultimate Parent: Chevron Corp. **SIC:** 2911—Petroleum Refining; 2951—Asphalt Paving Mixtures & Blocks.

★ 84782 ★ **Chevron USA Inc. El Paso Terminal**
6501 Trowbridge Dr.
El Paso, TX 79905
Ultimate Parent: Chevron Corp. **SIC:** 5171—Petroleum Bulk Stations & Terminals.

★ 84783 ★ **Circus World Toy**
8401 Gateway Blvd. W
El Paso, TX 79925
(915)779-6730
Ultimate Parent: Melville.

★ 84784 ★ **Circus World Toys**
8401 Cielo Vis
El Paso, TX 79925
(915)779-5493
Ultimate Parent: Melville. **SIC:** 5945—Hobby, Toy & Game Shops.

★ 84785 ★ **Coast to Coast Express**
1301 Horizon Blvd.
El Paso, TX 79927
(915)852-3577
Ultimate Parent: Servistar Corp. **SIC:** 4212—Local Trucking Without Storage.

★ 84786 ★ **Dale Electronics Inc.**
26728 PO Box
El Paso, TX 79926
Ultimate Parent: Vishay Intertechnology, Inc. **SIC:** 3679—Electronic Components Nec; 5065—Electronic Parts & Equipment Nec.

★ 84787 ★ **Delta Air Cargo**
6501 Convair Rd.
El Paso, TX 79925
(915)779-8050
Ultimate Parent: Delta Air Lines, Inc. **SIC:** 4513—Air Courier Services.

★ 84788 ★ **Delta Air Lines**
International Airport
El Paso, TX 79925
(915)779-2288
Ultimate Parent: Delta Air Lines, Inc. **SIC:** 4512—Air Transportation—Scheduled.

★ 84789 ★ **Dewalt Industrial Tool Co.**
6822 Gateway Blvd. E.
El Paso, TX 79915-1007
(915)778-9768
Ultimate Parent: Black & Decker Corp. **SIC:** 5085—Industrial Supplies.

★ 84790 ★ **Diesel Recon Co.**
20 Zane Grey
El Paso, TX 79906-4809
Ultimate Parent: Cummins Engine Co. **SIC:** 3714—Motor Vehicle Parts & Accessories.

★ 84791 ★ **Digital Equipment Corp.**
4100 Rio Bravo St.
El Paso, TX 79902
(915)544-6211
Ultimate Parent: Digital Equipment Corp. **SIC:** 5046—Commercial Equipment Nec.

★ 84792 ★ **EDUSA Corp.**
10830 Pellicano Dr.
El Paso, TX 79935-4602
(915)592-9425 **Fax:** (915)593-3591
Officer: Larry Lair, Plant Manager. **Ultimate Parent:** Minnesota Mining & Mfg.

★ 84793 ★ **El Paso Natural Gas Inc.**
304 Texas St., No. 1
El Paso, TX 79901
(915)541-2600
Officer: Richard M. Bressler, Chairman. **Ultimate Parent:** Burlington Resources. **SIC:** 2911—Petroleum Refining.

★ 84794 ★ **El Paso Refining Inc.**
6500 Trowbridge Dr.
El Paso, TX 79905
(915)772-1433
Officer: David Jones, President. **Ultimate Parent:** Burlington Resources. **SIC:** 2911—Petroleum Refining.

★ 84795 ★ **Emery Worldwide**
6501 Convair Rd.
El Paso, TX 79925
(915)779-7111
Ultimate Parent: Consolidated Freightways. **SIC:** 4512—Air Transportation—Scheduled.

★ 84796 ★ **Express**
750 Sunland Park Dr.
El Paso, TX 79912
(915)584-0038
Ultimate Parent: Limited. **SIC:** 5621—Women's Clothing Stores.

★ 84797 ★ **Express Ltd.**
8401 Gateway Blvd. W
El Paso, TX 79925
(915)779-2812
Ultimate Parent: Limited.

★ 84798 ★ **Exxon**
7770 Alabama St.
El Paso, TX 79904
(915)751-8741
Ultimate Parent: Exxon. **SIC:** 5541—Gasoline Service Stations.

★ 84799 ★ **Exxon Co. USA**
1042 Humble Pl
El Paso, TX 79915
(915)772-1409
Ultimate Parent: Exxon. **SIC:** 5541—Gasoline Service Stations.

★ 84800 ★ **Flowers Baking Co. of El Paso Inc.**
PO Box 1768
El Paso, TX 79949
(915)771-6262 **Fax:** (915)771-6262
Company Type: Subsidiary. **Officer:** Shelby Strickland, President. **Ultimate Parent:** Flowers Industries.

★ 84801 ★ **Foot Action**
750 Sunland Park Dr.
El Paso, TX 79912
(915)833-8112
Ultimate Parent: Melville. **SIC:** 5941—Sporting Goods & Bicycle Shops.

★ 84802 ★ **Foot Action for Kids**
8401 Cielo Vis
El Paso, TX 79925
(915)772-9655
Ultimate Parent: Melville. **SIC:** 5661—Shoe Stores.

★ 84803 ★ **Foot Action U S a**
8401 Cielo Vis
El Paso, TX 79925
(915)772-9661
Ultimate Parent: Melville. **SIC:** 5661—Shoe Stores.

★ 84804 ★ **The Gap**
8401 Gateway Blvd. W
El Paso, TX 79925
(915)778-9568
Ultimate Parent: GAP.

★ 84805 ★ **The Gap**
Cielo Vis
El Paso, TX 79925
(915)778-9568
Ultimate Parent: GAP. **SIC:** 5611—Men's & Boys' Clothing Stores.

★ 84806 ★ **Gap Stores**
Cielo Vis
El Paso, TX 79925
(915)778-9568
Ultimate Parent: GAP. **SIC:** 5611—Men's & Boys' Clothing Stores.

★ 84807 ★ **Greyhound Bus Lines**
111 San Francisco Ave.
El Paso, TX 79901
(915)544-7200
Ultimate Parent: Greyhound Lines Inc. **SIC:** 4111—Local & Suburban Transit; 4131—Intercity & Rural Bus Transportation.

★ 84808 ★ **Greyhound Bus Lines**
212 W. Main Dr.
El Paso, TX 79901
(915)533-9812
Ultimate Parent: Greyhound Lines Inc. **SIC:** 4111—Local & Suburban Transit.

★ 84809 ★ **Hertz**
Rent-A-Car Division
El Ps International Arpr
El Paso, TX 79925
(915)772-4255
Ultimate Parent: Hertz. **SIC:** 7514—Passenger Car Rental.

★ 84810 ★ **Hit or Miss**
Cielo Vis
El Paso, TX 79925
(915)779-9204
Ultimate Parent: TJX. **SIC:** 5621—Women's Clothing Stores.

★ 84811 ★ **Hit or Miss**
1323 N. Lee Trevino Dr.
El Paso, TX 79936
(915)595-0189
Ultimate Parent: TJX. **SIC:** 5621—Women's Clothing Stores; 5651—Family Clothing Stores.

★ 84812 ★ **International Paper**
9301 Billy the Kid
El Paso, TX 79901
Ultimate Parent: International Paper Co. **SIC:** 2653—Corrugated & Solid Fiber Boxes.

★ 84813 ★ **Johnson Controls Inc.**
900 Hawkins Blvd.
El Paso, TX 79915
(915)778-5255
Ultimate Parent: Johnson Controls Inc. **SIC:** 5075—Warm Air Heating & Air-Conditioning; 5084—Industrial Machinery & Equipment.

★ 84814 ★ **Kay Bee Toys**
750 Sunland Park Dr.
El Paso, TX 79912
(915)584-9376
Ultimate Parent: Melville. **SIC:** 5945—Hobby, Toy & Game Shops.

★ 84815 ★ **Kay Bee Toys**
8401 Cielo Vis
El Paso, TX 79925
(915)778-7216
Ultimate Parent: Melville. **SIC:** 5945—Hobby, Toy & Game Shops.

★ 84816 ★ **Kentucky Fried Chicken**
7100 Alameda Ave.
El Paso, TX 79915
(915)772-2628
Ultimate Parent: Pepsico. **SIC:** 5812—Eating Places.

★ 84817 ★ **Kentucky Fried Chicken**
427 Yarbrough Dr.
El Paso, TX 79915
(915)592-2418
Ultimate Parent: Pepsico. **SIC:** 5812—Eating Places.

★ 84818 ★ **Kentucky Fried Chicken**
7940 N. Mesa St.
El Paso, TX 79932
(915)833-8856
Ultimate Parent: Pepsico. **SIC:** 5812—Eating Places.

★ 84819 ★ **Kentucky Fried Chicken**
950 W. Main Dr.
El Paso, TX 79902
(915)886-3420
Ultimate Parent: Pepsico. **SIC:** 5812—Eating Places.

★ 84820 ★ **Kentucky Fried Chicken**
6840 Montana Ave.
El Paso, TX 79925
(915)778-6868
Ultimate Parent: Pepsico. **SIC:** 5812—Eating Places.

★ 84821 ★ **Kentucky Fried Chicken**
5905 N. Mesa St.
El Paso, TX 79912
(915)584-6161
Ultimate Parent: Pepsico. **SIC:** 5812—Eating Places.

★ 84822 ★ **Kentucky Fried Chicken**
3601 Gateway Blvd. W
El Paso, TX 79903
(915)566-0552
Ultimate Parent: Pepsico. **SIC:** 5812—Eating Places.

★ 84823 ★ **Kentucky Fried Chicken**
1202 Mcrae Blvd.
El Paso, TX 79925
(915)591-9098
Ultimate Parent: Pepsico. **SIC:** 5812—Eating Places.

★ 84824 ★ **Kentucky Fried Chicken**
9568 Dyer St.
El Paso, TX 79924
(915)751-7561
Ultimate Parent: Pepsico. **SIC:** 5812—Eating Places.

★ 84825 ★ **Kentucky Fried Chicken**
120 E. Paisano Dr.
El Paso, TX 79901
(915)532-8783
Ultimate Parent: Pepsico. **SIC:** 5812—Eating Places.

★ 84826 ★ **Kentucky Fried Chicken**
5419 Dyer St.
El Paso, TX 79904
(915)562-7414
Ultimate Parent: Pepsico. **SIC:** 5812—Eating Places.

★ 84827 ★ **Kids R US**
6404 N. Mesa St.
El Paso, TX 79912
(915)581-4986
Ultimate Parent: Toys "R" US. **SIC:** 8351—Child Day Care Services.

★ 84828 ★ **Lane Bryant**
8401 Cielo Vis
El Paso, TX 79925
(915)778-6811
Ultimate Parent: Limited. **SIC:** 5651—Family Clothing Stores.

★ 84829 ★ **Lane Bryant**
750 Sunland Park Dr.
El Paso, TX 79912
(915)584-0580
Ultimate Parent: Limited. **SIC:** 5651—Family Clothing Stores.

★ 84830 ★ **Lane Bryant**
6000 Bassett Ctr.
El Paso, TX 79925
(915)772-4425
Ultimate Parent: Limited. **SIC:** 5651—Family Clothing Stores.

★ 84831 ★ **Lens Crafters**
8401 Cielo Vis
El Paso, TX 79925
(915)772-6880
Ultimate Parent: United States Shoe. **SIC:** 5995—Optical Goods Stores.

★ 84832 ★ **Lerner Shop**
9350 Dyer St.
El Paso, TX 79924
(915)755-6769
Ultimate Parent: Limited. **SIC:** 5651—Family Clothing Stores; 5651—Family Clothing Stores.

★ 84833 ★ **Lerner Shop**
101 N. Mesa St.
El Paso, TX 79901
(915)533-6541
Ultimate Parent: Limited. **SIC:** 5651—Family Clothing Stores.

★ 84834 ★ **Lerner Shop**
6000 Bassett Ctr.
El Paso, TX 79925
(915)772-7518
Ultimate Parent: Limited. **SIC:** 5651—Family Clothing Stores.

★ 84835 ★ **Lerner Shop**
8401 Cielo Vis
El Paso, TX 79925
(915)779-0116
Ultimate Parent: Limited. **SIC:** 5651—Family Clothing Stores.

★ 84836 ★ **Lerner Shop**
Bassett Ctr.
El Paso, TX 79901
(915)772-7518
Ultimate Parent: Limited. **SIC:** 5621—Women's Clothing Stores.

★ 84837 ★ **Liberty Mutual Insurance Co.**
4150 Pinnacle St.
El Paso, TX 79902
(915)532-5681
Ultimate Parent: Liberty Mutual Group. **SIC:** 6411—Insurance Agents, Brokers & Service.

★ 84838 ★ **The Limited**
750 Sunland Park Dr.
El Paso, TX 79912
(915)833-5067
Ultimate Parent: Limited. **SIC:** 5651—Family Clothing Stores.

★ 84839 ★ **The Limited**
6000 Bassett Ctr.
El Paso, TX 79925
(915)772-6686
Ultimate Parent: Limited. **SIC:** 5651—Family Clothing Stores.

★ 84840 ★ The Limited
8401 Cielo Vis
El Paso, TX 79925
(915)772-5036
Ultimate Parent: Limited. SIC: 5651—
Family Clothing Stores.

★ 84841 ★ The Limited
8401 Gateway Blvd. W
El Paso, TX 79925
(915)772-5036
Ultimate Parent: Limited.

★ 84842 ★ The Limited Express
8401 Cielo Vis
El Paso, TX 79925
(915)779-2812
Ultimate Parent: Limited. SIC: 2339—
Women's/Misses' Outerwear Nec.

★ 84843 ★ The Limited Express
6000 Bassett Ctr.
El Paso, TX 79925
(915)778-1511
Ultimate Parent: Limited. SIC: 5651—
Family Clothing Stores.

★ 84844 ★ Magnetek Inc.
1168 Barranca Dr.
El Paso, TX 79935-5002
(915)593-1621
Officer: Richard D. Meyer. Ultimate
Parent: Magnetek Inc. SIC: 3621—Motors
& Generators.

★ 84845 ★ Manufacturers
Folding Carton
1100 Kessler Dr.
El Paso, TX 79907
Ultimate Parent: Stone Container Corp.
SIC: 2657—Folding Paperboard Boxes.

★ 84846 ★ Mary Kay Cosmetics
1200 Golden Key Cir.
El Paso, TX 79925
(915)591-5884
Ultimate Parent: Mary Kay Cosmetics. SIC:
5999—Miscellaneous Retail Stores Nec.

★ 84847 ★ Mary Kay Cosmetics
209 Mardi Gras Dr.
El Paso, TX 79912
(915)584-4070
Ultimate Parent: Mary Kay Cosmetics. SIC:
5999—Miscellaneous Retail Stores Nec.

★ 84848 ★ Massachusetts Mutual
Life Insurance
4150 Pinnacle St.
El Paso, TX 79902
(915)533-1656
Ultimate Parent: Massasucetts Mutual Life.
SIC: 6411—Insurance Agents, Brokers &
Service.

★ 84849 ★ McDonalds
625 N. Zaragosa Rd.
El Paso, TX 79907
(915)859-4910
Ultimate Parent: McDonald's.

★ 84850 ★ McDonalds
1274 Horizon Blvd.
El Paso, TX 79927
(915)858-6048
Ultimate Parent: McDonald's.

★ 84851 ★ Mcduff Electronics
750 Sunland Park Dr.
El Paso, TX 79912
(915)585-0499
Ultimate Parent: Tandy Corp.

★ 84852 ★ Mcduff Electronics
8401 Gateway Blvd. W
El Paso, TX 79925
(915)779-7900
Ultimate Parent: Tandy Corp.

★ 84853 ★ Metro Mobile CTS of
El Paso, Inc.
423 Executive Ctr. Blvd.
El Paso, TX 79902
(915)532-5559
Ultimate Parent: Bell Atlantic Corp. SIC:
4812—Radiotelephone Communications.

★ 84854 ★ Mutual of New York
Money
9440 Viscount Blvd.
El Paso, TX 79925
(915)592-9400
Ultimate Parent: Mutual of New York. SIC:
6411—Insurance Agents, Brokers &
Service.

★ 84855 ★ Navajo Refing Co.
897 Hawkins Blvd.
El Paso, TX 79915
(915)778-1028
Ultimate Parent: Holly Corp.

★ 84856 ★ Navajo Refining Co.
1000 Eastside Rd.
El Paso, TX 79915
(915)772-3161
Ultimate Parent: Holly Corp. SIC: 2911—
Petroleum Refining.

★ 84857 ★ Navajo Refining Co.
1810 N. Zaragosa Rd.
El Paso, TX 79936
(915)857-0011
Ultimate Parent: Holly Corp. SIC: 2911—
Petroleum Refining.

★ 84858 ★ New England Mutl
Life Insurance C
Bassett
El Paso, TX 79901
(915)544-8161
Ultimate Parent: New England Mutual Life.
SIC: 6411—Insurance Agents, Brokers &
Service.

★ 84859 ★ New York Life El Paso
General Office
Western Agencies
State National Plz.
221 N. Kansas St., Ste. 1000
El Paso, TX 79901
(915)534-3276 Fax: (915)534-3263
Officer: Albert C. Iovinelli, General
Manager. Ultimate Parent: New York Life.

★ 84860 ★ Otis Elevator Co.
611 N. Stanton St.
El Paso, TX 79901
(915)533-9533
Ultimate Parent: United Technologies. SIC:
5084—Industrial Machinery & Equipment.

★ 84861 ★ Otis Elevator Co.
9121 Airport Rd.
El Paso, TX 79925
(915)775-0847
Ultimate Parent: United Technologies. SIC:
1796—Installing Building Equipment Nec.

★ 84862 ★ Payless Shoesource
6022 Aztec Rd.
El Paso, TX 79925
(915)778-4940
Ultimate Parent: May Department Stores.
SIC: 5661—Shoe Stores.

★ 84863 ★ Payless Shoesource
6000 Bassett Ctr.
El Paso, TX 79925
(915)779-1134
Ultimate Parent: May Department Stores.
SIC: 5661—Shoe Stores.

★ 84864 ★ Payless Shoesource
7176 Alameda Ave.
El Paso, TX 79915
(915)778-6981
Ultimate Parent: May Department Stores.
SIC: 5632—Women's Accessory &
Specialty Stores; 5661—Shoe Stores.

★ 84865 ★ Payless Shoesource
9839 Dyer St.
El Paso, TX 79924
(915)755-7278
Ultimate Parent: May Department Stores.
SIC: 5661—Shoe Stores.

★ 84866 ★ Payless Shoesource
5523 Alameda Ave.
El Paso, TX 79905
(915)778-3719
Ultimate Parent: May Department Stores.
SIC: 5661—Shoe Stores.

★ 84867 ★ Payless Shoesource
725 Sunland Pk. Dr.
El Paso, TX 79912
Ultimate Parent: May Department Stores.
SIC: 5661—Shoe Stores.

★ 84868 ★ Payless Shoesource
119 S. Stanton St.
El Paso, TX 79901
(915)533-0371
Ultimate Parent: May Department Stores.
SIC: 5661—Shoe Stores.

★ 84869 ★ Payless Shoesource
8401 Dyer St.
El Paso, TX 79904
(915)755-6055
Ultimate Parent: May Department Stores.
SIC: 5661—Shoe Stores.

★ 84870 ★ Payless Shoesource
800 S. El Paso St.
El Paso, TX 79901
(915)544-1309
Ultimate Parent: May Department Stores.
SIC: 5661—Shoe Stores.

★ 84871 ★ Payless Shoesource
10501 Gateway Blvd. W
El Paso, TX 79925
(915)594-0722
Ultimate Parent: May Department Stores.
SIC: 5661—Shoe Stores.

★ 84872 ★ Payless Shoesource
2904 Alameda Ave.
El Paso, TX 79905
(915)542-0076
Ultimate Parent: May Department Stores.
SIC: 5661—Shoe Stores.

★ 84873 ★ Pepsi-Cola Bottling
Co.
401 Raynolds St.
El Paso, TX 79905
(915)532-6965
Ultimate Parent: Pepsico. SIC: 2086—
Bottled & Canned Soft Drinks.

★ 84874 ★ Peyton Packing Co.
PO Box 9066
El Paso, TX 79982
(915)858-6632 Fax: (915)858-8005
Company Type: Subsidiary. Officer: Keith
Veale, General Manager. Ultimate Parent:
American Financial. SIC: 2011—Meat
Packing Plants; 2013—Sausages & Other
Prepared Meats. Employee Count: 14.

★ 84875 ★ Peyton Packing Co.
Inc.
6930 Market Ave.
El Paso, TX 79915
(915)778-9524
Ultimate Parent: Chiquita Brands
International. SIC: 2011—Meat Packing
Plants.

★ 84876 ★ Phelps Dodge Copper
Products
897 Hawkins Blvd.
El Paso, TX 79915
Ultimate Parent: Phelps Dodge. SIC:
3351—Copper Rolling & Drawing; 3331—
Primary Copper.

★ 84877 ★ Phelps Dodge
Refining Corp.
North Loop Rd. PO Box 20001
El Paso, TX 79998
Ultimate Parent: Phelps Dodge. SIC:
3331—Primary Copper; 2819—Industrial
Inorganic Chemicals Nec; 3339—Primary
Nonferrous Metals Nec.

★ 84878 ★ Phelps Dodge
Refining Corp.
El Paso Works
6999 N. Loop Rd. PO Box 20001
El Paso, TX 79915
Company Type: Division. Ultimate Parent:
Phelps Dodge. SIC: 3331—Primary Copper;
2819—Industrial Inorganic Chemicals Nec;
3339—Primary Nonferrous Metals Nec.

★ 84879 ★ Pizza Hut
1071 N. Carolina Dr.
El Paso, TX 79915
(915)592-9929
Ultimate Parent: Pepsico. SIC: 5812—
Eating Places.

★ 84880 ★ Pizza Hut
3545 N. Yarbrough Dr.
El Paso, TX 79925
(915)591-2012
Ultimate Parent: Pepsico. SIC: 5812—
Eating Places.

★ 84881 ★ Pizza Hut
1626 N. Yarbough Dr.
El Paso, TX 79925
(915)591-8143
Ultimate Parent: Pepsico. SIC: 5812—
Eating Places.

★ 84882 ★ Pizza Hut
6115 N. Mesa St.
El Paso, TX 79912
Ultimate Parent: Pepsico. SIC: 5812—
Eating Places.

★ 84883 ★ Pizza Hut
7960 N. Mesa St.
El Paso, TX 79932
(915)584-5574
Ultimate Parent: Pepsico. SIC: 5812—
Eating Places.

★ 84884 ★ Pizza Hut
2000 N. Lee Trevino Dr.
El Paso, TX 79936
(915)593-8950
Ultimate Parent: Pepsico.

★ 84885 ★ Pizza Hut
2915 N. Mesa St.
El Paso, TX 79902
(915)544-9818
Ultimate Parent: Pepsico. SIC: 5812—
Eating Places.

★ 84886 ★ Pizza Hut
5201 Montana Ave.
El Paso, TX 79903
(915)562-1177
Ultimate Parent: Pepsico.

★ 84887 ★ Pizza Hut
6702 Montana Ave.
El Paso, TX 79925
(915)778-9103
Ultimate Parent: Pepsico. SIC: 5812—
Eating Places.

★ 84888 ★ Pizza Hut
1800 George Dieter Dr.
El Paso, TX 79936
(915)857-7663
Ultimate Parent: Pepsico. SIC: 5812—
Eating Places.

★ 84889 ★ Pizza Hut
1104 Mcrae Blvd.
El Paso, TX 79925
(915)591-2322
Ultimate Parent: Pepsico. SIC: 5812—
Eating Places.

★ 84890 ★ Pizza Hut
8100 Dyer St.
El Paso, TX 79904
(915)757-0323
Ultimate Parent: Pepsico. SIC: 5812—
Eating Places.

★ 84891 ★ Pizza Hut
9757 Dyer St.
El Paso, TX 79924
(915)757-0321
Ultimate Parent: Pepsico. SIC: 5812—
Eating Places.

★ 84892 ★ Pizza Hut
6940 Alameda Ave.
El Paso, TX 79915
(915)778-2775
Ultimate Parent: Pepsico. SIC: 5812—
Eating Places.

★ 84893 ★ Pizza Hut
8731 Alameda Ave.
El Paso, TX 79907
(915)859-4889
Ultimate Parent: Pepsico. SIC: 5812—
Eating Places.

★ 84894 ★ Pizza Hut
4201 Alabama St.
El Paso, TX 79930
(915)566-9613
Ultimate Parent: Pepsico. SIC: 5812—
Eating Places.

★ 84895 ★ Price's Creameries
600 N. Piedras St.
El Paso, TX 79903
(713)565-2711
Officer: Gene Carrejo, Vice President.
Ultimate Parent: Dean Foods. SIC: 2022—
Cheese—Natural & Processed; 2023—Dry,
Condensed & Evaporated Dairy Products;
2024—Ice Cream & Frozen Desserts.

★ 84896 ★ Radio Shack
8500 Sunrise Shopping Ctr.
El Paso, TX 79904
(915)757-0784
Company Type: Division. Ultimate Parent:
Tandy Corp. SIC: 5065—Electronic Parts &
Equipment Nec.

★ 84897 ★   Radio Shack
1214 Wedgewood Dr.
El Paso, TX 79925
(915)594-0756
Company Type: Division. Ultimate Parent:
Tandy Corp. SIC: 5731—Radio, Television
& Electronics Stores.

★ 84898 ★   Radio Shack
3315 Quanah Pl
El Paso, TX 79936
Company Type: Division. Ultimate Parent:
Tandy Corp. SIC: 5046—Commercial
Equipment Nec.

★ 84899 ★   Radio Shack
750 Sunland Park Dr.
El Paso, TX 79912
(915)581-4388
Company Type: Division. Ultimate Parent:
Tandy Corp. SIC: 5065—Electronic Parts &
Equipment Nec.

★ 84900 ★   Radio Shack
800 N. Zaragosa Rd.
El Paso, TX 79907
(915)859-1907
Company Type: Division. Ultimate Parent:
Tandy Corp. SIC: 5731—Radio, Television
& Electronics Stores.

★ 84901 ★   Radio Shack
Plaza Motor Htl
El Paso, TX 79949
(915)533-3209
Company Type: Division. Ultimate Parent:
Tandy Corp. SIC: 5731—Radio, Television
& Electronics Stores.

★ 84902 ★   Radio Shack
6524 N. Mesa St.
El Paso, TX 79912
(915)581-4908
Company Type: Division. Ultimate Parent:
Tandy Corp. SIC: 5731—Radio, Television
& Electronics Stores.

★ 84903 ★   Radio Shack
1188 N. Yarbrough Dr.
El Paso, TX 79925
(915)591-8101
Company Type: Division. Ultimate Parent:
Tandy Corp. SIC: 5065—Electronic Parts &
Equipment Nec.

★ 84904 ★   Radio Shack
222 N. Mesa St.
El Paso, TX 79901
(915)533-3209
Company Type: Division. Ultimate Parent:
Tandy Corp. SIC: 5065—Electronic Parts &
Equipment Nec.

★ 84905 ★   Radio Shack
3737 N. Mesa St.
El Paso, TX 79902
(915)532-5780
Company Type: Division. Ultimate Parent:
Tandy Corp. SIC: 5065—Electronic Parts &
Equipment Nec.

★ 84906 ★   Radio Shack
5014 Montana Ave.
El Paso, TX 79903
(915)779-5099
Company Type: Division. Ultimate Parent:
Tandy Corp. SIC: 5065—Electronic Parts &
Equipment Nec.

★ 84907 ★   Radio Shack
1443 N. Lee Trevino Dr.
El Paso, TX 79936
(915)592-4521
Company Type: Division. Ultimate Parent:
Tandy Corp. SIC: 5065—Electronic Parts &
Equipment Nec.

★ 84908 ★   Radio Shack
85 Charles Bassett Cent
El Paso, TX 79925
(915)778-7965
Company Type: Division. Ultimate Parent:
Tandy Corp. SIC: 5065—Electronic Parts &
Equipment Nec.

★ 84909 ★   Radio Shack
8401 Cielo Vis
El Paso, TX 79925
(915)779-3691
Company Type: Division. Ultimate Parent:
Tandy Corp. SIC: 5065—Electronic Parts &
Equipment Nec.

★ 84910 ★   Radio Shack
5521 Alameda Ave.
El Paso, TX 79905
(915)774-0303
Company Type: Division. Ultimate Parent:
Tandy Corp.

★ 84911 ★   Radio Shack
85 Bassett Ctr.
El Paso, TX 79925
(915)778-4247
Company Type: Division. Ultimate Parent:
Tandy Corp. SIC: 5734—Computer &
Software Stores.

★ 84912 ★   Radio Shack
3315 Quanah Pl
El Paso, TX 79936
Company Type: Division. Ultimate Parent:
Tandy Corp. SIC: 5065—Electronic Parts &
Equipment Nec.

★ 84913 ★   Raytheon Service Co.
7201 Lockheed Dr.
El Paso, TX 79925
(915)779-7666
Ultimate Parent: Raytheon Co. SIC:
7629—Electrical Repair Shops Nec.

★ 84914 ★   Rockwell
9566 Railroad Dr.
El Paso, TX 79924
Ultimate Parent: Rockwell International
Corp. SIC: 3679—Electronic Components
Nec.

★ 84915 ★   Rockwell International
9566 Railroad Dr.
El Paso, TX 79924
Ultimate Parent: Rockwell International
Corp. SIC: 3679—Electronic Components
Nec.

★ 84916 ★   Rockwell International
Corp.
6 Butterfield Trail
El Paso, TX 79906
Ultimate Parent: Rockwell International
Corp. SIC: 3663—Radio & T.V.
Communications Equipment.

★ 84917 ★   Rockwell International
Corp. Autonetic Electronics
System
9566 Railroad Dr.
El Paso, TX 79924
Ultimate Parent: Rockwell International
Corp. SIC: 3679—Electronic Components
Nec.

★ 84918 ★   Rockwell Int'l Spd/
Ntsd
6 Butterfield Tr.
El Paso, TX 79906
Ultimate Parent: Rockwell International
Corp. SIC: 3663—Radio & T.V.
Communications Equipment.

★ 84919 ★   Ryder Truck Rental
260 Montoya Ln.
El Paso, TX 79932
(915)833-7884
Ultimate Parent: Ryder System. SIC:
7513—Truck Rental & Leasing Without
Drivers.

★ 84920 ★   Ryder Truck Rental
6974 Gateway Blvd. E
El Paso, TX 79915
(915)778-9866
Ultimate Parent: Ryder System. SIC:
7513—Truck Rental & Leasing Without
Drivers.

★ 84921 ★   Ryder Truck Rental
1341 Lomaland Dr.
El Paso, TX 79935
(915)594-4935
Ultimate Parent: Ryder System. SIC:
7513—Truck Rental & Leasing Without
Drivers.

★ 84922 ★   Ryder Truck Rental
6127 N. Mesa St.
El Paso, TX 79912
(915)833-2949
Ultimate Parent: Ryder System.

★ 84923 ★   Ryder Truck Rental
10105 Dyer St.
El Paso, TX 79924
(915)751-1850
Ultimate Parent: Ryder System.

★ 84924 ★   Ryder Truck Rental
6121 Montana Ave.
El Paso, TX 79925
(915)779-7184
Ultimate Parent: Ryder System.

★ 84925 ★   Safety Kleen Corp.
900 Hawkins Blvd.
El Paso, TX 79915
(915)778-8773
Ultimate Parent: Safety-Kleen. SIC: 2899—
Chemical Preparations Nec; 7359—
Equipment Rental & Leasing Nec.

★ 84926 ★   Sam's Wholesale
Club
11360 Pellicano Dr.
El Paso, TX 79936
(915)591-6687
Ultimate Parent: Wal-Mart Stores, Inc. SIC:
5399—Miscellaneous General Merchandise
Store.

★ 84927 ★   Shell Oil Co.
6767 Gateway Blvd. W
El Paso, TX 79925
(915)778-3376
Ultimate Parent: Shell Oil Co. SIC: 1311—
Crude Petroleum & Natural Gas.

★ 84928 ★   Shell Pipeline Corp.
6767 Gateway Blvd. W
El Paso, TX 79925
(915)778-6497
Ultimate Parent: Shell Oil Co. SIC: 4619—
Pipelines Nec; 4789—Transportation
Services Nec; 5812—Eating Places.

★ 84929 ★   Shell Pipeline Corp.
6767 Gateway Blvd. W
El Paso, TX 79925
(915)778-6497
Ultimate Parent: Shell Oil Co. SIC: 4619—
Pipelines Nec; 4789—Transportation
Services Nec; 5812—Eating Places.

★ 84930 ★   Shell Self Serve
3232 W. Illinois
El Paso, TX 79930
(915)330-9511
Ultimate Parent: Shell Oil Co. SIC: 5541—
Gasoline Service Stations.

★ 84931 ★   Southwest Airlines
Co.
International Airport
El Paso, TX 79925
(915)779-7174
Ultimate Parent: Southwest Airlines. SIC:
4512—Air Transportation—Scheduled.

★ 84932 ★   Star-Kist Foods, Inc.
4707 Fred Wilson Rd.
El Paso, TX 79936
(915)562-8500
Company Type: Subsidiary. Location
Type: Facility. Officer: B. Bullock, Plant
General Manager. Ultimate Parent: H.J.
Heinz.

★ 84933 ★   Stop & Shop Grocery
6266 Alameda Ave.
El Paso, TX 79905
(915)772-8012
Ultimate Parent: Stop & Shop. SIC: 5411—
Grocery Stores.

★ 84934 ★   Sunwest Bank of El
Paso
1301 N. Lee Trevino Dr.
El Paso, TX 79936
(915)598-1200
Ultimate Parent: Boatmen's Bancshares.

★ 84935 ★   Sunwest Bank of El
Paso
416 N. Stanton St.
El Paso, TX 79901-1236
(915)544-1420
Company Type: Subsidiary. Officer: David
M. Graham, Chairman of the Board &
President. Ultimate Parent: Boatmen's
Bancshares. SIC: 6022—State Commercial
Banks. Employee Count: 134.

★ 84936 ★   Taco Bell
400 Montana Ave.
El Paso, TX 79902
(915)544-9777
Ultimate Parent: Pepsico. SIC: 5812—
Eating Places.

★ 84937 ★   Taco Bell
9505 Viscount Blvd.
El Paso, TX 79925
(915)592-3619
Ultimate Parent: Pepsico. SIC: 5812—
Eating Places.

★ 84938 ★   Taco Bell
2103 N. Mesa St.
El Paso, TX 79902
(915)533-9161
Ultimate Parent: Pepsico. SIC: 5812—
Eating Places.

★ 84939 ★   Taco Bell
6951 N. Mesa St.
El Paso, TX 79912
(915)581-1967
Ultimate Parent: Pepsico. SIC: 5812—
Eating Places.

★ 84940 ★   Taco Bell
9215 Montana Ave.
El Paso, TX 79925
(915)591-8187
Ultimate Parent: Pepsico. SIC: 5812—
Eating Places.

★ 84941 ★   Taco Bell
9620 Montana Ave.
El Paso, TX 79925
(915)591-8677
Ultimate Parent: Pepsico. SIC: 5812—
Eating Places.

★ 84942 ★   Taco Bell
9455 Dyer St.
El Paso, TX 79924
(915)751-4204
Ultimate Parent: Pepsico. SIC: 5812—
Eating Places.

★ 84943 ★   Taco Bell
6130 Montana Ave.
El Paso, TX 79925
(915)772-3574
Ultimate Parent: Pepsico. SIC: 5812—
Eating Places.

★ 84944 ★   Taco Bell
4901 Alameda Ave.
El Paso, TX 79905
(915)772-6768
Ultimate Parent: Pepsico. SIC: 5812—
Eating Places.

★ 84945 ★   Taco Bell
5620 Dyer St.
El Paso, TX 79904
(915)562-2935
Ultimate Parent: Pepsico. SIC: 5812—
Eating Places.

★ 84946 ★   Texaco
10299 Dyer St.
El Paso, TX 79924
(915)755-7891
Ultimate Parent: Texaco. SIC: 5541—
Gasoline Service Stations.

★ 84947 ★   Texas Engineered
Products
990 Kessler Dr.
El Paso, TX 79907-1843
(915)592-1181
Location Type: Branch office. Officer:
Donald Bartley. Ultimate Parent: Aluminum
Co. of America–Alcoa. SIC: 3354—
Aluminum Extruded Products.

★ 84948 ★   Thom Mcan Family
Shoe Store
5533 Alameda Ave.
El Paso, TX 79905
(915)779-9332
Ultimate Parent: Melville. SIC: 5661—Shoe
Stores.

★ 84949 ★   Tonka Corp.
9050 Viscount Blvd.
El Paso, TX 79925
(915)591-9300
Ultimate Parent: Hasbro. SIC: 3944—
Games, Toys & Children's Vehicles.

★ 84950 ★   Tonka Toys
9050 Viscount Blvd.
El Paso, TX 79925
Ultimate Parent: Hasbro. SIC: 3944—
Games, Toys & Children's Vehicles.

★ 84951 ★   Toys R US
801 S. Mesa Hills Dr.
El Paso, TX 79912
(915)833-3459
Ultimate Parent: Toys "R" US.

★ 84952 ★   Trailways Bus System
200 W. San Antonio Ave.
El Paso, TX 79901
(915)533-5921
Ultimate Parent: Greyhound Lines Inc. SIC:
4724—Travel Agencies.

★ 84953 ★   Trailways Inc.
1253 Lomaland Dr.
El Paso, TX 79907
(915)594-1957
Ultimate Parent: Greyhound Lines Inc. SIC:
4131—Intercity & Rural Bus Transportation.

★ 84954 ★   Underwriters
Adjusting Co.
444 Executive Ctr. Blvd.
El Paso, TX 79902
(915)544-1898
Ultimate Parent: Continental. SIC: 6411—
Insurance Agents, Brokers & Service.

★ 84955 ★   Unisys Corp.
4150 Rio Bravo St. 130
El Paso, TX 79902
Ultimate Parent: Unisys Corp.

★ 84956 ★   United Parcel Service
23 Spur Dr.
El Paso, TX 79906
(915)533-9301
Ultimate Parent: United Parcel Service of
America. SIC: 4215—Courier Services
Except by Air.

★ 84957 ★   US Fidelity
6044 Gateway Blvd. E
El Paso, TX 79905
(915)778-7981
Ultimate Parent: USF&G Corp. SIC:
6411—Insurance Agents, Brokers &
Service.

★ 84958 ★   Vickers Inc.
4421 Montana Ave.
El Paso, TX 79903
(915)565-4452
Ultimate Parent: Trinova Corp. SIC:
5541—Gasoline Service Stations.

★ 84959 ★   Vickers Inc.
2725 N. Mesa St.
El Paso, TX 79902
(915)533-1078
Ultimate Parent: Trinova Corp. SIC:
5541—Gasoline Service Stations.

★ 84960 ★   Victoria's Secret
8401 Cielo Vis
El Paso, TX 79925
(915)778-9959
Ultimate Parent: Limited. SIC: 5651—
Family Clothing Stores.

★ 84961 ★   Wal Mart Discount
201 S. Americas Ave.
El Paso, TX 79907
(915)858-2964
Ultimate Parent: Wal-Mart Stores, Inc. SIC:
5311—Department Stores.

★ 84962 ★   Wal Mart Discount
Store
1144 N. Yarbrough Dr.
El Paso, TX 79925
(915)594-0243
Ultimate Parent: Wal-Mart Stores, Inc. SIC:
5311—Department Stores; 5912—Drug
Stores & Proprietary Stores.

★ 84963 ★   Waldenbooks
8401 Cielo Vis
El Paso, TX 79925
(915)779-1677
Ultimate Parent: K-Mart. SIC: 5942—Book
Stores.

★ 84964 ★   Waldenbooks
750 Sunland Park Dr.
El Paso, TX 79912
(915)833-8506
Ultimate Parent: K-Mart. SIC: 5942—Book
Stores.

★ 84965 ★   Waldenbooks
6000 Bassett Ctr.
El Paso, TX 79925
(915)778-5074
Ultimate Parent: K-Mart. SIC: 5942—Book
Stores.

★ 84966 ★   Walgreen
1840 N. Lee Trevino Dr.
El Paso, TX 79936
(915)594-1127
Ultimate Parent: Walgreen Co. SIC:
7384—Photofinishing Laboratories.

★ 84967 ★   Walgreen
9155 Dyer St.
El Paso, TX 79924
(915)751-2494
Ultimate Parent: Walgreen Co. SIC:
5912—Drug Stores & Proprietary Stores.

★ 84968 ★   Walgreen Drug Stores
3355 N. Yarbrough Dr.
El Paso, TX 79925
(915)591-5112
Ultimate Parent: Walgreen Co. SIC:
5912—Drug Stores & Proprietary Stores.

★ 84969 ★   Walgreen Drug Stores
200 N. Mesa St.
El Paso, TX 79901
(915)542-1793
Ultimate Parent: Walgreen Co. SIC:
5912—Drug Stores & Proprietary Stores;
7384—Photofinishing Laboratories.

★ 84970 ★   Walgreen Drug Stores
3100 N. Mesa St.
El Paso, TX 79902
(915)533-5449
Ultimate Parent: Walgreen Co. SIC:
5912—Drug Stores & Proprietary Stores;
7384—Photofinishing Laboratories.

★ 84971 ★   Walgreen Drug Stores
20 Bassett Ctr.
El Paso, TX 79925
(915)778-3120
Ultimate Parent: Walgreen Co. SIC:
5812—Eating Places.

★ 84972 ★   Walgreen Drug Stores
9801 Gateway Blvd. W
El Paso, TX 79925
(915)591-9401
Ultimate Parent: Walgreen Co. SIC:
5812—Eating Places; 5912—Drug Stores &
Proprietary Stores.

★ 84973 ★   Walgreen Drug Stores
5150 Fairbanks Dr.
El Paso, TX 79924
(915)755-9506
Ultimate Parent: Walgreen Co.

★ 84974 ★   Walgreen Pharmacy
2900 Pershing Dr.
El Paso, TX 79903
(915)562-5588
Ultimate Parent: Walgreen Co. SIC:
5912—Drug Stores & Proprietary Stores.

★ 84975 ★   Walgreen Pharmacy
200 N. Mesa St.
El Paso, TX 79901
(915)532-4344
Ultimate Parent: Walgreen Co. SIC:
5912—Drug Stores & Proprietary Stores.

★ 84976 ★   Western Auto Supply
Co.
90 Bassett Ctr.
El Paso, TX 79925
(915)778-5365
Ultimate Parent: Sears Roebuck & Co.
SIC: 5531—Automobile & Home Supply
Stores.

★ 84977 ★   Western Auto Supply
Co. Del
7750 N. Loop Dr.
El Paso, TX 79915
(915)592-5915
Ultimate Parent: Sears Roebuck & Co.
SIC: 5251—Hardware Stores.

★ 84978 ★   Western Auto Supply
Co. No. 7
425 E. Paisano Dr.
El Paso, TX 79901
(915)544-4663
Ultimate Parent: Sears Roebuck & Co.
SIC: 5531—Automobile & Home Supply
Stores.

★ 84979 ★   Wrangler Menswear
7085 Alameda Ave.
El Paso, TX 79915
(915)778-5389
Officer: Dave Rush, Manager. Ultimate
Parent: VF Corp. SIC: 2325—Men's/Boys'
Trousers & Slacks; 2389—Apparel &
Accessories Nec.

★ 84980 ★   Xerox Corp.
7400 Viscount Blvd., Ste. 200
El Paso, TX 79925
(915)755-9400
Officer: Gary Derr, Manager. Ultimate
Parent: Xerox Corp. SIC: 3663—Radio &
T.V. Communications Equipment.

★ 84981 ★   Zenith Electronic
Corp. of T
Zane Grey Blvd.
El Paso, TX 79925
(915)775-1600
Ultimate Parent: Zenith Electronics Corp.

★ 84982 ★   Zenith Electronics
1155 Larry Mahan Dr.
El Paso, TX 79925
(915)593-0685
Ultimate Parent: Zenith Electronics Corp.
SIC: 5065—Electronic Parts & Equipment
Nec.

Eldorado

★ 84983 ★   Arco Oil & Gas Co.
PO Box 638
Eldorado, TX 76936-0638
(915)853-2323
Officer: L. Cook. Ultimate Parent: Atlantic
Richfield Co., Inc. SIC: 2911—Petroleum
Refining.

Electra

★ 84984 ★   Lone Star Gas Co.
108 W. Cleveland Ave.
Electra, TX 76360
(817)495-3702
Ultimate Parent: Enserch. SIC: 4925—Gas
Production & Distribution Nec.

★ 84985 ★   Mobil Credit Union
118 N. Waggoner St.
Electra, TX 76360
(817)495-2216
Ultimate Parent: Mobil. SIC: 6062—State
Credit Unions.

★ 84986 ★   Mobil Oil Co.
Wholesale Dept
600 E. Front Ave.
Electra, TX 76360
(817)495-2326
Ultimate Parent: Mobil. SIC: 5171—
Petroleum Bulk Stations & Terminals.

★ 84987 ★   Mobil Pipe Line Co.
13688 State Hwy. 240 W
Electra, TX 76360
(817)495-2224
Ultimate Parent: Mobil.

★ 84988 ★   Mobil Pipe Line Co.
13688 SH 240
Electra, TX 76360
(817)495-2224
Company Type: Branch. Ultimate Parent:
Mobil. SIC: 4612—Crude Petroleum
Pipelines.

★ 84989 ★   Mobil Pipe Line Co.
Electra, TX 76360
(817)495-2854
Ultimate Parent: Mobil. SIC: 4612—Crude
Petroleum Pipelines.

★ 84990 ★   Texaco Inc.
1 Mile Hwy. 287 W
Electra, TX 76360
(817)495-3694
Ultimate Parent: Texaco. SIC: 5172—
Petroleum Products Nec.

Elmendorf

★ 84991 ★   Golden Aluminum Co.
14555 Old Corpus Christi Rd.
Elmendorf, TX 78112
Ultimate Parent: ACX Technologies. SIC:
3353—Aluminum Sheet, Plate & Foil.

Emory

★ 84992 ★   Piggly Wiggly
Emory, TX 75440
(214)473-2231
Ultimate Parent: Bruno's. SIC: 5411—
Grocery Stores.

Ennis

★ 84993 ★   Ace Hardware Plus
201 SW Main St.
Ennis, TX 75119
(214)875-2721
Ultimate Parent: Ace Hardware. SIC:
5072—Hardware.

★ 84994 ★   Lone Star Gas Co.
2705 N. Kaufman St.
Ennis, TX 75119
(214)875-3876
Ultimate Parent: Enserch.

★ 84995 ★   Manville Sales Corp.
2705 N. Kaufman
Ennis, TX 75119
Ultimate Parent: Manville Corp. SIC:
2297—Nonwoven Fabrics.

★ 84996 ★   Piggly Wiggly
704 W. Ennis Ave.
Ennis, TX 75119
(214)875-5221
Ultimate Parent: Bruno's. SIC: 5411—
Grocery Stores.

★ 84997 ★   Pizza Hut
807 W. Ennis Ave.
Ennis, TX 75119
(214)875-8810
Ultimate Parent: Pepsico. SIC: 5812—
Eating Places.

★ 84998 ★   Press
113 S. Dallas St.
Ennis, TX 75119-4744
(214)878-9016
Ultimate Parent: Banta Corp. SIC: 2711—
Newspapers.

★ 84999 ★   Press Inc.
113 S. Dallas St.
Ennis, TX 75119-4744
(214)878-9016
Ultimate Parent: Banta Corp. SIC: 2711—
Newspapers.

★ 85000 ★   Ryder Truck Rental
208 Metro Park Blvd.
Ennis, TX 75119
(214)875-8646
Ultimate Parent: Ryder System.

★ 85001 ★   Schuller International
Inc.
2705 N. Kaufman Ave.
Ennis, TX 75119
Ultimate Parent: Manville Corp. SIC:
2297—Nonwoven Fabrics.

★ 85002 ★   Taco Bell
1107 E. Ennis Ave.
Ennis, TX 75119
(214)875-0208
Ultimate Parent: Pepsico.

★ 85003 ★   Wal Mart Discount
City
I 45
Ennis, TX 75119
(214)875-9671
Ultimate Parent: Wal-Mart Stores, Inc. SIC:
5311—Department Stores.

★ 85004 ★   Wal Mart Discount
Pharmacy
I 45
Ennis, TX 75119
(214)875-9636
Ultimate Parent: Wal-Mart Stores, Inc. SIC:
5912—Drug Stores & Proprietary Stores.

Euless

★ 85005 ★   Arco Pipe Line Co.
3301 N. Hwy. 157
Euless, TX 76040-7036
(817)267-3242
Ultimate Parent: Atlantic Richfield Co., Inc.
SIC: 4612—Crude Petroleum Pipelines.

★ 85006 ★ Arco Pipe Line Co.
Hwy. 157
Euless, TX 76039
(817)267-9451
Ultimate Parent: Atlantic Richfield Co., Inc.
SIC: 4612—Crude Petroleum Pipelines.

★ 85007 ★ Atchison, Topeka &
Santa Fe Railway Co.
1441 Airport Fwy.
Euless, TX 76040
(817)878-1414
Ultimate Parent: Santa Fe Pacific Corp.
SIC: 4119—Local Passenger Transportation
Nec.

★ 85008 ★ Coltec Industries
Menasco Aerospace
4000 S. Hwy. 157
Euless, TX 76040
(817)283-4471 Fax: (817)283-4591
Officer: Robert Grill, President. Ultimate
Parent: Coltec Industries.

★ 85009 ★ Herman Miller Inc.
15050 Trinity Blvd.
Euless, TX 76040
(817)545-3122
Ultimate Parent: Herman Miller. SIC:
2599—Furniture & Fixtures Nec.

★ 85010 ★ Jiffy Lube
840 S. Industrial Blvd.
Euless, TX 76040
(817)283-7037
Ultimate Parent: Pennzoil. SIC: 7539—
Automotive Repair Shops Nec.

★ 85011 ★ Jiffy Lube
1012 N. Industrial Blvd.
Euless, TX 76039
(817)571-2242
Ultimate Parent: Pennzoil.

★ 85012 ★ Kentucky Fried
Chicken
508 W. Euless Blvd.
Euless, TX 76040
(817)283-2591
Ultimate Parent: Pepsico. SIC: 5812—
Eating Places.

★ 85013 ★ Kmart
701 S. Industrial Blvd.
Euless, TX 76040
(817)283-5336
Ultimate Parent: K-Mart.

★ 85014 ★ Kroger Food Store
1060 N. Main St.
Euless, TX 76039
(817)571-1008
Ultimate Parent: Kroger. SIC: 5411—
Grocery Stores.

★ 85015 ★ Menasco
Aerosystems Div.
4000 Hwy. 157 S
Euless, TX 76040-7012
Company Type: Division. Ultimate Parent:
Coltec Industries. SIC: 3728—Aircraft Parts
& Equipment Nec.

★ 85016 ★ Pizza Hut
1001 W. Euless Blvd.
Euless, TX 76040
(817)283-2831
Ultimate Parent: Pepsico. SIC: 5812—
Eating Places.

★ 85017 ★ Pizza Hut
314 S. Industrial Blvd.
Euless, TX 76040
(817)283-7881
Ultimate Parent: Pepsico. SIC: 5812—
Eating Places.

★ 85018 ★ Radio Shack
104 S. Ector Dr.
Euless, TX 76040
(817)283-7951
Company Type: Division. Ultimate Parent:
Tandy Corp.

★ 85019 ★ Ryder Truck Rental
113 W. Euless Blvd.
Euless, TX 76040
(817)571-7854
Ultimate Parent: Ryder System.

★ 85020 ★ Taco Bell
100 W. Euless Blvd.
Euless, TX 76040
(817)283-2931
Ultimate Parent: Pepsico. SIC: 5812—
Eating Places.

★ 85021 ★ Total Petroleum Inc.
3520 S. Euless Main St.
Euless, TX 76040
(817)267-1296
Ultimate Parent: Total Petroleum Inc. SIC:
2911—Petroleum Refining.

★ 85022 ★ Total Petroleum Inc.
3520 S. Euless Main St.
Euless, TX 76040
(817)267-1296
Ultimate Parent: Total Petroleum Inc. SIC:
2911—Petroleum Refining.

★ 85023 ★ Trailways Bus Station
604 W. Euless Blvd.
Euless, TX 76040
(817)267-4911
Ultimate Parent: Greyhound Lines Inc. SIC:
4111—Local & Suburban Transit; 4131—
Intercity & Rural Bus Transportation; 4173—
Bus Terminal & Service Facilities.

Evadale

★ 85024 ★ Pulp & Paperboard
Operations
Hwy. 105 South
Evadale, TX 77615
Ultimate Parent: Temple-Inland. SIC:
2631—Paperboard Mills.

★ 85025 ★ Temple-Inland Inc.
Pulp & Paperboard Operations
Hwy. 105 S.
Evadale, TX 77615
Ultimate Parent: Temple-Inland. SIC:
2631—Paperboard Mills.

★ 85026 ★ Tifpc Bleached
Paperboard Pulp & Paperboard
Operations
Hwy. 105 S.
Evadale, TX 77615
Ultimate Parent: Temple-Inland. SIC:
2631—Paperboard Mills.

Fabens

★ 85027 ★ Greyhound Bus
Station
130 W. Main
Fabens, TX 79838
(915)764-3410
Ultimate Parent: Greyhound Lines Inc. SIC:
4731—Freight Transportation Arrangement.

★ 85028 ★ Wrangler
Access Rd.
Fabens, TX 79838
Ultimate Parent: VF Corp. SIC: 2326—
Men's/Boys' Work Clothing.

Fairfield

★ 85029 ★ Fairfield Memorial
Hospital
125 Newman St.
Fairfield, TX 75840-1499
(903)389-2121
Officer: Milton W. Meadows. Ultimate
Parent: Beverly Enterprises. SIC: 8062—
General Medical & Surgical Hospitals;
8093—Specialty Outpatient Facilities Nec;
8099—Health & Allied Services Nec.

Falfurrias

★ 85030 ★ Pizza Hut
915 S. Saint Marys St.
Falfurrias, TX 78355
(512)325-3923
Ultimate Parent: Pepsico. SIC: 5812—
Eating Places.

Farmers Branch

★ 85031 ★ Comerica Bank-Texas
13333 Midway Rd.
Farmers Branch, TX 75244
(214)392-7401
Company Type: Subsidiary. Location
Type: Branch office. Ultimate Parent:

Comerica Bank. SIC: 6021—National
Commercial Banks.

★ 85032 ★ Comerica Bank-Texas
4100 Spring Valley Rd.
Farmers Branch, TX 75244-3618
(214)661-1515
Company Type: Subsidiary. Location
Type: Branch office. Ultimate Parent:
Comerica Bank. SIC: 6021—National
Commercial Banks.

★ 85033 ★ National Hand Tool
Mechanics Tool Division
12827 Valley Branch Ln.
Farmers Branch, TX 75234
Ultimate Parent: Stanley Works. SIC:
3423—Hand & Edge Tools Nec.

★ 85034 ★ Pitney Bowes Credit
Corp.
1503 Lyndon B Johnson Fwy.
Farmers Branch, TX 75234
(214)241-0060
Ultimate Parent: Pitney Bowes. SIC:
6159—Miscellaneous Business Credit
Institutions.

★ 85035 ★ Tj Maxx
500 Park Forest Ctr.
Farmers Branch, TX 75234
(214)241-4288
Ultimate Parent: TJX. SIC: 7389—
Business Services Nec.

★ 85036 ★ Valley National
Financial Service Co.
4255 LBJ Fwy.
Farmers Branch, TX 75244
(214)458-9930
Ultimate Parent: Banc One Corp. SIC:
6141—Personal Credit Institutions.

Farmers Brnch

★ 85037 ★ Ryder Truck Rental
14026 Harry Hines Blvd.
Farmers Brnch, TX 75234
(214)243-1334
Ultimate Parent: Ryder System. SIC:
7513—Truck Rental & Leasing Without
Drivers.

Floresville

★ 85038 ★ Greyhound Bus Sta
1109 F St.
Floresville, TX 78114
(512)393-2722
Ultimate Parent: Greyhound Lines Inc.

★ 85039 ★ Wal Mart Discount
Cities
181 N
Floresville, TX 78114
(512)393-4417
Ultimate Parent: Wal-Mart Stores, Inc. SIC:
5311—Department Stores.

Floydada

★ 85040 ★ Mobil Chemical Co.
517 E. Houston St.
Floydada, TX 79235
(806)983-2400
Ultimate Parent: Mobil. SIC: 5191—Farm
Supplies.

Forney

★ 85041 ★ Texaco Pep Stop
Farm Rd. 740
Forney, TX 75126
(214)552-1160
Ultimate Parent: Texaco. SIC: 5541—
Gasoline Service Stations.

Forsan

★ 85042 ★ Exxon Co. USA
Forsan, TX 79733
(915)457-2331
Ultimate Parent: Exxon. SIC: 1389—Oil &
Gas Field Services Nec.

Fort Stockton

★ 85043 ★ Exxon Co. USA
404 W. 18th St.
Fort Stockton, TX 79735
(915)336-5029
Ultimate Parent: Exxon. SIC: 1382—Oil &
Gas Exploration Services.

★ 85044 ★ Exxon Co. USA
E Hwy. 290
Fort Stockton, TX 79735
(915)336-2912
Ultimate Parent: Exxon. SIC: 1382—Oil &
Gas Exploration Services.

★ 85045 ★ Kentucky Fried
Chicken
800 W. Dickinson Blvd.
Fort Stockton, TX 79735
(915)336-5841
Ultimate Parent: Pepsico. SIC: 5812—
Eating Places.

★ 85046 ★ Pizza Hut
909 W. Dickinson Blvd.
Fort Stockton, TX 79735
(915)336-5926
Ultimate Parent: Pepsico. SIC: 5812—
Eating Places.

★ 85047 ★ Radio Shack
1301 W. Dickinson Blvd.
Fort Stockton, TX 79735
(915)336-2308
Company Type: Division. Ultimate Parent:
Tandy Corp. SIC: 7373—Computer
Integrated Systems Design.

★ 85048 ★ Shell Hammond Oil
305 W. Dickinson Blvd.
Fort Stockton, TX 79735
(915)336-3852
Ultimate Parent: Shell Oil Co. SIC: 5541—
Gasoline Service Stations.

★ 85049 ★ Stop & Shop
101 W. Hornbeck Blvd.
Fort Stockton, TX 79735
(915)336-5091
Ultimate Parent: Stop & Shop. SIC: 5411—
Grocery Stores.

★ 85050 ★ Tranmission Systems
Inc.
3101 W. 9th St.
Fort Stockton, TX 79735-4510
(915)336-8553
Officer: Leonard Ledford. Ultimate Parent:
AT&T. SIC: 2813—Industrial Gases.

★ 85051 ★ Transwestern Pipeline
Co.
2101 W. Dickinson Blvd.
Fort Stockton, TX 79735
(915)336-2966
Ultimate Parent: Enron. SIC: 4923—Gas
Transmission & Distribution.

★ 85052 ★ Wal Mart
1700 W. Dickinson Blvd.
Fort Stockton, TX 79735
(915)336-3389
Ultimate Parent: Wal-Mart Stores, Inc. SIC:
5311—Department Stores.

Fort Worth

★ 85053 ★ Ace Hardware
3370 Mansfield Hwy.
Fort Worth, TX 76119
(817)534-0059
Ultimate Parent: Ace Hardware. SIC:
5251—Hardware Stores.

★ 85054 ★ Aerospace
Technologies Inc.
7445 E. Lancaster
Fort Worth, TX 76112
Ultimate Parent: Alco Standard Corp. SIC:
3728—Aircraft Parts & Equipment Nec.

★ 85055 ★ Aerospace
Technologies Inc.
PO Box 50727
Fort Worth, TX 76105-0727
(817)451-0620
Officer: James M Shortt. Ultimate Parent:
Alco Standard Corp. SIC: 3724—Aircraft
Engines & Engine Parts.

★ 85056 ★   **Aerospace Technologies Inc.**
PO Box 50727
Fort Worth, TX 76105-0727
(817)451-0620
Officer: James M Shortt. **Ultimate Parent:** Alco Standard Corp. **SIC:** 3724—Aircraft Engines & Engine Parts.

★ 85057 ★   **Albertson's Food & Drug**
6249 Rufe Snow Dr.
Fort Worth, TX 76148
(817)581-7233
Ultimate Parent: Albertson's Inc. **SIC:** 5411—Grocery Stores.

★ 85058 ★   **Albertson's Sew & Vacuum**
5631 Crowley Rd.
Fort Worth, TX 76134
(817)293-4059
Ultimate Parent: Albertson's Inc. **SIC:** 5722—Household Appliance Stores.

★ 85059 ★   **Ambac Indmnty Corp.**
5450 Doral Ct
Fort Worth, TX 76112
(817)654-2900
Ultimate Parent: AMBAC Inc.

★ 85060 ★   **American Airlines Cargo**
4330 Amon Carter Blvd.
Fort Worth, TX 76155
(817)963-1234
Company Type: Division. **Officer:** William Boesch, President. **Ultimate Parent:** AMR Corp. **SIC:** 4512—Air Transportation—Scheduled.

★ 85061 ★   **American Airlines Decision Technologies Inc.**
4255 Amon Carter Blvd.
Fort Worth, TX 76155-2603
(817)967-1000
Company Type: Subsidiary. **Officer:** Thomas M. Cook, President. **Ultimate Parent:** AMR Corp. **SIC:** 8748—Business Consulting Services Nec. **Employee Count:** 380. **Sales:** 41 M.

★ 85062 ★   **American Home Food Prods, Inc.**
1734 E. El Paso
Fort Worth, TX 76102
Ultimate Parent: American Home Products. **SIC:** 2032—Canned Specialties.

★ 85063 ★   **American Home Food Products Inc.**
1734 East El Paso
Fort Worth, TX 76101
Ultimate Parent: American Home Products. **SIC:** 2032—Canned Specialties.

★ 85064 ★   **AMR Corp.**
4333 Amon Carter Blvd.
Fort Worth, TX 76155-2605
(817)963-1234
Company Type: Headquarters. **Officer:** Robert L. Crandall, Chairman of the Board & President. **SIC:** 4512—Air Transportation—Scheduled; 4581—Airports, Flying Fields & Services; 7374—Data Processing & Preparation; 7359—Equipment Rental & Leasing Nec; 7389—Business Services Nec. **Employee Count:** 118900. **Sales:** 15816 M. **Fortune Service 500:** Ranking 2.

★ 85065 ★   **AMR Eagle, Inc.**
4200 American Blvd.
Fort Worth, TX 76155-2101
(817)355-1234
Officer: Robert E. Martens, President & CEO. **Ultimate Parent:** AMR Corp. **SIC:** 4512—Air Transportation—Scheduled. **Employee Count:** 5000. **Sales:** 584 M.

★ 85066 ★   **AMR Services Corp.**
4255 Amon Carter Blvd.
Fort Worth, TX 76155-2603
(817)963-2700
Company Type: Subsidiary. **Location Type:** Branch office. **Officer:** Thomas M. Metzler, President. **Ultimate Parent:** AMR Corp. **SIC:** 4581—Airports, Flying Fields & Services; 5172—Petroleum Products Nec; 4212—Local Trucking Without Storage. **Employee Count:** 5000. **Sales:** 247 M.

★ 85067 ★   **Armco**
Tex-Tube Div.
9003 Airport Fwy.
Fort Worth, TX 76180-7770
(817)498-3123
Company Type: Division. **Ultimate Parent:** Armco. **SIC:** 5074—Plumbing & Hydronic Heating Supplies.

★ 85068 ★   **Avnet**
Freeman Products
2310 Franklin Dr.
Fort Worth, TX 76106
(817)625-5181
Location Type: Branch office. **Ultimate Parent:** Avnet. **SIC:** 5099—Durable Goods Nec.

★ 85069 ★   **Bell Helicopter Textron Inc.**
600 E. Hurst Blvd.
Fort Worth, TX 76101
Ultimate Parent: Textron. **SIC:** 3721—Aircraft.

★ 85070 ★   **Bell Helicopter Textron Inc. Plant I**
600 E. Hurst Blvd.
Fort Worth, TX 76053
Ultimate Parent: Textron. **SIC:** 3721—Aircraft.

★ 85071 ★   **Borden Inc.**
3232 S. Main St.
Fort Worth, TX 76110
(817)429-8543
Officer: Dave Marrell, Manager. **Ultimate Parent:** Borden, Inc. **SIC:** 2024—Ice Cream & Frozen Desserts.

★ 85072 ★   **Burlington Northern**
777 Main St.
Fort Worth, TX 76102
(817)878-2000
Company Type: Headquarters. **Officer:** Gerald Grinstein. **Fortune Service 500:** Ranking 12.

★ 85073 ★   **Burlington Northern Inc.**
3800 Continental Plz.
777 Main St.
Fort Worth, TX 76102
(817)878-2000 **Fax:** (817)878-2377
Company Type: Headquarters. **Officer:** Gerald Grinstein, Chairman & CEO. **Ultimate Parent:** Burlington Northern. **Employee Count:** 32900.

★ 85074 ★   **Burlington Northern Railroad Co.**
3800 Continental Plz.
777 Main St.
Fort Worth, TX 76102
(817)878-2000 **Fax:** (817)878-2377
Company Type: Subsidiary. **Officer:** Gerald Grinstein, Chairman & CEO. **Ultimate Parent:** Burlington Northern.

★ 85075 ★   **Burlington Northern Railroad Co.**
Continental Plz.
777 Main St.
Fort Worth, TX 76102-5384
(817)878-2000 **Fax:** (817)878-2377
Officer: Gerald Grinstein, CEO. **Ultimate Parent:** Burlington Northern. **Employee Count:** 31204. **Sales:** 4699 M.

★ 85076 ★   **Casual Corner**
4800 S. Hulen St.
Fort Worth, TX 76132
(817)292-5190
Ultimate Parent: United States Shoe. **SIC:** 5651—Family Clothing Stores.

★ 85077 ★   **Casual Corner**
1 Tandy Ctr. Bldg.
Fort Worth, TX 76102
(817)332-4196
Ultimate Parent: United States Shoe. **SIC:** 5621—Women's Clothing Stores.

★ 85078 ★   **Casual Corner**
1978 Green Oaks Rd.
Fort Worth, TX 76116
(817)731-6447
Ultimate Parent: United States Shoe. **SIC:** 5651—Family Clothing Stores.

★ 85079 ★   **Ceramic Cooling Tower Co.**
1100 Northway Dr.
Fort Worth, TX 76131
(817)232-4661 **Fax:** (817)232-4703
Company Type: Division. **Officer:** Charles Bardo, President. **Ultimate Parent:** Amsted Industries Inc. **SIC:** 3585—Refrigeration & Heating Equipment; 1799—Special Trade Contractors Nec; 5084—Industrial Machinery & Equipment.

★ 85080 ★   **Champion International Corp.**
1901 Windsor Pl.
Fort Worth, TX 76110-1895
Ultimate Parent: Champion International. **SIC:** 2621—Paper Mills.

★ 85081 ★   **Circuit City**
4820 Southwest Blvd.
Fort Worth, TX 76116
(817)738-1796
Ultimate Parent: Circuit City Stores.

★ 85082 ★   **Citgo Quick Mart**
6820 Crowley Rd.
Fort Worth, TX 76134
(817)293-6301
Ultimate Parent: Citgo Petroleum. **SIC:** 5541—Gasoline Service Stations.

★ 85083 ★   **Coast to Coast Adj**
900 N. University Dr.
Fort Worth, TX 76114
(817)625-9407
Ultimate Parent: Servistar Corp.

★ 85084 ★   **Coast to Coast Hardware**
6513 Meadowbrook Dr.
Fort Worth, TX 76112
(817)451-5820
Ultimate Parent: Servistar Corp. **SIC:** 5251—Hardware Stores.

★ 85085 ★   **Coca Cola Bottling Co.**
2501 Great Pky. SW
Fort Worth, TX 76106
(817)625-0201
Ultimate Parent: Coca-Cola Enterprises. **SIC:** 5812—Eating Places.

★ 85086 ★   **Coca Cola Bottling Co.**
1405 E. Hattie St.
Fort Worth, TX 76104
(817)332-4087
Ultimate Parent: Coca-Cola Enterprises. **SIC:** 5812—Eating Places.

★ 85087 ★   **Coca-Cola Bottling Co. N. Texas**
3400 Fossil Creek Blvd.
Fort Worth, TX 76137
Ultimate Parent: Coca-Cola Enterprises. **SIC:** 2086—Bottled & Canned Soft Drinks.

★ 85088 ★   **Coca-Cola Bottling Co. of North Texas**
3400 Fossil Creek Blvd.
Fort Worth, TX 76161-3349
Ultimate Parent: Coca-Cola Enterprises. **SIC:** 2086—Bottled & Canned Soft Drinks.

★ 85089 ★   **Comerica Bank-Texas**
5701 Camp Bowie Blvd.
Fort Worth, TX 76107-5092
(817)763-5021
Company Type: Subsidiary. **Location Type:** Branch office. **Ultimate Parent:** Comerica Bank. **SIC:** 6021—National Commercial Banks.

★ 85090 ★   **Comerica Bank-Texas**
415 Throckmorton
Fort Worth, TX 76102-7495
(817)870-2718
Company Type: Subsidiary. **Location Type:** Branch office. **Ultimate Parent:** Comerica Bank. **SIC:** 6021—National Commercial Banks.

★ 85091 ★   **Composite Technologies Inc.**
1005 Blue Mound Rd.
Fort Worth, TX 76131
Ultimate Parent: W. R. Grace. **SIC:** 3089—Plastics Products Nec.

★ 85092 ★   **Composite Technology**
Polycel Div.
1005 Blue Mound Rd.
Fort Worth, TX 76131
Company Type: Division. **Ultimate Parent:** W. R. Grace. **SIC:** 3089—Plastics Products Nec.

★ 85093 ★   **Composite Technology Inc. Conn**
1005 Blue Mound Rd.
Fort Worth, TX 76131
Ultimate Parent: W. R. Grace. **SIC:** 3089—Plastics Products Nec.

★ 85094 ★   **Con-Way Intermodal Inc.**
2322 Gravel Dr.
Fort Worth, TX 76118-6950
(817)284-7800
Company Type: Subsidiary. **Officer:** James R. Hertwig, President, CEO. **Ultimate Parent:** Consolidated Freightways. **SIC:** 4213—Trucking Except Local. **Employee Count:** 330. **Sales:** 165 M.

★ 85095 ★   **Con-Way Southwest Express Inc.**
14500 Trinity Blvd.
Fort Worth, TX 76155-2528
(817)267-9959
Company Type: Subsidiary. **Officer:** John Hickerson, President. **Ultimate Parent:** Consolidated Freightways. **SIC:** 4213—Trucking Except Local. **Employee Count:** 1200. **Sales:** 70 M.

★ 85096 ★   **Delta Air Lines**
2 Tandy Ctr.
Fort Worth, TX 76103
(817)336-8341
Ultimate Parent: Delta Air Lines, Inc. **SIC:** 4724—Travel Agencies.

★ 85097 ★   **Delta Air Lines**
2450 E. 1st St.
Fort Worth, TX 76111
(817)336-0489
Ultimate Parent: Delta Air Lines, Inc. **SIC:** 4724—Travel Agencies.

★ 85098 ★   **Delta Air Lines Inc.**
2450 E. 1st St.
Fort Worth, TX 76111
(817)336-0489
Ultimate Parent: Delta Air Lines, Inc. **SIC:** 4724—Travel Agencies.

★ 85099 ★   **Delta Air Lines Inc.**
2 Tandy Ctr.
Fort Worth, TX 76103
(817)336-8341
Ultimate Parent: Delta Air Lines, Inc. **SIC:** 4724—Travel Agencies.

★ 85100 ★   **Design Foods**
3709 E. 1st St.
Fort Worth, TX 76111
Ultimate Parent: Sara Lee Corp. **SIC:** 2013—Sausages & Other Prepared Meats.

★ 85101 ★   **Diebold Inc.**
2430 Gravel St.
Fort Worth, TX 76118
(817)284-5104
Ultimate Parent: Diebold, Inc. **SIC:** 5063—Electrical Apparatus & Equipment.

★ 85102 ★   **Digital Equip Corp.**
6800 Manhattan Blvd.
Fort Worth, TX 76120
(817)457-1041
Ultimate Parent: Digital Equipment Corp. **SIC:** 5734—Computer & Software Stores.

★ 85103 ★   **Digital Equip Corp.**
8713 Airport Fwy.
Fort Worth, TX 76180
(817)577-6000
Ultimate Parent: Digital Equipment Corp.

★ 85104 ★   **Dillard Department Stores**
Fort Worth Division
4501 N. Beach St.
Fort Worth, TX 76111
(817)831-5111
Officer: James W. Sherburne Jr., Chairman of the Board. **Ultimate Parent:** Dillard Department Stores. **SIC:** 5311—Department Stores.

★ 85105 ★　Dr. Pepper Seven-Up Co. Inc.
2817 Braswell Dr.
Fort Worth, TX 76111
(817)625-4440
Officer: Michael Grant, Manager. **Ultimate Parent:** Dr. Pepper/Seven-Up. **SIC:** 2086—Bottled & Canned Soft Drinks.

★ 85106 ★　E/M Corp.
6525 Midway Rd.
Fort Worth, TX 76117-5306
Ultimate Parent: Great Lakes Chemical.
SIC: 3479—Metal Coating & Allied Services.

★ 85107 ★　E/M Corp.
Fort Worth Div. Processing
6525 Midway Rd.
Fort Worth, TX 76117-5386
Company Type: Division. **Ultimate Parent:** Great Lakes Chemical. **SIC:** 3479—Metal Coating & Allied Services.

★ 85108 ★　Emery Worldwide
2410 Minnis Ln.
Fort Worth, TX 76117
(817)831-4161
Ultimate Parent: Consolidated Freightways.
SIC: 4513—Air Courier Services.

★ 85109 ★　Express
2060 Green Oaks Rd.
Fort Worth, TX 76116
(817)732-0513
Ultimate Parent: Limited.

★ 85110 ★　Exxon
5728 E. Berry St.
Fort Worth, TX 76119
(817)451-6751
Ultimate Parent: Exxon. **SIC:** 5541—Gasoline Service Stations.

★ 85111 ★　Exxon
6001 Camp Bowie Blvd.
Fort Worth, TX 76116
(817)738-3020
Ultimate Parent: Exxon. **SIC:** 5541—Gasoline Service Stations.

★ 85112 ★　Exxon
2424 Azle Ave.
Fort Worth, TX 76106
(817)626-1622
Ultimate Parent: Exxon. **SIC:** 7538—General Automotive Repair Shops.

★ 85113 ★　Exxon Car Care Center
620 E. Berry St.
Fort Worth, TX 76110
(817)926-9206
Ultimate Parent: Exxon. **SIC:** 5541—Gasoline Service Stations.

★ 85114 ★　Exxon Motor Fuel Store
7900 South Fwy.
Fort Worth, TX 76134
(817)551-0870
Ultimate Parent: Exxon. **SIC:** 5411—Grocery Stores.

★ 85115 ★　Exxon Shop
8424 Hwy. 377 S
Fort Worth, TX 76126
(817)249-0545
Ultimate Parent: Exxon.

★ 85116 ★　Exxon Shop
920 E. Loop 820
Fort Worth, TX 76112
(817)451-6705
Ultimate Parent: Exxon.

★ 85117 ★　Farm & Home Savings Association
5017 S. Hulen St.
Fort Worth, TX 76132
(817)294-7283
Ultimate Parent: Farm & Home Financial Corp. **SIC:** 6035—Federal Savings Institutions.

★ 85118 ★　Federated Department Stores
7624 Grapevine Hwy.
Fort Worth, TX 76180
(817)589-2236
Ultimate Parent: Dillard Department Stores.
SIC: 5311—Department Stores.

★ 85119 ★　Foot Action
2032 Green Oaks Rd.
Fort Worth, TX 76116
(817)738-4461
Ultimate Parent: Melville. **SIC:** 5661—Shoe Stores.

★ 85120 ★　Footaction U S a
7624 Grapevine Hwy.
Fort Worth, TX 76180
(817)589-0059
Ultimate Parent: Melville. **SIC:** 5661—Shoe Stores.

★ 85121 ★　The Gap
2060 Green Oaks Rd.
Fort Worth, TX 76116
(817)731-0271
Ultimate Parent: GAP.

★ 85122 ★　The Gap
4800 S. Hulen St.
Fort Worth, TX 76132
(817)292-7291
Ultimate Parent: GAP. **SIC:** 5611—Men's & Boys' Clothing Stores.

★ 85123 ★　The Gap
2026 Green Oaks Rd.
Fort Worth, TX 76116
(817)731-0271
Ultimate Parent: GAP. **SIC:** 5651—Family Clothing Stores.

★ 85124 ★　The Gap
7624 Grapevine Hwy.
Fort Worth, TX 76180
(817)284-5056
Ultimate Parent: GAP. **SIC:** 5651—Family Clothing Stores.

★ 85125 ★　Greyhound Bus Line
2409 Cullen St.
Fort Worth, TX 76107
(817)335-1872
Ultimate Parent: Greyhound Lines Inc.

★ 85126 ★　Greyhound Bus Lines
2525 NE 28th St.
Fort Worth, TX 76106
(817)626-1967
Ultimate Parent: Greyhound Lines Inc. **SIC:** 4131—Intercity & Rural Bus Transportation.

★ 85127 ★　Halliburton Logging Services
1100 Everman Rd.
Fort Worth, TX 76140-4994
Ultimate Parent: Halliburton. **SIC:** 3533—Oil & Gas Field Machinery.

★ 85128 ★　Hertz Rent-A-Car
917 Taylor St.
Fort Worth, TX 76102
(817)332-5205
Ultimate Parent: Hertz. **SIC:** 7514—Passenger Car Rental.

★ 85129 ★　Hit or Miss
6080 S. Hulen St.
Fort Worth, TX 76132
(817)370-0255
Ultimate Parent: TJX.

★ 85130 ★　Innovative Office Systems Inc.
501 Jones St.
Fort Worth, TX 76102
(817)261-1106
Officer: Philip Fleming, Manager. **Ultimate Parent:** Alco Standard Corp. **SIC:** 3663—Radio & T.V. Communications Equipment.

★ 85131 ★　A & a International
5412 SE Loop
Fort Worth, TX 76119
(817)478-9251
Ultimate Parent: Tandy Corp. **SIC:** 7389—Business Services Nec.

★ 85132 ★　Jiffy Lube
6253 Mccart Ave.
Fort Worth, TX 76133
(817)346-1777
Ultimate Parent: Pennzoil. **SIC:** 7539—Automotive Repair Shops Nec.

★ 85133 ★　Jiffy Lube
6739 Rufe Snow Dr.
Fort Worth, TX 76148
(817)281-7966
Ultimate Parent: Pennzoil.

★ 85134 ★　Jiffy Lube
7343 Grapevine Hwy.
Fort Worth, TX 76180
(817)281-5188
Ultimate Parent: Pennzoil. **SIC:** 7539—Automotive Repair Shops Nec.

★ 85135 ★　Jiffy Lube
7601 Hwy. 80 W
Fort Worth, TX 76116
(817)244-0938
Ultimate Parent: Pennzoil. **SIC:** 7539—Automotive Repair Shops Nec.

★ 85136 ★　Jiffy Lube
5028 Davis Blvd.
Fort Worth, TX 76180
(817)581-0693
Ultimate Parent: Pennzoil. **SIC:** 7539—Automotive Repair Shops Nec.

★ 85137 ★　Kay Bee Toy & Hobby
7624 Grapevine Hwy.
Fort Worth, TX 76180
(817)284-8546
Ultimate Parent: Melville. **SIC:** 5945—Hobby, Toy & Game Shops.

★ 85138 ★　Kentucky Fried Chicken
5010 Trail Lake Dr.
Fort Worth, TX 76133
(817)292-1867
Ultimate Parent: Pepsico. **SIC:** 5812—Eating Places.

★ 85139 ★　Kentucky Fried Chicken
407 W. Rosedale St.
Fort Worth, TX 76104
(817)332-3564
Ultimate Parent: Pepsico. **SIC:** 5812—Eating Places.

★ 85140 ★　Kentucky Fried Chicken
5651 Rufe Snow Dr.
Fort Worth, TX 76180
(817)281-8630
Ultimate Parent: Pepsico. **SIC:** 5812—Eating Places.

★ 85141 ★　Kentucky Fried Chicken
1224 S. Ayers Ave.
Fort Worth, TX 76105
(817)535-6142
Ultimate Parent: Pepsico. **SIC:** 5812—Eating Places.

★ 85142 ★　Kentucky Fried Chicken
1000 N. Beach St.
Fort Worth, TX 76111
(817)838-3481
Ultimate Parent: Pepsico. **SIC:** 5812—Eating Places.

★ 85143 ★　Kentucky Fried Chicken
6150 Ramey Ave.
Fort Worth, TX 76112
(817)457-6586
Ultimate Parent: Pepsico. **SIC:** 5812—Eating Places.

★ 85144 ★　Kentucky Fried Chicken
2251 Jacksboro Hwy.
Fort Worth, TX 76114
(817)626-0562
Ultimate Parent: Pepsico. **SIC:** 5812—Eating Places.

★ 85145 ★　Kentucky Fried Chicken
3134 Mansfield Hwy.
Fort Worth, TX 76119
(817)531-2311
Ultimate Parent: Pepsico. **SIC:** 5812—Eating Places.

★ 85146 ★　Kentucky Fried Chicken
5510 E. Lancaster Ave.
Fort Worth, TX 76112
(817)451-1459
Ultimate Parent: Pepsico. **SIC:** 5812—Eating Places.

★ 85147 ★　Kentucky Fried Chicken
8725 Hwy. 80 W
Fort Worth, TX 76116
(817)560-0916
Ultimate Parent: Pepsico. **SIC:** 5812—Eating Places.

★ 85148 ★　Kentucky Fried Chicken
3529 Alta Mere Dr.
Fort Worth, TX 76116
(817)244-6861
Ultimate Parent: Pepsico. **SIC:** 5812—Eating Places.

★ 85149 ★　Kentucky Fried Chicken
3620 Altamesa Blvd.
Fort Worth, TX 76133
(817)294-1728
Ultimate Parent: Pepsico. **SIC:** 5812—Eating Places.

★ 85150 ★　Kmart Photography Studio
3316 Denton Hwy.
Fort Worth, TX 76117
(817)838-6503
Ultimate Parent: K-Mart.

★ 85151 ★　Kmart Portrait Studio
4812 South Fwy.
Fort Worth, TX 76115
(817)923-5584
Ultimate Parent: K-Mart.

★ 85152 ★　Kroger
1270 Woodhaven Blvd.
Fort Worth, TX 76112
(817)496-4151
Ultimate Parent: Kroger. **SIC:** 5411—Grocery Stores.

★ 85153 ★　Kroger Co
2215 S. Cooper St.
Fort Worth, TX 76104
(817)277-4201
Ultimate Parent: Kroger. **SIC:** 5411—Grocery Stores.

★ 85154 ★　Kroger Food & Drug
9114 Hwy. 80 W
Fort Worth, TX 76116
(817)244-2576
Ultimate Parent: Kroger. **SIC:** 5411—Grocery Stores.

★ 85155 ★　Kroger Food Store No 401
4812 South Fwy.
Fort Worth, TX 76115
(817)921-9771
Ultimate Parent: Kroger. **SIC:** 5411—Grocery Stores.

★ 85156 ★　Kroger Food Store No 694
3304 Denton Hwy.
Fort Worth, TX 76117
(817)838-6974
Ultimate Parent: Kroger. **SIC:** 5411—Grocery Stores.

★ 85157 ★　Kroger Food Store No 224
3510 Altamesa Blvd.
Fort Worth, TX 76133
(817)294-5911
Ultimate Parent: Kroger. **SIC:** 5411—Grocery Stores.

★ 85158 ★　Kroger Food Store Number 60
6009 Jacksboro Hwy.
Fort Worth, TX 76135
(817)237-1144
Ultimate Parent: Kroger. **SIC:** 5411—Grocery Stores.

★ 85159 ★　Kroger Phrmcy
6080 S. Hulen St.
Fort Worth, TX 76132
(817)346-0487
Ultimate Parent: Kroger.

★ 85160 ★　Kroger Phrmcy
3510 Altamesa Blvd.
Fort Worth, TX 76133
(817)292-3777
Ultimate Parent: Kroger.

★ 85161 ★ Kroger Phrmcy
6246 Rufe Snow Dr.
Fort Worth, TX 76148
(817)281-0778
Ultimate Parent: Kroger.

★ 85162 ★ Lafarge Corp.
3900 Angle Ave.
Fort Worth, TX 76106
(817)429-3764
Ultimate Parent: Lafarge.

★ 85163 ★ Lafarge Corp.
5050 South Fwy.
Fort Worth, TX 76115
(817)921-9356
Ultimate Parent: Lafarge.

★ 85164 ★ Lane Bryant
4800 S. Hulen St.
Fort Worth, TX 76132
(817)294-5666
Ultimate Parent: Limited.

★ 85165 ★ Lane Bryant
7624 Grapevine Hwy.
Fort Worth, TX 76180
(817)595-2971
Ultimate Parent: Limited. SIC: 5651—
Family Clothing Stores.

★ 85166 ★ Lane Bryant
2108 Green Oaks Rd.
Fort Worth, TX 76116
(817)738-5436
Ultimate Parent: Limited. SIC: 5651—
Family Clothing Stores.

★ 85167 ★ Lane Bryant
4200 Fort Worth Town Ctr.
Fort Worth, TX 76110
(817)927-1796
Ultimate Parent: Limited. SIC: 5651—
Family Clothing Stores.

★ 85168 ★ Lerner Shop
4800 S. Hulen St.
Fort Worth, TX 76132
(817)294-1860
Ultimate Parent: Limited.

★ 85169 ★ Lerner Shop
2020 Green Oaks Rd.
Fort Worth, TX 76116
(817)738-3442
Ultimate Parent: Limited. SIC: 5651—
Family Clothing Stores.

★ 85170 ★ Lerner Shop
601 Houston St.
Fort Worth, TX 76102
(817)336-7963
Ultimate Parent: Limited. SIC: 5621—
Women's Clothing Stores.

★ 85171 ★ Lerner Shop
4200 Fort Worth Town Ctr.
Fort Worth, TX 76110
(817)921-9921
Ultimate Parent: Limited. SIC: 5651—
Family Clothing Stores.

★ 85172 ★ The Limited
2018 Green Oaks Rd.
Fort Worth, TX 76116
(817)738-5468
Ultimate Parent: Limited. SIC: 5651—
Family Clothing Stores.

★ 85173 ★ The Limited
4800 S. Hulen St.
Fort Worth, TX 76132
(817)292-6941
Ultimate Parent: Limited. SIC: 5621—
Women's Clothing Stores; 5651—Family
Clothing Stores.

★ 85174 ★ The Limited
4200 Fort Worth Town Cent
Fort Worth, TX 76110
(817)921-9618
Ultimate Parent: Limited. SIC: 5651—
Family Clothing Stores.

★ 85175 ★ The Limited
7624 Grapevine Hwy.
Fort Worth, TX 76180
(817)284-4398
Ultimate Parent: Limited. SIC: 5651—
Family Clothing Stores.

★ 85176 ★ The Limited
2060 Green Oaks Rd.
Fort Worth, TX 76116
(817)732-2285
Ultimate Parent: Limited.

★ 85177 ★ The Limited Express
1988 Green Oaks Rd.
Fort Worth, TX 76116
(817)732-0513
Ultimate Parent: Limited. SIC: 5651—
Family Clothing Stores.

★ 85178 ★ Lockheed Fort Worth Co.
Lockheed Blvd.
Fort Worth, TX 76101-0748
(817)777-2000 Fax: (817)777-2115
Company Type: Operating unit. Ultimate
Parent: Lockheed Corp. SIC: 3721—
Aircraft.

★ 85179 ★ Lockheed Fort Worth Co.
PO Box 748
Fort Worth, TX 76101
(817)777-2000
Officer: Gordon R. England, President.
Ultimate Parent: Lockheed Corp.

★ 85180 ★ Lone Star Gas Co.
4500 Blue Mound Rd.
Fort Worth, TX 76106
(817)624-4681
Ultimate Parent: Enserch. SIC: 4939—
Combination Utility Nec.

★ 85181 ★ Lone Star Gas Co.
908 Monroe St.
Fort Worth, TX 76102
(817)336-8381
Ultimate Parent: Enserch. SIC: 4939—
Combination Utility Nec; 5992—Florists.

★ 85182 ★ M P I Inc.
1301 Cold Springs Rd.
Fort Worth, TX 76102
Ultimate Parent: Leggett & Platt Inc. SIC:
3000—Rubber & Miscellaneous Plastics
Products.

★ 85183 ★ Marshalls
5200 S. Hulen St.
Fort Worth, TX 76132
(817)294-0538
Ultimate Parent: Melville. SIC: 5311—
Department Stores.

★ 85184 ★ Mary Kay Cosmetics
6916 Quail Meadow Dr.
Fort Worth, TX 76148
(817)581-9408
Ultimate Parent: Mary Kay Cosmetics.

★ 85185 ★ Mary Kay Cosmetics
7400 Windhaven Rd.
Fort Worth, TX 76180
(817)581-6870
Ultimate Parent: Mary Kay Cosmetics.

★ 85186 ★ McDonalds Restaurant
6809 Mccart Ave.
Fort Worth, TX 76133
(817)370-1622
Ultimate Parent: McDonald's.

★ 85187 ★ Mervyn's
7624 Grapevine Hwy.
Fort Worth, TX 76180
(817)284-8008
Ultimate Parent: Dayton Hudson. SIC:
5311—Department Stores.

★ 85188 ★ Milcare
15050 Trinity Blvd. 400
Fort Worth, TX 76155
Ultimate Parent: Herman Miller. SIC:
5099—Durable Goods Nec.

★ 85189 ★ Miller Brewing Co.
7001 S. Freeway
Fort Worth, TX 76134
Ultimate Parent: Philip Morris. SIC: 2082—
Malt Beverages.

★ 85190 ★ Miller Brewing Co.
7001 S. Freeway
Fort Worth, TX 76134
Ultimate Parent: Philip Morris. SIC: 2082—
Malt Beverages.

★ 85191 ★ Miller Brewing Co.
Fort Worth Container Div.
6600 Will Rogers Blvd.
Fort Worth, TX 76140
Ultimate Parent: Philip Morris. SIC: 3411—
Metal Cans.

★ 85192 ★ Mitchell Energy Corp.
6000 Western Pl.
Fort Worth, TX 76107-4654
(817)731-5600
Officer: Wyndell Thomas. Ultimate Parent:
Mitchell Energy & Devel. SIC: 1382—Oil &
Gas Exploration Services.

★ 85193 ★ Mobil Gas Station No 12 a N
6700 Rufe Snow Dr.
Fort Worth, TX 76148
(817)656-3771
Ultimate Parent: Mobil. SIC: 5541—
Gasoline Service Stations.

★ 85194 ★ Mobil Oil Corp. (Terminal)
3600 N. Sylvania Ave.
Fort Worth, TX 76111
(817)429-6931
Ultimate Parent: Mobil. SIC: 5171—
Petroleum Bulk Stations & Terminals.

★ 85195 ★ Mobil Oil No 12
4351 Western Ctr. Blvd.
Fort Worth, TX 76137
(817)232-2187
Ultimate Parent: Mobil.

★ 85196 ★ Mobil Service Station
1801 E. Lancaster Ave.
Fort Worth, TX 76103
(817)338-0233
Ultimate Parent: Mobil. SIC: 5541—
Gasoline Service Stations.

★ 85197 ★ Mobil Service Station
5001 Old Granbury Rd.
Fort Worth, TX 76133
(817)292-7410
Ultimate Parent: Mobil. SIC: 5541—
Gasoline Service Stations.

★ 85198 ★ Mobil Service Station
4429 Bellaire Dr. S
Fort Worth, TX 76109
(817)924-6862
Ultimate Parent: Mobil. SIC: 5541—
Gasoline Service Stations.

★ 85199 ★ Mobil Slf Srv
1051 Bridgewood Dr.
Fort Worth, TX 76112
(817)457-7928
Ultimate Parent: Mobil.

★ 85200 ★ Monarch Paper Co.
1612 Summit Ave.
Fort Worth, TX 76102-5915
(817)335-4894
Ultimate Parent: Alco Standard Corp. SIC:
5113—Industrial & Personal Service Paper.

★ 85201 ★ MPI, Inc.
1301 Cold Springs Rd.
Fort Worth, TX 76102
Ultimate Parent: Leggett & Platt Inc. SIC:
3086—Plastics Foam Products.

★ 85202 ★ Ncr Corp.
5750 N. Riverside Dr.
Fort Worth, TX 76137
(817)847-2000
Ultimate Parent: AT&T.

★ 85203 ★ New England Mutl Life Insurance C
3112 W. 4th St.
Fort Worth, TX 76107
(817)429-0460
Ultimate Parent: New England Mutual Life.
SIC: 6411—Insurance Agents, Brokers &
Service.

★ 85204 ★ New York Life Fort Worth General Office
Western Agencies
1320 S. University 9th Fl.
University Center
Fort Worth, TX 76107
(817)336-2565 Fax: (817)878-3231
Officer: John E. Williams, General
Manager. Ultimate Parent: New York Life.

★ 85205 ★ Norwest Mortgage, Inc.
500 Grapevine Hwy.
Fort Worth, TX 76180
(817)498-2463
Ultimate Parent: Norwest Corp. SIC:
6141—Personal Credit Institutions.

★ 85206 ★ NTS
6100 Western Pl.
Fort Worth, TX 76121
(817)731-8721 Fax: (817)737-5493
Officer: Tommy L. Andrews, Senior Vice
President & General Manager. Ultimate
Parent: PHH.

★ 85207 ★ Otis Elevator Co. Inc.
1806 Hickory Dr.
Fort Worth, TX 76117
(817)831-4453
Ultimate Parent: United Technologies. SIC:
5084—Industrial Machinery & Equipment.

★ 85208 ★ Pactel Paging
2630 Freeway W
Fort Worth, TX 76102
(817)870-9855
Ultimate Parent: Pacific Telesis Group.
SIC: 4812—Radiotelephone
Communications.

★ 85209 ★ Payless Cashways Building M
8148 Interstate W. 30
Fort Worth, TX 76108
(817)246-0181
Ultimate Parent: Payless Cashways. SIC:
5039—Construction Materials Nec.

★ 85210 ★ Payless Cashways Inc.
8904 South Fwy.
Fort Worth, TX 76140
(817)293-5222
Ultimate Parent: Payless Cashways. SIC:
5039—Construction Materials Nec; 5211—
Lumber & Other Building Materials.

★ 85211 ★ Payless Cashways Inc.
1300 Blue Mound Rd.
Fort Worth, TX 76131
(817)625-1591
Ultimate Parent: Payless Cashways. SIC:
5211—Lumber & Other Building Materials.

★ 85212 ★ Payless Cashways Mtrls
5445 Blue Mound Rd.
Fort Worth, TX 76106
(817)625-1591
Ultimate Parent: Payless Cashways. SIC:
5211—Lumber & Other Building Materials.

★ 85213 ★ Payless Shoesource
4200 South Fwy.
Fort Worth, TX 76115
(817)921-1639
Ultimate Parent: May Department Stores.

★ 85214 ★ Payless Shoesource
5010 S. Hulen St.
Fort Worth, TX 76132
(817)292-7151
Ultimate Parent: May Department Stores.

★ 85215 ★ Payless Shoesource
3732 E. Rosedale St.
Fort Worth, TX 76105
(817)535-0636
Ultimate Parent: May Department Stores.
SIC: 5661—Shoe Stores.

★ 85216 ★ Pennzoil-Zippy Lube
836 S. Saginaw Blvd.
Fort Worth, TX 76179
(817)232-4721
Ultimate Parent: Pennzoil.

★ 85217 ★ Pepsi-Cola Bottling Co.
5201 Blue Mound Rd.
Fort Worth, TX 76106
(817)625-4101
Officer: Joe Giles, Manager. Ultimate
Parent: Pepsico. SIC: 2086—Bottled &
Canned Soft Drinks.

★ 85218 ★ Petite Sophisticate
4800 S. Hulen St.
Fort Worth, TX 76132
(817)346-1101
Ultimate Parent: United States Shoe. SIC:
5651—Family Clothing Stores.

★ 85219 ★ **Petite Sophisticate**
7624 Grapevine Hwy.
Fort Worth, TX 76180
(817)589-2759
Ultimate Parent: United States Shoe. **SIC:** 5651—Family Clothing Stores.

★ 85220 ★ **Piggly Wiggly**
3113 Walton Ave.
Fort Worth, TX 76133
(817)292-6475
Ultimate Parent: Bruno's. **SIC:** 5411—Grocery Stores.

★ 85221 ★ **Piggly Wiggly**
2005 N. Riverside Dr.
Fort Worth, TX 76111
(817)834-8173
Ultimate Parent: Bruno's. **SIC:** 5411—Grocery Stores.

★ 85222 ★ **Pizza Hut**
14500 Trinity Blvd.
Fort Worth, TX 76155
(817)737-6051
Ultimate Parent: Pepsico. **SIC:** 5812—Eating Places.

★ 85223 ★ **Pizza Hut**
500 University Dr.
Fort Worth, TX 76107
(817)335-1944
Ultimate Parent: Pepsico. **SIC:** 5812—Eating Places.

★ 85224 ★ **Pizza Hut**
6066 S. Hulen St.
Fort Worth, TX 76132
(817)370-1399
Ultimate Parent: Pepsico.

★ 85225 ★ **Pizza Hut**
616 S. Saginaw Blvd.
Fort Worth, TX 76179
(817)232-1571
Ultimate Parent: Pepsico. **SIC:** 5812—Eating Places.

★ 85226 ★ **Pizza Hut**
1701 McClellan Ct.
Fort Worth, TX 76112
(817)457-0072
Ultimate Parent: Pepsico. **SIC:** 5812—Eating Places.

★ 85227 ★ **Pizza Hut**
4705 River Oaks Blvd.
Fort Worth, TX 76114
(817)625-2383
Ultimate Parent: Pepsico. **SIC:** 5812—Eating Places.

★ 85228 ★ **Pizza Hut**
6059 Jacksboro Hwy.
Fort Worth, TX 76135
(817)237-8138
Ultimate Parent: Pepsico. **SIC:** 5812—Eating Places.

★ 85229 ★ **Pizza Hut**
3205 Mansfield Hwy.
Fort Worth, TX 76119
(817)531-2949
Ultimate Parent: Pepsico. **SIC:** 5812—Eating Places.

★ 85230 ★ **Pizza Hut**
9208 Hwy. 377 S
Fort Worth, TX 76126
(817)249-4530
Ultimate Parent: Pepsico. **SIC:** 5812—Eating Places.

★ 85231 ★ **Pizza Hut**
8048 Hwy. 80 W
Fort Worth, TX 76116
(817)244-5742
Ultimate Parent: Pepsico. **SIC:** 5812—Eating Places.

★ 85232 ★ **Pizza Hut**
3033 Cockrell Ave.
Fort Worth, TX 76109
(817)926-4117
Ultimate Parent: Pepsico. **SIC:** 5812—Eating Places.

★ 85233 ★ **Pizza Hut**
5912 Denton Hwy.
Fort Worth, TX 76148
(817)485-2010
Ultimate Parent: Pepsico. **SIC:** 5812—Eating Places.

★ 85234 ★ **Pizza Hut**
3801 Altamesa Blvd.
Fort Worth, TX 76133
(817)294-1560
Ultimate Parent: Pepsico. **SIC:** 5812—Eating Places.

★ 85235 ★ **Pizza Hut**
4200 South Fwy.
Fort Worth, TX 76115
(817)924-8339
Ultimate Parent: Pepsico.

★ 85236 ★ **PMS Consolidated**
9001 S. Freeway
Fort Worth, TX 76140
Ultimate Parent: M.A.Hanna. **SIC:** 3087—Custom Compound of Purchased Resins.

★ 85237 ★ **PMS Consolidated**
9001 South Freeway
Fort Worth, TX 76140
Ultimate Parent: M.A.Hanna. **SIC:** 3000—Rubber & Miscellaneous Plastics Products.

★ 85238 ★ **Polar Ice Co.**
601 N. Sylvania
Fort Worth, TX 76111
Ultimate Parent: Southland Corp. **SIC:** 2097—Manufactured Ice.

★ 85239 ★ **Pulte Home Corp.**
7504 Meadow Creek Dr.
Fort Worth, TX 76123
(817)294-1525
Ultimate Parent: Pulte.

★ 85240 ★ **R R Donnelley & Sons Co.**
2 Tandy Ctr.
Fort Worth, TX 76103
(817)335-6000
Ultimate Parent: R. R. Donnelley & Sons. **SIC:** 2759—Commercial Printing Nec.

★ 85241 ★ **Radio Shack**
4250 Mccart Ave.
Fort Worth, TX 76115
(817)927-7828
Company Type: Division. **Ultimate Parent:** Tandy Corp. **SIC:** 5065—Electronic Parts & Equipment Nec.

★ 85242 ★ **Radio Shack**
100 Tandy Ctr. 1
Fort Worth, TX 76103
(817)335-2078
Company Type: Division. **Ultimate Parent:** Tandy Corp. **SIC:** 5065—Electronic Parts & Equipment Nec.

★ 85243 ★ **Radio Shack**
5400 Woodway Dr.
Fort Worth, TX 76133
(817)292-3927
Company Type: Division. **Ultimate Parent:** Tandy Corp. **SIC:** 5065—Electronic Parts & Equipment Nec.

★ 85244 ★ **Radio Shack**
2525 W. 7th St.
Fort Worth, TX 76107
(817)336-4684
Company Type: Division. **Ultimate Parent:** Tandy Corp. **SIC:** 5065—Electronic Parts & Equipment Nec.

★ 85245 ★ **Radio Shack**
2900 W. Berry St.
Fort Worth, TX 76109
(817)923-7238
Company Type: Division. **Ultimate Parent:** Tandy Corp. **SIC:** 5065—Electronic Parts & Equipment Nec.

★ 85246 ★ **Radio Shack**
1000 Terminal Rd.
Fort Worth, TX 76106
Company Type: Division. **Ultimate Parent:** Tandy Corp. **SIC:** 5065—Electronic Parts & Equipment Nec.

★ 85247 ★ **Radio Shack**
100 Throckmorton St. 400
Fort Worth, TX 76102
Company Type: Division. **Ultimate Parent:** Tandy Corp. **SIC:** 5046—Commercial Equipment Nec.

★ 85248 ★ **Radio Shack**
7816 South Fwy.
Fort Worth, TX 76134
(817)293-2711
Company Type: Division. **Ultimate Parent:**

Tandy Corp. **SIC:** 5065—Electronic Parts & Equipment Nec.

★ 85249 ★ **Radio Shack**
1 Tandy Ctr.
Fort Worth, TX 76102
(817)390-3011
Company Type: Division. **Ultimate Parent:** Tandy Corp. **SIC:** 5731—Radio, Television & Electronics Stores.

★ 85250 ★ **Radio Shack**
1626 S. Cherry Ln.
Fort Worth, TX 76108
(817)246-7141
Company Type: Division. **Ultimate Parent:** Tandy Corp. **SIC:** 5065—Electronic Parts & Equipment Nec.

★ 85251 ★ **Radio Shack**
4800 S. Hulen St.
Fort Worth, TX 76132
(817)292-3781
Company Type: Division. **Ultimate Parent:** Tandy Corp. **SIC:** 5731—Radio, Television & Electronics Stores.

★ 85252 ★ **Radio Shack**
3075 Mansfield Hwy. A
Fort Worth, TX 76119
(817)531-2121
Company Type: Division. **Ultimate Parent:** Tandy Corp. **SIC:** 5065—Electronic Parts & Equipment Nec.

★ 85253 ★ **Radio Shack**
6242 Rufe Snow Dr.
Fort Worth, TX 76148
(817)656-2500
Company Type: Division. **Ultimate Parent:** Tandy Corp.

★ 85254 ★ **Radio Shack**
8111 Hwy. 80 W
Fort Worth, TX 76116
(817)244-7997
Company Type: Division. **Ultimate Parent:** Tandy Corp. **SIC:** 5734—Computer & Software Stores; 5731—Radio, Television & Electronics Stores.

★ 85255 ★ **Radio Shack**
6000 Jacksboro Hwy.
Fort Worth, TX 76135
(817)237-5531
Company Type: Division. **Ultimate Parent:** Tandy Corp. **SIC:** 5065—Electronic Parts & Equipment Nec.

★ 85256 ★ **Radio Shack**
7624 Grapevine Hwy.
Fort Worth, TX 76180
(817)284-5229
Company Type: Division. **Ultimate Parent:** Tandy Corp. **SIC:** 5065—Electronic Parts & Equipment Nec.

★ 85257 ★ **Radio Shack**
1726 Green Oaks Rd.
Fort Worth, TX 76116
(817)731-4185
Company Type: Division. **Ultimate Parent:** Tandy Corp. **SIC:** 5065—Electronic Parts & Equipment Nec.

★ 85258 ★ **Radio Shack**
900 E. Northside Dr.
Fort Worth, TX 76102
(817)870-5600
Company Type: Division. **Ultimate Parent:** Tandy Corp.

★ 85259 ★ **Radio Shack**
4200 Fort Worth Town Cent
Fort Worth, TX 76110
(817)927-7480
Company Type: Division. **Ultimate Parent:** Tandy Corp. **SIC:** 5065—Electronic Parts & Equipment Nec.

★ 85260 ★ **Radio Shack**
3901 E. Belknap St.
Fort Worth, TX 76111
(817)834-0951
Company Type: Division. **Ultimate Parent:** Tandy Corp. **SIC:** 5065—Electronic Parts & Equipment Nec.

★ 85261 ★ **Radio Shack**
4705 E. Lancaster Ave.
Fort Worth, TX 76103
(817)531-2551
Company Type: Division. **Ultimate Parent:** Tandy Corp. **SIC:** 3651—Household Audio & Video Equipment.

★ 85262 ★ **Radio Shack**
6387 Camp Bowie Blvd.
Fort Worth, TX 76116
(817)732-8168
Company Type: Division. **Ultimate Parent:** Tandy Corp. **SIC:** 5734—Computer & Software Stores.

★ 85263 ★ **Radio Shack**
3183 Denton Hwy.
Fort Worth, TX 76117
(817)831-1951
Company Type: Division. **Ultimate Parent:** Tandy Corp. **SIC:** 5063—Electrical Apparatus & Equipment; 5065—Electronic Parts & Equipment Nec.

★ 85264 ★ **Radio Shack**
3401 Altamesa Blvd.
Fort Worth, TX 76133
(817)346-0083
Company Type: Division. **Ultimate Parent:** Tandy Corp. **SIC:** 5065—Electronic Parts & Equipment Nec.

★ 85265 ★ **Ryder Truck Rental**
5604 River Oaks Blvd.
Fort Worth, TX 76114
(817)731-4864
Ultimate Parent: Ryder System.

★ 85266 ★ **Ryder Truck Rental**
4712 South Fwy.
Fort Worth, TX 76115
(817)921-3565
Ultimate Parent: Ryder System. **SIC:** 7513—Truck Rental & Leasing Without Drivers.

★ 85267 ★ **Ryder Truck Rental**
5608 Mccart Ave.
Fort Worth, TX 76133
(817)370-8681
Ultimate Parent: Ryder System.

★ 85268 ★ **Ryder Truck Rental**
7354 PO Box
Fort Worth, TX 76111
(817)878-8800
Ultimate Parent: Ryder System. **SIC:** 7513—Truck Rental & Leasing Without Drivers.

★ 85269 ★ **Ryder Truck Rental**
3021 Alta Mere Dr.
Fort Worth, TX 76116
(817)731-4843
Ultimate Parent: Ryder System.

★ 85270 ★ **Ryder Truck Rental**
8723 Hwy. 377 S
Fort Worth, TX 76126
(817)249-0692
Ultimate Parent: Ryder System.

★ 85271 ★ **SABRE Travel Information Network**
4330 Amon Carter Blvd.
Fort Worth, TX 76155
(817)963-1234
Company Type: Division. **Officer:** Kathy Misunar, President. **Ultimate Parent:** AMR Corp. **SIC:** 8742—Management Consulting Services.

★ 85272 ★ **Sam's Wholesale Club**
1451 S. Cherry Ln.
Fort Worth, TX 76108
(817)246-5501
Ultimate Parent: Wal-Mart Stores, Inc. **SIC:** 5399—Miscellaneous General Merchandise Store.

★ 85273 ★ **Sam's Wholesale Club**
7500 Baker Blvd.
Fort Worth, TX 76118
(817)589-1356
Ultimate Parent: Wal-Mart Stores, Inc. **SIC:** 5099—Durable Goods Nec.

★ 85274 ★ **Sav-On**
1657 PO Box
Fort Worth, TX 76101
Ultimate Parent: American Stores. **SIC:** 5044—Office Equipment.

★ 85275 ★ **Scott Polymers Inc.**
3607 N. Sylvania Ave.
Fort Worth, TX 76111
Ultimate Parent: Scott Paper Co. **SIC:** 2821—Plastics Materials & Resins.

★ 85276 ★   Service Merchandise
1600 Green Oaks Rd.
Fort Worth, TX 76116
(817)731-7581
Ultimate Parent: Service Merchandise Co.,
Inc. SIC: 5399—Miscellaneous General
Merchandise Store.

★ 85277 ★   Southwestern Bell
Yellow Pages
6707 Brentwood Stair Rd. 30
Fort Worth, TX 76112
(817)496-7000
Ultimate Parent: Southwestern Bell. SIC:
7313—Radio, T.V. & Publisher
Representatives.

★ 85278 ★   Star Telegram
6108 Bianca Cir. 210
Fort Worth, TX 76132
(817)292-1587
Ultimate Parent: Walt Disney . SIC:
8712—Architectural Services.

★ 85279 ★   Star Telegram
8220 Bedford Euless Rd.
Fort Worth, TX 76180
(817)656-8273
Ultimate Parent: Walt Disney SIC:
2711—Newspapers.

★ 85280 ★   Stevens Graphics
Corp.
5500 Airport Fwy.
Fort Worth, TX 76117-3911
(817)831-3911
Location Type: Headquarters. Officer:
Richard I. Stevens. Ultimate Parent:
BellSouth Corp. SIC: 3555—Printing Trades
Machinery; 5084—Industrial Machinery &
Equipment.

★ 85281 ★   Stop & Shop
2601 S. Riverside Dr.
Fort Worth, TX 76104
(817)531-3381
Ultimate Parent: Stop & Shop. SIC: 5411—
Grocery Stores.

★ 85282 ★   Stratoflex Inc.
Aerospace & Military Div.
220 Roberts Cut-Off Rd.
Fort Worth, TX 76114
Company Type: Division. Ultimate Parent:
Parker Hannifin. SIC: 3498—Fabricated
Pipe & Fittings; 3451—Screw Machine
Products; 3492—Fluid Power Valves &
Hose Fittings; 3494—Valves & Pipe Fittings
Nec.

★ 85283 ★   Structure
2116 Green Oaks Rd.
Fort Worth, TX 76116
(817)732-8725
Ultimate Parent: Limited.

★ 85284 ★   Sunrise Properties
500 W. Berry St.
Fort Worth, TX 76110
(817)921-2571
Ultimate Parent: Penn Traffic. SIC: 6531—
Real Estate Agents & Managers.

★ 85285 ★   Taco Bell
612 University Dr.
Fort Worth, TX 76107
(817)332-6585
Ultimate Parent: Pepsico. SIC: 5812—
Eating Places.

★ 85286 ★   Taco Bell
1405 S. Cherry Ln.
Fort Worth, TX 76108
(817)246-6006
Ultimate Parent: Pepsico. SIC: 5812—
Eating Places.

★ 85287 ★   Taco Bell
117 Sycamore School Rd.
Fort Worth, TX 76134
(817)293-3000
Ultimate Parent: Pepsico. SIC: 5812—
Eating Places.

★ 85288 ★   Taco Bell
4729 River Oaks Blvd.
Fort Worth, TX 76114
(817)624-1712
Ultimate Parent: Pepsico. SIC: 5812—
Eating Places.

★ 85289 ★   Taco Bell
6261 Rufe Snow Dr.
Fort Worth, TX 76148
(817)581-8804
Ultimate Parent: Pepsico. SIC: 5812—
Eating Places.

★ 85290 ★   Taco Bell
2824 N. Main St.
Fort Worth, TX 76106
(817)625-8313
Ultimate Parent: Pepsico. SIC: 5812—
Eating Places.

★ 85291 ★   Taco Bell
1221 Oakland Blvd.
Fort Worth, TX 76103
(817)457-2417
Ultimate Parent: Pepsico. SIC: 5812—
Eating Places.

★ 85292 ★   Taco Bell
1712 Montgomery St.
Fort Worth, TX 76107
(817)731-0581
Ultimate Parent: Pepsico. SIC: 5812—
Eating Places.

★ 85293 ★   Taco Bell
951 N. Beach St.
Fort Worth, TX 76111
(817)838-0351
Ultimate Parent: Pepsico. SIC: 5812—
Eating Places.

★ 85294 ★   Taco Bell
3351 Mansfield Hwy.
Fort Worth, TX 76119
(817)534-8301
Ultimate Parent: Pepsico. SIC: 5812—
Eating Places.

★ 85295 ★   Taco Bell
6162 Meadowbrook Dr.
Fort Worth, TX 76112
(817)496-1634
Ultimate Parent: Pepsico.

★ 85296 ★   Taco Bell
7417 Hwy. 80 W
Fort Worth, TX 76116
(817)244-4610
Ultimate Parent: Pepsico. SIC: 5812—
Eating Places.

★ 85297 ★   Taco Bell
6038 Jacksboro Hwy.
Fort Worth, TX 76135
(817)237-1311
Ultimate Parent: Pepsico. SIC: 5812—
Eating Places; 5812—Eating Places.

★ 85298 ★   Taco Bell
2076 Green Oaks Rd.
Fort Worth, TX 76116
(817)737-2207
Ultimate Parent: Pepsico. SIC: 5812—
Eating Places.

★ 85299 ★   Taco Bell
9481 Hwy. 377 S
Fort Worth, TX 76126
(817)249-1569
Ultimate Parent: Pepsico. SIC: 5812—
Eating Places.

★ 85300 ★   Taco Bell
5621 E. Belknap St.
Fort Worth, TX 76117
(817)834-8471
Ultimate Parent: Pepsico. SIC: 5812—
Eating Places.

★ 85301 ★   Taco Bell
4200 Fort Worth Town Ctr.
Fort Worth, TX 76110
(817)923-7861
Ultimate Parent: Pepsico. SIC: 5812—
Eating Places.

★ 85302 ★   Taco Bell
5737 Crowley Rd.
Fort Worth, TX 76134
(817)293-9580
Ultimate Parent: Pepsico. SIC: 5812—
Eating Places.

★ 85303 ★   Taco Bell
5000 Davis Blvd.
Fort Worth, TX 76180
(817)281-5692
Ultimate Parent: Pepsico. SIC: 5812—
Eating Places.

★ 85304 ★   Taco Bell
3767 Altamesa Blvd.
Fort Worth, TX 76133
(817)292-2721
Ultimate Parent: Pepsico. SIC: 5812—
Eating Places.

★ 85305 ★   Taco Bell
5733 Camp Bowie Blvd.
Fort Worth, TX 76107
(817)732-6489
Ultimate Parent: Pepsico. SIC: 5812—
Eating Places.

★ 85306 ★   Tandy Cabinet
701 N. Hampton St.
Fort Worth, TX 76102
(817)336-1777
Ultimate Parent: Tandy Corp. SIC: 2434—
Wood Kitchen Cabinets.

★ 85307 ★   Tandy Cabinets
701 N. Hampton St.
Fort Worth, TX 76102
(817)336-1777
Officer: Jerry Hawk, Manager. Ultimate
Parent: Tandy Corp. SIC: 2434—Wood
Kitchen Cabinets.

★ 85308 ★   Tandy Cable Products
1924 8th Ave.
Fort Worth, TX 76110
Ultimate Parent: Tandy Corp. SIC: 3357—
Nonferrous Wiredrawing & Insulating.

★ 85309 ★   Tandy Consumer Srv
7435 Airport Fwy.
Fort Worth, TX 76118
(817)284-8691
Ultimate Parent: Tandy Corp.

★ 85310 ★   Tandy Corp.
700 One Tandy Ctr.
Fort Worth, TX 76102
(817)390-3592
Ultimate Parent: Tandy Corp.

★ 85311 ★   Tandy Corp.
1800 One Tandy Ctr.
Fort Worth, TX 76102
(817)390-3700 Fax: (817)390-2774
Officer: John V. Roach, CEO. Ultimate
Parent: Tandy Corp. Employee Count:
37000. Sales: 4103 M.

★ 85312 ★   Tandy Crystal &
Consumer Mail
401 NE 38th St.
Fort Worth, TX 76106
(817)390-8255
Officer: Guy Davis, Manager. Ultimate
Parent: Tandy Corp.

★ 85313 ★   Tandy Electronics
801 NE 38th St.
Fort Worth, TX 76106
(817)390-8370
Ultimate Parent: Tandy Corp. SIC: 5065—
Electronic Parts & Equipment Nec.

★ 85314 ★   Tandy Electronics
Bus Computer
1001 NE Loop 820
Fort Worth, TX 76131
(817)232-5900
Officer: Rick Keyer, Manager. Ultimate
Parent: Tandy Corp. SIC: 3571—Electronic
Computers.

★ 85315 ★   Tandy Electronics
Warehouse
900 Terminal Rd.
Fort Worth, TX 76106
Ultimate Parent: Tandy Corp. SIC: 4225—
General Warehousing & Storage.

★ 85316 ★   Tandy Magnetics
401 NE 38th St.
Fort Worth, TX 76106
Ultimate Parent: Tandy Corp. SIC: 3694—
Engine Electrical Equipment.

★ 85317 ★   Tandy Manufacturing
Technology
5560 Blue Mound Rd.
Fort Worth, TX 76131
(817)847-7787
Officer: Kenji Nishikawa, Vice President.
Ultimate Parent: Tandy Corp. SIC: 3999—
Manufacturing Industries Nec.

★ 85318 ★   Tandy Software
Assembly
205 NW 7th St.
Fort Worth, TX 76106
(817)336-1330
Officer: Harry Mantooth, Manager. Ultimate
Parent: Tandy Corp. SIC: 3679—Electronic
Components Nec; 3695—Magnetic &
Optical Recording Media.

★ 85319 ★   Tandy Wire & Cable
3500 McCart Ave.
Fort Worth, TX 76110
(817)921-2023
Officer: David Schneider, Manager.
Ultimate Parent: Tandy Corp. SIC: 3317—
Steel Pipe & Tubes.

★ 85320 ★   Tandy Wire
Fabrication
1924 8th Ave.
Fort Worth, TX 76110
Ultimate Parent: Tandy Corp. SIC: 3357—
Nonferrous Wiredrawing & Insulating.

★ 85321 ★   Tandy Wire &
Specialty Cable
3500 McCart Ave.
Fort Worth, TX 76110-4696
Ultimate Parent: Tandy Corp. SIC: 3357—
Nonferrous Wiredrawing & Insulating.

★ 85322 ★   Target Stores
5020 S. Hulen St.
Fort Worth, TX 76132
(817)294-2140
Company Type: Subsidiary. Ultimate
Parent: Dayton Hudson. SIC: 5311—
Department Stores.

★ 85323 ★   Texaco Food Mart
6720 S. Hulen St.
Fort Worth, TX 76133
(817)370-2519
Ultimate Parent: Texaco. SIC: 5541—
Gasoline Service Stations.

★ 85324 ★   Texaco Food Mart
4600 SW Loop 820
Fort Worth, TX 76109
(817)732-8062
Ultimate Parent: Texaco.

★ 85325 ★   Texaco Food Mart
6720 S. Hulen St.
Fort Worth, TX 76133
(817)346-1609
Ultimate Parent: Texaco. SIC: 5912—Drug
Stores & Proprietary Stores.

★ 85326 ★   Texaco Food Mart
3070 S. University Dr.
Fort Worth, TX 76109
(817)924-5765
Ultimate Parent: Texaco.

★ 85327 ★   Texaco Food Mart
700 California Pkwy. N
Fort Worth, TX 76115
(817)921-6383
Ultimate Parent: Texaco.

★ 85328 ★   Texaco Food Mart
6051 Lake Worth Blvd.
Fort Worth, TX 76135
(817)237-6128
Ultimate Parent: Texaco.

★ 85329 ★   Texaco-Hanson
Hank's
5709 Denton Hwy.
Fort Worth, TX 76148
(817)581-1028
Ultimate Parent: Texaco. SIC: 5541—
Gasoline Service Stations.

★ 85330 ★   Texaco Refining &
Mktg
4901 E. California Pkwy.
Fort Worth, TX 76119
(817)534-7547
Ultimate Parent: Texaco. SIC: 5541—
Gasoline Service Stations.

★ 85331 ★   Texaco Serv Sta
6705 Meadowbrook Dr.
Fort Worth, TX 76112
(817)496-9116
Ultimate Parent: Texaco.

★ 85332 ★ **Texaco Service Station**
1602 N. Beach St.
Fort Worth, TX 76111
(817)831-6481
Ultimate Parent: Texaco. **SIC:** 5541—Gasoline Service Stations.

★ 85333 ★ **Texaco Service Station**
3901 Altamesa Blvd.
Fort Worth, TX 76133
(817)346-9214
Ultimate Parent: Texaco. **SIC:** 5541—Gasoline Service Stations.

★ 85334 ★ **Texaco Service Station**
6800 Hwy. 80 W
Fort Worth, TX 76116
(817)738-1771
Ultimate Parent: Texaco. **SIC:** 5541—Gasoline Service Stations.

★ 85335 ★ **Texaco Svce Sta**
3642 E. Berry St.
Fort Worth, TX 76105
(817)534-3262
Ultimate Parent: Texaco. **SIC:** 5541—Gasoline Service Stations.

★ 85336 ★ **Toys R US**
7606 West Fwy.
Fort Worth, TX 76108
(817)246-2251
Ultimate Parent: Toys "R" US.

★ 85337 ★ **Trailways Inc.**
901 Commerce St.
Fort Worth, TX 76102
(817)332-7611
Ultimate Parent: Greyhound Lines Inc. **SIC:** 4111—Local & Suburban Transit.

★ 85338 ★ **Underwriters Adjusting Co.**
301 Loop 820
Fort Worth, TX 76112
(817)284-3500
Ultimate Parent: Continental. **SIC:** 6411—Insurance Agents, Brokers & Service.

★ 85339 ★ **Union Equity**
425 Fairmount Ave.
Fort Worth, TX 76179
(817)232-5221
Ultimate Parent: Farmland Industries. **SIC:** 6411—Insurance Agents, Brokers & Service.

★ 85340 ★ **Union Pacific Resources Co.**
801 Cherry St.
Fort Worth, TX 76102
(817)877-6000
Officer: William L. Adams, Chairman of the Board. **Ultimate Parent:** Union Pacific Corp. **SIC:** 2911—Petroleum Refining.

★ 85341 ★ **United Parcel Service**
10155 Monroe
Fort Worth, TX 76102
(817)263-8661
Ultimate Parent: United Parcel Service of America. **SIC:** 7513—Truck Rental & Leasing Without Drivers.

★ 85342 ★ **US Sprint Communication Co.**
800 Cherry St.
Fort Worth, TX 76102
(817)332-2411
Ultimate Parent: Sprint.

★ 85343 ★ **Valley National Financial Service**
3880 Hulen St.
Fort Worth, TX 76107
(817)735-1631
Ultimate Parent: Banc One Corp. **SIC:** 6062—State Credit Unions.

★ 85344 ★ **Vandervoort**
900 S. Main St.
Fort Worth, TX 76104
Ultimate Parent: Kroger. **SIC:** 2026—Fluid Milk.

★ 85345 ★ **Vandervoort Dairy Foods Co.**
900 S. Main St.
Fort Worth, TX 76104
Ultimate Parent: Kroger. **SIC:** 2024—Ice Cream & Frozen Desserts; 2026—Fluid Milk; 2086—Bottled & Canned Soft Drinks.

★ 85346 ★ **Vandervoort's**
900 S. Main
Fort Worth, TX 76104
Ultimate Parent: Kroger. **SIC:** 2026—Fluid Milk; 2024—Ice Cream & Frozen Desserts.

★ 85347 ★ **Victoria's Secret**
4800 S. Hulen St.
Fort Worth, TX 76132
(817)292-0264
Ultimate Parent: Limited. **SIC:** 5651—Family Clothing Stores.

★ 85348 ★ **W. R. Grace & Co. Polycel Products**
1005 Blue Mound Rd.
Fort Worth, TX 76131
Ultimate Parent: W. R. Grace. **SIC:** 3089—Plastics Products Nec.

★ 85349 ★ **Wagner Brake Co.**
5125 Rondo Dr.
Fort Worth, TX 76106
Ultimate Parent: Cooper Industries. **SIC:** 3714—Motor Vehicle Parts & Accessories.

★ 85350 ★ **Wagner Electric Corp.**
51225 Rondo Dr.
Fort Worth, IX 76106
Ultimate Parent: Cooper Industries. **SIC:** 3714—Motor Vehicle Parts & Accessories.

★ 85351 ★ **Wal Mart**
1401 S. Cherry Ln.
Fort Worth, TX 76108
(817)246-6666
Ultimate Parent: Wal-Mart Stores, Inc. **SIC:** 5311—Department Stores.

★ 85352 ★ **Wal Mart**
9250 Hwy. 377 S
Fort Worth, TX 76126
(817)249-5931
Ultimate Parent: Wal-Mart Stores, Inc. **SIC:** 5311—Department Stores.

★ 85353 ★ **Wal Mart Discount Cities**
600 E. Loop 820
Fort Worth, TX 76112
(817)496-8700
Ultimate Parent: Wal-Mart Stores, Inc.

★ 85354 ★ **Wal Mart Discount Cities**
6801 NE Loop 820
Fort Worth, TX 76180
(817)498-4555
Ultimate Parent: Wal-Mart Stores, Inc.

★ 85355 ★ **Wal Mart Pharmacy**
1401 S. Cherry Ln.
Fort Worth, TX 76108
(817)246-4984
Ultimate Parent: Wal-Mart Stores, Inc. **SIC:** 5912—Drug Stores & Proprietary Stores.

★ 85356 ★ **Waldenbooks**
7624 Grapevine Hwy.
Fort Worth, TX 76180
(817)284-1504
Ultimate Parent: K-Mart. **SIC:** 5942—Book Stores.

★ 85357 ★ **Waldenbooks**
1724 Green Oaks Rd.
Fort Worth, TX 76116
(817)731-2911
Ultimate Parent: K-Mart. **SIC:** 5942—Book Stores.

★ 85358 ★ **Waldenbooks**
4200 Fort Worth Town Cent
Fort Worth, TX 76110
(817)923-8021
Ultimate Parent: K-Mart. **SIC:** 5942—Book Stores.

★ 85359 ★ **Warren Petroleum Co.**
6308 Ridglea Pl. No. 417
Fort Worth, TX 76116
(817)732-8895
Ultimate Parent: Chevron Corp. **SIC:** 5992—Florists.

★ 85360 ★ **Washington Inventory Servic**
5608 Malvey Ave. 103
Fort Worth, TX 76107
(817)732-3371
Ultimate Parent: Huffy. **SIC:** 7389—Business Services Nec.

★ 85361 ★ **Western Auto Supply Co.**
3149 Denton Hwy.
Fort Worth, TX 76117
(817)834-7411
Ultimate Parent: Sears Roebuck & Co. **SIC:** 5531—Automobile & Home Supply Stores.

★ 85362 ★ **Westronics**
5001 Blue Mound Rd.
Fort Worth, TX 76106
(817)625-2311
Ultimate Parent: Baker Hughes.

★ 85363 ★ **Westronics Inc.**
5050 Mark Iv Pky.
Fort Worth, TX 76106
Ultimate Parent: Baker Hughes. **SIC:** 3823—Process Control Instruments.

★ 85364 ★ **Witco Corp.**
611 E. Northside Dr.
Fort Worth, TX 76106
Location Type: Plant. **Ultimate Parent:** Witco Corp. **SIC:** 2841—Soap & Other Detergents.

★ 85365 ★ **W.R. Grace & Co. Conn**
1005 Blue Mound Rd.
Fort Worth, TX 76131
Ultimate Parent: W. R. Grace. **SIC:** 3089—Plastics Products Nec.

★ 85366 ★ **Xerox Corp.**
1200 Summit Ave.
Fort Worth, TX 76102
(817)882-1400
Officer: Gary Ivy, Manager. **Ultimate Parent:** Xerox Corp. **SIC:** 3663—Radio & T.V. Communications Equipment.

★ 85367 ★ **York Air Conditioning**
361 N. Beach St.
Fort Worth, TX 76111
(817)834-9675
Ultimate Parent: York International Corp. **SIC:** 3585—Refrigeration & Heating Equipment.

★ 85368 ★ **American Airlines**
4333 Amon Carter Blvd.
Forth Worth, TX 76155
(817)355-1234 **Fax:** (817)967-3816
Company Type: Subsidiary. **Officer:** Robert L. Crandall, Chairman of the Board & CEO. **Ultimate Parent:** AMR Corp. **SIC:** 4512—Air Transportation—Scheduled. **Employee Count:** 7200. **Sales:** 10,000,000,000 M.

★ 85369 ★ **SABRE Computer Services**
4330 Amon Carter Blvd.
Forth Worth, TX 76155
(817)963-1234
Company Type: Division. **Officer:** Tom Kiernan, President. **Ultimate Parent:** AMR Corp.

★ 85370 ★ **ABF Freight System Inc.**
1414 Baurline St.
Forthworth, TX 76111-1026
(817)335-6221
Ultimate Parent: Arkansas Best. **SIC:** 4212—Local Trucking Without Storage.

★ 85371 ★ **Radio Shack**
1400 1 Tandy Ctr.
Fortworth, TX 76102
(817)878-6697
Company Type: Division. **Ultimate Parent:** Tandy Corp.

Fredericksburg

★ 85372 ★ **Lone Star Gas Co.**
111 N. Llano St.
Fredericksbg, TX 78624
(512)997-2177
Ultimate Parent: Enserch. **SIC:** 4932—Gas & Other Services Combined.

★ 85373 ★ **Ryder Truck Rental**
323 W. Main St.
Fredericksbg, TX 78624
(512)997-9778
Ultimate Parent: Ryder System. **SIC:** 7359—Equipment Rental & Leasing Nec.

★ 85374 ★ **Wal Mart**
1511 E. Main St.
Fredericksbg, TX 78624
(512)997-2633
Ultimate Parent: Wal-Mart Stores, Inc. **SIC:** 5311—Department Stores.

★ 85375 ★ **Texaco Distrbtr**
109 E. Park St.
Fredericksbrg, TX 78624
(512)997-2059
Ultimate Parent: Texaco.

★ 85376 ★ **Mini Mart No 12**
120 W. Driftwood Dr.
Fredericksbg, TX 78624
(512)997-7407
Ultimate Parent: Kroger. **SIC:** 5411—Grocery Stores.

★ 85377 ★ **Pizza Hut**
1104 E. Main St.
Fredericksbg, TX 78624
(512)997-7222
Ultimate Parent: Pepsico. **SIC:** 5812—Eating Places.

Freeport

★ 85378 ★ **BASF Corp.**
602 Copper Rd.
Freeport, TX 77541
Ultimate Parent: BASF Corp. **SIC:** 2869—Industrial Organic Chemicals Nec.

★ 85379 ★ **Dow Chemical Co.**
Bldg. OC-708
Freeport, TX 77541
Ultimate Parent: Dow Chemical Co. USA. **SIC:** 2812—Alkalies & Chlorine; 2813—Industrial Gases; 2819—Industrial Inorganic Chemicals Nec; 2821—Alkalies & Chlorine; 2822—Synthetic Rubber; 2865—Cyclic Crudes & Intermediates.

★ 85380 ★ **Dow Chemical Co.**
Texas Division
PO Drawer K
Freeport, TX 77541
(409)238-2011
Company Type: Division. **Location Type:** Plant. **Officer:** R .L. Walzel, General Manager. **Ultimate Parent:** Dow Chemical Co. USA. **SIC:** 2821—Plastics Materials & Resins; 8731—Commercial Physical Research. **Employee Count:** 7300.

★ 85381 ★ **Dow Chemical Co. Texas Operations**
2301 Brazosport Blvd. Bldg. OC-708
Freeport, TX 77541-3257
Ultimate Parent: Dow Chemical Co. USA. **SIC:** 2812—Alkalies & Chlorine; 2813—Industrial Gases; 2819—Industrial Inorganic Chemicals Nec; 2821—Plastics Materials & Resins; 2822—Synthetic Rubber; 2865—Cyclic Crudes & Intermediates.

★ 85382 ★ **Dow Chemical Co. Texas Operations**
Building OC - 708
Freeport, TX 77541
Ultimate Parent: Dow Chemical Co. USA. **SIC:** 2812—Alkalies & Chlorine; 2813—Industrial Gases; 2819—Industrial Inorganic Chemicals Nec.

★ 85383 ★ **Exxon Pipeline Co.**
602 Copper Rd.
Freeport, TX 77541
(409)239-1400
Ultimate Parent: Exxon Pipeline.

★ 85384 ★ **Exxon Pipeline Co.**
602 Copper Rd.
Freeport, TX 77541
(409)239-1400
Ultimate Parent: Exxon.

★ 85385 ★ **Kentucky Fried Chicken**
1614 N. Brazosport Blvd.
Freeport, TX 77541
(409)233-8822
Ultimate Parent: Pepsico. **SIC:** 5812—
Eating Places.

★ 85386 ★ **Kroger Co.**
301 S. Brazosport Blvd.
Freeport, TX 77541
(409)233-7208
Ultimate Parent: Kroger. **SIC:** 5411—
Grocery Stores.

★ 85387 ★ **Mobil Oil Consignee**
Park Ave.
Freeport, TX 77541
(409)233-3291
Ultimate Parent: Mobil. **SIC:** 5172—
Petroleum Products Nec.

★ 85388 ★ **Mobil Petroleum Products**
Park Ave.
Freeport, TX 77541
(409)233-6022
Ultimate Parent: Mobil. **SIC:** 5171—
Petroleum Bulk Stations & Terminals.

★ 85389 ★ **Nalco Chemical Co.**
County Rd. 229
Freeport, TX 77541
Ultimate Parent: Nalco Chemical Co. **SIC:**
2869—Industrial Organic Chemicals Nec;
2899—Chemical Preparations Nec.

★ 85390 ★ **Rhone Poulenc Inc.**
6213 E. Hwy. 332
Freeport, TX 77541
(409)233-7871
Officer: Ron Miles, Manager. **Ultimate Parent:** Rhone-Poulenc Rorer. **SIC:** 2819—
Industrial Inorganic Chemicals Nec; 2869—
Industrial Organic Chemicals Nec.

★ 85391 ★ **Rhone-Poulenc Inc. Freeport Plant**
6213 Hwy. 332 E
Freeport, TX 77541
Location Type: Plant. **Ultimate Parent:**
Rhone-Poulenc Rorer. **SIC:** 2869—Industrial
Organic Chemicals Nec; 2819—Industrial
Inorganic Chemicals Nec.

★ 85392 ★ **Sentry Polymers Inc.**
5500 E. Hwy. 332
Freeport, TX 77541
Ultimate Parent: RPM, Inc. **SIC:** 2851—
Paints & Allied Products.

★ 85393 ★ **Shell Oil**
Surfside Rd.
Freeport, TX 77541
(409)233-3588
Ultimate Parent: Shell Oil Co. **SIC:** 1382—
Oil & Gas Exploration Services.

★ 85394 ★ **Tesoro Petroleum Distribution Co.**
1200 Brazos St.
Freeport, TX 77541
(409)233-7846
Ultimate Parent: Tesoro Petroleum Corp.
SIC: 5171—Petroleum Bulk Stations &
Terminals.

Freer

★ 85395 ★ **Exxon Co. USA**
Hwy. 16 N
Freer, TX 78357
(512)394-6861
Ultimate Parent: Exxon. **SIC:** 5171—
Petroleum Bulk Stations & Terminals.

Friendswood

★ 85396 ★ **Betz Process Chemicals, Inc.**
102 N. Friendswood Dr.
Friendswood, TX 77546
(713)482-2080
Ultimate Parent: Betz Laboratories Inc.
SIC: 5169—Chemicals & Allied Products
Nec.

★ 85397 ★ **Exxon Co. USA**
100 W. Parkwood Ave.
Friendswood, TX 77546
(713)996-7725
Ultimate Parent: Exxon. **SIC:** 5599—
Automotive Dealers Nec.

★ 85398 ★ **The Gap**
1054 Baybrook Mall
Friendswood, TX 77546
(713)480-8888
Ultimate Parent: GAP.

★ 85399 ★ **Kroger Co.**
110 W. Edgewood Dr.
Friendswood, TX 77546
(713)482-2466
Ultimate Parent: Kroger. **SIC:** 5411—
Grocery Stores.

★ 85400 ★ **Kroger Food Stores**
108 W. Edgewood Dr.
Friendswood, TX 77546
(713)482-9536
Ultimate Parent: Kroger.

★ 85401 ★ **Lerner Shop**
1098 Baybrook Mall
Friendswood, TX 77546
(713)488-3681
Ultimate Parent: Limited. **SIC:** 5621—
Women's Clothing Stores.

★ 85402 ★ **Lockwood National Bank of Houston**
203 Friendswood Dr.
Friendswood, TX 77546-3748
(713)996-9900
Location Type: Branch office. **Ultimate Parent:** Michigan National Corp. **SIC:**
6021—National Commercial Banks.

★ 85403 ★ **McDonalds Restaurant**
302 S. Friendswood Dr.
Friendswood, TX 77546
(713)996-8284
Ultimate Parent: McDonald's.

★ 85404 ★ **Mobil Mart**
1310 W. Bay Area Blvd.
Friendswood, TX 77546
(713)486-8737
Ultimate Parent: Mobil.

★ 85405 ★ **Payless Shoesource**
500 Baybrook Mall
Friendswood, TX 77546
(713)486-4109
Ultimate Parent: May Department Stores.

★ 85406 ★ **Pizza Hut**
108 W. Parkwood Ave.
Friendswood, TX 77546
Ultimate Parent: Pepsico. **SIC:** 5812—
Eating Places.

★ 85407 ★ **Radio Shack**
154 S. Friendswood Dr.
Friendswood, TX 77546
(713)482-4774
Company Type: Division. **Ultimate Parent:**
Tandy Corp. **SIC:** 5065—Electronic Parts &
Equipment Nec.

★ 85408 ★ **Waldenbooks**
1104 Baybrook Mall
Friendswood, TX 77546
(713)488-2330
Ultimate Parent: K-Mart. **SIC:** 5999—
Miscellaneous Retail Stores Nec.

Frisco

★ 85409 ★ **Burlington Northern Railroa**
Main St.
Frisco, TX 75034
(214)377-2431
Ultimate Parent: Burlington Northern. **SIC:**
4011—Railroads—Line-Haul Operating.

★ 85410 ★ **Comerica Bank-Texas**
2249 Preston Rd.
Frisco, TX 75034
(214)377-9751
Company Type: Subsidiary. **Location Type:** Branch office. **Ultimate Parent:**
Comerica Bank. **SIC:** 6021—National
Commercial Banks.

★ 85411 ★ **Compass Bank-Dallas**
8951 Main St.
Frisco, TX 75034-3810
(214)248-6840
Company Type: Subsidiary. **Location Type:** Branch office. **Ultimate Parent:** Robert
Jackson, Manager. **Ultimate Parent:**
Compass Bancshares. **SIC:** 6021—National
Commercial Banks.

Ft. Worth

★ 85412 ★ **Anvil Products Inc.**
1901 Terminal Rd.
Ft. Worth, TX 76106
(817)624-3107
Officer: Paul Harper, Manager. **Ultimate Parent:** Tyco International. **SIC:** 3462—Iron
& Steel Forgings.

★ 85413 ★ **Brazos Point, Inc.**
PO Box 7558
Ft. Worth, TX 76111
(817)834-8496 **Fax:** (817)834-2918
Officer: Thomas R. Crossett, President.
Ultimate Parent: Centex.

★ 85414 ★ **MPI, Inc.**
PO Box 2076
Ft. Worth, TX 76113
(817)347-7200 **Fax:** (817)870-0315
Officer: Larry Heppe, President. **Ultimate Parent:** Leggett & Platt Inc.

★ 85415 ★ **Savings of America, FSB**
915 Houston St.
Ft. Worth, TX 76102
(817)335-4721
Company Type: Division. **Location Type:**
Branch office. **Ultimate Parent:** H. F.
Ahmanson. **SIC:** 6021—National
Commercial Banks.

★ 85416 ★ **Southern Cotton Oil Co.**
PO Box 1837
Ft. Worth, TX 76101-1837
(817)922-0200
Officer: Mike Johnson. **Ultimate Parent:**
Archer Daniels Midland Co. **SIC:** 2074—
Cottonseed Oil Mills.

★ 85417 ★ **Tandy Corp.**
1800 One Tandy Ctr.
Ft. Worth, TX 76102
(817)390-3700
Company Type: Headquarters. **Officer:**
John V. Roach. **Employee Count:** 42000.
Sales: 4471 M. **Fortune Service 500:**
Ranking 30.

★ 85418 ★ **Tandy Corporation**
916 One Tandy Ctr.
Ft. Worth, TX 76102
(817)334-8134
Ultimate Parent: Tandy Corp.

Gainesville

★ 85419 ★ **Arco Oil & Gas Co.**
Walnut Bend Community
Gainesville, TX 76240
(817)665-7802
Location Type: Branch office. **Ultimate Parent:** Atlantic Richfield Co., Inc. **SIC:**
1311—Crude Petroleum & Natural Gas.

★ 85420 ★ **Arco Pipe Line Co.**
Walnut Bend Community
Gainesville, TX 76240
(817)665-5981
Location Type: Branch office. **Ultimate Parent:** Atlantic Richfield Co., Inc. **SIC:**
1311—Crude Petroleum & Natural Gas.

★ 85421 ★ **Arco Pipe Line Co.**
N I H 35
Gainesville, TX 76240
(817)665-3562
Ultimate Parent: Atlantic Richfield Co., Inc.
SIC: 4612—Crude Petroleum Pipelines.

★ 85422 ★ **Kentucky Fried Chicken**
1706 E. Hwy. 82
Gainesville, TX 76240
(817)665-3787
Ultimate Parent: Pepsico. **SIC:** 5812—
Eating Places.

★ 85423 ★ **Mary Kay Cosmetic Director**
714 S. Denton St.
Gainesville, TX 76240
(817)665-4505
Ultimate Parent: Mary Kay Cosmetics. **SIC:**
5999—Miscellaneous Retail Stores Nec.

★ 85424 ★ **Mobil Pipe Line Co.**
N. Gainesville Sta. Springs
Gainesville, TX 76240
(817)665-5944
Ultimate Parent: Mobil. **SIC:** 4612—Crude
Petroleum Pipelines.

★ 85425 ★ **Piggly Wiggly**
Gainesville Shopping Ctr.
Gainesville, TX 76240
(817)668-7243
Ultimate Parent: Bruno's. **SIC:** 5411—
Grocery Stores.

★ 85426 ★ **Pizza Hut**
738 N. Grand Ave.
Gainesville, TX 76240
(817)665-6292
Ultimate Parent: Pepsico. **SIC:** 5812—
Eating Places.

★ 85427 ★ **Ryder Truck Rental**
Hwy. 82 E
Gainesville, TX 76240
(817)668-8747
Ultimate Parent: Ryder System. **SIC:**
7513—Truck Rental & Leasing Without
Drivers.

★ 85428 ★ **Texaco Inc.**
Delaware
Gainesville, TX 76240
(817)665-9220
Ultimate Parent: Texaco. **SIC:** 3829—
Measuring & Controlling Devices Nec.

★ 85429 ★ **Wal Mart Discount Pharmacy**
1311 N. Grand Ave.
Gainesville, TX 76240
(817)665-2839
Ultimate Parent: Wal-Mart Stores, Inc. **SIC:**
5912—Drug Stores & Proprietary Stores.

★ 85430 ★ **Weber Aircraft Inc.**
2000 Weber Dr.
Gainesville, TX 76240-9699
Ultimate Parent: Hanson Industries. **SIC:**
2531—Public Building & Related Furniture.

Gainsville

★ 85431 ★ **Borden Packaging & Industrial Products**
1 Loadmaster Cir.
Gainsville, TX 76240
(817)665-8075
Location Type: Plant. **Officer:** Allison
Crabtree, Plant Manager. **Ultimate Parent:**
Borden, Inc. **SIC:** 3081—Unsupported
Plastics Film & Sheet; 3089—Plastics
Products Nec.

Galena Park

★ 85432 ★ **Amerada Hess Corp. Quality Assurance**
12901 American Petroleum
Galena Park, TX 77547
(713)453-6301
Ultimate Parent: Amerada Hess.

★ 85433 ★ **Kentucky Fried Chicken**
2215 Clinton Dr.
Galena Park, TX 77547
(713)671-2410
Ultimate Parent: Pepsico. **SIC:** 5812—
Eating Places.

★ 85434 ★ **Lockwood National Bank of Houston**
1515 Clinton Dr.
Galena Park, TX 77547-3337
(713)674-7661
Location Type: Branch office. **Ultimate Parent:** Michigan National Corp. **SIC:**
6021—National Commercial Banks.

Galveston

★ 85435 ★ **Burlington Northern Rr**
325 33rd St.
Galveston, TX 77550
(409)765-7717
Ultimate Parent: Burlington Northern. **SIC:**
4011—Railroads—Line-Haul Operating.

★ 85436 ★ **Capezio Factory**
2211 Strand St.
Galveston, TX 77550
(409)765-1718
Ultimate Parent: United States Shoe. **SIC:** 5699—Miscellaneous Apparel & Accessory Stores.

★ 85437 ★ **Dr. Pepper Seven-Up Co.**
8000 Broadway St.
Galveston, TX 77554
(409)744-5726
Officer: Charles King, Manager. **Ultimate Parent:** Dr. Pepper/Seven-Up. **SIC:** 2087—Flavoring Extracts & Syrups Nec.

★ 85438 ★ **Exxon Co. USA**
6026 Seawall Blvd.
Galveston, TX 77551
(409)740-0364
Ultimate Parent: Exxon. **SIC:** 5541—Gasoline Service Stations.

★ 85439 ★ **The Gap**
6402 Avenue J
Galveston, TX 77551
(409)740-1977
Ultimate Parent: GAP. **SIC:** 5651—Family Clothing Stores.

★ 85440 ★ **Hertz Rent-A-Car**
Scholes Field
Galveston, TX 77550
(409)744-0469
Ultimate Parent: Hertz. **SIC:** 7514—Passenger Car Rental.

★ 85441 ★ **Kay Bee Toys**
6402 Broadway St.
Galveston, TX 77551
(409)740-0442
Ultimate Parent: Melville.

★ 85442 ★ **Kentucky Fried Chicken**
2227 Butterowe St.
Galveston, TX 77551
(409)740-3416
Ultimate Parent: Pepsico. **SIC:** 5812—Eating Places.

★ 85443 ★ **Kentucky Fried Chicken**
3102 Seawall Blvd.
Galveston, TX 77550
(409)762-9097
Ultimate Parent: Pepsico. **SIC:** 5812—Eating Places.

★ 85444 ★ **Kentucky Fried Chicken**
2801 Broadway St.
Galveston, TX 77550
(409)762-5933
Ultimate Parent: Pepsico. **SIC:** 5812—Eating Places.

★ 85445 ★ **Kroger Store**
4523 Fort Crockett Blvd.
Galveston, TX 77551
(409)765-6614
Ultimate Parent: Kroger. **SIC:** 5411—Grocery Stores.

★ 85446 ★ **Kroger's Pharmacy**
4525 Fort Crockett Blvd.
Galveston, TX 77551
(409)762-6235
Ultimate Parent: Kroger. **SIC:** 5912—Drug Stores & Proprietary Stores.

★ 85447 ★ **Lane Bryant**
6402 Avenue J
Galveston, TX 77551
(409)744-9292
Ultimate Parent: Limited. **SIC:** 5651—Family Clothing Stores.

★ 85448 ★ **The Limited**
6402 Avenue J
Galveston, TX 77551
(409)744-5130
Ultimate Parent: Limited. **SIC:** 5651—Family Clothing Stores.

★ 85449 ★ **The Limited**
6402 Broadway St.
Galveston, TX 77551
(409)744-5130
Ultimate Parent: Limited.

★ 85450 ★ **M-I Drilling Fluids Brownsville**
4105 Port Industry Blvd.
Galveston, TX 77550
Ultimate Parent: Halliburton. **SIC:** 3295—Minerals—Ground or Treated.

★ 85451 ★ **M-I Drilling Fluids Co. Galveston**
4105 Port Industrial Blvd.
Galveston, TX 77550
Ultimate Parent: Halliburton. **SIC:** 3295—Minerals—Ground or Treated.

★ 85452 ★ **McDonalds Restaurant**
2912 Butterowe St.
Galveston, TX 77551
(409)744-0398
Ultimate Parent: McDonald's.

★ 85453 ★ **Milpark Drilling Fluids Galveston Barite Grinding Fac**
7501 Port Industrial Blvd. PO Box 2580
Galveston, TX 77553
Ultimate Parent: Baker Hughes. **SIC:** 3295—Minerals—Ground or Treated.

★ 85454 ★ **Milpark Drilling Fluids (Grinding Facility)**
7501 Prot Industrial Blvd., PO Box 2580
Galveston, TX 77553
Ultimate Parent: Baker Hughes. **SIC:** 3295—Minerals—Ground or Treated.

★ 85455 ★ **Mitchell Energy Corp.**
4700 Winnie
Galveston, TX 77550
(409)763-6100
Officer: Le Roy Pagel. **Ultimate Parent:** Mitchell Energy & Devel. **SIC:** 1311—Crude Petroleum & Natural Gas; 1389—Oil & Gas Field Services Nec.

★ 85456 ★ **Mobil Oil Bulk Plant**
1202 Water St.
Galveston, TX 77550
(409)765-5517
Ultimate Parent: Mobil. **SIC:** 5172—Petroleum Products Nec.

★ 85457 ★ **Mobil Oil Co.**
1202 A Ave.
Galveston, TX 77554
(409)765-5517
Ultimate Parent: Mobil. **SIC:** 5541—Gasoline Service Stations.

★ 85458 ★ **Otis Elevator Co.**
909 Moody Ave.
Galveston, TX 77550
(409)762-3321
Ultimate Parent: United Technologies. **SIC:** 3534—Elevators & Moving Stairways.

★ 85459 ★ **Payless Shoesource**
6106 Stewart Rd.
Galveston, TX 77551
(409)740-3296
Ultimate Parent: May Department Stores. **SIC:** 5661—Shoe Stores.

★ 85460 ★ **Payless Shoesource**
6402 Broadway Ave.
Galveston, TX 77551
(409)740-1533
Ultimate Parent: May Department Stores.

★ 85461 ★ **Pizza Hut**
2427 Butterowe St.
Galveston, TX 77551
(409)763-3780
Ultimate Parent: Pepsico. **SIC:** 5812—Eating Places.

★ 85462 ★ **Radio Shack**
4714 Seawall Blvd.
Galveston, TX 77551
(409)762-3186
Company Type: Division. **Ultimate Parent:** Tandy Corp. **SIC:** 5065—Electronic Parts & Equipment Nec.

★ 85463 ★ **Radio Shack**
6402 Avenue J
Galveston, TX 77551
(409)744-1645
Company Type: Division. **Ultimate Parent:** Tandy Corp. **SIC:** 5065—Electronic Parts & Equipment Nec.

★ 85464 ★ **Radio Shack**
5934 Avenue J
Galveston, TX 77551
(409)740-3566
Company Type: Division. **Ultimate Parent:** Tandy Corp. **SIC:** 7373—Computer Integrated Systems Design.

★ 85465 ★ **Red Arrow Freight Lines Inc.**
3002 Church St.
Galveston, TX 77550
(409)762-7009
Ultimate Parent: Carolina Freight. **SIC:** 4212—Local Trucking Without Storage.

★ 85466 ★ **Stop & Shop**
5201 Avenue J
Galveston, TX 77551
(409)744-8560
Ultimate Parent: Stop & Shop. **SIC:** 5541—Gasoline Service Stations.

★ 85467 ★ **Taco Bell**
6124 Stewart Rd.
Galveston, TX 77551
(409)744-7411
Ultimate Parent: Pepsico. **SIC:** 5812—Eating Places.

★ 85468 ★ **Taco Bell**
5701 Avenue J
Galveston, TX 77551
(409)740-1616
Ultimate Parent: Pepsico. **SIC:** 5812—Eating Places.

★ 85469 ★ **Tesoro Petroleum Distribution Co.**
Pelican is
Galveston, TX 77550
(409)744-5753
Ultimate Parent: Tesoro Petroleum Corp. **SIC:** 1389—Oil & Gas Field Services Nec; 5172—Petroleum Products Nec.

★ 85470 ★ **Wal Mart Discount Cities**
2711 61st St.
Galveston, TX 77551
(409)744-7134
Ultimate Parent: Wal-Mart Stores, Inc. **SIC:** 5311—Department Stores.

★ 85471 ★ **Walgreen Drug Stores**
Port Holiday Mall
Galveston, TX 77551
(409)763-4604
Ultimate Parent: Walgreen Co. **SIC:** 5912—Drug Stores & Proprietary Stores.

★ 85472 ★ **Walgreen Drug Stores**
2715 61st St.
Galveston, TX 77551
(409)744-8919
Ultimate Parent: Walgreen Co. **SIC:** 5912—Drug Stores & Proprietary Stores.

★ 85473 ★ **Western Geophysical Co.**
Pelican is
Galveston, TX 77550
(409)744-7121
Ultimate Parent: Litton Industries. **SIC:** 8713—Surveying Services.

Ganado

★ 85474 ★ **Citizens State Bank, Ganado**
201 S. 3rd St.
Ganado, TX 77962
(512)771-3391
Ultimate Parent: Liberty National Bancorp. **SIC:** 6022—State Commercial Banks.

Garland

★ 85475 ★ **Albertson's Food Centers**
5710 Broadway Blvd.
Garland, TX 75043
(214)240-7339
Ultimate Parent: Albertson's Inc. **SIC:** 5411—Grocery Stores.

★ 85476 ★ **AT&T Microelectronics Power**
2701 S. Shiloh Rd.
Garland, TX 75041-2412
(214)278-3233
Ultimate Parent: AT&T. **SIC:** 5063—Electrical Apparatus & Equipment.

★ 85477 ★ **Beneficial Texas Inc.**
1225 Belt Line Rd.
Garland, TX 75040-3294
(214)495-8118
Ultimate Parent: Beneficial. **SIC:** 6141—Personal Credit Institutions.

★ 85478 ★ **Betz Laboratories Inc.**
2222 Lonnecker Dr.
Garland, TX 75041
Ultimate Parent: Betz Laboratories Inc. **SIC:** 2899—Chemical Preparations Nec.

★ 85479 ★ **Betz Laboratories Inc.**
2222 Lonnecker Dr.
Garland, TX 75041
Ultimate Parent: Betz Laboratories Inc. **SIC:** 2899—Chemical Preparations Nec.

★ 85480 ★ **Borden Inc.**
2621 Industrial Ln.
Garland, TX 75041
(214)271-1536
Officer: Cynthia Tucker, Manager. **Ultimate Parent:** Borden, Inc. **SIC:** 2024—Ice Cream & Frozen Desserts.

★ 85481 ★ **E-Systems Inc.**
Garland Div.
1200 S. Jupiter Rd.
Garland, TX 75042
Company Type: Division. **Ultimate Parent:** E-Systems Inc. **SIC:** 3660—Communications Equipment.

★ 85482 ★ **E-Systems Inc.**
Garland Div.
1200 S. Jupiter Rd.
Garland, TX 75042
(214)272-0515
Company Type: Division. **Officer:** F. E. Stapp, President. **Ultimate Parent:** E-Systems Inc. **SIC:** 3663—Radio & T.V. Communications Equipment; 3679—Electronic Components Nec.

★ 85483 ★ **Eckerd Corp.**
Eckerd Drug Co.
4409 Action St.
Garland, TX 75042
(214)272-0411
Company Type: Headquarters. **Officer:** Oren Peacock, Sr. Vice President. **Ultimate Parent:** Eckerd Corp. **SIC:** 5912—Drug Stores & Proprietary Stores.

★ 85484 ★ **Ecolab, Inc.**
2305 Sherwin St.
Garland, TX 75041
(214)278-6121
Officer: Molly Cutting, Manager. **Ultimate Parent:** Ecolab Inc. **SIC:** 2842—Polishes & Sanitation Goods; 2841—Soap & Other Detergents.

★ 85485 ★ **Exxon**
2431 W. Walnut St.
Garland, TX 75042
(214)494-5800
Ultimate Parent: Exxon.

★ 85486 ★ **Garland Beverage Co.**
2750 Oakland Ave.
Garland, TX 75041
Ultimate Parent: Kroger. **SIC:** 2086—Bottled & Canned Soft Drinks.

★ 85487 ★ **Greyhound Bus Lines**
601 W. Ave.
Garland, TX 75040
(214)276-5663
Ultimate Parent: Greyhound Lines Inc. **SIC:** 4111—Local & Suburban Transit.

★ 85488 ★ **Gte Supply**
1718 N. 1st St.
Garland, TX 75040
(214)272-3535
Ultimate Parent: GTE.

★ 85489 ★ **Intercontinental Mfg. Co.**
1200 N. Glenbrook
Garland, TX 75046
Ultimate Parent: International Controls. **SIC:** 3463—Nonferrous Forgings; 3499—Fabricated Metal Products Nec.

★ 85490 ★ **Jiffy Lube**
2945 N. Garland Ave.
Garland, TX 75040
(214)530-4036
Ultimate Parent: Pennzoil.

★ 85491 ★   Jiffy Lube
530 N. Plano Rd.
Garland, TX 75042
(214)272-1392
Ultimate Parent: Pennzoil. **SIC:** 7538—
General Automotive Repair Shops.

★ 85492 ★   Johnson Controls Inc.
1111 Shiloh Rd.
Garland, TX 75046
Ultimate Parent: Johnson & Johnson. **SIC:**
3691—Storage Batteries.

★ 85493 ★   Kentucky Fried
Chicken
1929 S. 1st St.
Garland, TX 75040
(214)278-0130
Ultimate Parent: Pepsico. **SIC:** 5812—
Eating Places.

★ 85494 ★   Kentucky Fried
Chicken
3545 W. Walnut St.
Garland, TX 75042
(214)272-9888
Ultimate Parent: Pepsico. **SIC:** 5812—
Eating Places.

★ 85495 ★   Kmart Photography
Studio
1406 W. Walnut St.
Garland, TX 75042
(214)272-4656
Ultimate Parent: K-Mart. **SIC:** 7384—
Photofinishing Laboratories.

★ 85496 ★   Kmart Store
1406 W. Walnut St.
Garland, TX 75042
(214)276-9411
Ultimate Parent: K-Mart. **SIC:** 5311—
Department Stores; 5531—Automobile &
Home Supply Stores.

★ 85497 ★   Kmart Store
5701 Broadway Blvd.
Garland, TX 75043
(214)271-0007
Ultimate Parent: K-Mart. **SIC:** 5531—
Automobile & Home Supply Stores.

★ 85498 ★   Kraft Inc.
2340 Forest Ln.
Garland, TX 75042
Ultimate Parent: Philip Morris. **SIC:** 2033—
Canned Fruits & Vegetables; 2035—Pickles,
Sauces & Salad Dressings; 2064—Candy &
Other Confectionery Products; 2079—Edible
Fats & Oils Nec; 2099—Food Preparations
Nec.

★ 85499 ★   Kroger Food Stores
1040 W. Centerville Rd.
Garland, TX 75041
(214)270-7568
Ultimate Parent: Kroger.

★ 85500 ★   Kroger Stores
140 N. Star Rd.
Garland, TX 75040
(214)494-3456
Ultimate Parent: Kroger. **SIC:** 5411—
Grocery Stores.

★ 85501 ★   Lone Star Gas Co.
1310 Hwy. 66
Garland, TX 75040
(214)276-3147
Officer: Jan McCorstin, Executive Director.
Ultimate Parent: Ensearch. **SIC:** 2813—
Industrial Gases.

★ 85502 ★   Ltv Energy Products
2441 Forest Ln.
Garland, TX 75042
Ultimate Parent: LTV. **SIC:** 3533—Oil &
Gas Field Machinery; 3561—Pumps &
Pumping Equipment.

★ 85503 ★   LTV Energy Products
Co.
2441 Forest Ln.
Garland, TX 75042-7928
(214)487-3000 **Fax:** (214)276-8416
Officer: David E. Althoff, President & CEO.
Ultimate Parent: LTV.

★ 85504 ★   LTV Energy Products,
Plant 1
2441 Forest Ln.
Garland, TX 75042-6510
Ultimate Parent: LTV. **SIC:** 3533—Oil &
Gas Field Machinery; 3561—Pumps &
Pumping Equipment.

★ 85505 ★   LTV Energy Products,
Plant 2
2735 Forest Ln.
Garland, TX 75042-6510
Ultimate Parent: LTV. **SIC:** 3533—Oil &
Gas Field Machinery; 3561—Pumps &
Pumping Equipment.

★ 85506 ★   Mary Kay Cosmetics
4021 Amherst Dr.
Garland, TX 75042
(214)272-7166
Ultimate Parent: Mary Kay Cosmetics. **SIC:**
5999—Miscellaneous Retail Stores Nec.

★ 85507 ★   Mary Kay Cosmetics
5705 Bentley Dr.
Garland, TX 75043
Ultimate Parent: Mary Kay Cosmetics. **SIC:**
5999—Miscellaneous Retail Stores Nec.

★ 85508 ★   McDonalds
Hamburgers
2321 W. Walnut St.
Garland, TX 75042
(214)272-6198
Ultimate Parent: McDonald's.
SIC: 5812—Eating Places.

★ 85509 ★   McDonalds
Restaurant
3285 Broadway Blvd.
Garland, TX 75043
(214)278-8433
Ultimate Parent: McDonald's.

★ 85510 ★   McDonalds
Restaurant
6118 Broadway Blvd.
Garland, TX 75043
(214)240-8736
Ultimate Parent: McDonald's.

★ 85511 ★   Mobil Oil Corp.
6418 N. Jupiter Rd.
Garland, TX 75044
(214)530-8382
Ultimate Parent: Mobil.

★ 85512 ★   Mobil Self Serve
3036 Broadway Blvd.
Garland, TX 75041
(214)278-3071
Ultimate Parent: Mobil. **SIC:** 5541—
Gasoline Service Stations.

★ 85513 ★   Mobil Self Serve
1405 W. Buckingham Rd.
Garland, TX 75042
(214)495-7333
Ultimate Parent: Mobil. **SIC:** 5541—
Gasoline Service Stations.

★ 85514 ★   Mobil Self Serve
1401 Belt Line Rd.
Garland, TX 75044
(214)530-1883
Ultimate Parent: Mobil. **SIC:** 5541—
Gasoline Service Stations.

★ 85515 ★   Mobil Self Service
3501 Forest Ln.
Garland, TX 75042
(214)276-6205
Ultimate Parent: Mobil. **SIC:** 5599—
Automotive Dealers Nec.

★ 85516 ★   Mobil Self Service
6122 Broadway Blvd.
Garland, TX 75043
(214)271-0912
Ultimate Parent: Mobil. **SIC:** 5541—
Gasoline Service Stations.

★ 85517 ★   Optic-Electronic
Ni-Tec Div.
3414 Herrmann Dr.
Garland, TX 75041
Company Type: Division. **Ultimate Parent:**
Imo Industries. **SIC:** 3827—Optical
Instruments & Lenses.

★ 85518 ★   Payless Cashways
1734 Hwy. 66
Garland, TX 75040
(214)276-3409
Ultimate Parent: Payless Cashways.

★ 85519 ★   Payless Cashways
Bldg Matls
2906 W. Miller Rd.
Garland, TX 75041
(214)271-3571
Ultimate Parent: Payless Cashways. **SIC:**
5211—Lumber & Other Building Materials.

★ 85520 ★   Payless Shoesource
5986 Broadway Blvd.
Garland, TX 75043
(214)840-9094
Ultimate Parent: May Department Stores.
SIC: 5661—Shoe Stores.

★ 85521 ★   Payless Shoesource
1501 W. Buckingham Rd.
Garland, TX 75042
(214)530-3377
Ultimate Parent: May Department Stores.

★ 85522 ★   Pizza Hut
1449 W. Buckingham Rd.
Garland, TX 75042
(214)530-7100
Ultimate Parent: Pepsico.

★ 85523 ★   Pizza Hut
3725 W. Walnut St.
Garland, TX 75042
(214)276-8221
Ultimate Parent: Pepsico. **SIC:** 5812—
Eating Places.

★ 85524 ★   Praxair Inc.
2225 Lonnecker Dr.
Garland, TX 75041
Ultimate Parent: Praxair. **SIC:** 2813—
Industrial Gases.

★ 85525 ★   Praxair Inc.
Linde Div.
2225 Lonnecker Dr.
Garland, TX 75047
Company Type: Division. **Ultimate Parent:**
Union Carbide Corp. **SIC:** 2813—Industrial
Gases.

★ 85526 ★   Quick-To-Fix Foods
113 Range Dr.
Garland, TX 75040
Tyson Foods, Inc. **SIC:**
2013—Sausages & Other Prepared Meats.

★ 85527 ★   Radio Shack
3516 W. Walnut St.
Garland, TX 75042
(214)272-2620
Company Type: Division. **Ultimate Parent:**
Tandy Corp. **SIC:** 5065—Electronic Parts &
Equipment Nec.

★ 85528 ★   Radio Shack
552 W. Ih
Garland, TX 75043
(214)226-3321
Company Type: Division. **Ultimate Parent:**
Tandy Corp. **SIC:** 5719—Miscellaneous
Home Furnishings Stores.

★ 85529 ★   Radio Shack
1428 W. Buckingham Rd.
Garland, TX 75042
(214)272-8750
Company Type: Division. **Ultimate Parent:**
Tandy Corp. **SIC:** 5065—Electronic Parts &
Equipment Nec.

★ 85530 ★   Radio Shack
121 E. Kingsley Rd.
Garland, TX 75041
(214)278-3028
Company Type: Division. **Ultimate Parent:**
Tandy Corp. **SIC:** 5065—Electronic Parts &
Equipment Nec.

★ 85531 ★   Radio Shack
1542 Northwest Hwy.
Garland, TX 75041
(214)279-1632
Company Type: Division. **Ultimate Parent:**
Tandy Corp. **SIC:** 5731—Radio, Television
& Electronics Stores.

★ 85532 ★   Ryder Truck Rental
1231 S. Jupiter Rd.
Garland, TX 75042
(214)276-9431
Ultimate Parent: Ryder System. **SIC:**
7359—Equipment Rental & Leasing Nec.

★ 85533 ★   Shell Oil Co.
1214 W. Centerville Rd.
Garland, TX 75041
(214)270-6121
Ultimate Parent: Shell Oil Co. **SIC:** 7542—
Car Washes.

★ 85534 ★   Shell Self Serve
502 W. Interstate 30
Garland, TX 75043
(214)226-0067
Ultimate Parent: Shell Oil Co.

★ 85535 ★   Sherwin-Williams Co.
2802 W. Miller Rd.
Garland, TX 75041
(214)271-2541
Officer: John Davidson, Manager. **Ultimate
Parent:** Sherwin-Williams Co. **SIC:** 2851—
Paints & Allied Products.

★ 85536 ★   Silicon Materials
Service
2643 Industrial Ln.
Garland, TX 75041
Ultimate Parent: Air Products & Chemicals,
Inc. **SIC:** 3674—Semiconductors & Related
Devices.

★ 85537 ★   Silicon Materials
Service Inc.
2613 Industrial Ln.
Garland, TX 75041
Ultimate Parent: Air Products & Chemicals,
Inc. **SIC:** 3674—Semiconductors & Related
Devices.

★ 85538 ★   Taco Bell
2227 W. Walnut St.
Garland, TX 75042
(214)494-2167
Ultimate Parent: Pepsico. **SIC:** 5812—
Eating Places.

★ 85539 ★   Taco Bell
105 Main St.
Garland, TX 75040
(214)272-5710
Ultimate Parent: Pepsico. **SIC:** 5812—
Eating Places.

★ 85540 ★   Taco Bell
501 N. Plano Rd.
Garland, TX 75042
(214)272-5839
Ultimate Parent: Pepsico. **SIC:** 5812—
Eating Places.

★ 85541 ★   Taco Bell
3327 Broadway Blvd.
Garland, TX 75043
(214)271-7880
Ultimate Parent: Pepsico. **SIC:** 5812—
Eating Places.

★ 85542 ★   Taco Bell
5709 Broadway Blvd.
Garland, TX 75043
(214)240-6039
Ultimate Parent: Pepsico.

★ 85543 ★   Target Stores
3212 N. Jupiter Rd.
Garland, TX 75044
(903)530-1177
Company Type: Subsidiary. **Ultimate
Parent:** Dayton Hudson. **SIC:** 5311—
Department Stores.

★ 85544 ★   Texaco Instant Lube
1336 W. Kingsley Rd.
Garland, TX 75041
(214)840-0321
Ultimate Parent: Texaco. **SIC:** 7539—
Automotive Repair Shops Nec.

★ 85545 ★   Tyson Foods Inc.
113 Range Dr.
Garland, TX 75040
(214)272-5521
Officer: Rick Watson, Plant Manager.
Ultimate Parent: Tyson Foods, Inc. **SIC:**
2038—Frozen Specialties Nec.

★ 85546 ★   Tyson Foods Inc.
(Quik-To-Fix)
113 Range Dr.
Garland, TX 75040
Ultimate Parent: Tyson Foods, Inc. **SIC:**
2013—Sausages & Other Prepared Meats.

★ 85547 ★   Ucar Emulsion
Systems
2326 Lonnecker Dr.
Garland, TX 75041
Ultimate Parent: Union Carbide Corp. **SIC:**
2821—Plastics Materials & Resins.

★ 85548 ★   Union Carbide
Chemical Corp.
2326 Lonnecker Dr.
Garland, TX 75041
(214)864-6000
Officer: Lloyd Monroe, Manager. **Ultimate
Parent:** Union Carbide Corp. **SIC:** 2821—
Plastics Materials & Resins.

★ 85549 ★ **Union Carbide Chemicals & Plastics Inc.**
2326 Lonnecker Dr.
Garland, TX 75041
Ultimate Parent: Union Carbide Corp. **SIC:** 2821—Plastics Materials & Resins.

★ 85550 ★ **Union Carbide Corp.**
2326 Lonnecker Dr.
Garland, TX 75041
Ultimate Parent: Union Carbide Corp. **SIC:** 2810—Industrial Inorganic Chemicals.

★ 85551 ★ **Union Carbide Corp.**
Linde Div.
2225 Lonnecker Dr.
Garland, TX 75047-2404
Company Type: Division. **Ultimate Parent:** Union Carbide Corp. **SIC:** 2813—Industrial Gases.

★ 85552 ★ **Union Carbide Industrial Gases**
Linde Div.
2225 Lonnecker Dr.
Garland, TX 75047
Company Type: Division. **Ultimate Parent:** Union Carbide Corp. **SIC:** 2813—Industrial Gases.

★ 85553 ★ **Union Carbide Industrial Gases Inc.**
2225 Lonnecker Dr.
Garland, TX 75041
Ultimate Parent: Union Carbide Corp. **SIC:** 2813—Industrial Gases.

★ 85554 ★ **Valspar Corp.**
701 Shiloh Rd.
Garland, TX 75042
Ultimate Parent: Valspar Corp. **SIC:** 2851—Paints & Allied Products; 2521—Wood Office Furniture.

★ 85555 ★ **Valspar Corp.**
701 S. Shiloh Rd.
Garland, TX 75042
(214)276-5181
Officer: Valarie Reese, Vice President. **Ultimate Parent:** Valspar Corp. **SIC:** 2851—Paints & Allied Products.

★ 85556 ★ **Valspar Corp. Garland**
701 Shiloh Rd.
Garland, TX 75042
Ultimate Parent: Valspar Corp. **SIC:** 2851—Paints & Allied Products.

★ 85557 ★ **Varo, Inc.**
2203 W. Walnut St.
Garland, TX 75042
(214)487-4100
Ultimate Parent: Imo Industries. **SIC:** 3699—Electrical Equipment & Supplies Nec.

★ 85558 ★ **Varo, Inc.**
2800 W. Kingsley
PO Box 461426
Garland, TX 75046-1426
(214)840-5000 **Fax:** (214)840-5113
Company Type: Subsidiary. **Officer:** J. Dwayne Attaway, Executive Vice President. **Ultimate Parent:** Imo Industries. **SIC:** 3612—Transformers Except Electronic.

★ 85559 ★ **Varo Inc.**
3609 Marquis Dr.
Garland, TX 75046-2328
Ultimate Parent: Imo Industries. **SIC:** 3499—Fabricated Metal Products Nec.

★ 85560 ★ **Varo Inc.**
Ni-Tec Div.
3414 Herrmann Dr.
Garland, TX 75041
Company Type: Division. **Ultimate Parent:** Imo Industries. **SIC:** 3827—Optical Instruments & Lenses.

★ 85561 ★ **Varo Inc. Esd-Kingsley**
2800 W. Kingsley Rd.
Garland, TX 75041
Ultimate Parent: Imo Industries. **SIC:** 3671—Electron Tubes.

★ 85562 ★ **Varo Inc. Walnut**
2203 W. Walnut St.
Garland, TX 75046
Ultimate Parent: Imo Industries. **SIC:** 3671—Electron Tubes.

★ 85563 ★ **Varo Inc. Wds**
3609 Marquis Dr.
Garland, TX 75046-2328
Ultimate Parent: Imo Industries. **SIC:** 3499—Fabricated Metal Products Nec.

★ 85564 ★ **Varo Systems**
3609 Marquis Dr.
Garland, TX 75046-2328
Ultimate Parent: Imo Industries. **SIC:** 3499—Fabricated Metal Products Nec.

Georgetown

★ 85565 ★ **Citizens State Bank**
900 Austin Ave.
Georgetown, TX 78626
(512)863-2567
Ultimate Parent: Liberty National Bancorp. **SIC:** 6099—Functions Related to Deposit Banking.

★ 85566 ★ **Exxon Products**
301 Holly St.
Georgetown, TX 78626
(512)863-3341
Ultimate Parent: Exxon.

★ 85567 ★ **Greyhound Bus Lines**
403 W. 7th St.
Georgetown, TX 78626
(512)863-7462
Ultimate Parent: Greyhound Lines Inc. **SIC:** 7389—Business Services Nec.

★ 85568 ★ **Harris Calorific**
3026 Gabriel View Dr.
Georgetown, TX 78628
(512)863-8660
Ultimate Parent: Lincoln Electric Co. **SIC:** 5084—Industrial Machinery & Equipment.

★ 85569 ★ **Kentucky Fried Chicken**
121 N. Frontage Rd.
Georgetown, TX 78628
(512)863-6740
Ultimate Parent: Pepsico. **SIC:** 5812—Eating Places.

★ 85570 ★ **Mobil Oil Co.**
2300 N. Austin Ave.
Georgetown, TX 78626
(512)863-9549
Ultimate Parent: Mobil.

★ 85571 ★ **Piggly Wiggly**
2421 Williams Dr.
Georgetown, TX 78628
(512)863-6018
Ultimate Parent: Bruno's. **SIC:** 5411—Grocery Stores.

★ 85572 ★ **Pizza Hut**
928 N. Austin Ave.
Georgetown, TX 78626
(512)863-9556
Ultimate Parent: Pepsico.

★ 85573 ★ **Ryder Truck Rental**
408 N. Austin Ave.
Georgetown, TX 78626
(512)863-0877
Ultimate Parent: Ryder System. **SIC:** 7359—Equipment Rental & Leasing Nec.

★ 85574 ★ **Texaco Inc.**
1101 I Hwy. 35 N
Georgetown, TX 78626
(512)863-9971
Ultimate Parent: Texaco. **SIC:** 5541—Gasoline Service Stations.

Giddings

★ 85575 ★ **Citizens State Bank**
104 W. Austin St.
Giddings, TX 78942
(409)542-3136
Ultimate Parent: Liberty National Bancorp. **SIC:** 6022—State Commercial Banks.

★ 85576 ★ **Pizza Hut**
556 W. Austin St.
Giddings, TX 78942
(409)542-3011
Ultimate Parent: Pepsico. **SIC:** 5812—Eating Places.

★ 85577 ★ **Wal Mart Discount Cities**
Hwy. 290
Giddings, TX 78942
(409)542-1375
Ultimate Parent: Wal-Mart Stores, Inc. **SIC:** 5311—Department Stores.

Gilmer

★ 85578 ★ **Marshalls Department Store**
100 Buffalo St.
Gilmer, TX 75644
(214)843-2713
Ultimate Parent: Melville. **SIC:** 5311—Department Stores.

★ 85579 ★ **Piggly Wiggly**
N Wood
Gilmer, TX 75644
(903)843-2212
Ultimate Parent: Bruno's. **SIC:** 5411—Grocery Stores.

Gladewater

★ 85580 ★ **Exxon Co. USA**
Gilmer Hwy.
Gladewater, TX 75647
(214)845-2776
Ultimate Parent: Exxon. **SIC:** 1311—Crude Petroleum & Natural Gas.

★ 85581 ★ **Pizza Hut**
1210 Broadway Ave.
Gladewater, TX 75647
(903)845-5571
Ultimate Parent: Pepsico.

★ 85582 ★ **Texaco Inc. Producing Dept**
Longview Hwy.
Gladewater, TX 75647
(214)845-2124
Ultimate Parent: Texaco. **SIC:** 5171—Petroleum Bulk Stations & Terminals.

Glen Rose

★ 85583 ★ **Radio Shack**
Glen Rose, TX 76043
(817)897-4700
Company Type: Division. **Ultimate Parent:** Tandy Corp. **SIC:** 5065—Electronic Parts & Equipment Nec.

★ 85584 ★ **Sunrise Properties**
1210 Hwy. 67
Glen Rose, TX 76043
(817)897-3720
Ultimate Parent: Penn Traffic.

Goldthwaite

★ 85585 ★ **Stop & Shop Grocery**
1312 Fisher
Goldthwaite, TX 76844
(915)648-2455
Ultimate Parent: Stop & Shop. **SIC:** 5411—Grocery Stores.

Gonzales

★ 85586 ★ **American National Bank**
1606 Sarah Dewitt
Gonzales, TX 78629
(210)672-8585
Officer: John Paul Jones, Chairman of the Board. **Ultimate Parent:** First Chicago Corp. **SIC:** 6021—National Commercial Banks. **Employee Count:** 20.

★ 85587 ★ **Holly Farms Foods Inc. Tyson Foods Inc. Feed Mill**
Hwy. 90A Industrial Park
Gonzales, TX 78629
Ultimate Parent: Tyson Foods, Inc. **SIC:** 2048—Prepared Feeds Nec.

★ 85588 ★ **Holly Farms of Texas, Inc.**
Gonzales Feed Mill
Industrial Park, Hwy. 90A
PO Drawer 697
Gonzales, TX 78629
Location Type: Plant. **Ultimate Parent:** Tyson Foods, Inc. **SIC:** 2048—Prepared Feeds Nec.

★ 85589 ★ **Mobil Petroleum Co.**
Rural Route 1
Gonzales, TX 78629
(512)672-2018
Ultimate Parent: Mobil. **SIC:** 5172—Petroleum Products Nec.

★ 85590 ★ **Pizza Hut**
312 E. Hwy. 90A
Gonzales, TX 78629
(512)672-6924
Ultimate Parent: Pepsico. **SIC:** 5812—Eating Places.

★ 85591 ★ **Pizza Hut**
312 E. Hwy. 90A
Gonzales, TX 78629
(512)672-9616
Ultimate Parent: Pepsico.

★ 85592 ★ **Tyson Foods Feed Mill**
2504 Church St.
Gonzales, TX 78629
(210)672-6548
Officer: Harold Grauke, Manager. **Ultimate Parent:** Tyson Foods, Inc. **SIC:** 2048—Prepared Feeds Nec.

★ 85593 ★ **Tyson Foods Inc. Gonzales Feed Mill**
2504 Church St. Industrial Park
Gonzales, TX 78629
Ultimate Parent: Tyson Foods, Inc. **SIC:** 2048—Prepared Feeds Nec.

★ 85594 ★ **Tyson Foods Inc. Gonzales Feed Mill**
Industrial Park Hwy. 90A PO Box 697
Gonzales, TX 78629
Ultimate Parent: Tyson Foods, Inc. **SIC:** 2048—Prepared Feeds Nec.

★ 85595 ★ **Wal Mart Discount City**
Hwy. 90a E
Gonzales, TX 78629
(512)672-7301
Ultimate Parent: Wal-Mart Stores, Inc. **SIC:** 7538—General Automotive Repair Shops.

★ 85596 ★ **Wal Mart Discount Pharmacy**
Hwy. 90 Bypass
Gonzales, TX 78629
(512)672-2811
Ultimate Parent: Wal-Mart Stores, Inc. **SIC:** 5912—Drug Stores & Proprietary Stores.

Gorman

★ 85597 ★ **Citizens State Bank**
115 S. Fisher St.
Gorman, TX 76454
(817)734-2255
Ultimate Parent: Liberty National Bancorp. **SIC:** 6022—State Commercial Banks.

Granbury

★ 85598 ★ **Pizza Hut**
1006 S. Morgan St.
Granbury, TX 76048
(817)573-3765
Ultimate Parent: Pepsico.

★ 85599 ★ **Texaco Exprss Tube**
906 Hwy. 377 E
Granbury, TX 76048
(817)573-5218
Ultimate Parent: Texaco.

★ 85600 ★ **Trailways Bus Sys**
1512 W. Pearl St.
Granbury, TX 76048
(817)573-2174
Ultimate Parent: Greyhound Lines Inc. **SIC:** 4131—Intercity & Rural Bus Transportation.

★ 85601 ★ **United Parcel Service**
6 Briarwood St.
Granbury, TX 76048
(817)573-2616
Ultimate Parent: United Parcel Service of America.

★ 85602 ★ **Volunteer State Life Insurance Co.**
213 N. Crockett St.
Granbury, TX 76048
(817)573-4331
Ultimate Parent: Chubb. **SIC:** 8712—Architectural Services.

★ 85603 ★   Wal Mart Automotive
N Loop E. 377
Granbury, TX 76048
(817)573-4862
Ultimate Parent: Wal-Mart Stores, Inc. SIC:
7538—General Automotive Repair Shops.

Grand Praire

★ 85604 ★   Magnetek Universal
Electric
1330 W. N. Carrier Pky.
Grand Prairie, TX 75050-1203
Officer: Jerry Ritter. Ultimate Parent:
Magnetek Inc. SIC: 1731—Electrical Work;
3621—Motors & Generators.

Grand Prairie

★ 85605 ★   Avon Products Inc.
702 W. Springdale Ln.
Grand Prairie, TX 75051
(214)263-2971
Ultimate Parent: Avon Products, Inc. SIC:
5999—Miscellaneous Retail Stores Nec.

★ 85606 ★   Baker Hughes Mining
Tools Inc.
1600 S. Great Southwest Pky.
Grand Prairie, TX 75051
(214)988-3322
Officer: Robert W. Thomas, Vice President,
Sales. Ultimate Parent: Baker Hughes.
SIC: 3532—Mining Machinery; 3533—Oil &
Gas Field Machinery; 3542—Machine
Tools—Metal Forming Types.

★ 85607 ★   Baker Hughes Mining
Tools Inc.
1600 S. Great SW Pky.
Grand Prairie, TX 75051
Ultimate Parent: Baker Hughes. SIC:
3532—Mining Machinery.

★ 85608 ★   Baker Hughes
Process Equip.
Baker Hughes Mining Tools, Inc.
1600 S. Great Southwest Pky.
Grand Prairie, TX 75051
(214)988-3322
Company Type: Division. Officer: John A.
Alich Jr., President. Ultimate Parent: Baker
Hughes. SIC: 3532—Mining Machinery.

★ 85609 ★   Baxter Healthcare
Corp.
2501 N. Great SW Pky.
Grand Prairie, TX 75050-6429
(214)647-1633
Location Type: Branch office. Ultimate
Parent: Baxter International. SIC: 5122—
Drugs, Proprietaries & Sundries.

★ 85610 ★   Bell Helicopter
Textron Inc.
1700 N. Hwy. 360
Grand Prairie, TX 75050
Ultimate Parent: Textron. SIC: 3721—
Aircraft.

★ 85611 ★   Bristol Myers Co.
1301 Avenue T
Grand Prairie, TX 75050-1212
(214)641-5700
Officer: R. Johnson. Ultimate Parent:
Bristol-Myers Squibb. SIC: 5122—Drugs,
Proprietaries & Sundries.

★ 85612 ★   Brownell Electro Inc.
1130 W. North Carrier Pky.
Grand Prairie, TX 75050
(214)988-0821
Location Type: Branch office. Ultimate
Parent: Avnet. SIC: 5063—Electrical
Apparatus & Equipment.

★ 85613 ★   Challenger Electrical
Equipment
1102 Ave. T
Grand Prairie, TX 75050
Ultimate Parent: Westinghouse Electric
Corp. SIC: 3600—Electronic & Other
Electrical Equipment.

★ 85614 ★   Chase Home
Mortgage Corp.
2080 N. Hwy. 360
Grand Prairie, TX 75050
(214)988-3765
Ultimate Parent: Chase Manhattan Corp.
SIC: 6162—Mortgage Bankers &
Correspondents.

★ 85615 ★   D & S Plastics
International
1201 Ave. H E.
Grand Prairie, TX 75050
Ultimate Parent: Dexter Corp. SIC: 3087—
Custom Compound of Purchased Resins.

★ 85616 ★   D & S Plastics
International
1201 Ave. H. E.
Grand Prairie, TX 75050
Ultimate Parent: Dexter Corp. SIC: 2850—
Paints & Allied Products.

★ 85617 ★   Exxon
1501 NW 19th St.
Grand Prairie, TX 75050
(214)641-8274
Ultimate Parent: Exxon. SIC: 5599—
Automotive Dealers Nec.

★ 85618 ★   Heads & Threads Co.
923 Ave. N
Grand Prairie, TX 75050-1919
(214)660-2266
Ultimate Parent: Alleghany Corp. SIC:
5072—Hardware.

★ 85619 ★   Kentucky Fried
Chicken
402 E. Main St.
Grand Prairie, TX 75050
(214)262-7392
Ultimate Parent: Pepsico. SIC: 5812—
Eating Places.

★ 85620 ★   Kmart Discount
Stores
2602 SE 8th St.
Grand Prairie, TX 75051
(214)264-1523
Ultimate Parent: K-Mart.

★ 85621 ★   Kroger Financial
Center
313 E. Hwy. 303
Grand Prairie, TX 75051
(214)642-2148
Ultimate Parent: Kroger. SIC: 6411—
Insurance Agents, Brokers & Service.

★ 85622 ★   Kroger Food Stores
514 S. Carrier Pky.
Grand Prairie, TX 75051
(214)264-0301
Ultimate Parent: Kroger. SIC: 5912—Drug
Stores & Proprietary Stores.

★ 85623 ★   Loral Vought Systems
1701 W. Marshall
Grand Prairie, TX 75051
(214)603-1000 Fax: (214)603-7843
Company Type: Subsidiary. Ultimate
Parent: Loral Corp. SIC: 3711—Motor
Vehicles & Car Bodies; 3728—Aircraft Parts
& Equipment Nec; 3761—Guided Missiles &
Space Vehicles.

★ 85624 ★   Ltv Aerospace &
Defense
1701 W. Marshall Dr.
Grand Prairie, TX 75051
Ultimate Parent: LTV. SIC: 3761—Guided
Missiles & Space Vehicles; 3764—Space
Propulsion Units & Parts; 3769—Space
Vehicle Equipment Nec.

★ 85625 ★   Ltv Aerospace &
Defense Co.
1850 West Park Dr.
Grand Prairie, TX 75051
Ultimate Parent: LTV. SIC: 3721—Aircraft.

★ 85626 ★   Ltv Aerospace &
Defense Co.
1701 W. Marshall Dr.
Grand Prairie, TX 75051
Ultimate Parent: LTV. SIC: 3721—Aircraft.

★ 85627 ★   McDonalds Corp.
802 E. Main St.
Grand Prairie, TX 75050
(214)262-5171
Ultimate Parent: McDonald's.
SIC: 5812—Eating Places.

★ 85628 ★   McDonalds of Grand
Prairie
1401 NW 19th St.
Grand Prairie, TX 75050
(214)641-3394
Ultimate Parent: McDonald's.
SIC: 5812—Eating Places.

★ 85629 ★   Mercantile Mortgage
Corp.
12870 Hillcrest Rd.
Grand Prairie, TX 75051
(214)263-9630
Ultimate Parent: Mercantile Bankshares
Corp. SIC: 6162—Mortgage Bankers &
Correspondents.

★ 85630 ★   Mobil Oil Co.
305 NW 24th St.
Grand Prairie, TX 75050
(214)647-2289
Ultimate Parent: Mobil. SIC: 5172—
Petroleum Products Nec.

★ 85631 ★   Murdock Engineering
Co.
2006 South Great Southwest Pky.
Grand Prairie, TX 75051
Ultimate Parent: Lockheed Corp. SIC:
3728—Aircraft Parts & Equipment Nec.

★ 85632 ★   Pizza Hut
501 W. Hwy. 303
Grand Prairie, TX 75051
(214)647-0919
Ultimate Parent: Pepsico. SIC: 5812—
Eating Places.

★ 85633 ★   Pulte Home Corp.
513 Newberry St.
Grand Prairie, TX 75052
(214)263-7806
Ultimate Parent: Pulte. SIC: 1521—
Single-Family Housing Construction.

★ 85634 ★   Radio Shack
2501 S. Carrier Pky.
Grand Prairie, TX 75051
(214)262-4102
Company Type: Division. Ultimate Parent:
Tandy Corp. SIC: 5065—Electronic Parts &
Equipment Nec.

★ 85635 ★   Radio Shack
1026 N. Carrier Pky.
Grand Prairie, TX 75050
(214)262-2654
Company Type: Division. Ultimate Parent:
Tandy Corp. SIC: 5065—Electronic Parts &
Equipment Nec.

★ 85636 ★   Reynolds & Reynolds
Co.
1010 E. Ave. J
Grand Prairie, TX 75050
(214)647-1722
Officer: Ed Dilhoff, Manager. Ultimate
Parent: Reynolds & Reynolds. SIC: 2700—
Printing & Publishing; 2761—Manifold
Business Forms.

★ 85637 ★   Ryder Truck Rental
2501 109th St.
Grand Prairie, TX 75050
(214)602-1511
Ultimate Parent: Ryder System.

★ 85638 ★   Ryder Truck Rental
500 S. Great Pky. SW
Grand Prairie, TX 75051
(214)647-1261
Ultimate Parent: Ryder System. SIC:
7513—Truck Rental & Leasing Without
Drivers.

★ 85639 ★   Taco Bell
361 W. Hwy. 303
Grand Prairie, TX 75051
(214)262-7050
Ultimate Parent: Pepsico.

★ 85640 ★   Taco Bell
125 E. Main St.
Grand Prairie, TX 75050
(214)262-6096
Ultimate Parent: Pepsico. SIC: 5812—
Eating Places.

★ 85641 ★   Texaco Food Mart
730 W. Hwy. 303
Grand Prairie, TX 75051
(214)264-7128
Ultimate Parent: Texaco.

★ 85642 ★   Texaco Selfserv
Centers
730 E. Hwy. 303
Grand Prairie, TX 75051
(214)262-8989
Ultimate Parent: Texaco. SIC: 5541—
Gasoline Service Stations.

★ 85643 ★   Texas Fibers
1213 W. North Carrier Pky.
Grand Prairie, TX 75050-1250
Ultimate Parent: Leggett & Platt Inc. SIC:
3086—Plastics Foam Products.

★ 85644 ★   Trailways Group
Travel
1500 Jackson St.
Grand Prairie, TX 75051
(214)263-3800
Ultimate Parent: Greyhound Lines Inc. SIC:
4142—Bus Charter Service Except Local.

★ 85645 ★   Wal Mart Discount
Cities
2615 W. Hwy. 303
Grand Prairie, TX 75051
(214)660-4200
Ultimate Parent: Wal-Mart Stores, Inc.

★ 85646 ★   Warner Lambert Ltd
1102 N. Carrier Pky.
Grand Prairie, TX 75050
(214)641-1233
Ultimate Parent: Warner-Lambert Co. SIC:
5122—Drugs, Proprietaries & Sundries.

★ 85647 ★   Willamette Industries
Inc.
1200 W. Carrier Pky. N
Grand Prairie, TX 75050
(214)641-3891
Ultimate Parent: Willamette Industries, Inc.
SIC: 2221—Broadwoven Fabric Mills—
Manmade; 5113—Industrial & Personal
Service Paper.

Grand Saline

★ 85648 ★   Piggly Wiggly
Hwy. 80
Grand Saline, TX 75140
(214)962-3094
Ultimate Parent: Bruno's. SIC: 5411—
Grocery Stores.

★ 85649 ★   Ryder Truck Rental
322 Freeman
Grand Saline, TX 75140
(214)569-2134
Ultimate Parent: Ryder System.

Grandview

★ 85650 ★   Great Southwest
Telephone Corp.
PO Drawer 429
Grandview, TX 76050
(817)866-3377
Company Type: Subsidiary. Ultimate
Parent: ALLTEL Corp. SIC: 4812—
Radiotelephone Communications.

★ 85651 ★   Universal Forest Prod
447 PO Box
Grandview, TX 76050
(817)866-3356
Ultimate Parent: Universal Forest Products.
SIC: 2439—Structural Wood Members Nec.

★ 85652 ★   Universal Forest
Products
Hwy. 81 S.
Grandview, TX 76050
(817)866-3306
Officer: Dick Frazier, President. Ultimate
Parent: Universal Forest Products. SIC:
2439—Structural Wood Members Nec.

Grangerland

★ 85653 ★   Exxon Co., USA
RR 4
Box 1275
Grangerland, TX 77302
(409)231-2261
Officer: Johnny Sanze, Manager. Ultimate
Parent: Exxon. SIC: 2911—Petroleum
Refining.

Grapeland

★ 85654 ★   Mobil Pipeline Co.
Daly Rd.
Grapeland, TX 75844
(409)687-2313
Company Type: Branch. Ultimate Parent:
Mobil. SIC: 4612—Crude Petroleum
Pipelines.

★ 85655 ★ Nucor Corp.
Vulcraft Div.
Hwy. 287 N. N. Main Extension
Grapeland, TX 75844
Company Type: Division. Ultimate Parent:
Nucor Corp. SIC: 3341—Secondary
Nonferrous Metals.

Grapevine

★ 85656 ★ Avery Labels
Business System Div.
1025 S. Main St.
Grapevine, TX 76051-5542
(817)481-1900
Company Type: Division. Ultimate Parent:
Avery Dennison Corp. SIC: 2759—
Commercial Printing Nec.

★ 85657 ★ Four Seasons
500 Industrial Park Dr.
Grapevine, TX 76051
Ultimate Parent: Standard Products. SIC:
3585—Refrigeration & Heating Equipment.

★ 85658 ★ International Turbine
Corp.
1060 W. Northwest Hwy.
Grapevine, TX 76051
(817)488-8554
Officer: Tom Kincaid, President. Ultimate
Parent: Allied-Signal Inc. SIC: 3728—
Aircraft Parts & Equipment Nec.

★ 85659 ★ Pizza Hut
1111 W. Northwest Hwy.
Grapevine, TX 76051
(817)488-9521
Ultimate Parent: Pepsico. SIC: 5812—
Eating Places.

★ 85660 ★ Precision
Interconnect
1701 W. Northwest Hwy.
Grapevine, TX 76051
(817)488-2668
Ultimate Parent: AMP Inc.

★ 85661 ★ Ryder Truck Rental
1150 E. Northwest Hwy.
Grapevine, TX 76051
(817)481-3568
Ultimate Parent: Ryder System. SIC:
5113—Industrial & Personal Service Paper.

★ 85662 ★ Ryder Truck Rental
3613 W. Hwy. 26
Grapevine, TX 76051
(817)488-2192
Ultimate Parent: Ryder System.

★ 85663 ★ Ryder Truck Rental
1106 W. Northwest Hwy.
Grapevine, TX 76051
(817)488-8685
Ultimate Parent: Ryder System.

Greenville

★ 85664 ★ Dowbrands
1001 Ed Rutherford Dr.
Greenville, TX 75401
Ultimate Parent: Dow Chemical Co. USA.
SIC: 2841—Soap & Other Detergents.

★ 85665 ★ Dowbrands L.P.
1001 Ed Rutherford Dr.
Greenville, TX 75401
Ultimate Parent: Dow Chemical Co. USA.
SIC: 2841—Soap & Other Detergents.

★ 85666 ★ E-Systems Inc.
Majors Field Fm 1570
Greenville, TX 75403
Ultimate Parent: E-Systems Inc. SIC:
3721—Aircraft.

★ 85667 ★ E-Systems Inc.
Greenville Div.
FM 1570
Greenville, TX 75401
(903)455-3450
Company Type: Division. Officer: Brian
Cullen, President. Ultimate Parent:
E-Systems Inc. SIC: 3721—Aircraft.

★ 85668 ★ E-Systems Inc.
Greenville Division
POB 6056
Greenville, TX 75403-3450
(903)455-3450 Fax: (903)457-4413
Company Type: Subsidiary. Officer: Brian
D. Cullen, Vice President/General Manager.
Ultimate Parent: E-Systems Inc.

★ 85669 ★ Federal Express
Coroporatio
106 Rr 2
Greenville, TX 75402
Ultimate Parent: Federal Express. SIC:
4215—Courier Services Except by Air.

★ 85670 ★ Gillette Co. Inc.
Rutherford
Greenville, TX 75401
(214)454-7100
Ultimate Parent: Gillette. SIC: 2899—
Chemical Preparations Nec.

★ 85671 ★ Goodyear Tire &
Rubber Co.
6401 Hwy. 380 W.
Greenville, TX 75401
Ultimate Parent: Goodyear Tire & Rubber.
SIC: 3011—Tires & Inner Tubes.

★ 85672 ★ Kroger Co
5010 Wesley St.
Greenville, TX 75401
(214)454-3662
Ultimate Parent: Kroger. SIC: 5411—
Grocery Stores.

★ 85673 ★ Lone Star Gas Co.
1054 PO Box
Greenville, TX 75403
Ultimate Parent: Enserch. SIC: 4925—Gas
Production & Distribution Nec; 4939—
Combination Utility Nec.

★ 85674 ★ Pizza Hut
5202 Wesley St.
Greenville, TX 75401
(214)455-0934
Ultimate Parent: Pepsico. SIC: 5812—
Eating Places.

★ 85675 ★ Radio Shack
Cross
Greenville, TX 75401
(214)454-2601
Company Type: Division. Ultimate Parent:
Tandy Corp. SIC: 5046—Commercial
Equipment Nec.

★ 85676 ★ Rubbermaid Office
Products Inc.
7121 Shelby Ave.
Greenville, TX 75402
(903)455-0011
Ultimate Parent: Rubbermaid. SIC: 3089—
Plastics Products Nec; 3469—Metal
Stampings Nec.

★ 85677 ★ Serv - Air Inc.
POB 669,9315 FM 1570
Greenville, TX 75403-6669
(903)454-2000 Fax: (903)454-0332
Company Type: Subsidiary. Officer: R. J.
Zacny, Vice President/General Manager.
Ultimate Parent: E-Systems Inc.

★ 85678 ★ Serv-Air Inc.
9315 FM 1570
Greenville, TX 75043
(903)454-2000
Company Type: Subsidiary. Officer:
Robert J. Zacny, President. Ultimate
Parent: E-Systems Inc. SIC: 4581—
Airports, Flying Fields & Services.
Employee Count: 2800. Sales: 285 M.

★ 85679 ★ Trailways Bus System
2805 Mitchell St.
Greenville, TX 75401
(214)455-5440
Ultimate Parent: Greyhound Lines Inc. SIC:
4131—Intercity & Rural Bus Transportation.

★ 85680 ★ Trico Ind. Inc.
6325 Trico Ln.
Greenville, TX 75401
Ultimate Parent: Paccar. SIC: 3462—Iron
& Steel Forgings; 3398—Metal Heat
Treating; 3449—Miscellaneous Metal Work.

Gregory

★ 85681 ★ Occidental Chemical
Corp.
Corpus Christi Plant
Hwy. 361
Gregory, TX 78359
Location Type: Plant. Ultimate Parent:
Occidental Petroleum Corp. SIC: 2869—
Industrial Organic Chemicals Nec.

★ 85682 ★ Reynolds Metals Co.
Sherwin Plant
Hwy. 361
Gregory, TX 78359
Ultimate Parent: Reynolds Metals Co. SIC:
2819—Industrial Inorganic Chemicals Nec.

Groves

★ 85683 ★ Radio Shack
3701 Twin City Hwy.
Groves, TX 77619
(409)962-6011
Company Type: Division. Ultimate Parent:
Tandy Corp. SIC: 5734—Computer &
Software Stores.

★ 85684 ★ Savings of America,
FSB
3434 Twin City Hwy.
Groves, TX 77619-2837
(409)962-8457
Company Type: Division. Location Type:
Branch office. Ultimate Parent: H. F.
Ahmanson. SIC: 6021—National
Commercial Banks.

★ 85685 ★ Ucar Pipeline Inc.
6700 Hogaboom Rd.
Groves, TX 77619
(409)962-1655
Ultimate Parent: Union Carbide Corp.

★ 85686 ★ Union Carbide Corp.
Linde Div.
6710 Hogaboom Rd.
Groves, TX 77619
Company Type: Division. Ultimate Parent:
Union Carbide Corp. SIC: 2813—Industrial
Gases.

★ 85687 ★ Walgreen Drug Stores
3501 Twin City Hwy.
Groves, TX 77619
(409)962-5747
Ultimate Parent: Walgreen Co. SIC:
5912—Drug Stores & Proprietary Stores.

★ 85688 ★ Western Auto Supply
Co.
3637 Twin City Hwy.
Groves, TX 77619
(409)962-5741
Ultimate Parent: Sears Roebuck & Co.
SIC: 5531—Automobile & Home Supply
Stores.

Groveton

★ 85689 ★ First Bank
Corner Devn St. 1st
Groveton, TX 75845
(409)642-1444
Ultimate Parent: Shawmut National Corp.
SIC: 6022—State Commercial Banks.

★ 85690 ★ Mobil Pipe Line Co.
Groveton, TX 75845
(409)642-1636
Company Type: Branch. Ultimate Parent:
Mobil. SIC: 4612—Crude Petroleum
Pipelines.

Gruver

★ 85691 ★ Air Products
Manufacturing Corp.
Hwy. 136
Gruver, TX 79040
Ultimate Parent: Air Products & Chemicals,
Inc. SIC: 2813—Industrial Gases.

★ 85692 ★ Air Products
Manufacturing Corp.
Hwy. 136
Gruver, TX 79040
Ultimate Parent: Air Products & Chemicals,
Inc. SIC: 2813—Industrial Gases.

Hale Center

★ 85693 ★ Texaco Service
Station
612 D Ave.
Hale Center, TX 79041
(806)839-2565
Ultimate Parent: Texaco. SIC: 5541—
Gasoline Service Stations.

Hamilton

★ 85694 ★ Lone Star Gas Co.
900 S. Rice
Hamilton, TX 76531
(817)386-5511
Ultimate Parent: Enserch. SIC: 4932—Gas
& Other Services Combined.

★ 85695 ★ Texaco Inc.
300 E. Main St.
Hamilton, TX 76531
(817)386-8360
Ultimate Parent: Texaco. SIC: 5541—
Gasoline Service Stations.

Harlingen

★ 85696 ★ AMR Services
Valley International Airport
Harlingen, TX 78550
(210)430-8655
Ultimate Parent: AMR Corp. SIC: 4581—
Airports, Flying Fields & Services.

★ 85697 ★ BFI Waste Systems
W Expy. 83
Harlingen, TX 78552
(210)423-7316
Location Type: Branch office. Ultimate
Parent: Browning-Ferris Industries. SIC:
4953—Refuse Systems.

★ 85698 ★ Browning Ferris
Industries
2202 S. 77 Sunshine Strip
Harlingen, TX 78550-8332
(210)425-8960
Ultimate Parent: Browning-Ferris
Industries. SIC: 4953—Refuse Systems.

★ 85699 ★ Casual Corner
Valle Vis
Harlingen, TX 78550
(512)421-2594
Ultimate Parent: United States Shoe. SIC:
5611—Men's & Boys' Clothing Stores.

★ 85700 ★ Foot Action
Valle Vis
Harlingen, TX 78550
(512)423-0122
Ultimate Parent: Melville. SIC: 5661—Shoe
Stores.

★ 85701 ★ Hit or Miss
2000 S. Expy. 83
Harlingen, TX 78552
(512)423-9908
Ultimate Parent: TJX. SIC: 5621—
Women's Clothing Stores.

★ 85702 ★ IDS Financial
Services Inc.
1206 E. Tyler St.
Harlingen, TX 78550-7140
(210)423-1023
Ultimate Parent: American Express Co.
SIC: 6282—Investment Advice.

★ 85703 ★ Kentucky Fried
Chicken
201 S. 77th Sunshine St.
Harlingen, TX 78550
(512)425-5392
Ultimate Parent: Pepsico. SIC: 5812—
Eating Places.

★ 85704 ★ Lerner Shop
Valle Vis
Harlingen, TX 78550
(512)421-2390
Ultimate Parent: Limited. SIC: 5621—
Women's Clothing Stores.

★ 85705 ★ Mary Kay Cosmet
Indep Sales
2901 Jacaranda Dr.
Harlingen, TX 78550
(512)428-9151
Ultimate Parent: Mary Kay Cosmetics. SIC:
5999—Miscellaneous Retail Stores Nec.

★ 85706 ★ McDonalds
401 E. Jackson St.
Harlingen, TX 78550
(512)425-5555
Ultimate Parent: McDonald's.
SIC: 5812—Eating Places.

★ 85707 ★   Mutual of New York
1222 E. Tyler St.
Harlingen, TX 78550
(512)423-1100
Ultimate Parent: Mutual of New York. SIC:
6411—Insurance Agents, Brokers &
Service.

★ 85708 ★   NCR Corp.
1011 W. Harrison St.
Harlingen, TX 78550-6018
(210)423-6144
Ultimate Parent: AT&T. SIC: 2761—
Manifold Business Forms.

★ 85709 ★   Pizza Hut
1802 W. Tyler St.
Harlingen, TX 78550
(512)425-6520
Ultimate Parent: Pepsico. SIC: 5812—
Eating Places.

★ 85710 ★   Pizza Hut
920 Morgan Blvd.
Harlingen, TX 78550
(512)428-2191
Ultimate Parent: Pepsico. SIC: 5812—
Eating Places.

★ 85711 ★   Pizza Hut
1224 S. Commerce St.
Harlingen, TX 78550
(512)423-1900
Ultimate Parent: Pepsico. SIC: 5812—
Eating Places.

★ 85712 ★   Radio Shack
Valle Vis
Harlingen, TX 78550
(512)428-0844
Company Type: Division. Ultimate Parent:
Tandy Corp. SIC: 5065—Electronic Parts &
Equipment Nec.

★ 85713 ★   Radio Shack
601 S. Expressway 83
Harlingen, TX 78550
Company Type: Division. Ultimate Parent:
Tandy Corp. SIC: 5065—Electronic Parts &
Equipment Nec.

★ 85714 ★   Ryder Truck Rental
1702 N. 77 Sunshine Strip
Harlingen, TX 78550
(512)428-4833
Ultimate Parent: Ryder System. SIC:
7359—Equipment Rental & Leasing Nec.

★ 85715 ★   Ryder Truck Rental
621 S. 77 Sunshine Strip
Harlingen, TX 78550
(512)425-4274
Ultimate Parent: Ryder System. SIC:
7513—Truck Rental & Leasing Without
Drivers.

★ 85716 ★   Trailways Bus System
520 S. Commerce St.
Harlingen, TX 78550
(512)423-1451
Ultimate Parent: Greyhound Lines Inc. SIC:
4212—Local Trucking Without Storage.

★ 85717 ★   Trailways
Manufacturing Inc.
2800 Rebel Dr.
Harlingen, TX 78550
(512)428-3121
Ultimate Parent: Greyhound Lines Inc. SIC:
3711—Motor Vehicles & Car Bodies.

★ 85718 ★   Underwriters
Adjusting Co.
421 S. 77 Sunshine Strip
Harlingen, TX 78550
(512)423-4636
Ultimate Parent: Continental. SIC: 6411—
Insurance Agents, Brokers & Service.

★ 85719 ★   Wal Mart Discount
Cities
Dixieland Hwy. W
Harlingen, TX 78550
(512)421-2341
Ultimate Parent: Wal-Mart Stores, Inc. SIC:
5311—Department Stores.

★ 85720 ★   Waldenbooks
Valle Vis
Harlingen, TX 78550
(512)423-4286
Ultimate Parent: K-Mart. SIC: 5942—Book
Stores.

Hawkins

★ 85721 ★   Exxon Co. USA
Hwy. 14 NE 1795
Hawkins, TX 75765
(903)769-2161
Officer: Randy Morrison, Manager.
Ultimate Parent: Exxon SIC: 2911—
Petroleum Refining.

Hearne

★ 85722 ★   Greyhound Bus Lines
905 W. Brown St.
Hearne, TX 77859
(409)279-5221
Ultimate Parent: Greyhound Lines Inc. SIC:
4142—Bus Charter Service Except Local.

★ 85723 ★   Lone Star Gas Co.
307 3rd
Hearne, TX 77859
(409)279-3252
Ultimate Parent: Enserch. SIC: 4925—Gas
Production & Distribution Nec.

★ 85724 ★   Piggly Wiggly
Brown
Hearne, TX 77859
(409)279-5604
Ultimate Parent: Bruno's. SIC: 5411—
Grocery Stores.

★ 85725 ★   Pizza Hut Hearne
Office
907 Hwy. 79
Hearne, TX 77859
(409)279-6760
Ultimate Parent: Pepsico. SIC: 5812—
Eating Places.

★ 85726 ★   Radio Shack
201 S. Magnolia St.
Hearne, TX 77859
(409)279-5208
Company Type: Division. Ultimate Parent:
Tandy Corp. SIC: 5731—Radio, Television
& Electronics Stores.

★ 85727 ★   Texaco Distribution
Terminal Bryam Hwy.
Hearne, TX 77859
(409)279-2414
Ultimate Parent: Texaco. SIC: 5171—
Petroleum Bulk Stations & Terminals.

★ 85728 ★   Wal Mart Tire & Auto
Ctr
Hwy. 79
Hearne, TX 77859
(409)279-6530
Ultimate Parent: Wal-Mart Stores, Inc. SIC:
7538—General Automotive Repair Shops.

Hebbronville

★ 85729 ★   Union Texas
Petroleum Corp.
510 W. Beasley St.
Hebbronville, TX 78361
(512)527-4315
Ultimate Parent: Union Texas Petroleum.

Hemphill

★ 85730 ★   Arco Oil & Gas Co.
Hemphill, TX 75948
(409)579-3895
Ultimate Parent: Atlantic Richfield Co., Inc.
SIC: 1311—Crude Petroleum & Natural
Gas.

Hempstead

★ 85731 ★   Citizens State Bank
13th & Austin St.
Hempstead, TX 77445
(713)826-2431
Ultimate Parent: Liberty National Bancorp.
SIC: 6022—State Commercial Banks.

Henderson

★ 85732 ★   Arco Oil & Gas Co.
2400 Hwy. 322
Henderson, TX 75652-6630
(903)657-0600
Location Type: Branch office. Officer: Rex
Copeland. Ultimate Parent: Atlantic
Richfield Co., Inc. SIC: 1311—Crude
Petroleum & Natural Gas.

★ 85733 ★   Kentucky Fried
Chicken
301 Us Hwy. 79 N
Henderson, TX 75652
(214)657-9631
Ultimate Parent: Pepsico. SIC: 5812—
Eating Places.

★ 85734 ★   Wal Mart
2309 Us Hwy. 79 S
Henderson, TX 75652
(903)657-9528
Ultimate Parent: Wal-Mart Stores, Inc. SIC:
5311—Department Stores.

Henrietta

★ 85735 ★   Burlington Northern
Railroa
Jacksboro Hwy.
Henrietta, TX 76365
(817)538-4261
Ultimate Parent: Burlington Northern. SIC:
4011—Railroads—Line-Haul Operating.

★ 85736 ★   Lone Star Gas Co.
108 W. Ikard St.
Henrietta, TX 76365
(817)538-4811
Ultimate Parent: Enserch. SIC: 4925—Gas
Production & Distribution Nec.

★ 85737 ★   Mobil Oil Distributor
215 W. Omega St.
Henrietta, TX 76365
(817)538-5021
Ultimate Parent: Mobil. SIC: 5541—
Gasoline Service Stations.

Hereford

★ 85738 ★   American Family Life
Assurance
242 E. 3rd St.
Hereford, TX 79045
(806)364-6690
Ultimate Parent: American Family Life
Assurance Co. SIC: 6411—Insurance
Agents, Brokers & Service.

★ 85739 ★   Coast to Coast Home
& Auto
114 E. Park Ave.
Hereford, TX 79045
(806)364-0574
Ultimate Parent: Servistar Corp. SIC:
5531—Automobile & Home Supply Stores.

★ 85740 ★   Crown of Texas
Hospice
805 Main St.
Hereford, TX 79045-5263
(806)364-0182
Ultimate Parent: Beverly Enterprises. SIC:
8059—Nursing & Personal Care Nec.

★ 85741 ★   Farr Better Feeds
112 South Progressive Rd.
Hereford, TX 79045
Ultimate Parent: W. R. Grace. SIC: 2048—
Prepared Feeds Nec.

★ 85742 ★   Holly Sugar Corp.
Hereford Factory
Holly Sugar Rd.
Hereford, TX 79045
Ultimate Parent: Imperial Holly. SIC:
2063—Beet Sugar.

★ 85743 ★   Kentucky Fried
Chicken
437 N. 25 Mile Ave.
Hereford, TX 79045
(806)364-6431
Ultimate Parent: Pepsico. SIC: 5812—
Eating Places.

★ 85744 ★   Pizza Hut
611 Mckinley St.
Hereford, TX 79045
(806)364-8555
Ultimate Parent: Pepsico. SIC: 5812—
Eating Places.

★ 85745 ★   Pizza Hut
1304 W. 1st St.
Hereford, TX 79045
(806)364-5551
Ultimate Parent: Pepsico. SIC: 5812—
Eating Places.

★ 85746 ★   Red Arrow Freight
Lines Inc.
105 S. Blevins St.
Hereford, TX 79045
(806)364-2306
Ultimate Parent: Carolina Freight. SIC:
4213—Trucking Except Local.

Hewitt

★ 85747 ★   Ryder Truck Rental
525 Connie Dr.
Hewitt, TX 76643
(817)666-0366
Ultimate Parent: Ryder System.

Hidalgo

★ 85748 ★   Tara Foods Inc.
106 E. Coma Ave.
Hidalgo, TX 78557
(512)843-2503
Ultimate Parent: Kroger. SIC: 5142—
Packaged Frozen Foods.

Highlands

★ 85749 ★   Mobil Oil Corp.
409 E. Wallisville Rd.
Highlands, TX 77562-3827
(713)426-7137
Company Type: Branch. Ultimate Parent:
Mobil. SIC: 1311—Crude Petroleum &
Natural Gas; 1000—Metal Mining.

Hillsboro

★ 85750 ★   Greyhound Bus Lines
201 N. Waco St.
Hillsboro, TX 76645
(817)582-3762
Ultimate Parent: Greyhound Lines Inc. SIC:
4111—Local & Suburban Transit.

★ 85751 ★   Pizza Hut
I 35
Hillsboro, TX 76645
(817)582-8295
Ultimate Parent: Pepsico. SIC: 5812—
Eating Places.

Hondo

★ 85752 ★   Pizza Hut
801 19th St.
Hondo, TX 78861
(512)426-4965
Ultimate Parent: Pepsico. SIC: 5812—
Eating Places.

★ 85753 ★   Universal Rundle
Corp.
815 Carter St.
Hondo, TX 78861
(210)426-3371
Officer: Lloyd Witte, Manager. Ultimate
Parent: Nortek. SIC: 3261—Vitreous
Plumbing Fixtures.

★ 85754 ★   Universal-Rundle
Corp.
Hondo Airbase
Hondo, TX 78861
Ultimate Parent: Nortek. SIC: 3261—
Vitreous Plumbing Fixtures.

★ 85755 ★   Universal Rundle
Corp.
Airfield Rd.
Hondo, TX 78861
Ultimate Parent: Nortek. SIC: 3261—
Vitreous Plumbing Fixtures.

Honey Grove

★ 85756 ★   Piggly Wiggly
N Side Sq.
Honey Grove, TX 75446
(214)378-2691
Ultimate Parent: Bruno's. SIC: 5411—
Grocery Stores.

Houston

★ 85757 ★   Abercrombie & Fitch
2300 Maxwell Ln.
Houston, TX 77023
(713)924-5190
Ultimate Parent: Limited. SIC: 5941—
Sporting Goods & Bicycle Shops.

★ 85758 ★　ABF Freight System Inc.
200 Brisbane St.
Houston, TX 77061-5002
(713)644-9585
Location Type: Branch office. **Ultimate Parent:** Arkansas Best. **SIC:** 4212—Local Trucking Without Storage.

★ 85759 ★　Acco Waste Paper
403 Jensen Dr.
Houston, TX 77020-8497
(713)227-6541
Officer: Alan Stein. **Ultimate Parent:** Browning-Ferris Industries. **SIC:** 4953—Refuse Systems; 5093—Scrap & Waste Materials.

★ 85760 ★　Ace Hardware Stores
11655 Jones Rd.
Houston, TX 77070
(713)469-8020
Ultimate Parent: Ace Hardware. **SIC:** 3714—Motor Vehicle Parts & Accessories.

★ 85761 ★　Ace Hardware&Home Center
12130 Stuebner Airline Rd.
Houston, TX 77067
(713)537-0997
Ultimate Parent: Ace Hardware. **SIC:** 5251—Hardware Stores.

★ 85762 ★　Advanced Medical Systems
9919 S. Gessner Dr.
Houston, TX 77071
(713)772-6690
Ultimate Parent: Standard Register. **SIC:** 7372—Prepackaged Software.

★ 85763 ★　Advanced Micro Devices Inc.
2925 Briarpark Dr.
Houston, TX 77042
(713)785-9001
Ultimate Parent: Advanced Micro Devices Inc. **SIC:** 3699—Electrical Equipment & Supplies Nec.

★ 85764 ★　Advanced Micro Devices Inc.
20333 State Hwy. 249
Houston, TX 77070-2617
(713)376-8084
Ultimate Parent: Advanced Micro Devices Inc. **SIC:** 3679—Electronic Components Nec.

★ 85765 ★　Aero Service Corp.
3600 Briarpark
Houston, TX 77042-4299
(713)784-4299 **Fax:** (713)781-1806 **Telex:** 775909
Company Type: Division. **Officer:** Emil J. Mateker, President. **Ultimate Parent:** Litton Industries. **SIC:** 1382—Oil & Gas Exploration Services; 7335—Commercial Photography.

★ 85766 ★　Airborne Freight Corp.
3101 Igloo Rd.
Houston, TX 77032
(713)443-8510
Ultimate Parent: Airborne Freight Corp. **SIC:** 4512—Air Transportation—Scheduled.

★ 85767 ★　All American Pipeline Co.
333 Clay St., Ste. 2700
Houston, TX 77002
(713)750-4500
Company Type: Subsidiary. **Ultimate Parent:** Goodyear Tire & Rubber.

★ 85768 ★　All American Pipeline Co. Inc.
333 Clay St., Ste. 2600
Houston, TX 77002-4101
(713)750-4500
Company Type: Subsidiary. **Officer:** Robert Milk, President; Chief Executive Officer. **Ultimate Parent:** Goodyear Tire & Rubber. **SIC:** 4612—Crude Petroleum Pipelines. **Employee Count:** 167. **Sales:** 38.8000000 M.

★ 85769 ★　Allegheny Ludlum Steel Corp.
333 E. Belt N
Houston, TX 77060
(713)999-3700
Ultimate Parent: Allegheny Ludlum Corp.

SIC: 5051—Metals Service Centers & Offices.

★ 85770 ★　Allied Industries Inc.
2828 Clinton Dr.
Houston, TX 77028-8402
Ultimate Parent: Halliburton. **SIC:** 3443—Fabricated Plate Work—Boiler Shops.

★ 85771 ★　Allied Plywood Corp.
8925 Market St.
Houston, TX 77029
(713)676-2766
Ultimate Parent: Ply Gem. **SIC:** 5211—Lumber & Other Building Materials.

★ 85772 ★　Allied Signal Aerospace
501 Gemini St.
Houston, TX 77058
(713)486-9384
Ultimate Parent: Allied-Signal Inc.

★ 85773 ★　Allied-Signal Inc.
Uop Process Div.
11511 Katy Fwy.
Houston, TX 77079
(713)496-3600
Company Type: Division. **Ultimate Parent:** Allied-Signal Inc. **SIC:** 3861—Photographic Equipment & Supplies.

★ 85774 ★　Allstate Life Insurance Co.
7600 W. Tidwell Rd.
Houston, TX 77040
(713)462-0683
Ultimate Parent: Allstate Life. **SIC:** 6411—Insurance Agents, Brokers & Service.

★ 85775 ★　Amerada Hess Corp.
1200 Milam St.
Houston, TX 77002
(713)658-9770
Ultimate Parent: Amerada Hess. **SIC:** 5171—Petroleum Bulk Stations & Terminals.

★ 85776 ★　America West Airlines
2941 Airfreight Rd.
Houston, TX 78722-1237
(512)475-2250
Ultimate Parent: America West Airlines. **SIC:** 4513—Air Courier Services.

★ 85777 ★　American Financial Service Inc.
9630 Rockhurst Dr.
Houston, TX 77080-1202
(713)460-2952
Ultimate Parent: Bancorp Hawaii. **SIC:** 6141—Personal Credit Institutions.

★ 85778 ★　American General Corp.
PO Box 3247
Houston, TX 77253
Ultimate Parent: American General Corp.

★ 85779 ★　American General Corp.
2929 Allen Pky.
Houston, TX 77019-2119
(713)522-1111
Company Type: Headquarters. **Officer:** Harold S. Hook, CEO. **SIC:** 6311—Life Insurance; 5331—Variety Stores; 6141—Personal Credit Institutions; 6162—Mortgage Bankers & Correspondents; 6153—Short-Term Business Credit. **Employee Count:** 11531. **Sales:** 43982 M. **Fortune Service 500:** Ranking 15.

★ 85780 ★　American General Federal Credit Union
2919 Allen Pky.
Houston, TX 77019-2116
(713)831-2773
Location Type: Branch office. **Officer:** Pamela Cody, Manager. **Ultimate Parent:** American General Corp. **SIC:** 6061—Federal Credit Unions.

★ 85781 ★　American General Investment Corp.
PO Box 1375
Houston, TX 77251-1375
(713)522-1111
Location Type: Branch office. **Officer:** Howard York. **Ultimate Parent:** American General Corp. **SIC:** 6162—Mortgage Bankers & Correspondents; 6552—Subdividers & Developers Nec.

★ 85782 ★　American General Investment Corp.
2929 Allen Pkw.
Houston, TX 77019-2119
(713)522-1111
Location Type: Branch office. **Officer:** Howard A. York, President. **Ultimate Parent:** American General Corp. **SIC:** 6531—Real Estate Agents & Managers.

★ 85783 ★　American General Investment Corp.
PO Box 1375
Houston, TX 77251-1375
(713)522-1111
Location Type: Branch office. **Officer:** Howard York. **Ultimate Parent:** American General Corp. **SIC:** 6162—Mortgage Bankers & Correspondents; 6552—Subdividers & Developers Nec.

★ 85784 ★　American General Life Insurance Co.
PO Box 4382
Houston, TX 77210-4382
(713)522-1111
Location Type: Branch office. **Officer:** Robert M. Devlin. **Ultimate Parent:** American General Corp. **SIC:** 6311—Life Insurance; 6321—Accident & Health Insurance.

★ 85785 ★　American General Life Insurance Co.
2727 Allen Pky.
Houston, TX 77019-2115
(713)522-1111
Location Type: Branch office. **Officer:** Robert M. Devlin, President & CEO. **Ultimate Parent:** American General Corp. **SIC:** 6311—Life Insurance. **Employee Count:** 1076.

★ 85786 ★　American General Life Insurance Co.
PO Box 4382
Houston, TX 77210-4382
(713)522-1111
Location Type: Branch office. **Officer:** Robert M. Devlin. **Ultimate Parent:** American General Corp. **SIC:** 6311—Life Insurance; 6321—Accident & Health Insurance.

★ 85787 ★　American General Mortgage Co.
2777 Allen Pky.
Houston, TX 77019
(713)522-1111
Officer: Edward H. James, President & CEO. **Ultimate Parent:** American General Corp. **SIC:** 6162—Mortgage Bankers & Correspondents; 6531—Real Estate Agents & Managers.

★ 85788 ★　American General Mortgage Co.
2929 Allen Pky.
Houston, TX 77019-2119
(713)522-1111
Officer: Howard A. York, President. **Ultimate Parent:** American General Corp. **SIC:** 6162—Mortgage Bankers & Correspondents.

★ 85789 ★　American General Mortgage Co.
2929 Allen Pky.
Houston, TX 77019-2119
(713)522-1111
Location Type: Branch office. **Officer:** Howard A. York, President. **Ultimate Parent:** American General Corp. **SIC:** 6162—Mortgage Bankers & Correspondents.

★ 85790 ★　American General Realty Investment Corp.
2929 Allen Pky.
Houston, TX 77019-2119
(713)522-1111
Location Type: Branch office. **Officer:** Howard A. York, President. **Ultimate Parent:** American General Corp. **SIC:** 6798—Real Estate Investment Trusts; 6531—Real Estate Agents & Managers. **Sales:** 2 M.

★ 85791 ★　American General Securities Inc.
2727 Allen Pky.
Houston, TX 77019-2115
(713)522-1111
Location Type: Branch office. **Officer:** Larry K. Janney, President. **Ultimate**

Parent: American General Corp. **SIC:** 6211—Security Brokers & Dealers. **Employee Count:** 16. **Sales:** 1 M.

★ 85792 ★　American General Securities Inc.
2727 Allen Pky.
Houston, TX 77019-2115
(713)522-1111
Officer: Larry K. Janney, President. **Ultimate Parent:** American General Corp. **SIC:** 6211—Security Brokers & Dealers. **Employee Count:** 16. **Sales:** 1.1 M.

★ 85793 ★　American General Securities Inc.
Riviana Bldg., 2777 Allen Pky.
Houston, TX 77019
(713)831-3387
Officer: Robert M. Devlin, President. **Ultimate Parent:** American General Corp. **SIC:** 6211—Security Brokers & Dealers.

★ 85794 ★　American Parts System Inc.
3000 Pawnee St.
Houston, TX 77054-3301
(713)741-2470
Company Type: Subsidiary. **Officer:** Mark S. Hoffman, President. **Ultimate Parent:** Collins & Aikman Group. **SIC:** 5013—Motor Vehicle Supplies & New Parts. **Employee Count:** 662. **Sales:** 198 M.

★ 85795 ★　American Ref-Fuel Co.
777 N. Eldridge
Houston, TX 77079
(713)531-4233 **Fax:** (713)584-4696
Company Type: Subsidiary. **Officer:** Paul J. Varello, Chairman. **Ultimate Parent:** Brown-Forman.

★ 85796 ★　Ametek
Process & Analytical Instruments Div.
15311 Vantage Pky. W
Houston, TX 77032
(713)449-2596
Ultimate Parent: Ametek Inc.

★ 85797 ★　Ametek Inc.
330 E. Belt N
Houston, TX 77060
(713)445-9670
Ultimate Parent: Ametek Inc. **SIC:** 3498—Fabricated Pipe & Fittings.

★ 85798 ★　Analog Devices Inc.
6006 Bellaire Blvd.
Houston, TX 77081
(713)664-6704
Ultimate Parent: Analog Devices, Inc. **SIC:** 5065—Electronic Parts & Equipment Nec.

★ 85799 ★　Analog Devices Inc. Systems
9100 Southwest Fwy.
Houston, TX 77074
(713)664-5866
Ultimate Parent: Analog Devices, Inc.

★ 85800 ★　Anchor Glass Container Corp. Plant 18
4202 Fidelity
Houston, TX 77029
Ultimate Parent: Anchor Glass Container Corp. **SIC:** 3221—Glass Containers.

★ 85801 ★　Anchor Glass Container Plant 18
4202 Fidelity
Houston, TX 77029
Ultimate Parent: Anchor Glass Container Corp. **SIC:** 3221—Glass Containers.

★ 85802 ★　Anheuser-Busch, Inc.
775 Gellhorn Dr.
Houston, TX 77029
Ultimate Parent: Anheuser-Busch. **SIC:** 2082—Malt Beverages.

★ 85803 ★　APS Acquisition Corp.
3000 Pawnee St.
Houston, TX 77054-3301
(713)741-2470
Company Type: Subsidiary. **Officer:** Mark S. Hoffman, President. **Ultimate Parent:** Collins & Aikman Group. **SIC:** 5013—Motor Vehicle Supplies & New Parts; 5531—Automobile & Home Supply Stores. **Employee Count:** 2000. **Sales:** 404 M.

★ 85804 ★   **APS Holding Corp.**
3000 Pawnee St.
Houston, TX 77054-3301
(713)741-2470
Officer: Mark S. Hoffman, President.
Ultimate Parent: Collins & Aikman Group.
SIC: 5013—Motor Vehicle Supplies & New
Parts; 5531—Automobile & Home Supply
Stores. **Employee Count:** 2000. **Sales:** 404
M.

★ 85805 ★   **APS Inc.**
3000 Pawnee St.
Houston, TX 77054-3301
(713)741-2470
Company Type: Subsidiary. **Officer:** Mark
S. Hoffman, President. **Ultimate Parent:**
Collins & Aikman Group. **SIC:** 5013—Motor
Vehicle Supplies & New Parts; 5531—
Automobile & Home Supply Stores.
Employee Count: 2000. **Sales:** 404 M.

★ 85806 ★   **Archer Daniels
Midland**
6800 South Loop E
Houston, TX 77087-2306
(713)666-2306
Ultimate Parent: Archer Daniels Midland
Co. **SIC:** 5172—Petroleum Products Nec.

★ 85807 ★   **Arco**
15375 Memorial Dr.
Houston, TX 77079-4101
(713)584-6000
Officer: R. M. Malaise. **Ultimate Parent:**
Atlantic Richfield Co., Inc. **SIC:** 1311—
Crude Petroleum & Natural Gas.

★ 85808 ★   **ARCO Channelview,
Inc.**
1 Houston Center, 1221 McKinney St.
Houston, TX 77253-3646
(713)652-7200
Company Type: Subsidiary. **Ultimate
Parent:** Lyondell Petrochemical Co.

★ 85809 ★   **ARCO Lyondell, Inc.**
1 Houston Center, 1221 McKinney St.
Houston, TX 77253-3646
(713)652-7200
Company Type: Subsidiary. **Ultimate
Parent:** Lyondell Petrochemical Co.

★ 85810 ★   **ARCO Mont Belview
Corp.**
1 Houston Center, 121 McKinney St.
Houston, TX 77253-3646
Company Type: Subsidiary. **Ultimate
Parent:** Lyondell Petrochemical Co.

★ 85811 ★   **Arco Pipe Line Co.,
Inc.**
15600 John F. Kennedy Blvd.
Houston, TX 77032-2343
(713)987-0056
Company Type: Subsidiary. **Officer:**
Cynthia L. Claus, Secretary General
Counsel. **Ultimate Parent:** Atlantic Richfield
Co., Inc. **SIC:** 4612—Crude Petroleum
Pipelines; 4613—Refined Petroleum
Pipelines. **Employee Count:** 550. **Sales:**
116 M.

★ 85812 ★   **Armco**
Tex-Tube Div.
1503 N. Post Oak Rd.
Houston, TX 77055
(713)686-4351 **Fax:** (713)681-5256
Company Type: Division. **Officer:** C.G.
Farnsworth, General Manager. **Ultimate
Parent:** Armco. **SIC:** 3317—Steel Pipe &
Tubes.

★ 85813 ★   **Armco**
Tex-Tube Div.
PO Box 7705
Houston, TX 77270
(713)686-4351
Company Type: Division. **Officer:** Carl g.
Farnsworth, General Manager. **Ultimate
Parent:** Armco.

★ 85814 ★   **Armco**
Tex-Tube Div.
PO Box 7705
Houston, TX 77270-7705
(713)686-4351
Company Type: Division. **Officer:** Carl G.
Camsworth. **Ultimate Parent:** Armco. **SIC:**
3444—Sheet Metal Work.

★ 85815 ★   **Armco**
Tex-Tube Div.
1503 N. Post Oak Rd.
Houston, TX 77055-5492
(713)686-4351
Company Type: Division. **Location Type:**
Branch office. **Officer:** Debbie Sherrer.
Ultimate Parent: Armco. **SIC:** 3317—Steel
Pipe & Tubes; 5074—Plumbing & Hydronic
Heating Supplies.

★ 85816 ★   **Armco Inc.**
Tex Tube Div.
1503 N. Post Oak Rd.
Houston, TX 77055
Company Type: Division. **Ultimate Parent:**
Armco. **SIC:** 3400—Fabricated Metal
Products.

★ 85817 ★   **Arnet Computer**
1235 N. Loop W, Ste. 525
Houston, TX 77008
(713)867-8572
Location Type: Branch office. **Ultimate
Parent:** Avnet. **SIC:** 5045—Computers,
Peripherals & Software; 7379—Computer
Related Services Nec.

★ 85818 ★   **Arrow/Kieulft
Electronics**
Ste. 100, 10899 Kinghurst St.
Houston, TX 77099
(713)530-4700
Company Type: Division. **Location Type:**
Distribution center. **Officer:** Stephen Bober,
General Manager. **Ultimate Parent:** Arrow
Electronics. **SIC:** 5065—Electronic Parts &
Equipment Nec.

★ 85819 ★   **Ashland Chemical
Inc.**
8901 Old Galveston Rd.
Houston, TX 77034
(713)941-3403
Officer: Dan D'Antoni, Vice President.
Ultimate Parent: Ashland Oil. **SIC:** 2865—
Cyclic Crudes & Intermediates.

★ 85820 ★   **Ashland Chemical
Inc.**
Drew Div.
6121 Almeda-Genoa Rd.
Houston, TX 77048-4597
Company Type: Division. **Ultimate Parent:**
Ashland Oil. **SIC:** 2899—Chemical
Preparations Nec.

★ 85821 ★   **Ashland Exploration,
Inc.**
14701 St. Mary's Lane
Houston, TX 77079-2907
(713)531-2900
Company Type: Subsidiary. **Officer:** G.
Thomas Wikinson, President. **Ultimate
Parent:** Ashland Oil. **SIC:** 1382—Oil & Gas
Exploration Services. **Employee Count:**
318.

★ 85822 ★   **Ashland Exploration,
Inc.**
14701 St. Mary's Ln., Ste. 200
Houston, TX 77079-2907
(713)531-2900 **Fax:** (713)951-0008
Company Type: Subsidiary. **Officer:** G.
Thomas Wilkinson, President. **Ultimate
Parent:** Ashland Oil.

★ 85823 ★   **Atchison, Topeka &
Santa Fe Railway Co.**
1320 Houston Ave.
Houston, TX 77007
(713)229-7600
Ultimate Parent: Santa Fe Pacific Corp.
SIC: 4011—Railroads—Line-Haul
Operating.

★ 85824 ★   **Atlas Wire Services**
10205 Westheimer Rd.
Houston, TX 77042-4299
(713)972-4000 **Fax:** (713)963-2318 **Telex:**
6717084
Company Type: Division. **Officer:** Damiz
Skeri, President. **Ultimate Parent:** Litton
Industries. **SIC:** 3533—Oil & Gas Field
Machinery; 1381—Drilling Oil & Gas Wells.

★ 85825 ★   **Autoparts Finance
Co. Inc.**
3000 Pawnee St.
Houston, TX 77054-3301
(713)741-2470
Company Type: Subsidiary. **Officer:** Mark
Hoffman, President. **Ultimate Parent:**
Collins & Aikman Group. **SIC:** 6159—

Miscellaneous Business Credit Institutions.
Employee Count: 6.

★ 85826 ★   **Avon Products Inc.**
6231 Westward St.
Houston, TX 77081
(713)772-6677
Ultimate Parent: Avon Products, Inc. **SIC:**
5999—Miscellaneous Retail Stores Nec.

★ 85827 ★   **Avon Products West
Houston**
2718 Crossview Dr.
Houston, TX 77063-4205
(713)780-1112
Ultimate Parent: Avon Products, Inc. **SIC:**
5122—Drugs, Proprietaries & Sundries.

★ 85828 ★   **Baker, Baker Hughes
Process Equi.**
BJ-Titan Services Co. (Partnership)
PO Box 4442
5500 Northwest Central Dr.
Houston, TX 77092
(713)462-4239
Company Type: Division. **Officer:** J.W.
Stewart, President. **Ultimate Parent:** Baker
Hughes. **SIC:** 1389—Oil & Gas Field
Services Nec. **Sales:** 336000000 M.

★ 85829 ★   **Baker-CAC, Inc.**
Hughes Tool Div. B-1 Baker Hughes Drilling
Equipment
PO Box 2539
Houston, TX 77252
(713)363-6000 **Fax:** (713)363-6009
Company Type: Division. **Officer:** Andy
Szescila, President. **Ultimate Parent:** Baker
Hughes. **SIC:** 3533—Oil & Gas Field
Machinery. **Employee Count:** 12700.
Sales: 1,260,000,000 M.

★ 85830 ★   **Baker Hughes**
3900 Essex Ln.
Houston, TX 77027
(713)439-8600
Company Type: Headquarters. **Officer:**
James D. Woods. **Sales:** 2701.7 M.
Fortune 500: Largest U.S. Industrial
Corporations: Ranking 175.

★ 85831 ★   **Baker Hughes Drilling
Equipment Co.**
3900 Essex Ln., Ste. 800
PO Box 800
Houston, TX 77027
(713)439-8600
Ultimate Parent: Baker Hughes.

★ 85832 ★   **Baker Hughes Drilling
Technologies**
Exlog Div.
7000 Hollister Rd.
Houston, TX 77040
(713)744-3640
Company Type: Division. **Officer:** J. Will
Honeyborne, President. **Ultimate Parent:**
Baker Hughes. **SIC:** 1389—Oil & Gas Field
Services Nec. **Employee Count:** 1231.

★ 85833 ★   **Baker Hughes Inc.**
3900 Essex Ln., No. 1200
Houston, TX 77027
(713)439-8600
Officer: James D. Woods, Chairman.
Ultimate Parent: Baker Hughes.

★ 85834 ★   **Baker Hughes Inc.**
3900 Essex Lane Ste. 1200
Houston, TX 77027
(713)439-8600 **Fax:** (713)439-8699
Company Type: Headquarters. **Officer:**
James D. Woods, Chairman. **Ultimate
Parent:** Baker Hughes. **Employee Count:**
20000.

★ 85835 ★   **Baker Hughes Inc.**
PO Box 4740
Houston, TX 77210-4740
(713)439-8600
Officer: Philip A. Rice, Vice President of
Human Resources. **Ultimate Parent:** Baker
Hughes. **SIC:** 3533—Oil & Gas Field
Machinery; 3532—Mining Machinery;
7359—Equipment Rental & Leasing Nec.
Employee Count: 20400. **Sales:** 260 M.

★ 85836 ★   **Baker Hughes Inc.**
Baker Hughes Process Equipment Group
3900 Essex Ln., Ste. 1200
Houston, TX
Ultimate Parent: Baker Hughes.

★ 85837 ★   **Baker Hughes Inc.,
Baker Hughes Drilling
Technologies**
Baker Hughes Inteq
15355 Vantage Pky. W. 300
Houston, TX 77032
(713)442-0800 **Fax:** (713)985-3920
Officer: Tim J. Probert, President. **Ultimate
Parent:** Baker Hughes. **SIC:** 3533—Oil &
Gas Field Machinery. **Employee Count:**
1800.

★ 85838 ★   **Baker Hughes Inc.
Baker Hughes Drilling
Technologies**
Milpark Drilli Fluids
PO Box 27111, 3900 Essex Ln.
Houston, TX 77277
(713)439-8000 **Telex:** 775455
Officer: John P. Laulette, President.
Ultimate Parent: Baker Hughes. **SIC:**
1499—Miscellaneous Nonmetallic Minerals;
2899—Chemical Preparations Nec; 1389—
Oil & Gas Field Services Nec. **Employee
Count:** 824.

★ 85839 ★   **Baker Hughes
Process Equipment Group**
3900 Essex Ln.
PO Box 4740
Houston, TX 77027
(713)439-8600
Company Type: Division. **Ultimate Parent:**
Baker Hughes.

★ 85840 ★   **baker Hughes Prod**
Baker Performance Chemicals
3920 Essex Ln.
Houston, TX 77027
(713)599-7400
Company Type: Division. **Officer:** M. Glen
Bassett, President. **Ultimate Parent:** Baker
Hughes. **SIC:** 2842—Polishes & Sanitation
Goods.

★ 85841 ★   **Baker Hughes Prod
Tools**
Bakekr Sand Control
1010 Rankin Rd.
Houston, TX 77073
(713)443-7590
Company Type: Division. **Officer:** Jay P.
Trahan, President. **Ultimate Parent:** Baker
Hughes. **SIC:** 3533—Oil & Gas Field
Machinery.

★ 85842 ★   **Baker Hughes Prod.
Tools**
Baker-CAC Inc.
17015 A Aldine-Westfield Rd.
Houston, TX 77073
(713)625-4200 **Fax:** (713)230-6250
Officer: Christopher K. Mahauni, President.
Ultimate Parent: Baker Hughes. **SIC:**
3625—Relays & Industrial Controls.

★ 85843 ★   **Baker Hughes Prod.
Tools**
Baker Oil Tools
6023 Navigation Blvd.
Houston, TX 77011
(713)923-9351
Company Type: Division. **Officer:** A.G.
Avant, President. **Ultimate Parent:** Baker
Hughes. **SIC:** 3533—Oil & Gas Field
Machinery.

★ 85844 ★   **Baker Hughes Prod.
Tools**
Baker Service Tools
9100 Emmott Rd.
Houston, TX 77040
(713)466-1322
Company Type: Division. **Officer:** Edwin C.
Howell, President. **Ultimate Parent:** Baker
Hughes. **SIC:** 3533—Oil & Gas Field
Machinery.

★ 85845 ★   **Baker Hughes Prod.
Tools**
Centrilift
3900 Essex Ln., Ste. 640
Houston, TX 77027
(713)439-8930
Company Type: Division. **Ultimate Parent:**
Baker Hughes. **SIC:** 3533—Oil & Gas Field
Machinery.

★ 85846 ★ Baker Hughes Prod. Tools
Tri-State Oil Tools
365 N. Sam Houston Pkwy E.
Houston, TX 77060
(713)999-4200 Telex: 6821282
Company Type: Division. Officer: Andrew Schmidt, President. Ultimate Parent: Baker Hughes. SIC: 3533—Oil & Gas Field Machinery; 1389—Oil & Gas Field Services Nec.

★ 85847 ★ Baker Hughes Production Tools, Inc.
3900 Essex Ln., Ste. 12000
Houston, TX 77027
(713)439-8600
Officer: Mary L. Lukens, President. Ultimate Parent: Baker Hughes. SIC: 3533—Oil & Gas Field Machinery. Sales: 630,000,000 M.

★ 85848 ★ Baker Hughes Production Tools Inc.
3900 Essex Ln. Ste. 800
PO Box 4740
Houston, TX 77027
(713)439-8600
Ultimate Parent: Baker Hughes.

★ 85849 ★ Baker Hughes Treatment Services
17015 Aldine Westfield
Houston, TX
(713)230-6300 Fax: (713)233-6633
Company Type: Subsidiary. Officer: Todd Matherne, COO. Ultimate Parent: Baker Hughes.

★ 85850 ★ Baker Hughes Tubular Services
12100 W. Little York
Houston, TX 77041
Ultimate Parent: Baker Hughes. SIC: 3479—Metal Coating & Allied Services.

★ 85851 ★ Baker Hughes Vetco Services
12100 W. Little York
Houston, TX 77041
Ultimate Parent: Baker Hughes. SIC: 3479—Metal Coating & Allied Services.

★ 85852 ★ Baker Huhes Inc.
3900 Essex Ln.
Houston, TX 77027-5177
(713)439-8600 Fax: (713)439-8699
Officer: James D. Woods, CEO. Ultimate Parent: Baker Hughes. Employee Count: 1840. Sales: 2702 M.

★ 85853 ★ Baker Oil Tool
6023 Navigation
Houston, TX 77011
Ultimate Parent: Baker Hughes. SIC: 3533—Oil & Gas Field Machinery.

★ 85854 ★ Baker Oil Tools
9100 Emmott Rd.
Houston, TX 77040
(713)466-1322
Officer: Ed Howell, President. Ultimate Parent: Baker Hughes. SIC: 3533—Oil & Gas Field Machinery; 3599—Industrial Machinery Nec.

★ 85855 ★ Baker Oil Tools Inc.
6023 Navigation Blvd.
Houston, TX 77011
(713)923-9351
Ultimate Parent: Baker Hughes. SIC: 3533—Oil & Gas Field Machinery; 3823—Process Control Instruments.

★ 85856 ★ Baker Performance Chemicals
3920 Essex Ln.
Houston, TX 77027
(713)599-7400
Officer: M. Glen Bassett, President. Ultimate Parent: Baker Hughes. SIC: 2819—Industrial Inorganic Chemicals Nec; 2843—Surface Active Agents; 2899—Chemical Preparations Nec.

★ 85857 ★ Baker Sand Control
1010 Rankin Rd.
Houston, TX 77073
(713)443-7590
Officer: Jay P. Trahan, President. Ultimate Parent: Baker Hughes.

★ 85858 ★ Baker Sand Control Houston Manufacturing
1010 Rankin Rd.
Houston, TX 77073
Ultimate Parent: Baker Hughes. SIC: 3533—Oil & Gas Field Machinery.

★ 85859 ★ Baker Sand Control Houston Mfg.
1010 Rankin Rd.
Houston, TX 77070
Ultimate Parent: Baker Hughes. SIC: 3533—Oil & Gas Field Machinery.

★ 85860 ★ Baltimore Specialty Steele Corp.
17314 Tomball Pky.
Houston, TX 77064-1100
(713)890-6626
Ultimate Parent: Armco. SIC: 3312—Blast Furnaces & Steel Mills.

★ 85861 ★ Banana Republic
5015 Westheimer Rd.
Houston, TX 77056
(713)621-4451
Ultimate Parent: GAP.

★ 85862 ★ BancBoston Mortgage Corp.
9430 Old Katy Rd.
Houston, TX 77055-6368
(713)973-1229
Ultimate Parent: Bank of Boston Corp. SIC: 6162—Mortgage Bankers & Correspondents.

★ 85863 ★ Bankers Trust
909 Fannin St.
Houston, TX 77010-1003
(713)759-6700
Officer: Robert D. Wagner Jr. Ultimate Parent: Bankers Trust New York Corp. SIC: 6211—Security Brokers & Dealers; 6021—National Commercial Banks.

★ 85864 ★ Bankers Trust Co.
1100 Milam St.
Houston, TX 77002
(713)651-1777
Ultimate Parent: Bankers Trust New York Corp. SIC: 6141—Personal Credit Institutions.

★ 85865 ★ Bankers Trust Co.
3000 Houston Ave.
Houston, TX 77009
(713)651-1777
Ultimate Parent: Bankers Trust New York Corp. SIC: 6159—Miscellaneous Business Credit Institutions.

★ 85866 ★ Bear Stearn Co. Inc.
5 Post Oak Park
Houston, TX 77027-3413
(713)960-0304
Officer: Bruce N. Calvin. Ultimate Parent: Bear Stearns. SIC: 6221—Commodity Contracts Brokers & Dealers.

★ 85867 ★ Beckman Instruments Inc.
9630 Clarewood Dr.
Houston, TX 77036
(713)988-0030
Ultimate Parent: Beckman Instruments. SIC: 3911—Jewelry & Precious Metal.

★ 85868 ★ Bell Atlantic Business Systems Services
10900 Northwest Fwy.
Houston, TX 77092-7309
(713)680-4620
Ultimate Parent: Bell Atlantic Corp. SIC: 7378—Computer Maintenance & Repair.

★ 85869 ★ Beneficial Texas Inc.
11703 Bellaire Blvd.
Houston, TX 77072
(713)933-3202
Ultimate Parent: Beneficial. SIC: 6141—Personal Credit Institutions.

★ 85870 ★ Beneficial Texas Inc.
13186 Stuebner Airline Rd.
Houston, TX 77014
(713)580-0421
Ultimate Parent: Beneficial. SIC: 6141—Personal Credit Institutions.

★ 85871 ★ Beneficial Texas Inc.
15534 W. Hardy Rd.
Houston, TX 77060-3604
(713)847-1804
Ultimate Parent: Beneficial. SIC: 6141—Personal Credit Institutions.

★ 85872 ★ Beneficial Texas Inc.
15462 FM 529 Rd.
Houston, TX 77095
(713)859-2621
Ultimate Parent: Beneficial. SIC: 6141—Personal Credit Institutions.

★ 85873 ★ Beneficial Texas Inc.
13160 Veterans Memorial Dr.
Houston, TX 77014-1904
(713)580-0421
Location Type: Branch office. Ultimate Parent: Beneficial. SIC: 6141—Personal Credit Institutions.

★ 85874 ★ Beneficial Texas Inc.
3218 S. Loop W
Houston, TX 77025-5232
(713)661-1056
Location Type: Branch office. Ultimate Parent: Beneficial. SIC: 6141—Personal Credit Institutions.

★ 85875 ★ Bethlehem Steel Corp.
3 Riverway 1420
Houston, TX 77056-1910
(713)626-2200
Location Type: Branch office. Officer: J. L. Biddle. Ultimate Parent: Bethlehem Steel Corp. SIC: 3312—Blast Furnaces & Steel Mills.

★ 85876 ★ Betz Laboratories Inc.
6900 Nelms Ave.
Houston, TX 77061
Ultimate Parent: Betz Laboratories Inc. SIC: 2389—Apparel & Accessories Nec.

★ 85877 ★ Betz Laboratories Inc.
6900 Nelms Ave.
Houston, TX 77061
Ultimate Parent: Betz Laboratories Inc. SIC: 2899—Chemical Preparations Nec.

★ 85878 ★ Beverly Enterprises
2626 South Loop W.
Houston, TX 77054-2654
(713)661-3567
Ultimate Parent: Beverly Enterprises. SIC: 8059—Nursing & Personal Care Nec.

★ 85879 ★ BFI International Inc.
757 N. Eldridge
PO Box 3151
Houston, TX 77253
(713)870-8100 Fax: (713)870-7844
Company Type: Subsidiary. Ultimate Parent: Browning-Ferris Industries.

★ 85880 ★ BFI International Inc.
757 N. Eldridge
PO Box 3151
Houston, TX 77253
(713)870-8100 Fax: (713)870-7844
Company Type: Subsidiary. Ultimate Parent: Brown-Forman.

★ 85881 ★ BFI Medical Waste Systems
8101 Little York Rd.
Houston, TX 77016
(713)635-6666
Officer: Randy Farmer, Manager. Ultimate Parent: Browning-Ferris Industries. SIC: 3589—Service Industry Machinery Nec.

★ 85882 ★ Big A Auto Parts Inc.
3000 Pawnee St.
Houston, TX 77054-3301
(713)741-2470
Officer: Mark S. Hoffman, President. Ultimate Parent: Collins & Aikman Group. SIC: 5013—Motor Vehicle Supplies & New Parts; 5531—Automobile & Home Supply Stores. Employee Count: 830. Sales: 84.7 M.

★ 85883 ★ Bindley Western Drug Co.
Houston, Texas
3562 E. T C Jester
Houston, TX 77018
(713)683-0453 Fax: (713)956-7767
Company Type: Subsidiary. Officer: Cletus B. Jarboe, Vice President & Division Manager. Ultimate Parent: Bindley-Western Industries, Inc.

★ 85884 ★ Boeing Co
1300 Bay Area Blvd.
Houston, TX 77058
(713)488-0910
Ultimate Parent: Boeing. SIC: 8712—Architectural Services.

★ 85885 ★ Borden Inc.
4494 Campbell Rd.
Houston, TX 77041
(713)744-3700
Officer: Dan Doty, Manager. Ultimate Parent: Borden, Inc. SIC: 2026—Fluid Milk; 2024—Ice Cream & Frozen Desserts.

★ 85886 ★ Borden Inc.
Dairy
2020 Texas Ave.
Houston, TX 77003
Company Type: Division. Ultimate Parent: Borden, Inc. SIC: 2026—Fluid Milk.

★ 85887 ★ Borden Inc.
Dairy
2020 Texas Ave.
Houston, TX 77003
Company Type: Division. Ultimate Parent: Borden, Inc. SIC: 5143—Dairy Products Except Dried or Canned.

★ 85888 ★ Britt Airways Inc.
15333 John F. Kennedy Blvd., Ste. 600
Houston, TX 77032
(713)985-2700
Company Type: Subsidiary. Officer: Dennis Crabtree, President. Ultimate Parent: Continental Airlines. SIC: 4512—Air Transportation—Scheduled. Employee Count: 2369. Sales: 384 M.

★ 85889 ★ Brown & Root Civil
4100 Clinton Dr.
Houston, TX 77020-6299
(713)676-7091 Fax: (713)676-4543
Company Type: Subsidiary. Officer: Stephen A. Zander, President. Ultimate Parent: Halliburton.

★ 85890 ★ Brown & Root Environmental
10200 Bellaire Blvd.
Houston, TX 77072-5299
(713)676-3011 Fax: (713)575-4660
Company Type: Subsidiary. Officer: Peter D. Arrowsmith, President. Ultimate Parent: Halliburton.

★ 85891 ★ Brown & Root Forest Products
1500 City West Blvd.
Houston, TX 77042-2343
(713)267-9432 Fax: (713)267-9423
Company Type: Subsidiary. Officer: John W. Redmon, President. Ultimate Parent: Halliburton.

★ 85892 ★ Brown & Root Holdings Inc.
4100 Clinton Dr.
Houston, TX 77020-6237
(713)676-3011
Company Type: Subsidiary. Ultimate Parent: Halliburton. SIC: 8711—Engineering Services; 1629—Heavy Construction Nec; 1541—Industrial Buildings & Warehouses; 1542—Nonresidential Construction Nec; 1611—Highway & Street Construction; 8742—Management Consulting Services.

★ 85893 ★ Brown & Root Inc.
4100 Clinton Dr.
Houston, TX 77020-6237
(713)676-3011
Company Type: Subsidiary. Ultimate Parent: Halliburton. SIC: 1629—Heavy Construction Nec; 8711—Engineering Services; 1611—Highway & Street Construction.

★ 85894 ★ Brown & Root Inc.
4100 Clinton Dr.
PO Box 3
Houston, TX 77001
(713)676-3011 Fax: (713)676-4109
Company Type: Subsidiary. Officer: Tommy E. Knight, President & CEO. Ultimate Parent: Halliburton.

★ 85895 ★   Brown & Root Inc.
Marine Fabrication Yard
14035 Industrial Rd.
Houston, TX 77015
Ultimate Parent: Halliburton. **SIC:** 3731—
Ship Building & Repairing; 3498—
Fabricated Pipe & Fittings; 1629—Heavy
Construction Nec.

★ 85896 ★   Brown & Root
Industrial Services Inc.
4100 Clinton Dr.
Houston, TX 77020-6299
(713)676-5774 **Fax:** (713)676-7941
Company Type: Subsidiary. **Officer:** R.
Randall Harl, President. **Ultimate Parent:**
Halliburton.

★ 85897 ★   Brown & Root
Industrial Services Inc.
4100 Clinton Dr.
Houston, TX 77020-6237
(713)676-4870
Company Type: Subsidiary. **Ultimate
Parent:** Halliburton. **SIC:** 7699—Repair
Services Nec; 8711—Engineering Services.

★ 85898 ★   Brown & Root
Manufacturing & Process
Industries
1500 City West Blvd.
Houston, TX 77042-2343
(713)267-9432 **Fax:** (713)267-9423
Company Type: Subsidiary. **Officer:** John
W. Redmon, President. **Ultimate Parent:**
Halliburton.

★ 85899 ★   Brown & Root
Petroleum & Chemical
4100 Clinton Dr.
Houston, TX 77020-6299
(713)676-5000 **Fax:** (713)676-3769
Company Type: Subsidiary. **Officer:** Larry
D. Pope, President. **Ultimate Parent:**
Halliburton.

★ 85900 ★   Brown & Root Power
4100 Clinton Dr.
Houston, TX 77020-6299
(713)676-3631 **Fax:** (713)676-8094
Company Type: Subsidiary. **Officer:** Jack
F. Browder, President. **Ultimate Parent:**
Halliburton.

★ 85901 ★   Brown & Root
Services Corp.
4100 Clinton Dr.
Houston, TX 77020-6299
(713)676-8000 **Fax:** (713)676-5174
Company Type: Subsidiary. **Officer:** Arthur
E. Stephens, President. **Ultimate Parent:**
Halliburton.

★ 85902 ★   Brownell Electro Inc.
421 Blueberry St., Ste. 5
Houston, TX 77018
(713)699-1981
Location Type: Branch office. **Ultimate
Parent:** Avnet. **SIC:** 5063—Electrical
Apparatus & Equipment.

★ 85903 ★   Browning-Ferris
Industrial
757 N. Eldridge
PO Box 3151
Houston, TX 77253
(713)870-8100 **Fax:** (713)870-7844
Company Type: Headquarters. **Ultimate
Parent:** Browning-Ferris Industries.

★ 85904 ★   Browning-Ferris
Industrial
757 N. Eldridge
PO Box 3151
Houston, TX 77253
(713)870-8100 **Fax:** (713)870-7844
Company Type: Headquarters. **Officer:**
William D. Ruckelshaus, Chairman & CEO.
Ultimate Parent: Browning-Ferris
Industries. **Employee Count:** 29000.

★ 85905 ★   Browning-Ferris
Industries
11013 Old Beaumont Hwy.
Houston, TX 77078
(713)675-6101
Ultimate Parent: Browning-Ferris
Industries. **SIC:** 4953—Refuse Systems.

★ 85906 ★   Browning-Ferris
Industries
Landfill
Houston, TX 77079
(713)675-6101
Ultimate Parent: Browning-Ferris
Industries. **SIC:** 4953—Refuse Systems.

★ 85907 ★   Browning-Ferris
Industries
757 N. Eldridge
Houston, TX 77079
(713)870-8100
Company Type: Headquarters. **Officer:**
William D. Ruckelshaus. **Fortune Service
500:** Ranking 33.

★ 85908 ★   Browning Ferris
Industries of Fall Township Inc.
757 S. Eldridge
PO Box 3151
Houston, TX 77079
(713)870-8100 **Fax:** (713)870-7844
Officer: Jeffrey E. Curtiss, CEO. **Ultimate
Parent:** Browning-Ferris Industries.
Employee Count: 31600. **Sales:** 3495 M.

★ 85909 ★   Browning Ferris
Industries Inc.
757 N. Eldridge
PO Box 3151
Houston, TX 77079
(713)870-8100 **Fax:** (713)870-7844
Officer: William D. Ruckelshaus, CEO.
Ultimate Parent: Browning-Ferris
Industries. **Employee Count:** 31600. **Sales:**
3495 M.

★ 85910 ★   Browning-Ferris
Industries Inc.
757 N. Eldridge
Houston, TX 77079-4435
(713)870-8100
Location Type: Headquarters. **Officer:**
Bruce E. Ranck. **Ultimate Parent:**
Browning-Ferris Industries. **SIC:** 4953—
Refuse Systems; 4959—Sanitary Services
Nec.

★ 85911 ★   Builders Square
13328 W. FM 1960
Houston, TX 77065
(713)955-5282
Company Type: Subsidiary. **Ultimate
Parent:** K-Mart. **SIC:** 5211—Lumber &
Other Building Materials.

★ 85912 ★   Builders Square
1010 N. Belt Dr. E
Houston, TX 77032
(713)973-6411
Company Type: Subsidiary. **Ultimate
Parent:** K-Mart.

★ 85913 ★   Builders Square
11402 East Fwy.
Houston, TX 77029
(713)451-1382
Company Type: Subsidiary. **Ultimate
Parent:** K-Mart. **SIC:** 5211—Lumber &
Other Building Materials.

★ 85914 ★   Burlington Resources
5051 Westheimer
Houston, TX 77056
(713)831-1600
Company Type: Headquarters. **Officer:**
Thomas H. O'Leary. **Employee Count:**
1729. **Sales:** 1249 M. **Fortune 500:** Largest
U.S. Industrial Corporations: Ranking 30.

★ 85915 ★   Business Week
601 Jefferson St.
Houston, TX 77002
(713)659-6004
Ultimate Parent: McGraw-Hill. **SIC:** 2721—
Periodicals.

★ 85916 ★   Capezio Shoes
1304 Bay Brook Mall
Houston, TX 77004
(713)486-8483
Ultimate Parent: United States Shoe. **SIC:**
5661—Shoe Stores.

★ 85917 ★   Career Image
716 Westwood Mall
Houston, TX 77036
(713)995-6080
Ultimate Parent: United States Shoe. **SIC:**
5621—Women's Clothing Stores.

★ 85918 ★   Career Image
1000 W. Oaks Mall
Houston, TX 77082
(713)497-6008
Ultimate Parent: United States Shoe. **SIC:**
6512—Nonresidential Building Operators.

★ 85919 ★   Career Image
5085 Westheimer Rd.
Houston, TX 77056
(713)960-1049
Ultimate Parent: United States Shoe. **SIC:**
5621—Women's Clothing Stores.

★ 85920 ★   Career Image
432 NW Mall
Houston, TX 77092
(713)957-4693
Ultimate Parent: United States Shoe. **SIC:**
5611—Men's & Boys' Clothing Stores.

★ 85921 ★   Career Image
Town
Houston, TX 77024
(713)461-4530
Ultimate Parent: United States Shoe. **SIC:**
5611—Men's & Boys' Clothing Stores.

★ 85922 ★   Career Image
1348 Baybrook Mall
Houston, TX 77004
(713)480-2101
Ultimate Parent: United States Shoe. **SIC:**
5621—Women's Clothing Stores.

★ 85923 ★   Casual Corner
277 Westwood Mall
Houston, TX 77036
(713)771-3325
Ultimate Parent: United States Shoe. **SIC:**
5611—Men's & Boys' Clothing Stores.

★ 85924 ★   Casual Corner
1400 Willowbrook Mall
Houston, TX 77070
(713)890-6706
Ultimate Parent: United States Shoe. **SIC:**
5611—Men's & Boys' Clothing Stores.

★ 85925 ★   Casual Corner
1000 W. Oaks Mall
Houston, TX 77082
(713)493-3020
Ultimate Parent: United States Shoe. **SIC:**
5651—Family Clothing Stores.

★ 85926 ★   Casual Corner
5085 Westheimer Rd.
Houston, TX 77056
(713)961-4802
Ultimate Parent: United States Shoe. **SIC:**
5611—Men's & Boys' Clothing Stores.

★ 85927 ★   Casual Corner
220 Sharpstown Ctr.
Houston, TX 77036
(713)776-9567
Ultimate Parent: United States Shoe. **SIC:**
5651—Family Clothing Stores.

★ 85928 ★   Casual Corner
800 W. Belt Dr. N
Houston, TX 77024
(713)461-4025
Ultimate Parent: United States Shoe. **SIC:**
5611—Men's & Boys' Clothing Stores.

★ 85929 ★   Casual Corner
409 Meyerland Plz.
Houston, TX 77096
(713)661-3954
Ultimate Parent: United States Shoe. **SIC:**
5621—Women's Clothing Stores.

★ 85930 ★   Casual Corner
226 NW Mall
Houston, TX 77092
(713)688-1378
Ultimate Parent: United States Shoe. **SIC:**
5651—Family Clothing Stores.

★ 85931 ★   Casual Corner
1200 McKinney St. 413
Houston, TX 77010
(713)694-3544
Ultimate Parent: United States Shoe. **SIC:**
5611—Men's & Boys' Clothing Stores.

★ 85932 ★   Casual Corner
752 Mem City Shopping Ctr.
Houston, TX 77024
(713)468-2689
Ultimate Parent: United States Shoe. **SIC:**
5611—Men's & Boys' Clothing Stores.

★ 85933 ★   Casual Corner
125 Gulfgate Mall
Houston, TX 77087
(713)643-0621
Ultimate Parent: United States Shoe. **SIC:**
5611—Men's & Boys' Clothing Stores.

★ 85934 ★   Casual Corner
226 Almeda Mall
Houston, TX 77075
(713)944-2410
Ultimate Parent: United States Shoe. **SIC:**
5621—Women's Clothing Stores.

★ 85935 ★   Casual Corner
1038 Baybrook Mall
Houston, TX 77004
(713)488-9077
Ultimate Parent: United States Shoe. **SIC:**
5611—Men's & Boys' Clothing Stores.

★ 85936 ★   Cathodic Protection
Services Co.
PO Box 36409
7211 Regency Square
Houston, TX 77036
(713)974-7211
Company Type: Subsidiary. **Ultimate
Parent:** Lukens. **SIC:** 7549—Automotive
Services Nec.

★ 85937 ★   CBI Co. Ltd.
8900 Fairbanks N. Houston Rd.
Houston, TX 77064
(713)466-7581
Company Type: Subsidiary. **Officer:**
Donald E. Weinmann, President. **Ultimate
Parent:** CBI Industries, Inc. **SIC:** 1791—
Structural Steel Erection. **Employee Count:**
250. **Sales:** 56 M.

★ 85938 ★   CBI Co. Ltd.
PO Box 692001
Houston, TX 77269
(713)466-7581
Company Type: Subsidiary. **Officer:** D. E.
Weinmann, President. **Ultimate Parent:** CBI
Industries, Inc. **SIC:** 1629—Heavy
Construction Nec.

★ 85939 ★   Cbi Na-Con
8900 N. Fairbanks
Houston, TX 77064
Ultimate Parent: CBI Industries, Inc. **SIC:**
3443—Fabricated Plate Work—Boiler
Shops.

★ 85940 ★   Cbi Na-Con_Inc.
8900 N. Fairbanks
Houston, TX 77064
Ultimate Parent: CBI Industries, Inc. **SIC:**
3443—Fabricated Plate Work—Boiler
Shops.

★ 85941 ★   Celeron Corp.
2600 Mcorp Plz.
333 Clay St.
PO Box 53270
Houston, TX 77052-3270
(713)750-4500 **Fax:** (713)750-4504
Company Type: Subsidiary. **Officer:**
George Hargreaves Jr., President & CEO.
Ultimate Parent: Goodyear Tire & Rubber.

★ 85942 ★   Centri Marc
9919 Steelman Ave.
Houston, TX 77017
(713)473-6208 **Fax:** (713)473-6496
Company Type: Subsidiary. **Officer:**
Stephen W Jadney, General Manager.
Ultimate Parent: Imo Industries.

★ 85943 ★   Chevron U.S.A.
Production Co.
1301 McKinney
Houston, TX 77010
(713)754-2000 **Fax:** (713)754-2016
Officer: Raymond E. Galvin, President.
Ultimate Parent: Chevron Corp.

★ 85944 ★   Circus World Toy
Stores
329 Westwood Mall
Houston, TX 77036
(713)981-4327
Ultimate Parent: Melville. **SIC:** 5945—
Hobby, Toy & Game Shops.

★ 85945 ★   Circus World Toy
Stores
1256 Willowbrook Mall
Houston, TX 77070
(713)469-2652
Ultimate Parent: Melville. **SIC:** 5945—
Hobby, Toy & Game Shops.

★ 85946 ★　Circus World Toy Stores
Sharpstown Ctr.
Houston, TX 77036
(713)774-7338
Ultimate Parent: Melville. **SIC:** 5945—Hobby, Toy & Game Shops.

★ 85947 ★　Circus World Toy Stores
800 W. Belt Dr. N
Houston, TX 77024
(713)465-4725
Ultimate Parent: Melville. **SIC:** 5945—Hobby, Toy & Game Shops.

★ 85948 ★　Circus World Toy Stores
308 Northline Mall
Houston, TX 77022
(713)692-8129
Ultimate Parent: Melville. **SIC:** 5945—Hobby, Toy & Game Shops.

★ 85949 ★　Circus World Toy Stores
Northwest Mall
Houston, TX 77092
(713)686-2127
Ultimate Parent: Melville. **SIC:** 5945—Hobby, Toy & Game Shops.

★ 85950 ★　Circus World Toy Stores
211 Gulfgate Mall
Houston, TX 77087
(713)643-0442
Ultimate Parent: Melville. **SIC:** 5945—Hobby, Toy & Game Shops.

★ 85951 ★　Circus World Toy Stores
Meyerland Court Apts
Houston, TX 77096
(713)668-3651
Ultimate Parent: Melville. **SIC:** 5945—Hobby, Toy & Game Shops.

★ 85952 ★　Circus World Toy Stores
Galleria
Houston, TX 77056
(713)623-6192
Ultimate Parent: Melville. **SIC:** 5945—Hobby, Toy & Game Shops.

★ 85953 ★　Circus World Toy Stores
Greenspoint Mall
Houston, TX 77060
(713)447-6548
Ultimate Parent: Melville. **SIC:** 5945—Hobby, Toy & Game Shops.

★ 85954 ★　Circus World Toy Stores
Almeda Mall
Houston, TX 77075
(713)944-1470
Ultimate Parent: Melville. **SIC:** 5945—Hobby, Toy & Game Shops.

★ 85955 ★　Cisco Systems
8323 Southwest Fwy.
Houston, TX 77074
(713)779-4757
Ultimate Parent: Cisco Systems Inc.

★ 85956 ★　Citgo Petroleum Corp.
2525 N. Loop W
Houston, TX 77008
(713)861-1853
Ultimate Parent: Citgo Petroleum. **SIC:** 1382—Oil & Gas Exploration Services.

★ 85957 ★　Citgo Pipeline Co.
6402 Uvalde Rd.
Houston, TX 77049
(713)458-1434
Ultimate Parent: Citgo Petroleum.

★ 85958 ★　Citgo Pipeline Co.
6402 Uvalde Rd.
Houston, TX 77049
(713)458-1434
Ultimate Parent: Citgo Petroleum.

★ 85959 ★　Citgo Quick Mart
10096 Veterans Memorial Dr.
Houston, TX 77038
(713)448-5136
Ultimate Parent: Citgo Petroleum. **SIC:** 5541—Gasoline Service Stations.

★ 85960 ★　Citibank International
1200 Smith St.
Houston, TX 77002
(713)654-2800
Company Type: Subsidiary. **Location Type:** Branch office. **Ultimate Parent:** Citicorp. **SIC:** 6021—National Commercial Banks.

★ 85961 ★　Citrus Corp.
PO Box 1188
Houston, TX 77251-1188
(713)853-6159
Officer: William V. Allison, Chairman of the Board & CEO. **Ultimate Parent:** Enron. **SIC:** 4922—Natural Gas Transmission; 4924—Natural Gas Distribution.

★ 85962 ★　Citrus Corp.
Florida Gas Transmission Co.
PO Box 1188
Houston, TX 77251
(713)853-6159
Officer: William V. Allison, President. **Ultimate Parent:** Fort Howard. **SIC:** 4922—Natural Gas Transmission.

★ 85963 ★　Clereon Corp.
333 Clay St., Ste. 2700
Houston, TX 77002
(713)750-4500
Company Type: Subsidiary. **Ultimate Parent:** Goodyear Tire & Rubber. **SIC:** 1382—Oil & Gas Exploration Services; 4924—Natural Gas Distribution.

★ 85964 ★　Clorox Co. Household Products Co.
5822 Armour Dr.
Houston, TX 77020
Ultimate Parent: Clorox Co. **SIC:** 2842—Polishes & Sanitation Goods.

★ 85965 ★　Clorox Co. Houston Plant
5822 Armour Dr.
Houston, TX 77020
Ultimate Parent: Clorox Co. **SIC:** 2842—Polishes & Sanitation Goods.

★ 85966 ★　Coastal Catalyst Technology, Inc.
Coastal Tower, 9 Greenway Plz.
Houston, TX 77046-0995
(713)877-7700 **Fax:** (713)877-3874
Officer: Alan T. Rowe, President & CEO. **Ultimate Parent:** Coastal Corp.

★ 85967 ★　Coastal Corp.
Coastal Tower, 9 Greenway Plz.
Houston, TX 77046-0995
(713)877-1400 **Fax:** (713)877-6752 **Telex:** 166008/166228
Officer: Oscar S. Wyatt Jr., Chairman & CEO. **Ultimate Parent:** Coastal Corp. **Employee Count:** 16500.

★ 85968 ★　Coastal Corp.
9 Greenway Plz.
Houston, TX 77046
(713)877-1400
Officer: David A. Arledge. **Employee Count:** 16000. **Sales:** 10 M. **Fortune 500:** Largest U.S. Industrial Corporations: Ranking 47.

★ 85969 ★　Coastal Dril, Inc.
Coastal Tower, 9 Greenway Plz.
Houston, TX 77046-0995
(713)877-6088
Officer: Jerry D. Bullock, President. **Ultimate Parent:** Coastal Corp.

★ 85970 ★　Coastal Finance Corp.
Coastal Tower, 9 Greenway Plz.
Houston, TX 77046-0995
(713)877-7043
Officer: David A. Arledge, President. **Ultimate Parent:** Coastal Corp.

★ 85971 ★　Coastal Gas Service Co.
Coastal Tower, 9 Greenway Plz.
Houston, TX 77046-0995
(713)877-7976
Officer: Charles M. Oglesby, President & CEO. **Ultimate Parent:** Coastal Corp.

★ 85972 ★　Coastal Holding Corp.
Coastal Tower, 9 Greenway Plz.
Houston, TX 77046-0995
(713)877-7981
Officer: Kenneth O. Johnson, Executive Vice President. **Ultimate Parent:** Coastal Corp.

★ 85973 ★　Coastal Ltd. Ventures, Inc.
Coastal Tower, 9 Greenway Plz.
Houston, TX 77046-0995
(713)877-6088
Officer: Jerry D. Bullock, President. **Ultimate Parent:** Coastal Corp.

★ 85974 ★　Coastal Mart, Inc.
Coastal Tower, 9 Greenway Plz.
Houston, TX 77045-0995
(713)877-7034 **Fax:** (713)877-6271
Officer: Jack C. Pester, Chairman & CEO. **Ultimate Parent:** Coastal Corp.

★ 85975 ★　Coastal Multi-Fuels, Inc.
Coastal Tower, 9 Greenway Plz.
Houston, TX 77046-0995
(713)877-6404 **Fax:** (713)877-3714
Officer: Clark C. Smith, President. **Ultimate Parent:** Coastal Corp.

★ 85976 ★　Coastal Natural Gas Co.
9 E. Greenway Plz.
Houston, TX 77046-0901
(713)877-1400
Company Type: Subsidiary. **Officer:** Harold Burrow, Chairman of the Board, CEO. **Ultimate Parent:** Coastal Corp. **SIC:** 4922—Natural Gas Transmission; 1382—Oil & Gas Exploration Services; 1311—Crude Petroleum & Natural Gas; 1221—Bituminous Coal & Lignite—Surface; 4213—Trucking Except Local; 4212—Local Trucking Without Storage. **Employee Count:** 5000. **Sales:** 2 M.

★ 85977 ★　Coastal Oil & Gas Corp.
9 E. Greenway Plz.
Houston, TX 77046-0902
(713)877-1400
Officer: James R. Paul, Chairman of the Board, CEO. **Ultimate Parent:** Coastal Corp. **SIC:** 1311—Crude Petroleum & Natural Gas. **Employee Count:** 648. **Sales:** 145 M.

★ 85978 ★　Coastal Oil & Gas Corp.
Coastal Tower, 9 Greenway Plz.
Houston, TX 77046-0995
(713)877-6088 **Fax:** (713)877-7230
Officer: Jerry D. Bullock, President. **Ultimate Parent:** Coastal Corp.

★ 85979 ★　Coastal Power Production Co.
9 E. Greenway Plz.
Houston, TX 77046-0902
(713)877-1400
Company Type: Subsidiary. **Officer:** James L. Van Lanen, Chairman of the Board, CEO. **Ultimate Parent:** Coastal Corp. **SIC:** 8742—Management Consulting Services. **Employee Count:** 20. **Sales:** 30 M.

★ 85980 ★　Coastal States Gas Transmission Co.
9 E. Greenway Plz.
Houston, TX 77046-0902
(713)877-1400
Company Type: Subsidiary. **Officer:** Clark C. Smith, President. **Ultimate Parent:** Coastal Corp. **SIC:** 4923—Gas Transmission & Distribution. **Employee Count:** 9. **Sales:** 3 M.

★ 85981 ★　Coastal States Gas Transmission Co.
Coastal Tower, 9 Greenway Plz.
Houston, TX 77046-0995
(713)877-6464 **Fax:** (713)877-7132
Officer: Clark C. Smith, President. **Ultimate Parent:** Coastal Corp.

★ 85982 ★　Coastal States Trading, Inc.
Coastal Tower, 9 Greenway Plz.
Houston, TX 77046-0995
(713)877-7976
Officer: Oscar S. Wyatt Jr., Chairman. **Ultimate Parent:** Coastal Corp.

★ 85983 ★　Coca-Cola Foods
2000 St. James Pl.
Houston, TX
(713)888-5000
Officer: Timothy J. Haas, President & CEO. **Ultimate Parent:** Coca-Cola.

★ 85984 ★　Coca Cola USA
9000 Southwest Fwy.
Houston, TX 77074
(713)772-2881
Ultimate Parent: Coca-Cola. **SIC:** 5149—Groceries & Related Products Nec.

★ 85985 ★　Columbia Gas Development Corp.
1 Riverway, 1st Fl.
Houston, TX 77056
(713)871-3400 **Fax:** (713)871-3683
Officer: John P. Bornman Jr., President. **Ultimate Parent:** Columbia Gas System.

★ 85986 ★　Columbia Gas Development Corp.
1 Riverway, Ste. 100
Houston, TX 77056-1902
(713)871-3406
Company Type: Subsidiary. **Officer:** John P. Bornman Jr, President & CEO. **Ultimate Parent:** Columbia Gas System. **SIC:** 1382—Oil & Gas Exploration Services; 1311—Crude Petroleum & Natural Gas. **Employee Count:** 206.

★ 85987 ★　Columbia Gulf Transmission Co.
2603 Augusta, Ste. 125
Houston, TX 77057
(713)267-4100 **Fax:** (713)267-4110
Officer: James P. Holland, Chairman & CEO. **Ultimate Parent:** Columbia Gas System.

★ 85988 ★　Comerica Bank-Texas
9100 Airport Blvd.
Houston, TX 77061-3404
(713)946-2265
Company Type: Subsidiary. **Location Type:** Branch office. **Ultimate Parent:** Comerica Bank. **SIC:** 6021—National Commercial Banks.

★ 85989 ★　Comerica Bank-Texas
14606 Memorial Dr.
Houston, TX 77079-7502
(713)531-9300
Company Type: Subsidiary. **Location Type:** Branch office. **Ultimate Parent:** Comerica Bank. **SIC:** 6021—National Commercial Banks.

★ 85990 ★　Comerica Bank-Texas
2215 Gessner
Houston, TX 77080-5003
(713)467-8200
Company Type: Subsidiary. **Location Type:** Branch office. **Ultimate Parent:** Comerica Bank. **SIC:** 6021—National Commercial Banks.

★ 85991 ★　Compaq Computer
20555 State Hwy. 249
Houston, TX 77070
(713)370-0670
Company Type: Headquarters. **Officer:** Eckherd Pfeiffer. **Employee Count:** 10541. **Sales:** 7191 M. **Fortune 500:** Largest U.S. Industrial Corporations: Ranking 76.

★ 85992 ★　Compaq Computer Corp.
12344 Perry Rd.
Houston, TX 77070
(713)890-6350
Ultimate Parent: Compaq Computer. **SIC:** 5112—Stationery & Office Supplies.

★ 85993 ★　Compaq Computer Corp.
20555 Sh249 Ms 09020
Houston, TX 77070
(713)374-0952
Ultimate Parent: Compaq Computer.

★ 85994 ★　Compaq Computer Corp.
20555 State Hwy. 249
Houston, TX 77070
Ultimate Parent: Compaq Computer.

★ 85995 ★　Compaq Computer Corp.
20555 FM 149
Houston, TX 77070
Ultimate Parent: Compaq Computer. **SIC:** 5046—Commercial Equipment Nec.

★ 85996 ★   **Compass Bank**
24 E. Greenway Plz.
Houston, TX 77046
(713)621-3336
Ultimate Parent: Compass Bancshares.
SIC: 6022—State Commercial Banks.

★ 85997 ★   **Compass Bank-Houston**
9191 N. Loop E
Houston, TX 77029-1221
(713)676-2265
Company Type: Subsidiary. **Location Type:** Branch office. **Ultimate Parent:** Comerica Bank. **SIC:** 6021—National Commercial Banks.

★ 85998 ★   **Compass Bank-Houston**
2001 Kirby Dr.
Houston, TX 77019-6015
(713)526-2211
Company Type: Subsidiary. **Location Type:** Branch office. **Officer:** Bob Hewell, Manager. **Ultimate Parent:** Compass Bancshares. **SIC:** 6021—National Commercial Banks.

★ 85999 ★   **Compass Bank-Houston**
5030 Westheimer Rd.
Houston, TX 77056-5601
(713)867-5601 **Fax:** (713)867-1190
Company Type: Subsidiary. **Location Type:** Branch office. **Ultimate Parent:** Compass Bancshares. **SIC:** 6021—National Commercial Banks.

★ 86000 ★   **Compass Bank-Houston**
2900 N. Loop W
Houston, TX 77092-8809
(713)867-1370
Company Type: Subsidiary. **Location Type:** Branch office. **Ultimate Parent:** Compass Bancshares. **SIC:** 6021—National Commercial Banks.

★ 86001 ★   **Compass Bank-Houston**
14255 I-45 N
Houston, TX 77090-6503
(713)872-6100
Company Type: Subsidiary. **Location Type:** Branch office. **Ultimate Parent:** Compass Bancshares. **SIC:** 6021—National Commercial Banks.

★ 86002 ★   **Compass Bank-Houston**
3646 University Blvd. & Edloe
Houston, TX 77005-3360
(713)867-1350
Company Type: Subsidiary. **Location Type:** Branch office. **Ultimate Parent:** Compass Bancshares. **SIC:** 6021—National Commercial Banks.

★ 86003 ★   **Compass Bank-Houston**
9601 Daty Fwy. & Bunker Hill
Houston, TX 77024-1330
(713)867-1300
Company Type: Subsidiary. **Location Type:** Branch office. **Ultimate Parent:** Compass Bancshares. **SIC:** 6021—National Commercial Banks.

★ 86004 ★   **Compass Bank-Houston**
10898 Westheimer Rd.
Houston, TX 77042
(713)867-1340
Company Type: Subsidiary. **Location Type:** Branch office. **Ultimate Parent:** Compass Bancshares. **SIC:** 6021—National Commercial Banks.

★ 86005 ★   **Compass Bank-Houston**
12649 Memorial Dr.
Houston, TX 77024-4800
(713)867-1320
Company Type: Subsidiary. **Location Type:** Branch office. **Ultimate Parent:** Compass Bancshares. **SIC:** 6021—National Commercial Banks.

★ 86006 ★   **Compass Bank-Houston**
24 Greenway Plz., Ste. 1402
PO Box 4444
Houston, TX 77210-4444
(713)621-3336 **Fax:** (713)993-8500
Company Type: Subsidiary. **Location Type:** Branch office. **Ultimate Parent:** Compass Bancshares. **SIC:** 6021—National Commercial Banks.

★ 86007 ★   **Compass Bank Na**
4004 Richmond Ave.
Houston, TX 77027
(713)621-7884
Ultimate Parent: Compass Bancshares.

★ 86008 ★   **Compass Bank Na**
9669 Katy Fwy.
Houston, TX 77024
(713)461-3648
Ultimate Parent: Compass Bancshares.

★ 86009 ★   **Compass Bank Na**
12697 Memorial Dr.
Houston, TX 77024
(713)968-8209
Ultimate Parent: Compass Bancshares.

★ 86010 ★   **Continental Airlines**
2929 Allen Pky.
Houston, TX 77019
(713)834-5000
Company Type: Headquarters. **Officer:** Robert R. Ferguson III. **Employee Count:** 43140. **Fortune Service 500:** Ranking 10.

★ 86011 ★   **Continental Airlines Inc.**
2929 Allen Pky., Ste. 1100
Houston, TX 77019-2119
Officer: David Bonderman, Chairman of the Board. **Ultimate Parent:** Continental Airlines. **SIC:** 4512—Air Transportation—Scheduled. **Employee Count:** 38300. **Sales:** 5.4 M.

★ 86012 ★   **Continental Group Inc.**
104 N. Norwood St.
Houston, TX 77011
(713)928-7300
Ultimate Parent: Continental Assurance Co. Inc. **SIC:** 3411—Metal Cans.

★ 86013 ★   **Continental Ind Inc.**
1303 Upland Dr.
Houston, TX 77043
(713)932-8015
Ultimate Parent: Handy & Harman. **SIC:** 5075—Warm Air Heating & Air-Conditioning.

★ 86014 ★   **Cooper Industries**
1001 Fannin St.
Houston, TX 77002
(713)739-5400
Company Type: Headquarters. **Officer:** Robert Cizik. **Sales:** 6273.8 M. **Fortune 500:** Largest U.S. Industrial Corporations: Ranking 87.

★ 86015 ★   **Cosbel Petroleum Corp.**
9 E. Greenway Plz.
Houston, TX 77046-0902
(713)877-1400
Company Type: Subsidiary. **Officer:** James R. Paul, Chairman of the Board, CEO. **Ultimate Parent:** Coastal Corp. **SIC:** 5171—Petroleum Bulk Stations & Terminals; 5983—Fuel Oil Dealers; 5172—Petroleum Products Nec; 4226—Special Warehousing & Storage Nec. **Employee Count:** 826. **Sales:** 173 M.

★ 86016 ★   **Coscol Marine Corp.**
Coastal Tower, 9 Greenway Plz.
Houston, TX 77046-0995
(713)877-3370 **Fax:** (713)877-7949
Officer: Edward W. Knutsen, President.
Ultimate Parent: Coastal Corp.

★ 86017 ★   **Coscol Petroleum Corp.**
Coastal Tower, 9 Greenway Plz.
Houston, TX 77046-0995
(713)877-6600
Officer: Sam F. Willson Jr., President.
Ultimate Parent: Coastal Corp.

★ 86018 ★   **Criterion Catalyst Co.**
16825 N. Chase Dr., 1000
Houston, TX 77060
(713)874-2600
Company Type: Joint venture. **Ultimate Parent:** American Cyanamid Co. **SIC:** 2819—Industrial Inorganic Chemicals Nec.

★ 86019 ★   **Criterion Catalyst Co. LP**
16825 Northchase Dr.
Houston, TX 77060-6024
(713)874-2600
Ultimate Parent: American Cyanamid Co.
SIC: 8741—Management Services.

★ 86020 ★   **CSC Credit Services**
652 E.N. Belt, Ste. 400
Houston, TX 77060
(713)878-1900 **Fax:** (713)878-1949
Officer: Dale B. Elam, President. **Ultimate Parent:** Computer Sciences.

★ 86021 ★   **Csc Credit Services**
Bill Hiller
Houston, TX 77056
(713)878-4978
Ultimate Parent: Computer Sciences. **SIC:** 6159—Miscellaneous Business Credit Institutions.

★ 86022 ★   **Csc Credit Services**
7909 Parkwood Circle
Houston, TX 77036
(713)995-3518
Ultimate Parent: Computer Sciences.

★ 86023 ★   **CSC Industry Services Group**
652 N. Belt E, Ste. 400
Houston, TX 77060
(713)615-0311 **Fax:** (713)878-1905
Officer: Dale B. Elam, Group President.
Ultimate Parent: Computer Sciences.

★ 86024 ★   **Cyprus Minerals**
17509 Van Rd.
Houston, TX 77049
(713)456-0133
Ultimate Parent: Cyprus Amax Minerals.

★ 86025 ★   **Daniel Radiator Corp.**
5606 Harvey Wilson Dr.
Houston, TX 77020
Ultimate Parent: Handy & Harman. **SIC:** 3714—Motor Vehicle Parts & Accessories; 5013—Motor Vehicle Supplies & New Parts.

★ 86026 ★   **Delta Air Lines**
5150 Westheimer Rd.
Houston, TX 77056
(713)629-9020
Ultimate Parent: Delta Air Lines, Inc.

★ 86027 ★   **Delta Air Lines**
340 N. Belt Dr. E
Houston, TX 77060
(713)448-3000
Ultimate Parent: Delta Air Lines, Inc.

★ 86028 ★   **Delta Air Lines**
216 N. Belt Pl
Houston, TX 77060
(713)878-3233
Ultimate Parent: Delta Air Lines, Inc.

★ 86029 ★   **Delta Air Lines**
255 N. Belt Dr. E
Houston, TX 77060
(713)875-3156
Ultimate Parent: Delta Air Lines, Inc.

★ 86030 ★   **Delta Air Lines**
2 E. Greenway Plz.
Houston, TX 77046
(713)621-7262
Ultimate Parent: Delta Air Lines, Inc. **SIC:** 4522—Air Transportation—Nonscheduled.

★ 86031 ★   **Delta Air Lines Inc.**
2 E. Greenway Plz.
Houston, TX 77046
(713)621-7262
Ultimate Parent: Delta Air Lines, Inc. **SIC:** 4522—Air Transportation—Nonscheduled.

★ 86032 ★   **Deltex/Pro Mac**
PO Box 12878
Houston, TX 77217
(713)641-2211 **Fax:** (713)641-1428
Company Type: Subsidiary. **Officer:** Thomas W. Smith, Acting General Manager. **Ultimate Parent:** Imo Industries.

★ 86033 ★   **Deluxe Check Printers Inc.**
3900 Dacoma St.
Houston, TX 77092-8720
Ultimate Parent: Deluxe Corp. **SIC:** 2752—Commercial Printing—Lithographic; 2782—Blankbooks & Looseleaf Binders.

★ 86034 ★   **Deluxe Check Printers Inc.**
3900 Dacoma
Houston, TX 77092-8720
Ultimate Parent: Deluxe Corp. **SIC:** 2782—Blankbooks & Looseleaf Binders; 2752—Commercial Printing—Lithographic.

★ 86035 ★   **Diamond M Offshore, Inc.**
15415 Katy Fwy.
Houston, TX 77094
(713)492-5300
Company Type: Subsidiary. **Officer:** Robert E. Rose, President. **Ultimate Parent:** Loews. **SIC:** 1389—Oil & Gas Field Services Nec. **Employee Count:** 2700. **Sales:** 217713000 M.

★ 86036 ★   **Diamond Offshore Drilling, Inc.**
PO Box 4558
Houston, TX 77210
(713)492-5300 **Fax:** (713)492-5316
Officer: Robert E. Rose, President & CEO.
Ultimate Parent: Loews.

★ 86037 ★   **Diebold Inc.**
10325 Landsbury Dr.
Houston, TX 77099
(713)495-3999
Ultimate Parent: Diebold, Inc. **SIC:** 5021—Furniture.

★ 86038 ★   **Digital Equipment Corp.**
6200 Savoy Dr.
Houston, TX 77036
(713)953-3500
Ultimate Parent: Digital Equipment Corp. **SIC:** 5046—Commercial Equipment Nec.

★ 86039 ★   **Dillard Department Stores**
Dilliard's Galleria
Houston, TX 77056
(713)622-6950
Ultimate Parent: Dillard Department Stores. **SIC:** 4789—Transportation Services Nec.

★ 86040 ★   **Dillard Department Stores**
Town Country
Houston, TX 77024
(713)464-1851
Ultimate Parent: Dillard Department Stores. **SIC:** 5311—Department Stores.

★ 86041 ★   **Dillards**
4925 Westheimer Rd.
Houston, TX 77056
(713)877-1836
Ultimate Parent: Dillard Department Stores.

★ 86042 ★   **Dillards**
7925 Fm 1960 Rd. W
Houston, TX 77070
(713)894-7518
Ultimate Parent: Dillard Department Stores.

★ 86043 ★   **Dr. Pepper Bottling Co.**
2400 Holly Hall St.
Houston, TX 77054
(713)799-1024
Officer: Joe Lombardo, President. **Ultimate Parent:** Dr. Pepper/Seven-Up. **SIC:** 2086—Bottled & Canned Soft Drinks; 2087—Flavoring Extracts & Syrups Nec.

★ 86044 ★   **Dole Foods of America**
2115 Briarstem Dr.
Houston, TX 77077
(713)589-2331
Ultimate Parent: Dole Food.

★ 86045 ★   **Donnelley Publishing**
1415 North Blvd.
Houston, TX 77006
(713)880-1007
Ultimate Parent: R. R. Donnelley & Sons. **SIC:** 7313—Radio, T.V. & Publisher Representatives.

★ 86046 ★   Dow Chemical Co.
Engineering & Construction Services
Division
PO Box 3387
Houston, TX 77001
(713)978-2971
Company Type: Division. Officer: G. O.
McDaniel, General Manager. Ultimate
Parent: Dow Chemical Co. USA. SIC:
8711—Engineering Services; 1521—
Single-Family Housing Construction.

★ 86047 ★   Downhole Seismic
Services
3600 Briarpark
Houston, TX 77042-4299
(713)952-1133 Fax: (713)785-9008 Telex:
166214
Company Type: Division. Officer: Peter
Aronstam, President. Ultimate Parent:
Litton Industries. SIC: 1389—Oil & Gas
Field Services Nec.

★ 86048 ★   Dresser Industries
Inc.
Trading Division
3 Greenway Plaza
Houston, TX 77046
(713)297-2229 Fax: (713)297-2232
Company Type: Subsidiary. Ultimate
Parent: Dresser Industries Inc.

★ 86049 ★   Dresser Industries
Inc.
Waukesha Engine Division
14505 Torrey Chase Blvd.
Houston, TX 77014
(713)893-4170
Company Type: Division. Ultimate Parent:
Dresser Industries Inc. SIC: 3714—Motor
Vehicle Parts & Accessories.

★ 86050 ★   Drew Chemical Corp.
6121 Almeda Genoa Rd.
Houston, TX 77048
Ultimate Parent: Ashland Oil. SIC: 2899—
Chemical Preparations Nec.

★ 86051 ★   E. R. Carpenter Co.
Inc.
2802 Canal St.
Houston, TX 77223
Ultimate Parent: Carpenter. SIC: 3086—
Plastics Foam Products.

★ 86052 ★   E. R. Carpenter Co.
Inc.
PO Box 230026
Houston, TX 77223
Ultimate Parent: Carpenter. SIC: 3086—
Plastics Foam Products.

★ 86053 ★   E. R. Carpenter Co.
Inc.
1702 Dowling
Houston, TX 77003
Ultimate Parent: Carpenter. SIC: 2392—
Housefurnishings Nec.

★ 86054 ★   Eaton Corp. Ion Beam
8323 Shadow Wind Dr.
Houston, TX 77040
(713)466-1011
Ultimate Parent: Eaton Corp. SIC: 5065—
Electronic Parts & Equipment Nec.

★ 86055 ★   Emery Worldwide
24007 PO Box
Houston, TX 77229
(409)639-4063
Ultimate Parent: Consolidated Freightways.
SIC: 4215—Courier Services Except by Air.

★ 86056 ★   Energy Coatings Co.
7211 Regency Sq., Ste. 104
Houston, TX 77036
(713)974-7211
Company Type: Subsidiary. Ultimate
Parent: Lukens. SIC: 3479—Metal Coating
& Allied Services.

★ 86057 ★   Engelhard Corp.
Engelhard Di
1800 Saint James Pl
Houston, TX 77056
(713)627-2160
Ultimate Parent: Engelhard Corp. SIC:
2819—Industrial Inorganic Chemicals Nec.

★ 86058 ★   Enron
1400 Smith St.
Houston, TX 77002
(713)853-6161
Company Type: Headquarters. Officer:

Kenneth L. Lay. Fortune Service 500:
Ranking 11.

★ 86059 ★   Enron
1400 Smith St.
Houston, TX 77002
(713)853-6161
Company Type: Headquarters. Officer:
Kenneth L. Lay. Ultimate Parent: Enron.
Employee Count: 7100. Fortune 500:
Largest U.S. Industrial Corporations:
Ranking 11.

★ 86060 ★   Enron Americas Inc.
PO Box 1188
Houston, TX 77251
(713)853-6161
Officer: William C. Horwitz, President.
Ultimate Parent: Enron. SIC: 8741—
Management Services.

★ 86061 ★   Enron Americas Inc.
1400 Smith St., Ste. 1565
Houston, TX 77002-7338
(713)853-6161
Company Type: Subsidiary. Officer:
William C. Horwitz, COO, Executive Vice
President. Ultimate Parent: Enron. SIC:
5172—Petroleum Products Nec. Employee
Count: 4107. Sales: 73.9 M.

★ 86062 ★   Enron Corp.
1400 Smith St.
Houston, TX 77002
(713)853-6161 Fax: (713)856-6790
Company Type: Headquarters. Officer:
Kenneth L. Lay, Chairman of the Board &
CEO. Ultimate Parent: Enron. SIC: 1311—
Crude Petroleum & Natural Gas; 4922—
Natural Gas Transmission; 5813—Drinking
Places; 4613—Refined Petroleum Pipelines;
1321—Natural Gas Liquids; 6331—Fire,
Marine & Casualty Insurance; 5171—
Petroleum Bulk Stations & Terminals;
5984—Liquefied Petroleum Gas Dealers;
5172—Petroleum Products Nec. Employee
Count: 7000. Sales: 13520000000 M.

★ 86063 ★   Enron Corp.
PO Box 1188
Houston, TX 77257-1188
Company Type: Headquarters. Ultimate
Parent: Enron.

★ 86064 ★   Enron Corp.
PO Box 1188
Houston, TX 77251-1188
(713)853-6161 Fax: (713)853-3129
Company Type: Headquarters. Ultimate
Parent: Enron. Employee Count: 7800.
Sales: 10000000000 M.

★ 86065 ★   Enron Gas Gathering
Inc.
1400 Smith St.
Houston, TX 77002-7337
(713)654-6167
Company Type: Subsidiary. Officer: John
J. Easlinger, President, COO. Ultimate
Parent: Enron. SIC: 4924—Natural Gas
Distribution. Sales: 1.1 M.

★ 86066 ★   Enron Gas Liquids
Inc.
1400 Smith St.
Houston, TX 77002-7337
(713)853-6161
Company Type: Subsidiary. Officer: J.
Michael Muckleroy, Chairman of the Board,
CEO. Ultimate Parent: Enron. SIC: 4925—
Gas Production & Distribution Nec.

★ 86067 ★   Enron Gas Liquids
Inc.
PO Box 1188
Houston, TX 77251
(713)853-5100
Officer: William C. Horwitz, Executive Vice
President & COO. Ultimate Parent: Enron.
SIC: 5172—Petroleum Products Nec.

★ 86068 ★   Enron Gas
Processing
PO Box 1188
Houston, TX 77251-1188
(713)853-5595
Company Type: Subsidiary. Ultimate
Parent: Enron.

★ 86069 ★   Enron Gas
Processing Co.
PO Box 1188
Houston, TX 77251
(713)853-7875
Officer: David C. Roussel, President.

Ultimate Parent: Enron. SIC: 1321—
Natural Gas Liquids.

★ 86070 ★   Enron Gas
Processing Co. Inc.
1400 Smith St.
Houston, TX 77002-7337
(713)853-6161
Company Type: Subsidiary. Officer: J.
Michael Muckleroy, Chairman of the Board,
CEO. Ultimate Parent: Enron. SIC: 1321—
Natural Gas Liquids. Employee Count:
560. Sales: 258 M.

★ 86071 ★   Enron Gas Services
Corp.
1400 Smith St.
Houston, TX 77002-7337
(713)853-7500
Company Type: Subsidiary. Officer:
Jeffrey K. Skilling, Chairman of the Board,
CEO. Ultimate Parent: Enron. SIC: 4924—
Natural Gas Distribution. Employee Count:
1200. Sales: 323 (est) M.

★ 86072 ★   Enron Gas Services
Group
PO Box 1188
Houston, TX 77251-1188
Company Type: Subsidiary. Ultimate
Parent: Enron.

★ 86073 ★   Enron Interstate
Pipeline Co.
PO Box 1188
Houston, TX 77251
(713)853-6161
Officer: R. J. Burns, President. Ultimate
Parent: Enron. SIC: 4924—Natural Gas
Distribution. Employee Count: 349.

★ 86074 ★   Enron Liquid Fuels
PO Box 1188
Houston, TX 77251
Officer: J. M. Muckleroy, Chairman of the
Board & CEO. Ultimate Parent: Enron.
SIC: 1311—Crude Petroleum & Natural
Gas; 2869—Industrial Organic Chemicals
Nec.

★ 86075 ★   Enron Liquids
Pipeline Co.
PO Box 1188
Houston, TX 77251-1188
(713)853-3119
Company Type: Subsidiary. Ultimate
Parent: Enron.

★ 86076 ★   Enron Liquids
Pipeline Group
PO Box 1188
Houston, TX 77251
(713)853-6161
Officer: James E. Spencer, President.
Ultimate Parent: Enron. SIC: 1311—Crude
Petroleum & Natural Gas; 2813—Industrial
Gases; 2911—Petroleum Refining; 5171—
Petroleum Bulk Stations & Terminals;
5172—Petroleum Products Nec.

★ 86077 ★   Enron Oil & Gas Co.
PO Box 1188
Houston, TX 77251-1188
Company Type: Subsidiary. Ultimate
Parent: Enron.

★ 86078 ★   Enron Oil & Gas Co.
Inc.
1400 Smith St., Ste. 2180
Houston, TX 77002-7339
(713)853-6161
Company Type: Subsidiary. Officer:
Forrest E. Hoglund, Chairman of the Board,
President. Ultimate Parent: Enron. SIC:
1382—Oil & Gas Exploration Services;
1311—Crude Petroleum & Natural Gas.
Employee Count: 610. Sales: 452 M.

★ 86079 ★   Enron Oil & Gas
Marketing Inc.
1400 Smith St.
Houston, TX 77002-7337
(713)654-6161
Company Type: Subsidiary. Officer:
Forrest E. Hoglund, President. Ultimate
Parent: Enron. SIC: 1382—Oil & Gas
Exploration Services; 1311—Crude
Petroleum & Natural Gas. Sales: 123 M.

★ 86080 ★   Enron Oil Trading &
Transportation
PO Box 1188
Houston, TX 77251
(713)993-5203
Officer: Charles D. Emel, President.

Ultimate Parent: Enron. SIC: 4612—Crude
Petroleum Pipelines.

★ 86081 ★   Enron Operating Co.
1400 Smith St.
Houston, TX 77002-7337
(713)853-6161
Company Type: Subsidiary. Officer: T.
White, President. Ultimate Parent: Enron.
SIC: 4922—Natural Gas Transmission.
Employee Count: 2932. Sales: 1.5 (est) M.

★ 86082 ★   Enron Operations
Corp.
PO Box 1188
Houston, TX 77251-1188
(713)853-6394
Company Type: Subsidiary. Ultimate
Parent: Enron.

★ 86083 ★   Enron Power Corp.
PO Box 1188
Houston, TX 77251-1188
(713)646-6012
Company Type: Subsidiary. Ultimate
Parent: Enron.

★ 86084 ★   Enron Power
Development Corp.
333 Clay St., Ste. 400
Houston, TX 77002-4004
(713)646-6000
Company Type: Subsidiary. Officer: R.
Mark, Chairman of the Board, CEO.
Ultimate Parent: Enron. SIC: 4911—
Electric Services. Sales: 79.2 M.

★ 86085 ★   Eron Exploration Co.
PO Box 1188
Houston, TX 77251-1188
(713)853-5566
Company Type: Subsidiary. Ultimate
Parent: Enron.

★ 86086 ★   Eron Gas Liquids
International Ltd.
PO Box 1188
Houston, TX 77251-1188
(713)853-7985
Company Type: Subsidiary. Ultimate
Parent: Enron.

★ 86087 ★   Eron International Inc.
PO Box 1188
Houston, TX 77251-1188
(713)853-5917
Company Type: Subsidiary. Ultimate
Parent: Enron.

★ 86088 ★   Express
7355 Alabonson Rd.
Houston, TX 77088
(713)937-9232
Ultimate Parent: Limited. SIC: 5411—
Grocery Stores.

★ 86089 ★   Exxon
8550 S. Braeswood Blvd.
Houston, TX 77071
(713)271-5082
Ultimate Parent: Exxon.

★ 86090 ★   Exxon
10801 Eastex Fwy.
Houston, TX 77093
(713)449-0393
Ultimate Parent: Exxon. SIC: 5599—
Automotive Dealers Nec.

★ 86091 ★   Exxon
5601 Southwest Fwy.
Houston, TX 77057
(713)667-3940
Ultimate Parent: Exxon. SIC: 5411—
Grocery Stores.

★ 86092 ★   Exxon
2111 Southmore Blvd.
Houston, TX 77004
(713)527-8043
Ultimate Parent: Exxon. SIC: 5541—
Gasoline Service Stations.

★ 86093 ★   Exxon
1003 Nasa Rd. 1
Houston, TX 77058
(713)488-0032
Ultimate Parent: Exxon. SIC: 5541—
Gasoline Service Stations.

★ 86094 ★　Exxon
14101 Northwest Fwy.
Houston, TX 77040
(713)462-0102
Ultimate Parent: Exxon. SIC: 5541—
Gasoline Service Stations.

★ 86095 ★　Exxon
7102 Tidwell Rd.
Houston, TX 77016
(713)633-6476
Ultimate Parent: Exxon. SIC: 5411—
Grocery Stores.

★ 86096 ★　Exxon
13643 W. Montgomery Rd.
Houston, TX 77086
(713)820-4748
Ultimate Parent: Exxon. SIC: 5541—
Gasoline Service Stations.

★ 86097 ★　Exxon
5138 San Felipe St.
Houston, TX 77056
(713)621-2300
Ultimate Parent: Exxon. SIC: 5541—
Gasoline Service Stations.

★ 86098 ★　Exxon
9605 Stella Link Rd.
Houston, TX 77025
(713)668-0843
Ultimate Parent: Exxon. SIC: 5411—
Grocery Stores.

★ 86099 ★　Exxon
8930 North Fwy.
Houston, TX 77037
(713)448-5519
Ultimate Parent: Exxon. SIC: 5541—
Gasoline Service Stations.

★ 86100 ★　Exxon
2521 S. Post Oak Rd.
Houston, TX 77056
(713)850-9900
Ultimate Parent: Exxon. SIC: 5541—
Gasoline Service Stations.

★ 86101 ★　Exxon
5710 Memorial Dr.
Houston, TX 77007
(713)861-9363
Ultimate Parent: Exxon. SIC: 5411—
Grocery Stores.

★ 86102 ★　Exxon
6901 Navigation Blvd.
Houston, TX 77011
(713)926-3715
Ultimate Parent: Exxon. SIC: 5541—
Gasoline Service Stations.

★ 86103 ★　Exxon
9602 Main St.
Houston, TX 77025
(713)661-1944
Ultimate Parent: Exxon. SIC: 5541—
Gasoline Service Stations.

★ 86104 ★　Exxon
14001 Main St.
Houston, TX 77035
(713)723-7060
Ultimate Parent: Exxon. SIC: 5541—
Gasoline Service Stations.

★ 86105 ★　Exxon
3003 Ella Blvd.
Houston, TX 77018
(713)862-3991
Ultimate Parent: Exxon. SIC: 5541—
Gasoline Service Stations.

★ 86106 ★　Exxon
12355 Katy Fwy.
Houston, TX 77079
(713)497-1270
Ultimate Parent: Exxon. SIC: 5411—
Grocery Stores.

★ 86107 ★　Exxon
2121 Cullen Blvd.
Houston, TX 77004
(713)741-2700
Ultimate Parent: Exxon. SIC: 5541—
Gasoline Service Stations.

★ 86108 ★　Exxon
11656 Eastex Fwy.
Houston, TX 77093
(713)442-0541
Ultimate Parent: Exxon. SIC: 5541—
Gasoline Service Stations.

★ 86109 ★　Exxon
5402 North Fwy.
Houston, TX 77076
(713)697-3129
Ultimate Parent: Exxon. SIC: 5541—
Gasoline Service Stations.

★ 86110 ★　Exxon
102 Cavalcade St.
Houston, TX 77009
(713)692-8422
Ultimate Parent: Exxon. SIC: 5541—
Gasoline Service Stations.

★ 86111 ★　Exxon
4729 PO Box
Houston, TX 77210
(903)584-3112
Ultimate Parent: Exxon.

★ 86112 ★　Exxon
2227 W. Fm 1960
Houston, TX 77090
(713)444-5382
Ultimate Parent: Exxon. SIC: 5541—
Gasoline Service Stations.

★ 86113 ★　Exxon Car Wash
2525 S. Shepherd Dr.
Houston, TX 77019
(713)529-1622
Ultimate Parent: Exxon. SIC: 7542—Car
Washes.

★ 86114 ★　Exxon Car Wash
6825 Fondren Rd.
Houston, TX 77036
(713)777-2008
Ultimate Parent: Exxon. SIC: 7542—Car
Washes.

★ 86115 ★　Exxon Chemical Co.
16850 Saturn Ln.
Houston, TX 77058
(713)488-3559
Ultimate Parent: Exxon.

★ 86116 ★　Exxon Chemical Co.
13501 Katy Fwy.
Houston, TX 77079
(713)870-6000
Ultimate Parent: Exxon. SIC: 2824—
Organic Fibers—Noncellulosic.

★ 86117 ★　Exxon Chemical Co.
16000 Barkers Point Ln.
Houston, TX 77079
(713)870-1162
Ultimate Parent: Exxon.

★ 86118 ★　Exxon Chemical Co.
13105 Northwest Fwy.
Houston, TX 77040
(713)460-6800
Ultimate Parent: Exxon.

★ 86119 ★　Exxon Chemical Co.
8230 Stedman St.
Houston, TX 77029
(713)672-0748
Officer: John Cross, Manager. Ultimate
Parent: Ethyl. SIC: 2819—Industrial
Inorganic Chemicals Nec; 2899—Chemical
Preparations Nec.

★ 86120 ★　Exxon Chemical Co.
13501 Katy Fwy.
Houston, TX 77079
(713)584-7600
Officer: Ray B. Nesbitt, President. Ultimate
Parent: Exxon SIC: 2819—Industrial
Inorganic Chemicals Nec; 2911—Petroleum
Refining.

★ 86121 ★　Exxon Chemical Co.
580 Westlake Plz.
Houston, TX 77079-1398
(713)584-7600 Fax: (713)584-7600
Company Type: Subsidiary. Officer: R. B.
Nesbitt, President. Ultimate Parent: Exxon.

★ 86122 ★　Exxon Chemical
Fertilizer Co.
800 Bell St.
Houston, TX 77002-7426
Company Type: Subsidiary. Officer:
Lawrence G. Rawl, Chairman of the Board.
Ultimate Parent: Exxon. SIC: 1311—Crude
Petroleum & Natural Gas.

★ 86123 ★　Exxon Coal &
Minerals Co.
2401 S. Glessner
Houston, TX 77063-2005
(713)978-5333 Fax: (713)978-5618
Company Type: Subsidiary. Officer: R. P.
Larkins, President. Ultimate Parent: Exxon.

★ 86124 ★　Exxon Coal USA Inc.
2401 S. Gessner Rd.
Houston, TX 77063-2005
(713)978-5333
Company Type: Subsidiary. Officer: R. P.
Larkins, President. Ultimate Parent: Exxon.
SIC: 1241—Coal Mining Services.
Employee Count: 1400. Sales: 116 M.

★ 86125 ★　Exxon Co.
4692 PO Box
Houston, TX 77210
(713)656-4267
Ultimate Parent: Exxon.

★ 86126 ★　Exxon Co. USA
16945 Northchase Dr.
Houston, TX 77060
(713)874-5100
Ultimate Parent: Exxon.

★ 86127 ★　Exxon Co. USA
7414 Alabonson Rd.
Houston, TX 77088
(713)445-1340
Ultimate Parent: Exxon.

★ 86128 ★　Exxon Co. USA
13200 Bellaire Blvd.
Houston, TX 77083
(713)568-5971
Ultimate Parent: Exxon.

★ 86129 ★　Exxon Co. USA
12000 Greenspoint Dr.
Houston, TX 77060
(713)875-6430
Ultimate Parent: Exxon.

★ 86130 ★　Exxon Co. USA
5702 Westheimer Rd.
Houston, TX 77057
(713)781-6644
Ultimate Parent: Exxon. SIC: 7538—
General Automotive Repair Shops.

★ 86131 ★　Exxon Co. USA
4255 Hawn 6
Houston, TX 77091
(713)859-8426
Ultimate Parent: Exxon. SIC: 5541—
Gasoline Service Stations.

★ 86132 ★　Exxon Co. USA
932 N. Wilcrest Dr.
Houston, TX 77079
(713)464-5437
Ultimate Parent: Exxon. SIC: 7542—Car
Washes.

★ 86133 ★　Exxon Co. USA
2405 Bay Area Blvd.
Houston, TX 77058
(713)486-9630
Ultimate Parent: Exxon. SIC: 5541—
Gasoline Service Stations.

★ 86134 ★　Exxon Co. USA
1531 Gessner Dr.
Houston, TX 77080
(713)468-7324
Ultimate Parent: Exxon. SIC: 5541—
Gasoline Service Stations.

★ 86135 ★　Exxon Co. USA
6060 Wilcrest Dr.
Houston, TX 77072
(713)879-0615
Ultimate Parent: Exxon.

★ 86136 ★　Exxon Co. USA
9670 Westheimer Rd.
Houston, TX 77063
(713)780-4843
Ultimate Parent: Exxon.

★ 86137 ★　Exxon Co. USA
10595 Westpark Dr.
Houston, TX 77042
(713)974-0558
Ultimate Parent: Exxon.

★ 86138 ★　Exxon Co. USA
3140 Southwest Fwy.
Houston, TX 77098
(713)528-4756
Ultimate Parent: Exxon.

★ 86139 ★　Exxon Co. USA
5302 W. Bellfort St.
Houston, TX 77035
(713)723-1283
Ultimate Parent: Exxon.

★ 86140 ★　Exxon Co. USA
3902 S. Shaver St.
Houston, TX 77034
(713)943-1048
Ultimate Parent: Exxon.

★ 86141 ★　Exxon Co. USA
2402 S. Wayside Dr.
Houston, TX 77023
(713)926-8695
Ultimate Parent: Exxon.

★ 86142 ★　Exxon Co. USA
2800 Reed Rd.
Houston, TX 77051
(713)734-6342
Ultimate Parent: Exxon.

★ 86143 ★　Exxon Co. USA
3803 S. Gessner Rd.
Houston, TX 77063
(713)974-5411
Ultimate Parent: Exxon.

★ 86144 ★　Exxon Co. USA
1290 Pinemont Dr.
Houston, TX 77018
(713)686-9663
Ultimate Parent: Exxon.

★ 86145 ★　Exxon Co. USA
290 Rankin Rd.
Houston, TX 77073
(713)876-3775
Ultimate Parent: Exxon.

★ 86146 ★　Exxon Co. USA
2211 North Fwy.
Houston, TX 77009
(713)861-5233
Ultimate Parent: Exxon.

★ 86147 ★　Exxon Co. USA
17503 North Fwy.
Houston, TX 77090
(713)444-3171
Ultimate Parent: Exxon.

★ 86148 ★　Exxon Co. USA
12585 N. Bammel Houston Rd.
Houston, TX 77066
(713)583-5539
Ultimate Parent: Exxon.

★ 86149 ★　Exxon Co. USA
6901 Navigation Blvd.
Houston, TX 77011
(713)928-2021
Ultimate Parent: Exxon.

★ 86150 ★　Exxon Co. USA
6802 Kirby Dr.
Houston, TX 77030
(713)667-9293
Ultimate Parent: Exxon.

★ 86151 ★　Exxon Co. USA
6015 Long Dr.
Houston, TX 77087
(713)644-3415
Ultimate Parent: Exxon.

★ 86152 ★　Exxon Co. USA
9998 Hempstead Rd.
Houston, TX 77092
(713)683-7323
Ultimate Parent: Exxon.

★ 86153 ★　Exxon Co. USA
17438 Hempstead Rd.
Houston, TX 77040
(713)937-6692
Ultimate Parent: Exxon.

★ 86154 ★　Exxon Co. USA
12602 East Fwy.
Houston, TX 77015
(713)453-3288
Ultimate Parent: Exxon.

★ 86155 ★　Exxon Co. USA
16750 El Camino Real
Houston, TX 77062
(713)488-1180
Ultimate Parent: Exxon.

★ 86156 ★   Exxon Co. USA
3102 Buffalo Speedway
Houston, TX 77098
(713)621-9434
Ultimate Parent: Exxon.

★ 86157 ★   Exxon Co. USA
9150 Chimney Rock Rd.
Houston, TX 77096
(713)729-5498
Ultimate Parent: Exxon.

★ 86158 ★   Exxon Co. USA
9322 Bissonnet St.
Houston, TX 77074
(713)981-8435
Ultimate Parent: Exxon.

★ 86159 ★   Exxon Co. USA
10831 Bissonnet St.
Houston, TX 77099
(713)568-7891
Ultimate Parent: Exxon.

★ 86160 ★   Exxon Co. USA
3924 Bellaire Blvd.
Houston, TX 77025
(713)664-2498
Ultimate Parent: Exxon.

★ 86161 ★   Exxon Co. USA
7470 Bellfort St.
Houston, TX 77087
(713)644-9534
Ultimate Parent: Exxon.

★ 86162 ★   Exxon Co. USA
13350 Almeda Rd.
Houston, TX 77045
(713)433-1024
Ultimate Parent: Exxon.

★ 86163 ★   Exxon Co. USA
233 Benmar Dr.
Houston, TX 77060
(713)775-7301
Officer: L. Bryant Williams Jr., Manager.
Ultimate Parent: Exxon SIC: 2911—
Petroleum Refining.

★ 86164 ★   Exxon Co. USA
800 Bell St.
Houston, TX 77002-7426
(713)656-3636 Fax: (713)656-3514
Company Type: Subsidiary. Officer: H. J.
Longwell, President. Ultimate Parent:
Exxon.

★ 86165 ★   Exxon Computing
Services Co.
800 Bell St.
Houston, TX 77002-7426
(713)656-3636
Company Type: Subsidiary. Officer: P. C.
Hewlett, Manager. Ultimate Parent: Exxon.

★ 86166 ★   Exxon Exploration
Co.
233 Benmar Dr., Ste. 10
Houston, TX 77060-3105
(713)775-7771 Fax: (713)775-7500
Officer: J. L. Thompson, President.
Ultimate Parent: Exxon.

★ 86167 ★   Exxon Gas
Accounting Service
4496 PO Box
Houston, TX 77210
(713)656-4769
Ultimate Parent: Exxon.

★ 86168 ★   Exxon Gas System
4550 Dacoma St.
Houston, TX 77092
(713)224-0429
Ultimate Parent: Exxon.

★ 86169 ★   Exxon Gas System
Inc.
800 Bell St.
Houston, TX 77002-7426
(713)656-7866
Company Type: Subsidiary. Officer: B. L.
Noble, President. Ultimate Parent: Exxon.
SIC: 4923—Gas Transmission &
Distribution. Employee Count: 51. Sales:
165 M.

★ 86170 ★   Exxon Pipeline
800 Bell St.
Houston, TX 77002
(713)656-3636
Company Type: Headquarters. Officer:
Otto R. Harrison. Ultimate Parent: Exxon

Pipeline. Employee Count: 565. Fortune
Service 500: Ranking 46.

★ 86171 ★   Exxon Pipeline
800 Bell St.
Houston, TX 77002
(713)656-3636
Company Type: Headquarters. Officer:
Otto R. Harrison. Fortune Service 500:
Ranking 46.

★ 86172 ★   Exxon Pipeline Co.
11005 Fairmont Pky.
Houston, TX 77024
(713)471-6045
Ultimate Parent: Exxon Pipeline. SIC:
5599—Automotive Dealers Nec.

★ 86173 ★   Exxon Pipeline Co.
2050 Fuel Storage Rd.
Houston, TX 77073
(713)443-2575
Ultimate Parent: Exxon Pipeline.

★ 86174 ★   Exxon Pipeline Co.
11005 Fairmont Pky.
Houston, TX 77024
(713)471-6045
Ultimate Parent: Exxon. SIC: 5599—
Automotive Dealers Nec.

★ 86175 ★   Exxon Pipeline Co.
2050 Fuel Storage Rd.
Houston, TX 77073
(713)443-2575
Ultimate Parent: Exxon.

★ 86176 ★   Exxon Pipeline Co.
10255 Fm 1960 Rd. W
Houston, TX 77070
(713)469-8904
Ultimate Parent: Exxon.

★ 86177 ★   Exxon Pipeline Co.
800 Bell St.
Houston, TX 77002
(713)656-3636
Officer: Otto R. Harrison, CEO. Ultimate
Parent: Exxon SIC: 2911—Petroleum
Refining.

★ 86178 ★   Exxon Pipeline Co.
Inc.
800 Bell St.
Houston, TX 77002
(713)656-3636
Company Type: Subsidiary. Officer: D. G.
Warner, Principal. Ultimate Parent: Exxon.
SIC: 4612—Crude Petroleum Pipelines;
4613—Refined Petroleum Pipelines.
Employee Count: 611. Sales: 551 M.

★ 86179 ★   Exxon Pipeline Co.,
Inc.
800 Bell St.
Houston, TX 77002
(713)656-3636
Company Type: Subsidiary. Officer: D. G.
Warner, Principal. Ultimate Parent: Exxon.
SIC: 4612—Crude Petroleum Pipelines;
4613—Refined Petroleum Pipelines.
Employee Count: 611. Sales: 551 M.

★ 86180 ★   Exxon Production
Research Co.
3120 Buffalo Speedway
Houston, TX 77098-1806
(713)965-4222
Company Type: Subsidiary. Officer: F. M.
Perkins, President & CEO. Ultimate Parent:
Exxon. SIC: 8731—Commercial Physical
Research. Employee Count: 1000. Sales:
200 M.

★ 86181 ★   Exxon Production
Research Co.
3120 Buffalo Speedway
Houston, TX 77001
(713)965-4222 Fax: (713)966-6026
Company Type: Subsidiary. Officer: Dan
Mendell III, President. Ultimate Parent:
Exxon.

★ 86182 ★   Exxon Production
Research Co.
3120 Buffalo Speedway
Houston, TX 77098-1806
(713)965-4222
Company Type: Subsidiary. Officer: F. M.
Perkins, President & CEO. Ultimate Parent:
Exxon. SIC: 8731—Commercial Physical
Research. Employee Count: 1000. Sales:
200 M.

★ 86183 ★   Exxon Shipping Co.
800 Bell St.
Houston, TX 77002-7426
(713)656-3636
Company Type: Subsidiary. Officer:
Augustus Elmer III, President. Ultimate
Parent: Exxon. SIC: 4449—Water
Transportation of Freight Nec. Employee
Count: 1000. Sales: 104 M.

★ 86184 ★   Exxon Shipping Co.
800 Bell St.
Houston, TX 77002-7426
(713)656-3636
Company Type: Subsidiary. Officer:
Augustus Elmer III, President. Ultimate
Parent: Exxon. SIC: 4449—Water
Transportation of Freight Nec. Employee
Count: 1000. Sales: 104 M.

★ 86185 ★   Exxon Supply Co.
800 Bell St.
Houston, TX 77002-7426
(713)656-3636
Company Type: Subsidiary. Officer: H. E.
Collier, President. Ultimate Parent: Exxon.
SIC: 5172—Petroleum Products Nec.
Employee Count: 35. Sales: 9.3 M.

★ 86186 ★   Exxon Supply Co.
800 Bell St.
Houston, TX 77002-7426
(713)656-3636
Company Type: Subsidiary. Officer: H. E.
Collier, President. Ultimate Parent: Exxon.
SIC: 5172—Petroleum Products Nec.
Employee Count: 35. Sales: 9000000 M.

★ 86187 ★   Exxon Upstream
Technical Computing Co.
3616 Richmond Ave.
Houston, TX 77046
(713)965-4908 Fax: (713)965-7310
Company Type: Subsidiary. Officer: C. T.
McCombs, Manager. Ultimate Parent:
Exxon.

★ 86188 ★   Farm & Home
Savings Association
130587 PO Box
Houston, TX 77219
(713)529-4491
Ultimate Parent: Farm & Home Financial
Corp. SIC: 6035—Federal Savings
Institutions.

★ 86189 ★   Farm & Home
Savings Association
744907 PO Box
Houston, TX 77274
(713)529-4491
Ultimate Parent: Farm & Home Financial
Corp. SIC: 6035—Federal Savings
Institutions.

★ 86190 ★   Farm & Home
Savings Association
6945 Fm 1960 Rd. W
Houston, TX 77069
(713)529-4491
Ultimate Parent: Farm & Home Financial
Corp. SIC: 6035—Federal Savings
Institutions.

★ 86191 ★   Farm & Home
Savings Association
9326 N. Fwy.
Houston, TX 77074
(713)529-4491
Ultimate Parent: Farm & Home Financial
Corp. SIC: 6035—Federal Savings
Institutions.

★ 86192 ★   Farm & Home
Savings Association
813 Dallas St.
Houston, TX 77002
(713)529-4491
Ultimate Parent: Farm & Home Financial
Corp. SIC: 6035—Federal Savings
Institutions.

★ 86193 ★   Federal Express Corp.
8229 Travelair St.
Houston, TX 77061
(713)667-2500
Ultimate Parent: Federal Express. SIC:
4512—Air Transportation—Scheduled.

★ 86194 ★   Ferro Corp.
5300 Hollister St.
Houston, TX 77040
(713)462-7444
Ultimate Parent: Ferro Corp. SIC: 5169—
Chemicals & Allied Products Nec.

★ 86195 ★   First Bank
2824 Hillcroft St.
Houston, TX 77057
(713)785-5500
Ultimate Parent: Shawmut National Corp.
SIC: 6022—State Commercial Banks.

★ 86196 ★   First Interstate Bank
of Texas
1000 Louisiana St.
Houston, TX 77002-5008
(713)224-6611
Company Type: Subsidiary. Officer: Linnet
F. Deily, Chairman of the Board &
President. Ultimate Parent: First Interstate
Bancorp. SIC: 6022—State Commercial
Banks. Employee Count: 3479.

★ 86197 ★   First Mutual Financial
Corp.
1980 Post Oak Blvd.
Houston, TX 77056-3807
(713)850-0991
Ultimate Parent: Bank of Boston Corp.
SIC: 6141—Personal Credit Institutions.

★ 86198 ★   First Mutual Financial
Corp.
8507 North Fwy.
Houston, TX 77037-2809
(713)445-1080
Ultimate Parent: Bank of Boston Corp.
SIC: 6141—Personal Credit Institutions.

★ 86199 ★   Florida Gas
Transmission Co.
1400 Smith St., Ste. 3842
Houston, TX 77002-7342
Company Type: Subsidiary. Officer:
William V. Allison, President, CEO. Ultimate
Parent: Enron. SIC: 4923—Gas
Transmission & Distribution. Employee
Count: 500. Sales: 258 M.

★ 86200 ★   Florida Gas
Transmission Co.
PO Box 1188
Houston, TX 77251-1188
Company Type: Subsidiary. Ultimate
Parent: Enron.

★ 86201 ★   FMC Energy &
Transmission Equipment Group
1777 Gears Rd.
Houston, TX 77067
(713)448-0211
Officer: Joe Netherland, Manager. Ultimate
Parent: FMC. SIC: 3494—Valves & Pipe
Fittings Nec; 3533—Oil & Gas Field
Machinery; 3568—Power Transmission
Equipment Nec.

★ 86202 ★   Foot Action
1398 Willowbrook Mall
Houston, TX 77070
(713)890-4980
Ultimate Parent: Melville. SIC: 5661—Shoe
Stores.

★ 86203 ★   Foot Action
408 Greenspoint Mall
Houston, TX 77060
(713)874-9290
Ultimate Parent: Melville. SIC: 5661—Shoe
Stores.

★ 86204 ★   Foot Action Inc.
305 Northline Mall
Houston, TX 77022
(713)695-9313
Ultimate Parent: Melville.

★ 86205 ★   Foot Action Inc.
216 Gulfgate Mall
Houston, TX 77087
(713)643-3525
Ultimate Parent: Melville.

★ 86206 ★   Foot Action USA
900 Gessner Rd.
Houston, TX 77024
(713)464-3889
Ultimate Parent: Melville.

★ 86207 ★   Foster Prods. Corp.
6107 Industrial Way
Houston, TX 77011
Ultimate Parent: H. B. Fuller. SIC: 2891—
Adhesives & Sealants.

★ 86208 ★   Foster Products Corp.
6107 Industrial Way
Houston, TX 77011
Ultimate Parent: H. B. Fuller. SIC: 2891—
Adhesives & Sealants.

★ 86209 ★ Friendswood
Development Com
17001 Northchase Dr.
Houston, TX 77060
Ultimate Parent: Exxon.

★ 86210 ★ Friendswood
Development Co.
3322 Richmond Ave.
Houston, TX 77098
(713)527-0518
Ultimate Parent: Exxon. SIC: 6552—
Subdividers & Developers Nec.

★ 86211 ★ Friendswood
Development Co.
12450 Greenspoint Dr.
Houston, TX 77060
(713)875-7900
Ultimate Parent: Exxon.

★ 86212 ★ Friendswood
Development Co.
17001 Northchase Dr.
Houston, TX 77060-2139
(713)423-4000
Officer: John E. Walsh Jr., President &
CEO. Ultimate Parent: Exxon. SIC: 1531—
Operative Builders; 6552—Subdividers &
Developers Nec; 6512—Nonresidential
Building Operators. Employee Count: 170.
Sales: 170 M.

★ 86213 ★ H.B. Fuller Co.
Foster Div.
6107 Industrial Way
Houston, TX 77011
Company Type: Division. Ultimate Parent:
H. B. Fuller. SIC: 2900—Petroleum & Coal
Products.

★ 86214 ★ The Gap
11245 Fondren Rd.
Houston, TX 77096
(713)988-9435
Ultimate Parent: GAP.

★ 86215 ★ The Gap
1000 W. Oaks Mall
Houston, TX 77082
(713)496-2695
Ultimate Parent: GAP.

★ 86216 ★ The Gap
5015 Westheimer Rd.
Houston, TX 77056
(713)626-8191
Ultimate Parent: GAP. SIC: 5611—Men's &
Boys' Clothing Stores.

★ 86217 ★ The Gap
208 Memorial City
Houston, TX 77024
(713)932-7000
Ultimate Parent: GAP. SIC: 5651—Family
Clothing Stores.

★ 86218 ★ The Gap
W Oaks Mall
Houston, TX 77082
(713)496-2695
Ultimate Parent: GAP. SIC: 5611—Men's &
Boys' Clothing Stores.

★ 86219 ★ The Gap
7500 Bellaire Blvd.
Houston, TX 77036
(713)981-0335
Ultimate Parent: GAP.

★ 86220 ★ The Gap
7519 Westheimer Rd.
Houston, TX 77063
(713)789-4989
Ultimate Parent: GAP. SIC: 5621—
Women's Clothing Stores.

★ 86221 ★ The Gap
313 Westwood Mall
Houston, TX 77036
(713)772-8535
Ultimate Parent: GAP. SIC: 5611—Men's &
Boys' Clothing Stores.

★ 86222 ★ The Gap
242 Sharpstown Ctr.
Houston, TX 77036
(713)771-7219
Ultimate Parent: GAP. SIC: 5611—Men's &
Boys' Clothing Stores.

★ 86223 ★ The Gap
800 W. Belt Dr. N
Houston, TX 77024
(713)984-1036
Ultimate Parent: GAP. SIC: 5621—
Women's Clothing Stores.

★ 86224 ★ The Gap
322 Northline Mall
Houston, TX 77022
(713)697-9772
Ultimate Parent: GAP. SIC: 5611—Men's &
Boys' Clothing Stores.

★ 86225 ★ The Gap
252 NW Mall
Houston, TX 77092
(713)686-1620
Ultimate Parent: GAP. SIC: 5611—Men's &
Boys' Clothing Stores.

★ 86226 ★ The Gap
1200 Mckinney St. 321
Houston, TX 77010
Ultimate Parent: GAP. SIC: 5651—Family
Clothing Stores.

★ 86227 ★ The Gap
7925 Fm 1960 Rd. W
Houston, TX 77070
(713)890-0493
Ultimate Parent: GAP. SIC: 5611—Men's &
Boys' Clothing Stores.

★ 86228 ★ The Gap
467 Greenspoint Mall
Houston, TX 77060
(713)445-1900
Ultimate Parent: GAP. SIC: 5621—
Women's Clothing Stores.

★ 86229 ★ The Gap
555 Almeda Mall
Houston, TX 77075
(713)941-2293
Ultimate Parent: GAP. SIC: 5651—Family
Clothing Stores.

★ 86230 ★ The Gap Kids
5175 Westheimer Rd.
Houston, TX 77056
(713)965-9929
Ultimate Parent: GAP.

★ 86231 ★ Gap Stores
7519 Westheimer Rd.
Houston, TX 77063
(713)789-4989
Ultimate Parent: GAP. SIC: 5621—
Women's Clothing Stores.

★ 86232 ★ Gap Stores
313 Westwood Mall
Houston, TX 77036
(713)772-8535
Ultimate Parent: GAP. SIC: 5611—Men's &
Boys' Clothing Stores.

★ 86233 ★ Gap Stores
800 W. Belt Dr. N
Houston, TX 77024
(713)984-1036
Ultimate Parent: GAP. SIC: 5621—
Women's Clothing Stores.

★ 86234 ★ Gap Stores
4689 W. F M 1960
Houston, TX 77069
(713)440-6512
Ultimate Parent: GAP. SIC: 5621—
Women's Clothing Stores.

★ 86235 ★ Gap Stores
252 NW Mall
Houston, TX 77092
(713)686-1620
Ultimate Parent: GAP. SIC: 5611—Men's &
Boys' Clothing Stores.

★ 86236 ★ Gap Stores
242 Sharpstown Ctr.
Houston, TX 77036
(713)771-7219
Ultimate Parent: GAP. SIC: 5611—Men's &
Boys' Clothing Stores.

★ 86237 ★ Gap Stores
11245 Fondren Rd.
Houston, TX 77096
(713)988-9435
Ultimate Parent: GAP. SIC: 5611—Men's &
Boys' Clothing Stores.

★ 86238 ★ Gap Stores
322 Northline Mall
Houston, TX 77022
(713)697-9772
Ultimate Parent: GAP. SIC: 5611—Men's &
Boys' Clothing Stores.

★ 86239 ★ Gap Stores
1054 Baybrook Mall
Houston, TX 77004
(713)480-8888
Ultimate Parent: GAP. SIC: 5611—Men's &
Boys' Clothing Stores.

★ 86240 ★ Gap Stores
1200 McKinney St. 321
Houston, TX 77010
Ultimate Parent: GAP. SIC: 5651—Family
Clothing Stores.

★ 86241 ★ Gap Stores
7925 Fm 1960 Rd. W
Houston, TX 77070
(713)890-0493
Ultimate Parent: GAP. SIC: 5611—Men's &
Boys' Clothing Stores.

★ 86242 ★ Gap Stores
467 Greenspoint Mall
Houston, TX 77060
(713)445-1900
Ultimate Parent: GAP. SIC: 5621—
Women's Clothing Stores.

★ 86243 ★ Gap Stores
555 Almeda Mall
Houston, TX 77075
(713)941-2293
Ultimate Parent: GAP. SIC: 5651—Family
Clothing Stores.

★ 86244 ★ General American Life
Insurance C
3701 Kirby Dr.
Houston, TX 77098
(713)526-8713
Ultimate Parent: General American Life.
SIC: 6411—Insurance Agents, Brokers &
Service.

★ 86245 ★ General Electric Co.
9204 Emmott Rd.
Houston, TX 77040
(713)896-0334
Officer: Kay Coffey, Manager. Ultimate
Parent: General Electric. SIC: 3844—X-Ray
Apparatus & Tubes.

★ 86246 ★ General Electric Co.
8800 Wallisville Rd.
Houston, TX 77029
(713)672-3500
Officer: Paul Desmarais, Manager.
Ultimate Parent: General Electric. SIC:
3511—Turbines & Turbine Generator Sets;
3599—Industrial Machinery Nec.

★ 86247 ★ General Electric Co.
3530 W. 12th St.
Houston, TX 77008
(713)864-4431
Officer: Tom Harris, Manager. Ultimate
Parent: General Electric. SIC: 3613—
Switchgear & Switchboard Apparatus;
3699—Electrical Equipment & Supplies Nec.

★ 86248 ★ General Electric Ed&C
3530 West 12th St.
Houston, TX 77008
Ultimate Parent: General Electric. SIC:
3600—Electronic & Other Electrical
Equipment.

★ 86249 ★ General Foods Corp.
Maxwell House Div.
3900 Harrisburg
Houston, TX 77001
Company Type: Division. Ultimate Parent:
Philip Morris. SIC: 2095—Roasted Coffee.

★ 86250 ★ General Foods Mfg.
Corp.
Maxwell Div.
3900 Harrisburg
Houston, TX 77001
Company Type: Division. Ultimate Parent:
Philip Morris. SIC: 2095—Roasted Coffee.

★ 86251 ★ Georgia Gulf Corp.
2900 N. Loop W
Houston, TX 77092
(713)956-3900
Ultimate Parent: Georgia Gulf.

★ 86252 ★ Georgia-Pacific
Resins Inc.
1503 Haden Rd.
Houston, TX 77015
Ultimate Parent: Georgia-Pacific. SIC:
2869—Industrial Organic Chemicals Nec.

★ 86253 ★ Goodyear Tire &
Rubber Co. Houston Chemical
Plant
2000 Goodyear Dr.
Houston, TX 77017
Ultimate Parent: Goodyear Tire & Rubber.
SIC: 2822—Synthetic Rubber.

★ 86254 ★ Greyhound Bus Lines
500 St. Marys
Houston, TX 77001
(713)222-2317
Ultimate Parent: Greyhound Lines Inc.

★ 86255 ★ Greyhound Bus Lines
9750 Hempstead Rd.
Houston, TX 77092
(713)686-9929
Ultimate Parent: Greyhound Lines Inc. SIC:
4131—Intercity & Rural Bus Transportation.

★ 86256 ★ Greyhound Bus Lines
10203 Market St.
Houston, TX 77029
(713)674-3030
Ultimate Parent: Greyhound Lines Inc. SIC:
4111—Local & Suburban Transit.

★ 86257 ★ Grinnell Corp.
6999 Old Clinton Rd.
Houston, TX 77020
(713)675-6371
Officer: Bill Moser, Manager. Ultimate
Parent: Tyco International. SIC: 3494—
Valves & Pipe Fittings Nec.

★ 86258 ★ Gulf Printing Co.
8100 Kempwood Dr.
Houston, TX 77055
Ultimate Parent: Southwestern Bell. SIC:
2752—Commercial Printing—Lithographic.

★ 86259 ★ Halliburton Energy
Services
2500 Halliburton Ctr.
S. 151 San Felipe
Houston, TX 77210
(713)840-2700 Fax: (713)840-2707
Company Type: Subsidiary. Officer: Alan
A. Baker, Chairman & CEO. Ultimate
Parent: Halliburton.

★ 86260 ★ Halliburton
Geophysical Services Inc.
6909 SW Freeway
Houston, TX 77074
Ultimate Parent: Halliburton. SIC: 1382—
Oil & Gas Exploration Services; 3429—
Hardware Nec; 3699—Electrical Equipment
& Supplies Nec; 8999—Services Nec.

★ 86261 ★ Halliburton
Geophysical Services Inc.
6909 Southwest Fwy.
Houston, TX 77074-2105
(713)774-7561
Company Type: Subsidiary. Ultimate
Parent: Halliburton. SIC: 1382—Oil & Gas
Exploration Services; 3829—Measuring &
Controlling Devices Nec.

★ 86262 ★ Halliburton Logging
Services Inc.
2135 Hwy. 6 S
Houston, TX 77077-4319
(713)496-8100
Company Type: Subsidiary. Ultimate
Parent: Halliburton. SIC: 1389—Oil & Gas
Field Services Nec; 1382—Oil & Gas
Exploration Services; 3533—Oil & Gas Field
Machinery.

★ 86263 ★ Halliburton Nus Corp.
10200 Bellaire Blvd.
Houston, TX 77072-5206
(713)575-3087
Company Type: Subsidiary. Ultimate
Parent: Halliburton. SIC: 8711—
Engineering Services; 8734—Testing
Laboratories.

★ 86264 ★ Heads & Threads Co.
3647 Willowbend Blvd.
Houston, TX 77054-1103
(713)668-1854
Ultimate Parent: Alleghany Corp. SIC:
5072—Hardware.

★ 86265 ★ Herman Miller Inc.
1980 Post Oak Blvd.
Houston, TX 77056-3807
(713)627-7670
Ultimate Parent: Herman Miller. SIC: 2599—Furniture & Fixtures Nec; 5021—Furniture.

★ 86266 ★ Hertz Rent-A-Car
1910 Nasa Rd. 1
Houston, TX 77058
(713)333-2405
Ultimate Parent: Hertz. SIC: 7514—Passenger Car Rental.

★ 86267 ★ Hertz Rent-A-Car
13210 Katy Fwy.
Houston, TX 77079
(713)497-3443
Ultimate Parent: Hertz. SIC: 7514—Passenger Car Rental.

★ 86268 ★ Hertz Rent-A-Car
12401 Katy Fwy.
Houston, TX 77079
(713)531-5491
Ultimate Parent: Hertz.

★ 86269 ★ Hertz Rent-A-Car
5060 W. Alabama St.
Houston, TX 77056
(713)629-0190
Ultimate Parent: Hertz.

★ 86270 ★ Hertz Rent-A-Car
8100 Monroe Rd.
Houston, TX 77061
(713)943-1246
Ultimate Parent: Hertz.

★ 86271 ★ Hertz Rent-A-Car
2900 Briarpark Dr.
Houston, TX 77042
(713)977-0036
Ultimate Parent: Hertz. SIC: 7514—Passenger Car Rental.

★ 86272 ★ Hertz Rent-A-Car
6 E. Greenway Plz.
Houston, TX 77046
(713)840-8415
Ultimate Parent: Hertz. SIC: 7514—Passenger Car Rental.

★ 86273 ★ Hertz Rent-A-Car
Hobby Airport
Houston, TX 77012
(713)645-5101
Ultimate Parent: Hertz.

★ 86274 ★ Hertz Rent-A-Car Local Rese
8100 Monroe Rd.
Houston, TX 77061
(713)941-6821
Ultimate Parent: Hertz.

★ 86275 ★ Hertz Rental Trucks
2305 Broadway St.
Houston, TX 77012
(713)645-9706
Ultimate Parent: Hertz.

★ 86276 ★ Highlands Insurance Co.
10370 Richmond Ave.
Houston, TX 77042-4123
(713)952-9555 Fax: (713)952-9977
Company Type: Subsidiary. Officer: Harold G. Duble, President. Ultimate Parent: Halliburton.

★ 86277 ★ Hit or Miss
9600 Westheimer Rd.
Houston, TX 77063
(713)266-2636
Ultimate Parent: TJX.

★ 86278 ★ Hit or Miss
10905 Westheimer Rd.
Houston, TX 77042
(713)972-0094
Ultimate Parent: TJX. SIC: 5621—Women's Clothing Stores.

★ 86279 ★ Hit or Miss
8616 Stella Link Rd.
Houston, TX 77025
(713)664-3158
Ultimate Parent: TJX. SIC: 5621—Women's Clothing Stores.

★ 86280 ★ Hit or Miss
5085 Westheimer Rd.
Houston, TX 77056
(713)621-1319
Ultimate Parent: TJX.

★ 86281 ★ Hit or Miss
800 N. Belt Dr. E
Houston, TX 77032
(713)468-7459
Ultimate Parent: TJX. SIC: 5621—Women's Clothing Stores.

★ 86282 ★ Hit or Miss
12159 North Fwy.
Houston, TX 77060
(713)872-6168
Ultimate Parent: TJX.

★ 86283 ★ Hit or Miss
1200 McKinney St.
Houston, TX 77010
(713)654-7880
Ultimate Parent: TJX. SIC: 5621—Women's Clothing Stores.

★ 86284 ★ Hit or Miss
14622 Memorial Dr.
Houston, TX 77079
(713)497-7169
Ultimate Parent: TJX.

★ 86285 ★ Hit or Miss
13821 Breck St.
Houston, TX 77066
(713)580-5597
Ultimate Parent: TJX.

★ 86286 ★ Hit or Miss
11267 Fondren Rd.
Houston, TX 77096
(713)271-9640
Ultimate Parent: TJX.

★ 86287 ★ Hormel Foods Corp.
16727 Park Row
Houston, TX 77084
(713)492-1770
Location Type: Plant. Officer: Brad Moschak, Plant Manager. Ultimate Parent: Hormel Foods. SIC: 2013—Sausages & Other Prepared Meats.

★ 86288 ★ Hosuton Industries Energy Inc.
611 Walker
Houston, TX 77001
(713)228-9211
Company Type: Subsidiary. Officer: Lee W. Hogan, President & CEO. Ultimate Parent: Houston Industries.

★ 86289 ★ Houston Coca-Cola Bottling Co.
2819 Berkley
Houston, TX 77012-3597
Ultimate Parent: Coca-Cola Enterprises. SIC: 2086—Bottled & Canned Soft Drinks.

★ 86290 ★ Houston Coca-Cola Bottling Co.
2800 Bissonnet
Houston, TX 77005
Ultimate Parent: Coca-Cola Enterprises. SIC: 2086—Bottled & Canned Soft Drinks.

★ 86291 ★ Houston Coca-Cola Bottling Co.
2800 Bissonnet
Houston, TX 77005
Ultimate Parent: Coca-Cola Enterprises. SIC: 2086—Bottled & Canned Soft Drinks.

★ 86292 ★ Houston Coca-Cola Bottling Co.
2819 Berkley
Houston, TX 77012
Ultimate Parent: Coca-Cola Enterprises. SIC: 2086—Bottled & Canned Soft Drinks.

★ 86293 ★ Houston Industries
4400 Post Oak Pky.
Houston, TX 77027
(713)629-3000
Company Type: Headquarters. Officer: Don D. Jordon. Employee Count: 11350. Fortune Service 500: Ranking 22.

★ 86294 ★ Houston Industries Inc.
4400 Post Oak Pk., Ste. 2700
Houston, TX 77027
(713)629-3000 Fax: (713)629-3129
Officer: Don D Jordan, Chairman & CEO. Ultimate Parent: Houston Industries.

Employee Count: 11576. Sales: 12 Billion M.

★ 86295 ★ Houston Lighting & Power Co.
PO Box 1700
Houston, TX 77001
(713)228-9211 Fax: (713)220-5503
Company Type: Subsidiary. Officer: Don D Jordan, Chairman & CEO. Ultimate Parent: Houston Industries.

★ 86296 ★ Houston Pipe Line Co.
PO Box 1188
Houston, TX 77251-1188
Company Type: Subsidiary. Ultimate Parent: Enron.

★ 86297 ★ Houston Pipe Line Co. Inc.
1400 Smith St.
Houston, TX 77002-7361
(713)853-6161
Company Type: Subsidiary. Officer: Ronald J. Burns, Chairman of the Board. Ultimate Parent: Enron. SIC: 4922—Natural Gas Transmission. Employee Count: 400. Sales: 991 M.

★ 86298 ★ Hudson Co.
801 N. Eldridge St.
Houston, TX 77218
(713)870-5000 Fax: (713)870-5045
Officer: Sidney P. Victory, President. Ultimate Parent: McDermott.

★ 86299 ★ Hudson Eng Corp. Mcdermott C
801 N. Eldridge Pky.
Houston, TX 77079
(713)870-5000
Ultimate Parent: McDermott. SIC: 8712—Architectural Services.

★ 86300 ★ Hughes Christensen Co. Hughes Tool Co.
5425 Polk Ave.
Houston, TX 77023
Ultimate Parent: Baker Hughes. SIC: 3533—Oil & Gas Field Machinery; 3533—Oil & Gas Field Machinery.

★ 86301 ★ Hughes Diamond Products
15815 Waverly Rd.
Houston, TX 77032
Ultimate Parent: Baker Hughes. SIC: 3533—Oil & Gas Field Machinery.

★ 86302 ★ Hughes-Mpd
4427 W. 12th St.
Houston, TX 77055
Ultimate Parent: Baker Hughes. SIC: 3533—Oil & Gas Field Machinery.

★ 86303 ★ Human Affairs Int'l Inc.
16010 Barkers Point Ln.
Houston, TX 77079
(713)558-6577
Ultimate Parent: Aetna Life & Annuity.

★ 86304 ★ IBM Corp. Nsd
1 Riverway
Houston, TX 77056
(713)940-1100
Ultimate Parent: IBM. SIC: 7379—Computer Related Services Nec.

★ 86305 ★ IDS Financial Services
9855 Sageaspen Ln.
Houston, TX 77089-3519
(713)485-6898
Ultimate Parent: American Express Co. SIC: 6282—Investment Advice.

★ 86306 ★ IDS Financial Services Inc.
8323 Southwest Fwy.
Houston, TX 77074-1609
(713)988-3106
Officer: Charles Calvin. Ultimate Parent: American Express Co. SIC: 6282—Investment Advice.

★ 86307 ★ IDS Financial Services Inc.
400 N. Sam Houston Pky. E
Houston, TX 77060-3548
(713)931-1900
Ultimate Parent: American Express Co. SIC: 6282—Investment Advice.

★ 86308 ★ Intel Corp.
1634 Imperial Crown Dr.
Houston, TX 77043
(713)461-7993
Ultimate Parent: Intel Corp.

★ 86309 ★ Intereal Co.
2777 Allen Pky.
Houston, TX 77019
(713)522-1111
Officer: Robert E. Conklin, President & CEO. Ultimate Parent: American General Corp. SIC: 6552—Subdividers & Developers Nec. Employee Count: 12.

★ 86310 ★ Intergrated Technologies
10205 Westheimer Rd.
Houston, TX 77084
(713)578-3210 Telex: 756154
Company Type: Division. Officer: James S. Nolen, President. Ultimate Parent: Litton Industries. SIC: 7372—Prepackaged Software.

★ 86311 ★ Intertel, Inc.
6955 Port West Dr., Ste. 190
Houston, TX 77024
(713)748-8700
Company Type: Subsidiary. Officer: Charles L. Zoi, President & CEO. Ultimate Parent: Bell Atlantic Corp. SIC: 4812—Radiotelephone Communications.

★ 86312 ★ J B Hunt Transport Inc.
350 Gellhorn Dr.
Houston, TX 77013
(713)671-6700
Ultimate Parent: J. B. Hunt Transport. SIC: 4213—Trucking Except Local.

★ 86313 ★ Jiffy Lube
71 Uvalde Rd.
Houston, TX 77015
(713)453-4964
Ultimate Parent: Pennzoil.

★ 86314 ★ Jiffy Lube
2413 W. Holcombe Blvd.
Houston, TX 77030
(713)665-6949
Ultimate Parent: Pennzoil.

★ 86315 ★ Jiffy Lube
2901 Chimney Rock Rd.
Houston, TX 77056
(713)953-7129
Ultimate Parent: Pennzoil.

★ 86316 ★ Jiffy Lube
18115 Kuykendahl
Houston, TX 77070
(713)320-0703
Ultimate Parent: Pennzoil.

★ 86317 ★ Jiffy Lube
6440 Antoine Dr.
Houston, TX 77091
(713)682-5383
Ultimate Parent: Pennzoil.

★ 86318 ★ Jiffy Lube
7546 Bellfort St.
Houston, TX 77061
(713)644-1927
Ultimate Parent: Pennzoil.

★ 86319 ★ Jiffy Lube
490 Addicks Howell Rd.
Houston, TX 77079
(713)589-1111
Ultimate Parent: Pennzoil.

★ 86320 ★ Jiffy Lube International, Inc.
Pennzoil Pl.
PO Box 2967
Houston, TX 77252-2967
Officer: Clyde W. Beahm, President. Ultimate Parent: Pennzoil.

★ 86321 ★ Johnson Controls Inc.
222 T C Jester Blvd.
Houston, TX 77007
(713)869-3603
Ultimate Parent: Johnson Controls Inc. SIC: 5099—Durable Goods Nec.

★ 86322 ★   Kaiser Aluminum
Corp.
5847 San Felipe, Ste. 2600
PO Box 572887
Houston, TX 77257-2887
(713)267-3777 Fax: (713)267-3710
Officer: A. Stephens Hutchcraft Jr.,
Chairman of the Board & CEO. Ultimate
Parent: Maxxam.

★ 86323 ★   Kay Bee Toy and
Hobbys
7925 Fm 1960 Rd. W
Houston, TX 77070
(713)955-8030
Ultimate Parent: Melville.

★ 86324 ★   KBLCOM Inc.
1200 Smith, Ste. 1800
Houston, TX 77002
(713)659-7503 Fax: (713)651-2700
Company Type: Subsidiary. Officer: Don D
Jordan, Chairman & CEO. Ultimate Parent:
Houston Industries.

★ 86325 ★   Kentucky Fried
Chicken
963 Nasa Rd. 1
Houston, TX 77058
(713)488-9072
Ultimate Parent: Pepsico. SIC: 5812—
Eating Places.

★ 86326 ★   Kentucky Fried
Chicken
5865 Westheimer Rd.
Houston, TX 77057
(713)780-2057
Ultimate Parent: Pepsico. SIC: 5812—
Eating Places.

★ 86327 ★   Kentucky Fried
Chicken
2002 Yale St.
Houston, TX 77008
(713)869-5695
Ultimate Parent: Pepsico. SIC: 5812—
Eating Places.

★ 86328 ★   Kentucky Fried
Chicken
622 W. Little York Rd.
Houston, TX 77091
(713)694-5992
Ultimate Parent: Pepsico. SIC: 5812—
Eating Places.

★ 86329 ★   Kentucky Fried
Chicken
739 W. Mount Houston Rd.
Houston, TX 77038
(713)448-5569
Ultimate Parent: Pepsico. SIC: 5812—
Eating Places.

★ 86330 ★   Kentucky Fried
Chicken
4410 W. Fuqua St.
Houston, TX 77045
(713)433-4731
Ultimate Parent: Pepsico. SIC: 5812—
Eating Places.

★ 86331 ★   Kentucky Fried
Chicken
2265 W. Holcombe Blvd.
Houston, TX 77030
(713)661-6823
Ultimate Parent: Pepsico. SIC: 5812—
Eating Places.

★ 86332 ★   Kentucky Fried
Chicken
7701 W. Bellfort St.
Houston, TX 77071
(713)728-4610
Ultimate Parent: Pepsico. SIC: 5812—
Eating Places.

★ 86333 ★   Kentucky Fried
Chicken
927 W. Belt Dr. N
Houston, TX 77024
(713)464-9061
Ultimate Parent: Pepsico. SIC: 5812—
Eating Places.

★ 86334 ★   Kentucky Fried
Chicken
4701 W. 34th St.
Houston, TX 77092
(713)683-6534
Ultimate Parent: Pepsico. SIC: 5812—
Eating Places.

★ 86335 ★   Kentucky Fried
Chicken
5355 W. Bellfort St.
Houston, TX 77035
(713)726-0800
Ultimate Parent: Pepsico. SIC: 5812—
Eating Places.

★ 86336 ★   Kentucky Fried
Chicken
1216 Uvalde Rd.
Houston, TX 77015
(713)453-2614
Ultimate Parent: Pepsico. SIC: 5812—
Eating Places.

★ 86337 ★   Kentucky Fried
Chicken
1203 W. 11th St.
Houston, TX 77008
(713)862-6574
Ultimate Parent: Pepsico. SIC: 5812—
Eating Places.

★ 86338 ★   Kentucky Fried
Chicken
4667 Telephone Rd.
Houston, TX 77087
(713)649-3633
Ultimate Parent: Pepsico. SIC: 5812—
Eating Places.

★ 86339 ★   Kentucky Fried
Chicken
8787 Tidwell Rd.
Houston, TX 77028
(713)635-5465
Ultimate Parent: Pepsico. SIC: 5812—
Eating Places.

★ 86340 ★   Kentucky Fried
Chicken
2359 S. Shepherd Dr.
Houston, TX 77019
(713)522-0970
Ultimate Parent: Pepsico. SIC: 5812—
Eating Places.

★ 86341 ★   Kentucky Fried
Chicken
4702 Scott St.
Houston, TX 77004
(713)524-1534
Ultimate Parent: Pepsico. SIC: 5812—
Eating Places.

★ 86342 ★   Kentucky Fried
Chicken
3619 Old Spanish Trl
Houston, TX 77021
(713)747-8365
Ultimate Parent: Pepsico. SIC: 5812—
Eating Places.

★ 86343 ★   Kentucky Fried
Chicken
14202 S. Post Oak Rd.
Houston, TX 77045
(713)433-2031
Ultimate Parent: Pepsico. SIC: 5812—
Eating Places.

★ 86344 ★   Kentucky Fried
Chicken
4005 Montrose Blvd.
Houston, TX 77006
(713)529-3203
Ultimate Parent: Pepsico. SIC: 5812—
Eating Places.

★ 86345 ★   Kentucky Fried
Chicken
3701 N. Main St.
Houston, TX 77009
(713)880-8076
Ultimate Parent: Pepsico. SIC: 5812—
Eating Places.

★ 86346 ★   Kentucky Fried
Chicken
9510 Main St.
Houston, TX 77025
(713)668-6820
Ultimate Parent: Pepsico. SIC: 5812—
Eating Places.

★ 86347 ★   Kentucky Fried
Chicken
14490 Memorial Dr.
Houston, TX 77079
(713)497-0061
Ultimate Parent: Pepsico. SIC: 5812—
Eating Places.

★ 86348 ★   Kentucky Fried
Chicken
7800 Long Point Rd.
Houston, TX 77055
(713)686-0221
Ultimate Parent: Pepsico. SIC: 5812—
Eating Places.

★ 86349 ★   Kentucky Fried
Chicken
5913 Lyons Ave.
Houston, TX 77020
(713)674-3872
Ultimate Parent: Pepsico. SIC: 5812—
Eating Places.

★ 86350 ★   Kentucky Fried
Chicken
8601 Jensen Dr.
Houston, TX 77093
(713)695-5869
Ultimate Parent: Pepsico. SIC: 5812—
Eating Places.

★ 86351 ★   Kentucky Fried
Chicken
7074 Lawndale St.
Houston, TX 77023
(713)921-0544
Ultimate Parent: Pepsico. SIC: 5812—
Eating Places.

★ 86352 ★   Kentucky Fried
Chicken
7501 Harrisburg Blvd.
Houston, TX 77012
(713)924-5015
Ultimate Parent: Pepsico. SIC: 5812—
Eating Places.

★ 86353 ★   Kentucky Fried
Chicken
9855 Homestead Rd.
Houston, TX 77016
(713)633-4392
Ultimate Parent: Pepsico. SIC: 5812—
Eating Places.

★ 86354 ★   Kentucky Fried
Chicken
4845 Fm 1960 Rd. W
Houston, TX 77069
(713)583-7424
Ultimate Parent: Pepsico. SIC: 5812—
Eating Places.

★ 86355 ★   Kentucky Fried
Chicken
10934 Fm 1960 Rd. W
Houston, TX 77070
(713)469-9230
Ultimate Parent: Pepsico. SIC: 5812—
Eating Places.

★ 86356 ★   Kentucky Fried
Chicken
810 Fm 1960 Rd. W
Houston, TX 77090
(713)583-7317
Ultimate Parent: Pepsico. SIC: 5812—
Eating Places.

★ 86357 ★   Kentucky Fried
Chicken
3130 Fm 1960 Rd. W
Houston, TX 77068
(713)821-3725
Ultimate Parent: Pepsico. SIC: 5812—
Eating Places.

★ 86358 ★   Kentucky Fried
Chicken
905 Edgebrook Dr.
Houston, TX 77034
(713)947-2072
Ultimate Parent: Pepsico. SIC: 5812—
Eating Places.

★ 86359 ★   Kentucky Fried
Chicken
3330 Ella Blvd.
Houston, TX 77018
(713)686-9920
Ultimate Parent: Pepsico. SIC: 5812—
Eating Places.

★ 86360 ★   Kentucky Fried
Chicken
9201 Cullen Blvd.
Houston, TX 77051
(713)733-9171
Ultimate Parent: Pepsico. SIC: 5812—
Eating Places.

★ 86361 ★   Kentucky Fried
Chicken
10518 Eastex Fwy.
Houston, TX 77093
(713)694-5207
Ultimate Parent: Pepsico. SIC: 5812—
Eating Places.

★ 86362 ★   Kentucky Fried
Chicken
11570 Bellaire Blvd.
Houston, TX 77072
(713)498-1069
Ultimate Parent: Pepsico. SIC: 5812—
Eating Places.

★ 86363 ★   Kentucky Fried
Chicken
7806 Bellfort St.
Houston, TX 77061
(713)645-9184
Ultimate Parent: Pepsico. SIC: 5812—
Eating Places.

★ 86364 ★   Kentucky Fried
Chicken
8595 Beechnut St.
Houston, TX 77036
(713)774-4734
Ultimate Parent: Pepsico. SIC: 5812—
Eating Places.

★ 86365 ★   Kentucky Fried
Chicken
5945 Bellaire Blvd.
Houston, TX 77081
(713)666-4503
Ultimate Parent: Pepsico. SIC: 5812—
Eating Places.

★ 86366 ★   Kentucky Fried
Chicken
5322 Antoine Dr.
Houston, TX 77091
(713)688-0006
Ultimate Parent: Pepsico. SIC: 5812—
Eating Places.

★ 86367 ★   Kentucky Fried
Chicken
7069 Beechnut St.
Houston, TX 77074
(713)988-2258
Ultimate Parent: Pepsico. SIC: 5812—
Eating Places.

★ 86368 ★   Kentucky Fried
Chicken
11106 Airline Dr.
Houston, TX 77037
(713)820-9454
Ultimate Parent: Pepsico. SIC: 5812—
Eating Places.

★ 86369 ★   Kentucky Fried
Chicken
5010 Aldine Mail Rd.
Houston, TX 77039
(713)442-5344
Ultimate Parent: Pepsico. SIC: 5812—
Eating Places.

★ 86370 ★   Keystone
International Inc.
9600 W. Gulf Bank Dr.
Houston, TX 77040
(713)466-1176 Fax: (713)937-8453
Officer: Raymond A. Le Blanc, CEO.
Ultimate Parent: Ralston Purina. Employee
Count: 4100. Sales: 516 M.

★ 86371 ★   Kids R US
15201 Philippine St.
Houston, TX 77040
(713)937-1885
Ultimate Parent: Toys "R" US. SIC: 8351—
Child Day Care Services.

★ 86372 ★   Kids R US Inc.
15201 Philippine St.
Houston, TX 77040
(713)937-1885
Ultimate Parent: Toys "R" US. SIC: 8351—
Child Day Care Services.

★ 86373 ★   Kitchen Collection
Inc.
431 Air Texas Dr.
Houston, TX 77073
(713)821-4415
Ultimate Parent: Nacco Industries. SIC:
5719—Miscellaneous Home Furnishings
Stores.

★ 86374 ★ **Kmart Discount Stores**
10261 North Fwy.
Houston, TX 77037
Ultimate Parent: K-Mart.

★ 86375 ★ **Kmart Discount Stores**
5607 Uvalde Rd.
Houston, TX 77049
(713)458-2471
Ultimate Parent: K-Mart.

★ 86376 ★ **Kmart Discount Stores**
4815 Hwy. 6 N
Houston, TX 77084
(713)463-6721
Ultimate Parent: K-Mart.

★ 86377 ★ **Kmart Discount Stores**
8230 Kirby Dr.
Houston, TX 77054
(713)668-2866
Ultimate Parent: K-Mart.

★ 86378 ★ **Kmart Discount Stores**
10955 W. FM 1960
Houston, TX 77070
(713)469-7400
Ultimate Parent: K-Mart. **SIC:** 5311—Department Stores; 5912—Drug Stores & Proprietary Stores.

★ 86379 ★ **Kmart Discount Stores**
5702 Van Fleet St.
Houston, TX 77033
(713)644-1761
Ultimate Parent: K-Mart. **SIC:** 5311—Department Stores.

★ 86380 ★ **Kmart Discount Stores**
1431 W. 20th St.
Houston, TX 77008
(713)869-7186
Ultimate Parent: K-Mart. **SIC:** 5311—Department Stores; 5912—Drug Stores & Proprietary Stores.

★ 86381 ★ **Kmart Discount Stores**
10261 North Fwy.
Houston, TX 77037
Ultimate Parent: K-Mart. **SIC:** 5531—Automobile & Home Supply Stores; 5912—Drug Stores & Proprietary Stores.

★ 86382 ★ **Kmart Discount Stores**
8150 Southwest Fwy.
Houston, TX 77074
(713)771-3656
Ultimate Parent: K-Mart. **SIC:** 5311—Department Stores.

★ 86383 ★ **Kmart Discount Stores**
8315 Long Point Rd.
Houston, TX 77055
(713)468-7695
Ultimate Parent: K-Mart. **SIC:** 5311—Department Stores; 5912—Drug Stores & Proprietary Stores.

★ 86384 ★ **Kroger**
2877 S. Richey St.
Houston, TX 77017
(713)944-0611
Ultimate Parent: Kroger. **SIC:** 5411—Grocery Stores.

★ 86385 ★ **Kroger**
1309 PO Box
Houston, TX 77251
Ultimate Parent: Kroger. **SIC:** 5411—Grocery Stores.

★ 86386 ★ **Kroger Bakery**
24700 PO Box
Houston, TX 77229
(713)672-5348
Ultimate Parent: Kroger.

★ 86387 ★ **Kroger Comapny No 289**
1309 PO Box
Houston, TX 77251
Ultimate Parent: Kroger. **SIC:** 5411—Grocery Stores.

★ 86388 ★ **Kroger Company**
1309 PO Box
Houston, TX 77251
Ultimate Parent: Kroger. **SIC:** 5411—Grocery Stores.

★ 86389 ★ **Kroger Co.**
14710 Wood Forest Blvd.
Houston, TX 77015
(713)453-1175
Ultimate Parent: Kroger. **SIC:** 5411—Grocery Stores.

★ 86390 ★ **Kroger Co.**
200 W. Greens Rd.
Houston, TX 77067
(713)893-6651
Ultimate Parent: Kroger. **SIC:** 5411—Grocery Stores.

★ 86391 ★ **Kroger Co.**
12580 Westheimer Rd.
Houston, TX 77077
(713)496-1882
Ultimate Parent: Kroger. **SIC:** 5411—Grocery Stores.

★ 86392 ★ **Kroger Co.**
601 S. Wayside Dr.
Houston, TX 77011
(713)928-3724
Ultimate Parent: Kroger. **SIC:** 5411—Grocery Stores.

★ 86393 ★ **Kroger Co.**
13121 Stuebner Airline Rd.
Houston, TX 77014
(713)440-0522
Ultimate Parent: Kroger. **SIC:** 5411—Grocery Stores.

★ 86394 ★ **Kroger Co.**
961 Nasa Rd. 1
Houston, TX 77058
(713)488-4605
Ultimate Parent: Kroger. **SIC:** 5411—Grocery Stores.

★ 86395 ★ **Kroger Co.**
2455 S. Braeswood Blvd.
Houston, TX 77030
(713)666-9643
Ultimate Parent: Kroger. **SIC:** 5912—Drug Stores & Proprietary Stores.

★ 86396 ★ **Kroger Co.**
3300 Montrose Blvd.
Houston, TX 77006
(713)524-3015
Ultimate Parent: Kroger. **SIC:** 5411—Grocery Stores.

★ 86397 ★ **Kroger Co.**
1035 N. Shepherd Dr.
Houston, TX 77008
(713)862-4448
Ultimate Parent: Kroger. **SIC:** 5411—Grocery Stores.

★ 86398 ★ **Kroger Co.**
9402 Hwy. 6 S
Houston, TX 77083
(713)495-1375
Ultimate Parent: Kroger. **SIC:** 5411—Grocery Stores.

★ 86399 ★ **Kroger Co.**
12340 Jones Rd.
Houston, TX 77070
(713)955-1757
Ultimate Parent: Kroger. **SIC:** 5411—Grocery Stores.

★ 86400 ★ **Kroger Co.**
4114 Fulton St.
Houston, TX 77009
(713)694-7775
Ultimate Parent: Kroger. **SIC:** 5411—Grocery Stores.

★ 86401 ★ **Kroger Co.**
1099 Gessner Dr.
Houston, TX 77055
(713)464-8291
Ultimate Parent: Kroger. **SIC:** 5411—Grocery Stores.

★ 86402 ★ **Kroger Co.**
1918 El Dorado Blvd.
Houston, TX 77062
(713)480-2678
Ultimate Parent: Kroger. **SIC:** 5411—Grocery Stores.

★ 86403 ★ **Kroger Co.**
148 Fm 1960 Rd.
Houston, TX 77073
(713)443-7245
Ultimate Parent: Kroger. **SIC:** 5411—Grocery Stores.

★ 86404 ★ **Kroger Co.**
13210 Bellaire Blvd.
Houston, TX 77083
(713)879-4889
Ultimate Parent: Kroger. **SIC:** 5411—Grocery Stores.

★ 86405 ★ **Kroger Co.**
11873 Bissonnet St.
Houston, TX 77099
(713)498-8832
Ultimate Parent: Kroger. **SIC:** 5411—Grocery Stores.

★ 86406 ★ **Kroger Co.**
6749 Airline Dr.
Houston, TX 77076
(713)699-5980
Ultimate Parent: Kroger. **SIC:** 5411—Grocery Stores.

★ 86407 ★ **Kroger Co.**
10796 Bellaire Blvd.
Houston, TX 77072
(713)933-7755
Ultimate Parent: Kroger. **SIC:** 5411—Grocery Stores.

★ 86408 ★ **Kroger Co. Inc.**
701 Gellhorn Dr.
Houston, TX 77029
(713)672-5331
Ultimate Parent: Kroger. **SIC:** 2051—Bread, Cake & Related Products.

★ 86409 ★ **Kroger Company No 323**
1309 PO Box
Houston, TX 77251
Ultimate Parent: Kroger. **SIC:** 5411—Grocery Stores.

★ 86410 ★ **Kroger Company No 291**
1309 PO Box
Houston, TX 77251
Ultimate Parent: Kroger. **SIC:** 5411—Grocery Stores.

★ 86411 ★ **Kroger Company No 292**
1309 PO Box
Houston, TX 77251
Ultimate Parent: Kroger. **SIC:** 5411—Grocery Stores.

★ 86412 ★ **Kroger Distribution Inc.**
701 Gellhorn Dr.
Houston, TX 77029
(713)672-5280
Ultimate Parent: Kroger. **SIC:** 5141—Groceries—General Line.

★ 86413 ★ **Kroger Food & Drugs Store N**
1309 PO Box
Houston, TX 77251
Ultimate Parent: Kroger. **SIC:** 5411—Grocery Stores.

★ 86414 ★ **Kroger Food Stores**
9795 Westheimer Rd.
Houston, TX 77042
(713)783-4430
Ultimate Parent: Kroger. **SIC:** 5411—Grocery Stores.

★ 86415 ★ **Kroger Food Stores**
641 W. Crosstimbers St.
Houston, TX 77018
(713)697-3301
Ultimate Parent: Kroger.

★ 86416 ★ **Kroger Food Stores**
200 W. Greens Rd.
Houston, TX 77067
(713)873-6651
Ultimate Parent: Kroger. **SIC:** 5411—Grocery Stores.

★ 86417 ★ **Kroger Food Stores**
2455 S. Braeswood Blvd.
Houston, TX 77030
(713)666-6800
Ultimate Parent: Kroger.

★ 86418 ★ **Kroger Food Stores**
13749 Tomball Pky.
Houston, TX 77086
(713)820-0550
Ultimate Parent: Kroger. **SIC:** 5411—Grocery Stores.

★ 86419 ★ **Kroger Food Stores**
8120 Long Point Rd.
Houston, TX 77055
(713)468-6500
Ultimate Parent: Kroger.

★ 86420 ★ **Kroger Food Stores**
3300 Montrose Blvd.
Houston, TX 77006
(713)526-7865
Ultimate Parent: Kroger.

★ 86421 ★ **Kroger Food Stores**
12355 Fondren Rd.
Houston, TX 77035
(713)728-8429
Ultimate Parent: Kroger. **SIC:** 5411—Grocery Stores.

★ 86422 ★ **Kroger Food Stores**
8500 Hwy. 6 N
Houston, TX 77095
(713)463-2409
Ultimate Parent: Kroger. **SIC:** 5912—Drug Stores & Proprietary Stores.

★ 86423 ★ **Kroger Food Stores**
5153 Antoine Dr.
Houston, TX 77092
(713)683-8331
Ultimate Parent: Kroger. **SIC:** 5411—Grocery Stores.

★ 86424 ★ **Kroger Pharmacies**
5155 Antoine Dr.
Houston, TX 77092
(713)683-0205
Ultimate Parent: Kroger. **SIC:** 5912—Drug Stores & Proprietary Stores.

★ 86425 ★ **Kroger Pharmacy**
14340 Memorial Dr.
Houston, TX 77079
(713)497-3565
Ultimate Parent: Kroger. **SIC:** 5912—Drug Stores & Proprietary Stores.

★ 86426 ★ **Kroger Pharmacy**
10998 Fuqua St.
Houston, TX 77089
(713)481-0231
Ultimate Parent: Kroger. **SIC:** 5912—Drug Stores & Proprietary Stores.

★ 86427 ★ **Kroger Store**
3541 Palmer St.
Houston, TX 77004
(713)480-3304
Ultimate Parent: Kroger. **SIC:** 5411—Grocery Stores.

★ 86428 ★ **Kroger Store**
4025 W. Fuqua St.
Houston, TX 77045
(713)433-4588
Ultimate Parent: Kroger. **SIC:** 5411—Grocery Stores.

★ 86429 ★ **Kroger Store**
11035 E. Fwy.
Houston, TX 77031
(713)673-5166
Ultimate Parent: Kroger. **SIC:** 5411—Grocery Stores.

★ 86430 ★ **Kroger Transportation**
1309 PO Box
Houston, TX 77251
(713)672-5326
Ultimate Parent: Kroger.

★ 86431 ★ **Lafarge Corp.**
152 PO Box
Houston, TX 77001
Ultimate Parent: Lafarge.

★ 86432 ★ **Lane Bryant**
NW Massachusetts
Houston, TX 77092
(713)681-4671
Ultimate Parent: Limited. **SIC:** 5621—Women's Clothing Stores.

★ 86433 ★   Lane Bryant
Willowbrook Mall
Houston, TX 77061
(713)955-5034
Ultimate Parent: Limited. SIC: 5621—
Women's Clothing Stores.

★ 86434 ★   Lane Bryant
1128 Willowbrook Mall
Houston, TX 77070
(713)955-5036
Ultimate Parent: Limited. SIC: 5621—
Women's Clothing Stores.

★ 86435 ★   Lane Bryant
1000 W. Oaks Mall
Houston, TX 77082
(713)497-2159
Ultimate Parent: Limited. SIC: 5621—
Women's Clothing Stores.

★ 86436 ★   Lane Bryant
251 Westwood Mall
Houston, TX 77036
(713)271-7157
Ultimate Parent: Limited. SIC: 5611—
Men's & Boys' Clothing Stores.

★ 86437 ★   Lane Bryant
323 Northline Mall
Houston, TX 77022
(713)691-6007
Ultimate Parent: Limited. SIC: 5621—
Women's Clothing Stores.

★ 86438 ★   Lane Bryant
800 W. Belt Dr. N
Houston, TX 77024
(713)461-7295
Ultimate Parent: Limited. SIC: 5621—
Women's Clothing Stores.

★ 86439 ★   Lane Bryant
471 Greenspoint Mall
Houston, TX 77060
(713)875-9740
Ultimate Parent: Limited.

★ 86440 ★   Lane Bryant
219 Gulfgate Mall
Houston, TX 77087
(713)644-6619
Ultimate Parent: Limited. SIC: 5621—
Women's Clothing Stores.

★ 86441 ★   Lane Bryant
1314 Baybrook Mall
Houston, TX 77004
(713)280-9919
Ultimate Parent: Limited. SIC: 5621—
Women's Clothing Stores.

★ 86442 ★   Lane Bryant
7500 Bellaire Blvd.
Houston, TX 77036
(713)270-0800
Ultimate Parent: Limited.

★ 86443 ★   Lehman Brothers
1 Allen Ctr.
Houston, TX 77002
(713)757-9100
Ultimate Parent: American Express Co.
SIC: 6211—Security Brokers & Dealers.

★ 86444 ★   Lerner Shop
9700 Bissonnet St.
Houston, TX 77036
(713)541-0784
Ultimate Parent: Limited.

★ 86445 ★   Lerner Shop
438 NW Mall
Houston, TX 77092
(713)686-4101
Ultimate Parent: Limited. SIC: 5621—
Women's Clothing Stores.

★ 86446 ★   Lerner Shop
500 Westwood Mall
Houston, TX 77036
(713)774-3374
Ultimate Parent: Limited. SIC: 5621—
Women's Clothing Stores.

★ 86447 ★   Lerner Shop
770 Memorial City
Houston, TX 77024
(713)461-8079
Ultimate Parent: Limited. SIC: 5621—
Women's Clothing Stores.

★ 86448 ★   Lerner Shop
213 Northline Mall
Houston, TX 77022
(713)694-7981
Ultimate Parent: Limited. SIC: 5621—
Women's Clothing Stores.

★ 86449 ★   Lerner Shop
Gulfgate Mall
Houston, TX 77087
(713)644-0812
Ultimate Parent: Limited. SIC: 5621—
Women's Clothing Stores.

★ 86450 ★   Lerner Shop
814 Main St.
Houston, TX 77002
(713)227-0996
Ultimate Parent: Limited. SIC: 5621—
Women's Clothing Stores.

★ 86451 ★   Lerner Shop
438 Almeda Mall
Houston, TX 77075
(713)944-1064
Ultimate Parent: Limited. SIC: 5621—
Women's Clothing Stores.

★ 86452 ★   Lerner Shop
626 Greenspoint Mall
Houston, TX 77060
(713)931-0146
Ultimate Parent: Limited. SIC: 5621—
Women's Clothing Stores.

★ 86453 ★   Lerner Shop
438 NW Massachusetts
Houston, TX 77029
(713)686-4101
Ultimate Parent: Limited. SIC: 5621—
Women's Clothing Stores.

★ 86454 ★   Lerner Shop
Sharpstown Ctr.
Houston, TX 77036
(713)776-3134
Ultimate Parent: Limited. SIC: 5621—
Women's Clothing Stores.

★ 86455 ★   Lerner Shop
1650 Willowbrook Mall
Houston, TX 77070
(713)890-3018
Ultimate Parent: Limited. SIC: 5621—
Women's Clothing Stores.

★ 86456 ★   Liberty Mutual
Insurance Co.
13201 N. Southwest Fwy.
Houston, TX 77031
(713)460-4650
Ultimate Parent: Liberty Mutual Group.
SIC: 6411—Insurance Agents, Brokers &
Service.

★ 86457 ★   Liberty Mutual
Insurance Co.
8588 Katy Fwy.
Houston, TX 77024
(713)827-0101
Ultimate Parent: Liberty Mutual Group.
SIC: 6411—Insurance Agents, Brokers &
Service.

★ 86458 ★   Lifeco/American
Express
2901 Wilcrest
Houston, TX 77042
(713)789-3424 Fax: (713)954-7733
Company Type: Subsidiary. Ultimate
Parent: American Express Co. SIC: 4724—
Travel Agencies; 4725—Tour Operators.

★ 86459 ★   Lifeco/American
Express Corp.
2901 Wilcrest Dr., Ste. 600
Houston, TX 77042-6014
(713)954-7500
Company Type: Subsidiary. Officer: Brian
P. Froelich, President. Ultimate Parent:
American Express Co. SIC: 4724—Travel
Agencies. Employee Count: 2000. Sales:
607 M.

★ 86460 ★   The Limited
5510 W. F M1960
Houston, TX 77069
(713)893-1351
Ultimate Parent: Limited. SIC: 5621—
Women's Clothing Stores.

★ 86461 ★   The Limited
209 Sharpstown Ctr.
Houston, TX 77036
(713)777-0325
Ultimate Parent: Limited. SIC: 5621—
Women's Clothing Stores.

★ 86462 ★   The Limited
555 NW Mall
Houston, TX 77092
(713)688-6957
Ultimate Parent: Limited. SIC: 5621—
Women's Clothing Stores.

★ 86463 ★   The Limited
Park
Houston, TX 77010
(713)951-9334
Ultimate Parent: Limited. SIC: 5621—
Women's Clothing Stores.

★ 86464 ★   The Limited
226 Gulfgate Mall
Houston, TX 77087
(713)641-6813
Ultimate Parent: Limited. SIC: 5621—
Women's Clothing Stores.

★ 86465 ★   The Limited
204 Memorial City
Houston, TX 77024
(713)932-7009
Ultimate Parent: Limited. SIC: 5621—
Women's Clothing Stores.

★ 86466 ★   The Limited
1162 Baybrook Mall
Houston, TX 77058
(713)488-4955
Ultimate Parent: Limited. SIC: 5621—
Women's Clothing Stores.

★ 86467 ★   The Limited
Almeda Mall
Houston, TX 77075
(713)947-8040
Ultimate Parent: Limited. SIC: 5621—
Women's Clothing Stores.

★ 86468 ★   The Limited
5085 Westheimer Rd.
Houston, TX 77056
(713)961-5301
Ultimate Parent: Limited.

★ 86469 ★   The Limited
373 Westwood Fashion Pl
Houston, TX 77036
(713)777-5334
Ultimate Parent: Limited. SIC: 5621—
Women's Clothing Stores.

★ 86470 ★   The Limited
555 Almeda Mall
Houston, TX 77075
(713)947-8040
Ultimate Parent: Limited.

★ 86471 ★   The Limited
1000 W. Oaks Mall
Houston, TX 77082
(713)556-6032
Ultimate Parent: Limited. SIC: 5621—
Women's Clothing Stores.

★ 86472 ★   The Limited Express
714 NW Mall
Houston, TX 77092
(713)683-8434
Ultimate Parent: Limited. SIC: 5621—
Women's Clothing Stores.

★ 86473 ★   The Limited Express
1130 Willowbrook Mall
Houston, TX 77070
(713)890-2533
Ultimate Parent: Limited. SIC: 5621—
Women's Clothing Stores.

★ 86474 ★   The Limited Express
12200 Gulf Fwy.
Houston, TX 77034
(713)946-7003
Ultimate Parent: Limited. SIC: 5621—
Women's Clothing Stores.

★ 86475 ★   The Limited Express
1322 Baybrook Mall
Houston, TX 77004
(713)486-7613
Ultimate Parent: Limited. SIC: 5621—
Women's Clothing Stores.

★ 86476 ★   The Limited Express
291 Westwood Mall
Houston, TX 77036
(713)270-4451
Ultimate Parent: Limited. SIC: 5621—
Women's Clothing Stores.

★ 86477 ★   The Limited Express
Town
Houston, TX 77024
(713)461-1332
Ultimate Parent: Limited. SIC: 5621—
Women's Clothing Stores.

★ 86478 ★   The Limited Express
1000 W. Oaks Mall
Houston, TX 77082
(713)556-6059
Ultimate Parent: Limited. SIC: 5621—
Women's Clothing Stores.

★ 86479 ★   The Limited Express
7500 Bellaire Blvd.
Houston, TX 77036
(713)270-8667
Ultimate Parent: Limited. SIC: 5621—
Women's Clothing Stores.

★ 86480 ★   The Limited Express
208 Greenspoint Mall
Houston, TX 77060
(713)445-2214
Ultimate Parent: Limited. SIC: 5621—
Women's Clothing Stores.

★ 86481 ★   The Limited Express
257 Mem City Shopping Ctr.
Houston, TX 77024
(713)467-4897
Ultimate Parent: Limited. SIC: 5621—
Women's Clothing Stores.

★ 86482 ★   Lockheed
Engineering & Sciences Co.
Corporate Plaza 2
2625 Bay Area Blvd.
Houston, TX 77058
(713)283-4400 Fax: (713)283-4660
Officer: Richard P. Parten, President.
Ultimate Parent: Lockheed Corp.

★ 86483 ★   Lockheed
Engineering & Services Co., Inc.
2625 Bay Area Blvd.
Houston, TX 77058
(713)283-4400 Fax: (713)283-4660
Company Type: Division. Ultimate Parent:
Lockheed Corp. SIC: 8711—Engineering
Services.

★ 86484 ★   Lockheed
Environmental Systems &
Technologies Co.
Citicorp Ctr.
1200 Smith St., Ste. 900
Houston, TX 77002-3400
(713)659-3332
Company Type: Division. Ultimate Parent:
Lockheed Corp.

★ 86485 ★   Lockheed
Environmental Systems &
Technologies Co.
Citicorp Ctr.
1200 Smith St., Ste. 800
Houston, TX 77002-4309
(713)659-3332 Fax: (713)654-4850
Officer: William J. Denson, President.
Ultimate Parent: Lockheed Corp.

★ 86486 ★   Lockwood National
Bank of Houston
2424 Bay Area Blvd.
Houston, TX 77058
(713)286-6800
Location Type: Branch office. Ultimate
Parent: Michigan National Corp. SIC:
6021—National Commercial Banks.

★ 86487 ★   Lockwood National
Bank of Houston
755 Podt Oak Blvd.
Houston, TX 77056-3203
(713)674-7661
Location Type: Branch office. Ultimate
Parent: Michigan National Corp. SIC:
6021—National Commercial Banks.

★ 86488 ★　Lockwood National
Bank of Houston
14200 Gulf Fwy.
Houston, TX 77034-5361
(713)484-7000
Location Type: Branch office. Ultimate
Parent: Michigan National Corp. SIC:
6021—National Commercial Banks.

★ 86489 ★　Lockwood National
Bank of Houston
PO Box 15104
Houston, TX 77220-5104
Location Type: Headquarters. Ultimate
Parent: Michigan National Corp. SIC:
6021—National Commercial Banks.

★ 86490 ★　Lockwood National
Bank of Houston
800 Lockwood
Houston, TX 77020-7918
(713)674-7661 Fax: (713)674-1084 Telex:
775792
Location Type: Branch office. Ultimate
Parent: Michigan National Corp. SIC:
6021—National Commercial Banks.

★ 86491 ★　Lone Star Gas Co.
Houston Natural Gas Bldg.
Houston, TX 77002
(713)658-9963
Ultimate Parent: Enserch. SIC: 4925—Gas
Production & Distribution Nec.

★ 86492 ★　Lone Star Gas Co.
8543 Market St.
Houston, TX 77029
(713)672-6636
Ultimate Parent: Enserch. SIC: 4925—Gas
Production & Distribution Nec.

★ 86493 ★　Lone Star Lead
Construction
PO Box 24038
Houston, TX 77229-4038
(713)674-7611
Officer: Robert Ray. Ultimate Parent:
Asarco. SIC: 3295—Minerals—Ground or
Treated.

★ 86494 ★　Lone Star Lead
Construction Co. Inc.
9200 Market Street Rd.
Houston, TX 77029-3428
(713)674-7611
Company Type: Subsidiary. Officer:
Richard De J. Osborne, President. Ultimate
Parent: Asarco. SIC: 1799—Special Trade
Contractors Nec. Employee Count: 20.
Sales: 4 M.

★ 86495 ★　Lone Star Lead
Construction Corp.
9200 Market Street Rd.
Houston, TX 77029
(713)674-7611
Company Type: Subsidiary. Officer: R.S.
Ray, President. Ultimate Parent: Asarco.
SIC: 5051—Metals Service Centers &
Offices.

★ 86496 ★　Loral Space
Information Stysems
901 Bay Area Blvd.
Houston, TX 77058
(713)335-5090 Fax: (713)335-5010
Officer: Clinton H. Denny, President.
Ultimate Parent: Loral Corp.

★ 86497 ★　Loral Space
Information Systems
901 Bay Area Blvd.
Houston, TX 77058
(713)335-5090 Fax: (713)335-5010
Company Type: Division. Ultimate Parent:
Loral Corp. SIC: 8711—Engineering
Services.

★ 86498 ★　Louisiana Land &
Exploration
Houston Div.
2950 N. Loop W. Ste. 1200
Brookhollow 3
Houston, TX 77092
(713)957-6400 Fax: (713)957-1108
Company Type: Division. Officer: Ernest J.
Leidner Jr., Vice President & General
Manager. Ultimate Parent: Louisiana Land
& Exploration.

★ 86499 ★　Lubrizol Corp
12941 North Fwy.
Houston, TX 77060
(713)583-2264
Ultimate Parent: Lubrizol. SIC: 5159—
Farm-Product Raw Materials Nec.

★ 86500 ★　Lyondell Licensing,
Inc.
1 Houston Center, 1221 McKinney St.
Houston, TX 77253-3646
(713)652-7200
Company Type: Subsidiary. Ultimate
Parent: Lyondell Petrochemical Co.

★ 86501 ★　Lyondell
Petrochemical
1221 McKinney St.
Houston, TX 77010
(713)652-7200
Company Type: Headquarters. Officer:
Bob G. Gower. Ultimate Parent: Lyondell
Petrochemical Co. Employee Count: 2283.
Sales: 3850.0 M. Fortune 500: Largest
U.S. Industrial Corporations: Ranking 133.

★ 86502 ★　Lyondell
Petrochemical Co.
1 Houston Center, 1221 McKinney St.
Houston, TX 77253-3646
(713)652-7200
Company Type: Headquarters. Ultimate
Parent: Lyondell Petrochemical Co. SIC:
2911—Petroleum Refining; 5172—
Petroleum Products Nec.

★ 86503 ★　Lyondell
Petrochemical Co.
1221 McKinney St.
Houston, TX 77010
(713)652-7200
Company Type: Headquarters. Officer:
Bob G. Gower. SIC: 2911—Petroleum
Refining. Sales: 3850 M. Fortune 500:
Largest U.S. Industrial Corporations:
Ranking 133.

★ 86504 ★　Lyondell
Petrochemical Co.
Houston Refinery
12000 Lawndale
Houston, TX 77252-2451
Company Type: Division. Ultimate Parent:
Atlantic Richfield Co., Inc. SIC: 2911—
Petroleum Refining; 2869—Industrial
Organic Chemicals Nec; 2992—Lubricating
Oils & Greases.

★ 86505 ★　Lyondell
Petrochemical deMexico, Inc.
1 Houston Center, 1221 McKinney St.
Houston, TX 77253-3646
(713)652-7200
Company Type: Subsidiary. Ultimate
Parent: Lyondell Petrochemical Co.

★ 86506 ★　Lyondell Polymers
Corp.
1 Houston Center, 1221 McKinney St.
Houston, TX 77253-3646
(713)652-7200
Company Type: Subsidiary. Ultimate
Parent: Lyondell Petrochemical Co.

★ 86507 ★　Lyondell Refining Co.
1 Houston Center, 1221 McKinney St.
Houston, TX 77253-3646
(713)652-7200
Company Type: Subsidiary. Ultimate
Parent: Lyondell Petrochemical Co.

★ 86508 ★　M-1 Drilling Fluids Co.
3 Greenway Plz.
Houston, TX 77046
(713)972-1310 Fax: (713)297-3908
Company Type: Subsidiary. Ultimate
Parent: Dresser Industries Inc.

★ 86509 ★　Magic Chef Inc.
8020 Katy Fwy.
Houston, TX 77024
(713)686-7860
Ultimate Parent: Maytag. SIC: 5064—
Electrical Appliances—Television & Radio.

★ 86510 ★　Magnetek Ohio
Transformer
7501 Schneider St.
Houston, TX 77093
Ultimate Parent: Magnetek Inc. SIC:
3612—Transformers Except Electronic.

★ 86511 ★　Magnetek/Ohio
Transformer
10010 Gulf Fwy.
Houston, TX 77034-1045
(713)695-0666
Officer: Paul Few. Ultimate Parent:
Magnetek Inc. SIC: 3612—Transformers
Except Electronic; 5063—Electrical
Apparatus & Equipment; 7694—Armature
Rewinding Shops.

★ 86512 ★　Marathon Oil Co.
17281 John F Kennedy Blvd.
Houston, TX 77032
(713)443-2905
Ultimate Parent: USX Corp.

★ 86513 ★　Marathon Oil Co.
17281 John F Kennedy Blvd.
Houston, TX 77032
(713)443-2905
Ultimate Parent: USX Corp.

★ 86514 ★　Marathon Petroleum
Co.
431 N. S. Ave.
Houston, TX 77011
(713)473-6663
Ultimate Parent: USX Corp. SIC: 5172—
Petroleum Products Nec.

★ 86515 ★　Marshalls Inc.
10010 Kleckley Dr.
Houston, TX 77075
(713)946-9192
Ultimate Parent: Melville. SIC: 5311—
Department Stores.

★ 86516 ★　Marshalls Inc.
12175 North Fwy.
Houston, TX 77060
(713)873-4200
Ultimate Parent: Melville.

★ 86517 ★　Mary Kay Cosmetics
6411 Sutter Pk. Ln.
Houston, TX 77066
(713)440-1767
Ultimate Parent: Mary Kay Cosmetics. SIC:
5999—Miscellaneous Retail Stores Nec.

★ 86518 ★　Mary Kay Cosmetics
1208 Castlewood
Houston, TX 77025
(713)482-8849
Ultimate Parent: Mary Kay Cosmetics. SIC:
5999—Miscellaneous Retail Stores Nec.

★ 86519 ★　Mary Kay Cosmetics
8003 St. Louis St.
Houston, TX 77028
(713)734-4548
Ultimate Parent: Mary Kay Cosmetics. SIC:
8661—Religious Organizations.

★ 86520 ★　Mary Kay Cosmitcs
10918 Bob White Dr.
Houston, TX 77096
(713)995-0553
Ultimate Parent: Mary Kay Cosmetics. SIC:
5999—Miscellaneous Retail Stores Nec.

★ 86521 ★　Matco Manufacturing
12000 Eastex Fwy.
Houston, TX 77039
(713)449-0361
Officer: Rick Bullitt, President. Ultimate
Parent: Danaher Corp. SIC: 3533—Oil &
Gas Field Machinery; 3545—Machine Tool
Accessories.

★ 86522 ★　Maxxam
5847 San Felipe
Houston, TX 77057
(713)975-7600
Company Type: Headquarters. Officer:
Charles E. Hurwitz. Sales: 2031.1 M.
Fortune 500: Largest U.S. Industrial
Corporations: Ranking 218.

★ 86523 ★　MAXXAM Group Inc.
5847 San Felipe, Ste. 2600
PO Box 572887
Houston, TX 77257-2887
(713)267-3777 Fax: (713)267-3710
Officer: Charles E. Hurwitz, Chairman of
the Board & CEO. Ultimate Parent:
Maxxam.

★ 86524 ★　Maxxam Inc.
5847 San Felipe
Houston, TX 77257-2887
(713)975-7600 Fax: (713)267-3710
Company Type: Headquarters. Officer:
Charles E. Hurwitz, Chairman of the Board,

President & Chief Executive Officer.
Ultimate Parent: Maxxam. SIC: 3334—
Primary Aluminum; 2421—Sawmills &
Planing Mills—General; 6552—Subdividers
& Developers Nec. Employee Count:
12700. Sales: 2202600 M.

★ 86525 ★　Maxxam, Inc.
P O Box 572887
Houston, TX 77257-2887
Company Type: Headquarters. Ultimate
Parent: Maxxam.

★ 86526 ★　MAXXAM Property
Co.
P O Box 572887,
5847 San Felipe, Ste. 2600
Houston, TX 77257-2887
(713)975-7600 Fax: (713)267-3710
Company Type: Subsidiary. Officer: James
D. Noteware, President & Chief Executive
Officer. Ultimate Parent: Maxxam. SIC:
6552—Subdividers & Developers Nec.

★ 86527 ★　MAXXAM Property
Co.
5847 San Felipe, Ste. 2600
PO Box 572887
Houston, TX 77257-2887
(713)267-3777 Fax: (713)267-3710
Officer: James D. Noteware, President.
Ultimate Parent: Maxxam.

★ 86528 ★　McCullough, an Atlas
Wireline Service Operation
PO Box 1407
10205 Westheimer Rd.
Houston, TX 77251-1407
(713)972-4000
Officer: J.R. DallaPezze, Senior Vice
President & General Manager. Ultimate
Parent: Anchor Bancorp. SIC: 3533—Oil &
Gas Field Machinery; 1381—Drilling Oil &
Gas Wells.

★ 86529 ★　McDonalds
17250 Fm 149 Rd.
Houston, TX 77064
(713)890-2633
Ultimate Parent: McDonald's.
SIC: 5812—Eating Places.

★ 86530 ★　McDonalds
Restaurant
185 West Rd.
Houston, TX 77037
(713)448-1644
Ultimate Parent: McDonald's.

★ 86531 ★　McDonalds
Restaurant
1302 Westheimer Rd.
Houston, TX 77006
(713)528-0016
Ultimate Parent: May Department Stores.

★ 86532 ★　McDonalds
Restaurant
6615 Tidwell Rd.
Houston, TX 77016
(713)635-7730
Ultimate Parent: McDonald's.

★ 86533 ★　McDonalds
Restaurant
6509 Washington Ave.
Houston, TX 77007
(713)880-3930
Ultimate Parent: May Department Stores.

★ 86534 ★　McDonalds
Restaurant
5930 S. Gessner Dr.
Houston, TX 77036
(713)541-9538
Ultimate Parent: McDonald's.

★ 86535 ★　McDonalds
Restaurant
14405 S. Post Oak Rd.
Houston, TX 77045
(713)963-0647
Ultimate Parent: McDonald's.

★ 86536 ★　McDonalds
Restaurant
12020 Northwest Fwy.
Houston, TX 77092
(713)681-9460
Ultimate Parent: McDonald's.

★ 86537 ★ McDonalds
Restaurant
5888 Richmond Ave.
Houston, TX 77057
(713)781-8085
Ultimate Parent: McDonald's.

★ 86538 ★ McDonalds
Restaurant
9203 Main St.
Houston, TX 77025
(713)666-6122
Ultimate Parent: McDonald's.

★ 86539 ★ McDonalds
Restaurant
5608 N. Shepherd Dr.
Houston, TX 77091
(713)695-8595
Ultimate Parent: McDonald's.

★ 86540 ★ McDonalds
Restaurant
7302 Hwy. 6 N
Houston, TX 77095
(713)859-9936
Ultimate Parent: McDonald's.

★ 86541 ★ McDonalds
Restaurant
8147 Katy Fwy.
Houston, TX 77024
(713)686-3342
Ultimate Parent: McDonald's.

★ 86542 ★ McDonalds
Restaurant
255 Greens Rd.
Houston, TX 77060
(713)872-6742
Ultimate Parent: McDonald's.

★ 86543 ★ McDonalds
Restaurant
6815 Harrisburg Blvd.
Houston, TX 77011
(713)928-5335
Ultimate Parent: McDonald's.

★ 86544 ★ McDonalds
Restaurant
7121 Fondren Rd.
Houston, TX 77036
(713)774-9433
Ultimate Parent: McDonald's.

★ 86545 ★ McDonalds
Restaurant
900 Gessner Rd.
Houston, TX 77024
(713)973-1035
Ultimate Parent: McDonald's.

★ 86546 ★ McDonalds
Restaurant
6621 Fannin St.
Houston, TX 77030
(713)795-4638
Ultimate Parent: McDonald's.

★ 86547 ★ McDonalds
Restaurant
4803 Fm 1960 Rd. W
Houston, TX 77069
(713)893-1136
Ultimate Parent: McDonald's.
SIC: 5812—Eating Places.

★ 86548 ★ McDonalds
Restaurant
1409 Brittmoore Rd.
Houston, TX 77043
(713)464-1409
Ultimate Parent: McDonald's.

★ 86549 ★ McDonalds
Restaurant
5085 Westheimer Rd.
Houston, TX 77056
(713)840-8646
Ultimate Parent: McDonald's.
SIC: 5812—Eating Places.

★ 86550 ★ McDonalds
Restaurant
7719 W. Bellfort St.
Houston, TX 77071
(713)728-3233
Ultimate Parent: McDonald's.
SIC: 5812—Eating Places.

★ 86551 ★ McDonalds
Restaurant
10610 W. F M1960
Houston, TX 77070
(713)469-8317
Ultimate Parent: McDonald's.
SIC: 5812—Eating Places.

★ 86552 ★ McDonalds
Restaurant
5915 S. Braeswood Blvd.
Houston, TX 77096
(713)721-4925
Ultimate Parent: McDonald's.
SIC: 5812—Eating Places.

★ 86553 ★ McDonalds
Restaurant
12979 Scarsdale Blvd.
Houston, TX 77089
(713)484-3404
Ultimate Parent: McDonald's.
SIC: 5812—Eating Places.

★ 86554 ★ McDonalds
Restaurant
7702 N. Shepherd Dr.
Houston, TX 77088
(713)448-9444
Ultimate Parent: McDonald's.
SIC: 5812—Eating Places.

★ 86555 ★ McDonalds
Restaurant
10450 Northwest Fwy.
Houston, TX 77092
(713)686-9781
Ultimate Parent: McDonald's.
SIC: 5812—Eating Places.

★ 86556 ★ McDonalds
Restaurant
15700 Kuykendahl Rd.
Houston, TX 77090
(713)444-1047
Ultimate Parent: McDonald's.
SIC: 5812—Eating Places.

★ 86557 ★ McDonalds
Restaurant
14450 Memorial Dr.
Houston, TX 77079
(713)493-1882
Ultimate Parent: McDonald's.
SIC: 5812—Eating Places.

★ 86558 ★ McDonalds
Restaurant
16002 Hempstead Rd.
Houston, TX 77040
(713)937-8011
Ultimate Parent: McDonald's.
SIC: 5812—Eating Places.

★ 86559 ★ McDonalds
Restaurant
10323 I E. 10
Houston, TX 77029
(713)673-5074
Ultimate Parent: McDonald's.
SIC: 5812—Eating Places.

★ 86560 ★ McDonalds
Restaurant
339 Fm 1960 Rd. W
Houston, TX 77090
(713)444-5871
Ultimate Parent: McDonald's.
SIC: 5812—Eating Places.

★ 86561 ★ McDonalds
Restaurant
3110 Fm 1960 Rd. W
Houston, TX 77068
(713)821-3346
Ultimate Parent: McDonald's.
SIC: 5812—Eating Places.

★ 86562 ★ McDonalds
Restaurant
6115 Downwood Forest Dr.
Houston, TX 77088
(713)440-9099
Ultimate Parent: McDonald's.
SIC: 5812—Eating Places.

★ 86563 ★ McDonalds
Restaurant
5301 E. Fwy.
Houston, TX 77056
(713)674-0016
Ultimate Parent: McDonald's.
SIC: 5812—Eating Places.

★ 86564 ★ McDonalds
Restaurant
7814 Bellfort St.
Houston, TX 77061
(713)645-2041
Ultimate Parent: McDonald's.
SIC: 5812—Eating Places.

★ 86565 ★ McDonalds
Restaurant
8920 Clearwood St.
Houston, TX 77075
(713)941-2204
Ultimate Parent: McDonald's.
SIC: 5812—Eating Places.

★ 86566 ★ McDonalds
Restaurant
6924 Antoine Dr.
Houston, TX 77091
(713)683-0752
Ultimate Parent: McDonald's.
SIC: 5812—Eating Places.

★ 86567 ★ McDonalds
Restaurant
11825 Bellaire Blvd.
Houston, TX 77072
(713)495-0120
Ultimate Parent: McDonald's.
SIC: 5812—Eating Places.

★ 86568 ★ McDonalds
Restaurant
13402 Almeda Genoa
Houston, TX 77034
(713)434-2574
Ultimate Parent: McDonald's.
SIC: 5812—Eating Places.

★ 86569 ★ McDonalds
Restaurant
406 Almeda Mall
Houston, TX 77075
(713)944-7908
Ultimate Parent: McDonald's.
SIC: 5812—Eating Places.

★ 86570 ★ McDonalds
Restaurants
9601 Westheimer Rd.
Houston, TX 77063
(713)789-0082
Ultimate Parent: McDonald's.
SIC: 5812—Eating Places.

★ 86571 ★ McDonalds
Restaurants
4650 Hawn 6
Houston, TX 77091
(713)463-4022
Ultimate Parent: McDonald's.
SIC: 5812—Eating Places.

★ 86572 ★ Mcduff Electronics
6805 Southwest Fwy.
Houston, TX 77074
(713)772-1218
Ultimate Parent: Tandy Corp.

★ 86573 ★ Mcduff Electronics
13302 Westheimer Rd.
Houston, TX 77077
(713)558-6375
Ultimate Parent: Tandy Corp.

★ 86574 ★ Mcduff Electronics
567 Garden Oaks Blvd.
Houston, TX 77018
(713)692-4785
Ultimate Parent: Tandy Corp.

★ 86575 ★ Mcduff Electronics
173 Greenspoint Mall
Houston, TX 77060
Ultimate Parent: Tandy Corp.

★ 86576 ★ Mead Data Central
Inc.
5444 Westheimer Rd.
Houston, TX 77056
(713)850-1156
Ultimate Parent: Mead.

★ 86577 ★ Metals Operations
3 Greenway Plz.
Houston, TX 77046
(713)297-2659
Company Type: Subsidiary. Ultimate
Parent: Dresser Industries Inc.

★ 86578 ★ Metlife Capital Corp.
515 W. Greens Rd.
Houston, TX 77067
(713)874-9200
Ultimate Parent: Metropolitan Life. SIC:
7389—Business Services Nec.

★ 86579 ★ Microsoft Corp.
4731 Pinebrook Ln.
Houston, TX 77053
(713)433-0318
Ultimate Parent: Microsoft.

★ 86580 ★ Microsoft Corp.
5151 San Felipe St.
Houston, TX 77056
(713)960-1418
Ultimate Parent: Microsoft. SIC: 7372—
Prepackaged Software.

★ 86581 ★ Mirex Corp. of Texas
Service
7250 Wynnpark Dr.
Houston, TX 77008-6030
(713)868-6900
Ultimate Parent: Alco Standard Corp. SIC:
5044—Office Equipment.

★ 86582 ★ Mobil Chemical Co.
9822 La Porte Fwy.
Houston, TX 77017
(713)475-6000
Ultimate Parent: Mobil.

★ 86583 ★ Mobil Chemical Co.
2025 Turning Basin Dr.
Houston, TX 77029
(713)672-0544
Ultimate Parent: Mobil. SIC: 2833—
Medicinals & Botanicals.

★ 86584 ★ Mobil Chemical Co.
9822 LaPorte Fwy.
Houston, TX 77017-2721
(713)475-6000
Officer: Ken Cary. Ultimate Parent: Mobil.
SIC: 2869—Industrial Organic Chemicals
Nec.

★ 86585 ★ Mobil Chemical
Packaging Di
3737 Westheimer Rd.
Houston, TX 77027
(713)526-1595
Ultimate Parent: Mobil. SIC: 5085—
Industrial Supplies.

★ 86586 ★ Mobil Explrn &
Prdcng US Inc.
12450 Greenspoint Dr.
Houston, TX 77060-1905
(713)775-2000
Officer: G. R. Still. Ultimate Parent: Mobil.
SIC: 1311—Crude Petroleum & Natural
Gas.

★ 86587 ★ Mobil Gas
510 Fm 1960 Rd. W
Houston, TX 77090
(713)583-7256
Ultimate Parent: Mobil.

★ 86588 ★ Mobil Mart
5800 S. Gessner Dr.
Houston, TX 77036
(713)779-3525
Ultimate Parent: Mobil.

★ 86589 ★ Mobil Mart
13300 Northwest Fwy.
Houston, TX 77040
(713)462-6540
Ultimate Parent: Mobil.

★ 86590 ★ Mobil Mining &
Minerals
2001 Jackson St.
Houston, TX 77003-5841
(713)920-5300
Ultimate Parent: Mobil. SIC: 1499—
Miscellaneous Nonmetallic Minerals.

★ 86591 ★ Mobil Natural Gas,
Inc.
1605 Beaconshire Dr.
Houston, TX 77077
(713)775-2641
Ultimate Parent: Mobil.

★ 86592 ★ Mobil Natural Gas Inc.
12450 Greenspoint Dr.
Houston, TX 77060
(713)775-2636
Ultimate Parent: Mobil.

★ 86593 ★   **Mobil Oil Corp.**
12450 Greenspoint Dr.
Houston, TX 77060
Ultimate Parent: Mobil. **SIC:** 5171—
Petroleum Bulk Stations & Terminals.

★ 86594 ★   **Mobil Oil Corp.**
9 E. Greenway Plz.
Houston, TX 77046
(713)871-5000
Ultimate Parent: Mobil. **SIC:** 2833—
Medicinals & Botanicals.

★ 86595 ★   **Mobil Pipe Line Co.**
15215 Hardy Rd.
Houston, TX 77032
(713)591-3700
Company Type: Branch. **Ultimate Parent:**
Mobil. **SIC:** 4612—Crude Petroleum
Pipelines.

★ 86596 ★   **Mobil Pipe Line Co.
Inc.**
505 Aldine Bender Rd.
Houston, TX 77060
(713)447-8983
Ultimate Parent: Mobil. **SIC:** 4612—Crude
Petroleum Pipelines.

★ 86597 ★   **Mobil Self Serve**
11503 Southwest Fwy.
Houston, TX 77031
(713)933-9348
Ultimate Parent: Mobil. **SIC:** 5599—
Automotive Dealers Nec.

★ 86598 ★   **Mobil Self Serve**
11110 Westheimer Rd.
Houston, TX 77042
(713)782-1471
Ultimate Parent: Mobil. **SIC:** 5599—
Automotive Dealers Nec.

★ 86599 ★   **Mobil Self Serve**
3835 Louetta Rd.
Houston, TX 77069
(713)350-4995
Ultimate Parent: Mobil.

★ 86600 ★   **Mobil Self Serve**
3141 Southwest Fwy.
Houston, TX 77098
(713)529-3723
Ultimate Parent: Mobil.

★ 86601 ★   **Mobil Self Serve**
8497 Hwy. 6 N
Houston, TX 77095
(713)855-0193
Ultimate Parent: Mobil.

★ 86602 ★   **Mobil Self Serve**
9461 Jones Rd.
Houston, TX 77065
(713)955-8505
Ultimate Parent: Mobil.

★ 86603 ★   **Mobil Steel Corp.**
13830 S. Wayside Dr.
Houston, TX 77048-5296
(713)991-0450
Officer: Dottie Manhart. **Ultimate Parent:**
Mobil. **SIC:** 3441—Fabricated Structural
Metal; 1791—Structural Steel Erection.

★ 86604 ★   **Molex Inc.**
13231 Champions Dr.
Houston, TX 77069
(713)586-9112
Ultimate Parent: Molex.

★ 86605 ★   **Monarch Paper Co.**
4414 Hollister St.
Houston, TX 77040
(713)744-5600
Company Type: Division. **Ultimate Parent:**
Alco Standard Corp. **SIC:** 5111—Printing &
Writing Paper; 5113—Industrial & Personal
Service Paper.

★ 86606 ★   **MW Kellogg Co.**
601 Jefferson
Houston, TX 77002
(713)753-2000 **Fax:** (713)753-2144
Company Type: Subsidiary. **Ultimate
Parent:** Dresser Industries Inc.

★ 86607 ★   **Nabisco Inc. Nabisco
Biscuit Co.**
6803 Almeda Rd.
Houston, TX 77021
Ultimate Parent: RJR Nabisco Holdings.
SIC: 2052—Cookies & Crackers.

★ 86608 ★   **National Chemsearch
Corp.**
2200 Southwest Fwy.
Houston, TX 77098
(713)528-7063
Ultimate Parent: NCH. **SIC:** 5087—Service
Establishment Equipment.

★ 86609 ★   **National-Oilwell**
PO Box 4638
Houston, TX 77210-4638
(713)960-5100 **Fax:** (713)960-5428 **Telex:**
4223976 & 762128
Company Type: Joint venture. **Officer:**
D.A. Higbee, President. **Ultimate Parent:**
Armco. **SIC:** 3533—Oil & Gas Field
Machinery. **Employee Count:** 2800.

★ 86610 ★   **National Oilwell**
555 San Felipe
Houston, TX 77056
(713)960-5100
Company Type: Subsidiary. **Officer:** David
A. Higbee, Presidet. **Ultimate Parent:**
Armco.

★ 86611 ★   **National Steel Corp.**
363 E. Belt N
Houston, TX 77060
(713)591-0075
Ultimate Parent: National Intergroup. **SIC:**
3312—Blast Furnaces & Steel Mills.

★ 86612 ★   **Ncr Corp.**
3200 Wilcrest Dr. 600
Houston, TX 77042
Ultimate Parent: AT&T. **SIC:** 5046—
Commercial Equipment Nec.

★ 86613 ★   **New York Life Gulf
Coast Houston General Office**
Western Agencies
Union Texas Petroleum Tower
Four Oaks Place, Ste. 1700
1330 Post Oak Blvd.
Houston, TX 77056
(713)961-0100 **Fax:** (713)963-4295
Officer: Patricia A. Golub, General
Manager. **Ultimate Parent:** New York Life.

★ 86614 ★   **New York Life
Houston General Office**
Western Agencies
Interfin Bldg.
1400 Post Oak Blvd., Ste. 700
Houston, TX 77056
(713)961-4545 **Fax:** (713)961-0321
Officer: Carl M. Carter Jr., General
Manager. **Ultimate Parent:** New York Life.

★ 86615 ★   **New York Life
Houston Group Sales Office**
Western Group Marketing Zone Office
9 Greenway Plz. Ste. 3030
Houston, TX 77046
(713)624-5300 **Fax:** (713)624-5330
Officer: Kim Vannatter, Group Manager.
Ultimate Parent: New York Life.

★ 86616 ★   **Nike International**
12418 Shepherds Ridge Dr.
Houston, TX 77077
(713)870-8433
Ultimate Parent: Nike.

★ 86617 ★   **Northern Mich
Exploration Co.**
507 W. Belt N
Houston, TX 77024
(713)448-9185
Ultimate Parent: CMS Energy Corp. **SIC:**
1382—Oil & Gas Exploration Services.

★ 86618 ★   **Northern National Gas
Co.**
PO Box 1188
Houston, TX 77251-1188
(409)398-7070
Company Type: Subsidiary. **Ultimate
Parent:** Enron.

★ 86619 ★   **Northern Natural Gas
Co.**
1400 Smith St.
Houston, TX 77002-7337
(713)853-6161
Company Type: Subsidiary. **Officer:** Stan
Korton, President. **Ultimate Parent:** Enron.
SIC: 4922—Natural Gas Transmission.
Sales: 1.1 M.

★ 86620 ★   **Northern Trust Bank
of Texas, NA**
2701 Kirby Dr.
Houston, TX 77098
(713)521-1171
Location Type: Branch office. **Ultimate
Parent:** Northern Trust Corp. **SIC:** 6021—
National Commercial Banks.

★ 86621 ★   **Northern Trust Bank
of Texas, NA**
700 Rusk St., Ste. 5120
Houston, TX 77002
(713)225-5900
Location Type: Branch office. **Ultimate
Parent:** Northern Trust Corp. **SIC:** 6021—
National Commercial Banks.

★ 86622 ★   **Norwest Mortgage
Inc.**
2500 E. T C Jester Blvd.
Houston, TX 77008
(713)864-8600
Ultimate Parent: Norwest Corp. **SIC:**
6159—Miscellaneous Business Credit
Institutions.

★ 86623 ★   **O & M Manufacturing
Co.**
8203 Market St.
Houston, TX 77029
Ultimate Parent: Handy & Harman. **SIC:**
3443—Fabricated Plate Work—Boiler
Shops.

★ 86624 ★   **O & M Manufacturing
Co.**
8203 Market St.
Houston, TX 77029
Ultimate Parent: Handy & Harman. **SIC:**
3443—Fabricated Plate Work—Boiler
Shops.

★ 86625 ★   **O & M Manufacturing
Co.**
8203 Market St.
Houston, TX 77029
Ultimate Parent: Handy & Harman. **SIC:**
3443—Fabricated Plate Work—Boiler
Shops.

★ 86626 ★   **Oak Farms Inc.**
2006 Westheimer
Houston, TX 77098
Ultimate Parent: Southland Corp. **SIC:**
2024—Ice Cream & Frozen Desserts.

★ 86627 ★   **Oilfield Service Corp.
Amer**
3935 Westheimer Rd.
Houston, TX 77027
(713)960-8850
Ultimate Parent: Great Lakes Chemical.
SIC: 5169—Chemicals & Allied Products
Nec.

★ 86628 ★   **OTC Co.**
227 N. Lenox St.
Houston, TX 77011
(713)926-6144
Ultimate Parent: SPX Corp. **SIC:** 5084—
Industrial Machinery & Equipment.

★ 86629 ★   **Otis Elevator Co.**
3033 W. Alabama St.
Houston, TX 77098
(713)524-8486
Ultimate Parent: United Technologies.

★ 86630 ★   **Owens Corning**
8360 Market Street Rd.
Houston, TX 77029
(713)672-7371
Officer: Bill Moore, Manager. **Ultimate
Parent:** Owens-Corning. **SIC:** 2952—
Asphalt Felts & Coatings.

★ 86631 ★   **Owens Corning
Fiberglass**
256 N. Belt Dr. E. 100
Houston, TX 77060
(713)872-0671
Ultimate Parent: Owens-Corning. **SIC:**
3999—Manufacturing Industries Nec.

★ 86632 ★   **Owens Corning
Fiberglass Co.**
256 E. Belt N
Houston, TX 77060
(713)445-6100
Ultimate Parent: Owens-Corning. **SIC:**
1742—Plastering, Drywall & Insulation.

★ 86633 ★   **Panhandle Eastern**
5400 Westheimer Ct.
Houston, TX 77056
(713)627-5400
Company Type: Headquarters. **Officer:**
Dennis R. Hendrix. **Employee Count:** 4900.
Fortune Service 500: Ranking 23.

★ 86634 ★   **Panhandle Eastern
Corp.**
5400 Westheimer Ct.
PO Box 1642
Houston, TX 77251-1642
(713)627-5400 **Fax:** (713)627-4145
Officer: Dennis R. Hendrix, Chairman,
President & CEO. **Ultimate Parent:**
Panhandle Eastern. **Employee Count:**
6000.

★ 86635 ★   **Panhandle Eastern
Pipe Line Co.**
5400 Westheimer Ct.
PO Box 1642
Houston, TX 77251-1642
(713)627-5500
Officer: Paul M. Anderson, President.
Ultimate Parent: Panhandle Eastern.

★ 86636 ★   **Pappagallo**
1000 W. Oaks Mall
Houston, TX 77082
(713)960-0366
Ultimate Parent: United States Shoe. **SIC:**
5661—Shoe Stores.

★ 86637 ★   **Pappagallo**
1370 Bay Brook Mall
Houston, TX 77004
(713)486-1577
Ultimate Parent: United States Shoe. **SIC:**
5661—Shoe Stores.

★ 86638 ★   **Park Plaza Hospital**
1313 Hermann Dr.
Houston, TX 77004
(713)527-5000
Officer: Paul Crafts, Executive Director.
Ultimate Parent: American Medical
Holdings. **SIC:** 8062—General Medical &
Surgical Hospitals.

★ 86639 ★   **Patrick Media Group**
1313 West Loop N
Houston, TX 77055
(713)688-8651
Officer: Jerry McCarver, President.
Ultimate Parent: General Electric. **SIC:**
3993—Signs & Advertising Displays.

★ 86640 ★   **Payless Shoesource**
8321 Jensen Dr.
Houston, TX 77093
(713)697-6077
Ultimate Parent: May Department Stores.
SIC: 5661—Shoe Stores.

★ 86641 ★   **Payless Shoesource**
1421 Little York Rd.
Houston, TX 77093
(713)987-9394
Ultimate Parent: May Department Stores.
SIC: 5661—Shoe Stores.

★ 86642 ★   **Payless Shoesource**
10148 Hammerly Blvd.
Houston, TX 77080
(713)468-5478
Ultimate Parent: May Department Stores.

★ 86643 ★   **Payless Shoesource**
2204 FM 1960 Rd. W
Houston, TX 77090
(713)537-2039
Ultimate Parent: May Department Stores.
SIC: 5661—Shoe Stores.

★ 86644 ★   **Payless Shoesource**
113 Greenspoint Mall
Houston, TX 77060
(713)873-4825
Ultimate Parent: May Department Stores.

★ 86645 ★   **Payless Shoesource**
5556 North Fwy.
Houston, TX 77076
(713)692-5604
Ultimate Parent: May Department Stores.

★ 86646 ★   **Payless Shoesource**
8132 Kirby Dr.
Houston, TX 77054
(713)661-9624
Ultimate Parent: May Department Stores.

★ 86647 ★   Payless Shoesource
8554 Long Point Rd.
Houston, TX 77055
(713)467-1200
Ultimate Parent: May Department Stores.
SIC: 5661—Shoe Stores.

★ 86648 ★   Payless Shoesource
500 Westwood Mall
Houston, TX 77036
(713)995-6892
Ultimate Parent: May Department Stores.

★ 86649 ★   Payless Shoesource
7500 Bellaire Blvd.
Houston, TX 77036
(713)778-1947
Ultimate Parent: May Department Stores.

★ 86650 ★   Payless Shoesource
11003 Market St.
Houston, TX 77029
(713)450-1433
Ultimate Parent: May Department Stores.
SIC: 5661—Shoe Stores.

★ 86651 ★   Payless Shoesource
7425 Martin Luther King Blvd.
Houston, TX 77033
(713)649-7722
Ultimate Parent: May Department Stores.
SIC: 5661—Shoe Stores.

★ 86652 ★   Payless Shoesource
9401 Katy Fwy.
Houston, TX 77024
(713)461-2714
Ultimate Parent: May Department Stores.

★ 86653 ★   Payless Shoesource
8600 Mesa Dr.
Houston, TX 77028
(713)633-6667
Ultimate Parent: May Department Stores.
SIC: 5661—Shoe Stores.

★ 86654 ★   Payless Shoesource
1229 W. 43rd St.
Houston, TX 77018
(713)682-3467
Ultimate Parent: May Department Stores.
SIC: 5661—Shoe Stores.

★ 86655 ★   Payless Shoesource
720 Telephone Rd.
Houston, TX 77023
(713)921-7770
Ultimate Parent: May Department Stores.
SIC: 5661—Shoe Stores.

★ 86656 ★   Payless Shoesource
13502 East Fwy.
Houston, TX 77015
(713)451-1583
Ultimate Parent: May Department Stores.

★ 86657 ★   Payless Shoesource
9520 Homestead Rd.
Houston, TX 77016
(713)631-7329
Ultimate Parent: May Department Stores.
SIC: 5661—Shoe Stores.

★ 86658 ★   Payless Shoesource
2225 N. Shepherd Dr.
Houston, TX 77008
(713)862-7332
Ultimate Parent: May Department Stores.
SIC: 5661—Shoe Stores.

★ 86659 ★   Payless Shoesource
1016 Quitman St.
Houston, TX 77009
(713)227-1059
Ultimate Parent: May Department Stores.

★ 86660 ★   Payless Shoesource
912 Main
Houston, TX 77002
(713)655-8273
Ultimate Parent: May Department Stores.

★ 86661 ★   Payless Shoesource
11160 Fondren Rd.
Houston, TX 77096
(713)776-3790
Ultimate Parent: May Department Stores.

★ 86662 ★   Payless Shoesource
7555 Bellaire Blvd.
Houston, TX 77036
(713)779-4507
Ultimate Parent: May Department Stores.

★ 86663 ★   Payless Shoesource
10941 W. FM 1960
Houston, TX 77070
(713)469-2712
Ultimate Parent: May Department Stores.
SIC: 5661—Shoe Stores.

★ 86664 ★   Payment Services Co.
720 N. Post Oak Rd.
Houston, TX 77024
(713)599-7700
Ultimate Parent: First Financial
Management Corp.

★ 86665 ★   Pennzoil
700 Milam St.
Houston, TX 77002
(713)546-4000
Company Type: Headquarters. **Officer:**
James L. Pate. **Employee Count:** 9901.
Sales: 2742 M. **Fortune 500:** Largest U.S.
Industrial Corporations: Ranking 170.

★ 86666 ★   Pennzoil
2967 PO Box
Houston, TX 77252
(713)546-4521
Ultimate Parent: Pennzoil.

★ 86667 ★   Pennzoil
17001 J F Kennedy Blvd.
Houston, TX 77032
(713)443-0721
Ultimate Parent: Pennzoil. **SIC:** 1311—
Crude Petroleum & Natural Gas.

★ 86668 ★   Pennzoil Co.
Pennzoil Pl.
PO Box 2967
Houston, TX 77252-2967
(713)546-4000 **Fax:** (713)546-6639 **Telex:**
762170
Officer: James L. Pate, President & CEO.
Ultimate Parent: Pennzoil. **Employee
Count:** 6100.

★ 86669 ★   Pennzoil Corp.
2 Riverway
Houston, TX 77056
(713)993-9684
Ultimate Parent: Pennzoil.

★ 86670 ★   Pennzoil Exploration
& Production Co.
Pennzoil Pl.
PO Box 2967
Houston, TX 77252-2967
Officer: Thomas M. Hamilton, President.
Ultimate Parent: Pennzoil.

★ 86671 ★   Pennzoil Products Co.
Pennzoil Pl.
PO Box 2967
Houston, TX 77252-2967
Officer: James L. Pate, President. **Ultimate
Parent:** Pennzoil.

★ 86672 ★   Pennzoil Sulphur Co.
Pennzoil Pl.
PO Box 2967
Houston, TX 77252-2967
Officer: John L. Davis, President. **Ultimate
Parent:** Pennzoil.

★ 86673 ★   Pepsi-Cola Co.
9300 La Porte Fwy.
Houston, TX 77017
(713)845-3236
Ultimate Parent: Pepsico. **SIC:** 2086—
Bottled & Canned Soft Drinks.

★ 86674 ★   Pepsi-Cola South
9300 La Porte Fwy.
Houston, TX 77017
(713)645-7630
Ultimate Parent: Pepsico.

★ 86675 ★   Personal Performance
Consultants
6100 Richmond Ave.
Houston, TX 77057
(713)266-0371
Ultimate Parent: Medco Containment
Services. **SIC:** 8742—Management
Consulting Services.

★ 86676 ★   Pest Elimination
Services
13940 N. Bammel Houston Rd.
Houston, TX 77066
(713)447-7378
Ultimate Parent: Ecolab Inc.

★ 86677 ★   Petite Sophisticate
800 W. Belt Dr. N
Houston, TX 77024
(713)984-1640
Ultimate Parent: United States Shoe. **SIC:**
5621—Women's Clothing Stores.

★ 86678 ★   Petite Sophisticate
147 Greenspoint Mall
Houston, TX 77060
(713)999-5388
Ultimate Parent: United States Shoe. **SIC:**
5621—Women's Clothing Stores.

★ 86679 ★   Petite Sophisticate
Memorial City Mall
Houston, TX 77024
(713)465-6037
Ultimate Parent: United States Shoe. **SIC:**
5621—Women's Clothing Stores.

★ 86680 ★   Petite Sophisticate
7925 Fm 1960 Rd. W
Houston, TX 77070
(713)894-9144
Ultimate Parent: United States Shoe. **SIC:**
5621—Women's Clothing Stores.

★ 86681 ★   Petrocorp
16800 Greenspoint Park Dr.
Houston, TX 77069-2304
(713)875-2500
Company Type: Subsidiary. **Officer:** Lee
Sargent, President. **Ultimate Parent:** Cigna
Corp. **SIC:** 1382—Oil & Gas Exploration
Services; 1311—Crude Petroleum & Natural
Gas. **Employee Count:** 44. **Sales:** 11 M.

★ 86682 ★   Phibro Energy USA
Inc.
9701 Manchester
Houston, TX 77262
Ultimate Parent: Salomon, Inc. **SIC:**
2911—Petroleum Refining.

★ 86683 ★   Phibro Refining Inc.
9701 Manchester
Houston, TX 77012
Ultimate Parent: Salomon, Inc. **SIC:**
2911—Petroleum Refining.

★ 86684 ★   Phillips Fruitland Gas
Corp.
PO Box 1967
Houston, TX 77251-1967
(713)669-7088 **Fax:** (713)669-3541
Ultimate Parent: Phillips Petroleum.

★ 86685 ★   Phillips Gas Co.
1300 Post Oak Blvd.
Houston, TX 77056
(713)297-6001 **Fax:** (713)297-6015
Ultimate Parent: Phillips Petroleum.

★ 86686 ★   Pitney Bowes
Management Services
600 Jefferson St., Ste. 125
Houston, TX 77002
(713)759-1700
Officer: Don Hennig, Manager. **Ultimate
Parent:** Pitney Bowes. **SIC:** 2752—
Commercial Printing—Lithographic; 2759—
Commercial Printing Nec.

★ 86687 ★   Pizza Hut
11040 Westheimer Rd.
Houston, TX 77042
(713)784-0298
Ultimate Parent: Pepsico. **SIC:** 5812—
Eating Places.

★ 86688 ★   Pizza Hut
403 Winkler Dr.
Houston, TX 77087
(713)643-0783
Ultimate Parent: Pepsico. **SIC:** 5812—
Eating Places.

★ 86689 ★   Pizza Hut
2400 W. Holcombe Blvd.
Houston, TX 77030
(713)664-1391
Ultimate Parent: Pepsico. **SIC:** 5812—
Eating Places.

★ 86690 ★   Pizza Hut
17254 W. Montgomery Rd.
Houston, TX 77064
(713)820-1566
Ultimate Parent: Pepsico. **SIC:** 5812—
Eating Places.

★ 86691 ★   Pizza Hut
335 FM 1960 Rd. W
Houston, TX 77090
(713)440-9190
Ultimate Parent: Pepsico. **SIC:** 5812—
Eating Places.

★ 86692 ★   Pizza Hut
6009 FM 1960 Rd. W
Houston, TX 77069
(713)440-1087
Ultimate Parent: Pepsico. **SIC:** 5812—
Eating Places.

★ 86693 ★   Pizza Hut
10904 Scarsdale Blvd.
Houston, TX 77089
Ultimate Parent: Pepsico. **SIC:** 5812—
Eating Places.

★ 86694 ★   Pizza Hut
10703 W. Bellfort St.
Houston, TX 77099
(713)495-2176
Ultimate Parent: Pepsico. **SIC:** 5812—
Eating Places.

★ 86695 ★   Pizza Hut
2600 S. Richey St.
Houston, TX 77017
(713)943-9420
Ultimate Parent: Pepsico. **SIC:** 5812—
Eating Places.

★ 86696 ★   Pizza Hut
2230 S. Shepherd Dr.
Houston, TX 77019
(713)526-7536
Ultimate Parent: Pepsico. **SIC:** 5812—
Eating Places.

★ 86697 ★   Pizza Hut
10333 Richmond Ave. 340
Houston, TX 77042
(713)467-2486
Ultimate Parent: Pepsico. **SIC:** 5812—
Eating Places.

★ 86698 ★   Pizza Hut
6605 S. Gessner Dr.
Houston, TX 77036
(713)777-0338
Ultimate Parent: Pepsico. **SIC:** 5812—
Eating Places.

★ 86699 ★   Pizza Hut
5011 N. Shepherd Dr.
Houston, TX 77018
(713)692-3908
Ultimate Parent: Pepsico. **SIC:** 5812—
Eating Places.

★ 86700 ★   Pizza Hut
11381 Meadowglen Ln.
Houston, TX 77082
(713)531-6709
Ultimate Parent: Pepsico. **SIC:** 5812—
Eating Places.

★ 86701 ★   Pizza Hut
11230 N. Fwy.
Houston, TX 77031
(713)447-8373
Ultimate Parent: Pepsico. **SIC:** 5812—
Eating Places.

★ 86702 ★   Pizza Hut
9410 Homestead Rd.
Houston, TX 77016
(713)633-6418
Ultimate Parent: Pepsico. **SIC:** 5812—
Eating Places.

★ 86703 ★   Pizza Hut
8401 Long Point Rd.
Houston, TX 77055
(713)465-5080
Ultimate Parent: Pepsico. **SIC:** 1521—
Single-Family Housing Construction.

★ 86704 ★   Pizza Hut
1940 Fry Rd.
Houston, TX 77084
(713)578-7461
Ultimate Parent: Pepsico.

★ 86705 ★   Pizza Hut
4385 Hwy. 6 N
Houston, TX 77084
(713)463-7272
Ultimate Parent: Pepsico. **SIC:** 5812—
Eating Places.

★ 86706 ★ Pizza Hut
743 Dairy Ashford St.
Houston, TX 77079
(713)497-0420
Ultimate Parent: Pepsico. **SIC:** 5812—
Eating Places.

★ 86707 ★ Pizza Hut
7025 Fondren Rd.
Houston, TX 77036
(713)771-0386
Ultimate Parent: Pepsico. **SIC:** 5812—
Eating Places.

★ 86708 ★ Pizza Hut
5302 Chimney Rock Rd.
Houston, TX 77081
(713)661-6096
Ultimate Parent: Pepsico. **SIC:** 5812—
Eating Places.

★ 86709 ★ Pizza Hut
8925 Clearwood St.
Houston, TX 77075
(713)946-4201
Ultimate Parent: Pepsico. **SIC:** 5812—
Eating Places.

★ 86710 ★ Pizza Hut
7815 Bellfort St.
Houston, TX 77061
(713)649-3089
Ultimate Parent: Pepsico. **SIC:** 5812—
Eating Places.

★ 86711 ★ Pizza Hut
12775 Bissonnet St.
Houston, TX 77099
(713)495-4393
Ultimate Parent: Pepsico.

★ 86712 ★ Pizza Hut
11828 Bellaire Blvd.
Houston, TX 77072
(713)495-4090
Ultimate Parent: Pepsico.

★ 86713 ★ Pizza Hut
2117 Bellfort
Houston, TX 77035
(713)443-7851
Ultimate Parent: Pepsico. **SIC:** 5812—
Eating Places.

★ 86714 ★ Pizza Hut
8090 Antoine Dr.
Houston, TX 77088
(713)591-0753
Ultimate Parent: Pepsico. **SIC:** 5812—
Eating Places.

★ 86715 ★ Pizza Hut
1227 Bay Area Blvd.
Houston, TX 77058
(713)488-1649
Ultimate Parent: Pepsico. **SIC:** 5812—
Eating Places.

★ 86716 ★ Pizza Hut
2117 Aldine
Houston, TX 77090
(713)946-4201
Ultimate Parent: Pepsico. **SIC:** 5812—
Eating Places.

★ 86717 ★ Ppg Industries Inc.
7240 Wynnpark Dr.
Houston, TX 77008
(713)675-4261
Ultimate Parent: PPG Industries Inc. **SIC:**
5013—Motor Vehicle Supplies & New Parts.

★ 86718 ★ Ppg Industries Inc.
3812 Ace St.
Houston, TX 77063
(713)782-9212
Ultimate Parent: PPG Industries Inc.

★ 86719 ★ Provident National
Assurance
20405 Tomball Pky.
Houston, TX 77070
(713)376-6637
Ultimate Parent: Provident Life & Accident.

★ 86720 ★ Pulte Home Corp.
16906 River Wlw Dr.
Houston, TX 77069
(713)370-0254
Ultimate Parent: Pulte.

★ 86721 ★ Pulte Home Corp.
7815 Pebble Run Ct
Houston, TX 77095
(713)855-8150
Ultimate Parent: Pulte.

★ 86722 ★ Pulte Home Corp.
10519 Goldfield Ln.
Houston, TX 77064
(713)890-6284
Ultimate Parent: Pulte. **SIC:** 1521—
Single-Family Housing Construction.

★ 86723 ★ Pulte Home Corp.
5518 Forest Trails Dr.
Houston, TX 77084
(713)855-4100
Ultimate Parent: Pulte.

★ 86724 ★ Pulte Home Corp.
13955 Beckwith Dr.
Houston, TX 77014
(713)873-0130
Ultimate Parent: Pulte.

★ 86725 ★ Pulte Home Corp.
13343 Somersworth Dr.
Houston, TX 77041
(713)937-6869
Ultimate Parent: Pulte. **SIC:** 1521—
Single-Family Housing Construction.

★ 86726 ★ Pulte Home Corp.
Cons
10203 Tablerock Dr.
Houston, TX 77064
(713)890-8048
Ultimate Parent: Pulte.

★ 86727 ★ Puritan Sportswear
2620 Fountain View Dr.
Houston, TX 77057
(713)780-0693
Ultimate Parent: Warnaco Group. **SIC:**
5136—Men's/Boys' Clothing.

★ 86728 ★ Quanex
1900 West Loop S
Houston, TX 77027
(713)961-4600
Company Type: Headquarters. **Officer:**
Robert C. Snyder. **Employee Count:** 2536.
Sales: 616.1 M. **Fortune 500:** Largest U.S.
Industrial Corporations: Ranking 499.

★ 86729 ★ Quincy Compressor
Colt Indu
2302 Eaglerock Dr.
Houston, TX 77080
(713)461-8619
Ultimate Parent: Coltec Industries. **SIC:**
5084—Industrial Machinery & Equipment.

★ 86730 ★ Radio Shack
7950 Westheimer Rd.
Houston, TX 77063
(713)781-4042
Company Type: Division. **Ultimate Parent:**
Tandy Corp.

★ 86731 ★ Radio Shack
W Oaks Mall
Houston, TX 77082
(713)493-0582
Company Type: Division. **Ultimate Parent:**
Tandy Corp. **SIC:** 5065—Electronic Parts &
Equipment Nec.

★ 86732 ★ Radio Shack
1214 Westheimer Rd.
Houston, TX 77006
(713)526-2188
Company Type: Division. **Ultimate Parent:**
Tandy Corp. **SIC:** 5734—Computer &
Software Stores.

★ 86733 ★ Radio Shack
6316 Telephone Rd.
Houston, TX 77087
(713)645-3013
Company Type: Division. **Ultimate Parent:**
Tandy Corp. **SIC:** 5065—Electronic Parts &
Equipment Nec.

★ 86734 ★ Radio Shack
1403 W. Mount Houston Rd.
Houston, TX 77038
(713)445-0390
Company Type: Division. **Ultimate Parent:**
Tandy Corp. **SIC:** 3699—Electrical
Equipment & Supplies Nec.

★ 86735 ★ Radio Shack
9400 Richmond Ave.
Houston, TX 77063
(713)781-5405
Company Type: Division. **Ultimate Parent:**
Tandy Corp.

★ 86736 ★ Radio Shack
6813 Southwest Fwy.
Houston, TX 77074
(713)776-0513
Company Type: Division. **Ultimate Parent:**
Tandy Corp. **SIC:** 5065—Electronic Parts &
Equipment Nec.

★ 86737 ★ Radio Shack
8329 Mesa Dr.
Houston, TX 77028
(713)453-0600
Company Type: Division. **Ultimate Parent:**
Tandy Corp. **SIC:** 5046—Commercial
Equipment Nec.

★ 86738 ★ Radio Shack
5900 N. Fwy.
Houston, TX 77057
(713)699-1932
Company Type: Division. **Ultimate Parent:**
Tandy Corp. **SIC:** 5046—Commercial
Equipment Nec.

★ 86739 ★ Radio Shack
2900 Hillcroft St.
Houston, TX 77057
(713)780-7449
Company Type: Division. **Ultimate Parent:**
Tandy Corp.

★ 86740 ★ Radio Shack
625 Mem City Shopping Ctr.
Houston, TX 77024
(713)464-4165
Company Type: Division. **Ultimate Parent:**
Tandy Corp. **SIC:** 5065—Electronic Parts &
Equipment Nec.

★ 86741 ★ Radio Shack
5462 Fm 1960 Rd. W
Houston, TX 77069
(713)580-1404
Company Type: Division. **Ultimate Parent:**
Tandy Corp. **SIC:** 5046—Commercial
Equipment Nec.

★ 86742 ★ Radio Shack
610 Greenspoint Mall
Houston, TX 77060
(713)875-4787
Company Type: Division. **Ultimate Parent:**
Tandy Corp.

★ 86743 ★ Radio Shack
15158 Bellaire Blvd.
Houston, TX 77083
(713)568-4396
Company Type: Division. **Ultimate Parent:**
Tandy Corp.

★ 86744 ★ Radio Shack
12222 Bissonnet St.
Houston, TX 77099
(713)495-2954
Company Type: Division. **Ultimate Parent:**
Tandy Corp.

★ 86745 ★ Radio Shack
Astrodome
Houston, TX 77054
(713)661-5212
Company Type: Division. **Ultimate Parent:**
Tandy Corp. **SIC:** 5734—Computer &
Software Stores.

★ 86746 ★ Radio Shack
5655 Beechnut St.
Houston, TX 77096
(713)779-1327
Company Type: Division. **Ultimate Parent:**
Tandy Corp.

★ 86747 ★ Radio Shack
6161 Savoy Dr. 920
Houston, TX 77036
(512)657-3958
Company Type: Division. **Ultimate Parent:**
Tandy Corp. **SIC:** 5046—Commercial
Equipment Nec.

★ 86748 ★ Radio Shack
720 Westwood Fashion Pl
Houston, TX 77036
(713)772-9000
Company Type: Division. **Ultimate Parent:**
Tandy Corp. **SIC:** 3699—Electrical
Equipment & Supplies Nec.

★ 86749 ★ Radio Shack
Willowbrook Mall
Houston, TX 77061
(713)890-6551
Company Type: Division. **Ultimate Parent:**
Tandy Corp. **SIC:** 3699—Electrical
Equipment & Supplies Nec.

★ 86750 ★ Radio Shack
13628 W. Montgomery Rd.
Houston, TX 77086
(713)445-3668
Company Type: Division. **Ultimate Parent:**
Tandy Corp. **SIC:** 3699—Electrical
Equipment & Supplies Nec.

★ 86751 ★ Radio Shack
10953 Westheimer Rd.
Houston, TX 77042
(713)975-7095
Company Type: Division. **Ultimate Parent:**
Tandy Corp. **SIC:** 5065—Electronic Parts &
Equipment Nec.

★ 86752 ★ Radio Shack
5328 W. 34th St.
Houston, TX 77092
(713)682-5694
Company Type: Division. **Ultimate Parent:**
Tandy Corp. **SIC:** 5065—Electronic Parts &
Equipment Nec.

★ 86753 ★ Radio Shack
1232 W. 43rd St.
Houston, TX 77018
(713)682-7713
Company Type: Division. **Ultimate Parent:**
Tandy Corp. **SIC:** 5065—Electronic Parts &
Equipment Nec.

★ 86754 ★ Radio Shack
440 Uvalde Rd.
Houston, TX 77015
Company Type: Division. **Ultimate Parent:**
Tandy Corp. **SIC:** 3699—Electrical
Equipment & Supplies Nec.

★ 86755 ★ Radio Shack
1507 W. 18th St.
Houston, TX 77008
(713)861-9343
Company Type: Division. **Ultimate Parent:**
Tandy Corp. **SIC:** 5065—Electronic Parts &
Equipment Nec.

★ 86756 ★ Radio Shack
5858 S. Gessner Dr. 102
Houston, TX 77036
(713)772-4842
Company Type: Division. **Ultimate Parent:**
Tandy Corp. **SIC:** 3699—Electrical
Equipment & Supplies Nec.

★ 86757 ★ Radio Shack
9119 Stella Link Rd.
Houston, TX 77025
(713)665-5219
Company Type: Division. **Ultimate Parent:**
Tandy Corp. **SIC:** 5065—Electronic Parts &
Equipment Nec.

★ 86758 ★ Radio Shack
Park Houston Ctr.
Houston, TX 77002
(713)652-9070
Company Type: Division. **Ultimate Parent:**
Tandy Corp. **SIC:** 5065—Electronic Parts &
Equipment Nec.

★ 86759 ★ Radio Shack
2405 Rice Blvd.
Houston, TX 77005
(713)524-2512
Company Type: Division. **Ultimate Parent:**
Tandy Corp. **SIC:** 5065—Electronic Parts &
Equipment Nec.

★ 86760 ★ Radio Shack
17478 Northwest Fwy.
Houston, TX 77040
(713)937-1580
Company Type: Division. **Ultimate Parent:**
Tandy Corp. **SIC:** 3699—Electrical
Equipment & Supplies Nec.

★ 86761 ★ Radio Shack
506 NW Mall
Houston, TX 77092
(713)686-9264
Company Type: Division. **Ultimate Parent:**
Tandy Corp. **SIC:** 5065—Electronic Parts &
Equipment Nec.

★ 86762 ★   Radio Shack
1022 N. Shepherd Dr.
Houston, TX 77008
(713)861-3795
Company Type: Division. Ultimate Parent:
Tandy Corp. SIC: 5065—Electronic Parts &
Equipment Nec.

★ 86763 ★   Radio Shack
325 Northline Mall
Houston, TX 77022
(713)697-7914
Company Type: Division. Ultimate Parent:
Tandy Corp. SIC: 5046—Commercial
Equipment Nec.

★ 86764 ★   Radio Shack
5458 N. Fwy.
Houston, TX 77056
(713)695-0211
Company Type: Division. Ultimate Parent:
Tandy Corp. SIC: 5065—Electronic Parts &
Equipment Nec.

★ 86765 ★   Radio Shack
10938 N. Fwy.
Houston, TX 77037
(713)448-4908
Company Type: Division. Ultimate Parent:
Tandy Corp. SIC: 3699—Electrical
Equipment & Supplies Nec.

★ 86766 ★   Radio Shack
8319 Mesa Dr.
Houston, TX 77028
(713)631-6494
Company Type: Division. Ultimate Parent:
Tandy Corp. SIC: 5065—Electronic Parts &
Equipment Nec.

★ 86767 ★   Radio Shack
Meyerland
Houston, TX 77096
(713)664-5645
Company Type: Division. Ultimate Parent:
Tandy Corp. SIC: 5065—Electronic Parts &
Equipment Nec.

★ 86768 ★   Radio Shack
625 Memorial City
Houston, TX 77024
(713)464-6165
Company Type: Division. Ultimate Parent:
Tandy Corp. SIC: 5046—Commercial
Equipment Nec.

★ 86769 ★   Radio Shack
14356 Memorial Dr.
Houston, TX 77079
Company Type: Division. Ultimate Parent:
Tandy Corp. SIC: 3699—Electrical
Equipment & Supplies Nec.

★ 86770 ★   Radio Shack
8211 Long Point Rd.
Houston, TX 77055
(713)932-0233
Company Type: Division. Ultimate Parent:
Tandy Corp. SIC: 5065—Electronic Parts &
Equipment Nec.

★ 86771 ★   Radio Shack
1105 Main St.
Houston, TX 77002
(713)759-0826
Company Type: Division. Ultimate Parent:
Tandy Corp. SIC: 5065—Electronic Parts &
Equipment Nec.

★ 86772 ★   Radio Shack
9417 Jensen Dr.
Houston, TX 77093
(713)694-4266
Company Type: Division. Ultimate Parent:
Tandy Corp. SIC: 5065—Electronic Parts &
Equipment Nec.

★ 86773 ★   Radio Shack
9427 Kempwood Dr.
Houston, TX 77080
(713)462-0190
Company Type: Division. Ultimate Parent:
Tandy Corp. SIC: 5731—Radio, Television
& Electronics Stores.

★ 86774 ★   Radio Shack
223 Gulfgate Mall
Houston, TX 77087
(713)649-5090
Company Type: Division. Ultimate Parent:
Tandy Corp. SIC: 5065—Electronic Parts &
Equipment Nec.

★ 86775 ★   Radio Shack
2900 Hillcroft St.
Houston, TX 77057
(713)465-3013
Company Type: Division. Ultimate Parent:
Tandy Corp. SIC: 5731—Radio, Television
& Electronics Stores.

★ 86776 ★   Radio Shack
2551 Gessner Dr.
Houston, TX 77080
(713)462-2459
Company Type: Division. Ultimate Parent:
Tandy Corp. SIC: 3699—Electrical
Equipment & Supplies Nec.

★ 86777 ★   Radio Shack
8456 Gulf Fwy.
Houston, TX 77017
(713)643-4731
Company Type: Division. Ultimate Parent:
Tandy Corp. SIC: 5065—Electronic Parts &
Equipment Nec.

★ 86778 ★   Radio Shack
11163 Fondren Rd.
Houston, TX 77096
(713)774-7257
Company Type: Division. Ultimate Parent:
Tandy Corp. SIC: 5046—Commercial
Equipment Nec.

★ 86779 ★   Radio Shack
3425 Galleria Mall
Houston, TX 77056
(713)626-7352
Company Type: Division. Ultimate Parent:
Tandy Corp. SIC: 5046—Commercial
Equipment Nec.

★ 86780 ★   Radio Shack
3040 Fm 1960 Rd.
Houston, TX 77073
(713)443-3041
Company Type: Division. Ultimate Parent:
Tandy Corp. SIC: 3699—Electrical
Equipment & Supplies Nec.

★ 86781 ★   Radio Shack
10880 Fm 1960 Rd. W
Houston, TX 77070
(713)469-6202
Company Type: Division. Ultimate Parent:
Tandy Corp. SIC: 3699—Electrical
Equipment & Supplies Nec.

★ 86782 ★   Radio Shack
11717 Eastex Fwy.
Houston, TX 77039
(713)442-4215
Company Type: Division. Ultimate Parent:
Tandy Corp. SIC: 5065—Electronic Parts &
Equipment Nec.

★ 86783 ★   Radio Shack
152 Fm 1960 Rd.
Houston, TX 77073
(713)443-1026
Company Type: Division. Ultimate Parent:
Tandy Corp. SIC: 5065—Electronic Parts &
Equipment Nec.

★ 86784 ★   Radio Shack
11107 Bellaire Blvd.
Houston, TX 77072
(713)495-7619
Company Type: Division. Ultimate Parent:
Tandy Corp. SIC: 3699—Electrical
Equipment & Supplies Nec.

★ 86785 ★   Radio Shack
Cypress Station Shopping
Houston, TX 77017
(713)444-7006
Company Type: Division. Ultimate Parent:
Tandy Corp. SIC: 5731—Radio, Television
& Electronics Stores.

★ 86786 ★   Radio Shack
510 Almeda Mall
Houston, TX 77075
(713)943-1780
Company Type: Division. Ultimate Parent:
Tandy Corp. SIC: 5065—Electronic Parts &
Equipment Nec.

★ 86787 ★   Radio Shack
4741 Hawn 6
Houston, TX 77091
(713)463-6865
Company Type: Division. Ultimate Parent:
Tandy Corp. SIC: 3699—Electrical
Equipment & Supplies Nec.

★ 86788 ★   Radio Shack
1018 Memorl Cnty Shopping Cent
Houston, TX 77024
(713)464-9120
Company Type: Division. Ultimate Parent:
Tandy Corp. SIC: 5065—Electronic Parts &
Equipment Nec.

★ 86789 ★   Radio Shack
1002 Federal Rd.
Houston, TX 77015
(713)453-2022
Company Type: Division. Ultimate Parent:
Tandy Corp. SIC: 3699—Electrical
Equipment & Supplies Nec.

★ 86790 ★   Radio Shack
6815 Southwest Fwy.
Houston, TX 77074
Company Type: Division. Ultimate Parent:
Tandy Corp. SIC: 5046—Commercial
Equipment Nec.

★ 86791 ★   Radio Shack
10543 Gulf Fwy.
Houston, TX 77034
(713)943-9310
Company Type: Division. Ultimate Parent:
Tandy Corp. SIC: 5046—Commercial
Equipment Nec.

★ 86792 ★   Ralph Wilson Plastics
Co.
552 Garden Oaks Blvd.
Houston, TX 77018
(713)699-4043
Officer: Gary Allison, Manager. Ultimate
Parent: Premark International. SIC: 3083—
Laminated Plastics Plate & Sheet; 3089—
Plastics Products Nec.

★ 86793 ★   Reliance Insurance
Co.
2500 Wilcrest Dr.
Houston, TX 77042
(713)780-2500
Ultimate Parent: Reliance Group Holdings.
SIC: 6411—Insurance Agents, Brokers &
Service.

★ 86794 ★   Reynolds Metals Co.
10000 N. Loop E.
Houston, TX 77029
Ultimate Parent: Reynolds Metals Co. SIC:
3411—Metal Cans.

★ 86795 ★   Reynolds Metals Co.
10, 000 North Loop East
Houston, TX 77029
Ultimate Parent: Reynolds Metals Co. SIC:
3411—Metal Cans.

★ 86796 ★   Rhone-Poulenc Basic
Chemicals Co.
8615 Manchester Blvd.
Houston, TX 77012
Ultimate Parent: Rhone-Poulenc Rorer.
SIC: 2819—Industrial Inorganic Chemicals
Nec.

★ 86797 ★   Richland
Development Corp.
Pennzoil Pl.
PO Box 2967
Houston, TX 77252-2967
Officer: James L. Pate, President. Ultimate
Parent: Pennzoil.

★ 86798 ★   Ring Around
Products Inc.
2001 Sabine St.
Houston, TX 77007
(713)869-1407
Ultimate Parent: Occidental Petroleum
Corp. SIC: 5191—Farm Supplies.

★ 86799 ★   River Oaks Trust Co.
2001 Kirby
PO Box 4886
Houston, TX 77210-4886
(713)526-2211 Fax: (713)831-5750
Company Type: Subsidiary. Location
Type: Branch office. Ultimate Parent:
Compass Bancshares. SIC: 6021—National
Commercial Banks.

★ 86800 ★   Ryder Truck Rental
707 Wayside Dr.
Houston, TX 77011
(713)921-5393
Ultimate Parent: Ryder System. SIC:
7359—Equipment Rental & Leasing Nec.

★ 86801 ★   Ryder Truck Rental
6250 Westward St.
Houston, TX 77081
(713)778-0383
Ultimate Parent: Ryder System. SIC:
7359—Equipment Rental & Leasing Nec.

★ 86802 ★   Ryder Truck Rental
6834 W. Little York Rd.
Houston, TX 77040
(713)896-1884
Ultimate Parent: Ryder System. SIC:
7359—Equipment Rental & Leasing Nec;
7513—Truck Rental & Leasing Without
Drivers.

★ 86803 ★   Ryder Truck Rental
3141 W. Loop S
Houston, TX 77027
(713)623-4115
Ultimate Parent: Ryder System. SIC:
7359—Equipment Rental & Leasing Nec.

★ 86804 ★   Ryder Truck Rental
1850 W. 43rd St.
Houston, TX 77018
(713)688-9771
Ultimate Parent: Ryder System. SIC:
7359—Equipment Rental & Leasing Nec.

★ 86805 ★   Ryder Truck Rental
1138 W. Belt Dr. N
Houston, TX 77043
(713)464-0579
Ultimate Parent: Ryder System. SIC:
7359—Equipment Rental & Leasing Nec.

★ 86806 ★   Ryder Truck Rental
14120 Stuebner Airline Rd.
Houston, TX 77069
(713)537-7899
Ultimate Parent: Ryder System. SIC:
7359—Equipment Rental & Leasing Nec.

★ 86807 ★   Ryder Truck Rental
9814 Veterans Memorial Dr.
Houston, TX 77038
(713)448-3476
Ultimate Parent: Ryder System.

★ 86808 ★   Ryder Truck Rental
10890 Sabo Rd.
Houston, TX 77089
(713)944-7088
Ultimate Parent: Ryder System.

★ 86809 ★   Ryder Truck Rental
7302 Senate St.
Houston, TX 77040
(713)896-1387
Ultimate Parent: Ryder System. SIC:
7359—Equipment Rental & Leasing Nec.

★ 86810 ★   Ryder Truck Rental
3555 S. Loop W
Houston, TX 77025
(713)661-6674
Ultimate Parent: Ryder System. SIC:
7359—Equipment Rental & Leasing Nec.

★ 86811 ★   Ryder Truck Rental
11526 S. Post Oak Rd.
Houston, TX 77035
(713)721-8183
Ultimate Parent: Ryder System. SIC:
7359—Equipment Rental & Leasing Nec.

★ 86812 ★   Ryder Truck Rental
4816 N. Shepherd Dr.
Houston, TX 77018
(713)692-4799
Ultimate Parent: Ryder System. SIC:
7359—Equipment Rental & Leasing Nec.

★ 86813 ★   Ryder Truck Rental
17050 North Fwy.
Houston, TX 77090
(713)452-1765
Ultimate Parent: Ryder System. SIC:
7359—Equipment Rental & Leasing Nec.

★ 86814 ★   Ryder Truck Rental
11200 Hempstead Rd.
Houston, TX 77092
(713)956-4074
Ultimate Parent: Ryder System.

★ 86815 ★   Ryder Truck Rental
9223 Long Point Rd.
Houston, TX 77055
(713)827-0503
Ultimate Parent: Ryder System. SIC:
7359—Equipment Rental & Leasing Nec.

★ 86816 ★ Ryder Truck Rental
8530 Gulf Fwy.
Houston, TX 77017
(713)472-0703
Ultimate Parent: Ryder System. **SIC:** 7359—Equipment Rental & Leasing Nec.

★ 86817 ★ Ryder Truck Rental
5200 Gulfton St.
Houston, TX 77081
(713)661-7794
Ultimate Parent: Ryder System. **SIC:** 7359—Equipment Rental & Leasing Nec.

★ 86818 ★ Ryder Truck Rental
7814 Fulton St.
Houston, TX 77022
(713)691-5701
Ultimate Parent: Ryder System. **SIC:** 7359—Equipment Rental & Leasing Nec.

★ 86819 ★ Ryder Truck Rental
1111 Goodnight Trl
Houston, TX 77060
(713)821-1501
Ultimate Parent: Ryder System.

★ 86820 ★ Ryder Truck Rental
8110 East Fwy.
Houston, TX 77029
(713)672-2300
Ultimate Parent: Ryder System.

★ 86821 ★ Ryder Truck Rental
12903 East Fwy.
Houston, TX 77015
(713)450-3373
Ultimate Parent: Ryder System.

★ 86822 ★ Ryder Truck Rental
6901 Ashcroft Dr.
Houston, TX 77081
(713)772-2180
Ultimate Parent: Ryder System.

★ 86823 ★ Ryder Truck Rental
9110 Blueberry St.
Houston, TX 77049
(713)452-1133
Ultimate Parent: Ryder System. **SIC:** 7359—Equipment Rental & Leasing Nec.

★ 86824 ★ Ryder Truck Rental
10600 Almeda Genoa Rd.
Houston, TX 77034
(713)472-6132
Ultimate Parent: Ryder System. **SIC:** 7359—Equipment Rental & Leasing Nec.

★ 86825 ★ Ryder Truck Rental
7789 Katy Fwy.
Houston, TX 77024
(713)670-2885
Ultimate Parent: Ryder System. **SIC:** 7513—Truck Rental & Leasing Without Drivers.

★ 86826 ★ Ryder Truck Rental
90009 N. Loop E
Houston, TX 77008
(713)670-2735
Ultimate Parent: Ryder System. **SIC:** 7359—Equipment Rental & Leasing Nec.

★ 86827 ★ Ryder Truck Rental
10730 Jones Rd.
Houston, TX 77065
(713)890-9619
Ultimate Parent: Ryder System. **SIC:** 7359—Equipment Rental & Leasing Nec.

★ 86828 ★ Ryder Truck Rental
11527 Jones Rd.
Houston, TX 77070
(713)469-6998
Ultimate Parent: Ryder System. **SIC:** 7513—Truck Rental & Leasing Without Drivers.

★ 86829 ★ Ryder Truck Rental
6211 Bellaire Blvd.
Houston, TX 77081
(713)771-4262
Ultimate Parent: Ryder System. **SIC:** 7359—Equipment Rental & Leasing Nec; 7359—Equipment Rental & Leasing Nec.

★ 86830 ★ Ryder Truck Rental
17007 Fm M M M M Rd. 1960
Houston, TX 77073
(713)591-6552
Ultimate Parent: Ryder System. **SIC:** 7359—Equipment Rental & Leasing Nec.

★ 86831 ★ Ryder Truck Rental
3684 Eastex Fwy.
Houston, TX 77026
(713)671-2026
Ultimate Parent: Ryder System. **SIC:** 7359—Equipment Rental & Leasing Nec.

★ 86832 ★ Ryder Truck Rental
14900 Chrisman Rd.
Houston, TX 77039
(713)449-3955
Ultimate Parent: Ryder System. **SIC:** 7359—Equipment Rental & Leasing Nec.

★ 86833 ★ Ryder Truck Rental
8950 Westpark Dr.
Houston, TX 77063
(713)780-2762
Ultimate Parent: Ryder System. **SIC:** 7359—Equipment Rental & Leasing Nec.

★ 86834 ★ Ryder Truck Rental
6615 S. Gessner Dr.
Houston, TX 77036
(713)995-1052
Ultimate Parent: Ryder System. **SIC:** 7359—Equipment Rental & Leasing Nec.

★ 86835 ★ Ryder Truck Rental
6120 S. Loop E
Houston, TX 77087
(713)644-6260
Ultimate Parent: Ryder System. **SIC:** 7359—Equipment Rental & Leasing Nec.

★ 86836 ★ Ryder Truck Rental
9710 Plainfield St.
Houston, TX 77036
(713)995-8053
Ultimate Parent: Ryder System. **SIC:** 7359—Equipment Rental & Leasing Nec.

★ 86837 ★ Ryder Truck Rental
2850 Rogerdale Rd.
Houston, TX 77042
(713)784-3893
Ultimate Parent: Ryder System. **SIC:** 7359—Equipment Rental & Leasing Nec.

★ 86838 ★ Ryder Truck Rental
9115 North Fwy.
Houston, TX 77037
(713)447-0996
Ultimate Parent: Ryder System. **SIC:** 7513—Truck Rental & Leasing Without Drivers.

★ 86839 ★ Ryder Truck Rental
11900 Old Katy Rd.
Houston, TX 77079
(713)493-0981
Ultimate Parent: Ryder System. **SIC:** 7359—Equipment Rental & Leasing Nec.

★ 86840 ★ Ryder Truck Rental
9330 Gulf Fwy.
Houston, TX 77017
(713)472-7371
Ultimate Parent: Ryder System. **SIC:** 7513—Truck Rental & Leasing Without Drivers.

★ 86841 ★ Ryder Truck Rental
14253 Lee Rd.
Houston, TX 77032
(713)442-0356
Ultimate Parent: Ryder System. **SIC:** 7359—Equipment Rental & Leasing Nec.

★ 86842 ★ Ryder Truck Rental
2610 Broadway St.
Houston, TX 77012
(713)643-7778
Ultimate Parent: Ryder System. **SIC:** 7359—Equipment Rental & Leasing Nec.

★ 86843 ★ Ryder Truck Rental
14700 El Cam
Houston, TX 77054
(713)480-4765
Ultimate Parent: Ryder System. **SIC:** 7513—Truck Rental & Leasing Without Drivers.

★ 86844 ★ Ryder Truck Rental
2129 Aldine Bender Rd.
Houston, TX 77032
(713)449-6012
Ultimate Parent: Ryder System. **SIC:** 7359—Equipment Rental & Leasing Nec.

★ 86845 ★ Ryder Truck Rental
1860 Blalock Rd.
Houston, TX 77080
(713)984-1316
Ultimate Parent: Ryder System. **SIC:** 7513—Truck Rental & Leasing Without Drivers.

★ 86846 ★ Ryder Truck Rental
11820 Airline Dr.
Houston, TX 77037
(713)445-1070
Ultimate Parent: Ryder System. **SIC:** 7359—Equipment Rental & Leasing Nec.

★ 86847 ★ Ryder Truck Rental
914 N. Shepherd Dr.
Houston, TX 77008
(713)671-3405
Ultimate Parent: Ryder System. **SIC:** 7389—Business Services Nec.

★ 86848 ★ Ryder Truck Rental
621 Fm 1960 Rd. E
Houston, TX 77073
(713)670-2840
Ultimate Parent: Ryder System. **SIC:** 7389—Business Services Nec.

★ 86849 ★ Ryder Truck Rental
9420 Main St.
Houston, TX 77025
(713)670-2733
Ultimate Parent: Ryder System. **SIC:** 7389—Business Services Nec.

★ 86850 ★ Ryder Truck Rental
11100 Beechnut St.
Houston, TX 77072
(713)670-2848
Ultimate Parent: Ryder System. **SIC:** 7389—Business Services Nec.

★ 86851 ★ Ryder Truck Rental
7535 Wynlea St.
Houston, TX 77061
(713)645-4991
Ultimate Parent: Ryder System. **SIC:** 7359—Equipment Rental & Leasing Nec.

★ 86852 ★ Ryder Truck Rental
400 N. Sam Houston Pky. E. 400
Houston, TX 77060
(713)445-1070
Ultimate Parent: Ryder System. **SIC:** 7513—Truck Rental & Leasing Without Drivers.

★ 86853 ★ Ryder Truck Rental
96529 PO Box
Houston, TX 77213
(713)688-0241
Ultimate Parent: Ryder System. **SIC:** 7359—Equipment Rental & Leasing Nec.

★ 86854 ★ Salomon Brothers Inc.
2727 Allen Pky.
Houston, TX 77019
(713)527-8815
Ultimate Parent: Salomon, Inc. **SIC:** 6211—Security Brokers & Dealers.

★ 86855 ★ Sam's Wholesale Club
17211 North Fwy.
Houston, TX 77090
(713)586-8930
Ultimate Parent: Wal-Mart Stores, Inc.

★ 86856 ★ Sam's Wholesale Club
13600 East Fwy.
Houston, TX 77015
(713)450-1900
Ultimate Parent: Wal-Mart Stores, Inc.

★ 86857 ★ Sam's Wholesale Club
12205 West Rd.
Houston, TX 77065
(713)955-2071
Ultimate Parent: Wal-Mart Stores, Inc.

★ 86858 ★ Savings of America, A Division of Home Savings of America FSB
12802 Memorial Dr.
Houston, TX 77024-4899
(713)932-1133
Company Type: Division. **Location Type:** Branch office. **Ultimate Parent:** H. F. Ahmanson. **SIC:** 6021—National Commercial Banks.

★ 86859 ★ Savings of America, A Division of Home Savings of America FSB
1934 W. Gray
Houston, TX 77019
(713)529-4491
Company Type: Division. **Location Type:** Branch office. **Ultimate Parent:** H. F. Ahmanson. **SIC:** 6021—National Commercial Banks.

★ 86860 ★ Savings of America, A Division of Home Savings of America FSB
5884 Westheimer Rd.
Houston, TX 77057-5641
(713)974-6346
Company Type: Division. **Location Type:** Branch office. **Ultimate Parent:** H. F. Ahmanson. **SIC:** 6021—National Commercial Banks.

★ 86861 ★ Savings of America, FSB
929 E. Little York Rd.
Houston, TX 77076-1630
(713)692-5133
Company Type: Division. **Location Type:** Branch office. **Ultimate Parent:** H. F. Ahmanson. **SIC:** 6021—National Commercial Banks.

★ 86862 ★ Savings of America, FSB
3003 S. Loop W.
Houston, TX 77054-1301
(713)663-5151
Company Type: Division. **Location Type:** Branch office. **Ultimate Parent:** H. F. Ahmanson. **SIC:** 6021—National Commercial Banks.

★ 86863 ★ Savings of America, FSB
5401 S. Braeswood Blvd.
Houston, TX 77096-4001
(713)729-6401
Company Type: Division. **Location Type:** Branch office. **Ultimate Parent:** H. F. Ahmanson. **SIC:** 6021—National Commercial Banks.

★ 86864 ★ Savings of America, FSB
991 NASA Rd. 1
Houston, TX 77058-3039
(713)488-4673
Company Type: Division. **Location Type:** Branch office. **Ultimate Parent:** H. F. Ahmanson. **SIC:** 6021—National Commercial Banks.

★ 86865 ★ Savings of America, FSB
9819-V Bissonnet
Houston, TX 77036-9912
(713)981-6126
Company Type: Division. **Location Type:** Branch office. **Ultimate Parent:** H. F. Ahmanson. **SIC:** 6021—National Commercial Banks.

★ 86866 ★ Savings of America, FSB
3000 Woodridge Dr.
Houston, TX 77087-2516
(713)644-2791
Company Type: Division. **Location Type:** Branch office. **Ultimate Parent:** H. F. Ahmanson. **SIC:** 6021—National Commercial Banks.

★ 86867 ★ Savings of America, FSB
14565 Memorial Dr.
Houston, TX 77079-5407
(713)493-5901
Company Type: Division. **Location Type:** Branch office. **Ultimate Parent:** H. F. Ahmanson. **SIC:** 6021—National Commercial Banks.

★ 86868 ★ Savings of America, FSB
8550 Broadway Blvd.
Houston, TX 77061-2226
(713)644-8492
Company Type: Division. **Location Type:** Branch office. **Ultimate Parent:** H. F. Ahmanson. **SIC:** 6021—National Commercial Banks.

★ 86869 ★ **Savings of America, FSB**
4081 FM 1960 W
Houston, TX 77068-3431
(713)444-7767
Company Type: Division. **Location Type:**
Branch office. **Ultimate Parent:** H. F.
Ahmanson. **SIC:** 6021—National
Commercial Banks.

★ 86870 ★ **Savings of America, FSB**
10850 Bellaire Blvd.
Houston, TX 77072-2736
(713)498-2233
Company Type: Division. **Location Type:**
Branch office. **Ultimate Parent:** H. F.
Ahmanson. **SIC:** 6021—National
Commercial Banks.

★ 86871 ★ **Schott's Bakery Inc.**
3000 Washington Ave.
Houston, TX 77007-6029
(713)869-5701
Company Type: Subsidiary. **Officer:** Dan
Harrison, President. **Ultimate Parent:**
Flowers Industries. **SIC:** 2051—Bread, Cake
& Related Products; 5149—Groceries &
Related Products Nec. **Employee Count:**
140. **Sales:** 40 M.

★ 86872 ★ **Scurlock Permian Corp.**
333 Clay St., Ste. 2900
Houston, TX 77042
(713)739-4100 **Fax:** (713)787-2503
Company Type: Subsidiary. **Officer:** D.
Duane Gilliam, President. **Ultimate Parent:**
Ashland Oil. **SIC:** 1311—Crude Petroleum &
Natural Gas; 5172—Petroleum Products
Nec.

★ 86873 ★ **Sekin Transport Internation**
16058 Vickery Dr.
Houston, TX 77032
(713)442-8470
Ultimate Parent: Harsco. **SIC:** 4789—
Transportation Services Nec.

★ 86874 ★ **Shell Co.**
14531 Westheimer Rd.
Houston, TX 77077
(713)497-4360
Ultimate Parent: Shell Oil Co.

★ 86875 ★ **Shell Co.**
5401 Telephone Rd.
Houston, TX 77087
(713)649-5470
Ultimate Parent: Shell Oil Co. **SIC:** 7542—
Car Washes.

★ 86876 ★ **Shell Co.**
2400 W. Looscan Ln.
Houston, TX 77019
(713)621-0330
Ultimate Parent: Shell Oil Co. **SIC:** 5172—
Petroleum Products Nec.

★ 86877 ★ **Shell Co.**
1202 N. Belt
Houston, TX 77060
(713)449-0373
Ultimate Parent: Shell Oil Co. **SIC:** 5541—
Gasoline Service Stations.

★ 86878 ★ **Shell Co.**
11500 Southwest Fwy.
Houston, TX 77031
(713)495-8124
Ultimate Parent: Shell Oil Co. **SIC:** 5541—
Gasoline Service Stations.

★ 86879 ★ **Shell Co.**
14304 Gulf Fwy.
Houston, TX 77034
(713)481-0791
Ultimate Parent: Shell Oil Co. **SIC:** 5541—
Gasoline Service Stations.

★ 86880 ★ **Shell Co.**
3333 Hwy. 6 S
Houston, TX 77082
(713)493-7171
Ultimate Parent: Shell Oil Co. **SIC:** 3861—
Photographic Equipment & Supplies.

★ 86881 ★ **Shell Oil Co.**
200 Dairy Ashford Village
Houston, TX 77077
(713)531-0129
Ultimate Parent: Shell Oil Co.

★ 86882 ★ **Shell Oil Co.**
2463 PO Box
Houston, TX 77252
(713)241-6161
Ultimate Parent: Shell Oil Co.

★ 86883 ★ **Shell Oil Co.**
3100 Fm 1960 Rd. W
Houston, TX 77068
(713)443-0002
Ultimate Parent: Shell Oil Co. **SIC:** 1311—
Crude Petroleum & Natural Gas.

★ 86884 ★ **Shell Oil Co.**
12777 E. Fairway
Houston, TX 77087
(713)451-6011
Ultimate Parent: Shell Oil Co. **SIC:** 5541—
Gasoline Service Stations.

★ 86885 ★ **Shell Oil Co.**
1 Shell Plz.
Houston, TX 77002
(713)241-6161 **Fax:** (713)241-6781
Officer: Philip J. Carroll, CEO. **Ultimate
Parent:** Shell Oil Co. **Employee Count:**
133000. **Sales:** 83364 M.

★ 86886 ★ **Shell Oil Co.**
900 Louisiana St.
Houston, TX 77002
(713)241-6161
Company Type: Headquarters. **Officer:**
Philip J. Carroll. **Employee Count:** 22212.
Sales: 20853.0 M. **Fortune 500:** Largest
U.S. Industrial Corporations: Ranking 17.

★ 86887 ★ **Shell Oil Legal Library**
2463 PO Box
Houston, TX 77252
(713)241-3514
Ultimate Parent: Shell Oil Co. **SIC:** 8231—
Libraries.

★ 86888 ★ **Shell Pipe Line Corp.**
2 Shell Plz.
Houston, TX 77002
(713)241-6161
Ultimate Parent: Shell Oil Co. **SIC:** 5172—
Petroleum Products Nec.

★ 86889 ★ **Shell Pipeline Corp.**
12730 Zavalla St.
Houston, TX 77085
(713)729-8730
Ultimate Parent: Shell Oil Co.

★ 86890 ★ **Shell Pipeline Corp.**
12730 Zavalla St.
Houston, TX 77085
(713)729-8730
Ultimate Parent: Shell Oil Co.

★ 86891 ★ **Shell Pipeline Corp.**
2 Shell Plz.
Houston, TX 77002
(713)241-6161
Ultimate Parent: Shell Oil Co. **SIC:** 5172—
Petroleum Products Nec.

★ 86892 ★ **Shell Self Serve**
12546 E. Fairway
Houston, TX 77087
(713)453-6147
Ultimate Parent: Shell Oil Co. **SIC:** 5541—
Gasoline Service Stations.

★ 86893 ★ **Sigma Coatings Inc.**
8979 Market St.
Houston, TX 77029
(713)672-1175
Ultimate Parent: Fina. **SIC:** 5198—Paints,
Varnishes & Supplies.

★ 86894 ★ **Sigma Coatings Inc.**
1701 Crosspoint Ave.
Houston, TX 77054
(713)799-9259
Ultimate Parent: Fina. **SIC:** 5198—Paints,
Varnishes & Supplies.

★ 86895 ★ **Signature Travel Inc.**
8 E. Greenway Plz.
Houston, TX 77046
(713)850-1455
Ultimate Parent: Washington Mutual
Savings Bank. **SIC:** 4724—Travel Agencies.

★ 86896 ★ **Smith Barney Harris Upham & Co.**
5065 Westheimer Rd.
Houston, TX 77056-5612
(713)960-9669
Officer: Frank Maggio. **Ultimate Parent:**
Automatic Data Processing, Inc. **SIC:**

6211—Security Brokers & Dealers; 6221—
Commodity Contracts Brokers & Dealers.

★ 86897 ★ **Solar Turbines Inc.**
13105 Northwest Fwy.
Houston, TX 77040
(713)895-2305
Ultimate Parent: Carter-Wallace. **SIC:**
5084—Industrial Machinery & Equipment.

★ 86898 ★ **Solar Turbines Inc.**
7600 W. Tidwell Rd.
Houston, TX 77040
(713)895-2300
Ultimate Parent: Carter-Wallace. **SIC:**
3511—Turbines & Turbine Generator Sets.

★ 86899 ★ **Sonoco Semi-Bulk Packaging**
9280 Baythorne Dr.
Houston, TX 77041
(713)462-0073
Officer: Tom Meyer, Manager. **Ultimate
Parent:** Sonoco Products. **SIC:** 3412—
Metal Barrels, Drums & Pails.

★ 86900 ★ **Sonoco Semi-Bulk Packaging**
8610 Wellisville Rd.
Houston, TX 77029
(713)675-8241
Officer: Richard Crosby, Manager. **Ultimate
Parent:** Sonoco Products. **SIC:** 2655—Fiber
Cans, Drums & Similar Products; 3412—
Metal Barrels, Drums & Pails.

★ 86901 ★ **South Padre Land Co.**
2727 Allen Pky.
Houston, TX 77019
(713)522-1111
Officer: Robert E. Conklin, President &
CEO. **Ultimate Parent:** American General
Corp. **SIC:** 6531—Real Estate Agents &
Managers.

★ 86902 ★ **Southland Corp.**
6412 N. Main St.
Houston, TX 77009
(713)869-1372
Ultimate Parent: Southland Corp. **SIC:**
2097—Manufactured Ice.

★ 86903 ★ **Southland Royalty Co. Inc.**
5251 Westheimer Rd.
Houston, TX 77056
(713)629-8390
Ultimate Parent: Burlington Resources.
SIC: 1311—Crude Petroleum & Natural
Gas.

★ 86904 ★ **Southwest Airlines Co.**
Houston
Houston, TX 77205
(713)443-6100
Ultimate Parent: Southwest Airlines. **SIC:**
4512—Air Transportation—Scheduled.

★ 86905 ★ **Southwestern Bell Printing Co.**
8100 Kempwood Dr.
Houston, TX 77055
(713)895-...
Ultimate Parent: Southwestern Bell. **SIC:**
2752—Commercial Printing—Lithographic.

★ 86906 ★ **Sparkletts Water Sys. Aqua Vend**
4540 W. 34th St. Ste. F
Houston, TX 77092
Ultimate Parent: McKesson. **SIC:** 7389—
Business Services Nec.

★ 86907 ★ **Sparkletts Water Systems Aqua Vend**
4540 W. 34th St. Ste. F
Houston, TX 77092
Ultimate Parent: McKesson. **SIC:** 7389—
Business Services Nec.

★ 86908 ★ **Sparkletts Water Systems Aquavend**
4540 W. 34th St. Ste. F
Houston, TX 77092
Ultimate Parent: McKesson. **SIC:** 7389—
Business Services Nec.

★ 86909 ★ **Specialized Transportation Inc.**
4807 Wakeforest St.
Houston, TX 77005
(713)666-0789
Ultimate Parent: Ryder System. **SIC:**
4212—Local Trucking Without Storage.

★ 86910 ★ **Specialty Metal Products**
6915 Penny Ct.
Houston, TX 77069-1109
(713)893-3863
Officer: Ronald S. Palma. **Ultimate Parent:**
Ametek Inc. **SIC:** 5051—Metals Service
Centers & Offices.

★ 86911 ★ **Standard Register Houston Div.**
1201 Bonner St.
Houston, TX 77007
(713)864-2611
Officer: Charles Parker, Manager. **Ultimate
Parent:** Standard Register. **SIC:** 2752—
Commercial Printing—Lithographic; 2759—
Commercial Printing Nec; 2761—Manifold
Business Forms.

★ 86912 ★ **Stewart & Stevenson**
2707 N. Loop W.
Houston, TX 77008
(713)868-7700
Company Type: Headquarters. **Officer:**
Bob H. O'Neal. **Employee Count:** 2850.
Sales: 813 M. **Fortune 500:** Largest U.S.
Industrial Corporations: Ranking 406.

★ 86913 ★ **Stewart & Stevenson Inc.**
4516 Harrisburg St.
Houston, TX 77011
(713)923-2161
Officer: Fred Mace, Manager. **Ultimate
Parent:** Stewart & Stevenson. **SIC:** 3519—
Internal Combustion Engines Nec; 3533—
Oil & Gas Field Machinery; 3621—Motors &
Generators.

★ 86914 ★ **Stewart & Stevenson Services Inc.**
2707 N. Loop
Houston, TX 77008
(713)868-7700 **Fax:** (713)868-7692
Officer: C. Jim Steward III, CEO. **Ultimate
Parent:** Stewart & Stevenson. **Employee
Count:** 2850. **Sales:** 982 M.

★ 86915 ★ **Stewart & Stevenson SVC**
8631 East Fwy.
Houston, TX 77029
(713)671-6220
Officer: Aart Suter, Manager. **Ultimate
Parent:** Stewart & Stevenson. **SIC:** 3511—
Turbines & Turbine Generator Sets.

★ 86916 ★ **Stewart & Stevenson SVC**
2707 North Loop W. Fl. 8
Houston, TX 77008
(713)868-7700
Officer: C. Jim Stewart II, Chairman.
Ultimate Parent: Stewart & Stevenson.
SIC: 3511—Turbines & Turbine Generator
Sets; 3519—Internal Combustion Engines
Nec; 3533—Oil & Gas Field Machinery.

★ 86917 ★ **Stewart & Stevenson SVC**
16415 Jacintoport Blvd.
Houston, TX 77015
(713)452-3610
Officer: Rick Stewart, President. **Ultimate
Parent:** Stewart & Stevenson. **SIC:** 3511—
Turbines & Turbine Generator Sets.

★ 86918 ★ **Stop & Shop**
510 Charlie Voix St.
Houston, TX 77015
(713)451-0809
Ultimate Parent: Stop & Shop. **SIC:** 5411—
Grocery Stores.

★ 86919 ★ **Subsea Venture Inc.**
5819 Almeda Genoa Rd.
Houston, TX 77048
(713)991-5621
Officer: Werner Kief, Chairman. **Ultimate
Parent:** FMC. **SIC:** 3533—Oil & Gas Field
Machinery.

★ 86920 ★ **Sun Refining & Marketing Co.**
3730 Fm 1960 Rd. W
Houston, TX 77068
(713)893-7780
Ultimate Parent: Sun. **SIC:** 5199—
Nondurable Goods Nec.

★ 86921 ★ **Sunbeam Appliance Co.**
5156 Richmond Ave.
Houston, TX 77056
(713)626-0190
Ultimate Parent: Sunbeam/Oster. **SIC:** 5722—Household Appliance Stores.

★ 86922 ★ **Swaco Geolograph Operations**
3 Greenway Plz.
Houston, TX 77046
(713)297-3900 **Fax:** (713)297-2563
Company Type: Subsidiary. **Ultimate Parent:** Dresser Industries Inc.

★ 86923 ★ **Sysco**
1390 Enclave Pky.
Houston, TX 77077
(713)584-1390
Company Type: Headquarters. **Officer:** John F. Woodhouse. **Employee Count:** 24200. **Sales:** 10022 M. **Fortune Service 500:** Ranking 7.

★ 86924 ★ **Sysco Corp.**
1390 Enclave Pky.
Houston, TX 77077-2094
(713)584-1390 **Fax:** (713)584-1188
Officer: John W. F. Woodhouse, CEO.
Ultimate Parent: Sysco. **Employee Count:** 24200. **Sales:** 10022 M.

★ 86925 ★ **Sysco Food Services Inc.**
15316 PO Box
Houston, TX 77220
(713)672-8080
Ultimate Parent: Sysco. **SIC:** 5046—Commercial Equipment Nec.

★ 86926 ★ **System One Information Management Inc.**
1301 Fannin St., Ste. 1800
Houston, TX 77002-7011
Company Type: Subsidiary. **Officer:** William S. Diffenderffer, President. **Ultimate Parent:** Continental Airlines. **Employee Count:** 950. **Sales:** 206 M.

★ 86927 ★ **Systems Control Inc.**
550 Westlake Park Blvd.
Houston, TX 77079
(713)558-4066
Ultimate Parent: Snap-on Tools. **SIC:** 7379—Computer Related Services Nec.

★ 86928 ★ **SYTECH Corp.**
7110 Harwin Dr.
Houston, TX 77036
(713)783-9540
Ultimate Parent: Cummins Engine Co. **SIC:** 7372—Prepackaged Software.

★ 86929 ★ **T J Maxx**
10717 Jones Rd.
Houston, TX 77065
(713)955-9876
Ultimate Parent: TJX.

★ 86930 ★ **T J Maxx**
13188 Memorial Dr.
Houston, TX 77079
(713)973-2692
Ultimate Parent: TJX. **SIC:** 5651—Family Clothing Stores.

★ 86931 ★ **T J Maxx No Two Seventy Fiv**
9607 Fondren Rd.
Houston, TX 77096
(713)981-9191
Ultimate Parent: TJX. **SIC:** 5621—Women's Clothing Stores.

★ 86932 ★ **Taco Bell**
1033 Bay Area Blvd.
Houston, TX 77058
(713)488-4760
Ultimate Parent: Pepsico. **SIC:** 5812—Eating Places.

★ 86933 ★ **Taco Bell**
6525 Westheimer Rd.
Houston, TX 77057
(713)780-8101
Ultimate Parent: Pepsico. **SIC:** 5812—Eating Places.

★ 86934 ★ **Taco Bell**
10701 W. Bellfort St.
Houston, TX 77099
(713)495-8681
Ultimate Parent: Pepsico. **SIC:** 5812—Eating Places.

★ 86935 ★ **Taco Bell**
4202 W. Fuqua St.
Houston, TX 77045
(713)433-3923
Ultimate Parent: Pepsico. **SIC:** 5812—Eating Places.

★ 86936 ★ **Taco Bell**
2521 Southmore Blvd.
Houston, TX 77004
(713)475-9187
Ultimate Parent: Pepsico. **SIC:** 5812—Eating Places.

★ 86937 ★ **Taco Bell**
546 Uvalde Rd.
Houston, TX 77015
(713)453-3636
Ultimate Parent: Pepsico. **SIC:** 5812—Eating Places.

★ 86938 ★ **Taco Bell**
10906 Scarsdale Blvd.
Houston, TX 77089
(713)484-8501
Ultimate Parent: Pepsico. **SIC:** 5812—Eating Places.

★ 86939 ★ **Taco Bell**
5802 Renwick Dr.
Houston, TX 77081
(713)668-0281
Ultimate Parent: Pepsico. **SIC:** 5812—Eating Places.

★ 86940 ★ **Taco Bell**
330 S. 69th St.
Houston, TX 77011
(713)926-2179
Ultimate Parent: Pepsico. **SIC:** 5812—Eating Places.

★ 86941 ★ **Taco Bell**
14129 Memorial Dr.
Houston, TX 77079
(713)496-4840
Ultimate Parent: Pepsico. **SIC:** 5812—Eating Places.

★ 86942 ★ **Taco Bell**
7473 N. Shepherd Dr.
Houston, TX 77091
(713)699-3825
Ultimate Parent: Pepsico. **SIC:** 5812—Eating Places.

★ 86943 ★ **Taco Bell**
9600 Main St.
Houston, TX 77025
(713)661-9918
Ultimate Parent: Pepsico. **SIC:** 5812—Eating Places.

★ 86944 ★ **Taco Bell**
2049 Mangum Rd.
Houston, TX 77092
(713)956-5624
Ultimate Parent: Pepsico. **SIC:** 5812—Eating Places.

★ 86945 ★ **Taco Bell**
12303 John F Kennedy Blvd.
Houston, TX 77039
(713)449-2310
Ultimate Parent: Pepsico. **SIC:** 5812—Eating Places.

★ 86946 ★ **Taco Bell**
8825 Knight Rd.
Houston, TX 77054
(713)799-9195
Ultimate Parent: Pepsico. **SIC:** 5812—Eating Places.

★ 86947 ★ **Taco Bell**
6907 Hwy. 6 S
Houston, TX 77083
(713)879-9882
Ultimate Parent: Pepsico. **SIC:** 5812—Eating Places.

★ 86948 ★ **Taco Bell**
4970 Hwy. 6 N
Houston, TX 77084
(713)855-8006
Ultimate Parent: Pepsico.

★ 86949 ★ **Taco Bell**
900 Gessner Rd.
Houston, TX 77024
(713)461-6267
Ultimate Parent: Pepsico. **SIC:** 5812—Eating Places.

★ 86950 ★ **Taco Bell**
132 Greenspoint Mall
Houston, TX 77060
(713)876-3920
Ultimate Parent: Pepsico.

★ 86951 ★ **Taco Bell**
11002 Fuqua St.
Houston, TX 77089
(713)484-1400
Ultimate Parent: Pepsico. **SIC:** 5812—Eating Places.

★ 86952 ★ **Taco Bell**
2022 Gessner Dr.
Houston, TX 77080
(713)468-3793
Ultimate Parent: Pepsico. **SIC:** 5812—Eating Places.

★ 86953 ★ **Taco Bell**
1082 Edgebrook Dr.
Houston, TX 77034
Ultimate Parent: Pepsico. **SIC:** 5812—Eating Places.

★ 86954 ★ **Taco Bell**
8101 Fondren Rd.
Houston, TX 77074
(713)981-8478
Ultimate Parent: Pepsico. **SIC:** 5812—Eating Places.

★ 86955 ★ **Taco Bell**
10 E. Crosstimbers St.
Houston, TX 77022
(713)694-0189
Ultimate Parent: Pepsico.

★ 86956 ★ **Taco Bell**
2960 E. F M1960
Houston, TX 77073
(713)443-1277
Ultimate Parent: Pepsico. **SIC:** 5812—Eating Places.

★ 86957 ★ **Taco Bell**
7540 Bellfort St.
Houston, TX 77061
(713)643-5945
Ultimate Parent: Pepsico. **SIC:** 5812—Eating Places.

★ 86958 ★ **Taco Bell**
11825 Chimney Rock Rd.
Houston, TX 77035
(713)729-5250
Ultimate Parent: Pepsico. **SIC:** 5812—Eating Places.

★ 86959 ★ **Taco Bell**
5600 Bellaire Blvd.
Houston, TX 77081
Ultimate Parent: Pepsico. **SIC:** 5812—Eating Places.

★ 86960 ★ **Taco Bell**
7500 Bellaire Blvd.
Houston, TX 77036
(713)772-9681
Ultimate Parent: Pepsico.

★ 86961 ★ **Taco Bell**
6701 Airline Dr.
Houston, TX 77076
(713)691-3139
Ultimate Parent: Pepsico. **SIC:** 5812—Eating Places.

★ 86962 ★ **Taco Bell**
5800 Antoine Dr.
Houston, TX 77091
(713)680-0840
Ultimate Parent: Pepsico. **SIC:** 5812—Eating Places.

★ 86963 ★ **Tandy Corp. Del**
9647 S. Gessner Dr.
Houston, TX 77071
(713)777-6998
Ultimate Parent: Tandy Corp. **SIC:** 5945—Hobby, Toy & Game Shops.

★ 86964 ★ **Target Stores**
14485 Bellaire Blvd.
Houston, TX 77083
(713)568-9290
Company Type: Subsidiary. **Ultimate Parent:** Dayton Hudson.

★ 86965 ★ **Target Stores**
6059 S. Loop E
Houston, TX 77087
(713)645-4811
Ultimate Parent: Dayton Hudson. **SIC:** 5311—Department Stores.

★ 86966 ★ **Target Stores**
7051 Southwest Fwy.
Houston, TX 77074
(713)771-8321
Company Type: Subsidiary. **Ultimate Parent:** Dayton Hudson. **SIC:** 5311—Department Stores.

★ 86967 ★ **Target Stores**
10000 Kleckley Dr.
Houston, TX 77075
(713)941-3800
Company Type: Subsidiary. **Ultimate Parent:** Dayton Hudson. **SIC:** 5311—Department Stores.

★ 86968 ★ **Target Stores**
205 W. Greens Rd.
Houston, TX 77067
(713)847-2161
Company Type: Subsidiary. **Ultimate Parent:** Dayton Hudson. **SIC:** 5311—Department Stores.

★ 86969 ★ **Target Stores**
4701 W. F M 1960
Houston, TX 77069
(713)444-0600
Ultimate Parent: Dayton Hudson. **SIC:** 5311—Department Stores.

★ 86970 ★ **Target Stores**
10801 Westheimer Rd.
Houston, TX 77042
(713)782-9950
Company Type: Subsidiary. **Ultimate Parent:** Dayton Hudson. **SIC:** 5311—Department Stores.

★ 86971 ★ **Target Stores**
10701 Jones Rd.
Houston, TX 77065
(713)890-8440
Company Type: Subsidiary. **Ultimate Parent:** Dayton Hudson. **SIC:** 5311—Department Stores.

★ 86972 ★ **Target Stores**
9429 Katy Fwy.
Houston, TX 77024
(713)464-9461
Company Type: Subsidiary. **Ultimate Parent:** Dayton Hudson. **SIC:** 5311—Department Stores.

★ 86973 ★ **Target Stores**
7801 Main St.
Houston, TX 77030
(713)795-4735
Ultimate Parent: Dayton Hudson. **SIC:** 5311—Department Stores.

★ 86974 ★ **Target Stores**
3900 Spencer St.
Houston, TX 77007
(713)943-7700
Company Type: Subsidiary. **Ultimate Parent:** Dayton Hudson. **SIC:** 5311—Department Stores.

★ 86975 ★ **Target Stores**
Hedwig
Houston, TX 77024
(713)465-0093
Ultimate Parent: Dayton Hudson. **SIC:** 5311—Department Stores.

★ 86976 ★ **Target Stores I 10 East**
12001 East Fwy.
Houston, TX 77029
(713)451-2111
Ultimate Parent: Dayton Hudson. **SIC:** 5311—Department Stores.

★ 86977 ★ **Tejas Gas**
1301 McKinney
Houston, TX 77010
(713)658-0509
Company Type: Headquarters. **Officer:** Jay A. Precourt. **Employee Count:** 366. **Fortune Service 500:** Ranking 39.

★ 86978 ★   Tenneco Inc.
1010 Milam St.
Houston, TX 77002
(713)757-2131
Company Type: Headquarters. Officer:
Dana G. Mead. Employee Count: 750000.
Sales: 13255 M. Fortune 500: Largest U.S.
Industrial Corporations: Ranking 34.

★ 86979 ★   Tenneco Inc.
Tenneco Bldg.
PO Box 2511
Houston, TX 77252-2511
(713)757-2131 Fax: (713)757-1410
Officer: Dana G. Mead, CEO. Ultimate
Parent: Tenneco Inc. Employee Count:
79000. Sales: 13255 M.

★ 86980 ★   Tesoro Petroleum
Distribution Co.
9426 Telephone Rd.
Houston, TX 77075
(713)991-0990
Ultimate Parent: Tesoro Petroleum Corp.
SIC: 5172—Petroleum Products Nec.

★ 86981 ★   Texaco
13210 Veterans Memorial Dr.
Houston, TX 77014
(713)580-8586
Ultimate Parent: Texaco.

★ 86982 ★   Texaco
5750 Royalton St.
Houston, TX 77081
(713)666-2658
Ultimate Parent: Texaco.

★ 86983 ★   Texaco
1107 Upland Dr.
Houston, TX 77043
(713)467-7512
Ultimate Parent: Texaco. SIC: 5541—
Gasoline Service Stations.

★ 86984 ★   Texaco
11001 Fuqua St.
Houston, TX 77089
(713)946-4559
Ultimate Parent: Texaco.

★ 86985 ★   Texaco
9201 N. Loop E
Houston, TX 77029
(713)446-2703
Ultimate Parent: Texaco. SIC: 5947—Gift,
Novelty & Souvenir Shops.

★ 86986 ★   Texaco
634 Allen Genoa Rd.
Houston, TX 77017
(713)641-6285
Ultimate Parent: Texaco. SIC: 5541—
Gasoline Service Stations.

★ 86987 ★   Texaco
2709 Broadway St.
Houston, TX 77017
(713)643-1615
Ultimate Parent: Texaco. SIC: 5541—
Gasoline Service Stations.

★ 86988 ★   Texaco Car Care
Center
10202 Westheimer Rd.
Houston, TX 77042
(713)781-0611
Ultimate Parent: Texaco. SIC: 5541—
Gasoline Service Stations.

★ 86989 ★   Texaco Food Mart
2103 Westheimer Rd.
Houston, TX 77098
(713)528-1040
Ultimate Parent: Texaco.

★ 86990 ★   Texaco Food Mart
10999 Scarsdale Blvd.
Houston, TX 77089
(713)484-1940
Ultimate Parent: Texaco.

★ 86991 ★   Texaco Food Mart
6690 W. Airport Blvd.
Houston, TX 77035
(713)721-8140
Ultimate Parent: Texaco.

★ 86992 ★   Texaco Food Mart
17435 North Fwy.
Houston, TX 77090
(713)537-0658
Ultimate Parent: Texaco.

★ 86993 ★   Texaco Food Mart
675 Rankin Rd.
Houston, TX 77073
(713)873-2811
Ultimate Parent: Texaco.

★ 86994 ★   Texaco Food Mart
10355 Huffmeister Rd.
Houston, TX 77065
(713)894-0629
Ultimate Parent: Texaco.

★ 86995 ★   Texaco Food Mart
9502 Jones Rd.
Houston, TX 77065
(713)469-5802
Ultimate Parent: Texaco.

★ 86996 ★   Texaco Food Mart
5103 Farb Dr.
Houston, TX 77016
(713)583-0119
Ultimate Parent: Texaco.

★ 86997 ★   Texaco Food Mart
8402 Hillcroft St.
Houston, TX 77096
(713)270-7270
Ultimate Parent: Texaco.

★ 86998 ★   Texaco Food Mart
8702 Bellaire Blvd.
Houston, TX 77036
(713)271-5737
Ultimate Parent: Texaco.

★ 86999 ★   Texaco Food Mart
11905 Bissonnet St.
Houston, TX 77099
(713)495-0608
Ultimate Parent: Texaco.

★ 87000 ★   Texaco Inc.
2661 Stevens St.
Houston, TX 77026
(713)225-5039
Ultimate Parent: Texaco.

★ 87001 ★   Texaco Inc.
Texaco Rd.
Houston, TX 77013
(713)453-7501
Ultimate Parent: Texaco. SIC: 8641—Civic
& Social Associations.

★ 87002 ★   Texaco Inc.
1222 Park Ln.
Houston, TX 77079
(713)578-7219
Ultimate Parent: Texaco.

★ 87003 ★   Texaco Inc.
6464 Savoy Dr.
Houston, TX 77036
(713)975-4000
Ultimate Parent: Texaco. SIC: 1311—
Crude Petroleum & Natural Gas.

★ 87004 ★   Texaco Inc.
3936 Dunvale Rd.
Houston, TX 77063
(713)781-7124
Ultimate Parent: Texaco.

★ 87005 ★   Texaco Lubracants
Co.
1111 Bugby
Houston, TX 77002
(713)752-3017
Ultimate Parent: Texaco.

★ 87006 ★   Texaco Lubricants
PO Box 4427
Houston, TX 77210
(713)752-3180
Ultimate Parent: Texaco.

★ 87007 ★   Texaco Pipeline Inc.
Aldine Bender House
Houston, TX 77009
(713)448-3103
Ultimate Parent: Texaco.

★ 87008 ★   Texaco & Service
Center
9492 Kempwood Dr.
Houston, TX 77080
(713)661-7119
Ultimate Parent: Texaco.

★ 87009 ★   Texaco USA
780 Clinton Dr.
Houston, TX 77013
(713)450-3216
Ultimate Parent: Texaco.

★ 87010 ★   Texaco USA
1 Allen Ctr.
Houston, TX 77002
(713)651-4609
Ultimate Parent: Texaco. SIC: 1311—
Crude Petroleum & Natural Gas.

★ 87011 ★   Texaco USA
1404 PO Box
Houston, TX 77251
Ultimate Parent: Texaco. SIC: 1311—
Crude Petroleum & Natural Gas.

★ 87012 ★   Texaco USA
2000 N. Loop W
Houston, TX 77018
(713)686-1311
Ultimate Parent: Texaco. SIC: 5172—
Petroleum Products Nec.

★ 87013 ★   Texas Commerce
BancShares
712 Main St.
Houston, TX 77002-3206
(713)236-4865
Company Type: Subsidiary. Officer: Walter
Shirley, Chairman of the Board. Ultimate
Parent: Chemical Banking Corp. SIC:
6021—National Commercial Banks.
Employee Count: 7900.

★ 87014 ★   Texas Commerce
Bank National
7545 Bellfort St.
Houston, TX 77061
(713)641-0291
Ultimate Parent: Chemical Banking Corp.
SIC: 6021—National Commercial Banks;
6022—State Commercial Banks.

★ 87015 ★   Texas Commerce
Bank National
5702 Airline Dr.
Houston, TX 77076
(713)696-7000
Ultimate Parent: Chemical Banking Corp.
SIC: 6099—Functions Related to Deposit
Banking.

★ 87016 ★   Texas Commerce
Bank National
10411 Westheimer Rd.
Houston, TX 77042
(713)783-8700
Ultimate Parent: Chemical Banking Corp.
SIC: 6021—National Commercial Banks;
6022—State Commercial Banks.

★ 87017 ★   Texas Commerce
Bank National
5 E. Greenway Plz.
Houston, TX 77046
(713)627-3250
Ultimate Parent: Chemical Banking Corp.
SIC: 6021—National Commercial Banks;
6022—State Commercial Banks.

★ 87018 ★   Texas Commerce
Bank National
801 W. Greens Rd.
Houston, TX 77067
(713)775-5300
Ultimate Parent: Chemical Banking Corp.
SIC: 6099—Functions Related to Deposit
Banking.

★ 87019 ★   Texas Commerce
Bank National
5177 Richmond Ave.
Houston, TX 77056
(713)840-1130
Ultimate Parent: Chemical Banking Corp.
SIC: 6021—National Commercial Banks;
6022—State Commercial Banks.

★ 87020 ★   Texas Commerce
Bank National
712 Main St.
Houston, TX 77002
(713)236-4865
Ultimate Parent: Chemical Banking Corp.
SIC: 6021—National Commercial Banks;
6022—State Commercial Banks.

★ 87021 ★   Texas Eastern Corp.
PO Box 2521
Houston, TX 77252
(713)759-3131
Ultimate Parent: Panhandle Eastern.

★ 87022 ★   Texas Eastern
Transmission Corp.
5400 Westheimer Ct.
PO Box 1642
Houston, TX 77251-1642
Officer: Dennis R. Hendrix, Chairman.
Ultimate Parent: Panhandle Eastern.

★ 87023 ★   Thermacote Welco
Inc.
6309 Long Dr.
Houston, TX 77087
(713)644-1805
Ultimate Parent: Foster Wheeler Corp.
SIC: 5084—Industrial Machinery &
Equipment; 5084—Industrial Machinery &
Equipment.

★ 87024 ★   Thom Mcan Shoe
Stores
214 Gulfgate Mall a
Houston, TX 77087
(713)645-8491
Ultimate Parent: Melville. SIC: 5661—Shoe
Stores.

★ 87025 ★   Thom Mcan Store No
7141
7925 Fm 1960 Rd. W
Houston, TX 77070
(713)890-0843
Ultimate Parent: Melville. SIC: 5661—Shoe
Stores.

★ 87026 ★   Thomas & Betts Corp.
Meyer Ind.
8700 Fairbanks-N. Houston Rd. Rd.
Houston, TX 77064
Ultimate Parent: Thomas & Betts. SIC:
3441—Fabricated Structural Metal.

★ 87027 ★   Time Electronics
10450 Stancliff Rd.
Houston, TX 77099
(713)530-0800
Ultimate Parent: Avnet. SIC: 5065—
Electronic Parts & Equipment Nec.

★ 87028 ★   TNI Inc.
6630 Harwin Dr.
Houston, TX 77036
(713)783-8446
Ultimate Parent: Tyco Toys, Inc. SIC:
8641—Civic & Social Associations.

★ 87029 ★   Torrington Co
10500 Richmond Ave.
Houston, TX 77042
(713)780-8009
Ultimate Parent: Ingersoll-Rand. SIC:
5085—Industrial Supplies.

★ 87030 ★   Toys R US
2703 Hwy. 6 S
Houston, TX 77082
(713)556-5369
Ultimate Parent: Toys "R" US.

★ 87031 ★   Toys R US
Katy Fwy.
Houston, TX 77024
(713)465-0087
Ultimate Parent: Toys "R" US. SIC: 5641—
Children's & Infants' Wear Stores.

★ 87032 ★   Toys R US
North Fwy.
Houston, TX 77022
(713)695-8873
Ultimate Parent: Toys "R" US. SIC: 5641—
Children's & Infants' Wear Stores.

★ 87033 ★   Toys R US
7323 Fm 1960 Rd. W
Houston, TX 77070
(713)583-7733
Ultimate Parent: Toys "R" US. SIC: 5641—
Children's & Infants' Wear Stores.

★ 87034 ★   Toys R US
10220 Almeda Genoa Rd.
Houston, TX 77075
(713)941-1920
Ultimate Parent: Toys "R" US. SIC: 5641—
Children's & Infants' Wear Stores.

★ 87035 ★   Trailways Bus System
1600 Nagle St.
Houston, TX 77003
(713)224-7826
Ultimate Parent: Greyhound Lines Inc. SIC:
4212—Local Trucking Without Storage.

657

★ 87036 ★   Trailways Bus System
6892 Southwest Fwy.
Houston, TX 77074
(713)785-5460
Ultimate Parent: Greyhound Lines Inc. SIC:
4212—Local Trucking Without Storage.

★ 87037 ★   Trailways Bus System
6519 Long Point Rd.
Houston, TX 77055
(713)688-9845
Ultimate Parent: Greyhound Lines Inc. SIC:
4212—Local Trucking Without Storage.

★ 87038 ★   Trailways Business
Systems
2121 Main St.
Houston, TX 77002
(713)759-6500
Ultimate Parent: Greyhound Lines Inc. SIC:
4111—Local & Suburban Transit.

★ 87039 ★   Trailways Inc.
7011 Main St.
Houston, TX 77030
(713)790-9160
Ultimate Parent: Greyhound Lines Inc. SIC:
4131—Intercity & Rural Bus Transportation.

★ 87040 ★   Trans World Airlines
Inc.
Houston
Houston, TX 77205
(713)443-2416
Ultimate Parent: Trans World Airlines. SIC:
9721—International Affairs.

★ 87041 ★   Transamerica
Occidental Life Insurance
7322 Southwest Fwy.
Houston, TX 77074
(713)271-1887
Ultimate Parent: Transamerica Occidental
Life Insurance. SIC: 6411—Insurance
Agents, Brokers & Service.

★ 87042 ★   Transco Energy Co.
2800 Post Oak Blvd.
Houston, TX 77056
(713)439-4400 Fax: (713)439-2440
Company Type: Headquarters. Officer:
John P. DesBarres, CEO. Employee
Count: 4583. Sales: 2938.1 M. Fortune
500: Largest U.S. Industrial Corporations:
Ranking 42.

★ 87043 ★   Transwestern Pipeline
Co.
PO Box 1188
Houston, TX 77251-1188
(713)853-7173
Company Type: Subsidiary. Ultimate
Parent: Enron.

★ 87044 ★   Transwestern Pipeline
Co. Inc.
1400 Smith St.
Houston, TX 77002-7337
(713)853-6161
Company Type: Subsidiary. Officer:
Ronald J. Burns, Chairman of the Board.
Ultimate Parent: Enron. Employee Count:
535. Sales: 248 M.

★ 87045 ★   Trico Industries Inc.
1020 Fennell St.
Houston, TX 77012
(713)923-6603
Ultimate Parent: Paccar. SIC: 5084—
Industrial Machinery & Equipment.

★ 87046 ★   Trunkline Gas Co.
5400 Westheimer Ct.
PO Box 1642
Houston, TX 77251-1642
Ultimate Parent: Panhandle Eastern.

★ 87047 ★   Trw Inc. Mission
Drilling Products
8760 Clay Rd.
Houston, TX 77080
Ultimate Parent: TRW, Inc. SIC: 3533—Oil
& Gas Field Machinery; 3532—Mining
Machinery.

★ 87048 ★   Twelve Oaks Hospital
4200 Portsmouth
Houston, TX 77027
(713)623-2500
Officer: Walter J. Ornsteen, Executive
Director. Ultimate Parent: American
Medical Holdings. SIC: 8062—General
Medical & Surgical Hospitals.

★ 87049 ★   Txt a Brunswick Co.
1020 Rankin Rd.
Houston, TX 77073
Ultimate Parent: Brunswick Corp. SIC:
3491—Industrial Valves; 3494—Valves &
Pipe Fittings Nec.

★ 87050 ★   Ungermann-Bass Inc.
4550 Post Oak Pl
Houston, TX 77027
(713)622-5672
Ultimate Parent: Tandem.

★ 87051 ★   Union Camp Corp.
3120 Southwest Fwy.
Houston, TX 77098
(713)529-4704
Ultimate Parent: Union Camp Corp. SIC:
5113—Industrial & Personal Service Paper.

★ 87052 ★   Union Camp Corp.
3851 Yale St.
Houston, TX 77018
(713)692-3511
Officer: Phil Warzon, Manager. Ultimate
Parent: Union Camp Corp. SIC: 2621—
Paper Mills; 2678—Stationery Products.

★ 87053 ★   Union Carbide
Coating Service Corp.
9200 Telephone Rd.
Houston, TX 77075
Ultimate Parent: Union Carbide Corp. SIC:
3479—Metal Coating & Allied Services.

★ 87054 ★   Union Oil Co. of
California
4635 Southwest Fwy.
Houston, TX 77027
(713)623-8000
Ultimate Parent: Unocal Corp. SIC: 1311—
Crude Petroleum & Natural Gas.

★ 87055 ★   Union Texas Petro
Holding Co.
1330 Post Oak Blvd.
Houston, TX 77056
(713)623-6544
Officer: A. Clark Johnson, Chairman.
Ultimate Parent: Union Texas Petroleum.
SIC: 2869—Industrial Organic Chemicals
Nec; 2911—Petroleum Refining.

★ 87056 ★   Union Texas
Petroleum
8888 W. Monroe Rd.
Houston, TX 77061
(713)645-2925
Ultimate Parent: Union Texas Petroleum.

★ 87057 ★   Union Texas
Petroleum
1330 Post Oak Blvd.
Houston, TX 77056
(713)623-6544 Fax: (713)968-2771
Company Type: Headquarters. Officer: A.
Clark Johnson, CEO. Employee Count:
1000. Sales: 681.9 M. Fortune 500:
Largest U.S. Industrial Corporations:
Ranking 463.

★ 87058 ★   Union Texas
Petroleum Holdings Inc.
1330 Post Oak Blvd.
Houston, TX 77056
(713)623-6544 Fax: (713)968-2771
Officer: A. Clark Johnson, CEO. Ultimate
Parent: Union Texas Petroleum. Employee
Count: 1000. Sales: 694 M.

★ 87059 ★   Unisys Corp.
16811 El Camino Real
Houston, TX 77058
(713)488-3300
Ultimate Parent: Unisys Corp.

★ 87060 ★   Unisys Corp.
555 Gemini St.
Houston, TX 77058
(713)488-3901
Ultimate Parent: Unisys Corp.

★ 87061 ★   Universal Foods
Corp.
1201 Oliver St.
Houston, TX 77007
(713)227-7479
Ultimate Parent: Universal Foods Corp.
SIC: 5149—Groceries & Related Products
Nec.

★ 87062 ★   US Concord, Inc.
4420 W. F M1960
Houston, TX 77068
(713)444-5206
Ultimate Parent: Marine Midland Banks.
SIC: 7359—Equipment Rental & Leasing
Nec.

★ 87063 ★   US Fidelity & Gu
4477 PO Box
Houston, TX 77210
Ultimate Parent: USF&G Corp. SIC:
6411—Insurance Agents, Brokers &
Service.

★ 87064 ★   US Fidelity & Gu
1000 Bay Area Blvd.
Houston, TX 77058
(713)480-7600
Ultimate Parent: USF&G Corp. SIC:
6411—Insurance Agents, Brokers &
Service.

★ 87065 ★   US Fleet Leasing
2040 North Blvd.
Houston, TX 77098
(713)682-9913
Ultimate Parent: Ford Motor Co. SIC:
7514—Passenger Car Rental.

★ 87066 ★   Utility Fuels Inc.
24 E. Greenway Plz.
Houston, TX 77046
(713)552-1612
Ultimate Parent: Houston Industries. SIC:
4731—Freight Transportation Arrangement.

★ 87067 ★   Valero Refining &
Marketing Co.
1200 Smith St., No. 900
Houston, TX 77002
(713)951-2000
Officer: Bill Greehey, President. Ultimate
Parent: Valero Energy Corp. SIC: 2911—
Petroleum Refining.

★ 87068 ★   Valley Line Co. Inc
9801 Westheimer Rd.
Houston, TX 77042
(713)266-7373
Ultimate Parent: CSF Holdings. SIC:
4449—Water Transportation of Freight Nec.

★ 87069 ★   Valspar Corp
2503 W. 11th St.
Houston, TX 77008
(713)861-6192
Ultimate Parent: Valspar Corp. SIC:
2851—Paints & Allied Products.

★ 87070 ★   Valspar Corp.
2503 West 11 St.
Houston, TX 77008
Ultimate Parent: Valspar Corp. SIC:
2851—Paints & Allied Products.

★ 87071 ★   Van Waters & Rogers
Inc.
777 Brisbane St.
Houston, TX 77061
(713)644-1601
Ultimate Parent: Univar Corp.

★ 87072 ★   Variable Annuity Life
3929 Allen Pky.
Houston, TX 77019
(713)831-5251
Company Type: Headquarters. Officer:
Stephen D. Bickel. Employee Count: 1976.
Fortune Service 500: Ranking 18.

★ 87073 ★   Variable Annuity Life
Insur
800 Gessner Rd.
Houston, TX 77024
(713)465-2253
Ultimate Parent: Variable Annuity Life.

★ 87074 ★   Variable Annuity Life
Insurance Co.
2929 Allen Pky.
Houston, TX 77019
(713)526-5251
Officer: Stephen D. Bickel, President.
Ultimate Parent: American General Corp.
SIC: 6311—Life Insurance; 6411—
Insurance Agents, Brokers & Service.

★ 87075 ★   Variable Annuity Life
Insurance Co.
2929 Allen Pky. W, 8th Fl.
Houston, TX 77019-2119
(713)526-5251
Location Type: Branch office. Officer:
Stephen D. Bickel, President. Ultimate

Parent: American General Corp. SIC:
6311—Life Insurance. Employee Count:
926.

★ 87076 ★   Variable Annuity
Marketing Co.
2929 Allen Pky.
Houston, TX 77019
(713)526-5251
Officer: Joe C. Osborne, President.
Ultimate Parent: American General Corp.
SIC: 6411—Insurance Agents, Brokers &
Service.

★ 87077 ★   Verex Assurance Inc.
12700 Northborough Dr.
Houston, TX 77067
(713)583-0424
Ultimate Parent: Dial Corp. SIC: 6411—
Insurance Agents, Brokers & Service.

★ 87078 ★   Victoria's Secret
Willowbrook Mall
Houston, TX 77061
(713)890-1572
Ultimate Parent: Limited. SIC: 5632—
Women's Accessory & Specialty Stores.

★ 87079 ★   Victoria's Secret
Town
Houston, TX 77024
(713)827-7414
Ultimate Parent: Limited. SIC: 5632—
Women's Accessory & Specialty Stores.

★ 87080 ★   Victoria's Secret
346 Greenspoint Mall
Houston, TX 77060
(713)820-0282
Ultimate Parent: Limited. SIC: 4512—Air
Transportation—Scheduled.

★ 87081 ★   W. R. Grace & Co.
Connecticut Construction Products Div.
4323 Crites St.
Houston, TX 77003
Company Type: Division. Ultimate Parent:
W. R. Grace Co. SIC: 2899—Chemical
Preparations Nec.

★ 87082 ★   Wal Mart Discnt Cy
10750 Westview Dr.
Houston, TX 77043
(713)984-2773
Ultimate Parent: Wal-Mart Stores, Inc.

★ 87083 ★   Wal Mart Discount
Cities
7080 Hwy. 6 N
Houston, TX 77095
(713)855-1604
Ultimate Parent: Wal-Mart Stores, Inc. SIC:
5311—Department Stores.

★ 87084 ★   Wal Mart Discount
City
13350 East Fwy.
Houston, TX 77015
(713)453-3196
Ultimate Parent: Wal-Mart Stores, Inc.

★ 87085 ★   Wal Mart Discount
City
8103 Fondren Rd.
Houston, TX 77074
(713)988-4495
Ultimate Parent: Wal-Mart Stores, Inc.

★ 87086 ★   Wal Mart Discount
City
14550 Beechnut St.
Houston, TX 77083
(713)561-0866
Ultimate Parent: Wal-Mart Stores, Inc.

★ 87087 ★   Wal Mart Pharmacy
22420 W. Montgomery Rd.
Houston, TX 77070
(713)251-3010
Ultimate Parent: Wal-Mart Stores, Inc.

★ 87088 ★   Wald Moving &
Storage Service
5205 S. Rice Ave.
Houston, TX 77081
(713)666-2121
Ultimate Parent: Mayflower Group. SIC:
4214—Local Trucking With Storage.

★ 87089 ★   Waldenbooks
Westwood Mall
Houston, TX 77036
(713)777-5196
Ultimate Parent: K-Mart. SIC: 5942—Book
Stores.

★ 87090 ★　Waldenbooks
Willowbrook Mall
Houston, TX 77070
(713)469-1901
Ultimate Parent: K-Mart. **SIC:** 5942—Book
Stores.

★ 87091 ★　Waldenbooks
W Oaks Mall
Houston, TX 77082
(713)558-2585
Ultimate Parent: K-Mart. **SIC:** 5942—Book
Stores.

★ 87092 ★　Waldenbooks
10001 Westheimer Rd.
Houston, TX 77042
(713)789-0226
Ultimate Parent: K-Mart.

★ 87093 ★　Waldenbooks
Northwest Mall
Houston, TX 77092
(713)682-2237
Ultimate Parent: K-Mart. **SIC:** 5942—Book
Stores.

★ 87094 ★　Waldenbooks
Sharpstown Shopping Ctr.
Houston, TX 77036
(713)771-3200
Ultimate Parent: K-Mart. **SIC:** 5942—Book
Stores.

★ 87095 ★　Waldenbooks
Memorial County Shopping Ctr.
Houston, TX 77024
(713)468-7142
Ultimate Parent: K-Mart. **SIC:** 5942—Book
Stores.

★ 87096 ★　Waldenbooks
800 N. Belt Dr. E
Houston, TX 77032
(713)973-0622
Ultimate Parent: K-Mart.

★ 87097 ★　Waldenbooks
Greenspoint Mall
Houston, TX 77060
(713)447-0281
Ultimate Parent: K-Mart. **SIC:** 5942—Book
Stores.

★ 87098 ★　Waldenbooks
Gulfgate Mall
Houston, TX 77087
(713)649-3880
Ultimate Parent: K-Mart. **SIC:** 5942—Book
Stores.

★ 87099 ★　Waldenbooks
Baybrook
Houston, TX 77058
(713)488-2330
Ultimate Parent: K-Mart. **SIC:** 5942—Book
Stores.

★ 87100 ★　Waldenbooks
Galleria
Houston, TX 77056
(713)871-1689
Ultimate Parent: K-Mart. **SIC:** 5942—Book
Stores.

★ 87101 ★　Waldenbooks
280 Almeda Mall
Houston, TX 77075
(713)944-7465
Ultimate Parent: K-Mart. **SIC:** 5942—Book
Stores.

★ 87102 ★　Walgreen
300 Main St.
Houston, TX 77002
(713)522-5194
Ultimate Parent: Walgreen Co. **SIC:**
5912—Drug Stores & Proprietary Stores.

★ 87103 ★　Walgreen Answering
Service
4335 Hanley Ln.
Houston, TX 77093
(713)987-9484
Ultimate Parent: Walgreen Co. **SIC:**
7389—Business Services Nec.

★ 87104 ★　Walgreen
Construction Co. in
15622 Magee St.
Houston, TX 77032
(713)449-6513
Ultimate Parent: Walgreen Co. **SIC:**
1623—Water, Sewer & Utility Lines.

★ 87105 ★　Walgreen Drug Stores
142 E. FM 1960
Houston, TX 77073
(713)443-7946
Ultimate Parent: Walgreen Co. **SIC:**
5912—Drug Stores & Proprietary Stores.

★ 87106 ★　Walgreen Drug Stores
11025 East Fwy.
Houston, TX 77029
(713)674-3682
Ultimate Parent: Walgreen Co. **SIC:**
5912—Drug Stores & Proprietary Stores.

★ 87107 ★　Walgreen Drug Stores
9410 Cullen Blvd.
Houston, TX 77051
(713)733-4306
Ultimate Parent: Walgreen Co. **SIC:**
5912—Drug Stores & Proprietary Stores.

★ 87108 ★　Walgreen Drug Stores
8231 Broadway St.
Houston, TX 77061
(713)641-0659
Ultimate Parent: Walgreen Co. **SIC:**
5912—Drug Stores & Proprietary Stores.

★ 87109 ★　Walgreen Drug Stores
175 Camino Shopping Ctr.
Houston, TX 77062
(713)488-3424
Ultimate Parent: Walgreen Co. **SIC:**
5912—Drug Stores & Proprietary Stores.

★ 87110 ★　Walgreen Drug Stores
6616 Antoine Dr.
Houston, TX 77091
(713)957-8185
Ultimate Parent: Walgreen Co. **SIC:**
5912—Drug Stores & Proprietary Stores.

★ 87111 ★　Walgreen Drug Stores
8105 Antoine Dr.
Houston, TX 77088
(713)445-7939
Ultimate Parent: Walgreen Co. **SIC:**
5912—Drug Stores & Proprietary Stores.

★ 87112 ★　Walgreen Drug Stores
12 Uvalde Rd.
Houston, TX 77015
(713)455-9942
Ultimate Parent: Walgreen Co. **SIC:**
5912—Drug Stores & Proprietary Stores.

★ 87113 ★　Walgreen Drug Stores
9378 Richmond Ave.
Houston, TX 77063
(713)789-6433
Ultimate Parent: Walgreen Co. **SIC:**
5912—Drug Stores & Proprietary Stores.

★ 87114 ★　Walgreen Drug Stores
203 Sharpstown Ctr.
Houston, TX 77036
(713)774-6381
Ultimate Parent: Walgreen Co. **SIC:**
5912—Drug Stores & Proprietary Stores.

★ 87115 ★　Walgreen Drug Stores
9499 Main St.
Houston, TX 77025
(713)663-7778
Ultimate Parent: Walgreen Co.

★ 87116 ★　Walgreen Drug Stores
822 Main
Houston, TX 77002
(713)223-4243
Ultimate Parent: Walgreen Co.

★ 87117 ★　Walgreen Drug Stores
11894 Wilcrest Dr.
Houston, TX 77031
(713)495-1021
Ultimate Parent: Walgreen Co. **SIC:**
5912—Drug Stores & Proprietary Stores.

★ 87118 ★　Walgreen Drug Stores
8644 S. Braeswood Blvd.
Houston, TX 77031
(713)988-7989
Ultimate Parent: Walgreen Co. **SIC:**
7389—Business Services Nec.

★ 87119 ★　Walgreen Drug Stores
6320 Telephone Rd.
Houston, TX 77087
(713)644-1354
Ultimate Parent: Walgreen Co. **SIC:**
7389—Business Services Nec.

★ 87120 ★　Walgreen Drug Stores
8540 Long Point Rd.
Houston, TX 77055
(713)468-7815
Ultimate Parent: Walgreen Co. **SIC:**
5912—Drug Stores & Proprietary Stores.

★ 87121 ★　Walgreen Drug Stores
550 Memorial City Shopping Ctr.
Houston, TX 77024
(713)468-7961
Ultimate Parent: Walgreen Co. **SIC:**
7389—Business Services Nec.

★ 87122 ★　Walgreen Drug Stores
9492 Hammerly Blvd.
Houston, TX 77080
(713)468-3601
Ultimate Parent: Walgreen Co. **SIC:**
5999—Miscellaneous Retail Stores Nec.

★ 87123 ★　Walgreen Drug Stores
9329 Katy Fwy.
Houston, TX 77024
(713)461-8800
Ultimate Parent: Walgreen Co. **SIC:**
7389—Business Services Nec.

★ 87124 ★　Walgreen Drug Stores
910 E. Tidwell Rd.
Houston, TX 77022
(713)699-8211
Ultimate Parent: Walgreen Co. **SIC:**
7389—Business Services Nec.

★ 87125 ★　Walgreen Drug Stores
5207 Fm 1960 Rd. W
Houston, TX 77069
(713)440-1550
Ultimate Parent: Walgreen Co. **SIC:**
7389—Business Services Nec.

★ 87126 ★　Walgreen Drug Stores
10790 Bellaire Blvd.
Houston, TX 77072
(713)495-0601
Ultimate Parent: Walgreen Co. **SIC:**
5912—Drug Stores & Proprietary Stores.

★ 87127 ★　Walgreen Drug Stores
10311 Club Creek Dr.
Houston, TX 77036
(713)772-8544
Ultimate Parent: Walgreen Co. **SIC:**
5912—Drug Stores & Proprietary Stores.

★ 87128 ★　Walgreen Drug Stores
5560 Weslayan St.
Houston, TX 77005
(713)667-7870
Ultimate Parent: Walgreen Co.

★ 87129 ★　Walgreen Drug Stores
7525 Westheimer Rd.
Houston, TX 77063
(713)785-3394
Ultimate Parent: Walgreen Co.

★ 87130 ★　Walgreen Drug Stores
215 W. 20th St.
Houston, TX 77008
(713)861-2331
Ultimate Parent: Walgreen Co.

★ 87131 ★　Walgreen Drug Stores
1940 W. Gray St.
Houston, TX 77019
(713)526-2161
Ultimate Parent: Walgreen Co.

★ 87132 ★　Walgreen Drug Stores
10903 Scarsdale Blvd.
Houston, TX 77089
(713)484-1292
Ultimate Parent: Walgreen Co.

★ 87133 ★　Walgreen Drug Stores
8624 Stella Link Rd.
Houston, TX 77025
(713)666-8061
Ultimate Parent: Walgreen Co.

★ 87134 ★　Walgreen Drug Stores
5300 N. Braeswood Blvd.
Houston, TX 77096
(713)721-0654
Ultimate Parent: Walgreen Co.

★ 87135 ★　Walgreen Drug Stores
300 Northline Mall
Houston, TX 77022
(713)695-2919
Ultimate Parent: Walgreen Co.

★ 87136 ★　Walgreen Drug Stores
17551 Imperial Valley Dr.
Houston, TX 77060
(713)876-3820
Ultimate Parent: Walgreen Co.

★ 87137 ★　Walgreen Drug Stores
10066 Long Point Rd.
Houston, TX 77055
(713)464-0436
Ultimate Parent: Walgreen Co.

★ 87138 ★　Walgreen Drug Stores
133 Gulfgate Mall
Houston, TX 77087
(713)649-2726
Ultimate Parent: Walgreen Co.

★ 87139 ★　Walgreen Drug Stores
9520 Homestead Rd.
Houston, TX 77016
(713)633-5600
Ultimate Parent: Walgreen Co.

★ 87140 ★　Walgreen Drug Stores
10826 Beechnut St.
Houston, TX 77072
(713)530-6205
Ultimate Parent: Walgreen Co.

★ 87141 ★　Walgreen Drug Stores
9600 Westheimer Rd.
Houston, TX 77063
(713)783-2961
Ultimate Parent: Walgreen Co.

★ 87142 ★　Walgreen Drug Stores
12522 Westheimer Rd.
Houston, TX 77077
(713)870-9240
Ultimate Parent: Walgreen Co. **SIC:**
5912—Drug Stores & Proprietary Stores.

★ 87143 ★　Walgreen Drug Stores
420 W. Little York Rd.
Houston, TX 77076
(713)448-6361
Ultimate Parent: Walgreen Co. **SIC:**
5912—Drug Stores & Proprietary Stores.

★ 87144 ★　Walgreen Drug Stores
11051 Westheimer Rd.
Houston, TX 77042
(713)789-4872
Ultimate Parent: Walgreen Co. **SIC:**
5912—Drug Stores & Proprietary Stores.

★ 87145 ★　Walgreen Drug Stores
11315 Veterans Memorial Dr.
Houston, TX 77067
(713)444-1458
Ultimate Parent: Walgreen Co. **SIC:**
7389—Business Services Nec.

★ 87146 ★　Walgreen Drug Stores
5306 W. 34th St.
Houston, TX 77092
(713)683-8125
Ultimate Parent: Walgreen Co. **SIC:**
5912—Drug Stores & Proprietary Stores.

★ 87147 ★　Walgreen Drug Stores
13131 Stuebner Airline Rd.
Houston, TX 77014
(713)537-9210
Ultimate Parent: Walgreen Co. **SIC:**
5912—Drug Stores & Proprietary Stores.

★ 87148 ★　Walgreen Drug Stores
190 Town
Houston, TX 77024
(713)464-8264
Ultimate Parent: Walgreen Co. **SIC:**
5912—Drug Stores & Proprietary Stores.

★ 87149 ★　Walgreen Drug Stores
1265 Pinemont Dr.
Houston, TX 77018
(713)688-7913
Ultimate Parent: Walgreen Co. **SIC:**
5912—Drug Stores & Proprietary Stores.

★ 87150 ★　Walgreen Drug Stores
2885 S. Richey St.
Houston, TX 77017
(713)943-1091
Ultimate Parent: Walgreen Co. **SIC:**
5912—Drug Stores & Proprietary Stores.

★ 87151 ★　Walgreen Drug Stores
514 Normandy St.
Houston, TX 77015
(713)453-3825
Ultimate Parent: Walgreen Co. **SIC:**
5912—Drug Stores & Proprietary Stores.

★ 87152 ★   **Walgreen Drug Stores**
10826 North Fwy.
Houston, TX 77037
(713)445-1300
Ultimate Parent: Walgreen Co. **SIC:**
5912—Drug Stores & Proprietary Stores.

★ 87153 ★   **Walgreen Drug Stores**
10066 Long Point Rd.
Houston, TX 77055
(713)468-6596
Ultimate Parent: Walgreen Co. **SIC:**
5912—Drug Stores & Proprietary Stores.

★ 87154 ★   **Walgreen Drug Stores**
10826 North Fwy.
Houston, TX 77037
(713)445-1308
Ultimate Parent: Walgreen Co. **SIC:**
5912—Drug Stores & Proprietary Stores.

★ 87155 ★   **Walgreen Drug Stores**
13606 Kuykendahl Rd.
Houston, TX 77090
Ultimate Parent: Walgreen Co. **SIC:**
5912—Drug Stores & Proprietary Stores.

★ 87156 ★   **Walgreen Drug Stores**
1421 Little York Rd.
Houston, TX 77093
(713)449-2913
Ultimate Parent: Walgreen Co. **SIC:**
5912—Drug Stores & Proprietary Stores.

★ 87157 ★   **Walgreen Drug Stores**
8110 Kempwood Dr.
Houston, TX 77055
(713)468-9611
Ultimate Parent: Walgreen Co. **SIC:**
5912—Drug Stores & Proprietary Stores.

★ 87158 ★   **Walgreen Drug Stores**
9433 Kempwood Dr.
Houston, TX 77080
(713)939-9206
Ultimate Parent: Walgreen Co. **SIC:**
5912—Drug Stores & Proprietary Stores.

★ 87159 ★   **Walgreen Drug Stores**
11121 Huffmeister Rd.
Houston, TX 77065
(713)955-8346
Ultimate Parent: Walgreen Co. **SIC:**
5912—Drug Stores & Proprietary Stores.

★ 87160 ★   **Walgreen Drug Stores**
10787 Jones Rd.
Houston, TX 77065
(713)890-3801
Ultimate Parent: Walgreen Co. **SIC:**
5912—Drug Stores & Proprietary Stores.

★ 87161 ★   **Walgreen Drug Stores**
4707 Hawn 6
Houston, TX 77091
(713)463-6358
Ultimate Parent: Walgreen Co. **SIC:**
5912—Drug Stores & Proprietary Stores.

★ 87162 ★   **Walgreen Drug Stores**
6730 Hillcroft St.
Houston, TX 77081
(713)988-6405
Ultimate Parent: Walgreen Co. **SIC:**
5912—Drug Stores & Proprietary Stores.

★ 87163 ★   **Walgreen Drug Stores**
5086 Griggs Rd.
Houston, TX 77021
(713)741-6737
Ultimate Parent: Walgreen Co. **SIC:**
5912—Drug Stores & Proprietary Stores.

★ 87164 ★   **Walgreen Drug Stores**
10527 Gulf Fwy.
Houston, TX 77034
(713)941-3641
Ultimate Parent: Walgreen Co. **SIC:**
5912—Drug Stores & Proprietary Stores.

★ 87165 ★   **Walgreen Drug Stores**
241 Fm 1960 Rd.
Houston, TX 77073
(713)444-1203
Ultimate Parent: Walgreen Co. **SIC:**
5912—Drug Stores & Proprietary Stores.

★ 87166 ★   **Walgreen Drug Stores**
11234 Fondren Rd.
Houston, TX 77096
Ultimate Parent: Walgreen Co. **SIC:**
5912—Drug Stores & Proprietary Stores.

★ 87167 ★   **Walgreen Drug Stores**
13345 East Fwy.
Houston, TX 77015
(713)455-2336
Ultimate Parent: Walgreen Co. **SIC:**
5912—Drug Stores & Proprietary Stores.

★ 87168 ★   **Walgreen Drug Stores**
1954 El Dorado Blvd.
Houston, TX 77062
(713)486-5872
Ultimate Parent: Walgreen Co. **SIC:**
5912—Drug Stores & Proprietary Stores.

★ 87169 ★   **Wall Street Journal**
3040 Post Oak Blvd.
Houston, TX 77056
(713)664-8606
Ultimate Parent: Dow Jones. **SIC:** 2711—
Newspapers.

★ 87170 ★   **Warren Petroleum Co.**
Shoppe
Houston, TX 77034
(713)453-7173
Ultimate Parent: Chevron Corp. **SIC:**
5984—Liquefied Petroleum Gas Dealers.

★ 87171 ★   **Watkins Manufacturing**
3148 Almeda Genoa Rd.
Houston, TX 77047
(713)434-8788
Ultimate Parent: Masco. **SIC:** 5063—
Electrical Apparatus & Equipment.

★ 87172 ★   **Welex**
2135 Hwy. 6 South
Houston, TX 77077
Ultimate Parent: Halliburton. **SIC:** 3533—
Oil & Gas Field Machinery.

★ 87173 ★   **Wells Fargo Guard Servs Co.**
6234 Richmond Ave.
Houston, TX 77057
(713)974-3407
Ultimate Parent: Borg Warner Automotive.
SIC: 7381—Detective & Armored Car
Services.

★ 87174 ★   **Western Atlas International Inc.**
10205 Westheimer
Houston, TX 77042
(713)266-5700 **Fax:** (713)972-4909
Company Type: Subsidiary. **Ultimate
Parent:** Dresser Industries Inc.

★ 87175 ★   **Western Atlas Software**
10205 Westheimer
Houston, TX 77042
(713)266-5700
Company Type: Division. **Ultimate Parent:**
Litton Industries.

★ 87176 ★   **Western Auto Supply Co.**
12406 S. Post Oak Rd.
Houston, TX 77045
(713)721-4440
Ultimate Parent: Sears Roebuck & Co.
SIC: 5531—Automobile & Home Supply
Stores.

★ 87177 ★   **Western Auto Supply Co.**
1409 Little York Rd.
Houston, TX 77093
(713)449-0176
Ultimate Parent: Sears Roebuck & Co.
SIC: 5531—Automobile & Home Supply
Stores.

★ 87178 ★   **Western Auto Supply Co.**
1019 N. Shepherd Dr.
Houston, TX 77008
(713)869-6656
Ultimate Parent: Sears Roebuck & Co.
SIC: 5531—Automobile & Home Supply
Stores.

★ 87179 ★   **Western Auto Supply Co.**
11743 Eastex Fwy.
Houston, TX 77039
(713)449-2334
Ultimate Parent: Sears Roebuck & Co.
SIC: 5531—Automobile & Home Supply
Stores.

★ 87180 ★   **Western Auto Supply Co.**
1910 John Ralston Rd.
Houston, TX 77013
(713)672-1616
Ultimate Parent: Sears Roebuck & Co.
SIC: 5531—Automobile & Home Supply
Stores.

★ 87181 ★   **Western Auto Supply Co.**
5323 Antoine Dr.
Houston, TX 77091
(713)681-7528
Ultimate Parent: Sears Roebuck & Co.
SIC: 5531—Automobile & Home Supply
Stores.

★ 87182 ★   **Western Auto Supply Co.**
11698 Bellaire Blvd.
Houston, TX 77072
(713)495-2060
Ultimate Parent: Sears Roebuck & Co.
SIC: 5531—Automobile & Home Supply
Stores.

★ 87183 ★   **Western Geophysical**
10001 Richmond Ave.
Houston, TX 77042-4299
(713)789-9600 **Fax:** (713)789-0172 **Telex:**
762-406
Company Type: Division. **Officer:** Neal
Cramer, President. **Ultimate Parent:** Litton
Industries. **SIC:** 1382—Oil & Gas
Exploration Services.

★ 87184 ★   **Western Geophysical Co.**
3630 Westchase Dr.
Houston, TX 77042
(713)789-5191
Ultimate Parent: Litton Industries. **SIC:**
1382—Oil & Gas Exploration Services.

★ 87185 ★   **Western Geophysical Co. Libr**
10001 Richmond Ave.
Houston, TX 77042
(713)789-9600
Ultimate Parent: Litton Industries. **SIC:**
1382—Oil & Gas Exploration Services.

★ 87186 ★   **Western National Life**
5555 San Felipe
Houston, TX 77056
(713)888-7800
Company Type: Headquarters. **Officer:**
Michael J. Poulos. **Employee Count:** 160.
Fortune Service 500: Ranking 42.

★ 87187 ★   **Western Union International**
5444 Westheimer Rd.
Houston, TX 77056
(713)552-1429
Ultimate Parent: MCI Communications.

★ 87188 ★   **Western Union International**
1415 N. Loop
Houston, TX 77022
(713)861-6575
Ultimate Parent: MCI Communications.

★ 87189 ★   **Western Union International**
11900 Spears Rd.
Houston, TX 77067
(713)580-6654
Ultimate Parent: MCI Communications.

★ 87190 ★   **Westinghouse Electric**
5730 Clinton Dr.
Houston, TX 77020
(713)675-9686
Officer: Allen Schuler, Manager. **Ultimate
Parent:** Westinghouse Electric Corp. **SIC:**
3511—Turbines & Turbine Generator Sets.

★ 87191 ★   **Westinghouse Electric**
10510 Harwin Dr.
Houston, TX 77036
(713)778-4400
Officer: Sander Campbell, Manager.
Ultimate Parent: Westinghouse Electric
Corp. **SIC:** 3511—Turbines & Turbine
Generator Sets; 3699—Electrical Equipment
& Supplies Nec.

★ 87192 ★   **Westinghouse Electric**
5722 Clinton Dr.
Houston, TX 77020
(713)675-9629
Officer: James Morris, Manager. **Ultimate
Parent:** Westinghouse Electric Corp. **SIC:**
3511—Turbines & Turbine Generator Sets.

★ 87193 ★   **Westvaco Corp.**
8337 Long Point Rd.
Houston, TX 77055
(713)465-3253
Ultimate Parent: WestVaco Corp.

★ 87194 ★   **Westvaco Corp.**
7207 Wynnwood Ln.
Houston, TX 77008
(713)880-3222
Ultimate Parent: WestVaco Corp.

★ 87195 ★   **Wheeling Corrugating Co.**
4204 Fidelity St.
Houston, TX 77029
(713)674-6737
Ultimate Parent: Wheeling-Pittsburgh Steel
Corp. **SIC:** 3444—Sheet Metal Work.

★ 87196 ★   **Wheeling Corrugating Co. Inc.**
4204 Fidelity St.
Houston, TX 77029
(713)674-6737
Ultimate Parent: Wheeling-Pittsburgh Steel
Corp. **SIC:** 5039—Construction Materials
Nec.

★ 87197 ★   **Wheeling Machine Products**
12047 Proctor St.
Houston, TX 77038
(713)999-6230
Ultimate Parent: Cooper Industries. **SIC:**
5085—Industrial Supplies.

★ 87198 ★   **Wilsonart**
552 Garden Oaks Blvd.
Houston, TX 77018
(713)699-2840
Ultimate Parent: Premark International.
SIC: 3089—Plastics Products Nec.

★ 87199 ★   **Wingfoot Ventures Seven Inc.**
333 Clay St., Ste. 2600
Houston, TX 77002-4101
(713)750-4500
Company Type: Subsidiary. **Officer:** Mike
Latistaes. **Ultimate Parent:** Goodyear Tire
& Rubber. **SIC:** 4612—Crude Petroleum
Pipelines; 8741—Management Services;
1311—Crude Petroleum & Natural Gas.
Sales: 38.8000000 M.

★ 87200 ★   **Witco Corp.**
3230 Brookfield Dr.
Houston, TX 77045
(713)433-7281
Officer: Connie Roland, Manager. **Ultimate
Parent:** Witco Corp. **SIC:** 2843—Surface
Active Agents; 2879—Agricultural Chemicals
Nec; 2899—Chemical Preparations Nec.

★ 87201 ★   **Witco Corp.**
Oleo-Surfactant Organics
15200 Almeda Rd.
Houston, TX 77053-4920
Ultimate Parent: Witco Corp. **SIC:** 2843—
Surface Active Agents.

★ 87202 ★   **Witco Corp.**
Organics
15200 Almeda Rd.
Houston, TX 77053
Ultimate Parent: Witco Corp. **SIC:** 2843—
Surface Active Agents.

★ 87203 ★   **W.R. Grace & Co.**
Construction Production Div.
4323 Crites St.
Houston, TX 77003
Company Type: Division. **Ultimate Parent:**
W. R. Grace. **SIC:** 2899—Chemical
Preparations Nec.

★ 87204 ★   **Xerox Corp.**
5151 San Felipe St.
Houston, TX 77056
(713)961-5511
Officer: Doug Buller, Manager. **Ultimate
Parent:** Xerox Corp. **SIC:** 3663—Radio &
T.V. Communications Equipment.

★ 87205 ★   XI Datacomp
4130 Directors Row
Houston, TX 77092
(713)956-6100
Ultimate Parent: Storage Technology.

★ 87206 ★   Xomox Corp.
9454 Kirby Dr.
Houston, TX 77054
(713)668-6300
Ultimate Parent: Emerson Electric Co. Inc.

★ 87207 ★   Zenger-Miller &
Associates
510 Bering Dr.
Houston, TX 77057
(713)785-6364
Ultimate Parent: Times Mirror Co.

★ 87208 ★   Zenger-Miller &
Associates Inc.
730 N. Post Oak Rd.
Houston, TX 77024
(713)956-2834
Ultimate Parent: Times Mirror Co. SIC:
8742—Management Consulting Services.

★ 87209 ★   Zeno Systems of
Houston
8601 Jameel Rd.
Houston, TX 77040
(713)895-8238
Ultimate Parent: Alco Standard Corp. SIC:
5044—Office Equipment.

★ 87210 ★   Zeno Systems of
Houston Inc.
8601 Jameel, Ste. 190
Houston, TX 77040
Company Type: Subsidiary. Officer: Milo
C. Bump, President. Ultimate Parent: Alco
Standard Corp. SIC: 5044—Office
Equipment; 7359—Equipment Rental &
Leasing Nec.

★ 87211 ★   ZEP Manufacturing
Co.
6827 Wynnwood Dr.
Houston, TX 77008
(713)869-3636
Officer: Michael Gilmore, Manager.
Ultimate Parent: National Service
Industries. SIC: 2842—Polishes &
Sanitation Goods.

Hughes Springs

★ 87212 ★   Piggly Wiggly
111 W. 2nd
Hughes Springs, TX 75656
(214)639-2021
Ultimate Parent: Bruno's. SIC: 5411—
Grocery Stores.

Hull

★ 87213 ★   Mobil Pipe Line Co.
Hull, TX 77564
(409)536-6880
Ultimate Parent: Mobil. SIC: 4612—Crude
Petroleum Pipelines.

★ 87214 ★   Texaco Inc.
Hull, TX 77564
(409)536-3020
Ultimate Parent: Texaco. SIC: 1389—Oil &
Gas Field Services Nec.

Humble

★ 87215 ★   Ace Hardware
5815 E. F M 1960
Humble, TX 77338
(713)852-2730
Ultimate Parent: Ace Hardware. SIC:
5251—Hardware Stores.

★ 87216 ★   Capezio Shoes
20131 Hwy. 59 N
Humble, TX 77338
(713)446-0318
Ultimate Parent: United States Shoe. SIC:
5661—Shoe Stores.

★ 87217 ★   Casual Corner
20131 Hwy. 59 N
Humble, TX 77338
(713)446-2979
Ultimate Parent: United States Shoe. SIC:
5651—Family Clothing Stores.

★ 87218 ★   Comerica Bank-Texas
19506 Eastex Fwy.
Humble, TX 77338-4302
(713)446-8133
Company Type: Subsidiary. Location
Type: Branch office. Ultimate Parent:
Comerica Bank. SIC: 6021—National
Commercial Banks.

★ 87219 ★   Eckerd Drug Co.
7064 E. F M1960
Humble, TX 77338
(713)852-4700
Ultimate Parent: Eckerd Corp. SIC: 5912—
Drug Stores & Proprietary Stores.

★ 87220 ★   Exxon Co. USA
21502 Aldine Westfield Rd.
Humble, TX 77338
(713)821-8808
Ultimate Parent: Exxon.

★ 87221 ★   Footaction USA
20131 Hwy. 59 N
Humble, TX 77338
(713)446-6521
Ultimate Parent: Melville. SIC: 5941—
Sporting Goods & Bicycle Shops.

★ 87222 ★   Friendswood
Development Co.
Rockmead Dr.
Humble, TX 77339
(713)358-2111
Ultimate Parent: Exxon. SIC: 6531—Real
Estate Agents & Managers.

★ 87223 ★   The Gap
20131 Hwy. 59 N
Humble, TX 77338
(713)540-1042
Ultimate Parent: GAP.

★ 87224 ★   The Gap
19755 Hwy. 59 N
Humble, TX 77338
(713)540-1096
Ultimate Parent: GAP. SIC: 5621—
Women's Clothing Stores.

★ 87225 ★   Jiffy Lube
1622 FM 1960 Bypass E
Humble, TX 77338
(713)446-5823
Ultimate Parent: Pennzoil.

★ 87226 ★   Jiffy Lube
1890 Northpark Dr.
Humble, TX 77339
(713)359-5823
Ultimate Parent: Pennzoil.

★ 87227 ★   Kay Bee Toy&Hobby
Shop
20131 Hwy. 59 N
Humble, TX 77338
(713)446-1977
Ultimate Parent: Melville. SIC: 5945—
Hobby, Toy & Game Shops.

★ 87228 ★   Kentucky Fried
Chicken
1524 1st St. E
Humble, TX 77338
(713)446-3188
Ultimate Parent: Pepsico. SIC: 5812—
Eating Places.

★ 87229 ★   Kentucky Fried
Chicken
1712 Kingwood Dr.
Humble, TX 77339
(713)358-1997
Ultimate Parent: Pepsico. SIC: 5812—
Eating Places.

★ 87230 ★   Kroger Food Stores
19611 Eastex Fwy.
Humble, TX 77338
(713)446-2620
Ultimate Parent: Kroger. SIC: 5912—Drug
Stores & Proprietary Stores.

★ 87231 ★   Lerner Shop
20131 Hwy. 59 N
Humble, TX 77338
(713)446-7551
Ultimate Parent: Limited. SIC: 5611—
Men's & Boys' Clothing Stores.

★ 87232 ★   The Limited
20131 Hwy. 59 N
Humble, TX 77338
(713)446-8487
Ultimate Parent: Limited.

★ 87233 ★   The Limited Express
20131 Hwy. 59 N
Humble, TX 77338
(713)446-7503
Ultimate Parent: Limited. SIC: 5621—
Women's Clothing Stores.

★ 87234 ★   Marshalls Dept Str
9592 Fm 1960 Rd. W
Humble, TX 77338
(713)540-2711
Ultimate Parent: Melville.

★ 87235 ★   McDonalds Corp.
20131 Hwy. 59 N
Humble, TX 77338
(713)446-1530
Ultimate Parent: McDonald's.
SIC: 5812—Eating Places.

★ 87236 ★   Mcduff Electronics
20131 Hwy. 59 N
Humble, TX 77338
(713)446-6085
Ultimate Parent: Tandy Corp.

★ 87237 ★   Mobil Oil Corp.
520 Northpark Dr.
Humble, TX 77339
(713)358-4703
Ultimate Parent: Mobil.

★ 87238 ★   Petite Sophisticate
20131 Hwy. 59 N
Humble, TX 77338
(713)540-2444
Ultimate Parent: United States Shoe. SIC:
5621—Women's Clothing Stores.

★ 87239 ★   Pizza Hut
150 1st St. W
Humble, TX 77338
(713)446-1711
Ultimate Parent: Pepsico. SIC: 5812—
Eating Places.

★ 87240 ★   Pizza Hut
4122 Lake Houston Pky.
Humble, TX 77339
(713)360-3322
Ultimate Parent: Pepsico.

★ 87241 ★   Radio Shack
Deerbrook Mall
Humble, TX 77338
(713)446-2928
Company Type: Division. Ultimate Parent:
Tandy Corp. SIC: 5065—Electronic Parts &
Equipment Nec.

★ 87242 ★   Radio Shack
142 1st St. W
Humble, TX 77338
(713)446-0932
Company Type: Division. Ultimate Parent:
Tandy Corp. SIC: 5065—Electronic Parts &
Equipment Nec.

★ 87243 ★   Radio Shack
19300 Hwy. 59 N
Humble, TX 77338
(713)446-6314
Company Type: Division. Ultimate Parent:
Tandy Corp. SIC: 5734—Computer &
Software Stores.

★ 87244 ★   Savings of America, A
Division of Home Savings of
America, FSB
10011 FM 1960 Bypass
Humble, TX 77338
(713)446-1800
Company Type: Division. Location Type:
Branch office. Ultimate Parent: H. F.
Ahmanson. SIC: 6021—National
Commercial Banks.

★ 87245 ★   Taco Bell
20131 Hwy. 59 N
Humble, TX 77338
(713)540-7400
Ultimate Parent: Pepsico.

★ 87246 ★   Taco Bell
10019 Fm 1960 Rd. W
Humble, TX 77338
(713)540-7420
Ultimate Parent: Pepsico.

★ 87247 ★   Texaco Exprss Lube
3319 Lake Houston Pky.
Humble, TX 77339
(713)360-2838
Ultimate Parent: Texaco.

★ 87248 ★   Texaco Food Mart
8435 Fm 1960 Rd. W
Humble, TX 77338
(713)446-3406
Ultimate Parent: Texaco.

★ 87249 ★   Texaco Inc.
4103 E. FM 1960
Humble, TX 77338
(713)852-3614
Ultimate Parent: Texaco. SIC: 5171—
Petroleum Bulk Stations & Terminals.

★ 87250 ★   Texaco Pep Stop
18040 Hwy. 59 N
Humble, TX 77396
(713)446-5458
Ultimate Parent: Texaco. SIC: 5411—
Grocery Stores.

★ 87251 ★   Texas Commerce
Bank National
1075 Kingwood Dr.
Humble, TX 77339
(713)358-3111
Ultimate Parent: Chemical Banking Corp.
SIC: 6021—National Commercial Banks;
6022—State Commercial Banks.

★ 87252 ★   Tyson Foods Inc.
7611 Live Oak Dr.
Humble, TX 77396
(713)446-5868
Ultimate Parent: Tyson Foods, Inc. SIC:
5141—Groceries—General Line.

★ 87253 ★   Victoria's Secret
20131 Hwy. 59 N
Humble, TX 77338
(713)540-1941
Ultimate Parent: Limited. SIC: 5632—
Women's Accessory & Specialty Stores.

★ 87254 ★   Wal Mart Discount
City
Deerbrook Mall
Humble, TX 77338
(713)446-4165
Ultimate Parent: Wal-Mart Stores, Inc. SIC:
5912—Drug Stores & Proprietary Stores.

★ 87255 ★   Waldenbooks
Deerbrook
20131 Hwy. 59 N
Humble, TX 77338
(713)446-0243
Ultimate Parent: K-Mart. SIC: 5942—Book
Stores.

★ 87256 ★   Walgreen Drug Stores
23902 Hwy. 59 N
Humble, TX 77339
(713)358-9848
Ultimate Parent: Walgreen Co.

★ 87257 ★   Walgreen Drug Stores
4307 Kingwood Dr.
Humble, TX 77339
(713)360-4692
Ultimate Parent: Walgreen Co. SIC:
5912—Drug Stores & Proprietary Stores.

Hungerford

★ 87258 ★   M-I Drilling Fluids,
Wharton Chemical Plant
             Hwy. 59, 9 Miles East of
Wharton
Hungerford, TX 77448
Location Type: Plant. Ultimate Parent:
Halliburton. SIC: 2899—Chemical
Preparations Nec.

★ 87259 ★   M-I Drilling Fluids,
Wharton Chemical Plant
PO Box 1000
Hungerford, TX 77448
Location Type: Plant. Ultimate Parent:
Halliburton. SIC: 2899—Chemical
Preparations Nec.

Huntsville

★ 87260 ★   IBM Corp.
1704 Avenue O
Huntsville, TX 77340
(409)295-6434
Ultimate Parent: IBM. SIC: 5112—
Stationery & Office Supplies.

★ 87261 ★　Kentucky Fried
Chicken
3020 11th St.
Huntsville, TX 77340
(409)291-7511
Ultimate Parent: Pepsico. **SIC:** 5812—
Eating Places.

★ 87262 ★　Louisiana Pacific
Corp.
Hwy. 75 S
Huntsville, TX 77340
(409)295-5471
Ultimate Parent: Louisiana-Pacific. **SIC:**
5031—Lumber, Plywood & Millwork.

★ 87263 ★　Pizza Hut
1700 11th St.
Huntsville, TX 77340
(409)295-5586
Ultimate Parent: Pepsico. **SIC:** 5812—
Eating Places.

★ 87264 ★　Pizza Hut
2505 Lake Rd.
Huntsville, TX 77340
(409)294-9191
Ultimate Parent: Pepsico. **SIC:** 5812—
Eating Places.

★ 87265 ★　Taco Bell
2103 Sam Houston Ave.
Huntsville, TX 77340
(409)295-6888
Ultimate Parent: Pepsico. **SIC:** 5812—
Eating Places.

★ 87266 ★　Trailways Bus System
Inc.
1421 Sam Houston Ave.
Huntsville, TX 77340
(409)295-3732
Ultimate Parent: Greyhound Lines Inc. **SIC:**
4131—Intercity & Rural Bus Transportation.

★ 87267 ★　Walgreen Drug Stores
I Hwy. 30 45th
Huntsville, TX 77340
(409)291-6743
Ultimate Parent: Walgreen Co. **SIC:**
7384—Photofinishing Laboratories.

Hurst

★ 87268 ★　Allergan Optical
500 Grapevine Hwy.
Hurst, TX 76054
(817)581-6492
Ultimate Parent: Allergan Inc. **SIC:** 5995—
Optical Goods Stores.

★ 87269 ★　Casual Corner
1101 Melbourne Rd.
Hurst, TX 76053
(817)589-1374
Ultimate Parent: United States Shoe. **SIC:**
5651—Family Clothing Stores.

★ 87270 ★　Circus World
1101 Melbourne Rd.
Hurst, TX 76053
(817)595-1068
Ultimate Parent: Melville. **SIC:** 5945—
Hobby, Toy & Game Shops.

★ 87271 ★　Clark Equipment Co.
305 NE Loop 820
Hurst, TX 76053
(817)595-3737
Ultimate Parent: Clark Equipment Co. **SIC:**
3537—Industrial Trucks & Tractors.

★ 87272 ★　Delta Air Lines
8704 Airport Fwy.
Hurst, TX 76053
(817)589-2839
Ultimate Parent: Delta Air Lines, Inc.

★ 87273 ★　Express
1101 Melbourne Rd.
Hurst, TX 76053
(817)595-3502
Ultimate Parent: Limited. **SIC:** 5651—
Family Clothing Stores.

★ 87274 ★　Hoechst Roussel
Pharmaceutc
301 NE Loop 820
Hurst, TX 76053
(817)284-5155
Ultimate Parent: Hoechst Celanese Corp.
SIC: 5122—Drugs, Proprietaries &
Sundries.

★ 87275 ★　Kentucky Fried
Chicken
645 W. Harwood Rd.
Hurst, TX 76054
(817)498-7957
Ultimate Parent: Pepsico. **SIC:** 5812—
Eating Places.

★ 87276 ★　Kentucky Fried
Chicken
324 W. Pipeline Rd.
Hurst, TX 76053
(817)282-4641
Ultimate Parent: Pepsico. **SIC:** 5812—
Eating Places.

★ 87277 ★　Kentucky Fried
Chicken
6385 Grapevine Hwy.
Hurst, TX 76054
(817)284-1241
Ultimate Parent: Pepsico. **SIC:** 5812—
Eating Places.

★ 87278 ★　Lane Bryant
1101 Melbourne Rd.
Hurst, TX 76053
(817)595-2774
Ultimate Parent: Limited. **SIC:** 5651—
Family Clothing Stores.

★ 87279 ★　The Limited
1101 Melbourne Rd.
Hurst, TX 76053
(817)284-1958
Ultimate Parent: Limited. **SIC:** 5651—
Family Clothing Stores.

★ 87280 ★　Marshalls Inc.
1432 N. Precinct Line Rd.
Hurst, TX 76053
(817)282-5562
Ultimate Parent: Melville. **SIC:** 5311—
Department Stores.

★ 87281 ★　Mary Kay Cosmetics
1050 W. Pipeline Rd.
Hurst, TX 76053
(817)589-1338
Ultimate Parent: Mary Kay Cosmetics. **SIC:**
5999—Miscellaneous Retail Stores Nec.

★ 87282 ★　Massachusetts Mutual
Life Insurance
8701 W. Bedford Euless Rd.
Hurst, TX 76053
(817)595-0056
Ultimate Parent: Massasucetts Mutual Life.
SIC: 6411—Insurance Agents, Brokers &
Service.

★ 87283 ★　Massachusetts Mutual
Life Insurance
1800 N. Norwood Dr.
Hurst, TX 76054
(817)282-6211
Ultimate Parent: Massasucetts Mutual Life.
SIC: 6411—Insurance Agents, Brokers &
Service.

★ 87284 ★　McDonalds
Restaurant
450 Grapevine Hwy.
Hurst, TX 76054
(817)498-7776
Ultimate Parent: May Department Stores.

★ 87285 ★　Mobil Self Serve
1397 W. Pipeline Rd.
Hurst, TX 76053
(817)284-0259
Ultimate Parent: Mobil. **SIC:** 5541—
Gasoline Service Stations.

★ 87286 ★　Mobil Service Station
1397 W. Pipeline Rd.
Hurst, TX 76053
(817)595-1915
Ultimate Parent: Mobil. **SIC:** 5541—
Gasoline Service Stations.

★ 87287 ★　Noxell Corp.
1241 Southridge Ct
Hurst, TX 76053
(817)268-1666
Ultimate Parent: Procter & Gamble Co.
SIC: 5999—Miscellaneous Retail Stores
Nec.

★ 87288 ★　Payless Shoesource
860 Airport Fwy.
Hurst, TX 76054
(817)485-7273
Ultimate Parent: McDonald's.

★ 87289 ★　Payless Shoesource
1101 Melbourne Rd.
Hurst, TX 76053
(817)595-1013
Ultimate Parent: May Department Stores.
SIC: 5661—Shoe Stores.

★ 87290 ★　Pizza Hut
7901 Grapevine Hwy.
Hurst, TX 76054
(817)281-8560
Ultimate Parent: Pepsico. **SIC:** 5812—
Eating Places.

★ 87291 ★　Radio Shack
235 NE Loop 820
Hurst, TX 76053
(817)284-1988
Company Type: Division. **Ultimate Parent:**
Tandy Corp. **SIC:** 5065—Electronic Parts &
Equipment Nec.

★ 87292 ★　Radio Shack
664 Grapevine Hwy.
Hurst, TX 76054
(817)581-4385
Company Type: Division. **Ultimate Parent:**
Tandy Corp. **SIC:** 7373—Computer
Integrated Systems Design.

★ 87293 ★　Radio Shack
1009 Melbourne Rd.
Hurst, TX 76053
(817)284-4531
Company Type: Division. **Ultimate Parent:**
Tandy Corp. **SIC:** 5065—Electronic Parts &
Equipment Nec.

★ 87294 ★　Radio Shack
1011 Melbourne Rd.
Hurst, TX 76053
Company Type: Division. **Ultimate Parent:**
Tandy Corp. **SIC:** 7373—Computer
Integrated Systems Design.

★ 87295 ★　Ryder Truck Rental
10712 S. Pipeline Rd.
Hurst, TX 76053
(817)571-7647
Ultimate Parent: Ryder System.

★ 87296 ★　Savings of America, A
Division of Home Savings of
America, FSB
123313 Melbourne Rd.
Hurst, TX 76053-6219
(817)268-5238
Company Type: Division. **Location Type:**
Branch office. **Ultimate Parent:** H. F.
Ahmanson. **SIC:** 6021—National
Commercial Banks.

★ 87297 ★　Service Merchandise
1101 Melbourne Rd.
Hurst, TX 76053
(817)284-4751
Ultimate Parent: Service Merchandise Co.,
Inc. **SIC:** 3911—Jewelry & Precious Metal.

★ 87298 ★　Taco Bell
301 W. Pipeline Rd.
Hurst, TX 76053
(817)282-4542
Ultimate Parent: Pepsico. **SIC:** 5812—
Eating Places.

★ 87299 ★　Texaco Gas Station
1200 W. Hurst Blvd.
Hurst, TX 76053
(817)595-2233
Ultimate Parent: Texaco. **SIC:** 5541—
Gasoline Service Stations.

★ 87300 ★　Underwriters
Adjusting Co.
305 NE Loop 820
Hurst, TX 76053
(817)589-7816
Ultimate Parent: Continental. **SIC:** 4812—
Radiotelephone Communications.

Hutchins

★ 87301 ★　Browning-Ferris
Industries
450 E. Cleveland Rd.
Hutchins, TX 75141
(214)225-8181
Officer: Lee Solheid, Manager. **Ultimate
Parent:** Browning-Ferris Industries. **SIC:**
3594—Fluid Power Pumps & Motors.

★ 87302 ★　Exxon
I 45
Hutchins, TX 75141
(214)225-7089
Ultimate Parent: Exxon. **SIC:** 5541—
Gasoline Service Stations.

Ingleside

★ 87303 ★　Arco Oil & Gas Co.
Ingleside, TX 78362
(512)776-3538
Ultimate Parent: Atlantic Richfield Co., Inc.
SIC: 1311—Crude Petroleum & Natural
Gas.

★ 87304 ★　Arco Oil & Gas Co.
FM Rd. 1069
Ingleside, TX 78362
(512)758-8220
Location Type: Branch office. **Ultimate
Parent:** Atlantic Richfield Co., Inc. **SIC:**
1311—Crude Petroleum & Natural Gas.

Ingram

★ 87305 ★　Mini Mart 7
Skyview
Ingram, TX 78025
(512)367-5565
Ultimate Parent: Kroger. **SIC:** 5411—
Grocery Stores.

Iowa Park

★ 87306 ★　Lone Star Gas Co.
406 W. Park Ave.
Iowa Park, TX 76367
(817)592-4261
Ultimate Parent: Enserch. **SIC:** 4925—Gas
Production & Distribution Nec.

★ 87307 ★　Lone Star Gas Co.
Trans Division
Electra Rd.
Iowa Park, TX 76367
(817)592-2191
Ultimate Parent: Enserch. **SIC:** 4932—Gas
& Other Services Combined.

★ 87308 ★　W. R. Grace & Co.
Cryovac Div.
1301 W. Magnolia Ave.
Iowa Park, TX 76367
Company Type: Division. **Ultimate Parent:**
W. R. Grace. **SIC:** 3089—Plastics Products
Nec.

★ 87309 ★　Wal Mart Discount
City
370th
Iowa Park, TX 76367
(817)592-4104
Ultimate Parent: Wal-Mart Stores, Inc. **SIC:**
5311—Department Stores.

★ 87310 ★　Wal Mart Pharmacy
Loop 370
Iowa Park, TX 76367
(817)592-4157
Ultimate Parent: Wal-Mart Stores, Inc. **SIC:**
5912—Drug Stores & Proprietary Stores.

★ 87311 ★　W.R. Grace & Co.
Cryovac Div.
1301 Magnolia Ave.
Iowa Park, TX 76367
Company Type: Division. **Ultimate Parent:**
W. R. Grace. **SIC:** 3089—Plastics Products
Nec.

Ira

★ 87312 ★　Trico Industries Inc.
Ira, TX 79527
(915)573-1151
Ultimate Parent: Paccar. **SIC:** 1389—Oil &
Gas Field Services Nec.

Iraan

★ 87313 ★　Marathon Oil Co.
W Town
Iraan, TX 79744
(915)639-2553
Ultimate Parent: USX Corp. **SIC:** 1311—
Crude Petroleum & Natural Gas.

★ 87314 ★　Marathon Oil Co.
W Town
Iraan, TX 79744
(915)639-2553
Ultimate Parent: USX Corp. SIC: 1311—
Crude Petroleum & Natural Gas.

Irving

★ 87315 ★　Abbott Laboratories
Diagnostic Div.
PO Box 152020
Irving, TX 75015-2020
(214)518-6000
Company Type: Division. Officer: Mark S.
Peccarelli. Ultimate Parent: Abbott
Laboratories. SIC: 3841—Surgical &
Medical Instruments.

★ 87316 ★　Abbott Laboratories
Diagnostics Division
1921 Hurd Dr.
Irving, TX 75015
Ultimate Parent: Abbott Laboratories. SIC:
2895—Carbon Black; 3826—Analytical
Instruments.

★ 87317 ★　Abbott Manufacturing
Inc.
1921 Hurd Dr.
Irving, TX 75038
Ultimate Parent: Abbott Laboratories. SIC:
2895—Carbon Black; 3826—Analytical
Instruments.

★ 87318 ★　Ace Hardware
2333 W. Shady Grove Rd.
Irving, TX 75060
(214)986-5825
Ultimate Parent: Ace Hardware. SIC:
5251—Hardware Stores.

★ 87319 ★　Air Products &
Chemicals Inc.
8505 Freeport Pky., Ste. 280
Irving, TX 75063-2505
(214)929-8180
Officer: A. D. Marek. Ultimate Parent: Air
Products & Chemicals, Inc. SIC: 2813—
Industrial Gases; 5169—Chemicals & Allied
Products Nec.

★ 87320 ★　Air Treads Inc.
Dallas Div.
3419 Royalty Row
Irving, TX 75062
Ultimate Parent: Goodyear Tire & Rubber.
SIC: 3911—Jewelry & Precious Metal.

★ 87321 ★　Auto Data
Processing, Inc.
Dealer Services Div.
2300 Valley View Ln.
Irving, TX 75062-5058
(214)255-1447
Company Type: Division. Ultimate Parent:
Automatic Data Processing, Inc. SIC:
8243—Data Processing Schools.

★ 87322 ★　Bellsouth
Communication Systems Inc.
9150 W. Royal Ln.
Irving, TX 75063-2437
(214)929-0900
Officer: Pegi Lair. Ultimate Parent:
BellSouth Corp. SIC: 5999—Miscellaneous
Retail Stores Nec.

★ 87323 ★　Beneficial Texas
1111 W. Airport Fwy.
Irving, TX 75062
(214)255-3770
Ultimate Parent: Beneficial.

★ 87324 ★　Boeing Electronics
Irving Co.
3131 Story Rd. W
Irving, TX 75038
Ultimate Parent: Boeing. SIC: 3679—
Electronic Components Nec.

★ 87325 ★　Bristol-Myers Squibb
Co.
6125 Campus Cir. Dr. W
Irving, TX 75063-2610
(214)518-5600
Ultimate Parent: Bristol-Myers Squibb. SIC:
5122—Drugs, Proprietaries & Sundries.

★ 87326 ★　Burlington Northern
Railroa
525 E. Airport Fwy.
Irving, TX 75062
(214)252-8525
Ultimate Parent: Burlington Northern. SIC:
4011—Railroads—Line-Haul Operating.

★ 87327 ★　Caltex Petroleum
Corp.
125 E. John Carpenter Fwy.
Irving, TX 75062-2750
(214)830-1000
Officer: Patrick J. Ward, Chairman of the
Board. Ultimate Parent: Chevron Corp.
SIC: 2911—Petroleum Refining; 4731—
Freight Transportation Arrangement; 5172—
Petroleum Products Nec. Employee Count:
8000. Sales: 5 M.

★ 87328 ★　Casual Corner
3718 Irving Mall
Irving, TX 75062
(214)252-8411
Ultimate Parent: United States Shoe. SIC:
5621—Women's Clothing Stores.

★ 87329 ★　Cigna Insurance Co.
of Texas
600 Las Colinas Blvd. E
Irving, TX 75039-5616
(214)869-8500
Company Type: Subsidiary. Officer:
Charels McCullough, President. Ultimate
Parent: Cigna Corp. SIC: 6321—Accident &
Health Insurance; 6331—Fire, Marine &
Casualty Insurance; 6351—Surety
Insurance.

★ 87330 ★　Circus World Toys
Inc.
2417 Irving Mall
Irving, TX 75062
(214)258-1542
Ultimate Parent: Melville. SIC: 5945—
Hobby, Toy & Game Shops.

★ 87331 ★　City National Bank of
Irvin
301 W. Irving Blvd.
Irving, TX 75060
(214)254-6000
Ultimate Parent: City National Corp. SIC:
6021—National Commercial Banks.

★ 87332 ★　City National Bank of
Irving
222 Las Colinas Blvd. W.
Irving, TX 75039-5421
(214)401-4044
Ultimate Parent: City National Corp. SIC:
6021—National Commercial Banks.

★ 87333 ★　City National Bank of
Irving
301 W. Irving Blvd.
Irving, TX 75060-2920
(214)259-3445
Ultimate Parent: City National Corp. SIC:
6021—National Commercial Banks.

★ 87334 ★　Comerica Bank-Texas
301 W. Irving Blvd.
Irving, TX 75060-2920
(214)841-2004
Company Type: Subsidiary. Location
Type: Branch office. Ultimate Parent:
Comerica Bank. SIC: 6021—National
Commercial Banks.

★ 87335 ★　Compass Bank-Dallas
4925 N. O'Conner Blvd.
Irving, TX 75062-2760
(214)541-2265
Company Type: Subsidiary. Location
Type: Branch office. Officer: Bill Wood,
Manager. Ultimate Parent: Compass
Bancshares. SIC: 6021—National
Commercial Banks.

★ 87336 ★　Computer Associates
909 E. Las Colinas Blvd.
Irving, TX 75039
(214)556-7435
Ultimate Parent: Computer Associates
International.

★ 87337 ★　Crestar Food
Products Inc.
2240 E. Union Bower Rd.
Irving, TX 75061
(214)554-8804 Fax: (214)554-7930
Company Type: Subsidiary. Location
Type: Plant. Officer: John MacArthy, Dir.
Southern Opns. Ultimate Parent: H.J.

Heinz. SIC: 2032—Canned Specialties;
2035—Pickles, Sauces & Salad Dressings.

★ 87338 ★　Critikon Inc.
9425 N. MacArthur Blvd.
Irving, TX 75063-4706
(214)401-2100
Ultimate Parent: Johnson & Johnson. SIC:
5251—Hardware Stores; 7372—
Prepackaged Software; 7374—Data
Processing & Preparation.

★ 87339 ★　Dr. Pepper Bottling
Co.
2304 Century Ctr. Blvd.
Irving, TX 75062
(214)579-1024
Officer: Jim L. Turner, President. Ultimate
Parent: Dr. Pepper/Seven-Up. SIC: 2086—
Bottled & Canned Soft Drinks; 2087—
Flavoring Extracts & Syrups Nec.

★ 87340 ★　Exxon
225 E. John Carpenter Fwy.
Irving, TX 75062
(214)444-1000
Company Type: Headquarters. Officer: L.
R. Raymond. Sales: 97825 M. Fortune
500: Largest U.S. Industrial Corporations:
Ranking 3.

★ 87341 ★　Exxon Capital Holding
Corp.
225 E. John W. Carpenter Fwy.
Irving, TX 75062
(214)444-1000
Company Type: Subsidiary. Officer: E. A.
Robinson, President. Ultimate Parent:
Exxon. SIC: 1382—Oil & Gas Exploration
Services; 1311—Crude Petroleum & Natural
Gas. Sales: 179 M.

★ 87342 ★　Exxon Co. USA
1201 E. Airport Fwy.
Irving, TX 75062
(214)579-3840
Ultimate Parent: Exxon.

★ 87343 ★　Exxon Co. USA
Irving, TX 75015
(214)650-7088
Ultimate Parent: Exxon.

★ 87344 ★　Exxon Corp.
225 E. John W. Carpenter Fwy.
Irving, TX 75062-2298
(214)444-1000 Fax: (214)444-1350
Company Type: Headquarters. Officer:
Lee R. Raymond, Chairman & CEO.
Ultimate Parent: Exxon. Employee Count:
95000.

★ 87345 ★　First Gibraltar Bank
1925 W. John Carpenter Fwy.
Irving, TX 75063
(214)225-5342 Fax: (214)960-4500
Company Type: Subsidiary. Officer:
Gerald J. Ford, Chairman of the Board.
Ultimate Parent: Bankamerica Corp. SIC:
6022—State Commercial Banks.

★ 87346 ★　Footaction U S a
Irving Mall
Irving, TX 75062
(214)570-0996
Ultimate Parent: Melville. SIC: 7699—
Repair Services Nec.

★ 87347 ★　Fresh Foods
3250 International Pl
Irving, TX 75062
(214)438-2801
Ultimate Parent: Dole Food. SIC: 5148—
Fresh Fruits & Vegetables.

★ 87348 ★　The Gap
3712 Irving Mall
Irving, TX 75062
(214)659-1970
Ultimate Parent: GAP. SIC: 5611—Men's &
Boys' Clothing Stores.

★ 87349 ★　Greystone Realty
Corp.
400 E. Las Colinas Blvd.
Irving, TX 75039
(214)556-0222
Ultimate Parent: New York Life. SIC:
6552—Subdividers & Developers Nec.

★ 87350 ★　GTE Southwest Inc.
500 E. Carpenter Fwy.
Irving, TX 75062
(214)717-7900 Fax: (214)717-6347
Company Type: Subsidiary. Ultimate

Parent: GTE. SIC: 4812—Radiotelephone
Communications.

★ 87351 ★　GTE Southwest Inc.
500 E. John W. Carpenter Fwy.
Irving, TX 75062
(214)717-7900
Company Type: Subsidiary. Officer:
Michael Esstman, President. Ultimate
Parent: GTE. SIC: 4813—Telephone
Communications Except Radiotelephone;
6519—Real Property Lessors Nec; 8721—
Accounting, Auditing & Bookkeeping;
5065—Electronic Parts & Equipment Nec;
7629—Electrical Repair Shops Nec.
Employee Count: 7809. Sales: 282 M.

★ 87352 ★　GTE Supply
5615 High Point Dr.
Irving, TX 75038
(214)751-4100 Fax: (214)751-4933
Company Type: Division. Ultimate Parent:
GTE. SIC: 4813—Telephone
Communications Except Radiotelephone.

★ 87353 ★　GTE Telephone
Operations
600 Hidden Ridge
Irving, TX 75038
(214)718-5600 Fax: (214)718-6374
Company Type: Subsidiary. Officer: Kent
B. Foster, President. Ultimate Parent: GTE.

★ 87354 ★　Hit or Miss
3517 N. Belt Line Rd.
Irving, TX 75062
(214)252-8832
Ultimate Parent: TJX.

★ 87355 ★　Jiffy Lube
1528 N. Belt Line Rd.
Irving, TX 75061
(214)986-1006
Ultimate Parent: Pennzoil.

★ 87356 ★　Kentucky Fried
Chicken
3410 W. Rochelle Rd.
Irving, TX 75062
(214)252-2213
Ultimate Parent: Pepsico. SIC: 5812—
Eating Places.

★ 87357 ★　Kentucky Fried
Chicken
1812 N. Story Rd.
Irving, TX 75061
(214)790-2902
Ultimate Parent: Pepsico. SIC: 5812—
Eating Places.

★ 87358 ★　Kentucky Fried
Chicken
2125 Vanco Dr.
Irving, TX 75061
(214)438-3616
Ultimate Parent: Pepsico. SIC: 5812—
Eating Places.

★ 87359 ★　Kimberly-Clark
545 E. John Carpenter Fwy.
Irving, TX 75062
(214)830-1200
Company Type: Headquarters. Officer:
Wayne R. Sanders. Employee Count:
42131. Sales: 6973 M. Fortune 500:
Largest U.S. Industrial Corporations:
Ranking 79.

★ 87360 ★　Kroger Co.
1331 E. Airport Frwy.
Irving, TX 75062
Ultimate Parent: Kroger. SIC: 5411—
Grocery Stores.

★ 87361 ★　Kroger Co.
Airport Freeway
Irving, TX 75062
(214)721-4700
Ultimate Parent: Kroger. SIC: 5141—
Groceries—General Line.

★ 87362 ★　Kroger Food Stores
2201 W. Grauwyler Rd.
Irving, TX 75061
(214)790-5747
Ultimate Parent: Kroger. SIC: 5411—
Grocery Stores.

★ 87363 ★　Kroger Food Stores
3612 N. Belt Line Rd.
Irving, TX 75062
(214)252-7413
Ultimate Parent: Kroger.

★ 87364 ★   **Kroger Food Stores**
515 S. Macarthur Blvd.
Irving, TX 75060
(214)254-9105
Ultimate Parent: Kroger. **SIC:** 5912—Drug
Stores & Proprietary Stores.

★ 87365 ★   **Kroger Food Stores**
1901 Gateway Dr.
Irving, TX 75038
(214)580-3000
Ultimate Parent: Kroger. **SIC:** 5411—
Grocery Stores.

★ 87366 ★   **Lane Bryant**
3945 Irving Mall
Irving, TX 75062
(214)252-3547
Ultimate Parent: Limited. **SIC:** 5621—
Women's Clothing Stores.

★ 87367 ★   **Lerner Shop**
Irving Mall
Irving, TX 75062
(214)252-4744
Ultimate Parent: Limited. **SIC:** 5621—
Women's Clothing Stores.

★ 87368 ★   **The Limited**
2417 Irving Mall
Irving, TX 75062
(214)255-1055
Ultimate Parent: Limited. **SIC:** 5621—
Women's Clothing Stores.

★ 87369 ★   **The Limited Express**
3924 Irving Mall
Irving, TX 75062
(214)255-0350
Ultimate Parent: Limited. **SIC:** 5621—
Women's Clothing Stores.

★ 87370 ★   **Logistics Data
System**
104 E. Decker Ct., Ste. 700
Irving, TX 75062
(214)717-0630 **Fax:** (214)402-9891
Company Type: Subsidiary. **Ultimate
Parent:** Dun & Bradstreet. **SIC:** 7372—
Prepackaged Software; 7379—Computer
Related Services Nec; 8742—Management
Consulting Services.

★ 87371 ★   **Lone Star Gas Co.**
1931 E. 6th St.
Irving, TX 75060
(214)579-0232
Ultimate Parent: Enserch. **SIC:** 4932—Gas
& Other Services Combined.

★ 87372 ★   **Lone Star Gas Co.**
205 S. Jefferson St.
Irving, TX 75060
(214)253-5102
Ultimate Parent: Enserch. **SIC:** 4932—Gas
& Other Services Combined.

★ 87373 ★   **Mary Kay Cosmetics**
2707 W. Royal Ln.
Irving, TX 75063
(214)401-0375
Ultimate Parent: Mary Kay Cosmetics.

★ 87374 ★   **McCormick & Co. Inc.**
Flavor Group-Industrial Products
3300 Century Cir.
Irving, TX 75062
(214)554-1354
Company Type: Division. **Location Type:**
Plant. **Officer:** George Winchester, Plant
Manager. **Ultimate Parent:** McCormick &
Co. Inc.

★ 87375 ★   **McDonalds**
4098 N. Belt Line Rd.
Irving, TX 75038
(214)255-1387
Ultimate Parent: McDonald's.

★ 87376 ★   **McDonalds
Restaurants**
302 W. Irving Blvd.
Irving, TX 75060
(214)253-4492
Ultimate Parent: McDonald's.
SIC: 5812—Eating Places.

★ 87377 ★   **Mcduff Electronics**
3301 W. Airport Fwy.
Irving, TX 75062
(214)255-2996
Ultimate Parent: Tandy Corp.

★ 87378 ★   **Milwaukee
Seasonings**
3241 W. Story Rd.
Irving, TX 75038
(214)570-1510
Ultimate Parent: CPC International.

★ 87379 ★   **Mobil Self Service**
1300 Airport Fwy.
Irving, TX 75062
(214)438-1026
Ultimate Parent: Mobil. **SIC:** 5541—
Gasoline Service Stations.

★ 87380 ★   **Murdock Engineering
Co.**
5100 Airport Freeway W.
Irving, TX 75062-5805
Ultimate Parent: Lockheed Corp. **SIC:**
3728—Aircraft Parts & Equipment Nec.

★ 87381 ★   **Murdock Engineering
Co.**
5100 Airport Frwy. West
Irving, TX 75062-5805
Ultimate Parent: Lockheed Corp. **SIC:**
3728—Aircraft Parts & Equipment Nec.

★ 87382 ★   **NCH**
2727 Chemsearch Blvd.
Irving, TX 75062
(214)438-0211
Company Type: Headquarters. **Officer:**
Irvin L. Levy. **Employee Count:** 10098.
Sales: 680 M.

★ 87383 ★   **NCH Corp.**
2727 Chemsearch Blvd.
PO Box 152170
Irving, TX 75015
(214)438-0211 **Fax:** (214)438-0186 **Telex:**
73336
Officer: Lester A. Levy, Chairman of the
Board. **Ultimate Parent:** NCH. **Employee
Count:** 1000.

★ 87384 ★   **NCH Corp.**
Mohawk Labratories Div.
2730 Carl Rd.
Irving, TX 75062
Company Type: Division. **Ultimate Parent:**
NCH. **SIC:** 2842—Polishes & Sanitation
Goods.

★ 87385 ★   **NCH Corp.**
Mohawk Labratories Div.
2730 Carl Rd.
Irving, TX 75062
Company Type: Division. **Ultimate Parent:**
NCH. **SIC:** 2842—Polishes & Sanitation
Goods.

★ 87386 ★   **Owens-Corning
Fiberglas Corp.**
201 N. Nursery Rd.
Irving, TX 75061
(214)438-1050
Officer: Jeff Zureick, Manager. **Ultimate
Parent:** Owens-Corning. **SIC:** 2952—
Asphalt Felts & Coatings.

★ 87387 ★   **Payless Cashways
Inc.**
100 S. Belt Line Rd.
Irving, TX 75060
(214)790-0502
Ultimate Parent: Payless Cashways. **SIC:**
5211—Lumber & Other Building Materials.

★ 87388 ★   **Payless Shoesource**
3049 N. Belt Line Rd.
Irving, TX 75062
(214)255-9213
Ultimate Parent: May Department Stores.
SIC: 5661—Shoe Stores.

★ 87389 ★   **Payless Shoesource**
103 Plymouth Pk. Shopping
Irving, TX 75061
(214)790-2296
Ultimate Parent: May Department Stores.
SIC: 5661—Shoe Stores.

★ 87390 ★   **Pizza Hut**
3302 W. Rochelle Rd.
Irving, TX 75062
(214)659-0074
Ultimate Parent: Pepsico. **SIC:** 5812—
Eating Places.

★ 87391 ★   **Pizza Hut**
4835 N. O Connor Rd.
Irving, TX 75062
(214)717-1199
Ultimate Parent: Pepsico.

★ 87392 ★   **Pizza Hut**
942 W. Airport Fwy.
Irving, TX 75062
(214)438-5411
Ultimate Parent: Pepsico. **SIC:** 5812—
Eating Places.

★ 87393 ★   **Price Pfister Inc.**
1939 Hereford Dr.
Irving, TX 75038-4317
(214)550-8889
Ultimate Parent: Black & Decker Corp.
SIC: 5074—Plumbing & Hydronic Heating
Supplies.

★ 87394 ★   **Radio Shack**
229 Plymouth Park Shoppi
Irving, TX 75061
(214)986-6811
Company Type: Division. **Ultimate Parent:**
Tandy Corp. **SIC:** 5065—Electronic Parts &
Equipment Nec.

★ 87395 ★   **Radio Shack**
1001 W. Rochelle Rd.
Irving, TX 75062
(214)255-5156
Company Type: Division. **Ultimate Parent:**
Tandy Corp. **SIC:** 5065—Electronic Parts &
Equipment Nec.

★ 87396 ★   **Radio Shack**
Irving Mall
Irving, TX 75062
(214)659-1765
Company Type: Division. **Ultimate Parent:**
Tandy Corp. **SIC:** 5065—Electronic Parts &
Equipment Nec.

★ 87397 ★   **Radio Shack**
2019 W. Airport Fwy.
Irving, TX 75062
(214)252-6543
Company Type: Division. **Ultimate Parent:**
Tandy Corp. **SIC:** 5731—Radio, Television
& Electronics Stores.

★ 87398 ★   **Ryder Truck Rental**
1122 W. Airport Fwy.
Irving, TX 75062
(214)438-5388
Ultimate Parent: Ryder System. **SIC:**
7359—Equipment Rental & Leasing Nec;
7513—Truck Rental & Leasing Without
Drivers.

★ 87399 ★   **Ryder Truck Rental**
3906 W. Airport Fwy.
Irving, TX 75062
(214)986-9516
Ultimate Parent: Ryder System.

★ 87400 ★   **Savings of America, A
Division of Home Savings of
America, FSB**
1307 Airport Fwy. W.
Irving, TX 75062-6222
(214)255-4114
Company Type: Division. **Location Type:**
Branch office. **Ultimate Parent:** H. F.
Ahmanson. **SIC:** 6021—National
Commercial Banks.

★ 87401 ★   **Shell Oil Co.**
412 E. Airport Fwy.
Irving, TX 75062
(214)445-1207
Ultimate Parent: Shell Oil Co. **SIC:** 2821—
Plastics Materials & Resins.

★ 87402 ★   **Shipley Co. Inc.**
2020 Century Blvd.
Irving, TX 75062
(214)438-2400
Ultimate Parent: Rohm & Haas. **SIC:**
3861—Photographic Equipment & Supplies.

★ 87403 ★   **T J Maxx**
3445 N. Belt Line Rd.
Irving, TX 75062
(214)255-5630
Ultimate Parent: TJX.

★ 87404 ★   **Taco Bell**
2300 Valley View Ln. 400
Irving, TX 75062
(214)327-7630
Ultimate Parent: Pepsico. **SIC:** 5812—
Eating Places.

★ 87405 ★   **Taco Bell**
1105 W. Shady Grove Rd.
Irving, TX 75060
(214)986-8042
Ultimate Parent: Pepsico. **SIC:** 5812—
Eating Places.

★ 87406 ★   **Taco Bell**
801 S. Belt Line Rd.
Irving, TX 75060
(214)986-2041
Ultimate Parent: Pepsico. **SIC:** 5812—
Eating Places.

★ 87407 ★   **Taco Bell**
101 W. Airport Fwy.
Irving, TX 75062
(214)570-4438
Ultimate Parent: Pepsico.

★ 87408 ★   **Taco Bell**
2821 N. Belt Line Rd.
Irving, TX 75062
(214)570-5065
Ultimate Parent: Pepsico. **SIC:** 5812—
Eating Places.

★ 87409 ★   **Taco Bell**
1601 N. Story Rd.
Irving, TX 75061
(214)790-3313
Ultimate Parent: Pepsico. **SIC:** 5812—
Eating Places.

★ 87410 ★   **Taco Bell**
3840 Irving Mall
Irving, TX 75062
(214)252-2755
Ultimate Parent: Pepsico. **SIC:** 5812—
Eating Places.

★ 87411 ★   **Target Stores**
3333 W. Airport Fwy.
Irving, TX 75062
(214)252-9888
Company Type: Subsidiary. **Ultimate
Parent:** Dayton Hudson.

★ 87412 ★   **Texaco Food Mart**
4055 N. Belt Line Rd.
Irving, TX 75038
(214)258-6889
Ultimate Parent: Texaco. **SIC:** 5411—
Grocery Stores.

★ 87413 ★   **Texaco Food Mrt**
2112 N. O Connor Rd.
Irving, TX 75061
(214)721-1014
Ultimate Parent: Texaco.

★ 87414 ★   **Texaco Lubricants**
4500 Fuller Dr.
Irving, TX 75038
(214)717-4440
Ultimate Parent: Texaco.

★ 87415 ★   **Trailway Tours Inc.**
127 S. Jefferson St.
Irving, TX 75060
(214)254-8412
Ultimate Parent: Greyhound Lines Inc. **SIC:**
4131—Intercity & Rural Bus Transportation.

★ 87416 ★   **Willamette Industries
Inc.**
8800 Sterling St.
Irving, TX 75063
(214)258-6262
Ultimate Parent: Willamette Industries, Inc.
SIC: 1521—Single-Family Housing
Construction.

★ 87417 ★   **World Savings &
Loan**
4040 N. MacArthur Blvd.
Irving, TX 75038
(214)717-9217
Ultimate Parent: Golden West Financial
Corp. **SIC:** 6159—Miscellaneous Business
Credit Institutions.

★ 87418 ★   **Zeno Systems Inc.**
3000 Gateway Dr.
Irving, TX 75063-2674
(214)751-8000
Ultimate Parent: Alco Standard Corp. **SIC:**
5044—Office Equipment.

★ 87419 ★   **Zeno Systems Inc.**
3000 Gateway Dr.
Irving, TX 75063-2674
(214)751-8000
Ultimate Parent: Alco Standard Corp. **SIC:**
5044—Office Equipment.

Jacksboro

★ 87420 ★   Arco Pipe Line Co.
Pump Station Rd.
Jacksboro, TX 76458
(817)567-2703
Ultimate Parent: Atlantic Richfield Co., Inc.
SIC: 4612—Crude Petroleum Pipelines;
1389—Oil & Gas Field Services Nec.

Jacksonville

★ 87421 ★   Baxter Healthcare
Corp.
PO Box 2046
Jacksonville, TX 75766-2046
(903)586-6502
Officer: Dave Garber. Ultimate Parent:
Baxter International. SIC: 3841—Surgical &
Medical Instruments.

★ 87422 ★   Kentucky Fried
Chicken
411 S. Jackson St.
Jacksonville, TX 75766
(214)586-1341
Ultimate Parent: Pepsico. SIC: 5812—
Eating Places; 5812—Eating Places.

★ 87423 ★   Kids R US
315 N. Ragsdale St.
Jacksonville, TX 75766
(214)586-7210
Ultimate Parent: Toys "R" US. SIC: 8211—
Elementary & Secondary Schools.

★ 87424 ★   Pizza Hut
1602 S. Jackson St.
Jacksonville, TX 75766
(903)586-6531
Ultimate Parent: Pepsico.

★ 87425 ★   Plastics, Inc.
1800 N. Bolton St.
Jacksonville, TX 75766
(214)586-2408
Ultimate Parent: Newell. SIC: 3089—
Plastics Products Nec.

★ 87426 ★   Ryder Truck Rental
439 Frankston St.
Jacksonville, TX 75766
(903)586-4703
Ultimate Parent: Ryder System.

★ 87427 ★   Wal Mart Discnt
1631 S. Jackson St.
Jacksonville, TX 75766
(903)586-1516
Ultimate Parent: Wal-Mart Stores, Inc.

★ 87428 ★   Wal Mart Discount
Center
1612 S. Jackson St.
Jacksonville, TX 75766
(214)586-1516
Ultimate Parent: Wal-Mart Stores, Inc. SIC:
5311—Department Stores; 5932—Used
Merchandise Stores.

Jarrell

★ 87429 ★   Exxon Truck Stop
Jarrell, TX 76537
(512)746-4172
Ultimate Parent: Exxon. SIC: 5541—
Gasoline Service Stations.

Jasper

★ 87430 ★   Coca-Cola Bottling
Co.
710 W. Gibson St.
Jasper, TX 75951
(409)384-2272
Ultimate Parent: Coca-Cola Enterprises.
SIC: 2086—Bottled & Canned Soft Drinks.

★ 87431 ★   Exxon Distributor
Kirbyville Hwy.
Jasper, TX 75951
(409)384-2441
Ultimate Parent: Exxon. SIC: 5171—
Petroleum Bulk Stations & Terminals.

★ 87432 ★   Kentucky Fried
Chicken
405 E. Gibson St.
Jasper, TX 75951
(409)384-8701
Ultimate Parent: Pepsico. SIC: 5812—
Eating Places; 5812—Eating Places.

★ 87433 ★   Louisiana-Pacific
Corp., Plywood
Hwy. 63 E
Jasper, TX 75951
Ultimate Parent: Louisiana-Pacific. SIC:
2436—Softwood Veneer & Plywood.

★ 87434 ★   Pizza Hut
410 E. Gibson St.
Jasper, TX 75951
(409)384-5495
Ultimate Parent: Pepsico. SIC: 5812—
Eating Places.

★ 87435 ★   Wal Mart Discount
City
450 E. Gibson St.
Jasper, TX 75951
(409)384-4691
Ultimate Parent: Wal-Mart Stores, Inc. SIC:
5912—Drug Stores & Proprietary Stores.

★ 87436 ★   Wal Mart Pharmacy
450 E. Gibson St.
Jasper, TX 75951
(409)384-7200
Ultimate Parent: Wal-Mart Stores, Inc. SIC:
5912—Drug Stores & Proprietary Stores.

Jayton

★ 87437 ★   Mobil Exploration &
Producing US
Jayton, TX 79528
(806)237-5300
Ultimate Parent: Mobil. SIC: 1311—Crude
Petroleum & Natural Gas.

★ 87438 ★   Mobil Oil Drilling
Department
Jayton, TX 79528
(806)237-9160
Ultimate Parent: Mobil. SIC: 1311—Crude
Petroleum & Natural Gas.

Jefferson

★ 87439 ★   Piggly Wiggly
404 E. Broadway St.
Jefferson, TX 75657
(214)665-3601
Ultimate Parent: Bruno's. SIC: 5411—
Grocery Stores.

★ 87440 ★   Texaco Jobber
Warehouse
301 E. Lafayette St.
Jefferson, TX 75657
(214)665-2261
Ultimate Parent: Texaco. SIC: 5171—
Petroleum Bulk Stations & Terminals.

Jewett

★ 87441 ★   Nucor Corp.
Nucor Steel Div.
Hwy. 79 S.
Jewett, TX 75846
Company Type: Division. Ultimate Parent:
Nucor Corp. SIC: 3310—Blast Furnace &
Basic Steel Products.

★ 87442 ★   Nucor Steel
Texas Div.
Hwy. 79 S.
Jewett, TX 75846
Company Type: Division. Ultimate Parent:
Nucor Corp. SIC: 3312—Blast Furnaces &
Steel Mills.

Joaquin

★ 87443 ★   Piggly Wiggly
Joaquin, TX 75954
(409)269-3130
Ultimate Parent: Bruno's. SIC: 5421—Meat
& Fish Markets.

Johnson City

★ 87444 ★   Texaco
Hwy. 289
Johnson City, TX 78636
(512)868-7056
Ultimate Parent: Texaco. SIC: 5541—
Gasoline Service Stations.

Jones Creek

★ 87445 ★   Phillips 66
Jones Creek Terminal
SH 36 S
Jones Creek, TX 77480-0866
Company Type: Division. Ultimate Parent:
Phillips Petroleum. SIC: 5171—Petroleum
Bulk Stations & Terminals; 2911—Petroleum
Refining.

★ 87446 ★   Phillips 66 Co.
Jones Creek Terminal
S.H. 36 S
Jones Creek, TX 77480-0866
Company Type: Division. Ultimate Parent:
Phillips Petroleum. SIC: 5171—Petroleum
Bulk Stations & Terminals; 2911—Petroleum
Refining.

Katy

★ 87447 ★   Cameron Elastomer
Technology Inc.
29501 Katy Freeway
Katy, TX 77450
Ultimate Parent: Cooper Industries. SIC:
3053—Gaskets, Packing & Sealing Devices.

★ 87448 ★   Cooper Elastomer
Technology Inc.
29501 Katy Freeway
Katy, TX 77450
Ultimate Parent: Cooper Industries. SIC:
3053—Gaskets, Packing & Sealing Devices.

★ 87449 ★   Kentucky Fried
Chicken
908 S. Mason Rd.
Katy, TX 77450
(713)392-3715
Ultimate Parent: Pepsico. SIC: 5812—
Eating Places.

★ 87450 ★   Lone Star Gas Co.
28801 Morton Rd.
Katy, TX 77493
(713)391-1300
Ultimate Parent: Enserch. SIC: 4932—Gas
& Other Services Combined.

★ 87451 ★   McDonalds
22003 Katy Fwy.
Katy, TX 77450
(713)392-9990
Ultimate Parent: McDonald's.

★ 87452 ★   Payless Shoesource
1741 N. Fry Rd.
Katy, TX 77449
(713)579-2560
Ultimate Parent: May Department Stores.

★ 87453 ★   Pizza Hut
390 S. Mason Rd.
Katy, TX 77450
(713)392-9057
Ultimate Parent: Pepsico. SIC: 5812—
Eating Places.

★ 87454 ★   Radio Shack
22511 Katy Fwy.
Katy, TX 77450
(713)392-0747
Company Type: Division. Ultimate Parent:
Tandy Corp.

★ 87455 ★   Radio Shack
20031 Katy Fwy.
Katy, TX 77450
(713)492-2338
Company Type: Division. Ultimate Parent:
Tandy Corp.

★ 87456 ★   Super Saver
653 Pin Oak Rd.
Katy, TX 77494
(713)391-4424
Ultimate Parent: Wal-Mart Stores, Inc.

★ 87457 ★   Taco Bell
601 S. Mason Rd.
Katy, TX 77450
(713)578-1342
Ultimate Parent: Pepsico.

★ 87458 ★   Walgreen Drug Stores
599 S. Mason Rd.
Katy, TX 77450
(713)579-1400
Ultimate Parent: Walgreen Co.

Kaufman

★ 87459 ★   Pizza Hut
2250 S. Washington St.
Kaufman, TX 75142
(214)932-3919
Ultimate Parent: Pepsico. SIC: 5812—
Eating Places.

Keller

★ 87460 ★   Ball Corp.
Efratom Regional Office
1445 Melody Ln.
Keller, TX 76248
(817)379-6070
Location Type: Branch office. Ultimate
Parent: Ball Corp. SIC: 5065—Electronic
Parts & Equipment Nec.

★ 87461 ★   Mobil Oil
104 S. Main St.
Keller, TX 76248
(817)431-6171
Ultimate Parent: Mobil. SIC: 5599—
Automotive Dealers Nec.

★ 87462 ★   Mobil Pipe Line Co.
2955 Keller Hicks Rd.
Keller, TX 76248-9542
(817)431-1181
Ultimate Parent: Mobil. SIC: 4612—Crude
Petroleum Pipelines.

Kemah

★ 87463 ★   Wilmer Service Line
4719 Broadmoore Dr.
Kemah, TX 77565
(800)537-7793
Ultimate Parent: Reynolds & Reynolds.

Kemp

★ 87464 ★   Ace Hardware
Hwy. 175
Kemp, TX 75143
(903)498-2301
Ultimate Parent: Ace Hardware. SIC:
5211—Lumber & Other Building Materials.

Kenedy

★ 87465 ★   Aqualon Co.
1 Mill St.
Kenedy, TX 78119
Ultimate Parent: Hercules. SIC: 2899—
Chemical Preparations Nec.

★ 87466 ★   Pizza Hut
Hwy. 181 Bypass
Kenedy, TX 78119
(512)583-9818
Ultimate Parent: Pepsico. SIC: 5812—
Eating Places.

★ 87467 ★   Wal Mart Pharmacy
337 N. Sunset Strip St.
Kenedy, TX 78119
(512)583-9832
Ultimate Parent: Wal-Mart Stores, Inc. SIC:
5912—Drug Stores & Proprietary Stores.

Kermit

★ 87468 ★   Mobil Pipeline Co.
Halley Sta.
Kermit, TX 79745
(915)586-6208
Company Type: Branch. Ultimate Parent:
Mobil. SIC: 4612—Crude Petroleum
Pipelines.

★ 87469 ★   Oryx Energy Co.
Monahans Hwy.
Kermit, TX 79745
(915)586-3891
Ultimate Parent: Oryx Energy. SIC: 1389—
Oil & Gas Field Services Nec.

★ 87470 ★   Pizza Hut
226 E. Hwy. 302
Kermit, TX 79745
(915)586-2255
Ultimate Parent: Pepsico. SIC: 5812—
Eating Places.

Kerrville

★ 87471 ★   Allstate Life
Insurance Co.
838 Sidney Baker St.
Kerrville, TX 78028
(512)896-2055
Ultimate Parent: Allstate Life. SIC: 6411—
Insurance Agents, Brokers & Service.

★ 87472 ★   Exxon Products
206 Mcfarland Dr.
Kerrville, TX 78028
(512)257-6944
Ultimate Parent: Exxon.

★ 87473 ★   IBM Corp.
236 A St.
Kerrville, TX 78028
(512)896-8870
Ultimate Parent: IBM. SIC: 5999—
Miscellaneous Retail Stores Nec.

★ 87474 ★   Kentucky Fried
Chicken
102 Plaza Dr.
Kerrville, TX 78028
(512)895-5522
Ultimate Parent: Pepsico. SIC: 5812—
Eating Places.

★ 87475 ★   Mary Kay Cosmetics
575 Rimrock Rd.
Kerrville, TX 78028
(512)257-7098
Ultimate Parent: Mary Kay Cosmetics. SIC:
5999—Miscellaneous Retail Stores Nec.

★ 87476 ★   Mini Mart Grcry
816 Ranchero Rd.
Kerrville, TX 78028
(512)257-2566
Ultimate Parent: Kroger.

★ 87477 ★   Mini Mart Grocery
San Antonio Hwy.
Kerrville, TX 78028
(512)896-3884
Ultimate Parent: Kroger. SIC: 5411—
Grocery Stores.

★ 87478 ★   Mini Mart Grocery
1001 Sidney Baker St. S
Kerrville, TX 78028
(512)896-2994
Ultimate Parent: Kroger. SIC: 5411—
Grocery Stores.

★ 87479 ★   Mini Mart Grocery
1805 Broadway
Kerrville, TX 78028
(512)257-8644
Ultimate Parent: Kroger. SIC: 5411—
Grocery Stores.

★ 87480 ★   Mini Mart Grocery
1698 Jct Hwy.
Kerrville, TX 78028
(512)895-2996
Ultimate Parent: Kroger. SIC: 5411—
Grocery Stores.

★ 87481 ★   Pizza Hut
1018 Sidney Baker St.
Kerrville, TX 78028
(512)896-0440
Ultimate Parent: Pepsico.

★ 87482 ★   Radio Shack
410 Main St.
Kerrville, TX 78028
(512)257-7011
Company Type: Division. Ultimate Parent:
Tandy Corp.

★ 87483 ★   Ryder Truck Rental
528 Main St.
Kerrville, TX 78028
(512)896-2464
Ultimate Parent: Ryder System. SIC:
7359—Equipment Rental & Leasing Nec.

★ 87484 ★   Wal Mart Discnt
1305 Sidney Baker St.
Kerrville, TX 78028
(512)896-2900
Ultimate Parent: Wal-Mart Stores, Inc.

Kilgore

★ 87485 ★   City National Bank
1006 Stone Rd.
Kilgore, TX 75662
(903)983-1584
Ultimate Parent: City National Corp.

★ 87486 ★   City National Bank of
Kilgore
1006 Stone Rd.
Kilgore, TX 75662-5476
(903)983-1584
Company Type: Headquarters. Officer:
James E. Wallace, President. Ultimate
Parent: City National Corp. SIC: 6021—
National Commercial Banks; 6141—
Personal Credit Institutions; 6162—
Mortgage Bankers & Correspondents.

★ 87487 ★   Exxon Chemical Co.
2550 N. Longview St.
Kilgore, TX 75662
(903)983-2483
Ultimate Parent: Exxon.

★ 87488 ★   Kentucky Fried
Chicken
800 Hwy. 259 N
Kilgore, TX 75662
(214)984-0136
Ultimate Parent: Pepsico. SIC: 5812—
Eating Places.

★ 87489 ★   Kilgore Plumbing
Products Inc.
Hwy. 259
Kilgore, TX 75662-9022
(903)984-3525
Company Type: Subsidiary. Officer: Paul
Fischer, President. Ultimate Parent: Great
American Management & Investment. SIC:
3261—Vitreous Plumbing Fixtures; 3431—
Metal Sanitary Ware; 7513—Truck Rental &
Leasing Without Drivers. Employee Count:
400. Sales: 22.9 (est) M.

★ 87490 ★   McDonalds
Restaurant
906 Us Hwy. 259 N
Kilgore, TX 75662
(903)984-1666
Ultimate Parent: McDonald's.

★ 87491 ★   Mini Mart
Fm Rd. 1252
Kilgore, TX 75662
(214)983-3862
Ultimate Parent: Kroger. SIC: 5411—
Grocery Stores.

★ 87492 ★   Mobil Oil Corp.
Hwy. 42
Kilgore, TX 75662
(214)984-2512
Ultimate Parent: Mobil. SIC: 1311—Crude
Petroleum & Natural Gas.

★ 87493 ★   Mobil Pipe Line Co.
Norris Rd.
Kilgore, TX 75662
(903)984-7541
Company Type: Branch. Ultimate Parent:
Mobil. SIC: 4612—Crude Petroleum
Pipelines.

★ 87494 ★   Mobil Producing TX &
NM
Hwy. 42
Kilgore, TX 75662
(903)984-2512
Ultimate Parent: Mobil. SIC: 1311—Crude
Petroleum & Natural Gas.

★ 87495 ★   Nalco Chemical Co.
3212 N. Hwy. 135
Kilgore, TX 75662
(214)984-1580
Ultimate Parent: Nalco Chemical Co. SIC:
5169—Chemicals & Allied Products Nec.

★ 87496 ★   Pizza Hut
1213 N. Kilgore St.
Kilgore, TX 75662
(903)984-4026
Ultimate Parent: Pepsico. SIC: 5812—
Eating Places.

★ 87497 ★   Radio Shack
1014 N. Kilgore St.
Kilgore, TX 75662
(903)984-4425
Company Type: Division. Ultimate Parent:
Tandy Corp.

★ 87498 ★   Shell Oil Co.
700 Hwy. 31
Kilgore, TX 75662
(214)984-3086
Ultimate Parent: Shell Oil Co. SIC: 1311—
Crude Petroleum & Natural Gas.

★ 87499 ★   Tesoro Petroleum
Distribution Co.
Laird Hill Rd.
Kilgore, TX 75662
(903)984-5524
Ultimate Parent: Tesoro Petroleum Corp.
SIC: 5171—Petroleum Bulk Stations &
Terminals.

★ 87500 ★   Texaco Incorporated
Getty Camp
Kilgore, TX 75662
(903)984-1561
Ultimate Parent: Texaco. SIC: 1311—
Crude Petroleum & Natural Gas.

★ 87501 ★   Trailways Bus System
214 E. South St.
Kilgore, TX 75662
(214)984-3411
Ultimate Parent: Greyhound Lines Inc. SIC:
4131—Intercity & Rural Bus Transportation.

★ 87502 ★   Wal Mart
1811 Hwy. 259 N
Kilgore, TX 75662
(214)983-1494
Ultimate Parent: Wal-Mart Stores, Inc. SIC:
5311—Department Stores.

★ 87503 ★   Wal Mart Discount
1811 Us Hwy. 259 N
Kilgore, TX 75662
(903)983-1494
Ultimate Parent: Wal-Mart Stores, Inc.

★ 87504 ★   Warren Petroleum
Corp.
Gulf Hercules Rd.
Kilgore, TX 75662
(214)984-5047
Ultimate Parent: Chevron Corp. SIC:
2911—Petroleum Refining.

★ 87505 ★   Waste Disposal, Inc.
215 N. Kilgore St.
Kilgore, TX 75662
(214)984-1446
Ultimate Parent: Browning-Ferris
Industries. SIC: 4953—Refuse Systems.

Killeen

★ 87506 ★   Beneficial Income Tax
Service
870 S. FM 440
Killeen, TX 76541
(817)634-0206
Ultimate Parent: Bemis Co., Inc. SIC:
7291—Tax Return Preparation Services.

★ 87507 ★   Casual Corner
2100 Killeen Mall
Killeen, TX 76541
(817)699-5329
Ultimate Parent: United States Shoe. SIC:
5651—Family Clothing Stores.

★ 87508 ★   Circus World Toy
Store
2100 Killeen Mall N
Killeen, TX 76543
(817)699-3714
Ultimate Parent: Melville. SIC: 5945—
Hobby, Toy & Game Shops.

★ 87509 ★   Dataserve Inc.
603 Estes Dr.
Killeen, TX 76541-8001
(817)634-1311
Ultimate Parent: BellSouth Corp. SIC:
5065—Electronic Parts & Equipment Nec.

★ 87510 ★   Exxon
401 Us 190 E
Killeen, TX 76541
(817)256-7025
Ultimate Parent: Exxon. SIC: 5541—
Gasoline Service Stations.

★ 87511 ★   Foot Action
2100 Killeen Mall
Killeen, TX 76541
(817)699-5730
Ultimate Parent: Melville. SIC: 5661—Shoe
Stores.

★ 87512 ★   Foot Action
2100 Killeen Mall N
Killeen, TX 76543
(817)699-5730
Ultimate Parent: Melville. SIC: 5661—Shoe
Stores; 7221—Photographic Studios—
Portrait.

★ 87513 ★   Kay-Bee Toy & Hobby
Shop
2100 Killeen Mall
Killeen, TX 76541
(817)699-4294
Ultimate Parent: Melville. SIC: 5945—
Hobby, Toy & Game Shops.

★ 87514 ★   Kentucky Fried
Chicken
904 Fort Hood St.
Killeen, TX 76541
(817)526-4333
Ultimate Parent: Pepsico. SIC: 5812—
Eating Places.

★ 87515 ★   Lane Bryant
2100 Killeen Mall
Killeen, TX 76541
(817)699-3727
Ultimate Parent: Limited. SIC: 5651—
Family Clothing Stores.

★ 87516 ★   Lerner Shop
Killeen
Killeen, TX 76541
(817)699-4936
Ultimate Parent: Limited. SIC: 5621—
Women's Clothing Stores.

★ 87517 ★   Lone Star Gas Co.
501 N. 2nd St.
Killeen, TX 76541
(817)634-2185
Ultimate Parent: Enserch. SIC: 4925—Gas
Production & Distribution Nec.

★ 87518 ★   Pizza Hut
903 W. Rancier Ave.
Killeen, TX 76541
(817)526-2302
Ultimate Parent: Pepsico. SIC: 5812—
Eating Places.

★ 87519 ★   Pizza Hut
523 E. Us 190
Killeen, TX 76541
(817)699-2233
Ultimate Parent: Pepsico. SIC: 5812—
Eating Places.

★ 87520 ★   Pizza Hut
1215 S. Fort Hood St.
Killeen, TX 76542
(817)634-7019
Ultimate Parent: Pepsico. SIC: 5812—
Eating Places.

★ 87521 ★   Pizza Hut
2503 E. Rancier Ave.
Killeen, TX 76543
(817)526-6888
Ultimate Parent: Pepsico. SIC: 5812—
Eating Places.

★ 87522 ★   Radio Shack
2100 S. Young Dr. S
Killeen, TX 76543
(817)699-0357
Company Type: Division. Ultimate Parent:
Tandy Corp.

★ 87523 ★   Radio Shack
2100 Killeen Mall
Killeen, TX 76541
(817)699-5107
Company Type: Division. Ultimate Parent:
Tandy Corp. SIC: 5065—Electronic Parts &
Equipment Nec.

★ 87524 ★   Taco Bell
1313 S. Fort Hood St.
Killeen, TX 76542
(817)526-7618
Ultimate Parent: Pepsico. SIC: 5812—
Eating Places.

★ 87525 ★   Taco Bell
417 E. Rancier Ave.
Killeen, TX 76541
(817)634-8883
Ultimate Parent: Pepsico. SIC: 5812—
Eating Places.

★ 87526 ★ **Taco Bell**
408 N. Fort Hood St.
Killeen, TX 76541
(817)526-2084
Ultimate Parent: Pepsico. **SIC:** 5812—
Eating Places.

★ 87527 ★ **Wal Mart Discount City No 4**
2002 E. Central Texas Expy.
Killeen, TX 76541
(817)526-4102
Ultimate Parent: Wal-Mart Stores, Inc. **SIC:**
5311—Department Stores.

★ 87528 ★ **Waldenbooks**
Killeen
Killeen, TX 76541
(817)699-4866
Ultimate Parent: K-Mart. **SIC:** 5942—Book
Stores.

★ 87529 ★ **Waldenbooks**
2100 Killeen Mall N
Killeen, TX 76543
(817)699-4866
Ultimate Parent: K-Mart. **SIC:** 5942—Book
Stores.

★ 87530 ★ **Walgreen**
2100 Killeen Mall
Killeen, TX 76541
(817)699-3132
Ultimate Parent: Walgreen Co. **SIC:**
5912—Drug Stores & Proprietary Stores.

Kingsbury

★ 87531 ★ **Texaco Inc.**
F M 1150
Kingsbury, TX 78638
(512)639-4448
Ultimate Parent: Texaco. **SIC:** 1311—
Crude Petroleum & Natural Gas.

Kingsville

★ 87532 ★ **Exxon**
201 S. 6th St.
Kingsville, TX 78363
(512)592-3521
Ultimate Parent: Exxon.

★ 87533 ★ **Hertz Rent-A-Car Licensee**
213 S. 6th St.
Kingsville, TX 78363
(512)592-7406
Ultimate Parent: Hertz. **SIC:** 7514—
Passenger Car Rental.

★ 87534 ★ **Kroger Family Center**
S 14th
Kingsville, TX 78363
(512)592-8551
Ultimate Parent: Kroger. **SIC:** 4724—Travel
Agencies.

Kingwood

★ 87535 ★ **Baker Hughes Prod. Tools**
Westronics, Inc.
22001 North Park Dr.
Kingwood, TX 77339-3804
(713)348-1000 **Fax:** (713)348-1285
Company Type: Division. **Officer:** Donald
L. Clarke, President & General Manager.
Ultimate Parent: Baker Hughes. **SIC:**
3825—Instruments to Measure Electricity.
Employee Count: 160. **Sales:** 17000000
M.

★ 87536 ★ **Comerica Bank-Texas**
2240 Northpark Dr., Ste. 102
Kingwood, TX 77339-1747
(713)358-6700
Company Type: Subsidiary. **Location
Type:** Branch office. **Ultimate Parent:**
Comerica Bank. **SIC:** 6021—National
Commercial Banks.

★ 87537 ★ **Compass Bank-Houston**
200 Northpark
Kingwood, TX 77339-1509
(713)867-1271
Company Type: Subsidiary. **Location
Type:** Branch office. **Officer:** Sheryl
McKellar, Manager. **Ultimate Parent:**
Compass Bancshares. **SIC:** 6021—National
Commercial Banks.

Knox City

★ 87538 ★ **Trico Industries Inc.**
109 N. 2nd
Knox City, TX 79529
(817)658-3821
Ultimate Parent: Paccar. **SIC:** 1389—Oil &
Gas Field Services Nec.

La Grange

★ 87539 ★ **Wal Mart Discount Cities**
Hwy. 71
La Grange, TX 78945
(409)968-8426
Ultimate Parent: Wal-Mart Stores, Inc.

★ 87540 ★ **Wal Mart Discount Pharmacy**
Rural Route 1
La Grange, TX 78945
(409)968-8465
Ultimate Parent: Wal-Mart Stores, Inc.

La Marque

★ 87541 ★ **Capezio Factory Direct**
12003 Delaney
La Marque, TX 77568
(409)938-7595
Ultimate Parent: United States Shoe.

★ 87542 ★ **Marathon Oil Co.**
Loop S
La Marque, TX 77568
(409)945-7021
Ultimate Parent: USX Corp.

★ 87543 ★ **Marathon Oil Co.**
Loop S
La Marque, TX 77568
(409)945-7021
Ultimate Parent: USX Corp.

★ 87544 ★ **Mary Kay Cosmetics**
1005 Laura Ave.
La Marque, TX 77568
Ultimate Parent: Mary Kay Cosmetics. **SIC:**
5999—Miscellaneous Retail Stores Nec.

★ 87545 ★ **Radio Shack**
2412 Perthuis Dr.
La Marque, TX 77568
Company Type: Division. **Ultimate Parent:**
Tandy Corp. **SIC:** 1711—Plumbing, Heating
& Air-Conditioning; 5065—Electronic Parts &
Equipment Nec; 5731—Radio, Television &
Electronics Stores.

★ 87546 ★ **Ryder Truck Rental**
2116 Palm St.
La Marque, TX 77568
(409)935-1404
Ultimate Parent: Ryder System. **SIC:**
7389—Business Services Nec.

★ 87547 ★ **United Parcel Service**
8 Main St.
La Marque, TX 77568
(409)938-4801
Ultimate Parent: United Parcel Service of
America. **SIC:** 4215—Courier Services
Except by Air.

★ 87548 ★ **United Parcel Service**
10 Main St.
La Marque, TX 77568
(409)938-0979
Ultimate Parent: United Parcel Service of
America. **SIC:** 4215—Courier Services
Except by Air.

★ 87549 ★ **United Parcel Service Inc.**
10 Main St.
La Marque, TX 77568
(409)938-0979
Ultimate Parent: United Parcel Service of
America. **SIC:** 4215—Courier Services
Except by Air.

★ 87550 ★ **United Parcel Service Inc.**
8 Main St.
La Marque, TX 77568
(409)938-4801
Ultimate Parent: United Parcel Service of
America. **SIC:** 4215—Courier Services
Except by Air.

★ 87551 ★ **Walgreen Drugs**
5416 Hwy. 1765
La Marque, TX 77568
(409)938-7263
Ultimate Parent: Walgreen Co. **SIC:**
5912—Drug Stores & Proprietary Stores.

La Porte

★ 87552 ★ **Air Products & Chemicals Inc.**
Rte. 1 10202
La Porte, TX 77571
Ultimate Parent: Air Products & Chemicals,
Inc. **SIC:** 2813—Industrial Gases.

★ 87553 ★ **Air Products Manufacturing Corp.**
Strang Rd.
La Porte, TX 77571
Ultimate Parent: Air Products & Chemicals,
Inc. **SIC:** 2813—Industrial Gases.

★ 87554 ★ **Air Products Manufacturing Corp.**
Rte. 1, 10202
La Porte, TX 77571
Ultimate Parent: Air Products & Chemicals,
Inc. **SIC:** 2813—Industrial Gases.

★ 87555 ★ **Dow Chemical Co.**
Battleground Rd. PO Box 685
La Porte, TX 77571
Ultimate Parent: Dow Chemical Co. USA.
SIC: 2821—Plastics Materials & Resins;
2869—Industrial Organic Chemicals Nec.

★ 87556 ★ **Dow Chemical Co. La Porte Plant**
Battleground Road, PO Box 685
La Porte, TX 77572-0685
Ultimate Parent: Dow Chemical Co. USA.
SIC: 2821—Plastics Materials & Resins;
2869—Industrial Organic Chemicals Nec.

★ 87557 ★ **Dow Chemical Co. La Porte Site**
Battleground Rd.
La Porte, TX 77571
Ultimate Parent: Dow Chemical Co. USA.
SIC: 2821—Plastics Materials & Resins;
2869—Industrial Organic Chemicals Nec.

★ 87558 ★ **Egp Fuels Co.**
1200 N. Broadway
La Porte, TX 77571
Ultimate Parent: Enron. **SIC:** 2869—
Industrial Organic Chemicals Nec.

★ 87559 ★ **Enron Corp.**
1200 N. Broadway
La Porte, TX 77571
(713)470-4900
Officer: Jerry Lockie, Manager. **Ultimate
Parent:** Enron. **SIC:** 2911—Petroleum
Refining.

★ 87560 ★ **Fina Oil & Chemical Co. La Porte Plant**
1818 Battleground Rd.
La Porte, TX 77571
Ultimate Parent: Fina. **SIC:** 2821—Plastics
Materials & Resins.

★ 87561 ★ **Kroger**
N Alexander Dr.
La Porte, TX 77571
(713)471-2030
Ultimate Parent: Kroger. **SIC:** 5411—
Grocery Stores.

★ 87562 ★ **Occidental Chemical Corp.**
Battleground Site
1800 Vista Rd.
La Porte, TX 77571
Company Type: Division. **Ultimate Parent:**
Occidental Petroleum Corp. **SIC:** 2812—
Alkalies & Chlorine.

★ 87563 ★ **Ppg Industries**
1901 Ave. H & 16th St.
La Porte, TX 77571-0995
Ultimate Parent: PPG Industries Inc. **SIC:**
2869—Industrial Organic Chemicals Nec.

★ 87564 ★ **Praxair Inc.**
Linde
100 Strang Rd.
La Porte, TX 77571
Ultimate Parent: Praxair. **SIC:** 2813—
Industrial Gases.

★ 87565 ★ **Pulte Home Corp.**
Meadow Park
La Porte, TX 77571
(713)471-3858
Ultimate Parent: Pulte. **SIC:** 1521—
Single-Family Housing Construction.

★ 87566 ★ **Pulte Home Corp.**
1505 Brook Meadow Dr.
La Porte, TX 77571
(713)471-3853
Ultimate Parent: Pulte. **SIC:** 1521—
Single-Family Housing Construction.

★ 87567 ★ **Radio Shack**
1126 Baybrook Mall
La Porte, TX 77571
(713)486-8630
Company Type: Division. **Ultimate Parent:**
Tandy Corp. **SIC:** 3699—Electrical
Equipment & Supplies Nec.

★ 87568 ★ **Reliance Electric Co.**
1500 E. Main St.
La Porte, TX
(713)471-4611
Officer: Tom Cell, Manager. **Ultimate
Parent:** Reliance Electric. **SIC:** 3621—
Motors & Generators.

★ 87569 ★ **Rohm & Haas Bayport Inc.**
13300 Bay Area Blvd.
La Porte, TX 77571
Ultimate Parent: Rohm & Haas. **SIC:**
2879—Agricultural Chemicals Nec; 2869—
Industrial Organic Chemicals Nec.

★ 87570 ★ **Rohm & Haas Inc. Bayport**
13300 Bay Area Blvd.
La Porte, TX 77571
Ultimate Parent: Rohm & Haas. **SIC:**
2869—Industrial Organic Chemicals Nec;
2879—Agricultural Chemicals Nec.

★ 87571 ★ **Union Carbide Corp.**
Linde Div.
100 Strang Rd.
La Porte, TX 77571
Company Type: Division. **Ultimate Parent:**
Union Carbide Corp. **SIC:** 2813—Industrial
Gases.

★ 87572 ★ **Union Carbide Industrial Gases Inc.**
100 Strang Rd.
La Porte, TX 77571
Ultimate Parent: Union Carbide Corp. **SIC:**
2813—Industrial Gases.

★ 87573 ★ **Walgreen Drug Stores**
1102 S. Broadway St.
La Porte, TX 77571
Ultimate Parent: Walgreen Co. **SIC:**
5912—Drug Stores & Proprietary Stores.

★ 87574 ★ **Witco Corp.**
Argus
9401 Strang Rd.
La Porte, TX 77571
Ultimate Parent: Witco Corp. **SIC:** 2819—
Industrial Inorganic Chemicals Nec.

La Vernia

★ 87575 ★ **Skinner Macroni Co.**
103 Oak Creek Dr.
La Vernia, TX 78121
Ultimate Parent: Hershey Foods.

Lake Dallas

★ 87576 ★ **Boeing Aerospace & Electronics**
7801 S. Stemmons
Lake Dallas, TX 75065-9119
Ultimate Parent: Boeing. **SIC:** 3679—
Electronic Components Nec.

★ 87577 ★ **Payless Cashways**
500 N. Stemmons Fwy.
Lake Dallas, TX 75065
(817)497-4061
Ultimate Parent: Payless Cashways. **SIC:**
5211—Lumber & Other Building Materials.

Lake Jackson

★ 87578 ★ Albertson's Food Centers, Inc.
604 Hwy. 332
Lake Jackson, TX 77566
(409)297-0164
Ultimate Parent: Albertson's Inc. SIC: 5411—Grocery Stores.

★ 87579 ★ Casual Corner
100 Brazos Mall
Lake Jackson, TX 77566
(409)297-7241
Ultimate Parent: United States Shoe. SIC: 5651—Family Clothing Stores.

★ 87580 ★ Foot Action
Brazos Mall
Lake Jackson, TX 77566
(409)297-0025
Ultimate Parent: Melville. SIC: 5661—Shoe Stores.

★ 87581 ★ Lerner Shop
Brazos Mall
Lake Jackson, TX 77566
(409)297-2311
Ultimate Parent: Limited. SIC: 5621—Women's Clothing Stores.

★ 87582 ★ The Limited
100 Brazos Mall N
Lake Jackson, TX 77566
(409)297-0129
Ultimate Parent: Limited. SIC: 5651—Family Clothing Stores.

★ 87583 ★ Pizza Hut
120 Circle Way
Lake Jackson, TX 77566
(409)297-5281
Ultimate Parent: Pepsico. SIC: 5812—Eating Places.

★ 87584 ★ Radio Shack
1550 PO Box
Lake Jackson, TX 77566
(409)849-0049
Company Type: Division. Ultimate Parent: Tandy Corp. SIC: 5065—Electronic Parts & Equipment Nec.

★ 87585 ★ Radio Shack
120 Circle Way
Lake Jackson, TX 77566
(409)297-3681
Company Type: Division. Ultimate Parent: Tandy Corp. SIC: 5065—Electronic Parts & Equipment Nec; 7622—Radio & T.V. Repair.

★ 87586 ★ Service Merchandise
100 Brazos Mall N
Lake Jackson, TX 77566
(409)297-8051
Ultimate Parent: Service Merchandise Co., Inc. SIC: 5311—Department Stores.

★ 87587 ★ Wal Mart Discount Cities
120 Hwy. 332 W
Lake Jackson, TX 77566
(409)297-9757
Ultimate Parent: Wal-Mart Stores, Inc. SIC: 5311—Department Stores.

★ 87588 ★ Waldenbooks
100 Brazos Mall N
Lake Jackson, TX 77566
(409)297-8412
Ultimate Parent: K-Mart. SIC: 5942—Book Stores.

Lamesa

★ 87589 ★ Exxon Co. USA
407 N. Lynn Ave.
Lamesa, TX 79331
(806)872-3900
Ultimate Parent: Exxon. SIC: 5199—Nondurable Goods Nec.

★ 87590 ★ Kentucky Fried Chicken
501 N. Dallas Ave.
Lamesa, TX 79331
(806)872-3775
Ultimate Parent: Pepsico. SIC: 5812—Eating Places.

★ 87591 ★ Pizza Hut
305 N. 4th St.
Lamesa, TX 79331
(806)872-8309
Ultimate Parent: Pepsico. SIC: 5812—Eating Places.

Lampasas

★ 87592 ★ Lone Star Gas Co.
215 E. 3rd St.
Lampasas, TX 76550
(512)556-3841
Ultimate Parent: Enserch. SIC: 4932—Gas & Other Services Combined.

★ 87593 ★ Pizza Hut
1602 S. Key Ave.
Lampasas, TX 76550
(512)556-8211
Ultimate Parent: Pepsico. SIC: 5812—Eating Places.

★ 87594 ★ Ryder Truck Rental
607 E. 4th St.
Lampasas, TX 76550
(512)556-8867
Ultimate Parent: Ryder System. SIC: 7513—Truck Rental & Leasing Without Drivers.

★ 87595 ★ Ryder Truck Rental
1423 S. Key Ave.
Lampasas, TX 76550
(512)556-2311
Ultimate Parent: Ryder System. SIC: 5541—Gasoline Service Stations.

Lancaster

★ 87596 ★ Brass Craft Western Co.
300 E. Pecan St.
Lancaster, TX 75146
Ultimate Parent: Masco. SIC: 3432—Plumbing Fixtures Fittings & Trim.

★ 87597 ★ Dana Corp.
600 W. Belt Line Rd.
Lancaster, TX 75146
(214)227-2221
Ultimate Parent: Dana Corp. SIC: 3599—Industrial Machinery Nec.

★ 87598 ★ Dana Corp.
Mobile Fluid Products Div.
600 W. Beltline Rd.
Lancaster, TX 75146-3019
Company Type: Division. Ultimate Parent: Dana Corp. SIC: 3599—Industrial Machinery Nec.

★ 87599 ★ Exxon Shop
1458 W. Pleasant Run Rd.
Lancaster, TX 75146
(214)227-0167
Ultimate Parent: Exxon.

★ 87600 ★ Lone Star Gas Co.
114 N. State St.
Lancaster, TX 75146
(214)227-2158
Ultimate Parent: Enserch. SIC: 4932—Gas & Other Services Combined.

★ 87601 ★ Power Systems
939 E. Pleasant Run Rd.
Lancaster, TX 75146
(214)227-2961
Officer: Bob Borden, Manager. Ultimate Parent: Sundstrand. SIC: 3444—Sheet Metal Work; 3523—Farm Machinery & Equipment; 3559—Special Industry Machinery Nec.

LaPorte

★ 87602 ★ Air Products Manufacturing Corp.
10202 Strang Rd.
LaPorte, TX 77571-9721
(713)479-5901
Officer: Justin L. Shuck. Ultimate Parent: Air Products & Chemicals, Inc. SIC: 2813—Industrial Gases.

★ 87603 ★ Fina Oil & Chemical Co.
1818 Battleground Rd.
LaPorte, TX 77571
(713)476-3700
Officer: Joe Monk, Manager. Ultimate Parent: Fina.

★ 87604 ★ PPG Industries Inc.
1901 Ave. H
LaPorte, TX 77571
(713)471-0943
Officer: Henry Hack, Manager. Ultimate Parent: PPG Industries Inc. SIC: 2819—Industrial Inorganic Chemicals Nec; 2865—Cyclic Crudes & Intermediates; 2869—Industrial Organic Chemicals Nec.

★ 87605 ★ Witco Corp.
9401 Strang Rd.
LaPorte, TX 77571
(713)476-4321
Officer: Jerry Vail, Manager. Ultimate Parent: Witco Corp. SIC: 2819—Industrial Inorganic Chemicals Nec; 2899—Chemical Preparations Nec.

Laredo

★ 87606 ★ American Brokerage Co.
Mann
Laredo, TX 78041
(512)723-7821
Ultimate Parent: Phoenix Home Life Mutual. SIC: 4225—General Warehousing & Storage.

★ 87607 ★ Circus World Toy
144 Mall Del Norte
Laredo, TX 78041
(512)722-0013
Ultimate Parent: Melville.

★ 87608 ★ City National Bank Laredo
Mann Rd.
Laredo, TX 78041
(512)724-2424
Ultimate Parent: City National Corp. SIC: 6141—Personal Credit Institutions.

★ 87609 ★ Emery Worldwide
Laredo
Laredo, TX 78040
(512)723-7391
Ultimate Parent: Consolidated Freightways. SIC: 4212—Local Trucking Without Storage.

★ 87610 ★ First Choice
1304 Zaragoza St.
Laredo, TX 78040-5905
(210)722-2229
Ultimate Parent: Bindley-Western Industries, Inc. SIC: 5651—Family Clothing Stores; 5137—Women's/Children's Clothing.

★ 87611 ★ Foot Action
Mall Delnorte
Laredo, TX 78041
(512)723-2166
Ultimate Parent: Melville. SIC: 5661—Shoe Stores.

★ 87612 ★ Hertz Rent-A-Car Licensee
104 Laredo St.
Laredo, TX 78040
(512)722-7607
Ultimate Parent: Hertz. SIC: 7514—Passenger Car Rental; 7514—Passenger Car Rental.

★ 87613 ★ Lerner Shop
N Ih 35
Laredo, TX 78041
(512)722-1633
Ultimate Parent: Limited. SIC: 5621—Women's Clothing Stores.

★ 87614 ★ Mccaw Communicatns
1112 Calle Del Norte
Laredo, TX 78041
(512)723-2893
Ultimate Parent: McCaw Cellular Communications.

★ 87615 ★ McDonalds Restaurant
2301 Guadalupe St.
Laredo, TX 78043
(512)722-7605
Ultimate Parent: McDonald's.

★ 87616 ★ Pizza Hut
2106 Santa Ursula Ave.
Laredo, TX 78040
(512)722-1234
Ultimate Parent: Pepsico.

★ 87617 ★ Pizza Hut
5303 Mcpherson Ave.
Laredo, TX 78041
(512)727-8988
Ultimate Parent: Pepsico.

★ 87618 ★ Pizza Hut
4821 San Bernardo Ave.
Laredo, TX 78041
(512)722-3682
Ultimate Parent: Pepsico. SIC: 5812—Eating Places.

★ 87619 ★ Pizza Hut
2619 E. Saunders St.
Laredo, TX 78041
(512)727-1354
Ultimate Parent: Pepsico. SIC: 5812—Eating Places.

★ 87620 ★ Pizza Hut
1519 Guadalupe St.
Laredo, TX 78040
(512)722-0222
Ultimate Parent: Pepsico. SIC: 5812—Eating Places.

★ 87621 ★ Radio Shack
102 E. Calton Rd.
Laredo, TX 78041
(512)727-4678
Company Type: Division. Ultimate Parent: Tandy Corp. SIC: 5734—Computer & Software Stores.

★ 87622 ★ Radio Shack
Riverdrive Mall
Laredo, TX 78040
(512)727-5308
Company Type: Division. Ultimate Parent: Tandy Corp. SIC: 5065—Electronic Parts & Equipment Nec.

★ 87623 ★ Radio Shack
Mall Del Norte
Laredo, TX 78041
(512)724-8581
Company Type: Division. Ultimate Parent: Tandy Corp. SIC: 5065—Electronic Parts & Equipment Nec.

★ 87624 ★ Texaco Inc.
1300 E. Saunders St.
Laredo, TX 78041
(512)723-3626
Ultimate Parent: Texaco.

★ 87625 ★ Thom Mcan Shoe Store
1111 Hidalgo St.
Laredo, TX 78040
(512)722-9239
Ultimate Parent: Melville. SIC: 5661—Shoe Stores.

Larue

★ 87626 ★ Target Stores Inc.
305 W. 281st
Larue, TX 75770
(903)663-4921
Ultimate Parent: Dayton Hudson. SIC: 5311—Department Stores.

League City

★ 87627 ★ GTE Center
PO Box 899
League City, TX 77574-0899
(713)338-8330
Location Type: Branch office. Ultimate Parent: GTE.

★ 87628 ★ Kentucky Fried Chicken
1601 W. Main St.
League City, TX 77573
(713)332-3037
Ultimate Parent: Pepsico. SIC: 5812—Eating Places.

★ 87629 ★ Krogers
200 Gulf Fwy. S
League City, TX 77573
(713)332-5323
Ultimate Parent: Kroger. SIC: 5912—Drug Stores & Proprietary Stores.

★ 87630 ★   **Radio Shack**
227 W. Main St.
League City, TX 77573
(713)332-5611
Company Type: Division. **Ultimate Parent:** Tandy Corp. **SIC:** 5065—Electronic Parts & Equipment Nec.

★ 87631 ★   **Ryder Truck Rental**
1211 E. Main St.
League City, TX 77573
(713)332-6125
Ultimate Parent: Ryder System.

★ 87632 ★   **Space Industries International**
101 Courageous Dr.
League City, TX 77573
(713)538-6000 **Fax:** (713)334-1010
Company Type: Subsidiary. **Officer:** James K. Baker, Chairman & President. **Ultimate Parent:** Arvin Industries Inc.

★ 87633 ★   **Taco Bell**
1755 W. Main St.
League City, TX 77573
(713)332-1969
Ultimate Parent: Pepsico.

★ 87634 ★   **Union Carbide Corp.**
2525 S. Shore Blvd., No. 300
League City, TX 77573
(713)334-3527
Officer: Larry Calvert, Manager. **Ultimate Parent:** Union Carbide Corp. **SIC:** 2869—Industrial Organic Chemicals Nec.

★ 87635 ★   **Walgreen Drug Stores**
196 Gulf Fwy. N
League City, TX 77573
(713)332-0625
Ultimate Parent: Walgreen Co.

Leesburg

★ 87636 ★   **Exxon Pipeline**
Fm 1975
Leesburg, TX 75451
(903)856-6821
Ultimate Parent: Exxon Pipeline.

★ 87637 ★   **Exxon Pipeline Co.**
Fm 1975
Leesburg, TX 75451
(903)856-6821
Ultimate Parent: Exxon.

Levelland

★ 87638 ★   **Levelland Vegetable Oil**
Hwy. 114 East (Lubbock Hwy.)
Levelland, TX 79336
Ultimate Parent: Procter & Gamble Co. **SIC:** 2074—Cottonseed Oil Mills; 2079—Edible Fats & Oils Nec.

★ 87639 ★   **Mary Kay Cosmetics**
2021 Longhorn Dr.
Levelland, TX 79336
(806)894-4480
Ultimate Parent: Mary Kay Cosmetics. **SIC:** 5999—Miscellaneous Retail Stores Nec.

★ 87640 ★   **Procter & Gamble Oilseed Products Co.**
Hwy. 114 East (Lubbock Hwy.)
Levelland, TX 79336
Ultimate Parent: Procter & Gamble Co. **SIC:** 2074—Cottonseed Oil Mills; 2079—Edible Fats & Oils Nec.

★ 87641 ★   **Ryder Truck Rental**
809 11th St.
Levelland, TX 79336
(806)894-2383
Ultimate Parent: Ryder System. **SIC:** 7359—Equipment Rental & Leasing Nec.

★ 87642 ★   **Southern Cotton Oil Co.**
PO Drawer N
Levelland, TX 79336-1633
(806)894-4931
Officer: Mike Tomlinson. **Ultimate Parent:** Archer Daniels Midland Co. **SIC:** 2079—Edible Fats & Oils Nec; 2074—Cottonseed Oil Mills; 5199—Nondurable Goods Nec.

★ 87643 ★   **Southern Cotton Oil Co. Inc.**
Lubbock Hwy.
Levelland, TX 79336
(806)894-4931
Officer: Mike Tomlinson, Manager. **Ultimate Parent:** Archer Daniels Midland Co. **SIC:** 2074—Cottonseed Oil Mills; 2079—Edible Fats & Oils Nec.

Lewisville

★ 87644 ★   **Albertson's**
1087 W. Main St.
Lewisville, TX 75067-3517
(214)420-1969
Ultimate Parent: Albertson's Inc. **SIC:** 5411—Grocery Stores.

★ 87645 ★   **Albertson's**
2434 I Hwy. 35E
Lewisville, TX 75067
(214)434-1703
Ultimate Parent: Albertson's Inc. **SIC:** 5411—Grocery Stores.

★ 87646 ★   **Allergan Optical**
1422 W. Main St.
Lewisville, TX 75067
(214)219-0560
Ultimate Parent: Allergan Inc.

★ 87647 ★   **Allergan Pharmaceuticals**
131 Degan Ave.
Lewisville, TX 75057-3664
(214)221-2361
Ultimate Parent: Allergan Inc. **SIC:** 5122—Drugs, Proprietaries & Sundries.

★ 87648 ★   **Comerica Bank-Texas**
1686 S. Hwy. 121
Lewisville, TX 75067-8907
(214)434-3671
Company Type: Subsidiary. **Location Type:** Branch office. **Ultimate Parent:** Comerica Bank. **SIC:** 6021—National Commercial Banks.

★ 87649 ★   **Kroger Food Stores**
1305 S. Hwy. 121
Lewisville, TX 75067
(214)436-1006
Ultimate Parent: Kroger.

★ 87650 ★   **Kroger Food Stores**
128 Lakeland Shopping Ctr.
Lewisville, TX 75067
(214)436-7523
Ultimate Parent: Kroger. **SIC:** 5411—Grocery Stores.

★ 87651 ★   **Kroger Pharmacies**
1280 W. Main St.
Lewisville, TX 75067
(214)221-9886
Ultimate Parent: Kroger.

★ 87652 ★   **Kroger Pharmacies**
1305 S. Hwy. 121
Lewisville, TX 75067
(214)436-1607
Ultimate Parent: Kroger.

★ 87653 ★   **Mary Kay Cosmetics**
428 Remington Dr.
Lewisville, TX 75067
(214)317-6650
Ultimate Parent: Mary Kay Cosmetics.

★ 87654 ★   **McDonalds**
4915 Main St.
Lewisville, TX 75056
(214)625-7710
Ultimate Parent: McDonald's.

★ 87655 ★   **McDonalds**
1598 W. Main St.
Lewisville, TX 75067
(214)434-2549
Ultimate Parent: McDonald's.

★ 87656 ★   **Mcduff Elctrncs Ct**
598 E. Round Grove Rd.
Lewisville, TX 75067
(214)315-7304
Ultimate Parent: Tandy Corp.

★ 87657 ★   **Mobil Self Service**
1298 W. Main St.
Lewisville, TX 75067
(214)436-0923
Ultimate Parent: Mobil. **SIC:** 5541—Gasoline Service Stations.

★ 87658 ★   **Payless Cashways Bldg Matls**
900 S. Mill St.
Lewisville, TX 75057
(214)221-3777
Ultimate Parent: Payless Cashways. **SIC:** 5211—Lumber & Other Building Materials.

★ 87659 ★   **Piggly Wiggly**
225 S. Charles St.
Lewisville, TX 75057-3903
(214)221-1626
Location Type: Branch office. **Ultimate Parent:** Bruno's. **SIC:** 5411—Grocery Stores.

★ 87660 ★   **Pizza Hut**
1567 W. Main St.
Lewisville, TX 75067
(214)436-2866
Ultimate Parent: Pepsico.

★ 87661 ★   **PPG Industries**
1660 S. Stemmons Fwy.
Lewisville, TX 75067
(214)436-7870
Ultimate Parent: PPG Industries Inc.

★ 87662 ★   **Radio Shack**
724 W. Main St.
Lewisville, TX 75067
(214)436-4505
Company Type: Division. **Ultimate Parent:** Tandy Corp. **SIC:** 5731—Radio, Television & Electronics Stores.

★ 87663 ★   **Radio Shack**
5000 Main St.
Lewisville, TX 75056
(214)625-9409
Company Type: Division. **Ultimate Parent:** Tandy Corp.

★ 87664 ★   **Ryder Truck Rental**
7513 Main St.
Lewisville, TX 75056
(214)370-5008
Ultimate Parent: Ryder System.

★ 87665 ★   **Taco Bell**
5005 Main St.
Lewisville, TX 75056
(214)625-6978
Ultimate Parent: Pepsico.

★ 87666 ★   **Taco Bell**
1286 W. Main St.
Lewisville, TX 75067
(214)436-7472
Ultimate Parent: Pepsico. **SIC:** 5812—Eating Places.

★ 87667 ★   **Taco Bell**
1233 E. Hwy. 121
Lewisville, TX 75057
(214)221-4399
Ultimate Parent: Pepsico.

★ 87668 ★   **Texaco Food Mart**
802 S. Stemmons Fwy.
Lewisville, TX 75067
(214)221-8390
Ultimate Parent: Texaco.

★ 87669 ★   **Wal Mart**
5000 E. Hwy. 121
Lewisville, TX 75056
(214)370-1161
Ultimate Parent: Wal-Mart Stores, Inc. **SIC:** 5912—Drug Stores & Proprietary Stores.

★ 87670 ★   **Wal Mart Discount Cities**
1171 S. Old Orchard Ln.
Lewisville, TX 75067
(214)436-9597
Ultimate Parent: Wal-Mart Stores, Inc. **SIC:** 5311—Department Stores.

Liberty

★ 87671 ★   **Coast to Coast Home**
334 Main St.
Liberty, TX 77575
(409)336-3861
Ultimate Parent: Servistar Corp.

★ 87672 ★   **Greyhound Bus Lines**
1910 Commerce St.
Liberty, TX 77575
(409)336-7431
Ultimate Parent: Greyhound Lines Inc. **SIC:** 4111—Local & Suburban Transit.

★ 87673 ★   **Kentucky Fried Chicken**
1829 Us 90
Liberty, TX 77575
(409)336-2474
Ultimate Parent: Pepsico. **SIC:** 5812—Eating Places.

★ 87674 ★   **Mobil Pipeline Sta.**
FM 563
Liberty, TX 77575
(409)336-2114
Ultimate Parent: Mobil. **SIC:** 4612—Crude Petroleum Pipelines.

★ 87675 ★   **Mobil Pipeline Sta.**
Hwy. 90
Liberty, TX 77575
(409)336-2112
Ultimate Parent: Mobil. **SIC:** 4612—Crude Petroleum Pipelines.

★ 87676 ★   **Nalco Chemical Co.**
229 Industrial Pl
Liberty, TX 77575
(409)336-8937
Ultimate Parent: Nalco Chemical Co. **SIC:** 5169—Chemicals & Allied Products Nec.

★ 87677 ★   **Payless Shoesource**
2333 N. Main St.
Liberty, TX 77575
(409)336-9655
Ultimate Parent: May Department Stores. **SIC:** 5661—Shoe Stores.

★ 87678 ★   **Pizza Hut**
1012 Main St.
Liberty, TX 77575
(409)336-8708
Ultimate Parent: Pepsico. **SIC:** 5812—Eating Places.

★ 87679 ★   **Radio Shack**
108 Shady Lane St.
Liberty, TX 77575
Company Type: Division. **Ultimate Parent:** Tandy Corp. **SIC:** 5731—Radio, Television & Electronics Stores; 7622—Radio & T.V. Repair.

★ 87680 ★   **Ryder Truck Rental**
2001 Hwy. 90
Liberty, TX 77575
(409)336-4122
Ultimate Parent: Ryder System. **SIC:** 7359—Equipment Rental & Leasing Nec.

★ 87681 ★   **Texaco**
105 Crockett
Liberty, TX 77575
(409)336-6163
Ultimate Parent: Texaco. **SIC:** 5172—Petroleum Products Nec.

★ 87682 ★   **Wal Mart**
2801 N. Main St.
Liberty, TX 77575
(409)336-5601
Ultimate Parent: Wal-Mart Stores, Inc. **SIC:** 5311—Department Stores.

Lindale

★ 87683 ★   **Piggly Wiggly**
2724 W. Gentry Pky.
Lindale, TX 75771
(214)592-7251
Ultimate Parent: Bruno's. **SIC:** 5411—Grocery Stores.

Linden

★ 87684 ★   **Piggly Wiggly**
105 S. Kaufman
Linden, TX 75563
(214)756-5641
Ultimate Parent: Bruno's. **SIC:** 5411—Grocery Stores.

Livingston

★ 87685 ★   **Exxon Co. USA**
Hwy. 146
Livingston, TX 77351
(409)327-8309
Ultimate Parent: Exxon. **SIC:** 1311—Crude Petroleum & Natural Gas.

★ 87686 ★   Kentucky Fried
Chicken
N Washington
Livingston, TX 77351
(409)327-8979
Ultimate Parent: Pepsico. SIC: 5812—
Eating Places.

★ 87687 ★   Mary Kay Cosmetics
205 White Oak St.
Livingston, TX 77351
(409)327-3484
Ultimate Parent: Mary Kay Cosmetics. SIC:
5999—Miscellaneous Retail Stores Nec.

★ 87688 ★   McDonalds
1601 W. Church St. 59
Livingston, TX 77351
(409)327-7676
Ultimate Parent: McDonald's.
SIC: 5812—Eating Places.

★ 87689 ★   Piggly Wiggly
1400 N. Washington Ave.
Livingston, TX 77351
(409)327-3490
Ultimate Parent: Bruno's. SIC: 5411—
Grocery Stores.

★ 87690 ★   Pizza Hut
1501 W. Church St.
Livingston, TX 77351
(409)327-2503
Ultimate Parent: Pepsico. SIC: 5812—
Eating Places.

★ 87691 ★   Shell Pipeline Corp.
Hwy. 146
Livingston, TX 77351
(409)327-5512
Ultimate Parent: Shell Oil Co. SIC: 1311—
Crude Petroleum & Natural Gas.

★ 87692 ★   Trailways Bus Stop
209 S. Washington Ave.
Livingston, TX 77351
(409)327-4224
Ultimate Parent: Greyhound Lines Inc. SIC:
4131—Intercity & Rural Bus Transportation.

Llano

★ 87693 ★   Piggly Wiggly
201 E. Main St.
Llano, TX 78643
(915)247-5059
Ultimate Parent: Bruno's. SIC: 5411—
Grocery Stores.

★ 87694 ★   Pizza Hut
308 W. Young St.
Llano, TX 78643
(915)247-4032
Ultimate Parent: Pepsico. SIC: 5812—
Eating Places.

Lockhart

★ 87695 ★   Pizza Hut
610 S. Colorado St.
Lockhart, TX 78644
(512)398-3451
Ultimate Parent: Pepsico. SIC: 5812—
Eating Places.

★ 87696 ★   Ryder Truck Rental
E Walnut
Lockhart, TX 78644
(512)398-2309
Ultimate Parent: Ryder System. SIC:
7513—Truck Rental & Leasing Without
Drivers.

Lolita

★ 87697 ★   Arco Pipe Line Co.
Lolita, TX 77971
(512)874-4419
Location Type: Branch office. Ultimate
Parent: Atlantic Richfield Co., Inc. SIC:
4612—Crude Petroleum Pipelines.

Lometa

★ 87698 ★   Citizens State Bank
PO Box 130
Lometa, TX 76853
(512)752-3613
Ultimate Parent: Liberty National Bancorp.
SIC: 6081—Foreign Banks—Branches &
Agencies.

Lone Star

★ 87699 ★   Air Products &
Chemicals, Inc.
Farm Rd. 250
Lone Star, TX 75668
(214)656-2506
Ultimate Parent: Air Products & Chemicals,
Inc. SIC: 3548—Welding Apparatus.

Long Mott

★ 87700 ★   Gaf Chemicals Corp.
Seadrift Plant
Hwy. 185
Long Mott, TX 77972
Ultimate Parent: GAF Corp. SIC: 2869—
Industrial Organic Chemicals Nec.

Longview

★ 87701 ★   Anvil Products Inc.
305 Simms St.
Longview, TX 75604
(903)759-4417
Officer: Charles A. Stull, Plant Manager.
Ultimate Parent: Tyco International. SIC:
3494—Valves & Pipe Fittings Nec.

★ 87702 ★   Arco Oil & Gas Co.
2100 Sinclair Rd.
Longview, TX 75604-9519
(903)759-2422
Officer: Steve Tink. Ultimate Parent:
Atlantic Richfield Co., Inc. SIC: 2911—
Petroleum Refining.

★ 87703 ★   Arco Oil & Gas Co.
Old Hwy. 80
Longview, TX 75604
(903)759-2785
Location Type: Branch office. Ultimate
Parent: Atlantic Richfield Co., Inc. SIC:
1311—Crude Petroleum & Natural Gas.

★ 87704 ★   Betz Process
Chemicals
414 E. Loop 281
Longview, TX 75601
(903)753-8119
Ultimate Parent: Betz Laboratories Inc.
SIC: 2899—Chemical Preparations Nec;
3861—Photographic Equipment & Supplies.

★ 87705 ★   Butler Paper Co.
Longview, TX 75604
(903)753-7655
Ultimate Parent: Alco Standard Corp. SIC:
5113—Industrial & Personal Service Paper.

★ 87706 ★   Butler Paper Co.
Longview, TX 75604
(903)753-7655
Ultimate Parent: Alco Standard Corp. SIC:
5113—Industrial & Personal Service Paper.

★ 87707 ★   Casual Corner
3500 Longview Mall N
Longview, TX 75604
(214)758-6361
Ultimate Parent: United States Shoe. SIC:
5651—Family Clothing Stores.

★ 87708 ★   Circus World Toy
Stores Inc.
3500 Longview Mall N
Longview, TX 75604
(214)753-2852
Ultimate Parent: Melville. SIC: 5945—
Hobby, Toy & Game Shops.

★ 87709 ★   Coca-Cola Bottling
Co.
340 W. Tyler St.
Longview, TX 75601
(903)753-7609
Ultimate Parent: Coca-Cola Enterprises.
SIC: 2086—Bottled & Canned Soft Drinks;
5149—Groceries & Related Products Nec.

★ 87710 ★   Coltec Industries
Stemco Truck Products
300 E. Industrial Blvd.
Box 1989
Longview, TX 75606
Officer: Paul Norton, President. Ultimate
Parent: Coltec Industries.

★ 87711 ★   Crown Beverage
Packaging
901 Fisher Rd.
Longview, TX 75604
Ultimate Parent: Crown Cork & Seal. SIC:
3411—Metal Cans.

★ 87712 ★   Crown Beverage
Packaging Inc.
901 Fisher Rd.
Longview, TX 75604
Ultimate Parent: Crown Cork & Seal. SIC:
3411—Metal Cans.

★ 87713 ★   Diebold Inc.
3417 W. Marshall Ave.
Longview, TX 75604
(214)759-1361
Ultimate Parent: Diebold, Inc. SIC: 5046—
Commercial Equipment Nec.

★ 87714 ★   Exxon Gas System
Eastman Blvd.
Longview, TX 75601
(214)753-1025
Ultimate Parent: Exxon. SIC: 4925—Gas
Production & Distribution Nec.

★ 87715 ★   Fleetwood Travel
Trailers of Texas Inc.
810 Prowler Dr.
Longview, TX 75607
Ultimate Parent: Fleetwood Enterprises,
Inc. SIC: 3792—Travel Trailers & Campers.

★ 87716 ★   Footaction U S a
3500 Longview Mall N
Longview, TX 75604
(214)753-8733
Ultimate Parent: Melville. SIC: 5661—Shoe
Stores.

★ 87717 ★   Hertz Rent-A-Car
Licensee
Hwy. 322
Longview, TX 75603
(214)643-2291
Ultimate Parent: Hertz. SIC: 7514—
Passenger Car Rental.

★ 87718 ★   Kentucky Fried
Chicken
300 N. Standard St.
Longview, TX 75604
(214)759-2401
Ultimate Parent: Pepsico. SIC: 5812—
Eating Places.

★ 87719 ★   Lerner Shop
3500 Longview Mall N
Longview, TX 75604
(214)757-7481
Ultimate Parent: Limited. SIC: 5651—
Family Clothing Stores.

★ 87720 ★   Lone Star Gas Co.
7037 PO Box
Longview, TX 75607
(214)758-0611
Ultimate Parent: Enserch. SIC: 4939—
Combination Utility Nec.

★ 87721 ★   McDonalds
Restaurant
128 W. Loop 281
Longview, TX 75604
(903)757-9235
Ultimate Parent: McDonald's.

★ 87722 ★   McDonalds
Restaurant
408 E. Marshall Ave.
Longview, TX 75601
(903)753-1622
Ultimate Parent: McDonald's.

★ 87723 ★   Mobil Pipe Line Co.
500 Rockdale Dr.
Longview, TX 75604-4917
(903)759-2791
Company Type: Branch. Officer: David
Clay. Ultimate Parent: Mobil. SIC: 4612—
Crude Petroleum Pipelines; 4619—Pipelines
Nec.

★ 87724 ★   Ncr Corp.
101 W. Hawkins Pky. 5
Longview, TX 75605
Ultimate Parent: AT&T.

★ 87725 ★   Payless Cashways
Bldg Mtrls
Loop W. 281
Longview, TX 75601
(214)297-1005
Ultimate Parent: Payless Cashways. SIC:
5211—Lumber & Other Building Materials.

★ 87726 ★   Payless Cashways
Building M
1102 W. Loop 281
Longview, TX 75604
(903)297-1005
Ultimate Parent: Payless Cashways. SIC:
5211—Lumber & Other Building Materials.

★ 87727 ★   Pepsi-Cola Co.
1501 Hwy. 31 S
Longview, TX 75604
(903)753-8688
Ultimate Parent: Pepsico. SIC: 2086—
Bottled & Canned Soft Drinks.

★ 87728 ★   Performance Friction
Products
PO Box 8326
Longview, TX 75607
Ultimate Parent: Coltec Industries. SIC:
5100—Wholesale Trade—Nondurable
Goods.

★ 87729 ★   Pizza Hut
1100 W. Marshall Ave.
Longview, TX 75604
(214)758-3411
Ultimate Parent: Pepsico. SIC: 5812—
Eating Places.

★ 87730 ★   Pizza Hut
2100 Gilmer Rd.
Longview, TX 75604
(903)297-4771
Ultimate Parent: Pepsico.

★ 87731 ★   Pizza Hut
1906 E. Marshall Ave.
Longview, TX 75601
(903)758-8899
Ultimate Parent: Pepsico.

★ 87732 ★   Radio Shack
3500 Longview Mall N
Longview, TX 75604
(214)758-9811
Company Type: Division. Ultimate Parent:
Tandy Corp. SIC: 5065—Electronic Parts &
Equipment Nec.

★ 87733 ★   Ryder Truck Rental
212 N. Standard St.
Longview, TX 75604
(214)759-8219
Ultimate Parent: Ryder System. SIC:
5113—Industrial & Personal Service Paper.

★ 87734 ★   Ryder Truck Rental
350 W. Tyler St.
Longview, TX 75601
Ultimate Parent: Ryder System.

★ 87735 ★   Service Merchandise
3500 Longview Mall N
Longview, TX 75604
(214)757-5162
Ultimate Parent: Service Merchandise Co.,
Inc. SIC: 5944—Jewelry Stores.

★ 87736 ★   Stemco Inc.
300 Industrial Blvd.
Longview, TX 75606
Ultimate Parent: Coltec Industries. SIC:
3499—Fabricated Metal Products Nec.

★ 87737 ★   Texas Eastman Co.
Off Hwy. 149
PO Box 7444
Longview, TX 75607-7444
Ultimate Parent: Eastman Kodak. SIC:
2869—Industrial Organic Chemicals Nec;
2821—Plastics Materials & Resins.

★ 87738 ★   Texas Eastman Co.
Kodak Blvd.
Longview, TX 75602
(903)237-5000
Officer: Paul Folzenlogan, President.
Ultimate Parent: Eastman Kodak. SIC:
2819—Industrial Inorganic Chemicals Nec;
2821—Plastics Materials & Resins; 2869—
Industrial Organic Chemicals Nec.

★ 87739 ★ Transamerica
Occidental Life Insurance
201 E. Methvin St.
Longview, TX 75601
(214)758-9702
Ultimate Parent: Transamerica Occidental
Life Insurance. SIC: 6411—Insurance
Agents, Brokers & Service.

★ 87740 ★ Trinity Ind. Inc.
1111 W. Harrison Rd.
Longview, TX 75604
Ultimate Parent: Trinity Industries. SIC:
3443—Fabricated Plate Work—Boiler
Shops.

★ 87741 ★ Trinity Industries Inc.
R 7 Box 175
Longview, TX 75602
Ultimate Parent: Trinity Industries. SIC:
3743—Railroad Equipment.

★ 87742 ★ Trinity Industries Inc.
East
Rte. 7 Box 175
Longview, TX 75602
Ultimate Parent: Trinity Industries. SIC:
3400—Fabricated Metal Products.

★ 87743 ★ United Parcel Service
1709 E. Whaley St.
Longview, TX 75601
(214)758-7832
Ultimate Parent: United Parcel Service of
America. SIC: 4215—Courier Services
Except by Air.

★ 87744 ★ Wal Mart Tire &
Battery Ctr
1905 W. Loop 281
Longview, TX 75604
(903)297-6261
Ultimate Parent: Wal-Mart Stores, Inc. SIC:
5311—Department Stores.

★ 87745 ★ Waldenbooks
3500 Longview Mall N
Longview, TX 75604
(214)753-9602
Ultimate Parent: K-Mart. SIC: 5942—Book
Stores.

Lubbock

★ 87746 ★ ABF Freight System
Inc.
402 E. 14th St.
Lubbock, TX 79403-4906
(806)744-2381
Location Type: Branch office. Ultimate
Parent: Arkansas Best. SIC: 4212—Local
Trucking Without Storage.

★ 87747 ★ Bell Atlantic Business
Systems
4601 S. Loop 289
Lubbock, TX 79414-1403
(806)797-2373
Ultimate Parent: Bell Atlantic Corp. SIC:
7378—Computer Maintenance & Repair.

★ 87748 ★ Bell Dairy Products
Inc.
201 University Dr.
Lubbock, TX 79408
(806)765-8833
Officer: Noble Anderson, Vice President.
Ultimate Parent: Dean Foods. SIC: 2023—
Dry, Condensed & Evaporated Dairy
Products; 2024—Ice Cream & Frozen
Desserts; 2026—Fluid Milk.

★ 87749 ★ Borden Inc.
519 Ave. J
Lubbock, TX 79401
(806)763-2892
Officer: Tom Locke, Manager. Ultimate
Parent: Borden, Inc. SIC: 2026—Fluid Milk;
2086—Bottled & Canned Soft Drinks.

★ 87750 ★ Brownell Electro Inc.
331 E. 40th St.
Lubbock, TX 79404
(806)747-0211
Location Type: Branch office. Ultimate
Parent: Avnet. SIC: 3679—Electronic
Components Nec.

★ 87751 ★ Browning-Ferris
Industries
405 30th St.
Lubbock, TX 79404-1519
(806)763-8124
Location Type: Branch office. Officer:

Denny Graham. Ultimate Parent:
Browning-Ferris Industries. SIC: 4953—
Refuse Systems; 4212—Local Trucking
Without Storage.

★ 87752 ★ Browning-Ferris
Industries
Landfill N. of City
Lubbock, TX 79408
(806)744-4580
Ultimate Parent: Browning-Ferris
Industries. SIC: 4953—Refuse Systems.

★ 87753 ★ Burlington Northern
Railroa
222 34th St.
Lubbock, TX 79404
(806)744-2321
Ultimate Parent: Burlington Northern. SIC:
4011—Railroads-Line-Haul Operating;
4119—Local Passenger Transportation Nec.

★ 87754 ★ Delta Air Lines
Lubbock International Airport
Lubbock, TX 79401
(806)763-7262
Ultimate Parent: Delta Air Lines, Inc. SIC:
4512—Air Transportation—Scheduled.

★ 87755 ★ Delta Air Lines Inc.
Lubbck International Arp
Lubbock, TX 79401
(806)763-7262
Ultimate Parent: Delta Air Lines, Inc. SIC:
4512—Air Transportation—Scheduled.

★ 87756 ★ Eagle-Picher
Construction
1802 E. 50th St.
Lubbock, TX 79404
(806)747-4663
Officer: James E. Lowder, President.
Ultimate Parent: Eagle-Picher Industries
Inc. SIC: 3531—Construction Machinery.

★ 87757 ★ Eagle-Picher Ind. Inc.
Construction Equipment Div.
1802 E. 50th St.
Lubbock, TX 79404
Company Type: Division. Ultimate Parent:
Eagle-Picher Industries Inc. SIC: 3531—
Construction Machinery.

★ 87758 ★ Eagle Picher
Industries
Construction Equipment Div.
1802 E. 50th
Lubbock, TX 79404
(806)747-4663 Fax: (806)747-8931
Company Type: Headquarters. Officer:
James Lowder, Chairman of the Board.
Ultimate Parent: Eagle-Picher Industries
Inc.

★ 87759 ★ Eagle-Picher
Industries Inc.
Construction Equipment Div.
1802 E. 50th St.
Lubbock, TX 79408
Company Type: Division. Ultimate Parent:
Eagle-Picher Industries Inc. SIC: 3531—
Construction Machinery.

★ 87760 ★ Eagle-Picher
Industries Inc.
Construction Equipment Div.
1802 E. 50th St.
Lubbock, TX 79408
Company Type: Division. Ultimate Parent:
Eagle-Picher Industries Inc. SIC: 3531—
Construction Machinery.

★ 87761 ★ Eagle-Picher
Industries Inc.
Construction Equipment Div.
1802-E. 50th St.
Lubbock, TX 79408
Company Type: Division. Ultimate Parent:
Eagle-Picher Industries Inc. SIC: 3531—
Construction Machinery.

★ 87762 ★ Emery Worldwide
818 Avenue G
Lubbock, TX 79401
(806)763-6337
Ultimate Parent: Consolidated Freightways.
SIC: 4512—Air Transportation—Scheduled.

★ 87763 ★ First Colony Life
5201 Indiana Ave.
Lubbock, TX 79413
(806)792-7707
Ultimate Parent: First Colony Life. SIC:
6411—Insurance Agents, Brokers &
Service.

★ 87764 ★ GroAgriseed Co.
PO Box 1656
Lubbock, TX 79408
(806)747-6225
Company Type: Division. Ultimate Parent:
Lubrizol. SIC: 5191—Farm Supplies.

★ 87765 ★ Hertz Rent-A-Car
Lubbck International Arp
Lubbock, TX 79401
(806)762-0222
Ultimate Parent: Hertz. SIC: 7514—
Passenger Car Rental.

★ 87766 ★ Johnson Controls Inc.
4801 Frankford Ave.
Lubbock, TX 79424
(806)795-8800
Ultimate Parent: Johnson Controls Inc.
SIC: 5084—Industrial Machinery &
Equipment.

★ 87767 ★ Johnson Controls Inc.
1603 W. Loop
Lubbock, TX 79407
(806)795-8800
Ultimate Parent: Johnson Controls Inc.
SIC: 7373—Computer Integrated Systems
Design.

★ 87768 ★ Kerr Mcgee Refining
Corp.
4209 50th St.
Lubbock, TX 79413
(806)792-6454
Ultimate Parent: Kerr-McGee. SIC: 5172—
Petroleum Products Nec.

★ 87769 ★ Liberty Mutual
Insurance Co.
1515 Avenue J
Lubbock, TX 79401
(806)762-5401
Ultimate Parent: Liberty Mutual Group.
SIC: 6411—Insurance Agents, Brokers &
Service.

★ 87770 ★ The Limited
6002 Slide Rd.
Lubbock, TX 79414
(806)793-0270
Ultimate Parent: Limited.

★ 87771 ★ Lubrizol
Agrigenetics Southern Div.
624 27th St.
Lubbock, TX 79404
(806)744-1408
Company Type: Division. Officer: James
O. Gilbreath, Vice President - Southern
Division. Ultimate Parent: Lubrizol. SIC:
5191—Farm Supplies.

★ 87772 ★ Mary Kay Cosmetics
5728 90th St.
Lubbock, TX 79424
(806)794-4392
Ultimate Parent: Mary Kay Cosmetics. SIC:
5999—Miscellaneous Retail Stores Nec.

★ 87773 ★ Payless Cashways
5921 34th St.
Lubbock, TX 79407
(806)793-7451
Ultimate Parent: Payless Cashways. SIC:
5211—Lumber & Other Building Materials.

★ 87774 ★ Payless Shoesource
4821 34th St.
Lubbock, TX 79410
(806)795-9140
Ultimate Parent: May Department Stores.
SIC: 5632—Women's Accessory &
Specialty Stores.

★ 87775 ★ Pepsi-Cola Co.
115 S. Loop 289
Lubbock, TX 79404
(806)745-7711
Officer: Bill Rutledge, Manager. Ultimate
Parent: Pepsico. SIC: 2086—Bottled &
Canned Soft Drinks.

★ 87776 ★ Pizza Hut
4401 82nd St.
Lubbock, TX 79424
(806)794-6600
Ultimate Parent: Pepsico. SIC: 5812—
Eating Places.

★ 87777 ★ Pizza Hut
3311 82nd St.
Lubbock, TX 79423
(806)797-0865
Ultimate Parent: Pepsico. SIC: 5812—
Eating Places.

★ 87778 ★ Radio Shack
S Plains Mall
Lubbock, TX 79414
(806)792-4180
Company Type: Division. Ultimate Parent:
Tandy Corp. SIC: 5065—Electronic Parts &
Equipment Nec.

★ 87779 ★ Radio Shack
2504 82nd St.
Lubbock, TX 79423
(915)332-1761
Company Type: Division. Ultimate Parent:
Tandy Corp. SIC: 5065—Electronic Parts &
Equipment Nec.

★ 87780 ★ Ryder Truck Rental
6602 Avenue H
Lubbock, TX 79404
(806)745-5326
Ultimate Parent: Ryder System. SIC:
5113—Industrial & Personal Service Paper.

★ 87781 ★ Southern Cotton Oil
Co. Inc.
2300 E. 50th St.
Lubbock, TX 79404
(806)763-4371
Officer: Bill Quatteldanm, Manager.
Ultimate Parent: Archer Daniels Midland
Co. SIC: 2074—Cottonseed Oil Mills.

★ 87782 ★ Southland Corp.
7412 University Ave.
Lubbock, TX 79423
(806)743-8711
Ultimate Parent: Southland Corp. SIC:
5411—Grocery Stores.

★ 87783 ★ Taco Bell
2312 19th St.
Lubbock, TX 79401
(806)799-8765
Ultimate Parent: Pepsico. SIC: 5812—
Eating Places.

★ 87784 ★ Taco Bell
E St. 50th
Lubbock, TX 79404
(806)763-3558
Ultimate Parent: Pepsico. SIC: 5812—
Eating Places.

★ 87785 ★ Texaco Food Mart
1415 University Ave.
Lubbock, TX 79401
(806)741-1072
Ultimate Parent: Texaco. SIC: 5411—
Grocery Stores.

★ 87786 ★ Texaco Food Marts
7201 Indiana Ave.
Lubbock, TX 79423
(806)795-2386
Ultimate Parent: Texaco.

★ 87787 ★ Texas Instruments
Inc.
2301 N. University Ave.
Lubbock, TX 79415
Ultimate Parent: Texas Instruments. SIC:
3674—Semiconductors & Related Devices;
3578—Calculating & Accounting Equipment.

★ 87788 ★ Texas Instruments
Inc.
2301 North University
Lubbock, TX 79415
Ultimate Parent: Texas Instruments. SIC:
3674—Semiconductors & Related Devices;
3500—Industrial Machinery & Equipment.

★ 87789 ★ Texas New Mexico &
Oklahoma Coaches, Inc.
1313 13th St.
Lubbock, TX 79401-3915
(806)763-5389
Company Type: Subsidiary. Officer: Fred
G. Currey, Chairman of the Board. Ultimate
Parent: Greyhound Lines Inc. SIC: 4131—
Intercity & Rural Bus Transportation.
Employee Count: 177. Sales: 9 M.

★ 87790 ★ Tj Maxx
7020 Quaker Ave.
Lubbock, TX 79424
(806)797-0851
Ultimate Parent: TJX.

★ 87791 ★   Treadco
701 N. I H 27
Lubbock, TX 79403
(806)762-6194
Officer: Larry Wright. Ultimate Parent:
Arkansas Best. SIC: 5531—Automobile &
Home Supply Stores; 7534—Tire
Retreading & Repair Shops.

★ 87792 ★   United Parcel Service
1601 Avenue N
Lubbock, TX 79401
(806)747-5111
Ultimate Parent: United Parcel Service of
America. SIC: 4212—Local Trucking
Without Storage; 4215—Courier Services
Except by Air.

★ 87793 ★   United Parcel Service
515 E. 44th St.
Lubbock, TX 79404
(806)747-5111
Ultimate Parent: United Parcel Service of
America. SIC: 4215—Courier Services
Except by Air.

★ 87794 ★   Wal Mart Discount
Cities
5206 4th St.
Lubbock, TX 79416
(806)792-7122
Ultimate Parent: Wal-Mart Stores, Inc.

★ 87795 ★   Waste Management
Inc.
1408 N. Quirt Ave.
Lubbock, TX 79403
(806)762-2650
Officer: Jim Blakeley, Manager. Ultimate
Parent: WMX Technologies, Inc. SIC:
3443—Fabricated Plate Work—Boiler
Shops; 3469—Metal Stampings Nec;
3499—Fabricated Metal Products Nec.

Lufkin

★ 87796 ★   Albertson's Food &
Drug Store
111 N. Timberland Dr.
Lufkin, TX 75901
(409)637-7449
Ultimate Parent: Albertson's Inc. SIC:
5411—Grocery Stores.

★ 87797 ★   Butler Paper
480 Regal Row
Lufkin, TX 75904
(409)632-7703
Officer: Dennis Miller. Ultimate Parent:
Alco Standard Corp. SIC: 5113—Industrial
& Personal Service Paper; 5111—Printing &
Writing Paper.

★ 87798 ★   Champion
International Corp.
3201 Atkinson Dr.
Lufkin, TX 75901
(409)634-8811
Ultimate Parent: Champion International.
SIC: 2621—Paper Mills.

★ 87799 ★   Champion
International Corp. Lufkin
Newsprint Operations
Hwy. 103 E.
Lufkin, TX 75902-0149
Ultimate Parent: Champion International.
SIC: 2621—Paper Mills.

★ 87800 ★   Champion
International Lufkin Newsprint
Operation
Hwy. 103 East
Lufkin, TX 75902-0149
Ultimate Parent: Champion International.
SIC: 2621—Paper Mills.

★ 87801 ★   Circus World
4600 S. Medford Dr.
Lufkin, TX 75901
(409)639-4700
Ultimate Parent: Melville. SIC: 5945—
Hobby, Toy & Game Shops.

★ 87802 ★   Exxon
1507 S. 1st St.
Lufkin, TX 75901
(409)634-4514
Ultimate Parent: Exxon. SIC: 5541—
Gasoline Service Stations.

★ 87803 ★   Foot Action U S a
4600 S. Medford Dr. 1266
Lufkin, TX 75901
(409)639-4866
Ultimate Parent: Melville. SIC: 5661—Shoe
Stores.

★ 87804 ★   Georgia Pacific
Resins Inc.
1429 E. Lufkin Ave.
Lufkin, TX 75901
Ultimate Parent: Georgia-Pacific. SIC:
2821—Plastics Materials & Resins; 2869—
Industrial Organic Chemicals Nec.

★ 87805 ★   Georgia-Pacific
Resins Inc.
300 E. Lufkin Ave.
Lufkin, TX 75901
Ultimate Parent: Georgia-Pacific. SIC:
2821—Plastics Materials & Resins; 2869—
Industrial Organic Chemicals Nec.

★ 87806 ★   Hertz Rent-A-Car
Licensee
Angelina
Lufkin, TX 75901
(409)632-2822
Ultimate Parent: Hertz. SIC: 7514—
Passenger Car Rental.

★ 87807 ★   Lerner Shop
4600 Lufkin Mall N. 1316
Lufkin, TX 75901
(409)639-4800
Ultimate Parent: Limited. SIC: 5651—
Family Clothing Stores.

★ 87808 ★   Louisiana Pacific
Corp.
Old Mill Rd.
Lufkin, TX 75901
(409)639-1321
Ultimate Parent: Louisiana-Pacific. SIC:
2436—Softwood Veneer & Plywood.

★ 87809 ★   Louisiana-Pacific
Corp. Plywood
Old Mill Rd.
Lufkin, TX 75901
Ultimate Parent: Louisiana-Pacific. SIC:
2436—Softwood Veneer & Plywood.

★ 87810 ★   Mary Kay Cosmetics
704 Mantooth Ave.
Lufkin, TX 75901
(409)639-3060
Ultimate Parent: Mary Kay Cosmetics. SIC:
5999—Miscellaneous Retail Stores Nec.

★ 87811 ★   Pilgrim's Pride Corp.
Hwy. 94
Lufkin, TX 75901
(409)639-1174
Ultimate Parent: Pilgrim's Pride Corp. SIC:
5499—Miscellaneous Food Stores.

★ 87812 ★   Pilgrim's Pride Corp.
Corner of Franks & Webber
Lufkin, TX 75901
Ultimate Parent: Pilgrim's Pride Corp. SIC:
2000—Food & Kindred Products.

★ 87813 ★   Pilgrim's Pride Corp.
Lufkin Processing
Corner of Frank & Webber
Lufkin, TX 75901
Company Type: Division. Ultimate Parent:
Pilgrim's Pride Corp. SIC: 2015—Poultry
Slaughtering & Processing.

★ 87814 ★   Pizza Hut
318 S. Chestnut St.
Lufkin, TX 75901
(409)632-5210
Ultimate Parent: Pepsico. SIC: 5812—
Eating Places.

★ 87815 ★   Radio Shack
113 N. Timberland Dr. A
Lufkin, TX 75901
(409)632-1801
Company Type: Division. Ultimate Parent:
Tandy Corp. SIC: 5065—Electronic Parts &
Equipment Nec.

★ 87816 ★   Radio Shack
4600 S. Medford Dr.
Lufkin, TX 75901
(409)639-4777
Company Type: Division. Ultimate Parent:
Tandy Corp. SIC: 5065—Electronic Parts &
Equipment Nec.

★ 87817 ★   Ryder Truck Rental
1902 E. Denman Ave.
Lufkin, TX 75901
(409)639-3800
Ultimate Parent: Ryder System. SIC:
7359—Equipment Rental & Leasing Nec.

★ 87818 ★   Shell Service Station
1500 Atkinson Dr.
Lufkin, TX 75901
(409)634-9938
Ultimate Parent: Shell Oil Co. SIC: 5541—
Gasoline Service Stations.

★ 87819 ★   Sullivan Graphics Inc.
1029 PO Box
Lufkin, TX 75902
(409)634-3357
Ultimate Parent: Morgan Stanley Group.
SIC: 2732—Book Printing.

★ 87820 ★   US Sprint
Communication Co.
8253rd
Lufkin, TX 75901
(214)387-4686
Ultimate Parent: Sprint. SIC: 7389—
Business Services Nec.

★ 87821 ★   Waldenbooks
4600 S. Medford Dr.
Lufkin, TX 75901
(409)639-4143
Ultimate Parent: K-Mart. SIC: 5942—Book
Stores.

Luling

★ 87822 ★   Arco Pipe Line Co.
FM 2984
Luling, TX 78648
(210)875-5214
Ultimate Parent: Atlantic Richfield Co., Inc.
SIC: 4612—Crude Petroleum Pipelines.

★ 87823 ★   Arco Pipe Line Co.
F M 2984
Luling, TX 78648
(210)875-5214
Ultimate Parent: Atlantic Richfield Co., Inc.
SIC: 4612—Crude Petroleum Pipelines.

★ 87824 ★   Mobil Pipe Line Co.
Houston Hwy.
Luling, TX 78648
(210)875-9228
Company Type: Branch. Ultimate Parent:
Mobil. SIC: 4612—Crude Petroleum
Pipelines.

Mabank

★ 87825 ★   McDonalds
104 W. Main St.
Mabank, TX 75147
(903)887-0054
Ultimate Parent: McDonald's.

Madisonville

★ 87826 ★   Coca Cola Bottling
Co.
601 E. Magnolia St.
Madisonville, TX 77864
(409)348-2202
Ultimate Parent: Coca-Cola Enterprises.
SIC: 5149—Groceries & Related Products
Nec.

★ 87827 ★   Exxon Co. USA
509 S. Elm St.
Madisonville, TX 77864
(409)348-2616
Ultimate Parent: Exxon. SIC: 5172—
Petroleum Products Nec; 5531—Automobile
& Home Supply Stores.

★ 87828 ★   Texaco Distributor
608 S. Elm St.
Madisonville, TX 77864
(409)348-2232
Ultimate Parent: Texaco. SIC: 5172—
Petroleum Products Nec.

Malakoff

★ 87829 ★   Ace Hardware
202 W. Royall Blvd.
Malakoff, TX 75148
(903)489-1529
Ultimate Parent: Ace Hardware. SIC:
5251—Hardware Stores.

★ 87830 ★   Citizens State Bank
115 W. Royall Blvd.
Malakoff, TX 75148
(214)489-0530
Ultimate Parent: Liberty National Bancorp.
SIC: 6022—State Commercial Banks.

★ 87831 ★   Malakoff Ind. Inc.
State Hwy. 31 W.
Malakoff, TX 75148
Ultimate Parent: Reynolds Metals Co. SIC:
2899—Chemical Preparations Nec.

Mansfield

★ 87832 ★   Kroger Phrmcy
1740 Hwy. 157 N
Mansfield, TX 76063
(817)473-4485
Ultimate Parent: Kroger.

★ 87833 ★   McDonalds
Restaurant
1001 Hwy. 287 N
Mansfield, TX 76063
(817)473-3260
Ultimate Parent: May Department Stores.

★ 87834 ★   Mobil Mart
1901 Hwy. 157 N
Mansfield, TX 76063
(817)477-1047
Ultimate Parent: Mobil.

★ 87835 ★   Pizza Hut
1351 Hwy. 157 N
Mansfield, TX 76063
(817)473-1108
Ultimate Parent: Pepsico. SIC: 5812—
Eating Places.

★ 87836 ★   Ryder Truck Rental
2440 Hwy. 287 N
Mansfield, TX 76063
(817)473-8215
Ultimate Parent: Ryder System.

★ 87837 ★   Wal Mart Discount
City
Hwy. 287
Mansfield, TX 76063
(817)473-1189
Ultimate Parent: Wal-Mart Stores, Inc. SIC:
5331—Variety Stores.

Marble Falls

★ 87838 ★   Exxon Products
2403 Commerce St.
Marble Falls, TX 78654
(512)693-3991
Ultimate Parent: Exxon. SIC: 5171—
Petroleum Bulk Stations & Terminals.

★ 87839 ★   Mary Kay Cosmetics
Independent
328 Columbine Cir.
Marble Falls, TX 78654
(512)693-3357
Ultimate Parent: Mary Kay Cosmetics. SIC:
5999—Miscellaneous Retail Stores Nec.

★ 87840 ★   Ryder Truck Rental
Hwy. 281 N
Marble Falls, TX 78654
(512)693-5972
Ultimate Parent: Ryder System. SIC:
7513—Truck Rental & Leasing Without
Drivers.

★ 87841 ★   Wal Mart Discount
Cities
2510 N. Hwy. 281
Marble Falls, TX 78654
(512)693-3682
Ultimate Parent: Wal-Mart Stores, Inc. SIC:
5311—Department Stores.

Marfa

★ 87842 ★   Texaco Inc.
203 E. El Paco
Marfa, TX 79843
(915)729-4242
Ultimate Parent: Texaco. SIC: 5172—
Petroleum Products Nec.

★ 87843 ★   **West Texas Utilities Co.**
120 N. Highland
Marfa, TX 79843
(915)729-4321
Ultimate Parent: Central & South West.
SIC: 4911—Electric Services.

Marietta

★ 87844 ★   **Shell Oil Co.**
Marietta, TX 75566
(214)835-3752
Ultimate Parent: Shell Oil Co. **SIC:** 5171—
Petroleum Bulk Stations & Terminals.

Markham

★ 87845 ★   **Marathon Oil Co.**
Farm Rd.
Markham, TX 77456
(409)245-9186
Ultimate Parent: USX Corp.

★ 87846 ★   **Marathon Oil Co.**
Markham, TX 77456
(409)843-5521
Ultimate Parent: USX Corp. **SIC:** 1311—
Crude Petroleum & Natural Gas.

★ 87847 ★   **Marathon Oil Co.**
Markham, TX 77456
(409)843-5521
Ultimate Parent: USX Corp. **SIC:** 1311—
Crude Petroleum & Natural Gas.

★ 87848 ★   **Marathon Oil Co.**
Farm Rd.
Markham, TX 77456
(409)245-9186
Ultimate Parent: USX Corp.

★ 87849 ★   **Texaco Pipeline Inc.**
128th
Markham, TX 77456
(409)843-5112
Ultimate Parent: Texaco.

Marlin

★ 87850 ★   **Lone Star Gas Co.**
151 Coleman St.
Marlin, TX 76661
(817)883-3551
Ultimate Parent: Enserch. **SIC:** 4925—Gas
Production & Distribution Nec.

★ 87851 ★   **Pizza Hut**
219 Craik St.
Marlin, TX 76661
(817)883-9262
Ultimate Parent: Pepsico.

Marshall

★ 87852 ★   **Aluminum Co. of America**
Us 80 E
Marshall, TX 75670
(214)938-5151
Ultimate Parent: Aluminum Co. of America-
-Alcoa. **SIC:** 2241—Narrow Fabric Mills.

★ 87853 ★   **Freeman Resins**
Scottsville Rd., Fm 1998
Marshall, TX 75670
Ultimate Parent: Georgia Gulf. **SIC:** 2821—
Plastics Materials & Resins.

★ 87854 ★   **Kentucky Fried Chicken**
2100 Victory Dr.
Marshall, TX 75670
(214)938-2727
Ultimate Parent: Pepsico. **SIC:** 5812—
Eating Places.

★ 87855 ★   **Kroger Family Cntr**
300 E. End Blvd. N
Marshall, TX 75670
(214)938-7711
Ultimate Parent: Kroger. **SIC:** 5411—
Grocery Stores.

★ 87856 ★   **Kroger Food Store**
300 S. End Blvd. E
Marshall, TX 75670
(903)938-7711
Ultimate Parent: Kroger.

★ 87857 ★   **Lewis Engineering Co.**
1608 E. Houston St.
Marshall, TX 75670-4442
(903)938-6754
Ultimate Parent: Coltec Industries. **SIC:**
3599—Industrial Machinery Nec; 7692—
Welding Repair; 3489—Ordnance &
Accessories Nec.

★ 87858 ★   **McDonalds**
5408 E. End Blvd. S
Marshall, TX 75670
(903)938-6411
Ultimate Parent: McDonald's.

★ 87859 ★   **McDonalds**
2000 Victory Dr.
Marshall, TX 75670
(903)938-7031
Ultimate Parent: McDonald's.

★ 87860 ★   **Pizza Hut**
1601 E. End Blvd. S
Marshall, TX 75670
Ultimate Parent: Pepsico.

★ 87861 ★   **R. W. Snyder Co. Inc.**
1401 Central Rte. 6
Marshall, TX 75670
Ultimate Parent: Quaker Oates. **SIC:**
2087—Flavoring Extracts & Syrups Nec.

★ 87862 ★   **Radio Shack**
1300 E. Pinecrest Dr.
Marshall, TX 75670
(903)938-4821
Company Type: Division. **Ultimate Parent:**
Tandy Corp.

★ 87863 ★   **Radio Shack**
120 N. End Blvd. E
Marshall, TX 75670
(903)935-9871
Company Type: Division. **Ultimate Parent:**
Tandy Corp.

★ 87864 ★   **Radio Shack**
Marshall
Marshall, TX 75670
(214)938-4821
Company Type: Division. **Ultimate Parent:**
Tandy Corp. **SIC:** 5065—Electronic Parts &
Equipment Nec.

★ 87865 ★   **Radio Shack**
120 E. End Blvd. N
Marshall, TX 75670
(214)935-9871
Company Type: Division. **Ultimate Parent:**
Tandy Corp. **SIC:** 5065—Electronic Parts &
Equipment Nec.

★ 87866 ★   **Ryder Truck Rental**
2602 W. Grand Ave.
Marshall, TX 75670
(903)935-1114
Ultimate Parent: Ryder System. **SIC:**
7513—Truck Rental & Leasing Without
Drivers.

★ 87867 ★   **Ryder Truck Rental**
303 S. End Blvd. E
Marshall, TX 75670
(903)935-1862
Ultimate Parent: Ryder System.

★ 87868 ★   **Taco Bell**
628 S. End Blvd. E
Marshall, TX 75670
(903)935-0207
Ultimate Parent: Pepsico.

★ 87869 ★   **Trailways Bus Terminal**
201 S. Bolivar St.
Marshall, TX 75670
(214)938-6763
Ultimate Parent: Greyhound Lines Inc. **SIC:**
4111—Local & Suburban Transit.

★ 87870 ★   **Wal Mart Disc Cits**
105 S. End Blvd. E
Marshall, TX 75670
(903)938-5123
Ultimate Parent: Wal-Mart Stores, Inc.

★ 87871 ★   **Waldenbooks**
Marshall
Marshall, TX 75670
(214)938-2491
Ultimate Parent: K-Mart. **SIC:** 5942—Book
Stores.

★ 87872 ★   **Witco Corp.**
Hwy. 59 N. & Bussey Rd.
PO Box 1439
Marshall, TX 75670
Ultimate Parent: Witco Corp. **SIC:** 2869—
Industrial Organic Chemicals Nec.

★ 87873 ★   **Witco Corp.**
Off Hwy. 59, N. Bussey Rd.
PO Box 1439
Marshall, TX 75670
Ultimate Parent: Witco Corp. **SIC:** 2869—
Industrial Organic Chemicals Nec.

★ 87874 ★   **Witco Corp.**
Argus
Off Hwy. 59 Bussey Rd.
Marshall, TX 75670
Ultimate Parent: Witco Corp. **SIC:** 2869—
Industrial Organic Chemicals Nec.

★ 87875 ★   **Witco Corp.**
Argus
Off Hwy. 59, North of Marshall
Marshall, TX 75670
Ultimate Parent: Witco Corp. **SIC:** 2869—
Industrial Organic Chemicals Nec.

★ 87876 ★   **Witco Corp.**
Argus Chemcial Div.
Hwy. 59 & Bussey Rd.
Marshall, TX 75670
(903)938-5141
Company Type: Division. **Officer:** Paul
Martin, Manager. **Ultimate Parent:** Witco
Corp. **SIC:** 2819—Industrial Inorganic
Chemicals Nec; 2869—Industrial Organic
Chemicals Nec.

Martindale

★ 87877 ★   **GTE Center**
PO Box 39
Martindale, TX 78655-0039
(512)357-6115
Location Type: Branch office. **Ultimate
Parent:** GTE.

Maryneal

★ 87878 ★   **Lone Star Industries Inc.**
FM Rd. 608
Maryneal, TX 79535
(915)288-4221
Location Type: Plant. **Officer:** Richard S.
Franklin, Plant Manager. **Ultimate Parent:**
Enserch. **SIC:** 3241—Cement—Hydraulic.

Mathis

★ 87879 ★   **Pizza Hut**
517 N. Old Hwy. 9
Mathis, TX 78368
(512)547-6111
Ultimate Parent: Pepsico. **SIC:** 5812—
Eating Places.

★ 87880 ★   **Pizza Hut**
517 N. State Hwy. 9
Mathis, TX 78368
(512)547-9127
Ultimate Parent: Pepsico.

★ 87881 ★   **Trailways Bus System**
423 W. Hwy. 9
Mathis, TX 78368
(512)547-5261
Ultimate Parent: Greyhound Lines Inc. **SIC:**
4131—Intercity & Rural Bus Transportation.

Mc Allen

★ 87882 ★   **Aviall - Mcallen**
6200 S. 42nd St.
Mc Allen, TX 78503
Ultimate Parent: Ryder System. **SIC:**
3728—Aircraft Parts & Equipment Nec.

★ 87883 ★   **Hertz Rent-A-Car Licensee**
Mac Allen International Airport
Mc Allen, TX 78501
(512)686-7443
Ultimate Parent: Hertz. **SIC:** 7514—
Passenger Car Rental.

★ 87884 ★   **Hertz Rent-A-Car Svc Dept**
2800 N. Main St.
Mc Allen, TX 78503
(512)687-1731
Ultimate Parent: Hertz. **SIC:** 7514—
Passenger Car Rental.

★ 87885 ★   **Hewlett Packard Co.**
224 Nolana St.
Mc Allen, TX 78504
(512)630-3030
Ultimate Parent: Hewlett-Packard. **SIC:**
5046—Commercial Equipment Nec.

★ 87886 ★   **Hit or Miss**
2200 S. 10th St.
Mc Allen, TX 78503
(512)687-9224
Ultimate Parent: TJX. **SIC:** 5621—
Women's Clothing Stores.

★ 87887 ★   **Kentucky Fried Chicken**
707 Nolana St.
Mc Allen, TX 78504
(512)682-5241
Ultimate Parent: Pepsico. **SIC:** 5812—
Eating Places.

★ 87888 ★   **Kmart Pharmacy**
1801 S. 10th St.
Mc Allen, TX 78503
(512)682-4339
Ultimate Parent: K-Mart. **SIC:** 5531—
Automobile & Home Supply Stores.

★ 87889 ★   **McDonalds**
2808 N. 10th St.
Mc Allen, TX 78501
(512)687-5898
Ultimate Parent: McDonald's.
SIC: 5812—Eating Places.

★ 87890 ★   **Mobil Oils Distributor**
2401 W. Hwy. 83
Mc Allen, TX 78501
(512)686-5466
Ultimate Parent: Mobil. **SIC:** 5172—
Petroleum Products Nec.

★ 87891 ★   **Mutual of New York**
309 Nolana St.
Mc Allen, TX 78504
(512)682-6363
Ultimate Parent: Mutual of New York. **SIC:**
6411—Insurance Agents, Brokers &
Service.

★ 87892 ★   **National Medical Care**
Medical Products Div.
6620 S. 33rd St.
Mc Allen, TX 78503
Company Type: Division. **Ultimate Parent:**
W. R. Grace. **SIC:** 3841—Surgical &
Medical Instruments.

★ 87893 ★   **National Medical Care Inc.**
Medical Products Div.
6620 S. 23rd St.
Mc Allen, TX 78503
Company Type: Division. **Ultimate Parent:**
W. R. Grace. **SIC:** 3841—Surgical &
Medical Instruments.

★ 87894 ★   **Pennzoil Producing Co. Inc.**
801 Quince Ave.
Mc Allen, TX 78501
(512)686-0297
Ultimate Parent: Pennzoil. **SIC:** 5171—
Petroleum Bulk Stations & Terminals.

★ 87895 ★   **Pizza Hut**
2101 N. 23rd St.
Mc Allen, TX 78501
(512)682-1521
Ultimate Parent: Pepsico. **SIC:** 5812—
Eating Places.

★ 87896 ★   **Red Arrow Freight Lines Inc.**
N Mac Coll Rd.
Mc Allen, TX 78501
(512)687-5137
Ultimate Parent: Carolina Freight. **SIC:**
4213—Trucking Except Local.

★ 87897 ★   **Rio Grande Foods Inc.**
3701 W. Military Hwy.
Mc Allen, TX 78501
Ultimate Parent: Flowers Industries. **SIC:**
2037—Frozen Fruits & Vegetables.

★ 87898 ★   **Ryder Airline Services Mcallen**
6200 S. 42nd St.
Mc Allen, TX 78503-8895
(512)682-8895
Ultimate Parent: Ryder System. **SIC:** 3724—Aircraft Engines & Engine Parts.

★ 87899 ★   **Safety Kleen Corp.**
N Jackson
Mc Allen, TX 78501
(512)682-1951
Ultimate Parent: Safety-Kleen. **SIC:** 5085—Industrial Supplies.

★ 87900 ★   **Stokely USA Inc.**
2100 Trophy Dr.
Mc Allen, TX 78504
(210)686-1533
Officer: Arnold Bolman, Manager. **Ultimate Parent:** Quaker Oates. **SIC:** 2038—Frozen Specialties Nec.

★ 87901 ★   **Thom Mcan Shoe Store No 141**
218 S. Main St.
Mc Allen, TX 78501
(512)630-9748
Ultimate Parent: Melville. **SIC:** 5661—Shoe Stores.

★ 87902 ★   **Trailways Bus Systems**
100 N. Broadway St.
Mc Allen, TX 78501
(512)682-5513
Ultimate Parent: Greyhound Lines Inc. **SIC:** 4111—Local & Suburban Transit.

★ 87903 ★   **Valley Coca-Cola Bottling Co.**
2400 Expressway 83
Mc Allen, TX 78501
Ultimate Parent: Coca-Cola Enterprises. **SIC:** 2086—Bottled & Canned Soft Drinks.

★ 87904 ★   **Waldenbooks**
La Plz.
Mc Allen, TX 78503
(512)631-1292
Ultimate Parent: K-Mart. **SIC:** 5942—Book Stores.

Mc Gregor

★ 87905 ★   **Hercules Inc. US Naval Weapons Indl. Res. Plant**
1101 Johnson Dr.
Mc Gregor, TX 76657-1999
Ultimate Parent: Hercules. **SIC:** 3764—Space Propulsion Units & Parts; 2892—Explosives.

★ 87906 ★   **Hercules Inc. US Naval Weapons Plant**
1101 Johnson Dr.
Mc Gregor, TX 76657-1999
Ultimate Parent: Hercules. **SIC:** 3764—Space Propulsion Units & Parts; 2892—Explosives.

★ 87907 ★   **Trane Co. Wshpbu**
Hwy. 84 & Cotton Belt Pky.
Mc Gregor, TX 76657
Ultimate Parent: American Standard. **SIC:** 3585—Refrigeration & Heating Equipment.

Mc Kinney

★ 87908 ★   **Cincinnati Shoe Co.**
800 Shelby Dr.
Mc Kinney, TX 75069
(214)542-5381
Ultimate Parent: United States Shoe. **SIC:** 5661—Shoe Stores.

★ 87909 ★   **Coast to Coast Store**
Westgate Shopping Ctr.
Mc Kinney, TX 75069
(214)542-9459
Ultimate Parent: Servistar Corp. **SIC:** 5251—Hardware Stores.

★ 87910 ★   **Fisher Controls International Inc.**
310 E. University PO Box 8004
Mc Kinney, TX 75069-8004
Ultimate Parent: Monsanto. **SIC:** 3491—Industrial Valves; 3823—Process Control Instruments.

★ 87911 ★   **Fisher Controls International Inc.**
E. Hwy. 380
Mc Kinney, TX 75069
Ultimate Parent: Monsanto. **SIC:** 3494—Valves & Pipe Fittings Nec; 3823—Process Control Instruments.

★ 87912 ★   **Greyhound Bus Lines**
202 S. Tennessee St.
Mc Kinney, TX 75069
(214)542-5621
Ultimate Parent: Greyhound Lines Inc. **SIC:** 4111—Local & Suburban Transit.

★ 87913 ★   **Kentucky Fried Chicken**
204 W. University Dr.
Mc Kinney, TX 75069
(214)542-5271
Ultimate Parent: Pepsico. **SIC:** 5812—Eating Places.

★ 87914 ★   **Kroger**
1707 W. University Dr.
Mc Kinney, TX 75069
(214)548-9053
Ultimate Parent: Kroger. **SIC:** 5411—Grocery Stores.

★ 87915 ★   **Mary Kay Cosmetics Dir**
4433 Santa Cruz Ln.
Mc Kinney, TX 75070
(214)548-0116
Ultimate Parent: Mary Kay Cosmetics. **SIC:** 7231—Beauty Shops.

★ 87916 ★   **McDonalds of Mckinney**
402 N. Central Expy.
Mc Kinney, TX 75069
(214)542-3441
Ultimate Parent: McDonald's. **SIC:** 5812—Eating Places.

★ 87917 ★   **Piggly Wiggly**
Hwy. 380
Mc Kinney, TX 75069
(214)542-7381
Ultimate Parent: Bruno's. **SIC:** 5411—Grocery Stores.

★ 87918 ★   **Pizza Hut**
208 W. University Dr.
Mc Kinney, TX 75069
(214)542-3368
Ultimate Parent: Pepsico. **SIC:** 5812—Eating Places.

★ 87919 ★   **Radio Shack**
Westgate Shopping Ctr.
Mc Kinney, TX 75069
(214)542-6214
Company Type: Division. **Ultimate Parent:** Tandy Corp. **SIC:** 5065—Electronic Parts & Equipment Nec.

★ 87920 ★   **Ryder Truck Rental**
Hwy. 75
Mc Kinney, TX 75069
(214)542-0422
Ultimate Parent: Ryder System. **SIC:** 7359—Equipment Rental & Leasing Nec.

★ 87921 ★   **Taco Bell**
404 N. Central Expy.
Mc Kinney, TX 75070
(214)548-0649
Ultimate Parent: Pepsico.

★ 87922 ★   **Texas Instruments**
2501 West University
Mc Kinney, TX 75069
Ultimate Parent: Texas Instruments. **SIC:** 3812—Search & Navigation Equipment.

★ 87923 ★   **Texas Instruments Inc.**
2501 W. University
Mc Kinney, TX 75069
Ultimate Parent: Texas Instruments. **SIC:** 3812—Search & Navigation Equipment.

★ 87924 ★   **Trailways Bus System**
1600 S. Mcdonald St.
Mc Kinney, TX 75069
(214)542-3152
Ultimate Parent: Greyhound Lines Inc. **SIC:** 4212—Local Trucking Without Storage.

★ 87925 ★   **Wal Mart**
1670 W. University Dr.
Mc Kinney, TX 75069
(214)542-4493
Ultimate Parent: Wal-Mart Stores, Inc.

★ 87926 ★   **Wal Mart Pharmacy**
1670 W. University Dr.
Mc Kinney, TX 75069
(214)542-2619
Ultimate Parent: Wal-Mart Stores, Inc. **SIC:** 5912—Drug Stores & Proprietary Stores.

Mc Queeney

★ 87927 ★   **Exxon**
W Old Farm Rd.
Mc Queeney, TX 78123
(512)557-6720
Ultimate Parent: Exxon. **SIC:** 5541—Gasoline Service Stations.

McAllen

★ 87928 ★   **Casual Corner**
2200 S. 10th St.
McAllen, TX 78503
(512)631-8701
Ultimate Parent: United States Shoe.

★ 87929 ★   **Circus World Toy**
2200 S. 10th St.
Mcallen, TX 78503
(512)682-7644
Ultimate Parent: Melville.

★ 87930 ★   **Foot Action USA**
2200 S. 10th St.
Mcallen, TX 78503
(512)630-2360
Ultimate Parent: Melville.

★ 87931 ★   **Lane Bryant**
2200 S. 10th St.
Mcallen, TX 78503
(512)682-8228
Ultimate Parent: Limited.

★ 87932 ★   **Lerner Shop**
2200 S. 10th St.
Mcallen, TX 78503
(512)687-4161
Ultimate Parent: Limited.

★ 87933 ★   **Mccaw Communctns**
4405 N. 22nd St.
Mcallen, TX 78504
(512)682-3171
Ultimate Parent: McCaw Cellular Communications.

★ 87934 ★   **Mcduff Elctrncs**
801 Savannah Ave.
Mcallen, TX 78503
(512)630-2922
Ultimate Parent: Tandy Corp.

★ 87935 ★   **Payless Shoesource**
Hwy. 83
Mcallen, TX 78501
(512)686-0152
Ultimate Parent: May Department Stores. **SIC:** 5661—Shoe Stores.

★ 87936 ★   **Pizza Hut**
1116 Pecan Blvd.
McAllen, TX 78501
(512)630-3077
Ultimate Parent: Pepsico. **SIC:** 5812—Eating Places.

★ 87937 ★   **Radio Shack**
1001 S. 10th St.
Mcallen, TX 78501
(512)631-0147
Company Type: Division. **Ultimate Parent:** Tandy Corp.

★ 87938 ★   **Radio Shack**
Gateway Plz.
Mcallen, TX 78501
(512)631-2262
Company Type: Division. **Ultimate Parent:** Tandy Corp. **SIC:** 5734—Computer & Software Stores.

★ 87939 ★   **Radio Shack**
1303 S. 10th St.
Mcallen, TX 78501
Company Type: Division. **Ultimate Parent:** Tandy Corp. **SIC:** 5065—Electronic Parts & Equipment Nec.

★ 87940 ★   **Rio Grande Foods**
3701 W. Military Hwy.
McAllen, TX 78503
(210)682-1368
Company Type: Subsidiary. **Location Type:** Plant. **Officer:** Dale Robins, Vice President of Production. **Ultimate Parent:** Flowers Industries. **SIC:** 2033—Canned Fruits & Vegetables; 2038—Frozen Specialties Nec.

★ 87941 ★   **Sysco Food Services**
1301 E. Hackberry Ave.
Mcallen, TX 78501
(512)682-6145
Ultimate Parent: Sysco. **SIC:** 5961—Catalog & Mail-Order Houses.

★ 87942 ★   **Texaco**
1521 N. 10th St.
Mcallen, TX 78501
(512)682-6811
Ultimate Parent: Texaco.

★ 87943 ★   **TRW Automotive Products Remfg.**
2705 Ebony Ave.
McAllen, TX 78501
(210)687-7717
Officer: Charles Pestow, Manager. **Ultimate Parent:** TRW, Inc. **SIC:** 3714—Motor Vehicle Parts & Accessories.

★ 87944 ★   **TRW Vehicle Safety Systems**
2701 Ebony Ave., No. A
McAllen, TX 75801
(210)632-8100
Officer: Dave Beal, President. **Ultimate Parent:** TRW, Inc. **SIC:** 2399—Fabricated Textile Products Nec.

★ 87945 ★   **Valley Coca-Cola Bottling Co., Inc.**
2400 W. Expwy. 83
McAllen, TX 78503-7768
(210)632-3700
Officer: Henry A. Schimberg, President. **Ultimate Parent:** Coca-Cola Enterprises. **SIC:** 2086—Bottled & Canned Soft Drinks. **Employee Count:** 1400.

★ 87946 ★   **Wal Mart Discount City**
4001 N. 23rd St.
McAllen, TX 78504
Ultimate Parent: Wal-Mart Stores, Inc. **SIC:** 5311—Department Stores.

★ 87947 ★   **Weyerhaeuser Paper**
200 N. 26th St.
McAllen, TX 78501
(512)968-3611
Ultimate Parent: Weyerhaeuser Co.

Memphis

★ 87948 ★   **Lone Star Gas Co.**
515 W. Main St.
Memphis, TX 79245
(806)259-2526
Ultimate Parent: Enserch. **SIC:** 4925—Gas Production & Distribution Nec.

★ 87949 ★   **Mobil Oil Co. Consignee**
221 W. Main St.
Memphis, TX 79245
(806)259-2531
Ultimate Parent: Mobil. **SIC:** 5171—Petroleum Bulk Stations & Terminals.

★ 87950 ★   **Texaco Service Center**
415 N. Boykin Dr.
Memphis, TX 79245
(806)259-2047
Ultimate Parent: Texaco. **SIC:** 5541—Gasoline Service Stations.

★ 87951 ★ Trailways Bus System
705 W. Noel St.
Memphis, TX 79245
(806)259-3045
Ultimate Parent: Greyhound Lines Inc. SIC:
4131—Intercity & Rural Bus Transportation.

Menard

★ 87952 ★ Exxon Co. USA
Menard, TX 76859
(915)396-4651
Ultimate Parent: Exxon. SIC: 5172—
Petroleum Products Nec.

Mercedes

★ 87953 ★ Pizza Hut
826 W. 2nd St.
Mercedes, TX 78570
(512)565-6319
Ultimate Parent: Pepsico. SIC: 5812—
Eating Places.

Mertzon

★ 87954 ★ Compass Bank-Dallas
3111 N. Galloway
Mertzon, TX 75150-4753
(214)681-5500
Company Type: Subsidiary. Location
Type: Branch office. Ultimate Parent:
Compass Bancshares. SIC: 6021—National
Commercial Banks.

★ 87955 ★ Conoco Inc.
Hwy. 67
Mertzon, TX 76941
(915)835-2101
Officer: Bill Way, Manager. Ultimate
Parent: E.I. DuPont De Nemours. SIC:
2992—Lubricating Oils & Greases.

Mesquite

★ 87956 ★ Casual Corner
2072 Town Mall E
Mesquite, TX 75150
(214)270-4451
Ultimate Parent: United States Shoe. SIC:
5621—Women's Clothing Stores.

★ 87957 ★ Express Ltd.
1246 Town Mall E
Mesquite, TX 75150
(214)613-9591
Ultimate Parent: Limited.

★ 87958 ★ Exxon
Oates Dr.
Mesquite, TX 75150
(214)270-1132
Ultimate Parent: Exxon. SIC: 5541—
Gasoline Service Stations.

★ 87959 ★ Exxon
12600 Lake June Rd.
Mesquite, TX 75180
(214)285-4396
Ultimate Parent: Exxon. SIC: 5541—
Gasoline Service Stations.

★ 87960 ★ Exxon Shop
1015 N. Town Blvd. E
Mesquite, TX 75150
(214)613-8808
Ultimate Parent: Exxon. SIC: 5599—
Automotive Dealers Nec.

★ 87961 ★ Exxon Shop
3828 E. Hwy. 80
Mesquite, TX 75149
(214)288-0596
Ultimate Parent: Exxon. SIC: 5599—
Automotive Dealers Nec.

★ 87962 ★ First Bank
3636 Shepherd Ln.
Mesquite, TX 75180
(214)286-3636
Ultimate Parent: Shawmut National Corp.
SIC: 6022—State Commercial Banks.

★ 87963 ★ Foamex L.P.
3210 Curtis Blvd.
Mesquite, TX 75149
Ultimate Parent: Foamex. SIC: 3086—
Plastics Foam Products.

★ 87964 ★ The Gap
1012 Town Mall E
Mesquite, TX 75150
(214)270-7625
Ultimate Parent: GAP.

★ 87965 ★ Jiffy Lube
110 S. Galloway Ave.
Mesquite, TX 75149
(214)285-8305
Ultimate Parent: Pennzoil. SIC: 7539—
Automotive Repair Shops Nec.

★ 87966 ★ Jiffy Lube
2214 N. Town Blvd. E
Mesquite, TX 75150
(214)681-3484
Ultimate Parent: Pennzoil.

★ 87967 ★ Kmart Apparel Corp.
199 Planters Rd.
Mesquite, TX 75182
(214)226-0295
Ultimate Parent: K-Mart.

★ 87968 ★ Kmart Discount
Stores
12005 Elam Rd.
Mesquite, TX 75180
(214)286-1112
Ultimate Parent: K-Mart.

★ 87969 ★ Kroger Financial Ctrs
505 N. Galloway Ave.
Mesquite, TX 75149
(214)289-1807
Ultimate Parent: Kroger. SIC: 6411—
Insurance Agents, Brokers & Service.

★ 87970 ★ Kroger Food Stores
3600 Gus Thomasson Rd.
Mesquite, TX 75150
(214)270-2401
Ultimate Parent: Kroger.

★ 87971 ★ Kroger Food Stores
11925 Elam Rd.
Mesquite, TX 75180
(214)557-2567
Ultimate Parent: Kroger.

★ 87972 ★ Kroger Stores
3600 Gus Thomasson Rd.
Mesquite, TX 75150
(214)270-3589
Ultimate Parent: Kroger. SIC: 5411—
Grocery Stores.

★ 87973 ★ Lane Bryant
1026 Town Mall E
Mesquite, TX 75150
(214)270-5213
Ultimate Parent: Limited. SIC: 5621—
Women's Clothing Stores.

★ 87974 ★ Lerner Shop
900 Big Town Shopping Ctr.
Mesquite, TX 75149
(214)327-1413
Ultimate Parent: Limited.

★ 87975 ★ Lerner Shop
1014 Town Mall E
Mesquite, TX 75150
(214)270-4649
Ultimate Parent: Limited. SIC: 5621—
Women's Clothing Stores.

★ 87976 ★ The Limited
Town Shopping Ctr. E
Mesquite, TX 75150
(214)270-6506
Ultimate Parent: Limited. SIC: 5621—
Women's Clothing Stores.

★ 87977 ★ Lone Star Gas Co.
300 W. Kearney St.
Mesquite, TX 75149
(214)285-6342
Ultimate Parent: Enserch. SIC: 4932—Gas
& Other Services Combined.

★ 87978 ★ Marshalls Inc.
1515 N. Town Blvd. E
Mesquite, TX 75150
(214)681-9757
Ultimate Parent: Melville. SIC: 5651—
Family Clothing Stores.

★ 87979 ★ McDonalds
1531 N. Town Blvd. E
Mesquite, TX 75150
(214)270-0766
Ultimate Parent: McDonald's.

★ 87980 ★ McDonalds
2012 W. Scyene Rd.
Mesquite, TX 75149
(214)289-2950
Ultimate Parent: McDonald's.

★ 87981 ★ Payless Cashways
Bldg Matls
103 Gross Rd.
Mesquite, TX 75149
(214)288-5461
Ultimate Parent: Payless Cashways. SIC:
5211—Lumber & Other Building Materials.

★ 87982 ★ Pepsi-Cola Co.
4532 N. Hwy. 67
Mesquite, TX 75150
(214)324-8500
Ultimate Parent: Pepsico. SIC: 2086—
Bottled & Canned Soft Drinks.

★ 87983 ★ Pepsi-Cola Co.
South
4532 Hwy. 67 E
Mesquite, TX 75150
Company Type: Division. Ultimate Parent:
Pepsico. SIC: 2086—Bottled & Canned Soft
Drinks.

★ 87984 ★ Pizza Hut
1912 Oates Dr.
Mesquite, TX 75150
(214)681-4295
Ultimate Parent: Pepsico.

★ 87985 ★ Pizza Hut
1730 Military Pky.
Mesquite, TX 75149
(214)285-8826
Ultimate Parent: Pepsico.

★ 87986 ★ Pizza Hut
2202 N. Galloway Ave.
Mesquite, TX 75150
(214)270-8729
Ultimate Parent: Pepsico. SIC: 5812—
Eating Places.

★ 87987 ★ Pizza Hut
11922 Elam Rd.
Mesquite, TX 75180
(214)557-3530
Ultimate Parent: Pepsico.

★ 87988 ★ Pulte Home Corp.
506 Pioneer Rd.
Mesquite, TX 75149
(214)285-8179
Ultimate Parent: Pulte. SIC: 1521—
Single-Family Housing Construction.

★ 87989 ★ Radio Shack
2110 N. Galloway Ave.
Mesquite, TX 75150
(214)289-9948
Company Type: Division. Ultimate Parent:
Tandy Corp.

★ 87990 ★ Radio Shack
2021 N. Town Blvd. E
Mesquite, TX 75150
(214)686-0100
Company Type: Division. Ultimate Parent:
Tandy Corp. SIC: 5734—Computer &
Software Stores.

★ 87991 ★ Radio Shack
919 Big Town Shopping Ctr.
Mesquite, TX 75149
(214)328-3591
Company Type: Division. Ultimate Parent:
Tandy Corp.

★ 87992 ★ Radio Shack
4434 Gus Thomasson Rd.
Mesquite, TX 75150
(214)270-2792
Company Type: Division. Ultimate Parent:
Tandy Corp.

★ 87993 ★ Radio Shack
150 Broadmoor Plz.
Mesquite, TX 75149
(214)285-4610
Company Type: Division. Ultimate Parent:
Tandy Corp. SIC: 5065—Electronic Parts &
Equipment Nec.

★ 87994 ★ Radio Shack
3330 N. Galloway Ave.
Mesquite, TX 75150
(214)681-8845
Company Type: Division. Ultimate Parent:
Tandy Corp. SIC: 5065—Electronic Parts &
Equipment Nec.

★ 87995 ★ Ryder Truck Rental
1101 E. Hwy. 80
Mesquite, TX 75150
(214)216-7609
Ultimate Parent: Ryder System. SIC:
7513—Truck Rental & Leasing Without
Drivers.

★ 87996 ★ Ryder Truck Rental
3527 E. Hwy. 80
Mesquite, TX 75150
(214)681-3331
Ultimate Parent: Ryder System. SIC:
7513—Truck Rental & Leasing Without
Drivers.

★ 87997 ★ Sam's Wholesale
Club
12110 Garland Rd.
Mesquite, TX 75149
(214)328-6362
Ultimate Parent: Wal-Mart Stores, Inc.

★ 87998 ★ Shell Self Service
502 W. I 30
Mesquite, TX 75150
(214)226-2410
Ultimate Parent: Shell Oil Co. SIC: 5541—
Gasoline Service Stations.

★ 87999 ★ Taco Bell
302 S. Galloway Ave.
Mesquite, TX 75149
(214)288-0855
Ultimate Parent: Pepsico. SIC: 5812—
Eating Places.

★ 88000 ★ Taco Bell
3018 Town Mall E
Mesquite, TX 75150
(214)613-2195
Ultimate Parent: Pepsico.

★ 88001 ★ Taco Bell
4555 Gus Thomasson Rd.
Mesquite, TX 75150
(214)270-6807
Ultimate Parent: Pepsico.

★ 88002 ★ Taco Bell
2114 N. Galloway Ave.
Mesquite, TX 75150
(214)285-0080
Ultimate Parent: Pepsico. SIC: 5812—
Eating Places.

★ 88003 ★ Taco Bell
12002 Elam Rd.
Mesquite, TX 75180
(214)557-3895
Ultimate Parent: Pepsico.

★ 88004 ★ Tandy
2000 Town Mall E
Mesquite, TX 75150
(214)279-6161
Ultimate Parent: Tandy Corp.

★ 88005 ★ Target Stores
1629 N. Town Blvd. E
Mesquite, TX 75150
(214)681-9071
Company Type: Subsidiary. Ultimate
Parent: Dayton Hudson. SIC: 5311—
Department Stores.

★ 88006 ★ Texaco
3601 Hwy. 67 Hyde Park
Mesquite, TX 75150
(214)279-5518
Ultimate Parent: Texaco. SIC: 5541—
Gasoline Service Stations.

★ 88007 ★ Texaco Food Mart
106 E. Hwy. 80
Mesquite, TX 75149
(214)216-0014
Ultimate Parent: Texaco.

★ 88008 ★ Thom Mcan Shoe
Store
1084 Town Mall E
Mesquite, TX 75150
(214)279-5589
Ultimate Parent: Melville. SIC: 5661—Shoe
Stores.

★ 88009 ★ Trailways Bus System
3633 E. Hwy. 80
Mesquite, TX 75150
(214)270-8190
Ultimate Parent: Greyhound Lines Inc. SIC:
4131—Intercity & Rural Bus Transportation.

★ 88010 ★   Wal Mart
200 E. Hwy. 80
Mesquite, TX 75149
Ultimate Parent: Wal-Mart Stores, Inc. **SIC:**
5311—Department Stores.

★ 88011 ★   Wal Mart Discount
Cities
12300 Lake June Rd.
Mesquite, TX 75180
(214)286-8600
Ultimate Parent: Wal-Mart Stores, Inc.

★ 88012 ★   Waldenbooks
Town Mall E
Mesquite, TX 75150
(214)270-4595
Ultimate Parent: K-Mart. **SIC:** 5942—Book
Stores.

★ 88013 ★   Western Auto Supply
Co.
44 Broadmoor Plz.
Mesquite, TX 75149
(214)285-0201
Ultimate Parent: Sears Roebuck & Co.
SIC: 5531—Automobile & Home Supply
Stores.

Mexia

★ 88014 ★   Pizza Hut
601 N. Hwy. 14
Mexia, TX 76667
(817)562-6861
Ultimate Parent: Pepsico. **SIC:** 5812—
Eating Places.

★ 88015 ★   Radio Shack
Hwy. 171
Mexia, TX 76667
(817)562-2727
Company Type: Division. **Ultimate Parent:**
Tandy Corp. **SIC:** 5731—Radio, Television
& Electronics Stores.

★ 88016 ★   Ryder Truck Rental
507 E. Milam St.
Mexia, TX 76667
(817)562-7838
Ultimate Parent: Ryder System. **SIC:**
7359—Equipment Rental & Leasing Nec.

Midkiff

★ 88017 ★   Mobil Exploration &
Prodcng
2200 PO Box
Midkiff, TX 79755
(915)563-0193
Ultimate Parent: Mobil. **SIC:** 1321—Natural
Gas Liquids.

★ 88018 ★   Mobil Exploration
Producting U
PO Box 2200
Midkiff, TX 79755
(915)563-0193
Officer: H. E. Dornack. **Ultimate Parent:**
Mobil. **SIC:** 2911—Petroleum Refining.

Midland

★ 88019 ★   Amerada Hess Corp.
2207 W. Industrial Ave.
Midland, TX 79701
(915)684-5531
Ultimate Parent: Amerada Hess. **SIC:**
1311—Crude Petroleum & Natural Gas;
5171—Petroleum Bulk Stations & Terminals.

★ 88020 ★   Arco Oil & Gas Co.
19801 S. F M 1788
Midland, TX 79703
(915)563-0347
Ultimate Parent: Atlantic Richfield Co., Inc.
SIC: 1311—Crude Petroleum & Natural
Gas.

★ 88021 ★   Arco Pipe Line Co.
4500 E. US Hwy. 80
Midland, TX 79706
(915)682-2576
Ultimate Parent: Atlantic Richfield Co., Inc.
SIC: 4612—Crude Petroleum Pipelines.

★ 88022 ★   Bell Atlantic Corp.
3610 W. Wall St. No. 107
Midland, TX 79701-7134
(915)520-2039
Ultimate Parent: Bell Atlantic Corp. **SIC:**
4813—Telephone Communications Except
Radiotelephone.

★ 88023 ★   Beneficial Texas Inc.
1028 Andrews Hwy.
Midland, TX 79701
(915)694-9639
Ultimate Parent: Beneficial. **SIC:** 6062—
State Credit Unions.

★ 88024 ★   Betz Laboratory
3325 W. Wadley Ave., Ste. B18
Midland, TX 79707-5751
(915)694-0119
Ultimate Parent: Betz Laboratories Inc.
SIC: 8734—Testing Laboratories.

★ 88025 ★   Burlington Air
Express
Midland Air Trm
Midland, TX 79701
(915)563-1354
Ultimate Parent: Pittston. **SIC:** 4513—Air
Courier Services.

★ 88026 ★   Casual Corner
4511 Midland Park Mall N
Midland, TX 79701
(915)697-2154
Ultimate Parent: United States Shoe. **SIC:**
5651—Family Clothing Stores.

★ 88027 ★   Centrilift Co.
2065 Market St.
Midland, TX 79703
(915)694-9676
Officer: Ed Peet, Manager. **Ultimate
Parent:** Baker Hughes. **SIC:** 3561—Pumps
& Pumping Equipment.

★ 88028 ★   Charles Schwab &
Co. Inc.
200 N. Loraine St. 110
Midland, TX 79701
(915)686-9814
Ultimate Parent: Charles Schwab Corp.
SIC: 6211—Security Brokers & Dealers.

★ 88029 ★   Citgo Petroleum Corp.
1031 Andrews Hwy.
Midland, TX 79701
(915)699-7002
Ultimate Parent: Citgo Petroleum. **SIC:**
5172—Petroleum Products Nec.

★ 88030 ★   Coca Cola Bottling
Co.
305 E. Texas Ave.
Midland, TX 79701
(915)684-6401
Ultimate Parent: Coca-Cola Enterprises.
SIC: 5149—Groceries & Related Products
Nec.

★ 88031 ★   Digital Equipment
Corp.
3415 W. Illinois Ave.
Midland, TX 79703
(915)563-9132
Ultimate Parent: Digital Equipment Corp.
SIC: 7373—Computer Integrated Systems
Design.

★ 88032 ★   Dillard Department
Stores
4511 N. Midkiff Rd.
Midland, TX 79705
(915)697-4106
Ultimate Parent: Dillard Department Stores.

★ 88033 ★   Dillard Department
Stores
4511 N. Midland Dr.
Midland, TX 79707
(915)694-7182
Ultimate Parent: Dillard Department Stores.
SIC: 7221—Photographic Studios—Portrait.

★ 88034 ★   Exxon Chemical Co.
1030 Andrews Hwy.
Midland, TX 79701
(915)699-3400
Ultimate Parent: Exxon.

★ 88035 ★   Exxon Co. USA
5101 Truck St.
Midland, TX 79701
(915)563-4621
Ultimate Parent: Exxon.

★ 88036 ★   Exxon Co. USA
Mobile Service
Midland, TX 79701
(915)683-1204
Ultimate Parent: Exxon.

★ 88037 ★   Exxon Corp.
Exxon Bldg.
Midland, TX 79701
(915)683-0101
Ultimate Parent: Exxon. **SIC:** 1311—Crude
Petroleum & Natural Gas.

★ 88038 ★   Greyhound Bus
Terminal
1308 W. Front St.
Midland, TX 79701
(915)682-2761
Ultimate Parent: Greyhound Lines Inc. **SIC:**
4111—Local & Suburban Transit; 4173—
Bus Terminal & Service Facilities.

★ 88039 ★   Hertz Rent-A-Car
202 Pilot Rd.
Midland, TX 79701
(915)563-0110
Ultimate Parent: Hertz. **SIC:** 7514—
Passenger Car Rental.

★ 88040 ★   Hit or Miss
4511 N. Midkiff Rd.
Midland, TX 79705
(915)694-9189
Ultimate Parent: TJX. **SIC:** 5621—
Women's Clothing Stores.

★ 88041 ★   Kentucky Fried
Chicken
2311 N. Big Spring St.
Midland, TX 79705
(915)685-1383
Ultimate Parent: Pepsico. **SIC:** 5812—
Eating Places.

★ 88042 ★   Liberty Mutual
Insurance Companie
Texas
Midland, TX 79701
(915)683-5341
Ultimate Parent: Liberty Mutual Group.
SIC: 6411—Insurance Agents, Brokers &
Service.

★ 88043 ★   Lone Star Gas Co.
6 Desta Dr.
Midland, TX 79705
(915)683-5561
Ultimate Parent: Enserch.

★ 88044 ★   Lone Star Gas Co.
1 County National Bank
Midland, TX 79701
(915)683-5561
Ultimate Parent: Enserch. **SIC:** 4932—Gas
& Other Services Combined.

★ 88045 ★   Marathon Oil Co.
125 W. Missouri Ave.
Midland, TX 79701
(915)682-1626
Ultimate Parent: USX Corp.

★ 88046 ★   Marathon Oil Co.
125 W. Missouri Ave.
Midland, TX 79701
(915)682-1626
Ultimate Parent: USX Corp.

★ 88047 ★   Marathon Petroleum
Co.
200 N. Loraine St.
Midland, TX 79701
(915)687-8514
Ultimate Parent: USX Corp. **SIC:** 5199—
Nondurable Goods Nec.

★ 88048 ★   Mary Kay Cosmetic
706 Boyd Ave.
Midland, TX 79705
(915)682-4596
Ultimate Parent: Mary Kay Cosmetics. **SIC:**
5999—Miscellaneous Retail Stores Nec.

★ 88049 ★   McDonalds Ofifce
4427 Norwood St.
Midland, TX 79707
(915)687-4545
Ultimate Parent: McDonald's.
SIC: 5812—Eating Places.

★ 88050 ★   Mobil Exploration &
Product
500 W. Illinois Ave.
Midland, TX 79701
(915)688-2000
Ultimate Parent: Mobil. **SIC:** 2911—
Petroleum Refining.

★ 88051 ★   Mobil Explrn &
Prdcng U S Inc.
500 W. Illinois Ave.
Midland, TX 79701-4319
(915)688-2000
Ultimate Parent: Mobil. **SIC:** 1311—Crude
Petroleum & Natural Gas.

★ 88052 ★   Mobil Oil Co. Inc.
2200 E. County Rd. 90
Midland, TX 79706-4356
(915)458-3344
Ultimate Parent: Mobil. **SIC:** 4612—Crude
Petroleum Pipelines.

★ 88053 ★   Mobil Oil Corp.
Wall
Midland, TX 79701
(915)684-8211
Ultimate Parent: Mobil. **SIC:** 1311—Crude
Petroleum & Natural Gas.

★ 88054 ★   Mobil Pipe Line
2200 E. County Rd. 90
Midland, TX 79701
(915)686-1943
Ultimate Parent: Mobil.

★ 88055 ★   Mobil Pipe Line Co.
2200 E. County Rd. 90
Midland, TX 79706-4356
(915)686-1943
Ultimate Parent: Mobil. **SIC:** 4612—Crude
Petroleum Pipelines.

★ 88056 ★   Mobil Pipeline
Sprayberry Pump Stat
Midland, TX 79701
(915)682-7727
Ultimate Parent: Mobil.

★ 88057 ★   Mobil Pipeline Co.
3300 N. a St.
Midland, TX 79705
(915)688-1482
Ultimate Parent: Mobil. **SIC:** 4619—
Pipelines Nec.

★ 88058 ★   Mobil Pipeline Co.
3300 N. A St. Ste. 100
Midland, TX 79705-5421
(915)686-1482
Officer: Jack H. Jouette. **Ultimate Parent:**
Mobil. **SIC:** 4619—Pipelines Nec.

★ 88059 ★   New York Life West
Texas General Office
Western Agencies
PO Box 2375
Midland, TX 79701
(915)688-3170 **Fax:** (915)688-3150
Officer: Gary Phillips, General Manager.
Ultimate Parent: New York Life.

★ 88060 ★   New York Life West
Texas General Office
Western Agencies
Clay Desta National Bank Bldg.
6 Desta Dr., Ste. 2550
Midland, TX 79705
(915)688-3170 **Fax:** (915)688-3150
Officer: Gary Phillips, General Manager.
Ultimate Parent: New York Life.

★ 88061 ★   Otis Elevator Co.
3312 Bankhead Hwy.
Midland, TX 79701
(915)563-5747
Ultimate Parent: United Technologies. **SIC:**
3534—Elevators & Moving Stairways.

★ 88062 ★   Pactel Paging
710 W. Washington Ave.
Midland, TX 79701
(915)683-2711
Ultimate Parent: Pacific Telesis Group.

★ 88063 ★   Payless Shoesource
4511 Midland Pk. Mall N
Midland, TX 79701
(915)699-7709
Ultimate Parent: May Department Stores.
SIC: 5661—Shoe Stores.

★ 88064 ★   Payless Shoesource
900 N. Midkiff Rd.
Midland, TX 79701
(915)694-2981
Ultimate Parent: May Department Stores.
SIC: 5661—Shoe Stores.

★ 88065 ★   Pennzoil Co.
200 N. Loraine St.
Midland, TX 79701
(915)682-7316
Ultimate Parent: Pennzoil. SIC: 1311—
Crude Petroleum & Natural Gas.

★ 88066 ★   Pizza Hut
4400 N. Midland Dr.
Midland, TX 79707
(915)694-7225
Ultimate Parent: Pepsico.

★ 88067 ★   Pizza Hut
427 Andrews Hwy.
Midland, TX 79701
(915)682-3302
Ultimate Parent: Pepsico. SIC: 5812—
Eating Places.

★ 88068 ★   Pizza Hut
4320 Andrews Hwy.
Midland, TX 79703
(915)697-5581
Ultimate Parent: Pepsico. SIC: 5812—
Eating Places.

★ 88069 ★   Pizza Hut Inc.
2200 W. Wadley Ave.
Midland, TX 79705
(915)683-2240
Ultimate Parent: Pepsico. SIC: 5812—
Eating Places.

★ 88070 ★   Radio Shack
4511 N. Midland Dr.
Midland, TX 79707
(915)697-7971
Company Type: Division. Ultimate Parent:
Tandy Corp. SIC: 5065—Electronic Parts &
Equipment Nec.

★ 88071 ★   Radio Shack
9 Meta Dr.
Midland, TX 79701
(915)682-7001
Company Type: Division. Ultimate Parent:
Tandy Corp. SIC: 5065—Electronic Parts &
Equipment Nec.

★ 88072 ★   Safety Kleen Corp.
10627 W. County Rd. 127
Midland, TX 79701
(915)563-2305
Ultimate Parent: Safety-Kleen. SIC: 7389—
Business Services Nec.

★ 88073 ★   Sam's Wholesale
Club
1500 Tradewinds Blvd.
Midland, TX 79703
(915)694-1615
Ultimate Parent: Wal-Mart Stores, Inc.

★ 88074 ★   Service Merchandise
Midkiff Pl
Midland, TX 79705
(915)699-8008
Ultimate Parent: Service Merchandise Co.,
Inc. SIC: 5944—Jewelry Stores.

★ 88075 ★   Shell Pipe Line Corp.
Centra
200 Briercroft Bldg.
Midland, TX 79701
(915)686-5200
Ultimate Parent: Shell Oil Co. SIC: 4619—
Pipelines Nec.

★ 88076 ★   Shell Pipeline Corp.
200 Briercroft Bldg.
Midland, TX 79701
(915)686-5200
Ultimate Parent: Shell Oil Co. SIC: 4619—
Pipelines Nec.

★ 88077 ★   Shell Self Service
2404 N. Big Spring St.
Midland, TX 79705
(915)686-9397
Ultimate Parent: Shell Oil Co. SIC: 7542—
Car Washes.

★ 88078 ★   Shell Self Service
N Big Spring St.
Midland, TX 79701
(915)686-9397
Ultimate Parent: Shell Oil Co. SIC: 7542—
Car Washes.

★ 88079 ★   Southland Royalty
Co.
3501 W. Stokes
Midland, TX 79701
(915)682-4031
Ultimate Parent: Burlington Resources.
SIC: 1311—Crude Petroleum & Natural
Gas.

★ 88080 ★   Southwest Airlines
Co.
8008 Aviation Dallas Texa
Midland, TX 79701
(915)563-5711
Ultimate Parent: Southwest Airlines.

★ 88081 ★   Sun Refining &
Marketing
2415 E. Us Hwy. 80
Midland, TX 79701
(915)687-1741
Ultimate Parent: Sun. SIC: 5172—
Petroleum Products Nec.

★ 88082 ★   Texaco
500 N. Loraine St.
Midland, TX 79701
(915)688-4100
Ultimate Parent: Texaco. SIC: 2911—
Petroleum Refining.

★ 88083 ★   Texaco Inc.
Hermitage Ctr.
Midland, TX 79705
(915)688-4100
Ultimate Parent: Texaco. SIC: 4612—
Crude Petroleum Pipelines.

★ 88084 ★   Texaco Self Service
3300 N. Midkiff Rd.
Midland, TX 79705
(915)699-5807
Ultimate Parent: Texaco. SIC: 5541—
Gasoline Service Stations.

★ 88085 ★   Texacopep
3301 Andrews Hwy.
Midland, TX 79703
(915)694-9319
Ultimate Parent: Texaco. SIC: 5541—
Gasoline Service Stations.

★ 88086 ★   Texas Instruments
Fm 1788 & I-20
Midland, TX 79711
Ultimate Parent: Texas Instruments. SIC:
3674—Semiconductors & Related Devices.

★ 88087 ★   Texas Instruments
Inc. Midland Odessa Site
Fm 1788 & I-20 Ms:3014
Midland, TX 79711-0448
Ultimate Parent: Texas Instruments. SIC:
3674—Semiconductors & Related Devices.

★ 88088 ★   Thom Mcan Shoes
Midland
Midland, TX 79705
(915)689-9016
Ultimate Parent: Melville. SIC: 5661—Shoe
Stores.

★ 88089 ★   Toys R US
3109 N. Loop W. 250
Midland, TX 79707
(915)689-9821
Ultimate Parent: Toys "R" US.

★ 88090 ★   Transamerica
Occidental Life Insurance
308 N. a St.
Midland, TX 79701
(915)683-4851
Ultimate Parent: Transamerica Occidental
Life Insurance. SIC: 6411—Insurance
Agents, Brokers & Service.

★ 88091 ★   Trico Industries Inc.
4500 W. Illinois Ave.
Midland, TX 79703
(915)699-5128
Ultimate Parent: Paccar. SIC: 5084—
Industrial Machinery & Equipment.

★ 88092 ★   Union Oil Co. of
California
300 N. Carrizo St.
Midland, TX 79701
(915)684-8231
Ultimate Parent: Unocal Corp. SIC: 1311—
Crude Petroleum & Natural Gas.

★ 88093 ★   United Parcel Service
2701 Market St.
Midland, TX 79703
(915)697-2401
Ultimate Parent: United Parcel Service of
America. SIC: 4215—Courier Services
Except by Air.

★ 88094 ★   US Fidelity & Gu
700 Andrews Hwy.
Midland, TX 79701
(915)685-1191
Ultimate Parent: USF&G Corp. SIC:
5074—Plumbing & Hydronic Heating
Supplies; 6411—Insurance Agents, Brokers
& Service.

★ 88095 ★   Western Geophysical
300 W. Texas Ave.
Midland, TX 79701
(915)687-2413
Ultimate Parent: Litton Industries. SIC:
1081—Metal Mining Services.

★ 88096 ★   Western Geophysical
Co.
300 W. United Life Bldg.
Midland, TX 79701
(915)682-9247
Ultimate Parent: Litton Industries. SIC:
1081—Metal Mining Services.

Midlothian

★ 88097 ★   Air Products &
Chemicals Inc.
310 Ward Rd.
Midlothian, TX 76065
Ultimate Parent: Air Products & Chemicals,
Inc. SIC: 2813—Industrial Gases.

★ 88098 ★   Air Products &
Chemicals Inc.
310 Ward Rd.
Midlothian, TX 76065
(214)775-2365
Officer: Ronnie Foster, Manager. Ultimate
Parent: Air Products & Chemicals, Inc. SIC:
2813—Industrial Gases; 5172—Petroleum
Products Nec.

★ 88099 ★   Air Products
Manufacturing Corp.
310 Ward Rd.
Midlothian, TX 76065
Ultimate Parent: Air Products & Chemicals,
Inc. SIC: 2813—Industrial Gases.

★ 88100 ★   Chaparral Steel Co.
300 Ward Rd.
Midlothian, TX 76065
Ultimate Parent: Texas Industries. SIC:
3312—Blast Furnaces & Steel Mills.

★ 88101 ★   Lone Star Gas Co.
816 W. Ave.
Midlothian, TX 76065
(214)775-3081
Ultimate Parent: Enserch. SIC: 4932—Gas
& Other Services Combined.

★ 88102 ★   Texas Industries Inc.
245 Ward Rd.
Midlothian, TX 76065
Ultimate Parent: Texas Industries. SIC:
3241—Cement—Hydraulic.

Midway

★ 88103 ★   Lone Star Gas Co.
204 Trinity W
Midway, TX 75852
(409)348-2285
Ultimate Parent: Enserch.

Millsap

★ 88104 ★   Vulcan Materials Co.
RR 1 Box 286
Millsap, TX 76066
(817)594-4524
Officer: Ron Kelley, Manager. Ultimate
Parent: Vulcan Materials Co. SIC: 2951—
Asphalt Paving Mixtures & Blocks; 3281—
Cut Stone & Stone Products; 3295—
Minerals—Ground or Treated.

Mineola

★ 88105 ★   Eagle Picher
Industries Inc.
Hwy. 80 W
Mineola, TX 75773
(214)569-3855
Ultimate Parent: Eagle-Picher Industries
Inc. SIC: 2873—Nitrogenous Fertilizers.

★ 88106 ★   International Paper
Co.
701 Freeman St.
Mineola, TX 75773
Ultimate Parent: International Paper Co.
SIC: 2491—Wood Preserving.

★ 88107 ★   Trailways Bus System
810 S. Johnson St.
Mineola, TX 75773
(214)569-3955
Ultimate Parent: Greyhound Lines Inc. SIC:
4131—Intercity & Rural Bus Transportation.

Mineral Wells

★ 88108 ★   City National Bank
the
1800 E. Hubbard St.
Mineral Wells, TX 76067
(817)325-0761
Ultimate Parent: City National Corp. SIC:
6022—State Commercial Banks.

★ 88109 ★   Coast to Coast
2900 E. Hubbard St.
Mineral Wells, TX 76067
(817)325-5952
Ultimate Parent: Servistar Corp. SIC:
5251—Hardware Stores.

★ 88110 ★   Itw Shakeproof Indl.
Prods. Products
501 Garrett Morris Pky.
Mineral Wells, TX 76067-9675
Ultimate Parent: Illinois Tool Works. SIC:
3452—Bolts, Nuts, Rivets & Washers.

★ 88111 ★   ITW Shakeproof
Industrial Products
201 Garrett Morris Pky.
Mineral Wells, TX 76067-9675
Ultimate Parent: Illinois Tool Works. SIC:
3452—Bolts, Nuts, Rivets & Washers.

★ 88112 ★   Kentucky Fried
Chicken
2703 E. Hubbard St.
Mineral Wells, TX 76067
(817)325-1196
Ultimate Parent: Pepsico. SIC: 5812—
Eating Places.

★ 88113 ★   Piggly Wiggly
201 SE 1st Ave.
Mineral Wells, TX 76067
(817)325-5801
Ultimate Parent: Bruno's. SIC: 5411—
Grocery Stores.

★ 88114 ★   Pizza Hut
100 SE 10th Ave.
Mineral Wells, TX 76067
(817)325-4461
Ultimate Parent: Pepsico.

★ 88115 ★   Radio Shack
211 SE 1st
Mineral Wells, TX 76067
(817)325-5211
Company Type: Division. Ultimate Parent:
Tandy Corp.

★ 88116 ★   Ryder Truck Rental
701 Lincoln Ave.
Mineral Wells, TX 76067
(817)325-9448
Ultimate Parent: Ryder System. SIC:
5113—Industrial & Personal Service Paper.

★ 88117 ★   Ryder Truck Rental
4501 E. Hubbard St.
Mineral Wells, TX 76067
(817)325-2481
Ultimate Parent: Ryder System. SIC:
7513—Truck Rental & Leasing Without
Drivers.

★ 88118 ★   Ryder Truck Rental
2900 E. Hubbard St.
Mineral Wells, TX 76067
(817)325-2820
Ultimate Parent: Ryder System.

★ 88119 ★   Taco Bell
1907 E. Hubbard St.
Mineral Wells, TX 76067
(817)325-0641
Ultimate Parent: Pepsico. **SIC:** 5812—
Eating Places.

Mirando City

★ 88120 ★   Arco Oil & Gas Co.
Mirando City, TX 78369
(512)568-4416
Location Type: Branch office. **Ultimate
Parent:** Atlantic Richfield Co., Inc. **SIC:**
1311—Crude Petroleum & Natural Gas.

Mission

★ 88121 ★   Arco Oil & Gas Co.
W. Loop 374 & Hwy. 83
Mission, TX 78572
(210)585-1667
Location Type: Branch office. **Ultimate
Parent:** Atlantic Richfield Co., Inc. **SIC:**
4924—Natural Gas Distribution.

★ 88122 ★   First State Bank &
Trust Co.
900 N. Conway Ave.
Mission, TX 78572
(512)585-4801
Ultimate Parent: Michigan National Corp.
SIC: 6022—State Commercial Banks.

★ 88123 ★   Kentucky Fried
Chicken
901 E. Hwy. 83
Mission, TX 78572
(512)585-7922
Ultimate Parent: Pepsico. **SIC:** 5812—
Eating Places.

★ 88124 ★   Kmart Discount
Stores
1405 E. Expressway 83
Mission, TX 78572
Ultimate Parent: K-Mart.

★ 88125 ★   Pizza Hut
821 E. 9th St.
Mission, TX 78572
(512)581-7466
Ultimate Parent: Pepsico. **SIC:** 5812—
Eating Places.

★ 88126 ★   Radio Shack
1605 E. Expy. 83
Mission, TX 78572
(512)581-2765
Company Type: Division. **Ultimate Parent:**
Tandy Corp.

Missouri City

★ 88127 ★   Cooper Industries
Flow Control Div.
16500 South Main
Missouri City, TX 77459
Company Type: Division. **Ultimate Parent:**
Cooper Industries. **SIC:** 3494—Valves &
Pipe Fittings Nec.

★ 88128 ★   Cooper Industries Inc.
Flow Control Div.
16500 South Main
Missouri City, TX 77459
Company Type: Division. **Ultimate Parent:**
Cooper Industries. **SIC:** 3494—Valves &
Pipe Fittings Nec.

★ 88129 ★   Mary Kay Cosmetics
2111 Masters Ln.
Missouri City, TX 77459
(713)438-0832
Ultimate Parent: Mary Kay Cosmetics.

★ 88130 ★   Pizza Hut
2710 Cypress Point Dr.
Missouri City, TX 77459
(713)499-8313
Ultimate Parent: Pepsico. **SIC:** 5812—
Eating Places.

★ 88131 ★   Pulte Home Corp.
4402 Crow Valley Dr.
Missouri City, TX 77459
(713)438-6521
Ultimate Parent: Pulte.

★ 88132 ★   Radio Shack
1617 Cartwright Rd.
Missouri City, TX 77489
(713)438-0527
Company Type: Division. **Ultimate Parent:**
Tandy Corp.

★ 88133 ★   Safety Kleen Corp.
1570 Industrial Dr.
Missouri City, TX 77489
(713)261-0221
Ultimate Parent: Safety-Kleen.

★ 88134 ★   Walgreen Drug Stores
1657 Cartwright Rd.
Missouri City, TX 77489
(713)438-5225
Ultimate Parent: Walgreen Co. **SIC:**
5912—Drug Stores & Proprietary Stores.

Monahans

★ 88135 ★   Citgo Pipeline Co.
1604 S. Ike St.
Monahans, TX 79756
(915)943-8466
Ultimate Parent: Citgo Petroleum.

★ 88136 ★   Citgo Pipeline Co.
1604 S. Ike St.
Monahans, TX 79756
(915)943-8466
Ultimate Parent: Citgo Petroleum.

★ 88137 ★   Exxon Chemical Co.
400 N. Ruth St.
Monahans, TX 79756
(915)943-7991
Ultimate Parent: Exxon.

★ 88138 ★   Exxon Co. USA
303 S. Gary St.
Monahans, TX 79756
(915)943-4131
Ultimate Parent: Exxon.

★ 88139 ★   Greyhound Bus Lines
2113 S. Stockton St.
Monahans, TX 79756
(915)943-4993
Ultimate Parent: Greyhound Lines Inc. **SIC:**
4111—Local & Suburban Transit.

★ 88140 ★   Lone Star Gas Co.
1308 E. Sealy Ave.
Monahans, TX 79756
(915)943-3261
Ultimate Parent: Enserch.

★ 88141 ★   McDonalds
1905 S. Stockton St.
Monahans, TX 79756
(915)943-3264
Ultimate Parent: McDonald's.

★ 88142 ★   Pizza Hut
501 S. Main St.
Monahans, TX 79756
(915)943-2772
Ultimate Parent: Pepsico. **SIC:** 5812—
Eating Places.

★ 88143 ★   Ryder Truck Rental
2101 S. Stockton St.
Monahans, TX 79756
(915)943-3665
Ultimate Parent: Ryder System. **SIC:**
7513—Truck Rental & Leasing Without
Drivers.

★ 88144 ★   Trailways Bus System
2113 S. Stockton St.
Monahans, TX 79756
(915)943-5651
Ultimate Parent: Greyhound Lines Inc. **SIC:**
4131—Intercity & Rural Bus Transportation.

Mont Belvieu

★ 88145 ★   Diamond Shamrock
Mont Belvieu E.
316 S. Main Loop 207
Mont Belvieu, TX 77580
Ultimate Parent: Diamond Shamrock. **SIC:**
2869—Industrial Organic Chemicals Nec.

★ 88146 ★   Mobil Pipe Line Co.
FM Rd. 1942
Mont Belvieu, TX 77580
(713)576-2124
Company Type: Branch. **Ultimate Parent:**
Mobil. **SIC:** 4612—Crude Petroleum
Pipelines.

Montgomery

★ 88147 ★   Mary Kay Cosmetics
16 April Pt.
Montgomery, TX 77356
(409)588-1765
Ultimate Parent: Mary Kay Cosmetics. **SIC:**
5999—Miscellaneous Retail Stores Nec.

Mount Pleasant

★ 88148 ★   Pilgrim's Pride Corp.
FM Rd.
Mount Pleasant, TX 75455
(903)572-8921
Ultimate Parent: Pilgrim's Pride Corp.

★ 88149 ★   Pilgrims Pride Corp.
1000 S. O'Tyson
Mount Pleasant, TX 75455
Ultimate Parent: Pilgrim's Pride Corp. **SIC:**
2000—Food & Kindred Products.

★ 88150 ★   Pilgrim's Pride Corp.
East Processing Plant
Monticello Rd. & O'Tyson St.
Mount Pleasant, TX 75455
Location Type: Plant. **Ultimate Parent:**
Pilgrim's Pride Corp. **SIC:** 2015—Poultry
Slaughtering & Processing.

★ 88151 ★   Pilgrim's Pride Corp.
Protein Conversion
Monticello Rd. & O'Tyson St.
Mount Pleasant, TX 75455
Company Type: Division. **Ultimate Parent:**
Pilgrim's Pride Corp. **SIC:** 2077—Animal &
Marine Fats & Oils.

★ 88152 ★   Pilgrim's Pride Corp.
Wastewater Treatment
Monticello Rd. & O'Tyson St.
Mount Pleasant, TX 75455
Company Type: Division. **Ultimate Parent:**
Pilgrim's Pride Corp. **SIC:** 2077—Animal &
Marine Fats & Oils.

★ 88153 ★   Pilgrim's Pride Corp.
West Processing Plant
Monticello Rd. & O'Tyson St.
Mount Pleasant, TX 75455
Location Type: Plant. **Ultimate Parent:**
Pilgrim's Pride Corp. **SIC:** 2015—Poultry
Slaughtering & Processing.

★ 88154 ★   Pilgrim's Pride Corp.
Prepared Foods
Monticello Rd. & O'tyson
Mount Pleasant, TX 75455
Ultimate Parent: Pilgrim's Pride Corp. **SIC:**
2015—Poultry Slaughtering & Processing.

Mount Vernon

★ 88155 ★   Mobil Pipe Line Co.
Mount Vernon, TX 75457
(903)860-2177
Ultimate Parent: Mobil. **SIC:** 4612—Crude
Petroleum Pipelines.

★ 88156 ★   Texaco Inc.
Cypress Springs
Mount Vernon, TX 75457
(903)860-3600
Ultimate Parent: Texaco. **SIC:** 1389—Oil &
Gas Field Services Nec.

Mt Pleasant

★ 88157 ★   Kentucky Fried
Chicken
N Jeffrson
Mt Pleasant, TX 75455
(214)572-2086
Ultimate Parent: Pepsico. **SIC:** 5812—
Eating Places.

★ 88158 ★   Piggly Wiggly
601 N. Jefferson Ave.
Mt Pleasant, TX 75455
(214)572-3752
Ultimate Parent: Bruno's. **SIC:** 5411—
Grocery Stores.

★ 88159 ★   Pilgrim's Pride Corp.
Pittsburg Hwy.
Mt Pleasant, TX 75455
(903)572-4932
Ultimate Parent: Pilgrim's Pride Corp.

★ 88160 ★   Pizza Hut
1902 S. Jefferson Ave.
Mt Pleasant, TX 75455
(214)572-1871
Ultimate Parent: Pepsico. **SIC:** 5812—
Eating Places.

★ 88161 ★   Shell Oil Co.
Hwy. 271
Mt Pleasant, TX 75455
(214)572-1301
Ultimate Parent: Shell Oil Co. **SIC:** 5541—
Gasoline Service Stations.

★ 88162 ★   Wal Mart Discount
Pharmacy
Hwy. 271 S
Mt Pleasant, TX 75455
(214)572-7924
Ultimate Parent: Wal-Mart Stores, Inc. **SIC:**
5912—Drug Stores & Proprietary Stores.

Muenster

★ 88163 ★   Associated Milk
Producers Inc.
115 N. Elm
Muenster, TX 76252
(817)759-2266
Ultimate Parent: Associated Milk Producers
Inc. **SIC:** 5143—Dairy Products Except
Dried or Canned.

★ 88164 ★   Mary Kay Cosmetics
213 S. Main St.
Muenster, TX 76252
(817)759-4408
Ultimate Parent: Mary Kay Cosmetics. **SIC:**
5999—Miscellaneous Retail Stores Nec.

Muleshoe

★ 88165 ★   ADM Specialty Grain
Clovis Hwy.
Muleshoe, TX 79347
(806)272-4231
Officer: Duane Anddreas, President.
Ultimate Parent: Archer Daniels Midland
Co.

★ 88166 ★   Pizza Hut
1412 W. American Blvd.
Muleshoe, TX 79347
(806)272-4213
Ultimate Parent: Pepsico. **SIC:** 5812—
Eating Places.

Nacogdoches

★ 88167 ★   Holly Farms of Texas
Nacogdoches Feed Mill
2208 SE Stallings Dr., S. Loop 224
Nacogdoches, TX 75961
Ultimate Parent: Tyson Foods, Inc. **SIC:**
2048—Prepared Feeds Nec.

★ 88168 ★   Holly Farms of Texas
Inc. Nacogdoches Mill
2208 SE Stallings Dr. S. Loop 224
Nacogdoches, TX 75961
Ultimate Parent: Tyson Foods, Inc. **SIC:**
2015—Poultry Slaughtering & Processing.

★ 88169 ★   International Paper
2301 SE Stallings Dr.
Nacogdoches, TX 75963-2750
Ultimate Parent: International Paper Co.
SIC: 2493—Reconstructed Wood Products.

★ 88170 ★   Kentucky Fried
Chicken
630608 PO Box
Nacogdoches, TX 75963
(409)935-2424
Ultimate Parent: Pepsico. **SIC:** 5812—
Eating Places.

★ 88171 ★   Manville Sales Corp.
403 Industrial Dr.
Nacogdoches, TX 75961
Ultimate Parent: Manville Corp. **SIC:**
3053—Gaskets, Packing & Sealing Devices.

★ 88172 ★   Mobil Oil Co.
301 Bremond St.
Nacogdoches, TX 75964-5149
(409)564-4881
Officer: W. Perry. **Ultimate Parent:** Mobil.
SIC: 5172—Petroleum Products Nec;
1311—Crude Petroleum & Natural Gas.

★ 88173 ★　Nacogdoches Medical Center
4920 NE Stallings
Nacogdoches, TX 75963
(409)569-9481
Officer: Bryant Krenek, Executive Director.
Ultimate Parent: American Medical Holdings. **SIC:** 8062—General Medical & Surgical Hospitals.

★ 88174 ★　Pilgrim's Pride Corp.
Nacogdoches Feed Mill
Fm Rd. 1275 S.
Nacogdoches, TX 75963
Company Type: Division. **Ultimate Parent:** Pilgrim's Pride Corp. **SIC:** 2048—Prepared Feeds Nec.

★ 88175 ★　Taco Bell
1525 North St.
Nacogdoches, TX 75961
(409)560-2758
Ultimate Parent: Pepsico. **SIC:** 5812—Eating Places.

★ 88176 ★　Tyson Foods Inc. Nacogdoches Mill
2208 SE Stallings Dr. S. Loop 224
Nacogdoches, TX 75961
Ultimate Parent: Tyson Foods, Inc. **SIC:** 2048—Prepared Feeds Nec.

Navasota

★ 88177 ★　First Bank
400 E. Washington Ave.
Navasota, TX 77868
(409)825-6401
Ultimate Parent: Shawmut National Corp. **SIC:** 6022—State Commercial Banks.

★ 88178 ★　Holsum Foods
202 W. McAlpine St.
Navasota, TX 77868
(409)825-6563
Ultimate Parent: Harvest States Coops. **SIC:** 5411—Grocery Stores.

★ 88179 ★　Mobil Pipeline Co.
Navasota, TX 77868
(409)825-7811
Company Type: Branch. **Ultimate Parent:** Mobil. **SIC:** 4612—Crude Petroleum Pipelines.

★ 88180 ★　Pizza Hut
501 S. La Salle St.
Navasota, TX 77868
(409)825-7273
Ultimate Parent: Pepsico. **SIC:** 5812—Eating Places.

★ 88181 ★　Pizza Hut
701 Brosig Ave.
Navasota, TX 77868
(409)825-6688
Ultimate Parent: Pepsico. **SIC:** 5411—Grocery Stores.

★ 88182 ★　Wal Mart Discount City
Hwy. 6 Loop S
Navasota, TX 77868
(409)825-7541
Ultimate Parent: Wal-Mart Stores, Inc. **SIC:** 5331—Variety Stores.

Nederland

★ 88183 ★　BFI Medical Waste Systems
Hwy. 69
Nederland, TX 77627
(409)724-2371
Location Type: Branch office. **Ultimate Parent:** Browning-Ferris Industries. **SIC:** 4953—Refuse Systems.

★ 88184 ★　Continental Express
Jefferson County Airport
Nederland, TX 77627
(409)727-7289
Ultimate Parent: Continental Airlines. **SIC:** 4512—Air Transportation—Scheduled.

★ 88185 ★　Exxon
109 N. Twin City Hwy.
Nederland, TX 77627
(409)727-4716
Ultimate Parent: Exxon. **SIC:** 7542—Car Washes.

★ 88186 ★　Kentucky Fried Chicken
1404 Nederland Ave.
Nederland, TX 77627
(409)722-8144
Ultimate Parent: Pepsico. **SIC:** 5812—Eating Places.

★ 88187 ★　Mid-Jefferson County Hospital
Hwy. 365 & 27th St.
Nederland, TX 77627
(409)727-2321
Officer: Luis Silvaf, Executive Director.
Ultimate Parent: American Medical Holdings. **SIC:** 8062—General Medical & Surgical Hospitals.

★ 88188 ★　Mobil Pipe Line Co.
W. Port Arthur Rd.
Nederland, TX 77627
(409)722-8432
Company Type: Branch. **Ultimate Parent:** Mobil. **SIC:** 4612—Crude Petroleum Pipelines.

★ 88189 ★　Pizza Hut
7849 Twin City
Nederland, TX 77627
(409)727-6024
Ultimate Parent: Pepsico. **SIC:** 5812—Eating Places.

★ 88190 ★　Radio Shack
1027 Nederland Ave.
Nederland, TX 77627
(409)727-3205
Company Type: Division. **Ultimate Parent:** Tandy Corp. **SIC:** 5065—Electronic Parts & Equipment Nec.

★ 88191 ★　Savings of America, A Division of Home Savings of America, FSB
1022 Nederland Ave.
Nederland, TX 77627-2897
(409)727-2152
Company Type: Division. **Location Type:** Branch office. **Ultimate Parent:** H. F. Ahmanson. **SIC:** 6021—National Commercial Banks.

★ 88192 ★　Shell Food Mart
2704 Hwy. 365
Nederland, TX 77627
(409)724-7171
Ultimate Parent: Shell Oil Co.

★ 88193 ★　Sun Refining & Marketing Co.
166 Hilldale Dr.
Nederland, TX 77627
(409)724-1637
Ultimate Parent: Sun. **SIC:** 2911—Petroleum Refining.

★ 88194 ★　Taco Bell
1624 Nederland Ave.
Nederland, TX 77627
(409)722-4200
Ultimate Parent: Pepsico. **SIC:** 5812—Eating Places.

★ 88195 ★　Union Oil of California Dba Unocal
Hwy. 366 1/2 Mile East of Intersection W/Hwy. 347
Nederland, TX 77627
Ultimate Parent: Unocal Corp. **SIC:** 2911—Petroleum Refining; 2865—Cyclic Crudes & Intermediates; 2992—Lubricating Oils & Greases.

★ 88196 ★　Union Oil Co. of California Dba Unocal Chem.
Hwy. 366-One Half Mile E. of Intersection with Hwy. 347
Nederland, TX 77627-0237
Ultimate Parent: Unocal Corp. **SIC:** 2911—Petroleum Refining; 2865—Cyclic Crudes & Intermediates; 2992—Lubricating Oils & Greases.

★ 88197 ★　Wal Mart Discount Cities
2004 Hwy. 365
Nederland, TX 77627
(409)727-4667
Ultimate Parent: Wal-Mart Stores, Inc. **SIC:** 5311—Department Stores.

★ 88198 ★　Walgreen Drug Stores
1011 Nederland Ave.
Nederland, TX 77627
(409)727-0728
Ultimate Parent: Walgreen Co. **SIC:** 5912—Drug Stores & Proprietary Stores.

New Berlin

★ 88199 ★　Holly Farms Foods Inc. Seguin Plant
1200 West Kingsbury St.
New Berlin, TX 78155
Ultimate Parent: Tyson Foods, Inc. **SIC:** 2015—Poultry Slaughtering & Processing.

New Boston

★ 88200 ★　Exxon Co. USA
202 E. Main St.
New Boston, TX 75570
(214)628-2761
Ultimate Parent: Exxon. **SIC:** 5171—Petroleum Bulk Stations & Terminals.

★ 88201 ★　Piggly Wiggly
Hwy. 82 W
New Boston, TX 75570
(214)628-2361
Ultimate Parent: Bruno's. **SIC:** 5411—Grocery Stores.

★ 88202 ★　Pizza Hut
N Hwy. 8
New Boston, TX 75570
(214)628-3808
Ultimate Parent: Pepsico. **SIC:** 5812—Eating Places.

★ 88203 ★　Wal Mart Discount
401 N. State Hwy. 8
New Boston, TX 75570
(903)628-5557
Ultimate Parent: Wal-Mart Stores, Inc.

★ 88204 ★　Wal Mart Discount City
401 N. Hwy. 8
New Boston, TX 75570
(214)628-5557
Ultimate Parent: Wal-Mart Stores, Inc. **SIC:** 5311—Department Stores.

★ 88205 ★　Wal Mart Pharmacy
401 N. State Hwy. 8
New Boston, TX 75570
(903)628-6561
Ultimate Parent: Wal-Mart Stores, Inc.

New Braunfels

★ 88206 ★　Coleman Co.
766 N. Hwy. 306
New Braunfels, TX 78130
(210)625-6943
Officer: Randy Kuntz, Manager. **Ultimate Parent:** Fleetwood Enterprises, Inc. **SIC:** 3732—Boat Building & Repairing.

★ 88207 ★　E R Carpenter Co.
483 N. End Ave. W
New Braunfels, TX 78130
(512)629-5991
Ultimate Parent: Carpenter.

★ 88208 ★　E. R. Carpenter Co. Inc. New Braunfels
483 N. West End St.
New Braunfels, TX 78130
Ultimate Parent: Carpenter. **SIC:** 3086—Plastics Foam Products.

★ 88209 ★　Greyhound Bus Lines
275 S. Seguin St.
New Braunfels, TX 78130
(512)625-4111
Ultimate Parent: Greyhound Lines Inc. **SIC:** 4142—Bus Charter Service Except Local.

★ 88210 ★　Kentucky Fried Chicken
690 S. Walnut Ave.
New Braunfels, TX 78130
(512)625-1791
Ultimate Parent: Pepsico. **SIC:** 5812—Eating Places.

★ 88211 ★　Kroger Co. Store
601 Hwy. 46 S
New Braunfels, TX 78130
(512)629-5003
Ultimate Parent: Kroger. **SIC:** 5411—Grocery Stores.

★ 88212 ★　Kroger Pharmacy
601 Hwy. 46 S
New Braunfels, TX 78130
(512)629-4040
Ultimate Parent: Kroger. **SIC:** 5912—Drug Stores & Proprietary Stores.

★ 88213 ★　Lafarge Corp. -Balcones
Solms Rd. & Wald Rd.
New Braunfels, TX 78132
Ultimate Parent: Lafarge. **SIC:** 3241—Cement—Hydraulic.

★ 88214 ★　Lafarge Corp. Balcones Cement Plant
Solm & Wald Roads PO Box 311507
New Braunfels, TX 78131
Ultimate Parent: Lafarge. **SIC:** 3241—Cement—Hydraulic.

★ 88215 ★　Lafarge Corp. Balcones Plant
Solms Rd. & Wald Rd.
New Braunfels, TX 78131-1507
Ultimate Parent: Lafarge. **SIC:** 3241—Cement—Hydraulic.

★ 88216 ★　Mary Kay Cosmetics Independent
RR 8
New Braunfels, TX 78132
(512)625-5218
Ultimate Parent: Mary Kay Cosmetics. **SIC:** 5999—Miscellaneous Retail Stores Nec.

★ 88217 ★　Payless Shoesource
696 S. Walnut Ave.
New Braunfels, TX 78130
(512)625-4380
Ultimate Parent: May Department Stores. **SIC:** 5661—Shoe Stores.

★ 88218 ★　Pizza Hut
220 S. Seguin St.
New Braunfels, TX 78130
(512)625-6930
Ultimate Parent: Pepsico. **SIC:** 5812—Eating Places.

★ 88219 ★　Radio Shack
636 W. Walnut Sq.
New Braunfels, TX 78130
(512)625-7201
Company Type: Division. **Ultimate Parent:** Tandy Corp. **SIC:** 5065—Electronic Parts & Equipment Nec.

★ 88220 ★　Taco Bell
249 N. Loop 337
New Braunfels, TX 78130
(512)625-0293
Ultimate Parent: Pepsico.

★ 88221 ★　Trailways
684 S. Walnut Ave.
New Braunfels, TX 78130
(512)629-3013
Ultimate Parent: Greyhound Lines Inc. **SIC:** 4142—Bus Charter Service Except Local.

★ 88222 ★　US Gypsum Co.
Wald Rd.
New Braunfels, TX 78130
(512)625-2327
Ultimate Parent: USG Corp. **SIC:** 5039—Construction Materials Nec.

★ 88223 ★　West Point Pepperell Mission Valley Mill
555 Porter St.
New Braunfels, TX 78130
Ultimate Parent: West Point Stevens. **SIC:** 2211—Broadwoven Fabric Mills—Cotton; 2261—Finishing Plants—Cotton.

New London

★ 88224 ★　Exxon Co. USA
FM 1513
New London, TX 75682
(903)895-4433
Officer: J. D. Foremen, Manager. **Ultimate Parent:** Exxon. **SIC:** 2911—Petroleum Refining.

New Waverly

★ 88225 ★ Louisiana Pacific Corp.
Hwy. 75 N
New Waverly, TX 77358
Ultimate Parent: Louisiana-Pacific. SIC: 2421—Sawmills & Planing Mills—General; 2436—Softwood Veneer & Plywood; 2491—Wood Preserving; 2493—Reconstituted Wood Products.

Newcastle

★ 88226 ★ Stop & Shop Grocery
Hwy. 380
Newcastle, TX 76372
(817)846-3512
Ultimate Parent: Stop & Shop. SIC: 5411—Grocery Stores.

Nocona

★ 88227 ★ ALLTEL Texas Inc.
117 E. Oak St.
PO Box 120
Nocona, TX 76255
(817)825-3231
Ultimate Parent: ALLTEL Corp. SIC: 4812—Radiotelephone Communications.

★ 88228 ★ Lone Star Gas Co.
115 Cooke St.
Nocona, TX 76255
(817)825-6327
Ultimate Parent: Enserch. SIC: 4925—Gas Production & Distribution Nec.

★ 88229 ★ Piggly Wiggly
303 W. Walnut St.
Nocona, TX 76255
(817)825-6813
Ultimate Parent: Bruno's. SIC: 5411—Grocery Stores.

Nordheim

★ 88230 ★ Shell Oil Co.
Nordheim, TX 78141
(512)938-5401
Ultimate Parent: Shell Oil Co. SIC: 1389—Oil & Gas Field Services Nec.

Normangee

★ 88231 ★ Lone Star Gas Co.
Normangee, TX 77871
(409)396-2491
Ultimate Parent: Enserch. SIC: 4925—Gas Production & Distribution Nec.

North Zulch

★ 88232 ★ Lone Star Gas Co.
North Zulch, TX 77872
(409)399-4311
Ultimate Parent: Enserch. SIC: 4932—Gas & Other Services Combined.

Novice

★ 88233 ★ Southland Royalty Co.
Novice, TX 79538
(915)625-2877
Ultimate Parent: Burlington Resources. SIC: 1311—Crude Petroleum & Natural Gas.

★ 88234 ★ Southland Royalty Co.
Novice, TX 79538
(915)625-2877
Ultimate Parent: Burlington Resources. SIC: 1311—Crude Petroleum & Natural Gas.

Odem

★ 88235 ★ Texaco Inc.
Odem, TX 78370
(512)368-9556
Ultimate Parent: Texaco. SIC: 1311—Crude Petroleum & Natural Gas.

Odessa

★ 88236 ★ Arco Oil & Gas Co.
520 Elliott Ave.
Odessa, TX 79763-4145
(915)334-4400
Location Type: Branch office. Ultimate Parent: Atlantic Richfield Co., Inc. SIC: 1311—Crude Petroleum & Natural Gas.

★ 88237 ★ Avon Products Inc.
2535 N. Jackson Ave.
Odessa, TX 79761
(915)332-4771
Ultimate Parent: Avon Products, Inc. SIC: 5999—Miscellaneous Retail Stores Nec.

★ 88238 ★ Coca-Cola Botlg Co.
2700 Van St.
Odessa, TX 79763
(915)332-9119
Ultimate Parent: Coca-Cola Enterprises.

★ 88239 ★ Compressor Components
2605 W. 42nd St.
Odessa, TX 79764
(915)367-7786
Officer: Wayne Elder, President. Ultimate Parent: Dover Corp. SIC: 3053—Gaskets, Packing & Sealing Devices.

★ 88240 ★ Exxon Chemical Co.
2126 Maurice Rd.
Odessa, TX 79763
(915)332-4338
Ultimate Parent: Exxon. SIC: 5199—Nondurable Goods Nec.

★ 88241 ★ Exxon Motor Fuel Store
2544 Andrews Hwy.
Odessa, TX 79761
(915)333-6532
Ultimate Parent: Exxon. SIC: 5172—Petroleum Products Nec.

★ 88242 ★ Exxon Pipeline Co.
1300 W. 10th St.
Odessa, TX 79763
(915)337-2301
Ultimate Parent: Exxon. SIC: 1521—Single-Family Housing Construction.

★ 88243 ★ Exxon Pipeline Co.
1300 W. 10th St.
Odessa, TX 79763
(915)337-2301
Ultimate Parent: Exxon Pipeline. SIC: 1521—Single-Family Housing Construction.

★ 88244 ★ Foot Action
Permian
Odessa, TX 79762
(915)362-0965
Ultimate Parent: Melville. SIC: 5661—Shoe Stores.

★ 88245 ★ Fruehauf Trailer Corp.
11112 W. US Hwy. 80 E
Odessa, TX 79765-9422
(915)563-0923
Officer: Jim Boyd. Ultimate Parent: Terex Corp. SIC: 5012—Automobiles & Other Motor Vehicles; 5013—Motor Vehicle Supplies & New Parts; 7519—Utility Trailer Rental; 7539—Automotive Repair Shops Nec.

★ 88246 ★ Fruehauf Trailers
11112 W. US Hwy. 80 E
Odessa, TX 79765-9422
(915)563-0923
Officer: Jim Boyd. Ultimate Parent: Terex Corp. SIC: 5012—Automobiles & Other Motor Vehicles; 5013—Motor Vehicle Supplies & New Parts; 7519—Utility Trailer Rental; 7539—Automotive Repair Shops Nec.

★ 88247 ★ Greyhound Bus Lines
500 N. Jackson Ave.
Odessa, TX 79761
(915)332-5302
Ultimate Parent: Greyhound Lines Inc. SIC: 4111—Local & Suburban Transit; 4131—Intercity & Rural Bus Transportation.

★ 88248 ★ Greyhound Bus Lins
500 N. Jackson Ave.
Odessa, TX 79761
(915)332-5711
Ultimate Parent: Greyhound Lines Inc.

★ 88249 ★ Kay Bee Toy and Hobby Shop
4101 E. 42nd St.
Odessa, TX 79762
(915)363-9202
Ultimate Parent: Melville.

★ 88250 ★ Kay Bee Toy&Hobby
4101 E. 42nd St.
Odessa, TX 79762
(915)368-4274
Ultimate Parent: Melville.

★ 88251 ★ Kentucky Fried Chicken
2217 N. County Rd. W
Odessa, TX 79763
(915)332-6902
Ultimate Parent: Pepsico. SIC: 5812—Eating Places.

★ 88252 ★ Kentucky Fried Chicken
2604 N. Grandview Ave.
Odessa, TX 79761
(915)366-2846
Ultimate Parent: Pepsico. SIC: 5812—Eating Places.

★ 88253 ★ Lane Bryant
4101 E. 42nd St.
Odessa, TX 79762
(915)362-1946
Ultimate Parent: Limited.

★ 88254 ★ Lerner Shop
4101 E. 42nd St.
Odessa, TX 79762
(915)367-4551
Ultimate Parent: Limited. SIC: 5621—Women's Clothing Stores.

★ 88255 ★ McDonalds Restaurant
5023 E. Hwy. 80
Odessa, TX 79761
(915)333-3551
Ultimate Parent: McDonald's. SIC: 5812—Eating Places.

★ 88256 ★ McDonalds Restaurant
1347 W. University Blvd.
Odessa, TX 79764
(915)333-4112
Ultimate Parent: May Department Stores.

★ 88257 ★ Mobil Oil Distrbtr
9421 Andrews Hwy.
Odessa, TX 79765
(915)362-0285
Ultimate Parent: Mobil.

★ 88258 ★ Odesa Women's & Children's Hospital
520 E. 6th St.
Odessa, TX 79760
(915)334-8200
Officer: Tom Shapiro, Executive Director. Ultimate Parent: American Medical Holdings. SIC: 8062—General Medical & Surgical Hospitals.

★ 88259 ★ Otis Elevator Co.
700 N. Grant Ave.
Odessa, TX 79761
(915)332-7477
Ultimate Parent: United Technologies. SIC: 1796—Installing Building Equipment Nec.

★ 88260 ★ Payless Shoesource
4101 E. 42nd St.
Odessa, TX 79762
(915)367-6534
Ultimate Parent: May Department Stores.

★ 88261 ★ Payless Shoesource
3134 Andrews Hwy.
Odessa, TX 79762
(915)362-0760
Ultimate Parent: May Department Stores.

★ 88262 ★ Pizza Hut
2625 N. County Rd. W
Odessa, TX 79763
(915)332-7222
Ultimate Parent: Pepsico. SIC: 5812—Eating Places.

★ 88263 ★ Pizza Hut
2131 E. 8th St.
Odessa, TX 79761
(915)333-4422
Ultimate Parent: Pepsico. SIC: 5812—Eating Places.

★ 88264 ★ Pizza Hut
4960 E. University Blvd.
Odessa, TX 79762
(915)367-6505
Ultimate Parent: Pepsico. SIC: 5812—Eating Places.

★ 88265 ★ Pizza Hut
3824 E. 42nd St.
Odessa, TX 79762
(915)362-4011
Ultimate Parent: Pepsico. SIC: 5812—Eating Places.

★ 88266 ★ Radio Shack
3310 Andrews Hwy.
Odessa, TX 79762
(915)367-7111
Company Type: Division. Ultimate Parent: Tandy Corp. SIC: 5065—Electronic Parts & Equipment Nec.

★ 88267 ★ Radio Shack
Permian
Odessa, TX 79762
(915)362-6348
Company Type: Division. Ultimate Parent: Tandy Corp. SIC: 5065—Electronic Parts & Equipment Nec.

★ 88268 ★ Radio Shack
1613 E. 8th St.
Odessa, TX 79761
(915)334-8355
Company Type: Division. Ultimate Parent: Tandy Corp. SIC: 5046—Commercial Equipment Nec.

★ 88269 ★ Radio Shack
901 N. Grandview Ave.
Odessa, TX 79761
(915)332-9322
Company Type: Division. Ultimate Parent: Tandy Corp. SIC: 5065—Electronic Parts & Equipment Nec.

★ 88270 ★ Ryder Truck Rental
400 S. Grandview Ave.
Odessa, TX 79761
(915)563-1241
Ultimate Parent: Ryder System. SIC: 7359—Equipment Rental & Leasing Nec.

★ 88271 ★ Ryder Truck Rental
5040 Andrews Hwy.
Odessa, TX 79762
(915)362-8688
Ultimate Parent: Ryder System. SIC: 7359—Equipment Rental & Leasing Nec.

★ 88272 ★ Shell Oil Co.
2700 N. Grandview Ave.
Odessa, TX 79762
(915)337-5321
Ultimate Parent: Shell Oil Co. SIC: 2911—Petroleum Refining.

★ 88273 ★ Shell Oil Co.
S Grandview
Odessa, TX 79763
(915)337-5321
Ultimate Parent: Shell Oil Co. SIC: 2911—Petroleum Refining.

★ 88274 ★ Shell Oil Co.
Odessa, TX 79760
(915)381-2130
Ultimate Parent: Shell Oil Co.

★ 88275 ★ Shell Oil Co.
Odessa Refinery
2700 S. Grandview Ave.
Odessa, TX 79766
Ultimate Parent: Shell Oil Co. SIC: 2911—Petroleum Refining.

★ 88276 ★ Shell Oil Co.
Odessa Refinery
S. Grandview St.
Odessa, TX 79760
Ultimate Parent: Shell Oil Co. SIC: 2911—Petroleum Refining.

★ 88277 ★ Shell Pipeline Corp.
S Grandview
Odessa, TX 79763
(915)333-3900
Ultimate Parent: Shell Oil Co. SIC: 4612—Crude Petroleum Pipelines.

★ **88278** ★ **Shell Pipeline Corp.**
S Grandview
Odessa, TX 79763
(915)333-3900
Ultimate Parent: Shell Oil Co. **SIC:** 4612—
Crude Petroleum Pipelines.

★ **88279** ★ **Solar Turbines Inc.**
4526 E. University Blvd.
Odessa, TX 79762
(915)367-4145
Ultimate Parent: Carter-Wallace. **SIC:**
3511—Turbines & Turbine Generator Sets.

★ **88280** ★ **Taco Bell**
1927 E. 8th St.
Odessa, TX 79761
(915)333-1891
Ultimate Parent: Pepsico. **SIC:** 5812—
Eating Places.

★ **88281** ★ **Taco Bell**
3601 Andrews Hwy.
Odessa, TX 79762
(915)362-8502
Ultimate Parent: Pepsico. **SIC:** 5812—
Eating Places.

★ **88282** ★ **Texaco Inc.**
501 E. Loop 338
Odessa, TX 79762
(915)366-8801
Ultimate Parent: Texaco.

★ **88283** ★ **Texaco Inc.**
Cities Ser Rd.
Odessa, TX 79760
(915)332-0517
Ultimate Parent: Texaco.

★ **88284** ★ **Texaco Inc.
Producingdepartm**
Notrees Texas
Odessa, TX 79760
(915)332-4011
Ultimate Parent: Texaco.

★ **88285** ★ **Texaco Jpep**
4200 Andrews Hwy.
Odessa, TX 79762
(915)362-9387
Ultimate Parent: Texaco. **SIC:** 5541—
Gasoline Service Stations.

★ **88286** ★ **Trailways Bus
Systems**
300 N. Texas Ave.
Odessa, TX 79761
(915)332-1414
Ultimate Parent: Greyhound Lines Inc. **SIC:**
4131—Intercity & Rural Bus Transportation.

★ **88287** ★ **Trico Ind. Inc.**
3218 Kermit Hwy.
Odessa, TX 79764
Ultimate Parent: Paccar.

★ **88288** ★ **Trico Industries Inc.**
3310 W. Loop 338
Odessa, TX 79764
(915)332-8206
Ultimate Parent: Paccar. **SIC:** 5084—
Industrial Machinery & Equipment.

★ **88289** ★ **Union Oil Co. of
California**
County Rd. S
Odessa, TX 79763
(915)332-8228
Ultimate Parent: Unocal Corp. **SIC:** 5171—
Petroleum Bulk Stations & Terminals.

★ **88290** ★ **Wal Mart Discount
City**
3800 E. 42nd St.
Odessa, TX 79762
(915)368-4006
Ultimate Parent: Wal-Mart Stores, Inc. **SIC:**
5311—Department Stores.

★ **88291** ★ **Waldenbooks**
Permian
Odessa, TX 79762
(915)366-3498
Ultimate Parent: K-Mart. **SIC:** 5942—Book
Stores.

★ **88292** ★ **Walgreen**
801 Maple Ave.
Odessa, TX 79761
(915)337-5224
Ultimate Parent: Walgreen Co. **SIC:**
5912—Drug Stores & Proprietary Stores.

Olden

★ **88293** ★ **Liberty Mutual Insco**
2227 Division St. E
Olden, TX 76466
(817)652-0726
Ultimate Parent: Liberty Mutual Group.

Olney

★ **88294** ★ **Lone Star Gas Co.**
401 E. Payne St.
Olney, TX 76374
(817)564-5250
Ultimate Parent: Enserch. **SIC:** 4932—Gas
& Other Services Combined.

★ **88295** ★ **Lone Star Gas Co.**
116 S. Ave.
Olney, TX 76374
(817)564-2822
Ultimate Parent: Enserch. **SIC:** 4932—Gas
& Other Services Combined.

★ **88296** ★ **Texaco Inc.**
401 S. Ave.
Olney, TX 76374
(817)564-2066
Ultimate Parent: Texaco. **SIC:** 5171—
Petroleum Bulk Stations & Terminals.

Orange

★ **88297** ★ **A. Schulman Inc.**
Thomas St/Foreman Rd.
Orange, TX 77630
Ultimate Parent: A. Schulman, Inc. **SIC:**
3089—Plastics Products Nec.

★ **88298** ★ **A. Schulman Inc.**
Thomas St. Near Foreman Rd.
Orange, TX 77630
Ultimate Parent: A. Schulman, Inc. **SIC:**
3087—Custom Compound of Purchased
Resins.

★ **88299** ★ **A. Schulman Inc.**
Dispersion
Thomas St. Near Foreman Rd.
Orange, TX 77630
Company Type: Division. **Ultimate Parent:**
A. Schulman, Inc. **SIC:** 3087—Custom
Compound of Purchased Resins.

★ **88300** ★ **Aid Association for
Luthera**
601 4th St.
Orange, TX 77630
(409)883-8553
Ultimate Parent: Aid Association for
Lutherans. **SIC:** 6411—Insurance Agents,
Brokers & Service.

★ **88301** ★ **Allied-Signal Inc.**
F.M. 1006
Orange, TX 77630
Ultimate Parent: Allied-Signal Inc. **SIC:**
2821—Plastics Materials & Resins.

★ **88302** ★ **Allied-Signal Inc.**
F.M. 1006
Orange, TX 77630
Location Type: Plant. **Ultimate Parent:**
Allied-Signal Inc. **SIC:** 2821—Plastics
Materials & Resins.

★ **88303** ★ **Allied-Signal, Inc.**
PO Box 640
Orange, TX 77631-0640
(409)886-7445
Officer: Darrell B. Reed. **Ultimate Parent:**
Allied-Signal Inc. **SIC:** 2821—Plastics
Materials & Resins.

★ **88304** ★ **Allied-Signal Inc.**
FM Rd. 1006
Orange, TX 77630
(409)886-7445
Officer: Darrell B. Beed, Manager. **Ultimate
Parent:** Allied-Signal Inc. **SIC:** 2821—
Plastics Materials & Resins; 2822—
Synthetic Rubber; 3089—Plastics Products
Nec.

★ **88305** ★ **Allied-Signal Inc.**
PO Box 640
Orange, TX 77631-0640
(409)886-7445
Officer: Darrell B. Reed. **Ultimate Parent:**
Allied-Signal Inc. **SIC:** 2821—Plastics
Materials & Resins.

★ **88306** ★ **Allied-Signal Inc.**
FM Rd. 1006
Orange, TX 77630
(409)886-7445
Officer: Darrell B. Beed, Manager. **Ultimate
Parent:** Allied-Signal Inc. **SIC:** 2821—
Plastics Materials & Resins; 2822—
Synthetic Rubber; 3089—Plastics Products
Nec.

★ **88307** ★ **Cain Chemical Inc.**
FM 1006
Orange, TX 77630
Ultimate Parent: Occidental Petroleum
Corp. **SIC:** 2821—Plastics Materials &
Resins.

★ **88308** ★ **Chevron Chemical
Co.**
Farm Rd. 1006
Orange, TX 77630
Ultimate Parent: Chevron Corp. **SIC:**
2821—Plastics Materials & Resins.

★ **88309** ★ **Chevron Chemical
Co.**
Fm 1006
Orange, TX 77630
Ultimate Parent: Chevron Corp. **SIC:**
2821—Plastics Materials & Resins.

★ **88310** ★ **Chevron Chemical
Co.**
Olefins & Derivatives Div.
Fm Rd. 1006
Orange, TX 77630
Company Type: Division. **Ultimate Parent:**
Chevron Corp. **SIC:** 2821—Plastics
Materials & Resins.

★ **88311** ★ **Exxon**
1415 16th St.
Orange, TX 77630
(409)883-2768
Ultimate Parent: Exxon.

★ **88312** ★ **Giant Food Store**
319 W. Park Ave.
Orange, TX 77630
(409)886-7344
Ultimate Parent: Giant Food. **SIC:** 5411—
Grocery Stores.

★ **88313** ★ **Greyhound Bus Lines**
411 4th St.
Orange, TX 77630
(409)883-4353
Ultimate Parent: Greyhound Lines Inc. **SIC:**
4111—Local & Suburban Transit; 4173—
Bus Terminal & Service Facilities.

★ **88314** ★ **Gulf States Utilities
Co.**
1088 PO Box
Orange, TX 77631
Ultimate Parent: Gulf State Utilities Co.
SIC: 4911—Electric Services.

★ **88315** ★ **Hertz Rent-A-Car
Licensee**
3001 MacArthur Dr.
Orange, TX 77630
(409)883-3392
Ultimate Parent: Hertz. **SIC:** 7514—
Passenger Car Rental.

★ **88316** ★ **Inland-Orange Inc.**
Old Hwy. 87 N.
Orange, TX 77632
Ultimate Parent: Temple-Inland. **SIC:**
2621—Paper Mills; 2631—Paperboard Mills;
2600—Paper & Allied Products.

★ **88317** ★ **J. M. Huber Corp.
Echo Carbon Plant**
Fm 736
Orange, TX 77630
Ultimate Parent: J. M. Huber. **SIC:** 2895—
Carbon Black.

★ **88318** ★ **James River Corp.**
Flexible Packaging Group
Farm Rd. 1006
Orange, TX 77630
Ultimate Parent: James River Corp. of
Virginia. **SIC:** 3081—Unsupported Plastics
Film & Sheet.

★ **88319** ★ **J.M. Huber Corp.
Echo Carbon Plant**
Fm 736
Orange, TX 77630
Ultimate Parent: J. M. Huber. **SIC:** 2895—
Carbon Black.

★ **88320** ★ **J.M. Huber Echo
Carbon Plant**
Fm 736
Orange, TX 77630
Ultimate Parent: J. M. Huber. **SIC:** 2895—
Carbon Black.

★ **88321** ★ **Kentucky Fried
Chicken**
1501 Green Ave.
Orange, TX 77630
(409)883-8555
Ultimate Parent: Pepsico. **SIC:** 5812—
Eating Places.

★ **88322** ★ **Marathon Oil Co.**
Childers
Orange, TX 77630
(409)883-8436
Ultimate Parent: USX Corp. **SIC:** 1311—
Crude Petroleum & Natural Gas.

★ **88323** ★ **Marathon Oil Co.**
Childers
Orange, TX 77630
(409)883-8436
Ultimate Parent: USX Corp. **SIC:** 1311—
Crude Petroleum & Natural Gas.

★ **88324** ★ **Miles Inc.**
Polysar Rubber Div.
Fm 1006
Orange, TX 77631-2000
Company Type: Division. **Ultimate Parent:**
Miles. **SIC:** 2822—Synthetic Rubber.

★ **88325** ★ **Occidental Chemical
Corp.**
Fm 1006
Orange, TX 77631-3870
Ultimate Parent: Occidental Petroleum
Corp. **SIC:** 2821—Plastics Materials &
Resins.

★ **88326** ★ **Pizza Hut**
Northway Shopping Ctr.
Orange, TX 77630
(409)886-7717
Ultimate Parent: Pepsico. **SIC:** 5812—
Eating Places.

★ **88327** ★ **Radio Shack**
Northway Shopping Ctr.
Orange, TX 77630
(409)883-0110
Company Type: Division. **Ultimate Parent:**
Tandy Corp. **SIC:** 5065—Electronic Parts &
Equipment Nec.

★ **88328** ★ **Radio Shack**
2674 Macarthur Dr.
Orange, TX 77630
(409)886-0787
Company Type: Division. **Ultimate Parent:**
Tandy Corp. **SIC:** 5065—Electronic Parts &
Equipment Nec.

★ **88329** ★ **Ryder Truck Rental**
101 Green Ave.
Orange, TX 77630
(409)883-0989
Ultimate Parent: Ryder System. **SIC:**
7513—Truck Rental & Leasing Without
Drivers.

★ **88330** ★ **Taco Bell**
1803 16th St.
Orange, TX 77630
(409)883-5470
Ultimate Parent: Pepsico. **SIC:** 5812—
Eating Places.

★ **88331** ★ **Texas-Lehigh Cement
Co.**
Womack Rd.
Orange, TX 77630
(409)883-8850
Ultimate Parent: Centex. **SIC:** 5099—
Durable Goods Nec.

★ **88332** ★ **Walgreen Drug Stores**
2280 MacArthur Dr.
Orange, TX 77630
(409)883-0876
Ultimate Parent: Walgreen Co. **SIC:**
5912—Drug Stores & Proprietary Stores.

Orla

★ **88333** ★ **Texaco Inc.**
Orla, TX 79770
(915)273-4661
Ultimate Parent: Texaco. **SIC:** 1311—
Crude Petroleum & Natural Gas.

Overton

★ 88334 ★   Exxon Co., USA
RR 1
Box 94
Overton, TX 75684
(903)834-3663
Officer: Dave Fullman, Manager. **Ultimate Parent:** Exxon. **SIC:** 2911—Petroleum Refining.

★ 88335 ★   Exxon Credit Union
107 S. Rusk St.
Overton, TX 75684
(214)834-3119
Ultimate Parent: Exxon. **SIC:** 6062—State Credit Unions.

Ozona

★ 88336 ★   Radio Shack
303 D Ave.
Ozona, TX 76943
(915)392-3605
Company Type: Division. **Ultimate Parent:** Tandy Corp. **SIC:** 5731—Radio, Television & Electronics Stores.

★ 88337 ★   Texaco Gasoline Plant
S City
Ozona, TX 76943
(915)392-3308
Ultimate Parent: Texaco. **SIC:** 2813—Industrial Gases.

Paducah

★ 88338 ★   Lone Star Gas Co.
817 Richards
Paducah, TX 79248
(806)492-3828
Ultimate Parent: Enserch. **SIC:** 4925—Gas Production & Distribution Nec.

★ 88339 ★   West Texas Utilities Co.
710 10th
Paducah, TX 79248
(806)492-3040
Ultimate Parent: Central & South West. **SIC:** 5722—Household Appliance Stores.

Palacios

★ 88340 ★   Trailways Bus Station
317 Commerce St.
Palacios, TX 77465
(512)972-2419
Ultimate Parent: Greyhound Lines Inc. **SIC:** 4131—Intercity & Rural Bus Transportation.

Palestine

★ 88341 ★   Kentucky Fried Chicken
1717 W. Palestine Ave.
Palestine, TX 75801
(214)729-6222
Ultimate Parent: Pepsico. **SIC:** 5812—Eating Places.

★ 88342 ★   Kroger Food Store
703 N. Mallard St.
Palestine, TX 75801
(214)729-5233
Ultimate Parent: Kroger. **SIC:** 5411—Grocery Stores.

★ 88343 ★   Mini Mart
321 W. Palestine Ave.
Palestine, TX 75801
(214)729-1594
Ultimate Parent: Kroger. **SIC:** 5411—Grocery Stores.

★ 88344 ★   Pizza Hut
402 E. Palestine Ave.
Palestine, TX 75801
(903)723-5109
Ultimate Parent: Pepsico. **SIC:** 5812—Eating Places.

★ 88345 ★   Radio Shack
Palestine
Palestine, TX 75801
(214)729-2614
Company Type: Division. **Ultimate Parent:** Tandy Corp. **SIC:** 5065—Electronic Parts & Equipment Nec.

★ 88346 ★   Texaco Petroleum Prod Dist
507 W. Reagan St.
Palestine, TX 75801
(214)729-5036
Ultimate Parent: Texaco. **SIC:** 5171—Petroleum Bulk Stations & Terminals.

★ 88347 ★   Trailways Bus Depot
310 W. Palestine Ave.
Palestine, TX 75801
(214)729-2832
Ultimate Parent: Greyhound Lines Inc. **SIC:** 4131—Intercity & Rural Bus Transportation.

★ 88348 ★   Wal Mart Distribution Center
Old Elkhart Rd.
Palestine, TX 75801
(214)723-4412
Ultimate Parent: Wal-Mart Stores, Inc. **SIC:** 4225—General Warehousing & Storage.

Pampa

★ 88349 ★   Halliburton Resource Mgt
114 Western
Pampa, TX 79065
(806)669-7651
Ultimate Parent: Halliburton. **SIC:** 5084—Industrial Machinery & Equipment.

★ 88350 ★   Hoechst-Celanese Corp. Pampa Plant
U.S. Hwy. 60 5 Miles W. of Pampa
Pampa, TX 79065
Ultimate Parent: Hoechst Celanese Corp. **SIC:** 2869—Industrial Organic Chemicals Nec.

★ 88351 ★   Hoechst Celanese - Pampa Plant
5 Miles West of Pampa on U.S. Hwy. 60
Pampa, TX 79066-0937
Ultimate Parent: Hoechst Celanese Corp. **SIC:** 2869—Industrial Organic Chemicals Nec.

★ 88352 ★   Hoechst Celanese Pampa Plant
Five Miles West of Pampa on U.S. Hwy. 60
Pampa, TX 79066-0937
Ultimate Parent: Hoechst Celanese Corp. **SIC:** 2869—Industrial Organic Chemicals Nec.

★ 88353 ★   IRI International Corp.
Hwy. 60 West
Pampa, TX 79065
(806)665-3701 **Fax:** (806)665-3216
Company Type: Subsidiary. **Ultimate Parent:** Dresser Industries Inc.

★ 88354 ★   Pizza Hut
1500 N. Banks St.
Pampa, TX 79065
(806)665-0887
Ultimate Parent: Pepsico. **SIC:** 5812—Eating Places.

★ 88355 ★   Pizza Hut
855 W. Kingsmill Ave.
Pampa, TX 79065
(806)665-5971
Ultimate Parent: Pepsico. **SIC:** 5812—Eating Places.

★ 88356 ★   Radio Shack
1820 N. Hobart St.
Pampa, TX 79065
(806)669-2253
Company Type: Division. **Ultimate Parent:** Tandy Corp. **SIC:** 5065—Electronic Parts & Equipment Nec.

★ 88357 ★   Trailways Bus System
115 S. Russell St.
Pampa, TX 79065
(806)669-3317
Ultimate Parent: Greyhound Lines Inc. **SIC:** 4131—Intercity & Rural Bus Transportation.

★ 88358 ★   Wal Mart Inc.
2225 N. Hobart St.
Pampa, TX 79065
(806)665-0727
Ultimate Parent: Wal-Mart Stores, Inc. **SIC:** 5311—Department Stores.

★ 88359 ★   Waldenbooks
2545 Perryton Pky.
Pampa, TX 79065
(806)669-6462
Ultimate Parent: K-Mart. **SIC:** 5942—Book Stores.

Paris

★ 88360 ★   Anheuser-Busch Inc.
Earth Grains Div.
2020 19th NW
Paris, TX 75460
Company Type: Division. **Ultimate Parent:** Anheuser-Busch. **SIC:** 2051—Bread, Cake & Related Products.

★ 88361 ★   Beverly Enterprises
610 Deshong Dr.
Paris, TX 75462-1931
(903)784-4525
Ultimate Parent: Beverly Enterprises. **SIC:** 8059—Nursing & Personal Care Nec.

★ 88362 ★   Burlington Northern Railroa
1264 Main
Paris, TX 75460
(214)784-3155
Ultimate Parent: Burlington Northern. **SIC:** 4011—Railroads—Line-Haul Operating.

★ 88363 ★   Campbell Soup Co.
500 NW
Paris, TX 75460
Ultimate Parent: Campbell Soup. **SIC:** 2032—Canned Specialties.

★ 88364 ★   Campbell Soup Co. Texas Inc.
Loop 286
Paris, TX 75461-9016
Ultimate Parent: Campbell Soup. **SIC:** 2033—Canned Fruits & Vegetables.

★ 88365 ★   Campbell Soup (Texas) Inc.
PO Box 9016
Paris, TX 75461-9016
(214)784-3341 **Fax:** (214)784-0327
Officer: Ross Kelly, Plant Manager. **Ultimate Parent:** Campbell Soup.

★ 88366 ★   First Federal S & L
630 Clarksville St.
Paris, TX 75460-5934
(903)784-0881
Company Type: Headquarters. **Officer:** Richard M. Amis. **Ultimate Parent:** Bancorp Hawaii. **SIC:** 6035—Federal Savings Institutions.

★ 88367 ★   Kentucky Fried Chicken
3110 Clarksville St.
Paris, TX 75460
(214)784-8593
Ultimate Parent: Pepsico. **SIC:** 5812—Eating Places; 8721—Accounting, Auditing & Bookkeeping.

★ 88368 ★   Kids R US
2535 Lamar Ave.
Paris, TX 75460
(214)784-7123
Ultimate Parent: Toys "R" US. **SIC:** 8351—Child Day Care Services.

★ 88369 ★   Kimberly-Clark Corp. Paris Tx Plant
Loop 286 Fm 137 Intersection
Paris, TX 75461
Ultimate Parent: Kimberly-Clark. **SIC:** 2676—Sanitary Paper Products.

★ 88370 ★   Kroger Family Center
1310 Clarksville St.
Paris, TX 75460
(214)785-5591
Ultimate Parent: Kroger. **SIC:** 5399—Miscellaneous General Merchandise Store; 5411—Grocery Stores.

★ 88371 ★   Lone Star Gas Co.
355 13th St. SW
Paris, TX 75460
Ultimate Parent: Enserch. **SIC:** 4939—Combination Utility Nec.

★ 88372 ★   Oliver Rubber Co.
2305 NW Loop 286
Paris, TX 75460
(214)785-1637
Ultimate Parent: Standard Products. **SIC:** 3069—Fabricated Rubber Products Nec.

★ 88373 ★   Oliver Rubber Co.
2305 NW Loop 286 PO Drawer 309
Paris, TX 75461-0309
Ultimate Parent: Standard Products. **SIC:** 3011—Tires & Inner Tubes; 3069—Fabricated Rubber Products Nec.

★ 88374 ★   Payless Shoesource
3562 Lamar Ave.
Paris, TX 75460
(214)785-5463
Ultimate Parent: May Department Stores. **SIC:** 5661—Shoe Stores.

★ 88375 ★   Pizza Hut
1610 Clarksville St.
Paris, TX 75460
(214)784-5051
Ultimate Parent: Pepsico. **SIC:** 5812—Eating Places.

★ 88376 ★   Radio Shack
3528 Lamar Ave.
Paris, TX 75460
(214)784-0144
Company Type: Division. **Ultimate Parent:** Tandy Corp. **SIC:** 5065—Electronic Parts & Equipment Nec.

★ 88377 ★   Sesame Prods. Inc.
700 W. Center St.
Paris, TX 75460
Ultimate Parent: McCormick & Co. Inc. **SIC:** 2099—Food Preparations Nec.

★ 88378 ★   Sesame Products Inc.
700 W. Ctr. St.
Paris, TX 75460
(214)784-7419
Ultimate Parent: McCormick & Co. Inc. **SIC:** 3556—Food Products Machinery; 5046—Commercial Equipment Nec.

★ 88379 ★   Taco Bell
1210 Lamar Ave.
Paris, TX 75460
(214)785-7731
Ultimate Parent: Pepsico. **SIC:** 5812—Eating Places.

★ 88380 ★   Wal Mart Discount Cities
3100 Clarksville St.
Paris, TX 75460
(903)785-9555
Ultimate Parent: Wal-Mart Stores, Inc. **SIC:** 5311—Department Stores.

Pasadena

★ 88381 ★   Air Products & Chemicals Inc.
1423 Hwy. 225
Pasadena, TX 77506
Ultimate Parent: Air Products & Chemicals, Inc. **SIC:** 2865—Cyclic Crudes & Intermediates; 2873—Nitrogenous Fertilizers; 2869—Industrial Organic Chemicals Nec.

★ 88382 ★   Air Products Manufacturing Corp.
1423 Hwy. 225
Pasadena, TX 77506
Ultimate Parent: Air Products & Chemicals, Inc. **SIC:** 2865—Cyclic Crudes & Intermediates; 2873—Nitrogenous Fertilizers; 2869—Industrial Organic Chemicals Nec.

★ 88383 ★   Air Products Manufacturing Corp.
PO Box 3326
Pasadena, TX 77501-3326
(713)477-6841
Officer: R. Brad Chandler. **Ultimate Parent:** Air Products & Chemicals, Inc. **SIC:** 2819—Industrial Inorganic Chemicals Nec.

★ 88384 ★   Air Products
Manufacturing Corp.
1423 Pasadena Blvd.
Pasadena, TX 77502
(713)477-6841
Officer: Brad Chandler, Manager. Ultimate
Parent: Air Products & Chemicals, Inc. SIC:
2819—Industrial Inorganic Chemicals Nec;
2821—Plastics Materials & Resins.

★ 88385 ★   Arco Chemical Co.
10801 Choate Rd.
Pasadena, TX 77507-1503
(713)474-4191
Officer: Douglas Mathera. Ultimate Parent:
Atlantic Richfield Co., Inc. SIC: 2899—
Chemical Preparations Nec; 2869—
Industrial Organic Chemicals Nec.

★ 88386 ★   Arco Chemical Co.
Bayport Div.
10801 Choate Rd.
Pasadena, TX 77507
Company Type: Division. Ultimate Parent:
Atlantic Richfield Co., Inc. SIC: 2869—
Industrial Organic Chemicals Nec.

★ 88387 ★   Atlantic Richfield
Credit Union
PO Box 1538
Pasadena, TX 77501-1538
(713)477-3164
Location Type: Headquarters. Officer:
Royce Phares. Ultimate Parent: Atlantic
Richfield Co., Inc. SIC: 6061—Federal
Credit Unions.

★ 88388 ★   Beneficial Texas, Inc.
714 Southmore Ave.
Pasadena, TX 77502
(713)473-4493
Ultimate Parent: Beneficial. SIC: 6141—
Personal Credit Institutions.

★ 88389 ★   Beneficial Texas Inc.
714 Southmore Ave.
Pasadena, TX 77502
(713)473-4493
Ultimate Parent: Beneficial. SIC: 6141—
Personal Credit Institutions.

★ 88390 ★   Builders Square
3316 Shaver St.
Pasadena, TX 77504
(713)941-0910
Company Type: Subsidiary. Ultimate
Parent: K-Mart. SIC: 5063—Electrical
Apparatus & Equipment.

★ 88391 ★   Cain Chemical Inc.
Bayport Site
5757 Underwood Rd.
Pasadena, TX 77507
Ultimate Parent: Occidental Petroleum
Corp. SIC: 2869—Industrial Organic
Chemicals Nec.

★ 88392 ★   Calgon Corp.
9640 Bayport Blvd.
Pasadena, TX 77507
Ultimate Parent: Merck. SIC: 2899—
Chemical Preparations Nec.

★ 88393 ★   Carpenter Chemical
Co.
11002 Choate Rd.
Pasadena, TX 77507
Ultimate Parent: Carpenter. SIC: 2869—
Industrial Organic Chemicals Nec.

★ 88394 ★   Casual Corner
143 Pasadena Fwy.
Pasadena, TX 77506
(713)472-5054
Ultimate Parent: United States Shoe. SIC:
5611—Men's & Boys' Clothing Stores.

★ 88395 ★   Catalyst Resources
Inc.
10001 Chemical Rd.
Pasadena, TX 77507
Ultimate Parent: Phillips Petroleum. SIC:
2819—Industrial Inorganic Chemicals Nec.

★ 88396 ★   Circus World Toy
Stores
Pasadena Sq.
Pasadena, TX 77506
(713)475-8070
Ultimate Parent: Melville. SIC: 5945—
Hobby, Toy & Game Shops.

★ 88397 ★   Colonial Pipeline Co.
Laporte Rd.
Pasadena, TX 77502
(713)473-5401
Ultimate Parent: Colonial Pipeline. SIC:
4612—Crude Petroleum Pipelines.

★ 88398 ★   An Corp. Bayport
Plant
12000 Bay Area Blvd.
Pasadena, TX 77507
Ultimate Parent: FMC. SIC: 2819—
Industrial Inorganic Chemicals Nec; 2869—
Industrial Organic Chemicals Nec.

★ 88399 ★   Crown Central
Petroleum Corp.
111 Red Bluff Rd.
Pasadena, TX 77506
Ultimate Parent: Crown Central Petroleum
Corp. SIC: 2911—Petroleum Refining.

★ 88400 ★   Crown Central
Petroleum Corp. Houston Refinery
111 Red Bluff Rd.
Pasadena, TX 77506
Ultimate Parent: Crown Central Petroleum
Corp. SIC: 2911—Petroleum Refining.

★ 88401 ★   Enron Methanol Co.
4403 Laporte Rd.
Pasadena, TX 77503
Ultimate Parent: Enron. SIC: 2869—
Industrial Organic Chemicals Nec.

★ 88402 ★   Ethyl Corp.
1000 N. South St.
Pasadena, TX 77503
(713)740-1000
Officer: Charlie B. Hunt, Manager. Ultimate
Parent: Ethyl. SIC: 2819—Industrial
Inorganic Chemicals Nec; 2865—Cyclic
Crudes & Intermediates; 2869—Industrial
Organic Chemicals Nec.

★ 88403 ★   Ethyl Corp.
Houston Plant
1000 N. South Ave.
Pasadena, TX 77501-0472
Location Type: Plant. Ultimate Parent:
Ethyl. SIC: 2869—Industrial Organic
Chemicals Nec; 2819—Industrial Inorganic
Chemicals Nec.

★ 88404 ★   Exxon
950 Pasadena Fwy.
Pasadena, TX 77506
(713)473-3110
Ultimate Parent: Exxon. SIC: 5541—
Gasoline Service Stations.

★ 88405 ★   Exxon
5501 Fairmont Pky.
Pasadena, TX 77505
(713)998-0849
Ultimate Parent: Exxon.

★ 88406 ★   Exxon Co. USA
4651 Spencer Hwy.
Pasadena, TX 77504
(713)941-7693
Ultimate Parent: Exxon.

★ 88407 ★   Fina Oil & Chemical
Co.
12212 Port Rd.
Pasadena, TX 77507
(713)474-6000
Officer: Darrell Bailey, Plant Manager.
Ultimate Parent: Fina. SIC: 2821—Plastics
Materials & Resins; 2865—Cyclic Crudes &
Intermediates; 3087—Custom Compound of
Purchased Resins.

★ 88408 ★   FMC Corp.
12000 Bay Area Blvd.
Pasadena, TX 77507
(713)474-4171
Officer: Whitman Hopkins, Manager.
Ultimate Parent: FMC. SIC: 2819—
Industrial Inorganic Chemicals Nec; 2869—
Industrial Organic Chemicals Nec; 2899—
Chemical Preparations Nec.

★ 88409 ★   FMC Corp.
Peroxygen Chemicals Div.
12000 Bay Area Blvd.
Pasadena, TX 77507
Company Type: Division. Ultimate Parent:
FMC. SIC: 2819—Industrial Inorganic
Chemicals Nec.

★ 88410 ★   Fmc Corp.-Bayport
Plant
12000 Bay Area Blvd.
Pasadena, TX 77507
Ultimate Parent: FMC. SIC: 2819—
Industrial Inorganic Chemicals Nec; 2869—
Industrial Organic Chemicals Nec.

★ 88411 ★   The Gap
327 Pasadena Town Sq.
Pasadena, TX 77506
(713)472-4115
Ultimate Parent: GAP.

★ 88412 ★   The Gap
327 Pasadena Plz.
Pasadena, TX 77504
(713)472-4115
Ultimate Parent: GAP. SIC: 5611—Men's &
Boys' Clothing Stores.

★ 88413 ★   Gap Stores
327 Pasadena Plz.
Pasadena, TX 77504
(713)472-4115
Ultimate Parent: GAP. SIC: 5611—Men's &
Boys' Clothing Stores.

★ 88414 ★   Goodyear Bayport
Chem. Plant
13441 Bay Area Blvd.
Pasadena, TX 77507
Ultimate Parent: Goodyear Tire & Rubber.
SIC: 2865—Cyclic Crudes & Intermediates;
2869—Industrial Organic Chemicals Nec.

★ 88415 ★   Goodyear Bayport
Chemcial Plant
13441 Bay Area Blvd.
Pasadena, TX 77507
Ultimate Parent: Goodyear Tire & Rubber.
SIC: 2865—Cyclic Crudes & Intermediates;
2869—Industrial Organic Chemicals Nec.

★ 88416 ★   Goodyear Tire &
Rubber Co. Bayport Chemical Plant
13441 Bay Area Blvd.
Pasadena, TX 77507
Ultimate Parent: Goodyear Tire & Rubber.
SIC: 2865—Cyclic Crudes & Intermediates;
2869—Industrial Organic Chemicals Nec.

★ 88417 ★   Hoechst Celanese
Chamical Group Inc. Clear Lake
Plant
9502 Bayport Rd.
Pasadena, TX 77507-1498
Ultimate Parent: Hoechst Celanese Corp.
SIC: 2869—Industrial Organic Chemicals
Nec.

★ 88418 ★   Hoechst-Celanese
Chemical Group Inc. Clear Lake
Plant
9502 Bayport Rd.
Pasadena, TX 77507-1498
Ultimate Parent: Hoechst Celanese Corp.
SIC: 2869—Industrial Organic Chemicals
Nec.

★ 88419 ★   Hoechst-Celanese
Corp.
Bayport Works
12212 Port Rd.
Pasadena, TX 77507
Location Type: Plant. Ultimate Parent:
Hoechst Celanese Corp. SIC: 2821—
Plastics Materials & Resins.

★ 88420 ★   Kentucky Fried
Chicken
6839 Spencer Hwy.
Pasadena, TX 77505
(713)487-3412
Ultimate Parent: Pepsico. SIC: 5812—
Eating Places.

★ 88421 ★   Kentucky Fried
Chicken
802 W. Southmore Ave.
Pasadena, TX 77502
(713)472-7698
Ultimate Parent: Pepsico. SIC: 5812—
Eating Places.

★ 88422 ★   Kentucky Fried
Chicken
1202 South St.
Pasadena, TX 77503
(713)472-7621
Ultimate Parent: Pepsico. SIC: 5812—
Eating Places.

★ 88423 ★   Kentucky Fried
Chicken
3207 Spencer Hwy.
Pasadena, TX 77504
(713)943-0150
Ultimate Parent: Pepsico. SIC: 5812—
Eating Places.

★ 88424 ★   Kroger Co.
2619 Red Bluff Rd.
Pasadena, TX 77506
(713)475-0925
Ultimate Parent: Kroger. SIC: 5411—
Grocery Stores.

★ 88425 ★   Kroger Co.
6835 Spencer Hwy.
Pasadena, TX 77505
(713)487-4476
Ultimate Parent: Kroger. SIC: 5411—
Grocery Stores.

★ 88426 ★   Kroger Co.
118 Fairmont Pky.
Pasadena, TX 77504
(713)941-8926
Ultimate Parent: Kroger. SIC: 5411—
Grocery Stores.

★ 88427 ★   Kroger Food Stores
6835 Spencer Hwy.
Pasadena, TX 77505
(713)487-7112
Ultimate Parent: Kroger.

★ 88428 ★   Kroger Pharmacy
118 Fairmont Pky.
Pasadena, TX 77504
(713)941-0192
Ultimate Parent: Kroger. SIC: 5912—Drug
Stores & Proprietary Stores.

★ 88429 ★   Lane Bryant
236 Pasadena Town Sq.
Pasadena, TX 77506
(713)475-8009
Ultimate Parent: Limited.

★ 88430 ★   Lerner Shop
337 Pasadena Town Sq.
Pasadena, TX 77506
(713)473-4783
Ultimate Parent: Limited.

★ 88431 ★   Lerner Shop
2024 Pasadena Plz.
Pasadena, TX 77504
(713)946-3674
Ultimate Parent: Limited. SIC: 5611—
Men's & Boys' Clothing Stores.

★ 88432 ★   Liquid Carbonic
Specialty Gas Corp.
9950 Chemical Rd.
Pasadena, TX 77507
Ultimate Parent: CBI Industries, Inc. SIC:
2813—Industrial Gases.

★ 88433 ★   Lockwood National
Bank of Houston
722 Fairmont Pky.
Pasadena, TX 77504-2825
(713)947-2000
Location Type: Branch office. Ultimate
Parent: Michigan National Corp. SIC:
6021—National Commercial Banks.

★ 88434 ★   Lockwood National
Bank of Houston
2222 S. Shaver
Pasadena, TX 77502-3640
(713)477-8888
Location Type: Branch office. Ultimate
Parent: Michigan National Corp. SIC:
6021—National Commercial Banks.

★ 88435 ★   Lubrizol Corp. the
12801 Bay Area Blvd.
Pasadena, TX 77507
(713)474-5171
Ultimate Parent: Lubrizol.

★ 88436 ★   Lubrizol Petroleum
Chemicals, Bayport Plant
12801 Bay Area Blvd.
Pasadena, TX 77507
Location Type: Plant. Ultimate Parent:
Lubrizol. SIC: 2869—Industrial Organic
Chemicals Nec.

★ 88437 ★ Lubrizol Petroleum Chemicals Co. Bayport Plant
12801 Bay Area Blvd.
Pasadena, TX 77507
Ultimate Parent: Lubrizol. SIC: 2869—Industrial Organic Chemicals Nec.

★ 88438 ★ Lyondell Polymers Corp.
9802 Fairmont Pky.
Pasadena, TX 77507
Ultimate Parent: Lyondell Petrochemical Co. SIC: 2821—Plastics Materials & Resins.

★ 88439 ★ Marathon Pipeline Co.
539 South St.
Pasadena, TX 77503
(713)472-3625
Ultimate Parent: USX Corp. SIC: 4612—Crude Petroleum Pipelines.

★ 88440 ★ McDonalds of Red Bluff
3815 Red Bluff Rd.
Pasadena, TX 77503
(713)920-2128
Ultimate Parent: McDonald's. SIC: 5812—Eating Places.

★ 88441 ★ McDonalds Restaurant
407 W. Southmore Ave.
Pasadena, TX 77502
(713)472-5313
Ultimate Parent: McDonald's. SIC: 5812—Eating Places.

★ 88442 ★ McDonalds Restaurant
3223 Spencer Hwy.
Pasadena, TX 77504
(713)941-7410
Ultimate Parent: McDonald's. SIC: 5812—Eating Places.

★ 88443 ★ Mcduff Electronics
3322 Spencer Hwy.
Pasadena, TX 77504
(713)943-2555
Ultimate Parent: Tandy Corp.

★ 88444 ★ Mobil Mining & Minerals Co.
PO Box 3447
Pasadena, TX 77501-3447
(713)920-5311
Officer: David E. Thomas. Ultimate Parent: Mobil. SIC: 2874—Phosphatic Fertilizers.

★ 88445 ★ Ocapi
Houston Ammonia Terminal
4403 Laporte Rd. PO Box 46
Pasadena, TX 77501
Company Type: Division. Ultimate Parent: Occidental Petroleum Corp. SIC: 2873—Nitrogenous Fertilizers.

★ 88446 ★ Ocapi
Houston Ammonia Terminal
4403 Laporte Rd. PO Box 46
Pasadena, TX 77501
Company Type: Division. Ultimate Parent: Occidental Petroleum Corp. SIC: 2873—Nitrogenous Fertilizers.

★ 88447 ★ Occidental Chemical Corp.
4403 Pasadena Fwy.
Pasadena, TX 77503
Ultimate Parent: Occidental Petroleum Corp. SIC: 2821—Plastics Materials & Resins.

★ 88448 ★ Occidental Chemical Corp.
4403 La Porte Rd.
Pasadena, TX 77501
Ultimate Parent: Occidental Petroleum Corp. SIC: 2821—Plastics Materials & Resins.

★ 88449 ★ Occidental Chemical Corp.
Houston Ammonia Terminal
4403 Laporte Rd. PO Box 46
Pasadena, TX 77501-0046
Location Type: Plant. Ultimate Parent: Occidental Petroleum Corp. SIC: 2873—Nitrogenous Fertilizers.

★ 88450 ★ Oxychem Petrochemicals
Bayport Plant
5761 Underwood Rd.
Pasadena, TX 77507
Location Type: Plant. Ultimate Parent: Occidental Petroleum Corp. SIC: 2869—Industrial Organic Chemicals Nec.

★ 88451 ★ Payless Shoesource
336 Pasadena Town Sq.
Pasadena, TX 77506
(713)920-2654
Ultimate Parent: May Department Stores.

★ 88452 ★ Payless Shoesource
2701 Red Bluff Rd.
Pasadena, TX 77506
(713)472-2073
Ultimate Parent: May Department Stores. SIC: 5661—Shoe Stores.

★ 88453 ★ Payless Shoesource
3800 Spencer Hwy.
Pasadena, TX 77504
(713)946-4527
Ultimate Parent: May Department Stores. SIC: 5661—Shoe Stores.

★ 88454 ★ Payless Shoesource
6808 Spencer Hwy.
Pasadena, TX 77505
(713)487-6044
Ultimate Parent: May Department Stores. SIC: 5661—Shoe Stores.

★ 88455 ★ Payless Shoesource
1701 Richey St.
Pasadena, TX 77502
(713)473-2136
Ultimate Parent: May Department Stores. SIC: 5661—Shoe Stores.

★ 88456 ★ Phillips Petroleum Co.
Houston Chemical Complex
1400 Jefferson Rd.
Pasadena, TX 77506
Company Type: Division. Ultimate Parent: Phillips Petroleum. SIC: 2821—Plastics Materials & Resins; 2869—Industrial Organic Chemicals Nec.

★ 88457 ★ Pizza Hut
6918 Spencer Hwy.
Pasadena, TX 77505
(713)479-0777
Ultimate Parent: Pepsico.

★ 88458 ★ Pizza Hut
3017 Red Bluff Rd.
Pasadena, TX 77503
(713)472-8698
Ultimate Parent: Pepsico. SIC: 5812—Eating Places.

★ 88459 ★ Pizza Hut
3342 Spencer Hwy.
Pasadena, TX 77504
(713)941-5588
Ultimate Parent: Pepsico.

★ 88460 ★ Radio Shack
100 Fairmont Pky.
Pasadena, TX 77504
(713)941-2325
Company Type: Division. Ultimate Parent: Tandy Corp. SIC: 5065—Electronic Parts & Equipment Nec.

★ 88461 ★ Radio Shack
2125 Southmore Ave.
Pasadena, TX 77502
(713)473-5342
Company Type: Division. Ultimate Parent: Tandy Corp. SIC: 5065—Electronic Parts & Equipment Nec.

★ 88462 ★ Radio Shack
276 Pasadena Town Sq.
Pasadena, TX 77506
(713)475-2946
Company Type: Division. Ultimate Parent: Tandy Corp. SIC: 5065—Electronic Parts & Equipment Nec.

★ 88463 ★ Reddy Ice
409 E. Pasadena Freeway
Pasadena, TX 77506
Ultimate Parent: Southland Corp. SIC: 2097—Manufactured Ice.

★ 88464 ★ Ryder Truck Rental
901 Pasadena Fwy.
Pasadena, TX 77506
(713)473-4710
Ultimate Parent: Ryder System. SIC: 7513—Truck Rental & Leasing Without Drivers.

★ 88465 ★ Ryder Truck Rental
941 Fairmont Pky.
Pasadena, TX 77504
(713)944-4880
Ultimate Parent: Ryder System.

★ 88466 ★ Ryder Truck Rental
7333 Spencer Hwy.
Pasadena, TX 77505
(713)476-4402
Ultimate Parent: Ryder System. SIC: 7359—Equipment Rental & Leasing Nec.

★ 88467 ★ Safety Kleen Corp.
3333 Federal Rd.
Pasadena, TX 77504
(713)941-8184
Ultimate Parent: Safety-Kleen. SIC: 2842—Polishes & Sanitation Goods.

★ 88468 ★ Savings of America, A Division of Home Savings of America, FSB
817 E. Southmore Ave.
Pasadena, TX 77502
(713)473-0800
Company Type: Division. Location Type: Branch office. Ultimate Parent: H. F. Ahmanson. SIC: 6021—National Commercial Banks.

★ 88469 ★ Shell Oil
12212 Port Dr.
Pasadena, TX 77507
(713)474-9359
Ultimate Parent: Shell Oil Co.

★ 88470 ★ Taco Bell
2611 Strawberry Rd.
Pasadena, TX 77502
(713)941-3119
Ultimate Parent: Pepsico. SIC: 5812—Eating Places.

★ 88471 ★ Taco Bell
120 N. Tatar St.
Pasadena, TX 77506
(713)472-8721
Ultimate Parent: Pepsico. SIC: 5812—Eating Places.

★ 88472 ★ Taco Bell
3816 Red Bluff Rd.
Pasadena, TX 77503
(713)472-5505
Ultimate Parent: Pepsico. SIC: 5812—Eating Places.

★ 88473 ★ Taco Bell
4860 Fairmont Pky.
Pasadena, TX 77505
(713)487-1848
Ultimate Parent: Pepsico.

★ 88474 ★ Tenneco Methanol Co.
4403 LaPorte Hwy.
Pasadena, TX 77501
Ultimate Parent: Tenneco Inc. SIC: 2819—Industrial Inorganic Chemicals Nec.

★ 88475 ★ Waldenbooks
Pasadena Sq.
Pasadena, TX 77506
(713)473-4439
Ultimate Parent: K-Mart. SIC: 5942—Book Stores.

★ 88476 ★ Walgreen Drug Stores
1201 Strawberry Rd.
Pasadena, TX 77506
Ultimate Parent: Walgreen Co. SIC: 5912—Drug Stores & Proprietary Stores.

★ 88477 ★ Walgreen Drug Stores
108 Pasadena Fwy.
Pasadena, TX 77506
(713)472-1786
Ultimate Parent: Walgreen Co. SIC: 5912—Drug Stores & Proprietary Stores.

★ 88478 ★ Walgreen Drug Stores
3620 Spencer Hwy.
Pasadena, TX 77504
(713)946-1200
Ultimate Parent: Walgreen Co. SIC: 5912—Drug Stores & Proprietary Stores.

★ 88479 ★ Walgreen Drug Stores
116 Fairmont Pky.
Pasadena, TX 77504
(713)944-3891
Ultimate Parent: Walgreen Co. SIC: 5912—Drug Stores & Proprietary Stores.

Pearland

★ 88480 ★ Exxon Gas Pipe Line
988 PO Box
Pearland, TX 77588
(713)485-4334
Ultimate Parent: Exxon. SIC: 4619—Pipelines Nec.

★ 88481 ★ Kentucky Fried Chicken
2326 N. Main St.
Pearland, TX 77581
(713)485-0007
Ultimate Parent: Pepsico. SIC: 5812—Eating Places.

★ 88482 ★ Kmart Discount Stores
3265 E. Broadway St.
Pearland, TX 77581
(713)485-6923
Ultimate Parent: K-Mart.

★ 88483 ★ Kroger Company
3245 E. Broadway St.
Pearland, TX 77581
(713)485-6229
Ultimate Parent: Kroger. SIC: 5411—Grocery Stores.

★ 88484 ★ Payless Shoesource
3205 E. Broadway St.
Pearland, TX 77581
(713)485-1399
Ultimate Parent: May Department Stores. SIC: 5661—Shoe Stores.

★ 88485 ★ Pearland Lumber Co. Inc.
2027 N. Main St.
Pearland, TX 77581-3307
(713)485-1474
Officer: Larry Loeisin, President & Treasure. Ultimate Parent: Ace Hardware. SIC: 5211—Lumber & Other Building Materials; 5251—Hardware Stores. Employee Count: 25.

★ 88486 ★ Pizza Hut
2334 N. Main St.
Pearland, TX 77581
(713)485-5373
Ultimate Parent: Pepsico. SIC: 5812—Eating Places.

★ 88487 ★ Pulte Home Corp.
2718 Glendale Dr.
Pearland, TX 77584
Ultimate Parent: Pulte.

★ 88488 ★ Pulte Home Corp.
2504 Shady Bend Dr.
Pearland, TX 77581
(713)485-0006
Ultimate Parent: Pulte. SIC: 1521—Single-Family Housing Construction.

★ 88489 ★ Radio Shack
3254 E. Broadway St.
Pearland, TX 77581
(713)485-5617
Company Type: Division. Ultimate Parent: Tandy Corp. SIC: 5065—Electronic Parts & Equipment Nec.

★ 88490 ★ Wal Mart
1928 N. Main St.
Pearland, TX 77581
(713)485-0877
Ultimate Parent: Wal-Mart Stores, Inc. SIC: 5311—Department Stores.

★ 88491 ★ Walgreen Drug Stores
3235 E. Broadway St.
Pearland, TX 77581
(713)485-7796
Ultimate Parent: Walgreen Co. SIC: 5912—Drug Stores & Proprietary Stores.

Pearsall

★ 88492 ★   Pizza Hut
814 N. Oak St.
Pearsall, TX 78061
(512)334-2568
Ultimate Parent: Pepsico. SIC: 5812—
Eating Places.

Pecos

★ 88493 ★   ABF Freight Systems
Pecos, TX 79772
(915)447-2312
Ultimate Parent: Arkansas Best. SIC:
4213—Trucking Except Local.

★ 88494 ★   Exxon Products
2323 Tolivar St.
Pecos, TX 79772
(915)447-2346
Ultimate Parent: Exxon. SIC: 5171—
Petroleum Bulk Stations & Terminals.

★ 88495 ★   Kentucky Fried
Chicken
1420 S. Eddy St.
Pecos, TX 79772
(915)445-2906
Ultimate Parent: Pepsico. SIC: 5812—
Eating Places.

★ 88496 ★   Pizza Hut
524 S. Cedar St.
Pecos, TX 79772
(915)445-2929
Ultimate Parent: Pepsico. SIC: 5812—
Eating Places.

★ 88497 ★   Ryder Truck Rental
505 E. 3rd St.
Pecos, TX 79772
(915)445-2761
Ultimate Parent: Ryder System. SIC:
7359—Equipment Rental & Leasing Nec.

★ 88498 ★   Texaco Inc.
2325 Stafford
Pecos, TX 79772
(915)445-5594
Ultimate Parent: Texaco. SIC: 1389—Oil &
Gas Field Services Nec.

★ 88499 ★   Trailways Bus System
202 W. 3rd St.
Pecos, TX 79772
(915)445-5016
Ultimate Parent: Greyhound Lines Inc. SIC:
4111—Local & Suburban Transit.

Perryton

★ 88500 ★   Kentucky Fried
Chicken
1222 S. Main St.
Perryton, TX 79070
(806)435-3811
Ultimate Parent: Pepsico. SIC: 5812—
Eating Places.

★ 88501 ★   Mobil Pipe Line
Beaver Sta.
Perryton, TX 79070
(806)435-5240
Company Type: Branch. Ultimate Parent:
Mobil. SIC: 4612—Crude Petroleum
Pipelines.

★ 88502 ★   Pizza Hut
1518 S. Main St.
Perryton, TX 79070
(806)435-4061
Ultimate Parent: Pepsico. SIC: 5812—
Eating Places.

★ 88503 ★   Radio Shack
707 S. Ash St.
Perryton, TX 79070
(806)435-6862
Company Type: Division. Ultimate Parent:
Tandy Corp. SIC: 5084—Industrial
Machinery & Equipment.

★ 88504 ★   Transwestern Pipeline
Co.
1201 S. Ash St.
Perryton, TX 79070
(806)435-4068
Ultimate Parent: Enron. SIC: 1623—Water,
Sewer & Utility Lines.

Petersburg

★ 88505 ★   Burlington Northern
Railroad
Petersburg, TX 79250
(806)667-3361
Ultimate Parent: Burlington Northern. SIC:
4011—Railroads—Line-Haul Operating.

Pflugerville

★ 88506 ★   Comerica Bank-Texas
116 FM 1825
Pflugerville, TX 78660
(512)251-3454
Company Type: Subsidiary. Location
Type: Branch office. Ultimate Parent:
Comerica Bank. SIC: 6021—National
Commercial Banks.

★ 88507 ★   Mary Kay Cosmetics
13610 Long Meadow Dr.
Pflugerville, TX 78660
(512)251-3514
Ultimate Parent: Mary Kay Cosmetics. SIC:
7231—Beauty Shops.

Pharr

★ 88508 ★   Kentucky Fried
Chicken
707 W. Hwy. 83
Pharr, TX 78577
(512)787-8291
Ultimate Parent: Pepsico. SIC: 5812—
Eating Places.

★ 88509 ★   Pizza Hut
1001 W. Hwy. 83
Pharr, TX 78577
(512)787-1593
Ultimate Parent: Pepsico. SIC: 5812—
Eating Places.

★ 88510 ★   Radio Shack
920 E. Us Hwy. 83
Pharr, TX 78577
(512)781-0968
Company Type: Division. Ultimate Parent:
Tandy Corp.

★ 88511 ★   Radio Shack
El Centro Mall
Pharr, TX 78577
(512)787-7771
Company Type: Division. Ultimate Parent:
Tandy Corp. SIC: 5065—Electronic Parts &
Equipment Nec.

★ 88512 ★   Ryder Truck Rental
4800 N. Cage Blvd.
Pharr, TX 78577
(512)781-3551
Ultimate Parent: Ryder System. SIC:
7359—Equipment Rental & Leasing Nec.

★ 88513 ★   Trailways Bus System
120 E. Hwy. 83
Pharr, TX 78577
(512)787-1862
Ultimate Parent: Greyhound Lines Inc. SIC:
4111—Local & Suburban Transit.

Pilot Point

★ 88514 ★   Ace Hardware &
Lumber
104 E. Main St.
Pilot Point, TX 76258
(817)686-5330
Ultimate Parent: Ace Hardware. SIC:
5231—Paint, Glass & Wallpaper Stores.

Pineland

★ 88515 ★   Mobil Pipeline Co.
Pineland, TX 75968
(409)584-2328
Company Type: Branch. Ultimate Parent:
Mobil. SIC: 4612—Crude Petroleum
Pipelines.

★ 88516 ★   Temple-Inland Forest
Prods. Corp. Pineland Ops.
1 Denning St.
Pineland, TX 75968
Ultimate Parent: Temple-Inland. SIC:
2436—Softwood Veneer & Plywood.

Pittsburg

★ 88517 ★   Coca Cola Bottling
Co. Inc.
143 Marshall
Pittsburg, TX 75686
(214)856-2861
Ultimate Parent: Coca-Cola Enterprises.
SIC: 5149—Groceries & Related Products
Nec.

★ 88518 ★   Marshalls Department
Store
106 Quitman St.
Pittsburg, TX 75686
(214)856-2221
Ultimate Parent: Melville. SIC: 5651—
Family Clothing Stores.

★ 88519 ★   Pilgrim's Pride Corp.
110 S. Texas St.
Pittsburg, TX 75686
(903)855-1000
Company Type: Headquarters. Officer:
Lonnie A. Pilgrim. Employee Count: 10900.
Sales: 888 M. Fortune 500: Largest U.S.
Industrial Corporations: Ranking 385.

★ 88520 ★   Pilgrim's Pride Corp.
PO Box 93
Pittsburg, TX 75686
(214)856-7901
Officer: Monty Henderson, President.
Ultimate Parent: Pilgrim's Pride Corp. SIC:
2013—Sausages & Other Prepared Meats.

★ 88521 ★   Pilgrim's Pride Corp.
Pittsburg Feed Mill
110 S. Texas St.
Pittsburg, TX 75686
Company Type: Division. Ultimate Parent:
Pilgrim's Pride Corp. SIC: 2048—Prepared
Feeds Nec.

Plains

★ 88522 ★   Amerada Hess Corp.
Roswell Rd.
Plains, TX 79355
(806)456-5522
Ultimate Parent: Amerada Hess. SIC:
5171—Petroleum Bulk Stations & Terminals.

Plainview

★ 88523 ★   Adm Milling
Harvest Queen Mill & Elevator Div.
1208 N. Columbia
Plainview, TX 79072
Company Type: Division. Ultimate Parent:
Archer Daniels Midland Co. SIC: 2041—
Flour & Other Grain Mill Products.

★ 88524 ★   Adm Milling Co.
Harvest Queen Mill & Elevator Div.
1208 N. Columbia
Plainview, TX 79072
Company Type: Division. Ultimate Parent:
Archer Daniels Midland Co. SIC: 2041—
Flour & Other Grain Mill Products.

★ 88525 ★   Beneficial Texas Inc.
305 W. 7th St.
Plainview, TX 79072
(806)293-4311
Ultimate Parent: Beneficial. SIC: 6062—
State Credit Unions; 6141—Personal Credit
Institutions.

★ 88526 ★   Burlington Northern
Railroa
1121 Ash
Plainview, TX 79072
(806)296-2345
Ultimate Parent: Burlington Northern. SIC:
4011—Railroads—Line-Haul Operating.

★ 88527 ★   City National Bank
211 W. 7th St.
Plainview, TX 79072
(806)293-1311
Ultimate Parent: City National Corp. SIC:
6029—Commercial Banks Nec.

★ 88528 ★   Coca-Cola Bottling
Co. of Pl
105 Hwy. 87 Byp
Plainview, TX 79072
(806)293-4381
Ultimate Parent: Coca-Cola Enterprises.
SIC: 2086—Bottled & Canned Soft Drinks;
5046—Commercial Equipment Nec.

★ 88529 ★   Harvest Queen Mill &
Elevator Co.
1208 Columbia St.
Plainview, TX 79072-5424
(806)293-1331
Company Type: Division. Location Type:
Branch office. Officer: Gabriel Lopez,
Manager. Ultimate Parent: Archer Daniels
Midland Co. SIC: 2041—Flour & Other
Grain Mill Products; 2046—Wet Corn
Milling; 4221—Farm Product Warehousing &
Storage; 5153—Grain & Field Beans.

★ 88530 ★   Kentucky Fried
Chicken
1900 W. 5th St.
Plainview, TX 79072
(806)293-1245
Ultimate Parent: Pepsico. SIC: 5812—
Eating Places.

★ 88531 ★   Pizza Hut
2909 Olton Rd.
Plainview, TX 79072
(806)293-5334
Ultimate Parent: Pepsico. SIC: 5812—
Eating Places.

★ 88532 ★   Ring Around
Products Inc.
Dimmitt Hwy.
Plainview, TX 79072
(806)283-2676
Ultimate Parent: Occidental Petroleum
Corp. SIC: 5999—Miscellaneous Retail
Stores Nec.

★ 88533 ★   Ryder Truck Rental
416 Ash St.
Plainview, TX 79072
(806)293-8825
Ultimate Parent: Ryder System. SIC:
7359—Equipment Rental & Leasing Nec.

★ 88534 ★   Taco Bell
2910 Olton Rd.
Plainview, TX 79072
(806)296-6228
Ultimate Parent: Pepsico. SIC: 5812—
Eating Places.

★ 88535 ★   Wal Mart Discount
City
1001 N. I Hwy. 27th
Plainview, TX 79072
(806)293-4278
Ultimate Parent: Wal-Mart Stores, Inc. SIC:
5311—Department Stores.

★ 88536 ★   Wal Mart Discount
Pharmacy
1001 N. I Hwy. 27th
Plainview, TX 79072
(806)293-4219
Ultimate Parent: Wal-Mart Stores, Inc. SIC:
5912—Drug Stores & Proprietary Stores.

Plano

★ 88537 ★   Beneficial Texas
151 W. Spring Creek Pky.
Plano, TX 75023
(214)517-5284
Ultimate Parent: Beneficial.

★ 88538 ★   BFI Waste Systems
4200 14th St.
Plano, TX 75074-7102
(214)422-2341
Ultimate Parent: Browning-Ferris
Industries. SIC: 4953—Refuse Systems.

★ 88539 ★   Bowater Computer
Forms
3000 E. Plano Pky.
PO Box 869020
Plano, TX 75086-9020
(214)578-2000 Fax: (214)424-7493
Company Type: Subsidiary. Officer:
Shelley Saidman, President. Ultimate
Parent: Bowater.

★ 88540 ★   Bowater Computer
Forms Inc.
3000 E. Plano Pky.
Plano, TX 75074
(214)578-2000
Ultimate Parent: Bowater. SIC: 2761—
Manifold Business Forms.

★ 88541 ★ Burlington Coat Factory
2049 Coit Rd.
Plano, TX 75075-3701
(214)964-2628
Ultimate Parent: Burlington Industries, Equity. SIC: 5311—Department Stores; 5137—Women's/Children's Clothing.

★ 88542 ★ Butler Paper Co.
2321 Coit Rd.
Plano, TX 75075-3707
(214)596-5040
Location Type: Branch office. Ultimate Parent: Alco Standard Corp. SIC: 5113—Industrial & Personal Service Paper.

★ 88543 ★ Butler Paper Co.
2321 Coit Rd.
Plano, TX 75075-3707
(214)596-5040
Location Type: Branch office. Ultimate Parent: Alco Standard Corp. SIC: 5113—Industrial & Personal Service Paper.

★ 88544 ★ Casual Corner
1045 Collin Creek Mall
Plano, TX 75075
(214)423-3707
Ultimate Parent: United States Shoe. SIC: 5621—Women's Clothing Stores.

★ 88545 ★ Cincinnati Shoe Co.
2049 Coit Rd.
Plano, TX 75075
(214)519-0368
Ultimate Parent: United States Shoe.

★ 88546 ★ Circus World Toy Store
1004 Collin Creek Mall
Plano, TX 75075
(214)423-8353
Ultimate Parent: Melville. SIC: 5945—Hobby, Toy & Game Shops.

★ 88547 ★ Comerica Bank-Texas
3310 Premier Dr.
Plano, TX 75023-7099
(214)422-7100
Company Type: Subsidiary. Location Type: Branch office. Ultimate Parent: Comerica Bank. SIC: 6021—National Commercial Banks.

★ 88548 ★ Compass Bank-Dallas
1409 Shiloh Rd.
Plano, TX 75074-8200
(214)705-8650
Company Type: Subsidiary. Location Type: Branch office. Ultimate Parent: Compass Bancshares. SIC: 6021—National Commercial Banks.

★ 88549 ★ Compass Bank-Dallas
4901 W. Pk. Blvd.
Plano, TX 75093-5144
(214)985-6000
Company Type: Subsidiary. Location Type: Branch office. Officer: Judy Alvarado, Manager. Ultimate Parent: Compass Bancshares. SIC: 6021—National Commercial Banks.

★ 88550 ★ Compass Bank-Dallas
5501 Independence Pky.
Plano, TX 75023
(214)681-5500
Company Type: Subsidiary. Location Type: Branch office. Ultimate Parent: Compass Bancshares. SIC: 6021—National Commercial Banks.

★ 88551 ★ Compass Bank-Dallas
1201 E. 14th St.
Plano, TX 75074-6203
(214)705-4452
Company Type: Subsidiary. Location Type: Branch office. Ultimate Parent: Compass Bancshares. SIC: 6021—National Commercial Banks.

★ 88552 ★ Compass Bank-Dallas
2521 E. 14th St.
Plano, TX 75074-6526
(214)422-0440
Company Type: Subsidiary. Location Type: Branch office. Officer: Reha Bartlett, Manager. Ultimate Parent: Compass Bancshares. SIC: 6021—National Commercial Banks.

★ 88553 ★ Compass Bank-Dallas
848 Springcreek Pky.
Plano, TX 75023-4607
(214)681-5500
Company Type: Subsidiary. Location Type: Branch office. Ultimate Parent: Compass Bancshares. SIC: 6021—National Commercial Banks.

★ 88554 ★ Compass Bank-Dallas
1420 Independence Pky.
Plano, TX 75075-7543
(214)705-4400
Company Type: Subsidiary. Location Type: Branch office. Ultimate Parent: Compass Bancshares. SIC: 6021—National Commercial Banks.

★ 88555 ★ Compass Bank-Dallas
5201 W. Pk. Blvd.
Plano, TX 75093-2542
(214)964-0222
Company Type: Subsidiary. Location Type: Branch office. Officer: Judy Alvarado, Manager. Ultimate Parent: Compass Bancshares. SIC: 6021—National Commercial Banks.

★ 88556 ★ DSC Communication Corp.
1000 Coit Rd.
Plano, TX 75075-5813
(214)519-3000 Fax: (214)519-2322
Company Type: Headquarters. Officer: James L. Donald, Chairman President & CEO. Ultimate Parent: DSC Communications. Employee Count: 3300. Sales: Exceeds 500 ill M.

★ 88557 ★ DSC Communications
1000 Coit Rd.
Plano, TX 75075-5802
(214)519-3000
Company Type: Headquarters. Officer: James L. Donald. Employee Count: 4041. Sales: 730.8 M. Fortune 500: Largest U.S. Industrial Corporations: Ranking 433.

★ 88558 ★ DSC International Corp.
1000 Coio Rd.
Plano, TX 75075-5813
(214)519-3000 Fax: (214)519-2322
Company Type: Subsidiary. Officer: Frank G. Cummiskey, Chairman. Ultimate Parent: DSC Communications.

★ 88559 ★ Eds
5400 Legacy Dr.5-1g
Plano, TX 75024
(214)604-0386
Ultimate Parent: Electronic Data Systems.

★ 88560 ★ Electronic Data Systems
3865 Beaumont Ln.
Plano, TX 75023
(214)604-4443
Ultimate Parent: Electronic Data Systems.

★ 88561 ★ Electronic Data Systems
540 Legacy Dr.
Plano, TX 75024
(214)604-6000
Company Type: Headquarters. Officer: Lester M. Alberthal Jr. Fortune Service 500: Ranking 10.

★ 88562 ★ Electronic Data Systems Corp.
5400 Legacy Dr.
Plano, TX 75024
Ultimate Parent: Electronic Data Systems. SIC: 3579—Office Machines Nec; 7374—Data Processing & Preparation.

★ 88563 ★ Exxon
4001 W. Park Blvd.
Plano, TX 75093
(214)867-0247
Ultimate Parent: Exxon. SIC: 5541—Gasoline Service Stations.

★ 88564 ★ Exxon Car Care
2913 Legacy Dr.
Plano, TX 75023
(214)618-6725
Ultimate Parent: Exxon.

★ 88565 ★ Exxon Co. USA
3040 W. Parker Rd.
Plano, TX 75075
(214)596-7410
Ultimate Parent: Exxon. SIC: 5541—Gasoline Service Stations.

★ 88566 ★ Exxon Shop
5940 W. Park Blvd.
Plano, TX 75093
(214)250-6196
Ultimate Parent: Exxon.

★ 88567 ★ Farm & Home Savings Association
3115 W. Parker Rd.
Plano, TX 75023
(214)596-3535
Ultimate Parent: Farm & Home Financial Corp. SIC: 6036—Savings Institutions Except Federal.

★ 88568 ★ Foot Action
2148 Collin Creek Mall
Plano, TX 75075
(214)424-0171
Ultimate Parent: Melville. SIC: 5661—Shoe Stores.

★ 88569 ★ Frito-Lay, Inc.
7701 Legacy Dr.
Plano, TX 75024-4099
(214)334-7000 Fax: (214)353-2045
Officer: Steven S. Reinemund, President & CEO. Ultimate Parent: Pepsico.

★ 88570 ★ The Gap
2107 Collin Creek Mall
Plano, TX 75075
(214)424-0777
Ultimate Parent: GAP.

★ 88571 ★ The Gap Kids
811 N. Central Expy.
Plano, TX 75075
(214)881-9550
Ultimate Parent: GAP.

★ 88572 ★ Georgia-Pacific Corp.
1800 E. Plano Pky.
Plano, TX 75074
Ultimate Parent: Georgia-Pacific. SIC: 2653—Corrugated & Solid Fiber Boxes.

★ 88573 ★ Hit or Miss
1717 E. Spring Creek Pky.
Plano, TX 75074
(214)422-7738
Ultimate Parent: TJX.

★ 88574 ★ J.C. Penney
6501 Legacy Dr.
Plano, TX 75024
(214)431-1000
Company Type: Headquarters. Officer: William R. Howell. Employee Count: 192097. Sales: 19578 M. Fortune Service 500: Ranking 5.

★ 88575 ★ J.C. Penney Life Insurance Co.
2700 W. Plano Pky.
Plano, TX 75075
(214)881-6000 Fax: (214)881-6782
Officer: John E. Fesperman, Director, Insurance. Ultimate Parent: J.C. Penney.

★ 88576 ★ Jiffy Lube
5401 Alma Dr.
Plano, TX 75023
(214)881-7314
Ultimate Parent: Pennzoil.

★ 88577 ★ Kroger Food&Drug Store
3101 W. Parker Rd.
Plano, TX 75023
(214)596-6868
Ultimate Parent: Kroger. SIC: 5411—Grocery Stores.

★ 88578 ★ Lane Bryant
1176 Collin Creek Mall
Plano, TX 75075
(214)423-5033
Ultimate Parent: Limited. SIC: 5621—Women's Clothing Stores.

★ 88579 ★ Lerner Shop
2091 Collin Creek Mall
Plano, TX 75075
(214)423-1448
Ultimate Parent: Limited. SIC: 5621—Women's Clothing Stores.

★ 88580 ★ The Limited
2043 Collin Creek Mall
Plano, TX 75075
(214)578-9316
Ultimate Parent: Limited. SIC: 5621—Women's Clothing Stores.

★ 88581 ★ The Limited
811 N. Central Expy.
Plano, TX 75075
(214)578-1867
Ultimate Parent: Limited. SIC: 5651—Family Clothing Stores.

★ 88582 ★ The Limited Express
2075 Collin Creek Mall
Plano, TX 75075
(214)424-9742
Ultimate Parent: Limited. SIC: 5621—Women's Clothing Stores.

★ 88583 ★ Lone Star Gas Co.
1406 J Ave.
Plano, TX 75074
(214)424-8531
Ultimate Parent: Enserch. SIC: 4925—Gas Production & Distribution Nec.

★ 88584 ★ Louisiana Pacific Corp.
2729 Northcrest Dr.
Plano, TX 75075
(214)596-3204
Ultimate Parent: Louisiana-Pacific. SIC: 5031—Lumber, Plywood & Millwork.

★ 88585 ★ Luminator
1200 E. Plano Pky.
Plano, TX 75074
Ultimate Parent: Mark IV Industries. SIC: 3647—Vehicular Lighting Equipment; 3993—Signs & Advertising Displays; 3999—Manufacturing Industries Nec.

★ 88586 ★ McDonalds
1 Preston Park
Plano, TX 75093
(214)867-8887
Ultimate Parent: McDonald's. SIC: 7299—Miscellaneous Personal Services Nec.

★ 88587 ★ McDonalds of Plano
701 W. Spring Creek Pky.
Plano, TX 75023
(214)517-7095
Ultimate Parent: McDonald's.

★ 88588 ★ Mobil Oil
2000 Preston Rd.
Plano, TX 75093
(214)867-5266
Ultimate Parent: Mobil.

★ 88589 ★ Mobil Oil
3960 Legacy Dr.
Plano, TX 75023
(214)618-4395
Ultimate Parent: Mobil. SIC: 5599—Automotive Dealers Nec.

★ 88590 ★ Mobil Self Service
1129 Preston Rd.
Plano, TX 75093
(214)250-0135
Ultimate Parent: Mobil.

★ 88591 ★ Morton Salt Co.
5068 W. Plano Pky.
Plano, TX 75093
(214)380-9506
Ultimate Parent: Morton International.

★ 88592 ★ Nalco Chemical Co.
1400 Preston Rd.
Plano, TX 75093
(214)867-5156
Ultimate Parent: Nalco Chemical Co.

★ 88593 ★ Pappagallo
1900 Preston Rd.
Plano, TX 75093
(214)985-7500
Ultimate Parent: United States Shoe.

★ 88594 ★ Payless Cashways Bldg Matls
850 E. Parker Rd.
Plano, TX 75074
(214)578-0526
Ultimate Parent: Payless Cashways. SIC: 5211—Lumber & Other Building Materials.

★ 88595 ★ PepsiCo Foods International
7701 Legacy Dr.
Plano, TX 75024-4099
(214)334-7000
Ultimate Parent: Pepsico.

★ 88596 ★ **Pepsico Worldwide Foods**
7701 Legacy Dr.
Plano, TX 75024
(214)334-7000
Officer: Roger Enrico, Chairman. **Ultimate Parent:** Pepsico. **SIC:** 2099—Food Preparations Nec.

★ 88597 ★ **Phoenix Packaging**
1865 Summit Ave.
Plano, TX 75074
(214)578-0161
Ultimate Parent: Savannah Foods & Industries, Inc.

★ 88598 ★ **Pizza Hut**
1409 Shiloh Rd.
Plano, TX 75074
(214)881-8885
Ultimate Parent: Pepsico.

★ 88599 ★ **Pizza Hut**
2600 14th St.
Plano, TX 75074
(214)422-7772
Ultimate Parent: Pepsico. **SIC:** 5812—Eating Places.

★ 88600 ★ **Pizza Hut**
1600 Independence Pky.
Plano, TX 75075
(214)596-5606
Ultimate Parent: Pepsico. **SIC:** 5812—Eating Places.

★ 88601 ★ **Radio Shack**
4909 W. Park Blvd.
Plano, TX 75093
(214)985-1773
Company Type: Division. **Ultimate Parent:** Tandy Corp.

★ 88602 ★ **Radio Shack**
1834 K Ave.
Plano, TX 75074
(214)424-1789
Company Type: Division. **Ultimate Parent:** Tandy Corp. **SIC:** 5065—Electronic Parts & Equipment Nec.

★ 88603 ★ **Radio Shack**
Spring
Plano, TX 75074
(214)423-9113
Company Type: Division. **Ultimate Parent:** Tandy Corp. **SIC:** 5065—Electronic Parts & Equipment Nec.

★ 88604 ★ **Radio Shack**
Collin Creek Mall
Plano, TX 75075
(214)424-2511
Company Type: Division. **Ultimate Parent:** Tandy Corp. **SIC:** 5065—Electronic Parts & Equipment Nec.

★ 88605 ★ **Ryder Truck Rental**
1518 N. Central Expy.
Plano, TX 75074
(214)422-1089
Ultimate Parent: Ryder System. **SIC:** 7513—Truck Rental & Leasing Without Drivers.

★ 88606 ★ **Safeco Insurance Co. of America**
869012 PO Box
Plano, TX 75086
Ultimate Parent: Safeco. **SIC:** 6411—Insurance Agents, Brokers & Service.

★ 88607 ★ **Savings of America, A Division of Home Savings of America, FSB**
3041 W. Parker Rd.
Plano, TX 75023
(214)985-7939
Company Type: Division. **Location Type:** Branch office. **Ultimate Parent:** H. F. Ahmanson. **SIC:** 6021—National Commercial Banks.

★ 88608 ★ **Simco Co. Inc.**
3401 Custer Rd.
Plano, TX 75023
(214)867-5500
Ultimate Parent: Illinois Tool Works.

★ 88609 ★ **T J Maxx Dept Stor**
1717 E. Spring Creek Pky.
Plano, TX 75074
(214)578-1539
Ultimate Parent: TJX.

★ 88610 ★ **Taco Bell**
150 W. Parker Rd.
Plano, TX 75075
(214)423-0036
Ultimate Parent: Pepsico.

★ 88611 ★ **Target Stores**
4817 W. Park Blvd.
Plano, TX 75093
(214)596-8499
Company Type: Subsidiary. **Ultimate Parent:** Dayton Hudson.

★ 88612 ★ **Target Stores**
120 W. Parker Rd.
Plano, TX 75075
(214)424-9575
Company Type: Subsidiary. **Ultimate Parent:** Dayton Hudson. **SIC:** 5311—Department Stores.

★ 88613 ★ **Texaco Food Mart**
6925 Independence Pky.
Plano, TX 75023
(214)618-2877
Ultimate Parent: Texaco.

★ 88614 ★ **Texaco Food Mart**
4001 W. Parker Rd.
Plano, TX 75093
(214)867-3260
Ultimate Parent: Texaco.

★ 88615 ★ **US Clinical Products, Inc.**
PO Box 940129
2552 Summit Ave., Ste. 406
Plano, TX 75094-0129
(214)424-6268
Company Type: Subsidiary. **Officer:** C.E. Hart, President. **Ultimate Parent:** American Home Products. **SIC:** 2834—Pharmaceutical Preparations.

★ 88616 ★ **Victoria's Secret**
811 N. Central Expy.
Plano, TX 75075
(214)423-6299
Ultimate Parent: Limited.

★ 88617 ★ **Wal Mart Discount**
1300 Custer Rd.
Plano, TX 75075
(214)422-9926
Ultimate Parent: Wal-Mart Stores, Inc.

★ 88618 ★ **Waldenbooks**
Collin Creek Mall
Plano, TX 75075
(214)423-2429
Ultimate Parent: K-Mart. **SIC:** 5942—Book Stores.

★ 88619 ★ **Waldenbooks & More**
1900 Preston Rd.
Plano, TX 75093
(214)867-2644
Ultimate Parent: K-Mart.

Plantersville

★ 88620 ★ **Arco Pipe Line Co.**
F M Rd. 1774
Plantersville, TX 77363
(409)894-2321
Ultimate Parent: Atlantic Richfield Co., Inc. **SIC:** 4612—Crude Petroleum Pipelines.

Pleasanton

★ 88621 ★ **Golden Peanut Co.**
704 2nd St.
Pleasanton, TX 78064-3104
(210)569-8794
Ultimate Parent: Archer Daniels Midland Co. **SIC:** 5159—Farm-Product Raw Materials Nec.

★ 88622 ★ **Pizza Hut**
615 2nd St.
Pleasanton, TX 78064
(512)569-3189
Ultimate Parent: Pepsico. **SIC:** 5812—Eating Places.

Point Comfort

★ 88623 ★ **Aluminum Co. of America**
US Hwy. 35
Point Comfort, TX 77978-9998
(512)987-2631
Location Type: Branch office. **Officer:** J.E.

Vasquez. **Ultimate Parent:** Aluminum Co. of America–Alcoa. **SIC:** 2819—Industrial Inorganic Chemicals Nec.

★ 88624 ★ **Aluminum Co. of America**
US Hwy. 35
Point Comfort, TX 77978-9998
(512)987-2631
Location Type: Branch office. **Officer:** J.E. Vasquez. **Ultimate Parent:** Aluminum Co. of America–Alcoa. **SIC:** 2819—Industrial Inorganic Chemicals Nec.

★ 88625 ★ **Aluminum Co. of America**
Alcoa Site
Point Comfort, TX 77978
(512)987-2631
Ultimate Parent: Aluminum Co. of America-Alcoa. **SIC:** 5051—Metals Service Centers & Offices.

Pollok

★ 88626 ★ **Coast to Coast Shops**
Hwy. 69 N
Pollok, TX 75969
(409)853-2218
Ultimate Parent: Servistar Corp. **SIC:** 7538—General Automotive Repair Shops.

Port Arthur

★ 88627 ★ **Bethlehem Steel Beth-Ship**
Hwy. 82
Port Arthur, TX 77641
(409)985-0571
Officer: M. L. White. **Ultimate Parent:** Bethlehem Steel Corp. **SIC:** 3731—Ship Building & Repairing.

★ 88628 ★ **Bethlehem Steel Corp.**
Sabine Yard
2500 Martin Luther King Dr.
Port Arthur, TX 77641
Ultimate Parent: Bethlehem Steel Corp. **SIC:** 3731—Ship Building & Repairing.

★ 88629 ★ **Casual Corner**
3100 Central Mall Dr.
Port Arthur, TX 77642
(409)724-1034
Ultimate Parent: United States Shoe. **SIC:** 5651—Family Clothing Stores.

★ 88630 ★ **Chevron USA Inc.**
Port Arthur Refinery
End of W. 7th St.
Port Arthur, TX 77640
Ultimate Parent: Chevron Corp. **SIC:** 2911—Petroleum Refining.

★ 88631 ★ **Chevron USA Products Co. Port Arthur Refinery**
End of W. 7th St.
Port Arthur, TX 77641
Ultimate Parent: Chevron Corp. **SIC:** 2911—Petroleum Refining.

★ 88632 ★ **Greyhound Bus Lines**
2737 Memorial Blvd.
Port Arthur, TX 77640
(409)985-4356
Ultimate Parent: Greyhound Lines Inc. **SIC:** 4131—Intercity & Rural Bus Transportation.

★ 88633 ★ **Kentucky Fried Chicken**
3749 N. Twin City Hwy.
Port Arthur, TX 77642
(409)962-4323
Ultimate Parent: Pepsico. **SIC:** 5812—Eating Places.

★ 88634 ★ **Lane Bryant**
3100 Central Mall Dr.
Port Arthur, TX 77642
(409)724-6297
Ultimate Parent: Limited. **SIC:** 5651—Family Clothing Stores.

★ 88635 ★ **Lerner Shop**
3100 Central Mall Dr.
Port Arthur, TX 77642
(409)727-1816
Ultimate Parent: Limited. **SIC:** 5651—Family Clothing Stores.

★ 88636 ★ **Lubrizol Corp**
4801 53rd St.
Port Arthur, TX 77642
(409)963-1111
Ultimate Parent: Lubrizol. **SIC:** 3861—Photographic Equipment & Supplies.

★ 88637 ★ **Mary Kay Cosmetics**
244 Mills Ave.
Port Arthur, TX 77642
(409)962-0905
Ultimate Parent: Mary Kay Cosmetics. **SIC:** 5999—Miscellaneous Retail Stores Nec.

★ 88638 ★ **Mini Mart No 2**
3453 25th St.
Port Arthur, TX 77642
(409)983-4061
Ultimate Parent: Kroger. **SIC:** 5411—Grocery Stores.

★ 88639 ★ **Mobil Mart No 3**
8196 9th Ave.
Port Arthur, TX 77642
(409)727-3334
Ultimate Parent: Mobil. **SIC:** 5411—Grocery Stores.

★ 88640 ★ **North End Houston Avenue**
Port Arthur
Port Arthur, TX 77640
Ultimate Parent: Texaco. **SIC:** 2911—Petroleum Refining.

★ 88641 ★ **Park Place Hospital**
3050 39th St.
Port Arthur, TX 77642
(409)983-4951
Officer: Luis Silva, Executive Director. **Ultimate Parent:** American Medical Holdings. **SIC:** 8062—General Medical & Surgical Hospitals.

★ 88642 ★ **Pizza Hut**
7849 N. Twin City Hwy.
Port Arthur, TX 77642
(409)727-6024
Ultimate Parent: Pepsico. **SIC:** 5812—Eating Places.

★ 88643 ★ **Pizza Hut**
5250 Gulfway Dr.
Port Arthur, TX 77642
(409)985-2513
Ultimate Parent: Pepsico. **SIC:** 5812—Eating Places.

★ 88644 ★ **Radio Shack**
3701 N. Twin City Hwy.
Port Arthur, TX 77642
(409)963-1129
Company Type: Division. **Ultimate Parent:** Tandy Corp. **SIC:** 5731—Radio, Television & Electronics Stores.

★ 88645 ★ **Radio Shack**
3100 Central Mall Dr.
Port Arthur, TX 77642
(409)963-7099
Company Type: Division. **Ultimate Parent:** Tandy Corp. **SIC:** 5065—Electronic Parts & Equipment Nec.

★ 88646 ★ **Taco Bell**
3966 Gulfway Dr.
Port Arthur, TX 77642
(409)983-1979
Ultimate Parent: Pepsico. **SIC:** 5812—Eating Places.

★ 88647 ★ **Texaco Chemical Co.**
Port Arthur Chemical Plant
Gate 22 Savannah Ave.
Port Arthur, TX 77641
Location Type: Plant. **Ultimate Parent:** Texaco. **SIC:** 2869—Industrial Organic Chemicals Nec; 2865—Cyclic Crudes & Intermediates; 2819—Industrial Inorganic Chemicals Nec.

★ 88648 ★ **Texaco Express Lub**
5221 N. Twin City Hwy.
Port Arthur, TX 77642
(409)963-2860
Ultimate Parent: Texaco.

★ 88649 ★ **Texaco Inc.**
401 W. 19th St.
Port Arthur, TX 77640
(409)982-6406
Ultimate Parent: Texaco. **SIC:** 4449—Water Transportation of Freight Nec.

★ 88650 ★ Texaco Inc. Research & Development
4545 Savannah Ave.
Port Arthur, TX 77640
Ultimate Parent: Texaco. SIC: 2911—Petroleum Refining; 2992—Lubricating Oils & Greases; 2899—Chemical Preparations Nec.

★ 88651 ★ Texaco P a W Employees Fede
4401 Hwy. 73
Port Arthur, TX 77642
(409)962-8793
Ultimate Parent: Texaco. SIC: 6062—State Credit Unions.

★ 88652 ★ Texaco Port Arthur Research Laboratories
Savannah Ave. & Hwy. 73
Port Arthur, TX 77641
Ultimate Parent: Texaco. SIC: 2911—Petroleum Refining; 2992—Lubricating Oils & Greases; 2899—Chemical Preparations Nec.

★ 88653 ★ Texaco Ref. & Mktg. Inc. Port Arthur Plant
North End Houston Ave.
Port Arthur, TX 77640
Ultimate Parent: Texaco. SIC: 2911—Petroleum Refining.

★ 88654 ★ Texaco Ref. & Mktg. Inc. Port Arthur Terminal
Texaco Island West End of 7th St.
Port Arthur, TX 77640
Ultimate Parent: Texaco. SIC: 5171—Petroleum Bulk Stations & Terminals.

★ 88655 ★ Texaco Refining & Marketing Inc. Pap
North End of Houston Ave.
Port Arthur, TX 77641-0712
Ultimate Parent: Texaco. SIC: 2911—Petroleum Refining.

★ 88656 ★ Texaco Refining & Marketing Inc. Pat
Texaco Island West of 7th St.
Port Arthur, TX 77640
Ultimate Parent: Texaco. SIC: 5171—Petroleum Bulk Stations & Terminals.

★ 88657 ★ Wal Mart Tire
6701 Gulfway
Port Arthur, TX 77642
(409)962-3553
Ultimate Parent: Wal-Mart Stores, Inc. SIC: 7538—General Automotive Repair Shops.

★ 88658 ★ Waldenbooks
3100 Central Mall St.
Port Arthur, TX 77642
(409)727-4933
Ultimate Parent: K-Mart. SIC: 5942—Book Stores.

★ 88659 ★ Walgreen Drug Stores
435 Procter St.
Port Arthur, TX 77640
(409)983-2021
Ultimate Parent: Walgreen Co. SIC: 5912—Drug Stores & Proprietary Stores.

★ 88660 ★ Walgreen Drug Stores
8797 9th Ave.
Port Arthur, TX 77642
(409)724-1912
Ultimate Parent: Walgreen Co. SIC: 5912—Drug Stores & Proprietary Stores.

★ 88661 ★ Walgreen Drug Stores
3501 N. Twin City Hwy.
Port Arthur, TX 77642
(409)962-1313
Ultimate Parent: Walgreen Co. SIC: 5912—Drug Stores & Proprietary Stores.

Port Isabel

★ 88662 ★ Pizza Hut
1905 Padre Blvd.
Port Isabel, TX 78597
(512)761-1361
Ultimate Parent: Pepsico.

★ 88663 ★ Pizza Hut
1202 State Hwy. 100
Port Isabel, TX 78578
Ultimate Parent: Pepsico.

★ 88664 ★ Radio Shack
1710 Hwy. 100
Port Isabel, TX 78578
(512)943-7121
Company Type: Division. Ultimate Parent: Tandy Corp. SIC: 5731—Radio, Television & Electronics Stores.

★ 88665 ★ Ryder Truck Rental
Hwy. 100
Port Isabel, TX 78578
(512)943-9407
Ultimate Parent: Ryder System. SIC: 7359—Equipment Rental & Leasing Nec.

Port Lavaca

★ 88666 ★ First State Bank & Trust Co.
311 N. Virginia
Port Lavaca, TX 77979-3495
(512)552-9771 Fax: (512)552-8937
Location Type: Branch office. Ultimate Parent: Michigan National Corp. SIC: 6021—National Commercial Banks.

★ 88667 ★ First State Bank & Trust Co.
PO Box 228
Port Lavaca, TX 77979-0228
Location Type: Branch office. Ultimate Parent: Michigan National Corp. SIC: 6021—National Commercial Banks.

★ 88668 ★ Mobil Exploration & Producing US Inc.
Port Lavaca, TX 77979
(512)284-7400
Ultimate Parent: Mobil. SIC: 1311—Crude Petroleum & Natural Gas.

★ 88669 ★ Pizza Hut
425 N. Hwy. 35
Port Lavaca, TX 77979
(512)552-6868
Ultimate Parent: Pepsico. SIC: 5812—Eating Places.

★ 88670 ★ Seadrift Plant
PO Box 186
Port Lavaca, TX 77979
Ultimate Parent: Union Carbide Corp. SIC: 2869—Industrial Organic Chemicals Nec.

★ 88671 ★ Union Carbide Chemicals Plastics Co. Seadrift Plant
PO Box 186
Port Lavaca, TX 77979
Ultimate Parent: Union Carbide Corp. SIC: 2869—Industrial Organic Chemicals Nec.

★ 88672 ★ Union Carbide Chemicals Plastics Inc. Seadrift Plant
PO Box 186
Port Lavaca, TX 77979
Ultimate Parent: Union Carbide Corp. SIC: 2869—Industrial Organic Chemicals Nec.

Port Neches

★ 88673 ★ Gulf States Utilities Co.
2645 Nall St.
Port Neches, TX 77651
(409)722-0222
Ultimate Parent: Gulf State Utilities Co. SIC: 4911—Electric Services.

★ 88674 ★ Mobil Mart No 2
1309 Magnolia Ave.
Port Neches, TX 77651
(409)727-8198
Ultimate Parent: Mobil. SIC: 5541—Gasoline Service Stations.

★ 88675 ★ Mobil Oil Co. Terminal
PT Neches
Port Neches, TX 77651
(409)722-1968
Ultimate Parent: Mobil. SIC: 2911—Petroleum Refining.

★ 88676 ★ Texaco Chemical Co.
Hwy. 366 & Hogaboom Rd.
Port Neches, TX 77651
Ultimate Parent: Texaco. SIC: 2869—Industrial Organic Chemicals Nec.

★ 88677 ★ Texaco Inc.
Grisby
Port Neches, TX 77651
(409)722-4331
Ultimate Parent: Texaco. SIC: 2911—Petroleum Refining.

★ 88678 ★ Texaco Ref. & Mktg. Inc. Port Arthur Asphalt
Corner Spur 136 & Grigsby Dr.
Port Neches, TX 77651
Ultimate Parent: Texaco. SIC: 2911—Petroleum Refining.

★ 88679 ★ Texaco Refining & Marketing Inc. Paac
Corner Spur 136 & Grigsby Dr.
Port Neches, TX 77651
Ultimate Parent: Texaco. SIC: 2911—Petroleum Refining.

★ 88680 ★ Wal Mart Discount Pharmacy
2004 Fm Hwy. 365
Port Neches, TX 77651
(409)724-0054
Ultimate Parent: Wal-Mart Stores, Inc. SIC: 5912—Drug Stores & Proprietary Stores.

Porter

★ 88681 ★ McDonalds of Porter
103 Farm Rd. 1314
Porter, TX 77365
(713)354-4090
Ultimate Parent: May Department Stores.

★ 88682 ★ Pizza Hut
857 Fm 1314 Rd.
Porter, TX 77365
(713)354-5100
Ultimate Parent: Pepsico. SIC: 5812—Eating Places.

★ 88683 ★ Radio Shack
14 Porter Ln.
Porter, TX 77365
(713)354-3866
Company Type: Division. Ultimate Parent: Tandy Corp. SIC: 5734—Computer & Software Stores.

★ 88684 ★ Wal Mart Discount City
Hwy. 59
Porter, TX 77365
(713)354-5166
Ultimate Parent: Wal-Mart Stores, Inc. SIC: 5311—Department Stores.

★ 88685 ★ Wal Mart Pharmacy
33285 Hwy. 59
Porter, TX 77365
(713)354-5125
Ultimate Parent: Wal-Mart Stores, Inc.

Portland

★ 88686 ★ Beneficial Texas Inc.
410 W. Hwy. 181
Portland, TX 78374
(512)643-4565
Ultimate Parent: Beneficial. SIC: 6141—Personal Credit Institutions.

★ 88687 ★ Exxon Co. USA
206 Us 181 W
Portland, TX 78374
(512)643-9974
Ultimate Parent: Exxon.

★ 88688 ★ Jiffy Lube
1306 Wildcat Dr.
Portland, TX 78374
(512)643-4658
Ultimate Parent: Pennzoil.

★ 88689 ★ Kentucky Fried Chicken
1304 Wildcat Dr.
Portland, TX 78374
(512)643-3000
Ultimate Parent: Pepsico. SIC: 5812—Eating Places.

★ 88690 ★ Payless Shoesource
1522 Wilcat Dr.
Portland, TX 78374
(512)643-1410
Ultimate Parent: May Department Stores. SIC: 5661—Shoe Stores.

★ 88691 ★ Payless Shoesource No. 2132
1522 Wildcat Dr.
Portland, TX 78374
(512)643-1490
Ultimate Parent: May Department Stores. SIC: 5661—Shoe Stores.

★ 88692 ★ Pennzoil Exploration
1037 W. Us Hwy. 181
Portland, TX 78374
(512)643-4561
Ultimate Parent: Pennzoil.

★ 88693 ★ Pizza Hut
1003 Wildcat Dr.
Portland, TX 78374
(512)643-7544
Ultimate Parent: Pepsico. SIC: 5812—Eating Places.

★ 88694 ★ Ryder Truck Rental
809 Market St.
Portland, TX 78374
(512)643-2330
Ultimate Parent: Ryder System. SIC: 7359—Equipment Rental & Leasing Nec.

★ 88695 ★ Texaco Self Serv
1000 Us 181
Portland, TX 78374
(512)643-3304
Ultimate Parent: Texaco. SIC: 5541—Gasoline Service Stations.

Poynor

★ 88696 ★ Exxon
Poynor, TX 75782
(903)876-2201
Ultimate Parent: Exxon. SIC: 5541—Gasoline Service Stations.

★ 88697 ★ Mobil Pipe Line Co.
Poynor
Poynor, TX 75782
(903)876-2831
Ultimate Parent: Mobil. SIC: 4612—Crude Petroleum Pipelines.

Premont

★ 88698 ★ Mobil Exploration & Producing Inc.
Premont, TX 78375
(512)348-3585
Officer: A. H. Hunter. Ultimate Parent: Mobil. SIC: 1311—Crude Petroleum & Natural Gas.

★ 88699 ★ Oryx Energy Co.
668th
Premont, TX 78375
(512)348-3582
Ultimate Parent: Oryx Energy.

Quanah

★ 88700 ★ Pizza Hut
334 PO Box
Quanah, TX 79252
(817)663-2402
Ultimate Parent: Pepsico. SIC: 5812—Eating Places.

★ 88701 ★ Southern Cotton Oil Co. Inc.
600 E. Nelson St.
Quanah, TX 79252
(817)663-5323
Officer: Robert R. Riggs, Manager. Ultimate Parent: Archer Daniels Midland Co. SIC: 2048—Prepared Feeds Nec; 2074—Cottonseed Oil Mills; 2076—Vegetable Oil Mills Nec.

★ 88702 ★ West Texas Utilities Co.
223 Main St.
Quanah, TX 79252
(817)663-5346
Ultimate Parent: Central & South West. SIC: 5722—Household Appliance Stores.

Quann

★ 88703 ★   Southern Cotton Oil Co.
PO Box 180
Quann, TX 79252-0180
(817)663-5323
Officer: Robert R. Riggs. Ultimate Parent: Archer Daniels Midland Co. SIC: 2048—Prepared Feeds Nec; 2074—Cottonseed Oil Mills; 5083—Farm & Garden Machinery; 5131—Piece Goods & Notions; 5999—Miscellaneous Retail Stores Nec.

Quitman

★ 88704 ★   Mobil Pipe Line Co.
Quitman, TX 75783
(903)878-2912
Ultimate Parent: Mobil. SIC: 4612—Crude Petroleum Pipelines.

★ 88705 ★   Union Carbide Industrial Gases Inc.
Linde Div.
Hwy. 37 5 Miles NE of Quitman
Quitman, TX 75783
Company Type: Division. Ultimate Parent: Union Carbide Corp. SIC: 2813—Industrial Gases.

Ranger

★ 88706 ★   GE Capital Railcar Service
Tiffin Rd.
Ranger, TX 76470
(817)647-3223
Officer: Rudy Espinoza, Manager. Ultimate Parent: General Electric. SIC: 3743—Railroad Equipment.

Raymondville

★ 88707 ★   McDonalds Restaurant
1105 E. State Hwy. 186
Raymondville, TX 78580
(512)689-5546
Ultimate Parent: McDonald's.

★ 88708 ★   Pizza Hut
501 E. Hidalgo Ave.
Raymondville, TX 78580
(512)689-5564
Ultimate Parent: Pepsico. SIC: 5812—Eating Places.

★ 88709 ★   Rio Grande Valley Gas Co.
471 W. Main Ave.
Raymondville, TX 78580
(512)689-2436
Ultimate Parent: Valero Energy Corp. SIC: 4925—Gas Production & Distribution Nec.

★ 88710 ★   Ryder Truck Rental
905 S. 7th St.
Raymondville, TX 78580
(512)689-3054
Ultimate Parent: Ryder System. SIC: 7513—Truck Rental & Leasing Without Drivers.

Raywood

★ 88711 ★   Texaco Svc Ctr
603 PO Box
Raywood, TX 77582
Ultimate Parent: Texaco.

Red Oak

★ 88712 ★   Ryder Truck Rental
501 N. Hwy. 342
Red Oak, TX 75154
(214)576-0053
Ultimate Parent: Ryder System. SIC: 7513—Truck Rental & Leasing Without Drivers.

Refugia

★ 88713 ★   Exxon Co. USA Production
Greta
Refugia, TX 78377
(512)526-4122
Officer: J. D. Yeary, Manager. Ultimate Parent: Exxon SIC: 2911—Petroleum Refining.

Refugio

★ 88714 ★   Arco Pipe Line Co.
Austwell Rd.
Refugio, TX 78377
(512)526-4666
Location Type: Branch office. Ultimate Parent: Atlantic Richfield Co., Inc. SIC: 4612—Crude Petroleum Pipelines.

★ 88715 ★   Exxon Co. USA
Greta
Refugio, TX 78377
(512)526-2994
Ultimate Parent: Exxon. SIC: 2911—Petroleum Refining.

★ 88716 ★   Lone Star Gas Co.
Old Beeville Rd.
Refugio, TX 78377
(512)526-4612
Ultimate Parent: Enserch. SIC: 4925—Gas Production & Distribution Nec.

★ 88717 ★   Pennzoil Producing Co.
100 1st St.
Refugio, TX 78377
(512)526-2308
Ultimate Parent: Pennzoil. SIC: 5171—Petroleum Bulk Stations & Terminals.

★ 88718 ★   Pizza Hut
208 N. Alamo St.
Refugio, TX 78377
(512)526-4601
Ultimate Parent: Pepsico.

★ 88719 ★   Trailways Inc.
706 Commerce St.
Refugio, TX 78377
(512)526-4890
Ultimate Parent: Greyhound Lines Inc. SIC: 4131—Intercity & Rural Bus Transportation.

Richardson

★ 88720 ★   American Cyanamid Co.
650 N. Glenville Dr.
Richardson, TX 75081-2832
(214)235-4658
Location Type: Branch office. Ultimate Parent: American Cyanamid Co. SIC: 5169—Chemicals & Allied Products Nec.

★ 88721 ★   Avery Dennison Corp.
333 W. Campbell Rd.
Richardson, TX 75080-3623
(214)918-0290
Ultimate Parent: Avery Dennison Corp. SIC: 5085—Industrial Supplies.

★ 88722 ★   Avery Dennison Corp.
333 W. Campbell Rd.
Richardson, TX 75080-3623
(214)918-0290
Ultimate Parent: Avery Dennison Corp. SIC: 5085—Industrial Supplies.

★ 88723 ★   Bowater Computer Forms
2350 Lakeside Blvd., Ste. 850
Richardson, TX 75082-4342
Officer: Gary Newell. Ultimate Parent: Bowater. SIC: 5045—Computers, Peripherals & Software; 7371—Computer Programming Services.

★ 88724 ★   Business Systems Tech. Inc.
885 E. Collins Blvd.
Richardson, TX 75081-2251
(214)783-1326
Ultimate Parent: Avery Dennison Corp. SIC: 7374—Data Processing & Preparation.

★ 88725 ★   Business Systems Technology Inc.
885 E. Collins Blvd.
Richardson, TX 75081-2251
(214)783-1326
Ultimate Parent: Avery Dennison Corp. SIC: 7374—Data Processing & Preparation.

★ 88726 ★   Casual Corner
Richardson Sq.
Richardson, TX 75081
(214)234-5862
Ultimate Parent: United States Shoe. SIC: 5621—Women's Clothing Stores.

★ 88727 ★   Circus World Toy Stores
501 S. Plano Rd.
Richardson, TX 75081
(214)783-7003
Ultimate Parent: Melville. SIC: 5945—Hobby, Toy & Game Shops.

★ 88728 ★   Comerica Bank-Texas
801 E. Campbell Rd.
Richardson, TX 75801-4110
(214)818-2353
Company Type: Subsidiary. Location Type: Branch office. Ultimate Parent: Comerica Bank. SIC: 6021—National Commercial Banks.

★ 88729 ★   Comerica Bank-Texas
811 S. Central Expy.
Richardson, TX 75080-7415
(214)997-9900
Company Type: Subsidiary. Location Type: Branch office. Ultimate Parent: Comerica Bank. SIC: 6021—National Commercial Banks.

★ 88730 ★   Comerica Bank-Texas
12014 E. Belt Line Rd.
Richardson, TX 75081
(214)828-5812
Company Type: Subsidiary. Location Type: Branch office. Ultimate Parent: Comerica Bank. SIC: 6021—National Commercial Banks.

★ 88731 ★   Compass Bank
1500 Promenade Ctr.
Richardson, TX 75080
(214)705-4200
Company Type: Subsidiary. Officer: Eugene Weimer, Vice Chairman. Ultimate Parent: Compass Bancshares. SIC: 6022—State Commercial Banks. Employee Count: 38.

★ 88732 ★   Compass Bank-Dallas
1600 Promenade Ctr.
Richardson, TX 75080-5400
(214)705-4200
Company Type: Subsidiary. Location Type: Branch office. Ultimate Parent: Compass Bancshares. SIC: 6021—National Commercial Banks.

★ 88733 ★   Eds
1800 Jay Drive
Richardson, TX 75081
(214)470-5053
Ultimate Parent: Electronic Data Systems.

★ 88734 ★   Electrospace Systems inc.
1301 E. Collins Blvd.
Richardson, TX 75081-2404
(214)470-2000
Company Type: Subsidiary. Officer: Paul Wright, Chairman of the Board. Ultimate Parent: Chrysler Corp. SIC: 3663—Radio & T.V. Communications Equipment; 3661—Telephone & Telegraph Apparatus. Employee Count: 900. Sales: 133 M.

★ 88735 ★   Exxon
940 N. Central Expy.
Richardson, TX 75080
(214)234-3752
Ultimate Parent: Exxon. SIC: 5541—Gasoline Service Stations.

★ 88736 ★   Greyhound Bus Lines
400 N. Greenville Ave.
Richardson, TX 75081
(214)231-1763
Ultimate Parent: Greyhound Lines Inc. SIC: 4111—Local & Suburban Transit.

★ 88737 ★   Hanover Lloyd's Insurance Co.
801 E. Campbell Rd.
Richardson, TX 75081
(214)680-3399
Company Type: Subsidiary. Officer: Stephen Williams, General Manager. Ultimate Parent: Allmerica Property & Casualty Companies Inc. SIC: 6331—Fire, Marine & Casualty Insurance. Sales: 3.3 M.

★ 88738 ★   Hanover Texas Insurance Management Co., Inc.
801 E. Campbell Rd.
Richardson, TX 75081
Company Type: Subsidiary. Ultimate Parent: Allmerica Property & Casualty Companies Inc.

★ 88739 ★   Honeywell Inc. Optoelectronics
830 E. Arapaho Rd.
Richardson, TX 75081
Ultimate Parent: Honeywell. SIC: 3674—Semiconductors & Related Devices.

★ 88740 ★   Honeywell Optoelectronics
830 E. Arapaho Rd.
Richardson, TX 75081
Ultimate Parent: Honeywell. SIC: 3674—Semiconductors & Related Devices.

★ 88741 ★   IDS Financial Services
801 E. Campbell Rd., Ste. 250
Richardson, TX 75801-1866
(214)437-9311
Location Type: Branch office. Officer: Allen Gibson. Ultimate Parent: American Express Co. SIC: 6211—Security Brokers & Dealers; 6141—Personal Credit Institutions; 6282—Investment Advice.

★ 88742 ★   Itt Life Insurance Corp.
777 N. Central Expy.
Richardson, TX 75080
(214)699-0121
Ultimate Parent: ITT. SIC: 6411—Insurance Agents, Brokers & Service.

★ 88743 ★   Jiffy Lube
890 W. Arapaho Rd.
Richardson, TX 75080
(214)235-2543
Ultimate Parent: Pennzoil. SIC: 5541—Gasoline Service Stations.

★ 88744 ★   Jiffy Lube
687 W. Campbell Rd.
Richardson, TX 75080
(214)234-8738
Ultimate Parent: Pennzoil.

★ 88745 ★   Kroger Financial Centers
1750 E. Belt Line Rd.
Richardson, TX 75081
(214)234-0246
Ultimate Parent: Kroger. SIC: 6411—Insurance Agents, Brokers & Service.

★ 88746 ★   Kroger Food&Drug
1400 W. Spring Valley Rd.
Richardson, TX 75080
(214)231-2739
Ultimate Parent: Kroger. SIC: 5411—Grocery Stores.

★ 88747 ★   Kroger Stores
1750 E. Belt Line Rd.
Richardson, TX 75081
(214)690-0120
Ultimate Parent: Kroger.

★ 88748 ★   The Limited
501 S. Plano Rd.
Richardson, TX 75081
(214)234-8506
Ultimate Parent: Limited. SIC: 5621—Women's Clothing Stores.

★ 88749 ★   McDonalds Restaurant
2041 N. Central Expy.
Richardson, TX 75080
(214)690-9821
Ultimate Parent: McDonald's. SIC: 5812—Eating Places.

★ 88750 ★   Mcduff Electronics
501 S. Plano Rd.
Richardson, TX 75081
(214)783-1545
Ultimate Parent: Tandy Corp.

★ 88751 ★   Mobil Oil Corp.
1436 W. Spring Valley Rd.
Richardson, TX 75080
(214)234-6631
Ultimate Parent: Mobil.

★ 88752 ★   Ncr Corp.
1201 Richardson Dr.
Richardson, TX 75080
(214)783-2313
Ultimate Parent: AT&T.

★ 88753 ★ **Payless Cashways Bldg Matl**
4803 Belt Line Rd.
Richardson, TX 75080
(214)233-1096
Ultimate Parent: Payless Cashways. **SIC:** 5211—Lumber & Other Building Materials.

★ 88754 ★ **Payless Shoesource**
501 S. Plano Rd.
Richardson, TX 75081
(214)783-4541
Ultimate Parent: May Department Stores.

★ 88755 ★ **Pentastar Support Services Inc.**
1301 E. Collins Blvd.
Richardson, TX 75081-2404
(214)470-2000
Company Type: Subsidiary. **Officer:** Michael D. McAnally, President. **Ultimate Parent:** Chrysler Corp. **SIC:** 8711—Engineering Services. **Employee Count:** 150. **Sales:** 6 M.

★ 88756 ★ **Phillips Coal Co.**
2929 N. Central Expwy., Ste. 200
Richardson, TX 75080
(214)669-1200 **Fax:** (214)669-5900
Ultimate Parent: Phillips Petroleum.

★ 88757 ★ **Phillips Driscopipe Inc.**
2929 N. Central Expwy., Ste. 100
Richardson, TX 75080
(214)783-2666 **Fax:** (214)783-2678
Ultimate Parent: Phillips Petroleum.

★ 88758 ★ **Pizza Hut**
108 University Village Dr.
Richardson, TX 75081
(214)690-9857
Ultimate Parent: Pepsico. **SIC:** 5812—Eating Places.

★ 88759 ★ **Pizza Hut**
515 W. Campbell Rd.
Richardson, TX 75080
(214)907-2900
Ultimate Parent: Pepsico.

★ 88760 ★ **Pizza Hut**
1602 E. Belt Line Rd.
Richardson, TX 75081
(214)783-7000
Ultimate Parent: Pepsico.

★ 88761 ★ **Radio Shack**
202 W. Campbell Rd.
Richardson, TX 75080
(214)669-1210
Company Type: Division. **Ultimate Parent:** Tandy Corp. **SIC:** 5065—Electronic Parts & Equipment Nec.

★ 88762 ★ **Radio Shack**
Richardson Sq.
Richardson, TX 75081
(214)783-7052
Company Type: Division. **Ultimate Parent:** Tandy Corp. **SIC:** 5719—Miscellaneous Home Furnishings Stores.

★ 88763 ★ **Ram Mobile Data**
258 E. Arapaho Rd.
Richardson, TX 75081-2775
(214)705-0750
Ultimate Parent: BellSouth Corp. **SIC:** 4813—Telephone Communications Except Radiotelephone.

★ 88764 ★ **Rockwell International**
3200 E. Renner Rd.
Richardson, TX 75081
Ultimate Parent: Rockwell International Corp. **SIC:** 3600—Electronic & Other Electrical Equipment.

★ 88765 ★ **Rockwell International Corp.**
3200 E. Renner Rd.
Richardson, TX 75081
Ultimate Parent: Rockwell International Corp. **SIC:** 3600—Electronic & Other Electrical Equipment.

★ 88766 ★ **Rockwell International Corp.**
NTSD Div.
1200 N. Alma Rd.
Richardson, TX 75081
Company Type: Division. **Ultimate Parent:** Rockwell International Corp. **SIC:** 3663—Radio & T.V. Communications Equipment.

★ 88767 ★ **Rockwell International Ntsd**
1200 N. Alma Rd.
Richardson, TX 75081
Ultimate Parent: Rockwell International Corp. **SIC:** 3663—Radio & T.V. Communications Equipment.

★ 88768 ★ **Russell Associates Inc.**
13777 N. Central Expy.
Richardson, TX 75080
(214)699-0383
Ultimate Parent: Pall.

★ 88769 ★ **Ryder Truck Rental**
140 Centennial Blvd.
Richardson, TX 75081
(214)231-7582
Ultimate Parent: Ryder System. **SIC:** 7513—Truck Rental & Leasing Without Drivers.

★ 88770 ★ **Ryder Truck Rental**
1310 W. Spring Valley Rd.
Richardson, TX 75080
(214)437-1476
Ultimate Parent: Ryder System. **SIC:** 7359—Equipment Rental & Leasing Nec.

★ 88771 ★ **Ryder Truck Rental**
9330 Hillcrest Rd.
Richardson, TX 75081
(214)783-8738
Ultimate Parent: Ryder System. **SIC:** 7359—Equipment Rental & Leasing Nec.

★ 88772 ★ **Ryder Truck Rental**
505 W. Arapaho Rd.
Richardson, TX 75080
(214)690-8300
Ultimate Parent: Ryder System.

★ 88773 ★ **Ryder Truck Rental**
747 S. Central Expy.
Richardson, TX 75080
(214)644-1613
Ultimate Parent: Ryder System.

★ 88774 ★ **Savings of America, A Division of Home Savings of America, FSB**
1225 E. Belt Line Rd.
Richardson, TX 75081-3708
(214)234-1527
Company Type: Division. **Location Type:** Branch office. **Ultimate Parent:** H. F. Ahmanson. **SIC:** 6021—National Commercial Banks.

★ 88775 ★ **Savings of America, A Division of Home Savings of America, FSB**
110 N. Coit
Richardson, TX 75080
(214)231-9400
Company Type: Division. **Location Type:** Branch office. **Ultimate Parent:** H. F. Ahmanson. **SIC:** 6021—National Commercial Banks.

★ 88776 ★ **Shell Service Station**
5304 Arapaho
Richardson, TX 75081
(214)233-7968
Ultimate Parent: Shell Oil Co. **SIC:** 5541—Gasoline Service Stations.

★ 88777 ★ **Sun Diamond Growers**
1219 Chesterton Dr.
Richardson, TX 75080
(214)644-1499
Ultimate Parent: Sun-Diamond Growers. **SIC:** 5145—Confectionery.

★ 88778 ★ **T J Maxx**
Richardson
Richardson, TX 75080
(214)437-1842
Ultimate Parent: TJX. **SIC:** 5311—Department Stores.

★ 88779 ★ **Taco Bell**
517 W. Arapaho Rd.
Richardson, TX 75080
(214)783-6442
Ultimate Parent: Pepsico. **SIC:** 5812—Eating Places.

★ 88780 ★ **Taco Bell**
1606 E. Belt Line Rd.
Richardson, TX 75081
(214)783-4689
Ultimate Parent: Pepsico.

★ 88781 ★ **Taco Bell**
160 E. Spring Valley Rd.
Richardson, TX 75081
(214)235-7942
Ultimate Parent: Pepsico. **SIC:** 5812—Eating Places.

★ 88782 ★ **Texaco**
401 S. Sherman St.
Richardson, TX 75081
(214)231-3878
Ultimate Parent: Texaco. **SIC:** 3149—Footwear Except Rubber Nec.

★ 88783 ★ **Thom Mcan Shoe Stores**
2214 N. Plano Rd.
Richardson, TX 75082
(214)233-9618
Ultimate Parent: Melville. **SIC:** 5661—Shoe Stores.

★ 88784 ★ **Thom Mcan Shoe Stores**
501 S. Plano Rd.
Richardson, TX 75081
(214)231-8982
Ultimate Parent: Melville. **SIC:** 5661—Shoe Stores.

★ 88785 ★ **Time Electronics**
1876 Firman Dr.
Richardson, TX 75081
(214)644-4644
Location Type: Branch office. **Ultimate Parent:** Avnet. **SIC:** 5065—Electronic Parts & Equipment Nec.

★ 88786 ★ **US Clinical Prods. Inc.**
1900 Jay Ell Dr.
Richardson, TX 75083
Ultimate Parent: American Home Products. **SIC:** 3841—Surgical & Medical Instruments.

★ 88787 ★ **Varian Associates**
13531 N. Central
Richardson, TX 75080
(214)235-2385
Ultimate Parent: Varian Associates, Inc. **SIC:** 3699—Electrical Equipment & Supplies Nec.

★ 88788 ★ **Varian Associates Inc.**
405 International Pky.
Richardson, TX 75081
(214)235-2385
Officer: Sam Barlow, Manager. **Ultimate Parent:** Varian Associates, Inc. **SIC:** 3679—Electronic Components Nec.

★ 88789 ★ **Waldenbooks**
Richardson Sq.
Richardson, TX 75081
(214)234-0449
Ultimate Parent: K-Mart. **SIC:** 5942—Book Stores.

★ 88790 ★ **Western Union ATS**
2400 N. Glenville Dr.
Richardson, TX 75082
(214)918-6750 **Fax:** (214)918-6711
Officer: H. P. Scott, President. **Ultimate Parent:** MCI Communications.

★ 88791 ★ **Wolf Brand Product**
1755 N. Collins Blvd.
Richardson, TX 75080
(214)680-0460
Ultimate Parent: Quaker Oates.

★ 88792 ★ **Yoplait USA Inc.**
15100 Midway Rd.
Richardson, TX 75081
(214)991-1200
Ultimate Parent: General Mills. **SIC:** 5451—Dairy Products Stores.

Richmond

★ 88793 ★ **BASF Tpu Marketing**
3418 Apple Orchard Dr.
Richmond, TX 77469-6858
(713)341-0449
Ultimate Parent: BASF Corp. **SIC:** 2821—Plastics Materials & Resins.

★ 88794 ★ **Cooper Industries**
Flow Control Div.
126 Collins Rd.
Richmond, TX 77469
Company Type: Division. **Ultimate Parent:** Cooper Industries. **SIC:** 3325—Steel Foundries Nec.

★ 88795 ★ **Cooper Industries**
Flow Control Div.
126 Collins Rd.
Richmond, TX 77469-0396
Company Type: Division. **Ultimate Parent:** Cooper Industries. **SIC:** 3325—Steel Foundries Nec.

★ 88796 ★ **Exxon Co. USA**
Skinner Rd.
Richmond, TX 77469
(713)342-1919
Ultimate Parent: Exxon. **SIC:** 5172—Petroleum Products Nec.

★ 88797 ★ **Southern Cotton Oil Co.**
PO Box 489
Richmond, TX 77406-0489
(214)342-4606
Officer: David Winters. **Ultimate Parent:** Archer Daniels Midland Co. **SIC:** 2074—Cottonseed Oil Mills.

★ 88798 ★ **Southern Cotton Oil Co. Inc.**
1805 Liberty St.
Richmond, TX 77469
(713)342-4606
Officer: David Winters, Manager. **Ultimate Parent:** Archer Daniels Midland Co. **SIC:** 2074—Cottonseed Oil Mills; 2076—Vegetable Oil Mills Nec; 2911—Petroleum Refining.

Ringgold

★ 88799 ★ **Mobil Pipe Line Co.**
Ringgold, TX 76261
(817)934-6231
Company Type: Branch. **Ultimate Parent:** Mobil. **SIC:** 4612—Crude Petroleum Pipelines.

Rio Grande City

★ 88800 ★ **Pizza Hut**
4300 E. US Hwy. 83
Rio Grande City, TX 78582
(512)487-2551
Ultimate Parent: Pepsico.

★ 88801 ★ **Pizza Hut**
430 Hwy. 83 E
Rio Grande City, TX 78582
(512)487-9946
Ultimate Parent: Pepsico.

★ 88802 ★ **Pizza Hut**
4300 E. Hwy. 83
Rio Grande City, TX 78582
(512)487-5172
Ultimate Parent: Pepsico. **SIC:** 5812—Eating Places.

★ 88803 ★ **Trailways Bus Station**
1116 E. Hwy. 83
Rio Grande City, TX 78582
(512)487-2620
Ultimate Parent: Greyhound Lines Inc. **SIC:** 4131—Intercity & Rural Bus Transportation.

Robinson Plz

★ 88804 ★ **Pizza Hut**
1111 S. 8th St.
Robinson Plz, TX 76706
(817)756-2320
Ultimate Parent: Pepsico. **SIC:** 5812—Eating Places.

Robstown

★ 88805 ★ **Exxon Co. USA**
Hwy. 77 S
Robstown, TX 78380
(512)387-5585
Ultimate Parent: Exxon. **SIC:** 1389—Oil & Gas Field Services Nec.

★ 88806 ★ **Exxon Gas System**
Fm Rd. 2826
Robstown, TX 78380
(512)387-5736
Ultimate Parent: Exxon.

★ 88807 ★ **GTE Center**
1889 Farm Rd.
Robstown, TX 78380
Location Type: Branch office. **Ultimate Parent:** GTE.

★ 88808 ★	Halliburton Resource Mgt
Hwy. 77
Robstown, TX 78380
(512)387-7650
Ultimate Parent: Halliburton. **SIC:** 7359—Equipment Rental & Leasing Nec.

★ 88809 ★	Pizza Hut
419 W. Ave.
Robstown, TX 78380
(512)387-1587
Ultimate Parent: Pepsico. **SIC:** 5812—Eating Places.

Roby

★ 88810 ★	Citizens State Bank
1st
Roby, TX 79543
(915)776-2261
Ultimate Parent: Liberty National Bancorp. **SIC:** 6022—State Commercial Banks.

★ 88811 ★	West Texas Utilities Co.
Roby, TX 79543
(915)776-2421
Ultimate Parent: Central & South West. **SIC:** 1731—Electrical Work.

Rockdale

★ 88812 ★	Alcoa
FM Rd. 1786
Rockdale, TX 76567
(512)446-5811
Officer: Jack Drake, Plant Manager. **Ultimate Parent:** Aluminum Co. of America-Alcoa. **SIC:** 3334—Primary Aluminum; 3355—Aluminum Rolling & Drawing Nec; 3399—Primary Metal Products Nec.

★ 88813 ★	Alcoa
FM Rd. 1786
Rockdale, TX 76567
(512)446-5811
Officer: Jack Drake, Plant Manager. **Ultimate Parent:** Aluminum Co. of America-Alcoa. **SIC:** 3334—Primary Aluminum; 3355—Aluminum Rolling & Drawing Nec; 3399—Primary Metal Products Nec.

★ 88814 ★	Alcoa Rockdale Works
Sandow Near Rockdale PO Box 472
Rockdale, TX 76567
Ultimate Parent: Aluminum Co. of America-Alcoa. **SIC:** 3334—Primary Aluminum.

★ 88815 ★	Aluminum Co. of America
Airport Rd.
Rockdale, TX 76567
(512)446-3872
Ultimate Parent: Aluminum Co. of America-Alcoa. **SIC:** 5051—Metals Service Centers & Offices.

★ 88816 ★	Aluminum Co. of America
PO Box 472
Rockdale, TX 76567-0472
(512)446-8346
Location Type: Branch office. **Officer:** W. J. Drake. **Ultimate Parent:** Aluminum Co. of America-Alcoa. **SIC:** 3334—Primary Aluminum.

★ 88817 ★	Lone Star Gas Co.
43 PO Box
Rockdale, TX 76567
(512)446-5251
Ultimate Parent: Enserch. **SIC:** 4925—Gas Production & Distribution Nec.

★ 88818 ★	Pizza Hut
1212 W. Cameron Ave.
Rockdale, TX 76567
(512)446-6131
Ultimate Parent: Pepsico. **SIC:** 5812—Eating Places.

Rockport

★ 88819 ★	Pizza Hut
Hwy. 35 N
Rockport, TX 78382
(512)729-7270
Ultimate Parent: Pepsico. **SIC:** 5812—Eating Places.

★ 88820 ★	Ryder Truck Rental
1102 E. Wharf St.
Rockport, TX 78382
(512)729-9300
Ultimate Parent: Ryder System. **SIC:** 7513—Truck Rental & Leasing Without Drivers.

★ 88821 ★	Tesoro Petroleum Distribution Co.
Caspry Wndll Dc
Rockport, TX 78382
(512)729-6108
Ultimate Parent: Tesoro Petroleum Corp. **SIC:** 5172—Petroleum Products Nec.

Rockwall

★ 88822 ★	Ace Hardware
1013 S. Goliad St.
Rockwall, TX 75087
(214)722-3341
Ultimate Parent: Ace Hardware.

★ 88823 ★	McDonalds Restaurant
610 Interstate 30
Rockwall, TX 75087
(214)771-0635
Ultimate Parent:	McDonald's.

★ 88824 ★	Pizza Hut
2000 S. Goliad St.
Rockwall, TX 75087
(214)722-6512
Ultimate Parent: Pepsico. **SIC:** 5812—Eating Places.

★ 88825 ★	Radio Shack
445 Interstate 30
Rockwall, TX 75087
(214)771-9276
Company Type: Division. **Ultimate Parent:** Tandy Corp.

Roma

★ 88826 ★	Citizens State Bank
1709 Grant St.
Roma, TX 78584
(512)849-2311
Ultimate Parent: Liberty National Bancorp. **SIC:** 6022—State Commercial Banks.

Rosenberg

★ 88827 ★	Jiffy Lube
5131 Avenue H
Rosenberg, TX 77471
(713)272-3085
Ultimate Parent: Pennzoil.

★ 88828 ★	Kentucky Fried Chicken
3620 Avenue H
Rosenberg, TX 77471
(713)342-2305
Ultimate Parent: Pepsico. **SIC:** 5812—Eating Places.

★ 88829 ★	Kmart Discount Stores
3803 Avenue H
Rosenberg, TX 77471
(713)342-6101
Ultimate Parent: K-Mart.

★ 88830 ★	McDonalds
3627 Avenue H
Rosenberg, TX 77471
(713)342-8373
Ultimate Parent: McDonald's. **SIC:** 5812—Eating Places.

★ 88831 ★	Payless Shoesource
4605 Ave. H
Rosenberg, TX 77471
(713)232-3352
Ultimate Parent: May Department Stores. **SIC:** 5661—Shoe Stores.

★ 88832 ★	Pizza Hut
4420 Avenue H
Rosenberg, TX 77471
(713)342-4350
Ultimate Parent: Pepsico. **SIC:** 5812—Eating Places.

★ 88833 ★	Quanex Corp.
Gulf States Tube
Scott Rd. & Spur 529
PO Box 952
Rosenberg, TX 77471-0952
Company Type: Division. **Ultimate Parent:** Quanex. **SIC:** 3317—Steel Pipe & Tubes.

★ 88834 ★	Quanex Gulf States Tube
PO Box 952
Rosenberg, TX 77471
Company Type: Division. **Ultimate Parent:** Quanex. **SIC:** 3317—Steel Pipe & Tubes.

★ 88835 ★	Radio Shack
5028 Avenue H
Rosenberg, TX 77471
(713)342-4526
Company Type: Division. **Ultimate Parent:** Tandy Corp. **SIC:** 5065—Electronic Parts & Equipment Nec.

★ 88836 ★	Ryder Truck Rental
1501 Avenue H
Rosenberg, TX 77471
(713)232-0807
Ultimate Parent: Ryder System. **SIC:** 7513—Truck Rental & Leasing Without Drivers.

★ 88837 ★	Shell Self Service Station
2420 Avenue H
Rosenberg, TX 77471
(713)232-9243
Ultimate Parent: Shell Oil Co. **SIC:** 5541—Gasoline Service Stations.

★ 88838 ★	Taco Bell
3827 Avenue H
Rosenberg, TX 77471
(713)342-0130
Ultimate Parent: Pepsico. **SIC:** 5812—Eating Places.

★ 88839 ★	Texaco Food Mart
3417 1st St.
Rosenberg, TX 77471
(713)341-9372
Ultimate Parent: Texaco.

★ 88840 ★	Texaco Pep Stop
3417 1st St.
Rosenberg, TX 77471
(713)342-0370
Ultimate Parent: Texaco. **SIC:** 5541—Gasoline Service Stations.

★ 88841 ★	Wal Mart
4520 Reading Rd.
Rosenberg, TX 77471
(713)232-8581
Ultimate Parent: Wal-Mart Stores, Inc. **SIC:** 5311—Department Stores.

Round Rock

★ 88842 ★	AMP Packaging Systems Inc.
700 E. Jeffrey Way
Round Rock, TX 78664
(512)244-5100 **Fax:** (512)244-5112
Company Type: Subsidiary. **Officer:** Christopher Doggett, General Manager. **Ultimate Parent:** AMP Inc.

★ 88843 ★	AMP Packaging Systems Inc.
700 Jeffrey Way, Ste. E
Round Rock, TX 78664
(512)388-7444
Officer: Chris Doggett, Manager. **Ultimate Parent:** AMP Inc. **SIC:** 3672—Printed Circuit Boards; 3679—Electronic Components Nec. **Sales:** 20 M.

★ 88844 ★	AMP Packaging Systems, Inc.
700 E. Jeffrey Way
Round Rock, TX 78664-2425
(512)244-5100 (800)522-6752 **Fax:** (512)986-7575
Company Type: Subsidiary. **Officer:** Tim Heidelbaugh, General Manager. **Ultimate Parent:** AMP Inc. **SIC:** 3679—Electronic Components Nec. **Sales:** 20 M.

★ 88845 ★	Carroll Touch
811 Paloma Dr.
Round Rock, TX 78664-2402
(512)244-3500
Location Type: Branch office. **Officer:** Joe Williams. **Ultimate Parent:** AMP Inc. **SIC:**

3571—Electronic Computers; 5045—Computers, Peripherals & Software.

★ 88846 ★	Carroll Touch Inc.
700 E. Jeffrey Way
Round Rock, TX 78664
(512)244-3500 **Fax:** (512)244-7040
Company Type: Subsidiary. **Officer:** Joe Williamson, General Manager. **Ultimate Parent:** AMP Inc.

★ 88847 ★	Carroll Touch Inc.
811 Paloma Dr.
Round Rock, TX 78664
(512)244-3500
Company Type: Subsidiary. **Officer:** Joe Williamson, Manager. **Ultimate Parent:** AMP Inc. **SIC:** 3577—Computer Peripheral Equipment Nec. **Employee Count:** 83. **Sales:** 20 M.

★ 88848 ★	Hit or Miss Austin
Outlet Mall
Round Rock, TX 78664
(512)244-0931
Ultimate Parent: TJX. **SIC:** 5621—Women's Clothing Stores.

★ 88849 ★	Jim Walter Homes Inc.
16000 N. I 35
Round Rock, TX 78664
(512)251-4187
Ultimate Parent: Walter Industries, Inc. **SIC:** 1521—Single-Family Housing Construction.

★ 88850 ★	Mcneil Consumer Products Co.
4001 N. I-35
Round Rock, TX 78664
Ultimate Parent: Johnson & Johnson. **SIC:** 2834—Pharmaceutical Preparations.

★ 88851 ★	Pizza Hut
1237 Round Rock Ave.
Round Rock, TX 78681
(512)388-2288
Ultimate Parent: Pepsico.

★ 88852 ★	Radio Shack
214 W. Taylor Ave.
Round Rock, TX 78664
(512)255-6600
Company Type: Division. **Ultimate Parent:** Tandy Corp. **SIC:** 5065—Electronic Parts & Equipment Nec.

★ 88853 ★	Ryder Truck Rental
807 S. Mays St.
Round Rock, TX 78664
(512)244-3488
Ultimate Parent: Ryder System.

★ 88854 ★	Taco Bell
1108 I N
Round Rock, TX 78681
(512)244-1264
Ultimate Parent: Pepsico.

★ 88855 ★	Tn Tech. Inc.
2555 N. I-35
Round Rock, TX 78664
Ultimate Parent: Baker Hughes. **SIC:** 3823—Process Control Instruments.

★ 88856 ★	Wal Mart Tire & Battery Ctr
2400 I N. 35
Round Rock, TX 78664
(512)244-1026
Ultimate Parent: Wal-Mart Stores, Inc. **SIC:** 5531—Automobile & Home Supply Stores.

★ 88857 ★	Westinghouse Motor Co.
Interstate Hwy. 35 N. at Westinghouse Rd.
Round Rock, TX 78680-0277
Ultimate Parent: Westinghouse Electric Corp. **SIC:** 3621—Motors & Generators.

★ 88858 ★	Westinghouse Power Systems
Westinghouse Rd.
Round Rock, TX 78680
(512)255-4141
Officer: Robert Tianchon, President. **Ultimate Parent:** Westinghouse Electric Corp. **SIC:** 3511—Turbines & Turbine Generator Sets; 3533—Oil & Gas Field Machinery; 3621—Motors & Generators.

★ 88859 ★ Westinghouse Specialty
Westinghouse Rd.
Round Rock, TX 78618
(512)459-9400
Officer: Bill Whitehead, Manager. Ultimate Parent: Westinghouse Electric Corp. SIC: 3317—Steel Pipe & Tubes; 3356—Nonferrous Rolling & Drawing Nec.

Rowlett

★ 88860 ★ Mobil Oil Corp.
3430 Hwy. 66
Rowlett, TX 75088
(214)475-3084
Ultimate Parent: Mobil. SIC: 5541—Gasoline Service Stations.

Sabinal

★ 88861 ★ Texaco Inc.
300 N. Front W
Sabinal, TX 78881
(512)988-2514
Ultimate Parent: Texaco. SIC: 5172—Petroleum Products Nec.

Sabine Pass

★ 88862 ★ Oryx Energy Co.
1266 S. 1st Ave.
Sabine Pass, TX 77655
(409)971-2332
Ultimate Parent: Oryx Energy. SIC: 1382—Oil & Gas Exploration Services.

Saginaw

★ 88863 ★ Scott Polymers Inc.
400 E. Minton Rd.
Saginaw, TX 76179
Ultimate Parent: Scott Paper Co. SIC: 2821—Plastics Materials & Resins.

★ 88864 ★ Scott Polymers Inc.
2760 Peden Rd.
Saginaw, TX 76179
Ultimate Parent: Scott Paper Co. SIC: 2821—Plastics Materials & Resins.

★ 88865 ★ Tank Lining & Rail Car Repair
Business Hwy. 287 North Peden Rd.
Saginaw, TX 76179
Ultimate Parent: Trinity Industries. SIC: 3743—Railroad Equipment.

San Angelo

★ 88866 ★ Albertson's
1852 Sherwood Way
San Angelo, TX 76901
(915)944-1547
Ultimate Parent: Albertson's Inc. SIC: 5411—Grocery Stores; 5912—Drug Stores & Proprietary Stores.

★ 88867 ★ American Family Life Assurance
103 W. Beauregard Ave.
San Angelo, TX 76903
(915)944-4148
Ultimate Parent: American Family Life Assurance Co. SIC: 6411—Insurance Agents, Brokers & Service.

★ 88868 ★ Associated Milk Producers Inc.
309 Pulliam St.
San Angelo, TX 76903
(915)653-4879
Ultimate Parent: Associated Milk Producers Inc. SIC: 5143—Dairy Products Except Dried or Canned.

★ 88869 ★ Butler Paper Co.
3315 Cumberland Dr.
San Angelo, TX 76904-6003
(915)942-6428
Ultimate Parent: Alco Standard Corp. SIC: 5111—Printing & Writing Paper; 5113—Industrial & Personal Service Paper.

★ 88870 ★ Casual Corner
1032 Sunset Mall
San Angelo, TX 76904
(915)949-3784
Ultimate Parent: United States Shoe. SIC: 5651—Family Clothing Stores.

★ 88871 ★ Circus World
1130 Sunset Mall
San Angelo, TX 76904
(915)949-6464
Ultimate Parent: Melville. SIC: 5945—Hobby, Toy & Game Shops.

★ 88872 ★ Ethicon Inc.
3348 Pulliam
San Angelo, TX 76905
Ultimate Parent: Johnson & Johnson. SIC: 3841—Surgical & Medical Instruments; 3842—Surgical Appliances & Supplies.

★ 88873 ★ Foot Action
1180 Sunset Mall
San Angelo, TX 76904
(915)949-6371
Ultimate Parent: Melville. SIC: 5661—Shoe Stores.

★ 88874 ★ Foot Action for Kids
1180 Sunset Mall
San Angelo, TX 76904
(915)944-2501
Ultimate Parent: Melville. SIC: 5661—Shoe Stores.

★ 88875 ★ Gandy's Dairies
332 Pulliam St.
San Angelo, TX 76903
Ultimate Parent: Dean Foods. SIC: 2026—Fluid Milk; 2024—Ice Cream & Frozen Desserts; 2022—Cheese—Natural & Processed.

★ 88876 ★ Gandy's Dairies Inc.
332 Pulliam St.
San Angelo, TX 76903
Ultimate Parent: Dean Foods. SIC: 2026—Fluid Milk; 2024—Ice Cream & Frozen Desserts.

★ 88877 ★ Hertz Rent-A-Car
Mathis Field
San Angelo, TX 76903
(915)944-1221
Ultimate Parent: Hertz. SIC: 7514—Passenger Car Rental.

★ 88878 ★ Kentucky Fried Chicken
1514 Pulliam St.
San Angelo, TX 76903
(915)658-7503
Ultimate Parent: Pepsico. SIC: 5812—Eating Places.

★ 88879 ★ Kentucky Fried Chicken
1705 S. Bryant Blvd.
San Angelo, TX 76903
(915)653-2444
Ultimate Parent: Pepsico. SIC: 5812—Eating Places.

★ 88880 ★ Kentucky Fried Chicken
2302 N. Bryant Blvd.
San Angelo, TX 76903
(915)655-8924
Ultimate Parent: Pepsico. SIC: 5812—Eating Places.

★ 88881 ★ Lane Bryant
1280 Sunset Mall
San Angelo, TX 76904
(915)949-5899
Ultimate Parent: Limited. SIC: 5651—Family Clothing Stores.

★ 88882 ★ Lone Star Gas Co.
1730 N. Main St.
San Angelo, TX 76903
Ultimate Parent: Enserch. SIC: 4932—Gas & Other Services Combined; 4939—Combination Utility Nec.

★ 88883 ★ Marathon Oil Co.
9661 N. Us Hwy. 67
San Angelo, TX 76905
(915)949-4750
Ultimate Parent: USX Corp.

★ 88884 ★ Marathon Oil Co.
9661 N. Us Hwy. 67
San Angelo, TX 76905
(915)949-4750
Ultimate Parent: USX Corp.

★ 88885 ★ Matco Tools
921 Baker St.
San Angelo, TX 76903
(915)658-5604
Ultimate Parent: Danaher Corp. SIC: 5072—Hardware.

★ 88886 ★ Mini Mart
3302 N. Bryant Blvd.
San Angelo, TX 76903
(915)653-5952
Ultimate Parent: Kroger. SIC: 5411—Grocery Stores.

★ 88887 ★ Mutual of New York
302 S. David St.
San Angelo, TX 76903
(915)655-3909
Ultimate Parent: Mutual of New York.

★ 88888 ★ Ncr Corp.
3194 Executive Dr. A
San Angelo, TX 76903
Ultimate Parent: AT&T. SIC: 5099—Durable Goods Nec; 8099—Health & Allied Services Nec.

★ 88889 ★ Otis Elevator Co.
36 W. Beauregard Ave.
San Angelo, TX 76903
(915)655-3208
Ultimate Parent: United Technologies. SIC: 5084—Industrial Machinery & Equipment.

★ 88890 ★ Payless Shoesource
1020 Sunset Mall
San Angelo, TX 76904
(915)949-4167
Ultimate Parent: May Department Stores. SIC: 5661—Shoe Stores.

★ 88891 ★ Payless Shoesource
3950 Sunset Dr.
San Angelo, TX 76904
(915)944-9938
Ultimate Parent: May Department Stores. SIC: 5661—Shoe Stores.

★ 88892 ★ Pizza Hut
1425 N. Chadboure St.
San Angelo, TX 76903
(915)653-4239
Ultimate Parent: Pepsico. SIC: 5812—Eating Places.

★ 88893 ★ Pizza Hut
3029 Sherwood Way
San Angelo, TX 76901
(915)949-0597
Ultimate Parent: Pepsico. SIC: 5812—Eating Places.

★ 88894 ★ Pizza Hut
3510 Knickerbocker Rd.
San Angelo, TX 76904
(915)949-8509
Ultimate Parent: Pepsico. SIC: 5812—Eating Places.

★ 88895 ★ Pizza Hut
1701 Pulliam St.
San Angelo, TX 76905
(915)653-1233
Ultimate Parent: Pepsico. SIC: 5812—Eating Places.

★ 88896 ★ Pizza Hut Office
1807 S. Bryant Blvd.
San Angelo, TX 76903
(915)655-0101
Ultimate Parent: Pepsico.

★ 88897 ★ Radio Shack
1152 Sunset Mall
San Angelo, TX 76904
(915)942-0946
Company Type: Division. Ultimate Parent: Tandy Corp. SIC: 5065—Electronic Parts & Equipment Nec.

★ 88898 ★ Radio Shack
2432 Sherwood Way
San Angelo, TX 76901
(915)949-6929
Company Type: Division. Ultimate Parent: Tandy Corp. SIC: 5065—Electronic Parts & Equipment Nec.

★ 88899 ★ Ryder Truck Rental
2615 N. Bryant Blvd.
San Angelo, TX 76903
(915)655-3995
Ultimate Parent: Ryder System. SIC: 7359—Equipment Rental & Leasing Nec.

★ 88900 ★ Ryder Truck Rental
1809 W. N. Ave.
San Angelo, TX 76904
(915)942-6572
Ultimate Parent: Ryder System. SIC: 7359—Equipment Rental & Leasing Nec.

★ 88901 ★ Service Merchandise
5000 Sunset Mall
San Angelo, TX 76904
(915)944-8581
Ultimate Parent: Service Merchandise Co., Inc. SIC: 5399—Miscellaneous General Merchandise Store.

★ 88902 ★ Taco Bell
3336 Sherwood Way
San Angelo, TX 76901
(915)949-0216
Ultimate Parent: Pepsico. SIC: 5812—Eating Places.

★ 88903 ★ Target Stores
4235 Sunset Dr.
San Angelo, TX 76904
(915)949-5555
Ultimate Parent: Dauphin Deposit Corp. SIC: 5311—Department Stores.

★ 88904 ★ Underwriters Adjusting Co.
103 City Savings Bldg.
San Angelo, TX 76903
(915)942-9272
Ultimate Parent: Continental. SIC: 6411—Insurance Agents, Brokers & Service.

★ 88905 ★ Waldenbooks
1284 Sunset Mall
San Angelo, TX 76904
(915)949-7040
Ultimate Parent: K-Mart. SIC: 5942—Book Stores.

★ 88906 ★ West Texas Utilities Co.
106 S. Chadbourne St.
San Angelo, TX 76903
(915)653-1451
Ultimate Parent: Central & South West. SIC: 4911—Electric Services; 5722—Household Appliance Stores.

★ 88907 ★ Winn-Dixie Texas Inc. No. 248
2020 W. Beauregard Ave.
San Angelo, TX 76901
(915)949-9719
Ultimate Parent: Winn-Dixie Stores, Inc. SIC: 5411—Grocery Stores.

San Antoino

★ 88908 ★ Comerica Bank-Texas
4625 Centerview
San Antoino, TX 78228-1278
(210)737-1000
Company Type: Subsidiary. Location Type: Branch office. Ultimate Parent: Comerica Bank. SIC: 6021—National Commercial Banks.

San Antonia

★ 88909 ★ Dillard Department Stores
San Antonio Division
9315 N. Broadway
San Antonia, TX 78217
(210)821-7611
Officer: Charles E. Franzke, Chairman. Ultimate Parent: Dillard Department Stores. SIC: 5311—Department Stores.

San Antonio

★ 88910 ★ Ace Hardware Store
13909 Nacogdoches Rd.
San Antonio, TX 78217
(512)655-9772
Ultimate Parent: Ace Hardware. SIC: 5251—Hardware Stores.

★ 88911 ★ Advanced Micro Devices Inc.
8611 W. Military Dr.
San Antonio, TX 78245
(512)681-9000
Ultimate Parent: Advanced Micro Devices Inc. SIC: 3674—Semiconductors & Related Devices.

★ 88912 ★ **Albertson's Drug Store**
5538 Walzem Rd.
San Antonio, TX 78218
(512)656-7900
Ultimate Parent: Albertson's Inc. **SIC:** 5311—Department Stores; 5411—Grocery Stores; 5912—Drug Stores & Proprietary Stores.

★ 88913 ★ **Albertson's Drug Store**
5707 Bandera Rd.
San Antonio, TX 78238
(512)684-8795
Ultimate Parent: Albertson's Inc. **SIC:** 5311—Department Stores; 5411—Grocery Stores; 5912—Drug Stores & Proprietary Stores.

★ 88914 ★ **Albertson's Food & Drug Store**
999 E. Basse Rd.
San Antonio, TX 78209
(512)829-7417
Ultimate Parent: Albertson's Inc. **SIC:** 5411—Grocery Stores.

★ 88915 ★ **Albertson's Food Store, No. 4**
16648 San Pedro Ave.
San Antonio, TX 78232
(512)496-7191
Ultimate Parent: Albertson's Inc. **SIC:** 5411—Grocery Stores.

★ 88916 ★ **Albertson's Inc.**
Texas Div.
10515 Gulfdale Dr., Ste. 111
San Antonio, TX 78216
(210)349-6431
Company Type: Division. **Officer:** William Emmons, Vice President. **Ultimate Parent:** Albertson's Inc. **SIC:** 5411—Grocery Stores.

★ 88917 ★ **Alliant Tech Systems**
6810 Alamo Downs Pky.
San Antonio, TX 78238-4516
(210)647-8231
Ultimate Parent: Alliant Techsystems Inc. **SIC:** 8731—Commercial Physical Research; 7692—Welding Repair.

★ 88918 ★ **Associated Milk Producers Inc.**
6609 Blanco Rd.
San Antonio, TX 78216
(210)340-9100
Company Type: Headquarters. **Officer:** Noble Anderson. **SIC:** 2026—Fluid Milk. **Employee Count:** 4199. **Sales:** 2692 M.

★ 88919 ★ **Associated Milk Producers Inc.**
1475 Ackerman Rd.
San Antonio, TX 78219
(512)661-8494
Ultimate Parent: Associated Milk Producers Inc. **SIC:** 5731—Radio, Television & Electronics Stores.

★ 88920 ★ **AT&T Capital Small Business Lending**
9311 San Pedro Ave.
San Antonio, TX 78216-4458
(210)524-7787
Ultimate Parent: AT&T. **SIC:** 4813—Telephone Communications Except Radiotelephone.

★ 88921 ★ **Automatic Data Processing**
1044 Central Pky. S
San Antonio, TX 78232-5021
(210)490-4984
Officer: Paul Alvarez. **Ultimate Parent:** Automatic Data Processing, Inc. **SIC:** 7374—Data Processing & Preparation.

★ 88922 ★ **Avon Products Inc.**
301 S. Frio St.
San Antonio, TX 78207
(512)270-4565
Ultimate Parent: Avon Products, Inc. **SIC:** 5999—Miscellaneous Retail Stores Nec.

★ 88923 ★ **Banana Republic**
7400 N. Star Mall
San Antonio, TX 78216
(512)340-1766
Ultimate Parent: GAP. **SIC:** 5651—Family Clothing Stores.

★ 88924 ★ **Banana Republic**
849 E. Commerce St.
San Antonio, TX 78205
(512)271-0525
Ultimate Parent: GAP. **SIC:** 5651—Family Clothing Stores.

★ 88925 ★ **Bell Atlantic Corp.**
11847 Starcrest Dr.
San Antonio, TX 78247-4114
(210)491-9471
Location Type: Branch office. **Officer:** Gene Greer. **Ultimate Parent:** Bell Atlantic Corp. **SIC:** 7378—Computer Maintenance & Repair; 7371—Computer Programming Services.

★ 88926 ★ **Beneficial Texas Inc.**
1739 SW Loop 410
San Antonio, TX 78227-1668
(210)673-7360
Location Type: Branch office. **Ultimate Parent:** Beneficial. **SIC:** 6141—Personal Credit Institutions.

★ 88927 ★ **Beneficial Texas Inc.**
502 Embassy Oaks Ste. 125
San Antonio, TX 78216-2070
(210)491-0431
Officer: Eloy Ozuna. **Ultimate Parent:** Beneficial. **SIC:** 6141—Personal Credit Institutions.

★ 88928 ★ **Beneficial Texas Inc.**
5374 Walzem Rd.
San Antonio, TX 78218-2123
(210)656-2410
Location Type: Branch office. **Officer:** Don Flynn. **Ultimate Parent:** Beneficial. **SIC:** 6141—Personal Credit Institutions.

★ 88929 ★ **Bergen Brunswig Drug Co.**
1949 Hormel Dr.
San Antonio, TX 78219
(512)222-1231
Ultimate Parent: Bergen Brunswig Corp. **SIC:** 2834—Pharmaceutical Preparations.

★ 88930 ★ **BFI Waste Systems**
7790 Tessman Rd.
San Antonio, TX 78210
(210)661-4104
Location Type: Branch office. **Ultimate Parent:** Browning-Ferris Industries. **SIC:** 4953—Refuse Systems.

★ 88931 ★ **Borden Inc.**
875 E. Ashby Pl.
San Antonio, TX 78212
(210)736-3101
Officer: James Wolf, Manager. **Ultimate Parent:** Borden, Inc. **SIC:** 2021—Creamery Butter; 2024—Ice Cream & Frozen Desserts; 2026—Fluid Milk.

★ 88932 ★ **Borden Inc.**
Dairy
875 E. Ashby Pl.
San Antonio, TX 78212
Company Type: Division. **Ultimate Parent:** Borden, Inc. **SIC:** 2026—Fluid Milk.

★ 88933 ★ **Borden Inc.**
Dairy
875 E. Ashby Pl.
San Antonio, TX 78212
Company Type: Division. **Ultimate Parent:** Borden, Inc. **SIC:** 2026—Fluid Milk.

★ 88934 ★ **Borden Inc.**
Grocery & Specialty Products
875 E. Ashby Pl.
San Antonio, TX 78212
Company Type: Division. **Ultimate Parent:** Borden, Inc. **SIC:** 2026—Fluid Milk.

★ 88935 ★ **Browning Ferris Inc. Waste System**
4542 SE Loop 410
San Antonio, TX 78222-3925
(210)648-5222
Location Type: Branch office. **Officer:** James W. Baker. **Ultimate Parent:** Browning-Ferris Industries. **SIC:** 4953—Refuse Systems; 4212—Local Trucking Without Storage.

★ 88936 ★ **Builders Square**
96 Crossroads Blvd.
San Antonio, TX 78201
(512)735-6126
Company Type: Subsidiary. **Ultimate Parent:** K-Mart. **SIC:** 6062—State Credit Unions.

★ 88937 ★ **Builders Square**
9725 Datapoint Dr.
San Antonio, TX 78229
Company Type: Subsidiary. **Ultimate Parent:** K-Mart. **SIC:** 5044—Office Equipment.

★ 88938 ★ **Builders Square**
8109 Meadow Leaf Dr.
San Antonio, TX 78227
(512)675-4440
Company Type: Subsidiary. **Ultimate Parent:** K-Mart. **SIC:** 5039—Construction Materials Nec.

★ 88939 ★ **Builders Square**
527 Fair Ave.
San Antonio, TX 78223
(512)533-6581
Company Type: Subsidiary. **Ultimate Parent:** K-Mart. **SIC:** 1521—Single-Family Housing Construction.

★ 88940 ★ **Builders Square**
9725 Datapoint Dr.
San Antonio, TX 78229
Company Type: Subsidiary. **Ultimate Parent:** K-Mart. **SIC:** 5231—Paint, Glass & Wallpaper Stores.

★ 88941 ★ **Builders Square Corporate Office**
98 Crossroads Blvd.
San Antonio, TX 78201
(512)731-0500
Company Type: Subsidiary. **Ultimate Parent:** K-Mart. **SIC:** 6512—Nonresidential Building Operators.

★ 88942 ★ **Builders Square Inc.**
9725 Data Paint Dr.
San Antonio, TX 78229-2029
(210)616-8000
Company Type: Division. **Ultimate Parent:** K-Mart. **SIC:** 5211—Lumber & Other Building Materials; 5251—Hardware Stores; 5261—Retail Nurseries & Garden Stores; 5231—Paint, Glass & Wallpaper Stores.

★ 88943 ★ **Burlington Air Express**
5711 Bus Park Dr.
San Antonio, TX 78218
(512)661-5006
Ultimate Parent: Pittston. **SIC:** 4215—Courier Services Except by Air.

★ 88944 ★ **Burlington Northern Railroa**
1222 N. Main Ave.
San Antonio, TX 78212
(512)223-6515
Ultimate Parent: Burlington Northern. **SIC:** 4011—Railroads—Line-Haul Operating.

★ 88945 ★ **Butler Paper Co.**
5410 Rittiman Plz.
San Antonio, TX 78218-5211
(210)828-8897
Location Type: Branch office. **Officer:** Bill Lancaster. **Ultimate Parent:** Alco Standard Corp. **SIC:** 5111—Printing & Writing Paper; 5113—Industrial & Personal Service Paper.

★ 88946 ★ **Butler Paper Co.**
5410 Rittiman Plz.
San Antonio, TX 78218-5211
(210)828-8897
Location Type: Branch office. **Officer:** Bill Lancaster. **Ultimate Parent:** Alco Standard Corp. **SIC:** 5111—Printing & Writing Paper; 5113—Industrial & Personal Service Paper.

★ 88947 ★ **Casual Corner**
7400 N. Star Mall
San Antonio, TX 78216
(512)349-8798
Ultimate Parent: United States Shoe. **SIC:** 5651—Family Clothing Stores.

★ 88948 ★ **Casual Corner**
Windsor
San Antonio, TX 78218
(512)654-1402
Ultimate Parent: United States Shoe. **SIC:** 8661—Religious Organizations.

★ 88949 ★ **Casual Corner**
849 E. Commerce St.
San Antonio, TX 78205
(512)224-2023
Ultimate Parent: United States Shoe. **SIC:** 5651—Family Clothing Stores.

★ 88950 ★ **Casual Corner**
6301 Ingram Rd.
San Antonio, TX 78238
(512)684-5300
Ultimate Parent: United States Shoe. **SIC:** 2339—Women's/Misses' Outerwear Nec.

★ 88951 ★ **Casual Corner**
622 Central Park Shopping Ctr.
San Antonio, TX 78216
(512)344-9254
Ultimate Parent: United States Shoe. **SIC:** 5651—Family Clothing Stores.

★ 88952 ★ **Cincinnati Shoe Co.**
999 E. Basse Rd.
San Antonio, TX 78209
(512)824-2669
Ultimate Parent: United States Shoe.

★ 88953 ★ **Circus World**
Loop N
San Antonio, TX 78252
(512)651-6553
Ultimate Parent: Melville. **SIC:** 5945—Hobby, Toy & Game Shops.

★ 88954 ★ **Citgo Petroleum Corp.**
2643 NW Loop 410
San Antonio, TX 78230
(512)340-2171
Ultimate Parent: Citgo Petroleum. **SIC:** 5541—Gasoline Service Stations.

★ 88955 ★ **Citgo Quick Mart**
6104 Montgomery
San Antonio, TX 78239
(512)655-2840
Ultimate Parent: Citgo Petroleum. **SIC:** 5541—Gasoline Service Stations.

★ 88956 ★ **Citgo Quick Mart Sales Office**
431 Isom Rd.
San Antonio, TX 78216
(512)341-2699
Ultimate Parent: Citgo Petroleum. **SIC:** 5541—Gasoline Service Stations.

★ 88957 ★ **Citizens State Bank**
1300 W. Hildebrand Ave.
San Antonio, TX 78201
(512)732-6201
Ultimate Parent: Liberty National Bancorp. **SIC:** 6022—State Commercial Banks.

★ 88958 ★ **Coast to Coast Imprinted Sp**
12007 Radium St.
San Antonio, TX 78216
Ultimate Parent: Servistar Corp. **SIC:** 7389—Business Services Nec.

★ 88959 ★ **Coca-Cola Bottling Co. of San Antonio**
1 Coca Cola Pl.
San Antonio, TX 78219
(512)225-2601
Ultimate Parent: Coca-Cola Enterprises. **SIC:** 2086—Bottled & Canned Soft Drinks.

★ 88960 ★ **Comerica Bank-Texas**
16500 San Pedro Ave.
San Antonio, TX 78232-2241
(210)496-7900
Company Type: Subsidiary. **Location Type:** Branch office. **Ultimate Parent:** Comerica Bank. **SIC:** 6021—National Commercial Banks.

★ 88961 ★ **Comerica Bank-Texas**
2800 Thousand Oaks
San Antonio, TX 78232-4108
(210)496-7999
Company Type: Subsidiary. **Location Type:** Branch office. **Ultimate Parent:** Comerica Bank. **SIC:** 6021—National Commercial Banks.

★ 88962 ★ **Courtyard by Marriott**
8585 Marriott Dr.
San Antonio, TX 78229
(512)696-7100
Ultimate Parent: Marriott International. **SIC:** 7011—Hotels & Motels; 8742—Management Consulting Services.

★ 88963 ★ **Courtyard by Marriott**
8615 Broadway St.
San Antonio, TX 78217
(512)828-7240
Ultimate Parent: Marriott International. **SIC:** 7011—Hotels & Motels.

★ 88964 ★ **Decker Food Co.**
1000 H.F. McCarty Dr.
San Antonio, TX 78210
Ultimate Parent: Conagra. **SIC:** 2013—
Sausages & Other Prepared Meats.

★ 88965 ★ **Delta Air Lines**
9830 Colonnade Blvd.
San Antonio, TX 78230
(512)222-2354
Ultimate Parent: Delta Air Lines, Inc. **SIC:**
4512—Air Transportation—Scheduled.

★ 88966 ★ **Delta Air Lines**
International Airport Terminal
San Antonio, TX 78216
(512)222-2354
Ultimate Parent: Delta Air Lines, Inc. **SIC:**
4512—Air Transportation—Scheduled.

★ 88967 ★ **Delta Air Lines**
San Antonio International Airport
San Antonio, TX 78216
(512)828-3151
Ultimate Parent: Delta Air Lines, Inc. **SIC:**
4512—Air Transportation—Scheduled.

★ 88968 ★ **Delta Air Lines Inc.**
San Antonio International Airport
San Antonio, TX 78216
(512)828-3151
Ultimate Parent: Delta Air Lines, Inc. **SIC:**
4512—Air Transportation—Scheduled.

★ 88969 ★ **Diamond Shamrock**
9830 Colonnade Blvd.
San Antonio, TX 78230
(210)641-6800
Company Type: Headquarters. **Officer:**
Roger R. Hemminghaus. **Employee Count:**
6000. **Sales:** 2555 M. **Fortune 500:** Largest
U.S. Industrial Corporations: Ranking 181.

★ 88970 ★ **Diebold, Inc.**
5692 Randolph Blvd.
San Antonio, TX 78233
(512)656-9385
Ultimate Parent: Diebold, Inc. **SIC:** 7382—
Security Systems Services.

★ 88971 ★ **Digital Equipment
Corporation**
8200 W. I-10
San Antonio, TX 78230
(512)524-2800
Ultimate Parent: Digital Equipment Corp.
SIC: 7373—Computer Integrated Systems
Design.

★ 88972 ★ **Dillard Department
Stores**
7900 N. Ih 35
San Antonio, TX 78218
(512)654-3131
Ultimate Parent: Dillard Department Stores.
SIC: 5311—Department Stores.

★ 88973 ★ **Dillard Department
Stores**
6301 NW Loop 410
San Antonio, TX 78238
(512)681-7970
Ultimate Parent: Dillard Department Stores.
SIC: 8021—Offices & Clinics of Dentists.

★ 88974 ★ **Dillard Department
Stores**
622 Central Park Shopping Ctr.
San Antonio, TX 78216
(512)341-5151
Ultimate Parent: Dillard Department Stores.
SIC: 5311—Department Stores.

★ 88975 ★ **Dillard Department
Stores**
102 Alamo Plz.
San Antonio, TX 78205
(512)227-4343
Ultimate Parent: Dillard Department Stores.
SIC: 5311—Department Stores.

★ 88976 ★ **Electronic Data
Systems**
6061 Northwest Expy.
San Antonio, TX 78201
(512)734-7700
Ultimate Parent: Electronic Data Systems.
SIC: 7374—Data Processing & Preparation.

★ 88977 ★ **Electronic Data
Systems Corp.**
Hemisfair Plz.
San Antonio, TX 78205
(512)226-3198
Ultimate Parent: Electronic Data Systems.
SIC: 7374—Data Processing & Preparation.

★ 88978 ★ **Electronic Data
Systems Dat**
106 Alamo Plz. 1
San Antonio, TX 78205
(512)271-6300
Ultimate Parent: EG & G.

★ 88979 ★ **Exxon**
1527 N. New Braunfels Ave.
San Antonio, TX 78208
(512)223-9391
Ultimate Parent: Exxon. **SIC:** 5541—
Gasoline Service Stations.

★ 88980 ★ **Exxon**
12202 Jones Maltsberger Rd.
San Antonio, TX 78247
(512)494-0987
Ultimate Parent: Exxon. **SIC:** 5541—
Gasoline Service Stations.

★ 88981 ★ **Exxon**
1702 SW Loop 410
San Antonio, TX 78227
(512)674-1861
Ultimate Parent: Exxon. **SIC:** 5541—
Gasoline Service Stations.

★ 88982 ★ **Exxon**
3926 W. Commerce St.
San Antonio, TX 78207
(512)432-4771
Ultimate Parent: Exxon. **SIC:** 5541—
Gasoline Service Stations.

★ 88983 ★ **Exxon**
822 Hot Wells Blvd.
San Antonio, TX 78223
(512)532-6590
Ultimate Parent: Exxon. **SIC:** 5541—
Gasoline Service Stations.

★ 88984 ★ **Exxon**
12011 San Pedro Ave.
San Antonio, TX 78216
(512)494-6329
Ultimate Parent: Exxon. **SIC:** 5541—
Gasoline Service Stations.

★ 88985 ★ **Exxon**
7930 Callaghan Rd.
San Antonio, TX 78229
(512)349-0411
Ultimate Parent: Exxon. **SIC:** 5541—
Gasoline Service Stations.

★ 88986 ★ **Exxon**
4623 S. Panam Expy.
San Antonio, TX 78225
(512)927-4970
Ultimate Parent: Exxon. **SIC:** 5541—
Gasoline Service Stations.

★ 88987 ★ **Exxon**
403 Fair Ave.
San Antonio, TX 78223
(512)533-5635
Ultimate Parent: Exxon. **SIC:** 5541—
Gasoline Service Stations.

★ 88988 ★ **Exxon**
12210 Nacogdoches Rd.
San Antonio, TX 78217
(512)657-1901
Ultimate Parent: Exxon. **SIC:** 5541—
Gasoline Service Stations.

★ 88989 ★ **Exxon**
5801 Babcock Rd.
San Antonio, TX 78240
(512)691-0843
Ultimate Parent: Exxon. **SIC:** 5541—
Gasoline Service Stations.

★ 88990 ★ **Exxon**
2299 NW Military Hwy.
San Antonio, TX 78213
(512)366-2693
Ultimate Parent: Exxon. **SIC:** 5541—
Gasoline Service Stations.

★ 88991 ★ **Exxon**
1063 SE Military Dr.
San Antonio, TX 78214
(512)922-5414
Ultimate Parent: Exxon.

★ 88992 ★ **Exxon**
7203 NW Loop 410
San Antonio, TX 78238
(512)684-6675
Ultimate Parent: Exxon.

★ 88993 ★ **Exxon**
4645 W. Commerce St.
San Antonio, TX 78237
(512)432-2153
Ultimate Parent: Exxon. **SIC:** 5541—
Gasoline Service Stations.

★ 88994 ★ **Exxon Car Care
Center**
1000 NW Loop 410
San Antonio, TX 78213
(512)341-6288
Ultimate Parent: Exxon.

★ 88995 ★ **Exxon Car Care
Center**
1038 Culebra Rd.
San Antonio, TX 78201
(512)736-2623
Ultimate Parent: Exxon. **SIC:** 5541—
Gasoline Service Stations.

★ 88996 ★ **Exxon Car Care
Center**
2302 West Ave.
San Antonio, TX 78201
(512)732-9672
Ultimate Parent: Exxon. **SIC:** 5541—
Gasoline Service Stations.

★ 88997 ★ **Exxon Car Wash**
6523 San Pedro Ave.
San Antonio, TX 78216
(512)341-2102
Ultimate Parent: Exxon. **SIC:** 5411—
Grocery Stores.

★ 88998 ★ **Exxon Car Wash**
2102 SW Military Dr.
San Antonio, TX 78224
(512)924-7781
Ultimate Parent: Exxon. **SIC:** 5541—
Gasoline Service Stations.

★ 88999 ★ **Exxon Co.**
13939 Nacogdoches Rd.
San Antonio, TX 78217
(512)656-4583
Ultimate Parent: Exxon. **SIC:** 5541—
Gasoline Service Stations.

★ 89000 ★ **Exxon Co. USA**
2302 West Ave.
San Antonio, TX 78201
(512)732-2413
Ultimate Parent: Exxon. **SIC:** 7538—
General Automotive Repair Shops.

★ 89001 ★ **Exxon Corp.**
N Panam Expy.
San Antonio, TX 78219
(512)220-3401
Ultimate Parent: Exxon. **SIC:** 5541—
Gasoline Service Stations.

★ 89002 ★ **Exxon Shop**
1303 W. Hildebrand Ave.
San Antonio, TX 78201
(512)736-6302
Ultimate Parent: Exxon. **SIC:** 5541—
Gasoline Service Stations.

★ 89003 ★ **Exxon Shop**
9445 Bandera Rd.
San Antonio, TX 78250
(512)684-1680
Ultimate Parent: Exxon.

★ 89004 ★ **Exxon Shop**
1527 N. New Braunfels Ave.
San Antonio, TX 78208
(512)222-9391
Ultimate Parent: Exxon.

★ 89005 ★ **Farm & Home
Savings Associa**
6310 N. New Braunfels Ave.
San Antonio, TX 78209
(512)822-8646
Ultimate Parent: Farm & Home Financial
Corp. **SIC:** 6035—Federal Savings
Institutions.

★ 89006 ★ **Farm & Home
Savings Associa**
202 Jefferson St.
San Antonio, TX 78205
(512)225-6771
Ultimate Parent: Farm & Home Financial

Corp. **SIC:** 6035—Federal Savings
Institutions.

★ 89007 ★ **Farm & Home
Savings Association**
615 NW Loop 410
San Antonio, TX 78216
(512)349-3131
Ultimate Parent: Farm & Home Financial
Corp. **SIC:** 6035—Federal Savings
Institutions.

★ 89008 ★ **First Data Resources**
4241 E. Piedras Dr.
San Antonio, TX 78228
(512)732-4268
Ultimate Parent: First Data Corp. **SIC:**
7378—Computer Maintenance & Repair.

★ 89009 ★ **Foot Action**
4522 Crossroads of a S
San Antonio, TX 78201
(512)734-6819
Ultimate Parent: Melville. **SIC:** 5661—Shoe
Stores.

★ 89010 ★ **Foot Action**
849 E. Commerce St.
San Antonio, TX 78205
(512)271-7530
Ultimate Parent: Melville. **SIC:** 5661—Shoe
Stores.

★ 89011 ★ **Foot Action**
622 Central Park Shopping Ctr.
San Antonio, TX 78216
(512)342-0032
Ultimate Parent: Melville. **SIC:** 5661—Shoe
Stores.

★ 89012 ★ **Foot Action U S a**
Loop N
San Antonio, TX 78252
(512)651-5970
Ultimate Parent: Melville. **SIC:** 5661—Shoe
Stores.

★ 89013 ★ **Footaction U S a**
7900 N. Ih 35
San Antonio, TX 78218
(512)653-2777
Ultimate Parent: Melville. **SIC:** 5661—Shoe
Stores.

★ 89014 ★ **The Gap**
6301 NW Loop 410
San Antonio, TX 78238
(512)647-1177
Ultimate Parent: GAP.

★ 89015 ★ **The Gap**
849 E. Commerce St. 313
San Antonio, TX 78205
(512)222-9581
Ultimate Parent: GAP. **SIC:** 5651—Family
Clothing Stores.

★ 89016 ★ **The Gap**
N Star Mall
San Antonio, TX 78216
(512)340-1433
Ultimate Parent: GAP. **SIC:** 5611—Men's &
Boys' Clothing Stores.

★ 89017 ★ **The Gap**
Central Park Shopping Ctr.
San Antonio, TX 78216
(512)349-9304
Ultimate Parent: GAP. **SIC:** 5611—Men's &
Boys' Clothing Stores.

★ 89018 ★ **The Gap Kids**
7400 N. Star Mall
San Antonio, TX 78216
(512)349-9010
Ultimate Parent: GAP. **SIC:** 5137—
Women's/Children's Clothing.

★ 89019 ★ **Gap Stores**
Central Park Shopping Ctr.
San Antonio, TX 78216
(512)349-9304
Ultimate Parent: GAP. **SIC:** 5611—Men's &
Boys' Clothing Stores.

★ 89020 ★ **Gap Stores**
N Star Mall
San Antonio, TX 78216
(512)340-1433
Ultimate Parent: GAP. **SIC:** 5611—Men's &
Boys' Clothing Stores.

★ 89021 ★　**General Electric Co.**
1210 Arion Pky.
San Antonio, TX 78216
(210)491-9085
Officer: Mike Koester, Manager. **Ultimate Parent:** General Electric. **SIC:** 3844—X-Ray Apparatus & Tubes.

★ 89022 ★　**Greyhound Bus Lines**
1025 Dewhurst Rd.
San Antonio, TX 78213
(512)732-7441
Ultimate Parent: Greyhound Lines Inc. **SIC:** 4111—Local & Suburban Transit.

★ 89023 ★　**Greyhound Bus Lines**
1505 E. Houston St.
San Antonio, TX 78202
(512)270-5841
Ultimate Parent: Greyhound Lines Inc. **SIC:** 4131—Intercity & Rural Bus Transportation.

★ 89024 ★　**Harris Corp.**
Farion Div. San Antonio Operations
5727 Farinon Dr.
San Antonio, TX 78249
Company Type: Division. **Ultimate Parent:** Harris. **SIC:** 3672—Printed Circuit Boards.

★ 89025 ★　**Hertz Rent-A-Car**
101 Bowie St.
San Antonio, TX 78205
(512)222-1695
Ultimate Parent: Hertz. **SIC:** 7514—Passenger Car Rental.

★ 89026 ★　**Hewlett-Packard Co.**
14100 San Pedro Ave. 100
San Antonio, TX 78232
(512)494-9336
Ultimate Parent: Hewlett-Packard. **SIC:** 5699—Miscellaneous Apparel & Accessory Stores; 7373—Computer Integrated Systems Design.

★ 89027 ★　**Hibernia National Bank**
16500 San Pedro Ave.
San Antonio, TX 78232
(512)496-7900
Ultimate Parent: Hibernia Corp.

★ 89028 ★　**Hit or Miss**
8513 Blanco Rd.
San Antonio, TX 78216
(512)349-4529
Ultimate Parent: TJX. **SIC:** 5621—Women's Clothing Stores; 5651—Family Clothing Stores.

★ 89029 ★　**Hit or Miss**
14050 Nacogdoches Rd.
San Antonio, TX 78247
(512)656-9005
Ultimate Parent: TJX. **SIC:** 5651—Family Clothing Stores.

★ 89030 ★　**Hit or Miss**
7012 Bandera Rd.
San Antonio, TX 78238
(512)680-6840
Ultimate Parent: TJX. **SIC:** 5651—Family Clothing Stores.

★ 89031 ★　**Industrial Lubricants Co.**
434 Riverside Dr.
San Antonio, TX 78210
Ultimate Parent: Diamond Shamrock. **SIC:** 2992—Lubricating Oils & Greases; 5172—Petroleum Products Nec.

★ 89032 ★　**Jiffy Lube**
11505 Toepperwein Rd.
San Antonio, TX 78233
(512)655-5244
Ultimate Parent: Pennzoil. **SIC:** 7549—Automotive Services Nec.

★ 89033 ★　**Jiffy Lube**
12903 Nacogdoches Rd.
San Antonio, TX 78217
(512)590-7244
Ultimate Parent: Pennzoil. **SIC:** 5172—Petroleum Products Nec.

★ 89034 ★　**Jiffy Lube**
15703 San Pedro Ave.
San Antonio, TX 78232
(512)496-2548
Ultimate Parent: Pennzoil.

★ 89035 ★　**Jiffy Lube**
7083 Bandera Rd.
San Antonio, TX 78238
(512)680-6581
Ultimate Parent: Pennzoil.

★ 89036 ★　**Jiffy Lube**
7626 Culebra Rd.
San Antonio, TX 78251
(512)521-1400
Ultimate Parent: Pennzoil.

★ 89037 ★　**Kay Bee Toy & Hobby Shop**
2310 SW Military Dr.
San Antonio, TX 78224
(512)921-2974
Ultimate Parent: Melville. **SIC:** 5945—Hobby, Toy & Game Shops.

★ 89038 ★　**Kay Bee Toy & Hobby Shop**
6301 Ingram Rd.
San Antonio, TX 78238
(512)680-8759
Ultimate Parent: Melville. **SIC:** 5945—Hobby, Toy & Game Shops.

★ 89039 ★　**Kay Bee Toy & Hobby Shop**
7900 N. Ih 35
San Antonio, TX 78218
(512)653-6317
Ultimate Parent: Melville. **SIC:** 5945—Hobby, Toy & Game Shops.

★ 89040 ★　**Kay Bee Toy & Hobby Shop**
622 Central Park Shopping Ctr.
San Antonio, TX 78216
(512)340-2326
Ultimate Parent: Melville. **SIC:** 5945—Hobby, Toy & Game Shops.

★ 89041 ★　**Kay Bee Toy&Hobby Shop**
Ingram
San Antonio, TX 78238
(512)680-8579
Ultimate Parent: Melville. **SIC:** 5945—Hobby, Toy & Game Shops.

★ 89042 ★　**Kay Bee Toy&Hobby Shop**
Mercado
San Antonio, TX 78227
(512)673-6260
Ultimate Parent: Melville. **SIC:** 5945—Hobby, Toy & Game Shops.

★ 89043 ★　**Kentucky Fried Chicken**
4711 W. Commerce St.
San Antonio, TX 78237
(512)433-0195
Ultimate Parent: Pepsico. **SIC:** 5812—Eating Places.

★ 89044 ★　**Kentucky Fried Chicken**
4310 Vance Jackson Rd.
San Antonio, TX 78230
(512)344-9561
Ultimate Parent: Pepsico. **SIC:** 1741—Masonry & Other Stonework; 5812—Eating Places.

★ 89045 ★　**Kentucky Fried Chicken**
10857 Vandale St.
San Antonio, TX 78216
(512)341-3321
Ultimate Parent: Pepsico. **SIC:** 1741—Masonry & Other Stonework.

★ 89046 ★　**Kentucky Fried Chicken**
2622 Rockgate St.
San Antonio, TX 78227
(512)674-2991
Ultimate Parent: Pepsico. **SIC:** 1741—Masonry & Other Stonework; 5812—Eating Places.

★ 89047 ★　**Kentucky Fried Chicken**
1404 SW Military Dr.
San Antonio, TX 78221
(512)923-2047
Ultimate Parent: Pepsico. **SIC:** 1741—Masonry & Other Stonework; 5812—Eating Places; 5812—Eating Places.

★ 89048 ★　**Kentucky Fried Chicken**
531 N. New Braunfels Ave.
San Antonio, TX 78202
(512)223-1238
Ultimate Parent: Pepsico. **SIC:** 5812—Eating Places; 5812—Eating Places.

★ 89049 ★　**Kentucky Fried Chicken**
2525 Nogalitos
San Antonio, TX 78225
(512)921-0721
Ultimate Parent: Pepsico. **SIC:** 5812—Eating Places.

★ 89050 ★　**Kentucky Fried Chicken**
530 Fair Ave.
San Antonio, TX 78223
(512)534-9190
Ultimate Parent: Pepsico. **SIC:** 1741—Masonry & Other Stonework; 5812—Eating Places; 5812—Eating Places.

★ 89051 ★　**Kentucky Fried Chicken**
3018 Fredericksburg Rd.
San Antonio, TX 78201
(512)735-9453
Ultimate Parent: Pepsico. **SIC:** 1741—Masonry & Other Stonework; 5812—Eating Places.

★ 89052 ★　**Kentucky Fried Chicken**
1264 Austin Hwy.
San Antonio, TX 78209
(512)824-0720
Ultimate Parent: Pepsico. **SIC:** 3429—Hardware Nec; 5812—Eating Places.

★ 89053 ★　**Kentucky Fried Chicken**
14075 Nacogdoches Rd.
San Antonio, TX 78247
(512)653-8814
Ultimate Parent: Pepsico. **SIC:** 5812—Eating Places.

★ 89054 ★　**Kentucky Fried Chicken**
8510 Fredericksburg Rd.
San Antonio, TX 78229
(512)697-8650
Ultimate Parent: Pepsico. **SIC:** 5812—Eating Places.

★ 89055 ★　**Kentucky Fried Chicken**
2110 Goliad Rd.
San Antonio, TX 78223
(512)337-2214
Ultimate Parent: Pepsico. **SIC:** 5812—Eating Places.

★ 89056 ★　**Kroger Co.**
4958 Stout Dr.
San Antonio, TX 78219
(512)661-4657
Ultimate Parent: Kroger. **SIC:** 5411—Grocery Stores.

★ 89057 ★　**Kroger Co.**
5004 Stout Dr.
San Antonio, TX 78219
(512)661-8775
Ultimate Parent: Kroger. **SIC:** 5411—Grocery Stores.

★ 89058 ★　**Kroger Co.**
1246 Austin Hwy.
San Antonio, TX 78209
(512)828-0007
Ultimate Parent: Kroger. **SIC:** 5411—Grocery Stores.

★ 89059 ★　**Kroger Company No 286**
5254 Blanco Rd.
San Antonio, TX 78216
(512)349-3773
Ultimate Parent: Kroger. **SIC:** 5411—Grocery Stores.

★ 89060 ★　**Kroger Pharmacy**
5254 Blanco Rd.
San Antonio, TX 78216
(512)349-3491
Ultimate Parent: Kroger. **SIC:** 5912—Drug Stores & Proprietary Stores.

★ 89061 ★　**Kroger Pharmacy**
2321 SW Military Dr.
San Antonio, TX 78224
(512)923-7425
Ultimate Parent: Kroger. **SIC:** 5912—Drug Stores & Proprietary Stores.

★ 89062 ★　**Kroger Pharmacy**
1246 Austin Hwy.
San Antonio, TX 78209
(512)828-4895
Ultimate Parent: Kroger. **SIC:** 5912—Drug Stores & Proprietary Stores.

★ 89063 ★　**Lane Bryant**
7900 N. Interstate 35
San Antonio, TX 78218
(512)650-9337
Ultimate Parent: Limited. **SIC:** 5651—Family Clothing Stores.

★ 89064 ★　**Lane Bryant**
7400 N. Star Mall
San Antonio, TX 78216
(512)342-5103
Ultimate Parent: Limited. **SIC:** 5651—Family Clothing Stores.

★ 89065 ★　**Lane Bryant**
Loop N
San Antonio, TX 78252
(512)651-6204
Ultimate Parent: Limited. **SIC:** 5651—Family Clothing Stores.

★ 89066 ★　**Lane Bryant**
4100 Mac Creless Mall N
San Antonio, TX 78223
(512)534-7600
Ultimate Parent: Limited. **SIC:** 5651—Family Clothing Stores.

★ 89067 ★　**Lane Bryant**
849 E. Commerce St. 337
San Antonio, TX 78205
(512)223-4308
Ultimate Parent: Limited. **SIC:** 5651—Family Clothing Stores.

★ 89068 ★　**Lane Bryant**
6301 Ingram Rd.
San Antonio, TX 78238
(512)681-3117
Ultimate Parent: Limited. **SIC:** 5651—Family Clothing Stores.

★ 89069 ★　**Lane Bryant**
622 Central Park Shopping Ctr.
San Antonio, TX 78216
(512)349-4037
Ultimate Parent: Limited. **SIC:** 5651—Family Clothing Stores.

★ 89070 ★　**Lens Crafters**
4522 Crossroads of a S
San Antonio, TX 78201
(512)733-3766
Ultimate Parent: United States Shoe. **SIC:** 5995—Optical Goods Stores.

★ 89071 ★　**Lens Crafters**
7900 N. I-35
San Antonio, TX 78218
(512)590-0041
Ultimate Parent: United States Shoe. **SIC:** 8042—Offices & Clinics of Optometrists.

★ 89072 ★　**Lerner Shop**
7900 N. Ih 35
San Antonio, TX 78218
(512)654-0110
Ultimate Parent: Limited. **SIC:** 5651—Family Clothing Stores.

★ 89073 ★　**Lerner Shop**
N Star Mall
San Antonio, TX 78216
(512)344-6279
Ultimate Parent: Limited. **SIC:** 5621—Women's Clothing Stores.

★ 89074 ★　**Lerner Shop**
915 Mccreless Mall
San Antonio, TX 78223
(512)534-7391
Ultimate Parent: Limited. **SIC:** 5621—Women's Clothing Stores.

★ 89075 ★　**Lerner Shop**
849 E. Commerce St. 383
San Antonio, TX 78205
(512)223-8991
Ultimate Parent: Limited. **SIC:** 5651—Family Clothing Stores.

★ **89076** ★　　**Lerner Shop**
Ingram
San Antonio, TX 78238
(512)681-6750
Ultimate Parent: Limited. **SIC:** 5621—
Women's Clothing Stores.

★ **89077** ★　　**Lerner Shop**
1401 SW Loop 410
San Antonio, TX 78227
(512)675-8180
Ultimate Parent: Limited. **SIC:** 5651—
Family Clothing Stores.

★ **89078** ★　　**Lerner Shop**
7400 N. Star Mall
San Antonio, TX 78216
(512)340-5377
Ultimate Parent: Limited. **SIC:** 5651—
Family Clothing Stores.

★ **89079** ★　　**Lerner Shop**
211 S. Park Mall
San Antonio, TX 78224
(512)922-9508
Ultimate Parent: Limited. **SIC:** 5621—
Women's Clothing Stores.

★ **89080** ★　　**The Limited**
124 Wonderland Shopping
San Antonio, TX 78201
(512)732-3393
Ultimate Parent: Limited. **SIC:** 5621—
Women's Clothing Stores.

★ **89081** ★　　**The Limited**
N Star Mall
San Antonio, TX 78216
(512)340-1019
Ultimate Parent: Limited. **SIC:** 5621—
Women's Clothing Stores.

★ **89082** ★　　**The Limited**
7900 N. Ih 35
San Antonio, TX 78218
(512)653-2013
Ultimate Parent: Limited. **SIC:** 5651—
Family Clothing Stores.

★ **89083** ★　　**The Limited**
4522 S. Crossroads of a a
San Antonio, TX 78201
(512)734-6471
Ultimate Parent: Limited. **SIC:** 5651—
Family Clothing Stores.

★ **89084** ★　　**The Limited**
849 E. Commerce St.
San Antonio, TX 78205
(512)223-3839
Ultimate Parent: Limited. **SIC:** 5651—
Family Clothing Stores.

★ **89085** ★　　**The Limited**
7900 N. Interstate 35
San Antonio, TX 78218
(512)653-2013
Ultimate Parent: Limited.

★ **89086** ★　　**The Limited Express**
7900 N. Ih 35
San Antonio, TX 78218
(512)653-6514
Ultimate Parent: Limited. **SIC:** 5651—
Family Clothing Stores.

★ **89087** ★　　**The Limited Express**
7400 N. Star Mall
San Antonio, TX 78216
(512)377-0734
Ultimate Parent: Limited. **SIC:** 5651—
Family Clothing Stores.

★ **89088** ★　　**The Limited Express**
6301 Ingram Rd.
San Antonio, TX 78238
(512)684-0008
Ultimate Parent: Limited. **SIC:** 5651—
Family Clothing Stores.

★ **89089** ★　　**The Limited Express**
Loop N
San Antonio, TX 78252
(512)651-9460
Ultimate Parent: Limited. **SIC:** 8221—
Colleges & Universities.

★ **89090** ★　　**The Limited Express**
849 E. Commerce St. 479
San Antonio, TX 78205
(512)223-6567
Ultimate Parent: Limited. **SIC:** 5651—
Family Clothing Stores.

★ **89091** ★　　**Marshalls**
5455 Evers Rd.
San Antonio, TX 78238
Ultimate Parent: Melville. **SIC:** 5311—
Department Stores.

★ **89092** ★　　**Mary Kay Cosmetics**
306 Westwind Cir.
San Antonio, TX 78239
(512)655-2925
Ultimate Parent: Mary Kay Cosmetics.

★ **89093** ★　　**Mary Kay Cosmetics**
9481 Old Tezel Rd.
San Antonio, TX 78250
(512)681-4543
Ultimate Parent: Mary Kay Cosmetics. **SIC:**
5999—Miscellaneous Retail Stores Nec.

★ **89094** ★　　**Mary Kay Cosmetics**
10302 Quail Meadow St.
San Antonio, TX 78230
(512)691-8448
Ultimate Parent: Mary Kay Cosmetics.

★ **89095** ★　　**Mary Kay Cosmetics**
2518 Old Orchard Ln.
San Antonio, TX 78230
(512)340-1477
Ultimate Parent: Mary Kay Cosmetics.

★ **89096** ★　　**Mary Kay Cosmetics**
767 Utopia Ave.
San Antonio, TX 78223
(512)333-2231
Ultimate Parent: Mary Kay Cosmetics. **SIC:**
7231—Beauty Shops.

★ **89097** ★　　**McDonalds
Restaurant**
3502 Roosevelt Ave.
San Antonio, TX 78214
(512)927-5273
Ultimate Parent: McDonald's.

★ **89098** ★　　**McDonalds
Restaurant**
2935 Roosevelt Ave.
San Antonio, TX 78214
(512)927-9913
Ultimate Parent: McDonald's.

★ **89099** ★　　**McDonalds
Restaurant**
148 Interloop Rd.
San Antonio, TX 78216
(512)344-0077
Ultimate Parent: McDonald's.

★ **89100** ★　　**McDonalds
Restaurant**
7267 Wurzbach Rd.
San Antonio, TX 78240
(512)692-9886
Ultimate Parent: McDonald's.

★ **89101** ★　　**McDonalds
Restaurants**
7300 Blanco Rd.
San Antonio, TX 78216
(512)344-9707
Ultimate Parent: McDonald's.
SIC: 5812—Eating Places.

★ **89102** ★　　**Mcduff Electrncs**
1922 SW Military Dr.
San Antonio, TX 78221
(512)921-0926
Ultimate Parent: Tandy Corp.

★ **89103** ★　　**Mcduff Electrncs**
7101 San Pedro Ave.
San Antonio, TX 78216
(512)341-8625
Ultimate Parent: Tandy Corp.

★ **89104** ★　　**Meyer Machine Co.**
3528 Fredericksburg Rd.
San Antonio, TX 78201
(512)736-1811
Ultimate Parent: Tele-Communications.
SIC: 3523—Farm Machinery & Equipment;
3534—Elevators & Moving Stairways.

★ **89105** ★　　**Mobil Gas Station**
10110 San Pedro Ave.
San Antonio, TX 78216
(512)341-1771
Ultimate Parent: Mobil. **SIC:** 5541—
Gasoline Service Stations.

★ **89106** ★　　**Mobil Mart**
16707 Nacogdoches Rd.
San Antonio, TX 78266
(512)651-5346
Ultimate Parent: Mobil.

★ **89107** ★　　**Mobil Mart**
2914 Thousand Oaks Dr.
San Antonio, TX 78247
(512)494-1892
Ultimate Parent: Mobil.

★ **89108** ★　　**Mobil Mart**
9355 Culebra Rd.
San Antonio, TX 78251
(512)523-5665
Ultimate Parent: Mobil.

★ **89109** ★　　**Mobil Mart**
12350 N. Interstate 35
San Antonio, TX 78233
(512)650-8019
Ultimate Parent: Mobil.

★ **89110** ★　　**Mobil Mart**
8426 Broadway St.
San Antonio, TX 78209
(512)828-8700
Ultimate Parent: Mobil. **SIC:** 5541—
Gasoline Service Stations.

★ **89111** ★　　**Mobil Mart**
7203 Culebra Rd.
San Antonio, TX 78251
(512)681-2721
Ultimate Parent: Mobil.

★ **89112** ★　　**Mobil Mart**
2223 Lockhill Selma Rd.
San Antonio, TX 78230-3001
(210)366-4244
Officer: David Menkennett. **Ultimate
Parent:** Mobil. **SIC:** 5541—Gasoline Service
Stations.

★ **89113** ★　　**Mobil Oil Corp. S a
Terminal**
242 W. White
San Antonio, TX 78214
(512)333-5510
Ultimate Parent: Mobil. **SIC:** 2911—
Petroleum Refining.

★ **89114** ★　　**Mobil Oil Self Serve**
5770 Babcock Rd.
San Antonio, TX 78240
(512)697-0089
Ultimate Parent: Mobil. **SIC:** 5541—
Gasoline Service Stations.

★ **89115** ★　　**Mobil Oil Service
Station N**
4535 Rittiman Rd.
San Antonio, TX 78218
(512)655-9216
Ultimate Parent: Mobil. **SIC:** 5541—
Gasoline Service Stations.

★ **89116** ★　　**Monarch Crown Corp.**
13750 San Pedro Ave.
San Antonio, TX 78232-4332
(210)491-9408
Ultimate Parent: Bristol-Myers Squibb. **SIC:**
5141—Groceries—General Line.

★ **89117** ★　　**National Chemsearch**
910 San Pedro Ave.
San Antonio, TX 78212
(512)342-4311
Ultimate Parent: NCH. **SIC:** 5087—Service
Establishment Equipment.

★ **89118** ★　　**New York Life San
Antonio General Office**
Western Agencies
8000 IH-10 W., Ste. 1100
San Antonio, TX 78230
(512)342-7878 **Fax:** (512)342-0235
Officer: Michael L. Jackson, General
Manager. **Ultimate Parent:** New York Life.

★ **89119** ★　　**Newell Ind. Inc.**
530 Steves Ave.
San Antonio, TX 78210
Ultimate Parent: Newell. **SIC:** 3589—
Service Industry Machinery Nec.

★ **89120** ★　　**North American Van
Lines Inc.**
931 S. Flores St.
San Antonio, TX 78204
(512)226-8224
Ultimate Parent: Norfolk Southern. **SIC:**
4783—Packing & Crating.

★ **89121** ★　　**Otis Elevator Co. Inc.**
539 4th St.
San Antonio, TX 78205
(512)224-6623
Ultimate Parent: United Technologies. **SIC:**
1796—Installing Building Equipment Nec.

★ **89122** ★　　**Owens Corning
Fiberglas Cor**
3011 N. Panam Expy.
San Antonio, TX 78219
(512)222-9544
Ultimate Parent: Owens-Corning. **SIC:**
5039—Construction Materials Nec.

★ **89123** ★　　**PacifiCare of Texas**
8200 I.H. 10 W., Ste. 1000
San Antonio, TX 78230-3878
(512)524-9800 **Fax:** (512)979-6311
Officer: Jon Wampler, President. **Ultimate
Parent:** Pacificare Health Systems.

★ **89124** ★　　**Payless Shoesource**
2118 S. Zarzamora St.
San Antonio, TX 78207
(512)222-9589
Ultimate Parent: May Department Stores.
SIC: 5661—Shoe Stores.

★ **89125** ★　　**Payless Shoesource**
District Office
2118 S. Zarzamora St.
San Antonio, TX 78207
(512)222-9589
Ultimate Parent: May Department Stores.
SIC: 5661—Shoe Stores.

★ **89126** ★　　**Payless Shoesource**
6080 Ingram Rd.
San Antonio, TX 78238
(512)680-0017
Ultimate Parent: May Department Stores.
SIC: 5661—Shoe Stores.

★ **89127** ★　　**Payless Shoesource**
6963 Bandera Rd.
San Antonio, TX 78238
(512)684-7303
Ultimate Parent: May Department Stores.
SIC: 5661—Shoe Stores.

★ **89128** ★　　**Payless Shoesource**
6301 Ingram Rd.
San Antonio, TX 78238
(512)680-2561
Ultimate Parent: May Department Stores.
SIC: 5661—Shoe Stores.

★ **89129** ★　　**Payless Shoesource**
7167 W. Hwy. 90
San Antonio, TX 78227
(512)675-0391
Ultimate Parent: May Department Stores.
SIC: 5661—Shoe Stores.

★ **89130** ★　　**Payless Shoesource**
904 Bandera Rd.
San Antonio, TX 78228
(512)434-4360
Ultimate Parent: May Department Stores.
SIC: 5661—Shoe Stores.

★ **89131** ★　　**Payless Shoesource**
1020 SW Military Dr.
San Antonio, TX 78221
(512)923-8351
Ultimate Parent: May Department Stores.
SIC: 5661—Shoe Stores.

★ **89132** ★　　**Payless Shoesource**
3602 S. New Braunfels Ave.
San Antonio, TX 78223
(512)534-2002
Ultimate Parent: May Department Stores.
SIC: 5661—Shoe Stores.

★ **89133** ★　　**Payless Shoesource**
935 N. NW White Rd.
San Antonio, TX 78219
(512)337-2002
Ultimate Parent: May Department Stores.
SIC: 5661—Shoe Stores.

★ **89134** ★　　**Payless Shoesource**
711 SW Military Dr.
San Antonio, TX 78221
(512)921-2733
Ultimate Parent: May Department Stores.
SIC: 5661—Shoe Stores.

★ **89135** ★   **Payless Shoesource**
4414 Blanco Rd.
San Antonio, TX 78212
(512)733-5582
Ultimate Parent: May Department Stores.
SIC: 5661—Shoe Stores.

★ **89136** ★   **Payless Shoesource**
7900 N. IH 35
San Antonio, TX 78218
(512)656-9427
Ultimate Parent: May Department Stores.
SIC: 5661—Shoe Stores.

★ **89137** ★   **Payless Shoesource**
314 E. Houston St.
San Antonio, TX 78205
(512)222-8566
Ultimate Parent: May Department Stores.
SIC: 5661—Shoe Stores.

★ **89138** ★   **Payless Shoesource**
100 S. Zarzamora St.
San Antonio, TX 78207
(512)432-1900
Ultimate Parent: May Department Stores.

★ **89139** ★   **Payless Shoesource**
601 N. New Braunfels Ave.
San Antonio, TX 78202
(512)223-2150
Ultimate Parent: May Department Stores.
SIC: 5661—Shoe Stores.

★ **89140** ★   **Payless Shoesource**
2927 Nogalitos
San Antonio, TX 78225
(512)923-3362
Ultimate Parent: May Department Stores.
SIC: 5661—Shoe Stores.

★ **89141** ★   **Payless Shoesource**
1401 SW Loop 410
San Antonio, TX 78227
(512)675-0680
Ultimate Parent: May Department Stores.
SIC: 5661—Shoe Stores.

★ **89142** ★   **Payless Shoesource**
2310 SW Military Dr.
San Antonio, TX 78224
(512)924-1489
Ultimate Parent: May Department Stores.
SIC: 5661—Shoe Stores.

★ **89143** ★   **Pepsi-Cola Bottling Co.**
6100 NE Loop 410
San Antonio, TX 78218
Ultimate Parent: Pepsico. **SIC:** 2086—
Bottled & Canned Soft Drinks.

★ **89144** ★   **Pepsi-Cola Co.**
6100 NE Loop 410
San Antonio, TX 78209
(210)661-5311
Ultimate Parent: Pepsico. **SIC:** 2086—
Bottled & Canned Soft Drinks.

★ **89145** ★   **Petite Sophisticate**
7400 N. Star Mall
San Antonio, TX 78216
(512)344-9214
Ultimate Parent: United States Shoe. **SIC:**
5651—Family Clothing Stores.

★ **89146** ★   **Petite Sophisticate**
849 E. Commerce St. 281
San Antonio, TX 78205
(512)227-1610
Ultimate Parent: United States Shoe. **SIC:**
5651—Family Clothing Stores.

★ **89147** ★   **Pizza Hut**
65100 PO Box
San Antonio, TX 78265
Ultimate Parent: Pepsico. **SIC:** 5812—
Eating Places.

★ **89148** ★   **Pizza Hut**
1727 SW Military Dr.
San Antonio, TX 78221
Ultimate Parent: Pepsico. **SIC:** 5812—
Eating Places.

★ **89149** ★   **Pizza Hut**
9415 Wurzbach Rd.
San Antonio, TX 78240
(512)696-4670
Ultimate Parent: Pepsico. **SIC:** 5812—
Eating Places.

★ **89150** ★   **Pizza Hut**
110 W. White
San Antonio, TX 78214
(512)337-0047
Ultimate Parent: Pepsico. **SIC:** 5812—
Eating Places.

★ **89151** ★   **Pizza Hut**
11725 West Ave.
San Antonio, TX 78216
(512)342-7052
Ultimate Parent: Pepsico. **SIC:** 5812—
Eating Places.

★ **89152** ★   **Pizza Hut**
1749 W. Loop N
San Antonio, TX 78251
(512)673-6133
Ultimate Parent: Pepsico.

★ **89153** ★   **Pizza Hut**
1749 SW Loop 410
San Antonio, TX 78227
(512)670-1555
Ultimate Parent: Pepsico.

★ **89154** ★   **Pizza Hut**
2511 SW Military Dr.
San Antonio, TX 78224
(512)922-6910
Ultimate Parent: Pepsico. **SIC:** 5812—
Eating Places.

★ **89155** ★   **Pizza Hut**
611 San Pedro Ave.
San Antonio, TX 78212
(512)222-2540
Ultimate Parent: Pepsico. **SIC:** 5812—
Eating Places.

★ **89156** ★   **Pizza Hut**
16100 San Pedro Ave.
San Antonio, TX 78232
(512)494-7351
Ultimate Parent: Pepsico. **SIC:** 5812—
Eating Places.

★ **89157** ★   **Pizza Hut**
2035 S. Hackberry
San Antonio, TX 78210
(512)532-8042
Ultimate Parent: Pepsico. **SIC:** 5812—
Eating Places.

★ **89158** ★   **Pizza Hut**
1322 S. Laredo St.
San Antonio, TX 78204
(512)227-4911
Ultimate Parent: Pepsico. **SIC:** 5812—
Eating Places.

★ **89159** ★   **Pizza Hut**
5970 Old Pearsall Rd.
San Antonio, TX 78242
(512)623-5570
Ultimate Parent: Pepsico. **SIC:** 5812—
Eating Places.

★ **89160** ★   **Pizza Hut**
1820 S. Gen C Macmullen Dr.
San Antonio, TX 78237
(512)433-3371
Ultimate Parent: Pepsico. **SIC:** 5812—
Eating Places.

★ **89161** ★   **Pizza Hut**
9055 Marbach Rd.
San Antonio, TX 78245
(512)673-9933
Ultimate Parent: Pepsico. **SIC:** 5812—
Eating Places.

★ **89162** ★   **Pizza Hut**
14614 Nacogdoches Rd.
San Antonio, TX 78247
(512)636-9344
Ultimate Parent: Pepsico. **SIC:** 5812—
Eating Places.

★ **89163** ★   **Pizza Hut**
1926 Goliad Rd.
San Antonio, TX 78223
(512)333-3942
Ultimate Parent: Pepsico. **SIC:** 5812—
Eating Places.

★ **89164** ★   **Pizza Hut**
8754 Grissom Rd.
San Antonio, TX 78251
(512)680-4531
Ultimate Parent: Pepsico. **SIC:** 5812—
Eating Places.

★ **89165** ★   **Pizza Hut**
2364 E. Southcross Blvd.
San Antonio, TX 78223
(512)532-9988
Ultimate Parent: Pepsico. **SIC:** 5812—
Eating Places.

★ **89166** ★   **Pizza Hut**
3663 Fredericksburg Rd.
San Antonio, TX 78201
(512)736-2721
Ultimate Parent: Pepsico. **SIC:** 5812—
Eating Places.

★ **89167** ★   **Pizza Hut**
10555 Culebra Rd.
San Antonio, TX 78251
(512)680-3892
Ultimate Parent: Pepsico.

★ **89168** ★   **Pizza Hut**
4500 De Zavala Rd.
San Antonio, TX 78249
(512)493-3101
Ultimate Parent: Pepsico.

★ **89169** ★   **Pizza Hut**
217 Alamo Plz.
San Antonio, TX 78205
(512)299-1220
Ultimate Parent: Pepsico. **SIC:** 5812—
Eating Places.

★ **89170** ★   **Pizza Hut**
12146 Nacogdoches Rd.
San Antonio, TX 78217
(512)655-1101
Ultimate Parent: Pepsico. **SIC:** 5812—
Eating Places.

★ **89171** ★   **Pizza Hut**
5731 Babcock Rd.
San Antonio, TX 78240
(512)696-6053
Ultimate Parent: Pepsico. **SIC:** 5812—
Eating Places.

★ **89172** ★   **Pizza Hut**
1008 SW Military Dr.
San Antonio, TX 78221
(512)927-4661
Ultimate Parent: Pepsico. **SIC:** 5812—
Eating Places.

★ **89173** ★   **Pizza Hut**
3323 Roosevelt Ave.
San Antonio, TX 78214
(512)924-7898
Ultimate Parent: Pepsico. **SIC:** 5812—
Eating Places.

★ **89174** ★   **Pizza Hut**
2621 Rockgate St.
San Antonio, TX 78227
(512)674-2407
Ultimate Parent: Pepsico. **SIC:** 5812—
Eating Places.

★ **89175** ★   **Pizza Hut**
6418 Callaghan Rd.
San Antonio, TX 78229
(512)341-6811
Ultimate Parent: Pepsico. **SIC:** 5812—
Eating Places.

★ **89176** ★   **Pizza Hut**
4511 Rigsby Ave.
San Antonio, TX 78222
(512)333-1616
Ultimate Parent: Pepsico. **SIC:** 5812—
Eating Places.

★ **89177** ★   **Pizza Hut**
310 Valley Hi Dr.
San Antonio, TX 78227
(512)675-6666
Ultimate Parent: Pepsico. **SIC:** 5812—
Eating Places.

★ **89178** ★   **Pizza Hut**
7319 N. Loop W
San Antonio, TX 78249
(512)695-2205
Ultimate Parent: Pepsico. **SIC:** 5812—
Eating Places.

★ **89179** ★   **Pizza Hut**
7031 Bandera Rd.
San Antonio, TX 78238
(512)681-3358
Ultimate Parent: Pepsico. **SIC:** 5812—
Eating Places.

★ **89180** ★   **Pizza Hut**
4001 W. Commerce St.
San Antonio, TX 78207
(512)432-4766
Ultimate Parent: Pepsico. **SIC:** 5812—
Eating Places.

★ **89181** ★   **Pizza Hut**
5331 Walzem Rd.
San Antonio, TX 78218
(512)655-6141
Ultimate Parent: Pepsico. **SIC:** 5812—
Eating Places.

★ **89182** ★   **Pizza Hut**
6630 San Pedro Ave.
San Antonio, TX 78216
(512)826-1181
Ultimate Parent: Pepsico. **SIC:** 5812—
Eating Places.

★ **89183** ★   **Pizza Hut**
700 Walgreen Plz.
San Antonio, TX 78207
(512)436-9933
Ultimate Parent: Pepsico. **SIC:** 5812—
Eating Places.

★ **89184** ★   **Pizza Hut Inc.**
2511 SW Military Dr.
San Antonio, TX 78224
(512)924-9473
Ultimate Parent: Pepsico. **SIC:** 5812—
Eating Places.

★ **89185** ★   **Radio Shack**
13440 San Pedro Ave.
San Antonio, TX 78216
Company Type: Division. **Ultimate Parent:**
Tandy Corp. **SIC:** 5065—Electronic Parts &
Equipment Nec.

★ **89186** ★   **Radio Shack**
8131 W. Ih 10
San Antonio, TX 78230
(512)342-5540
Company Type: Division. **Ultimate Parent:**
Tandy Corp. **SIC:** 5065—Electronic Parts &
Equipment Nec.

★ **89187** ★   **Radio Shack**
211 W. Market St.
San Antonio, TX 78205
(512)225-0345
Company Type: Division. **Ultimate Parent:**
Tandy Corp. **SIC:** 5046—Commercial
Equipment Nec.

★ **89188** ★   **Radio Shack**
2310 SW Military Dr.
San Antonio, TX 78224
(512)924-9110
Company Type: Division. **Ultimate Parent:**
Tandy Corp. **SIC:** 5065—Electronic Parts &
Equipment Nec.

★ **89189** ★   **Radio Shack**
310 Valley Hi Dr.
San Antonio, TX 78227
(512)674-2443
Company Type: Division. **Ultimate Parent:**
Tandy Corp. **SIC:** 5731—Radio, Television
& Electronics Stores.

★ **89190** ★   **Radio Shack**
7119 San Pedro Ave.
San Antonio, TX 78216
(512)341-3391
Company Type: Division. **Ultimate Parent:**
Tandy Corp. **SIC:** 5065—Electronic Parts &
Equipment Nec.

★ **89191** ★   **Radio Shack**
1401 SW Loop 410
San Antonio, TX 78227
(512)675-3880
Company Type: Division. **Ultimate Parent:**
Tandy Corp. **SIC:** 5731—Radio, Television
& Electronics Stores.

★ **89192** ★   **Radio Shack**
7400 N. Star Mall
San Antonio, TX 78216
(512)366-0217
Company Type: Division. **Ultimate Parent:**
Tandy Corp. **SIC:** 5731—Radio, Television
& Electronics Stores.

★ **89193** ★   **Radio Shack**
945 N. Ww White Rd.
San Antonio, TX 78219
(512)333-6711
Company Type: Division. **Ultimate Parent:**
Tandy Corp. **SIC:** 5065—Electronic Parts &
Equipment Nec.

★ 89194 ★   Radio Shack
Loop N
San Antonio, TX 78252
(512)651-3048
Company Type: Division. **Ultimate Parent:**
Tandy Corp. **SIC:** 5065—Electronic Parts &
Equipment Nec.

★ 89195 ★   Radio Shack
4100 Mac Creless Mall N
San Antonio, TX 78223
(512)533-9869
Company Type: Division. **Ultimate Parent:**
Tandy Corp. **SIC:** 5065—Electronic Parts &
Equipment Nec.

★ 89196 ★   Radio Shack
999 E. Basse Rd.
San Antonio, TX 78209
(512)822-1639
Company Type: Division. **SIC:** 7373—Computer
Integrated Systems Design.

★ 89197 ★   Radio Shack
6301 Ingram Rd.
San Antonio, TX 78238
(512)681-1421
Company Type: Division. **Ultimate Parent:**
Tandy Corp. **SIC:** 5065—Electronic Parts &
Equipment Nec.

★ 89198 ★   Radio Shack
5164 Broadway St.
San Antonio, TX 78209
(512)822-1965
Company Type: Division. **Ultimate Parent:**
Tandy Corp. **SIC:** 5731—Radio, Television
& Electronics Stores.

★ 89199 ★   Radio Shack
622 Central Park Shopping Ctr.
San Antonio, TX 78216
(512)342-9547
Company Type: Division. **Ultimate Parent:**
Tandy Corp. **SIC:** 5731—Radio, Television
& Electronics Stores.

★ 89200 ★   Radio Shack
5815 Babcock Rd.
San Antonio, TX 78240
(512)684-6351
Company Type: Division. **Ultimate Parent:**
Tandy Corp. **SIC:** 5063—Electrical
Apparatus & Equipment.

★ 89201 ★   Radio Shack
6955 Bandera Rd.
San Antonio, TX 78238
(512)684-9322
Company Type: Division. **Ultimate Parent:**
Tandy Corp. **SIC:** 7373—Computer
Integrated Systems Design.

★ 89202 ★   Radio Shack
1201 Austin Hwy.
San Antonio, TX 78209
(512)822-3186
Company Type: Division. **Ultimate Parent:**
Tandy Corp. **SIC:** 5731—Radio, Television
& Electronics Stores.

★ 89203 ★   Radio Shack
409 Mccreless Mall
San Antonio, TX 78223
(512)653-9869
Company Type: Division. **Ultimate Parent:**
Tandy Corp. **SIC:** 5734—Computer &
Software Stores.

★ 89204 ★   Radio Shack
138 N. Star Mall
San Antonio, TX 78216
(512)366-1179
Company Type: Division. **Ultimate Parent:**
Tandy Corp. **SIC:** 5065—Electronic Parts &
Equipment Nec.

★ 89205 ★   Radio Shack
3021 West Ave.
San Antonio, TX 78201
(512)341-9411
Company Type: Division. **Ultimate Parent:**
Tandy Corp. **SIC:** 5611—Men's & Boys'
Clothing Stores.

★ 89206 ★   Radio Shack
Mercado Sq.
San Antonio, TX 78207
(512)675-3880
Company Type: Division. **Ultimate Parent:**
Tandy Corp. **SIC:** 5046—Commercial
Equipment Nec.

★ 89207 ★   Radio Shack
5402 Glen Ridge Dr.
San Antonio, TX 78229
(512)684-6351
Company Type: Division. **Ultimate Parent:**
Tandy Corp. **SIC:** 5611—Men's & Boys'
Clothing Stores.

★ 89208 ★   Radio Shack
945 E. White
San Antonio, TX 78223
(512)333-6711
Company Type: Division. **Ultimate Parent:**
Tandy Corp. **SIC:** 5611—Men's & Boys'
Clothing Stores.

★ 89209 ★   Radio Shack
409 Mccreless Mall
San Antonio, TX 78223
(512)533-4341
Company Type: Division. **Ultimate Parent:**
Tandy Corp. **SIC:** 5046—Commercial
Equipment Nec.

★ 89210 ★   Radio Shack
7900 N. IH 35
San Antonio, TX 78218
(512)653-1437
Company Type: Division. **Ultimate Parent:**
Tandy Corp. **SIC:** 5065—Electronic Parts &
Equipment Nec.

★ 89211 ★   Radio Shack
5378 Walzem Rd.
San Antonio, TX 78218
Company Type: Division. **Ultimate Parent:**
Tandy Corp. **SIC:** 5065—Electronic Parts &
Equipment Nec.

★ 89212 ★   Reliance Insurance
Co.
10999 W. I-10
San Antonio, TX 78230
(512)690-0800
Ultimate Parent: Reliance Group Holdings.
SIC: 6411—Insurance Agents, Brokers &
Service.

★ 89213 ★   Reliance Insurance
Co.
4100 E. Piedras Dr.
San Antonio, TX 78228
(512)734-5321
Ultimate Parent: Reliance Group Holdings.
SIC: 6411—Insurance Agents, Brokers &
Service.

★ 89214 ★   Rollins Burdick
Hunter
8023 Vantage Dr.
San Antonio, TX 78230
(512)377-3200
Ultimate Parent: Aon Corp. **SIC:** 6411—
Insurance Agents, Brokers & Service.

★ 89215 ★   Ryder Truck Rental
927 Coliseum Rd.
San Antonio, TX 78219
(512)224-6146
Ultimate Parent: Ryder System. **SIC:**
5113—Industrial & Personal Service Paper;
7513—Truck Rental & Leasing Without
Drivers.

★ 89216 ★   Ryder Truck Rental
5834 Joiner
San Antonio, TX 78238
(512)681-8533
Ultimate Parent: Ryder System. **SIC:**
5541—Gasoline Service Stations.

★ 89217 ★   Ryder Truck Rental
7325 Broadway St.
San Antonio, TX 78209
(512)821-5739
Ultimate Parent: Ryder System. **SIC:**
5541—Gasoline Service Stations.

★ 89218 ★   Ryder Truck Rental
10157 N. Interstate 35
San Antonio, TX 78233
(512)655-2789
Ultimate Parent: Ryder System.

★ 89219 ★   Safeco Insurance Co.
of America
84 NE Loop Uite
San Antonio, TX 78216
(512)366-2036
Ultimate Parent: Safeco. **SIC:** 6411—
Insurance Agents, Brokers & Service.

★ 89220 ★   Safety Kleen Corp.
5243 Sinclair Rd.
San Antonio, TX 78222
(512)648-0744
Ultimate Parent: Safety-Kleen.

★ 89221 ★   Sam's Wholesale
Club
3150 SW Military Dr.
San Antonio, TX 78224
(512)927-3595
Ultimate Parent: Wal-Mart Stores, Inc. **SIC:**
5099—Durable Goods Nec.

★ 89222 ★   Sani-Fresh
International
4702 Goldfield Dr.
San Antonio, TX 78218
Ultimate Parent: Scott Paper Co. **SIC:**
2841—Soap & Other Detergents.

★ 89223 ★   Savings of America, A
Division of Home Savings of
America, FSB
2201 NW Military Hwy.
San Antonio, TX 78213-1864
(210)366-0617
Company Type: Division. **Location Type:**
Branch office. **Ultimate Parent:** H. F.
Ahmanson. **SIC:** 6021—National
Commercial Banks.

★ 89224 ★   Savings of America, A
Division of Home Savings of
America, FSB
5401 Walzem Rd.
San Antonio, TX 78218-2126
(210)646-9986
Company Type: Division. **Location Type:**
Branch office. **Ultimate Parent:** H. F.
Ahmanson. **SIC:** 6021—National
Commercial Banks.

★ 89225 ★   Savings of America, A
Division of Home Savings of
America, FSB
5900 Broadway
San Antonio, TX 78209-5236
(210)829-7125
Company Type: Division. **Location Type:**
Branch office. **Ultimate Parent:** H. F.
Ahmanson. **SIC:** 6021—National
Commercial Banks.

★ 89226 ★   Sea World of Texax,
Inc.
10500 Sea World Dr.
San Antonio, TX 78251
(210)523-3000 **Fax:** (210)523-3199
Company Type: Subsidiary. **Officer:** Robin
Carson, General Manager. **Ultimate Parent:**
Agway Inc. **SIC:** 7999—Amusement &
Recreation Nec. **Employee Count:** 1300.

★ 89227 ★   Service Merchandise
5482 Walzem Rd.
San Antonio, TX 78218
(512)657-6091
Ultimate Parent: Service Merchandise Co.,
Inc. **SIC:** 5399—Miscellaneous General
Merchandise Store.

★ 89228 ★   Service Merchandise
6161 NW Loop 410
San Antonio, TX 78238
(512)647-8435
Ultimate Parent: Service Merchandise Co.,
Inc. **SIC:** 5399—Miscellaneous General
Merchandise Store.

★ 89229 ★   Seven Up U S a Inc.
120 W. Josephine St.
San Antonio, TX 78212
(512)733-7102
Ultimate Parent: Dr. Pepper/Seven-Up.
SIC: 5149—Groceries & Related Products
Nec.

★ 89230 ★   Southwest Airlines
Co.
3635 Medical Dr.
San Antonio, TX 78229
(512)699-1204
Ultimate Parent: Southwest Airlines.

★ 89231 ★   Southwestern Bell
175 E. Houston
San Antonio, TX 78205
(210)821-4105
Company Type: Headquarters. **Officer:**
Edward E. Whitacre Jr. **Employee Count:**
58400. **Fortune Service 500:** Ranking 7.

★ 89232 ★   Southwestern Bell
Corp.
175 E. Houston
San Antonio, TX 78294-2933
(210)821-4105 **Fax:** (210)351-2071
Officer: Edward E. Whitacre Jr., CEO.
Ultimate Parent: Southwestern Bell.
Employee Count: 59310. **Sales:** 10690 M.

★ 89233 ★   Stanhome Inc.
4266 Dividend
San Antonio, TX 78219
(512)337-8841
Ultimate Parent: Stanhome. **SIC:** 5199—
Nondurable Goods Nec.

★ 89234 ★   Sullivan Graphics
310 Yosemite Dr.
San Antonio, TX 78232
(512)490-4105
Ultimate Parent: Morgan Stanley Group.

★ 89235 ★   Systems Research
Labs Inc.
Brook
San Antonio, TX 78235
(512)534-8512
Ultimate Parent: Arvin Industries Inc. **SIC:**
8731—Commercial Physical Research.

★ 89236 ★   Systems Research
Labs Inc.
1182 Brooks AFB
San Antonio, TX 78235
(210)534-8776
Ultimate Parent: Arvin Industries Inc. **SIC:**
8731—Commercial Physical Research.

★ 89237 ★   Systems Research
Labs Inc.
9601 McAllister Fwy.
San Antonio, TX 78216-4605
(210)308-7388
Ultimate Parent: Arvin Industries Inc. **SIC:**
8713—Surveying Services.

★ 89238 ★   Taco Bell
17890 Blanco Rd.
San Antonio, TX 78232
(512)493-3505
Ultimate Parent: Pepsico.

★ 89239 ★   Taco Bell
5299 Walzem Rd.
San Antonio, TX 78218
(512)655-3505
Ultimate Parent: Pepsico. **SIC:** 5812—
Eating Places.

★ 89240 ★   Taco Bell
7243 San Pedro Ave.
San Antonio, TX 78216
(512)342-9664
Ultimate Parent: Pepsico. **SIC:** 5812—
Eating Places.

★ 89241 ★   Taco Bell
9323 Wurzbach Rd.
San Antonio, TX 78240
(512)696-7152
Ultimate Parent: Pepsico. **SIC:** 5812—
Eating Places.

★ 89242 ★   Taco Bell
4407 Vance Jackson Rd.
San Antonio, TX 78230
(512)341-4763
Ultimate Parent: Pepsico. **SIC:** 5812—
Eating Places.

★ 89243 ★   Taco Bell
11615 West Ave.
San Antonio, TX 78213
(512)341-4205
Ultimate Parent: Pepsico.

★ 89244 ★   Taco Bell
615 San Pedro Ave.
San Antonio, TX 78212
(512)223-4882
Ultimate Parent: Pepsico. **SIC:** 5812—
Eating Places.

★ 89245 ★   Taco Bell
1304 SW Military Dr.
San Antonio, TX 78221
(512)922-3441
Ultimate Parent: Pepsico. **SIC:** 5812—
Eating Places; 5812—Eating Places.

★ 89246 ★   Taco Bell
11827 Radium St.
San Antonio, TX 78216
(512)349-6439
Ultimate Parent: Pepsico. SIC: 5812—
Eating Places.

★ 89247 ★   Taco Bell
2619 Rockgate St.
San Antonio, TX 78227
(512)673-6467
Ultimate Parent: Pepsico. SIC: 5812—
Eating Places.

★ 89248 ★   Taco Bell
809 Pat Booker
San Antonio, TX 78233
(512)658-3110
Ultimate Parent: Pepsico. SIC: 5812—
Eating Places.

★ 89249 ★   Taco Bell
11470 Perrin Beitel Rd.
San Antonio, TX 78217
(512)655-6921
Ultimate Parent: Pepsico. SIC: 5812—
Eating Places.

★ 89250 ★   Taco Bell
1602 Bandera Rd.
San Antonio, TX 78228
(512)436-0033
Ultimate Parent: Pepsico. SIC: 5812—
Eating Places.

★ 89251 ★   Taco Bell
14320 Nacogdoches Rd.
San Antonio, TX 78247
(512)560-0316
Ultimate Parent: Pepsico. SIC: 5812—
Eating Places.

★ 89252 ★   Taco Bell
1450 Austin Hwy.
San Antonio, TX 78209
(512)822-5760
Ultimate Parent: Pepsico. SIC: 5812—
Eating Places.

★ 89253 ★   Tektronix Inc.
1831 S. General Mcmullen Dr.
San Antonio, TX 78226
(512)432-1341
Ultimate Parent: Tektronix, Inc.

★ 89254 ★   Tektronix Inc.
3311 Roselawn Rd.
San Antonio, TX 78226
(512)434-4334
Ultimate Parent: Tektronix, Inc. SIC:
5065—Electronic Parts & Equipment Nec.

★ 89255 ★   Tesoro Petroleum
Corp.
8700 Tesoro Dr.
San Antonio, TX 78217
(210)828-8484
Company Type: Headquarters. Officer:
Michael D. Burke. Employee Count: 900.
Sales: 831 M. Fortune 500: Largest U.S.
Industrial Corporations: Ranking 401.

★ 89256 ★   Tesoror Petroleum
Corp.
8700 Tesoro Dr.
San Antonio, TX 78217
(210)828-8484 Fax: (210)828-8600
Officer: Michael D Burke, CEO. Ultimate
Parent: Tesoro Petroleum Corp. Employee
Count: 900. Sales: 835 M.

★ 89257 ★   Texaco
2506 Commercial Ave.
San Antonio, TX 78221
(512)922-7926
Ultimate Parent: Texaco. SIC: 5541—
Gasoline Service Stations.

★ 89258 ★   Texaco & Food Gas
Mart
2310 Babcock Rd.
San Antonio, TX 78229
(512)696-5829
Ultimate Parent: Texaco. SIC: 5541—
Gasoline Service Stations.

★ 89259 ★   Texaco Food Mart
719 Palo Alto Rd.
San Antonio, TX 78211
(512)922-9393
Ultimate Parent: Texaco. SIC: 5411—
Grocery Stores.

★ 89260 ★   Texaco Food Mart
1615 SW Loop 410
San Antonio, TX 78227
(512)673-2810
Ultimate Parent: Texaco. SIC: 5541—
Gasoline Service Stations.

★ 89261 ★   Texaco Food Mart
3101 Nacogdoches Rd.
San Antonio, TX 78217
(512)653-5610
Ultimate Parent: Texaco. SIC: 5411—
Grocery Stores.

★ 89262 ★   Texaco Food Mart No
71
14400 Nacogdoches Rd.
San Antonio, TX 78247
(512)646-7215
Ultimate Parent: Texaco. SIC: 5541—
Gasoline Service Stations.

★ 89263 ★   Texaco & J & L
Snacks
606 W. Theo Ave.
San Antonio, TX 78225
(512)532-4126
Ultimate Parent: Texaco. SIC: 5541—
Gasoline Service Stations.

★ 89264 ★   Texaco Self Serve
2002 SW Military Dr.
San Antonio, TX 78221
(512)922-5764
Ultimate Parent: Texaco. SIC: 5541—
Gasoline Service Stations.

★ 89265 ★   Texaco Self Serve
4825 Walzem Rd.
San Antonio, TX 78218
(512)655-8877
Ultimate Parent: Texaco. SIC: 5541—
Gasoline Service Stations.

★ 89266 ★   Texaco Self Serve
3719 SE Military Dr.
San Antonio, TX 78223
(512)337-2418
Ultimate Parent: Texaco.

★ 89267 ★   Texaco Self Serve
5245 SW Loop 410
San Antonio, TX 78227
(512)675-9540
Ultimate Parent: Texaco. SIC: 5541—
Gasoline Service Stations.

★ 89268 ★   Texaco Self Serve
6202 N. Panam Expy.
San Antonio, TX 78218
(512)654-1824
Ultimate Parent: Texaco. SIC: 5541—
Gasoline Service Stations.

★ 89269 ★   Texaco Self Serve
2347 Nacogdoches Rd.
San Antonio, TX 78209
(512)828-9142
Ultimate Parent: Texaco. SIC: 5541—
Gasoline Service Stations.

★ 89270 ★   Texaco Self Serve
1526 N. New Braunfels Ave.
San Antonio, TX 78208
(512)224-4880
Ultimate Parent: Texaco. SIC: 5171—
Petroleum Bulk Stations & Terminals.

★ 89271 ★   Texaco Self Serve
Crwsh
13363 Blanco Rd.
San Antonio, TX 78216
(512)492-0514
Ultimate Parent: Texaco. SIC: 5541—
Gasoline Service Stations.

★ 89272 ★   Texaco Self-Service
8501 Broadway St.
San Antonio, TX 78217
(512)822-6851
Ultimate Parent: Texaco. SIC: 5541—
Gasoline Service Stations.

★ 89273 ★   Texaco Service
Station
11911 San Pedro Ave.
San Antonio, TX 78216
(512)494-7914
Ultimate Parent: Texaco. SIC: 5541—
Gasoline Service Stations.

★ 89274 ★   Texaco Service
Station
5815 S. Panam Expy.
San Antonio, TX 78211
(512)923-1249
Ultimate Parent: Texaco. SIC: 5541—
Gasoline Service Stations.

★ 89275 ★   Thom Mcan Shoe
Store
145 Plaza Del Sol St.
San Antonio, TX 78237
(512)433-4560
Ultimate Parent: Melville. SIC: 5661—Shoe
Stores.

★ 89276 ★   Trailways Bus
Systems
301 Broadway St.
San Antonio, TX 78205
(512)226-2259
Ultimate Parent: Greyhound Lines Inc. SIC:
4111—Local & Suburban Transit.

★ 89277 ★   Trailways Package
Express
301 Broadway St.
San Antonio, TX 78205
(512)226-2250
Ultimate Parent: Greyhound Lines Inc. SIC:
4212—Local Trucking Without Storage.

★ 89278 ★   Trailways Texas Inc.
301 Broadway St.
San Antonio, TX 78205
(512)226-6136
Ultimate Parent: Greyhound Lines Inc. SIC:
4111—Local & Suburban Transit.

★ 89279 ★   Trico Industries Inc.
8620 N. New Braunfels Ave.
San Antonio, TX 78217
(512)822-8676
Ultimate Parent: Paccar. SIC: 5084—
Industrial Machinery & Equipment.

★ 89280 ★   Underwriters
Adjusting Co.
792427 PO Box
San Antonio, TX 78279
(512)854-4781
Ultimate Parent: Continental. SIC: 6411—
Insurance Agents, Brokers & Service.

★ 89281 ★   Union Bank
3570 SW Military Dr.
San Antonio, TX 78211
(512)923-3451
Ultimate Parent: Union Bank. SIC: 6022—
State Commercial Banks.

★ 89282 ★   Union Camp Corp.
610 Pop Gunn St.
San Antonio, TX 78219
(210)661-8543
Officer: Stan Lenge, Manager. Ultimate
Parent: Union Camp Corp. SIC: 2653—
Corrugated & Solid Fiber Boxes.

★ 89283 ★   United Parcel Service
84 Loop St.
San Antonio, TX 78212
(512)340-1001
Ultimate Parent: United Parcel Service of
America. SIC: 7513—Truck Rental &
Leasing Without Drivers.

★ 89284 ★   United Parcel Service
84 Loop St.
San Antonio, TX 78212
(512)340-1001
Ultimate Parent: United Parcel Service of
America. SIC: 7513—Truck Rental &
Leasing Without Drivers.

★ 89285 ★   United Parcel Service
922 Mallard St.
San Antonio, TX 78224
(512)340-1001
Ultimate Parent: United Parcel Service of
America. SIC: 4215—Courier Services
Except by Air.

★ 89286 ★   United Parcel Service
7129 Eckhert Rd.
San Antonio, TX 78238
(512)520-2010
Ultimate Parent: United Parcel Service of
America. SIC: 4215—Courier Services
Except by Air.

★ 89287 ★   United Services Auto
Association
U.S. Bldg.
San Antonio, TX 78218
(512)690-6835
Ultimate Parent: USAA. SIC: 6399—
Insurance Carriers Nec.

★ 89288 ★   Universal Foods
Corp.
5024 Service Ctr. Dr.
San Antonio, TX 78218
(512)666-2720
Ultimate Parent: Universal Foods Corp.
SIC: 4783—Packing & Crating.

★ 89289 ★   USAA
9800 Fredericksburg Rd.
San Antonio, TX 78288
(210)498-2211 Fax: (210)498-9940
Company Type: Headquarters. Officer:
Robert T. Herres, CEO. Employee Count:
15905. Sales: 5989 M. Fortune Service
500: Ranking 23.

★ 89290 ★   Valero Energy Corp.
530 McCullough Ave.
San Antonio, TX 78215
(210)246-2000
Company Type: Headquarters. Officer:
William E. Greehey. Employee Count:
1740. Sales: 1222.2 M. Fortune 500:
Largest U.S. Industrial Corporations:
Ranking 319.

★ 89291 ★   Valley National
Financial Service
70 Loop St.
San Antonio, TX 78212
(512)340-5994
Ultimate Parent: Banc One Corp. SIC:
6062—State Credit Unions.

★ 89292 ★   Victoria's Secret
7400 N. Star Mall
San Antonio, TX 78216
(512)344-9831
Ultimate Parent: Limited. SIC: 5651—
Family Clothing Stores.

★ 89293 ★   Victoria's Secret
849 E. Commerce St.
San Antonio, TX 78205
(512)224-7072
Ultimate Parent: Limited. SIC: 5651—
Family Clothing Stores.

★ 89294 ★   Victoria's Secret
Loop N
San Antonio, TX 78252
(512)651-5806
Ultimate Parent: Limited. SIC: 5651—
Family Clothing Stores.

★ 89295 ★   Volunteer State Life
Insurance Co.
National Bank Commerce
San Antonio, TX 78205
(512)226-0361
Ultimate Parent: Chubb. SIC: 6411—
Insurance Agents, Brokers & Service.

★ 89296 ★   Vulcan Materials Co.
800 Isom Rd.
San Antonio, TX 78216
(210)349-3311
Officer: William L. Glusac, President.
Ultimate Parent: Vulcan Materials Co. SIC:
2951—Asphalt Paving Mixtures & Blocks;
3273—Ready-Mixed Concrete; 3281—Cut
Stone & Stone Products.

★ 89297 ★   Wal Mart
7702 N. Panam Expy.
San Antonio, TX 78218
(512)637-1700
Ultimate Parent: Wal-Mart Stores, Inc. SIC:
5311—Department Stores.

★ 89298 ★   Wal Mart Discount
Cities
286 Bitters Rd.
San Antonio, TX 78216
(512)491-9450
Ultimate Parent: Wal-Mart Stores, Inc.

★ 89299 ★   Wal Mart Discount
City
5025 NW Loop 410
San Antonio, TX 78229
(512)523-1091
Ultimate Parent: Wal-Mart Stores, Inc. SIC:
5311—Department Stores.

★ **89300** ★ **Waldenbooks**
1401 SW Loop 410
San Antonio, TX 78227
(512)673-6510
Ultimate Parent: K-Mart. **SIC:** 5942—Book Stores.

★ **89301** ★ **Waldenbooks**
Windsor
San Antonio, TX 78218
(512)655-0591
Ultimate Parent: K-Mart. **SIC:** 5942—Book Stores.

★ **89302** ★ **Waldenbooks**
Mercado Sq.
San Antonio, TX 78207
(512)673-6510
Ultimate Parent: K-Mart. **SIC:** 5942—Book Stores.

★ **89303** ★ **Waldenbooks**
N Star Mall
San Antonio, TX 78216
(512)344-0037
Ultimate Parent: K-Mart. **SIC:** 5942—Book Stores.

★ **89304** ★ **Waldenbooks**
Ingram
San Antonio, TX 78238
(512)681-2955
Ultimate Parent: K-Mart. **SIC:** 5942—Book Stores.

★ **89305** ★ **Waldenbooks**
Loop N
San Antonio, TX 78252
(512)651-5304
Ultimate Parent: K-Mart. **SIC:** 5942—Book Stores.

★ **89306** ★ **Walgreen**
5282 Medical Dr.
San Antonio, TX 78229
(512)641-6429
Ultimate Parent: Walgreen Co. **SIC:** 5912—Drug Stores & Proprietary Stores.

★ **89307** ★ **Walgreen Data Terminal**
10427 Perrin Beitel Rd.
San Antonio, TX 78217
(512)637-1736
Ultimate Parent: Walgreen Co. **SIC:** 3679—Electronic Components Nec.

★ **89308** ★ **Walgreen Drug Stores**
4210 McCullough Ave.
San Antonio, TX 78212
(512)829-7811
Ultimate Parent: Walgreen Co. **SIC:** 5912—Drug Stores & Proprietary Stores.

★ **89309** ★ **Walgreen Drug Stores**
139 Plaza D Las Palmas
San Antonio, TX 78237
(512)434-4101
Ultimate Parent: Walgreen Co. **SIC:** 7384—Photofinishing Laboratories.

★ **89310** ★ **Walgreen Drug Stores**
3600 Fredericksburg Rd.
San Antonio, TX 78201
(512)734-7229
Ultimate Parent: Walgreen Co. **SIC:** 5912—Drug Stores & Proprietary Stores.

★ **89311** ★ **Walgreen Drug Stores**
700 Walgreen Plz. N
San Antonio, TX 78207
(512)434-4101
Ultimate Parent: Walgreen Co. **SIC:** 5912—Drug Stores & Proprietary Stores.

★ **89312** ★ **Walgreen Drug Stores**
5740 Walzem Rd.
San Antonio, TX 78218
(512)657-7761
Ultimate Parent: Walgreen Co. **SIC:** 5912—Drug Stores & Proprietary Stores; 7384—Photofinishing Laboratories.

★ **89313** ★ **Walgreen Drug Stores**
605 SW Military Dr.
San Antonio, TX 78221
(512)924-6575
Ultimate Parent: Walgreen Co. **SIC:** 5912—Drug Stores & Proprietary Stores; 7384—Photofinishing Laboratories.

★ **89314** ★ **Walgreen Drug Stores**
4811 W. Commerce St.
San Antonio, TX 78237
(512)434-3181
Ultimate Parent: Walgreen Co. **SIC:** 5912—Drug Stores & Proprietary Stores; 7384—Photofinishing Laboratories.

★ **89315** ★ **Walgreen Drug Stores**
2361 NW Military Hwy.
San Antonio, TX 78231
(512)349-4277
Ultimate Parent: Walgreen Co. **SIC:** 5912—Drug Stores & Proprietary Stores; 7384—Photofinishing Laboratories.

★ **89316** ★ **Walgreen Drug Stores**
13430 San Pedro Ave.
San Antonio, TX 78216
(512)496-1116
Ultimate Parent: Walgreen Co. **SIC:** 5912—Drug Stores & Proprietary Stores.

★ **89317** ★ **Walgreen Drug Stores**
7400 N. Star Mall
San Antonio, TX 78216
(512)342-2358
Ultimate Parent: Walgreen Co. **SIC:** 5912—Drug Stores & Proprietary Stores.

★ **89318** ★ **Walgreen Drug Stores**
13930 Nacogdoches Rd.
San Antonio, TX 78217
(512)656-5043
Ultimate Parent: Walgreen Co. **SIC:** 5912—Drug Stores & Proprietary Stores; 7384—Photofinishing Laboratories.

★ **89319** ★ **Walgreen Drug Stores**
3638 Fredericksburg Rd.
San Antonio, TX 78201
(512)732-8291
Ultimate Parent: Walgreen Co. **SIC:** 5912—Drug Stores & Proprietary Stores.

★ **89320** ★ **Walgreen Drug Stores**
6020 Ingram Rd.
San Antonio, TX 78238
(512)680-2960
Ultimate Parent: Walgreen Co. **SIC:** 5912—Drug Stores & Proprietary Stores; 7384—Photofinishing Laboratories.

★ **89321** ★ **Walgreen Drug Stores**
5246 Blanco Rd.
San Antonio, TX 78216
(512)349-9807
Ultimate Parent: Walgreen Co. **SIC:** 5912—Drug Stores & Proprietary Stores; 7384—Photofinishing Laboratories.

★ **89322** ★ **Walgreen Drug Stores**
300 E. Houston St.
San Antonio, TX 78205
(512)225-2619
Ultimate Parent: Walgreen Co. **SIC:** 5912—Drug Stores & Proprietary Stores; 7384—Photofinishing Laboratories.

★ **89323** ★ **Walgreen Drug Stores**
7058 Bandera Rd.
San Antonio, TX 78238
(512)681-8530
Ultimate Parent: Walgreen Co. **SIC:** 5912—Drug Stores & Proprietary Stores; 7384—Photofinishing Laboratories.

★ **89324** ★ **Walgreen Drug Stores**
3600 Fredericksburg Rd.
San Antonio, TX 78201
Ultimate Parent: Walgreen Co. **SIC:** 5912—Drug Stores & Proprietary Stores; 7384—Photofinishing Laboratories.

★ **89325** ★ **Western Auto Supply Co.**
125 Plaza D
Las Palmas Dr.
San Antonio, TX 78237
(512)433-1421
Ultimate Parent: Sears Roebuck & Co. **SIC:** 5531—Automobile & Home Supply Stores.

★ **89326** ★ **Weyerhaeuser Paper**
611 Pop Gunn St.
San Antonio, TX 78219
(512)662-0600
Ultimate Parent: Weyerhaeuser Co.

★ **89327** ★ **Xerox Corp.**
7810 Jones Maltsberger Rd.
San Antonio, TX 78216
(210)821-6688
Officer: John Oldham, Manager. **Ultimate**

Parent: Xerox Corp. **SIC:** 2759—Commercial Printing Nec.

★ **89328** ★ **Xerox Corp.**
100 N. Loop 410, Ste. 1200
San Antonio, TX 78216
(210)524-5600
Officer: Jill Kinney, Manager. **Ultimate Parent:** Xerox Corp. **SIC:** 3663—Radio & T.V. Communications Equipment.

★ **89329** ★ **Zep Manufacturing**
10727 I N
San Antonio, TX 78233
(512)650-9111
Ultimate Parent: National Service Industries. **SIC:** 5087—Service Establishment Equipment.

San Benito

★ **89330** ★ **McDonalds**
Sam Houston Blvd.
San Benito, TX 78586
(512)399-4033
Ultimate Parent: McDonald's. **SIC:** 5812—Eating Places.

★ **89331** ★ **Pizza Hut**
1110 W. Hwy. 77
San Benito, TX 78586
(512)399-1612
Ultimate Parent: Pepsico. **SIC:** 5812—Eating Places.

★ **89332** ★ **Wal Mart Discnt**
850 W. Hwy. 77
San Benito, TX 78586
(512)399-1373
Ultimate Parent: Wal-Mart Stores, Inc.

San Isidro

★ **89333** ★ **Texaco Inc.**
San Isidro, TX 78588
(512)481-3222
Ultimate Parent: Texaco. **SIC:** 5171—Petroleum Bulk Stations & Terminals.

San Juan

★ **89334** ★ **Piggly Wiggly**
600 S. Nebraska Ave.
San Juan, TX 78589
(512)787-9009
Ultimate Parent: Bruno's. **SIC:** 5411—Grocery Stores.

★ **89335** ★ **Stewart & Stevenson Service Inc.**
W State Hwy.
San Juan, TX 78589
(512)787-2769
Ultimate Parent: Stewart & Stevenson. **SIC:** 5084—Industrial Machinery & Equipment; 7538—General Automotive Repair Shops.

San Marcos

★ **89336** ★ **Capezio Factory**
3939 S. Interstate 35
San Marcos, TX 78666
(512)392-5066
Ultimate Parent: United States Shoe.

★ **89337** ★ **Hta Aerostructures Inc.**
2005 Technology Way
San Marcos, TX 78666
Ultimate Parent: Rohr. **SIC:** 3728—Aircraft Parts & Equipment Nec.

★ **89338** ★ **Kentucky Fried Chicken**
1204 S. I H35
San Marcos, TX 78666
(512)392-3150
Ultimate Parent: Pepsico. **SIC:** 5812—Eating Places.

★ **89339** ★ **Pizza Hut**
720 Bugg Ln.
San Marcos, TX 78666
(512)396-3696
Ultimate Parent: Pepsico. **SIC:** 5812—Eating Places.

★ **89340** ★ **Pizza Hut**
403 N. Guadalupe St.
San Marcos, TX 78666
(512)392-5900
Ultimate Parent: Pepsico. **SIC:** 5812—Eating Places.

★ **89341** ★ **Ryder Truck Rental**
1108 N. I H 35
San Marcos, TX 78666
(512)754-0202
Ultimate Parent: Ryder System.

★ **89342** ★ **Taco Bell**
415 N. L B J Dr.
San Marcos, TX 78666
(512)392-0929
Ultimate Parent: Pepsico. **SIC:** 5812—Eating Places.

★ **89343** ★ **Texaco Station**
205 W. Hopkins St.
San Marcos, TX 78666
(512)396-4111
Ultimate Parent: Texaco.

★ **89344** ★ **Trylon Corp. Inc.**
Country Estates
San Marcos, TX 78666
(512)396-2954
Ultimate Parent: Mascotech, Inc. **SIC:** 1731—Electrical Work.

★ **89345** ★ **Wal Mart Pharmacy**
San Mar Plz.
San Marcos, TX 78666
(512)353-3000
Ultimate Parent: Wal-Mart Stores, Inc. **SIC:** 5122—Drugs, Proprietaries & Sundries.

San Saba

★ **89346** ★ **City National Bank of San Saba**
209 E. Brown St.
San Saba, TX 76877-3501
(915)372-5721
Company Type: Headquarters. **Officer:** Douglas P. Hayes, President. **Ultimate Parent:** City National Corp. **SIC:** 6021—National Commercial Banks; 6141—Personal Credit Institutions.

★ **89347** ★ **Mobil Oil**
412 E. Commerce St.
San Saba, TX 76877
(915)372-5223
Ultimate Parent: Mobil. **SIC:** 5172—Petroleum Products Nec.

Sandow

★ **89348** ★ **Alcoa Rockdale Works**
5 Miles S. of Hwy. 79 on Fm 1786
Sandow, TX 76567
Ultimate Parent: Aluminum Co. of America-Alcoa. **SIC:** 3334—Primary Aluminum.

Santa Anna

★ **89349** ★ **Lone Star Gas Co.**
104 S. 2nd
Santa Anna, TX 76878
(915)348-3615
Ultimate Parent: Enserch. **SIC:** 4925—Gas Production & Distribution Nec.

Santa Fe

★ **89350** ★ **Radio Shack**
12406 Hwy. 6
Santa Fe, TX 77510
(409)925-1038
Company Type: Division. **Ultimate Parent:** Tandy Corp.

Saratoga

★ **89351** ★ **Mobil Pipeline**
Saratoga, TX 77585
(409)274-5211
Company Type: Branch. **Ultimate Parent:** Mobil. **SIC:** 4612—Crude Petroleum Pipelines.

Schulenburg

★ 89352 ★ Mid-America
Dairymen Inc.
PO Box 176
Schulenburg, TX 78956-0176
(409)743-4161
Officer: Edwin Orsak. Ultimate Parent:
Mid-America Dairymen. SIC: 2022—
Cheese—Natural & Processed; 5143—Dairy
Products Except Dried or Canned.

★ 89353 ★ Mobil Pipe Line Co.
Flatonia Hwy.
Schulenburg, TX 78956
(409)743-3857
Company Type: Branch. Ultimate Parent:
Mobil. SIC: 4612—Crude Petroleum
Pipelines.

Scottsville

★ 89354 ★ Conductor Products
Inc.
Hwy. 80 8 Miles East of Marshall
Scottsville, TX 75688
Ultimate Parent: Reynolds Metals Co. SIC:
3355—Aluminum Rolling & Drawing Nec.

★ 89355 ★ Tank Lining & Rail
Car Repair
Fm 2199
Scottsville, TX 75688
Ultimate Parent: Trinity Industries. SIC:
3743—Railroad Equipment.

Scroggins

★ 89356 ★ New Hope Plant
Rte. 1, Box 36-A8
Scroggins, TX 75480
Ultimate Parent: Texaco. SIC: 2819—
Industrial Inorganic Chemicals Nec.

Seabrook

★ 89357 ★ Hoechst Celanese
Chemical Group Inc. Bayport
11807 Port Rd.
Seabrook, TX 77586
Ultimate Parent: Hoechst Celanese Corp.
SIC: 5100—Wholesale Trade—Nondurable
Goods.

★ 89358 ★ Hoechst Celanese
Chemical Group Inc. Bayport
Terminal
11807 Port Rd.
Seabrook, TX 77586
Ultimate Parent: Hoechst Celanese Corp.
SIC: 5100—Wholesale Trade—Nondurable
Goods.

★ 89359 ★ Radio Shack
4620 Nasa Rd. 1
Seabrook, TX 77586
(713)326-3111
Company Type: Division. Ultimate Parent:
Tandy Corp.

★ 89360 ★ Southwest Chemical
Services
PO Drawer 478
Seabrook, TX 77586
(713)474-2831 Fax: (713)474-2043
Company Type: Subsidiary. Officer:
Everette Hayes, General Manager. Ultimate
Parent: M.A.Hanna.

★ 89361 ★ Southwest Chemical
Services Inc.
5306 Hwy. 146 S.
Seabrook, TX 77586
Ultimate Parent: M.A.Hanna. SIC: 3087—
Custom Compound of Purchased Resins.

★ 89362 ★ Southwest Chemical
Services Inc.
5306 Hwy. North
Seabrook, TX 77586
Ultimate Parent: M.A.Hanna. SIC: 3087—
Custom Compound of Purchased Resins.

Seagoville

★ 89363 ★ Enthone-OMI
1317 Bryan Pl.
Seagoville, TX 75159-1256
(214)287-8738
Ultimate Parent: Asarco. SIC: 5169—
Chemicals & Allied Products Nec.

Sealy

★ 89364 ★ Citizens State Bank
222 Main St.
Sealy, TX 77474
(409)885-3571
Ultimate Parent: Liberty National Bancorp.
SIC: 6022—State Commercial Banks.

★ 89365 ★ Wal Mart Discount
Cities
2200 Hwy. 36 S
Sealy, TX 77474
(409)885-7478
Ultimate Parent: Wal-Mart Stores, Inc. SIC:
5311—Department Stores.

Seguin

★ 89366 ★ Air Products &
Chemicals
733 N. Hwy. 123 Byp.
Seguin, TX 78155
(512)372-4090
Ultimate Parent: Air Products & Chemicals,
Inc. SIC: 5169—Chemicals & Allied
Products Nec.

★ 89367 ★ Greyhound Bus Lines
1009 W. Court St.
Seguin, TX 78155
(512)372-0272
Ultimate Parent: Greyhound Lines Inc. SIC:
4111—Local & Suburban Transit; 4131—
Intercity & Rural Bus Transportation.

★ 89368 ★ Holly Farms of Texas
Inc.
Sequin Texas Plant
1200 West Kingsbury St.
PO Box 191
Seguin, TX 78155
Location Type: Plant. Ultimate Parent:
Tyson Foods, Inc. SIC: 0251—Broiler, Fryer
& Roaster Chickens.

★ 89369 ★ Kentucky Fried
Chicken
1479 E. Court St.
Seguin, TX 78155
(512)379-8880
Ultimate Parent: Pepsico. SIC: 5812—
Eating Places.

★ 89370 ★ Mobil Oil Co.
2525 N. Austin St.
Seguin, TX 78155
(512)379-1937
Ultimate Parent: Mobil.

★ 89371 ★ Mobil Service Sta
6042 Stockdale Hwy.
Seguin, TX 78155
(512)379-7380
Ultimate Parent: Mobil. SIC: 5541—
Gasoline Service Stations.

★ 89372 ★ Pizza Hut
1006 E. Kingsbury St.
Seguin, TX 78155
(512)379-7051
Ultimate Parent: Pepsico. SIC: 5812—
Eating Places.

★ 89373 ★ Radio Shack
1355 E. Court St.
Seguin, TX 78155
(512)379-3623
Company Type: Division. Ultimate Parent:
Tandy Corp. SIC: 5065—Electronic Parts &
Equipment Nec.

★ 89374 ★ Ryder Truck Rental
2506 N. Austin St.
Seguin, TX 78155
(512)372-5360
Ultimate Parent: Ryder System. SIC:
5012—Automobiles & Other Motor Vehicles.

★ 89375 ★ Structural Metals Inc.
Mill Rd.
Seguin, TX 78155
(512)379-7520
Ultimate Parent: Commercial Federal Corp.
SIC: 3499—Fabricated Metal Products Nec.

★ 89376 ★ Taco Bell
1494 E. Court St.
Seguin, TX 78155
(512)372-2710
Ultimate Parent: Pepsico. SIC: 5812—
Eating Places.

★ 89377 ★ Texaco Number One
1810 W. I
Seguin, TX 78155
(512)379-0876
Ultimate Parent: Texaco. SIC: 5541—
Gasoline Service Stations.

★ 89378 ★ Trailways Bus Station
1024 E. Court St.
Seguin, TX 78155
(512)379-8450
Ultimate Parent: Greyhound Lines Inc. SIC:
4111—Local & Suburban Transit.

★ 89379 ★ Tyson Foods Inc.
Seguin Plant
1200 W. Kingsbury St. PO Box 191
Seguin, TX 78156
Ultimate Parent: Tyson Foods, Inc. SIC:
2000—Food & Kindred Products.

★ 89380 ★ Wal Mart
1500 E. Court St.
Seguin, TX 78155
(512)372-3740
Ultimate Parent: Wal-Mart Stores, Inc. SIC:
5311—Department Stores.

Seminole

★ 89381 ★ Arco Pipeline Co.
NW Seminole
Seminole, TX 79360
(915)758-2227
Location Type: Branch office. Ultimate
Parent: Atlantic Richfield Co., Inc. SIC:
4612—Crude Petroleum Pipelines.

★ 89382 ★ Arco Pipline Co.
NW Seminole
Seminole, TX 79360
(915)758-2227
Location Type: Branch office. Ultimate
Parent: Atlantic Richfield Co., Inc. SIC:
4612—Crude Petroleum Pipelines.

★ 89383 ★ Mobil Pipe Line Co.
Andrews Hwy.
Seminole, TX 79360
(915)758-2346
Company Type: Branch. Ultimate Parent:
Mobil. SIC: 4612—Crude Petroleum
Pipelines.

★ 89384 ★ Pizza Hut
619 S. Main St.
Seminole, TX 79360
(915)758-3481
Ultimate Parent: Pepsico. SIC: 5812—
Eating Places.

★ 89385 ★ Radio Shack
108 S. Main St.
Seminole, TX 79360
(915)758-2764
Company Type: Division. Ultimate Parent:
Tandy Corp. SIC: 5731—Radio, Television
& Electronics Stores.

Sequin

★ 89386 ★ Holly Farms Foods
Inc.
Sequin Texas Plant
1200 W. Kingsbury St.
PO Box 191
Sequin, TX 78155
Location Type: Plant. Ultimate Parent:
Tyson Foods, Inc. SIC: 0251—Broiler, Fryer
& Roaster Chickens.

★ 89387 ★ Tyson Foods Inc.
1200 W. Kingsbury St.
Sequin, TX 78155
(210)379-5151
Officer: Bill W. Lovette, Manager. Ultimate
Parent: Tyson Foods, Inc. SIC: 2015—
Poultry Slaughtering & Processing; 2048—
Prepared Feeds Nec.

Seymour

★ 89388 ★ Texaco Inc.
202 W. Pecan St.
Seymour, TX 76380
(817)888-3537
Ultimate Parent: Texaco. SIC: 5171—
Petroleum Bulk Stations & Terminals.

Sheldon

★ 89389 ★ Champion
International Corp.
11611 Fifth St.
Sheldon, TX 77044
Ultimate Parent: Champion International. SIC: 2621—Paper Mills.

Sherman

★ 89390 ★ Burlington Northern R
R
Frisco Rd.
Sherman, TX 75090
(214)868-1011
Ultimate Parent: Burlington Northern. SIC:
4011—Railroads—Line-Haul Operating.

★ 89391 ★ Burlington Northern
Railway
1200 N. Frisco Rd.
Sherman, TX 75090
(214)892-8174
Ultimate Parent: Burlington Northern. SIC:
4119—Local Passenger Transportation Nec.

★ 89392 ★ Casual Corner
4800 Texoma Pky.
Sherman, TX 75090
(214)893-7161
Ultimate Parent: United States Shoe. SIC:
5651—Family Clothing Stores.

★ 89393 ★ Circus World
208 Sher Den Mall
Sherman, TX 75090
(903)893-7922
Ultimate Parent: Melville. SIC: 5945—
Hobby, Toy & Game Shops.

★ 89394 ★ Emery Worldwide
RR 1
Sherman, TX 75090
(214)893-4206
Ultimate Parent: Consolidated Freightways.
SIC: 4512—Air Transportation—Scheduled.

★ 89395 ★ Fabricated Prods.
Plant
Hwy. 75 S.
P O Box 1215
Sherman, TX 75091
(903)893-5566
Ultimate Parent: Maxxam. SIC: 3354—
Aluminum Extruded Products.

★ 89396 ★ Folger Coffee Co.
300 W. FM 1417
Sherman, TX 75090
Ultimate Parent: Procter & Gamble Co.
SIC: 2095—Roasted Coffee.

★ 89397 ★ Foot Action U S a
428 Sher Den Mall
Sherman, TX 75090
(214)868-1166
Ultimate Parent: Melville. SIC: 5661—Shoe
Stores.

★ 89398 ★ Greyhound Bus Lnes
311 W. Houston St.
Sherman, TX 75090
(903)892-3131
Ultimate Parent: Greyhound Lines Inc.

★ 89399 ★ Greyhound Bus
Station
311 W. Houston St.
Sherman, TX 75090
(214)892-3131
Ultimate Parent: Greyhound Lines Inc. SIC:
4173—Bus Terminal & Service Facilities;
4212—Local Trucking Without Storage.

★ 89400 ★ Johnson & Johnson
Medical, Inc.
Hwy. 75 S. & 1417 W
Sherman, TX 75091
Ultimate Parent: Johnson & Johnson. SIC:
3842—Surgical Appliances & Supplies;
3069—Fabricated Rubber Products Nec.

★ 89401 ★ Kaiser Aluminum &
Chemical Corp.
4300 Hwy. 75 S.
Sherman, TX 75090
Ultimate Parent: Maxxam. SIC: 3354—
Aluminum Extruded Products.

★ 89402 ★ **Kay Bee Toys**
4800 Texoma Pky.
Sherman, TX 75090
(214)893-6676
Ultimate Parent: Melville. **SIC:** 5945—
Hobby, Toy & Game Shops.

★ 89403 ★ **Kentucky Fried Chicken**
1439 PO Box
Sherman, TX 75091
(214)892-1325
Ultimate Parent: Pepsico. **SIC:** 5812—
Eating Places.

★ 89404 ★ **Kraft Food Ingredients Corp.**
1201 E. Pecan St.
Sherman, TX 75090
Ultimate Parent: Philip Morris. **SIC:** 2079—
Edible Fats & Oils Nec.

★ 89405 ★ **Kraft Food Ingredients Corp.**
1201 E. Pecan
Sherman, TX 75090
Ultimate Parent: Philip Morris. **SIC:** 2079—
Edible Fats & Oils Nec.

★ 89406 ★ **Kroger Co.**
721 E. Taylor St.
Sherman, TX 75090
(214)868-9552
Ultimate Parent: Kroger. **SIC:** 5912—Drug
Stores & Proprietary Stores.

★ 89407 ★ **Kroger Food Store**
721 E. Taylor St.
Sherman, TX 75090
(903)893-6788
Ultimate Parent: Kroger.

★ 89408 ★ **Kroger Pharmacy**
721 E. Taylor St.
Sherman, TX 75090
(214)892-3850
Ultimate Parent: Kroger. **SIC:** 5912—Drug
Stores & Proprietary Stores.

★ 89409 ★ **Lane Bryant**
4800 Texoma Pky.
Sherman, TX 75090
(214)893-1744
Ultimate Parent: Limited. **SIC:** 5651—
Family Clothing Stores.

★ 89410 ★ **The Limited**
4800 Texoma Pky. 306
Sherman, TX 75090
(903)892-4866
Ultimate Parent: Limited. **SIC:** 5651—
Family Clothing Stores.

★ 89411 ★ **Lone Star Gas Co.**
5111 Blue Flame Rd.
Sherman, TX 75090
(214)892-9166
Ultimate Parent: Enserch. **SIC:** 4932—Gas
& Other Services Combined.

★ 89412 ★ **McDonalds Restaurant**
2217 Texoma Pky.
Sherman, TX 75090
(903)893-5927
Ultimate Parent: McDonald's.

★ 89413 ★ **Mcduff Elec Applnc**
719 E. Taylor St.
Sherman, TX 75090
(903)893-4262
Ultimate Parent: Tandy Corp.

★ 89414 ★ **Mervyn's**
4800 Texoma Pky.
Sherman, TX 75090
(214)868-1990
Ultimate Parent: Dayton Hudson. **SIC:**
5311—Department Stores.

★ 89415 ★ **Oscar Mayer Foods Corp.**
4700 Hwy. 75 S
Sherman, TX 75090-0100
Ultimate Parent: Philip Morris. **SIC:** 2013—
Sausages & Other Prepared Meats.

★ 89416 ★ **Payless Cashways**
2500 Texoma Pky.
Sherman, TX 75090
(214)893-9611
Ultimate Parent: Payless Cashways. **SIC:**
5039—Construction Materials Nec.

★ 89417 ★ **Piggly Wiggly**
220 Sunset Blvd.
Sherman, TX 75090
(903)892-9095
Ultimate Parent: Bruno's.

★ 89418 ★ **Piggly Wiggly**
699 PO Box
Sherman, TX 75091
Ultimate Parent: Bruno's. **SIC:** 5411—
Grocery Stores.

★ 89419 ★ **Piggly Wiggly Corp.**
220 Sunset Blvd.
Sherman, TX 75090
(214)892-9095
Ultimate Parent: Bruno's. **SIC:** 5411—
Grocery Stores.

★ 89420 ★ **Pizza Hut**
2020 Texoma Pky.
Sherman, TX 75090
(903)892-0303
Ultimate Parent: Pepsico.

★ 89421 ★ **Pizza Hut**
901 E. Lamar St.
Sherman, TX 75090
(214)892-1122
Ultimate Parent: Pepsico. **SIC:** 5812—
Eating Places.

★ 89422 ★ **Radio Shack**
1610 N. Hwy. 75
Sherman, TX 75090
(214)892-6553
Company Type: Division. **Ultimate Parent:**
Tandy Corp. **SIC:** 5065—Electronic Parts &
Equipment Nec.

★ 89423 ★ **Radio Shack**
1610 Texoma Pky.
Sherman, TX 75090
(903)892-6553
Company Type: Division. **Ultimate Parent:**
Tandy Corp.

★ 89424 ★ **Southern Pacific Railroad**
N Music
Sherman, TX 75090
(214)893-8028
Ultimate Parent: Southern Pacific Rail.
SIC: 4011—Railroads—Line-Haul
Operating.

★ 89425 ★ **Southern Pacific Railroad**
429 N. East St.
Sherman, TX 75090
(214)892-9168
Ultimate Parent: Southern Pacific Rail.
SIC: 4011—Railroads—Line-Haul
Operating.

★ 89426 ★ **Taco Bell**
3210 Texoma Pky.
Sherman, TX 75090
(903)868-2464
Ultimate Parent: Pepsico.

★ 89427 ★ **Texas Instruments Inc. Sherman**
6400 U.S. Hwy. 75 S.
Sherman, TX 75090
Ultimate Parent: Texas Instruments. **SIC:**
3674—Semiconductors & Related Devices;
3812—Search & Navigation Equipment;
2819—Industrial Inorganic Chemicals Nec.

★ 89428 ★ **Trailways Bus Systems**
210 E. Houston St.
Sherman, TX 75090
(214)892-9245
Ultimate Parent: Greyhound Lines Inc. **SIC:**
4131—Intercity & Rural Bus Transportation.

★ 89429 ★ **Wal Mart Discount Cities**
3201 S. Hwy. 75
Sherman, TX 75090
(903)893-5050
Ultimate Parent: Wal-Mart Stores, Inc.

Sierra Blanca

★ 89430 ★ **Southern Pacific Railroad**
Sierra Blanca, TX 79851
(915)369-2831
Ultimate Parent: Southern Pacific Rail.
SIC: 4011—Railroads—Line-Haul
Operating.

Silsbee

★ 89431 ★ **Arco Oil & Gas Co.**
PO Box 517
Silsbee, TX 77656-0517
Officer: Ray Allen. **Ultimate Parent:**
Atlantic Richfield Co., Inc. **SIC:** 2911—
Petroleum Refining.

★ 89432 ★ **Kentucky Fried Chicken**
815 Hwy. 96 S
Silsbee, TX 77656
(409)385-4961
Ultimate Parent: Pepsico. **SIC:** 5812—
Eating Places.

★ 89433 ★ **Kirby Forest Industries Inc. Trt./Osb**
Hwy. 92 N.
Silsbee, TX 77656
Ultimate Parent: Louisiana-Pacific. **SIC:**
2100—Tobacco Products; 2493—
Reconstituted Wood Products.

★ 89434 ★ **Pizza Hut**
720 Hwy. 96 S
Silsbee, TX 77656
(409)385-3431
Ultimate Parent: Pepsico. **SIC:** 5812—
Eating Places.

★ 89435 ★ **Radio Shack**
295 Hwy. 96 S
Silsbee, TX 77656
(409)385-5480
Company Type: Division. **Ultimate Parent:**
Tandy Corp.

★ 89436 ★ **Trailways Bus Station**
120 S. 3rd St.
Silsbee, TX 77656
(409)385-7606
Ultimate Parent: Greyhound Lines Inc. **SIC:**
4131—Intercity & Rural Bus Transportation.

★ 89437 ★ **Wal Mart Discount City**
Texas Hwy. 327
Silsbee, TX 77656
(409)385-0782
Ultimate Parent: Wal-Mart Stores, Inc. **SIC:**
5311—Department Stores.

★ 89438 ★ **Wal Mart Pharmacy**
1010 Hwy. 327 E
Silsbee, TX 77656
(409)385-1437
Ultimate Parent: Wal-Mart Stores, Inc.

Sinton

★ 89439 ★ **Marathon Oil Co.**
Plymouth Field
Sinton, TX 78387
(512)364-2150
Ultimate Parent: USX Corp. **SIC:** 1382—Oil
& Gas Exploration Services.

★ 89440 ★ **Marathon Oil Co.**
Plymouth Field
Sinton, TX 78387
(512)364-2150
Ultimate Parent: USX Corp. **SIC:** 1382—Oil
& Gas Exploration Services.

★ 89441 ★ **Pizza Hut**
210 E. Sinton St.
Sinton, TX 78387
(512)364-4796
Ultimate Parent: Pepsico. **SIC:** 5812—
Eating Places.

★ 89442 ★ **Wal Mart Discount City**
1300 E. Sinton St.
Sinton, TX 78387
(512)364-5011
Ultimate Parent: Wal-Mart Stores, Inc.

Slaton

★ 89443 ★ **Piggly Wiggly**
140 E. Panhandle St.
Slaton, TX 79364
(806)828-3818
Ultimate Parent: Bruno's. **SIC:** 5421—Meat
& Fish Markets.

★ 89444 ★ **Pizza Hut**
23rd
Slaton, TX 79364
(806)828-5888
Ultimate Parent: Pepsico. **SIC:** 5812—
Eating Places.

Snyder

★ 89445 ★ **Exxon Co. USA**
1920 6th St.
Snyder, TX 79549
(915)573-2656
Ultimate Parent: Exxon. **SIC:** 1311—Crude
Petroleum & Natural Gas.

★ 89446 ★ **Lone Star Gas Co.**
3501 37th St.
Snyder, TX 79549
(915)573-6941
Ultimate Parent: Enserch. **SIC:** 4939—
Combination Utility Nec.

★ 89447 ★ **Lone Star Gas Co.**
1712 27th St.
Snyder, TX 79549
(915)573-3594
Ultimate Parent: Enserch. **SIC:** 4932—Gas
& Other Services Combined; 4939—
Combination Utility Nec.

★ 89448 ★ **Mobil Oil Co.**
7 St.
Snyder, TX 79549
(915)573-5476
Ultimate Parent: Mobil. **SIC:** 2911—
Petroleum Refining.

★ 89449 ★ **Piggly Wiggly**
Big Spring Hwy.
Snyder, TX 79549
(915)573-1971
Ultimate Parent: Bruno's. **SIC:** 5461—
Retail Bakeries.

★ 89450 ★ **Pizza Hut**
3909 College Ave.
Snyder, TX 79549
(915)573-4919
Ultimate Parent: Pepsico. **SIC:** 5812—
Eating Places.

★ 89451 ★ **Radio Shack**
2201 25th St.
Snyder, TX 79549
(915)573-0515
Company Type: Division. **Ultimate Parent:**
Tandy Corp. **SIC:** 5065—Electronic Parts &
Equipment Nec.

★ 89452 ★ **Ryder Truck Rental**
3800 College Ave.
Snyder, TX 79549
(915)573-4826
Ultimate Parent: Ryder System. **SIC:**
7359—Equipment Rental & Leasing Nec.

★ 89453 ★ **Texaco Inc.**
Clairemont Rd.
Snyder, TX 79549
(915)573-3036
Ultimate Parent: Texaco. **SIC:** 1311—
Crude Petroleum & Natural Gas.

★ 89454 ★ **Union Oil Co. of California**
1907 40th St.
Snyder, TX 79549
(915)573-1833
Ultimate Parent: Unocal Corp. **SIC:** 1311—
Crude Petroleum & Natural Gas.

Somerville

★ 89455 ★ **Citizens State Bank**
PO Box 518
Somerville, TX 77879
(409)596-1421
Ultimate Parent: Liberty National Bancorp.
SIC: 6022—State Commercial Banks.

Sonora

★ 89456 ★ **Lone Star Gas Co.**
510 S. Crockett Ave.
Sonora, TX 76950
(915)387-2661
Ultimate Parent: Enserch.

Sour Lake

★ 89457 ★ Texaco
Shoestring Rd.
Sour Lake, TX 77659
(409)287-3946
Ultimate Parent: Texaco. **SIC:** 5172—
Petroleum Products Nec.

★ 89458 ★ Texaco Pipeline Inc.
Hwy. 105
Sour Lake, TX 77659
(409)287-3232
Ultimate Parent: Texaco.

South Houston

★ 89459 ★ Kmart Discount Stores
1402 Spencer Hwy.
South Houston, TX 77587
(713)946-6950
Ultimate Parent: K-Mart.

★ 89460 ★ Radio Shack
1407 Spencer Hwy.
South Houston, TX 77587
(713)944-5575
Company Type: Division. **Ultimate Parent:**
Tandy Corp. **SIC:** 5065—Electronic Parts &
Equipment Nec.

Spearman

★ 89461 ★ Pizza Hut
Hwy. 207 S
Spearman, TX 79081
(806)659-2547
Ultimate Parent: Pepsico. **SIC:** 5812—
Eating Places.

Spring

★ 89462 ★ Ace Hardware&Home Center Inc.
16852 Stuebner Airline Rd.
Spring, TX 77379
(713)376-4565
Ultimate Parent: Ace Hardware. **SIC:**
5251—Hardware Stores.

★ 89463 ★ Betz Laboratories Inc.
9669 Grogans Mill Rd.
Spring, TX 77380-1026
(713)367-6201
Location Type: Branch office. **Officer:**
Debby West. **Ultimate Parent:** Betz
Laboratories Inc. **SIC:** 8731—Commercial
Physical Research.

★ 89464 ★ Compass Bank-Houston
1530 Spring Cypress Rd.
Spring, TX 77388-3608
(713)867-1160
Company Type: Subsidiary. **Location
Type:** Branch office. **Ultimate Parent:**
Compass Bancshares. **SIC:** 6021—National
Commercial Banks.

★ 89465 ★ Dr. Pepper Bottling Co.
21500 Spring West Dr.
Spring, TX 77388
(713)350-0058
Officer: Stan Noviski, Manager. **Ultimate
Parent:** Dr. Pepper/Seven-Up. **SIC:** 2086—
Bottled & Canned Soft Drinks.

★ 89466 ★ Dresser Valve&Cntr
10077 Grogans Mill Rd.
Spring, TX 77380
(713)367-5741
Ultimate Parent: Dresser Industries Inc.

★ 89467 ★ Exxon
16803 Stuebner Airline Rd.
Spring, TX 77379
(713)376-8058
Ultimate Parent: Exxon. **SIC:** 5541—
Gasoline Service Stations.

★ 89468 ★ Exxon Car Care Center
2300 Buckthorne Pl
Spring, TX 77380
(713)367-4116
Ultimate Parent: Exxon. **SIC:** 7538—
General Automotive Repair Shops.

★ 89469 ★ Exxon Co. USA
16803 Stuebner Airline Rd.
Spring, TX 77379
(713)370-7524
Ultimate Parent: Exxon.

★ 89470 ★ Exxon Co. USA
21334 Interstate 45
Spring, TX 77373
(713)353-3875
Ultimate Parent: Exxon.

★ 89471 ★ McDonalds Restaurant
18604 Kuykendahl Rd.
Spring, TX 77379
(713)350-2590
Ultimate Parent: McDonald's.

★ 89472 ★ Mitchell Energy Prod Corp.
PO Box 4000
Spring, TX 77387-4000
(713)363-5500
Company Type: Headquarters. **Officer:**
George P Mitchell. **Ultimate Parent:**
Mitchell Energy & Devel. **SIC:** 1311—Crude
Petroleum & Natural Gas; 1321—Natural
Gas Liquids; 1381—Drilling Oil & Gas Wells;
1382—Oil & Gas Exploration Services;
1389—Oil & Gas Field Services Nec;
4922—Natural Gas Transmission; 6552—
Subdividers & Developers Nec; 6792—Oil
Royalty Traders.

★ 89473 ★ Mitchell Energy&Development
2201 Timberloch Pl
Spring, TX 77380
(713)363-5500
Ultimate Parent: Mitchell Energy & Devel.
SIC: 4932—Gas & Other Services
Combined.

★ 89474 ★ Mobil Mart
8253 Louetta Rd.
Spring, TX 77379
(713)370-2685
Ultimate Parent: Mobil.

★ 89475 ★ Mobil Mart
21327 Interstate 45
Spring, TX 77388
(713)353-3037
Ultimate Parent: Mobil.

★ 89476 ★ Mobil Station No 12468
25029 N. Hwy. 75
Spring, TX 77373
(713)363-1863
Ultimate Parent: Mobil. **SIC:** 5541—
Gasoline Service Stations.

★ 89477 ★ Payless Shoesource
1417 Spring Cypress Rd.
Spring, TX 77373
(713)353-7698
Ultimate Parent: May Department Stores.

★ 89478 ★ Pennzoil Co.
1440 Lake Front Cir.
Spring, TX 77380
(713)367-0353
Ultimate Parent: Pennzoil.

★ 89479 ★ Pennzoil Products Co.
1520 Lake Front Cir.
Spring, TX 77380
(713)363-9085
Ultimate Parent: Pennzoil. **SIC:** 8731—
Commercial Physical Research.

★ 89480 ★ Pennzoil Products Co.
1520 Lake Front Cir.
Spring, TX 77380
(713)363-9085
Ultimate Parent: Pennzoil. **SIC:** 8731—
Commercial Physical Research.

★ 89481 ★ Pizza Hut
1491 Spring
Spring, TX 77373
(713)353-8869
Ultimate Parent: Pepsico. **SIC:** 5812—
Eating Places.

★ 89482 ★ Pizza Hut
16670 Stuebner-Airline Rd.
Spring, TX 77373
(713)376-8019
Ultimate Parent: Pepsico. **SIC:** 5812—
Eating Places.

★ 89483 ★ Pizza Hut
21127 Aldine Westfield
Spring, TX 77373
(713)443-7851
Ultimate Parent: Pepsico. **SIC:** 5812—
Eating Places.

★ 89484 ★ Radio Shack
7110 Louetta Rd.
Spring, TX 77379
(713)376-0700
Company Type: Division. **Ultimate Parent:**
Tandy Corp. **SIC:** 5065—Electronic Parts &
Equipment Nec.

★ 89485 ★ Radio Shack
Northland Shopping Ctr.
Spring, TX 77373
(713)353-7834
Company Type: Division. **Ultimate Parent:**
Tandy Corp. **SIC:** 5065—Electronic Parts &
Equipment Nec.

★ 89486 ★ Ryder Truck Rental
23114 Interstate 45
Spring, TX 77373
(713)350-2480
Ultimate Parent: Ryder System. **SIC:**
7359—Equipment Rental & Leasing Nec.

★ 89487 ★ Ryder Truck Rental
26460 Interstate 45
Spring, TX 77386
(713)367-9338
Ultimate Parent: Ryder System.

★ 89488 ★ Ryder Truck Rental
7613 Spring Cypress Rd.
Spring, TX 77379
(713)370-3365
Ultimate Parent: Ryder System.

★ 89489 ★ Shell Co.
21403 Interstate 45
Spring, TX 77388
(713)367-8144
Ultimate Parent: Shell Oil Co. **SIC:** 5541—
Gasoline Service Stations.

★ 89490 ★ Taco Bell
1509 Spring Cypress Rd.
Spring, TX 77388
(713)353-7667
Ultimate Parent: Pepsico.

★ 89491 ★ Taco Bell
7100 Louetta Rd.
Spring, TX 77379
(713)376-6835
Ultimate Parent: Pepsico.

★ 89492 ★ Texaco Food Mart
25103 Interstate 45
Spring, TX 77380
(713)363-9790
Ultimate Parent: Texaco.

★ 89493 ★ Texaco Food Mart
18603 Kuykendahl Rd.
Spring, TX 77379
(713)370-2266
Ultimate Parent: Texaco.

★ 89494 ★ Texaco Food Mart
22560 Aldine Westfield Rd.
Spring, TX 77373
(713)350-3836
Ultimate Parent: Texaco.

★ 89495 ★ Thom Mcan Family Shoes
1420 Spring Cypress Rd.
Spring, TX 77373
(713)353-4127
Ultimate Parent: Melville. **SIC:** 5661—Shoe
Stores.

★ 89496 ★ Walgreen Drug Stores
1469 Spring Cypress Rd.
Spring, TX 77373
(713)350-1629
Ultimate Parent: Walgreen Co.

Springtown

★ 89497 ★ Lone Star Gas Co.
Springtown, TX 76082
(817)523-7417
Ultimate Parent: Enserch. **SIC:** 4932—Gas
& Other Services Combined.

Spur

★ 89498 ★ Piggly Wiggly
611 Burlington Ave.
Spur, TX 79370
(806)271-4372
Ultimate Parent: Bruno's. **SIC:** 5421—Meat
& Fish Markets.

Stafford

★ 89499 ★ Exxon Co. USA
12411 Murphy Rd.
Stafford, TX 77477
(713)561-9585
Ultimate Parent: Exxon.

★ 89500 ★ Hamilton Hallmark
4850 Wright Rd., Ste. 190
Stafford, TX 77477
(713)240-7733
Location Type: Branch office. **Ultimate
Parent:** Avnet. **SIC:** 5065—Electronic Parts
& Equipment Nec.

★ 89501 ★ Kroger Co.
220 Fm 1092 Rd.
Stafford, TX 77477
(713)499-5535
Ultimate Parent: Kroger. **SIC:** 5411—
Grocery Stores.

★ 89502 ★ McDonalds Restaurant
12705 S. Kirkwood Rd. 130
Stafford, TX 77477
(713)271-0311
Ultimate Parent: May Department Stores.
SIC: 5812—Eating Places.

★ 89503 ★ Pizza Hut
3307 S. Main St.
Stafford, TX 77477
(713)499-4414
Ultimate Parent: Pepsico. **SIC:** 5812—
Eating Places.

★ 89504 ★ Radio Shack
231 Fm 1092 Rd.
Stafford, TX 77477
(713)499-8944
Company Type: Division. **Ultimate Parent:**
Tandy Corp. **SIC:** 5065—Electronic Parts &
Equipment Nec.

★ 89505 ★ Schott's Bakery
2207 S. Main St.
Stafford, TX 77477
(713)499-9897
Officer: Dan Harrison, President. **Ultimate
Parent:** Flowers Industries. **SIC:** 2051—
Bread, Cake & Related Products.

★ 89506 ★ Taco Bell
503 Fm 1092 Rd.
Stafford, TX 77477
(713)499-2245
Ultimate Parent: Pepsico. **SIC:** 5812—
Eating Places.

★ 89507 ★ Ten Minute Oil Change
13770 Murphy Rd.
Stafford, TX 77477
(713)499-7144
Ultimate Parent: Pennzoil. **SIC:** 7539—
Automotive Repair Shops Nec.

★ 89508 ★ Texaco Food Mart
13102 Murphy Rd.
Stafford, TX 77477
(713)240-3666
Ultimate Parent: Texaco.

★ 89509 ★ United Parcel Service
13922 Stafford Rd.
Stafford, TX 77477
(713)261-1704
Ultimate Parent: United Parcel Service of
America. **SIC:** 4213—Trucking Except
Local.

Stamford

★ 89510 ★ Burlington Northern Railroa
1072 PO Box
Stamford, TX 79553
(915)673-3151
Ultimate Parent: Burlington Northern. **SIC:**
4011—Railroads—Line-Haul Operating;
4119—Local Passenger Transportation Nec.

★ 89511 ★   **Piggly Wiggly**
210 E. Mcharg St.
Stamford, TX 79553
(915)773-2152
Ultimate Parent: Bruno's. **SIC:** 5421—Meat
& Fish Markets.

★ 89512 ★   **Pizza Hut**
530 PO Box
Stamford, TX 79553
Ultimate Parent: Pepsico. **SIC:** 5812—
Eating Places.

Stephenville

★ 89513 ★   **Appleton Electric Co.**
2150 S. Loop Ave.
Stephenville, TX 76401-3984
Ultimate Parent: Emerson Electric Co. Inc.
SIC: 3699—Electrical Equipment & Supplies
Nec.

★ 89514 ★   **FMC Corp. Fluid
Control**
2825 W. Washington St.
Stephenville, TX 76401
(817)968-2181
Officer: John Moore, Manager. **Ultimate
Parent:** FMC. **SIC:** 3494—Valves & Pipe
Fittings Nec.

★ 89515 ★   **Fmc Fluid Control
Stephenville**
2825 W. Washington
Stephenville, TX 76401
Ultimate Parent: FMC. **SIC:** 3533—Oil &
Gas Field Machinery.

★ 89516 ★   **Genuine Parts Co.**
Rayloc Div.
840 SE Loop 196
Box 908
Stephenville, TX 76401
Company Type: Division. **Ultimate Parent:**
Genuine Parts. **SIC:** 3714—Motor Vehicle
Parts & Accessories; 3465—Automotive
Stampings.

★ 89517 ★   **Kentucky Fried
Chicken**
1901 W. Washington St.
Stephenville, TX 76401
(817)968-3900
Ultimate Parent: Pepsico. **SIC:** 5812—
Eating Places.

★ 89518 ★   **Lone Star Gas Co.**
651 PO Box
Stephenville, TX 76401
Ultimate Parent: Enserch. **SIC:** 4932—Gas
& Other Services Combined.

★ 89519 ★   **Lone Star Gas Co.**
299 N. Belknap St.
Stephenville, TX 76401
(817)965-3918
Ultimate Parent: Enserch. **SIC:** 4932—Gas
& Other Services Combined.

★ 89520 ★   **McDonalds**
1416 W. Washington St.
Stephenville, TX 76401
(817)965-3777
Ultimate Parent: McDonald's.
SIC: 5812—Eating Places.

★ 89521 ★   **Piggly Wiggly**
555 W. Washington St.
Stephenville, TX 76401
(817)965-4518
Ultimate Parent: Bruno's. **SIC:** 5411—
Grocery Stores.

★ 89522 ★   **Pizza Hut**
2320 W. Washington St.
Stephenville, TX 76401
(817)968-3941
Ultimate Parent: Pepsico. **SIC:** 5812—
Eating Places.

★ 89523 ★   **Radio Shack**
202 S. Patrick
Stephenville, TX 76401
(817)445-2240
Company Type: Division. **Ultimate Parent:**
Tandy Corp. **SIC:** 5731—Radio, Television
& Electronics Stores.

★ 89524 ★   **Rayloc Industries, Inc.**
Hwy. 377
Stephenville, TX 76401
(817)965-5075
Officer: Boyd Phelps, Manager. **Ultimate**

Parent: Genuine Parts. **SIC:** 3714—Motor
Vehicle Parts & Accessories.

★ 89525 ★   **Ryder Truck Rental**
1479 S. Loop
Stephenville, TX 76401
(817)968-5859
Ultimate Parent: Ryder System. **SIC:**
7359—Equipment Rental & Leasing Nec.

★ 89526 ★   **Trailways Texas Inc.**
223 E. College St.
Stephenville, TX 76401
(817)965-3175
Ultimate Parent: Greyhound Lines Inc. **SIC:**
4111—Local & Suburban Transit.

★ 89527 ★   **Warner
Communications Inc.**
975 N. Lillian St.
Stephenville, TX 76401
(817)968-4189
Ultimate Parent: Time Warner, Inc. **SIC:**
4833—Television Broadcasting Stations.

Streetman

★ 89528 ★   **Aker Sulfur Recovery
Plant**
PO Box 128
Streetman, TX 75859
Ultimate Parent: Texaco. **SIC:** 2819—
Industrial Inorganic Chemicals Nec.

Sugar Land

★ 89529 ★   **Comerica Bank-Texas**
1 Sugar Creek Ctr. Blvd.
Sugar Land, TX 77478
(713)491-2265
Company Type: Subsidiary. **Location
Type:** Branch office. **Ultimate Parent:**
Comerica Bank. **SIC:** 6021—National
Commercial Banks.

★ 89530 ★   **Compass Bank-
Houston**
2520 Hwy. 6
Sugar Land, TX 77487
(713)867-1180
Company Type: Subsidiary. **Location
Type:** Branch office. **Ultimate Parent:**
Compass Bancshares. **SIC:** 6021—National
Commercial Banks.

★ 89531 ★   **Crown Beverage
Packaging Inc.**
12901 Jesse Pirtle Blvd.
Sugar Land, TX 77478
Ultimate Parent: Crown Cork & Seal. **SIC:**
3411—Metal Cans.

★ 89532 ★   **Imperial Holly**
8016 Hwy. 90 A
Sugar Land, TX 77478
(713)491-9181
Company Type: Headquarters. **Officer:**
James C. Kempner. **Employee Count:**
1840. **Sales:** 648 M. **Fortune 500:** Largest
U.S. Industrial Corporations: Ranking 482.

★ 89533 ★   **Kroger Food Stores**
3665 Hwy. 6
Sugar Land, TX 77478
(713)980-5400
Ultimate Parent: Kroger.

★ 89534 ★   **Marshalls Inc.**
2382 Eldridge Rd.
Sugar Land, TX 77478
(713)558-4600
Ultimate Parent: Melville.

★ 89535 ★   **Mary Kay Cosmetics**
13111 Georgetown Dr.
Sugar Land, TX 77478
(713)240-0438
Ultimate Parent: Mary Kay Cosmetics.

★ 89536 ★   **McDonalds
Restaurant**
3401 Hwy. 6
Sugar Land, TX 77478
(713)980-3553
Ultimate Parent: McDonald's.

★ 89537 ★   **Mobil Oil Self Sv**
3650 Hwy. 6
Sugar Land, TX 77478
(713)980-1151
Ultimate Parent: Mobil.

★ 89538 ★   **Nalco Chemical**
7701 Hwy. 90a
Sugar Land, TX 77478
(713)491-4500
Ultimate Parent: Nalco Chemical Co.

★ 89539 ★   **Nalco Chemical Co.**
7701 US Hwy. 90-A
Sugar Land, TX 77478
Ultimate Parent: Nalco Chemical Co. **SIC:**
2899—Chemical Preparations Nec; 2869—
Industrial Organic Chemicals Nec; 2843—
Surface Active Agents.

★ 89540 ★   **Pizza Hut**
3638 Hwy. 6
Sugar Land, TX 77478
(713)265-1000
Ultimate Parent: Pepsico.

★ 89541 ★   **Pulte Home Corp.**
2719 Old Fort Rd.
Sugar Land, TX 77479
(713)980-7886
Ultimate Parent: Pulte. **SIC:** 1521—
Single-Family Housing Construction.

★ 89542 ★   **Radio Shack**
3221 Hwy. 6
Sugar Land, TX 77478
(713)980-6884
Company Type: Division. **Ultimate Parent:**
Tandy Corp.

★ 89543 ★   **Sermatech
International Inc.**
12505 Reed Rd.
Sugar Land, TX 77478
Ultimate Parent: Teleflex. **SIC:** 3479—
Metal Coating & Allied Services.

★ 89544 ★   **Shell Oil Co.**
15145 Southwest Fwy.
Sugar Land, TX 77478
(713)242-1141
Ultimate Parent: Shell Oil Co.

★ 89545 ★   **Varian Associates**
505 Julie Rivers Dr.
Sugar Land, TX 77478
(713)240-7330
Ultimate Parent: Varian Associates, Inc.

★ 89546 ★   **Walgreen Drug Store**
3316 Hwy. 6
Sugar Land, TX 77478
(713)980-5780
Ultimate Parent: Walgreen Co. **SIC:**
5912—Drug Stores & Proprietary Stores.

Sugarland

★ 89547 ★   **Fort Bend Letilities**
PO Box 9
Sugarland, TX 77487-0009
(713)491-9181 **Fax:** (713)490-9530
Company Type: Subsidiary. **Officer:**
Robert C. Hanna, President & CEO.
Ultimate Parent: Imperial Holly.

★ 89548 ★   **Imperial Holly Corp.**
1 Imperial Sq., Ste. 200
PO Box 9
Sugarland, TX 77487-0009
(713)491-9181 **Fax:** (713)490-9530
Company Type: Headquarters. **Officer:** I.H.
Kempner III, Chairman. **Ultimate Parent:**
Imperial Holly. **Sales:** 600 illion M.

Sulphur Spring

★ 89549 ★   **City National Bank of
Sulphur Spring**
201 Connally St.
Sulphur Spring, TX 75482-2611
(903)885-7523
Company Type: Headquarters. **Officer:**
Lee Teetes, President. **Ultimate Parent:**
City National Corp. **SIC:** 6021—National
Commercial Banks; 6141—Personal Credit
Institutions.

★ 89550 ★   **City National Bank of
Sulphur Spring**
1108 S. Broadway St.
Sulphur Spring, TX 75482-4840
(903)885-5432
Company Type: Branch. **Ultimate Parent:**
City National Corp. **SIC:** 6021—National
Commercial Banks.

Sulphur Springs

★ 89551 ★   **Associated Milk
Producers Inc.**
1123 Main St.
Sulphur Springs, TX 75482
(214)885-6518
Ultimate Parent: Associated Milk Producers
Inc. **SIC:** 5143—Dairy Products Except
Dried or Canned.

★ 89552 ★   **Associated Milk
Producers Inc.**
1123 Main St.
Sulphur Springs, TX 75482
(214)885-2133
Ultimate Parent: Associated Milk Producers
Inc. **SIC:** 5143—Dairy Products Except
Dried or Canned.

★ 89553 ★   **Borden Inc.**
Dairy
500 N. Jackson St.
Sulphur Springs, TX 75482
Company Type: Division. **Ultimate Parent:**
Borden, Inc. **SIC:** 2026—Fluid Milk; 2086—
Bottled & Canned Soft Drinks.

★ 89554 ★   **Borden Inc.**
Grocery Division
500 N. Jackson St.
Sulphur Springs, TX 75482
Company Type: Division. **Ultimate Parent:**
Borden, Inc. **SIC:** 2026—Fluid Milk; 2086—
Bottled & Canned Soft Drinks.

★ 89555 ★   **City National Bank**
201 Connally St.
Sulphur Springs, TX 75482
(214)885-7523
Ultimate Parent: City National Corp. **SIC:**
6022—State Commercial Banks.

★ 89556 ★   **City National Bank**
1108 S. Broadway St.
Sulphur Springs, TX 75482
(214)885-5432
Location Type: Branch office. **Ultimate
Parent:** City National Corp. **SIC:** 6022—
State Commercial Banks.

★ 89557 ★   **Hon Co.**
906 Hillcrest Dr.
Sulphur Springs, TX 75482
Ultimate Parent: Hon Industries. **SIC:**
2522—Office Furniture Except Wood.

★ 89558 ★   **Kentucky Fried
Chicken**
425 Industrial Dr. E
Sulphur Springs, TX 75482
Ultimate Parent: Pepsico. **SIC:** 5812—
Eating Places.

★ 89559 ★   **Ocean Spray
Cranberries Inc.**
419 Industrial Dr. E
Sulphur Springs, TX 75482
(903)885-8676
Officer: Craig Miller, Manager. **Ultimate
Parent:** Ocean Spray. **SIC:** 2033—Canned
Fruits & Vegetables; 2035—Pickles, Sauces
& Salad Dressings; 2086—Bottled &
Canned Soft Drinks.

★ 89560 ★   **Ocean Spray
Cranberries, Inc.**
419 E. Industrial Dr.
Sulphur Springs, TX 75482
(904)885-8676
Officer: Craig Miller, Plant Manager.
Ultimate Parent: Ocean Spray. **SIC:**
2033—Canned Fruits & Vegetables; 2086—
Bottled & Canned Soft Drinks.

★ 89561 ★   **Ocean Spray
Cranberries Inc.**
419 Industrial Dr. E
Sulphur Springs, TX 75482
(214)885-8676
Ultimate Parent: Ocean Spray. **SIC:**
2099—Food Preparations Nec.

★ 89562 ★   **Pizza Hut**
113 Hodge St.
Sulphur Springs, TX 75482
(214)885-8668
Ultimate Parent: Pepsico. **SIC:** 5812—
Eating Places.

★ **89563** ★ **Radio Shack**
1402 Mockingbird Ln. 3
Sulphur Springs, TX 75482
(214)885-9494
Company Type: Division. **Ultimate Parent:** Tandy Corp. **SIC:** 5065—Electronic Parts & Equipment Nec; 5731—Radio, Television & Electronics Stores.

★ **89564** ★ **Rockwell International Corp.**
MF&C Div.
1511 Jefferson PO Box 501
Sulphur Springs, TX 75482
Company Type: Division. **Ultimate Parent:** Rockwell International Corp. **SIC:** 3494—Valves & Pipe Fittings Nec.

★ **89565** ★ **Wal Mart Auto Repair**
1401 Mockingbird Ln.
Sulphur Springs, TX 75482
(214)885-2941
Ultimate Parent: Wal-Mart Stores, Inc. **SIC:** 7538—General Automotive Repair Shops.

★ **89566** ★ **Wal Mart Discount Cities**
1401 Mockingbird Ln.
Sulphur Springs, TX 75482
(214)885-1566
Ultimate Parent: Wal-Mart Stores, Inc. **SIC:** 5331—Variety Stores.

Sundown

★ **89567** ★ **Exxon Corp.**
Sundown, TX 79372
(806)229-8661
Ultimate Parent: Exxon. **SIC:** 1311—Crude Petroleum & Natural Gas.

★ **89568** ★ **Texaco Inc.**
910 S. Texas
Sundown, TX 79372
(806)229-2961
Ultimate Parent: Texaco. **SIC:** 1311—Crude Petroleum & Natural Gas.

Sunray

★ **89569** ★ **Diamond Shamrock Inc. Mckee Plants**
Fm 119 & Fm 1284 PO Box 36
Sunray, TX 79086
Ultimate Parent: Diamond Shamrock. **SIC:** 2911—Petroleum Refining.

★ **89570** ★ **Diamond Shamrock Refining & Marketing Co.**
SR 1
PO Box 36
Sunray, TX 79086-9705
Ultimate Parent: Diamond Shamrock. **SIC:** 2911—Petroleum Refining.

★ **89571** ★ **Diamond Shamrock Refining & Marketing Co. Mckee Plants**
Star Rte. 1 PO Box 36
Sunray, TX 79086
Ultimate Parent: Diamond Shamrock. **SIC:** 2911—Petroleum Refining.

★ **89572** ★ **Mobil Producing TX & New Mex**
SE Of City
Sunray, TX 79086
(806)948-4450
Ultimate Parent: Mobil. **SIC:** 1311—Crude Petroleum & Natural Gas.

★ **89573** ★ **Witco Corp.**
Concarb
2 Miles N. Hwy. 119
Sunray, TX 79086
Ultimate Parent: Witco Corp. **SIC:** 2895—Carbon Black.

★ **89574** ★ **Witco Corp.**
Concarb Div.
Hwy. 1 - Box 15
Sunray, TX 79086
Company Type: Division. **Ultimate Parent:** Witco Corp. **SIC:** 2895—Carbon Black.

Suplhur Springs

★ **89575** ★ **Borden Inc.**
500 Jackson St. S
Suplhur Springs, TX 75482
(903)885-7573
Officer: John Starkey, Manager. **Ultimate Parent:** Borden, Inc. **SIC:** 2022—Cheese—

Natural & Processed; 2026—Fluid Milk; 2033—Canned Fruits & Vegetables.

Sweeny

★ **89576** ★ **Phillips 66**
Freeport Terminal Ii
Fm 1495
Sweeny, TX 77480-0866
Company Type: Division. **Ultimate Parent:** Phillips Petroleum. **SIC:** 5171—Petroleum Bulk Stations & Terminals.

★ **89577** ★ **Phillips 66 Co.**
State Hwy. 35 & Fm 524
Sweeny, TX 77480-0866
Ultimate Parent: Phillips Petroleum. **SIC:** 2911—Petroleum Refining; 2819—Industrial Inorganic Chemicals Nec.

★ **89578** ★ **Phillips 66 Co.**
Freeport Ii Terminal
Fm 1495
Sweeny, TX 77480-0866
Company Type: Division. **Ultimate Parent:** Phillips Petroleum. **SIC:** 5171—Petroleum Bulk Stations & Terminals.

★ **89579** ★ **Phillips 66 Co.**
Freeport Terminal
FM 1495
Sweeny, TX 77480-0866
Company Type: Division. **Ultimate Parent:** Phillips Petroleum. **SIC:** 5171—Petroleum Bulk Stations & Terminals; 2911—Petroleum Refining.

★ **89580** ★ **Phillips 66 Co.**
San Bernard Terminal
C.R. 372
Sweeny, TX 77480-0866
Company Type: Division. **Ultimate Parent:** Phillips Petroleum. **SIC:** 5171—Petroleum Bulk Stations & Terminals; 2911—Petroleum Refining.

Sweetwater

★ **89581** ★ **Archer Daniels Midland Co.**
FM Rd. 419
Sweetwater, TX 79556
(915)235-1721
Officer: Buford Patterson, Manager. **Ultimate Parent:** Archer Daniels Midland Co. **SIC:** 2048—Prepared Feeds Nec; 2074—Cottonseed Oil Mills.

★ **89582** ★ **Coca Cola Bottling Co.**
908 E. Broadway St.
Sweetwater, TX 79556
(915)235-2992
Ultimate Parent: Coca-Cola Enterprises. **SIC:** 5149—Groceries & Related Products Nec.

★ **89583** ★ **Exxon Energy Chemicals**
105 Mohawk St.
Sweetwater, TX 79556
(915)235-1431
Ultimate Parent: Exxon. **SIC:** 5169—Chemicals & Allied Products Nec.

★ **89584** ★ **Greyhound Bus Lins**
1901 E. Broadway St.
Sweetwater, TX 79556
(915)235-2742
Ultimate Parent: Greyhound Lines Inc.

★ **89585** ★ **Kentucky Fried Chicken**
2012 Lamar St.
Sweetwater, TX 79556
(915)235-8060
Ultimate Parent: Pepsico. **SIC:** 5812—Eating Places.

★ **89586** ★ **Lone Star Gas Co.**
307 Locust St.
Sweetwater, TX 79556
(915)236-6871
Ultimate Parent: Enserch.

★ **89587** ★ **Mobil Pipe Line Co.**
SW Of City
Sweetwater, TX 79556
(915)235-8150
Ultimate Parent: Mobil. **SIC:** 4612—Crude Petroleum Pipelines.

★ **89588** ★ **Piggly Wiggly**
2015 Lamar St.
Sweetwater, TX 79556
(915)236-6629
Ultimate Parent: Bruno's. **SIC:** 5411—Grocery Stores.

★ **89589** ★ **Pizza Hut**
800 E. Broadway St.
Sweetwater, TX 79556
(915)235-8673
Ultimate Parent: Pepsico. **SIC:** 5812—Eating Places.

★ **89590** ★ **Radio Shack**
1106 E. Broadway St.
Sweetwater, TX 79556
(915)235-4500
Company Type: Division. **Ultimate Parent:** Tandy Corp. **SIC:** 5065—Electronic Parts & Equipment Nec.

★ **89591** ★ **Southern Cotton Oil Co. INc.**
FM Rd. 419 N. of City
Sweetwater, TX 79556
(915)236-6661
Officer: Buford Patterson, Manager. **Ultimate Parent:** Archer Daniels Midland Co. **SIC:** 2048—Prepared Feeds Nec; 2079—Edible Fats & Oils Nec.

★ **89592** ★ **Southren Cotton Oil Co.**
PO Box 420
Sweetwater, TX 79556-0420
(915)236-6661
Officer: Buford Patterson. **Ultimate Parent:** Archer Daniels Midland Co. **SIC:** 2079—Edible Fats & Oils Nec; 5191—Farm Supplies.

★ **89593** ★ **Texaco Inc.**
W Hwy. 80
Sweetwater, TX 79556
(915)236-6651
Ultimate Parent: Texaco. **SIC:** 1382—Oil & Gas Exploration Services.

Taft

★ **89594** ★ **Greyhound Bus Lines Inc.**
Hwy. 181
Taft, TX 78390
(512)528-3609
Ultimate Parent: Greyhound Lines Inc. **SIC:** 4131—Intercity & Rural Bus Transportation.

★ **89595** ★ **Mobil Producing TX & NM Inc.**
Taft, TX 78390
(512)528-2441
Ultimate Parent: Mobil. **SIC:** 1311—Crude Petroleum & Natural Gas.

Talco

★ **89596** ★ **Exxon Co. USA**
U.S. a
Talco, TX 75487
(214)379-2401
Ultimate Parent: Exxon. **SIC:** 1311—Crude Petroleum & Natural Gas.

Taylor

★ **89597** ★ **City National Bank**
3200 N. Main St.
Taylor, TX 76574-1216
(512)352-9207
Ultimate Parent: City National Corp. **SIC:** 6021—National Commercial Banks.

★ **89598** ★ **City National Bank of Taylor**
116 W. 3rd St.
Taylor, TX 76574-3515
(512)352-8523
Company Type: Headquarters. **Officer:** Andrew D. LittleJohn, President. **Ultimate Parent:** City National Corp. **SIC:** 6021—National Commercial Banks; 6141—Personal Credit Institutions; 6211—Security Brokers & Dealers.

★ **89599** ★ **Intercraft Co., Inc.**
1 Intercraft Plz.
Taylor, TX 76574
(512)352-8501 **Fax:** (512)352-4880
Officer: Vincent J. Pasquale, President. **Ultimate Parent:** Newell.

★ **89600** ★ **Pizza Hut**
Hwy. 95 N
Taylor, TX 76574
(512)352-6680
Ultimate Parent: Pepsico. **SIC:** 5812—Eating Places.

★ **89601** ★ **Ryder Truck Rental**
Hwy. 95 N
Taylor, TX 76574
(512)352-8915
Ultimate Parent: Ryder System. **SIC:** 7359—Equipment Rental & Leasing Nec.

★ **89602** ★ **Texaco Inc.**
815 W. 2nd St.
Taylor, TX 76574
(512)352-2442
Ultimate Parent: Texaco. **SIC:** 5171—Petroleum Bulk Stations & Terminals.

★ **89603** ★ **Trailways Bus System**
517 N. Main St. 19
Taylor, TX 76574
(512)352-6355
Ultimate Parent: Greyhound Lines Inc. **SIC:** 4131—Intercity & Rural Bus Transportation.

Teague

★ **89604** ★ **Arco Pipe Line Co.**
Donie Rd.
Teague, TX 75860
(817)739-2271
Location Type: Branch office. **Ultimate Parent:** Atlantic Richfield Co., Inc. **SIC:** 4612—Crude Petroleum Pipelines.

Temple

★ **89605** ★ **AT&T**
702 E. Downs Ave.
Temple, TX 76501-4557
(817)774-9885
Ultimate Parent: AT&T. **SIC:** 4813—Telephone Communications Except Radiotelephone.

★ **89606** ★ **Butler Paper**
2010 Forest Trail
Temple, TX 76502-2616
(817)778-4475
Location Type: Branch office. **Ultimate Parent:** Alco Standard Corp. **SIC:** 5113—Industrial & Personal Service Paper.

★ **89607** ★ **Butler Paper**
2010 Forest Trail
Temple, TX 76502-2616
(817)778-4475
Location Type: Branch office. **Ultimate Parent:** Alco Standard Corp. **SIC:** 5113—Industrial & Personal Service Paper.

★ **89608** ★ **Casual Corner**
3111 S. 31st St.
Temple, TX 76502
(817)778-1907
Ultimate Parent: United States Shoe. **SIC:** 5651—Family Clothing Stores.

★ **89609** ★ **Casual Corner**
Temple Mall
Temple, TX 76501
(817)778-1907
Ultimate Parent: United States Shoe. **SIC:** 5621—Women's Clothing Stores.

★ **89610** ★ **Champion International Corp.**
1900 Industrial Blvd.
Temple, TX 76504
(817)778-4837
Ultimate Parent: Champion International. **SIC:** 5112—Stationery & Office Supplies.

★ **89611** ★ **Coca Cola Bottling Co.**
1401 N. 3rd St.
Temple, TX 76501
(817)773-6812
Ultimate Parent: Coca-Cola Enterprises. **SIC:** 5149—Groceries & Related Products Nec.

★ **89612** ★ **Dillard Department Stores**
Temple Mall
Temple, TX 76501
(817)778-1854
Ultimate Parent: Dillard Department Stores. **SIC:** 5311—Department Stores.

★ 89613 ★   E R Carpenter Co.
2611 S. General Bruce Dr.
Temple, TX 76504
(817)778-8991
Ultimate Parent: Carpenter.

★ 89614 ★   E. R. Carpenter Co.
Inc.
2611 N. General Bruce Dr.
Temple, TX 76501
Ultimate Parent: Carpenter. SIC: 3086—
Plastics Foam Products.

★ 89615 ★   E. R. Carpenter Co. of
Texas
2611 North General Bruce Dr.
Temple, TX 76501
Ultimate Parent: Carpenter. SIC: 3086—
Plastics Foam Products.

★ 89616 ★   E.R. Carpenter Co. of
Texas
2611 North General Bruce Dr.
Temple, TX 76501
Ultimate Parent: Carpenter. SIC: 2392—
Housefurnishings Nec.

★ 89617 ★   Foot Action
3111 S. 31st St.
Temple, TX 76502
(817)773-7337
Ultimate Parent: Melville. SIC: 5661—Shoe
Stores.

★ 89618 ★   Greyhound Bus Lines
20 S. 5th St.
Temple, TX 76501
(817)773-4123
Ultimate Parent: Greyhound Lines Inc. SIC:
4111—Local & Suburban Transit.

★ 89619 ★   Hertz Rent-A-Car
6800 Airport Rd.
Temple, TX 76501
(817)773-2269
Ultimate Parent: Hertz. SIC: 4522—Air
Transportation—Nonscheduled.

★ 89620 ★   Kay Bee Toy Store
3111 S. 31st St.
Temple, TX 76502
(817)770-0329
Ultimate Parent: Melville. SIC: 5945—
Hobby, Toy & Game Shops.

★ 89621 ★   Lane Bryant
3111 S. 31st St.
Temple, TX 76502
(817)773-7486
Ultimate Parent: Limited. SIC: 5651—
Family Clothing Stores.

★ 89622 ★   Lone Star Gas Co.
368 PO Box
Temple, TX 76503
Ultimate Parent: Enserch. SIC: 4932—Gas
& Other Services Combined; 4939—
Combination Utility Nec.

★ 89623 ★   Manpower, Inc.
401 W. Central Ave.
Temple, TX 76501
(817)778-6741
Ultimate Parent: Manpower, Inc. SIC:
7363—Help Supply Services.

★ 89624 ★   Mobil Chemical Co.
1000 Industrial Blvd.
Temple, TX 76501
(817)778-4851
Ultimate Parent: Mobil. SIC: 5162—
Plastics Materials & Basic Shapes.

★ 89625 ★   Mobil Chemical Co.
3000 Pegasus Dr.
Temple, TX 76501-1101
(817)770-4100
Company Type: Branch. Officer: Brad
Early. Ultimate Parent: Mobil. SIC: 3081—
Unsupported Plastics Film & Sheet; 2899—
Chemical Preparations Nec; 5162—Plastics
Materials & Basic Shapes.

★ 89626 ★   Mobil Chemical Co.
Foam
3000 Pegasus Dr.
Temple, TX 76503
Ultimate Parent: Mobil. SIC: 3086—
Plastics Foam Products.

★ 89627 ★   Mobil Chemical Co.
General Products
3000 Pegasus Dr.
Temple, TX 76503
Ultimate Parent: Mobil. SIC: 2673—Bags—
Plastics, Laminated & Coated; 3081—
Unsupported Plastics Film & Sheet.

★ 89628 ★   Payless Shoesource
3111 S. 31st St.
Temple, TX 76502
(817)773-6304
Ultimate Parent: May Department Stores.
SIC: 5661—Shoe Stores.

★ 89629 ★   Payless Shoesource
1308 W. Adams Ave.
Temple, TX 76504
(817)778-2811
Ultimate Parent: May Department Stores.
SIC: 5661—Shoe Stores.

★ 89630 ★   Piggly Wiggly
2905 S. Gen Bruce Dr.
Temple, TX 76504
(817)773-6730
Ultimate Parent: Bruno's. SIC: 5411—
Grocery Stores.

★ 89631 ★   Pizza Hut
1530 Thornton Ln.
Temple, TX 76504
(817)773-1122
Ultimate Parent: Pepsico. SIC: 5812—
Eating Places.

★ 89632 ★   Pizza Hut
420 Greenview Dr. 100
Temple, TX 76502
Ultimate Parent: Pepsico.

★ 89633 ★   Pizza Hut
603 N. Gen Bruce Dr.
Temple, TX 76504
(817)778-5512
Ultimate Parent: Pepsico. SIC: 5812—
Eating Places.

★ 89634 ★   Radio Shack
3111 S. 31st St.
Temple, TX 76502
(817)774-7887
Company Type: Division. Ultimate Parent:
Tandy Corp. SIC: 5731—Radio, Television
& Electronics Stores.

★ 89635 ★   Radio Shack
Temple Mall
Temple, TX 76501
(817)778-0058
Company Type: Division. Ultimate Parent:
Tandy Corp. SIC: 5065—Electronic Parts &
Equipment Nec.

★ 89636 ★   Ralph Wilson Plastic
North Plant
10501 NW Hk Dodgen Loop
Temple, TX 76503
Location Type: Plant. Ultimate Parent:
Premark International. SIC: 3083—
Laminated Plastics Plate & Sheet.

★ 89637 ★   Ralph Wilson Plastic
South Plant
600 General Bruce Dr.
Temple, TX 76504
Location Type: Plant. Ultimate Parent:
Premark International. SIC: 3083—
Laminated Plastics Plate & Sheet.

★ 89638 ★   Ralph Wilson Plastics
Co.
500 E. Ridge Dr.
Temple, TX 76503
(817)778-2322
Officer: Bill Reeb, President. Ultimate
Parent: Premark International. SIC: 3083—
Laminated Plastics Plate & Sheet.

★ 89639 ★   Ralph Wilson Plastics
Co.
600 S. General Bruce Dr.
Temple, TX 76504
(817)778-2711
Officer: William Reeb, President. Ultimate
Parent: Potomac Electric Power. SIC:
3083—Laminated Plastics Plate & Sheet;
3089—Plastics Products Nec.

★ 89640 ★   Ralph Wilson Plastics
Co.
North Plant
10501 NW H.K. Dodgen Loop
Temple, TX 76503
Location Type: Plant. Ultimate Parent:
Premark International. SIC: 3083—
Laminated Plastics Plate & Sheet.

★ 89641 ★   Ralph Wilson Plastics
Co.
South Plant
600 S. General Bruce
Temple, TX 76504
Location Type: Plant. Ultimate Parent:
Premark International. SIC: 3083—
Laminated Plastics Plate & Sheet.

★ 89642 ★   Red Arrow Freight
Lines Inc.
3600 Range Rd.
Temple, TX 76501
(817)773-2834
Ultimate Parent: Carolina Freight. SIC:
4213—Trucking Except Local.

★ 89643 ★   Ryder Truck Rental
1307 Industrial Blvd.
Temple, TX 76504
(817)778-5510
Ultimate Parent: Ryder System. SIC:
7359—Equipment Rental & Leasing Nec;
7513—Truck Rental & Leasing Without
Drivers.

★ 89644 ★   Ryder Truck Rental
2710 Thornton Ln.
Temple, TX 76502
(817)773-1971
Ultimate Parent: Ryder System. SIC:
7359—Equipment Rental & Leasing Nec.

★ 89645 ★   Service Merchandise
3111 S. 31st St.
Temple, TX 76502
(817)778-3511
Ultimate Parent: Service Merchandise Co.,
Inc. SIC: 5311—Department Stores.

★ 89646 ★   Taco Bell
1512 W. Adams Ave.
Temple, TX 76504
(817)773-6666
Ultimate Parent: Pepsico. SIC: 5812—
Eating Places.

★ 89647 ★   Texaco Food Mart No
One
919 N. Gen Bruce Dr.
Temple, TX 76504
(817)778-0184
Ultimate Parent: Texaco. SIC: 5541—
Gasoline Service Stations.

★ 89648 ★   Texaco Food Mart 2
3703 S. General Bruce Dr.
Temple, TX 76504
(817)778-8600
Ultimate Parent: Texaco.

★ 89649 ★   Texas Instruments
Inc. Temple Site
5701 Airport Rd. PO Box 6102
Temple, TX 76503-6102
Ultimate Parent: Texas Instruments. SIC:
3577—Computer Peripheral Equipment Nec.

★ 89650 ★   Underwriters
Adjusting Co.
4302 Cactus Trl
Temple, TX 76502
(817)771-0170
Ultimate Parent: Continental. SIC: 6411—
Insurance Agents, Brokers & Service.

★ 89651 ★   Waldenbooks
3111 S. 31st St.
Temple, TX 76502
(817)778-1928
Ultimate Parent: K-Mart. SIC: 5942—Book
Stores.

★ 89652 ★   Waldenbooks
Temple Mall
Temple, TX 76501
(817)778-1928
Ultimate Parent: K-Mart. SIC: 5942—Book
Stores.

★ 89653 ★   Western Auto Supply
Co.
3002 S. 31st St.
Temple, TX 76502
(817)773-8008
Ultimate Parent: Sears Roebuck & Co.

SIC: 5531—Automobile & Home Supply
Stores.

★ 89654 ★   World Savings &
Loan
3407 S. 31st St.
Temple, TX 76502
(817)773-4958
Ultimate Parent: Golden West Financial
Corp. SIC: 6035—Federal Savings
Institutions.

Tenaha

★ 89655 ★   Citizens State Bank
210 Main St.
Tenaha, TX 75974
(409)248-3991
Ultimate Parent: Liberty National Bancorp.
SIC: 6022—State Commercial Banks;
6029—Commercial Banks Nec.

★ 89656 ★   Tyson Foods Inc.
Feedmill
Hwy. 96
Tenaha, TX 75974
Ultimate Parent: Tyson Foods, Inc. SIC:
2048—Prepared Feeds Nec.

Terell

★ 89657 ★   American National
Bank
102 W. Moore Ave.
Terell, TX 75160-3129
(214)563-2611
Officer: Riter C. Hulsey, Chairman of the
Board. Ultimate Parent: First Chicago
Corp. SIC: 6021—National Commercial
Banks. Employee Count: 185.

Terrell

★ 89658 ★   Kentucky Fried
Chicken
502 W. Moore Ave.
Terrell, TX 75160
(214)563-3398
Ultimate Parent: Pepsico. SIC: 5812—
Eating Places.

★ 89659 ★   Kroger Food Stores
1418 W. Moore Ave.
Terrell, TX 75160
(214)563-7604
Ultimate Parent: Kroger.

★ 89660 ★   Pizza Hut
701 W. Moore Ave.
Terrell, TX 75160
(214)563-5541
Ultimate Parent: Pepsico. SIC: 5812—
Eating Places.

★ 89661 ★   Ryder Truck Rental
1132 S. Virginia St.
Terrell, TX 75160
(214)563-1016
Ultimate Parent: Ryder System. SIC:
7359—Equipment Rental & Leasing Nec.

★ 89662 ★   Texaco
108 N. Rockwall St.
Terrell, TX 75160
(214)563-2666
Ultimate Parent: Texaco.

★ 89663 ★   Trailways Bus System
815 E. Moore Ave.
Terrell, TX 75160
(214)563-7566
Ultimate Parent: Greyhound Lines Inc. SIC:
4142—Bus Charter Service Except Local;
7349—Building Maintenance Services Nec.

Texarkana

★ 89664 ★   ABF Freight System
Inc.
Hwy. 67 N
Texarkana, TX 75501
(903)774-4179
Ultimate Parent: Arkansas Best. SIC:
4212—Local Trucking Without Storage.

★ 89665 ★   Ace Hardware
Downtown
W Hwy. 7th
Texarkana, TX 75501
(214)838-7551
Ultimate Parent: Ace Hardware. SIC:
5211—Lumber & Other Building Materials.

★ 89666 ★ Albertson's Food & Drug
2315 Richmond Rd.
Texarkana, TX 75503
(214)832-2561
Ultimate Parent: Albertson's Inc. SIC: 5411—Grocery Stores.

★ 89667 ★ American National Bank
2000 Richmond Rd.
Texarkana, TX 75503-2448
(903)832-2551
Officer: Billy I. Crutchfield, Chairman of the Board, President. Ultimate Parent: First Chicago Corp. SIC: 6021—National Commercial Banks. Employee Count: 52.

★ 89668 ★ Borden Inc.
3123 Magnolia St.
Texarkana, TX 75503
(903)793-4676
Officer: James McBride, Manager. Ultimate Parent: Borden, Inc. SIC: 2024—Ice Cream & Frozen Desserts; 2026—Fluid Milk; 2033—Canned Fruits & Vegetables.

★ 89669 ★ Casual Corner
37 Central Mall
Texarkana, TX 75503
(903)832-4851
Ultimate Parent: United States Shoe.

★ 89670 ★ Casual Corner
2300 Richmond Rd.
Texarkana, TX 75503
(214)832-4851
Ultimate Parent: United States Shoe. SIC: 5651—Family Clothing Stores.

★ 89671 ★ Circus World
135 Central Mall
Texarkana, TX 75503
(903)838-5777
Ultimate Parent: Melville.

★ 89672 ★ Circus World
2300 Richmond Rd.
Texarkana, TX 75503
(214)838-5777
Ultimate Parent: Melville. SIC: 5945—Hobby, Toy & Game Shops.

★ 89673 ★ Colgate-Palmolive Co.
Institutional Products Div.
303 Falvey Ave.
Texarkana, TX 75501
Company Type: Division. Ultimate Parent: Colgate-Palmolive. SIC: 3411—Metal Cans; 2899—Chemical Preparations Nec.

★ 89674 ★ E. R. Carpenter Co. Inc.
41 Globe Union Ave.
Texarkana, TX 75504-0989
Ultimate Parent: Carpenter. SIC: 3086—Plastics Foam Products.

★ 89675 ★ Foot Action
83 Central Mall
Texarkana, TX 75503
(214)832-2494
Ultimate Parent: Melville. SIC: 5661—Shoe Stores.

★ 89676 ★ GE Capital Railcar Service
PO Box 580
Texarkana, TX 75504
(903)773-5641
Officer: Rich Carter, Manager. Ultimate Parent: General Electric. SIC: 3743—Railroad Equipment.

★ 89677 ★ Greyhound Bus Lines
721 Spruce St.
Texarkana, TX 75501
(214)794-6171
Ultimate Parent: Greyhound Lines Inc. SIC: 4131—Intercity & Rural Bus Transportation.

★ 89678 ★ International Paper Texarkana Mill
PO Box 870
Texarkana, TX 75504
Ultimate Parent: International Paper Co. SIC: 2611—Pulp Mills; 2621—Paper Mills.

★ 89679 ★ Kentucky Fried Chicken
4100 Summerhill Rd.
Texarkana, TX 75503
(214)793-4100
Ultimate Parent: Pepsico. SIC: 5812—Eating Places.

★ 89680 ★ Kentucky Fried Chicken
2839 New Boston Rd.
Texarkana, TX 75501
(214)832-6511
Ultimate Parent: Pepsico. SIC: 5812—Eating Places.

★ 89681 ★ Kerr-McGee Chemical Corp.
2513 Buchanan Rd.
Texarkana, TX 75501
Ultimate Parent: Kerr-McGee. SIC: 2491—Wood Preserving.

★ 89682 ★ Kerr Mcgee Chemical Corp.
155 Buchanan Rd.
Texarkana, TX 75503
Ultimate Parent: Kerr-McGee. SIC: 2491—Wood Preserving.

★ 89683 ★ Lane Bryant
51 Central Mall
Texarkana, TX 75503
(903)832-5684
Ultimate Parent: Limited.

★ 89684 ★ Lane Bryant
2300 Central Mall N
Texarkana, TX 75503
(214)832-5684
Ultimate Parent: Limited. SIC: 5651—Family Clothing Stores.

★ 89685 ★ Lerner Shop
49 Central Mall
Texarkana, TX 75503
(903)832-3086
Ultimate Parent: Limited.

★ 89686 ★ Lerner Shop
2300 Richmond Rd.
Texarkana, TX 75503
(214)832-3086
Ultimate Parent: Limited. SIC: 5651—Family Clothing Stores.

★ 89687 ★ Mary Kay Cosmetics
RR 5
Texarkana, TX 75501
(903)838-5629
Ultimate Parent: Mary Kay Cosmetics.

★ 89688 ★ McDonalds Hamburgers
63 Central Mall
Texarkana, TX 75503
(903)832-5491
Ultimate Parent: McDonald's.

★ 89689 ★ McDonalds Hamburgers
3402 Texas Blvd.
Texarkana, TX 75503
(903)794-3761
Ultimate Parent: McDonald's.

★ 89690 ★ McDonalds Restaurant
2105 Richmond Rd.
Texarkana, TX 75503
(903)838-0599
Ultimate Parent: McDonald's.

★ 89691 ★ Mobil Mart
4402 S. Lake Dr.
Texarkana, TX 75501
(214)838-5511
Ultimate Parent: Mobil. SIC: 5271—Mobile Home Dealers.

★ 89692 ★ Otis Elevator Co.
201 W. 3rd St.
Texarkana, TX 75501
(903)792-5411
Ultimate Parent: United Technologies.

★ 89693 ★ Payless Cashways
927 N. Robison Rd.
Texarkana, TX 75501
(903)838-5546
Ultimate Parent: Payless Cashways.

★ 89694 ★ Piggly Wiggly
Richmond Sq.
Texarkana, TX 75503
(903)832-6936
Ultimate Parent: Bruno's. SIC: 5499—Miscellaneous Food Stores.

★ 89695 ★ Piggly Wiggly
26 SW Mall
Texarkana, TX 75501
(214)793-1474
Ultimate Parent: Bruno's. SIC: 5411—Grocery Stores.

★ 89696 ★ Piggly Wiggly
1721 W. 7th St.
Texarkana, TX 75501
(214)792-7498
Ultimate Parent: Bruno's. SIC: 5411—Grocery Stores.

★ 89697 ★ Piggly Wiggly
14 Oaklawn Village
Texarkana, TX 75501
(214)838-0391
Ultimate Parent: Bruno's. SIC: 5411—Grocery Stores.

★ 89698 ★ Piggly Wiggly
3315 N. State Line Ave.
Texarkana, TX 75503
(214)792-8136
Ultimate Parent: Bruno's. SIC: 5411—Grocery Stores.

★ 89699 ★ Pizza Hut
1617 New Boston Rd.
Texarkana, TX 75501
(903)792-7336
Ultimate Parent: Pepsico.

★ 89700 ★ Radio Shack
16 Central Mall
Texarkana, TX 75503
(903)838-8444
Company Type: Division. Ultimate Parent: Tandy Corp.

★ 89701 ★ Radio Shack
2011 Summerhill Rd.
Texarkana, TX 75501
(903)794-3100
Company Type: Division. Ultimate Parent: Tandy Corp.

★ 89702 ★ Radio Shack
2300 Central Mall N
Texarkana, TX 75503
(214)838-8444
Company Type: Division. Ultimate Parent: Tandy Corp. SIC: 5065—Electronic Parts & Equipment Nec.

★ 89703 ★ Radio Shack
5101 N. State Line Ave.
Texarkana, TX 75503
(214)792-4341
Company Type: Division. Ultimate Parent: Tandy Corp. SIC: 5065—Electronic Parts & Equipment Nec.

★ 89704 ★ Radio Shack
23 K Mart Plz.
Texarkana, TX 75503
(903)792-4341
Company Type: Division. Ultimate Parent: Tandy Corp.

★ 89705 ★ Radio Shack
34 Oaklawn Village
Texarkana, TX 75501
(214)832-5100
Company Type: Division. Ultimate Parent: Tandy Corp. SIC: 5065—Electronic Parts & Equipment Nec.

★ 89706 ★ Ryder Truck Rental
2317 Richmond Rd.
Texarkana, TX 75503
(903)838-4592
Ultimate Parent: Ryder System.

★ 89707 ★ Ryder Truck Rental
1624 W. 7th St.
Texarkana, TX 75501
(903)793-1234
Ultimate Parent: Ryder System.

★ 89708 ★ Sam's Wholesale Club
3610 Hampton Rd.
Texarkana, TX 75503
(214)838-4338
Ultimate Parent: Wal-Mart Stores, Inc. SIC: 5099—Durable Goods Nec.

★ 89709 ★ Taco Bell
5021 N. State Line Ave.
Texarkana, TX 75503
(903)794-0358
Ultimate Parent: Pepsico.

★ 89710 ★ Taco Bell
1609 New Boston Rd.
Texarkana, TX 75501
(214)794-2900
Ultimate Parent: Pepsico. SIC: 5812—Eating Places.

★ 89711 ★ Target Stores
2315 Richmond Rd.
Texarkana, TX 75503
(214)838-6555
Company Type: Subsidiary. Ultimate Parent: Dayton Hudson. SIC: 5311—Department Stores.

★ 89712 ★ Texaco Inc.
4310 McKnight Rd.
Texarkana, TX 75501
(214)832-8080
Ultimate Parent: Texaco. SIC: 5171—Petroleum Bulk Stations & Terminals.

★ 89713 ★ Texas Fibers
114 S. Lelia
Texarkana, TX 75501
Ultimate Parent: Leggett & Platt Inc. SIC: 3086—Plastics Foam Products.

★ 89714 ★ Thom Mcan Shoes
41 Central Mall
Texarkana, TX 75503
(903)838-9271
Ultimate Parent: Melville.

★ 89715 ★ Waldenbooks
2300 Richmond Rd.
Texarkana, TX 75503
(214)832-4286
Ultimate Parent: K-Mart. SIC: 5942—Book Stores.

Texas City

★ 89716 ★ Amoco Transport Co.
2501 Emmett F Lowry Expy.
Texas City, TX 77590
(409)948-9191
Ultimate Parent: Amoco Corp. SIC: 4231—Trucking Terminal Facilities.

★ 89717 ★ Exxon
2102 9th Ave. N
Texas City, TX 77590
(409)945-3477
Ultimate Parent: Exxon. SIC: 7538—General Automotive Repair Shops.

★ 89718 ★ Exxon Car Wash
2104 Palmer Hwy.
Texas City, TX 77590
(409)945-5131
Ultimate Parent: Exxon. SIC: 7542—Car Washes.

★ 89719 ★ Exxon Shop
2102 Palmer Hwy.
Texas City, TX 77590
(409)948-6220
Ultimate Parent: Exxon. SIC: 5541—Gasoline Service Stations.

★ 89720 ★ Gaf Chemicals Corp.
PO Box 2141
Texas City, TX 77598
Ultimate Parent: GAF Corp. SIC: 2869—Industrial Organic Chemicals Nec.

★ 89721 ★ Kentucky Fried Chicken
3013 Palmer Hwy.
Texas City, TX 77590
(409)945-3424
Ultimate Parent: Pepsico. SIC: 5812—Eating Places.

★ 89722 ★ Kroger Pharmacy
3541 Palmer Hwy.
Texas City, TX 77590
(409)945-3436
Ultimate Parent: Kroger. SIC: 5411—Grocery Stores.

★ 89723 ★ Kroger Store No 108
3541 Palmer Hwy.
Texas City, TX 77590
(409)948-3471
Ultimate Parent: Kroger. SIC: 5411—Grocery Stores.

★ 89724 ★   Lowe's
3302 Palmer Hwy.
Texas City, TX 77590
(409)945-9522
Ultimate Parent: Lowe's. SIC: 5651—
Family Clothing Stores.

★ 89725 ★   Marathon Oil Co.
6 St.
Texas City, TX 77590
(409)945-2331
Ultimate Parent: USX Corp. SIC: 2911—
Petroleum Refining.

★ 89726 ★   Marathon Oil Co.
6 St.
Texas City, TX 77590
(409)945-2331
Ultimate Parent: USX Corp. SIC: 2911—
Petroleum Refining.

★ 89727 ★   Marathon Petroleum Co.
1320 Loop 197 S.
Texas City, TX 77590
(409)945-2331
Officer: Lloyd Nordhausen. Ultimate Parent: USX Corp. SIC: 2911—Petroleum Refining.

★ 89728 ★   Mobil Self Serv Co.
3551 Palmer Hwy.
Texas City, TX 77590
(409)948-9622
Ultimate Parent: Mobil. SIC: 5541—
Gasoline Service Stations.

★ 89729 ★   Phibro Energy USA Inc.
1301 Loop 197 S. & 14th St.
Texas City, TX 77590
Ultimate Parent: Salomon, Inc. SIC: 2911—Petroleum Refining.

★ 89730 ★   Phibro Refining Inc.
1301 Loop 197 S. at 14th St.
Texas City, TX 77592
Ultimate Parent: Salomon, Inc. SIC: 2911—Petroleum Refining.

★ 89731 ★   Pizza Hut
2305 Palmer Hwy.
Texas City, TX 77590
(409)948-4327
Ultimate Parent: Pepsico. SIC: 5812—
Eating Places.

★ 89732 ★   Praxair Inc.
703 6th St. S.
Texas City, TX 77592-3777
Ultimate Parent: Praxair. SIC: 2813—
Industrial Gases.

★ 89733 ★   Radio Shack
915 20th St. N
Texas City, TX 77590
(409)945-3581
Company Type: Division. Ultimate Parent: Tandy Corp. SIC: 5065—Electronic Parts & Equipment Nec.

★ 89734 ★   Safeway Inc.
915 6th St. N
Texas City, TX 77590
(409)948-2181
Ultimate Parent: Safeway. SIC: 5411—
Grocery Stores.

★ 89735 ★   Shell Pipeline Corp.
Fm 519 E
Texas City, TX 77590
(409)948-4009
Ultimate Parent: Shell Oil Co.

★ 89736 ★   Shell Pipeline Corp.
Fm 519 E
Texas City, TX 77590
(409)948-4009
Ultimate Parent: Shell Oil Co.

★ 89737 ★   Sterling Chemicals Inc.
201 Bay St. S
Texas City, TX 77590
(409)945-4431
Officer: Gordon A. Cain, Chairman. Ultimate Parent: Eastman Kodak. SIC: 2819—Industrial Inorganic Chemicals Nec; 2865—Cyclic Crudes & Intermediates; 2869—Industrial Organic Chemicals Nec.

★ 89738 ★   Taco Bell
3028 Palmer Hwy.
Texas City, TX 77590
(409)945-3221
Ultimate Parent: Pepsico. SIC: 5812—
Eating Places.

★ 89739 ★   Texas City Refining Inc.
Loop 197 East at 14th St.
Texas City, TX 775921271
Ultimate Parent: Agway Inc. SIC: 2911—
Petroleum Refining.

★ 89740 ★   Union Carbide Chemicals & Plastics Co. Marine Terminal
2800 Loop 197 South
Texas City, TX 77592-0471
Ultimate Parent: Union Carbide Corp. SIC: 2821—Plastics Materials & Resins; 2899—Chemical Preparations Nec.

★ 89741 ★   Union Carbide Chemicals & Plastics Co. Texas City Plt.
3301 5th Ave. South
Texas City, TX 77592-0471
Ultimate Parent: Union Carbide Corp. SIC: 2821—Plastics Materials & Resins; 2869—Industrial Organic Chemicals Nec.

★ 89742 ★   Union Carbide Corp.
3301 5th Ave. South
Texas City, TX 77592-0471
Ultimate Parent: Union Carbide Corp. SIC: 2821—Plastics Materials & Resins; 2869—Industrial Organic Chemicals Nec.

★ 89743 ★   Union Carbide Corp. Marine Terminal
2800 Loop 197 South
Texas City, TX 77592-0471
Ultimate Parent: Union Carbide Corp. SIC: 4400—Water Transportation.

★ 89744 ★   Union Carbide Marine Terminal
2800 Loop 197 South
Texas City, TX 77592-0471
Ultimate Parent: Union Carbide Corp. SIC: 4400—Water Transportation.

★ 89745 ★   Union Carbide Texas City Plant
3301 5th Ave. South
Texas City, TX 77592-0471
Ultimate Parent: Union Carbide Corp. SIC: 2821—Plastics Materials & Resins; 2869—Industrial Organic Chemicals Nec.

★ 89746 ★   Wal Mart Auto Repair
3401 Palmer Hwy.
Texas City, TX 77590
(409)945-2081
Ultimate Parent: Wal-Mart Stores, Inc. SIC: 7538—General Automotive Repair Shops.

★ 89747 ★   Wal Mart Discount Store
3401 Emmett F Lowry Expy.
Texas City, TX 77590
(409)945-0800
Ultimate Parent: Wal-Mart Stores, Inc. SIC: 5311—Department Stores.

Texline

★ 89748 ★   Peoples Natural Gas Co.
111 N. 2nd
Texline, TX 79087
(806)362-4220
Ultimate Parent: Consolidated Natural Gas. SIC: 4932—Gas & Other Services Combined.

The Woodlands

★ 89749 ★   Ace Hardware
7636 PO Box
The Woodlands, TX 77387
Ultimate Parent: Ace Hardware.

★ 89750 ★   Betz Process Chemicals Inc.
9669 Grogans Mill Rd.
The Woodlands, TX 77380-1026
(713)367-2442
Company Type: Subsidiary. Officer: Ronald A. Kutsche, President. Officer: Joan Matas. Ultimate Parent: Betz Laboratories Inc. SIC: 2899—Chemical Preparations

Nec; 5169—Chemicals & Allied Products Nec. Employee Count: 200. Sales: 55 M.

★ 89751 ★   Dresser Industries Inc.
Valve & Controls Division
10077 Grogans Mill Rd.
The Woodlands, TX 77380
(713)367-5741 Fax: (713)363-8244
Company Type: Subsidiary. Ultimate Parent: Dresser Industries Inc.

★ 89752 ★   Mitchell Energy Corp.
2001 Timberloch Pl.
PO Box 4000
The Woodlands, TX 77387-4000
Officer: George P. Mitchell, Chairman of the Board & President. Ultimate Parent: Mitchell Energy & Devel.

★ 89753 ★   Mitchell Energy & Devel.
2001 Timberloch Pl.
The Woodlands, TX 77380
(713)377-5500
Company Type: Headquarters. Officer: George P. Mitchell. Employee Count: 2825. Sales: 903 M. Fortune 500: Largest U.S. Industrial Corporations: Ranking 380.

★ 89754 ★   Mitchell Energy & Development
Exploration & Production Div.
2001 Timberloch Pl.
PO Box 4000
The Woodlands, TX 77387-4000
Company Type: Division. Officer: F. D. Covey, President. Ultimate Parent: Mitchell Energy & Devel.

★ 89755 ★   Mitchell Energy & Development
Transmission & Processing Div.
2001 Timberloch Pl.
PO Box 4000
The Woodlands, TX 77387-4000
Officer: Allen J. Tarbutton Jr., President. Ultimate Parent: Mitchell Energy & Devel.

★ 89756 ★   Mitchell Energy & Development Corp.
2001 Timberloch Pl.
PO Box 4000
The Woodlands, TX 77387-4000
(713)377-5500 Fax: (713)377-6910
Officer: George P. Mitchell, Chairman of the Board, President & CEO. Ultimate Parent: Mitchell Energy & Devel. Employee Count: 2825.

★ 89757 ★   Woodlands Corp.
2001 Timberloch Pl.
PO Box 4000
The Woodlands, TX 77387-4000
Officer: George P. Mitchell, Chairman of the Board. Ultimate Parent: Mitchell Energy & Devel.

Thorndale

★ 89758 ★   Mobil Oil Co.
N Main
Thorndale, TX 76577
(512)898-2511
Ultimate Parent: Mobil. SIC: 4131—
Intercity & Rural Bus Transportation.

★ 89759 ★   Southern Cotton Oil Co.
Thorndale, TX 76577
(512)898-5209
Ultimate Parent: Archer Daniels Midland Co. SIC: 2074—Cottonseed Oil Mills.

Three Rivers

★ 89760 ★   Diamond Shamrock Refining & Marketing Co.
301 Leroy St.
Three Rivers, TX 78071
Ultimate Parent: Diamond Shamrock. SIC: 2911—Petroleum Refining.

★ 89761 ★   Diamond Shamrock Refining & Marketing Co. Three Rivers
301 Leroy St.
Three Rivers, TX 78071
Ultimate Parent: Diamond Shamrock. SIC: 2911—Petroleum Refining.

★ 89762 ★   Mobil Oil Co.
3 Rivers Texas
Three Rivers, TX 78071
(512)786-3737
Ultimate Parent: Mobil. SIC: 5171—
Petroleum Bulk Stations & Terminals.

Tilden

★ 89763 ★   Shell Oil Co.
Tilden, TX 78072
(512)274-3665
Ultimate Parent: Shell Oil Co. SIC: 5171—
Petroleum Bulk Stations & Terminals.

Timpson

★ 89764 ★   Ace Hardware
101 1st
Timpson, TX 75975
(409)254-3320
Ultimate Parent: Ace Hardware. SIC: 5251—Hardware Stores.

Tomball

★ 89765 ★   Amerada Hess Corp.
28903 Tomball Pky.
Tomball, TX 77375
(713)255-8730
Ultimate Parent: Amerada Hess.

★ 89766 ★   Amerada Hess Corp.
28903 W. Montgomery Rd.
Tomball, TX 77375
(713)351-1143
Ultimate Parent: Amerada Hess. SIC: 1311—Crude Petroleum & Natural Gas.

★ 89767 ★   Copier Consultants
1231 Alma St.
Tomball, TX 77375-4520
(713)351-6460
Ultimate Parent: Alco Standard Corp. SIC: 5044—Office Equipment.

★ 89768 ★   Exxon Co.
1475 E. Main St.
Tomball, TX 77375
(713)351-2356
Ultimate Parent: Exxon. SIC: 5499—
Miscellaneous Food Stores.

★ 89769 ★   Exxon Co. USA
Tomball Field Rd. 149
Tomball, TX 77375
(713)351-5866
Ultimate Parent: Exxon. SIC: 1311—Crude Petroleum & Natural Gas.

★ 89770 ★   Kentucky Fried Chicken
905 W. Main St.
Tomball, TX 77375
(713)255-9427
Ultimate Parent: Pepsico. SIC: 5812—
Eating Places.

★ 89771 ★   Kroger
25506 Fm 149 Rd.
Tomball, TX 77375
(713)370-8946
Ultimate Parent: Kroger. SIC: 5411—
Grocery Stores.

★ 89772 ★   Mini Mart Rosehill Inc.
18402 Fm Rd. 2920
Tomball, TX 77375
(713)351-1471
Ultimate Parent: Kroger. SIC: 5411—
Grocery Stores.

★ 89773 ★   Mobil Oil Consignee
203 N. Live Oak St.
Tomball, TX 77375
(713)351-0447
Ultimate Parent: Mobil. SIC: 5172—
Petroleum Products Nec.

★ 89774 ★   Payless Shoesource
28435 Tomball Pky.
Tomball, TX 77375
(713)351-8814
Ultimate Parent: May Department Stores.

★ 89775 ★   Pizza Hut
1211 W. Main St.
Tomball, TX 77375
(713)255-2536
Ultimate Parent: Pepsico. SIC: 5812—
Eating Places.

★ 89776 ★　Pulte Home Corp.
17214 Colony Creek Rd.
Tomball, TX 77375
(713)370-9651
Ultimate Parent: Pulte. SIC: 1521—
Single-Family Housing Construction.

★ 89777 ★　Radio Shack
28105 Fm 149 Rd.
Tomball, TX 77375
(713)351-6103
Company Type: Division. Ultimate Parent:
Tandy Corp. SIC: 5065—Electronic Parts &
Equipment Nec.

★ 89778 ★　Ryder Truck Rental
27202 Tomball Pky.
Tomball, TX 77375
(713)255-9214
Ultimate Parent: Ryder System.

★ 89779 ★　Shell Co.
1432 W. Main St.
Tomball, TX 77375
(713)351-4005
Ultimate Parent: Shell Oil Co. SIC: 5541—
Gasoline Service Stations.

★ 89780 ★　Taco Bell
27760 Tomball Pky.
Tomball, TX 77375
(713)351-2409
Ultimate Parent: Pepsico.

★ 89781 ★　Walgreen Drug Stores
18433 Kuykendahl
Tomball, TX 77375
(713)370-8090
Ultimate Parent: Walgreen Co. SIC:
5912—Drug Stores & Proprietary Stores.

★ 89782 ★　Walgreen Drug Stores
22490 Fm 149
Tomball, TX 77375
(713)376-7336
Ultimate Parent: Walgreen Co. SIC:
5912—Drug Stores & Proprietary Stores.

Trinity

★ 89783 ★　Louisiana Pacific
Corp.
Mf 356
Trinity, TX 75862
(409)594-2823
Ultimate Parent: Louisiana-Pacific. SIC:
2421—Sawmills & Planing Mills—General.

★ 89784 ★　Radio Shack
934 Robb
Trinity, TX 75862
(409)594-6911
Company Type: Division. Ultimate Parent:
Tandy Corp. SIC: 5065—Electronic Parts &
Equipment Nec.

Troup

★ 89785 ★　Mini Mart
302 W. Duval St.
Troup, TX 75789
(214)842-3156
Ultimate Parent: Kroger. SIC: 5411—
Grocery Stores.

Tulia

★ 89786 ★　Pizza Hut
811 SW 2nd St.
Tulia, TX 79088
(806)995-4010
Ultimate Parent: Pepsico. SIC: 5812—
Eating Places.

★ 89787 ★　Taylor-Erans Seed
Co.
PO Box 68
Tulia, TX 79088
(806)995-4111
Company Type: Division. Ultimate Parent:
Mayflower Group. SIC: 5191—Farm
Supplies.

★ 89788 ★　Texas New Mexico &
Oklahoma
120 S. Maxwell Ave.
Tulia, TX 79088
(806)995-4138
Ultimate Parent: Greyhound Lines Inc. SIC:
4173—Bus Terminal & Service Facilities.

Turkey

★ 89789 ★　Texaco Warehouse
Turkey, TX 79261
(806)423-1334
Ultimate Parent: Texaco. SIC: 5172—
Petroleum Products Nec.

Tyler

★ 89790 ★　Avon Products Inc.
310 S. Vine Ave.
Tyler, TX 75702
(214)597-4558
Ultimate Parent: Avon Products, Inc. SIC: .
5999—Miscellaneous Retail Stores Nec.

★ 89791 ★　Beneficial Texas Inc.
500 W. Front St.
Tyler, TX 75702
(903)593-6485
Ultimate Parent: Beneficial. SIC: 6062—
State Credit Unions.

★ 89792 ★　Borden Inc.
805 W. Front St.
Tyler, TX 75702
(903)595-4461
Officer: Mike Woods, Manager. Ultimate
Parent: Borden, Inc. SIC: 2026—Fluid Milk;
2086—Bottled & Canned Soft Drinks.

★ 89793 ★　Butler Paper
4706 Chandler Hwy.
Tyler, TX 75709
(903)592-1685
Location Type: Branch office. Ultimate
Parent: Alco Standard Corp. SIC: 5113—
Industrial & Personal Service Paper; 5111—
Printing & Writing Paper.

★ 89794 ★　Butler Paper
4706 Chandler Hwy.
Tyler, TX 75709
(903)592-1685
Location Type: Branch office. Ultimate
Parent: Alco Standard Corp. SIC: 5113—
Industrial & Personal Service Paper; 5111—
Printing & Writing Paper.

★ 89795 ★　Carrier Corp.
1700 E. Duncan St.
Tyler, TX 75702
Ultimate Parent: United Technologies. SIC:
3585—Refrigeration & Heating Equipment.

★ 89796 ★　Coca Cola Bottling
Co.
60 PO Box
Tyler, TX 75710
(214)586-8833
Ultimate Parent: Coca-Cola Enterprises.
SIC: 5046—Commercial Equipment Nec;
5149—Groceries & Related Products Nec.

★ 89797 ★　Dearborn Brass
St. Hwy. 155 at Fm 3270 East Texas Ctr.
Tyler, TX 75710
Ultimate Parent: American Brands Inc.
SIC: 3470—Metal Services Nec.

★ 89798 ★　Dearborn Brass
St. Hwy. 155 & Fm 3720
Tyler, TX 75710
Ultimate Parent: American Brands Inc.
SIC: 3471—Plating & Polishing.

★ 89799 ★　Dearborn Brass
East Texas Ctr.
3270 East Texas Ctr.
Hwy. 155 N
Tyler, TX 75708
Ultimate Parent: American Brands Inc.

★ 89800 ★　Ferro Corp.
1812 E. Duncan St.
Tyler, TX 75702
Ultimate Parent: Ferro Corp. SIC: 3255—
Clay Refractories.

★ 89801 ★　First Federal S & L
1200 S. Beckham Ave.
Tyler, TX 75701-3319
(903)593-1767
Company Type: Headquarters. Officer:
Gerald W. Free. Ultimate Parent: Bancorp
Hawaii. SIC: 6035—Federal Savings
Institutions; 1521—Single-Family Housing
Construction; 6162—Mortgage Bankers &
Correspondents.

★ 89802 ★　Flowers Baking Co.
1200 W. Erwin St.
Tyler, TX 75702
(903)595-2421
Officer: C. Steve Green, President.
Ultimate Parent: Flowers Industries. SIC:
2051—Bread, Cake & Related Products.

★ 89803 ★　Flowers Baking Co. of
Tyler Inc.
1200 W. Erwin St.
PO Box 360
Tyler, TX 75702
(903)595-2421 Fax: (903)593-8368
Company Type: Subsidiary. Officer: Steve
Green, President. Ultimate Parent: Flowers
Industries.

★ 89804 ★　Greyhound Bus Lins
303 N. Bois D Arcade Ave.
Tyler, TX 75702
(903)597-7441
Ultimate Parent: Greyhound Lines Inc.

★ 89805 ★　Kelly Springfield Tire
Co.
Hwy. 31 W.
Tyler, TX 75712-4670
Ultimate Parent: Goodyear Tire & Rubber.
SIC: 3011—Tires & Inner Tubes.

★ 89806 ★　Kelly-Springfield Tire
Co. T
Chandler Hwy.
Tyler, TX 75702
(214)535-1500
Ultimate Parent: Goodyear Tire & Rubber.
SIC: 3011—Tires & Inner Tubes; 5531—
Automobile & Home Supply Stores.

★ 89807 ★　Kentucky Fried
Chicken
2215 W. Gentry Pky.
Tyler, TX 75702
(214)592-6184
Ultimate Parent: Pepsico. SIC: 5812—
Eating Places.

★ 89808 ★　Kids R US
635 S. Vine Ave.
Tyler, TX 75701
(903)592-7305
Ultimate Parent: Toys "R" US. SIC: 7231—
Beauty Shops.

★ 89809 ★　Kmart Discount Store
1909 E. Southeast Loop 323
Tyler, TX 75701
Ultimate Parent: K-Mart.

★ 89810 ★　La Gloria Oil & Gas
Co.
1702 E. Commerce St.
Tyler, TX 75702
Ultimate Parent: Crown Central Petroleum
Corp. SIC: 2911—Petroleum Refining.

★ 89811 ★　Lane Bryant
4601 S. Broadway Ave.
Tyler, TX 75703
(214)534-0765
Ultimate Parent: Limited. SIC: 5651—
Family Clothing Stores.

★ 89812 ★　Liberty Mutual
Insurance Co.
1101 E. Loop SE 323
Tyler, TX 75701
(214)561-7070
Ultimate Parent: Liberty Mutual Group.
SIC: 6411—Insurance Agents, Brokers &
Service.

★ 89813 ★　The Limited
4601 S. Broadway Ave.
Tyler, TX 75703
(903)581-8288
Ultimate Parent: Limited.

★ 89814 ★　Marshalls
2125 S. Broadway Ave.
Tyler, TX 75701
(903)595-4383
Ultimate Parent: Melville.

★ 89815 ★　McDonalds
Restaurant
3109 W. Gentry Pky.
Tyler, TX 75702
(903)593-0018
Ultimate Parent: McDonald's.

★ 89816 ★　McDonalds
Restaurant
4014 S. Broadway Ave.
Tyler, TX 75701
(903)561-7204
Ultimate Parent: May Department Stores.

★ 89817 ★　Mini Mart
Hwy. 155 S
Tyler, TX 75701
(214)561-2700
Ultimate Parent: Kroger. SIC: 5541—
Gasoline Service Stations.

★ 89818 ★　New York Life Tyler
Sales Office
Dallas General Office
11 American Ctr., Ste. 500
Tyler, TX 75701
(903)561-5055
Ultimate Parent: New York Life.

★ 89819 ★　Oryx Energy Co.
S Farm Rd. 14
Tyler, TX 75707
(903)593-1915
Ultimate Parent: Oryx Energy.

★ 89820 ★　Otis Elevator Co.
Blackstone Hotl
Tyler, TX 75701
(214)592-7611
Ultimate Parent: United Technologies. SIC:
3534—Elevators & Moving Stairways.

★ 89821 ★　Payless Cashways
Bldg Matls
1817 W. Loop SW 323
Tyler, TX 75701
(214)561-3700
Ultimate Parent: Payless Cashways. SIC:
5211—Lumber & Other Building Materials.

★ 89822 ★　Pizza Hut
209 NE Loop N. 323
Tyler, TX 75708
(214)561-7774
Ultimate Parent: Pepsico. SIC: 5812—
Eating Places.

★ 89823 ★　Pizza Hut
1733 S. Beckham Ave.
Tyler, TX 75701
(214)597-3461
Ultimate Parent: Pepsico. SIC: 5812—
Eating Places.

★ 89824 ★　Radio Shack
4601 S. Broadway Ave.
Tyler, TX 75703
(903)561-5106
Company Type: Division. Ultimate Parent:
Tandy Corp.

★ 89825 ★　Ryder Truck Rental
3111 W. Gentry Pky.
Tyler, TX 75702
(214)593-5544
Ultimate Parent: Ryder System. SIC:
5113—Industrial & Personal Service Paper.

★ 89826 ★　Ryder Truck Rental
3210 W. Gentry Pky.
Tyler, TX 75702
(903)593-5544
Ultimate Parent: Ryder System.

★ 89827 ★　Ryder Truck Rental
2624 E. Erwin St.
Tyler, TX 75702
(214)595-3705
Ultimate Parent: Ryder System. SIC:
7359—Equipment Rental & Leasing Nec;
7513—Truck Rental & Leasing Without
Drivers.

★ 89828 ★　Sam's Wholesale
Club
2025 S. Loop SW
Tyler, TX 75701
(214)597-2296
Ultimate Parent: Wal-Mart Stores, Inc. SIC:
5141—Groceries—General Line.

★ 89829 ★　Taco Bell
2611 W. Gentry Pky.
Tyler, TX 75702
(903)597-1766
Ultimate Parent: Pepsico.

★ 89830 ★ Taco Bell
2603 W. Gentry Pky.
Tyler, TX 75702
(214)597-1766
Ultimate Parent: Pepsico. SIC: 5812—
Eating Places.

★ 89831 ★ Taco Bell
1224 E. 5th St.
Tyler, TX 75701
(214)592-6391
Ultimate Parent: Pepsico. SIC: 5141—
Groceries—General Line; 5812—Eating
Places.

★ 89832 ★ Taco Bell
121 NE Loop N. 323
Tyler, TX 75708
(214)561-7408
Ultimate Parent: Pepsico. SIC: 5812—
Eating Places.

★ 89833 ★ Target Stores
5001 S. Broadway Ave.
Tyler, TX 75703
(214)561-0044
Company Type: Subsidiary. Ultimate
Parent: Dayton Hudson. SIC: 5311—
Department Stores.

★ 89834 ★ Texaco Auto Service
Ctr
1106 E. 5th St.
Tyler, TX 75701
(214)592-2594
Ultimate Parent: Texaco. SIC: 7538—
General Automotive Repair Shops.

★ 89835 ★ Texaco Express Lube
1305 S. Beckham Ave.
Tyler, TX 75701
(214)573-7036
Ultimate Parent: Texaco. SIC: 7532—Top
& Body Repair & Paint Shops; 7539—
Automotive Repair Shops Nec.

★ 89836 ★ Texaco Food Mart
1106 E. 5th St.
Tyler, TX 75701
(214)593-1936
Ultimate Parent: Texaco. SIC: 5411—
Grocery Stores.

★ 89837 ★ Trane Co.
6200 Troup Hwy.
Tyler, TX 75711
Ultimate Parent: American Standard. SIC:
3585—Refrigeration & Heating Equipment.

★ 89838 ★ Unisys Corp.
1121 NE Loop E. 323
Tyler, TX 75708
(214)561-6670
Ultimate Parent: Unisys Corp. SIC: 7372—
Prepackaged Software.

★ 89839 ★ Unitary Products
Group Residential
6200 Troup Hwy.
Tyler, TX 75711
(903)581-3200
Officer: H. Thompson Smith, President.
Ultimate Parent: American Standard. SIC:
3585—Refrigeration & Heating Equipment.

★ 89840 ★ United Parcel Service
740 S. Lyons Ave.
Tyler, TX 75702
(214)595-4343
Ultimate Parent: United Parcel Service of
America. SIC: 4215—Courier Services
Except by Air.

Universal City

★ 89841 ★ Jiffy Lube
2217 Pat Booker Rd.
Universal City, TX 78148
(512)658-2721
Ultimate Parent: Pennzoil.

★ 89842 ★ Mobil Mart
12003 E. Loop N. 1604
Universal City, TX 78148
(512)659-8711
Ultimate Parent: Mobil.

★ 89843 ★ Mobil Mart
3100 Pat Booker Rd.
Universal City, TX 78148
(512)658-8491
Ultimate Parent: Mobil.

★ 89844 ★ Pizza Hut
1530 Pat Booker Rd.
Universal City, TX 78148
(512)659-5881
Ultimate Parent: Pepsico.

★ 89845 ★ Trailways
Transportation
420 Pat Booker Rd.
Universal City, TX 78148
(512)658-6316
Ultimate Parent: Greyhound Lines Inc. SIC:
4131—Intercity & Rural Bus Transportation.

Universal Cty

★ 89846 ★ Pizza Hut
1200 Farm Rd. 78
Universal Cty, TX 78148
(512)658-4440
Ultimate Parent: Pepsico. SIC: 5812—
Eating Places.

★ 89847 ★ Radio Shack
1705 Pat Booker Rd.
Universal Cty, TX 78148
(512)658-5005
Company Type: Division. Ultimate Parent:
Tandy Corp. SIC: 5065—Electronic Parts &
Equipment Nec.

Uvalde

★ 89848 ★ Asgrow Seed Co.
Hacienda Rd.
Uvalde, TX 78801
(512)278-6117
Ultimate Parent: Upjohn Co. SIC: 5191—
Farm Supplies.

★ 89849 ★ Dean Foods
Vegetable Co.
PO Box 367
Uvalde, TX 78801
(210)278-4525 Fax: (210)278-1094
Location Type: Plant. Officer: Roy Joe
Ham, Plant Manager. Ultimate Parent:
Dean Foods. SIC: 2037—Frozen Fruits &
Vegetables.

★ 89850 ★ Diebold Inc.
103 S. Piper Ln.
Uvalde, TX 78801
(512)278-8494
Ultimate Parent: Diebold, Inc. SIC: 5044—
Office Equipment.

★ 89851 ★ Frio Foods Inc.
2369 Hacienda Rd.
Uvalde, TX 78801
(210)278-4525
Company Type: Subsidiary. Officer: Ron
Trine, President. Ultimate Parent: Dean
Foods. SIC: 5142—Packaged Frozen
Foods. Employee Count: 300. Sales: 98.5
M.

★ 89852 ★ Kentucky Fried
Chicken
728 E. Main St.
Uvalde, TX 78801
(512)278-7508
Ultimate Parent: Pepsico. SIC: 5812—
Eating Places.

★ 89853 ★ Larsen Co. Dba Frio
Foods
Fm 2369 W.
Uvalde, TX 78801
Ultimate Parent: Dean Foods. SIC: 2037—
Frozen Fruits & Vegetables.

★ 89854 ★ Pizza Hut
502 E. Main St.
Uvalde, TX 78801
(512)278-1181
Ultimate Parent: Pepsico. SIC: 5812—
Eating Places.

★ 89855 ★ Radio Shack
114 W. North St.
Uvalde, TX 78801
(512)278-2593
Company Type: Division. Ultimate Parent:
Tandy Corp. SIC: 5065—Electronic Parts &
Equipment Nec.

★ 89856 ★ Ryder Truck Rental
1412 N. Getty St.
Uvalde, TX 78801
(512)278-4983
Ultimate Parent: Ryder System. SIC:
7359—Equipment Rental & Leasing Nec.

★ 89857 ★ Sierra Industries Inc.
Garner Field Rd.
Uvalde, TX 78801
(210)278-4381
Officer: Mark Huffstutler, President.
Ultimate Parent: Echlin. SIC: 3724—
Aircraft Engines & Engine Parts.

★ 89858 ★ Vulcan Materials Co.
Del Rio Hwy.
Uvalde, TX 78802
(210)278-6205
Officer: Kim Duke, Manager. Ultimate
Parent: Vulcan Materials Co. SIC: 2951—
Asphalt Paving Mixtures & Blocks.

★ 89859 ★ Wal Mart
2340 E. Main St.
Uvalde, TX 78801
(512)278-9117
Ultimate Parent: Wal-Mart Stores, Inc. SIC:
5399—Miscellaneous General Merchandise
Store.

Van Horn

★ 89860 ★ Greyhound Bus Lines
210 E. Broadway
Van Horn, TX 79855
(915)283-2112
Ultimate Parent: Greyhound Lines Inc. SIC:
4111—Local & Suburban Transit.

★ 89861 ★ Radio Shack
Van Horn, TX 79855
(915)283-2920
Company Type: Division. Ultimate Parent:
Tandy Corp. SIC: 2761—Manifold Business
Forms; 7231—Beauty Shops.

Vanderbilt

★ 89862 ★ Meridian Oil Inc.
Mobil Camp
Vanderbilt, TX 77991
(512)284-3281
Officer: F.D. Hendricks, Manager. Ultimate
Parent: Burlington Resources. SIC: 2911—
Petroleum Refining.

★ 89863 ★ Mobil Pipe Line Co.
Vanderbilt, TX 77991
(512)284-3269
Company Type: Branch. Ultimate Parent:
Mobil. SIC: 4612—Crude Petroleum
Pipelines.

★ 89864 ★ Mobil Producing TX &
New
PO Box 308
Vanderbilt, TX 77991-0308
(512)284-3281
Officer: J. L. Kempton. Ultimate Parent:
Mobil. SIC: 2911—Petroleum Refining.

Vernon

★ 89865 ★ Hi-Tek Polymers Inc.
Vernon Plant
201 Harrison St.
Vernon, TX 76384
Ultimate Parent: Rhone-Poulenc Rorer.
SIC: 2041—Flour & Other Grain Mill
Products; 2079—Edible Fats & Oils Nec;
2899—Chemical Preparations Nec.

★ 89866 ★ Kentucky Fried
Chicken
Hillcrest
Vernon, TX 76384
(817)552-2221
Ultimate Parent: Pepsico. SIC: 5812—
Eating Places.

★ 89867 ★ Lone Star Gas Co.
1680 PO Box
Vernon, TX 76384
(817)552-6216
Ultimate Parent: Enserch. SIC: 4932—Gas
& Other Services Combined; 4939—
Combination Utility Nec.

★ 89868 ★ Pizza Hut
2230 Wilbarger St.
Vernon, TX 76384
(817)553-1806
Ultimate Parent: Pepsico. SIC: 5812—
Eating Places.

★ 89869 ★ Rhone Poulenc Inc.
201 Harrison St.
Vernon, TX 76384
(817)552-9911
Ultimate Parent: Rhone-Poulenc Rorer.
SIC: 2048—Prepared Feeds Nec; 2861—
Gum & Wood Chemicals; 3533—Oil & Gas
Field Machinery.

★ 89870 ★ Rhone-Poulenc Inc.
Rhone-Poulenc Specialty Chemicals Div.
201 Harrison St.
Vernon, TX 76384
Company Type: Division. Ultimate Parent:
Rhone-Poulenc Rorer. SIC: 2041—Flour &
Other Grain Mill Products; 2048—Prepared
Feeds Nec; 2899—Chemical Preparations
Nec.

★ 89871 ★ Ryder Truck Rental
1426 Wilbarger St.
Vernon, TX 76384
(817)553-1191
Ultimate Parent: Ryder System. SIC:
7359—Equipment Rental & Leasing Nec.

★ 89872 ★ Texaco
930 Main St.
Vernon, TX 76384
(817)553-1051
Ultimate Parent: Texaco. SIC: 5411—
Grocery Stores.

★ 89873 ★ Texaco Incorporated
926 Bowie St.
Vernon, TX 76384
(817)553-1843
Ultimate Parent: Texaco. SIC: 5172—
Petroleum Products Nec.

★ 89874 ★ Trailways Inc.
1510 Pease St.
Vernon, TX 76384
(817)553-3316
Ultimate Parent: Greyhound Lines Inc. SIC:
4173—Bus Terminal & Service Facilities.

★ 89875 ★ United Parcel Service
1301 Frontage Rd.
Vernon, TX 76384
(817)552-5431
Ultimate Parent: United Parcel Service of
America. SIC: 4215—Courier Services
Except by Air.

Victoria

★ 89876 ★ Albertson's Drug &
Food
1309 E. Red River St.
Victoria, TX 77901
(512)578-9841
Ultimate Parent: Albertson's Inc. SIC:
5912—Drug Stores & Proprietary Stores.

★ 89877 ★ Butler Paper Co.
208 Lakeshore Dr.
Victoria, TX 77901-2402
(512)576-0528
Location Type: Branch office. Ultimate
Parent: Alco Standard Corp. SIC: 5113—
Industrial & Personal Service Paper.

★ 89878 ★ Butler Paper Co.
208 Lakeshore Dr.
Victoria, TX 77901-2402
(512)576-0528
Location Type: Branch office. Ultimate
Parent: Alco Standard Corp. SIC: 5113—
Industrial & Personal Service Paper.

★ 89879 ★ Casual Corner
7800 Victoria Mall
Victoria, TX 77901
(512)572-3796
Ultimate Parent: United States Shoe. SIC:
5651—Family Clothing Stores.

★ 89880 ★ Circus World
7800 Victoria Mall N
Victoria, TX 77901
(512)576-9821
Ultimate Parent: Melville. SIC: 5945—
Hobby, Toy & Game Shops.

★ 89881 ★ Coca Cola Bottling
Co.
212 N. Main St.
Victoria, TX 77901
(512)578-9704
Ultimate Parent: Coca-Cola Enterprises.
SIC: 2086—Bottled & Canned Soft Drinks.

★ 89882 ★ **Coca-Cola Bottling Co.**
2604 N. Navarro St.
Victoria, TX 77901
Ultimate Parent: Coca-Cola Enterprises.
SIC: 5149—Groceries & Related Products Nec.

★ 89883 ★ **Diebold Inc.**
806 E. North St.
Victoria, TX 77901
(512)575-4391
Ultimate Parent: Diebold, Inc. **SIC:** 5044—Office Equipment.

★ 89884 ★ **Dillard Department Stores**
Victoria Mall
Victoria, TX 77904
(512)576-5261
Ultimate Parent: Dillard Department Stores.
SIC: 5311—Department Stores.

★ 89885 ★ **Electronic Data Systems**
3708 N. Navarro St. D
Victoria, TX 77901
Ultimate Parent: Electronic Data Systems.
SIC: 7374—Data Processing & Preparation.

★ 89886 ★ **Exxon Co.**
1810 S. Laurent St.
Victoria, TX 77901
(512)573-7443
Ultimate Parent: Exxon. **SIC:** 5172—Petroleum Products Nec.

★ 89887 ★ **Hertz Rent-A-Car**
Houston Hwy.
Victoria, TX 77901
(512)575-6502
Ultimate Parent: Hertz. **SIC:** 7514—Passenger Car Rental.

★ 89888 ★ **Jiffy Lube**
5905 Hallettsville Hwy.
Victoria, TX 77904
(512)572-0379
Ultimate Parent: Pennzoil.

★ 89889 ★ **Kay Bee Toy & Hobby**
7800 Victoria Mall N
Victoria, TX 77901
(512)576-2271
Ultimate Parent: Melville. **SIC:** 5945—Hobby, Toy & Game Shops.

★ 89890 ★ **Kay Bee Toy&Hobby Shop**
Victoria Mall
Victoria, TX 77904
(512)576-2271
Ultimate Parent: Melville. **SIC:** 5945—Hobby, Toy & Game Shops.

★ 89891 ★ **Kentucky Fried Chicken**
1002 E. Rio Grande St.
Victoria, TX 77901
(512)573-6111
Ultimate Parent: Pepsico. **SIC:** 5812—Eating Places.

★ 89892 ★ **Kroger Family Center**
2805 N. Navarro St.
Victoria, TX 77901
(512)575-0456
Ultimate Parent: Kroger. **SIC:** 5411—Grocery Stores.

★ 89893 ★ **Kroger Pharmacy**
2805 N. Navarro St.
Victoria, TX 77901
(512)575-0563
Ultimate Parent: Kroger. **SIC:** 5912—Drug Stores & Proprietary Stores.

★ 89894 ★ **Lane Bryant**
7800 Victoria Mall N
Victoria, TX 77901
(512)576-0500
Ultimate Parent: Limited. **SIC:** 5651—Family Clothing Stores.

★ 89895 ★ **Lerner Shop**
7800 Victoria Mall N
Victoria, TX 77901
(512)576-2001
Ultimate Parent: Limited. **SIC:** 5651—Family Clothing Stores.

★ 89896 ★ **Lone Star Gas Co.**
3804 John Stockbauer Dr.
Victoria, TX 77904
(512)573-3286
Ultimate Parent: Enserch. **SIC:** 4932—Gas & Other Services Combined; 4939—Combination Utility Nec.

★ 89897 ★ **Occidental Chemical Co.**
Old Bloomington Hwy.
Victoria, TX 77902
Ultimate Parent: Occidental Petroleum Corp. **SIC:** 2821—Plastics Materials & Resins.

★ 89898 ★ **Occidental Chemical Corp.**
Old Bloomington Hwy.
Victoria, TX 77901
Ultimate Parent: Occidental Petroleum Corp. **SIC:** 2821—Plastics Materials & Resins.

★ 89899 ★ **Payless Shoesource**
701 E. Rio Grande St.
Victoria, TX 77901
(512)575-6201
Ultimate Parent: May Department Stores.
SIC: 5661—Shoe Stores.

★ 89900 ★ **Payless Shoesource**
7800 Victoria Mall
Victoria, TX 77901
(512)578-7203
Ultimate Parent: May Department Stores.
SIC: 5661—Shoe Stores.

★ 89901 ★ **Pizza Hut**
3406 N. Navarro St.
Victoria, TX 77901
(512)573-9137
Ultimate Parent: Pepsico. **SIC:** 5812—Eating Places.

★ 89902 ★ **Radio Shack**
Victoria Mall
Victoria, TX 77904
(512)575-0694
Company Type: Division. **Ultimate Parent:** Tandy Corp. **SIC:** 5065—Electronic Parts & Equipment Nec.

★ 89903 ★ **Radio Shack**
7800 Victoria Mall N
Victoria, TX 77901
(512)575-0694
Company Type: Division. **Ultimate Parent:** Tandy Corp. **SIC:** 5065—Electronic Parts & Equipment Nec.

★ 89904 ★ **Sears Mortgage Co.**
3904 John Stockbauer Dr.
Victoria, TX 77904
(512)578-2372
Ultimate Parent: PNC Bank Corp.

★ 89905 ★ **Sonoco Products Co.**
1 E. Sonoco Dr.
Victoria, TX 77901
(512)575-0999
Officer: George Freiji, Manager. **Ultimate Parent:** Sonoco Products. **SIC:** 2673—Bags—Plastics, Laminated & Coated.

★ 89906 ★ **Taco Bell**
3101 N. Navarro St.
Victoria, TX 77901
(512)573-4228
Ultimate Parent: Pepsico. **SIC:** 5812—Eating Places.

★ 89907 ★ **Texaco Seismic Party**
906 E. Red River St.
Victoria, TX 77901
(512)572-3085
Ultimate Parent: Texaco. **SIC:** 1389—Oil & Gas Field Services Nec.

★ 89908 ★ **United Parcel Service**
3002 S. Laurent St.
Victoria, TX 77901
(512)573-1364
Ultimate Parent: United Parcel Service of America. **SIC:** 4215—Courier Services Except by Air.

★ 89909 ★ **Wal Mart**
8402 N. Navarro St.
Victoria, TX 77904
(512)576-6189
Ultimate Parent: Wal-Mart Stores, Inc. **SIC:** 5311—Department Stores.

★ 89910 ★ **Wal Mart Discount Pharmacy**
8402 Hallettsville Hwy.
Victoria, TX 77904
(512)576-2132
Ultimate Parent: Wal-Mart Stores, Inc. **SIC:** 5311—Department Stores; 5912—Drug Stores & Proprietary Stores.

★ 89911 ★ **Waldenbooks**
7800 Victoria Mall N
Victoria, TX 77901
(512)576-1990
Ultimate Parent: K-Mart. **SIC:** 5942—Book Stores.

★ 89912 ★ **Waldenbooks**
Victoria Mall
Victoria, TX 77904
(512)576-1990
Ultimate Parent: K-Mart. **SIC:** 5942—Book Stores.

★ 89913 ★ **Walgreen Drug Stores**
1502 Town Plz.
Victoria, TX 77901
(512)572-0288
Ultimate Parent: Walgreen Co. **SIC:** 5912—Drug Stores & Proprietary Stores.

★ 89914 ★ **Western Geophysical Co.**
302 E. Industrial Dr.
Victoria, TX 77901
(512)578-4191
Ultimate Parent: Litton Industries. **SIC:** 1382—Oil & Gas Exploration Services.

Vidor

★ 89915 ★ **Gulf States Utilities Co.**
355 N. Main St.
Vidor, TX 77662
(409)769-2478
Ultimate Parent: Gulf State Utilities Co.
SIC: 4911—Electric Services.

★ 89916 ★ **Kentucky Fried Chicken**
425 N. Main St.
Vidor, TX 77662
(409)769-5491
Ultimate Parent: Pepsico. **SIC:** 5812—Eating Places.

★ 89917 ★ **Pizza Hut**
580 N. Main St.
Vidor, TX 77662
(409)769-6922
Ultimate Parent: Pepsico. **SIC:** 5812—Eating Places.

★ 89918 ★ **Radio Shack**
872 N. Main St.
Vidor, TX 77662
(409)769-9733
Company Type: Division. **Ultimate Parent:** Tandy Corp. **SIC:** 5731—Radio, Television & Electronics Stores.

★ 89919 ★ **Taco Bell**
455 N. Main St.
Vidor, TX 77662
(409)769-5022
Ultimate Parent: Pepsico. **SIC:** 5812—Eating Places.

★ 89920 ★ **Texaco Food Mart**
2598 N. Main St.
Vidor, TX 77662
(409)769-8920
Ultimate Parent: Texaco. **SIC:** 5541—Gasoline Service Stations.

★ 89921 ★ **Wal Mart Auto Center**
1350 N. Main St.
Vidor, TX 77662
(409)769-0572
Ultimate Parent: Wal-Mart Stores, Inc. **SIC:** 7538—General Automotive Repair Shops.

★ 89922 ★ **Wal Mart Pharmacy**
1350 N. Main St.
Vidor, TX 77662
(409)769-1691
Ultimate Parent: Wal-Mart Stores, Inc. **SIC:** 5912—Drug Stores & Proprietary Stores.

Vinton

★ 89923 ★ **Cal-Compack Foods**
200 Valley Chili Dr.
Vinton, TX 79821
(915)886-3777
Company Type: Division. **Location Type:** Plant. **Officer:** Sam Blount, Plant Manager.
Ultimate Parent: Conagra. **SIC:** 2033—Canned Fruits & Vegetables.

Voca

★ 89924 ★ **Vulcan Materials Co.**
PO Box 8
Voca, TX 76887
(915)239-5491
Officer: Jimmy Bradshaw, Manager.
Ultimate Parent: Vulcan Materials Co. **SIC:** 3295—Minerals—Ground or Treated.

Waco

★ 89925 ★ **Allergan Inc.**
PO Box 2675
Waco, TX 76702-2675
(817)666-3331
Officer: Declan Finan. **Ultimate Parent:** Allergan Inc. **SIC:** 2834—Pharmaceutical Preparations.

★ 89926 ★ **Allergan Inc.**
8301 Mars Dr.
Waco, TX 76712
(817)666-3331
Officer: Declan Finan, Plant Manager.
Ultimate Parent: Allergan Inc. **SIC:** 3827—Optical Instruments & Lenses.

★ 89927 ★ **American-Amicable Life Insurance Co. of Texas**
425 Austin Ave.
Waco, TX 76701
(817)753-7311 **Fax:** (817)750-7733
Officer: S. Land Peavy, President. **Ultimate Parent:** American General Corp. **SIC:** 6311—Life Insurance.

★ 89928 ★ **Avery Dennison Corp.**
Aigner Products Div.
1001 Jewel Dr.
Waco, TX 76702
(817)776-7800
Company Type: Division. **Ultimate Parent:** Avery Dennison Corp. **SIC:** 2759—Commercial Printing Nec.

★ 89929 ★ **Avon Products Inc.**
725 Lake Air Dr.
Waco, TX 76710
(817)772-3910
Ultimate Parent: Avon Products, Inc. **SIC:** 8661—Religious Organizations.

★ 89930 ★ **Borden Inc.**
4541 W. Waco Dr.
Waco, TX 76710
(817)772-6200
Officer: Rick Dill, Manager. **Ultimate Parent:** Borden, Inc. **SIC:** 2024—Ice Cream & Frozen Desserts.

★ 89931 ★ **Cast Products Corp.**
4530 Speight Ave.
Waco, TX 76711
(817)752-9853
Ultimate Parent: Harvard Industries. **SIC:** 5271—Mobile Home Dealers.

★ 89932 ★ **Chrysler Technologies Airborne Systems Inc.**
7500 Maehr Rd.
Waco, TX 76705-1647
(817)799-5533
Company Type: Subsidiary. **Officer:** R. H. Pacey, CEO. **Ultimate Parent:** Chrysler Corp. **SIC:** 3728—Aircraft Parts & Equipment Nec; 7699—Repair Services Nec. **Employee Count:** 1500. **Sales:** 200 M.

★ 89933 ★ **Diebold Inc.**
725 Lake Air Dr.
Waco, TX 76710
(817)772-8652
Ultimate Parent: Diebold, Inc. **SIC:** 5044—Office Equipment.

★ **89934** ★ **Dr. Pepper Seven-Up Co. Inc.**
120 Villa Dr.
Waco, TX 76710
(817)772-4600
Officer: Dale Ochs, Manager. **Ultimate Parent:** Dr. Pepper/Seven-Up. **SIC:** 2086—Bottled & Canned Soft Drinks.

★ **89935** ★ **Fleetwood Homes**
2801 Gholson Rd.
Waco, TX 76704
(817)799-4986
Officer: Richard Carlson, Manager. **Ultimate Parent:** Fleetwood Enterprises, Inc. **SIC:** 2451—Mobile Homes.

★ **89936** ★ **The Gap**
6001 W. Waco Dr.
Waco, TX 76710
(817)772-8244
Ultimate Parent: GAP.

★ **89937** ★ **Greyhound Bus Lines**
700 Columbus Ave.
Waco, TX 76701
(817)754-3574
Ultimate Parent: Greyhound Lines Inc. **SIC:** 4111—Local & Suburban Transit.

★ **89938** ★ **Hertz Rent-A-Car**
2828 Franklin Ave.
Waco, TX 76710
(817)756-5191
Ultimate Parent: Hertz. **SIC:** 7514—Passenger Car Rental.

★ **89939** ★ **Hertz Rent-A-Car Licensee**
New
Waco, TX 76708
(817)753-1311
Ultimate Parent: Hertz. **SIC:** 7514—Passenger Car Rental.

★ **89940** ★ **Huck International**
PO Box 8117
Waco, TX 76714
(817)776-2000
Ultimate Parent: Thiokol Corp.

★ **89941** ★ **Huck International Inc.**
8001 Imperial Dr.
Waco, TX 76714-8117
Ultimate Parent: Thiokol Corp. **SIC:** 3452—Bolts, Nuts, Rivets & Washers.

★ **89942** ★ **Huck International Inc.**
8001 Imperial Dr.
Waco, TX 76714
Ultimate Parent: Thiokol Corp. **SIC:** 3452—Bolts, Nuts, Rivets & Washers.

★ **89943** ★ **Huck Manufacturing Co.**
8001 Imperial Dr.
Waco, TX 76714-8117
Ultimate Parent: Federal-Mogul Corp. **SIC:** 3452—Bolts, Nuts, Rivets & Washers.

★ **89944** ★ **Huck Mfg. Co.**
8001 Imperial Dr.
Waco, TX 76714
Ultimate Parent: Federal-Mogul Corp. **SIC:** 3452—Bolts, Nuts, Rivets & Washers.

★ **89945** ★ **JMA Inc.**
Plastics Div.
1700 Austin Ave.
Waco, TX 76701-1742
(817)752-7842
Ultimate Parent: Ball Corp. **SIC:** 5162—Plastics Materials & Basic Shapes.

★ **89946** ★ **Kmart Corp.**
105 E. Loop 340
Waco, TX 76705
(817)799-0216
Ultimate Parent: K-Mart.

★ **89947** ★ **Kmart Corp.**
4324 W. Waco Dr.
Waco, TX 76710
(817)772-8440
Ultimate Parent: K-Mart.

★ **89948** ★ **Lone Star Gas Co.**
1500 W. Loop 340
Waco, TX 76712
(817)662-2350
Ultimate Parent: Enserch.

★ **89949** ★ **Lone Star Gas Co. Transmissi**
210 N. 9th St.
Waco, TX 76701
(817)752-2642
Ultimate Parent: Enserch. **SIC:** 4932—Gas & Other Services Combined.

★ **89950** ★ **Mary Kay Cosmetics**
433 Cranbrook St.
Waco, TX 76712
(817)772-0881
Ultimate Parent: Mary Kay Cosmetics. **SIC:** 5999—Miscellaneous Retail Stores Nec.

★ **89951** ★ **Mary Kay Cosmetics**
4601 Anlo Ave.
Waco, TX 76710
(817)753-1110
Ultimate Parent: Mary Kay Cosmetics.

★ **89952** ★ **Mary Kay Cosmetics**
502 Camp Round Rd.
Waco, TX 76710
(817)799-8170
Ultimate Parent: Mary Kay Cosmetics. **SIC:** 7231—Beauty Shops.

★ **89953** ★ **Mutual of New York**
3004 Deerwood Dr.
Waco, TX 76710
(817)751-0036
Ultimate Parent: Mutual of New York.

★ **89954** ★ **National Public Service Isurance Co.**
425 Austin Ave.
Waco, TX 76701
(817)752-6142
Officer: Robert M. Devlin, Chairman, President & CEO. **Ultimate Parent:** American General Corp. **SIC:** 6311—Life Insurance.

★ **89955** ★ **Owens-Brockway Glass Container**
5200 Beverly Dr.
Waco, TX 76711
Ultimate Parent: Owens-Illinois. **SIC:** 3221—Glass Containers.

★ **89956** ★ **Owens-Brockway Glass Container Inc.**
5200 Beverly Dr.
Waco, TX 76711
Ultimate Parent: Owens-Illinois. **SIC:** 3221—Glass Containers.

★ **89957** ★ **Owens-Illinois Glass Container Inc.**
5200 Beverley Dr.
Waco, TX 76711-0728
Ultimate Parent: Owens-Illinois. **SIC:** 3221—Glass Containers; 2653—Corrugated & Solid Fiber Boxes.

★ **89958** ★ **Owens Illinois Inc.**
Plant 15 Waco
5200 Beverly
Waco, TX 76711-0728
Location Type: Plant. **Ultimate Parent:** Owens-Illinois. **SIC:** 3221—Glass Containers.

★ **89959** ★ **Pennzoil Co.**
3103 Mary Ave.
Waco, TX 76710
(817)756-1764
Ultimate Parent: Pennzoil. **SIC:** 5172—Petroleum Products Nec.

★ **89960** ★ **Pepsi-Cola Co.**
2000 La Salle Ave.
Waco, TX 76706
(817)752-9725
Officer: Gary Richards, Manager. **Ultimate Parent:** Pepsico. **SIC:** 2086—Bottled & Canned Soft Drinks.

★ **89961** ★ **Piggly Wiggly**
3407 Memorial Dr.
Waco, TX 76711
(817)754-1775
Ultimate Parent: Bruno's. **SIC:** 5411—Grocery Stores.

★ **89962** ★ **Piggly Wiggly**
1917 Park Lake Dr.
Waco, TX 76708
(817)754-1211
Ultimate Parent: Bruno's. **SIC:** 5411—Grocery Stores.

★ **89963** ★ **Piggly Wiggly**
1711 Herring Ave.
Waco, TX 76708
(817)754-1681
Ultimate Parent: Bruno's. **SIC:** 5411—Grocery Stores.

★ **89964** ★ **Piggly Wiggly**
400 N. Robinson Dr.
Waco, TX 76706
(817)662-3303
Ultimate Parent: Bruno's. **SIC:** 5411—Grocery Stores.

★ **89965** ★ **Piggly Wiggly**
581 N. Valley Mills Dr.
Waco, TX 76710
(817)776-4281
Ultimate Parent: Bruno's. **SIC:** 5411—Grocery Stores.

★ **89966** ★ **Pioneer Security Life Insurance**
425 Austin Ave.
Waco, TX 76701-2104
(817)753-4092
Location Type: Branch office. **Officer:** S. Land Peavy, President. **Ultimate Parent:** American General Corp. **SIC:** 6311—Life Insurance. **Employee Count:** 124.

★ **89967** ★ **Pioneer Security Life Insurance Co.**
425 Austin Ave.
Waco, TX 76701
(817)753-4092
Officer: S. Lanny Peavy, President. **Ultimate Parent:** American General Corp. **SIC:** 6311—Life Insurance.

★ **89968** ★ **Precise Hard Chrome**
6613 N. 19th St.
Waco, TX 76708
Ultimate Parent: Dover Corp. **SIC:** 3471—Plating & Polishing.

★ **89969** ★ **Radio Shack**
119 Eastgate Plz.
Waco, TX 76705
(817)751-0380
Company Type: Division. **Ultimate Parent:** Tandy Corp. **SIC:** 7378—Computer Maintenance & Repair.

★ **89970** ★ **Radio Shack**
4300 W. Waco Dr.
Waco, TX 76710
(817)772-6046
Company Type: Division. **Ultimate Parent:** Tandy Corp. **SIC:** 5734—Computer & Software Stores.

★ **89971** ★ **Reddy Ice**
421 S. 9th St.
Waco, TX 76706
Ultimate Parent: Southland Corp. **SIC:** 2097—Manufactured Ice.

★ **89972** ★ **Ryder Truck Rental**
4217 W. Waco Dr.
Waco, TX 76710
(817)755-6147
Ultimate Parent: Ryder System.

★ **89973** ★ **Ryder Truck Rental**
2880 Franklin Ave.
Waco, TX 76710
(817)755-7351
Ultimate Parent: Ryder System.

★ **89974** ★ **Ryder Truck Rental**
811 Lake Air Dr.
Waco, TX 76710
(817)751-0378
Ultimate Parent: Ryder System.

★ **89975** ★ **Ryder Truck Rental**
4716 Bosque Blvd.
Waco, TX 76710
(817)751-7755
Ultimate Parent: Ryder System.

★ **89976** ★ **Safety Kleen Corp.**
22006 Woodway Dr.
Waco, TX 76712
(817)772-4419
Ultimate Parent: Safety-Kleen.

★ **89977** ★ **Spenco Medical Corp.**
6301 Imperial Dr.
PO Box 2501
Waco, TX 76702-2501
Ultimate Parent: Kimberly-Clark. **SIC:** 5047—Medical & Hospital Equipment; 3086—Plastics Foam Products; 3842—Surgical Appliances & Supplies; 3949—Sporting & Athletic Goods Nec.

★ **89978** ★ **Spenco Medical Corp.**
6301 Imperial Dr.
PO Box 2501
Waco, TX 76702-2501
Ultimate Parent: Kimberly-Clark. **SIC:** 5047—Medical & Hospital Equipment; 3086—Plastics Foam Products; 3842—Surgical Appliances & Supplies; 3949—Sporting & Athletic Goods Nec.

★ **89979** ★ **Spenco Medical Corp.**
2501 PO Box
Waco, TX 76702
(817)772-6000
Ultimate Parent: Kimberly-Clark. **SIC:** 5049—Professional Equipment Nec.

★ **89980** ★ **Texaco Inc.**
420 S. Lacy Dr.
Waco, TX 76705
(817)799-2403
Ultimate Parent: Texaco. **SIC:** 5172—Petroleum Products Nec.

★ **89981** ★ **Unisys Corp.**
209 Old Hewitt Rd. 3
Waco, TX 76712
Ultimate Parent: Unisys Corp.

★ **89982** ★ **Weyerhaeuser Co.**
4920 Franklin Ave.
Waco, TX 76710
Ultimate Parent: Weyerhaeuser Co. **SIC:** 2676—Sanitary Paper Products.

Wadsworth

★ **89983** ★ **Cain Chemical Inc.**
Matagorda Operation
13 Miles South of Bay City on Hwy. 60
Wadsworth, TX 77483
Company Type: Division. **Ultimate Parent:** Occidental Petroleum Corp. **SIC:** 2821—Plastics Materials & Resins.

★ **89984** ★ **Cain Chemical Inc.**
Matagorda Operations
13 Miles S. of Bay City on Hwy. 60
Wadsworth, TX 77483
Company Type: Division. **Ultimate Parent:** Occidental Petroleum Corp. **SIC:** 2821—Plastics Materials & Resins.

★ **89985** ★ **Occidental Chemical Corp.**
13 Miles S. of Bay City on Hwy. 60
Wadsworth, TX 77483
Ultimate Parent: Occidental Petroleum Corp. **SIC:** 2821—Plastics Materials & Resins.

Waller

★ **89986** ★ **Big Bear Super Market**
2503 Washington St.
Waller, TX 77484
(409)372-2318
Ultimate Parent: Penn Traffic. **SIC:** 5421—Meat & Fish Markets.

Walnut Springs

★ **89987** ★ **Mobil Pipe Line Co.**
Walnut Springs, TX 76690
(817)797-2441
Company Type: Branch. **Ultimate Parent:** Mobil. **SIC:** 4612—Crude Petroleum Pipelines.

Waskom

★ **89988** ★ **Mobil Oil Corp.**
F M S. 9
Waskom, TX 75692
(214)687-3314
Ultimate Parent: Mobil. **SIC:** 5171—Petroleum Bulk Stations & Terminals.

★ **89989** ★ **Mobil Pipe Line Co.**
FM 9 S.
Waskom, TX 75692
(903)687-3319
Company Type: Branch. **Ultimate Parent:** Mobil. **SIC:** 4612—Crude Petroleum Pipelines.

★ 89990 ★   **Texaco Inc.**
Waskom
Waskom, TX 75692
(214)687-3320
Ultimate Parent: Texaco. SIC: 4226—Special Warehousing & Storage Nec.

★ 89991 ★   **Trailways Bus System**
Waskom, TX 75692
(214)687-9347
Ultimate Parent: Greyhound Lines Inc. SIC: 4131—Intercity & Rural Bus Transportation.

Waxachachie

★ 89992 ★   **Owens-Corning Fiberglas Corp.**
3700 N. Interstate Hwy. 35
Waxachachie, TX 75165
(214)937-1340
Officer: Dick Le Bouef, Manager. Ultimate Parent: Owens-Corning. SIC: 3089—Plastics Products Nec; 3296—Mineral Wool.

Waxahachie

★ 89993 ★   **Exxon Products**
307 Ferris Ave.
Waxahachie, TX 75165
(214)937-3920
Ultimate Parent: Exxon.

★ 89994 ★   **Greyhound Bus**
1436 Brookside Rd.
Waxahachie, TX 75165
(214)937-4893
Ultimate Parent: Greyhound Lines Inc.

★ 89995 ★   **Kroger Food Stores**
500 N. Hwy. 77
Waxahachie, TX 75165
(214)937-7843
Ultimate Parent: Kroger.

★ 89996 ★   **Lone Star Gas Co.**
709 Ferris Ave.
Waxahachie, TX 75165
(214)937-1410
Ultimate Parent: Enserch. SIC: 4932—Gas & Other Services Combined.

★ 89997 ★   **Mobil Oil Co.**
101 Waco Rd.
Waxahachie, TX 75165
(214)937-1951
Ultimate Parent: Mobil.

★ 89998 ★   **Owens-Corning Fiberglass Corp.**
Hwy. 35 E
Waxahachie, TX 75165
Ultimate Parent: Owens-Corning. SIC: 3296—Mineral Wool.

★ 89999 ★   **Pizza Hut**
905 Ferris Ave.
Waxahachie, TX 75165
(214)937-2013
Ultimate Parent: Pepsico.

★ 90000 ★   **Wal Mart Discount Pharmacy**
Us 77
Waxahachie, TX 75165
(214)937-6152
Ultimate Parent: Wal-Mart Stores, Inc. SIC: 5912—Drug Stores & Proprietary Stores.

Waxahacie

★ 90001 ★   **Press**
821 Ferris Ave.
Waxahacie, TX 75165-2553
(214)938-1440
Ultimate Parent: Banta Corp. SIC: 2711—Newspapers.

★ 90002 ★   **Press Inc.**
821 Ferris Ave.
Waxahacie, TX 75165-2553
(214)938-1440
Ultimate Parent: Banta Corp. SIC: 2711—Newspapers.

Waxahochie

★ 90003 ★   **Comerica Bank-Texas**
800 Ferris Ave.
Waxahochie, TX 75165-2554
(214)299-5355
Company Type: Subsidiary. Location Type: Branch office. Ultimate Parent: Comerica Bank. SIC: 6021—National Commercial Banks.

Weatherford

★ 90004 ★   **Exxon Co. USA Wholesale**
133 W. Water St.
Weatherford, TX 76086
(817)599-8331
Ultimate Parent: Exxon.

★ 90005 ★   **Exxon Petroleum Products**
133 W. Water St.
Weatherford, TX 76086
(817)683-4250
Ultimate Parent: Exxon.

★ 90006 ★   **Greyhound Bus Liens**
1508 Mineral Wells Hwy.
Weatherford, TX 76086
Ultimate Parent: Greyhound Lines Inc. SIC: 4111—Local & Suburban Transit.

★ 90007 ★   **Kentucky Fried Chicken**
820 S. Main St.
Weatherford, TX 76086
(817)594-1391
Ultimate Parent: Pepsico. SIC: 5812—Eating Places.

★ 90008 ★   **Kroger Food**
102 College Ave.
Weatherford, TX 76086
(817)498-0524
Ultimate Parent: Kroger.

★ 90009 ★   **McDonalds Restaurant**
2407 S. Main St.
Weatherford, TX 76086
(817)594-2891
Ultimate Parent: May Department Stores.

★ 90010 ★   **Pizza Hut**
710 Fort Worth St.
Weatherford, TX 76086
(817)599-4134
Ultimate Parent: Pepsico. SIC: 5812—Eating Places.

★ 90011 ★   **Radio Shack**
1418 S. Main St.
Weatherford, TX 76086
(817)599-9621
Company Type: Division. Ultimate Parent: Tandy Corp. SIC: 5065—Electronic Parts & Equipment Nec; 5731—Radio, Television & Electronics Stores.

★ 90012 ★   **Ryder Truck Rental**
914 Fort Worth St.
Weatherford, TX 76086
(817)599-7689
Ultimate Parent: Ryder System.

★ 90013 ★   **Ryder Truck Rental**
814 Palo Pinto St.
Weatherford, TX 76086
(817)594-5271
Ultimate Parent: Ryder System. SIC: 7359—Equipment Rental & Leasing Nec.

★ 90014 ★   **Taco Bell**
1002 S. Main St.
Weatherford, TX 76086
(817)594-4295
Ultimate Parent: Pepsico. SIC: 5812—Eating Places.

★ 90015 ★   **Texaco Oil Co.**
406 N. Alamo St.
Weatherford, TX 76086
(817)594-3393
Ultimate Parent: Texaco. SIC: 5171—Petroleum Bulk Stations & Terminals.

★ 90016 ★   **Wal Mart Discnt**
1817 S. Main St.
Weatherford, TX 76086
(817)599-4188
Ultimate Parent: Wal-Mart Stores, Inc.

Webster

★ 90017 ★   **Builders Square**
20091 Gulf Fwy.
Webster, TX 77598
(713)338-6692
Company Type: Subsidiary. Ultimate Parent: K-Mart.

★ 90018 ★   **Digital Equipment Corp.**
100 E. Nasa Blvd.
Webster, TX 77598
(713)332-9524
Ultimate Parent: Digital Equipment Corp. SIC: 7378—Computer Maintenance & Repair.

★ 90019 ★   **Grumman Houston Corp.**
12130 Galveston Rd.
Webster, TX 77598-1504
(713)484-2141
Company Type: Subsidiary. Ultimate Parent: Grumman. SIC: 3728—Aircraft Parts & Equipment Nec. Employee Count: 300. Sales: 24.9 (est) M.

★ 90020 ★   **Jiffy Lube**
471 W. Bay Area Blvd.
Webster, TX 77598
(713)338-2329
Ultimate Parent: Pennzoil.

★ 90021 ★   **Mcduff Electrncs**
20610 Gulf Fwy.
Webster, TX 77598
(713)332-1800
Ultimate Parent: Tandy Corp.

★ 90022 ★   **Payless Shoesource**
20740 Gulf Fwy.
Webster, TX 77598
(713)332-8947
Ultimate Parent: May Department Stores.

★ 90023 ★   **Ryder Truck Rental**
1007 W. Nasa Blvd.
Webster, TX 77598
(713)332-1431
Ultimate Parent: Ryder System. SIC: 5541—Gasoline Service Stations.

★ 90024 ★   **Savings of America, A Division of Home Savings of America, FSB**
1441 W. Bay Area Blvd.
Webster, TX 77598-3831
(713)338-1960
Company Type: Division. Location Type: Branch office. Ultimate Parent: H. F. Ahmanson. SIC: 6021—National Commercial Banks.

★ 90025 ★   **Target Stores Inc.**
1425 W. Bay Area Blvd.
Webster, TX 77598
(713)338-1514
Ultimate Parent: Dayton Hudson. SIC: 5311—Department Stores.

★ 90026 ★   **Toys R US**
1449 W. Bay Area Blvd.
Webster, TX 77598
(713)338-2915
Ultimate Parent: Toys "R" US. SIC: 5945—Hobby, Toy & Game Shops.

★ 90027 ★   **Wal Mart Discount Cities**
20810 I Hwy. 45
Webster, TX 77598
(713)338-1208
Ultimate Parent: Wal-Mart Stores, Inc. SIC: 5311—Department Stores.

Weimar

★ 90028 ★   **Texaco Inc.**
400 W. Main St.
Weimar, TX 78962
(409)725-6745
Ultimate Parent: Texaco. SIC: 5171—Petroleum Bulk Stations & Terminals.

Wellington

★ 90029 ★   **Ace Hardware**
801 West Ave.
Wellington, TX 79095
(806)447-2141
Ultimate Parent: Ace Hardware. SIC: 5251—Hardware Stores.

★ 90030 ★   **Lone Star Gas Co.**
817 West Ave.
Wellington, TX 79095
(806)447-2990
Ultimate Parent: Enserch. SIC: 4925—Gas Production & Distribution Nec.

★ 90031 ★   **West Texas Util Co.**
903 9th St.
Wellington, TX 79095
(806)447-5414
Ultimate Parent: Central & South West.

Weslaco

★ 90032 ★   **City National Bank**
400 N. Texas Blvd.
Weslaco, TX 78596-5308
Company Type: Branch. Ultimate Parent: City National Corp. SIC: 6021—National Commercial Banks.

★ 90033 ★   **City National Bank**
401 S. Kansas Ave.
Weslaco, TX 78596-6213
(210)968-1511
Company Type: Headquarters. Officer: Robert J. Dyer, President. Ultimate Parent: City National Corp. SIC: 6021—National Commercial Banks; 6141—Personal Credit Institutions; 6162—Mortgage Bankers & Correspondents.

★ 90034 ★   **Gaylord Container Corp.**
715 W. Pike Blvd.
Weslaco, TX 78596
(210)968-3115
Officer: Minnie Galvan, Manager. Ultimate Parent: Gaylord Container. SIC: 2652—Setup Paperboard Boxes.

★ 90035 ★   **McDonalds Restaurant**
1025 N. Texas Blvd.
Weslaco, TX 78596
(512)968-6554
Ultimate Parent: McDonald's. SIC: 5812—Eating Places.

★ 90036 ★   **Pizza Hut**
623 W. Hwy. 83
Weslaco, TX 78596
(512)969-1444
Ultimate Parent: Pepsico. SIC: 5812—Eating Places.

★ 90037 ★   **Rio Grande Valley Gas Co.**
805 W. Pike Blvd.
Weslaco, TX 78596
(512)968-2464
Ultimate Parent: Valero Energy Corp. SIC: 4925—Gas Production & Distribution Nec.

★ 90038 ★   **Rio Grande Valley Gas Co.**
313 S. Texas Blvd.
Weslaco, TX 78596
(512)968-2176
Ultimate Parent: Valero Energy Corp. SIC: 4925—Gas Production & Distribution Nec.

★ 90039 ★   **Texaco Inc.**
Rural Route 1
Weslaco, TX 78596
(512)968-2321
Ultimate Parent: Texaco. SIC: 5172—Petroleum Products Nec.

★ 90040 ★   **Trailways Bus System**
112 E. 3rd St.
Weslaco, TX 78596
(512)968-3814
Ultimate Parent: Greyhound Lines Inc. SIC: 4131—Intercity & Rural Bus Transportation; 4212—Local Trucking Without Storage.

★ 90041 ★   **Wal Mart Dict Cty**
1310 N. Texas Blvd.
Weslaco, TX 78596
(512)968-6357
Ultimate Parent: Wal-Mart Stores, Inc.

West

★ 90042 ★   **Exxon Co. USA**
501 S. Washington St.
West, TX 76691
(817)826-5392
Ultimate Parent: Exxon. SIC: 5172—Petroleum Products Nec.

★ 90043 ★   **Lone Star Gas Co.**
310 PO Box
West, TX 76691
Ultimate Parent: Enserch. SIC: 4932—Gas & Other Services Combined.

★ 90044 ★ **Radio Shack**
109 E. Oak St.
West, TX 76691
(817)826-5432
Company Type: Division. **Ultimate Parent:**
Tandy Corp.

West Columbia

★ 90045 ★ **Mini Mart**
902 E. Brazos Ave.
West Columbia, TX 77486
(409)345-4700
Ultimate Parent: Kroger. **SIC:** 6022—State
Commercial Banks.

★ 90046 ★ **Radio Shack**
Columbia Plz.
West Columbia, TX 77486
(409)345-4544
Company Type: Division. **Ultimate Parent:**
Tandy Corp. **SIC:** 5731—Radio, Television
& Electronics Stores.

★ 90047 ★ **Texaco Inc. Prod Dept**
Damon Hwy.
West Columbia, TX 77486
(409)345-3525
Ultimate Parent: Texaco. **SIC:** 1389—Oil &
Gas Field Services Nec.

West Orange

★ 90048 ★ **Betz Laboratories Inc.**
3901 Williams Dr.
West Orange, TX 77630
Ultimate Parent: Betz Laboratories Inc.
SIC: 2899—Chemical Preparations Nec.

★ 90049 ★ **Betz Laboratories Inc.**
3901 Williams Dr.
West Orange, TX 77630
Ultimate Parent: Betz Laboratories Inc.
SIC: 2899—Chemical Preparations Nec.

Westbrook

★ 90050 ★ **Union Texas
Petroleum**
Westbrook, TX 79565
(915)644-3121
Ultimate Parent: Union Texas Petroleum.
SIC: 1389—Oil & Gas Field Services Nec.

Wharton

★ 90051 ★ **Trailways Bus Station**
2111 N. Richmond Rd.
Wharton, TX 77488
(409)532-5540
Ultimate Parent: Greyhound Lines Inc. **SIC:**
4131—Intercity & Rural Bus Transportation.

White Oak

★ 90052 ★ **Amerada Hess Corp.**
White Oak
White Oak, TX 75693
(214)759-4441
Ultimate Parent: Amerada Hess. **SIC:**
1311—Crude Petroleum & Natural Gas.

★ 90053 ★ **Citgo Pipeline Co.**
1708 State Hwy. 42 S
White Oak, TX 75693
(903)759-2522
Ultimate Parent: Citgo Petroleum.

★ 90054 ★ **Citgo Pipeline Co.**
1708 State Hwy. 42 S
White Oak, TX 75693
(903)759-2522
Ultimate Parent: Citgo Petroleum.

★ 90055 ★ **Mini Mart No 413**
209 W. Hwy. 80
White Oak, TX 75693
(214)297-2959
Ultimate Parent: Kroger. **SIC:** 5411—
Grocery Stores.

Whiteface

★ 90056 ★ **Exxon Co. USA**
126th
Whiteface, TX 79379
(806)287-1185
Ultimate Parent: Exxon.

Whitehouse

★ 90057 ★ **City National Bank**
1125 State Hwy. 110 N.
Whitehouse, TX 75791-3027
(903)839-6000
Company Type: Headquarters. **Officer:**
Betty L. Sizemore, President. **Ultimate
Parent:** City National Corp. **SIC:** 6021—
National Commercial Banks.

★ 90058 ★ **City National Bank**
1125 N. Hwy. 110
Whitehouse, TX 75791
(214)839-6000
Ultimate Parent: City National Corp. **SIC:**
6021—National Commercial Banks.

Whitesboro

★ 90059 ★ **Coast to Coast**
140 E. Main St.
Whitesboro, TX 76273
(903)564-3241
Ultimate Parent: Servistar Corp.

★ 90060 ★ **Lone Star Gas Co.**
107 E. Main St.
Whitesboro, TX 76273
(903)564-3221
Ultimate Parent: Enserch.

★ 90061 ★ **Pizza Hut**
1000 Hwy. 82 E
Whitesboro, TX 76273
(903)564-3539
Ultimate Parent: Pepsico. **SIC:** 5812—
Eating Places.

Wichita Fall

★ 90062 ★ **Dana Corp.**
2800 Fisher Rd.
Wichita Fall, TX 76302
(817)767-2000
Ultimate Parent: Dana Corp. **SIC:** 3586—
Measuring & Dispensing Pumps; 3714—
Motor Vehicle Parts & Accessories.

Wichita Falls

★ 90063 ★ **Albertson's**
2720 Southwest Pky.
Wichita Falls, TX 76308
(817)691-0420
Ultimate Parent: Albertson's Inc. **SIC:**
5411—Grocery Stores.

★ 90064 ★ **Albertson's**
2720 Southwest Pky.
Wichita Falls, TX 76308
(817)691-0420
Ultimate Parent: Albertson's Inc. **SIC:**
5411—Grocery Stores.

★ 90065 ★ **American National
Bank**
2732 Midwestern Pky.
Wichita Falls, TX 76308-2904
(817)691-1221
Officer: John B. Stahler, President.
Ultimate Parent: First Chicago Corp. **SIC:**
6021—National Commercial Banks.
Employee Count: 51.

★ 90066 ★ **Arco Pipe Line Co.**
4309 Jacksboro Hwy.
Wichita Falls, TX 76302-2745
(817)322-6937
Officer: M. A. Schmidt. **Ultimate Parent:**
Atlantic Richfield Co., Inc. **SIC:** 4619—
Pipelines Nec.

★ 90067 ★ **Beverly Enterprise**
3101 10th St.
Wichita Falls, TX 76309-2103
(817)766-0425
Ultimate Parent: Beverly Enterprises. **SIC:**
8059—Nursing & Personal Care Nec.

★ 90068 ★ **Burlington Northern
Railroa**
503 10th St.
Wichita Falls, TX 76301
(817)723-1426
Ultimate Parent: Burlington Northern. **SIC:**
4011—Railroads—Line-Haul Operating.

★ 90069 ★ **Casual Corner**
3111 Sikes Senter
Wichita Falls, TX 76302
(817)691-1431
Ultimate Parent: United States Shoe. **SIC:**
5651—Family Clothing Stores.

★ 90070 ★ **City National Bank**
800 Scott Ave.
Wichita Falls, TX 76301
(817)723-2771
Ultimate Parent: City National Corp. **SIC:**
6029—Commercial Banks Nec.

★ 90071 ★ **Exxon**
2317 Jacksboro Hwy.
Wichita Falls, TX 76302
(817)766-2034
Ultimate Parent: Exxon. **SIC:** 5541—
Gasoline Service Stations.

★ 90072 ★ **Exxon Co. USA**
Henrietta Rd.
Wichita Falls, TX 76301
(817)767-4356
Ultimate Parent: Exxon. **SIC:** 5172—
Petroleum Products Nec.

★ 90073 ★ **Hertz Rent-A-Car
Licensee**
Municipal Airport
Wichita Falls, TX 76304
(817)723-2280
Ultimate Parent: Hertz. **SIC:** 7514—
Passenger Car Rental.

★ 90074 ★ **IBM Corp.**
2115 Kemp Blvd.
Wichita Falls, TX 76309
(817)761-1091
Ultimate Parent: IBM. **SIC:** 5046—
Commercial Equipment Nec.

★ 90075 ★ **Kentucky Fried
Chicken**
503 E. Scott Ave.
Wichita Falls, TX 76301
(817)767-1723
Ultimate Parent: Pepsico. **SIC:** 5812—
Eating Places.

★ 90076 ★ **Kentucky Fried
Chicken**
4020 Kemp Blvd.
Wichita Falls, TX 76308
(817)692-5693
Ultimate Parent: Pepsico. **SIC:** 5142—
Packaged Frozen Foods; 5812—Eating
Places.

★ 90077 ★ **Kentucky Fried
Chicken**
801 Brook Ave.
Wichita Falls, TX 76301
(817)322-2380
Ultimate Parent: Pepsico. **SIC:** 5142—
Packaged Frozen Foods; 5812—Eating
Places.

★ 90078 ★ **Lerner Shop**
Sikes Ctr.
Wichita Falls, TX 76308
(817)692-8681
Ultimate Parent: Limited. **SIC:** 5621—
Women's Clothing Stores.

★ 90079 ★ **Lone Star Gas Co.**
3704 Gregory St.
Wichita Falls, TX 76308
(817)766-4151
Ultimate Parent: Enserch.

★ 90080 ★ **Lone Star Gas Co.**
5328 PO Box
Wichita Falls, TX 76307
Ultimate Parent: Enserch. **SIC:** 1711—
Plumbing, Heating & Air-Conditioning;
4920—Gas Production & Distribution;
4939—Combination Utility Nec.

★ 90081 ★ **Mary Kay Cosmetics**
2313 Ellingham Dr.
Wichita Falls, TX 76308
(817)322-5457
Ultimate Parent: Mary Kay Cosmetics. **SIC:**
5999—Miscellaneous Retail Stores Nec.

★ 90082 ★ **McDonalds
Restaurant**
3103 Kemp Blvd.
Wichita Falls, TX 76308
(817)691-0525
Ultimate Parent: McDonald's.

★ 90083 ★ **McDonalds
Restaurants**
1 Parker Sq.
Wichita Falls, TX 76308
(817)766-0922
Ultimate Parent: McDonald's.
SIC: 5812—Eating Places.

★ 90084 ★ **Mobil Prdcng. TX &
New Mex Inc.**
1730 City View Dr.
Wichita Falls, TX 76305-1104
(817)855-7200
Ultimate Parent: Mobil. **SIC:** 1311—Crude
Petroleum & Natural Gas.

★ 90085 ★ **Otis Elevator Co.**
708 8th St.
Wichita Falls, TX 76301
(817)767-4025
Ultimate Parent: United Technologies. **SIC:**
1796—Installing Building Equipment Nec.

★ 90086 ★ **Payless Cashways
Building M**
4401 Seymour Hwy.
Wichita Falls, TX 76309
(817)696-5021
Ultimate Parent: Payless Cashways. **SIC:**
5211—Lumber & Other Building Materials.

★ 90087 ★ **Pgg Industries Inc.**
I 44 E. East Rd. Exit
Wichita Falls, TX 76307
Ultimate Parent: PPG Industries Inc. **SIC:**
3211—Flat Glass.

★ 90088 ★ **Pizza Hut**
4311 Kemp Blvd.
Wichita Falls, TX 76308
(817)692-0731
Ultimate Parent: Pepsico. **SIC:** 5812—
Eating Places.

★ 90089 ★ **Pizza Hut**
4000 Sheppard Access Rd.
Wichita Falls, TX 76304
(817)855-0872
Ultimate Parent: Pepsico. **SIC:** 5812—
Eating Places.

★ 90090 ★ **Pizza Hut**
504 Galveston St.
Wichita Falls, TX 76301
(817)767-3212
Ultimate Parent: Pepsico. **SIC:** 5812—
Eating Places.

★ 90091 ★ **Pizza Hut**
4201 Jacksboro Hwy.
Wichita Falls, TX 76302
(817)761-2222
Ultimate Parent: Pepsico.

★ 90092 ★ **Pizza Hut**
2501 5th St.
Wichita Falls, TX 76301
(817)322-5757
Ultimate Parent: Pepsico. **SIC:** 5812—
Eating Places.

★ 90093 ★ **PPG Industries Inc.**
I-44 E. East Rd. Exit
Wichita Falls, TX 76307
Ultimate Parent: PPG Industries Inc. **SIC:**
3211—Flat Glass.

★ 90094 ★ **PPG Industries Inc.**
7400 Central Fwy. N
Wichita Falls, TX 76307
(817)855-3804
Officer: Joel Ellett, Manager. **Ultimate
Parent:** PPG Industries Inc. **SIC:** 3211—
Flat Glass; 3231—Products of Purchased
Glass.

★ 90095 ★ **Ppg Industries Inc.**
Century Fwy.
Wichita Falls, TX 76311
(817)855-3804
Ultimate Parent: PPG Industries Inc. **SIC:**
3211—Flat Glass.

★ 90096 ★ **Radio Shack**
3118 5th St.
Wichita Falls, TX 76301
(817)322-1093
Company Type: Division. **Ultimate Parent:**
Tandy Corp. **SIC:** 5065—Electronic Parts &
Equipment Nec.

★ **90097** ★ **Radio Shack**
2800 Garnett St.
Wichita Falls, TX 76308
(817)322-2220
Ultimate Parent: M.A.Hanna. **SIC:** 3251—Brick & Structural Clay Tile. **Company Type:** Division. **Ultimate Parent:** Tandy Corp. **SIC:** 5065—Electronic Parts & Equipment Nec.

★ **90098** ★ **Ryder Truck Rental**
3612 Iowa Park Rd.
Wichita Falls, TX 76305
(817)855-5848
Ultimate Parent: Ryder System. **SIC:** 7513—Truck Rental & Leasing Without Drivers.

★ **90099** ★ **Ryder Truck Rental**
4312 Jacksboro Hwy.
Wichita Falls, TX 76302
(817)322-3201
Ultimate Parent: Ryder System. **SIC:** 7359—Equipment Rental & Leasing Nec.

★ **90100** ★ **Ryder Truck Rental**
406 4th St.
Wichita Falls, TX 76301
(817)766-2137
Ultimate Parent: Ryder System. **SIC:** 7359—Equipment Rental & Leasing Nec.

★ **90101** ★ **Ryder Truck Rental**
2403 Grant St.
Wichita Falls, TX 76309
(817)723-1470
Ultimate Parent: Ryder System. **SIC:** 7359—Equipment Rental & Leasing Nec.

★ **90102** ★ **Stanley Proto Industrial Tools**
2801 Production Blvd.
Wichita Falls, TX 76302
Ultimate Parent: Stanley Works. **SIC:** 3471—Plating & Polishing.

★ **90103** ★ **Stanley Works**
Mechanics Tool Division
2801 Production Blvd.
Wichita Falls, TX 76302
Ultimate Parent: Stanley Works. **SIC:** 3471—Plating & Polishing; 3423—Hand & Edge Tools Nec.

★ **90104** ★ **Taco Bell**
2512 Kemp Blvd.
Wichita Falls, TX 76309
(817)766-4859
Ultimate Parent: Pepsico. **SIC:** 5812—Eating Places.

★ **90105** ★ **Taco Bell**
4601 Kemp Blvd.
Wichita Falls, TX 76308
(817)692-9592
Ultimate Parent: Pepsico. **SIC:** 5812—Eating Places.

★ **90106** ★ **Tandy**
3401 Kemp Blvd.
Wichita Falls, TX 76308
Ultimate Parent: Tandy Corp. **SIC:** 5948—Luggage & Leather Goods Stores.

★ **90107** ★ **Target Stores**
4317 Kemp Blvd.
Wichita Falls, TX 76308
(817)691-3310
Ultimate Parent: Dayton Hudson. **SIC:** 5311—Department Stores.

★ **90108** ★ **Texaco Food Mart**
726 Scott Ave. 815
Wichita Falls, TX 76301
Ultimate Parent: Texaco.

★ **90109** ★ **Texaco Food Mart**
4601 Southwest Pky.
Wichita Falls, TX 76310
(817)692-1421
Ultimate Parent: Texaco. **SIC:** 5411—Grocery Stores.

★ **90110** ★ **Texaco Food Mart**
3701 Kell Blvd.
Wichita Falls, TX 76308
(817)696-9034
Ultimate Parent: Texaco.

★ **90111** ★ **Texaco Pipeline**
2110 Harding St.
Wichita Falls, TX 76303
(817)766-2221
Ultimate Parent: Texaco.

★ **90112** ★ **Texaco Service Station**
13 Spring Park Ln.
Wichita Falls, TX 76308
Ultimate Parent: Texaco. **SIC:** 5541—Gasoline Service Stations.

★ **90113** ★ **Texaco Svc Sta**
2515 5th St.
Wichita Falls, TX 76301
(817)322-8397
Ultimate Parent: Texaco.

★ **90114** ★ **Texaco USA Marketing**
2629 Plaza Pky.
Wichita Falls, TX 76308
(817)692-6266
Ultimate Parent: Texaco. **SIC:** 1742—Plastering, Drywall & Insulation.

★ **90115** ★ **Trailways Bus Systems**
512 Lamar St.
Wichita Falls, TX 76301
(817)322-5408
Ultimate Parent: Greyhound Lines Inc. **SIC:** 4731—Freight Transportation Arrangement.

★ **90116** ★ **Tranter Inc.**
1900 Old Burk Hwy.
Wichita Falls, TX 76304
(817)723-7125
Officer: Feroz Patel, President. **Ultimate Parent:** Dover Corp. **SIC:** 3443—Fabricated Plate Work—Boiler Shops; 3567—Industrial Furnaces & Ovens.

★ **90117** ★ **Trico Industries Inc.**
6013 Jacksboro Hwy.
Wichita Falls, TX 76302
(817)767-2081
Ultimate Parent: Paccar. **SIC:** 5084—Industrial Machinery & Equipment.

★ **90118** ★ **Underwriters Adjusting Co.**
1508 10th St.
Wichita Falls, TX 76301
(817)766-0229
Ultimate Parent: Continental. **SIC:** 6411—Insurance Agents, Brokers & Service.

★ **90119** ★ **United Parcel Service**
310 Petrolia Rd.
Wichita Falls, TX 76303
(817)767-1311
Ultimate Parent: United Parcel Service of America. **SIC:** 4215—Courier Services Except by Air.

★ **90120** ★ **Wal Mart Discount City**
3705 Kell Blvd.
Wichita Falls, TX 76308
(817)692-0771
Ultimate Parent: Wal-Mart Stores, Inc.

★ **90121** ★ **Walgreen Drug Stores**
112 Sikes Ctr. Shopping
Wichita Falls, TX 76308
(817)692-0911
Ultimate Parent: Walgreen Co. **SIC:** 5999—Miscellaneous Retail Stores Nec.

Wickett

★ **90122** ★ **Trico Industries Inc.**
104 O Brien
Wickett, TX 79788
(915)943-4411
Ultimate Parent: Paccar. **SIC:** 5084—Industrial Machinery & Equipment.

Winnie

★ **90123** ★ **Radio Shack**
PO Box
Winnie, TX 77665
(409)296-4765
Company Type: Division. **Ultimate Parent:** Tandy Corp. **SIC:** 5065—Electronic Parts & Equipment Nec.

★ **90124** ★ **Texaco Inc. Prod Dept**
238 PO Box
Winnie, TX 77665
(409)296-2831
Ultimate Parent: Texaco. **SIC:** 1311—Crude Petroleum & Natural Gas.

Winnsboro

★ **90125** ★ **City National Bank**
Winnsboro, TX 75494
(903)342-3791
Ultimate Parent: City National Corp. **SIC:** 6021—National Commercial Banks.

★ **90126** ★ **Whispering Pines Nursing Home**
910 Beech St. S
Winnsboro, TX 75494
(214)342-5243
Ultimate Parent: Beverly Enterprises. **SIC:** 8051—Skilled Nursing Care Facilities.

Winters

★ **90127** ★ **Exxon Co. USA**
1015 N. Main St.
Winters, TX 79567
(915)754-4218
Ultimate Parent: Exxon.

★ **90128** ★ **Piggly Wiggly**
339 S. Main St.
Winters, TX 79567
(915)754-4418
Ultimate Parent: Bruno's. **SIC:** 5039—Construction Materials Nec.

★ **90129** ★ **Pizza Hut**
710 N. Main St.
Winters, TX 79567
(915)754-5543
Ultimate Parent: Pepsico.

Woodville

★ **90130** ★ **Citizens State Bank**
102 W. Bluff St.
Woodville, TX 75979
(409)283-2561
Ultimate Parent: Liberty National Bancorp. **SIC:** 6022—State Commercial Banks.

★ **90131** ★ **Radio Shack**
719 S. Magnolia St.
Woodville, TX 75979
(409)283-2282
Company Type: Division. **Ultimate Parent:** Tandy Corp. **SIC:** 5065—Electronic Parts & Equipment Nec.

★ **90132** ★ **Wal Mart Discount City**
S Magnolia
Woodville, TX 75979
(409)283-2278
Ultimate Parent: Wal-Mart Stores, Inc. **SIC:** 5311—Department Stores.

Wylie

★ **90133** ★ **McDonalds Restaurant**
415 S. Hwy. 78
Wylie, TX 75098
(214)442-3952
Ultimate Parent: McDonald's.

★ **90134** ★ **Shell Service**
1300 Martinez Ln.
Wylie, TX 75098
(214)442-6988
Ultimate Parent: Shell Oil Co. **SIC:** 5541—Gasoline Service Stations.

Yoakum

★ **90135** ★ **Arco Pipe Line**
RR 2
Yoakum, TX 77995-9801
(512)293-5074
Location Type: Branch office. **Ultimate Parent:** Atlantic Richfield Co., Inc. **SIC:** 4612—Crude Petroleum Pipelines.

★ **90136** ★ **Pizza Hut**
1201 W. Grand Ave.
Yoakum, TX 77995
(512)293-6521
Ultimate Parent: Pepsico. **SIC:** 5812—Eating Places.

★ **90137** ★ **Tandy Brands Accessories**
107 W. Gonzales St.
Yoakum, TX 77995
(512)293-2311
Officer: Britt Jenkins, President. **Ultimate Parent:** Tandy Corp. **SIC:** 2387—Apparel Belts; 2389—Apparel & Accessories Nec; 3172—Personal Leather Goods Nec.

Zapata

★ **90138** ★ **Pizza Hut**
S Hwy. 83
Zapata, TX 78076
(512)765-4882
Ultimate Parent: Pepsico. **SIC:** 5812—Eating Places.

Zavalla

★ **90139** ★ **M-I Drilling Fluids Zavalla**
Hwy. 69, 5 Miles South of Zavalla
Zavalla, TX 75980
Ultimate Parent: Halliburton. **SIC:** 3251—Brick & Structural Clay Tile.

VIRGIN ISLANDS

Charlotte Amalie

★ 90140 ★   Banco Popular de Puerto Rico
Fort Mylner Shopping Ctr.
Charlotte Amalie, VI 00801
(809)775-0400
Company Type: Subsidiary. **Location Type:** Branch office. **Ultimate Parent:** Banponce Corp. **SIC:** 6022—State Commercial Banks.

★ 90141 ★   Banco Popular de Puerto Rico
Veterans Dr.
Charlotte Amalie, VI 00801
(809)774-2300
Company Type: Subsidiary. **Location Type:** Branch office. **Ultimate Parent:** Banponce Corp. **SIC:** 6022—State Commercial Banks.

★ 90142 ★   Banco Popular de Puerto Rico
Red Hook Plaza Shopping Ctr.
Charlotte Amalie, VI 00802-3401
(809)775-0657
Company Type: Subsidiary. **Location Type:** Branch office. **Ultimate Parent:** Banponce Corp. **SIC:** 6022—State Commercial Banks.

★ 90143 ★   Banco Popular de Puerto Rico
Lockhard Garden Shopping Ctr.
Charlotte Amalie, VI 00801
(809)774-7085
Company Type: Subsidiary. **Location Type:** Branch office. **Ultimate Parent:** Banponce Corp. **SIC:** 6022—State Commercial Banks.

★ 90144 ★   Banco Popular de Puerto Rico
70B Kronprindsens Gate Quarter
Charlotte Amalie, VI 00801
(809)776-7800
Company Type: Subsidiary. **Location Type:** Branch office. **Ultimate Parent:** Banponce Corp. **SIC:** 6022—State Commercial Banks.

★ 90145 ★   Bell Atlantic Foreign Sales Corp.
CitiBank Bldg., Veteran's Dr., Ste. 208
Charlotte Amalie, VI 00801
Company Type: Subsidiary. **Ultimate Parent:** Bell Atlantic Corp.

Christiansted

★ 90146 ★   Banco Popular de Puerto Rico
17 Church St.
Christiansted, VI 00820
(809)773-0077
Company Type: Subsidiary. **Location Type:** Branch office. **Ultimate Parent:** Banponce Corp. **SIC:** 6022—State Commercial Banks.

★ 90147 ★   Banco Popular de Puerto Rico
Sunny Isle Shopping Ctr.
Christiansted, VI 00820
(809)778-5955
Company Type: Subsidiary. **Location Type:** Branch office. **Ultimate Parent:** Banponce Corp. **SIC:** 6022—State Commercial Banks.

Kingshill

★ 90148 ★   Hess Oil Virgin Islands Corp. (Hovic)
Estate Hope
Kingshill, VI 00851-0127
Ultimate Parent: Amerada Hess. **SIC:** 2911—Petroleum Refining.

St. Croix

★ 90149 ★   Hess Oil Virgin Islands Corp. (Hovic)
Limetree Bay
St. Croix, VI 00851
Company Type: Division. **Ultimate Parent:** Amerada Hess. **SIC:** 2911—Petroleum Refining.

St. Thomas

★ 90150 ★   Air Products World Trade, Inc.
c/oChase Trade, Inc.
PO Box 6220
11A & 11B Curacao Gade
St. Thomas, VI 00804-6220
(809)778-8700
Company Type: Subsidiary. **Ultimate Parent:** Air Products & Chemicals, Inc. **SIC:** 5169—Chemicals & Allied Products Nec.

VIRGINIA

Abingdon

★ 90152 ★ First Union National Bank of Virginia
332 Cummins St.
PO Box 1357
Abingdon, VA 24210-1310
(703)676-6125
Location Type: Branch office. Ultimate Parent: First Union Corp. SIC: 6021—National Commercial Banks.

★ 90153 ★ Food Lion
Cummings St. SW
Abingdon, VA 24210
(703)628-8196
Ultimate Parent: Food Lion. SIC: 5411—Grocery Stores.

★ 90154 ★ Kroger Co.
Cummings
Abingdon, VA 24210
(703)628-6015
Ultimate Parent: Kroger. SIC: 5411—Grocery Stores.

★ 90155 ★ New York Life Insurance
458 E. Main St.
Abingdon, VA 24210
(703)628-5511
Ultimate Parent: New York Life. SIC: 6411—Insurance Agents, Brokers & Service.

★ 90156 ★ Overnite Transportation Co.
Kingsport Hwy.
Abingdon, VA 24210
(703)628-7823
Ultimate Parent: Union Pacific Corp. SIC: 4212—Local Trucking Without Storage.

★ 90157 ★ Piggly Wiggly
263 W. Main St.
Abingdon, VA 24210
(703)628-2151
Ultimate Parent: Bruno's. SIC: 5411—Grocery Stores.

★ 90158 ★ Ryder Truck Rental Inc.
Abingdon, VA 24210
(703)628-7771
Ultimate Parent: Ryder System. SIC: 7513—Truck Rental & Leasing Without Drivers.

★ 90159 ★ Westinghouse Electric
18259 Westinghouse Rd.
Abingdon, VA 24210
(703)676-9100
Officer: Roy Thomas, Manager. Ultimate Parent: Westinghouse Electric Corp. SIC: 3351—Copper Rolling & Drawing; 3357—Nonferrous Wiredrawing & Insulating.

★ 90160 ★ Westinghouse Electric Corp.
Rte. 11 Box 100 Westinghouse Rd.
Abingdon, VA 24210
Ultimate Parent: Westinghouse Electric Corp. SIC: 3357—Nonferrous Wiredrawing & Insulating.

★ 90161 ★ Westinghouse Electric Corp.
Wire Div.
Hwy. 11 Westinghouse Rd.
Abingdon, VA 24210
Company Type: Division. Ultimate Parent: Westinghouse Electric Corp. SIC: 3357—Nonferrous Wiredrawing & Insulating.

Accomac

★ 90162 ★ Crestar Bank
23364 Front St.
Accomac, VA 23301
(804)858-3048
Location Type: Branch office. Ultimate Parent: Crestar Financial Corp. SIC: 6021—National Commercial Banks.

Alexandra

★ 90163 ★ Beneficial Virginia Inc.
6911 Richmond Hwy.
Alexandra, VA 22306-1803
(703)765-0900
Location Type: Branch office. Ultimate Parent: Beneficial. SIC: 6141—Personal Credit Institutions; 6162—Mortgage Bankers & Correspondents.

★ 90164 ★ Signet Bank, Virginia
6300 Richmond Hwy.
Alexandra, VA 22306-6499
(703)768-0047
Ultimate Parent: Signet Banking Corp. SIC: 6021—National Commercial Banks.

Alexandria

★ 90165 ★ Atlantic Research Corp.
5321 Shawnee Rd.
Alexandria, VA 22312
Ultimate Parent: Sequa Corp. SIC: 3764—Space Propulsion Units & Parts.

★ 90166 ★ Atlantic Research Corp.
5390 Cherokee Ave.
Alexandria, VA 22312
Ultimate Parent: Sequa Corp. SIC: 3764—Space Propulsion Units & Parts.

★ 90167 ★ Coca-Cola Bottling Co. Mid Atlantic
5401 Seminary Rd.
Alexandria, VA 22313
Ultimate Parent: Coca-Cola Enterprises. SIC: 2086—Bottled & Canned Soft Drinks.

★ 90168 ★ Columbia First Bank, FSB
203 N. Washington St.
Alexandria, VA 22314
(703)684-7807
Company Type: Subsidiary. Location Type: Branch office. Ultimate Parent: Columbia First Bank, FSB. SIC: 6021—National Commercial Banks.

★ 90169 ★ Crestar Bank
2111 Eisenhower Ave.
Alexandria, VA 22314-4679
Location Type: Branch office. Ultimate Parent: Crestar Financial Corp. SIC: 6021—National Commercial Banks.

★ 90170 ★ Crestar Bank
1460 N. Beauregard
Alexandria, VA 22311-5800
Location Type: Branch office. Ultimate Parent: Crestar Financial Corp. SIC: 6021—National Commercial Banks.

★ 90171 ★ Crestar Bank
3610 H King St.
Alexandria, VA 22302-1991
Location Type: Branch office. Ultimate Parent: Crestar Financial Corp. SIC: 6021—National Commercial Banks.

★ 90172 ★ Crestar Bank
2809 Mount Vernon Ave.
Alexandria, VA 22301-1125
Location Type: Branch office. Ultimate Parent: Crestar Financial Corp. SIC: 6021—National Commercial Banks.

★ 90173 ★ Crestar Bank
5701-B Duke St.
Alexandria, VA 22304-3293
Location Type: Branch office. Ultimate Parent: Crestar Financial Corp. SIC: 6021—National Commercial Banks.

★ 90174 ★ Crestar Bank
5922 Richmond Hwy.
Alexandria, VA 22303-9998
(703)838-3201
Location Type: Branch office. Ultimate Parent: Crestar Financial Corp. SIC: 6021—National Commercial Banks.

★ 90175 ★ Crestar Bank
901 N. Washington St.
Alexandria, VA 22314-1535
Location Type: Branch office. Ultimate Parent: Crestar Financial Corp. SIC: 6021—National Commercial Banks.

★ 90176 ★ Crestar Bank
1650 King St.
Alexandria, VA 22314-2786
Location Type: Branch office. Ultimate Parent: Crestar Financial Corp. SIC: 6021—National Commercial Banks.

★ 90177 ★ Crestar Bank
4616 Kenmore Ave.
Alexandria, VA 22304-1321
Location Type: Branch office. Ultimate Parent: Crestar Financial Corp. SIC: 6021—National Commercial Banks.

★ 90178 ★ Crestar Bank
515 King St.
Alexandria, VA 22314-3194
(800)451-2435
Location Type: Branch office. Ultimate Parent: Crestar Financial Corp. SIC: 6021—National Commercial Banks.

★ 90179 ★ Electronic Data Systems
1600 N. Beauregard St.
Alexandria, VA 22311
(703)578-5177
Ultimate Parent: Electronic Data Systems.

★ 90180 ★ First American Bank
1501 Duke St.
Alexandria, VA 22314
(703)739-3481
Ultimate Parent: First American Corp. SIC: 6099—Functions Related to Deposit Banking.

★ 90181 ★ First American Bank
8770 Richmond Hwy.
Alexandria, VA 22309
(703)739-3552
Ultimate Parent: First American Corp. SIC: 6099—Functions Related to Deposit Banking.

★ 90182 ★ First American Bank
8306 Richmond Hwy.
Alexandria, VA 22309
(703)739-3566
Ultimate Parent: First American Corp. SIC: 6099—Functions Related to Deposit Banking.

★ 90183 ★ First American Bank
1711 Fern St.
Alexandria, VA 22302
(703)284-6439
Ultimate Parent: First American Corp. SIC: 6099—Functions Related to Deposit Banking.

★ 90184 ★ First American Bank
6911 Richmond Hwy.
Alexandria, VA 22306
(703)739-3543
Ultimate Parent: First American Corp. SIC: 6099—Functions Related to Deposit Banking.

★ 90185 ★ First American Bank Virginia
833 S. Washington St.
Alexandria, VA 22314
(703)827-8573
Ultimate Parent: First American Corp. SIC: 6022—State Commercial Banks.

★ 90186 ★ First American Bank Virginia
1705 Fern St.
Alexandria, VA 22302
(703)827-8531
Ultimate Parent: First American Corp. SIC: 6022—State Commercial Banks.

★ 90187 ★ First American Bank Virginia
326 King St.
Alexandria, VA 22314
(703)827-8793
Ultimate Parent: First American Corp. SIC: 6022—State Commercial Banks.

★ 90188 ★ First American Bank Virginia
Washington National
Alexandria, VA 22301
(703)827-8527
Ultimate Parent: First American Corp. SIC: 6022—State Commercial Banks.

★ 90189 ★ First American Bank of Virginia
1501 Duke St.
Alexandria, VA 22314
Ultimate Parent: First American Corp. SIC: 6022—State Commercial Banks.

★ 90190 ★ First American Bank of Virginia
330 N. Washington St.
Alexandria, VA 22314
(703)827-8502
Ultimate Parent: First American Corp. SIC: 6022—State Commercial Banks; 6029—Commercial Banks Nec.

★ 90191 ★ First American Bank of Virginia
6911 Richmond Hwy.
Alexandria, VA 22306
(703)241-4000
Ultimate Parent: First American Corp. SIC: 6022—State Commercial Banks.

★ 90192 ★ First American Bank of Virginia
8306 Richmond Hwy.
Alexandria, VA 22309
(703)827-8581
Ultimate Parent: First American Corp. SIC: 6022—State Commercial Banks.

★ 90193 ★ First American Bank of Virginia
4651 King St.
Alexandria, VA 22302
(703)827-8554
Ultimate Parent: First American Corp. SIC: 6022—State Commercial Banks.

★ 90194 ★ First Union National Bank of Virginia
326 King & Royal Sts.
Alexandria, VA 22314-3239
(703)739-3444
Location Type: Branch office. Ultimate Parent: First Union Corp. SIC: 6021—National Commercial Banks.

★ 90195 ★ First Union National Bank of Virginia
4651 King St.
Alexandria, VA 22302-1298
(703)284-6463
Location Type: Branch office. Ultimate Parent: First Union Corp. SIC: 6021—National Commercial Banks.

★ **90196** ★ **First Union National Bank of Virginia**
1711 Fern St.
Alexandria, VA 22302-2606
(703)284-6439
Location Type: Branch office. **Ultimate Parent:** First Union Corp. **SIC:** 6021—National Commercial Banks.

★ **90197** ★ **First Union National Bank of Virginia**
8770 Richmond Hwy.
Alexandria, VA 22309-4204
(703)739-3552
Location Type: Branch office. **Ultimate Parent:** First Union Corp. **SIC:** 6021—National Commercial Banks.

★ **90198** ★ **First Union National Bank of Virginia**
833 S. Washington St.
Alexandria, VA 22314-4295
(703)739-3469
Location Type: Branch office. **Ultimate Parent:** First Union Corp. **SIC:** 6021—National Commercial Banks.

★ **90199** ★ **First Union National Bank of Virginia**
4601 Duke St.
Alexandria, VA 22304-2505
(703)739-3495
Location Type: Branch office. **Ultimate Parent:** First Union Corp. **SIC:** 6021—National Commercial Banks.

★ **90200** ★ **First Union National Bank of Virginia**
1501 Duke St.
Alexandria, VA 22314-3449
(703)739-3480
Location Type: Branch office. **Ultimate Parent:** First Union Corp. **SIC:** 6021—National Commercial Banks.

★ **90201** ★ **First Union National Bank of Virginia**
6565 Little River Tpke.
Alexandria, VA 22312-1488
(703)739-3519
Location Type: Branch office. **Ultimate Parent:** First Union Corp. **SIC:** 6021—National Commercial Banks.

★ **90202** ★ **First Union National Bank of Virginia**
330 N. Washington St.
Alexandria, VA 22314-2554
(703)739-3400
Location Type: Branch office. **Ultimate Parent:** First Union Corp. **SIC:** 6021—National Commercial Banks.

★ **90203** ★ **First Union National Bank of Virginia**
1805 Belleview Blvd.
Alexandria, VA 22307-6731
(703)442-3505
Location Type: Branch office. **Ultimate Parent:** First Union Corp. **SIC:** 6021—National Commercial Banks.

★ **90204** ★ **First Union National Bank of Virginia**
6259 Little River Tpke.
Alexandria, VA 22312-1764
(703)442-3634
Location Type: Branch office. **Ultimate Parent:** First Union Corp. **SIC:** 6021—National Commercial Banks.

★ **90205** ★ **First Union National Bank of Virginia**
6110 Franconia Rd.
Alexandria, VA 22310-2544
(703)442-3613
Location Type: Branch office. **Ultimate Parent:** First Union Corp. **SIC:** 6021—National Commercial Banks.

★ **90206** ★ **First Union National Bank of Virginia**
7524 Richmond Hwy.
Alexandria, VA 22306-2305
(703)442-3619
Location Type: Branch office. **Ultimate Parent:** First Union Corp. **SIC:** 6021—National Commercial Banks.

★ **90207** ★ **First Union National Bank of Virginia**
7920 Fort Hunt Rd.
Alexandria, VA 22308-1203
(703)442-3616
Location Type: Branch office. **Ultimate Parent:** First Union Corp. **SIC:** 6021—National Commercial Banks.

★ **90208** ★ **First Union National Bank of Virginia**
3506 Mt. Vernon Ave.
Alexandria, VA 22305-2498
(703)442-3649
Location Type: Branch office. **Ultimate Parent:** First Union Corp. **SIC:** 6021—National Commercial Banks.

★ **90209** ★ **First Union National Bank of Virginia**
3690 King St.
Alexandria, VA 22302-1908
(703)442-3508
Location Type: Branch office. **Ultimate Parent:** First Union Corp. **SIC:** 6021—National Commercial Banks.

★ **90210** ★ **First Virginia Bank**
233 S. Van Dorn St.
Alexandria, VA 22304-4303
(703)241-3344
Location Type: Branch office. **Ultimate Parent:** First Virginia Banks Inc. **SIC:** 6021—National Commercial Banks.

★ **90211** ★ **First Virginia Bank**
7025-A Manchester Lakes Blvd.
Alexandria, VA 22310
(703)241-3587
Location Type: Branch office. **Ultimate Parent:** First Virginia Banks Inc. **SIC:** 6021—National Commercial Banks.

★ **90212** ★ **First Virginia Bank**
7960 Fort Hunt Rd.
Alexandria, VA 22308-1292
(703)241-3455
Location Type: Branch office. **Ultimate Parent:** First Virginia Banks Inc. **SIC:** 6021—National Commercial Banks.

★ **90213** ★ **First Virginia Bank**
7716 Telegraph Rd.
Alexandria, VA 22310-3896
(703)241-3431
Location Type: Branch office. **Ultimate Parent:** First Virginia Banks Inc. **SIC:** 6021—National Commercial Banks.

★ **90214** ★ **First Virginia Bank**
5203 Franconia Rd.
Alexandria, VA 22310-1930
(703)241-3465
Location Type: Branch office. **Ultimate Parent:** First Virginia Banks Inc. **SIC:** 6021—National Commercial Banks.

★ **90215** ★ **First Virginia Bank**
5838-C N. Kings Hwy.
Alexandria, VA 22303-2021
(703)241-3422
Location Type: Branch office. **Ultimate Parent:** First Virginia Banks Inc. **SIC:** 6021—National Commercial Banks.

★ **90216** ★ **First Virginia Bank**
1642 Belle View Blvd.
Alexandria, VA 22307-6531
Location Type: Branch office. **Ultimate Parent:** First Virginia Banks Inc. **SIC:** 6021—National Commercial Banks.

★ **90217** ★ **First Virginia Bank**
6618 Richmond Hwy.
Alexandria, VA 22306-6601
(703)241-3435
Location Type: Branch office. **Ultimate Parent:** First Virginia Banks Inc. **SIC:** 6021—National Commercial Banks.

★ **90218** ★ **First Virginia Bank**
8650 Richmond Hwy.
Alexandria, VA 22309-4205
(703)241-4681
Location Type: Branch office. **Ultimate Parent:** First Virginia Banks Inc. **SIC:** 6021—National Commercial Banks.

★ **90219** ★ **First Virginia Bank**
300 S. Washington St.
Alexandria, VA 22314-3672
(703)241-3311
Location Type: Branch office. **Ultimate Parent:** First Virginia Banks Inc.

★ **90220** ★ **First Virginia Bank**
4999 Seminary Rd.
Alexandria, VA 22311-1835
(703)241-3195
Location Type: Branch office. **Ultimate Parent:** First Virginia Banks Inc. **SIC:** 6021—National Commercial Banks.

★ **90221** ★ **Fruit Growers Express Co. Inc.**
1650 King St., Ste. 401
Alexandria, VA 22314-2747
(703)838-5560
Company Type: Subsidiary. **Officer:** Edward h. Latchford, President. **Ultimate Parent:** CSX Corp. **SIC:** 4741—Rental of Railroad Cars; 4789—Transportation Services Nec. **Employee Count:** 180. **Sales:** 20 M.

★ **90222** ★ **The Gap 1024**
622 King St.
Alexandria, VA 22314
(703)683-0181
Ultimate Parent: GAP. **SIC:** 5699—Miscellaneous Apparel & Accessory Stores.

★ **90223** ★ **Greyhound Bus Lines**
1519 N. Quaker Ln.
Alexandria, VA 22302
(703)998-6312
Ultimate Parent: Greyhound Lines Inc. **SIC:** 4724—Travel Agencies.

★ **90224** ★ **Harris Data Services Corp.**
1201 E. Abington Dr.
Alexandria, VA 22314
(703)739-1885 **Fax:** (703)739-1991
Company Type: Subsidiary. **Officer:** Paul Patch, Vice President. **Ultimate Parent:** Harris.

★ **90225** ★ **Hit or Miss**
6208 Little River Tpke.
Alexandria, VA 22312
(703)354-3334
Ultimate Parent: TJX. **SIC:** 5699—Miscellaneous Apparel & Accessory Stores.

★ **90226** ★ **Mary Kay Cosmetics**
6101 Edsall Rd.
Alexandria, VA 22304
(703)370-5256
Ultimate Parent: Mary Kay Cosmetics.

★ **90227** ★ **Mid-Atlantic Coca-Cola Bottling Co. Inc.**
5401 Seminary Rd.
Alexandria, VA 22313
Ultimate Parent: Coca-Cola Enterprises. **SIC:** 2086—Bottled & Canned Soft Drinks.

★ **90228** ★ **Otis Elevator Co.**
30 S. Quaker Ln.
Alexandria, VA 22314
(703)461-3400
Officer: Wayne Lamkin, Manager. **Ultimate Parent:** United Technologies. **SIC:** 3721—Aircraft.

★ **90229** ★ **Radio Shack**
Belle View Shopping Ctr.
Alexandria, VA 22307
(703)768-7575
Company Type: Division. **Ultimate Parent:** Tandy Corp. **SIC:** 5065—Electronic Parts & Equipment Nec.

★ **90230** ★ **Radio Shack**
604 King St.
Alexandria, VA 22314
(703)549-3999
Company Type: Division. **Ultimate Parent:** Tandy Corp. **SIC:** 5731—Radio, Television & Electronics Stores.

★ **90231** ★ **Radio Shack**
4660 King St.
Alexandria, VA 22302
Company Type: Division. **Ultimate Parent:** Tandy Corp. **SIC:** 5046—Commercial Equipment Nec.

★ **90232** ★ **Radio Shack**
676 S. Pickett St.
Alexandria, VA 22304
(703)370-5494
Company Type: Division. **Ultimate Parent:** Tandy Corp. **SIC:** 5251—Hardware Stores.

★ **90233** ★ **Radio Shack**
4660 King St.
Alexandria, VA 22302
Company Type: Division. **Ultimate Parent:** Tandy Corp. **SIC:** 5046—Commercial Equipment Nec.

★ **90234** ★ **Radio Shack**
Belle View Shopping Ctr.
Alexandria, VA 22307
(703)768-7575
Company Type: Division. **Ultimate Parent:** Tandy Corp. **SIC:** 5065—Electronic Parts & Equipment Nec.

★ **90235** ★ **Radio Shack**
Woodlawn Shopping Ctr.
Alexandria, VA 22309
(703)360-2666
Company Type: Division. **Ultimate Parent:** Tandy Corp. **SIC:** 5065—Electronic Parts & Equipment Nec.

★ **90236** ★ **Radio Shack**
604 King St.
Alexandria, VA 22314
(703)549-3999
Company Type: Division. **Ultimate Parent:** Tandy Corp. **SIC:** 5731—Radio, Television & Electronics Stores.

★ **90237** ★ **Radio Shack**
676 S. Pickett St.
Alexandria, VA 22304
(703)370-5494
Company Type: Division. **Ultimate Parent:** Tandy Corp. **SIC:** 5251—Hardware Stores.

★ **90238** ★ **Rite Aid**
Brightonplz
Alexandria, VA 22305
(703)354-4441
Ultimate Parent: Rite Aid. **SIC:** 5912—Drug Stores & Proprietary Stores.

★ **90239** ★ **Signet Bank, Virginia**
133 N. Fairfax St.
Alexandria, VA 22314-3272
(703)683-6371
Ultimate Parent: Signet Banking Corp. **SIC:** 6021—National Commercial Banks.

★ **90240** ★ **Tandy Electronics**
6142 Rose Hill Dr.
Alexandria, VA 22310
(703)971-4154
Ultimate Parent: Tandy Corp. **SIC:** 5719—Miscellaneous Home Furnishings Stores.

★ **90241** ★ **Turner Corp.**
6634 Elk Park Ct
Alexandria, VA 22310
(703)922-7774
Ultimate Parent: Turner Corp. **SIC:** 6531—Real Estate Agents & Managers.

★ **90242** ★ **Unijax Inc.**
828 N. Henry St.
Alexandria, VA 22314-1691
(703)684-0120
Ultimate Parent: Alco Standard Corp. **SIC:** 5113—Industrial & Personal Service Paper.

★ **90243** ★ **United Parcel Service**
1000 S. Van Dorn St.
Alexandria, VA 22304
(703)370-9840
Ultimate Parent: United Parcel Service of America.

★ **90244** ★ **United Services Automobile**
2402 Oakville St.
Alexandria, VA 22301
(703)739-2478
Ultimate Parent: USAA.

Altavista

★ **90245** ★ **Burlington Industries Inc.**
401 Amherst Ave.
Altavista, VA 24517
(804)369-4751
Officer: Graham Pope, President. **Ultimate Parent:** Burlington Industries, Equity. **SIC:** 2221—Broadwoven Fabric Mills—Manmade.

★ **90246** ★ **Lane Co. Inc.**
E. Franklin Ave.
Altavista, VA 24517
Ultimate Parent: Interco. **SIC:** 2511—Wood Household Furniture.

★ 90247 ★ **Lane Co. Inc. the**
5 St.
Altavista, VA 24517
(804)369-5641
Ultimate Parent: Interco. **SIC:** 2511—Wood Household Furniture; 2599—Furniture & Fixtures Nec.

★ 90248 ★ **Magnetek/Altavista**
201 Ogden Rd.
Altavista, VA 24517-1040
(804)369-4794
Officer: Donald A. Marr. **Ultimate Parent:** Magnetek Inc. **SIC:** 3621—Motors & Generators; 5063—Electrical Apparatus & Equipment.

★ 90249 ★ **Magnetek Universal Electric**
Altavista Works
201 Ogden Rd.
Altavista, VA 24517
Company Type: Division. **Ultimate Parent:** Magnetek Inc. **SIC:** 3621—Motors & Generators.

★ 90250 ★ **Magnetek Universal Electric Co.**
Altavista Works
201 Ogden Rd.
Altavista, VA 24517
Company Type: Division. **Ultimate Parent:** Magnetek Inc. **SIC:** 3621—Motors & Generators.

★ 90251 ★ **New York Life**
517 Main St.
Altavista, VA 24517
(804)369-7788
Ultimate Parent: New York Life. **SIC:** 6411—Insurance Agents, Brokers & Service.

★ 90252 ★ **Ross Laboratories**
Rte. 29 - Business
Altavista, VA 245170479
Ultimate Parent: Abbott Laboratories. **SIC:** 2023—Dry, Condensed & Evaporated Dairy Products.

Amherst

★ 90253 ★ **New York Life Insurance Co.**
Main St.
Amherst, VA 24521
(804)946-7987
Ultimate Parent: New York Life. **SIC:** 6411—Insurance Agents, Brokers & Service.

Annandale

★ 90254 ★ **Casual Corner**
5801 Duke St.
Annandale, VA 22003
(703)354-3202
Ultimate Parent: United States Shoe. **SIC:** 5621—Women's Clothing Stores.

★ 90255 ★ **Columbia First Bank, FSB**
6960 E. Bradlick Shopping Ctr.
Annandale, VA 22003-6090
(703)914-1205
Company Type: Subsidiary. **Location Type:** Branch office. **Ultimate Parent:** Columbia First Bank, FSB. **SIC:** 6021—National Commercial Banks.

★ 90256 ★ **Commonwealth Mortgage Assurance**
4306 Evergreen Ln.
Annandale, VA 22003
(703)642-2240
Ultimate Parent: Reliance Group Holdings. **SIC:** 6411—Insurance Agents, Brokers & Service.

★ 90257 ★ **Crestar Bank**
4250 John Marr Dr.
Annandale, VA 22003-3291
(703)813-4110
Location Type: Branch office. **Ultimate Parent:** Crestar Financial Corp. **SIC:** 6021—National Commercial Banks.

★ 90258 ★ **Crestar Bank**
7617 Little River Tpke.
Annandale, VA 22003-2603
(800)451-2435
Location Type: Branch office. **Ultimate**

Parent: Crestar Financial Corp. **SIC:** 6021—National Commercial Banks.

★ 90259 ★ **First American Bank**
4260 John Marr Dr.
Annandale, VA 22003
(703)739-3529
Ultimate Parent: First American Corp. **SIC:** 6099—Functions Related to Deposit Banking.

★ 90260 ★ **First American Bank Virginia**
6565 Little Rv Tpke.
Annandale, VA 22003
(703)827-8567
Ultimate Parent: First American Corp. **SIC:** 6022—State Commercial Banks.

★ 90261 ★ **First American Bank of Virginia**
4260 John Marr Dr.
Annandale, VA 22003
(703)827-8750
Ultimate Parent: First American Corp. **SIC:** 6022—State Commercial Banks.

★ 90262 ★ **First American Bank of Virginia**
7879 Heritage Dr.
Annandale, VA 22003
(703)821-7761
Ultimate Parent: First American Corp. **SIC:** 6022—State Commercial Banks.

★ 90263 ★ **First Union National Bank of Virginia**
7879 Heritage Dr.
Annandale, VA 22003-5394
(703)934-1860
Location Type: Branch office. **Ultimate Parent:** First Union Corp. **SIC:** 6021—National Commercial Banks.

★ 90264 ★ **First Union National Bank of Virginia**
4260 John Marr Dr.
Annandale, VA 22003-3289
(703)739-3529
Location Type: Branch office. **Ultimate Parent:** First Union Corp. **SIC:** 6021—National Commercial Banks.

★ 90265 ★ **First Union National Bank of Virginia**
7000 Bradlick Shopping Ctr.
Annandale, VA 22003-6036
(703)442-3511
Location Type: Branch office. **Ultimate Parent:** First Union Corp. **SIC:** 6021—National Commercial Banks.

★ 90266 ★ **First Virginia Bank**
7205 Little River Tpke.
Annandale, VA 22003-3375
(703)241-3333
Location Type: Branch office. **Ultimate Parent:** First Virginia Banks Inc. **SIC:** 6021—National Commercial Banks.

★ 90267 ★ **The Gap Stores**
Landmark Ctr.
Annandale, VA 22003
(703)642-9532
Ultimate Parent: GAP. **SIC:** 5699—Miscellaneous Apparel & Accessory Stores.

★ 90268 ★ **Mobil Oil Corp.**
8280 Willow Oaks Corpor
Annandale, VA 22003
(703)876-1700
Ultimate Parent: Mobil.

★ 90269 ★ **Radio Shack**
7408 Little River Tpke.
Annandale, VA 22003
(703)256-1600
Company Type: Division. **Ultimate Parent:** Tandy Corp. **SIC:** 5065—Electronic Parts & Equipment Nec.

★ 90270 ★ **Radio Shack**
7408 Little River Tpke.
Annandale, VA 22003
(703)256-1600
Company Type: Division. **Ultimate Parent:** Tandy Corp. **SIC:** 5065—Electronic Parts & Equipment Nec.

Appomattox

★ 90271 ★ **Armstrong Furniture Inc.**
Hwy. 460 E
Appomattox, VA 24522
(804)352-7181
Officer: Bruce Cowan, Manager. **Ultimate Parent:** Armstrong World Industries. **SIC:** 2511—Wood Household Furniture; 2599—Furniture & Fixtures Nec.

Arlington

★ 90272 ★ **BAII/NZ, Inc.**
1300 N. 17th St., 15th Fl.
Arlington, VA
Company Type: Division. **Ultimate Parent:** Bell Atlantic Corp.

★ 90273 ★ **Ball Corp.**
2200 Clarendon Blvd.
Arlington, VA 22201
(703)284-5400
Officer: Laurie Chiperfield, Manager. **Ultimate Parent:** Ball Corp. **SIC:** 3812—Search & Navigation Equipment.

★ 90274 ★ **Bell Atlantic Argentina, Inc.**
1300 N. 17th St., Ste. 1510
Arlington, VA 22209
Company Type: Subsidiary. **Ultimate Parent:** Bell Atlantic Corp.

★ 90275 ★ **Bell Atlantic Asia, Inc.**
1300 N. 17th St., Ste. 1510
Arlington, VA 22209
Company Type: Subsidiary. **Ultimate Parent:** Bell Atlantic Corp.

★ 90276 ★ **Bell Atlantic International, Inc.**
1300 N. 17th St., Ste. 1510
Arlington, VA 22209
(703)875-8800
Company Type: Subsidiary. **Officer:** Edgar Brown Jr., President. **Ultimate Parent:** Bell Atlantic Corp. **SIC:** 5065—Electronic Parts & Equipment Nec.

★ 90277 ★ **Bell Atlantic Network SErvices Inc.**
1310 N. Court House Rd.
Arlington, VA 22201
(703)974-3000
Company Type: Subsidiary. **Ultimate Parent:** Bell Atlantic Corp. **SIC:** 4813—Telephone Communications Except Radiotelephone.

★ 90278 ★ **Bell Atlantic Puerto Rico, Inc.**
1300 N. 17th St., Ste. 1510
Arlington, VA 22209
Company Type: Subsidiary. **Ultimate Parent:** Bell Atlantic Corp.

★ 90279 ★ **Bell Atlantic Software & Systems Solutions, Inc.**
1550 Wilson Blvd., 5th Fl.
Arlington, VA 22209
(703)516-2900 **Fax:** (703)516-2930
Company Type: Subsidiary. **Officer:** Jeffrey S. McDermott, Chm. Bd. & CEO. **Ultimate Parent:** Bell Atlantic Corp. **SIC:** 7373—Computer Integrated Systems Design.

★ 90280 ★ **Boeing Co**
1700 N. Moore St.
Arlington, VA 22209
(703)558-9600
Ultimate Parent: Boeing. **SIC:** 7374—Data Processing & Preparation.

★ 90281 ★ **Casual Corner**
Crystal Sq.
Arlington, VA 22202
(703)920-7950
Ultimate Parent: United States Shoe. **SIC:** 5621—Women's Clothing Stores.

★ 90282 ★ **Centech Group**
4200 Wilson Blvd.
Arlington, VA 22203-1800
(703)525-5818
Officer: Fernando V. Galaviz. **Ultimate Parent:** Bethlehem Steel Corp. **SIC:** 7374—Data Processing & Preparation.

★ 90283 ★ **Chrysler Technologies Corp.**
1725 Jefferson Davis Hwy.
Arlington, VA 22202
(703)521-8540
Officer: Paul E. Wright, Chairman & President. **Ultimate Parent:** Chrysler Corp.

★ 90284 ★ **Columbia First Bank, FSB**
1560 Wilson Blvd.
Arlington, VA 22209
(703)247-5000
Company Type: Headquarters. **Officer:** Thomas J. Schaefer. **SIC:** 6159—Miscellaneous Business Credit Institutions; 6036—Savings Institutions Except Federal. **Employee Count:** 504. **Fortune Service 500:** Ranking 43.

★ 90285 ★ **Columbia 1st Bank FSB**
1560 Wilson Blvd.
Arlington, VA 22209-2409
(703)247-5000
Officer: Thomas J. Schaefer, Pr CEO. **Ultimate Parent:** Columbia First Bank, FSB. **SIC:** 6035—Federal Savings Institutions. **Employee Count:** 445.

★ 90286 ★ **Crestar Bank**
4710 Lee Hwy.
Arlington, VA 22207-3486
(703)838-3360
Location Type: Branch office. **Ultimate Parent:** Crestar Financial Corp. **SIC:** 6021—National Commercial Banks.

★ 90287 ★ **Crestar Bank**
6711 Lee Hwy.
Arlington, VA 22205-1999
(703)838-3344
Location Type: Branch office. **Ultimate Parent:** Crestar Financial Corp. **SIC:** 6021—National Commercial Banks.

★ 90288 ★ **Crestar Bank**
4259 Wilson Blvd.
Arlington, VA 22203-1859
(703)838-3430
Location Type: Branch office. **Ultimate Parent:** Crestar Financial Corp. **SIC:** 6021—National Commercial Banks.

★ 90289 ★ **Crestar Bank**
2050 Wilson Blvd.
Arlington, VA 22203
(703)838-3430
Location Type: Branch office. **Ultimate Parent:** Crestar Financial Corp. **SIC:** 6021—National Commercial Banks.

★ 90290 ★ **Crestar Bank**
3141 Lee Hwy.
Arlington, VA 22201-4294
Location Type: Branch office. **Ultimate Parent:** Crestar Financial Corp. **SIC:** 6021—National Commercial Banks.

★ 90291 ★ **Crestar Bank**
3108 Columbia Pke.
Arlington, VA 22204-4397
(703)838-3410
Location Type: Branch office. **Ultimate Parent:** Crestar Financial Corp. **SIC:** 6021—National Commercial Banks.

★ 90292 ★ **Crestar Bank**
5335 Lee Hwy.
Arlington, VA 22207-1607
Location Type: Branch office. **Ultimate Parent:** Crestar Financial Corp. **SIC:** 6021—National Commercial Banks.

★ 90293 ★ **Crestar Bank**
4601 N. Fairfax Dr.
Arlington, VA 22203-1500
Location Type: Branch office. **Ultimate Parent:** Crestar Financial Corp. **SIC:** 6021—National Commercial Banks.

★ 90294 ★ **Crestar Bank**
1000 Wilson Blvd.
Arlington, VA 22209-2230
Location Type: Branch office. **Ultimate Parent:** Crestar Financial Corp. **SIC:** 6021—National Commercial Banks.

★ 90295 ★ **Crestar Bank**
249 N. Glebe Rd.
Arlington, VA 22203-3789
Location Type: Branch office. **Ultimate Parent:** Crestar Financial Corp. **SIC:** 6021—National Commercial Banks.

★ 90296 ★ Cretar Bank
3040 N. Clarenden Blvd.
Arlington, VA 22201-2804
Location Type: Branch office. Ultimate
Parent: Crestar Financial Corp. SIC:
6021—National Commercial Banks.

★ 90297 ★ Exxon Car Care
Center
6730 Lee Hwy.
Arlington, VA 22205
(703)536-6401
Ultimate Parent: Exxon. SIC: 7538—
General Automotive Repair Shops.

★ 90298 ★ Exxon Car Care
Center
Columbia Pike
Arlington, VA 22204
(703)920-2220
Ultimate Parent: Exxon. SIC: 7538—
General Automotive Repair Shops.

★ 90299 ★ Exxon Car Wash
6720 Lee Hwy.
Arlington, VA 22205
(703)536-2778
Ultimate Parent: Exxon. SIC: 7542—Car
Washes.

★ 90300 ★ Federal Home Loan
Mortgage Corp. (Freddic Mac)-
Northeast Region
2231 Crystal Dr., Ste. 900
Arlington, VA 22202
(703)685-4500
Location Type: Branch office. Ultimate
Parent: Federal Home Loan Mortgage. SIC:
6111—Federal & Federally-Sponsored
Credit.

★ 90301 ★ First American Bank
Big North Post
Arlington, VA 22211
(703)284-6428
Ultimate Parent: First American Corp. SIC:
6099—Functions Related to Deposit
Banking.

★ 90302 ★ First American Bank
951 S. George Mason Dr.
Arlington, VA 22204
(703)284-6492
Ultimate Parent: First American Corp. SIC:
6099—Functions Related to Deposit
Banking.

★ 90303 ★ First American Bank
1701 N. Mckinley Rd.
Arlington, VA 22205
(703)284-6552
Ultimate Parent: First American Corp. SIC:
6099—Functions Related to Deposit
Banking.

★ 90304 ★ First American Bank
1111 Army Navy Dr.
Arlington, VA 22202
(703)284-6540
Ultimate Parent: First American Corp. SIC:
6099—Functions Related to Deposit
Banking.

★ 90305 ★ First American Bank
2001 Jeff Davis Hwy.
Arlington, VA 22202
(703)284-6523
Ultimate Parent: First American Corp. SIC:
6099—Functions Related to Deposit
Banking.

★ 90306 ★ First American Bank
1515 N. Court House Rd.
Arlington, VA 22201
(703)284-6310
Ultimate Parent: First American Corp. SIC:
6099—Functions Related to Deposit
Banking.

★ 90307 ★ First American Bank
1011 N. Stafford St.
Arlington, VA 22201
(703)284-6384
Ultimate Parent: First American Corp. SIC:
6099—Functions Related to Deposit
Banking.

★ 90308 ★ First American Bank
Virginia
Navy Annex
Arlington, VA 22217
(703)827-8684
Ultimate Parent: First American Corp. SIC:
6022—State Commercial Banks.

★ 90309 ★ First American Bank
Virginia
Fort Myer Bldg.
Arlington, VA 22209
(703)821-7641
Ultimate Parent: First American Corp. SIC:
6022—State Commercial Banks.

★ 90310 ★ First American Bank
Virginia
1501 Wilson Blvd.
Arlington, VA 22209
(703)821-7671
Ultimate Parent: First American Corp. SIC:
6022—State Commercial Banks.

★ 90311 ★ First American Bank
of Virginia
1930 Jeff Davis Hwy.
Arlington, VA 22202
(703)821-7631
Ultimate Parent: First American Corp. SIC:
6022—State Commercial Banks.

★ 90312 ★ First American Bank
of Virginia
2001 Jeff Davis Hwy.
Arlington, VA 22202
(703)827-8660
Ultimate Parent: First American Corp. SIC:
6022—State Commercial Banks.

★ 90313 ★ First American Bank
of Virginia
1200 Wilson Blvd.
Arlington, VA 22209
(703)827-8708
Ultimate Parent: First American Corp. SIC:
6022—State Commercial Banks.

★ 90314 ★ First American Bank
of Virginia
1701 N. Mckinley Rd.
Arlington, VA 22205
(703)821-7681
Ultimate Parent: First American Corp. SIC:
6022—State Commercial Banks; 6029—
Commercial Banks Nec.

★ 90315 ★ First American Bank
of Virginia
2213 N. Glebe Rd.
Arlington, VA 22207
(703)827-8672
Ultimate Parent: First American Corp. SIC:
6022—State Commercial Banks.

★ 90316 ★ First American Bank
of Virginia
2300 9th St. S
Arlington, VA 22204
(703)827-8650
Ultimate Parent: First American Corp. SIC:
6022—State Commercial Banks.

★ 90317 ★ First American Bank
of Virginia
951 S. George Mason Dr.
Arlington, VA 22204
(703)827-8630
Ultimate Parent: First American Corp. SIC:
6022—State Commercial Banks.

★ 90318 ★ First American Bank
of Virginia
3140 Washington Blvd.
Arlington, VA 22201
(703)821-7516
Ultimate Parent: First American Corp. SIC:
6022—State Commercial Banks.

★ 90319 ★ First American Bank
of Virginia
1111 Army Navy Dr.
Arlington, VA 22202
(703)827-8645
Ultimate Parent: First American Corp. SIC:
6022—State Commercial Banks.

★ 90320 ★ First American Bank
of Virginia
1515 N. Court House Rd.
Arlington, VA 22201
(703)827-8765
Ultimate Parent: First American Corp. SIC:
6022—State Commercial Banks.

★ 90321 ★ First American Bank
of Virginia
1011 N. Stafford St.
Arlington, VA 22201
(703)827-8620
Ultimate Parent: First American Corp. SIC:
6022—State Commercial Banks.

★ 90322 ★ First Union Natinal
Bank of Virginia
6500 Williamsburg Blvd.
Arlington, VA 22213-1329
(703)284-6557
Location Type: Branch office. Ultimate
Parent: First Union Corp. SIC: 6021—
National Commercial Banks.

★ 90323 ★ First Union National
Bank of Virginia
951 S. George Mason Dr.
Arlington, VA 22204-1566
(703)284-6492
Location Type: Branch office. Ultimate
Parent: First Union Corp. SIC: 6021—
National Commercial Banks.

★ 90324 ★ First Union National
Bank of Virginia
3140 N. Washington Blvd.
Arlington, VA 22201-4616
(703)284-6371
Location Type: Branch office. Ultimate
Parent: First Union Corp. SIC: 6021—
National Commercial Banks.

★ 90325 ★ First Union National
Bank of Virginia
1515 N. Courthouse Rd.
Arlington, VA 22201-2909
(703)284-6310
Location Type: Branch office. Ultimate
Parent: First Union Corp. SIC: 6021—
National Commercial Banks.

★ 90326 ★ First Union National
Bank of Virginia
2001 Jefferson Davis Hwy.
Arlington, VA 22202-3604
(703)284-6520
Location Type: Branch office. Ultimate
Parent: First Union Corp. SIC: 6021—
National Commercial Banks.

★ 90327 ★ First Union National
Bank of Virginia
567 S. 23rd St.
Arlington, VA 22202-2517
(703)284-6473
Location Type: Branch office. Ultimate
Parent: First Union Corp. SIC: 6021—
National Commercial Banks.

★ 90328 ★ First Union National
Bank of Virginia
2300 S. 9th St.
Arlington, VA 22204-2320
(703)284-6508
Location Type: Branch office. Ultimate
Parent: First Union Corp. SIC: 6021—
National Commercial Banks.

★ 90329 ★ First Union National
Bank of Virginia
1701 N. McKinley Rd.
Arlington, VA 22205-2940
(703)284-6552
Location Type: Branch office. Ultimate
Parent: First Union Corp. SIC: 6021—
National Commercial Banks.

★ 90330 ★ First Union National
Bank of Virginia
1011 N. Stafford St.
Arlington, VA 22201-4695
(703)284-6384
Location Type: Branch office. Ultimate
Parent: First Union Corp. SIC: 6021—
National Commercial Banks.

★ 90331 ★ First Union Nationl
Bank of Virginia
2213 N. Glebe Rd.
Arlington, VA 22207-3499
(703)284-6395
Location Type: Branch office. Ultimate
Parent: First Union Corp. SIC: 6021—
National Commercial Banks.

★ 90332 ★ First Virginia Bank
2947 S. Glebe Rd.
Arlington, VA 22206-2710
(703)241-3161
Location Type: Branch office. Ultimate
Parent: First Virginia Banks Inc. SIC:
6021—National Commercial Banks.

★ 90333 ★ First Virginia Bank
Arlington Courthouse
2200 Wilson Blvd.
Arlington, VA 22201-3324
(703)241-3211
Location Type: Branch office. Ultimate

Parent: First Virginia Banks Inc. SIC:
6021—National Commercial Banks.

★ 90334 ★ First Virginia Bank
920 N. Taylor St.
Arlington, VA 22203-1818
(703)241-3222
Location Type: Branch office. Ultimate
Parent: First Virginia Banks Inc. SIC:
6021—National Commercial Banks.

★ 90335 ★ First Virginia Bank
2221 S. Eads St.
Arlington, VA 22202-4606
(703)241-3151
Location Type: Branch office. Ultimate
Parent: First Virginia Banks Inc. SIC:
6021—National Commercial Banks.

★ 90336 ★ First Virginia Bank
5515 Lee Hwy.
Arlington, VA 22207-1613
(703)241-3141
Location Type: Branch office. Ultimate
Parent: First Virginia Banks Inc. SIC:
6021—National Commercial Banks.

★ 90337 ★ First Virginia Bank
1469 Jefferson Daris Hwy.
Arlington, VA 22202-3229
(703)241-3275
Location Type: Branch office. Ultimate
Parent: First Virginia Banks Inc. SIC:
6021—National Commercial Banks.

★ 90338 ★ First Virginia Bank
4707 Lee Hwy.
Arlington, VA 22207-3487
(703)241-3244
Location Type: Branch office. Ultimate
Parent: First Virginia Banks Inc. SIC:
6021—National Commercial Banks.

★ 90339 ★ First Virginia Bank
5037 Columbia Pke.
Arlington, VA 22204-2906
(703)241-3111
Location Type: Branch office. Ultimate
Parent: First Virginia Banks Inc. SIC:
6021—National Commercial Banks.

★ 90340 ★ First Virginia Bank
3001 N. Washington Blvd.
Arlington, VA 22201-2117
(703)241-3271
Location Type: Branch office. Ultimate
Parent: First Virginia Banks Inc. SIC:
6021—National Commercial Banks.

★ 90341 ★ First Virginia Bank
6745 Lee Hwy.
Arlington, VA 22205-1925
(703)241-3555
Location Type: Branch office. Ultimate
Parent: First Virginia Banks Inc. SIC:
6021—National Commercial Banks.

★ 90342 ★ First Virginia Bank
2700 S. Quincy St.
Arlington, VA 22206-2226
(703)241-3288
Location Type: Branch office. Ultimate
Parent: First Virginia Banks Inc. SIC:
6021—National Commercial Banks.

★ 90343 ★ First Virginia Bank
1901 N. Fort Myer Dr.
Arlington, VA 22209-1604
(703)241-3131
Location Type: Branch office. Ultimate
Parent: First Virginia Banks Inc. SIC:
6021—National Commercial Banks.

★ 90344 ★ First Virginia Bank
2113 Grystal Plz. Arcade
Arlington, VA 22202
(703)241-3275
Location Type: Branch office. Ultimate
Parent: First Virginia Banks Inc. SIC:
6021—National Commercial Banks.

★ 90345 ★ Gannett
1100 Wilson Blvd.
Arlington, VA 22234
(703)284-6000
Company Type: Headquarters. Officer:
John J. Curley. Sales: 3641.6 M. Fortune
500: Largest U.S. Industrial Corporations:
Ranking 138.

★ 90346 ★ Gannett
Newspaper Division
1100 Wilson Blvd.
Arlington, VA 22234
(703)284-6777
Officer: Gary L. Watson, President.
Ultimate Parent: Gannett.

★ 90347 ★ Gannett Broadcasting
1100 Wilson Blvd.
Arlington, VA 22234
(703)284-6767
Officer: Cecil L. Walker, President & CEO.
Ultimate Parent: Gannett.

★ 90348 ★ Gannett Co., Inc.
1100 Wilson Blvd.
Arlington, VA 22234
(703)284-6000
Officer: John J. Curley, Chairman,
President & CEO. Ultimate Parent:
Gannett. Employee Count: 36700.

★ 90349 ★ Gannett New Media
Services
1000 Wilson Blvd.
Arlington, VA 22229
(703)276-5357 Fax: (703)276-5357
Officer: Thomas J. Ferrell, President.
Ultimate Parent: Gannett.

★ 90350 ★ Gannett News Service
1000 Wilson Blvd.
Arlington, VA 22229
(703)284-5800 Fax: (703)243-0190
Officer: Robert Ritter, Editor. Ultimate
Parent: Gannett.

★ 90351 ★ Gannett Supply Corp.
1100 Wilson Blvd.
Arlington, VA 22234
(703)284-6701 Fax: (703)524-8427
Officer: William Metzfield, President.
Ultimate Parent: Gannett.

★ 90352 ★ Gannett
Telemarketing Inc.
1100 Wilson Blvd.
Arlington, VA 22234
(703)284-6660
Officer: Robert T. Burns, President &
General Manager. Ultimate Parent:
Gannett.

★ 90353 ★ Gannett Television
1100 Wilson Blvd.
Arlington, VA 22234
(703)284-6789
Officer: Ronald Townsend, President.
Ultimate Parent: Gannett.

★ 90354 ★ General Dynamics
Corp.
1745 Jefferson Davis, No. 1000
Arlington, VA 22202
(703)553-1200
Officer: Alan C. Chase, President. Ultimate
Parent: General Dynamics. SIC: 3721—
Aircraft.

★ 90355 ★ Grumman Corp.
1000 Wilson Blvd.
Arlington, VA 22209
(703)276-4900
Ultimate Parent: Northrop Corp. SIC:
3721—Aircraft.

★ 90356 ★ Macy's
1000 S. Hayes St.
Arlington, VA 22202
(703)418-4488
Ultimate Parent: R. H. Macy.

★ 90357 ★ Mary Kay Cosmetics
716 22nd St. S
Arlington, VA 22202
(703)979-7528
Ultimate Parent: Mary Kay Cosmetics. SIC:
5999—Miscellaneous Retail Stores Nec.

★ 90358 ★ McDonald's
Hamburgers
1823 N. Moore St.
Arlington, VA 22209
(703)528-1259
Ultimate Parent: McDonald's. SIC: 5812—
Eating Places.

★ 90359 ★ MCI Consumer
Markets
1200 S. Hayes St.
Arlington, VA 22202
(703)415-6000 Fax: (703)415-6976
Officer: Gerald H. Taylor, President.
Ultimate Parent: MCI Communications.

★ 90360 ★ Metropolitan Federal
Saving
2930 Wilson Blvd.
Arlington, VA 22201
(703)524-6880
Ultimate Parent: Metropolitan Financial.
SIC: 6035—Federal Savings Institutions.

★ 90361 ★ Mobil Oil Corp.
Washington Blvd.
Arlington, VA 22201
(703)528-0646
Ultimate Parent: Mobil.

★ 90362 ★ New York Life
Insurance Co.
1655 Fort Myer Dr.
Arlington, VA 22209
(703)525-1088
Ultimate Parent: New York Life. SIC:
6411—Insurance Agents, Brokers &
Service.

★ 90363 ★ New York Life
Insurance Co.
1000 Wilson Blvd.
Arlington, VA 22209
(703)841-4500
Ultimate Parent: New York Life. SIC:
6411—Insurance Agents, Brokers &
Service.

★ 90364 ★ Nordstrom
1400 S. Hayes St.
Arlington, VA 22202
(703)415-1121
Ultimate Parent: Nordstrom.

★ 90365 ★ Oracle Complex
Systems Corp.
1110 N. Glebe Rd., Ste. 1100
Arlington, VA 22201
(703)875-7660 Fax: (703)875-0489
Officer: George Dreyer, President. Ultimate
Parent: Oracle Systems.

★ 90366 ★ Payless Shoesource
4238 Wilson Blvd. 2180
Arlington, VA 22203
(703)243-0515
Ultimate Parent: May Department Stores.
SIC: 5661—Shoe Stores.

★ 90367 ★ Radio Shack
Virginia Sq.
Arlington, VA 22206
(703)524-5541
Company Type: Division. Ultimate Parent:
Tandy Corp. SIC: 5734—Computer &
Software Stores.

★ 90368 ★ Radio Shack
1117 17th St. S
Arlington, VA 22202
(703)524-8535
Company Type: Division. Ultimate Parent:
Tandy Corp. SIC: 5065—Electronic Parts &
Equipment Nec.

★ 90369 ★ Radio Shack
3441 Fairfax Dr.
Arlington, VA 22201
(703)524-5540
Company Type: Division. Ultimate Parent:
Tandy Corp. SIC: 5065—Electronic Parts &
Equipment Nec.

★ 90370 ★ Radio Shack
1735 Jefferson Davis Hwy.
Arlington, VA 22202
(703)979-5585
Company Type: Division. Ultimate Parent:
Tandy Corp. SIC: 5065—Electronic Parts &
Equipment Nec.

★ 90371 ★ Radio Shack
1735 Jeff Davis Hwy.
Arlington, VA 22202
(703)979-5585
Company Type: Division. Ultimate Parent:
Tandy Corp. SIC: 5065—Electronic Parts &
Equipment Nec.

★ 90372 ★ Radio Shack
1911 Fort Myer Dr.
Arlington, VA 22209
(703)243-5955
Company Type: Division. Ultimate Parent:
Tandy Corp. SIC: 5046—Commercial
Equipment Nec.

★ 90373 ★ Radio Shack
Ballston Commons Mall
Arlington, VA 22203
(703)522-2087
Company Type: Division. Ultimate Parent:
Tandy Corp. SIC: 5734—Computer &
Software Stores.

★ 90374 ★ Radio Shack
Virginia Sq.
Arlington, VA 22206
(703)524-5541
Company Type: Division. Ultimate Parent:
Tandy Corp. SIC: 5734—Computer &
Software Stores.

★ 90375 ★ Radio Shack
Crystal
Arlington, VA 22202
(703)521-0520
Company Type: Division. Ultimate Parent:
Tandy Corp. SIC: 5065—Electronic Parts &
Equipment Nec.

★ 90376 ★ Radio Shack
1117 17th St. S
Arlington, VA 22202
(703)524-8535
Company Type: Division. Ultimate Parent:
Tandy Corp. SIC: 5065—Electronic Parts &
Equipment Nec.

★ 90377 ★ Radio Shack
3441 Fairfax Dr.
Arlington, VA 22201
(703)524-5540
Company Type: Division. Ultimate Parent:
Tandy Corp. SIC: 5065—Electronic Parts &
Equipment Nec.

★ 90378 ★ Raychem Corp.
2341 Jeff Davis Hwy.
Arlington, VA 22202
(703)979-4000
Ultimate Parent: Raychem Corp. SIC:
5065—Electronic Parts & Equipment Nec.

★ 90379 ★ Raytheon Corporate
Jets
1101 Wilson Blvd. 1200
Arlington, VA 22209
(703)243-3939
Officer: Peter Boxer, President. Ultimate
Parent: Raytheon Co. SIC: 3721—Aircraft.

★ 90380 ★ Rite Aid
1667 Crystal Sq.
Arlington, VA 22202
(703)920-5218
Ultimate Parent: Rite Aid.

★ 90381 ★ Rite Aid
2503 N. Harrisonst
Arlington, VA 22207
(703)536-7333
Ultimate Parent: Rite Aid. SIC: 7384—
Photofinishing Laboratories.

★ 90382 ★ Signet Bank, Virginia
4736 Lee Hwy.
Arlington, VA 22207-3416
(703)750-7134
Ultimate Parent: Signet Banking Corp. SIC:
6021—National Commercial Banks.

★ 90383 ★ Signet Bank, Virginia
2200 Claredon Blvd.
Arlington, VA 22201
(703)525-6621
Ultimate Parent: Signet Banking Corp. SIC:
6021—National Commercial Banks.

★ 90384 ★ Signet Bank, Virginia
1755 Jefferson Davis Hwy.
Arlington, VA 22202-3501
(703)750-7111
Ultimate Parent: Signet Banking Corp. SIC:
6021—National Commercial Banks.

★ 90385 ★ Signet Bank, Virginia
6045 Wilson Blvd.
Arlington, VA 22205-1526
(703)536-3036
Ultimate Parent: Signet Banking Corp. SIC:
6021—National Commercial Banks.

★ 90386 ★ Signet Bank, Virginia
2011 Crystal Park Dr.
Arlington, VA 22202-3709
(703)797-7004
Ultimate Parent: Signet Banking Corp. SIC:
6021—National Commercial Banks.

★ 90387 ★ Signet Bank, Virginia
901 N. Stuart St.
Arlington, VA 22203
(703)525-7726
Ultimate Parent: Signet Banking Corp. SIC:
6021—National Commercial Banks.

★ 90388 ★ Signet Bank, Virginia
1815 N. Fort Myer Dr.
Arlington, VA 22209-2401
(703)525-4355
Ultimate Parent: Signet Banking Corp. SIC:
6021—National Commercial Banks.

★ 90389 ★ TRW Information Svc.
1001 19th St. N, No. 800
Arlington, VA 22209
(703)276-5000
Officer: John Castellani, Vice President.
Ultimate Parent: TRW, Inc. SIC: 3999—
Manufacturing Industries Nec.

★ 90390 ★ USA Today
1100 Wilson Blvd.
Arlington, VA 22234
Officer: Thomas Curley, Publisher &
President. Ultimate Parent: Gannett.

★ 90391 ★ USAIR Group
2345 Crystal Dr.
Arlington, VA 22227
(703)418-7000
Company Type: Headquarters. Officer:
Seth E. Schofield. Employee Count:
48500. Sales: 7083 M. Fortune Service
500: Ranking 9.

★ 90392 ★ Waldenbooks
Ballston Commons
Arlington, VA 22203
(703)527-2442
Ultimate Parent: K-Mart. SIC: 5942—Book
Stores.

★ 90393 ★ Washington D.C.
Government Affairs Office
1901 N. Moore St., Ste. 609
Arlington, VA 22209-1772
(703)524-2310 Fax: (703)524-5575
Company Type: Subsidiary. Officer: Harry
Foulkrod, Vice President of Operations.
Ultimate Parent: E-Systems Inc.

★ 90394 ★ Xerox Corp.
1616 Fort Myers Dr.
Arlington, VA 22209
(703)527-6400
Officer: Dave Garnett, Vice President.
Ultimate Parent: Xerox Corp. SIC: 3577—
Computer Peripheral Equipment Nec;
3663—Radio & T.V. Communications
Equipment.

★ 90395 ★ Xerox Corp.
1530 Wilson Blvd.
Arlington, VA 22209
(703)841-0900
Officer: Art Corrales, Manager. Ultimate
Parent: Xerox Corp. SIC: 2759—
Commercial Printing Nec.

★ 90396 ★ Wall Street Journal
Pentagon Bldg. Roo
Arlington Vir, VA 22202
(703)892-4251
Ultimate Parent: Dow Jones.

Ashburn

★ 90397 ★ E-Systems Inc.
44983 Knoll Sq.
Ashburn, VA 22011
(703)729-6000
Officer: Talbot S. Huff, President. Ultimate
Parent: E-Systems Inc. SIC: 3612—
Transformers Except Electronic.

Ashland

★ 90398 ★ Baxter Healthcare
Corp. Prescr
98 Lakeridge Pky.
Ashland, VA 23005-9460
(804)550-4100
Officer: Olaf Berghiem. Ultimate Parent:
Baxter International. SIC: 5122—Drugs,
Proprietaries & Sundries.

★ 90399 ★ Bear Island Paper Co.
Rte. 738 E
Ashland, VA 23005
(804)227-3394
Ultimate Parent: Dow Jones. SIC: 2621—
Paper Mills.

★ 90400 ★ Bear Island Paper Co.
PO Box 2119
Ashland, VA 23005
(804)227-3394
Officer: Gary Graham, General Manager.
Ultimate Parent: Dow Jones. SIC: 2621—
Paper Mills.

★ 90401 ★ Crestar Bank
101 England St.
Ashland, VA 23005
(804)273-7510
Location Type: Branch office. Ultimate
Parent: Crestar Financial Corp. SIC:
6021—National Commercial Banks.

★ 90402 ★ Food Lion
3327 Kings Charter Dr.
Ashland, VA 23005
(804)550-2502
Ultimate Parent: Food Lion. SIC: 5499—
Miscellaneous Food Stores.

★ 90403 ★ Food Lion Inc.
3327 Kings Charter Dr.
Ashland, VA 23005
(804)550-2502
Ultimate Parent: Food Lion. SIC: 5499—
Miscellaneous Food Stores.

★ 90404 ★ Mobil Chemical Co.
Atlee Rd. I95
Ashland, VA 23005
(804)798-4291
Ultimate Parent: Mobil. SIC: 1011—Iron
Ores.

★ 90405 ★ Mobil Mining &
Minerals Compan
96 Lakeridge Pky.
Ashland, VA 23005-9460
(804)550-2636
Company Type: Branch. Officer: F. Max
Merrell. Ultimate Parent: Mobil. SIC:
2874—Phosphatic Fertilizers; 1221—
Bituminous Coal & Lignite—Surface; 1499—
Miscellaneous Nonmetallic Minerals; 2879—
Agricultural Chemicals Nec.

★ 90406 ★ Penske Truck Leasing
115 Sylvia Rd.
Ashland, VA 23005
(804)798-0083
Ultimate Parent: Penske Truck Leasing.
SIC: 7514—Passenger Car Rental.

★ 90407 ★ Radio Shack
109 N. Washington Hwy.
Ashland, VA 23005
(804)798-5451
Company Type: Division. Ultimate Parent:
Tandy Corp. SIC: 5065—Electronic Parts &
Equipment Nec.

Assawoman

★ 90408 ★ Syscon Corp.
180 Rural Route 1
Assawoman, VA 23302
(804)824-0130
Ultimate Parent: Harnischfeger Industries.

Atkins

★ 90409 ★ Lowe's
Bear Creek Rd.
Atkins, VA 24311
(703)228-2100
Ultimate Parent: Lowe's. SIC: 5722—
Household Appliance Stores.

★ 90410 ★ Merillat Ind. Inc.
PO Box 259 Rte. 11
Atkins, VA 24311
Ultimate Parent: Masco. SIC: 2426—
Hardwood Dimension & Flooring Mills.

★ 90411 ★ Merillat Industries Inc.
Rte. 11
Atkins, VA 24311
Ultimate Parent: Masco. SIC: 2426—
Hardwood Dimension & Flooring Mills.

Bailey Crossroads

★ 90412 ★ First Virginia Bank
5871 Leesburg Pke.
Bailey Crossroads, VA 22041-2310
(703)241-3375
Location Type: Branch office. Ultimate
Parent: First Virginia Banks Inc. SIC:
6021—National Commercial Banks.

★ 90413 ★ Rite Aid
1700 N. Moore St.
Baileys Crossroad, VA 22042
(703)527-2201
Ultimate Parent: Rite Aid.

Bassett

★ 90414 ★ Aeroquip Corp.
Rivermont Rd.
Bassett, VA 24055
(703)629-5317
Officer: Terry Cundiff, Manager. Ultimate
Parent: Trinova Corp. SIC: 3089—Plastics
Products Nec.

★ 90415 ★ First Union National
Bank of Virginia
210-211 Main St.
Bassett, VA 24055
(703)629-5311
Location Type: Branch office. Ultimate
Parent: First Union Corp. SIC: 6021—
National Commercial Banks.

★ 90416 ★ New York Life
Insurance
RR 1
Bassett, VA 24055
(703)629-3311
Ultimate Parent: New York Life. SIC:
6311—Life Insurance; 6411—Insurance
Agents, Brokers & Service.

Beaverdam

★ 90417 ★ Crestar Bank
Rte. 739
Beaverdam, VA 23015-0068
(804)449-6275
Location Type: Branch office. Ultimate
Parent: Crestar Financial Corp. SIC:
6021—National Commercial Banks.

Bedford

★ 90418 ★ First Union National
Bank of Virginia
1621 Forrest Rd.
Bedford, VA 24523-2307
(703)586-8733
Location Type: Branch office. Ultimate
Parent: First Union Corp. SIC: 6021—
National Commercial Banks.

★ 90419 ★ First Union National
Bank of Virginia
101 N. Bridge St.
Bedford, VA 24523-1923
(703)586-8292
Location Type: Branch office. Ultimate
Parent: First Union Corp. SIC: 6021—
National Commercial Banks.

★ 90420 ★ Food Lion
1515 Longwood Ave.
Bedford, VA 24523
(703)586-3867
Ultimate Parent: Food Lion. SIC: 5411—
Grocery Stores.

★ 90421 ★ Food Lion Inc.
1515 Longwood Ave.
Bedford, VA 24523
(703)586-3867
Ultimate Parent: Food Lion. SIC: 5411—
Grocery Stores.

★ 90422 ★ Golden West Foods,
Inc.
PO Box 334
Bedford, VA 24523
(703)586-8284 Fax: (703)586-1072
Officer: Steen A. Metz, President. Ultimate
Parent: McCormick & Co. Inc.

★ 90423 ★ Golden West Foods,
Inc.
940 Orange St.
Bedford, VA 24523
(703)586-8284 Fax: (703)586-5101
Company Type: Subsidiary. Location
Type: Plant. Officer: Steve Metz, President.
Ultimate Parent: McCormick & Co. Inc.
SIC: 2038—Frozen Specialties Nec; 2013—
Sausages & Other Prepared Meats.

★ 90424 ★ Wal-Mart Discount
Store
109 Us 460 E
Bedford, VA 24523
(703)586-6171
Ultimate Parent: Wal-Mart Stores, Inc. SIC:
5311—Department Stores.

★ 90425 ★ Westvaco Corp.
1587 Dawn Dr.
Bedford, VA 24523
(703)586-2251
Ultimate Parent: WestVaco Corp. SIC:
2631—Paperboard Mills.

Bee

★ 90426 ★ Riverside Grocery
Rural Route a
Bee, VA 24217
(703)859-2211
Ultimate Parent: Penn Traffic. SIC: 5411—
Grocery Stores.

Belle Haven

★ 90427 ★ Farmers & Merchants
Bank-Eastern Shore
36344 Lankford Hwy.
Belle Haven, VA 23306
(804)442-2000
Location Type: Branch office. Officer:
Paula M. Chapman, President. Ultimate
Parent: Mercantile Bankshares Corp. SIC:
6021—National Commercial Banks.

★ 90428 ★ McDonald's
Hamburgers
Rural Route 13
Belle Haven, VA 23306
(804)442-3534
Ultimate Parent: McDonald's. SIC: 5812—
Eating Places.

Berryville

★ 90429 ★ Radio Shack
107 W. Main St.
Berryville, VA 22611
(703)955-2130
Company Type: Division. Ultimate Parent:
Tandy Corp. SIC: 5013—Motor Vehicle
Supplies & New Parts.

★ 90430 ★ Radio Shack
Div. of Tandy Corp.
107 W. Main St.
Berryville, VA 22611
(703)955-2130
Company Type: Division. Ultimate Parent:
Tandy Corp. SIC: 5013—Motor Vehicle
Supplies & New Parts.

Big Island

★ 90431 ★ Nekoosa Packaging
Hwy. 501
Big Island, VA 24526
Ultimate Parent: Georgia-Pacific. SIC:
2631—Paperboard Mills.

Big Stone Gap

★ 90432 ★ First Union National
Bank of Virginia
216 Wood Ave.
Big Stone Gap, VA 24219-2732
(703)523-1132
Location Type: Branch office. Ultimate
Parent: First Union Corp. SIC: 6021—
National Commercial Banks.

★ 90433 ★ Flowers Baking Co.
Big Stone Gap, VA 24219
(703)523-2713
Ultimate Parent: Flowers Industries. SIC:
2051—Bread, Cake & Related Products.

★ 90434 ★ Food Lion
Wall Mart Shopping. Ctr.
Big Stone Gap, VA 24219
(703)523-5380
Ultimate Parent: Food Lion. SIC: 5411—
Grocery Stores.

★ 90435 ★ Wal Mart Discount
Cities
Powell Valley Ctr.
Big Stone Gap, VA 24219
(703)523-5026
Ultimate Parent: Wal-Mart Stores, Inc. SIC:
5311—Department Stores.

Big Stonegap

★ 90436 ★ Rite Aid
Norton Plz.
Big Stonegap, VA 24219
(703)679-2110
Ultimate Parent: Rite Aid.

Blacksburg

★ 90437 ★ Eagle-Picher
Industries Inc.
Wolverine Gasket Div. Blacksburg Div.
201 Industrial Park Rd. SE
Blacksburg, VA 24060
Company Type: Division. Ultimate Parent:
Eagle-Picher Industries Inc. SIC: 3053—
Gaskets, Packing & Sealing Devices;
3479—Metal Coating & Allied Services.

★ 90438 ★ Federal Mogul
300 Industrial Park Rd. SE
Blacksburg, VA 24060
(703)951-1211
Location Type: Plant. Officer: Peter
Bonafede, Plant Manager. Ultimate Parent:
Federal-Mogul Corp. SIC: 3568—Power
Transmission Equipment Nec.

★ 90439 ★ Federal Mogul Corp.
Us 460 S
Blacksburg, VA 24060
(703)951-1211
Ultimate Parent: Federal-Mogul Corp. SIC:
5085—Industrial Supplies.

★ 90440 ★ Federal Mogul Corp.
Rte. 460, South Main St.
Blacksburg, VA 24060
Ultimate Parent: Federal-Mogul Corp. SIC:
3714—Motor Vehicle Parts & Accessories.

★ 90441 ★ Federal-Mogul Corp.
300 Industrial Park Rd. SE
Blacksburg, VA 24060-6699
Ultimate Parent: Federal-Mogul Corp. SIC:
3714—Motor Vehicle Parts & Accessories.

★ 90442 ★ Federal-Mogul Corp.
Rte. 460 S. Main St.
Blacksburg, VA 24060
Ultimate Parent: Federal-Mogul Corp. SIC:
3714—Motor Vehicle Parts & Accessories.

★ 90443 ★ Federal-Mogul Corp.
Blacksburg Plant
300 Industrial Park Rd. SE
Blacksburg, VA 24060-0669
Ultimate Parent: Federal-Mogul Corp. SIC:
3714—Motor Vehicle Parts & Accessories.

★ 90444 ★ First Union National
Bank of Virginia
1114 S. Main St.
Blacksburg, VA 24060-5545
(703)951-8215
Location Type: Branch office. Ultimate
Parent: First Union Corp. SIC: 6021—
National Commercial Banks.

★ 90445 ★ Food Lion
1413 N. Main St.
Blacksburg, VA 24060
(703)552-1445
Ultimate Parent: Food Lion. SIC: 5411—
Grocery Stores.

★ 90446 ★ Food Lion
801 Hethwood Blvd.
Blacksburg, VA 24060
(703)953-2671
Ultimate Parent: Food Lion. SIC: 5411—
Grocery Stores.

★ 90447 ★ **Food Lion Inc. Store No. 425**
1413 N. Main St.
Blacksburg, VA 24060
(703)552-1445
Ultimate Parent: Food Lion. **SIC:** 5411—Grocery Stores.

★ 90448 ★ **Kroger Co.**
903 University City Blvd.
Blacksburg, VA 24060
(703)951-3045
Ultimate Parent: Kroger. **SIC:** 5411—Grocery Stores.

★ 90449 ★ **Litton Clifton Precision**
1213 N. Main St.
Blacksburg, VA 24060
(703)552-3011 (800)336-2112 **Fax:** (703)953-1841
Company Type: Division. **Officer:** L.A. Bowman, President. **Ultimate Parent:** Litton Industries. **SIC:** 3621—Motors & Generators.

★ 90450 ★ **Litton Industries**
Poly-Scientific Div.
1213 N. Main St.
Blacksburg, VA 24060-3127
(703)552-3011
Company Type: Division. **Ultimate Parent:** Litton Industries. **SIC:** 3728—Aircraft Parts & Equipment Nec; 3621—Motors & Generators.

★ 90451 ★ **Rite Aid**
Prices Frank Rd.
Blacksburg, VA 24061
(703)951-0166
Ultimate Parent: Rite Aid.

★ 90452 ★ **Wolverine Gasket Co.**
Blacksburg Div.
201 Industrial Park Rd. SE
Blacksburg, VA 24060
Company Type: Division. **Ultimate Parent:** Eagle-Picher Industries Inc. **SIC:** 3053—Gaskets, Packing & Sealing Devices.

★ 90453 ★ **Wolverine Gasket & Mfg Co.**
201 Industrial Park Rd. SE
Blacksburg, VA 24060
Ultimate Parent: Eagle-Picher Industries Inc. **SIC:** 3053—Gaskets, Packing & Sealing Devices.

Blackstone

★ 90454 ★ **Radio Shack**
Church
Blackstone, VA 23824
(804)292-5615
Company Type: Division. **Ultimate Parent:** Tandy Corp. **SIC:** 5731—Radio, Television & Electronics Stores.

★ 90455 ★ **Radio Shack**
122 N. Main St.
Blackstone, VA 23824
(804)292-1390
Company Type: Division. **Ultimate Parent:** Tandy Corp. **SIC:** 5211—Lumber & Other Building Materials.

★ 90456 ★ **Radio Shack**
122 N. Main St.
Blackstone, VA 23824
(804)292-1390
Company Type: Division. **Ultimate Parent:** Tandy Corp. **SIC:** 5211—Lumber & Other Building Materials.

Bluefield

★ 90457 ★ **American La France**
600 Mountain Ln.
Bluefield, VA 24605
(703)326-1121 **Fax:** (703)322-3666
Company Type: Subsidiary. **Officer:** Arnold J. Heller, President. **Ultimate Parent:** Figgie International.

★ 90458 ★ **American LaFrance**
600 Mountain Ln.
Bluefield, VA 24605
(703)326-1121
Company Type: Division. **Ultimate Parent:** Figgie International. **SIC:** 3532—Mining Machinery; 5044—Office Equipment. **Employee Count:** 180.

★ 90459 ★ **Brownell Electro Inc.**
Rte. 2.
PO Box 1736
Bluefield, VA 24605
Location Type: Branch office. **Ultimate Parent:** Avnet. **SIC:** 5063—Electrical Apparatus & Equipment.

★ 90460 ★ **First Union National Bank of Virginia**
108 Spruce St.
Bluefield, VA 24605-1738
(703)322-4611
Location Type: Branch office. **Ultimate Parent:** First Union Corp. **SIC:** 6021—National Commercial Banks.

★ 90461 ★ **Rite Aid**
Twin City Shopping.Ctr.
Bluefield, VA 24605
(703)322-4882
Ultimate Parent: Rite Aid. **SIC:** 5912—Drug Stores & Proprietary Stores.

★ 90462 ★ **Sealy Mattress Co.**
Furnace
Bluefield, VA 24605
(703)326-1193
Ultimate Parent: Sealy. **SIC:** 5712—Furniture Stores.

★ 90463 ★ **Virginia Foods of Bluefield**
Falls Mill Rd.
Bluefield, VA 24605
(703)326-2654
Ultimate Parent: Nash Finch. **SIC:** 5141—Groceries—General Line.

Bowling Green

★ 90464 ★ **Radio Shack**
327 PO Box
Bowling Green, VA 22427
(804)633-4500
Company Type: Division. **Ultimate Parent:** Tandy Corp. **SIC:** 5945—Hobby, Toy & Game Shops.

Boydton

★ 90465 ★ **Signet Bank, Virginia**
Bank St.
Boydton, VA 23917
(804)738-6155
Ultimate Parent: Signet Banking Corp. **SIC:** 6021—National Commercial Banks.

Bridgewater

★ 90466 ★ **First American Bank**
516 N. Main St.
Bridgewater, VA 22812
(703)828-6010
Ultimate Parent: First American Corp. **SIC:** 6099—Functions Related to Deposit Banking.

★ 90467 ★ **First Union National Bank of Virginia**
500 N. Main St.
Bridgewater, VA 22812-1625
(703)828-2564
Location Type: Branch office. **Ultimate Parent:** First Union Corp. **SIC:** 6021—National Commercial Banks.

★ 90468 ★ **First Virginia Bank**
Planters
111 N. Main St.
Bridgewater, VA 22812-0085
(703)828-2571
Company Type: Subsidiary. **Officer:** Wayne F. Geisert, Chairman of the Board. **Ultimate Parent:** First Virginia Banks Inc. **SIC:** 6022—State Commercial Banks.

★ 90469 ★ **First Virginia Bank - Planters**
111 N. Main St.
Bridgewater, VA 22812-1303
(703)828-2571
Company Type: Subsidiary. **Officer:** Mark McNeil, Chairman of the Board. **Ultimate Parent:** First Virginia Banks Inc. **SIC:** 6022—State Commercial Banks. **Employee Count:** 63.

Bristol

★ 90470 ★ **Bristol Compressors Inc.**
649 Industrial Park Rd.
Bristol, VA 24201-8199
Ultimate Parent: York International Corp. **SIC:** 3499—Fabricated Metal Products Nec; 3585—Refrigeration & Heating Equipment; 5075—Warm Air Heating & Air-Conditioning.

★ 90471 ★ **Dana Corp.**
Spicer Universal Joint Div.
110 Thomas Rd.
Bristol, VA 24201
Company Type: Division. **Ultimate Parent:** Dana Corp. **SIC:** 3714—Motor Vehicle Parts & Accessories.

★ 90472 ★ **Eckerd Drugs**
1315 Euclid Ave.
Bristol, VA 24201
(703)466-5708
Ultimate Parent: Eckerd Corp. **SIC:** 5912—Drug Stores & Proprietary Stores.

★ 90473 ★ **Facet Fuel Systems**
1048 Industrial Park Rd.
Bristol, VA 24201
Ultimate Parent: Pennzoil. **SIC:** 3592—Carburetors, Pistons, Rings & Valves.

★ 90474 ★ **First American National Bank**
PO Box 368
Bristol, VA 24201
(703)968-4122
Ultimate Parent: First American Corp. **SIC:** 6099—Functions Related to Deposit Banking; 6022—State Commercial Banks.

★ 90475 ★ **First Union National Bank of Virginia**
1465 Lee Hwy.
Bristol, VA 24201-2861
(703)645-1280
Location Type: Branch office. **Ultimate Parent:** First Union Corp. **SIC:** 6021—National Commercial Banks.

★ 90476 ★ **First Union National Bank of Virginia**
3375 Lee Hwy.
Bristol, VA 24201-8321
(703)645-1295
Location Type: Branch office. **Ultimate Parent:** First Union Corp. **SIC:** 6021—National Commercial Banks.

★ 90477 ★ **First Union National Bank of Virginia**
601 State St.
Bristol, VA 24201-4315
(703)645-1200
Location Type: Branch office. **Ultimate Parent:** First Union Corp. **SIC:** 6021—National Commercial Banks.

★ 90478 ★ **First Union National Bank of Virginia**
18 Midway St.
Bristol, VA 24201-3247
(703)645-1285
Location Type: Branch office. **Ultimate Parent:** First Union Corp. **SIC:** 6021—National Commercial Banks.

★ 90479 ★ **Food Lion**
1061 Old Abingdon Wy
Bristol, VA 24201
(703)669-7341
Ultimate Parent: Food Lion. **SIC:** 5411—Grocery Stores.

★ 90480 ★ **J C Penney Co.**
629 State St.
Bristol, VA 24201
(703)669-3184
Ultimate Parent: J.C. Penney. **SIC:** 5311—Department Stores.

★ 90481 ★ **Kroger Co.**
2006 Lee Hwy.
Bristol, VA 24201
(703)669-5532
Ultimate Parent: Kroger. **SIC:** 5411—Grocery Stores.

★ 90482 ★ **Moore's Quality Snack Food Inc.**
Commonwealth Ave. Ext.
Bristol, VA 24201
Ultimate Parent: Borden, Inc. **SIC:** 2099—Food Preparations Nec.

★ 90483 ★ **Morrison Molded Fiber Glass Co.**
400 Commonwealth Ave.
Bristol, VA 24203-0508
Ultimate Parent: Shell Oil Co. **SIC:** 3083—Laminated Plastics Plate & Sheet; 3089—Plastics Products Nec; 3544—Special Dies, Tools, Jigs & Fixtures.

★ 90484 ★ **Piggly Wiggly**
Euclid Ave.
Bristol, VA 24201
(703)466-5021
Ultimate Parent: Bruno's. **SIC:** 5411—Grocery Stores.

★ 90485 ★ **Radio Shack**
510 Gate City Hwy.
Bristol, VA 24201
(703)466-8872
Company Type: Division. **Ultimate Parent:** Tandy Corp. **SIC:** 5731—Radio, Television & Electronics Stores.

★ 90486 ★ **Reynolds Metals Co.**
750 Old Abingdon Hwy.
Bristol, VA 24201-1899
Ultimate Parent: Reynolds Metals Co. **SIC:** 3411—Metal Cans.

★ 90487 ★ **Reynolds Metals Co. Bristol End Plant**
750 Old Abingdon Hwy.
Bristol, VA 24201-1899
Ultimate Parent: Reynolds Metals Co. **SIC:** 3411—Metal Cans.

★ 90488 ★ **Signet Bank, Virginia**
1700 Euclid Ave.
Bristol, VA 24201-3736
Ultimate Parent: Signet Banking Corp. **SIC:** 6021—National Commercial Banks.

★ 90489 ★ **Signet Bank, Virginia**
3000 Lee Hwy.
Bristol, VA 24201-8316
Ultimate Parent: Signet Banking Corp. **SIC:** 6021—National Commercial Banks.

★ 90490 ★ **Signet Bank, Virginia**
Bristol Mall
Bristol, VA 24201-2352
(703)466-4422
Ultimate Parent: Signet Banking Corp. **SIC:** 6021—National Commercial Banks.

★ 90491 ★ **Signet Bank, Virginia**
425 State St.
Bristol, VA 24201-4313
Ultimate Parent: Signet Banking Corp. **SIC:** 6021—National Commercial Banks.

★ 90492 ★ **Vulcan Materials Co.**
PO Box 1209
Bristol, VA 24203
(703)669-5033
Officer: Harold Lambert, President. **Ultimate Parent:** Vulcan Materials Co. **SIC:** 3273—Ready-Mixed Concrete.

★ 90493 ★ **Vulcan Materials Co.**
Shakesville Rd.
Bristol, VA 24201
(703)669-5033
Ultimate Parent: Vulcan Materials Co. **SIC:** 5032—Brick, Stone & Related Materials.

★ 90494 ★ **Vulcan Materials Co.**
Shakesville Rd.
Bristol, VA 24201
(703)669-5033
Ultimate Parent: Vulcan Materials Co. **SIC:** 5032—Brick, Stone & Related Materials.

Broadway

★ 90495 ★ **Wampler Long Acre Inc.**
PO Box 7275
Broadway, VA 22815-7275
(703)896-7000 **Fax:** (703)896-5127
Company Type: Division. **Ultimate Parent:** WLR Foods. **SIC:** 2013—Sausages & Other Prepared Meats.

Brookneal

★ 90496 ★ Thomasville Furniture Ind. Inc.
Hwy. 501
Brookneal, VA 24528
Ultimate Parent: Armstrong World Industries. **SIC:** 2511—Wood Household Furniture.

Buena Vista

★ 90497 ★ Ace Hardware
2122 Magnolia Ave.
Buena Vista, VA 24416
(703)261-3155
Ultimate Parent: Ace Hardware. **SIC:** 5251—Hardware Stores.

Burgess

★ 90498 ★ Signet Bank, Virginia
State Rte. 360
Burgess, VA 22432-9718
(804)453-4181
Ultimate Parent: Signet Banking Corp. **SIC:** 6021—National Commercial Banks.

Burke

★ 90499 ★ Crestar Bank
6052 Burke Commons Rd.
Burke, VA 22015
(800)451-2435
Location Type: Branch office. **Ultimate Parent:** Crestar Financial Corp. **SIC:** 6021—National Commercial Banks.

★ 90500 ★ First American Bank
5703 Burke Centre Pky.
Burke, VA 22015
(703)934-1817
Ultimate Parent: First American Corp. **SIC:** 6099—Functions Related to Deposit Banking.

★ 90501 ★ First Union National Bank of Virginia
5703 Burke Ctr. Pky.
Burke, VA 22015-2204
(703)934-1817
Location Type: Branch office. **Ultimate Parent:** First Union Corp. **SIC:** 6021—National Commercial Banks.

★ 90502 ★ First Virginia Bank
6401-B Shiplett Blvd.
Burke, VA 22015
(703)241-3514
Location Type: Branch office. **Ultimate Parent:** First Virginia Banks Inc. **SIC:** 6021—National Commercial Banks.

★ 90503 ★ First Virginia Bank
6045-A Burke Ctr. Pky.
Burke, VA 22015-3751
(703)241-3690
Location Type: Branch office. **Ultimate Parent:** First Virginia Banks Inc. **SIC:** 6021—National Commercial Banks.

★ 90504 ★ First Virginia Bank
9502 Burke Rd.
Burke, VA 22015-3132
(703)241-3261
Location Type: Branch office. **Ultimate Parent:** First Virginia Banks Inc. **SIC:** 6021—National Commercial Banks.

★ 90505 ★ Mary Kay Cosmetics
5926 New England Woods Dr.
Burke, VA 22015
(703)978-9228
Ultimate Parent: Mary Kay Cosmetics. **SIC:** 5999—Miscellaneous Retail Stores Nec.

★ 90506 ★ Mary Kay Cosmetics
5914 Crossin Ct.
Burke, VA 22015
(703)569-9793
Ultimate Parent: Mary Kay Cosmetics. **SIC:** 5999—Miscellaneous Retail Stores Nec.

Burkeville

★ 90507 ★ Greyhound Bus Lines
Burkeville, VA 23922
(804)767-4148
Ultimate Parent: Greyhound Lines Inc. **SIC:** 4131—Intercity & Rural Bus Transportation.

Callao

★ 90508 ★ First Virginia Bank
State Rtes. 202 & 360
Callao, VA 22435
(804)529-6161
Location Type: Branch office. **Ultimate Parent:** First Virginia Banks Inc. **SIC:** 6021—National Commercial Banks.

Castlewood

★ 90509 ★ Stop & Shop Superette
176 PO Box
Castlewood, VA 24224
(703)762-7711
Ultimate Parent: Stop & Shop. **SIC:** 5411—Grocery Stores.

★ 90510 ★ Stop & Shop Supermarket
176 PO Box
Castlewood, VA 24224
(703)762-7711
Ultimate Parent: Stop & Shop. **SIC:** 5411—Grocery Stores.

Catlett

★ 90511 ★ Agri Services Inc.
Catlett, VA 22019
(703)788-4646
Ultimate Parent: Agway Inc. **SIC:** 3993—Signs & Advertising Displays.

Cedar Bluff

★ 90512 ★ Simmons-Rand Co.
St.Rte. 719
Cedar Bluff, VA 24609
Ultimate Parent: Ingersoll-Rand. **SIC:** 3532—Mining Machinery; 3537—Industrial Trucks & Tractors.

★ 90513 ★ United Parcel Service
68 PO Box
Cedar Bluff, VA 24609
(703)964-5912
Ultimate Parent: United Parcel Service of America. **SIC:** 4215—Courier Services Except by Air.

Centreville

★ 90514 ★ Crestar Bank
14200 E. Centreville Sq.
Centreville, VA 22020-2300
(800)451-2435
Location Type: Branch office. **Ultimate Parent:** Crestar Financial Corp. **SIC:** 6021—National Commercial Banks.

★ 90515 ★ First Union National Bank of Virginia
13880 Braddock Rd.
Centreville, VA 22020-2412
(703)934-1975
Location Type: Branch office. **Ultimate Parent:** First Union Corp. **SIC:** 6021—National Commercial Banks.

★ 90516 ★ First Virginia Bank
14175 St. Germain Dr.
Centreville, VA 22020-2310
(703)241-4781
Location Type: Branch office. **Ultimate Parent:** First Virginia Banks Inc. **SIC:** 6021—National Commercial Banks.

★ 90517 ★ Fluor Daniel Inc.
1607 PO Box
Centreville, VA 22020
(703)968-1234
Ultimate Parent: Fluor.

★ 90518 ★ Rite Aid
Manassas Park Shopping.Ctr.
Centreville, VA 22020
(703)631-9453
Ultimate Parent: Rite Aid. **SIC:** 5999—Miscellaneous Retail Stores Nec.

Chantilly

★ 90519 ★ Crestar Bank
13900 Lee Jackson Memorial Hwy.
Chantilly, VA 22021-3202
(703)749-8565
Location Type: Branch office. **Ultimate Parent:** Crestar Financial Corp. **SIC:** 6021—National Commercial Banks.

★ 90520 ★ Crestar Bank
13655 Lee Jackson Memorial Hwy.
Chantilly, VA 22021-3502
(800)451-2435
Location Type: Branch office. **Ultimate Parent:** Crestar Financial Corp. **SIC:** 6021—National Commercial Banks.

★ 90521 ★ Delta Air Lines Inc.
Airport
Chantilly, VA 22021
(703)471-0489
Ultimate Parent: Delta Air Lines, Inc.

★ 90522 ★ First Union National Bank of Virginia
13960 Lee Jackson Memorial Hwy.
Chantilly, VA 22021
(703)934-1823
Location Type: Branch office. **Ultimate Parent:** First Union Corp. **SIC:** 6021—National Commercial Banks.

★ 90523 ★ Rite Aid
Pines Shopping.Ctr.
Chantilly, VA 22021
(703)471-7440
Ultimate Parent: Rite Aid.

★ 90524 ★ Rite Aid
696 Edenway
Chantilly, VA 22021
(703)471-6841
Ultimate Parent: Rite Aid.

★ 90525 ★ Trans World Airlines, Inc.
Washington Dulles
Chantilly, VA 22030
(703)471-5098
Ultimate Parent: Trans World Airlines.

Charlottesville

★ 90526 ★ Cedars
1242 Cedars Ct.
Charlottesville, VA 22903-4800
(804)296-5611
Officer: Brian Carlton. **Ultimate Parent:** Beverly Enterprises. **SIC:** 8361—Residential Care; 8051—Skilled Nursing Care Facilities; 8059—Nursing & Personal Care Nec.

★ 90527 ★ Cincinnati Insurance Co.
1102 Little High St.
Charlottesville, VA 22901
(804)296-4696
Ultimate Parent: Cincinnati Financial. **SIC:** 6411—Insurance Agents, Brokers & Service.

★ 90528 ★ Crestar Bank
1980 Rio Hill
Charlottesville, VA 22901
Location Type: Branch office. **Ultimate Parent:** Crestar Financial Corp. **SIC:** 6021—National Commercial Banks.

★ 90529 ★ Crestar Bank
1202 Emmet St.
Charlottesville, VA 22903
Location Type: Branch office. **Ultimate Parent:** Crestar Financial Corp. **SIC:** 6021—National Commercial Banks.

★ 90530 ★ Crestar Bank
1904 Emmet St.
Charlottesville, VA 22901
Location Type: Branch office. **Ultimate Parent:** Crestar Financial Corp. **SIC:** 6021—National Commercial Banks.

★ 90531 ★ Crestar Bank
1643 Seminole Trl.
Charlottesville, VA 22901
(804)973-0651
Location Type: Branch office. **Ultimate Parent:** Crestar Financial Corp. **SIC:** 6021—National Commercial Banks.

★ 90532 ★ Crestar Bank
29 N. Rio Rd.
Charlottesville, VA 22901
Location Type: Branch office. **Ultimate Parent:** Crestar Financial Corp. **SIC:** 6021—National Commercial Banks.

★ 90533 ★ Crestar Bank
2117 Ivy Rd.
Charlottesville, VA 22903-1715
Location Type: Branch office. **Ultimate Parent:** Crestar Financial Corp. **SIC:** 6021—National Commercial Banks.

★ 90534 ★ Crestar Bank
402 Park St.
Charlottesville, VA 22901-4659
Location Type: Branch office. **Ultimate Parent:** Crestar Financial Corp. **SIC:** 6021—National Commercial Banks.

★ 90535 ★ Figgie Fire Protection Systems
Rte. 29 N
PO Box 7146
Charlottesville, VA 22906
(804)973-4361
Company Type: Subsidiary. **Officer:** C. Michael Dempsey, President. **Ultimate Parent:** Figgie International.

★ 90536 ★ First Virginia Bank Central
305 E. Jefferson St.
Charlottesville, VA 22906-7466
(804)978-3000
Company Type: Subsidiary. **Officer:** William W. Stevenson, Chairman of the Board. **Ultimate Parent:** First Virginia Banks Inc. **SIC:** 6022—State Commercial Banks.

★ 90537 ★ First Virginia Bank Central
305 E. Jefferson St.
Charlottesville, VA 22902-5106
(804)978-3024
Company Type: Subsidiary. **Officer:** Edward S. Yates III, President. **Ultimate Parent:** First Virginia Banks Inc. **SIC:** 6022—State Commercial Banks. **Employee Count:** 54.

★ 90538 ★ Flowers Baking Co.
360 Greenbrier Dr.
Charlottesville, VA 22901
(804)978-4104
Ultimate Parent: Flowers Industries. **SIC:** 5141—Groceries—General Line.

★ 90539 ★ GE Fanuc
Rte. 29 N. & Rte. 606
Charlottesville, VA 22901
(804)978-5000
Officer: Robert P. Collins, President. **Ultimate Parent:** General Electric. **SIC:** 3549—Metalworking Machinery Nec; 3569—General Industrial Machinery Nec; 3612—Transformers Except Electronic.

★ 90540 ★ GE Fanuc Automation North America
US 29 N. at Rte. 606
Charlottesville, VA 22901
Ultimate Parent: General Electric. **SIC:** 3625—Relays & Industrial Controls.

★ 90541 ★ Hertz Rent-A-Car
1283 Seminole Trl.
Charlottesville Airport
Charlottesville, VA 22901
(804)973-8349
Ultimate Parent: Hertz. **SIC:** 7514—Passenger Car Rental.

★ 90542 ★ Mary Kay Cosmetics
326 Carrsbrook Dr.
Charlottesville, VA 22901
(804)973-7104
Ultimate Parent: Mary Kay Cosmetics. **SIC:** 5999—Miscellaneous Retail Stores Nec.

★ 90543 ★ McDonald's Hamburgers
Shoppers World
Charlottesville, VA 22901
(804)973-3055
Ultimate Parent: McDonald's. **SIC:** 5812—Eating Places.

★ 90544 ★ New York Life Insurance
1113 W. Main St.
Charlottesville, VA 22903
(804)977-4898
Ultimate Parent: New York Life. **SIC:** 6311—Life Insurance.

★ 90545 ★ **Northwestern Mutual Life Inc.**
2250 Old Ivy Rd.
Charlottesville, VA 22901
(804)293-5154
Ultimate Parent: Northwestern Mutual Life. **SIC:** 6411—Insurance Agents, Brokers & Service.

★ 90546 ★ **Pepsi-Cola Bottling Co.**
1150 Pepsi Pl.
Charlottesville, VA 22901
(804)978-2140
Officer: Jesse L. Jessup Jr., President. **Ultimate Parent:** Pepsico. **SIC:** 2086—Bottled & Canned Soft Drinks.

★ 90547 ★ **Radio Shack**
1432 Shoppers World
Charlottesville, VA 22903
(804)973-7330
Company Type: Division. **Ultimate Parent:** Tandy Corp. **SIC:** 5731—Radio, Television & Electronics Stores.

★ 90548 ★ **Reuben H. Donnelley Corp.**
1150 Pepsi Pl., No. 300
Charlottesville, VA 22901
(804)973-3373
Officer: Sue Fansarillo, Manager. **Ultimate Parent:** E.I. DuPont De Nemours. **SIC:** 2741—Miscellaneous Publishing.

★ 90549 ★ **Sperry Marine Inc.**
1070 Seminole Trail
Charlottesville, VA 22901
Ultimate Parent: Tenneco Inc. **SIC:** 3699—Electrical Equipment & Supplies Nec.

★ 90550 ★ **Wall Street Journal**
1930 Stillhouse Rd.
Charlottesville, VA 22901
(804)293-7771
Ultimate Parent: Dow Jones. **SIC:** 2711—Newspapers.

Charlottesvle

★ 90551 ★ **Food Lion**
Pantops Shopping Ctr.
Charlottesvle, VA 22901
(804)971-8451
Ultimate Parent: Food Lion. **SIC:** 5411—Grocery Stores.

Chase City

★ 90552 ★ **New York Life Insurance Co.**
420 N. Main St.
Chase City, VA 23924
(804)372-5553
Ultimate Parent: New York Life. **SIC:** 6411—Insurance Agents, Brokers & Service.

Chatham

★ 90553 ★ **Freeman Resins**
Pittsylvania Industrial Park Hwy. 29
Chatham, VA 24531
Ultimate Parent: Georgia Gulf. **SIC:** 2821—Plastics Materials & Resins.

★ 90554 ★ **Westvaco Corp.**
State Rte. 703
Chatham, VA 24531
(804)432-0372
Ultimate Parent: WestVaco Corp. **SIC:** 2679—Converted Paper Products Nec.

Cheriton

★ 90555 ★ **Crestar Bank**
21263 Langford Hwy.
Cheriton, VA 23316
(804)858-3049
Location Type: Branch office. **Ultimate Parent:** Crestar Financial Corp. **SIC:** 6021—National Commercial Banks.

Chesapeake

★ 90556 ★ **Beneficial Virginia Inc.**
Woodford Sq. Shopping Ctr.
Chesapeake, VA 23320
(804)547-1002
Location Type: Branch office. **Officer:**
Glenn Hafner. **Ultimate Parent:** Beneficial. **SIC:** 6141—Personal Credit Institutions; 6162—Mortgage Bankers & Correspondents; 6282—Investment Advice.

★ 90557 ★ **Beneficial Virgnia Inc.**
Stonebridge Plz.
Chesapeake, VA 23321
(804)488-1700
Officer: A. T. Yost. **Ultimate Parent:** Beneficial. **SIC:** 6141—Personal Credit Institutions; 6162—Mortgage Bankers & Correspondents.

★ 90558 ★ **BFI Waste Systems**
3821 Cook Blvd.
Chesapeake, VA 23323-1605
(804)487-2220
Location Type: Branch office. **Officer:** Robert Tingley. **Ultimate Parent:** Browning-Ferris Industries. **SIC:** 4953—Refuse Systems; 4952—Sewerage Systems.

★ 90559 ★ **Casual Corner**
1172 Greenbrier Pky.
Chesapeake, VA 23320
(804)420-7482
Ultimate Parent: United States Shoe. **SIC:** 5651—Family Clothing Stores.

★ 90560 ★ **Citgo**
3801 Indian River Rd.
Chesapeake, VA 23325
(804)420-1866
Ultimate Parent: Citgo Petroleum. **SIC:** 5541—Gasoline Service Stations.

★ 90561 ★ **Citgo Gas Mart**
2753 Campostella Rd.
Chesapeake, VA 23324
(804)543-4807
Ultimate Parent: Citgo Petroleum. **SIC:** 5541—Gasoline Service Stations.

★ 90562 ★ **Citgo Petroleum Corp.**
110 Freeman Ave.
Chesapeake, VA 23324
(804)543-3514
Ultimate Parent: Citgo Petroleum. **SIC:** 1311—Crude Petroleum & Natural Gas.

★ 90563 ★ **Colonial Pipeline Co.**
100 Republic Rd.
Chesapeake, VA 23324
(804)543-2988
Ultimate Parent: Colonial Pipeline. **SIC:** 1629—Heavy Construction Nec.

★ 90564 ★ **Colonial Pipeline Co.**
513 Barnes Rd.
Chesapeake, VA 23324
(804)545-7004
Ultimate Parent: Colonial Pipeline. **SIC:** 4619—Pipelines Nec.

★ 90565 ★ **Crestar Bank**
4113 Portsmouth Blvd.
Chesapeake, VA 23321
(804)858-3259
Location Type: Branch office. **Ultimate Parent:** Crestar Financial Corp. **SIC:** 6021—National Commercial Banks.

★ 90566 ★ **Crestar Bank**
1122 George Washington Hwy. N
Chesapeake, VA 23323
(804)858-3186
Location Type: Branch office. **Ultimate Parent:** Crestar Financial Corp. **SIC:** 6021—National Commercial Banks.

★ 90567 ★ **Crestar Bank**
2211 S. Military Hwy.
Chesapeake, VA 23320
(804)858-3451
Location Type: Branch office. **Ultimate Parent:** Crestar Financial Corp. **SIC:** 6021—National Commercial Banks.

★ 90568 ★ **Crestar Bank**
911 S. Military Hwy.
Virginia Beach
Chesapeake, VA 23464
(804)858-3273
Location Type: Branch office. **Ultimate Parent:** Crestar Financial Corp. **SIC:** 6021—National Commercial Banks.

★ 90569 ★ **Crestar Bank**
320 Battlefield Blvd. S
Chesapeake, VA 23320
(804)858-3369
Location Type: Branch office. **Ultimate Parent:** Crestar Financial Corp. **SIC:** 6021—National Commercial Banks.

★ 90570 ★ **Crestar Bank**
2421 Bainbridge Blvd.
Chesapeake, VA 23324
(804)858-3300
Location Type: Branch office. **Ultimate Parent:** Crestar Financial Corp. **SIC:** 6021—National Commercial Banks.

★ 90571 ★ **Exxon Co.**
4115 Buell St.
Chesapeake, VA 23324
(804)494-0464
Ultimate Parent: Exxon. **SIC:** 2911—Petroleum Refining.

★ 90572 ★ **First American Bank**
1401 Greenbrier Pky. 100
Chesapeake, VA 23320
Ultimate Parent: First American Corp.

★ 90573 ★ **First American Bank of Virginia**
1401 Greenbrier Pky. 100
Chesapeake, VA 23320
Ultimate Parent: First American Corp.

★ 90574 ★ **First Union National Bank of Virginia**
1401 Greenbrier Pky.
Chesapeake, VA 23320
(804)424-6622
Location Type: Branch office. **Ultimate Parent:** First Union Corp. **SIC:** 6021—National Commercial Banks.

★ 90575 ★ **First Union National Bank of Virginia**
3114 Western Branch Blvd.
Chesapeake, VA 23321-5517
(804)483-2900
Location Type: Branch office. **Ultimate Parent:** First Union Corp. **SIC:** 6021—National Commercial Banks.

★ 90576 ★ **First Union National Bank of Virginia**
3936 Portsmouth Blvd.
Chesapeake, VA 23321-3625
(804)488-4610
Location Type: Branch office. **Ultimate Parent:** First Union Corp. **SIC:** 6021—National Commercial Banks.

★ 90577 ★ **Food Lion**
717 Battlefield Blvd. S
Chesapeake, VA 23320
(804)482-5259
Ultimate Parent: Food Lion. **SIC:** 5411—Grocery Stores.

★ 90578 ★ **Food Lion**
Parkview Shopping. Ctr.
Chesapeake, VA 23320
(804)424-1077
Ultimate Parent: Food Lion. **SIC:** 5411—Grocery Stores.

★ 90579 ★ **Food Lion**
801 Volvo Pky.
Chesapeake, VA 23320
(804)436-9304
Ultimate Parent: Food Lion. **SIC:** 5411—Grocery Stores.

★ 90580 ★ **Food Lion**
1745 Greenbrier Pky.
Chesapeake, VA 23320
(804)424-1197
Ultimate Parent: Food Lion. **SIC:** 5411—Grocery Stores.

★ 90581 ★ **Gap the**
1224 Greenbrier Pky.
Chesapeake, VA 23320
(804)424-4103
Ultimate Parent: GAP. **SIC:** 5651—Family Clothing Stores.

★ 90582 ★ **Hecht's**
1401 Greenbrier Pky.
Chesapeake, VA 23320
(804)424-6260
Ultimate Parent: May Department Stores. **SIC:** 5311—Department Stores.

★ 90583 ★ **Hit or Miss**
Greenbriar Mall
Chesapeake, VA 23323
(804)420-8811
Ultimate Parent: TJX. **SIC:** 5621—Women's Clothing Stores.

★ 90584 ★ **Hit or Miss**
1236 Greenbrier Pky.
Chesapeake, VA 23320
(804)424-4684
Ultimate Parent: TJX. **SIC:** 5651—Family Clothing Stores.

★ 90585 ★ **Huntsman Chemical Corp.**
5100 Bainbridge Blvd.
Chesapeake, VA 23320
(804)494-2500
Ultimate Parent: Great American Management & Investment. **SIC:** 3089—Plastics Products Nec.

★ 90586 ★ **Lenscrafters**
2112 Greenbrier Mall
Chesapeake, VA 23320
(804)420-3032
Ultimate Parent: United States Shoe. **SIC:** 5995—Optical Goods Stores.

★ 90587 ★ **Mary Kay Cosmetics**
2100 Hollins Ct
Chesapeake, VA 23320
(804)424-5413
Ultimate Parent: Mary Kay Cosmetics. **SIC:** 5999—Miscellaneous Retail Stores Nec.

★ 90588 ★ **Mobil Service Station**
2154 S. Military Hwy.
Chesapeake, VA 23320
(804)545-3361
Ultimate Parent: Mobil. **SIC:** 5541—Gasoline Service Stations.

★ 90589 ★ **Mobil Service Station**
3715 Bainbridge Blvd.
Chesapeake, VA 23324
(804)545-9667
Ultimate Parent: Mobil. **SIC:** 5541—Gasoline Service Stations.

★ 90590 ★ **Otis Elevator Co. Inc.**
840 Juniper Cres
Chesapeake, VA 23320
(804)524-5035
Ultimate Parent: United Technologies. **SIC:** 1796—Installing Building Equipment Nec.

★ 90591 ★ **Overnite Transportation Co.**
2053 S. Military Hwy.
Chesapeake, VA 23320
(804)545-8401
Ultimate Parent: Union Pacific Corp. **SIC:** 4213—Trucking Except Local.

★ 90592 ★ **Radio Shack**
1961 S. Military Hwy.
Chesapeake, VA 23320
(804)543-3711
Company Type: Division. **Ultimate Parent:** Tandy Corp. **SIC:** 5731—Radio, Television & Electronics Stores.

★ 90593 ★ **Radio Shack**
4309 Indian River Rd.
Chesapeake, VA 23325
(804)420-0838
Company Type: Division. **Ultimate Parent:** Tandy Corp. **SIC:** 5731—Radio, Television & Electronics Stores.

★ 90594 ★ **Radio Shack**
2188 Greenbrier Rd.
Chesapeake, VA 23320
(804)420-8251
Company Type: Division. **Ultimate Parent:** Tandy Corp. **SIC:** 5065—Electronic Parts & Equipment Nec.

★ 90595 ★ **Radio Shack**
Greenbriar Mall
Chesapeake, VA 23323
(804)420-8251
Company Type: Division. **Ultimate Parent:** Tandy Corp. **SIC:** 5065—Electronic Parts & Equipment Nec.

★ 90596 ★ **Radio Shack**
Greenbriar Mall
Chesapeake, VA 23323
(804)420-8251
Company Type: Division. **Ultimate Parent:** Tandy Corp. **SIC:** 5065—Electronic Parts & Equipment Nec.

★ 90597 ★ **Rite Aid**
649 Newton Dr.
Chesapeake, VA 23320
(804)490-3262
Ultimate Parent: Rite Aid.

★ 90598 ★ Rite Aid
717 Battlefield Blvd. S
Chesapeake, VA 23320
(804)482-9801
Ultimate Parent: Rite Aid. SIC: 5912—Drug
Stores & Proprietary Stores.

★ 90599 ★ Ryder Truck Rental Inc.
1950 Old Greenbrier Rd.
Chesapeake, VA 23320
(804)523-1965
Ultimate Parent: Ryder System. SIC:
7513—Truck Rental & Leasing Without
Drivers.

★ 90600 ★ Shell Oil Co.
501 Hill St.
Chesapeake, VA 23324
(804)545-2427
Ultimate Parent: Shell Oil Co. SIC: 5172—
Petroleum Products Nec.

★ 90601 ★ Shell Oil Co.
501 Hill St.
Chesapeake, VA 23324
(804)545-2427
Ultimate Parent: Shell Oil Co. SIC: 5172—
Petroleum Products Nec.

★ 90602 ★ Signet Bank, Virginia
1510 S. Military Hwy.
Chesapeake, VA 23320-2608
(804)640-4404
Location Type: Branch office. Ultimate
Parent: Signet Banking Corp. SIC: 6021—
National Commercial Banks.

★ 90603 ★ Signet Bank, Virginia
205 Battlefield Blvd. South
Chesapeake, VA 23320-3913
(804)640-4242
Location Type: Branch office. Ultimate
Parent: Signet Banking Corp. SIC: 6021—
National Commercial Banks.

★ 90604 ★ Signet Bank, Virginia
3216 Western Branch Blvd.
Chesapeake, VA 23321-5293
(804)640-4333
Ultimate Parent: Signet Banking Corp. SIC:
6021—National Commercial Banks.

★ 90605 ★ Southern States Co-Op. Inc.
2651 S. Military Hwy.
Chesapeake, VA 23324
Ultimate Parent: Southern. SIC: 2875—
Fertilizers—Mixing Only.

★ 90606 ★ Spartan Express Inc.
1720 S. Military Hwy.
Chesapeake, VA 23320
(804)424-9567
Ultimate Parent: Roadway Services. SIC:
4213—Trucking Except Local.

★ 90607 ★ Texaco Lubricants Co. Inc.
Foot of Rosemont Ave.
Chesapeake, VA 23324
Ultimate Parent: Texaco. SIC: 2992—
Lubricating Oils & Greases.

★ 90608 ★ Waldenbooks
Greenbriar Mall
Chesapeake, VA 23323
(804)424-7984
Ultimate Parent: K-Mart. SIC: 5942—Book
Stores.

★ 90609 ★ Waldenbooks
1248 Greenbrier Pky.
Chesapeake, VA 23320
(804)424-7984
Ultimate Parent: K-Mart. SIC: 5942—Book
Stores.

★ 90610 ★ Warwick Mfg. Co.
1112 Cavalier Blvd.
Chesapeake, VA 23323
Ultimate Parent: Maytag. SIC: 3632—
Household Refrigerators & Freezers.

★ 90611 ★ Weyerhaeuser Co.
201 Dexter St. West
Chesapeake, VA 23324-3023
Ultimate Parent: Weyerhaeuser Co. SIC:
2435—Hardwood Veneer & Plywood.

★ 90612 ★ Weyerhaeuser Co.
201 Dexter Street, West
Chesapeake, VA 23324-3023
Ultimate Parent: Weyerhaeuser Co. SIC:
2436—Softwood Veneer & Plywood.

★ 90613 ★ Zippy Mart
2141 Campostella Rd.
Chesapeake, VA 23324
(804)545-3460
Ultimate Parent: Crown Central Petroleum
Corp. SIC: 5411—Grocery Stores.

Chester

★ 90614 ★ Allied-Signal Inc.
4101 Bermuda Hundred Rd.
Chester, VA 23831
Ultimate Parent: Allied-Signal Inc. SIC:
2821—Plastics Materials & Resins; 2824—
Organic Fibers—Noncellulosic.

★ 90615 ★ American Tobacco Co.
13203 N. Enon Church Rd.
Chester, VA 23831-3122
(804)751-2100
Company Type: Subsidiary. Ultimate
Parent: American Brands Inc. SIC: 2121—
Cigars; 2141—Tobacco Stemming &
Redrying; 2110—Cigarettes.

★ 90616 ★ American Tobacco Co.
13101 N. Enon Church Rd.
Chester, VA 23831-3120
(804)751-7500
Officer: W.H. Kramer. Ultimate Parent:
American Brands Inc. SIC: 2141—Tobacco
Stemming & Redrying; 2131—Chewing &
Smoking Tobacco.

★ 90617 ★ Citgo Self Service Station
701 S. Crater Rd.
Chester, VA 23831
(804)748-6358
Ultimate Parent: Citgo Petroleum. SIC:
5541—Gasoline Service Stations.

★ 90618 ★ Crestar Bank
12551 Jefferson Davis Hwy.
Chester, VA 23831-5305
(804)782-5476
Location Type: Branch office. Ultimate
Parent: Crestar Financial Corp. SIC:
6021—National Commercial Banks.

★ 90619 ★ Hon Co.
11200 Old Stage Rd.
Chester, VA 23831-2445
Ultimate Parent: Hon Industries. SIC:
2522—Office Furniture Except Wood.

★ 90620 ★ McDonald's Hamburgers
12530 Jefferson Davis Hwy.
Chester, VA 23831
(804)748-9328
Ultimate Parent: McDonald's. SIC: 5812—
Eating Places.

★ 90621 ★ New York Life
4209 Hidden Valley Rd.
Chester, VA 23831
(804)748-7083
Ultimate Parent: New York Life. SIC:
6411—Insurance Agents, Brokers &
Service.

★ 90622 ★ Philip Morris USA
Park 500
4100 Bermuda Hundred Rd.
Chester, VA 23831
Company Type: Division. Ultimate Parent:
Philip Morris. SIC: 2141—Tobacco
Stemming & Redrying.

★ 90623 ★ Phillip Morris USA
Park 500
4100 Bermuda Hundred Rd.
Chester, VA 23831
Company Type: Division. Ultimate Parent:
Philip Morris. SIC: 2141—Tobacco
Stemming & Redrying.

★ 90624 ★ Rite Aid
12633 Jefferson Davishwy
Chester, VA 23831
(804)748-9042
Ultimate Parent: Rite Aid. SIC: 5912—Drug
Stores & Proprietary Stores.

★ 90625 ★ Safety-Kleen Corp.
1200 Hundred Rd. W
Chester, VA 23831
(804)748-3767
Ultimate Parent: Safety-Kleen. SIC: 7349—
Building Maintenance Services Nec.

★ 90626 ★ Signet Bank, Virginia
4221 W. Hundred Rd.
Chester, VA 23831-9810
(804)748-2265
Location Type: Branch office. Ultimate
Parent: Signet Banking Corp. SIC: 6021—
National Commercial Banks.

★ 90627 ★ Sonoco Products Co.
1701 W. Hundred Rd.
Chester, VA 23831
(804)748-8166
Officer: Lee Foster, Manager. Ultimate
Parent: Sonoco Products. SIC: 2655—Fiber
Cans, Drums & Similar Products.

Chesterfield

★ 90628 ★ Allied-Signal Inc.
Technical Center
15801 Woods Edge Rd.
Chesterfield, VA 23832
Ultimate Parent: Allied-Signal Inc. SIC:
2824—Organic Fibers—Noncellulosic.

★ 90629 ★ Allied-Signal Inc.
Technical Center
Exit 5 Interstate 95
Chesterfield, VA 23832
Ultimate Parent: Allied-Signal Inc. SIC:
2824—Organic Fibers—Noncellulosic.

★ 90630 ★ First Union National Bank of Virginia
10101 Hull St.
Chesterfield, VA 23236-1405
(804)788-9635
Location Type: Branch office. Ultimate
Parent: First Union Corp. SIC: 6021—
National Commercial Banks.

★ 90631 ★ Signet Bank, Virginia
10001 Court View Ln.
Chesterfield, VA 23832-6567
(804)771-7500
Location Type: Branch office. Ultimate
Parent: Signet Banking Corp. SIC: 6021—
National Commercial Banks.

Chilhowie

★ 90632 ★ GTE Valenite Corp.
Kendall Rd.
Chilhowie, VA 24319
Ultimate Parent: GTE. SIC: 3532—Mining
Machinery.

Chinco Teague

★ 90633 ★ Farmers & Merchants Bank-Eastern Shore
6204 Maddox Blvd.
Chinco Teague, VA 23336
(804)336-3101
Location Type: Branch office. Officer:
Wesley E. Hughes Jr., President & CEO.
Ultimate Parent: Mercantile Bankshares
Corp. SIC: 6021—National Commercial
Banks. Employee Count: 66. Sales: Na M.

Christiansburg

★ 90634 ★ First Union National Bank of Virginia
16 N. Franklin St.
Christiansburg, VA 24073-2951
(703)382-6184
Location Type: Branch office. Ultimate
Parent: First Union Corp. SIC: 6021—
National Commercial Banks.

★ 90635 ★ Food Lion
1530 Franklin St. N
Christiansburg, VA 24073
(703)382-5215
Ultimate Parent: Food Lion. SIC: 5411—
Grocery Stores.

★ 90636 ★ Hubbell
Lighting Division
Electric Way
Christiansburg, VA 24073
(703)382-6111 Fax: (703)382-1526
Company Type: Subsidiary. Officer: G.M.
Grunewald, Vice President & General
Manager. Ultimate Parent: Hubbell.

Clarksville

★ 90637 ★ Burlington Industries Inc.
Hwy. 722
Clarksville, VA 23927
(804)374-8111
Officer: Junior Waldo. Ultimate Parent:
Burlington Industries, Equity. SIC: 2211—
Broadwoven Fabric Mills—Cotton; 2221—
Broadwoven Fabric Mills—Manmade;
5131—Piece Goods & Notions.

★ 90638 ★ Burlington Menswear
State Rd. 722
Clarksville, VA 23927
(804)374-8111
Officer: Steve Herman, Manager. Ultimate
Parent: Burlington Industries, Equity. SIC:
2231—Broadwoven Fabric Mills—Wool;
2297—Nonwoven Fabrics.

★ 90639 ★ Stop & Shop
Hwy. 58
Clarksville, VA 23927
(804)374-4258
Ultimate Parent: Stop & Shop. SIC: 5411—
Grocery Stores.

Clifton Forge

★ 90640 ★ Crestar Bank
540 Main St.
Clifton Forge, VA 24422-1167
Location Type: Branch office. Ultimate
Parent: Crestar Financial Corp. SIC:
6021—National Commercial Banks.

★ 90641 ★ Crestar Bank
1501 Main St.
Clifton Forge, VA 24422-1837
Location Type: Branch office. Ultimate
Parent: Crestar Financial Corp. SIC:
6021—National Commercial Banks.

★ 90642 ★ Greyhound Bus Lines
411 E. Ridgeway St.
Clifton Forge, VA 24422
(703)862-4116
Ultimate Parent: Greyhound Lines Inc. SIC:
4121—Taxicabs.

★ 90643 ★ Kroger Co.
1618 Main St.
Clifton Forge, VA 24422
(703)863-5591
Ultimate Parent: Kroger. SIC: 5411—
Grocery Stores.

Clinchco

★ 90644 ★ Riverside Grocery
Rural Route 1
Clinchco, VA 24226
(703)762-7670
Ultimate Parent: Penn Traffic. SIC: 5399—
Miscellaneous General Merchandise Store.

Clintwood

★ 90645 ★ First Union National Bank of Virginia
80 Main St.
Clintwood, VA 24228
(703)926-4651
Location Type: Branch office. Ultimate
Parent: First Union Corp. SIC: 6021—
National Commercial Banks.

Coeburn

★ 90646 ★ Piggly Wiggly
Marty Shopping Ctr.
Coeburn, VA 24230
(703)395-2047
Ultimate Parent: Bruno's. SIC: 5421—Meat
& Fish Markets.

Collinsville

★ 90647 ★ Crestar Bank
243 Virginia Ave.
Collinsville, VA 24078-2219
(703)666-8205
Location Type: Branch office. Ultimate
Parent: Crestar Financial Corp. SIC:
6021—National Commercial Banks.

★ 90648 ★   First Union National
Bank of Virginia
115 S. Virginia Ave.
Collinsville, VA 24078-2221
(703)647-3737
Location Type: Branch office. Ultimate
Parent: First Union Corp. SIC: 6021—
National Commercial Banks.

Colonial Beach

★ 90649 ★   First Virginia Bank
416 Colonial Ave.
Colonial Beach, VA 22443-2298
(804)224-0151
Location Type: Branch office. Ultimate
Parent: First Virginia Banks Inc. SIC:
6021—National Commercial Banks.

★ 90650 ★   Signet Bank, Virginia
State Rte. 205
Colonial Beach, VA 22443-1861
(804)224-0101
Location Type: Branch office. Ultimate
Parent: Signet Banking Corp. SIC: 6021—
National Commercial Banks.

Colonial Heights

★ 90651 ★   Colonial Heights
Packaging Inc.
1106 W. Roslyn Rd.
Colonial Heights, VA 23834
Ultimate Parent: Philip Morris. SIC: 2754—
Commercial Printing—Gravure.

★ 90652 ★   Signet Bank, Virginia
45 Colonial Sq.
Colonial Heights, VA 23834-2406
(804)526-6650
Location Type: Branch office. Ultimate
Parent: Signet Banking Corp. SIC: 6021—
National Commercial Banks.

Columbia

★ 90653 ★   Reliance Insurance
Co.
5565 Sterrett Pl.
Columbia, VA 23038
(804)643-3209
Ultimate Parent: Reliance Group Holdings.
SIC: 6411—Insurance Agents, Brokers &
Service.

Courtland

★ 90654 ★   First Union National
Bank of Virginia
305 S. Main St.
Courtland, VA 23837-1126
(804)653-2642
Location Type: Branch office. Ultimate
Parent: First Union Corp. SIC: 6021—
National Commercial Banks.

Covington

★ 90655 ★   Exxon Co.
909 S. Lexington Ave.
Covington, VA 24426
(703)965-5386
Ultimate Parent: Exxon. SIC: 5172—
Petroleum Products Nec.

★ 90656 ★   First Union National
Bank of Virginia
246 W. Main St.
Covington, VA 24426-1543
(703)962-6111
Location Type: Branch office. Ultimate
Parent: First Union Corp. SIC: 6021—
National Commercial Banks.

★ 90657 ★   First Virginia Bank
Highlands
450 W. Main St.
Covington, VA 24426-1554
(703)962-6131
Company Type: Subsidiary. Officer:
Fletcher D. Watson, Chairman of the Board.
Ultimate Parent: First Virginia Banks Inc.
SIC: 6022—State Commercial Banks.

★ 90658 ★   First Virginia Bank -
Highlands
450 W. Main St.
Covington, VA 24426-1554
(703)962-6131
Company Type: Subsidiary. Officer: F. D.
Watson, Chairman of the Board. Ultimate

Parent: First Virginia Banks Inc. SIC:
6022—State Commercial Banks. Employee
Count: 35.

★ 90659 ★   Food Lion
1252 S. Craig Ave.
Covington, VA 24426
(703)962-5232
Ultimate Parent: Food Lion. SIC: 5411—
Grocery Stores.

★ 90660 ★   Greyhound Bus Lines
804 S. Highland Ave.
Covington, VA 24426
(703)962-5022
Ultimate Parent: Greyhound Lines Inc. SIC:
4111—Local & Suburban Transit.

★ 90661 ★   Hercules Inc.
Edgemont Dr.
Covington, VA 24426
Ultimate Parent: Hercules. SIC: 3081—
Unsupported Plastics Film & Sheet.

★ 90662 ★   Kroger Co.
1015 S. Craig Ave.
Covington, VA 24426
(703)965-9306
Ultimate Parent: Kroger. SIC: 5411—
Grocery Stores.

★ 90663 ★   New York Life
Insurance Co.
203 W. Locust St.
Covington, VA 24426
(703)962-7579
Ultimate Parent: New York Life. SIC:
6411—Insurance Agents, Brokers &
Service.

★ 90664 ★   Radio Shack
Mallow Mall
Covington, VA 24426
(703)962-3248
Company Type: Division. Ultimate Parent:
Tandy Corp. SIC: 5065—Electronic Parts &
Equipment Nec; 5731—Radio, Television &
Electronics Stores.

★ 90665 ★   Thrift Drug
Mallow Mall
Covington, VA 24426
(703)962-3438
Ultimate Parent: J.C. Penney. SIC: 5049—
Professional Equipment Nec; 5912—Drug
Stores & Proprietary Stores.

★ 90666 ★   Westvaco Corp.
Bleached Board
104 E. Riverside Ave.
Covington, VA 24426-0950
Ultimate Parent: WestVaco Corp. SIC:
2631—Paperboard Mills; 2836—Biological
Products Except Diagnostic.

★ 90667 ★   Westvaco Corp.
Chemicals
Washington St.
Covington, VA 24426
Ultimate Parent: WestVaco Corp. SIC:
2819—Industrial Inorganic Chemicals Nec.

★ 90668 ★   Westvaco Corp.
Carbon Dept.
104 E. Riverside St.
Covington, VA 24426
(703)969-5000
Officer: Bill Small, Vice President. Ultimate
Parent: WestVaco Corp. SIC: 2621—Paper
Mills; 2631—Paperboard Mills; 2819—
Industrial Inorganic Chemicals Nec.

Crewe

★ 90669 ★   Tyson Foods Inc.
Hwy. 360
Crewe, VA 23930
(804)645-7791
Officer: Chip Miller, Manager. Ultimate
Parent: Tyson Foods, Inc. SIC: 2015—
Poultry Slaughtering & Processing.

Cross Junction

★ 90670 ★   McDonald's
Hamburgers
Hcr 1
Cross Junction, VA 22625
(703)888-3656
Ultimate Parent: McDonald's. SIC: 5947—
Gift, Novelty & Souvenir Shops.

Crozet

★ 90671 ★   ConAgra Frozen
Foods
Rte. 240 W
RR 1, Box 24A
Crozet, VA 22932
(804)823-3200 Fax: (804)823-3255
Company Type: Division. Officer: Gary
Bartolacci, Plant Manager. Ultimate Parent:
Conagra.

Culpeper

★ 90672 ★   Blazer Financial
Services
162 E. Davis St.
Culpeper, VA 22701
(703)825-0761
Ultimate Parent: Great Western Financial
Corp. SIC: 6141—Personal Credit
Institutions.

★ 90673 ★   Chesapeake &
Potomac Telephone Co.
502 E. Piedmont St.
Culpeper, VA 22701-2830
(703)543-4788
Company Type: Subsidiary. Location
Type: Branch office. Officer: Dougalss T.
Pinkard. Ultimate Parent: Bell Atlantic
Corp. SIC: 4813—Telephone
Communications Except Radiotelephone.

★ 90674 ★   First Union National
Bank of Virginia
633 Meadowbrook Ctr.
Culpeper, VA 22701-3949
(703)825-2740
Location Type: Branch office. Ultimate
Parent: First Union Corp. SIC: 6021—
National Commercial Banks.

★ 90675 ★   Food Lion
509 Meadowbrook Dr.
Culpeper, VA 22701
(703)825-9448
Ultimate Parent: Food Lion. SIC: 5411—
Grocery Stores.

★ 90676 ★   Hudson's
806 N. Main St.
Culpeper, VA 22701
(703)825-2110
Ultimate Parent: Dayton Hudson. SIC:
5941—Sporting Goods & Bicycle Shops.

★ 90677 ★   Radio Shack
515 Madison Rd.
Culpeper, VA 22701
(703)825-3054
Company Type: Division. Ultimate Parent:
Tandy Corp. SIC: 5063—Electrical
Apparatus & Equipment.

★ 90678 ★   Rite Aid
701 James Madisonhwy
Culpeper, VA 22701
(703)825-0704
Ultimate Parent: Rite Aid. SIC: 5912—Drug
Stores & Proprietary Stores.

Dahlgren

★ 90679 ★   Citgo
RR 301
Dahlgren, VA 22448
(703)663-2431
Ultimate Parent: Citgo Petroleum.

★ 90680 ★   First Virginia Bank
Rte. 206
Dahlgren, VA 22448
(703)663-2101
Location Type: Branch office. Ultimate
Parent: First Virginia Banks Inc. SIC:
6021—National Commercial Banks.

Dale City

★ 90681 ★   Crestar Bank
4150 Dale Blvd.
Dale City, VA 22193-2286
(800)451-2435
Location Type: Branch office. Ultimate
Parent: Crestar Financial Corp. SIC:
6021—National Commercial Banks.

★ 90682 ★   First Union National
Bank of Virginia
13870 Smoketown Rd.
Dale City, VA 22193
(703)934-1851
Location Type: Branch office. Ultimate
Parent: First Union Corp. SIC: 6021—
National Commercial Banks.

Damascus

★ 90683 ★   First Virginia Bank
Mountain Empire
PO Box 368
Laurel Ave.
Damascus, VA 24236-0368
(703)475-3112
Company Type: Subsidiary. Officer: Clyde
T. Combs, Chairman of the Board. Ultimate
Parent: First Virginia Banks Inc. SIC:
6022—State Commercial Banks.

Danville

★ 90684 ★   APAC
239 Eastwood Dr.
Danville, VA 24540
(804)792-4211
Officer: John Conway, President. Ultimate
Parent: Ashland Oil. SIC: 2951—Asphalt
Paving Mixtures & Blocks.

★ 90685 ★   Blazer Financial
Services
113 Market St. N
Danville, VA 24541
(804)792-3232
Ultimate Parent: Great Western Financial
Corp. SIC: 6141—Personal Credit
Institutions.

★ 90686 ★   Carter Machinery Co.,
Inc.
RR 58
Danville, VA 24541
(804)793-7900
Ultimate Parent: Carter-Wallace. SIC:
5082—Construction & Mining Machinery.

★ 90687 ★   Corning Glass Works
Rte. 4 Box 495
Danville, VA 24541
Ultimate Parent: Corning. SIC: 3229—
Pressed & Blown Glass Nec.

★ 90688 ★   Corning Inc.
265 Corning Dr.
Danville, VA 24541
Ultimate Parent: Corning.

★ 90689 ★   Dibrell Brothers
512 Bridge St.
Danville, VA 24543
(804)792-7511
Company Type: Headquarters. Officer:
Claude B. Owen Jr. Employee Count:
4600. Sales: 1065 M. Fortune 500: Largest
U.S. Industrial Corporations: Ranking 356.

★ 90690 ★   Eckerd Drugs
2 Piedmont Massachusetts
Danville, VA 24541
(804)792-1469
Ultimate Parent: Eckerd Corp. SIC: 5912—
Drug Stores & Proprietary Stores.

★ 90691 ★   Eckerd Drugs
20 Piedmont Mall
Danville, VA 24540
(804)792-1469
Ultimate Parent: Eckerd Corp. SIC: 5912—
Drug Stores & Proprietary Stores.

★ 90692 ★   First Virginia Bank -
Moutain Empire
1017 W. Main St.
Danville, VA 24541-4712
(703)475-3112
Company Type: Subsidiary. Officer: Larry
Richardson, President. Ultimate Parent:
First Virginia Banks Inc. SIC: 6022—State
Commercial Banks. Employee Count: 63.

★ 90693 ★   Flowers Baking Co.
1276 S. Boston Rd.
Danville, VA 24540
(804)791-4100
Ultimate Parent: Flowers Industries. SIC:
5149—Groceries & Related Products Nec;
5461—Retail Bakeries.

★ **90694** ★ **Food Lion**
3311 Riverside Dr.
Danville, VA 24541
(804)792-2002
Ultimate Parent: Food Lion. **SIC:** 5411—Grocery Stores.

★ **90695** ★ **Food Lion**
540 Westover Dr.
Danville, VA 24541
(804)793-1513
Ultimate Parent: Food Lion. **SIC:** 5411—Grocery Stores.

★ **90696** ★ **Food Lion**
703 Piney Forest Rd.
Danville, VA 24540
(804)792-3091
Ultimate Parent: Food Lion. **SIC:** 5411—Grocery Stores.

★ **90697** ★ **Goodyear Tire & Rubber Co.**
1901 Goodyear Blvd.
Danville, VA 24541-9473
Ultimate Parent: Goodyear Tire & Rubber. **SIC:** 3011—Tires & Inner Tubes.

★ **90698** ★ **Goodyear Tire & Rubber Co.**
Goodyear Blvd.
Danville, VA 24541-9473
Ultimate Parent: Goodyear Tire & Rubber. **SIC:** 3011—Tires & Inner Tubes.

★ **90699** ★ **Goodyear Tire & Rubber Co.**
1435 Goodyear Blvd.
Danville, VA 24541-9473
Ultimate Parent: Goodyear Tire & Rubber. **SIC:** 3011—Tires & Inner Tubes.

★ **90700** ★ **J C Penney Catalog Sales**
33 Piedmont Mall
Danville, VA 24540
(804)793-7741
Ultimate Parent: J.C. Penney. **SIC:** 5961—Catalog & Mail-Order Houses.

★ **90701** ★ **Kroger Co.**
Kings Plz.
Danville, VA 24541
(804)797-2742
Ultimate Parent: Kroger. **SIC:** 5411—Grocery Stores.

★ **90702** ★ **Kroger Co.**
1350 W. Main St.
Danville, VA 24541
(804)791-1601
Ultimate Parent: Kroger. **SIC:** 5411—Grocery Stores.

★ **90703** ★ **Kroger Co.**
119 Piney Forest Rd.
Danville, VA 24540
(804)793-2351
Ultimate Parent: Kroger. **SIC:** 5411—Grocery Stores.

★ **90704** ★ **Life Insurance Co. Virginia**
610 N. Ridge St.
Danville, VA 24541
(804)792-1913
Ultimate Parent: Life Insurance Co. of Virginia. **SIC:** 6411—Insurance Agents, Brokers & Service.

★ **90705** ★ **New York Life**
2420 Riverside Dr.
Danville, VA 24540
(804)792-0636
Ultimate Parent: New York Life. **SIC:** 6411—Insurance Agents, Brokers & Service.

★ **90706** ★ **New York Life Insurance Co.**
Masonic Temple
Danville, VA 24541
(804)792-0851
Ultimate Parent: New York Life. **SIC:** 6411—Insurance Agents, Brokers & Service.

★ **90707** ★ **Overnite Transportation Co.**
101 Mount Cross Rd.
Danville, VA 24540
(804)792-4822
Ultimate Parent: Union Pacific Corp. **SIC:** 4213—Trucking Except Local.

★ **90708** ★ **Overnite Transportation Co.**
Old Riverside Dr.
Danville, VA 24541
(804)792-4822
Ultimate Parent: Union Pacific Corp. **SIC:** 4213—Trucking Except Local.

★ **90709** ★ **Piggly Wiggly**
1304 S. Boston Rd.
Danville, VA 24540
(804)793-8355
Ultimate Parent: Bruno's. **SIC:** 5411—Grocery Stores.

★ **90710** ★ **Radio Shack**
3 Piedmont Massachusetts
Danville, VA 24541
(804)799-4006
Company Type: Division. **Ultimate Parent:** Tandy Corp. **SIC:** 7373—Computer Integrated Systems Design.

★ **90711** ★ **Radio Shack**
3 Piedmont Dr.
Danville, VA 24541
(804)799-4006
Company Type: Division. **Ultimate Parent:** Tandy Corp. **SIC:** 7373—Computer Integrated Systems Design.

★ **90712** ★ **Radio Shack**
36 Piedmont Mall
Danville, VA 24540
(804)799-4006
Company Type: Division. **Ultimate Parent:** Tandy Corp. **SIC:** 7373—Computer Integrated Systems Design.

★ **90713** ★ **Radio Shack**
211 Nordan Dr.
Danville, VA 24540
(804)793-4568
Company Type: Division. **Ultimate Parent:** Tandy Corp. **SIC:** 5731—Radio, Television & Electronics Stores.

★ **90714** ★ **Radio Shack**
Riverside Shopping Ctr.
Danville, VA 24541
(804)799-3516
Company Type: Division. **Ultimate Parent:** Tandy Corp. **SIC:** 5065—Electronic Parts & Equipment Nec.

★ **90715** ★ **Radio Shack**
36 Piedmont Mall
Danville, VA 24540
(804)799-3516
Company Type: Division. **Ultimate Parent:** Tandy Corp. **SIC:** 5731—Radio, Television & Electronics Stores.

★ **90716** ★ **Signet Bank, VA**
530 Main St.
Danville, VA 24541-1318
(804)791-6813
Location Type: Branch office. **Ultimate Parent:** Signet Banking Corp. **SIC:** 6021—National Commercial Banks.

★ **90717** ★ **Signet Bank, VA**
1500 Piney Forest Rd.
Danville, VA 24541-1706
(804)791-6850
Location Type: Branch office. **Ultimate Parent:** Signet Banking Corp. **SIC:** 6021—National Commercial Banks.

★ **90718** ★ **Signet Bank, Virginia**
3320 Riverside Dr.
Danville, VA 24541-3429
(804)791-6840
Location Type: Branch office. **Ultimate Parent:** Signet Banking Corp. **SIC:** 6021—National Commercial Banks.

★ **90719** ★ **Signet Bank, Virginia**
Ballou Shopping Ctr.
Danville, VA 24541
(804)791-6830
Location Type: Branch office. **Ultimate Parent:** Signet Banking Corp. **SIC:** 6021—National Commercial Banks.

★ **90720** ★ **Southern Processors Inc.**
State Rd. 729
Danville, VA 24540
(804)797-4414
Officer: Bryant Gravitte, Vice President. **Ultimate Parent:** Universal Corp. **SIC:** 2141—Tobacco Stemming & Redrying.

★ **90721** ★ **Thrift Drug**
Danville Plz.
Danville, VA 24541
(804)793-5092
Ultimate Parent: J.C. Penney. **SIC:** 5049—Professional Equipment Nec.

★ **90722** ★ **United Parcel Service**
Mt Crs Rd.
Danville, VA 24543
(804)522-3908
Ultimate Parent: United Parcel Service of America. **SIC:** 4215—Courier Services Except by Air.

★ **90723** ★ **Winn-Dixie Stores**
211 Dan Ln.
Danville, VA 24540
(804)793-9886
Ultimate Parent: Winn-Dixie Stores, Inc. **SIC:** 5411—Grocery Stores.

★ **90724** ★ **Winn-Dixie Stores**
3360 Riverside Dr.
Danville, VA 24541
(804)792-9748
Ultimate Parent: Winn-Dixie Stores, Inc. **SIC:** 5411—Grocery Stores.

★ **90725** ★ **Wood Fiber Industries**
Masonite Dr.
Danville, VA 24543
Ultimate Parent: International Paper Co. **SIC:** 2493—Reconstituted Wood Products.

Dinwiddie

★ **90726** ★ **Signet Bank, Virginia**
14003 Boydton Plank Rd.
Dinwiddie, VA 23841-9801
(804)469-3761
Location Type: Branch office. **Ultimate Parent:** Signet Banking Corp. **SIC:** 6021—National Commercial Banks.

Doswell

★ **90727** ★ **Circuit City**
Rr 1
Doswell, VA 23047
(804)876-3330
Ultimate Parent: Circuit City Stores. **SIC:** 5719—Miscellaneous Home Furnishings Stores.

★ **90728** ★ **Crestar Bank**
US Rte. 1 & Rte. 602
Doswell, VA 23047-9801
(804)876-3611
Location Type: Branch office. **Ultimate Parent:** Crestar Financial Corp. **SIC:** 6021—National Commercial Banks.

Dublin

★ **90729** ★ **Signet Bank, Virginia**
US Rte. 11
Dublin, VA 24084-9501
(703)674-8886
Location Type: Branch office. **Ultimate Parent:** Signet Banking Corp. **SIC:** 6021—National Commercial Banks.

Duffield

★ **90730** ★ **Cyprus Foote Mineral Co.**
State Rte. 871
Duffield, VA 24244-0087
Ultimate Parent: Cyprus Amax Minerals. **SIC:** 2891—Adhesives & Sealants.

Dumfries

★ **90731** ★ **Signet Bank, Virginia**
201 Graham Pk. Rd.
US Rte. 1
Dumfries, VA 22026-2598
(703)221-4101
Location Type: Branch office. **Ultimate Parent:** Signet Banking Corp. **SIC:** 6021—National Commercial Banks.

Earlysville

★ **90732** ★ **Cooper Industries Ded**
Rte. 660
Earlysville, VA 22936
Ultimate Parent: Cooper Industries. **SIC:** 3643—Current-Carrying Wiring Devices.

★ **90733** ★ **Cooper Industries Edp**
Hwy. Rte. 660
Earlysville, VA 22936
Ultimate Parent: Cooper Industries. **SIC:** 3643—Current-Carrying Wiring Devices.

★ **90734** ★ **Cooper Industries Inc. Electrical Distrib. Products**
Rte. 660
Earlysville, VA 22936
Ultimate Parent: Cooper Industries. **SIC:** 3643—Current-Carrying Wiring Devices.

★ **90735** ★ **Teledyne Avionics**
Rte. 743 Earlysville Rd.
Earlysville, VA 22936
Ultimate Parent: Teledyne. **SIC:** 3800—Instruments & Related Products.

Eastville

★ **90736** ★ **Eastville Bank**
16485 Lankford Hwy.
Eastville, VA 23347
(804)678-5187 **Fax:** (804)678-9046
Location Type: Headquarters. **Ultimate Parent:** Mercantile Bankshares Corp. **SIC:** 6021—National Commercial Banks.

★ **90737** ★ **Eastville Bank**
PO Box 7
Eastville, VA 23347-0007
Location Type: Headquarters. **Officer:** Carl A. Tenhoopen Jr., Chairman of the Board. **Ultimate Parent:** Mercantile Bankshares Corp. **SIC:** 6021—National Commercial Banks. **Employee Count:** 123.

★ **90738** ★ **Eastville Banks**
U S. Rte. 13
Eastville, VA 23347
(804)678-5187
Officer: Robert L. Sempson, President & CEO. **Ultimate Parent:** Mercantile Bankshares Corp. **SIC:** 6022—State Commercial Banks. **Employee Count:** 10. **Sales:** Na M.

Edinberg

★ **90739** ★ **Crestar Bank**
300 Stoney Creek Blvd.
Edinberg, VA 22824
(703)984-4165
Location Type: Branch office. **Ultimate Parent:** Crestar Financial Corp. **SIC:** 6021—National Commercial Banks.

★ **90740** ★ **First Union National Bank of Virginia**
120 S. Main St.
Edinburg, VA 22824
(703)984-4128
Location Type: Branch office. **Ultimate Parent:** First Union Corp. **SIC:** 6021—National Commercial Banks.

Elk Creek

★ **90741** ★ **Camcar Elk Creek Paycarl Prods. Div.**
Elk Creek Paycarl Products Division
PO Box 106 Hwy. 21
Elk Creek, VA 24326
Ultimate Parent: Textron. **SIC:** 3452—Bolts, Nuts, Rivets & Washers.

★ **90742** ★ **Camcar/Textron Inc.**
Elk Creek Raycarl Products Division
Hwy. 21 PO Box 106
Elk Creek, VA 24326-0106
Ultimate Parent: Textron. **SIC:** 3452—Bolts, Nuts, Rivets & Washers.

Elkton

★ **90743** ★ **Adolph Coors Co.**
Rte. 340, PO Box 25
Elkton, VA 22827
Ultimate Parent: Adolph Coors. **SIC:** 2082—Malt Beverages; 4222—Refrigerated Warehousing & Storage; 5181—Beer & Ale.

★ 90744 ★   **Coors Brewing Co.**
Rte. 340 S. PO Box 25
Elkton, VA 22827
Ultimate Parent: Adolph Coors. **SIC:**
2082—Malt Beverages; 4222—Refrigerated
Warehousing & Storage; 5181—Beer & Ale.

★ 90745 ★   **Coors Brewing Co.**
Rte. 340 PO Box 25
Elkton, VA 22827
Ultimate Parent: Adolph Coors. **SIC:**
2082—Malt Beverages; 4222—Refrigerated
Warehousing & Storage; 5181—Beer & Ale.

★ 90746 ★   **Merck & Co. Inc.**
Hwy. 340 S.
Elkton, VA 22827-7000
Ultimate Parent: Merck. **SIC:** 2834—
Pharmaceutical Preparations.

★ 90747 ★   **Rite Aid**
Shen Elk Plz.
Elkton, VA 22827
(703)298-2234
Ultimate Parent: Rite Aid. **SIC:** 5912—Drug
Stores & Proprietary Stores.

Emporia

★ 90748 ★   **Georgia-Pacific Corp.
Emporia Pine Plywood**
Davis Rd.
Emporia, VA 23847
Ultimate Parent: Georgia-Pacific. **SIC:**
2436—Softwood Veneer & Plywood.

★ 90749 ★   **Mary Kay Cosmetics**
412 PO Box
Emporia, VA 23847
(804)634-5426
Ultimate Parent: Mary Kay Cosmetics.

Exmore

★ 90750 ★   **Asgrow Seed Co.**
Exmore, VA 23350
(804)442-5451
Ultimate Parent: Upjohn Co.

★ 90751 ★   **Radio Shack**
RR 1
Exmore, VA 23350
(804)787-2491
Company Type: Division. **Ultimate Parent:**
Tandy Corp. **SIC:** 7231—Beauty Shops.

★ 90752 ★   **Radio Shack**
Rural Route 1
Exmore, VA 23350
(804)787-2491
Company Type: Division. **Ultimate Parent:**
Tandy Corp. **SIC:** 7231—Beauty Shops.

Fairfax

★ 90753 ★   **Atlantic Richfield Co.**
9601 Colonial Ave.
Fairfax, VA 22031
(703)323-8230
Ultimate Parent: Atlantic Richfield Co., Inc.
SIC: 5172—Petroleum Products Nec.

★ 90754 ★   **Beneficial Virginia
Inc.**
10201 Lee Hwy.
Fairfax, VA 22030-2222
(703)591-8360
Location Type: Branch office. **Ultimate
Parent:** Beneficial. **SIC:** 6141—Personal
Credit Institutions; 6162—Mortgage Bankers
& Correspondents.

★ 90755 ★   **Browning-Ferris
Industries**
2813 Juniper St.
Fairfax, VA 22031
(703)560-8866
Officer: Randy Bergeson, Manager.
Ultimate Parent: Browning-Ferris
Industries. **SIC:** 3589—Service Industry
Machinery Nec.

★ 90756 ★   **Business Systems**
4009 Williamsburg Ct.
Fairfax, VA 22032-1139
(703)352-4555
Ultimate Parent: Avery Dennison Corp.
SIC: 7371—Computer Programming
Services.

★ 90757 ★   **Career Image**
Fair Oaks Mall
Fairfax, VA 22033
(703)352-8098
Ultimate Parent: United States Shoe. **SIC:**
5621—Women's Clothing Stores.

★ 90758 ★   **Centex-Simpson
Construction Co., Inc.**
10300 Eaton Pl., Ste. 300
Fairfax, VA 22030
(703)698-6886 **Fax:** (703)934-5520
Officer: Michael A. Wagner, President &
CEO. **Ultimate Parent:** Centex.

★ 90759 ★   **Circuit City**
19060 Lee Hwy.
Fairfax, VA 22030
(703)591-3142
Ultimate Parent: Circuit City Stores. **SIC:**
5731—Radio, Television & Electronics
Stores.

★ 90760 ★   **Citgo Petroleum Corp.**
9600 Colonial Ave.
Fairfax, VA 22031
(703)323-1100
Ultimate Parent: Citgo Petroleum. **SIC:**
5983—Fuel Oil Dealers.

★ 90761 ★   **Citgo Petroleum Corp.**
9600 Colonial Ave.
Fairfax, VA 22031
(703)323-1100
Ultimate Parent: Citgo Petroleum. **SIC:**
5983—Fuel Oil Dealers.

★ 90762 ★   **Crestar Bank**
13033 Lee Jackson Memorial Hwy.
Fairfax, VA 22033-2001
(703)838-3570
Location Type: Branch office. **Ultimate
Parent:** Crestar Financial Corp. **SIC:**
6021—National Commercial Banks.

★ 90763 ★   **Crestar Bank**
10641 W. Lee Hwy.
Fairfax, VA 22030-4309
(703)838-3560
Location Type: Branch office. **Ultimate
Parent:** Crestar Financial Corp. **SIC:**
6021—National Commercial Banks.

★ 90764 ★   **Crestar Bank**
9401 Lee Hwy.
Fairfax, VA 22031-1803
(800)451-2435
Location Type: Branch office. **Ultimate
Parent:** Crestar Financial Corp. **SIC:**
6021—National Commercial Banks.

★ 90765 ★   **Crestar Bank**
4020 University Dr.
Fairfax, VA 22030-6802
(703)691-4520
Location Type: Branch office. **Ultimate
Parent:** Crestar Financial Corp. **SIC:**
6021—National Commercial Banks.

★ 90766 ★   **E-Systems Inc.**
Melpar Div.
11225 Waples Mill Rd.
Fairfax, VA 22030
Company Type: Division. **Ultimate Parent:**
E-Systems Inc. **SIC:** 3663—Radio & T.V.
Communications Equipment.

★ 90767 ★   **First American Bank**
10695 Braddock Rd.
Fairfax, VA 22032
(703)934-1931
Ultimate Parent: First American Corp. **SIC:**
6099—Functions Related to Deposit
Banking.

★ 90768 ★   **First American Bank**
11944 L Fair Oaks
Fairfax, VA 22033
(703)934-1825
Ultimate Parent: First American Corp. **SIC:**
6099—Functions Related to Deposit
Banking.

★ 90769 ★   **First American Bank**
3090 Williams Dr.
Fairfax, VA 22031
(703)934-1811
Ultimate Parent: First American Corp. **SIC:**
6099—Functions Related to Deposit
Banking.

★ 90770 ★   **First American Bank
of Virginia**
4021 University Dr., No. 100
Fairfax, VA 22030
(703)827-8720
Ultimate Parent: First American Corp. **SIC:**
6022—State Commercial Banks.

★ 90771 ★   **First American Bank
of Virginia**
3090 Williams Dr.
Fairfax, VA 22031
(703)821-7721
Ultimate Parent: First American Corp. **SIC:**
6022—State Commercial Banks.

★ 90772 ★   **First Federal S & L**
3554 Chain Bridge Rd., Ste. 201
Fairfax, VA 22030-2709
(703)273-5400
Company Type: Branch. **Ultimate Parent:**
Bancorp Hawaii. **SIC:** 6035—Federal
Savings Institutions.

★ 90773 ★   **First Union National
Bank of Virginia**
12735 Shops Ln.
Fairfax, VA 22033
(703)934-1865
Location Type: Branch office. **Ultimate
Parent:** First Union Corp. **SIC:** 6021—
National Commercial Banks.

★ 90774 ★   **First Union National
Bank of Virginia**
3040 Williams Dr.
Fairfax, VA 22031-4613
(703)934-1810
Location Type: Branch office. **Ultimate
Parent:** First Union Corp. **SIC:** 6021—
National Commercial Banks.

★ 90775 ★   **First Union National
Bank of Virginia**
10697 Braddock Rd.
Fairfax, VA 22032-2237
(703)934-1931
Location Type: Branch office. **Ultimate
Parent:** First Union Corp. **SIC:** 6021—
National Commercial Banks.

★ 90776 ★   **First Union National
Bank of Virginia**
4021 University Dr.
Fairfax, VA 22030-3408
Location Type: Branch office. **Ultimate
Parent:** First Union Corp. **SIC:** 6021—
National Commercial Banks.

★ 90777 ★   **First Union National
Bank of Virginia**
3019 Nutley St.
Fairfax, VA 22031-1931
(703)442-3654
Location Type: Branch office. **Ultimate
Parent:** First Union Corp. **SIC:** 6021—
National Commercial Banks.

★ 90778 ★   **First Union National
Bank of Virginia**
501 Main St.
Fairfax, VA 22030-3301
(703)442-3603
Location Type: Branch office. **Ultimate
Parent:** First Union Corp. **SIC:** 6021—
National Commercial Banks.

★ 90779 ★   **First Virginia Bank**
8920 Village Shops Dr.
Fairfax, VA 22039
(703)241-4742
Location Type: Branch office. **Ultimate
Parent:** First Virginia Banks Inc. **SIC:**
6021—National Commercial Banks.

★ 90780 ★   **First Virginia Bank**
8416 Arlington Blvd.
Fairfax, VA 22031-4615
(703)241-3485
Location Type: Branch office. **Ultimate
Parent:** First Virginia Banks Inc. **SIC:**
6021—National Commercial Banks.

★ 90781 ★   **First Virginia Bank**
5700 Union Mill Rd.
Fairfax, VA 22024
(703)241-4463
Location Type: Branch office. **Ultimate
Parent:** First Virginia Banks Inc. **SIC:**
6021—National Commercial Banks.

★ 90782 ★   **First Virginia Bank**
9521 Braddock Rd.
Fairfax, VA 22032-2539
(703)241-3471
Location Type: Branch office. **Ultimate
Parent:** First Virginia Banks Inc. **SIC:**
6021—National Commercial Banks.

★ 90783 ★   **First Virginia Bank**
13045 Lee Jackson Memorial Hwy.
Fairfax, VA 22033-2001
(703)241-3322
Location Type: Branch office. **Ultimate
Parent:** First Virginia Banks Inc. **SIC:**
6021—National Commercial Banks.

★ 90784 ★   **First Virginia Bank**
10302 Willard Way
Fairfax, VA 22030-2578
(703)241-3411
Location Type: Branch office. **Ultimate
Parent:** First Virginia Banks Inc. **SIC:**
6021—National Commercial Banks.

★ 90785 ★   **First Virginia Bank**
11230 Waples Mill Rd.
Fairfax, VA 22030-6087
(703)241-3611
Location Type: Branch office. **Ultimate
Parent:** First Virginia Banks Inc. **SIC:**
6021—National Commercial Banks.

★ 90786 ★   **Friendswood Dev Co.**
12500 Fair Lakes Cir.
Fairfax, VA 22033
(703)818-2708
Ultimate Parent: Exxon.

★ 90787 ★   **Gap Stores**
Fair Oaks Mall
Fairfax, VA 22033
(703)385-9708
Ultimate Parent: GAP. **SIC:** 5699—
Miscellaneous Apparel & Accessory Stores.

★ 90788 ★   **Gap Stores**
Fair Oaks Mll
Fairfax, VA 22033
(703)385-9708
Ultimate Parent: GAP. **SIC:** 5699—
Miscellaneous Apparel & Accessory Stores.

★ 90789 ★   **Hit or Miss**
Faircity Mall
Fairfax, VA 22031
(703)425-3872
Ultimate Parent: TJX. **SIC:** 5621—
Women's Clothing Stores.

★ 90790 ★   **Liberty Mutual
Insurance Co.**
12011 Lee Jackson Hwy.
Fairfax, VA 22033
(703)385-4444
Ultimate Parent: Liberty Mutual Group.
SIC: 6411—Insurance Agents, Brokers &
Service.

★ 90791 ★   **Life Insurance Co. of
Virginia**
10600 Arrowhead Dr.
Fairfax, VA 22030
Ultimate Parent: Life Insurance Co. of
Virginia. **SIC:** 6411—Insurance Agents,
Brokers & Service.

★ 90792 ★   **Lincoln Electric Co.**
2832 Dorr Ave.
Fairfax, VA 22031
(703)573-9225
Ultimate Parent: Lincoln Electric Co. **SIC:**
5063—Electrical Apparatus & Equipment.

★ 90793 ★   **Mary Kay Cosmetics**
5209 Grinnell St.
Fairfax, VA 22032
(703)978-4361
Ultimate Parent: Mary Kay Cosmetics.

★ 90794 ★   **Mary Kay Cosmetics
Independ**
4612 Lawn Ct
Fairfax, VA 22032
(703)323-9593
Ultimate Parent: Mary Kay Cosmetics. **SIC:**
5999—Miscellaneous Retail Stores Nec.

★ 90795 ★   **Mobil**
3225 Gallows Rd.
Fairfax, VA 22037
(703)846-3000
Company Type: Headquarters. **Officer:**
Lucio R. Noto. **Employee Count:** 61900.
Sales: 56576 M. **Fortune 500:** Largest U.S.
Industrial Corporations: Ranking 6.

★ 90796 ★　Mobil Chemical
3225 Gallows Rd.
Fairfax, VA 22037-0001
Officer: Philip W. Matos, President.
Ultimate Parent: Mobil.

★ 90797 ★　Mobil Corp.
3225 Gallows Rd.
Fairfax, VA 22037
(703)846-3000
Company Type: Headquarters. **Officer:**
Lucio A. Noto. **Ultimate Parent:** Mobil. **SIC:**
6719—Holding Companies Nec; 1311—
Crude Petroleum & Natural Gas; 1382—Oil
& Gas Exploration Services; 2869—
Industrial Organic Chemicals Nec; 2911—
Petroleum Refining; 3089—Plastics
Products Nec; 5172—Petroleum Products
Nec.

★ 90798 ★　Mobil Land
Development Corp.
3225 Gallows Rd.
Fairfax, VA 22037-0001
Officer: W. D. Deihl, General Manager.
Ultimate Parent: Mobil.

★ 90799 ★　Mobil Oil Corp.
3225 Gallows Rd.
Fairfax, VA 22037-0001
Officer: Allen E. Murray, Chairman of the
Board & CEO. **Ultimate Parent:** Mobil.

★ 90800 ★　Mobil Oil Corp.
3225 Gallows Rd.
Fairfax, VA 22037
(703)883-4242
Ultimate Parent: Mobil. **SIC:** 5172—
Petroleum Products Nec.

★ 90801 ★　Mobil Service Center
10619 Braddock Rd.
Fairfax, VA 22032
(703)471-0018
Ultimate Parent: Mobil. **SIC:** 5541—
Gasoline Service Stations.

★ 90802 ★　Radio Shack
Fair Oaks Mall
Fairfax, VA 22033
(703)591-2043
Company Type: Division. **Ultimate Parent:**
Tandy Corp. **SIC:** 5065—Electronic Parts &
Equipment Nec.

★ 90803 ★　Radio Shack
3242 Pickett Rd.
Fairfax, VA 22031
(703)591-3783
Company Type: Division. **Ultimate Parent:**
Tandy Corp. **SIC:** 5065—Electronic Parts &
Equipment Nec.

★ 90804 ★　Radio Shack
Fair Oaks Mall
Fairfax, VA 22033
(703)591-2043
Company Type: Division. **Ultimate Parent:**
Tandy Corp. **SIC:** 5065—Electronic Parts &
Equipment Nec.

★ 90805 ★　Radio Shack
3242 Pickett Rd.
Fairfax, VA 22031
(703)591-3783
Company Type: Division. **Ultimate Parent:**
Tandy Corp. **SIC:** 5065—Electronic Parts &
Equipment Nec.

★ 90806 ★　Rite Aid
Fair Oaksmall
Fairfax, VA 22033
(703)591-0334
Ultimate Parent: Rite Aid. **SIC:** 5912—Drug
Stores & Proprietary Stores.

★ 90807 ★　Signet Bank, Virginia
4087 University Dr.
Fairfax, VA 22030-3415
(703)691-8969
Location Type: Branch office. **Ultimate
Parent:** Signet Banking Corp. **SIC:** 6021—
National Commercial Banks.

★ 90808 ★　Southland Corp.
Fairfax, VA 22031
(703)550-9641
Ultimate Parent: Southland Corp.

★ 90809 ★　Texas Instruments
3001 Prosperity Ave.
Fairfax, VA 22031
(703)849-1400
Ultimate Parent: Texas Instruments. **SIC:**
5734—Computer & Software Stores.

★ 90810 ★　Title Insurance Co. of
Minn
3900 University Dr.
Fairfax, VA 22030
(703)591-1310
Ultimate Parent: Old Republic International.
SIC: 6541—Title Abstract Offices.

★ 90811 ★　Toys R US
11151 Lee Hwy.
Fairfax, VA 22030
(703)273-0444
Ultimate Parent: Toys "R" US. **SIC:** 5641—
Children's & Infants' Wear Stores.

★ 90812 ★　TRW System
Integration Group
1 Federal Systems Park Dr.
Fairfax, VA 22033
(703)968-1000
Officer: John Stenbit, Manager. **Ultimate
Parent:** TRW, Inc. **SIC:** 3812—Search &
Navigation Equipment.

★ 90813 ★　United State Lime &
Minerals, Inc.
8300 Arlington Blvd.
Fairfax, VA 22031
(703)207-9702
Officer: Robert T. Kizer, CEO. **Ultimate
Parent:** USG Corp. **Sales:** 32 M.

★ 90814 ★　Western Resources
3851 Zelkova Ct.
Fairfax, VA 22033
(703)378-2192
Ultimate Parent: Bay View Capital Corp.

Fairfax Station

★ 90815 ★　Crestar Bank
5616-A Ox Rd.
Fairfax Station, VA 22039-9998
(703)749-8515
Location Type: Branch office. **Ultimate
Parent:** Crestar Financial Corp. **SIC:**
6021—National Commercial Banks.

Falls Church

★ 90816 ★　American General
Finance
2230 Gallows Rd.
Falls Church, VA 22042
(703)698-4333
Ultimate Parent: American General Corp.
SIC: 6141—Personal Credit Institutions.

★ 90817 ★　American General
Finance Inc.
2230 Gallows Rd.
Falls Church, VA 22042
(703)698-4333
Location Type: Branch office. **Ultimate
Parent:** American General Corp. **SIC:**
6141—Personal Credit Institutions.

★ 90818 ★　Arco Mini Market
5757 Seminary Rd.
Falls Church, VA 22041
(703)671-0867
Ultimate Parent: Atlantic Richfield Co., Inc.
SIC: 5411—Grocery Stores.

★ 90819 ★　Blazer Financial
Services
7115 Leesburg Pike 102
Falls Church, VA 22043
(703)237-8288
Ultimate Parent: Great Western Financial
Corp. **SIC:** 6141—Personal Credit
Institutions.

★ 90820 ★　Central Fidelity
National Bank
5127 A. Leesburg Pike
Falls Church, VA 22041-3207
(703)824-1510
Company Type: Subsidiary. **Location
Type:** Branch office. **Officer:** Stephanie L.
Robinson, Manger. **Ultimate Parent:**
Central Fidelity Bank. **SIC:** 6021—National
Commercial Banks.

★ 90821 ★　Circuit City
5520 Leesburg Pke.
Falls Church, VA 22041
(703)671-2700
Ultimate Parent: Circuit City Stores. **SIC:**
5731—Radio, Television & Electronics
Stores.

★ 90822 ★　Circuit City
1905 Chain Bridge Rd.
Falls Church, VA 22043
(703)893-1941
Ultimate Parent: Circuit City Stores.

★ 90823 ★　Computer Sciences
Applied Technology
6565 Arlington Blvd.
Falls Church, VA 22046
(703)237-2000 **Fax:** (703)237-0752
Officer: Edward P. Boykin, President.
Ultimate Parent: Computer Sciences.

★ 90824 ★　Computer Sciences
Business Development
3160 Fairview Park Dr.
Falls Church, VA 22042
(703)876-1000 **Fax:** (703)849-1000
Officer: Sterling E. Phillips, President.
Ultimate Parent: Computer Sciences.

★ 90825 ★　Computer Sciences
System Sciences
3160 Fairview Park Dr.
Falls Church, VA 22042
(703)876-1000 **Fax:** (703)876-4072
Officer: Thomas C. Robinson, President.
Ultimate Parent: Computer Sciences.

★ 90826 ★　Computer Sciences
Technology Management
3160 Fairview Park Dr.
Falls Church, VA 22042
(703)876-1000 **Fax:** (703)876-4072
Officer: Thomas William, President.
Ultimate Parent: Computer Sciences.

★ 90827 ★　Crestar Bank
603 W. Broad St.
Falls Church, VA 22046-3218
(703)838-3264
Location Type: Branch office. **Ultimate
Parent:** Crestar Financial Corp. **SIC:**
6021—National Commercial Banks.

★ 90828 ★　Crestar Bank
633 Leesburg Pke.
Falls Church, VA 22044-2403
(703)838-3310
Location Type: Branch office. **Ultimate
Parent:** Crestar Financial Corp. **SIC:**
6021—National Commercial Banks.

★ 90829 ★　CSC Systems Group
3160 Fairview Park Dr.
Falls Church, VA 22042
(703)641-2111 **Fax:** (703)849-1000
Officer: Milton E. Cooper, Group President.
Ultimate Parent: Computer Sciences.

★ 90830 ★　E-Systems Inc.
Melpar Div.
7700 Arlington Blvd.
Falls Church, VA 22042
(703)560-5000
Company Type: Division. **Officer:** Talbot S.
Huff, Vice President. **Ultimate Parent:**
E-Systems Inc. **SIC:** 3669—
Communications Equipment Nec.

★ 90831 ★　E-Systems Inc.
Melpar Div.
7700 Arlington Blvd.
Falls Church, VA 22046
Company Type: Division. **Ultimate Parent:**
E-Systems Inc. **SIC:** 3663—Radio & T.V.
Communications Equipment.

★ 90832 ★　First American Bank
133 S. Washington St.
Falls Church, VA 22046
(703)284-6565
Ultimate Parent: First American Corp. **SIC:**
6099—Functions Related to Deposit
Banking.

★ 90833 ★　First American Bank
of Virginia
133 S. Washington St.
Falls Church, VA 22046
(703)827-2622
Ultimate Parent: First American Corp. **SIC:**
6022—State Commercial Banks.

★ 90834 ★　First General
Mortgage Co.
6402 Arlington Blvd.
Falls Church, VA 22042
(703)241-4678
Company Type: Subsidiary. **Officer:**
Joseph J. Kilty, President. **Ultimate Parent:**
First Virginia Banks Inc. **SIC:** 6162—
Mortgage Bankers & Correspondents.

★ 90835 ★　First General
Mortgage Co. Inc.
6402 Arlington Blvd.
Falls Church, VA 22042-2300
(703)241-4695
Company Type: Subsidiary. **Officer:**
Robert Zalokar, Chairman of the Board.
Ultimate Parent: First Virginia Banks Inc.
SIC: 6162—Mortgage Bankers &
Correspondents. **Employee Count:** 31.

★ 90836 ★　First Union National
Bank of Virginia
6045 Leesburg Pke.
Falls Church, VA 22041-2297
(703)442-3606
Location Type: Branch office. **Ultimate
Parent:** First Union Corp. **SIC:** 6021—
National Commercial Banks.

★ 90837 ★　First Union National
Bank of Virginia
930 W. Broad St.
Falls Church, VA 22046-3170
(703)442-3610
Location Type: Branch office. **Ultimate
Parent:** First Union Corp. **SIC:** 6021—
National Commercial Banks.

★ 90838 ★　First Union National
Bank of Virginia
2928 Annandale Rd.
Falls Church, VA 22042-2250
(703)442-3627
Location Type: Branch office. **Ultimate
Parent:** First Union Corp. **SIC:** 6021—
National Commercial Banks.

★ 90839 ★　First Virginia Bank
6400 Arlington Blvd.
Falls Church, VA 22042-2336
(703)241-4000
Company Type: Subsidiary. **Officer:**
Robert H. Zalokar, Chairman of the Board.
Ultimate Parent: First Virginia Banks Inc.
SIC: 6022—State Commercial Banks.

★ 90840 ★　First Virginia Bank
6172 Arlington Blvd.
Falls Church, VA 22044
Location Type: Branch office. **Ultimate
Parent:** First Virginia Banks Inc. **SIC:**
6021—National Commercial Banks.

★ 90841 ★　First Virginia Bank
7202 Arlington Blvd.
Falls Church, VA 22042
Location Type: Branch office. **Ultimate
Parent:** First Virginia Banks Inc. **SIC:**
6021—National Commercial Banks.

★ 90842 ★　First Virginia Bank
3010 Annandale Rd.
Falls Church, VA 22042
Location Type: Branch office. **Ultimate
Parent:** First Virginia Banks Inc. **SIC:**
6021—National Commercial Banks.

★ 90843 ★　First Virginia Bank
191 W. Broad St.
Falls Church, VA 22046
Location Type: Branch office. **Ultimate
Parent:** First Virginia Banks Inc. **SIC:**
6021—National Commercial Banks.

★ 90844 ★　First Virginia Bank
1224 W. Broad St.
Falls Church, VA 22046
Location Type: Branch office. **Ultimate
Parent:** First Virginia Banks Inc. **SIC:**
6021—National Commercial Banks.

★ 90845 ★　First Virginia Bank
7393 A. Lee Hwy.
Falls Church, VA 22042
Location Type: Branch office. **Ultimate
Parent:** First Virginia Banks Inc. **SIC:**
6021—National Commercial Banks.

★ 90846 ★　First Virginia Bank
6400 Arlington Blvd.
Falls Church, VA 22042-2336
(703)241-4000
Company Type: Subsidiary. **Officer:**
Robert . Zalokar, Chairman of the Board.
Ultimate Parent: First Virginia Banks Inc.
SIC: 6022—State Commercial Banks.
Employee Count: 1435.

★ 90847 ★ **First Virginia Banks**
6400 Arlington Blvd.
Falls Church, VA 22042
(703)241-4000
Company Type: Headquarters. **Officer:**
Robert H. Zalokar. **Ultimate Parent:** First
Virginia Banks Inc.

★ 90848 ★ **First Virginia Banks
Inc.**
1 1st Virginia Plz.
6400 Arlington Blvd.
Falls Church, VA 22042-2336
(703)241-4000 **Fax:** (703)241-3090
Company Type: Headquarters. **Officer:**
Robert H. Zalokar, Chairman of the Board.
Ultimate Parent: First Virginia Banks Inc.
SIC: 6712—Bank Holding Companies;
6022—State Commercial Banks.

★ 90849 ★ **First Virginia Banks
Inc.**
6400 Arlington Blvd.
Falls Church, VA 22042-2336
(703)241-4000
Officer: Robert H. Zalokar, Chairman of the
Board. **SIC:** 6022—State Commercial
Banks. **Employee Count:** 4576.

★ 90850 ★ **First Virginia
Insurance Services Inc.**
6402 Arlington Blvd.
Falls Church, VA 22042-2398
(703)241-4444
Company Type: Subsidiary. **Officer:** Edwin
D. Pierce, President. **Ultimate Parent:** First
Virginia Insurance Services. **SIC:** 6331—Fire, Marine
& Casualty Insurance.

★ 90851 ★ **First Virginia Life
Insurance Co.**
6400 Arlington Blvd.
Falls Church, VA 22042
(703)241-4401
Company Type: Subsidiary. **Officer:** Paul
H. Geithner Jr., President. **Ultimate Parent:**
First Virginia Banks Inc. **SIC:** 6311—Life
Insurance.

★ 90852 ★ **First Virginia
Mortgage Co.**
6402 Arlington Blvd., Ste. 1030
Falls Church, VA 22042
(703)241-3201
Company Type: Subsidiary. **Officer:**
William S. Corish, Chairman of the Board &
CEO. **Ultimate Parent:** First Virginia Banks
Inc. **SIC:** 6162—Mortgage Bankers &
Correspondents.

★ 90853 ★ **First Virginia
Mortgage Co.**
6402 Arlington Blvd.
Falls Church, VA 22042-2300
(703)241-3201
Company Type: Subsidiary. **Officer:**
William S. Corish, Chairman of the Board,
CEO. **Ultimate Parent:** First Virginia Banks
Inc. **SIC:** 6162—Mortgage Bankers &
Correspondents. **Employee Count:** 136.

★ 90854 ★ **First Virginia Services
Inc.**
6402 Arlington Blvd.
Falls Church, VA 22042-2398
(703)241-3360
Company Type: Subsidiary. **Officer:**
Shirley C. Beavers, President & CEO.
Ultimate Parent: First Virginia Banks Inc.
SIC: 7374—Data Processing & Preparation.

★ 90855 ★ **General Dynamics**
3190 Fairview Park Dr.
Falls Church, VA 22042
(703)876-3000
Fortune 500: Largest U.S. Industrial
Corporations: Ranking 112.

★ 90856 ★ **General Dynamics
Corp.**
3190 Fairview Park Dr.
Falls Church, VA 22042-4501
(703)876-3000
Officer: William A. Anders, Chairman of the
Board. **Ultimate Parent:** General Dynamics.
SIC: 3731—Ship Building & Repairing;
3795—Tanks & Tank Components; 3769—
Space Vehicle Equipment Nec; 3271—
Concrete Block & Brick; 3273—
Ready-Mixed Concrete; 3274—Lime.
Employee Count: 51500. **Sales:** 3.4 M.

★ 90857 ★ **Hit or Miss**
6035 Leesburg Pike
Falls Church, VA 22041
(703)671-0227
Ultimate Parent: TJX. **SIC:** 5621—
Women's Clothing Stores.

★ 90858 ★ **Lord & Taylor**
Lord Taylor Rd.
Falls Church, VA 22044
(703)536-5000
Ultimate Parent: May Department Stores.
SIC: 5311—Department Stores.

★ 90859 ★ **Mary Kay Cosmetics**
206 W. Rosemary Ln.
Falls Church, VA 22046
(703)534-5939
Ultimate Parent: Mary Kay Cosmetics. **SIC:**
5999—Miscellaneous Retail Stores Nec.

★ 90860 ★ **Mobil Oil Corp.**
8411 Leesburg Pke
Falls Church, VA 22043
(703)893-5530
Ultimate Parent: Mobil.

★ 90861 ★ **New York Life Fairfax
General Office**
Southeastern Agencies
5109 Leesburg Pke., Ste. 900
Falls Church, VA 22041
(703)820-2100 **Fax:** (703)578-3711
Officer: James J. Torrell, General Manager.
Ultimate Parent: New York Life.

★ 90862 ★ **Northern Operations
Center Inc.**
6402 Arlington Blvd.
Falls Church, VA 22042-2398
(703)241-4816
Company Type: Subsidiary. **Officer:** J.
Patrick Francis, President. **Ultimate Parent:**
First Virginia Banks Inc. **SIC:** 7374—Data
Processing & Preparation.

★ 90863 ★ **Radio Shack**
6600 Arlington Blvd.
Falls Church, VA 22042
(703)532-2441
Company Type: Division. **Ultimate Parent:**
Tandy Corp. **SIC:** 5065—Electronic Parts &
Equipment Nec.

★ 90864 ★ **Radio Shack**
3521 S. Jefferson St.
Falls Church, VA 22041
(703)931-0320
Company Type: Division. **Ultimate Parent:**
Tandy Corp. **SIC:** 5065—Electronic Parts &
Equipment Nec.

★ 90865 ★ **Radio Shack**
7395 Lee Hwy. I
Falls Church, VA 22042
(703)573-8035
Company Type: Division. **Ultimate Parent:**
Tandy Corp. **SIC:** 5719—Miscellaneous
Home Furnishings Stores.

★ 90866 ★ **Radio Shack**
7395 Lee Hwy.
Falls Church, VA 22042
(703)573-8035
Company Type: Division. **Ultimate Parent:**
Tandy Corp. **SIC:** 5065—Electronic Parts &
Equipment Nec.

★ 90867 ★ **Radio Shack**
3521 S. Jefferson St.
Falls Church, VA 22041
(703)931-0320
Company Type: Division. **Ultimate Parent:**
Tandy Corp. **SIC:** 5065—Electronic Parts &
Equipment Nec.

★ 90868 ★ **Radio Shack**
6600 Arlington Blvd.
Falls Church, VA 22042
(703)532-2441
Company Type: Division. **Ultimate Parent:**
Tandy Corp. **SIC:** 5065—Electronic Parts &
Equipment Nec.

★ 90869 ★ **Signet Bank, Virginia**
5205 Leesburg Pke.
Falls Church, VA 22041-3802
(703)931-1590
Location Type: Branch office. **Ultimate
Parent:** Signet Banking Corp. **SIC:** 6021—
National Commercial Banks.

★ 90870 ★ **Signet Bank, Virginia**
225 W. Broad St.
Falls Church, VA 22046-4292
(703)532-7876
Location Type: Branch office. **Ultimate
Parent:** Signet Banking Corp. **SIC:** 6021—
National Commercial Banks.

★ 90871 ★ **Springdale
Advertising Agency Inc.**
6400 Arlington Blvd.
Falls Church, VA 22042
(703)241-4896
Company Type: Subsidiary. **Officer:**
Douglas M. Church Jr., President. **Ultimate
Parent:** First Virginia Banks Inc. **SIC:**
7311—Advertising Agencies.

★ 90872 ★ **Toys R US**
5521 Leesburg Pike
Falls Church, VA 22041
(703)820-2428
Ultimate Parent: Toys "R" US. **SIC:** 5641—
Children's & Infants' Wear Stores.

★ 90873 ★ **WSA**
350 S. Washington St.
Falls Church, VA 22046
(703)241-0687
Officer: Bob Bocek, President. **Ultimate
Parent:** Data General. **SIC:** 3669—
Communications Equipment Nec.

Farmerville

★ 90874 ★ **Central Fidelity
National Bank**
127 N. Main St.
Farmerville, VA 23901-1305
(804)392-6121
Company Type: Subsidiary. **Location
Type:** Branch office. **Officer:** Jay S. Fulton,
Manger. **Ultimate Parent:** Central Fidelity
Bank. **SIC:** 6021—National Commercial
Banks.

★ 90875 ★ **First Virginia Bank**
200 N. Main St.
PO Box 467
Farmville, VA 23901-0467
(804)392-3126
Company Type: Subsidiary. **Officer:**
Landon G. Atkins, Chairman of the Board.
Ultimate Parent: First Virginia Banks Inc.
SIC: 6022—State Commercial Banks.

★ 90876 ★ **First Virginia Bank -
Southside**
200 N. Main St.
Farmville, VA 23901-1308
(804)392-3126
Company Type: Subsidiary. **Officer:** John
M. Lee, President, CEO. **Ultimate Parent:**
First Virginia Banks Inc. **SIC:** 6022—State
Commercial Banks; 6162—Mortgage
Bankers & Correspondents. **Employee
Count:** 66.

★ 90877 ★ **Flowers Baking Co.**
RR 15
Farmville, VA 23901
(804)392-8580
Ultimate Parent: Flowers Industries. **SIC:**
5149—Groceries & Related Products Nec.

Fieldale

★ 90878 ★ **Crestar Bank**
Marshall Way
Fieldale, VA 24089
(703)673-6751
Location Type: Branch office. **Ultimate
Parent:** Crestar Financial Corp. **SIC:**
6021—National Commercial Banks.

★ 90879 ★ **Dumaine Towel Mill**
Mill Dr.
Fieldale, VA 24089
Ultimate Parent: Fieldcrest Cannon. **SIC:**
2211—Broadwoven Fabric Mills—Cotton.

★ 90880 ★ **Fieldale Towel Mill**
Mill Dr.
Fieldale, VA 24089
Ultimate Parent: Fieldcrest Cannon. **SIC:**
2241—Narrow Fabric Mills.

Fishersville

★ 90881 ★ **Carter Machinery Co.
Inc.**
Hwy. 608
Fishersville, VA 22939
(703)949-8111
Ultimate Parent: Carter-Wallace. **SIC:**
5082—Construction & Mining Machinery.

Floyd

★ 90882 ★ **Stop & Shop**
N Locust
Floyd, VA 24091
(703)745-4561
Ultimate Parent: Stop & Shop. **SIC:** 5949—
Sewing, Needlework & Piece Goods.

Forest

★ 90883 ★ **Central Fidelity
National Bank**
Rte. 221 & Graves Mill Rd.
Forest, VA 24551-9768
(804)385-0085
Company Type: Subsidiary. **Location
Type:** Branch office. **Officer:** Brian K.
Blankinship, Manger. **Ultimate Parent:**
Central Fidelity Bank. **SIC:** 6021—National
Commercial Banks.

★ 90884 ★ **Structures Unlimited**
Rural Route 2
Forest, VA 24551
(804)239-7151
Ultimate Parent: Limited. **SIC:** 1521—
Single-Family Housing Construction.

Fort Belvoir

★ 90885 ★ **Central Fidelity
National Bank**
Fort Belvoir, VA 22060
(703)781-5804
Company Type: Subsidiary. **Location
Type:** Branch office. **Officer:** Virginia Lattig,
Manger. **Ultimate Parent:** Central Fidelity
Bank. **SIC:** 6021—National Commercial
Banks.

★ 90886 ★ **Crestar Bank**
12 & Gunston Rd.
Fort Belvoir, VA 22060
Location Type: Branch office. **Ultimate
Parent:** Crestar Financial Corp. **SIC:**
6021—National Commercial Banks.

★ 90887 ★ **Crestar Bank**
1801 Goethals Rd.
Fort Belvoir, VA 22060-1201
Location Type: Branch office. **Ultimate
Parent:** Crestar Financial Corp. **SIC:**
6021—National Commercial Banks.

Fort Lee

★ 90888 ★ **Crestar Bank**
4305 Mahone Ave.
Fort Lee, VA 23801
(804)862-2500
Location Type: Branch office. **Ultimate
Parent:** Crestar Financial Corp. **SIC:**
6021—National Commercial Banks.

Fort Union

★ 90889 ★ **Armstrong Furniture**
Carysbrook
Fort Union, VA 23055
(804)842-2020
Officer: Donald F. Williams, Manager.
Ultimate Parent: Armstrong World
Industries. **SIC:** 2511—Wood Household
Furniture; 2599—Furniture & Fixtures Nec.

Fortbelvoir

★ 90890 ★ **Rite Aid**
8244 Richmond Hwy.
Fortbelvoir, VA 22060
(703)360-7166
Ultimate Parent: Rite Aid.

Franklin

★ 90891 ★   Central Fidelity
National Bank
510 N. Main St.
Franklin, VA 23851-1438
(804)562-2163
Company Type: Subsidiary. Location
Type: Branch office. Officer: Kandy S.
Lewis, Manger. Ultimate Parent: Central
Fidelity Bank. SIC: 6021—National
Commercial Banks.

★ 90892 ★   Crestar Bank
117 W. 2nd Ave.
Franklin, VA 23851
(804)858-3264
Location Type: Branch office. Ultimate
Parent: Crestar Financial Corp. SIC:
6021—National Commercial Banks.

★ 90893 ★   First Union National
Bank of Virginia
200 N. Main St.
Franklin, VA 23851-1754
(804)562-2116
Location Type: Branch office. Ultimate
Parent: First Union Corp. SIC: 6021—
National Commercial Banks.

★ 90894 ★   Hercules Inc.
27123 Shady Brook Trail PO Box 656
Franklin, VA 23851-0656
Ultimate Parent: Hercules. SIC: 2861—
Gum & Wood Chemicals; 2869—Industrial
Organic Chemicals Nec; 2899—Chemical
Preparations Nec.

★ 90895 ★   Hercules Inc.
Rte. 671 & Rte. 650 PO Box 656
Franklin, VA 23851-0656
Ultimate Parent: Hercules. SIC: 2861—
Gum & Wood Chemicals; 2869—Industrial
Organic Chemicals Nec; 2899—Chemical
Preparations Nec.

★ 90896 ★   New York Life
Insurance Co.
403 Main St. N
Franklin, VA 23851
(804)569-8171
Ultimate Parent: New York Life. SIC:
6411—Insurance Agents, Brokers &
Service.

★ 90897 ★   Radio Shack
Hwy. 58 E
Franklin, VA 23851
(804)562-6217
Company Type: Division. Ultimate Parent:
Tandy Corp. SIC: 5065—Electronic Parts &
Equipment Nec.

★ 90898 ★   Radio Shack
Hwy. 58 E
Franklin, VA 23851
(804)562-6217
Company Type: Division. Ultimate Parent:
Tandy Corp. SIC: 5065—Electronic Parts &
Equipment Nec.

★ 90899 ★   Union Camp Corp.
E. 2nd Ave.
Franklin, VA 23851
(804)569-4623
Officer: Rick Malm, Manager. Ultimate
Parent: Union Camp Corp. SIC: 2411—
Logging.

★ 90900 ★   Union Camp Corp.
Building Products Div.
Hwy. 58 E.
Franklin, VA 23851
Company Type: Division. Ultimate Parent:
Union Camp Corp. SIC: 2400—Lumber &
Wood Products.

★ 90901 ★   Union Camp Corp.
Building Products Div.
Hwy. 58 East
Franklin, VA 23851-0178
Company Type: Division. Ultimate Parent:
Union Camp Corp. SIC: 2400—Lumber &
Wood Products.

★ 90902 ★   Union Camp Corp.
Fine Paper Div.
Hwy. 58 E.
Franklin, VA 23851-0178
Company Type: Division. Ultimate Parent:
Union Camp Corp. SIC: 2621—Paper Mills;
2611—Pulp Mills; 2631—Paperboard Mills;
2679—Converted Paper Products Nec.

★ 90903 ★   Union Camp Corp.
Fine Paper Div.
Hwy. 58 East
Franklin, VA 23851-0178
Company Type: Division. Ultimate Parent:
Union Camp Corp. SIC: 2400—Lumber &
Wood Products.

★ 90904 ★   Union Camp Corp.
Fine Paper Div.
U.S. Hwy. 58 E
Franklin, VA 23851
(804)569-4321
Company Type: Division. Officer: Charlie
Greiner, President. Ultimate Parent: Union
Camp Corp. SIC: 2421—Sawmills & Planing
Mills—General; 2426—Hardwood Dimension
& Flooring Mills; 2493—Reconstituted Wood
Products.

★ 90905 ★   Vulcan Material Co.
2001 Whitley Ln.
Franklin, VA 23851
Ultimate Parent: Vulcan Materials Co. SIC:
5082—Construction & Mining Machinery.

Fredericksbg

★ 90906 ★   United Parcel Service
432 Lee Hill Dr.
Fredericksburg, VA 22408
(703)371-8666
Ultimate Parent: United Parcel Service of
America. SIC: 4215—Courier Services
Except by Air.

Fredericksbrg

★ 90907 ★   Food Lion
1030 Woodlawn Village C S
Fredericksbrg, VA 22405
(703)371-3258
Ultimate Parent: Food Lion. SIC: 5411—
Grocery Stores.

★ 90908 ★   Food Lion
10611 Courthouse Rd.
Fredericksbrg, VA 22407
(703)898-1771
Ultimate Parent: Food Lion. SIC: 5411—
Grocery Stores.

★ 90909 ★   Food Lion Inc.
10611 Courthouse Rd.
Fredericksbrg, VA 22407
(703)898-1771
Ultimate Parent: Food Lion. SIC: 5411—
Grocery Stores.

★ 90910 ★   Food Lion Inc. Store
No. 358
1030 Woodlawn Village C S
Fredericksbrg, VA 22405
(703)371-3258
Ultimate Parent: Food Lion. SIC: 5411—
Grocery Stores.

★ 90911 ★   The Gap
3102 Plank Rd.
Fredericksbrg, VA 22407
(703)786-4776
Ultimate Parent: GAP. SIC: 5651—Family
Clothing Stores.

★ 90912 ★   J C Penney Co.
41126 PO Box
Fredericksbrg, VA 22404
Ultimate Parent: J.C. Penney. SIC: 7231—
Beauty Shops.

Fredericksburg

★ 90913 ★   Casual Corner
3102 Plank Rd.
Fredericksburg, VA 22407
(703)786-7001
Ultimate Parent: United States Shoe. SIC:
5651—Family Clothing Stores.

★ 90914 ★   Central Fidelity
National Bank
614 Princess Anne St.
Fredericksburg, VA 22401-5915
(703)899-0131
Company Type: Subsidiary. Location
Type: Branch office. Officer: Sharon P.
Dunnavant, Manger. Ultimate Parent:
Central Fidelity Bank. SIC: 6021—National
Commercial Banks.

★ 90915 ★   Crestar Bank
5101 Jefferson Davis Hwy.
Fredericksburg, VA 22401-4264
(800)451-2435
Location Type: Branch office. Ultimate
Parent: Crestar Financial Corp. SIC:
6021—National Commercial Banks.

★ 90916 ★   Exxon Service Station
375 Warrenton Rd.
Fredericksburg, VA 22405
(703)371-5544
Ultimate Parent: Exxon. SIC: 5541—
Gasoline Service Stations.

★ 90917 ★   First Union National
Bank of Virginia
3406 Plank Rd.
Fredericksburg, VA 22401-4931
(804)899-9231
Location Type: Branch office. Ultimate
Parent: First Union Corp. SIC: 6021—
National Commercial Banks.

★ 90918 ★   First Union National
Bank of Virginia
2004 Augustine Ave.
Fredericksburg, VA 22401-4419
(703)899-9200
Location Type: Branch office. Ultimate
Parent: First Union Corp. SIC: 6021—
National Commercial Banks.

★ 90919 ★   First Virginia Bank
1016 Princess Anne St.
Fredericksburg, VA 22401-3836
(703)373-3120
Location Type: Branch office. Ultimate
Parent: First Virginia Banks Inc. SIC:
6021—National Commercial Banks.

★ 90920 ★   First Virginia Bank
2062 Plank Rd.
Fredericksburg, VA 22401-5104
(703)373-3124
Location Type: Branch office. Ultimate
Parent: First Virginia Banks Inc. SIC:
6021—National Commercial Banks.

★ 90921 ★   First Virginia Bank
3400 Plank Rd.
Fredericksburg, VA 22401
(703)373-3123
Location Type: Branch office. Ultimate
Parent: First Virginia Banks Inc. SIC:
6021—National Commercial Banks.

★ 90922 ★   First Virginia Bank
401 Jefferson Davis Hwy.
Fredericksburg, VA 22401-3118
(703)373-3113
Location Type: Branch office. Ultimate
Parent: First Virginia Banks Inc. SIC:
6021—National Commercial Banks.

★ 90923 ★   First Virginia Bank
2609 Lafayette Blvd.
Fredericksburg, VA 22401-3915
(703)373-2121
Location Type: Branch office. Ultimate
Parent: First Virginia Banks Inc. SIC:
6021—National Commercial Banks.

★ 90924 ★   First Virginia Bank
1001 Princess Anne St.
Fredericksburg, VA 22401-3835
(703)373-3117
Location Type: Branch office. Ultimate
Parent: First Virginia Banks Inc. SIC:
6021—National Commercial Banks.

★ 90925 ★   Food Lion
4153 Plank Rd.
Fredericksburg, VA 22407
(703)786-5122
Ultimate Parent: Food Lion. SIC: 5411—
Grocery Stores.

★ 90926 ★   Friction Inc.
1000 Falls Run Dr.
Fredericksburg, VA 22406
(703)371-8010
Officer: Joe Berry, Manager. Ultimate
Parent: Echlin. SIC: 3714—Motor Vehicle
Parts & Accessories.

★ 90927 ★   Greyhound Bus Lines
Rural Route 1
Fredericksburg, VA 22401
(703)373-2103
Ultimate Parent: Greyhound Lines Inc. SIC:
4111—Local & Suburban Transit.

★ 90928 ★   Hertz Rent-A-Car
1400 Jefferson Davis Hwy.
Fredericksburg, VA 22401
(703)371-8525
Ultimate Parent: Hertz. SIC: 7514—
Passenger Car Rental.

★ 90929 ★   Life Insurance Co. of
Virginia
4810 Jeff Davis
Fredericksburg, VA 22401
(703)898-8392
Ultimate Parent: Life Insurance Co. of
Virginia. SIC: 8742—Management
Consulting Services.

★ 90930 ★   Mast Advertising &
Publishing
104 Westwood Park Office
Fredericksburg, VA 22401
(703)371-7122
Ultimate Parent: Southwestern Bell. SIC:
7311—Advertising Agencies.

★ 90931 ★   Mast Advertising &
Publishing
5444 Jefferson Davis Hwy.
Fredericksburg, VA 22407
(703)891-5366
Ultimate Parent: Southwestern Bell. SIC:
7311—Advertising Agencies.

★ 90932 ★   New York Life
Insurance Co.
1619 Jefferson Davis Hwy.
Fredericksburg, VA 22401
(703)373-0225
Ultimate Parent: New York Life. SIC:
6411—Insurance Agents, Brokers &
Service.

★ 90933 ★   Pennzoil Products
2309 Airport Ave.
Fredericksburg, VA 22401
(703)371-3244
Ultimate Parent: Pennzoil. SIC: 5172—
Petroleum Products Nec.

★ 90934 ★   Radio Shack
5065 Jefferson Davis Hwy.
Fredericksburg, VA 22408
(703)898-6330
Company Type: Division. Ultimate Parent:
Tandy Corp. SIC: 5731—Radio, Television
& Electronics Stores.

★ 90935 ★   Radio Shack
2012 Plank Rd.
Fredericksburg, VA 22401
(703)371-1277
Company Type: Division. Ultimate Parent:
Tandy Corp. SIC: 5719—Miscellaneous
Home Furnishings Stores; 5731—Radio,
Television & Electronics Stores.

★ 90936 ★   Radio Shack
3102 Plank Rd.
Fredericksburg, VA 22407
(703)786-6254
Company Type: Division. Ultimate Parent:
Tandy Corp. SIC: 5731—Radio, Television
& Electronics Stores.

★ 90937 ★   Rite Aid
2028 Plankrd
Fredericksburg, VA 22401
(703)371-2771
Ultimate Parent: Rite Aid. SIC: 5912—Drug
Stores & Proprietary Stores.

★ 90938 ★   Rite Aid
439 Jefferson Davis Hwy.
Fredericksburg, VA 22401
(703)373-6262
Ultimate Parent: Rite Aid. SIC: 5912—Drug
Stores & Proprietary Stores.

★ 90939 ★   Rite Aid
3102 Plank Rd.
Fredericksburg, VA 22407
(703)786-9176
Ultimate Parent: Rite Aid. SIC: 5912—Drug
Stores & Proprietary Stores.

★ 90940 ★   Signet Bank, Virginia
2101 Plank Rd.
Fredericksburg, VA 22401-4420
(703)371-9331
Location Type: Branch office. Ultimate
Parent: Signet Banking Corp. SIC: 6021—
National Commercial Banks.

★ **90941** ★ **Signet Bank, Virginia**
1014 Charles St.
Fredericksburg, VA 22401-3830
(703)371-4040
Location Type: Branch office. **Ultimate Parent:** Signet Banking Corp. **SIC:** 6021—National Commercial Banks.

★ **90942** ★ **Signet Bank, Virginia**
501-1/2 Jefferson Davis Hwy.
Fredericksburg, VA 22401-4420
(703)371-6010
Location Type: Branch office. **Ultimate Parent:** Signet Banking Corp. **SIC:** 6021—National Commercial Banks.

★ **90943** ★ **Stop & Shop**
104 Olde Greenwich Dr.
Fredericksburg, VA 22408
(703)898-4309
Ultimate Parent: Stop & Shop. **SIC:** 5411—Grocery Stores.

★ **90944** ★ **Structures Unlimited**
122 Early St.
Fredericksburg, VA 22408
(703)898-5385
Ultimate Parent: Limited.

★ **90945** ★ **Waldenbooks**
3102 Plank Rd.
Fredericksburg, VA 22407
(703)786-2897
Ultimate Parent: K-Mart. **SIC:** 5942—Book Stores.

Fredricksberg

★ **90946** ★ **Crestar Bank**
3557 Ploank Rd.
Fredricksberg, VA 22401-6800
Location Type: Branch office. **Ultimate Parent:** Crestar Financial Corp. **SIC:** 6021—National Commercial Banks.

Front Royal

★ **90947** ★ **Cincinnati Insurance Co.**
110 S. Royal Ave.
Front Royal, VA 22630
(703)636-3303
Ultimate Parent: Cincinnati Financial. **SIC:** 8062—General Medical & Surgical Hospitals.

★ **90948** ★ **First American Bank**
200 Gateway Plz.
Front Royal, VA 22630
(703)635-6832
Ultimate Parent: First American Corp. **SIC:** 6022—State Commercial Banks.

★ **90949** ★ **First Federal S&L of America**
1 S. Royal Ave.
Front Royal, VA 22630
(703)635-4112
Ultimate Parent: Bancorp Hawaii. **SIC:** 6035—Federal Savings Institutions.

★ **90950** ★ **First Union National Bank of Virginia**
200 Remount Rd.
Front Royal, VA 22630
(703)635-6832
Location Type: Branch office. **Ultimate Parent:** First Union Corp. **SIC:** 6021—National Commercial Banks.

★ **90951** ★ **Mary Kay Cosmetics**
1204 Ripple Ct
Front Royal, VA 22630
Ultimate Parent: Mary Kay Cosmetics. **SIC:** 5999—Miscellaneous Retail Stores Nec.

★ **90952** ★ **Mary Kay Cosmetics**
RR 3
Front Royal, VA 22630
(703)636-2392
Ultimate Parent: Mary Kay Cosmetics. **SIC:** 5999—Miscellaneous Retail Stores Nec.

★ **90953** ★ **Radio Shack**
Royal Plz.
Front Royal, VA 22630
(703)635-7686
Company Type: Division. **Ultimate Parent:** Tandy Corp. **SIC:** 5731—Radio, Television & Electronics Stores.

★ **90954** ★ **Rite Aid**
Royal Plz.
Front Royal, VA 22630
(703)635-4136
Ultimate Parent: Rite Aid. **SIC:** 1799—Special Trade Contractors Nec.

★ **90955** ★ **Signet Bank, Virginia**
305-7 E. Main St.
Front Royal, VA 22630
(703)635-7111
Location Type: Branch office. **Ultimate Parent:** Signet Banking Corp. **SIC:** 6021—National Commercial Banks.

★ **90956** ★ **Signet Bank, Virginia**
610 N. Royal Ave.
Front Royal, VA 22630-2712
(703)635-7144
Location Type: Branch office. **Ultimate Parent:** Signet Banking Corp. **SIC:** 6021—National Commercial Banks.

★ **90957** ★ **United Parcel Service**
Rural Route 3
Front Royal, VA 22630
(703)635-7151
Ultimate Parent: United Parcel Service of America. **SIC:** 4215—Courier Services Except by Air.

★ **90958** ★ **United Parcel Service**
RR 3
Front Royal, VA 22630
(703)635-7151
Ultimate Parent: United Parcel Service of America. **SIC:** 4215—Courier Services Except by Air.

Frontroyal

★ **90959** ★ **Rite Aid**
449 Royal Plz.
Frontroyal, VA 22630
(703)636-9193
Ultimate Parent: Rite Aid. **SIC:** 5912—Drug Stores & Proprietary Stores.

Gainesville

★ **90960** ★ **Atlantic Research Corp.**
5945 Wellington Rd.
Gainesville, VA 22065
Ultimate Parent: Sequa Corp. **SIC:** 3764—Space Propulsion Units & Parts; 3480—Ordnance & Accessories Nec.

Galax

★ **90961** ★ **Kroger Co.**
Galax Plz.
Galax, VA 24333
(703)236-2841
Ultimate Parent: Kroger. **SIC:** 5411—Grocery Stores.

★ **90962** ★ **Piggly Wiggly**
Oldtown
Galax, VA 24333
(703)236-3280
Ultimate Parent: Bruno's. **SIC:** 5411—Grocery Stores.

★ **90963** ★ **Radio Shack**
964 Stuart Dr. E
Galax, VA 24333
(703)236-8863
Company Type: Division. **Ultimate Parent:** Tandy Corp. **SIC:** 5731—Radio, Television & Electronics Stores.

★ **90964** ★ **Sara Lee Knit Products**
Galax Plant
1012 Glendale Rd.
Galax, VA 24333
Location Type: Plant. **Ultimate Parent:** Sara Lee Corp. **SIC:** 2322—Men's/Boys' Underwear & Nightwear.

★ **90965** ★ **Signet Bank, Virginia**
E. Stuart Dr.
Galax, VA 24333
Location Type: Branch office. **Ultimate Parent:** Signet Banking Corp. **SIC:** 6021—National Commercial Banks.

★ **90966** ★ **Signet Bank, Virginia**
200 N. Main St.
Galax, VA 24333-2910
(703)236-6181
Location Type: Branch office. **Ultimate**

Parent: Signet Banking Corp. **SIC:** 6021—National Commercial Banks.

Gate City

★ **90967** ★ **Food Lion**
101 Hwy. 23
Gate City, VA 24251
(703)386-6650
Ultimate Parent: Food Lion. **SIC:** 5411—Grocery Stores.

★ **90968** ★ **Food Lion Inc.**
101 Hwy. 23
Gate City, VA 24251
(703)386-6650
Ultimate Parent: Food Lion. **SIC:** 5411—Grocery Stores.

★ **90969** ★ **Signet Bank, Virginia**
E. Jackson St.
Gate City, VA 24251
(703)386-3123
Location Type: Branch office. **Ultimate Parent:** Signet Banking Corp. **SIC:** 6021—National Commercial Banks.

Glade Spring

★ **90970** ★ **Piggly Wiggly**
Glade Spring, VA 24340
(703)429-5311
Ultimate Parent: Bruno's. **SIC:** 5411—Grocery Stores.

Gladstone

★ **90971** ★ **Warren Transport**
716 Rural Route 1
Gladstone, VA 24553
(804)933-8212
Ultimate Parent: Federal Express.

Glasgow

★ **90972** ★ **Lees Carpet**
404 Anderson St.
Glasgow, VA 24555-2802
(703)258-2811
Officer: Neal Yeargin. **Ultimate Parent:** Burlington Industries, Equity. **SIC:** 2273—Carpets & Rugs.

★ **90973** ★ **Lees Carpet Burlington**
499 Rural Route 1
Glasgow, VA 24555
(703)258-2811
Ultimate Parent: Burlington Industries, Equity. **SIC:** 2281—Yarn Spinning Mills.

Glen Allen

★ **90974** ★ **Bergen Brunswig Corp.**
4800 Cox Rd.
Glen Allen, VA 23060
(804)682-6571
Ultimate Parent: Bergen Brunswig Corp. **SIC:** 5049—Professional Equipment Nec.

★ **90975** ★ **Cardinal Casualty Co. Inc.**
1063 Technology Park Dr.
Glen Allen, VA 23060-4500
(804)261-7000
Company Type: Subsidiary. **Ultimate Parent:** Figgie International. **SIC:** 6411—Insurance Agents, Brokers & Service.

★ **90976** ★ **Circuit City**
3800 Deep Rock Rd.
Glen Allen, VA 23060
(804)346-5064
Ultimate Parent: Circuit City Stores.

★ **90977** ★ **Colony Insurance Co. Inc.**
1063 Technology Park Dr.
Glen Allen, VA 23060-4500
(804)261-7000
Company Type: Subsidiary. **Ultimate Parent:** Figgie International. **SIC:** 6331—Fire, Marine & Casualty Insurance; 6411—Insurance Agents, Brokers & Service.

★ **90978** ★ **Hamilton Beach/Protor-Silex, Inc.**
4421 Waterfront Dr.
Glen Allen, VA 23060
(804)273-9777 **Fax:** (804)747-5318
Officer: George C. Nebel, President & CEO. **Ultimate Parent:** Nacco Industries.

★ **90979** ★ **Hamilton Insurance Co.**
1063 Technology Park Dr.
Glen Allen, VA 23060
(804)261-7000
Company Type: Division. **Ultimate Parent:** Figgie International. **SIC:** 6211—Security Brokers & Dealers.

★ **90980** ★ **Holly Farms Foods Inc.**
3301 US 33
Glen Allen, VA 23060
Ultimate Parent: Tyson Foods, Inc. **SIC:** 0251—Broiler, Fryer & Roaster Chickens.

★ **90981** ★ **Holly Farms Foods Inc.**
Richmond Plant
3301 US-33
Glen Allen, VA 23060
Location Type: Plant. **Ultimate Parent:** Tyson Foods, Inc. **SIC:** 0251—Broiler, Fryer & Roaster Chickens.

★ **90982** ★ **Holly Farms Foods Inc. Waste Water Treatment Plant**
3301 Us Hwy. 33 W.
Glen Allen, VA 23060
Ultimate Parent: Tyson Foods, Inc. **SIC:** 2015—Poultry Slaughtering & Processing.

★ **90983** ★ **Price Club**
9650 W. Broad St.
Glen Allen, VA 23060
Ultimate Parent: Price. **SIC:** 5399—Miscellaneous General Merchandise Store.

★ **90984** ★ **Signet Bank, Virginia**
4101 Dominion Blvd.
Glen Allen, VA 23060
(804)747-3061
Location Type: Branch office. **Ultimate Parent:** Signet Banking Corp. **SIC:** 6021—National Commercial Banks.

★ **90985** ★ **Tyson Foods Inc.**
3301 US Hwy. 33
Glen Allen, VA 23060
(804)798-8357
Officer: Claude Owens, Manager. **Ultimate Parent:** Tyson Foods, Inc. **SIC:** 2015—Poultry Slaughtering & Processing.

★ **90986** ★ **Tyson/Holly Farms Foods Inc. Waste Water Treatment Plant**
3301 U.S. Hwy. 33
Glen Allen, VA 23060
Ultimate Parent: Tyson Foods, Inc. **SIC:** 2015—Poultry Slaughtering & Processing.

★ **90987** ★ **Waite Hill Holdings Inc.**
1063 Technology Park Dr.
Glen Allen, VA 23060
(804)261-7000 **Fax:** (804)266-4458
Company Type: Subsidiary. **Officer:** John K. Latham Jr., President. **Ultimate Parent:** Figgie International.

★ **90988** ★ **Waite Hill Holdings Inc.**
1063 Technology Park Dr.
Glen Allen, VA 23060
(804)261-7000
Company Type: Division. **Ultimate Parent:** Figgie International. **SIC:** 6211—Security Brokers & Dealers.

★ **90989** ★ **Waite Hill Holdings Inc.**
1063 Technology Dr.
Glen Allen, VA 23060
(804)261-7000
Ultimate Parent: Figgie International.

Gloucester

★ **90990** ★ **Crestar Bank**
Main St.
Gloucester, VA 23061
(804)693-1500
Location Type: Branch office. **Ultimate Parent:** Crestar Financial Corp. **SIC:** 6021—National Commercial Banks.

★ 90991 ★   **First Union National Bank of Virginia**
US Hwy. 17 & State Hwy. 14
Gloucester, VA 23061-9712
(804)693-3040
Location Type: Branch office. **Ultimate Parent:** First Union Corp. **SIC:** 6021—National Commercial Banks.

★ 90992 ★   **Virginia Electric & Power C**
Gloucester
Gloucester, VA 23061
(804)843-3322
Ultimate Parent: Dominion Resources.

Gloucester Point

★ 90993 ★   **Crestar Bank**
US Rte. 17
Gloucester Point, VA 23062-8955
(804)642-2141
Location Type: Branch office. **Ultimate Parent:** Crestar Financial Corp. **SIC:** 6021—National Commercial Banks.

Gordonsville

★ 90994 ★   **Potomac Edison Co.**
Gordonsville, VA 22942
(703)832-7457
Ultimate Parent: Allegheny Power System. **SIC:** 4911—Electric Services.

Grafton

★ 90995 ★   **Crestar Bank**
Rte. 17
Grafton, VA 23692
(804)873-7826
Location Type: Branch office. **Ultimate Parent:** Crestar Financial Corp. **SIC:** 6021—National Commercial Banks.

★ 90996 ★   **First Union National Bak of Virginia**
5208 George Washington Memorial Hwy.
Grafton, VA 23692-9702
(804)728-2120
Location Type: Branch office. **Ultimate Parent:** First Union Corp. **SIC:** 6021—National Commercial Banks.

★ 90997 ★   **Signet Bank, Virginia**
5030 George Washington Memorial Hwy.
Grafton, VA 23690
(804)825-7697
Location Type: Branch office. **Ultimate Parent:** Signet Banking Corp. **SIC:** 6021—National Commercial Banks.

Great Falls

★ 90998 ★   **Crestar Bank**
9883 Georgetown Pke.
Great Falls, VA 22066-2617
(800)451-2435
Location Type: Branch office. **Ultimate Parent:** Crestar Financial Corp. **SIC:** 6021—National Commercial Banks.

★ 90999 ★   **First Virginia Bank**
9915 Georgetown Pke.
Great Falls, VA 22066-2826
(703)241-4706
Location Type: Branch office. **Ultimate Parent:** First Virginia Banks Inc. **SIC:** 6021—National Commercial Banks.

★ 91000 ★   **McDonald's Hamburgers**
10201 Brennanhill Ct
Great Falls, VA 22066
(703)556-9088
Ultimate Parent: McDonald's.

★ 91001 ★   **Signet Bank, Virginia**
750 Walker Rd.
Great Falls, VA 22066-2611
(703)759-4088
Location Type: Branch office. **Ultimate Parent:** Signet Banking Corp. **SIC:** 6021—National Commercial Banks.

Gretna

★ 91002 ★   **Crestar Bank**
109 Main St.
Gretna, VA 24557
(804)656-1246
Location Type: Branch office. **Ultimate**

Parent: Crestar Financial Corp. **SIC:** 6021—National Commercial Banks.

★ 91003 ★   **Raco Inc.**
Gretna, VA 24557
(804)656-6676
Ultimate Parent: Hubbell. **SIC:** 1623—Water, Sewer & Utility Lines.

Grottoes

★ 91004 ★   **First Union National Bank of Virginia**
40 - 6th St.
Grottoes, VA 24441
(703)249-5723
Location Type: Branch office. **Ultimate Parent:** First Union Corp. **SIC:** 6021—National Commercial Banks.

★ 91005 ★   **Reynolds Metals Co.**
Caverns Blvd.
Grottoes, VA 24441
(703)249-5711
Officer: Ronald Layne, Manager. **Ultimate Parent:** Reynolds Metals Co. **SIC:** 3081—Unsupported Plastics Film & Sheet; 3089—Plastics Products Nec.

★ 91006 ★   **Reynolds Metals Co. Plastics Plant**
Caverns Blvd.
Grottoes, VA 24441
Ultimate Parent: Reynolds Metals Co. **SIC:** 3081—Unsupported Plastics Film & Sheet.

★ 91007 ★   **Reynolds Metals Co. Plastics Plant**
Caverns Blvd. (Route 884)
Grottoes, VA 24441
Ultimate Parent: Reynolds Metals Co. **SIC:** 3000—Rubber & Miscellaneous Plastics Products.

Grundy

★ 91008 ★   **First Union National Bank of Virginia**
212 Riverside Ave.
Grundy, VA 24614-9615
(703)935-8151
Location Type: Branch office. **Ultimate Parent:** First Union Corp. **SIC:** 6021—National Commercial Banks.

Hague

★ 91009 ★   **First Virginia Bank**
State Rte. 202
Hague, VA 22469-9610
(804)472-3100
Location Type: Branch office. **Ultimate Parent:** First Virginia Banks Inc. **SIC:** 6021—National Commercial Banks.

Halifax

★ 91010 ★   **Burlington Menswear Halifax**
Cowford Rd.
Halifax, VA 24558
(804)476-6501
Location Type: Branch office. **Officer:** Lott Rogers. **Ultimate Parent:** Burlington Industries, Equity. **SIC:** 2211—Broadwoven Fabric Mills—Cotton; 2221—Broadwoven Fabric Mills—Manmade.

Hampton

★ 91011 ★   **American General Finance**
3007 W. Mercury Blvd.
Hampton, VA 23666-2296
(804)826-2296
Location Type: Branch office. **Officer:** Debra Bailey. **Ultimate Parent:** American General Corp. **SIC:** 6141—Personal Credit Institutions.

★ 91012 ★   **American General Finance**
2101 Executive Dr.
Hampton, VA 23666-2404
(804)826-4926
Location Type: Branch office. **Officer:** Donna Gray. **Ultimate Parent:** American General Corp. **SIC:** 6141—Personal Credit Institutions.

★ 91013 ★   **American General Finance Inc.**
2101 Executive Dr.
Hampton, VA 23666-2404
(804)826-4926
Location Type: Branch office. **Officer:** Donna Gray. **Ultimate Parent:** American General Corp. **SIC:** 6141—Personal Credit Institutions.

★ 91014 ★   **American General Finance Inc.**
3007 W. Mercury Blvd.
Hampton, VA 23666-2296
(804)826-2296
Location Type: Branch office. **Officer:** Debra Bailey. **Ultimate Parent:** American General Corp. **SIC:** 6141—Personal Credit Institutions.

★ 91015 ★   **Avon Products Inc.**
2021 Cunningham Dr.
Hampton, VA 23666
(804)826-8011
Ultimate Parent: Avon Products, Inc. **SIC:** 5999—Miscellaneous Retail Stores Nec.

★ 91016 ★   **Bell Atlantic Business Systems Services**
2101 Executive Dr.
Hampton, VA 23666-2404
(804)838-2649
Ultimate Parent: Bell Atlantic Corp. **SIC:** 5045—Computers, Peripherals & Software.

★ 91017 ★   **Boeing Co. the**
2101 Executive Dr.
Hampton, VA 23666
(804)838-2176
Ultimate Parent: Boeing. **SIC:** 3721—Aircraft.

★ 91018 ★   **Casual Corner**
Coliseum Mall
Hampton, VA 23666
(804)827-6552
Ultimate Parent: United States Shoe. **SIC:** 5621—Women's Clothing Stores; 5651—Family Clothing Stores.

★ 91019 ★   **Circuit City**
2525 W. Mercury Blvd.
Hampton, VA 23666
(804)826-1921
Ultimate Parent: Circuit City Stores. **SIC:** 5731—Radio, Television & Electronics Stores.

★ 91020 ★   **Circuit City**
2207 W. Mercury Blvd.
Hampton, VA 23666
(804)838-3570
Ultimate Parent: Circuit City Stores. **SIC:** 5731—Radio, Television & Electronics Stores.

★ 91021 ★   **Crestar Bank**
2155 Coliseum Dr.
Hampton, VA 23666-3183
(804)873-7561
Location Type: Branch office. **Ultimate Parent:** Crestar Financial Corp. **SIC:** 6021—National Commercial Banks.

★ 91022 ★   **Crestar Bank**
Willow Oaks Blvd.
Hampton, VA 23669
(804)873-7822
Location Type: Branch office. **Ultimate Parent:** Crestar Financial Corp. **SIC:** 6021—National Commercial Banks.

★ 91023 ★   **Crestar Bank**
Mercury Plz. Shopping Ctr.
Hampton, VA 23666-3130
(804)873-7811
Location Type: Branch office. **Ultimate Parent:** Crestar Financial Corp. **SIC:** 6021—National Commercial Banks.

★ 91024 ★   **Crestar Bank**
2 E. Queen St.
Hampton, VA 23669-4002
(804)873-7845
Location Type: Branch office. **Ultimate Parent:** Crestar Financial Corp. **SIC:** 6021—National Commercial Banks.

★ 91025 ★   **First American Bank**
1 S. Armistead Ave.
Hampton, VA 23669
(804)728-2250
Ultimate Parent: First American Corp. **SIC:** 6099—Functions Related to Deposit Banking.

★ 91026 ★   **First American Bank**
2050 Coliseum Dr.
Hampton, VA 23666
Ultimate Parent: First American Corp. **SIC:** 6099—Functions Related to Deposit Banking.

★ 91027 ★   **First American Bank**
1304 Todds Ln.
Hampton, VA 23666
(804)728-2290
Ultimate Parent: First American Corp. **SIC:** 6099—Functions Related to Deposit Banking.

★ 91028 ★   **First American Bank of Virginia**
4910 W. Mercury Blvd.
Hampton, VA 23666
(804)728-2260
Ultimate Parent: First American Corp.

★ 91029 ★   **First American Bank of Virginia**
30 S. Mallory St.
Hampton, VA 23663
(804)728-2285
Ultimate Parent: First American Corp.

★ 91030 ★   **First American Bank of Virginia**
2050 Coliseum Dr.
Hampton, VA 23666
(804)728-2225
Ultimate Parent: First American Corp. **SIC:** 6099—Functions Related to Deposit Banking.

★ 91031 ★   **First Union National Bank of Virginia**
30 S. Mallory St.
Hampton, VA 23663-1798
(804)728-2285
Location Type: Branch office. **Ultimate Parent:** First Union Corp. **SIC:** 6021—National Commercial Banks.

★ 91032 ★   **First Union National Bank of Virginia**
1 S. Armistead
Hampton, VA 23669-4016
(804)728-2250
Location Type: Branch office. **Ultimate Parent:** First Union Corp. **SIC:** 6021—National Commercial Banks.

★ 91033 ★   **First Union National Bank of Virginia**
2050 Coliseum Dr.
Hampton, VA 23666-3220
(804)728-2225
Location Type: Branch office. **Ultimate Parent:** First Union Corp. **SIC:** 6021—National Commercial Banks.

★ 91034 ★   **Food Lion**
2070 Nickerson Blvd.
Hampton, VA 23663
(804)850-0302
Ultimate Parent: Food Lion. **SIC:** 5411—Grocery Stores.

★ 91035 ★   **Food Lion**
2137 Coliseum Dr.
Hampton, VA 23666
(804)827-1304
Ultimate Parent: Food Lion. **SIC:** 5411—Grocery Stores.

★ 91036 ★   **Food Lion**
2900 Hampton Hwy.
Hampton, VA 23666
(804)865-0848
Ultimate Parent: Food Lion. **SIC:** 3433—Heating Equipment Except Electric.

★ 91037 ★   **Gap the**
Coliseum Mall
Hampton, VA 23666
(804)826-6200
Ultimate Parent: GAP. **SIC:** 5651—Family Clothing Stores.

★ 91038 ★   **General Electric Co.**
2101 Executive Dr.
Hampton, VA 23666
(804)827-4500
Officer: Bruce Matthias, Manager. **Ultimate Parent:** General Electric. **SIC:** 3699—Electrical Equipment & Supplies Nec.

★ 91039 ★ **Greyhound Bus Lines**
22 S. Armistead Ave.
Hampton, VA 23669
(804)722-9861
Ultimate Parent: Greyhound Lines Inc. **SIC:**
4111—Local & Suburban Transit.

★ 91040 ★ **Hit or Miss**
4031 W. Mercury Blvd.
Hampton, VA 23666
(804)826-9767
Ultimate Parent: TJX. **SIC:** 5621—
Women's Clothing Stores.

★ 91041 ★ **Home Savings Bank**
550 Settlers Landing Rd.
Hampton, VA 23669
(804)722-5655
Ultimate Parent: H. F. Ahmanson. **SIC:**
6159—Miscellaneous Business Credit
Institutions.

★ 91042 ★ **J C Penney Co.**
2023 Coliseum Dr.
Hampton, VA 23666
(804)838-7470
Ultimate Parent: J.C. Penney. **SIC:** 5311—
Department Stores.

★ 91043 ★ **Lenscrafters**
Coliseum Mall
Hampton, VA 23666
(804)825-3044
Ultimate Parent: United States Shoe. **SIC:**
8042—Offices & Clinics of Optometrists.

★ 91044 ★ **Martin Marietta Corp.**
2101 Executive Dr.
Hampton, VA 23666
(804)827-7620
Ultimate Parent: Martin Marietta. **SIC:**
8731—Commercial Physical Research.

★ 91045 ★ **McDonald's
Hamburgers**
4104 W. Mercury Blvd.
Hampton, VA 23666
(804)826-6900
Ultimate Parent: McDonald's. **SIC:** 5812—
Eating Places.

★ 91046 ★ **Price Club**
2120 Coliseum Dr.
Hampton, VA 23666
(804)838-0769
Ultimate Parent: Price. **SIC:** 5399—
Miscellaneous General Merchandise Store.

★ 91047 ★ **Radio Shack**
Mercury
Hampton, VA 23666
(804)838-5200
Company Type: Division. **Ultimate Parent:**
Tandy Corp. **SIC:** 5065—Electronic Parts &
Equipment Nec; 5731—Radio, Television &
Electronics Stores.

★ 91048 ★ **Radio Shack**
51 W. Mercury Blvd.
Hampton, VA 23669
(804)723-6656
Company Type: Division. **Ultimate Parent:**
Tandy Corp. **SIC:** 5731—Radio, Television
& Electronics Stores.

★ 91049 ★ **Radio Shack**
Coliseum Mall
Hampton, VA 23666
(804)826-7411
Company Type: Division. **Ultimate Parent:**
Tandy Corp. **SIC:** 5731—Radio, Television
& Electronics Stores.

★ 91050 ★ **Radio Shack**
Coliseum Shopping Ctr.
Hampton, VA 23666
(804)826-7593
Company Type: Division. **Ultimate Parent:**
Tandy Corp. **SIC:** 5046—Commercial
Equipment Nec.

★ 91051 ★ **Radio Shack**
Coliseum Shopping Ctr.
Hampton, VA 23666
(804)826-7593
Company Type: Division. **Ultimate Parent:**
Tandy Corp. **SIC:** 5046—Commercial
Equipment Nec.

★ 91052 ★ **Rite Aid**
2900 Hampton Hwy.
Hampton, VA 23666
(804)865-1694
Ultimate Parent: Rite Aid. **SIC:** 5912—Drug
Stores & Proprietary Stores.

★ 91053 ★ **Rite Aid**
Coliseum Mall
Hampton, VA 23666
(804)838-9907
Ultimate Parent: Rite Aid. **SIC:** 5912—Drug
Stores & Proprietary Stores.

★ 91054 ★ **Rite Aid**
227 Fox Hillrd
Hampton, VA 23669
(804)851-9260
Ultimate Parent: Rite Aid. **SIC:** 5912—Drug
Stores & Proprietary Stores.

★ 91055 ★ **Service Merchandise**
2330 W. Mercury Blvd.
Hampton, VA 23666
(804)827-9507
Ultimate Parent: Service Merchandise Co.,
Inc. **SIC:** 5311—Department Stores.

★ 91056 ★ **Signet Bank, Virginia**
4100 W. Mercury Blvd.
Hampton, VA 23666-3783
(804)825-7677
Location Type: Branch office. **Ultimate
Parent:** Signet Banking Corp. **SIC:** 6021—
National Commercial Banks.

★ 91057 ★ **Toys R US**
4019 W. Mercury Blvd.
Hampton, VA 23666
(804)838-4787
Ultimate Parent: Toys "R" US. **SIC:** 5641—
Children's & Infants' Wear Stores; 5945—
Hobby, Toy & Game Shops.

★ 91058 ★ **Weight Watchers
Internation**
5013 W. Mercury Blvd.
Hampton, VA 23666
(804)441-7171
Ultimate Parent: H.J. Heinz. **SIC:** 7299—
Miscellaneous Personal Services Nec.

★ 91059 ★ **Mary Kay Cosmetics**
7 Honeysucklehill
Hampton Virgi, VA 23669
(804)851-1965
Ultimate Parent: Mary Kay Cosmetics. **SIC:**
5999—Miscellaneous Retail Stores Nec.

Hanover

★ 91060 ★ **Crestar Bank**
Rtes. 301 & 646
Hanover, VA 23069
(804)782-5681
Location Type: Branch office. **Ultimate
Parent:** Crestar Financial Corp.

Harman Junction

★ 91061 ★ **First Union National
Bank of Virginia**
Rte. 460 E
Harman Junction, VA 24614-9615
(703)935-8151
Location Type: Branch office. **Ultimate
Parent:** First Union Corp. **SIC:** 6021—
National Commercial Banks.

Harrisonburg

★ 91062 ★ **Agri-Services of
Harrisonburg**
103 Greystone St.
Harrisonburg, VA 22801
(703)564-6030
Location Type: Branch office. **Officer:**
James Mason. **Ultimate Parent:** Agway Inc.
SIC: 5169—Chemicals & Allied Products
Nec.

★ 91063 ★ **American Family Life
Assurance**
1341 Smithland Rd.
Harrisonburg, VA 22801
(703)433-9764
Ultimate Parent: American Family Life
Assurance Co. **SIC:** 6411—Insurance
Agents, Brokers & Service.

★ 91064 ★ **AMP Inc.**
1175 N. Main St.
Harrisonburg, VA 22801
(703)433-3200
Officer: Wayne Faber, Manager. **Ultimate
Parent:** AMP Inc. **SIC:** 3699—Electrical
Equipment & Supplies Nec.

★ 91065 ★ **AMP Inc.**
1175 N. Main St.
Harrisonburg, VA 22801-4630
Ultimate Parent: AMP Inc. **SIC:** 3471—
Plating & Polishing; 3678—Electronic
Connectors.

★ 91066 ★ **AMP Inc.**
1175 N. Main St.
Harrisonburg, VA 22801-4630
Ultimate Parent: AMP Inc. **SIC:** 3678—
Electronic Connectors.

★ 91067 ★ **Banta Co.**
3330 Willow Spring Rd.
Harrisonburg, VA 22801-9729
(703)564-3900
Location Type: Branch office. **Officer:**
Robert Engle. **Ultimate Parent:** Banta Corp.
SIC: 3732—Boat Building & Repairing.

★ 91068 ★ **Banta Co., Inc.**
3330 Willow Spring Rd.
Harrisonburg, VA 22801
(703)433-2571
Company Type: Subsidiary. **Officer:**
Robert Engell, Vice President & General
Manager. **Ultimate Parent:** Banta Corp.
SIC: 2732—Book Printing; 2759—
Commercial Printing Nec. **Employee
Count:** 230.

★ 91069 ★ **Banta Co., Inc.
Harrisonburg**
3330 Willow Spring Rd.
Harrisonburg, VA 22801
(703)433-2571
Company Type: Subsidiary. **Officer:**
Robert Engell, Vice President & General
Manager. **Ultimate Parent:** Banta Corp.
SIC: 2732—Book Printing; 2759—
Commercial Printing Nec. **Employee
Count:** 230.

★ 91070 ★ **Banta Corp.**
3330 Willow Spring Rd.
Harrisonburg, VA 22801-9729
(703)564-3900
Location Type: Branch office. **Officer:**
Robert Engle. **Ultimate Parent:** Banta Corp.
SIC: 3732—Boat Building & Repairing.

★ 91071 ★ **Cassco Ice & Cola
Inc.**
PO Box 548
Harrisonburg, VA 22801
Ultimate Parent: WLR Foods. **SIC:** 2097—
Manufactured Ice.

★ 91072 ★ **Crestar Bank**
1905 E. Market St.
Harrisonburg, VA 22801-3401
Location Type: Branch office. **Ultimate
Parent:** Crestar Financial Corp. **SIC:**
6021—National Commercial Banks.

★ 91073 ★ **Crestar Bank**
1300 S. Main St.
Harrisonburg, VA 22801-3028
Location Type: Branch office. **Ultimate
Parent:** Crestar Financial Corp. **SIC:**
6021—National Commercial Banks.

★ 91074 ★ **Crestar Bank**
180 E. Market St.
Harrisonburg, VA 22801-4129
Location Type: Branch office. **Ultimate
Parent:** Crestar Financial Corp. **SIC:**
6021—National Commercial Banks.

★ 91075 ★ **R.R. Donnelley &
Sons Co.**
Harrisonburg Manufacturing Div.
1400 Kratzer Rd.
Harrisonburg, VA 22801
Company Type: Division. **Ultimate Parent:**
R. R. Donnelley & Sons. **SIC:** 2732—Book
Printing.

★ 91076 ★ **R.R. Donnelley &
Sons Co.**
Harrisonburg Manufacturing Div.
1400 Kratzer Rd.
Harrisonburg, VA 22801
Company Type: Division. **Ultimate Parent:**
R. R. Donnelley & Sons. **SIC:** 2732—Book
Printing.

★ 91077 ★ **Eckerd Drugs**
1755 S. High St.
Harrisonburg, VA 22801
(703)433-1158
Ultimate Parent: Eckerd Corp. **SIC:** 5912—
Drug Stores & Proprietary Stores.

★ 91078 ★ **Eckerd Drugs**
1663 E. Market St.
Harrisonburg, VA 22801
(703)433-5393
Ultimate Parent: Eckerd Corp. **SIC:** 5912—
Drug Stores & Proprietary Stores.

★ 91079 ★ **First American Bank
of Virginia**
8 Pleasant Hill Rd.
Harrisonburg, VA 22801
(703)433-2741
Ultimate Parent: First American Corp. **SIC:**
6022—State Commercial Banks.

★ 91080 ★ **First American Bank
of Virginia**
932 W. Market St.
Harrisonburg, VA 22801
(703)433-6693
Ultimate Parent: First American Corp. **SIC:**
6022—State Commercial Banks.

★ 91081 ★ **First American Bank
of Virginia**
75 N. Mason St.
Harrisonburg, VA 22801
(703)432-3000
Ultimate Parent: First American Corp. **SIC:**
6022—State Commercial Banks.

★ 91082 ★ **First Union National
Bank of Virginia**
1600 S. Main St.
Harrisonburg, VA 22801-2729
(703)564-5393
Location Type: Branch office. **Ultimate
Parent:** First Union Corp. **SIC:** 6021—
National Commercial Banks.

★ 91083 ★ **First Union National
Bank of Virginia**
932 W. Market St.
Harrisonburg, VA 22801-2136
(703)432-3050
Location Type: Branch office. **Ultimate
Parent:** First Union Corp. **SIC:** 6021—
National Commercial Banks.

★ 91084 ★ **First Union National
Bank of Virginia**
10 E. Gay St.
Harrisonburg, VA 22801-4108
Location Type: Branch office. **Ultimate
Parent:** First Union Corp. **SIC:** 6021—
National Commercial Banks.

★ 91085 ★ **First Union National
Bank of Virginia**
1600 S. Main St.
Harrisonburg, VA 22801-2729
(703)564-5393
Location Type: Branch office. **Ultimate
Parent:** First Union Corp. **SIC:** 6021—
National Commercial Banks.

★ 91086 ★ **First Union National
Bank of Virginia**
141 E. Market St.
Harrisonburg, VA 22801-4128
Location Type: Branch office. **Ultimate
Parent:** First Union Corp. **SIC:** 6021—
National Commercial Banks.

★ 91087 ★ **First Union National
Bank of Virginia**
2005 E. Market St.
Harrisonburg, VA 22801
(703)433-8383
Location Type: Branch office. **Ultimate
Parent:** First Union Corp. **SIC:** 6021—
National Commercial Banks.

★ 91088 ★ **Food Lion**
1751 S. High St.
Harrisonburg, VA 22801
(703)433-8099
Ultimate Parent: Food Lion. **SIC:** 5411—
Grocery Stores.

★ 91089 ★ **Food Lion**
924 W. Market St.
Harrisonburg, VA 22801
(703)433-8365
Ultimate Parent: Food Lion. **SIC:** 5411—
Grocery Stores.

★ 91090 ★ **Food Lion Inc.**
1751 S. High St.
Harrisonburg, VA 22801
(703)433-8099
Ultimate Parent: Food Lion. **SIC:** 5411—
Grocery Stores.

★ 91091 ★   Holly Farms Foods Inc.
501 N. Liberty St.
Harrisonburg, VA 22801
Ultimate Parent: Tyson Foods, Inc. SIC: 0251—Broiler, Fryer & Roaster Chickens.

★ 91092 ★   Holly Farms Foods Inc. Wastewater Processing Plant
501 North Liberty St. PO Box 589
Harrisonburg, VA 22801
Ultimate Parent: Tyson Foods, Inc. SIC: 2015—Poultry Slaughtering & Processing.

★ 91093 ★   Kroger Co.
Hwy. 33
Harrisonburg, VA 22801
(703)432-1830
Ultimate Parent: Kroger. SIC: 5411—Grocery Stores.

★ 91094 ★   New York Life Insurance Co.
270 S. Liberty St.
Harrisonburg, VA 22801
(703)433-0522
Ultimate Parent: New York Life. SIC: 6411—Insurance Agents, Brokers & Service.

★ 91095 ★   Office Products Inc.
4011 S. Main St.
Harrisonburg, VA 22801-9771
(703)434-8958
Officer: William Lam, President. Ultimate Parent: Avery Dennison Corp. SIC: 5021—Furniture. Employee Count: 16. Sales: 2.6 M.

★ 91096 ★   Packaging Corp. of America
400 Pleasant Valley Rd.
Harrisonburg, VA 22801
Ultimate Parent: Tenneco Inc. SIC: 2653—Corrugated & Solid Fiber Boxes.

★ 91097 ★   Radio Shack
4 Valley Mall
Harrisonburg, VA 22801
(703)434-9838
Company Type: Division. Ultimate Parent: Tandy Corp. SIC: 5731—Radio, Television & Electronics Stores.

★ 91098 ★   Radio Shack
Vly Mall
Harrisonburg, VA 22801
(703)434-3667
Company Type: Division. Ultimate Parent: Tandy Corp. SIC: 5065—Electronic Parts & Equipment Nec.

★ 91099 ★   Rite Aid
109 S. Carlton St.
Harrisonburg, VA 22801
(703)434-7341
Ultimate Parent: Rite Aid. SIC: 5912—Drug Stores & Proprietary Stores.

★ 91100 ★   Southern States Co-Op. Inc.
421 Chesapeake Ave.
Harrisonburg, VA 22801
Ultimate Parent: Southern. SIC: 2048—Prepared Feeds Nec.

★ 91101 ★   Tyson Foods Inc.
501 N. Liberty St.
Harrisonburg, VA 22801
(703)433-0720
Officer: Danny Sutton, Manager. Ultimate Parent: Tyson Foods, Inc. SIC: 2015—Poultry Slaughtering & Processing.

★ 91102 ★   Tyson Foods Inc. Shenandoah Valley Complex
501 N. Liberty St. PO Box 589
Harrisonburg, VA 22801
Ultimate Parent: Tyson Foods, Inc. SIC: 2015—Poultry Slaughtering & Processing.

★ 91103 ★   Tyson Foods Inc. Wastewater Treatment Plant
501 N. Liberty St. PO Box 589
Harrisonburg, VA 22801
Ultimate Parent: Tyson Foods, Inc. SIC: 2015—Poultry Slaughtering & Processing.

★ 91104 ★   Walker Manufacturing Co.
I 81
Harrisonburg, VA 22801
(703)434-2561
Ultimate Parent: Tenneco Inc. SIC: 3714—Motor Vehicle Parts & Accessories.

★ 91105 ★   Walker Mfg. Co.
3160 Abbott Ln.
Harrisonburg, VA 22801
Ultimate Parent: Tenneco Inc. SIC: 3714—Motor Vehicle Parts & Accessories.

★ 91106 ★   Wampler Foods Inc.
590 Mt. Clinton Pike
Harrisonburg, VA 22801
Ultimate Parent: WLR Foods. SIC: 2048—Prepared Feeds Nec.

★ 91107 ★   Wampler Longacre Inc.
862 N. Liberty St.
Harrisonburg, VA 22801
(703)564-6000
Company Type: Division. Location Type: Facility. Officer: Tim Ranion, Plant Mgr. Ultimate Parent: WLR Foods. SIC: 2013—Sausages & Other Prepared Meats.

★ 91108 ★   Wampler-Longacre Turkey Inc.
590 Mt. Clinton Pke.
Harrisonburg, VA 22801
Ultimate Parent: WLR Foods. SIC: 2048—Prepared Feeds Nec.

★ 91109 ★   Wampler-Longacre Turkey Inc.
862 N. Liberty St.
Harrisonburg, VA 22801
Ultimate Parent: WLR Foods. SIC: 2015—Poultry Slaughtering & Processing.

Hartwood

★ 91110 ★   Teledyne Total Power
1127 International Pky.
Hartwood, VA 22471
(703)752-9395
Ultimate Parent: Teledyne. SIC: 3714—Motor Vehicle Parts & Accessories.

Hayes

★ 91111 ★   Ace Hardware
334 PO Box
Hayes, VA 23072
(804)642-5300
Ultimate Parent: Ace Hardware. SIC: 5719—Miscellaneous Home Furnishings Stores.

Haymarket

★ 91112 ★   First Virginia Bank
14901 Washington St.
Haymarket, VA 22069-2921
(703)241-3250
Location Type: Branch office. Ultimate Parent: First Virginia Banks Inc. SIC: 6021—National Commercial Banks.

Haysi

★ 91113 ★   First Union National Bank of Virginia
Main St.
Haysi, VA 24556
(703)935-8151
Location Type: Branch office. Ultimate Parent: First Union Corp. SIC: 6021—National Commercial Banks.

Heathsville

★ 91114 ★   First Virginia Bank
US Rte. 360 & State Rte. 634
Heathsville, VA 22473-9701
(804)580-2211
Location Type: Branch office. Ultimate Parent: First Virginia Banks Inc. SIC: 6021—National Commercial Banks.

Henton

★ 91115 ★   W L R Foods
PO Box 228
Henton, VA 22831
(703)867-4001 Fax: (703)867-4098
Officer: James L. Keeler, CEO. Ultimate Parent: WLR Foods. Employee Count: 6850. Sales: 617 M.

★ 91116 ★   Wampler Longacre Inc.
Rte. 33 W.
Henton, VA 22831
(703)867-4000
Company Type: Division. Location Type: Facility. Officer: Keith Grogg, Plant Mgr. Ultimate Parent: WLR Foods. SIC: 2013—Sausages & Other Prepared Meats.

Herndon

★ 91117 ★   Collins International Service Co.
13651 Mclearen Rd.
Herndon, VA 22071
(703)318-7780
Ultimate Parent: Rockwell International Corp.

★ 91118 ★   Computer Sciences
Network Integration
3001 Centreville Rd.
Herndon, VA 22071
(703)471-3112 Fax: (703)471-9082
Officer: Werner Schaer, President. Ultimate Parent: Computer Sciences.

★ 91119 ★   Crestar Bank
2401 Centreville Rd.
Herndon, VA 22071
(703)838-3180
Location Type: Branch office. Ultimate Parent: Crestar Financial Corp. SIC: 6021—National Commercial Banks.

★ 91120 ★   Electronic Data Systems Cor
13600 Eds Dr.
Herndon, VA 22071
(703)897-9250
Ultimate Parent: Electronic Data Systems. SIC: 7374—Data Processing & Preparation.

★ 91121 ★   First American Bank
1099 Elden St.
Herndon, VA 22070
(703)934-1860
Ultimate Parent: First American Corp. SIC: 6099—Functions Related to Deposit Banking.

★ 91122 ★   First American Bank of Virginia
1099 Elden St.
Herndon, VA 22070
(703)827-8718
Ultimate Parent: First American Corp. SIC: 6022—State Commercial Banks.

★ 91123 ★   First American Bank of Virginia
11260 Roger Bacon Dr.
Herndon, VA 22090
(703)827-8812
Ultimate Parent: First American Corp. SIC: 6022—State Commercial Banks.

★ 91124 ★   First Union National Bank of Virginia
1099 Elden St.
Herndon, VA 22070-3802
(703)934-1860
Location Type: Branch office. Ultimate Parent: First Union Corp. SIC: 6021—National Commercial Banks.

★ 91125 ★   First Union National Bank of Virginia
13350 Franklin Farms Rd.
Herndon, VA 22070-4036
(703)934-1944
Location Type: Branch office. Ultimate Parent: First Union Corp. SIC: 6021—National Commercial Banks.

★ 91126 ★   First Virginia Bank
2148 Centreville Rd.
Herndon, VA 22070-4308
(703)241-4861
Location Type: Branch office. Ultimate Parent: First Virginia Banks Inc. SIC: 6021—National Commercial Banks.

★ 91127 ★   First Virginia Bank
13360 Franklin Farm Rd.
Herndon, VA 22071
(703)533-6207
Location Type: Branch office. Ultimate Parent: First Virginia Banks Inc. SIC: 6021—National Commercial Banks.

★ 91128 ★   First Virginia Bank
2513 Fox Mill Rd.
Herndon, VA 22071-2552
(703)241-3491
Location Type: Branch office. Ultimate Parent: First Virginia Banks Inc. SIC: 6021—National Commercial Banks.

★ 91129 ★   Pulse Communications Inc.
2900 Towerview Rd.
Herndon, VA 22071
(703)471-2900 Fax: (703)471-2951
Company Type: Subsidiary. Officer: F.E. Glave, Vice President & General Manager. Ultimate Parent: Hubbell.

★ 91130 ★   Radio Shack
Fox Mill Ctr.
Herndon, VA 22071
(703)620-9090
Company Type: Division. Ultimate Parent: Tandy Corp. SIC: 5065—Electronic Parts & Equipment Nec.

★ 91131 ★   Radio Shack
Fox Mill Ctr.
Herndon, VA 22071
(703)620-9090
Company Type: Division. Ultimate Parent: Tandy Corp. SIC: 5065—Electronic Parts & Equipment Nec.

★ 91132 ★   Signet Bank
13021 Worldgate Dr.
Herndon, VA 22070-2527
(703)471-1517
Location Type: Branch office. Ultimate Parent: Signet Banking Corp. SIC: 6021—National Commercial Banks.

★ 91133 ★   Signet Bank, Virginia
199 Elden St.
Herndon, VA 22070-4810
(703)471-0022
Location Type: Branch office. Ultimate Parent: Signet Banking Corp. SIC: 6021—National Commercial Banks.

★ 91134 ★   Signet Bank, Virginia
2575 John Milton Dr.
Herndon, VA 22071-2527
(703)620-4500
Location Type: Branch office. Ultimate Parent: Signet Banking Corp. SIC: 6021—National Commercial Banks.

★ 91135 ★   Washington Federal Savings Bank
570 Herndon Pky.
Herndon, VA 22070
(804)478-9100 Fax: (804)624-2334
Officer: Carroll E. Amos, CEO. Ultimate Parent: Washington Federal S&L. Employee Count: 198. Sales: 63 M.

★ 91136 ★   Westvaco Corp.
607 Herndon Pky.
Herndon, VA 22070
(703)834-3680
Ultimate Parent: WestVaco Corp. SIC: 5943—Stationery Stores.

★ 91137 ★   Westvaco Corp.
11800 Sunrise Valley Dr.
Herndon, VA 22091
(703)620-4090
Ultimate Parent: WestVaco Corp. SIC: 5112—Stationery & Office Supplies.

★ 91138 ★   Xerox Corp.
607 Herndon Pky.
Herndon, VA 22070
(703)787-2000
Officer: Janet Wylie, Manager. Ultimate Parent: Xerox Corp. SIC: 3579—Office Machines Nec.

Hillsville

★ 91139 ★   Burlington Industries Inc.
Hwy. 221
Hillsville, VA 24343
(703)728-2141
Officer: Craig Vandeventer, Manager. Ultimate Parent: Burlington Industries, Equity. SIC: 2399—Fabricated Textile Products Nec.

★ 91140 ★　　**Food Lion**
Main
Hillsville, VA 24343
(703)728-9111
Ultimate Parent: Food Lion. **SIC:** 5411—
Grocery Stores.

★ 91141 ★　　**Greyhound Bus Lines**
S Main
Hillsville, VA 24343
(703)728-9333
Ultimate Parent: Greyhound Lines Inc. **SIC:**
4111—Local & Suburban Transit.

★ 91142 ★　　**Mary Kay Cosmetics**
Northview Hts.
Hillsville, VA 24343
(703)236-9532
Ultimate Parent: Mary Kay Cosmetics. **SIC:**
5999—Miscellaneous Retail Stores Nec.

★ 91143 ★　　**Mini Mart**
Rural Route 3
Hillsville, VA 24343
(703)728-4914
Ultimate Parent: Kroger. **SIC:** 5521—Used
Car Dealers.

Hinton

★ 91144 ★　　**Wampler Foods Inc.**
US Rte. 33 West
Hinton, VA 22831
Ultimate Parent: WLR Foods. **SIC:** 2048—
Prepared Feeds Nec.

★ 91145 ★　　**Wampler-Longacre
Turkey Inc.**
US Rte. 33 W
Hinton, VA 22831
Ultimate Parent: WLR Foods. **SIC:** 2015—
Poultry Slaughtering & Processing.

Hollins

★ 91146 ★　　**First Union National
Bank of Virginia**
PO Box 13327, Roanoke
Hollins, VA 24040-0001
Location Type: Branch office. **Ultimate
Parent:** First Union Corp. **SIC:** 6021—
National Commercial Banks.

★ 91147 ★　　**First Union National
Bank of Virginia**
7711 Plantation Rd. NW
Hollins, VA 24019-3224
(703)563-7000 **Telex:** 829-484
Location Type: Headquarters. **Ultimate
Parent:** First Union Corp. **SIC:** 6021—
National Commercial Banks.

★ 91148 ★　　**Pepsi-Cola Bottling
Co.**
Rte. 11 Lee Hwy.
Hollins, VA 24019
Ultimate Parent: Pepsico. **SIC:** 2086—
Bottled & Canned Soft Drinks.

Honaker

★ 91149 ★　　**Piggly Wiggly**
Honaker, VA 24260
(703)873-4221
Ultimate Parent: Bruno's. **SIC:** 5399—
Miscellaneous General Merchandise Store.

★ 91150 ★　　**Signet Bank, Virginia**
Albert Dr. & Fairmount Ave.
Honaker, VA 24260
(703)873-6811
Location Type: Branch office. **Ultimate
Parent:** Signet Banking Corp. **SIC:** 6021—
National Commercial Banks.

Hopewell

★ 91151 ★　　**Allied-Signal
Communications Systems**
905 E. Randolph Rd.
Hopewell, VA 23860
(804)541-5000
Officer: Andre Tremper, Manager. **Ultimate
Parent:** Allied-Signal Inc. **SIC:** 2819—
Industrial Inorganic Chemicals Nec; 2824—
Organic Fibers—Noncellulosic; 2869—
Industrial Organic Chemicals Nec.

★ 91152 ★　　**Allied-Signal
Hopewell Plant**
PO Box 761, Rte. 10
Hopewell, VA 23860
Ultimate Parent: Allied-Signal Inc. **SIC:**
2869—Industrial Organic Chemicals Nec;
2819—Industrial Inorganic Chemicals Nec;
2873—Nitrogenous Fertilizers.

★ 91153 ★　　**Allied-Signal Inc.**
Rte. 10 & Industrial St.
Hopewell, VA 23860
Location Type: Plant. **Ultimate Parent:**
Allied-Signal Inc. **SIC:** 2869—Industrial
Organic Chemicals Nec; 2819—Industrial
Inorganic Chemicals Nec; 2873—
Nitrogenous Fertilizers.

★ 91154 ★　　**Allied-Signal Inc.**
PO Box 761 Rte. 10
Hopewell, VA 23860
Location Type: Plant. **Ultimate Parent:**
Allied-Signal Inc. **SIC:** 2869—Industrial
Organic Chemicals Nec; 2819—Industrial
Inorganic Chemicals Nec; 2873—
Nitrogenous Fertilizers.

★ 91155 ★　　**Allied-Signal Inc.**
Rte. 10
Hopewell, VA 23860
Location Type: Plant. **Ultimate Parent:**
Allied-Signal Inc. **SIC:** 2869—Industrial
Organic Chemicals Nec; 2819—Industrial
Inorganic Chemicals Nec; 2873—
Nitrogenous Fertilizers.

★ 91156 ★　　**Aqualon Co.**
1111 Hercules Rd.
Hopewell, VA 23860
Ultimate Parent: Hercules. **SIC:** 2869—
Industrial Organic Chemicals Nec.

★ 91157 ★　　**Browning-Ferris
Industries**
Hopewell, VA 23860
(804)788-8126
Ultimate Parent: Browning-Ferris
Industries. **SIC:** 4953—Refuse Systems.

★ 91158 ★　　**Carbon Dioxide Corp.
Liquid Carbonic**
PO Box 937
Hopewell, VA 23860
Ultimate Parent: CBI Industries, Inc. **SIC:**
2813—Industrial Gases.

★ 91159 ★　　**Chesapeake &
Potomac Telephone Co.**
204 W. Poythress St.
Hopewell, VA 23860-2725
(804)458-1514
Company Type: Subsidiary. **Ultimate
Parent:** Bell Atlantic Corp. **SIC:** 4813—
Telephone Communications Except
Radiotelephone.

★ 91160 ★　　**Crestar Bank**
200-204 N. Main St.
Hopewell, VA 23860-2720
(804)541-2940
Location Type: Branch office. **Ultimate
Parent:** Crestar Financial Corp. **SIC:**
6021—National Commercial Banks.

★ 91161 ★　　**Liquid Carbonic
Carbon Dioxide Corp.**
221 Hopewell St.
Hopewell, VA 23860
Ultimate Parent: CBI Industries, Inc. **SIC:**
2813—Industrial Gases.

★ 91162 ★　　**Radio Shack**
402 Cavalier Sq.
Hopewell, VA 23860
(804)452-0805
Company Type: Division. **Ultimate Parent:**
Tandy Corp. **SIC:** 5731—Radio, Television
& Electronics Stores.

★ 91163 ★　　**Radio Shack**
Lee Plz.
Hopewell, VA 23860
(804)458-0018
Company Type: Division. **Ultimate Parent:**
Tandy Corp. **SIC:** 5731—Radio, Television
& Electronics Stores.

★ 91164 ★　　**Rite Aid**
205 Cavaliersq
Hopewell, VA 23860
(804)458-1233
Ultimate Parent: Rite Aid. **SIC:** 5912—Drug
Stores & Proprietary Stores.

★ 91165 ★　　**Stone Container Corp.**
910 Industrial St.
Hopewell, VA 23860
(804)541-9600
Officer: Milton I. Hargrave, Manager.
Ultimate Parent: Stone Container Corp.
SIC: 2621—Paper Mills; 2631—Paperboard
Mills; 2673—Bags—Plastics, Laminated &
Coated.

★ 91166 ★　　**Stone Hopewell Inc.**
910 Industrial St.
Hopewell, VA 23860
Ultimate Parent: Stone Container Corp.
SIC: 2631—Paperboard Mills; 2611—Pulp
Mills.

Hot Springs

★ 91167 ★　　**Hertz Rent-A-Car**
Independent Lvry.
Hot Springs, VA 24445
(703)839-2752
Ultimate Parent: Hertz. **SIC:** 7514—
Passenger Car Rental.

Hurt

★ 91168 ★　　**Burlington Industries
Inc.**
Rte. 29 S
Hurt, VA 24563
(804)324-4211
Officer: Kate Karoly. **Ultimate Parent:**
Burlington Industries, Equity. **SIC:** 2262—
Finishing Plants—Manmade; 2221—
Broadwoven Fabric Mills—Manmade;
2269—Finishing Plants Nec; 4225—General
Warehousing & Storage.

Independence

★ 91169 ★　　**Nautilis International**
709 Powerhouse Rd.
Independence, VA 24348
(703)773-2881
Officer: Dan D. Baldwin, Chairman.
Ultimate Parent: Delta Woodside
Industries. **SIC:** 3949—Sporting & Athletic
Goods Nec.

Ivor

★ 91170 ★　　**Golden Peanut Co.**
Hwy. 460 W
Ivor, VA 23866
(804)859-6466
Ultimate Parent: Archer Daniels Midland
Co. **SIC:** 5159—Farm-Product Raw
Materials Nec.

Ivy

★ 91171 ★　　**Westvaco Corp.**
Ivy Wood Yard
Ivy, VA 22945
(804)293-5949
Ultimate Parent: WestVaco Corp. **SIC:**
2679—Converted Paper Products Nec.

Jarratt

★ 91172 ★　　**Georgia-Pacific Corp.
Jarratt Softboard**
Allen Road.
Jarratt, VA 23867
Ultimate Parent: Georgia-Pacific. **SIC:**
2493—Reconstituted Wood Products.

Jetersville

★ 91173 ★　　**Holly Farms Foods
Inc.**
US Hwy. 360
Jetersville, VA 23083
Ultimate Parent: Tyson Foods, Inc. **SIC:**
2048—Prepared Feeds Nec.

Keller

★ 91174 ★　　**Crestar Bank**
18255 1st St.
Keller, VA 23401
(804)858-3287
Location Type: Branch office. **Ultimate
Parent:** Crestar Financial Corp. **SIC:**
6021—National Commercial Banks.

Kenbridge

★ 91175 ★　　**Commonwealth
Tobacco Co. Inc.**
138 Main
Kenbridge, VA 23944
(804)676-8251
Ultimate Parent: Dibrell Brothers. **SIC:**
2141—Tobacco Stemming & Redrying.

Keysville

★ 91176 ★　　**Crestar Bank**
King St.
Keysville, VA 23947
(804)736-8421
Location Type: Branch office. **Ultimate
Parent:** Crestar Financial Corp. **SIC:**
6021—National Commercial Banks.

★ 91177 ★　　**West Point Pepperell**
Hwy. 40 West
Keysville, VA 23947
Location Type: Plant. **Ultimate Parent:**
West Point Stevens. **SIC:** 2273—Carpets &
Rugs.

★ 91178 ★　　**Westpoint Pepperell**
Hwy. 40 West
Keysville, VA 23947
Location Type: Plant. **Ultimate Parent:**
West Point Stevens. **SIC:** 2200—Textile Mill
Products.

Kilmarnock

★ 91179 ★　　**Signet Bank, Virginia**
248 N. Main St.
Kilmarnock, VA 22482
(804)435-2681
Location Type: Branch office. **Ultimate
Parent:** Signet Banking Corp. **SIC:** 6021—
National Commercial Banks.

King George

★ 91180 ★　　**First Virginia Bank**
States Rtes. 3 & 610
King George, VA 22485
(703)775-2930
Location Type: Branch office. **Ultimate
Parent:** First Virginia Banks Inc. **SIC:**
6021—National Commercial Banks.

★ 91181 ★　　**Syscon Corp.**
RR 3 E
King George, VA 22485
(703)775-3200
Ultimate Parent: Harnischfeger Industries.
SIC: 7374—Data Processing & Preparation.

La Crosse

★ 91182 ★　　**Signet Bank, Virginia**
Main St.
La Crosse, VA 23950
(804)757-7301
Location Type: Branch office. **Ultimate
Parent:** Signet Banking Corp. **SIC:** 6021—
National Commercial Banks.

Langley AFB

★ 91183 ★　　**Crestar Bank**
Langley Air Force Base, Bldg. 268
Langley AFB, VA 23665
(804)873-7820
Location Type: Branch office. **Ultimate
Parent:** Crestar Financial Corp. **SIC:**
6021—National Commercial Banks.

Lawrenceville

★ 91184 ★　　**Jones Store**
229 N. Main St.
Lawrenceville, VA 23868
(804)848-2812
Ultimate Parent: Mercantile Stores. **SIC:**
5331—Variety Stores.

★ 91185 ★　　**Life Insurance Co. of
Virginia**
102 N. Hicks St.
Lawrenceville, VA 23868
(804)848-2235
Ultimate Parent: Life Insurance Co. of
Virginia. **SIC:** 6411—Insurance Agents,
Brokers & Service.

★ 91186 ★ **Vulcan Materials Co.**
Hwy. 756
Lawrenceville, VA 23868
(804)848-4775
Ultimate Parent: Vulcan Materials Co. **SIC:** 1429—Crushed & Broken Stone Nec.

★ 91187 ★ **Vulcan Materials Co.**
Hwy. 756
Lawrenceville, VA 23868
(804)848-4775
Ultimate Parent: Vulcan Materials Co. **SIC:** 1429—Crushed & Broken Stone Nec.

Lebanon

★ 91188 ★ **First Union National Bank of Virginia**
16-18 Main St.
Lebanon, VA 24266
(703)889-2141
Location Type: Branch office. **Ultimate Parent:** First Union Corp. **SIC:** 6021—National Commercial Banks.

★ 91189 ★ **Piggly Wiggly**
Russell City Shopping Ctr.
Lebanon, VA 24266
(703)889-3296
Ultimate Parent: Bruno's. **SIC:** 5461—Retail Bakeries.

★ 91190 ★ **Rite Aid**
Lebanoncenter
Lebanon, VA 24266
(703)889-9873
Ultimate Parent: Rite Aid. **SIC:** 5912—Drug Stores & Proprietary Stores.

★ 91191 ★ **Signet Bank, Virginia**
Main St. & Mill Ave.
Lebanon, VA 24266-9705
(703)889-3331
Location Type: Branch office. **Ultimate Parent:** Signet Banking Corp. **SIC:** 6021—National Commercial Banks.

Leesburg

★ 91192 ★ **First Union National Bank of Virginia**
13 N. King St.
Leesburg, VA 22075-2819
(703)771-7520
Location Type: Branch office. **Ultimate Parent:** First Union Corp. **SIC:** 6021—National Commercial Banks.

★ 91193 ★ **First Union National Bank of Virginia**
20 Catoctin Cir. SE
Leesburg, VA 22075-3612
(703)771-7617
Location Type: Branch office. **Ultimate Parent:** First Union Corp. **SIC:** 6021—National Commercial Banks.

★ 91194 ★ **First Virginia Bank**
504 E. Market St.
Leesburg, VA 22075-4112
(703)241-4436
Location Type: Branch office. **Ultimate Parent:** First Virginia Banks Inc. **SIC:** 6021—National Commercial Banks.

★ 91195 ★ **McDonald's Hamburgers**
157 E. Market St.
Leesburg, VA 22075
(703)777-9600
Ultimate Parent: McDonald's. **SIC:** 5812—Eating Places.

★ 91196 ★ **Mutual of New York Insurance Co.**
F Bldg.
Leesburg, VA 22075
(703)777-2920
Ultimate Parent: Mutual of New York. **SIC:** 6411—Insurance Agents, Brokers & Service.

★ 91197 ★ **Signet Bank, Virginia**
701-A E. Market St.
Leesburg, VA 22705
Location Type: Branch office. **Ultimate Parent:** Signet Banking Corp. **SIC:** 6021—National Commercial Banks.

Lexington

★ 91198 ★ **Crestar Bank**
708 S. Main St.
Lexington, VA 24450-2235
(703)463-8228
Location Type: Branch office. **Ultimate Parent:** Crestar Financial Corp. **SIC:** 6021—National Commercial Banks.

★ 91199 ★ **Crestar Bank**
US Rte. 11 N
Lexington, VA 24450-8842
(703)463-8230
Ultimate Parent: Crestar Financial Corp. **SIC:** 6021—National Commercial Banks.

★ 91200 ★ **Crestar Bank**
45 S. Main St.
Lexington, VA 24450-2522
(703)463-2126
Location Type: Branch office. **Ultimate Parent:** Crestar Financial Corp. **SIC:** 6021—National Commercial Banks.

★ 91201 ★ **Exxon Co.**
402 W. Nelson St.
Lexington, VA 24450
(703)463-2511
Ultimate Parent: Exxon. **SIC:** 5075—Warm Air Heating & Air-Conditioning; 5172—Petroleum Products Nec.

★ 91202 ★ **First American Bank of Virginia**
22 S. Main St.
Lexington, VA 24450
(703)463-3171
Ultimate Parent: First American Corp. **SIC:** 6022—State Commercial Banks.

★ 91203 ★ **First American Bank of Virginia**
102 Walker St.
Lexington, VA 24450
(703)463-3174
Ultimate Parent: First American Corp. **SIC:** 6022—State Commercial Banks.

★ 91204 ★ **First Union National Bank of Virginia**
102 Walker St.
Lexington, VA 24450-2432
Location Type: Branch office. **Ultimate Parent:** First Union Corp. **SIC:** 6021—National Commercial Banks.

★ 91205 ★ **First Union National Bank of Virginia**
22 S. Main St.
Lexington, VA 24450-2523
(703)463-3171
Location Type: Branch office. **Ultimate Parent:** First Union Corp. **SIC:** 6021—National Commercial Banks.

★ 91206 ★ **First Union National Bank of Virginia**
101 S. Main St.
Lexington, VA 24450-2315
(703)463-7321
Location Type: Branch office. **Ultimate Parent:** First Union Corp. **SIC:** 6021—National Commercial Banks.

★ 91207 ★ **Greyhound Bus Lines**
614 S. Main St.
Lexington, VA 24450
(703)463-2424
Ultimate Parent: Greyhound Lines Inc. **SIC:** 4111—Local & Suburban Transit.

★ 91208 ★ **Kroger Co.**
Rural Route 11
Lexington, VA 24450
(703)463-3231
Ultimate Parent: Kroger. **SIC:** 5411—Grocery Stores.

★ 91209 ★ **Northwestern Mutual Life Inc.**
2 E. Washington St.
Lexington, VA 24450
(703)463-9489
Ultimate Parent: Northwestern Mutual Life. **SIC:** 6411—Insurance Agents, Brokers & Service.

★ 91210 ★ **Pappagallo**
23 N. Main St.
Lexington, VA 24450
(703)463-5988
Ultimate Parent: United States Shoe. **SIC:** 5661—Shoe Stores.

★ 91211 ★ **Radio Shack**
Us 11 N
Lexington, VA 24450
(703)463-1020
Company Type: Division. **Ultimate Parent:** Tandy Corp. **SIC:** 5731—Radio, Television & Electronics Stores.

★ 91212 ★ **Radio Shack**
US 11 N
Lexington, VA 24450
(703)463-1020
Company Type: Division. **Ultimate Parent:** Tandy Corp. **SIC:** 5731—Radio, Television & Electronics Stores.

★ 91213 ★ **Wal-Mart Discount Cities**
Us 11 N
Lexington, VA 24450
(703)464-3535
Ultimate Parent: Wal-Mart Stores, Inc. **SIC:** 5311—Department Stores.

★ 91214 ★ **Westvaco Corp.**
17 N. Randolph St.
Lexington, VA 24450
(703)463-9578
Ultimate Parent: WestVaco Corp. **SIC:** 5099—Durable Goods Nec.

Lorton

★ 91215 ★ **Browning-Ferris Industries**
8397 Terminal Rd.
Lorton, VA 22079-1423
(703)550-2421
Ultimate Parent: Browning-Ferris Industries. **SIC:** 4953—Refuse Systems.

Luray

★ 91216 ★ **Potomac Edison Co.**
2 Mechanic St.
Luray, VA 22835-1132
(703)743-4582
Officer: Harry G. Saufley. **Ultimate Parent:** Allegheny Power System. **SIC:** 4911—Electric Services.

★ 91217 ★ **Rite Aid**
12 Luray Shopping Ctr.
Luray, VA 22835
(703)743-6576
Ultimate Parent: Rite Aid. **SIC:** 5912—Drug Stores & Proprietary Stores.

★ 91218 ★ **Wrangler**
101 Blue Bell Ave.
Luray, VA 22835
(703)743-5147
Officer: Tom LaFrance, Manager. **Ultimate Parent:** VF Corp. **SIC:** 2325—Men's/Boys' Trousers & Slacks; 2369—Girls'/Children's Outerwear Nec.

Lynchburg

★ 91219 ★ **ABF Freight Systems Inc.**
132 Tomahawk Industrial Pk.
Lynchburg, VA 24502-4151
(804)237-1604
Officer: Franklin D. Terminal. **Ultimate Parent:** Arkansas Best. **SIC:** 4212—Local Trucking Without Storage; 4731—Freight Transportation Arrangement.

★ 91220 ★ **Air Products & Chemicals Inc.**
3310 Mayflower Dr., Ste. A
Lynchburg, VA 24501-4946
(804)528-2780
Location Type: Branch office. **Officer:** Elizabeth Draper. **Ultimate Parent:** Air Products & Chemicals, Inc. **SIC:** 5169—Chemicals & Allied Products Nec; 5047—Medical & Hospital Equipment.

★ 91221 ★ **American Family Life Assurance**
7701 Timberlake Rd.
Lynchburg, VA 24502
(804)239-8850
Ultimate Parent: American Family Life Assurance Co. **SIC:** 6411—Insurance Agents, Brokers & Service.

★ 91222 ★ **Babcock & Wilcox Co.**
Mt. Athos Rd.
Lynchburg, VA 24504
Ultimate Parent: McDermott. **SIC:** 3443—Fabricated Plate Work—Boiler Shops.

★ 91223 ★ **Ball Efratom Corp.**
725 Church St.
Lynchburg, VA 24504-1440
(804)846-1400
Ultimate Parent: Ball Corp. **SIC:** 5065—Electronic Parts & Equipment Nec.

★ 91224 ★ **Bell Atlantic Services**
104 Oakdale Circle
Lynchburg, VA 24502-3422
(804)239-3003
Ultimate Parent: Bell Atlantic Corp. **SIC:** 7378—Computer Maintenance & Repair.

★ 91225 ★ **BFI Waste Systems**
Holcomb Path Rd.
Lynchburg, VA 24506
(804)846-6800
Ultimate Parent: Browning-Ferris Industries. **SIC:** 4953—Refuse Systems.

★ 91226 ★ **Casual Corner**
River Ridge Shopping Ctr.
Lynchburg, VA 24502
(804)239-0130
Ultimate Parent: United States Shoe. **SIC:** 5621—Women's Clothing Stores.

★ 91227 ★ **Circuit City**
2834 Candlers Mountain Rd.
Lynchburg, VA 24502
(804)239-2083
Ultimate Parent: Circuit City Stores. **SIC:** 5065—Electronic Parts & Equipment Nec.

★ 91228 ★ **Crestar Bank**
6001 Fort Ave.
Lynchburg, VA 24502-1931
(804)847-2331
Location Type: Branch office. **Ultimate Parent:** Crestar Financial Corp. **SIC:** 6021—National Commercial Banks.

★ 91229 ★ **Crestar Bank**
4710 Boonsboro Rd.
Lynchburg, VA 24503-2243
(804)847-2324
Location Type: Branch office. **Ultimate Parent:** Crestar Financial Corp. **SIC:** 6021—National Commercial Banks.

★ 91230 ★ **Crestar Bank**
2482 Rivermont Ave.
Lynchburg, VA 24503-1546
(804)847-2271
Location Type: Branch office. **Ultimate Parent:** Crestar Financial Corp. **SIC:** 6021—National Commercial Banks.

★ 91231 ★ **Crestar Bank**
No. 1 The Plz.
Lynchburg, VA 24501
(804)847-2281
Location Type: Branch office. **Ultimate Parent:** Crestar Financial Corp. **SIC:** 6021—National Commercial Banks.

★ 91232 ★ **Crestar Bank**
1010 Main St.
Lynchburg, VA 24504-1712
(804)847-2200
Location Type: Branch office. **Ultimate Parent:** Crestar Financial Corp. **SIC:** 6021—National Commercial Banks.

★ 91233 ★ **Crestar Bank**
9604 Timberlake Rd.
Lynchburg, VA 24502-3744
(804)847-2337
Location Type: Branch office. **Ultimate Parent:** Crestar Financial Corp. **SIC:** 6021—National Commercial Banks.

★ 91234 ★ **Ecco**
32 Arrowhead Dr.
Lynchburg, VA 24502
(804)239-3226
Ultimate Parent: Itel. **SIC:** 1731—Electrical Work.

★ 91235 ★ **Electro Mechanical Holding Inc.**
4900 Wards Rd.
Lynchburg, VA 24501
(804)237-2966
Ultimate Parent: Ametek Inc. **SIC:** 5063—Electrical Apparatus & Equipment; 5021—Furniture; 5084—Industrial Machinery & Equipment.

★ 91236 ★   **Exxon Co.**
Parkwood St.
Lynchburg, VA 24501
(804)845-3862
Ultimate Parent: Exxon. **SIC:** 5541—Gasoline Service Stations.

★ 91237 ★   **Exxon Service Center**
3028 Memorial Ave.
Lynchburg, VA 24501
(804)846-2607
Ultimate Parent: Exxon. **SIC:** 5541—Gasoline Service Stations.

★ 91238 ★   **First Colony Life**
700 Main St.
Lynchburg, VA 24504
(804)845-0911
Company Type: Headquarters. **Officer:** Ronald V. Dolan. **Employee Count:** 850. **Fortune Service 500:** Ranking 49.

★ 91239 ★   **First Colony Life Insurance**
700 Main St.
Lynchburg, VA 24504
(804)845-0911
Ultimate Parent: First Colony Life. **SIC:** 6411—Insurance Agents, Brokers & Service.

★ 91240 ★   **First Colony Life Insurance Co.**
700 Main St.
Lynchburg, VA 24504
(804)845-0911 **Fax:** (804)528-3488
Company Type: Subsidiary. **Ultimate Parent:** Ethyl.

★ 91241 ★   **First Colony Life Insurance Co.**
7700 Main St.
Lynchburg, VA 24504-1412
(804)845-0911
Company Type: Subsidiary. **Officer:** Ronald V. Dolan, President & CEO. **Ultimate Parent:** Ethyl. **SIC:** 6311—Life Insurance; 6321—Accident & Health Insurance. **Employee Count:** 811.

★ 91242 ★   **First Federal S&L of America**
925 Main St.
Lynchburg, VA 24504
(804)845-2371
Ultimate Parent: Bancorp Hawaii. **SIC:** 6035—Federal Savings Institutions; 6035—Federal Savings Institutions.

★ 91243 ★   **First Federal S&L of America**
9515 Timberlake Rd.
Lynchburg, VA 24502
(804)948-1241
Ultimate Parent: Bancorp Hawaii. **SIC:** 6035—Federal Savings Institutions.

★ 91244 ★   **First Virginia Bank**
Piedmont
7901 Timberlake Rd.
Lynchburg, VA 24502
(804)239-2958
Company Type: Subsidiary. **Officer:** Herbert W. Guthrie, Chairman of the Board. **Ultimate Parent:** First Virginia Banks Inc. **SIC:** 6022—State Commercial Banks.

★ 91245 ★   **First Virginia Bank - Piedmont**
7901 Timberlake Rd.
Lynchburg, VA 24502-2603
(804)237-2958
Company Type: Subsidiary. **Officer:** B. T. Corish, President. **Ultimate Parent:** First Virginia Banks Inc. **SIC:** 6022—State Commercial Banks. **Employee Count:** 105.

★ 91246 ★   **Flowers Baking Co.**
1905 Hollins Mill Rd.
Lynchburg, VA 24503
(804)528-0441
Officer: Lewis J. Forrest, President, **Ultimate Parent:** Flowers Industries. **SIC:** 2051—Bread, Cake & Related Products.

★ 91247 ★   **Flowers Baking Co. of Lynchburg**
10301 Timberlake Rd.
Lynchburg, VA 24502
(804)237-5993
Ultimate Parent: Flowers Industries. **SIC:** 5149—Groceries & Related Products Nec.

★ 91248 ★   **Flowers Baking Co. of Lynchburg**
2120 Lakeside Dr.
Lynchburg, VA 24501
(804)385-5044
Ultimate Parent: Flowers Industries. **SIC:** 5149—Groceries & Related Products Nec; 5461—Retail Bakeries.

★ 91249 ★   **Flowers Baking Co. of Lynchburg Inc.**
1905 Hollins Mill Rd.
PO Box 3307
Lynchburg, VA 24503-3307
(804)528-0441 **Fax:** (804)528-2642
Officer: Lewis J. Forrest, President. **Ultimate Parent:** Flowers Industries.

★ 91250 ★   **Food Lion**
9201 Timberlake Rd.
Lynchburg, VA 24502
(804)237-6655
Ultimate Parent: Food Lion. **SIC:** 5411—Grocery Stores.

★ 91251 ★   **Food Lion**
3410 Old Forest Rd.
Lynchburg, VA 24501
(804)385-7411
Ultimate Parent: Food Lion. **SIC:** 5411—Grocery Stores.

★ 91252 ★   **Food Lion**
Memorial Ave.
Lynchburg, VA 24501
(804)846-0022
Ultimate Parent: Food Lion. **SIC:** 5411—Grocery Stores.

★ 91253 ★   **General Electric Co.**
Mountain View Rd.
Lynchburg, VA 24502
(804)528-7000
Officer: John Wilkins, Vice President. **Ultimate Parent:** General Electric. **SIC:** 3663—Radio & T.V. Communications Equipment; 3699—Electrical Equipment & Supplies Nec.

★ 91254 ★   **General Electric Co. Mobile Communications**
Mountain View Rd.
Lynchburg, VA 24502
Ultimate Parent: General Electric. **SIC:** 3600—Electronic & Other Electrical Equipment.

★ 91255 ★   **General Electric Co. Mobile Communications Business**
Mountain View Rd.
Lynchburg, VA 24502
Ultimate Parent: General Electric. **SIC:** 3679—Electronic Components Nec.

★ 91256 ★   **Griffin Pipe Products Co.**
Adams St. Upper Basin
Lynchburg, VA 24505
Ultimate Parent: Amsted Industries Inc. **SIC:** 3321—Gray & Ductile Iron Foundries.

★ 91257 ★   **Griffin Pipe Products Co.**
203 9th St.
Lynchburg, VA 24504
(804)528-8000
Ultimate Parent: Amsted Industries Inc. **SIC:** 5051—Metals Service Centers & Offices.

★ 91258 ★   **Griffin Pipe Products Co.**
10 Adams St.
Lynchburg, VA 24504
(804)845-8021
Officer: Thomas Fitzgerald, President. **Ultimate Parent:** Amsted Industries Inc. **SIC:** 3321—Gray & Ductile Iron Foundries.

★ 91259 ★   **Hanson Porcelain Co. Inc.**
3300 John Capron Rd.
Lynchburg, VA 24506
Ultimate Parent: Premark International. **SIC:** 3469—Metal Stampings Nec.

★ 91260 ★   **Hertz Rent-A-Car**
2009 Airport Rd.
Lynchburg, VA 24502
(804)237-6284
Ultimate Parent: Hertz. **SIC:** 7514—Passenger Car Rental.

★ 91261 ★   **J C Penney Co.**
River Ridge Shopping
Lynchburg, VA 24502
(804)847-7708
Ultimate Parent: J.C. Penney. **SIC:** 5399—Miscellaneous General Merchandise Store.

★ 91262 ★   **Kroger Co.**
2009 Wards Rd.
Lynchburg, VA 24502
(804)239-6244
Ultimate Parent: Kroger. **SIC:** 5411—Grocery Stores.

★ 91263 ★   **Kroger Co.**
2820 Linkhorne Dr.
Lynchburg, VA 24503
(804)384-0642
Ultimate Parent: Kroger. **SIC:** 5411—Grocery Stores.

★ 91264 ★   **Kroger Co.**
2029 Fort Ave.
Lynchburg, VA 24501
(804)846-0861
Ultimate Parent: Kroger. **SIC:** 5411—Grocery Stores.

★ 91265 ★   **Kroger Co.**
Timbrook Sq.
Lynchburg, VA 24502
(804)239-1084
Ultimate Parent: Kroger. **SIC:** 5411—Grocery Stores.

★ 91266 ★   **Liberty Mutual Insurance Co.**
2316 Atherholt Rd.
Lynchburg, VA 24501
(804)845-2368
Ultimate Parent: Liberty Mutual Group. **SIC:** 6411—Insurance Agents, Brokers & Service.

★ 91267 ★   **Lowe's**
7401 Timberlake Rd.
Lynchburg, VA 24502
(804)239-9271
Ultimate Parent: Lowe's. **SIC:** 5722—Household Appliance Stores.

★ 91268 ★   **Mead Paperboard Products**
1801 Concord Turnpike
Lynchburg, VA 24505-0980
Ultimate Parent: Mead. **SIC:** 2631—Paperboard Mills.

★ 91269 ★   **Meredith/Burda**
4201 Murray Pl.
Lynchburg, VA 24501
Ultimate Parent: Meredith. **SIC:** 2754—Commercial Printing—Gravure.

★ 91270 ★   **New York Life Insurance**
508 Leesville Rd.
Lynchburg, VA 24502
(804)237-1900
Ultimate Parent: New York Life. **SIC:** 6411—Insurance Agents, Brokers & Service.

★ 91271 ★   **New York Life Insurance Co.**
Fort
Lynchburg, VA 24505
(804)846-7349
Ultimate Parent: New York Life. **SIC:** 6411—Insurance Agents, Brokers & Service.

★ 91272 ★   **New York Life Insurance Co.**
7315 Timberlake Rd.
Lynchburg, VA 24502
(804)239-3534
Ultimate Parent: New York Life. **SIC:** 6411—Insurance Agents, Brokers & Service.

★ 91273 ★   **New York Life Insurance Co.**
Allied Arts Bldg.
Lynchburg, VA 24505
(804)845-9231
Ultimate Parent: New York Life. **SIC:** 6411—Insurance Agents, Brokers & Service.

★ 91274 ★   **Northwestern Mutual Life Inc.**
1001 PO Box
Lynchburg, VA 24505
(804)528-4090
Ultimate Parent: Northwestern Mutual Life. **SIC:** 6411—Insurance Agents, Brokers & Service.

★ 91275 ★   **Overnite Transportation Co.**
4640 Murray Pl
Lynchburg, VA 24502
(804)845-9001
Ultimate Parent: Union Pacific Corp. **SIC:** 4231—Trucking Terminal Facilities.

★ 91276 ★   **R. R. Donnelley Printing**
4201 Murray Pl.
Lynchburg, VA 24501-5099
Ultimate Parent: R. R. Donnelley & Sons. **SIC:** 2754—Commercial Printing—Gravure.

★ 91277 ★   **R. R. Donnelley Printing Co.**
4201 Murray Pl.
Lynchburg, VA 24506
Ultimate Parent: R. R. Donnelley & Sons. **SIC:** 2754—Commercial Printing—Gravure.

★ 91278 ★   **Radio Shack**
Forest Plz. W
Lynchburg, VA 24501
(804)384-0932
Company Type: Division. **Ultimate Parent:** Tandy Corp. **SIC:** 5731—Radio, Television & Electronics Stores.

★ 91279 ★   **Radio Shack**
3405 Candlers Mountain Rd.
Lynchburg, VA 24502
(804)239-1414
Company Type: Division. **Ultimate Parent:** Tandy Corp. **SIC:** 5731—Radio, Television & Electronics Stores.

★ 91280 ★   **Radio Shack**
Hills Plz.
Lynchburg, VA 24502
(804)237-1664
Company Type: Division. **Ultimate Parent:** Tandy Corp. **SIC:** 5046—Commercial Equipment Nec.

★ 91281 ★   **Radio Shack**
12 Plaza
Lynchburg, VA 24501
(804)845-3089
Company Type: Division. **Ultimate Parent:** Tandy Corp. **SIC:** 5731—Radio, Television & Electronics Stores.

★ 91282 ★   **Radio Shack**
Forest Plz. W
Lynchburg, VA 24501
(804)384-0932
Company Type: Division. **Ultimate Parent:** Tandy Corp. **SIC:** 5731—Radio, Television & Electronics Stores.

★ 91283 ★   **Rite Aid**
3225 Old Forest Rd.
Lynchburg, VA 24501
(804)385-7827
Ultimate Parent: Rite Aid. **SIC:** 5912—Drug Stores & Proprietary Stores.

★ 91284 ★   **Rite Aid**
Timbrook Sq.
Lynchburg, VA 24502
(804)239-9279
Ultimate Parent: Rite Aid. **SIC:** 5912—Drug Stores & Proprietary Stores.

★ 91285 ★   **Rite Aid**
3405 Candlers Mountainrd
Lynchburg, VA 24502
(804)239-9382
Ultimate Parent: Rite Aid. **SIC:** 5311—Department Stores; 5912—Drug Stores & Proprietary Stores.

★ 91286 ★   **R.R. Donnelley Printing Co.**
1011 Creekside Dr.
Lynchburg, VA 24502
(804)582-4500
Company Type: Subsidiary. **Ultimate Parent:** R. R. Donnelley & Sons. **SIC:** 2752—Commercial Printing—Lithographic; 2759—Commercial Printing Nec.

★ **91287** ★ **Ryder Truck Rental Inc.**
3229 John Capron Rd.
Lynchburg, VA 24501
(804)528-0044
Ultimate Parent: Ryder System. **SIC:** 7513—Truck Rental & Leasing Without Drivers.

★ **91288** ★ **Southeast Vinyl Co.**
6222 Logans Ln.
Lynchburg, VA 24502
Ultimate Parent: Reynolds Metals Co. **SIC:** 3089—Plastics Products Nec.

★ **91289** ★ **Starmark of Virginia**
1 Millrace Dr.
Lynchburg, VA 24502
Ultimate Parent: Masco. **SIC:** 2434—Wood Kitchen Cabinets.

★ **91290** ★ **Travelers Insurance**
4849 Fort Ave.
Lynchburg, VA 24502
(804)237-5050
Ultimate Parent: Travelers Inc. **SIC:** 6411—Insurance Agents, Brokers & Service.

★ **91291** ★ **United Parcel Service**
5235 Woodall Rd.
Lynchburg, VA 24502
(804)237-6659
Ultimate Parent: United Parcel Service of America. **SIC:** 4215—Courier Services Except by Air.

★ **91292** ★ **Westover Dairy**
2801 Fort Ave.
Lynchburg, VA 24501
Ultimate Parent: Kroger. **SIC:** 2026—Fluid Milk.

Lynchburgh

★ **91293** ★ **ITW Pactron**
1205 McConville Rd.
Lynchburgh, VA 24502
(804)239-6941 **Fax:** (804)237-4930
Company Type: Subsidiary. **Officer:** Ian Clelland, General Manager. **Ultimate Parent:** Illinois Tool Works.

Madison

★ **91294** ★ **Wrangler**
PO Box 36
Madison, VA 22727
(703)948-4504
Officer: Andy Caviness, Manager. **Ultimate Parent:** VF Corp. **SIC:** 2325—Men's/Boys' Trousers & Slacks.

Madison Heights

★ **91295** ★ **Crestar Bank**
Rte. 29 N. & Dillard Rd.
Madison Heights, VA 24572
(804)847-2370
Location Type: Branch office. **Ultimate Parent:** Crestar Financial Corp. **SIC:** 6021—National Commercial Banks.

★ **91296** ★ **Eckerd Drugs**
N. Madison
Madison Heights, VA 24572
(804)846-7351
Ultimate Parent: Eckerd Corp. **SIC:** 5912—Drug Stores & Proprietary Stores.

★ **91297** ★ **Food Lion**
1613 Amherst Hwy.
Madison Heights, VA 24572
(804)528-2632
Ultimate Parent: Food Lion. **SIC:** 5411—Grocery Stores.

★ **91298** ★ **Food Lion Inc.**
1613 Amherst Hwy.
Madison Heights, VA 24572
(804)528-2632
Ultimate Parent: Food Lion. **SIC:** 5411—Grocery Stores.

★ **91299** ★ **Mary Kay Cosmetics**
Madison Hts
Madison Heights, VA 24572
(804)528-4847
Ultimate Parent: Mary Kay Cosmetics. **SIC:** 5999—Miscellaneous Retail Stores Nec.

★ **91300** ★ **New York Life**
RR 6
Madison Heights, VA 24572
(804)846-0163
Ultimate Parent: New York Life. **SIC:** 6411—Insurance Agents, Brokers & Service.

★ **91301** ★ **Radio Shack**
James Rv Shopping Ctr.
Madison Heights, VA 24572
(804)528-3982
Company Type: Division. **Ultimate Parent:** Tandy Corp. **SIC:** 5731—Radio, Television & Electronics Stores.

★ **91302** ★ **Rite Aid**
1765 Seminole Shopping. Ctr.
Madison Heights, VA 24572
(804)528-9404
Ultimate Parent: Rite Aid. **SIC:** 5912—Drug Stores & Proprietary Stores.

Manassas

★ **91303** ★ **APAC**
8737 Wellington Rd.
Manassas, VA 22110
(703)690-1156
Officer: John Conway, President. **Ultimate Parent:** Ashland Oil. **SIC:** 2951—Asphalt Paving Mixtures & Blocks.

★ **91304** ★ **Courtyard by Marriott**
10701 Battleview Pky.
Manassas, VA 22110
(703)335-1300
Ultimate Parent: Marriott International. **SIC:** 7011—Hotels & Motels.

★ **91305** ★ **Crestar Bank**
7915 Sudley Rd.
Manassas, VA 22110-2802
Location Type: Branch office. **Ultimate Parent:** Crestar Financial Corp. **SIC:** 6021—National Commercial Banks.

★ **91306** ★ **Crestar Bank**
8885 Centreville Rd.
Manassas, VA 22110-5203
Location Type: Branch office. **Ultimate Parent:** Crestar Financial Corp. **SIC:** 6021—National Commercial Banks.

★ **91307** ★ **Exxon Service Station**
8905 Centreville Rd.
Manassas, VA 22110
(703)368-9443
Ultimate Parent: Exxon. **SIC:** 5541—Gasoline Service Stations.

★ **91308** ★ **Finance Co.**
7000 Infantry Ridge Rd. 200
Manassas, VA 22110-2370
(703)361-1699
Officer: Sandra J. Rabatin. **Ultimate Parent:** Beneficial. **SIC:** 6141—Personal Credit Institutions.

★ **91309** ★ **First Union National Bank of Virginia**
7900 Sudley Rd.
Manassas, VA 22110
(703)934-1953
Location Type: Branch office. **Ultimate Parent:** First Union Corp. **SIC:** 6021—National Commercial Banks.

★ **91310** ★ **First Virginia Bank**
8650 Centreville Rd.
Manassas, VA 22110-5264
(703)241-3668
Location Type: Branch office. **Ultimate Parent:** First Virginia Banks Inc. **SIC:** 6021—National Commercial Banks.

★ **91311** ★ **First Virginia Bank**
9100 Ctr. St.
Manassas, VA 22110-5409
(703)241-3210
Location Type: Branch office. **Ultimate Parent:** First Virginia Banks Inc. **SIC:** 6021—National Commercial Banks.

★ **91312** ★ **First Virginia Bank**
10420 Portsmouth Rd.
Manassas, VA 22110-2806
(703)241-4459
Location Type: Branch office. **Ultimate Parent:** First Virginia Banks Inc. **SIC:** 6021—National Commercial Banks.

★ **91313** ★ **First Virginia Bank**
11670 Sudley Manor Rd.
Manassas, VA 22110-2856
(703)241-3676
Location Type: Branch office. **Ultimate Parent:** First Virginia Banks Inc. **SIC:** 6021—National Commercial Banks.

★ **91314** ★ **Hit or Miss**
Manor Ct
Manassas, VA 22111
(703)330-7331
Ultimate Parent: TJX. **SIC:** 5621—Women's Clothing Stores.

★ **91315** ★ **Mobil Oil Corp.**
10315 Balls Ford Rd.
Manassas, VA 22110
(703)368-9141
Ultimate Parent: Mobil. **SIC:** 5172—Petroleum Products Nec.

★ **91316** ★ **Mobil Oil Corp.**
10315 Balls Ford Rd.
Manassas, VA 22110-2603
(703)368-9141
Company Type: Branch. **Officer:** B. L. Williams. **Ultimate Parent:** Mobil. **SIC:** 5172—Petroleum Products Nec.

★ **91317** ★ **New York Life Insurance Co.**
9379 Forestwood Ln.
Manassas, VA 22110
(703)369-7888
Ultimate Parent: New York Life. **SIC:** 6411—Insurance Agents, Brokers & Service.

★ **91318** ★ **Radio Shack**
10768 Sudley Manor Dr.
Manassas, VA 22110
(703)369-1847
Company Type: Division. **Ultimate Parent:** Tandy Corp. **SIC:** 5734—Computer & Software Stores.

★ **91319** ★ **Radio Shack**
Manassas
Manassas, VA 22111
(703)369-6666
Company Type: Division. **Ultimate Parent:** Tandy Corp. **SIC:** 5065—Electronic Parts & Equipment Nec.

★ **91320** ★ **Radio Shack**
Manassas
Manassas, VA 22111
(703)369-6666
Company Type: Division. **Ultimate Parent:** Tandy Corp. **SIC:** 5065—Electronic Parts & Equipment Nec.

★ **91321** ★ **Rite Aid**
8300 Sudley Rd.
Manassas, VA 22110
(703)361-9922
Ultimate Parent: Rite Aid. **SIC:** 5311—Department Stores.

★ **91322** ★ **Ryder Truck Rental Inc.**
12001 Balls Ford Rd.
Manassas, VA 22110
(703)369-3900
Ultimate Parent: Ryder System. **SIC:** 7513—Truck Rental & Leasing Without Drivers.

★ **91323** ★ **Safeco Insurance Co. of America**
7900 Sudley Rd.
Manassas, VA 22110
(703)369-5200
Ultimate Parent: Safeco. **SIC:** 8712—Architectural Services.

★ **91324** ★ **Signet Bank, Virginia**
8091 Sudley Rd.
Westgate Shopping Ctr.
Manassas, VA 22110
Location Type: Branch office. **Ultimate Parent:** Signet Banking Corp. **SIC:** 6021—National Commercial Banks.

★ **91325** ★ **Signet Bank, Virginia**
9166 Mathis Ave.
Manassas, VA 22110-5291
(703)368-9121
Location Type: Branch office. **Ultimate Parent:** Signet Banking Corp. **SIC:** 6021—National Commercial Banks.

★ **91326** ★ **Southland Corp.**
8708 Liberia Ave.
Manassas, VA 22110
(703)335-2012
Ultimate Parent: Southland Corp. **SIC:** 5411—Grocery Stores.

★ **91327** ★ **Vulcan Materials Co.**
509 PO Box
Manassas, VA 22110
(703)368-3135
Ultimate Parent: Vulcan Materials Co. **SIC:** 5039—Construction Materials Nec.

★ **91328** ★ **Vulcan Materials Co.**
509 PO Box
Manassas, VA 22110
(703)368-3135
Ultimate Parent: Vulcan Materials Co. **SIC:** 5039—Construction Materials Nec.

Mappsville

★ **91329** ★ **Signet Bank, Virginia**
Rtes. 13 & 691
Mappsville, VA 23407
(804)824-3483
Location Type: Branch office. **Ultimate Parent:** Signet Banking Corp. **SIC:** 6021—National Commercial Banks.

Marion

★ **91330** ★ **Brunswick Composites Defense Facility**
150 Johnston Rd.
Marion, VA 24354
Ultimate Parent: Brunswick Corp. **SIC:** 3728—Aircraft Parts & Equipment Nec; 3724—Aircraft Engines & Engine Parts; 3448—Prefabricated Metal Buildings.

★ **91331** ★ **Brunswick Corp.**
150 Johnston Rd.
Marion, VA 24354
(703)783-3121
Officer: H. Dwight Byrd, Manager. **Ultimate Parent:** Brunswick Corp. **SIC:** 3089—Plastics Products Nec; 3448—Prefabricated Metal Buildings.

★ **91332** ★ **First Union National Bank of Virginia**
102 E. Main St.
Marion, VA 24354-3106
(703)783-7141
Location Type: Branch office. **Ultimate Parent:** First Union. **SIC:** 6021—National Commercial Banks.

★ **91333** ★ **Greyhound Bus Lines**
435 S. Main St.
Marion, VA 24354
(703)783-7114
Ultimate Parent: Greyhound Lines Inc. **SIC:** 4131—Intercity & Rural Bus Transportation.

★ **91334** ★ **Mary Kay Cosmetics**
704 Dover St.
Marion, VA 24354
(703)783-7977
Ultimate Parent: Mary Kay Cosmetics. **SIC:** 7231—Beauty Shops.

★ **91335** ★ **New York Life Insurance Co.**
1319 N. Main St.
Marion, VA 24354
(703)783-8869
Ultimate Parent: New York Life. **SIC:** 6411—Insurance Agents, Brokers & Service.

★ **91336** ★ **Pepsi Cola General Bottlers**
211 Washington Ave.
Marion, VA 24354
(703)783-7232
Officer: Dan Starsky, Manager. **Ultimate Parent:** Pepsico. **SIC:** 2086—Bottled & Canned Soft Drinks.

★ **91337** ★ **Piggly Wiggly**
E Main St.
Marion, VA 24354
(703)783-2712
Ultimate Parent: Bruno's. **SIC:** 6512—Nonresidential Building Operators.

★ 91338 ★   **Radio Shack**
1 Marion Plz.
Marion, VA 24354
(703)783-4341
Company Type: Division. **Ultimate Parent:**
Tandy Corp. **SIC:** 5731—Radio, Television
& Electronics Stores.

★ 91339 ★   **Wal-Mart Store**
1193 N. Main St.
Marion, VA 24354
(703)783-4244
Ultimate Parent: Wal-Mart Stores, Inc. **SIC:**
5932—Used Merchandise Stores.

Martinsville

★ 91340 ★   **American General Finance Inc.**
5 E. Church St.
Martinsville, VA 24112-6207
(703)666-2100
Location Type: Branch office. **Ultimate Parent:** American General Corp. **SIC:**
6141—Personal Credit Institutions; 2000—
Food & Kindred Products.

★ 91341 ★   **American General Finance Inc.**
5 E. Church St.
Martinsville, VA 24112-6207
(703)666-2100
Ultimate Parent: American General Corp.
SIC: 6141—Personal Credit Institutions;
2000—Food & Kindred Products.

★ 91342 ★   **AT & T Family Federal Credit Union**
135 E. Market St.
Martinsville, VA 24112
(703)632-0926
Location Type: Branch office. **Officer:**
Jerry Minter, Manager. **Ultimate Parent:**
AT&T. **SIC:** 6061—Federal Credit Unions.

★ 91343 ★   **Bassett-Walker Inc.**
Walker Rd. PO Box 5423
Martinsville, VA 24115
Ultimate Parent: VF Corp. **SIC:** 2253—Knit
Outerwear Mills.

★ 91344 ★   **Bassett-Walker Inc.**
Walker Rd.
Martinsville, VA 24115
Ultimate Parent: VF Corp. **SIC:** 2253—Knit
Outerwear Mills.

★ 91345 ★   **Crestar Bank**
Rte. 58 E
Martinsville, VA 24112
(703)666-8221
Location Type: Branch office. **Ultimate Parent:** Crestar Financial Corp. **SIC:**
6021—National Commercial Banks.

★ 91346 ★   **Crestar Bank**
1105 Spruce St.
Martinsville, VA 24112-4508
(703)666-8208
Location Type: Branch office. **Ultimate Parent:** Crestar Financial Corp. **SIC:**
6021—National Commercial Banks.

★ 91347 ★   **Crestar Bank**
Rte. 220 S. & Fontaine Rd.
Martinsville, VA 24112-9522
(703)666-8278
Location Type: Branch office. **Ultimate Parent:** Crestar Financial Corp. **SIC:**
6021—National Commercial Banks.

★ 91348 ★   **Crestar Bank**
900 Memorial Blvd.
Martinsville, VA 24112
(703)666-8228
Location Type: Branch office. **Ultimate Parent:** Crestar Financial Corp. **SIC:**
6021—National Commercial Banks.

★ 91349 ★   **Crestar Bank**
134 - 138 E. Church St.
Martinsville, VA 24112-2806
(703)666-8200
Location Type: Branch office. **Ultimate Parent:** Crestar Financial Corp. **SIC:**
6021—National Commercial Banks.

★ 91350 ★   **First Union National Bank of Virginia**
231 E. Church St.
Martinsville, VA 24112-2840
(703)632-6130
Location Type: Branch office. **Ultimate**

Parent: First Union Corp. **SIC:** 6021—
National Commercial Banks.

★ 91351 ★   **Food Lion**
Commonwealth Blvd.
Martinsville, VA 24112
(703)638-2373
Ultimate Parent: Food Lion. **SIC:** 5411—
Grocery Stores.

★ 91352 ★   **Food Lion Inc.**
Commonwealth Blvd.
Martinsville, VA 24112
(703)638-2373
Ultimate Parent: Food Lion. **SIC:** 5411—
Grocery Stores.

★ 91353 ★   **J C Penney Co.**
Liberty Fair Massach
Martinsville, VA 24112
(703)638-2401
Ultimate Parent: J.C. Penney. **SIC:** 5311—
Department Stores.

★ 91354 ★   **Kroger Co.**
Commonwealth
Martinsville, VA 24112
(703)638-3127
Ultimate Parent: Kroger. **SIC:** 5411—
Grocery Stores.

★ 91355 ★   **New York Life Insurance Agt**
107 Chief Tassel Bldg.
Martinsville, VA 24112
(703)632-2697
Ultimate Parent: New York Life. **SIC:**
6311—Life Insurance.

★ 91356 ★   **Ryder Truck Rental Inc.**
708 Memorial Blvd. N
Martinsville, VA 24112
(703)638-1166
Ultimate Parent: Ryder System. **SIC:**
7389—Business Services Nec.

★ 91357 ★   **Sara Lee Knit Products**
202 Cleveland Ave.
Martinsville, VA 24112
Ultimate Parent: Sara Lee Corp. **SIC:**
2300—Apparel & Other Textile Products.

★ 91358 ★   **Sara Lee Knit Products**
202 Cleveland Ave.
Martinsville, VA 24115
Ultimate Parent: Sara Lee Corp. **SIC:**
2300—Apparel & Other Textile Products.

★ 91359 ★   **Stone Container Corp.**
220 Industrial Park
Martinsville, VA 24112
(703)632-2176
Officer: Bob Davis, Manager. **Ultimate Parent:** Stone Container Corp. **SIC:** 2652—
Setup Paperboard Boxes.

Mc Lean

★ 91360 ★   **Allied-Signal Inc.**
Bendix Communications
1768 Old Meadow Rd.
Mc Lean, VA 22102
Ultimate Parent: Allied-Signal Inc.

★ 91361 ★   **Allied-Signal Inc.**
Communication Systems
1768 Old Meadow Rd.
Mc Lean, VA 22102
Ultimate Parent: Allied-Signal Inc. **SIC:**
3669—Communications Equipment Nec.

★ 91362 ★   **Boeing Co.**
1945 Old Gallows Rd.
Mc Lean, VA 22102
(703)761-0730
Ultimate Parent: Boeing.

★ 91363 ★   **Casual Corner**
Tysons Corner
Mc Lean, VA 22102
(703)790-8880
Ultimate Parent: United States Shoe. **SIC:**
5621—Women's Clothing Stores.

★ 91364 ★   **Equitable Life Insurance Co.**
8300 Greensboro Dr.
Mc Lean, VA 22102
(703)448-5992
Ultimate Parent: American General Corp.

SIC: 6311—Life Insurance; 6411—
Insurance Agents, Brokers & Service.

★ 91365 ★   **First American Bank**
6635 Old Dominion Dr.
Mc Lean, VA 22101
(703)760-5070
Ultimate Parent: First American Corp. **SIC:**
6099—Functions Related to Deposit
Banking.

★ 91366 ★   **Gap Stores**
Tysons Corner Ctr.
Mc Lean, VA 22102
(703)893-4546
Ultimate Parent: GAP. **SIC:** 5621—
Women's Clothing Stores.

★ 91367 ★   **Gap Stores**
Tysons Corner Ctr.
Mc Lean, VA 22102
(703)893-4546
Ultimate Parent: GAP. **SIC:** 5621—
Women's Clothing Stores.

★ 91368 ★   **Hertz Rent-A-Car**
1955 Chain Bridge Rd.
Mc Lean, VA 22102
(703)893-8262
Ultimate Parent: Hertz. **SIC:** 7514—
Passenger Car Rental.

★ 91369 ★   **Macy's**
1651 International Dr.
Mc Lean, VA 22102-3907
Company Type: Branch. **Ultimate Parent:**
R. H. Macy. **SIC:** 5311—Department Stores.

★ 91370 ★   **Mary Kay Cosmetics**
6513 Smoot Dr.
Mc Lean, VA 22101
(703)356-3211
Ultimate Parent: Mary Kay Cosmetics. **SIC:**
5999—Miscellaneous Retail Stores Nec.

★ 91371 ★   **Radio Shack**
Tysons Corner Ctr.
Mc Lean, VA 22102
(703)790-1438
Company Type: Division. **Ultimate Parent:**
Tandy Corp. **SIC:** 5065—Electronic Parts &
Equipment Nec.

★ 91372 ★   **Radio Shack**
6242 Old Dominion Dr.
Mc Lean, VA 22101
(703)534-0533
Company Type: Division. **Ultimate Parent:**
Tandy Corp. **SIC:** 5065—Electronic Parts &
Equipment Nec.

★ 91373 ★   **Radio Shack**
Tysons Corner Ctr.
Mc Lean, VA 22102
(703)790-1438
Company Type: Division. **Ultimate Parent:**
Tandy Corp. **SIC:** 5065—Electronic Parts &
Equipment Nec.

★ 91374 ★   **Radio Shack**
6242 Old Dominion Dr.
Mc Lean, VA 22101
(703)534-0533
Company Type: Division. **Ultimate Parent:**
Tandy Corp. **SIC:** 5065—Electronic Parts &
Equipment Nec.

★ 91375 ★   **Verex Assurance Inc.**
1304 Old Chain Bridge Rd.
Mc Lean, VA 22101
(703)790-1880
Ultimate Parent: Dial Corp. **SIC:** 6411—
Insurance Agents, Brokers & Service.

★ 91376 ★   **Signet Bank, Virginia**
1300 Chain Bridge Rd.
Mc Leen, VA 22101-3978
(703)448-0583
Location Type: Branch office. **Ultimate Parent:** Signet Banking Corp. **SIC:** 6021—
National Commercial Banks.

McKenny

★ 91377 ★   **Maclin Zimmer McGill Tobacco**
20052 Unico Rd.
McKenny, VA 23872
(804)768-0081
Ultimate Parent: Universal Corp. **SIC:**
2121—Cigars.

McLean

★ 91378 ★   **Crestar Bank**
1301 Chain Bridge Rd.
McLean, VA 22101-3998
Location Type: Branch office. **Ultimate Parent:** Crestar Financial Corp. **SIC:**
6021—National Commercial Banks.

★ 91379 ★   **Crestar Bank**
1449-A Chain Bridge Rd.
McLean, VA 22101-3722
Location Type: Branch office. **Ultimate Parent:** Crestar Financial Corp. **SIC:**
6021—National Commercial Banks.

★ 91380 ★   **Crestar Bank**
7900 Westpark Dr., Ste. T114
McLean, VA 22102-4203
Location Type: Branch office. **Ultimate Parent:** Crestar Financial Corp. **SIC:**
6021—National Commercial Banks.

★ 91381 ★   **Crestar Bank**
1430 Spring Hill Rd.
McLean, VA 22102-3000
Location Type: Branch office. **Ultimate Parent:** Crestar Financial Corp. **SIC:**
6021—National Commercial Banks.

★ 91382 ★   **Federal Home Loan Mortgage**
8200 Jones Branch Dr.
McLean, VA 22102
(703)903-2000
Company Type: Headquarters. **Officer:**
Leland C. Brendsel. **SIC:** 6159—
Miscellaneous Business Credit Institutions.
Fortune Service 500: Ranking 10.

★ 91383 ★   **Federal Home Loan Mortgage Corp.**
8200 Jones Branch Dr.
McLean, VA 22101-3107
(703)903-2200 **Fax:** (703)903-2447
Company Type: Headquarters. **Officer:**
Leland C. Brendsel, Chairman of the Board
& CEO. **Ultimate Parent:** Federal Home
Loan Mortgage. **SIC:** 6111—Federal &
Federally-Sponsored Credit. **Sales:** 622 M.

★ 91384 ★   **First American Metro Corp.**
1751 Pinnacle Dr.
McLean, VA 22102
(703)821-7777
Company Type: Subsidiary. **Officer:** Fred
L. Ballurer, Chairman of the Board & CEO.
Ultimate Parent: First Union Corp. **SIC:**
6021—National Commercial Banks.

★ 91385 ★   **First Union National Bank, Capital Area**
1650 Tysons Blvd., 17th Fl.
McLean, VA 22102
(703)827-1610 **Fax:** (703)760-6355
Company Type: Subsidiary. **Officer:** Hugh
Long, Regional President. **Ultimate Parent:**
First Union Corp. **SIC:** 6022—State
Commercial Banks.

★ 91386 ★   **First Union National Bank of Virginia**
1970 Chain Bridge Rd.
McLean, VA 22102-4000
(703)760-5343
Location Type: Branch office. **Ultimate Parent:** First Union Corp. **SIC:** 6021—
National Commercial Banks.

★ 91387 ★   **First Union National Bank of Virginia**
6844 Old Dominion Dr.
McLean, VA 22101-3715
(703)442-3637
Location Type: Branch office. **Ultimate Parent:** First Union Corp. **SIC:** 6021—
National Commercial Banks.

★ 91388 ★   **First Virginia Bank**
6220 Old Dominion Dr.
McLean, VA 22101-4217
(703)241-3366
Location Type: Branch office. **Ultimate Parent:** First Virginia Banks Inc. **SIC:**
6021—National Commercial Banks.

★ 91389 ★   **First Virginia Bank**
1455 Chain Bridge Rd.
McLean, VA 22101-4559
(703)241-3385
Location Type: Branch office. **Ultimate Parent:** First Virginia Banks Inc. **SIC:**
6021—National Commercial Banks.

★ 91390 ★　GTE Spacenet
1700 Old Meadow Rd.
McLean, VA 22102
(703)848-1000 **Fax:** (703)848-0004
Company Type: Subsidiary. **Officer:**
Howard M. Svigals, Acting President.
Ultimate Parent: GTE.

★ 91391 ★　GTE Spacenet Corp.
1700 Old Meadow Rd.
McLean, VA 22102-4304
(703)848-1000
Company Type: Subsidiary. **Officer:** C.J.
Waylar, President. **Ultimate Parent:** GTE.
SIC: 8711—Engineering Services; 3663—
Radio & T.V. Communications Equipment;
7373—Computer Integrated Systems
Design. **Employee Count:** 1200. **Sales:**
76.6 (est) M.

★ 91392 ★　GTE Spacenet Corp.
1700 Old Meadow Rd.
McLean, VA 22102
(703)848-1000 **Fax:** (703)848-0004
Company Type: Subsidiary. **Ultimate
Parent:** GTE. **SIC:** 4899—Communications
Services Nec; 5065—Electronic Parts &
Equipment Nec.

★ 91393 ★　New York Life
Northern Virginia General Office
Southeastern Agencies
2000 Corporate Ridge, Ste. 750
Mclean, VA 22102
(703)749-3700 **Fax:** (703)749-3746
Officer: William E. Babcock, General
Manager. **Ultimate Parent:** New York Life.

★ 91394 ★　PRC
1500 Planning Research Dr.
McLean, VA 22102
(703)556-1111
Company Type: Subsidiary. **Officer:** Gary
D. Kennedy, Chairman of the Board &
President. **Ultimate Parent:** Black & Decker
Corp. **SIC:** 7371—Computer Programming
Services; 7374—Data Processing &
Preparation; 8742—Management Consulting
Services. **Employee Count:** 7200. **Sales:**
685 M.

★ 91395 ★　PRC Inc.
15000 Planning Research Dr.
McLean, VA 22102-5001
(703)556-1111 **Fax:** (703)556-1174
Company Type: Subsidiary. **Location
Type:** Branch office. **Officer:** James J. Leto,
President & CEO. **Ultimate Parent:** Black &
Decker Corp. **SIC:** 7379—Computer Related
Services Nec; 2731—Book Publishing;
7371—Computer Programming Services;
7374—Data Processing & Preparation; 7389—
Business Services Nec; 8711—
Engineering Services; 8741—Management
Services.

★ 91396 ★　PRC Public Sector
Inc.
1500 Planning Research Dr.
McLean, VA 22102-5001
(703)556-2500
Company Type: Subsidiary. **Officer:** Mark
C. Filteau, President. **Ultimate Parent:**
Black & Decker Corp. **SIC:** 7373—Computer
Integrated Systems Design. **Employee
Count:** 170. **Sales:** 45 M.

★ 91397 ★　PRC Realty Systems
Inc.
1500 PRC Dr.
McLean, VA 22102
(703)556-2500
Company Type: Subsidiary. **Officer:**
Robert B. Laurence, Chairman of the Board
& CEO. **Ultimate Parent:** Black & Decker
Corp. **SIC:** 7374—Data Processing &
Preparation; 6531—Real Estate Agents &
Managers.

★ 91398 ★　Professional
Assistance, Inc.
8251 Greensboro Dr., Rm. 630
McLean, VA 22102
Company Type: Subsidiary. **Ultimate
Parent:** Bell Atlantic Corp.

★ 91399 ★　Rite Aid
1312 Chain Bridge Rd.
Mclean, VA 22101
(703)356-5824
Ultimate Parent: Rite Aid. **SIC:** 5912—Drug
Stores & Proprietary Stores.

Mechanicsville

★ 91400 ★　Crestar Bank
6008 Mechanicsville Tpke.
Mechanicsville, VA 23111-1728
(804)782-5524
Location Type: Branch office. **Ultimate
Parent:** Crestar Financial Corp. **SIC:**
6021—National Commercial Banks.

★ 91401 ★　Eastern Operations
Center Inc.
923 Battlehill Dr.
PO Box 668
Mechanicsville, VA 23111
(804)746-6800
Company Type: Subsidiary. **Officer:**
Patricia R. Ryan, President. **Ultimate
Parent:** First Virginia Banks Inc. **SIC:**
7374—Data Processing & Preparation.

★ 91402 ★　First Union National
Bank of Virginia
5701 Mechanicsville Tpke.
Mechanicsville, VA 23111-1220
(804)730-8390
Location Type: Branch office. **Ultimate
Parent:** First Union Corp. **SIC:** 6021—
National Commercial Banks.

★ 91403 ★　Signet Bank, Virginia
7117 Mechanicsville Tpke.
Mechanicsville, VA 23111
(804)343-6610
Location Type: Branch office. **Ultimate
Parent:** Signet Banking Corp. **SIC:** 6021—
National Commercial Banks.

★ 91404 ★　Diebold Inc.
Ellerson
Mechanicsvl, VA 23111
(804)730-9250
Ultimate Parent: Diebold, Inc. **SIC:** 5044—
Office Equipment.

★ 91405 ★　Food Lion
6551 Mechanicsville Pike
Mechanicsvl, VA 23111
(804)746-7829
Ultimate Parent: Food Lion. **SIC:** 5411—
Grocery Stores.

Middleburg

★ 91406 ★　TNI Inc.
3 Washington St.
Middleburg, VA 22117
(703)687-6345
Ultimate Parent: Tyco Toys, Inc. **SIC:**
8742—Management Consulting Services.

Middletown

★ 91407 ★　Technicon
Instruments Corp.
Rte. 11 S.
Middletown, VA 22645
Ultimate Parent: Miles. **SIC:** 2835—
Diagnostic Substances.

Midlothian

★ 91408 ★　Atchinson, Topeka, &
Santa Fe Railway Co.
10610 Copperfield Pl
Midlothian, VA 23113
(804)320-5474
Ultimate Parent: Santa Fe Pacific Corp.
SIC: 4011—Railroads—Line-Haul
Operating.

★ 91409 ★　Avery Dennison
Manufacturing Corp.
4403 Heritage Woods Ln.
Midlothian, VA 23112-4871
(804)744-8176
Ultimate Parent: Avery Dennison Corp.
SIC: 2679—Converted Paper Products Nec.

★ 91410 ★　Avery Dennison Mfg.
Corp.
4403 Heritage Woods Ln.
Midlothian, VA 23112-4871
(804)744-8176
Ultimate Parent: Avery Dennison Corp.
SIC: 2679—Converted Paper Products Nec.

★ 91411 ★　Citgo Whiting Self
Service
Huguenot
Midlothian, VA 23113
(804)794-7633
Ultimate Parent: Citgo Petroleum. **SIC:**
5541—Gasoline Service Stations.

★ 91412 ★　Crestar Bank
11601 Midlothian Tpke.
Midlothian, VA 23113-2620
(804)378-1206
Location Type: Branch office. **Ultimate
Parent:** Crestar Financial Corp. **SIC:**
6021—National Commercial Banks.

★ 91413 ★　Crestar Bank
Midlothian Tpke. & Crowder Dr.
Midlothian, VA 23113
(804)782-5616
Location Type: Branch office. **Ultimate
Parent:** Crestar Financial Corp. **SIC:**
6021—National Commercial Banks.

★ 91414 ★　Food Lion
Ashbys Sq.
Midlothian, VA 23113
(804)379-1135
Ultimate Parent: Food Lion. **SIC:** 5411—
Grocery Stores.

★ 91415 ★　Food Lion Inc. Store
623
8006 Buford Ct
Midlothian, VA 23113
(804)330-7866
Ultimate Parent: Food Lion.

★ 91416 ★　Food Lion Inc. 256
Ashbys Sq.
Midlothian, VA 23113
(804)379-1135
Ultimate Parent: Food Lion. **SIC:** 5411—
Grocery Stores.

★ 91417 ★　Hormel&Co/George a
1915 Huguenot Rd.
Midlothian, VA 23113
(804)794-3935
Ultimate Parent: Hormel Foods. **SIC:**
5141—Groceries—General Line.

★ 91418 ★　Life Insurance Co. of
Va
713 N. Courthouse Rd.
Midlothian, VA 23113
(804)794-8195
Ultimate Parent: Life Insurance Co. of
Virginia. **SIC:** 6411—Insurance Agents,
Brokers & Service.

★ 91419 ★　Mary Kay Cosmetic's
10604 Royal Cres
Midlothian, VA 23113
(804)231-9007
Ultimate Parent: Mary Kay Cosmetics. **SIC:**
5999—Miscellaneous Retail Stores Nec.

★ 91420 ★　New York Life
Insurance
1915 Huguenot Rd.
Midlothian, VA 23113
(804)379-2077
Ultimate Parent: New York Life. **SIC:**
6411—Insurance Agents, Brokers &
Service.

★ 91421 ★　Radio Shack
Midlothian Mall Shopping
Midlothian, VA 23113
(804)233-7400
Company Type: Division. **Ultimate Parent:**
Tandy Corp. **SIC:** 5731—Radio, Television
& Electronics Stores.

★ 91422 ★　Radio Shack
Chesterfield Mall
Midlothian, VA 23113
(804)794-4931
Company Type: Division. **Ultimate Parent:**
Tandy Corp. **SIC:** 5065—Electronic Parts &
Equipment Nec.

★ 91423 ★　Radio Shack
Midlothian Mall
Midlothian, VA 23113
(804)233-7400
Company Type: Division. **Ultimate Parent:**
Tandy Corp. **SIC:** 5731—Radio, Television
& Electronics Stores.

★ 91424 ★　Rite Aid
2011 Huguenotrd
Midlothian, VA 23113
(804)320-7182
Ultimate Parent: Rite Aid. **SIC:** 5912—Drug
Stores & Proprietary Stores.

★ 91425 ★　Signet Bank, Virginia
Hull St. Rd. & Genito Rd.
Midlothian, VA 23113
(804)771-7888
Location Type: Branch office. **Ultimate
Parent:** Signet Banking Corp. **SIC:** 6021—
National Commercial Banks.

★ 91426 ★　Signet Bank, Virginia
13700 Midlothian Tpke.
Midlothian, VA 23113-4317
(804)771-7971
Location Type: Branch office. **Ultimate
Parent:** Signet Banking Corp. **SIC:** 6021—
National Commercial Banks.

★ 91427 ★　Signet Bank, Virginia
4900 Millridge Pky. E.
Midlothian, VA 23112-4828
(804)771-7556
Location Type: Branch office. **Ultimate
Parent:** Signet Banking Corp. **SIC:** 6021—
National Commercial Banks.

★ 91428 ★　Gap
Chesterfield Towne
Midlothian Vi, VA 23113
(804)794-2602
Ultimate Parent: GAP.

★ 91429 ★　XI Datacomp
300 Arboretum Pl
Midlothian Vi, VA 23113
(804)330-5836
Ultimate Parent: Storage Technology.

Milford

★ 91430 ★　Hoover Treated Wood
Prods. Inc.
Caroline Industrial Park, Rte. 640
Milford, VA 22514
Ultimate Parent: Ply Gem. **SIC:** 2491—
Wood Preserving.

★ 91431 ★　Hoover Treated Wood
Products
Caroline Industrial Park Rte. 640
Milford, VA 22514
Ultimate Parent: Ply Gem. **SIC:** 2491—
Wood Preserving.

Moneta

★ 91432 ★　First Union National
Bank of Virginia
6 Village Sq.
Moneta, VA 24121
(703)297-1333
Location Type: Branch office. **Ultimate
Parent:** First Union Corp. **SIC:** 6021—
National Commercial Banks.

Montross

★ 91433 ★　Signet Bank, Virginia
Rte. 3, Kings Hwy.
Montross, VA 22520-9803
(804)493-8071
Location Type: Branch office. **Ultimate
Parent:** Signet Banking Corp. **SIC:** 6021—
National Commercial Banks.

Moseley

★ 91434 ★　Stone Container Corp.
5700 Lewis Rd.
Moseley, VA 23120
(804)222-5433
Officer: Jim Yarnell, Manager. **Ultimate
Parent:** Stone Container Corp. **SIC:** 2679—
Converted Paper Products Nec.

Mount Jackson

★ 91435 ★ **Merillat Ind. Inc.**
State Rte. 950
Mount Jackson, VA 22842
Ultimate Parent: Masco. **SIC:** 2426—
Hardwood Dimension & Flooring Mills.

★ 91436 ★ **Merillat Industries**
State Rte. 950
Mount Jackson, VA 22842
Ultimate Parent: Masco. **SIC:** 2434—Wood
Kitchen Cabinets.

N Tazewell

★ 91437 ★ **Food Lion**
612 Market St.
N Tazewell, VA 24630
(703)988-2584
Ultimate Parent: Food Lion. **SIC:** 5411—
Grocery Stores.

Narrows

★ 91438 ★ **Hoechst Celanese**
Rte. 460
Narrows, VA 24124
Ultimate Parent: Hoechst Celanese Corp.
SIC: 2869—Industrial Organic Chemicals
Nec; 2821—Plastics Materials & Resins;
2823—Cellulosic Manmade Fibers.

★ 91439 ★ **Hoechst-Celanese Corp.**
Rte. 460
Narrows, VA 24124
Ultimate Parent: Hoechst Celanese Corp.
SIC: 2869—Industrial Organic Chemicals
Nec; 2821—Plastics Materials & Resins;
2823—Cellulosic Manmade Fibers.

Nassawa Dox

★ 91440 ★ **Crestar Bank**
10233 Rogers Ave.
Nassawa Dox, VA 23413
(804)853-3169
Location Type: Branch office. **Ultimate
Parent:** Crestar Financial Corp. **SIC:**
6021—National Commercial Banks.

New Market

★ 91441 ★ **Crestar Bank**
Congress St.
New Market, VA 22844
(703)740-3121
Location Type: Branch office. **Ultimate
Parent:** Crestar Financial Corp. **SIC:**
6021—National Commercial Banks.

★ 91442 ★ **Holly Farms Foods Inc.**
New Market Feed Mill
State Rte. 730
PO Box 279
New Market, VA 22844
Ultimate Parent: Tyson Foods, Inc. **SIC:**
2048—Prepared Feeds Nec.

★ 91443 ★ **Tyson Foods Inc. Feed Mill**
State Rd. 730
New Market, VA 22844
Ultimate Parent: Tyson Foods, Inc. **SIC:**
2048—Prepared Feeds Nec.

★ 91444 ★ **Tyson Foods Inc. Feed Mill**
State Rte. 730 PO Box 279
New Market, VA 22844
Ultimate Parent: Tyson Foods, Inc. **SIC:**
2048—Prepared Feeds Nec.

New Post

★ 91445 ★ **Chesapeake Corp. Fredericksburg Wood Treating**
Rte. 2 & Rte. 17
New Post, VA 22401
Ultimate Parent: Chesapeake. **SIC:** 2400—
Lumber & Wood Products.

★ 91446 ★ **Chesapeake Wood Treating Co.**
Rte. 2 & US Hwy. 17 S
New Post, VA 22401
Ultimate Parent: Chesapeake. **SIC:** 2491—
Wood Preserving.

Newington

★ 91447 ★ **Plantation Pipe Line**
8204 Terminal Rd.
Newington, VA 22122
(703)550-9330
Ultimate Parent: Chevron Corp. **SIC:**
4612—Crude Petroleum Pipelines.

Newport News

★ 91448 ★ **ADP Dealers Services**
711 Gum Rock Ct.
Newport News, VA 23606-2523
(804)873-1336
Ultimate Parent: Automatic Data
Processing, Inc. **SIC:** 7374—Data
Processing & Preparation.

★ 91449 ★ **Allied-Signal Corp.**
615 Bland Blvd.
Newport News, VA 23602
Ultimate Parent: Allied-Signal Inc. **SIC:**
3714—Motor Vehicle Parts & Accessories.

★ 91450 ★ **American General Finance**
459 Orleans Rd.
Newport News, VA 23602-3717
(804)874-1906
Officer: Mark Gray. **Ultimate Parent:**
American General Corp. **SIC:** 6141—
Personal Credit Institutions.

★ 91451 ★ **American General Finance Inc.**
459 Orleans Rd.
Newport News, VA 23602-3717
(804)874-1906
Officer: Mark Gray. **Ultimate Parent:**
American General Corp. **SIC:** 6141—
Personal Credit Institutions.

★ 91452 ★ **Beneficial Virginia Inc.**
14501 Warwick Blvd., Ste. I
Newport News, VA 23602-3752
(804)875-0400
Officer: Larry Tocco. **Ultimate Parent:**
Beneficial. **SIC:** 6141—Personal Credit
Institutions; 6162—Mortgage Bankers &
Correspondents.

★ 91453 ★ **Casual Corner**
Newmarket
Newport News, VA 23605
(804)838-9600
Ultimate Parent: United States Shoe. **SIC:**
5621—Women's Clothing Stores; 5651—
Family Clothing Stores.

★ 91454 ★ **Chesapeake & Potomac Tel Co.**
12805 Jefferson Ave.
Newport News, VA 23602-3017
(804)874-9931
Ultimate Parent: Bell Atlantic Corp. **SIC:**
4813—Telephone Communications Except
Radiotelephone.

★ 91455 ★ **Crestar Bank**
10814 Warwick Blvd.
Newport News, VA 23601-9998
(804)873-7801
Location Type: Branch office. **Ultimate
Parent:** Crestar Financial Corp.

★ 91456 ★ **Crestar Bank**
14500 Warwick Blvd.
Newport News, VA 23602-9998
(804)873-7806
Location Type: Branch office. **Ultimate
Parent:** Crestar Financial Corp. **SIC:**
6021—National Commercial Banks.

★ 91457 ★ **Crestar Bank**
12227 Jefferson Ave.
Newport News, VA 23602
(804)873-7853
Location Type: Branch office. **Ultimate
Parent:** Crestar Financial Corp. **SIC:**
6021—National Commercial Banks.

★ 91458 ★ **Crestar Bank**
11817 Canon Blvd.
Newport News, VA 23606
(804)873-7930
Location Type: Branch office. **Ultimate
Parent:** Crestar Financial Corp. **SIC:**
6021—National Commercial Banks.

★ 91459 ★ **Crestar Bank**
2501 Washington Ave.
Newport News, VA 23607-4327
(804)873-7569
Location Type: Branch office. **Ultimate
Parent:** Crestar Financial Corp. **SIC:**
6021—National Commercial Banks.

★ 91460 ★ **Edwards Co., Inc.**
2406 G. Ave.
Newport News, VA 23602-4352
(804)874-7335
Officer: James Boyce Edwards, President &
Vice President. **Ultimate Parent:** General
Signal. **SIC:** 5983—Fuel Oil Dealers;
0782—Lawn & Garden Services; 7342—
Disinfecting & Pest Control Services.
Employee Count: 14. **Sales:** 844000 M.

★ 91461 ★ **Exxon Corp. Gas Station**
3102 Big Bethel Rd.
Newport News, VA 23602
(804)865-1665
Ultimate Parent: Exxon. **SIC:** 5541—
Gasoline Service Stations.

★ 91462 ★ **First American Bank**
2015 25th St.
Newport News, VA 23607
Ultimate Parent: First American Corp. **SIC:**
6099—Functions Related to Deposit
Banking.

★ 91463 ★ **First American Bank**
12300 Jefferson Ave. 422
Newport News, VA 23602
(804)728-2130
Ultimate Parent: First American Corp. **SIC:**
6099—Functions Related to Deposit
Banking.

★ 91464 ★ **First Union National Bank of Virginia**
2015 25th St.
Newport News, VA 23607-5511
(804)728-2240
Location Type: Branch office. **Ultimate
Parent:** First Union Corp. **SIC:** 6021—
National Commercial Banks.

★ 91465 ★ **First Union National Bank of Virginia**
441 Denbigh Blvd.
Newport News, VA 23602-3897
(804)728-2230
Location Type: Branch office. **Ultimate
Parent:** First Union Corp. **SIC:** 6021—
National Commercial Banks.

★ 91466 ★ **First Union National Bank of Virginia**
776 J. Clyde Morris Blvd.
Newport News, VA 23601-1510
(804)595-6881
Location Type: Branch office. **Ultimate
Parent:** First Union Corp. **SIC:** 6021—
National Commercial Banks.

★ 91467 ★ **First Union National Bank of Virginia**
12300 Jefferson Ave., Ste. 422
Newport News, VA 23602-6900
(804)728-2130
Location Type: Branch office. **Ultimate
Parent:** First Union Corp. **SIC:** 6021—
National Commercial Banks.

★ 91468 ★ **First Union National Bank of Virginia**
11006 Warwick Blvd.
Newport News, VA 23601-3212
(804)728-2295
Location Type: Branch office. **Ultimate
Parent:** First Union Corp. **SIC:** 6021—
National Commercial Banks.

★ 91469 ★ **Flowers Baking Co.**
13269 Warwick Blvd.
Newport News, VA 23602
(804)874-0518
Ultimate Parent: Flowers Industries. **SIC:**
5149—Groceries & Related Products Nec.

★ 91470 ★ **J C Penney Catalog Center**
308 Oyster Point Rd.
Newport News, VA 23602
(804)249-1394
Ultimate Parent: J.C. Penney. **SIC:** 5961—
Catalog & Mail-Order Houses.

★ 91471 ★ **J C Penney Co.**
2023 W. Mercury Blvd.
Newport News, VA 23605
(804)838-9684
Ultimate Parent: J.C. Penney.

★ 91472 ★ **Jim Walter Homes Inc.**
101 Production Dr.
Newport News, VA 23602
(804)591-0063
Ultimate Parent: Walter Industries, Inc.
SIC: 1521—Single-Family Housing
Construction.

★ 91473 ★ **McDonald's Hamburgers**
2607 Jefferson Ave.
Newport News, VA 23607
(804)380-8735
Ultimate Parent: McDonald's. **SIC:** 5812—
Eating Places.

★ 91474 ★ **New York Life**
13302 Preakness Dr. A
Newport News, VA 23602
(804)874-9489
Ultimate Parent: New York Life. **SIC:**
6411—Insurance Agents, Brokers &
Service.

★ 91475 ★ **Newport News Shipbuilding & Dry Dock Co.**
4101 Washington Ave.
Newport News, VA 23607-2770
Ultimate Parent: Tenneco Inc. **SIC:** 3731—
Ship Building & Repairing.

★ 91476 ★ **Newport News Shipbuilding & Drydock Co.**
4101 Washington Ave.
Newport News, VA 23607-2770
Ultimate Parent: Tenneco Inc. **SIC:** 3731—
Ship Building & Repairing.

★ 91477 ★ **Pepsi-Cola Bottling Co.**
17200 Warwick Blvd.
Newport News, VA 23603
(804)887-2310
Ultimate Parent: Pepsico. **SIC:** 2086—
Bottled & Canned Soft Drinks.

★ 91478 ★ **Radio Shack**
Heritage Sq.
Newport News, VA 23602
(804)898-9454
Company Type: Division. **Ultimate Parent:**
Tandy Corp. **SIC:** 5731—Radio, Television
& Electronics Stores.

★ 91479 ★ **Radio Shack**
120145 PO Box
Newport News, VA 23612
Company Type: Division. **Ultimate Parent:**
Tandy Corp. **SIC:** 5046—Commercial
Equipment Nec.

★ 91480 ★ **Radio Shack**
10868 Warwick Blvd.
Newport News, VA 23601
(804)595-7755
Company Type: Division. **Ultimate Parent:**
Tandy Corp. **SIC:** 5731—Radio, Television
& Electronics Stores.

★ 91481 ★ **Radio Shack**
283 Newmarket Fair
Newport News, VA 23605
(804)838-5611
Company Type: Division. **Ultimate Parent:**
Tandy Corp. **SIC:** 5065—Electronic Parts &
Equipment Nec.

★ 91482 ★ **Radio Shack**
Heritage Sq.
Newport News, VA 23602
(804)898-9454
Company Type: Division. **Ultimate Parent:**
Tandy Corp. **SIC:** 5731—Radio, Television
& Electronics Stores.

★ 91483 ★ **Signet Bank, Virginia**
Hidenwood Shopping Ctr.
Newport News, VA 23606-2359
(804)825-7648
Location Type: Branch office. **Ultimate
Parent:** Signet Banking Corp. **SIC:** 6021—
National Commercial Banks.

★ **91484** ★   **Signet Bank, Virginia**
96 Main St.
Newport News, VA 23601-4042
(804)825-7655
Location Type: Branch office. **Ultimate Parent:** Signet Banking Corp. **SIC:** 6021—National Commercial Banks.

★ **91485** ★   **Signet Bank, Virginia**
Beechmont Shopping Ctr.
Newport News, VA 23602-3658
(804)825-7638
Location Type: Branch office. **Ultimate Parent:** Signet Banking Corp. **SIC:** 6021—National Commercial Banks.

★ **91486** ★   **Signet Bank, Virginia**
618 Denbigh Blvd.
Newport News, VA 23603
(804)825-7630
Location Type: Branch office. **Ultimate Parent:** Signet Banking Corp. **SIC:** 6021—National Commercial Banks.

★ **91487** ★   **Signet Bank, Virginia**
11742 Jefferson Ave.
Newport News, VA 23606-2557
(804)825-7664
Location Type: Branch office. **Ultimate Parent:** Signet Banking Corp. **SIC:** 6021—National Commercial Banks.

★ **91488** ★   **Signet Bank, Virginia**
3101 Wahington Ave.
Newport News, VA 23607-3345
(804)825-7603
Location Type: Branch office. **Ultimate Parent:** Signet Banking Corp. **SIC:** 6021—National Commercial Banks.

★ **91489** ★   **Tandy Corp.**
2511 W. Mercury Blvd.
Newport News, VA 23605
(804)838-5071
Ultimate Parent: Tandy Corp. **SIC:** 5731—Radio, Television & Electronics Stores.

★ **91490** ★   **Turner Corp.**
13195 Warwick Blvd.
Newport News, VA 23602
(804)872-9800
Ultimate Parent: Turner Corp. **SIC:** 6531—Real Estate Agents & Managers.

★ **91491** ★   **World Book**
Childcraft
52 Sweetbriar Dr.
Newport News, VA 23606-3907
(804)874-7373
Location Type: Branch office. **Ultimate Parent:** Berkshire Hathaway. **SIC:** 5963—Direct Selling Establishments.

★ **91492** ★   **World Book**
Childcraft
11828 Canon Blvd., Ste. E
Newport News, VA 23606-2554
(804)873-3662
Location Type: Branch office. **Officer:** Ardith G. Shivar. **Ultimate Parent:** Berkshire Hathaway. **SIC:** 5963—Direct Selling Establishments; 5942—Book Stores.

★ **91493** ★   **Rite Aid**
11712 Jefferson Ave. G
Newportnews, VA 23606
(804)599-9723
Ultimate Parent: Rite Aid. **SIC:** 5912—Drug Stores & Proprietary Stores.

★ **91494** ★   **Rite Aid**
2 Newmarket Sq.
Newportnews, VA 23605
(804)245-0207
Ultimate Parent: Rite Aid. **SIC:** 5912—Drug Stores & Proprietary Stores.

★ **91495** ★   **Crestar Bank**
6060 Jefferson Ave.
Newprot News, VA 23605-3066
(804)873-7831
Location Type: Branch office. **Ultimate Parent:** Crestar Financial Corp. **SIC:** 6021—National Commercial Banks.

Newsoms

★ **91496** ★   **First Union National Bank of Virginia**
22334 General Thomas Hwy.
Newsoms, VA 23874-9703
(804)654-6210
Location Type: Branch office. **Ultimate Parent:** First Union Corp. **SIC:** 6021—National Commercial Banks.

Nokesville

★ **91497** ★   **Signet Bank, Virginia**
12912 Fitzwater Dr.
Nokesville, VA 22123-2241
(703)594-2101
Location Type: Branch office. **Ultimate Parent:** Signet Banking Corp. **SIC:** 6021—National Commercial Banks.

Norfolk

★ **91498** ★   **American General Finance Inc.**
5329 E. Virginia Beach Blvd.
Norfolk, VA 23502-3408
(804)461-5737
Officer: Barry Brown. **Ultimate Parent:** American General Corp. **SIC:** 6141—Personal Credit Institutions; 6162—Mortgage Bankers & Correspondents.

★ **91499** ★   **American General Finance Inc.**
5329 E. Virginia Beach Blvd.
Norfolk, VA 23502-3408
(804)461-5737
Location Type: Branch office. **Officer:** Barry Brown. **Ultimate Parent:** American General Corp. **SIC:** 6141—Personal Credit Institutions; 6162—Mortgage Bankers & Correspondents.

★ **91500** ★   **Brownell Electro Inc.**
4575 A Progress Rd.
Norfolk, VA 23502
(804)855-2400
Location Type: Branch office. **Ultimate Parent:** Avnet. **SIC:** 5063—Electrical Apparatus & Equipment.

★ **91501** ★   **Casual Corner**
Military Cir.
Norfolk, VA 23502
(804)461-3822
Ultimate Parent: United States Shoe. **SIC:** 5621—Women's Clothing Stores.

★ **91502** ★   **Circuit City**
843 E. Little Creek Rd.
Norfolk, VA 23518
(804)480-6677
Ultimate Parent: Circuit City Stores. **SIC:** 5521—Used Car Dealers; 5731—Radio, Television & Electronics Stores.

★ **91503** ★   **Circuit City**
90 Janaf Shopping. Ctr.
Norfolk, VA 23502
Ultimate Parent: Circuit City Stores. **SIC:** 5065—Electronic Parts & Equipment Nec; 5731—Radio, Television & Electronics Stores.

★ **91504** ★   **Citgo Service Station**
8595 Chesapeake Blvd.
Norfolk, VA 23503
(804)480-2958
Ultimate Parent: Citgo Petroleum. **SIC:** 5541—Gasoline Service Stations.

★ **91505** ★   **Crestar Bank**
777 W. 21st St.
Norfolk, VA 23517
(804)858-3282
Location Type: Branch office. **Ultimate Parent:** Crestar Financial Corp. **SIC:** 6021—National Commercial Banks.

★ **91506** ★   **Crestar Bank**
Janaf Shopping Ctr.
5800 Virginia Beach Blvd.
Norfolk, VA 23502
(804)858-3228
Location Type: Branch office. **Ultimate Parent:** Crestar Financial Corp. **SIC:** 6021—National Commercial Banks.

★ **91507** ★   **Crestar Bank**
3351 Princess Anne Rd.
Norfolk, VA 23502
(804)858-3222
Location Type: Branch office. **Ultimate Parent:** Crestar Financial Corp. **SIC:** 6021—National Commercial Banks.

★ **91508** ★   **Crestar Bank**
129 W. Little Creek Rd.
Norfolk, VA 23505
(804)858-3250
Location Type: Branch office. **Ultimate Parent:** Crestar Financial Corp. **SIC:** 6021—National Commercial Banks.

★ **91509** ★   **Crestar Bank**
Medical Tower Bldg.
400 Gresham Dr.
Norfolk, VA 23507
(804)858-3252
Location Type: Branch office. **Ultimate Parent:** Crestar Financial Corp. **SIC:** 6021—National Commercial Banks.

★ **91510** ★   **Crestar Bank**
1221 E. Little Creek Rd.
Norfolk, VA 23518
(804)858-3240
Location Type: Branch office. **Ultimate Parent:** Crestar Financial Corp. **SIC:** 6021—National Commercial Banks.

★ **91511** ★   **Crestar Bank**
120 W. York St.
Norfolk, VA 23510
(804)858-3268
Location Type: Branch office. **Ultimate Parent:** Crestar Financial Corp. **SIC:** 6021—National Commercial Banks.

★ **91512** ★   **Crestar Bank**
500 Main St.
Norfolk, VA 23510
(804)624-5550
Location Type: Branch office. **Ultimate Parent:** Crestar Financial Corp. **SIC:** 6021—National Commercial Banks.

★ **91513** ★   **Delta Air Lines Inc.**
Norfolk International Airport
Norfolk, VA 23518
(804)857-3313
Ultimate Parent: Delta Air Lines, Inc. **SIC:** 4512—Air Transportation—Scheduled.

★ **91514** ★   **Dover Elevator Co.**
5365 Robin Hood Rd.
Norfolk, VA 23513
(804)853-4563
Officer: Keith Moore, President. **Ultimate Parent:** Dover Corp. **SIC:** 3534—Elevators & Moving Stairways.

★ **91515** ★   **Exxon Corp.**
8201 Hampton Blvd.
Norfolk, VA 23505
(804)489-6257
Ultimate Parent: Exxon. **SIC:** 5099—Durable Goods Nec.

★ **91516** ★   **Exxon Service Station**
4528 E. Princess Anne Rd.
Norfolk, VA 23502
(804)857-0781
Ultimate Parent: Exxon. **SIC:** 7231—Beauty Shops.

★ **91517** ★   **Exxon Service Station**
3801 Hampton Blvd.
Norfolk, VA 23508
(804)451-0224
Ultimate Parent: Exxon. **SIC:** 5541—Gasoline Service Stations.

★ **91518** ★   **First American Bank of Virginia**
2300 PO Box
Norfolk, VA 23501
Ultimate Parent: First American Corp. **SIC:** 6022—State Commercial Banks.

★ **91519** ★   **First American Bank of Virginia**
5832 E. Virginia Beach Blvd.
Norfolk, VA 23502
(804)858-5220
Ultimate Parent: First American Corp. **SIC:** 6022—State Commercial Banks.

★ **91520** ★   **First American Bank of Virginia**
448 Boush St.
Norfolk, VA 23510
(804)858-5225
Ultimate Parent: First American Corp. **SIC:** 6022—State Commercial Banks.

★ **91521** ★   **First American Bank of Virginia**
1636 S. Military Hwy.
Norfolk, VA 23502
(804)455-7887
Ultimate Parent: First American Corp. **SIC:** 6099—Functions Related to Deposit Banking.

★ **91522** ★   **First Union National Bank of Virginia**
5832 Virginia Beach Blvd.
Norfolk, VA 23502-2424
(804)455-7820
Location Type: Branch office. **Ultimate Parent:** First Union Corp. **SIC:** 6021—National Commercial Banks.

★ **91523** ★   **First Union National Bank of Virginia**
200 Monticello Ave.
Norfolk, VA 23510-2301
(804)622-7259
Location Type: Branch office. **Ultimate Parent:** First Union Corp. **SIC:** 6021—National Commercial Banks.

★ **91524** ★   **First Union National Bank of Virginia**
7912 Halprin Dr.
Norfolk, VA 23518-3097
(804)455-7830
Location Type: Branch office. **Ultimate Parent:** First Union Corp. **SIC:** 6021—National Commercial Banks.

★ **91525** ★   **First Union National Bank of Virginia**
7627 Granby St.
Norfolk, VA 23505-2508
(804)489-2265
Location Type: Branch office. **Ultimate Parent:** First Union Corp. **SIC:** 6021—National Commercial Banks.

★ **91526** ★   **First Union National Bank of Virginia**
4500 E. Princess Anne Rd.
Norfolk, VA 23513-2356
(804)855-3683
Location Type: Branch office. **Ultimate Parent:** First Union Corp. **SIC:** 6021—National Commercial Banks.

★ **91527** ★   **First Union National Bank of Virginia**
999 Waterside Dr.
Norfolk, VA 23510-3300
(804)628-0458
Location Type: Branch office. **Ultimate Parent:** First Union Corp. **SIC:** 6021—National Commercial Banks.

★ **91528** ★   **First Virginia Bank**
of Tidewater
555 Main St.
Norfolk, VA 23510-2713
(804)628-6600
Company Type: Subsidiary. **Officer:** James F. Babcock, Chairman of the Board & CEO. **Ultimate Parent:** First Virginia Banks Inc. **SIC:** 6022—State Commercial Banks.

★ **91529** ★   **First Virginia Bank - Tidewater**
555 E. Main St.
Norfolk, VA 23510-2207
(804)628-6600
Company Type: Subsidiary. **Officer:** James F. Babcock, Chairman of the Board, CEO. **Ultimate Parent:** First Virginia Banks Inc. **SIC:** 6029—Commercial Banks Nec. **Employee Count:** 339.

★ **91530** ★   **Flowers Baking Co.**
1209 Corprew Ave.
Norfolk, VA 23504
(804)622-6317
Ultimate Parent: Flowers Industries. **SIC:** 2051—Bread, Cake & Related Products.

★ **91531** ★ **Flowers Baking Co. of Norfolk Inc.**
1209 Corprew Ave.
PO Box 2860
Norfolk, VA 23501-2860
(804)622-6317 **Fax:** (804)640-1308
Officer: Joseph Toshie, President. **Ultimate Parent:** Flowers Industries.

★ **91532** ★ **Food Lion**
6203 E. Virginia Beach Blvd.
Norfolk, VA 23502
(804)461-4333
Ultimate Parent: Food Lion. **SIC:** 5411—Grocery Stores.

★ **91533** ★ **Food Lion**
5 South Shopping Ctr.
Norfolk, VA 23505
(804)588-7791
Ultimate Parent: Food Lion. **SIC:** 5411—Grocery Stores.

★ **91534** ★ **Food Lion**
6206 N. Military Hwy.
Norfolk, VA 23518
(804)853-2850
Ultimate Parent: Food Lion. **SIC:** 5411—Grocery Stores.

★ **91535** ★ **Food Lion**
1859 E. Little Creek Rd.
Norfolk, VA 23518
(804)588-0423
Ultimate Parent: Food Lion. **SIC:** 5411—Grocery Stores.

★ **91536** ★ **Ford Motor Co. Norfolk Assembly Plant**
2424 Springfield Ave.
Norfolk, VA 23523
Ultimate Parent: Ford Motor Co. **SIC:** 3711—Motor Vehicles & Car Bodies.

★ **91537** ★ **Gap Stores Inc.**
Military Cir.
Norfolk, VA 23502
(804)461-7613
Ultimate Parent: GAP. **SIC:** 5611—Men's & Boys' Clothing Stores.

★ **91538** ★ **Gap Stores Inc.**
Military Cir.
Norfolk, VA 23502
(804)461-7613
Ultimate Parent: GAP. **SIC:** 5611—Men's & Boys' Clothing Stores.

★ **91539** ★ **Greyhound Bus Lines**
701 Monticello Ave.
Norfolk, VA 23510
(804)625-7500
Ultimate Parent: Greyhound Lines Inc. **SIC:** 4111—Local & Suburban Transit; 4131—Intercity & Rural Bus Transportation; 4141—Local Bus Charter Service.

★ **91540** ★ **Greyhound Bus Lines**
101 W. Ocean View Ave.
Norfolk, VA 23503
(804)480-1092
Ultimate Parent: Greyhound Lines Inc. **SIC:** 4131—Intercity & Rural Bus Transportation.

★ **91541** ★ **Greyhound Bus Lines**
Naval Air Station
Norfolk, VA 23511
(804)423-8471
Ultimate Parent: Greyhound Lines Inc. **SIC:** 4131—Intercity & Rural Bus Transportation.

★ **91542** ★ **Harris Technical Service Co.**
5365 Robin Hood Rd.
Norfolk, VA 23513
(804)857-0099
Ultimate Parent: Harris. **SIC:** 2899—Chemical Preparations Nec.

★ **91543** ★ **Hertz Rent-A-Car**
3323 N. Military Hwy.
Norfolk, VA 23518
(804)855-1961
Ultimate Parent: Hertz. **SIC:** 7514—Passenger Car Rental.

★ **91544** ★ **Hertz Rent-A-Car System**
Norfolk International Airport
Norfolk, VA 23518
(804)857-1261
Ultimate Parent: Hertz. **SIC:** 7514—Passenger Car Rental.

★ **91545** ★ **Hit or Miss**
148 Janaf Shopping Ctr.
Norfolk, VA 23502
(804)466-7881
Ultimate Parent: TJX. **SIC:** 5621—Women's Clothing Stores; 5651—Family Clothing Stores.

★ **91546** ★ **Huntsman Chemical**
5100 Bainridge Blvd.
Norfolk, VA 23523
(804)532-5200
Ultimate Parent: Great American Management & Investment. **SIC:** 5051—Metals Service Centers & Offices.

★ **91547** ★ **J C Penney Co.**
26 Military Cir.
Norfolk, VA 23502
(804)461-9490
Ultimate Parent: J.C. Penney. **SIC:** 5311—Department Stores.

★ **91548** ★ **Kids R US**
5957 E. Virginia Beach Blvd.
Norfolk, VA 23502
(804)466-1299
Ultimate Parent: Toys "R" US. **SIC:** 5651—Family Clothing Stores.

★ **91549** ★ **Liberty Mutual Insurance Co.**
20 Koger Executive Ctr.
Norfolk, VA 23502
(804)461-6831
Ultimate Parent: Liberty Mutual Group. **SIC:** 6411—Insurance Agents, Brokers & Service.

★ **91550** ★ **Life Insurance Co. of Virginia**
5 Koger Executive Cent
Norfolk, VA 23502
(804)461-3500
Ultimate Parent: Life Insurance Co. of Virginia. **SIC:** 6411—Insurance Agents, Brokers & Service.

★ **91551** ★ **Manpower Inc.**
733 Boush St.
Norfolk, VA 23510
(804)622-6581
Ultimate Parent: Manpower, Inc. **SIC:** 7349—Building Maintenance Services Nec.

★ **91552** ★ **Mary Kay Cosmetics**
7427 Gleneagles Rd.
Norfolk, VA 23505
(804)440-1464
Ultimate Parent: Mary Kay Cosmetics. **SIC:** 5999—Miscellaneous Retail Stores Nec.

★ **91553** ★ **Mary Kay Cosmetics**
406 N. Shore Rd.
Norfolk, VA 23505
(804)440-7538
Ultimate Parent: Mary Kay Cosmetics. **SIC:** 5999—Miscellaneous Retail Stores Nec.

★ **91554** ★ **Mary Kay Cosmetics**
255 E. 39th St.
Norfolk, VA 23504
(804)623-7318
Ultimate Parent: Mary Kay Cosmetics. **SIC:** 5999—Miscellaneous Retail Stores Nec.

★ **91555** ★ **New York Life Insurance**
5 E. Main Plz.
Norfolk, VA 23510
(804)628-1800
Ultimate Parent: New York Life. **SIC:** 6411—Insurance Agents, Brokers & Service.

★ **91556** ★ **New York Life Insurance Co.**
142 W. York St.
Norfolk, VA 23510
(804)628-1842
Ultimate Parent: New York Life. **SIC:** 6411—Insurance Agents, Brokers & Service.

★ **91557** ★ **New York Life Insurance Co.**
United Virginia Bank
Norfolk, VA 23514
(804)628-1800
Ultimate Parent: New York Life. **SIC:** 6411—Insurance Agents, Brokers & Service.

★ **91558** ★ **New York Life Norfolk General Office**
Southeastern Agencies
Box 3068
Norfolk, VA 23514
(804)628-1800 **Fax:** (804)628-1821
Officer: Harold C. Bullard, General Manager. **Ultimate Parent:** New York Life.

★ **91559** ★ **New York Life Norfolk General Office**
Southeastern Agencies
900 Crestar Bank Bldg.
Norfolk, VA 23514
(804)628-1800 **Fax:** (804)628-1821
Officer: Harold C. Bullard. **Ultimate Parent:** New York Life.

★ **91560** ★ **Norfolk Southern**
3 Commercial Pl.
Norfolk, VA 23510
(804)629-2600
Company Type: Headquarters. **Officer:** David R. Goode. **Employee Count:** 29304. **Fortune Service 500:** Ranking 13.

★ **91561** ★ **Norfolk Southern Corp.**
3 Commercial Pl.
Norfolk, VA 23510-2191
(804)629-2600 **Fax:** (804)629-2344
Officer: David R. Goode, Chairman of the Board, President & CEO. **Ultimate Parent:** Norfolk Southern. **Employee Count:** 33270.

★ **91562** ★ **Norfolk Southern Railway Co.**
3 Commercial Pl.
Norfolk, VA 23510-2191
(804)629-2610
Officer: David R. Goode, President & CEO. **Ultimate Parent:** Norfolk Southern.

★ **91563** ★ **Norfolk & Western Railway Co.**
3 Commercial Pl.
Norfolk, VA 23510-2191
(804)629-2610
Officer: David R. Goode, President & CEO. **Ultimate Parent:** Norfolk Southern.

★ **91564** ★ **Otis Elevator Co.**
1721 Cromwell Dr.
Norfolk, VA 23509
(804)622-4005
Ultimate Parent: United Technologies. **SIC:** 1521—Single-Family Housing Construction.

★ **91565** ★ **Pittston Coal Export Co.**
World Trade Ctr.
Norfolk, VA 23510
(804)622-3393
Ultimate Parent: Pittston. **SIC:** 7389—Business Services Nec.

★ **91566** ★ **PPG Industries Inc.**
5618 E. Virginia Beach Blvd.
Norfolk, VA 23502
(804)466-1811
Ultimate Parent: PPG Industries Inc. **SIC:** 1731—Electrical Work.

★ **91567** ★ **Price Club**
850 Glenrock Rd.
Norfolk, VA 23502
(804)461-0777
Ultimate Parent: Price. **SIC:** 5399—Miscellaneous General Merchandise Store.

★ **91568** ★ **Radio Shack**
2401 Colley Ave.
Norfolk, VA 23517
(804)623-3826
Company Type: Division. **Ultimate Parent:** Tandy Corp. **SIC:** 5065—Electronic Parts & Equipment Nec; 5731—Radio, Television & Electronics Stores.

★ **91569** ★ **Radio Shack**
4241 E. Little Creek Rd.
Norfolk, VA 23518
(804)587-0888
Company Type: Division. **Ultimate Parent:** Tandy Corp. **SIC:** 5731—Radio, Television & Electronics Stores.

★ **91570** ★ **Radio Shack**
31 South Shopping Ctr.
Norfolk, VA 23505
(804)480-9405
Company Type: Division. **Ultimate Parent:** Tandy Corp. **SIC:** 5065—Electronic Parts & Equipment Nec.

★ **91571** ★ **Radio Shack**
7530 Granby St.
Norfolk, VA 23505
(804)588-6661
Company Type: Division. **Ultimate Parent:** Tandy Corp. **SIC:** 5065—Electronic Parts & Equipment Nec; 5731—Radio, Television & Electronics Stores.

★ **91572** ★ **Radio Shack**
19 Military Cir.
Norfolk, VA 23502
(804)461-8995
Company Type: Division. **Ultimate Parent:** Tandy Corp. **SIC:** 5065—Electronic Parts & Equipment Nec.

★ **91573** ★ **Radio Shack**
167 W. Ocean View Ave.
Norfolk, VA 23503
(804)588-7319
Company Type: Division. **Ultimate Parent:** Tandy Corp. **SIC:** 5065—Electronic Parts & Equipment Nec.

★ **91574** ★ **Radio Shack**
234 Janaf Shopping Ctr.
Norfolk, VA 23502
(804)461-1078
Company Type: Division. **Ultimate Parent:** Tandy Corp. **SIC:** 5734—Computer & Software Stores.

★ **91575** ★ **Rite Aid**
7720 Hampton Blvd.
Norfolk, VA 23505
(804)451-3282
Ultimate Parent: Rite Aid.

★ **91576** ★ **Ryder Truck Rental Inc.**
4600 E. Princess Anne Rd.
Norfolk, VA 23502
(804)473-5500
Ultimate Parent: Ryder System. **SIC:** 7513—Truck Rental & Leasing Without Drivers; 7514—Passenger Car Rental.

★ **91577** ★ **Serv Air Inc.**
Norfolk, VA 23505
(804)489-4886
Ultimate Parent: E-Systems Inc.

★ **91578** ★ **Signet Bank, Virginia**
2014 Granby St.
Norfolk, VA 23517-2396
(804)640-4385
Location Type: Branch office. **Ultimate Parent:** Signet Banking Corp. **SIC:** 6021—National Commercial Banks.

★ **91579** ★ **Signet Bank, Virginia**
Webb Ctr.
5201 Hampton Blvd.
Norfolk, VA 23508
(804)640-4468
Location Type: Branch office. **Ultimate Parent:** Signet Banking Corp. **SIC:** 6021—National Commercial Banks.

★ **91580** ★ **Signet Bank, Virginia**
6330 Newton Rd.
Norfolk, VA 23502-4802
(804)640-4665
Location Type: Branch office. **Ultimate Parent:** Signet Banking Corp. **SIC:** 6021—National Commercial Banks.

★ **91581** ★ **Signet Bank, Virginia**
870 Military Hwy.
Norfolk, VA 23502-3638
(804)640-4371
Location Type: Branch office. **Ultimate Parent:** Signet Banking Corp. **SIC:** 6021—National Commercial Banks.

★ **91582** ★ **Signet Bank, Virginia**
500 Plume St. East
Norfolk, VA 23510-2310
(804)640-4209
Location Type: Branch office. **Ultimate Parent:** Signet Banking Corp. **SIC:** 6021—National Commercial Banks.

★ **91583** ★ **Smithfield Packing Co.**
435 E. Indian River Rd.
Norfolk, VA 23523
(804)543-6780
Officer: George E. Hamilton, President. **Ultimate Parent:** Smithfield Foods Inc. **SIC:** 2011—Meat Packing Plants.

★ 91584 ★ **Smithfield Packing Co. Inc.**
435 East Indian River Rd.
Norfolk, VA 23523
Ultimate Parent: Smithfield Foods Inc. **SIC:** 2010—Meat Products.

★ 91585 ★ **Specialty Products Inc.**
5660 E. Virginia Beach Blvd.
Norfolk, VA 23502-2428
(804)461-6301
Officer: Leonard Swann Jr. **Ultimate Parent:** Avery Dennison Corp. **SIC:** 5084—Industrial Machinery & Equipment; 5085—Industrial Supplies.

★ 91586 ★ **Toys R US**
400 N. Military Hwy.
Norfolk, VA 23502
(804)461-0440
Ultimate Parent: Toys "R" US. **SIC:** 5641—Children's & Infants' Wear Stores; 5945—Hobby, Toy & Game Shops.

★ 91587 ★ **Trans World Airlines, Inc.**
Norfolk International Airport
Norfolk, VA 23518
(804)461-6116
Ultimate Parent: Trans World Airlines. **SIC:** 4512—Air Transportation—Scheduled.

★ 91588 ★ **Transamerica Occidental Life Insurance**
700 Newtown Rd.
Norfolk, VA 23502
(804)461-1480
Ultimate Parent: Transamerica Occidental Life Insurance. **SIC:** 6411—Insurance Agents, Brokers & Service.

★ 91589 ★ **Underwriters Adjusting Co.**
7 Koger Executive Ctr.
Norfolk, VA 23502
(804)461-1379
Ultimate Parent: Continental. **SIC:** 6411—Insurance Agents, Brokers & Service.

★ 91590 ★ **United Parcel Service**
3313 Croft St.
Norfolk, VA 23513
(804)857-4876
Ultimate Parent: United Parcel Service of America. **SIC:** 7389—Business Services Nec.

★ 91591 ★ **US Gypsum Co.**
1217 Appomattox St.
Norfolk, VA 23523
(804)545-2461
Ultimate Parent: USG Corp. **SIC:** 5039—Construction Materials Nec.

★ 91592 ★ **Virginia Electric & Power C**
329 PO Box
Norfolk, VA 23501
(804)857-2000
Ultimate Parent: Dominion Resources. **SIC:** 4911—Electric Services.

★ 91593 ★ **Virginia Natural Gas Co. Inc.**
5100 E. Virginia Beach Blvd.
Norfolk, VA 23502
(804)466-5400
Ultimate Parent: Consolidated Natural Gas. **SIC:** 4939—Combination Utility Nec; 5714—Drapery & Upholstery Stores.

★ 91594 ★ **Virginia Natural Gas, Inc.**
5100 E. Virginia Beach Blvd.
Norfolk, VA 23502-3488
(804)466-5400 **Fax:** (804)466-5437
Officer: William F. Fritsche Jr., President. **Ultimate Parent:** Consolidated Natural Gas.

★ 91595 ★ **Waldenbooks**
Military Cir.
Norfolk, VA 23502
(804)461-1758
Ultimate Parent: K-Mart. **SIC:** 5942—Book Stores.

★ 91596 ★ **Waldenbooks**
333 Waterside Dr.
Norfolk, VA 23510
(804)625-7827
Ultimate Parent: K-Mart. **SIC:** 5942—Book Stores.

★ 91597 ★ **Western Auto Supply Co.**
7460 Tidewater Dr.
Norfolk, VA 23505
(804)480-3011
Ultimate Parent: Sears Roebuck & Co. **SIC:** 5531—Automobile & Home Supply Stores.

North Garden

★ 91598 ★ **Martin Marietta Corp.**
RR 29
North Garden, VA 22959
(804)296-5561
Ultimate Parent: Martin Marietta. **SIC:** 2899—Chemical Preparations Nec.

North Tazewell

★ 91599 ★ **Acme Markets**
246 PO Box
North Tazewell, VA 24630
(703)988-2561
Ultimate Parent: American Stores. **SIC:** 5411—Grocery Stores.

★ 91600 ★ **ACME Markets of Virginia Inc.**
PO Box 246
North Tazewell, VA 24630-0246
(703)988-2561
Company Type: Headquarters. **Officer:** J. William Crowe. **Ultimate Parent:** American Stores. **SIC:** 5411—Grocery Stores; 5141—Groceries—General Line.

Norton

★ 91601 ★ **Carter Machinery Co. Inc.**
Kentucky Ave.
Norton, VA 24273
(703)679-1010
Ultimate Parent: Carter-Wallace. **SIC:** 5082—Construction & Mining Machinery.

★ 91602 ★ **Eckerd Drugs**
Square Shopping Ctr. N
Norton, VA 24273
(703)679-4362
Ultimate Parent: Eckerd Corp. **SIC:** 5912—Drug Stores & Proprietary Stores.

★ 91603 ★ **First Union National Bank of Virginia**
701 Park Ave.
Norton, VA 24273-1007
(703)328-8031
Location Type: Branch office. **Ultimate Parent:** First Union Corp. **SIC:** 6021—National Commercial Banks.

★ 91604 ★ **Kroger Co.**
Norton Sq.
Norton, VA 24273
(703)679-2771
Ultimate Parent: Kroger. **SIC:** 5411—Grocery Stores.

★ 91605 ★ **McDonald's Hamburgers**
1400 Ark Ave. NW
Norton, VA 24273
(703)679-1481
Ultimate Parent: McDonald's. **SIC:** 5812—Eating Places.

★ 91606 ★ **Piggly Wiggly**
206 Coeburn Ave. SW
Norton, VA 24273
(703)679-5205
Ultimate Parent: Bruno's. **SIC:** 5411—Grocery Stores.

★ 91607 ★ **Piggly Wiggly**
Kentucky Ave.
Norton, VA 24273
(703)679-3311
Ultimate Parent: Bruno's. **SIC:** 5411—Grocery Stores.

★ 91608 ★ **Radio Shack**
736 Park Ave.
Norton, VA 24273
(703)679-5184
Company Type: Division. **Ultimate Parent:** Tandy Corp. **SIC:** 5731—Radio, Television & Electronics Stores.

★ 91609 ★ **Radio Shack**
736 Park Ave.
Norton, VA 24273
(703)679-5184
Company Type: Division. **Ultimate Parent:** Tandy Corp. **SIC:** 5731—Radio, Television & Electronics Stores.

Oak Hall

★ 91610 ★ **Farmers & Merchants Bank-Eastern Shore**
6461 Landford Hwy.
Oak Hall, VA 23416
(804)824-3424
Location Type: Branch office. **Officer:** Harold J. Kahl, Chairman of the Board & President. **Ultimate Parent:** Mercantile Bankshares Corp. **SIC:** 6021—National Commercial Banks. **Employee Count:** 64. **Sales:** Na M.

Oakton

★ 91611 ★ **First Virginia Bank**
2941 Chain Bridge Rd.
Oakton, VA 22124-3004
(703)241-3495
Location Type: Branch office. **Ultimate Parent:** First Virginia Banks Inc. **SIC:** 6021—National Commercial Banks.

Oakwood

★ 91612 ★ **Carter Machinery Co., Inc.**
RR 460
Oakwood, VA 24631
(703)498-4586
Ultimate Parent: Carter-Wallace. **SIC:** 5082—Construction & Mining Machinery.

★ 91613 ★ **First Union National Bank of Virginia**
U.S. 460 E
Oakwood, VA 24631-9601
(703)935-8151
Location Type: Branch office. **Ultimate Parent:** First Union Corp. **SIC:** 6021—National Commercial Banks.

Onancock

★ 91614 ★ **Crestar Bank**
62 Market St.
Onancock, VA 23417
(804)858-3014
Location Type: Branch office. **Ultimate Parent:** Crestar Financial Corp. **SIC:** 6021—National Commercial Banks.

Onley

★ 91615 ★ **Farmers & Merchants Bank-Eastern Shore**
PO Box 623
Onley, VA 23418-0623
Location Type: Headquarters. **Officer:** J Donald Henyon, Chairman of the Board. **Ultimate Parent:** Mercantile Bankshares Corp. **SIC:** 6021—National Commercial Banks. **Employee Count:** 187. **Sales:** Na M.

★ 91616 ★ **Farmers Merchants Bank-Eastern Shore**
25275 Lankford Hwy.
Onley, VA 23418-2821
(804)787-4111
Company Type: Division. **Officer:** H B Rew Jr., President. **Ultimate Parent:** Mercantile Bankshares Corp. **SIC:** 6022—State Commercial Banks. **Employee Count:** 65. **Sales:** Na M.

Orange

★ 91617 ★ **Crestar Bank**
101 E. Main St.
Orange, VA 22960
(804)672-1084
Location Type: Branch office. **Ultimate Parent:** Crestar Financial Corp. **SIC:** 6021—National Commercial Banks.

★ 91618 ★ **Food Lion**
367 Madison Rd.
Orange, VA 22960
(703)672-0866
Ultimate Parent: Food Lion. **SIC:** 5411—Grocery Stores.

★ 91619 ★ **Radio Shack**
Rural Route 20
Orange, VA 22960
(703)672-5552
Company Type: Division. **Ultimate Parent:** Tandy Corp. **SIC:** 5731—Radio, Television & Electronics Stores.

★ 91620 ★ **Radio Shack**
RR 20
Orange, VA 22960
(703)672-5552
Company Type: Division. **Ultimate Parent:** Tandy Corp. **SIC:** 5731—Radio, Television & Electronics Stores.

Painter

★ 91621 ★ **Crestar Bank**
Edmunds St. & Railroad Ave.
Painter, VA 23420
(804)858-3129
Location Type: Branch office. **Ultimate Parent:** Crestar Financial Corp. **SIC:** 6021—National Commercial Banks.

Pearisburg

★ 91622 ★ **First Union National Bank of Virginia**
605 Wenonah Ave.
Pearisburg, VA 24134-1635
(703)921-3611
Location Type: Branch office. **Ultimate Parent:** First Union Corp. **SIC:** 6021—National Commercial Banks.

★ 91623 ★ **Food Lion**
New River Shopping Ctr.
Pearisburg, VA 24134
(703)921-2571
Ultimate Parent: Food Lion. **SIC:** 5411—Grocery Stores.

★ 91624 ★ **Kroger Co.**
Wenonah Ave.
Pearisburg, VA 24134
(703)921-2147
Ultimate Parent: Kroger. **SIC:** 5411—Grocery Stores.

★ 91625 ★ **New York Life Insurance Co.**
621 S. Main St.
Pearisburg, VA 24134
(703)921-1457
Ultimate Parent: New York Life. **SIC:** 6411—Insurance Agents, Brokers & Service.

Pembroke

★ 91626 ★ **First Union National Bank of Virginia**
27 State Hwy. & Cascade Dr.
Pembroke, VA 24136
(703)626-7272
Location Type: Branch office. **Ultimate Parent:** First Union Corp. **SIC:** 6021—National Commercial Banks.

Petersburg

★ 91627 ★ **Batesville Casket Co. Inc.**
2031 Puddledock Rd.
Petersburg, VA 23803
(804)861-3030
Ultimate Parent: Hillenbrand Industries. **SIC:** 3995—Burial Caskets.

★ 91628 ★ **Blazer Financial Services**
123 N. Sycamore St.
Petersburg, VA 23803
(804)732-6722
Ultimate Parent: Great Western Financial Corp. **SIC:** 6141—Personal Credit Institutions.

★ **91629** ★   **Circuit City**
3330 S. Crater Rd. 23
Petersburg, VA 23805
(804)733-1943
Ultimate Parent: Circuit City Stores. **SIC:**
5065—Electronic Parts & Equipment Nec.

★ **91630** ★   **Crestar Bank**
898 E. Washington St.
Petersburg, VA 23803-3452
(804)541-2905
Location Type: Branch office. **Ultimate
Parent:** Crestar Financial Corp. **SIC:**
6021—National Commercial Banks.

★ **91631** ★   **Crestar Bank**
1941 S. Sycamore St.
Petersburg, VA 23805-2728
(804)541-2954
Location Type: Branch office. **Ultimate
Parent:** Crestar Financial Corp. **SIC:**
6021—National Commercial Banks.

★ **91632** ★   **Lee Laboratories, Inc.**
Petersburg Industrial Park
PO Box 1658
Petersburg, VA 23805
(804)862-2534
Ultimate Parent: American Home Products.

★ **91633** ★   **Mary Kay Cosmetics**
2305 Chemin Rd.
Petersburg, VA 23805
(804)733-1922
Ultimate Parent: Mary Kay Cosmetics. **SIC:**
5999—Miscellaneous Retail Stores Nec.

★ **91634** ★   **Pepsi-Cola Bottling
Co.**
1501 W. Washington St.
Petersburg, VA 23803
(804)732-0333
Ultimate Parent: Pepsico. **SIC:** 2086—
Bottled & Canned Soft Drinks.

★ **91635** ★   **Signet Bank, Virginia**
Walnut Hill Plz.
1963 S. Crater Rd.
Petersburg, VA 23803-2765
(804)732-5395
Location Type: Branch office. **Ultimate
Parent:** Signet Banking Corp. **SIC:** 6021—
National Commercial Banks.

★ **91636** ★   **Signet Bank, Virginia**
20 Franklin St.
Petersburg, VA 23803-4515
(804)732-5099
Location Type: Branch office. **Ultimate
Parent:** Signet Banking Corp. **SIC:** 6021—
National Commercial Banks.

Pocahontas

★ **91637** ★   **First Union National
Bank of Virginia**
19A Ctr. St.
Pocahontas, VA 24635
(703)945-2102
Location Type: Branch office. **Ultimate
Parent:** First Union Corp. **SIC:** 6021—
National Commercial Banks.

Portsmouth

★ **91638** ★   **Ace Hardware**
3619 High St.
Portsmouth, VA 23707
(804)397-0703
Ultimate Parent: Ace Hardware. **SIC:**
5251—Hardware Stores.

★ **91639** ★   **American General
Finance Inc.**
4552 George Washington Hwy.
Portsmouth, VA 23702-2404
(804)485-5050
Officer: Ruby Davidson. **Ultimate Parent:**
American General Corp. **SIC:** 6141—
Personal Credit Institutions; 6162—
Mortgage Bankers & Correspondents.

★ **91640** ★   **American General
Finance Inc.**
4552 George Washington Hwy.
Portsmouth, VA 23702-2404
(804)485-5050
Location Type: Branch office. **Officer:**
Ruby Davidson. **Ultimate Parent:** American
General Corp. **SIC:** 6141—Personal Credit
Institutions; 6162—Mortgage Bankers &
Correspondents.

★ **91641** ★   **Avon Products Inc.**
505 Washington St.
Portsmouth, VA 23704
(804)393-7503
Ultimate Parent: Avon Products, Inc. **SIC:**
5999—Miscellaneous Retail Stores Nec.

★ **91642** ★   **Circuit City**
3939 Turnpike Rd.
Portsmouth, VA 23701
(804)490-0099
Ultimate Parent: Circuit City Stores. **SIC:**
5722—Household Appliance Stores.

★ **91643** ★   **Crestar Bank**
2860 Airline Blvd.
Portsmouth, VA 23701-2705
(804)858-3362
Location Type: Branch office. **Ultimate
Parent:** Crestar Financial Corp. **SIC:**
6021—National Commercial Banks.

★ **91644** ★   **Crestar Bank**
303 County St.
Portsmouth, VA 23705
(804)858-3351
Location Type: Branch office. **Ultimate
Parent:** Crestar Financial Corp. **SIC:**
6021—National Commercial Banks.

★ **91645** ★   **Crestar Bank**
5800 High St.
Portsmouth, VA 23703-4504
(804)858-3344
Location Type: Branch office. **Ultimate
Parent:** Crestar Financial Corp. **SIC:**
6021—National Commercial Banks.

★ **91646** ★   **First American Bank
of Virginia**
5798 Churchland Blvd.
Portsmouth, VA 23703
(804)455-7840
Ultimate Parent: First American Corp.

★ **91647** ★   **First American Bank
of Virginia**
3315 High St.
Portsmouth, VA 23707
(804)858-5245
Ultimate Parent: First American Corp.

★ **91648** ★   **First Union National
Bank of Virginia**
2400 Airline Blvd.
Portsmouth, VA 23701-2912
(804)488-1481
Location Type: Branch office. **Ultimate
Parent:** First Union Corp. **SIC:** 6021—
National Commercial Banks.

★ **91649** ★   **First Union National
Bank of Virginia**
430 Crawford St.
Portsmouth, VA 23704-3813
(804)396-6548
Location Type: Branch office. **Ultimate
Parent:** First Union Corp. **SIC:** 6021—
National Commercial Banks.

★ **91650** ★   **First Union National
Bank of Virginia**
1901 Victory Blvd.
Portsmouth, VA 23702
(804)485-0738
Location Type: Branch office. **Ultimate
Parent:** First Union Corp. **SIC:** 6021—
National Commercial Banks.

★ **91651** ★   **First Union National
Bank of Virginia**
600 Loudoun Ave.
Portsmouth, VA 23707-3200
(804)397-4426
Location Type: Branch office. **Ultimate
Parent:** First Union Corp. **SIC:** 6021—
National Commercial Banks.

★ **91652** ★   **Food Lion**
1907 Victory Blvd.
Portsmouth, VA 23702
(804)487-4252
Ultimate Parent: Food Lion. **SIC:** 5411—
Grocery Stores.

★ **91653** ★   **Food Lion**
1238 Cedar Rd.
Portsmouth, VA 23703
(804)547-8170
Ultimate Parent: Food Lion. **SIC:** 5411—
Grocery Stores.

★ **91654** ★   **Food Lion**
3100 Airline Blvd.
Portsmouth, VA 23701
(804)488-7464
Ultimate Parent: Food Lion. **SIC:** 5411—
Grocery Stores.

★ **91655** ★   **Food Lion**
5606 Portsmouth Blvd.
Portsmouth, VA 23701
(804)488-8014
Ultimate Parent: Food Lion. **SIC:** 5411—
Grocery Stores.

★ **91656** ★   **Food Lion**
5917 High St. W
Portsmouth, VA 23703
(804)484-6435
Ultimate Parent: Food Lion. **SIC:** 5411—
Grocery Stores.

★ **91657** ★   **Greyhound Bus Lines**
701 Court St.
Portsmouth, VA 23704
(804)399-2434
Ultimate Parent: Greyhound Lines Inc. **SIC:**
4111—Local & Suburban Transit.

★ **91658** ★   **Gwaltney of
Smithfield Ltd.**
2175 Elmhurst Ln.
Portsmouth, VA 23701
Ultimate Parent: Smithfield Foods Inc. **SIC:**
2011—Meat Packing Plants.

★ **91659** ★   **Hoechst Celanese**
3340 West Norfork Rd.
Portsmouth, VA 23703
Ultimate Parent: Hoechst Celanese Corp.
SIC: 2869—Industrial Organic Chemicals
Nec; 2819—Industrial Inorganic Chemicals
Nec; 2821—Plastics Materials & Resins.

★ **91660** ★   **Hoechst-Celanese
Corp.**
3340 W. Norfolk Rd.
Portsmouth, VA 23703
Ultimate Parent: Hoechst Celanese Corp.
SIC: 2821—Plastics Materials & Resins;
2869—Industrial Organic Chemicals Nec.

★ **91661** ★   **Life Insurance Co. of
Virginia**
303 Wavy St.
Portsmouth, VA 23704
(804)399-6386
Ultimate Parent: Life Insurance Co. of
Virginia. **SIC:** 6411—Insurance Agents,
Brokers & Service.

★ **91662** ★   **New York Life
Insurance Co.**
355 Crawford St.
Portsmouth, VA 23704
(804)393-7673
Ultimate Parent: New York Life. **SIC:**
6411—Insurance Agents, Brokers &
Service.

★ **91663** ★   **Pet Inc. Dairy**
2320 Turnpike Rd.
Portsmouth, VA 23704
(804)722-1997
Ultimate Parent: Pet. **SIC:** 2013—
Sausages & Other Prepared Meats.

★ **91664** ★   **Radio Shack**
1036 Frederick Blvd.
Portsmouth, VA 23707
(804)397-0026
Company Type: Division. **Ultimate Parent:**
Tandy Corp. **SIC:** 5731—Radio, Television
& Electronics Stores.

★ **91665** ★   **Radio Shack**
4020 Victory Blvd.
Portsmouth, VA 23701
(804)488-6026
Company Type: Division. **Ultimate Parent:**
Tandy Corp. **SIC:** 5065—Electronic Parts &
Equipment Nec.

★ **91666** ★   **Radio Shack**
5780 Churchland Blvd.
Portsmouth, VA 23703
(804)484-7825
Company Type: Division. **Ultimate Parent:**
Tandy Corp. **SIC:** 5731—Radio, Television
& Electronics Stores; 5065—Electronic Parts
& Equipment Nec.

★ **91667** ★   **Rite Aid**
1130 London Blvd.
Portsmouth, VA 23704
(804)393-6048
Ultimate Parent: Rite Aid. **SIC:** 5912—Drug
Stores & Proprietary Stores.

★ **91668** ★   **Rite Aid**
5616 Portsmouth Blvd.
Portsmouth, VA 23701
(804)488-9819
Ultimate Parent: Rite Aid. **SIC:** 5912—Drug
Stores & Proprietary Stores.

★ **91669** ★   **Signet Bank, Virginia**
5700 Portsmouth Blvd.
Portsmouth, VA 23701-1442
(804)640-4656
Location Type: Branch office. **Ultimate
Parent:** Signet Banking Corp. **SIC:** 6021—
National Commercial Banks.

★ **91670** ★   **Signet Bank, Virginia**
3201 High St.
Portsmouth, VA 23707
(804)640-4629
Location Type: Branch office. **Ultimate
Parent:** Signet Banking Corp. **SIC:** 6021—
National Commercial Banks.

★ **91671** ★   **Signet Bank, Virginia**
355 Crawford St.
Portsmouth, VA 23704-2816
(804)640-4602
Location Type: Branch office. **Ultimate
Parent:** Signet Banking Corp. **SIC:** 6021—
National Commercial Banks.

★ **91672** ★   **Virginia Chemicals
Co.**
3340 West Norfolk Rd.
Portsmouth, VA 23703
Ultimate Parent: Hoechst Celanese Corp.
SIC: 2869—Industrial Organic Chemicals
Nec; 2819—Industrial Inorganic Chemicals
Nec; 2821—Plastics Materials & Resins.

★ **91673** ★   **Waldenbooks**
45 Tower Mall Shopping
Portsmouth, VA 23701
(804)488-6430
Ultimate Parent: K-Mart. **SIC:** 5942—Book
Stores.

Pound

★ **91674** ★   **Rite Aid**
Main St.
Pound, VA 24279
(703)796-9825
Ultimate Parent: Rite Aid. **SIC:** 5912—Drug
Stores & Proprietary Stores.

Pounding Mill

★ **91675** ★   **Lowe's**
Us 19-460 Northeast
Pounding Mill, VA 24637
(703)964-9151
Ultimate Parent: Lowe's. **SIC:** 5039—
Construction Materials Nec.

Prince George

★ **91676** ★   **New York Life
Insurance Co.**
Seberas County Sq.
Prince George, VA 23875
(804)861-8732
Ultimate Parent: New York Life. **SIC:**
6411—Insurance Agents, Brokers &
Service.

Pulaski

★ **91677** ★   **Piggly Wiggly**
Maple Shopping Ctr.
Pulaski, VA 24301
(703)980-0549
Ultimate Parent: Bruno's. **SIC:** 5411—
Grocery Stores.

★ **91678** ★   **Signet Bank, Virginia**
1000 E. Mian St.
Pulaski, VA 24301-5281
(703)980-6206
Location Type: Branch office. **Ultimate
Parent:** Signet Banking Corp. **SIC:** 6021—
National Commercial Banks.

★ **91679** ★ **Signet Bank, Virginia**
1 Main St.
Pulaski, VA 24301-5013
(703)980-2840
Location Type: Branch office. **Ultimate Parent:** Signet Banking Corp. **SIC:** 6021—National Commercial Banks.

★ **91680** ★ **West Point Pepperell**
Burgiss Ave.
Pulaski, VA 24301
Location Type: Plant. **Ultimate Parent:** West Point Stevens. **SIC:** 2295—Coated Fabrics—Not Rubberized.

Purcellville

★ **91681** ★ **First American Bank**
431 W. Main St.
Purcellville, VA 22132
(703)338-4134
Ultimate Parent: First American Corp. **SIC:** 6099—Functions Related to Deposit Banking.

★ **91682** ★ **First Union National Bank of Virginia**
611 E. Main St.
Purcellville, VA 22132-3012
(703)338-4102
Location Type: Branch office. **Ultimate Parent:** First Union Corp. **SIC:** 6021—National Commercial Banks.

★ **91683** ★ **First Virginia Bank**
120 N. Maple Ave.
Purcellville, VA 22132-3101
(703)241-4655
Location Type: Branch office. **Ultimate Parent:** First Virginia Banks Inc. **SIC:** 6021—National Commercial Banks.

★ **91684** ★ **First Virginia Bank**
115 E. Main St.
Purcellville, VA 22132
(703)241-4658
Location Type: Branch office. **Ultimate Parent:** First Virginia Banks Inc. **SIC:** 6021—National Commercial Banks.

★ **91685** ★ **Rite Aid**
Loudoun Valley Shopping.Ctr.
Purcellville, VA 22132
(703)338-4195
Ultimate Parent: Rite Aid. **SIC:** 5912—Drug Stores & Proprietary Stores.

Quantico

★ **91686** ★ **Mary Kay Cosmetics**
414 Quarters
Quantico, VA 22134
(703)640-7396
Ultimate Parent: Mary Kay Cosmetics.

Radford

★ **91687** ★ **ACME Markets**
RR 2
Radford, VA 24141
(703)639-1244
Ultimate Parent: American Stores. **SIC:** 5411—Grocery Stores.

★ **91688** ★ **AT & T Family Federal Credit Union**
Hwy. 14 & Hwy. 630
Radford, VA 24141
(703)731-8599
Location Type: Branch office. **Officer:** Susan Rooney, Manager. **Ultimate Parent:** AT&T. **SIC:** 6061—Federal Credit Unions.

★ **91689** ★ **Avon Products**
926 1st St.
Radford, VA 24141-4510
(703)731-4435
Ultimate Parent: Avon Products, Inc. **SIC:** 5122—Drugs, Proprietaries & Sundries; 5999—Miscellaneous Retail Stores Nec; 9999—Nonclassifiable Establishments.

★ **91690** ★ **Brad Ragan Inc.**
1905 1st & Ingles St.
Radford, VA 24141
Ultimate Parent: Goodyear Tire & Rubber. **SIC:** 3011—Tires & Inner Tubes.

★ **91691** ★ **Brad Ragan Inc.**
1905 First & Ingles Sts.
Radford, VA 24141
Ultimate Parent: Goodyear Tire & Rubber. **SIC:** 3011—Tires & Inner Tubes.

★ **91692** ★ **Brad Regan Inc.**
Rubber Div.
1905 First & Ingles Sts.
Radford, VA 24141
Company Type: Division. **Ultimate Parent:** Goodyear Tire & Rubber. **SIC:** 3011—Tires & Inner Tubes.

★ **91693** ★ **Crestar Bank**
1st & Kent Sts.
Radford, VA 24141
(703)731-9240
Location Type: Branch office. **Ultimate Parent:** Crestar Financial Corp. **SIC:** 6021—National Commercial Banks.

★ **91694** ★ **Crestar Bank**
Rtes. 114 & 600
Radford, VA 24141
(703)731-9230
Location Type: Branch office. **Ultimate Parent:** Crestar Financial Corp. **SIC:** 6021—National Commercial Banks.

★ **91695** ★ **Crestar Bank**
1000 Norwood St.
Radford, VA 24141-4743
(703)731-9200
Location Type: Branch office. **Ultimate Parent:** Crestar Financial Corp. **SIC:** 6021—National Commercial Banks.

★ **91696** ★ **Eckerd Drugs**
Village Oak Shopping. Ctr.
Radford, VA 24141
(703)639-9363
Ultimate Parent: Eckerd Corp. **SIC:** 5912—Drug Stores & Proprietary Stores.

★ **91697** ★ **Greyhound Bus Lines**
Norwood St.
Radford, VA 24141
(703)639-3311
Ultimate Parent: Greyhound Lines Inc. **SIC:** 4111—Local & Suburban Transit.

★ **91698** ★ **Kroger Co.**
Radford Shopping Plz.
Radford, VA 24141
(703)639-0311
Ultimate Parent: Kroger. **SIC:** 5411—Grocery Stores.

★ **91699** ★ **Radford Army Ammunition Plant**
State Rte. 114 PO Box 1
Radford, VA 24141-0299
Ultimate Parent: Hercules. **SIC:** 2892—Explosives.

★ **91700** ★ **Radford Army Ammunition Plant**
PO Box 1 State Rte. 114
Radford, VA 24141
Ultimate Parent: Hercules. **SIC:** 2892—Explosives.

★ **91701** ★ **Radio Shack**
Radford Shopping Plz.
Radford, VA 24141
(703)731-1333
Company Type: Division. **Ultimate Parent:** Tandy Corp. **SIC:** 5065—Electronic Parts & Equipment Nec; 5731—Radio, Television & Electronics Stores.

Ranoke

★ **91702** ★ **Crestar Bank**
510 S. Jefferson St.
Ranoke, VA 24011-2417
(703)982-3179
Location Type: Branch office. **Ultimate Parent:** Crestar Financial Corp. **SIC:** 6021—National Commercial Banks.

Reston

★ **91703** ★ **Amdahl Federal Service Corp.**
12020 Sunrise Valley Dr.
Reston, VA 22091-3429
(703)648-0301
Company Type: Subsidiary. **Officer:** John Notaro, President. **Ultimate Parent:** Amdahl Corp. **SIC:** 7378—Computer Maintenance & Repair. **Employee Count:** 46. **Sales:** 13 M.

★ **91704** ★ **Crestar Bank**
11180 S. Lakes Dr.
Reston, VA 22091-4327
Location Type: Branch office. **Ultimate Parent:** Crestar Financial Corp. **SIC:** 6021—National Commercial Banks.

★ **91705** ★ **Crestar Bank**
1601 WAshington Plz.
Reston, VA 22090-4304
Location Type: Branch office. **Ultimate Parent:** Crestar Financial Corp. **SIC:** 6021—National Commercial Banks.

★ **91706** ★ **Crestar Bank**
1900 Centenial Pk. Dr.
Reston, VA 22091-1510
Location Type: Branch office. **Ultimate Parent:** Crestar Financial Corp. **SIC:** 6021—National Commercial Banks.

★ **91707** ★ **First Union National Bank of Virginia**
11260 Roger Bacon Dr.
Reston, VA 22090-5203
(703)934-1881
Location Type: Branch office. **Ultimate Parent:** First Union Corp. **SIC:** 6021—National Commercial Banks.

★ **91708** ★ **First Union National Bank of Virginia**
11911 Freedom Dr., Ste. 100
Reston, VA 22090
(703)442-3730
Location Type: Branch office. **Ultimate Parent:** First Union Corp. **SIC:** 6021—National Commercial Banks.

★ **91709** ★ **First Virginia Bank**
11100 South Lakes Dr.
Reston, VA 22091-4327
(703)241-3680
Location Type: Branch office. **Ultimate Parent:** First Virginia Banks Inc. **SIC:** 6021—National Commercial Banks.

★ **91710** ★ **Grumman**
Space Station Integration Division
1760 Business Ctr. Dr.
Reston, VA 22090
(703)834-1244 **Fax:** (703)438-5140
Company Type: Subsidiary. **Officer:** M. C. Blyseth, Senior Vice President & General Manager. **Ultimate Parent:** Grumman.

★ **91711** ★ **Lafarge**
11130 Sunrise Valley Dr.
Reston, VA 22091
(703)264-3600
Company Type: Headquarters. **Officer:** Michel A. Rose. **Employee Count:** 7400. **Sales:** 1495 M. **Fortune 500:** Largest U.S. Industrial Corporations: Ranking 280.

★ **91712** ★ **Lafarge Corp.**
11130 Sunrise Valley Dr., Ste. 300
PO Box 4600
Reston, VA 22090
(703)264-3600 **Fax:** (703)264-0634
Officer: Michel Rose, President & CEO. **Ultimate Parent:** Lafarge. **Employee Count:** 7600.

★ **91713** ★ **Litton Computer Services-Eastern Regional Data Center**
1831 Michael Faraday Dr.
Reston, VA 22090-5298
(703)471-9200 **Fax:** (703)478-2439
Company Type: Division. **Ultimate Parent:** Litton Industries. **SIC:** 7374—Data Processing & Preparation.

★ **91714** ★ **Loral Advanced Projects**
1761 Business Ctr. Dr., Ste. 300
Reston, VA 22090
(703)759-1400 **Fax:** (703)759-1450
Company Type: Division. **Ultimate Parent:** Loral Corp. **SIC:** 3812—Search & Navigation Equipment.

★ **91715** ★ **New York Life Central Atlantic Pension Reg.**
Eatern Pension Zone
11400 Commerce Park Dr., Ste. 250
Reston, VA 22091
(703)264-9700 **Fax:** (703)264-3906
Officer: Michael W. Anderson, Regional Manager. **Ultimate Parent:** New York Life.

★ **91716** ★ **Paramax Systems Corp.**
12010 Sunrise Valley Dr.
Reston, VA 22091
(703)620-7000
Officer: Larry R. Sadler, President. **Ultimate Parent:** Unisys Corp. **SIC:** 3663—Radio & T.V. Communications Equipment; 3679—Electronic Components Nec.

★ **91717** ★ **PRC Engineering Systems, Inc.**
12005 Sunrise Valley Dr.
Reston, VA 22091-3406
(703)620-8423
Company Type: Subsidiary. **Officer:** Joe Grosson, President. **Ultimate Parent:** Black & Decker Corp. **SIC:** 8711—Engineering Services. **Employee Count:** 170. **Sales:** 12 M.

★ **91718** ★ **Sprint**
12490 Sunrise Valley Dr.
Reston, VA 22091
(703)689-6000
Officer: Paolo Guidi, President. **Ultimate Parent:** Sprint. **SIC:** 3661—Telephone & Telegraph Apparatus.

Richlands

★ **91719** ★ **First Union National Bank of Virginia**
201 Suffolk Ave.
Richlands, VA 24641-2436
(703)963-1041
Location Type: Branch office. **Ultimate Parent:** First Union Corp. **SIC:** 6021—National Commercial Banks.

★ **91720** ★ **First Virginia Bank**
Clinch Valley
501 Railroad Ave.
PO Drawer 878
Richlands, VA 24641-0878
(703)963-1051
Officer: Harmon P. Hess, Chairman of the Board. **Ultimate Parent:** First Virginia Banks Inc. **SIC:** 6022—State Commercial Banks.

★ **91721** ★ **First Virginia Bank Clinch Valley**
501 Railroad Ave.
Richlands, VA 24641-2513
(703)963-1051
Company Type: Subsidiary. **Officer:** Michael J. Firecetz, President, CEO. **Ultimate Parent:** First Virginia Banks Inc. **SIC:** 6022—State Commercial Banks. **Employee Count:** 33.

★ **91722** ★ **Kroger Co.**
320 Richlands Mall
Richlands, VA 24641
(703)964-2985
Ultimate Parent: Kroger. **SIC:** 5411—Grocery Stores.

Richmond

★ **91723** ★ **ABF Freight System Inc.**
2501 Turner Rd.
Richmond, VA 23224-2537
(804)745-2881
Location Type: Branch office. **Officer:** Jim Riendeau. **Ultimate Parent:** Arkansas Best. **SIC:** 4212—Local Trucking Without Storage; 4213—Trucking Except Local.

★ **91724** ★ **A.H. Robins Co.**
Operations
1407 Cummings Dr.
Richmond, VA 23220
(804)257-2000
Company Type: Subsidiary. **Officer:** Daniel E. French, Sr. V.P. **Ultimate Parent:** American Home Products. **SIC:** 8741—Management Services.

★ **91725** ★ **A.H. Robins Co., Inc.**
1407 Cummings
PO Box 26604
Richmond, VA 23261-6609
(804)257-2000 **Fax:** (804)257-2670
Company Type: Subsidiary. **Officer:** Bernard Canavan M.D., President. **Ultimate Parent:** American Home Products.

★ **91726** ★ **Airborne Freight Corp.**
Byrd
Richmond, VA 23231
(804)222-3804
Ultimate Parent: Airborne Freight Corp. **SIC:** 4512—Air Transportation—Scheduled.

★ 91727 ★ **American Family Life Assurance**
3212 Cutshaw Ave.
Richmond, VA 23230
(804)359-9092
Ultimate Parent: American Family Life Assurance. **SIC:** 6411—Insurance Agents, Brokers & Service.

★ 91728 ★ **American General Finance**
5312 Chamberlayne Rd.
Richmond, VA 23227-2958
(804)264-6600
Location Type: Branch office. **Officer:** Tony Lewis. **Ultimate Parent:** American General Corp. **SIC:** 6141—Personal Credit Institutions; 6162—Mortgage Bankers & Correspondents.

★ 91729 ★ **American General Finance Inc.**
5245 S. Laburnum Ave.
Richmond, VA 23231-4437
(804)649-9031
Location Type: Branch office. **Officer:** Barbara Heisler. **Ultimate Parent:** American General Corp. **SIC:** 6141—Personal Credit Institutions; 6162—Mortgage Bankers & Correspondents.

★ 91730 ★ **American General Finance Inc.**
9022 W. Broad St.
Richmond, VA 23294-6475
(804)270-6475
Location Type: Branch office. **Officer:** Willie Mitchell. **Ultimate Parent:** American General Corp. **SIC:** 6141—Personal Credit Institutions; 6162—Mortgage Bankers & Correspondents.

★ 91731 ★ **American General Finance Inc.**
5245 S. Laburnum Ave.
Richmond, VA 23231-4437
(804)649-9031
Location Type: Branch office. **Officer:** Barbara Heisler. **Ultimate Parent:** American General Corp. **SIC:** 6141—Personal Credit Institutions; 6162—Mortgage Bankers & Correspondents.

★ 91732 ★ **American General Finance Inc.**
9022 W. Broad St.
Richmond, VA 23294-6475
(804)270-6475
Location Type: Branch office. **Officer:** Willie Mitchell. **Ultimate Parent:** American General Corp. **SIC:** 6141—Personal Credit Institutions; 6162—Mortgage Bankers & Correspondents.

★ 91733 ★ **American General Finance Inc.**
5312 Chamberlayne Rd.
Richmond, VA 23227-2958
(804)264-6600
Location Type: Branch office. **Officer:** Tony Lewis. **Ultimate Parent:** American General Corp. **SIC:** 6141—Personal Credit Institutions; 6162—Mortgage Bankers & Correspondents.

★ 91734 ★ **APAC**
3600 Warbro Rd.
Richmond, VA 23235
(804)744-1130
Officer: C. Gray Hilton, President. **Ultimate Parent:** Ashland Oil.

★ 91735 ★ **Arrow Electronics Inc.**
8002 Discovery Dr.
Richmond, VA 23229
(804)282-0413
Ultimate Parent: Arrow Electronics. **SIC:** 5065—Electronic Parts & Equipment Nec.

★ 91736 ★ **AT & T Family Federal Credit Union**
4500 Labamum Ave.
Richmond, VA 23231
(804)226-5151
Location Type: Branch office. **Officer:** Mel Siple, Manager. **Ultimate Parent:** AT&T. **SIC:** 6061—Federal Credit Unions.

★ 91737 ★ **AT&T**
703 E. Grace St.
Richmond, VA 23219-1843
(804)225-1576
Location Type: Branch office. **Ultimate Parent:** AT&T. **SIC:** 4813—Telephone Communications Except Radiotelephone.

★ 91738 ★ **Atlantic Richfield Co.**
5500 Old Osborne Tpke.
Richmond, VA 23231
(804)226-1940
Ultimate Parent: Atlantic Richfield Co., Inc. **SIC:** 5172—Petroleum Products Nec.

★ 91739 ★ **August Max**
225 Regency Sq.
Richmond, VA 23229
(804)740-4107
Ultimate Parent: United States Shoe. **SIC:** 5651—Family Clothing Stores.

★ 91740 ★ **Avon Products Inc.**
7635 Hull St.
Richmond, VA 23235
(804)745-4934
Ultimate Parent: Avon Products, Inc. **SIC:** 5999—Miscellaneous Retail Stores Nec.

★ 91741 ★ **BASF Corp.**
3435 W. Leigh St.
Richmond, VA 23230
Ultimate Parent: BASF Corp. **SIC:** 2893—Printing Ink.

★ 91742 ★ **Bell Atlantic Business Systems Services**
3619 Saunders Ave.
Richmond, VA 23227-4354
(804)355-2643
Officer: Mary Lee Clark. **Ultimate Parent:** Bell Atlantic Corp. **SIC:** 7378—Computer Maintenance & Repair; 4813—Telephone Communications Except Radiotelephone; 5112—Stationery & Office Supplies.

★ 91743 ★ **Bell Atlantic Paging**
8400 W. Broad St. A
Richmond, VA 23294-6202
(804)346-0540
Officer: Scott Medvetz. **Ultimate Parent:** Bell Atlantic Corp. **SIC:** 5065—Electronic Parts & Equipment Nec.

★ 91744 ★ **Bellwood Printing Plant**
2001 Reymet Rd.
Richmond, VA 23237-3798
Ultimate Parent: Reynolds Metals Co. **SIC:** 2754—Commercial Printing—Gravure.

★ 91745 ★ **BFI-Richmond Landfill**
2325 Charles City Rd.
Richmond, VA 23231-4303
(804)222-9229
Location Type: Branch office. **Officer:** Danny Smith. **Ultimate Parent:** Browning-Ferris Industries. **SIC:** 8742—Management Consulting Services; 4212—Local Trucking Without Storage; 4953—Refuse Systems.

★ 91746 ★ **Blazer Financial Services**
320 E. Grace St.
Richmond, VA 23219
(804)648-6566
Ultimate Parent: Great Western Financial Corp. **SIC:** 6141—Personal Credit Institutions.

★ 91747 ★ **Brookhollow Corp.**
6800 Paragon Pl
Richmond, VA 23230
(804)288-9333
Ultimate Parent: Texas Industries. **SIC:** 6531—Real Estate Agents & Managers.

★ 91748 ★ **C. F. Sauer Co. Inc.**
2000 W. Broad St.
Richmond, VA 23220-2006
(804)359-5786
Officer: Conrad F. Sauer II, Ch. Bd. Sec. **Ultimate Parent:** Dean Foods. **SIC:** 2079—Edible Fats & Oils Nec; 2035—Pickles, Sauces & Salad Dressings; 2099—Food Preparations Nec; 5072—Hardware. **Employee Count:** 700. **Sales:** 218 M.

★ 91749 ★ **Carolina Surgical Supply Corp.**
300 Arboretum Pl., Ste. 140
Richmond, VA 23236-3465
(804)872-9960
Company Type: Subsidiary. **Officer:** Jack Herrington, President. **Ultimate Parent:** Bergen Brunswig Corp. **SIC:** 5047—Medical & Hospital Equipment. **Employee Count:** 47. **Sales:** 9 M.

★ 91750 ★ **Carpenter**
5016 Monument Ave.
Richmond, VA 23230
(804)359-0800
Company Type: Headquarters. **Officer:** S. F. Pauley. **Sales:** 619 M. **Fortune 500:** Largest U.S. Industrial Corporations: Ranking 495.

★ 91751 ★ **Casual Corner**
138 Regency Sq.
Richmond, VA 23229
(804)740-1391
Ultimate Parent: United States Shoe. **SIC:** 5651—Family Clothing Stores.

★ 91752 ★ **Casual Corner**
Cloverleaf Mall
Richmond, VA 23225
(804)276-0083
Ultimate Parent: United States Shoe. **SIC:** 5651—Family Clothing Stores.

★ 91753 ★ **Cedars Guest Homes The**
1607 Jefferson Davis Hwy.
Richmond, VA 23224-7207
(804)233-4111
Officer: Jeanne Taroissien. **Ultimate Parent:** Beverly Enterprises. **SIC:** 8059—Nursing & Personal Care Nec; 8051—Skilled Nursing Care Facilities; 8361—Residential Care.

★ 91754 ★ **Central Fidelity Bank**
1021 E. Cary St.
Richmond, VA 23219
(804)782-4000
Company Type: Headquarters. **Officer:** Carroll L. Saine. **Fortune Service 500:** Ranking 63.

★ 91755 ★ **Central Fidelity Bank NA**
1021 E. Cary St.
Richmond, VA 23219-4000
(804)782-4000
Company Type: Subsidiary. **Officer:** Lewis N. Miller Jr., President. **Ultimate Parent:** Central Fidelity Bank. **SIC:** 6021—National Commercial Banks. **Employee Count:** 3.

★ 91756 ★ **Central Fidelity Banks Inc.**
1021 E. Cary St.
Richmond, VA 23219-4000
(804)782-4000
Officer: Carroll Saine, Chairman of the Board. **Ultimate Parent:** Alberto-Culver Co. Inc. **SIC:** 6022—State Commercial Banks. **Employee Count:** 3200.

★ 91757 ★ **Chesapeak Corp.**
1021 E. Cary St.
Richmond, VA 23219-4000
(804)697-1000
Officer: J. Carter Fox, Chairman of the Board. **Ultimate Parent:** Chesapeake. **SIC:** 2621—Paper Mills; 2611—Pulp Mills; 2631—Paperboard Mills; 2653—Corrugated & Solid Fiber Boxes; 2421—Sawmills & Planing Mills—General; 2426—Hardwood Dimension & Flooring Mills.

★ 91758 ★ **Chesapeake**
1021 E. Cary St.
Richmond, VA 23218
(804)697-1000
Company Type: Headquarters. **Officer:** J. Carter Fox. **Sales:** 885 M. **Fortune 500:** Largest U.S. Industrial Corporations: Ranking 388.

★ 91759 ★ **Chesapeake**
Packaging
2104 W. Laburnum Ave., Ste. 209
Richmond, VA 23227
(804)353-6400 **Fax:** (804)355-4968
Officer: Robert F. Schick, President. **Ultimate Parent:** Chesapeake.

★ 91760 ★ **Chesapeake Consumer Products Co.**
1021 E. Cary St., 22nd Floor
PO Box 2350
Richmond, VA 23218-2350
Officer: William A. Raaths, President. **Ultimate Parent:** Chesapeake.

★ 91761 ★ **Chesapeake Corp.**
1021 E. Cary St., 22nd Floor
PO Box 2350
Richmond, VA 23218-2350
(804)697-1000 **Fax:** (804)697-1199
Officer: J. Carter Fox, President & CEO.

Ultimate Parent: Chesapeake. **Employee Count:** 5000.

★ 91762 ★ **Chesapeake Forest Products Co.**
1021 E. Cary St., 22nd Floor
PO Box 2350
Richmond, VA 23218-2350
(804)843-5466
Officer: Thomas Blackburn, President. **Ultimate Parent:** Chesapeake.

★ 91763 ★ **Chesapeake Packaging Co.**
2104 W. Laburnum Ave.
Richmond, VA 23227-4357
(804)353-6500
Officer: Samuel Taylor, President. **Ultimate Parent:** Chesapeake. **SIC:** 2653—Corrugated & Solid Fiber Boxes.

★ 91764 ★ **Chesapeake & Patomac Telephone Co. of Virginia**
600 E. Main St.
Richmond, VA 23219
(804)225-6300 **Fax:** (804)772-2796
Company Type: Subsidiary. **Officer:** Hugh R. Stallard, President & CEO. **Ultimate Parent:** Bell Atlantic Corp.

★ 91765 ★ **Chesapeake & Potomac Telephone Co.**
3805 Cutshaw Ave. 400
Richmond, VA 23230-3939
(804)358-5200
Company Type: Subsidiary. **Location Type:** Headquarters. **Officer:** Lew Slusher. **Ultimate Parent:** Bell Atlantic Corp. **SIC:** 6061—Federal Credit Unions.

★ 91766 ★ **Chesapeake & Potomac Telephone Co.**
6917 Patterson AV
Richmond, VA 23226-3627
(804)772-5606
Company Type: Subsidiary. **Location Type:** Branch office. **Ultimate Parent:** Bell Atlantic Corp. **SIC:** 4813—Telephone Communications Except Radiotelephone.

★ 91767 ★ **Chesapeake & Potomac Telephone Co.**
600 E. Main St.
Richmond, VA 23219-2441
(804)772-2000
Company Type: Subsidiary. **Location Type:** Branch office. **Officer:** Hubert R. Stallard. **Ultimate Parent:** Bell Atlantic Corp. **SIC:** 4812—Radiotelephone Communications; 4813—Telephone Communications Except Radiotelephone.

★ 91768 ★ **The Chesapeake & Potomac Telephone Co. of Virginia**
600 E. Main St.
Richmond, VA 23219-2441
(804)225-6300
Company Type: Subsidiary. **Officer:** Hubert R. Stallard, President & CEO. **Ultimate Parent:** Bell Atlantic Corp. **SIC:** 4813—Telephone Communications Except Radiotelephone; 7389—Business Services Nec. **Employee Count:** 7626. **Sales:** 2 M.

★ 91769 ★ **The Chesapeake & Potomic Co. of Virginia**
600 E. Main St.
Richmond, VA 23219
(804)772-2000
Company Type: Subsidiary. **Officer:** Hobert R. Stallard, President & CEO. **Ultimate Parent:** Bell Atlantic Corp. **SIC:** 4812—Radiotelephone Communications. **Employee Count:** 10000. **Sales:** 1545000000 M.

★ 91770 ★ **Chesapeake Wood Treating Co.**
1021 E. Cary St., 22nd Floor
PO Box 2350
Richmond, VA 23218-2350
Officer: Michael H. Sloane, President. **Ultimate Parent:** Chesapeake.

★ 91771 ★ **Circuit City**
8401 Midlothian Tpke.
Richmond, VA 23235
(804)320-8888
Ultimate Parent: Circuit City Stores. **SIC:** 5722—Household Appliance Stores; 7622—Radio & T.V. Repair.

★ 91772 ★　Circuit City
2040 Thalbro St.
Richmond, VA 23230
(804)527-4000
Ultimate Parent: Circuit City Stores. SIC:
5722—Household Appliance Stores.

★ 91773 ★　Circuit City
PO Box 14836
Richmond, VA 23221
(804)747-9953
Ultimate Parent: Circuit City Stores. SIC:
7629—Electrical Repair Shops Nec.

★ 91774 ★　Circuit City
9950 Mayland Drive
Richmond, VA 23233
(804)527-4000
Ultimate Parent: Circuit City Stores.

★ 91775 ★　Circuit City Stores
9950 Mayland Dr.
Richmond, VA 23233
(804)527-4000
Company Type: Headquarters. Officer:
Richard L. Sharp. Fortune Service 500:
Ranking 41.

**★ 91776 ★　Circuit City Stores,
Inc.**
9950 Maryland Dr.
Richmond, VA 23233-4164
(804)527-4000 Fax: (804)527-4173
Officer: Richard L. Sharp, President &
CEO. Ultimate Parent: Circuit City Stores.
Employee Count: 19848.

★ 91777 ★　Citgo Petroleum Corp.
6824 Forest Hill Ave.
Richmond, VA 23225
(804)320-7252
Ultimate Parent: Citgo Petroleum. SIC:
1311—Crude Petroleum & Natural Gas.

★ 91778 ★　Citgo Petroleum Corp.
6824 Forest Hill Ave.
Richmond, VA 23225
(804)320-7252
Ultimate Parent: Citgo Petroleum. SIC:
1311—Crude Petroleum & Natural Gas.

**★ 91779 ★　Citgo Self Service
Station**
3600 W. Cary St.
Richmond, VA 23221
(804)359-4805
Ultimate Parent: Citgo Petroleum. SIC:
5541—Gasoline Service Stations.

★ 91780 ★　Citgo Service Station
2109 Jefferson Davis Hwy.
Richmond, VA 23224
(804)231-5797
Ultimate Parent: Citgo Petroleum. SIC:
5541—Gasoline Service Stations.

★ 91781 ★　Colonial Pipeline Co.
2607 Willard Rd.
Richmond, VA 23294
(804)288-3077
Ultimate Parent: Colonial Pipeline. SIC:
4619—Pipelines Nec.

**★ 91782 ★　Colonial Pipeline Co.
Inc.**
5001 W. Broad St.
Richmond, VA 23230
(804)282-9771
Ultimate Parent: Colonial Pipeline. SIC:
1623—Water, Sewer & Utility Lines.

★ 91783 ★　Colony Insurance Co.
33 Lambert Hwy.
Richmond, VA 23234
(804)732-0890
Company Type: Subsidiary. Ultimate
Parent: Figgie International. SIC: 6211—
Security Brokers & Dealers.

★ 91784 ★　Color Response Inc.
705 Twinridge Ln.
Richmond, VA 23235-5270
(804)330-0200
Ultimate Parent: Banta Corp. SIC: 2752—
Commercial Printing—Lithographic; 2796—
Platemaking Services.

**★ 91785 ★　Columbia Propane
Corp.**
800 Moorefield Park Dr.
Richmond, VA 23236-3659
(804)323-5394
Company Type: Subsidiary. Officer:
Mason Brent, President. Ultimate Parent:
Columbia Gas System. SIC: 5984—

Liquefied Petroleum Gas Dealers.
Employee Count: 43.

**★ 91786 ★　Commonwealth Gas
Services Inc.**
800 Moorefield Park Dr.
Richmond, VA 23236-3659
(804)323-5300
Company Type: Subsidiary. Officer: C.
Ronald Tilley, Chairman of the Board.
Ultimate Parent: Columbia Gas System.
SIC: 4924—Natural Gas Distribution.
Employee Count: 401.

**★ 91787 ★　Commonwealth
Propane, Inc.**
800 Moorefield Park Dr.
Richmond, VA 23236
(804)323-5300 Fax: (804)323-5307
Officer: A. Mason Brent, President.
Ultimate Parent: Columbia Gas System.

**★ 91788 ★　Conagra Pet Products
Co.**
2258 Darbytown Rd.
Richmond, VA 23231
Ultimate Parent: Conagra. SIC: 2879—
Agricultural Chemicals Nec.

★ 91789 ★　Copy Van, Inc.
2211 Dickens Rd.
Richmond, VA 23230
(804)285-7841 Fax: (804)285-4549
Company Type: Division. Officer: Thomas
J. Kemp, President. Ultimate Parent: Alco
Standard Corp. SIC: 5044—Office
Equipment; 5046—Commercial Equipment
Nec.

★ 91790 ★　Copy Van Inc.
2211 Dickens Rd.
Richmond, VA 23230-2005
(804)285-7841
Officer: Tom Kemp. Ultimate Parent: Alco
Standard Corp. SIC: 5044—Office
Equipment; 5084—Industrial Machinery &
Equipment; 5999—Miscellaneous Retail
Stores Nec.

★ 91791 ★　Copy Van Inc.
2211 Dickens Rd.
Richmond, VA 23230
(804)285-7841
Officer: Tom Kemp, President. Ultimate
Parent: Alco Standard Corp. SIC: 2761—
Manifold Business Forms.

★ 91792 ★　Courtyard by Marriott
6400 W. Broad St.
Richmond, VA 23230
(804)282-1881
Ultimate Parent: Marriott International. SIC:
7011—Hotels & Motels.

★ 91793 ★　Crestar Bank
919 E. Main St.
Richmond, VA 23219-4625
(804)782-5000
Company Type: Subsidiary. Ultimate
Parent: Crestar Financial Corp. SIC:
6022—State Commercial Banks; 6162—
Mortgage Bankers & Correspondents.

★ 91794 ★　Crestar Bank
1131 Gaskins Rd.
Richmond, VA 23233-5227
(804)782-7276
Location Type: Branch office. Ultimate
Parent: Crestar Financial Corp. SIC:
6021—National Commercial Banks.

★ 91795 ★　Crestar Bank
2694 Williamsburg Rd.
Richmond, VA 23231-2031
(804)782-5736
Location Type: Branch office. Ultimate
Parent: Crestar Financial Corp. SIC:
6021—National Commercial Banks.

★ 91796 ★　Crestar Bank
1601 Willow Lawn Dr.
Richmond, VA 23230-3403
(804)782-5535
Location Type: Branch office. Ultimate
Parent: Crestar Financial Corp. SIC:
6021—National Commercial Banks.

★ 91797 ★　Crestar Bank
6501 W. Broad St.
Richmond, VA 23230-2013
(804)782-5533
Location Type: Branch office. Ultimate
Parent: Crestar Financial Corp. SIC:
6021—National Commercial Banks.

★ 91798 ★　Crestar Bank
4307 williamsburg Rd.
Richmond, VA 23231-2798
(804)782-7316
Location Type: Branch office. Ultimate
Parent: Crestar Financial Corp. SIC:
6021—National Commercial Banks.

★ 91799 ★　Crestar Bank
9072 W. Broad St.
Richmond, VA 23294
(804)782-7396
Location Type: Branch office. Ultimate
Parent: Crestar Financial Corp. SIC:
6021—National Commercial Banks.

★ 91800 ★　Crestar Bank
Staples Mill Rd. & 1601 Glenside Dr.
Richmond, VA 23228
(804)782-5141
Location Type: Branch office. Ultimate
Parent: Crestar Financial Corp. SIC:
6021—National Commercial Banks.

★ 91801 ★　Crestar Bank
1500 Parham Rd.
Richmond, VA 23229-4675
(804)782-7203
Location Type: Branch office. Ultimate
Parent: Crestar Financial Corp. SIC:
6021—National Commercial Banks.

★ 91802 ★　Crestar Bank
3022 W. Broad St.
Richmond, VA 23230-5105
(804)782-5587
Location Type: Branch office. Ultimate
Parent: Crestar Financial Corp. SIC:
6021—National Commercial Banks.

★ 91803 ★　Crestar Bank
8201 Brook Rd.
Richmond, VA 23227-1309
(804)782-5802
Location Type: Branch office. Ultimate
Parent: Crestar Financial Corp. SIC:
6021—National Commercial Banks.

★ 91804 ★　Crestar Bank
11501 E. Broad St.
Richmond, VA 23233
(804)273-7416
Location Type: Branch office. Ultimate
Parent: Crestar Financial Corp. SIC:
6021—National Commercial Banks.

★ 91805 ★　Crestar Bank
1810 W. Broad St.
Richmond, VA 23220-2192
(804)782-5301
Location Type: Branch office. Ultimate
Parent: Crestar Financial Corp. SIC:
6021—National Commercial Banks.

★ 91806 ★　Crestar Bank
424 E. Grace St.
Richmond, VA 23219-1838
(804)782-5462
Location Type: Branch office. Ultimate
Parent: Crestar Financial Corp. SIC:
6021—National Commercial Banks.

★ 91807 ★　Crestar Bank
2500 E. Broad St.
Richmond, VA 23223-7131
(804)782-5387
Location Type: Branch office. Ultimate
Parent: Crestar Financial Corp. SIC:
6021—National Commercial Banks.

★ 91808 ★　Crestar Bank
1101 Azalea Ave.
Richmond, VA 23227-3411
(804)782-5492
Location Type: Branch office. Ultimate
Parent: Crestar Financial Corp. SIC:
6021—National Commercial Banks.

★ 91809 ★　Crestar Bank
1518 Hull St.
Richmond, VA 23224-3898
(804)782-5422
Location Type: Branch office. Ultimate
Parent: Crestar Financial Corp. SIC:
6021—National Commercial Banks.

★ 91810 ★　Crestar Bank
7133 Forest Hill Ave.
Richmond, VA 23225-1588
(804)782-5673
Location Type: Branch office. Ultimate
Parent: Crestar Financial Corp. SIC:
6021—National Commercial Banks.

★ 91811 ★　Crestar Bank
3513 W. Cary St.
Richmond, VA 23221-2728
(804)782-5161
Location Type: Branch office. Ultimate
Parent: Crestar Financial Corp. SIC:
6021—National Commercial Banks.

★ 91812 ★　Crestar Bank
5419 Lakeside Ave.
Richmond, VA 23228-6009
(804)378-1202
Location Type: Branch office. Ultimate
Parent: Crestar Financial Corp.

★ 91813 ★　Crestar Bank
4708 Forest Hill Ave.
Richmond, VA 23225-3180
(804)782-5561
Location Type: Branch office. Ultimate
Parent: Crestar Financial Corp. SIC:
6021—National Commercial Banks.

★ 91814 ★　Crestar Bank
2613 Parham Rd.
Richmond, VA 23294-4650
(804)378-1207
Location Type: Branch office. Ultimate
Parent: Crestar Financial Corp. SIC:
6021—National Commercial Banks.

★ 91815 ★　Crestar Bank
5601 Patterson Ave.
Richmond, VA 23226-2007
(804)378-1204
Location Type: Branch office. Ultimate
Parent: Crestar Financial Corp. SIC:
6021—National Commercial Banks.

★ 91816 ★　Crestar Bank
1624 Hull St.
Richmond, VA 23224-3806
(804)378-1203
Location Type: Branch office. Ultimate
Parent: Crestar Financial Corp. SIC:
6021—National Commercial Banks.

★ 91817 ★　Crestar Bank
14 N. Laburnum Ave.
Richmond, VA 23223-5702
(804)378-1208
Location Type: Branch office. Ultimate
Parent: Crestar Financial Corp. SIC:
6021—National Commercial Banks.

★ 91818 ★　Crestar Bank
10710 Midlothian Tpke.
Richmond, VA 23235-0811
(804)378-1201
Location Type: Branch office. Ultimate
Parent: Crestar Financial Corp. SIC:
6021—National Commercial Banks.

★ 91819 ★　Crestar Bank
550 E. Marshall St.
Richmond, VA 23219
(804)378-1200
Location Type: Branch office. Ultimate
Parent: Crestar Financial Corp. SIC:
6021—National Commercial Banks.

★ 91820 ★　Crestar Bank
4830 Jefferson Davis Hwy.
Richmond, VA 23234
(804)782-5621
Location Type: Branch office. Ultimate
Parent: Crestar Financial Corp. SIC:
6021—National Commercial Banks.

★ 91821 ★　Crestar Bank
10300 Midlothian Tpke.
Richmond, VA 23235-4406
(804)782-7090
Location Type: Branch office. Ultimate
Parent: Crestar Financial Corp. SIC:
6021—National Commercial Banks.

★ 91822 ★　Crestar Bank
13001 Hull St. Rd.
Richmond, VA 23112-2617
(804)782-5036
Location Type: Branch office. Ultimate
Parent: Crestar Financial Corp. SIC:
6021—National Commercial Banks.

★ 91823 ★　Crestar Bank
2065 Huguenot Rd.
Richmond, VA 23235-4358
(804)782-7393
Location Type: Branch office. Ultimate
Parent: Crestar Financial Corp. SIC:
6021—National Commercial Banks.

★ 91824 ★ Crestar Bank
1206 Willow Lawn Dr.
Richmond, VA 23230
(804)273-7515
Location Type: Branch office. Ultimate Parent: Crestar Financial Corp. SIC: 6021—National Commercial Banks.

★ 91825 ★ Crestar Bank
12199 Grayton Rd.
Richmond, VA 23233
(804)273-7520
Location Type: Branch office. Ultimate Parent: Crestar Financial Corp. SIC: 6021—National Commercial Banks.

★ 91826 ★ Crestar Bank
901 E. Byrd St., Ste. 130
Richmond, VA 23219-3319
(804)782-9102
Location Type: Branch office. Ultimate Parent: Crestar Financial Corp. SIC: 6021—National Commercial Banks.

★ 91827 ★ Crestar Bank
6845 Midlothian Tpke.
Richmond, VA 23225-5809
(804)782-5130
Location Type: Branch office. Ultimate Parent: Crestar Financial Corp. SIC: 6021—National Commercial Banks.

★ 91828 ★ Crestar Bank
3631 Mechanicsville Tpke.
Richmond, VA 23223
(804)343-9129
Location Type: Branch office. Ultimate Parent: Crestar Financial Corp. SIC: 6021—National Commercial Banks.

★ 91829 ★ Crestar Bank
5801 Patterson Ave.
Richmond, VA 23226
(804)273-7530
Location Type: Branch office. Ultimate Parent: Crestar Financial Corp. SIC: 6021—National Commercial Banks.

★ 91830 ★ Crestar Bank
PO Box 26665
Richmond, VA 23261-6665
Location Type: Branch office. Ultimate Parent: Crestar Financial Corp. SIC: 6021—National Commercial Banks.

★ 91831 ★ Crestar Financial Corp.
PO Box 26665
Richmond, VA 23261-6665
Location Type: Branch office. Ultimate Parent: Crestar Financial Corp.

★ 91832 ★ Crestar Financial Corp.
919 E. Main St.
Richmond, VA 23261
(804)782-5000
Company Type: Headquarters. Officer: Richard G. Tilghman. Employee Count: 6500. Fortune Service 500: Ranking 49.

★ 91833 ★ Crestar Morgage Corp.
2108 W. Laburnum Ave.
Richmond, VA 23227-4342
(804)254-1741
Company Type: Subsidiary. Ultimate Parent: Crestar Financial Corp. SIC: 6162—Mortgage Bankers & Correspondents.

★ 91834 ★ Crestar Securities Corp.
919 E. Main St., Ste. 19
Richmond, VA 23219-4625
(804)782-7036
Company Type: Subsidiary. Ultimate Parent: Crestar Financial Corp. SIC: 6211—Security Brokers & Dealers.

★ 91835 ★ CSX Corp.
1 James Ctr., 901 E. Cary St.
PO Box 85629
Richmond, VA 23285-5629
(804)782-1400 Fax: (804)782-1409
Officer: John W. Snow, Chairman of the Board, President & CEO. Ultimate Parent: CSX Corp. Employee Count: 47598.

★ 91836 ★ CSX Corp.
901 E. Cary St.
Richmond, VA 23219
(804)782-1400
Company Type: Headquarters. Officer:

John W. Snow. Employee Count: 47063. Fortune Service 500: Ranking 5.

★ 91837 ★ CSX Corp.
1 James Ctr.
Richmond, VA 23219
(804)782-1400
Officer: John W. Snow, Chairman of the Board & President. Ultimate Parent: CSX Corp. SIC: 4011—Railroads—Line-Haul Operating; 4412—Deep Sea Foreign Transportation of Freight; 4424—Deep Sea Domestic Transportation of Freight; 4491—Marine Cargo Handling; 4214—Local Trucking With Storage; 4449—Water Transportation of Freight Nec. Employee Count: 47598. Sales: 9 M.

★ 91838 ★ CSX Realty Inc.
901 E. Cary St.
Richmond, VA 23219-1442
(804)782-1442
Company Type: Subsidiary. Officer: richard L. Beadles, President. Ultimate Parent: CSX Corp. SIC: 6531—Real Estate Agents & Managers. Employee Count: 12. Sales: 610 M.

★ 91839 ★ Dean Foods Co.
2000 W. Broad St.
Richmond, VA 23220-2006
(804)359-5786
Company Type: Subsidiary. Officer: Conrad F. Sauer IV, President. Ultimate Parent: Dean Foods. SIC: 2079—Edible Fats & Oils Nec. Employee Count: 56. Sales: 34 M.

★ 91840 ★ Delta Air Lines Inc.
5004 Monument Ave.
Richmond, VA 23230
(804)358-7661
Ultimate Parent: Delta Air Lines, Inc. SIC: 4513—Air Courier Services; 4729—Passenger Transportation Arrangement Nec.

★ 91841 ★ Delta Air Lines Inc.
Byrd International Airport
Richmond, VA 23231
(804)222-3677
Ultimate Parent: Delta Air Lines, Inc. SIC: 4512—Air Transportation—Scheduled.

★ 91842 ★ Deluxe Check Printers
3405 Commerce Rd.
Richmond, VA 23234
Ultimate Parent: Deluxe Corp. SIC: 2782—Blankbooks & Looseleaf Binders; 2752—Commercial Printing—Lithographic.

★ 91843 ★ Deluxe Check Printers Inc.
3405 Commerce Rd.
Richmond, VA 23234-1814
Ultimate Parent: Deluxe Corp. SIC: 2782—Blankbooks & Looseleaf Binders; 2752—Commercial Printing—Lithographic.

★ 91844 ★ Digital Equipment Corp.
2809 Emerywood Pky.
Richmond, VA 23294
(804)756-1700
Ultimate Parent: Digital Equipment Corp. SIC: 5046—Commercial Equipment Nec; 7373—Computer Integrated Systems Design.

★ 91845 ★ Dominion Capital Inc.
Riverfront Plz. W.
901 E. Byrd St.
Ste. 1700
Richmond, VA
(804)775-5700 Fax: (804)775-5819
Company Type: Subsidiary. Officer: O. James Peterson III, President. Ultimate Parent: Dominion Resources.

★ 91846 ★ Dominion Capital Inc.
PO Box 26532
Richmond, VA 23261
(804)775-5700
Company Type: Subsidiary. Ultimate Parent: Dominion Resources. SIC: 6159—Miscellaneous Business Credit Institutions.

★ 91847 ★ Dominion Energy Inc.
Riverfront Plz. W.
901 E. Byrd St.
Ste. 1700
Richmond, VA 23219
(804)775-5700 Fax: (804)775-5819
Company Type: Subsidiary. Officer:

Lyndall L. Baucon, President & CEO. Ultimate Parent: Dominion Resources.

★ 91848 ★ Dominion Energy Inc.
PO Box 23261
Richmond, VA 23261
(804)775-5814
Company Type: Subsidiary. Ultimate Parent: Dominion Resources. SIC: 1382—Oil & Gas Exploration Services.

★ 91849 ★ Dominion Energy Services Co.
PO Box 26532
Richmond, VA 23261
(804)775-5814
Company Type: Subsidiary. Ultimate Parent: Dominion Resources.

★ 91850 ★ Dominion Financing Inc.
PO Box 26532
Richmond, VA 23261
(804)775-5700
Company Type: Subsidiary. Ultimate Parent: Dominion Resources. SIC: 6159—Miscellaneous Business Credit Institutions.

★ 91851 ★ Dominion Lands Inc.
Riverfront Plz. W.
901 E. Byrd St.
Ste. 1700
Richmond, VA 23219
(804)775-5700 Fax: (804)775-5819
Company Type: Subsidiary. Officer: Donald T. Herrick Jr., President. Ultimate Parent: Dominion Resources.

★ 91852 ★ Dominion Lands Inc.
PO Box 26532
Richmond, VA 23261
(804)775-5893
Company Type: Subsidiary. Ultimate Parent: Dominion Resources. SIC: 6531—Real Estate Agents & Managers.

★ 91853 ★ Dominion Lands Inc.
901 E. Byrd St.
Richmond, VA 23219-4069
(804)775-5700
Company Type: Subsidiary. Ultimate Parent: Dominion Resources. SIC: 6552—Subdividers & Developers Nec.

★ 91854 ★ Dominion Resources
Riverfront Plz. W.
901 E. Byrd St.
Ste. 1700
Richmond, VA 23219
(804)775-5700 Fax: (804)775-5819
Company Type: Headquarters. Officer: Thos. E. Capps, Chairman, President & CEO. Ultimate Parent: Dominion Resources. Employee Count: 12217. Sales: Exceeds12Bill. M.

★ 91855 ★ Dominion Resources
901 E. Byrd St.
Richmond, VA 23219
(804)775-5700
Company Type: Headquarters. Officer: Thomas E. Capps. Employee Count: 12057. Fortune Service 500: Ranking 20.

★ 91856 ★ Dominion Resources Inc.
Riverfront Plz., W. Tower, 901 E. Byrd St.
Richmond, VA 23219
(804)775-5700 Fax: (804)775-5819
Company Type: Headquarters. Ultimate Parent: Dominion Resources. SIC: 6719—Holding Companies Nec; 4931—Electric & Other Services Combined.

★ 91857 ★ Dominion Resources Inc.
PO Box 26532
Richmond, VA 23261
Company Type: Headquarters. Ultimate Parent: Dominion Resources.

★ 91858 ★ Dominion Resources Inc.
901 E. Byrd St.
Richmond, VA 23219-4069
(804)775-5700
Ultimate Parent: Dominion Resources. SIC: 4911—Electric Services; 1311—Crude Petroleum & Natural Gas; 6552—Subdividers & Developers Nec; 8741—Management Services; 6799—Investors Nec.

★ 91859 ★ Dominion Resources Inc. VA
901 E. Byrd St.
Richmond, VA 23219-6532
(804)775-5700
Ultimate Parent: Dominion Resources. SIC: 4911—Electric Services; 6719—Holding Companies Nec.

★ 91860 ★ E. R. Carpenter Co. Inc.
2400 Jefferson Davis Hwy.
Richmond, VA 23234
Ultimate Parent: Carpenter. SIC: 3086—Plastics Foam Products; 2297—Nonwoven Fabrics.

★ 91861 ★ Ethyl
330 S. 4th St.
Richmond, VA 23217
(804)788-5000
Company Type: Headquarters. Officer: Bruce C. Gottwald. Employee Count: 5500. Sales: 2676 M. Fortune 500: Largest U.S. Industrial Corporations: Ranking 177.

★ 91862 ★ Ethyl Corp.
330 S. 4th St.
PO Box 2189
Richmond, VA 23219-4304
(804)788-5000
Officer: Floyd D. Gottwald Jr., Chairman of the Board. Ultimate Parent: Ethyl. SIC: 2869—Industrial Organic Chemicals Nec; 2865—Cyclic Crudes & Intermediates; 2812—Alkalies & Chlorine; 2819—Industrial Inorganic Chemicals Nec; 2911—Petroleum Refining; 6311—Life Insurance; 2824—Organic Fibers—Noncellulosic; 2899—Chemical Preparations Nec.

★ 91863 ★ Ethyl Corp.
330 S. Fourth St.
POB 2189
Richmond, VA 23217
(804)788-5000 Fax: (804)788-5688
Company Type: Headquarters. Officer: Floyd D. Gottwald Jr., Chairman. Ultimate Parent: Ethyl. Employee Count: 6300.

★ 91864 ★ Ethyl Petroleum Additives Inc.
203 E. Cary St.
Richmond, VA 23219-3736
(804)788-6400
Company Type: Subsidiary. Officer: Thomas E. Gottwald, President. Ultimate Parent: Ethyl. SIC: 2899—Chemical Preparations Nec. Employee Count: 460. Sales: 762 M.

★ 91865 ★ Exxon Car Care Center
8601 Patterson Ave.
Richmond, VA 23229
(804)740-7226
Ultimate Parent: Exxon. SIC: 7538—General Automotive Repair Shops.

★ 91866 ★ Exxon Co.
2000 Trenton Ave.
Richmond, VA 23234
(804)743-0100
Ultimate Parent: Exxon. SIC: 2911—Petroleum Refining.

★ 91867 ★ Exxon Corp.
4810 Forest Hill Ave.
Richmond, VA 23225
(804)232-0237
Ultimate Parent: Exxon. SIC: 5541—Gasoline Service Stations.

★ 91868 ★ Exxon Self Service Station
10031 Hull St.
Richmond, VA 23236
(804)276-1667
Ultimate Parent: Exxon. SIC: 5541—Gasoline Service Stations.

★ 91869 ★ Exxon Self Service Station
Willis Rd.
Richmond, VA 23237
(804)275-2176
Ultimate Parent: Exxon. SIC: 5541—Gasoline Service Stations.

★ 91870 ★ Exxon Shop
4900 W. Broad St.
Richmond, VA 23230
(804)359-8651
Ultimate Parent: Exxon. SIC: 5541—Gasoline Service Stations.

★ 91871 ★ **Federal Paper Board Co. Inc.**
1850 E. Commerce Rd.
Richmond, VA 23224
(804)233-5411
Ultimate Parent: Federal Paper Board.
SIC: 5093—Scrap & Waste Materials;
5084—Industrial Machinery & Equipment.

★ 91872 ★ **Ffrl Re Corp.**
6610 W. Broad St.
Richmond, VA 23230-1702
(804)281-6000
Officer: Dennis a. Catanzano, President.
Ultimate Parent: Aon Corp. **SIC:** 6411—
Insurance Agents, Brokers & Service.

★ 91873 ★ **First Colony Life**
Riverfront Plz., W. Tower, Ste. 1350
901 E. Byrd St.
Richmond, VA 23219
Officer: Bruce C. Gottwald, CEO. **Ultimate
Parent:** First Colony Life. **SIC:** 6311—Life
Insurance; 6719—Holding Companies Nec.

★ 91874 ★ **First Union National Bank of Virginia**
5630 Hopkins Rd.
Richmond, VA 23234-6612
(804)788-9630
Location Type: Branch office. **Ultimate
Parent:** First Union Corp. **SIC:** 6021—
National Commercial Banks.

★ 91875 ★ **First Union National Bank of Virginia**
901 E. Cary St.
Richmond, VA 23219-4057
(804)788-9601
Location Type: Branch office. **Ultimate
Parent:** First Union Corp. **SIC:** 6021—
National Commercial Banks.

★ 91876 ★ **First Union National Bank of Virginia**
5001 W. Broad St.
Richmond, VA 23230-3003
(804)281-7120
Location Type: Branch office. **Ultimate
Parent:** First Union Corp. **SIC:** 6021—
National Commercial Banks.

★ 91877 ★ **First Union National Bank of Virginia**
3508 W. Cary St.
Richmond, VA 23221-2729
(804)788-9772
Location Type: Branch office. **Ultimate
Parent:** First Union Corp. **SIC:** 6021—
National Commercial Banks.

★ 91878 ★ **First Union National Bank of Virginia**
5900 Midlothian Tpke.
Richmond, VA 23225-5918
(804)233-1696
Location Type: Branch office. **Ultimate
Parent:** First Union Corp. **SIC:** 6021—
National Commercial Banks.

★ 91879 ★ **First Union National Bank of Virginia**
8727 Staples Mill Rd.
Richmond, VA 23228-2730
(804)261-5430
Location Type: Branch office. **Ultimate
Parent:** First Union Corp. **SIC:** 6021—
National Commercial Banks.

★ 91880 ★ **First Union National Bank of Virginia**
1701 Parham Rd.
Richmond, VA 23229-4606
(804)281-7130
Location Type: Branch office. **Ultimate
Parent:** First Union Corp. **SIC:** 6021—
National Commercial Banks.

★ 91881 ★ **First Union National Bank of Virginia**
10831 Midlothian Tpke.
Richmond, VA 23235-4705
(804)378-9690
Location Type: Branch office. **Ultimate
Parent:** First Union Corp. **SIC:** 6021—
National Commercial Banks.

★ 91882 ★ **First Virginia Bank**
Colonial
700 E. Main St.
Richmond, VA 23219-2053
(804)697-5200
Company Type: Subsidiary. **Officer:** L. H.
Ginn III, Chairman of the Board. **Ultimate**

Parent: First Virginia Banks Inc. **SIC:**
6022—State Commercial Banks.

★ 91883 ★ **First Virginia Bank - Colonial**
700 E. Main St.
Richmond, VA 23219-2619
(804)697-5200
Company Type: Subsidiary. **Officer:**
William H. McFaddin, President, CEO.
Ultimate Parent: First Virginia Banks Inc.
SIC: 6022—State Commercial Banks.
Employee Count: 207.

★ 91884 ★ **Fluor Daniel Inc.**
9200 Arboretum Pky.
Richmond, VA 23236
(804)330-5200
Ultimate Parent: Fluor. **SIC:** 8712—
Architectural Services.

★ 91885 ★ **Food Lion**
9033 W. Broad St.
Richmond, VA 23294
(804)270-0693
Ultimate Parent: Food Lion. **SIC:** 5411—
Grocery Stores.

★ 91886 ★ **Food Lion**
6201 Belmont Rd.
Richmond, VA 23234
(804)745-1095
Ultimate Parent: Food Lion. **SIC:** 5411—
Grocery Stores.

★ 91887 ★ **Food Lion**
8006 Buford Ct
Richmond, VA 23235
(804)330-7866
Ultimate Parent: Food Lion. **SIC:** 5411—
Grocery Stores.

★ 91888 ★ **Food Lion**
9157 Staples Mill Rd.
Richmond, VA 23228
(804)261-7977
Ultimate Parent: Food Lion. **SIC:** 5411—
Grocery Stores.

★ 91889 ★ **Food Lion**
11304 Midlothian Tpke.
Richmond, VA 23235
(804)379-1135
Ultimate Parent: Food Lion. **SIC:** 5411—
Grocery Stores.

★ 91890 ★ **Food Lion**
8910 Quioccasin Rd.
Richmond, VA 23229
(804)741-0600
Ultimate Parent: Food Lion. **SIC:** 5411—
Grocery Stores.

★ 91891 ★ **Food Lion**
6425 Iron Bridge Rd.
Richmond, VA 23234
(804)271-9885
Ultimate Parent: Food Lion. **SIC:** 5411—
Grocery Stores.

★ 91892 ★ **Food Lion Inc.**
8006 Buford Ct
Richmond, VA 23235
(804)330-7866
Ultimate Parent: Food Lion. **SIC:** 5411—
Grocery Stores.

★ 91893 ★ **Forth Financial Resources Ltd. Inc.**
6610 W. Broad St.
Richmond, VA 23230-1702
Officer: David O'Maley, President. **Ultimate
Parent:** Aon Corp. **SIC:** 6411—Insurance
Agents, Brokers & Service. **Employee
Count:** 15.

★ 91894 ★ **Fruehauf Corp.**
3210 W. Marshall St.
Richmond, VA 23230-4612
(804)355-7476
Location Type: Branch office. **Officer:**
John B. Throupe. **Ultimate Parent:** Terex
Corp. **SIC:** 5012—Automobiles & Other
Motor Vehicles; 5012—Automobiles & Other
Motor Vehicles.

★ 91895 ★ **Fruehauf Trailer Corp.**
3210 W. Marshall St.
Richmond, VA 23230-4612
(804)355-7476
Location Type: Branch office. **Officer:**
John B. Throupe. **Ultimate Parent:** Terex
Corp. **SIC:** 5012—Automobiles & Other
Motor Vehicles; 5012—Automobiles & Other
Motor Vehicles.

★ 91896 ★ **General American Life Insur**
1001 Chinaberry Blvd.
Richmond, VA 23225
(804)323-1990
Ultimate Parent: General American Life.
SIC: 6411—Insurance Agents, Brokers &
Service.

★ 91897 ★ **General Electric Co.**
9030 Stony Point Pky.
Richmond, VA 23235
(804)560-8600
Officer: Sherry Martin, Manager. **Ultimate
Parent:** General Electric. **SIC:** 3699—
Electrical Equipment & Supplies Nec.

★ 91898 ★ **General Electric Medical Sy**
2513 Grenoble Rd.
Richmond, VA 23294
(804)672-7551
Ultimate Parent: General Electric. **SIC:**
5047—Medical & Hospital Equipment.

★ 91899 ★ **Gravure Packaging Inc.**
4500 Savellen Rd.
Richmond, VA 23231
(804)222-1016
Officer: John S. Waring, President.
Ultimate Parent: Bemis Co., Inc. **SIC:**
2652—Setup Paperboard Boxes; 2657—
Folding Paperboard Boxes.

★ 91900 ★ **Greyhound Bus Lines**
412 E. Broad St.
Richmond, VA 23219
(804)643-0173
Ultimate Parent: Greyhound Lines Inc. **SIC:**
4131—Intercity & Rural Bus Transportation.

★ 91901 ★ **Greyhound Bus Lines**
2910 N. Blvd.
Richmond, VA 23230
(804)254-5904
Ultimate Parent: Greyhound Lines Inc. **SIC:**
4111—Local & Suburban Transit.

★ 91902 ★ **Hertz Rent-A-Car**
11 N. 4th St.
Richmond, VA 23219
(804)643-5055
Ultimate Parent: Hertz. **SIC:** 7514—
Passenger Car Rental.

★ 91903 ★ **Hit or Miss**
7516 W. Broad St.
Richmond, VA 23294
(804)282-4699
Ultimate Parent: TJX. **SIC:** 5621—
Women's Clothing Stores; 5651—Family
Clothing Stores.

★ 91904 ★ **Hit or Miss**
501 E. Grace St.
Richmond, VA 23219
(804)225-0858
Ultimate Parent: TJX. **SIC:** 5651—Family
Clothing Stores.

★ 91905 ★ **Hit or Miss**
7425 Midlothian Tpke.
Richmond, VA 23225
(804)745-6025
Ultimate Parent: TJX. **SIC:** 5621—
Women's Clothing Stores; 5651—Family
Clothing Stores.

★ 91906 ★ **Humana Health Care Plans**
4114 E. Parham Rd.
Richmond, VA 23228
(804)499-4131
Ultimate Parent: Humana. **SIC:** 6411—
Insurance Agents, Brokers & Service.

★ 91907 ★ **Huntington Mortgage Co.**
7275 Glen Forest Dr.
Richmond, VA 23226
(804)288-2700
Ultimate Parent: Huntington Bancshares.
SIC: 6162—Mortgage Bankers &
Correspondents.

★ 91908 ★ **Intel Corp.**
1504 Santa Rosa Rd.
Richmond, VA 23229
(804)282-5668
Ultimate Parent: Intel Corp. **SIC:** 7373—
Computer Integrated Systems Design.

★ 91909 ★ **Jafra Cosmetics**
1103 Hill Cir.
Richmond, VA 23229
(804)288-3482
Ultimate Parent: Gillette. **SIC:** 5999—
Miscellaneous Retail Stores Nec.

★ 91910 ★ **James River Corp.**
Filtration Products Div. Richmond
Tredegar St.
Richmond, VA 23219
Company Type: Division. **Ultimate Parent:**
James River Corp. of Virginia. **SIC:** 2621—
Paper Mills.

★ 91911 ★ **James River Corp.**
Filtration Products Div. Richmond
Tredegar St.
Richmond, VA 23219
Company Type: Division. **Ultimate Parent:**
James River Corp. of Virginia. **SIC:** 2621—
Paper Mills.

★ 91912 ★ **James River Corp. of Virginia**
120 Tredegar St.
Richmond, VA 23219
(804)644-5411
Company Type: Headquarters. **Officer:**
Robert C. Williams. **Employee Count:**
27000. **Sales:** 4650 M. **Fortune 500:**
Largest U.S. Industrial Corporations:
Ranking 113.

★ 91913 ★ **Kraft General Foods**
Frozen Foods Div.
3031 Norfolk St.
Richmond, VA 23230-4850
Company Type: Division. **Ultimate Parent:**
Philip Morris. **SIC:** 2024—Ice Cream &
Frozen Desserts.

★ 91914 ★ **Kraft General Foods Inc.**
National Dairy Products Corp.
3031 Norfolk St.
Richmond, VA 23230
Company Type: Division. **Ultimate Parent:**
Philip Morris. **SIC:** 2024—Ice Cream &
Frozen Desserts.

★ 91915 ★ **Lawyers Title Corp.**
6630 W. Broad St.
Richmond, VA 23260
(804)281-6700 **Fax:** (804)282-5453
Officer: Charles H. Faster Jr., CEO.
Ultimate Parent: Universal Corp.
Employee Count: 2800. **Sales:** 504 M.

★ 91916 ★ **Lenscrafters**
254 Willow Lawn
Richmond, VA 23230
(804)288-8938
Ultimate Parent: United States Shoe. **SIC:**
5995—Optical Goods Stores.

★ 91917 ★ **Lenscrafters**
Cloverleaf Mall
Richmond, VA 23225
(804)745-0173
Ultimate Parent: United States Shoe. **SIC:**
5995—Optical Goods Stores.

★ 91918 ★ **Life Insurance Co. of Virgin**
6604 W. Broad St.
Richmond, VA 23230
(804)288-3100
Ultimate Parent: Life Insurance Co. of
Virginia. **SIC:** 6411—Insurance Agents,
Brokers & Service.

★ 91919 ★ **Life Insurance Co. of Virginia**
6610 W. Broad St.
Richmond, VA 23261
(804)281-6000
Company Type: Headquarters. **Location
Type:** Branch office. **Officer:** Daniel T. Cox.
SIC: 6311—Life Insurance; 6231—Security
& Commodity Exchanges; 6411—Insurance
Agents, Brokers & Service. **Employee
Count:** 1101. **Fortune Service 500:**
Ranking 48.

★ 91920 ★ **Manville Sales Corp.**
7400 Ranco Rd.
Richmond, VA 23228
Ultimate Parent: Manville Corp. **SIC:**
2600—Paper & Allied Products.

★ 91921 ★   Mapco Coal Inc.
9603 Gayton Rd.
Richmond, VA 23233
(804)741-3900
Ultimate Parent: Mapco. **SIC:** 1221—
Bituminous Coal & Lignite—Surface; 5989—
Fuel Dealers Nec.

★ 91922 ★   Mapco Coals Inc.
1501 Santa Rosa Rd.
Richmond, VA 23229
(804)282-9064
Ultimate Parent: Mapco. **SIC:** 1221—
Bituminous Coal & Lignite—Surface.

★ 91923 ★   Mary Kay Cosmetics
7056 Mosswood Rd.
Richmond, VA 23231
(804)795-5569
Ultimate Parent: Mary Kay Cosmetics. **SIC:**
5999—Miscellaneous Retail Stores Nec.

★ 91924 ★   Mary Kay Cosmetics
6722 Carnation St. G
Richmond, VA 23225
(804)320-3802
Ultimate Parent: Mary Kay Cosmetics.

★ 91925 ★   Mary Kay Cosmetics
7644 Comanche Dr.
Richmond, VA 23225
(804)272-5297
Ultimate Parent: Mary Kay Cosmetics.

★ 91926 ★   Mary Kay Cosmetics
3430 Floyd Ave.
Richmond, VA 23221
(804)353-2668
Ultimate Parent: Mary Kay Cosmetics.

**★ 91927 ★   Mary Kay Cosmetics
Sr Direc**
8203 Lydell Dr.
Richmond, VA 23228
(804)266-5188
Ultimate Parent: Mary Kay Cosmetics. **SIC:**
5999—Miscellaneous Retail Stores Nec.

**★ 91928 ★   McDonald's
Hamburgers**
Stony Point Shopping Ctr.
Richmond, VA 23235
(804)323-4115
Ultimate Parent: McDonald's.

**★ 91929 ★   McDonald's
Hamburgers**
11280 Patterson Ave.
Richmond, VA 23233
(804)740-3094
Ultimate Parent: McDonald's. **SIC:** 5812—
Eating Places.

★ 91930 ★   Mead
Packaging Division
3105 W. Marshall St.
Richmond, VA 23230
(804)320-7085
Ultimate Parent: Mead. **SIC:** 5113—
Industrial & Personal Service Paper.

★ 91931 ★   Mil-Mor Media, Inc.
1407 Sherwood Ave.
Richmond, VA 23220
(804)257-2875 **Fax:** (804)257-2109
Company Type: Subsidiary. **Officer:** Carl
D. O'Hallahan, President. **Ultimate Parent:**
American Home Products. **SIC:** 8741—
Management Services.

★ 91932 ★   Mini Mart
3610 E. Broad Rock Rd.
Richmond, VA 23224
(804)230-9503
Ultimate Parent: Kroger. **SIC:** 5411—
Grocery Stores.

★ 91933 ★   Nabisco Biscuit Co.
6002 S. Laburnum Ave.
Richmond, VA 23231
Ultimate Parent: RJR Nabisco Holdings.
SIC: 2052—Cookies & Crackers.

★ 91934 ★   National Vendors
2325 W. Broad St.
Richmond, VA 23220
(804)358-7839
Ultimate Parent: Crane. **SIC:** 5046—
Commercial Equipment Nec.

**★ 91935 ★   New York Life
Insurance**
701 E. Franklin St.
Richmond, VA 23219
(804)643-0192
Ultimate Parent: New York Life. **SIC:**
6411—Insurance Agents, Brokers &
Service.

**★ 91936 ★   New York Life
Richmond General Office**
Southeastern Agencies
9100 Arboretum Pky., Ste. 350
Richmond, VA 23236
(804)320-7575 **Fax:** (804)320-6295
Officer: Peter B. Crane, General Manager.
Ultimate Parent: New York Life.

**★ 91937 ★   Northwestern Mutual
Life**
5009 PO Box
Richmond, VA 23220
(804)861-9301
Ultimate Parent: Northwestern Mutual Life.
SIC: 6411—Insurance Agents, Brokers &
Service.

**★ 91938 ★   Overnite
Transportation Co.**
1000 Semmes Ave.
Richmond, VA 23224
(804)231-8000
Ultimate Parent: Union Pacific Corp. **SIC:**
4213—Trucking Except Local; 4231—
Trucking Terminal Facilities; 4789—
Transportation Services Nec.

**★ 91939 ★   Owens-Corning
Fiberglass Corp.**
10800 Midlothian Tpke.
Richmond, VA 23235
(804)379-9127
Ultimate Parent: Owens-Corning. **SIC:**
5039—Construction Materials Nec.

★ 91940 ★   Parker Services Inc.
8533 Elm Rd.
Richmond, VA 23235
(804)272-4596
Ultimate Parent: Parker Hannifin. **SIC:**
0783—Ornamental Shrub & Tree Services.

**★ 91941 ★   Pepsi-Cola Bottling
Co.**
3008 Mechanicsville Tpke.
Richmond, VA 23223
(804)644-7032
Ultimate Parent: Pepsico. **SIC:** 2086—
Bottled & Canned Soft Drinks.

★ 91942 ★   Petite Sophisticate
Cloverleaf Mall
Richmond, VA 23225
(804)276-0117
Ultimate Parent: United States Shoe. **SIC:**
5651—Family Clothing Stores.

★ 91943 ★   Philip Morris USA
3601 Commerce Rd.
Richmond, VA 23234
(804)274-2000
Ultimate Parent: Philip Morris. **SIC:** 2131—
Chewing & Smoking Tobacco; 8231—
Libraries.

★ 91944 ★   Philip Morris USA
BI Plant
2301 Everett St.
Richmond, VA 23224
Location Type: Plant. **Ultimate Parent:**
Philip Morris. **SIC:** 2141—Tobacco
Stemming & Redrying.

**★ 91945 ★   Philip Morris USA
Mfg. Center**
3601 Commerce Rd.
Richmond, VA 23234
Ultimate Parent: Philip Morris. **SIC:** 2111—
Cigarettes.

★ 91946 ★   Phillip Morris USA
BI Plant
2301 Everett St.
Richmond, VA 23224
Location Type: Plant. **Ultimate Parent:**
Philip Morris. **SIC:** 2141—Tobacco
Stemming & Redrying.

★ 91947 ★   Phillip Morris USA
Westab Annex
702 Everett St.
Richmond, VA 23224
Company Type: Division. **Ultimate Parent:**
Philip Morris. **SIC:** 2111—Cigarettes.

**★ 91948 ★   Phillip Morris USA
Manufacturing Center**
3601 Commerce Rd.
Richmond, VA 23234
Ultimate Parent: Philip Morris. **SIC:** 2111—
Cigarettes.

★ 91949 ★   Phillips Investments
13 Dove Cove
Richmond, VA 23233
(804)784-3036
Ultimate Parent: Phillips Petroleum. **SIC:**
6531—Real Estate Agents & Managers.

★ 91950 ★   Pitney Bowes
1570 E. Parham Rd.
Richmond, VA 23228
(804)266-4187
Officer: Larry Killmeier, Manager. **Ultimate
Parent:** Pitney Bowes. **SIC:** 3554—Paper
Industries Machinery.

★ 91951 ★   Porter-Cable Corp.
1705 Dabney Rd.
Richmond, VA 23230
(804)257-7348
Ultimate Parent: Pentair. **SIC:** 5063—
Electrical Apparatus & Equipment; 5072—
Hardware.

**★ 91952 ★   Progressive Casualty
Insurance Co.**
1503 Santa Rosa Rd.
Richmond, VA 23229
(804)282-1422
Ultimate Parent: Progressive. **SIC:** 6411—
Insurance Agents, Brokers & Service.

★ 91953 ★   Radio Shack
7728 Midlothian Tpke.
Richmond, VA 23235
(804)272-8840
Company Type: Division. **Ultimate Parent:**
Tandy Corp. **SIC:** 5065—Electronic Parts &
Equipment Nec.

★ 91954 ★   Radio Shack
7514 W. Broad St.
Richmond, VA 23294
(804)672-7684
Company Type: Division. **Ultimate Parent:**
Tandy Corp. **SIC:** 5065—Electronic Parts &
Equipment Nec.

★ 91955 ★   Radio Shack
5748 Hopkins Rd.
Richmond, VA 23234
(804)271-9311
Company Type: Division. **Ultimate Parent:**
Tandy Corp. **SIC:** 5731—Radio, Television
& Electronics Stores.

★ 91956 ★   Radio Shack
7110 Hull St.
Richmond, VA 23235
(804)745-2135
Company Type: Division. **Ultimate Parent:**
Tandy Corp. **SIC:** 5731—Radio, Television
& Electronics Stores.

★ 91957 ★   Radio Shack
4795 Bethlehem Rd.
Richmond, VA 23230
(804)353-0794
Company Type: Division. **Ultimate Parent:**
Tandy Corp. **SIC:** 5065—Electronic Parts &
Equipment Nec; 7379—Computer Related
Services Nec.

★ 91958 ★   Radio Shack
11244 Patterson Ave.
Richmond, VA 23233
(804)740-2716
Company Type: Division. **Ultimate Parent:**
Tandy Corp. **SIC:** 5065—Electronic Parts &
Equipment Nec.

★ 91959 ★   Radio Shack
Merchants Walk Ctr.
Richmond, VA 23229
(804)672-7686
Company Type: Division. **Ultimate Parent:**
Tandy Corp. **SIC:** 5065—Electronic Parts &
Equipment Nec.

★ 91960 ★   Radio Shack
105 Regency Sq.
Richmond, VA 23229
(804)740-2139
Company Type: Division. **Ultimate Parent:**
Tandy Corp. **SIC:** 5731—Radio, Television
& Electronics Stores.

★ 91961 ★   Radio Shack
4826 Azalea Mall Shop Ctr.
Richmond, VA 23227
(804)262-0542
Company Type: Division. **Ultimate Parent:**
Tandy Corp. **SIC:** 5731—Radio, Television
& Electronics Stores.

★ 91962 ★   Radio Shack
7115 Staples Mill Rd.
Richmond, VA 23228
(804)262-0608
Company Type: Division. **Ultimate Parent:**
Tandy Corp. **SIC:** 5065—Electronic Parts &
Equipment Nec; 5731—Radio, Television &
Electronics Stores.

★ 91963 ★   Radio Shack
614 W. Southside Plz.
Richmond, VA 23224
(804)232-8280
Company Type: Division. **Ultimate Parent:**
Tandy Corp. **SIC:** 5065—Electronic Parts &
Equipment Nec.

★ 91964 ★   Radio Shack
Cloverleaf Mall
Richmond, VA 23225
(804)276-2062
Company Type: Division. **Ultimate Parent:**
Tandy Corp. **SIC:** 5731—Radio, Television
& Electronics Stores.

★ 91965 ★   Radio Shack
3822 Mechanicsville Pike
Richmond, VA 23223
(804)329-5531
Company Type: Division. **Ultimate Parent:**
Tandy Corp. **SIC:** 5731—Radio, Television
& Electronics Stores.

★ 91966 ★   Radio Shack
4709 Nine Mile Rd.
Richmond, VA 23223
(804)226-0725
Company Type: Division. **Ultimate Parent:**
Tandy Corp. **SIC:** 5065—Electronic Parts &
Equipment Nec; 5731—Radio, Television &
Electronics Stores.

★ 91967 ★   Radio Shack
7728 Midlothian Tpke.
Richmond, VA 23235
(804)272-8803
Company Type: Division. **Ultimate Parent:**
Tandy Corp. **SIC:** 7373—Computer
Integrated Systems Design.

★ 91968 ★   Radio Shack
102 Willow Lawn
Richmond, VA 23230
(804)282-3453
Company Type: Division. **Ultimate Parent:**
Tandy Corp. **SIC:** 7373—Computer
Integrated Systems Design.

★ 91969 ★   Radio Shack
1557 N. Parham Rd.
Richmond, VA 23229
(804)285-0734
Company Type: Division. **Ultimate Parent:**
Tandy Corp. **SIC:** 5731—Radio, Television
& Electronics Stores.

★ 91970 ★   Radio Shack
7801 W. Broad St. 23
Richmond, VA 23294
(804)282-3453
Company Type: Division. **Ultimate Parent:**
Tandy Corp. **SIC:** 5046—Commercial
Equipment Nec.

★ 91971 ★   Radio Shack
Chesterfield Mall
Richmond, VA 23225
(804)794-4931
Company Type: Division. **Ultimate Parent:**
Tandy Corp. **SIC:** 5731—Radio, Television
& Electronics Stores.

★ 91972 ★   Radio Shack
Regency Sq.
Richmond, VA 23229
(804)741-0589
Company Type: Division. **Ultimate Parent:**
Tandy Corp. **SIC:** 5046—Commercial
Equipment Nec.

★ 91973 ★   Radio Shack
Chesterfield Mall
Richmond, VA 23225
(804)794-4931
Company Type: Division. **Ultimate Parent:**
Tandy Corp. **SIC:** 5731—Radio, Television
& Electronics Stores.

★ 91974 ★ Radio Shack
4826 Azalea Mall Shopping Ctr.
Richmond, VA 23227
(804)262-0542
Company Type: Division. **Ultimate Parent:** Tandy Corp. **SIC:** 5731—Radio, Television & Electronics Stores.

★ 91975 ★ Radio Shack
102 Willow Lawn
Richmond, VA 23230
(804)282-3453
Company Type: Division. **Ultimate Parent:** Tandy Corp. **SIC:** 7373—Computer Integrated Systems Design.

★ 91976 ★ Radio Shack
1557 N. Parham Rd.
Richmond, VA 23229
(804)285-0734
Company Type: Division. **Ultimate Parent:** Tandy Corp. **SIC:** 5731—Radio, Television & Electronics Stores.

★ 91977 ★ Radio Shack
7801 W. Broad St. 23
Richmond, VA 23294
(804)282-3453
Company Type: Division. **Ultimate Parent:** Tandy Corp. **SIC:** 5046—Commercial Equipment Nec.

★ 91978 ★ Residence Inn by Marriott
2121 Dickens Rd.
Richmond, VA 23230
(804)285-8200
Ultimate Parent: Marriott International. **SIC:** 7011—Hotels & Motels.

★ 91979 ★ Reynolds Aluminum Bellwood Extrusion Plant
1901 Reymet Rd.
Richmond, VA 23237
Ultimate Parent: Reynolds Metals Co. **SIC:** 3354—Aluminum Extruded Products.

★ 91980 ★ Reynolds Bellwood Extrusion Plant
1901 Reymet Rd.
Richmond, VA 23237
Location Type: Plant. **Ultimate Parent:** Reynolds Metals Co. **SIC:** 3354—Aluminum Extruded Products.

★ 91981 ★ Reynolds Metals Co.
2001 Reymer Rd.
Richmond, VA 23237
(804)743-6730
Officer: Eugene Voss, Manager. **Ultimate Parent:** Reynolds Metals Co. **SIC:** 2671—Paper Coated & Laminated—Packaging.

★ 91982 ★ Reynolds Metals Co.
8310 Shell Rd.
Richmond, VA 23237
(804)743-5149
Location Type: Plant. **Officer:** Robert Messenger, Manager. **Ultimate Parent:** Reynolds Metals Co. **SIC:** 3444—Sheet Metal Work.

★ 91983 ★ Reynolds Metals Co.
2101 Reymet Rd.
Richmond, VA 23237
(804)743-6648
Ultimate Parent: Reynolds Metals Co. **SIC:** 2754—Commercial Printing—Gravure; 2759—Commercial Printing Nec; 3341—Secondary Nonferrous Metals.

★ 91984 ★ Reynolds Metals Co.
7th & Bainbridge
Richmond, VA 23224
(804)230-5299
Officer: Kerry Dean, Manager. **Ultimate Parent:** Reynolds Metals Co. **SIC:** 3353—Aluminum Sheet, Plate & Foil.

★ 91985 ★ Reynolds Metals Co.
6601 W. Broad St.
Richmond, VA 23230
(804)281-2000 **Fax:** (804)281-3695
Officer: Richard S. Halder, CEO. **Ultimate Parent:** Reynolds Metals Co. **Employee Count:** 29300. **Sales:** 5294 M.

★ 91986 ★ Reynolds Metals Co.
6601 W. Broad St.
Richmond, VA 23230
(804)281-2000
Company Type: Headquarters. **Officer:** Richard G. Holder. **Employee Count:** 29100. **Sales:** 5269 M. **Fortune 500:**

Largest U.S. Industrial Corporations: Ranking 101.

★ 91987 ★ Reynolds Metals Co. Bellwood Development Center
1941 Reymet Rd.
Richmond, VA 23237
Ultimate Parent: Reynolds Metals Co. **SIC:** 3300—Primary Metal Industries.

★ 91988 ★ Reynolds Metals Co. Bellwood Reclamation Plant
1711 Reymet Rd.
Richmond, VA 23237
Location Type: Plant. **Ultimate Parent:** Reynolds Metals Co. **SIC:** 3341—Secondary Nonferrous Metals.

★ 91989 ★ Reynolds Metals Co. Can Fabrication Plant
3001 Space Rd.
Richmond, VA 23234
Ultimate Parent: Reynolds Metals Co. **SIC:** 3411—Metal Cans.

★ 91990 ★ Reynolds Metals Co. Plant 44
1701 Reymet Rd.
Richmond, VA 23237
Ultimate Parent: Reynolds Metals Co. **SIC:** 3353—Aluminum Sheet, Plate & Foil.

★ 91991 ★ Reynolds Metals Co. Transition Laboratory
1801 Reymet Rd.
Richmond, VA 23237
Ultimate Parent: Reynolds Metals Co. **SIC:** 3334—Primary Aluminum.

★ 91992 ★ Reynolds Metals Extrusion Div.
1901 Reymet Rd.
Richmond, VA 23237
(804)743-6459
Company Type: Division. **Ultimate Parent:** Reynolds Metals Co. **SIC:** 3354—Aluminum Extruded Products.

★ 91993 ★ Richmond Foil Plant
7th & Bainbridge Sts.
Richmond, VA 23224-0688
Location Type: Plant. **Ultimate Parent:** Reynolds Metals Co. **SIC:** 3497—Metal Foil & Leaf.

★ 91994 ★ Richmond Gravure
Folding Carton Div.
3400 Deepwater Terminal Rd.
Richmond, VA 23234
Company Type: Division. **Ultimate Parent:** International Paper Co. **SIC:** 2657—Folding Paperboard Boxes.

★ 91995 ★ Richmond Gravure Inc.
3400 Deepwater Terminal Rd.
Richmond, VA 23234
Ultimate Parent: International Paper Co. **SIC:** 2657—Folding Paperboard Boxes.

★ 91996 ★ Rincon Securities Inc.
PO Box 26532
Richmond, VA 23219
(804)775-5708
Company Type: Subsidiary. **Ultimate Parent:** Dominion Resources. **SIC:** 6282—Investment Advice.

★ 91997 ★ Rite Aid
102 Regencysq
Richmond, VA 23229
(804)740-9761
Ultimate Parent: Rite Aid. **SIC:** 5912—Drug Stores & Proprietary Stores.

★ 91998 ★ Rite Aid
1517 N. Parhamrd
Richmond, VA 23229
(804)288-0009
Ultimate Parent: Rite Aid. **SIC:** 5912—Drug Stores & Proprietary Stores.

★ 91999 ★ Rite Aid
810 W. Gracest
Richmond, VA 23220
(804)355-9536
Ultimate Parent: Rite Aid. **SIC:** 5912—Drug Stores & Proprietary Stores.

★ 92000 ★ Rite Aid
4209 Beulahrd
Richmond, VA 23237
(804)275-9825
Ultimate Parent: Rite Aid. **SIC:** 5912—Drug Stores & Proprietary Stores.

★ 92001 ★ Rite Aid
5724 Hopkinsrd
Richmond, VA 23234
(804)271-0100
Ultimate Parent: Rite Aid. **SIC:** 5912—Drug Stores & Proprietary Stores.

★ 92002 ★ Rite Aid
6023 9 Mile Rd.
Richmond, VA 23223
(804)328-1167
Ultimate Parent: Rite Aid.

★ 92003 ★ Rite Aid
1354 Gaskins Rd. N
Richmond, VA 23233
(804)740-9862
Ultimate Parent: Rite Aid. **SIC:** 5912—Drug Stores & Proprietary Stores.

★ 92004 ★ Rite Aid
7218 Hull St.
Richmond, VA 23235
(804)276-5101
Ultimate Parent: Rite Aid. **SIC:** 5912—Drug Stores & Proprietary Stores.

★ 92005 ★ A.H. Robins
Finance
1407 Cummings Dr.
Richmond, VA 23220
(804)257-2000
Company Type: Subsidiary. **Officer:** G.E.R. Stiles, Sr. V.P. **Ultimate Parent:** American Home Products. **SIC:** 8741—Management Services.

★ 92006 ★ A.H. Robins Co.
Administration
1407 Cummings Dr.
Richmond, VA 23220
(804)257-2000
Company Type: Division. **Officer:** Howard L. Hall, Sr. V.P. **Ultimate Parent:** American Home Products. **SIC:** 8741—Management Services.

★ 92007 ★ Ryder Truck Rental Inc.
35776 PO Box
Richmond, VA 23235
(804)355-1761
Ultimate Parent: Ryder System. **SIC:** 7359—Equipment Rental & Leasing Nec; 7513—Truck Rental & Leasing Without Drivers.

★ 92008 ★ Ryder Truck Rental Inc.
4116 Charles City Rd.
Richmond, VA 23231
(804)222-0300
Ultimate Parent: Ryder System. **SIC:** 7513—Truck Rental & Leasing Without Drivers.

★ 92009 ★ Ryder Truck Rental Inc.
2200 Station Rd.
Richmond, VA 23234
(804)275-6434
Ultimate Parent: Ryder System. **SIC:** 7513—Truck Rental & Leasing Without Drivers.

★ 92010 ★ Schuller International Inc.
7400 Ranco Rd.
Richmond, VA 23228
Ultimate Parent: Manville Corp. **SIC:** 2672—Coated & Laminated Paper Nec.

★ 92011 ★ Shell Co.
Shell Rd.
Richmond, VA 23237
(804)275-1457
Ultimate Parent: Shell Oil Co. **SIC:** 5172—Petroleum Products Nec.

★ 92012 ★ Shipley Co. Inc.
7206 Hull St.
Richmond, VA 23235
(804)276-8415
Ultimate Parent: Rohm & Haas. **SIC:** 2819—Industrial Inorganic Chemicals Nec.

★ 92013 ★ Signet Bank, Virginia
2230 E. Parham Rd.
Richmond, VA 23228
(804)747-2000
Location Type: Branch office. **Ultimate Parent:** Signet Banking Corp. **SIC:** 6021—National Commercial Banks.

★ 92014 ★ Signet bank, Virginia
Azales Mall Shopping Ctr.
4824 Brook Rd.
Richmond, VA 23227
(804)771-7776
Location Type: Branch office. **Ultimate Parent:** Signet Banking Corp. **SIC:** 6021—National Commercial Banks.

★ 92015 ★ Signet Bank, Virginia
11 S. 12th St.
Richmond, VA 23219
(804)771-7006
Location Type: Branch office. **Ultimate Parent:** Signet Banking Corp. **SIC:** 6021—National Commercial Banks.

★ 92016 ★ Signet Bank, Virginia
906 Branchway Way
Richmond, VA 23236-4718
(804)771-7717
Location Type: Branch office. **Ultimate Parent:** Signet Banking Corp. **SIC:** 6021—National Commercial Banks.

★ 92017 ★ Signet Bank, Virginia
7202 Midlothian Tpke.
Richmond, VA 23235-5502
(804)771-7609
Location Type: Branch office. **Ultimate Parent:** Signet Banking Corp. **SIC:** 6021—National Commercial Banks.

★ 92018 ★ Signet Bank, Virginia
4th & Grace Sts.
Richmond, VA 23219
(804)771-7775
Location Type: Branch office. **Ultimate Parent:** Signet Banking Corp. **SIC:** 6021—National Commercial Banks.

★ 92019 ★ Signet Bank, Virginia
11th & Marshall Sts.
Richmond, VA 23219
(804)771-7737
Location Type: Branch office. **Ultimate Parent:** Signet Banking Corp. **SIC:** 6021—National Commercial Banks.

★ 92020 ★ Signet Bank, Virginia
9700 Grayton Rd.
Richmond, VA 23233-4907
(804)771-7992
Location Type: Branch office. **Ultimate Parent:** Signet Banking Corp. **SIC:** 6021—National Commercial Banks.

★ 92021 ★ Signet Bank, Virginia
4840 S. Labrum Ave.
Richmond, VA 23231-2714
(804)771-7288
Location Type: Branch office. **Ultimate Parent:** Signet Banking Corp. **SIC:** 6021—National Commercial Banks.

★ 92022 ★ Signet Bank, Virginia
6922 Lakeside Ave.
Richmond, VA 23228-5235
(804)771-7712
Location Type: Branch office. **Ultimate Parent:** Signet Banking Corp. **SIC:** 6021—National Commercial Banks.

★ 92023 ★ Signet Bank, Virginia
800 E. Main St.
Richmond, VA 23219-6001
(804)771-7375
Location Type: Branch office. **Ultimate Parent:** Signet Banking Corp. **SIC:** 6021—National Commercial Banks.

★ 92024 ★ Signet Bank, Virginia
4025 Mechanicsville Pke.
Richmond, VA 23223-1117
(804)771-7706
Location Type: Branch office. **Ultimate Parent:** Signet Banking Corp. **SIC:** 6021—National Commercial Banks.

★ 92025 ★ Signet Bank, Virginia
8215 W. Broad St.
Richmond, VA 23229-4126
(804)771-7266
Location Type: Branch office. **Ultimate Parent:** Signet Banking Corp. **SIC:** 6021—National Commercial Banks.

★ 92026 ★ Signet Bank, Virginia
1415 Eastridge Rd.
Richmond, VA 23229
(804)771-7726
Location Type: Branch office. **Ultimate Parent:** Signet Banking Corp. **SIC:** 6021—National Commercial Banks.

★ **92027** ★ **Signet Bank, Virginia**
3301 Jeff Davis Hwy.
Petersburg Pke. & Ruffin Rd.
Richmond, VA 23224
(804)771-7212
Location Type: Branch office. **Ultimate Parent:** Signet Banking Corp. **SIC:** 6021—National Commercial Banks.

★ **92028** ★ **Signet Bank, Virginia**
141 E. Belt Blvd.
Richmond, VA 23224-9998
(804)771-7330
Location Type: Branch office. **Ultimate Parent:** Signet Banking Corp. **SIC:** 6021—National Commercial Banks.

★ **92029** ★ **Signet Bank, Virginia**
Staples Mill Rd. & Broad St.
Richmond, VA 23230
(804)771-7788
Location Type: Branch office. **Ultimate Parent:** Signet Banking Corp. **SIC:** 6021—National Commercial Banks.

★ **92030** ★ **Signet Bank, Virginia**
Stratford Hills Shopping Ctr.
Richmond, VA 23225
(804)771-7318
Location Type: Branch office. **Ultimate Parent:** Signet Banking Corp. **SIC:** 6021—National Commercial Banks.

★ **92031** ★ **Signet Bank, Virginia**
7017 3 Chopt Rd.
Richmond, VA 23226-3606
(804)771-7276
Location Type: Branch office. **Ultimate Parent:** Signet Banking Corp. **SIC:** 6021—National Commercial Banks.

★ **92032** ★ **Signet Bank, Virginia**
315 Libbie Ave.
Richmond, VA 23226-2613
(804)771-7782
Location Type: Branch office. **Ultimate Parent:** Signet Banking Corp. **SIC:** 6021—National Commercial Banks.

★ **92033** ★ **Signet Bank, Virginia**
11011 W. Broad St.
Richmond, VA 23060
(804)747-2037
Location Type: Branch office. **Ultimate Parent:** Signet Banking Corp. **SIC:** 6021—National Commercial Banks.

★ **92034** ★ **Signet Bank, Virginia**
5445 Glenside Dr.
Richmond, VA 23228
(804)343-6600
Location Type: Branch office. **Ultimate Parent:** Signet Banking Corp. **SIC:** 6021—National Commercial Banks.

★ **92035** ★ **Signet Bank, Virginia**
PO Box 25970
Richmond, VA 23260-5970
Location Type: Headquarters. **Ultimate Parent:** Signet Banking Corp. **SIC:** 6021—National Commercial Banks.

★ **92036** ★ **Signet Bank, Virginia**
2810 Buford Rd.
Richmond, VA 23235-2426
(804)771-7410
Location Type: Branch office. **Ultimate Parent:** Signet Banking Corp. **SIC:** 6021—National Commercial Banks.

★ **92037** ★ **Signet Bank, Virginia**
7 N. 8th St.
Richmond, VA 23219-6003
(804)747-2000 **Fax:** (804)771-7599 **Telex:** RCA 24935 RANVA UR
Location Type: Headquarters. **Ultimate Parent:** Signet Banking Corp. **SIC:** 6021—National Commercial Banks.

★ **92038** ★ **Signet Banking Corp.**
PO Box
Richmond, VA 23260-5970
Ultimate Parent: Signet Banking Corp. **SIC:** 6021—National Commercial Banks.

★ **92039** ★ **Signet Banking Corp.**
7 N. 8th St.
Richmond, VA 23219
(804)747-2000 **Fax:** (804)771-7594
Company Type: Headquarters. **Officer:** Robert M. Freeman, CEO. **Employee Count:** 5733. **Sales:** 1169 M. **Fortune Service 500:** Ranking 54.

★ **92040** ★ **Signet Trust Co.**
PO Box 26311
Richmond, VA 23260-6311
Ultimate Parent: Signet Banking Corp. **SIC:** 6021—National Commercial Banks.

★ **92041** ★ **Snap On Tools Corp.**
601 Johnston Willis Dr.
Richmond, VA 23236
(804)794-2416
Officer: Gary Fisher, Manager. **Ultimate Parent:** Snap-on Tools. **SIC:** 3544—Special Dies, Tools, Jigs & Fixtures.

★ **92042** ★ **Sonoco Products Co.**
1850 Commerce Rd.
Richmond, VA 23224
(804)233-5411
Officer: Garris Bacon, Plant Manager. **Ultimate Parent:** Sonoco Products. **SIC:** 2621—Paper Mills; 2631—Paperboard Mills; 2679—Converted Paper Products Nec.

★ **92043** ★ **Southern Gravure Service**
2891 Sprouse Dr.
Richmond, VA 23231
Ultimate Parent: Reynolds Metals Co. **SIC:** 2796—Platemaking Services.

★ **92044** ★ **Southern States Co-Op. Inc. Richmond Feed Mill**
1st & Hull St.
Richmond, VA 23224
Ultimate Parent: Southern. **SIC:** 2048—Prepared Feeds Nec.

★ **92045** ★ **Southland Corp.**
11 Erich Rd.
Richmond, VA 23225
(804)231-4711
Ultimate Parent: Southland Corp. **SIC:** 5411—Grocery Stores.

★ **92046** ★ **Southland Corp.**
4009 Macarthur Ave.
Richmond, VA 23227
(804)730-2500
Ultimate Parent: Southland Corp. **SIC:** 5411—Grocery Stores.

★ **92047** ★ **Stanley Works**
Stanley Hardware Division
5700 S. Laburnum Ave.
Richmond, VA 23231
Ultimate Parent: Stanley Works. **SIC:** 3429—Hardware Nec.

richmond

★ **92048** ★ **Stevens Graphics**
1910 Byrd Ave.
richmond, VA 23230-3016
(804)285-9205
Ultimate Parent: BellSouth Corp. **SIC:** 5112—Stationery & Office Supplies.

Richmond

★ **92049** ★ **Stone Container Corp.**
2900 Sprouse Dr.
Richmond, VA 23231
Ultimate Parent: Stone Container Corp. **SIC:** 2653—Corrugated & Solid Fiber Boxes.

★ **92050** ★ **Stone Container Corp.**
4301 Carolina Ave.
Richmond, VA 23222
(804)329-3775
Officer: Roger Linbille, Manager. **Ultimate Parent:** Stone Container Corp. **SIC:** 2671—Paper Coated & Laminated—Packaging; 2672—Coated & Laminated Paper Nec; 2673—Bags—Plastics, Laminated & Coated.

★ **92051** ★ **Structured Management Syste**
2807 N. Parham Rd.
Richmond, VA 23294
(804)273-0033
Ultimate Parent: Limited. **SIC:** 7372—Prepackaged Software.

★ **92052** ★ **Structured Management Syste**
2317 Westwood Ave.
Richmond, VA 23230
(804)358-6472
Ultimate Parent: Limited. **SIC:** 7374—Data Processing & Preparation.

★ **92053** ★ **Structured Mgt Systems Inc.**
8814 Fargo Rd.
Richmond, VA 23229
(804)288-8428
Ultimate Parent: Limited. **SIC:** 7374—Data Processing & Preparation.

★ **92054** ★ **Structured Shelt Richmond**
8601 Mayland Dr.
Richmond, VA 23294
(804)346-0755
Ultimate Parent: Limited. **SIC:** 6282—Investment Advice.

★ **92055** ★ **A T Massey Coal Co. Inc.**
4 N. 4th St.
Richmond, VA 23219
(804)788-1800 **Fax:** (804)788-1870
Company Type: Subsidiary. **Officer:** Don L. Blankenship, Chairman & CEO. **Ultimate Parent:** Fluor.

★ **92056** ★ **This End Up, Inc.**
1309 Exchange Alley
Richmond, VA 23219
(804)644-1248 **Fax:** (804)783-2159
Officer: Douglas McEllhinney III, President. **Ultimate Parent:** Melville.

★ **92057** ★ **Toys R US**
7545 Midlothian Tpke.
Richmond, VA 23225
(804)276-1544
Ultimate Parent: Toys "R" US. **SIC:** 5945—Hobby, Toy & Game Shops.

★ **92058** ★ **Toys R US**
Midlothian
Richmond, VA 23224
(804)276-1544
Ultimate Parent: Toys "R" US. **SIC:** 5012—Automobiles & Other Motor Vehicles.

★ **92059** ★ **Transco Coal Co.**
629 E. Main St.
Richmond, VA 23219
(804)780-3000
Ultimate Parent: Transco Energy Co. **SIC:** 5052—Coal, Other Minerals & Ores.

★ **92060** ★ **Tredegar Industries Inc.**
1100 Boulders Pky.
Richmond, VA 23225-4000
(804)330-1000
Officer: John D. Gotwald, President. **Ultimate Parent:** Ethyl. **SIC:** 3089—Plastics Products Nec; 3081—Unsupported Plastics Film & Sheet; 3354—Aluminum Extruded Products; 6519—Real Property Lessors Nec; 1382—Oil & Gas Exploration Services. **Employee Count:** 3500. **Sales:** 480 M.

★ **92061** ★ **Union Camp Corp.**
2801 Cofer Rd.
Richmond, VA 23224
(804)231-5781
Officer: Richard Evans, Manager. **Ultimate Parent:** Union Camp Corp. **SIC:** 2673—Bags—Plastics, Laminated & Coated; 2674—Bags—Uncoated Paper & Multiwall.

★ **92062** ★ **Union Camp Corp.**
Container Div.
2811 Cofer Rd.
Richmond, VA 23224
Company Type: Division. **Ultimate Parent:** Union Camp Corp. **SIC:** 2653—Corrugated & Solid Fiber Boxes.

★ **92063** ★ **Union Camp Corp. Richmond Bag**
2801 Cofer Rd.
Richmond, VA 23224
Ultimate Parent: Union Camp Corp. **SIC:** 2600—Paper & Allied Products.

★ **92064** ★ **Union Envelope Co.**
Sherwd Ave.
Richmond, VA 23220
(804)358-5555
Ultimate Parent: International Paper Co. **SIC:** 2677—Envelopes; 5112—Stationery & Office Supplies.

★ **92065** ★ **United Parcel Service**
RR 7
Richmond, VA 23231
(804)743-8400
Ultimate Parent: United Parcel Service of America. **SIC:** 4215—Courier Services Except by Air.

★ **92066** ★ **United Parcel Service**
9601 Coach Rd.
Richmond, VA 23237
(804)743-8400
Ultimate Parent: United Parcel Service of America. **SIC:** 4212—Local Trucking Without Storage; 4215—Courier Services Except by Air.

★ **92067** ★ **United Parcel Service**
6282 PO Box
Richmond, VA 23230
Ultimate Parent: United Parcel Service of America. **SIC:** 4215—Courier Services Except by Air.

★ **92068** ★ **United Parcel Service**
Rural Route 7
Richmond, VA 23231
(804)743-8400
Ultimate Parent: United Parcel Service of America. **SIC:** 4215—Courier Services Except by Air.

★ **92069** ★ **United Parcel Service**
6224 PO Box
Richmond, VA 23230
Ultimate Parent: United Parcel Service of America. **SIC:** 4215—Courier Services Except by Air.

★ **92070** ★ **United Van Lines Inc.**
2314 Dabney Rd.
Richmond, VA 23230
(804)359-5959
Ultimate Parent: Unigroup. **SIC:** 7389—Business Services Nec.

★ **92071** ★ **Universal Corp.**
1501 N. Hamilton
Richmond, VA 23230
(804)359-9311 **Fax:** (804)254-3584
Company Type: Headquarters. **Officer:** Henry H. Harrell, CEO. **Employee Count:** 25000. **Sales:** 3047.2 M. **Fortune 500:** Largest U.S. Industrial Corporations: Ranking 160.

★ **92072** ★ **US Fidelity & Gu**
2819 N. Parham Rd.
Richmond, VA 23294
(804)747-0300
Ultimate Parent: USF&G Corp. **SIC:** 6411—Insurance Agents, Brokers & Service.

★ **92073** ★ **Van Waters & Rogers Inc.**
Rural Route 7
Richmond, VA 23231
(804)743-0540
Ultimate Parent: Univar Corp. **SIC:** 2899—Chemical Preparations Nec.

★ **92074** ★ **Variable Annuity Life Insurance**
7633 Hull St.
Richmond, VA 23235
(804)276-1910
Ultimate Parent: Variable Annuity Life. **SIC:** 6411—Insurance Agents, Brokers & Service.

★ **92075** ★ **Victor Products Corp.**
328 N. 18th St.
Richmond, VA 23223
(804)643-9091
Ultimate Parent: Dana Corp. **SIC:** 2087—Flavoring Extracts & Syrups Nec.

★ **92076** ★ **Virginia Electric And Power Co.**
1 James River Plz.
Richmond, VA 23219
(804)771-3000
Company Type: Subsidiary. **Ultimate Parent:** Dominion Resources. **SIC:** 4931—Electric & Other Services Combined.

★ **92077** ★ **Virginia Electric & Power Co.**
PO Box 26666
Richmond, VA 23261
(804)771-3000 **Fax:** (804)771-4066
Company Type: Subsidiary. **Officer:** James T. Rhodes, President & CEO. **Ultimate Parent:** Dominion Resources.

★ 92078 ★   **Virginia Electric & Power Co.**
1 James River Plz.
Richmond, VA 23219-3229
(804)771-3000
Company Type: Subsidiary. **Ultimate Parent:** Dominion Resources. **SIC:** 4911—Electric Services.

★ 92079 ★   **Waldenbooks**
Regency Sq.
Richmond, VA 23229
(804)740-1253
Ultimate Parent: K-Mart. **SIC:** 5942—Book Stores.

★ 92080 ★   **Waldenbooks**
Chesterfield Town Ctr.
Richmond, VA 23225
(804)794-0556
Ultimate Parent: K-Mart. **SIC:** 5942—Book Stores.

★ 92081 ★   **Washington Inventory Servic**
6010 W. Broad St.
Richmond, VA 23230
(804)285-9995
Ultimate Parent: Huffy. **SIC:** 7374—Data Processing & Preparation.

★ 92082 ★   **Westvaco**
403 Stockton St.
Richmond, VA 23224
Ultimate Parent: WestVaco Corp. **SIC:** 2754—Commercial Printing—Gravure.

★ 92083 ★   **Westvaco**
3001 Cofer Rd.
Richmond, VA 23224
Location Type: Plant. **Ultimate Parent:** WestVaco Corp. **SIC:** 2754—Commercial Printing—Gravure.

★ 92084 ★   **Westvaco**
Folding Carton
3001 Cofer Rd.
Richmond, VA 23224
Location Type: Plant. **Ultimate Parent:** WestVaco Corp. **SIC:** 2754—Commercial Printing—Gravure.

★ 92085 ★   **Westvaco**
Folding Carton
403 Stockton St.
Richmond, VA 23224
Location Type: Plant. **Ultimate Parent:** WestVaco Corp. **SIC:** 2754—Commercial Printing—Gravure.

★ 92086 ★   **Westvaco Corp.**
2300 Jefferson Davis Hwy.
Richmond, VA 23234
(804)232-5691
Ultimate Parent: WestVaco Corp. **SIC:** 5113—Industrial & Personal Service Paper.

★ 92087 ★   **Westvaco Corp.**
320 Hull St.
Richmond, VA 23224
(804)233-9205
Ultimate Parent: WestVaco Corp. **SIC:** 2652—Setup Paperboard Boxes; 2657—Folding Paperboard Boxes.

★ 92088 ★   **Westvaco Corp.**
2828 Cofer Rd.
Richmond, VA 23224
(804)232-6746
Officer: Dick Lawson, Manager. **Ultimate Parent:** WestVaco Corp. **SIC:** 2656—Sanitary Food Containers.

★ 92089 ★   **Westvaco Corp.**
3001 Cofer Rd.
Richmond, VA 23224
(804)233-6949
Officer: Norman Maddox, Manager. **Ultimate Parent:** WestVaco Corp. **SIC:** 2652—Setup Paperboard Boxes.

★ 92090 ★   **Westvaco Corp.**
Liquid Packaging
2828 Cofer Rd.
Richmond, VA 23224
Ultimate Parent: WestVaco Corp. **SIC:** 2656—Sanitary Food Containers.

★ 92091 ★   **Westvaco Corp.**
Milk Carton
2828 Cofer Rd.
Richmond, VA 23224
Ultimate Parent: WestVaco Corp. **SIC:** 2600—Paper & Allied Products.

★ 92092 ★   **Weyerhaeuser Paper Co.**
1308 Jefferson Davis Hwy.
Richmond, VA 23224
(804)232-2386
Officer: Ashley Weatherford, Manager. **Ultimate Parent:** Weyerhaeuser Co. **SIC:** 3589—Service Industry Machinery Nec.

★ 92093 ★   **Whitby Inc.**
2801 Reserve Rd.
Richmond, VA 23220
(804)254-4400 **Fax:** (804)254-4035
Company Type: Subsidiary. **Officer:** William M. Gottwald MD, President. **Ultimate Parent:** Ethyl.

★ 92094 ★   **Whitby Inc.**
1211 Sherwood Ave.
Richmond, VA 23220-1212
(804)254-4400
Company Type: Subsidiary. **Officer:** Dr. William M. Gottwald, President & Chairman of the Board. **Ultimate Parent:** Ethyl. **SIC:** 5122—Drugs, Proprietaries & Sundries; 8731—Commercial Physical Research. **Employee Count:** 390. **Sales:** 65 M.

★ 92095 ★   **Xerox Corp.**
6620 W. Broad St.
Richmond, VA 23230
(804)289-5400
Officer: Joe Dougherty, Manager. **Ultimate Parent:** Xerox Corp. **SIC:** 3554—Paper Industries Machinery; 3663—Radio & T.V. Communications Equipment.

Ringgold

★ 92096 ★   **O-I Brockway Glass Inc.**
Plant 29
Rte. 3 Box 190
Ringgold, VA 24586
Location Type: Plant. **Ultimate Parent:** Owens-Illinois. **SIC:** 3221—Glass Containers.

★ 92097 ★   **Owens-Brockway Glass Container**
State Rd. No. 730
Ringgold, VA 24586
Ultimate Parent: Owens-Illinois. **SIC:** 3221—Glass Containers.

★ 92098 ★   **Owens-Brockway Glass Container**
Plant 29
State Rd. No. 730
Ringgold, VA 24586
Location Type: Plant. **Ultimate Parent:** Owens-Illinois. **SIC:** 3221—Glass Containers.

Roanoke

★ 92099 ★   **Air Products & Chemicals Inc.**
603 Centre Ave. NW
Roanoke, VA 24016-2308
(703)343-3683
Officer: W. Ed McCollum. **Ultimate Parent:** Air Products & Chemicals, Inc. **SIC:** 5085—Industrial Supplies; 2813—Industrial Gases; 5169—Chemicals & Allied Products Nec.

★ 92100 ★   **AMP Inc.**
520 Kimball Ave. NE
Roanoke, VA 24016
(703)342-5033
Officer: Harold McInnes, Chairman. **Ultimate Parent:** AMP Inc. **SIC:** 3571—Electronic Computers.

★ 92101 ★   **ANR Coal Co.**
Crestar Bank Bldg., 310 1st. St.
Roanoke, VA 24011
(703)983-0222 **Fax:** (703)983-0267
Officer: James L. Van Lanen, President & CEO. **Ultimate Parent:** Coastal Corp.

★ 92102 ★   **AT & T**
341 Reserve Ave. SW
Roanoke, VA 24016
(703)982-0672
Officer: J. G. Meador, Manager. **Ultimate Parent:** AT&T. **SIC:** 3661—Telephone & Telegraph Apparatus.

★ 92103 ★   **Banister Shoe Factory Outlet**
3645 Thirlane Rd. NW
Roanoke, VA 24019
(703)563-4147
Ultimate Parent: United States Shoe. **SIC:** 5661—Shoe Stores.

★ 92104 ★   **Bell Atlantic Business Systems Services**
6701 Peters Creek Rd. NW
Roanoke, VA 24019-4014
(703)362-1907
Officer: Don Harrison. **Ultimate Parent:** Bell Atlantic Corp. **SIC:** 7378—Computer Maintenance & Repair; 5065—Electronic Parts & Equipment Nec; 5112—Stationery & Office Supplies.

★ 92105 ★   **BellSouth Communication Systems, Inc.**
1936 Blue Hills Dr. NE
Roanoke, VA 24014
(703)983-6000
Company Type: Subsidiary. **Ultimate Parent:** BellSouth Corp.

★ 92106 ★   **Bellsouth Communications Systems, Inc.**
1936 Blue Hills Dr. NE
Roanoke, VA 24012-8608
(703)983-6000
Company Type: Subsidiary. **Officer:** Fredrick K. Shaftman, President & CEO. **Ultimate Parent:** BellSouth Corp. **SIC:** 5999—Miscellaneous Retail Stores Nec. **Employee Count:** 2500. **Sales:** 163 M.

★ 92107 ★   **Casual Corner**
212 Valleyview Mall
Roanoke, VA 24017
(703)362-8282
Ultimate Parent: United States Shoe. **SIC:** 5651—Family Clothing Stores.

★ 92108 ★   **Chesapeake & Potomac Telephone Co.**
5415 Airport Rd. NW
Roanoke, VA 24012-1303
(703)561-1000
Company Type: Subsidiary. **Location Type:** Branch office. **Ultimate Parent:** Bell Atlantic Corp. **SIC:** 4813—Telephone Communications Except Radiotelephone.

★ 92109 ★   **Cincinnati Insurance Co.**
5002 Bruceton Rd. SW
Roanoke, VA 24018
(703)774-2796
Ultimate Parent: Cincinnati Financial. **SIC:** 6411—Insurance Agents, Brokers & Service.

★ 92110 ★   **Cincinnati Insurance Co.**
6700 Shingle Ridge Rd.
Roanoke, VA 24018
(703)774-2537
Ultimate Parent: Cincinnati Financial. **SIC:** 6411—Insurance Agents, Brokers & Service.

★ 92111 ★   **Circuit City**
26 Crossroads Mall
Roanoke, VA 24017
(703)563-2864
Ultimate Parent: Circuit City Stores. **SIC:** 7841—Video Tape Rental.

★ 92112 ★   **Circuit City Stores Inc.**
26 Crossroads Mall
Roanoke, VA 24017
(703)563-2864
Ultimate Parent: Circuit City Stores. **SIC:** 7841—Video Tape Rental.

★ 92113 ★   **Coastal Coal Sales, Inc.**
Crestar Bank Bldg., 310 1st. St.
Roanoke, VA 24011
(703)983-0222 **Fax:** (703)983-0267
Officer: Robert A. Feilner, President. **Ultimate Parent:** Coastal Corp.

★ 92114 ★   **Coastal Power Production Co.**
310 1st. St., 5th Fl.
Roanoke, VA 24011
(703)983-0222 **Fax:** (703)983-4399
Officer: James L. Van Lanen, Chairman & CEO. **Ultimate Parent:** Coastal Corp.

★ 92115 ★   **Coastal Remediation Co.**
Crestar Bank Bldg., 4th Fl.
310 1st. St.
Roanoke, VA 24011
(703)983-0282 **Fax:** (703)983-4363
Officer: James L. Van Lanen, President & CEO. **Ultimate Parent:** Coastal Corp.

★ 92116 ★   **Coastal Technology Inc.**
310 1st. St.
Roanoke, VA 24011
(703)983-0222 **Fax:** (703)983-0267
Officer: James L. Van Lanen, Chairman & CEO. **Ultimate Parent:** Coastal Corp.

★ 92117 ★   **Coastal Technology Inc.**
310 1st. St. SW, 5th Fl.
Roanoke, VA 24011-1922
(703)983-0222
Company Type: Subsidiary. **Officer:** James L. Van Lanen, Chairman of the Board, CEO. **Ultimate Parent:** Coastal Corp. **SIC:** 4911—Electric Services. **Employee Count:** 75. **Sales:** 5 M.

★ 92118 ★   **Coca-Cola Bottling Co.**
235 Shenandoah Ave.
Roanoke, VA 24016
(703)343-8041
Company Type: Subsidiary. **Officer:** Jim Moore, Pr. **Ultimate Parent:** Coca-Cola Bottling Consol. **SIC:** 2086—Bottled & Canned Soft Drinks. **Employee Count:** 475. **Sales:** 71000 M.

★ 92119 ★   **Coca-Cola Bottling Co. Consolidated**
235 Shenandoah Ave. NW
Roanoke, VA 24016-2046
Ultimate Parent: Coca-Cola Bottling Consol. **SIC:** 2086—Bottled & Canned Soft Drinks.

★ 92120 ★   **Cooper Industries**
Gardner Denver M&C Div.
1700 Blue Hills Dr. NE
Roanoke, VA 24012-8601
Company Type: Division. **Ultimate Parent:** Cooper Industries. **SIC:** 3500—Industrial Machinery & Equipment.

★ 92121 ★   **Crestar Bank**
7227 Williamson Rd.
Roanoke, VA 24019-4234
(703)985-5251
Location Type: Branch office. **Ultimate Parent:** Crestar Financial Corp. **SIC:** 6021—National Commercial Banks.

★ 92122 ★   **Crestar Bank**
4025 Brambleton Ave.
Roanoke, VA 24018-3426
(703)985-5231
Location Type: Branch office. **Ultimate Parent:** Crestar Financial Corp. **SIC:** 6021—National Commercial Banks.

★ 92123 ★   **Crestar Bank**
3407 Orange Ave. NE
Roanoke, VA 24012-6452
(703)982-3475
Location Type: Branch office. **Ultimate Parent:** Crestar Financial Corp. **SIC:** 6021—National Commercial Banks.

★ 92124 ★   **Crestar Bank**
3504 Electric Rd. SW
Roanoke, VA 24018-4451
(703)985-5230
Location Type: Branch office. **Ultimate Parent:** Crestar Financial Corp. **SIC:** 6021—National Commercial Banks.

★ 92125 ★   **Crestar Bank**
2730 Ogden Rd.
Roanoke, VA 24014-2808
(703)982-3428
Location Type: Branch office. **Ultimate Parent:** Crestar Financial Corp. **SIC:** 6021—National Commercial Banks.

★ 92126 ★   **Crestar Bank**
3403 Williamson Rd.
Roanoke, VA 24012-4050
(703)982-3435
Location Type: Branch office. **Ultimate Parent:** Crestar Financial Corp. **SIC:** 6021—National Commercial Banks.

★ **92127** ★ **Crestar Bank**
4203 Melrose Ave. NW
Roanoke, VA 24017-5813
(703)982-3418
Location Type: Branch office. **Ultimate Parent:** Crestar Financial Corp. **SIC:** 6021—National Commercial Banks.

★ **92128** ★ **Crestar Bank**
112 McClanahan St.
Roanoke, VA 24014-1708
(703)982-3425
Location Type: Branch office. **Ultimate Parent:** Crestar Financial Corp. **SIC:** 6021—National Commercial Banks.

★ **92129** ★ **Crestar BAnk**
1535 Hershberger Rd. NW
Roanoke, VA 24012-7319
(703)982-3096
Location Type: Branch office. **Ultimate Parent:** Crestar Financial Corp. **SIC:** 6021—National Commercial Banks.

★ **92130** ★ **Crestar Bank**
2230 Melrose Ave. NW
Roanoke, VA 24017-6204
(703)982-3415
Location Type: Branch office. **Ultimate Parent:** Crestar Financial Corp. **SIC:** 6021—National Commercial Banks.

★ **92131** ★ **Crestar Bank**
37 W. Church Ave.
Roanoke, VA 24011-2103
(703)985-5274
Location Type: Branch office. **Ultimate Parent:** Crestar Financial Corp. **SIC:** 6021—National Commercial Banks.

★ **92132** ★ **Crestar Bank**
2112 Colonial Ave. SW
Roanoke, VA 24015-3205
(703)982-3404
Location Type: Branch office. **Ultimate Parent:** Crestar Financial Corp. **SIC:** 6021—National Commercial Banks.

★ **92133** ★ **Crestar Bank**
2929 Keagy Rd. & Rte. 419
Roanoke, VA 24018
(703)982-3357
Location Type: Branch office. **Ultimate Parent:** Crestar Financial Corp.

★ **92134** ★ **Digital Equipment Corp.**
3807 Brandon Ave. SW
Roanoke, VA 24018
(703)989-9087
Ultimate Parent: Digital Equipment Corp. **SIC:** 3579—Office Machines Nec.

★ **92135** ★ **Digital Equipment Corp. Bran**
5221 Valley Park Dr. 7
Roanoke, VA 24019
(703)237-6262
Ultimate Parent: Digital Equipment Corp. **SIC:** 3579—Office Machines Nec.

★ **92136** ★ **Dominion Bankshare Corp.**
PO Box 13327
Roanoke, VA 24033
Company Type: Subsidiary. **Ultimate Parent:** First Union Corp.

★ **92137** ★ **Eckerd Drug Co.**
Market Sq. N
Roanoke, VA 24012
(703)366-2905
Ultimate Parent: Eckerd Corp. **SIC:** 5912—Drug Stores & Proprietary Stores.

★ **92138** ★ **Eckerd Drugs**
Market Sq. N.
Roanoke, VA 24012
(703)366-2905
Ultimate Parent: Eckerd Corp. **SIC:** 5912—Drug Stores & Proprietary Stores.

★ **92139** ★ **First Union National Bank of Virginia**
3625 Williamson Rd., NW
Roanoke, VA 24012-3327
(703)362-7231
Location Type: Branch office. **Ultimate Parent:** First Union Corp. **SIC:** 6021—National Commercial Banks.

★ **92140** ★ **First Union National Bank of Virginia**
3442 Orange Ave., NE
Roanoke, VA 24012-9604
(703)563-7837
Location Type: Branch office. **Ultimate Parent:** First Union Corp. **SIC:** 6021—National Commercial Banks.

★ **92141** ★ **First Union National Bank of Virginia**
301 McClanahan St.
Roanoke, VA 24014-1774
(703)563-7741
Location Type: Branch office. **Ultimate Parent:** First Union Corp. **SIC:** 6021—National Commercial Banks.

★ **92142** ★ **First Union National Bank of Virginia**
2201 Colonial Ave., SW
Roanoke, VA 24015-3208
(703)563-7751
Location Type: Branch office. **Ultimate Parent:** First Union Corp. **SIC:** 6021—National Commercial Banks.

★ **92143** ★ **First Union National Bank of Virginia**
2657 Peters Creek Rd.
Roanoke, VA 24017-1648
(703)563-7248
Location Type: Branch office. **Ultimate Parent:** First Union Corp. **SIC:** 6021—National Commercial Banks.

★ **92144** ★ **First Union National Bank of Virginia**
616 9th St., SE
Roanoke, VA 24013-1808
(703)563-7205
Location Type: Branch office. **Ultimate Parent:** First Union Corp. **SIC:** 6021—National Commercial Banks.

★ **92145** ★ **First Union National Bank of Virginia**
3862 Electric Rd.
Roanoke, VA 24018-4511
(703)563-7168
Location Type: Branch office. **Ultimate Parent:** First Union Corp. **SIC:** 6021—National Commercial Banks.

★ **92146** ★ **First Union National Bank of Virginia**
4202 Melrose Ave., NW
Roanoke, VA 24017-5814
(703)362-7221
Location Type: Branch office. **Ultimate Parent:** First Union Corp. **SIC:** 6021—National Commercial Banks.

★ **92147** ★ **First Union National Bank of Virginia**
1323 Grendin Rd. SW
Roanoke, VA 24015-2315
(703)362-7711
Location Type: Branch office. **Ultimate Parent:** First Union Corp. **SIC:** 6021—National Commercial Banks.

★ **92148** ★ **First Union National Bank of Virginia**
1518 Hershberger Rd.
Roanoke, VA 24012-7320
(703)563-7268
Location Type: Branch office. **Ultimate Parent:** First Union Corp. **SIC:** 6021—National Commercial Banks.

★ **92149** ★ **First Union National Bank of Virginia**
201 S. Jefferson St.
Roanoke, VA 24011-1701
(703)563-7000
Location Type: Branch office. **Ultimate Parent:** First Union Corp. **SIC:** 6021—National Commercial Banks.

★ **92150** ★ **First Union National Bank of Virginia**
213 S. Jefferson St.
Roanoke, VA 24011-1705
(703)563-7757
Location Type: Branch office. **Ultimate Parent:** First Union Corp. **SIC:** 6021—National Commercial Banks.

★ **92151** ★ **First Virginia Bank Southwest**
601 S. Jefferson St.
Roanoke, VA 24011-2414
(703)561-8600
Company Type: Subsidiary. **Officer:** Joseph C. Thomas, Chairman of the Board. **Ultimate Parent:** First Virginia Banks Inc. **SIC:** 6022—State Commercial Banks.

★ **92152** ★ **First Virginia Bank - Southwest**
601 S. Jefferson St.
Roanoke, VA 24011-2415
(703)561-8600
Company Type: Subsidiary. **Officer:** James N. Hinson Jr., President. **Ultimate Parent:** First Virginia Banks Inc. **SIC:** 6022—State Commercial Banks. **Employee Count:** 223.

★ **92153** ★ **Flowers Baking Co.**
523 Shenandoah Ave. NW
Roanoke, VA 24016
(703)343-8165
Ultimate Parent: Flowers Industries. **SIC:** 5461—Retail Bakeries.

★ **92154** ★ **Food Lion**
2631 Peters Creek Rd. NW
Roanoke, VA 24017
(703)362-2246
Ultimate Parent: Food Lion. **SIC:** 5411—Grocery Stores.

★ **92155** ★ **Gardner Denver Mc**
1700 Blue Hills Dr.
Roanoke, VA 24012
Ultimate Parent: Cooper Industries. **SIC:** 3532—Mining Machinery.

★ **92156** ★ **Greyhound Bus Lines**
13324 PO Box
Roanoke, VA 24033
(703)343-5436
Ultimate Parent: Greyhound Lines Inc. **SIC:** 4111—Local & Suburban Transit.

★ **92157** ★ **Hit or Miss**
1919 Hershberger Rd. NW
Roanoke, VA 24012
(703)366-9687
Ultimate Parent: TJX. **SIC:** 5621—Women's Clothing Stores.

★ **92158** ★ **Ingersoll-Rand Co.**
7500 Shadwell Dr.
Roanoke, VA 24019
Ultimate Parent: Ingersoll-Rand. **SIC:** 3532—Mining Machinery.

★ **92159** ★ **Intel Corp.**
3807 Brandon Ave. SW
Roanoke, VA 24018
(703)989-0437
Ultimate Parent: Intel Corp. **SIC:** 5812—Eating Places.

★ **92160** ★ **J C Penney Co.**
4832 Valleyview Blvd. NW
Roanoke, VA 24012
(703)362-1251
Ultimate Parent: J.C. Penney. **SIC:** 5311—Department Stores.

★ **92161** ★ **Kroger Co.**
44 Crossroads Mall
Roanoke, VA 24012
(703)362-0925
Ultimate Parent: Kroger. **SIC:** 5411—Grocery Stores.

★ **92162** ★ **Kroger Co.**
3631 Peters Creek Rd. NW
Roanoke, VA 24019
(703)563-3500
Ultimate Parent: Kroger. **SIC:** 5411—Grocery Stores.

★ **92163** ★ **Kroger Co.**
14002 PO Box
Roanoke, VA 24038
(703)563-3500
Ultimate Parent: Kroger. **SIC:** 5411—Grocery Stores.

★ **92164** ★ **Kroger Co.**
1489 Main St. SW
Roanoke, VA 24015
(703)986-0009
Ultimate Parent: Kroger. **SIC:** 5411—Grocery Stores.

★ **92165** ★ **Kroger Co.**
Orange Ave. E
Roanoke, VA 24016
(703)982-3509
Ultimate Parent: Kroger. **SIC:** 5411—Grocery Stores.

★ **92166** ★ **Kroger Co.**
Lake Dr.
Roanoke, VA 24018
(703)345-7017
Ultimate Parent: Kroger. **SIC:** 5411—Grocery Stores.

★ **92167** ★ **Kroger Zone Office**
Tanglewood
Roanoke, VA 24014
(703)989-6615
Ultimate Parent: Kroger. **SIC:** 5411—Grocery Stores.

★ **92168** ★ **Liberty Mutual Insurance Co.**
3223 Brandon Ave. SW
Roanoke, VA 24018
(703)344-4371
Ultimate Parent: Liberty Mutual Group. **SIC:** 6411—Insurance Agents, Brokers & Service.

★ **92169** ★ **Life Insurance Co. of Virgin**
2727 Electric Rd. 102
Roanoke, VA 24018
(703)774-1649
Ultimate Parent: Life Insurance Co. of Virginia. **SIC:** 6411—Insurance Agents, Brokers & Service.

★ **92170** ★ **Life Insurance Co. of Virginia**
4502 Starkey Rd. SW
Roanoke, VA 24014
(703)774-1649
Ultimate Parent: Life Insurance Co. of Virginia. **SIC:** 6411—Insurance Agents, Brokers & Service.

★ **92171** ★ **Manpower Inc.**
123 Franklin Rd. SE
Roanoke, VA 24011
(703)345-0957
Ultimate Parent: Manpower, Inc. **SIC:** 7338—Secretarial & Court Reporting.

★ **92172** ★ **Mary Kay Cosmetics Dist.**
1530 Lawrence Ave. SE
Roanoke, VA 24013
(703)345-0611
Ultimate Parent: Mary Kay Cosmetics. **SIC:** 5999—Miscellaneous Retail Stores Nec.

★ **92173** ★ **Minnesota Mutual Life Insurance C**
Shenandoah
Roanoke, VA 24011
(703)343-7244
Ultimate Parent: Minnesota Mutual Life. **SIC:** 6411—Insurance Agents, Brokers & Service.

★ **92174** ★ **New York Life Roanoke General Office**
Southeasten Agnecies
PO Box 14207
Roanoke, VA 24038
(703)982-2241 **Fax:** (703)981-9358
Officer: Victor Schendel, General Manager. **Ultimate Parent:** New York Life.

★ **92175** ★ **New York Life Roanoke General Office**
Southeastern Agencies
111 Franklin Plz., 5th Fl.
Roanoke, VA 24011
(703)982-2241 **Fax:** (703)981-9358
Officer: Victor W. Schendel, General Manager. **Ultimate Parent:** New York Life.

★ **92176** ★ **Overnite Transportation Co.**
4668 Peters Creek Rd. NW
Roanoke, VA 24019
(703)563-4000
Ultimate Parent: Union Pacific Corp. **SIC:** 4212—Local Trucking Without Storage.

★ **92177** ★ **Pitney Bowes**
3825 Electric Rd. SW
Roanoke, VA 24018
(703)989-1211
Officer: Martha Ryan, Manager. **Ultimate Parent:** Pitney Bowes. **SIC:** 3554—Paper Industries Machinery.

★ 92178 ★ Radio Shack
Roanoke Salem Plz.
Roanoke, VA 24017
(703)362-2779
Company Type: Division. Ultimate Parent:
Tandy Corp. SIC: 5065—Electronic Parts &
Equipment Nec; 5731—Radio, Television &
Electronics Stores.

★ 92179 ★ Radio Shack
3561 Franklin Rd. SW
Roanoke, VA 24014
(703)342-6335
Company Type: Division. Ultimate Parent:
Tandy Corp. SIC: 5046—Commercial
Equipment Nec.

★ 92180 ★ Radio Shack
35 Crossroads Mall
Roanoke, VA 24017
(703)563-4411
Company Type: Division. Ultimate Parent:
Tandy Corp. SIC: 5731—Radio, Television
& Electronics Stores.

★ 92181 ★ Radio Shack
3561 Franklin Rd. SW
Roanoke, VA 24014
(703)342-6335
Company Type: Division. Ultimate Parent:
Tandy Corp. SIC: 5046—Commercial
Equipment Nec.

★ 92182 ★ Radio Shack
Roanoke Salem Plz.
Roanoke, VA 24017
(703)362-2779
Company Type: Division. Ultimate Parent:
Tandy Corp. SIC: 5065—Electronic Parts &
Equipment Nec; 5731—Radio, Television &
Electronics Stores.

★ 92183 ★ Radio Shack
35 Crossroads Mall
Roanoke, VA 24017
(703)563-4411
Company Type: Division. Ultimate Parent:
Tandy Corp. SIC: 5731—Radio, Television
& Electronics Stores.

★ 92184 ★ Sav on Food & Drug
3631 Peters Creek Rd. NW
Roanoke, VA 24019
(703)568-2727
Ultimate Parent: Kroger. SIC: 5912—Drug
Stores & Proprietary Stores.

★ 92185 ★ Sav on Food & Drug
14002 PO Box
Roanoke, VA 24038
(703)527-5470
Ultimate Parent: Kroger. SIC: 5411—
Grocery Stores.

★ 92186 ★ Shenandoah Life
Insurance Co.
2301 Brableton Ave. SW
Roanoke, VA 24015-4701
(703)985-4400
Company Type: Headquarters. Officer:
William R. Battle. Ultimate Parent: Black &
Decker Corp. SIC: 6311—Life Insurance;
6411—Insurance Agents, Brokers &
Service.

★ 92187 ★ Signet Bank, Virginia
3615 Franklin Rd.
Roanoke, VA 24014-2203
(703)985-3285
Location Type: Branch office. Ultimate
Parent: Signet Banking Corp. SIC: 6021—
National Commercial Banks.

★ 92188 ★ Signet Bank, Virginia
1959 Valley View Rd.
Roanoke, VA 24012-2025
(703)985-3270
Location Type: Branch office. Ultimate
Parent: Signet Banking Corp. SIC: 6021—
National Commercial Banks.

★ 92189 ★ Signet Bank, Virginia
3132 Electric Rd.
Roanoke, VA 24018-6441
(703)985-3231
Location Type: Branch office. Ultimate
Parent: Signet Banking Corp. SIC: 6021—
National Commercial Banks.

★ 92190 ★ Signet Bank, Virginia
1st & Church Sts.
Roanoke, VA 24011
(703)985-3334
Location Type: Branch office. Ultimate

Parent: Signet Banking Corp. SIC: 6021—
National Commercial Banks.

★ 92191 ★ Skyline Coal Co.
310 1st St.
Roanoke, VA 24011
(703)983-0222 Fax: (703)983-0267
Officer: James L. Van Lanen, President &
CEO. Ultimate Parent: Coastal Corp.

★ 92192 ★ Southern Utah Fuel
Co.
310 1st St.
Roanoke, VA 24011
(703)983-0222
Officer: James L. Van Lanen, President &
CEO. Ultimate Parent: Coastal Corp.

★ 92193 ★ Southern Utah Fuel
Co. Inc.
310 1st St. SW, Ste. 10
Roanoke, VA 24011-1922
(703)983-0222
Company Type: Subsidiary. Officer: James
R. Paul, Chairman of the Board. Ultimate
Parent: Coastal Corp. SIC: 1221—
Bituminous Coal & Lignite—Surface.
Employee Count: 253. Sales: 45000 M.

★ 92194 ★ Southern Utah Fuel
Co. Inc.
310 1st St. SW, Ste. 10
Roanoke, VA 24011-1922
(703)983-0222
Company Type: Subsidiary. Officer: James
R. Paul, Chairman of the Board. Ultimate
Parent: Coastal Corp. SIC: 1221—
Bituminous Coal & Lignite—Surface.
Employee Count: 253. Sales: 45 M.

★ 92195 ★ Southwest Operations
Center Inc.
1410 Coulter Dr. NW
Roanoke, VA 24012
(703)561-8600
Company Type: Subsidiary. Officer: A.
Leon Tomblin, President. Ultimate Parent:
First Virginia Banks Inc. SIC: 7374—Data
Processing & Preparation.

★ 92196 ★ Utah Fuel Co. Inc.
310 1st St. SW
Roanoke, VA 24011-1922
(703)983-0222
Company Type: Subsidiary. Officer: James
L. Van Lanen, President, Treasury. Ultimate
Parent: Coastal Corp. SIC: 1222—
Bituminous Coal—Underground. Employee
Count: 350. Sales: 53 M.

★ 92197 ★ Vitramon Inc.
3435 Chip Dr.
Roanoke, VA 24012
Ultimate Parent: Thomas & Betts. SIC:
3675—Electronic Capacitors.

★ 92198 ★ Waldenbooks Inc. (Br)
31 Crossroads Mall
Roanoke, VA 24017
(703)366-3666
Ultimate Parent: K-Mart. SIC: 5942—Book
Stores.

Rocky Mount

★ 92199 ★ First Virginia Bank
Franklin County
228 Franklin St.
Rocky Mount, VA 24151-1329
(703)483-5284
Company Type: Subsidiary. Officer: T.
Keister Greer, Chairman of the Board.
Ultimate Parent: First Virginia Banks Inc.
SIC: 6022—State Commercial Banks.

★ 92200 ★ First Virginia Bank
Franklin County
228 Franklin St.
Rocky Mount, VA 24151-1329
(703)483-5284
Company Type: Subsidiary. Officer: T.
Keister Greer, Chairman of the Board.
Ultimate Parent: First Virginia Banks Inc.
SIC: 6022—State Commercial Banks.
Employee Count: 51.

★ 92201 ★ Fleetwood Homes of
Virginia Inc. No. 19
Hwy. 40 West Rfd 4 PO Box 100
Rocky Mount, VA 24151
Ultimate Parent: Fleetwood Enterprises,
Inc. SIC: 2451—Mobile Homes.

★ 92202 ★ Kroger Co.
Tanyard Sq.
Rocky Mount, VA 24151
(703)483-2557
Ultimate Parent: Kroger. SIC: 5411—
Grocery Stores.

★ 92203 ★ Lane Co. Inc.
129 Pell Ave.
Rocky Mount, VA 24151
Ultimate Parent: Interco. SIC: 2511—Wood
Household Furniture.

★ 92204 ★ Standard Register Co.
Industrial Ave.
Rocky Mount, VA 24151
(703)483-9281
Officer: J L Galbraith, Manager. Ultimate
Parent: Standard Register. SIC: 2761—
Manifold Business Forms.

Rocky Mountain

★ 92205 ★ Fleetwood Homes of
Virginia
RR 4
Box 100
Rocky Mountain, VA 24151
(703)483-5171
Officer: Walter K. Hughes, Manager.
Ultimate Parent: Fleetwood Enterprises,
Inc. SIC: 2451—Mobile Homes.

Rose Hill

★ 92206 ★ Piggly Wiggly
Rose Hill, VA 24281
(703)445-4701
Ultimate Parent: Bruno's. SIC: 5411—
Grocery Stores.

Rosslyn

★ 92207 ★ New York Life
Washington General Office
Southeastern Agencies
1001 19th St. N., Ste. 1010
Rosslyn, VA 22209
(703)908-8900 Fax: (703)908-8850
Officer: Hwa Tran, General Manager.
Ultimate Parent: New York Life.

Salem

★ 92208 ★ Crestar Bank
1499 W. Main St.
Salem, VA 24153-3120
(703)985-5271
Location Type: Branch office. Ultimate
Parent: Crestar Financial Corp. SIC:
6021—National Commercial Banks.

★ 92209 ★ Drive Systems
Operations
1501 Roanoke Blvd.
Salem, VA 24153
Ultimate Parent: General Electric. SIC:
3679—Electronic Components Nec.

★ 92210 ★ Eckerd Drugs
1227 W. Main St.
Salem, VA 24153
(703)389-8221
Ultimate Parent: Eckerd Corp. SIC: 5912—
Drug Stores & Proprietary Stores.

★ 92211 ★ First Union National
Bank of Virginia
14 W. Main St.
Salem, VA 24153-3890
(703)387-3917
Location Type: Branch office. Ultimate
Parent: First Union Corp. SIC: 6021—
National Commercial Banks.

★ 92212 ★ First Union National
Bank of Virginia
1432 Apperson Dr.
Salem, VA 24153-7299
(703)387-1700
Location Type: Branch office. Ultimate
Parent: First Union Corp. SIC: 6021—
National Commercial Banks.

★ 92213 ★ General Electric Drive
Systems
1501 Roanoke Blvd.
Salem, VA 24153
(703)387-7000
Officer: Tom Brock Jr., Manager. Ultimate
Parent: General Electric. SIC: 3699—
Electrical Equipment & Supplies Nec.

★ 92214 ★ Kroger Co.
Rte. 3 Garman Rd.
Salem, VA 24153
Ultimate Parent: Kroger. SIC: 4226—
Special Warehousing & Storage Nec.

★ 92215 ★ Kroger Co.
2161 Apperson Dr.
Salem, VA 24153
(703)774-7879
Ultimate Parent: Kroger. SIC: 5411—
Grocery Stores.

★ 92216 ★ Kroger Co.
Garman Rd.
Salem, VA 24153
(703)387-5260
Ultimate Parent: Kroger. SIC: 5411—
Grocery Stores.

★ 92217 ★ Marriott Hotels
900 Prices Fork Rd.
Salem, VA 24153
(703)389-6700
Ultimate Parent: Marriott International. SIC:
7011—Hotels & Motels.

★ 92218 ★ McDonald's
Hamburgers Office
320 Wildwood Rd.
Salem, VA 24153
(703)389-8306
Ultimate Parent: McDonald's.

★ 92219 ★ Medeco Security
Locks Inc.
Us 11 & 460 West at Alleghany Dr.
Salem, VA 24153
Ultimate Parent: Hillenbrand Industries.
SIC: 3429—Hardware Nec.

★ 92220 ★ Medeco Security
Locks Inc.
3625 Alleghany Dr. Dr.
Salem, VA 24153
Ultimate Parent: Hillenbrand Industries.
SIC: 3429—Hardware Nec.

★ 92221 ★ Medeco Security
Locks Inc.
PO Box 3075
Salem, VA 24153
(703)380-5000 Fax: (703)380-5010
Company Type: Subsidiary. Officer: Tim
W. Layton, President & CEO. Ultimate
Parent: Hillenbrand Industries.

★ 92222 ★ PPG Industries Inc.
1814 Jefferson S
Salem, VA 24153
(703)345-7787
Ultimate Parent: PPG Industries Inc. SIC:
1793—Glass & Glazing Work.

★ 92223 ★ Seven-Up Bottling Co.
2103 Industrial Dr.
Salem, VA 24153
(703)389-7770
Officer: Jim Schneeloch, Manager.
Ultimate Parent: Dr. Pepper/Seven-Up.
SIC: 2086—Bottled & Canned Soft Drinks.

★ 92224 ★ Signet Bank, Virginia
W. Salem Plz.
Salem, VA 24153-5587
(703)985-3336
Location Type: Branch office. Ultimate
Parent: Signet Banking Corp. SIC: 6021—
National Commercial Banks.

★ 92225 ★ Valleydale Inc.
1013 Iowa St.
Salem, VA 24153
Ultimate Parent: Smithfield Foods Inc. SIC:
2011—Meat Packing Plants.

Saltville

★ 92226 ★ Piggly Wiggly
Saltville, VA 24370
(703)496-4051
Ultimate Parent: Bruno's. SIC: 5411—
Grocery Stores.

★ 92227 ★ Piggly Wiggly
Palmer Ave.
Saltville, VA 24370
(703)496-4051
Ultimate Parent: Bruno's. SIC: 5411—
Grocery Stores.

★ 92228 ★   **Rite Aid**
Main
Saluda, VA 24370
(703)496-5289
Ultimate Parent: Rite Aid. **SIC:** 5912—Drug Stores & Proprietary Stores.

Saluda

★ 92229 ★   **First Union National Bank of Virginia**
Rte. 33, Cooks Cnr.
Saluda, VA 23149
(804)758-2317
Location Type: Branch office. **Ultimate Parent:** First Union Corp. **SIC:** 6021—National Commercial Banks.

Sandston

★ 92230 ★   **Dean Foods Co.**
1595 Mary St.
Sandston, VA 23150
(804)737-8272
Officer: T. E. A. Sauer, President. **Ultimate Parent:** Dean Foods. **SIC:** 2079—Edible Fats & Oils Nec.

★ 92231 ★   **Delta Air Lines Inc.**
Krouse Rd.
Sandston, VA 23150
(804)222-2989
Ultimate Parent: Delta Air Lines, Inc. **SIC:** 4512—Air Transportation—Scheduled.

★ 92232 ★   **Hertz Rent-A-Car**
Krouse Rd.
Sandston, VA 23150
(804)222-7228
Ultimate Parent: Hertz. **SIC:** 7514—Passenger Car Rental.

★ 92233 ★   **Mid-Atlantic Coca-Cola Bottling Co. Inc.**
500 E. Park Ct.
Sandston, VA 23150
Ultimate Parent: Coca-Cola Enterprises. **SIC:** 2086—Bottled & Canned Soft Drinks.

★ 92234 ★   **Union Electric Co. Inc.**
606 PO Box
Sandston, VA 23150
Ultimate Parent: Union Electric Co. **SIC:** 1731—Electrical Work.

Shenandoah

★ 92235 ★   **Wrangler**
323 Pulaski Ave.
Shenandoah, VA 22849
(703)652-8149
Officer: Rick Vercellone, Manager. **Ultimate Parent:** VF Corp. **SIC:** 2325—Men's/Boys' Trousers & Slacks; 2326—Men's/Boys' Work Clothing.

Skippers

★ 92236 ★   **Georgia-Pacific Corp. Skippers Osb**
U.S. 301
Skippers, VA 23879
Ultimate Parent: Georgia-Pacific. **SIC:** 2493—Reconstituted Wood Products.

Smithfield

★ 92237 ★   **First Union National Bank of Virginia**
115 Main St.
Smithfield, VA 23430-1322
(804)357-4381
Location Type: Branch office. **Ultimate Parent:** First Union Corp. **SIC:** 6021—National Commercial Banks.

★ 92238 ★   **Gwaltney of Smithfield Ltd.**
Hwy. 10
Smithfield, VA 23430
Ultimate Parent: Smithfield Foods Inc. **SIC:** 2011—Meat Packing Plants.

★ 92239 ★   **Radio Shack**
Smithfield Sq.
Smithfield, VA 23430
(804)357-3000
Company Type: Division. **Ultimate Parent:** Tandy Corp. **SIC:** 5065—Electronic Parts & Equipment Nec.

★ 92240 ★   **Radio Shack**
Smithfield Sq.
Smithfield, VA 23430
(804)357-3000
Company Type: Division. **Ultimate Parent:** Tandy Corp. **SIC:** 5065—Electronic Parts & Equipment Nec.

★ 92241 ★   **Smithfield Foods Inc.**
501 N. Church St.
Smithfield, VA 23430
(804)357-4321
Company Type: Headquarters. **Officer:** Joseph Luter III, CEO. **Sales:** 1142 M. **Fortune 500:** Largest U.S. Industrial Corporations: Ranking 335.

★ 92242 ★   **Smithfield Ham Products**
401 N. Church St.
Smithfield, VA 23430
(804)357-2121
Officer: Alton Gwaltney, President. **Ultimate Parent:** Smithfield Foods Inc. **SIC:** 2011—Meat Packing Plants; 2013—Sausages & Other Prepared Meats; 2033—Canned Fruits & Vegetables.

★ 92243 ★   **Smithfield Packing Co.**
501 N. Church St.
Smithfield, VA 23430
(804)357-4321
Officer: Joseph W. Luter III, Chairman. **Ultimate Parent:** Smithfield Foods Inc. **SIC:** 2011—Meat Packing Plants.

★ 92244 ★   **Smithfield Packing Co. Inc.**
Hwy. 10
Smithfield, VA 23430
Ultimate Parent: Smithfield Foods Inc. **SIC:** 2011—Meat Packing Plants.

South Boston

★ 92245 ★   **C-K Co.**
State Rd. 919
South Boston, VA 24592
Ultimate Parent: Teledyne. **SIC:** 3312—Blast Furnaces & Steel Mills.

★ 92246 ★   **Coca Cola Bottling Co. Conso**
Hwy. 58 W
South Boston, VA 24592
(804)575-7944
Ultimate Parent: Coca-Cola Bottling Consol. **SIC:** 5149—Groceries & Related Products Nec.

★ 92247 ★   **Crestar Bank**
4027 Halifax Rd.
South Boston, VA 24592-4831
(804)575-0430
Location Type: Branch office. **Ultimate Parent:** Crestar Financial Corp. **SIC:** 6021—National Commercial Banks.

★ 92248 ★   **Crestar Bank**
410 Main St.
South Boston, VA 24592-3284
(804)575-0400
Location Type: Branch office. **Ultimate Parent:** Crestar Financial Corp. **SIC:** 6021—National Commercial Banks.

★ 92249 ★   **First Federal S&L of America**
4018 Halifax Rd.
South Boston, VA 24592
(804)572-8961
Ultimate Parent: Bancorp Hawaii. **SIC:** 6035—Federal Savings Institutions.

★ 92250 ★   **Food Lion**
Us 58 E
South Boston, VA 24592
(804)572-1960
Ultimate Parent: Food Lion. **SIC:** 5411—Grocery Stores.

★ 92251 ★   **Georgia-Pacific Corp. S. Boston Particleboard**
Rte. 879 Hwy. 80 E.
South Boston, VA 24592
Ultimate Parent: Georgia-Pacific. **SIC:** 2493—Reconstituted Wood Products.

★ 92252 ★   **Georgia Pacific Corp. South Boston Particleboard**
Rte. 879 Hwy. 360 West
South Boston, VA 24592
Ultimate Parent: Georgia-Pacific. **SIC:** 2493—Reconstituted Wood Products.

★ 92253 ★   **Greyhound Bus Lines**
1104 Seymour Dr.
South Boston, VA 24592
(804)572-3304
Ultimate Parent: Greyhound Lines Inc. **SIC:** 4131—Intercity & Rural Bus Transportation; 4173—Bus Terminal & Service Facilities.

★ 92254 ★   **New York Life Insurance Co.**
554 N. Main St.
South Boston, VA 24592
(804)575-7276
Ultimate Parent: New York Life. **SIC:** 6411—Insurance Agents, Brokers & Service.

★ 92255 ★   **Northwestern Mutual Life Inc.**
106 Security Bldg.
South Boston, VA 24592
(804)572-2569
Ultimate Parent: Northwestern Mutual Life. **SIC:** 6411—Insurance Agents, Brokers & Service.

★ 92256 ★   **O'sullivan Ind. Inc. of Virginia**
Hwy. 58 Halifax County Industrial Park
South Boston, VA 24592
Ultimate Parent: Tandy Corp. **SIC:** 2511—Wood Household Furniture.

★ 92257 ★   **Radio Shack**
2213 Hwy. 501 N
South Boston, VA 24592
(804)575-5411
Company Type: Division. **Ultimate Parent:** Tandy Corp. **SIC:** 5731—Radio, Television & Electronics Stores.

★ 92258 ★   **Radio Shack**
2213 Hwy. 501 N
South Boston, VA 24592
(804)575-5411
Company Type: Division. **Ultimate Parent:** Tandy Corp. **SIC:** 5731—Radio, Television & Electronics Stores.

★ 92259 ★   **Teledyne Allvac/ Vasco S. Boston Plant**
919 State Rd.
PO Box 447
South Boston, VA 24592
Ultimate Parent: Teledyne. **SIC:** 3315—Steel Wire & Related Products.

★ 92260 ★   **Vulcan Materials Co.**
Hwy. 304
South Boston, VA 24592
(804)572-3967
Ultimate Parent: Vulcan Materials Co. **SIC:** 1429—Crushed & Broken Stone Nec.

★ 92261 ★   **Vulcan Materials Co.**
Hwy. 304
South Boston, VA 24592
(804)572-3967
Ultimate Parent: Vulcan Materials Co. **SIC:** 1429—Crushed & Broken Stone Nec.

★ 92262 ★   **Westinghouse/Abb Power T&D Co.**
Hwy. 58 West
South Boston, VA 24592
Ultimate Parent: Westinghouse Electric Corp. **SIC:** 3612—Transformers Except Electronic.

★ 92263 ★   **Westinghouse Electric Corp.**
Hwy. 58 West
South Boston, VA 24592
Ultimate Parent: Westinghouse Electric Corp. **SIC:** 3612—Transformers Except Electronic.

South Hill

★ 92264 ★   **First Virginia Bank**
111 E. Danville St.
South Hill, VA 23970-2611
(804)447-7141
Company Type: Subsidiary. **Officer:** James H. Wells, President, CEO. **Ultimate Parent:** First Virginia Banks Inc. **SIC:** 6022—State Commercial Banks. **Employee Count:** 24.

★ 92265 ★   **First Virginia Bank**
111 E. Danville St.
PO Box 30
South Hill, VA 23970-0030
(804)447-7141
Company Type: Subsidiary. **Officer:** Thomas J. Fitzgerald, Chairman of the Board. **Ultimate Parent:** First Virginia Banks Inc. **SIC:** 6022—State Commercial Banks.

★ 92266 ★   **Rite Aid**
Town Sq.
South Hill, VA 23970
(804)447-3417
Ultimate Parent: Rite Aid. **SIC:** 5912—Drug Stores & Proprietary Stores.

★ 92267 ★   **Signet Bank, Virginia**
US Rte. 58
South Hill, VA 23970
Location Type: Branch office. **Ultimate Parent:** Signet Banking Corp. **SIC:** 6021—National Commercial Banks.

★ 92268 ★   **Signet Bank, Virginia**
122 W. Atlantic St.
South Hill, VA 23970-1943
(804)447-3171
Location Type: Branch office. **Ultimate Parent:** Signet Banking Corp. **SIC:** 6021—National Commercial Banks.

★ 92269 ★   **Watkins Manufacturing Co.**
Hwy. 1 S
South Hill, VA 23970
(804)447-7611
Ultimate Parent: Masco. **SIC:** 5012—Automobiles & Other Motor Vehicles.

Southboston

★ 92270 ★   **Rite Aid**
3340 Hwy. 501 N
Southboston, VA 24592
(804)575-0144
Ultimate Parent: Rite Aid. **SIC:** 5912—Drug Stores & Proprietary Stores.

Spotsylvania

★ 92271 ★   **Crestar Bank**
8970 Courthouse Rd.
Spotsylvania, VA 22553
(800)451-2435
Location Type: Branch office. **Ultimate Parent:** Crestar Financial Corp. **SIC:** 6021—National Commercial Banks.

★ 92272 ★   **Hit or Miss**
Spotsylvania Mall
Spotsylvania, VA 22553
(703)786-9024
Ultimate Parent: TJX. **SIC:** 5621—Women's Clothing Stores.

Springfield

★ 92273 ★   **Avon Corp.**
5241-A Rolling Rd.
Springfield, VA 22151
(703)978-8300
Ultimate Parent: Avon Products, Inc. **SIC:** 3272—Concrete Products Nec; 0782—Lawn & Garden Services; 1741—Masonry & Other Stonework.

★ 92274 ★   **Crestar Bank**
6720 Commerce
Springfield, VA 22150-2557
(703)838-3260
Location Type: Branch office. **Ultimate Parent:** Crestar Financial Corp. **SIC:** 6021—National Commercial Banks.

★ 92275 ★   **Crestar Bank**
8098 Rolling Rd.
Springfield, VA 22153-2928
(703)838-3440
Location Type: Branch office. **Ultimate Parent:** Crestar Financial Corp. **SIC:** 6021—National Commercial Banks.

★ 92276 ★   **Crestar Bank**
7205 Commerce St.
Springfield, VA 22150-3411
Location Type: Branch office. **Ultimate Parent:** Crestar Financial Corp. **SIC:** 6021—National Commercial Banks.

★ 92277 ★ **Crestar Bank**
6216 Rolling Rd.
Springfield, VA 22152-2307
Location Type: Branch office. **Ultimate Parent:** Crestar Financial Corp. **SIC:** 6021—National Commercial Banks.

★ 92278 ★ **First American Bank**
6592 Springfield Mall
Springfield, VA 22150
(703)739-3583
Ultimate Parent: First American Corp. **SIC:** 6099—Functions Related to Deposit Banking.

★ 92279 ★ **First American Bank**
6949 Commerce St.
Springfield, VA 22150
(703)934-1899
Ultimate Parent: First American Corp. **SIC:** 6099—Functions Related to Deposit Banking.

★ 92280 ★ **First American Bank Virginia**
6592 Springfield Mall
Springfield, VA 22150
(703)827-8606
Ultimate Parent: First American Corp. **SIC:** 6022—State Commercial Banks.

★ 92281 ★ **First American Bank Virginia**
5703 Buke Ctr. Pky.
Springfield, VA 22015
(703)821-7600
Ultimate Parent: First American Corp. **SIC:** 6022—State Commercial Banks.

★ 92282 ★ **First Union National Bank of Virginia**
6949 Commerce St.
Springfield, VA 22150-2605
(703)934-1899
Location Type: Branch office. **Ultimate Parent:** First Union Corp. **SIC:** 6021—National Commercial Banks.

★ 92283 ★ **First Union National Bank of Virginia**
8401 Old Keene Mill Rd.
Springfield, VA 22152-2899
(703)442-4656
Location Type: Branch office. **Ultimate Parent:** First Union Corp. **SIC:** 6021—National Commercial Banks.

★ 92284 ★ **First Union National Bank of Virginia**
6592 Springfield Mall
Springfield, VA 22150-1781
(703)739-3583
Location Type: Branch office. **Ultimate Parent:** First Union Corp. **SIC:** 6021—National Commercial Banks.

★ 92285 ★ **First Union National Bank of Virginia**
8900 Burke Lake Rd.
Springfield, VA 22151-1079
(703)442-3630
Location Type: Branch office. **Ultimate Parent:** First Union Corp. **SIC:** 6021—National Commercial Banks.

★ 92286 ★ **First Virginia Bank**
7000 Bland St.
Springfield, VA 22150-3432
(703)241-3395
Location Type: Branch office. **Ultimate Parent:** First Virginia Banks Inc. **SIC:** 6021—National Commercial Banks.

★ 92287 ★ **Greyhound Bus Lines**
7025 Brookfield Plz.
Springfield, VA 22150
(703)451-6322
Ultimate Parent: Greyhound Lines Inc. **SIC:** 4111—Local & Suburban Transit.

★ 92288 ★ **Macy's**
Springfield Mall
Springfield, VA 22150
(703)719-6100
Ultimate Parent: R. H. Macy. **SIC:** 5311—Department Stores.

★ 92289 ★ **Pitney Bowes**
5580 Port Royal Rd.
Springfield, VA 22151
(703)321-4995
Officer: Tom Shaughnessy, Manager. **Ultimate Parent:** Pitney Bowes. **SIC:** 3663—Radio & T.V. Communications Equipment.

★ 92290 ★ **Radio Shack**
Saratoga Shopping Ctr.
Springfield, VA 22153
(703)455-5144
Company Type: Division. **Ultimate Parent:** Tandy Corp. **SIC:** 5731—Radio, Television & Electronics Stores.

★ 92291 ★ **Radio Shack**
Saratoga Shopping Ctr.
Springfield, VA 22153
(703)455-5144
Company Type: Division. **Ultimate Parent:** Tandy Corp. **SIC:** 5731—Radio, Television & Electronics Stores.

★ 92292 ★ **Signet Bank, Virginia**
7030 Old Keene Mill Rd.
Springfield, VA 22150-3440
(703)750-7161
Location Type: Branch office. **Ultimate Parent:** Signet Banking Corp. **SIC:** 6021—National Commercial Banks.

★ 92293 ★ **Systems Control Inc.**
6501 Loisdale Ct
Springfield, VA 22150
(703)922-7267
Ultimate Parent: Snap-on Tools. **SIC:** 7377—Computer Rental & Leasing.

★ 92294 ★ **Teledyne Total Power**
7943 Angus Ct.
Springfield, VA 22153
(703)569-9397
Ultimate Parent: Teledyne. **SIC:** 3714—Motor Vehicle Parts & Accessories.

★ 92295 ★ **Vulcan Materials Co.**
Industrial Rd.
Springfield, VA 22151
(703)354-5783
Ultimate Parent: Vulcan Materials Co. **SIC:** 1429—Crushed & Broken Stone Nec.

★ 92296 ★ **Vulcan Materials Co.**
Industrial Rd.
Springfield, VA 22151
(703)354-5783
Ultimate Parent: Vulcan Materials Co. **SIC:** 1429—Crushed & Broken Stone Nec.

St. Paul

★ 92297 ★ **First Union National Bank of Virginia**
28 Russell St.
St. Paul, VA 24283
(703)762-5551
Location Type: Branch office. **Ultimate Parent:** First Union Corp. **SIC:** 6021—National Commercial Banks.

★ 92298 ★ **Signet Bank, Virginia**
3052 4th Ave.
St. Paul, VA 24283
(703)762-5531
Location Type: Branch office. **Ultimate Parent:** Signet Banking Corp. **SIC:** 6021—National Commercial Banks.

Stafford

★ 92299 ★ **First Virginia Bank**
300 Butler Rd.
Chatham Sq. Shopping Ctr.
Stafford, VA 22405-2514
(703)373-3114
Location Type: Branch office. **Ultimate Parent:** First Virginia Banks Inc. **SIC:** 6021—National Commercial Banks.

★ 92300 ★ **First Virginia Bank**
289 Garrisonville Rd.
Stafford, VA 22554-1527
(703)241-3118
Location Type: Branch office. **Ultimate Parent:** First Virginia Banks Inc. **SIC:** 6021—National Commercial Banks.

★ 92301 ★ **Vulcan Materials Co.**
1590 PO Box
Stafford, VA 22554
(703)631-2070
Ultimate Parent: Vulcan Materials Co. **SIC:** 1429—Crushed & Broken Stone Nec.

★ 92302 ★ **Vulcan Materials Co.**
Garrisonville
Stafford, VA 22554
(703)659-3003
Ultimate Parent: Vulcan Materials Co. **SIC:** 5039—Construction Materials Nec.

★ 92303 ★ **Vulcan Materials Co.**
Garrisonville
Stafford, VA 22554
(703)659-3003
Ultimate Parent: Vulcan Materials Co. **SIC:** 5039—Construction Materials Nec.

★ 92304 ★ **Vulcan Materials Corp.**
1590 PO Box
Stafford, VA 22554
(703)631-2070
Ultimate Parent: Vulcan Materials Co. **SIC:** 1429—Crushed & Broken Stone Nec.

Standardsville

★ 92305 ★ **AT&T**
Standardsville, VA 22973
(804)985-2941
Location Type: Branch office. **Ultimate Parent:** AT&T. **SIC:** 4813—Telephone Communications Except Radiotelephone.

Stanley

★ 92306 ★ **Rockingham Poultry Inc.**
Rte. 340
Stanley, VA 22851
Ultimate Parent: WLR Foods. **SIC:** 2015—Poultry Slaughtering & Processing.

★ 92307 ★ **Wampler Longacre Inc.**
Rte. 340
Stanley, VA 22851
(703)778-2291
Company Type: Division. **Location Type:** Facility. **Officer:** Tom Mallalieu, Plant Mgr. **Ultimate Parent:** WLR Foods. **SIC:** 2013—Sausages & Other Prepared Meats.

Staunton

★ 92308 ★ **Beneficial Income Tax Service**
1373 Greenville Ave.
Staunton, VA 24401
(703)886-0781
Ultimate Parent: Beneficial. **SIC:** 7291—Tax Return Preparation Services.

★ 92309 ★ **Chesapeake & Potomac Telephone Co.**
115 Fillmore St.
Staunton, VA 24401-3316
(703)887-6101
Company Type: Subsidiary. **Officer:** Mike Riley. **Ultimate Parent:** Bell Atlantic Corp. **SIC:** 4813—Telephone Communications Except Radiotelephone.

★ 92310 ★ **Crestar Bank**
1111 Greenville Ave.
Staunton, VA 24401-5020
(703)887-0158
Location Type: Branch office. **Ultimate Parent:** Crestar Financial Corp. **SIC:** 6021—National Commercial Banks.

★ 92311 ★ **Crestar Bank**
1410 Churchville Ave.
Staunton, VA 24401-1718
(703)887-0136
Location Type: Branch office. **Ultimate Parent:** Crestar Financial Corp. **SIC:** 6021—National Commercial Banks.

★ 92312 ★ **Crestar Bank**
2-14 W. Beverly St.
Staunton, VA 24402-1269
(703)887-0100
Location Type: Branch office. **Ultimate Parent:** Crestar Financial Corp. **SIC:** 6021—National Commercial Banks.

★ 92313 ★ **Crestar Bank**
638 N. Coalter St.
Staunton, VA 24401-3403
(703)887-0151
Location Type: Branch office. **Ultimate Parent:** Crestar Financial Corp. **SIC:** 6021—National Commercial Banks.

★ 92314 ★ **First American Bank**
833 Springhill Rd.
Staunton, VA 24401
(703)885-7583
Ultimate Parent: First American Corp. **SIC:** 6099—Functions Related to Deposit Banking.

★ 92315 ★ **First American Bank**
239 N. Central Ave.
Staunton, VA 24401
(703)886-0774
Ultimate Parent: First American Corp. **SIC:** 6099—Functions Related to Deposit Banking.

★ 92316 ★ **First American Bank of Virginia**
833 Springhill Rd.
Staunton, VA 24401
(703)887-1340
Ultimate Parent: First American Corp. **SIC:** 6022—State Commercial Banks.

★ 92317 ★ **First Union National Bank of Virginia**
239 N. Central Ave.
Staunton, VA 24401-3310
(703)887-1300
Location Type: Branch office. **Ultimate Parent:** First Union Corp. **SIC:** 6021—National Commercial Banks.

★ 92318 ★ **First Virginia Bank Augusta**
125 N. Central Ave.
Staunton, VA 24401-3308
(703)885-1561
Company Type: Subsidiary. **Officer:** Richard W. Smith, Chairman of the Board. **Ultimate Parent:** First Virginia Banks Inc. **SIC:** 6022—State Commercial Banks.

★ 92319 ★ **First Virginia Bank - Augusta**
125 N. Central Ave.
Staunton, VA 24401-3308
(703)885-1561
Company Type: Subsidiary. **Officer:** Richard W. Smith, Chairman of the Board. **Ultimate Parent:** First Virginia Banks Inc. **SIC:** 6022—State Commercial Banks. **Employee Count:** 52.

★ 92320 ★ **Food Lion**
2411 W. Beverley St.
Staunton, VA 24401
(703)885-8022
Ultimate Parent: Food Lion. **SIC:** 5411—Grocery Stores.

★ 92321 ★ **Food Lion**
Orchard Hill Shopping Ctr.
Staunton, VA 24401
(703)886-6308
Ultimate Parent: Food Lion. **SIC:** 5411—Grocery Stores.

★ 92322 ★ **J C Penney Co.**
1349 Staunton Massachuset
Staunton, VA 24401
(703)885-1511
Ultimate Parent: J.C. Penney. **SIC:** 5311—Department Stores.

★ 92323 ★ **Kroger Co.**
850 Statler Blvd.
Staunton, VA 24401
(703)885-0363
Ultimate Parent: Kroger. **SIC:** 5411—Grocery Stores.

★ 92324 ★ **Kroger Co.**
2030 W. Beverley St.
Staunton, VA 24401
(703)885-0778
Ultimate Parent: Kroger. **SIC:** 5411—Grocery Stores.

★ 92325 ★ **Life Insur Co. of Virginia**
11 Terry Ct
Staunton, VA 24401
(703)886-4111
Ultimate Parent: Life Insurance Co. of Virginia. **SIC:** 6411—Insurance Agents, Brokers & Service.

★ 92326 ★ **New York Life Insurance Co.**
1105 Greenville Ave.
Staunton, VA 24401
(703)886-3138
Ultimate Parent: New York Life. **SIC:** 6411—Insurance Agents, Brokers & Service.

★ 92327 ★ **Radio Shack**
1309 Greenville Ave.
Staunton, VA 24401
(703)886-6460
Company Type: Division. **Ultimate Parent:** Tandy Corp. **SIC:** 7629—Electrical Repair Shops Nec.

★ 92328 ★ **Rite Aid**
600 N. Coalter St.
Staunton, VA 24401
(703)885-7276
Ultimate Parent: Rite Aid. **SIC:** 5912—Drug Stores & Proprietary Stores.

★ 92329 ★ **Southern Electric Corp.**
818 Greenville Ave.
Staunton, VA 24401
(703)886-6218
Officer: Herbert H. Walge, Manager. **Ultimate Parent:** Sonoco Products.

★ 92330 ★ **UNIFI**
PO Box 2525
Staunton, VA 24402
(703)885-1211
Ultimate Parent: UNIFI, Inc. **SIC:** 2282—Throwing & Winding Mills.

★ 92331 ★ **Unifi Inc.**
Morris Mill Rd.
Staunton, VA 24401
Ultimate Parent: UNIFI, Inc. **SIC:** 2282—Throwing & Winding Mills.

★ 92332 ★ **Waldenbooks**
1309 Greenville Ave.
Staunton, VA 24401
(703)885-5839
Ultimate Parent: K-Mart. **SIC:** 5942—Book Stores.

★ 92333 ★ **Westvaco Corp.**
305 Hudson Ave.
Staunton, VA 24401
(703)886-7107
Ultimate Parent: WestVaco Corp. **SIC:** 5113—Industrial & Personal Service Paper.

★ 92334 ★ **World Book**
Childcraft
319 Rainbow Dr.
Staunton, VA 24401-2134
(703)886-5443
Location Type: Branch office. **Ultimate Parent:** Berkshire Hathaway. **SIC:** 5963—Direct Selling Establishments.

Stephens city

★ 92335 ★ **First Union National Bank of Virginia**
382 Fairfax Pke.
Stephens city, VA 22655
(703)665-6738
Location Type: Branch office. **Ultimate Parent:** First Union Corp. **SIC:** 6021—National Commercial Banks.

Stephens City

★ 92336 ★ **Rite Aid**
Stephens City Plz.
Stephens City, VA 22655
(703)869-9831
Ultimate Parent: Rite Aid. **SIC:** 5912—Drug Stores & Proprietary Stores.

Sterling

★ 92337 ★ **Browning-Ferris Industries**
13 Douglas Ct.
Sterling, VA 20166
(703)471-1320
Officer: Mark Oderkirk, Manager. **Ultimate Parent:** Browning-Ferris Industries. **SIC:** 3589—Service Industry Machinery Nec.

★ 92338 ★ **Crestar Bank**
46910 Community Plz.
Sterling, VA 22170-1888
(703)838-3040
Location Type: Branch office. **Ultimate Parent:** Crestar Financial Corp. **SIC:** 6021—National Commercial Banks.

★ 92339 ★ **Crestar Bank**
11 Pidgeon Hill Dr.
Sterling, VA 22170-6102
(800)451-2435
Location Type: Branch office. **Ultimate**

Parent: Crestar Financial Corp. **SIC:** 6021—National Commercial Banks.

★ 92340 ★ **First Union National Bank of Virginia**
1201 W. Church Rd., Rte. 28
Sterling, VA 22170-9302
(703)430-6110
Location Type: Branch office. **Ultimate Parent:** First Union Corp. **SIC:** 6021—National Commercial Banks.

★ 92341 ★ **First Union National Bank of Virginia**
209 Harry Flood Byrd Hwy.
Sterling, VA 22170-1812
(703)442-3694
Location Type: Branch office. **Ultimate Parent:** First Union Corp. **SIC:** 6021—National Commercial Banks.

★ 92342 ★ **First Union National Bank of Virginia**
209 Leesburg Pke.
Sterling, VA 22170-2228
(703)430-2800
Location Type: Branch office. **Ultimate Parent:** First Union Corp. **SIC:** 6021—National Commercial Banks.

★ 92343 ★ **First Virginia Bank**
20921 Davenport Dr., Ste. 105
Sterling, VA 22170-6132
(703)241-4722
Location Type: Branch office. **Ultimate Parent:** First Virginia Banks Inc. **SIC:** 6021—National Commercial Banks.

★ 92344 ★ **First Virginia Bank**
101 Enterprise St.
Sterling, VA 22170-3219
(703)241-4621
Location Type: Branch office. **Ultimate Parent:** First Virginia Banks Inc. **SIC:** 6021—National Commercial Banks.

★ 92345 ★ **Hit or Miss**
21800 Towncenter Plz. 268
Sterling, VA 22170
(703)444-3446
Ultimate Parent: TJX. **SIC:** 5699—Miscellaneous Apparel & Accessory Stores.

★ 92346 ★ **Price Club 218**
21398 Price Cascades Plz.
Sterling, VA 22170
(703)406-7004
Ultimate Parent: Price. **SIC:** 5399—Miscellaneous General Merchandise Store.

★ 92347 ★ **Raytheon Corporate Jets**
22070 Broderick Dr.
Sterling, VA 20166
(703)406-2000
Officer: Robert L. Kirk, Chairman. **Ultimate Parent:** Raytheon Co. **SIC:** 3721—Aircraft.

Strasburg

★ 92348 ★ **Borden Inc.**
Dairy
E. King St.
Strasburg, VA 22657
Company Type: Division. **Ultimate Parent:** Borden, Inc. **SIC:** 2026—Fluid Milk; 2021—Creamery Butter; 2023—Dry, Condensed & Evaporated Dairy Products.

★ 92349 ★ **Borden Inc.**
Dairy
329 E. King St.
Strasburg, VA 22657-0271
Company Type: Division. **Ultimate Parent:** Borden, Inc. **SIC:** 2026—Fluid Milk; 2021—Creamery Butter; 2023—Dry, Condensed & Evaporated Dairy Products.

★ 92350 ★ **Star Market**
Rural Route 1
Strasburg, VA 22657
(703)465-3013
Ultimate Parent: American Stores. **SIC:** 5411—Grocery Stores.

Stuart

★ 92351 ★ **Clark Gas & Oil Co.**
Commerce
Stuart, VA 24171
(703)694-3772
Ultimate Parent: Exxon. **SIC:** 5983—Fuel Oil Dealers.

★ 92352 ★ **Crestar Bank**
Blue Ridge St.
Stuart, VA 24171
(703)694-1100
Location Type: Branch office. **Ultimate Parent:** Crestar Financial Corp. **SIC:** 6021—National Commercial Banks.

★ 92353 ★ **Masonite Corp. Stuart Plant**
Commerce St.
Stuart, VA 24171
Ultimate Parent: International Paper Co. **SIC:** 2499—Wood Products Nec.

★ 92354 ★ **Rite Aid**
Store Village Shopping Ctr.
Stuart, VA 24171
(703)694-7386
Ultimate Parent: Rite Aid. **SIC:** 5912—Drug Stores & Proprietary Stores.

★ 92355 ★ **Rite Aid**
Pharmacy Village Shopping Ctr.
Stuart, VA 24171
(703)694-4034
Ultimate Parent: Rite Aid. **SIC:** 5912—Drug Stores & Proprietary Stores.

Stuarts Draft

★ 92356 ★ **Alcoa Building Products**
Rte. 909 PO Box 538
Stuarts Draft, VA 24477
Ultimate Parent: Aluminum Co. of America--Alcoa. **SIC:** 3089—Plastics Products Nec.

★ 92357 ★ **Alcoa Building Products Inc.**
Route 909
Stuarts Draft, VA 24477
(703)337-3663
Officer: David Barker, Plant Manager. **Ultimate Parent:** Aluminum Co. of America--Alcoa. **SIC:** 3952—Lead Pencils & Art Goods.

★ 92358 ★ **Alcoa Building Products Inc.**
Route 909
Stuarts Draft, VA 24477
(703)337-3663
Officer: David Barker, Plant Manager. **Ultimate Parent:** Aluminum Co. of America--Alcoa. **SIC:** 3952—Lead Pencils & Art Goods.

Suffolk

★ 92359 ★ **Butler Paper Co.**
324 Newport St.
Suffolk, VA 23434
(804)539-2351
Officer: James E. Butler III, President. **Ultimate Parent:** Alco Standard Corp. **SIC:** 2621—Paper Mills.

★ 92360 ★ **Butler Paper Co.**
324 Newport St.
Suffolk, VA 23434
(804)539-2351
Officer: James E. Butler III, President. **Ultimate Parent:** Alco Standard Corp. **SIC:** 2621—Paper Mills.

★ 92361 ★ **Chesapeake & Potomac Telephone Co.**
206 N. Main St.
Suffolk, VA 23434-4421
(804)539-5036
Company Type: Subsidiary. **Officer:** Charles E. Gwaltney. **Ultimate Parent:** Bell Atlantic Corp. **SIC:** 4813—Telephone Communications Except Radiotelephone.

★ 92362 ★ **Crestar Bank**
123 N. Main St.
Suffolk, VA 23434
(804)925-6514
Location Type: Branch office. **Ultimate Parent:** Crestar Financial Corp. **SIC:** 6021—National Commercial Banks.

★ 92363 ★ **Crestar Bank**
6617 HOLLAND RD.
Suffolk, VA 23437
(804)858-3063
Location Type: Branch office. **Ultimate Parent:** Crestar Financial Corp. **SIC:** 6021—National Commercial Banks.

★ 92364 ★ **Exxon Service Station**
2109 N. Main St.
Suffolk, VA 23434
(804)539-9538
Ultimate Parent: Exxon. **SIC:** 5541—Gasoline Service Stations.

★ 92365 ★ **Exxon Service Station**
809 E. Pinner St.
Suffolk, VA 23434
(804)539-9516
Ultimate Parent: Exxon. **SIC:** 5541—Gasoline Service Stations.

★ 92366 ★ **Flowers Baking Co.**
810 E. Pinner St.
Suffolk, VA 23434
(804)539-2898
Ultimate Parent: Flowers Industries. **SIC:** 5461—Retail Bakeries.

★ 92367 ★ **Food Lion**
1242 Holland Rd.
Suffolk, VA 23434
(804)934-2121
Ultimate Parent: Food Lion. **SIC:** 5411—Grocery Stores.

★ 92368 ★ **Food Lion**
1226 White Marsh Rd.
Suffolk, VA 23434
(804)539-3565
Ultimate Parent: Food Lion. **SIC:** 5411—Grocery Stores.

★ 92369 ★ **Golden Peanut Co.**
303 S. Saratoga St.
Suffolk, VA 23434-5836
(804)934-6700
Officer: L. C. Umphlette. **Ultimate Parent:** Archer Daniels Midland Co. **SIC:** 5159—Farm-Product Raw Materials Nec; 2076—Vegetable Oil Mills Nec; 2064—Candy & Other Confectionery Products.

★ 92370 ★ **Life Insurance Co. of Va**
211 Market St.
Suffolk, VA 23434
(804)539-3321
Ultimate Parent: Life Insurance Co. of Virginia. **SIC:** 8742—Management Consulting Services.

★ 92371 ★ **Planters Lifesavers Co.**
200 Johnson Ave.
Suffolk, VA 23434
Ultimate Parent: RJR Nabisco Holdings. **SIC:** 2064—Candy & Other Confectionery Products; 2068—Salted & Roasted Nuts & Seeds; 2099—Food Preparations Nec.

★ 92372 ★ **Radio Shack**
Suffolk Shopping Ctr. W
Suffolk, VA 23434
(804)539-2490
Company Type: Division. **Ultimate Parent:** Tandy Corp. **SIC:** 1521—Single-Family Housing Construction; 5731—Radio, Television & Electronics Stores.

★ 92373 ★ **Rite Aid**
1226 White Marshrd
Suffolk, VA 23434
(804)539-9732
Ultimate Parent: Rite Aid. **SIC:** 5912—Drug Stores & Proprietary Stores.

Tappahannock

★ 92374 ★ **First Union National Bank of Virginia**
Essex Sq. Shopping Ctr., Rte. 7
Tappahannock, VA 22560
(804)443-5385
Location Type: Branch office. **Ultimate Parent:** First Union Corp. **SIC:** 6021—National Commercial Banks.

★ 92375 ★ **Food Lion**
1850 Tappahannock Blvd.
Tappahannock, VA 22560
(804)443-5518
Ultimate Parent: Food Lion. **SIC:** 5411—Grocery Stores.

★ 92376 ★ **Food Lion Inc.**
1850 Tappahannock Blvd.
Tappahannock, VA 22560
(804)443-5518
Ultimate Parent: Food Lion. **SIC:** 5411—Grocery Stores.

★ 92377 ★   **Greyhound Bus Lines**
Rappahannock Shopping Ctr.
Tappahannock, VA 22560
(804)443-5970
Ultimate Parent: Greyhound Lines Inc. **SIC:**
4111—Local & Suburban Transit.

Tazewell

★ 92378 ★   **Acme Markets**
Tazewell Mall
Tazewell, VA 24651
(703)988-2561
Ultimate Parent: American Stores. **SIC:**
5331—Variety Stores.

★ 92379 ★   **Food Lion**
61 Market
Tazewell, VA 24651
(703)988-2584
Ultimate Parent: Food Lion. **SIC:** 5411—
Grocery Stores.

Temperanceville

★ 92380 ★   **Holly Farms Foods Inc.**
Temperanceville Plant
US Hwy. 13
PO Box 8
Temperanceville, VA 23442
Location Type: Plant. **Ultimate Parent:**
Tyson Foods, Inc. **SIC:** 2010—Meat
Products.

★ 92381 ★   **Holly Farms/Tyson Foods Inc. Tyson Foods Inc.**
U.S. Hwy. 13 PO Box 8
Temperanceville, VA 23442
Ultimate Parent: Tyson Foods, Inc. **SIC:**
2015—Poultry Slaughtering & Processing.

★ 92382 ★   **Tyson Foods Inc.**
11224 Lankford Hwy.
Temperanceville, VA 23442
(804)824-3471
Officer: Carl A. Cold, Manager. **Ultimate Parent:** Tyson Foods, Inc. **SIC:** 2015—
Poultry Slaughtering & Processing.

Timberville

★ 92383 ★   **Rockingham Poultry Inc.**
Co-Op Dr.
Timberville, VA 22853
Ultimate Parent: WLR Foods. **SIC:** 2015—
Poultry Slaughtering & Processing.

★ 92384 ★   **Wampler Longacre Inc.**
Co-Op Dr.
Timberville, VA 22853
(703)896-7000
Company Type: Division. **Location Type:**
Facility. **Officer:** Hobert Hovey, Plant Mgr.
Ultimate Parent: WLR Foods. **SIC:** 2013—
Sausages & Other Prepared Meats.

★ 92385 ★   **WLR Foods**
800 Co-op Dr.
Timberville, VA 22853
(703)896-7001
Company Type: Headquarters. **Officer:**
James L. Keeler. **Employee Count:** 6850.
Sales: 616.7 M. **Fortune 500:** Largest U.S.
Industrial Corporations: Ranking 498.

Toano

★ 92386 ★   **Owens-Illinois Glass Container Inc.**
150 Industrial Blvd.
Toano, VA 23168
Ultimate Parent: Owens-Illinois. **SIC:**
3221—Glass Containers.

Triangle

★ 92387 ★   **Greyhound Bus Lines**
18518 Jefferson Davis Hwy.
Triangle, VA 22172
(703)221-4080
Ultimate Parent: Greyhound Lines Inc. **SIC:**
4111—Local & Suburban Transit.

★ 92388 ★   **Radio Shack**
124 Graham Park Rd.
Triangle, VA 22172
(703)221-2164
Company Type: Division. **Ultimate Parent:**
Tandy Corp. **SIC:** 5065—Electronic Parts &
Equipment Nec.

★ 92389 ★   **Radio Shack**
124 Graham Park Rd.
Triangle, VA 22172
(703)221-2164
Company Type: Division. **Ultimate Parent:**
Tandy Corp. **SIC:** 5065—Electronic Parts &
Equipment Nec.

Vansant

★ 92390 ★   **Shell Mart**
Vansant, VA 24656
(703)935-5840
Ultimate Parent: Shell Oil Co. **SIC:** 5983—
Fuel Oil Dealers.

Verona

★ 92391 ★   **Dr. Pepper Bottling Co.**
Rte. 11
Verona, VA 24482
(703)248-0095
Officer: Bo Wilson, Manager. **Ultimate
Parent:** Dr. Pepper/Seven-Up. **SIC:** 2086—
Bottled & Canned Soft Drinks.

★ 92392 ★   **First Union National Bank of Virginia**
Rte. 11 N
Verona, VA 24482
(703)248-6276
Location Type: Branch office. **Ultimate
Parent:** First Union Corp. **SIC:** 6021—
National Commercial Banks.

★ 92393 ★   **Food Lion**
820 PO Box
Verona, VA 24482
(703)248-4122
Ultimate Parent: Food Lion. **SIC:** 5411—
Grocery Stores.

★ 92394 ★   **New York Life Insurance**
997 PO Box
Verona, VA 24482
(703)248-0515
Ultimate Parent: New York Life. **SIC:**
6411—Insurance Agents, Brokers &
Service.

Vienna

★ 92395 ★   **Boeing Co.**
7980 Boeing Ct
Vienna, VA 22182
(703)821-6000
Ultimate Parent: Boeing. **SIC:** 7374—Data
Processing & Preparation.

★ 92396 ★   **Crestar Bank**
501 Maple Ave. W
Vienna, VA 22180-4288
(703)749-8530
Location Type: Branch office. **Ultimate
Parent:** Crestar Financial Corp. **SIC:**
6021—National Commercial Banks.

★ 92397 ★   **Crestar Bank**
515 Maple Ave. E
Vienna, VA 22180-4781
(800)451-2435
Location Type: Branch office. **Ultimate
Parent:** Crestar Financial Corp. **SIC:**
6021—National Commercial Banks.

★ 92398 ★   **Crestar Bank**
8219 Leesburg Pke.
Vienna, VA 22182-2625
(703)749-8500
Location Type: Branch office. **Ultimate
Parent:** Crestar Financial Corp. **SIC:**
6021—National Commercial Banks.

★ 92399 ★   **Engineering Research Associates**
1595 Springhill Rd.
Vienna, VA 22182-2235
(703)734-8800 **Fax:** (703)734-8862
Company Type: Subsidiary. **Officer:** Dr.
Terry Collins, Vice President/General
Manager. **Ultimate Parent:** E-Systems Inc.

★ 92400 ★   **Engineering Research Associates Inc.**
1595 Spring Hill Rd.
Vienna, VA 22182-2228
(703)734-8800
Company Type: Subsidiary. **Officer:** Bill

Hanelly, Secretary. **Ultimate Parent:**
E-Systems Inc. **SIC:** 7373—Computer
Integrated Systems Design. **Employee
Count:** 350. **Sales:** 51 M.

★ 92401 ★   **First American Bank**
440 Maple Ave. E
Vienna, VA 22180
(703)934-1915
Ultimate Parent: First American Corp. **SIC:**
6099—Functions Related to Deposit
Banking.

★ 92402 ★   **First American Bank**
200 Dominion Rd. NE
Vienna, VA 22180
(703)934-1925
Ultimate Parent: First American Corp. **SIC:**
6099—Functions Related to Deposit
Banking.

★ 92403 ★   **First American Bank of Virginia**
440 Maple Ave. E
Vienna, VA 22180
(703)827-8730
Ultimate Parent: First American Corp. **SIC:**
6022—State Commercial Banks.

★ 92404 ★   **First American Bank of Virginia**
200 Dominion Rd. NE
Vienna, VA 22180
(703)827-8741
Ultimate Parent: First American Corp. **SIC:**
6022—State Commercial Banks.

★ 92405 ★   **First Union National Bank of Virginia**
133 Maple Ave. E
Vienna, VA 22180-5780
(703)255-3400
Location Type: Branch office. **Ultimate
Parent:** First Union Corp. **SIC:** 6021—
National Commercial Banks.

★ 92406 ★   **First Union National Bank of Virginia**
440 Maple Ave. E
Vienna, VA 22180-4723
(703)934-1915
Location Type: Branch office. **Ultimate
Parent:** First Union Corp. **SIC:** 6021—
National Commercial Banks.

★ 92407 ★   **First Virginia Bank**
8385 A. Leesburg Pke.
Vienna, VA 22182-2402
(703)241-3475
Location Type: Branch office. **Ultimate
Parent:** First Virginia Banks Inc. **SIC:**
6021—National Commercial Banks.

★ 92408 ★   **First Virginia Bank**
1953 Gallows Rd.
Vienna, VA 22182-3934
(703)241-3315
Location Type: Branch office. **Ultimate
Parent:** First Virginia Banks Inc. **SIC:**
6021—National Commercial Banks.

★ 92409 ★   **First Virginia Bank**
415 Maple Ave. W
Vienna, VA 22180-4222
(703)241-3191
Location Type: Branch office. **Ultimate
Parent:** First Virginia Banks Inc. **SIC:**
6021—National Commercial Banks.

★ 92410 ★   **First Virginia Bank**
260 Cedar Ln.
Vienna, VA 22180-6613
(703)241-3544
Location Type: Branch office. **Ultimate
Parent:** First Virginia Banks Inc. **SIC:**
6021—National Commercial Banks.

★ 92411 ★   **Hazleton Corp.**
9200 Leesburg Pke.
Vienna, VA 22182-1656
(703)759-7806
Company Type: Subsidiary. **Officer:**
Gerald Faiche, CEO. **Ultimate Parent:**
Corning. **SIC:** 8731—Commercial Physical
Research; 0279—Animal Specialties Nec.
Employee Count: 2193. **Sales:** 165 M.

★ 92412 ★   **Lees Car Wash**
159 Maple Ave. W
Vienna, VA 22180
(703)255-3434
Ultimate Parent: Burlington Industries,
Equity. **SIC:** 7542—Car Washes.

★ 92413 ★   **Radio Shack**
Tysons Plz.
Vienna, VA 22180
(703)821-0808
Company Type: Division. **Ultimate Parent:**
Tandy Corp. **SIC:** 5734—Computer &
Software Stores.

★ 92414 ★   **Radio Shack**
320 Maple Ave. W
Vienna, VA 22180
(703)281-1510
Company Type: Division. **Ultimate Parent:**
Tandy Corp. **SIC:** 5065—Electronic Parts &
Equipment Nec.

★ 92415 ★   **Radio Shack**
8500 Leesburg Pike 308
Vienna, VA 22182
Company Type: Division. **Ultimate Parent:**
Tandy Corp. **SIC:** 5065—Electronic Parts &
Equipment Nec.

★ 92416 ★   **Radio Shack**
Tysons Plz.
Vienna, VA 22180
(703)821-0808
Company Type: Division. **Ultimate Parent:**
Tandy Corp. **SIC:** 5734—Computer &
Software Stores.

★ 92417 ★   **Radio Shack**
8500 Leesburg Pike 308
Vienna, VA 22182
Company Type: Division. **Ultimate Parent:**
Tandy Corp. **SIC:** 5065—Electronic Parts &
Equipment Nec.

★ 92418 ★   **Radio Shack**
320 Maple Ave. W
Vienna, VA 22180
(703)281-1510
Company Type: Division. **Ultimate Parent:**
Tandy Corp. **SIC:** 5065—Electronic Parts &
Equipment Nec.

★ 92419 ★   **Residence Inn by Marriott**
Westwood Ctr. Dr.
Vienna, VA 22182
(703)893-0120
Ultimate Parent: Marriott International. **SIC:**
7011—Hotels & Motels.

★ 92420 ★   **Signet Bank, Virginia**
8330 Boone Blvd.
Vienna, VA 22182
(703)734-7435
Location Type: Branch office. **Ultimate
Parent:** Signet Banking Corp. **SIC:** 6021—
National Commercial Banks.

★ 92421 ★   **Signet Bank, Virginia**
374 Maple Ave. East
Vienna, VA 22180-4718
(703)281-2200
Location Type: Branch office. **Ultimate
Parent:** Signet Banking Corp. **SIC:** 6021—
National Commercial Banks.

★ 92422 ★   **Sun Microsystems Inc.**
2650 Park Tower Dr.
Vienna, VA 22180
(703)204-4100
Officer: Dick Bowman, Vice President.
Ultimate Parent: Sun Microsystems Inc.
SIC: 3571—Electronic Computers.

★ 92423 ★   **Systems Engineering Solutions Inc.**
2301 Gallows Rd.
Vienna, VA 22027-1117
(703)573-4366
Ultimate Parent: Ball Corp. **SIC:** 7371—
Computer Programming Services.

Vinton

★ 92424 ★   **Crestar Bank**
210 E. Washington Ave.
Vinton, VA 24179-4514
(703)982-3431
Location Type: Branch office. **Ultimate
Parent:** Crestar Financial Corp. **SIC:**
6021—National Commercial Banks.

★ 92425 ★   First Union National
Bank of Virginia
120 Virginia Ave.
Vinton, VA 24179-3402
(703)563-7116
Location Type: Branch office. **Ultimate
Parent:** First Union Corp. **SIC:** 6021—
National Commercial Banks.

★ 92426 ★   Signet Bank, Virginia
901 Hardy Rd.
Vinton, VA 24179
(703)985-3291
Location Type: Branch office. **Ultimate
Parent:** Signet Banking Corp. **SIC:** 6021—
National Commercial Banks.

★ 92427 ★   Southern States
Co-Op. Inc. Roanoke Feed Mill
1003 Walnut Ave.
Vinton, VA 24179
Ultimate Parent: Southern. **SIC:** 2048—
Prepared Feeds Nec.

Virgilina

★ 92428 ★   Crestar Bank
7th St.
Virgilina, VA 24598
(804)585-2567
Location Type: Branch office. **Ultimate
Parent:** Crestar Financial Corp. **SIC:**
6021—National Commercial Banks.

Virginia Beach

★ 92429 ★   American Family Life
Assurance
412 Oakmears Cres
Virginia Beach, VA 23462
(804)671-7354
Ultimate Parent: American Family Life
Assurance Co. **SIC:** 6411—Insurance
Agents, Brokers & Service.

★ 92430 ★   American Family Life
Assurance
256 N. Witchduck Rd.
Virginia Beach, VA 23462
(804)490-7674
Ultimate Parent: American Family Life
Assurance Co. **SIC:** 6411—Insurance
Agents, Brokers & Service.

★ 92431 ★   American General
Finance
829 Lynnhaven Pky., Ste. 120
Virginia Beach, VA 23452-7224
(804)486-0567
Location Type: Branch office. **Officer:** Lori
Cummings. **Ultimate Parent:** American
General Corp. **SIC:** 6162—Mortgage
Bankers & Correspondents; 6141—Personal
Credit Institutions.

★ 92432 ★   Automated Office
Systems
4510 Holland Office Park
Virginia Beach, VA 23452-1127
(804)499-8813
Ultimate Parent: Alco Standard Corp. **SIC:**
7378—Computer Maintenance & Repair.

★ 92433 ★   Avon Products Inc.
4857 Bonney Rd.
Virginia Beach, VA 23462
(804)497-4220
Ultimate Parent: Avon Products, Inc. **SIC:**
5999—Miscellaneous Retail Stores Nec.

★ 92434 ★   Banc One Mortgage
Corp.
4534 Bonney Rd.
Virginia Beach, VA 23462
(804)490-3101
Ultimate Parent: Banc One Corp. **SIC:**
6162—Mortgage Bankers &
Correspondents.

★ 92435 ★   BancBoston Mortgage
Corp.
621 Lynnhaven Pky.
Virginia Beach, VA 23452-7313
(804)431-0023
Officer: Kim Curtis. **Ultimate Parent:** Bank
of Boston Corp. **SIC:** 6141—Personal Credit
Institutions.

★ 92436 ★   Beneficial Virginia
Inc.
New Pointe Shopping Ctr.
Virginia Beach, VA 23462
(804)456-5300
Location Type: Branch office. **Officer:**
Ronald Morecock. **Ultimate Parent:**
Beneficial. **SIC:** 6141—Personal Credit
Institutions; 6162—Mortgage Bankers &
Correspondents; 7323—Credit Reporting
Services.

★ 92437 ★   Beverly Enterprises
Inc.
3284 Virginia Beach Blvd.
Virginia Beach, VA 23452-5724
(804)431-7000
Company Type: Headquarters. **Officer:**
Charles Chamberlain. **Ultimate Parent:**
Beverly Enterprises. **SIC:** 8051—Skilled
Nursing Care Facilities.

★ 92438 ★   Beverly Enterprises
Inc.
4820 Columbus St.
Virginia Beach, VA 23468
Ultimate Parent: Beverly Enterprises. **SIC:**
8051—Skilled Nursing Care Facilities.

★ 92439 ★   Beverly Enterprises
Inc.
3284 Virginia Beach Blvd.
Virginia Beach, VA 23452
(804)431-7000
Ultimate Parent: Beverly Enterprises. **SIC:**
8051—Skilled Nursing Care Facilities.

★ 92440 ★   Blazer Financial
Services
1105 N. Newtown Rd.
Virginia Beach, VA 23462
(804)490-3106
Ultimate Parent: Great Western Financial
Corp. **SIC:** 6141—Personal Credit
Institutions.

★ 92441 ★   Blazer Financial
Services I
3809 Princess Anne Rd.
Virginia Beach, VA 23456
(804)471-0900
Ultimate Parent: Great Western Financial
Corp. **SIC:** 6062—State Credit Unions.

★ 92442 ★   Builder's Square
4725 Virginia Beach Blvd.
Virginia Beach, VA 23462
(804)473-1701
Ultimate Parent: K-Mart. **SIC:** 5039—
Construction Materials Nec.

★ 92443 ★   Capezio
4000 Virginia Beach Blvd.
Virginia Beach, VA 23452
(804)486-2424
Ultimate Parent: United States Shoe. **SIC:**
5651—Family Clothing Stores.

★ 92444 ★   Casual Corner
701 Lynnhaven Pky.
Virginia Beach, VA 23452
(804)486-7296
Ultimate Parent: United States Shoe. **SIC:**
5621—Women's Clothing Stores; 5651—
Family Clothing Stores.

★ 92445 ★   Circuit City
110 S. Independence Blvd.
Virginia Beach, VA 23462
(804)499-0099
Ultimate Parent: Circuit City Stores. **SIC:**
2731—Book Publishing; 5065—Electronic
Parts & Equipment Nec.

★ 92446 ★   Copy Data Group, Inc.
5361 Cleveland St.
Virginia Beach, VA 23462
(804)285-7841 **Fax:** (804)499-9329
Company Type: Division. **Officer:** Joseph
M. Gianascoll, President. **Ultimate Parent:**
Alco Standard Corp. **SIC:** 5044—Office
Equipment; 5046—Commercial Equipment
Nec.

★ 92447 ★   Courtyard by Marriott
5700 Greenwich Rd.
Virginia Beach, VA 23462
(804)490-2002
Ultimate Parent: Marriott International. **SIC:**
7011—Hotels & Motels.

★ 92448 ★   Crestar Bank
711 1st Colonial Rd.
Virginia Beach, VA 23451
(804)858-3309
Location Type: Branch office. **Ultimate
Parent:** Crestar Financial Corp. **SIC:**
6021—National Commercial Banks.

★ 92449 ★   Crestar Bank
3322 Holland Rd.
Virginia Beach, VA 23452
(804)858-3303
Location Type: Branch office. **Ultimate
Parent:** Crestar Financial Corp. **SIC:**
6021—National Commercial Banks.

★ 92450 ★   Crestar Bank
Pembroke Mall Shopping Ctr.
4550 VA Beach Blvd.
Virginia Beach, VA 23462
(804)858-3332
Location Type: Branch office. **Ultimate
Parent:** Crestar Financial Corp. **SIC:**
6021—National Commercial Banks.

★ 92451 ★   Crestar Bank
3330 Pacific Ave.
Virginia Beach, VA 23451-2939
(804)858-3326
Location Type: Branch office. **Ultimate
Parent:** Crestar Financial Corp. **SIC:**
6021—National Commercial Banks.

★ 92452 ★   Crestar Bank
1625 General Booth Blvd.
Virginia Beach, VA 23454
(804)858-3035
Location Type: Branch office. **Ultimate
Parent:** Crestar Financial Corp. **SIC:**
6021—National Commercial Banks.

★ 92453 ★   Crestar Bank
635 Lynnhaven Pky.
Virginia Beach, VA 23452
(804)858-3512
Location Type: Branch office. **Ultimate
Parent:** Crestar Financial Corp. **SIC:**
6021—National Commercial Banks.

★ 92454 ★   Crestar Bank
2260 Sunstates Ct.
Virginia Beach, VA 23451
(804)858-3441
Location Type: Branch office. **Ultimate
Parent:** Crestar Financial Corp. **SIC:**
6021—National Commercial Banks.

★ 92455 ★   Crestar Bank
750 Independence Blvd.
Virginia Beach, VA 23455
(804)858-3385
Location Type: Branch office. **Ultimate
Parent:** Crestar Financial Corp. **SIC:**
6021—National Commercial Banks.

★ 92456 ★   Crestar Bank
849 Kempsville Rd.
Virginia Beach, VA 23464
(804)858-3082
Location Type: Branch office. **Ultimate
Parent:** Crestar Financial Corp. **SIC:**
6021—National Commercial Banks.

★ 92457 ★   Diebold Inc.
4940 Rutherford Rd.
Virginia Beach, VA 23455
(804)460-1131
Ultimate Parent: Diebold, Inc. **SIC:** 5046—
Commercial Equipment Nec; 7382—Security
Systems Services.

★ 92458 ★   Digital Equipment
Corp.
4417 Corporation Ln.
Virginia Beach, VA 23462
(804)490-0555
Ultimate Parent: Digital Equipment Corp.
SIC: 7373—Computer Integrated Systems
Design.

★ 92459 ★   Electronic Systems
Inc.
361 Southport Cir.
Virginia Beach, VA 23452-1144
(804)497-8000
Officer: William G. Kamarek, President.
Ultimate Parent: Imo Industries. **SIC:**
5999—Miscellaneous Retail Stores Nec;
7629—Electrical Repair Shops Nec.

★ 92460 ★   Exxon Car Care
Center
841 S. Military Hwy.
Virginia Beach, VA 23464
(804)424-2400
Ultimate Parent: Exxon. **SIC:** 5541—
Gasoline Service Stations.

★ 92461 ★   Exxon Car Care
Center
3653 Virginia Beach Blvd.
Virginia Beach, VA 23452
(804)486-6161
Ultimate Parent: Exxon. **SIC:** 7538—
General Automotive Repair Shops.

★ 92462 ★   Exxon Self Service
Station
3597 Holland Rd.
Virginia Beach, VA 23452
(804)340-6263
Ultimate Parent: Exxon. **SIC:** 5541—
Gasoline Service Stations.

★ 92463 ★   Exxon Self Service
Station
4172 Princess Anne Rd.
Virginia Beach, VA 23456
(804)467-0628
Ultimate Parent: Exxon. **SIC:** 5541—
Gasoline Service Stations.

★ 92464 ★   First American Bank
of Virginia
405 S. Witchduck Rd.
Virginia Beach, VA 23462
(804)858-5260
Ultimate Parent: First American Corp. **SIC:**
6022—State Commercial Banks.

★ 92465 ★   First American Bank
of Virginia
1645 Independence Blvd.
Virginia Beach, VA 23455
(804)858-5255
Ultimate Parent: First American Corp. **SIC:**
6022—State Commercial Banks.

★ 92466 ★   First American Bank
of Virginia
304 Kellam Rd.
Virginia Beach, VA 23462
(804)455-7850
Ultimate Parent: First American Corp. **SIC:**
6022—State Commercial Banks.

★ 92467 ★   First American Bank
of Virginia
64 Princess Anne Plz.
Virginia Beach, VA 23452
(804)858-5265
Ultimate Parent: First American Corp. **SIC:**
6022—State Commercial Banks.

★ 92468 ★   First Union National
Bank of Virginia
304 Kellam Rd.
Virginia Beach, VA 23462-2712
(804)455-7850
Location Type: Branch office. **Ultimate
Parent:** First Union Corp. **SIC:** 6021—
National Commercial Banks.

★ 92469 ★   First Union National
Bank of Virginia
4287 Holland Rd.
Virginia Beach, VA 23452-1937
(804)467-6365
Location Type: Branch office. **Ultimate
Parent:** First Union Corp. **SIC:** 6021—
National Commercial Banks.

★ 92470 ★   First Union National
Bank of Virginia
5300 Kemps River Dr., Ste. 100
Virginia Beach, VA 23464-5348
(804)420-3535
Location Type: Branch office. **Ultimate
Parent:** First Union Corp. **SIC:** 6021—
National Commercial Banks.

★ 92471 ★   First Union National
Bank of Virginia
2888 Virginia Beach Blvd.
Virginia Beach, VA 23452-7614
(804)486-3720
Location Type: Branch office. **Ultimate
Parent:** First Union Corp. **SIC:** 6021—
National Commercial Banks.

★ 92472 ★ First Union National Bank of Virginia
1068 Independence Blvd.
Virginia Beach, VA 23455-5503
(804)460-3757
Location Type: Branch office. Ultimate Parent: First Union Corp. SIC: 6021—National Commercial Banks.

★ 92473 ★ First Union National Bank of Virginia
1613 Laskin Rd.
Virginia Beach, VA 23451-6113
(804)422-3350
Location Type: Branch office. Ultimate Parent: First Union Corp. SIC: 6021—National Commercial Banks.

★ 92474 ★ First Union National Bank of Virginia
5393 Princess Anne Rd.
Virginia Beach, VA 23462-6307
(804)490-9807
Location Type: Branch office. Ultimate Parent: First Union Corp. SIC: 6021—National Commercial Banks.

★ 92475 ★ First Union National Bank of Virginia
6563 College Park Sq.
Virginia Beach, VA 23464-3605
(804)424-0861
Location Type: Branch office. Ultimate Parent: First Union Corp. SIC: 6021—National Commercial Banks.

★ 92476 ★ Food Lion
Cape Henry Towers
Virginia Beach, VA 23451
(804)481-7480
Ultimate Parent: Food Lion. SIC: 5411—Grocery Stores.

★ 92477 ★ Food Lion
8 Aragona Shopping. Ctr.
Virginia Beach, VA 23462
(804)497-1397
Ultimate Parent: Food Lion. SIC: 5411—Grocery Stores.

★ 92478 ★ Food Lion
544 Newtown Rd.
Virginia Beach, VA 23462
(804)499-0852
Ultimate Parent: Food Lion. SIC: 5411—Grocery Stores.

★ 92479 ★ Food Lion
3770 Virginia Beach Blvd.
Virginia Beach, VA 23452
(804)340-7920
Ultimate Parent: Food Lion. SIC: 5411—Grocery Stores.

★ 92480 ★ Food Lion
325 Kempsville Plz.
Virginia Beach, VA 23462
(804)490-1808
Ultimate Parent: Food Lion. SIC: 5411—Grocery Stores.

★ 92481 ★ Food Lion
880 S. Military Hwy.
Virginia Beach, VA 23464
(804)523-0217
Ultimate Parent: Food Lion. SIC: 5411—Grocery Stores.

★ 92482 ★ Food Lion
1505 Lynnhaven Pky. 1349
Virginia Beach, VA 23456
(804)427-9130
Ultimate Parent: Food Lion. SIC: 5411—Grocery Stores.

★ 92483 ★ Food Lion
4318 Holland Rd.
Virginia Beach, VA 23452
(804)463-5943
Ultimate Parent: Food Lion. SIC: 5411—Grocery Stores.

★ 92484 ★ Food Lion Inc.
544 Newtown Rd.
Virginia Beach, VA 23462
(804)499-0852
Ultimate Parent: Food Lion. SIC: 5411—Grocery Stores.

★ 92485 ★ Greyhound Bus Lines
1017 Laskin Rd.
Virginia Beach, VA 23451
(804)422-2998
Ultimate Parent: Greyhound Lines Inc. SIC: 4131—Intercity & Rural Bus Transportation; 4131—Intercity & Rural Bus Transportation.

★ 92486 ★ Hit or Miss
11 Pembroke Mall
Virginia Beach, VA 23462
(804)499-4063
Ultimate Parent: TJX. SIC: 5651—Family Clothing Stores.

★ 92487 ★ Hit or Miss
701 Lynnhaven Pky.
Virginia Beach, VA 23452
(804)463-8294
Ultimate Parent: TJX. SIC: 5621—Women's Clothing Stores; 5651—Family Clothing Stores.

★ 92488 ★ Kelly Assisted Living Service
281 Independence Blvd.
Virginia Beach, VA 23462
(804)490-1203
Ultimate Parent: Kelly Services. SIC: 8099—Health & Allied Services Nec.

★ 92489 ★ Kids R US
2701 N. Mall Dr.
Virginia Beach, VA 23452
(804)431-1743
Ultimate Parent: Toys "R" US. SIC: 5651—Family Clothing Stores.

★ 92490 ★ Lorillard Inc.
6200 Pardue Ct.
Virginia Beach, VA 23464
(804)420-1280
Ultimate Parent: Loews. SIC: 7832—Motion Picture Theaters Except Drive-In.

★ 92491 ★ Mobil
1405 N. Great Neck Rd.
Virginia Beach, VA 23454
(804)481-5116
Ultimate Parent: Mobil. SIC: 7549—Automotive Services Nec.

★ 92492 ★ National City Mortgage Co.
484 Viking Dr.
Virginia Beach, VA 23452
(804)498-1200
Ultimate Parent: National City Corp. SIC: 6162—Mortgage Bankers & Correspondents.

★ 92493 ★ New York Life Insurance Co.
505 S. Independence Blvd.
Virginia Beach, VA 23452
(804)856-9000
Ultimate Parent: New York Life. SIC: 6411—Insurance Agents, Brokers & Service.

★ 92494 ★ Pappagallo
701 Lynnhaven Pky.
Virginia Beach, VA 23452
(804)463-5006
Ultimate Parent: United States Shoe. SIC: 5661—Shoe Stores.

★ 92495 ★ Radio Shack
116 S. Independence Blvd.
Virginia Beach, VA 23462
(804)473-1909
Company Type: Division. Ultimate Parent: Tandy Corp. SIC: 7373—Computer Integrated Systems Design.

★ 92496 ★ Radio Shack
5234 Fairfield Shopping Ctr.
Virginia Beach, VA 23464
(804)495-0895
Company Type: Division. Ultimate Parent: Tandy Corp. SIC: 5065—Electronic Parts & Equipment Nec.

★ 92497 ★ Radio Shack
6537 College Park Sq.
Virginia Beach, VA 23464
(804)424-4240
Company Type: Division. Ultimate Parent: Tandy Corp. SIC: 5065—Electronic Parts & Equipment Nec; 5731—Radio, Television & Electronics Stores.

★ 92498 ★ Radio Shack
1037 Independence Blvd.
Virginia Beach, VA 23455
(804)460-2979
Company Type: Division. Ultimate Parent: Tandy Corp. SIC: 5731—Radio, Television & Electronics Stores.

★ 92499 ★ Radio Shack
12 Pembroke Mall
Virginia Beach, VA 23462
(804)497-9211
Company Type: Division. Ultimate Parent: Tandy Corp. SIC: 5731—Radio, Television & Electronics Stores.

★ 92500 ★ Radio Shack
701 Lynnhaven Pky.
Virginia Beach, VA 23452
(804)463-5010
Company Type: Division. Ultimate Parent: Tandy Corp. SIC: 5065—Electronic Parts & Equipment Nec.

★ 92501 ★ Radio Shack
2152 Great Neck Sq.
Virginia Beach, VA 23454
(804)481-1684
Company Type: Division. Ultimate Parent: Tandy Corp. SIC: 5731—Radio, Television & Electronics Stores.

★ 92502 ★ Radio Shack
754 N. Hilltop Shopping Ctr.
Virginia Beach, VA 23451
(804)428-3392
Company Type: Division. Ultimate Parent: Tandy Corp. SIC: 5731—Radio, Television & Electronics Stores.

★ 92503 ★ Radio Shack
4326 Holland Rd.
Virginia Beach, VA 23452
(804)486-1652
Company Type: Division. Ultimate Parent: Tandy Corp. SIC: 5065—Electronic Parts & Equipment Nec; 5731—Radio, Television & Electronics Stores.

★ 92504 ★ Radio Shack
116 S. Independence Blvd.
Virginia Beach, VA 23462
(804)473-1909
Company Type: Division. Ultimate Parent: Tandy Corp. SIC: 7373—Computer Integrated Systems Design.

★ 92505 ★ Rite Aid
963 Providence Sq.
Virginia Beach, VA 23462
(804)495-0934
Ultimate Parent: Rite Aid. SIC: 5912—Drug Stores & Proprietary Stores.

★ 92506 ★ Rite Aid
3501 Holland Rd.
Virginia Beach, VA 23452
(804)498-3150
Ultimate Parent: Rite Aid. SIC: 5912—Drug Stores & Proprietary Stores.

★ 92507 ★ Rite Aid
320 Laskin Rd.
Virginia Beach, VA 23451
(804)422-0331
Ultimate Parent: Rite Aid. SIC: 5912—Drug Stores & Proprietary Stores.

★ 92508 ★ Ryder Truck Rental Inc.
700 Baker Rd.
Virginia Beach, VA 23462
(804)473-5520
Ultimate Parent: Ryder System. SIC: 7513—Truck Rental & Leasing Without Drivers.

★ 92509 ★ Schwab Charles & Co. Inc.
291 Independence Blvd.
Virginia Beach, VA 23462
(804)490-9600
Ultimate Parent: Charles Schwab Corp. SIC: 6211—Security Brokers & Dealers.

★ 92510 ★ Sherwin Williams Paint Stor
3800 Holland Rd.
Virginia Beach, VA 23452
(804)498-1182
Ultimate Parent: Sherwin-Williams Co. SIC: 5231—Paint, Glass & Wallpaper Stores.

★ 92511 ★ Signet Bank, Virginia
4460 Corporation Ln.
Virginia Beach, VA 23462-2822
(804)640-4366
Location Type: Branch office. Ultimate Parent: Signet Banking Corp. SIC: 6021—National Commercial Banks.

★ 92512 ★ Signet Bank, Virginia
2821 Shore Dr.
Virginia Beach, VA 23451-1367
(804)640-4338
Location Type: Branch office. Ultimate Parent: Signet Banking Corp. SIC: 6021—National Commercial Banks.

★ 92513 ★ Signet Bank, Virginia
1705 Baltic Ave.
Virginia Beach, VA 23451-3427
(804)640-4322
Location Type: Branch office. Ultimate Parent: Signet Banking Corp. SIC: 6021—National Commercial Banks.

★ 92514 ★ Signet Bank, Virginia
5241 Providence Rd.
Virginia Beach, VA 23464-4201
(804)640-4330
Location Type: Branch office. Ultimate Parent: Signet Banking Corp. SIC: 6021—National Commercial Banks.

★ 92515 ★ Signet Bank, Virginia
925 Diamond Springs Rd.
Virginia Beach, VA 23462
(804)640-4456
Location Type: Branch office. Ultimate Parent: Signet Banking Corp. SIC: 6021—National Commercial Banks.

★ 92516 ★ Signet Bank, Virginia
996 1st. Colonial Rd.
Virginia Beach, VA 23451-3427
(804)640-4344
Location Type: Branch office. Ultimate Parent: Signet Banking Corp. SIC: 6021—National Commercial Banks.

★ 92517 ★ Signet Bank, Virginia
675 Lynnhaven Pky.
Virginia Beach, VA 23452-7320
(804)640-4430
Location Type: Branch office. Ultimate Parent: Signet Banking Corp. SIC: 6021—National Commercial Banks.

★ 92518 ★ Syscon Corp.
3500 Virginia Beach Blvd.
Virginia Beach, VA 23452
(804)486-4411
Ultimate Parent: Harnischfeger Industries. SIC: 8742—Management Consulting Services.

★ 92519 ★ United Parcel Service
501 Viking Dr.
Virginia Beach, VA 23452
(804)340-6227
Ultimate Parent: United Parcel Service of America. SIC: 4215—Courier Services Except by Air.

★ 92520 ★ Washington Inventory Servic
5541 Parliament Dr.
Virginia Beach, VA 23462
(804)490-1121
Ultimate Parent: Huffy. SIC: 8721—Accounting, Auditing & Bookkeeping.

★ 92521 ★ Western Auto Supply Co.
2346 Virginia Beach Blvd.
Virginia Beach, VA 23454
(804)486-6900
Ultimate Parent: Sears Roebuck & Co. SIC: 5531—Automobile & Home Supply Stores.

Warrenton

★ 92522 ★ Carter Machinery Co. Inc.
1 PO Box
Warrenton, VA 22186
(703)349-1100
Ultimate Parent: Carter-Wallace. SIC: 5082—Construction & Mining Machinery.

★ 92523 ★ First Virginia Bank
Vint Hill Farms Sta.
Warrenton, VA 22186-5001
(703)241-3258
Location Type: Branch office. Ultimate Parent: First Virginia Banks Inc. SIC: 6021—National Commercial Banks.

★ 92524 ★   **First Virginia Bank**
11047 Marsh Rd.
Warrenton, VA 22186
(703)241-4767
Location Type: Branch office. **Ultimate Parent:** First Virginia Banks Inc. **SIC:** 6021—National Commercial Banks.

★ 92525 ★   **First Virginia Bank**
530 Blackwell Rd.
Warrenton, VA 22186-2600
(703)241-4478
Location Type: Branch office. **Ultimate Parent:** First Virginia Banks Inc. **SIC:** 6021—National Commercial Banks.

★ 92526 ★   **New York Life Insurance Co.**
751 PO Box
Warrenton, VA 22186
(703)349-1800
Ultimate Parent: New York Life. **SIC:** 6411—Insurance Agents, Brokers & Service.

★ 92527 ★   **Pepsi-Cola Bottling Co.**
RR 6, Box 302A
Warrenton, VA 22186
(703)347-3112
Officer: Francis Burns, Manager. **Ultimate Parent:** Pepsico. **SIC:** 2086—Bottled & Canned Soft Drinks.

★ 92528 ★   **Radio Shack**
Warrenton Ctr.
Warrenton, VA 22186
(703)347-0077
Company Type: Division. **Ultimate Parent:** Tandy Corp. **SIC:** 5734—Computer & Software Stores.

Warsaw

★ 92529 ★   **Flowers Baking Co.**
Warsaw, VA 22572
(804)333-3725
Ultimate Parent: Flowers Industries. **SIC:** 2051—Bread, Cake & Related Products; 5149—Groceries & Related Products Nec.

★ 92530 ★   **Signet Bank, Virginia**
610 W. Richmond Rd.
Warsaw, VA 22572
(804)333-3692
Location Type: Branch office. **Ultimate Parent:** Signet Banking Corp. **SIC:** 6021—National Commercial Banks.

Waverly

★ 92531 ★   **Masonite Corp.**
721 West Main St.
Waverly, VA 23890
Ultimate Parent: USG Corp. **SIC:** 2400—Lumber & Wood Products.

Waynesboro

★ 92532 ★   **Crestar Bank**
1100 W. Broad St.
Waynesboro, VA 22980-4325
(703)943-2100
Location Type: Branch office. **Ultimate Parent:** Crestar Financial Corp. **SIC:** 6021—National Commercial Banks.

★ 92533 ★   **Crestar Bank**
230 S. Wayne St.
Waynesboro, VA 22980
(703)943-5226
Location Type: Branch office. **Ultimate Parent:** Crestar Financial Corp. **SIC:** 6021—National Commercial Banks.

★ 92534 ★   **First Union National Bank of Virginia**
216 S. Wayne Ave.
Waynesboro, VA 22980-4622
(703)946-2100
Location Type: Branch office. **Ultimate Parent:** First Union Corp. **SIC:** 6021—National Commercial Banks.

★ 92535 ★   **New York Life Insur Co.**
336 Chestnut Ave.
Waynesboro, VA 22980
(703)943-5155
Ultimate Parent: New York Life. **SIC:** 6411—Insurance Agents, Brokers & Service.

Weber City

★ 92536 ★   **Signet Bank, Virginia**
Hwy. 23
Weber City, VA 24251-8907
(703)386-7028
Location Type: Branch office. **Ultimate Parent:** Signet Banking Corp. **SIC:** 6021—National Commercial Banks.

West Point

★ 92537 ★   **Chesapeake Land Development Operations**
PO Box 1700
West Point, VA 23181
(804)843-5300 **Fax:** (804)843-4152
Officer: Joel Mostrom, President. **Ultimate Parent:** Chesapeake.

★ 92538 ★   **Chesapeake Paper Products Co.**
19th & Main Sts.
West Point, VA 23181
(804)843-5000
Officer: Paul Dresser, Chairman of the Board. **Ultimate Parent:** Chesapeake. **SIC:** 2631—Paperboard Mills; 2611—Pulp Mills; 2621—Paper Mills.

★ 92539 ★   **Chesapeake Wood Treating Co.**
15th & Main Sts.
West Point, VA 23181
(804)843-5680
Officer: Michael Sloane, President. **Ultimate Parent:** Chesapeake. **SIC:** 2491—Wood Preserving.

★ 92540 ★   **Crestar Bank**
14th & Lee Sts.
West Point, VA 23181
(804)843-3061
Location Type: Branch office. **Ultimate Parent:** Crestar Financial Corp. **SIC:** 6021—National Commercial Banks.

★ 92541 ★   **Delmarva Properties, Inc.**
PO Box 1700
West Point, VA 23181
(804)843-5300 **Fax:** (804)843-4152
Officer: Robert F. Brake, President. **Ultimate Parent:** Chesapeake.

★ 92542 ★   **First Union National Bank of Virginia**
16th & Main St.
West Point, VA 23181
(804)843-2233
Location Type: Branch office. **Ultimate Parent:** First Union Corp. **SIC:** 6021—National Commercial Banks.

★ 92543 ★   **Stonehouse Inc.**
PO Box 1700
West Point, VA 23181
(804)220-6800 **Fax:** (804)843-4152
Officer: Jim Franklin, Vice President. **Ultimate Parent:** Chesapeake.

Weyers Cave

★ 92544 ★   **First Union National Bank of Virginia**
Rtes. 256 & 276
Weyers Cave, VA 24486
(703)234-9216
Location Type: Branch office. **Ultimate Parent:** First Union Corp. **SIC:** 6021—National Commercial Banks.

White Stone

★ 92545 ★   **Signet Bank, Virginia**
Rte. 695
White Stone, VA 22578-9616
(804)435-1626
Location Type: Branch office. **Ultimate Parent:** Signet Banking Corp. **SIC:** 6021—National Commercial Banks.

Williamsberg

★ 92546 ★   **Crestar Bank**
1222 Richmond Rd.
Williamsberg, VA 23185-2891
(804)229-5363
Location Type: Branch office. **Ultimate Parent:** Crestar Financial Corp. **SIC:** 6021—National Commercial Banks.

★ 92547 ★   **Crestar Bank**
James York Plz.
Williamsberg, VA 23185
(804)253-9275
Location Type: Branch office. **Ultimate Parent:** Crestar Financial Corp. **SIC:** 6021—National Commercial Banks.

★ 92548 ★   **Crestar Bank**
120 Monticello Ave.
Williamsberg, VA 23185-2813
(804)253-9269
Location Type: Branch office. **Ultimate Parent:** Crestar Financial Corp. **SIC:** 6021—National Commercial Banks.

★ 92549 ★   **Crestar Bank**
1186 Jamestown Rd.
Williamsberg, VA 23185
(804)253-9254
Location Type: Branch office. **Ultimate Parent:** Crestar Financial Corp. **SIC:** 6021—National Commercial Banks.

★ 92550 ★   **Crestar Bank**
Duke of Gloucester St.
Williamsberg, VA 23185
(804)253-9200
Location Type: Branch office. **Ultimate Parent:** Crestar Financial Corp. **SIC:** 6021—National Commercial Banks.

Williamsburg

★ 92551 ★   **Anheuser-Busch Inc.**
7801 Pocahontas Trl.
Williamsburg, VA 23185
Ultimate Parent: Anheuser-Busch. **SIC:** 2082—Malt Beverages.

★ 92552 ★   **Ball Corp.**
3000 Pocahontas Trl
Williamsburg, VA 23185
(804)887-2061
Ultimate Parent: Ball Corp. **SIC:** 3221—Glass Containers.

★ 92553 ★   **Ball Corp. Ball Metal Container**
Metal Beverage Container Group
8935 Pocahontas Trl.
Williamsburg, VA 23185-6249
(804)887-2061 **Fax:** (804)883-1669
Company Type: Division. **Ultimate Parent:** Ball Corp.

★ 92554 ★   **Ball Metal Container**
8935 Pocahontas Trl.
Williamsburg, VA 23185-6249
(804)887-2061
Location Type: Branch office. **Ultimate Parent:** Ball Corp. **SIC:** 3411—Metal Cans; 5085—Industrial Supplies.

★ 92555 ★   **Ball Metal Container Group**
8935 Pocahontas Trl.
Williamsburg, VA 23185
(804)887-2061
Officer: David J. Kolb, Manager. **Ultimate Parent:** Ball Corp. **SIC:** 3411—Metal Cans.

★ 92556 ★   **Ball Metal Container Operations**
8935 Pocahontas Trail
Williamsburg, VA 23185-6249
Ultimate Parent: Ball Corp. **SIC:** 3411—Metal Cans.

★ 92557 ★   **Ball Packaging Products Group**
Metal Container Div.
8935 Pocahontas Trail
Williamsburg, VA 23185-6249
Company Type: Division. **Ultimate Parent:** Ball Corp. **SIC:** 3411—Metal Cans.

★ 92558 ★   **Ball Packaging Products Group**
Metal Container Div.
8935 Pocahontas Trail
Williamsburg, VA 23185-6249
Company Type: Division. **Ultimate Parent:** Ball Corp. **SIC:** 3411—Metal Cans.

★ 92559 ★   **Ball Packaging Products Group Mcd**
8935 Pocahontas Trail
Williamsburg, VA 23185-6249
Ultimate Parent: Ball Corp. **SIC:** 3411—Metal Cans.

★ 92560 ★   **Banister Shoe Factory Outlet**
Rural Route 60
Williamsburg, VA 23185
(804)564-9788
Ultimate Parent: United States Shoe. **SIC:** 5661—Shoe Stores.

★ 92561 ★   **BASF Corp.**
Rte. 60 E.
Williamsburg, VA 23185
Ultimate Parent: BASF Corp. **SIC:** 2821—Plastics Materials & Resins; 2824—Organic Fibers—Noncellulosic.

★ 92562 ★   **BASF Corp.**
Fiber Products
Drawer D
Williamsburg, VA 23187
(804)887-6000
Company Type: Subsidiary. **Officer:** Werner Burget, President. **Ultimate Parent:** BASF Corp.

★ 92563 ★   **BASF Corp.**
Fibers
Rte. 60 E.
Williamsburg, VA 23187
Company Type: Division. **Ultimate Parent:** BASF Corp. **SIC:** 2824—Organic Fibers—Noncellulosic; 2281—Yarn Spinning Mills.

★ 92564 ★   **BASF Corp.**
Fibers Div.
PO Drawer D
Williamsburg, VA 23187
(804)887-6000
Ultimate Parent: BASF Corp. **SIC:** 3695—Magnetic & Optical Recording Media. **Employee Count:** 7000.

★ 92565 ★   **BASF Fibers**
Rte. 60
Williamsburg, VA 23185
(804)887-6000
Officer: Werner Burgert, President. **Ultimate Parent:** BASF Corp. **SIC:** 2655—Fiber Cans, Drums & Similar Products; 2823—Cellulosic Manmade Fibers.

★ 92566 ★   **Busch Gardens Williamsburg**
PO Box 8785, One Busch Gardens Blvd.
Williamsburg, VA 23187-8785
(804)253-3358
Company Type: Subsidiary. **Officer:** Keith Kasen, General Manager. **Ultimate Parent:** Agway Inc. **SIC:** 7996—Amusement Parks.

★ 92567 ★   **Crestar Bank**
496 McLaws Cir.
Williamsburg, VA 23185-5646
(804)253-9294
Location Type: Branch office. **Ultimate Parent:** Crestar Financial Corp. **SIC:** 6021—National Commercial Banks.

★ 92568 ★   **Crestar Bank**
Rte. 60 & Centerville Rd.
Williamsburg, VA 23185
(804)253-9278
Location Type: Branch office. **Ultimate Parent:** Crestar Financial Corp. **SIC:** 6021—National Commercial Banks.

★ 92569 ★   **First Union National Bank of Virginia**
133 Waller Mill Rd.
Williamsburg, VA 23185
(804)253-2265
Location Type: Branch office. **Ultimate Parent:** First Union Corp. **SIC:** 6021—National Commercial Banks.

★ 92570 ★   **First Virginia Bank**
Commonwealth
171 Monticello Ave.
Williamsburg, VA 23185-2812
(804)253-2816
Company Type: Subsidiary. **Officer:** Jon A. Nystrom, Chairman, President & CEO. **Ultimate Parent:** First Virginia Banks Inc. **SIC:** 6022—State Commercial Banks.

★ 92571 ★   **Food Lion**
5251 John Tyler Hwy.
Williamsburg, VA 23185
(804)220-1473
Ultimate Parent: Food Lion. **SIC:** 5411—Grocery Stores.

★ 92572 ★ Greyhound Bus Lines
468 N. Boundary St.
Williamsburg, VA 23185
(804)229-1460
Ultimate Parent: Greyhound Lines Inc. SIC:
4111—Local & Suburban Transit; 4173—
Bus Terminal & Service Facilities.

★ 92573 ★ Hertz Rent-A-Car
1351 Richmond Rd.
Williamsburg, VA 23185
(804)229-5115
Ultimate Parent: Hertz. SIC: 7514—
Passenger Car Rental.

★ 92574 ★ Hit or Miss
Richmond Rd.
Williamsburg, VA 23185
(804)565-0390
Ultimate Parent: TJX. SIC: 5651—Family
Clothing Stores.

★ 92575 ★ Life Insurance Co. of
Va
161 John Jefferson Rd.
Williamsburg, VA 23185
(804)229-2977
Ultimate Parent: Life Insurance Co. of
Virginia. SIC: 6411—Insurance Agents,
Brokers & Service.

★ 92576 ★ McDonald's
Hamburgers
1991 PO Box
Williamsburg, VA 23187
Ultimate Parent: McDonald's. SIC: 5812—
Eating Places.

★ 92577 ★ New York Life
Insurance Co.
Parkway Bldg.
Williamsburg, VA 23185
(804)229-2900
Ultimate Parent: New York Life. SIC:
8742—Management Consulting Services.

★ 92578 ★ Radio Shack
159 Monticello Ave.
Williamsburg, VA 23185
(804)229-4157
Company Type: Division. Ultimate Parent:
Tandy Corp. SIC: 5065—Electronic Parts &
Equipment Nec; 5731—Radio, Television &
Electronics Stores.

★ 92579 ★ Syscon Corp.
309 Mac Laws Cir.
Williamsburg, VA 23185
(804)253-5700
Ultimate Parent: Harnischfeger Industries.
SIC: 7372—Prepackaged Software; 8742—
Management Consulting Services.

★ 92580 ★ Water Country USA
176 Water Country Pky.
Williamsburg, VA 23185
(804)229-9300 Fax: (804)220-2816
Company Type: Subsidiary. Officer: Tim
Cuddihy, General Manager. Ultimate
Parent: Agway Inc. SIC: 7999—Amusement
& Recreation Nec.

Winchester

★ 92581 ★ BFI Waste Systems
403 Lenoir Dr.
Winchester, VA 22603-4605
(703)667-7474
Ultimate Parent: Browning-Ferris
Industries. SIC: 4953—Refuse Systems.

★ 92582 ★ Crown Cork & Seal
Co. Inc.
Rte. 11 Martinsburg Pike
Winchester, VA 22601
Ultimate Parent: Crown Cork & Seal. SIC:
3411—Metal Cans.

★ 92583 ★ First Union National
Bank of Virginia
2505 Valley Ave.
Winchester, VA 22601-2761
(703)665-6724
Location Type: Branch office. Ultimate
Parent: First Union Corp. SIC: 6021—
National Commercial Banks.

★ 92584 ★ First Union National
Bank of Virginia
320 Westside Sta. Dr.
Winchester, VA 22601-3856
(703)665-6713
Location Type: Branch office. Ultimate

Parent: First Union Corp. SIC: 6021—
National Commercial Banks.

★ 92585 ★ First Union National
Bank of Virginia
Millwood Ave. & US Rte. 50 E
Winchester, VA 22601-9218
(703)665-6746
Location Type: Branch office. Ultimate
Parent: First Union Corp. SIC: 6021—
National Commercial Banks.

★ 92586 ★ First Union National
Bank of Virginia
828 Berryville Ave.
Winchester, VA 22601-5914
(703)665-6759
Location Type: Branch office. Ultimate
Parent: First Union Corp. SIC: 6021—
National Commercial Banks.

★ 92587 ★ First Union National
Bank of Virginia
186 N. Loudoun St.
Winchester, VA 22601-4718
(703)667-6100
Location Type: Branch office. Ultimate
Parent: First Union Corp. SIC: 6021—
National Commercial Banks.

★ 92588 ★ First Union National
Bank of Virginia
201 N. Londoun St.
Winchester, VA 22601-4800
(703)667-2000
Location Type: Branch office. Ultimate
Parent: First Union Corp. SIC: 6021—
National Commercial Banks.

★ 92589 ★ Fleetwood Travel
Trailer Inc.
380 Battaile Dr.
Winchester, VA 22601
(703)662-3436
Officer: Bill Cook, Manager. Ultimate
Parent: Fleetwood Enterprises, Inc. SIC:
3711—Motor Vehicles & Car Bodies;
3792—Travel Trailers & Campers.

★ 92590 ★ Fleetwood Travel
Trailers of Virginia Inc.
380 Battaile Dr.
Winchester, VA 22601
Ultimate Parent: Fleetwood Enterprises,
Inc. SIC: 3711—Motor Vehicles & Car
Bodies.

★ 92591 ★ Food Lion
South Park Ctr.
Winchester, VA 22601
(703)665-3090
Ultimate Parent: Food Lion. SIC: 5411—
Grocery Stores.

★ 92592 ★ Food Lion Inc.
South Park Ctr.
Winchester, VA 22601
(703)665-3090
Ultimate Parent: Food Lion. SIC: 5411—
Grocery Stores.

★ 92593 ★ General Electric Co.
125 Apple Valley Rd.
Winchester, VA 22602
(703)667-5990
Officer: Carl Mosher, Manager. Ultimate
Parent: General Electric. SIC: 3641—
Electric Lamps.

★ 92594 ★ General Electric Co.
Winchester Lamp Plant
Rte. 3 Box 310
Winchester, VA 22601
Ultimate Parent: General Electric. SIC:
3641—Electric Lamps.

★ 92595 ★ Hertz Rent-A-Car
216 S. Loudoun St.
Winchester, VA 22601
(703)662-1121
Ultimate Parent: Hertz. SIC: 7514—
Passenger Car Rental.

★ 92596 ★ J C Penney Co.
701 Millwood Ave.
Winchester, VA 22601
(703)667-2334
Ultimate Parent: J.C. Penney. SIC: 5311—
Department Stores.

★ 92597 ★ Life Insurance Co. of
Va
2816 Valley Ave.
Winchester, VA 22601
(703)667-5300
Ultimate Parent: Life Insurance Co. of
Virginia. SIC: 6411—Insurance Agents,
Brokers & Service.

★ 92598 ★ Mobil Service Center
613 Millwood Ave.
Winchester, VA 22601
(703)662-7799
Ultimate Parent: Mobil. SIC: 5541—
Gasoline Service Stations.

★ 92599 ★ Northwestern Mutual
Life
10 W. Boscawen St.
Winchester, VA 22601
(703)667-0203
Ultimate Parent: Northwestern Mutual Life.
SIC: 6411—Insurance Agents, Brokers &
Service.

★ 92600 ★ Potomac Edison Co.
RR 11
Winchester, VA 22603-9846
(703)665-0115
Ultimate Parent: Allegheny Power System.
SIC: 4911—Electric Services.

★ 92601 ★ Radio Shack
2246 Valley Ave.
Winchester, VA 22601
(703)667-3643
Company Type: Division. Ultimate Parent:
Tandy Corp. SIC: 5065—Electronic Parts &
Equipment Nec.

★ 92602 ★ Radio Shack
2246 Valley Ave.
Winchester, VA 22601
(703)667-3643
Company Type: Division. Ultimate Parent:
Tandy Corp. SIC: 5065—Electronic Parts &
Equipment Nec.

★ 92603 ★ Rubbermaid
Commercial Products
3124 Valley Ave.
Winchester, VA 22601
(703)667-8700
Ultimate Parent: Rubbermaid. SIC: 3089—
Plastics Products Nec.

★ 92604 ★ Rubbermaid Inc.
Commerical Products
3124 Valley Ave.
Winchester, VA 22601
Ultimate Parent: Rubbermaid. SIC: 3089—
Plastics Products Nec.

★ 92605 ★ Southland Corp.
128 S. Loudoun St.
Winchester, VA 22601
(703)667-3840
Ultimate Parent: Southland Corp. SIC:
5411—Grocery Stores.

★ 92606 ★ Waldenbooks
Apple Blossom Mall
Winchester, VA 22601
(703)665-0070
Ultimate Parent: K-Mart. SIC: 5942—Book
Stores.

★ 92607 ★ Westvaco Corp.
2737 Valley Ave.
Winchester, VA 22601
(703)662-4756
Ultimate Parent: WestVaco Corp.

Woodbridge

★ 92608 ★ Banister Shoe
2700 Potomac Mills Cir. 607
Woodbridge, VA 22192
(703)494-4190
Ultimate Parent: United States Shoe. SIC:
5661—Shoe Stores.

★ 92609 ★ Business Systems
Inc.
14205 Telegraph Rd.
Woodbridge, VA 22192-4615
(703)494-3447
Ultimate Parent: Avery Dennison Corp.
SIC: 7371—Computer Programming
Services.

★ 92610 ★ Crestar Bank
13408 Jefferson Davis Hwy.
Woodbridge, VA 22191-1295
(703)838-3371
Location Type: Branch office. Ultimate
Parent: Crestar Financial Corp. SIC:
6021—National Commercial Banks.

★ 92611 ★ Crestar Bank
12417 Dillinham Sq.
Woodbridge, VA 22192
(703)838-3905
Location Type: Branch office. Ultimate
Parent: Crestar Financial Corp. SIC:
6021—National Commercial Banks.

★ 92612 ★ FICON Corp.
14011 Telegraph Rd.
Woodbridge, VA 22192-4611
(703)494-2218
Officer: Clement Mitchell, President & CEO.
Ultimate Parent: American International
Group, Inc. SIC: 1711—Plumbing, Heating
& Air-Conditioning; 1731—Electrical Work;
1629—Heavy Construction Nec. Employee
Count: 400. Sales: 47 M.

★ 92613 ★ First Union National
Bank of Virginia
1476 Davis Ford Rd.
Woodbridge, VA 22192-2711
(703)878-7398
Location Type: Branch office. Ultimate
Parent: First Union Corp. SIC: 6021—
National Commercial Banks.

★ 92614 ★ First Virginia Bank
2089 Daniel Stuart Sq.
Woodbridge, VA 22191
(703)241-3508
Location Type: Branch office. Ultimate
Parent: First Virginia Banks Inc. SIC:
6021—National Commercial Banks.

★ 92615 ★ First Virginia Bank
14000 Jefferson Davis Hwy.
Woodbridge, VA 22191-2102
(703)241-3584
Location Type: Branch office. Ultimate
Parent: First Virginia Banks Inc. SIC:
6021—National Commercial Banks.

★ 92616 ★ First Virginia Bank
12435 Dillingham Sq.
Woodbridge, VA 22192
(703)241-4637
Location Type: Branch office. Ultimate
Parent: First Virginia Banks Inc. SIC:
6021—National Commercial Banks.

★ 92617 ★ Greyhound Bus Lines
14010 Jefferson Davis Hwy.
Woodbridge, VA 22191
(703)494-6718
Ultimate Parent: Greyhound Lines Inc. SIC:
4111—Local & Suburban Transit; 4131—
Intercity & Rural Bus Transportation.

★ 92618 ★ Mary Kay Cosmetics
1292 Bayside Ave. 9
Woodbridge, VA 22191
(703)490-1159
Ultimate Parent: Mary Kay Cosmetics.

★ 92619 ★ Mast Advertising &
Publishing
14525 Telegraph Rd.
Woodbridge, VA 22192
(703)494-0219
Ultimate Parent: Southwestern Bell. SIC:
7313—Radio, T.V. & Publisher
Representatives; 7311—Advertising
Agencies.

★ 92620 ★ Pulte Home Corp.
2887 Burgundy Pl
Woodbridge, VA 22192
(703)491-1775
Ultimate Parent: Pulte. SIC: 1521—
Single-Family Housing Construction.

★ 92621 ★ Radio Shack
Woodbridge Shopping Ctr.
Woodbridge, VA 22191
(703)494-1717
Company Type: Division. Ultimate Parent:
Tandy Corp. SIC: 5719—Miscellaneous
Home Furnishings Stores.

★ 92622 ★ **Radio Shack**
Forestdale Plz.
Woodbridge, VA 22193
(804)898-5466 (703)670-9144
Ultimate Parent: Rite Aid. **SIC:** 5912—Drug Stores & Proprietary Stores. **Company Type:** Division. **Ultimate Parent:** Tandy Corp. **SIC:** 5731—Radio, Television & Electronics Stores.

★ 92623 ★ **Radio Shack**
Forestdale Plz.
Woodbridge, VA 22193
(703)670-9144
Company Type: Division. **Ultimate Parent:** Tandy Corp. **SIC:** 5731—Radio, Television & Electronics Stores.

★ 92624 ★ **Radio Shack**
Woodbridge Shopping Ctr.
Woodbridge, VA 22191
(703)494-1717
Company Type: Division. **Ultimate Parent:** Tandy Corp. **SIC:** 5719—Miscellaneous Home Furnishings Stores.

★ 92625 ★ **Rite Aid**
14422 Jefferson Davis Hwy.
Woodbridge, VA 22191
(703)491-1151
Ultimate Parent: Rite Aid. **SIC:** 5912—Drug Stores & Proprietary Stores.

★ 92626 ★ **Signet Bank, Virginia**
13927 Jefferson Davis Hwy.
Woodbridge, VA 22191-2086
(703)494-1161
Location Type: Branch office. **Ultimate Parent:** Signet Banking Corp. **SIC:** 6021—National Commercial Banks.

★ 92627 ★ **Signet Bank, Virginia**
2876 Dale Blvd.
Woodbridge, VA 22193-1196
(703)670-2121
Location Type: Branch office. **Ultimate Parent:** Signet Banking Corp. **SIC:** 6021—National Commercial Banks.

★ 92628 ★ **Southland Corp.**
12506 Lake Ridge Dr.
Woodbridge, VA 22192
(703)491-6505
Ultimate Parent: Southland Corp. **SIC:** 5411—Grocery Stores.

Woodstock

★ 92629 ★ **First Union National Bank of Virginia**
161 S. Main St.
Woodstock, VA 22664-1422
(703)459-3707
Location Type: Branch office. **Ultimate Parent:** First Union Corp. **SIC:** 6021—National Commercial Banks.

★ 92630 ★ **First Virginia Bank - Shenandoah Valley**
200 N. Main St.
Woodstock, VA 22664-1419
(703)459-3771
Company Type: Subsidiary. **Officer:**

Charles R. Cash, President. **Ultimate Parent:** First Virginia Banks Inc. **SIC:** 6021—National Commercial Banks. **Employee Count:** 88.

★ 92631 ★ **Food Lion**
1029 S. Main St.
Woodstock, VA 22664
(703)459-8381
Ultimate Parent: Food Lion. **SIC:** 5411—Grocery Stores.

★ 92632 ★ **Rite Aid**
486 N. Main St.
Woodstock, VA 22664
(703)459-9934
Ultimate Parent: Rite Aid. **SIC:** 5912—Drug Stores & Proprietary Stores.

★ 92633 ★ **Wrangler**
113 Indian Spring Rd.
Woodstock, VA 22664
(703)459-2181
Officer: Charles Sours, Manager. **Ultimate Parent:** VF Corp. **SIC:** 2325—Men's/Boys' Trousers & Slacks.

Wytheville

★ 92634 ★ **Camcar Inc.**
Amsco Division
345 East Marshall St.
Wytheville, VA 24382
Ultimate Parent: Textron. **SIC:** 3452—Bolts, Nuts, Rivets & Washers.

★ 92635 ★ **Camcar/Textron Inc.**
Amsco Products Division
345 E. Marshall St.
Wytheville, VA 24382
Ultimate Parent: Textron. **SIC:** 3452—Bolts, Nuts, Rivets & Washers.

★ 92636 ★ **Eckerd Drugs**
Evansham Shopping Ctr.
Wytheville, VA 24382
(703)228-7158
Ultimate Parent: Eckerd Corp. **SIC:** 5912—Drug Stores & Proprietary Stores.

★ 92637 ★ **Emerson Electric Co.**
Alco Controls Div.
555 Peppers Ferry Rd.
Wytheville, VA 24382
Company Type: Division. **Ultimate Parent:** Emerson Electric Co. Inc. **SIC:** 3491—Industrial Valves.

★ 92638 ★ **Emerson Electric Co. Inc.**
Alco Controls Div.
555 Peppers Ferry Rd.
Wytheville, VA 24382
Company Type: Division. **Ultimate Parent:** Emerson Electric Co. Inc. **SIC:** 3634—Electric Housewares & Fans; 3822—Environmental Controls.

★ 92639 ★ **First Union National Bank of Virginia**
320 W. Main St.
Wytheville, VA 24382-2205
(703)228-5433
Location Type: Branch office. **Ultimate Parent:** First Union Corp. **SIC:** 6021—National Commercial Banks.

★ 92640 ★ **Greyhound Bus Lines**
385 E. Main St.
Wytheville, VA 24382
(703)228-2161
Ultimate Parent: Greyhound Lines Inc. **SIC:** 4111—Local & Suburban Transit.

★ 92641 ★ **Kingston-Warren Corp.**
1150 S. 3rd St.
Wytheville, VA 24382-0758
Ultimate Parent: Harvard Industries. **SIC:** 3069—Fabricated Rubber Products Nec.

★ 92642 ★ **Kroger Co.**
130 W. Lee Hwy.
Wytheville, VA 24382
(703)228-2241
Ultimate Parent: Kroger. **SIC:** 5411—Grocery Stores.

★ 92643 ★ **Morton International Inc.**
2460 N. 4th St.
Wytheville, VA 24382-4418
(703)228-1500
Officer: Chuck Lanigan. **Ultimate Parent:** Morton International. **SIC:** 3479—Metal Coating & Allied Services.

★ 92644 ★ **Morton International Inc.**
2460 N. Fourth St.
Wytheville, VA 24382
Ultimate Parent: Morton International. **SIC:** 2851—Paints & Allied Products.

★ 92645 ★ **Morton International Inc.**
Rte. 1 Box A-57
Wytheville, VA 24382
Ultimate Parent: Morton International. **SIC:** 2851—Paints & Allied Products.

★ 92646 ★ **Radio Shack**
100 W. Main St.
Wytheville, VA 24382
(703)228-4231
Company Type: Division. **Ultimate Parent:** Tandy Corp. **SIC:** 5065—Electronic Parts & Equipment Nec.

★ 92647 ★ **Textron**
Amsco Products Division
345 East Marshall St.
Wytheville, VA 24382
Ultimate Parent: Textron. **SIC:** 3452—Bolts, Nuts, Rivets & Washers.

Yarina

★ 92648 ★ **Signet Bank, Virginia**
1320 New Market Rd.
Yarina, VA 23231-9802
(804)771-7711
Location Type: Branch office. **Ultimate Parent:** Signet Banking Corp. **SIC:** 6021—National Commercial Banks.

Yorktown

★ 92649 ★ **Browning-Ferris Industries**
124 Greene Dr.
Yorktown, VA 23692-4800
(804)728-5488
Location Type: Branch office. **Officer:** Bill Lacy. **Ultimate Parent:** Browning-Ferris Industries. **SIC:** 4953—Refuse Systems; 4212—Local Trucking Without Storage.

★ 92650 ★ **Exxon Service Station**
8017 Washington Memorial Hwy.
Yorktown, VA 23692
(804)898-4225
Ultimate Parent: Exxon. **SIC:** 5541—Gasoline Service Stations.

★ 92651 ★ **First American Bank**
5208 Washington Sq.
Yorktown, VA 23692
(804)728-2120
Ultimate Parent: First American Corp. **SIC:** 6022—State Commercial Banks.

★ 92652 ★ **Food Lion**
5210 Washington Sq.
Yorktown, VA 23692
(804)898-5023
Ultimate Parent: Food Lion. **SIC:** 5411—Grocery Stores.

★ 92653 ★ **Greyhound Bus Lines**
Fort Eustis Terminal
Yorktown, VA 23690
(804)887-2626
Ultimate Parent: Greyhound Lines Inc. **SIC:** 4111—Local & Suburban Transit.

★ 92654 ★ **New York Life Insurance Co.**
5731 Washington Mem Hwy.
Yorktown, VA 23692
(804)898-8086
Ultimate Parent: New York Life. **SIC:** 6411—Insurance Agents, Brokers & Service.

★ 92655 ★ **Radio Shack**
4326 Washington Mem Hwy.
Yorktown, VA 23692
(804)898-9454
Company Type: Division. **Ultimate Parent:** Tandy Corp. **SIC:** 5731—Radio, Television & Electronics Stores.

★ 92656 ★ **Rite Aid**
5234 Washington Sq.
Yorktown, VA 23692
(804)898-5466
Ultimate Parent: Rite Aid. **SIC:** 5912—Drug Stores & Proprietary Stores.

WEST VIRGINIA

Alma

★ 92657 ★ Quaker State Oil
Refining Co.
Alma, WV 26320
(304)758-2653
Ultimate Parent: Quaker State. SIC:
1311—Crude Petroleum & Natural Gas.

Alum Creek

★ 92658 ★ Cranberry Pipeline
Corp.
Lick Creek Rd.
Alum Creek, WV 25003
(304)756-9642
Ultimate Parent: Cabot. SIC: 4925—Gas
Production & Distribution Nec.

Anmoore

★ 92659 ★ Ucar Carbon Co. Inc.
Rte. 58 Philippi Pike
Anmoore, WV 26323
Ultimate Parent: Union Carbide Corp. SIC:
3624—Carbon & Graphite Products.

★ 92660 ★ Union Carbide Corp.
Philippi Pk.
Anmoore, WV 26323
(304)624-7651
Officer: Herman A. Overcash, Manager.
Ultimate Parent: Union Carbide Corp. SIC:
3295—Minerals—Ground or Treated;
3624—Carbon & Graphite Products; 3643—
Current-Carrying Wiring Devices.

Ansted

★ 92661 ★ Rite Aid Discount
Pharmacy
Main St.
Ansted, WV 25812
(304)658-4426
Ultimate Parent: Rite Aid.

Apple Grove

★ 92662 ★ Goodyear Tire &
Rubber Co.
State Rte. 2
Apple Grove, WV 25502
Ultimate Parent: Goodyear Tire & Rubber.
SIC: 2821—Plastics Materials & Resins.

★ 92663 ★ Goodyear Tire &
Rubber Co.
St. Rte. 2
Apple Grove, WV 25502
Ultimate Parent: Goodyear Tire & Rubber.
SIC: 2821—Plastics Materials & Resins.

★ 92664 ★ Shell Chemical Co.
Point Pleasant Polyester Plant
State Rte. 2
Apple Grove, WV 25502
Location Type: Plant. Ultimate Parent:
Shell Oil Co. SIC: 2821—Plastics Materials
& Resins.

Arnoldsburg

★ 92665 ★ Pennzoil Co.
Rural Route 3
Arnoldsburg, WV 25234
(304)354-6818
Ultimate Parent: Pennzoil. SIC: 1389—Oil
& Gas Field Services Nec.

Augusta

★ 92666 ★ Potomac Edison Co.
Augusta, WV 26704
(304)496-8129
Ultimate Parent: Allegheny Power System.
SIC: 4911—Electric Services.

Ballengee

★ 92667 ★ Kroger Co.
RR 107
Ballengee, WV 24919
(304)466-4888
Ultimate Parent: Kroger. SIC: 5411—
Grocery Stores.

Barboursville

★ 92668 ★ Casual Corner
455 Huntington Mall
Barboursville, WV 25504
(304)733-0073
Ultimate Parent: United States Shoe. SIC:
5651—Family Clothing Stores.

★ 92669 ★ Fitness World
3677 Us 60 E
Barboursville, WV 25504
(304)733-1600
Ultimate Parent: New York Times. SIC:
7299—Miscellaneous Personal Services
Nec.

★ 92670 ★ Layne Bryant
780 Huntington Mall
Barboursville, WV 25504
(304)733-3672
Ultimate Parent: Limited. SIC: 5621—
Women's Clothing Stores.

★ 92671 ★ McDonald's
Hamburgers
102 Mall Rd.
Barboursville, WV 25504
(304)733-0455
Ultimate Parent: McDonald's. SIC: 5812—
Eating Places.

★ 92672 ★ Victoria's Secret
265 Huntington Mall
Barboursville, WV 25504
(304)736-9660
Ultimate Parent: Limited. SIC: 5621—
Women's Clothing Stores.

Beaver

★ 92673 ★ Kroger Co.
Beaver Plz.
Beaver, WV 25813
(304)255-5525
Ultimate Parent: Kroger. SIC: 5411—
Grocery Stores.

Beckley

★ 92674 ★ Chesapeake &
Potomac Telephone Co.
200 Woodlawn Ave.
Beckley, WV 25801-5407
(304)255-9786
Company Type: Subsidiary. Ultimate
Parent: Bell Atlantic Corp. SIC: 4813—
Telephone Communications Except
Radiotelephone.

★ 92675 ★ Dr. Pepper Seven-Up
Co. Inc.
4419 Robert C. Byrd Dr.
Beckley, WV 25801
(304)253-3532
Officer: Letia Drewry, Owner. Ultimate
Parent: Dr. Pepper/Seven-Up. SIC: 2086—
Bottled & Canned Soft Drinks.

★ 92676 ★ Kroger Co.
Raleigh Mall
Beckley, WV 25801
(304)253-5688
Ultimate Parent: Kroger. SIC: 5411—
Grocery Stores.

★ 92677 ★ Lerner Shops
77 Crossroads Mall
Beckley, WV 25801
(304)253-9700
Ultimate Parent: Limited. SIC: 5621—
Women's Clothing Stores.

★ 92678 ★ Mary Kay Cosmetics
Sales Di
102 Lilly St.
Beckley, WV 25801
(304)253-1833
Ultimate Parent: Mary Kay Cosmetics.

★ 92679 ★ Northwestern Mutual
Life Inc.
103 Virginia St.
Beckley, WV 25801
(304)255-1521
Ultimate Parent: Northwestern Mutual Life.
SIC: 6411—Insurance Agents, Brokers &
Service.

★ 92680 ★ Pennzoil Oil Change
Center
100 S. Eisenhower Dr.
Beckley, WV 25801
(304)253-7738
Ultimate Parent: Pennzoil. SIC: 5541—
Gasoline Service Stations.

★ 92681 ★ Pennzoil Self Service
Station
1209 Johnstown Rd.
Beckley, WV 25801
(304)252-4546
Ultimate Parent: Pennzoil. SIC: 5541—
Gasoline Service Stations.

★ 92682 ★ Rite Aid Discount
Pharmacy
Beckley Plz.
Beckley, WV 25801
(304)252-7313
Ultimate Parent: Rite Aid. SIC: 5912—Drug
Stores & Proprietary Stores.

★ 92683 ★ Rite Aid Discount
Pharmacy
322 Neville St.
Beckley, WV 25801
(304)252-9110
Ultimate Parent: Rite Aid. SIC: 5912—Drug
Stores & Proprietary Stores.

★ 92684 ★ Rite Aid Discount
Pharmacy
Town Country Shopping Ctr.
Beckley, WV 25801
(304)252-2074
Ultimate Parent: Rite Aid.

★ 92685 ★ Rite Aid Discount
Pharmacy
Beckley Plz.
Beckley, WV 25801
(304)252-9126
Ultimate Parent: Rite Aid. SIC: 5912—Drug
Stores & Proprietary Stores.

★ 92686 ★ Rite Aid Discount
Pharmacy
79 Crossroads Mall
Beckley, WV 25801
(304)255-6045
Ultimate Parent: Rite Aid. SIC: 5912—Drug
Stores & Proprietary Stores.

★ 92687 ★ Underwriters
Adjusting Co.
112 Mcclure St.
Beckley, WV 25801
(304)253-7177
Ultimate Parent: Continental. SIC: 6411—
Insurance Agents, Brokers & Service.

★ 92688 ★ Underwriters
Adjusting Co.
107 Lewis St.
Beckley, WV 25801
(304)253-5144
Ultimate Parent: Continental. SIC: 6411—
Insurance Agents, Brokers & Service.

★ 92689 ★ United Parcel Service
201 George St.
Beckley, WV 25801
(304)253-1327
Ultimate Parent: United Parcel Service of
America. SIC: 4215—Courier Services
Except by Air.

Beech Bottom

★ 92690 ★ Wheeling-Pittsburgh
Steel
Rte. 2
Beech Bottom, WV 26030
Ultimate Parent: Wheeling-Pittsburgh Steel
Corp. SIC: 3312—Blast Furnaces & Steel
Mills.

★ 92691 ★ Wheeling-Pittsburgh
Steel Corp.
Rte. 2
Beech Bottom, WV 26030
Ultimate Parent: Wheeling-Pittsburgh Steel
Corp. SIC: 3312—Blast Furnaces & Steel
Mills.

★ 92692 ★ Wheeling Pittsburgh
Steel Corp.
RR 2 PO 37
Beech Bottom, WV 26030
(304)234-4275
Officer: Steven Beecoft, Manager. Ultimate
Parent: Wheeling-Pittsburgh Steel Corp.
SIC: 2952—Asphalt Felts & Coatings;
3316—Cold-Finishing of Steel Shapes.

Belle

★ 92693 ★ Kroger Co.
2700 E. Dupont Ave.
Belle, WV 25015
(304)949-2147
Ultimate Parent: Kroger. SIC: 5411—
Grocery Stores.

★ 92694 ★ Occidental Chemical
Corp.
Dupont Ave. PO Box 615
Belle, WV 25015
Ultimate Parent: Occidental Petroleum
Corp. SIC: 2869—Industrial Organic
Chemicals Nec.

★ 92695 ★ Occidental Chemical
Corp.
Dupont Ave. PO Box 615
Belle, WV 25015-1599
Ultimate Parent: Occidental Petroleum
Corp. SIC: 2869—Industrial Organic
Chemicals Nec.

★ 92696 ★ Rite Aid Discount
Pharmacy
2305 W. Dupont Ave.
Belle, WV 25015
(304)949-9820
Ultimate Parent: Rite Aid. SIC: 5912—Drug
Stores & Proprietary Stores.

★ 92697 ★ Superamerica 5086
524 Campbells Creek Rd.
Belle, WV 25015
(304)925-5808
Ultimate Parent: Ashland Oil.

Benwood

★ 92698 ★　Kroger Co.
211 Marshall Station
Benwood, WV 26031
(304)232-1342
Ultimate Parent: Kroger. **SIC:** 5411—
Grocery Stores.

Bluefield

★ 92699 ★　Acme Markets of Tazewell Va
N. Tazewell
Bluefield, WV 24701
(304)988-2561
Ultimate Parent: American Stores. **SIC:**
5411—Grocery Stores.

★ 92700 ★　Flowers Baking Co.
Rte. 52 N
Bluefield, WV 24701
(304)327-3561
Officer: Bill Gasperson, President. **Ultimate Parent:** Flowers Industries. **SIC:** 2051—
Bread, Cake & Related Products.

★ 92701 ★　Flowers Baking Co. of West Virginia Inc.
US Rte. 52 N
PO Drawer 308
Bluefield, WV 24701-0308
(304)327-3561 **Fax:** (304)327-5027
Company Type: Subsidiary. **Officer:** Bill
Gasperson, President. **Ultimate Parent:**
Flowers Industries.

★ 92702 ★　Greyhound Bus Lines
1332 Bland St.
Bluefield, WV 24701
(304)327-1805
Ultimate Parent: Greyhound Lines Inc. **SIC:**
4142—Bus Charter Service Except Local;
4111—Local & Suburban Transit; 4131—
Intercity & Rural Bus Transportation.

★ 92703 ★　Ryder Truck Rental One Way
2415 Washington St.
Bluefield, WV 24701
(304)325-9452
Ultimate Parent: Ryder System. **SIC:**
7359—Equipment Rental & Leasing Nec.

★ 92704 ★　Thrift Drugs
Blue Prince Plz.
Bluefield, WV 24701
(304)327-5022
Ultimate Parent: J.C. Penney. **SIC:** 5912—
Drug Stores & Proprietary Stores.

Bolt

★ 92705 ★　Eimco Coal Machinery Inc.
RR 99
Bolt, WV 25817
(304)934-5351
Officer: Perk Kidd, Manager. **Ultimate
Parent:** Baker Hughes. **SIC:** 3532—Mining
Machinery; 3599—Industrial Machinery Nec.

Bridgeport

★ 92706 ★　Casual Corner
Meadowbrook Mall
Bridgeport, WV 26330
(304)842-5515
Ultimate Parent: United States Shoe. **SIC:**
5621—Women's Clothing Stores.

★ 92707 ★　Kroger Co.
104 Thompson Dr.
Bridgeport, WV 26330
(304)842-6141
Ultimate Parent: Kroger. **SIC:** 5411—
Grocery Stores.

★ 92708 ★　P&Wc Aircraft Services Inc.
Benedum Industrial Park Rte. 3 Box 16
Bridgeport, WV 26330-9506
Ultimate Parent: United Technologies. **SIC:**
3724—Aircraft Engines & Engine Parts.

★ 92709 ★　Pratt & Whitney Aircraft of West Virginia
Benedum Industrial Pk.
Rte. 3, Box 16
Bridgeport, WV 26330
Ultimate Parent: United Technologies. **SIC:**
3724—Aircraft Engines & Engine Parts.

★ 92710 ★　Rite Aid Discount Pharmacy
Meadowbrook Mall
Bridgeport, WV 26330
(304)842-6089
Ultimate Parent: Rite Aid. **SIC:** 5912—Drug
Stores & Proprietary Stores.

★ 92711 ★　Rite Aid Discount Pharmacy
300 W. Main St.
Bridgeport, WV 26330
(304)842-6098
Ultimate Parent: Rite Aid. **SIC:** 5912—Drug
Stores & Proprietary Stores.

★ 92712 ★　Unisys Corp.
106 Hill St.
Bridgeport, WV 26330
Ultimate Parent: Unisys Corp. **SIC:** 7373—
Computer Integrated Systems Design.

Buckhannon

★ 92713 ★　Kroger Co.
RR 20
Buckhannon, WV 26201
(304)472-0918
Ultimate Parent: Kroger. **SIC:** 5411—
Grocery Stores.

★ 92714 ★　Rite Aid Discount Pharmacy
20 S. Florida St.
Buckhannon, WV 26201
(304)472-3782
Ultimate Parent: Rite Aid. **SIC:** 5912—Drug
Stores & Proprietary Stores.

★ 92715 ★　Rite Aid Discount Pharmacy
23 E. Main St.
Buckhannon, WV 26201
(304)472-9896
Ultimate Parent: Rite Aid.

★ 92716 ★　Ryder Truck Rental
222 S. Kanawha St.
Buckhannon, WV 26201
(304)472-1760
Ultimate Parent: Ryder System.

★ 92717 ★　Ryder Truck Rental
Buckhannon, WV 26201
(304)269-5342
Ultimate Parent: Ryder System. **SIC:**
7513—Truck Rental & Leasing Without
Drivers.

★ 92718 ★　Superamerica
33 S. Locust St.
Buckhannon, WV 26201
(304)472-0826
Ultimate Parent: Ashland Oil. **SIC:** 5541—
Gasoline Service Stations.

Caldwell

★ 92719 ★　United Parcel Service
Harts Run Rd.
Caldwell, WV 24925
(304)536-4614
Ultimate Parent: United Parcel Service of
America.

Charles Town

★ 92720 ★　Denny's Restaurant
903 E. Washington St.
Charles Town, WV 25414
(304)728-8522
Ultimate Parent: Flagstar Co. **SIC:** 5812—
Eating Places.

★ 92721 ★　Minnesota Mining & Mfg Co.
Middleway
Charles Town, WV 25414
(304)725-2031
Ultimate Parent: Minnesota Mining & Mfg.
SIC: 2796—Platemaking Services.

★ 92722 ★　Peoples Bank
W Washington
Charles Town, WV 25414
(304)725-7018
Ultimate Parent: People's Bank. **SIC:**
6022—State Commercial Banks.

★ 92723 ★　Peoples Bank
106 W. Washington St.
Charles Town, WV 25414
(304)728-8000
Ultimate Parent: People's Bank. **SIC:**
6022—State Commercial Banks.

Charleston

★ 92724 ★　AT&T Network System
3224 Pennsylvania Ave.
Charleston, WV 25302
(304)343-2694
Ultimate Parent: AT&T. **SIC:** 4813—
Telephone Communications Except
Radiotelephone.

★ 92725 ★　Borden Inc.
508 Roane St.
Charleston, WV 25302
(304)422-2401
Officer: Sandy Rhoades, Manager.
Ultimate Parent: Borden, Inc. **SIC:** 2024—
Ice Cream & Frozen Desserts.

★ 92726 ★　Borden Inc. Valley Bell Dairy
508 Roane St.
Charleston, WV 25302
Ultimate Parent: Borden, Inc. **SIC:** 2026—
Fluid Milk.

★ 92727 ★　Casual Corner
Town Ctr. Mall
Charleston, WV 25389
(304)342-3909
Ultimate Parent: United States Shoe. **SIC:**
5621—Women's Clothing Stores.

★ 92728 ★　The Chesapeak & Potomae Co. of West Virginia
1500 MacCorkle Ave. SE
Charleston, WV 25314
(304)343-9911
Company Type: Subsidiary. **Officer:** David
K. Hall, V.P. Gen. Counsel & Sec. **Ultimate
Parent:** Bell Atlantic Corp. **SIC:** 4812—
Radiotelephone Communications.
Employee Count: 3350. **Sales:** 500000000
M.

★ 92729 ★　Chesapeake & Patomac Telephone Co. of West Virginia
1500 MacCorkle Ave. SE
Charleston, WV 25314
(304)343-9911
Company Type: Subsidiary. **Officer:** David
E. Lowe, President & CEO. **Ultimate
Parent:** Bell Atlantic Corp.

★ 92730 ★　Chesapeake & Potomac Telephone Co.
1500 MacCorkle Ave. SE
Charleston, WV 25314-1596
(304)343-9911
Company Type: Subsidiary. **Officer:** David
E. Lowe, President & CEO. **Ultimate
Parent:** Bell Atlantic Corp. **SIC:** 4813—
Telephone Communications Except
Radiotelephone. **Employee Count:** 2552.
Sales: 560 M.

★ 92731 ★　Circuit City
233 Virginia St. E
Charleston, WV 25301
(304)345-0411
Ultimate Parent: Circuit City Stores. **SIC:**
5571—Motorcycle Dealers.

★ 92732 ★　Circuit City
3716 Maccorkle Ave. SE
Charleston, WV 25304
(304)925-6911
Ultimate Parent: Circuit City Stores. **SIC:**
5731—Radio, Television & Electronics
Stores.

★ 92733 ★　City National Bank
715 Lee St. E.
Charleston, WV 25301-1706
(304)926-3348
Ultimate Parent: City National Corp. **SIC:**
6021—National Commercial Banks.

★ 92734 ★　City National Bank
4168 PO Box
Charleston, WV 25364
Ultimate Parent: City National Corp. **SIC:**
6099—Functions Related to Deposit
Banking.

★ 92735 ★　City National Bank of Charleston
308 Goff Mountain Rd.
Charleston, WV 25313-1415
(304)926-3300
Company Type: Branch. **Ultimate Parent:**
City National Corp. **SIC:** 6022—State
Commercial Banks.

★ 92736 ★　City National Bank of Charleston
1004 Bridge Rd.
Charleston, WV 25314-1306
Company Type: Branch. **Ultimate Parent:**
City National Corp. **SIC:** 6021—National
Commercial Banks.

★ 92737 ★　City National Bank of Charleston
715 Lee St. E.
Charleston, WV 25301-1706
Company Type: Branch. **Ultimate Parent:**
City National Corp.

★ 92738 ★　Columbia Gas Transmission Corp.
1700 MacCorkle Ave. SE
Charleston, WV 25314-1518
(304)357-2000
Company Type: Subsidiary. **Officer:** James
P. Holland, Chairman of the Board & CEO.
Ultimate Parent: Columbia Gas System.
SIC: 4922—Natural Gas Transmission.
Employee Count: 3065.

★ 92739 ★　Columbia Natural Resources Inc.
900 Pennsylvania Ave.
Charleston, WV 25302-3531
(304)353-5000
Company Type: Subsidiary. **Officer:** J. R.
Henning, President. **Ultimate Parent:**
Columbia Gas System. **SIC:** 1311—Crude
Petroleum & Natural Gas. **Employee
Count:** 390.

★ 92740 ★　Commerce Banc Corp.
1 Commerce Sq.
Charleston, WV 25301-1721
(304)348-5000
Ultimate Parent: Huntington Bancshares.
SIC: 6021—National Commercial Banks;
6022—State Commercial Banks.

★ 92741 ★　Dean Witter Reynolds Inc.
Charleston National Plz.
Charleston, WV 25301
(304)344-1969
Location Type: Branch office. **Ultimate
Parent:** Dean Witter Discover. **SIC:** 6211—
Security Brokers & Dealers.

★ 92742 ★　Dean Witter Reynolds Inc.
500 Virginia St. E
Charleston, WV 25301
(304)357-4550
Location Type: Branch office. **Ultimate
Parent:** Dean Witter Discover. **SIC:** 6211—
Security Brokers & Dealers.

★ 92743 ★　Eastman Kodak Co.
1 Commerce Sq.
Charleston, WV 25301
(304)343-9437
Ultimate Parent: Eastman Kodak. **SIC:**
5044—Office Equipment; 5046—
Commercial Equipment Nec.

★ 92744 ★　Eastman Kodak Co.
1420 Kanawha Blvd. W
Charleston, WV 25312
(304)346-3291
Ultimate Parent: Eastman Kodak. **SIC:**
5046—Commercial Equipment Nec.

★ 92745 ★　Exxon Chemicals Americas
1018 Kanawha Blvd. W
Charleston, WV 25302
(304)344-2500
Ultimate Parent: Exxon. **SIC:** 3861—
Photographic Equipment & Supplies.

★ 92746 ★　Exxon Co.
Thayer St.
Charleston, WV 25314
(304)347-1053
Ultimate Parent: Exxon. **SIC:** 1311—Crude
Petroleum & Natural Gas.

★ 92747 ★ **Exxon Co. U S a**
1410 Maccorkle Ave. SW
Charleston, WV 25303
(304)347-1000
Ultimate Parent: Exxon. **SIC:** 5172—
Petroleum Products Nec.

★ 92748 ★ **Greyhound Bus Lines**
300 Reynolds St.
Charleston, WV 25301
(304)357-0057
Ultimate Parent: Greyhound Lines Inc. **SIC:**
4111—Local & Suburban Transit; 4131—
Intercity & Rural Bus Transportation; 4142—
Bus Charter Service Except Local.

★ 92749 ★ **Greyhound Lines Inc.**
300 Reynolds St.
Charleston, WV 25301
(304)357-0057
Ultimate Parent: Greyhound Lines Inc. **SIC:**
4111—Local & Suburban Transit; 4131—
Intercity & Rural Bus Transportation.

★ 92750 ★ **J C Penney Co. Inc.**
401 Lee St. E
Charleston, WV 25301
(304)345-9075
Ultimate Parent: J.C. Penney. **SIC:** 5311—
Department Stores.

★ 92751 ★ **Jiffy Lube Oil Change**
121 Virginia St. W
Charleston, WV 25302
(304)343-4961
Ultimate Parent: Pennzoil. **SIC:** 7539—
Automotive Repair Shops Nec.

★ 92752 ★ **Kroger Co.**
Oakwood Rd.
Charleston, WV 25320
(304)346-1043
Ultimate Parent: Kroger. **SIC:** 5411—
Grocery Stores.

★ 92753 ★ **Kroger Co.**
Smith St.
Charleston, WV 25301
(304)344-3103
Ultimate Parent: Kroger. **SIC:** 5411—
Grocery Stores.

★ 92754 ★ **Kroger Co.**
Kanawha Mall
Charleston, WV 25303
(304)925-5447
Ultimate Parent: Kroger. **SIC:** 5411—
Grocery Stores.

★ 92755 ★ **Kroger Co.**
10635 Maccorkle Ave.
Charleston, WV 25315
(304)949-6124
Ultimate Parent: Kroger. **SIC:** 5411—
Grocery Stores.

★ 92756 ★ **Kroger Co.**
5450 Big Tylerrd
Charleston, WV 25313
(304)776-5063
Ultimate Parent: Kroger. **SIC:** 5411—
Grocery Stores.

★ 92757 ★ **Kroger Co.**
1100 Fledder John Rd.
Charleston, WV 25314
(304)346-1043
Ultimate Parent: Kroger. **SIC:** 5411—
Grocery Stores.

★ 92758 ★ **Kroger Co.**
6313 Maccorkle Avese
Charleston, WV 25304
(304)347-2600
Ultimate Parent: Kroger. **SIC:** 5411—
Grocery Stores.

★ 92759 ★ **Kroger Co.**
6313 Maccorkle Ave. SE
Charleston, WV 25304
Ultimate Parent: Kroger. **SIC:** 4226—
Special Warehousing & Storage Nec.

★ 92760 ★ **Lane Bryant**
Charleston National Plz.
Charleston, WV 25301
(304)343-6270
Ultimate Parent: Limited. **SIC:** 5621—
Women's Clothing Stores.

★ 92761 ★ **Lane Bryant**
1034 Charleston Town Cent
Charleston, WV 25389
(304)343-6270
Ultimate Parent: Limited. **SIC:** 5621—
Women's Clothing Stores.

★ 92762 ★ **Lerner Shops**
208 Capitol St.
Charleston, WV 25301
(304)342-6353
Ultimate Parent: Limited. **SIC:** 5621—
Women's Clothing Stores.

★ 92763 ★ **Lerner Shops**
1085 Charleston Town Cent
Charleston, WV 25389
(304)344-8540
Ultimate Parent: Limited. **SIC:** 5621—
Women's Clothing Stores.

★ 92764 ★ **Life Insurance Co. of Va**
1123 Virginia St. E
Charleston, WV 25301
(304)343-7688
Ultimate Parent: Life Insurance Co. of
Virginia. **SIC:** 6411—Insurance Agents,
Brokers & Service.

★ 92765 ★ **The Limited**
Charleston Town Cent
Charleston, WV 25389
(304)344-5127
Ultimate Parent: Limited. **SIC:** 5621—
Women's Clothing Stores.

★ 92766 ★ **Limited the**
680 Charleston Town Cent
Charleston, WV 25389
(304)344-5128
Ultimate Parent: Limited. **SIC:** 5621—
Women's Clothing Stores.

★ 92767 ★ **Mary Kay Cosmetics**
1518 Mount Vernon Rd.
Charleston, WV 25314
(304)343-1396
Ultimate Parent: Mary Kay Cosmetics. **SIC:**
7231—Beauty Shops; 7231—Beauty Shops.

★ 92768 ★ **Mary Kay Cosmetics**
210 Branchfield Dr.
Charleston, WV 25314
(304)342-5404
Ultimate Parent: Mary Kay Cosmetics. **SIC:**
5999—Miscellaneous Retail Stores Nec.

★ 92769 ★ **NCR Corp.**
515 Central Ave.
Charleston, WV 25302-1909
(304)344-2416
Ultimate Parent: AT&T. **SIC:** 2761—
Manifold Business Forms.

★ 92770 ★ **New York Life West Virginia General Office**
Southeastern Agencies
Box 2186
Charleston, WV 25328
(304)340-4350
Officer: John Purdum, General Manager.
Ultimate Parent: New York Life.

★ 92771 ★ **New York Life West Virginia General Office**
Southeastern Agencies
Charleston National Plz.
Charleston, WV 25301
(304)340-4350
Officer: John H. Purdum, GeneralManager.
Ultimate Parent: New York Life.

★ 92772 ★ **Pappagallo**
Charleston Town Cent
Charleston, WV 25389
(304)346-3000
Ultimate Parent: United States Shoe. **SIC:**
5661—Shoe Stores.

★ 92773 ★ **Pappagallo**
Charleston National Plz.
Charleston, WV 25301
(304)346-3000
Ultimate Parent: United States Shoe. **SIC:**
5661—Shoe Stores.

★ 92774 ★ **Payless Shoe Source**
1077 Charleston Town Cent
Charleston, WV 25389
(304)344-0866
Ultimate Parent: May Department Stores.
SIC: 5661—Shoe Stores.

★ 92775 ★ **Payless Shoe Source**
113 Kanawha Mall
Charleston, WV 25387
(304)925-8657
Ultimate Parent: May Department Stores.
SIC: 5661—Shoe Stores.

★ 92776 ★ **Payless Shoe Source**
Charleston National Plz.
Charleston, WV 25301
(304)344-0866
Ultimate Parent: May Department Stores.
SIC: 5661—Shoe Stores.

★ 92777 ★ **Penn Mutual Life Insurance**
1012 Kanawha Blvd. E
Charleston, WV 25301
(304)345-2050
Ultimate Parent: Penn Mutual Life. **SIC:**
6411—Insurance Agents, Brokers &
Service.

★ 92778 ★ **Pennzoil Products Co.**
1015 Barlow Dr.
Charleston, WV 25311
(304)342-8161
Ultimate Parent: Pennzoil. **SIC:** 5172—
Petroleum Products Nec.

★ 92779 ★ **Pennzoil Products Co.**
1015 Barlow Dr.
Charleston, WV 25311
(304)342-8161
Ultimate Parent: Pennzoil. **SIC:** 5172—
Petroleum Products Nec.

★ 92780 ★ **Pennzoil 10 Minute Oil Change**
1300 Bigley Ave.
Charleston, WV 25302
(304)343-2023
Ultimate Parent: Pennzoil. **SIC:** 5541—
Gasoline Service Stations.

★ 92781 ★ **Rite Aid Discount Pharmacy**
9106 Maccorkle Ave.
Charleston, WV 25315
(304)949-8880
Ultimate Parent: Rite Aid. **SIC:** 5912—Drug
Stores & Proprietary Stores.

★ 92782 ★ **Rite Aid Discount Pharmacy**
209 Capitol St.
Charleston, WV 25301
(304)344-3131
Ultimate Parent: Rite Aid. **SIC:** 5912—Drug
Stores & Proprietary Stores.

★ 92783 ★ **Rite Aid Discount Pharmacy**
1011 Bridge Rd.
Charleston, WV 25314
(304)342-9364
Ultimate Parent: Rite Aid. **SIC:** 5912—Drug
Stores & Proprietary Stores.

★ 92784 ★ **Rite Aid Discount Pharmacy**
4708 Maccorkle Ave. SW
Charleston, WV 25309
(304)768-6426
Ultimate Parent: Rite Aid. **SIC:** 5912—Drug
Stores & Proprietary Stores.

★ 92785 ★ **Rite Aid Discount Pharmacy**
306 7th Ave. SW
Charleston, WV 25303
(304)744-9205
Ultimate Parent: Rite Aid. **SIC:** 5912—Drug
Stores & Proprietary Stores.

★ 92786 ★ **Rite Aid Discount Pharmacy**
1627 Bigley Ave.
Charleston, WV 25302
(304)342-9928
Ultimate Parent: Rite Aid. **SIC:** 5912—Drug
Stores & Proprietary Stores.

★ 92787 ★ **Rite Aid Discount Pharmacy**
6401 Sissonville Dr.
Charleston, WV 25312
Ultimate Parent: Rite Aid. **SIC:** 5912—Drug
Stores & Proprietary Stores.

★ 92788 ★ **Rite Aid Discount Pharmacy**
1598 Washington St. E
Charleston, WV 25311
(304)342-7117
Ultimate Parent: Rite Aid. **SIC:** 5912—Drug
Stores & Proprietary Stores.

★ 92789 ★ **Rite Aid Discount Pharmacy**
200 Capitol St.
Charleston, WV 25301
(304)342-9873
Ultimate Parent: Rite Aid. **SIC:** 5912—Drug
Stores & Proprietary Stores.

★ 92790 ★ **Rite Aid Discount Pharmacy**
222 Washington St. W
Charleston, WV 25302
(304)342-9575
Ultimate Parent: Rite Aid. **SIC:** 5912—Drug
Stores & Proprietary Stores.

★ 92791 ★ **Rite Aid Discount Pharmacy**
302 7th Ave. SW
Charleston, WV 25303
(304)744-4621
Ultimate Parent: Rite Aid. **SIC:** 5912—Drug
Stores & Proprietary Stores.

★ 92792 ★ **Rite Aid Discount Pharmacy**
2002 Charleston Town Cent
Charleston, WV 25389
(304)342-9377
Ultimate Parent: Rite Aid. **SIC:** 5912—Drug
Stores & Proprietary Stores.

★ 92793 ★ **Ryder Truck Rental**
512 Capitol St.
Charleston, WV 25301
(304)346-9454
Ultimate Parent: Ryder System. **SIC:**
7359—Equipment Rental & Leasing Nec;
7513—Truck Rental & Leasing Without
Drivers.

★ 92794 ★ **Transamerica Occidental Life Insurance**
245 Peoples Bldg.
Charleston, WV 25301
(304)342-0144
Ultimate Parent: Transamerica Occidental
Life Insurance. **SIC:** 6411—Insurance
Agents, Brokers & Service.

★ 92795 ★ **Underwriters Adjusting Co.**
611 3rd Ave.
Charleston, WV 25312
(304)744-4636
Ultimate Parent: Continental. **SIC:** 6411—
Insurance Agents, Brokers & Service.

★ 92796 ★ **Unisys Corp.**
400 Allen Dr. 401
Charleston, WV 25302
Ultimate Parent: Unisys Corp. **SIC:** 8712—
Architectural Services.

★ 92797 ★ **United Parcel Service**
3100 Maccorkle Ave. SW
Charleston, WV 25303
(304)746-3302
Ultimate Parent: United Parcel Service of
America. **SIC:** 4215—Courier Services
Except by Air.

★ 92798 ★ **United Parcel Service**
Drive
Charleston, WV 25313
(304)776-1916
Ultimate Parent: United Parcel Service of
America. **SIC:** 4215—Courier Services
Except by Air.

★ 92799 ★ **Victoria's Secret**
2087 Charleston Town Cent
Charleston, WV 25389
(304)345-2061
Ultimate Parent: Limited. **SIC:** 5621—
Women's Clothing Stores.

★ 92800 ★ **Xerox Corp.**
1 Valley Sq., Ste. 900
Charleston, WV 25301
(304)245-0110
Officer: C. R. Howdyshell, Manager.
Ultimate Parent: Xerox Corp. **SIC:** 3663—
Radio & T.V. Communications Equipment.

Chattaroy

★ 92801 ★   Tramco Inc.
Chattaroy, WV 25667
(304)235-5370
Ultimate Parent: B.F. Goodrich. **SIC:**
5063—Electrical Apparatus & Equipment.

Chester

★ 92802 ★   Quaker State Oil Refining
Congo Rd.
Chester, WV 26034
(304)387-9792
Ultimate Parent: Quaker State. **SIC:**
5172—Petroleum Products Nec.

Clarksburg

★ 92803 ★   Anchor Hocking Corp.
N Sycamore St.
Clarksburg, WV 26301
(304)623-3671
Ultimate Parent: Newell. **SIC:** 5023—
Homefurnishings.

★ 92804 ★   Chesapeake & Potomac Telephone Co.
425 S. Holden St.
Clarksburg, WV 26301-3736
(304)626-9911
Company Type: Subsidiary. **Ultimate Parent:** Bell Atlantic Corp. **SIC:** 4813—
Telephone Communications Except Radiotelephone.

★ 92805 ★   CNG Transmission Corp.
445 W. Main St.
Clarksburg, WV 26301
(304)623-8000
Officer: L. J. Timms Jr., President. **Ultimate Parent:** Consolidated Natural Gas.

★ 92806 ★   Hope Gas, Inc.
Union Bank Ctr.
Clarksburg, WV 26301-2868
(304)623-8600 **Fax:** (304)623-8659
Officer: Ralph J. Bean Jr., President.
Ultimate Parent: Consolidated Natural Gas.

★ 92807 ★   Kroger Co.
770 W. Pike St.
Clarksburg, WV 26301
(304)622-0131
Ultimate Parent: Kroger. **SIC:** 5411—
Grocery Stores.

★ 92808 ★   Kroger Co.
198 Emily Dr.
Clarksburg, WV 26301
(304)623-1015
Ultimate Parent: Kroger. **SIC:** 5411—
Grocery Stores.

★ 92809 ★   Lerner Shops
330 W. Main St.
Clarksburg, WV 26301
(304)622-2191
Ultimate Parent: Limited. **SIC:** 5621—
Women's Clothing Stores.

★ 92810 ★   Lockheed Aeronautical Systems Co.
Bridge Port Hill Rd.
Clarksburg, WV 26301
Ultimate Parent: Lockheed Corp. **SIC:**
3271—Concrete Block & Brick.

★ 92811 ★   Mary Kay Cosmetics
28 Gardens Cir.
Clarksburg, WV 26301
(304)624-4984
Ultimate Parent: Mary Kay Cosmetics.

★ 92812 ★   Monongahela Power Co.
Armory Rd.
Clarksburg, WV 26301
(304)624-7521
Officer: Dana L. Rogers. **Ultimate Parent:** Allegheny Power System. **SIC:** 4911—
Electric Services.

★ 92813 ★   Northwestern Mutual Life Inc.
516 W. Main St.
Clarksburg, WV 26301
(304)624-6373
Ultimate Parent: Northwestern Mutual Life.
SIC: 6411—Insurance Agents, Brokers & Service.

★ 92814 ★   Otis Elevator Co.
209 N. 4th St.
Clarksburg, WV 26301
(304)622-4691
Ultimate Parent: United Technologies. **SIC:**
1796—Installing Building Equipment Nec;
5084—Industrial Machinery & Equipment.

★ 92815 ★   Penn Mutual Life Insurance
516 W. Main St.
Clarksburg, WV 26301
(304)624-5000
Ultimate Parent: Penn Mutual Life. **SIC:**
6411—Insurance Agents, Brokers & Service.

★ 92816 ★   Penn Mutual Life Insurance Co.
516 W. Main St.
Clarksburg, WV 26301
(304)624-5548
Ultimate Parent: Penn Mutual Life. **SIC:**
6411—Insurance Agents, Brokers & Service.

★ 92817 ★   Rite Aid Discount Pharmacy
312 W. Main St.
Clarksburg, WV 26301
(304)622-9356
Ultimate Parent: Rite Aid. **SIC:** 5912—Drug Stores & Proprietary Stores.

★ 92818 ★   Rite Aid Discount Pharmacy
Rose Plz.
Clarksburg, WV 26301
(304)622-9193
Ultimate Parent: Rite Aid. **SIC:** 5946—
Camera & Photographic Supply Stores.

★ 92819 ★   Ryder Truck Rental
Rural Route 2
Clarksburg, WV 26301
(304)842-2234
Ultimate Parent: Ryder System. **SIC:**
7513—Truck Rental & Leasing Without Drivers.

★ 92820 ★   Texaco U S a
225 S. 3rd St.
Clarksburg, WV 26301
(304)624-5295
Ultimate Parent: Texaco. **SIC:** 2911—
Petroleum Refining.

★ 92821 ★   Unisys Corp.
629 W. Main St.
Clarksburg, WV 26301
(304)624-6379
Ultimate Parent: Unisys Corp. **SIC:** 7372—
Prepackaged Software.

★ 92822 ★   United Parcel Service
411 Water St.
Clarksburg, WV 26301
(304)624-4100
Ultimate Parent: United Parcel Service of America. **SIC:** 4215—Courier Services Except by Air.

Congo

★ 92823 ★   Quaker State Corp. Congo Plant
Rte. 2
Congo, WV 26050
Ultimate Parent: Quaker State. **SIC:**
2911—Petroleum Refining.

Culloden

★ 92824 ★   Sonoco Fibre Drum Co.
2423 Virginia Ave.
Culloden, WV 25510
(304)743-9046
Officer: J. Randy Kelley, Executive Vice President. **Ultimate Parent:** Sonoco Products. **SIC:** 2655—Fiber Cans, Drums & Similar Products.

Dorothy

★ 92825 ★   Rite Aid Discount Pharmacy
Whitesville Acros Rd.
Dorothy, WV 25060
(304)854-2373
Ultimate Parent: Rite Aid.

Dunbar

★ 92826 ★   Diebold Inc.
1317 Dunbar Ave.
Dunbar, WV 25064
(304)768-0071
Ultimate Parent: Diebold, Inc. **SIC:** 3914—
Silverware & Plated Ware.

★ 92827 ★   Digital Equipment Corp.
Dunbar, WV 25064
(304)766-6137
Ultimate Parent: Digital Equipment Corp.
SIC: 5045—Computers, Peripherals & Software.

★ 92828 ★   Kroger Co.
1000 Dunbar Ave.
Dunbar, WV 25064
(304)768-6481
Ultimate Parent: Kroger. **SIC:** 5411—
Grocery Stores.

★ 92829 ★   Rite Aid Discount Pharmacy
100 21st St.
Dunbar, WV 25064
(304)768-1284
Ultimate Parent: Rite Aid. **SIC:** 5912—Drug Stores & Proprietary Stores.

★ 92830 ★   Ryder Truck Rental
2815 Fairlawn Ave.
Dunbar, WV 25064
(304)768-7336
Ultimate Parent: Ryder System. **SIC:**
7359—Equipment Rental & Leasing Nec.

Eleanor

★ 92831 ★   Rite Aid Discount Pharmacy
Eleanor Plz.
Eleanor, WV 25070
(304)586-9937
Ultimate Parent: Rite Aid. **SIC:** 5912—Drug Stores & Proprietary Stores.

★ 92832 ★   Rite Aid Discount Pharmacy
St
Eleanor, WV 25070
(304)586-9064
Ultimate Parent: Rite Aid. **SIC:** 5912—Drug Stores & Proprietary Stores.

Elkins

★ 92833 ★   Community Bank & Trust of Randolph County
Davis Ave. at 5th
Elkins, WV 26241
(304)636-6033
Ultimate Parent: Huntington Bancshares.
SIC: 6036—Savings Institutions Except Federal.

★ 92834 ★   Ryder Truck Rental-Oneway
Grant
Elkins, WV 26241
(304)636-8680
Ultimate Parent: Ryder System. **SIC:**
7359—Equipment Rental & Leasing Nec.

Elkview

★ 92835 ★   Rite Aid Discount Pharmacy
Us V
Elkview, WV 25071
(304)965-1111
Ultimate Parent: Rite Aid. **SIC:** 5912—Drug Stores & Proprietary Stores.

★ 92836 ★   Rite Aid Discount Pharmacy
5068 Elk Rv Rd. S
Elkview, WV 25071
(304)965-3003
Ultimate Parent: Rite Aid. **SIC:** 5912—Drug Stores & Proprietary Stores.

Fairmont

★ 92837 ★   City National Bank of Fairmont
120 Fairmont Ave.
Fairmont, WV 26554-2848
(304)363-5500
Company Type: Headquarters. **Officer:**
Mike Hudnall, President. **Ultimate Parent:**
City National Corp. **SIC:** 6021—National Commercial Banks; 6141—Personal Credit Institutions; 6153—Short-Term Business Credit; 6162—Mortgage Bankers & Correspondents.

★ 92838 ★   Community Bank & Trust National Association
103 Adams St.
Fairmont, WV 26554-2823
(304)363-5800
Ultimate Parent: Huntington Bancshares.
SIC: 6021—National Commercial Banks.

★ 92839 ★   First Fidelity Bancorp
301 Adams St.
Fairmont, WV 26554-3103
(304)363-1300
Officer: Robert Martin, Chairman of the Board. **Ultimate Parent:** First Fidelity Bancorp. **SIC:** 6022—State Commercial Banks. **Employee Count:** 124.

★ 92840 ★   Greyhound Bus Lines
308 Adams St.
Fairmont, WV 26554
(304)363-0420
Ultimate Parent: Greyhound Lines Inc. **SIC:**
4111—Local & Suburban Transit; 4142—
Bus Charter Service Except Local; 4131—
Intercity & Rural Bus Transportation.

★ 92841 ★   Kroger Co.
Country Clubrd
Fairmont, WV 26554
(304)366-7300
Ultimate Parent: Kroger. **SIC:** 5411—
Grocery Stores.

★ 92842 ★   Monogahela Power Co.
1310 Fairmont Ave.
Fairmont, WV 26554-3526
(304)366-3000
Officer: Benjamin H. Hayes, President.
Ultimate Parent: Allegheny Power System.
SIC: 4911—Electric Services. **Employee Count:** 1957. **Sales:** 625 M.

★ 92843 ★   Monongahela Power Co.
PO Box 1392
Fairmont, WV 26555-1392
(304)366-3000
Location Type: Branch office. **Officer:** B.
H. Hayes. **Ultimate Parent:** Allegheny Power System. **SIC:** 4911—Electric Services.

★ 92844 ★   Monongahela Power Co.
1310 Fairmont Ave.
Fairmont, WV 26554
(304)366-3000 **Fax:** (304)366-3000
Company Type: Subsidiary. **Ultimate Parent:** Allegheny Power System. **SIC:**
4911—Electric Services.

★ 92845 ★   Payless Shoe Source
14 Middletown Mall
Fairmont, WV 26554
(304)366-9492
Ultimate Parent: May Department Stores.
SIC: 5661—Shoe Stores.

★ 92846 ★   Quaker State Oil Refining
737 Merchant St.
Fairmont, WV 26554
(304)363-1410
Ultimate Parent: Quaker State. **SIC:**
5983—Fuel Oil Dealers.

★ 92847 ★   Ryder Truck Rental
2035 Fairmont Ave.
Fairmont, WV 26554
(304)366-4171
Ultimate Parent: Ryder System. **SIC:**
7338—Secretarial & Court Reporting;
7513—Truck Rental & Leasing Without Drivers.

★ 92848 ★　Thrift Drugs
23 Middletown Mall
Fairmont, WV 26554
(304)366-4110
Ultimate Parent: J.C. Penney. SIC: 5912—Drug Stores & Proprietary Stores.

★ 92849 ★　United Parcel Service
2040 Pleasant Valley Rd.
Fairmont, WV 26554
(304)366-6026
Ultimate Parent: United Parcel Service of America. SIC: 4215—Courier Services Except by Air.

Falling Rock

★ 92850 ★　Pennzoil Co.
Falling Rock, WV 25079
(304)457-5255
Ultimate Parent: Pennzoil. SIC: 2911—Petroleum Refining.

Farmington

★ 92851 ★　City National Bank of Fairmont
PO Box 39
Farmington, WV 26571
(304)825-6565
Company Type: Branch. Officer: Tammy Muzichuck, Manager. Ultimate Parent: City National Corp. SIC: 6022—State Commercial Banks; 6021—National Commercial Banks.

Follansbee

★ 92852 ★　Wheeling-Pittsburgh Steel
Rte. 2
Follansbee, WV 26037
Ultimate Parent: Wheeling-Pittsburgh Steel Corp. SIC: 3312—Blast Furnaces & Steel Mills.

Franklin

★ 92853 ★　Monongahela Power Co.
Franklin, WV 26807
(304)358-2383
Ultimate Parent: Allegheny Power System. SIC: 4911—Electric Services.

Gassaway

★ 92854 ★　Kroger Co.
RR 4 N
Gassaway, WV 26624
(304)364-2332
Ultimate Parent: Kroger. SIC: 5411—Grocery Stores.

Gauley Bridge

★ 92855 ★　Greyhound Bus Lines
Gauley Bridge, WV 25085
(304)632-2555
Ultimate Parent: Greyhound Lines Inc. SIC: 4111—Local & Suburban Transit; 4142—Bus Charter Service Except Local; 4131—Intercity & Rural Bus Transportation.

Gauleybridge

★ 92856 ★　Kroger Co.
Gauleybridge, WV 25085
(304)632-1139
Ultimate Parent: Kroger. SIC: 5411—Grocery Stores.

Glenville

★ 92857 ★　Rite Aid Discount Pharmacy
Glenville Shopping Ctr.
Glenville, WV 26351
(304)462-5888
Ultimate Parent: Rite Aid. SIC: 5912—Drug Stores & Proprietary Stores.

Grafton

★ 92858 ★　Rite Aid Discount Pharmacy
28 W. Main St.
Grafton, WV 26354
(304)265-1217
Ultimate Parent: Rite Aid. SIC: 5912—Drug Stores & Proprietary Stores.

★ 92859 ★　Rite Aid Discount Pharmacy
2 W. Main St.
Grafton, WV 26354
(304)265-9820
Ultimate Parent: Rite Aid. SIC: 5912—Drug Stores & Proprietary Stores.

Grantsville

★ 92860 ★　B. F. Goodrich Co.
Rte. 1 Box 7
Grantsville, WV 26147-9707
Ultimate Parent: B.F. Goodrich. SIC: 3069—Fabricated Rubber Products Nec.

Harrisvile

★ 92861 ★　Community Bank & Trust of Ritchie County
121 N. Court St.
Harrisvile, WV 26362-1225
(304)643-2901
Ultimate Parent: Huntington Bancshares.

Hinton

★ 92862 ★　Coast to Coast Motel
Hinton, WV 25951
(304)466-2040
Ultimate Parent: Servistar Corp.

★ 92863 ★　Rite Aid Discount Pharmacy
Country Rd.
Hinton, WV 25951
(304)466-5069
Ultimate Parent: Rite Aid. SIC: 5912—Drug Stores & Proprietary Stores.

Holden Wv

★ 92864 ★　Ryder Truck Rental
Rd
Holden Wv, WV 25625
(304)239-3206
Ultimate Parent: Ryder System. SIC: 7513—Truck Rental & Leasing Without Drivers.

Hugheston

★ 92865 ★　Texaco Inc.
Hugheston
Hugheston, WV 25110
(304)442-2439
Ultimate Parent: Texaco. SIC: 5171—Petroleum Bulk Stations & Terminals.

Hundred

★ 92866 ★　Bank of Hundred
Rte. 250
Hundred, WV 26575-9712
(304)775-4411
Ultimate Parent: Huntington Bancshares. SIC: 6022—State Commercial Banks.

Huntington

★ 92867 ★　Ashland Coal, Inc.
2205 Fifth Street Rd.
Huntington, WV 25701
(304)526-3333 Fax: (304)526-3678
Company Type: Division. Officer: William C. Payne, President & CEO. Ultimate Parent: Ashland Oil. SIC: 1221—Bituminous Coal & Lignite—Surface; 1222—Bituminous Coal—Underground. Employee Count: 1090. Sales: 579,724,000 M.

★ 92868 ★　BASF Corp.
5th Ave. & 24th St.
Huntington, WV 25703
(304)528-2300
Officer: Thomas M. Boggs, Manager. Ultimate Parent: BASF Corp. SIC: 2816—Inorganic Pigments; 2865—Cyclic Crudes &

Intermediates; 2899—Chemical Preparations Nec.

★ 92869 ★　BASF Corp.
24th St. & 5th Ave.
Huntington, WV 25722
(304)529-1311
Officer: Thomas Boggs, Manager. Ultimate Parent: BASF Corp. SIC: 2865—Cyclic Crudes & Intermediates.

★ 92870 ★　BASF Corp.
Chemicals
24th St. & 5th Ave.
Huntington, WV 25722
Ultimate Parent: BASF Corp. SIC: 2865—Cyclic Crudes & Intermediates.

★ 92871 ★　Casual Corner
Huntington
Huntington, WV 25705
(304)733-0073
Ultimate Parent: United States Shoe. SIC: 5621—Women's Clothing Stores.

★ 92872 ★　Exxon Station
1413 Rte. 60
Huntington, WV 25705
(304)522-3110
Ultimate Parent: Exxon. SIC: 5541—Gasoline Service Stations.

★ 92873 ★　Fitness World
1321 4th Ave.
Huntington, WV 25701
(304)529-0100
Ultimate Parent: New York Times. SIC: 7991—Physical Fitness Facilities.

★ 92874 ★　Hit or Miss
Huntington
Huntington, WV 25705
(304)733-0943
Ultimate Parent: TJX. SIC: 5621—Women's Clothing Stores.

★ 92875 ★　Inland Gas Co. Inc.
340 17th St. W
Huntington, WV 25704
(304)523-5775
Ultimate Parent: Columbia Gas System. SIC: 8099—Health & Allied Services Nec.

★ 92876 ★　J. H. Fletcher & Co.
402 High St.
Huntington, WV 25705
Ultimate Parent: H.J. Heinz. SIC: 3532—Mining Machinery.

★ 92877 ★　Jiffy Lube Oil Change
1 Washington Ave.
Huntington, WV 25701
(304)522-1991
Ultimate Parent: Pennzoil. SIC: 5541—Gasoline Service Stations; 7539—Automotive Repair Shops Nec.

★ 92878 ★　Kroger Co.
Huntington
Huntington, WV 25705
(304)525-6851
Ultimate Parent: Kroger. SIC: 5411—Grocery Stores.

★ 92879 ★　Kroger Co.
5636 Rte. 60 E
Huntington, WV 25705
(304)736-1577
Ultimate Parent: Kroger. SIC: 5411—Grocery Stores.

★ 92880 ★　Layne Bryant
Huntington
Huntington, WV 25705
(304)733-3672
Ultimate Parent: Limited. SIC: 5621—Women's Clothing Stores.

★ 92881 ★　Lerner Shops
919 3rd Ave.
Huntington, WV 25701
(304)525-6791
Ultimate Parent: Limited. SIC: 5621—Women's Clothing Stores.

★ 92882 ★　Lerner Shops
Huntington
Huntington, WV 25705
(304)733-0439
Ultimate Parent: Limited. SIC: 5621—Women's Clothing Stores.

★ 92883 ★　Life Insurance Co. of Va
Frederick Hotel Bldg.
Huntington, WV 25701
(304)522-8351
Ultimate Parent: Life Insurance Co. of Virginia. SIC: 8742—Management Consulting Services.

★ 92884 ★　Limited
Huntington
Huntington, WV 25705
(304)733-0734
Ultimate Parent: Limited. SIC: 5621—Women's Clothing Stores.

★ 92885 ★　New England Mutual Life Insurance
910 4th Ave.
Huntington, WV 25701
(304)522-7676
Ultimate Parent: New England Mutual Life. SIC: 6411—Insurance Agents, Brokers & Service.

★ 92886 ★　Northwestern Mutual Life Inc.
1009 5th Ave.
Huntington, WV 25701
(304)522-7326
Ultimate Parent: Northwestern Mutual Life. SIC: 6411—Insurance Agents, Brokers & Service.

★ 92887 ★　Otis Elevator Co.
549 Washington Ave.
Huntington, WV 25705
(304)523-7253
Ultimate Parent: United Technologies. SIC: 3534—Elevators & Moving Stairways; 5084—Industrial Machinery & Equipment.

★ 92888 ★　Owens-Brockway Glass Container Inc.
8th Ave. & 5th St. W.
Huntington, WV 25711
Ultimate Parent: Owens-Illinois. SIC: 3221—Glass Containers.

★ 92889 ★　Owens Illinois Glass Container Inc.
Plant 2
8th Ave. & 5th St. W.
Huntington, WV 25701
Location Type: Plant. Ultimate Parent: Owens-Illinois. SIC: 3221—Glass Containers; 2653—Corrugated & Solid Fiber Boxes.

★ 92890 ★　Pepsi-Cola Co.
1531 Monroe Ave.
Huntington, WV 25704
(304)429-6767
Officer: Jim Moore, Manager. Ultimate Parent: Pepsico. SIC: 2086—Bottled & Canned Soft Drinks.

★ 92891 ★　Rite Aid Discount Pharamacy
Rural Route 60
Huntington, WV 25705
(304)736-9007
Ultimate Parent: Rite Aid. SIC: 5912—Drug Stores & Proprietary Stores.

★ 92892 ★　Rite Aid Discount Pharmacy
900 4th Ave.
Huntington, WV 25701
(304)696-9113
Ultimate Parent: Rite Aid. SIC: 5912—Drug Stores & Proprietary Stores.

★ 92893 ★　Rite Aid Discount Pharmacy
Huntington
Huntington, WV 25705
(304)733-0931
Ultimate Parent: Rite Aid. SIC: 5912—Drug Stores & Proprietary Stores.

★ 92894 ★　Rite Aid Discount Pharmacy
2620 5th Ave.
Huntington, WV 25702
(304)696-9152
Ultimate Parent: Rite Aid. SIC: 5912—Drug Stores & Proprietary Stores.

★ **92895** ★   **Rite Aid Discount Pharmacy**
902 4th Ave.
Huntington, WV 25701
(304)529-0180
Ultimate Parent: Rite Aid. **SIC:** 5912—Drug Stores & Proprietary Stores.

★ **92896** ★   **Ryder Truck Rental**
2593 5th Ave.
Huntington, WV 25703
(304)525-6558
Ultimate Parent: Ryder System. **SIC:** 7513—Truck Rental & Leasing Without Drivers.

★ **92897** ★   **Thrift Drugs**
810 14th St. W
Huntington, WV 25704
(304)525-5741
Ultimate Parent: J.C. Penney. **SIC:** 5912—Drug Stores & Proprietary Stores.

★ **92898** ★   **Thrift Drugs**
Ern Hts Shopping Ctr.
Huntington, WV 25705
(304)736-3406
Ultimate Parent: J.C. Penney. **SIC:** 5912—Drug Stores & Proprietary Stores.

★ **92899** ★   **Unijax Inc.**
550 27th St.
Huntington, WV 25702-1333
(304)522-0331
Officer: Robin Reed. **Ultimate Parent:** Alco Standard Corp. **SIC:** 2842—Polishes & Sanitation Goods; 5087—Service Establishment Equipment.

★ **92900** ★   **Unijax Inc.**
550 27th St.
Huntington, WV 25702-1333
(304)522-0331
Officer: Robin Reed. **Ultimate Parent:** Alco Standard Corp. **SIC:** 2842—Polishes & Sanitation Goods; 5087—Service Establishment Equipment.

Institute

★ **92901** ★   **Arco Chemical Co.**
Institute West Virginia Plant
Rte. 25
Institute, WV 25112
Location Type: Plant. **Ultimate Parent:** Atlantic Richfield Co., Inc. **SIC:** 2869—Industrial Organic Chemicals Nec; 2879—Agricultural Chemicals Nec.

★ **92902** ★   **FMC Corp., Institute Plant**
Rte. 25
Institute, WV 25112-0579
Location Type: Plant. **Ultimate Parent:** FMC. **SIC:** 2879—Agricultural Chemicals Nec; 2869—Industrial Organic Chemicals Nec.

★ **92903** ★   **Rhone-Poulenc Ag Co. Institute Wv Plant**
Rte. 25
Institute, WV 25112
Ultimate Parent: Rhone-Poulenc Rorer. **SIC:** 2879—Agricultural Chemicals Nec.

★ **92904** ★   **Rhone-Poulenc Ag Co. Institute Wv Plant Operations**
Rte. 25
Institute, WV 25112
Ultimate Parent: Rhone-Poulenc Rorer. **SIC:** 2869—Industrial Organic Chemicals Nec; 2879—Agricultural Chemicals Nec.

★ **92905** ★   **Rhone Poulenc Inc. Industrial Plant**
Rte. 25
Institute, WV 25112
(304)747-6774
Location Type: Plant. **Ultimate Parent:** Rhone-Poulenc Rorer. **SIC:** 2819—Industrial Inorganic Chemicals Nec.

★ **92906** ★   **Union Carbide C & P Co. Institute Wv Plant Ops.**
Rte. 25
Institute, WV 25112
Ultimate Parent: Union Carbide Corp. **SIC:** 2869—Industrial Organic Chemicals Nec.

★ **92907** ★   **Union Carbide C&P Co. Institute Wv Plant Operations**
Rte. 25
Institute, WV 25112
Ultimate Parent: Union Carbide Corp. **SIC:** 2869—Industrial Organic Chemicals Nec; 2879—Agricultural Chemicals Nec.

★ **92908** ★   **Union Carbide Corp.**
Rte. 25
Institute, WV 25112
(304)747-1683
Officer: D.G. Mashier, Manager. **Ultimate Parent:** Union Carbide Corp. **SIC:** 2879—Agricultural Chemicals Nec.

Kearneysville

★ **92909** ★   **3M Co.**
Brucetown Rd.
Kearneysville, WV 25430
(304)725-2031
Company Type: Branch. **Officer:** Mark D. Pugh. **Ultimate Parent:** Minnesota Mining & Mfg. **SIC:** 3555—Printing Trades Machinery.

Keyser

★ **92910** ★   **Allegany Ballistics Lab.**
West Virginia Secondary Rte. 956
Keyser, WV 26726
Ultimate Parent: Hercules. **SIC:** 3764—Space Propulsion Units & Parts; 3089—Plastics Products Nec.

★ **92911** ★   **Anchor Glass Container Corp.**
Waxler Rd.
Keyser, WV 26726
(304)788-4055
Officer: Eugene Savieo, Manager. **Ultimate Parent:** Anchor Glass Container Corp. **SIC:** 3221—Glass Containers.

★ **92912** ★   **Rite Aid Discount Pharmacy**
77 Armstrong St.
Keyser, WV 26726
(304)788-9836
Ultimate Parent: Rite Aid. **SIC:** 5912—Drug Stores & Proprietary Stores.

Kopperston

★ **92913** ★   **Stop & Shop**
Kopperston, WV 24854
(304)682-8857
Ultimate Parent: Stop & Shop. **SIC:** 5411—Grocery Stores.

Le Roy

★ **92914** ★   **Rite Aid Discount Pharmacy**
431 Washington St.
Le Roy, WV 25252
(304)273-5961
Ultimate Parent: Rite Aid.

Lewisburg

★ **92915** ★   **Greyhound Bus Lines**
111 N. Jefferson St.
Lewisburg, WV 24901
(304)645-7506
Ultimate Parent: Greyhound Lines Inc. **SIC:** 4111—Local & Suburban Transit; 4142—Bus Charter Service Except Local; 4131—Intercity & Rural Bus Transportation.

★ **92916** ★   **Greyhound Bus Lines**
Lewisburg, WV 24901
(304)645-7505
Ultimate Parent: Greyhound Lines Inc. **SIC:** 4142—Bus Charter Service Except Local; 4111—Local & Suburban Transit; 4131—Intercity & Rural Bus Transportation.

★ **92917** ★   **Northwestern Mutual Life Inc.**
103 W. Washington St.
Lewisburg, WV 24901
(304)645-1331
Ultimate Parent: Northwestern Mutual Life. **SIC:** 6411—Insurance Agents, Brokers & Service.

★ **92918** ★   **Rite Aid Discount Pharmacy**
Red Oak Shopping Ctr.
Lewisburg, WV 24901
(304)645-2096
Ultimate Parent: Rite Aid. **SIC:** 5912—Drug Stores & Proprietary Stores.

★ **92919** ★   **Rite Aid Discount Pharmacy**
202 E. Washington St.
Lewisburg, WV 24901
(304)645-9878
Ultimate Parent: Rite Aid. **SIC:** 5912—Drug Stores & Proprietary Stores.

Logan

★ **92920** ★   **Trailways Bus Lines**
60 Water St.
Logan, WV 25601
(304)752-7541
Ultimate Parent: Greyhound Lines Inc. **SIC:** 4142—Bus Charter Service Except Local; 4111—Local & Suburban Transit; 4131—Intercity & Rural Bus Transportation.

Madison

★ **92921** ★   **Hobert Mining, Inc.**
PO Box 305
Madison, WV 25130
(304)369-6780
Company Type: Subsidiary. **Officer:** Raymond Smallwood, President. **Ultimate Parent:** Ashland Oil. **SIC:** 1221—Bituminous Coal & Lignite—Surface; 1222—Bituminous Coal—Underground.

★ **92922** ★   **Kroger Co.**
RR 119
Madison, WV 25130
(304)369-5955
Ultimate Parent: Kroger. **SIC:** 5411—Grocery Stores.

★ **92923** ★   **Rite Aid Discount Pharmacy**
417 Main St.
Madison, WV 25130
(304)369-9828
Ultimate Parent: Rite Aid. **SIC:** 5912—Drug Stores & Proprietary Stores.

Mannington

★ **92924** ★   **Pennzoil Co.**
109 Railroad St.
Mannington, WV 26582
(304)986-1800
Ultimate Parent: Pennzoil. **SIC:** 4932—Gas & Other Services Combined.

Marlinton

★ **92925** ★   **Monongahela Power Co.**
Marlinton, WV 24954
(304)799-4515
Ultimate Parent: Allegheny Power System. **SIC:** 4911—Electric Services.

Martinsburg

★ **92926** ★   **Acme Markets**
103 Berkeley Plz.
Martinsburg, WV 25401
(304)263-9075
Ultimate Parent: American Stores. **SIC:** 5411—Grocery Stores.

★ **92927** ★   **Corning Consumer Products Co.**
Rte. 11 S. PO Box 100
Martinsburg, WV 25401
Ultimate Parent: Corning. **SIC:** 3229—Pressed & Blown Glass Nec.

★ **92928** ★   **Corning Consumer Products Co.**
Rte. 11 S. Rte. 11 S.
Martinsburg, WV 25401
Ultimate Parent: Corning. **SIC:** 3229—Pressed & Blown Glass Nec.

★ **92929** ★   **Corning Inc.**
PO Box 100 Rte. 11 S.
Martinsburg, WV 25401
Ultimate Parent: Corning. **SIC:** 3229—Pressed & Blown Glass Nec.

★ **92930** ★   **Corning Inc.**
Rte. 11 S.
Martinsburg, WV 25401
Ultimate Parent: Corning. **SIC:** 3229—Pressed & Blown Glass Nec.

★ **92931** ★   **Greyhound Bus Lines**
531 W. King St.
Martinsburg, WV 25401
(304)263-8141
Ultimate Parent: Greyhound Lines Inc. **SIC:** 4111—Local & Suburban Transit; 4142—Bus Charter Service Except Local; 4131—Intercity & Rural Bus Transportation.

★ **92932** ★   **Jiffy Lube Oil Change**
1109 N. Queen St.
Martinsburg, WV 25401
(304)263-5516
Ultimate Parent: Pennzoil. **SIC:** 7538—General Automotive Repair Shops.

★ **92933** ★   **Payless Shoe Source**
1347 Edwin Miller Blvd.
Martinsburg, WV 25401
(304)267-6675
Ultimate Parent: May Department Stores. **SIC:** 5661—Shoe Stores.

★ **92934** ★   **Potomac Edison Co.**
Berkeley County
Martinsburg, WV 25401
(304)263-3700
Ultimate Parent: Allegheny Power System. **SIC:** 4911—Electric Services.

★ **92935** ★   **Rite Aid Discount Pharmacy**
601 Winchester Ave. 609
Martinsburg, WV 25401
(304)267-9802
Ultimate Parent: Rite Aid. **SIC:** 5912—Drug Stores & Proprietary Stores.

★ **92936** ★   **Variform Inc.**
1403 Charles Town Rd.
Martinsburg, WV 25401
Ultimate Parent: Ply Gem. **SIC:** 3089—Plastics Products Nec.

Masontown

★ **92937** ★   **Mountain State Telephone Co.**
Depot St.
Masontown, WV 26542
(304)864-3131
Company Type: Subsidiary. **Ultimate Parent:** ALLTEL Corp. **SIC:** 4812—Radiotelephone Communications.

Matewan

★ **92938** ★   **Energy Development Corp.**
Matewan, WV 25678
(304)426-4698
Ultimate Parent: Public Service Enterprise Group. **SIC:** 5052—Coal, Other Minerals & Ores.

Montgomery

★ **92939** ★   **Mobil Oil Products**
Eagle
Montgomery, WV 25136
(304)442-5644
Ultimate Parent: Mobil. **SIC:** 5171—Petroleum Bulk Stations & Terminals.

★ **92940** ★   **Rite Aid Discount Pharmacy**
506 3rd Ave.
Montgomery, WV 25136
(304)442-2445
Ultimate Parent: Rite Aid. **SIC:** 5912—Drug Stores & Proprietary Stores.

Moore Field

★ **92941** ★   **Wampler Longacre Inc.**
129 Potomac Ave.
Moore Field, WV 26836
(304)538-7811
Company Type: Division. **Location Type:** Facility. **Officer:** Walt Shafer, Plant Mgr. **Ultimate Parent:** WLR Foods. **SIC:** 2013—Sausages & Other Prepared Meats.

Moorefield

★ 92942 ★ **Rockingham Poultry Inc.**
Potomac Ave.
Moorefield, WV 26836
Ultimate Parent: WLR Foods. **SIC:** 2015—Poultry Slaughtering & Processing.

Morgantown

★ 92943 ★ **EG & G Washington Analytical Service Center**
Morgantown Energy Tech Ctr.
3610 Collins Ferry Rd.
PO Box 880, Mail Stop 003
Morgantown, WV 26507-0880
(304)291-4587 **Fax:** (304)291-4035
Company Type: Subsidiary. **Officer:** A.L. Rice, Manager. **Ultimate Parent:** EG & G.

★ 92944 ★ **GE Specialty Chemicals**
Morgantown Industrial Park
Morgantown, WV 26505
(304)296-2554
Officer: Phil Johnson, Plant Manager. **Ultimate Parent:** General Electric. **SIC:** 2869—Industrial Organic Chemicals Nec.

★ 92945 ★ **GE Specialty Chemicals North Plant**
1000 Dupont Rd. Bldg. 816
Morgantown, WV 26505
Ultimate Parent: General Electric. **SIC:** 2869—Industrial Organic Chemicals Nec; 2819—Industrial Inorganic Chemicals Nec.

★ 92946 ★ **Monongahela Power Co.**
237 Hartman Run Rd.
Morgantown, WV 26505-5377
(304)292-9404
Officer: B. H. Hayes. **Ultimate Parent:** Allegheny Power System. **SIC:** 4911—Electric Services.

★ 92947 ★ **Pennzoil Co.**
Star City
Morgantown, WV 26505
(304)599-0130
Ultimate Parent: Pennzoil. **SIC:** 5171—Petroleum Bulk Stations & Terminals.

★ 92948 ★ **Rite Aid Discount Pharmacy**
327 Holland Ave.
Morgantown, WV 26505
(304)292-9162
Ultimate Parent: Rite Aid. **SIC:** 5912—Drug Stores & Proprietary Stores.

★ 92949 ★ **Rite Aid Discount Pharmacy**
250 High St.
Morgantown, WV 26505
(304)296-4419
Ultimate Parent: Rite Aid. **SIC:** 5912—Drug Stores & Proprietary Stores.

★ 92950 ★ **Rite Aid Discount Pharmacy**
378 Patterson Dr.
Morgantown, WV 26505
(304)598-2265
Ultimate Parent: Rite Aid. **SIC:** 5912—Drug Stores & Proprietary Stores.

Moundsville

★ 92951 ★ **Chesapeake & Potomac Telephone Co.**
720 7th St.
Moundsville, WV 26041-2102
(304)845-9974
Company Type: Subsidiary. **Officer:** David Ranson. **Ultimate Parent:** Bell Atlantic Corp. **SIC:** 4813—Telephone Communications Except Radiotelephone.

★ 92952 ★ **Columbian Chemicals Co.**
Rte. 2 S.
Moundsville, WV 26041
Ultimate Parent: Phelps Dodge. **SIC:** 2895—Carbon Black.

★ 92953 ★ **Rite Aid Discount Pharmacy**
120 Jefferson Ave.
Moundsville, WV 26041
Ultimate Parent: Rite Aid. **SIC:** 5912—Drug Stores & Proprietary Stores.

★ 92954 ★ **Ryder Truck Rental**
1108 Purdy Ave.
Moundsville, WV 26041
(304)845-7132
Ultimate Parent: Ryder System. **SIC:** 7389—Business Services Nec.

Mount Alto

★ 92955 ★ **Kroger Co.**
966 Dunbar Village Shopping Ctr.
Mount Alto, WV 25264
(304)768-6481
Ultimate Parent: Kroger. **SIC:** 5411—Grocery Stores.

Mullens

★ 92956 ★ **Peoples Bank of Mullens**
200 1st St.
Mullens, WV 25882
(304)294-7115
Ultimate Parent: People's Bank. **SIC:** 6022—State Commercial Banks.

★ 92957 ★ **Rite Aid Discount Pharmacy**
101 4th St.
Mullens, WV 25882
(304)294-0343
Ultimate Parent: Rite Aid. **SIC:** 5912—Drug Stores & Proprietary Stores.

N. Martinsville

★ 92958 ★ **PPG Industries Inc.**
191 PO Box
N. Martinsville, WV 26155
(304)455-2200
Ultimate Parent: PPG Industries Inc. **SIC:** 2812—Alkalies & Chlorine.

Neal

★ 92959 ★ **Ashland Chemical Co.**
Big Sandy River Rd.
Neal, WV 25530
Ultimate Parent: Ashland Oil. **SIC:** 2865—Cyclic Crudes & Intermediates.

★ 92960 ★ **Ashland Chemical Inc.**
Big Sandy River Rd.
Neal, WV 25530
Ultimate Parent: Ashland Oil. **SIC:** 2865—Cyclic Crudes & Intermediates.

New Martinsville

★ 92961 ★ **Fitness Connection**
200 North St.
New Martinsville, WV 26155
(304)455-3476
Ultimate Parent: New York Times.

★ 92962 ★ **Ppg Industries Inc.**
State Rte. 2
New Martinsville, WV 26155
Ultimate Parent: PPG Industries Inc. **SIC:** 2812—Alkalies & Chlorine; 2819—Industrial Inorganic Chemicals Nec; 2865—Cyclic Crudes & Intermediates.

★ 92963 ★ **PPG Industries Inc.**
RR 2 Box 191
New Martinsville, WV 26155
(304)845-5300
Officer: Robert Eakin, Manager. **Ultimate Parent:** PPG Industries Inc. **SIC:** 2869—Industrial Organic Chemicals Nec.

Newell

★ 92964 ★ **Quaker State Corp. Congo Plant**
State Rte. 2 PO Box 336
Newell, WV 26050-1397
Ultimate Parent: Quaker State. **SIC:** 2911—Petroleum Refining; 2992—Lubricating Oils & Greases.

★ 92965 ★ **Quaker State Corp. Congo Plant**
PO Box 336 Rte. 2
Newell, WV 26050
Ultimate Parent: Quaker State. **SIC:** 2911—Petroleum Refining.

★ 92966 ★ **Quaker State Oil Refining Co.**
Congo Rd.
Newell, WV 26050
(304)387-3530
Ultimate Parent: Quaker State. **SIC:** 5172—Petroleum Products Nec.

★ 92967 ★ **Thiokol Corp.**
State
Newell, WV 26050
(304)387-3554
Ultimate Parent: Thiokol Corp. **SIC:** 2911—Petroleum Refining.

Nitor

★ 92968 ★ **Pepsi-Cola Co.**
100 Independence Ave.
Nitor, WV 25143
(304)755-4393
Officer: Chris Furman, Vice President. **Ultimate Parent:** Pepsico. **SIC:** 2086—Bottled & Canned Soft Drinks.

Nitro

★ 92969 ★ **FMC Corp.**
Pickerns Rd.
Nitro, WV 25143
(304)755-6300
Officer: Dennis Miller, Manager. **Ultimate Parent:** FMC. **SIC:** 2819—Industrial Inorganic Chemicals Nec; 2869—Industrial Organic Chemicals Nec.

★ 92970 ★ **Fmc Corp. Nitro Plant**
Pickens Rd. PO Box 2000
Nitro, WV 25143
Ultimate Parent: FMC. **SIC:** 2869—Industrial Organic Chemicals Nec.

★ 92971 ★ **Fmc Corp. - Nitro Plant**
Plant Rd.
Nitro, WV 25143-0547
Ultimate Parent: FMC. **SIC:** 2869—Industrial Organic Chemicals Nec.

★ 92972 ★ **Monsanto Co.**
1 Monsanto Rd.
Nitro, WV 25143-2526
(304)759-4400
Company Type: Headquarters. **Officer:** Tom J. Mckean. **Ultimate Parent:** Monsanto. **SIC:** 2869—Industrial Organic Chemicals Nec; 5169—Chemicals & Allied Products Nec; 6061—Federal Credit Unions.

★ 92973 ★ **Rite Aid Discount Pharmacy**
Tyler Plz.
Nitro, WV 25143
(304)776-3276
Ultimate Parent: Rite Aid. **SIC:** 5912—Drug Stores & Proprietary Stores.

★ 92974 ★ **Rite Aid Discount Pharmacy**
21 St. St
Nitro, WV 25143
(304)755-9021
Ultimate Parent: Rite Aid. **SIC:** 5912—Drug Stores & Proprietary Stores.

★ 92975 ★ **Wetterau Inc.**
West Virginia
James Rv Tpke.
Nitro, WV 25143
(304)755-9186
Ultimate Parent: Supervalu. **SIC:** 5141—Groceries—General Line.

North Parkers

★ 92976 ★ **Digital Equipment Corp.**
4421 Emerson Ave.
North Parkers, WV 26104
(304)428-1772
Ultimate Parent: Digital Equipment Corp. **SIC:** 7379—Computer Related Services Nec.

Northfork

★ 92977 ★ **Casual Corner**
Northfork, WV 24868
(304)862-2226
Ultimate Parent: United States Shoe. **SIC:** 5311—Department Stores.

Oak Hill

★ 92978 ★ **Rite Aid Discount Pharmacy**
Store Fountain Ctr.
Oak Hill, WV 25901
(304)469-9042
Ultimate Parent: Rite Aid. **SIC:** 5912—Drug Stores & Proprietary Stores.

Oakhill

★ 92979 ★ **Kroger Co.**
US 19 Lochgelly Rd.
Oakhill, WV 25901
(304)469-2921
Ultimate Parent: Kroger. **SIC:** 5411—Grocery Stores.

Paden City

★ 92980 ★ **Corning Inc.**
First Ave.
Paden City, WV 26159
Ultimate Parent: Corning. **SIC:** 3229—Pressed & Blown Glass Nec.

Parkersburg

★ 92981 ★ **Challenger Electrical Equipment Corp.**
3401 Camden Ave.
Parkersburg, WV 26101
Ultimate Parent: Westinghouse Electric Corp. **SIC:** 3644—Noncurrent-Carrying Wiring Devices.

★ 92982 ★ **Chesapeake & Potomac Telephone Co.**
921 Market St.
Parkersburg, WV 26101-4736
(304)485-7926
Company Type: Subsidiary. **Ultimate Parent:** Bell Atlantic Corp. **SIC:** 4813—Telephone Communications Except Radiotelephone.

★ 92983 ★ **Corning Inc.**
1624 Staunton Ave.
Parkersburg, WV 26101
Ultimate Parent: Corning. **SIC:** 3229—Pressed & Blown Glass Nec.

★ 92984 ★ **GE Plastics**
5th & Avery St.
Parkersburg, WV 26102
(304)424-5411
Officer: Craig Morrison, Manager. **Ultimate Parent:** General Electric. **SIC:** 2821—Plastics Materials & Resins.

★ 92985 ★ **Hit or Miss**
100 Grand Central Mall
Parkersburg, WV 26101
(304)485-9935
Ultimate Parent: TJX. **SIC:** 5621—Women's Clothing Stores.

★ 92986 ★ **Jiffy Lube Oil Change**
905 Grand Central Ave.
Parkersburg, WV 26105
(304)295-9671
Ultimate Parent: Pennzoil. **SIC:** 7538—General Automotive Repair Shops.

★ 92987 ★ **Kroger Co.**
RR 2
Parkersburg, WV 26101
(304)428-8534
Ultimate Parent: Kroger. **SIC:** 5411—Grocery Stores.

★ 92988 ★ **Kroger Co.**
Murdochave
Parkersburg, WV 26101
(304)422-3641
Ultimate Parent: Kroger. **SIC:** 5411—Grocery Stores.

★ 92989 ★ **Kroger Co.**
1030 Division St.
Parkersburg, WV 26101
(304)428-8533
Ultimate Parent: Kroger. **SIC:** 5411—Grocery Stores.

★ 92990 ★ **Lane Bryant**
330 Grand Central Mall
Parkersburg, WV 26101
(304)422-5529
Ultimate Parent: Limited. **SIC:** 5621—Women's Clothing Stores.

★ 92991 ★　Lerner Shops
260 Grand Central Mall
Parkersburg, WV 26101
(304)485-2382
Ultimate Parent: Limited. **SIC:** 5621—
Women's Clothing Stores.

★ 92992 ★　Mary Kay Cosmetics
1020 51st St.
Parkersburg, WV 26105
(304)295-7511
Ultimate Parent: Mary Kay Cosmetics. **SIC:**
5999—Miscellaneous Retail Stores Nec.

★ 92993 ★　Monogahela Power
Co.
1803 Murdoch Ave.
Parkersburg, WV 26101-3229
(304)422-6421
Ultimate Parent: Allegheny Power System.
SIC: 4911—Electric Services.

★ 92994 ★　Payless Shoe Source
410 Grand Central Mall
Parkersburg, WV 26101
(304)422-0716
Ultimate Parent: May Department Stores.
SIC: 5661—Shoe Stores.

★ 92995 ★　Pennzoil Co.
49 Hall St.
Parkersburg, WV 26101
(304)485-3011
Ultimate Parent: Pennzoil. **SIC:** 5171—
Petroleum Bulk Stations & Terminals.

★ 92996 ★　Rite Aid Discount
Pharmacy
3934 Murdoch Ave.
Parkersburg, WV 26101
(304)422-4151
Ultimate Parent: Rite Aid. **SIC:** 5912—
Drug Stores & Proprietary Stores.

★ 92997 ★　Thrift Drugs
277 Grand Central Mall
Parkersburg, WV 26101
(304)485-3846
Ultimate Parent: J.C. Penney. **SIC:** 5912—
Drug Stores & Proprietary Stores.

★ 92998 ★　United Parcel Service
2500 Gihon Rd.
Parkersburg, WV 26101
(304)642-9180
Ultimate Parent: United Parcel Service of
America. **SIC:** 4215—Courier Services
Except by Air.

★ 92999 ★　Westvaco Corp.
Larkmead Rd.
Parkersburg, WV 26101
(304)863-5051
Ultimate Parent: WestVaco Corp.

★ 93000 ★　Westvaco Corp.
Rural Route 95
Parkersburg, WV 26101
(304)428-4739
Ultimate Parent: WestVaco Corp. **SIC:**
2611—Pulp Mills.

Parsons

★ 93001 ★　Monongahela Power
Co.
Parsons, WV 26287
(304)478-2031
Ultimate Parent: Allegheny Power System.
SIC: 4911—Electric Services.

Petersburg

★ 93002 ★　Potomac Valley Bank
7 Park St.
Petersburg, WV 26847
(304)257-1551
Ultimate Parent: Mercantile Bankshares
Corp. **SIC:** 6022—State Commercial Banks.

★ 93003 ★　Potomac Valley Bank
4 N. Main St.
Petersburg, WV 26847
(304)257-1244
Ultimate Parent: Mercantile Bankshares
Corp. **SIC:** 6022—State Commercial Banks.

★ 93004 ★　Ryder Truck Rental
308 Virginia Ave.
Petersburg, WV 26847
(304)257-2488
Ultimate Parent: Ryder System. **SIC:**
7513—Truck Rental & Leasing Without
Drivers.

Philippi

★ 93005 ★　Rite Aid Discount
Pharmacy
101103 S. Main St.
Philippi, WV 26416
(304)457-4911
Ultimate Parent: Rite Aid. **SIC:** 5912—Drug
Stores & Proprietary Stores.

Pineville

★ 93006 ★　National Mines Corp.
Pineville, WV 24874
(304)732-7070
Ultimate Parent: National Steel. **SIC:**
5052—Coal, Other Minerals & Ores.

Pointe Pleasant

★ 93007 ★　People's Bank
PO Box 518
Pointe Pleasant, WV 25550
(304)675-1121
Ultimate Parent: People's Bank. **SIC:**
6099—Functions Related to Deposit
Banking.

Princeton

★ 93008 ★　Kroger Co.
1213 Stafford Dr.
Princeton, WV 24740
(304)487-6136
Ultimate Parent: Kroger. **SIC:** 5411—
Grocery Stores.

★ 93009 ★　Kroger Co.
Bluefield Plz.
Princeton, WV 24740
(304)325-3786
Ultimate Parent: Kroger. **SIC:** 5411—
Grocery Stores.

★ 93010 ★　Lowe's Home Centers
Inc.
250 Oakvale Rd.
Princeton, WV 24740
Ultimate Parent: Lowe's. **SIC:** 5211—
Lumber & Other Building Materials; 5251—
Hardware Stores.

★ 93011 ★　Northwestern Mutual
Life Inc.
1422 E. Main St.
Princeton, WV 24740
(304)487-6171
Ultimate Parent: Northwestern Mutual Life.
SIC: 6411—Insurance Agents, Brokers &
Service.

★ 93012 ★　Pepsi Cola General
Bottlers
Rogers St.
Princeton, WV 24740
(304)425-9525
Officer: Charlie Powers, Manager. **Ultimate
Parent:** Pepsico. **SIC:** 2086—Bottled
& Canned Soft Drinks.

★ 93013 ★　Rite Aid Discount
Pharmacy
1121 Stafford Dr.
Princeton, WV 24740
(304)425-9024
Ultimate Parent: Rite Aid. **SIC:** 5912—Drug
Stores & Proprietary Stores.

Proctor

★ 93014 ★　McDonald's
Hamburgers Office
509 Kent Ln.
Proctor, WV 26055
(304)455-5925
Ultimate Parent: McDonald's. **SIC:** 5812—
Eating Places.

Pt Pleasant

★ 93015 ★　Rite Aid Discount
Pharmacy
2418 Jackson Ave.
Pt Pleasant, WV 25550
(304)675-9790
Ultimate Parent: Rite Aid. **SIC:** 5912—Drug
Stores & Proprietary Stores.

★ 93016 ★　Superamerica
2725 Jackson Ave.
Pt Pleasant, WV 25550
(304)675-7167
Ultimate Parent: Ashland Oil. **SIC:** 5411—
Grocery Stores.

Rainelle

★ 93017 ★　Greyhound Bus Lines
705 Main St.
Rainelle, WV 25962
(304)438-6175
Ultimate Parent: Greyhound Lines Inc. **SIC:**
4131—Intercity & Rural Bus Transportation;
4111—Local & Suburban Transit; 4142—
Bus Charter Service Except Local.

★ 93018 ★　Rite Aid Discount
Pharmacy
Park Ctr.
Rainelle, WV 25962
(304)438-9204
Ultimate Parent: Rite Aid. **SIC:** 5912—Drug
Stores & Proprietary Stores.

Ranson

★ 93019 ★　Dixie-Narco Inc.
N. Lawrence St.
Ranson, WV 25438
Ultimate Parent: Maytag. **SIC:** 3581—
Automatic Vending Machines.

★ 93020 ★　Dixie Narco Inc.
North Lawrence St.
Ranson, WV 25438
Ultimate Parent: Maytag. **SIC:** 3581—
Automatic Vending Machines.

★ 93021 ★　Figgie Fire Protection
Systems
N. Mildred
Ranson, WV 25438
(304)725-9721 **Fax:** (304)728-8481
Location Type: Plant. **Ultimate Parent:**
Figgie International. **SIC:** 3569—General
Industrial Machinery Nec. **Employee Count:**
350. **Sales:** 20000000 M.

Ravenswood

★ 93022 ★　First Federal S & L
234 Washington St.
Ravenswood, WV 26164-1842
(304)273-4212
Company Type: Headquarters. **Ultimate
Parent:** Bancorp Hawaii. **SIC:** 6035—
Federal Savings Institutions; 6141—
Personal Credit Institutions.

★ 93023 ★　Rite Aid Discount
Pharmacy
Ravenswood Shopping Ctr.
Ravenswood, WV 26164
(304)273-9339
Ultimate Parent: Rite Aid. **SIC:** 5049—
Professional Equipment Nec.

Richwood

★ 93024 ★　Peoples Bank
Oakford Ave.
Richwood, WV 26261
(304)846-2581
Ultimate Parent: People's Bank. **SIC:**
6029—Commercial Banks Nec.

★ 93025 ★　Peoples Bank of
Richwood Inc.
30 PO Box
Richwood, WV 26261
(304)846-2654
Ultimate Parent: People's Bank. **SIC:**
6022—State Commercial Banks.

★ 93026 ★　Rite Aid Discount
Pharmacy
Cherry Rv Plz.
Richwood, WV 26261
(304)846-2406
Ultimate Parent: Rite Aid. **SIC:** 5912—Drug
Stores & Proprietary Stores.

Ripley

★ 93027 ★　Exxon Co.
Pinnell St.
Ripley, WV 25271
(304)372-5925
Ultimate Parent: Exxon. **SIC:** 5541—
Gasoline Service Stations.

★ 93028 ★　McDonald's
Hamburgers
101 New Stone Ridge Rd.
Ripley, WV 25271
(304)372-9611
Ultimate Parent: McDonald's. **SIC:** 5812—
Eating Places.

★ 93029 ★　Rite Aid Discount
Pharmacy
33 Miller
Ripley, WV 25271
(304)372-6005
Ultimate Parent: Rite Aid. **SIC:** 5912—Drug
Stores & Proprietary Stores.

★ 93030 ★　Rite Aid Discount
Pharmacy
Rural Route 33
Ripley, WV 25271
(304)372-9009
Ultimate Parent: Rite Aid. **SIC:** 5912—Drug
Stores & Proprietary Stores.

★ 93031 ★　Rite Aid Discount
Pharmacy
106 North St. E
Ripley, WV 25271
(304)372-9058
Ultimate Parent: Rite Aid.

Rocket Center

★ 93032 ★　Allegany Ballistics
Laboratory
Wv Secondary Rte. 956
Rocket Center, WV 26726
Ultimate Parent: Hercules. **SIC:** 3764—
Space Propulsion Units & Parts; 3089—
Plastics Products Nec.

Romney

★ 93033 ★　Rite Aid Discount
Pharmacy
111 W. Main St.
Romney, WV 26757
(304)822-5984
Ultimate Parent: Rite Aid. **SIC:** 5912—Drug
Stores & Proprietary Stores.

★ 93034 ★　Rite Aid Discount
Pharmacy
74 W. Main St.
Romney, WV 26757
(304)822-3313
Ultimate Parent: Rite Aid. **SIC:** 5912—Drug
Stores & Proprietary Stores.

Ronceverte

★ 93035 ★　Rite Aid Discount
Pharmacy
Washington St.
Ronceverte, WV 24970
(304)647-4699
Ultimate Parent: Rite Aid. **SIC:** 5912—Drug
Stores & Proprietary Stores.

S Charleston

★ 93036 ★　Hudsons
3200 Maccorkle Ave. SW
S Charleston, WV 25303
(304)746-1542
Ultimate Parent: Dayton Hudson.

Salem

★ 93037 ★　Chesapeake &
Potomac Telephone Co.
179 W. Main St.
Salem, WV 26426-1229
(304)782-9972
Company Type: Subsidiary. **Ultimate
Parent:** Bell Atlantic Corp. **SIC:** 4813—
Telephone Communications Except
Radiotelephone.

Scharleston

★ 93038 ★   Kroger Co.
Maccorkle Southwest Ave.
Scharleston, WV 25303
(304)744-1472
Ultimate Parent: Kroger. SIC: 5411—
Grocery Stores.

Scott Depot

★ 93039 ★   Bird Machine Co.
Erskine Ln.
Scott Depot, WV 25560
(304)757-2678
Officer: Bruce Welling, Manager. Ultimate
Parent: Baker Hughes. SIC: 3599—
Industrial Machinery Nec.

★ 93040 ★   Kroger Co.
Putnam Village Shopping Ctr.
Scott Depot, WV 25560
(304)757-7317
Ultimate Parent: Kroger. SIC: 5411—
Grocery Stores.

Seth

★ 93041 ★   Stop & Shop
Seth, WV 25181
(304)837-3633
Ultimate Parent: Stop & Shop. SIC: 5411—
Grocery Stores.

Sharples

★ 93042 ★   Dal-Tex Coal Co.
PO Box D
Sharples, WV 25183
(304)369-0666
Company Type: Subsidiary. Officer: Allen
Workman, President. Ultimate Parent:
Ashland Oil. SIC: 1221—Bituminous Coal &
Lignite—Surface; 1222—Bituminous Coal—
Underground.

Shinnston

★ 93043 ★   Rite Aid Discount
Pharmacy
210 S. Pike St.
Shinnston, WV 26431
(304)592-5482
Ultimate Parent: Rite Aid. SIC: 5912—Drug
Stores & Proprietary Stores.

Sistersville

★ 93044 ★   Union Carbide
Chemicals & Plastics Co. Inc.
State Rte. 2 PO Box 180
Sistersville, WV 26175
Ultimate Parent: Union Carbide Corp. SIC:
2869—Industrial Organic Chemicals Nec.

Skelton

★ 93045 ★   Fitness Concepts Hlth
Club
434 PO Box
Skelton, WV 25919
Ultimate Parent: New York Times. SIC:
7997—Membership Sports & Recreation
Clubs.

South Charleston

★ 93046 ★   Arco Chemical Co.
437 Maccorkle Ave.
South Charleston, WV 25303-0004
Ultimate Parent: Atlantic Richfield Co., Inc.
SIC: 2869—Industrial Organic Chemicals
Nec.

★ 93047 ★   FMC Corp.
3200 MacCorkle Ave. SW
South Charleston, WV 25303
(304)746-1500
Officer: Scott Johnson, Manager. Ultimate
Parent: FMC. SIC: 2819—Industrial
Inorganic Chemicals Nec.

★ 93048 ★   FMC Corp.
Ashbe St. & MacCorkle Ave.
South Charleston, WV 25303
(304)746-2300
Officer: E. L. Perry, Manager. Ultimate
Parent: FMC. SIC: 2813—Industrial Gases.

★ 93049 ★   Fmc Corp. Spring Hill
Plant
3200 Maccorkle Ave.
South Charleston, WV 25303-1448
Ultimate Parent: FMC. SIC: 2819—
Industrial Inorganic Chemicals Nec.

★ 93050 ★   Kroger Co.
5 Ave. D
South Charleston, WV 25303
(304)744-9844
Ultimate Parent: Kroger. SIC: 5411—
Grocery Stores.

★ 93051 ★   Olin Corp.
95 Maccorkle Ave. SW
South Charleston, WV 25303
Ultimate Parent: Olin Corp. SIC: 2819—
Industrial Inorganic Chemicals Nec.

★ 93052 ★   Olin Corp.
95 MacCorkle Ave. SW
South Charleston, WV 25303
(304)746-3000
Officer: Mike Murray, Manager. Ultimate
Parent: Olin Corp. SIC: 2819—Industrial
Inorganic Chemicals Nec.

★ 93053 ★   Pitney Bowes
527 2nd Ave. SW
South Charleston, WV 25303
Officer: Larry Edmonds, Manager. Ultimate
Parent: Pitney Bowes. SIC: 3554—Paper
Industries Machinery.

★ 93054 ★   Union Carbide
Chemical & Plastics Co. Technical
Center
3200-3300 Kanawha Turnpike PO Box 8361
South Charleston, WV 25303
Ultimate Parent: Union Carbide Corp. SIC:
2869—Industrial Organic Chemicals Nec;
2821—Plastics Materials & Resins.

★ 93055 ★   Union Carbide
Chemicals & Plastics Co. Holz
Impoundment
Adjacent Rte. 214 PO Box 8004
South Charleston, WV 25303-0004
Ultimate Parent: Union Carbide Corp. SIC:
2869—Industrial Organic Chemicals Nec;
4953—Refuse Systems.

★ 93056 ★   Union Carbide
Chemicals & Plastics Co. Inc.
437 MacCorkle Ave. PO Box 8004
South Charleston, WV 25303-0004
Ultimate Parent: Union Carbide Corp. SIC:
2869—Industrial Organic Chemicals Nec.

★ 93057 ★   Union Carbide Corp.
437 MacCorkle Ave.
South Charleston, WV 25303-0004
Ultimate Parent: Union Carbide Corp. SIC:
2869—Industrial Organic Chemicals Nec.

★ 93058 ★   Union Carbide Corp.
South Charleston Plant
3200-3300 Kanawha Turnpike
South Charleston, WV 25303-0004
Location Type: Plant. Ultimate Parent:
Union Carbide Corp. SIC: 2869—Industrial
Organic Chemicals Nec.

★ 93059 ★   Union Carbide Corp.
Holz Impoundment
Adjacent Rte. 214
PO Box 8004
South Charleston, WV 25303
Ultimate Parent: Union Carbide Corp. SIC:
2869—Industrial Organic Chemicals Nec;
4953—Refuse Systems.

★ 93060 ★   Union Carbide Corp.
South Charleston Plant
437 MacCorkle Avenue, SW (PO Box 8004)
South Charleston, WV 25303-0004
Ultimate Parent: Union Carbide Corp. SIC:
2869—Industrial Organic Chemicals Nec.

★ 93061 ★   Union Carbide Corp.
Tech Nical Center
3200-3300 Kanawha Turnpike
South Charleston, WV 25303
Ultimate Parent: Union Carbide Corp. SIC:
2869—Industrial Organic Chemicals Nec.

Spencer

★ 93062 ★   B. F. Goodrich Co.
Roane County Industrial Park
Spencer, WV 25276-0128
Ultimate Parent: B.F. Goodrich. SIC:
3069—Fabricated Rubber Products Nec.

★ 93063 ★   Pennzoil Co.
801 Capitol St.
Spencer, WV 25276
(304)927-3400
Ultimate Parent: Pennzoil. SIC: 5171—
Petroleum Bulk Stations & Terminals.

★ 93064 ★   Pennzoil Co.
Otto Rd.
Spencer, WV 25276
(304)927-4097
Ultimate Parent: Pennzoil. SIC: 5171—
Petroleum Bulk Stations & Terminals.

★ 93065 ★   Rite Aid Discount
Pharmacy
408 Main St.
Spencer, WV 25276
(304)927-4166
Ultimate Parent: Rite Aid. SIC: 5912—Drug
Stores & Proprietary Stores.

St. Albans

★ 93066 ★   City National Bank of
Charleston
560 4th St.
St. Albans, WV 25177-2819
Company Type: Branch. Ultimate Parent:
City National Corp.

★ 93067 ★   Kroger Co.
1500 MacCorkle Ave.
St. Albans, WV 25177
(304)722-4248
Ultimate Parent: Kroger. SIC: 5411—
Grocery Stores.

★ 93068 ★   Kroger Co.
201 Great Teays Blvd.
St. Albans, WV 25177
(304)757-7915
Ultimate Parent: Kroger. SIC: 5411—
Grocery Stores.

★ 93069 ★   Rite Aid Discount
Pharmacy
Gateway Shopping Ctr.
St. Albans, WV 25177
(304)727-9019
Ultimate Parent: Rite Aid. SIC: 5912—Drug
Stores & Proprietary Stores.

★ 93070 ★   Summit Corp.
6416 Maccorkle Ave.
St. Albans, WV 25177
(304)766-6204
Ultimate Parent: American Greetings. SIC:
1629—Heavy Construction Nec.

★ 93071 ★   Texaco Inc.
51 Main St.
St. Albans, WV 25177
(304)722-2784
Ultimate Parent: Texaco. SIC: 5541—
Gasoline Service Stations.

St. Marys

★ 93072 ★   Quaker State Oil
Refining Co.
201 Barkwill St.
St. Marys, WV 26170
(304)684-2222
Ultimate Parent: Quaker State. SIC:
2911—Petroleum Refining.

★ 93073 ★   Rite Aid Discount
Pharmacy
313 2nd St.
St. Marys, WV 26170
(304)684-2297
Ultimate Parent: Rite Aid. SIC: 7384—
Photofinishing Laboratories.

Summersville

★ 93074 ★   Rite Aid Discount
Pharmacy
Nicholas Village Shopping Ctr.
Summersville, WV 26651
(304)872-5650
Ultimate Parent: Rite Aid. SIC: 5912—Drug
Stores & Proprietary Stores.

★ 93075 ★   Ryder Truck Rental
Rural Route 41
Summersville, WV 26651
(304)872-5016
Ultimate Parent: Ryder System. SIC:
7513—Truck Rental & Leasing Without
Drivers.

Tariff

★ 93076 ★   Pennzoil Co.
Tariff, WV 25281
(304)565-7731
Ultimate Parent: Pennzoil. SIC: 5171—
Petroleum Bulk Stations & Terminals.

Vienna

★ 93077 ★   Business Systems &
Service Inc.
Vienna, WV 26105
(304)295-4151
Ultimate Parent: Avery Dennison Corp.
SIC: 7378—Computer Maintenance &
Repair; 5045—Computers, Peripherals &
Software; 5734—Computer & Software
Stores; 5999—Miscellaneous Retail Stores
Nec; 7371—Computer Programming
Services.

★ 93078 ★   Manville Sales Corp.
2905 3rd Ave.
Vienna, WV 26105-5130
Ultimate Parent: Manville Corp. SIC:
3296—Mineral Wool.

★ 93079 ★   Schuller
Manufacturing Corp.
2905 3rd Ave.
Vienna, WV 26105-5130
Ultimate Parent: Manville Corp. SIC:
3296—Mineral Wool.

Washington

★ 93080 ★   GE Chemicals Inc.
State Rte. 892
Washington, WV 26181
Ultimate Parent: General Electric. SIC:
2821—Plastics Materials & Resins.

★ 93081 ★   Westvaco Corp.
41 Rural Route 1
Washington, WV 26181
(304)863-9073
Ultimate Parent: WestVaco Corp. SIC:
0831—Forest Products.

Webster Springs

★ 93082 ★   Rite Aid Discount
Pharmacy
139 Baker St.
Webster Springs, WV 26288
(304)847-9600
Ultimate Parent: Rite Aid. SIC: 5912—Drug
Stores & Proprietary Stores.

Weirton

★ 93083 ★   Air Products &
Chemicals Inc.
4th & St. Johns Rd.
Weirton, WV 26062
Ultimate Parent: Air Products & Chemicals,
Inc. SIC: 2813—Industrial Gases.

★ 93084 ★   Air Products &
Chemicals, Inc.
4th St. & Johns Rd.
Weirton, WV 26062
(304)797-1810
Officer: Terry Grant, Manager. Ultimate
Parent: Air Products & Chemicals, Inc. SIC:
2813—Industrial Gases.

★ 93085 ★   Anchor Hocking
Packaging
Weirton Plant 33
3011 Birch Dr.
Weirton, WV 26062
Location Type: Plant. Ultimate Parent:
Newell. SIC: 3466—Crowns & Closures.

★ 93086 ★   Anchor Hocking
Packaging Co.
Weirton Plant
3011 Birch Dr.
Weirton, WV 26062
Location Type: Plant. Ultimate Parent:
Newell. SIC: 3400—Fabricated Metal
Products.

★ 93087 ★   Fitness World
1707 Pennsylvania Ave.
Weirton, WV 26062
(304)723-3035
Ultimate Parent: New York Times. SIC:
7991—Physical Fitness Facilities.

★ 93088 ★   **Greyhound Bus Lines**
3075 Main St.
Weirton, WV 26062
(304)665-2422 (304)282-3608
Officer: David Chatfield. **Ultimate Parent:**
American Cyanamid Co. **SIC:** 2869—
Industrial Organic Chemicals Nec. **Ultimate
Parent:** Greyhound Lines Inc. **SIC:** 4131—
Intercity & Rural Bus Transportation; 4111—
Local & Suburban Transit; 4142—Bus
Charter Service Except Local.

★ 93089 ★   **H. J. Heinz**
Pet Products Div.
3030 Birch Dr., Halfmoon Industrial Park
Weirton, WV 26062
Company Type: Division. **Ultimate Parent:**
H.J. Heinz. **SIC:** 3411—Metal Cans.

★ 93090 ★   **H. J. Heinz Co.**
Heinz Pet Products Div.
3030 Birch Dr., Halfmoon Industrial Park
Weirton, WV 26062
Company Type: Division. **Ultimate Parent:**
H.J. Heinz. **SIC:** 3411—Metal Cans.

★ 93091 ★   **Heekin Can Co.**
3010 Birch Dr.
Weirton, WV 26062-5133
(304)797-0062
Officer: Eileen W. Klakos. **Ultimate Parent:**
Ball Corp. **SIC:** 3411—Metal Cans.

★ 93092 ★   **Heinz Pet Prods.
Weirton Plant**
3030 Birch Dr. Halfmoon Industrial Park
Weirton, WV 26062
Ultimate Parent: H.J. Heinz. **SIC:** 3411—
Metal Cans.

★ 93093 ★   **Kroger Co.**
290 Three Springs Dr.
Weirton, WV 26062
(304)723-5130
Ultimate Parent: Kroger. **SIC:** 5411—
Grocery Stores.

★ 93094 ★   **Kroger Co.**
3558 Main St.
Weirton, WV 26062
(304)748-6230
Ultimate Parent: Kroger. **SIC:** 5411—
Grocery Stores.

★ 93095 ★   **Mobil Service Station**
981 Cove Rd.
Weirton, WV 26062
(304)748-9625
Ultimate Parent: Mobil. **SIC:** 5541—
Gasoline Service Stations.

★ 93096 ★   **Monongahela Power
Co.**
217 3 Springs Dr.
Weirton, WV 26062-3814
(304)723-4500
Officer: D. L. Riggleman. **Ultimate Parent:**
Allegheny Power System. **SIC:** 4911—
Electric Services.

★ 93097 ★   **National Steel Corp.**
Hamilton Rd.
Weirton, WV 26062
(304)748-8520
Ultimate Parent: National Intergroup. **SIC:**
5051—Metals Service Centers & Offices;
8231—Libraries.

★ 93098 ★   **Peoples Bank**
3425 Main St.
Weirton, WV 26062
(304)748-7373
Ultimate Parent: People's Bank. **SIC:**
6029—Commercial Banks Nec.

★ 93099 ★   **Signode Supply Corp.**
3015 Birch Dr.
Weirton, WV 26062
Ultimate Parent: Illinois Tool Works. **SIC:**
3479—Metal Coating & Allied Services.

★ 93100 ★   **Starkist Foods Inc.**
Pet Food Div.
3030 Birch Dr. Halfmoon Industrial Park
Weirton, WV 26062
Company Type: Division. **Ultimate Parent:**
H.J. Heinz. **SIC:** 3411—Metal Cans.

★ 93101 ★   **Thrift Drugs**
263 Penco Rd.
Weirton, WV 26062
(304)723-2110
Ultimate Parent: J.C. Penney. **SIC:** 5912—
Drug Stores & Proprietary Stores.

★ 93102 ★   **Thrift Drugs**
3549 Main St.
Weirton, WV 26062
(304)748-4322
Ultimate Parent: J.C. Penney. **SIC:** 5912—
Drug Stores & Proprietary Stores.

★ 93103 ★   **Weirton Steel Corp.**
400 3 Springs Dr.
Weirton, WV 26062
(304)797-2000 **Fax:** (304)797-2821
Company Type: Headquarters. **Officer:**
Herbert Elish, CEO. **Employee Count:**
6026. **Sales:** 1201.1 M. **Fortune 500:**
Largest U.S. Industrial Corporations:
Ranking 325.

Wellsburg

★ 93104 ★   **Stone Container Corp.**
2333 Commerce St.
Wellsburg, WV 26070
(304)737-3311
Officer: Richard E. Harrison, Manager.
Ultimate Parent: Stone Container Corp.
SIC: 2652—Setup Paperboard Boxes;
2673—Bags—Plastics, Laminated &
Coated.

★ 93105 ★   **Westvaco Corp.**
2333 Commerce St.
Wellsburg, WV 26070
(304)737-3311
Ultimate Parent: WestVaco Corp. **SIC:**
2621—Paper Mills.

Weston

★ 93106 ★   **Kroger Co.**
Arnold Rd.
Weston, WV 26452
(304)269-5293
Ultimate Parent: Kroger. **SIC:** 5411—
Grocery Stores.

★ 93107 ★   **Louie Glass Co. Inc.**
631 E. 3rd St.
Weston, WV 26452
Ultimate Parent: Colgate-Palmolive. **SIC:**
3229—Pressed & Blown Glass Nec.

★ 93108 ★   **Rite Aid Discount
Pharmacy**
161 Main Ave.
Weston, WV 26452
(304)269-9885
Ultimate Parent: Rite Aid. **SIC:** 5912—Drug
Stores & Proprietary Stores.

★ 93109 ★   **Ryder Truck Rental**
326 PO Box
Weston Wv, WV 26452
(304)269-5342
Ultimate Parent: Ryder System. **SIC:**
7513—Truck Rental & Leasing Without
Drivers.

Wharncliffe

★ 93110 ★   **Mingo Logan Coal Co.**
1000 Mingo Logan Ave.
Wharncliffe, WV 25651
(304)664-3873
Company Type: Subsidiary. **Officer:**
Markus Ladd, President. **Ultimate Parent:**
Ashland Oil. **SIC:** 1221—Bituminous Coal &
Lignite—Surface; 1222—Bituminous Coal—
Underground.

Wheeling

★ 93111 ★   **Emery Worldwide
(ACF Co.)**
3027 PO Box
Wheeling, WV 26003
(304)232-2570
Ultimate Parent: Consolidated Freightways.

SIC: 4731—Freight Transportation
Arrangement.

★ 93112 ★   **Genuine Parts Co.**
2347 Main St.
Wheeling, WV 26003
(304)233-0300
Officer: William King Jr., Owner. **Ultimate
Parent:** Genuine Parts. **SIC:** 3599—
Industrial Machinery Nec; 3694—Engine
Electrical Equipment.

★ 93113 ★   **Greyhound Bus Lines**
1109 Main St.
Wheeling, WV 26003
(304)232-1500
Ultimate Parent: Greyhound Lines Inc. **SIC:**
4131—Intercity & Rural Bus Transportation;
4111—Local & Suburban Transit; 4142—
Bus Charter Service Except Local.

★ 93114 ★   **Kroger Co.**
1201 National Rd.
Wheeling, WV 26003
(304)243-1470
Ultimate Parent: Kroger. **SIC:** 5411—
Grocery Stores.

★ 93115 ★   **Kroger Co.**
1211 Warwood Ave.
Wheeling, WV 26003
(304)277-3260
Ultimate Parent: Kroger. **SIC:** 5411—
Grocery Stores.

★ 93116 ★   **Northwestern Mutual
Life Inc.**
1060 Chapline St.
Wheeling, WV 26003
(304)232-2340
Ultimate Parent: Northwestern Mutual Life.
SIC: 6411—Insurance Agents, Brokers &
Service.

★ 93117 ★   **Ohio Valley-
Clarksburg Inc.**
71 Mill-Acres Dr.
Wheeling, WV 26003-5042
(304)242-9526
Officer: Robert D. Walter, Chairman.
Ultimate Parent: Cardinal Health. **SIC:**
5122—Drugs, Proprietaries & Sundries.
Employee Count: 165.

★ 93118 ★   **Rite Aid Discount
Pharmacy**
1227 Warwood Ave.
Wheeling, WV 26003
(304)277-9895
Ultimate Parent: Rite Aid. **SIC:** 5912—Drug
Stores & Proprietary Stores.

★ 93119 ★   **Rite Aid Discount
Pharmacy**
Elm Ter
Wheeling, WV 26003
(304)242-9169
Ultimate Parent: Rite Aid. **SIC:** 5912—Drug
Stores & Proprietary Stores.

★ 93120 ★   **Safety-Kleen Corp.**
10 Industrial Park Dr.
Wheeling, WV 26003
(304)233-6567
Ultimate Parent: Safety-Kleen. **SIC:** 2899—
Chemical Preparations Nec.

★ 93121 ★   **Union Oil Co.**
439 River Rd.
Wheeling, WV 26003
(304)277-2610
Ultimate Parent: Unocal Corp. **SIC:** 5983—
Fuel Oil Dealers.

★ 93122 ★   **Wheeling Corrugating
Co.**
31st & Wood St.
Wheeling, WV 26003
(304)234-2773
Officer: James W. Raymond, Manager.
Ultimate Parent: Wheeling-Pittsburgh Steel
Corp. **SIC:** 3315—Steel Wire & Related
Products; 3441—Fabricated Structural
Metal.

★ 93123 ★   **Wheeling Pittsburgh
Steel Corp.**
1134 Market St.
Wheeling, WV 26003
(304)234-3430
Officer: James L. Wareham, Chm. **Ultimate
Parent:** Wheeling-Pittsburgh Steel Corp.
SIC: 3312—Blast Furnaces & Steel Mills;
3316—Cold-Finishing of Steel Shapes;
3317—Steel Pipe & Tubes.

★ 93124 ★   **Wheeling-Pittsburgh
Steel Corp. Labelle**
31st St.
Wheeling, WV 26003
Ultimate Parent: Wheeling-Pittsburgh Steel
Corp. **SIC:** 3312—Blast Furnaces & Steel
Mills.

White Sulphur Springs

★ 93125 ★   **Greenbrier Resort
Management Co.**
Sta. A
White Sulphur Springs, WV 24986
(304)536-1110 **Fax:** (304)536-7819
Officer: Theodore J. Kleisner, President &
Managing Director. **Ultimate Parent:** CSX
Corp.

★ 93126 ★   **Greenbrier Resort
Management Co. Inc.**
Rte. 60
White Sulphur Springs, WV 24986
(304)536-1110
Company Type: Subsidiary. **Officer:**
Theodore Kleisner, President. **Ultimate
Parent:** CSX Corp. **SIC:** 8741—
Management Services. **Employee Count:**
2500. **Sales:** 85 M.

★ 93127 ★   **Kroger Co.**
45 W. Main St.
White Sulphur Springs, WV 24986
(304)536-1070
Ultimate Parent: Kroger. **SIC:** 5411—
Grocery Stores.

Whitesville

★ 93128 ★   **Rite Aid Discount
Pharmacy**
Rural Route 3
Whitesville, WV 25209
(304)854-9842
Ultimate Parent: Rite Aid. **SIC:** 5999—
Miscellaneous Retail Stores Nec.

Williamson

★ 93129 ★   **Kroger Co.**
Southside Mall
Williamson, WV 25661
(304)237-5680
Ultimate Parent: Kroger. **SIC:** 5411—
Grocery Stores.

★ 93130 ★   **Rite Aid Discount
Pharmacy**
2 E. 2nd Ave. 6
Williamson, WV 25661
(304)235-2944
Ultimate Parent: Rite Aid. **SIC:** 5912—Drug
Stores & Proprietary Stores.

Willow Island

★ 93131 ★   **American Cyanamid
Co.**
State Rte. 2
Willow Island, WV 26140
Ultimate Parent: American Cyanamid Co.
SIC: 2819—Industrial Inorganic Chemicals
Nec; 2833—Medicinals & Botanicals;
2843—Surface Active Agents; 2869—
Industrial Organic Chemicals Nec; 2899—
Chemical Preparations Nec.

★ 93132 ★   **American Cyanamid
Co.**
S R 2
Willow Island, WV 26134
(304)665-2422
Officer: David Chatfield. **Ultimate Parent:**
American Cyanamid Co. **SIC:** 2869—
Industrial Organic Chemicals Nec.

SIC Index

0111 Wheat
Farmland Green Division (Enid, OK) 77048

0119 Cash Grains Nec
Farmland Green Division (Enid, OK) 77048

0132 Tobacco
Taylor J P Co. (Goldsboro, NC) 74737

0139 Field Crops Except Cash Grains Nec
Golden Peanut (Dothan, AL) 55651
Golden Peanuts Co. (Atlanta, GA) 64514

0174 Citrus Fruits
FPL Group Inc. (West Palm Beach, FL) 63866
Turner Food Corp. (Parrish, FL) 62360
Turner Foods Corp. (Punta Gorda, FL) 62722

0181 Ornamental Nursery Products
Southland (Plymouth, FL) 62577

0191 General Farms—Primarily Crop
Dixon Hardware & Furniture Co. Inc. (Camilla, GA) 65478

0251 Broiler, Fryer & Roaster Chickens
Conagra Poultry Co. (Dalton, GA) 65778
Conagra Poultry Co. (Gainesville, GA) 66272
Gold Kist Inc. (Atlanta, GA) 64511
Herider Farms Inc. (Fayetteville, AR) 56979
Holly Farms Food Service Inc. (Wilkesboro, NC) 76507
Holly Farms Foods Inc. (Harmony, NC) 75004
Holly Farms Foods Inc. (Wilkesboro, NC) 76509
Holly Farms Foods Inc. (Glen Allen, VA) 90980
Holly Farms Foods Inc. (Harrisonburg, VA) 91091
Holly Farms Foods Inc. Center Texas Plant (Center, TX) 83536
Holly Farms Foods Inc. Harmony Rendering (Harmony, NC) 75005
Holly Farms Foods Inc. Richmond Plant (Glen Allen, VA) 90981
Holly Farms Foods Inc. Sequin Texas Plant (Sequin, TX) 89386
Holly Farms of Texas Inc. Center Texas Plant (Center, TX) 83537
Holly Farms of Texas Inc. Sequin Texas Plant (Seguin, TX) 89368

0253 Turkeys & Turkey Eggs
Herider Farms Inc. (Fayetteville, AR) 56979

0254 Poultry Hatcheries
Gold Kist Inc. (Atlanta, GA) 64511
Hudson Farms Inc. (Muskogee, OK) 77222
Tyson Foods Inc. (Decherd, TN) 80729

0279 Animal Specialties Nec
Hazleton Corp. (Vienna, VA) 92411

0723 Crop Preparation Services for Market
Blue Goose Growers Inc. (Vero Beach, FL) 63744
Ocean Spray Cranberries Inc. (Vero Beach, FL) 63762

0751 Livestock Services
Associated Milk Producers Inc. (Arlington, TX) 82634

0782 Lawn & Garden Services
Avon Corp. (Springfield, VA) 92273
Edwards Co., Inc. (Newport News, VA) 91460
Mapco Natural Gas Liquids Inc. (Tulsa, OK) 78010

0783 Ornamental Shrub & Tree Services
Lawn Boy (Morehead City, NC) 75623
Parker Services Inc. (Richmond, VA) 91940

0811 Timber Tracts
Blue Grass Cooperage Co., Inc. (Benton, KY) 68124
Bowater Southern Div. (Newnan, GA) 67078
Bowater Inc. (Duluth, GA) 66027
Bowater Inc. (Aiken, SC) 78645
Bowater Inc. South Div. (Cullman, AL) 55538
Bowater Inc. Southern Div. (Albertville, AL) 54960
Bowater Woodlands (Harriman, TN) 80899
Bowater Woodlands (Kingston, TN) 81126
Champion International Corp. (Courtland, AL) 55532
Crescent Resources Inc. (Charlotte, NC) 73920; 73921
Duke Power Co. (Charlotte, NC) 73939
Duke Power Co. Inc. (Charlotte, NC) 73940
Federal Paper Board Co. (Four Oaks, NC) 74621
Federal Paper Board Co., Inc. (Bolton, NC) 73705
Louisiana Pacific Corp. (Grenada, MS) 72843
Willamette Industries, Inc. (Moncure, NC) 75571
Willamette Industries Inc. (Chester, SC) 78946

0831 Forest Products
Champion International Corp. (Canton, NC) 73777
Champion International Corp. (Newberry, SC) 79724
Westvaco Corp. (Washington, WV) 93081

0919 Miscellaneous Marine Products
American Brokerage Co. (Miami, FL) 61155
Litton Industries C. Plath North American Div. (Annapolis, MD) 71015
Texaco (Larose, LA) 70188

0921 Fish Hatcheries & Preserves
Farm Fresh Catfish Co. (Lake Village, AR) 57239
Turner Foods Corp. (Punta Gorda, FL) 62722

1000 Metal Mining
Mobil Oil Corp. (Highlands, TX) 85749
Unijax Inc. (Atlanta, GA) 65229

1011 Iron Ores
Eagle Picher Industries Inc. (Miami, OK) 77203
Mobil Chemical Co. (Ashland, VA) 90404

1021 Copper Ores
P. T. Freeport Indonesia Co. (New Orleans, LA) 70458
Freeport-McMoran Copper & Gold Co., Inc. (New Orleans, LA) 70461
Freeport-McMoran Inc. (New Orleans, LA) 70462

1031 Lead & Zinc Ores
Asarco Inc. (Knoxville, TN) 81143
Asarco Inc. (Straw Plains, TN) 82362

1041 Gold Ores
P. T. Freeport Indonesia Co. (New Orleans, LA) 70458
Freeport-McMoran Copper & Gold Co., Inc. (New Orleans, LA) 70461
Freeport-McMoran Inc. (New Orleans, LA) 70462

1044 Silver Ores
P. T. Freeport Indonesia Co. (New Orleans, LA) 70458

1081 Metal Mining Services
Western Geophysical (Midland, TX) 88095
Western Geophysical Co. (Midland, TX) 88096

1094 Uranium, Radium & Vanadium Ores
Imc Fertilizer Inc. Plant City Uranium Recovery (Plant City, FL) 62546; 62547

1200 Coal Mining
Grace Energy Corp. (Dallas, TX) 84094

1221 Bituminous Coal & Lignite—Surface
Ashland Coal, Inc. (Huntington, WV) 92867
Coal-Mac, Inc. (Pikeville, KY) 69224
Coastal Natural Gas Co. (Houston, TX) 85976
Cyprus Mountain Coals Corp. (Hazard, KY) 68424
Dal-Tex Coal Co. (Sharples, WV) 93042
Hobert Mining, Inc. (Madison, WV) 92921
Mapco Coal Inc. (Tulsa, OK) 78007
Mapco Coal Inc. (Richmond, VA) 91921

Mapco Coals Inc. (Richmond, VA) 91922
Mapco Inc. (Tulsa, OK) 78009
Mingo Logan Coal Co. (Wharncliffe, WV) 93110
Mobil Mining & Minerals Compan (Ashland, VA) 90405
Southern Utah Fuel Co. Inc. (Roanoke, VA) 92193; 92194

1222 Bituminous Coal—Underground
Ashland Coal, Inc. (Huntington, WV) 92867
Coal-Mac, Inc. (Pikeville, KY) 69224
Dal-Tex Coal Co. (Sharples, WV) 93042
Hobert Mining, Inc. (Madison, WV) 92921
Mapco Inc. (Tulsa, OK) 78009
Mingo Logan Coal Co. (Wharncliffe, WV) 93110
Utah Fuel Co. Inc. (Roanoke, VA) 92196

1231 Anthracite Mining
National Mines Corp. (Wayland, KY) 69336

1241 Coal Mining Services
Cyprus Mountain Coals Corp. (Hazard, KY) 68424
Exxon Coal USA Inc. (Houston, TX) 86124

1311 Crude Petroleum & Natural Gas
Amerada Hess Corp. (Atlanta, GA) 64218
Amerada Hess Corp. (Des Allemads, LA) 69835
Amerada Hess Corp. (Lafayette, LA) 70040
Amerada Hess Corp. (Lockport, LA) 70194
Amerada Hess Corp. (Quitman, MS) 73311
Amerada Hess Corp. (Tulsa, OK) 77875
Amerada Hess Corp. (Midland, TX) 88019
Amerada Hess Corp. (Tomball, TX) 89766
Amerada Hess Corp. (White Oak, TX) 90052
Arco (Houston, TX) 85807
Arco Oil & Gas Co. (Vencie, LA) 70921
Arco Oil & Gas Co. (Magnolia, AR) 57328
Arco Oil & Gas Co. (Abbeville, LA) 69360; 69361
Arco Oil & Gas Co. (Amelia, LA) 69419
Arco Oil & Gas Co. (Crowley, LA) 69800
Arco Oil & Gas Co. (Lafayette, LA) 70042
Arco Oil & Gas Co. (Venice, LA) 70922
Arco Oil & Gas Co. (Woodward, OK) 78256
Arco Oil & Gas Co. (Andrews, TX) 82593
Arco Oil & Gas Co. (Dallas, TX) 83857
Arco Oil & Gas Co. (Denver City, TX) 84646
Arco Oil & Gas Co. (Gainesville, TX) 85419
Arco Oil & Gas Co. (Hemphill, TX) 85730
Arco Oil & Gas Co. (Henderson, TX) 85732
Arco Oil & Gas Co. (Ingleside, TX) 87303; 87304

Arco Oil & Gas Co. (Longview, TX) 87703
Arco Oil & Gas Co. (Midland, TX) 88020
Arco Oil & Gas Co. (Mirando City, TX) 88120
Arco Oil & Gas Co. (Odessa, TX) 88236
Arco Pipe Line Co. (Natchitoches, LA) 70399
Arco Pipe Line Co. (Gainesville, TX) 85420
Atlantic Richfield Co. (St. Landry, LA) 70868
Citgo Petroleum Corp. (Birmingham, AL) 55193
Citgo Petroleum Corp. (Chesapeake, VA) 90562
Citgo Petroleum Corp. (Richmond, VA) 91777; 91778
Coastal Natural Gas Co. (Houston, TX) 85976
Coastal Oil & Gas Corp. (Houston, TX) 85977
Columbia Gas Development Corp. (Houston, TX) 85986
Columbia Natural Resources Inc. (Charleston, WV) 92739
Dominion Resources Inc. (Richmond, VA) 91858
Enron Corp. (Houston, TX) 86062
Enron Liquid Fuels (Houston, TX) 86074
Enron Liquids Pipeline Group (Houston, TX) 86076
Enron Oil & Gas Co. Inc. (Houston, TX) 86078
Enron Oil & Gas Marketing Inc. (Houston, TX) 86079
Ensearch Corp. (Dallas, TX) 84010; 84011
Ensearch Exploration Partners Ltd. (Dallas, TX) 84013
Exxon Capital Holding Corp. (Irving, TX) 87341
Exxon Chemical Fertilizer Co. (Houston, TX) 86122
Exxon Co. (Charleston, WV) 92746
Exxon Co. USA (Baton Rouge, LA) 69527
Exxon Co. USA (Centerville, LA) 69760; 69761; 69762
Exxon Co. USA (Jackson, MS) 72983
Exxon Co. USA (Hennessey, OK) 77123
Exxon Co. USA (Baytown, TX) 83118; 83119
Exxon Co. USA (Conroe, TX) 83659
Exxon Co. USA (Gladewater, TX) 85580
Exxon Co. USA (Livingston, TX) 87685
Exxon Co. USA (Snyder, TX) 89445
Exxon Co. USA (Talco, TX) 89596
Exxon Co. USA (Tomball, TX) 89769
Exxon Corp. (Oklahoma City, OK) 77356
Exxon Corp. (Midland, TX) 88037
Exxon Corp. (Sundown, TX) 89567
Exxon Distributor (Vinemont, AL) 56703
Fina Inc. (Dallas, TX) 84064
Fina Oil & Chemical Co. (Dallas, TX) 84066
Inland Gas Co. Inc. (Ashland, KY) 68098
La Gloria Oil & Gas Co. Inc. (Bellaire, TX) 83265
Louisiana Land & Exploratio (Oklahoma City, OK) 77432
Marathon Oil Co. (Oklahoma City, OK) 77433; 77434
Marathon Oil Co. (Bay City, TX) 83102; 83103
Marathon Oil Co. (Iraan, TX) 87313; 87314
Marathon Oil Co. (Markham, TX) 87846; 87847

Marathon Oil Co. (Orange, TX) 88322; 88323
Mitchell Energy Corp. (Alba, TX) 82481
Mitchell Energy Corp. (Galveston, TX) 85455
Mitchell Energy Prod Corp. (Spring, TX) 89472
Mobil Alaska Pipeline Co. (Dallas, TX) 84238
Mobil Corp. (Fairfax, VA) 90797
Mobil Exploration & Producing Inc. (Premont, TX) 88698
Mobil Exploration & Producing US (Jayton, TX) 87437
Mobil Exploration & Producing US Inc. (Port Lavaca, TX) 88668
Mobil Explrn & Prdcng U S Inc. (Midland, TX) 88051
Mobil Explrn & Prdcng US Inc. (Houston, TX) 86586
Mobil Oil (Houma, LA) 69962
Mobil Oil Co. (Nacogdoches, TX) 88172
Mobil Oil Corp. (Cement, OK) 76912
Mobil Oil Corp. (Lindsay, OK) 77179
Mobil Oil Corp. (Thomas, OK) 77868
Mobil Oil Corp. (Avinger, TX) 83078
Mobil Oil Corp. (Dallas, TX) 84248
Mobil Oil Corp. (Highlands, TX) 85749
Mobil Oil Corp. (Kilgore, TX) 87492
Mobil Oil Corp. (Midland, TX) 88053
Mobil Oil Corp. Offshore Production (Cameron, LA) 69752
Mobil Oil Drilling Department (Jayton, TX) 87438
Mobil Oil Explor&Produc Se (Natchez, MS) 73203
Mobil Oil Exploring & Producing (Cameron, LA) 69753
Mobil Oil Exploring & Producing SE (Lake Charles, LA) 70150
Mobil Oil Hughes Station (Alex, OK) 76792
Mobil Oil Inc/E&P S (Kaplan, LA) 69991
Mobil Pipe Line (Andrews, TX) 82599
Mobil Prdcng. TX & New Mex Inc. (Wichita Falls, TX) 90084
Mobil Producing TX & New Mex (Andrews, TX) 82600
Mobil Producing TX & New Mex (Sunray, TX) 89572
Mobil Producing TX & NM (Kilgore, TX) 87494
Mobil Producing TX & NM Inc. (Taft, TX) 89595
Oryx Energy (Oklahoma City, OK) 77459
Pennzoil (Houston, TX) 86667
Pennzoil Co. (Baton Rouge, LA) 69595
Pennzoil Co. (Houma, LA) 69963
Pennzoil Co. (Midland, TX) 88065
Pennzoil Explor&Prod Co. (Corpus Christi, TX) 83746
Pennzoil Products Co. (Tinsley, MS) 73381
Petrocorp (Houston, TX) 86681
Quaker State Oil Refining Co. (Alma, WV) 92657
Scurlock Permian Corp. (Houston, TX) 86872
Shell Oil Co. (Morgan City, LA) 70393
Shell Oil Co. (New Orleans, LA) 70555
Shell Oil Co. (Edinburg, TX) 84737
Shell Oil Co. (El Paso, TX) 84927
Shell Oil Co. (Houston, TX) 86883
Shell Oil Co. (Kilgore, TX) 87498
Shell Pipeline Corp. (Montegut, LA) 70384; 70385
Shell Pipeline Corp. (Livingston, TX) 87691
Southland Royalty Co. (Midland, TX) 88079
Southland Royalty Co. (Novice, TX) 88233; 88234
Southland Royalty Co. Inc. (Houston, TX) 86903
Tesoro Petroleum Distribution Co. (Morgan City, LA) 70395
Texaco Inc. (Morgan City, LA) 70396
Texaco Inc. (Venice, LA) 70926
Texaco Inc. (Charlotte, NC) 74169
Texaco Inc. (Ardmore, OK) 76822
Texaco Inc. (Houston, TX) 87003
Texaco Incorporated (Kilgore, TX) 87500
Texaco Inc. (Kingsbury, TX) 87531
Texaco Inc. (Odem, TX) 88235
Texaco Inc. (Orla, TX) 88333
Texaco Inc. (Snyder, TX) 89453
Texaco Inc. (Sundown, TX) 89568
Texaco Inc. Prod Dept (Edinburg, TX) 84738
Texaco Inc. Prod Dept (Winnie, TX) 90124
Texaco Inc. Sales Office (Nashville, TN) 82106
Texaco Oil Co. (Guymon, OK) 77113
Texaco USA (Jackson, MS) 73075
Texaco USA (Houston, TX) 87010; 87011
Total Petroleum Inc. (Memphis, TN) 81712
Total Service Station (Memphis, TN) 81713
Trico Industries Inc. (Oklahoma City, OK) 77636
Union Oil Co. of California (Amelia, LA) 69423
Union Oil Co. of California (Oklahoma City, OK) 77640
Union Oil Co. of California (Pauls Valley, OK) 77694
Union Oil Co. of California (Andrews, TX) 82607
Union Oil Co. of California (Houston, TX) 87054
Union Oil Co. of California (Midland, TX) 88092
Union Oil Co. of California (Snyder, TX) 89454
Union Texas Petroleum (Baton Rouge, LA) 69679; 69680
Union Texas Petroleum Corp. (Noble, OK) 77246
Union Texas Petroleum Corp. (Oklahoma City, OK) 77643
Warren Petroleum Co. (Louisville, KY) 69036
Wingfoot Ventures Seven Inc. (Houston, TX) 87199

1321 Natural Gas Liquids

Arco Oil & Gas Co. (Dallas, TX) 83857
Enron Corp. (Houston, TX) 86062
Enron Gas Processing Co. (Houston, TX) 86069
Enron Gas Processing Co. Inc. (Houston, TX) 86070
Enserch Corp. (Dallas, TX) 84010; 84011
Mapco Inc. (Tulsa, OK) 78009
Marathon Oil Co. (Cotton Valley, LA) 69788; 69790
Mitchell Energy Prod Corp. (Spring, TX) 89472
Mobil Exploration & Prodcng (Midkiff, TX) 88017
Union Texas Petroleum (Haughton, LA) 69944
Warren Petroleum Co. (Marlow, OK) 77187

1381 Drilling Oil & Gas Wells

Atlas Wire Services (Houston, TX) 85824
Grace Energy Corp. (Dallas, TX) 84094
McCullough, an Atlas Wireline Service Operation (Houston, TX) 86528
Mitchell Energy Prod Corp. (Spring, TX) 89472
Quarles Drilling Corp. (Belle Chasse, LA) 69694
Quarles Drilling & Exploration, Inc. (Tulsa, OK) 78071
Southland Royalty Co. (Seiling, OK) 77802; 77803
Texaco Inc. (Enid, OK) 77071

1382 Oil & Gas Exploration Services

Aero Service Corp. (Houston, TX) 85765
Amerada Hess Corp. (Tulsa, OK) 77875
Arco Oil & Gas Co. (Lafayette, LA) 70042
Ashland Exploration, Inc. (Houston, TX) 85821
Citgo Petroleum Corp. (Houston, TX) 85956
Clereon Corp. (Houston, TX) 85963
Coastal Natural Gas Co. (Houston, TX) 85976
Columbia Gas Development Corp. (Houston, TX) 85986
Comdisco Resources Inc. (Tulsa, OK) 77921
Dominion Energy Inc. (Richmond, VA) 91848
Enron Oil & Gas Co. Inc. (Houston, TX) 86078
Enron Oil & Gas Marketing Inc. (Houston, TX) 86079
Enserch Exlporation Partners Ltd. (Dallas, TX) 84013
Exxon Capital Holding Corp. (Irving, TX) 87341
Exxon Co. USA (Hattiesburg, MS) 72889
Exxon Co. USA (Stigler, OK) 77830
Exxon Co. USA (Fort Stockton, TX) 85043; 85044
Halliburton Geophysical Services Inc. (Houston, TX) 86260; 86261
Halliburton Logging Services Inc. (Houston, TX) 86262
La Gloria Oil & Gas Co. Inc. (Bellaire, TX) 83265
Marathon Oil Co. (Sinton, TX) 89439; 89440
Marathon Petroleum Co. (Stephens, AR) 57659
Mitchell Energy Corp. (Fort Worth, TX) 85192
Mitchell Energy Prod Corp. (Spring, TX) 89472
Mobil Corp. (Fairfax, VA) 90797
Mobil Exploring & Producing US (Morgan City, LA) 70388
Mobil Oil Corp. (Chickasha, OK) 76932
Mobil Oil Corporation (Chickasha Ok, OK) 76942
Mobil Oil Corp. (Dayton, TX) 84522
Mobil Oil Exploration & Pro (Dallas, TX) 84249
Mobil Oil Exploring & Producing SE (Lake Charles, LA) 70150
Northern Mich Exploration Co. (Houston, TX) 86617
Oryx Energy Co. (Sabine Pass, TX) 88862
Pennzoil Producing Co. (Monroe, LA) 70365
Pennzoil Producing Co. (Tylertown, MS) 73430
Petrocorp (Houston, TX) 86681
Shell Oil (Freeport, TX) 85393
Shell Oil Co. (Mc Comb, MS) 73150
Shell Oil Co. (Yukon, OK) 78281
Shell Pipeline Corp. (Denver City, TX) 84648; 84649
Southland Royalty Co. (Oklahoma City, OK) 77558
Tenax Corp. (Oklahoma City, OK) 77599
Texaco Inc. (Lafayette, LA) 70114
Texaco Inc. (Paradis, LA) 70610
Texaco Inc. (Tulsa, OK) 78149
Texaco Inc. (Sweetwater, TX) 89593
Transco Exploration Co. (New Orleans, LA) 70580
Tredegar Industries Inc. (Richmond, VA) 92060
Trico Industries Inc. (Woodward, OK) 78268
Union Oil Co. of California (Houma, LA) 69973
Union Oil Co. of California (Oklahoma City, OK) 77641; 77642
Union Texas Petroleum Corp. (Oklahoma City, OK) 77644
Western Geophysical (Houston, TX) 87183
Western Geophysical Co. (Metairie, LA) 70334
Western Geophysical Co. (Woodward, OK) 78270
Western Geophysical Co. (Houston, TX) 87184
Western Geophysical Co. (Victoria, TX) 89914
Western Geophysical Co. Amer (Beeville, TX) 83263
Western Geophysical Co. Libr (Houston, TX) 87185

1389 Oil & Gas Field Services Nec

Arco Pipe Line Co. (Jacksboro, TX) 87420
Baker, Baker Hughes Process Equi. BJ-Titan Services Co. (Partnership) (Houston, TX) 85828
Baker Hughes Drilling Technologies Exlog Inc. (Houston, TX) 85832
Baker Hughes Inc. Baker Hughes Drilling Technologies Milpark Drilli Fluids (Houston, TX) 85838
Baker Hughes Prod. Tools Tri-State Oil Tools (Houston, TX) 85846
Diamond M Offshore, Inc. (Houston, TX) 86035
Downhole Seismic Services (Houston, TX) 86047
Exxon Co. USA (Andrews, TX) 82596; 82597
Exxon Co. USA (Forsan, TX) 85042
Exxon Co. USA (Robstown, TX) 88805
Grace Energy Corp. (Dallas, TX) 84094
Halliburton Co. Inc. (Dallas, TX) 84110
Halliburton Holdings Inc. (Dallas, TX) 84111
Halliburton Logging Services Inc. (Houston, TX) 86262
Marathon Oil Co. (Venice, LA) 70923; 70924
Mitchell Energy Corp. (Galveston, TX) 85455
Mitchell Energy Prod Corp. (Spring, TX) 89472
Nalco Chemical Co. (Guymon, OK) 77105
Oilfield Service Corp. of Am (Lafayette, LA) 70078
Oilfield Service Corp. Amer (Oklahoma City, OK) 77456
Oryx Energy Co. (Kermit, TX) 87469
Osca Inc. (Lafayette, LA) 70080
Pennzoil Co. (Abbeville, LA) 69362
Pennzoil Co. (Arnoldsburg, WV) 92665
Shell Oil Co. (Donaldsonville, LA) 69842
Shell Oil Co. (Nordheim, TX) 88230
Shell Oil Offshore Inc. (Golden Meadow, LA) 69889
Tesoro Petroleum Distribution Co. (Galveston, TX) 85469
Texaco Inc. (Drumright, OK) 76990
Texaco Inc. (Hull, TX) 87214
Texaco Inc. (Mount Vernon, TX) 88156
Texaco Inc. (Pecos, TX) 88498
Texaco Inc. Prod Dept (West Columbia, TX) 90047
Texaco Seismic Party (Victoria, TX) 89907
Total Petroleum Inc. (Healdton, OK) 77121; 77122
Trico Industries Inc. (Ira, TX) 87312
Trico Industries Inc. (Knox City, TX) 87538
Union Texas Petroleum (Westbrook, TX) 90050
Vista Energy Inc. (Lafayette, LA) 70122
Western Geophysical Co. (Gulfport, MS) 72883

1411 Dimension Stone

Martin Marietta Aggregates (Charlotte, NC) 74079
Martin Marietta Aggregates (West Columbia, SC) 80098

1422 Crushed & Broken Limestone

Agrico Chemical Co. (Union City, TN) 82381
American Limestone Co. Inc. (Knoxville, TN) 81139
American Limestone Co. Inc. (Pleasant View, TN) 82231
American Limestone Co. Inc. (Springfield, TN) 82354
American Limestone Co. Inc. (Watauga, TN) 82403
American Limestone Co. Inc. (Dallas, TX) 83847
Asarco Inc. (Mascot, TN) 81430
Harper Brothers, Inc. (Fort Myers, FL) 59703
Martin Marietta Aggregates (Leesburg, GA) 66549
Vulcan Materials Co. (Louisville., KY) 69045

1429 Crushed & Broken Stone Nec

American Limestone Co. Inc. (Springfield, TN) 82354
Martin Marietta Aggregates (Hickory, NC) 75088
Vulcan Materials Co. (Knoxville., TN) 81278
Vulcan Materials Co. (Nashville., TN) 82148
Vulcan Materials Co. (S. Pittsburg, TN) 82288
Vulcan Materials Co. (Sevierville., TN) 82299
Vulcan Materials Co. (Lawrenceville, VA) 91186; 91187
Vulcan Materials Co. (South Boston, VA) 92260; 92261
Vulcan Materials Co. (Springfield, VA) 92295; 92296
Vulcan Materials Co. (Stafford, VA) 92301
Vulcan Materials Corp. (Stafford, VA) 92304
Westvaco Corp. (Camden, TN) 80277

1442 Construction Sand & Gravel

American Limestone Co. Inc. (Watauga, TN) 82403
APAC Holdings, Inc. (Atlanta, GA) 64234

1455 Kaolin & Ball Clay

Cyprus Mines Corp. (Gleason, TN) 80860
Engelhard Corp. (Mc Intyre, GA) 66960
Engelhard Corp. McIntyre-Toddville Plant (McIntyre, GA) 66971
Engelhard Corp. Daveyville Plant (Mc Intyre, GA) 66961
Engelhard Corp. Dixie Mine (Toomsboro, GA) 67839
Engelhard Corp. Edgar Plant (Mc Intyre, GA) 66962
Engelhard Corp. Gardner Plant (Oconee, GA) 67217
Engelhard Corp. Gibraltar Mine (Toomsboro, GA) 67840
Engelhard Corp. Gordon Plant (Gordon, GA) 66307
Engelhard Corp. Klondyke Mine (Mc Intyre, GA) 66963
Engelhard Corp. Mcintyre-Edgars Plant (Mc Intyre, GA) 66964
Engelhard Corp. Toddville Plant (Mc Intyre, GA) 66965
Engelhard Corp. Washington Co. Mine (Deepstep, GA) 65913
Engelhard Kaolin Co. Griffin Mine (Dry Branch, GA) 66006
Engelhard Kaolin Co. Scott Mine (Deepstep, GA) 65914
Engelhard Kaolin Corp. Griffin Mine (Dry Branch, GA) 66007

1475 Phosphate Rock

Freeport-McMoran Inc. (New Orleans, LA) 70462
Freeport-McMoran Resource Partners (New Orleans, LA) 70464

1479 Chemical & Fertilizer Mining Nec

Exxon Corp. (Cookeville, TN) 80650
Freeport-McMoran Inc. (New Orleans, LA) 70462
Freeport-McMoran Resource Partners (New Orleans, LA) 70464

1481 Nonmetallic Minerals Services

Asarco Inc. (Washington, DC) 58128
US Gypsum Co. Inc. (Heflin, AL) 55866

1490 Miscellaneous Nonmetallic Minerals

ADM Milling (Knobel, AR) 57237

1499 Miscellaneous Nonmetallic Minerals

American Cyanamid Co. (Montezuma, GA) 66996
Asarco Inc. (Jefferson City, TN) 81020
Asarco Inc. (Maryville, TN) 81401
Asarco Inc. (New Market, TN) 82152; 82153
Baker Hughes Inc. Baker Hughes Drilling Technologies Milpark Drilli Fluids (Houston, TX) 85838
Harper Brothers, Inc. (Fort Myers, FL) 59703
Mobil Mining & Minerals (Houston, TX) 86590
Mobil Mining & Minerals Compan (Ashland, VA) 90405
US Gypsum Co. (Spruce Pine, NC) 76304

1521 Single-Family Housing Construction

Blount Inc. (Montgomery, AL) 56284
Browning-Ferris Industries (Lake Charles, LA) 70133
Builders Square (Casselberry, FL) 58930
Builders Square (Tulsa, OK) 77895

Builders Square (San Antonio, TX) 88939
Chase Home Mortgage Corp. (Jacksonville, FL) 60242
Cole Engineering Corp. (Clearwater, FL) 58989
Dolphin Construction Co. (Alexandria, LA) 69374
Dolphin Construction Co. Inc. (Melbourne, FL) 61052
Dow Chemical Co. Engineering & Construction Services Division (Houston, TX) 86046
Exxon Co. USA (Anahuac, TX) 82592
Exxon Pipeline Co. (Odessa, TX) 88242; 88243
First Alabama Bank (Huntsville, AL) 55924
First Federal S & L (Tyler, TX) 89801
Fleet Finance Inc. (Metairie, LA) 70263
Jim Walter Homes Inc. (Greenville, SC) 79373
Jim Walter Homes Inc. (Round Rock, TX) 88849
Jim Walter Homes Inc. (Newport News, VA) 91472
Kitchen Collection Inc. (Boaz, AL) 55469
Kroger (Savannah, GA) 67494
Lorillard Inc. (Tulsa, OK) 78002

Parker Properties (Mary Esther, FL) 61020

Pulte Home Corp. (Clg Pkwy, FL) 59064
Pulte Home Corp. (Tampa, FL) 63554; 63555; 63556; 63557
Pulte Home Corp. (Laurel, MD) 72083
Pulte Home Corp. (Grand Prairie, TX) 85633
Pulte Home Corp. (Houston, TX) 86722; 86725
Pulte Home Corp. (La Porte, TX) 87565; 87566
Pulte Home Corp. (Mesquite, TX) 87988
Pulte Home Corp. (Pearland, TX) 88488
Pulte Home Corp. (Sugar Land, TX) 89541
Pulte Home Corp. (Tomball, TX) 89776
Pulte Home Corp. (Woodbridge, VA) 92620

Sico Inc. (Ruston, LA) 70672
Structures Unlimited (Forest, VA) 90884

Willamette Industries Inc. (Irving, TX) 87416
Williams Brothers Engineering (Pensacola Fl, FL) 62493
Winchester Homes Inc. (Severna Park, MD) 72379

1522 Residential Construction Nec
Hudson's (Hendersonville, NC) 75042

1531 Operative Builders
Friendswood Development Co. (Houston, TX) 86212
Peco Inc. (Jupiter, FL) 60544

1541 Industrial Buildings & Warehouses
Blount Inc. (Montgomery, AL) 56284; 56285
Brown & Root Holdings Inc. (Houston, TX) 85892
Coast to Coast Welding & Fa (Flatwoods, KY) 68306
Dolphin Construction Co. (Alexandria, LA) 69373
Fischbach & Moore International Group (Dallas, TX) 84070
National Projects Inc. (Key West, FL) 60576
National Projects Inc. (Dallas, TX) 84259
Pulte Home Corp. (Matthews, NC) 75528
Sico Inc. (Tampa, FL) 63594; 63596

Superamerica Design & Const (Louisville, KY) 69011
U S Design (Tulsa, OK) 78183

1542 Nonresidential Construction Nec
Blount Inc. (Montgomery, AL) 56284; 56285
Brown & Root Holdings Inc. (Houston, TX) 85892
Enserch Corp. (Dallas, TX) 84011
Fischbach & Moore International Group (Dallas, TX) 84070
KMS Group (Columbia, MD) 71594
Radio Shack (Merritt is, FL) 61131
Structures Inc. (Baltimore, MD) 71315

1611 Highway & Street Construction
APAC Holdings, Inc. (Atlanta, GA) 64234
Blount Construction Co. Inc. (Atlanta, GA) 64329
Brown & Root Holdings Inc. (Houston, TX) 85892
Brown & Root Inc. (Houston, TX) 85893
Dolphin Construction Co. (Alexandria, LA) 69373
Halliburton Co. Inc. (Dallas, TX) 84110
Halliburton Holdings Inc. (Dallas, TX) 84111
Harper Brothers, Inc. (Fort Myers, FL) 59703
Marathon Petroleum (Louisville, KY) 68879

1622 Bridge, Tunnel & Elevated Highway
Halliburton Co. Inc. (Dallas, TX) 84110
Halliburton Holdings Inc. (Dallas, TX) 84111

1623 Water, Sewer & Utility Lines
Blount Inc. (Montgomery, AL) 56284
Colonial Pipeline Co. Inc. (Richmond, VA) 91782
Exxon Pipeline Co. (Franklin, LA) 69858; 69859
Raco Inc. (Gretna, VA) 91003
Transwestern Pipeline Co. (Perryton, TX) 88504
Walgreen Construction Co. in (Houston, TX) 87104

1629 Heavy Construction Nec
Blount Inc. (Montgomery, AL) 56284; 56285
Brown & Root Holdings Inc. (Houston, TX) 85892
Brown & Root Inc. (Houston, TX) 85893
Brown & Root Inc. Marine Fabrication Yard (Houston, TX) 85895
CBI Co. Ltd. (Houston, TX) 85938
Colonial Pipeline Co. (Chesapeake, VA) 90563
Duke/Fluor Daniel (Charlotte, NC) 73937
Enserch Corp. (Dallas, TX) 84010; 84011
FICON Corp. (Woodbridge, VA) 92612
Halliburton Co. Inc. (Dallas, TX) 84110
Halliburton Holdings Inc. (Dallas, TX) 84111
Harper Brothers, Inc. (Fort Myers, FL) 59703
Lockheed Corp. Austin Div. (Austin, TX) 82930
Summit Corp. (St. Albans, WV) 93070

1711 Plumbing, Heating & Air-Conditioning
Ace Hardware (Greenville, NC) 74945
Blount Inc. (Montgomery, AL) 56284
FICON Corp. (Woodbridge, VA) 92612
Fischbach & Moore International Corp. (Dallas, TX) 84069
Fischbach & Moore International Group (Dallas, TX) 84070

Johnson Controls Inc. (Mobile, AL) 56190
Johnson Controls Inc. (Shreveport, LA) 70734; 70735
Johnson Controls Inc. (Jackson, MS) 72993
Johnson Controls Inc. (Carrollton, TX) 83476
Lone Star Gas Co. (Denton, TX) 84620
Lone Star Gas Co. (Wichita Falls, TX) 90080
May Supply Co. (Beaumont, TX) 83176

Stewart & Stevenson Services (Austin, TX) 83007
Taylor Rental Corp. (Altamonte Springs, FL) 58564

Trane Co. (Mobile, AL) 56250
Trane Co. (Jessup, MD) 71986
Wilsons (Durham, NC) 74442

1721 Painting & Paper Hanging
Flour City Architectural (Johnson City, TN) 81037
Tandy Signs (Arlington, TX) 82764

1731 Electrical Work
Diebold Inc. (Fort Smith, AR) 57047
Diebold, Inc. (Oklahoma City, OK) 77345
Dolphin Construction (Dallas, TX) 83981
Ecco (Lynchburg, VA) 91234
FICON Corp. (Woodbridge, VA) 92612
Fischbach & Moore International Corp. (Dallas, TX) 84069
Fischbach & Moore International Group (Dallas, TX) 84070
Magnetek Universal Electric (Grand Praire, TX) 85604
PPG Industries Inc. (Norfolk, VA) 91566
Tektronix Inc. (Fort Lauderdale, FL) 59617
Trylon Corp. Inc. (San Marcos, TX) 89344
Union Electric Co. (Maryville, TN) 81424; 81425
Union Electric Co. Inc. (Sandston, VA) 92234
West Texas Utilities Co. (Roby, TX) 88811

1741 Masonry & Other Stonework
Avon Corp. (Springfield, VA) 92273

1742 Plastering, Drywall & Insulation
Ball Corp. (North Charleston, SC) 79744
Lapp Insulator Co. (Birmingham, AL) 55305
Owens Corning Fiberglas (Mobile, AL) 56217
Owens Corning Fiberglas Cor (W Palm Beach, FL) 63798
Owens Corning Fiberglas Cor (Raleigh, NC) 55934
Owens Corning Fiberglass Co. (Shreveport, LA) 70759
Owens Corning Fiberglass Co. (Houston, TX) 86632
Specialty Products (Tampa, FL) 63601
Texaco USA Marketing (Wichita Falls, TX) 90114

1751 Carpentry Work
Maison Blanche Home Improve (Metairie, LA) 70291

1761 Roofing, Siding & Sheet Metal Work
AMR Co. (Chattanooga, TN) 80297
Charter Co. (Brenham, TX) 83334

1791 Structural Steel Erection
AMR Co. (Chattanooga, TN) 80297
CBI Co. Ltd. (Houston, TX) 85937
Mobil Steel Corp. (Houston, TX) 86603

1793 Glass & Glazing Work
PPG Industries (Hunt Valley, MD) 71944
Ppg Industries Inc. (Orlando, FL) 62100
PPG Industries Inc. (Nashville, TN) 82084
PPG Industries Inc. (Salem, VA) 92222

1796 Installing Building Equipment Nec
Dover Elevator International Inc. (Memphis, TN) 81513
Otis Elevator Co. (Huntsville, AL) 55983
Otis Elevator Co. (Montgomery, AL) 56359
Otis Elevator Co. (Sheffield, AL) 56554
Otis Elevator Co. (Daytona Beach, FL) 59195
Otis Elevator Co. (Fort Myers, FL) 59728
Otis Elevator Co. (Miami, FL) 61384; 61385
Otis Elevator Co. (Pensacola, FL) 62453
Otis Elevator Co. (Savannah, GA) 67502
Otis Elevator Co. (Ocean City, MD) 72163
Otis Elevator Co. (Long Beach, MS) 73118
Otis Elevator Co. (Wilmington, NC) 76584
Otis Elevator Co. (Columbia, SC) 79058
Otis Elevator Co. (Nashville, TN) 82074
Otis Elevator Co. (Austin, TX) 82949
Otis Elevator Co. (Dallas, TX) 84286; 84287
Otis Elevator Co. (El Paso, TX) 84861
Otis Elevator Co. (Odessa, TX) 88259
Otis Elevator Co. (Wichita Falls, TX) 90085
Otis Elevator Co. (Clarksburg, WV) 92814
Otis Elevator Co. Inc. (San Antonio, TX) 89121
Otis Elevator Co. Inc. (Chesapeake, VA) 90590

1799 Special Trade Contractors Nec
Blount Inc. (Montgomery, AL) 56284
Ceramic Cooling Tower Co. (Fort Worth, TX) 85079
Coast to Coast Fence Co. (Fort Myers, FL) 59691
Lone Star Lead Construction Co. Inc. (Houston, TX) 86494

2000 Food & Kindred Products
American General Finance Inc. (Martinsville, VA) 91340; 91341
Campbell Soup Co. Chestertown Plant (Chestertown, MD) 71519
Carolina Coca-Cola Bottling Co. (Sumter, SC) 80013
Champlin Refining Co. (Corpus Christi, TX) 83709
Chick-N-Quick (Rogers, AR) 57560
Coca-Cola Bottling Co. of South Arkansas (Monticello, AR) 57373
Conagra Foodservice Companies (Birmingham, AL) 55208
Conangra Poultry Co. (Dalton, GA) 65779
Farm Fresh Catfish Co. (Hollandale, MS) 72904
Fayetteville Freezer (Fayetteville, AR) 56977
Geo. A. Hormel & Co. (Oklahoma City, OK) 77374
Gold Kist Inc. Poultry (Boaz, AL) 55467

Golden Poultry Co. (Douglas, GA) 65968
Hudson Foods Inc. (Springdale, AR) 57635
Jim Dandy Co. Inc. (Decatur, AL) 55593
Life Savers Inc. (Las Piedras, PR) 78483
Pilgrim's Pride Corp. (De Queen, AR) 56893
Pilgrim's Pride Corp. (Dallas, TX) 84306
Pilgrim's Pride Corp. (Lufkin, TX) 87812
Pilgrims Pride Corp. (Mount Pleasant, TX) 88149
Quaker Oats Co. (Jackson, TN) 80999
Rudys Farm Co. (Nashville, TN) 82091
Rudys Farm Co. (Newbern, TN) 82156
Seaboard Farms of Canton Inc. (Canton, GA) 65487
Tyson Distribution Center (Rogers, AR) 57571
Tyson Food Chick'n Quick (Rogers, AR) 57572
Tyson Foods (Shelbyville, TN) 82319
Tyson Foods of Bentonville (Bentonville, AR) 56790
Tyson Foods Inc. (Ashland, AL) 55032; 55033
Tyson Foods Inc. (Clarksville, AR) 56853
Tyson Foods Inc. (North Little Rock, AR) 57478
Tyson Foods Inc. (Springdale, AR) 57650
Tyson Foods Inc. (Van Buren, AR) 57696
Tyson Foods Inc. (Waldron, AR) 57703
Tyson Foods Inc. (Broken Bow, OK) 76896
Tyson Foods Inc. (Shelbyville, TN) 82321
Tyson Foods Inc. (Carthage, TX) 83523
Tyson Foods Inc. of Bentonville (Bentonville, AR) 56792
Tyson Foods Inc. of Berryville (Berryville, AR) 56800
Tyson Foods Inc. Berryville of Berryville (Berryville, AR) 56801
Tyson Foods Inc. Bloountsville Plant (Blountsville, AL) 55465
Tyson Foods Inc. Krispy Kitchens (Bentonville, AR) 56793
Tyson Foods Inc. Seguin Plant (Seguin, TX) 89379
Tyson Foods Inc. Tyler Road Plant (Russellville, AR) 57594
Tyson Garrett Plant (Rogers, AR) 57574
Tyson of Nashville (Nashville, AR) 57445

2010 Meat Products
Holly Farms Foods Inc. (Wilkesboro, NC) 76508
Holly Farms Foods Inc. Temperanceville Plant (Temperanceville, VA) 92380
Smithfield Packing Co. Inc. (Norfolk, VA) 91584

2011 Meat Packing Plants
Armour Food Co. (Louisville, KY) 68692
Bryan Foods Inc. (West Point, MS) 73479
Esskay (Baltimore, MD) 71114
Flavorland Beef (Amarillo, TX) 82547
Gold Kist Inc. (Atlanta, GA) 64511
Gwaltney of Smithfield Ltd. (Portsmouth, VA) 91658
Gwaltney of Smithfield Ltd. (Smithfield, VA) 92238
Hillshire Farm & Kahn's Co. (Alexandria, KY) 68078
IBP Inc. (Amarillo, TX) 82554
Monfort Beef Dumas Plant Fka-Sipco-D-B-A (Cactus, TX) 83430
Monfort Inc. (Louisville, KY) 68889
Montgomery Food Processing Inc. (Montgomery, AL) 56356
Peyton Packing Co. (El Paso, TX) 84874
Peyton Packing Co. Inc. (El Paso, TX) 84875
Rudys Farm (Florence, AL) 55744
Sara Lee Sausage Newbern Facility (Newbern, TN) 82157
Smithfield Ham Products (Smithfield, VA) 92242
Smithfield Packing Co. (Kinston, NC) 75329

Smithfield Packing Co. (Wilson, NC) 76643
Smithfield Packing Co. (Norfolk, VA) 91583
Smithfield Packing Co. (Smithfield, VA) 92243
Smithfield Packing Co. Inc. (Kinston, NC) 75330
Smithfield Packing Co. Inc. (Smithfield, VA) 92244
Swift Independent Packing Co. (Nashville, TN) 82105
Tyson Foods Inc. was Tysons Foods Inc. (Springdale, AR) 57655
Valleydale Inc. (Salem, VA) 92225
Wilson Foods Corp. (Shreveport, LA) 70807
Wilson Foods Corp. (Wilson, NC) 76654
Wilson Foods Corp. (Oklahoma City, OK) 77665; 77666; 77667

2013 Sausages & Other Prepared Meats

Albertson's Wholesale Meats (Oklahoma City, OK) 77295
Bryan Foods Inc. (West Point, MS) 73477; 73478
Buring Foods (Memphis, TN) 81486
Circle T Foods Co. Inc. (Dallas, TX) 83911
Dean Sausage Co. (Attalla, AL) 55054
Decker Food Co. (San Antonio, TX) 88964
Design Foods (Fort Worth, TX) 85100
Gold Kist Inc. Poultry Division (Athens, GA) 64168
Gold Kist Inc. Poultry Division (Atlanta, GA) 64512
Golden West Foods, Inc. (Bedford, VA) 90423
Hormel Foods Corp. (Oklahoma City, OK) 77386
Hormel Foods Corp. (Houston, TX) 86287
Oscar Mayer Foods Corp. (Goodlettsville, TN) 80870
Oscar Mayer Foods Corp. (Sherman, TX) 89415
Pet Inc. Dairy (Portsmouth, VA) 91663
Peyton Packing Co. (El Paso, TX) 84874
Pilgrim's Pride Corp. (Pittsburg, TX) 88520
Powell Valley Foods Co. (Caryville, TN) 80280
Quick-To-Fix Foods (Garland, TX) 85526
Sara Lee Sausage Newbern Facility (Newbern, TN) 82157
Smithfield Ham Products (Smithfield, VA) 92242
Smoky Hollow Foods (Little Rock, AR) 57312
Star-Kist Foods, Inc. (Newport, KY) 69145
Sweet Sue Kitchens Inc. (Athens, AL) 55048
Thorn Apple Valley Inc. Carolina Div. (Holly Ridge, NC) 75191
Tyson Foods Inc. (Quik-To-Fix) (Garland, TX) 85546
Tyson Foods Inc. was Tysons Foods Inc. (Springdale, AR) 57655
Wampler Long Acre Inc. (Broadway, VA) 90495
Wampler Longacre Inc. (Harrisonburg, VA) 91107
Wampler Longacre Inc. (Henton, VA) 91116
Wampler Longacre Inc. (Stanley, VA) 92307
Wampler Longacre Inc. (Timberville, VA) 92384
Wampler Longacre Inc. (Moore Field, WV) 92941
Wilson Brands Corp. (Birmingham, AL) 55458
Wilson Brands Corp. (Oklahoma City, OK) 77664

2015 Poultry Slaughtering & Processing

Borden City Foods, Inc. (Fort Smith, AR) 57032
Campbell Soup Co. Swanson Div. (Fayetteville, AR) 56971
Carolina Golden Products Co. (Sumpter, SC) 79998
Conagra Broiler Co. (Enterprise, AL) 55681
Conagra Broiler Co. (El Dorado, AR) 56930
Conagra Broiler Co. (Dalton, GA) 65777
Conagra Broiler Co. (Gainesville, GA) 66270; 66271
Conagra Broiler Co. (Farmerville, LA) 69851
Conagra Broiler Co. (Natchitoches, LA) 70400
Conagra Broiler Co. Arcadia Div. (Arcadia, LA) 69427
Conagra Broiler Co. Hurlock Processing Plant (Hurlock, MD) 71950
Conagra Broiler Co. Milford Processing Plant (Milford, DE) 57842
Conagra Frozen Foods Processing Plant (Batesville, AR) 56749
Gold Kist Inc. (Atlanta, GA) 64511
Gold Kist Inc. Poultry (Guntersville, AL) 55827
Gold Kist Inc. Poultry (Trussville, AL) 56628
Gold Kist Inc. Poultry (Live Oak, FL) 60912
Gold Kist Inc. Poultry (Athens, GA) 64169
Gold Kist Inc. Poultry (Carrollton, GA) 65495
Gold Kist Inc. Poultry (Ellijay, GA) 66170
Golden Poultry Co. (Russellville, AL) 56507
Golden Poultry Co. (Sanford, NC) 76195
Golden Poultry Co. Inc. (Atlanta, GA) 64515
Holly Farms Foods Inc. Cooked Products Plant (Wilkesboro, NC) 76510
Holly Farms Foods Inc. Seguin Plant (New Berlin, TX) 88199
Holly Farms Foods Inc. Tyson Foods Pretreatment Plant (Wilkesboro, NC) 76511
Holly Farms Foods Inc. Tyson Foods Processing Plant (Monroe, NC) 75578
Holly Farms Foods Inc. Waste Water Treatment Plant (Glen Allen, VA) 90982
Holly Farms Foods Inc. Wastewater Processing Plant (Harrisonburg, VA) 91092
Holly Farms of Texas Inc. Nacogdoches Mill (Nacogdoches, TX) 88168
Holly Farms/Tyson Foods Inc. Pre-Treatment Plant (Wilkesboro, NC) 76512
Holly Farms/Tyson Foods Inc. Processing Plant (Wilkesboro, NC) 76513
Holly Farms/Tyson Foods Inc. Processing Plant (Center, TX) 83538
Holly Farms/Tyson Foods Inc. Tyson Foods Inc. (Temperanceville, VA) 92381
Holly Farms/Tyson Foods Inc. Tyson Foods Pretreatment Plant (Wilkesboro, NC) 76514
Holly Farms/Tyson Foods Inc. Tyson Foods Processing Plant (Monroe, NC) 75579
Holly Farms/Tyson Foods Inc. Waste Water Treatment (Wilkesboro, NC) 76515
Hudson Foods Inc. (Albertville, AL) 54967
Joseph Campbell Co. (Douglas, GA) 65970
Louis Rich Co. (Newberry, SC) 79727
Pet Poultry Products Inc. (Bridgeville, DE) 57754
Pilgrim's Pride Corp. Dallas Processing (Dallas, TX) 84307
Pilgrim's Pride Corp. Dequeen Processing (De Queen, AR) 56894
Pilgrim's Pride Corp. East Processing Plant (Mount Pleasant, TX) 88150
Pilgrim's Pride Corp. Lufkin Processing (Lufkin, TX) 87813
Pilgrim's Pride Corp. West Processing Plant (Mount Pleasant, TX) 88153
Pilgrim's Pride Corp. Prepared Foods (Mount Pleasant, TX) 88154
Rockingham Poultry Inc. (Stanley, VA) 92306
Rockingham Poultry Inc. (Timberville, VA) 92383
Rockingham Poultry Inc. (Moorefield, WV) 92942
Seaboard Farms of Athens Inc. Processing Plant (Athens, GA) 64177
Seaboard Farms of Canton Inc. Feedmill (Canton, GA) 65488
Seaboard Farms of Chattanooga Inc. (Chattanooga, TN) 80487
Seaboard Farms of Chattanooga Inc. Processing Plant (Chattanooga, TN) 80488
Seaboard Farms of KY Inc. (Hickory, KY) 68462
Tyson Food Service (Wilkesboro, NC) 76521
Tyson Foods (Boaz, AL) 55478
Tyson Foods (Waldron, AR) 57701
Tyson Foods Bloomer Plant (Charleston, AR) 56845
Tyson Foods Cornish Cornish Plant (Springdale, AR) 57646
Tyson Foods Inc. (Ashland, AL) 55034
Tyson Foods, Inc. (Blountsville, AL) 55464
Tyson Foods Inc. (Gadsden, AL) 55793
Tyson Foods Inc. (Heflin, AL) 55863; 55864
Tyson Foods Inc. (Oxford, AL) 56440
Tyson Foods Inc. (Bentonville, AR) 56791
Tyson Foods Inc. (Berryville, AR) 56799
Tyson Foods Inc. (Clarksville, AR) 56854
Tyson Foods Inc. (Dardanelle, AR) 56889
Tyson Foods Inc. (Fayetteville, AR) 56997
Tyson Foods Inc. (Fort Smith, AR) 57111
Tyson Foods Inc. (Grannis, AR) 57121
Tyson Foods, Inc. (Green Forest, AR) 57122
Tyson Foods Inc. (Nashville, AR) 57443
Tyson Foods Inc. (Paris, AR) 57503
Tyson Foods Inc. (Pine Bluff, AR) 57533; 57534
Tyson Foods Inc. (Rogers, AR) 57573
Tyson Foods Inc. (Springdale, AR) 57648; 57649
Tyson Foods Inc. (Van Buren, AR) 57697
Tyson Foods Inc. (Waldron, AR) 57702; 57704
Tyson Foods Inc. (Ball Ground, GA) 65377
Tyson Foods Inc. (Cumming, GA) 65751
Tyson Foods Inc. (Snow Hills, MD) 72453
Tyson Foods Inc. (Monroe, NC) 75594
Tyson Foods Inc. (Wilkesboro, NC) 76522
Tyson Foods Inc. (Broken Bow, OK) 76895
Tyson Foods Inc. (Shelbyville, TN) 82320; 82322
Tyson Foods Inc. (Carthage, TX) 83524
Tyson Foods Inc. (Sequin, TX) 89387
Tyson Foods Inc. (Crewe, VA) 90669
Tyson Foods Inc. (Glen Allen, VA) 90985
Tyson Foods Inc. (Harrisonburg, VA) 91101
Tyson Foods Inc. (Temperanceville, VA) 92382
Tyson Foods Inc. Cooked Products Div. (Wilkesboro, NC) 76523
Tyson Foods, Inc.- Berry St. Plant (Springdale, AR) 57653
Tyson Foods Inc. Broken Bow Processing (Broken Bow, OK) 76897
Tyson Foods Inc. Dardanelle Complex (Dardanelle, AR) 56890
Tyson Foods Inc. Gadsden Processing Plant (Gadsden, AL) 55794
Tyson Foods Inc. N. Litle Rock Plant (North Little Rock, AR) 57479
Tyson Foods Inc. Pine Bluff Further Processing (Pine Bluff, AR) 57537
Tyson Foods Inc. Processing Plant (Carthage, TX) 83525
Tyson Foods Inc. Shenandoah Valley Complex (Harrisonburg, VA) 91102
Tyson Foods Inc. Tyler Rd. Plant (Russellville, AR) 57593
Tyson Foods Inc. (was Tysons Foods Inc.) (Springdale, AR) 57655
Tyson Foods Inc. Wastewater Treatment Plant (Harrisonburg, VA) 91103
Tyson/Holly Farms Foods Inc. Waste Water Treatment Plant (Glen Allen, VA) 90986
Tyson & ORG Holly Farms Inc. (Center, TX) 83543
Tyson's Chick'n Quick (Rogers, AR) 57575
Tyson's & ORG Rogers (Rogers, AR) 57576
Wampler-Longacre Turkey Inc. (Harrisonburg, VA) 91109
Wampler-Longacre Turkey Inc. (Hinton, VA) 91145

2021 Creamery Butter

Borden Inc. (Oklahoma City, OK) 77309
Borden Inc. (San Antonio, TX) 88931
Borden Inc. Dairy (Strasburg, VA) 92348; 92349

2022 Cheese—Natural & Processed

Borden Inc. (Dallas, TX) 83884
Borden Inc. (Suplhur Springs, TX) 89575
Gandy's Dairies (San Angelo, TX) 88875
Kraft General Foods Inc. (Lawrenceburg, KY) 68507
Kraft Inc. (Bentonville, AR) 56786
Kraft USA Fayetteville (Fayetteville, TN) 80797
Mid-America Dairymen Inc. (Schulenburg, TX) 89352
Price's Creameries (El Paso, TX) 84895

2023 Dry, Condensed & Evaporated Dairy Products

Armour Dairy & Food Oils Co. (Springfield, KY) 69300
Armour Food Ingredients Co. (Springfield, KY) 69301
Bell Dairy Products Inc. (Lubbock, TX) 87748
Borden Inc. (Jackson, MS) 72951
Borden Inc. (Starkville, MS) 73361
Borden Inc. (Chester, SC) 78931
Borden Inc. (Corpus Christi, TX) 83703
Borden Inc. Dairy (Strasburg, VA) 92348; 92349
Borden Inc. Grocery (Starkville, MS) 73362
Borden Inc. Grocery & Specialty Products (Starkville, MS) 73363
Borden Inc. Meadow Gold Dairy (Tulsa, OK) 77890
Pet, Inc. (Greeneville, TN) 80887
Price's Creameries (El Paso, TX) 84895
Ross Laboratories (Altavista, VA) 90252

2024 Ice Cream & Frozen Desserts

Bell Dairy Products Inc. (Lubbock, TX) 87748
Borden Inc. (Augusta, GA) 65315
Borden Inc. (Macon, GA) 66675
Borden Inc. (Baton Rouge, LA) 69474
Borden Inc. (Lake Charles, LA) 70132
Borden Inc. (Biloxi, MS) 72615
Borden Inc. (Jackson, MS) 72951
Borden Inc. (Oklahoma City, OK) 77309
Borden Inc. (Amarillo, TX) 82526
Borden Inc. (El Paso, TX) 84771
Borden Inc. (Fort Worth, TX) 85071
Borden Inc. (Garland, TX) 85480
Borden Inc. (Houston, TX) 85885
Borden Inc. (San Antonio, TX) 88931
Borden Inc. (Texarkana, TX) 89668
Borden Inc. (Waco, TX) 89930
Borden Inc. (Charleston, WV) 92725
Borden Inc. Dairy (Miami, FL) 61205; 61206
Borden Inc. Dairy (Tampa, FL) 63367; 63368
Borden Inc. Dairy (Tupelo, MS) 73386; 73387
Borden Inc. Dairy (High Point, NC) 75113; 75114
Borden Inc. Dairy (Greenville, SC) 79305; 79306
Borden Inc. Dairy (Amarillo, TX) 82527; 82530
Borden Inc. Dairy Div. (Miami, FL) 61207
Borden Inc. Dairy Division (Dothan, AL) 55626
Borden Inc. Dairy Division (Orlando, FL) 61939
Borden Inc. Grocery & Specialty Products (Tupelo, MS) 73388
Borden Inc. Meadow Gold Dairy (Tulsa, OK) 77890
Borden Inc. Dairy (Dothan, AL) 55627
Borden Inc. Diary (Dothan, AL) 55628
Borden Inc. Diary (Nashville, TN) 81907
Borden Inc. Grocery & Speciality Prds. (Miami, FL) 61208
Borden Inc. Grocery & Specialty Prds. (Nashville, TN) 81908
Borden Inc. Grocery & Specialty Products (Nashville, TN) 81909
Borden Inc. Refrigerated Products (Dothan, AL) 55629
Borden Milk & Ice Cream (Shreveport, LA) 70692
Borden Milk & Ice Cream (Tupelo, MS) 73389
Borden Superior Dairies Inc. (Austin, TX) 82831
Dean Milk Co. (Louisville, KY) 68741
Gandy's Dairies (San Angelo, TX) 88875
Gandy's Dairies Inc. (San Angelo, TX) 88876
Gilt Edge Farms (Norman, OK) 77253
Kraft General Foods (Charlotte, NC) 74062
Kraft General Foods Frozen Foods Div. (Richmond, VA) 91913
Kraft General Foods Frozen Products (Charlotte, NC) 74063
Kraft General Foods Inc. Frozen Dairy Group (Memphis, TN) 81634
Kraft General Foods Inc. National Dairy Products Corp. (Richmond, VA) 91914
Lakeland Indl. Center & Bakery & Bakery (Lakeland, FL) 60742
T. G. Lee Foods (Fort Myers, FL) 59715
T. G. Lee Foods (Orlando, FL) 62033
Mantecados Nevada (Bayamon, PR) 78339
Mayfield Dairy Farms Inc. (Marietta, GA) 66831
Mayfield Dairy Farms Inc. (Athens, TN) 80190; 80191
Mayfield Dairy Farms Inc. (Concord Farragut, TN) 80641
McArthur Dairy Inc. (Ft. Lauderdale, FL) 59854
Meadow Gold Dairy (Dothan, AL) 55656
Meadow Gold Dairy (Huntsville, AL) 55974
Meadow Gold Dairy (Lexington, KY) 68578
Meadow Gold Dairy (Nashville, TN) 82062
National Dairy Products Corp. (Charlotte, NC) 74087
Oak Farms Inc. (Houston, TX) 86626
Pet Dairy (Hickory, NC) 75092
Pet Inc. Pet Dairy Group (Greenville, SC) 79402
Price's Creameries (El Paso, TX) 84895
Publix Deerfield Beach Facility (Deerfield Beach, FL) 59284
Vandervoort Dairy Foods Co. (Fort Worth, TX) 85345
Vandervoort's (Fort Worth, TX) 85346

2026 Fluid Milk

Associated Milk Producers Inc. (San Antonio, TX) 88918
Bell Dairy Products Inc. (Lubbock, TX) 87748
Borden Inc. (Augusta, GA) 65315
Borden Inc. (Macon, GA) 66675
Borden Inc. (Baton Rouge, LA) 69474
Borden Inc. (Lafayette, LA) 70044
Borden Inc. (Jackson, MS) 72951
Borden Inc. (Meridian, MS) 73160
Borden Inc. (Oklahoma City, OK) 77309
Borden Inc. (Amarillo, TX) 82526
Borden Inc. (Corpus Christi, TX) 83703
Borden Inc. (Dallas, TX) 83884
Borden Inc. (El Paso, TX) 84771
Borden Inc. (Houston, TX) 85885
Borden Inc. (Lubbock, TX) 87749
Borden Inc. (San Antonio, TX) 88931
Borden Inc. (Suplhur Springs, TX) 89575
Borden Inc. (Texarkana, TX) 89668
Borden Inc. (Tyler, TX) 89792

Borden Inc. Dairy (Gadsden, AL) 55774; 55775
Borden Inc. Dairy (Huntsville, AL) 55892; 55893
Borden Inc. Dairy (Tuscaloosa, AL) 56635; 56636
Borden Inc. Dairy (Asher, AR) 56730
Borden Inc. Dairy (Little Rock, AR) 57260
Borden Inc. Dairy (Miami, FL) 61205; 61206
Borden Inc. Dairy (Pennsacola, FL) 62375
Borden Inc. Dairy (Macon, GA) 66676; 66677
Borden Inc. Dairy (Lexington, KY) 68528; 68529
Borden Inc. Dairy (Baton Rouge, LA) 69475
Borden Inc. Dairy (Lafayette, LA) 70045; 70046
Borden Inc. Dairy (High Point, NC) 75113; 75114
Borden Inc. Dairy (Oklahoma City, OK) 77310; 77311
Borden Inc. Dairy (Nashville, TN) 81905; 81906
Borden Inc. Dairy (Amarillo, TX) 82528; 82529
Borden Inc. Dairy (Austin, TX) 82828; 82829
Borden Inc. Dairy (Corpus Christi, TX) 83704
Borden Inc. Dairy (Dallas, TX) 83885
Borden Inc. Dairy (Houston, TX) 85886
Borden Inc. Dairy (San Antonio, TX) 88932; 88933
Borden Inc. Dairy (Sulphur Springs, TX) 89553
Borden Inc. Dairy (Strasburg, VA) 92348; 92349
Borden Inc. Dairy Div. (Miami, FL) 61207
Borden Inc. Dairy Div. (Metairie, LA) 70254
Borden Inc. Dairy Division (Jackson, MS) 72952
Borden Inc. Grocery Division (Sulphur Springs, TX) 89554
Borden Inc. Grocery & Specialty Products (Little Rock, AR) 57261
Borden Inc. Grocery & Specialty Products (Macon, GA) 66678
Borden Inc. Grocery & Specialty Products (Corpus Christi, TX) 83705
Borden Inc. Grocery & Specialty Products (San Antonio, TX) 88934
Borden Inc. Meadow Gold Dairy (Tulsa, OK) 77890
Borden Inc. Dairy (Gadsden, AL) 55776
Borden Inc. Dairy (Monroe, LA) 70350
Borden Inc. Dairy (Jackson, MS) 72953
Borden Inc. Grocery & Speciality (Austin, TX) 82830
Borden Inc. Grocery & Speciality Prds. (Miami, FL) 61208
Borden Inc. Grocery & Speciality Prds. (Baton Rouge, LA) 69476
Borden Inc. Grocery & Speciality Prds. (Dallas, TX) 83888
Borden Inc. Grocery & Specialty Products (Conroe, TX) 83653
Borden Inc. Grocery & Specialty Products (Oklahoma City, OK) 77312
Borden Inc. Valley Bell Dairy (Charleston, WV) 92726
Borden Milk & Ice Cream (Tupelo, MS) 73389
Dean Foods Co. (Louisville, KY) 68740
Dean Foods Co. (Memphis, TN) 81501
Dean Milk Co. (Louisville, KY) 68741
Gandy's Dairies (San Angelo, TX) 88875
Gandy's Dairies Inc. (San Angelo, TX) 88876
Giant Food (Landover, MD) 72020
Giant Food Dairy (Landover, MD) 72021
Gilt Edge Farms (Norman, OK) 77253
Gilt Edge Farms Inc. (Norman, OK) 77254
Harts Dairy (Fort Myers, FL) 59704
Heritage Farms Dairy (Murfreesboro, TN) 81851
Lakeland Indl. Center & Bakery & Bakery (Lakeland, FL) 60742
T. G. Lee Foods (Fort Myers, FL) 59715
T. G. Lee Foods (Orlando, FL) 62033
T. G. Lee Lifestyle (Orange City, FL) 61874
Mayfield Dairy Farms Inc. (Athens, TN) 80190; 80191
McArthur Dairy, Inc. (Miami, FL) 61370
Meadow Gold Dairy (Huntsville, AL) 55974
Meadow Gold Dairy Inc. (Tulsa, OK) 78019
Meadow Gold Dairy Products (Gadsden, AL) 55785
Meadowland Creamery (Conroe, TX) 83668
Pet Dairy (Charlotte, NC) 74105
Publix Deerfield Beach Facility (Deerfield Beach, FL) 59284
Ryan Milk Co. (Murray, KY) 69129; 69130; 69131
Ryan Milk Co. Inc. (Murray, KY) 69133
T. G. Lee Foods Inc. (Orange City, FL) 61875
T. G. Lee Foods Inc. (Orlando, FL) 62151; 62152
T.G. Lee Foods Inc. (Orange City, FL) 61876
T.G. Lee Foods Inc. (Orlando, FL) 62164
Vandervoort (Fort Worth, TX) 85344
Vandervoort Dairy Foods Co. (Fort Worth, TX) 85345
Vandervoort's (Fort Worth, TX) 85346
Westover Dairy (Lynchburg, VA) 91292
Winchester Farms Dairy (Winchester, KY) 69356

2032 Canned Specialties

American Home Food Prods, Inc. (Fort Worth, TX) 85062
American Home Food Products Inc. (Fort Worth, TX) 85063
Campbell Soup Co. (Maxton, NC) 75534
Campbell Soup Co. (Paris, TX) 88363
Crestar Food Products Inc. (Irving, TX) 87337
Del Monte Corp. (Cambridge, MD) 71485
Hershey Chocolate USA (Savannah, GA) 67485
Hormel Foods Corp. (Tucker, GA) 67857
Lucks, Inc. (Seagrove, NC) 76215
Mountain Pass Canning (Anthony, TX) 82617
Old El Paso Foods Mountain Pass Canning (Anthony, TX) 82619
Pet Inc. Mountain Pass Canning (Anthony, TX) 82620
Quaker Oats Co. (Dallas, TX) 84326
Sweet Sue Kitchens (Athens, AL) 55047
Tyson Foods Inc. was Tysons Foods Inc. (Springdale, AR) 57655
Wolf Brand Products Inc. (Corsicana, TX) 83798

2033 Canned Fruits & Vegetables

Aunt Nellie's Farm Kitchens (Covington, KY) 68214
Bama Food Products (Birmingham, AL) 55158
Best Foods Caribbean Inc. (San Juan, PR) 78576
Borden Inc. (Macon, GA) 66675
Borden Inc. (Lafayette, LA) 70044
Borden Inc. (Suplhur Springs, TX) 89575
Borden Inc. (Texarkana, TX) 89668
Borden Inc. Foodservice (Jackson, MS) 72954
Cal-Compack Foods (Vinton, TX) 89923
Campbell Soup Co. Texas Inc. (Paris, TX) 88364
Casere Foods Inc. (Barceloneta, PR) 78326
Coca-Cola Foods Auburndale Facility (Auburndale, FL) 58594
Coca-Cola Foods Food Service Group (Dunedin, FL) 59357
Coca-Cola Foods Plymouth Chilled Juice (Plymouth, FL) 62573
CPC Foodservice (Asheboro, NC) 73583
Del Monte Corp. (Crystal City, TX) 83817
Del Monte Foods Plant No. 250 (Crystal City, TX) 83818
Del Monte Foods Plants 250 & 255 (Crystal City, TX) 83820
Industrias La Famosa (Toa Baja, PR) 78611
Juice Bowl Products Inc. (Lakeland, FL) 60737
Kraft Inc. (Decatur, GA) 65841
Kraft Inc. (Garland, TX) 85498
T. G. Lee Foods (Orange City, FL) 61873
Lucks, Inc. (Seagrove, NC) 76215
Mccormick & Co. Inc. Food Service Div. (Cockeysville, MD) 71551
Meadow Gold Dairy (Huntsville, AL) 55974
Meadow Gold Dairy Products (Gadsden, AL) 55785
Mountain Pass Canning Co. (Anthony, TX) 82618
Ocean Spray Cranberries Inc. (Sulphur Springs, TX) 89559; 89560
Pet, Inc. (Greeneville, TN) 80887
PYA Monarch Inc. (Greenville, SC) 79411
Quaker Oats Co. (Newport, TN) 82170
Rio Grande Foods (McAllen, TX) 87940
Smithfield Ham Products (Smithfield, VA) 92242
Stilwell Foods Inc. (Stilwell, OK) 77851
Tropicana Products Inc. (Bradenton, FL) 58853
Tyson Foods Inc. (Berryville, AR) 56799

2034 Dehydrated Fruits, Vegetables & Soups

Golden Peanut Co. (Anadarko, OK) 76802; 76804
Tyson Foods Inc. (Fort Smith, AR) 57110

2035 Pickles, Sauces & Salad Dressings

Atkins Pickle Co. (Atkins, AR) 56731
Bama Food Products (Birmingham, AL) 55158
Best Foods Caribbean Inc. (San Juan, PR) 78576
Borden Inc. Foodservice (Jackson, MS) 72954
C. F. Sauer Co. Inc. (Richmond, VA) 91748
Campbell Soup Co. Chestertown Plant (Chestertown, MD) 71518
Cates Charles F. & Sons Inc. (Faison, NC) 74513
Charles F. Cates & Son Inc. (Faison, NC) 74514
Charles F. Cates & Sons (Faison, NC) 74515
Crestar Food Products Inc. (Irving, TX) 87337
Flavorite Labs. Inc. (Horn Lake, MS) 72915
Green Bay Food Co. (Atkins, AR) 56733
Green Bay Food Co. Atkins Plant (Atkins, AR) 56734
Kraft General Foods Inc. (Decatur, GA) 65840
Kraft Inc. (Decatur, GA) 65841
Kraft Inc. (Garland, TX) 85498
McCormick & Co. Inc. Flavor Group (Hunt Valley, MD) 71930; 71931
Mccormick & Co. Inc. Food Service Div. (Cockeysville, MD) 71551
McCormick & Co. Inc. Hunt Valley Condiment Plant (Cockeysville, MD) 71552
Mountain Pass Canning Co. (Anthony, TX) 82618
Ocean Spray Cranberries Inc. (Sulphur Springs, TX) 89559
Pilgrim Farms, Inc. (Sanford, FL) 62770
Portion Pac, Inc. (Dallas, TX) 84321
W. B. Roddenbery Co., Inc. (Cairo, GA) 65450
W. B. Roddenbery Co., Inc. Pickle Division (Cairo, GA) 65452
Specialty Food Products (Jackson, MS) 73066
Vlasic Foods (Greenville, MS) 72825
Vlasic Foods Inc. (Millsboro, DE) 57850; 57851
Vlasic Foods Inc. (Greenville, MS) 72826; 72827

2037 Frozen Fruits & Vegetables

Ardmore Farms Inc. (De Land, FL) 59246
Citrus Hill Manufacturing Co. (Frostproof, FL) 59845
Citrus Hill Mfg. Co. (Frostproof, FL) 59846
Coca-Cola Foods Auburndale (Auburndale, FL) 58593
Coca-Cola Foods Auburndale Facility (Auburndale, FL) 58594
Coca-Cola Foods Food Service Group (Dunedin, FL) 59357
Coca-Cola Foods Leesburg (Leesburg, FL) 60882
Coca-Cola Plymouth (Plymouth, FL) 62575
Dean Foods Vegetable Co. (Uvalde, TX) 89849
Juice Bowl Products Inc. (Lakeland, FL) 60737
Larsen Co. Dba Frio Foods (Uvalde, TX) 89853
Pet Inc. Frozen Foods Div. (Chickasha, OK) 76935
Rio Grande Foods Inc. (Mc Allen, TX) 87897

2038 Frozen Specialties Nec

All American Gourmet Co. Inc. (Atlanta, GA) 64216
Bagel Bites (Fort Myers, FL) 59662
Campbell Soup Co. (Pocomoke City, MD) 72218
Campbell Soup Co. (Salisbury, MD) 72337; 72338; 72339
Campbell Soup Co. (Sumter, SC) 80011
Campbell Soup Co. Swanson Div. (Fayetteville, AR) 56971
Campbell Soup Co. (Sumter Plant) (Sumter, SC) 80012
Conagra Frozen Foods Cooking Plant (Batesville, AR) 56745
Eagle Crest Foods, Inc. (Dallas, TX) 83995
Eagle Crest Inc. (Dallas, TX) 83996
Flowers Baking Co. (Fountain Inn, SC) 79246
Golden West Foods, Inc. (Bedford, VA) 90423
Grocery USA (Chickasha, OK) 76926
Heinz Bakery Products (Vinita, OK) 78224
Kim Products (Clarksville, AR) 56848
Pet, Inc. (Lithonia, GA) 66602
Pet, Inc. (Chickasha, OK) 76934
Pet Inc. Frozen Foods Div. (Chickasha, OK) 76935
Pet Inc. Grocery Operations (Lithonia, GA) 66603
Quaker Oats Co. (Jackson, TN) 80998
Rio Grande Foods (McAllen, TX) 87940
Stilwell Foods Inc. (Stilwell, OK) 77851
Stokely USA Inc. (Mc Allen, TX) 87900
Thomas' Frozen Foods Inc. (Frederick, MD) 71750
Tyson Foods Inc. (Garland, TX) 85545
Tyson Foods Inc. Entree Div. (Fayetteville, AR) 56999
Tyson's Chick'n Quick (Rogers, AR) 57575
Tyson's of Fayetteville Entree (Fayetteville, AR) 57000

2041 Flour & Other Grain Mill Products

ADM Miling Co. (Crowley, LA) 69799
ADM Milling Co. (Charlottte, NC) 74232
Adm Milling Harvest Queen Mill & Elevator Div. (Plainview, TX) 88523
ADM Milling Co. (Destrehan, LA) 69836
ADM Milling Co. (Enid, OK) 77042
ADM Milling Co. (Chatanooga, TN) 80291
ADM Milling Co. (Cleveland, TN) 80563
Adm Milling Co. Harvest Queen Mill & Elevator Div. (Plainview, TX) 88524
Adm Milling Co. Interstate Div. (Charlotte, NC) 73827
Archer Daniels Midland (Destrehan, LA) 69837
Archer Daniels Midland Co. (Kershaw, SC) 79547
Crestar Food Products Inc. (Brentwood, TN) 80223
Farmland Industries Grain Div. (Enid, OK) 77049
General Mills Inc. (Johnson City, TN) 81043
Harvest Queen Mill & Elevator Co. (Plainview, TX) 88529
Hi-Tek Polymers Inc. Vernon Plant (Vernon, TX) 89865
Rhone-Poulenc Inc. Rhone-Poulenc Specialty Chemicals Div. (Vernon, TX) 89870
Universal Foods Corp. (Baltimore, MD) 71318

2043 Cereal Breakfast Foods

Gold Kist Inc. Agri-Service Feed Mill (Flowery Branch, GA) 66218

2044 Rice Milling

ADM Miling Co. (Crowley, LA) 69799
ADM Milling Co. (Weiner, AR) 57712
Corning Grain Drying Co. (Delaplaine, AR) 56903
Riceland Foods Inc. (Dumas, AR) 56914
Riceland Foods Inc. (Jonesboro, AR) 57229
Ring Around Prdts Inc. (East Bernard, TX) 84725
Southern Cotton Oil Co. (North Little Rock, AR) 57473
Southern Cotton Oil Co. Inc. (North Little Rock, AR) 57475

2045 Prepared Flour Mixes & Doughs

Conagra Flour Mill (Macon, GA) 66681
Merico Inc. (Forest Park, GA) 66243
Procter & Gamble Mfg. Co. (Jackson, TN) 80997

2046 Wet Corn Milling

ADM Milling Co. (Cleveland, TN) 80563
Corn Products (Winston-Salem, NC) 76722
Corn Products Winston-Salem Plant (Winston-Salem, NC) 76723
Harvest Queen Mill & Elevator Co. (Plainview, TX) 88529

2047 Dog & Cat Food

Delight Prods. Co. (Springfield, TN) 82355
Heinz Pet Prods. (Biloxi, MS) 72618; 72619
Heinz Pet Prods. (Pascagoula, MS) 73257
Heinz Pet Products (Biloxi, MS) 72620; 72621
Heinz Pet Products (Pascagoula, MS) 73258
Hill's Pet Nutrition Inc. (Bowling Green, KY) 68144
Hills Pet Products (Bowling Green, KY) 68145
Jim Dandy Co. Inc. (Decatur, AL) 55593
Pet Specialties Inc. (Hanceville, AL) 55851
Ralston Purina Co. (Fairburn, GA) 66181
Ralston Purina Co. (Edmond, OK) 77016
River Valley By-Products (Scranton, AR) 57598; 57599
Star Kist Caribe Inc. (Mayaguez, PR) 78513; 78514
Tyson Foods Inc. (Shelbyville, TN) 82320; 82321
Tyson Foods Inc. Cornish Plant-Protein (Springdale, AR) 57654

2048 Prepared Feeds Nec

ADM Milling Co. (Enid, OK) 77042
ADM Milling Co. (Chatanooga, TN) 80291
Archer Daniels Midland Co. (Sweetwater, TX) 89581
Carolina Golden Products Feed Mill (Sumter, SC) 80014
Central Soya Co. Inc. (Tifton, GA) 67819
Central Soya Co. Inc. (Chattanooga, TN) 80338
Central Soya Del Norte Inc. (Hatillo, PR) 78446; 78447
Central Soya Feed Co. Inc. (Tifton, GA) 67820
Central Soya Feed Co. Inc. (Orangeburg, SC) 79770
Conagra Broiler (El Dorado, AR) 56929
Conagra Broiler Co. (El Dorado, AR) 56931

Conagra Broiler Co. (Many, LA) 70219
Conagra Broiler Co. Arcadia Feedmill (Arcadia, LA) 69428
Conagra Broiler Co. Feed Mill (Hurlock, MD) 71949
Conagra Broiler Co. Feedmill (Choudrant, LA) 69777; 69778
Conagra Feed Mill (Enterprise, AL) 55682
Conagra Feed Mill (Tunnel Hill, GA) 67910
Conagra Frozen Foods (Atkins, AR) 56732
Conagra Frozen Foods Cooking Plant (Batesville, AR) 56746
Conagra Frozen Foods Feed Mill (Batesville, AR) 56747
Conagra Frozen Foods Feedmill (Batesville, AR) 56748
Coors Biotech Inc. (Winchester, KY) 69342
Farmland Industries Inc. (Chickasha, OK) 76924
Farr Better Feeds (Guymon, OK) 77102
Farr Better Feeds (Hereford, TX) 85741
Gold Kist Inc. Feed Mill (Jasper, AL) 56086
Gold Kist Inc. Feed Mill (Live Oak, FL) 60911
Gold Kist Inc. Feed Mill (Calhoun, GA) 65465
Gold Kist Inc. Feed Mill (Cartersville, GA) 65501
Gold Kist Inc. Feed Mill (Commerce, GA) 65660
Gold Kist Inc. Feed Mill (Flowery Branch, GA) 66219
Gold Kist Inc. Feed Mill (Valdosta, GA) 67959
Gold Kist Inc. Poultry Feed Mill (Guntersville, AL) 55828
Golden Peanut Co. (DeLeon, TX) 84590
Golden Poultry (Bonlee, NC) 73706
Golden Poultry Co. (Bonlee, NC) 73707
Golden Poultry Co. Feedmill (Tuscumbia, AL) 56683
Golden Poultry Feed Mill (Bonlee, NC) 73708
H. J. Baker & Bro. Inc. (Fort Smith, AR) 57054
Holly Farms Foods Inc. (Roaring River, NC) 76048
Holly Farms Foods Inc. (Jetersville, VA) 91173
Holly Farms Foods Inc. Monroe Plant (Monroe, NC) 75577
Holly Farms Foods Inc. New Market Feed Mill (New Market, VA) 91442
Holly Farms Foods Inc. Roaring River Mill (Roaring River, NC) 76049
Holly Farms Foods, Inc.-Snow Hill Feed Mill (Snow Hill, MD) 72452
Holly Farms Foods Inc. Tyson Foods Inc. Feed Mill (Gonzales, TX) 85587
Holly Farms of Texas Nacogdoches Feed Mill (Nacogdoches, TX) 88167
Holly Farms of Texas, Inc. Gonzales Feed Mill (Gonzales, TX) 85588
Holly Farms/Tyson Foods Inc. Roaring River Feed Mill (Roaring River, NC) 76050
Hudson Farms Inc. (Albertville, AL) 54966
Hudson Foods Inc. Feedmill (Westville, OK) 78246
IMC Fertilizer Inc. New Wales Operation (Mulberry, FL) 61574
Jim Beam Brands Co. (Boston, KY) 68129
Jim Beam Brands Co. (Clermont, KY) 68203
Nutri Basics Co. (Chattanooga, TN) 80457
Pilgrim's Pride Corp. Hope Feed Mill (Hope, AR) 57158
Pilgrim's Pride Corp. Nacogdoches Feed Nill (Nacogdoches, TX) 88174
Pilgrim's Pride Corp. Nashville Feed Mill (Nashville, AR) 57440
Pilgrim's Pride Corp. Pittsburg Feed Mill (Pittsburg, TX) 88521
Precision Microblenders Inc. (Ciales, PR) 78390
Rhone Poulenc Inc. (Vernon, TX) 89869
Rhone-Poulenc Inc. Rhone-Poulenc Specialty Chemicals Div. (Vernon, TX) 89870
River Valley By-Products (Scranton, AR) 57598; 57599
Roaring River Feed Mill Holly Farms Foods/Tyson Foods Inc. (Roaring River, NC) 76051
Seaboard Farms of Athens Inc. Feed Mill (Athens, GA) 64176
Seaboard Farms of Chattanooga Inc. (Chattanooga, TN) 80486
Seaboard Farms of KY Inc. (Mayfield, KY) 69081
Southern Cotton Oil Co. (Quann, TX) 88703
Southern Cotton Oil Co. INc. (Sweetwater, TX) 89591
Southern Cotton Oil Co. Inc. (Quanah, TX) 88701
Southern States Co-Op. Inc. (Harrisonburg, VA) 91100
Southern States Co-Op. Inc. Feed Div. (Park City, KY) 69221
Southern States Co-Op. Inc. Feed Div. (Baltimore, MD) 71310
Southern States Co-Op. Inc. Barber Feed Mill (Barber, NC) 73661
Southern States Co-Op Inc. Feed Mill (Winchester, KY) 69355
Southern States Co-Op. Inc. Feed Mill (Durham, NC) 74429
Southern States Co-Op. Inc. Feed Mill (Farmville, NC) 74522
Southern States Co-Op. Inc. Richmond Feed Mill (Richmond, VA) 92044
Southern States Co-Op. Inc. Roanoke Feed Mill (Vinton, VA) 92427
Star Kist Caribe Inc. (Mayaguez, PR) 78513; 78514
Tyson E. Feed Mill (Springdale, AR) 57645
Tyson Feed Mill (Attalla, AL) 55058
Tyson Feed Mill (Cullman, AL) 55553
Tyson Feed Mill (Estill Springs, TN) 80777
Tyson Feed Mills (Roaring River, NC) 76052
Tyson Fods Inc. (Cullman, AL) 55554
Tyson Foods (Waldron, AR) 57701
Tyson Foods Feed Mill (Springdale, AR) 57647
Tyson Foods Feed Mill (Gonzales, TX) 85592
Tyson Foods Inc. (Oxford, AL) 56440; 56441
Tyson Foods Inc. (Clarksville, AR) 56853
Tyson Foods Inc. (Dardanelle, AR) 56889
Tyson Foods Inc. (Fort Smith, AR) 57111
Tyson Foods Inc. (Paris, AR) 57501; 57502; 57503
Tyson Foods Inc. (Springdale, AR) 57648
Tyson Foods Inc. (Waldron, AR) 57703
Tyson Foods Inc. (Ball Ground, GA) 65378
Tyson Foods Inc. (Snow Hills, MD) 72453
Tyson Foods Inc. (Sequin, TX) 89387
Tyson Foods Inc. Bergman Feed Mill (Bergman, AR) 56798
Tyson Foods Inc. Cornish Plant-Protein (Springdale, AR) 57654
Tyson Foods Inc. Craig Feed Mill (Broken Bow, OK) 76898
Tyson Foods Inc. Dardanelle Complex (Dardanelle, AR) 56890
Tyson Foods Inc. Feed Mill (Pine Bluff, AR) 57535
Tyson Foods Inc. Feed Mill (New Market, VA) 91443; 91444
Tyson Foods Inc. Feedmill (Tenaha, TX) 89656
Tyson Foods Inc. Gonzales Feed Mill (Gonzales, TX) 85593; 85594
Tyson Foods Inc. Nacogdoches Mill (Nacogdoches, TX) 88176
Tyson Foods Inc. Nashville Feed Mill (Nashville, AR) 57444
Tyson Foods Inc. Pine Bluff Feed Mill (Pine Bluff, AR) 57536
Tyson Foods Inc. Tyson Feed Mill (Cullman, AL) 55555
Tyson Johnson Rd. Mill (Springdale, AR) 57657
Tyson & ORG Holly Farms Inc. (Center, TX) 83543
W. R. Grace & Co. Farr Better Feeds (Guymon, OK) 77118
Wampler Foods Inc. (Harrisonburg, VA) 91106
Wampler Foods Inc. (Hinton, VA) 91144
Wampler-Longacre Turkey Inc. (Harrisonburg, VA) 91108
Zeagen Inc. (Winchester, KY) 69357

2051 Bread, Cake & Related Products

Anheuser-Busch Inc. Earth Grains Div. (Fort Payne, AL) 55755
Anheuser-Busch Inc. Earth Grains Div. (Paris, TX) 88360
Atlanta Baking Co., Inc. (Atlanta, GA) 64242
Bama Pies (Tulsa, OK) 77884
Betts Baking Co. (Dallas, TX) 83880
Bunny Bread Co. (New Orleans, LA) 70436
Colonial Baking Co. (Dallas, TX) 83925
European Bakers, Ltd. (Tucker, GA) 67854
Flowers Baking Co. (Montgomery, AL) 56336
Flowers Baking Co. (Opelika, AL) 56417
Flowers Baking Co. (Jacksonville, FL) 60304
Flowers Baking Co. (Miami, FL) 61312
Flowers Baking Co. (Orlando, FL) 61987
Flowers Baking Co. (Thomasville, GA) 67794
Flowers Baking Co. (Baton Rouge, LA) 69536
Flowers Baking Co. (Jamestown, NC) 75238
Flowers Baking Co. (Fountain Inn, SC) 79246
Flowers Baking Co. (Spartanburg, SC) 79904
Flowers Baking Co. (Morristown, TN) 81798
Flowers Baking Co. (Tyler, TX) 89802
Flowers Baking Co. (Big Stone Gap, VA) 90433
Flowers Baking Co. (Lynchburg, VA) 91246
Flowers Baking Co. (Norfolk, VA) 91530
Flowers Baking Co. (Warsaw, VA) 92529
Flowers Baking Co. (Bluefield, WV) 92700
Flowers Baking Co. of Chatanooga Inc. (Crossville, TN) 80701
Flowers Baking Co. of S.C., Inc. (Spartanburg, SC) 79905
Flowers Distributing Co. (Baton Rouge, LA) 69538
Flowers Holding Co. of South Carolina Inc. (Thomasville, GA) 67796
Flowers Snack of Tennessee Inc. (Crossville, TN) 80702
Flowers Specialty Baked Foods (Tucker, GA) 67856
Flowers Specialty Foods Inc. (Montgomery, AL) 56338
Flowers Thrift & Distribution (Hixson, TN) 80933
Fort Howard Cup Corp. (Owings Mills, MD) 72187
Griffin Pie Co. (London, KY) 68660
Griffin Pie Co. Inc. (London, KY) 68661
Hardin's Bakery (Tuscaloosa, AL) 56657
Huval Bakeries Inc. (Lafayette, LA) 70062
Kilpatrick's Bakeries, Inc. (Dallas, TX) 84173
Kroger Co. Inc. (Houston, TX) 86408
Lakeland Indl. Center & Bakery & Bakery (Lakeland, FL) 60742
Liqui Dri Foods Inc. (Louisville, KY) 68868
Manor Baking Co. (Dallas, TX) 84215
Pet Bakery (Rome, GA) 67346
Pet Inc. (Atlanta, GA) 65011
Pet Inc. (Federalsburg, MD) 71683
Protein Technologies International (Pryor, OK) 77745
Rainbo Baking Co. (Dallas, TX) 84349
Schott's Bakery (Stafford, TX) 89505
Schott's Bakery Inc. (Houston, TX) 86871
Stilwell Foods Inc. (Stilwell, OK) 77851
Tyson Mexican Original (Sanford, NC) 76207

2052 Cookies & Crackers

Holsum Bakers of Puerto Rico (Toa Baja, PR) 78609
Lakeland Indl. Center & Bakery & Bakery (Lakeland, FL) 60742
Nabisco Biscuit Co. (Richmond, VA) 91933
Nabisco Brands Inc. (Atlanta, GA) 64740
Nabisco Inc. Nabisco Biscuit Co. (Houston, TX) 86607
Procter & Gamble Mfg. Co. (Jackson, TN) 80997

2053 Frozen Bakery Products Except Bread

Mrs. Smith's Frozen Foods (Atlanta, GA) 64735
Mrs. Smith's Frozen Foods Co. (Atlanta, GA) 64736
Mrs. Smith's Frozen Foods Co. (Rossville, TN) 82285
Sara Lee Bakery (Forest, MS) 72777
Sara Lee Bakery (Tarboro, NC) 76365

2061 Raw Cane Sugar

Raceland Sugars Inc. (Raceland, LA) 70655
Supreme Sugar Co., Inc. (Labadieville, LA) 70032; 70033
Supreme Sugar Co., Inc. (Metairie, LA) 70312
Valhi, Inc. (Dallas, TX) 84484

2062 Cane Sugar Refining

Colonial Sugars Inc. (Gramercy, LA) 69894; 69895; 69896; 69897
Everglades Sugar Refinery Inc. (Clewiston, FL) 59059
Savannah Sugar Refinery (Port Wentworth, GA) 67276
Supreme Sugar Co. (New Orleans, LA) 70562
Supreme Sugar Co. Inc. (Labadieville, LA) 70033; 70034; 70035
Supreme Sugar Co., Inc. (New Orleans, LA) 70564
Valhi, Inc. (Dallas, TX) 84484

2063 Beet Sugar

Holly Sugar Corp. Hereford Factory (Hereford, TX) 85742
Valhi, Inc. (Dallas, TX) 84484

2064 Candy & Other Confectionery Products

Golden Peanut Co. (Aulander, NC) 73644
Golden Peanut Co. (DeLeon, TX) 84590; 84591
Golden Peanut Co. (Suffolk, VA) 92369
Kraft Inc. (Garland, TX) 85498
Planters Lifesavers Co. (Suffolk, VA) 92371

2067 Chewing Gum

Life Savers Mfg. Inc. (Las Piedras, PR) 78484
William Wrigley Co. (Flowery Branch, GA) 66221

2068 Salted & Roasted Nuts & Seeds

Eagle Snacks Inc. (Robersonville, NC) 76054
Golden Peanut Co. (Ozark, AL) 56444
Golden Peanut Co. (Cordele, GA) 65711
Golden Peanut Co. (Aulander, NC) 73644
Golden Peanut Co. (De Leon, TX) 84528
Golden Peanut Co. (DeLeon, TX) 84590
Planters Lifesavers Co. (Suffolk, VA) 92371

2074 Cottonseed Oil Mills

Archer Daniels Southern Cotton Oil Co. (North Little Rock, AR) 57453
Archer Daniels Midland Co. (Little Rock, AR) 57251
Archer Daniels Midland Co. (Sweetwater, TX) 89581
Levelland Vegetable Oil (Levelland, TX) 87638
Procter & Gamble Oilseed Products Co. (Levelland, TX) 87640
Southern Cotton Oil (Montgomery, AL) 56380
Southern Cotton Oil Co. (North Little Rock, AR) 57473; 57474
Southern Cotton Oil Co. (Memphis, TN) 81697; 81698
Southern Cotton Oil Co. (Ft. Worth, TX) 85416
Southern Cotton Oil Co. (Levelland, TX) 87642
Southern Cotton Oil Co. (Quann, TX) 88703
Southern Cotton Oil Co. (Richmond, TX) 88797
Southern Cotton Oil Co. (Thorndale, TX) 89759
Southern Cotton Oil Co. Inc. (North Little Rock, AR) 57475
Southern Cotton Oil Co. Inc. (Memphis, TN) 81699
Southern Cotton Oil Co. Inc. (Levelland, TX) 87643
Southern Cotton Oil Co. Inc. (Lubbock, TX) 87781
Southern Cotton Oil Co. Inc. (Quanah, TX) 88701
Southern Cotton Oil Co. Inc. (Richmond, TX) 88798

2075 Soybean Oil Mills

ADM Co. (Clarksdale, MS) 72665
Archer Daniels Southern Cotton Oil Co. (North Little Rock, AR) 57453
Archer Daniels Midland Co. (Little Rock, AR) 57250; 57251
Archer Daniels Midland Co. (Augusta, GA) 65314
Archer Daniels Midland Co. (Macon, GA) 66651
Archer Daniels Midland Co. (Valdosta, GA) 67941; 67942
Archer Daniels Midland Co. (Clarksdale, MS) 72667
Archer Daniels Midland Co. (Kershaw, SC) 79547
Archer Daniels Midland Co. (Adm) (Clarksdale, MS) 72668
Central Soya Co. Inc. (Chattanooga, TN) 80338
Protein Tech. International International (Pryor, OK) 77743
Protein Tech. International International (Memphis, TN) 81674
Protein Technologies International (Louisville, KY) 68984
Protein Technologies International (Pryor, OK) 77744
Protein Technologies International (Memphis, TN) 81675
Riceland Foods Inc. (Dumas, AR) 56914
Riceland Foods Inc. (Jonesboro, AR) 57229
Riceland Foods Inc. Soybean Plant (Stuttgart, AR) 57668
Riceland Foods Soybean Plant (Stuttgart, AR) 57669
Southern Cotton Oil Co. (North Little Rock, AR) 57474
Southern Cotton Oil Co. Inc. (North Little Rock, AR) 57475
Southern Cotton Oil Co. Inc. (Memphis, TN) 81699

2076 Vegetable Oil Mills Nec

Archer Daniels Midland Co. (Augusta, GA) 65314
Golden Peanut (Dothan, AL) 55651
Golden Peanut Co. (Atlanta, GA) 64513
Golden Peanut Co. (Camilla, GA) 65479; 65480
Golden Peanut Co. (Suffolk, VA) 92369
Golden Peanuts Co. (Atlanta, GA) 64514
River Valley By-Products (Scranton, AR) 57599
Southern Cotton Oil Co. Inc. (Quanah, TX) 88701
Southern Cotton Oil Co. Inc. (Richmond, TX) 88798

2077 Animal & Marine Fats & Oils

Carolina Golden Products Co. (Sumpter, SC) 79998
Conagra Broiler Co. (Enterprise, AL) 55681
Conagra Broiler Co. (El Dorado, AR) 56930
Conagra Broiler Co. (Farmerville, LA) 69851
Conagra Broiler Co. (Natchitoches, LA) 70400
Conagra Broiler Co. Arcadia Div. (Arcadia, LA) 69427
Gold Kist Inc. By-Products Plant (Ball Ground, GA) 65376

Gold Kist Inc. Poultry (Trussville, AL) 56628
Gold Kist Inc. Poultry (Live Oak, FL) 60912
IBP Inc. (Amarillo, TX) 82554
Pilgrim's Pride Corp. Protein Conversion (Mount Pleasant, TX) 88151
Pilgrim's Pride Corp. Wastewater Treatment (Mount Pleasant, TX) 88152
River Valley By-Products (Scranton, AR) 57598
Tyson Foods Inc. (Harmony, NC) 75006
Tyson Foods Inc. Cornish Plant-Protein (Springdale, AR) 57654

2079 Edible Fats & Oils Nec

Archer Daniels Midland Co. (Augusta, GA) 65314
Beatrice/Hunt-Wesson Inc. Savannah Refinery (Savannah, GA) 67455
C. F. Sauer Co. Inc. (Richmond, VA) 91748
Dean Foods Co. (Richmond, VA) 91839
Dean Foods Co. (Sandston, VA) 92230
Hi-Tek Polymers Inc. Vernon Plant (Vernon, TX) 89865
Hunt-Wesson, Inc. (Memphis, TN) 81628
Hunt-Wesson Inc. Savannah Refinery (Savannah, GA) 67488
Kraft Food Ingredients Corp. (Sherman, TX) 89404; 89405
Kraft General Foods Inc. (Decatur, GA) 65840
Kraft Inc. (Decatur, GA) 65841
Kraft Inc. (Garland, TX) 85498
Levelland Vegetable Oil (Levelland, TX) 87638
Procter & Gamble Mfg. Co. (Jackson, TN) 80997
Procter & Gamble Oilseed Products Co. (Levelland, TX) 87640
Riceland Foods Inc. (Dumas, AR) 56914
Riceland Foods Inc. (Jonesboro, AR) 57229
Southern Cotton Oil Co. (Levelland, TX) 87642
Southern Cotton Oil Co. INc. (Sweetwater, TX) 89591
Southern Cotton Oil Co. Inc. (Levelland, TX) 87643
Southren Cotton Oil Co. (Sweetwater, TX) 89592
Wesson/Peter Pan Foods Co. (Memphis, TN) 81756

2080 Beverages

Coca-Cola (Auburndale, FL) 58591
Coca-Cola Foods (Auburndale, FL) 58592
Coca-Cola Foods (Leesburg, FL) 60881
Coca-Cola Foods Foodservice Product Group (Dunedin, FL) 59358
Coca-Cola Foods Plymouth (Plymouth, FL) 62572
Coca-Cola Plymouth (Plymouth, FL) 62575

2082 Malt Beverages

Adolph Coors Co. (Elkton, VA) 90743
Anheuser-Busch Inc. (Jacksonville, FL) 60182
Anheuser-Busch Inc. (Tampa, FL) 63328
Anheuser-Busch, Inc. (Houston, TX) 85802
Anheuser-Busch Inc. (Williamsburg, VA) 92551
Coors Brewing Co. (Elkton, VA) 90744; 90745
Miller Brewing Co. (Albany, GA) 64083
Miller Brewing Co. (Eden, NC) 74462
Miller Brewing Co. (Fort Worth, TX) 85189; 85190

2084 Wines, Brandy & Brandy Spirits

Brown-Forman Corp. (Louisville, KY) 68715; 68718; 68719

2085 Distilled & Blended Liquors

Brown-Forman Corp. (Louisville, KY) 68715; 68718; 68719
Coca-Cola Bottling Co. of Jackson Inc. (Jackson, TN) 80967
Early Times Distillers Co. (Louisville, KY) 68756
House of Seagram (Lawrenceburg, KY) 68506
Jack Daniel Distillery (Lynchburg, TN) 81365; 81366; 81367
Jack Daniel Distillery (Nashville, TN) 82038
Jack Daniel Distillery Lem Motlow Prop. (Lynchburg, TN) 81368
Jack Daniel Distillery Lem Motlow Prop. Inc. (Lynchburg, TN) 81369
Jim Beam Brands Co. (Bardstown, KY) 68115; 68116
Jim Beam Brands Co. (Boston, KY) 68129; 68130
Jim Beam Brands Co. (Clermont, KY) 68203; 68204
Jim Beam Brands Co. (Frankfort, KY) 68361; 68362
Seagram Sons Inc. Joseph E (Lawrenceburg, KY) 68508

2086 Bottled & Canned Soft Drinks

Ask. Coca-Cola Bottling Co. (Little Rock, AR) 57253
Atlanta Coca-Cola Bottling Co. (Marietta, GA) 66737
Atlanta Coca-Cola Bottling Co. - College Park Plant (College Park, GA) 65576
Atlanta Coca-Cola Bottling Co. - Marietta Plant (Marietta, GA) 66738
Atlanta Coca-Cola Bottling Co. Oxford Al Plant (Oxford, AL) 56438
Atlantic Soft Drink Co. Inc. (Columbia, SC) 78973
Austin Coca-Cola Bottling Co. Austin Bottling (Austin, TX) 82820
Baton Rouge Coca-Cola Bottling Co. (Baton Rouge, LA) 69470
Birmingham Coca-Cola (Birmingham, AL) 55167
Birmingham Coca-Cola Bottling Co. (Birmingham, AL) 55168
Bluegrass Coca Cola Inc. (Louisville, KY) 68707
Borden Inc. (Amarillo, TX) 82526
Borden Inc. (Corpus Christi, TX) 83703
Borden Inc. (El Paso, TX) 84771
Borden Inc. (Lubbock, TX) 87749
Borden Inc. (Tyler, TX) 89792
Borden Inc. Dairy (Sulphur Springs, TX) 89553
Borden Inc. Grocery Division (Sulphur Springs, TX) 89554
Canners of Eastern Arkansas Inc. (West Memphis, AR) 57718
Coca Cola Bot Co. Laurens (Laurens, SC) 79589
Coca-Cola Botting Co. of Bat (Baton Rouge, LA) 69500
Coca-Cola Botting Co. of Miami (Hollywood, FL) 60053
Coca Cola Bottling Austin (Austin, TX) 82840
Coca-Cola Bottling Co. (Andalusia, AL) 54985
Coca Cola Bottling Co. (Dothan, AL) 55635
Coca Cola Bottling Co. (Batesville, AR) 56743
Coca Cola Bottling Co. (Monticello, AR) 57372
Coca-Cola Bottling Co. of so (Pine Bluff, AR) 57512
Coca Cola Bottling Co. (Leesburg, FL) 60880
Coca Cola Bottling Co. (Vero Beach, FL) 63748
Coca-Cola Bottling Co. (Sylvania, GA) 67766
Coca-Cola Bottling Co. (Warner Robins, GA) 68013
Coca Cola Bottling Co. (Jennings, LA) 69978
Coca Cola Bottling Co. (Lafayette, LA) 70050
Coca Cola Bottling Co. (Leesville, LA) 70189
Coca Cola Bottling Co. (Bessemer City, NC) 73686
Coca-Cola Bottling Co. (Altus, OK) 76793
Coca Cola Bottling Co. (Ripley, OK) 77767
Coca Cola Bottling Co. (Walterboro, SC) 80067
Coca Cola Bottling Co. (Amarillo, TX) 82541
Coca Cola Bottling Co. (Collinsville, TX) 83633
Coca Cola Bottling Co. (Conroe, TX) 83654
Coca Cola Bottling Co. (Cuero, TX) 83823
Coca-Cola Bottling Co. (Jasper, TX) 87430
Coca-Cola Bottling Co. (Longview, TX) 87709
Coca Cola Bottling Co. (Victoria, TX) 89881
Coca-Cola Bottling Co. (Roanoke, VA) 92118
Coca-Cola Bottling Co. of Arkansas (Little Rock, AR) 57265
Coca-Cola Bottling Co. of Arkansas (Morrilton, AR) 57377
Coca-Cola Bottling Co. Blue Grass (Louisville, KY) 68734
Coca-Cola Bottling Co. Bluegrass (Louisville, KY) 68735
Coca Cola Bottling Co. Conso (Gastonia, NC) 74672
Coca Cola Bottling Co. Consolidated (Mobile, AL) 56152
Coca-Cola Bottling Co. Consolidated (Charlotte, NC) 73908
Coca-Cola Bottling Co. Consolidated (Roanoke, VA) 92119
Coca Cola Bottling Co. of Fr (Frisco City, AL) 55769
Coca Cola Bottling Co. Inc. (Lucedale, MS) 73127
Coca-Cola Bottling Co. Johnston (Cleveland, TN) 80573
Coca-Cola Bottling Co. Louisiana Ltd. (New Orleans, LA) 70440
Coca-Cola Bottling Co. of Memphis (Memphis, TN) 81496
Coca-Cola Bottling Co. of Memphis Tennessee Inc. (Memphis, TN) 81497
Coca-Cola Bottling Co. of Miami (Hollywood, FL) 60054
Coca-Cola Bottling Co. of Miami Inc. (Hollywood, FL) 60055
Coca-Cola Bottling Co. Mid Atlantic (Alexandria, VA) 90167
Coca-Cola Bottling Co. N. Texas (Fort Worth, TX) 85087
Coca-Cola Bottling Co. of Nashville (Nashville, TN) 81924
Coca-Cola Bottling Co. of North Texas (Dallas, TX) 83920; 83921
Coca-Cola Bottling Co. of North Texas (Fort Worth, TX) 85088
Coca-Cola Bottling Co. Of Mobile Inc. (Mobile, AL) 56153
Coca-Cola Bottling Co. Of Nashville Inc. (Nashville, TN) 81925
Coca-Cola Bottling Co. Orlando (Orlando, FL) 61954
Coca-Cola Bottling Co. of Pl (Plainview, TX) 88528
Coca-Cola Bottling Co. of San Antonio (San Antonio, TX) 88959
Coca-Cola Bottling Co. of Sherveport (Shreveport, LA) 70699
Coca-Cola Bottling Co. of Shreveprot Inc. (Atlanta, GA) 64373
Coca-Cola Bottling Co. of Tu (Tulsa, OK) 77919
Coca-Cola Bottling of Miami Inc. (Hollywood, FL) 60056
Coca Cola U S a (Altamonte Spg, FL) 58536
Coca-Cola U S a (New Orleans, LA) 70441
Coca Cola U S a (Dallas, TX) 83922
Coca Cola U S A (Dallas, TX) 83923
Coca Cola U S a Fnt Sales (Little Rock, AR) 57266
Dr. Pepper Bottling Co. (Hot Springs, AR) 57162
Dr. Pepper Bottling Co. (Madisonville, KY) 69047
Dr. Pepper Bottling Co. (Gulfport, MS) 72853
Dr. Pepper Bottling Co. (West Jefferson, NC) 76485
Dr. Pepper Bottling Co. (Mt. Minnville, TN) 81831
Dr. Pepper Bottling Co. (Houston, TX) 86043
Dr. Pepper Bottling Co. (Irving, TX) 87339
Dr. Pepper Bottling Co. (Spring, TX) 89465
Dr. Pepper Bottling Co. (Verona, VA) 92391
Dr. Pepper Pepsi-Cola Bottling (Dyersburg, TN) 80746
Dr. Pepper/Seven-Up (Catonsville, MD) 71505
Dr. Pepper Seven-Up Co. Inc. (Fort Worth, TX) 85105
Dr. Pepper Seven-Up Co. Inc. (Waco, TX) 89934
Dr. Pepper Seven-Up Co. Inc. (Beckley, WV) 92675
Florida Coca-Cola Bottling Co. (Hollywood, FL) 60060
Florida Coca-Cola Bottling Co. (Jacksonville, FL) 60303
Florida Coca-Cola Bottling Co. (Orlando, FL) 61986
Florida Coca-Cola Bottling Co. (Tampa, FL) 63432
Garland Beverage Co. (Garland, TX) 85486
Houston Coca-Cola Bottling Co. (Houston, TX) 86289; 86290; 86291; 86292
Hygeia Coca-Cola Bottling Co. (Pensacola, FL) 62437
Industrias La Famosa (Toa Baja, PR) 78610
Johnston Coca-Cola Bottling Co. (Cleveland, TN) 80589
Johnston Coca-Cola Bottling Group Inc. (Atlanta, GA) 64562
Juice Bowl Prods. Inc. (Lakeland, FL) 60735
Juice Bowl Products Inc. (Lakeland, FL) 60736
Lakeland Indl. Center & Bakery & Bakery (Lakeland, FL) 60742
Louisiana Coca-Cola Bottling Co. (New Orleans, LA) 70516
Louisiana Coca-Cola Bottling Co. Ltd. (Gretna, LA) 69907
Louisiana Coca-Cola Bottling Co. Ltd. (New Orleans, LA) 70517
Mid-Atlantic Coca-Cola Bottling Co. (Baltimore, MD) 71207
Mid-Atlantic Coca-Cola Bottling Co. Inc. (Baltimore, MD) 71208
Mid-Atlantic Coca-Cola Bottling Co. Inc. (Silver Spring, MD) 72419
Mid-Atlantic Coca-Cola Bottling Co. Inc. (Alexandria, VA) 90227
Mid-Atlantic Coca-Cola Bottling Co. Inc. (Sandston, VA) 92233
Ocean Spray Cranberries Inc. (Sulphur Springs, TX) 89559; 89560
Oklahoma Canning Co. (Oklahoma City, OK) 77457
Orlando Coca-Cola Bottling Co. (Orlando, FL) 62070
Ouachita Coca-Cola Bottling Co. Inc. (Monroe, LA) 70364
Pepsi-Cola Knoxville (Knoxville, TN) 81237
Pepsi-Cola South North America (Conroe, TX) 83676
Pepsi-Cola Bottlers of Miami (Miami, FL) 61388
Pepsi-Cola Bottling (Asheville, NC) 73631
Pepsi-Cola Bottling Co. (Decatur, AL) 55601
Pepsi-Cola Bottling Co. (Huntsville, AL) 55992
Pepsi-Cola Bottling Co. (Luverne, AL) 56116
Pepsi-Cola Bottling Co. (Selma, AL) 56533
Pepsi-Cola Bottling Co. (Tuscaloosa, AL) 56665
Pepsi-Cola Bottling Co. (Batesville, AR) 56759
Pepsi-Cola Bottling Co. (Jonesboro, AR) 57227
Pepsi-Cola Bottling Co. (Springdale, AR) 57639
Pepsi-Cola Bottling Co. (Wilmington, DE) 58092
Pepsi-Cola Bottling Co. (Fort Walton Beach, FL) 59832
Pepsi-Cola Bottling Co. (Gainesville, FL) 59897
Pepsi-Cola Bottling Go. (Jacksonville, FL) 60388
Pepsi-Cola Bottling Co. (Orlando, FL) 62074; 62075
Pepsi-Cola Bottling Co. (Riviera Beach, FL) 62741
Pepsi-Cola Bottling Co. (Atlanta, GA) 65007
Pepsi-Cola Bottling Co. (Augusta, GA) 65344
Pepsi-Cola Bottling Co. (Bainbridge, GA) 65368
Pepsi-Cola Bottling Co. (Bogart, GA) 65386
Pepsi-Cola Bottling Co. (Gainsville, GA) 66300
Pepsi-Cola Bottling Co. (Macon, GA) 66702
Pepsi-Cola Bottling Co. (Newnan, GA) 67084
Pepsi-Cola Bottling Co. (Savannah, GA) 67505
Pepsi-Cola Bottling Co. (Valdosta, GA) 67966
Pepsi-Cola Bottling Co. (Corbin, KY) 68210; 68211
Pepsi-Cola Bottling Co. (Hazard, KY) 68428
Pepsi-Cola Bottling Co. (Lexington, KY) 68602
Pepsi-Cola Bottling Co. (Winchester, KY) 69349
Pepsi-Cola Bottling Co. (Lake Charles, LA) 70155
Pepsi-Cola Bottling Co. (Cheverly, MD) 71526
Pepsi-Cola Bottling Co. (Havre DeGrace, MD) 71918
Pepsi-Cola Bottling Co. (Salisbury, MD) 72357
Pepsi-Cola Bottling Co. (Columbus, MS) 72720
Pepsi-Cola Bottling Co. (Greenville, MS) 72811
Pepsi-Cola Bottling Co. (Jackson, MS) 73030
Pepsi Cola Bottling Co. (McComb, MS) 73155
Pepsi-Cola Bottling Co. (Tupelo, MS) 73416
Pepsi-Cola Bottling Co. (Charlette, NC) 73825
Pepsi-Cola Bottling Co. (Cherryville, NC) 74249
Pepsi-Cola Bottling Co. (Durham, NC) 74421
Pepsi-Cola Bottling Co. (Elizabeth City, NC) 74483
Pepsi-Cola Bottling Co. (Goldsboro, NC) 74728
Pepsi-Cola Bottling Co. (Greenville, NC) 74970
Pepsi-Cola Bottling Co. (Hickory, NC) 75091
Pepsi-Cola Bottling Co. (Jonesville, NC) 75252
Pepsi-Cola Bottling Co. (Kinston, NC) 75326
Pepsi-Cola Bottling Co. (Lumberton, NC) 75469
Pepsi-Cola Bottling Co. (Marion, NC) 75506
Pepsi-Cola Bottling Co. (Midland, NC) 75559
Pepsi-Cola Bottling Co. (New Bern, NC) 75731
Pepsi-Cola Bottling Co. (Rockingham, NC) 76065
Pepsi-Cola Bottling Co. (Rocky Mountain, NC) 76113
Pepsi-Cola Bottling Co. (Roxboro, NC) 76130
Pepsi-Cola Bottling Co. (Enid, OK) 77059
Pepsi-Cola Bottling Co. (Lawton, OK) 77170
Pepsi-Cola Bottling Co. (Oklahoma City, OK) 77483
Pepsi-Cola Bottling Co. (Tulsa, OK) 78055
Pepsi-Cola Bottling Co. (Anderson, SC) 78685
Pepsi-Cola Bottling Co. (Bennettsville, SC) 78729
Pepsi-Cola Bottling Co. (Conway, SC) 79133
Pepsi-Cola Bottling Co. (Greenville, SC) 79401
Pepsi-Cola Bottling Co. (Kingstree, SC) 79557
Pepsi-Cola Bottling Co. (Jackson, TN) 80994
Pepsi-Cola Bottling Co. (Knoxville, TN) 81238
Pepsi-Cola Bottling Co. (Nashville, TN) 82081
Pepsi-Cola Bottling Co. (Austin, TX) 82955
Pepsi-Cola Bottling Co. (Beaumont, TX) 83197
Pepsi Cola Bottling Co. (Corpus Christi, TX) 83747
Pepsi-Cola Bottling Co. (El Paso, TX) 84873
Pepsi-Cola Bottling Co. (Fort Worth, TX) 85217
Pepsi-Cola Bottling Co. (San Antonio, TX) 89143
Pepsi-Cola Bottling Co. (Charlottesville, VA) 90546
Pepsi-Cola Bottling Co. (Hollins, VA) 91148
Pepsi-Cola Bottling Co. (Newport News, VA) 91477
Pepsi-Cola Bottling Co. (Petersburg, VA) 91634
Pepsi-Cola Bottling Co. (Richmond, VA) 91941
Pepsi-Cola Bottling Co. (Warrenton, VA) 92527
Pepsi-Cola Bottling Co. Knoxville (Knoxville, TN) 81239
Pepsi-Cola Bottling Co. Tampa (Tampa, FL) 63516
Pepsi-Cola Bottling Co. Winston-Salem (Winston-Salem, NC) 76737
Pepsi-Cola Co. (Mobile, AL) 56219
Pepsi-Cola Co. (Fort Smith, AR) 57081
Pepsi-Cola Co. (Daytona Beach, FL) 59196

Pepsi-Cola Co. (Tallahassee, FL) 63254
Pepsi-Cola Co. (Tampa, FL) 63517
Pepsi-Cola Co. (Codele, GA) 65573
Pepsi-Cola Co. (Columbus, GA) 65647
Pepsi-Cola Co. (Rome, GA) 67345
Pepsi-Cola Co. (Vidalia, GA) 67988
Pepsi-Cola Co. (Louisville, KY) 68945
Pepsi-Cola Co. (Shreveport, LA) 70762
Pepsi-Cola Co. (Baltimore, MD) 71219
Pepsi-Cola Co. (Hattiesburg, MS) 72894
Pepsi-Cola Co. (Wilmington, NC) 76586
Pepsi-Cola Co. (Columbia, SC) 79060
Pepsi-Cola Co. (Summerville, SC) 79990
Pepsi-Cola Co. (Chattanooga, TN) 80470
Pepsi-Cola Co. (Cookeville, TN) 80663
Pepsi-Cola Co. (Bryan, TX) 83400
Pepsi-Cola Co. (Conroe, TX) 83677
Pepsi-Cola Co. (Houston, TX) 86673
Pepsi-Cola Co. (Longview, TX) 87727
Pepsi-Cola Co. (Lubbock, TX) 87775
Pepsi-Cola Co. (Mesquite, TX) 87982
Pepsi-Cola Co. (San Antonio, TX) 89144
Pepsi-Cola Co. (Waco, TX) 89960
Pepsi-Cola Co. (Huntington, WV) 92890
Pepsi-Cola Co. (Nitor, WV) 92968
Pepsi-Cola Co. South (Mesquite, TX) 87983
Pepsi-Cola Co. West Columbia Plant (West Columbia, SC) 80099
Pepsi-Cola Distributing Co. (Albany, GA) 64085
Pepsi-Cola Distributing Co. (Corinth, MS) 72741
Pepsi-Cola Distributing Co. (Washington, NC) 76458
Pepsi Cola General Bottlers (Bowling Green, KY) 68159
Pepsi-Cola General Bottlers (Covington, KY) 68230
Pepsi-Cola General Bottlers (Elizabethtown, KY) 68289
Pepsi Cola General Bottlers (Hopkinsville, KY) 68482
Pepsi Cola General Bottlers (Owensboro, KY) 69190
Pepsi Cola General Bottlers (Marion, VA) 91336
Pepsi Cola General Bottlers (Princeton, WV) 93012
Pepsi-Cola Seven-Up (Fayetteville, NC) 74570
Pepsi-Cola Seven-Up Bottling (Montgomery, AL) 56363
Pepsi-Cola Seven-Up Bottling (Monroe, LA) 70366
Pepsi-Cola Seven-Up Bottling (Pineville, LA) 70624
Pepsi-Cola Seven-Up Bottling (Batesville, MS) 72600
Pepsi-Cola Seven-Up Group (Baton Rouge, LA) 69596
Pepsi-Cola South (Dallas, TX) 84298
Pepsi-Cola South Bottling Co. (Burton, SC) 78753
Pepsi South (Johnson City, TN) 81053
Pepsico Food Systems Inc. (Oklahoma City, OK) 77484
Premier Beverage Co. (Dallas, TX) 84323
Publix Deerfield Beach Facility (Deerfield Beach, FL) 59284
Roddy Coca-Cola Bottling Co. Inc. (Knoxville, TN) 81243
Royal Crown Cola Co. (Columbus, GA) 65650
Seven-Up Bottling Co. (Bayamon, PR) 78340
Seven-Up Bottling Co. (Union City, TN) 82390
Seven-Up Bottling Co. (Salem, VA) 92223
Seven Up Bottling Co. Inc. (Bayamon, PR) 78341
Seven-Up-RC-Big Red Bottling (Austin, TX) 83001
Seven-Up Royal Crown Cola (Tulsa, OK) 78111
Snyder Production Center Consolidated (Charlotte, NC) 74160
Southwest Coca Cola (Abilene, TX) 82458
Southwest Coca-Cola Bottling Co. (Amarillo, TX) 82580
Sparkletts Drinking Water Corp. (Dallas, TX) 84396
Tampa Coca-Cola Bottling Co. (Tampa, FL) 63611
Valley Coca-Cola Bottling Co. (Mc Allen, TX) 87903
Valley Coca-Cola Bottling Co., Inc. (McAllen, TX) 87945
Vandervoort Dairy Foods Co. (Fort Worth, TX) 85345

2087 Flavoring Extracts & Syrups Nec

Caribbean Refrescos Inc. (Cidra, PR) 78395; 78396
Coca Cola Bottling Co. (Greensboro, NC) 74800
Coca-Cola Foods Special Products Dept. (Plymouth, FL) 62574
Coca-Cola USA (Atlanta, GA) 64379; 64380; 64381
Coca-Cola USA (Harahan, LA) 69936
Coca-Cola USA (Baltimore, MD) 71090
Coca-Cola USA (Dallas, TX) 83924
Dr. Pepper Bottling Co. (Houston, TX) 86043
Dr. Pepper Bottling Co. (Irving, TX) 87339
Dr. Pepper/Seven-Up (Dallas, TX) 83978
Dr. Pepper/7-Up Companies Inc. (Dallas, TX) 83979
Dr. Pepper Seven-Up Co. (Galveston, TX) 85437
Dr. Pepper/7-Up Corp. (Dallas, TX) 83980
Fantasy-Blankebaer Corp. (Winter Haven, FL) 63933
Pepsi-Cola Bottling (Asheville, NC) 73631
Pepsi-Cola Manufacturing (Arlington, TX) 82719
Pepsi Cola Manufacturing Co. Inc. (Cidra, PR) 78398
Pepsi-Cola Mfg. Co. Inc. (Cidra, PR) 78399
Pepsico Inc. (Arlington, TX) 82720
Phillips Research Ctr. (Bartlesville, OK) 76845
Premier Beverage Co. (Dallas, TX) 84323
Procter & Gamble Mfg. Co. (Jackson, TN) 80997
R. J. Reynolds Tobacco Co. Whitaker Park (Winston-Salem, NC) 76753
R. W. Snyder Co. Inc. (Marshall, TX) 87861
R.J. Reynolds Tobacco Co. Avoca Div. (Merry Hill, NC) 75555
Victor Products Corp. (Richmond, VA) 92075

2091 Canned & Cured Fish & Seafoods

Farm Fresh Catfish Co. (Lake Village, AR) 57238
Farm Fresh Catfish Co. (Hollandale, MS) 72906
National Packing Co. (Playa Ponce, PR) 78527
Star Kist Caribe Inc. (Mayaguez, PR) 78513; 78514
Star-Kist Caribe Inc. (Mayaquez, PR) 78518
Star-Kist Foods, Inc. (Newport, KY) 69145

2092 Fresh or Frozen Prepared Fish

Farm Fresh Catfish Co. (Lake Village, AR) 57238
Farm Fresh Catfish Co. (Hollandale, MS) 72905; 72906
Farm Fresh Catfish Co. Inc. (Hollandale, MS) 72907
Star-Kist Caribe Inc. (Mayaquez, PR) 78518
Star-Kist Foods, Inc. (Newport, KY) 69145
Tyson Foods Inc. was Tysons Foods Inc. (Springdale, AR) 57655

2095 Roasted Coffee

Folger Coffee Co. (Sherman, TX) 89396
General Foods Corp. Maxwell House Div. (Houston, TX) 86249
General Foods Mfg. Corp. Maxwell Div. (Houston, TX) 86250
Maxwell House Coffee Co. (Jacksonville, FL) 60373
Maxwell House Coffee Co. International Div. (Jacksonville, FL) 60374

2096 Potato Chips & Similar Snacks

Borden Inc. Wise Foods (St Augustine, FL) 62939
Eagle Snacks Inc. (Robersonville, NC) 76054
Eagle Snacks Inc. (Fayetteville, TN) 80792
Golden Peanut Co. (DeLeon, TX) 84591
Golden Peanut Co. Ashburn Plant (Ashburn, GA) 64151
Golden Peanut Processing Plant (De Leon, TX) 84529
Wise Foods (Atlanta, GA) 65290

2097 Manufactured Ice

Cassco Ice & Cola Inc. (Harrisonburg, VA) 91071
Polar Ice Co. (Fort Worth, TX) 85238
Reddy Ice (Davie, FL) 59159
Reddy Ice (Pasadena, TX) 88463
Reddy Ice (Waco, TX) 89971
Southland Corp. (Fort Lauderdale, FL) 59612
Southland Corp. (Houston, TX) 86902

2098 Macaroni & Spaghetti

Hershey Pasta Group Louisville Kentucky Plant (Louisville, KY) 68771

2099 Food Preparations Nec

Archer Daniels Midland Co. (Macon, GA) 66651
Bama Food Products (Birmingham, AL) 55158
Borden Inc. Snacks & International Products (Dallas, TX) 83886
Borden Inc. Southwest Snacks (Dallas, TX) 83887
Borden Snacks Inc. (Spartanburg, SC) 79881
C. F. Sauer Co. Inc. (Richmond, VA) 91748
Flavorite Labs. Inc. (Horn Lake, MS) 72915
General Foods USA (Dover, DE) 57789
Gilt Edge Farms (Norman, OK) 77253
Herby's Foods (Dallas, TX) 84114
Hercules, Inc. (Vero Beach, FL) 63758; 63759
Kraft General Foods Inc. (Decatur, GA) 65840
Kraft Inc. (Decatur, GA) 65841
Kraft Inc. (Garland, TX) 85498
Lakeland Indl. Center & Bakery & Bakery (Lakeland, FL) 60742
McCormick Ingredients Spice Mill (Hunt Valley, MD) 71937
Moore's Quality Snack Food Inc. (Bristol, VA) 90482
Ocean Spray Cranberries Inc. (Sulphur Springs, TX) 89561
Pepsico Worldwide Foods (Plano, TX) 88596
Planters Lifesavers Co. (Suffolk, VA) 92371
Premier Beverage Co. (Dallas, TX) 84323
Procter & Gamble Mfg. Co. (Jackson, TN) 80997
Red Star Yeast (Baltimore, MD) 71236; 71237
Red Star Yeast (Dallas, TX) 84353; 84354
Red Star Yeast & Products (Baltimore, MD) 71238
Sesame Prods. Inc. (Paris, TX) 88377
Taco Bell (Austin, TX) 83011
Tyson Foods Inc. (Heflin, AL) 55865
Tyson Foods Inc. (Fayetteville, AR) 56998
Wise Foods (St. Augustine, FL) 63063
Witco Corp. Humko Chemical (Memphis, TN) 81760
Wolf Brand Products Inc. (Dallas, TX) 84498

2100 Tobacco Products

Kirby Forest Industries Inc. Trt./Osb (Silsbee, TX) 89433

2110 Cigarettes

American Tobacco Co. (Chester, VA) 90615

2111 Cigarettes

American Tobacco Co. (Reidsville, NC) 75994; 75995
Lorillard Inc. (Statesboro, GA) 67639
Lorillard Inc. (Greensboro, NC) 74867
Lorillard Tobacco Co. (Greensboro, NC) 74868
Philip Morris USA Cabarrus Manufacturing Center (Concord, NC) 74317
Philip Morris USA MS Complex (Louisville, KY) 68948
Philip Morris USA Mfg. Center (Richmond, VA) 91945
Phillip Morris USA Cabarrus (Concord, NC) 74318
Phillip Morris USA Westab Annex (Richmond, VA) 91947
Phillip Morris USA Manufacturing Center (Richmond, VA) 91948
R. J. Reynolds Tobacco Co. Downtown (Winston-Salem, NC) 76740; 76741
R. J. Reynolds Tobacco Co. Downtown 91-1 (Winston-Salem, NC) 76742
R. J. Reynolds Tobacco Co. Downtown 93-7 (Winston-Salem, NC) 76743
R. J. Reynolds Tobacco Co. Downtown 92-2 (Winston-Salem, NC) 76744; 76745
R. J. Reynolds Tobacco Co. Downtown 64 (Winston-Salem, NC) 76746
R. J. Reynolds Tobacco Co. Downtown 26 (Winston-Salem, NC) 76747
R. J. Reynolds Tobacco Co. Downtown 23-1 (Winston-Salem, NC) 76748; 76749
R. J. Reynolds Tobacco Co. Dt 95-1 (Winston-Salem, NC) 76750
R. J. Reynolds Tobacco Co. Dt 90-3 (Winston-Salem, NC) 76751
R. J. Reynolds Tobacco Co. Dt 63-1 (Winston-Salem, NC) 76752
R. J. Reynolds Tobacco Co. Tobaccoville (King, NC) 75292
R. J. Reynolds Tobacco Co. Whitaker Park (Winston-Salem, NC) 76753
R. J. Reynolds Tobacco Co. Whitaker Park 605-1 (Winston-Salem, NC) 76754
R. J. Reynolds Tobacco Co. Whitaker Park 641 (Winston-Salem, NC) 76755
R. J. Reynolds Tobacco Co. Whitaker Park 604-1 (Winston-Salem, NC) 76757
R. J. Reynolds Tobacco Co. Wp 631-1 (Winston-Salem, NC) 76758
R.J. Reynolds Tobacco Co. (Winston-Salem, NC) 76759

2121 Cigars

American Tobacco Co. (Reidsville, NC) 75994
American Tobacco Co. (Chester, VA) 90615
Maclin Zimmer McGill Tobacco (McKenny, VA) 91377

2131 Chewing & Smoking Tobacco

American Tobacco Co. (Chester, VA) 90616
Lorillard Inc. (Huntsville, AL) 55969
Philip Morris USA (Richmond, VA) 91943
RJ Reynolds Tobacco Co. (Mobile, AL) 56233
RJ Reynolds Tobacco Co. (Lafayette, LA) 70099
Southwestern Tobacco Co. (Lexington, KY) 68630

2141 Tobacco Stemming & Redrying

American Tobacco Co. (Lexington, KY) 68522
American Tobacco Co. (Chester, VA) 90615; 90616
Commonwealth Tobacco Co. Inc. (Kenbridge, VA) 91175
J.P. Taylor Co. (Henderson, NC) 75024
Philip Morris USA Bl Plant (Richmond, VA) 91944
Philip Morris USA Park 500 (Chester, VA) 90622
Phillip Morris USA Bl Plant (Richmond, VA) 91946
Phillip Morris USA Park 500 (Chester, VA) 90623
Southern Processors Inc. (Danville, VA) 90720
Tobacco Processors, Inc. (Wilson, NC) 76649

2200 Textile Mill Products

Kendall Co. (Augusta, GA) 65334
Westpoint Pepperell (Keysville, VA) 91178
Witco Corp. Kendall-Amalie (East Houston, TX) 84726

2211 Broadwoven Fabric Mills—Cotton

Avondale Mills Inc. (Sylacauga, AL) 56575
Brunswick Corp. (DeLand, FL) 59297
Burlington Industries Inc. (Asheboro, NC) 73582
Burlington Industries Inc. (Greensboro, NC) 74796
Burlington Industries Inc. (Liberty, NC) 75427
Burlington Industries Inc. (Mooresville, NC) 75599
Burlington Industries Inc. (Clarksville, VA) 90637
Burlington Industries Inc. Pine (Dahlonega, GA) 65754
Burlington Menswear Halifax (Halifax, VA) 91010
Burlington Sportswear (Stonewall, MS) 73373; 73374
Chicopee (Gainesville, GA) 66268; 66269
Cliffside Plant (Cliffside, NC) 74274
Columbus Towel (Columbus, GA) 65639
Cone Mills Corp. (Greensboro, NC) 74803
Cone Mills Corp. Cliffside Plant (Cliffside, NC) 74275
Cone Mills Corp. Salisbury Plant (Salisbury, NC) 76157
Cone Mills Corp. White Oak Plant (Greensboro, NC) 74804
Delta Mills Marketing (Piedmont, SC) 79794
Delta Woodside Estes Plant (Piedmont, SC) 79795
Delta Woodside Industries Inc. (Greenville, SC) 79342
Dumaine Towel Mill (Fieldale, VA) 90879
Fieldcrest/Cannon, Inc. (Eden, NC) 74454
Fieldcrest Cannon, Inc. (Kannapolis, NC) 75254; 75255; 75256
Fieldcrest Canon Inc. (Kannapolis, NC) 75257
Guilford Mills Inc. (Kenansville, NC) 75270
J. P. Stevens & Co. Inc. Seneca Plant (Seneca, SC) 79861
Klopman Burlington Fabrics (Rockingham, NC) 76064
Russell Corp. (Alexander City, AL) 54979
Russell Corp. (Lafayette, AL) 56100
Southern Cotton Oil Co. (Memphis, TN) 81698
Southern Cotton Oil Co. Inc. (Memphis, TN) 81699
Southern Phenix Textiles Inc. (Phenix City, AL) 56473; 56474
Springs Industrial Products (Honea Path, SC) 79530
Springs Industries, Inc. (Laurel Hill, NC) 75346
Springs Industries, Inc. (Anderson, SC) 78693
Springs Industries, Inc. (Chester, SC) 78944
Springs Industries, Inc. (Fort Lawn, SC) 79230
Springs Industries, Inc. (Fort Mill, SC) 79238
Springs Industries, Inc. (Lyman, SC) 79627
UNIFI, Inc. (Mayodan, NC) 75539
UNIFI, Inc. (Stoneville, NC) 76344
Union Camp Corp. (Opelika, AL) 56427
West Point Pepperell (Valley, AL) 56691; 56692; 56693; 56694; 56695
West Point Pepperell (Columbus, GA) 65657
West Point Pepperell Mission Valley Mill (New Braunfels, TX) 88223
Woodside Mills Inc. (Fountain Inn, SC) 79251

Woodside Mills Inc. Beattie Plant (Fountain Inn, SC) 79252; 79253
Woodside Mills Inc. Furman Plant (Fountain Inn, SC) 79255

2221 Broadwoven Fabric Mills—Manmade

Burlington Industries (Mount Olive, NC) 75694
Burlington Industries Inc. (Dahlonega, GA) 65753
Burlington Industries Inc. (Asheboro, NC) 73581
Burlington Industries Inc. (Cordova, NC) 74344
Burlington Industries Inc. (Greensboro, NC) 74796
Burlington Industries Inc. (Mooresville, NC) 75599
Burlington Industries Inc. (Oxford, NC) 75777
Burlington Industries Inc. (Rocky Mount, NC) 76080
Burlington Industries Inc. (Smithfield, NC) 76257
Burlington Industries Inc. (Johnson City, TN) 81026
Burlington Industries Inc. (Altavista, VA) 90245
Burlington Industries Inc. (Clarksville, VA) 90637
Burlington Industries Inc. (Hurt, VA) 91168
Burlington Industries/Sheffield Plant (Rocky Mount, NC) 76081
Burlington Industries William G. Lord (Belmont, NC) 73673
Burlington Madison Yarn Co. (Mayodan, NC) 75537
Burlington Menswear Halifax (Halifax, VA) 91010
Clark-Schwebel Fiber Glass Corp. (Statesville, NC) 76324
Clark-Schwebel Fiber Glass Corp. (Anderson, SC) 78672
Clark-Schwebel Fiberglass Corp. (Anderson, SC) 78674
Collins & Aiken Holding II Corp. (Charlotte, NC) 73910
Collins Aikman Corp. (Charlotte, NC) 73912
Collins & Aikman Holdings Corp. (Charlotte, NC) 73915
Cone Mills Corp. (Greensboro, NC) 74803
Delta Woodside Industries Inc. (Greenville, SC) 79342
Ferro Corp. (Miami, FL) 61282
Fieldcrest/Cannon, Inc. (Eden, NC) 74454
Louisiana Pacific Corp. (Clayton, AL) 55522
Russell Corp. (Alexander City, AL) 54979; 54980
Russell Corp. (Niceville, FL) 61717
Scottsboro Rug Mill (Scottsboro, AL) 56523
Sedgefield Specialties (Greensboro, NC) 74906
Springs Industires Inc. (Fort Lawn, SC) 79229
Springs Industries, Inc. (Chester, SC) 78944
Springs Industries, Inc. (Fort Lawn, SC) 79230
Springs Industries, Inc. (Fort Mill, SC) 79238
Springs Industries, Inc. (Gaffney, SC) 79265
Springs Industries, Inc. (Lyman, SC) 79627
Steiner Liff Textile Produc (Nashville, TN) 82101
UNIFI, Inc. (Mayodan, NC) 75539
UNIFI, Inc. (Stoneville, NC) 76344
Union Underwear Co. (St. Martinville, LA) 70871
Willamette Industries Inc. (Grand Prairie, TX) 85647
Woodside Mills Inc. (Anderson, SC) 78696
Woodside Mills Inc. Beattie Plant (Fountain Inn, SC) 79252; 79253
Woodside Mills Inc. Furman Plant (Fountain Inn, SC) 79254
Woodside Mills Inc. Haynsworth Plant (Anderson, SC) 78697

2231 Broadwoven Fabric Mills—Wool

Burlington Industries Inc. (Forest city, NC) 74603
Burlington Industries Inc. (Greensboro, NC) 74796
Burlington Menswear (Clarksville, VA) 90638
Delta Woodside Industries Inc. (Greenville, SC) 79342
Springs Industries, Inc. (Fort Mill, SC) 79238
UNIFI, Inc. (Mayodan, NC) 75539

2241 Narrow Fabric Mills

Aluminum Co. of America (Marshall, TX) 87852
Ametek, Inc. Heaveg Div. (Wilmington, DE) 57985
Fieldale Towel Mill (Fieldale, VA) 90880
Magnetek Hesgon (Brownsville, TX) 83370
Playtex Apparel Inc. (Dover, DE) 57798
Taco Bell (Birmingham, AL) 55409

2251 Women's Hosiery Except Socks

Burlington Industries Inc. (Greensboro, NC) 74796
Collins & Aiken Holding II Corp. (Charlotte, NC) 73910
Fruit of the Loom Hosiery Star Div. (Star, NC) 76314
Kayser-Roth Corp. (Greensboro, NC) 74856
Kayser-Roth Corp. (Arecibo, PR) 78313
Kayser-Roth Corp. (Prosperity, SC) 79805
Kayser-Roth Corp. (Dayton, TN) 80719; 80720
Kayser-Roth Corp. Sheer Hosiery Div. (Lumberton, NC) 75466
Rice Hosiery (High Point, NC) 75160
Sara Lee Hosiery (Lumberton, NC) 75473
Sara Lee Hosiery (Rockingham, NC) 76069
Sara Lee Hosiery (Winston-Salem, NC) 76764
Sara Lee Hosiery (Yadkinville, NC) 76781
Sara Lee Hosiery (Bennettsville, SC) 78731; 78732
Sara Lee Hosiery (Florence, SC) 79225
Sara Lee Hosiery (Hartsville, SC) 79502
Sara Lee Hosiery (Marion, SC) 79644

2252 Hosiery Nec

Adams-Millis Drexel Knitting (Drexel, NC) 74363
Adams-Millis Hoisery (Hickory, NC) 75054
Adams-Millis Hoisery (Kernersville, NC) 75273
Adams-Millis Hoisery (Mount Airy, NC) 75671
Adams Millis Hoisery Corp. (Kernersville, NC) 75274
Adams Millis Hosiery Corp. (Mount Airy, NC) 75672
Adams-Millis Influential (High Point, NC) 75109
Adams Millis Influential (Mebane, NC) 75548
Adams-Millis Influential No. 2 (Mebane, NC) 75549
Adams-Millis Wrangler (High Point, NC) 75110
Adams Millis Wranlger (High Point, NC) 75111
Burlington Industries Inc. (Greensboro, NC) 74796
Burlington Maid Enterprises II (Haw River, NC) 75011
Camp Hosiery Inc. (Lenoir City, TN) 81320
Cluett Hosiery Annedeen Hosiery Mill (Burlington, NC) 73752
Collins & Aiken Holding II Corp. (Charlotte, NC) 73910
Collins & Aikman Holdings Corp. (Charlotte, NC) 73915
Kayser-Roth Corp. (Graham, NC) 74749
Kayser-Roth Corp. (Greensboro, NC) 74856
Kayser-Roth Corp. (Rockwood, TN) 82269
Kayser-Roth Corp. Asheboro Plant (Asheboro, NC) 73588
Silver Knit Industries, Inc. (High Point, NC) 75171
UNIFI (Madison, NC) 75485
West Point Pepperell Newton Knitting Mills (Newton, NC) 75756

2253 Knit Outerwear Mills

Bassett-Walker Inc. (Martinsville, VA) 91343; 91344
Burlington Industries Inc. (Greensboro, NC) 74796
Cross Creek Apparel Inc. Dyeing Finishing (Mount Airy, NC) 75675
Delta Apparel (Tellico Plains, TN) 82368
Fruit of the Loom Inc. Martin Mills Inc. (St. Martinville, LA) 70870
Pannill Knitting Co. (Eden, NC) 74463
Russell Corp. (Alexander City, AL) 54978
Russell Corp. (Crestview, FL) 59125
Russell Corp. (Marianna, FL) 61010
Sara Lee Knit Products (Forest City, NC) 74611
Sara Lee Knit Products (Morganton, NC) 75655
Sara Lee Knit Products Dyeing & Finishing Plant (Eden, NC) 74468
Spring City Knitting Co. (Gaffney, SC) 79264
Westpoint Pepperell (Hamilton, NC) 74995
Westpoint Pepperell (Lumberton, NC) 75477
Wrangler (Greensboro, NC) 74944

2254 Knit Underwear Mills

Delta Apparel Maiden Plant (Maiden, NC) 75490
Duck Head Apparel Co. (Winder, GA) 68059
Fruit of the Loom (Campbellsvlle, KY) 68185; 68186
Fruit of the Loom Inc. Martin Mills Inc. (St. Martinville, LA) 70870
Hanes Menswear Inc. (Ponce, PR) 78536
Spring City Knitting Co. (Gaffney, SC) 79264
Stevcoknit Fabric Co. Maiden (Maiden, NC) 75495

2257 Weft Knit Fabric Mills

Burlington Industries Inc. (Denton, NC) 74360
Burlington Industries Inc. (Greensboro, NC) 74796
Burlington Industries Inc. (Statesville, NC) 76320
Burlington Industries Inc. (Wake Forest, NC) 76430
Delta Apparel Maiden Plant (Maiden, NC) 75490
Hanes Menswear Inc. (Ponce, PR) 78536
Russell Corp. (Alexander City, AL) 54980
Sara Lee Knit Products (Lumberton, NC) 75474
Stevcoknit Fabric Co. Maiden (Maiden, NC) 75495
Stevcoknit Fabrics Co. (Fayetteville, NC) 74576
Stevcoknit Fabrics Co. Carter Plant (Wallace, NC) 76445

2258 Lace & Warp Knit Fabric Mills

Burlington Industries Inc. (Denton, NC) 74360
Burlington Industries Inc. (Greensboro, NC) 74796
Collins Aikman Corp. (Charlotte, NC) 73912
Collins & Aikman Corp. Specialty Fabrics Div. (Farmville, NC) 74520
Duck Head Apparel Co. (Maiden, NC) 75492
Guilford Mills Inc. Industrial Fabrics Div. (Greensboro, NC) 74845
Guilford Mills Inc. Guilford E. Plant (Kenansville, NC) 75271
Guilford Mills Inc. Oak Ridge Plant (Greensboro, NC) 74846; 74847
Guilford Mills Inc. W. Market St. Plant (Greensboro, NC) 74848
Stevcoknit Fabrics Co. Carter Plant (Wallace, NC) 76445

2259 Knitting Mills Nec

Collins & Aikman Corp. Cavel Div. (Roxboro, NC) 76122
Fieldcrest Cannon Inc. (Eden, NC) 74453
Russell Corp. (Alexander City, AL) 54979
Veratec (Bethune, SC) 78737
West Point Pepperell (Elizabethtown, NC) 74494
West Point Pepperell (Lumberton, NC) 75476

2261 Finishing Plants—Cotton

Avondale Mills Inc. (Sylacauga, AL) 56575
Blanket Finishing (Eden, NC) 74449
Burlington Industries Inc. (Burlington, NC) 73746
Burlington Industries/Sheffield Plant (Rocky Mount, NC) 76081
Carlisle Finishing Plant (Carlisle, SC) 78764
Carlisle Finishing Plant Carlisle Finishing Plant (Carlisle, SC) 78765
Cheraw Dyeing & Finishing Plant (Cheraw, SC) 78918
Cliffside Plant (Cliffside, NC) 74274
Cone Mills Corp. (Greensboro, NC) 74803
Cone Mills Corp. Cliffside Plant (Cliffside, NC) 74275
Cone Mills Corp. Granite Finishing Plant (Haw River, NC) 75012
Cone Mills Corp. Granite Plant (Haw River, NC) 75013
Cone Mills Corp. Salisbury Plant (Salisbury, NC) 76157
Cone Mills Corp. White Oak Plant (Greensboro, NC) 74804
Delta Mills Marketing (Wallace, SC) 80059
Fieldcrest Cannon Inc. (Kannapolis, NC) 75255
Granite Plant (Haw River, NC) 75014
J. P. Stevens & Co. (Clemson, SC) 78950
Monroe Industries Inc. (Greenville, SC) 79397
North Carolina Finishing Co. (Salisbury, NC) 76169
Springs Industries, Inc. (Piedmont, AL) 56482
Springs Industries, Inc. (Lyman, SC) 79627
West Point Pepperell Mission Valley Mill (New Braunfels, TX) 88223

2262 Finishing Plants—Manmade

Ametek Corp. Haveg Div. (Wilmington, DE) 57983
Ametek, Inc. Heaveg Div. (Wilmington, DE) 57985
Blanket Finishing (Eden, NC) 74449
Burlington Industries Inc. (Forest city, NC) 74603
Burlington Industries Inc. (Mooresville, NC) 75599
Burlington Industries Inc. (Rocky Mount, NC) 76080
Burlington Industries Inc. (Wake Forest, NC) 76430
Burlington Industries Inc. (Hurt, VA) 91168
Carlisle Finishing Plant (Carlisle, SC) 78764
Carlisle Finishing Plant Carlisle Finishing Plant (Carlisle, SC) 78765
Cheraw Dyeing & Finishing Plant (Cheraw, SC) 78918
Clark-Schwebel Fiber Glass Corp. (Statesville, NC) 76324
Clark-Schwebel Fiber Glass Corp. (Anderson, SC) 78672
Clark-Schwebel Fiberglass Corp. (Anderson, SC) 78674
Collins & Aikman Corp. Cavel Div. (Roxboro, NC) 76122
Collins & Aikman Corp. Albemarle Plant (Albemarle, NC) 73526; 73527
Cone Mills Corp. (Greensboro, NC) 74803
Cone Mills Corp. Granite Finishing Plant (Haw River, NC) 75012
Cone Mills Corp. Granite Plant (Haw River, NC) 75013
Delta Mills Marketing (Wallace, SC) 80059
Granite Plant (Haw River, NC) 75014
Mastercraft Fabric Corp. Concord Plant (Concord, NC) 74316
Monroe Industries Inc. (Greenville, SC) 79397
North Carolina Finishing Co. (Salisbury, NC) 76169
Springs Industries Grace Finishing (Lancaster, SC) 79577
Springs Industries Lyman Filter Plant (Lyman, SC) 79628

2269 Finishing Plants Nec

Burlington Industries Inc. (Hurt, VA) 91168
Burlington Industries/Lakewood Plant (Cramerton, NC) 74351
Burlington Menswear/Plant 17 (Raeford, NC) 75846
Carisbrook Templon Div. (Mooresville, NC) 75600
Carisbrook Yarns Franklin Div. (Greenville, SC) 79324
Delta Mills Marketing Co. (Wallace, SC) 80060
Delta Mills Marketing Co., Delta No. 3 (Wallace, SC) 80061
Delta Mills Marketing Co. Delta Plant No. 2 (Wallace, SC) 80062
Delta Mills Marketing Delta Plant No. 2 (Wallace, SC) 80063
Fibertec Co. (Bethune, SC) 78736
Fieldcrest Cannon (Pheonix City, AL) 56479
Fieldcrest Cannon Inc. (Kannapolis, NC) 75255; 75256
Fieldcrest Canon Inc. (Kannapolis, NC) 75257
North Carolina Finishing Co. (Salisbury, NC) 76169
Rock Hill Printing & Finishing (Rock Hill, SC) 79841
Russell Corp. (Alexander City, AL) 54979
Shaw Industries Inc. (Decatur, TN) 80727
Spring City Knitting Co. (Gaffney, SC) 79264
Unifi, Inc. (Yadkinville, NC) 76782
Veratec (Bethune, SC) 78737
West Point Pepperell (Opelika, AL) 56432

2270 Carpets & Rugs

Collins & Aikman Corp. (Salisbury, NC) 76156

2273 Carpets & Rugs

Burlington Industries Inc. (Monticello, AR) 57370
Burlington Industries Inc. (Rahun Gap, GA) 67293
Burlington Industries Inc. (Greensboro, NC) 74796
Collins & Aiken Holding II Corp. (Charlotte, NC) 73910
Collins Aikman Corp. (Charlotte, NC) 73912
Collins & Aikman Corp. Floor Covering Div. (Dalton, GA) 65774; 65775
Collins & Aikman Corp. Old Fort Plant (Old Fort, NC) 75773
Collins & Aikman Holdings Corp. (Charlotte, NC) 73915
Color-Tech Plant (Dalton, GA) 65776
Fieldcrest Cannon Inc. (Eden, NC) 74453
Fieldcrest Cannon Inc. Landrum Mills (Landrum, SC) 79583
Georgia Rug Mill (Summerville, GA) 67737
Interface Flooring Sys. Inc. Inc. (La Grange, GA) 66479
Interface Flooring Systems Inc. (La Grange, GA) 66480; 66481
Karastan Bigelow (Greenville, SC) 79376
Karastan Rug Mill (Eden, NC) 74458
Karastan Spinning (Greenville, NC) 74965
Laurel Hill Carpet Mill (Laurel Hill, NC) 75345
Lees Carpet (Glasgow, VA) 90972
Lyerly Rug Mill (Lyerly, GA) 66630; 66631
Shaw Industries Inc. (Dalton, GA) 65789
Shaw Industries Inc. (Trenton, SC) 80046
Shaw Industries Inc. (Winchester, TN) 82421
Shaw Industries Plant (Charlotte, NC) 74157
Springs Industries Bath Fashions (Calhoun, GA) 65475
Springs Industries, Inc. (Calhoun, GA) 65476
Springs Industries, Inc. (Dalton, GA) 65791
West Point Pepperell (Keysville, VA) 91177

2281 Yarn Spinning Mills

Avondale Mills Inc. (Sylacauga, AL) 56575
BASF Corp. Fibers (Sylvania, GA) 67764
BASF Corp. Fibers (Williamsburg, VA) 92563
BASF Corp. Fibers Division (Lowland, TN) 81362
BASF Fibers (Sylvania, GA) 67765
BASF Fibers (Lowland, TN) 81363

Burlington Industries Inc. (Monticello, AR) 57370
Burlington Industries Inc. (Dahlonega, GA) 65753
Burlington Industries Inc. (Caroleen, NC) 73782
Burlington Industries Inc. (Forest city, NC) 74603
Burlington Industries Inc. (Gastonia, NC) 74668; 74669
Burlington Industries Inc. (Graham, NC) 74747
Burlington Industries Inc. (Greensboro, NC) 74796
Burlington Industries Inc. (Mount Holly, NC) 75689
Burlington Industries Inc. (Mt. Holly, NC) 75699
Burlington Industries Inc. (Oxford, NC) 75776
Burlington Industries Inc. (Smithfield, NC) 76256; 76257
Burlington Industries/Pioneer Plant (Burlington, NC) 73747
Burlington Industries/Ranlo Plant (Gastonia, NC) 74670
Burlington Madison Yarn Co. (Mayodan, NC) 75537
Burlington Madison Yarn Co. (St. Pauls, NC) 76306
Burlington Menswear/Plant 17 (Raeford, NC) 75846
Collins Aikman Corp. (Charlotte, NC) 73912
Delta Mills Marketing (Maiden, NC) 75491
Fieldcrest/Cannon, Inc. (Eden, NC) 74454
Fieldcrest Cannon Inc. Carpet & Rug (Calhoun Falls, SC) 78754
Karastan (Calhoun Falls, SC) 78755
Karastan Bigelow (Calhoun Falls, SC) 78756
Karastan-Bigolon (Calhoun Falls, SC) 78757
Lees Carpet Burlington (Glasgow, VA) 90973
Russell Corp. (Alexander City, AL) 54978; 54979; 54980
Shaw Industries Co. (Millendgeville, GA) 66987
Shaw Industries Inc. (Stevenson, AL) 56573
Shaw Industries Inc. (Valley Head, AL) 56696
Shaw Industries Inc. (Blue Ridge, GA) 65383
Shaw Industries Inc. (Calhoun, GA) 65474
Shaw Industries Inc. (Chatsworth, GA) 65558; 65559
Shaw Industries Inc. (Dallas, GA) 65767
Shaw Industries Inc. (Fitzgerald, GA) 66213
Shaw Industries Inc. (La Fayette, GA) 66472
Shaw Industries Inc. (Newnan, GA) 67085
Shaw Industries Inc. (Tifton, GA) 67829
Shaw Industries Inc. (Toccoa, GA) 67838
Shaw Industries Inc. (Trenton, GA) 67843
Shaw Industries Inc. (Trenton, SC) 80046
Shaw Industries Inc. (Decatur, TN) 80727
Shaw Industries Inc. (South Pittsburg, TN) 82340
Stevcoknit Fabrics Co. (Edgefield, SC) 79185
UNIFI, Inc. (Archdale, NC) 73562
UNIFI, Inc. (Reidsville, NC) 76015

2282 Throwing & Winding Mills
BASF Corp. (Central, SC) 78781
BASF Corp.-Clemson Plant (Central, SC) 78784
Burlington Industries Inc. (Greensboro, NC) 74796
Burlington Industries Inc. (Mt. Holly, NC) 75699
Collins Aikman Corp. (Charlotte, NC) 73912
Fieldcrest Cannon Inc. Carpet & Rug (Calhoun Falls, SC) 78754
Karastan Bigelow (Calhoun Falls, SC) 78756
Russell Corp. (Alexander City, AL) 54978
Shaw Industries Inc. (Stevenson, AL) 56573
UNIFI (Madison, NC) 75485
UNIFI (Staunton, VA) 92330
UNIFI, Inc. (Madison, NC) 75486
Unifi, Inc. (Yadkinville, NC) 76782
Unifi Inc. (Staunton, VA) 92331

Unifi Inc. Plant 1 (Mayodan, NC) 75540

2295 Coated Fabrics—Not Rubberized
American Cyanamid Co. (Havre De Grace, MD) 71914
Ametek Corp. Haveg Div. (Wilmington, DE) 57983
Collins & Aikman Corp. Cavel Div. (Roxboro, NC) 76122
Diversitech General (Columbus, MS) 72708
Dow Corning Corp. Norcross Plant (Norcross, GA) 67112
Gencorp Inc. (Columbus, MS) 72710
Gencorp Polymer Prods. (Columbus, MS) 72711
Gencorp Polymer Products (Columbus, MS) 72712
United Technologies Automotive Thomson Plant (Thomson, GA) 67817
West Point Pepperell (Pulaski, VA) 91680

2296 Tire Cord & Fabrics
Goodyear Cartersville Mill (Cartersville, GA) 65502
Goodyear Tire & Rubber Co. (Decatur, AL) 55588; 55589; 55590
Goodyear Tire & Rubber Co. (Scottsboro, AL) 56521
Oliver Rubber Co. (Athens, GA) 64173

2297 Nonwoven Fabrics
Automatic Blanket (Smithfield, NC) 76253; 76254
Berkeley Mills (Balfour, NC) 73656
Burlington Menswear (Clarksville, VA) 90638
Central Filter (Eden, NC) 74451
E. R. Carpenter Co. Inc. (Russellville, KY) 69259
E. R. Carpenter Co. Inc. (Richmond, VA) 91860
Fibertec Co. (Bethune, SC) 78736
Fieldcrest Cannon Inc. Non-Woven (Eden, NC) 74455
Fort Howard Paper Co. (Muskogee, OK) 77221
Fort Howard Paper Corp. (Rincon, GA) 67301
Hoechst Celanese Corp. (Spartanburg, SC) 79913
Hoechst-Celanese Corp. Spartanburg (Spartanburg, SC) 79914
Hoechst Celanese Corp. Spartanburg Plant (Spartanburg, SC) 79915
James River Corp. (Cantonment, FL) 58909
Kimberly-Clark (La Grange, GA) 66483
Kimberly-Clark Corp. (Corinth, MS) 72740
Kimberly-Clark Corp. (Lexington, NC) 75406
Kimberly-Clark Corp. Lagrange Mill (La Grange, GA) 66484
Kimberly-Clark Corp. Lexington Mill (Lexington, NC) 75407
Manville Corp. (Etowah, TN) 80781
Manville Sales Corp. (Etowah, TN) 80782
Manville Sales Corp. (Ennis, TX) 84995
Schuller International Inc. (Ennis, TX) 85001
United Technologies Automotive Thomson Plant (Thomson, GA) 67817
Veratec (Bethune, SC) 78737

2299 Textile Goods Nec
Allied-Signal Inc. (Dalton, GA) 65770
BASF Corp. (Dalton, GA) 65772
BASF Corp. Fibers Division (Dalton, GA) 65773
Burlington Industries (Bishopville, SC) 78738
Burlington Industries Inc. (Greensboro, NC) 74796
Burlington Industries Inc. (Bishopville, SC) 78739
Collins & Aikman Corp. Cavel Div. (Roxboro, NC) 76122
Cone Mills Corp. (Greensboro, NC) 74803
J. P. Stevens & Co. Bob Stevens Plant (Wagram, NC) 76428
Quality Mills Inc. Cloth Plant (Mount Airy, NC) 75682

Shaw Industries Inc. (Toccoa, GA) 67838
Sonoco Products Co. (Memphis, TN) 81694
Stevcoknit Fabrics Co. (Wallace, NC) 76444
Stevcoknit Fabrics Co. (Greer, SC) 79482
West Point Pepperell Bob Stevens Facility (Wagram, NC) 76429
West Point Pepperell Grifftex Chemicals (Opelika, AL) 56433

2300 Apparel & Other Textile Products
Pineland (Diboll, TX) 84657
Sara Lee Knit Products (Martinsville, VA) 91357; 91358
Union Underwear Co. Inc. (Jamestown, KY) 68491; 68492
Union Underwear Co. Inc. (Kings Mountain, NC) 75310
Union Underwear Co. Inc. (Rockingham, NC) 76070

2311 Men's/Boys' Suits & Coats
Duck Head Apparel Co. (Monroe, GA) 66989; 66990
Wrangler (Greensboro, NC) 74944

2321 Men's/Boys' Shirts
Delta Apparel (Decatur, TN) 80726
Duck Head Apparel Co. (Sandersville, GA) 67429
Duck Head Apparel Co. (Washington, GA) 68021
Duck Head Apparel Co. (Jellico, TN) 81023
Fruit of the Loom Inc. Richmond Apparel (Rockingham, NC) 76061
Red Kap Ind. (Baldwyn, MS) 72592
Red Kap Ind. (Dickson, TN) 80736
Russell Corp. (Marianna, FL) 61008; 61010
Russell Corp. (Cumming, GA) 65749
Wemco Inc. (New Orleans, LA) 70589
White County Industries Inc. (Sparta, TN) 82348
Wrangler (Hackleburg, AL) 55840
Wrangler (Greensboro, NC) 74944

2322 Men's/Boys' Underwear & Nightwear
Delta Apparel (Duluth, GA) 66033
Delta Apparel (Tellico Plains, TN) 82368
Fruit of the Loom Inc. (Jamestown, KY) 68490
Fruit of the Loom Inc. Arkansas (Osceola, AR) 57482
Fruit of the Loom Inc. Union Underwear (Campbellsville, KY) 68180
Russell Corp. (Columbia, AL) 55525
Russell Corp. (Dadeville, AL) 55560
Russell Corp. (Montgomery, AL) 56373
Russell Corp. (Sylacauga, AL) 56589
Sara Lee Knit Products (Asheboro, NC) 73597
Sara Lee Knit Products (Gastonia, NC) 74689
Sara Lee Knit Products (Winston-Salem, NC) 76769
Sara Lee Knit Products Galax Plant (Galax, VA) 90964
Sara Lee Knit Products Hanes Menswear (Ponce, PR) 78537

2323 Men's/Boys' Neckwear
Wemco Inc. (New Orleans, LA) 70589

2325 Men's/Boys' Trousers & Slacks
Duck Head Apparel Co. (Baldwin, GA) 65375
Duck Head Apparel Co. (Monroe, GA) 66989; 66990
Duck Head Apparel Co. (Sparta, GA) 67616
Duck Head Apparel Co. (Winder, GA) 68059
Duck Head Apparel Co. (Jellico, TN) 81023
Red Kap (Clarksville, TX) 83572
Red Kap Ind. (Vienna, GA) 68000

Red Kap Ind. (Amory, MS) 72586; 72587
Red Kap Ind. (Baldwyn, MS) 72592
Red Kap Ind. (Booneville, MS) 72648
Red Kap Ind. (Columbus, MS) 72727
Red Kap Ind. (Mathiston, MS) 73142
Red Kap Ind. (Tupelo, MS) 73423
Red Kap Ind. (Antlers, OK) 76806
Red Kap Ind. (Dickson, TN) 80736
Red Kap Ind. (Erwin, TN) 80776
Red Kap Ind. (Harriman, TN) 80902
Red Kap Ind. (Sparta, TN) 82347
Red Kap Ind. (Wartburg, TN) 82402
Wemco Inc. (New Orleans, LA) 70589
Wrangler (Arab, AL) 55028
Wrangler (Hanceville, AL) 55852
Wrangler (Oneonta, AL) 56414
Wrangler (Red Bay, AL) 56497
Wrangler (Greensboro, NC) 74943
Wrangler (Colgate, OK) 76968
Wrangler (Okemah, OK) 77288
Wrangler (Prague, OK) 77731
Wrangler (Seminole, OK) 77807
Wrangler (Newbern, TN) 82159
Wrangler (Troy, TN) 82375
Wrangler (Luray, VA) 91218
Wrangler (Madison, VA) 91294
Wrangler (Shenandoah, VA) 92235
Wrangler (Woodstock, VA) 92633
Wrangler Menswear (El Paso, TX) 84979

2326 Men's/Boys' Work Clothing
Baxter Healthcare (McDonough, GA) 66967
Red Kap Ind. (Cookeville, TN) 80665
Red Kap Ind. (Dickson, TN) 80736
Red Kap Ind. (Erwin, TN) 80776
Red Kap Ind. (Harriman, TN) 80902
Red Kap Ind. (Sparta, TN) 82347
Red Kap Ind. (Wartburg, TN) 82402
Wrangler (Hanceville, AL) 55852
Wrangler (Oneonta, AL) 56414
Wrangler (Greensboro, NC) 74943
Wrangler (Fabens, TX) 85028
Wrangler (Shenandoah, VA) 92235

2329 Men's/Boys' Clothing Nec
California Manufacturing Co. (Macon, MS) 73134
Delta Apparel (Duluth, GA) 66033
Delta Apparel (Decatur, TN) 80726
Duck Head Apparel Co. (Monroe, GA) 66990
Fruit of the Loom Inc. Martin Mills Inc. (St. Martinville, LA) 70870
Fruit of the Loom Inc. Richmond Apparel (Rockingham, NC) 76061
J. Schoeneman Wiltex (Wilmington, DE) 58077
Red Kap (Clarksville, TX) 83572
Red Kap Ind. (Lillington, NC) 75434
Russell Corp. (Alexander City, AL) 54979
Russell Corp. (Ashland, AL) 55031
Russell Corp. (Crestview, FL) 59125
Russell Corp. (Marianna, FL) 61009
Russell Corp. D.C. & Ind. Park (Marianna, FL) 61011
Wrangler (Hackleburg, AL) 55840
Wrangler (Red Bay, AL) 56497
Wrangler (Newbern, TN) 82159

2330 Women's/Misses' Outerwear
Buster Brown Apparel Inc. (La Fayette, GA) 66468
Buster Brown Apparel Inc. (Chattanooga, TN) 80336

2331 Women's/Misses' Blouses & Shirts
Duck Head Apparel Co. (Sandersville, GA) 67429
Red Kap Ind. (Lillington, NC) 75434
Warner's (Sylvania, GA) 67773

2335 Women's/Misses' Dresses
Wells Manufacturing Co. (Hendersonvl, NC) 75051

2337 Women's/Misses' Suits & Coats
Red Kap Ind. (Baldwyn, MS) 72592
Warner's (Sylvania, GA) 67773

2339 Women's/Misses' Outerwear Nec
Burlington Coat Factory Warehouse (Huntsville, AL) 55895
Casual Corner (Oklahoma City, OK) 77324
Casual Corner (San Antonio, TX) 88950
Delta Apparel (Duluth, GA) 66033
Hit or Miss (Covington, KY) 68222
Lane Bryant (Oklahoma City, OK) 77417
The Limited (Oklahoma City, OK) 77426
The Limited Express (El Paso, TX) 84842
Olga (Checotah, OK) 76915
Red Kap Ind. (Maysville, KY) 69089
Red Kap Ind. (Columbus, MS) 72727
Vanity Fair Mills Inc. (Monroeville, AL) 56269
Warner's (Sylvania, GA) 67773
Warner's Distribution Center (Murfreesboro, TN) 81874
Warner's Warnaco Inc. (Barbourville, KY) 68111
Wrangler (Windsor, NC) 76658
Wrangler (Newbern, TN) 82159
Wrangler (Troy, TN) 82375

2341 Women's/Children's Underwear
Vanity Fair Mills Inc. (Atmore, AL) 55053
Vanity Fair Mills Inc. (Butler, AL) 55497
Vanity Fair Mills Inc. (Jackson, AL) 56070
Vanity Fair Mills Inc. (Monroeville, AL) 56269
Vanity Fair Mills Inc. (Robertsdale, AL) 56504
Warner Co. (Thomasvile, GA) 67786

2342 Bras, Girdles & Allied Garments
Vanity Fair Mills Inc. (Atmore, AL) 55053
Vanity Fair Mills Inc. (Butler, AL) 55497
Vanity Fair Mills Inc. (Monroeville, AL) 56269
Vanity Fair Mills Inc. (Robertsdale, AL) 56504
Warner Co. (Thomasvile, GA) 67786

2369 Girls'/Children's Outerwear Nec
Wrangler (Troy, TN) 82375
Wrangler (Luray, VA) 91218

2387 Apparel Belts
Tandy Brands Accessories (Yoakum, TX) 90137

2389 Apparel & Accessories Nec
Betz Laboratories Inc. (Houston, TX) 85876
Champion Products Inc. (Clayton, NC) 74258; 74259
Champion Products Inc. (Dunn, NC) 74370
Red Kap Ind. (Russellville, KY) 69264
Red Kap Ind. (Tompkinsville, KY) 69318
Russell Corp. (Marianna, FL) 61010
Tandy Brands Accessories (Yoakum, TX) 90137
Wrangler Menswear (El Paso, TX) 84979

2391 Curtains & Draperies
Burlington Industries (Mount Olive, NC) 75694
Burlington Industries Inc. (Greensboro, NC) 74796
Burlington Industries Inc. (Mt. Olive, NC) 75700

Springs Industries, Inc. (Fort Lawn, SC) 79230

2392 Housefurnishings Nec
Brown Forman Corp. (Louisville, KY) 68718; 68719
Burlington Industries Inc. (Greensboro, NC) 74796
Burlington Industries Inc. (Reidsville, NC) 75997
E. R. Carpenter Co. Inc. (Russellville, KY) 69258
E. R. Carpenter Co. Inc. (Niota, TN) 82176
E. R. Carpenter Co. Inc. (Houston, TX) 86053
E.R. Carpenter Co. Inc. (Pontotoc, MS) 73300
E.R. Carpenter Co. Inc. (Cleveland, TN) 80581
E.R. Carpenter Co. Inc. (Dallas, TX) 84016
E.R. Carpenter Co. of Texas (Temple, TX) 89616
Fieldcrest Cannon, Inc. (Kannapolis, NC) 75254
Gold Medal Inc. (Cookeville, TN) 80659
Rubbermaid Commercial Proudcts (Cleveland, TN) 80598
Sealy Mattress Co. (Memphis, TN) 81691
Springs Industries, Inc. (Piedmont, AL) 56482

2393 Textile Bags
Mead Ink Products (Atlanta, GA) 64722

2396 Automotive & Apparel Trimmings
Gold Medal Inc. (Cookeville, TN) 80659

2399 Fabricated Textile Products Nec
Allied-Signal Safety Restraint (Greenville, AL) 55815; 55816
Allied-Signal Safety Restraint (Knoxville, TN) 81134
BASF Corp. (Central, SC) 78781
BASF Corp. Fibers Division (Anderson, SC) 78664
BASF Corp.-Clemson Plant (Central, SC) 78784
BASF Fibers (Anderson, SC) 78666
Baxter Healthcare Corp. (El Paso, TX) 84765
Burlington Industries (Denton, NC) 74359
Burlington Industries (Mount Olive, NC) 75694
Burlington Industries Fabrics Inc. (Franklinton, NC) 74630
Burlington Industries Inc. (Monticello, AR) 57370
Burlington Industries Inc. (Atlanta, GA) 64335
Burlington Industries Inc. (Belmont, NC) 73672
Burlington Industries Inc. (Caroleen, NC) 73782
Burlington Industries Inc. (Cordova, NC) 74344
Burlington Industries Inc. (Denton, NC) 74360
Burlington Industries Inc. (Gastonia, NC) 74669
Burlington Industries Inc. (Gibsonville, NC) 74697
Burlington Industries Inc. (Greensboro, NC) 74796
Burlington Industries Inc. (Mount Holly, NC) 75690
Burlington Industries Inc. (Mt. Holly, NC) 75699
Burlington Industries Inc. (Mt. Olive, NC) 75700
Burlington Industries Inc. (Oxford, NC) 75776; 75777
Burlington Industries Inc. (Rocky Mount, NC) 76079; 76080
Burlington Industries Inc. (Smithfield, NC) 76256; 76257
Burlington Industries Inc. (St. Pauls, NC) 76305
Burlington Industries Inc. (Statesville, NC) 76320
Burlington Industries Inc. (Wake Forest, NC) 76430
Burlington Industries Inc. (Johnson City, TN) 81026
Burlington Industries Inc. (Hillsville, VA) 91139
Burlington Industries/Ranlo Plant (Gastonia, NC) 74670
Burlington Industries Richmond Plant (Cordova, NC) 74345
Burlington Industries/Sheffield Plant (Rocky Mount, NC) 76081
Burlington Industries William G. Lord (Belmont, NC) 73673
Burlington Madison Yarn Co. (St. Pauls, NC) 76306
Burlington Menswear/Plant 17 (Raeford, NC) 75846
Delta Apparel (Decatur, TN) 80726
Delta Mills Marketing (Maiden, NC) 75491
Delta Mills Marketing (Pamplico, SC) 79785
Delta Mills Marketing (Piedmont, SC) 79794
Duck Head Apparel Co. (Maiden, NC) 75492
Owens-Corning Fiberglas Corp. (Aiken, SC) 78653
Quality Mills Inc. Cloth Plant (Mount Airy, NC) 75682
Russell Corp. (Columbia, AL) 55525
Russell Corp. (Dadeville, AL) 55560
Russell Corp. (Lafayette, AL) 56099
Russell Corp. (Montgomery, AL) 56373
Russell Corp. (Sylacauga, AL) 56589
Russell Corp. D.C. & Ind. Park (Marianna, FL) 61011
Shaw Industries Co. (Millendgeville, GA) 66987
Shaw Industries Inc. (Newnan, GA) 67085
Springs Industrial Products (Honea Path, SC) 79530
Springs Industries, Inc. (Anderson, SC) 78693
Springs Industries, Inc. (Chester, SC) 78944
Springs Industries, Inc. (Gaffney, SC) 79265
Springs Industries, Inc. (Kershaw, SC) 79548
Springs Industries, Inc. Eureka (Chester, SC) 78945
Stevcoknit Fabrics Co. (Fayetteville, NC) 74576
Stevcoknit Fabrics Co. (Wallace, NC) 76444
Stevcoknit Fabrics Co. (Edgefield, SC) 79185
TRW Seat Belt Systems (Louisville, MS) 73125
TRW Vehicle Safety Systems (McAllen, TX) 87944
UNIFI, Inc. (Reidsville, NC) 76015
Wellman Inc. (Charlotte, NC) 74224; 74225
Wellman Inc. (Marion, SC) 79645
Woodside Mills Inc. (Anderson, SC) 78696
Woodside Mills Inc. (Fountain Inn, SC) 79251
Wrangler (Wilson, NC) 76655

2400 Lumber & Wood Products
Chesapeake Corp. Fredericksburg Wood Treating (New Post, VA) 91445
Georgia-Pacific Corp. (Palatka, FL) 62228
Louisiana-Pacific Corp. Eufaula Mdf Mill (Clayton, AL) 55523
Louisiana-Pacific Mdf (Clayton, AL) 55524
Masonite Corp. (Waverly, VA) 92531
Union Camp Corp. Building Products Div. (Franklin, VA) 90900; 90901
Union Camp Corp. Fine Paper Div. (Franklin, VA) 90903
Willamette Ind. Lillie (Lillie, LA) 70192
Willamette Industries, Inc. Surepine (Simsboro, LA) 70813

2411 Logging
Blue Grass Cooperage Co., Inc. (Honenwald, TN) 80948
Bowater Carolina Div. (Catawba, SC) 78768
Bowater Inc. (Calhoun, GA) 65460
Bowater Inc. (Lilesville, NC) 75430
Bowater, Inc. (Etowah, TN) 80778
Bowater Inc. (Kingston, TN) 81125
Bowater Inc. Southern Div. (Calhoun, TN) 80269
Champion International Corp. (Cullman, AL) 55539
Federal Paper Board Co. (Lumberton, NC) 75464
Federal Paper Board Co. (Johnston, SC) 79545
Georgia Pacific Corp. (Brunswick, GA) 65409
Mobil Oil Company (Springhill, LA) 70852
Three Rivers Timber Co. Inc. (Simmesport, LA) 70810
Union Camp Corp. (Brent, AL) 55479
Union Camp Corp. (Chapman, AL) 55506; 55507
Union Camp Corp. (Louisville, GA) 66625; 66626
Union Camp Corp. (Swainsboro, GA) 67760
Union Camp Corp. (Waycross, GA) 68042
Union Camp Corp. (Gray Court, SC) 79288
Union Camp Corp. (Franklin, VA) 90899
Westvaco Corp. (Summerville, SC) 79995; 79996
Westvaco Corp. (Walterboro, SC) 80079
Westvaco Corp. (Winnsboro, SC) 80135
Weyeerhaeuser Co. (Plymouth, NC) 75837
Weyerhaeuser Co. (Dierks, AR) 56907
Weyerhaeuser Co. (Hot Springs, AR) 57167

2421 Sawmills & Planing Mills—General
Boise Cascade (Jackson, AL) 56062
Boise Cascade Jackson Operations (Jackson, AL) 56063
Boise Cascade Corp. (Florien, LA) 69854
Boise Cascade Corp. (Oakdale, LA) 70597
Boise Cascade Paper Group (Jackson, AL) 56065
Bowater Inc. (Albertville, AL) 54959
Bowater Inc. (Greenville, SC) 79310
Bowater Lumber Co. (Albertville, AL) 54961; 54962
Champion International Corp. (Jacksonville, FL) 60241
Champion International Corp. (Waycross, GA) 68031
Chesapeak Corp. (Richmond, VA) 91757
Container Corp. of America (Stone Mountain, GA) 67688
Federal Paper Board Co. (Augusta, GA) 65320
Federal Paper Board Co. (Washington, GA) 68022
Federal Paper Board Co. (Rieglewood, NC) 76031
Federal Paper Board Co. (Newberry, SC) 79725
Federal Paper Board Co. Inc. (Riegelwood, NC) 76029
Georgia Pacific Corp. (Belk, AL) 55079; 55080
Georgia Pacific Corp. (Bellamy, AL) 55081
Georgia Pacific Corp. (Monroeville, AL) 56261
Georgia Pacific Corp. (El Dorado, AR) 56943
Georgia Pacific Corp. (Fordyce, AR) 57005
Georgia Pacific Corp. (Cross City, FL) 59128
Georgia Pacific Corp. (Ellabell, GA) 66167
Georgia Pacific Corp. (Hagan, GA) 66328
International Paper Co. Gurdon Wood Products (Gurdon, AR) 57124
International Paper Gurdon Wood Products (Gurdon, AR) 57125
Louisiana Pacific Corp. (Baker, FL) 58615
Louisiana Pacific Corp. (De Funiak Springs, FL) 59243
Louisiana Pacific Corp. (Panama City, FL) 62330
Louisiana Pacific Corp. (Statesboro, GA) 67640
Louisiana Pacific Corp. (Grenada, MS) 72843
Louisiana Pacific Corp. (Bon Wier, TX) 83310
Louisiana Pacific Corp. (New Waverly, TX) 88225
Louisiana Pacific Corp. (Trinity, TX) 89783
Louisiana-Pacific Corp. Kirby Forest Industries (Bon Wier, TX) 83311
Manville Forest Products Joyce Facility (Joyce, LA) 69988
Maxxam Inc. (Houston, TX) 86524
Potlatch Corp. Southern Unit (Warren, AR) 57711
Stone Container Corp. (Orangeburg, SC) 79778
Tibbals Flooring Co. West Plant (Oneida, TN) 82215
Union Camp Corp. (Chapman, AL) 55506; 55507
Union Camp Corp. (Opelika, AL) 56429
Union Camp Corp. (Folkston, GA) 66224
Union Camp Corp. (Vidalia, GA) 67996
Union Camp Corp. Fine Paper Div. (Franklin, VA) 90904
Union Camp Corp. Sawmill Div. (Meldrim, GA) 66973
Universal Forest Products, Inc. (Auburndale, FL) 58603
Universal Forest Products, Inc. (Mouetrie, GA) 67053
Weyeerhaeuser Co. (Plymouth, NC) 75837
Weyerhaeuser Co. (Millport, AL) 56129
Weyerhaeuser Co. (De Queen, AR) 56898
Weyerhaeuser Co. (Dierks, AR) 56906; 56907
Weyerhaeuser Co. (Mountain Pine, AR) 57394; 57395
Weyerhaeuser Co. (Bruce, MS) 72659; 72660
Weyerhaeuser Co. (Philadelphia, MS) 73285; 73286
Weyerhaeuser Co. (Elkin, NC) 74498
Weyerhaeuser Co. (Wright City, OK) 78271
Weyerhaeuser Forest Prods. Co. (Plymouth, NC) 75839
Weyerhaeuser Forest Products Co. (Plymouth, NC) 75840; 75841
Willamette Industries, Inc. Chester (Chester, SC) 78947
Willamette Industries Inc. Dodson (Dodson, LA) 69840
Willamette Industries Inc. Emerson (Emerson, AR) 56965
Willamette Industries, Inc. Moncure (Moncure, NC) 75572

2426 Hardwood Dimension & Flooring Mills
Aristokraft Inc. (Crossville, TN) 80689
Chesapeak Corp. (Richmond, VA) 91757
Fayette Enterprises, Inc. (Fayette, MS) 72769
Georgia Pacific Corp. (El Dorado, AR) 56943
Gold Medal (Houston, MS) 72918
Kimball Furniture Reproductions Inc. (Montgomery, AL) 56349
Merillat Ind. Inc. (Atkins, VA) 90410
Merillat Ind. Inc. (Mount Jackson, VA) 91435
Merillat Industries Inc. (Atkins, VA) 90411
Potlatch Corp. Townsend Unit (Stuttgart, AR) 57664
Riverside Furniture (Russellville, AR) 57586
Sonoco Products Co. (Hartsville, SC) 79505
Thomasville Upholstery, Inc. (Troutman, NC) 76409
Tibbals Flooring Co. (Oneida, TN) 82213
Tibbals Flooring Co. East Plant (Oneida, TN) 82214
Tyson Foods Inc. (Rison, AR) 57557
Union Camp Corp. Fine Paper Div. (Franklin, VA) 90904
West Jefferson Wood Product (W Jefferson, NC) 76421
Weyerhaeuser Co. (Wright City, OK) 78271
Wood Products Co. (Newport, TN) 82175

2429 Special Product Sawmills Nec
Blue Grass Cooperage Co. (Byrdstown, TN) 80264
Blue Grass Cooperage Co., Inc. (Benton, KY) 68124
Sonoco Products Co. (Hartsville, SC) 79505

2430 Millwork, Plywood & Structural Members
Weyerhaeuser Co. (Mountain Pine, AR) 57395

2431 Millwork
Abitibi-Price Corp. (Lumberton, NC) 75458; 75459
Ace Hardware Store (Winston Salem, NC) 76659
GAF Building Materials Corp. (Garden City, GA) 66301
Georgia-Pacific Corp. (Atlantic, GA) 65305
Georgia Pacific Corp. (Doraville, GA) 65930
Master Lock Co. (Auburn, AL) 55066
Potlatch Corp. Townsend Unit (Stuttgart, AR) 57664
Short & Paulk Supply Co. Inc. (Tifton, GA) 67830
Stanley Door Systems (Orlando, FL) 62148
Taylor Building Products of (Auburndale, FL) 58602
Universal Forest Products, Inc. (Salisbury, NC) 76180
Weyerhaeuser Co. (Memphis, TN) 81758

2434 Wood Kitchen Cabinets
Merillat Industries (Mount Jackson, VA) 91436
Starmark of Virginia (Lynchburg, VA) 91289
Tandy Cabinet (Fort Worth, TX) 85306
Tandy Cabinets (Fort Worth, TX) 85307
Walker Manufacturing (Punta Gorda, FL) 62726

2435 Hardwood Veneer & Plywood
Boise Cascade Corp. (Oakdale, LA) 70597
Georgia Pacific Corp. (Monroeville, AL) 56261
Georgia Pacific Corp. (Hawthorne, FL) 59970
Georgia Pacific Corp. (Cedar Springs, GA) 65509
Georgia-Pacific Corp. Savannah Plywood (Savannah, GA) 67479
Ingram Plywoods Inc. (Thomasville, NC) 76378
Masonite Corp. (Thomasville, NC) 76379
Union Camp Corp. (Seaboard, NC) 76214
Universal Forest Products, Inc. (Mouetrie, GA) 67053
Weyeerhaeuser Co. (Plymouth, NC) 75837
Weyerhaeuser Co. (Chesapeake, VA) 90611

2436 Softwood Veneer & Plywood
Boise Cascade Corp. (Oakdale, LA) 70597
Champion Forest Products (Silverstreet, SC) 79867
Champion International Corp. (Waycross, GA) 68031
Champion International Corp. (Camden, TX) 83434; 83435
Champion International Corp. (Corrigan, TX) 83775
Fisher Sawmill (Florien, LA) 69855
Florien Plywood Plant (Florien, LA) 69856
Georgia Pacific Corp. (Monroeville, AL) 56261
Georgia Pacific Corp. (Cedar Springs, GA) 65509
Georgia-Pacific Corp. Warm Springs Pine Plywood (Warm Springs, GA) 68003
Georgia-Pacific Corp. Emporia Pine Plywood (Emporia, VA) 90748
Georgia-Pacific Corp. Hawthorne Plywood (Hawthorne, FL) 59971
Georgia-Pacific Corp. Madison Plywood (Madison, GA) 66728
Georgia-Pacific Corp. Monticello Plywood (Monticello, GA) 67002
Georgia Pacific Corp. Peterman Pine Plywood (Monroeville, AL) 56262
Georgia-Pacific Corp. Plywood (Crossett, AR) 56883
Georgia-Pacific Corp. Plywood Plant (Louisville, MS) 73119
Georgia-Pacific Corp. Prosperity Pine Plywood (Prosperity, SC) 79803
Georgia-Pacific Corp. Prosperity Plywood (Prosperity, SC) 79804
Georgia Pacific Corp. Russellville Pine Plywood (Russellville, SC) 79845

Georgia-Pacific Corp. Russellville Plywood (Russellville, SC) 79846
Georgia-Pacific Corp. Whiteville Plywood (Whiteville, NC) 76501
Georgia-Pacific Resins Inc. Resins (Crossett, AR) 56885
Ingram Plywoods Inc. (Thomasville, NC) 76378
International Paper Springhill Wood Products Plt. (Springhill, LA) 70850
Kirby Forest Ind. Inc. Bon Wier Plywood (Bon Wier, TX) 83308; 83308
Kirby Forest Industries Plywood (Bon Wier, TX) 83309
Kirby Forest Industries Plywood (Cleveland, TX) 83593
Louisiana Pacific Corp. (Bon Wier, TX) 83310
Louisiana Pacific Corp. (Lufkin, TX) 87808
Louisiana Pacific Corp. (New Waverly, TX) 88225
Louisiana-Pacific Corp. Kirby Forest Industries (Bon Wier, TX) 83311
Louisiana Pacific Corp., OSB (Urania, LA) 70920
Louisiana-Pacific Corp., Plywood (Logansport, LA) 70199
Louisiana-Pacific Corp., Plywood (Jasper, TX) 87433
Louisiana-Pacific Corp. Plywood (Lufkin, TX) 87809
Manville Forest Products Joyce Facility (Joyce, LA) 69988
Masonite Corp. (Thomasville, NC) 76379
Oakdale Plywood Plant (Oakdale, LA) 70598
Temple-Inland Forest Prods. Corp. Pineland Ops. (Pineland, TX) 88516
Union Camp Corp. (Chapman, AL) 55506; 55507
Union Camp Corp. (Thorsby, AL) 56612; 56613; 56614
Weyerhaeuser Co. (Millport, AL) 56129
Weyerhaeuser Co. (Dierks, AR) 56906; 56907
Weyerhaeuser Co. (Mountain Pine, AR) 57394; 57395
Weyerhaeuser Co. (Philadelphia, MS) 73285; 73286
Weyerhaeuser Co. (Wright City, OK) 78271
Weyerhaeuser Co. (Chesapeake, VA) 90612
Weyerhaeuser Forest Prods. Co. (Plymouth, NC) 75839
Weyerhaeuser Forest Products Co. (Plymouth, NC) 75840; 75841
Willamette Industries, Inc. Chester (Chester, SC) 78947
Willamette Industries, Inc. Dodson (Dodson, LA) 69839; 69840
Willamette Industries Inc. Emerson (Emerson, AR) 56965
Willamette Industries, Inc. Moncure (Moncure, NC) 75572
Willamette Industries Inc. Ruston (Ruston, LA) 70676; 70677
Willamette Industries Inc. Taylor (Taylor, LA) 70911
Willamette Industries Inc. Zwolle (Zwolle, LA) 70990

2439 Structural Wood Members Nec

Georgia Pacific Corp. (Ocala, FL) 61800
Georgia-Pacific Corp. Ocala Wood-I-Beam (Ocala, FL) 61801
Short & Paulk Supply Co. Inc. (Tifton, GA) 67830
Universal Forest Prod (Grandview, TX) 85651
Universal Forest Products (Grandview, TX) 85652
Universal Forest Products, Inc. (Auburndale, FL) 58603
Universal Forest Products, Inc. (Mouetrie, GA) 67053

2441 Nailed Wood Boxes & Shook

Piper/Casepro (Clarendon, AR) 56847

2449 Wood Containers Nec

Blue Grass Cooperage Co. (Louisville, KY) 68703; 68704; 68705

2451 Mobile Homes

Fleetwood Homes (Auburndale, FL) 58597
Fleetwood Homes (Plant City, FL) 62543
Fleetwood Homes (Alma, GA) 64100
Fleetwood Homes (Broxton, GA) 65396
Fleetwood Homes (Douglas, GA) 65967
Fleetwood Homes (Lexington, MS) 73114
Fleetwood Homes (Pembroke, NC) 75792
Fleetwood Homes (Roxboro, NC) 76127
Fleetwood Homes (Westmoreland, TN) 82409
Fleetwood Homes (Waco, TX) 89935
Fleetwood Homes Florida Inc. (Haines City, FL) 59947
Fleetwood Homes of Florida Inc. No. 70 (Auburndale, FL) 58598
Fleetwood Homes of North Carolina Inc. No. 41 (Pembroke, NC) 75793
Fleetwood Homes of Tennessee Inc. 27 (Westmoreland, TN) 82411
Fleetwood Homes of Tennessee Inc. 26 (Westmoreland, TN) 82412
Fleetwood Homes of Virginia (Rocky Mountain, VA) 92205
Fleetwood Homes of Virginia Inc. No. 19 (Rocky Mount, VA) 92201
Fleetwood Motor Homes of Florida Inc. (Haines City, FL) 59948
Fleetwood Motor Homes of Florida Inc. (Lakeland, FL) 60726
Fleetwood Motor Homes of North Carolina Inc. (Roxboro, NC) 76128
Fleetwood Motor Homes of Tennessee Inc. (Westmoreland, TN) 82413
Wells Manufacturing Co. Inc. (Fayetteville, NC) 74584
Westfield Homes of Georgia (Douglas, GA) 65982

2452 Prefabricated Wood Buildings

Fleetwood Homes (Douglas, GA) 65967
Fleetwood Homes (Roxboro, NC) 76127
Georgia Pacific Corp. (Lake City, FL) 60620
Westfield Homes of Georgia (Douglas, GA) 65982

2491 Wood Preserving

Borden Inc. Chemical (Alexandria, LA) 69368
Caribbean Lumber Co. (Savannah, GA) 67458
Carolina Wood Preserving (Scotland Neck, NC) 76211
Chesapeake Corp. Wood Treating (Elizabeth City, NC) 74476
Chesapeake Wood Treating (Pocomoke City, MD) 72219; 72220
Chesapeake Wood Treating (Eutawville, SC) 79191
Chesapeake Wood Treating Co. (North East, MD) 72153
Chesapeake Wood Treating Co. (Pocomoke City, MD) 72221
Chesapeake Wood Treating Co. (Elizabeth City, NC) 74477
Chesapeake Wood Treating Co. (New Post, VA) 91446
Chesapeake Wood Treating Co. (West Point, VA) 92539
Federal Paper Board Co. Inc. (Riegelwood, NC) 76029
Georgia Pacific Corp. (Cross City, FL) 59128
Georgia Pacific Corp. (Hawthorne, FL) 59970
Georgia Pacific Corp. (Lake City, FL) 60620
Georgia-Pacific Corp. Pearson Sawmill (Pearson, GA) 67255
Georgia-Pacific Corp. Sterling Sawmill (Brunswick, GA) 65412
Georgia-Pacific Corp. Sterling Sawmill (Sterling, GA) 67655
Gilbert & Bennett Mfg. Co. Carolina Wood Preserving Div. (Scotland Neck, NC) 76213
Hoover Treated Wood Prods. Inc. (Pine Bluff, AR) 57518
Hoover Treated Wood Prods. Inc. (Thomson, GA) 67810
Hoover Treated Wood Prods. Inc. (Milford, VA) 91430
Hoover Treated Wood Products (Pine Bluff, AR) 57519
Hoover Treated Wood Products (Thomson, GA) 67811
Hoover Treated Wood Products (Milford, VA) 91431
International Paper (Wiggins, MS) 73489; 73490; 73491
International Paper Co. (Mineola, TX) 88106
International Paper Co. De Ridder (De Ridder, LA) 69813
International Paper De Ridder (De Ridder, LA) 69814
Kerr-Mcgee Chemical Corp. (Columbus, MS) 72717
Kerr-Mcgee Chemical Corp. (Texarkana, TX) 89681; 89682
Louisiana Pacific Corp. (Statesboro, GA) 67640
Louisiana Pacific Corp. (Grenada, MS) 72843
Louisiana Pacific Corp. (New Waverly, TX) 88225
Southern Wood Piedmont Co. (Baldwin, FL) 58616
Southern Wood Piedmont Co. (Augusta, GA) 65347
Southern Wood Piedmont Co. (Inman, SC) 79536
Southern Wood Piedmont Co. (Spartanburg, SC) 79951
Southern Wood Piedmont Co. (Chattanooga, TN) 80494
Thomasville Forest Prods. (Thomasville, NC) 76386
Thomasville Forest Products (Thomasville, NC) 76387
Universal Forest Products, Inc. (Auburndale, FL) 58603
Weyerhaeuser Co. (Millport, AL) 56128; 56129
Weyerhaeuser Co. (De Queen, AR) 56898
Weyerhaeuser Co. Wood Treating Plant (De Queen, AR) 56899
Weyerhaeuser Forest Prods. Co. (Plymouth, NC) 75839
Weyerhaeuser Forest Products Co. (Plymouth, NC) 75840; 75841
Weyerhaeuser Wood Treating Plant (De Queen, AR) 56900
Willamette Industries Inc. Dodson (Dodson, LA) 69840
Willamette Industries Inc. Zwolle (Zwolle, LA) 70990

2493 Reconstituted Wood Products

Abitibi-Price Building Products (Roaring River, NC) 76045
Diboll Particleboard Plant (Diboll, TX) 84655; 84656
Georgia Pacific Corp. (North Little Rock, AR) 57463
Georgia-Pacific Corp. Catawba Hardboard (Catawba, SC) 78773; 78774
Georgia-Pacific Corp. Conway Hardboard (Conway, NC) 74341
Georgia-Pacific Corp. Dudley Comply (Dudley, NC) 74368
Georgia-Pacific Corp. Holly Hill Fiberboard (Holly Hill, SC) 79522
Georgia-Pacific Corp. Jarratt Softboard (Jarratt, VA) 91172
Georgia-Pacific Corp. Monticello Panelboard (Monticello, GA) 67000
Georgia-Pacific Corp. Monticello Pine Plywood (Monticello, GA) 67001
Georgia-Pacific Corp. Particleboard (Taylorsville, MS) 73377
Georgia- Pacific Corp. Russellville Particleboard (Russellville, SC) 79844
Georgia-Pacific Corp. S. Boston Particleboard (South Boston, VA) 92251
Georgia-Pacific Corp. Skippers Osb (Skippers, VA) 92236
Georgia Pacific Corp. South Boston Particleboard (South Boston, VA) 92252
Georgia-Pacific Corp. Vienna Particleboard (Vienna, GA) 67998
Goergia Pacific Corp. (North Little Rock, AR) 57465
International Paper (Nacogdoches, TX) 88169
J. M. Huber Corp. (Commerce, GA) 65661; 65662
Kirby Forest Industries Inc. Trt./Osb (Silsbee, TX) 89433
Louisiana Pacific Corp. (New Waverly, TX) 88225
Louisiana Pacific Corp., OSB (Athens, GA) 64170
Louisiana Pacific Corp., OSB (Urania, LA) 70920
Louisiana Pacific Corp., OSB (Corrigan, TX) 83776
Louisiana-Pacific Osb (Athens, GA) 64171
Masonite Corp. Bldg. Products Group (Laurel, MS) 73104
Masonite Corp. Hardboard Group (Laurel, MS) 73105
Monroeville Particleboard Plant (Monroeville, AL) 56264; 56265
Temple-Inland Forest Products Corp. (Thomson, GA) 67813
Union Camp Corp. Fine Paper Div. (Franklin, VA) 90904
Weyerhaeuser Co. (Adel, GA) 64058
Weyerhaeuser Co. (Elkin, NC) 74499
Weyerhaeuser Co. (Moncure, NC) 75570
Weyerhaeuser Co. (Broken Bow, OK) 76901
Weyerhaeuser Particleboard Mill (Adel, GA) 64059
Willamette Industries Inc. (Bennettsville, SC) 78734
Willamette Industries, Inc. Malvern (Malvern, AR) 57344
Willamette Industries Inc. Surepine (Simsboro, LA) 70812
Wood Fiber Industries (Danville, VA) 90725

2499 Wood Products Nec

Abitibi-Price Corp. (Roaring River, NC) 76046; 76047
ACME Frame Products (Harrisburg, AR) 57135
ACME Frame Products of Mississippi (Tutwiler, MS) 73429
Crown Cork & Seal Co. Inc. (Arlington, TX) 82644
Fayette Enterprise Inc. (Fayette, MS) 72768
Federal Paper Board Co. (Newberry, SC) 79725
Georgia-Pacific Corp. (Little Rock, AR) 57285
Georgia Pacific Corp. (North Little Rock, AR) 57463; 57464
Goergia Pacific Corp. (North Little Rock, AR) 57465
Housing Supply Inc. (Americus, GA) 64139
Louisville Ladder Corp. (Louisville, KY) 68871
Magee Co. (Piggott, AR) 57506; 57507
Magee Co. (Pocahontas, AR) 57542
Masonite Corp. (Thomasville, NC) 76379
Masonite Corp. International Paper (Spring Hope, NC) 76296
Masonite Corp. Stuart Plant (Stuart, VA) 92353
Sonoco Products Co. (Hartsville, SC) 79505
Stanley Hardware Wondura Products (Tupelo, MS) 73426
Stone Container Corp. (Orangeburg, SC) 79778
Superwood Corp. (North Little Rock, AR) 57476
Textone Inc. (Charleston, SC) 78904
True Temper Sports Division (Memphis, TN) 81719
Universal Forest Prods Inc. (Moultrie, GA) 67065
Weyerhaeuser Co. (Moncure, NC) 75569
Williamette Industries Inc. Malvern (Malvern, AR) 57345
Woodtek/Textone (North Charleston, SC) 79759
Woodtek/Textone Inc. (Charleston, SC) 78916

2500 Furniture & Fixtures

Dennison Transoceanic Corp. (Rogersville, TN) 82273
Orchard Decorative Prods. (Blythewood, SC) 78749

2511 Wood Household Furniture

Arkansas Best Corp. (Fort Smith, AR) 57023
Armstrong Furniture (Fort Union, VA) 90889
Armstrong Furniture Inc. (Appomattox, VA) 90271
Armstrong World Industries Furniture Div. (Thomasville, NC) 76371
Broyhill Furniture Ind., Inc. Lenoir Furn. Plant (Lenoir, NC) 75365
Broyhill Furniture Ind. Inc. Complex (Lenoir, NC) 75366
Broyhill Furniture Ind. Inc. Conover Plant (Conover, NC) 74327
Broyhill Furniture Ind. Inc. Harper Plant (Lenoir, NC) 75367
Broyhill Furniture Ind. Inc. Newton Plant (Newton, NC) 75742
Broyhill Furniture Ind., Inc. P Pacemaker Plant (Lenoir, NC) 75368
Broyhill Furniture Ind. Inc. Rutherford Plant (Rutherfordton, NC) 76143
Broyhill Furniture Ind. Inc. Wall Systems Plt. (Lenoir, NC) 75369
Broyhill Furniture Industries Inc. (Lenoir, NC) 75371
Dixie Furniture Co. (Lexington, NC) 75399
Dixie Furniture Co. Inc. (Asheboro, NC) 73584
Dixie Furniture Co. Inc. (Linwood, NC) 75444
Dixie Furniture Co. Inc. Dining Room Div. (Lexington, NC) 75400; 75401
Drexel Heritage Furnishings Plant 6 (Morganton, NC) 75635
Drexel Heritage Furnishings Plant 33 (Morganton, NC) 75636
Drexel Heritage Furnishings Plant 3/5 (Morganton, NC) 75637
Drexel Heritage Furnishings Plant 2 (Marion, NC) 75501
Drexel Heritage Furnishings Inc. Plant 43 (Hildebran, NC) 75185
Drexel Heritage Furnishings Inc. Plant 6 (Morganton, NC) 75638
Drexel Heritage Furnishings Inc. Plant 33 (Morganton, NC) 75639
Drexel Heritage Furnishings Inc. Plant 3/5 (Morganton, NC) 75640
Drexel Heritage Furnishings Inc. Plant 2 (Marion, NC) 75502
Drexel Heritage Furniture Plant 43 (Hildebran, NC) 75186
Drexel Heritage Furniture Plant 1 (Drexel, NC) 74366; 74367
Drexel Heritage Furniture Plant 6 (Morganton, NC) 75641
Drexel Heritage Furniture Plant 60 (Morganton, NC) 75642
Drexel Heritage Furniture Plant 33 (Morganton, NC) 75643
Drexel Heritage Furniture Plant 315 (Morganton, NC) 75644
Drexel Heritage Furniture Plant 2 (Marion, NC) 75503
Gordon Inc. (Johnson City, TN) 81046
Gordon's Inc. (Johnson City, TN) 81047
Hammary Furniture Co. Plant 15 (Lenoir, NC) 75379
Hammary Furniture Co. Plant 14 (Granite Falls, NC) 74755
Henredon Furn. Ind. Inc. (Morganton, NC) 75648
Henredon Furn. Ind. Inc. (Spruce Pine, NC) 76301
Henredon Furniture Ind. Inc. (Morganton, NC) 75649
Henredon Furniture Ind. Inc. (Spruce Pine, NC) 76302
Kimball Furniture Reproductions Inc. (Montgomery, AL) 56349
Kincaid Furniture Co. (Hudson, NC) 75201
Kincaid Furniture Co. Inc. Plant 8 (Lenoir, NC) 75382
Kincaid Furniture Co. Inc. Plant 1 (Hudson, NC) 75202; 75203
Kincaid Furniture Co. Inc. Plant 6 (Hudson, NC) 75204; 75205
Kincaid Furniture Co. Plant 8 (Gamewell, NC) 74643
Lane Co. Inc. (Altavista, VA) 90246; 90247
Lane Co. Inc. (Rocky Mount, VA) 92203
Lexington Furniture Ind. Plant 8 (Lexington, NC) 75411
Lexington Furniture Ind. Plant 11 (Mocksville, NC) 75566
Lexington Furniture Ind. Plant 1 (Lexington, NC) 75412
Lexington Furniture Ind. Plant 10 (Hildebran, NC) 75187
Lexington Furniture Ind. Plant 3 (Lexington, NC) 75413
Lexington Furniture Ind. Plant 12 (Lexington, NC) 75414
Lexington Furniture Ind. Plant 2 (Linwood, NC) 75447
Lexington Furniture Ind. Plants 4 & 5 (Lexington, NC) 75415
Lexington Furniture Ind. Inc. Plant 9 (Lexington, NC) 75416
Lexington Furniture Ind. Inc. Plant 7 (Lexington, NC) 75417

Lexington Furniture Industries Plant Plant 2 (Lexington, NC) 75419
Okla Homer Smith Furniture Co. Inc. (Fort Smith, AR) 57070
Broyhill Furniture Ind. Inc. Lenoir Furniture & Occ.1 Plts (Lenoir, NC) 75383
O'sullivan Ind. Inc. of Virginia (South Boston, VA) 92256
Riverside Furniture Corp. (Fort Smith, AR) 57095
Sico Inc. (Conway, AR) 56871
Southern Furniture Co. Conover Inc. (Conover, NC) 74336
Southern Furniture Co. of Conover Inc. -Catawba Plant (Claremont, NC) 74256
This End Up Furniture Co. (Raleigh, NC) 75964
This End Up Furniture Co. (Columbia, SC) 79108
Thomasville Furniture Ind. Inc. (Lenoir, NC) 75389
Thomasville Furniture Ind. Inc. (Pleasant Garden, NC) 75833
Thomasville Furniture Ind. Inc. (Thomasville, NC) 76388
Thomasville Furniture Ind. Inc. (West Jefferson, NC) 76489
Thomasville Furniture Ind. Inc. (Brookneal, VA) 90496
Thomasville Furniture Ind. Inc. Plant A (Thomasville, NC) 76389
Thomasville Furniture Ind. Inc. Plant B (Thomasville, NC) 76390
Thomasville Furniture Ind. Inc. Plant C (Thomasville, NC) 76391
Thomasville Furniture Ind. Inc. Plant D (Thomasville, NC) 76392
Thomasville Furniture Ind. Inc. Plant H (Winston-Salem, NC) 76772
Thomasville Furniture Industries Inc. (Lenoir, NC) 75390; 75391
Thomasville Furniture Industries Inc. (Thomasville, NC) 76393; 76394; 76395
Thomasville Furniture Industries Inc. (Winston-Salem, NC) 76773
Thomasville Furniture Industries, Inc. Plant A (Thomasville, NC) 76397
Thomasville Furniture Industries, Inc. Plant B (Thomasville, NC) 76398
Thomasville Furniture Industries Inc. Plant C (Thomasville, NC) 76399
Thomasville Furniture Industries Inc. Plant D (Thomasville, NC) 76400
Thomasville Furniture Industries Inc. Plant E (Thomasville, NC) 76401
Thomasville Furniture Industries Inc. Plant H (Winston-Salem, NC) 76774
Thomasville Furniture Industries Inc. Plant L (Thomasville, NC) 76402
Universal Bedroom Furniture Ltd. (Morristown, TN) 81815

2512 Upholstered Household Furniture

Aaron Rents (Atlanta, GA) 64187
Action Industries Inc. (Tupelo, MS) 73384
Arkansas Best Corp. (Fort Smith, AR) 57023
Avon Manufacturing Co. Inc. (Okolona, MS) 73224
Broyhill Furniture Ind. Inc. Taylorsville Plant (Taylorsville, NC) 76366
Broyhill Furniture Ind. Inc. Whitnel Plant (Lenoir, NC) 75370
Broyhill Furniture Industries Inc. (Lenoir, NC) 75371
Conover Inc. Southern Furniture Co. Main Pl (Conover, NC) 74328
Conover Inc. Southern Furniture Co.-Plant 2 (Conover, NC) 74329
Drexel Heritage Furniture Plant 45 (Hickory, NC) 75066
Kimball Furniture Reproductions (Montgomery, AL) 56348
Kimball Furniture Reproductions Inc. (Montgomery, AL) 56349
La-Z-Boy Chair Co. (Siloam Springs, AR) 57620
La-Z-Boy Chair Co. Chair Co. (Siloam Springs, AR) 57621
La-Z-Boy East (Florence, SC) 79213
La-Z-Boy East East (Florence, SC) 79214
La-Z-Boy S. South (Newton, MS) 73219
La-Z-Boy Tennessee (Dayton, TN) 80721
Riverside Furniture Plant 4 (Fort Smith, AR) 57092
Riverside Furniture Plant 1 (Fort Smith, AR) 57093
Riverside Furniture Plants 2, 6, & 7 (Fort Smith, AR) 57094
Riverside Furniture Corp. (Fort Smith, AR) 57095
Southern Furniture Co. of Conover Inc. (Conover, NC) 74337
This End Up Furniture Co. (Raleigh, NC) 75964
Thomasville Upholstery, Inc. (Statesville, NC) 76339
Thomasville Upholstery, Inc. (Troutman, NC) 76409

2514 Metal Household Furniture

Gordon's Inc. (Johnson City, TN) 81047
Leggett & Platt Inc. (Simpsonville, KY) 69290
Leggett & Platt Inc. (Winchester, KY) 69346; 69347
Leggett & Platt Inc. (Linwood, NC) 75445
Leggett & Platt Inc. Cotton Grove Plant (Lexington, NC) 75409
Leggett & Platt Sleeper Comp-O Nents (High Point, NC) 75146
Leggett & Platt Sleeper Components (High Point, NC) 75147
Sunbeam Outdoor Products (Waynesboro, GA) 68047
Sunbeam Outdoor Products (Portland, TN) 82235

2515 Mattresses & Bedsprings

Cone Mills Prelude Co. (Thomasville, NC) 76375
Sealy Mattress Co. (Orlando, FL) 62140
Sealy Mattress Co. (Lexington, NC) 75424
Sealy Mattress Co. (Memphis, TN) 81691
Sealy Mattress Co. (Brenham, TX) 83342
Sealy Stearns & Foster Bedding (Conyers, GA) 65704
Stearns & Foster Co. (Brenham, TX) 83343

2519 Household Furniture Nec

Riverside Furniture Corp. (Fort Smith, AR) 57095
Rubbermaid Specialty Products Inc. (Stanley, NC) 76311
Sunbeam Outdoor Products (Portland, TN) 82235

2521 Wood Office Furniture

Helikon Furniture Co. Inc. (Sanford, NC) 76197
Hon Co. (Owensboro, KY) 69172
La-Z-Boy Leland (Leland, MS) 73113
Riverside Furniture Corp. (Fort Smith, AR) 57095
Tesco Industries Inc. (Bellville, TX) 83275
Valspar Corp. (Garland, TX) 85554

2522 Office Furniture Except Wood

Flour City Architectural (Johnson City, TN) 81037
Hon Co. (Cedartown, GA) 65511
Hon Co. (Sulphur Springs, TX) 89557
Hon Co. (Chester, VA) 90619
Riverside Furniture Corp. (Fort Smith, AR) 57095
United Chair Co. Leeds Facility (Leeds, AL) 56109
United Chair - Irondale Plant (Irondale, AL) 56060

2531 Public Building & Related Furniture

Johnson Controls Inc. (Belcamp, MD) 71343
Johnson Controls Inc. (Pulaski, TN) 82243
National Seating Co. (Vonore, TN) 82395
Tesco Industries Inc. (Bellville, TX) 83275
Weber Aircraft Inc. (Gainesville, TX) 85430

2541 Wood Partitions & Fixtures

A. G. Industries, Inc. (Forest City, NC) 74595; 74595
A G Industries Inc. (Forest City, NC) 74606
Ralph Wilson Plastics Co. (Dallas, TX) 84350
Tesco Industries Inc. (Bellville, TX) 83275

2542 Partitions & Fixtures Except Wood

A G Industries Inc. (Forest City, NC) 74606
Leggett & Platt Inc. Masterack Div. (Atlanta, GA) 64636; 64637; 64638
Patrick Media Group (Arlington, TX) 82714
Waterloo Industries Inc. (Pocahontas, AR) 57548

2591 Drapery Hardware, Blinds & Shades

Kirsch (Scottsville, KY) 69267

2599 Furniture & Fixtures Nec

Armstrong Furniture (Fort Union, VA) 90889
Armstrong Furniture Inc. (Appomattox, VA) 90271
Avon Manufacturing Co. Inc. (Okolona, MS) 73224
Bard C R Inc. (Moncks Corner, SC) 79658
Black & Decker Corp. (Towson, MD) 72506
Ecco Inc. (High Point, NC) 75123
Gold Medal Inc. (Houston, MS) 72918
Gold Medal Inc. (Cookeville, TN) 80659
Gordon Inc. (Johnson City, TN) 81046
Herman Miller Inc. (New Castle, DE) 57865
Herman Miller Inc. (Euless, TX) 85009
Herman Miller Inc. (Houston, TX) 86265
Lane Co. Inc. the (Altavista, VA) 90247
Riverside Furniture (Atlanta, GA) 65080
Rubbermaid Specialty Products Inc. (Stanley, NC) 76311
Sunbeam Outdoor Products (Portland, TN) 82235
This End Up-Furniture Co. (N Little Rock, AR) 57431
Thomasville Upholstery, Inc. (Hickory, NC) 75102
Thomasville Upholstery, Inc. (Statesville, NC) 76339
Varian Associates Inc. (Covington, KY) 68240
Walker Manufacturing Co. (Pocahontas, AR) 57546
Waterloo Industries Inc. (Pocahontas, AR) 57548

2600 Paper & Allied Products

Armstrong Worldindustries Inc. (Pensacola, FL) 62392
Camvac International Inc. (Morristown, TN) 81791
Collins & Aikman Corp. Auto Div. Clinton Plant (Clinton, OK) 76964
Daniels Packaging Co. Inc. (Hendersonville, NC) 75032
Federal Paper Board Co. Inc. Riegelwood Operations (Riegelwood, NC) 76030
Inland-Orange Inc. (Orange, TX) 88316
International Paper Masonite Plant (Sellers, SC) 79854
James River Corp. (Lexington, KY) 68560
James River Corp. (Shreveport, LA) 70733
James River Corp. Dixie Products Group (Fort Smith, AR) 57058
James River Dixie Products (Darlington, SC) 79149
James River Paper Co. (Lexington, KY) 68561
James River Paper Products Inc. (Darlington, SC) 79152
Manville Forest Products Corp. (Clinton, MS) 72689
Manville Forest Products Corp. Packaging (Memphis, TN) 81653
Manville Sales Corp. (Richmond, VA) 91920
Mead Packaging Div. Atlanta Plant (Atlanta, GA) 64720
Procter & Gamble Co. Paper Products (Albany, GA) 64087
Rexham Corp. Memphis Plant (Memphis, TN) 81678
Stone Hodge Inc. (Hodge, LA) 69947
Union Camp Corp. (Spartanburg, SC) 79961
Union Camp Corp. Richmond Bag (Richmond, VA) 92063
Westvaco Corp. Folding Carton (Newark, DE) 57935
Westvaco Corp. Milk Carton (Richmond, VA) 92091

2611 Pulp Mills

Boise Cascade (Jackson, AL) 56062
Boise Cascade Jackson Operations (Jackson, AL) 56063
Boise Cascade Corp. Deridder Mill (De Ridder, LA) 69809
Boise Cascade Corp. White Paper (Jackson, AL) 56064
Boise Cascade Paper Group (Jackson, AL) 56065
Boise Southern Deridder Mill (De Ridder, LA) 69810
Boise Southern Deridder Paper Mill (De Ridder, LA) 69811
Bowater Carolina Div. (Catawba, SC) 78768
Bowater Southern Div. (Newnan, GA) 67078
Bowater Carolina Co. (Catawba, SC) 78769
Bowater Inc. (Albertville, AL) 54959
Bowater Inc. (Lilesville, NC) 75430
Bowater Inc. (Greenville, SC) 79310
Bowater Inc. (White Oak, SC) 80121
Bowater Inc. Carolina Div. Woodlands (Blythewood, SC) 78748
Bowater Inc. Carolina Division (Catawba, SC) 78772
Bowater Inc. South Div. (Cullman, AL) 55538
Bowater Inc. South Div. (Elgin, TN) 80767
Bowater Inc. Southern Div. (Albertville, AL) 54960
Bowater Inc. Southern Division (Calhoun, TN) 80270; 80271
Bowater Lumber Co. (Albertville, AL) 54961; 54962
Bowater Southern Paper Co. (Calhoun, TN) 80272
Bowater Southern Paper Co. Southern Division (Calhoun, TN) 80273
Buckeye Cellulose Corp. (Perry, FL) 62497; 62498
Buckeye Cellulose Corp. (Oglethorpe, GA) 67218
Chesapeak Corp. (Richmond, VA) 91757
Chesapeake Paper Products Co. (West Point, VA) 92538
Columbus Pulp & Paper Complex (Columbus, MS) 72707
Federal Paper Board Co. (Riegelwood, NC) 76031
Federal Paper Board Co. (Prosperity, SC) 79801
Federal Paper Board Co. Inc. (Riegelwood, NC) 76028
Federal Paper Board Co. Inc. Riegelwood Operations (Riegelwood, NC) 76030
Federal Paperboard Co. Inc. (New Bern, NC) 75722
Georgia Pacific Corp. (Ashdown, AR) 56727
Georgia Pacific Corp. (Cross City, FL) 59128
Georgia-Pacific Corp. (Palatka, FL) 62227; 62228
Georgia-Pacific Corp. (Atlantic, GA) 65305
Georgia Pacific Corp. (Brunswick, GA) 65409
Georgia-Pacific Corp. (Monticello, MS) 73186; 73187
Georgia-Pacific Corp. Brunswick Operations (Brunswick, GA) 65411
Georgia Pacific Corp. Monticello Mill (Monticello, MS) 73188
Georgia-Pacific Corp. Paper Operations (Crossett, AR) 56881
Georgia-Pacific Corp. Paper Ops. (Crossett, AR) 56882
Georgia-Pacific Corp. Port Hudson (Zachary, LA) 70983
Georgia-Pacific Corp. Port Hudson Operations (Zachary, LA) 70984; 70985
Hammermill Papers Riverdale Plant (Selma, AL) 56531
Inland-Rome, Inc. (Rome, GA) 67344
International Paper Aerated Stabilization Basins (Bastrop, LA) 69441
International Paper Camden Facility (Camden, AR) 56833
International Paper Clarifiers & Fiber Reclaimer (Bastrop, LA) 69442
International Paper Cmpany Natchez Mill (Natchez, MS) 73199
International Paper Co. Camden Mill (Camden, AR) 56834
International Paper Co. Moss Point Mill (Moss Point, MS) 73192
International Paper Co. Pine Bluff Mill (Pine Bluff, AR) 57520
International Paper Georgetown Mill (Georgetown, SC) 79275; 79276
International Paper Hammermill Riverdale Mill (Selma, AL) 56532
International Paper Louisiana Mill (Bastrop, LA) 69443; 69444
International Paper-Moss Point Mill (Moss Point, MS) 73193
International Paper Natchez Mill (Natchez, MS) 73200; 73201
International Paper - Pine Bluff Mill (Pine Bluff, AR) 57521
International Paper Texarkana Mill (Texarkana, TX) 89678
Itt Rayonier (Fernandina, FL) 59404
ITT Rayonier Inc.. Jessup Div. (Jesup, GA) 66370
ITT Rayonier Inc. Jesup Pulp Div. (Jesup, GA) 66371
James River Corp. Naheola Mill (Pennington, AL) 56455
James River Corp.-Naheola Mill (Silas, AL) 56568
James River Paper Co. Inc. St. Francisville (St. Francisville, LA) 70861
Mead Corp. Kingsport Mill (Kingsport, TN) 81112
Mead Paper (Kingsport, TN) 81113
Nalco Chemical Co. (Mt Pleasant, SC) 79675; 79676
Packaging Corp. of America Tennessee River Pulp Division (Counce, TN) 80681
Procter & Gamble Cellulose Co. (Perry, FL) 62502; 62503; 62504
Procter & Gamble Cellulose Co. (Oglethorpe, GA) 67219
Procter & Gamble Cellulose Co. Memphis Plant (Memphis, TN) 81673
Stone Container Corp. (Panama City, FL) 62351
Stone Container Corp. (Orangeburg, SC) 79778
Stone Hopewell Inc. (Hopewell, VA) 91166
Tennessee River Pulp & Paper Co. Packaging Division (Counce, TN) 80682
Union Camp Corp. (Opelika, AL) 56427
Union Camp Corp. (Prattville, AL) 56493
Union Camp Corp. (Savannah, GA) 67530; 67531
Union Camp Corp. Fine Paper Div. (Franklin, VA) 90902
US Pulp & Newsprint (Coosa Pines, AL) 55527
Westvaco Corp. (Parkersburg, WV) 93000
Westvaco Corp. Fine Papers Div. (Wickliffe, KY) 69340
Westvaco Corp. Kraft Div. (North Charleston, SC) 79756
Westvaco Corp. Research (Ravenel, SC) 79807
Weyerhaeuser (Oglethorpe, GA) 67220
Weyerhaeuser Co. (Hot Springs, AR) 57167
Weyerhaeuser Co. (Oglethorpe, GA) 67221
Weyerhaeuser Co. Plymouth Mill (Plymouth, NC) 75838
Weyerhaeuser Paper Co. (New Bern, NC) 75739
Weyerhaeuser Paper Co. (Vanceboro, NC) 76416
Willamette Industries Inc. (Hawesville, KY) 68419; 68420
Willamette Industries Inc. (Campti, LA) 69755

2621 Paper Mills

Abitibi Price Sales Corp. (Atlanta, GA) 64190; 64191
Avery Dennison (Meridian, MS) 73159
Bear Island Paper Co. (Ashland, VA) 90399; 90400

Boise Cascade (Jackson, AL) 56062
Boise Cascade Jackson Operations (Jackson, AL) 56063
Boise Cascade Corp. (DeRidder, LA) 69834
Boise Cascade Corp. Deridder Mill (De Ridder, LA) 69809
Boise Cascade Corp. White Paper (Jackson, AL) 56064
Boise Cascade Paper Group (Jackson, AL) 56065
Boise Southern Deridder Mill (De Ridder, LA) 69810
Boise Southern Deridder Paper Mill (De Ridder, LA) 69811
Bowater Carolina Div. (Catawba, SC) 78768
Bowater Data Processing Division (Greenville, SC) 79308
Bowater Carolina Co. (Catawba, SC) 78769
Bowater Communications Papers (Lakeland, FL) 60717
Bowater Inc. (Greenville, SC) 79310
Bowater Inc. Carolina Div. (Catawba, SC) 78771
Bowater Inc. Carolina Division (Catawba, SC) 78772
Bowater Inc. Southern Div. (Calhoun, TN) 80268; 80269
Bowater Inc. Southern Division (Calhoun, TN) 80270; 80271
Bowater Lumber Co. (Albertville, AL) 54961
Bowater Southern Paper Co. (Calhoun, TN) 80272
Bowater Southern Paper Co. Southern Division (Calhoun, TN) 80273
Butler Paper (Mobile, AL) 56147; 56148
Butler Paper Co. (Baton Rouge, LA) 69478
Butler Paper Co. (Lafayette, LA) 70047; 70048
Butler Paper Co. (Shreveport, LA) 70695
Butler Paper Co. (West Monroe, LA) 70943
Butler Paper Co. (Suffolk, VA) 92359; 92360
Carpenter Paper Co. (Amarillo, TX) 82536; 82537
Champion International Corp. (Dallas, TX) 83908
Champion International Corp. (Fort Worth, TX) 85080
Champion International Corp. (Lufkin, TX) 87798
Champion International Corp. (Sheldon, TX) 89389
Champion International Corp. Courtland Mill (Courtland, AL) 55533; 55534
Champion International Corp. Lufkin Newsprint Operations (Lufkin, TX) 87799
Champion International Courtland Mill (Courtland, AL) 55535
Champion International Lufkin Newsprint Operation (Lufkin, TX) 87800
Chesapeak Corp. (Richmond, VA) 91757
Chesapeake Paper Products Co. (West Point, VA) 92538
Columbus Pulp & Paper Complex (Columbus, MS) 72707
Federal Paper Board (Pineville, NC) 75814
Federal Paper Board Co. (Louisville, KY) 68762
Federal Paper Board Co. (East Flat Rock, NC) 74448
Federal Paper Board Co. (Riegelwood, NC) 76031
Federal Paper Board Co. (Wilmington, NC) 76556
Federal Paper Board Co. Inc. (Riegelwood, NC) 76028
Fort Howard Corp. (Rincon, GA) 67299; 67300
Fort Howard Corp. (Owings Mills, MD) 72186
Fort Howard Corp. (Muskogee, OK) 77219; 77220
Fort Howard Paper Co. (Muskogee, OK) 77221
Fort Howard Paper Corp. (Rincon, GA) 67301
Gaylord Container Corp. (Pine Bluff, AR) 57514; 57515
Gaylord Container Corp. (Bogalusa, LA) 69704
Gaylord Container Corp. Formerly Known as Mid-America (Pine Bluff, AR) 57516
Georgia Pacific Corp. (Ashdown, AR) 56727
Georgia-Pacific Corp. (Palatka, FL) 62227; 62228
Georgia-Pacific Corp. (Atlantic, GA) 65305
Georgia Pacific Corp. (Cedar Springs, GA) 65509
Georgia-Pacific Corp. Port Hudson (Zachary, LA) 70983
Georgia-Pacific Corp. Port Hudson Operations (Zachary, LA) 70984; 70985
Hammermill Papers Riverdale Plant (Selma, AL) 56531
Inland-Orange Inc. (Orange, TX) 88316
International Paper Aerated Stabilization Basins (Bastrop, LA) 69441
International Paper Camden Facility (Camden, AR) 56833
International Paper Clarifiers & Fiber Reclaimer (Bastrop, LA) 69442
International Paper Co. Camden Mill (Camden, AR) 56834
International Paper Co. Moss Point Mill (Moss Point, MS) 73192
International Paper Co. Pine Bluff Mill (Pine Bluff, AR) 57520
International Paper Co. Pineville Mill (Pineville, LA) 70618
International Paper Georgetown Mill (Georgetown, SC) 79275; 79276
International Paper Hammermill Riverdale Mill (Selma, AL) 56532
International Paper Louisiana Mill (Bastrop, LA) 69443; 69444
International Paper Mobile Mill (Mobile, AL) 56187
International Paper-Moss Point Mill (Moss Point, MS) 73193
International Paper - Pine Bluff Mill (Pine Bluff, AR) 57521
International Paper Pineville Mill (Pineville, LA) 70619; 70620
International Paper Texarkana Mill (Texarkana, TX) 89678
James River Corp. Curtis Div. (Newark, DE) 57912; 57913
James River Corp. Filtration Products Div. Richmond (Richmond, VA) 91910; 91911
James River Corp. Naheola Mill (Pennington, AL) 56455
James River Corp.-Naheola Mill (Silas, AL) 56568
James River Paper Co. Inc. Curtis Div. (Newark, DE) 57914
James River Paper Co. Inc. St. Francisville (St. Francisville, LA) 70861
Kimberly-Clark Corp. Beech Island Mill (Beech Island, SC) 78721
Manville Corp. Packaging Div. (Atlanta, GA) 64669
Manville Corp. Paperboard Div. (West Monroe, LA) 70945
Manville Corp. Wood Products/ Forest Resources/Energy Resources Div. (West Monroe, LA) 70946
Mead Corp. Kingsport Mill (Kingsport, TN) 81112
Mead Paper (Kingsport, TN) 81113
Packaging Corp. of America Tennessee River Pulp Division (Counce, TN) 80681
Potlatch Corp. (Arkansas City, AR) 56724
Procter & Gamble Paper Product Co. (Albany, GA) 64088
Riverwood International Corp. (Atlanta, GA) 65082
Scott Paper Co. (Mobile, AL) 56237
Scott Paper Co. (Dover, DE) 57808
Seminole Kraft Corp. (Jacksonville, FL) 60455
Sloan Paper Co. Inc. (Birmingham, AL) 55390
Sonoco Products Co. (Richmond, VA) 92042
Stone Container Corp. (Panama City, FL) 62351
Stone Container Corp. (Savannah, GA) 67515
Stone Container Corp. (Hodge, LA) 69946
Stone Container Corp. (Florence, SC) 79227
Stone Container Corp. (Hopewell, VA) 91165
Stone Container Corp. Containerboard & Paper Division (Florence, SC) 79228
3M Adhesive Technology Corp. (Burlington, NC) 73762
Unijax Inc. (Atlanta, GA) 65229
Unijax Inc. (Columbus, GA) 65655; 65656
Unijax Inc. (Macon, GA) 66720
Unijax Inc. (Valdosta, GA) 67976; 67977
Union Camp Corp. (Tucker, GA) 67899
Union Camp Corp. (Eastover, SC) 79182; 79183
Union Camp Corp. (Houston, TX) 87052
Union Camp Corp. Fine Paper Div. (Franklin, VA) 90902
Union Camp Corp. Woodlands Div. (Savannah, GA) 67532
US Pulp & Newsprint (Coosa Pines, AL) 55527
Valentine Paper Co. Lockport Div. (Lockport, LA) 70198
W. R. Grace & Co. (Owensboro, KY) 69196
Westvaco Corp. (Dallas, TX) 84494
Westvaco Corp. (Wellsburg, WV) 93105
Westvaco Corp. Fine Paper (Luke, MD) 72116
Westvaco Corp. Fine Papers Div. (Wickliffe, KY) 69340
WestVaco Corp. Kraft Div. (North Charleston, SC) 79755; 79756
Westvaco Corp. Carbon Dept. (Covington, VA) 90668
Weyerhaeuser (Oglethorpe, GA) 67220
Weyerhaeuser Co. (Columbus, MS) 72733
Weyerhaeuser Co. Plymouth Mill (Plymouth, NC) 75838
Weyerhaeuser Paper Co. (Charlotte, NC) 74229
Weyerhaeuser Paper Co. (Valliant, OK) 78221
Willamette Industries Inc. (Hawesville, KY) 68421
Wisconsin Tissue Mills (Louisville, KY) 69043
W.R. Grace & Co. (Owensboro, KY) 69199

2630 Paperboard Mills

Jefferson Smurfit Corp. (Jacksonville, FL) 60337

2631 Paperboard Mills

Boise Cascade Corp. (DeRidder, LA) 69834
Chesapeak Corp. (Richmond, VA) 91757
Chesapeake Paper Products Co. (West Point, VA) 92538
Container Corp. of America (Stone Mountain, GA) 67688
Federal Paper Board Co. (Augusta, GA) 65320
Federal Paper Board Co. Inc. (Charlotte, NC) 73950
Federal Paper Board Co. Inc. (Riegelwood, NC) 76028
Federal Paper Board Co. Inc. Augusta (Augusta, GA) 65321
Federal Paper Board Co. Inc.-Augusta Operations (Augusta, GA) 65322
Federal Paper Board Co. Inc. Riegelwood Operations (Riegelwood, NC) 76030
Gaylord Container Corp. (Bogalusa, LA) 69704
Georgia Pacific Corp. (Brunswick, GA) 65409
Georgia-Pacific Corp. (Monticello, MS) 73186; 73187
Georgia-Pacific Corp. (Pryor, OK) 77739
Georgia-Pacific Corp. Brunswick Operations (Brunswick, GA) 65411
Georgia Pacific Corp. Monticello Mill (Monticello, MS) 73188
Great Southern Paper (Cedar Springs, GA) 65510
Inland-Orange Inc. (Orange, TX) 88316
Inland-Rome, Inc. (Rome, GA) 67344
International Paper Co. Mansfield Mill (Mansfield, LA) 70212
International Paper Co. Moss Point Mill (Moss Point, MS) 73192
International Paper Co. Pineville Mill (Pineville, LA) 70618
International Paper Co. Vicksburg Mill (Vicksburg, MS) 73453
International Paper Mansfield Mill (Mansfield, LA) 70213
International Paper-Moss Point Mill (Moss Point, MS) 73193
International Paper Pineville Mill (Pineville, LA) 70619; 70620
International Paper Vicksburg Mill (Redwood, MS) 73314
International Paper Vicksburg Mill (Vicksburg, MS) 73454
James River Corp. Naheola Mill (Pennington, AL) 56455
Jefferson Smurfit Corp. Containerboard Mill Div. (Jacksonville, FL) 60338
Manville Forest Products Corp. Plant 31 (West Monroe, LA) 70951
Manville Forest Products Corp. Plant 20 (West Monroe, LA) 70953
Mead Coated Board Inc. (Cottonton, AL) 55531
Mead Containerboard (Stevenson, AL) 56572
Mead Paperboard Products (Lynchburg, VA) 91268
Mid America Packaging Inc. (Pine Bluff, AR) 57526
Nekoosa Packaging (Big Island, VA) 90431
Packaging Corp. of America Valdosta (Clyattville, GA) 65567
Packaging Corp. of America Valdosta Facility (Clyattville, GA) 65568
Potlatch Corp. (Mc Gehee, AR) 57357
Potlatch Corp. (McGehee, AR) 57362
Pulp & Paperboard Operations (Evadale, TX) 85024
Riverwood International Corp. (Atlanta, GA) 65082
Riverwood International USA Inc. (West Monroe, LA) 70958; 70959
Seminole Kraft Corp. (Jacksonville, FL) 60455
Sonoco Products Co. (Newport, TN) 82171; 82172
Sonoco Products Co. (Richmond, VA) 92042
Sonoco Products Co. Hartsville (Hartsville, SC) 79506
Stone Container Corp. (Birmingham, AL) 55399
Stone Container Corp. (Panama City, FL) 62351
Stone Container Corp. (Port Wentworth, GA) 67277
Stone Container Corp. (Savannah, GA) 67515
Stone Container Corp. (Hodge, LA) 69946
Stone Container Corp. (Florence, SC) 79227
Stone Container Corp. (Hopewell, VA) 91165
Stone Container Corp. Containerboard & Paper Division (Florence, SC) 79228
Stone Hodge Inc. (Hodge, LA) 69947
Stone Hopewell Inc. (Hopewell, VA) 91166
Stone Savannah River Pulp & Paper (Port Wentworth, GA) 67278
Temple-Inland Inc. Pulp & Paperboard Operations (Evadale, TX) 85025
Tifpc Bleached Paperboard Pulp & Paperboard Operations (Evadale, TX) 85026
Union Camp Corp. (Prattville, AL) 56493
Union Camp Corp. (Savannah, GA) 67530; 67531
Union Camp Corp. Fine Paper Div. (Franklin, VA) 90902
Union Camp Corp. Woodlands Div. (Savannah, GA) 67532
Westvaco Corp. (Bedford, VA) 90425
Westvaco Corp. Bleached Board (Covington, VA) 90666
WestVaco Corp. Kraft Div. (North Charleston, SC) 79755; 79756
Westvaco Corp. Carbon Dept. (Covington, VA) 90668
Weyerhaeuser Co. Plymouth Mill (Plymouth, NC) 75838
Weyerhaeuser Paper Co. (Valliant, OK) 78220; 78221
Willamette Industries Inc. (Hawesville, KY) 68419; 68420
Willamette Industries Inc. (Campti, LA) 69755

2650 Paperboard Containers & Boxes

James River Corp. Dixie Products (Darlington, SC) 79148
James River Paper Products Inc. (Darlington, SC) 79151

2652 Setup Paperboard Boxes

Federal Paper Board Co. (Thomaston, GA) 67785
Gaylord Container Corp. (Newark, DE) 57909
Gaylord Container Corp. (Weslaco, TX) 90034
Gravure Packaging Inc. (Richmond, VA) 91899
Perma Products Co. (Duncanville, TX) 84702
Rexham Corp. Pineville Plant (Pineville, NC) 75823
Stone Container Corp. (Lexington, NC) 75425
Stone Container Corp. (Martinsville, VA) 91359
Stone Container Corp. (Wellsburg, WV) 93104
Westvaco Corp. (Cleveland, TN) 80608
Westvaco Corp. (Richmond, VA) 92087; 92089
WestVaco Corp. Folding Carton Div. (Newark, DE) 57936
Weyerhaeuser Paper Co. (Lithonia, GA) 66613
Weyerhaeuser Paper Co. (Memphis, TN) 81759

2653 Corrugated & Solid Fiber Boxes

Boise Cascade Corp. Container (West Memphis, AR) 57717
Chesapeak Corp. (Richmond, VA) 91757
Chesapeak Display & Packaging Co. Inc. (Winston-Salem, NC) 76720
Chesapeake Packaging Co. (Richmond, VA) 91763
Gaylord Container Corp. (Bogalusa, LA) 69703; 69704
Georgia Pacific Corp. (Lake Placid, FL) 60643
Georgia-Pacific Corp. (Albany, GA) 64075
Georgia-Pacific Corp. (Plano, TX) 88572
Georgia-Pacific Corp. Packaging Div. (Asheboro, NC) 73587
Inland Container Corp. (Rome, GA) 67343
Inland Container Corp. (Louisville, KY) 68780
Inland Container Corp. (Minden, LA) 70341
Inland Container Corp. (Hattiesburg, MS) 72892
Inland Container Corp. (Vega Alta, PR) 78622
Inland Container Corp. (Carrollton, TX) 83471
Inland Container Corp. No. 33 (Fort Smith, AR) 57057
Inland Container Corp. No. 24 (Hattiesburg, MS) 72893
International Paper (Bay Minette, AL) 55075
International Paper (Edinburg, TX) 84733
International Paper (El Paso, TX) 84812
International Paper Container Div. (Carrollton, TX) 83472
International Paper Co. Container Div. (Statesville, NC) 76331
International Paper Co. Container Div. (Georgetown, SC) 79274
Jefferson Smurfit Corp. (Bryant, AR) 56823
Owens-Illinois Glass Container Inc. (Waco, TX) 89957
Owens Illinois Glass Container Inc. Plant 2 (Huntington, WV) 92889
Packaging Corp. of America (Arlington, TX) 82713
Packaging Corp. of America (Harrisonburg, VA) 91096
Perma Products (Atlanta, GA) 65008
Perma Products Co. (Duncanville, TX) 84702
Perma Products Inc. (Atlanta, GA) 65009
Perma Products Inc. (Duncanville, TX) 84705
Ryder Truck Rental (Batesville, AR) 56762
Sonoco Products Co. (Marietta, GA) 66917
Stone Container Corp. (Tupelo, MS) 73427
Stone Container Corp. (Collierville, TN) 80622
Stone Container Corp. (Nashville, TN) 82103
Stone Container Corp. (Richmond, VA) 92049
Stone Container Corp. Corrugated Container Div. (Pineville, NC) 75827
Temple-Inland Forest Production Co. (Diboll, TX) 84659
Union Camp Corp. (Decatur, AL) 55609
Union Camp Corp. (Forest Park, GA) 66251
Union Camp Corp. (Savannah, GA) 67530
Union Camp Corp. (Statesboro, GA) 67651

Union Camp Corp. (Houston, MS) 72924
Union Camp Corp. (Spartanburg, SC) 79969
Union Camp Corp. (Wellford, SC) 80082
Union Camp Corp. (Morristown, TN) 81814
Union Camp Corp. (San Antonio, TX) 89282
Union Camp Corp. Container Div. (Richmond, VA) 92062
Union Camp Corp. Woodlands Div. (Savannah, GA) 67532
Weyerhaeuser Paper Co. (Richland, MS) 73315
Weyerhaeuser Paper Co. (Amarillo, TX) 82590

2655 Fiber Cans, Drums & Similar Products

Allied-Signal Fiber (Moncure, NC) 75567
Allied-Signal Inc. (Dalton, GA) 65769; 65770
BASF Corp. (Dalton, GA) 65772
BASF Corp. Fibers Division (Dalton, GA) 65773
BASF Corp. Fibers Division (Anderson, SC) 78664
BASF Fibers (Anderson, SC) 78666
BASF Fibers (Williamsburg, VA) 92565
BASF Structural Materials (Rock Hill, SC) 79811
Owens Corning Fiberglass (Meridian, MS) 73172
Sonoco Fibre Drum Co. (Culloden, WV) 92824
Sonoco Fibre Drum Inc. (Charlotte, NC) 74162
Sonoco Products Co. (Canden, AR) 56842
Sonoco Products Co. (Atlanta, GA) 65159
Sonoco Products Co. (Forest Park, GA) 66249
Sonoco Products Co. (Lincolnton, NC) 75442
Sonoco Products Co. (Fountain Inn, SC) 79249
Sonoco Products Co. (Chattanooga, TN) 80493
Sonoco Products Co. (Jackson, TN) 81002
Sonoco Products Co. (Memphis, TN) 81695
Sonoco Products Co. (Newport, TN) 82171
Sonoco Products Co. (Arlington, TX) 82752
Sonoco Products Co. (Denison, TX) 84609
Sonoco Products Co. (Chester, VA) 90627
Sonoco Products Co. Hartsville (Hartsville, SC) 79506
Sonoco Semi-Bulk Packaging (Saraland, LA) 56519
Sonoco Semi-Bulk Packaging (Houston, TX) 86900
Sunoco Products Co. (Orlando, FL) 62150

2656 Sanitary Food Containers

Champion International Corp. (Athens, GA) 64165
Fort Howard Cup Corp. (Owings Mills, MD) 72187
Imperial Bondware (Lafayette, GA) 66492
International Paper (East Point, GA) 66145
International Paper Liquid Packaging Div. (Bastrop, LA) 69440
James River Paper Co. Inc. Dixie Products (Fort Smith, AR) 57060
James River Paper Co. Inc. Dixie Products (Darlington, SC) 79150
Westvaco Corp. (Chamblee, GA) 65552
Westvaco Corp. (Dallas, TX) 84495
Westvaco Corp. (Richmond, VA) 92088
Westvaco Corp. Liquid Packaging (Richmond, VA) 92090

2657 Folding Paperboard Boxes

Coors Packaging Co. (Lawrenceburg, TN) 81288
Federal Paper Board Co. (Thomaston, GA) 67785
Federal Paper Board Co. (Louisville, KY) 68762
Federal Paper Board Co. (Durham, NC) 74392

Federal Paper Board Co. (East Flat Rock, NC) 74448
Federal Paper Board Co. (Wilmington, NC) 76556
Federal Paper Board Co. Inc. (Durham, NC) 74393
Federal Paper Board Co. Inc. (Wilmington, NC) 76557
Federal Paper Board Co. Inc. Plant 49 (Durham, NC) 74394
Federal Paper Board Co. Inc., Plant 24 (Wilmington, NC) 76558
Graphic Packaging Corp. (Lawrenceburg, TN) 81289
Gravure Packaging Inc. (Richmond, VA) 91899
International Paper Co. Richmond Gravure (Raleigh, NC) 75917
International Paper Richmond Gravure (Raleigh, NC) 75918
James River Corp. (Newnan, GA) 67082
Manufacturers Folding Carton (El Paso, TX) 84845
Manville Forest Products Corp. Plant 70 (West Monroe, LA) 70948; 70949; 70950
Manville Forest Products Corp. Plant 31 (West Monroe, LA) 70952
Nekoosa Packaging (Winter Haven, FL) 63947
Rexham Corp. (Pineville, NC) 75822
Rexham Packaging (Pineville, NC) 75824; 75825
Richmond Gravure Folding Carton Div. (Richmond, VA) 91994
Richmond Gravure Inc. (Richmond, VA) 91995
Riverwood International USA Inc. (West Monroe, LA) 70957
Stone Container Corp. (Jeffersontown, KY) 68500
Stone Container Corp. (Lexington, NC) 75425
Union Camp Corp. (Jamestown, NC) 75244
Westvaco Corp. (Gastonia, NC) 74693
Westvaco Corp. (Cleveland, TN) 80608
Westvaco Corp. (Richmond, VA) 92087
WestVaco Corp. Folding Carton Div. (Newark, DE) 57936

2671 Paper Coated & Laminated—Packaging

Avery Dennison-Avery International Business Systems Div. (Flowery Branch, GA) 66216
Avery Dennison Co. (Gastonia, NC) 74656
Avery Dennison Soabar (Greensboro, NC) 74782
International Paper Container Div. (Shreveport, LA) 70732
James River Corp. (Jackson, TN) 80986
James River Paper Co. Inc. (Jackson, TN) 80987
Manville Corp. Packaging Div. (Atlanta, GA) 64669
Manville Forest Products Plant 20 (West Monroe, LA) 70947
Materials Group Fasson Roll Materials Div. (Peachtree, GA) 67232
R. J. Reynolds Tobacco Co. Whitaker Park 641 (Winston-Salem, NC) 76755
Rexham Corp. Memphis Plant (Memphis, TN) 81678
Reynolds Metals Co. (Louisville, KY) 68989
Reynolds Metals Co. (Richmond, VA) 91981
Riverwood International USA Inc. (West Monroe, LA) 70960
Schuylkill Metals Corp. (Baton Rouge, LA) 69658
Stone Container Corp. (Sheridan, AR) 57614
Stone Container Corp. (Arcadia, LA) 69430
Stone Container Corp. (Richmond, VA) 92050

International Paper Uniwood Div. (Statesville, NC) 76330
International Paper Co. Uniwood Div. (Statesville, NC) 76332
International Paper-Moss Point Mill (Moss Point, MS) 73193
Ludlow Corp. Laminating (Meridian, MS) 73171
Rexham Corp. (Greensboro, NC) 74891
Reynolds Metals Co. Plant 1 (Louisville, KY) 68991
Schuller International Inc. (Richmond, VA) 92010
Standard Register Co. (Tampa, FL) 63602
Stone Container Corp. (Richmond, VA) 92050
3M (Dallas, TX) 84451
3M Co. (Brownwood, TX) 83390
3M Co. Tape Manufacturing Div. (Greenville, SC) 79440
3M Co. Telecom Markets Div. (Austin, TX) 83046
Union Camp Corp. (Conway, AR) 56875
W. R. Grace & Co. (Owensboro, KY) 69196
W.R. Grace & Co. (Owensboro, KY) 69199

2673 Bags—Plastics, Laminated & Coated

Bemis Co. (Crossett, AR) 56879
Bemis Co. (Memphis, TN) 81472
First Brands Corp. (Rogers, AR) 57563
First Brands Corp. (Cartersville, GA) 65499
First Brands Puerto Rico (Hato Rey, PR) 78455
Mid America Packaging Inc. (Pine Bluff, AR) 57526
Mobil Chemical Co. General Products (Temple, TX) 89627
Plastic Packaging Inc. (Hickory, NC) 75095
Sonoco Products Co. (Victoria, TX) 89905
Stone Container Corp. (Jacksonville, AR) 57202
Stone Container Corp. (Yulee, FL) 64005
Stone Container Corp. (Louisville, KY) 69010
Stone Container Corp. (Hodge, LA) 69946
Stone Container Corp. (Hopewell, VA) 91165
Stone Container Corp. (Richmond, VA) 92050
Stone Container Corp. (Wellsburg, WV) 93104
Union Camp Corp. (La Grange, GA) 66490
Union Camp Corp. (Lifton, GA) 66551
Union Camp Corp. (Shelbyville, KY) 69278
Union Camp Corp. (Richmond, VA) 92061

2674 Bags—Uncoated Paper & Multiwall

Bemis Co. (Crossett, AR) 56879
Bemis Co. (Memphis, TN) 81472
International Paper (Mobile, AL) 56185
International Paper Kraft Packaging Div. (Mobile, AL) 56186
International Paper Camden Facility (Camden, AR) 56833
Mid America Packaging Inc. (Pine Bluff, AR) 57526
Moen Inc. (Durham, NC) 74419
Stone Container Corp. (Jacksonville, AR) 57202
Stone Container Corp. (Sheridan, AR) 57614
Stone Container Corp. (Yulee, FL) 64005
Stone Container Corp. (Savannah, GA) 67515
Stone Container Corp. (Louisville, KY) 69010
Stone Container Corp. (Arcadia, LA) 69430
Union Camp Corp. (Lifton, GA) 66551
Union Camp Corp. (Savannah, GA) 67530
Union Camp Corp. (Spartanburg, SC) 79960
Union Camp Corp. (Richmond, VA) 92061
Union Camp Corp. Bag (Spartanburg, SC) 79962

2675 Die-Cut Paper & Board

Sonoco Products Co. (Broken Arrow, OK) 76889
Unijax, Inc. (Jacksonville, FL) 60482
Wolverine Gasket Co. (Leesburg, FL) 60889

2676 Sanitary Paper Products

Fort Howard Cup Corp. (Owings Mills, MD) 72187
Fort Howard Paper Corp. (Rincon, GA) 67301
James River Co. (Lexington, KY) 68559
Kimberly-Clark Corp. Paris Tx Plant (Paris, TX) 88369
Procter & Gamble Paper Product Co. (Albany, GA) 64088
Weyerhaeuser Co. (Waco, TX) 89982
Weyerhaeuser Co. Bowling Green (Bowling Green, KY) 68165

2677 Envelopes

American Business Machines Inc. (Atlanta, GA) 64219
American Greetings Corp. (Lafayette, TN) 81286
Garrett-Buchanan Co. (Jessup, MD) 71984
Quality Park Product (Atlanta, GA) 65050; 65051
Quality Park Products (Atlanta, GA) 65052
Unijax, Inc. (Jacksonville, FL) 60482
Unijax Inc. (Miami, FL) 61487; 61488
Unijax, Inc. (Charlotte, NC) 74183
Unijax Inc. (Garner, NC) 74649
Union Envelope Co. (Richmond, VA) 92064
Westvaco Corp. (Chamblee, GA) 65552
Westvaco Corp. (Charlotte, NC) 74228
Westvaco Corp. (Dallas, TX) 84495
Westvaco Corp. Envelope (Dallas, TX) 84496

2678 Stationery Products

American Greetings Corp. (Lafayette, TN) 81286
Quality Park Product (Atlanta, GA) 65050; 65051
Quality Park Products (Atlanta, GA) 65052
Union Camp Corp. (Houston, TX) 87052
Union Camp Corp. School Supplies Div. (Birmingham, AL) 55435

2679 Converted Paper Products Nec

American Greetings Corp. (Osceola, AR) 57480
Armstrong World Industries Inc. (Pensacola, FL) 62391
Avery Dennison Corp. (Flowery Br, GA) 66214
Avery Dennison Manufacturing Corp. (Midlothian, VA) 91409
Avery Dennison Mfg. Corp. (Midlothian, VA) 91410
Avery Dennison Soabar (Greensboro, NC) 74782
Avery Dennison Soabar Production Group (Charlotte, NC) 73847
Avery Dennison Soabar Systems (Atlanta, GA) 64245
BASF (Charlotte, NC) 73849
Berkeley Mills (Balfour, NC) 73656
Boise Cascade Corp. White Paper (Jackson, AL) 56064
Bowater Inc. (Albertville, AL) 54959
Bowater Lumber Co. (Albertville, AL) 54962
Butler Paper Co. (Shreveport, LA) 70695
Champion International Corp. (Cantonment, FL) 58908
Champion International Corp. (Edgefield, SC) 79184
Collins Aikman Corp. (Charlotte, NC) 73912
Collins & Aikman Holdings Corp. (Charlotte, NC) 73915
Federal Paper Board Co. (East Flat Rock, NC) 74448
Federal Paper Board Co. (Prosperity, SC) 79800
Fort Howard Cup Corp. (Owings Mills, MD) 72187

Georgia-Pacific Corp. Port Hudson (Zachary, LA) 70983
Golden Belt Manufacturing (Durham, NC) 74403
James River Corp. Naheola Mill (Pennington, AL) 56455
James River Paper Co. Dixie Products (Fort Smith, AR) 57059
Label Systems International (Jacksonville, FL) 60358
Mead Packaging Div. Atlanta Plant (Atlanta, GA) 64719
Minnesota Mining & Mfg. Co. (Cynthiana, KY) 68249
NCR Corp. (Morristown, TN) 81806
Orchard Decorative Products (Blythewood, SC) 78750
Quality Park Product (Atlanta, GA) 65050; 65051
Quality Park Products (Atlanta, GA) 65052
Ryder Truck Rental (Lake Placid, FL) 60650
Sonoco Products Co. (Broken Arrow, OK) 76889
Sonoco Products Co. (Richmond, VA) 92042
Stone Container Corp. (Lexington, NC) 75425
Stone Container Corp. (Sand Springs, OK) 77785
Stone Container Corp. (Moseley, VA) 91434
3M Adhesive Technology Corp. (Burlington, NC) 73762
3M Co. (Cynthiana, KY) 68250
Union Camp Corp. (Townsend, GA) 67841
Union Camp Corp. (Tucker, GA) 67899
Union Camp Corp. (Jamestown, NC) 75245
Union Camp Corp. Fine Paper Div. (Franklin, VA) 90902
Union Camp Corp. School Supplies Div. (Birmingham, AL) 55435
Westvaco Corp. (Chatham, VA) 90554
Westvaco Corp. (Ivy, VA) 91171
Westvaco Corp. Research (Ravenel, SC) 79807
Weyerhaeuser (Oglethorpe, GA) 67220

2700 Printing & Publishing

Avery Dennison (Flowery Branch, GA) 66215
Reynolds & Reynolds Co. (Grand Prairie, TX) 85636

2711 Newspapers

Dow Jones & Co. (Silver Spring, MD) 72391
Dow Jones & Co. (Charlotte, NC) 73933
Dow Jones & Co. (Beaumont, TX) 83149
Dow Jones & Co. (Dallas, TX) 83982
Drinnon Inc. (Milledgeville, GA) 66974

Kentucky Post (Covington, KY) 68223

Press (Ennis, TX) 84998
Press (Waxahacie, TX) 90001
Press Inc. (Johnson City, TN) 81054
Press Inc. (Ennis, TX) 84999
Press Inc. (Waxahacie, TX) 90002
Star Telegram (Fort Worth, TX) 85279
Wall Street Journal (Birmingham, AL) 55453
Wall Street Journal (Washington, DC) 58517
Wall Street Journal (Miami, FL) 61512; 61513
Wall Street Journal (Orlando, FL) 62188
Wall Street Journal (Atlanta, GA) 65276
Wall Street Journal the (Oklahoma City, OK) 77662
Wall Street Journal (Memphis, TN) 81755
Wall Street Journal (Bellaire, TX) 83274
Wall Street Journal (Houston, TX) 87169
Wall Street Journal (Charlottesville, VA) 90550
Washington Post Newspaper (Washington, DC) 58519
Washington Post Newspaper (Austin, TX) 83068

2721 Periodicals
Business Week (Houston, TX) 85915
D Magazine (Dallas, TX) 83966
Dow Jones & Co. (Beaumont, TX) 83149
Dupont Publishing (Tampa, FL) 63411
Holt Rinehart & Winston Inc. (Orlando, FL) 62009
New Woman Magazine (Hendersonville, NC) 75043
Techsouth Publishing Services (Atlanta, GA) 65200
Travel Publications Inc. (Miami, FL) 61485
Washington Post Newspaper (Washington, DC) 58519

2731 Book Publishing
American Business Machines Inc. (Atlanta, GA) 64219
Circuit City (Virginia Beach, VA) 92445
Holt Rinehart & Winston Inc. (Orlando, FL) 62009
PRC Inc. (McLean, VA) 91395
Western Publishing Co. (Cambridge, MD) 71488

2732 Book Printing
American Business Machines Inc. (Atlanta, GA) 64219
Banta Co., Inc. (Harrisonburg, VA) 91068
Banta Co., Inc. Harrisonburg (Harrisonburg, VA) 91069
Clark Printing Inc. (Oklahoma City, OK) 77336
R.R. Donnelley & Sons Co. Harrisonburg Manufacturing Div. (Harrisonburg, VA) 91075; 91076
Golden Belt Manufacturing Co. (Reidsville, NC) 76000
Graphic Systems Inc. (Memphis, TN) 81617
R R Donnelley & Sons Co. (Charlotte, NC) 74124
Sloan Paper Co. (Tampa, FL) 63599
Stevens Graphics Inc. (Atlanta, GA) 65170
Sullivan Graphics Inc. (Lufkin, TX) 87819
Tylor Publishing Co. (Dallas, TX) 84467

2741 Miscellaneous Publishing
ALLTEL Corp. (Little Rock, AR) 57245
Bell Atlantic Bus Syst Servs. (Louisville, KY) 68700
Bell Atlantic Business System Services (Birmingham, AL) 55161
Bell Atlantic Tricon Lease Corp. (Ft. Lauderdale, FL) 59852
Bell South Enterprises, Inc. (Atlanta, GA) 64304
Bellsouth Advertising & Publishing (Charlotte, NC) 73858; 73859
Bellsouth Advertising & Publishing Corp. (Atlanta, GA) 64312; 64313
BellSouth Corp. (Atlanta, GA) 64317
BellSouth Telecommunications Inc. (Atlanta, GA) 64325
Berry L M & Co. (Louisville, KY) 68702
Chesapeake & Potomac Tel Co. (Washington, DC) 58149
The Chesapeake & Potomac Telephone Co. (Washington, DC) 58150
Donnelley Directory (Maitland, FL) 60976
GTE Directories Corp. (Dallas, TX) 84101
GTE Directories Service Corp. (Dallas, TX) 84103
GTE Information Services Inc. (Dallas, TX) 84105
Holt Rinehart & Winston Inc. (Orlando, FL) 62009
Mead Ink Products (Anniston, AL) 55004
Mead Ink Products (Atlanta, GA) 64722
Reuben H. Donnelley Corp. (Charlottesville, VA) 90548
Southwestern Bell Yellow Pages (Amarillo, TX) 82581
Southwestern Bell Yellow Pages (Austin, TX) 83005
Steiner Liff Textile Produc (Nashville, TN) 82101
Stevens Graphics, Inc. (Atlanta, GA) 65172
Studio W (Nashville, TN) 82104
Western Publishing Co. (Cambridge, MD) 71488

2752 Commercial Printing—Lithographic
Associated Business Products (Warner Robins, GA) 68006
Avery Dennison (Charlotte, NC) 73846
Avery Dennison Soabar (Greensboro, NC) 74782
Ball Metal Decorating & Service (Trussville, AL) 56626
Ball Metal Decorating & Services (Baltimore, MD) 71049
Bristol-Myers Squibb Co. (Atlanta, GA) 64332; 64333
Brookshore Lithographers (Cary, NC) 73792
Brookshore Lithographers Corp. (Cary, NC) 73793
Clark Printing Co. (Louisville, KY) 68732
Clark Printing Co. (Shelbyville, KY) 69271
Clark Printing Co. (Marion, MS) 73141
Color Response Inc. (Richmond, VA) 91784
Deluxe Check Printers (Jacksonville, FL) 60258
Deluxe Check Printers (Plantation, FL) 62566
Deluxe Check Printers (Tucker, GA) 67852
Deluxe Check Printers (Memphis, TN) 81508
Deluxe Check Printers (Richmond, VA) 91842
Deluxe Check Printers Inc. (Jacksonville, FL) 60259
Deluxe Check Printers Inc. (Plantation, FL) 62567
Deluxe Check Printers Inc. (Tampa, FL) 63405; 63406
Deluxe Check Printers Inc. (Tucker, GA) 67853
Deluxe Check Printers Inc. (New Orleans, LA) 70443
Deluxe Check Printers Inc. (Greensboro, NC) 74810; 74811
Deluxe Check Printers Inc. (Broken Arrow, OK) 76882
Deluxe Check Printers Inc. (Memphis, TN) 81509
Deluxe Check Printers Inc. (Dallas, TX) 83975; 83976
Deluxe Check Printers Inc. (Houston, TX) 86033; 86034
Deluxe Check Printers Inc. (Richmond, VA) 91843
Deluxe Corp. (Hanover, MD) 71910
R.R. Donnelley & Sons Co. Danville Manufacturing Div. (Danville, KY) 68255; 68256
R.R. Donnelley & Sons Co. Glasgow Manufacturing Div. (Glasgow, KY) 68391
R.R. Donnelley & Sons Co. Kentucky E. Manufacturing Div. (Danville, KY) 68257
R.R. Donnelley & Sons Co. Kentucky W. Div. (Glasgow, KY) 68392
Dow Jones & Co. (Beaumont, TX) 83149
Drinnon Inc. (Milledgeville, GA) 66974
GB Labels (Burlington, NC) 73755
Golden Belt Manufacturing Co. (Randleman, NC) 75988
Golden Belt Manufacturing Co. (Reidsville, NC) 76000
Golden Belt Mfg. Co. (Randleman, NC) 75989
Gulf Printing Co. (Houston, TX) 86258
Kerox Business Services (Austin, TX) 82911
Manville Forest Products Corp. Packaging (Memphis, TN) 81653
Pitney Bowes Management Services (Houston, TX) 86686
Plough Inc. Printing Plant (Memphis, TN) 81671
Plough Printing Plant (Memphis, TN) 81672
Press (Hilton Head, SC) 79509
Press Inc. (Johnson City, TN) 81054
Ripley Graphies (Ripley, TN) 82264
R.R. Donnelley Printing Co. (Newton, NC) 75753
R.R. Donnelley Printing Co. (Lynchburg, VA) 91286
Sara Lee Graphics (Winston-Salem, NC) 76763
Soabar Group Soabar Graphics Div. (Greensboro, NC) 74912
Southwestern Bell Printing Co. (Houston, TX) 86905
Springs Industries (Lancaster, SC) 79576
Springs Industries Marketing Materials (Lancaster, SC) 79579
Standard Register Houston Div. (Houston, TX) 86911
Stevens Graphics Inc. (Birmingham, AL) 55398
Stevens Graphics Inc. (Atlanta, GA) 65170; 65172
3M Co. (Westminster, MD) 72545
TRW Inc. Redi Property Data (Fort Lauderdale, FL) 59624
Union Camp Corp. (Conway, AR) 56875
Western Publishing Co. (Annapolis, MD) 71023
Western Publishing Co. (Cambridge, MD) 71488
Xeroc Corp. (Miami, FL) 61517
Xerox Business Services (Austin, TX) 83072

2754 Commercial Printing—Gravure
Austill Packaging (Jacksonville, FL) 60186
Austill Packaging Inc. (Jacksonville, FL) 60187
Avery Dennison (Clinton, SC) 78958
Avery Dennison Corp. Security Printing Div. (Clinton, SC) 78959
Avery Dennison Ipc (Rogersville, TN) 82271
Bellwood Printing Plant (Richmond, VA) 91744
Chase Packaging Corp. (Asheville, NC) 73609
Colonial Heights Packaging Inc. (Colonial Heights, VA) 90651
D-Graphics Inc. (Jacksonville, FL) 60251
Donnelley Printing Co. (Gallatin, TN) 80839
R.R. Donnelley & Sons Co. Gallatin Manufacturing Div. (Gallatin, TN) 80840
Golden Belt Manufacturing (Durham, NC) 74403
Golden Belt Manufacturing Co. (Reidsville, NC) 76000; 76001
Golden Belt Mfg. Co. (Durham, NC) 74405
Golden Belt Mfg. Co. (Randleman, NC) 75989
Golden Belt Mfg. Co. (Reidsville, NC) 76002
Ipc Avery Dennison (Rogersville, TN) 82278
Jsc/Cca D-Graphics (Jacksonville, FL) 60342
Meredith/Burda (Lynchburg, VA) 91269
Meredith/Burda Corp. (Newton, NC) 75750
Moen Inc. (Durham, NC) 74419
Occidental Chemical (Salisbury, MD) 72351
Occidental Chemical Corp. (Salisbury, MD) 72352
R. J. Reynolds Tobacco Co. Archer 200 (Winston-Salem, NC) 76739
R. J. Reynolds Tobacco Co. Whitaker Park 604 (Winston-Salem, NC) 76756
R. J. Reynolds Tobacco Co. Whitaker Park 604-1 (Winston-Salem, NC) 76757
R. R. Donnelley Printing (Lynchburg, VA) 91276
R. R. Donnelley Printing Co. (Newton, NC) 75752
R. R. Donnelley Printing Co. (Lynchburg, VA) 91277
R. R. Donnelley & Sons Co. (Spartanburg, SC) 79930
R. R. Donnelley & Sons Co. (Gallatin, TN) 80850
R. R. Donnelley & Sons Co. Lakeside Press (Spartanburg, SC) 79931
Reynolds Metals Co. (Richmond, VA) 91983
R.R. Donnelley & Sons Co. (Spartanburg, SC) 79948
Stevens Graphics Inc. (Atlanta, GA) 65170
Westvaco (Richmond, VA) 92082; 92083
Westvaco Folding Box Div. (Cleveland, TN) 80605
Westvaco Folding Carton (Richmond, VA) 92084; 92085
Westvaco Corp. (Luke, MD) 72115
Westvaco Corp. Folding Carton (Cleveland, TN) 80609

2759 Commercial Printing Nec
Avery Dennison (Clinton, SC) 78957
Avery Dennison Corp. (Flowery Br, GA) 66214
Avery Dennison Corp. (Greensboro, NC) 74781
Avery Dennison Corp. Aigner Products Div. (Marietta, GA) 66739
Avery Dennison Corp. Aigner Products Div. (Waco, TX) 89928
Avery Dennison Soabar (Greensboro, NC) 74782
Avery Labels Business System Div. (Grapevine, TX) 85656
Banta Co., Inc. (Harrisonburg, VA) 91068
Banta Co., Inc. Harrisonburg (Harrisonburg, VA) 91069
BCT International Inc. (Fort Lauderdale, FL) 59456
Bell South Advertising & Publishing Corp. (Metairie, LA) 70251
Bellsouth Adv & Publishing Corp. ALA (Birmingham, AL) 55162
Clark Printing Co. (Shelbyville, KY) 69271
Clark Printing Inc. (Oklahoma City, OK) 77336
Golden Belt Manufacturing Co. (Randleman, NC) 75988
Golden Belt Manufacturing Co. (Reidsville, NC) 76000
James River Corp Advance Film Div. (New Castle, DE) 57867
James River Corp. Advanced Film Div. (New Castle, DE) 57868
L M Berry & Co. (Shreveport, LA) 70746
Moen Inc. (Durham, NC) 74419
NCR Corp. (Corbin, KY) 68209
Pitney Bowes (Washington, DC) 58406
Pitney Bowes Management Services (Dallas, TX) 84308
Pitney Bowes Management Services (Houston, TX) 86686
Qualex Inc. (Memphis, TN) 81677
R R Donnelley & Sons Co. (Fort Worth, TX) 85240
Rayloc (Morganfield, KY) 69106
Reynolds Metals Co. (Richmond, VA) 91983
R.R. Donnelley Printing Co. (Newton, NC) 75753
R.R. Donnelley Printing Co. (Lynchburg, VA) 91286
Soabar Group Soabar Graphics Div. (Greensboro, NC) 74912
Standard Register Co. (Tampa, FL) 63602
Standard Register Co. (Cockysville Hunt Valley, MD) 71559
Standard Register Co. (Beaumont, TX) 83214
Standard Register Houston Div. (Houston, TX) 86911
Stevens Graphics Business (Green Springs, FL) 59930
Stevens Graphics Inc. (Atlanta, GA) 65170
Unijax Inc. (Miami, FL) 61487; 61488
Unijax Sloan Paper (Hollywood, FL) 60102
Union Camp Corp. (Conway, AR) 56875
Wall Street Journal (Orlando, FL) 62188
Washington Post Newspaper (Washington, DC) 58519
Xeroc Corp. (Miami, FL) 61517
Xerox Business Services (New Orleans, LA) 70591
Xerox Corp. (San Antonio, TX) 89327
Xerox Corp. (Arlington, VA) 90395

2761 Manifold Business Forms
Associated Business Products (Warner Robins, GA) 68006
Bowater Computer Forms Inc. (Plano, TX) 88540
Bowater Inc. (Greenville, SC) 79310
Business Systems Inc. (Shreveport, LA) 70694
Copy Van Inc. (Richmond, VA) 91791
NCR Corp. (Atlanta, GA) 64968
NCR Corp. (Peachtree City, GA) 67249
NCR Corp. (Louisville, KY) 68928
NCR Corp. (Metairie, LA) 70295
NCR Corp. (Columbia, MD) 71598
Ncr Corp. (Greenville, NC) 74968; 74969
NCR Corp. (Brentwood, TN) 80232
NCR Corp. (Jackson, TN) 80991
Ncr Corp. (Arlington, TX) 82712
NCR Corp. (Harlingen, TX) 85708
NCR Corp. (Charleston, WV) 92769
Radio Shack (Van Horn, TX) 89861
Reynolds & Reynolds Co. (Lithia Springs, GA) 66590
Reynolds & Reynolds Co. (Hagerstown, MD) 71894
Reynolds & Reynolds Co. (Memphis, TN) 81679
Reynolds & Reynolds Co. (Grand Prairie, TX) 85636
Standard Register Business (Raleigh, NC) 75956
Standard Register Co. (Fayetteville, AR) 56992
Standard Register Co. (Atlanta, GA) 65167
Standard Register Co. (St. Matthews, KY) 69309
Standard Register Co. (Salisbury, MD) 72362
Standard Register Co. (Charlotte, NC) 74163
Standard Register Co. (Murfreesboro, TN) 81868
Standard Register Co. (Beaumont, TX) 83214
Standard Register Co. (Rocky Mount, VA) 92204
Standard Register Houston Div. (Houston, TX) 86911
Stanfast Inc. (Carrollton, TX) 83506
Wells Fargo Armored Services (Columbia, MD) 71605
Wells Fargo Armored SVC (Columbia, MD) 71606

2771 Greeting Cards
American Greetings (Bardstown, KY) 68112
American Greetings Corp. (McCrory, AR) 57360
American Greetings Corp. (Osceola, AR) 57480; 57481
American Greetings Corp. (Bardstown, KY) 68113
American Greetings Corp. (Corbin, KY) 68208
Plus Mark Inc. (Afton, TN) 80145
Plus Mark, Inc. (Greenville, TN) 80897

2782 Blankbooks & Looseleaf Binders
Deluxe Check Printers (Jacksonville, FL) 60258
Deluxe Check Printers (Plantation, FL) 62566
Deluxe Check Printers (Memphis, TN) 81508
Deluxe Check Printers (Richmond, VA) 91842
Deluxe Check Printers Inc. (Jacksonville, FL) 60259
Deluxe Check Printers Inc. (Plantation, FL) 62567
Deluxe Check Printers Inc. (Tampa, FL) 63405; 63406
Deluxe Check Printers Inc. (Tucker, GA) 67853
Deluxe Check Printers Inc. (New Orleans, LA) 70443
Deluxe Check Printers Inc. (Greensboro, NC) 74810; 74811
Deluxe Check Printers Inc. (Broken Arrow, OK) 76882
Deluxe Check Printers Inc. (Memphis, TN) 81509
Deluxe Check Printers Inc. (Dallas, TX) 83975; 83976
Deluxe Check Printers Inc. (Houston, TX) 86033; 86034
Deluxe Check Printers Inc. (Richmond, VA) 91843
Deluxe Corp. (Hanover, MD) 71910
Perma Products Inc. (Duncanville, TX) 84705

2791 Typesetting
Pappagallo (Hilton Head Island, SC) 79519

2796 Platemaking Services
Color Response Inc. (Charlotte, NC) 73917
Color Response Inc. (Richmond, VA) 91784
Jostens Inc. (Shelbyville, TN) 82315
Mackay/Gravure Systems (Louisville, KY) 68873
Mackey/Gravure Systems (Florence, KY) 68323
Minnesota Mining & Mfg Co. (Charles Town, WV) 92721
Southern Gravure Service (Richmond, VA) 92043

Southern Gravure Service Inc. (Louisville, KY) 69009
Southern Gravure Service Inc. (Wilmington, NC) 76595

2800 Chemicals & Allied Products

Alkaril Chemicals (Winder, GA) 68052; 68053
Alkaril Chemicals Inc. (Winder, GA) 68054
Arizona Chemical Co. (Picayune, MS) 73291
Ball Metal Decorating (Trussville, AL) 56625
Dial Corp. (Auburndale, FL) 58595
J.M. Huber Solem Ind. (Benton, AR) 56772
Martin Marietta Paducah Gaseous Diffusion Plant (Paducah, KY) 69208
Philips P. R. Core Inc. Durand/ Learned Plant (Guayama, PR) 78425
Phillips P.R. Core/P.P. Inc. Duran/ Learned Plant (Guayama, PR) 78429
Rhone-Poulenc Inc. Surfactants & Specialties (Winder, GA) 68062
Shell Oil Co. Norco Manufacturing Complex (Norco, LA) 70596
Solem Industries Inc. (Benton, AR) 56775
Solem Industries Inc. (Fairmount, GA) 66185
Sylvachem Corp. (Picayune, MS) 73295

2810 Industrial Inorganic Chemicals

Union Carbide Corp. (Garland, TX) 85550

2812 Alkalies & Chlorine

Bio-Lab Inc. (Decatur, GA) 65801
Dow Chemical Co. (Freeport, TX) 85379; 85379
Dow Chemical Co. Louisiana Div. (Plaquemine, LA) 70637
Dow Chemical Co. Grand Bayou Plant (Paincourtville, LA) 70607
Dow Chemical Co. Texas Operations (Freeport, TX) 85381; 85382
Ethyl Corp. (Richmond, VA) 91862
FMC Corp. (Newark, DE) 57904
GE Plastics Burkville Div. (Lowndesboro, AL) 56114
Georgia Gulf Corp. (Delaware City, DE) 57769
Georgia Gulf Corp. (Atlanta, GA) 64507
Georgia Gulf Corp. (Plaquemine, LA) 70639
Occidental Chemical Corp. (Mobile, AL) 56215
Occidental Chemical Corp. (Muscle Shoals, AL) 56403
Occidental Chemical Corp. (Sheffield, AL) 56553
Occidental Chemical Corp. (Delaware City, DE) 57772
Occidental Chemical Corp. (Convent, LA) 69782; 69783
Occidental Chemical Corp. (Taft, LA) 70898
Occidental Chemical Corp. (Deer Park, TX) 84557
Occidental Chemical Corp. Battleground Site (La Porte, TX) 87562
Occidental Chemical Corp. Deer Park (Deer Park, TX) 84558
Occidental Chemical Corp. Taft Ammonia Terminal (Taft, LA) 70899
Olin Augusta Plant (Augusta, GA) 65339; 65340
Olin Chemicals Group (Charleston, TN) 80289
Olin Corp. (Mc Intosh, AL) 56125; 56126; 56127
Olin Corp. (Augusta, GA) 65341
Olin Corp. Augusta Plant (Augusta, GA) 65342; 65343
Olin Corp. Charleston Facility (Charleston, TN) 80290
Olin Corp. Hackberry Plant (Hackberry, LA) 69921
Olin Corp. Lake Charles Plant (Lake Charles, LA) 70152; 70153
PPG Industries Inc. (Lake Charles, LA) 70159
PPG Industries Inc. (N. Martinsville, WV) 92958
Ppg Industries Inc. (New Martinsville, WV) 92962
Thomasville Upholstery, Inc. (Conover, NC) 74339

2813 Industrial Gases

Air Products (Guayanilla, PR) 78430
Air Products & Chemicals (Decatur, AL) 55570
Air Products & Chemicals Inc. (Decatur, AL) 55571; 55572
Air Products & Chemicals Inc. (Sheffield, AL) 56543
Air Products & Chemicals, Inc. (Fayetteville, AR) 56968
Air Products & Chemicals, Inc. (Fort Smith, AR) 57019
Air Products & Chemicals Inc. (New Castle, DE) 57853; 57854
Air Products & Chemicals Inc. (Orlando, FL) 61903
Air Products & Chemicals Inc. (Albany, GA) 64061; 64062
Air Products & Chemicals Inc. (Conyers, GA) 65666
Air Products & Chemicals Inc. (Ashland, KY) 68083
Air Products & Chemicals Inc. (Addis, LA) 69364
Air Products & Chemicals Inc. (Convent, LA) 69781
Air Products & Chemicals Inc. (New Orleans, LA) 70425; 70426
Air Products & Chemicals Inc. (Baltimore, MD) 71031
Air Products & Chemicals Inc. (Hyattsville, MD) 71952
Air Products & Chemicals Inc. (Greensboro, NC) 74759
Air Products & Chemicals, Inc. (Pryor, OK) 77732; 77733; 77734; 77735; 77736
Air Products & Chemicals Inc. (Kingsport, TN) 81069; 81070; 81071; 81072
Air Products & Chemicals Inc. (Memphis, TN) 81446
Air Products & Chemicals Inc. (Austin, TX) 82805
Air Products & Chemicals Inc. (Deer Park, TX) 84546
Air Products & Chemicals Inc. (Irving, TX) 87319
Air Products & Chemicals Inc. (La Porte, TX) 87552
Air Products & Chemicals Inc. (Midlothian, TX) 88097; 88098
Air Products & Chemicals Inc. (Roanoke, VA) 92099
Air Products & Chemicals Inc. (Weirton, WV) 93083; 93084
Air Products Manufacturing Corp. (Gruver, TX) 85691; 85692
Air Products Manufacturing Corp. (La Porte, TX) 87553; 87554
Air Products Manufacturing Corp. (LaPorte, TX) 87602
Air Products Manufacturing Corp. (Midlothian, TX) 88099
Air Products of Puerto Rico (Guayanilla, PR) 78431
Allied-Signal Inc. (Geismar, LA) 69868; 69869
Arcadian Corp. (Memphis, TN) 81463
Arcadian Fertilizer LP (Millington, TN) 81774
At&T (Norcross, GA) 67098
At&T Network Systems (Norcross, GA) 67099
Borden Chemicals & Plastics (Geismar, LA) 69879
Carbon Dioxide Corp. Liquid Carbonic (Hopewell, VA) 91158
Dow Chemical Co. (Freeport, TX) 85379
Dow Chemical Co. Texas Operations (Freeport, TX) 85381; 85382
Enron Liquids Pipeline Group (Houston, TX) 86076
FMC Corp. (South Charleston, WV) 93048
Liquid Carbonic Carbon Dioxide Corp. (Loudon, TN) 81352
Liquid Carbonic Carbon Dioxide Corp. (Hopewell, VA) 91161
Liquid Carbonic Specialty Gas Corp. (Orlando, FL) 62040
Liquid Carbonic Specialty Gas Corp. (Gonzales, LA) 69892
Liquid Carbonic Specialty Gas Corp. (Pasadena, TX) 88432
Lone Star Gas Co. (Garland, TX) 85501
Merritt-Holland Co. (Knoxville, TN) 81230
Olin Corp. (Mc Intosh, AL) 56125; 56127
Praxair Inc. (Mims, FL) 61553
Praxair Inc. (Deer Park, TX) 84560
Praxair Inc. (Garland, TX) 85524
Praxair Inc. (Texas City, TX) 89732
Praxair Inc. Linde (La Porte, TX) 87564
Praxair Inc. Linde Div. (Garland, TX) 85525
Texaco Gasoline Plant (Ozona, TX) 88337
Tranmission Systems Inc. (Fort Stockton, TX) 85050
UCIG Inc. Linde Div. (Big Spring, TX) 83297
Union Carbide Corp. Linde Div. (Gadsden, AL) 55795
Union Carbide Corp. Linde Div. (Mims, FL) 61554
Union Carbide Corp. Linde Div. (Hahnville, LA) 69923
Union Carbide Corp. Linde Div. (Baltimore, MD) 71316
Union Carbide Corp. Linde Div. (Big Spring, TX) 83298
Union Carbide Corp. Linde Div. (Dallas, TX) 84469
Union Carbide Corp. Linde Div. (Garland, TX) 85551
Union Carbide Corp. Linde Div. (Groves, TX) 85686
Union Carbide Corp. Linde Div. (La Porte, TX) 87571
Union Carbide Corp. Indl. Gases Inc. (Baltimore, MD) 71317
Union Carbide Corp. Industrial Gases (Deer Park, TX) 84572
Union Carbide Ind. Gases Inc. Linde Div. (Mims, FL) 61555
Union Carbide Industrial Gases Linde Div. (Garland, TX) 85552
Union Carbide Industrial Gases Inc. (Mims, FL) 61556
Union Carbide Industrial Gases Inc. (Deer Park, TX) 84573
Union Carbide Industrial Gases Inc. (Garland, TX) 85553
Union Carbide Industrial Gases Inc. (La Porte, TX) 87572
Union Carbide Industrial Gases Inc. Linde Div. (Quitman, TX) 88705

2816 Inorganic Pigments

BASF Corp. (Huntington, WV) 92868
Engelhard Corp. (Louisville, KY) 68759
Engelhard Corp. Pigments & Additives Div. (Louisville, KY) 68760
Ferro Corp. (Arlington, TX) 82652; 82653
Ferro Corp. Color Div. (Toccoa, GA) 67836
Harshaw Chemical Co. (Louisville, KY) 68770
Kerr-Mcgee Chemical Corp. (Theodore, AL) 56606
Kerr-Mcgee Chemical Corp. (Hamilton, MS) 72884; 72885
Kerr-Mcgee Chemical Corp. Pigment Plant (Hamilton, MS) 72887
Scm Chemicals (Baltimore, MD) 71273
SCM Chemicals Inc. (Baltimore, MD) 71274
Scm Glidco Organics Corp. (Baltimore, MD) 71275

2819 Industrial Inorganic Chemicals Nec

Agrico Chemical Co. Uncle Sam Plant (Uncle Sam, LA) 70916
Air Products & Chemicals (New Orleans, LA) 70424
Air Products & Chemicals (St. Gabriel, LA) 70862
Air Products Manufacturing Corp. (Pasadena, TX) 88383; 88384
Aker Sulfur Recovery Plant (Streetman, TX) 89528
Albright & Wilson Americas Inc. (Charleston, SC) 78786
Albright & Wilson Americas Inc.- Charleston Plant (Charleston, SC) 78787
Alcoa (Fort Meade, FL) 59646
Allied-Signal Communications Systems (Hopewell, VA) 91151
Allied-Signal Hopewell Plant (Hopewell, VA) 91152
Allied-Signal Inc. (Claymont, DE) 57758
Allied-Signal Inc. (Baton Rouge, LA) 69458; 69459; 69460
Allied-Signal Inc. (Carville, LA) 69756
Allied-Signal Inc. (Geismar, LA) 69870; 69871
Allied-Signal Inc. (Hopewell, VA) 91153; 91154; 91155
Allied-Signal Inc. Environmental Catalysts (Catoosa, OK) 76908
Aluminum Co. of America (Bauxite, AR) 56765
Aluminum Co. of America (Fort Meade, FL) 59647; 59648
Aluminum Co. of America (Vidalia, LA) 70927
Aluminum Co. of America (Point Comfort, TX) 88623; 88624
Amax Metals Recovery Inc. (Braithwaite, LA) 69738; 69739
Amax Potash Corp. (Dumas, TX) 84683; 84684; 84685
American Cyanamid Co. (Mobile, AL) 56132; 56134
American Cyanamid Co. (Westwego, LA) 70968; 70969
American Cyanamid Co. (Havre De Grace, MD) 71915
American Cyanamid Co. (Willow Island, WV) 93131
Anchor/Lithkemko Inc. (Orange Park, FL) 61877
Arkansas Chemicals Inc. (El Dorado, AR) 56925; 56926
Arkansas Chemicals Inc. (Eldorado, AR) 56963
Ashland Chemical Co. (Dallas, TX) 83859
Ashland Chemical E & Lp (Dallas, TX) 83860
Baker Performance Chemicals (Dayton, TX) 84519
Baker Performance Chemicals (Houston, TX) 85856
BASF Corp. (Geismar, LA) 69874; 69876
Betz Laboratories Inc. (Beaumont, TX) 83144
Borden Inc. Chemical (Fayetteville, NC) 74535
Borden Inc. Package & Industrial Products (Fayetteville, NC) 74536; 74537
Catalyst Resources Inc. (Pasadena, TX) 88395
Central Products Inc. (Montgomery, AL) 56291; 56292
Conoco Inc. (Westlake, LA) 70963
An Corp. Bayport Plant (Pasadena, TX) 88398
Criterion Catalyst Co. (Houston, TX) 86018
Cyprus Foote Mineral Co. (Kings Mountain, NC) 75295; 75296
Dalton Plant (Dalton, GA) 65780
Dow Chemical Co. (Magnolia, AR) 57329
Dow Chemical Co. (Freeport, TX) 85379
Dow Chemical Co. Texas Operations (Freeport, TX) 85381; 85382
Eagle-Picher Ind. Inc. Boron Dept. (Quapaw, OK) 77753
Eagle Picher Ind. Inc. Electro-Optic Materials Dept. (Quapaw, OK) 77754
Eagle Picher Ind. Inc. Electro-Optics Mat. 1 (Quapaw, OK) 77755
Eagle-Picher Ind. Inc. Electro-Optics Materials Dept. (Quapaw, OK) 77756
Eagle-Picher Industries Inc. Boron Dept. (Quapaw, OK) 77759; 77760; 77761
Eagle Picher Industries Inc. Boron Dept (Quapaw, OK) 77762
Engelhard Catalyst & Chemicals Div. (Huntsville, AL) 55910
Engelhard Corp. (Huntsville, AL) 55911
Engelhard Corp. (Attapulgus, GA) 65307; 65308
Engelhard Corp. (Louisville, KY) 68759
Engelhard Corp. (Jackson, MS) 72980
Engelhard Corp. (Seneca, SC) 79856; 79857
Engelhard Corp. Catalysts & Chemicals Div. (Seneca, SC) 79858
Engelhard Corp. Environmental Catalysts Div. (Huntsville, AL) 55912
Engelhard Corp. Pigments & Additives Div. (Louisville, KY) 68760
Engelhard Corp. Catalyst & Chemical (Huntsville, AL) 55913
Engelhard Corp. Engelhard Di (Houston, TX) 86057
Engelhard Corp. Environmental Catalyst Group (Huntsville, AL) 55914
Engelhard Specialty Chemicals (Huntsville, AL) 55915
Ethyl Corp. (Magnolia, AR) 57330
Ethyl Corp. (Pasadena, TX) 88402
Ethyl Corp. (Richmond, VA) 91862
Ethyl Corp. Houston Plant (Pasadena, TX) 88403
Exxon Chemical Co. (Houston, TX) 86119; 86120
Exxon Co. USA (Baytown, TX) 83120
Exxon Corp. (Summerville, SC) 79983
Fabricated Products Plant (Tulsa, OK) 77939
Farmland Industries Inc. (Enid, OK) 77050
Ferro Corp. Grant Chemical Div. (Zachary, LA) 70982
FMC Corp. (Gastonia, NC) 74680
FMC Corp. (Pasadena, TX) 88408
FMC Corp. (Nitro, WV) 92969
FMC Corp. (South Charleston, WV) 93047
FMC Corp. Lithium Div. (Bessemer City, NC) 73688
FMC Corp. Peroxygen Chemicals Div. (Pasadena, TX) 88409
Fmc Corp. Agricultural Chemical Group (Baltimore, MD) 71153
FMC Corp., Baltimore Plant (Baltimore, MD) 71154
Fmc Corp.-Bayport Plant (Pasadena, TX) 88410
Fmc Corp. Spring Hill Plant (South Charleston, WV) 93049
Freeport Mcmoran Agrico Chemical Co. Div. (Uncle Sam, LA) 70917
Freeport-McMoran Resource Partners (New Orleans, LA) 70464
Gaf Chemical Corp. (Huntsville, AL) 55943
Gaf Chemicals Corp. (Huntsville, AL) 55944; 55945
GE Specialty Chemicals North Plant (Morgantown, WV) 92945
General Electric Co. (Wilmington, NC) 76573
Georgia Gulf Corp. (Atlanta, GA) 64507
Great Lakes Chemical Co. El Dorado-Main Plant (El Dorado, AR) 56944
Great Lakes Chemical Co. El Dorado Plant (El Dorado, AR) 56945
Great Lakes Chemical Co. (West Plant) (Marysville, AR) 57352
Great Lakes Chemical Corp. (Newport, TN) 82166; 82167
Great Lakes Chemical Corp. El Dorado Plant (El Dorado, AR) 56946
Great Lakes Chemical Corp. Marysville Plant (Marysville, AR) 57353
Great Lakes Chemical Corp. South Plant (El Dorado, AR) 56947; 56948
Harshaw Chemical Co. (Louisville, KY) 68770
Hoechst Celanese (Carlisle, SC) 78766
Hoechst Celanese (Portsmouth, VA) 91659
Hoechst-Celanese Corp. (Bucks, AL) 55489
Hoechst Celanese Corp. (Bishop, TX) 83302
Hoechst-Celanese Corp. Leeds Plant (Leeds, SC) 79599
Hoechst Celanese Corp. Virginia Chemicals Co. (Bucks, AL) 55490
Hoechst Celanese Corp. Virginia Chemicals Co. (Bishop, TX) 83303
Hoechst Celanese Specialty Chemicals Group (Bishop, TX) 83304
IMC Fertilizer Inc. New Wales Operation (Mulberry, FL) 61574
Industrial & Specialty Chemicals Plant (Mulberry, FL) 61575
J. M. Huber Corp. (Etowah, TN) 80779
Katalistiks Inc. (Savannah, GA) 67492
Kerr-Mcgee Chemical Corp. Electrolytic Plant (Hamilton, MS) 72886
Lithium Corp. of America (Bessemer City, NC) 73689
Lithium Corp. of America FMC Lithium Div. (Bessemer City, NC) 73690
Mallinckrodt Specialty Chemicals Co. (Paris, KY) 69219
Marathon Oil Co. (Garyville, LA) 69862
Martin Marietta US Doe Y-12 Plant (Oak Ridge, TN) 82196
Miles Inc. Pemco Products (Baltimore, MD) 71209
Mobil Chemical Co. Bcsp (Beaumont, TX) 83180
Mobil Mining & Minerals (Nichols, FL) 61722
Monsanto Co. (Anniston, AL) 55006
Monsanto Co. (Decatur, AL) 55597
Monsanto Co. (Augusta, GA) 65336; 65337
Monsanto Co. (Luling, LA) 70203; 70204

Monsanto Co. (Columbia, TN) 80632; 80633
Monsanto Co. (Alvin, TX) 82509
Morton International Specialty (Greenville, SC) 79398
Nalco Chemical Co. (Garyville, LA) 69865; 69866
New Hope Plant (Scroggins, TX) 89356
Occidental Chemical Corp. (Mobile, AL) 56215
Occidental Chemical Corp. (White Springs, FL) 63912
Occidental Chemical Corp. (Taft, LA) 70898
Occidental Chemical Corp. (Columbia, TN) 80634; 80635; 80636
Occidental Chemical Corp. (Dallas, TX) 84278
Occidental Chemical Corp. Agricultural Products (White Springs, FL) 63913
Occidental Chemical Corp. Castle Hayne Plant (Castle Hayne, NC) 73803; 73804
Occidental Chemical Corp. Taft Ammonia Terminal (Taft, LA) 70899
Olin Augusta Plant (Augusta, GA) 65339; 65340
Olin Chemicals Group (Charleston, TN) 80289
Olin Chemicals Group (Beaumont, TX) 83191
Olin Corp. (Mc Intosh, AL) 56126
Olin Corp. (St. Marks, FL) 63072
Olin Corp. (Augusta, GA) 65341
Olin Corp. (Brandenburg, KY) 68169
Olin Corp. (Shreveport, LA) 70755
Olin Corp. (Westlake, LA) 70966
Olin Corp. (Beaumont, TX) 83192
Olin Corp. (South Charleston, WV) 93051; 93052
Olin Corp. Augusta Plant (Augusta, GA) 65342; 65343
Olin Corp. Beaumont Plant (Beaumont, TX) 83193
Olin Corp. Charleston Facility (Charleston, TN) 80290
Olin Corp. Hackberry Plant (Hackberry, LA) 69921
Olin Corp. Lake Charles Plant (Lake Charles, LA) 70152; 70153
Olin Corp. Shreveport Plant (Shreveport, LA) 70756; 70757
Pfizer Specialty Minerals Inc. (Chickasaw, AL) 55512
Phelps Dodge Refining Corp. (El Paso, TX) 84877
Phelps Dodge Refining Corp. El Paso Works (El Paso, TX) 84878
Phillips 66 Co. (Borger, TX) 83321
Phillips 66 Co. (Sweeny, TX) 89577
Porocel Corp. (Little Rock, AR) 57299
PPG Industries Inc. (Lake Charles, LA) 70159
Ppg Industries Inc. (Beaumont, TX) 83204
PPG Industries Inc. (LaPorte, TX) 87604
Ppg Industries Inc. (New Martinsville, WV) 92962
Reynolds Metals Co. Sherwin Plant (Gregory, TX) 85682
Rhone Poulenc Basic Chemical (Baton Rouge, LA) 69649
Rhone Poulenc Basic Chemical (Mt. Pleasant, TN) 81833
Rhone Poulenc Basic Chemical (Baytown, TX) 83136
Rhone-Poulenc Basic Chemical Co. (Bastrop, LA) 69448
Rhone-Poulenc Basic Chemicals (Geismar, LA) 69882
Rhone-Poulenc Basic Chemicals Co. (Baton Rouge, LA) 69650; 69651
Rhone-Poulenc Basic Chemicals Co. (Springhill, LA) 70857
Rhone-Poulenc Basic Chemicals Co. (Mount Pleasant, TN) 81826
Rhone-Poulenc Basic Chemicals Co. (Nashville, TN) 82090
Rhone-Poulenc Basic Chemicals Co. (Baytown, TX) 83137
Rhone-Poulenc Basic Chemicals Co. (Houston, TX) 86796
Rhone Poulenc Inc. (Marietta, GA) 66905
Rhone Poulenc Inc. (Baltimore, MD) 71239
Rhone Poulenc Inc. (Freeport, TX) 85390
Rhone-Poulenc Inc. Freeport Plant (Freeport, TX) 85391
Rhone Poulenc Inc. Industrial Plant (Institute, WV) 92905
Rohm & Haas Kentucky Inc. (Louisville, KY) 68999
Scm Glidco Organics Corp. (Baltimore, MD) 71275
Sequa Chemicals Inc. (Chester, SC) 78943
Shell Chemical Co. Geismar Plant (Geismar, LA) 69884
Shell Oil Co. (Florence, MS) 72772
Shell Oil Co. (Deer Park, TX) 84567
Shell Oil Co. (Douglassville, TX) 84681
Shell Oil Co. Norco Manufacturing Complex (Norco, LA) 70594; 70595; 70596
Shipley Co. Inc. (Richmond, VA) 92012
Solem Ind. (Fairmount, GA) 66184
Stauffer Chemical Co. (Bastrop, LA) 69451
Stauffer Chemical Co. Furnace Plant (Mount Pleasant, TN) 81828
Sterling Chemicals Inc. (Texas City, TX) 89737
Tenneco Methanol Co. (Pasadena, TX) 88474
Texaco Chemical Co. Port Arthur Chemical Plant (Port Arthur, TX) 88647
Texaco Ref. & Mktg. Inc. (Union, LA) 70918
Texaco Refining & Marketing Inc. (Convent, LA) 69784
Texas Eastman Co. (Longview, TX) 87738
Texas Instruments Inc. Sherman (Sherman, TX) 89427
Union Carbide Corp. (Haknville, LA) 69928
Union Carbide Corp. Molecular Sieve Plant (Chickasaw, AL) 55513
UOP Inc. (Blanchard, LA) 69700
UOP Inc. (Shreveport, LA) 70801
Virginia Chemicals Co. (Carlisle, SC) 78767
Virginia Chemicals Co. (Portsmouth, VA) 91672
W. R. Grace & Co. (Sulphur, LA) 70893
W. R. Grace & Co. Davison Chemical Div. (Sulphur, LA) 70894
W. R. Grace & Co. Davison Chemical Div. (Baltimore, MD) 71324
W. R. Grace & Co. Davison Chemical Div. (Chattanooga, TN) 80524
Westinghouse Commercial Nuclear Fuel (Columbia, SC) 79124; 79125
Westinghouse Electric (Columbia, SC) 79126
Westvaco Corp. Chemicals (Covington, VA) 90667
Westvaco Corp. Carbon Dept. (Covington, VA) 90668
Witco Corp. (LaPorte, TX) 87605
Witco Corp. Argus (La Porte, TX) 87574
Witco Corp. Argus Chemcial Div. (Marshall, TX) 87876
Witco Corp. Humko Chemical Div. (Memphis, TN) 81763
W.R. Grace & Co. (Sulphur, LA) 70897
W.R. Grace & Co. Davison Chemical Div. (Baltimore, MD) 71330

2821 Plastics Materials & Resins

Air Products & Chemicals, Inc. (Milton, FL) 61541
Air Products & Chemicals Inc. (Pace, FL) 62218; 62219
Air Products & Chemicals Inc. (Calvert City, KY) 68175
Air Products & Chemicals, Inc. (Elkton, MD) 71670
Air Products & Chemicals Inc. (Langley, SC) 79584; 79585
Air Products & Chemicals, Inc. (Piedmont, SC) 79792
Air Products Manufacturing Corp. (Pasadena, TX) 88384
Albright & Wilson Americas Inc. (Charleston, SC) 78786
Albright & Wilson Americas Inc.- Charleston Plant (Charleston, SC) 78787
Allied-Signal, Inc. (Baton Rouge, LA) 69461
Allied-Signal Inc. (Orange, TX) 88301; 88302; 88303; 88304; 88305; 88306
Allied-Signal Inc. (Chester, VA) 90614
Allied-Signal Inc. Fibers (Moncure, NC) 75568
Allied-Signal Inc. Fibers (Columbia, SC) 78966; 78967
Allied-Signal Inc. Paxon Polymer (Baton Rouge, LA) 69462
American Cyanamid Co. (Mobile, AL) 56134
American Cyanamid Co. (Westwego, LA) 70968
American Cyanamid Co. (Havre De Grace, MD) 71915
American Cyanamid Co. (Charlotte, NC) 73834; 73835
Ametek Corp. Haveg Div. (Wilmington, DE) 57983
Ametek, Inc. Heaveg Div. (Wilmington, DE) 57985
Ametek Inc. Westchester Plastics Div. (Dallas, TX) 83852
Ashland Oil Inc. (Ashland, KY) 68090
Astro Industries Inc. Astro Industries Division (Morganton, NC) 75629
BASF Corp. (Stone Mountain, GA) 67686
BASF Corp. (Geismar, LA) 69875; 69876
BASF Corp. (Durham, NC) 74386
BASF Corp. (Chattanooga, TN) 80325
BASF Corp. (Lowland, TN) 81358
BASF Corp. (Carrollton, TX) 83452
BASF Corp. (Williamsburg, VA) 92561
BASF Corp. Fibers (Enka, NC) 74506
BASF Corp. Fibers (Central, SC) 78782; 78783
BASF Corp. Fibers (Lowland, TN) 81359; 81360
BASF Corp. Engineering Plastics (Marietta, GA) 66757
BASF Corp. Engineering Plastics (Louisville, KY) 68697
BASF Tpu Marketing (Richmond, TX) 88793
Bemis Co. Custom Resins Div. (Henderson, KY) 68440
Bf Goodrich Co. Geon Vinyl Div. Deer Park Plant (Deer Park, TX) 84547
Borden Inc. Astro Industries Division (Morganton, NC) 75633
Borden Inc. Chemical (Demopolis, AL) 55613
Borden Inc. Chemical (Louisville, KY) 68708
Borden Inc. Chemical (Fayetteville, NC) 74535
Borden Inc. Chemical (Diboll, TX) 84652
Borden Inc. Package & Industrial Products (Fayetteville, NC) 74536; 74537
Borden Inc. Packaging & Industrial Products (Alexandria, LA) 69369
Borden Inc. Packaging & Industrial Prods. (Diboll, TX) 84653
Borden Packaging & Industrial Products (Demopolis, AL) 55614
Borden Packaging & Industrial Products (Louisville, KY) 68709
Borden Packaging & Industrial Products (Fayetteville, NC) 74538
Borden Packaging & Industrial Products (Diboll, TX) 84654
Cain Chemical Inc. (Orange, TX) 88307
Cain Chemical Inc. Matagorda Operation (Wadsworth, TX) 89983
Cain Chemical Inc. Matagorda Operations (Wadsworth, TX) 89984
Capco Pipe Co. Inc. (Birmingham, AL) 55178; 55180
Carolina Eastman Co. (Columbia, SC) 78993; 78994; 78995
Celanese Engineering Resins Inc. (Bishop, TX) 83300
Celanese Engineering Resins Inc. Resins Div. (Bishop, TX) 83301
Chevron Chemical Co. (Baytown, TX) 83109
Chevron Chemical Co. (Orange, TX) 88308; 88309
Chevron Chemical Co. Olefins & Derivatives Div. (Orange, TX) 88310
Custom Resins (Henderson, KY) 68441
Dexter Corp. Midland Div. (Birmingham, AL) 55218
Dexter Corp. Packaging Products Div. (Birmingham, AL) 55219
Dexter Packaging Products (Birmingham, AL) 55220
Dow Chemical Co. (La Porte, TX) 87555
Dow Chemical Co. Louisiana Div. (Plaquemine, LA) 70637
Dow Chemical Co. Louisiana Division (Plaquemine, LA) 70633
Dow Chemical Co. Texas Division (Freeport, TX) 85380
Dow Chemical Co. La Porte Plant (La Porte, TX) 87556
Dow Chemical Co. La Porte Site (La Porte, TX) 87557
Dow Chemical Co. Texas Operations (Freeport, TX) 85381
Dow Chemical Dalton Site (Dalton, GA) 65781; 65782
Eastman Chemical Co. (Kingsport, TN) 81075
Eastman Kodak Co. Tennessee Div. (Kingsport, TN) 81076
Eastman Kodak Co. Tennessee Eastman Div. (Kingsport, TN) 81077
Echota Cushion (Calhoun, GA) 65462
Exxon Chemical Americas (Baytown, TX) 83112
Exxon Chemical Co. (Baton Rouge, LA) 69521; 69522
Exxon Chemical Co. (Baytown, TX) 83114
Exxon Chemical Plant (Baytown, TX) 83116
Ferro Corp. (Wildwood, FL) 63915
Fina Inc. (Dallas, TX) 84064; 84065
Fina Oil & Chemical Co. (Dallas, TX) 84066
Fina Oil & Chemical Co. (Pasadena, TX) 88407
Fina Oil & Chemical Co. La Porte Plant (La Porte, TX) 87560
Freeman Resins (Marshall, TX) 87853
Freeman Resins (Chatham, VA) 90553
GE Chemicals Inc. (Washington, WV) 93080
GE Co. Plastics (Sparta, TN) 82343
GE Plastics (Parkersburg, WV) 92984
GE Plastics Burkville Div. (Lowndesboro, AL) 56114
GE Plastics-Burkville Operation (Burkville, AL) 55491
General Electric Co. (Norcross, GA) 67120
General Electric Co. (Dallas, TX) 84089
General Electric Plastics Baymar (Bay St. Louis, MS) 72607
General Polymers (Charlotte, NC) 74030
Georgia Gulf Corp. (Delaware City, DE) 57769; 57770; 57771
Georgia Gulf Corp. (Atlanta, GA) 64507
Georgia Gulf Corp. (Plaquemine, LA) 70639; 70640
Georgia Gulf Corp. (Gallman, MS) 72781
Georgia Gulf Corp. (Tiptonville, TN) 82370
Georgia-Pacific Corp. Resins Div. (Taylorsville, MS) 73376
Georgia-Pacific Corp. Resins Plant (Louisville, MS) 73120
Georgia Pacific Resins Inc. (Crossett, AR) 56884
Georgia-Pacific Resins Inc. (Peachtree City, GA) 67243
Georgia-Pacific Resins Inc. (Port Wentworth, GA) 67275
Georgia-Pacific Resins Inc. (Vienna, GA) 67999
Georgia Pacific Resins Inc. (Louisville, MS) 73121
Georgia Pacific Resins Inc. (Conway, NC) 74342
Georgia-Pacific Resins Inc. (Russellville, SC) 79847; 79848
Georgia Pacific Resins Inc. (Lufkin, TX) 87804; 87805
Georgia-Pacific Resins Inc. Conway Hardboard (Conway, NC) 74343
Georgia-Pacific Resins Inc. Particleboard (Taylorsville, MS) 73378
Georgia-Pacific Resins Inc. Resins Plant (Louisville, MS) 73122
Goodyear Tire & Rubber Co. (Gadsden, AL) 55782
Goodyear Tire & Rubber Co. (Calhoun, GA) 65466
Goodyear Tire & Rubber Co. (Beaumont, TX) 83154
Goodyear Tire & Rubber Co. (Cheek, TX) 83557
Goodyear Tire & Rubber Co. (Apple Grove, WV) 92662; 92663
Goodyear Tire & Rubber Co. Beaumont Chemical Plant (Beaumont, TX) 83155
H. B. Fuller Co. (Covington, GA) 65727
H.B. Fuller Co. Asc Div. (Covington, GA) 65728
Hercules Inc. (Middletown, DE) 57832
Hercules Inc. (Hattiesburg, MS) 72890
Hercules Inc. Specialty Chemicals Div. (Savannah, GA) 67483
Hercules Inc. Hercules Research Center (Wilmington, DE) 58071
Hercules Inc. Research Center (Wilmington, DE) 58072; 58073
Hercules Specialty Chemicals Co. (Savannah, GA) 67484
Hi-Tek Polymers Inc. Plant 2700 (Louisville, KY) 68772
Hoechst Celanese (Shelby, NC) 76240
Hoechst Celanese (Narrows, VA) 91438
Hoechst Celanese (Portsmouth, VA) 91659
Hoechst-Celanese Corp. (Greer, SC) 79475; 79476
Hoechst Celanese Corp. (Spartanburg, SC) 79913
Hoechst-Celanese Corp. (Narrows, VA) 91439
Hoechst-Celanese Corp. (Portsmouth, VA) 91660
Hoechst-Celanese Corp. Bayport Works (Pasadena, TX) 88419
Hoechst Celanese Corp. Baton Rouge Works (Baton Rouge, LA) 69557
Hoechst-Celanese Corp. Dreyfus Research Park (Charlotte, NC) 74045
Hoechst-Celanese Corp. Salisbury Plant (Salisbury, NC) 76167
Hoechst-Celanese Corp. Shelby Plant (Shelby, NC) 76241
Hoechst-Celanese Corp. Spartanburg (Spartanburg, SC) 79914
Hoechst Celanese Corp. Spartanburg Plant (Spartanburg, SC) 79915
Hoechst Celanese Shelby Plant (Shelby, NC) 76242
Lyondell Petrochemical Co. (Channelview, TX) 83550
Lyondell Polymers Corp. (Pasadena, TX) 88438
Mobil Chemical Co. Bcsp (Beaumont, TX) 83180
Monsanto Chemical Group-Fibers (Greenwood, SC) 79459
Monsanto Co. (Cantonment, FL) 58910
Monsanto Co. (Pensacola, FL) 62450
Morton International Polmer Systems (Moss Point, MS) 73195
Morton International Specialty (Greenville, SC) 79398
Occidental Chemical Co. (Victoria, TX) 89897
Occidental Chemical Corp. (Addis, LA) 69365; 69366
Occidental Chemical Corp. (Orange, TX) 88325
Occidental Chemical Corp. (Pasadena, TX) 88447; 88448
Occidental Chemical Corp. (Victoria, TX) 89898
Occidental Chemical Corp. (Wadsworth, TX) 89985
Occidental Petroleum Corp. Alathon Polymers Div. (Ponca City, OK) 77708
Occidental Petroleum Corp. Alathon Polymers Div. Technology Dept. (Ponca City, OK) 77709
Owens-Corning Fiberglas Corp. (Anderson, SC) 78682
Owens Corning Fiberglass (Anderson, SC) 78683
Owens-Corning Fiberglass Corp. (Anderson, SC) 78684
Performance Plastics Business Unit (Kingsport, TN) 81115
Phillips Petroleum Co. Houston Chemical Complex (Pasadena, TX) 88456
Phillips Research Ctr. (Bartlesville, OK) 76845
Phillips 66 Co. (Borger, TX) 83321
Phillips 66 Co. Philtex/Ryton Complex (Borger, TX) 83322
Reneer Films Corp. (Dallas, TX) 84356
Rhone Poulenc Inc. (Jeffersontown, KY) 68499
Rhone-Poulenc Inc. Walsh Div. (Gastonia, NC) 74685
Rhone-Poulenc Inc. Plant 2700 (Louisville, KY) 68995
Rhone-Poulenc Performance Resins & Coatings (New Castle, DE) 57873
Rohm & Haas Unocal Chemical Div. (Charlotte, NC) 74149; 74150; 74151
Rohm & Haas Co. (Charlotte, NC) 74152

Rohm & Haas Inc. Kentucky (Louisville, KY) 68998
Rohm & Haas Inc. Tennessee (Knoxville, TN) 81244
Rohm & Haas Kentucky Inc. (Louisville, KY) 68999
Rohm & Haas Tennessee Inc. (Knoxville, TN) 81245
Scott Polymers Inc. (Fort Worth, TX) 85275
Scott Polymers Inc. (Saginaw, TX) 88863; 88864
Sequa Chemicals Inc. (Chester, SC) 78943
Shell Chemical Co. Point Pleasure Polyester Plant (Apple Grove, WV) 92664
Shell Chemical Co. Taft Plant (Taft, LA) 70900; 70901
Shell Oil Co. (Deer Park, TX) 84567
Shell Oil Co. (Irving, TX) 87401
Shell Oil Co. Deer Park Manufacturing Complex (Deer Park, TX) 84568
Texas Eastman Co. (Longview, TX) 87737; 87738
3M Co. Tape Manufacturing Div. (Greenville, SC) 79440
3M Co. Telecom Markets Div. (Austin, TX) 83046
Tremco Inc. (Barbourville, KY) 68110
Ucar Emulsion Systems (Garland, TX) 85547
Ucar Resinas Caribe Inc. (Bayamon, PR) 78342
Union Camp Corp. (Savannah, GA) 67530
Union Camp Corp. (Valdosta, GA) 67978
Union Carbide Carbibe, Inc. (Bayamon, PR) 78343
Union Carbide Chemical Corp. (Garland, TX) 85548
Union Carbide Chemical & Plastics Co. Technical Center (South Charleston, WV) 93054
Union Carbide Chemicals & Plastics (Tucker, GA) 67906
Union Carbide Chemicals & Plastics Co. Marine Terminal (Texas City, TX) 89740
Union Carbide Chemicals & Plastics Co. Texas City Plt. (Texas City, TX) 89741
Union Carbide Chemicals & Plastics Inc. (Garland, TX) 85549
Union Carbide Corp. (Tucker, GA) 67907
Union Carbide Corp. (Haknville, LA) 69928
Union Carbide Corp. (Texas City, TX) 89742
Union Carbide Corp., Star Plant (Taft, LA) 70902
Union Carbide Texas City Plant (Texas City, TX) 89745
Union Caride Corp. Star Plant (Taft, LA) 70903
Unocal Corp. Unocal Chemicals Div. (Charlotte, NC) 74191; 74192
Virginia Chemicals Co. (Portsmouth, VA) 91672
W. R. Grace & Co. (Atlanta, GA) 65247
W. R. Grace & Co. (Owensboro, KY) 69196
Wellman Inc. (Charlotte, NC) 74225
Wellman Inc. (Fayetteville, NC) 74583
Westvaco Corp. (De Ridder, LA) 69821
Westvaco Corp. Chemicals (De Ridder, LA) 69822
WestVaco Corp. Kraft Div. (North Charleston, SC) 79755
Wilmington Plant (New Castle, DE) 57878
Witco Corp. (Hahnville, LA) 69926
W.R. Grace & Co. (Atlanta, GA) 65291

2822 Synthetic Rubber

Allied-Signal Inc. (Orange, TX) 88304; 88306
BASF Corp. (Chattanooga, TN) 80325; 80326
BASF Corp. Chemicals (Chattanooga, TN) 80329
BASF Corp.-Clemson Plant (Central, SC) 78784
Bf Goodrich Co. Hattiesburg Plant (Hattiesburg, MS) 72888
Carpenter Co. Inc. (Russellville, KY) 69257
Carpenter Co. Inc. (Cleveland, TN) 80572
Dow Chemical Co. (Freeport, TX) 85379
Dow Chemical Co. Texas Operations (Freeport, TX) 85381
Dow Chemical Dalton Site (Dalton, GA) 65781; 65782
Dow Corning Corp. Elizabethtown Plant (Elizabethtown, KY) 68276
Eastman Chemical Co. (Kingsport, TN) 81075
Exxon Chemical Co. (Baton Rouge, LA) 69523
Exxon Chemical Co. (Baytown, TX) 83114
Goodyear Tire & Rubber Co. (Beaumont, TX) 83154
Goodyear Tire & Rubber Co. (Cheek, TX) 83557
Goodyear Tire & Rubber Co. Beaumont Chemical Plant (Beaumont, TX) 83155
Goodyear Tire & Rubber Co. Houston Chemical Plant (Houston, TX) 86253
Miles Inc. Polysar Rubber Div. (Orange, TX) 88324
Morton International Polmer Systems (Moss Point, MS) 73195
Rhone-Poulenc Inc. Walsh Div. (Gastonia, NC) 74685
Union Lake Petroleum Corp. (Carville, LA) 69758

2823 Cellulosic Manmade Fibers

BASF Corp. (Lowland, TN) 81358
BASF Corp. Fibers (Lowland, TN) 81359
BASF Fibers (Williamsburg, VA) 92565
Eastman Chemical Co. (Kingsport, TN) 81075
Eastman Kodak Co. Tennessee Div. (Kingsport, TN) 81076
Eastman Kodak Co. Tennessee Eastman Div. (Kingsport, TN) 81077
Hoechst Celanese (Narrows, VA) 91438
Hoechst Celanese Celriver Plant (Rock Hill, SC) 79828
Hoechst-Celanese Corp. (Narrows, VA) 91439
Hoechst-Celanese Corp. Celriver Plant (Rock Hill, SC) 79829
Hoechst-Celanese Corp. Dreyfus Research Park (Charlotte, NC) 74045

2824 Organic Fibers—Noncellulosic

Allied-Signal Communications Systems (Hopewell, VA) 91151
Allied-Signal Fiber (Moncure, NC) 75567
Allied-Signal Inc. (Chester, VA) 90614
Allied-Signal Inc. Fibers (Moncure, NC) 75568
Allied-Signal Inc. Fibers (Columbia, SC) 78966; 78967
Allied-Signal Inc. Technical Center (Chesterfield, VA) 90628; 90629
American Cyanamid Co. (Milton, FL) 61543
American Cyanamid Co. (Westwego, LA) 70968
BASF Corp. (Lowland, TN) 81358
BASF Corp. (Williamsburg, VA) 92561
BASF Corp. Fibers (Enka, NC) 74506
BASF Corp. Fibers (Anderson, SC) 78663
BASF Corp. Fibers (Central, SC) 78782; 78783
BASF Corp. Fibers (Lowland, TN) 81359
BASF Corp. Fibers (Williamsburg, VA) 92563
BASF Corp. Fibers Division (Anderson, SC) 78664
BASF Corp. Fibers Division (Lowland, TN) 81362
BASF Corp. Fibers & Products (Anderson, SC) 78665
BASF Fibers (Lowland, TN) 81363
BASF Structural Materials Inc. Celion Carbon Fibers (Rock Hill, SC) 79813
Carolina Eastman Co. (Columbia, SC) 78993; 78995
Ethyl Corp. (Richmond, VA) 91862
Exxon Chemical Co. (Houston, TX) 86116
Goodyear Tire & Rubber Co. (Scottsboro, AL) 56521
Hercules Inc. (Covington, GA) 65729
Hispan Corp. (Decatur, AL) 55592
Hoechst Celanese (Shelby, NC) 76240
Hoechst Celanese Corp. (Spartanburg, SC) 79913
Hoechst-Celanese Corp. Celriver Plant (Rock Hill, SC) 79829
Hoechst-Celanese Corp. Dreyfus Research Park (Charlotte, NC) 74045
Hoechst-Celanese Corp. Greenville Plant (Greenville, SC) 79369
Hoechst-Celanese Corp. Salisbury Plant (Salisbury, NC) 76167
Hoechst-Celanese Corp. Shelby Plant (Shelby, NC) 76241
Hoechst-Celanese Corp. Spartanburg (Spartanburg, SC) 79914
Hoechst Celanese Corp. Spartanburg Plant (Spartanburg, SC) 79915
Hoechst Celanese Dreyfus Research Park (Charlotte, NC) 74046
Hoechst Celanese Salisbury Plant (Salisbury, NC) 76168
Hoechst Celanese Shelby Plant (Shelby, NC) 76242
Monsanto Co. (Decatur, AL) 55598
Monsanto Co. (Cantonment, FL) 58910
Monsanto Co. (Greenwood, SC) 79460
Monsanto Co. Chemical Group (Decatur, AL) 55599
Phillips Fibers Corp. Spartanburg Plant (Spartanburg, SC) 79923
Technical Fibers Group Salisbury Plant (Salisbury, NC) 76179

2833 Medicinals & Botanicals

Abbott Chemical Inc. (Barceloneta, PR) 78319
Abbott Chemicals Inc. (Barceloneta, PR) 78320; 78321
Adm (Southport, NC) 76281
Agri-Bio Corp. (Gainesville, GA) 66265
Allergan Medical Optics (Lenoir, NC) 75364
American Cyanamid Co. (Pearl, MS) 73274
American Cyanamid Co. (Willow Island, WV) 93131
American Cyanamid Co. Shulton (Pearl, MS) 73275
BASF Corp. Chemicals Division (Spartanburg, SC) 79878
Bristol-Myers Products (Morrisville, NC) 75662; 75663
Clorox Co. (Pearl, MS) 73276
Eli Lilly Ind. Inc. (Mayaguez, PR) 78511
Eli Lilly Industries, Inc. (Mayaguez, PR) 78512
Kaiser Aluminum & Chemical (Tifton, GA) 67826
Merck & Co. Inc. Flint River Plant (Albany, GA) 64082
Merck Sharp & Dohme Quimica De P.R. (Barceloneta, PR) 78328
Merck Sharp & Dohme Quimica De Puerto Rico (Barceloneta, PR) 78329
Mobil Chemical Co. (Houston, TX) 86583
Mobil Oil Corp. (Houston, TX) 86594
Noramco of Delaware Inc. (Wilmington, DE) 58091
Noramco Inc. (Athens, GA) 64172
Pfizer Inc. (Southport, NC) 76287
Pfizer Pharmaceuticals Inc. (Barceloneta, PR) 78330
Schering Industrial Development Corp. (Manati, PR) 78503
Schering-Plough Products Inc. Development (Manati, PR) 78504
Xomed Inc. (Jacksonville, FL) 60514

2834 Pharmaceutical Preparations

Abbott Chemical Inc. (Barceloneta, PR) 78319
Abbott Chemicals Inc. (Barceloneta, PR) 78320; 78321
Abbott Laboratories (Rocky Mount, NC) 76071; 76072
Abbott Laboratories (Austin, TX) 82799
Abbott Laboratories International Co. (New Orleans, LA) 70423
Agri-Bio Corp. (Gainesville, GA) 66265
A.H. Robins Manufacturing Co. (Barceloneta, PR) 78322
Allergan Inc. (Waco, TX) 89925
American Cyanamid Co. Lederle Laboratories Division (Sanford, NC) 76186
Arbrook Manufacturing Corp. (Caguas, PR) 78348
Arbrook Mfg. Corp. (Caguas, PR) 78349
Ayerst-Wyeth Pharmaceuticals Inc. (Guayama, PR) 78418; 78419; 78420
Ayerst Wyeth Pharmaceuticals Whitehall Laboratories (Guayama, PR) 78421
Barcroft Co. (Lewes, DE) 57827
Bausch & Lomb Inc. (Greenville, SC) 79297; 79298
Bausch & Lomb Inc. Pharmaceutical Div. (Tampa, FL) 63361
Baxter Healthcare (Marion, NC) 75496
Baxter Healthcare Corp. (Cleveland, MS) 72682
Baxter Healthcare Corp. (Marion, NC) 75497
Baxter Healthcare Corp. of Puerto Rico (Jayuya, PR) 78466
Bergen Brunswig Drug Co. (Tulsa, OK) 77886
Bergen Brunswig Drug Co. (San Antonio, TX) 88929
Bio-Lab, Inc. (Decatur, GA) 65802
Block Drug Co. Inc. (Memphis, TN) 81480; 81481
Bristol Myers (Arlington, TX) 82638
Bristol-Myers Barceloneta Inc. (Barceloneta, PR) 78325
Bristol-Myers Products (Morrisville, NC) 75663
Bristol-Myers-Squibb Co. (Morrisville, NC) 75665
Cyanamid Agricultural De Puerto Rico Inc. (Manati, PR) 78494; 78495; 78496
Cynamid Agricultural De Puerto Rico Inc. (Manati, PR) 78497
E. R. Squibb & Sons Inc. (Kenly, NC) 75272
Eaton Laboratories, Inc. (Manati, PR) 78499
Eli Lilly Ind. Inc. (Carolina, PR) 78376
Eli Lilly Ind. Inc. (Mayaguez, PR) 78511
Eli Lilly Industries, Inc. (Carolina, PR) 78377
Eli Lilly Industries, Inc. (Mayaguez, PR) 78512
Ethyl Corp. (Orangeburg, SC) 79771
FMC Corp. (Newark, DE) 57904
G. D. Searle & Co. (Augusta, GA) 65331
GAF Chemicals Corp. (Calvert City, KY) 68176
Hoechst Roussel Pharmaceuti (Tampa, FL) 63457
Ivax Industry Inc. Textile Products (Rock Hill, SC) 79832
Key Pharmaceuticals Puerto Rico Inc. (Las Piedras, PR) 78482
Lederle Parentelas Lederle Piperacillin Inc. (Carolina, PR) 78378
Lederle Parenterals Inc.-Lederle Piperacillin Inc. (Carolina, PR) 78379
Lederle Parenterals & Lederle Piperacillin Inc. (Carolina, PR) 78380
Lederle Piperacillin Inc.; Lederle Parenterals Inc.- (Carolina, PR) 78379
Lederle-Praxis Biologics Inc. (Sanford, NC) 76198
Mcneil Consumer Products Co. (Round Rock, TX) 88850
Mcneil Pharmaceutical Co. (Dorado, PR) 78411; 78412
Merck & Co. Inc. (Elkton, VA) 90746
Merck Sharp & Dohme Quimica De P.R. (Barceloneta, PR) 78328
Merck Sharp & Dohme Quimica De Puerto Rico (Barceloneta, PR) 78329
Miles Cutter Biological Division (Daphne, AL) 55567
Monsanto Co. (Luling, LA) 70204
Olay Co. Inc. (Cayey, PR) 78385; 78386; 78387
Omb Pharmaceutical Partners (Gurabo, PR) 78444
Ortho Biologics, Inc. (Manati, PR) 78500
Ortho Pharmaceuticals Inc. (Manati, PR) 78501
Plough Inc. (Memphis, TN) 81669; 81670
Procter & Gamble Mfg. Co. (Greenville, SC) 79409; 79410
Proctor & Gamble Pharmaceuticals Pr Inc. (Manati, PR) 78502
Rhone Poulenc Inc. (Baltimore, MD) 71239
Richardson - Vick Inc. (Greensboro, NC) 74892
Richardson - Vicks Inc. USA (Greensboro, NC) 74893
Schering-Plough Healthcare Products (Cleveland, TN) 80600
Schering-Plough Healthcare Products Inc. (Memphis, TN) 81690
Schering-Plough Prodsucts Inc. Key Pharmaceuticals (Las Piedras, PR) 78487
Schering-Plough Products Inc. Key Pharmaceuticals (Las Piedras, PR) 78488
Searle & Co. (Caguas, PR) 78358; 78359
Squibb Mfg. Inc. (Humacao, PR) 78463
Sterling Drug Inc. (Gulfport, MS) 72876
Sterling Health (Gulfport, MS) 72877
Sterling Pharmaceuticals Inc. (Barceloneta, PR) 78331
Upjohn Co. (Barceloneta, PR) 78332
Upjohn Manufacturing Co. (Barceloneta, PR) 78333
Upjohn Mfg. Co. (Barceloneta, PR) 78334
US Clinical Products, Inc. (Plano, TX) 88615

2835 Diagnostic Substances

Baxter Healthcare Corp. Dade (Miami, FL) 61202
Baxter International Baxter Diagnostics Div. (Miami, FL) 61203
Becton Dickinson, Diagnostics Inc. (Cayey, PR) 78383; 78384
Technicon Instruments Corp. (Middletown, VA) 91407

2836 Biological Products Except Diagnostic

Baxter International Baxter Diagnostics Div. (Miami, FL) 61203
Miles Inc. Cutter Biological (Clayton, NC) 74265
Ortho Biologics, Inc. (Manati, PR) 78500
Sterwin Laboratories Inc. (Auburn, AL) 55071
Westvaco Corp. Bleached Board (Covington, VA) 90666

2841 Soap & Other Detergents

Burlington Industries Inc. (Greensbor, NC) 74758
Central Products Co., Inc. (Montgomery, AL) 56289; 56290
Clorox Co. Dyersburg Plant (Dyersburg, TN) 80743
Colgate-Palmolive Co. (Bethune, SC) 78735
Dial Corp. (Memphis, TN) 81510
Douglas/Quikut (Germantown, TN) 80855
Dow Consumer Products Inc. (Mauldin, SC) 79647
Dowbrands (Greenville, TX) 85664
Dowbrands Inc. (Mauldin, SC) 79649
Dowbrands Lp (Mauldin, SC) 79650
Dowbrands L.P. (Greenville, TX) 85665
Ecolab Inc. (Dorado, PR) 78408
Ecolab, Inc. (Garland, TX) 85484
Ecolab Inc. Mc Donough Plant (Mc Donough, GA) 66955
Ecolab Manufacturing Inc. (Dorado, PR) 78409
Ethicon, Inc. (Cornelia, GA) 65722
Hunter Zep (Baton Rouge, LA) 69559
Ivax Industries Inc. Textile Products (Rock Hill, SC) 79830
Ivax Industry Inc. Textile Products (Rock Hill, SC) 79832
Monsanto Co. (Alvin, TX) 82509
Olin Corp. (Brandenburg, KY) 68170
Procter & Gamble Manuf. Co. (Augusta, GA) 65345
Procter & Gamble Manufacturing (Lexington, KY) 68612
Procter & Gamble Mfg. Co. (Augusta, GA) 65346
Procter & Gamble Mfg. Co. (Pineville, LA) 70625
Procter & Gamble Mfg. Co. (Baltimore, MD) 71220
Procter & Gamble Mfg. Co. (Dallas, TX) 84325
Procter & Gamble Mfg. Co. Co. (Pineville, LA) 70626

Rhone Poulenc Inc. (Baltimore, MD) 71239
Sani-Fresh International (San Antonio, TX) 89222
Schering-Plough Healthcare Products (Cleveland, TN) 80600
Sequa Chemicals Inc. (Chester, SC) 78943
Sherwin-Williams Co. (Morrow, GA) 67044
Westvaco Corp. Chemical (Mulberry, FL) 61581
Witco Corp. (Fort Worth, TX) 85364
Witco Corp. Humko Chemical (Memphis, TN) 81760; 81761
ZEP Manufacturing Co. (Atlanta, GA) 65301
Zep Mfg. Co. (Atlanta, GA) 65303
Zep Mfg. Co. (De Soto, TX) 84542

2842 Polishes & Sanitation Goods

Arcadian Corp. (Lake Charles, LA) 70129
baker Hughes Prod Baker Performance Chemicals (Houston, TX) 85840
Borden Inc. Chemical (Diboll, TX) 84652
Borden Inc. Packaging & Industrial Prods. (Diboll, TX) 84653
Boyle-Midway Household Products Inc. (Atlanta, GA) 64331
Central Products Co., Inc. (Montgomery, AL) 56289; 56290
Chemical Specialties Manufacturing Corp. (Baltimore, MD) 71079
Chemspec Inc. (Baltimore, MD) 71080
Clorox Co. (Forest Park, GA) 66232
Clorox Co. (Frederick, MD) 71717
Clorox Co. (Charlotte, NC) 73904
Clorox Co. Charlotte Plant (Charlotte, NC) 73905
Clorox Co. Frederick Plant (Frederick, MD) 71718
Clorox Co. Household Products Co. (Houston, TX) 85964
Clorox Co. Houston Plant (Houston, TX) 85965
Clorox Co. Jackson Plant (Pearl, MS) 73277
Clorox Co. of Puerto Rico (Caguas, PR) 78356; 78357
Clorox Co., Tampa Plant (Tampa, FL) 63394
Davis & Geck, Inc. (Manati, PR) 78498
Dowbrands (Mauldin, SC) 79648
Ecolab, Inc. (Garland, TX) 85484
Ecolab Inc. Mc Donough Plant (Mc Donough, GA) 66955
Ethicon, Inc. (Cornelia, GA) 65722
Hunter Zep (Baton Rouge, LA) 69559
Mac's Oil & Chemicals, Inc. (Lexington, KY) 68575
NCH Corp. Mohawk Labratories Div. (Irving, TX) 87384; 87385
Safety Kleen Corp. (Lexington, SC) 79608
Safety Kleen Corp. (Pasadena, TX) 88467
Selig Chemical Ind. (Atlanta, GA) 65147
Selig Chemical Industries (Atlanta, GA) 65148
Specialty Products of America (Miami, FL) 61464
Unijax Inc. (Huntington, WV) 92899; 92900
ZEP Manufacturing Co. (Hialeah, FL) 60021
ZEP Manufacturing Co. (Atlanta, GA) 65301
ZEP Manufacturing Co. (Smyrna, GA) 67585
ZEP Manufacturing Co. (Jessup, MD) 71988
Zep Manufacturing Co. (Austin, TX) 83075
ZEP Manufacturing Co. (De Soto, TX) 84541
ZEP Manufacturing Co. (Houston, TX) 87211
Zep Mfg. Co. (Atlanta, GA) 65303
Zep Mfg. Co. (De Soto, TX) 84542

2843 Surface Active Agents

Air Products & Chemicals, Inc. (Piedmont, SC) 79792
Alkaril Chemicals (Winder, GA) 68052; 68053
Alkaril Chemicals Inc. (Winder, GA) 68054
American Cyanamid Co. (Charlotte, NC) 73834
American Cyanamid Co. (Willow Island, WV) 93131
American Emulsions Co. Inc. (Dalton, GA) 65771
Baker Performance Chemicals (Houma, LA) 69950
Baker Performance Chemicals (Houston, TX) 85856
BASF Corp. (Spartanburg, SC) 79876
BASF Corp. Chemicals (Spartanburg, SC) 79877
BASF Corp. Chemicals Division (Spartanburg, SC) 79878
Borden Packaging & Industrial Products (Fayetteville, NC) 74538
Burlington Industries Inc. (Greensbor, NC) 74758
Caribe G.E. Products Inc. Arecibo Plant (Arecibo, PR) 78312
Enenco Inc. (Memphis, TN) 81519
Gaf Chemical Corp. (Spartanburg, SC) 79907
GAF Chemicals Corp. (Calvert City, KY) 68176
Gaf Chemicals Corp. (Spartanburg, SC) 79908
Hercules Specialty Chemicals Co. (Savannah, GA) 67484
Hoechst-Celanese Charlotte Specialty Chemicals Group (Charlotte, NC) 74042
Hoechst Celanese Charlotte Spg (Charlotte, NC) 74043
Hunter Zep (Baton Rouge, LA) 69559
Ivax Industries Inc. Textile Products (Rock Hill, SC) 79830
Nalco Chemical Co. (Jonesboro, GA) 66389
Nalco Chemical Co. (Garyville, LA) 69865; 69866
Nalco Chemical Co. (Sugar Land, TX) 89539
Olin Corp. (Brandenburg, KY) 68170
Rhone-Poulenc (Reserve, LA) 70663
Rhone-Poulenc Inc. Surfactants & Specialties (Winder, GA) 68062
Rhone-Poulenc Inc. Surfactants & Specialties (Spartanburg, SC) 79937
Rhone-Poulenc Specialty Chemicals Co. (Marietta, GA) 66906
Rhone-Poulenc Surfactants & Specialties LP (Baltimore, MD) 71240
Rohm & Haas Inc. Tennessee (Knoxville, TN) 81244
Rohne Poulenc Inc. (Winder, GA) 68063
Sequa Chemicals Inc. (Chester, SC) 78943
Shell Chemical Co. Reserve Plant (Reserve, LA) 70664
Westvaco Corp. Chemicals (Mulberry, FL) 61578; 61579; 61580
Witco Corp. (Harvey, LA) 69943
Witco Corp. (New Orleans, LA) 70590
Witco Corp. (Houston, TX) 87200
Witco Corp. Harahan (Harahan, LA) 69937
Witco Corp. Humko Chemical (Memphis, TN) 81760
Witco Corp. Oleo-Surfactant Organics (Houston, TX) 87201
Witco Corp. Organics (Houston, TX) 87202
ZEP Manufacturing Co. (Atlanta, GA) 65301
Zep Mfg. Co. (Atlanta, GA) 65303
Zep Mfg. Co. (De Soto, TX) 84542

2844 Toilet Preparations

Avon Products Inc. (Newark, DE) 57890
Avon Products Inc. (Washington, DC) 58130
Block Drug Co. (Memphis, TN) 81479
Block Drug Co. Inc. (Memphis, TN) 81480; 81482
Carter P. D. Inc. (Rincon, PR) 78542
Dial Corp. (Memphis, TN) 81510
Hunter Zep (Baton Rouge, LA) 69559
Maybelline USA (North Little Rock, AR) 57469
Noxell Corp. (Hunt Valley, MD) 71939; 71940
Pfizer Inc. Coty Div. (Sanford, NC) 76200
Plough Inc. (Memphis, TN) 81669; 81670
Procter & Gamble Manufacturing Co. (Browns Summit, NC) 73729
Procter & Gamble Mfg. Co. (Browns Summit, NC) 73730
Schering-Plough Healthcare Products (Cleveland, TN) 80600
Sterling Drug Inc. (Gulfport, MS) 72876
Union Camp Corp. (Jacksonville, FL) 60483
ZEP Manufacturing Co. (Atlanta, GA) 65301
Zep Mfg. Co. (Atlanta, GA) 65303
Zep Mfg. Co. (De Soto, TX) 84542

2850 Paints & Allied Products

D & S Plastics International (Grand Prairie, TX) 85616

2851 Paints & Allied Products

BASF Corp. (Morganton, NC) 75630
BASF Corp. (Morgantown, NC) 75660
BASF Corp. Coatings & Inks (Morganton, NC) 75631
BASF Corp. Industrial Coatings Morganton (Morganton, NC) 75632
Carboline Co. (Lake Charles, LA) 70134
Chemical Coatings Inc. (Hudson, NC) 75198
Crown Metro Aerospace (Greenville, SC) 79333
Dexter Corp. Midland Div. (Birmingham, AL) 55218
Dexter Corp. Packaging Products Div. (Birmingham, AL) 55219
Dexter Crown Metro Aerospace (Greenville, SC) 79343
Dexter Packaging Products (Birmingham, AL) 55220
Evodex (Birmingham, AL) 55232
Ferro Corp. (Arlington, TX) 82655
Ferro Corp. Coating Div. (Nashville, TN) 81962
Fina Inc. (Dallas, TX) 84064
H. B. Fuller Co. (Conyers, GA) 65682
Hi-Tek Polymers Inc. Plant 2700 (Louisville, KY) 68772
Kurfees Coatings Inc. (Louisville, KY) 68816
Mccorquodale Process Inc. (Whiteford, MD) 72571
Mobil Oil (Louisville, KY) 68886
Mobil Oil Corp. (Louisville, KY) 68887
Morton International Inc. (Decatur, AL) 55600
Morton International Inc. (Wytheville, VA) 92644; 92645
Olympic Homecare Products Co. (Louisville, KY) 68933
Ppg Architectural Finishes (East Point, GA) 66153
Ppg Architectural Finishes (Louisville, KY) 68981
PPG Industries Inc. (Dover, DE) 57799
PPG Industries Inc. (Atlanta, GA) 65043
Rhone Poulenc Inc. (Marietta, GA) 66905
Rhone-Poulenc Inc. Plant 2700 (Louisville, KY) 68995
Rhone-Poulenc Performance Resins & Coatings (New Castle, DE) 57873
Sentry Polymers Inc. (Freeport, TX) 85392
Sherwin-Williams Co. (Orlando, FL) 62143
Sherwin-Williams Co. (Morrow, GA) 67044
Sherwin-Williams Co. (Tucker, GA) 67888
Sherwin-Williams Co. (Baltimore, MD) 71279
Sherwin-Williams Co. (Greensboro, NC) 74909; 74910
Sherwin-Williams Co. (Garland, TX) 85535
Sigma Coatings Inc. (Harvey, LA) 69941
Thompson & Formby Inc. (Olive Branch, MS) 73230
Thompson & Formby Inc. (Memphis, TN) 81709
Thompson & Formby's Inc. (Olive Branch, MS) 73231
Valaspar Corp. (High Point, NC) 75177
Valspar Corp (Houston, TX) 87069
Valspar Corp. (Tampa, FL) 63642
Valspar Corp. (Covington, GA) 65742
Valspar Corp. (Louisville, KY) 69032
Valspar Corp. (New Orleans, LA) 70583
Valspar Corp. (Baltimore, MD) 71321
Valspar Corp. (High Point, NC) 75178
Valspar Corp. (Beaumont, TX) 83230
Valspar Corp. (Garland, TX) 85554; 85555
Valspar Corp. (Houston, TX) 87070
Valspar Corp. Beaumont (Beaumont, TX) 83231
Valspar Corp. Fed (Tampa, FL) 63643
Valspar Corp. Garland (Garland, TX) 85556
Valspar Corp. Jackson (Jackson, TN) 81014
Wilmington Plant (New Castle, DE) 57878

2860 Industrial Organic Chemicals

Searle & Co. (Caguas, PR) 78359

2861 Gum & Wood Chemicals

Arizona Chemical (Port St. Joe, FL) 62692
Arizona Chemical Co. (Panama City, FL) 62318
Arizona Chemical Co. (Springhill, LA) 70847; 70848; 70849
Arizona Chemical Co. (Picayune, MS) 73290
Arizona Chemical Co. Sylvachem Corp. (Port St. Joe, FL) 62693
Georgia-Pacific Corp. (Monticello, MS) 73186; 73187
Georgia Pacific Corp. Monticello Mill (Monticello, MS) 73188
Hercules Inc. (Hattiesburg, MS) 72890
Hercules Inc. (Franklin, VA) 90894; 90895
Hercules Inc. Brunswick Plant (Brunswick, GA) 65414
Qualex Inc. (Durham, NC) 74425
Rhone Poulenc Inc. (Marietta, GA) 66905
Rhone Poulenc Inc. (Vernon, TX) 89869
Sylvachem Corp. (Port St. Joe, FL) 62694
Union Camp Corp. (Prattville, AL) 56493
Union Camp Corp. (Jacksonville, FL) 60483
Union Camp Corp. (Savannah, GA) 67530
Union Camp Corp. (Valdosta, GA) 67978
Westpoint Pepperell (Elizabethtown, NC) 74495
Westvaco Corp. (De Ridder, LA) 69821
Westvaco Corp. Charleston Chemical (North Charleston, SC) 79753
Westvaco Corp. Chemicals (Mulberry, FL) 61578; 61579; 61580
Westvaco Corp. Chemicals (De Ridder, LA) 69822
Westvaco Corp. Polychemicals (North Charleston, SC) 79757; 79758
Wood Products Inc. (Oakland, MD) 72159

2865 Cyclic Crudes & Intermediates

Air Products & Chemicals, Inc. (Pace, FL) 62217; 62218; 62219
Air Products & Chemicals Inc. (Pasadena, TX) 88381
Air Products Manufacturing Corp. (Pasadena, TX) 88382
Allied-Signal (Birmingham, AL) 55115
Allied-Signal Inc. (Birmingham, AL) 55117; 55118; 55119
Arco Chemical Co. (Channelview, TX) 83546
Arkansas Eastman Co. (Batesville, AR) 56740
Ashland Chemical Co. (Neal, WV) 92959
Ashland Chemical Inc. (Houston, TX) 85819
Ashland Chemical Inc. (Neal, WV) 92960
Ashland Oil Inc. (Ashland, KY) 68090
Avecor Inc. (Vonore, TN) 82394
Baker Performance Chemicals (Houma, LA) 69950
BASF Corp. (Geismar, LA) 69874; 69875
BASF Corp. (Charlotte, NC) 73849
BASF Corp. (Huntington, WV) 92868; 92869
BASF Corp. Chemicals (Huntington, WV) 92870
Brunswick Corp. (DeLand, FL) 59297
Cape Ind. (Wilmington, NC) 76546
Carolina Eastman Co. (Columbia, SC) 78994; 78995
Chevron Chemical Co. (St. James, LA) 70866; 70867
Cos-Mar Inc. (Carville, LA) 69757
Dow Chemical Co. (Freeport, TX) 85379
Dow Chemical Co. Texas Operations (Freeport, TX) 85381
Eastman Kodak Co. Arkansas Eastman Co. (Batesville, AR) 56752
Eastman Kodak Co. Arkansas Eastman Div. (Batesville, AR) 56753
Eastman Kodak Co. Tennessee Div. (Kingsport, TN) 81076
Eastman Kodak Co. Tennessee Eastman Div. (Kingsport, TN) 81077
Engelhard Corp. (Louisville, KY) 68759
Engelhard Corp. Pigments & Additives Div. (Louisville, KY) 68760
Ethyl Corp. (Pasadena, TX) 88402
Ethyl Corp. (Richmond, VA) 91862
Ferro Corp. Coating Div. (Nashville, TN) 81962
Fina Oil & Chemical Co. (Pasadena, TX) 88407
GAF Chemicals Corp. (Calvert City, KY) 68176
Goodyear Bayport Chem. Plant (Pasadena, TX) 88414
Goodyear Bayport Chemcial Plant (Pasadena, TX) 88415
Goodyear Tire & Rubber Co. Bayport Chemical Plant (Pasadena, TX) 88416
Harshaw Chemical Co. (Louisville, KY) 68770
Hoechst-Celanese Charlotte Specialty Chemicals Group (Charlotte, NC) 74042
Hoechst Celanese Charlotte Spg (Charlotte, NC) 74043
Miles Inc. Organic Products Div. (Rock Hill, SC) 79835
Monsanto Co. (Cantonment, FL) 58910
Monsanto Co. (Luling, LA) 70204
Olin Corp. (Westlake, LA) 70966
Olin Corp. Lake Charles Plant (Lake Charles, LA) 70152; 70153
PPG Industries Inc. (LaPorte, TX) 87604
Ppg Industries Inc. (New Martinsville, WV) 92962
Shell Oil Co. Deer Park Manufacturing Complex (Deer Park, TX) 84568
Sterling Chemicals Inc. (Texas City, TX) 89737
Texaco Chemical Co. Port Arthur Chemical Plant (Port Arthur, TX) 88647
Union Oil of California Dba Unocal (Nederland, TX) 88195
Union Oil Co. of California Dba Unocal Chem. (Nederland, TX) 88196
Witco Corp. Harahan (Harahan, LA) 69937

2869 Industrial Organic Chemicals Nec

Air Products & Chemicals, Inc. (Milton, FL) 61541
Air Products & Chemicals, Inc. (Pace, FL) 62217; 62218; 62219
Air Products & Chemicals Inc. (Calvert City, KY) 68175
Air Products & Chemicals, Inc. (St. Gabriel, LA) 70863; 70864; 70865
Air Products & Chemicals Inc. (Travelers Rest, SC) 80041; 80042
Air Products & Chemicals Inc. (Pasadena, TX) 88381
Air Products Manufacturing Corp. (Pasadena, TX) 88382
Albright & Wilson Americas Inc. (Charleston, SC) 78786
Albright & Wilson Americas Inc.-Charleston Plant (Charleston, SC) 78787
Allied-Signal Communications Systems (Hopewell, VA) 91151
Allied-Signal Hopewell Plant (Hopewell, VA) 91152
Allied-Signal Inc. (Claymont, DE) 57758

Allied-Signal Inc. (Baton Rouge, LA) 69458; 69460
Allied-Signal Inc. (Hopewell, VA) 91153; 91154; 91155
Amerchol Corp. (Greensburg, LA) 69899
American Cyanamid Co. (Westwego, LA) 70969
American Cyanamid Co. (Charlotte, NC) 73834; 73835
American Cyanamid Co. (Willow Island, WV) 93131; 93132
Aqualon Co. (Hopewell, VA) 91156
Arcadian Corp. (Memphis, TN) 81461
Arcadian Fertilizer, LP (Memphis, TN) 81464
Arcadian Partners Ltd. Partnership (Memphis, TN) 81465
Archer Daniels Midland Co. (Southport, NC) 76282; 76283
Arco Chemical Co. (Channelview, TX) 83546; 83547
Arco Chemical Co. (Pasadena, TX) 88385
Arco Chemical Co. (South Charleston, WV) 93046
Arco Chemical Co. Bayport Div. (Pasadena, TX) 88386
Arco Chemical Co. Institute West Virginia Plant (Institute, WV) 92901
Baker Performance Chemicals (Laurel, MS) 73099
BASF Corp. (Geismar, LA) 69874; 69875
BASF Corp. (Charlotte, NC) 73850
BASF Corp. (Freeport, TX) 85378
BASF Corp. Chemical (Charlotte, NC) 73852
BASF Structural Materials (Rock Hill, SC) 79811
Borden Inc. Chemical (Demopolis, AL) 55613
Borden Inc. Chemical (Louisville, KY) 68708
Borden Inc. Chemical (Fayetteville, NC) 74535
Borden Inc. Chemical (Diboll, TX) 84652
Borden Inc. Package & Industrial Products (Fayetteville, NC) 74536; 74537
Borden Inc. Packaging & Industrial Prods. (Diboll, TX) 84653
Borden Packaging & Industrial Products (Demopolis, AL) 55614
Borden Packaging & Industrial Products (Louisville, KY) 68709
Borden Packaging & Industrial Products (Fayetteville, NC) 74538
Borden Packaging & Industrial Products (Diboll, TX) 84654
Cain Chemical Inc. Bayport Site (Pasadena, TX) 88391
Cain Chemical Inc. Chocolate Bayou Plant (Alvin, TX) 82505
Cain Chemical Inc. Corpus Christi Plant (Corpus Christi, TX) 83706
Cape Industries (Wilmington, NC) 76547
Carolina Eastman Co. (Columbia, SC) 78993
Carpenter Chemical Co. (Pasadena, TX) 88393
Ccpc Chemical Inc. (Corpus Christi, TX) 83707
Celanese Engineering Resins Inc. (Bishop, TX) 83300
Celanese Engineering Resins Inc. Resins Div. (Bishop, TX) 83301
Cellulosic Products Inc. (Greensburg, LA) 69900
Chemtronics Inc. (Swannanoa, NC) 76349
Chevron Chemical Co. (Baytown, TX) 83109
Chevron Chemical Co. Oak Point Plant (Belle Chasse, LA) 69690; 69691; 69692
Chevron Products Co. Pascagoula Refinery (Pascagoula, MS) 73252; 73252
Chevron USA Inc. Pascagoula Refinery (Pascagoula, MS) 73253
Chevron USA Inc. Pascagoula Refinery (Pascagoula, MS) 73254
An Corp. Bayport Plant (Pasadena, TX) 88398
Cyanamid Agricultural De Puerto Rico Inc. (Manati, PR) 78494; 78495; 78496
Cyprus Foote Mineral Co. (New Johnsonville, TN) 82150
Diamond Shamrock Mont Belvieu E. (Mont Belvieu, TX) 88145
Dow Chemical Co. (La Porte, TX) 87555
Dow Chemical Co. Louisiana Div. (Plaquemine, LA) 70637
Dow Chemical Co. Grand Bayou Plant (Paincourtville, LA) 70606
Dow Chemical Co. La Porte Plant (La Porte, TX) 87556
Dow Chemical Co. La Porte Site (La Porte, TX) 87557
Dow Chemical Grand Bayou Plant (Paincourtville, LA) 70608
Dow Corning Corp. (Carrollton, KY) 68189
Eastman Kodak Co. Arkansas Eastman Div. (Batesville, AR) 56753
Eastman Kodak Co. Tennessee Div. (Kingsport, TN) 81076
Eastman Kodak Co. Tennessee Eastman Div. (Kingsport, TN) 81077
Egp Fuels Co. (La Porte, TX) 87558
Engelhard Corp. (Louisville, KY) 68759
Engelhard Corp. Pigments & Additives Div. (Louisville, KY) 68760
Enron Liquid Fuels (Houston, TX) 86074
Enron Methanol Co. (Pasadena, TX) 88401
Ethyl Corp. (Magnolia, AR) 57330; 57331
Ethyl Corp. (Baton Rouge, LA) 69512
Ethyl Corp. (Orangeburg, SC) 79771
Ethyl Corp. (Pasadena, TX) 88402
Ethyl Corp. (Richmond, VA) 91862
Ethyl Corp. Houston Plant (Pasadena, TX) 88403
Ethyl Corp. Chemicals (Baton Rouge, LA) 69513
Ethyl Corp. Pao Facility (Deer Park, TX) 84549
Ethyl Process Development Center (Baton Rouge, LA) 69514
Exxon Chemical Co. (Baton Rouge, LA) 69523
Exxon Chemical Co. (Baytown, TX) 83114
Ferro Corp. Grant Chemical Div. (Zachary, LA) 70982
FMC Corp. (Baltimore, MD) 71152
FMC Corp. (Pasadena, TX) 88408
FMC Corp. (Nitro, WV) 92969
FMC Corp. Lithium Div. (Bessemer City, NC) 73688
Fmc Corp. Agricultural Chemical Group (Baltimore, MD) 71153
FMC Corp., Baltimore Plant (Baltimore, MD) 71154
Fmc Corp.-Bayport Plant (Pasadena, TX) 88410
FMC Corp., Institute Plant (Institute, WV) 92902
Fmc Corp. Newark (Newark, DE) 57905
Fmc Corp.-Newark De. (Newark, DE) 57906
Fmc Corp. Newark Delaware Plant (Newark, DE) 57907
Fmc Corp. Nitro Plant (Nitro, WV) 92970; 92971
GAF Chemicals Corp. (Calvert City, KY) 68176
Gaf Chemicals Corp. (Texas City, TX) 89720
Gaf Chemicals Corp. Seadrift Plant (Long Mott, TX) 87700
Gaylord Chemical Corp. (Bogalusa, LA) 69702
GE Plastics (Pearlington, MS) 73278
GE Plastics Burkville Div. (Lowndesboro, AL) 56114
GE Specialty Chemicals (Morgantown, WV) 92944
GE Specialty Chemicals North Plant (Morgantown, WV) 92945
General Electric Co. (Wilmington, NC) 76572
Georgia Gulf Corp. (Plaquemine, LA) 70639
Georgia-Pacific Corp. Resins Div. (Taylorsville, MS) 73376
Georgia Pacific Resins Inc. (Crossett, AR) 56884
Georgia-Pacific Resins Inc. (Vienna, GA) 67999
Georgia Pacific Resins Inc. (Conway, NC) 74342
Georgia-Pacific Resins Inc. (Hampton, SC) 79492
Georgia-Pacific Resins Inc. (Russellville, SC) 79847; 79848
Georgia-Pacific Resins Inc. (Houston, TX) 86252
Georgia Pacific Resins Inc. (Lufkin, TX) 87804; 87805
Georgia-Pacific Resins Inc. Conway Hardboard (Conway, NC) 74343
Georgia-Pacific Resins Inc. Particleboard (Taylorsville, MS) 73378
Goodyear Bayport Chem. Plant (Pasadena, TX) 88414
Goodyear Bayport Chemcial Plant (Pasadena, TX) 88415
Goodyear Tire & Rubber Co. (Beaumont, TX) 83154
Goodyear Tire & Rubber Co. (Cheek, TX) 83557
Goodyear Tire & Rubber Co. Bayport Chemical Plant (Pasadena, TX) 88416
Goodyear Tire & Rubber Co. Beaumont Chemical Plant (Beaumont, TX) 83155
Great Lakes Chemical Co. El Dorado-Main Plant (El Dorado, AR) 56944
Great Lakes Chemical Co. El Dorado Plant (El Dorado, AR) 56945
Great Lakes Chemical Corp. (Newport, TN) 82166; 82167
Great Lakes Chemical Corp. El Dorado Plant (El Dorado, AR) 56946
Great Lakes Chemical Corp. South Plant (El Dorado, AR) 56947; 56948
Haarmann & Reimer Corp. (Goose Creek, SC) 79283
Hardwicke Chemical Co. (Elgin, SC) 79189
Harshaw Chemical Co. (Louisville, KY) 68770
Hercules Inc. (Hattiesburg, MS) 72890
Hercules Inc. (Franklin, VA) 90894; 90895
Hercules Inc. Specialty Chemicals Div. (Savannah, GA) 67483
Hercules Inc. Brunswick Plant (Brunswick, GA) 65414
Hercules Specialty Chemicals Co. (Savannah, GA) 67484
Hoechst Celanese (Narrows, VA) 91438
Hoechst Celanese (Portsmouth, VA) 91659
Hoechst Celanese Chamical Group Inc. Clear Lake Plant (Pasadena, TX) 88417
Hoechst-Celanese Chemical Group Inc. (Bay City, TX) 83099; 83100
Hoechst-Celanese Chemical Group Inc. Clear Lake Plant (Pasadena, TX) 88418
Hoechst-Celanese Corp. (Bucks, AL) 55489
Hoechst-Celanese Corp. (Narrows, VA) 91439
Hoechst-Celanese Corp. (Portsmouth, VA) 91660
Hoechst Celanese Corp. Baton Rouge Works (Baton Rouge, LA) 69557
Hoechst-Celanese Corp. Celriver Plant (Rock Hill, SC) 79829
Hoechst Celanese Corp. Corpus Christi Technical Ctr. (Corpus Christi, TX) 83722
Hoechst-Celanese Corp. Pampa Plant (Pampa, TX) 88350
Hoechst Celanese Corp. Sou-Tex Works (Mount Holly, NC) 75692
Hoechst-Celanese Corp. Technical Center (Corpus Christi, TX) 83723
Hoechst Celanese Corp. Virginia Chemicals Co. (Bucks, AL) 55490
Hoechst Celanese - Pampa Plant (Pampa, TX) 88351; 88352
Ivax Industries Inc. Textile Products (Rock Hill, SC) 79830; 79831
Ivax Industry Inc. Textile Products (Rock Hill, SC) 79832
Jetco Chemicals (Corsicana, TX) 83779
Lithium Corp. of America (Bessemer City, NC) 73689
Lithium Corp. of America FMC Lithium Div. (Bessemer City, NC) 73690
Lubrizol Corp. Deer Park Plant (Deer Park, TX) 84554
Lubrizol Petroleum Chemicals, Bayport Plant (Pasadena, TX) 88436
Lubrizol Petroleum Chemicals Co. Bayport Plant (Pasadena, TX) 88437
Lubrizol Petroleum Chemicals Co.-Deer Park Plant (Deer Park, TX) 84555
Lyondell Petrochemical Co. (Channelview, TX) 83550
Lyondell Petrochemical Co. Houston Refinery (Houston, TX) 86504
Mallinckrodt Specialty Chemicals Co. (Paris, KY) 69219
Merck & Co. Inc. Kelco Div. (Okmulgee, OK) 77681; 77682
Mobil Chemical Co. (Beaumont, TX) 83178
Mobil Chemical Co. (Houston, TX) 86584
Mobil Chemical Co. Olefins/ Aromatics Plant (Beaumont, TX) 83179
Mobil Chemical Co. Bcsp (Beaumont, TX) 83180
Mobil Corp. (Fairfax, VA) 90797
Monsanto Co. (Decatur, AL) 55598
Monsanto Co. (Cantonment, FL) 58910
Monsanto Co. (Luling, LA) 70204
Monsanto Co. (Alvin, TX) 82509
Monsanto Co. (Nitro, WV) 92972
Monsanto Co. Chemical Group (Decatur, AL) 55599
Morton International Polmer Systems (Moss Point, MS) 73195
Nalco Chemical Co. (Jonesboro, GA) 66389
Nalco Chemical Co. (Garyville, LA) 69865; 69866
Nalco Chemical Co. (Freeport, TX) 85389
Nalco Chemical Co. (Sugar Land, TX) 89539
Neches River Treatment Corp. Lower Neches Valley Authority (Beaumont, TX) 83189
Noramco Inc. (Athens, GA) 64172
Nutrasweet Co. (Augusta, GA) 65338
Occidental Chemical Corp. (Convent, LA) 69782; 69783
Occidental Chemical Corp. (Alvin, TX) 82510
Occidental Chemical Corp. (Deer Park, TX) 84557
Occidental Chemical Corp. (Belle, WV) 92694; 92695
Occidental Chemical Corp. Corpus Christi Plant (Gregory, TX) 85681
Occidental Chemical Corp. Deer Park (Deer Park, TX) 84558
Occidental Chemical Corp. Vcm Plant (Deer Park, TX) 84559
Olin Corp. (Mc Intosh, AL) 56126
Olin Corp. (Brandenburg, KY) 68169; 68170
Olin Corp. Lake Charles Plant (Lake Charles, LA) 70152; 70153
Oxy Petrochemical Inc. Corpus Christi Plant (Corpus Christi, TX) 83744
Oxy Petrochemicals Chorpus Christi Plant (Corpus Christi, TX) 83745
Oxy Petrochemicals Inc. (Sulphur, LA) 70886
Oxychem Petrochemicals Bayport Plant (Pasadena, TX) 88450
Oxychem Petrochemicals Lake Charles Plant (Sulphur, LA) 70887
Oxychem Petrochemicals Inc. (Alvin, TX) 82512
P D Glycol (Beaumont, TX) 83194
Pd Glycol (Beaumont, TX) 83195
Phillips Petroleum Co. Houston Chemical Complex (Pasadena, TX) 88456
Phillips Research Center (Bartlesville, OK) 76844
Phillips Research Ctr. (Bartlesville, OK) 76845
Phillips 66 Co. (Borger, TX) 83321
Phillips 66 Co. Philtex/Ryton Complex (Borger, TX) 83322
Plastics Inc. Seadrift Plant; Union Carbide Chemicals (Port Lavaca, TX) 88672
Ppg Industries (La Porte, TX) 87563
PPG Industries Inc. (Lake Charles, LA) 70159
PPG Industries Inc. (LaPorte, TX) 87604
PPG Industries Inc. (New Martinsville, WV) 92963
Qo Chemicals Inc. (Memphis, TN) 81676
QO Chemicals Inc. Belle Glade Plant (Belle Glade, FL) 58646
Rhone-Poulenc Ag Co. Institute Wv Plant Operations (Institute, WV) 92904
Rhone Poulenc Basic Chemical (Nashville, TN) 82089
Rhone-Poulenc Basic Chemicals Co. (Baton Rouge, LA) 69650; 69651
Rhone-Poulenc Inc. (Rock Hill, SC) 79839
Rhone Poulenc Inc. (Freeport, TX) 85390
Rhone-Poulenc Inc. Freeport Plant (Freeport, TX) 85391
Rhone-Poulenc Inc. Lyndal Chemicals (Dalton, GA) 65787
Rhone-Poulenc Inc. Surfactants & Specialties (Winder, GA) 68062
Rhone-Poulenc Specialty Chemicals Co. (Jacksonville, FL) 60437
Rhone-Poulenc Surfactants & Specialties LP (Baltimore, MD) 71240
Rockland React-Rite Inc. (Chatom, AL) 55510
Rockland React-Rite Inc. (Cartersville, GA) 65507
Rockland React-Rite Inc. (Rockmart, GA) 67333
Rohm &. Haas Inc. Texas (Deer Park, TX) 84563
Rohm & Haas Bayport Inc. (La Porte, TX) 87569
Rohm & Haas Inc. Bayport (La Porte, TX) 87570
Rohm & Haas Inc. Tennessee (Knoxville, TN) 81244
Rohm & Haas Inc. Texas (Deer Park, TX) 84564
Rohm & Haas of Texas Inc. (Deer Park, TX) 84565
Scm Glidco Organics Corp. (Jacksonville, FL) 60454
Scm Glidco Organics Corp. (Brunswick, GA) 65426; 65427
Seadrift Plant (Port Lavaca, TX) 88670
Sequa Chemicals Inc. (Chester, SC) 78943
Shell Chemical Co. Geismar (Geismar, LA) 69883
Shell Chemical Co. Geismar Plant (Geismar, LA) 69884
Shell Oil Co. Deer Park Manufacturing Complex (Deer Park, TX) 84568; 84569
Shell Oil Co. Norco Manufacturing Complex (Norco, LA) 70593; 70594; 70595; 70596
Sloss Industries Corp. Ariton Facility (Ariton, AL) 55030
Sloss Industries Corp. Birmingham Facility (Birmingham, AL) 55391
Sterling Chemicals Inc. (Texas City, TX) 89737
Texaco Chemical Co. (Austin, TX) 83027
Texaco Chemical Co. (Conroe, TX) 83686
Texaco Chemical Co. (Port Neches, TX) 88676
Texaco Chemical Co. Port Arthur Chemical Plant (Port Arthur, TX) 88647
Texas Eastman Co. (Longview, TX) 87737; 87738
Union Carbide C & P Co. Institute Wv Plant Ops. (Institute, WV) 92906
Union Carbide C&P Co. Institute Wv Plant Operations (Institute, WV) 92907
Union Carbide Chemical & Plastics Co. Technical Center (South Charleston, WV) 93054
Union Carbide Chemicals & Plastics Co. Holz Impoundment (South Charleston, WV) 93055
Union Carbide Chemicals & Plastics Co. Inc. (Sistersville, WV) 93044
Union Carbide Chemicals & Plastics Co. Inc. (South Charleston, WV) 93056
Union Carbide Chemicals Plastics Co. Seadrift Plant (Port Lavaca, TX) 88671
Union Carbide Chemicals & Plastics Co. Texas City Plt. (Texas City, TX) 89741
Union Carbide Chemicals Plastics Inc. Seadrift Plant (Port Lavaca, TX) 88672
Union Carbide Corp. (Haknville, LA) 69928
Union Carbide Corp. (League City, TX) 87634
Union Carbide Corp. (Texas City, TX) 89742
Union Carbide Corp. (South Charleston, WV) 93057
Union Carbide Corp. South Charleston Plant (South Charleston, WV) 93058
Union Carbide Corp. Holz Impoundment (South Charleston, WV) 93059
Union Carbide Corp. Indl. Chemicals (Hahnville, LA) 69924
Union Carbide Corp. Industrial Chemicals (Hahnville, LA) 69925
Union Carbide Corp. South Charleston Plant (South Charleston, WV) 93060
Union Carbide Corp. Tech Nical Center (South Charleston, WV) 93061
Union Carbide Texas City Plant (Texas City, TX) 89745

Union Lake Petroleum Corp. (Carville, LA) 69758
Union Texas Petro Holding Co. (Houston, TX) 87055
Union Texas Prods. Corp. Geismar Ethylene Plant (Geismar, LA) 69885
Union Texas Products Corp. Geismar Ethylene Plant (Geismar, LA) 69886
UOP Inc. (Blanchard, LA) 69700
UOP Inc. (Shreveport, LA) 70801
Virginia Chemicals Co. (Portsmouth, VA) 91672
W. R. Grace & Co. Deer Park Facility (Deer Park, TX) 84574
Westvaco Corp. (Mulberry, FL) 61577
Westvaco Corp. (De Ridder, LA) 69821
Westvaco Corp. Chemicals (De Ridder, LA) 69822
Westvaco Corp. Chemical (Mulberry, FL) 61581
Witco Corp. (Hahnville, LA) 69926
Witco Corp. (Marshall, TX) 87872; 87873
Witco Corp. Argus (Hahnville, LA) 69927
Witco Corp. Argus (Marshall, TX) 87874; 87875
Witco Corp. Argus Chemcial Div. (Marshall, TX) 87876
Witco Corp. Argus Chemical (Taft, LA) 70904
Witco Corp. Harahan (Harahan, LA) 69937
Witco Corp. Humko Chemical (Memphis, TN) 81760; 81761
Witco Corp. Humko Chemical Div. (Memphis, TN) 81762
Witco Corp. Polymer Additives (Taft, LA) 70905
W.R. Grace & Co. -Deer Park (Deer Park, TX) 84576
W.R. Grace & Co. Deer Park Facility (Deer Park, TX) 84577

2873 Nitrogenous Fertilizers

Agrico Chemical Co. (Henderson, KY) 68439
Air Products & Chemicals, Inc. (Milton, FL) 61541
Air Products & Chemicals, Inc. (Pace, FL) 62217; 62218; 62219
Air Products & Chemicals Inc. (New Orleans, LA) 70425
Air Products & Chemicals Inc. (Pasadena, TX) 88381
Air Products Manufacturing Corp. (Pasadena, TX) 88382
Allied-Signal Hopewell Plant (Hopewell, VA) 91152
Allied-Signal Inc. (Hopewell, VA) 91153; 91154; 91155
Arcadian Corp. (Lake Charles, LA) 70127
Arcadian Corp. (Wilmington, NC) 76539
Arcadian Corp. (Memphis, TN) 81461; 81463
Arcadian Corp. Augusta Plant (Augusta, GA) 65312
Arcadian Corp. Savannah Plant (Port Wentworth, GA) 67273; 67274
Arcadian Fertilizer L.P. (Geismar, LA) 69873
Arcadian Fertilizer, LP (Memphis, TN) 81464
Arcadian Fertilizer LP (Millington, TN) 81774
Arcadian Partners Ltd. Partnership (Memphis, TN) 81465
Borden Chemicals & Plastics (Geismar, LA) 69879
Chevron Products Co. Pascagoula Refinery (Pascagoula, MS) 73252; 73252
Chevron USA Inc. Pascagoula Refinery (Pascagoula, MS) 73253
Chevron USA Inc. Pascagoula Refinery (Pascagoula, MS) 73254
Eagle Picher Industries Inc. (Mineola, TX) 88105
Farmland Industries Inc. (Enid, OK) 77051
Farmland Industries Inc. Pollock Nitrogen Plant (Pollock, LA) 70646
Freeport Mcmoran Agrico Chemical Co. Div. (Blytheville, AR) 56804
Freeport-McMoran Resource Partners (New Orleans, LA) 70464
Hoechst-Celanese Corp. (Bucks, AL) 55489
Imc Fertilizer Inc. (Sterlington, LA) 70880
Monsanto Co. (Luling, LA) 70204
Ocapi Houston Ammonia Terminal (Pasadena, TX) 88445; 88446
Occidental Chemical Corp. (Taft, LA) 70898
Occidental Chemical Corp. Houston Ammonia Terminal (Pasadena, TX) 88449
Olin Corp. (Westlake, LA) 70966
Olin Corp. (Beaumont, TX) 83192
Olin Corp. Beaumont Plant (Beaumont, TX) 83193
Olin Corp. Lake Charles Plant (Lake Charles, LA) 70153
US Agri-Chemicals Bartow Plant (Bartow, FL) 58632

2874 Phosphatic Fertilizers

Agrico Chemical Co. S. Pierce (Mulberry, FL) 61571; 61572
Agrico Chemical Co. Taft Plant (Hahnville, LA) 69922
Agrico Chemical Co. Uncle Sam Plant (Uncle Sam, LA) 70916
Arcadian Corp. (Memphis, TN) 81461
Arcadian Fertilizer L.P. (Geismar, LA) 69873
Arcadian Fertilizer, LP (Memphis, TN) 81464
Arcadian Partners Ltd. Partnership (Memphis, TN) 81465
Central Phosphates Inc. (Plant City, FL) 62541; 62542
Cf Chemicals Inc. (Bartow, FL) 58625
Freeport Mcmoran Agrico Chemical Co. Div. (Uncle Sam, LA) 70917
Freeport-McMoran Inc. (New Orleans, LA) 70462
Freeport-McMoran Resource Partners (New Orleans, LA) 70464
Imc Fertilizer Inc. (Florence, AL) 55737
Imc Fertilizer Inc. (Americus, GA) 64140
Imc Fertilizer Inc. (Hartsville, SC) 79498
IMC Fertilizer Inc. New Wales Operation (Mulberry, FL) 61574
Mobil Mining & Minerals Compan (Ashland, VA) 90405
Mobil Mining & Minerals Co. (Pasadena, TX) 88444
Monsanto Co. (Augusta, GA) 65336
Occidental Chemical Corp. (White Springs, FL) 63912
Occidental Chemical Corp. (Dallas, TX) 84279
Occidental Chemical Corp. Agricultural Products (White Springs, FL) 63913
Seminole Fertilizer Corp. (Bartow, FL) 58630
US Agri-Chemicals Bartow Facility (Bartow, FL) 58631
US Agri-Chemicals Bartow Plant (Bartow, FL) 58632
US Agri-Chemicals Fort Meade Chemical Plant (Fort Meade, FL) 59653
US Agri-Chemicals Ft. Meade Facility (Fort Meade, FL) 59654
W.R. Grace & Co. Bartow Chemical Complex (Bartow, FL) 58635

2875 Fertilizers—Mixing Only

Air Products & Chemicals, Inc. (Milton, FL) 61540
Arcadian Corp. (Savannah, GA) 67446
Arcadian Corp. (Geismar, LA) 69872
Arcadian Fertilizer LP (Augusta, GA) 65313
Imc Fertilizer Inc. (Indiantown, FL) 60142
Imc Fertilizer Inc. (Mulberry, FL) 61573
Imc Fertilizer Inc. (Winston-Salem, NC) 76733
Mapco Inc. (Tulsa, OK) 78009
Ochoa Fertilizer Co., Inc. (Guanica, PR) 78417
Southern States Co-Op. Inc. Inc. (Baltimore, MD) 71311
Southern States Co-Op. Inc. Inc. (Statesville, NC) 76338
Southern States Co-Op. Inc. Inc. (Chesapeake, VA) 90605

2879 Agricultural Chemicals Nec

Arcadian Corp. (Wilmington, NC) 76540
Arcadian Corp. (Wilson, NC) 76618
Arco Chemical Co. Institute West Virginia Plant (Institute, WV) 92901
Asgrow Florida Co. (Belle Glade, FL) 58641
Asgrow Florida Co. (Plant City, FL) 62535
Baker Performance Chemicals (Houma, LA) 69950
BASF Corp. (Geismar, LA) 69876
Boyle-Midway Household Products Inc. (Atlanta, GA) 64331
Conagra Pet Products Co. (Richmond, VA) 91788
Cynamid Agricultural De Puerto Rico Inc. (Manati, PR) 78497
FMC Corp. (Newark, DE) 57904
FMC Corp. (Jacksonville, FL) 60306
FMC Corp. (Baltimore, MD) 71152
Fmc Corp. Agricultural Chemical Group (Baltimore, MD) 71153
FMC Corp., Baltimore Plant (Baltimore, MD) 71154
FMC Corp., Institute Plant (Institute, WV) 92902
Fmc Corp. Jacksonville Plant (Jacksonville, FL) 60307
Great Lakes Chemical Corp. (Newport, TN) 82166; 82167
Mobil Mining & Minerals Compan (Ashland, VA) 90405
Monsanto Co. (Luling, LA) 70204
Monsanto Co. (Fayetteville, NC) 74567
Monsanto Co. (Alvin, TX) 82509
Monsanto Co./Agricultural Grp (Fayetteville, NC) 74568
Phillips Research Center (Bartlesville, OK) 76844
Phillips Research Ctr. (Bartlesville, OK) 76845
Platte Chemical Co. (Greenville, MS) 72816; 72817
Rhone-Poulenc Ag Co. (Woodbine, GA) 68065
Rhone-Poulenc Ag Co. (Mount Pleasant, TN) 81824; 81825
Rhone-Poulenc Ag Co. Institute Wv Plant (Institute, WV) 92903
Rhone-Poulenc Ag Co. Institute Wv Plant Operations (Institute, WV) 92904
Rhone-Poulenc Ag Co. Woodbine Plant (Woodbine, GA) 68066
Rhone Poulenc Inc. (Mt. Pleasant, TN) 81834
Rhone-Poulenc Inc. Ag Co. (Woodbine, GA) 68067
Rhone-Poulenc Inc. Ag Co. (Mount Pleasant, TN) 81827
Rohm & Haas Bayport Inc. (La Porte, TX) 87569
Rohm & Haas Inc. Bayport (La Porte, TX) 87570
Rohne Poulenc Ag Co. (Research Triangle Pk., NC) 76024
Union Carbide C&P Co. Institute Wv Plant Operations (Institute, WV) 92907
Union Carbide Corp. (Institute, WV) 92908
Van Waters & Rogers Inc. (New Orleans, LA) 70584
Vulcan Materials Co. (Fairfield, AL) 55719
Witco Corp. (Houston, TX) 87200

2890 Miscellaneous Chemical Products

Dow Corning Corp. (Greensboro, NC) 74813
Dow Corning Corp. Atlanta Plant (Norcross, GA) 67111
Dow Corning Corp. Norcross Plant (Norcross, GA) 67112

2891 Adhesives & Sealants

Air Products & Chemicals, Inc. (Elkton, MD) 71670
Air Products & Chemicals, Inc. (Langley, SC) 79585
American Cyanamid Co. (Havre De Grace, MD) 71914; 71915
American Cyanamid Co. (Charlotte, NC) 73834
Avery Dennison (Crossville, TN) 80690
Borden Inc. (Shively, KY) 69286
Borden Inc. Chemical (Louisville, KY) 68708
Borden Inc. Chemical (High Point, NC) 75112
Borden Inc. Package & Industrial Products (High Point, NC) 75115
Borden Inc. Packaging & Industrial Products (High Point, NC) 75116
Borden Packaging & Industrial Products (Fayetteville, NC) 74538
Borden Packaging & Industrial Products (Diboll, TX) 84654
Cyprus Foote Mineral Co. (Duffield, VA) 90730
DAP Inc. (Conyers, GA) 65678
Dap Inc. (Baltimore, MD) 71109
Dennison Stationery Prods. Co. Inc. (Crossville, TN) 80691
Dennison Stationery Products Co., Inc. (Crossville, TN) 80692
Dow Corning Corp. (Elizabethtown, KY) 68275
Dow Corning Corp. Elizabethtown Plant (Elizabethtown, KY) 68276
E. R. Carpenter Co. Inc. (Russellville, KY) 69259
Foster Prods. Corp. (Houston, TX) 86207
Foster Products Corp. (Houston, TX) 86208
H. B. Fuller Co. (Forest Park, GA) 66234
H. B. Fuller Co. (Paducah, KY) 69203
H. B. Fuller Co. (Greensboro, NC) 74849
H. B. Fuller Co. (Bayamon, PR) 78336; 78337; 78338
H. B. Fuller Co. (Memphis, TN) 81625
H.B. Fuller Co. (Forest Park, GA) 66235
H.B. Fuller Co. (Memphis, TN) 81626
International Paper Co. Nevamar Div. (Odenton, MD) 72167
Morton International Specialty (Greenville, SC) 79398
PCI Industries Inc. (Riviera Beach, FL) 62740
Pci Industries Inc. (West Palm Beach, FL) 63890
Protein Tech. International International (Louisville, KY) 68982
Protein Technologies Intern. (Louisville, KY) 68983
Ralph Wilson Plastics Denham Springs (Denham Springs, LA) 69832
Ralph Wilson Plastics Co. Denham Springs Adhesive (Denham Springs, LA) 69833
Sherwin-Williams Co. (Baltimore, MD) 71279
Tremco Inc. (Barbourville, KY) 68110
W. R. Grace & Co. Container Products Div. (Atlanta, GA) 65248
W. R. Grace & Co. Dewey & Almy Chemical Div. (Atlanta, GA) 65249
W. R. Grace & Co. Inc. Connecticut (Boca Raton, FL) 58750
W. W. Henry Co. (Arlington, TX) 82779
W.R. Grace & Co. Dewey & Almy Chemical Div. (Atlanta, GA) 65292
Ww Henry Co. (Dallas, GA) 65768

2892 Explosives

Chemtronics Inc. (Swannanoa, NC) 76349
Flight Systems Inc. (Burns Flat, OK) 76903
Hercules Inc. US Naval Weapons Indl. Res. Plant (Mc Gregor, TX) 87905
Hercules Inc. US Naval Weapons Plant (Mc Gregor, TX) 87906
Jet Research Center Inc. Defense & Aerospace Div. (Swannanoa, NC) 76350
Olin Corp. (St. Marks, FL) 63073
Radford Army Ammunition Plant (Radford, VA) 91699; 91700

2893 Printing Ink

BASF Corp. (Charlotte, NC) 73849; 73851
BASF Corp. (Richmond, VA) 91741
BASF Corp. Coatings & Inks (Louisville, KY) 68695; 68696
BASF Corp. Coatings & Inks (Charlotte, NC) 73853; 73854
BASF Corp. Coatings & Inks (Morganton, NC) 75631
BASF Graphic Systems (Louisville, KY) 68698
Hoechst-Celanese Charlotte Specialty Chemicals Group (Charlotte, NC) 74042
Hoechst Celanese Charlotte Spg (Charlotte, NC) 74043
J.M. Huber Corp. (Macon, GA) 66694
Johnson & Bloy America Inc. (Baltimore, MD) 71170
Johnson & Bloy Inc. (Baltimore, MD) 71171
Mead Ink Products (Atlanta, GA) 64722
Plus Mark Inc. (Afton, TN) 80145
Plus Mark, Inc. (Greenville, TN) 80897
Ppg Printing Inks (Spartanburg, SC) 79928
Vera Imported Parts Corp. (Jacksonville, FL) 60490

2895 Carbon Black

Abbott Laboratories Diagnostics Division (Irving, TX) 87316
Abbott Manufacturing Inc. (Irving, TX) 87317
Ashland Chemical Co. (Louisa/ Ivanhoe, LA) 70201
Ashland Chemical Co. Carbon Black Div. (Aransas Pass, TX) 82623
Chevron Chemical Co. (Baytown, TX) 83109
Columbian Chemicals Co. (El Dorado, AR) 56927; 56928
Columbian Chemicals Co. (Centerville, LA) 69759
Columbian Chemicals Co. (Moundsville, WV) 92952
Columbian Chemicals Co. Inc. (Tulsa, OK) 77920
Fina Inc. (Dallas, TX) 84065
J. M. Huber Corp. Baytown Carbon Plant (Baytown, TX) 83126
J. M. Huber Corp. Borger Carbon Plant (Borger, TX) 83317
J. M. Huber Corp. Echo Carbon Plant (Orange, TX) 88317
J.M. Huber Baytown Carbon Plant (Baytown, TX) 83127
J.M. Huber Borger Carbon Plant (Borger, TX) 83318
J.M. Huber Carbon Plant (Baytown, TX) 83128
J.M. Huber Corp. Echo Carbon Plant (Orange, TX) 88319
J.M. Huber Echo Carbon Plant (Orange, TX) 88320
Witco Corp. (Phenix City, AL) 56476
Witco Corp. Concarb (Phenix City, AL) 56477; 56478
Witco Corp. Concarb (Ponca City, OK) 77717; 77718; 77719
Witco Corp. Concarb (Sunray, TX) 89573
Witco Corp. Concarb Div. (Sunray, TX) 89574

2899 Chemical Preparations Nec

Air Products & Chemicals (New Orleans, LA) 70424
Air Products & Chemicals, Inc. (Milton, FL) 61540; 61542
Air Products & Chemicals, Inc. (Atlanta, GA) 64209
Air Products & Chemicals, Inc. (St. Gabriel, LA) 70863
Air Products & Chemicals, Inc. (Columbia, SC) 78965
Allied Signal (Baton Rouge, LA) 69457
Allied-Signal Corp. (Birmingham, AL) 55116
Allied-Signal, Inc. (Claymont, DE) 57759
Allied-Signal Inc. (Baton Rouge, LA) 69458
Allied-Signal Inc. (Carville, LA) 69756
American Cyanamid Co. (Mobile, AL) 56133; 56134
American Cyanamid Co. (Willow Island, WV) 93131
Aqualon Co. (Kenedy, TX) 87465
Arcadian Corp. (Lake Charles, LA) 70128
Arco Chemical Co. (Pasadena, TX) 88385
Arizona Chemical Co. (Panama City, FL) 62318
Arkansas Eastman Co. (Batesville, AR) 56741
Ashland Chemical Inc. (Plaquemine, LA) 70636
Ashland Chemical Inc. Drew Div. (Houston, TX) 85820
Baker Hughes Inc. Baker Hughes Drilling Technologies Milpark Drilli Fluids (Houston, TX) 85838
Baker Performance Chemicals (Sand Springs, OK) 77778
Baker Performance Chemicals (Houston, TX) 85856
Baker Performance Chemicals Inc. (Dayton, TX) 84520
BASF Corp. (Central, SC) 78781
BASF Corp. (Spartanburg, SC) 79876

BASF Corp. (Huntington, WV) 92868
BASF Corp. Chemical Division (Geidmar, LA) 69867
BASF Corp. Chemicals (Spartanburg, SC) 79877
Betz Laboratories (Macon, GA) 66670
Betz Laboratories Inc. (Macon, GA) 66671; 66672
Betz Laboratories Inc. (Reserve, LA) 70660
Betz Laboratories Inc. (Beaumont, TX) 83143; 83144
Betz Laboratories Inc. (Garland, TX) 85478; 85479
Betz Laboratories Inc. (Houston, TX) 85877
Betz Laboratories Inc. (West Orange, TX) 90048; 90049
Betz Labs (Macon, GA) 66673
Betz PaperChem, Inc. (Jacksonville, FL) 60231
Betz Process Chemicals (Sulphur, LA) 70881
Betz Process Chemicals (Longview, TX) 87704
Betz Process Chemicals Inc. (Beaumont, TX) 83145; 83147
Betz Process Chemicals Inc. (The Woodlands, TX) 89750
Biolab Inc. (Conyers, GA) 65676
Borden Chemicals & Plastics (Geismar, LA) 69879
Borden Inc. (Shively, KY) 69286
Burlington Industries Inc. (Greensbor, NC) 74758
Calgon Corp. (Pasadena, TX) 88392
Cannon Chemical Co. (Concord, NC) 74308
Coastal Unilube Inc. (West Memphis, AR) 57720
Colgate-Palmolive Co. Institutional Products Div. (Texarkana, TX) 89673
Dexter Corp. Mogul Div. (Charlotte, NC) 73927
Dexter Corp. Mogul Div. (Arlington, TX) 82645
Dexter Water Management Sys. Mogul Corp. (Charlotte, NC) 73929
Dexter Water Management Systems (Arlington, TX) 82646
Dowell Schlumberger Inc. (Tulsa, OK) 77933
Drew Chemical Corp. (Houston, TX) 86050
Drilling Specialties Co. Alamo Plant (Conroe, TX) 83657
Engelhard Corp. (Jackson, MS) 72980
Ethyl Corp. (Baton Rouge, LA) 69512
Ethyl Corp. (Richmond, VA) 91862
Ethyl Petroleum Additives Inc. (Richmond, VA) 91864
Exxon Chemical Co. (Baton Rouge, LA) 69519; 69520
Exxon Chemical Co. (New Orleans, LA) 70451
Exxon Chemical Co. (Big Spring, TX) 83285
Exxon Chemical Co. (Houston, TX) 86119
Ferro Corp. Coating Div. (Nashville, TN) 81962
FMC Corp. (Gastonia, NC) 74680
FMC Corp. (Pasadena, TX) 88408
Fmc Corp. Lakeland Facility (Lakeland, FL) 60729
Fmc Corp. Lakeland Plant (Lakeland, FL) 60730
Georgia Gulf Corp. (Tiptonville, TN) 82370
Gillette Co. Inc. (Greenville, TX) 85670
Gli Inc. (Newport, TN) 82164; 82165
Harris Technical Service Co. (Norfolk, VA) 91542
Hercules Inc. (Hattiesburg, MS) 72890
Hercules Inc. (Franklin, VA) 90894; 90895
Hercules Inc. Specialty Chemicals Div. (Savannah, GA) 67483
Hi-Tek Polymers Inc. Vernon Plant (Vernon, TX) 89865
Hoechst Celanese Corp. Baton Rouge Works (Baton Rouge, LA) 69557
M-I Drilling Fluids, Wharton Chemical Plant (Hungerford, TX) 87258; 87259
Malakoff Ind. Inc. (Malakoff, TX) 87831
Martin Marietta Corp. (North Garden, VA) 91598
McCormick & Co. Inc. Tac Cleaning Products Group (Dallas, TX) 84231
Merck Sharp & Dohme Quimica De P.R. (Barceloneta, PR) 78328
Merck Sharp & Dohme Quimica De Puerto Rico (Barceloneta, PR) 78329
Millpark Drilling Fluids Inc. (Houma, LA) 69961
Mobil Chemical Co. (Temple, TX) 89625
Monsanto Co. (Anniston, AL) 55006
Monsanto Co. (Atlanta, GA) 64733
Monsanto Co. (Luling, LA) 70202
Monsanto Co. (Columbia, TN) 80632
Morton International Inc. (Weeks Island, LA) 70940
Morton International Inc. Morton Salt Div. (New Iberia, LA) 70413
Morton Salt (Conroe, TX) 83670
Nalco Chemical Co. (Mobile, AL) 56211
Nalco Chemical Co. (Jonesboro, GA) 66389
Nalco Chemical Co. (Baton Rouge, LA) 69590
Nalco Chemical Co. (Garyville, LA) 69865; 69866
Nalco Chemical Co. (Freeport, TX) 85389
Nalco Chemical Co. (Sugar Land, TX) 89539
Olin Chemicals Group (Charleston, TN) 80289
Olin Chemicals Group (Beaumont, TX) 83191
Olin Corp. (Mc Intosh, AL) 56125
Phillips Research Center (Bartlesville, OK) 76844
Rhone Poulenc Basic Chemical (Baton Rouge, LA) 69649
Rhone Poulenc Basic Chemical (Geismar, LA) 69881
Rhone Poulenc Basic Chemical (Mt. Pleasant, TN) 81833
Rhone Poulenc Basic Chemical (Nashville, TN) 82089
Rhone Poulenc Inc. (Jeffersontown, KY) 68499
Rhone Poulenc Inc. (Mt. Pleasant, TN) 81834
Rhone-Poulenc Inc. Rhone-Poulenc Specialty Chemicals Div. (Vernon, TX) 89870
Rhone-Poulenc Inc. Walsh Div. (Gastonia, NC) 74685
Rhone-Poulenc Specialty Chemicals Co. (Jacksonville, FL) 60437
Rhone-Poulenc Specialty Chemicals Co. (Marietta, GA) 66906
Rhone Poulenc Surfactants (Spartanburg, SC) 79938
Rohm & Haas Co. Latin America (Corel Gables, FL) 59118
Rohm & Haas Kentucky Inc. (Louisville, KY) 68999
Safety Kleen Corp. (Kenner, LA) 70012
Safety Kleen Corp. (El Paso, TX) 84925
Safety-Kleen Corp. (Wheeling, WV) 93120
Sedgefield Specialties (Greensboro, NC) 74906
Sequa Chemicals (Chester, SC) 78942
Sequa Chemicals Inc. (Chester, SC) 78943
Shell Oil Co. Deer Park Manufacturing Complex (Deer Park, TX) 84569
A.O. Smith Corp. P.C. Div. (Florence, KY) 68335
A.O. Smith Corp. Protective Coatings Div. (Florence, KY) 68336
Texaco Inc. Research & Development (Port Arthur, TX) 88650
Texaco Port Arthur Research Laboratories (Port Arthur, TX) 88652
Thompson & Formby Inc. (Memphis, TN) 81709
Thompson & Formby's Inc. (Olive Branch, MS) 73231
3M Co. (Decatur, AL) 55607
3M Co. Telecom Markets Div. (Austin, TX) 83046
Union Camp Corp. (Jacksonville, FL) 60483
Union Carbide Chemicals & Plastics Co. Marine Terminal (Texas City, TX) 89740
Uniroyal Chemical (Gastonia, NC) 74690
Unison Transformer Services Inc. (Henderson, KY) 68458
UOP Inc. (Shreveport, LA) 70801
Van Waters & Rogers Inc. (Birmingham, AL) 55445
Van Waters & Rogers Inc. (Richmond, VA) 92073
W. R. Grace & Co. Connecticut Construction Products Div. (Pompano Beach, FL) 62638
W. R. Grace & Co. Connecticut Construction Products Div. (Zellwood, FL) 64007
W. R. Grace & Co. Connecticut Construction Products Div. (Lithonia, GA) 66612
W. R. Grace & Co. Connecticut Construction Products Div. (Houston, TX) 87081
Westvaco Corp. Chemical Div. (North Charleston, SC) 79754
Witco Corp. (Hahnville, LA) 69926
Witco Corp. (Harvey, LA) 69943
Witco Corp. (Houston, TX) 87200
Witco Corp. (LaPorte, TX) 87605
Witco Corp. Humko Chemical (Memphis, TN) 81760; 81761
Witco Corp. Humko Chemical Div. (Memphis, TN) 81763
W.R. Grace & Co. Construction Production Div. (Houston, TX) 87203
W.R. Grace & Co. Construction Products Div. (Pompano Beach, FL) 62646
W.R. Grace & Co.-Conn. Cpd (Pompano Beach, FL) 62647
X-Chem Inc. (Harahan, LA) 69938
ZEP Manufacturing Co. (Hialeah, FL) 60021
ZEP Manufacturing Co. (Atlanta, GA) 65301
ZEP Manufacturing Co. (Baton Rouge, LA) 69689
Zep Manufacturing Co. (Oklahoma City, OK) 77675

2900 Petroleum & Coal Products

H.B. Fuller Co. Foster Div. (Houston, TX) 86213
L L & E Petroleum Mtg. Inc. (Saraland, AL) 56516
Murphy Oil USA Inc. Meraux Refinery (Meraux, LA) 70243
Temple-Inland Forest Products Corp. Fiber Products (Diboll, TX) 84660

2911 Petroleum Refining

Amerada Hess Corp. (Jacksonville, FL) 60163
Amerada Hess Corp. (Collins, MS) 72693
Amerada Hess Corp. (Purvis, MS) 73308; 73309
Amerada Hess Corp. (Wilmington, NC) 76538
Amerada Hess Corp. (Brownfield, TX) 83350
Amerada Hess Corp. Purvis Refinery (Purvis, MS) 73310
Arco Oil & Gas Co. (Lindsay, OK) 77178
Arco Oil & Gas Co. (Eldorado, TX) 84983
Arco Oil & Gas Co. (Longview, TX) 87702
Arco Oil & Gas Co. (Silsbee, TX) 89431
Arco Pipe Line Co. (Copan, OK) 76971; 76972
Arco Pipe Line Co. (Shawnee, OK) 77813
Ashland Oil Inc. (Ashland, KY) 68090
Ashland Petroleum Co. (Russell, KY) 69254
Ashland Petroleum Co. Catlettsburg Refinery (Ashland, KY) 68092
Ashland Petroleum Co. Catlettsburg Refinery (Catlettsburg, KY) 68195
Atlas Processing Co. (Shreveport, LA) 70690
Belcher Refining Co. (Mobile, AL) 56142
Caltex Petroleum Corp. (Irving, TX) 87327
Champlin Refining Co. (Corpus Christi, TX) 83710
Chevron Products Co. Pascagoula Refinery (Pascagoula, MS) 73252; 73252
Chevron USA Inc. El Paso Refinery (El Paso, TX) 84781
Chevron USA Inc. Pascagoula Refinery (Pascagoula, MS) 73253
Chevron USA Inc. Port Arthur Refinery (Port Arthur, TX) 88630
Chevron USA Inc. Pascagoula Refinery (Pascagoula, MS) 73254
Chevron USA Products Co. Port Arthur Refinery (Port Arthur, TX) 88631
Citgo Petroleum Corp. (Lake Charles, LA) 70135
Citgo Petroleum Corp. (Sulphur, LA) 70882
Citgo Petroleum Corp. (Tulsa, OK) 77907
Citgo Refining & Chemicals Inc. (Tulsa, OK) 77917
Coastal Mobile Refining Co. (Chickasaw, AL) 55511
Coastal Refining & Marketing Inc. (Corpus Christi, TX) 83711
Conoco In. (Ponca City, OK) 77703
Conoco Inc. (Westlake, LA) 70963
Crown Central Petroleum Corp. (Pasadena, TX) 88399
Crown Central Petroleum Corp. Houston Refinery (Pasadena, TX) 88400
Diamond Shamrock Inc. Mckee Plants (Sunray, TX) 89569
Diamond Shamrock Refining & Marketing Co. (Sunray, TX) 89570
Diamond Shamrock Refining & Marketing Co. (Three Rivers, TX) 89760
Diamond Shamrock Refining & Marketing Co. Mckee Plants (Sunray, TX) 89571
Diamond Shamrock Refining & Marketing Co. Three Rivers (Three Rivers, TX) 89761
El Paso Natural Gas Inc. (El Paso, TX) 84793
El Paso Refining Inc. (El Paso, TX) 84794
Enron Corp. (Geismar, LA) 69880
Enron Corp. (La Porte, TX) 87559
Enron Liquids Pipeline Group (Houston, TX) 86076
Ethyl Corp. (Richmond, VA) 91862
Exxon Chemical Co. (Baton Rouge, LA) 69523
Exxon Chemical Co. (Baytown, TX) 83113
Exxon Chemical Co. (Houston, TX) 86120
Exxon Co. (Chesapeake, VA) 90571
Exxon Co. (Richmond, VA) 91866
Exxon Co. USA (Atmore, AL) 55050
Exxon Co. USA (Mobile, AL) 56160
Exxon Co. USA (Jay, FL) 60523
Exxon Co. USA (Pensacola, FL) 62422
Exxon Co. USA (Baton Rouge, LA) 69526
Exxon Co. USA (Charlotte, NC) 73946
Exxon Co. USA (Durham, NC) 74391
Exxon Co. USA (Greensboro, NC) 74816
Exxon Co. USA (Baytown, TX) 83120
Exxon Co., USA (Grangerland, TX) 85653
Exxon Co. USA (Hawkins, TX) 85721
Exxon Co. USA (Houston, TX) 86163
Exxon Co. USA (New London, TX) 88224
Exxon Co., USA (Overton, TX) 88334
Exxon Co. USA (Refugio, TX) 88715
Exxon Co. USA Production (Refugia, TX) 88713
Exxon Corp. (Baytown, TX) 83122
Exxon Pipeline Co. (Houston, TX) 86177
Fina Inc. (Dallas, TX) 84064; 84065
Fina Oil & Chemical Co. (Big Springs, TX) 83299
Fina Oil & Chemical Co. (Dallas, TX) 84066
Great Lakes Research Corp. (Elizabethton, TN) 80768
Hess Oil Virgin Islands Corp. (Hovic) (Kingshill, VI) 90148
Hess Oil Virgin Islands Corp. (Hovic) (St. Croix, VI) 90149
Hill Petroleum Co. Krotz Springs Refinery (Krotz Springs, LA) 70028
Hill Petroleum Co. St. Rose Refinery (St. Rose, LA) 70874
Kerr-Mcgee Refining Corp. (Cotton Valley, LA) 69785; 69786
Kerr-Mcgee Refining Corp. (Wynnewood, OK) 78272; 78273
Kerr-Mcgee Refining Corp. Corp. (Cotton Valley, LA) 69787
La Gloria Oil & Gas Co. (Tyler, TX) 89810
La Gloria Oil & Gas Co. Inc. (Bellaire, TX) 83265
Ll & E Petroleum Mtg. Inc. (Saraland, AL) 56517
Ll&E Mobile River Terminal (Mobile, AL) 56202
Ll&E Petroleum Marketing Inc. Mobile Refinery (Saraland, AL) 56518
Lyondell Petrochemical Co. (Houston, TX) 86502; 86503
Lyondell Petrochemical Co. Houston Refinery (Houston, TX) 86504
Mapco Inc. (Tulsa, OK) 78009
Mapco Petroleum Tennessee Refinary (Memphis, TN) 81654
Mapco Petroleum Inc. (Tulsa, OK) 78011
Mapco Petroleum Inc. (Memphis, TN) 81655
Marathon Oil (Louisville, KY) 68875
Marathon Oil Co. (Louisville, KY) 68878
Marathon Oil Co. (Garyville, LA) 69862
Marathon Oil Co. (Texas City, TX) 89725; 89726
Marathon Oil Co. Louisiana Refining Div. (Garyville, LA) 69863
Marathon Oil Co. Louisiana Refinery (Garyville, LA) 69864
Marathon Petroleum Co. (Birmingham, AL) 55312
Marathon Petroleum Co. (Charleston, SC) 78843
Marathon Petroleum Co. (Texas City, TX) 89727
Meridian Oil Inc. (Vanderbilt, TX) 89862
Mobil Chemical Petroleum Div. (Beaumont, TX) 83177
Mobil Corp. (Fairfax, VA) 90797
Mobil Exploration & Product (Midland, TX) 88050
Mobil Exploration Producting U (Midkiff, TX) 88018
Mobil Oil (Metairie, LA) 70292
Mobil Oil Beaumont Refinery (Beaumont, TX) 83181
Mobil Oil Chalmette Refinery (Chalmette, LA) 69765
Mobil Oil Co. (Snyder, TX) 89448
Mobil Oil Co. Terminal (Port Neches, TX) 88675
Mobil Oil Corp. (Lake Worth, FL) 60684
Mobil Oil Corp. (Thomas, OK) 77868
Mobil Oil Corp. (Beaumont, TX) 83182; 83183
Mobil Oil Corp. (Bedford, TX) 83246
Mobil Oil Corp. (Dallas, TX) 84247; 84248
Mobil Oil Corp. Chalmette Refinery (Chalmette, LA) 69766
Mobil Oil Corp. S a Terminal (San Antonio, TX) 89113
Mobil Oil Refining Div (Beaumont, TX) 83185
Mobil Producing TX & New (Vanderbilt, TX) 89864
Mobile River Terminal (Mobile, AL) 56209
Murphy Oil USA Inc. Meraux Louisiana Refinery (Meraux, LA) 70241
Murphy Oil USA Inc. Meraux Refinery (Meraux, LA) 70242
National Coop Refinery Association (Oklahoma City, OK) 77450
Navajo Refining Co. (El Paso, TX) 84856; 84857
Neches River Treatment Corp. Lower Neches Valley Authority (Beaumont, TX) 83189
North End Houston Avenue (Port Arthur, TX) 88640
Pennzoil Co. (Jacksonville, FL) 60387
Pennzoil Co. (Carthage, TX) 83520
Pennzoil Co. (Falling Rock, WV) 92850
Pennzoil Products (Gainesville, FL) 59896
Phibro Energy USA Inc. (Houston, TX) 86682
Phibro Energy USA Inc. (Texas City, TX) 89729
Phibro Refinery Krotz Springs Refinery (Krotz Springs, LA) 70029
Phibro Refining (Krotz Springs, LA) 70030
Phibro Refining St. Rose Refinery (St. Rose, LA) 70875
Phibro Refining Inc. (Houston, TX) 86683
Phibro Refining Inc. (Texas City, TX) 89730
Phibro Refining Inc. St. Rose Refinery (St. Rose, LA) 70877

Philips P. R. Core Inc. Durand/ Learned Plant (Guayama, PR) 78425
Philips P.R. Core Inc. Durand/ Learned Plant (Guayama, PR) 78426
Phillips P. R. Core Inc. Phillips Paraxylene Inc. (Guayama, PR) 78427
Phillips P.R. Core Inc. Phillips Paraxylene Inc. (Guayama, PR) 78428
Phillips P.R. Core/P.P. Inc. Duran/ Learned Plant (Guayama, PR) 78429
Phillips 66 Jones Creek Terminal (Jones Creek, TX) 87445
Phillips 66 Co. (Borger, TX) 83321
Phillips 66 Co. (Sweeny, TX) 89577
Phillips 66 Co. Clemens Terminal (Brazoria, TX) 83333
Phillips 66 Co. Freeport Terminal (Sweeny, TX) 89579
Phillips 66 Co. Jones Creek Terminal (Jones Creek, TX) 87446
Phillips 66 Co. San Bernard Terminal (Sweeny, TX) 89580
Pyroil Performance Products (Hernando, MS) 72903
Quaker State Corp. Congo Plant (Congo, WV) 92823
Quaker State Corp. Congo Plant (Newell, WV) 92964; 92965
Quaker State Oil Refining Co. (St. Marys, WV) 93072
Shell Oil Co. (Birmingham, AL) 55388
Shell Oil Co. (Guntersville, AL) 55833
Shell Oil Co. (Tampa, FL) 63590
Shell Oil Co. (Gibson, LA) 69887; 69888
Shell Oil Co. (Jefferson, LA) 69975
Shell Oil Co. (Tulsa, OK) 78112
Shell Oil Co. (Deer Park, TX) 84567
Shell Oil Co. (Douglassville, TX) 84681
Shell Oil Co. (Odessa, TX) 88272; 88273
Shell Oil Co. Deer Park Manufacturing Complex (Deer Park, TX) 84568; 84569
Shell Oil Co. Norco Manufacturing Complex (Norco, LA) 70593; 70595; 70596
Shell Oil Co. Odessa Refinery (Odessa, TX) 88275; 88276
Shell Oil Co. Library (Deer Park, TX) 84570
Southern Cotton Oil Co. Inc. (Richmond, TX) 88798
Southland Oil Co. (Jackson, MS) 73065
Southland Oil Co. (Sandersville, MS) 73336
Southland Oil Co. Lumberton (Lumberton, MS) 73132; 73132
Southland Oil Co. Sandersville (Sandersville, MS) 73337
Southwestern Refining Co. Inc. (Corpus Christi, TX) 83752
Southwestern Refining Co. Inc. Inc. (Corpus Christi, TX) 83753
Star Enterprise Delaware City Refinery (Delaware City, DE) 57773
Stratton Field Office (Bishop, TX) 83305
Sun Refining & Marketing (Tulsa, OK) 78117
Sun Refining & Marketing Co. (Tulsa, OK) 78118; 78119
Sun Refining & Marketing Co. (Nederland, TX) 88193
Tenneco Oil Co. (Chalmette, LA) 69770
Tesoro Petroleum Distribution (New Orleans, LA) 70566
Texaco (Montgomery, AL) 56384
Texaco (Midland, TX) 88082
Texaco Delaware City Plant (Delaware City, DE) 57774
Texaco Fuel Man (Shreveport, LA) 70791
Texaco Inc. (Amarillo, TX) 82583
Texaco Inc. (Port Neches, TX) 88677
Texaco Inc. Research & Development (Port Arthur, TX) 88650
Texaco Port Arthur Research Laboratories (Port Arthur, TX) 88652
Texaco Ref. & Mktg. Inc. (Union, LA) 70918
Texaco Ref. & Mktg. Inc. Port Arthur Asphalt (Port Neches, TX) 88678
Texaco Ref. & Mktg. Inc. Port Arthur Plant (Port Arthur, TX) 88653
Texaco Refining & Marketing (Birmingham, AL) 55421
Texaco Refining & Marketing Inc. (Convent, LA) 69784
Texaco Refining & Marketing Inc. Paac (Port Neches, TX) 88679
Texaco Refining & Marketing Inc. Pap (Port Arthur, TX) 88655
Texaco U S a (Clarksburg, WV) 92820
Texas City Refining Inc. (Texas City, TX) 89739
Thiokol Corp. (Newell, WV) 92967
Total Petroleum Inc. (Ardmore, OK) 76823; 76824; 76825
Total Petroleum Inc. (Euless, TX) 85021; 85022
Union Oil of California Dba Unocal (Nederland, TX) 88195
Union Oil Co. of California Dba Unocal Chem. (Nederland, TX) 88196
Union Pacific Resources Co. (Fort Worth, TX) 85340
Union Texas Petro Holding Co. (Houston, TX) 87055
Union Texas Petroleum Corp. (Lafayette, LA) 70120; 70120
Valero Refining Co. (Corpus Christi, TX) 83763
Valero Refining & Marketing Co. (Houston, TX) 87067
Warren Petroleum Co. (Tampa, FL) 63662
Warren Petroleum Corp. (Kilgore, TX) 87504
Witco Corp. (Harvey, LA) 69943

2950 Asphalt Paving & Roofing Materials

Apac Georgia Inc. MacDougald Warren Div. (Smyrna, GA) 67539

2951 Asphalt Paving Mixtures & Blocks

APAC (Birmingham, AL) 55157
APAC (Fort Myers, FL) 59661
APAC (Port Charlotte, FL) 62652
APAC (Sarasota, FL) 62786
APAC (Augusta, GA) 65311
APAC (Fortson, GA) 66261
APAC (Savannah, GA) 67445
APAC (Smyrna, GA) 67538
APAC (Columbus, MS) 72702
APAC (Greenville, MS) 72789
APAC (Jackson, MS) 72945
APAC (Meridan, MS) 73158
APAC (Enka, NC) 74504
APAC (Tulsa, OK) 77879
APAC (Darlington, SC) 79142
APAC (Knoxville, TN) 81142
APAC (McMinnville, TN) 81441
APAC (Memphis, TN) 81459
APAC (Danville, VA) 90684
APAC (Manassas, VA) 91303
Blount Construction Co. Inc. (Atlanta, GA) 64329
Chevron Corp. El Paso Asphalt Refinery (El Paso, TX) 84780
Chevron USA Inc. El Paso Refinery (El Paso, TX) 84781
Chevron USA Inc. Baltimore Asphalt Terminal (Baltimore, MD) 71085
Mobile Asphalt Terminal (Mobile, AL) 56208
Owens-Corning Fiberglass Roofing Plant (Atlanta, GA) 64987
Owens-Corning Fiberglass Trumbull Plant (Atlanta, GA) 64988
Shell Chemical Co. Geismar (Geismar, LA) 69883
Southern States Asphalt Co. (Nashville, TN) 82100
Vulcan Materials Co. (Chattanooga, TN) 80520
Vulcan Materials Co. (Brownwood, TX) 83391
Vulcan Materials Co. (Millsap, TX) 88104
Vulcan Materials Co. (San Antonio, TX) 89296
Vulcan Materials Co. (Uvalde, TX) 89858

2952 Asphalt Felts & Coatings

GAF Building Materials Corp. (Mobile, AL) 56181
GAF Building Materials Corp. (Garden City, GA) 66301
GAF Building Materials Corp. (Baltimore, MD) 71155
GAF Building Materials Corp. (Dallas, TX) 84079
GAF Corp. (Tampa, FL) 63437
Georgia Pacific Corp. (Hampton, GA) 66331
Manville/Schuller Inc. (Savannah, GA) 67499
Owens Corning (Houston, TX) 86630
Owens-Corning Fiberglas Corp. (Atlanta, GA) 64986
Owens-Corning Fiberglas Corp. (Irving, TX) 87386
Owens-Corning Fiberglass Roofing Plant (Jacksonville, FL) 60385
Owens-Corning Fiberglass Roofing Plant (Atlanta, GA) 64987
Owens-Corning Fiberglass Trumbull Plant (Atlanta, GA) 64988
Sigma Coatings Inc. (Harvey, LA) 69941
Wheeling Pittsburgh Steel Corp. (Beech Bottom, WV) 92692

2992 Lubricating Oils & Greases

Belcher Co. of Tennessee (West Memphis, AR) 57716
Cato Oil & Grease Co. (Atlanta, GA) 64347
Cato Oil & Grease Co. (Oklahoma City, OK) 77326
Coastal Unilube Inc. (West Memphis, AR) 57720; 57721; 57722; 57723
Coastal Unilube Inc. (Perryville, MD) 72215
Coastal Unilube Inc. (Charlotte, NC) 73907
Conoco Inc. (Mertzon, TX) 87955
Exxon Co. USA (Baytown, TX) 83120
Farmland Industries Lube Oil Blend Plant (Amarillo, TX) 82545
Heekin Can Inc. (Newport, TN) 82169
Industrial Lubricants Co. (San Antonio, TX) 89031
Lyondell Petrochemical Co. Houston Refinery (Houston, TX) 86504
Mobil Chemical Co. Bcsp (Beaumont, TX) 83180
Mobil Oil Corp. (Beaumont, TX) 83182
Nalco Chemical Co. (Jonesboro, GA) 66389
Pennzoil Products Co. (Shreveport, LA) 70760
Pennzoil Products Co. Dickinson (Dickinson, TX) 84667
Pennzoil Products Co. Shreveport Packaging Plant (Shreveport, LA) 70761
Phibro Refining St. Rose Refinery (St. Rose, LA) 70876
Quaker State Corp. Congo Plant (Newell, WV) 92964
Shell Oil Co. Metairie Plant (Jefferson, LA) 69976
Texaco Inc. Research & Development (Port Arthur, TX) 88650
Texaco Industries Inc. (Guayanilla, PR) 78433
Texaco Lubricants Co. (North Charleston, SC) 79750
Texaco Lubricants Co. Inc. (Chesapeake, VA) 90607
Texaco Port Arthur Research Laboratories (Port Arthur, TX) 88652
Texaco Ref. & Mktg. Inc. (N. Charleston, SC) 79721
Texaco Ref. & Mktg. Ing (North Charleston, SC) 79751
Texaco Refining & Marketing Texaco Lubricants Division (North Charleston, SC) 79752
Thompson & Formby's Inc. (Olive Branch, MS) 73231
Union Oil of California Dba Unocal (Nederland, TX) 88195
Union Oil Co. of California Dba Unocal Chem. (Nederland, TX) 88196
Witco Corp. Kendall-Amalie (Jacksonville, FL) 60512

2999 Petroleum & Coal Products Nec

Clean Coal Research Center (Wilsonville, AL) 56705
Clean Coal Research Center Southern Co. Services Inc. (Wilsonville, AL) 56706
Engelhard Corp. (Louisville, KY) 68759
Engelhard Corp. Pigments & Additives Div. (Louisville, KY) 68760
Harshaw Chemical Co. (Louisville, KY) 68770
Pennzoil Products Co. Dickinson Plant (Penreco) (Dickinson, TX) 84668
Penreco Dickinson Pennzoil Products Co. (Dickinson, TX) 84669
Reynolds Metals Co. (Baton Rouge, LA) 69648
Shell Oil Co. (Norco, LA) 70592

3000 Rubber & Miscellaneous Plastics Products

Aeroquip Corp. Middlesex Plant (Middlesex, NC) 75558
Chicopee (Gainesville, GA) 66268; 66269
Davidson Interior Trim Textron (Athens, TN) 80186
Dayco Products Inc. (Walterboro, SC) 80069
Dexter Corp. Pistisols Div. (Pineville, NC) 75810
Dexter Corp. Plastisols Div. (Pineville, NC) 75811
Dexter Plastisols Rutland Plastics Inc. (Pineville, NC) 75812
Federal Express Corp. (Memphis, TN) 81535
Fisher-Price (Murray, KY) 69123; 69125
Foam Molding Co. of Arkansas (Rogers, AR) 57564
Loral Engineered Fabrics (Rockmart, GA) 67332
M P I Inc. (Fort Worth, TX) 85182
Mpi Inc. (Coldwater, MS) 72692
Mpi Inc. (Houston, MS) 72919
Occidental Chemical Corp. (Salisbury, MD) 72353
Owens Corning Fiberglas (Conroe, TX) 83673
Owens-Corning Fiberglas Corp. (Auburndale, FL) 58600
Owens-Corning Fiberglas Corp. (Conroe, TX) 83674
Plexco (Abbeville, SC) 78643
Plexco (Knoxville, TN) 81240
Plexco (Corsicana, TX) 83788
PMS Consolidated (Fort Worth, TX) 85237
Porelon Inc. (Cookeville, TN) 80664
Raychem Corp. (Fuquay-Varina, NC) 74642
Reynolds Metals Co. Plastics Plant (Grottoes, VA) 91007
Sterling Engineered Products (Mooresville, NC) 75609
Summitt Insulators Pc (Memphis, TN) 81700
United Technologies Automative Inc. (Mount Airy, NC) 75685
Universal Rundle Corp. (Union Point, GA) 67936
Westinghouse Electric Corp. (Hampton, SC) 79494
Westinghouse Electric Corp. Micarta Div. (Pendleton, SC) 79789

3011 Tires & Inner Tubes

Air Treads Inc. (Atlanta, GA) 64211
Arkansas Best Corp. (Fort Smith, AR) 57023; 57023
Brad Ragan Inc. (Radford, VA) 91690; 91691
Brad Regan Inc. Rubber Div. (Radford, VA) 91692
Cooper Tire Co. (Texarkana, AR) 57671
Cooper Tire Co. (Albany, GA) 64065
Cooper Tire Co. (Clarksdale, MS) 72669
Cooper Tire Co. (Tupelo, MS) 73393
Cooper Tire Co. Cooper Tire & Rubber Co. Div. (Texarkana, AR) 57672
Cooper Tire & Rubber Co. (Texarkana, AR) 57673
Cooper Tire & Rubber Co. (Clarksdale, MS) 72670
Cooper Tire & Rubber Co. (Tupelo, MS) 73394
Goodyear Tire & Rubber Co. (Gadsden, AL) 55782
Goodyear Tire & Rubber Co. (Madisonville, KY) 69053; 69054
Goodyear Tire & Rubber Co. (Lawton, OK) 77159
Goodyear Tire & Rubber Co. (Spartanburg, SC) 79909
Goodyear Tire & Rubber Co. (Union City, TN) 82382
Goodyear Tire & Rubber Co. (Greenville, TX) 85671
Goodyear Tire & Rubber Co. (Danville, VA) 90697; 90698; 90699
Goodyear Tire & Rubber Co. Union City Plant (Union City, TN) 82383
Kelly-Springfield Tire Co. (Fayetteville, NC) 74561
Kelly Springfield Tire Co. (Tyler, TX) 89805
Kelly Springfield Tire Co. Associate Brands Div. (Cumberland, MD) 71627
Kelly-Springfield Tire Co. Custom Brands Div. (Cumberland, MD) 71628
Kelly-Springfield Tire Co. Inc. (Cumberland, MD) 71629
Kelly Springfield Tire Co. T (Cumberland, MD) 71630
Kelly-Springfield Tire Co. T (Tyler, TX) 89806
Long Mile Rubber Co. (Miami, FL) 61363
Long Mile Rubber Co. (Spartanburg, SC) 79918
Long Mile Rubber Co. (Dallas, TX) 84211
Oliver Rubber Co. (Athens, GA) 64173
Oliver Rubber Co. (Asheboro, NC) 73590
Oliver Rubber Co. (Dallas, TX) 84280
Oliver Rubber Co. (Paris, TX) 88373
Oliver Rubber Co. Asheboro (Asheboro, NC) 73591
Oliver Rubber Co. Athens (Athens, GA) 64174

3050 Hose & Belting & Gaskets & Packing

Colonial Rubber Works Inc. (Kingstree, SC) 79553
Colonial Rubber Works Inc. (Dyersburg, TN) 80744; 80745

3052 Rubber & Plastics Hose & Belting

Aeroquip Corp. (Mountain Home, AR) 57381; 57382; 57383
Aeroquip Corp. (Forest City, NC) 74596; 74597; 74598
Aeroquip Corp. (Norwood, NC) 75768; 75769
Aeroquip Corp. Industrial Products Group (Norwood, NC) 75770
Anchor Swan Inc. Anchor Swan Div. (Lexington, TN) 81334
Boston Industrial Products (Paragould, AR) 57488; 57489
Boston Industrial Products (Brentwood, TN) 80220
Boston Industrial Products (Hohenwald, TN) 80939; 80940; 80941
Dana Corp. Boston Industrial Products Div. (Paragould, AR) 57490
Dana Corp. Boston Industrial Products Div. (Hohenwald, TN) 80942
Dana Corp. Boston Industrial Products Division (Brentwood, TN) 80224
Dayco Prods. Inc. (Waynesville, NC) 76463
Dayco Prods. Inc. (Walterboro, SC) 80068
Dayco Prods. Inc. (Williston, SC) 80125
Dayco Products Inc. (Ocala, FL) 61793
Dayco Products Inc. (Waynesville, NC) 76464
Dayco Products Inc. (Williston, SC) 80126
Federal Mogul Corp. (Manning, SC) 79630
Harvard Industries Anchor Swan (Lexington, TN) 81337
Owens Corning Fiberglass (Conroe, TX) 83675

3053 Gaskets, Packing & Sealing Devices

Boston Industrial Products (Paragould, AR) 57488
Boston Industrial Products (Brentwood, TN) 80220
Cameron Elastomer Technology Inc. (Katy, TX) 87447
Compressor Components (Odessa, TX) 88239
Cooper Elastomer Technology Inc. (Katy, TX) 87448
Cooper Industrial Products (El Dorado, AR) 56936

Cooper Tire & Rubber Co. Engineered Products Div. (El Dorado, AR) 56937
Copper Industrial Products (El Dorado, AR) 56938
Copper Tire & Rubber Co. Engineered Products Div. (El Dorado, AR) 56939
Dana Corp. Boston Industrial Products Div. (Paragould, AR) 57490
Dana Corp. Victor Products Div. (Danville, KY) 68254
Eagle-Picher Industries Inc. Wolverine Gasket Div. (Lisbon, FL) 60905
Eagle-Picher Industries Inc. Wolverine Gasket Div. Blacksburg Div. (Blacksburg, VA) 90437
EG & G Pressure Science Inc. (Beltsville, MD) 71351
Federal Mogul (Summerton, SC) 79978
GemStone Gasket Co. (Danville, KY) 68258
Gencorp Polymer Products (Fort Smith, AR) 57053
Manville Sales Corp. (Nacogdoches, TX) 88171
Wolverine Gasket Co. (Leesburg, FL) 60889; 60890
Wolverine Gasket Co. Blacksburg Div. (Blacksburg, VA) 90452
Wolverine Gasket & Mfg Co. (Blacksburg, VA) 90453

3061 Mechanical Rubber Goods

Cooper Industrial Products (El Dorado, AR) 56936
Cooper Tire & Rubber Co. Engineered Products Div. (El Dorado, AR) 56937
Copper Industrial Products (El Dorado, AR) 56938
Copper Tire & Rubber Co. Engineered Products Div. (El Dorado, AR) 56939
Dana Corp. Boston Industrial Products Div. (Paragould, AR) 57490
Gencorp Automotive Inc. Dba Gencorp Automotive (Batesville, AR) 56756
Oliver Rubber Co. (Dallas, TX) 84280
Waycross Molded Products Inc. (Waycross, GA) 68045

3069 Fabricated Rubber Products Nec

AGR Co. (Charlotte, NC) 73828
Allied-Signal Inc. Bendix Friction Materials (Lynn Haven, FL) 60955
B. F. Goodrich Aerospace Epp (Jacksonville, FL) 60188
B. F. Goodrich Co. (Grantsville, WV) 92860
B. F. Goodrich Co. (Spencer, WV) 93062
BASF Corp. (Chattanooga, TN) 80327; 80328
Baxter Healthcare Corp. (Kingstree, SC) 79552
Becton Dickinson & Co. (Honea Path, SC) 79526
BF Goodrich Co. (Jacksonville, FL) 60232
Boston Industrial Products (Paragould, AR) 57488
Boston Industrial Products (Newbern, TN) 82155
Burton Rubber Processing Inc. (Jonesborough, TN) 81064
Cone Mills Corp. (Greensboro, NC) 74803
Cooper Industrial Products (El Dorado, AR) 56936
Cooper Tire & Rubber Co. Engineered Products Div. (El Dorado, AR) 56937
Copper Industrial Products (El Dorado, AR) 56938
Copper Tire & Rubber Co. Engineered Products Div. (El Dorado, AR) 56939
Dana Corp. Boston Industrial Products Div. (Paragould, AR) 57490
Day International (Arden, NC) 73565
Day International Inc. (Arden, NC) 73566
Diversitech General Dba Gencorp Automotive (Batesville, AR) 56750
Diversitech General Inc. Dba Gencorp Automotive (Batesville, AR) 56751
Dresser Industries Inc. Guiberson Div. (Dallas, TX) 83985
Eagle-Picher Industries Inc. Molding Orthane Div. (Denton, TX) 84616
Eaton Corp. (Laurinburg, NC) 75351
Eaton Corp. Golf Grip Div. (Laurinburg, NC) 75352
Eaton Corp. Golf Group Div. (Laurinburg, NC) 75353
Gencorp Automotive Dba Gencorp Automotive (Batesville, AR) 56755
Goodyear Tire & Rubber Co. (Gadsden, AL) 55782
Johnson & Johnson Medical Inc. (Arlington, TX) 82669
Johnson & Johnson Medical, Inc. (Sherman, TX) 89400
Kingston-Warren Corp. (Church Hill, TN) 80531; 80532
Kingston-Warren Corp. (Wytheville, VA) 92641
L & P Foam Inc. (Tupelo, MS) 73409
Lagrange Molded Products Inc. (La Grange, GA) 66486
LaGrange Molded Products, Inc. (LaGrange, GA) 66494
L&P Foam Inc. (Tupelo, MS) 73410
L&P Foam Inc. (High Point, NC) 75144
L&P Foam Inc. (Newton, NC) 75748
Long Mile Rubber Co. (Dallas, TX) 84211
Loral Engineered Fabrics (Rockmart, GA) 67332
Ohio Rubber Co. Orthane Div. (Denton, TX) 84624
Oliver Rubber Co. (Athens, GA) 64173
Oliver Rubber Co. (Asheboro, NC) 73590
Oliver Rubber Co. (Dallas, TX) 84280
Oliver Rubber Co. (Paris, TX) 88372; 88373
Oliver Rubber Co. Asheboro (Asheboro, NC) 73591
Oliver Rubber Co. Athens (Athens, GA) 64174
Schering-Plough Healthcare Products (Cleveland, TN) 80600
Scott Aviation (Monroe, NC) 75591
Standard Products Co. (Goldsboro, NC) 74735
Standard Products Co. (Rocky Mountain, NC) 76114
Standard Products Co. Goldsboro Division (Goldsboro, NC) 74736
Teledyne Monarch Rubber Lewisburg (Lewisburg, TN) 81332
United Brake Systems Inc. (Charlotte, NC) 74189
W. R. Grace & Co. (Morristown, TN) 81817
Waycross Molded Products, Inc. (Waycross, GA) 68044
W.R. Grace & Co. (Morristown, TN) 81819

3081 Unsupported Plastics Film & Sheet

Ametek Inc. (Greenup, KY) 68405
Borden Chemical Inc. (Griffin, GA) 66311
Borden Inc. Packaging & Industrial Products (Griffin, GA) 66313
Borden Packaging & Industrial Products (Gainsville, TX) 85431
E. R. Carpenter Co. Inc. (Russellville, KY) 69259
First Brands Corp. (Rogers, AR) 57563
Gencorp Inc. (Columbus, MS) 72710
General Electric Co. (Dallas, TX) 84089
Hercules Inc. (Covington, VA) 90661
Hoechst-Celanese Corp. Seperations Products Div. (Charlotte, NC) 74044
James River Corp Advance Film Div. (New Castle, DE) 57867
James River Corp. Advanced Film Div. (New Castle, DE) 57868
James River Corp. Flexible Packaging Group (Orange, TX) 88318
Mobil Chemical Co. (Shawnee, OK) 77822
Mobil Chemical Co. (Temple, TX) 89625
Mobil Chemical Co. General Products (Temple, TX) 89627
Occidental Chemical (Salisbury, MD) 72351
Occidental Chemical Corp. (Salisbury, MD) 72352
Rexham Corp. Lancaster Plant (Lancaster, SC) 79573
Rexham Corp. Matthews (Matthews, NC) 75530
Rexham Inc. Industrial Division Spartanburg Plant (Spartanburg, SC) 79936
Rexham Inc. Industrial Div. Matthews Plant Industrial Division Matthews Plant (Matthews, NC) 75531
Rexham Inc. Lancaster Plant (Lancaster, SC) 79574
Reynolds Metals Co. (Grottoes, VA) 91005
Reynolds Metals Co. Plastics Plant (Grottoes, VA) 91006
Rohm & Haas Tennessee Inc. (Knoxville, TN) 81245
3M Co. Tape Manufacturing Div. (Greenville, SC) 79440
Tredegar Industries Inc. (Richmond, VA) 92060
W. R. Grace & Co. (Owensboro, KY) 69196
W. R. Grace & Co. Inc. Connecticut (Boca Raton, FL) 58750
W.R. Grace & Co. (Owensboro, KY) 69199

3082 Unsupported Plastics Profile Shapes

Amsted Industries Inc. Plexco Div. (Knoxville, TN) 81141
Boston Industrial Products (Hohenwald, TN) 80939
Gencorp Polymer Prods. (Fort Smith, AR) 57052
James River Co. (Lexington, KY) 68559

3083 Laminated Plastics Plate & Sheet

Aeroquip Corp. (Fitzgerald, GA) 66205
Aeroquip Corp. (Franklin, TN) 80806
Aeroquip Corp. Diversified Products Div. (Franklin, TN) 80807
Ametek Corp. Haveg Div. (Wilmington, DE) 57983
Ametek, Inc. Heaveg Div. (Wilmington, DE) 57985
International Paper Co. Nevamar Div. (Memphis, TN) 81630
Morrison Molded Fiber Glass Co. (Bristol, VA) 90483
Occidental Chemical Corp. (Salisbury, MD) 72352
Phillips Research Center (Bartlesville, OK) 76844
Phillips Research Ctr. (Bartlesville, OK) 76845
Ralph Wilson Plastic North Plant (Temple, TX) 89636
Ralph Wilson Plastic South Plant (Temple, TX) 89637
Ralph Wilson Plastics Co. (Miami, FL) 61439
Ralph Wilson Plastics Co. (Decatur, GA) 65891
Ralph Wilson Plastics Co. (Fletcher, NC) 74592; 74593
Ralph Wilson Plastics Co. (Houston, TX) 86792
Ralph Wilson Plastics Co. (Temple, TX) 89638; 89639
Ralph Wilson Plastics Co. North Plant (Temple, TX) 89640
Ralph Wilson Plastics Co. South Plant (Temple, TX) 89641
Rexham Corp. Lancaster Plant (Lancaster, SC) 79573
Rexham Corp. Matthews (Matthews, NC) 75530
Rexham Inc. Industrial Division Spartanburg Plant (Spartanburg, SC) 79936
Rexham Inc. Industrial Div. Matthews Plant Industrial Division Matthews Plant (Matthews, NC) 75531
Rexham Inc. Lancaster Plant (Lancaster, SC) 79574
Rohm & Haas Tennessee Inc. (Knoxville, TN) 81245
Sterling Engineered Products (Morristown, TN) 81810

3084 Plastics Pipe

Ametek Corp. Haveg Div. (Wilmington, DE) 57983
AMP, Inc. (Winston-Salem, NC) 76701
Capco Pipe Co. Inc. (Birmingham, AL) 55178; 55179
Capco Pipe Co. Inc. (Van Buren, AR) 57689
Chevron Chemical Co. Plexco Div. (Knoxville, TN) 81154

3085 Plastics Bottles

Baxter Healthcare Corp. (Cleveland, MS) 72682
Belcher Co. of Tennessee (West Memphis, AR) 57716
Borden Inc. (Lafayette, LA) 70044
Clorox Co. (Forest Park, GA) 66232
Clorox Co. of Puerto Rico (Caguas, PR) 78356; 78357
Clorox Co., Tampa Plant (Tampa, FL) 63394
Coastal Unilube Inc. (West Memphis, AR) 57720; 57721
Coastal Unilube Inc. (Perryville, MD) 72215
Coastal Unilube Inc. (Charlotte, NC) 73907
Constar International Inc. (Atlanta, GA) 64392
Owens Illinois Inc. (Dallas, TX) 84288
Thoroughbred Plastics Corp. (Louisville, KY) 69021

3086 Plastics Foam Products

Ametek Inc. Microfoam Div. Inc. (Wurtland, KY) 69359
Ametek Microfoam (Worthington, KY) 69358
Armstrong World Industries Inc. (Dallas, GA) 65757
E. R. Carpenter Co. (Texarkana, AR) 57675
E. R. Carpenter Co. Inc. (Birmingham, AL) 55228
E. R. Carpenter Co. Inc. (Fort Smith, AR) 57048
E. R. Carpenter Co. Inc. (Russellville, KY) 69259
E. R. Carpenter Co. Inc. (Booneville, MS) 72643
E. R. Carpenter Co. Inc. (Pontotoc, MS) 73299
E. R. Carpenter Co. Inc. (Saltillo, MS) 73335
E. R. Carpenter Co. Inc. (Conover, NC) 74330
E. R. Carpenter Co. Inc. (Hickory, NC) 75067
E. R. Carpenter Co. Inc. (High Point, NC) 75121; 75122
E. R. Carpenter Co. Inc. (Lenoir, NC) 75372; 75373; 75374
E. R. Carpenter Co. Inc. (Longview, NC) 75451
E. R. Carpenter Co. Inc. (Morganton, NC) 75645
E. R. Carpenter Co. Inc. (Taylorsville, NC) 76368
E. R. Carpenter Co. Inc. (Cleveland, TN) 80576
E. R. Carpenter Co. Inc. (Cookeville, TN) 80648; 80649
E. R. Carpenter Co. Inc. (Morristown, TN) 81792
E. R. Carpenter Co. Inc. (Dallas, TX) 83989
E. R. Carpenter Co. Inc. (Houston, TX) 86051; 86052
E. R. Carpenter Co. Inc. (Temple, TX) 89614
E. R. Carpenter Co. Inc. (Texarkana, TX) 89674
E. R. Carpenter Co. Inc. (Richmond, VA) 91860
E. R. Carpenter Co. Inc. New Braunfels (New Braunfels, TX) 88208
E. R. Carpenter Co. Inc. Tupelo (Verona, MS) 73445
E. R. Carpenter Co. of Texas (Temple, TX) 89615
Echota Cushion Inc. (Calhoun, GA) 65463; 65464
E.R. Carpenter Co. Inc. (Birmingham, AL) 55231
E.R. Carpenter Co., Inc. (Verona, MS) 73446
E.R. Carpenter Co. Inc. (Conover, NC) 74331
E.R. Carpenter Co. Inc. (Lenoir, NC) 75375; 75376
E.R. Carpenter Co. Inc. (Longview, NC) 75452
E.R. Carpenter Co. Inc. (Morristown, TN) 81793
Foamax Products Inc. (Verona, MS) 73447
Foamex Foamex L.P. (Conover, NC) 74332
Foamex Kihi Foamex (Tupelo, MS) 73402
Foamex L.P. (Conyers, GA) 65681
Foamex L.P. (Conover, NC) 74333
Foamex LP (High Point, NC) 75131
Foamex LP (Cookeville, TN) 80658
Foamex LP (Milan, TN) 81768
Foamex LP (Morristown, TN) 81800
Foamex L.P. (Mesquite, TX) 87963
Foamex L.P. Curon (Tampa, FL) 63433
Foamex L.P. Foamex Division (Cornelius, NC) 74347
Foamex LP Kihi Foamex (Verona, MS) 73448; 73449
Foamex L.P. Vahala (Bogart, GA) 65385
Foamex L.P. Plant 1 (Morristown, TN) 81801
Foamex L.P. Plant 3 (Morristown, TN) 81802
Knoll International Holdings Foames L.P. (Orlando, FL) 62027
Knoll International Holdings Foamex LP (Opa-Locka, FL) 61864; 61865
Leggett & Platt Foam Inc. (High Point, NC) 75145
Leggett & Platt Inc. (Newton, NC) 75749
Leggett & Platt Inc. Urethane Foam Div. (Tupelo, MS) 73411
Mobil Chemical (Covington, GA) 65736
Mobil Chemical Co. (Covington, GA) 65737
Mobil Chemical Co. Foam (Temple, TX) 89626
Mpi Inc. (Lakeland, FL) 60755
MPI, Inc. (Fort Worth, TX) 85201
Nashville Foam (Nashville, TN) 82068
Olympic Prods. Co. (Tupelo, MS) 73414
Olympic Prods. Co. (Greensboro, NC) 74872
Olympic Prods. Co. Rebond Plant (Greensboro, NC) 74873
Plastic Packaging Inc. (Hickory, NC) 75095
Prelude Co. (Thomasville, NC) 76382
Raychem Corp. (Fuquay Varina, NC) 74639
Schering-Plough Healthcare Products (Chatsworth, GA) 65557; 65557; 65557; 65557; 65557; 65557
Spenco Medical Corp. (Waco, TX) 89977; 89978
Texas Fibers (Brenham, TX) 83344
Texas Fibers (Grand Prairie, TX) 85643
Texas Fibers (Texarkana, TX) 89713
USG Interiors Inc. (Birmingham, AL) 55444

3087 Custom Compound of Purchased Resins

A. Schulman Inc. (Orange, TX) 88298
A. Schulman Inc. Dispersion (Orange, TX) 88299
Allied Color Ind. (Greenville, SC) 79292
Avecor Inc. (Vonore, TN) 82392
Chevron Chemical Co. (Channelview, TX) 83548
D & S Plastics International (Grand Prairie, TX) 85615
Evtech a Kodak Co. (Charlotte, NC) 73945
Fina Oil & Chemical Co. (Pasadena, TX) 88407
PMS Consolidated (Buford, GA) 65441
PMS Consolidated (Florence, KY) 68327
PMS Consolidated (Gastonia, NC) 74684
PMS Consolidated (Fort Worth, TX) 85236
Rutland Plastics (Pineville, NC) 75826
Southwest Chemical Services Inc. (Seabrook, TX) 89361; 89362
Stanley Works Stanley Tools Division (Cheraw, SC) 78926

3088 Plastics Plumbing Fixtures

Morgantown Plastics Co. (Morgantown, KY) 69110
Universal-Rundle Corp. Fiberglass Div. (Union Point, GA) 67937

3089 Plastics Products Nec

A. O. Smith Automotive Prods. Co. (Bowling Green, KY) 68131
A. Schulman Inc. (Orange, TX) 88297

Aeroquip Corp. (Fitzgerald, GA) 66205
Aeroquip Corp. (Henderson, KY) 68438
Aeroquip Corp. (Williamsport, MD) 72572
Aeroquip Corp. (Mooresville, NC) 75596; 75597
Aeroquip Corp. (Livingston, TN) 81347
Aeroquip Corp. (Bassett, VA) 90414
Aeroquip Corp. Sterling Div. (Mooresville, NC) 75598
Alcoa Building Products (Denison, TX) 84592
Alcoa Building Products (Stuarts Draft, VA) 92356
Allegany Ballistics Lab. (Keyser, WV) 92910
Allegany Ballistics Laboratory (Rocket Center, WV) 93032
Allied-Signal Inc. (Orange, TX) 88304; 88306
Ameritech Plastics (Boca Raton, FL) 58668
Ametek Corp. Haveg Div. (Wilmington, DE) 57983
Ball Corp. (Fort Smith, AR) 57026
Ball Corp. (Okmulgee, OK) 77676
Ball Corp. Unimark Plastics Division (Greer, SC) 79469
BASF Corp. (Geismar, LA) 69876
Baxter Healthcare Corp. (Cleveland, MS) 72682
Bemis Co. Custom Resins Div. (Henderson, KY) 68440
Bonny Products Inc. (Washington, NC) 76452
Borden Inc. (Griffin, GA) 66312
Borden Packaging & Industrial Products (Gainsville, TX) 85431
Boston Industrial Products (Hohenwald, TN) 80939
Brunswick Corp. (Marion, VA) 91331
Capco Pipe Co. Inc. (Birmingham, AL) 55178
Cellwood Products (Gaffney, SC) 79257
Central Moloney Transformer Components Operation (Pine Bluff, AR) 57510
Composite Technologies Inc. (Fort Worth, TX) 85091
Composite Technology Polycel Div. (Fort Worth, TX) 85092
Composite Technology Inc. Conn (Fort Worth, TX) 85093
Conitron (Trinity, NC) 76406
Constar International Inc. (Atlanta, GA) 64392
Continental Group Inc. (Olive Branch, MS) 73226
Continental Industries Inc. (Broken Arrow, OK) 76881
Continental Industries Inc. (Tulsa, OK) 77923
Crane Resistoflex Co. (Marion, NC) 75499; 75500
Danaher Corp. (Washington, DC) 58209
Exxon Chemical Americas (Baytown, TX) 83112
Exxon Chemical Co. (Dallas, TX) 84049
Exxon Co. USA (Baton Rouge, LA) 69528
Fina Inc. (Dallas, TX) 84065
Fort Howard Cup Corp. (Owings Mills, MD) 72187
Gencorp Inc. (Columbus, MS) 72710
Gencorp Polymer Products (Fort Smith, AR) 57053
General Electric Co. (Burkville, AL) 55492
General Electric Co. Frankfort Plant (Frankfort, KY) 68360
H C Industries Inc. (Olive Branch, MS) 73228
H.C. Industries Inc. Closure Systems (Olive Branch, MS) 73229
Hoechst Celanese Engineering Plastics Div. (Florence, KY) 68308
Hoechst Celanese Seperations Products Div. (Charlotte, NC) 74041
Hoechst-Celanese Corp. Specialty Prods. Facility (Florence, KY) 68309
Hoechst Celanese Eng. Plastics (Florence, KY) 68310
Hoov-R-Line (Providence, KY) 69235
Huntsman Chemical Corp. (Chesapeake, VA) 90585
Imperial Bondware (Lafayette, GA) 66492
Lagrange Molded Products Inc. (La Grange, GA) 66485
Louisville Ladder Corp. (Louisville, KY) 68871
Mercury Marine (St. Cloud, FL) 63067
Mercury Marine Plant 7 (St. Cloud, FL) 63068
Mobil Chemical (Covington, GA) 65736
Mobil Chemical Co. (Shawnee, OK) 77822
Mobil Corp. (Fairfax, VA) 90797
Mobil Oil Corp. (Covington, GA) 65738
Morrison Molded Fiber Glass Co. (Bristol, VA) 90483
O/C Tanks Corp. (Conroe, TX) 83671
Olympic Products Co. (Tupelo, MS) 73415
Olympic Products Co. (Pleasant Garden, NC) 75832
Olympic Rebond Plant (Greensboro, NC) 74874
Owens Corning (Conroe, TX) 83672
Owens-Corning Fiberglas Corp. (Memphis, TN) 81662
Owens-Corning Fiberglas Corp. (Amarillo, TX) 82571
Owens-Corning Fiberglas Corp. (Waxachachie, TX) 89992
Owens Corning Fiberglass (Huntsville, AL) 55984
Owens Illinois Inc. (Atlanta, GA) 64990
Owens Illinois Inc. (Bardstown, KY) 68117
Owens Illinois Inc. (Baltimore, MD) 71214
Owens-Illinois Inc. (Hamlet, NC) 74999
Owens Illinois Inc. (Dallas, TX) 84288
Owens-Illinois Labels Inc. Products Inc. (Bardstown, KY) 68118
Parkson Aeration & Fiberglass Corp. Inc. (Medley, FL) 61030
Plastic Packaging Inc. (Hickory, NC) 75095
Plastics Inc. (Greensboro, AL) 55813
Plastics Inc. (Rayne, LA) 70657
Plastics, Inc. (Jacksonville, TX) 87425
Porex Technologies Corp. (Fairburn, GA) 66179
Porex Technologies Corp. of Georgia (Fairburn, GA) 66180
Quazite (Lenoir City, TN) 81322; 81323
Ralph Wilson Plastics Co. (Miami, FL) 61439
Ralph Wilson Plastics Co. (Decatur, GA) 65891
Ralph Wilson Plastics Co. (Fletcher, NC) 74593
Ralph Wilson Plastics Co. (Houston, TX) 86792
Ralph Wilson Plastics Co. (Temple, TX) 89639
Raychem Corp. (Fuquay Varina, NC) 74639
Raychem Industries (Vega Baja, PR) 78629
Reynolds Metals Co. (Grottoes, VA) 91005
Rubbermaid Commercial Prods. Inc. (Cleburne, TX) 83583
Rubbermaid Commercial Products (Cleburne, TX) 83584
Rubbermaid Commercial Products (Winchester, VA) 92603
Rubbermaid Commercial Products Inc. (Cleburne, TX) 83585
Rubbermaid Inc. Commerical Products (Winchester, VA) 92604
Rubbermaid Office Products Inc. (Statesville, NC) 76336
Rubbermaid Office Products Inc. (Maryville, TN) 81423
Rubbermaid Office Products Inc. (Greenville, TX) 85676
Sigmaform Corp. (Vicksburg, MS) 73463
Slocomb Industries Inc. (Wilmington, DE) 58112
Smith Fiberglass Products Inc. (Little Rock, AR) 57311
Sonoco Products Co. (Forest Park, GA) 66249
Sonoco Products Co. (Greenville, SC) 79436
Sonoco Semi-Bulk Packaging (Marietta, GA) 66918
Southeast Vinyl Co. (Lynchburg, VA) 91288
Specialty Products (Wynnewood, OK) 78274
Standard Products Co. (Spartanburg, SC) 79953
Standard Products Co. (Winnsboro, SC) 80133
Stanley Hardware Wondura Products (Tupelo, MS) 73426
Stanley Works Stanley Tools Division (Cheraw, SC) 78926
Sterling Eng. Prods. Inc. (Franklin, TN) 80824
Stone Container Corp. (Sheridan, AR) 57614
Texas Instruments Inc. (Versailles, KY) 69332
Thoroughbred Plastics Corp. (Jonesboro, GA) 66406
Thoroughbred Plastics Corp. (Louisville, KY) 69021
3M Co. Telecom Markets Div. (Austin, TX) 83046
Tredegar Industries Inc. (Richmond, VA) 92060
Twentieth Century Companies Inc. Hoov-R-Line (Providence, KY) 69236
Unimark Plastics (Greer, SC) 79491
Union Camp Corp. (Griffin, GA) 66327
United Technologies Automotive Engineered Systems Div. (Dayton, TN) 80723
United Technologies Auto (Thomson, GA) 67816
United Technologies Automotive Inc. (Mount Airy, NC) 75686
Universal Rundle Corp. (Union Point, GA) 67935
Variform Inc. (Martinsburg, WV) 92936
W. R. Grace & Co. Cryovac Div. (Simpsonville, SC) 79870
W. R. Grace & Co. Cryovac Div. (Iowa Park, TX) 87308
W. R. Grace & Co. Polycel Products (Fort Worth, TX) 85348
Waterloo Industries Inc. (Pocahontas, AR) 57548
Whirlpool Corp. (Columbia, SC) 79127
Wilsonart (Dallas, TX) 84497
Wilsonart (Houston, TX) 87198
Witco Corp. (Philadelphia, MS) 73287
Witco Corp. Richardson Battery Parts (Philadelphia, MS) 73288; 73289
W.R. Grace & Co. Cryovac Div. (Simpsonville, SC) 79871
W.R. Grace & Co. Cryovac Div. (Iowa Park, TX) 87311
W.R. Grace & Co. Conn (Fort Worth, TX) 85365

3111 Leather Tanning & Finishing

Tandy Brands Accessories Inc. (Arlington, TX) 82761

3143 Men's Footwear Except Athletic

Georgia Boot Inc. Blairsville Plant (Blairsville, GA) 65382
Georgia Boot Inc. Franklin Plant (Franklin, TN) 80819
Pan-Am Shoe Co. Inc. (Camuy, PR) 78361; 78362
Thom Mcan Manufacturing (Wilkesboro, NC) 76519
Thom Mcan Mfg. Inc. (Wilkesboro, NC) 76520

3144 Women's Footwear Except Athletic

Thom Mcan Mfg. Inc. (Wilkesboro, NC) 76520

3149 Footwear Except Rubber Nec

Air Products & Chemicals Inc. (Calvert City, KY) 68174
Texaco (Richardson, TX) 88782

3161 Luggage

Brown Forman Corp. (Louisville, KY) 68718; 68719
Hartman Luggage Co. (Lebanon, TN) 81300
Hartmann Luggage Co. (Lebanon, TN) 81301
Tandy Brands Accessories Inc. (Arlington, TX) 82761

3171 Women's Handbags & Purses

Tandy Brands Accessories Inc. (Arlington, TX) 82761

3172 Personal Leather Goods Nec

Brown Forman Corp. (Louisville, KY) 68718; 68719
Hartman Luggage Co. (Lebanon, TN) 81300
Hartmann Luggage Co. (Lebanon, TN) 81301
Tandy Brands Accessories (Yoakum, TX) 90137

3200 Stone, Clay & Glass Products

Ball-Icon Glass Packaging (Asheville, NC) 73602

3211 Flat Glass

Ball-Icon Glass Packaging (Okmulgee, OK) 77677
Ball-Incon Glass Packaging (Asheville, NC) 73604
Ford Motor Co. (Nashville, TN) 82012
Ford Motor Co. Nashville Glass (Nashville, TN) 82013
Ford Motor Co., Tulsa Glass Plant (Tulsa, OK) 77941
Owens-Brockway Glass Container (Muskogee, OK) 77227
Pgg Industries Inc. (Wichita Falls, TX) 90087
PPG Industries Inc. (Wichita Falls, TX) 90093; 90094; 90095

3221 Glass Containers

Anchor Glass Container Corp. (Jacksonville, FL) 60179
Anchor Glass Container Corp. (Henrietta, OK) 77125
Anchor Glass Container Corp. (Keyser, WV) 92911
Anchor Glass Container Corp. Plant 18 (Houston, TX) 85800
Anchor Glass Container Corp. (02) Plant (Corsicana, TX) 83777
Anchor Glass Container Plant 18 (Houston, TX) 85801
Ball-Ball-InCon Glass Ball-Incon (Henderson, NC) 75016
Ball-Ball InCon Glass Ball-Incon (Laurens, SC) 79586
Ball Corp. (Williamsburg, VA) 92552
Ball-Icon Glass Packaging (Okmulgee, OK) 77677
Ball Incon Glass Packaging (Simmesport, LA) 70809
Ball Incon Glass Packaging (Asheville, NC) 73603
Ball Incon Glass Packaging (Henderson, NC) 75017; 75018; 75019
Ball Incon Glass Packaging (Okmulgee, OK) 77678
Ball - Incon Glass Packaging Corp. (Asheville, NC) 73605
Ball-Incon Glass Packaging Corp. (Henderson, NC) 75020
Ball-Incon Glass Packaging Corp. (Okmulgee, OK) 77679
Ball-Incon Glass Packaging Corp. (Laurens, SC) 79587
Carr-Lowrey Glass Co. (Baltimore, MD) 71076
O-I Brockway Glass Inc. Plant 13 (Montgomery, AL) 56358
O-I Brockway Glass Inc. Plant 3 (Muskogee, OK) 77225
O-I Brockway Glass Inc. Plant 29 (Ringgold, VA) 92096
Owens-Brockway Glass Container (Montgomery, AL) 56360
Owens-Brockway Glass Container (Ada, OK) 76786
Owens-Brockway Glass Container (Muskogee, OK) 77226
Owens-Brockway Glass Container (Waco, TX) 89955
Owens-Brockway Glass Container (Ringgold, VA) 92097
Owens-Brockway Glass Container Plant 29 (Ringgold, VA) 92098
Owens-Brockway Glass Container Inc. (Lakeland, FL) 60758
Owens-Brockway Glass Container Inc. (Atlanta, GA) 64985
Owens-Brockway Glass Container Inc. (Waco, TX) 89956
Owens-Brockway Glass Container Inc. (Huntington, WV) 92888
Owens Illinois De Puerto Rico Plant 138 (Vega Alta, PR) 78623
Owens Illinois Glass Co. (Winston Salem, NC) 76678
Owens-Illinois Glass Container Inc. (Atlanta, GA) 64989
Owens-Illinois Glass Container Inc. (Waco, TX) 89957
Owens-Illinois Glass Container Inc. (Toano, VA) 92386
Owens-Illinois Glass Container Inc. Plant 16 (Lakeland, FL) 60759
Owens Illinois Glass Container Inc. Plant 2 (Huntington, WV) 92889
Owens Illinois Inc. Plant 15 Waco (Waco, TX) 89958
Pepsi-Cola Bottling Co. (Rockingham, NC) 76065
Sonoco Products Co. (Memphis, TN) 81694

3229 Pressed & Blown Glass Nec

Ametek Corp. Haveg Div. (Wilmington, DE) 57983
Anchor Glass Container Corp. (Tampa, FL) 63322
Anchor Glass Container Corp. (Chattanooga, TN) 80323
Ball-Icon Glass Packaging (Okmulgee, OK) 77677
Corning Consumer Products Co. (Martinsburg, WV) 92927; 92928
Corning Glass Works (Danville, VA) 90687
Corning, Inc. (Harrodsburg, KY) 68410
Corning Inc. (Martinsburg, WV) 92929; 92930
Corning Inc. (Paden City, WV) 92980
Corning Inc. (Parkersburg, WV) 92983
GAF Building Materials Corp. (Chester, SC) 78937
GAF Building Materials Corp. (Nashville, TN) 82015
GTE Prods. Corp. Versailles Glass Plant (Versailles, KY) 69326
GTE Products Corp. Versailles Class Plant (Versailles, KY) 69327
GTE Products Corp., Versailles Glass Plant (Versailles, KY) 69328
Indiana Glass Co. (Sapulpa, OK) 77791
Indiana Glass Co. Bartlett-Collins (Sapulpa, OK) 77792
Kentucky Glass Plant - General Electric (Lexington, KY) 68564
Libbey Glass Co. (Shreveport, LA) 70749
Louie Glass Co. Inc. (Weston, WV) 93107
Manville Corp. (Etowah, TN) 80780
Owens Corning Fiberglas Corp. (Fort Smith, AR) 57076
Owens-Corning Fiberglas Corp. (Aiken, SC) 78653; 78654
Owens-Corning Fiberglas Corp. (Anderson, SC) 78682
Owens-Corning Fiberglas Corp. (Amarillo, TX) 82571
Owens Corning Fiberglass (Anderson, SC) 78683
Owens-Corning Fiberglass (Amarillo, TX) 82572
Owens-Corning Fiberglass Roofing Mat Plant (Fort Smith, AR) 57078
Owens-Corning Fiberglas Corp. (Anderson, SC) 78684
Palmetto Prods. Inc. (Columbia, SC) 79059
Ppg Industries Inc. (Shelby, NC) 76244; 76245
Schuller International Inc. (Etowah, TN) 80783

3231 Products of Purchased Glass

GAF Building Materials Corp. (Chester, SC) 78937
Gaf Corp. (Chester, SC) 78938
General Electric Co. (Lexington, KY) 68555
General Electric Co. (Somerset, KY) 69293
Harman Automotive Puerto Rico Inc. (Vega Alta, PR) 78620; 78621
PPG Industries Inc. (Huntsville, AL) 56000
PPG Industries Inc. (Knoxville, TN) 81242
PPG Industries Inc. (Wichita Falls, TX) 90094
Stanley Hardware Wondura Products (Tupelo, MS) 73426

3241 Cement—Hydraulic

Lafarge Corp. (Demopolis, AL) 55616
Lafarge Corp. -Balcones (New Braunfels, TX) 88213
Lafarge Corp. Balcones Cement Plant (New Braunfels, TX) 88214
Lafarge Corp. Balcones Plant (New Braunfels, TX) 88215

3251 Brick & Structural Clay Tile

Lone Star Industries Inc. (Pryor, OK) 77741
Lone Star Industries Inc. (Maryneal, TX) 87878
Systech Corp. (Demopolis, AL) 55618
Systech Environmental Corp. (Demopolis, AL) 55619
Texas Industries Inc. (Midlothian, TX) 88102
United Cement Co. (Artesia, MS) 72590

3251 Brick & Structural Clay Tile

American Olean Tile Co. (Fayette, AL) 55727
Athens Brick Co. (Athens, TX) 82786
J. L. Anderson Co. Inc. Palmetto Brick Co. (Wallace, SC) 80064
M-I Drilling Fluids Zavalla (Zavalla, TX) 90139
Maryland Clay Products (Beltsville, MD) 71357

3253 Ceramic Wall & Floor Tile

American Olean Tile Co. (Lewisport, KY) 68516; 68517
American Olean Tile Co. (Jackson, TN) 80964
Florida Tile Industries Inc. Florida Tile Div. (Lakeland, FL) 60727
Reynolds Metals Co. (Sheffield, AL) 56556
Reynolds Metals Co. Sheffield Plant (Sheffield, AL) 56562

3255 Clay Refractories

Ferro Corp. (Tyler, TX) 89800
Harbison Walker Refractories Dresser Industries Inc. (Bessemer, AL) 55095
Harbison-Walker Refractories Dresser Industries Inc. (Fairfield, AL) 55713

3261 Vitreous Plumbing Fixtures

Kilgore Plumbing Products Inc. (Kilgore, TX) 87489
Universal Rundle Corp. (Monroe, GA) 66994; 66995
Universal Rundle Corp. (Hondo, TX) 85753; 85754; 85755

3262 Vitreous China Table & Kitchenware

Brown Forman Corp. (Louisville, KY) 68718; 68719
Lenox China (Oxford, NC) 75782; 75783
Lenox China Shop (Kinston, NC) 75325

3264 Porcelain Electrical Supplies

Coors Electronic Package Co. (Chattanooga, TN) 80343
General Electric Ceramics Inc. (Laurens, SC) 79593
General Electric Ceramics Inc. (Chattanooga, TN) 80410

3269 Pottery Products Nec

ACI (Benton, AR) 56770
Lenox China Shop (Oxford, NC) 75784; 75785

3271 Concrete Block & Brick

General Dynamics Corp. (Falls Church, VA) 90856
Lockheed Aeronautical Sys. Co. Charleston Adhesive Bond Plan (Charleston, SC) 78840
Lockheed Aeronautical Systems Co. (Charleston, SC) 78841
Lockheed Aeronautical Systems Co. (Clarksburg, WV) 92810
Lockheed Aeronautical Systems Co.-Charleston (Charleston, SC) 78842
Lockheed Aeronautical Systems Co.-Georgia (Afp 6) (Marietta, GA) 66822
Radio Shack (Berlin, MD) 71367
Shaw Industries Inc. (Dalton, GA) 65789

3272 Concrete Products Nec

Avon Corp. (Springfield, VA) 92273
Browning-Ferris Industries (Metarie, LA) 70337
Capco Pipe Co. Inc. (Birmingham, AL) 55178; 55179; 55180
GAF Building Materials Corp. (Mobile, AL) 56181
Shaw Industries Inc. (Dalton, GA) 65789
US Gypsum Co. (Nashville, TN) 82133
US Gypsum Co. (Bellaire, TX) 83272
Willamette Industries Inc. (Simsboro, LA) 70811

3273 Ready-Mixed Concrete

American Limestone Co. Inc. (Springfield, TN) 82354
APAC (Columbus, MS) 72702
General Dynamics Corp. (Falls Church, VA) 90856
Lone Star Industries Inc. (Pryor, OK) 77741
Vulcan Materials Co. (Chattanooga, TN) 80520
Vulcan Materials Co. (San Antonio, TX) 89296
Vulcan Materials Co. (Bristol, VA) 90492
Vulcan Materials Co. Mideast Div. (Winston Salem, NC) 76690

3274 Lime

American Limestone Co. (Springfield, TN) 82353
American Limestone Co. Inc. (Springfield, TN) 82354
General Dynamics Corp. (Falls Church, VA) 90856
US Gypsum Co. (Chamblee, GA) 65549
Vulcan Materials Co. (Iuka, MS) 72936
Vulcan Materials Co. (Blacksburg, SC) 78747
Vulcan Materials Co. (S. Pittsburg, TN) 82289
Vulcan Materials Midsouth (Franklin, TN) 80827

3275 Gypsum Products

Georgia Pacific Corp. (Wilmington, DE) 58064
Georgia Pacific Corp. (Miami, FL) 61317
Georgia Pacific Corp. (Tampa, FL) 63443
Georgia Pacific Corp. (Augusta, GA) 65332
Georgia Pacific Corp. (Brunswick, GA) 65410
US Gypsum Co. (Baltimore, MD) 71319
US Gypsum Co. (Kings Mountain, NC) 75311

3281 Cut Stone & Stone Products

APAC (Savannah, GA) 67445
Vulcan Materials Co. (Birmingham, AL) 55447
Vulcan Materials Co. (Dalton, GA) 65792
Vulcan Materials Co. (Fortson, GA) 66262
Vulcan Materials Co. (Kennesaw, GA) 66462
Vulcan Materials Co. (La Grange, GA) 66491
Vulcan Materials Co. (Lithia Springs, GA) 66591
Vulcan Materials Co. (Norcross, GA) 67209
Vulcan Materials Co. (Red Oak, GA) 67294
Vulcan Materials Co. (Stockbridge, GA) 67671
Vulcan Materials Co. (Pacolet, SC) 79782
Vulcan Materials Co. (Maryville, TN) 81428
Vulcan Materials Co. (Brownwood, TX) 83391
Vulcan Materials Co. (Millsap, TX) 88104
Vulcan Materials Co. (San Antonio, TX) 89296

3291 Abrasive Products

Litton Industrial Automation Disc Abrasives Grinders (Calhoun, GA) 65468
Litton Industrial Automation Disc Grinders & Abrasives (Calhoun, GA) 65469
Safety Kleen Corp. (Wheatland, OK) 78251
3M Co. (High Point, NC) 75173

3292 Asbestos Products

Allied-Signal Automotive (Cleveland, TN) 80564
Allied-Signal Inc. Bendix Friction Materials (Cleveland, TN) 80565
Capco Pipe Co. (Van Buren, AR) 57688
Capco Pipe Co. Inc. (Birmingham, AL) 55178; 55180
Capco Pipe Co. Inc. (Van Buren, AR) 57689

3295 Minerals—Ground or Treated

American Cyanamid Co. (Andersonville, GA) 64147
APAC (Columbus, MS) 72702
APAC (Greenville, MS) 72789
APAC (Jackson, MS) 72945
APAC (Tulsa, OK) 77879
Eagle Picher Industries Specialty Materials Div. (Quapaw, OK) 77757
Engelhard Corp. (Attapulgus, GA) 65307
Engelhard Corp. (Gordon, GA) 66306
Engelhard Corp. (Jackson, MS) 72980
Great Lakes Research Corp. (Elizabethton, TN) 80768
Lone Star Lead Construction (Houston, TX) 86493
M-I Drilling Fluids, Brownsville (Brownsville, TX) 83367; 83368
M-I Drilling Fluids Brownsville (Galveston, TX) 85450
M-I Drilling Fluids Co. Brownsville (Brownsville, TX) 83369
M-I Drilling Fluids Co. Galveston (Galveston, TX) 85451
M-I Drilling Fluids Co. New Orleans (New Orleans, LA) 70522
M-I Drilling Fluids Co. Westlake Grinding Plant (Westlake, LA) 70964
M-I Drilling Fluids New Orleans (New Orleans, LA) 70523
M-I Drilling Fluids, Westlake (Westlake, LA) 70965
Martin Marietta Aggregates (Lemon Springs, NC) 75361
Millpark Drilling Fluids Inc. (Houma, LA) 69961
Millpark Drilling Fluids Corpus Christi Barite Grinding (Corpus Christi, TX) 83733
Millpark Drilling Fluids Galveston Barite Grinding Fac (Galveston, TX) 85453
Millpark Drilling Fluids (Grinding Facility) (New Orleans, LA) 70536
Millpark Drilling Fluids (Grinding Facility) (Corpus Christi, TX) 83734
Millpark Drilling Fluids (Grinding Facility) (Galveston, TX) 85454
Millpark Drilling Fluids New Orleans Barite Grmdg. Fac. (New Orleans, LA) 70537
Millpark Drlg. Fluids (Corpus Christi Barite Grinding Facility) (Corpus Christi, TX) 83735
Millpark Drlg. Fluids (New Orleans Barite) Grinding Faci (New Orleans, LA) 70538
Mobil Mining & Minerals Co. (Wauchula, FL) 63828
3M Co. (Little Rock, AR) 57316
Union Carbide Corp. (Anmoore, WV) 92660
Vulcan Materials Co. (Birmingham, AL) 55447
Vulcan Materials Co. (Calera, AL) 55499
Vulcan Materials Co. (Fairfield, AL) 55719
Vulcan Materials Co. (Iuka, MS) 72936
Vulcan Materials Co. (Henderson, NC) 75029
Vulcan Materials Co. (Hendersonville, NC) 75044
Vulcan Materials Co. (North Wilkesboro, NC) 75767
Vulcan Materials Co. (Blacksburg, SC) 78747
Vulcan Materials Co. (Liberty, SC) 79612
Vulcan Materials Co. (Pacolet, SC) 79781
Vulcan Materials Co. (Piedmont, SC) 79798
Vulcan Materials Co. (Chattanooga, TN) 80520
Vulcan Materials Co. (Brownwood, TX) 83391
Vulcan Materials Co. (Millsap, TX) 88104
Vulcan Materials Co. (Voca, TX) 89924
Vulcan Materials Co. Mideast Div. (Winston Salem, NC) 76690
W.R. Grace & Co. Construction Products Div. (Pompano Beach, FL) 62646
W.R. Grace & Co.-Conn. Cpd (Pompano Beach, FL) 62647

3296 Mineral Wool

Aqua Glass Corp. Main Plant (Adamsville, TN) 80142
Armstrong World Ind. Inc. (Macon, GA) 66652
Armstrong World Industries Inc. (Mobile, AL) 56141
Armstrong World Industries Inc. (Macon, GA) 66653
GAF Building Materials Corp. (Baltimore, MD) 71155
GAF Building Materials Corp. (Nashville, TN) 82015
Manville Sales Corp. (Winder, GA) 68061
Manville Sales Corp. (Cleburne, TX) 83576
Manville Sales Corp. (Vienna, WV) 93078
Owens Corning (Conroe, TX) 83672
Owens-Corning Fiberglas Corp. (Fort Smith, AR) 57077
Owens-Corning Fiberglas Corp. (Fairburn, GA) 66177
Owens-Corning Fiberglas Corp. (Memphis, TN) 81662
Owens-Corning Fiberglas Corp. (Waxachachie, TX) 89992
Owens-Corning Fiberglass (Fairburn, GA) 66178
Owens-Corning Fiberglass Corp. (Waxahachie, TX) 89998
Schuller International Inc. (Cleburne, TX) 83588
Schuller Manufacturing Corp. (Vienna, WV) 93079
US Gypsum Co. (Dallas, TX) 84480
USG Interiors Inc. (Birmingham, AL) 55444
Vulcan Materials Co. (Birmingham, AL) 55447

3297 Nonclay Refractories

Harbison-Walker Refractories Dresser Industries Inc. (Calhoun, GA) 65467
Permatech Inc. (Graham, NC) 74750; 74751

3299 Nonmetallic Mineral Products Nec

A.P. Green Industries Inc. (Pryor, OK) 77737
Armstar (Lenoir City, TN) 81318; 81319
Ceramx Corp. (Laurens, SC) 79588
Chi-Vit Corp. (Leesburg, AL) 56111
Federal Mogul Corp. (Summerton, SC) 79979

3300 Primary Metal Industries

Asarco Inc. Amarillo Plant (Amarillo, TX) 82523
Assured Castings Corp. (Rogersville, TN) 82270
Gorham Bronze (Aiken, SC) 78649
Reynolds Metals Co. Bellwood Development Center (Richmond, VA) 91987
Rockwell International Corp. Russellville Plant Measurement (Russellville, KY) 69262
Sunbean Outdoor Prods. (Paragould, AR) 57497

3310 Blast Furnace & Basic Steel Products

Nucor Corp. Nucor Steel Div. (Jewett, TX) 87441

3312 Blast Furnaces & Steel Mills

Allegheny Ludlum Corp. (Norcross, GA) 67091
Allegheny Ludlum Corp. (Claremore, OK) 76944; 76945
Allegheny Ludlum Corp. Tubular (Claremore, OK) 76946
Armco Ashland Works West Works (Ashland, KY) 68084
Armco Stainless & Alloy Prods. (Baltimore, MD) 71040
Armco Stainless & Alloy Products (Baltimore, MD) 71041; 71042
Armco Steel Co. L.P. Coke Plant (Ashland, KY) 68085
Armco Steel Co. L.P. Grey Iron Foundry (Ashland, KY) 68086
Armco Steel Co. L.P. West Works (Ashland, KY) 68087; 68088
Armco Steel Co. LP (Ashland, KY) 68089
Armco Steel Co. LP (Dallas, TX) 83858
Armco Steel Inc. (Brentwood, TN) 80215
Baltimore Specialty Steele Corp. (Houston, TX) 85860
Baltimore Specialty Steele Corps. (Baltimore, MD) 71059
Baltimore Specialty Steels Corp. (Baltimore, MD) 71060
Bethlehem Steel Corp. Sales OFC (Jacksonville, FL) 60230
Bethlehem Steel Corp. (Baltimore, MD) 71065
Bethlehem Steel Corp. (Columbia, SC) 78976
Bethlehem Steel Corp. (Brentwood, TN) 80218
Bethlehem Steel Corp. (Houston, TX) 85875
Bethlehem Steel Corp. Sparrows Point Div. (Sparrows Point, MD) 72466
Bethlehem Steel Corp. Sparrows Point Plant (Sparrows Point, MD) 72468
C-K Co. (South Boston, VA) 92245
Chaparral Steel Co. (Midlothian, TX) 88100
Cooper Steel (Greenville, MS) 72794
Copper Steel Co. (Greenville, MS) 72795
Eastern Stainless Corp. (Baltimore, MD) 71111
Empire Detroit Steel Div. (Cary, NC) 73794
Griffin Wheel Co. (Bessemer, AL) 55092
Mobil Oil Corp. Chitwood Gas (Ninnekah, OK) 77244
National Steel Corp. (Houston, TX) 86611
Nucor Corp. (Darlington Sc, SC) 79158
Nucor Steel (Darlington, SC) 79154
Nucor Steel Texas Div. (Jewett, TX) 87442
Nucor Steel Arkansas (Blytheville, AR) 56810; 56810
Nucor-Yamato Steel Co. (Armorel, AR) 56725
Nucor-Yamato Steel Co. (Barfield, AR) 56739
Nucor-Yamato Steel Co. (Blytheville, AR) 56811
Quanex Co. Macsteel Division (Fort Smith, AR) 57086
Quanex Corp. Macsteel Div. (Fort Smith, AR) 57087; 57088
Sloss Industries Corp. Birmingham Facility (Birmingham, AL) 55391
Teledyne Allvac/Vasco (Richburg, SC) 79808
Uss Fairfield Works Fairfield Works (Fairfield, AL) 55717
USX Fairfield Works (Fairfield, AL) 55718
Weirton Steel Corp. (Antioch, TN) 80179
Wheeling-Pittsburgh Steel (Beech Bottom, WV) 92690
Wheeling-Pittsburgh Steel (Follansbee, WV) 92852
Wheeling-Pittsburgh Steel Corp. (Beech Bottom, WV) 92691
Wheeling Pittsburgh Steel Corp. (Wheeling, WV) 93123
Wheeling-Pittsburgh Steel Corp. Labelle (Wheeling, WV) 93124

3313 Electrometallurgical Products

Gibson Electric of Pr. Inc. Cce Plant No. 2 (Luquillo, PR) 78490
Kerr-Mcgee Chemical Corp. Electrolytic Plant (Hamilton, MS) 72886
Quanex Corp. Macsteel Div. (Fort Smith, AR) 57088

3315 Steel Wire & Related Products

Adcom Wire Co. (Jacksonville, FL) 60159; 60159
Adcom Wire Co. (Nicholasville, KY) 69147; 69148; 69149; 69150; 69151
Alcoa Fujikura Ltd. (Brentwood, TN) 80213; 80214
Delta Wire Corp. (Clarksdale, MS) 72673
Goodyear Tire & Rubber Co. (Randleman, NC) 75990
Itw Paslode (Covington, TN) 80685
Teledyne Allvac/Vasco S. Boston Plant (South Boston, VA) 92259
Wheeling Corrugating Co. (Wheeling, WV) 93122

3316 Cold-Finishing of Steel Shapes

Armco Steel Co. LP (Ashland, KY) 68089
Bethlehem Steel Corp. Sparrows Point Div. (Sparrows Point, MD) 72466
Bethlehem Steel Corp. Sparrows Point Plant (Sparrows Point, MD) 72468
North American Stainless (Ghent, KY) 68389
Wheeling Pittsburgh Steel Corp. (Beech Bottom, WV) 92692
Wheeling Pittsburgh Steel Corp. (Wheeling, WV) 93123
Worthington Steel Co. (Baltimore, MD) 71329

3317 Steel Pipe & Tubes

Allegheny Ludlum Corp. Tubular (Claremore, OK) 76946
Armco Tex-Tube Div. (Houston, TX) 85812; 85815
Armco Advanced Materials Corp. (Wildwood, FL) 63914
Black & Decker Corp. True Temper Sports (Amory, MS) 72583
Camdel Metals Corp. (Camden, DE) 57756
Eaton International Corp. (Wilmington, DE) 58056
Quanex Corp. Gulf States Tube (Rosenberg, TX) 88833
Quanex Gulf States Tube (Rosenberg, TX) 88834
Tandy Wire & Cable (Fort Worth, TX) 85319
True Temper Sports Division (Amory, MS) 72589
True Temper Sports (Seneca, SC) 79866
Westinghouse Specialty (Round Rock, TX) 88859
Wheeling Pittsburgh Steel Corp. (Wheeling, WV) 93123

3321 Gray & Ductile Iron Foundries

American Standard Inc. (Louisville, KY) 68687; 68688
Bartlett-Collins (Sapulpa, OK) 77788
Cast Products Co. Inc. (Westminster, SC) 80115
Griffin Pipe Products Co. (Lynchburg, VA) 91256; 91258
Jacobs Manufacturing Co. (Bridgeport, AL) 55485
Manville Sales Corp. (Laurinburg, NC) 75354
Mueller Co. (Albertville, AL) 54968
Pryor Fndy. Inc. (Pryor, OK) 77746
Pryor Foundry Inc. (Pryor, OK) 77747
US Pipe & Foundry Co. (Chattanooga, TN) 80515
US Pipe & Foundry Co. Chattanooga Valve & Fittings (Chattanooga, TN) 80516

3322 Malleable Iron Foundries

Wheelabrator Corp. (Walterboro, SC) 80080

3324 Steel Investment Foundries

Chromalloy Castings Miami Corp. (Miami, FL) 61228
FMC Corp., Anniston Plant (Anniston, AL) 54999
Rmc Corp. Anniston Plant (Anniston, AL) 55011

3325 Steel Foundries Nec

Bellinger Shipyard (Jacksonville, FL) 60228
Cooper Industries Flow Control Div. (Richmond, TX) 88794; 88795
FMC Corp. (Anniston, AL) 54998
FMC Corp. Anniston Plant (Anniston, AL) 54999
Griffin Wheel Co. (Bessemer, AL) 55092; 55093
Griffin Wheel Co. Bessemer Plant (Bessemer, AL) 55094
Jacobs Manufacturing Co. (Bridgeport, AL) 55485
OMC Industries Inc. (Bryan, TX) 83399
Rmc Corp. Anniston Plant (Anniston, AL) 55011
Wheelabrator Corp. (Walterboro, SC) 80080

3331 Primary Copper

Asarco Inc. (Amarillo, TX) 82520
Asarco Inc. Amarillo Copper Refinery (Amarillo, TX) 82521
Asarco Inc. Amarillo Plant (Amarillo, TX) 82522
Asarco Inc. El Paso (El Paso, TX) 84760; 84761
Phelps Dodge Copper Products (El Paso, TX) 84876
Phelps Dodge Refining Corp. (El Paso, TX) 84877
Phelps Dodge Refining Corp. El Paso Works (El Paso, TX) 84878

3334 Primary Aluminum

Alcoa (Badin, NC) 73648; 73649
Alcoa (Alcoa, TN) 80148
Alcoa (Rockdale, TX) 88812; 88813
Alcoa Badin Works (Badin, NC) 73650
Alcoa Rockdale Works (Rockdale, TX) 88814
Alcoa Rockdale Works (Sandow, TX) 89348
Alcoa Tennessee Operations (Alcoa, TN) 80149
Alumax Inc. (Norcross, GA) 67095
Aluminum Co. of America (Mobile, AL) 56130; 56131
Aluminum Co. of America (Benton, AR) 56771
Aluminum Co. of America (Badin, NC) 73651
Aluminum Co. of America (Alcoa, TN) 80150
Aluminum Co. of America (Rockdale, TX) 88816
Aluminum Co. of America Badin Works (Badin, NC) 73652; 73653
Kaiser Aluminum & Chemical (Baton Rouge, LA) 69565
Maxxam Inc. (Houston, TX) 86524
R. J. Reynolds Tobacco Co. Archer 200 (Winston-Salem, NC) 76739
Raw Materials & Reduction Plant (Gramercy, LA) 69898
Reynolds Metals Co. Listerhill Reduction (Muscle Shoals, AL) 56405
Reynolds Metals Co. Listerhill Reduction (Sheffield, AL) 56560; 56561
Reynolds Metals Co. Transition Laboratory (Richmond, VA) 91991

3339 Primary Nonferrous Metals Nec

Asarco Inc. (Corpus Christi, TX) 83701
Asarco Inc. (El Paso, TX) 84759
Browning-Ferris Industries (Capital Heights, MD) 71499
Browning-Ferris Industries Inc. (Hyattsville, MD) 71955
Eagle Picher Ind. Inc. Electro-Optic Materials Dept. (Quapaw, OK) 77754
Eagle Picher Ind. Inc. Electro-Optics Mat. 1 (Quapaw, OK) 77755
Eagle-Picher Ind. Inc. Electro-Optics Materials Dept. (Quapaw, OK) 77756
Eagle-Picher Industries Inc. (Quapaw, OK) 77758
Eagle-Picher Specialty Materials (Quapaw, OK) 77763
Federated Metals Corp. (Sand Springs, OK) 77780
GTE Kentucky Carbide (Madisonville, KY) 69056
Phelps Dodge Refining Corp. (El Paso, TX) 84877
Phelps Dodge Refining Corp. El Paso Works (El Paso, TX) 84878

3341 Secondary Nonferrous Metals

Alabama Reclamation Plant (Sheffield, AL) 56544; 56545
Alabama Reclamation Plant Alabama Reclamation Plant (Sheffield, AL) 56546
Aluminum Co. of America (Alcoa, TN) 80150
Asarco Inc. (Corpus Christi, TX) 83701
Ball Corp. Zinc Products Div. (Greeneville, TN) 80882; 80883
Culp Smelting & Refining Co. (Steele, AL) 56571
Eagle Picher Ind. Inc. Electro-Optic Materials Dept. (Quapaw, OK) 77754
Eagle Picher Ind. Inc. Electro-Optics Mat. 1 (Quapaw, OK) 77755
Eagle-Picher Ind. Inc. Electro-Optics Materials Dept. (Quapaw, OK) 77756
Engelhard Corp. (Seneca, SC) 79856
Engelhard Corp. Catalysts & Chemicals Div. (Seneca, SC) 79858
Freeport-McMoran Copper & Gold Co., Inc. (New Orleans, LA) 70461
Nucor Corp. Vulcraft Div. (Grapeland, TX) 85655
Reynolds Metals Co. (Sheffield, AL) 56557
Reynolds Metals Co. (Richmond, VA) 91983
Reynolds Metals Co. Alabama Reclamation Plant (Sheffield, AL) 56558
Reynolds Metals Co. Bellwood Reclamation Plant (Richmond, VA) 91988
Tifton Aluminum Co., Inc. (Delhi, LA) 69825
Vulcan Materials Co. (Baltimore, MD) 71323

3351 Copper Rolling & Drawing

Essex Group Inc. (Lithonia, GA) 66593
General Cable Corp. (Lawrenceburg, KY) 68505
Hudson International Conductors (Trenton, GA) 67842
Hudson International Conductors (Inman, SC) 79534
Phelps Dodge Copper Products (El Paso, TX) 84876
Westinghouse Electric (Abingdon, VA) 90159

3353 Aluminum Sheet, Plate & Foil

Alcoa Tennessee Operations (Alcoa, TN) 80149
Alumax Inc. (Norcross, GA) 67095
Decatur Aluminum Co. (Decatur, AL) 55577
Golden Aluminum Co. (Elmendorf, TX) 84991
Hot Spring Continuous Rolling Plant (Jones Mills, AR) 57204
Reynolds Metal Co. Alloys Plant (Sheffield, AL) 56555
Reynolds Metals Co. (Jones Mills, AR) 57206
Reynolds Metals Co. (Richmond, VA) 91984
Reynolds Metals Co. Alloys Plant (Muscle Shoals, AL) 56404
Reynolds Metals Co. Alloys Plant (Sheffield, AL) 56559
Reynolds Metals Co. Hot Spring Cont. Rolling Plant (Jones Mills, AR) 57207
Reynolds Metals Co. Plant 44 (Richmond, VA) 91990
Reynolds Metals Co. Plant 1 (Louisville, KY) 68991

3354 Aluminum Extruded Products

Alumax Extrusions Inc. (Plant City, FL) 62534
Alumax Extrusions Inc. (Hernando, MS) 72902
Alumax Inc. (Norcross, GA) 67095
American Cyanamid Co. (Havre De Grace, MD) 71915
El Campo Aluminum Co. (El Campo, TX) 84746; 84747
Fabricated Prods. Plant (Sherman, TX) 89395
Fruehauf Trailer Corp. (Decatur, AL) 55583

Halethorpe Extrusions Inc. (Baltimore, MD) 71164
Kaiser Aluminum & Chemical Corp. (Sherman, TX) 89401
Kawneer Co. Inc. (Jonesboro, GA) 66380
Reynolds Aluminum Bellwood Extrusion Plant (Richmond, VA) 91979
Reynolds Bellwood Extrusion Plant (Richmond, VA) 91980
Reynolds Metals Co. (Louisville, KY) 68987; 68988
Reynolds Metals Co. Plant 15 (Louisville, KY) 68990
Reynolds Metals Extrusion Div. (Richmond, VA) 91992
Texas Engineered Products (El Paso, TX) 84947
Tifton Aluminum Co., Inc. (Tifton, GA) 67831
Tifton Aluminum Co., Inc. (Delhi, LA) 69825
Tredegar Industries Inc. (Richmond, VA) 92060
William L. Bonnell Co. Inc. (Newnan, GA) 67087
William L. Bonnell Co., Inc. (Carthage, TN) 80279

3355 Aluminum Rolling & Drawing Nec

Alcoa (Rockdale, TX) 88812; 88813
Alcoa Tennessee Operations (Alcoa, TN) 80149
Conductor Products Inc. (Scottsville, TX) 89354
Decatur Aluminum Co. (Decatur, AL) 55577
Flour City Architectural (Johnson City, TN) 81037

3356 Nonferrous Rolling & Drawing Nec

Ball Corp. Zinc Products Div. (Greeneville, TN) 80882; 80883
General Electric Co. (Wilmington, NC) 76573
Martin Marietta US Doe Y-12 Plant (Oak Ridge, TN) 82196
Teledyne Allvac/Vasco (Monroe, NC) 75592
Teledyne Allvac/Vasco (Richburg, SC) 79808
Tesco Hi-Lift Inc. (Davie, FL) 59160
Westinghouse Specialty (Round Rock, TX) 88859

3357 Nonferrous Wiredrawing & Insulating

Alcoa Fujikura Ltd. (Brentwood, TN) 80213; 80214
At&T (Norcross, GA) 67098
At&T Network Systems (Norcross, GA) 67099
Belden Automotive Wire & Cable (Dumas, AR) 56909; 56910
Belden/Copper Industries Franklin Plant (Franklin, NC) 74623
Belden Wire & Cable (Clinton, AR) 56855
Belden Wire & Cable (Monticello, KY) 69097
Belden Wire & Cable Tompkinsville (Tompkinsville, KY) 69315
Capital Wire & Cable (Newport, AR) 57447
Centrilift Cable (Claremore, OK) 76950
Cooper Industries Inc. Belden Div. (Tompkinsville, KY) 69316
Dixie Wire Co. (Nashville, TN) 81936; 81937
Essex Group Inc. (Bennettsville, SC) 78725
General Cable Corp. (Bonham, TX) 83312
Guardian Products (Watkinsville, GA) 68024
Hudson International Conductors (Trenton, GA) 67842
Magnetek (Gallman, MS) 72782
Magnetek Universal Manufacturing (Gallman, MS) 72783
Molex Inc. (N. Little Rock, AR) 57438
Nichols Wire Inc. (Florence, AL) 55740
Phelps Dodge Magnet Wire Co. (Hopkinsville, KY) 68483; 68484
Reynolds Metal Co. Malvern Cable Plant (Jones Mills, AR) 57205
Reynolds Metals Co. Malvern Cable Plant (Jones Mills, AR) 57208
Siecor Corp. (Hickory, NC) 75100

Spd Magnet Wire Co. (Edmonton, KY) 68271
Tandy Cable Products (Fort Worth, TX) 85308
Tandy Wire Fabrication (Fort Worth, TX) 85320
Tandy Wire & Specialty Cable (Fort Worth, TX) 85321
Westinghouse Electric (Abingdon, VA) 90159
Westinghouse Electric Corp. (Abingdon, VA) 90160
Westinghouse Electric Corp. Wire Div. (Abingdon, VA) 90161

3363 Aluminum Die-Castings

General Electric Lighting Systems (Hendersonville, NC) 75040
Harvard Industries Diecast Div. (Ripley, TN) 82254
Harvard Industries Inc. Diecasting (Ripley, TN) 82256
Hayes Albion Corp. Diecasting (Ripley, TN) 82257
Prescolite (El Dorado, AR) 56957
SCI Manufacturing Inc. (Laceys Spring, AL) 56097
True Temper Sports Division (Olive Branch, MS) 73232

3364 Nonferrous Die-Castings Except Aluminum

Bird-Johnson Co. (Mobile, AL) 56143
Bird-Johnson Co. (Pascagoula, MS) 73251
Gamco Prods. Co. (Henderson, KY) 68449
Gamco Products Co. (Henderson, KY) 68449
Hayes Albion Corp. Diecasting (Ripley, TN) 82257

3365 Aluminum Foundries

OMC Industries Inc. (Bryan, TX) 83399
Omc Spruce Pine (Spruce Pine, NC) 76303

3366 Copper Foundries

OMC Industries Inc. (Bryan, TX) 83399
Reliance Electric Co. (Weaverville, NC) 76476

3369 Nonferrous Foundries Nec

Gencorp Aerojet (Jonesborough, TN) 81067
Harvard Industries Diecast Div. (Ripley, TN) 82254
Harvard Industries Diecasting (Ripley, TN) 82255
Harvard Industries Inc. Diecasting (Ripley, TN) 82256
Martin Marietta US Doe Y-12 Plant (Oak Ridge, TN) 82196

3398 Metal Heat Treating

FMC Corp. (Anniston, AL) 54998
Quanex Corp. Macsteel Div. (Fort Smith, AR) 57087; 57088
Roper Corp. (Swainsboro, GA) 67759
Stanley Works Stanley Tools Division (Cheraw, SC) 78926
Sts-Klock (Palm Beach Gardens, FL) 62274
Trico Ind. Inc. (Greenville, TX) 85680

3399 Primary Metal Products Nec

Alcoa (Rockdale, TX) 88812; 88813
Armco Steel Co. LP (Ashland, KY) 68089
Bada Co. (Bowling Green, KY) 68132
Belden Wire & Cable (Monticello, KY) 69096
Continental Industries Inc. (Tulsa, OK) 77922
Cooper Industries Belden Div. (Clinton, AR) 56856
Engineered Sintered Components Co. (Troutman, NC) 76408
Evtech (Charlotte, NC) 73944
Gaf Chemical Corp. (Huntsville, AL) 55943

Gaf Chemicals Corp. (Huntsville, AL) 55944; 55945
Greenback Industries, Inc. (Greenback, TN) 80877; 80878; 80879
Kaiser Aluminum & Chemical (Denison, TX) 84597
Reynolds Metals Co. (Sheffield, AL) 56557
Reynolds Metals Co. Plant 3 (Louisville, KY) 68992; 68993
Scm Metal Products Inc. (Research Triangle Park, NC) 76023
Teledyne (Huntsville, AL) 56032
Teledyne Wah Chang (Huntsville, AL) 56034

3400 Fabricated Metal Products

Anchor Hocking Packaging Co. Weirton Plant (Weirton, WV) 93086
Armco Inc. Tex Tube Div. (Houston, TX) 85816
Maremont Corp. (Pulaski, TN) 82244
Maremont Corp. Pulaski Plant (Pulaski, TN) 82245
Maxwell House Coffee Co. (Tarrant City, AL) 56604
Parker Hannifin Corp. Rac Div. (Longwood, FL) 60940
Trinity Industries Inc. East (Longview, TX) 87742

3410 Metal Cans & Shipping Containers

Crown Cork & Seal Co. (Fruitland, MD) 71758

3411 Metal Cans

Ball Corp. (Blytheville, AR) 56802
Ball Metal Container (Tampa, FL) 63329
Ball Metal Container (Williamsburg, VA) 92554
Ball Metal Container Group (Tampa, FL) 63330
Ball Metal Container Group (Williamsburg, VA) 92555
Ball Metal Container Operations (Tampa, FL) 63331
Ball Metal Container Operations (Williamsburg, VA) 92556
Ball Pack Prd. Grp. Conroe Plant (Conroe, TX) 83651
Ball Packaging Products Group Metal Container Div. (Williamsburg, VA) 92557; 92558
Ball Packaging Products Group Mcd (Williamsburg, VA) 92559
Ball Packaging Products Group Metal Container Operations (Conroe, TX) 83652
Ball Packaging Products Group Tampa Can Plant (Tampa, FL) 63332
Bayamon Can Co. (Toa Alta, PR) 78605; 78606
Colgate-Palmolive Co. Institutional Products Div. (Texarkana, TX) 89673
Continental Group Inc. (Houston, TX) 86012
Crown Beverage Packaging (Perry, GA) 67264
Crown Beverage Packaging (Longview, TX) 87711
Crown Beverage Packaging Inc. (Atlanta, GA) 64400
Crown Beverage Packaging Inc. (Perry, GA) 67265
Crown Beverage Packaging Inc. (Baltimore, MD) 71105
Crown Beverage Packaging Inc. (Longview, TX) 87712
Crown Beverage Packaging Inc. (Sugar Land, TX) 89531
Crown Beverage Packaging Inc. Plant 16 (Baltimore, MD) 71106
Crown Beverage Packaging Inc. Plant 24 (Hurlock, MD) 71951
Crown Cork De P.R. Inc. (Carolina, PR) 78373
Crown Cork De Puerto Rico Inc. (Carolina, PR) 78374; 78375
Crown Cork & Seal Co. Inc. (Atlanta, GA) 64401
Crown Cork & Seal Co. Inc. (Fruitland, MD) 71759
Crown Cork & Seal Co., Inc. (Batesville, MS) 72594; 72595
Crown Cork & Seal Co. Inc. (Arden, NC) 73564
Crown Cork & Seal Co. Inc. (Cheraw, SC) 78921
Crown Cork & Seal Co. Inc. (Spartanburg, SC) 79889
Crown Cork & Seal Co. Inc. (Abilene, TX) 82433
Crown Cork & Seal Co., Inc. (Conroe, TX) 83655
Crown Cork & Seal Co. Inc. (Winchester, VA) 92582
Crown Cork & Seal Co. Inc. Metals Div. (Plymouth, FL) 62576
Crown Cork & Seal Co. Inc. Winter Garden Can Div. (Winter Garden, FL) 63920
Crown Cork & Seal_Co. Inc. (Batesville, MS) 72596
Davies Can Co. (Fairdale, KY) 68300
Del Monte Foods Plants (Crystal City, TX) 83819
H. J. Heinz Pet Products Div. (Weirton, WV) 93089
H. J. Heinz Co. Heinz Pet Products Div. (Weirton, WV) 93090
Heekin Can Co. (Weirton, WV) 93091
Heekin Can, Inc. (Blytheville, AR) 56806
Heekin Can Inc. (Springdale, AR) 57632; 57633
Heekin Can Inc. (Dandridge, TN) 80713
Heekin Can Inc. (Newport, TN) 82169
Heinz Pet Prods. Weirton Plant (Weirton, WV) 93092
Kaiser Aluminum & Chemical (Jacksonville, FL) 60343
Latas De Aluminio Reynolds Inc. Reynolds Metals Co. (Guayama, PR) 78424
Metal Container Corp. (Gainesville, FL) 59894; 59895
Metal Container Corp. (Jacksonville, FL) 60375; 60376; 60377
Metal Container Corp. (Oklahoma City, OK) 77443; 77444
Miller Brewing Co. (Reidsville, NC) 76006
Miller Brewing Co. Container Div. (Reidsville, NC) 76007
Miller Brewing Co. Fort Worth Container Div. (Fort Worth, TX) 85191
Miller Brewing Co. Moultrie (Moultrie, GA) 67056
Miller Brewing Co. Moultrie Container Plant (Moultrie, GA) 67057; 67058
Reynolds Metal Co. (Tampa, FL) 63576
Reynolds Metals Co. (Salisbury, NC) 76173; 76174
Reynolds Metals Co. (Houston, TX) 86794; 86795
Reynolds Metals Co. (Bristol, VA) 90486
Reynolds Metals Co. Can Div. (Salisbury, NC) 76175
Reynolds Metals Co. Bristol End Plant (Bristol, VA) 90487
Reynolds Metals Co. Can Fabrication Plant (Richmond, VA) 91989
Reynolds Metals Co. Salisbury Can Plant (Salisbury, NC) 76176; 76177
Reynolds Metals Co. Tampa Can Plant (Tampa, FL) 63577
Sonoco Products Co. (Jackson, TN) 81002
Starkist Foods Inc. Pet Food Div. (Weirton, WV) 93100
Sunoco Products Co. (Orlando, FL) 62150
Del Monte Foods USA Plant 255 (Crystal City, TX) 83822
Van Dorn Co. (Fountain Inn, SC) 79250

3412 Metal Barrels, Drums & Pails

Blue Grass Cooperage Co. (Louisville, KY) 68703; 68705
Sonoco Fibre Drum Inc. (Charlotte, NC) 74162
Sonoco Semi-Bulk Packaging (Saraland, AL) 56519
Sonoco Semi-Bulk Packaging (Marietta, GA) 66918
Sonoco Semi-Bulk Packaging (Houston, TX) 86899; 86900
Sunoco Products Co. (Orlando, FL) 62150

3421 Cutlery

H. K. Porter/Wiss (Statesboro, GA) 67636
H.K. Porter/Wiss (Statesboro, GA) 67637

3423 Hand & Edge Tools Nec

Air Control Products (Roxboro, NC) 76120
Black & Decker Corp. True Temper Sports (Anderson, SC) 78668
Black & Decker US Inc. (Lutherville Timonium, MD) 72119
Black & Decker USA (Easton, MD) 71659
Cooper Industries Inc. Plumb Plant (Monroe, NC) 75573
Cooper Industries Inc. Weller Wire Wrap Plant (Cheraw, SC) 78919
Cooper Industries Weller/Wire Wrap Plt (Cheraw, SC) 78920
Crescent/Xcelite (Sumter, SC) 80017; 80018
Danaher Corp. (Washington, DC) 58209
Danaher Tool Group (Springdale, AR) 57628
Danaher Tool Group (Hanover, MD) 71909
Danaher Tool Group (Gastonia, NC) 74673
Danaher Tool Group Fayetteville Ar. Operation (Fayetteville, AR) 56974
Easco Hand Tools Inc. (Springdale, AR) 57629
Easco Hand Tools Inc. (Gastonia, NC) 74674
Eaton Air Controls Products (Roxboro, NC) 76123
Emhart Corp. (Baltimore, MD) 71112
Emhart Industries Inc. (Baltimore, MD) 71113
H.K. Porter/Wiss (Statesboro, GA) 67637
National Hand Tool Mechanics Tool Division (Farmers Branch, TX) 85033
Nicholson File (Cullman, AL) 55546
Snap-On Tools (Johnson City, TN) 81056
Snap On Tools Corp. (Elizabethton, TN) 80769
Snap On Tools Corp. (Johnson City, TN) 81057
Stanley Tools (Cheraw, SC) 78924
Stanley Tools (Shelbyville, TN) 82317
Stanley Works (Cheraw, SC) 78925
Stanley Works Mechanics Tool Division (Wichita Falls, TX) 90103
Stanley Works Stanley Tools Division (Cheraw, SC) 78926

3425 Saw Blades & Handsaws

American Emblem Tool Co. (Shelbyville, KY) 69270
Blount Inc. (Montgomery, AL) 56284
Nicholson Saw (Greenville, MS) 72809
Sabre Textron (Pontiac, SC) 79799

3429 Hardware Nec

Aeroquip Corp. (Gainesboro, TN) 80833
Allied-Signal Safety Restraint (Knoxville, TN) 81134
Collier Keyworth Co. (Liberty, NC) 75429
Corbin & Russwin Architectural (Clarksdale, MS) 72671
Corbin & Russwin Architectural Hardware (Clarksdale, MS) 72672
Dana Corp. Weatherhead Div. (Vinita, OK) 78223
Eaton Corp. Axle & Brake Div. (Gallatin, TN) 80841
Electrical Specialty Prods. Co. (Montevallo, AL) 56272
Emhart Corp. (Baltimore, MD) 71112
Emhart Industries Inc. (Baltimore, MD) 71113
Funk Manufacturing Inc/O D (N Little Rock, AR) 57402
Halliburton Geophysical Services Inc. (Houston, TX) 86260
Kentucky Fried Chicken (San Antonio, TX) 89052
Kwikset Corp. (Bristow, OK) 76871; 76872
Kwikset Corp. (Denison, TX) 84600; 84601
Leggett & Platt Inc. (Winchester, KY) 69346; 69347
Master Lock Co. (Auburn, AL) 55066
Medeco Security Locks Inc. (Salem, VA) 92219; 92220
Mueller Co. (Albertville, AL) 54968
National Cabinet Lock (Mauldin, SC) 79651
Pacer Industries Inc. (Pensacola, FL) 62454
Royal Development Co. (High Point, NC) 75167; 75168
Schlage Lock Co. (Rocky Mount, NC) 76102
Schrader Automotive Inc. (Monroe, NC) 75588
Stanley Works Stanley Hardware Division (Richmond, VA) 92047
Tipper Tie Inc. (Apex, NC) 73559

3431 Metal Sanitary Ware

American Standard Inc. (Louisville, KY) 68687; 68688
Continental Industries Inc. (Tulsa, OK) 77923
Kilgore Plumbing Products Inc. (Kilgore, TX) 87489

3432 Plumbing Fixtures Fittings & Trim

American Standard, Inc. (Paintsville, KY) 69216; 69217
Brass Craft Western Co. (Lancaster, TX) 87596
Dana Corp. Weatherhead Div. (Vinita, OK) 78223
Delta Faucet Co. (Chickasha, OK) 76921; 76922
Delta Faucet of Oklahoma (Chickasha, OK) 76923
Moen Inc. (New Bern, NC) 75730
Moen Inc. (Sanford, NC) 76199
Moen Inc. (Trent Woods, NC) 76404

3433 Heating Equipment Except Electric

Food Lion (Greensboro, NC) 74836
Food Lion (Hampton, VA) 91036
Trane Commercial Self-Contained Systems Business Unit (Macon, GA) 66718
Tranter Inc. (Edgefield, SC) 79186

3441 Fabricated Structural Metal

Anchor Metals Inc. Steel Structures Group (Anniston, AL) 54993
General Dynamics Corp. (Goose Creek, SC) 79282
Ingalls Shipbuilding Inc. (Pascagoula, MS) 73261; 73262
Latco, Inc.- Pro AG (Lincoln, AR) 57243
McDermott Marine Construction Fabricators Div. (Morgan City, LA) 70387
Mobil Steel Corp. (Houston, TX) 86603
Nucor Corp. Vulcraft Al. Div. (Fort Payne, AL) 55758
Nucor Corp. Vulcraft Div. (Fort Payne, AL) 55759; 55760
Sunbeam Outdoor Products (Waynesboro, GA) 68047
Thomas & Betts Anchor Metals Steel Structures Group (Anniston, AL) 55017
Thomas & Betts Corp. Meyer Ind. (Houston, TX) 87026
Thomas & Betts Lancaster (Lancaster, SC) 79581
Trinity Industries Structural Steel Div. No. 32 (Montgomery, AL) 56389
Trinity Industries Trinity Structural Div. (Montgomery, AL) 56390
Trinity Industries Inc. Plant 32 (Montgomery, AL) 56391
Trinity Industries, Plant 77 Structural Steel Div. (Montgomery, AL) 56392
Trinity Industries_Inc. Structural Steel Plant 64 (Bainbridge, GA) 65374
Wheeling Corrugating Co. (Wheeling, WV) 93122

3442 Metal Doors, Sash & Trim

Alumax Inc. (Norcross, GA) 67095
Howard Industries Inc. (Miami, FL) 61331
PPG Industries Inc. (Knoxville, TN) 81242

3443 Fabricated Plate Work—Boiler Shops

Allied Industries Inc. (Houston, TX) 85770
Ametek Corp. Haveg Div. (Wilmington, DE) 57983
Babcock & Wilcox Co. (West Point, MS) 73475
Babcock & Wilcox Co. (Lynchburg, VA) 91222
Bac-Pritchard, Inc. (Baltimore, MD) 71046
Beaird Industries (Shreveport, LA) 70691
Brighton Corp. (Pine Bluff, AR) 57508
Cbi Na-Con (Houston, TX) 85939
Cbi Na-Con_Inc. (Houston, TX) 85940
Electro Mechanical Services (Miami, FL) 61279
FMP-Rauma Co. (Birmingham, AL) 55273
Glitsch International Inc. (Dallas, TX) 84093
Heil Co. (Athens, TN) 80189
Hudson Products Corp. (Beasley, TX) 83142
Ingalls Shipbuilding Inc. (Pascagoula, MS) 73261; 73262
O & M Manufacturing Co. (Houston, TX) 86623; 86624; 86625
Parkson Corp. (Pompano Beach, FL) 62613
Tranter Inc. (Wichita Falls, TX) 90116
Trinity Ind. Inc. (Longview, TX) 87740
Trinity Industries Inc. (Jacksonville, FL) 60479
Trinity Industries Inc. (Rocky Mount, NC) 76107
Trinity Industries Inc. (Denton, TX) 84642
Vickers (Decatur, AL) 55611
Waste Management Inc. (Lubbock, TX) 87795
Westinghouse Electric (Pensacola, FL) 62490
Westinghouse Electric Corp. Pensacola (Pensacola, FL) 62491
Wheeling Corrugating Co. (Statesville, NC) 76341
Wheeling Corrugating Co. Inc. (Louisville, KY) 69040
Worthington Cylinders Corp. (Claremore, OK) 76960

3444 Sheet Metal Work

Alumax Inc. (Norcross, GA) 67095
Armco Tex-Tube Div. (Houston, TX) 85814
Ball Metal Decorating & Services (Baltimore, MD) 71049
Broward Hurricane Panel Co. (Fort Lauderdale, FL) 59457
Emerson Electric Co. White-Rodger Div. (Harrison, AR) 57136
Power Systems (Lancaster, TX) 87601
Reynolds Metals Co. (Eastman, GA) 66162
Reynolds Metals Co. (Richmond, VA) 91982
SCI Manufacturing Inc. (Laceys Spring, AL) 56097; 56098
Scott Aviation (Monroe, NC) 75591
3M Co. (Guin, AL) 55821
Vapor Corp. (Montgomery, AL) 56395
Wheeling Corrugating Co. (Fort Payne, AL) 55764
Wheeling Corrugating Co. (Wilmington, NC) 76614
Wheeling Corrugating Co. (Houston, TX) 87195
White-Rodgers (Harrison, AR) 57146
White-Rodgers Harrison Air (Harrison, AR) 57147

3446 Architectural Metal Work

Alumax Inc. (Norcross, GA) 67095
Flour City Architectural Metals (Johnson City, TN) 81038
Louisville Ladder Corp. (Louisville, KY) 68871
Piper/Casepro (Clarendon, AR) 56847

3448 Prefabricated Metal Buildings

Alumax Inc. (Norcross, GA) 67095
Broward Hurricane Panel Co. (Fort Lauderdale, FL) 59457
Browning Ferris Industries Service Group Inc. (Mobile, AL) 56145
Brunswick Composites Defense Facility (Marion, VA) 91330
Brunswick Corp. (Marion, VA) 91331

3449 Miscellaneous Metal Work

American Electric (Southaven, MS) 73346
Broward Hurricane Panel Co. (Fort Lauderdale, FL) 59457
Leggett & Platt Sleeper Comp-O Nents (High Point, NC) 75146
Leggett & Platt Sleeper Components (High Point, NC) 75147
R. J. Reynolds Tobacco Co. Downtown (Winston-Salem, NC) 76740; 76741
SCI Manufacturing Inc. (Laceys Spring, AL) 56098
Star Manufacturing Co. (Oklahoma City, OK) 77561
Sweco Inc. (Florence, KY) 68342
Trico Ind. Inc. (Greenville, TX) 85680
Vapor Corp. (Montgomery, AL) 56395

3451 Screw Machine Products

Aeroquip Corp. (Lancaster, SC) 79566
Aeroquip Corp. (Gainesboro, TN) 80831; 80832
Aeroquip Corp. Industrial Products Div. (Gainesboro, TN) 80834
Anchor Swan Inc. (Easley, SC) 79177
Danaher Corp. (Washington, DC) 58209
Eaton Corp. (Roxboro, NC) 76124; 76125
Emerson Electric Co. White-Rodger Div. (Harrison, AR) 57136
Harvard Industries Inc. Anchor Swan (Easley, SC) 79181
Maremont Corp. (Pulaski, TN) 82244
Maremont Corp. Pulaski Plant (Pulaski, TN) 82245
Parker Hannifin (Boaz, AL) 55471
Parker Hannifin Corp. (Mooresville, NC) 75606
Parker Hannifin Corp. Instrumentation Connectors Div. (Huntsville, AL) 55987
Parker Hannifin Corp. Icd (Boaz, AL) 55472
Parker Hannifin Icd (Huntsville, AL) 55988
Stratoflex Inc. Aerospace & Military Div. (Fort Worth, TX) 85282
Torrington Co. (Honea Path, SC) 79531
United Technologies Automotive Engineered Systems Div. (Lexington, TN) 81344
United Technologies Automotive Inc. (Lexington, TN) 81345
White-Rodgers (Harrison, AR) 57146
White-Rodgers Harrison Air (Harrison, AR) 57147

3452 Bolts, Nuts, Rivets & Washers

The Black & Decker Corp. (Hampstead, MD) 71899
Black & Decker Corp. PO Fastenr Division (Hopkinsville, KY) 68474
Black & Decker Corp. Pop Fasteners (Hopkinsville, KY) 68475
Camcar Elk Creek Paycarl Prods. Div. Elk Creek Paycarl Products Division (Elk Creek, VA) 90741
Camcar Inc. Amsco Division (Wytheville, VA) 92634
Camcar/Textron Inc. Amsco Products Division (Wytheville, VA) 92635
Camcar/Textron Inc. Elk Creek Raycarl Products Division (Elk Creek, VA) 90742
Danaher Corp. (Washington, DC) 58209
Emhart Corp. (Baltimore, MD) 71112
Emhart Industries Inc. (Baltimore, MD) 71113
Huck International Inc. (Waco, TX) 89941; 89942
Huck Manufacturing Co. (Waco, TX) 89943
Huck Mfg. Co. (Waco, TX) 89944
Illinois Tool Works Inc. Shakeproof Div. (Russellville, KY) 69261
Itw Shakeproof Indl. Prods. Products (Mineral Wells, TX) 88110
ITW Shakeproof Industrial Products (Mineral Wells, TX) 88111
Parker-Kalon (Campbellsville, KY) 68182
Paslode Corp. (Pontotoc, MS) 73303
Textron Amsco Products Division (Wytheville, VA) 92647

3460 Metal Forgings & Stampings

Stylelander Metal Stamping Inc. (Verona, MS) 73450

3462 Iron & Steel Forgings

Allied Signal (Conway, SC) 79130
Anvil Products Inc. (Ft. Worth, TX) 85412
Cooper Industries Inc. Plumb Plant (Monroe, NC) 75573
Dana Corp. (Montgomery, AL) 56295
FMC Corp. (Anniston, AL) 54998
FMC Corp., Anniston Plant (Anniston, AL) 54999
Hackney Inc. (Ackerman, MS) 72582
Parker Hannifin Corp. Icd (Boaz, AL) 55472
Rmc Corp. Anniston Plant (Anniston, AL) 55011
Stanley Tools (Cheraw, SC) 78924
Trico Ind. Inc. (Greenville, TX) 85680

3463 Nonferrous Forgings

Intercontinental Mfg. Co. (Garland, TX) 85489
Kaiser Aluminum & Chemical Corp. Greenwood Forge (Greenwood, SC) 79455
Parker Hannifin Corp. Icd (Boaz, AL) 55472

3465 Automotive Stampings

Beck/Arnley Worldparts Corp. (Nashville, TN) 81899
Genuine Parts Co. Rayloc Div. (Stephenville, TX) 89516
Johnson Controls Inc. (Lexington, TN) 81338
Johnson Controls Inc. (Linden, TN) 81346
Johnson Controls Inc. (Pikeville, TN) 82228; 82229
Randall Textron (Grenada, MS) 72846
Randall Textron Inc. (Grenada, MS) 72847
Standard Products Co. (Lexington, KY) 68631

3466 Crowns & Closures

Anchor Hocking Packaging Weirton Plant 33 (Weirton, WV) 93085
H C Industries Inc. (Olive Branch, MS) 73228

3469 Metal Stampings Nec

American Cyanamid Co. (Havre De Grace, MD) 71915
Bonny Products Inc. (Washington, NC) 76452; 76453
Dana Corp. Arab Hydraulic Plant (Arab, AL) 55019
Electro Mechanical Services (Miami, FL) 61279
Flour City Architectural (Johnson City, TN) 81037
Hanson Porcelain Co. Inc. (Lynchburg, VA) 91259
Marathon Equipment Co. (Vernon, AL) 56699
Metal Container Corp. (Oklahoma City, OK) 77443; 77444
Parker Hannifin Corp. Copper Products Div. (Greenfield, TN) 80893
Prescolite (El Dorado, AR) 56957
Randall Textron Inc. (Blytheville, AR) 56814
Reynolds Metals Co. Plant 1 (Louisville, KY) 68991
Royal Development Co. (High Point, NC) 75169
Rubbermaid Office Products Inc. (Greenville, TX) 85676
Waste Management Inc. (Lubbock, TX) 87795

3470 Metal Services Nec

Dearborn Brass (Tyler, TX) 89797
Nelson Electric (Tulsa, OK) 78030

3471 Plating & Polishing

AMP Inc. (Gastonia, NC) 74653
AMP Inc. (Greensboro, NC) 74773
AMP Inc. (Harrisonburg, VA) 91065
Amp Inc. Building 67 (Winston-Salem, NC) 76703
Avon Lomalinda Inc. (San Sebastian, PR) 78582
Avon-Mirabella Inc. (Aguadilla, PR) 78290
Ball Corp. Zinc Products Div. (Greeneville, TN) 80882; 80883
Caribe G.E. Products Inc. Arecibo Plant (Arecibo, PR) 78312
Combustion Technologies Inc. (Flowery Branch, GA) 66217
Cooper Industries Flow Control Demco Plant (Oklahoma City, OK) 77339
Cooper Industries Inc. Oil Tool Div. (Oklahoma City, OK) 77340
Dearborn Brass (Tyler, TX) 89798
Delta Faucet Co. (Chickasha, OK) 76921
Gamco Prods. Co. (Henderson, KY) 68449
Gamco Products Co. (Henderson, KY) 68450
Goodyear Tire & Rubber Co. (Randleman, NC) 75990
Johnson Controls Inc. (Lexington, TN) 81338
Johnson Controls Inc. (Linden, TN) 81346
Johnson Controls Inc. (Pikeville, TN) 82228; 82229
Kirk Stieff Co. Kirk Stieff Division (Baltimore, MD) 71175
Maremont Corp. (Pulaski, TN) 82244
Maremont Corp. Pulaski Plant (Pulaski, TN) 82245
Michoud Assembly Facility (New Orleans, LA) 70535
Motorola Inc. Portable Products Div. (Plantation, FL) 62571
Pamcor Inc. (Rio Piedras, PR) 78544
Pamcor Inc. Las Piedras Plant (Las Piedras, PR) 78486
Parker Hannifin Hose Products Div. (Cleburne, TX) 83578
Parker Hannifin Corp. (Mooresville, NC) 75606
Parker Hannifin Corp. Hose Products Div. (Cleburne, TX) 83579
Parker Hannifin Corp. Icd (Boaz, AL) 55472
Precise Hard Chrome (Waco, TX) 89968
Randall Textron (Grenada, MS) 72846
Randall Textron Inc. (Blytheville, AR) 56814
Randall Textron Inc. (Grenada, MS) 72847
SCI Manufacturing Inc. (Laceys Spring, AL) 56097; 56098
Snap-On Tools Corp. (Elizabethton, TN) 80770
Stanley Proto Industrial Tools (Wichita Falls, TX) 90102
Stanley Tools (Cheraw, SC) 78924
Stanley Works Mechanics Tool Division (Wichita Falls, TX) 90103
Stanley Works Stanley Tools Division (Cheraw, SC) 78926
Sunbeam-Oster Household Products (Holly Springs, MS) 72910
Thomas & Betts Corp. (Gaffney, SC) 79266
Thomas Mfg. Co. Inc. (Thomasville, NC) 76385
Tifton Aluminum Co., Inc. (Delhi, LA) 69825
True Temper Sports Division (Amory, MS) 72589
True Temper Sports (Seneca, SC) 79865; 79866
United Chair Co. Irondale Plant (Irondale, AL) 56059
United Chair - Irondale Plant (Irondale, AL) 56060
Westinghouse De Pr, Inc. Interruptores Div. (Toa Baja, PR) 78613

3479 Metal Coating & Allied Services

Adcom Wire Co. (Jacksonville, FL) 60159; 60159
Baker Hughes Tubular Services (Amelia, LA) 69420
Baker Hughes Tubular Services (Houston, TX) 85850
Baker Hughes Tubular Services Inc. (Amelia, LA) 69421
Baker Hughes Vetco Services (Amelia, LA) 69422
Baker Hughes Vetco Services (Houston, TX) 85851
Ball Corp. Decorating & Service Div. (Baltimore, MD) 71047
Ball Corp. Metal Decorating & Service Div. (Trussville, AL) 56622; 56623; 56624
Ball Metal Decorating & Service (Baltimore, MD) 71048
Ceramx Corp. (Laurens, SC) 79588
Coast to Coast Coatings (Dothan, AL) 55634
Dow Chemical Co. (Russellville, AR) 57581
Dow Chemical Co. USA (Russellville, AR) 57582
E/M Corp. (Fort Worth, TX) 85106
E/M Corp. Fort Worth Div. Processing (Fort Worth, TX) 85107
Eagle-Picher Industries Inc. Wolverine Gasket Div. (Lisbon, FL) 60905
Eagle-Picher Industries Inc. Wolverine Gasket Div. Blacksburg Div. (Blacksburg, VA) 90437
Encoat-North Arlington, Inc. (Wilmington, DE) 58058
Energy Coatings Co. (Houston, TX) 86056
Evtech (Charlotte, NC) 73944
Ferro Corp. (Arlington, TX) 82654
Maxwell House Coffee Co. (Tarrant City, AL) 56604
Metal Forge Co. Protective Coatings Div. (Albemarle, NC) 73541
Michoud Assembly Facility (New Orleans, LA) 70535
Morton International Inc. (Decatur, AL) 55600
Morton International Inc. (Wytheville, VA) 92643
Permatech Inc. (Graham, NC) 74751
PPG Industries Inc. (Knoxville, TN) 81241
Precoat Metals (Channelview, TX) 83553
Rockwell International Corp. (Texarkana, AR) 57679
Roper Corp. (Swainsboro, GA) 67759
Sermatech International Inc. (Boynton Beach, FL) 58793
Sermatech International Inc. (Sugar Land, TX) 89543
Shannon Industries Inc. (Knoxville, TN) 81252
Sherwin-Williams Co. (Richmond, KY) 69250
Sigma Coatings Inc. (Harvey, LA) 69941
Signode Corp. (Baltimore, MD) 71307
Signode Eastern Ops. (Baltimore, MD) 71308
Signode Supply Corp. (Weirton, WV) 93099
Thomas & Betts Anchor Metals Steel Structures Group (Anniston, AL) 55017
Thomas & Betts Lancaster (Lancaster, SC) 79581
Tifton Aluminum Co., Inc. (Delhi, LA) 69825
Union Carbide Coating Service Corp. (Houston, TX) 87053
Union Carbide Coatings Service Corp. (Charlotte, NC) 74185
Union Carbide Corp. (Charlotte, NC) 74186
Valspar Corp. (New Orleans, LA) 70583

3480 Ordnance & Accessories Nec

Atlantic Research Corp. (Gainesville, VA) 90960

3482 Small Arms Ammunition

Blount Inc. (Montgomery, AL) 56284
Remington Arms Co. (Lonoke, AR) 57323

3483 Ammunition Except for Small Arms

Aerojet Heavy Metals Co. (Jonesborough, TN) 81063
Brunswick Corp. Defense Div. (De Land, FL) 59249
Danaher Tool Group (Gastonia, NC) 74673
Martin Marietta Milan Army Ammunition Plant (Milan, TN) 81770
Martin Marietta US Doe Y-12 Plant (Oak Ridge, TN) 82196
Trane Air Handling Systems Business Unit (Lexington, KY) 68644

3489 Ordnance & Accessories Nec

Aerojet Heavy Metals Co. (Jonesborough, TN) 81063
Brunswick Corp. (Camden, AR) 56827
Lewis Engineering Co. (Marshall, TX) 87857
McDonnell Douglas Astronautics Co. (Titusville, FL) 63696
McDonnell Douglas Missile Systems Co. (Titusville, FL) 63697
Valentec Dayron (Orlando, FL) 62175
Valentec Dayron Inc. (Orlando, FL) 62176
Valentec International Corp. Valentec Dayron Div. (Orlando, FL) 62177

3491 Industrial Valves

Automatic Switch Co. (Aiken, SC) 78644
Crane Co. (Rogers, AR) 57562
Emerson Electric Co. Alco Controls Div. (Wytheville, VA) 92637
Fisher Controls International Inc. (Mc Kinney, TX) 87910
Mueller Co. (Albertville, AL) 54968
Mueller Co. & ORG Chattanooga Plant (Chattanooga, TN) 80438
Txt a Brunswick Co. (Houston, TX) 87049

3492 Fluid Power Valves & Hose Fittings

American Standard Wabco Fluid Power Div. (Lexington, KY) 68520
American Standard Inc. Wabco Fluid Power Div. (Lexington, KY) 68521
Automatic Switch Co. (Aiken, SC) 78644
Eaton International Corp. (Wilmington, DE) 58056
Parker Hannifin Corp. (Madison, MS) 73137
Parker Hannifin Corp. (Mooresville, NC) 75606
Parker Hannifin Corp. Hose Products Div. (Cleburne, TX) 83579
Schrader Automotive Inc. (Monroe, NC) 75588
Stratoflex Inc. Aerospace & Military Div. (Fort Worth, TX) 85282
Vickers (Searcy, AR) 57610
Vickers Inc. (Searcy, AR) 57611

3493 Steel Springs Except Wire

Webster Spring Co. Inc. (Cameron, TX) 83440

3494 Valves & Pipe Fittings Nec

Aeroquip Corp. (Forest City, NC) 74599
Aeroquip Corp. (Middlesex, NC) 75557
American Electric (Athens, TN) 80185
American Standard Wabco Fluid Power Div. (Lexington, KY) 68520
American Standard Inc. Wabco Fluid Power Div. (Lexington, KY) 68521
Anvil Products Inc. (Longview, TX) 87701
Baker Oil Tools Inc. (Broken Arrow, OK) 76878
Cooper Industries Flow Control Div. (Missouri City, TX) 88127
Cooper Industries Flow Control Demco Plant (Oklahoma City, OK) 77339
Cooper Industries Inc. Flow Control Div. (Missouri City, TX) 88128
Cooper Industries Inc. Oil Tool Div. (Oklahoma City, OK) 77340
Dana Corp. (Sarasota, FL) 62808
Dana Corp. Mobile Fluid Controls Div. (Sarasota, FL) 62809; 62810
Dana Corp. Weatherhead Div. (Vinita, OK) 78223
Fisher Controls International Inc. (Mc Kinney, TX) 87911

FMC Corp. Fluid Control (Stephenville, TX) 89514
FMC Energy & Transmission Equipment Group (Houston, TX) 86201
Grinnell Corp. (Henderson, TN) 80907
Grinnell Corp. (Houston, TX) 86257
Mueller Co. & ORG Chattanooga Plant (Chattanooga, TN) 80438
Parker Hannifan Corp. (Forest City, NC) 74609
Parker Hannifan Corp. Instr. Valve Div. (Jacksonville, AL) 56072
Parker Hannifin (Boaz, AL) 55471
Parker-Hannifin Corp. (Forest City, NC) 74610
Parker Hannifin Corp. Cyl. Div. (Hillsborough, NC) 75189
Parker Hannifin Corp. Cylinder Div. (Hillsborough, NC) 75190
Parker Hannifin Corp. Instr Valve Div. (Jacksonville, AL) 56073
Parker Hannifin Corp. Instrumentation Valve Div. (Jacksonville, AL) 56074
Parker Hannifin Icd (Huntsville, AL) 55988
Rockwell International Corp. MF&C Div. (Sulphur Springs, TX) 89564
Schrader Bellows (Wake Forest, NC) 76433; 76434
Stratoflex Inc. Aerospace & Military Div. (Fort Worth, TX) 85282
Txt a Brunswick Co. (Houston, TX) 87049
Vickers (Searcy, AR) 57610
Wheeling-Machine Products Cooper Industries (Pine Bluff, AR) 57540

3495 Wire Springs

Grinnell Corp. (Henderson, TN) 80907
Maremont Exhaust Products, Inc. (Loudon, TN) 81354

3496 Miscellaneous Fabricated Wire Products

Bea Fasteners Inc. (Hamlet, NC) 74996
Blount Inc. (Montgomery, AL) 56285
Brunswick Corp. Technetics Division (De Land, FL) 59250
Clairson International Corp. (Ocala, FL) 61790
Comm/Scope Inc. (Catawba, NC) 73806
Itw Paslode (Augusta, AR) 56735
Itw Paslode (Pontotoc, MS) 73301
Layne & Bowler Inc. (Memphis, TN) 81642
Maryland Specialty Wire Inc. (Cockeysville, MD) 71550
Piper/Casepro (Clarendon, AR) 56847
Stanley-Bostitch Inc. Hamlet Plant (Hamlet, NC) 75001
Technetics Corp. Technetics Div. (De Land, FL) 59260
United Technologies Auto (Bennettsville, SC) 78733

3497 Metal Foil & Leaf

Golden Belt Manufacturing Co. (Reidsville, NC) 76001
Golden Belt Mfg. Co. (Reidsville, NC) 76002
Moen Inc. (Durham, NC) 74419
Reynolds Metals Co. Plant 1 (Louisville, KY) 68991
Richmond Foil Plant (Richmond, VA) 91993

3498 Fabricated Pipe & Fittings

Aeroquip Corp. Industrial Products Div. (Gainesboro, TN) 80834
Allegheny Ludlum Corp. (Claremore, OK) 76944
Ametek Inc. (Houston, TX) 85797
Brown & Root Inc. Marine Fabrication Yard (Houston, TX) 85895
Capco Pipe Co. Inc. (Birmingham, AL) 55178
Continental Industries (Broken Arrow, OK) 76880
Continental Industries Inc. (Tulsa, OK) 77922; 77924
Grinnell Corp. (Henderson, TN) 80907
Hackney Inc. (Enid, OK) 77053
Shaw Co/Benjamin F (Wilmington, DE) 58110
Shaw Industries Inc. (Prairieville, LA) 70651
Stratoflex Inc. Aerospace & Military Div. (Fort Worth, TX) 85282

3499 Fabricated Metal Products Nec

A. O. Smith Water Prods. Co. (El Paso, TX) 84754
Accuride Corp. (Henderson, KY) 68437
American Cyanamid Co. (Havre De Grace, MD) 71914
American Standard Wabco Fluid Power Div. (Lexington, KY) 68520
American Standard Inc. Wabco Fluid Power Div. (Lexington, KY) 68521
Ametek Corp. Haveg Div. (Wilmington, DE) 57983
Ametek Corp. US Gauge Div. (Bartow, FL) 58621
Ametek US Gauge (Bartow, FL) 58624
Avm Inc. (Marion, SC) 79639
Bristol Compressors Inc. (Bristol, VA) 90470
Carrier Corp. (Collierville, TN) 80617
Chace Precision Materials Group (Carolina, PR) 78372
Combustion Technologies Inc. (Flowery Branch, GA) 66217
Dana Corp. Arab Hydraulics (Arab, AL) 55020; 55021
Dana Corp. Arab Hydraulics Plant (Arab, AL) 55022
Diebold Inc. (Fayetteville, NC) 74545
Dow Chemical Co. (Russellville, AR) 57581
Dow Chemical Co. USA (Russellville, AR) 57582
Dresser Industries Inc. Guiberson Div. (Dallas, TX) 83985
General Electric Co. (Wilmington, NC) 76573
GTE Technical Products Div. (Reidsville, NC) 76004
GTE Prods. Corp. Kentucky Carbide (Madisonville, KY) 69057
Intercontinental Mfg. Co. (Garland, TX) 85489
Johnson Controls Inc. (Lexington, TN) 81338
Johnson Controls Inc. (Pikeville, TN) 82228; 82229
Kwikset Corp. (Denison, TX) 84600
Leggett & Platt Inc. (Lexington, NC) 75408
Leggett & Platt Inc. 0700 (Linwood, NC) 75446
Leggett & Platt Inc. 0701 (Lexington, NC) 75410
Loral American Beryllium Corp. (Tallevast, FL) 63293
Louisville Ladder Corp. (Louisville, KY) 68871
Martin Marietta Oak Ridge Y-12 Plant Dept. of Energy (Oak Ridge, TN) 82194
Martin Marietta US Doe Oak Ridge Y-12 Palnt (Oak Ridge, TN) 82195
Martin Marietta US Doe Y-12 Plant (Oak Ridge, TN) 82196
Michoud Assembly Facility (New Orleans, LA) 70535
New Industrial Techniques, Inc. (Coral Springs, FL) 59116
Owens Corning (Conroe, TX) 83672
Piper/Casepro (Clarendon, AR) 56847
Randall Textron Inc. (Blytheville, AR) 56814
Sears Roebuck & Co. (Fort Lauderdale, FL) 59610
Signode Corp. (Bel Air, MD) 71339
Signode Supply Corp. (Baltimore, MD) 71309
Sonoco Products Co. (Orlando, FL) 62144
Sonoco Products Co. (Henderson, KY) 68456
Stemco Inc. (Longview, TX) 87736
Structural Metals Inc. (Seguin, TX) 89375
Teledyne Packaging (Carrollton, KY) 68193
Teledyne Wirz (Carrollton, KY) 68194
Torrington Co. (Clinton, SC) 78963
True Temper Sports Division (Memphis, TN) 81719
True Temper Sports (Seneca, SC) 79865; 79866
Varo Inc. (Garland, TX) 85559
Varo Inc. Wds (Garland, TX) 85563
Varo Systems (Garland, TX) 85564
Waste Management Inc. (Lubbock, TX) 87795
Waterloo Industries Inc. (Pocahontas, AR) 57547; 57548; 57549
Worthington Cylinder Corp. (Claremore, OK) 76959
Worthington Cylinders Corp. (Columbus, GA) 65658

3500 Industrial Machinery & Equipment

Ametek Inc. Houston Instrument Div. (Austin, TX) 82816
Ametek Inc. Houston Instruments Div. (Austin, TX) 82817
Cooper Industries Gardner Denver M&C Div. (Roanoke, VA) 92120
Data General Corp. (Apex, NC) 73554
Hewlett-Packard Co. (Aguadilla, PR) 78294
Imprimis Technology Inc. (Oklahoma City, OK) 77387
International Business Machines Corp. (Boca Raton, FL) 58715
Seagate Technology Inc. (Oklahoma City, OK) 77552
Texas Instruments Inc. (Austin, TX) 83044
Texas Instruments Inc. (Lubbock, TX) 87788
W. R. Grace & Co. Connecticut Cryovac Div. (Duncan, SC) 79175

3511 Turbines & Turbine Generator Sets

AMBAC International (Columbia, SC) 78968
AMBAC International Corp. (Columbia, SC) 78970
Dana Corp. Mobile Fluid (Greenville, SC) 79334
General Electric Co. (Homewood, AL) 55869
General Electric Co. (Greenville, SC) 79361
General Electric Co. (Houston, TX) 86246
Solar Turbines Inc. (De Soto, TX) 84538
Solar Turbines Inc. (Houston, TX) 86898
Solar Turbines Inc. (Odessa, TX) 88279
Stewart & Stevenson SVC (Harvey, LA) 69942
Stewart & Stevenson SVC (Dallas, TX) 84402
Stewart & Stevenson SVC (Houston, TX) 86915; 86916; 86917
Westinghouse Electric (Pensacola, FL) 62490
Westinghouse Electric (Charlotte, NC) 74226
Westinghouse Electric (Rural Hall, NC) 76136
Westinghouse Electric (Houston, TX) 87190; 87191; 87192
Westinghouse Electric Corp. (Fort Payne, AL) 55762
Westinghouse Electric Corp. (Winston-Salem, NC) 76777
Westinghouse Electric Corp. Turbine Generator (Charlotte, NC) 74227
Westinghouse Electric Corp. Electrical Components Plant Electrical Components (Fort Payne, AL) 55763
Westinghouse Power Systems (Round Rock, TX) 88858

3519 Internal Combustion Engines Nec

AMBAC International Corp. (Columbia, SC) 78969
Briggs & Stratton Corp. (Murray, KY) 69119; 69120; 69121
Brunswick Corp. (Stillwater, OK) 77835
Brunswick Mercury Marine Plant 14 (Stillwater, OK) 77836
Caterpillar Inc. (Corinth, MS) 72735
Caterpillar Remanufactured Products Group (Corinth, MS) 72736
Consolidated Diesel Co. (Whitakers, NC) 76490; 76491
Cummins Engine Co. Inc. (Charleston, SC) 78798; 78799
Danaher Corp. (Washington, DC) 58209
Diesel Recon Co. (Memphis, TN) 81512
Lawn-Boy Oxford (Oxford, MS) 73242
Mercury Marine (Stillwater, OK) 77839
Mercury Marine Mercruiser Div. (Stillwater, OK) 77840
Mercury Marine Plant 14 (Stillwater, OK) 77841
OMC Burnsville (Burnsville, NC) 73768; 73769; 73770
Omc Calhoun (Calhoun, GA) 65472
Omc Lexington (Lexington, TN) 81342; 81343
Omc Rutherfordton (Rutherfordton, NC) 76145
ONAN Corp. (Huntsville, AL) 55982
Outboard Marine Corp. (Oxford, MS) 73243
Outboard Marine Corp. (Andrews, NC) 73549
Outboard Marine Corp. (Rutherfordton, NC) 76146
Pacolet Industrial Supply Co. (Pacolet, SC) 79780
Power Systems Diesel Inc. (Belle Chasse, LA) 69693
Stewart & Stevenson Inc. (Houston, TX) 86913
Stewart & Stevenson SVC (Houston, TX) 86916
Textron Lycoming (Greer, SC) 79485; 79486
Textron Lycoming Greer Plant (Greer, SC) 79487
Union Texas Petroleum (St. Bernard, LA) 70860

3523 Farm Machinery & Equipment

FMC Agricultural Machinery Div. (Jonesboro, AR) 57216
FMC Corp. (Jonesboro, AR) 57217
FMC Corp. Agricultural Machinery Div. (Jonesboro, AR) 57218
Meyer Machine Co. (San Antonio, TX) 89104
Power Systems (Lancaster, TX) 87601

3524 Lawn & Garden Equipment

Lawn-Boy Oxford (Oxford, MS) 73242
Outboard Marine Corp. (Oxford, MS) 73243
Roper Corp. (Swainsboro, GA) 67759
Roper Corp. Outdoor Power Equipment (Mc Rae, GA) 66966

3531 Construction Machinery

APAC (Fort Myers, FL) 59661
APAC Holdings, Inc. (Atlanta, GA) 64234
Blount Inc. (Montgomery, AL) 56284; 56285
Braden Carco Gearmatic (Broken Arrow, OK) 76879
Clark Equipment Co. (Statesville, NC) 76321
Clark-Hurth Components Box 38 (Statesville, NC) 76322
Corpane Industries Inc. (Jeffersontown, KY) 68493
Eagle-Picher Construction (Lubbock, TX) 87756
Eagle-Picher Ind. Inc. Construction Equipment Div. (Lubbock, TX) 87757
Eagle-Picher Industries Inc. Construction Equipment Div. (Lubbock, TX) 87759; 87760; 87761
Midland Brake Inc. (Paris, TN) 82222
Terex (Southaven, MS) 73357
Terex Corp. (Southaven, MS) 73358
Terex Corp. Koehring Cranes & Excavators (Chattanooga, TN) 80501
Terex Corp. Koehring Cranes & Excavators Koehring Cranes (Chattanooga, TN) 80502

3532 Mining Machinery

American LaFrance (Bluefield, VA) 90458
Baker Hughes Inc. (Houston, TX) 85835
Baker Hughes Mining Tools Inc. (Grand Prairie, TX) 85606; 85607
Baker Hughes Process Equip. Baker Hughes Mining Tools, Inc. (Grand Prairie, TX) 85608
Eimco Coal Machinery Inc. (Bolt, WV) 92705
Gardner Denver Mc (Roanoke, VA) 92155
GTE Valenite Corp. (Madisonville, KY) 69058; 69059
GTE Valenite Corp. (Chilhowie, VA) 90632
Ingersoll-Rand Co. (Roanoke, VA) 92158
J. H. Fletcher & Co. (Huntington, WV) 92876
Simmons-Rand Co. (Cedar Bluff, VA) 90512
Terex Corp. (Tulsa, OK) 78135
Terex Corp. Terex Unit Rig (Tulsa, OK) 78136
Trw Inc. Mission Drilling Products (Houston, TX) 87047

3533 Oil & Gas Field Machinery

Ajax-Superior Compressor Packaging Plant (Oklahoma City, OK) 77294
Atlas Wire Services (Houston, TX) 85824
Baker-CAC, Inc. Hughes Tool Div. B-1 Baker Hughes Drilling Equipment (Houston, TX) 85829
Baker Hughes Cac Div. (Oklahoma City, OK) 77303
Baker Hughes Inc. (Houston, TX) 85835
Baker Hughes Inc., Baker Hughes Drilling Technologies Baker Hughes Inteq (Houston, TX) 85837
Baker Hughes Inteq. (Oklahoma City, OK) 77304
Baker Hughes Mining Tools Inc. (Grand Prairie, TX) 85606
Baker Hughes Prod Tools Bakekr Sand Control (Houston, TX) 85841
Baker Hughes Prod. Tools Baker Oil Tools (Houston, TX) 85843
Baker Hughes Prod. Tools Baker Service Tools (Houston, TX) 85844
Baker Hughes Prod. Tools Centrilift (Claremore, OK) 76947
Baker Hughes Prod. Tools Centrilift (Houston, TX) 85845
Baker Hughes Prod. Tools Tri-State Oil Tools (Houston, TX) 85846
Baker Hughes Production Tools, Inc. (Houston, TX) 85847
Baker Oil Tool (Houston, TX) 85853
Baker Oil Tools (Houston, TX) 85854
Baker Oil Tools Inc. (Houston, TX) 85855
Baker Sand Control Houston Manufacturing (Houston, TX) 85858
Baker Sand Control Houston Mfg. (Houston, TX) 85859
Baker Sand Control Lafayette Manufacturing (Broussard, LA) 69743
Baker Sand Control Lafayette Mfg. (Broussard, LA) 69744
Centrilift Co. (Claremore, OK) 76951
Cooper Industries Inc. Oil Tool Div. (Ville Platte, LA) 70933
Dresser Industries Inc. Guiberson Div. (Dallas, TX) 83985
Eastman Christensen (Oklahoma City, OK) 77349
Eastman Teleco (Oklahoma City, OK) 77350
FMC Energy & Transmission Equipment Group (Houston, TX) 86201
Fmc Fluid Control Stephenville (Stephenville, TX) 89515
Gemoco (Houma, LA) 69956
Grace Energy Corp. (Dallas, TX) 84094
Halliburton Logging Services (Fort Worth, TX) 85127
Halliburton Logging Services Inc. (Houston, TX) 86262
Halliburton Services Davis Mfg. (Davis, OK) 76986
Halliburton Services Manufacturing (Duncan, OK) 76991
Halliburton Services Manufacturing Facility (Davis, OK) 76987
Halliburton Services Manufacturing Facility (Duncan, OK) 76992
Hughes Christensen Co. Hughes Tool Co. (Houston, TX) 86300; 86300
Hughes Diamond Products (Houston, TX) 86301
Hughes-Mpd (Houston, TX) 86302
Ltv Energy Products (Garland, TX) 85502
LTV Energy Products, Plant 1 (Garland, TX) 85504

LTV Energy Products, Plant 2 (Garland, TX) 85505
Matco Manufacturing (Houston, TX) 86521
McCullough, an Atlas Wireline Service Operation (Houston, TX) 86528
National-Oilwell (Houston, TX) 86609
Norris & O'Bannon (Tulsa, OK) 78033
Otis Engineering Corp. (Carrollton, TX) 83494; 83495
Rhone Poulenc Inc. (Vernon, TX) 89869
Sequa Corp. Gemoco (Houma, LA) 69970; 69971
Stewart & Stevenson Inc. (Houston, TX) 86913
Stewart & Stevenson SVC (Houston, TX) 86916
Subsea Venture Inc. (Houston, TX) 86919
Trw Inc. Mission Drilling Products (Houston, TX) 87047
Welex (Houston, TX) 87172
Westinghouse Power Systems (Round Rock, TX) 88858

3534 Elevators & Moving Stairways

Dover Elevator Co. (Louisville, KY) 68755
Dover Elevator Co. (Charlotte, NC) 73932
Dover Elevator Co. (Greensboro, NC) 74812
Dover Elevator Co. (Raleigh, NC) 75887
Dover Elevator Co. (Knoxville, TN) 81165
Dover Elevator Co. (Middleton, TN) 81764
Dover Elevator Co. (Norfolk, VA) 91514
Dover Elevator International Inc. (Horn Lake, MS) 72913
Dover Elevator International Inc. (Memphis, TN) 81513
Dover Elevator Systems Inc. (Horn Lake, MS) 72914
Meyer Machine Co. (San Antonio, TX) 89104
Miami Elevator Co. (Miami, FL) 61378
Miami Elevator Co. (Riviera Beach, FL) 62739
Otis Elevator Co. (Birmingham, AL) 55327
Otis Elevator Co. (Mobile, AL) 56216
Otis Elevator Co. (Fayetteville, AR) 56985
Otis Elevator Co. (Fort Smith, AR) 57074
Otis Elevator Co. (Tampa, FL) 63514
Otis Elevator Co. (Louisville, KY) 68934
Otis Elevator Co. (Alexandria, LA) 69396
Otis Elevator Co. (Metairie, LA) 70296
Otis Elevator Co. (Jackson, MS) 73027
Otis Elevator Co. (Oklahoma City, OK) 77460
Otis Elevator Co. (Tulsa, OK) 78037
Otis Elevator Co. (Anderson, SC) 78681
Otis Elevator Co. (Amarillo, TX) 82570
Otis Elevator Co. (Corpus Chrsti, TX) 83768
Otis Elevator Co. (Dallas, TX) 84286; 84287
Otis Elevator Co. (Galveston, TX) 85458
Otis Elevator Co. (Midland, TX) 88061
Otis Elevator Co. (Tyler, TX) 89820
Otis Elevator Co. (Huntington, WV) 92887

3535 Conveyors & Conveying Equipment

Boeing Co. Inc (Dallas, TX) 83883
FMC Corp. (Tupelo, MS) 73400
FMC Corp., Tupelo Plant (Tupelo, MS) 73401
Litton Industrial Unit Handling Systems Div. (Hebron, KY) 68430
Litton Industrial Automation Systems Automated Systems Div. (Hebron, KY) 68431
Litton Industrial Automation Systems Engineered Systems Div. (Florence, KY) 68321

Litton Industrial Contracting (Florence, KY) 68322
Litton Material Handling Systems (Hebron, KY) 68323
Logan Guildepath (Louisville, KY) 68870
Process Conveyors (Salisbury, NC) 76172
Stock Equipment Co. (Lynn Haven, FL) 60957

3537 Industrial Trucks & Tractors

Blount Inc. (Montgomery, AL) 56285
Clark Equipment Co. (Hurst, TX) 87271
Clark Material Handling Co. (Danville, KY) 68253
Clark Material Handling Co. (Lexington, KY) 68534; 68536; 68537
Fmc Corp. Orlando (Orlando, FL) 61990
Palletizers (Montgomery, AL) 56361
Simmons-Rand Co. (Cedar Bluff, VA) 90512
Terex Corp. Clark Material Handling Co. (Lexington, KY) 68642
Yale Materials Handling Corp. (Lenoir, NC) 75393

3541 Machine Tools— Metal Cutting Types

Black & Decker Corp. (Towson, MD) 72506
Cincinnati Milacron Fountain Inn Div. (Fountain Inn, SC) 79240; 79241
Cincinnati Milacron-Heald Corp. Fountain Inn Div. (Fountain Inn, SC) 79242
Cincinnati Milacron Inc. Fountain Inn Div. (Fountain Inn, SC) 79243
Delta International Machinery Corp. (Tupelo, MS) 73396; 73397
General Electric Co. (Dallas, TX) 84090
GTE Valenite (Seneca, SC) 79859
GTE Valenite (Westminster, SC) 80116; 80117
GTE Valenite Corp. Plant 4 (Seneca, SC) 79860
Jacobs Chuck Manufacturing Co. (Clemson, SC) 78951; 78952
Jacobs Chuck Mfg. Co. (Clemson, SC) 78953
National-Oilwell (Woodward, OK) 78262
Northwest Industries Inc. (Newcastle, OK) 77242
Peco (Huntsville, AL) 55989
GTE Valenite Corp. Plant 3 (Westminster, SC) 80118

3542 Machine Tools— Metal Forming Types

Baker Hughes Mining Tools Inc. (Grand Prairie, TX) 85606
Ball Metal Decorating & Service (Trussville, AL) 56626
Eaton International Corp. (Wilmington, DE) 58056

3544 Special Dies, Tools, Jigs & Fixtures

Aeroquip Corp. (Fitzgerald, GA) 66205
AMP Inc. (Largo, FL) 60811
AMP, Inc. (Winston-Salem, NC) 76701
Black & Decker Corp. (Fayetteville, NC) 74532
Gamco Prods. Co. (Henderson, KY) 68449
Gamco Products Co. (Henderson, KY) 68450
Morrison Molded Fiber Glass Co. (Bristol, VA) 90483
Piggly Wiggly (Louisville, GA) 66620; 66622
Scott Aviation (Monroe, NC) 75591
Snap On Tools Corp. (Richmond, VA) 92041

3545 Machine Tool Accessories

Ametek Inc. (Bartow, FL) 58622
Black & Decker Inc. Facilities Group (Hampstead, MD) 71900
Cincinnati Milacron (Fountain Inn, SC) 79239

Jacobs Man Jacobs Chuck Manufacturing (Clemson, SC) 78954
Matco Manufacturing (Houston, TX) 86521
Snap-On Tools Corp. (Elizabethton, TN) 80770
Teledyne Firth Sterling (Grant, AL) 55811
Teledyne Firth Sterling (Gurley, AL) 55839
Teledyne Firth Sterling (La Vergne, TN) 81284
Union/Butterfield Straight Line (Gaffney, SC) 79267

3546 Power-Driven Handtools

Black & Decker Co. (Franklin, TN) 80809
Black & Decker Corp. (Towson, MD) 72506
Black & Decker Corp. (Fayetteville, NC) 74532
Black & Decker Corp. (Tarboro, NC) 76362
Black & Decker Corp. Power Tools Group (Easton, MD) 71658
Black & Decker Corp. Power Tools Group (Fayetteville, NC) 74533
Black & Decker Inc. Facilities Group (Hampstead, MD) 71900
Black & Decker Inc. Power Tools Group (Fayetteville, NC) 74534
Black & Decker U.S. Inc. (Baltimore, MD) 71066
Black & Decker US Inc. (Lutherville Timonium, MD) 72119
Black & Decker USA (Easton, MD) 71659
Cooper Industries Inc. Weller Wire Wrap Plant (Cheraw, SC) 78919
Cooper Industries Weller/Wire Wrap Plt (Cheraw, SC) 78920
Homelite (Gastonia, NC) 74683
Homelite (Greer, SC) 79477
Homelite Homelite Division (Greer, SC) 79478
Porter-Cable Corp. (Jackson, TN) 80995; 80996
Purolator Products Co. Air Filtration Co. (Henderson, NC) 75026
Skil Corp. (Heber Springs, AR) 57155
Skil Dremel Corp. (Walnut Ridge, AR) 57707
Textron Inc. Homelite Division (Greer, SC) 79484

3548 Welding Apparatus

Air Products & Chemicals Inc. (Greensboro, NC) 74759
Air Products & Chemicals, Inc. (Lone Star, TX) 87699
Harris Calorfic Co. (Gainesville, GA) 66275
Lincoln Electric Co. Harris Calorific Div. (Gainesville, GA) 66283

3549 Metalworking Machinery Nec

Black & Decker Corp. (Tarboro, NC) 76362
Cooper Industries Inc. Weller Wire Wrap Plant (Cheraw, SC) 78919
Cooper Industries Weller/Wire Wrap Plt (Cheraw, SC) 78920
FMC Corp., Conway Plant (Conway, AR) 56862
GE Fanuc (Charlottesville, VA) 90539
Harris Calorific (Gainesville, GA) 66277

3552 Textile Machinery

Allied-Signal Inc. (Dalton, GA) 65769; 65770
Avery Dennison Corp. (Flowery Br, GA) 66214
BASF Corp. (Dalton, GA) 65772
Southern Co. (Memphis, TN) 81696

3553 Woodworking Machinery

Black & Decker Corp. (Towson, MD) 72506
Blount Inc. (Zebulon, NC) 76783
Delta International Machinery Corp. (Tupelo, MS) 73396; 73397; 73398
Emerson Electric Co. Special Products Div. (Murphy, NC) 75701
Emerson Electric Co. Special Products Div. (Paris, TN) 82217; 82218

Emerson Electric Co. SPD (Murphy, NC) 75702
Ralph Wilson Plastics Co. (Miami, FL) 61439

3554 Paper Industries Machinery

Beloit Manhattan (Columbus, MS) 72703
Carthage Machine Co. Southern (Morton, MS) 73189
Dexter Packaging Products (Birmingham, AL) 55273
FMP-Rauma Co. (Birmingham, AL) 55273
Murray Machinery (Florence, AL) 55739
Pitney Bowes (Jacksonville, FL) 60391
Pitney Bowes (Jeffersontown, KY) 68496
Pitney Bowes (Lexington, KY) 68603
Pitney Bowes (Baton Rouge, LA) 69599
Pitney Bowes (Shreveport, LA) 70765
Pitney Bowes (West Columbia, SC) 80103
Pitney Bowes (Memphis, TN) 81668
Pitney Bowes (Nashville, TN) 82083
Pitney Bowes (Richmond, VA) 91950
Pitney Bowes (Roanoke, VA) 92177
Pitney Bowes (South Charleston, WV) 93053
Stone Container Corp. (Lithonia, GA) 66609
Xerox Corp. (Richmond, VA) 92095

3555 Printing Trades Machinery

Ball Metal Decorating & Service (Trussville, AL) 56626
Soabar Group Soabar Products Group (Charlotte, NC) 74161
Stevens Graphics Corp. (Fort Worth, TX) 85280
3M Co. (Kearneysville, WV) 92909
Wabco Co. (Dayton, TN) 80724

3556 Food Products Machinery

FMC Corp. (Lakeland, FL) 60728
Hobart Corp. Pmi Food Equipment Group (Richmond Hill, GA) 67297
Luker Inc. (Augusta, GA) 65335
George J. Meyer Manufacturing (Swainsboro, GA) 67754
Pmi Food Equipment Group Hobart Corp. (Richmond Hill, GA) 67298
Sesame Products Inc. (Paris, TX) 88378
Tipper Tie Inc. (Apex, NC) 73558

3559 Special Industry Machinery Nec

Air Control Products (Roxboro, NC) 76120
Air Products & Chemicals (Theodore, AL) 56605
Air Products & Chemicals (Charlotte, NC) 73829
Danaher Corp. (Washington, DC) 58209
Dow Chemical USA (Russellville, AR) 57583
Eaton Air Controls Products (Roxboro, NC) 76123
Emhart Corp. (Baltimore, MD) 71112
Figgie Packaging Systems (Goose Creek, SC) 79279
FMC Corp. (Conway, AR) 56861
FMC Corp., Conway Plant (Conway, AR) 56862
Hayssen Manufacturing Co. (Duncan, SC) 79172
Hennessey Industries Hennessy/Coats Div. (La Vergne, TN) 81282
Litton Material Handling Systems (Hebron, KY) 68323
Geo. J. Meyer Manufacturing (Goose Creek, SC) 79285
Owens-Corning Fiberglass Corp. (Duncan, SC) 79173
Power Systems (Lancaster, TX) 87601
Stanley-Bostitch Inc. (Atlanta, GA) 65168
Stone Container Corp. (Orlando, FL) 62149
Sweco Inc. (Florence, KY) 68341

Westinghouse Electric (Columbia, SC) 79126

3561 Pumps & Pumping Equipment

Baker Hughes Cac Div. (Oklahoma City, OK) 77303
Centrilift (Claremore, OK) 76948; 76949
Centrilift Co. (Claremore, OK) 76951
Centrilift Co. (Midland, TX) 88027
Dana Corp. Corinth Plant (Corinth, MS) 72737
Dana Corp. Mobile Fluid Products Div. (Corinth, MS) 72738
Emerson Electric Co. Brooks Instrument Div. (Statesboro, GA) 67634
Esp Products (Oklahoma City, OK) 77352
Imo Delaval Inc. (Monroe, NC) 75580
Layne & Bowler Inc. (Memphis, TN) 81642
Little Giant Pump Co. (Oklahoma City, OK) 77431
Ltv Energy Products (Garland, TX) 85502
LTV Energy Products, Plant 1 (Garland, TX) 85504
LTV Energy Products, Plant 2 (Garland, TX) 85505
Monarch Industries Inc. (Br) (Dallas, TX) 84258
Trico Submersible System (Oklahoma City, OK) 77637
TRW Inc. Reda Pump Div. (Bartlesville, OK) 76853
Vickers Inc. Aerospace Marine Defense (Jackson, MS) 73087
York International Corp. (Madisonville, KY) 69074

3562 Ball & Roller Bearings

N W Ball & Roller (Walterboro, SC) 80074
Nn Ball & Roller Inc. (Walterboro, SC) 80075
Nucor Bearing Prods. (Wilson, NC) 76635
Reliance Electric Co. (Rogersville, TN) 82280
Terrington/Fafnir (Calhoun, GA) 65477
Torrington Co (Charlotte, NC) 74174
Torrington Co. the (Birmingham, AL) 55429; 55430
Torrington Co. the (Tampa, FL) 63624
Torrington Co. (Sylvania, GA) 67771
Torrington Co. (Clinton, SC) 78963
Torrington Co. (Union, SC) 80049
Torrington Co. (Walhalla, SC) 80058
Torrington Co. Bearing Div. (Dahlonega, GA) 65755
Torrington Co. Shiloh Plant (Rutherfordton, NC) 76147
Torrington Co. Inc (Honea Path, SC) 79532
Torrington Co. Inc. (Sylvania, GA) 67772
Torrington Co. Shiloh Plant (Rutherfordton, NC) 76148
Torrington Co. Tyger River (Union, SC) 80050
Torrington Co. Tyger River Plant (Union, SC) 80051; 80052; 80053
Unitron Inc. (Dallas, TX) 84474

3563 Air & Gas Compressors

Dresser-Rand Compression Services (Broken Arrow, OK) 76883
General Electric Co. (Columbia, TN) 80628; 80629
Halliburton Resource Manage (Dallas, TX) 84112
Ingersoll Rand (Mocksville, NC) 75564
Ingersoll-Rand Centrifugal Compressor Div. (Mayfield, KY) 69077
Ingersoll Rand Small Compressor Div. (Davidson, NC) 74358
Ingersoll-Rand Co. (Mayfield, KY) 69078
Ingersoll-Rand Co. Portable Compressor Div. (Mocksville, NC) 75565
Midland Brake Inc. (Marion, NC) 75505

3564 Blowers & Fans
Air Products & Chemicals (Charlotte, NC) 73829
Air Products & Chemicals, Inc. (Atlanta, GA) 64209
Air Products & Chemicals, Inc. (Valdosta, GA) 84709
Carrier Corp. (Knoxville, TN) 81152
Trane Air Handling Systems Business Unit (Lexington, KY) 68644
Trane Commercial Self-Contained Systems Business Unit (Macon, GA) 66718

3565 Packaging Machinery
Figgie Packaging Systems (Goose Creek, SC) 79279
Geo. J. Meyer Manufacturing (Goose Creek, SC) 79285
Torrington Co. (Cairo, GA) 65455

3566 Speed Changers, Drives & Gears
Browning Manufacturing (Maysville, KY) 69083
Browning Mfg. Plant 1 (Maysville, KY) 69084
Browning Mfg. Plant 3 (Maysville, KY) 69085
Browning Mfg. Plant 2 (Maysville, KY) 69086
Centrilift Co. (Claremore, OK) 76951
OMC Andrews (Andrews, NC) 73547; 73548
Reliance Electric Co. (Greenville, SC) 79419
Reliance Electric Co. Gear Products Plant (Greenville, SC) 79420

3567 Industrial Furnaces & Ovens
Air Products & Chemicals (Greenville, SC) 79291
Browning-Ferris Industries (Greensboro, NC) 74791
Emerson Electric Co. E. L. Wiegnd Div. (Vernon, AL) 56698
Hevi Duty Nelson (Tulsa, OK) 77954
Tranter Inc. (Wichita Falls, TX) 90116

3568 Power Transmission Equipment Nec
Federal Mogul (Blacksburg, VA) 90438
FMC Energy & Transmission Equipment Group (Houston, TX) 86201
Reliance Electric Co. (Weaverville, NC) 76476
Reliance Electric Co. (Rogersville, TN) 82279; 82280
Reliance Electric Co. Co. (Rogersville, TN) 82281
Reliance Electric Co. Mechanical Drives Plant (Weaverville, NC) 76477
Reliance Electric Mechanical Drives Plant (Weaverville, NC) 76478
Seco Electronic (Lancaster, SC) 79575
Vickers Inc. Aerospace Marine Defense (Jackson, MS) 73087

3569 General Industrial Machinery Nec
Air Products & Chemicals, Inc. (Clarksdale, MS) 72666
Atlantic Richfield (Woodward, OK) 78257
Atlantic Richfield Co. (Woodward, OK) 78258
Avery Dennison-Avery International Business Systems Div. (Flowery Branch, GA) 66216
Baltimore Aircoil Co. (Jessup, MD) 71981
Blount Inc. (Montgomery, AL) 56284
Brunswick Corp. (DeLand, FL) 59297
Dana Corp. Corinth Plant (Corinth, MS) 72737
Dana Corp. Mobile Fluid Products (Greenville, SC) 79335
Dana Corp. Mobile Fluid Products Division (Greenville, SC) 79336
Dynapert (Roswell, GA) 67368

Eaton Corp. Hydraulics Div. (Shawnee, OK) 77816
Exxon (Travelers Rest, SC) 80043
Figgie Fire Protection Systems (Ranson, WV) 93021
Figgie Packaging Systems (Goose Creek, SC) 79279
Filterite, Plant 1 (Timonium, MD) 72502
Filterite, Plant 2 (Timonium, MD) 72503
Fleetguard Inc. (Nashville, TN) 82011
GE Fanuc (Charlottesville, VA) 90539
Industrial Systems Inc. (Nashville, TN) 82031
Lincoln (Jonesboro, AR) 57225
Geo. J. Meyer Manufacturing (Goose Creek, SC) 79285
Piper/Casepro (Clarendon, AR) 56847
Southern Co. (North Little Rock, AR) 57472
Southern Co. (Memphis, TN) 81696
Westinghouse Electric (Orlando, FL) 62193

3571 Electronic Computers
Advanced Micro Devices (Austin, TX) 82803
AMP Inc. (Roanoke, VA) 92100
AT & T Network Systems (Oklahoma City, OK) 77301
AT&T (Little Rock, AR) 57254; 57255
AT&T Paradyne Corp. (Largo, FL) 60818
Avex Electronics Inc. (Huntsville, AL) 55883; 55884; 55885
Avex Electronics Inc. (Pulaski, TN) 82240
Carroll Touch (Round Rock, TX) 88845
Data General Corp. (Apex, NC) 73555
Data General Corp. (Clayton, NC) 74263
Data General Puerto Rico Inc. (Hato Rey, PR) 78454
Dell Computer Corp. (Austin, TX) 82847
Digital Equip Corp. (Mobile, AL) 56156
Digital Equipment Corporati (Baton Rouge, LA) 69509
Digital Equipment Corp. (Melbourne, FL) 61050
E-Systems Inc. (Dallas, TX) 83992
Exxon Corp. (Oklahoma City, OK) 77355
Harris Computer Systems Div. (Fort Lauderdale, FL) 59500
Harris Corp. Computer Systems Div. (Fort Lauderdale, FL) 59502
Hewlett-Packard Co. (Oklahoma City, OK) 77382
Hewlett Packard Co. Inc. (Jacksonville, FL) 60326
Hewlett-Packard Oki Printed Circuits (Aguadilla, PR) 78295
NCR Corp. (Morristown, TN) 81806
Paramax Systems Corp. Clearwater (Oldsmar, FL) 61848
Radio Shack (Cumberland, MD) 71634
Storage Tek Printer Operations (Palm Bay, FL) 62244
Sun Microsystems Inc. (Vienna, VA) 92422
Tandem Computers Inc. (Austin, TX) 83024
Tandy Electronics Bus Computer (Fort Worth, TX) 85314
Teledyne Lewisburg (Lewisburg, TN) 81331
Texas Instruments Inc. (Memphis, TN) 81707
Unisys Clearwater (Oldsmar, FL) 61849
Unisys Corp. (Oldsmar, FL) 61851

3572 Computer Storage Devices
Data General Puerto Rico Inc. (Hato Rey, PR) 78454
US Design Corp. (Lanham Seabrook, MD) 72061

3575 Computer Terminals
AT&T (Little Rock, AR) 57254; 57255
Dell Computer Corp. (Austin, TX) 82847
E-Systems Inc. (Dallas, TX) 83992
Tandem Computers Inc. (Austin, TX) 83024

3577 Computer Peripheral Equipment Nec
AT&T (Little Rock, AR) 57254; 57255
AT&T Paradyne Corp. (Largo, FL) 60817; 60818
Belden Wire & Cable (Monticello, KY) 69096
Carroll Touch Inc. (Round Rock, TX) 88847
Casi-Rusco Inc. (Boca Raton, FL) 58687
Cooper Industries Inc. Belden Div. (Monticello, KY) 69099
Data General Corp. (Apex, NC) 73555
Data General Corp. (Clayton, NC) 74263
Data General Puerto Rico Inc. (Hato Rey, PR) 78454
Eaton Corp. Power Distribution Div. (Cleveland, TN) 80579
Litton Industrial Automation Systems Automated Systems Div. (Hebron, KY) 68431
Litton Industries Integrated Systems Div. (Hebron, KY) 68434
NCR Corp. (Morristown, TN) 81806
Texas Instruments Inc. Temple Site (Temple, TX) 89649
Xerox Corp. (Arlington, VA) 90394

3578 Calculating & Accounting Equipment
NCR Corp. (Brentwood, TN) 80232
Texas Instruments Inc. (Lubbock, TX) 87787

3579 Office Machines Nec
AT&T Paradyne Corp. (Largo, FL) 60817; 60818
Danaher Corp. (Washington, DC) 58209
Digital Equipment Corp. (Mobile, AL) 56157
Digital Equipment Corp. (Lexington, KY) 68546
Digital Equipment Corp. (Roanoke, VA) 92134
Digital Equipment Corp. Bran (Roanoke, VA) 92135
Electronic Data Systems Corp. (Plano, TX) 88562
Emhart Corp. (Baltimore, MD) 71112
Emhart Industries Inc. (Baltimore, MD) 71113
Pitney Bowes (Shreveport, LA) 70765
Pitney Bowes (St. Rose, LA) 70878
Unisys Corp. (St Petersburg, FL) 63040
Universal Data Systems (Winston Salem, NC) 76689
Xerox Corp. (Oklahoma City, OK) 77671
Xerox Corp. (Herndon, VA) 91138

3581 Automatic Vending Machines
Dixie-Narco Inc. (Williston, SC) 80128
Dixie-Narco Inc. (Ranson, WV) 93019; 93020

3582 Commercial Laundry Equipment
Speed Queen Co. (Madisonville, KY) 69071; 69072

3585 Refrigeration & Heating Equipment
Aeroquip Corp. (Heber Springs, AR) 57148; 57149
Amana Refrigeration Inc. (Fayetteville, TN) 80789
American Standard Trance Co. Div. (Clarksville, TN) 80534
American Standard Trane Co. (Clarksville, TN) 80535
American Standard Inc. Trane Co. Div. (Clarksville, TN) 80536
Bristol Compressors Inc. (Bristol, VA) 90470
Carrier Corp. (Maumelle, AR) 57354
Carrier Corp. (Collierville, TN) 80617
Carrier Corp. (Morrison, TN) 81783
Carrier Corp. (Tyler, TX) 89795
Carrier Transicold (Athens, GA) 64164

Ceramic Cooling Tower Co. (Fort Worth, TX) 85079
Copeland Corp. (Hartselle, AL) 55854
Copeland Corp. (Shelby, NC) 76237
Delfield Co. (Covington, TN) 80684
Emerson Electric Co. (Newport, TN) 82160
Four Seasons (Grapevine, TX) 85657
General Electric Co. (Columbia, TN) 80628; 80629
Governair (Oklahoma City, OK) 77375
Heil Co. (Chattanooga, TN) 80415
Hussmann Corp. (Montgomery, AL) 56344
Hussmann Corp. (Dumas, AR) 56911
Premark International (Montgomery, AL) 56370
Rooftop Systems Inc. (Carrollton, TX) 83504
Shannon Group (Parsons, TN) 82225
Tecumseh Products Co. Somerset Div. (Somerset, KY) 69298
Thermal Components Inc. (Montgomery, AL) 56387; 56388
Thermo King Corp. (Louisville, GA) 66624
Trane Air Handling Systems Business Unit (Lexington, KY) 68644
Trane Commercial Self-Contained Systems Business Unit (Macon, GA) 66718
Trane Co. (Fort Smith, AR) 57106; 57107
Trane Co. (Lexington, KY) 68645
Trane Co. (Tyler, TX) 89837
Trane Co. Wshpbu (Mc Gregor, TX) 87907
Trane/Service First (Charlotte, NC) 74177
Trane/Servicefirst Service First (Charlotte, NC) 74178
Trans Unitary Products Group Commercial (Clarksville, TN) 80559
Tyler Refrigeration Corp. (Olive Branch, MS) 73234
Unitary Products Group Residential (Tyler, TX) 89839
Vapor Corp. (Montgomery, AL) 56395
Westinghouse De P.R. Inc. Thermo King Caribbean (Ciales, PR) 78391
Westinghouse De Puerto Rico Thermo King De Puerto Rico (Arecibo, PR) 78314
Westinghouse De Puerto Rico Inc. Thermo King Carribbean (Ciales, PR) 78392
Westinghouse De Puerto Rico Inc. Thermo King Div. (Arecibo, PR) 78315
Westinghouse Electric Corp. Thermo King Carribean (Ciales, PR) 78393
Westinghouse Electric Corp. Thermo King Corp. (Montgomery, AL) 56396
Westinghouse Electric Corp. Thermo King Corp. (Louisville, GA) 66627; 66628
Westinghouse Electric Corp. Thermo King De Puerto Rico (Arecibo, PR) 78316
Whirlpool Corp. (La Vergne, TN) 81285
York Air Conditioning (Fort Worth, TX) 85367
York Heating & Air Conditioning (Norman, OK) 77281
York International Corp. (Norcross, GA) 67213
York International Corp. (Madisonville, KY) 69074
York International Corp. (Norman, OK) 77282; 77283

3586 Measuring & Dispensing Pumps
Dana Corp. (Wichita Fall, TX) 90062
Dresser Industries Inc. Wayne Div. (Salisbury, MD) 72341
Gilbarco Inc. (Greensboro, NC) 74842; 74843
Jiffy Lube Oil Change (Lexington, KY) 68562
Texaco Express Lube (Del Rio, TX) 84588

3589 Service Industry Machinery Nec
A. O. Smith Water Prods. Co. (El Paso, TX) 84754

BFI Medical Waste Systems (Houston, TX) 85881
BFI Waste Systems (Lakeland, FL) 60716
BFI Waste Systems (Cleveland, TN) 80570
BFI Waste Systems (Memphis, TN) 81475
Bio-Lab Inc. (Decatur, GA) 65801
Browning-Ferris Industries (Capitol Heights, MD) 71504
Browning-Ferris Industries (Hyattsville, MD) 71954
Browning-Ferris Industries (Fairfax, VA) 90755
Browning-Ferris Industries (Sterling, VA) 92337
Cecos International Inc. (Westlake, LA) 70962
Litton Industrial Automation Systems Inc. (Hebron, KY) 68432
Marathon Equipment Co. (Vernon, AL) 56699
Newell Ind. Inc. (San Antonio, TX) 89119
Waste Management Inc. (Jacksonville, FL) 60508
Weyerhaeuser Paper Co. (Richmond, VA) 92092
ZEP Manufacturing Co. (Hialeah, FL) 60021
ZEP Manufacturing Co. (Smyrna, GA) 67585

3592 Carburetors, Pistons, Rings & Valves
Borg Warner Automotive (Blytheville, AR) 56803
Combustion Technologies Inc. (Flowery Branch, GA) 66217
Cummins Engine Co. Inc. (Charleston, SC) 78798; 78799; 78800
Eaton Air Controls Products (Roxboro, NC) 76123
Facet Fuel Systems (Bristol, VA) 90473
Midland Brake Inc. (Marion, NC) 75505
Pacer Industries Inc. (Pensacola, FL) 62454
SPX Corp. Sealed Power Div. (Franklin, KY) 68372
TRW Inc. Fuji Valve Div. (Sevierville, TN) 82298
US Engine Valve Co. (Westminster, SC) 80119; 80120

3593 Fluid Power Cylinders & Actuators
American Standard Wabco Fluid Power Div. (Lexington, KY) 68520
Atlas Cylinder (Decatur, AL) 55575
Dana Corp. Arab Hydraulics (Arab, AL) 55020; 55021
Dana Corp. Arab Hydraulics Plant (Arab, AL) 55022
Maremont Exhaust Products, Inc. (Loudon, TN) 81354
Vickers (Decatur, AL) 55611

3594 Fluid Power Pumps & Motors
Browning-Ferris Industries (Hutchins, TX) 87301
Eaton Corp. Hydraulics Div. (Shawnee, OK) 77816
Vickers Inc. Aerospace Marine Defense (Jackson, MS) 73087

3596 Scales & Balances Except Laboratory
Stock Equipment Co. (Lynn Haven, FL) 60957
Sunbeam Oster (Shubuta, MS) 73344

3599 Industrial Machinery Nec
Air Products & Chemicals Inc. (Memphis, TN) 81447
Allied-Signal Aerospace Co. (Naples, FL) 61596; 61597
AMBAC International Corp. (Columbia, SC) 78970
APAC (Tulsa, OK) 77879
Baker Hughes Cac Div. (Oklahoma City, OK) 77303
Baker Oil Tools (Houston, TX) 85854
Beloit Manhattan (Columbus, MS) 72703
Bird Machine Co. (Scott Depot, WV) 93039

Blount Inc. (Montgomery, AL) 56284
Champion Laboratories Inc. (York, SC) 80138
Clark Material Handling Co. (Lexington, KY) 68534; 68537
Coors Ceramics Co. (Norman, OK) 77249
Dana Corp. (Dillon, SC) 79159
Dana Corp. (Lancaster, TX) 87597
Dana Corp. Arab Hydraulic Plant (Arab, AL) 55019
Dana Corp. Mobile Fluid Products Div. (Lancaster, TX) 87598
Dana Corp. Mobile Fluid Products Division (Greenville, SC) 79336
Eimco Coal Machinery Inc. (Bolt, WV) 92705
Electro Mechanical Devices Inc. (Cordova, AL) 55528
FMC Corp. (Aiken, SC) 78646
GE Electrical Distribution (Jacksonville, FL) 60319
General Electric Co. (Birmingham, AL) 55278
General Electric Co. (New Orleans, LA) 70468
General Electric Co. (Baltimore, MD) 71159
General Electric Co. (Charlotte, NC) 74028
General Electric Co. (Dallas, TX) 84090
General Electric Co. (Houston, TX) 86246
Genuine Parts Co. (Wheeling, WV) 93112
Ibm Corp. (Marietta, GA) 66788
Johnson Controls Inc. (Columbia, SC) 79036
Johnson Controls, Inc. (Greenville, SC) 79374
Lewis Engineering Co. (Marshall, TX) 87857
George J. Meyer Manufacturing (Swainsboro, GA) 67754
Residence Inn by Marriott (Cape St Clare, MD) 71491
Unisys Corp. (Boca Raton, FL) 58746
United Parcel Service (Shreveport, LA) 70799
United Technologies Auto (St. Matthews, SC) 79975
Vickers Inc. Aerospace Marine Defense (Jackson, MS) 73087
Walker Manufacturing Inc. (Walker, LA) 70939
Westinghouse Electric (Pensacola, FL) 62490
Wheeling Machine Products (Birmingham, AL) 55457
Whirlpool Corp. (Danville, KY) 68265

3600 Electronic & Other Electrical Equipment

Avnet Channel Master (Smithfield, NC) 76255
BASF Structural Materials Inc. (Charlotte, NC) 73855
Challenger Electrical Equipment (Grand Prairie, TX) 85613
Electronic Systems Group Materials Acquistion Center (Glen Burnie, MD) 71840
General Electric Co. (Mebane, NC) 75550
General Electric Co. Mobile Communications (Lynchburg, VA) 91254
General Electric Ed&C (Houston, TX) 86248
General Electric Simulation & Control Systems (Daytona Beach, FL) 59182
General Instrument Corp. Puerto Rico (Barceloneta, PR) 78327
Harris Corp. GSS (Malabar, FL) 60991
Harris Corp. GSS (Palm Bay, FL) 62239
Honeywell Inc. Dcpd (Tampa, FL) 63458
Motorola De Puerto Rico (Vega Baja, PR) 78626
Motorola Inc. Portable Products Div. (Plantation, FL) 62571
Rockwell International (Richardson, TX) 88764
Rockwell International Corp. (Richardson, TX) 88765
Rockwell International Corp. Msd (Duluth) (Duluth, GA) 66077
Texas Instruments Inc. (Abilene, TX) 82463
Texas Instruments Inc. (Dallas, TX) 84448
Westinghouse Electric Corp. Integrated Logistics Support (Hunt Valley, MD) 71947
Westinghouse de Purerto Rico Productos Electronicos Industriales (Santa Isabel, PR) 78591

3612 Transformers Except Electronic

Abb Power T&D Co. Inc. (Pinetops, NC) 75806
Berkshire Hathaway France (Fairview, TN) 80785
Berkshire Hathaway Franee (Fairview, TN) 80786
Central Moloney Transformer Div. (Pine Bluff, AR) 57509
Central Moloney Inc. Arcadia (Arcadia, FL) 58580
Central Moloney Transformer Arcadia (Arcadia, FL) 58581
Cooper Power Systems (Lumberton, MS) 73130
E-Systems Inc. (Ashburn, VA) 90397
GE Co. Component Products Operation (Greeneville, TN) 80885
GE Co. Medium Transformer Operation (Rome, GA) 67341
GE Fanuc (Charlottesville, VA) 90539
General Electric Co. (Rome, GA) 67342
General Electric Co. (Shreveport, LA) 70723; 70724
General Electric Co. (Hickory, NC) 75077
General Electric Co. (Selmer, TN) 82291
General Electric Co. Transformer Bus. Dept. (Hickory, NC) 75078
General Electric Co. Transformer Business Dept. (Hickory, NC) 75079
Hevi Duty Electric (Goldsbora, NC) 74699
Hevi-Duty Electric (Celina, TN) 80283
Hevi-Duty Electric Co. (Goldsboro, NC) 74724
Hevi-Duty Electric Co. (Celina, TN) 80284
Magnetek (Athens, AL) 55042
Magnetek (Mendenhall, MS) 73156
Magnetek Inc. (Blytheville, AR) 56808
Magnetek Jefferson Electric (Athens, AL) 55043
Magnetek National Electric Coil, Inc. (Brownsville, TX) 83371
Magnetek Ohio Transformer (Houston, TX) 86510; 86511
Magnetek Ohio Transformer Brandenton Plant (Palmetto, FL) 62311
Magnetek Universal Manufacturing (Blytheville, AR) 56809
Magnetek Universal Manufacturing (Mendenhall, MS) 73157
Mcgraw Edison (Lumberton, MS) 73131
Varo, Inc. (Garland, TX) 85558
Westinghouse/Abb Power T&D Co. (South Boston, VA) 92262
Westinghouse Controls (Coamo, PR) 78402
Westinghouse Controls Inc. (Coamo, PR) 78403; 78404
Westinghouse Electric (Greenwood, SC) 79466
Westinghouse Electric Corp. (Athens, GA) 64178
Westinghouse Electric Corp. (Pinetops, NC) 75807
Westinghouse Electric Corp. (Sumter, SC) 80034
Westinghouse Electric Corp. (Alamo, TN) 80147
Westinghouse Electric Corp. (South Boston, VA) 92263

3613 Switchgear & Switchboard Apparatus

Caribe GE Products Inc. (San German, PR) 78548; 78549
Caribe General Electric Products Inc. (Anasco, PR) 78306; 78307
Challenger Caribbean Corp. (Canovanas, PR) 78364
Challenger Electric Equipment Co. (Vidalia, GA) 67985
Cooper Industries Inc. Bussmann Div. (Black Mountain, NC) 73695; 73696
Cooper Industries Inc. Bussmann Div. (Goldsboro, NC) 74713
Eaton Corp. (Arab, AL) 55023
Eaton Corp. (Athens, AL) 55037
Eaton Corp. (Sarasota, FL) 62814
Eaton Corp. (Cleveland, TN) 80578
Eaton Corp. Heinemann Products (Salisbury, MD) 72343
Eaton Corp. Heinemann Products Commercial Controls Div. (Salisbury, MD) 72344
Eaton Corp. Power Control Div. (Bowling Green, KY) 68137
Eaton Corp. Power Distribution Div. (Cleveland, TN) 80579
Eaton Corp. Heinemann Products (Salisbury, MD) 72345
EMB Corp. (Elizabethtown, KY) 68278
GE Electrial Distribution & Control (Morristown, TN) 81803
GE Electrical Distribution & Control (Morristown, TN) 81804
General Electric Co. (Shreveport, LA) 70723
General Electric Co. (Mebane, NC) 75551
General Electric Co. (Salisbury, NC) 76166
General Electric Co. (Morristown, TN) 81805
General Electric Co. (Selmer, TN) 82292; 82293
General Electric Co. (Houston, TX) 86247
Hevi Duty Nelson (Tulsa, OK) 77954
Nelson Electric (Tulsa, OK) 78030
Westinghouse Abb (Mayaguez, PR) 78515
Westinghouse Corp. of Puerto Rico Interruptores Div. (Toa Baja, PR) 78612
Westinghouse De Pr, Inc. Interruptores Div. (Toa Baja, PR) 78613
Westinghouse De Puerto Rico Interruptores (Toa Baja, PR) 78614
Westinghouse Electric (London, KY) 68672
Westinghouse Electric (Greenwood, SC) 79466
Westinghouse Electric Corp. (Coral Springs, FL) 59117
Westinghouse Electric Corp. (Deerfield Beach, FL) 59293
Westinghouse Electric Corp. (Greenwood, SC) 79467
Westinghouse Productos (Mayaguez, PR) 78516
Westinghouse de Puerto Rico Productos Westinghouse (Mayaguez, PR) 78517

3620 Electrical Industrial Apparatus

Johnson Controls Inc. (Poteau, OK) 77720

3621 Motors & Generators

A. O. Smith Electrical Prods. Co. (Mount Sterling, KY) 69113
A. O. Smith Electrical Prods. Co. (Mebane, NC) 75547
Ametek Inc. Lamb Electric Div. (Graham, NC) 74744
A.O. Smith Electrical Products Co. (Mount Sterling, KY) 69114
Copeland Electric Corp. (Humboldt, TN) 80949
Emerson Electri Co. Inc. Emerson Motor Div. (Oxford, MS) 73235
Emerson Electric Co. (Paragould, AR) 57491
Emerson Electric Co. (Russellville, KY) 69260
Emerson Electric Co. Emerson Motor Div. (Oxford, MS) 73236; 73237
Emerson Motor Co. (Oxford, MS) 73238
Emerson Motor Co. (Humboldt, TN) 80952
General Electric Co. (Dothan, AL) 55650
General Electric Co. (Jonesboro, AR) 57219; 57220
General Electric Co. (Owensboro, KY) 69170
General Electric Co. (Scottsville, KY) 69266
General Electric Co. (Hendersonville, TN) 80917
General Electric Co. (Murfreesboro, TN) 81848
General Electric Motor Plant (Owensboro, KY) 69171
Honeywell Inc. (Durham, NC) 74406; 74407
Honeywell Inc. Electro Components (Durham, NC) 74408
Litton Clifton Precision (Blacksburg, VA) 90449
Litton Industries Poly-Scientific Div. (Blacksburg, VA) 90450
Magnetek (Tulsa, OK) 78004
Magnetek/Altavista (Altavista, VA) 90248
Magnetek Century Electric (Adamsville, TN) 80143
Magnetek/Century Electric (Lexington, TN) 81340
Magnetek Century Electric (Mc Minnville, TN) 81436
Magnetek Century Electric Inc. (Lexington, TN) 81341
Magnetek Century Electric Inc. (Mc Minnville, TN) 81437
Magnetek Inc. (El Paso, TX) 84844
Magnetek National Electric Coil Inc. (Orlando, FL) 62043
Magnetek National Electric Coil, Inc. (Brownsville, TX) 83371
Magnetek Ripley Co. (Ripley, TN) 82258
Magnetek Universal Electric (Prairie Grove, AR) 57550
Magnetek Universal Electric (Ripley, TN) 82259
Magnetek Universal Electric (Grand Praire, TX) 85604
Magnetek Universal Electric Altavista Works (Altavista, VA) 90249
Magnetek Universal Electric Co. (Ripley, TN) 82260; 82261
Magnetek Universal Electric Co. Altavista Works (Altavista, VA) 90250
Power Systems Diesel Inc. (Belle Chasse, LA) 69693
Reliance Electric Co. (Birmingham, AL) 55368
Reliance Electric Co. (Athens, GA) 64175
Reliance Electric Co. (Flowery Branch, GA) 66220
Reliance Electric Co. (Kings Mountain, NC) 75307
Reliance Electric Co. (La Porte, TX) 87568
Stewart & Stevenson Inc. (Houston, TX) 86913
TRW Inc. Reda Pump Div. (Bartlesville, OK) 76853
United Technologies Auto (Columbus, MS) 72731
United Technologies Electro Systems (Columbus, MS) 72732
US Electrical Motors (Mena, AR) 57367; 57368
US Electrical Motors (Philadelphia, MS) 73282
US Motors (Philadelphia, MS) 73283
Vickers (Maysville, KY) 69092
Westinghouse Electric (Fort Payne, AL) 55761
Westinghouse Electric (Charlotte, NC) 74226
Westinghouse Electric Corp. Productos Electronic (Santa Isabel, PR) 78588
Westinghouse Motor Co. (Round Rock, TX) 88857
Westinghouse Power Systems (Round Rock, TX) 88858
Whirlpool Corp. Danville Div. (Danville, KY) 68266

3624 Carbon & Graphite Products

Allen-Bradley Co. (El Paso, TX) 84755
BASF Structural Materials Inc. (Rock Hill, SC) 79812
Materials Technology Co. (Dallas, TX) 84224
Materials Technology Corp. (Dallas, TX) 84225
Ucar Carbon Co. Inc. (Columbia, TN) 80640
Ucar Carbon Co. Inc. (Lawrenceburg, TN) 81292
Ucar Carbon Co. Inc. (Anmoore, WV) 92659
Union Carbide Corp. (Lawrenceburg, TN) 81293
Union Carbide Corp. (Anmoore, WV) 92660
Uscar Carbon Co. Inc. (Clarksville, TN) 80560

3625 Relays & Industrial Controls

Amicon Inc. (Charlotte, NC) 73840
Baker Hughes Prod. Tools Baker-CAC Inc. (Houston, TX) 85842
Berkshire Hathaway France (Fairview, TN) 80785
Caribe General Electric Products Inc. (Arroyo, PR) 78318
Caribe General Electric Products Inc. (Manati, PR) 78493
Casi-Rusco (Boca Raton, FL) 58686
Dover Elevator Co. (Walnut, MS) 73465
Eaton Corp. (Arab, AL) 55023
Eaton Corp. (Doraville, GA) 65926
Eaton Corp. (Bowling Green, KY) 68136
Eaton Corp. (Arden, NC) 73567
Eaton Corp. (Cleveland, TN) 80577
Eaton Corp. Aerospace Commercial Controls Div. (Sarasota, FL) 62815
Eaton Corp. Florida Commercial Controls Div. (Sarasota, FL) 62817
Eaton Corp. Logic Control Div. (Arden, NC) 73568
Eaton Corp. Power Control Div. (Bowling Green, KY) 68137
Eaton International Corp. (Wilmington, DE) 58056
Electro Mechanical Devices Inc. (Cordova, AL) 55528
EMB Corp. (Elizabethtown, KY) 68278
GE Fanuc Automation North America (Charlottesville, VA) 90540
Johnson Controls Inc. Panel Unit (Poteau, OK) 77722
Power Systems Diesel Inc. (Belle Chasse, LA) 69693
Reliance Electric Co. (Athens, GA) 64175
Texas Instruments Inc. (Versailles, KY) 69332
TRW Inc. Transportation Electronics Div. (Knoxville, TN) 81262; 81263
Trw Inc. Carr Knoxville (Knoxville, TN) 81264
Westinghouse Electric (Arden, NC) 73573
Westinghouse Electric (Fayeteville, NC) 74523
Westinghouse Electric (Sumter, SC) 80033
Westinghouse Electric Corp. (Oldsmar, FL) 61853
Westinghouse Electric Corp. (Fayetteville, NC) 74585
Westinghouse Electric Corp. Electrical Components (Oldsmar, FL) 61854

3629 Electrical Industrial Apparatus Nec

Challenger Caribbean Corp. (Canovanas, PR) 78364
Emerson Electric Co. E. L. Wiegnd Div. (Vernon, AL) 56698
General Electric Co. (Wilmington, NC) 76572
SCI Manufacturing Inc. (Huntsville, AL) 56014; 56015
SCI Technology Inc. (Huntsville, AL) 56017
Unitron Inc. (Dallas, TX) 84474
Westinghouse Corp. of Puerto Rico Breakers Div. (Aguas Buenas, PR) 78297
Westinghouse De Pr Inc. Breakers (Aguas Buenas, PR) 78298
Westinghouse Electric Corp. (Oldsmar, FL) 61853
Westinghouse Electric Corp. (Arden, NC) 73574; 73575
Westinghouse Electric Corp. Beakers (Aguas Buenas, PR) 78299
Westinghouse Electric Corp. Breakers (Aguas Buenas, PR) 78300
Westinghouse Electric Corp. Cabo Rojo (Cabo Rojo, PR) 78347
Westinghouse Electric Corp. Copper Laminates (Pendleton, SC) 79788
Westinghouse Electric Corp. Electrical Components (Oldsmar, FL) 61854
Westinghouse Electric Corp. Productos Electronicos (Santa Isabel, PR) 78589
Westinghouse Puerto Rico Inc. Breakers Div. (Aguas Buenas, PR) 78301

3631 Household Cooking Equipment

Caloric Corp. (Florence, SC) 79195
General Electric Co. (Columbia, MD) 71591
General Electric Co. Columbia Plant Operations (Columbia, MD) 71592
Magic Chef Hardwick Enamel Plant (Cleveland, TN) 80590
Magic Chef Plant 1 (Cleveland, TN) 80591
Maytag Corp. Magic Chef Div. (Cleveland, TN) 80593
Rge Corp. (La Fayette, GA) 66470

Roper Corp. (La Fayette, GA) 66471
Roper Corp. (Chattanooga, TN) 80478
Sunbeam Outdoor Products (Paragould, AR) 57496
Teledyne Still-Man (Cookeville, TN) 80667
Whirlpool Corp. (Oxford, MS) 73249; 73250

3632 Household Refrigerators & Freezers

Dixie-Narco Inc. (Williston, SC) 80129
GE Appliances Manufacturing Division (Decatur, AL) 55585
General Electric Co. (Decatur, AL) 55586
Maytag Corp. Admiral Co. Div. (Williston, SC) 80130
Shannon Group (Parsons, TN) 82225
Tecumseh Products Co. (Verona, MS) 73451
Warwick Mfg. Co. (Chesapeake, VA) 90610
Whirlpool Corp. (Fort Smith, AR) 57119
Whirlpool Corp. (La Vergne, TN) 81285

3633 Household Laundry Equipment

Speed Queen Co. (Searcy, AR) 57609

3634 Electric Housewares & Fans

Black & Decker Corp. (Towson, MD) 72506
Black & Decker Corp. (Asheboro, NC) 73578
Black & Decker Corp. Household Products Group (Asheboro, NC) 73579
Black & Decker Housewares Group (Asheboro, NC) 73580
Black & Decker Inc. Facilities Group (Hampstead, MD) 71900
Black & Decker U.S. Inc. (Baltimore, MD) 71066
Emerson Electric Co. Inc. Alco Controls Div. (Wytheville, VA) 92638
Oster Specialty Prods. (Mc Minnville, TN) 81438
Sunbeam Oster Household Products (Holly Springs, MS) 72911

3635 Household Vacuum Cleaners

Black & Decker Corp. (Towson, MD) 72506
Douglas/Quikut (Germantown, TN) 80855
Whirlpool Corp. Danville Div. (Danville, KY) 68266

3639 Household Appliances Nec

A. O. Smith Water Prods. Co. (Mc Bee, SC) 79654
A. O. Smith Water Products Co. (Mc Bee, SC) 79655; 79656
A.O. Smith Water Products Co. (Mc Bee, SC) 79657
Black & Decker US Distr Ctr (Charlotte, NC) 73863
Emerson Electric Co. E. L. Wiegnd Div. (Vernon, AL) 56698
Emerson Electric Co. White-Rodger Div. (Harrison, AR) 57136
Kitchen Aid Inc. (Mount Sterling, KY) 69115
Kitchenaid Inc. (Mount Sterling, KY) 69116
Sunbeam-Oster Corp. (Coushatta, LA) 69792
Whirlpool Corp. (Danville, KY) 68264
Whirlpool Corp. (La Vergne, TN) 81285
Whirlpool Corp. Danville Div. (Danville, KY) 68266
White-Rodgers (Harrison, AR) 57146
White-Rodgers Harrison Air (Harrison, AR) 57147

3641 Electric Lamps

GE Lighting (Memphis, TN) 81610
General Electric Co. (Winchester, VA) 92593
General Electric Co. Winchester Lamp Plant (Winchester, VA) 92594
General Electric Memphis Lamp Plant (Memphis, TN) 81611
GTE Prods. Corp. (Versailles, KY) 69325
GTE Prods. Corp. (Winchester, KY) 69343
GTE Products Corp. (Winchester, KY) 69344
Lexington Lamp Plant (Lexington, KY) 68572

3643 Current-Carrying Wiring Devices

Alcoa Conductor Products Co. (Brentwood, TN) 80211; 80212
Alcoa Fujikura Ltd. Telecommunications (Spartanburg, SC) 79874
AMP Inc. (Gastonia, NC) 74652; 74654
AMP Inc. (Greensboro, NC) 74771; 74772
AMP, Inc. (Winston-Salem, NC) 76701; 76702
Amp Inc. - Bldg. 101 (Gastonia, NC) 74655
Bryloc Inc. (Aibonito, PR) 78303; 78304
Caribe G.E. Products Inc. (San German, PR) 78549
Caribe G.E. Products Inc. Arecibo Plant (Arecibo, PR) 78312
Caribe General Electric Products Inc. (Palmer, PR) 78524
Caribe General Electric Products Inc. Humacao P.R. (Humacao, PR) 78461
Challenger Electrical Equipment Corp. (Pageland, SC) 79783
Challenger Electrical Equipment Inc. (Pageland, SC) 79784
Cooper Industries Belden Div. (Clinton, AR) 56856
Cooper Industries Ded (Earlysville, VA) 90732
Cooper Industries Edp (Earlysville, VA) 90733
Cooper Industries Inc. Belden Div. (Clinton, AR) 56857
Cooper Industries Inc. Belden Div. (Monticello, KY) 69099
Cooper Industries Inc. Electrical Distrib. Products (Earlysville, VA) 90734
Crouse-Hinds Joy Molded Products (La Grange, NC) 75338; 75339
Crouse-Hinds Molded Products Joy Molded Products (La Grange, NC) 75340
Day-Brite Lighting Inc. (Tupelo, MS) 73395
Eaton Corp. Aerospace & Commercial Controls Div. (Arab, AL) 55024
Eaton Corp. Aerospace & Commercial Controls Div. (Sarasota, FL) 62816
Eaton Corp. Aerospace & Commercial Controls Div. (Selma, NC) 76221
Electrical Specialty Prods. Co. (Montevallo, AL) 56272
Emerson Electric Co. Terminal Products Div. (Hormigueros, PR) 78459
Essex Group Inc. (Bennettsville, SC) 78725
General Electric Co. (Goldsboro, NC) 74722
General Electric Co. (Selmer, TN) 82291
Honeywell Micro Switch Div. (Mars Hill, NC) 75508
Honeywell Inc. Micro Switch Div. (Mars Hill, NC) 75509
Molex Inc. (Huntsville, AL) 55976
Molex Inc. (N. Little Rock, AR) 57438
Pamcor, Inc. (Las Piedras, PR) 78485
Pamcor Inc. (Rio Piedras, PR) 78544
Pamcor Inc. Las Piedras Plant (Las Piedras, PR) 78486
Syltron Inc. Lighting Products (Luquillo, PR) 78491
Therm-O-Disc Inc. Micro Devices Div. (London, KY) 68668
Thomas & Betts Caribe Inc. Electrical Products Division (Vega Baja, PR) 78630
Thomas & Betts Caribe Plant I (Vega Baja, PR) 78631
Thomas & Betts Co. (Tulsa, OK) 78165
Thomas & Betts Corp. (Tulsa, OK) 78166
3M Co. Telecom Markets Div. (Austin, TX) 83046
Union Carbide Corp. (Anmoore, WV) 92660

3644 Noncurrent-Carrying Wiring Devices

Alcoa Fujikura Ltd. Telecommunications (Spartanburg, SC) 79874
American Electric (Athens, TN) 80185
Belden Wire & Cable (Monticello, KY) 69096
Challenger Electrical Equipment Corp. (Portland, TN) 82233
Challenger Electrical Equipment Corp. (Parkersburg, WV) 92981
Cooper Industries Inc. Belden Div. (Monticello, KY) 69099
General Electric Co. (Morristown, TN) 81805
Reliable Electric Products Co. (Greenville, MS) 72819
Thomas & Betts Caribe Plant I (Vega Baja, PR) 78631
Thomas & Betts Co. (Tulsa, OK) 78165
Thomas & Betts Corp. (Tulsa, OK) 78166
Thomas & Betts Corp. (Athens, TN) 80195; 80195
3M Co. Telecom Markets Div. (Austin, TX) 83046

3645 Residential Lighting Fixtures

Coast to Coast Engineering (Plain Dealing, LA) 70634
National Services Ind. Lithonia Lighting Div. (Cochran, GA) 65571
National Services Ind. Lithonia Lighting Div. (Conyers, GA) 65693
Nsi Inc. Lithonia Lighting Div. (Cochran, GA) 65572

3646 Commercial Lighting Fixtures

American Electric (Southaven, MS) 73346
Day-Brite Lighting Inc. (Tupelo, MS) 73395
General Electric Lighting Systems (Hendersonville, NC) 75040
National Services Ind. Lithonia Lighting Div. (Cochran, GA) 65571
National Services Ind. Lithonia Lighting Div. (Conyers, GA) 65693
Nsi Inc. Lithonia Lighting Div. (Cochran, GA) 65572
Prescolite (El Dorado, AR) 56957

3647 Vehicular Lighting Equipment

General Electric Co. (Lexington, KY) 68556
Luminator (Plano, TX) 88585

3648 Lighting Equipment Nec

Day-Brite Lighting Inc. (Tupelo, MS) 73395
GE Lighting (3010 Spartanburg Hwy., NC) 73508
Thomas & Betts Corp. (Bainbridge, GA) 65372

3651 Household Audio & Video Equipment

Harman International Industries Inc. (Washington, DC) 58297
Radio Shack (Fort Worth, TX) 85261

3660 Communications Equipment

E-Systems Inc. Garland Div. (Garland, TX) 85481

3661 Telephone & Telegraph Apparatus

ALLTEL Corp. (Little Rock, AR) 57245
ALLTEL Supply Inc. (Norcross, GA) 67093
AT & T (Roanoke, VA) 92102
AT & T Network Systems (Norcross, GA) 67097
AT & T Network Systems (Oklahoma City, OK) 77301
AT&T (Montgomery, AL) 56279
AT&T (Atlanta, GA) 64240
AT&T Paradyne Corp. (Largo, FL) 60818
At&T Technologies Inc. (Burlington, NC) 73742
E-Systems Inc. (Dallas, TX) 83992
Electrospace Systems inc. (Richardson, TX) 88734
General Instrument Corp. (Brownsville, TX) 83359
Litton Industries, Inc. Amercom Div. (College Park, MD) 71563
R-Tec Systems (Bedford, TX) 83248
Reliable Electric (St. Stephen, SC) 79976
Reliable Electric Co. (St. Stephen, SC) 79977
Reliance Comm/Tec Reliance Electric (Toccoa, GA) 67837
Seiscor Tech. Inc. (Tulsa, OK) 78107
Siecor Corp. (Hickory, NC) 75100
Sprint (Reston, VA) 91718
3M Co. Telecom Markets Div. (Austin, TX) 83046

3663 Radio & T.V. Communications Equipment

ABM Graphics (Birmingham, AL) 55109
Acme Business Product (Greenville, SC) 79290
Acme Business Products (Albany, GA) 64060
Acustar Inc. Huntsville Electronics Plant (Huntsville, AL) 55872
Alliant Techsystems Inc. (Annapolis, MD) 71000
Allied-Signal Aerospace Co. (Orangeburg, SC) 79766
AT&T (McLeansville, NC) 75546
AT&T Paradyne Corp. (Largo, FL) 60818
Avnet Channel Master (Smithfield, NC) 76255
Borg Warner Automotive (Gary, NC) 74651
Copy Corp. (Lexington, KY) 68538
Delta Business Systems (Boca Raton, FL) 58694
Delta Business Systems (Jacksonville, FL) 60155
Delta Business Systems (Jacksonville, FL) 60257
Delta Business Systems (Miami, FL) 61277
Delta Business Systems (Orlando, FL) 61960
E-Systems ECI Div. (St. Petersburg, FL) 63099
E Systems Inc. (Dallas, TX) 83990; 83992
E-Systems Inc. C. M. Div. (St. Petersburg, FL) 63100
E-Systems Inc. C.M. Div. (St. Petersburg, FL) 63101
E-Systems Inc. ECI Div. (St. Petersburg, FL) 63102
E-Systems Inc. Garland Div. (Garland, TX) 85482
E-Systems Inc. Go-Co. (Lexington, KY) 68547
E-Systems Inc. Melpar Div. (Fairfax, VA) 90766
E-Systems Inc. Melpar Div. (Falls Church, VA) 90831
Electrospace Systems inc. (Richardson, TX) 88734
General Dynamics Space Systems (Huntsville, AL) 55947
General Electric Co. (Lynchburg, VA) 91253
GTE Spacenet Corp. (McLean, VA) 91391
Innovative Office Systems (Shreveport, LA) 70731
Innovative Office Systems Inc. (Fort Worth, TX) 85130
Litton Industries, Inc. Amercom Div. (College Park, MD) 71563
Mirex Corp. (Tulsa, OK) 78026
Motorola P.R. Operations (Vega Baja, PR) 78627
Omni Business Systems, Inc. (Fort Myers, FL) 59726; 59727
Omni Business Systems, Inc. (Fort Pierce, FL) 59798
Omni Business Systems, Inc. (Melbourne, FL) 61082
Paramax Systems Corp. (Reston, VA) 91716
Pitney Bowes (Tampa, FL) 63519
Pitney Bowes (Norcross, GA) 67166
Pitney Bowes (Tulsa, OK) 78057
Pitney Bowes (Austin, TX) 82958
Pitney Bowes (Springfield, VA) 92289
Pitney Bowes Facsimile Systems (Brimingham, AL) 55487
Pitney Bowes Facsimile Systems (Orlando, FL) 62081
RFD Inc. (St. Petersburg, FL) 63132
Rockwell International Corp. (El Paso, TX) 84916
Rockwell International Corp. NTSD Div. (Richardson, TX) 88766
Rockwell International Ntsd (Richardson, TX) 88767
Rockwell Int'l Spd/Ntsd (El Paso, TX) 84918
Scientific Atlanta Inc. (Odenton, MD) 72171
Standard Office Systems, Inc. (Norcross, GA) 67187; 67188
Texas Copy Systems (College Station, TX) 83625
Uni-Copy Corp. (Morrisville, NC) 75669
Universal Data Systems (Huntsville, AL) 56050
Watkins-Johnson Co. (Gaithersburg, MD) 71819
Westinghouse Electric (College Station, TX) 83626
Xerox Business Services (Birmingham, AL) 55460
Xerox Corp. (Huntsville, AL) 56057
Xerox Corp. (Mobile, AL) 56257
Xerox Corp. (Little Rock, AR) 57321
Xerox Corp. (Wilmington, DE) 58120
Xerox Corp. (Coral Gables, FL) 59105
Xerox Corp. (Fort Lauderdale, FL) 59644
Xerox Corp. (Jacksonville, FL) 60513
Xerox Corp. (Pensacola, FL) 62492
Xerox Corp. (Tallahassee, FL) 63290
Xerox Corp. (Baton Rouge, LA) 69688
Xerox Corp. (Shreveport, LA) 70808
Xerox Corp. (Baltimore, MD) 71331
Xerox Corp. (Rideland, MS) 73316
Xerox Corp. (Tulsa, OK) 78212
Xerox Corp. (Charleston, SC) 78917
Xerox Corp. (Columbia, SC) 79128
Xerox Corp. (Greenville, SC) 79450
Xerox Corp. (Chattanooga, TN) 80528
Xerox Corp. (Knoxville, TN) 81277
Xerox Corp. (Nashville, TN) 82146
Xerox Corp. (Austin, TX) 83073
Xerox Corp. (El Paso, TX) 84980
Xerox Corp. (Fort Worth, TX) 85366
Xerox Corp. (Houston, TX) 87204
Xerox Corp. (San Antonio, TX) 89328
Xerox Corp. (Arlington, VA) 90394
Xerox Corp. (Richmond, VA) 92095
Xerox Corp. (Charleston, WV) 92800
Zeno Systems (Oklahoma City, OK) 77673

3669 Communications Equipment Nec

Allied-Signal Aerospace Co. (Orangeburg, SC) 79766
Allied-Signal Inc. Bendix Communications (Towson, MD) 72504
Allied-Signal Inc. Communication Systems (Towson, MD) 72505
Allied-Signal Inc. Communication Systems (Mc Lean, VA) 91361
Dictaphone Corp. (Melbourne, FL) 61048
E-Systems ECI Div. (St. Petersburg, FL) 63099
E-Systems Inc. Go-Co. (Lexington, KY) 68547
E-Systems Inc. Melpar Div. (Falls Church, VA) 90830
Eaton Corp. Power Control Div. (Bowling Green, KY) 68137
Harris Corp. Electronic Sys. Sector (Palm Bay, FL) 62236
Harris Corp. Electronic System Sector (Palm Bay, FL) 62237
Harris Corp. Ess Malabar (Malabar, FL) 60990
Harris Corp. Government Systems Sector (Palm Bay, FL) 62238
Litton Industries, Inc. Laser Systems (Apopka, FL) 58573
Timeplex Caribe Ltd. (Juncos, PR) 78472; 78473
WSA (Falls Church, VA) 90873

3671 Electron Tubes

AMP-AKZO Corp. (Newark, DE) 57888

Electro Mechanical Design Services (Gaithersburg, MD) 71770
Varo Inc. (Dallas, TX) 84487
Varo Inc. Esd-Kingsley (Garland, TX) 85561
Varo Inc. Walnut (Garland, TX) 85562
Westinghouse Electric (Oldsmar, FL) 61852

3672 Printed Circuit Boards

Advanced Micro Devices (Austin, TX) 82803
Advanced Micro Devices Inc. (Austin, TX) 82804
Allied-Signal Inc. Communications System Div. (Baltimore, MD) 71032
AMP Packaging Systems Inc. (Round Rock, TX) 88843
Atlantic Design Co. Inc. (Charlotte, NC) 73845
Data General Corp. (Apex, NC) 73555
Data General Corp. (Clayton, NC) 74260; 74263
Digital Equipment Corp. (San Antonio, PR) 78546
Digital Equipment Corp. (San German, PR) 78550
Digital Equipment Corp. (Greenville, SC) 79344
Harris Corp. Farion Div. San Antonio Operations (San Antonio, TX) 89024
Lika Southwest (Azle, TX) 83079
Loral Fairchild Corp. Loral Data Systems Div. (Sarasota, FL) 62842
Martin Marietta Electronics Information & Missile Systems (Ocala, FL) 61805
Productos Circuitos De P.R. (Juana Diaz, PR) 78468
SCI Technology Inc. (Huntsville, AL) 56018
Tandy Electronics (Azle, TX) 83083
Texas Instruments Inc. (Versailles, KY) 69332
Texas Instruments Inc. (Austin, TX) 83044
Texas Instruments Inc. (Dallas, TX) 84447
Westinghouse De Puerto Rico Computer & Instrumentation (Villalba, PR) 78637
Westinghouse De Puerto Rico Productos Circuitos De Puerto Rico (Juana Diaz, PR) 78469
Westinghouse Electric Corp. Electronic Assembly Plant (College Station, TX) 83628
Westinghouse Electric Corp. Productos Electronic (Santa Isabel, PR) 78588
Westinghouse de Puerto Rico Productos Circuitos De Puerto Rico (Juana Diaz, PR) 78470

3674 Semiconductors & Related Devices

Advanced Micro Devices (Austin, TX) 82803
Advanced Micro Devices Inc. (Austin, TX) 82804
Advanced Micro Devices Inc. (San Antonio, TX) 88911
Advanced Technology Lab (Linthicum Heights, MD) 72106
Advanced Technology Labroatories (Linthicum, MD) 72104
Allied-Signal Aerospace Co. Aerospace Technology & Micro. (Columbia, MD) 71572
Allied-Signal Aerospace Co. Technology & Microelectronics (Columbia, MD) 71573
Analog Devices Inc. (Greensboro, NC) 74775
Analog Devices Inc. Computer Laboratories (Greensboro, NC) 74776
At&T Microelectronics (Orlando, FL) 61920
Department of Defense Special Process Lab (Fort George G. Meade, MD) 71706
Eaton Corp. Power Control Div. (Bowling Green, KY) 68137
Eaton Corp. Semiconductor Equipment (Austin, TX) 82862
GE Microelectronics Center (Research Triangle Park, NC) 76020
General Electric Co. (Durham, NC) 74402
Harris Computer Systems Div. (Fort Lauderdale, FL) 59500
Harris Corp. Semiconductor Palm Bay (Palm Bay, FL) 62235
Harris Corp. Semiconductor (Palm Bay, FL) 62240
Harris Corp. Semiconductor Palm Bay (Palm Bay, FL) 62241
Harris Corp. Semiconductor Sector (Palm Bay, FL) 62242
Harris Microelectronics Center (Research Triangle Park, NC) 76021
Harris Semiconductor International Center (Research Triangle Park, NC) 76022
Honeywell Inc. (Clearwater, FL) 59023
Honeywell Inc. Optoelectronics (Richardson, TX) 88739
Honeywell Optoelectronics (Richardson, TX) 88740
Loral Information Display Systems (Atlanta, GA) 64664
Monsanto Co. (Moore, SC) 79667; 79668
National Semiconductor Corp. (Arlington, TX) 82710
Silicon Materials Service (Garland, TX) 85536
Silicon Materials Service Inc. (Garland, TX) 85537
Southern Controls (Montgomery, AL) 56379
Texas Instruments (Midland, TX) 88086
Texas Instruments Inc. (Johnson City, TN) 81059
Texas Instruments Inc. (Dallas, TX) 84446; 84447; 84448
Texas Instruments Inc. (Lubbock, TX) 87787; 87788
Texas Instruments Inc. Midland Odessa Site (Midland, TX) 88087
Texas Instruments Inc. Sherman (Sherman, TX) 89427
Westinghouse Electric Corp. Advanced Technology Laboratories (Linthicum Heights, MD) 72111
Westinghouse Electric Corp. Advanced Technology Laboratory (Linthicum Heights, MD) 72112

3675 Electronic Capacitors

Aero M Inc. (Glasgow, KY) 68390
K & L Microwave Inc. (Salisbury, MD) 72348
Vitramon Inc. (Roanoke, VA) 92197

3676 Electronic Resistors

Allen-Bradley Co. (Browns Summit, NC) 73728
Allen-Bradley Co. (Greensboro, NC) 74760
Allen-Bradley Co. (El Paso, TX) 84755

3677 Electronic Coils & Transformers

Berkshire Hathaway France (Fairview, TN) 80785
General Dynamics Space Systems (Huntsville, AL) 55947
Hevi Duty Electric (Celina, TN) 80282
Magnetek (Palmetto, FL) 62310
Westinghouse Electric Corp. Productos Electronic (Santa Isabel, PR) 78588

3678 Electronic Connectors

AMP Inc. (Charlotte, NC) 73841
AMP Inc. (Gastonia, NC) 74652; 74653; 74654
AMP Inc. (Greensboro, NC) 74770; 74771; 74773; 74774
AMP Inc. (Winston-Salem, NC) 76702
AMP Inc. (Harrisonburg, VA) 91065; 91066
Amp Inc. - Bldg. 101 (Gastonia, NC) 74655
Amp Inc. Building 67 (Winston-Salem, NC) 76703
Molex-Etc Inc. (Pinellas Pk., FL) 62532
Molex-Etc Inc. (St. Petersburg, FL) 63128
Molex Inc. (N. Little Rock, AR) 57438
Pamcor, Inc. (Las Piedras, PR) 78485
Pamcor Inc. (Rio Piedras, PR) 78544
Pamcor Inc. Las Piedras Plant (Las Piedras, PR) 78486
Raychem Corp. (Vega Baja, PR) 78628
3M Co. Telecom Markets Div. (Austin, TX) 83046

3679 Electronic Components Nec

Acustar Inc. Huntsville Electronics Plant (Huntsville, AL) 55872
Advanced Micro Devices (Austin, TX) 82802; 82803
Advanced Micro Devices Inc. (Austin, TX) 82804
Advanced Micro Devices Inc. (Houston, TX) 85764
Aero M Inc. (Huntsville, AL) 55874
Aerovox Mallory (Huntsville, AL) 55876
Allen-Bradley Co. (El Paso, TX) 84755
Allied-Signal Laminate Systems Micarta (Pendleton, SC) 79787
AMP AKZO Corp. Carolina (Greenville, SC) 79294
AMP-Azco Carolina Circuits (Greenville, SC) 79295
AMP Inc. (Charlotte, NC) 73841
AMP Inc. (Greensboro, NC) 74771
AMP Packaging Systems Inc. (Round Rock, TX) 88843; 88844
AT & T (Austin, TX) 82819
Avnet Channel Master (Smithfield, NC) 76255
Black & Decker (Austin, TX) 82827
Boeing Aerospace & Electronics (Lake Dallas, TX) 87576
Boeing Electronics Irving Co. (Irving, TX) 87324
Borg Warner Automotive (Gary, NC) 74651
Brownell Electro Inc. (Lubbock, TX) 87750
Channel Master (Smithfield, NC) 76259
Collins General Aviation (Melbourne, FL) 61044
Dale Electronics Inc. (El Paso, TX) 84786
Data General Corp. (Apex, NC) 73555
Data General Corp. (Clayton, NC) 74261; 74262; 74263
Digital Equipment Corp. (San German, PR) 78550
Drive Systems Operations (Salem, VA) 92209
E-Systems Inc. Garland Div. (Garland, TX) 85482
Eagle-Picher Industries (Grove, OK) 77090
Eaton Corp. Condura (Brownsville, TX) 83356
Electronic Systems Group Friendship Site (Linthicum, MD) 72105
Electronic Systems Group Frienship Site (Linthicum Heights, MD) 72110
EMB Corp. (Elizabethtown, KY) 68278
Fischbach & Moore International Group (Dallas, TX) 84070
General Electric Co. (Durham, NC) 74402
General Electric Co. Mobile Communications Business (Lynchburg, VA) 91255
General Electric Ndd Pinellas Plant (Largo, FL) 60839
Granger Associates of Puerto Rico Inc. (Aguada, PR) 78289
K & L Microwave Inc. (Salisbury, MD) 72348
Litton Industries Advanced Circuit Design Div. (Austin, TX) 82929
Loral Fairchild Corp. Loral Data Systems Div. (Sarasota, FL) 62842
Martin Marietta Speciality Co. US Doe Pinellas Plant (Largo, FL) 60846
Mercury Marine (St. Cloud, FL) 63067
Mercury Marine Plant 7 (St. Cloud, FL) 63068
Molex Inc. (N. Little Rock, AR) 57438
Motorola Inc. Portable Products Div. (Plantation, FL) 62571
NCR Corp. (Dallas, TX) 84260
Pamcor, Inc. (Las Piedras, PR) 78485
Pamcor Inc. (Rio Piedras, PR) 78544
Paramax Systems Corp. (Reston, VA) 91716
Pentastar Electronics Inc. (Huntsville, AL) 55990; 55991
Raychem Corp. (Vega Baja, PR) 78628
Rockwell (El Paso, TX) 84914
Rockwell International (El Paso, TX) 84915
Rockwell International Corp. Collins General Aviation Div. (Melbourne, FL) 61105
Rockwell International Corp. Autonetic Electronics System (El Paso, TX) 84917
Rockwell International Corp. Msd Duluth (Duluth, GA) 66077
SCI Manufacturing (Graham, NC) 74752
Tandy (Azle, TX) 83082
Tandy Sign Co. (Arlington, TX) 82763
Tandy Software Assembly (Fort Worth, TX) 85318
Teledyne Lewisburg (Lewisburg, TN) 81331
Texas Instruments Inc. (Abilene, TX) 82463
3M Co. Telecom Markets Div. (Austin, TX) 83046
TRW Seat Belt Systems (Louisville, MS) 73125
Uds/Motorola (Huntsville, AL) 56043
Unisys Corp. (Oldsmar, FL) 61851
United Technologies Auto (Tampa, FL) 63640
United Technologies Automotive (Tampa, FL) 63641
Varian Associates Inc. (Richardson, TX) 88788
Vulcan Materials Co. (Nashville, TN) 82136
Walgreen Data Terminal (San Antonio, TX) 89307
Westinghouse Electric (College Station, TX) 83626
Westinghouse Electric Corp. Advanced Technology Laboratories (Linthicum Heights, MD) 72111
Westinghouse Electric Corp. Electronic Assembly (College Station, TX) 83627

3691 Storage Batteries

Duracell USA (Cleveland, TN) 80575
Eagle-Picher Ind. Inc. (Grove, OK) 77089
Eaton Corp. Supercharger Div. (Athens, GA) 64167
Eveready Battery Co. Inc. (Greenville, NC) 74957
Johnson Controls Battery Group Inc. (Louisville, KY) 68786
Johnson Controls Inc. (Middletown, DE) 57833
Johnson Controls Inc. (Florence, KY) 68311
Johnson Controls Inc. (Garland, TX) 85492
Johnson Controls Inc. Battery Div. (Winston-Salem, NC) 76734
Johnson Controls Inc. Battery Group (Middletown, DE) 57834
Johnson Controls Inc. Battery Group Inc. (Florence, KY) 68312
Johnson Controls Inc. Battery Group (Tampa, FL) 63464
Johnson Controls Inc. Winston-Salem Plant (Winston-Salem, NC) 76736
Motorola De Puerto Rico (Vega Baja, PR) 78626

3692 Primary Batteries—Dry & Wet

Duracell USA (La Grange, GA) 66478
Duracell USA (Lexington, NC) 75403
Duracell USA (Lancaster, SC) 79571
Duracell USA (Cleveland, TN) 80574
Eveready Battery Co. Inc. (Asheboro, NC) 73585; 73586
Eveready Battery Co. Inc. (Greenville, NC) 74957
Motorola P.R. Operations (Vega Baja, PR) 78627

3694 Engine Electrical Equipment

Alcoa Fujikura Ltd. (Brentwood, TN) 80213; 80214
Allied-Signal Inc. Autolite (Duncan, SC) 79168
Allied-Signal Inc. Autolite-Elberton (Elberton, GA) 66165
Allied-Signal Inc. Filter & Sparkplug Group (Duncan, SC) 79169
Allied-Signal Inc. Filters & Spark Plug (Duncan, SC) 79170
Alliedsignal Autolite (Elberton, GA) 66166
Borg Warner Automotive (Blytheville, AR) 56803
Cooper Industries Inc. Champion Aviation Products Div. (Liberty, SC) 79610; 79611
Echlin Ponce Inc. (Ponce, PR) 78535
Genuine Parts Co. (Wheeling, WV) 93112
Stanric Inc. (Puerto Real, PR) 78538
Stanric Inc. Pto. Real Industrial Park (Fajardo, PR) 78415
Tandy Magnetics (Fort Worth, TX) 85316
United Technologies Electro Systems (Columbus, MS) 72732

3695 Magnetic & Optical Recording Media

BASF Corp. (Enka, NC) 74505
BASF Corp. Fibers Div. (Williamsburg, VA) 92564
Tandy Software Assembly (Fort Worth, TX) 85318

3699 Electrical Equipment & Supplies Nec

Advanced Micro Devices Inc. (Houston, TX) 85763
Allied-Signal Inc. Bendix Electric Power (Orangeburg, SC) 79767
American Electric (Bainbridge, GA) 65363
AMP Inc. (Harrisonburg, VA) 91064
Appleton Electric Co. (Stephenville, TX) 89513
Barfield Mfg Co. Inc. (Murfreesboro, TN) 81835
Belden/Cooper Industries Franklin Plant (Franklin, NC) 74622
Berkshire Hathaway France (Fairview, TN) 80785
Challenger Caribbean Corp. (Canovanas, PR) 78364
Challenger Electrical Equipment Corp. (Jackson, MS) 72959
Cooper Power Systems (Greenwood, SC) 79454
Crouse-Hinds (Amarillo, TX) 82542
Crouse-Hinds Cooper Industries Inc. (Amarillo, TX) 82543
Eaton Corp. (Bowling Green, KY) 68136
Electronic Systems Group Frienship Site (Linthicum Heights, MD) 72110
Emerson Electric Co. (Paris, TN) 82216
Emerson Electric Co. Chromalox Div. (Murfreesboro, TN) 81840
Emerson Electric Co. Wiegand Industrial Div. (Murfreesboro, TN) 81841
Exxon Corp. (Winter Park, FL) 63973
GE Consumer Service (Columbia, SC) 79027
General Electric Carolina Products Plant (Goldsboro, NC) 74721
General Electric Co. (Jonesboro, AR) 57220
General Electric Co. (Columbia, MD) 71590
General Electric Co. (Salisbury, NC) 76166
General Electric Co. (Morristown, TN) 81805
General Electric Co. (Dallas, TX) 84090
General Electric Co. (Houston, TX) 86247
General Electric Co. (Hampton, VA) 91038
General Electric Co. (Lynchburg, VA) 91253
General Electric Co. (Richmond, VA) 91897
General Electric Drive Systems (Salem, VA) 92213
Halliburton Geophysical Services Inc. (Houston, TX) 86260
Hevi Duty Electric (Celina, TN) 80282
Hevi Duty Nelson (Tulsa, OK) 77954
Intel Corp. (Dallas, TX) 84135
Molex-Etc Inc. (Roswell, GA) 67395
Molex Inc. (Austin, TX) 82945
Radio Shack (Alief, TX) 82493
Radio Shack (Channelview, TX) 83554
Radio Shack (Houston, TX) 86734; 86748; 86749; 86750; 86754; 86756; 86760; 86765; 86769; 86776; 86780; 86781; 86784; 86787; 86789
Radio Shack (La Porte, TX) 87567

Raychem Corp. (Fuquay-Varina, NC) 74641
Reliance Electric Co. (Weaverville, NC) 76476
SCI Systems Inc. (Graham, NC) 74753
SCI Technology Inc. (Huntsville, AL) 56018
Sperry Marine Inc. (Charlottesville, VA) 90549
Teledyne Lewisburg (Lewisburg, TN) 81331
Teleflex Inc. (Sarasota, FL) 62862
Unisys Clearwater (Oldsmar, FL) 61850
Varian Associates (Richardson, TX) 88787
Varo, Inc. (Garland, TX) 85557
Westinghouse Electric (Atlanta, GA) 65285
Westinghouse Electric (Arden, NC) 73573
Westinghouse Electric (Sumter, SC) 80033
Westinghouse Electric (Houston, TX) 87191
Westinghouse Electric Corp. Electronic Assembly (College Station, TX) 83627
Westinghouse Electric Corp. Integrated Logistics Support (Hunt Valley, MD) 71945; 71946
Westinghouse de Puerto Rico Productos Electronicos Industriales (Santa Isabel, PR) 78590

3700 Transportation Equipment

A. O. Smith Automotive Prods. Co. (Milan, TN) 81765
Trw Inc. Staton (Greenville, NC) 74983
W. R. Grace & Co. Connecticut Cryovac Div. (Duncan, SC) 79175

3711 Motor Vehicles & Car Bodies

Cummins Military Systems (Augusta, GA) 65318
Cummins Military Systems Co. (Augusta, GA) 65319
Eagle Bus Mfg. Inc. (Brownsville, TX) 83355
Fleetwood Homes of Fl. Inc. 33 (Haines City, FL) 59946
Fleetwood Homes of Ga. Inc. No. 54 (Pearson, GA) 67254
Fleetwood Homes of Tennessee Inc. No. 27 (Westmoreland, TN) 82410
Fleetwood Motor Homes of Florida Inc. (Lakeland, FL) 60725
Fleetwood Travel Trailer Inc. (Winchester, VA) 92589
Fleetwood Travel Trailers Inc. (Hancock, MD) 71901
Fleetwood Travel Trailers Inc. (Congview, TX) 83647
Fleetwood Travel Trailers of Virginia Inc. (Winchester, VA) 92590
Ford Motor Co., Atlanta Assembly Plant (Hapeville, GA) 66334
Ford Motor Co., Louisville Assembly Plant (Louisville, KY) 68765
Ford Motor Co. Norfolk Assembly Plant (Norfolk, VA) 91536
Loral Vought Systems (Camden, AR) 56836
Loral Vought Systems (Grand Prairie, TX) 85623
Mobil Tech Inc. (Sanford, FL) 62769
Newark Assembly Plant (Newark, DE) 57923; 57924
Oshkosh Truck Corp. Chassis Div. (Gaffney, SC) 79261
Peterbilt Motors Co. (Madison, TN) 81379
Peterbilt Motors Co. (Denton, TX) 84626; 84626
Trailways Manufacturing Inc. (Harlingen, TX) 85717

3713 Truck & Bus Bodies

Allied-Signal Automotive (Frankfort, KY) 68357
Dover Corp. Heil Bulk Trailer Div. (Athens, TN) 80187
Eagle Bus Mfg. Inc. (Brownsville, TX) 83355
Fmc Corp. Orlando (Orlando, FL) 61990
Ford Motor Co. Kentucky Truck Plant (Louisville, KY) 68764
Heil Co. (Fort Payne, AL) 55757
Heil Co. (Tishomingo, MS) 73382
Heil Co. (Chattanooga, TN) 80415
Peterbilt Motors Co. (Madison, TN) 81379
Tesco Hi-Lift Inc. (Davie, FL) 59160

3714 Motor Vehicle Parts & Accessories

Ace Hardware Stores (Houston, TX) 85760
Acustar Inc. Huntsville Electronics Plant (Huntsville, AL) 55873
Aeroquip Corp. (Henderson, KY) 68438
Aeroquip Corp. (Mooresville, NC) 75596
Aeroquip Corp. (Statesville, NC) 76315
Aeroquip Corp. (Livingston, TN) 81347
Air Control Products (Roxboro, NC) 76120
Alcoa Fujikura Ltd. (Houston, MS) 72916; 72917
Alcoa Fujikura Ltd. (Brentwood, TN) 80213; 80214
Allied Automotive Bendix (Charlotte, NC) 73830
Allied-Signal Allied Automotive (Frankfort, KY) 68356
Allied-Signal Allied Automotive (Salisbury, NC) 76153
Allied-Signal Automotive (Sumter, SC) 79999; 80000
Allied-Signal Automotive (Jackson, TN) 80962; 80963
Allied-Signal Automotive Bendix Heavy Vehicle Systems (Frankfort, KY) 68358
Allied-Signal Brake Systems (Gallatin, TN) 80835
Allied-Signal Corp. (Newport News, VA) 91449
Allied-Signal Inc. Bendix Automotive (Charlotte, NC) 73831
Allied-Signal Inc. Bendix Automotive Systems (Sumter, SC) 80001; 80002
Allied-Signal Inc. Bendix Automotive Systems (Clarksville, TN) 80533
Allied-Signal Inc. Braking Systems (Sumter, SC) 80003
Allied-Signal Inc. Braking Systems Bendix Automotive (Gallatin, TN) 80836
Allied-Signal Inc. Environmental Catalysts (Catoosa, OK) 76908
Allied-Signal Inc. Saftey Restraints Systems (Knoxville, TN) 81133
Ambrake Corp. (Elizabethtown, KY) 68272
Anchor Swan Inc. (Easley, SC) 79176; 79177
A.O. Smith Automotive Products Co. (Milan, TN) 81766
Arvin Industries Inc. Gabriel Ride Control Div. (Pulaski, TN) 82238
Arvin Industries Gabriel Div. (Pulaski, TN) 82239
Arvin Industries Inc. (Fayette, AL) 55728
Arvin Industries Inc. Gabriel Ride Control Div. (Pulsaski, TN) 82246; 82247
Arvin Industries Inc. Gabriel Ride Control Products Div. (Brentwood, TN) 80216
Arvin Industries Inc. Gabriel Shock Absorber Plant (Chickasha, OK) 76920
Arvin Industries Inc. Maremount Exhaust Systems Product Div. (Loudon, TN) 81351
Arvin North American Automotive (Fayette, AL) 55729
AVM Inc. (Marion, SC) 79638
Beck/Arnley Worldparts Corp. (Nashville, TN) 81899
Belden Automotive Wire & Cable (Dumas, AR) 56908
Borg Warner Automotive (Gary, NC) 74651
Clark Equipment Co. (Statesville, NC) 76321
Colt Industries Inc. Holley Automotive Div. (Water Valley, MS) 73466
Colt Industries Inc. Holley Replacement Parts Div. (Bowling Green, KY) 68135
Coltec Automotive Div. (Sallisaw, OK) 77768
Coltec Industries Inc. Holley Automotive Div. (Water Valley, MS) 73467
Cooper Industries Inc. Wagner Brake Subsidiary (Boaz, AL) 55466
Cummins Engine Co. Inc. (Charleston, SC) 78798; 78799
Dana Corp. (Montgomery, AL) 56295
Dana Corp. (Jonesboro, AR) 57211
Dana Corp. (Hopkinsville, KY) 68476
Dana Corp. (Olive Branch, MS) 73227
Dana Corp. (Morganton, NC) 75634
Dana Corp. (Oklahoma City, OK) 77341; 77342
Dana Corp. (Gordonsville, TN) 80873
Dana Corp. (Wichita Fall, TX) 90062
Dana Corp. Mobile Fluid (Greenville, SC) 79334
Dana Corp. Spicer Systems Assembly Div. (Lugoff, SC) 79617
Dana Corp. Spicer Transmission (Knoxville, TN) 81160
Dana Corp. Spicer Transmission Div. (Jonesboro, AR) 57212
Dana Corp. Spicer Transmission Div. Gear Plant (Jonesboro, AR) 57213
Dana Corp. Spicer Transmission Div. Jonesboro Gear Plant (Jonesboro, AR) 57214
Dana Corp. Spicer Universal (Charlotte, NC) 73922
Dana Corp. Spicer Universal Joint Div. (Bristol, VA) 90471
Dana Corp. Camshaft Plant (Russellville, AR) 57580
Dana Corp., Spicer Trailer Axle Plant (Montgomery, AL) 56296
Danaher Corp. (Washington, DC) 58209
Daniel Radiator Corp. (West Palm Beach, FL) 63854
Daniel Radiator Corp. (Atlanta, GA) 64402
Daniel Radiator Corp. (La Grange, GA) 66477
Daniel Radiator Corp. (Lexington, TN) 81336
Daniel Radiator Corp. (Houston, TX) 86025
Davidson Exterior Trim Textron (Americus, GA) 64137; 64138
Diesel Recon Co. (El Paso, TX) 84790
Dresser Industries Inc. Waukesha Engine Division (Houston, TX) 86049
Eaton Corp. (Athens, GA) 64166
Eaton Corp. (Glasgow, KY) 68393
Eaton Corp. (Henderson, KY) 68442
Eaton Corp. (Louisville, KY) 68758
Eaton Corp. (Fletcher, NC) 74589
Eaton Corp. (Laurinburg, NC) 75351
Eaton Corp. (Roxboro, NC) 76124; 76125
Eaton Corp. (Humboldt, TN) 80950
Eaton Corp. (Shelbyville, TN) 82301
Eaton Corp. Axel & Brake Div. (Henderson, KY) 68444
Eaton Corp. Axle & Brake Div. (Glasgow, KY) 68394
Eaton Corp. Axle & Brake Div. (Humboldt, TN) 80951
Eaton Corp. Fluid Power Div. (Fletcher, NC) 74590
Eaton Corp. Power Control Div. (Bowling Green, KY) 68137
Eaton Corp. Transmission (Kings Mountain, NC) 75297
Eaton Corp. Transmission Div. (Kings Mountain, NC) 75298; 75299
Eaton Corp. Transmission Div. (Shelbyville, TN) 82302
Eaton Corp. Transmission Div. Kings Mountain (Kings Mountain, NC) 75300
Eaton Corp. Transmission Div. Kings Moutain Plant (Kings Mountain, NC) 75301
Echlin Ponce Inc. (Ponce, PR) 78535
Engelhard Catalyst & Chemicals Div. (Huntsville, AL) 55910
Engelhard Corp. (Huntsville, AL) 55911
Engelhard Corp. Environmental Catalysts Div. (Huntsville, AL) 55912
Engelhard Corp. Catalyst & Chemical (Huntsville, AL) 55913
Engelhard Corp. Environmental Catalyst Group (Huntsville, AL) 55914
Engelhard Specialty Chemicals (Huntsville, AL) 55915
Engineered Sintered Components Co. (Troutman, NC) 76408
Fayette Tubular Products Inc. (Livingston, TN) 81349
Federal Mogul Corp. (Blacksburg, VA) 90440; 90441; 90442
Federal-Mogul Corp. Blacksburg Plant (Blacksburg, VA) 90443
Fleetguard Inc. (Cookeville, TN) 80657
Friction, Inc. (Dallas, TX) 84077; 84078
Friction Inc. (Fredericksburg, VA) 90926
Gabriel Ride Control Products Inc. (Brentwood, TN) 80230
Genuine Parts Rayloc Div. (Atlanta, GA) 64498
Genuine Parts Co. Rayloc Div. (Atlanta, GA) 64501; 64502
Genuine Parts Co. Rayloc Div. (Hancock, MD) 71903; 71904
Genuine Parts Co. Rayloc Div. (Memphis, TN) 81612; 81613
Genuine Parts Co. Rayloc Div. (Stephenville, TX) 89516
Harman Automotive Puerto Rico Inc. (Vega Alta, PR) 78619
Heil Co. (Chattanooga, TN) 80415
Hennessy Industries, Inc. Coast Operations (La Vergne, TN) 81283
Johnson Controls Inc. (Linden, TN) 81346
Lexington Tube Co. (Lexington, TN) 81339
Maremont Corp. (Chickasha, OK) 76929
Maremont Corp. (Ripley, TN) 82262
Maremont Exhaust Products, Inc. (Loudon, TN) 81354
Maremont Exhaust System (Loudon, TN) 81355
Maremont Exhaust Systems (Loudon, TN) 81356
Maremount Corp. Shock Absorber (Chickasha, OK) 76930
Metal Forge Co. (Albemarle, NC) 73540
Midland Brake Inc. (Marion, NC) 75505
Monroe Auto Equipment Co. (Paragould, AR) 57494; 57495
Monroe Auto Equipment Co. (Hartwell, GA) 66342
Motion Industries Midwest, Inc. (Birmingham, AL) 55324
Napa Auto Parts (Ocala, FL) 61810
Pacer Industries Inc. (Pensacola, FL) 62454
Parker Hannifin (Batesville, MS) 72597
Parker Hannifin Corp. (Trumann, AR) 57685
Parker Hannifin Corp. (Batesville, MS) 72598
Parker Hannifin Corp. Acd (Batesville, MS) 72599
Prattville Mfg. Inc. (Prattville, AL) 56491
Radio Shack (De Ridder, LA) 69818
Rayloc (Morganfield, KY) 69106
Rayloc Rayloc Div. (Hancock, MD) 71907
Rayloc Co. (Hancock, MD) 71908
Rayloc Industries, Inc. (Stephenville, TX) 89524
Rockwell International (Winchester, KY) 69353
Rockwell International (York, SC) 80140
Rockwell International Corp. (Morristown, TN) 81807
Rockwell International Corp. Plastics Div. (Louisville, KY) 68996
Rockwell International Corp. R.I. Plastics Div. Louisville Plastics Plant (Louisville, KY) 68997
Rockwell International Corp. Winchester Facility (Winchester, KY) 69354
Safety Kleen Corp. (Oklahoma City, OK) 77546
Schrader Automotive Inc. (Monroe, NC) 75588; 75589
Standard Products Co. (Goldsboro, NC) 74735
Stanric Inc. Pto. Real Industrial Park (Fajardo, PR) 78414
Teledyne Total Power (Hartwood, VA) 91110
Teledyne Total Power (Springfield, VA) 92294
Tesco Hi-Lift Inc. (Davie, FL) 59160
Texas Instruments Inc. (Versailles, KY) 69332
Torrington Co. (Honea Path, SC) 79531
Trim Masters Inc. (Bardstown, KY) 68121
TRW Automotive Products Remfg. (McAllen, TX) 87943
TRW Commercial Steering (Lebanon, TN) 81311
TRW Inc. (Greensboro, NC) 74925
TRW Inc. (Greenville, NC) 74980
TRW Inc. (Rogersville, TN) 82282
TRW Inc. Commercial Steering Div. (Greeneville, TN) 80890
TRW Inc. Commercial Steering Div. (Lebanon, TN) 81312
TRW Inc. Ross Gear Div. (Greeneville, TN) 80891
TRW Inc. Ross Gear Inc. (Lebanon, TN) 81313
TRW Inc. Station Plant Steering & Suspension Div. (Greenville, NC) 74981
Trw Inc. Koyo Steering Sys. Co. (Vonore, TN) 82397
Trw Inc. Station Plant (Greenville, NC) 74982
TRW Koyo Steering System (Vonove, TN) 82398
United Brake Sys. Inc. (Conley, GA) 65664
United Brake Sys. Inc. (Charlotte, NC) 74188
United Brake Sys. Inc. (Columbia, SC) 79115
United Brake Sys. Inc. (Nashville, TN) 82129
United Brake Systems Inc. (Birmingham, AL) 55439
United Brake Systems Inc. (Tampa, FL) 63638
United Brake Systems Inc. (Charlotte, NC) 74189
United Technologies Auto (Manfield, KY) 69075
United Technologies Auto (Columbus, MS) 72731
United Technologies Electro Systems (Columbus, MS) 72732
Wagner Brake Co. (Fort Worth, TX) 85349
Wagner Brake Subsidiary (Memphis, TN) 81752
Wagner Electric Corp. (Memphis, TN) 81753
Wagner Electric Corp. (Fort Worth, TX) 85350
Walker Manufacturing Co. (Aberdeen, MS) 72581
Walker Manufacturing Co. (Harrisonburg, VA) 91104
Walker Mfg. Co. (Harrisonburg, VA) 91105
Wix Corp. (Gustonia, NC) 74991
Wix Dana Corp. Air Refiner Div. Perry Plant (Oklahoma City, OK) 77669
Wix/Dana Corp. Allen Plant (Gastonia, NC) 74694
Wix/Dana Corp. Dixon Plant (Gastonia, NC) 74695
Wix Dana Corp. Perry Plant (Oklahoma City, OK) 77670

3715 Truck Trailers

Banta Corp. Freuhauf Div. (Charlotte, NC) 73848
Clark Material Handling Co. (Lexington, KY) 68535; 68537
Dover Corp. Heil Bulk Trailer Div. (Athens, TN) 80187
Fruehauf Trailer Corp. (Decatur, AL) 55582; 55584
Fruehauf Trailer Corp. (Charlotte, NC) 74024
Fruehauf Trailer Corp. (Huntsville, TN) 80961
Fruehauf Trailer Corp. (Memphis, TN) 81608; 81609
Great Dane Trailers Inc. (Savannah, GA) 67480; 67481
Great Dane Trailers Tennessee Inc. (Memphis, TN) 81618
Oshkosh Trailer Div. (Bradenton, FL) 58838

3720 Aircraft & Parts

Bell Helicopter Textron Inc. (Amarillo, TX) 82525
Pall Land & Marine Corp. (New Port Richey, FL) 61690; 61691

3721 Aircraft

Bell Helicopter Textron Inc. (Fort Worth, TX) 85069
Bell Helicopter Textron Inc. (Grand Prairie, TX) 85610
Bell Helicopter Textron Inc. Plant I (Fort Worth, TX) 85070
Boeing Co. (Miami, FL) 61204
Boeing Co. the (Hampton, VA) 91017
E Systems Inc. (Dallas, TX) 83990
E-Systems Inc. (Greenville, TX) 85666
E-Systems Inc. Greenville Div. (Greenville, TX) 85667
General Dynamics Corp. (Arlington, VA) 90354

Grumman Corp. (Arlington, VA) 90355
Grumman Corp. Aircraft Systems Div. (Stuart, FL) 63170
Grumman Corp. St. Augustine (St. Augustine, FL) 63058
Grumman St. Augustine Corp. (St. Augustine, FL) 63059; 63060
Gulfstream Aerospace Corp. (Savannah, GA) 67482
Lockheed Aeromod Centers Inc. (Greenville, SC) 79391
Lockheed Aeronautical Systems Co. (Marietta, GA) 66821
Lockheed Fort Worth Co. (Fort Worth, TX) 85178
Lockheed Systems Corp. Lasc-Georgia Div. (Meridian, MS) 73170
Ltv Aerospace & Defense Co. (Dallas, TX) 84213
Ltv Aerospace & Defense Co. (Grand Prairie, TX) 85625; 85626
McDonnell Douglas (Tulsa, OK) 78017
McDonnell Douglas Tulsa (Tulsa, OK) 78018
Northrop Corp. (Jackson, MS) 73026
Otis Elevator Co. (Alexandria, VA) 90228
Raytheon Corporate Jets (Arlington, VA) 90379
Raytheon Corporate Jets (Sterling, VA) 92347
Rohr Industries Inc. (Hagerstown, MD) 71898
United Technologies Auto (Washington, DC) 58510
US Navy Naval Weapons Industrial Reserve Plant (Dallas, TX) 84481

3724 Aircraft Engines & Engine Parts

Aerospace Technologies Inc. (Fort Worth, TX) 85055; 85056
Airfoil Textron Inc. (Orlando, FL) 61905
Allied Signal (Anniston, AL) 54989
Allied-Signal Aerospace Co. Engine Controls (Jacksonville, FL) 60162
Allied-Signal Aerospace Co. Engine Controls (Naples, FL) 61598
Allied-Signal Controls & Accessories (Rocky Mount, NC) 76073
Allied Signal Inc. (Anniston, AL) 54991
Allied Signal Inc. (Oxford, AL) 56436; 56437
Brunswick Composites Defense Facility (Marion, VA) 91330
Chromalloy Castings Tampa Corp. (Tampa, FL) 63388
Compressor Components Textron Inc. (Thomasville, GA) 67793
FMC Corp. (Orlando, FL) 61989
GE Aircraft Engines (Madisonville, KY) 69051
P&Wc Aircraft Services Inc. (Bridgeport, WV) 92708
Pratt & Whitney (Columbus, GA) 65648
Pratt & Whitney Aircraft of West Virginia (Bridgeport, WV) 92709
Rohr Inc. (Hagerstown, MD) 71896
Rohr Industries Foley Plant (Foley, AL) 55752
Rohr Industries Inc. (Heber Springs, AR) 57154
Rohr Industries Inc. (Sheridan, AR) 57613
Ryder Airline Services Mcallen (Mc Allen, TX) 87898
Sequa Corp. Chromalloy (Midwest City, OK) 77213; 77214
Sequa Corp. Chromalloy (Oklahoma City, OK) 77554
Sierra Industries Inc. (Uvalde, TX) 89857
Solar Turbines Inc. (Scott, LA) 70678
Teledyne Continental Motors Aircraft Products (Mobile, AL) 56245
Textron Lycoming (Greer, SC) 79485; 79486
Textron Lycoming Greer Plant (Greer, SC) 79487
Textron Lycoming Turbine Services Plant (Greer, SC) 79488; 79489
Textron Turbine Services (Greer, SC) 79490

3728 Aircraft Parts & Equipment Nec

Aeroquip Corp. (Toccoa, GA) 67835

Aeroquip Corp. (Lancaster, SC) 79566
Aerospace Technologies Inc. (Fort Worth, TX) 85054
Aircraft Porous Media Inc. (Pinellas Park, FL) 62508
Allied-Signal Aerospace Co. Engine Controls (Jacksonville, FL) 60162
Allied-Signal Aerospace Co. Engine Controls (Naples, FL) 61598
Allied-Signal Aerospace Co. Garrett Hydraulics (Fort Lauderdale, FL) 59429
Allied-Signal Airline Services Inc. (Anniston, AL) 54990
Allied-Signal Inc. (Oxford, AL) 56436; 56437
Allied-Signal Inc. Aerospace Controls & Accessories (Fort Lauderdale, FL) 59430
Allied-Signal Inc. Garrett Airline Repair (Anniston, AL) 54992
Aviall (Dallas, TX) 83865; 83866
Aviall Forest Park Facility (Dallas, TX) 83867
Aviall - Mcallen (Mc Allen, TX) 87882
Boeing Aerospace & Electronics (Oak Ridge, TN) 82180
Boeing Defense & Space Group (Oak Ridge, TN) 82181
Boeing Georgia Inc. (Macon, GA) 66674
Boeing Louisiana Inc. (Lake Charles, LA) 70130; 70131
Boeing Tennessee Inc. (Oak Ridge, TN) 82182
Brunswick Composites Defense Facility (Marion, VA) 91330
Chrysler Technologies Airborne Systems Inc. (Waco, TX) 89932
Collins & Aiken Holding II Corp. (Charlotte, NC) 73910
Collins & Aikman Holdings Corp. (Charlotte, NC) 73915
General Dynamics Corp. Abilene Facility (Abilene, TX) 82437
General Electric Co. (Madisonville, KY) 69052
General Electric Co. (Wilmington, NC) 76572
Grumman Aircraft Systems Div. (Milledgeville, GA) 66976; 66977
Grumman Aerospace & Electronics (Milledgeville, GA) 66978
Grumman Houston Corp. (Webster, TX) 90019
Grumman St. Augustine Corp. (St. Augustine, FL) 63061
Hta Aerostructures Inc. (San Marcos, TX) 89337
International Turbine Corp. (Grapevine, TX) 85658
Litton Industries Poly-Scientific Div. (Blacksburg, VA) 90450
Lockheed Abilene Facility (Abilene, TX) 82446
Lockheed Corp. Austin Div. (Austin, TX) 82930
Loral Engineered Fabrics (Rockmart, GA) 67332
Loral Vought Systems (Camden, AR) 56836
Loral Vought Systems (Grand Prairie, TX) 85623
Martin Marietta Aero & Naval Systems (Baltimore, MD) 71184
Menasco Aerosystems Div. (Euless, TX) 85015
Murdock Engineering Co. (Grand Prairie, TX) 85631
Murdock Engineering Co. (Irving, TX) 87380; 87381
Precision Fabrication Center (Columbus, GA) 65649
Rockwell International (Tulsa, OK) 78094
Rohr Inc. (Hagerstown, MD) 71896
Rohr Inc. Foley Facility (Foley, AL) 55751
Rohr Ind. Inc. (Heber Springs, AR) 57152
Rohr Ind. Inc. (Sheridan, AR) 57612
Rohr Industries Foley Plant (Foley, AL) 55752
Rohr Industries Inc. (Foley, AL) 55753
Rohr Industries Inc. (Heber Springs, AR) 57153; 57154
Rohr Industries Inc. (Hagerstown, MD) 71897
Textron Aerospace Prods. (Columbus, GA) 65653
Textron Aerostructures (Nashville, TN) 82107; 82108
Textron Aerostructures Inc. (Nashville, TN) 82109
Vickers (Jackson, MS) 73085
Vickers Inc. (Jackson, MS) 73086

3731 Ship Building & Repairing

Aluminum Boats Inc. (Crown Point, LA) 69804
Bellinger Shipyard (Jacksonville, FL) 60228
Bethlehem Steel Beth-Ship (Port Arthur, TX) 88627
Bethlehem Steel Corp. (Baltimore, MD) 71065
Bethlehem Steel Corp. Baltimore Marine (Sparrows Point, MD) 72463
Bethlehem Steel Corp. Bethship Div. (Sparrows Point, MD) 72464
Bethlehem Steel Corp. Marine (Sparrows Point, MD) 72465
Bethlehem Steel Corp. Sabine Yard (Port Arthur, TX) 88628
Brown & Root Inc. Marine Fabrication Yard (Houston, TX) 85895
Dover Corp. Heil Bulk Trailer Div. (Athens, TN) 80187
Equitable Halter Div. (New Orleans, LA) 70449
Equitable Madisonville (Madisonville, LA) 70206
General Dynamics Corp. (Goose Creek, SC) 79282
General Dynamics Corp. (Falls Church, VA) 90856
Gretna Machine & Iron Works (Harvey, LA) 69940
Halter Marine Inc. Moss Point Div. (Moss Point, MS) 73191
Ingalls Shipbuilding Inc. (Pascagoula, MS) 73261; 73262
Intermarine USA (Savannah, GA) 67491
Jacksonville Shipyards Inc. (Jacksonville, FL) 60332
Jacksonville Shipyards, Inc. Electro Lube Devices (Jacksonville, FL) 60333
Jacksonville Shipyards, Inc.-Electro Lube Devices (Jacksonville, FL) 60334
Jacksonville Shipyards, Inc.-Key Houston & Bellinger (Jacksonville, FL) 60335
Litton Ingalls Shipbuilding Div. (Pascagoula, MS) 73264
Moss Point Marine (Escatawpa, MS) 72758
Newport News Shipbuilding & Dry Dock Co. (Newport News, VA) 91475
Newport News Shipbuilding & Drydock Co. (Newport News, VA) 91476
Textron Marine Sys. Shipyard Ops. (New Orleans, LA) 70573
Textron Marine Systems/Bell Halter Inc. Shipyard (New Orleans, LA) 70574
Textron Marine Systems Shipyard Operations (New Orleans, LA) 70575
Trinity Industries Equitable Div. (New Orleans, LA) 70581
Trinity Industries Halter Marine Lockport Div. (Lockport, LA) 70196
Trinity Industries Halter Marine Moss Point Div. (Moss Point, MS) 73196
Trinity Industries Moss Point Marine Div. (Escatawpa, MS) 72761
Trinity Industries Inc. Lockport Div. (Lockport, LA) 70197

3732 Boat Building & Repairing

Banta Co. (Harrisonburg, VA) 91067
Banta Corp. (Harrisonburg, VA) 91070
Bellinger Shipyard (Jacksonville, FL) 60228
Brunswick Corp. Marine Div. (Delhi, LA) 69823
Brunswick Fishing Boat Div. (Murfreesboro, TN) 81837
Brunswick Marine (Murfreesboro, TN) 81838
Brunswick Marine/Fisher Plant (West Point, MS) 73476
Brunswick Sea Ray Div. (Knoxville, TN) 81149
Coleman Co. (New Braunfels, TX) 88206
Donzi Marine (Sarasota, FL) 62812; 62813
Donzi Marine (Tallevast, FL) 63291
Donzi Marine Inc. (Fort Lauderdale, FL) 59481
Fisher Marine (West Point, MS) 73480; 73481; 73482
Four Winns of Texas (Athens, TX) 82787

Four Winns of Texas Inc. (Athens, TX) 82788
Hydra-Sports Inc. (Nashville, TN) 82027
Javelin Boats (Murfreesboro, TN) 81853
Marine Group (Murfreesboro, TN) 81857
Marine Group Inc. (Murfreesboro, TN) 81858; 81859
Mercury Marine (St. Cloud, FL) 63067
Mercury Powerboat (Delhi, LA) 69824
Mercury Powerboats (Rockledge, FL) 62746
Omc Fishing Boat Group Engineering (Murfreesboro, TN) 81860
Omc Fishing Boat Group Inc. (Murfreesboro, TN) 81861
Omc Fishing Boat Group Inc. (Nashville, TN) 82073
Omc Chris Craft (Sarasota, FL) 62848; 62849
Omc Chris Craft Inc. (Sarasota, FL) 62850; 62851
Omc Chris-Craft Inc. (Hubert, NC) 75196
Omc Fishing Boat Group Inc. (Old Hickory, TN) 82205
Omc Inc. Boat Development Center (Sarasota, FL) 62852
Omc-Stratos Boats Inc. (Old Hickory, TN) 82206
Ome Hydra-Sports (Hubert, NC) 75197
Outboard Marine Corp. Four Winds Yacht Div. (Tampa, FL) 63515
Sea Ray Boats Florida Corp. (Palm Coast, FL) 62286
Sea Ray Boats Inc. (Merritt Island, FL) 61144; 61145
Sea Ray Boats Inc. (Fort Mill, SC) 79236
Sea Ray Boats Inc. (Knoxville, TN) 81246; 81247
Sea Ray Boats Inc. (Vonore, TN) 82396
Sea Ray Boats Inc. Cherokee Cove (Madisonville, TN) 81388
Sea Ray Boats Inc. Product Development (Merritt Island, FL) 61146
Sea Ray Boats Inc. Riverview (Knoxville, TN) 81248
Stratos Boats Inc. (Old Hickory, TN) 82207
Sunbird Boat Co. (Columbia, SC) 79100
Sunbird Boat Co. Inc. (Columbia, SC) 79101; 79102
Taco Bell (Russellville, AR) 57590
US Marine/Bayliner (Tallahassee, FL) 63284
US Marine/Bayliner (Salisbury, MD) 72365
US Marine/Bayliner (Dandridge, TN) 80714

3743 Railroad Equipment

Fitzgerald Railcar Services (Fitzgerald, GA) 66209
GE Capital Railcar Service (Camden, AR) 56831
GE Capital Railcar Service (Ranger, TX) 88706
GE Capital Railcar Service (Texarkana, TX) 89676
Tank Lining & Rail Car Repair (Saginaw, TX) 88865
Tank Lining & Rail Car Repair (Scottsville, TX) 89355
Trinity Industries Inc. (Bessemer, AL) 55107
Trinity Industries Inc. (Longview, TX) 87741

3751 Motorcycles, Bicycles & Parts

True Temper Sports Division (Olive Branch, MS) 73232

3761 Guided Missiles & Space Vehicles

Aerospace Products SE Inc. (Huntsville, AL) 55875
Alliant Techsystems (Huntsville, AL) 55877
Allied Signal Aerospace (Arlington, TX) 82632
Atlantic Research Corp. (East Camden, AR) 56916
Brunswick Defense Div. (East Camden, AR) 56918
Brunswick Composites Defense Div. (East Camden, AR) 56919
Brunswick Corp. (Camden, AR) 56827

Brunswick Corp. Defense Div. (East Camden, AR) 56920
Brunswick Corp. Defense Division (East Camden, AR) 56921
General Dynamics (East Camden, AR) 56922; 56923
General Dynamics Corp. Space Sys. (Cape Canaveral, FL) 58914
General Dynamics Space Systems (Cocoa Beach, FL) 59081
Hughes Missile Sys. Co. (East Camden, AR) 56924
Lockheed Missiles & Space Co. Austin Div. (Austin, TX) 82931
Loral Vought Systems (Camden, AR) 56836
Loral Vought Systems (Grand Prairie, TX) 85623
Ltv Aerospace & Defense (Grand Prairie, TX) 85624
Martin Marietta Corp. Electonic Systems Co. (Orlando, FL) 62044
Martin Marietta Electronics Information & Missile Systems (Ocala, FL) 61805
Martin Marietta Electronics Systems Co. (Orlando, FL) 62047
Martin Marietta Missile Systems (Orlando, FL) 62048; 62049
Martin Marietta Missile Systems Co. (Orlando, FL) 62050
Martin Marietta Ocala Operations (Ocala, FL) 61807
Martin Marietta Space Launch Systems (Cape Canaveral, FL) 58915
Martin Marietta Technologies Inc. (Orlando, FL) 62052
McDonnell Douglas Astronautics Co. (Titusville, FL) 63696
McDonnell Douglas Missile Systems Co. (Titusville, FL) 63697
Northrop Corp. (Huntsville, AL) 55981
Northrop Corp. (Shalimar, FL) 62914
Raytheon Co. (Huntsville, AL) 56009
Raytheon Co. (Bristol, TN) 80252
Teledyne Brown Engineering (Huntsville, AL) 56033
TRW Inc. (Huntsville, AL) 56042
United Technologies Advanced Systems Div. (Huntsville, AL) 56048
United Technologies Corp. Advanced Systems Div. (Huntsville, AL) 56049
Westinghouse Electric Corp. Oceanic Div. (Annapolis, MD) 71024

3764 Space Propulsion Units & Parts

Allegany Ballistics Lab. (Keyser, WV) 92910
Allegany Ballistics Laboratory (Rocket Center, WV) 93032
Allied-Signal Technical Service (Columbia, MD) 71574
Atlantic Research Corp. (East Camden, AR) 56916
Atlantic Research Corp. (Alexandria, VA) 90165; 90166
Atlantic Research Corp. (Gainesville, VA) 90960
Atlantic Research Corp. Arkansas Propulsion (East Camden, AR) 56917
Hercules Inc. US Naval Weapons Indl. Res. Plant (Mc Gregor, TX) 87905
Hercules Inc. US Naval Weapons Plant (Mc Gregor, TX) 87906
Ltv Aerospace & Defense (Grand Prairie, TX) 85624
Teledyne Gainesville Division (Gainesville, GA) 66293
Thiokol Corp. (Huntsville, AL) 56036; 56037
Thiokol Corp. Elkton Division (Elkton, MD) 71675

3769 Space Vehicle Equipment Nec

Allied-Signal Technical Service (Columbia, MD) 71574
Ametek Corp. Haveg Div. (Wilmington, DE) 57983
General Dynamics Corp. (Falls Church, VA) 90856
Honeywell Inc. (Clearwater, FL) 59023
Ltv Aerospace & Defense (Grand Prairie, TX) 85624
Martin Marietta Aero & Naval Systems (Baltimore, MD) 71184

Martin Marietta Corp. Electonic Systems Co. (Orlando, FL) 62044
Martin Marietta Electronic Systems (Orlando, FL) 62045
Martin Marietta Electronics Systems Co. (Orlando, FL) 62047
Martin Marietta Missile Systems (Orlando, FL) 62049
Martin Marietta Missile Systems Co. (Orlando, FL) 62050
Martin Marietta Ocala Operations (Ocala, FL) 61807
Michoud Assembly Facility (New Orleans, LA) 70535
Raytheon Co. Nwirp Bristol (Bristol, TN) 80253
Rockwell International (Tulsa, OK) 78094
Rockwell International Msd (Duluth) (Duluth, GA) 66078
Srb Assembly & Refurbishment Facility (Kennedy Space Center, FL) 60557
Textron Aerostructures (Nashville, TN) 82107; 82108
Textron Aerostructures Inc. (Nashville, TN) 82109
United Technologies Corp. Srb Assembly & Refurb. Fac. (Kennedy Space Center, FL) 60558
United Technologies Optical (Jupiter, FL) 60553
Vehicle Assembly Building (Kennedy Space Center, FL) 60559

3792 Travel Trailers & Campers

Coleman Co. (Lake City, SC) 79560
Fleetwood Travel Trailer Inc. (Winchester, VA) 92589
Fleetwood Travel Trailers Inc. (Hancock, MD) 71901
Fleetwood Travel Trailers Inc. (Congview, TX) 83647
Fleetwood Travel Trailers of Maryland Inc. 28 (Hancock, MD) 71902
Fleetwood Travel Trailers of Texas Inc. (Longview, TX) 87715
Fruehauf Inc. (Nashville, TN) 82014

3795 Tanks & Tank Components

Fmc Corp. Aiken Plant (Aiken, SC) 78647
General Dynamics Corp. (Falls Church, VA) 90856

3799 Transportation Equipment Nec

Brunswick Fishing Boat Div. (Murfreesboro, TN) 81837
Brunswick Marine (Murfreesboro, TN) 81838
Piper/Casepro (Clarendon, AR) 56847
Textron Inc. E-Z-Go Div. (Augusta, GA) 65348

3800 Instruments & Related Products

Dap Inc. (Dallas, TX) 83967
Rockwell International Corp. R.I. Plastics Div. Louisville Plastics Plant (Louisville, KY) 68997
Teledyne Avionics (Earlysville, VA) 90735
Vistakon Inc. (Jacksonville, FL) 60492

3812 Search & Navigation Equipment

Allied-Signal Inc. Bendix-King Air Transport (Fort Lauderdale, FL) 59431
Allied-Signal Inc. Bendix Transport Avionics (Fort Lauderdale, FL) 59432
Ametek US Gauge (Bartow, FL) 58624
Ball Corp. (Arlington, VA) 90273
Brunswick Corp. Defense Div. (Deland, FL) 59298
Collins General Aviation (Melbourne, FL) 61042; 61043
E Systems Inc. (Dallas, TX) 83990; 83992
Eaton Corp. (Sarasota, FL) 62814
Hercules Defense Electronics Systems Inc. (Clearwater, FL) 59018
Honeywell Inc. (Clearwater, FL) 59022
Honeywell Inc. (St. Petersburg, FL) 63126
Litton Industries, Inc. Amercom Div. (College Park, MD) 71563
Loral Advanced Projects (Reston, VA) 91714
Loral Data Systems (Sarasota, FL) 62841
Martin Marietta Electronic Systems (Orlando, FL) 62045
Martin Marietta Electronics Information & Missile Systems (Ocala, FL) 61805
Martin Marietta Missile Systems (Orlando, FL) 62048
Martin Marietta Missile Systems Building 7 Ocala (Ocala, FL) 61806
Martin Marietta Ocean Systems Operations (Glen Burnie, MD) 71844
Martin Marietta Technologies Inc. (Orlando, FL) 62052
Texas Instruments (Mc Kinney, TX) 87922
Texas Instruments Inc. (Mc Kinney, TX) 87923
Texas Instruments Inc. Sherman (Sherman, TX) 89427
TRW System Integration Group (Fairfax, VA) 90812
UTL Corp. (Dallas, TX) 84482
Westinghouse Electric Corp. Electronic Assembly Plant (College Station, TX) 83628
Westinghouse Electric Corp. Electronic Systems Group (Linthicum Heights, MD) 72113

3821 Laboratory Apparatus & Furniture

Baxter Diagnostics Inc. (Miami, FL) 61199; 61200
Baxter Healthcare Corp. Dade (Miami, FL) 61202
Baxter International Baxter Diagnostics Div. (Miami, FL) 61203
Emerson Electric Co. Brooks Instrument Div. (Statesboro, GA) 67634

3822 Environmental Controls

Eaton Corp. (Athens, AL) 55038
Emerson Electric Co. Alco Controls Div. (Hazlehurst, GA) 66346
Emerson Electric Co. Inc. Alco Controls Div. (Hazlehurst, GA) 66347
Emerson Electric Co. Inc. Alco Controls Div. (Wytheville, VA) 92638
Emerson Puerto Rico Inc. (Dorado, PR) 78410
Johnson Controls Inc. (Orlando, FL) 62016
Mallory Controls (Sparta, TN) 82345; 82346
Texas Instruments Inc. (Versailles, KY) 69332
White Rodgers Co. (Batesville, AR) 56764

3823 Process Control Instruments

Air Control Products (Roxboro, NC) 76120
Ametek Inc. US Gauge Div. (Bartow, FL) 58623
Baker Oil Tools Inc. (Houston, TX) 85855
Danaher Corp. (Washington, DC) 58209
Eaton Corp. Power Control Div. (Bowling Green, KY) 68137
Fisher Controls International Inc. (Mc Kinney, TX) 87910; 87911
Leeds & Northrup Instruments (St. Petersburg, FL) 63127
Olin Corp. (St. Marks, FL) 63072
Schrader Automotive Inc. (Monroe, NC) 75588
Texas Instruments Inc. (Johnson City, TN) 81060
Tn Tech. Inc. (Round Rock, TX) 88855
Westinghouse De Puerto Rico Computer & Instrumentation (Villalba, PR) 78637
Westinghouse Electric (Columbia, SC) 79126
Westinghouse Electric Corp. Advanced Technology Laboratories (Linthicum Heights, MD) 72111
Westronics Inc. (Fort Worth, TX) 85363
Wika Instrument Corp. (Lawrenceville, GA) 66548

3824 Fluid Meters & Counting Devices

Ametek-U S Gauge (Dallas, TX) 83853
Ametek US Gauge (Bartow, FL) 58624
Danaher Controls (Elizabethtown, NC) 74488
Veeder-Root Co. (Elizabethtown, NC) 74493

3825 Instruments to Measure Electricity

Alliant Techsystems Inc. (Annapolis, MD) 71000
Baker Hughes Prod. Tools Westronics, Inc. (Kingwood, TX) 87535
Elographics Inc. (Oak Ridge, TN) 82190
FMC Corp. (Conway, AR) 56861
General Electric Co. (New Orleans, LA) 70468
General Electric Co. (Dallas, TX) 84091
K & L Microwave Inc. (Salisbury, MD) 72348
Tektronix Inc. (Oklahoma City, OK) 77598
Westinghouse Electric Corp. (Raleigh, NC) 75984
Westinghouse Electric Corp. Advanced Technology Laboratories (Linthicum Heights, MD) 72111
Westinghouse Electric Corp. Integrated Logistics Support (Hunt Valley, MD) 71945; 71946

3826 Analytical Instruments

Abbott Laboratories Diagnostics Division (Irving, TX) 87316
Abbott Manufacturing Inc. (Irving, TX) 87317
EG & G Instruments (Oak Ridge, TN) 82186
Eg & G Ortec (Oak Ridge, TN) 82189

3827 Optical Instruments & Lenses

Allergan Inc. (Waco, TX) 89926
Bausch & Lomb Inc. (Sarasota, FL) 62799
Lens Crafters (Lafayette, LA) 70069
Lens Crafters (Columbia, SC) 79044
Optic-Electronic Ni-Tec Div. (Garland, TX) 85517
Varo Inc. Ni-Tec Div. (Garland, TX) 85560

3829 Measuring & Controlling Devices Nec

Air Control Products (Roxboro, NC) 76120
Air Products & Chemicals Inc. (Austin, TX) 82805
Allied Signal Aerospace (Fort Lauderdale, FL) 59428
Ametek Inc. Mansfield & Green (Largo, FL) 60810
Ametek US Gauge (Bartow, FL) 58624
Eaton Corp. Bowling Green Plant (Bowling Green, KY) 68138
EG & G Instruments (Oak Ridge, TN) 82186
Halliburton Geophysical Services Inc. (Houston, TX) 86261
Tandy Sign Co. (Arlington, TX) 82763
Texaco Inc. (Gainesville, TX) 85428
Westinghouse Nuclear Fuel Div. (Columbia, SC) 79123
Westinghouse Electric Corp. Integrated Logistics Support (Hunt Valley, MD) 71945; 71946

3841 Surgical & Medical Instruments

Abbott Chemical Inc. (Barceloneta, PR) 78319
Abbott Chemicals Inc. (Barceloneta, PR) 78320; 78321
Abbott Laboratories (Laurinburg, NC) 75347; 75348
Abbott Laboratories (Louisburg, NC) 75453
Abbott Laboratories (Austin, TX) 82799
Abbott Laboratories Diagnostic Div. (Irving, TX) 87315
Bard Cardiopulmonary Inc. (Las Piedras, PR) 78476; 78477; 78478
Baxter Diagnostics Inc. (Miami, FL) 61199
Baxter Diagnostics Inc. Dade Div. (Miami, FL) 61201
Baxter Health Care (Largo, FL) 60823
Baxter Healthcare Corp. (Mountain Home, AR) 57384
Baxter Healthcare Corp. (Largo, FL) 60824; 60825
Baxter Healthcare Corp. (Cleveland, MS) 72682
Baxter Healthcare Corp. (Kingstree, SC) 79552
Baxter Healthcare Corp. (Jacksonville, TX) 87421
Baxter Healthcare Corp. of Puerto Rico (Jayuya, PR) 78466
Baxter International Baxter Diagnostics Div. (Miami, FL) 61203
Becton Dickinson & Co. (Hunt Valley, MD) 71925
Becton Dickinson & Co. Vacutainer Systems (Sumter, SC) 80004
Becton Dickinson Systems (Sumter, SC) 80005
Becton Dickinson Vacutainer Systems (Sumter, SC) 80006
C. R. Bard Inc. (Moncks Corner, SC) 79659; 79660
C. R. Bard Inc. Bard Urological (Covington, GA) 65724
C.R. Bard Inc. (Moncks Corner, SC) 79661
Durr Medical Corp. (Chattanooga, TN) 80355
Ethicon, Inc. (Cornelia, GA) 65722
Ethicon Inc. (San Angelo, TX) 88872
Howmedica Inc. (Orlando, FL) 62010
Ivac Corp. (Creedmoor, NC) 74355
Linvatec (Largo, FL) 60844
Mallinckrodt Medical Inc. Interventional Products Plant (Angleton, TX) 82610
Med Rel, Inc. (Humacao, PR) 78462
Medtronic Inc. Puerto Rico (Villalba, PR) 78634
Medtronic Puerto Rico Inc. (Villalba, PR) 78636
National Medical Care Medical Products Div. (Mc Allen, TX) 87892
National Medical Care Inc. Medical Products Div. (Mc Allen, TX) 87893
Sherwood Medical Co. (De Land, FL) 59259
Sherwood Medical Co. (Commerce, TX) 83644
US Clinical Prods. Inc. (Richardson, TX) 88786
Xomed Inc. (Jacksonville, FL) 60514
Xomed-Treace Inc. (Jacksonville, FL) 60515

3842 Surgical Appliances & Supplies

Allied-Signal Inc. (Greenville, AL) 55814
Allied-Signal Safety Restraint (Greenville, AL) 55815; 55816
Baxter Healthcare (Kingstree, SC) 79550
Baxter Healthcare Corp. (Norcross, GA) 67104
Baxter Healthcare Corp. (Kingstree, SC) 79551
Bristol-Myers Squibb Zimmer Patient Care Div. (Statesville, NC) 76319
Davis & Geck, Inc. (Manati, PR) 78498
Dow Corning Wright (Arlington, TN) 80182
Durr-Fillauer Medical, Inc. (Montgomery, AL) 56303
Durr-Fillauer Medical Inc. (Memphis, TN) 81514
Durr Medical Corp. (Chattanooga, TN) 80355
Ethicon, Inc. (Cornelia, GA) 65722
Ethicon Inc. (San Angelo, TX) 88872
Johnson & Johnson Consumer Products Inc. (Las Piedras, PR) 78480
Johnson & Johnson Medical, Inc. (Sherman, TX) 89400
Johnson & Johnson Orthopaedics Products Inc. (Las Piedras, PR) 78481
Linvatec (Largo, FL) 60844
Schering-Plough Healthcare Products (Cleveland, TN) 80600
Scholl Inc. (Cleveland, TN) 80601
Spenco Medical Corp. (Waco, TX) 89977; 89978
Surgikos (Arlington, TX) 82753
Unijax Inc. (Columbia, SC) 79112; 79113
Xomed Inc. (Jacksonville, FL) 60514

3843 Dental Equipment & Supplies

Ivac Co. (Creedmoor, NC) 74354
Ivac Corp. (Creedmoor, NC) 74356
Professional Dental Inc. (Batesville, AR) 56761

3844 X-Ray Apparatus & Tubes

Durr-Fillauer Medical, Inc. (Montgomery, AL) 56303
Eaton Corp. Ion Beam Systems Div. (Austin, TX) 82861
GE Consumer Service (New Orleans, LA) 70467
GE Medical Systems (Fort Lauderdale, FL) 59497
GE Medical Systems (St. Rose, LA) 70873
GE Medical Systems (Hanover, MD) 71911
GE Medical Systems (Fort Mill, SC) 79233
General Electric Co. (Homewood, AL) 55869
General Electric Co. (Tampa, FL) 63442
General Electric Co. (Louisville, KY) 68768
General Electric Co. (Houston, TX) 86245
General Electric Co. (San Antonio, TX) 89021

3845 Electromedical Equipment

Med Rel, Inc. (Humacao, PR) 78462
Medtronic Pr Inc. (Villalba, PR) 78635

3851 Ophthalmic Goods

Allergan Medical Optics (Anasco, PR) 78305
Allergan Optical Inc. (Santa Isabel, PR) 78586
Bausch & Lomb Inc. (Sarasota, FL) 62799
Bausch & Lomb Inc. (Oakland, MD) 72157
Eckerd Corp. (Largo, FL) 60831
Schering-Plough Inc. El Jibaro Incustrial (Cidra, PR) 78400
Vistakon Inc. (Jacksonville, FL) 60493
Vistakon Johnson & Johnson Vision Products (Jacksonville, FL) 60494

3861 Photographic Equipment & Supplies

Agrico Chemical Co. (Melbourne, KY) 69093
Allied-Signal Inc. Uop Process Div. (Houston, TX) 85773
Betz Process Chemicals (Longview, TX) 87704
Betz Process Chemicals Inc. (Beaumont, TX) 83146
Exxon Chemicals Americas (Charleston, WV) 92745
Exxon Corp. (Baytown, TX) 83121
Jamieson Film Co. (Dallas, TX) 84137
Kit Chemicals Inc. (Carrollton, TX) 83478
Kti Chemicals Inc. (Carrollton, TX) 83480
Lubrizol Corp (Port Arthur, TX) 88636
Lubrizol Corp. the (Deer Park, TX) 84553
Nalco Chemical Co. (Corpus Christi, TX) 83741
Qualex Inc. (Charlotte, NC) 74123
Qualex Inc. (Durham, NC) 74425
Qualex Inc. (Fayetteville, NC) 74573
Shell Co. (Houston, TX) 86880
Shipley Co. Inc. (Irving, TX) 87402
Van Waters & Rogers Inc. (Charlotte, NC) 74193
Van Waters & Rogers Inc. (Amarillo, TX) 82588
Xerox Business Services (Birmingham, AL) 55460
Xerox Corp. (Huntsville, AL) 56057

Xerox Corp. (Oklahoma City, OK) 77672

3911 Jewelry & Precious Metal

Air Treads Inc. Atlanta Div. (Forest Park, GA) 66227
Air Treads Inc. Dallas Div. (Irving, TX) 87320
Avon Lomalinda Inc. (San Sebastian, PR) 78582
Avon-Mirabella Inc. (Aguadilla, PR) 78290
Beckman Instruments Inc. (Houston, TX) 85867
Jostens Inc. (Memphis, TN) 81633
Kirk Steiff Co. (Baltimore, MD) 71173
Service Merchandise (Hurst, TX) 87297

3914 Silverware & Plated Ware

Brown Forman Corp. (Louisville, KY) 68718; 68719
Caribe General Electric Products Inc. Humacao P.R. (Humacao, PR) 78461
Diebold Inc. (Dunbar, WV) 92826
Kirk Steiff Co. (Baltimore, MD) 71173
Kirk Steiff Co. (Baltimore, MD) 71174
Kirk Steiff Co. Kirk Steiff Division (Baltimore, MD) 71175

3931 Musical Instruments

Diebold Inc. (Nashville, TN) 81933

3944 Games, Toys & Children's Vehicles

Fisher-Price (Murray, KY) 69124
Kay Bee Toy & Hobby (Jonesboro, AR) 57222
Tonka Corp. (El Paso, TX) 84949
Tonka Toys (El Paso, TX) 84950
Toys R US (Miami, FL) 61479
Wewstern Publishing Co. (Fayetteville, NC) 74586

3949 Sporting & Athletic Goods Nec

Brunswick Bowling & Billiards (Eminence, KY) 68296; 68297
Douglas/Quikut (Germantown, TN) 80855
Emhart Corp. (Baltimore, MD) 71112
Emhart Industries Inc. (Baltimore, MD) 71113
Nautilis International (Independence, VA) 91169
Nike Inc. (Memphis, TN) 81660
Spenco Medical Corp. (Waco, TX) 89977; 89978
True Temper Sports Division (Amory, MS) 72589
True Temper Sports Division (Olive Branch, MS) 73232
True Temper Sports Division (Seneca, SC) 79864
True Temper Sports Division (Memphis, TN) 81719
True Temper Sports (Olive Branch, MS) 73233
Zebco Corp-A Brunswick Co. (Tulsa, OK) 78213
Zebco Corp. (Tulsa, OK) 78214; 78215; 78216

3951 Pens & Mechanical Pencils

APAC (Dallas, TX) 83855
Avery Dennison (Crossville, TN) 80690
Dennison Stationery Prods. Co. Inc. (Crossville, TN) 80691
Dennison Stationery Products Co., Inc. (Crossville, TN) 80692

3952 Lead Pencils & Art Goods

Alcoa Building Products Inc. (Stuarts Draft, VA) 92357; 92358

3953 Marking Devices

Avery Dennison (Crossville, TN) 80690
Dennison Stationery Prods. Co. Inc. (Crossville, TN) 80691

Dennison Stationery Products Co., Inc. (Crossville, TN) 80692

3961 Costume Jewelry

Avon Lomalinda Inc. (San Sebastian, PR) 78582; 78583; 78584
Avon-Mirabella Inc. (Aguadilla, PR) 78290
Avon Products Inc. (Washington, DC) 58130
Johnson Controls Inc. Battery Group (Winston-Salem, NC) 76735

3991 Brooms & Brushes

Douglas/Quikut (Germantown, TN) 80855
PPG Industries Inc. (Dover, DE) 57799

3993 Signs & Advertising Displays

Agri Services Inc. (Catlett, VA) 90511
Luminator (Plano, TX) 88585
Patrick Media Group (Arlington, TX) 82714
Patrick Media Group (Houston, TX) 86639
Pizza Hut (Monroe, LA) 70369
Tandy Sign Co. (Arlington, TX) 82763
Tandy Signs (Arlington, TX) 82764
3M Advertising (Sanford, FL) 62783
3M Co. (Westminster, MD) 72545

3995 Burial Caskets

Batesville Casket Co. (Campbellsville, KY) 68178
Batesville Casket Co. (Manchester, TN) 81390
Batesville Casket Co. Inc. (Campbellsville, KY) 68179
Batesville Casket Co. Inc. (Batesville, MS) 72593
Batesville Casket Co. Inc. (Manchester, TN) 81391
Batesville Casket Co. Inc. (Petersburg, VA) 91627
West Point Casket Co. (West Point, MS) 73488

3996 Hard Surface Floor Coverings Nec

Armstrong World Industries Stillwater Plant (Stillwater, OK) 77834
Armstrong World Industries Inc. (Jackson, MS) 72946; 72947
Armstrong World Industries Inc. Jackson Plant (Jackson, MS) 72948

3999 Manufacturing Industries Nec

Air Products & Chemicals, Inc. (Baytown, TX) 83106
Bada Co. (Bowling Green, KY) 68133
Capco Pipe Co. Inc. (Birmingham, AL) 55178
Cd Medical Inc. (Miami Lakes, FL) 61534
Coleman Co. (Lake City, SC) 79560
Corning Inc. (Wilmington, NC) 76550
Eaton Corp. Condura (Brownsville, TX) 83356
Engineered Polymers (Winston-Salem, NC) 76724
Genuine Parts Co. Rayloc Div. (Morganfield, KY) 69104
Johnson & Johnson Dental Care Co. (PR), Inc. (Gurabo, PR) 78442
Johnson & Johnson Medical Co. Pr Inc. (Gurabo, PR) 78443
Loral Vought Systems Corp. Missiles & Electronics Div. (Camden, AR) 56837
Lufkin (Apex, NC) 73557
Luminator (Plano, TX) 88585
Owens Corning Fiberglass (Houston, TX) 86631
Parker Hannifin Corp. (Booneville, MS) 72645
Permatech (Charlotte, NC) 74104
Rayloc (Morganfield, KY) 69105
Red Kap Ind. (White Creek, TN) 82415
Schering-Plough Healthcare Products (Cleveland, TN) 80600

Siecor Corp. Rocky Mount Plant (Rocky Mount, NC) 76103
Standard Products Co. (Winnsboro, SC) 80133
Tandy Manufacturing Technology (Fort Worth, TX) 85317
Temple Inland Forest Products Corp. Rigid Form (Diboll, TX) 84661
TRW Information Svc. (Arlington, VA) 90389
Unisy Corp. (Huntsville, AL) 56045
Unisys Corp. (Huntsville, AL) 56046
Unitron Inc. (Dallas, TX) 84474
Walt Disney World Co. Facilities Support (Lake Buena Vista, FL) 60615
Walter Kidde Inc. (Wilson, NC) 76653
Walter Kidde Portable Equipment Inc. (Mebane, NC) 75554
Western Digital Caribe Inc. (Mercedita, PR) 78519
Wrangler (Greensboro, NC) 74943
Yescor Telephony Cable Plant (Hickory, NC) 75108
ZEP Manufacturing Co. (Atlanta, GA) 65301

4000 Railroad Transportation

Fedex Customs Brokerage Corp. (Memphis, TN) 81547

4011 Railroads—Line-Haul Operating

Atchinson, Topeka, & Santa Fe Railway Co. (Midlothian, VA) 91408
Atchison, Topeka & Santa Fe Railway Co. (Charlotte, NC) 73844
Atchison, Topeka & Santa Fe Railway Co. (Amarillo, TX) 82524
Atchison, Topeka & Santa Fe Railway Co. (Cleburne, TX) 83574
Atchison, Topeka & Santa Fe Railway Co. (Conroe, TX) 83649
Atchison, Topeka & Santa Fe Railway Co. (Houston, TX) 85823
Burlington Northern R R (Sherman, TX) 89390
Burlington Northern R R Co. (Chandler, OK) 76913
Burlington Northern Rail Rd (Clarendon, TX) 83567
Burlington Northern Railroa (Aliceville, AL) 54982
Burlington Northern Railroa (Birmingham, AL) 55177
Burlington Northern Railroa (Jasper, AL) 56078
Burlington Northern Railroa (Monroeville, AL) 56258
Burlington Northern Railroa (Winfield, AL) 56707
Burlington Northern Railroa (Springdale, AR) 57627
Burlington Northern Railroa (Pensacola, FL) 62411
Burlington Northern Railroa (Tampa, FL) 63371
Burlington Northern Railroa (Columbus, MS) 72704
Burlington Northern Railroa (Henryetta, OK) 77127
Burlington Northern Railroa (Muskogee, OK) 77217
Burlington Northern Railroa (Pawnee, OK) 77699
Burlington Northern Railroa (Thomas, OK) 77866
Burlington Northern Railroa (Amarillo, TX) 82532
Burlington Northern Railroa (Frisco, TX) 85409
Burlington Northern Railroa (Henrietta, TX) 85735
Burlington Northern Railroa (Irving, TX) 87326
Burlington Northern Railroa (Lubbock, TX) 87753
Burlington Northern Railroa (Paris, TX) 88362
Burlington Northern Railroa (Plainview, TX) 88526
Burlington Northern Railroa (San Antonio, TX) 88944
Burlington Northern Railroa (Stamford, TX) 89510
Burlington Northern Railroa (Wichita Falls, TX) 90068
Burlington Northern Railroad (Thomaston, AL) 56607
Burlington Northern Railroad (Okeene, OK) 77287
Burlington Northern Railroad (Valliant, OK) 78219

Burlington Northern Railroad (Amarillo, TX) 82533
Burlington Northern Railroad (Petersburg, TX) 88505
Burlington Northern Rr (Tupelo, MS) 73390
Burlington Northern Rr (Galveston, TX) 85435
CSX Corp. (Richmond, VA) 91837
Illinois Central R R Co. (Aberdeen, MS) 72576
Illinois Central Railroad (Reserve, LA) 70662
Illinois Central Railroad (Mc Comb, MS) 73144
Illinois Central Railroad C (New Orleans, LA) 70507
South Central Florida Railroad (Clewiston, FL) 59062
Southern Pacific Railroad (Bacliff, TX) 83084
Southern Pacific Railroad (Sherman, TX) 89424; 89425
Southern Pacific Railroad (Sierra Blanca, TX) 89430

4013 Switching & Terminal Services

Burlington Northern Railroa (Birmingham, AL) 55176

4111 Local & Suburban Transit

Greyhound Bus Depot (Eutaw, AL) 55704
Greyhound Bus Depot (Milton, FL) 61547
Greyhound Bus Liens (Weatherford, TX) 90006
Greyhound Bus Line (Camden, AR) 56832
Greyhound Bus Lines (Bessemer, AL) 55091
Greyhound Bus Lines (Brundidge, AL) 55488
Greyhound Bus Lines (Clanton, AL) 55521
Greyhound Bus Lines (Dothan, AL) 55652
Greyhound Bus Lines (Jasper, AL) 56087
Greyhound Bus Lines (Mobile, AL) 56184
Greyhound Bus Lines (Montgomery, AL) 56342
Greyhound Bus Lines (Selma, AL) 56530
Greyhound Bus Lines (Tuscaloosa, AL) 56656
Greyhound Bus Lines (Winfield, AL) 56708
Greyhound Bus Lines (Blytheville, AR) 56805
Greyhound Bus Lines (Forrest City, AR) 57008
Greyhound Bus Lines (Osceola, AR) 57483
Greyhound Bus Lines (Wilmington, DE) 58065
Greyhound Bus Lines (Chipley, FL) 58954
Greyhound Bus Lines (Dade City, FL) 59139
Greyhound Bus Lines (Fort Lauderdale, FL) 59498; 59499
Greyhound Bus Lines (Hollywood, FL) 60063
Greyhound Bus Lines (Key West, FL) 60574
Greyhound Bus Lines (Lakeland, FL) 60732
Greyhound Bus Lines (Miami, FL) 61318; 61320
Greyhound Bus Lines (Ocala, FL) 61802
Greyhound Bus Lines (Punta Gorda, FL) 62709
Greyhound Bus Lines (Sebring, FL) 62882
Greyhound Bus Lines (Starke, FL) 63146
Greyhound Bus Lines (Brunswick, GA) 65413
Greyhound Bus Lines (Cordele, GA) 65713
Greyhound Bus Lines (Fitzgerald, GA) 66210
Greyhound Bus Lines (Tifton, GA) 67825
Greyhound Bus Lines (Waycross, GA) 68033
Greyhound Bus Lines (Allen, KY) 68080
Greyhound Bus Lines (Bowling Green, KY) 68143
Greyhound Bus Lines (Cave City, KY) 68198
Greyhound Bus Lines (Columbia, KY) 68207
Greyhound Bus Lines (Covington, KY) 68220

Greyhound Bus Lines (Danville, KY) 68259
Greyhound Bus Lines (Fort Campbell, KY) 68347
Greyhound Bus Lines (Harlan, KY) 68409
Greyhound Bus Lines (Harrodsburg, KY) 68412
Greyhound Bus Lines (Hazard, KY) 68426
Greyhound Bus Lines (Henderson, KY) 68451
Greyhound Bus Lines (Hopkinsville, KY) 68479
Greyhound Bus Lines (Lexington, KY) 68557
Greyhound Bus Lines (Louisville, KY) 68769
Greyhound Bus Lines (Madisonville, KY) 69055
Greyhound Bus Lines (Middlesboro, KY) 69094
Greyhound Bus Lines (Morehead, KY) 69101
Greyhound Bus Lines (Mt Sterling, KY) 69117
Greyhound Bus Lines (Pikeville, KY) 69225
Greyhound Bus Lines (Richmond, KY) 69242
Greyhound Bus Lines (Shelbyville, KY) 69272
Greyhound Bus Lines (Whitley City, KY) 69339
Greyhound Bus Lines (Baton Rouge, LA) 69541
Greyhound Bus Lines (Hammond, LA) 69929
Greyhound Bus Lines (Lafayette, LA) 70056
Greyhound Bus Lines (Metairie, LA) 70267
Greyhound Bus Lines (New Orleans, LA) 70470; 70471
Greyhound Bus Lines (Ponchatoula, LA) 70647
Greyhound Bus Lines (Baltimore, MD) 71162; 71163
Greyhound Bus Lines (Cumberland, MD) 71623
Greyhound Bus Lines (Fork, MD) 71701
Greyhound Bus Lines (Waldorf, MD) 72529
Greyhound Bus Lines (Brookhaven, MS) 72655
Greyhound Bus Lines (Cleveland, MS) 72683
Greyhound Bus Lines (Greenwood, MS) 72833
Greyhound Bus Lines (Laurel, MS) 73101
Greyhound Bus Lines (Meridian, MS) 73163
Greyhound Bus Lines (Picayune, MS) 73292
Greyhound Bus Lines (Ruleville, MS) 73333
Greyhound Bus Lines (Tupelo, MS) 73404
Greyhound Bus Lines (Vicksburg, MS) 73452
Greyhound Bus Lines (Charlotte, NC) 74032
Greyhound Bus Lines (Fayetteville, NC) 74558
Greyhound Bus Lines (Hendersonville, NC) 75041
Greyhound Bus Lines (Mount Airy, NC) 75679
Greyhound Bus Lines (Elk City, OK) 77037
Greyhound Bus Lines (Miami, OK) 77204
Greyhound Bus Lines (Norman, OK) 77255
Greyhound Bus Lines (Oklahoma City, OK) 77377
Greyhound Bus Lines (Weatherford, OK) 78241
Greyhound Bus Lines (Florence, SC) 79206
Greyhound Bus Lines (Rock Hill, SC) 79827
Greyhound Bus Lines (Spartanburg, SC) 79910
Greyhound Bus Lines (Summerville, SC) 79986
Greyhound Bus Lines (Walterboro, SC) 80071
Greyhound Bus Lines (Bristol, TN) 80249
Greyhound Bus Lines (Brownsville, TN) 80258
Greyhound Bus Lines (Chattanooga, TN) 80412
Greyhound Bus Lines (Clarksville, TN) 80551
Greyhound Bus Lines (Cleveland, TN) 80587
Greyhound Bus Lines (Columbia, TN) 80631
Greyhound Bus Lines (Dyersburg, TN) 80752

SIC Index 4131

Greyhound Bus Lines (Fayetteville, TN) 80796
Greyhound Bus Lines (Kingsport, TN) 81106
Greyhound Bus Lines (Knoxville, TN) 81215; 81216
Greyhound Bus Lines (Manchester, TN) 81392
Greyhound Bus Lines (Mc Minnville, TN) 81435
Greyhound Bus Lines (Memphis, TN) 81619; 81620; 81621; 81622; 81623
Greyhound Bus Lines (Milan, TN) 81769
Greyhound Bus Lines (Millington, TN) 81776
Greyhound Bus Lines (Murfreesboro, TN) 81850
Greyhound Bus Lines (Nashville, TN) 82017; 82018
Greyhound Bus Lines (Newport, TN) 82168
Greyhound Bus Lines (Oak Ridge, TN) 82193
Greyhound Bus Lines (Pulaski, TN) 82242
Greyhound Bus Lines (Ripley, TN) 82253
Greyhound Bus Lines (Springfield, TN) 82359
Greyhound Bus Lines (Tullahoma, TN) 82378
Greyhound Bus Lines (Union City, TN) 82384
Greyhound Bus Lines (Winchester, TN) 82420
Greyhound Bus Lines (Addison, TX) 82473
Greyhound Bus Lines (Cisco, TX) 83564
Greyhound Bus Lines (Corpus Christi, TX) 83719
Greyhound Bus Lines (Dallas, TX) 84097; 84099
Greyhound Bus Lines (Denison, TX) 84596
Greyhound Bus Lines (El Paso, TX) 84807; 84808
Greyhound Bus Lines (Garland, TX) 85487
Greyhound Bus Lines (Hillsboro, TX) 85750
Greyhound Bus Lines (Houston, TX) 86256
Greyhound Bus Lines (Liberty, TX) 87672
Greyhound Bus Lines (Mc Kinney, TX) 87912
Greyhound Bus Lines (Monahans, TX) 88139
Greyhound Bus Lines (Odessa, TX) 88247
Greyhound Bus Lines (Orange, TX) 88313
Greyhound Bus Lines (Richardson, TX) 88736
Greyhound Bus Lines (San Antonio, TX) 89022
Greyhound Bus Lines (Seguin, TX) 89367
Greyhound Bus Lines (Temple, TX) 89618
Greyhound Bus Lines (Van Horn, TX) 89860
Greyhound Bus Lines (Waco, TX) 89937
Greyhound Bus Lines (Covington, VA) 90660
Greyhound Bus Lines (Fredericksburg, VA) 90927
Greyhound Bus Lines (Hampton, VA) 91039
Greyhound Bus Lines (Hillsville, VA) 91141
Greyhound Bus Lines (Lexington, VA) 91207
Greyhound Bus Lines (Norfolk, VA) 91539
Greyhound Bus Lines (Portsmouth, VA) 91657
Greyhound Bus Lines (Radford, VA) 91697
Greyhound Bus Lines (Richmond, VA) 91901
Greyhound Bus Lines (Roanoke, VA) 92156
Greyhound Bus Lines (Springfield, VA) 92287
Greyhound Bus Lines (Tappahannock, VA) 92377
Greyhound Bus Lines (Triangle, VA) 92387
Greyhound Bus Lines (Williamsburg, VA) 92572
Greyhound Bus Lines (Woodbridge, VA) 92617
Greyhound Bus Lines (Wytheville, VA) 92640
Greyhound Bus Lines (Yorktown, VA) 92653
Greyhound Bus Lines (Bluefield, WV) 92702
Greyhound Bus Lines (Charleston, WV) 92748
Greyhound Bus Lines (Fairmont, WV) 92840
Greyhound Bus Lines (Gauley Bridge, WV) 92855
Greyhound Bus Lines (Lewisburg, WV) 92915; 92916
Greyhound Bus Lines (Martinsburg, WV) 92931
Greyhound Bus Lines (Rainelle, WV) 93017
Greyhound Bus Lines (Weirton, WV) 93088
Greyhound Bus Lines (Wheeling, WV) 93113
Greyhound Bus Lines Inc. (Crystal River, FL) 59133
Greyhound Bus Liwes (Tulsa, OK) 77949
Greyhound Bus Station (Flomaton, AL) 55733
Greyhound Bus Station (Greenville, AL) 55817
Greyhound Bus Station (Pine Bluff, AR) 57517
Greyhound Bus Station (Homestead, FL) 60114
Greyhound Bus Station (Live Oak, FL) 60913
Greyhound Bus Station (Gonzales, LA) 69890
Greyhound Bus Station (Aiken, SC) 78650
Greyhound Bus Station (Beaufort, SC) 78709
Greyhound Bus Stop (Evergreen, AL) 55707
Greyhound Bus Stop (Mooresville, NC) 75605
Greyhound Bus Terminal (Gainesville, FL) 59879
Greyhound Bus Terminal (Marianna, FL) 61003
Greyhound Bus Terminal (Yazoo City, MS) 73502
Greyhound Bus Terminal (Midland, TX) 88038
Greyhound Lines Inc. (Nashville, TN) 82019
Greyhound Lines Inc. (Dallas, TX) 84100
Greyhound Lines Inc. (Charleston, WV) 92749
Trailway Bus Station (Laurel, MS) 73109
Trailways Bus Lines (Lexington, KY) 68643
Trailways Bus Lines (London, KY) 68669
Trailways Bus Lines (Louisville, KY) 69023
Trailways Bus Lines (Williamsburg, KY) 69341
Trailways Bus Lines (Bristol, TN) 80255
Trailways Bus Lines (Cookeville, TN) 80668
Trailways Bus Lines (Crossville, TN) 80706
Trailways Bus Lines (Elizabethton, TN) 80771
Trailways Bus Lines (Fayetteville, TN) 80799
Trailways Bus Lines (Gallatin, TN) 80851
Trailways Bus Lines (Jackson, TN) 81003
Trailways Bus Lines (Kingsport, TN) 81119
Trailways Bus Lines (Knoxville, TN) 81261
Trailways Bus Lines (Lebanon, TN) 81310
Trailways Bus Lines (Lenoir City, TN) 81324
Trailways Bus Lines (Lewisburg, TN) 81333
Trailways Bus Lines (Martin, TN) 81398
Trailways Bus Lines (Memphis, TN) 81714; 81715
Trailways Bus Lines (Morristown, TN) 81813
Trailways Bus Lines (Nashville, TN) 82114
Trailways Bus Lines (Shelbyville, TN) 82318
Trailways Bus Lines (Logan, WV) 92920
Trailways Bus Station (El Dorado, AR) 56961
Trailways Bus Station (Cairo, GA) 65456
Trailways Bus Station (Euless, TX) 85023
Trailways Bus Station (Seguin, TX) 89378
Trailways Bus System (Huntsville, AL) 56041
Trailways Bus System (Little Rock, AR) 57317
Trailways Bus System (Fort Walton Beach, FL) 59841
Trailways Bus System (Jacksonville, FL) 60478
Trailways Bus System (Alexandria, LA) 69412
Trailways Bus System (New Orleans, LA) 70578
Trailways Bus System (Shreveport, LA) 70797
Trailways Bus System (Morganton, NC) 75656
Trailways Bus System (Alice, TX) 82488
Trailways Bus System (Brownsville, TX) 83382
Trailways Bus System (Corsicana, TX) 83794
Trailways Bus System (Dallas, TX) 84457
Trailways Bus System (Denton, TX) 84641
Trailways Bus System (Edinburg, TX) 84741
Trailways Bus System (Pecos, TX) 88499
Trailways Bus System (Pharr, TX) 88513
Trailways Bus Systems (Fayetteville, NC) 74577
Trailways Bus Systems (Lenoir, NC) 75392
Trailways Bus Systems (Muskogee, OK) 77230
Trailways Bus Systems (Tulsa, OK) 78177
Trailways Bus Systems (Mc Allen, TX) 87902
Trailways Bus Systems (San Antonio, TX) 89276
Trailways Bus Terminal (Tampa, FL) 63628
Trailways Bus Terminal (Marshall, TX) 87869
Trailways Bus Terminal&Gril (Winnsboro, SC) 80134
Trailways Business Systems (Houston, TX) 87038
Trailways Greyhound Bus Lines (Cleveland, TN) 80603
Trailways Inc. (Fort Worth, TX) 85337
Trailways Southern Lines in (New Orleans, LA) 70579
Trailways Texas Inc. (San Antonio, TX) 89278
Trailways Texas Inc. (Stephenville, TX) 89526

4119 Local Passenger Transportation Nec

Amtran (Fort Myers, FL) 59660
Atchison, Topeka & Santa Fe Railway Co. (Amarillo, TX) 82524
Atchison, Topeka & Santa Fe Railway Co. (El Paso, TX) 84762
Atchison, Topeka & Santa Fe Railway Co. (Euless, TX) 85007
Burlington Northern Railroa (Pensacola, FL) 62411
Burlington Northern Railroa (Amory, MS) 72584
Burlington Northern Railroa (Lubbock, TX) 87753
Burlington Northern Railroa (Stamford, TX) 89510
Burlington Northern Railway (Sapulpa, OK) 77789
Burlington Northern Railway (Sherman, TX) 89391
Coast to Coast Limousine (Orlando, FL) 61952; 61952
Illinois Central Railroad (Brookhaven, MS) 72656
Illinois Central Railroad C (New Orleans, LA) 70507

4121 Taxicabs

Greyhound Bus Lines (Clifton Forge, VA) 90642
Mobil Tire Service (Campton, KY) 68188

4131 Intercity & Rural Bus Transportation

Greyhound Bus (Boca Raton, FL) 58710
Greyhound Bus (Big Spring, TX) 83286
Greyhound Bus Center (Lake City, FL) 60621
Greyhound Bus Depot (Statesboro, GA) 67635
Greyhound Bus Line (Clarendon, AR) 56846
Greyhound Bus Line (Natchez, MS) 73197
Greyhound Bus Lines (Bessemer, AL) 55091
Greyhound Bus Lines (Birmingham, AL) 55279
Greyhound Bus Lines (Decatur, AL) 55591
Greyhound Bus Lines (Enterprise, AL) 55686
Greyhound Bus Lines (Fort Payne, AL) 55756
Greyhound Bus Lines (Gadsden, AL) 55783
Greyhound Bus Lines (Huntsville, AL) 55948
Greyhound Bus Lines (Opelika, AL) 56419
Greyhound Bus Lines (Selma, AL) 56530
Greyhound Bus Lines (Sheffield, AL) 56550
Greyhound Bus Lines (Tuscaloosa, AL) 56656
Greyhound Bus Lines (Brinkley, AR) 56819
Greyhound Bus Lines (Little Rock, AR) 57286
Greyhound Bus Lines (Magnolia, AR) 57332
Greyhound Bus Lines (Dover, DE) 57790
Greyhound Bus Lines (Chiefland, FL) 58951
Greyhound Bus Lines (Delray Beach, FL) 59318
Greyhound Bus Lines (Islamorada, FL) 60154
Greyhound Bus Lines (Jacksonville, FL) 60321
Greyhound Bus Lines (Jupiter, FL) 60540
Greyhound Bus Lines (Lake Wales, FL) 60654
Greyhound Bus Lines (Lake Worth, FL) 60676
Greyhound Bus Lines (Miami, FL) 61321; 61322; 61323
Greyhound Bus Lines (Mount Dora, FL) 61565
Greyhound Bus Lines (Ocala, FL) 61802
Greyhound Bus Lines (Pompano Beach, FL) 62599
Greyhound Bus Lines (Sebring, FL) 62883
Greyhound Bus Lines (Tampa, FL) 63444
Greyhound Bus Lines (Venice, FL) 63726
Greyhound Bus Lines (Zephyrhills, FL) 64012
Greyhound Bus Lines (Bremen, GA) 65395
Greyhound Bus Lines (Eastman, GA) 66157
Greyhound Bus Lines (Nahunta, GA) 67067
Greyhound Bus Lines (Allen, KY) 68080
Greyhound Bus Lines (Bowling Green, KY) 68143
Greyhound Bus Lines (Cave City, KY) 68198
Greyhound Bus Lines (Columbia, KY) 68207
Greyhound Bus Lines (Covington, KY) 68220
Greyhound Bus Lines (Danville, KY) 68259
Greyhound Bus Lines (Fort Campbell, KY) 68347
Greyhound Bus Lines (Harlan, KY) 68409
Greyhound Bus Lines (Harrodsburg, KY) 68412
Greyhound Bus Lines (Hazard, KY) 68426
Greyhound Bus Lines (Henderson, KY) 68451
Greyhound Bus Lines (Hopkinsville, KY) 68479
Greyhound Bus Lines (Lexington, KY) 68557
Greyhound Bus Lines (Louisville, KY) 68769
Greyhound Bus Lines (Madisonville, KY) 69055
Greyhound Bus Lines (Middlesboro, KY) 69094
Greyhound Bus Lines (Morehead, KY) 69101
Greyhound Bus Lines (Mt Sterling, KY) 69117
Greyhound Bus Lines (Pikeville, KY) 69225
Greyhound Bus Lines (Richmond, KY) 69242
Greyhound Bus Lines (Shelbyville, KY) 69272
Greyhound Bus Lines (Whitley City, KY) 69339
Greyhound Bus Lines (Amite, LA) 69424
Greyhound Bus Lines (Baton Rouge, LA) 69541
Greyhound Bus Lines (Covington, LA) 69794
Greyhound Bus Lines (Grambling, LA) 69893
Greyhound Bus Lines (Lafayette, LA) 70056
Greyhound Bus Lines (Thibodaux, LA) 70913
Greyhound Bus Lines (Cumberland, MD) 71623
Greyhound Bus Lines (Frostburg, MD) 71756
Greyhound Bus Lines (Hagerstown, MD) 71882
Greyhound Bus Lines (Salisbury, MD) 72346
Greyhound Bus Lines (Belzoni, MS) 72612
Greyhound Bus Lines (Brookhaven, MS) 72655
Greyhound Bus Lines (Crystal Springs, MS) 72748
Greyhound Bus Lines (Greenville, MS) 72800
Greyhound Bus Lines (Leland, MS) 73111
Greyhound Bus Lines (Pascagoula, MS) 73256
Greyhound Bus Lines (Shaw, MS) 73342
Greyhound Bus Lines (Shelby, MS) 73343
Greyhound Bus Lines (Fort Bragg, NC) 74618
Greyhound Bus Lines (Gastonia, NC) 74682
Greyhound Bus Lines (Mocksville, NC) 75563
Greyhound Bus Lines (Mount Olive, NC) 75695
Greyhound Bus Lines (Reidsville, NC) 76003
Greyhound Bus Lines (Wallace, NC) 76440
Greyhound Bus Lines (Warsaw, NC) 76451
Greyhound Bus Lines (Claremore, OK) 76952
Greyhound Bus Lines (El Reno, OK) 77031
Greyhound Bus Lines (Henryetta, OK) 77128
Greyhound Bus Lines (Miami, OK) 77204
Greyhound Bus Lines (Mustang, OK) 77237
Greyhound Bus Lines (Okmulgee, OK) 77680
Greyhound Bus Lines (Anderson, SC) 78676
Greyhound Bus Lines (Cheraw, SC) 78923
Greyhound Bus Lines (Greenville, SC) 79366
Greyhound Bus Lines (Kingstree, SC) 79556
Greyhound Bus Lines (Lake City, SC) 79562
Greyhound Bus Lines (Rock Hill, SC) 79827
Greyhound Bus Lines (St Stephen, SC) 79971
Greyhound Bus Lines (Sumter, SC) 80020
Greyhound Bus Lines (Bristol, TN) 80249
Greyhound Bus Lines (Brownsville, TN) 80258
Greyhound Bus Lines (Chattanooga, TN) 80412
Greyhound Bus Lines (Clarksville, TN) 80551
Greyhound Bus Lines (Cleveland, TN) 80587
Greyhound Bus Lines (Columbia, TN) 80631
Greyhound Bus Lines (Dyersburg, TN) 80752
Greyhound Bus Lines (Fayetteville, TN) 80796
Greyhound Bus Lines (Kingsport, TN) 81106
Greyhound Bus Lines (Knoxville, TN) 81215; 81216
Greyhound Bus Lines (Manchester, TN) 81392
Greyhound Bus Lines (Mc Minnville, TN) 81435
Greyhound Bus Lines (Memphis, TN) 81619; 81620; 81621; 81622; 81623
Greyhound Bus Lines (Milan, TN) 81769
Greyhound Bus Lines (Millington, TN) 81776
Greyhound Bus Lines (Murfreesboro, TN) 81850
Greyhound Bus Lines (Nashville, TN) 82017; 82018
Greyhound Bus Lines (Newport, TN) 82168
Greyhound Bus Lines (Oak Ridge, TN) 82193
Greyhound Bus Lines (Pulaski, TN) 82242
Greyhound Bus Lines (Ripley, TN) 82253

SIC Index

Greyhound Bus Lines (Springfield, TN) 82359
Greyhound Bus Lines (Tullahoma, TN) 82378
Greyhound Bus Lines (Union City, TN) 82384
Greyhound Bus Lines (Winchester, TN) 82420
Greyhound Bus Lines (Amarillo, TX) 82549
Greyhound Bus Lines (Bryan, TX) 83396
Greyhound Bus Lines (Cotulla, TX) 83800
Greyhound Bus Lines (Dalhart, TX) 83832
Greyhound Bus Lines (Dallas, TX) 84096; 84099
Greyhound Bus Lines (Denison, TX) 84596
Greyhound Bus Lines (Eastland, TX) 84728
Greyhound Bus Lines (El Paso, TX) 84807
Greyhound Bus Lines (Fort Worth, TX) 85126
Greyhound Bus Lines (Houston, TX) 86255
Greyhound Bus Lines (Odessa, TX) 88247
Greyhound Bus Lines (Port Arthur, TX) 88632
Greyhound Bus Lines (San Antonio, TX) 89023
Greyhound Bus Lines (Seguin, TX) 89367
Greyhound Bus Lines (Texarkana, TX) 89677
Greyhound Bus Lines (Burkeville, VA) 90507
Greyhound Bus Lines (Marion, VA) 91333
Greyhound Bus Lines (Norfolk, VA) 91539; 91540; 91541
Greyhound Bus Lines (Richmond, VA) 91900
Greyhound Bus Lines (South Boston, VA) 92253
Greyhound Bus Lines (Virginia Beach, VA) 92485; 92485
Greyhound Bus Lines (Woodbridge, VA) 92617
Greyhound Bus Lines (Bluefield, WV) 92702
Greyhound Bus Lines (Charleston, WV) 92748
Greyhound Bus Lines (Fairmont, WV) 92840
Greyhound Bus Lines (Gauley Bridge, WV) 92855
Greyhound Bus Lines (Lewisburg, WV) 92915; 92916
Greyhound Bus Lines (Martinsburg, WV) 92931
Greyhound Bus Lines (Rainelle, WV) 93017
Greyhound Bus Lines (Weirton, WV) 93088
Greyhound Bus Lines (Wheeling, WV) 93113
Greyhound Bus Lines E (Rayne, LA) 70656
Greyhound Bus Lines Inc. (Thomasville, AL) 56609
Greyhound Bus Lines Inc. (Taft, TX) 89594
Greyhound Bus Station (Lanett, AL) 56101
Greyhound Bus Station (Pine Bluff, AR) 57517
Greyhound Bus Station (Boynton Beach, FL) 58778
Greyhound Bus Station (Haines City, FL) 59949
Greyhound Bus Station (Jacksonville, FL) 60322
Greyhound Bus Station (Panama City, FL) 62323
Greyhound Bus Station (Starke, FL) 63147
Greyhound Bus Station (Titusville, FL) 63689
Greyhound Bus Station (Adel, GA) 64055
Greyhound Bus Station (Nashville, GA) 67068
Greyhound Bus Station (De Ridder, LA) 69812
Greyhound Bus Station (Sulphur, LA) 70884
Greyhound Bus Station (Oxford, NC) 75780
Greyhound Bus Station (Bishopville, SC) 78743
Greyhound Bus System (Rockingham, NC) 76062; 76062
Greyhound Bus Terminal (Fort Myers, FL) 59702
Greyhound Bus Terminial (Dublin, GA) 66010
Greyhound Lines Inc. (Covington, KY) 68221
Greyhound Lines Inc. (Memphis, TN) 81624
Greyhound Lines Inc. (Charleston, WV) 92749
Mobil Oil Co. (Thorndale, TX) 89758
Texas New Mexico & Oklahoma Coaches, Inc. (Lubbock, TX) 87789
Trailway Bus Station (Arab, AL) 55027
Trailway Bus Station (Kinder, LA) 70026
Trailway Bus Station (Corinth, MS) 72746
Trailway Bus Station (Roanoke Rapids, NC) 76039
Trailway Bus Terminal (Dawson, GA) 65794
Trailway Tours Inc. (Irving, TX) 87415
Trailways (Monticello, AR) 57375
Trailways (Murphy, NC) 75710
Trailways (Wilson, NC) 76650
Trailways American Bus Line (Oklahoma City, OK) 77634
Trailways Bus (Alpine, TX) 82502
Trailways Bus Depot (Clarksville, AR) 56852
Trailways Bus Depot (De Quincy, LA) 69808
Trailways Bus Depot (Delhi, LA) 69826
Trailways Bus Depot (Winona, MS) 73495
Trailways Bus Depot (Center, TX) 83542
Trailways Bus Depot (Palestine, TX) 88347
Trailways Bus Line (Rocky Mount, NC) 76106
Trailways Bus Lines (Ocala, FL) 61824
Trailways Bus Lines (Lexington, KY) 68643
Trailways Bus Lines (London, KY) 68669
Trailways Bus Lines (Louisville, KY) 69023
Trailways Bus Lines (Williamsburg, KY) 69341
Trailways Bus Lines (Black Mountain, NC) 73699
Trailways Bus Lines (Bristol, TN) 80255
Trailways Bus Lines (Cookeville, TN) 80668
Trailways Bus Lines (Crossville, TN) 80706
Trailways Bus Lines (Elizabethton, TN) 80771
Trailways Bus Lines (Fayetteville, TN) 80799
Trailways Bus Lines (Gallatin, TN) 80851
Trailways Bus Lines (Jackson, TN) 81003
Trailways Bus Lines (Kingsport, TN) 81119
Trailways Bus Lines (Knoxville, TN) 81261
Trailways Bus Lines (Lebanon, TN) 81310
Trailways Bus Lines (Lenoir City, TN) 81324
Trailways Bus Lines (Lewisburg, TN) 81333
Trailways Bus Lines (Martin, TN) 81398
Trailways Bus Lines (Memphis, TN) 81714; 81715
Trailways Bus Lines (Morristown, TN) 81813
Trailways Bus Lines (Nashville, TN) 82114
Trailways Bus Lines (Shelbyville, TN) 82318
Trailways Bus Lines (Logan, WV) 92920
Trailways Bus Lines Carolin (Sanford, NC) 76206
Trailways Bus Linescarolina (Greensboro, NC) 74924
Trailways Bus Station (Albertville, AL) 54971
Trailways Bus Station (Enterprise, AL) 55698
Trailways Bus Station (Reform, AL) 56498
Trailways Bus Station (Sylacauga, AL) 56590
Trailways Bus Station (Talladega, AL) 56600
Trailways Bus Station (Arkadelphia, AR) 56722
Trailways Bus Station (Bald Knob, AR) 56738
Trailways Bus Station (Hope, AR) 57160
Trailways Bus Station (Nashville, AR) 57442
Trailways Bus Station (Pocahontas, AR) 57544
Trailways Bus Station (Camilla, GA) 65483
Trailways Bus Station (Claxton, GA) 65566
Trailways Bus Station (Jesup, GA) 66374
Trailways Bus Station (Pearson, GA) 67256
Trailways Bus Station (Bogalusa, LA) 69709
Trailways Bus Station (Forest, MS) 72778
Trailways Bus Station (Greenville, MS) 72822
Trailways Bus Station (Oxford, MS) 73246
Trailways Bus Station (Aiken, SC) 78658
Trailways Bus Station (Manning, SC) 79636
Trailways Bus Station (Abilene, TX) 82464
Trailways Bus Station (Euless, TX) 85023
Trailways Bus Station (Palacios, TX) 88340
Trailways Bus Station (Rio Grande City, TX) 88803
Trailways Bus Station (Silsbee, TX) 89436
Trailways Bus Station (Wharton, TX) 90051
Trailways Bus Stop (Livingston, TX) 87692
Trailways Bus Sys (Granbury, TX) 85600
Trailways Bus System (Tuscaloosa, AL) 56678
Trailways Bus System (Conway, AR) 56874
Trailways Bus System (Mc Gehee, AR) 57359
Trailways Bus System (Russellville, AR) 57592
Trailways Bus System (Blountstown, FL) 58663
Trailways Bus System (Hollywood, FL) 60101
Trailways Bus System (Orlando, FL) 62172
Trailways Bus System (Panama City, FL) 62354
Trailways Bus System (Pensacola, FL) 62483
Trailways Bus System (W Palm Beach, FL) 63816
Trailways Bus System (Americus, GA) 64146
Trailways Bus System (Savannah, GA) 67517
Trailways Bus System (Arcadia, LA) 69431
Trailways Bus System (Bunkie, LA) 69746
Trailways Bus System (Many, LA) 70221
Trailways Bus System (Oakdale, LA) 70601
Trailways Bus System (Opelousas, LA) 70603
Trailways Bus System (Booneville, MS) 72649
Trailways Bus System (Carthage, MS) 72663
Trailways Bus System (Columbus, MS) 72730
Trailways Bus System (Grenada, MS) 72849
Trailways Bus System (Meridian, MS) 73182
Trailways Bus System (High Point, NC) 75174
Trailways Bus System (Newton, NC) 75755
Trailways Bus System (Spring Lake, NC) 76300
Trailways Bus System (Waynesville, NC) 76473
Trailways Bus System (Charleston, SC) 78905
Trailways Bus System (Greenville, SC) 79441
Trailways Bus System (Bowie, TX) 83328
Trailways Bus System (Childress, TX) 83562
Trailways Bus System (Cisco, TX) 83566
Trailways Bus System (Colorado City, TX) 83641
Trailways Bus System (Dallas, TX) 84459
Trailways Bus System (Del Rio, TX) 84589
Trailways Bus System (Donna, TX) 84680
Trailways Bus System (El Campo, TX) 84751
Trailways Bus System (Greenville, TX) 85679
Trailways Bus System (Kilgore, TX) 87501
Trailways Bus System (Mathis, TX) 87881
Trailways Bus System (Memphis, TX) 87951
Trailways Bus System (Mesquite, TX) 88009
Trailways Bus System (Mineola, TX) 88107
Trailways Bus System (Monahans, TX) 88144
Trailways Bus System (Pampa, TX) 88357
Trailways Bus System (Taylor, TX) 89603
Trailways Bus System (Waskom, TX) 89991
Trailways Bus System (Weslaco, TX) 90040
Trailways Bus System Inc. (Dallas, TX) 84460
Trailways Bus System Inc. (Huntsville, TX) 87266
Trailways Bus Systemm (Macon, GA) 66716
Trailways Bus Systems (Dothan, AL) 55672
Trailways Bus Systems (Miami, FL) 61482
Trailways Bus Systems (Panama City, FL) 62355
Trailways Bus Systems (Sandersville, GA) 67432
Trailways Bus Systems (Sylvester, GA) 67777
Trailways Bus Systems (De Ridder, LA) 69819
Trailways Bus Systems (Mansfield, LA) 70217
Trailways Bus Systems (Durant, MS) 72753
Trailways Bus Systems (Waynesboro, MS) 73474
Trailways Bus Systems (Monroe, NC) 75593
Trailways Bus Systems (Rutherfordton, NC) 76149
Trailways Bus Systems (Muskogee, OK) 77230
Trailways Bus Systems (Wagoner, OK) 78233
Trailways Bus Systems (Charleston, SC) 78906
Trailways Bus Systems (Union, SC) 80054
Trailways Bus Systems (Beaumont, TX) 83227
Trailways Bus Systems (Crockett, TX) 83802
Trailways Bus Systems (Odessa, TX) 88286
Trailways Bus Systems (Sherman, TX) 89428
Trailways Communter Transit (Dallas, TX) 84462
Trailways Greyhound Bus Lines (Cleveland, TN) 80603
Trailways & Greyhounds Bus (Corsicana, TX) 83795
Trailways Inc. (Macon, GA) 66717
Trailways Incorporated (Monroe, LA) 70381
Trailways Inc. (Rayville, LA) 70659; 70659
Trailways Inc. (Charlotte, NC) 74176
Trailways Inc. (Marion, NC) 75507
Trailways Inc. (Bay City, TX) 83105
Trailways Inc. (El Paso, TX) 84953
Trailways Inc. (Houston, TX) 87039
Trailways Inc. (Refugio, TX) 88719
Trailways Inc. Bus Station (Tahlequah, OK) 77861
Trailways Transportation (Universal City, TX) 89845

4141 Local Bus Charter Service

Greyhound Bus Lines (Naples, FL) 61628
Greyhound Bus Lines (Winder, GA) 68060
Greyhound Bus Lines (Baltimore, MD) 71161
Greyhound Bus Lines (Norfolk, VA) 91539
Trailways Bus System (Biloxi, MS) 72641
Trailways Bus System (Hattiesburg, MS) 72899
Trailways Hickory Bus Sta (Hickory, NC) 75103

4142 Bus Charter Service Except Local

Greyhound Bus Lines (Jackson, AL) 56067
Greyhound Bus Lines (Troy, AL) 56620
Greyhound Bus Lines (Lewisville, AR) 57242
Greyhound Bus Lines (De Funiak Springs, FL) 59242
Greyhound Bus Lines (Vero Beach, FL) 63757
Greyhound Bus Lines (Griffin, GA) 66317
Greyhound Bus Lines (Allen, KY) 68080
Greyhound Bus Lines (Bowling Green, KY) 68143
Greyhound Bus Lines (Cave City, KY) 68198
Greyhound Bus Lines (Columbia, KY) 68207
Greyhound Bus Lines (Covington, KY) 68220
Greyhound Bus Lines (Danville, KY) 68259
Greyhound Bus Lines (Fort Campbell, KY) 68347
Greyhound Bus Lines (Harlan, KY) 68409
Greyhound Bus Lines (Harrodsburg, KY) 68412
Greyhound Bus Lines (Hazard, KY) 68426
Greyhound Bus Lines (Henderson, KY) 68451
Greyhound Bus Lines (Hopkinsville, KY) 68479
Greyhound Bus Lines (Lexington, KY) 68557
Greyhound Bus Lines (Louisville, KY) 68769
Greyhound Bus Lines (Madisonville, KY) 69055
Greyhound Bus Lines (Middlesboro, KY) 69094
Greyhound Bus Lines (Morehead, KY) 69101
Greyhound Bus Lines (Mt Sterling, KY) 69117
Greyhound Bus Lines (Pikeville, KY) 69225
Greyhound Bus Lines (Richmond, KY) 69242
Greyhound Bus Lines (Shelbyville, KY) 69272
Greyhound Bus Lines (Whitley City, KY) 69339
Greyhound Bus Lines (Jennings, LA) 69979
Greyhound Bus Lines (Natchez, MS) 73198
Greyhound Bus Lines (High Point, NC) 75137
Greyhound Bus Lines (Mc Alester, OK) 77191
Greyhound Bus Lines (Spartanburg, SC) 79910
Greyhound Bus Lines (Bristol, TN) 80249
Greyhound Bus Lines (Brownsville, TN) 80258
Greyhound Bus Lines (Chattanooga, TN) 80412
Greyhound Bus Lines (Clarksville, TN) 80551
Greyhound Bus Lines (Cleveland, TN) 80587
Greyhound Bus Lines (Columbia, TN) 80631
Greyhound Bus Lines (Dyersburg, TN) 80752
Greyhound Bus Lines (Fayetteville, TN) 80796
Greyhound Bus Lines (Kingsport, TN) 81106
Greyhound Bus Lines (Knoxville, TN) 81215; 81216
Greyhound Bus Lines (Manchester, TN) 81392
Greyhound Bus Lines (Mc Minnville, TN) 81435
Greyhound Bus Lines (Memphis, TN) 81619; 81620; 81621; 81622; 81623
Greyhound Bus Lines (Milan, TN) 81769
Greyhound Bus Lines (Millington, TN) 81776
Greyhound Bus Lines (Murfreesboro, TN) 81850
Greyhound Bus Lines (Nashville, TN) 82017; 82018
Greyhound Bus Lines (Newport, TN) 82168
Greyhound Bus Lines (Oak Ridge, TN) 82193
Greyhound Bus Lines (Pulaski, TN) 82242
Greyhound Bus Lines (Ripley, TN) 82253
Greyhound Bus Lines (Springfield, TN) 82359
Greyhound Bus Lines (Tullahoma, TN) 82378
Greyhound Bus Lines (Union City, TN) 82384
Greyhound Bus Lines (Winchester, TN) 82420
Greyhound Bus Lines (Big Spring, TX) 83287
Greyhound Bus Lines (Hearne, TX) 85722
Greyhound Bus Lines (New Braunfels, TX) 88209

Pony Express Courier Corp. (Charlotte, NC) 74120
United Parcel Service (Birmingham, AL) 55440
United Parcel Service (Dothan, AL) 55673
United Parcel Service (Enterprise, AL) 55699
United Parcel Service (Opelika, AL) 56430
United Parcel Service (Selma, AL) 56540
United Parcel Service (Talladega, AL) 56601; 56602
United Parcel Service (Conway, AR) 56876
United Parcel Service (Fort Smith, AR) 57114
United Parcel Service (Jonesboro, AR) 57232; 57233; 57234
United Parcel Service (Boynton Beach, FL) 58794; 58795
United Parcel Service (Bradenton, FL) 58854
United Parcel Service (Daytona Beach, FL) 59223
United Parcel Service (Fort Pierce, FL) 59815
United Parcel Service (Fort Walton Beach, FL) 59842
United Parcel Service (Lake City, FL) 60634; 60635
United Parcel Service (Melbourne, FL) 61113
United Parcel Service (Rockledge, FL) 62749
United Parcel Service (St Petersburg, FL) 63042
United Parcel Service (Tallahassee, FL) 63283
United Parcel Service (Tampa, FL) 63639
United Parcel Service (Albany, GA) 64099
United Parcel Service (Cairo, GA) 65457; 65458
United Parcel Service (Macon, GA) 66722
United Parcel Service (Valdosta, GA) 67979
United Parcel Service (Lexington, KY) 68648
United Parcel Service (London, KY) 68670
United Parcel Service (Louisville, KY) 69026; 69027; 69028
United Parcel Service (Paducah, KY) 69213
United Parcel Service (Alexandria, LA) 69413
United Parcel Service (Baton Rouge, LA) 69682
United Parcel Service (Gretna, LA) 69917
United Parcel Service (Lake Charles, LA) 70178
United Parcel Service (Monroe, LA) 70382
United Parcel Service (Natchitoches, LA) 70405
United Parcel Service (New Orleans, LA) 70582
United Parcel Service (Opelousas, LA) 70604
United Parcel Service (Cumberland, MD) 71639
United Parcel Service (Batesville, MS) 72602; 72603
United Parcel Service (Jackson, MS) 73082
United Parcel Service (Natchez, MS) 73212
United Parcel Service (Charlotte, NC) 74190
United Parcel Service (Raleigh, NC) 75968; 75970
United Parcel Service (Rocky Mount, NC) 76108
United Parcel Service (Wilmington, NC) 76603
United Parcel Service (Altus, OK) 76797
United Parcel Service (Enid, OK) 77072
United Parcel Service (Guymon, OK) 77116
United Parcel Service (Lawton, OK) 77176
United Parcel Service (Mc Alester, OK) 77200
United Parcel Service (Muskogee, OK) 77231
United Parcel Service (Oklahoma City, OK) 77646
United Parcel Service (Tulsa, OK) 78185; 78186
United Parcel Service (Anderson, SC) 78694; 78695
United Parcel Service (Spartanburg, SC) 79963
United Parcel Service (West Columbia, SC) 80110
United Parcel Service (Dyersburg, TN) 80762

United Parcel Service (Arlington, TX) 82775
United Parcel Service (Austin, TX) 83052
United Parcel Service (Beaumont, TX) 83229
United Parcel Service (Bryan, TX) 83410
United Parcel Service (Dallas, TX) 84471; 84472; 84473
United Parcel Service (Denton, TX) 84644
United Parcel Service (El Paso, TX) 84956
United Parcel Service (La Marque, TX) 87547; 87548
United Parcel Service (Longview, TX) 87743
United Parcel Service (Lubbock, TX) 87792; 87793
United Parcel Service (Midland, TX) 88093
United Parcel Service (San Antonio, TX) 89285; 89286
United Parcel Service (Tyler, TX) 89840
United Parcel Service (Vernon, TX) 89875
United Parcel Service (Victoria, TX) 89908
United Parcel Service (Wichita Falls, TX) 90119
United Parcel Service (Cedar Bluff, VA) 90513
United Parcel Service (Danville, VA) 90722
United Parcel Service (Fredericksbg, VA) 90906
United Parcel Service (Front Royal, VA) 90957; 90958
United Parcel Service (Lynchburg, VA) 91291
United Parcel Service (Richmond, VA) 92065; 92066; 92067; 92068; 92069
United Parcel Service (Virginia Beach, VA) 92519
United Parcel Service (Beckley, WV) 92689
United Parcel Service (Charleston, WV) 92797; 92798
United Parcel Service (Clarksburg, WV) 92822
United Parcel Service (Fairmont, WV) 92849
United Parcel Service (Parkersburg, WV) 92998
United Parcel Service Inc. (Lexington, KY) 68649
United Parcel Service Inc. (La Marque, TX) 87549; 87550
United Parcel Services (Spartanburg, SC) 79964

4221 Farm Product Warehousing & Storage

American Tobacco Co. (Wilson, NC) 76617
Farmland Green Division (Enid, OK) 77048
Gold Kist Inc. (Huntingdon, TN) 80960
Harvest Queen Mill & Elevator Co. (Plainview, TX) 88529
Sherman County Grain Co. (Texhoma, OK) 77864

4222 Refrigerated Warehousing & Storage

Adolph Coors Co. (Elkton, VA) 90743
Coors Brewing Co. (Elkton, VA) 90744; 90745
Russellville Distribution Center (Russellville, AR) 57587
Tyson Valley Distribution Center (Russellville, AR) 57595

4225 General Warehousing & Storage

American Brokerage Co. (Laredo, TX) 87606
Burlington Coat Factory Warehouse (Jacksonville, FL) 60235
Burlington Industries Inc. (Hurt, VA) 91168
Citgo Petroleum Warehouse (Tulsa, OK) 77908
Coca Cola Bottling Co. (Daleville, AL) 55561
Costco Wholesale (Orlando, FL) 61958
Jack Eckerd Corp. (Largo, FL) 60834

Kroger Warehouse (Jackson, MS) 73012

Selig Chemical Industries (Atlanta, GA) 65148

Tandy Electronics Warehouse (Fort Worth, TX) 85315
Unit Distribution of Texas (Arlington, TX) 82774
Wal Mart Distribution Center (Palestine, TX) 88348

4226 Special Warehousing & Storage Nec

Agrico Chemical Co. Inc. (Newport, KY) 69136
Amerada Hess Corp. (Marrero, LA) 70224; 70225
Amerada Hess Corp. (Corpus Christi, TX) 83698
Cosbel Petroleum Corp. (Houston, TX) 86015
Diebold Inc. (Columbia, MD) 71584
Fruehauf Trailer Corp. (Greensboro, NC) 74840
Fruehauf Trailers (Greensboro, NC) 74841
Kroger Co. (Salem, VA) 92214
Kroger Co. (Charleston, WV) 92759
Service Merchandise (Orlando, FL) 62141
Texaco Inc. (Waskom, TX) 89990
Union Oil Co. (Nashville, TN) 82118

4231 Trucking Terminal Facilities

Amoco Transport Co. (Texas City, TX) 89716
Exxon (N Little Rock, AR) 57401
Overnite Transportation Co. (Lynchburg, VA) 91275
Overnite Transportation Co. (Richmond, VA) 91938
Trailway Enterprises (Bay St Louis, MS) 72606
United Van Lines Inc. (Rocky Mount, NC) 76109
Warren Petroleum Co. (Calvert City, KY) 68177

4400 Water Transportation

Texaco Ref. & Mktg. Inc. (Union, LA) 70918
Texaco Refining & Marketing Inc. (Convent, LA) 69784
Union Carbide Corp. Marine Terminal (Texas City, TX) 89743
Union Carbide Marine Terminal (Texas City, TX) 89744

4412 Deep Sea Foreign Transportation of Freight

CSX Corp. (Richmond, VA) 91837
Fina Inc. (Dallas, TX) 84065

4424 Deep Sea Domestic Transportation of Freight

CSX Corp. (Richmond, VA) 91837

4449 Water Transportation of Freight Nec

CSX Corp. (Richmond, VA) 91837
Exxon Shipping Co. (Houston, TX) 86183; 86184
Texaco Inc. (Port Arthur, TX) 88649
Valley Line Co. Inc (Houston, TX) 87068

4491 Marine Cargo Handling

Agrico Chemical Co. (Gibsonton, FL) 59926
CSX Corp. (Richmond, VA) 91837

4492 Towing & Tugboat Services

Indland Towing Co. (Ashland, KY) 68097

4499 Water Transportation Services Nec

CSX Intermodal Inc. (Hunt Valley, MD) 71927

4500 Transportation by Air

Ppm Inc. (Tucker, GA) 67885

4512 Air Transportation—Scheduled

Airborne Freight Corp. (Fort Lauderdale, FL) 59426
Airborne Freight Corp. (Jacksonville, FL) 60161
Airborne Freight Corp. (Tampa, FL) 63305
Airborne Freight Corp. (Shreveport, LA) 70680
Airborne Freight Corp. (Greenville, NC) 74946
Airborne Freight Corp. (Greer, SC) 79468
Airborne Freight Corp. (Hilton Head isLand, SC) 79510
Airborne Freight Corp. (Houston, TX) 85766
Airborne Freight Corp. (Richmond, VA) 91726
America West (Austin, TX) 82812
America West Airlines (Tampa, FL) 63308
America West Airlines (Austin, TX) 82813
American Airlines (Forth Worth, TX) 85368
American Airlines Cargo (Fort Worth, TX) 85060
AMR Corp. (Fort Worth, TX) 85064
AMR Eagle, Inc. (Fort Worth, TX) 85065
Boeing Co. the (Warner Robins, GA) 68009
Britt Airways Inc. (Houston, TX) 85888
Continental Airlines Inc. (Houston, TX) 86011
Continental Express (Gulfport, MS) 72852
Continental Express (Nederland, TX) 88184
Continental Express Airline (Sarasota, FL) 62806
Delta Air Lines (Birmingham, AL) 55213; 55214
Delta Air Lines (Montgomery, AL) 56297
Delta Air Lines (Little Rock, AR) 57269; 57270
Delta Air Lines (Daytona Beach, FL) 59171; 59172
Delta Air Lines (Fort Lauderdale, FL) 59479
Delta Air Lines (Jacksonville, FL) 60253; 60254
Delta Air Lines (Melbourne, FL) 61046
Delta Air Lines (Orlando, FL) 61959
Delta Air Lines (Pensacola, FL) 62418
Delta Air Lines (Sarasota, FL) 62811
Delta Air Lines (Tallahassee, FL) 63228; 63229; 63230; 63231
Delta Air Lines (Tampa, FL) 63399; 63400; 63401
Delta Air Lines (W Palm Beach, FL) 63786; 63787
Delta Air Lines (Savannah, GA) 67461
Delta Air Lines (Lexington, KY) 68543
Delta Air Lines (Louisville, KY) 68743; 68745
Delta Air Lines (Baton Rouge, LA) 69502; 69503; 69504
Delta Air Lines (New Orleans, LA) 70442
Delta Air Lines (Shreveport, LA) 70712
Delta Air Lines (Jackson, MS) 72964
Delta Air Lines (Charlotte, NC) 73924
Delta Air Lines (Greensboro, NC) 74807; 74808; 74808
Delta Air Lines (Oklahoma City, OK) 77344
Delta Air Lines (Tulsa, OK) 77926
Delta Air Lines (Charleston, SC) 78804
Delta Air Lines (Columbia, SC) 79008
Delta Air Lines (Greenville, SC) 79339
Delta Air Lines (Greer, SC) 79472

Delta Air Lines (West Columbia, SC) 80088
Delta Air Lines (Memphis, TN) 81506
Delta Air Lines (Nashville, TN) 81929
Delta Air Lines (Austin, TX) 82856
Delta Air Lines (Dallas, TX) 83972
Delta Air Lines (El Paso, TX) 84788
Delta Air Lines (Lubbock, TX) 87754
Delta Air Lines (San Antonio, TX) 88965; 88966; 88967
Delta Air Lines, Inc. (Montgomery, AL) 56299
Delta Air Lines Inc. (Little Rock, AR) 57271
Delta Air Lines Inc. (Fort Lauderdale, FL) 59480
Delta Air Lines Inc. (Jacksonville, FL) 60256
Delta Air Lines Inc. (Melbourne, FL) 61047
Delta Air Lines Inc. (Tallahassee, FL) 63232
Delta Air Lines Inc. (Tampa, FL) 63402
Delta Air Lines Inc. (W Palm Beach, FL) 63788
Delta Air Lines, Inc. (Atlanta, GA) 64412
Delta Air Lines Inc. (Savannah, GA) 67465
Delta Air Lines Inc. (Lexington, KY) 68544
Delta Air Lines Inc. (Louisville, KY) 68748
Delta Air Lines Inc. (Baton Rouge, LA) 69505; 69506
Delta Air Lines Inc. (Shreveport, LA) 70716
Delta Air Lines Inc. (Glen Burnie, MD) 71838
Delta Air Lines, Inc. (Charlotte, NC) 73925
Delta Air Lines Inc. (Greensboro, NC) 74809; 74809
Delta Air Lines Inc. (Charleston, SC) 78806
Delta Air Lines Inc. (Greenville, SC) 79340
Delta Air Lines Inc. (West Columbia, SC) 80089
Delta Air Lines Inc. (Nashville, TN) 81930
Delta Air Lines Inc. (Dallas, TX) 83973
Delta Air Lines Inc. (Lubbock, TX) 87755
Delta Air Lines Inc. (San Antonio, TX) 88968
Delta Air Lines Inc. (Norfolk, VA) 91513
Delta Air Lines Inc. (Richmond, VA) 91841
Delta Air Lines Inc. (Sandston, VA) 92231
Delta Air Lines Marketing Office (Mobile, AL) 56154
Delta Air Lines Marketing Office (Dallas, TX) 83974
Emery Worldwide (Madison, AL) 56119
Emery Worldwide (Montgomery, AL) 56308
Emery Worldwide (Little Rock, AR) 57281
Emery Worldwide (Jacksonville, FL) 60266
Emery Worldwide (W Palm Beach, FL) 63789
Emery Worldwide (Macon, GA) 66684
Emery Worldwide (Lafayette, LA) 70053
Emery Worldwide (Shreveport, LA) 70718
Emery Worldwide (Jackson, MS) 72979
Emery Worldwide (Charlotte, NC) 73943
Emery Worldwide (Fletcher, NC) 74591
Emery Worldwide (Raleigh, NC) 75888
Emery Worldwide (Wilmington, NC) 76552; 76553
Emery Worldwide (Charleston, SC) 78808
Emery Worldwide (N Myrtle Beach, SC) 79719
Emery Worldwide (West Columbia, SC) 80091
Emery Worldwide (Maryville, TN) 81403
Emery Worldwide (Abilene, TX) 82435
Emery Worldwide (El Paso, TX) 84795
Emery Worldwide (Lubbock, TX) 87762

Emery Worldwide (Sherman, TX) 89394
Federal Express Corp. (Greensboro, NC) 74818
Federal Express Corp. (Memphis, TN) 81535
Federal Express Corp. (Dallas, TX) 84061
Federal Express Corp. (Houston, TX) 86193
Northwest Airlines Inc. (Birmingham, AL) 55326
Northwest Airlines Inc. (Fort Myers, FL) 59725
Northwest Airlines Inc. (Miami, FL) 61382
Northwest Airlines Inc. (Tampa, FL) 63511
Northwest Airlines Inc. (Dallas, TX) 84274
Sabre Travel Information Network (Baton Rouge, LA) 69657
Southwest Airlines Co. (Oklahoma City, OK) 77559; 77560
Southwest Airlines Co. (Tulsa, OK) 78114
Southwest Airlines Co. (Amarillo, TX) 82579
Southwest Airlines Co. (Austin, TX) 83004
Southwest Airlines Co. (El Paso, TX) 84931
Southwest Airlines Co. (Houston, TX) 86904
Trans World Airlines (Fort Myers, FL) 59769
Trans World Airlines (W Palm Beach, FL) 63817
Trans World Airlines (Lexington, KY) 68646
Trans World Airlines (Charlotte, NC) 74179
Trans World Airlines (Tulsa, OK) 78179; 78180
Trans World Airlines (Memphis, TN) 81717
Trans World Airlines Inc. (Tampa, FL) 63629; 63630
Trans World Airlines Inc. (Louisville, KY) 69024
Trans World Airlines Inc. (Oklahoma City, OK) 77635
Trans World Airlines, Inc. (Norfolk, VA) 91587
Victoria's Secret (Houston, TX) 87080

4513 Air Courier Services

Airborne Freight Corp. (Baton Rouge, LA) 69454; 69455
Airborne Freight Corp. (Oklahoma City, OK) 77293
Airborne Freight Corp. (Dallas, TX) 83839
America West Airlines (Baltimore, MD) 71035
America West Airlines (Houston, TX) 85776
Burlington Air Express (Birmingham, AL) 55175
Burlington Air Express (Mobile, AL) 56146
Burlington Air Express (Jacksonville, FL) 60234
Burlington Air Express (Lexington, KY) 68530
Burlington Air Express (Louisville, KY) 68725
Burlington Air Express (Shreveport, LA) 70693
Burlington Air Express (Charlotte, NC) 73886; 73886
Burlington Air Express (Tulsa, OK) 77896
Burlington Air Express (Memphis, TN) 81487
Burlington Air Express (Nashville, TN) 81911
Burlington Air Express (Austin, TX) 82833
Burlington Air Express (El Paso, TX) 84776
Burlington Air Express (Midland, TX) 88025
Delta Air Cargo (Fort Myers, FL) 59692
Delta Air Cargo (Jacksonville, FL) 60252
Delta Air Cargo (Melbourne, FL) 61045
Delta Air Cargo (Baton Rouge, LA) 69501
Delta Air Cargo (Charleston, SC) 78801
Delta Air Cargo (Greenville, SC) 79338
Delta Air Cargo (El Paso, TX) 84787
Delta Air Freight (Daytona Beach, FL) 59170
Delta Air Freight (Charlotte, NC) 73923
Delta Air Lines (Miami, FL) 61273
Delta Air Lines (Lexington, KY) 68541
Delta Air Lines (Charlotte, NC) 73924
Delta Air Lines Air Cargo (Louisville, KY) 68747
Delta Air Lines Inc. (Miami, FL) 61275
Delta Air Lines, Inc. (Charlotte, NC) 73925
Delta Air Lines Inc. (Richmond, VA) 91840
Emery Worldwide (Baton Rouge, LA) 69511
Emery Worldwide (Oklahoma City, OK) 77351
Emery Worldwide (Greer, SC) 79473
Emery Worldwide (Dallas, TX) 84007
Emery Worldwide (Fort Worth, TX) 85108
Federal Express Aviation Services Inc. (Memphis, TN) 81531
Federal Express Corp. (Orlando, FL) 61967
Federal Express Corp. (West Columbia, SC) 80092
Federal Express Corp. (Memphis, TN) 81535
Federal Express Corp. (Amarillo, TX) 82546
Federal Express Europlex Inc. (Memphis, TN) 81536
Federal Express International Inc. (Memphis, TN) 81537; 81538
Federal Express Redevelopment Corp. (Memphis, TN) 81545
Fedex Customs Brokerage Corp. (Memphis, TN) 81547
Fedex International Transmission Corp. (Memphis, TN) 81548
United Parcel Service (Louisville, KY) 69029
United Parcel Service Air (Birmingham, AL) 55441

4522 Air Transportation—Nonscheduled

Delta Air Cargo (Tallahassee, FL) 63227
Delta Air Lines (Houston, TX) 86030
Delta Air Lines Inc. (Houston, TX) 86031
Executive Airlines Inc. (Fort Lauderdale, FL) 59483
Flagship Airlines (Nashville, TN) 82009
Hertz Rent-A-Car (Houma, LA) 69958
Hertz Rent-A-Car (Temple, TX) 89619

4581 Airports, Flying Fields & Services

Air Treads Inc. (Atlanta, GA) 64211
AMR Corp. (Fort Worth, TX) 85064
AMR Services (Baton Rouge, LA) 69469
AMR Services (Harlingen, TX) 85696
AMR Services Corp. (Dallas-Fort Worth Airport, TX) 84514
AMR Services Corp. (Fort Worth, TX) 85066
E Systems Inc. (Dallas, TX) 83990; 83992
Garrett Airlines Repair (Anniston, AL) 55000
Grumman Technical Services Corp. (Titusville, FL) 63690
Lockheed Aeromod Center, Inc. (Greenville, SC) 79390
Lockheed Support Systems, Inc. (Arlington, TX) 82693; 82695
Marshall Field (Georgetown, KY) 68385
Northrop Aircraft Inc. (Dierks, AR) 56905
Serv-Air Inc. (Greenville, TX) 85678
Wilsons (Hickory, NC) 75106; 75107

4610 Pipelines Except Natural Gas

Fina Inc. (Dallas, TX) 84064

4612 Crude Petroleum Pipelines

Agrico Chemical Co. (Tulsa, OK) 77873
All American Pipeline Co. Inc. (Houston, TX) 85768
Amerada Hess Corp. (Heidelberg, MS) 72901
Amerada Hess Corp. (McComb, MS) 73154
Arco (Channelview, TX) 83545
Arco Pipe Lie Vickers Station (Ardmore, OK) 76809
Arco Pipe Line (Maysville, OK) 77189
Arco Pipe Line (Yoakum, TX) 90135
Arco Pipe Line Co. (Cushing, OK) 76975; 76976
Arco Pipe Line Co. (Pauls Valley, OK) 77687; 77688
Arco Pipe Line Co. (Ringling, OK) 77765; 77766
Arco Pipe Line Co. (Shawnee, OK) 77811; 77812; 77813
Arco Pipe Line Co. (Skiatook, OK) 77825; 77826
Arco Pipe Line Co. (Euless, TX) 85005; 85006
Arco Pipe Line Co. (Gainesville, TX) 85421
Arco Pipe Line Co. (Jacksboro, TX) 87420
Arco Pipe Line Co. (Lolita, TX) 87697
Arco Pipe Line Co. (Luling, TX) 87822; 87823
Arco Pipe Line Co. (Midland, TX) 88021
Arco Pipe Line Co. (Plantersville, TX) 88620
Arco Pipe Line Co. (Refugio, TX) 88714
Arco Pipe Line Co. (Teague, TX) 89604
Arco Pipe Line Co., Inc. (Houston, TX) 85811
Arco Pipe Line Vickers Station (Ardmore, OK) 76812
Arco Pipeline (Bryan, TX) 83392
Arco Pipeline Co. (Ratliff City, OK) 77764
Arco Pipeline Co. (Stratford, OK) 77853; 77854
Arco Pipeline Co. (Thackerville, OK) 77865
Arco Pipeline Co. (Corpus Christi, TX) 83700
Arco Pipeline Co. (Seminole, TX) 89381
Arco Pipline Co. (Seminole, TX) 89382
Ashland Pipe Line Co. (Ashland, KY) 68093
Citgo Petroleum Corp. (Tulsa, OK) 77907
Citgo Pipeline Co. (Tulsa, OK) 77909
Colonial Pipeline Co. (Pasadena, TX) 88397
Colonial Pipeline Inc. (Collins, MS) 72694
Enron Oil Trading & Transportation (Houston, TX) 86080
Exxon Pipeline Co. (Baton Rouge, LA) 69531; 69532
Exxon Pipeline Co. (Raceland, LA) 70652
Exxon Pipeline Co. Inc. (Raceland, LA) 70653
Exxon Pipeline Co. Inc. (Houston, TX) 86178; 86179
Fina Inc. (Dallas, TX) 84065
Fina Oil & Chemical Co. (Dallas, TX) 84066
La Gloria Oil & Gas Co. Inc. (Bellaire, TX) 83265
Marathon Pipeline Co. (Zachary, LA) 70987
Marathon Pipeline Co. (Pasadena, TX) 88439
Mobil Alaska Pipeline Co. (Dallas, TX) 84238
Mobil Oil Co. Inc. (Midland, TX) 88052
Mobil Oil Corp. (Lindsay, OK) 77179
Mobil Pipe Line (Perryton, TX) 88501
Mobil Pipe Line Co. (Foreman, AR) 57007
Mobil Pipe Line Co. (Glenwood, AR) 57120
Mobil Pipe Line Co. (Saffell, AR) 57597
Mobil Pipe Line Co. (Corpus Christi, TX) 83739
Mobil Pipe Line Co. (Electra, TX) 84988; 84989
Mobil Pipe Line Co. (Gainesville, TX) 85424
Mobil Pipe Line Co. (Groveton, TX) 85690
Mobil Pipe Line Co. (Houston, TX) 86595
Mobil Pipe Line Co. (Hull, TX) 87213
Mobil Pipe Line Co. (Keller, TX) 87462
Mobil Pipe Line Co. (Kilgore, TX) 87493
Mobil Pipe Line Co. (Longview, TX) 87723
Mobil Pipe Line Co. (Luling, TX) 87824
Mobil Pipe Line Co. (Midland, TX) 88055
Mobil Pipe Line Co. (Mont Belvieu, TX) 88146
Mobil Pipe Line Co. (Mount Vernon, TX) 88155
Mobil Pipe Line Co. (Nederland, TX) 88188
Mobil Pipe Line Co. (Poynor, TX) 88697
Mobil Pipe Line Co. (Quitman, TX) 88704
Mobil Pipe Line Co. (Ringgold, TX) 88799
Mobil Pipe Line Co. (Schulenburg, TX) 89353
Mobil Pipe Line Co. (Seminole, TX) 89383
Mobil Pipe Line Co. (Sweetwater, TX) 89587
Mobil Pipe Line Co. (Vanderbilt, TX) 89863
Mobil Pipe Line Co. (Walnut Springs, TX) 89987
Mobil Pipe Line Co. (Waskom, TX) 89989
Mobil Pipe Line Co. Inc. (Houston, TX) 86596
Mobil Pipe Line Co. Sohio Plant (Elmore City, OK) 77039
Mobil Pipeline (Saratoga, TX) 89351
Mobil Pipeline Co. (Healdton, OK) 77120
Mobil Pipeline Co. (Center, TX) 83539
Mobil Pipeline Co. (Grapeland, TX) 85654
Mobil Pipeline Co. (Kermit, TX) 87468
Mobil Pipeline Co. (Navasota, TX) 88179
Mobil Pipeline Co. (Pineland, TX) 88515
Mobil Pipeline Co. Tec Techn (Alice, TX) 82486
Mobil Pipeline Sta. (Liberty, TX) 87674; 87675
Mobil Pipeline Stations (Dayton, TX) 84523
Plantation Pipe Line (Newington, VA) 91447
Shell Pipeline Corp. (Odessa, TX) 88277; 88278
Texaco Inc. (Midland, TX) 88083
Wingfoot Ventures Seven Inc. (Houston, TX) 87199

4613 Refined Petroleum Pipelines

Arco Pipe Line Co., Inc. (Houston, TX) 85811
Colonial Pipeline Co. Inc. (Atlanta, GA) 64386
Enron Corp. (Houston, TX) 86062
Exxon Pipeline Co. Inc. (Houston, TX) 86178; 86179
Mapco Inc. (Tulsa, OK) 78009
Mapco Natural Gas Liquids Inc. (Tulsa, OK) 78010
Mobil Alaska Pipeline Co. (Dallas, TX) 84238

4619 Pipelines Nec

Arco Pipe Line Co. (Wichita Falls, TX) 90066
Colonial Pipeline Co. (Tallahassee, FL) 63226
Colonial Pipeline Co. (Bainbridge, GA) 65364
Colonial Pipeline Co. (Greensboro, NC) 74801
Colonial Pipeline Co. (Nashville, TN) 81926
Colonial Pipeline Co. (Chesapeake, VA) 90564
Colonial Pipeline Co. (Richmond, VA) 91781
Exxon Gas Pipe Line (Pearland, TX) 88480
Exxon Pipeline Co. (Baton Rouge, LA) 69530; 69531; 69532; 69533
Exxon Pipeline Co. (Dallas, TX) 84051; 84052
Mobil Alaska Pipeline Co. (Dallas, TX) 84238
Mobil Pipe Line Co. (Guymon, OK) 77104
Mobil Pipe Line Co. (Beaumont, TX) 83187; 83188
Mobil Pipe Line Co. (Corpus Christi, TX) 83739
Mobil Pipe Line Co. (Corsicana, TX) 83785
Mobil Pipe Line Co. (Longview, TX) 87723
Mobil Pipeline Co. (Midland, TX) 88057; 88058
Shell Pipe Line Corp. Centra (Midland, TX) 88075
Shell Pipeline Corp. (New Orleans, LA) 70556
Shell Pipeline Corp. (El Paso, TX) 84928; 84929
Shell Pipeline Corp. (Midland, TX) 88076
Shell Pipeline Corp. (Ofc) (New Orleans, LA) 70557

4724 Travel Agencies

Burdines (St Petersburg, FL) 62965
Burdines Travel (Miami, FL) 61218
Burdines Travel Bureau (Gainesville, FL) 59864
Carnival Cruise Lines (Miami, FL) 61223
Coast to Coast Travel (Miami, FL) 61265
Delta Air Lines (Birmingham, AL) 55212
Delta Air Lines (Montgomery, AL) 56298
Delta Air Lines (Fort Myers, FL) 59693
Delta Air Lines (Miami, FL) 61274
Delta Air Lines (St Petersburg, FL) 62969
Delta Air Lines (Savannah, GA) 67462
Delta Air Lines (Lexington, KY) 68542
Delta Air Lines (Louisville, KY) 68746
Delta Air Lines (Shreveport, LA) 70713; 70714
Delta Air Lines (Jackson, MS) 72965; 72966
Delta Air Lines (Oklahoma City, OK) 77343
Delta Air Lines (Tulsa, OK) 77927
Delta Air Lines (Charleston, SC) 78802
Delta Air Lines (Columbia, SC) 79008
Delta Air Lines (Knoxville, TN) 81161
Delta Air Lines (Dallas, TX) 83972
Delta Air Lines (Fort Worth, TX) 85096; 85097
Delta Air Lines Inc. (Birmingham, AL) 55215
Delta Air Lines Inc. (Montgomery, AL) 56300
Delta Air Lines Inc. (Miami, FL) 61276
Delta Air Lines Inc. (St Petersburg, FL) 62970
Delta Air Lines Inc. (Savannah, GA) 67463
Delta Air Lines Inc. (Lexington, KY) 68545
Delta Air Lines Inc. (Louisville, KY) 68750
Delta Air Lines Inc. (Shreveport, LA) 70715
Delta Air Lines Inc. (Linthicum Heights, MD) 72107; 72108
Delta Air Lines Inc. (Jackson, MS) 72967
Delta Air Lines Inc. (Charleston, SC) 78805
Delta Air Lines Inc. (Knoxville, TN) 81162
Delta Air Lines Inc. (Dallas, TX) 83973
Delta Air Lines Inc. (Fort Worth, TX) 85098; 85099
Dillard Travel Inc. (Little Rock, AR) 57279
Greyhound Bus Lines (Alexandria, VA) 90223
Greyhound Bus Station (Asheville, NC) 73630
Kroger Family Center (Kingsville, TX) 87534
Lifeco/American Express (Houston, TX) 86458
Lifeco/American Express Corp. (Houston, TX) 86459
Northwest Airlines Inc. (Fort Lauderdale, FL) 59550
Northwest Airlines Inc. (Miami, FL) 61383
Signature Travel Inc. (Houston, TX) 86895
Taco Bell (Elizabeth Cty, NC) 74486
Texas Tank Ship Agency Inc. (Corpus Christi, TX) 83761
Trailways Bus System (St Petersburg, FL) 63038
Trailways Bus System (El Paso, TX) 84952
Walt Disney Travel Co. Inc. (Orlando, FL) 62189

4725 Tour Operators

Lifeco/American Express (Houston, TX) 86458

Walt Disney Travel Co. Inc. (Orlando, FL) 62189

4729 Passenger Transportation Arrangement Nec

Burdines Travel Bureau (Orlando, FL) 61942
Burdines Travel Bureau (W Palm Beach, FL) 63781
Delta Air Lines (Birmingham, AL) 55213; 55214
Delta Air Lines (Hartly, DE) 57821
Delta Air Lines (Fort Myers, FL) 59694
Delta Air Lines (Tampa, FL) 63399
Delta Air Lines (Macon, GA) 66682
Delta Air Lines (Savannah, GA) 67460
Delta Air Lines (Louisville, KY) 68744
Delta Air Lines (Baton Rouge, LA) 69503
Delta Air Lines (Charleston, SC) 78803
Delta Air Lines Inc. (Macon, GA) 66683
Delta Air Lines Inc. (Savannah, GA) 67464
Delta Air Lines Inc. (Louisville, KY) 68749
Delta Air Lines Inc. (Baton Rouge, LA) 69505
Delta Air Lines, Inc. (Columbia, SC) 79009
Delta Air Lines Inc. (Richmond, VA) 91840
Northwest Airlines Inc. (Fort Lauderdale, FL) 59549
Trans World Airlines Inc. (Memphis, TN) 81718

4731 Freight Transportation Arrangement

ABF Freight Systems Inc. (Lynchburg, VA) 91219
American Brokerage Co. (Miami, FL) 61154
Caltex Petroleum Corp. (Irving, TX) 87327
Coast to Coast Express (Calhoun, LA) 69748
Emery Worldwide (Birmingham, AL) 55230
Emery Worldwide (Fayetteville, AR) 56976
Emery Worldwide (Tampa, FL) 63413
Emery Worldwide (Lake Charles, LA) 70138
Emery Worldwide (Greensboro, NC) 74814
Emery Worldwide (Memphis, TN) 81518
Emery Worldwide (Austin, TX) 82863
Emery Worldwide (ACF Co.) (Wheeling, WV) 93111
First Union Transportation Services Inc. (Charlotte, NC) 74012
Greyhound Bus Station (Fabens, TX) 85027
Innovative Logistics Inc. (Fort Mill, SC) 79234
Sekin Transport International (Tulsa, OK) 78108
Trailways Bus System (Fort Myers, FL) 59768
Trailways Bus Systems (Wichita Falls, TX) 90115
Utility Fuels Inc. (Houston, TX) 87066

4741 Rental of Railroad Cars

Burlington Northern Railroad (Amarillo, TX) 82533
Fruit Growers Express Co. Inc. (Alexandria, VA) 90221
GSC Leasing Dr. (Claymont, DE) 57763

4783 Packing & Crating

North American Van Lines Inc. (San Antonio, TX) 89120
Phoenix Packaging Inc. (Winston-Salem, NC) 76738
Southern Companies (Nashville, TN) 82098
Universal Foods Corp. (San Antonio, TX) 89288

4789 Transportation Services Nec

Delta Air Lines, Inc. (Columbia, SC) 79009
Dillard Department Stores (Houston, TX) 86039
Fruit Growers Express Co. Inc. (Alexandria, VA) 90221
Overnite Transportation Co. (Richmond, VA) 91938
Sekin Transport Internation (Houston, TX) 86873
Shell Pipeline Corp. (El Paso, TX) 84928; 84929

4812 Radiotelephone Communications

ALLTEL Alabama (Leeds, AL) 56105
ALLTEL Arkansas Inc. (Little Rock, AR) 57244
ALLTEL Carolina (Matthews, NC) 75516
ALLTEL Corp. (Little Rock, AR) 57245
ALLTEL Florida (Live Oak, FL) 60906
ALLTEL Georgia Inc. (Commerce, GA) 65659
ALLTEL Kentucky Inc. (Shepherdsville, KY) 69280
ALLTEL Mississippi Inc. (Florence, MS) 72771
ALLTEL Mobile Communications Inc. (Little Rock, AR) 57248
ALLTEL Oklahoma Inc. (Burns Flat, OK) 76902
ALLTEL Services Inc. (Little Rock, AR) 57249
ALLTEL South Carolina Inc. (Lexington, SC) 79600
ALLTEL Tennessee Inc. (Powell, TN) 82236
ALLTEL Texas Inc. (Nocona, TX) 88227
American Cellular Communications Corp. (Atlanta, GA) 64222
Bell Atlantic Bus Syst Servs. (Louisville, KY) 68700
Bell Atlantic Business System Services (Birmingham, AL) 55161
Bell Atlantic Metro Mobile (Greenville, SC) 79300
Bell Atlantic Mobile (Hickory, NC) 75058
Bell Atlantic Mobile (El Paso, TX) 84767
Bell Atlantic Tricon Lease Corp. (Ft. Lauderdale, FL) 59852
Bell South Co. (Metairie, LA) 70252
Bell South Enterprises, Inc. (Atlanta, GA) 64304
Bellsouth mobility (Baton rouge, LA) 69472
BellSouth Corp. (Atlanta, GA) 64317
BellSouth Enterprises Inc. (Atlanta, GA) 64318
BellSouth Mobility (Birmingham, AL) 55165
BellSouth Mobility (West Palm Beach, FL) 63848
Bellsouth Mobility (Metairie, LA) 70253
BellSouth Mobility Inc. (Atlanta, GA) 64322
Centel Cellular Inc. (Atlanta, GA) 64348
The Chesapeak & Potomae Co. of West Virginia (Charleston, WV) 92728
The Chesapeake & Potomac Co. of Maryland (Baltimore, MD) 71082
Chesapeake & Potomac Tel Co. MD (Baltimore, MD) 71083
Chesapeake & Potomac Telephone Co. (Richmond, VA) 91767
The Chesapeake & Potomic Co. of Virginia (Richmond, VA) 91769
Great Southwest Telephone Corp. (Grandview, TX) 85650
GTE Cellular Communications Corp. (Atlanta, GA) 64522
GTE Florida Inc. (Tampa, FL) 63448
GTE Mobile Communications Inc. (Atlanta, GA) 64525
GTE Mobilnet Inc. (Atlanta, GA) 64528
GTE South Inc. (Tampa, FL) 63452
GTE Southwest Inc. (Irving, TX) 87350
GTE Telecom Inc. (Tampa, FL) 63453
Heins Telephone Co. (Sanford, NC) 76196
Intertel, Inc. (Houston, TX) 86311
Metro Mobile CTS of Charlotte, Inc. (Charlotte, NC) 74084
Metro Mobile CTS of El Paso, Inc. (El Paso, TX) 84853
Metro Mobile CTS of Greenville, Inc. (Greenville, SC) 79394
Mobil & Comm (Dallas, TX) 84241
Mobile Communications Corp. of America (Ridgeland, MS) 73326
Mobilecomm of Nashville Inc. (Nashville, TN) 82064
Mobilecomm of Ohio Inc. (Ridgeland, MS) 73327
Mountain State Telephone Co. (Masontown, WV) 92937
Oklahoma ALLTEL Inc. (Poteau, OK) 77724
Pactel Paging (Orlando, FL) 62072
Pactel Paging (Lexington, KY) 68597
Pactel Paging (Fort Worth, TX) 85208
Radio Shack (New Orleans, LA) 70549
Radio Shack (Baltimore, MD) 71230; 71233
Radio Shack (Denton, TX) 84634
Sandhill Telephone Co. (Aberdeen, NC) 73520
TheChesapeake & Potomac Telephone Co. (Washington, DC) 58504
Underwriters Adjusting Co. (Hurst, TX) 87300

4813 Telephone Communications Except Radiotelephone

ALLTEL Corp. (Little Rock, AR) 57245
AT&T (Athens, LA) 69434
AT&T (Hornbeck, LA) 69949
AT&T (Welsh, LA) 70941
AT&T (West Monroe, LA) 70942
AT&T (Greensboro, NC) 74780
AT&T (Huntersville, NC) 75206
AT&T (Sweetwater, TN) 82366
AT&T (Caldwell, TX) 83431
AT&T (Temple, TX) 89605
AT&T (Richmond, VA) 91737
AT&T (Standardsville, VA) 92305
AT&T Capital Small Business Lending (San Antonio, TX) 88920
At&T Fitel Co. (Carrollton, GA) 65489
AT&T Network System (Charleston, WV) 92724
Bell Atlantic Bus Syst Servs. (Louisville, KY) 68700
Bell Atlantic Business System Services (Birmingham, AL) 55161
Bell Atlantic Business Systems Services (Richmond, VA) 91742
Bell Atlantic Corp. (Dallas, TX) 83875
Bell Atlantic Corp. (Midland, TX) 88022
Bell Atlantic Mobile (Lanham, MD) 72049
Bell Atlantic Mobile (Westminster, MD) 72540
Bell Atlantic Mobile (El Paso, TX) 84767
Bell Atlantic Mobile Systems (Wilmington, DE) 58009
Bell Atlantic Network SErvices Inc. (Arlington, VA) 90277
Bell Atlantic Tricon Lease Corp. (Ft. Lauderdale, FL) 59852
Bell South Enterprises, Inc. (Atlanta, GA) 64304
Bell South Mobility Inc. (Louisville, KY) 68701
BellSouth Corp. (Atlanta, GA) 64317
BellSouth Enterprises Inc. (Atlanta, GA) 64318
Bellsouth Mobility (Franklin, TN) 80808
BellSouth Telecom Inc. (Atlanta, GA) 64324
BellSouth Telecommunications Inc. (Atlanta, GA) 64325
BellSouth /telecommunictions Inc. (Atlanta, GA) 64326
Chesapeake & Potomac Phone Co. (Leonardtown, MD) 72098
Chesapeake & Potomac Tel Co. (Washington, DC) 58149
Chesapeake & Potomac Tel Co. (Newport News, VA) 91454
Chesapeake & Potomac Tel Co. MD (Baltimore, MD) 71083
Chesapeake & Potomac Tel Co. MD (Cumberland, MD) 71620; 71621
Chesapeake & Potomac Tel Co. MD (Keedysville, MD) 71991
The Chesapeake & Potomac Telephone Co. (Washington, DC) 58150
Chesapeake & Potomac Telephone Co. (Culpeper, VA) 90673
Chesapeake & Potomac Telephone Co. (Hopewell, VA) 91159
Chesapeake & Potomac Telephone Co. (Richmond, VA) 91766; 91767
Chesapeake & Potomac Telephone Co. (Roanoke, VA) 92108
Chesapeake & Potomac Telephone Co. (Staunton, VA) 92309
Chesapeake & Potomac Telephone Co. (Suffolk, VA) 92361
Chesapeake & Potomac Telephone Co. (Beckley, WV) 92674
Chesapeake & Potomac Telephone Co. (Charleston, WV) 92730
Chesapeake & Potomac Telephone Co. (Clarksburg, WV) 92804
Chesapeake & Potomac Telephone Co. (Moundsville, WV) 92951
Chesapeake & Potomac Telephone Co. (Parkersburg, WV) 92982
Chesapeake & Potomac Telephone Co. (Salem, WV) 93037
Chesapeake & Potomac Telephone Co. of Maryland (Baltimore, MD) 71084
The Chesapeake & Potomac Telephone Co. of Virginia (Richmond, VA) 91768
Diamond State Telephone Co. (Wilmington, DE) 58051
The Diamond State Telephone Co. Inc. (Wilmington, DE) 58052
Diamond State Telephone Co. The (Wilmington, DE) 58053
GTE Florida Inc. (Tampa, FL) 63447
GTE South Inc. (Tampa, FL) 63451
GTE Southwest Inc. (Irving, TX) 87351
GTE Supply (Irving, TX) 87352
Ram Mobile Data (Richardson, TX) 88763

4822 Telegraph & Other Communications

Greyhound Bus Lines (Apopka, FL) 58571
Kroger Food Store (Alexandria, LA) 69388
Kroger Food Store (Denison, TX) 84599
Piggly Wiggly (Carthage, MS) 72662

4832 Radio Broadcasting Stations

American Family Life Assurance Co. (Columbus, GA) 65617

4833 Television Broadcasting Stations

American Family Life Assurance Co. Broadcast Div. (Columbus, GA) 65618
Tuner Broadcasting System, Inc. was Turner Communications Corp. (Atlanta, GA) 65225
Walgreen Drug Stores (Auburndale, FL) 58604
Warner Communications Inc. (Stephenville, TX) 89527
WCIX-TV (Miami, FL) 61514

4841 Cable & Other Pay Television Services

Coast to Coast (Cullman, AL) 55540
FPL Group Inc. (West Palm Beach, FL) 63866
Telesat Cable T V Inc. (Florence, KY) 68344
Tuner Broadcasting System, Inc. (was Turner Communications Corp.) (Atlanta, GA) 65225

4899 Communications Services Nec

Allied-Signal Technical Service (Columbia, MD) 71574
ALLTEL Corp. (Little Rock, AR) 57245
AT&T Easylink Services (Nashville, TN) 81898
GTE Customer Networks, Inc. (Atlanta, GA) 64523
GTE Spacenet Corp. (McLean, VA) 91392
Mobile Communications Corp. of America (Ridgeland, MS) 73326
Radio Shack (Hartsville, SC) 79501
Raytheon Service Co. (Greenville, MS) 72818

4911 Electric Services

ALLTEL Corp. (Little Rock, AR) 57245
Arkansas Power & Light Co. (Little Rock, AR) 57252
Baltimore Gas & Electric Co. (Baltimore, MD) 71051; 71056
Baltimore Gas & Electric Co. (Bel Air, MD) 71334
Carolina Power & Light Co. (Aberdeen, NC) 73512; 73513
Carolina Power & Light Co. (Clinton, NC) 74282; 74283
Carolina Power & Light Co. (Goldsboro, NC) 74710; 74711
Carolina Power & Light Co. (Morehead City, NC) 75614; 75615
Carolina Power & Light Co. (New Bern, NC) 75721
Carolina Power & Light Co. (Rockingham, NC) 76058; 76059
Carolina Power & Light Co. (Selma, NC) 76219; 76220
Carolina Power & Light Co. (Southern Pines, NC) 76275
Carolina Power & Light Co. (Southern Pnes, NC) 76279
Carolina Power & Light Co. (Wadesboro, NC) 76424; 76425
Carolina Power & Light Co. (Whiteville, NC) 76495; 76496; 76497; 76498
Carolina Power & Light Co. (Wilmington, NC) 76548
Carolina Power & Light Co. (Bishopville, SC) 78740; 78741
Carolina Power & Light Co. (Darlington, SC) 79144; 79145
Coastal Technology Inc. (Roanoke, VA) 92117
Dominion Resources Inc. (Richmond, VA) 91858
Dominion Resources Inc. VA (Richmond, VA) 91859
Duke Power Co. (Charlotte, NC) 73939
Duke Power Co. Inc. (Charlotte, NC) 73940
Enron Power Development Corp. (Houston, TX) 86084
Entergy Operations Inc. (Jackson, MS) 72981
Florida Power & Light Co., Inc. (West Palm Beach, FL) 63865
FPL Group Inc. (West Palm Beach, FL) 63866
Gulf States Utilities Co. (Denham Springs, LA) 69828
Gulf States Utilities Co. (Lake Charles, LA) 70139
Gulf States Utilities Co. (Zachary, LA) 70986
Gulf States Utilities Co. (Austin, TX) 82885
Gulf States Utilities Co. (Conroe, TX) 83662
Gulf States Utilities Co. (Dayton, TX) 84521
Gulf States Utilities Co. (Orange, TX) 88314
Gulf States Utilities Co. (Port Neches, TX) 88673
Gulf States Utilities Co. (Vidor, TX) 89915
Louisiana Power & Light Co. (New Orleans, LA) 70521
Mississippi Power & Light Co. (Jackson, MS) 73025
Monogahela Power Co. (Fairmont, WV) 92842
Monogahela Power Co. (Parkersburg, WV) 92993
Monongahela Power Co. (Clarksburg, WV) 92812
Monongahela Power Co. (Fairmont, WV) 92843; 92844
Monongahela Power Co. (Franklin, WV) 92853
Monongahela Power Co. (Marlinton, WV) 92925
Monongahela Power Co. (Morgantown, WV) 92946
Monongahela Power Co. (Parsons, WV) 93001
Monongahela Power Co. (Weirton, WV) 93096
Nantahala Power & Light Co. (Bryson City, NC) 73732
Nantahala Power Light Co. (Franklin, NC) 74628; 74629
New Orleans Public Service Inc. (New Orleans, LA) 70540
Potomac Edison Co. (Cumberland, MD) 71632
Potomac Edison Co. (Frederick, MD) 71739; 71740
The Potomac Edison Co. (Hagerstown, MD) 71888; 71889; 71890
Potomac Edison Co. (Oakland, MD) 72158
Potomac Edison Co. (Gordonsville, VA) 90994

Watkins Manufacturing Co. (South Hill, VA) 92269

5013 Motor Vehicle Supplies & New Parts

Allied-Signal Corp. (Salisbury, NC) 76154; 76155
American Parts System Inc. (Houston, TX) 85794
APS Acquisition Corp. (Houston, TX) 85803
APS Holding Corp. (Houston, TX) 85804
APS Inc. (Houston, TX) 85805
Arvin Industries Inc. Maremount Exhaust Systems Product Div. (Loudon, TN) 81351
Avnet Mechanics Choice (Lithonia, GA) 66592
Beck/Arnley Worldparts Corp. (Nashville, TN) 81899
Big A Auto Parts Inc. (Houston, TX) 85882
Briggs & Stratton Corp. (Perry, GA) 67262
Daniel Radiator Corp. (West Palm Beach, FL) 63854
Daniel Radiator Corp. (Atlanta, GA) 64402
Daniel Radiator Corp. (La Grange, GA) 66477
Daniel Radiator Corp. (Lexington, TN) 81336
Daniel Radiator Corp. (Houston, TX) 86025
Eaton Corp. (Henderson, KY) 68443
Eaton Corp., U.S. Engine Valve Corp. (Westminister, SC) 80113
Fruehauf Inc. (Nashville, TN) 82014
Fruehauf Trailer Corp. (Little Rock, AR) 57284
Fruehauf Trailer Corp. (Shreveport, LA) 70722
Fruehauf Trailer Corp. (Greensboro, NC) 74840
Fruehauf Trailer Corp. (Tulsa, OK) 77942
Fruehauf Trailer Corp. (Odessa, TX) 88245
Fruehauf Trailers (Greensboro, NC) 74841
Fruehauf Trailers (Tulsa, OK) 77943
Fruehauf Trailers (Odessa, TX) 88246
Genuine Parts Co., Inc. (Atlanta, GA) 64503
Heil Co. the (Kodak, TN) 81280
Lexington Tube Co. (Lexington, TN) 81339
Maremont Corp. (Brentwood, TN) 80231
Maremont Exhaust Products, Inc. (Loudon, TN) 81354
North Riverside Holding Inc. (Norcross, GA) 67165
Ppg Industries Inc. (Houston, TX) 86717
Radio Shack (Purcell, OK) 77751
Radio Shack (Berryville, VA) 90429
Radio Shack Div. of Tandy Corp. (Berryville, VA) 90430
Safety Kleen Corp. (Birmingham, AL) 55384
Safety Kleen Corp. (Montgomery, AL) 56377
Safety Kleen Corp. (West Memphis, AR) 57735
Safety Kleen Corp. (Jacksonville, FL) 60451
Safety Kleen Corp. (Macon, GA) 66712
Safety Kleen Corp. (Kenner, LA) 70012
Safety Kleen Corp. (Pineville, LA) 70631
Safety Kleen Corp. (Catoosa, OK) 76911
Snap-On Tools Corp. (Elizabethton, TN) 80770
United Brake Systems Inc. (Dallas, TX) 84470
United Parcel Service (Shreveport, LA) 70799
Wang Laboratories Inc. (Ripley, TN) 82266
Western Auto Supply Co. (College Sta, TX) 83615

5014 Tires & Tubes

First Choice Co. (Memphis, TN) 81565; 81565
Hertz Rent-A-Car (Cambridge, MD) 71486
Kelly-Springfield Tire Co. Inc. (Cumberland, MD) 71629
Texaco Service Sta/Wardens (Burnet, TX) 83429

5021 Furniture

Diebold Inc. (Houston, TX) 86037
Ecco Inc. (High Point, NC) 75123
Electro Mechanical Holding Inc. (Lynchburg, VA) 91235
Genuine Parts Co., Inc. (Atlanta, GA) 64503
Herman Miller Inc. (New Castle, DE) 57865
Herman Miller Inc. (Washington, DC) 58299
Herman Miller Inc. (Houston, TX) 86265
Leggett & Platt Inc. (Winchester, KY) 69347
Office Products Inc. (Harrisonburg, VA) 91095
S. P. Richards Co., Inc. (Smyrna, GA) 67575
Scoot-Rice Co. Inc. (Tulsa, OK) 78105

5023 Homefurnishings

ACME Frame Products of Mississippi (Tutwiler, MS) 73429
Anchor Hocking Corp. (Louisville, KY) 68690
Anchor Hocking Corp. (Clarksburg, WV) 92803
Ball-Incon Glass Packaging (Henderson, NC) 75018; 75019
Brown-Forman Corp. (Louisville, KY) 68715
Kaiser Aluminum & Chemical (Birmingham, AL) 55287
Lees Carpets (Dallas, TX) 84196
Lenox China (Oxford, NC) 75782
Sysco Food Services Inc. (Austin, TX) 83009
Taco Bell (Fort Myers, FL) 59766

5031 Lumber, Plywood & Millwork

Bowater Lumber Co. (Albertville, AL) 54961
Coast to Coast Lumber Co. Inc. (Louisville, KY) 68733
Louisiana Pacific Corp. (Evergreen, AL) 55709
Louisiana Pacific Corp. (Alexandria, LA) 69393
Louisiana Pacific Corp. (Urania, LA) 70919
Louisiana Pacific Corp. (Winnfield, LA) 70978
Louisiana Pacific Corp. (Carthage, TX) 83519
Louisiana Pacific Corp. (Cleveland, TX) 83594
Louisiana Pacific Corp. (Huntsville, TX) 87262
Louisiana Pacific Corp. (Plano, TX) 88584
Louisiana Pacific Corp., OSB (Urania, LA) 70920
Potlatch Corp. (Warren, AR) 57710
Union Camp Corp. (Opelika, AL) 56428
Willamette Industries Inc. (Taylor, LA) 70910

5032 Brick, Stone & Related Materials

Martin Marietta Aggregates (Charlotte, NC) 74080
Martin Marietta Aggregates (Jamestown, NC) 75240
Martin Marietta Aggregates (New Bern, NC) 75729
Piggly Wiggly 255 (Itta Bena, MS) 72933
Vulcan Materials Co. (Bristol, VA) 90493; 90494

5033 Roofing, Siding & Insulation

Owens Corning Fiberglas Cor (Charlotte, NC) 74100
Short & Paulk Supply Co. Inc. (Tifton, GA) 67830
Specialty Products (Tampa, FL) 63601

5039 Construction Materials Nec

Allied Plywood Corp. (Dallas, TX) 83841
American Limestone Co. Inc. (Springfield, TN) 82354
Anchor Glass Container Corp. (Metairie, LA) 70250
Builders Square (Casselberry, FL) 58929
Builders Square (Pensacola, FL) 62410
Builders Square (Tampa, FL) 63369
Builders Square (Tulsa, OK) 77894
Builders Square (El Paso, TX) 84775
Builders Square (San Antonio, TX) 88938
Builder's Square (Virginia Beach, VA) 92442
Home Depot (Madison, TN) 81377
Lowe's (Eustis, FL) 59400
Lowe's (Brunswick, GA) 65418
Lowe's (Gainesville, GA) 66284
Lowe's (Selma, NC) 76225
Lowe's (Smithfield, NC) 76263
Lowe's (Columbia, SC) 79050
Lowe's (Greenville, SC) 79392
Lowe's (Pounding Mill, VA) 91675
Lowe's Home Center (Clinton, MS) 72688
Lowe's Home Center (Jackson, MS) 73023
Martin Marietta Aggregates (Charlotte, NC) 74080
Martin Marietta Aggregates (Maysville, NC) 75542
Owens Corning Fiberglas (Jacksonville, FL) 60384
Owens Corning Fiberglas Cor (Oklahoma City, OK) 77461
Owens Corning Fiberglas Cor (San Antonio, TX) 89122
Owens Corning Fiberglass (Charlotte, NC) 74101
Owens Corning Fiberglass (Tulsa, OK) 78038
Owens-Corning Fiberglass Corp. (Richmond, VA) 91939
Payless Cashways (Oklahoma City, OK) 77464
Payless Cashways (Tulsa, OK) 78041
Payless Cashways (Sherman, TX) 89416
Payless Cashways Building M (Tulsa, OK) 78042
Payless Cashways Building M (Fort Worth, TX) 85209
Payless Cashways Inc. (Fort Smith, AR) 57079
Payless Cashways Inc. (Fort Worth, TX) 85210
Piggly Wiggly (Winters, TX) 90128
Specialty Products (Tampa, FL) 63601
US Gypsum Co. (Birmingham, AL) 55443
US Gypsum Co. (Jacksonville, FL) 60489
US Gypsum Co. (Miami, FL) 61491
US Gypsum Co. (Louisville, KY) 69031
US Gypsum Co. (Nashville, TN) 82133
US Gypsum Co. (Dallas, TX) 84479
US Gypsum Co. (New Braunfels, TX) 88222
US Gypsum Co. (Norfolk, VA) 91591
Vulcan Materials Co. (Lexington, KY) 68657
Vulcan Materials Co. (Franklin, TN) 80826
Vulcan Materials Co. (Jackson, TN) 81015
Vulcan Materials Co. (Kingsport, TN) 81121
Vulcan Materials Co. (Maryville., TN) 81429
Vulcan Materials Co. (Morristown, TN) 81816
Vulcan Materials Co. (Nashville., TN) 82147; 82149
Vulcan Materials Co. (Parsons, TN) 82226
Vulcan Materials Co. (Rogersville., TN) 82284
Vulcan Materials Co. (Waverly, TN) 82406
Vulcan Materials Co. (Manassas, VA) 91327; 91328
Vulcan Materials Co. (Stafford, VA) 92302; 92303
Wheeling Corrugating Co. Inc. (Houston, TX) 87196

5043 Photographic Equipment & Supplies

Eastman Kodak (Owensboro, KY) 69169
Polaroid Corp. (Miami, FL) 61400

5044 Office Equipment

ABM Graphics (Birmingham, AL) 55109
ACME Business Products (Athens, GA) 64152
ACME Business Products (Brunswick, GA) 65399; 65400
ACME Business Products (Valdosta, GA) 67938
ACME Business Products (Asheville, NC) 73601
ACME Business Products (Anderson, SC) 78661
Advanced Image Systems Inc. (Dallas, TX) 83837
American LaFrance (Bluefield, VA) 90458
Arnet Computer (St. Petersburg, FL) 63081
Builders Square (San Antonio, TX) 88937
Copier Consultants (Tomball, TX) 89767
Copier Consultants Inc. (Marietta, GA) 66765
Copy Data Group, Inc. (Virginia Beach, VA) 92446
Copy Van, Inc. (Richmond, VA) 91789; 91790
Delta Business Systems (Orlando, FL) 61960
Diebold Inc. (Montgomery, AL) 56301
Diebold Inc. (Pearcy, AR) 57505
Diebold Inc. (Baton Rouge, LA) 69508
Diebold Inc. (Brookhaven, MS) 72653
Diebold Inc. (Raleigh, NC) 75886
Diebold Inc. (Jackson, TN) 80969
Diebold Inc. (Knoxville, TN) 81163
Diebold Inc. (Abilene, TX) 82434
Diebold Inc. (Uvalde, TX) 89850
Diebold Inc. (Victoria, TX) 89883
Diebold Inc. (Waco, TX) 89933
Diebold Inc. (Mechanicsvl, VA) 91404
Digital Equipment Corporati (Warner Robins, GA) 68014
Eastman Kodak Co. (Nashville, TN) 81938
Eastman Kodak Co. (Charleston, WV) 92743
EBM Inc. (Gallatin, TN) 80842
EBM, Inc. (Nashville, TN) 81942
Hewlett Packard Co. (Bethany, OK) 76858
Hit or Miss (Austin, TX) 82890
Hon Co. (Cedartown, GA) 65511
Ibm Corp. (Greenwood, MS) 72835
Ibm Corp. (Wilkesboro, NC) 76516
Innovative Office Systems, Inc. (Dallas, TX) 84133; 84134
Minnesota Mining&Mfg Co. Inc. (Memphis, TN) 81657
Mirex Corp. of Texas Service (Houston, TX) 86581
Modern Business Systems (Harrison, AR) 57139
Modern Office Machines Inc. (Greenville, SC) 79395; 79396
Molex Inc. (Louisville, KY) 68888
NCR Corp. (Hagerstown, MD) 71885
Richards S P Co. (Birmingham, AL) 55371
Richards S P Co. (Austin, TX) 82992
Sav-On (Fort Worth, TX) 85274
Smith Corona Corp. (Arlington, TX) 82751
Southern Copy Machines, Inc. (Norcross, GA) 67185
System Devices & Supplies Inc. (Miami, FL) 61467
J. L. Teel Co., Inc. (Columbus, MS) 72729
Texas Copy Systems, Inc. (Austin, TX) 83043
Uni-Copy Corp. of North Carolina (Raleigh, NC) 75967
Unicopy Corp. of North Carolina (Durham, NC) 74431
Unisys Corp. (Cape Canavral, FL) 58917
Zeno Systems of Georgia Inc. (Atlanta, GA) 65299
Zeno Systems of Houston (Houston, TX) 87209
Zeno Systems of Houston Inc. (Houston, TX) 87210
Zeno Systems Inc. (Carrollton, TX) 83514
Zeno Systems Inc. (Irving, TX) 87418; 87419
Zeno Systems of Oklahoma Inc. (Oklahoma City, OK) 77674

5045 Computers, Peripherals & Software

Apple Computers Inc. (Dallas, TX) 83856
Arnet Computer (Fort Lauderdale, FL) 59442
Arnet Computer (Deluth, GA) 65915
Arnet Computer (Columbia, MD) 71576
Arnet Computer (Raleigh, NC) 75860
Arnet Computer (Addison, TX) 82470
Arnet Computer (Houston, TX) 85817
Arrow Electronics Commercial Systems Div. (Duluth, GA) 66018
Arrow Electronics MTI Systems Div. (Huntsville, AL) 55881
Avnet*Hamilton Hallmark (Dallas, TX) 83868
Bell Atlantic Business Systems Services (Hampton, VA) 91016
Bell Atlantic Systems Lease International (Dallas, TX) 83876
Bowater Computer Forms (Richardson, TX) 88723
Business Systems & Service Inc. (Vienna, WV) 93077
Carroll Touch (Round Rock, TX) 88845
Dell Computer Corp. (Austin, TX) 82847
Dell Computer USA Corp. (Austin, TX) 82848
Dell Marketing Corp. (Austin, TX) 82851; 82852
Digital Equipment Corp. (Knoxville, TN) 81164
Digital Equipment Corp. (Dunbar, WV) 92827
First Data Corp. (Dallas, TX) 84068
Modern Office Machines Inc. (Greenville, SC) 79395; 79396
NCR Corp. (Springdale, AR) 57638
Radio Shack (Wiggins, MS) 73493
Teradata (Tulsa, OK) 78134

5046 Commercial Equipment Nec

Acme Business Products (Macon, GA) 66643
Amdahl Corp. (Baltimore, MD) 71034
Archer Daniels Midland Co. (Chattanooga, TN) 80324
Avery Dennison Co. (Gastonia, NC) 74656
T. Talbott Bond (Baltimore, MD) 71073
Coca-Cola Bottling Co. of so (Pine Bluff, AR) 57512
Coca Cola Bottling Co. (Lafayette, LA) 70050
Coca Cola Bottling Co. (Asheville, NC) 73610
Coca Cola Bottling Co. (Tyler, TX) 89796
Coca-Cola Bottling Co. of Pl (Plainview, TX) 88528
Coca-Cola Bottling Co. of Shreveprot Inc. (Atlanta, GA) 64373
Compaq Computer Corp. (Houston, TX) 85995
Computer Associates (Dallas, TX) 83956
Copy Corp. (Louisville, KY) 68737
Copy Data Group, Inc. (Virginia Beach, VA) 92446
Copy Van, Inc. (Richmond, VA) 91789
Cray Research Inc. (Tulsa, OK) 77925
Diebold Inc. (Birmingham, AL) 55221
Diebold Inc. (Jacksonville, FL) 60261
Diebold Inc. (Orlando, FL) 61962
Diebold Inc. (Louisville, KY) 68753
Diebold Inc. (Alexandria, LA) 69372
Diebold Inc. (Owings Mills, MD) 72184
Diebold Inc. (Jackson, MS) 72976
Diebold Inc. (Charlotte, NC) 73930
Diebold Inc. (Tulsa, OK) 77928
Diebold Inc. (Nashville, TN) 81933
Diebold Inc. (Dallas, TX) 83977
Diebold Inc. (Longview, TX) 87713
Diebold Inc. (Virginia Beach, VA) 92457
Digital Equipment Corporati (Pensacola, FL) 62419
Digital Equipment Corporati (Baton Rouge, LA) 69509
Digital Equipment Corp. (Birmingham, AL) 55224
Digital Equipment Corp. (Huntsville, AL) 55908
Digital Equipment Corp. (Miami, FL) 61278
Digital Equipment Corp. (Warner Robins, GA) 68015
Digital Equipment Corp. (Metairie, LA) 70260
Digital Equipment Corp. (Linthicum Heights, MD) 72109
Digital Equipment Corp. (Jackson, MS) 72977
Digital Equipment Corp. (Winston Salem, NC) 76667
Digital Equipment Corp. (Oklahoma City, OK) 77346
Digital Equipment Corp. (Nashville, TN) 81934; 81935
Digital Equipment Corp. (Corpus Christi, TX) 83713

Bell Atlantic Mobile Systems (Vienna, MD) 72526
Bell Atlantic Paging (Richmond, VA) 91743
Bell South Mobility (Tuscaloosa, AL) 56634
Bellsouth Communications (Birmingham, AL) 55163; 55164
BellSouth Corp. (Atlanta, GA) 64317
BellSouth Mobility (Birmingham, AL) 55165
BellSouth Mobility (Huntsville, AL) 55889
BellSouth Mobility (Gainesville, GA) 66266
Bellsouth Mobility (Crowley, LA) 69801
Bellsouth Mobility (Nashville, TN) 81900
BellSouth Telecommunications Inc. (Atlanta, GA) 64325
Capstone Electronics Div. (Raleigh, NC) 75879
Capstone Electronics Div. (Carrollton, TX) 83456
Circuit City (Louisville, KY) 68729
Circuit City (Cape St. Claire, MD) 71493
Circuit City (Greenville, SC) 79328
Circuit City (Goodlettsville, TN) 80861
Circuit City (Nashville, TN) 81921; 81922
Circuit City (Lynchburg, VA) 91227
Circuit City (Norfolk, VA) 91503
Circuit City (Petersburg, VA) 91629
Circuit City (Virginia Beach, VA) 92445
Dale Electronics Inc. (El Paso, TX) 84786
Dataserve Inc. (Killeen, TX) 87509
Diebold Inc. (Greenville, NC) 74956
Digital Equipment Corp. (Oklahoma City, OK) 77346
Eaton Corp. (Nashville, TN) 81939
Eaton Corp. Ion Beam (Houston, TX) 86054
Electro Mechanical Design Services (Gaithersburg, MD) 71770
Electronic Systems Group (Glen Burnie, MD) 71839
GTE Customer Networks Inc. (Atlanta, GA) 64524
GTE Florida Inc. (Tampa, FL) 63447
GTE South Inc. (Tampa, FL) 63451
GTE Southwest Inc. (Irving, TX) 87351
GTE Spacenet Corp. (McLean, VA) 91392
Hamilton Hallmark (Huntsville, AL) 55949
Hamilton Hallmark (Ft. Lauderdale, FL) 59853
Hamilton Hallmark (Winter Park, FL) 63980
Hamilton Hallmark (Norcross, GA) 67121
Hamilton Hallmark (Columbia, MD) 71593
Hamilton Hallmark (Raleigh, NC) 75913
Hamilton Hallmark (Tulsa, OK) 77950
Hamilton Hallmark (Austria, TX) 83077
Hamilton Hallmark (Dallas, TX) 84113
Hamilton Hallmark (Stafford, TX) 89500
Hewlett-Packard Co. (Columbia, SC) 79029
Material Aquisition Center (Glen Burnie, MD) 71845
Mobil & Comm (Dallas, TX) 84241
National Semiconductor (Huntsville, AL) 55977
Radio Shack (Anniston, AL) 55009
Radio Shack (Auburn, AL) 55070
Radio Shack (Birmingham, AL) 55355; 55356; 55358; 55359; 55360; 55361; 55362; 55363; 55365; 55366; 55367
Radio Shack (Dothan, AL) 55663
Radio Shack (Enterprise, AL) 55691
Radio Shack (Gadsden, AL) 55787
Radio Shack (Huntsville, AL) 56007
Radio Shack (Mobile, AL) 56228; 56229; 56230; 56231
Radio Shack (Montgomery, AL) 56372
Radio Shack (Pelham, AL) 56450
Radio Shack (Pell City, AL) 56452
Radio Shack (Talladega, AL) 56598
Radio Shack (Tuscaloosa, AL) 56670; 56671; 56672
Radio Shack (Valley, AL) 56690
Radio Shack (Benton, AR) 56774
Radio Shack (Fayetteville, AR) 56989
Radio Shack (Fort Smith, AR) 57089; 57091
Radio Shack (H Spg Nat Pk, AR) 57128
Radio Shack (Jacksonville, AR) 57200
Radio Shack (Jonesboro, AR) 57228
Radio Shack (Little Rock, AR) 57300; 57301; 57302; 57303; 57304
Radio Shack (Mountain Home, AR) 57389
Radio Shack (N Little Rock, AR) 57420
Radio Shack (Pine Bluff, AR) 57529
Radio Shack (Van Buren, AR) 57692
Radio Shack (West Memphis, AR) 57731
Radio Shack (Claymont, DE) 57764
Radio Shack (Dover, DE) 57801; 57802; 57803; 57804; 57806; 57807
Radio Shack (Milford, DE) 57843; 57844
Radio Shack (New Castle, DE) 57872
Radio Shack (Newark, DE) 57926; 57927; 57928
Radio Shack (Seaford, DE) 57952
Radio Shack (Smyrna, DE) 57961; 57962
Radio Shack (Wilmington, DE) 58096; 58097; 58098
Radio Shack (Avon Park, FL) 58610
Radio Shack (Bonita Springs, FL) 58761
Radio Shack (Boynton Beach, FL) 58789
Radio Shack (Brandon, FL) 58879
Radio Shack (Brooksville, FL) 58894
Radio Shack (Cape Coral, FL) 58925
Radio Shack (Clearwater, FL) 59043
Radio Shack (Daytona Beach, FL) 59206
Radio Shack (Deerfield Beach, FL) 59285; 59286
Radio Shack (Fort Lauderdale, FL) 59580; 59583; 59584; 59585; 59586; 59587; 59589; 59592; 59593; 59594
Radio Shack (Fort Myers, FL) 59750; 59751; 59752
Radio Shack (Fort Pierce, FL) 59804
Radio Shack (Gainesville, FL) 59911; 59912
Radio Shack (Hallandale, FL) 59963
Radio Shack (Hialeah, FL) 60005; 60006
Radio Shack (Hollywood, FL) 60088; 60090; 60091
Radio Shack (Homestead, FL) 60119; 60120
Radio Shack (Jacksonville, FL) 60426; 60428; 60434
Radio Shack (Key West, FL) 60578
Radio Shack (La Belle, FL) 60608
Radio Shack (Lake Placid, FL) 60648
Radio Shack (Lake Worth, FL) 60691; 60692; 60693
Radio Shack (Lakeland, FL) 60773; 60775
Radio Shack (Largo, FL) 60860
Radio Shack (Longwood, FL) 60947; 60948
Radio Shack (Mary Esther, FL) 61022
Radio Shack (Miami, FL) 61420; 61426; 61428; 61429; 61430; 61431; 61434; 61435; 61436; 61437
Radio Shack (Naples, FL) 61659; 61660
Radio Shack (Ocala, FL) 61819
Radio Shack (Opa-Locka, FL) 61866
Radio Shack (Orlando, FL) 62126; 62127
Radio Shack (Panama City, FL) 62345
Radio Shack (Pensacola, FL) 62464; 62466; 62467
Radio Shack (Plant City, FL) 62554
Radio Shack (Pompano Beach, FL) 62627
Radio Shack (Pt Charlotte, FL) 62700
Radio Shack (Punta Gorda, FL) 62717; 62718
Radio Shack (Sebring, FL) 62893
Radio Shack (St Augustine, FL) 62955
Radio Shack (St Petersburg, FL) 63028
Radio Shack (Tallahassee, FL) 63260; 63261; 63263; 63265; 63267
Radio Shack (Tampa, FL) 63565; 63567; 63569; 63570; 63572
Radio Shack (Winter Park, FL) 63992
Radio Shack (Zephyrhills, FL) 64025
Radio Shack (Albany, GA) 64089; 64090
Radio Shack (Cordele, GA) 65718
Radio Shack (Dublin, GA) 66015
Radio Shack (Eastman, GA) 66161
Radio Shack (Gainesville, GA) 66289
Radio Shack (Macon, GA) 66707
Radio Shack (Moultrie, GA) 67063
Radio Shack (Valdosta, GA) 67972
Radio Shack (Waycross, GA) 68037
Radio Shack (Alexandria, LA) 69399; 69400
Radio Shack (Baker, LA) 69437
Radio Shack (Bastrop, LA) 69447
Radio Shack (Baton Rouge, LA) 69638; 69639; 69640; 69641; 69645
Radio Shack (Bogalusa, LA) 69708
Radio Shack (Bossier City, LA) 69728; 69729
Radio Shack (Crowley, LA) 69803
Radio Shack (Denham Springs, LA) 69831
Radio Shack (Greenwell Spg, LA) 69902
Radio Shack (Hammond, LA) 69933
Radio Shack (Houma, LA) 69966; 69967
Radio Shack (Jonesville, LA) 69987
Radio Shack (Kenner, LA) 70008; 70009
Radio Shack (Lake Charles, LA) 70169; 70170
Radio Shack (Marrero, LA) 70233
Radio Shack (Metairie, LA) 70305; 70308; 70309
Radio Shack (Minden, LA) 70346
Radio Shack (New Orleans, LA) 70550
Radio Shack (Patterson, LA) 70613
Radio Shack (Rayville, LA) 70658
Radio Shack (Shreveport, LA) 70772; 70773; 70774; 70775
Radio Shack (Slidell, LA) 70837; 70838; 70839
Radio Shack (Sulphur, LA) 70889
Radio Shack (Ville Platte, LA) 70934
Radio Shack (Westwego, LA) 70972
Radio Shack (Baltimore, MD) 71223; 71226; 71231; 71232; 71234; 71235
Radio Shack (Chase, MD) 71511; 71512
Radio Shack (Cockeysville, MD) 71554
Radio Shack (Dunkirk Md, MD) 71655
Radio Shack (Easton, MD) 71660
Radio Shack (Edgewood, MD) 71665; 71666
Radio Shack (Elkton, MD) 71673
Radio Shack (Ellicott City, MD) 71679; 71680
Radio Shack (Frederick, MD) 71742; 71743
Radio Shack (Hagerstown, MD) 71893
Radio Shack (Hancock, MD) 71905
Radio Shack (Lexington Pk, MD) 72103
Radio Shack (Owings Mills, MD) 72191
Radio Shack (Rockville, MD) 72316
Radio Shack (Severna Park, MD) 72377; 72378
Radio Shack (Westminster, MD) 72542
Radio Shack (Columbus, MS) 72725
Radio Shack (Corinth, MS) 72745
Radio Shack (Forest, MS) 72775
Radio Shack (Grenada, MS) 72845
Radio Shack (Gulfport, MS) 72870; 72871; 72873
Radio Shack (Hattiesburg, MS) 72895
Radio Shack (Jackson, MS) 73041; 73043; 73044; 73045; 73047; 73052
Radio Shack (Meridian, MS) 73177
Radio Shack (Ridgeland, MS) 73328
Radio Shack (Starkville, MS) 73371
Radio Shack (Tupelo, MS) 73421; 73422
Radio Shack (Utica, MS) 73441
Radio Shack (Yazoo City, MS) 73506
Radio Shack (Asheboro, NC) 73593
Radio Shack (Asheville, NC) 73634
Radio Shack (Boone, NC) 73716
Radio Shack (Burlington, NC) 73760
Radio Shack (Charlotte, NC) 74125; 74126; 74127; 74128; 74129; 74131; 74135; 74136; 74138; 74139
Radio Shack (Concord, NC) 74322
Radio Shack (Conover, NC) 74335
Radio Shack (Durham, NC) 74426; 74427
Radio Shack (Eden, NC) 74465
Radio Shack (Elizabeth Cy, NC) 74487
Radio Shack (Fayetteville, NC) 74575
Radio Shack (Greensboro, NC) 74883; 74884; 74886; 74888; 74890
Radio Shack (Henderson, NC) 75027
Radio Shack (Hickory, NC) 75096; 75097; 75098
Radio Shack (Jacksonville, NC) 75228; 75229
Radio Shack (Lenoir, NC) 75386
Radio Shack (Lexington, NC) 75422
Radio Shack (Lincolnton, NC) 75441
Radio Shack (Monroe, NC) 75587
Radio Shack (Morganton, NC) 75653
Radio Shack (Mount Airy, NC) 75683
Radio Shack (N Wilkesboro, NC) 75713
Radio Shack (New Bern, NC) 75732; 75733
Radio Shack (Raleigh, NC) 75942; 75943; 75944; 75945; 75948
Radio Shack (Reidsville, NC) 76010
Radio Shack (Roanoke Rpds, NC) 76041; 76042
Radio Shack (Rockingham, NC) 76067
Radio Shack (Shelby, NC) 76247
Radio Shack (Southport, NC) 76288
Radio Shack (Spring Lake, NC) 76299
Radio Shack (Statesville, NC) 76334
Radio Shack (Waynesville, NC) 76472
Radio Shack (Wilmington, NC) 76589; 76590
Radio Shack (Winston Salem, NC) 76680; 76681
Radio Shack (Ardmore, OK) 76818
Radio Shack (Bartlesville, OK) 76849; 76851
Radio Shack (Duncan, OK) 76997
Radio Shack (Enid, OK) 77064; 77066
Radio Shack (Mc Alester, OK) 77198
Radio Shack (Norman, OK) 77271; 77272
Radio Shack (Oklahoma City, OK) 77510; 77512; 77513; 77515; 77516; 77518; 77519; 77522; 77527; 77533; 77534
Radio Shack (Sapulpa, OK) 77797
Radio Shack (Shattuck, OK) 77810
Radio Shack (Tulsa, OK) 78074; 78075; 78078; 78079; 78080; 78081; 78082; 78083; 78084; 78085; 78086; 78091; 78092
Radio Shack (Yukon, OK) 78280
Radio Shack (Aiken, SC) 78656
Radio Shack (Anderson, SC) 78689; 78690
Radio Shack (Charleston, SC) 78872; 78873
Radio Shack (Clinton, SC) 78962
Radio Shack (Columbia, SC) 79082; 79083; 79084
Radio Shack (Dillon, SC) 79165
Radio Shack (Florence, SC) 79222
Radio Shack (Greenville, SC) 79413
Radio Shack (Greenwood, SC) 79464
Radio Shack (Mauldin, SC) 79653
Radio Shack (Myrtle Beach, SC) 79710
Radio Shack (Rock Hill, SC) 79838
Radio Shack (Spartanburg, SC) 79934; 79935
Radio Shack (West Columbia, SC) 80105
Radio Shack (Alice, TX) 82487
Radio Shack (Arlington, TX) 82733; 82734; 82735; 82736; 82738; 82739; 82740
Radio Shack (Austin, TX) 82975; 82976; 82978; 82979; 82981; 82982; 82983; 82984; 82985; 82986; 82987
Radio Shack (Azle, TX) 83081
Radio Shack (Baytown, TX) 83134; 83135
Radio Shack (Beaumont, TX) 83205; 83206; 83207; 83209
Radio Shack (Bedford, TX) 83249; 83250
Radio Shack (Big Spring, TX) 83293
Radio Shack (Brownsville, TX) 83378; 83380
Radio Shack (Brownwood, TX) 83388
Radio Shack (Bryan, TX) 83406; 83407
Radio Shack (Burleson, TX) 83424
Radio Shack (Canyon, TX) 83444
Radio Shack (Carrollton, TX) 83503
Radio Shack (College Sta, TX) 83612; 83613
Radio Shack (Conroe, TX) 83683
Radio Shack (Corpus Chrsti, TX) 83769
Radio Shack (Corsicana, TX) 83789
Radio Shack (Crosby, TX) 83807
Radio Shack (Dalhart, TX) 83835
Radio Shack (Dallas, TX) 84328; 84330; 84331; 84332; 84333; 84334; 84335; 84336; 84338; 84339; 84340; 84341; 84342; 84343; 84345; 84346; 84347
Radio Shack (De Soto, TX) 84537
Radio Shack (Deer Park, TX) 84561; 84562
Radio Shack (Del Rio, TX) 84585
Radio Shack (Denison, TX) 84606
Radio Shack (Denton, TX) 84631; 84633
Radio Shack (Dickinson, TX) 84671
Radio Shack (Duncanville, TX) 84709
Radio Shack (El Paso, TX) 84896; 84899; 84903; 84904; 84905; 84906; 84907; 84908; 84909; 84912
Radio Shack (Fort Worth, TX) 85241; 85242; 85243; 85244; 85245; 85246; 85248; 85250; 85252; 85255; 85256; 85257; 85259; 85260; 85263; 85264
Radio Shack (Friendswood, TX) 85407
Radio Shack (Galveston, TX) 85462; 85463
Radio Shack (Garland, TX) 85527; 85529; 85530
Radio Shack (Glen Rose, TX) 85583
Radio Shack (Grand Prairie, TX) 85634; 85635
Radio Shack (Harlingen, TX) 85712; 85713
Radio Shack (Houston, TX) 86731; 86733; 86736; 86740; 86751; 86752; 86753; 86755; 86757; 86758; 86759; 86761; 86762; 86764; 86766; 86767; 86770; 86771; 86772; 86774; 86777; 86782; 86783; 86786; 86788
Radio Shack (Humble, TX) 87241; 87242
Radio Shack (Hurst, TX) 87291; 87293
Radio Shack (Irving, TX) 87394; 87395; 87396
Radio Shack (Killeen, TX) 87523
Radio Shack (La Marque, TX) 87545
Radio Shack (Lake Jackson, TX) 87584; 87585
Radio Shack (Laredo, TX) 87622; 87623
Radio Shack (League City, TX) 87630
Radio Shack (Longview, TX) 87732
Radio Shack (Lubbock, TX) 87778; 87779
Radio Shack (Lufkin, TX) 87815; 87816
Radio Shack (Marshall, TX) 87864; 87865
Radio Shack (Mc Kinney, TX) 87919
Radio Shack (Mcallen, TX) 87939
Radio Shack (Mesquite, TX) 87993; 87994
Radio Shack (Midland, TX) 88070; 88071
Radio Shack (Nederland, TX) 88190
Radio Shack (New Braunfels, TX) 88219
Radio Shack (Odessa, TX) 88266; 88267; 88269
Radio Shack (Orange, TX) 88327; 88328
Radio Shack (Palestine, TX) 88345
Radio Shack (Pampa, TX) 88356
Radio Shack (Paris, TX) 88376
Radio Shack (Pasadena, TX) 88460; 88461; 88462
Radio Shack (Pearland, TX) 88489
Radio Shack (Pharr, TX) 88511

Radio Shack (Plano, TX) 88602; 88603; 88604
Radio Shack (Port Arthur, TX) 88645
Radio Shack (Richardson, TX) 88761
Radio Shack (Rosenberg, TX) 88835
Radio Shack (Round Rock, TX) 88852
Radio Shack (San Angelo, TX) 88897; 88898
Radio Shack (San Antonio, TX) 89185; 89186; 89188; 89190; 89193; 89194; 89195; 89197; 89204; 89210; 89211
Radio Shack (Seguin, TX) 89373
Radio Shack (Sherman, TX) 89422
Radio Shack (Snyder, TX) 89451
Radio Shack (South Houston, TX) 89460
Radio Shack (Spring, TX) 89484; 89485
Radio Shack (Stafford, TX) 89504
Radio Shack (Sulphur Springs, TX) 89563
Radio Shack (Sweetwater, TX) 89590
Radio Shack (Temple, TX) 89635
Radio Shack (Texarkana, TX) 89702; 89703; 89705
Radio Shack (Texas City, TX) 89733
Radio Shack (Tomball, TX) 89777
Radio Shack (Trinity, TX) 89784
Radio Shack (Universal Cty, TX) 89847
Radio Shack (Uvalde, TX) 89855
Radio Shack (Victoria, TX) 89902; 89903
Radio Shack (Weatherford, TX) 90011
Radio Shack (Wichita Falls, TX) 90096; 90097
Radio Shack (Winnie, TX) 90123
Radio Shack (Woodville, TX) 90131
Radio Shack (Alexandria, VA) 90229; 90234; 90235
Radio Shack (Annandale, VA) 90269; 90270
Radio Shack (Arlington, VA) 90368; 90369; 90370; 90371; 90375; 90376; 90377
Radio Shack (Ashland, VA) 90407
Radio Shack (Chesapeake, VA) 90594; 90595; 90596
Radio Shack (Covington, VA) 90664
Radio Shack (Danville, VA) 90714
Radio Shack (Fairfax, VA) 90802; 90803; 90804; 90805
Radio Shack (Falls Church, VA) 90863; 90864; 90866; 90867; 90868
Radio Shack (Franklin, VA) 90897; 90898
Radio Shack (Hampton, VA) 91047
Radio Shack (Harrisonburg, VA) 91098
Radio Shack (Herndon, VA) 91130; 91131
Radio Shack (Manassas, VA) 91319; 91320
Radio Shack (Mc Lean, VA) 91371; 91372; 91373; 91374
Radio Shack (Midlothian, VA) 91422
Radio Shack (Newport News, VA) 91481
Radio Shack (Norfolk, VA) 91568; 91570; 91571; 91572; 91573
Radio Shack (Portsmouth, VA) 91665; 91666
Radio Shack (Radford, VA) 91701
Radio Shack (Richmond, VA) 91953; 91954; 91957; 91958; 91959; 91962; 91963; 91966
Radio Shack (Roanoke, VA) 92178; 92182
Radio Shack (Smithfield, VA) 92239; 92240
Radio Shack (Triangle, VA) 92388; 92389
Radio Shack (Vienna, VA) 92414; 92415; 92417; 92418
Radio Shack (Virginia Beach, VA) 92496; 92497; 92500; 92503
Radio Shack (Williamsburg, VA) 92578
Radio Shack (Winchester, VA) 92601; 92602
Radio Shack (Wytheville, VA) 92646
Radio Shack Div. of Tandy Corp. (Hancock, MD) 71906
Radio Shack Div. of Tandy Corp. (Westminster, MD) 72543
RAM Mobile Data (Orlando, FL) 62130
Raychem Corp. (Arlington, VA) 90378
Tandy Electronics (Oklahoma City, OK) 77594
Tandy Electronics (Fort Worth, TX) 85313
Tektronix Inc. (Huntsville, AL) 56031
Tektronix Inc. (Miami, FL) 61473
Tektronix Inc. (San Antonio, TX) 89254
Time Electronics (Huntsville, AL) 56039
Time Electronics (Ft. Lauderdale, FL) 59856
Time Electronics (Orlando, FL) 62170
Time Electronics (Atlanta, GA) 65215
Time Electronics (Norcross, GA) 67203
Time Electronics (Smyrna, GA) 67582
Time Electronics (Columbia, MD) 71603
Time Electronics (Oxford, NC) 75789
Time Electronics (Raleigh, NC) 75965
Time Electronics (Austin, TX) 83047
Time Electronics (Houston, TX) 87027
Time Electronics (Richardson, TX) 88785
Universal Instruments Corp. (Raleigh, NC) 75972
Zenith Electronics (El Paso, TX) 84982

5072 Hardware

Ace Hardware (St Petersburg, FL) 62962
Ace Hardware (Guymon, OK) 77099
Ace Hardware Corp. (Arlington, TX) 82630
Ace Hardware P P (Plant City, FL) 62533
Ace Hardware Plus (Ennis, TX) 84993
Bethlehem Steel Corp. (Atlanta, GA) 64328
Black & Decker Corp. Pop Fastners Division (Coldwater, MS) 72691
Black & Decker US Inc. (Lutherville Timonium, MD) 72119
C. F. Sauer Co. Inc. (Richmond, VA) 91748
Douglas/Quikut (Germantown, TN) 80855
Heads & Threads Co. (Grand Prairie, TX) 85618
Heads & Threads Co. (Houston, TX) 86264
Kwikset Corp. (Denison, TX) 84600
Matco Tools (San Angelo, TX) 88885
Porter Cable Corp. (Charlotte, NC) 74121
Porter-Cable Corp. (Richmond, VA) 91951

5074 Plumbing & Hydronic Heating Supplies

Armco Tex-Tube Div. (Fort Worth, TX) 85067
Armco Tex-Tube Div. (Houston, TX) 85815
Capco Pipe Co. Inc. (Birmingham, AL) 55178
Capco Pipe Co. Inc. (Van Buren, AR) 57689
Dexter Water Management Inc. (Charlotte, NC) 73928
May Supply Co., Inc. (West Monroe, LA) 70954
Mobil Pipe Line Co. (Corpus Christi, TX) 83738
Moen Inc. (Trent Woods, NC) 76404
Nalco Chemical Co. (Jacksonville, FL) 60380
Price Pfister Inc. (Irving, TX) 87393
Solar Turbines Inc. (New Orleans, LA) 70559
Texas Instruments Inc. (Versailles, KY) 69332
US Fidelity & Gu (Midland, TX) 88094

5075 Warm Air Heating & Air-Conditioning

Bristol Compressors Inc. (Bristol, VA) 90470
Clark Equipment Co., Inc. (Winter Garden, FL) 63919
Continental Ind Inc. (Houston, TX) 86013
Delta Air Systems Corp. (Birmingham, AL) 55217
Exxon Co. (Lexington, VA) 91201
Johnson Controls Inc. (Georgetown, KY) 68383
Johnson Controls Inc. (Austin, TX) 82898
Johnson Controls Inc. (El Paso, TX) 84813
May Supply Co. (Beaumont, TX) 83176
Natkin Service Co. (Tucker, GA) 67878
Trane Co. (Miami, FL) 61483; 61484
Trane Co. (Jackson, MS) 73077

5082 Construction & Mining Machinery

BFI Services Group (Jessup, MD) 71982
Builders Square Inc. (Largo, FL) 60826
Carter Machinery Co., Inc. (Danville, VA) 90686
Carter Machinery Co. Inc. (Fishersville, VA) 90881
Carter Machinery Co. Inc. (Norton, VA) 91601
Carter Machinery Co., Inc. (Oakwood, VA) 91612
Carter Machinery Co. Inc. (Warrenton, VA) 92522
Caterpillar Inc. (Brentwood, TN) 80221
Clark Equipment Co. (Miami, FL) 61263
Dewalt Industrial Tool Co. (Smyrna, GA) 67548
Electro Mechanical Corp. (Knoxville, TN) 81168
Exxon Chemical Co. (Oklahoma City, OK) 77354
Fastening Systems Inc. (Jacksonville, FL) 60268
Grace Energy Corp. (Dallas, TX) 84094
Terex Corp. (Dallas, TX) 84424
Vulcan Material Co. (Franklin, VA) 90905

5083 Farm & Garden Machinery

Ace Hardware (Nags Head, NC) 75714
Ace Hardware&Home Center (Broken Arrow, OK) 76877
ESI Inc. (Gainesville, GA) 66273
Intertrade Corp. (Lakeland, FL) 60734
Southern Cotton Oil Co. (Quann, TX) 88703
Sterwin Laboratories (Millsboro, DE) 57849

5084 Industrial Machinery & Equipment

Ace Hardware (Delray Beach, FL) 59303
Air Products & Chemicals (Theodore, AL) 56605
Air Products & Chemicals, Inc. (Fayetteville, AR) 56968
Air Products & Chemicals, Inc. (Fort Smith, AR) 57019
Air Products & Chemicals, Inc. (Fort Walton Beach, FL) 59819
Air Products & Chemicals, Inc. (Pensacola, FL) 62377
Air Products & Chemicals, Inc. (Tampa, FL) 63304
Air Products & Chemicals Inc. (Albany, GA) 64061
Air Products & Chemicals, Inc. (Tupelo, MS) 73385
Air Products & Chemicals, Inc. (Oklahoma City, OK) 77292
Air Products & Chemicals, Inc. (Columbia, SC) 78965
Air Products & Chemicals Inc. (Memphis, TN) 81447
Allied-Signal Inc. (Dalton, GA) 65770
Allied-Signal Inc. Uop Process Div. (Blanchard, LA) 69699
Ametek US Gauge (Bartow, FL) 58624
AMR Co. (Chattanooga, TN) 80297
Analog Devices Inc. (New Orleans, LA) 70433
API (Huntsvile, AL) 55871
Avery Dennison Co. (Gastonia, NC) 74656
BASF Corp. Fibers Division (Dalton, GA) 65773
BASF Inmont Corp. (Corinth, MS) 72734
Betz PaperChem Inc. (Huntsville, AL) 55890
BFI Waste Systems (Nashville, TN) 81904
BFI Waste Systems (Rogersville, TN) 82272
Blount Inc. (Zebulon, NC) 76783
Browning-Ferris Industries (Capital Heights, MD) 71499
Central Products Inc. (Montgomery, AL) 56291; 56292
Ceramic Cooling Tower Co. (Fort Worth, TX) 85079
Cincinnati Milacron (Tulsa, OK) 77901
Clark Material Handling Co. (Lexington, KY) 68535; 68536; 68537
Copy Van Inc. (Richmond, VA) 91790
Eaton Corp. (Nashville, TN) 81941
Eaton Kenway Inc. (Claymont, DE) 57761
Electro Mechanical Holding Inc. (Lynchburg, VA) 91235
Electro Mechanical Services (Miami, FL) 61279
Federal Paper Board Co. Inc. (Richmond, VA) 91871
Gear Products Inc. (Catoosa, OK) 76909
Genuine Parts Co., Inc. (Atlanta, GA) 64503
Halliburton Resource Manage (Chickasha, OK) 76927
Halliburton Resource Mgt (Camargo, OK) 76904
Halliburton Resource Mgt (Cushing, OK) 76978
Halliburton Resource Mgt (Pampa, TX) 88349
Harris Calorific (Gainesville, GA) 66277
Harris Calorific (Georgetown, TX) 85568
Industrial Systems (Goodlettsville, TN) 80865
Jacksonville Welder Sup (Jacksonville, FL) 60336
Johnson Controls Inc. (Louisville, KY) 68787
Johnson Controls Inc. (Poteau, OK) 77721
Johnson Controls Inc. (Kingsport, TN) 81108
Johnson Controls Inc. (Austin, TX) 82898
Johnson Controls Inc. (El Paso, TX) 84813
Johnson Controls Inc. (Lubbock, TX) 87766
Little Giant Pump Co. (Oklahoma City, OK) 77431
Machinery Acceptance Corp. (Louisville, KY) 68872
Miami Elevator Co. Inc. (Miami, FL) 61379
Monarch Industries Inc. (Orlando, FL) 62065
Monarch Industries Inc. Br (Dallas, TX) 84258
National-Oilwell (Shreveport, LA) 70753
OTC Co. (Houston, TX) 86628
Otis Elevator Co. (Birmingham, AL) 55327
Otis Elevator Co. (Mobile, AL) 56216
Otis Elevator Co. (Jacksonville, FL) 60383
Otis Elevator Co. (Orlando, FL) 62071
Otis Elevator Co. (Tallahassee, FL) 63253
Otis Elevator Co. (Tampa, FL) 63514
Otis Elevator Co. (Macon, GA) 66701
Otis Elevator Co. (Louisville, KY) 68934
Otis Elevator Co. (Alexandria, LA) 69396
Otis Elevator Co. (Baton Rouge, LA) 69592
Otis Elevator Co. (Lake Charles, LA) 70154
Otis Elevator Co. (Metairie, LA) 70296
Otis Elevator Co. (Monroe, LA) 70363
Otis Elevator Co. (Hagerstown, MD) 71887
Otis Elevator Co. (Jackson, MS) 73027
Otis Elevator Co. (Long Beach, MS) 73118
Otis Elevator Co. (Kernersville, NC) 75282
Otis Elevator Co. (Raleigh, NC) 75933
Otis Elevator Co. (Anderson, SC) 78681
Otis Elevator Co. (Columbia, SC) 79058
Otis Elevator Co. (Spartanburg, SC) 79921
Otis Elevator Co. (Kingsport, TN) 81114
Otis Elevator Co. (Knoxville, TN) 81232
Otis Elevator Co. (Nashville, TN) 82074
Otis Elevator Co. (El Paso, TX) 84860
Otis Elevator Co. (San Angelo, TX) 88889
Otis Elevator Co. (Clarksburg, WV) 92814
Otis Elevator Co. (Huntington, WV) 92887
Otis Elevator Co. Inc. (Fort Worth, TX) 85207
Ppg Industries Inc. (Spartanburg, SC) 79927
Pyro Chem Inc. (Louisville, KY) 68985
Quincy Compressor Colt Indu (Houston, TX) 86729
Radio Shack (Perryton, TX) 88503
Ryder Truck Rental-Oneway (Cleveland, TN) 80599
Saxon Paper Florida (Hollywood, FL) 60095
Schrader Automotive Inc. (Monroe, NC) 75588
Solar Turbines Inc. (Houston, TX) 86897
Specialty Products Inc. (Norfolk, VA) 91585
Stevens Graphics Corp. (Fort Worth, TX) 85280
Stewart & Stevenson Service Inc. (San Juan, TX) 89335
Terex Corp. (Dallas, TX) 84424
Texaco Inc. (Centerville, LA) 69763
Texas Instruments Inc. (Memphis, TN) 81707
Thermacote-Welco (Birmingham, AL) 55427
Thermacote Welco Co. (Kings Mountain, NC) 75309
Thermacote Welco Inc. (Houston, TX) 87023; 87023
Trico Industries Inc. (Andrews, TX) 82606
Trico Industries Inc. (Big Spring, TX) 83296
Trico Industries Inc. (Houston, TX) 87045
Trico Industries Inc. (Midland, TX) 88091
Trico Industries Inc. (Odessa, TX) 88288
Trico Industries Inc. (San Antonio, TX) 89279
Trico Industries Inc. (Wichita Falls, TX) 90117
Trico Industries Inc. (Wickett, TX) 90122
Trinity Industries Transport (Montgomery, AL) 56393
Unijax Inc. (Savannah, GA) 67529
Varian Associates (Largo, FL) 60866
Waterloo Industries Inc. (Pocahontas, AR) 57548
Western Geophysical Co. (Hattiesburg, MS) 72900
Wheelabrator Corp. (Newnan, GA) 67086

5085 Industrial Supplies

Aerospace Products SE Inc. (Huntsville, AL) 55875
Air Products & Chemicals (Arden, NC) 73563
Air Products & Chemicals Inc. (Fayetteville, AR) 56967
Air Products & Chemicals Inc. (Fort Smith, AR) 57020
Air Products & Chemicals Inc. (Huntsville, AR) 57192
Air Products & Chemicals Inc. (Albany, GA) 64061
Air Products & Chemicals Inc. (Memphis, TN) 81447
Air Products & Chemicals Inc. (Roanoke, VA) 92099
American Emblem Tool Co. (Shelbyville, KY) 69270
Avery Dennison Corp. (Richardson, TX) 88721; 88722
Ball Metal Container (Williamsburg, VA) 92554
BFI Recycling Systems (Summerville, SC) 79981
Black & Decker US Inc. (Winston-Salem, NC) 76709
Blue Grass Cooperage Co. (Louisville, KY) 68704
Browning-Ferris Industries (Greensboro, NC) 74791
Butler Paper (Miami, FL) 61219
Coast to Coast Suppliers Inc. (Rockledge, FL) 62743
Coca-Cola Bottling Co. (Ocala, FL) 61792
Continental Group Inc. (Birmingham, AL) 55209
Delphax Systems (Baltimore, MD) 71110
Dewalt Industrial Tool Co. (El Paso, TX) 84789
Eaton Corp. (Memphis, TN) 81517

Fastening Systems Inc. (Jacksonville, FL) 60268
Federal Mogul Corp. (Blacksburg, VA) 90439
Federal Paper Board Co. (High Point, NC) 75124
Henry Co. Inc/W W (Arlington, TX) 82661
Industrial Systems Associates (Raleigh, NC) 75916
Industrial Systems Associates Inc. (Lenoir, NC) 75380
Mobil Chemical Packaging Di (Houston, TX) 86585
Monumental Paper Co. (Baltimore, MD) 71211
Motion Industries Inc. (Birmingham, AL) 55323
Safety Kleen Corp. (Mc Allen, TX) 87899
Seagram Sons Inc/Joseph E (Tampa, FL) 63587
Sonoco Products Co. (Henderson, TN) 80909
Specialty Products Inc. (Norfolk, VA) 91585
Thoroughbred Plastics Corp. (Louisville, KY) 69021
3M (Atlanta, GA) 65213
3M (Dallas, TX) 84451
3M Co. (High Point, NC) 75173
Torrington Co (Tulsa, OK) 78171
Torrington Co (Houston, TX) 87029
Torrington Co. (Birmingham, AL) 55430
Wheeling Machine Products (Houston, TX) 87197
Xomox Corp. (Tampa, FL) 63664

5087 Service Establishment Equipment

Batesville Casket Co. Inc. (Campbellsvl, KY) 68184
Batesville Casket Co. Inc. (Baltimore, MD) 71061
Batesville Casket Co. Inc. (Knoxville, TN) 81145
Beckman Instruments Inc. (Baton Rouge, LA) 69471
Central Products Inc. (Montgomery, AL) 56291; 56292
Electro Mechanical Services (Miami, FL) 61279
Nadco Inc. (Nashville, TN) 82067
National Chemsearch (San Antonio, TX) 89117
National Chemsearch Corp. (Houston, TX) 86608
Ryder Truck Rental Inc. (Baltimore, MD) 71270
Safety Kleen Corp. (Clair Mel City, FL) 58956
Sally Beauty Co., Inc. (Denton, TX) 84637
Specialty Products Co. (Griffin, GA) 66325
Unijax Inc. (Columbus, GA) 65655; 65656
Unijax Inc. (Macon, GA) 66720
Unijax Inc. (Savannah, GA) 67529
Unijax Inc. (Huntington, WV) 92899; 92900
Western Auto Supply C (Biloxi, MS) 72642
Zep Manuf Co. (Birmingham, AL) 55461
Zep Manufacturing (San Antonio, TX) 89329
Zep Manufacturing Co. (Louisville, KY) 69044

5088 Transportation Equipment & Supplies

Flight Systems Inc. (Shreveport, LA) 70721
Garrett Airlines Service (Miami, FL) 61316
Pizza Hut (Durham, NC) 74424
Rohr Aero Service Inc. (Fairhope, AL) 55725
Russell Associates Inc. (Plant City, FL) 62555
Russell Associates Inc. (Winter Park, FL) 63994
Sundstrand Service Corp. (Oklahoma City, OK) 77563
Textron Marine Systems (Panama City, FL) 62353
Trailer Train Co. Hamburg Di (North Augusta, SC) 79741

5091 Sporting & Recreational Goods

Brunswick Corp. Zebco Division (Tulsa, OK) 77893
Joslins Inc. (Dallas, TX) 84153

5092 Toys & Hobby Goods & Supplies

Toys R US (Fort Myers, FL) 59767

5093 Scrap & Waste Materials

Acco Waste Paper (Houston, TX) 85759
BFI Waste Systems (Kinston, NC) 75312
BFI Waste Systems (Nashville, TN) 81904
Browning-Ferris Industries (Huntsville, AL) 55894
Browning-Ferris Industries (Greensboro, NC) 74791
Browning Ferris Industries Service Group Inc. (Mobile, AL) 56145
Coca Cola Bottling Co. (Shreveport, LA) 70698
Federal Metals Co. (Miami, FL) 61280
Federal Paper Board Co. Inc. (Richmond, VA) 91871
First Recovery (Lexington, KY) 68552
Oryx Energy (Oklahoma City, OK) 77459

5094 Jewelry & Precious Stones

Pitney Bowes Credit Corp. (Metairie, LA) 70299
Service Merchandise (Baton Rouge, LA) 69659

5099 Durable Goods Nec

Ace Hardware (Fort Lauderdale, FL) 59423
Ace Hardware (Longwood, FL) 60924
Air Products & Chemicals, Inc. (Albany, GA) 64063
Amdahl Corp. (Baltimore, MD) 71033
Amdahl Corp. (Columbia, MD) 71575
Avnet Freeman Products (Clarkston, GA) 65561
Avnet Freeman Products (Fort Worth, TX) 85068
Bank of Boston International (Miami, FL) 61172
Bowater Inc. (Duluth, GA) 66027
Bowater Inc. Carolina Div. (Catawba, SC) 78771
Bowater Inc. Southern Div. (Albertville, AL) 54960
Bowater Inc. Southern Div. (Spring City, TN) 82349
Bowater Woodlands (Harriman, TN) 80899
Bowater Woodlands (Kingston, TN) 81126
Brown-Forman Corp. (Louisville, KY) 68715
Burlington Industries Inc. Pine (Dahlonega, GA) 65754
Central Soya Co. Inc. (Charlotte, NC) 73891
Champion International Corp. (Monroeville, AL) 56259
Champion International Corp. (De Funiak Spg, FL) 59238
Champion International Corp. (Jacksonville, FL) 60240
Champion International Corp. (Greenville, SC) 79327
Coca-Cola Bottling Co. (Wesleyan College, NC) 76483
Digital Equipment Corporati (Jacksonville, FL) 60262
Exxon Corp. (Norfolk, VA) 91515
Flour City Architectural (Johnson City, TN) 81037
Hewlett-Packard Co. (Fort Lauderdale, FL) 59507
Hewlett Packard Co. (Melbourne, FL) 61067
Ibm Corp. (Little Rock, AR) 57288
Ibm Corp. (Melbourne, FL) 61069
Ibm Corp. (Orlando, FL) 62011
Johnson Controls Inc. (Houston, TX) 86321
Matco Tools (Venice, FL) 63727
Milcare (Fort Worth, TX) 85188
Ncr Corp. (San Angelo, TX) 88888
Pactel Paging (Orlando, FL) 62072
Radio Shack (Albertville, AL) 54970
Radio Shack (Melbourne, FL) 61100
Radio Shack (Mustang, OK) 77239
Sam's Wholesale Club (Casselberry, FL) 58942
Sam's Wholesale Club (Jacksonville, FL) 60453
Sam's Wholesale Club (Lakeland, FL) 60782
Sam's Wholesale Club (Tallahassee, FL) 63270
Sam's Wholesale Club (Shreveport, LA) 70781
Sam's Wholesale Club (Jackson, MS) 73057
Sam's Wholesale Club (Tulsa, OK) 78103
Sam's Wholesale Club (Charleston, SC) 78888
Sam's Wholesale Club (Dallas, TX) 84374
Sam's Wholesale Club (Fort Worth, TX) 85273
Sam's Wholesale Club (San Antonio, TX) 89221
Sam's Wholesale Club (Texarkana, TX) 89708
Service Merchandise (Oklahoma City, OK) 77556
Specialty Products International (Camden, TN) 80275
Star Marketing Co. (Dallas, TX) 84399
Superior Pools Products Inc. (Fort Pierce, FL) 59814
Tektronix Inc. (Maitland, FL) 60985
Texas-Lehigh Cement Co. (Orange, TX) 88331
Unisys Corp. (Macon, GA) 66721
Unisys Corp. (Metairie, LA) 70322
Westvaco Corp. (Lexington, VA) 91214
Weyerhaeuser Paper (Carrollton, TX) 83513
Wjz-Tv Television Station (Baltimore, MD) 71328
Zep Manufacturing Co. (De Soto, TX) 84540

5100 Wholesale Trade—Nondurable Goods

Hoechst Celanese Chemical Group Inc. Bayport (Seabrook, TX) 89357
Hoechst Celanese Chemical Group Inc. Bayport Terminal (Seabrook, TX) 89358
Performance Friction Products (Longview, TX) 87728
Selig Chemical Ind. (Atlanta, GA) 65147

5111 Printing & Writing Paper

Avery International (De Soto, TX) 84531
Butler Paper (Fort Smith, AR) 57033; 57034
Butler Paper (Tallahassee, FL) 63219
Butler Paper (Tupelo, MS) 73391; 73392
Butler Paper (Tulsa, OK) 77897
Butler Paper (Memphis, TN) 81489; 81490
Butler Paper (Lufkin, TX) 87797
Butler Paper (Tyler, TX) 89793; 89794
Butler Paper Co. (Rogers, AR) 57558; 57559
Butler Paper Co. (Baton Rouge, LA) 69478
Butler Paper Co. (Lafayette, LA) 70047; 70048
Butler Paper Co. (Amarillo, TX) 82534; 82535
Butler Paper Co. (Austin, TX) 82834
Butler Paper Co. (San Angelo, TX) 88869
Butler Paper Co. (San Antonio, TX) 88945; 88946
Carpenter Paper Co. (Amarillo, TX) 82536; 82537
Champion International Corp. (Nw Smyrna Beach, FL) 61763
Monarch Paper Co. (Houston, TX) 86605
Monumental Paper Co. (Baltimore, MD) 71211
Saxon Paper Florida (Hollywood, FL) 60095
Saxon Paper-Florida (Miami, FL) 61456
Sloan Paper Co. (Birmingham, AL) 55389
Sloan Paper Co. (Huntsville, AL) 56023
Sloan Paper Co. (Doraville, GA) 65951
Sloan Paper Co. (Jackson, MS) 73064
Specialty Products Co. (Griffin, GA) 66325
Unijax, Inc. (Jacksonville, FL) 60482
Unijax Inc. (Tampa, FL) 63633
Unijax Inc. (Columbus, GA) 65655; 65656
Unijax Inc. (Macon, GA) 66720
Unijax, Inc. (Charlotte, NC) 74183; 74184
Weyerhaeuser Paper Co. (Jacksonville, FL) 60510

5112 Stationery & Office Supplies

American Greetings Corp. (Osceola, AR) 57480
American Greetings Corp. (Norcross, GA) 67096
American Greetings Corp. (Bardstown, KY) 68113
American Greetings Corp. (Lafayette, TN) 81286
American Greetings Corp. (Carrollton, TX) 83447
American Greetings Inc. (McCrory, AR) 57361
Bell Atlantic Bus System Svc. (Tampa, FL) 63363
Bell Atlantic Business Services (El Paso, TX) 84766
Bell Atlantic Business Systems Services (Richmond, VA) 91742
Bell Atlantic Business Systems Services (Roanoke, VA) 92104
Boise Cascade Office Products Division (Hialeah, FL) 59977
Business Systems Inc. (Shreveport, LA) 70694
Carlton Cards (Carrollton, TX) 83457
Champion International Corp. (Arlington, TX) 82640
Champion International Corp. (Temple, TX) 89610
Compaq Computer Corp. (Houston, TX) 85992
Garrett-Buchanan Co. (Jessup, MD) 71984
Genuine Parts Co., Inc. (Atlanta, GA) 64503
Graphic Systems Inc. (Memphis, TN) 81617
Ibm Corp. (Huntsville, TX) 87260
Modern Office Machines Inc. (Greenville, SC) 79396
Monumental Paper Co. (Baltimore, MD) 71211
NCR Corp. (Morristown, TN) 81806
Quality Park Products (Atlanta, GA) 65052
Radio Shack (Sapulpa, OK) 77797
Radio Shack (Beaumont, TX) 83206
Reynolds & Reynolds (Louisville, KY) 68994
Richards Co/S P (Oklahoma City, OK) 77537
Richards S P Co. (Birmingham, AL) 55371
S. P. Richards Co., Inc. (Smyrna, GA) 67575
Saxon Paper Florida (Hollywood, FL) 60095
Scoot-Rice Co. Inc. (Tulsa, OK) 78105
Stevens Graphics (richmond, VA) 92048
Unijax, Inc. (Jacksonville, FL) 60482
Union Camp Corp. (Pooler, GA) 67272
Union Envelope Co. (Richmond, VA) 92064
Unisys Corp. (Tampa, FL) 63635
Westvaco Corp. (Jessup, MD) 71987
Westvaco Corp. (Laurel, MD) 72095
Westvaco Corp. (Herndon, VA) 91137

5113 Industrial & Personal Service Paper

Avery Dennison Fasson Roll Div. (Carrollton, TX) 83450; 83451
Avery International Specialty Tape (Arlington, TX) 82635
Butler Paper (Mobile, AL) 56147; 56148
Butler Paper (Fort Smith, AR) 57033; 57034
Butler Paper (Miami, FL) 61219
Butler Paper (Tallahassee, FL) 63219
Butler Paper (New Orleans, LA) 70437; 70438
Butler Paper (Tulsa, OK) 77897
Butler Paper (Knoxville, TN) 81150; 81151
Butler Paper (Lufkin, TX) 87797
Butler Paper (Temple, TX) 89606; 89607
Butler Paper (Tyler, TX) 89793; 89794
Butler Paper Co. (Baton Rouge, LA) 69478
Butler Paper Co. (Upper Marlboro, MD) 72514; 72515
Butler Paper Co. (Abilene, TX) 82428
Butler Paper Co. (Amarillo, TX) 82534; 82535
Butler Paper Co. (Austin, TX) 82834
Butler Paper Co. (El Paso, TX) 84778
Butler Paper Co. (Longview, TX) 87705; 87706
Butler Paper Co. (Plano, TX) 88542; 88543
Butler Paper Co. (San Angelo, TX) 88869
Butler Paper Co. (San Antonio, TX) 88945; 88946
Butler Paper Co. (Victoria, TX) 89877; 89878
Carpenter Paper Co. (Siloam Spring, AR) 57615; 57616
Carpenter Paper Co. (Amarillo, TX) 82536; 82537
Central Products Inc. (Montgomery, AL) 56291; 56292
Federal Paper Board Co. (E Flat Rock, NC) 74446
Garrett-Buchanan Co. (Jessup, MD) 71984
Graphic Packing Corp. (St Petersburg, FL) 62974
Mead Packaging Division (Richmond, VA) 91930
Mead Corp (Oklahoma City, OK) 77441
Monarch Paper Co. (Fort Worth, TX) 85200
Monarch Paper Co. (Houston, TX) 86605
Phoenix Packaging Inc. (Winston-Salem, NC) 76738
Ryder Truck Rental (Mobile, AL) 56235
Ryder Truck Rental (Bentonville, AR) 56789
Ryder Truck Rental (Blytheville, AR) 56816
Ryder Truck Rental (Mountain Home, AR) 57390
Ryder Truck Rental (Searcy, AR) 57608
Ryder Truck Rental (Texarkana, AR) 57680
Ryder Truck Rental (Panama City, FL) 62348
Ryder Truck Rental (Pensacola, FL) 62468
Ryder Truck Rental (Punta Gorda, FL) 62721
Ryder Truck Rental (Baton Rouge, LA) 69652; 69656
Ryder Truck Rental (Lafayette, LA) 70105
Ryder Truck Rental (Hattiesburg, MS) 72897
Ryder Truck Rental (Jackson, MS) 73054
Ryder Truck Rental (Meridian, MS) 73178
Ryder Truck Rental (Tupelo, MS) 73424; 73425
Ryder Truck Rental (Oklahoma City, OK) 77541
Ryder Truck Rental (Poteau, OK) 77728
Ryder Truck Rental (Sallisaw, OK) 77774
Ryder Truck Rental (Tulsa, OK) 78100
Ryder Truck Rental (Woodward, OK) 78266
Ryder Truck Rental (Grapevine, TX) 85661
Ryder Truck Rental (Longview, TX) 87733
Ryder Truck Rental (Lubbock, TX) 87780
Ryder Truck Rental (Mineral Wells, TX) 88116
Ryder Truck Rental (San Antonio, TX) 89215
Ryder Truck Rental (Tyler, TX) 89825
Saxon Paper Florida (Hollywood, FL) 60095
Sloan Paper Co. (Huntsville, AL) 56023
Sloan Paper Co. (Tampa, FL) 63599
Sloan Paper Co. (Jackson, MS) 73064
Sloan Paper Co. (Knoxville, TN) 81253
3M (Dallas, TX) 84451
Unijax, Inc. (Jacksonville, FL) 60482
Unijax Inc. (Atlanta, GA) 65229
Unijax Inc. (Columbus, GA) 65655; 65656
Unijax Inc. (Macon, GA) 66720
Unijax Inc. (Savannah, GA) 67529
Unijax Inc. (Valdosta, GA) 67976; 67977
Unijax Inc. (Alexandria, VA) 90242

Union Camp Corp. (Decatur, AL) 55610
Union Camp Corp. (Tifton Georgi, GA) 67834
Union Camp Corp. (Broussard, LA) 69745
Union Camp Corp. (Houston, MS) 72925
Union Camp Corp. (Houston, TX) 87051
Universal Foods Corp. (Dallas, TX) 84476
Westvaco Corp. (Newark, DE) 57934
Westvaco Corp. (Burlington, NC) 73764
Westvaco Corp. (Cleveland, TN) 80606; 80607
Westvaco Corp. (Richmond, VA) 92086
Westvaco Corp. (Staunton, VA) 92333
Weyerhaeuser Paper Co. Inc. (Franklin, KY) 68373
Willamette Industries Inc. (Grand Prairie, TX) 85647

5122 Drugs, Proprietaries & Sundries

Abbott Laboratories (Laurinburg, NC) 75347
Abbott Laboratories (Rocky Mountain, NC) 76112
Abbott Laboratories (Austin, TX) 82799
Allergan Pharmaceuticals (Lewisville, TX) 87647
American Cyanamid Co. (Dallas, TX) 83845
Amgen Inc. Louisville Distributors (Louisville, KY) 68689
Avon Products (Radford, VA) 91689
Avon Products Inc. (Newark, DE) 57890
Avon Products Inc. (Washington, DC) 58130
Avon Products West Houston (Houston, TX) 85827
Avon Retail Group Avon Products, Inc. (San Juan, PR) 78551
Avon Sales & Distribution Branch (Newark, DE) 57891
Avon Sales & Distribution Branch (Atlanta, GA) 64248
Baxter Healthcare Corp. (Mountain Home, AR) 57384
Baxter Healthcare Corp. (Cleveland, MS) 72682
Baxter Healthcare Corp. (Marion, NC) 75497
Baxter Healthcare Corp. (Grand Prairie, TX) 85609
Baxter Healthcare Corp. Prescr (Ashland, VA) 90398
Bergen Brunswig Drug Co. (Carrollton, TX) 83455
Bindley Western Drug (Austell, GA) 65349; 65349
Bindley Western Drug Co. (Dallas, TX) 83881; 83881
Bristol Myers Co. (Grand Prairie, TX) 85611
Bristol Myers Products Co. (Morrisville, NC) 75664
Bristol Myers Squibb Co. (Morrow, GA) 67005
Bristol-Myers Squibb Co. (Irving, TX) 87325
Dr. T.C. Smith Co. (Asheville, NC) 73611
Durr Drug Co., Inc. (Montgomery, AL) 56302
Durr-Fillauer Medical, Inc. (Montgomery, AL) 56303; 56305
Durr-Fillauer Medical Inc. (Shreveport, LA) 70717
Hoechst Roussel Pharmaceutc (Hurst, TX) 87274
Krogers Pharmacy Kroger Co. the (Atlanta, GA) 64626
Lederle-Praxis Biologics Inc. (Sanford, NC) 76198
Mary Kay Cosmetics, Inc. (Dallas, TX) 84221; 84222
Ohio Valley-Clarksburg Inc. (Wheeling, WV) 93117
Publix Super Market (Marietta, GA) 66885
Publix Super Market (Norcross, GA) 67170
Publix Super Markets (Marietta, GA) 66889; 66891; 66892
Publix Super Markets (Norcross, GA) 67172
Rite Aid (Beltsville, MD) 71364
Rite Aid Discount Pharmacy (Melbourne, FL) 61103
Rite Aid Discount Pharmacy (Lexington, KY) 68615
Wal Mart Discount Pharmacy (Marietta, GA) 66947

Wal Mart Pharmacy (San Marcos, TX) 89345
Wal-Mart Stores Inc. (Lebanon, TN) 81317
Walgreen (Austin, TX) 83057; 83058
Walgreen Drug Stores (Bossier City, LA) 69736
Warner Lambert Ltd (Grand Prairie, TX) 85646
Whitby Inc. (Richmond, VA) 92094

5131 Piece Goods & Notions

Burlington House Fabrics (Dallas, TX) 83890
Burlington House Upholstery (High Point, NC) 75119
Burlington Industries (Calhoun, GA) 65461
Burlington Industries Inc. (Dallas, TX) 83891
Burlington Industries Inc. (Clarksville, VA) 90637
Burlington Klopman Fabrics (Bremen, GA) 65393
Burlington Madison Yarn Co. (Mayodan, NC) 75537
Owens Corning Fiberglas (Mobile, AL) 56217
Owens Corning Fiberglas (Fort Smith, AR) 57075
Owens Corning Fiberglas (Altamonte Springs, FL) 58560
Owens Corning Fiberglas (Jacksonville, FL) 60384
Russell Corp. (Nashville, TN) 82092
Southern Cotton Oil Co. (Quann, TX) 88703

5136 Men's/Boys' Clothing

Ellesse USA Inc. (Dallas, TX) 84006
Personal Sportswear (Dallas, TX) 84301
Puritan Sportswear (Houston, TX) 86727
3M & D Inc. (Hialeah, FL) 60014

5137 Women's/ Children's Clothing

Burlington Coat Factory (Plano, TX) 88541
Burlington Coat Factory Warehouse (Dallas, TX) 83889
California Manufacturing Co. (Macon, MS) 73134
First Choice (Laredo, TX) 87610
The Gap Kids (San Antonio, TX) 89018
Personal Sportswear (Dallas, TX) 84301
Petite Sophisticate (Oklahoma City, OK) 77486

5139 Footwear

Payless Shoesource (Oklahoma City, OK) 77472

5141 Groceries—General Line

ACME Markets of Virginia Inc. (North Tazewell, VA) 91600
Del Monte Corp. (Columbia, MD) 71583
Fleming Companies Inc. (Oklahoma City, OK) 77360
Fleming Cos. Inc. (Oklahoma City, OK) 77362
Fleming Foods of Texas Inc. (Dallas, TX) 84072
Flowers Baking Co. (Charlottesville, VA) 90538
Food Lion (Salisbury, NC) 76161
Food Lion Inc. (Salisbury, NC) 76163
Grand Union Co (Hialeah, FL) 59986
Hormel&Co/George a (Midlothian, VA) 91417
Kroger Co. (Irving, TX) 87361
Kroger Distribution Inc. (Houston, TX) 86412
Liqui Dri Foods Inc. (Louisville, KY) 68869
Monarch Crown Corp. (San Antonio, TX) 89116
Piggly Wiggly (Elba, AL) 55676
Piggly Wiggly (Swainsboro, GA) 67755
Piggly Wiggly (Shreveport, LA) 70764
Piggly Wiggly (Sumter, SC) 80027
Piggly Wiggly Alabama Distribution (Birmingham, AL) 55336

Sam's Wholesale Club (Pensacola, FL) 62471
Sam's Wholesale Club (Savannah, GA) 67511
Sam's Wholesale Club (Greenville, SC) 79432
Sam's Wholesale Club (Austin, TX) 83000
Sam's Wholesale Club (Tyler, TX) 89828
Skinner Macaroni Co. (Charlotte, NC) 74159
Southland Corp. (Austin, TX) 83003
Southland Corp. (Dallas, TX) 84391
Sysco Food Services (Palm Beach Gardens, FL) 62275
Taco Bell (Duncan, OK) 76998
Taco Bell (Lawton, OK) 77175
Taco Bell (Tyler, TX) 89831
Timberlake Grocery Co. (Thomasville, GA) 67806
Tyson Foods Inc. (Humble, TX) 87252
Unijax, Inc. (Jacksonville, FL) 60482
Virginia Foods of Bluefield (Bluefield, VA) 90463
Watco Inc. (Oklahoma City, OK) 77663
Wetterau Inc. (Charleston, SC) 78915
Wetterau Inc. West Virginia (Nitro, WV) 92975
Wolf Brand Products Inc. (Dallas, TX) 84498
Woodhaven Foods (Birmingham, AL) 55459

5142 Packaged Frozen Foods

Coca-Cola Foods Auburndale Facility (Auburndale, FL) 58594
Fleming Companies Inc. (Oklahoma City, OK) 77360
Frio Foods Inc. (Uvalde, TX) 89851
Kentucky Fried Chicken (Wichita Falls, TX) 90076; 90077
Southern Food Inc. (Greensboro, NC) 74913
Tara Foods Inc. (Hidalgo, TX) 85748
Tyson Foods Inc. (Springhill, LA) 70858

5143 Dairy Products Except Dried or Canned

Associated Milk Producers Inc. (Shattuck, OK) 77808
Associated Milk Producers Inc. (Tulsa, OK) 77882
Associated Milk Producers Inc. (Arlington, TX) 82634
Associated Milk Producers Inc. (Muenster, TX) 88163
Associated Milk Producers Inc. (San Angelo, TX) 88868
Associated Milk Producers Inc. (Sulphur Springs, TX) 89551; 89552
Borden Inc. Dairy (Miami, FL) 61205; 61206
Borden Inc. Dairy (Minden, LA) 70338; 70339
Borden Inc. Dairy (Oklahoma City, OK) 77310; 77311
Borden Inc. Dairy (Greenville, SC) 79305; 79306
Borden Inc. Dairy (El Paso, TX) 84772; 84773
Borden Inc. Dairy (Houston, TX) 85887
Borden Inc. Grocery & Specialty Products (El Paso, TX) 84774
Borden Inc. Grocery & Specialty Products (Oklahoma City, OK) 77312
Coca Cola Bottling Co. (Bryan, TX) 83394
Fleming Companies Inc. (Oklahoma City, OK) 77360
Mid-America Dairymen Inc. (Schulenburg, TX) 89352
Potlatch Corp. Dairy (Dallas, TX) 84322
Ryan Milk Co. Inc. (Murray, KY) 69133
Southland Corp. (Baltimore, MD) 71312

5144 Poultry & Poultry Products

Golden Poultry Co. Inc. (Douglas, GA) 65969
Sam's Wholesale Club (Macon, GA) 66713
Tyson Foods, Inc. (Green Forest, AR) 57122

5145 Confectionery

Golden Peanut Co. (Camilla, GA) 65479
Golden Peanut Co. Ashburn Plant (Ashburn, GA) 64151
NCR Corp. (Orlando, FL) 62066
Sun Diamond Growers (Richardson, TX) 88777

5146 Fish & Seafoods

Coast to Coast Seafood Inc. (Biloxi, MS) 72616
Coast to Coast Sfd Sales Inc. (Miami, FL) 61264
Pizza Hut (Pompano Beach, FL) 62615

5147 Meats & Meat Products

Albertson's Wholesale Meats (Oklahoma City, OK) 77295
Fleming Companies Inc. (Oklahoma City, OK) 77360
Hormel & Co/Geo (Baltimore, MD) 71169
Southern Food Inc. (Greensboro, NC) 74913
Swift Independent Packing Co. (Morristown, TN) 81812
Webber Farms Inc. (Orlando, FL) 62192
Wilson Foods Corp. (Fort Lauderdale, FL) 59642
Wilson Foods Corp. (Oklahoma City, OK) 77665

5148 Fresh Fruits & Vegetables

Blue Goose Growers Inc. (Cobbtown, GA) 65569
Fleming Companies Inc. (Oklahoma City, OK) 77360
Fresh Foods (Irving, TX) 87347
Hertz Rent-A-Car Dba (Pompano Beach, FL) 62600
Kroger Wesco Foods Co. (Pompano Beach, FL) 62604
Piggly Wiggly (Columbia, SC) 79062
Southern Food Inc. (Greensboro, NC) 74913

5149 Groceries & Related Products Nec

ADM Milling Co. Inc. (North Little Rock, AR) 57452
ADM Milling Co. Otwell (Jonesboro, AR) 57209
Archer Daniels Midland (Destrehan, LA) 69837
Atlanta Baking Co., Inc. (Atlanta, GA) 64242
Bluegrass Coca-Cola Bottling Co., Inc. (Louisville, KY) 68706
Coca-Cola Botting Co. of Bat (Baton Rouge, LA) 69500
Coca-Cola Bottling Co. (Andalusia, AL) 54985
Coca Cola Bottling Co. (Dothan, AL) 55635
Coca Cola Bottling Co. (Florence, AL) 55735
Coca Cola Bottling Co. (Sylacauga, AL) 56585
Coca Cola Bottling Co. (Camden, AR) 56828
Coca Cola Bottling Co. (Monticello, AR) 57372
Coca Cola Bottling Co. (Rogers, AR) 57561
Coca Cola Bottling Co. (Lafayette, LA) 70050
Coca Cola Bottling Co. (Lake Charles, LA) 70137
Coca Cola Bottling Co. (Leesville, LA) 70189
Coca Cola Bottling Co. (Winnsboro, LA) 70980
Coca Cola Bottling Co. (Goldsboro, NC) 74712
Coca-Cola Bottling Co. (Altus, OK) 76793
Coca Cola Bottling Co. (Guthrie, OK) 77096
Coca Cola Bottling Co. (Stillwater, OK) 77837
Coca-Cola Bottling Co. (Georgetown, SC) 79273
Coca Cola Bottling Co. (Lancaster, SC) 79570
Coca Cola Bottling Co. (Angleton, TX) 82609
Coca-Cola Bottling Co. (El Campo, TX) 84745
Coca-Cola Bottling Co. (Longview, TX) 87709
Coca Cola Bottling Co. (Madisonville, TX) 87826

Coca Cola Bottling Co. (Midland, TX) 88030
Coca Cola Bottling Co. (Sweetwater, TX) 89582
Coca Cola Bottling Co. (Temple, TX) 89611
Coca Cola Bottling Co. (Tyler, TX) 89796
Coca-Cola Bottling Co. (Victoria, TX) 89882
Coca Cola Bottling Co. of Ar (Morrilton, AR) 57376
Coca Cola Bottling Co. Conso (Statesville, NC) 76325
Coca Cola Bottling Co. Conso (South Boston, VA) 92246
Coca Cola Bottling Co. (Minden, LA) 70340
Coca Cola Bottling Co. Inc. (Washington, NC) 76454
Coca Cola Bottling Co. Inc. (Pittsburg, TX) 88517
Coca-Cola Bottling Co. of Tu (Tulsa, OK) 77919
Coca Cola U S A (Orlando, FL) 61955
Coca Cola U S a (Atlanta, GA) 64378
Coca Cola U S a Fountain Sl (Raleigh, NC) 75884
Coca Cola USA (Houston, TX) 85984
Columbus Coca-Cola Bottling Inc. (Columbus, GA) 65638
Crestar Food Products Inc. (Brentwood, TN) 80223
Deer Park Spring Water Co., Inc. (Destin, FL) 59342
Deer Park Spring Water Inc. (Frederick, MD) 71719
Dickson Coca Cola Bottling (Dickson, TN) 80731
First Choice, Inc. (Fayetteville, AR) 56978
Fleming Companies Inc. (Oklahoma City, OK) 77360
Flowers Baking Co. (Danville, VA) 90693
Flowers Baking Co. (Farmville, VA) 90877
Flowers Baking Co. (Newport News, VA) 91469
Flowers Baking Co. (Warsaw, VA) 92529
Flowers Baking Co. of Lynchburg (Lynchburg, VA) 91247; 91248
Golden Peanuts Co. (Atlanta, GA) 64514
Kroger Wesco Foods Co. (Vero Beach, FL) 63760
Malone & Hyde of Lafayette (Lafayette, LA) 70073
Panama City Coca Cola Btlg (Panama City, FL) 62335
Pepsi-Cola General Bottlers (Bowling Green, KY) 68160
Schott's Bakery Inc. (Houston, TX) 86871
Seven Up U S a Inc. (San Antonio, TX) 89229
Sparkletts Drinking Water (Amarillo, TX) 82582
Sysco Food Service (Ocoee, FL) 61839
Universal Foods Corp. (Houston, TX) 87061
Winn-Dixie Louisville Inc. (Louisville, KY) 69042

5153 Grain & Field Beans

ADM Milling (Knobel, AR) 57237
Central Soya Co. Inc. (Guntersville, AL) 55823
Collingwood Grain Inc. (Guymon, OK) 77101
Farmers Elevator Co., Inc. (Ames, OK) 76801
Farmland Green Division (Enid, OK) 77048
Gold Kist Inc. (Dyersburg, TN) 80751
Gold Kist Inc. (Greenback, TN) 80875
Gold Kist Inc. (Jackson, TN) 80985
Gold Kist Inc. (Somerville, TN) 82336
Gold Kist Inc. (Springfield, TN) 82358
Harvest Queen Mill & Elevator Co. (Plainview, TX) 88529
Ralston Purina International (Miami, FL) 61440
Sherman County Grain Co. (Texhoma, OK) 77864

5154 Livestock

Gwaltney of Smithfield (Dunn, NC) 74374

5159 Farm-Product Raw Materials Nec

American Tobacco Co. (Wilson, NC) 76617
Burlington Cotton Co. (Greenville, SC) 79322
Carolina Leaf Tobacco Co. (Greenville, NC) 74953
Golden Peanut (Dothan, AL) 55651
Golden Peanut Co. (Cottondale, FL) 59119
Golden Peanut Co. (Atlanta, GA) 64513
Golden Peanut Co. (Bainbridge, GA) 65365; 65366
Golden Peanut Co. (Donalsonville, GA) 65916
Golden Peanut Co. (McRae, GA) 66972
Golden Peanut Co. (Plains, GA) 67269
Golden Peanut Co. (Elizabethtown, NC) 74490
Golden Peanut Co. (Anadarko, OK) 76803
Golden Peanut Co. (Pleasanton, TX) 88621
Golden Peanut Co. (Ivor, VA) 91170
Golden Peanut Co. (Suffolk, VA) 92369
Golden Peanuts Co. (Atlanta, GA) 64514
Lubrizol Corp (Houston, TX) 86499
Southern Cotton Oil (Montgomery, AL) 56380
Southern Cotton Oil Co. (Memphis, TN) 81698
Winstead Co. Inc. (Lothian, MD) 72114

5162 Plastics Materials & Basic Shapes

JMA Inc. Plastics Div. (Waco, TX) 89945
Mobil Chemical Co. (Covington, GA) 65737
Mobil Chemical Co. (Temple, TX) 89624; 89625
Novacor Chemicals Inc. (Forest City, NC) 74608
Thoroughbred Plastics Corp. (Louisville, KY) 69021
Unijax, Inc. (Jacksonville, FL) 60482

5169 Chemicals & Allied Products Nec

Abbott Laboratories (Jackson, MS) 72937
Agri-Services of Harrisonburg (Harrisonburg, VA) 91062
Air Products & Chemicals (New Orleans, LA) 70424
Air Products & Chemicals (Beltsville, MD) 71347
Air Products & Chemicals (Durham, NC) 74380; 74381
Air Products & Chemicals (Seguin, TX) 89366
Air Products & Chemicals Co. (Orlando, FL) 61902
Air Products & Chemicals Inc. (Birmingham, AL) 55114
Air Products & Chemicals Inc. (Sheffield, AL) 56543
Air Products & Chemicals Inc. (Fayetteville, AR) 56967
Air Products & Chemicals Inc. (Delaware City, DE) 57768
Air Products & Chemicals Inc. (Newark, DE) 57884
Air Products & Chemicals Inc. (Jacksonville, FL) 60160
Air Products & Chemicals, Inc. (Tampa, FL) 63304
Air Products & Chemicals Inc. (Atlanta, GA) 64210
Air Products & Chemicals Inc. (Greensboro, NC) 74759
Air Products & Chemicals Inc. (Knoxville, TN) 81130
Air Products & Chemicals Inc. (Memphis, TN) 81447
Air Products & Chemicals Inc. (Nashville, TN) 81881
Air Products & Chemicals Inc. (Irving, TX) 87319
Air Products & Chemicals Inc. (Lynchburg, VA) 91220
Air Products & Chemicals Inc. (Roanoke, VA) 92099
Air Products World Trade, Inc. c/oChase Trade, Inc. (St. Thomas, VI) 90150
American Cyanamid Co. (Atlanta, GA) 64223
American Cyanamid Co. (Havre De Grace, MD) 71915
American Cyanamid Co. (Charlotte, NC) 73834
American Cyanamid Co. (Memphis, TN) 81448; 81449
American Cyanamid Co. (Richardson, TX) 88720
Arcadian Corp. (Memphis, TN) 81460; 81462
Archer Daniels Midland Co. (Southport, NC) 76283
Arco Chemical Co. (Channelview, TX) 83547
BASF Corp.-Clemson Plant (Central, SC) 78784
BASF Corp. Urethanes (Memphis, TN) 81469
Betz Labs (Macon, GA) 66673
Betz PaperChem, Inc. (Jacksonville, FL) 60231
Betz Process Chemicals, Inc. (Friendswood, TX) 85396
Betz Process Chemicals Inc. (The Woodlands, TX) 89750
Central Products Inc. (Montgomery, AL) 56291; 56292
Enthone-OMI (Seagoville, TX) 89363
Exxon Energy Chemicals (Sweetwater, TX) 89583
Ferro Corp. (Houston, TX) 86194
Gaylord Chemical Corp. (Slidell, LA) 70826
Kaiser Aluminum & Chemical (Mulberry, FL) 61576
Lilly Research Laboratories (Shellman, GA) 67537
Lubrizol Corp. (Wilmington, DE) 58079
Martin Marietta Magnesia (Knoxville, TN) 81228
Mobil Chemical Company (Dallas, TX) 84239
Monsanto Agricultural Co. (Marietta, GA) 66841
Monsanto Co. (Wilmington, DE) 58088
Monsanto Co. (Washington, DC) 58369
Monsanto Co. (Atlanta, GA) 64733
Monsanto Co. (Augusta, GA) 65337
Monsanto Co. (Nitro, WV) 92972
Monsanto Co./Agricultural Grp (Fayetteville, NC) 74568
Morton International Arspc Polymer (Lilburn, GA) 66572
Morton International Ind Chemls (Tucker, GA) 67869
Nalco Chemical (Duncan, OK) 76995
Nalco Chemical Co. (Mobile, AL) 56212
Nalco Chemical Co. (Jacksonville, FL) 60380
Nalco Chemical Co. (Jonesboro, GA) 66389
Nalco Chemical Co. (Garyville, LA) 69865; 69866
Nalco Chemical Co. (Kenner, LA) 70000
Nalco Chemical Co. (Lake Charles, LA) 70151
Nalco Chemical Co. (Charlotte, NC) 74086
Nalco Chemical Co. (Kilgore, TX) 87495
Nalco Chemical Co. (Liberty, TX) 87676
Nalco Chemical Co. Inc. (Shreveport, LA) 70752
Nalco Chemical Co. Inc. (Tulsa, OK) 78028
Oilfield Service Corp. Amer (Houston, TX) 86627
OSCA (Lafayette, LA) 70079
Osca Inc. (Lafayette, LA) 70080
P M C Inc. (Kevil, KY) 68501
Sigma Diagnostics (Farmerville, LA) 69852
Specialty Products Co. (Griffin, GA) 66325
Specialty Products & Insulation (Savannah, GA) 67514
3M (Atlanta, GA) 65213
3M Scotchtint Window Film (Norcross, GA) 67202
Unijax, Inc. (Jacksonville, FL) 60482
Uniroyal Chemical (Gastonia, NC) 74690
Watco Inc. (Little Rock, AR) 57320
Westvaco Corp. (De Ridder, LA) 69821
Zep Manufacturing Co. (Minden, LA) 70348

5171 Petroleum Bulk Stations & Terminals

Amerada Hess Corp. (Shreveport, LA) 70681
Amerada Hess Corp. (Houston, TX) 85775
Amerada Hess Corp. (Midland, TX) 88019
Amerada Hess Corp. (Plains, TX) 88522
Chevron USA Inc. El Paso Terminal (El Paso, TX) 84782
Citgo Petroleum Corp. (Tulsa, OK) 77907
Cosbel Petroleum Corp. (Houston, TX) 86015
Enron Corp. (Houston, TX) 86062
Enron Liquids Pipeline Group (Houston, TX) 86076
Exxon Co. (Batesville, AR) 56754
Exxon Co. (Baltimore, MD) 71115
Exxon Co. USA (Beaumont, TX) 83151
Exxon Co. USA (Crowell, TX) 83812
Exxon Co. USA (Freer, TX) 85395
Exxon Co. USA (New Boston, TX) 88200
Exxon Distributor (Jasper, TX) 87431
Exxon Products (Marble Falls, TX) 87838
Exxon Products (Pecos, TX) 88494
LI&E Mobile River Terminal (Mobile, AL) 56202
Mapco Natural Gas Liquids Inc. (Tulsa, OK) 78010
Mapco Petroleum Inc. (Tulsa, OK) 78011
Marathon Oil Co. (Berwick, LA) 69697; 69698
Marathon Oil Co. (Pauls Valley, OK) 77691; 77692
Mobil Oil Co. (Crosbyton, TX) 83809
Mobil Oil Co. (Del Rio, TX) 84581
Mobil Oil Co. (Three Rivers, TX) 89762
Mobil Oil Co. Consignee (Memphis, TX) 87949
Mobil Oil Co. Products (Cameron, TX) 83437
Mobil Oil Co. Wholesale Dept (Electra, TX) 84986
Mobil Oil Corp. (Jacksonville, FL) 60379
Mobil Oil Corp. (Oklahoma City, OK) 77447
Mobil Oil Corp. (Alvin, TX) 82508
Mobil Oil Corp. (Austin, TX) 82942
Mobil Oil Corp. (Houston, TX) 86593
Mobil Oil Corp. (Waskom, TX) 89988
Mobil Oil Corp. (Terminal) (Fort Worth, TX) 85194
Mobil Oil Products (Montgomery, WV) 92939
Mobil Petroleum Products (Freeport, TX) 85388
Mobile River Terminal (Mobile, AL) 56209
Pennzoil Co. (Beaumont, TX) 83196
Pennzoil Co. (Morgantown, WV) 92947
Pennzoil Co. (Parkersburg, WV) 92995
Pennzoil Co. (Spencer, WV) 93063; 93064
Pennzoil Co. (Tariff, WV) 93076
Pennzoil Producing Co. (Refugio, TX) 88717
Pennzoil Producing Co. Inc. (Mc Allen, TX) 87894
Phillips 66 Freeport Terminal Ii (Sweeny, TX) 89576
Phillips 66 Jones Creek Terminal (Jones Creek, TX) 87445
Phillips 66 Co. Freeport Ii Terminal (Sweeny, TX) 89578
Phillips 66 Co. Freeport Terminal (Sweeny, TX) 89579
Phillips 66 Co. Jones Creek Terminal (Jones Creek, TX) 87446
Phillips 66 Co. San Bernard Terminal (Sweeny, TX) 89580
Shell Oil (Charleston, SC) 78890
Shell Oil Co. (Cheneyville, LA) 69776
Shell Oil Co. (Corpus Christi, TX) 83750; 83751
Shell Oil Co. (Marietta, TX) 87844
Shell Oil Co. (Tilden, TX) 89763
Sun Refining & Marketing (Corpus Christi, TX) 83754
Sun Refining & Marketing Co. (Chickasha, OK) 76938
Tesoro Petroleum Distribution Co. (Freeport, TX) 85394
Tesoro Petroleum Distribution Co. (Kilgore, TX) 87499
Texaco Distribution (Hearne, TX) 85727
Texaco Distributor (Pawhuska, OK) 77697
Texaco Distributor (Caldwell, TX) 83432
Texaco Inc. (Marvell, AR) 57350
Texaco Inc. (Orlando, FL) 62163
Texaco Inc. (Morganfield, KY) 69108
Texaco Inc. (Greensboro, NC) 74922
Texaco Inc. (Aransas Pass, TX) 82625
Texaco Inc. (Corpus Christi, TX) 83760
Texaco Inc. (De Kalb, TX) 84527
Texaco Inc. (Humble, TX) 87249
Texaco Inc. (Olney, TX) 88296
Texaco Inc. (San Isidro, TX) 89333
Texaco Inc. (Seymour, TX) 89388
Texaco Inc. (Taylor, TX) 89602
Texaco Inc. (Texarkana, TX) 89712
Texaco Inc. (Weimar, TX) 90028
Texaco Inc. (Hugheston, WV) 92865
Texaco Inc. Producing Dept (Gladewater, TX) 85582
Texaco Incorporated Sales (Abilene, TX) 82461
Texaco Inc. Warehouse (Cameron, TX) 83439
Texaco Jobber Warehouse (Jefferson, TX) 87440
Texaco Oil Co. (Weatherford, TX) 90015
Texaco Petroleum Prod Dist (Palestine, TX) 88346
Texaco Ref. & Mktg. Inc. (Union, LA) 70918
Texaco Ref. & Mktg. Inc. Port Arthur Terminal (Port Arthur, TX) 88654
Texaco Refining & Marketing Inc. (Convent, LA) 69784
Texaco Refining & Marketing Inc. Pat (Port Arthur, TX) 88656
Texaco Self Serve (San Antonio, TX) 89270
Total Petroleum Inc. (Dallas, TX) 84453; 84454
Union Oil Co. of California (Mulga, AL) 56401
Union Oil Co. of California (Odessa, TX) 88289
Union Texas Petroleum (Morgan City, LA) 70397
Union Texas Petroleum Corp. (Okarche, OK) 77286
Warren Petroleum Corp. (Albany, TX) 82482

5172 Petroleum Products Nec

Air Products & Chemicals Inc. (Midlothian, TX) 88098
Amerada Hess Corp. (Fort Lauderdale, FL) 59433
Amerada Hess Corp. (Jacksonville, FL) 60163
Amerada Hess Corp. (Atlanta, GA) 64218
Amerada Hess Corp. (Charlotte, NC) 73832; 73833
Amerada Hess Corp. (Greensboro, NC) 74761; 74762
Amerada Hess Corp. (Wilmington, NC) 76537
Amerada Hess Corp. (Charleston, SC) 78788
Amerada Hess Corp. (Como, TX) 83646
AMR Services Corp. (Fort Worth, TX) 85066
Archer Daniels Midland (Houston, TX) 85806
Arco Oil & Gas Co. (Dallas, TX) 83857
Ashland Petroleum Co. (Russell, KY) 69254
Atlantic Richfield Co. (Fairfax, VA) 90753
Atlantic Richfield Co. (Richmond, VA) 91738
Caltex Petroleum Corp. (Irving, TX) 87327
Citgo Petroleum (Knoxville, TN) 81156
Citgo Petroleum Corp. (Birmingham, AL) 55193
Citgo Petroleum Corp. (Altamonte Springs, FL) 58553
Citgo Petroleum Corp. (Fort Lauderdale, FL) 59471
Citgo Petroleum Corp. (Meridian, MS) 73161
Citgo Petroleum Corp. (Tulsa, OK) 77906
Citgo Petroleum Corp. (Knoxville, TN) 81157
Citgo Petroleum Corp. (Bryan, TX) 83393
Citgo Petroleum Corp. (Midland, TX) 88029
Citgo Refining & Chemicals Inc. (Tulsa, OK) 77917
Coastal Fuels Marketing Inc. (Miami, FL) 61267
Coastal Unilube Inc. (West Memphis, AR) 57720
Cosbel Petroleum Corp. (Houston, TX) 86015
Delta Air Lines, Inc. (Atlanta, GA) 64412
Enron Americas Inc. (Houston, TX) 86061
Enron Corp. (Houston, TX) 86062
Enron Gas Liquids Inc. (Houston, TX) 86067
Enron Liquids Pipeline Group (Houston, TX) 86076
Exxon Co. (De Queen, AR) 56891
Exxon Co. (Orange Park, FL) 61879
Exxon Co. (Alexandria, LA) 69376
Exxon Co. (Florence, SC) 79198
Exxon Co. (Victoria, TX) 89886
Exxon Co. (Covington, VA) 90655
Exxon Co. (Lexington, VA) 91201
Exxon Co. Terminal (Collins, MS) 72695
Exxon Co. U S a (Henderson, KY) 68445
Exxon Co. U S a (Somerset, KY) 69292; 69292
Exxon Co. U S a (Kingsport, TN) 81083
Exxon Co. U S a (Memphis, TN) 81522
Exxon Co. U S a (Nashville, TN) 81959
Exxon Co. U S a (Charleston, WV) 92747
Exxon Co. U S A (Memphis, TN) 81523
Exxon Co. U S A (Nashville, TN) 81960
Exxon Co. U S a Marketing (Jackson, TN) 80970
Exxon Co. USA (Newport, AR) 57448
Exxon Co. USA (Gulf Breeze, FL) 59936
Exxon Co. USA (Meadows Village, FL) 61027
Exxon Co. USA (Sylvania, GA) 67768
Exxon Co. USA (Henderson, KY) 68446
Exxon Co. USA (Columbia, LA) 69780
Exxon Co. USA (Houma, LA) 69951; 69952
Exxon Co. USA (Columbia, MS) 72698
Exxon Co. USA (Asheville, NC) 73612
Exxon Co. USA (Greenville, NC) 74958
Exxon Co. USA (Roxboro, NC) 76126
Exxon Co. USA (Wilmington, NC) 76554; 76555
Exxon Co. USA (Edisto Island, SC) 79188
Exxon Co. USA (Spartanburg, SC) 79892
Exxon Co. USA (Madisonville, TX) 87827
Exxon Co. USA (Menard, TX) 87952
Exxon Co. USA (Richmond, TX) 88796
Exxon Co. USA (West, TX) 90042
Exxon Co. USA (Wichita Falls, TX) 90072
Exxon Co. USA Wholesale (Atlanta, TX) 82795
Exxon Distributor (Cordele, GA) 65710
Exxon Distributor (Kilbourne, LA) 70025
Exxon Distributor (Eastland, TX) 84727
Exxon Motor Fuel Store (Odessa, TX) 88241
Exxon Oil Marketers (Yazoo City, MS) 73501
Exxon Products (Sheffield, AL) 56548
Exxon Products (Eagle Pass, TX) 84715
Exxon Stanton Oil Co. (Mc Minnville, TN) 81434
Exxon Supply Co. (Houston, TX) 86185; 86186
Fina Inc. (Dallas, TX) 84065
Fina Oil & Chemical Co. (Dallas, TX) 84066
Industrial Lubricants Co. (San Antonio, TX) 89031
Jiffy Lube (Prattville, AL) 56489
Jiffy Lube (Tulsa, OK) 77961
Jiffy Lube (Anderson, SC) 78677
Jiffy Lube (Charleston, SC) 78822
Jiffy Lube (Mt Pleasant, SC) 79674
Jiffy Lube (San Antonio, TX) 89033
Jiffy Lube Oil Change (Louisville, KY) 68784
Kerr Mcgee Refining Corp. (Lubbock, TX) 87768
Lyondell Petrochemical Comp (Mulga, AL) 56400

Lyondell Petrochemical Co. (Houston, TX) 86502
Mapco Inc. (Tulsa, OK) 78009
Marathon Fuels Inc. (Owensboro, KY) 69185
Marathon Oil (Louisville, KY) 68875; 68876
Marathon Oil (Shelbyville, KY) 69275
Marathon Oil Co. (Fort Lauderdale, FL) 59527; 59528
Marathon Oil Co. (Louisville, KY) 68877; 68878
Marathon Oil Co. (Shelbyville, KY) 69276
Marathon Oil Co. (Cameron, LA) 69749; 69750
Marathon Oil Co. (Cotton Valley, LA) 69789; 69791
Marathon Oil Co. (Bradley, OK) 76867; 76868
Marathon Petroleum Co. (Birmingham, AL) 55312
Marathon Petroleum Co. (Tampa, FL) 63491
Marathon Petroleum Co. (Charleston, SC) 78843
Marathon Petroleum Co. (Houston, TX) 86514
Mobil Bulk Plant (Foreman, AR) 57006
Mobil Corp. (Fairfax, VA) 90797
Mobil Exploration&Prod Serv (Dallas, TX) 84243
Mobil Oil (San Saba, TX) 89347
Mobil Oil Bulk Plant (Galveston, TX) 85456
Mobil Oil Chalmette Refinery (Chalmette, LA) 69765
Mobil Oil Co. (Bogalusa, LA) 69705
Mobil Oil Co. (Anson, TX) 82616
Mobil Oil Co. (Corsicana, TX) 83784
Mobil Oil Co. (Grand Prairie, TX) 85630
Mobil Oil Co. (Nacogdoches, TX) 88172
Mobil Oil Consignee (Freeport, TX) 85387
Mobil Oil Consignee (Tomball, TX) 89773
Mobil Oil Corp. (Fort Lauderdale, FL) 59541
Mobil Oil Corp. (Baltimore, MD) 71210
Mobil Oil Corp. (Charlotte, NC) 74085
Mobil Oil Corp. (Oklahoma City, OK) 77448
Mobil Oil Corp. (Austin, TX) 82942
Mobil Oil Corp. (Corpus Christi, TX) 83736
Mobil Oil Corp. (Eagle Pass, TX) 84719
Mobil Oil Corp. (Fairfax, VA) 90800
Mobil Oil Corp. (Manassas, VA) 91315; 91316
Mobil Oil Products (Lake Village, AR) 57241
Mobil Oil Service Station (Allen, KY) 68081; 68082
Mobil Oils Distributor (Mc Allen, TX) 87890
Mobil Petroleum Co. (Gonzales, TX) 85589
Mobil Research Devlpmnt Cor (Addison, TX) 82474
Murphy Oil Corp. (Nashville, TN) 82065; 82066
Pennzoil Co. (Lexington, KY) 68601
Pennzoil Co. (New Orleans, LA) 70547
Pennzoil Co. (Waco, TX) 89959
Pennzoil Lube Stop (Nashville, TN) 82080
Pennzoil Prodcts Co. (Vero Beach, FL) 63764
Pennzoil Product Co. (Savannah, GA) 67503; 67504
Pennzoil Products (Fredericksburg, VA) 90933
Pennzoil Products Co. (Longwood, FL) 60941; 60942
Pennzoil Products Co. (Vero Beach, FL) 63765
Pennzoil Products Co. (Charleston, WV) 92778; 92779
Pennzoil Swifty Lube Center (Panama City, FL) 62336
Pennzoil Ten Minute Oil Change (Casselberry, FL) 58937
Quaker State Oil Refining (Chester, WV) 92802
Quaker State Oil Refining Co. (Joppa, MD) 71990
Quaker State Oil Refining Co. (Newell, WV) 92966
Safety Kleen Corp. (Denton, TX) 84636
Scurlock Permian Corp. (Houston, TX) 86872
Shell Chemical Co. (Memphis, TN) 81693
Shell Co. (Houston, TX) 86876
Shell Co. (Richmond, VA) 92011
Shell Oil (Charlotte, NC) 74158
Shell Oil (Chattanooga, TN) 80491
Shell Oil Co. (Guntersville, AL) 55833
Shell Oil Co. (Mobile, AL) 56239
Shell Oil Co. (Orlando, FL) 62142
Shell Oil Co. (Tampa, FL) 63591
Shell Oil Co. (Greensboro, NC) 74908
Shell Oil Co. (Chesapeake, VA) 90600; 90601
Shell Pipe Line Corp. (Houston, TX) 86888
Shell Pipeline Corp. (Donaldsonville, LA) 69843
Shell Pipeline Corp. (Donaldsonvl, LA) 69846
Shell Pipeline Corp. (Houston, TX) 86891
Sun Refining & Marketing (Midland, TX) 88081
Sun Refining & Marketing Co. (Tampa, FL) 63605
Sun Refining & Marketing Co. (Henderson, KY) 68457
Ten Minute Oil Change (Del Rio, TX) 84587
Tesoro Petroleum Distribution (New Orleans, LA) 70566
Tesoro Petroleum Distribution Co. (Oklahoma City, OK) 77600
Tesoro Petroleum Distribution Co. (El Campo, TX) 84750
Tesoro Petroleum Distribution Co. (Galveston, TX) 85469
Tesoro Petroleum Distribution Co. (Houston, TX) 86980
Tesoro Petroleum Distribution Co. (Rockport, TX) 88821
Texaco (Corpus Christi, TX) 83759
Texaco (Liberty, TX) 87681
Texaco (Sour Lake, TX) 89457
Texaco Bulk Plant (Murray, KY) 69134
Texaco Distributor (Greeneville, TN) 80889
Texaco Distributor (Madisonville, TX) 87828
Texaco Distributors (Aberdeen, MS) 72580
Texaco Express Lube (Jacksonville, FL) 60473
Texaco Inc. (Birmingham, AL) 55420
Texaco Inc. (Dade City, FL) 59143
Texaco Inc. (Fort Lauderdale, FL) 59619
Texaco Inc. (Jacksonville, FL) 60475
Texaco Inc. (Frankfort, KY) 68370
Texaco Inc. (Louisville, KY) 69019
Texaco Inc. (Owensboro, KY) 69195
Texaco Inc. (Paducah, KY) 69212
Texaco Inc. (Baton Rouge, LA) 69672
Texaco Inc. (Houma, LA) 69972
Texaco Inc. (Loreauville, LA) 70200
Texaco Inc. (New Iberia, LA) 70421
Texaco Inc. (Paradis, LA) 70609
Texaco Inc. (Yazoo City, MS) 73507
Texaco Inc. (Paw Creek, NC) 75791
Texaco Inc. (Oklahoma City, OK) 77611; 77612
Texaco Inc. (Stillwater, OK) 77845
Texaco Inc. (Tulsa, OK) 78148
Texaco Inc. (Charleston, SC) 78903
Texaco Inc. (Spartanburg, SC) 79957
Texaco Inc. (Knoxville, TN) 81258
Texaco Inc. (Ballinger, TX) 83092
Texaco Inc. (Benavides, TX) 83281
Texaco Inc. (Dallas, TX) 84430
Texaco Inc. (Electra, TX) 84990
Texaco Inc. (Marfa, TX) 87842
Texaco Inc. (Sabinal, TX) 88861
Texaco Incorporated (Vernon, TX) 89873
Texaco Inc. (Waco, TX) 89980
Texaco Inc. (Weslaco, TX) 90039
Texaco Inc. (Ofc) (Tulsa, OK) 78151
Texaco Latin Amer W African (Miami, FL) 61475
Texaco Oil Distributors (Houston, MS) 72923
Texaco Refining & Marketing (Tampa, FL) 63620; 63620
Texaco Self Serve (New Orleans, LA) 70570
Texaco USA (Jackson, MS) 73075
Texaco USA (Houston, TX) 87012
Texaco Warehouse (Turkey, TX) 89789
Tosco Corp. (Memphis, TN) 81711
Tosco Corp. (Nashville, TN) 82113
Total Petroleum Inc. (Ardmore, OK) 76823; 76825
Total Petroleum Inc. (Oklahoma City, OK) 77629; 77630
Total Petroleum Inc. (Dallas, TX) 84453; 84454
Union Oil Co. (Knoxville, TN) 81266
Union Oil Co. of Cal (Columbia, SC) 79114
Union Oil Co. of California (Jacksonville, FL) 60484
Union Oil Co. of California (Miami, FL) 61489
Union Oil Co. of California (Tampa, FL) 63634
Union Oil Co. of California (Albany, GA) 64098
Union Oil Co. of California (Jackson, MS) 73080
Union Oil Co. of California (Charlotte, NC) 74187
Union Oil Co. of California Inc. (Birmingham, AL) 55436
Union Texas Petroleum Corp. (Collinsville, TX) 83636
Valvoline Inc. (Lexington, KY) 68651
Valvoline Instant Oil Chang (Lexington, KY) 68654
Valvoline Oil Co. (Lexington, KY) 68656
Warren Petroleum Co. (Tampa, FL) 63661
Warren Petroleum Co. (Arcadia, LA) 69432

5181 Beer & Ale

Adolph Coors Co. (Elkton, VA) 90743
Coors Brewing Co. (Elkton, VA) 90744; 90745

5182 Wines & Distilled Beverages

Brown-Forman Corp. (Louisville, KY) 68715

5191 Farm Supplies

Ace Hardware at Newport (Rock Hill, SC) 79810
Agrico Chemical Co. (Cecilia, KY) 68199
Agrico Chemical Co. (Baltimore, MD) 71030
Agrico Chemical Co. (Catoosa, OK) 76907
Agrico Chemical Co., Inc. (Clarkson, KY) 68201
Asgrow Seed Co. (Uvalde, TX) 89848
Central Soya Co. Inc. (Wilson, NC) 76628
Farmers Elevator Co., Inc. (Ames, OK) 76801
GroAgriseed Co. (Lubbock, TX) 87764
Kaiser Aluminum & Chemical (Edison, GA) 66164
Kaiser Aluminum & Chemical (Elizabeth City, NC) 74481
Kmart Discount Stores (Zephyrhills, FL) 64016
Lubrizol Agrigenetics Southern Div. (Lubbock, TX) 87771
Mobil Chemical Co. (Floydada, TX) 85040
Mobil Mining & Minerals (Nichols, FL) 61722
Pizza Hut (De Ridder, LA) 69817
Ring Around Products Inc. (N Little Rock, AR) 57421
Ring Around Products Inc. (Houston, TX) 86798
Southland Royalty Co. (Vernon, AL) 56700; 56701
Southren Cotton Oil Co. (Sweetwater, TX) 89592
Taylor-Erans Seed Co. (Tulia, TX) 89787

5192 Books, Periodicals & Newspapers

E R Carpenter Co. Inc. (Hickory, NC) 75068
Waldenbooks (Jacksonville, FL) 60498

5194 Tobacco & Tobacco Products

American Tobacco Co. (Reidsville, NC) 75994
General Processors Inc. (Oxford, NC) 75779; 75779
Lorillard Inc. (Baton Rouge, LA) 69583
RJ Reynolds Tobacco Co. (Oxford, NC) 75788
RJ Reynolds Tobacco Co. (Greenville, SC) 79430
RJ Reynolds Tobacco Co. Inc. (Vidalia, GA) 67994
RJ Reynolds Tobacco Co. Inc. (New Orleans, LA) 70552
RJ Reynolds Tobacco Co. Inc. (Winston Salem, NC) 76684

5198 Paints, Varnishes & Supplies

PPG Industries Inc. (Hagerstown, MD) 71891
Sigma Coatings Inc. (Houston, TX) 86893; 86894

5199 Nondurable Goods Nec

Advanced Micro Devices Inc. (Fort Lauderdale, FL) 59425
Air Products & Chemicals, Inc. (Clearwater, FL) 58959
BASF Corp. Chemical Division (Geismar, LA) 69877
BASF Corp. Fibers Division (Dalton, GA) 65773
BASF Corp. Fibers Division (Lowland, TN) 81361
BASF Corp.-Clemson Plant (Central, SC) 78784
Coast to Coast Cap Co. (Jacksonville, FL) 60245; 60246
Coast to Coast Sales Inc. (Orlando, FL) 61953
Creative Expressions (Memphis, TN) 81500
Exxon Chemical Co. (Andrews, TX) 82595
Exxon Chemical Co. (Odessa, TX) 88240
Exxon Co. USA (Lamesa, TX) 87589
Johnson Products Co. (Memphis, TN) 81632
Lubrizol Corp. (Tulsa, OK) 78003
Marathon Petroleum Co. (Midland, TX) 88047
Mobil Cheml-Films Div (Dallas, TX) 84240
Nalco Chemical Co. (Longwood, FL) 60938
Pepsi-Cola South (Bay City, TX) 83104
Rite Aid Discount Pharmacie (Kinston, NC) 75328
Salem Carpet Mills Inc. (S Pittsburg, TN) 82287
Sam's Wholesale Club (Oklahoma City, OK) 77547
Schering Lab (Miami, FL) 61457
Service Merchandise (Nashville, TN) 82097
Southern Cotton Oil Co. (Levelland, TX) 87642
Stanhome Inc. (San Antonio, TX) 89233
Stop & Shop (Clewiston, FL) 59063
Sun Refining & Marketing Co. (Houston, TX) 86920
Tandy Corp. (Miami, FL) 61472
Tandy Corp. Del (Beaumont, TX) 83219
Texaco Inc. (Seminole, OK) 77806
Van Waters & Rogers Inc. (Murfreesboro, TN) 81872
Waldenbooks (Miami, FL) 61499
Waldenbooks (Pompano Beach, FL) 62640
Waldenbooks (Wilkesboro, NC) 76524
Watco Inc. (Little Rock, AR) 57320

5211 Lumber & Other Building Materials

Abitibi-Price Corp. (Roaring River, NC) 76046; 76047
Ace Hardware (Blountstown, FL) 58661
Ace Hardware (New Port Richey, FL) 61672
Ace Hardware (Woodward, OK) 78254
Ace Hardware (Kemp, TX) 87464
Ace Hardware of Butler Inc. (Butler, AL) 55493
Ace Hardware Co. (Jackson, AL) 56061
Ace Hardware Downtown (Texarkana, TX) 89665
Ace Hardware Reynolds Brothers (Foley, AL) 55747
Ace Hardware Stores (Hobe Sound, FL) 60025
Ace Hardware&Furniture Inc. (Fordyce, AR) 57004
Ace Hardware&Garden Center (Baton Rouge, LA) 69453
Allied Plywood Corp. (Houston, TX) 85771
American Limestone Co. Inc. (Springfield, TN) 82354
American Savings of Florida, FSB (Delray Beach, FL) 59307
Arrow Electronics Inc. (Baltimore, MD) 71044
Builders Square (Oklahoma City, OK) 77314
Builders Square (Houston, TX) 85911; 85913
Builders Square Inc. (San Antonio, TX) 88942
Champion International Corp. (Jacksonville, FL) 60239
Charter Co. (Brenham, TX) 83335
Coast to Coast Contractors (Pompano Beach, FL) 62592
Coast to Coast Hardware (Winston Salem, NC) 76666
Coast to Coast Hardware (Johnson City, TN) 81027
Collins & Aiken Holding II Corp. (Charlotte, NC) 73910
Collins & Aikman Holdings Corp. (Charlotte, NC) 73915
Federal Paper Board Co. Inc. (Newberry, SC) 79726; 79726
Home Depot Inc (St Petersburg, FL) 62976
Home Depot Inc. (Clearwater, FL) 59021
Home Depot Inc. (Fort Lauderdale, FL) 59510
Home Depot Inc. (West Palm Beach, FL) 63872
Home Depot Inc. (Carrollton, TX) 83470
Louisiana Pacific Corp. (Philadelphia, MS) 73279
Lowe's Home Centers Inc. (Owensboro, KY) 69184
Lowe's Home Centers Inc. (Richmond, KY) 69245
Lowe's Home Centers Inc. (Princeton, WV) 93010
Number One Building Supply Inc. (Mount Olive, NC) 75696
Ogden Project Inc. (Tulsa, OK) 78036
Payless Cashways (Oklahoma City, OK) 77464
Payless Cashways (Lake Dallas, TX) 87577
Payless Cashways (Lubbock, TX) 87773
Payless Cashways Bldg Matl (Richardson, TX) 88753
Payless Cashways Bldg Matls (Oklahoma City, OK) 77465; 77466
Payless Cashways Bldg Matls (Garland, TX) 85519
Payless Cashways Bldg Matls (Lewisville, TX) 87658
Payless Cashways Bldg Matls (Mesquite, TX) 87981
Payless Cashways Bldg Matls (Plano, TX) 88594
Payless Cashways Bldg Matls (Tyler, TX) 89821
Payless Cashways Bldg Matrl (Dallas, TX) 84292
Payless Cashways Bldg Mtrls (Longview, TX) 87725
Payless Cashways Building M (Tulsa, OK) 78042
Payless Cashways Building M (Longview, TX) 87726
Payless Cashways Building M (Wichita Falls, TX) 90086
Payless Cashways Inc. (Edmond, OK) 77009
Payless Cashways Inc. (Tulsa, OK) 78043
Payless Cashways Inc. (Fort Worth, TX) 85210; 85211
Payless Cashways Inc. (Irving, TX) 87387
Payless Cashways Mtrls (Fort Worth, TX) 85212
Pearland Lumber Co. Inc. (Pearland, TX) 88485
Ppg Industries (Lattimore, NC) 75344
Radio Shack (Blackstone, VA) 90455; 90456
Specialty Products (Wynnewood, OK) 78274
Specialty Products & Installation (Greensboro, NC) 74915
Specialty Products & Insulation (Savannah, GA) 67514
Strunk Lumberyard Inc. (Key West, FL) 60579
Union Camp Corp. (Chapman, AL) 55508
Vulcan Materials Co. (Knoxville., TN) 81279
Willamette Industries, Inc. (Emerson, AR) 56964

5231 Paint, Glass & Wallpaper Stores

Ace Hardware (Searcy, AR) 57600

Ace Hardware (New Port Richey, FL) 61672
Ace Hardware (Ville Platte, LA) 70932
Ace Hardware (Raleigh, NC) 75848
Ace Hardware & Home Center (Raleigh, NC) 75850; 75852
Ace Hardware & Lumber (Pilot Point, TX) 88514
Ace Hardware&Hm Improvement (Edmond, OK) 77004
Builders Square (San Antonio, TX) 88940
Builders Square Inc. (San Antonio, TX) 88942
Coast to Coast (Hinton, OK) 77131
Coast to Coast Hardware (Elizabethtown, KY) 68273
Coast to Coast Hardware (Georgetown, KY) 68380
Coast to Coast Hardware (Murray, KY) 69122
Coast to Coast Total Hdwe (Powell, TN) 82237
Sherwin Williams Paint Stor (Fernandina, FL) 59405
Sherwin Williams Paint Stor (Fort Pierce, FL) 59813
Sherwin Williams Paint Stor (Bossier City, LA) 69732
Sherwin Williams Paint Stor (Greensboro, NC) 74911
Sherwin Williams Paint Stor (Sanford, NC) 76205
Sherwin Williams Paint Stor (Virginia Beach, VA) 92510

5251 Hardware Stores

Ace Hardware (Birmingham, AL) 55110; 55111
Ace Hardware (Dothan, AL) 55623
Ace Hardware (Belleview, FL) 58652
Ace Hardware (Bradenton, FL) 58799
Ace Hardware (Cocoa Beach, FL) 59077
Ace Hardware (Destin, FL) 59337
Ace Hardware (Fort Myers, FL) 59657
Ace Hardware (Frnandina Beach, FL) 59844
Ace Hardware (Jensen Beach, FL) 60524
Ace Hardware (Lake Mary, FL) 60637
Ace Hardware (Lake Worth, FL) 60660; 60661
Ace Hardware (Lakeland, FL) 60703
Ace Hardware (Largo, FL) 60806
Ace Hardware (Longwood, FL) 60925
Ace Hardware (Melbourne, FL) 61031; 61032
Ace Hardware (Merritt Island, FL) 61136
Ace Hardware (Panama City, FL) 62312
Ace Hardware (Perry, FL) 62496
Ace Hardware (Pinellas Park, FL) 62507
Ace Hardware (St Petersburg, FL) 62963
Ace Hardware (St. Petersburg, FL) 63075
Ace Hardware (W Palm Beach, FL) 63775
Ace Hardware (Brunswick, GA) 65397
Ace Hardware (Gray, GA) 66308
Ace Hardware (Hinesville, GA) 66349
Ace Hardware (Breaux Bridge, LA) 69740
Ace Hardware (Eunice, LA) 69847
Ace Hardware (Folsom, LA) 69857
Ace Hardware (Monroe, LA) 70349
Ace Hardware (Pearl River, LA) 70614
Ace Hardware (Shreveport, LA) 70679
Ace Hardware (Ville Platte, LA) 70932
Ace Hardware (Edgewood, MD) 71664
Ace Hardware (Madison, MS) 73135
Ace Hardware (Ahoskie, NC) 73522
Ace Hardware (Hickory, NC) 75053
Ace Hardware (Lenoir, NC) 75363
Ace Hardware (Raleigh, NC) 75848; 75849
Ace Hardware (Selma, NC) 76218
Ace Hardware (Jenks, OK) 77148
Ace Hardware (Stillwater, OK) 77833
Ace Hardware (Woodward, OK) 78254
Ace Hardware (Florence, SC) 79192
Ace Hardware (Georgetown, SC) 79270
Ace Hardware (Spartanburg, SC) 79873
Ace Hardware (West Columbia, SC) 80083
Ace Hardware (Austin, TX) 82800; 82801
Ace Hardware (Bedford, TX) 83238
Ace Hardware (Crowley, TX) 83813
Ace Hardware (Denton, TX) 84614
Ace Hardware (Fort Worth, TX) 85053
Ace Hardware (Humble, TX) 87215
Ace Hardware (Irving, TX) 87318
Ace Hardware (Malakoff, TX) 87829
Ace Hardware (Timpson, TX) 89764
Ace Hardware (Wellington, TX) 90029
Ace Hardware (Buena Vista, VA) 90497
Ace Hardware (Portsmouth, VA) 91638
Ace Hardware & Building Sup (Clanton, AL) 55518
Ace Hardware & Building Sup (Fort Mill, SC) 79231
Ace Hardware of Charlotte (Charlotte, NC) 73826
Ace Hardware Co. (Opelika, AL) 56415
Ace Hardware Co. (Dunnellon, FL) 59369
Ace Hardware Co. Inc. (New Iberia, LA) 70407
Ace Hardware Co. Inc. (Greenwood, SC) 79451
Ace Hardware of Concord (Concord, NC) 74304
Ace Hardware Corp. (Arlington, TX) 82630
Ace Hardware & Farm Supply (Saluda, SC) 79849
Ace Hardware & Garden Cente (Starke, FL) 63142
Ace Hardware Garner (Jacksonville, FL) 60157
Ace Hardware & Home Center (Raleigh, NC) 75850; 75851; 75852
Ace Hardware, Inc. (Ocala, FL) 61764
Ace Hardware Inc. (Brunswick, GA) 65398
Ace Hardware Lacombe (Lacombe, LA) 70036
Ace Hardware & Locksmith (Tampa, FL) 63302
Ace Hardware & Locksmith (Temple Ter, FL) 63673
Ace Hardware Margate (Pompano Beach, FL) 62579
Ace Hardware Marine Eqot (Fort Myers, FL) 59658
Ace Hardware No. 2822a (Donaldsonvl, LA) 69844
Ace Hardware of Palm Bay (Palm Bay, FL) 62229
Ace Hardware of Salisbury (Salisbury, NC) 76152
Ace Hardware of Screven (Screven, GA) 67534
Ace Hardware of Slidell Inc. (Slidell, LA) 70814
Ace Hardware Store (Fort Lauderdale, FL) 59424
Ace Hardware Store (Newnan, GA) 67075
Ace Hardware Store (Hobart, OK) 77132
Ace Hardware Store (San Antonio, TX) 88910
Ace Hardware Store No. 540 (W Palm Beach, FL) 63777
Ace Hardware & Supply (Fultondale, AL) 55770
Ace Hardware Supply (Oklahoma City, OK) 77291
Ace Hardware of Villa Rica (Villa Rica, GA) 68001
Ace Hardware&Equipment Co. (Waynesboro, MS) 73472
Ace Hardware&Farm Supply (Rector, AR) 57553
Ace Hardware&Hm Imprvmt Center (Angleton, TX) 82608
Ace Hardware&Home Center (Houston, TX) 85761
Ace Hardware&Home Center Inc. (Raleigh, NC) 75853
Ace Hardware&Home Center Inc. (Spring, TX) 89462
Ace Hardware&Locksmith (Brandon, FL) 58863
Ace Hardware&Lumber (Pompano Beach, FL) 62580
Ace Hareware (Sanford, FL) 62763
Black & Decker Corp. (Tarboro, NC) 76362
Builders Square (Oklahoma City, OK) 77313
Builders Square (Austin, TX) 82832
Builders Square Inc. (San Antonio, TX) 88942
Coast to Coast (Brewton, AL) 55480
Coast to Coast (Cushing, OK) 76977
Coast to Coast (Grove, OK) 77088
Coast to Coast (Georgetown, SC) 79272
Coast to Coast (Rock Hill, SC) 79818
Coast to Coast (Covington, TN) 80683
Coast to Coast (Mineral Wells, TX) 88109
Coast to Coast Hardware (Batesville, AR) 56742
Coast to Coast Hardware (Cynthiana, KY) 68248
Coast to Coast Hardware (Frankfort, KY) 68359
Coast to Coast Hardware (Georgetown, KY) 68379; 68380
Coast to Coast Hardware (Leitchfield, KY) 68512
Coast to Coast Hardware (Maysville, KY) 69087
Coast to Coast Hardware (Paris, KY) 69218
Coast to Coast Hardware (Ada, OK) 76784
Coast to Coast Hardware (Alva, OK) 76798
Coast to Coast Hardware (Mc Kenzie, TN) 81431
Coast to Coast Hardware (Bedford, TX) 83240
Coast to Coast Hardware (Fort Worth, TX) 85084
Coast to Coast Store (Mountain Home, AR) 57385
Coast to Coast Store (Perry, OK) 77701
Coast to Coast Store (Mc Kinney, TX) 87909
Coast to Coast Total Hdwe (Vinita, OK) 78222
Coast to Coast Total Hdwe (Greeneville, TN) 80884
Critikon Inc. (Irving, TX) 87338
Dixon Hardware & Furniture Co. Inc. (Camilla, GA) 65478
Home Depot Inc. the (Jacksonville, FL) 60330
Home Depot Inc. (Port Richey, FL) 62674
Lowe's (Morehead City, NC) 75624
Lowe's Home Centers Inc. (Owensboro, KY) 69184
Lowe's Home Centers Inc. (Richmond, KY) 69245
Lowe's Home Centers Inc. (Princeton, WV) 93010
Pearland Lumber Co. Inc. (Pearland, TX) 88485

Sale James J III (Madison, FL) 60968
Short & Paulk Supply Co. Inc. (Tifton, GA) 67830
Strunk Lumberyard Inc. (Key West, FL) 60579
Super Saver Station (Tulsa, OK) 78120
Ten Minute Oil Change (Del Rio, TX) 84587
Western Auto Supply Co. (Edgewood, MD) 71667
Western Auto Supply Co. Del (El Paso, TX) 84977

5261 Retail Nurseries & Garden Stores

Ace Hardware (Jacksonville, FL) 60156
Ace Hardware (New Port Richey, FL) 61672
Ace Hardware Proctor (Jacksonville, FL) 60158
Ace Hardware 3141 a (Pensacola, FL) 62376
Ace Hardware&Garden Center (Baton Rouge, LA) 69453
Agrico Chemical Co. (Clay, KY) 68202
Agrico Chemical Co. Inc. (Madisonville, KY) 69046
Builders Square Inc. (San Antonio, TX) 88942
Coast to Coast (Siloam Springs, AR) 57617; 57617
Coast to Coast Hardware (Murray, KY) 69122
Coast to Coast Store (Weatherford, OK) 78240
Gold Kist Inc. (Atlanta, GA) 64511

Pest Elimination Service (Fairview, TN) 80787

Ring Around Products Inc. (Sebree, KY) 69269

5271 Mobile Home Dealers

Cast Products Corp. (Waco, TX) 89931
Mobil Mart (Texarkana, TX) 89691

5311 Department Stores

Albertson's (Melbourne, FL) 61033
Albertson's Drug Store (San Antonio, TX) 88912; 88913
Burdines (Fort Lauderdale, FL) 59459
Burdines (Fort Myers, FL) 59685
Burdines (Hollywood, FL) 60043
Burdines Department Store Division (Miami, FL) 61211
Burdines Department Store (Gainesville, FL) 59863
Burdines Department Store (Melbourne, FL) 61039
Burlington Coat Factory (Little Rock, AR) 57263
Burlington Coat Factory (Augusta, GA) 65316
Burlington Coat Factory (Macon, GA) 66679
Burlington Coat Factory (Savannah, GA) 67457
Burlington Coat Factory (Columbia, MD) 71579
Burlington Coat Factory (Glen Burnie, MD) 71836
Burlington Coat Factory (Greensboro, NC) 74792
Burlington Coat Factory (Oklahoma City, OK) 77315
Burlington Coat Factory (Columbia, SC) 78992
Burlington Coat Factory (Kingsport, TN) 81073
Burlington Coat Factory (Memphis, TN) 81488
Burlington Coat Factory (Plano, TX) 88541
Burlington Coat Factory Warehouse (Huntsville, AL) 55895
Burlington Coat Factory Warehouse (Duluth, GA) 66028
Burlington Coat Factory Warehouse (Marietta, GA) 66758
Burlington Coat Factory Warehouse (District Heights, MD) 71651
Burlington Coat Factory Warehouse (Burlington, NC) 73745
Burlington Coat Factory Warehouse (Antioch, TN) 80165
Burlington Coat Factory Warehouse (Nashville, TN) 81912
Burlington Coat Factory Warehouse (Corpis Christi, TX) 83697
Burlington Coat Factory Warehouse (El Paso, TX) 84777
Burlington Handbag Factory Str. (Conway, SC) 79132
Burlington Manufactures Outlet Center (Burlington, NC) 73748
Burlington Outlet Mall (Burlington, NC) 73749
Burlington Shoe Outlet (Burlington, NC) 73750
Castner Knott (Huntsville, AL) 55896
Casual Corner (Northfork, WV) 92977
D.H. Holmes Co. Limited, Inc. (Little Rock, AR) 57272
Dillard Department Stores (Little Rock, AR) 57275
Dillard Department Stores (North Little Rock, AR) 57455
Dillard Department Stores (Baton Rouge, LA) 69510
Dillard Department Stores (Norman, OK) 77251
Dillard Department Stores (Austin, TX) 82859
Dillard Department Stores (Houston, TX) 86040
Dillard Department Stores (San Antonio, TX) 88972; 88974; 88975
Dillard Department Stores (Temple, TX) 89612
Dillard Department Stores (Victoria, TX) 89884
Dillard Department Stores Fort Worth Division (Fort Worth, TX) 85104
Dillard Department Stores Little Rock Division (Little Rock, AR) 57276
Dillard Department Stores San Antonio Division (San Antonia, TX) 88909
Dillards (Little Rock, AR) 57280
Dillards (Lafayette, LA) 70052
Dillards (Enid, OK) 77046
Dillards (Tulsa, OK) 77930; 77931
Duck Head Outlet Stores (Greenville, SC) 79346
Federated Department Stores (Fort Worth, TX) 85118
Gayfers (Fort Walton Beach, FL) 59827
Gayfers (Jackson, MS) 72987
Gayfers Cordova Mall (Pensacola, FL) 62431
Gayfers Dept Store (Mobile, AL) 56182
Gaylords National Corp. (Newark, DE) 57910
Hecht's (Bel Air, MD) 71338
Hecht's (Chesapeake, VA) 90582
J C Penney Catalog Sales (Elizabethtown, KY) 68280
J C Penney Catalog Sales (Georgetown, KY) 68382
J C Penney Co. (Laurel, MD) 72078
J C Penney Co. (Bristol, VA) 90480
J C Penney Co. (Hampton, VA) 91042
J C Penney Co. (Martinsville, VA) 91353
J C Penney Co. (Norfolk, VA) 91547
J C Penney Co. (Roanoke, VA) 92160
J C Penney Co. (Staunton, VA) 92322
J C Penney Co. (Winchester, VA) 92596
J C Penney Co. Inc. (Elizabethtown, KY) 68281
J C Penney Co. Inc. (Clarksville, TN) 80552
J C Penney Co. Inc. (Cleveland, TN) 80588
J C Penney Co. Inc. (Dyersburg, TN) 80753
J C Penney Co. Inc. (Charleston, WV) 92750
J C Penney Insurance (Nashville, TN) 82037
Kmart Discount Store (Slidell, LA) 70831
Kmart Discount Stores (Sanford, FL) 62768
Kmart Discount Stores (New Orleans, LA) 70513
Kmart Discount Stores (Durham, NC) 74412
Kmart Discount Stores (Houston, TX) 86378; 86379; 86380; 86382; 86383
Kmart Store (Moultrie, GA) 67055
Kmart Store (Garland, TX) 85496
Kmart Store Auto Service (Moncks Corner, SC) 79664
Kroger Co. (Brownsville, TX) 83363
Lane Bryant (Shawnee, OK) 77821
Lerner Shop (Beaumont, TX) 83169
Lord & Taylor (Falls Church, VA) 90858
Macy's (Newark, DE) 57915
Macy's (West Palm Beach, FL) 63881
Macy's (Atlanta, GA) 64666; 64667; 64668
Macy's (Decatur, GA) 65854
Macy's (Duluth, GA) 66054
Macy's (Macon, GA) 66698
Macy's (Morrow, GA) 67025
Macy's (Baltimore, MD) 71182
Macy's (Glen Burnie, MD) 71843
Macy's (Owings Mills, MD) 72189
Macy's (Mc Lean, VA) 91369
Macy's (Springfield, VA) 92288
Macy's Close-Out (Fort Lauderdale, FL) 59526
Macy's Close-Out (Pinellas Pk., FL) 62531
Macy's Close-Out (Hixson, TN) 80935
Macy's Riverchase Galleria (Birmingham, AL) 55311
Maison Blanche (Altamonte Springs, FL) 58559
Maison Blanche (Clearwater, FL) 59032
Maison Blanche (Lakeland, FL) 60746
Maison Blanche Co. (Metairie, LA) 70290
Maison Blanche Department S (Naples, FL) 61639
Marshalls (Birmingham, AL) 55313
Marshalls (Daytona Beach, FL) 59192
Marshalls (Charleston, SC) 78844
Marshalls (Fort Worth, TX) 85183
Marshalls (San Antonio, TX) 89091
Marshalls Department Store (Delray Beach, FL) 59321

Marshalls Department Store (Lakeland, FL) 60747
Marshalls Department Store (Melbourne, FL) 61077
Marshalls Department Store (Sarasota, FL) 62843
Marshalls Department Store (St Petersburg, FL) 62994
Marshalls Department Store (Gretna, LA) 69908
Marshalls Department Store (Lafayette, LA) 70074
Marshalls Department Store (New Orleans, LA) 70526
Marshalls Department Store (Gilmer, TX) 85578
Marshalls Inc. (Miami, FL) 61365
Marshalls Inc. (Pompano Beach, FL) 62607
Marshalls Inc. (Houston, TX) 86515
Marshalls Inc. (Hurst, TX) 87280
Marshalls Incorporation (Tulsa, OK) 78013
Mervyn's (Lakeland, FL) 60753
Mervyn's (Alexandria, LA) 69394
Mervyn's (Baton Rouge, LA) 69589
Mervyn's (Gretna, LA) 69909
Mervyn's (Slidell, LA) 70835
Mervyn's (Tulsa, OK) 78022; 78023
Mervyn's (Amarillo, TX) 82568
Mervyn's (Fort Worth, TX) 85187
Mervyn's (Sherman, TX) 89414
Penney J C (Frankfort, KY) 68367
Penney J C (Antioch, TN) 80173
Rite Aid (Lynchburg, VA) 91285
Rite Aid (Manassas, VA) 91321
Sam's Wholesale Club (Birmingham, AL) 55385
Service Merchandise (Fort Pierce, FL) 59812
Service Merchandise (Jacksonville, FL) 60456
Service Merchandise (Largo, FL) 60863
Service Merchandise (Bossier City, LA) 69731
Service Merchandise (Oklahoma City, OK) 77557
Service Merchandise (Tulsa, OK) 78110
Service Merchandise (Charleston, SC) 78889
Service Merchandise (Nashville, TN) 82095
Service Merchandise (Clute, TX) 83602
Service Merchandise (Lake Jackson, TX) 87586
Service Merchandise (Temple, TX) 89645
Service Merchandise (Hampton, VA) 91055
Super Saver Wholesale Club (Shreveport, LA) 70786
T J Maxx (Birmingham, AL) 55401; 55402; 55403
T J Maxx (Montgomery, AL) 56383
T J Maxx (Gainesville, FL) 59919
T J Maxx (Miami, FL) 61468
T J Maxx (Charlotte, NC) 74165
T J Maxx (Oklahoma City, OK) 77568
T J Maxx (Charleston, SC) 78895; 78896
T J Maxx (Richardson, TX) 88778
T J Maxx Store (Raleigh, NC) 75957
T J Maxx Store (Winston Salem, NC) 76686
T J Maxx Store (Carrollton, TX) 83507
Target (Louisville, KY) 69013; 69014; 69015
Target (Antioch, TN) 80176
Target (Knoxville, TN) 81255
Target (Memphis, TN) 81701; 81702
Target Stores (North Little Rock, AR) 57477
Target Stores (Louisville, KY) 69016; 69017; 69018
Target Stores (Tulsa, OK) 78132; 78133
Target Stores (Antioch, TN) 80177
Target Stores (Knoxville, TN) 81256
Target Stores (Memphis, TN) 81703; 81704
Target Stores (Abilene, TX) 82459
Target Stores (Dallas, TX) 84422
Target Stores (Fort Worth, TX) 85322
Target Stores (Garland, TX) 85543
Target Stores (Houston, TX) 86965; 86966; 86967; 86968; 86969; 86970; 86971; 86972; 86973; 86974; 86975
Target Stores (Mesquite, TX) 88005
Target Stores (Plano, TX) 88612
Target Stores (San Angelo, TX) 88903
Target Stores (Texarkana, TX) 89711
Target Stores (Tyler, TX) 89833
Target Stores (Wichita Falls, TX) 90107
Target Stores I 10 East (Houston, TX) 86976
Target Stores Inc. (Oklahoma City, OK) 77595; 77596
Target Stores Inc. (Larue, TX) 87626
Target Stores Inc. (Webster, TX) 90025
Wal Mart (Alex City, AL) 54973
Wal Mart (Anniston, AL) 55018
Wal Mart (Birmingham, AL) 55450
Wal Mart (Demopolis, AL) 55620
Wal Mart (Oneonta, AL) 56413
Wal Mart (Opelika, AL) 56431
Wal Mart (Prattville, AL) 56494
Wal Mart (Sheffield, AL) 56566
Wal Mart (Tuscaloosa, AL) 56679
Wal Mart (Benton, AR) 56781
Wal Mart (Bentonville, AR) 56794
Wal Mart (Conway, AR) 56877
Wal Mart (Fayetteville, AR) 57001
Wal Mart (Harrison, AR) 57143
Wal Mart (Hot Springs National Park, AR) 57185
Wal Mart (Mountain Home, AR) 57392
Wal Mart (Paragould, AR) 57498
Wal Mart (Walnut Ridge, AR) 57708
Wal Mart (West Memphis, AR) 57737
Wal Mart (Bradenton, FL) 58855
Wal Mart (Fort Myers, FL) 59772
Wal Mart (Gainesville, FL) 59924
Wal Mart (Jacksonville, FL) 60495; 60496
Wal Mart (Lake City, FL) 60636
Wal Mart (Marianna, FL) 61012
Wal Mart (Mary Esther, FL) 61025
Wal Mart (Melbourne, FL) 61114
Wal Mart (Mount Dora, FL) 61569
Wal Mart (Panama City, FL) 62356; 62357
Wal Mart (Pensacola, FL) 62486
Wal Mart (St. Cloud, FL) 63071
Wal Mart (Tampa, FL) 63647
Wal Mart (Cairo, GA) 65459
Wal Mart (Covington, GA) 65743
Wal Mart (Statesboro, GA) 67652
Wal Mart (Vidalia, GA) 67997
Wal Mart (Waycross, GA) 68043
Wal Mart (Abbeville, LA) 69363
Wal Mart (Bastrop, LA) 69452
Wal Mart (Baton Rouge, LA) 69683
Wal Mart (Bogalusa, LA) 69710
Wal Mart (Chalmette, LA) 69772
Wal Mart (De Ridder, LA) 69820
Wal Mart (Eunice, LA) 69849
Wal Mart (Gretna, LA) 69918
Wal Mart (Lafayette, LA) 70123
Wal Mart (Lake Charles, LA) 70179; 70180
Wal Mart (Port Allen, LA) 70650
Wal Mart (Slidell, LA) 70845
Wal Mart (Clarksdale, MS) 72681
Wal Mart (Columbia, MS) 72701
Wal Mart (Greenville, MS) 72828; 72829
Wal Mart (Gulfport, MS) 72882
Wal Mart (Mc Comb, MS) 73153
Wal Mart (Meridian, MS) 73183; 73184
Wal Mart (Ridgeland, MS) 73330
Wal Mart (Southaven, MS) 73359
Wal Mart (Albemarle, NC) 73544
Wal Mart (Jacksonville, NC) 75234
Wal Mart (Blackwell, OK) 76866
Wal Mart (Checotah, OK) 76917
Wal Mart (Duncan, OK) 76999
Wal Mart (Edmond, OK) 77026
Wal Mart (Miami, OK) 77211
Wal Mart (Nowata, OK) 77285
Wal Mart (Oklahoma City, OK) 77650; 77651
Wal Mart (Poteau, OK) 77729
Wal Mart (Shawnee, OK) 77824
Wal Mart (Tulsa, OK) 78190
Wal Mart (Aiken, SC) 78659
Wal Mart (Camden, SC) 78763
Wal Mart (Cheraw, SC) 78927; 78928
Wal Mart (Conway, SC) 79139
Wal Mart (Dillon, SC) 79166
Wal Mart (Gaffney, SC) 79269
Wal Mart (Greenville, SC) 79445
Wal Mart (Lake City, SC) 79565
Wal Mart (Lancaster, SC) 79582
Wal Mart (Lexington, SC) 79609
Wal Mart (Newberry, SC) 79728; 79729
Wal Mart (Orangeburg, SC) 79779
Wal Mart (Spartanburg, SC) 79965
Wal Mart (Summerville, SC) 79994
Wal Mart (Taylors, SC) 80040
Wal Mart (Union, SC) 80055
Wal Mart (West Columbia, SC) 80111
Wal Mart (Athens, TX) 82794
Wal Mart (Austin, TX) 83053
Wal Mart (Carthage, TX) 83526
Wal Mart (Center, TX) 83544
Wal Mart (Clute, TX) 83603
Wal Mart (Conroe, TX) 83687; 83688
Wal Mart (Corsicana, TX) 83796
Wal Mart (Denison, TX) 84611
Wal Mart (Fort Stockton, TX) 85052
Wal Mart (Fort Worth, TX) 85351; 85352
Wal Mart (Fredericksbg, TX) 85374
Wal Mart (Henderson, TX) 85734
Wal Mart (Kilgore, TX) 87502
Wal Mart (Liberty, TX) 87682
Wal Mart (Mesquite, TX) 88010
Wal Mart (Pearland, TX) 88490
Wal Mart (Rosenberg, TX) 88841
Wal Mart (San Antonio, TX) 89297
Wal Mart (Seguin, TX) 89380
Wal Mart (Victoria, TX) 89909
Wal Mart Automotive (Sallisaw, OK) 77775
Wal Mart Department Store (Magee, MS) 73139
Wal Mart Department Store N (Mobile, AL) 56253
Wal Mart Dept Store (Guymon, OK) 77119
Wal Mart Discount (El Paso, TX) 84961
Wal Mart Discount Center (Jacksonville, TX) 87428
Wal Mart Discount Cities (Mobile, AL) 56254
Wal Mart Discount Cities (Batesville, AR) 56763
Wal Mart Discount Cities (Forrest City, AR) 57014
Wal Mart Discount Cities (Fort Smith, AR) 57116
Wal Mart Discount Cities (Magnolia, AR) 57337
Wal Mart Discount Cities (Mena, AR) 57369
Wal Mart Discount Cities (N Little Rock, AR) 57434
Wal Mart Discount Cities (Nashville, AR) 57446
Wal Mart Discount Cities (Pocahontas, AR) 57545
Wal Mart Discount Cities (Van Buren, AR) 57699
Wal Mart Discount Cities (Bushnell, FL) 58902
Wal Mart Discount Cities (Chiefland, FL) 58952
Wal Mart Discount Cities (Jacksonville, FL) 60497
Wal Mart Discount Cities (MacClenny, FL) 60962
Wal Mart Discount Cities (Spring Hill, FL) 62936
Wal Mart Discount Cities (Cordele, GA) 65721
Wal Mart Discount Cities (Eastman, GA) 66163
Wal Mart Discount Cities (Forsyth, GA) 66255
Wal Mart Discount Cities (Swainsboro, GA) 67761
Wal Mart Discount Cities (Jennings, LA) 69982
Wal Mart Discount Cities (Minden, LA) 70347
Wal Mart Discount Cities (Ruston, LA) 70675
Wal Mart Discount Cities (Vivian, LA) 70938
Wal Mart Discount Cities (Corinth, MS) 72747
Wal Mart Discount Cities (Houston, MS) 72926
Wal Mart Discount Cities (Natchez, MS) 73213
Wal Mart Discount Cities (Picayune, MS) 73296
Wal Mart Discount Cities (West Point, MS) 73487
Wal Mart Discount Cities (Hickory, NC) 75105
Wal Mart Discount Cities (Southern Pines, NC) 76278
Wal Mart Discount Cities (Ada, OK) 76790
Wal Mart Discount Cities (Ardmore, OK) 76826
Wal Mart Discount Cities (Bixby, OK) 76863
Wal Mart Discount Cities (Broken Arrow, OK) 76890
Wal Mart Discount Cities (Pawhuska, OK) 77698
Wal Mart Discount Cities (Sallisaw, OK) 77776
Wal Mart Discount Cities (Wagoner, OK) 78234
Wal Mart Discount Cities (Yukon, OK) 78286
Wal Mart Discount Cities (Alvin, TX) 82517
Wal Mart Discount Cities (Bonham, TX) 83314
Wal Mart Discount Cities (Conroe, TX) 83689
Wal Mart Discount Cities (Corpus Christi, TX) 83764
Wal Mart Discount Cities (Denton, TX) 84645
Wal Mart Discount Cities (Floresville, TX) 85039
Wal Mart Discount Cities (Galveston, TX) 85470
Wal Mart Discount Cities (Giddings, TX) 85577
Wal Mart Discount Cities (Harlingen, TX) 85719
Wal Mart Discount Cities (Houston, TX) 87083
Wal Mart Discount Cities (Lake Jackson, TX) 87587
Wal Mart Discount Cities (Lewisville, TX) 87670
Wal Mart Discount Cities (Marble Falls, TX) 87841
Wal Mart Discount Cities (Nederland, TX) 88197
Wal Mart Discount Cities (Paris, TX) 88380
Wal Mart Discount Cities (Sealy, TX) 89365
Wal Mart Discount Cities (Webster, TX) 90027
Wal Mart Discount Cities (Big Stone Gap, VA) 90435
Wal-Mart Discount Cities (Lexington, VA) 91213
Wal Mart Discount City (Alabaster, AL) 54957
Wal Mart Discount City (Cullman, AL) 55556
Wal Mart Discount City (Decatur, AL) 55612
Wal Mart Discount City (Dothan, AL) 55674
Wal Mart Discount City (Fairfield, AL) 55720
Wal Mart Discount City (Guntersville, AL) 55836
Wal Mart Discount City (Mobile, AL) 56255
Wal Mart Discount City (Phenix City, AL) 56475
Wal Mart Discount City (Talladega, AL) 56603
Wal Mart Discount City (Tuscaloosa, AL) 56680
Wal Mart Discount City (Alma, AR) 56715
Wal Mart Discount City (Arkadelphia, AR) 56723
Wal Mart Discount City (El Dorado, AR) 56962
Wal Mart Discount City (Hot Springs, AR) 57166
Wal Mart Discount City (Huntsville, AR) 57194
Wal Mart Discount City (Pine Bluff, AR) 57539
Wal Mart Discount City (Fort Myers, FL) 59773
Wal Mart Discount City (Lakeland, FL) 60793
Wal Mart Discount City (Merritt Island, FL) 61148
Wal Mart Discount City (Brunswick, GA) 65429
Wal Mart Discount City (Savannah, GA) 67533
Wal Mart Discount City (Alexandria, LA) 69414
Wal Mart Discount City (Lake Charles, LA) 70181
Wal Mart Discount City (Natchitoches, LA) 70406
Wal Mart Discount City (New Iberia, LA) 70422
Wal Mart Discount City (Plaquemine, LA) 70644
Wal Mart Discount City (Shreveport, LA) 70802; 70803; 70804
Wal Mart Discount City (St. Martinville, LA) 70872
Wal Mart Discount City (Sulphur, LA) 70895
Wal Mart Discount City (Winnfield, LA) 70979
Wal Mart Discount City (Zachary, LA) 70989
Wal Mart Discount City (Fulton, MS) 72780
Wal Mart Discount City (Greenville, MS) 72830
Wal Mart Discount City (Indianola, MS) 72931
Wal Mart Discount City (Jackson, MS) 73089
Wal Mart Discount City (Louisville, MS) 73126
Wal Mart Discount City (Oxford, MS) 73247
Wal Mart Discount City (Philadelphia, MS) 73284
Wal Mart Discount City (Alva, OK) 76800
Wal Mart Discount City (Atoka, OK) 76828
Wal Mart Discount City (Collinsville, OK) 76969
Wal Mart Discount City (El Reno, OK) 77035
Wal Mart Discount City (Enid, OK) 77073
Wal Mart Discount City (Holdenville, OK) 77136
Wal Mart Discount City (Mc Alester, OK) 77201
Wal Mart Discount City (Muskogee, OK) 77234; 77235
Wal Mart Discount City (Ponca City, OK) 77716
Wal Mart Discount City (Purcell, OK) 77752
Wal Mart Discount City (Sapulpa, OK) 77798
Wal Mart Discount City (Stillwater, OK) 77846
Wal Mart Discount City (Stilwell, OK) 77852
Wal Mart Discount City (Tulsa, OK) 78194
Wal Mart Discount City (Weatherford, OK) 78244
Wal Mart Discount City (Greenville, SC) 79446
Wal Mart Discount City (Rock Hill, SC) 79843
Wal Mart Discount City (Union, SC) 80056
Wal Mart Discount City (Angleton, TX) 82615
Wal Mart Discount City (Atlanta, TX) 82798
Wal Mart Discount City (Beeville, TX) 83262
Wal Mart Discount City (Bryan, TX) 83411
Wal Mart Discount City (Burkburnett, TX) 83419
Wal Mart Discount City (Burleson, TX) 83427
Wal Mart Discount City (Cuero, TX) 83826
Wal Mart Discount City (Eagle Pass, TX) 84723
Wal Mart Discount City (El Campo, TX) 84752
Wal Mart Discount City (Ennis, TX) 85003
Wal Mart Discount City (Iowa Park, TX) 87309
Wal Mart Discount City (McAllen, TX) 87946
Wal Mart Discount City (New Boston, TX) 88204
Wal Mart Discount City (Odessa, TX) 88290
Wal Mart Discount City (Plainview, TX) 88535
Wal Mart Discount City (Porter, TX) 88684
Wal Mart Discount City (San Antonio, TX) 89299
Wal Mart Discount City (Silsbee, TX) 89437
Wal Mart Discount City (Woodville, TX) 90132
Wal Mart Discount City 542 (Houma, LA) 69974
Wal Mart Discount City No 4 (Killeen, TX) 87527
Wal Mart Discount Co. (Bristow, OK) 76875
Wal Mart Discount Cty (Gainesville, GA) 66299
Wal Mart Discount Pharmacy (Broken Bow, OK) 76899
Wal Mart Discount Pharmacy (Collinsville, OK) 76970
Wal Mart Discount Pharmacy (Stigler, OK) 77832
Wal Mart Discount Pharmacy (Victoria, TX) 89910
Wal Mart Discount Store (Selma, AL) 56541
Wal Mart Discount Store (Ville Platte, LA) 70935
Wal Mart Discount Store (Tulsa, OK) 78195
Wal Mart Discount Store (El Paso, TX) 84962
Wal Mart Discount Store (Texas City, TX) 89747
Wal-Mart Discount Store (Bedford, VA) 90424
Wal Mart Discunt Cities (New Albany, MS) 73218
Wal Mart Distribution Center (Cullman, AL) 55557
Wal Mart Inc. (Columbia, SC) 79121
Wal Mart Inc. (Pampa, TX) 88358
Wal-Mart Stores Inc. (Beaver Dam, KY) 68122
Wal-Mart Stores Inc. (Bowling Green, KY) 68164
Wal-Mart Stores Inc. (Crestwood, KY) 68247
Wal-Mart Stores Inc. (Cynthiana, KY) 68251
Wal-Mart Stores Inc. (Danville, KY) 68263

Wal-Mart Stores Inc. (Elizabethtown, KY) 68294
Wal-Mart Stores Inc. (Glasgow, KY) 68398
Wal-Mart Stores Inc. (Hardinsburg, KY) 68408
Wal-Mart Stores Inc. (Harrodsburg, KY) 68417
Wal-Mart Stores Inc. (Henderson, KY) 68460
Wal-Mart Stores Inc. (Leitchfield, KY) 68515
Wal-Mart Stores Inc. (Louisville, KY) 69035
Wal-Mart Stores Inc. (Madisonville, KY) 69073
Wal-Mart Stores Inc. (Morganfield, KY) 69109
Wal-Mart Stores Inc. (Murray, KY) 69135
Wal-Mart Stores Inc. (Nicholasville, KY) 69153
Wal-Mart Stores Inc. (Owensboro, KY) 69197; 69198
Wal-Mart Stores Inc. (Paris, KY) 69220
Wal-Mart Stores Inc. (Pewee Valley, KY) 69223
Wal-Mart Stores Inc. (Princeton, KY) 69231
Wal-Mart Stores Inc. (Shelbyville, KY) 69279
Wal-Mart Stores Inc. (Athens, TN) 80196
Wal-Mart Stores Inc. (Bolivar, TN) 80209
Wal-Mart Stores Inc. (Brownsville, TN) 80261
Wal-Mart Stores Inc. (Camden, TN) 80276
Wal-Mart Stores Inc. (Carthage, TN) 80278
Wal-Mart Stores Inc. (Clarksville, TN) 80561; 80562
Wal-Mart Stores Inc. (Cleveland, TN) 80604
Wal-Mart Stores Inc. (Collierville, TN) 80624
Wal-Mart Stores Inc. (Cookeville, TN) 80670
Wal-Mart Stores Inc. (Covington, TN) 80688
Wal-Mart Stores Inc. (Dayton, TN) 80725
Wal-Mart Stores Inc. (Dyersburg, TN) 80763; 80764
Wal-Mart Stores Inc. (Franklin, TN) 80828; 80830
Wal-Mart Stores Inc. (Gallatin, TN) 80853
Wal-Mart Stores Inc. (Greeneville, TN) 80892
Wal-Mart Stores Inc. (Harriman, TN) 80903
Wal-Mart Stores Inc. (Hermitage, TN) 80927
Wal-Mart Stores Inc. (Hohenwald, TN) 80947
Wal-Mart Stores Inc. (Jackson, TN) 81017
Wal-Mart Stores Inc. (Johnson City, TN) 81061
Wal-Mart Stores Inc. (Kingsport, TN) 81122; 81123
Wal-Mart Stores Inc. (Lebanon, TN) 81316
Wal-Mart Stores Inc. (Lenoir City, TN) 81325
Wal-Mart Stores Inc. (Madisonville, TN) 81389
Wal-Mart Stores Inc. (Manchester, TN) 81395
Wal-Mart Stores Inc. (Martin, TN) 81400
Wal-Mart Stores Inc. (Mc Minnville, TN) 81439
Wal-Mart Stores Inc. (Memphis, TN) 81754
Wal-Mart Stores Inc. (Millington, TN) 81779
Wal-Mart Stores Inc. (Morristown, TN) 81818
Wal-Mart Stores Inc. (Murfreesboro, TN) 81873
Wal-Mart Stores Inc. (Nashville, TN) 82138; 82139
Wal-Mart Stores Inc. (Newport, TN) 82174
Wal-Mart Stores Inc. (Savannah, TN) 82290
Wal-Mart Stores Inc. (Smyrna, TN) 82330
Wal-Mart Stores Inc. (Soddy Daisy, TN) 82332
Wal-Mart Stores Inc. (Springfield, TN) 82360
Wal Mart Tire/Automotive (Chickasha, OK) 76941
Wal Mart Tire & Battery Ctr (Longview, TX) 87744
Wilsons (Quincy, FL) 62734
Wilsons Department Store (Delhi, LA) 69827
Wilsons Dept Store (Eupora, MS) 72767
Winmar Co. Inc. (Louisville, KY) 69041

5331 Variety Stores

Acme Markets (Tazewell, VA) 92378
American General Corp. (Houston, TX) 85779
Burdines Variety Store (W Palm Beach, FL) 63782
Jones Store (Lawrenceville, VA) 91184
Service Merchandise (Brentwood, TN) 80234
Super Saver (Wilmington, NC) 76596
Wal Mart (Gardendale, AL) 55801
Wal Mart (De Queen, AR) 56897
Wal Mart (Northwest Smyrna Beach, FL) 61759
Wal Mart (Franklin, LA) 69860
Wal Mart (Holly Springs, MS) 72912
Wal Mart (Winona, MS) 73496
Wal Mart (Spartanburg, SC) 79966
Wal Mart Discount Cities (Woodward, OK) 78269
Wal Mart Discount Cities (Sulphur Springs, TX) 89566
Wal Mart Discount City (Huntsville, AL) 56052; 56053
Wal Mart Discount City (Bradenton, FL) 58856
Wal Mart Discount City (Dade City, FL) 59144
Wal Mart Discount City (Merritt Island, FL) 61147
Wal Mart Discount City (Orlando, FL) 62179
Wal Mart Discount City (Kinder, LA) 70027
Wal Mart Discount City (Booneville, MS) 72650
Wal Mart Discount City (Crockett, TX) 83804
Wal Mart Discount City (Mansfield, TX) 87837
Wal Mart Discount City (Navasota, TX) 88182
Wal-Mart Stores Inc. (Fulton, KY) 68378
Wal-Mart Stores Inc. (Mayfield, KY) 69082
Wal-Mart Stores Inc. (Paducah, KY) 69214
Wal-Mart Stores Inc. (Alcoa, TN) 80157
Wal-Mart Stores Inc. (Covington, TN) 80687
Wal-Mart Stores Inc. (Jackson, TN) 81016
Wal-Mart Stores Inc. (Lawrenceburg, TN) 81294
Walgreen (Brooksville, FL) 58898
Walgreen (Naples, FL) 61669

5399 Miscellaneous General Merchandise Store

Burdines (Miami, FL) 61210
Burdines (West Palm Beach, FL) 63849
Costco Wholesale (Orlando, FL) 61957
Fruit of the Loom (Campbellsvlle, KY) 68187
J C Penney Co. (Westminster, MD) 72541
J C Penney Co. (Lynchburg, VA) 91261
Kmart Discount Stores (Cedar Hill, TX) 83528
Kroger Family Center (Paris, TX) 88370
Lerner Shop (Austin, TX) 82922
Linens 'n Things (Morrisville, NC) 75668
Marshalls (Colorado City, TX) 83638
Mervyn's (Kenner, LA) 69999
Penney J C (Murfreesboro, TN) 81864
Petite Sophisticate (Durham, NC) 74422
Piggly Wiggly (Honaker, VA) 91149
Price Club (Glen Allen, VA) 90983
Price Club (Hampton, VA) 91046
Price Club (Norfolk, VA) 91567
Price Club 218 (Sterling, VA) 92346
Radio Shack (Morgan City, LA) 70392
Riverside Grocery (Clinchco, VA) 90644
Sam's Wholesale Club (Oklahoma City, OK) 77549
Sam's Wholesale Club (El Paso, TX) 84926
Sam's Wholesale Club (Fort Worth, TX) 85272
Service Merchandise (North Little Rock, AR) 57471
Service Merchandise (Gainesville, FL) 59918
Service Merchandise (Jacksonville, FL) 60457
Service Merchandise (Lakeland, FL) 60783
Service Merchandise (Pensacola, FL) 62472
Service Merchandise (Port Richey, FL) 62681
Service Merchandise (Tallahassee, FL) 63271
Service Merchandise (Louisville, KY) 69002; 69003
Service Merchandise (Owensboro, KY) 69193
Service Merchandise (Lake Charles, LA) 70171
Service Merchandise (Frederick, MD) 71747
Service Merchandise (Escatawpa, MS) 72760
Service Merchandise (Tulsa, OK) 78109
Service Merchandise (Brentwood, TN) 80233; 80234
Service Merchandise (Madison, TN) 81380
Service Merchandise (Nashville, TN) 82096
Service Merchandise (Fort Worth, TX) 85276
Service Merchandise (San Angelo, TX) 88901
Service Merchandise (San Antonio, TX) 89227; 89228
Service Merchandise Catalog (Florence, KY) 68331
Service Merchandise Catalog (Lexington, KY) 68627
Service Merchandise Catalog Sales (Florence, KY) 68332
Service Merchandise Catalog Sales (Lexington, KY) 68628
Wal Mart (Birmingham, AL) 55449
Wal Mart (Huntsville, AL) 56051
Wal Mart (Leeds, AL) 56110
Wal Mart (Benton, AR) 56782
Wal Mart (Casselberry, FL) 58944
Wal Mart (Daytona Beach, FL) 59224
Wal Mart (Sebring, FL) 62896
Wal Mart (Starke, FL) 63154
Wal Mart (Baton Rouge, LA) 69684
Wal Mart (Pascagoula, MS) 73273
Wal Mart (Goldsboro, NC) 74742
Wal Mart (Gaffney, SC) 79268
Wal Mart (Greenville, SC) 79444
Wal Mart (Dumas, TX) 84692
Wal Mart (Uvalde, TX) 89859
Wal Mart Corp. (Tallahassee, FL) 63286
Wal Mart Discount Cities (Lakeland, FL) 60792
Wal Mart Discount Cities (Macon, GA) 66723
Wal Mart Discount Cities (Chickasha, OK) 76939
Wal Mart Discount City (N Little Rock, AR) 57435
Wal Mart Discount City (Breaux Bridge, LA) 69742
Wal Mart Discount City (Jackson, MS) 73090
Wal Mart Discount City (Kosciusko, MS) 73098
Wal Mart Discount City (Beaumont, TX) 83233
Wal Mart Properties Inc. (Bentonville, AR) 56795
Wal-Mart Stores Inc. (London, KY) 68671
Wal-Mart Stores Inc. (Louisville, KY) 69034
Wal Mart Warehouse (Douglas, GA) 65981
Walgreen (Fort Lauderdale, FL) 59627
Western Auto Supply Codel (Jackson, MS) 73095

5411 Grocery Stores

ACME Markets (Dover, DE) 57775; 57776; 57777; 57778
Acme Markets (Middletown, DE) 57830
Acme Markets (Milford, DE) 57835
ACME Markets (Newark, DE) 57880; 57881; 57882
ACME Markets (Wilmington, DE) 57965; 57966; 57967; 57968; 57969; 57970
Acme Markets (Cambridge, MD) 71484
ACME Markets (Easton, MD) 71657
Acme Markets (Elkton, MD) 71669
Acme Markets (Salisbury, MD) 72333; 72334
Acme Markets (North Tazewell, VA) 91599
ACME Markets (Radford, VA) 91687
Acme Markets (Martinsburg, WV) 92926
ACME Markets Inc. (Wilmington, DE) 57971; 57972
Acme Markets of Tazewell Va (Bluefield, WV) 92699
ACME Markets of Virginia Inc. (North Tazewell, VA) 91600
Albertson's (Fort Walton Beach, FL) 59820
Albertson's (Jupiter, FL) 60529
,Albertson's (Maitland, FL) 60971
Albertson's (Mount Dora, FL) 61560
Albertson's (Winter Park, FL) 63958
Albertson's (Baton Rouge, LA) 69456
Albertson's (Lafayette, LA) 70039
Albertson's (Austin, TX) 82806; 82807; 82808; 82809
Albertson's (Bedford, TX) 83239
Albertson's (Lewisville, TX) 87644; 87645
Albertson's (San Angelo, TX) 88866
Albertson's (Wichita Falls, TX) 90063; 90064
Albertson's Drug Store (San Antonio, TX) 88912; 88913
Albertson's Food Center (Daytona Beach, FL) 59162
Albertson's Food Centers (Daytona Beach, FL) 59163
Albertson's Food Centers (Fort Lauderdale, FL) 59427
Albertson's Food Centers (Garland, TX) 85475
Albertson's Food Centers, Inc. (Lake Jackson, TX) 87578
Albertson's Food & Drug (Arlington, TX) 82631
Albertson's Food & Drug (Fort Worth, TX) 85057
Albertson's Food & Drug (Texarkana, TX) 89666
Albertson's Food & Drug Store (Lufkin, TX) 87796
Albertson's Food & Drug Store (San Antonio, TX) 88914
Albertson's Food Store, No. 4 (San Antonio, TX) 88915
Albertson's Inc. (Alexandria, LA) 69367
Albertson's Inc. (De Soto, TX) 84530
Albertson's Inc. Florida Div. (Orlando, FL) 61906
Albertson's Inc. Southern Regional Office (Orlando, FL) 61907
Albertson's Inc. Texas Div. (San Antonio, TX) 88916
Albertson's, No. 4377 (Winter Haven, FL) 63927
Albertson's, No. 4250 (Conroe, TX) 83648
Albertson's, No. 4245 (Austin, TX) 82810
Albertson's Southco (Bradenton, FL) 58801
Albertson's Supermarket (Austin, TX) 82811
AMCE Markets Inc. (Newark, DE) 57885
Arco Mini Market (Falls Church, VA) 90818
Bi-Lo (Cartersville, GA) 65498
Bi-Lo (Cochran, GA) 65570
Bi-Lo (Charlotte, NC) 73860
Bi-Lo (Matthews, NC) 75518
Bi-Lo (Manning, SC) 79629
Bi-Lo (Mt Pleasant, SC) 79672
Bi-Lo (North Augusta, SC) 79731
Bi-Lo (Sumter, SC) 80007
Bi-Lo Food Stores (Chesnee, SC) 78929
Bi-Lo Food Warehouse (Sand Springs, OK) 77779
Bi-Lo Food Warehouse (Tulsa, OK) 77889
Bi-Lo Grocery (Concord, NC) 74307
Bi-Lo Inc. (Vidalia, GA) 67984
Bi-Lo Inc. (Anderson, SC) 78667
Bi-Lo Inc. (Greenville, SC) 79302; 79303
Bi-Lo Inc. (Lexington, SC) 79601
Bi-Lo Inc. (Taylors, SC) 80035
Bi-Lo Inc. No 196 (Columbia, SC) 78977
Bi-Lo Incorporation (Pelzer, SC) 79786
Bi-Lo No One Ninety-Five (Greenville, SC) 79304
Bi-Lo No 63 (Darlington, SC) 79143
Bi-Lo No 265 (Spartanburg, SC) 79879
Bi-Lo Store (Franklin, NC) 74624
Bi-Lo Store (Rockingham, NC) 76055
Bi-Lo Store (Honea Path, SC) 79527
Bi-Lo Store (Inman, SC) 79533
Bi-Lo Store No 216 (Gainesville, GA) 66267
Bi-Lo Super Market (Beaufort, SC) 78706
Bi-Lo Super Market One-Hund (Asheville, NC) 73606
Bi-Lo Supermarket No 225 (Rock Hill, SC) 79815
Big Bear (Tuskegee, AL) 56684
Big Bear (Spartanburg, SC) 79880
Big Bear Store (Prattville, AL) 56485
Big Bear Super Market (Enterprise, AL) 55679
Bruno S Inc. (Birmingham, AL) 55172
Citgo (Oklahoma City, OK) 77329; 77330; 77331
Citgo Food Mart (Pell City, AL) 56451
Citgo Food Mart (Arlington, GA) 64149
Citgo Food Mart (Oklahoma City, OK) 77332
Citgo Food Mart (Shawnee, OK) 77814; 77815
Citgo Mini Mart (Cocoa, FL) 59066
Citgo Mini Mart (Anderson, SC) 78671
Citgo Mini Mart (Gaffney, SC) 79258
Citgo Mini Mart (Spartanburg, SC) 79888
Citgo Quick Mart (Daphne, AL) 55564
Citgo Quick Mart (Lake Charles, LA) 70136
Citgo Quick Mart (Shreveport, LA) 70697
Citgo Quick Mart (Sulphur, LA) 70883
Citgo Quick Mart (Charlotte, NC) 73899
Citgo Quick Mart (Oklahoma City, OK) 77333; 77334; 77335
Citgo Quick Mart (Tulsa, OK) 77911; 77913
Citgo Quick Mart (Columbia, SC) 79004; 79005; 79006
Crown Central Holding Corp. (Baltimore, MD) 71107
Express (Houston, TX) 86088
Exxon (Somerville, AL) 56569
Exxon (Bentonville, AR) 56784
Exxon (Coinjock, NC) 74300
Exxon (Dallas, TX) 84023; 84029
Exxon (Houston, TX) 86091; 86095; 86098; 86101; 86106
Exxon Car Care Center (Arlington, TX) 82649
Exxon Car Care Centers (Nashville, TN) 81956
Exxon Car Wash (San Antonio, TX) 88997
Exxon Co. USA (Austin, TX) 82871
Exxon Express (Concord, NC) 74310
Exxon Express (Landis, NC) 75342
Exxon Food Mart (Springdale, AR) 57631
Exxon Food Mart (New Smyrna, FL) 61695
Exxon Motor Fuel Store (Fort Worth, TX) 85114
Exxon Self Service Station (Memphis, TN) 81525; 81527
Exxon Shop (Orlando, FL) 61964
Exxon Shop (Shreveport, LA) 70720
Exxon Shop (Charlotte, NC) 73948; 73949
Exxon Shop (Fayetteville, NC) 74546
Exxon Shop (Pineville, NC) 75813
Exxon Shop (Charleston, SC) 78812
F Z Corp. (Baltimore, MD) 71117
Fleming Cos. Inc. (Oklahoma City, OK) 77362
Food Lion (Rehoboth Beach, DE) 57944
Food Lion (Brooksville, FL) 58888
Food Lion (Daytona Beach, FL) 59179
Food Lion (Fernandina Beach, FL) 59411
Food Lion (Gainesville, FL) 59877
Food Lion (Jacksonville, FL) 60308; 60309; 60310; 60311; 60312
Food Lion (Lake Wales, FL) 60653
Food Lion (Live Oak, FL) 60910
Food Lion (Northwest Smyrna Beach, FL) 61757
Food Lion (Ocala, FL) 61799
Food Lion (Ocoee, FL) 61833
Food Lion (Orange Park, FL) 61884; 61885

Kroger Co. (Scott Depot, WV) 93040
Kroger Co. (South Charleston, WV) 93050
Kroger Co. (St. Albans, WV) 93067; 93068
Kroger Co. (Weirton, WV) 93093; 93094
Kroger Co. (Weston, WV) 93106
Kroger Co. (Wheeling, WV) 93114; 93115
Kroger Co. (White Sulphur Springs, WV) 93127
Kroger Co. (Williamson, WV) 93129
Kroger Co. Deli (Louisville, KY) 68814; 68815
Kroger Co. Inc (De Witt, AR) 56902
Kroger Co. Inc. (N Little Rock, AR) 57409
Kroger Co. Inc. (Summerville, SC) 79988
Kroger Co. No 642 (N Little Rock, AR) 57410
Kroger Co. No 346 (Jackson, MS) 73009
Kroger Company No 323 (Houston, TX) 86409
Kroger Company No 286 (San Antonio, TX) 89059
Kroger Company No 291 (Houston, TX) 86410
Kroger Company No 292 (Houston, TX) 86411
Kroger Co. Store (New Braunfels, TX) 88211
Kroger Deli&Bakery (Magnolia, AR) 57333
Kroger Delicatessen (El Dorado, AR) 56952
Kroger Delicatessen (Morrilton, AR) 57378
Kroger Delicatessen (Searcy, AR) 57605
Kroger Delicatessen (Stuttgart, AR) 57661
Kroger Family Center (Lake Charles, LA) 70144
Kroger Family Center (Alice, TX) 82484
Kroger Family Center (College Sta, TX) 83610
Kroger Family Center (Paris, TX) 88370
Kroger Family Center (Victoria, TX) 89892
Kroger Family Centers (Corpus Christi, TX) 83729
Kroger Family Cntr (Marshall, TX) 87855
Kroger Family Cntrs (Corpus Christi, TX) 83730
Kroger Food & Drug (Richmond, KY) 69244
Kroger Food & Drug (Arlington, TX) 82675
Kroger Food & Drug (Fort Worth, TX) 85154
Kroger Food & Drug Store (Arlington, TX) 82676
Kroger Food & Drugs Store N (Houston, TX) 86413
Kroger Food Store (Alexandria, LA) 69388
Kroger Food Store (Mc Comb, MS) 73147
Kroger Food Store (Oxford, MS) 73241
Kroger Food Store (Tupelo, MS) 73408
Kroger Food Store (North Augusta, SC) 79735
Kroger Food Store (Arlington, TX) 82677; 82678
Kroger Food Store (Collinsville, TX) 83634
Kroger Food Store (Dallas, TX) 84177
Kroger Food Store (Denison, TX) 84599
Kroger Food Store (Euless, TX) 85014
Kroger Food Store (Palestine, TX) 88342
Kroger Food Store No 401 (Fort Worth, TX) 85155
Kroger Food Store No 464 (Dallas, TX) 84178
Kroger Food Store No 694 (Fort Worth, TX) 85156
Kroger Food Store No 224 (Fort Worth, TX) 85157
Kroger Food Store Number 60 (Fort Worth, TX) 85158
Kroger Food Stores (Alief, TX) 82491
Kroger Food Stores (Houston, TX) 86414; 86416; 86418; 86421; 86423
Kroger Food Stores (Irving, TX) 87362; 87365
Kroger Food Stores (Lewisville, TX) 87650
Kroger Food&Drug (Richardson, TX) 88746
Kroger Food&Drug Store (Plano, TX) 88577
Kroger Food&Drug Stores (Dallas, TX) 84185
Kroger Food&Drug Stores (Duncanville, TX) 84697
Kroger Groc (Sheffield, AL) 56551; 56552
Kroger Grocery (Huntsville, AL) 55962
Kroger Grocery (Jackson, MS) 73010
Kroger No 305 (Raleigh, NC) 75923
Kroger No 395 (Biloxi, MS) 72627
Kroger Pharmacy (Huntsville, AL) 55963
Kroger Pharmacy (Batesville, AR) 56758
Kroger Pharmacy (Winston Salem, NC) 76674
Kroger Pharmacy (Texas City, TX) 89722
Kroger Sav on Food and Drug (Irmo, SC) 79539
Kroger Sav on Food&Drug (Charlotte, NC) 74065
Kroger Sav on Food&Drugs (West Columbia, SC) 80097
Kroger Sav-On (Savannah, GA) 67495
Kroger Sav-On (Charlotte, NC) 74066; 74067
Kroger Sav-On (Myrtle Beach, SC) 79703
Kroger Sav-On (Summerville, SC) 79989
Kroger Sav-On Food & Drugs (Myrtle Beach, SC) 79704
Kroger Savon Food&Drugs (Sumter, SC) 80023
Kroger Store (Sulphur, LA) 70885
Kroger Store (Galveston, TX) 85445
Kroger Store (Houston, TX) 86427; 86428; 86429
Kroger Store No 542 (Pine Bluff, AR) 57524
Kroger Store No 108 (Texas City, TX) 89723
Kroger Store No 632 (Dallas, TX) 84186
Kroger Stores (Dallas, TX) 84187
Kroger Stores (Duncanville, TX) 84698
Kroger Stores (Garland, TX) 85500
Kroger Stores (Mesquite, TX) 87972
Kroger Stores No 421 (Dallas, TX) 84188
Kroger Super Market (Bossier City, LA) 69721
Kroger Super Market (Shreveport, LA) 70743; 70744
Kroger Super Markets (Shreveport, LA) 70745
Kroger Supermarket (Savannah, GA) 67498
Kroger Supermarket (Jackson, MS) 73011
Kroger Supermarket (Dallas, TX) 84189
Kroger Zone Office (Roanoke, VA) 92167
Krogerco (Winchester, KY) 69345
Krogers (Hartselle, AL) 55857
Kroger's (Paragould, AR) 57493
Kroger's (West Memphis, AR) 57726
Kroger's (Macon, GA) 66697
Krogers (Lake Charles, LA) 70146
Kroger's (Grenada, MS) 72842
Kroger's (Gulfport, MS) 72861
Krogers (High Point, NC) 75143
Krogers (Shelbyville, TN) 82316
Mapco Express (Merritt, FL) 61127
Mini Mart (Eufaula, AL) 55701
Mini Mart (Gurley, AL) 55837
Mini Mart the (Huntsville, AL) 55975
Mini Mart (Trinity, AL) 56616
Mini Mart (Dumas, AR) 56913
Mini Mart (Brunswick, GA) 65419
Mini Mart (Kaplan, LA) 69989
Mini Mart (Lake Charles, LA) 70149
Mini Mart (Frederick, MD) 71733
Mini Mart (Laurinburg, NC) 75355
Mini Mart (Ardmore, OK) 76815
Mini Mart (Coweta, OK) 76974
Mini Mart (Fairview, OK) 77078
Mini Mart (Sallisaw, OK) 77771
Mini Mart (Wewoka, OK) 78247
Mini Mart (Columbia, SC) 79055
Mini Mart (Dillon, SC) 79162
Mini Mart (Spartanburg, SC) 79920
Mini Mart (Athens, TN) 80192
Mini Mart (Dyersburg, TN) 80755
Mini Mart (Helenwood, TN) 80906
Mini Mart (Conroe, TX) 83669
Mini Mart (Crosbyton, TX) 83808
Mini Mart (Kilgore, TX) 87491
Mini Mart (Palestine, TX) 88343
Mini Mart (San Angelo, TX) 88886
Mini Mart (Troup, TX) 89785
Mini Mart (Richmond, VA) 91932
Mini Mart Food Store (Choudrant, LA) 69779
Mini Mart Foods Inc. (Bowling Green, KY) 68148
Mini Mart Grocery (De Quincy, LA) 69807
Mini Mart Grocery (Kerrville, TX) 87477; 87478; 87479; 87480
Mini Mart No 413 (White Oak, TX) 90055
Mini Mart No 3 (Fayetteville, AR) 56983
Mini Mart No 12 (Fredericksburg, TX) 85376
Mini Mart No 2 (Sallisaw, OK) 77772
Mini Mart No 2 (Port Arthur, TX) 88638
Mini Mart Number Two (Stewart, MS) 73372
Mini Mart Rosehill Inc. (Tomball, TX) 89772
Mini Mart 7 (Ingram, TX) 87305
Mini Mart Shopping Center (Plaucheville, LA) 70645
Mini Mart 6 (Comfort, TX) 83643
Mini Mart&Service (Bonifay, FL) 58758
Mobil Mart (Pinellas Park, FL) 62522
Mobil Mart Inc. (Thomasville, NC) 76380
Mobil Mart (Mobil Oil Corp) (Orlando, FL) 62061
Mobil Mart No 3 (Port Arthur, TX) 88639
Mobil Oil Corp. (Fort Lauderdale, FL) 59540
Piggly Wiggly (Abbeville, AL) 54951
Piggly Wiggly (Atmore, AL) 55051
Piggly Wiggly (Auburn, AL) 55067
Piggly Wiggly (Bay Minette, AL) 55076
Piggly Wiggly (Birmingham, AL) 55331; 55332; 55333; 55335
Piggly Wiggly (Brewton, AL) 55483
Piggly Wiggly (Butler, AL) 55496
Piggly Wiggly (Citronelle, AL) 55517
Piggly Wiggly (Courtland, AL) 55536
Piggly Wiggly (Cullman, AL) 55547
Piggly Wiggly (Dadeville, AL) 55558
Piggly Wiggly (Dothan, AL) 55659; 55660
Piggly Wiggly (Enterprise, AL) 55689
Piggly Wiggly (Evergreen, AL) 55710
Piggly Wiggly (Florala, AL) 55734
Piggly Wiggly (Florence, AL) 55741
Piggly Wiggly (Geneva, AL) 55804
Piggly Wiggly (Greensboro, AL) 55812
Piggly Wiggly (Grove Hill, AL) 55820
Piggly Wiggly (Guntersville, AL) 55831
Piggly Wiggly (Haleyville, AL) 55843; 55844
Piggly Wiggly (Hamilton, AL) 55849
Piggly Wiggly (Hartford, AL) 55853
Piggly Wiggly (Hartselle, AL) 55860
Piggly Wiggly (Headland, AL) 55862
Piggly Wiggly (Huntsville, AL) 55993
Piggly Wiggly (Jackson, AL) 56068
Piggly Wiggly (Killen, AL) 56096
Piggly Wiggly (Lanett, AL) 56104
Piggly Wiggly (Monroeville, AL) 56267
Piggly Wiggly (Montevallo, AL) 56275
Piggly Wiggly (Moulton, AL) 56397; 56398
Piggly Wiggly (Opp, AL) 56434
Piggly Wiggly (Parrish, AL) 56446
Piggly Wiggly (Phenix City, AL) 56463; 56464; 56465; 56466; 56467; 56468; 56469
Piggly Wiggly (Phil Campbell, AL) 56480
Piggly Wiggly (Roanoke, AL) 56501
Piggly Wiggly (Rogersville, AL) 56506
Piggly Wiggly (Russellville, AL) 56509
Piggly Wiggly (Samson, AL) 56512
Piggly Wiggly (Selma, AL) 56534
Piggly Wiggly (Shelby, AL) 56567
Piggly Wiggly (Sulligent, AL) 56574
Piggly Wiggly (Tuscaloosa, AL) 56666; 56667
Piggly Wiggly (Union Springs, AL) 56687
Piggly Wiggly (Winfield, AL) 56709; 56710
Piggly Wiggly (Arkadelphia, AR) 56718; 56719
Piggly Wiggly (Bald Knob, AR) 56737
Piggly Wiggly (Camden, AR) 56838
Piggly Wiggly (Clarksville, AR) 56849
Piggly Wiggly (Conway, AR) 56867
Piggly Wiggly (De Queen, AR) 56892
Piggly Wiggly (Gurdon, AR) 57126
Piggly Wiggly (Hot Springs National Park, AR) 57178; 57179; 57180; 57181
Piggly Wiggly (Morrilton, AR) 57379
Piggly Wiggly (Mulberry, AR) 57398
Piggly Wiggly (Murfreesboro, AR) 57399
Piggly Wiggly (Osceola, AR) 57484
Piggly Wiggly (Ozark, AR) 57486
Piggly Wiggly (Stuttgart, AR) 57662
Piggly Wiggly (Wynne, AR) 57743
Piggly Wiggly (Brandon, FL) 58875
Piggly Wiggly (Cantonment, FL) 58911
Piggly Wiggly (Century, FL) 58947
Piggly Wiggly (Clearwater, FL) 59036
Piggly Wiggly (Cross City, FL) 59129
Piggly Wiggly (De Funiak Spring, FL) 59240
Piggly Wiggly (Dunedin, FL) 59364
Piggly Wiggly (Havana, FL) 59968
Piggly Wiggly (Lakeland, FL) 60761
Piggly Wiggly (Lynn Haven, FL) 60956
Piggly Wiggly (Marianna, FL) 61005
Piggly Wiggly (Miami, FL) 61390
Piggly Wiggly (Milton, FL) 61549
Piggly Wiggly (Ocoee, FL) 61835
Piggly Wiggly (Orlando, FL) 62080
Piggly Wiggly (Vero Beach, FL) 63766
Piggly Wiggly (Atlanta, GA) 65019
Piggly Wiggly (Brunswick, GA) 65420
Piggly Wiggly (Cairo, GA) 65447
Piggly-Wiggly (Calhoun, GA) 65473
Piggly Wiggly (Camilla, GA) 65481
Piggly Wiggly (Colquitt, GA) 65613
Piggly Wiggly (Cordele, GA) 65714; 65715
Piggly Wiggly (Douglas, GA) 65972
Piggly Wiggly (Dublin, GA) 66012
Piggly Wiggly (Eastman, GA) 66159
Piggly Wiggly (Fitzgerald, GA) 66211
Piggly Wiggly (Griffin, GA) 66319
Piggly Wiggly (Hazlehurst, GA) 66348
Piggly Wiggly (Hinesville, GA) 66355
Piggly Wiggly (Louisville, GA) 66621
Piggly Wiggly (Lyons, GA) 66632
Piggly Wiggly (Macon, GA) 66703
Piggly Wiggly (Milledgeville, GA) 66981; 66982
Piggly Wiggly (Moultrie, GA) 67059; 67060; 67061
Piggly Wiggly (Pelham, GA) 67257
Piggly Wiggly (Quitman, GA) 67289
Piggly Wiggly (Sandersville, GA) 67430
Piggly Wiggly (Savannah, GA) 67506; 67507
Piggly Wiggly (Statesboro, GA) 67641
Piggly Wiggly (Sylvania, GA) 67770
Piggly Wiggly (Sylvester, GA) 67775
Piggly Wiggly (Vidalia, GA) 67989; 67990
Piggly Wiggly (Warner Robins, GA) 68018
Piggly Wiggly (Waycross, GA) 68036
Piggly Wiggly (Ball, LA) 69439
Piggly Wiggly (Baton Rouge, LA) 69597; 69598
Piggly Wiggly (Bernice, LA) 69696
Piggly Wiggly (De Ridder, LA) 69816
Piggly Wiggly (Ferriday, LA) 69853
Piggly Wiggly (Haynesville, LA) 69945
Piggly Wiggly (Homer, LA) 69948
Piggly Wiggly (Jennings, LA) 69980
Piggly Wiggly (Jonesboro, LA) 69984
Piggly Wiggly (Jonesville, LA) 69986
Piggly Wiggly (Lafayette, LA) 70082; 70083
Piggly Wiggly (Mansfield, LA) 70215
Piggly Wiggly (Minden, LA) 70343; 70344
Piggly Wiggly (Plaquemine, LA) 70641
Piggly Wiggly (Ruston, LA) 70670
Piggly Wiggly (Shreveport, LA) 70763
Piggly Wiggly (Springhill, LA) 70853; 70855
Piggly Wiggly (Vivian, LA) 70936
Piggly Wiggly (West Monroe, LA) 70955
Piggly Wiggly (Amory, MS) 72585
Piggly Wiggly (Ashland, MS) 72591
Piggly Wiggly (Bay Springs, MS) 72604
Piggly Wiggly (Belmont, MS) 72610
Piggly Wiggly (Biloxi, MS) 72631
Piggly Wiggly (Booneville, MS) 72646
Piggly Wiggly (Charleston, MS) 72664
Piggly Wiggly (Clarksdale, MS) 72677
Piggly Wiggly (Columbia, MS) 72699
Piggly Wiggly (Crystal Springs, MS) 72750
Piggly Wiggly (Dennis, MS) 72751
Piggly Wiggly (Durant, MS) 72752
Piggly Wiggly (Fulton, MS) 72779
Piggly Wiggly (Greenwood, MS) 72837; 72838
Piggly Wiggly (Houston, MS) 72920
Piggly Wiggly (Indianola, MS) 72929
Piggly Wiggly (Laurel, MS) 73106
Piggly Wiggly (Leakesville, MS) 73110
Piggly Wiggly (Lexington, MS) 73115
Piggly Wiggly (Louisville, MS) 73124
Piggly Wiggly (Lucedale, MS) 73128
Piggly Wiggly (Morton, MS) 73190
Piggly Wiggly (Natchez, MS) 73206; 73207; 73208
Piggly Wiggly (Poplarville, MS) 73305
Piggly Wiggly (Prentiss, MS) 73307
Piggly Wiggly (Ruleville, MS) 73334
Piggly Wiggly (Sardis, MS) 73338
Piggly Wiggly (Smithville, MS) 73345
Piggly Wiggly (Sumrall, MS) 73375
Piggly Wiggly (Taylorsville, MS) 73379
Piggly Wiggly (Tunica, MS) 73383
Piggly Wiggly (Tylertown, MS) 73431
Piggly Wiggly (Union, MS) 73432
Piggly Wiggly (Vaiden, MS) 73444
Piggly Wiggly (Water Valley, MS) 73470
Piggly Wiggly (Wiggins, MS) 73492
Piggly Wiggly (Winona, MS) 73494
Piggly Wiggly (Benson, NC) 73685
Piggly Wiggly (Castle Hayne, NC) 73805
Piggly Wiggly (Clinton, NC) 74293; 74294; 74295
Piggly Wiggly (Dunn, NC) 74376
Piggly Wiggly (Faison, NC) 74516
Piggly Wiggly (Fayetteville, NC) 74571
Piggly Wiggly (Fuquay-Varina, NC) 74640
Piggly Wiggly (Garland, NC) 74644
Piggly Wiggly (Goldsboro, NC) 74729; 74730
Piggly Wiggly (Grantsboro, NC) 74756
Piggly Wiggly (Greenville, NC) 74971
Piggly Wiggly (Jacksonville, NC) 75223
Piggly Wiggly (Kinston, NC) 75327
Piggly Wiggly (Lumberton, NC) 75470
Piggly Wiggly (Maxton, NC) 75535
Piggly Wiggly (Midway Park, NC) 75560
Piggly Wiggly (Murphy, NC) 75706
Piggly Wiggly (Pembroke, NC) 75794
Piggly Wiggly (Pikeville, NC) 75797
Piggly Wiggly (Red Springs, NC) 75993
Piggly Wiggly (Reidsville, NC) 76008
Piggly Wiggly (Richlands, NC) 76027
Piggly Wiggly (Rocky Mount, NC) 76098
Piggly Wiggly (Roseboro, NC) 76117
Piggly Wiggly (Selma, NC) 76226
Piggly Wiggly (Smithfield, NC) 76264
Piggly Wiggly (St. Pauls, NC) 76307
Piggly Wiggly (Swansboro, NC) 76354; 76355
Piggly Wiggly (Tarboro, NC) 76364

Texaco Food Mart (Bessemer, AL) 55104
Texaco Food Mart (Birmingham, AL) 55419
Texaco Food Mart (Beebe, AR) 56769
Texaco Food Mart (Fort Walton Beach, FL) 59840
Texaco Food Mart (Haines City, FL) 59954; 59955
Texaco Food Mart (Kissimmee, FL) 60604; 60605
Texaco Food Mart (Lake City, FL) 60631
Texaco Food Mart (Lakeland, FL) 60786
Texaco Food Mart (Live Oak, FL) 60921
Texaco Food Mart (Sanford, FL) 62782
Texaco Food Mart (Sebring, FL) 62895
Texaco Food Mart (Starke, FL) 63153
Texaco Food Mart (Tallahassee, FL) 63279
Texaco Food Mart (Tampa, FL) 63612; 63613; 63614; 63615
Texaco Food Mart (Winter Garden, FL) 63925
Texaco Food Mart (Winter Park, FL) 63996
Texaco Food Mart (Bainbridge, GA) 65371
Texaco Food Mart (Hattiesburg, MS) 72898
Texaco Food Mart (Greensboro, NC) 74920
Texaco Food Mart (Raleigh, NC) 75962
Texaco-Food Mart (Smithfield, NC) 76269
Texaco Food Mart (Guymon, OK) 77112
Texaco Food Mart (Oklahoma City, OK) 77602
Texaco-Food Mart (Tulsa, OK) 78143
Texaco Food Mart (North Augusta, SC) 79740
Texaco Food Mart (Dyersburg, TN) 80761
Texaco Food Mart (Denton, TX) 84640
Texaco Food Mart (Irving, TX) 87412
Texaco Food Mart (Lubbock, TX) 87785
Texaco Food Mart (San Antonio, TX) 89259; 89261
Texaco Food Mart (Tyler, TX) 89836
Texaco Food Mart (Wichita Falls, TX) 90109
Texaco Food Mart No 4 (Jamestown, NC) 75243
Texaco Food Mart No 7 (Huntsville, AL) 56035
Texaco Food Mart No 6 (Sheffield, AL) 56564
Texaco Food Mart No 2 (Beaumont, TX) 83223
Texaco Food Mart 160 (Tulsa, OK) 78144
Texaco Foodmart (Temple Terrace, FL) 63679
Texaco Inc. (Mobile, AL) 56248
Texaco Inc. (Tampa, FL) 63618
Texaco Inc. (Memphis, TN) 81706
Texaco Kwik Mart No 19 (Goldsboro, NC) 74738
Texaco Mart (Tulsa, OK) 78152
Texaco Mini Mart (Aliceville, AL) 54984
Texaco Mini Mart Ii (Daytona Beach, FL) 59218
Texaco Mini Mart & Serv Sta (Metairie, LA) 70317
Texaco No 208 (Tampa, FL) 63619
Texaco Pep Stop (Humble, TX) 87250
Wal-Mart Stores Inc. (Gallatin, TN) 80854
West Foods (Arlington, GA) 64150
Wilsons (Conway, SC) 79140
Winn-Dixie Louisville Inc. (Louisville, KY) 69042
Winn-Dixie Stores (Danville, VA) 90723; 90724
Winn-Dixie Texas Inc. No. 248 (San Angelo, TX) 88907
Zippy Mart (Chesapeake, VA) 90613
Zippy Mart Inc. (Birmingham, AL) 55462
Zippy Mart Inc. (Grant, FL) 59929
Zippy Mart Inc. (Melbourne, FL) 61122; 61123
Zippy Mart Inc. (Rockledge, FL) 62750
Zippy Mart Inc. (Jesup, GA) 66375
Zippy Mart Inc. (Valdosta, GA) 67982; 67983

Zippy Mart Inc. (Allendale, SC) 78660
Zippy Mart Inc. (Beaufort, SC) 78720
Zippy Mart Inc. (Summerton, SC) 79980
Zippy Mart Inc. (West Columbia, SC) 80112
Zippy Mart Inc. No. 883 (Walterboro, SC) 80081
Zippy Mart Inc. No. 515 (Adamsville, AL) 54952
Zippy Mart Inc. No. 516 (Bessemer, AL) 55108

5421 Meat & Fish Markets

Big Bear Super Market (Waller, TX) 89986
Piggly Wiggly (Centre, AL) 55505
Piggly Wiggly (Chatom, AL) 55509
Piggly Wiggly (Dadeville, AL) 55559
Piggly Wiggly (Gurley, AL) 55838
Piggly Wiggly (Jemison, AL) 56093
Piggly Wiggly (Oakdale, LA) 70599
Piggly Wiggly (Ringgold, LA) 70665
Piggly Wiggly (Vidalia, LA) 70930
Piggly Wiggly (Collins, MS) 72696
Piggly Wiggly (Eupora, MS) 72765
Piggly Wiggly (Starkville, MS) 73368
Piggly Wiggly (Durant, OK) 77002
Piggly Wiggly (Idabel, OK) 77143
Piggly Wiggly (Loris, SC) 79616
Piggly Wiggly (Myrtle Beach, SC) 79707
Piggly Wiggly (Ballinger, TX) 83089
Piggly Wiggly (Cleburne, TX) 83581
Piggly Wiggly (Joaquin, TX) 87443
Piggly Wiggly (Slaton, TX) 89443
Piggly Wiggly (Spur, TX) 89498
Piggly Wiggly (Stamford, TX) 89511
Piggly Wiggly (Coeburn, VA) 90646
Stop & Shop (Shreveport, LA) 70785

5431 Fruit & Vegetable Markets

Eckerd Drug Co. (Birmingham, AL) 55229
Piggly Wiggly (Indianola, MS) 72929

5441 Candy, Nut & Confectionery Stores

Sun Diamond Growers (Robertsdale, AL) 56503
Wal Mart Discount Pharmacy (West Helena, AR) 57715

5451 Dairy Products Stores

Associated Milk Producers Inc. (Lawton, OK) 77154
Associated Milk Producers Inc. (Tulsa, OK) 77881
Associated Milk Producers Inc. (Arlington, TX) 82633
Borden Inc. Dairy (Oklahoma City, OK) 77310; 77311
Borden Inc. Grocery & Specialty Products (Oklahoma City, OK) 77312
Hiland Dairy Co. (Springdale, AR) 57634
Tg Lee Foods Inc. (Tampa, FL) 63621
Yoplait USA Inc. (Richardson, TX) 88792

5461 Retail Bakeries

Flowers Baking Co. (Danville, VA) 90693
Flowers Baking Co. (Roanoke, VA) 92153
Flowers Baking Co. (Suffolk, VA) 92366
Flowers Baking Co. of Lynchburg (Lynchburg, VA) 91248
Giant Food Deli (Memphis, TN) 81614
Giant Food Market Inc. Bakery & Deli (Memphis, TN) 81616
Kroger Co (Hot Springs National Park, AR) 57173
Piggly Wiggly (Springhill, LA) 70854
Piggly Wiggly (Snyder, TX) 89449
Piggly Wiggly (Lebanon, VA) 91189
Publix Super Market (Boca Raton, FL) 58731
Publix Super Market (Daytona Beach, FL) 59205

Publix Super Market (Fort Myers, FL) 59742; 59744
Publix Super Market (Fort Myers Fl, FL) 59784
Publix Super Market (Miami, FL) 61407; 61409
Publix Super Market (Palm Beach, FL) 62260
Publix Super Market (St Petersburg, FL) 63012
Publix Super Market (Tallahassee, FL) 63259
Publix Super Markets (Fort Myers, FL) 59745
Publix Super Markets (Fort Myers Fl, FL) 59785
Publix Super Markets (Miami, FL) 61417
Publix Super Markets (St. Petersburg, FL) 63131
Quality Bakery (Enid, OK) 77063

5499 Miscellaneous Food Stores

Ace Hardware & Marine (Morehead City, NC) 75610
Albertson's (Winter Park, FL) 63958
Bi-Lo Inc. (Kannapolis, NC) 75253
Exxon Co. (Tomball, TX) 89768
Food Lion (Ponte Vedra, FL) 62648
Food Lion (Ashland, VA) 90402
Food Lion Inc. (Ponte Vedra, FL) 62649
Food Lion Inc. (Ashland, VA) 90403
Golden Poultry Co. Inc. (Douglas, GA) 65969
Kentucky Fried Chicken (Fort Myers, FL) 59708
Kroger Co. (Lanett, AL) 56102
Kroger Co. (Gainesville, GA) 66279
Kroger Delicatessen (Cleveland, MS) 72684
Kroger Food Co. (Albany, GA) 64080
Kroger 950 (Greenville, MS) 72807
Kroger Sav on (Fayetteville, NC) 74563
Kroger Stores (Monroe, NC) 75583
Kroger 377 (Clinton, MS) 72687
Kroger 325 (Starkville, MS) 73366
Mini Mart Food Store (Arnaudville, LA) 69433
Piggly Wiggly (Birmingham, AL) 55334
Piggly Wiggly (Panama City, FL) 62337
Piggly Wiggly (Bowdon, GA) 65389
Piggly Wiggly (Donalsonville, GA) 65917
Piggly Wiggly (Fort Valley, GA) 66259
Piggly Wiggly (Tallulah, LA) 70908
Piggly Wiggly (Texarkana, TX) 89694
Piggly Wiggly Southern Inc. (Fort Valley, GA) 66260
Pilgrim's Pride Corp. (Lufkin, TX) 87811
Texaco Kwik Trip (Shreveport, LA) 70795
Universal Foods Corp. (Dallas, TX) 84475
Valspar Corp. (New Orleans, LA) 70583
Wal Mart Pharmacy (Edmond, OK) 77027

5500 Automotive Dealers & Service Stations

Hyster Co. (Berea, KY) 68127

5511 New & Used Car Dealers

Park Corp. (Williamsport, MD) 72573
Ryder Truck Rental & Leasing (Morristown, TN) 81808

5521 Used Car Dealers

Big Bear (Haines City, FL) 59943
Circuit City (Norfolk, VA) 91502
Coast to Coast Car Sales (Pensacola, FL) 62416
Hertz Rent-A-Car Licensee (Oklahoma City, OK) 77381
Mini Mart (Hillsville, VA) 91143
Pizza Hut (Smithfield, NC) 76266
Rite Aid Discount Pharmacy (Kingsport, TN) 81117
Ryder Truck Rental (Hinesville, GA) 66357
Texas Gas Transmission (Benton, KY) 68126
United Parcel Service (Daytona Beach, FL) 59223

5531 Automobile & Home Supply Stores

APS Acquisition Corp. (Houston, TX) 85803
APS Holding Corp. (Houston, TX) 85804
APS Inc. (Houston, TX) 85805
Arkansas Best (Fort Smith, AR) 57022
Arkansas Best Corp. (Fort Smith, AR) 57023
Bear Automotive Service Equipment (Louisville, KY) 68699
Big A Auto Parts Inc. (Houston, TX) 85882
Brad Ragan, Inc. (Charlotte, NC) 73864
Coast to Coast (Beebe, AR) 56767
Coast to Coast (Monticello, AR) 57371
Coast to Coast (Covington, GA) 65725
Coast to Coast (Sterlington, LA) 70879
Coast to Coast (Pryor, OK) 77738
Coast to Coast (Yale, OK) 78275
Coast to Coast (Andrews, TX) 82594
Coast to Coast (Borger, TX) 83316
Coast to Coast Auto (Butler, AL) 55494
Coast to Coast Auto (Alpine, TX) 82499
Coast to Coast Home & Auto (Carlisle, AR) 56843
Coast to Coast Home & Auto (Sandersville, GA) 67428
Coast to Coast Home & Auto (Oberlin, LA) 70602
Coast to Coast Home & Auto (Vidalia, LA) 70929
Coast to Coast Home & Auto (Indianola, MS) 72927
Coast to Coast Home & Auto (Cordell, OK) 76973
Coast to Coast Home & Auto (Lyles, TN) 81364
Coast to Coast Home & Auto (Hereford, TX) 85739
Coast to Coast Home&Auto (Alva, OK) 76799
Coast to Coastsupply (Tishomingo, OK) 77869
Duracell International Inc. (Jacksonville, FL) 60264
Eaton Corp. (Harrodsburg, KY) 68411
Exxon (Dierks, AR) 56904
Exxon (Hilton Head Island, SC) 79513
Exxon (Cushing, TX) 83827
Exxon Car Care Center (Memphis, TN) 81520
Exxon Co. USA (Madisonville, TX) 87827
Federal Mogul Corp. (Oklahoma City, OK) 77357
Kelly Springfield Tire (Hialeah, FL) 59991
Kelly-Springfield Tire Co. T (Tyler, TX) 89806
Kmart Automotive Center (Fort Lauderdale, FL) 59521
Kmart Discount Stores (Albany, GA) 64079; 64079
Kmart Discount Stores (De Soto, TX) 84535
Kmart Discount Stores (Houston, TX) 86381
Kmart Pharmacy (Mc Allen, TX) 87888
Kmart Store (Garland, TX) 85496; 85497
Maison Blanche Car Care Cen (Baton Rouge, LA) 69585
Mobil Station (Pensacola, FL) 62449
Oshkosh Truck Corp. (Alvin, TX) 82511
Pizza Hut (Statesville, NC) 76333
Texaco Service Station (Boaz, AL) 55477
Texaco Tire Center (Nettleton, MS) 73214
Trans State Lines, Inc. (Fort Smith, AR) 57108
Treadco (Lubbock, TX) 87791
Treadco, Inc. (Atlanta, GA) 65224
United Brake Systems Inc. (Birmingham, AL) 55438
United Brake Systems Inc. (Dallas, TX) 84470
Value Added Service Corp. (Georgetown, KY) 68387
Wal Mart (Harrison, AR) 57142
Wal Mart Auto Center (Tulsa, OK) 78191
Wal Mart Tire & Battery Ctr (Round Rock, TX) 88856
Western Auto Sup Co. (Gretna, LA) 69920
Western Auto Supply Co. (Birmingham, AL) 55454; 55455; 55456

Western Auto Supply Co. (N Little Rock, AR) 57437
Western Auto Supply Co. (Largo, FL) 60870
Western Auto Supply Co. (Pensacola, FL) 62488
Western Auto Supply Co. (Plant City, FL) 62560
Western Auto Supply Co. (Ruskin, FL) 62761
Western Auto Supply Co. (Zephyrhills, FL) 64032
Western Auto Supply Co. (Macon, GA) 66724; 66725
Western Auto Supply Co. (Statesboro, GA) 67653
Western Auto Supply Co. (Louisville, KY) 69037; 69038; 69039
Western Auto Supply Co. (Baton Rouge, LA) 69686; 69687
Western Auto Supply Co. (Marrero, LA) 70239
Western Auto Supply Co. (Westwego, LA) 70976
Western Auto Supply Co. (District Heights Forestville, MD) 71653
Western Auto Supply Co. (Edgewood, MD) 71667
Western Auto Supply Co. (Garner, NC) 74650
Western Auto Supply Co. (Spartanburg, SC) 79968
Western Auto Supply Co. (Oak Ridge, TN) 82202
Western Auto Supply Co. (Austin, TX) 83069; 83070
Western Auto Supply Co. (El Paso, TX) 84976
Western Auto Supply Co. (Fort Worth, TX) 85361
Western Auto Supply Co. (Groves, TX) 85688
Western Auto Supply Co. (Houston, TX) 87176; 87177; 87178; 87179; 87180; 87181; 87182
Western Auto Supply Co. (Mesquite, TX) 88013
Western Auto Supply Co. (San Antonio, TX) 89325
Western Auto Supply Co. (Temple, TX) 89653
Western Auto Supply Co. (Norfolk, VA) 91597
Western Auto Supply Co. (Virginia Beach, VA) 92521
Western Auto Supply Co. Dela (Pensacola, FL) 62489
Western Auto Supply Co. Inc. (Bossier City, LA) 69737
Western Auto Supply Co. Inc. (Wilmington, NC) 76613
Western Auto Supply Co. Inc. (Knoxville, TN) 81274
Western Auto Supply Co. No. 7 (El Paso, TX) 84978
Western Auto Supply Co. No. 3 (Lakeland, FL) 60800
Wilsons (Lexington, OK) 77177

5541 Gasoline Service Stations

Amerada Hess Corp. (Tampa, FL) 63307
Amerada Hess Corp. (W Palm Beach, FL) 63778
Amerada Hess Corp. No. 40242 (Greenville, SC) 79293
Citgo (Birmingham, AL) 55192
Citgo (North Little Rock, AR) 57454
Citgo (Ellicott City, MD) 71676
Citgo (Greenville, MS) 72793
Citgo (Oklahoma City, OK) 77328
Citgo (Chesapeake, VA) 90560
Citgo Food Mart (Tulsa, OK) 77904
Citgo Gas & Grill (Dyer, TN) 80742
Citgo Gas Mart (Chesapeake, VA) 90561
Citgo Mini Mart (Spartanburg, SC) 79887
Citgo Mini Mart (Union, SC) 80047
Citgo Oil Service Co. (Columbia, SC) 79003
Citgo Petroleum Corp. (Orlando, FL) 61951
Citgo Petroleum Corp. (San Antonio, TX) 88954
Citgo Quick Mart (Fort Lauderdale, FL) 59472
Citgo Quick Mart (Hialeah, FL) 59980
Citgo Quick Mart (Bossier City, LA) 69713; 69714
Citgo Quick Mart (Shreveport, LA) 70697
Citgo Quick Mart (Oklahoma City, OK) 77335
Citgo Quick Mart (Tulsa, OK) 77910; 77912; 77914; 77915
Citgo Quick Mart (Deer Park, TX) 84548

Texaco Corp. (Hawthorne, FL) 59973
Texaco Express Lube (Jacksonville, FL) 60474
Texaco Fastop (N Little Rock, AR) 57429
Texaco & Food Gas Mart (San Antonio, TX) 89258
Texaco Food Mart (Guntersville, AL) 55835
Texaco Food Mart (York, AL) 56713
Texaco Food Mart (New Port Richey, FL) 61692
Texaco Food Mart (New Smyrna, FL) 61697
Texaco Food Mart (Oviedo, FL) 62216
Texaco Food Mart (Tampa, FL) 63613
Texaco Food Mart (Winter Haven, FL) 63954
Texaco Food Mart (Macon, GA) 66715
Texaco Food Mart (Greensboro, NC) 74921
Texaco Food Mart (Wilmington, NC) 76599
Texaco Food Mart (Tulsa, OK) 78142
Texaco Food Mart (Arlington, TX) 82768
Texaco Food Mart (Austin, TX) 83028; 83029
Texaco Food Mart (Fort Worth, TX) 85323
Texaco Food Mart (San Antonio, TX) 89260
Texaco Food Mart (Vidor, TX) 89920
Texaco Food Mart & Car Wash (Oklahoma City, OK) 77603
Texaco Food Mart & Gas Stat (Tampa, FL) 63616
Texaco Food Mart No One (Temple, TX) 89647
Texaco Food Mart No 71 (San Antonio, TX) 89262
Texaco Food Mart 119 (New Port Rich, FL) 61671
Texaco Food Mart 160 (Tulsa, OK) 78144
Texaco Foodmart (Arlington, TX) 82770
Texaco Foods (Tampa, FL) 63617
Texaco Full Service (Oklahoma City, OK) 77604
Texaco Gas Bar (Oklahoma City, OK) 77605; 77606
Texaco Gas Bar & Food Mart (Oklahoma City, OK) 77607
Texaco Gas Mart (Montgomery, AL) 56385
Texaco Gas Sta (New Orleans, LA) 70568
Texaco Gas Station (Russellville, KY) 69263
Texaco Gas Station (Oklahoma City, OK) 77608
Texaco Gas Station (College Station, TX) 83624
Texaco Gas Station (Hurst, TX) 87299
Texaco Gas Station & Food M (Daytona Beach, FL) 59217
Texaco Gas Station South (Dallas, TX) 84428
Texaco Gasoline Station (Dallas, TX) 84429
Texaco Gass Barr (Tulsa, OK) 78145
Texaco-Hanson Hank's (Fort Worth, TX) 85329
Texaco Inc. (Mobile, AL) 56247
Texaco Inc. (Conway, AR) 56873
Texaco Inc. (Russellville, AR) 57591
Texaco Inc. (Lakeland, FL) 60787
Texaco Inc. (Bossier City, LA) 69734
Texaco Incorporated (Shreveport, LA) 70792; 70794
Texaco Incorporated (Oklahoma City, OK) 77609; 77610
Texaco Incorporated (Tulsa, OK) 78146; 78147; 78150
Texaco Inc. (Bogata, TX) 83307
Texaco Inc. (Georgetown, TX) 85574
Texaco Inc. (Hamilton, TX) 85695
Texaco Inc. (St. Albans, WV) 93071
Texaco Inc. Marketing Dept (Lake Charles, LA) 70176
Texaco Incorporated Service (Oklahoma City, OK) 77613
Texaco & J & L Snacks (San Antonio, TX) 89263
Texaco Jpep (Odessa, TX) 88285
Texaco Mart (Sheffield, AL) 56565
Texaco Mini Mart (Tulsa, OK) 78153
Texaco No 5 (Florence, AL) 55746
Texaco No 411 (Kissimmee, FL) 60606
Texaco No 320 (Largo, FL) 60865
Texaco Number One (Seguin, TX) 89377
Texaco Oil Co. (Merritt is, FL) 61134
Texaco Oil Company (Opa Locka, FL) 61863
Texaco Oil & Gas (Jackson, MS) 73074
Texaco 134 (Lakeland, FL) 60788
Texaco One Stop (Austin, TX) 83031; 83032
Texaco Pep Stop (Forney, TX) 85041
Texaco Pep Stop (Rosenberg, TX) 88840
Texaco Refining & Marketing (Dallas, TX) 84432
Texaco Refining & Mktg (Fort Worth, TX) 85330
Texaco Royal Mart (Lake Worth, FL) 60699
Texaco Self Serv (Bessemer, AL) 55105
Texaco Self Serv (Tuscaloosa, AL) 56677
Texaco Self Serv (Baton Rouge, LA) 69673; 69674
Texaco Self Serv (Lafayette, LA) 70116
Texaco Self Serv (Port Allen, LA) 70649
Texaco Self Serv (Westwego, LA) 70974
Texaco Self Serv (Dallas, TX) 84433; 84434; 84435
Texaco Self Serv (Portland, TX) 88695
Texaco Self Serv Sta (Gretna, LA) 69916
Texaco Self Serv Sta (Tulsa, OK) 78154
Texaco Self Serve (Birmingham, AL) 55422
Texaco Self Serve (Baton Rouge, LA) 69675
Texaco Self Serve (Metairie, LA) 70318
Texaco Self-Serve (New Orleans, LA) 70569; 70571
Texaco Self Serve (Austin, TX) 83036; 83038
Texaco Self Serve (San Antonio, TX) 89264; 89265; 89267; 89268; 89269
Texaco Self Serve Crwsh (San Antonio, TX) 89271
Texaco Self Service (Bessemer, AL) 55106
Texaco Self-Service (Birmingham, AL) 55423; 55424; 55425; 55426
Texaco Self-Service (Baton Rouge, LA) 69676; 69677
Texaco Self Service (Lafayette, LA) 70117
Texaco Self Service (Metairie, LA) 70319
Texaco Self Service (New Orleans, LA) 70572
Texaco Self Service (Slidell, LA) 70843; 70844
Texaco Self Service (Westwego, LA) 70975
Texaco Self Service (Edmond, OK) 77022
Texaco Self Service (Oklahoma City, OK) 77615
Texaco Self Service (Austin, TX) 83039
Texaco Self Service (Dallas, TX) 84436
Texaco Self Service (Midland, TX) 88084
Texaco Self-Service (San Antonio, TX) 89272
Texaco Self Service Center (Tulsa, OK) 78155
Texaco Self Service Gas (Baker, LA) 69438
Texaco Self Service Inc. (Edmond, OK) 77023
Texaco Self Service Inc. (Oklahoma City, OK) 77616
Texaco Self Service No 4 (Greenville, SC) 79438
Texaco Self Service Station (Winter Park, FL) 63997
Texaco Self Service Station (Metairie, LA) 70320
Texaco Self Service Station (Oklahoma City, OK) 77617; 77618
Texaco Self Service Station (Tulsa, OK) 78156; 78157
Texaco Self-Way (Spartanburg, SC) 79958
Texaco Selfserv Centers (Grand Prairie, TX) 85642
Texaco Selfservice (Chalmette, LA) 69771
Texaco Service Center (Memphis, TX) 87950
Texaco Service Center Inc. (Opelika, AL) 56426
Texaco Service Station (Mobile, AL) 56249
Texaco Service Station (Merritt is, FL) 61135
Texaco Service Station (Titusville, FL) 63707
Texaco Service Station (Venice, FL) 63737
Texaco Service Station (Amory, MS) 72588
Texaco Service Station (Eupora, MS) 72766
Texaco Service Station (Wesleyan Col, NC) 76482
Texaco Service Station (Oklahoma City, OK) 77625; 77626
Texaco Service Station (Tulsa, OK) 78158; 78159; 78160; 78161; 78162; 78163
Texaco Service Station (Collierville, TN) 80623
Texaco Service Station (Beaumont, TX) 83224
Texaco Service Station (Dallas, TX) 84438; 84439
Texaco Service Station (Edinburg, TX) 84739
Texaco Service Station (Fort Worth, TX) 85332; 85333; 85334
Texaco Service Station (Hale Center, TX) 85693
Texaco Service Station (San Antonio, TX) 89273; 89274
Texaco Service Station (Wichita Falls, TX) 90112
Texaco Service Station No 2 (Tulsa, OK) 78164
Texaco Service Stations (Edinburg, TX) 84740
Texaco Shoppers Mart (Austin, TX) 83041
Texaco Shoppers Mart No 10 (Austin, TX) 83042
Texaco South Service Center (Meridian, MS) 73181
Texaco on the Square (Lexington, MS) 73116
Texaco Station (Brilliant, AL) 55486
Texaco Station (St Augustine, FL) 62957
Texaco Station (Greenville, SC) 79439
Texaco Station (Abilene, TX) 82462
Texaco Station (Beaumont, TX) 83225
Texaco Station & Deli (Charlotte, NC) 74170
Texaco Station & Food Mart (Oklahoma City, OK) 77627
Texaco Svce Sta (Fort Worth, TX) 85335
Texaco USA Inc. (Bellaire, TX) 83270
Texaco USA Inc. Adiv (Bellaire, TX) 83271
Texacopep (Midland, TX) 88085
Total Petroleum Inc. (New Orleans, LA) 70576; 70577
Total Petroleum Inc. (Tulsa, OK) 78172; 78174
Union Oil Co. of California (Jacksonville, FL) 60485
Valvoline Instant Oil Change, Inc. (Lexington, KY) 68655
Vickers Inc. (El Paso, TX) 84958; 84959
Wal Mart Self Serve Sta. (Russellville, AR) 57596
Wal Mart Shoes (Harrison, AR) 57145

5561 Recreational Vehicle Dealers

Fruehauf Trailer Corp. (Shreveport, LA) 70722

5571 Motorcycle Dealers

Circuit City (Charleston, WV) 92731
Harley Davidson Motorcycles (Charleston, SC) 78819
Radio Shack (Sylacauga, AL) 56588

5599 Automotive Dealers Nec

Burdines (Merritt Island, FL) 61138
Citgo (Hialeah, FL) 59979
Citgo (Glen Burnie, MD) 71837
Coast to Coast Home & Aut (Centerville, TN) 80286
Exxon (Macon, GA) 66685
Exxon (Grand Prairie, TX) 85617
Exxon (Houston, TX) 86090
Exxon Co. (Cockeysville, MD) 71547
Exxon Co. USA (Tampa, FL) 63415
Exxon Co. USA (Friendswood, TX) 85397
Exxon Pipeline Co. (Houston, TX) 86172; 86174
Exxon Shop (Arlington, TX) 82651
Exxon Shop (Mesquite, TX) 87960; 87961
Harris Space Systems (Miami, FL) 61324
Mobil Marts (N Fort Myers, FL) 61588
Mobil Oil (West Palm Beach, FL) 63887
Mobil Oil (Keller, TX) 87461
Mobil Oil (Plano, TX) 88589
Mobil Oil Corp-10 Aer (Fort Lauderdale, FL) 59539
Mobil Oil Corp. (Bonita Springs, FL) 58760
Mobil Oil Corp. (Delray Beach, FL) 59322; 59323
Mobil Oil Corp. (Hollywood, FL) 60078; 60079
Mobil Oil Corp. (Lake Worth, FL) 60683
Mobil Oil Corp. (Naples, FL) 61645
Mobil Oil Corp. (Carrollton, TX) 83487
Mobil Oil Service Sta (Port St Lucie, FL) 62688
Mobil Self Serve (Houston, TX) 86597; 86598
Mobil Self Service (Garland, TX) 85515
Mobil Service Center (Fort Lauderdale, FL) 59543
Shell Station (Ellaville, GA) 66168
Texaco Food Mart (Arlington, TX) 82769
Texaco/Philadelphia (Bellaire, TX) 83268
Texaco Refining & Marketing (Lafayette, LA) 70115
Texaco Self Serve (Covington, LA) 69798
Texaco Service Inc. (Bedford, TX) 83256

5611 Men's & Boys' Clothing Stores

Banana Republic (Fort Lauderdale, FL) 59443
Career Image (Houston, TX) 85920; 85921
Casual Corner (Harlingen, TX) 85699
Casual Corner (Houston, TX) 85923; 85924; 85926; 85928; 85931; 85932; 85933; 85935
Casual Corner (Pasadena, TX) 88394
The Gap (Birmingham, AL) 55275
The Gap (Newark, DE) 57908
The Gap (Hollywood, FL) 60061
The Gap (Jacksonville, FL) 60316
The Gap (Tampa, FL) 63439; 63441
The Gap (Baton Rouge, LA) 69539
The Gap (Jackson, MS) 72986
The Gap (Oklahoma City, OK) 77365; 77366
The Gap (Charleston, SC) 78817
The Gap (Arlington, TX) 82658
The Gap (Dallas, TX) 84084
The Gap (El Paso, TX) 84805
The Gap (Fort Worth, TX) 85122
The Gap (Houston, TX) 86216; 86218; 86221; 86222; 86224; 86225; 86227
The Gap (Irving, TX) 87348
The Gap (Pasadena, TX) 88412
The Gap (San Antonio, TX) 89016; 89017
Gap Store (Oklahoma City, OK) 77369; 77372
Gap Stores (Jacksonville, FL) 60317
Gap Stores (El Paso, TX) 84806
Gap Stores (Houston, TX) 86232; 86235; 86236; 86237; 86238; 86239; 86241
Gap Stores (Pasadena, TX) 88413
Gap Stores (San Antonio, TX) 89019; 89020
Gap Stores Inc (Birmingham, AL) 55276
Gap Stores Inc. (Hollywood, FL) 60062
Gap Stores Inc. (Norfolk, VA) 91537; 91538
Lane Bryant (Houston, TX) 86436
Lerner Shop (Austin, TX) 82920
Lerner Shop (Humble, TX) 87231
Lerner Shop (Pasadena, TX) 88431
The Limited (Tulsa, OK) 77993
Radio Shack (San Antonio, TX) 89205; 89207; 89208
Richman Brothers Co. the (Tallahassee, FL) 63268
Wal Mart Discount City (Port Richey, FL) 62682
Wal-Mart Stores Inc. (Richmond, KY) 69251
Wrangler (Miami, FL) 61516

5621 Women's Clothing Stores

Banana Republic (Charleston, SC) 78790
Career Image (Oklahoma City, OK) 77316
Career Image (Abilene, TX) 82430
Career Image (Dallas, TX) 83894
Career Image (Houston, TX) 85917; 85919; 85922
Career Image (Fairfax, VA) 90757
Casual Corner (Birmingham, AL) 55183
Casual Corner (Huntsville, AL) 55897
Casual Corner (Fayetteville, AR) 56973
Casual Corner (Jonesboro, AR) 57210
Casual Corner (Dover, DE) 57787
Casual Corner (Newark, DE) 57901
Casual Corner (Wilmington, DE) 58030
Casual Corner (Altamonte Springs, FL) 58551
Casual Corner (Fort Myers, FL) 59688
Casual Corner (Hollywood, FL) 60048
Casual Corner (Jacksonville, FL) 60238
Casual Corner (Melbourne, FL) 61041
Casual Corner (Miami, FL) 61224
Casual Corner (Plant City, FL) 62540
Casual Corner (Pompano Beach, FL) 62590
Casual Corner (Tampa, FL) 63378; 63379
Casual Corner (W Palm Beach, FL) 63783; 63784
Casual Corner (Albany, GA) 64064
Casual Corner (Lexington, KY) 68532
Casual Corner (Lafayette, LA) 70049
Casual Corner (Annapolis, MD) 71009
Casual Corner (Cockeysville, MD) 71546
Casual Corner (Frederick, MD) 71716
Casual Corner (Laurel, MD) 72064
Casual Corner (Salisbury, MD) 72340
Casual Corner (Columbus, MS) 72705
Casual Corner (Jackson, MS) 72958
Casual Corner (Drexel, NC) 74364
Casual Corner (Durham, NC) 74388
Casual Corner (Gastonia, NC) 74671
Casual Corner (Bartlesville, OK) 76831
Casual Corner (Enid, OK) 77044
Casual Corner (Lawton, OK) 77155
Casual Corner (Norman, OK) 77247
Casual Corner (Oklahoma City, OK) 77321; 77322; 77323; 77325
Casual Corner (Charleston, SC) 78795; 78796
Casual Corner (Columbia, SC) 79000
Casual Corner (Florence, SC) 79196
Casual Corner (Greenville, SC) 79325
Casual Corner (Greenwood, SC) 79452
Casual Corner (Sumter, SC) 80015
Casual Corner (Antioch, TN) 80166
Casual Corner (Jackson, TN) 80966
Casual Corner (Knoxville, TN) 81153
Casual Corner (Memphis, TN) 81492; 81493
Casual Corner (Nashville, TN) 81913; 81915; 81916
Casual Corner (Arlington, TX) 82639
Casual Corner (Austin, TX) 82837
Casual Corner (Beaumont, TX) 83148
Casual Corner (Dallas, TX) 83896
Casual Corner (Denton, TX) 84615
Casual Corner (Duncanville, TX) 84694
Casual Corner (Fort Worth, TX) 85077
Casual Corner (Houston, TX) 85929; 85934
Casual Corner (Irving, TX) 87328

Casual Corner (Mesquite, TX) 87956
Casual Corner (Plano, TX) 88544
Casual Corner (Richardson, TX) 88726
Casual Corner (Temple, TX) 89609
Casual Corner (Annandale, VA) 90254
Casual Corner (Arlington, VA) 90281
Casual Corner (Hampton, VA) 91018
Casual Corner (Lynchburg, VA) 91226
Casual Corner (Mc Lean, VA) 91363
Casual Corner (Newport News, VA) 91453
Casual Corner (Norfolk, VA) 91501
Casual Corner (Virginia Beach, VA) 92444
Casual Corner (Bridgeport, WV) 92706
Casual Corner (Charleston, WV) 92727
Casual Corner (Huntington, WV) 92871
Casual Corner Corp. (Charlotte, NC) 73890
Casual Corner Corp. (Durham, NC) 74389
Casual Corner Inc. (Hialeah, FL) 59978
Coast to Coast of Monticell (Monticello, KY) 69098
Express (Hialeah, FL) 59983
Express (Gainesville, GA) 66274
Express (Chattanooga, TN) 80368
Express (El Paso, TX) 84796
Express Ltd. (Jacksonville, FL) 60267
Express Ltd. (Arlington, TX) 82647
The Gap (West Palm Beach, FL) 63867
The Gap (Oklahoma City, OK) 77367
The Gap (Baytown, TX) 83124
The Gap (Houston, TX) 86220; 86223; 86228
The Gap (Humble, TX) 87224
Gap Store (Oklahoma City, OK) 77370
Gap Stores (Houston, TX) 86231; 86233; 86234; 86242
Gap Stores (Mc Lean, VA) 91366; 91367
Hit or Miss (Boynton Beach, FL) 58779
Hit or Miss (Deerfield Beach, FL) 59279; 59280
Hit or Miss (Fort Lauderdale, FL) 59508; 59509
Hit or Miss (Hollywood, FL) 60064
Hit or Miss (Jacksonville, FL) 60327
Hit or Miss (Lake Worth, FL) 60677
Hit or Miss (Largo, FL) 60841
Hit or Miss (Miami, FL) 61329; 61330
Hit or Miss (Orlando, FL) 62007
Hit or Miss (Sarasota, FL) 62838
Hit or Miss (Louisville, KY) 68773; 68774; 68775
Hit or Miss (New Orleans, LA) 70506
Hit or Miss (Baltimore, MD) 71167; 71168
Hit or Miss (Owings Mills, MD) 72188
Hit or Miss (Charlotte, NC) 74038
Hit or Miss (Greensboro, NC) 74851
Hit or Miss (Raleigh, NC) 75915
Hit or Miss (Oklahoma City, OK) 77384; 77385
Hit or Miss (Columbia, SC) 79030
Hit or Miss (Greenville, SC) 79368
Hit or Miss (Amarillo, TX) 82552
Hit or Miss (Austin, TX) 82889
Hit or Miss (Beaumont, TX) 83160
Hit or Miss (College Station, TX) 83620
Hit or Miss (Dallas, TX) 84126; 84127
Hit or Miss (El Paso, TX) 84810; 84811
Hit or Miss (Harlingen, TX) 85701
Hit or Miss (Houston, TX) 86278; 86279; 86281; 86283
Hit or Miss (Mc Allen, TX) 87886
Hit or Miss (Midland, TX) 88040
Hit or Miss (San Antonio, TX) 89028
Hit or Miss (Chesapeake, VA) 90583
Hit or Miss (Fairfax, VA) 90789
Hit or Miss (Falls Church, VA) 90857
Hit or Miss (Hampton, VA) 91040
Hit or Miss (Manassas, VA) 91314
Hit or Miss (Norfolk, VA) 91545
Hit or Miss (Richmond, VA) 91903; 91905
Hit or Miss (Roanoke, VA) 92157
Hit or Miss (Spotsylvania, VA) 92272
Hit or Miss (Virginia Beach, VA) 92487
Hit or Miss (Huntington, WV) 92874
Hit or Miss (Parkersburg, WV) 92985
Hit or Miss Austin (Round Rock, TX) 88848
Hit or Miss Womens Apparel (Orlando, FL) 62008
Lane Bryant (Altamonte Spg, FL) 58539
Lane Bryant (Fort Lauderdale, FL) 59522
Lane Bryant (Gainesville, FL) 59889
Lane Bryant (Hollywood, FL) 60072
Lane Bryant (Kissimmee, FL) 60591
Lane Bryant (Lakeland, FL) 60743
Lane Bryant (Miami, FL) 61353; 61354; 61355
Lane Bryant (Orlando, FL) 62030; 62031
Lane Bryant (Plant City, FL) 62550
Lane Bryant (St Petersburg, FL) 62989
Lane Bryant (Tampa, FL) 63479
Lane Bryant (Elizabethtown, KY) 68285
Lane Bryant (Florence, KY) 68313
Lane Bryant (Lexington, KY) 68571
Lane Bryant (Louisville, KY) 68817
Lane Bryant (Owensboro, KY) 69177
Lane Bryant (Metairie, LA) 70284
Lane Bryant (Jackson, MS) 73013; 73014
Lane Bryant (Charlotte, NC) 74068
Lane Bryant (Hickory, NC) 75086
Lane Bryant (Raleigh, NC) 75924
Lane Bryant (Columbia, SC) 79042
Lane Bryant (Antioch, TN) 80171
Lane Bryant (Chattanooga, TN) 80418
Lane Bryant (Clarksville, TN) 80554
Lane Bryant (Goodlettsville, TN) 80866
Lane Bryant (Amarillo, TX) 82559
Lane Bryant (Arlington, TX) 82685
Lane Bryant (Austin, TX) 82917
Lane Bryant (Dallas, TX) 84192; 84195
Lane Bryant (Houston, TX) 86432; 86433; 86434; 86435; 86437; 86438; 86440; 86441
Lane Bryant (Irving, TX) 87366
Lane Bryant (Mesquite, TX) 87973
Lane Bryant (Plano, TX) 88578
Lane Bryant (Charleston, WV) 92760; 92761
Lane Bryant (Parkersburg, WV) 92990
Layne Bryant (Memphis, TN) 81643
Layne Bryant (Barboursville, WV) 92670
Layne Bryant (Huntington, WV) 92880
Lerner the (Chattanooga, TN) 80419
Lerner Shop (Birmingham, AL) 55306
Lerner Shop (Decatur, AL) 55596
Lerner Shop (Huntsville, AL) 55966
Lerner Shop (Mobile, AL) 56198
Lerner Shop (Hot Springs National Park, AR) 57174
Lerner Shop (Altamonte Spg, FL) 58540
Lerner Shop (Boynton Beach, FL) 58783
Lerner Shop (Bradenton, FL) 58832
Lerner Shop (Clearwater, FL) 59028
Lerner Shop (Fort Walton Beach, FL) 59829
Lerner Shop (Hialeah, FL) 59996
Lerner Shop (Hollywood, FL) 60073; 60074
Lerner Shop (Jacksonville, FL) 60362; 60363
Lerner Shop (Miami, FL) 61356; 61357; 61358
Lerner Shop (Ocala, FL) 61804
Lerner Shop (Orlando, FL) 62035; 62036
Lerner Shop (Pensacola, FL) 62445
Lerner Shop (Pompano Beach, FL) 62605
Lerner Shop (Winter Park, FL) 63986
Lerner Shop (Alexandria, LA) 69390
Lerner Shop (Baton Rouge, LA) 69578; 69579
Lerner Shop (Gretna, LA) 69904; 69905
Lerner Shop (Hammond, LA) 69931
Lerner Shop (Lake Charles, LA) 70148
Lerner Shop (Metairie, LA) 70286
Lerner Shop (Biloxi, MS) 72629
Lerner Shop (Gulfport, MS) 72862
Lerner Shop (Jackson, MS) 73015; 73017
Lerner Shop (Meridian, MS) 73169
Lerner Shop (Pascagoula, MS) 73263
Lerner Shop (Greenville, NC) 74966
Lerner Shop (High Point, NC) 75149
Lerner Shop (Jacksonville, NC) 75222
Lerner Shop (Wilmington, NC) 76582
Lerner Shop (Norman, OK) 77260
Lerner Shop (Oklahoma City, OK) 77419; 77420; 77423
Lerner Shop (Tulsa, OK) 77992
Lerner Shop (Charleston, SC) 78833
Lerner Shop (Columbia, SC) 79045
Lerner Shop (Florence, SC) 79216
Lerner Shop (Greenville, SC) 79385; 79386
Lerner Shop (Sumter, SC) 80024
Lerner Shop (Abilene, TX) 82442
Lerner Shop (Amarillo, TX) 82562
Lerner Shop (Arlington, TX) 82687
Lerner Shop (Baytown, TX) 83131
Lerner Shop (Beaumont, TX) 83170
Lerner Shop (Brownsville, TX) 83365; 83366
Lerner Shop (Denton, TX) 84619
Lerner Shop (Duncanville, TX) 84699
Lerner Shop (Eagle Pass, TX) 84718
Lerner Shop (El Paso, TX) 84836
Lerner Shop (Fort Worth, TX) 85170
Lerner Shop (Friendswood, TX) 85401
Lerner Shop (Harlingen, TX) 85704
Lerner Shop (Houston, TX) 86445; 86446; 86447; 86448; 86449; 86450; 86451; 86452; 86453; 86454; 86455
Lerner Shop (Irving, TX) 87367
Lerner Shop (Killeen, TX) 87516
Lerner Shop (Lake Jackson, TX) 87581
Lerner Shop (Laredo, TX) 87613
Lerner Shop (Mesquite, TX) 87975
Lerner Shop (Odessa, TX) 88254
Lerner Shop (Plano, TX) 88579
Lerner Shop (San Antonio, TX) 89073; 89074; 89076; 89079
Lerner Shop (Wichita Falls, TX) 90078
Lerner Shops (Covington, KY) 68227
Lerner Shops (Florence, KY) 68314
Lerner Shops (Louisville, KY) 68818; 68819; 68820
Lerner Shops (Chattanooga, TN) 80420
Lerner Shops (Clarksville, TN) 80555
Lerner Shops (Johnson City, TN) 81050
Lerner Shops (Kingsport, TN) 81110
Lerner Shops (Knoxville, TN) 81224; 81225
Lerner Shops (Maryville, TN) 81417
Lerner Shops (Memphis, TN) 81645; 81646; 81647
Lerner Shops (Nashville, TN) 82052; 82053
Lerner Shops (Beckley, WV) 92677
Lerner Shops (Charleston, WV) 92762; 92763
Lerner Shops (Clarksburg, WV) 92809
Lerner Shops (Huntington, WV) 92881; 92882
Lerner Shops (Parkersburg, WV) 92991
Lerner Woman (Paducah, KY) 69206
Lerner Woman (Clarksville, TN) 80556
Lerner Woman (Goodlettsville, TN) 80867
Lerner Woman (Memphis, TN) 81648
The Limited (Birmingham, AL) 55309
The Limited (Mobile, AL) 56200
The Limited (Tuscaloosa, AL) 56662
The Limited (Boca Raton, FL) 58718
The Limited (Bradenton, FL) 58833
The Limited (Clearwater, FL) 59029
The Limited (Fort Lauderdale, FL) 59524; 59525
The Limited (Hialeah, FL) 59997
The Limited (Lakeland, FL) 60745
The Limited (Melbourne, FL) 61076
The Limited (Miami, FL) 61360; 61361
The Limited (Pompano Beach, FL) 62606
The Limited (Tampa, FL) 63487
Limited the (Bowling Green, KY) 68147
Limited the (Florence, KY) 68319
Limited the (Lexington, KY) 68573
The Limited (Louisville, KY) 68865; 68866; 68867
The Limited (Baton Rouge, LA) 69580
The Limited (Marrero, LA) 70230
The Limited (Shreveport, LA) 70750
The Limited (Jackson, MS) 73018; 73020
The Limited (Charlotte, NC) 74073; 74075
The Limited (Durham, NC) 74414
The Limited (Hickory, NC) 75087
The Limited (Raleigh, NC) 75926
The Limited (Oklahoma City, OK) 77424
The Limited (Columbia, SC) 79048
The Limited (Greenville, SC) 79388
Limited the (Chattanooga, TN) 80421
Limited (Knoxville, TN) 81226
Limited the (Memphis, TN) 81649; 81650
Limited (Nashville, TN) 82055; 82056; 82057
The Limited (Austin, TX) 82925; 82926
The Limited (Dallas, TX) 84201; 84203; 84204
The Limited (Fort Worth, TX) 85173
The Limited (Houston, TX) 86460; 86461; 86462; 86463; 86464; 86465; 86466; 86467; 86469; 86471
The Limited (Irving, TX) 87368
The Limited (Mesquite, TX) 87976
The Limited (Plano, TX) 88580
The Limited (Richardson, TX) 88748
The Limited (San Antonio, TX) 89080; 89081
The Limited (Charleston, WV) 92765; 92766
Limited (Huntington, WV) 92884
The Limited Express (Altamonte Spg, FL) 58542
The Limited Express (Miami, FL) 61362
The Limited Express (Tampa, FL) 63489
Limited Express (Florence, KY) 68320
Limited Express (Paducah, KY) 69207
The Limited Express (Lafayette, LA) 70072
The Limited Express (Marrero, LA) 70231
The Limited Express (Jackson, MS) 73021
The Limited Express (Durham, NC) 74415
Limited Express (Antioch, TN) 80172
Limited Express (Goodlettsville, TN) 80868
Limited Express the (Memphis, TN) 81651
Limited Express (Nashville, TN) 82058
The Limited Express (Dallas, TX) 84208; 84209
The Limited Express (Houston, TX) 86472; 86473; 86474; 86475; 86476; 86477; 86478; 86479; 86480; 86481
The Limited Express (Humble, TX) 87233
The Limited Express (Irving, TX) 87369
The Limited Express (Plano, TX) 88582
Pappagallo (Birmingham, AL) 55328
Pappagallo (Dothan, AL) 55657
Pappagallo (Huntsville, AL) 55985
Pappagallo (Boca Raton, FL) 58725
Pappagallo (Fort Myers, FL) 59729; 59730
Pappagallo (Jacksonville, FL) 60386
Pappagallo (Longwood, FL) 60939
Pappagallo (Miami, FL) 61386
Pappagallo (Vero Beach, FL) 63763
Pappagallo (Gainesville, GA) 66285
Pappagallo (Baton Rouge, LA) 69593
Pappagallo (Jackson, MS) 73028
Pappagallo (Norman, OK) 77265
Pappagallo (Dallas, TX) 84290
Petite Sophisticate (Newark, DE) 57925
Petite Sophisticate (Altamonte Springs, FL) 58561
Petite Sophisticate (Boca Raton, FL) 58726
Petite Sophisticate (Fort Lauderdale, FL) 59552
Petite Sophisticate (Miami, FL) 61389
Petite Sophisticate (Orlando, FL) 62079
Petite Sophisticate (Tampa, FL) 63518
Petite Sophisticate (Dallas, TX) 84302
Petite Sophisticate (Houston, TX) 86677; 86678; 86679; 86680
Petite Sophisticate (Humble, TX) 87238
Radio Shack (West Columbia, SC) 80106
Stop & Shop (Prestonsburg, KY) 69229
T J Maxx (Fort Lauderdale, FL) 59614
T J Maxx No Two Seventy Fiv (Houston, TX) 86931
Texaco Service Station (Greensboro, NC) 74923
Victoria's Secret (Florence, KY) 68345
Victoria's Secret (Louisville, KY) 69033
Victoria's Secret (Memphis, TN) 81750; 81751
Victoria's Secret (Nashville, TN) 82135
Victoria's Secret (Barboursville, WV) 92672
Victoria's Secret (Charleston, WV) 92799

5632 Women's Accessory & Specialty Stores

Hit or Miss (Goodlettsville, TN) 80864
Hit or Miss (Nashville, TN) 82024
Kayser-Roth Corp. (Greensboro, NC) 74856
Maison Blanche (Miami, FL) 61364
Payless Shoesource (West Memphis, AR) 57729
Payless Shoesource (Austin, TX) 82954
Payless Shoesource (El Paso, TX) 84864
Payless Shoesource (Lubbock, TX) 87774
Victoria's Secret (Houston, TX) 87078; 87079
Victoria's Secret (Humble, TX) 87253

5641 Children's & Infants' Wear Stores

The Gap Kids (Orlando, FL) 61993
Toys R US (Birmingham, AL) 55432
Toys R US (Fort Myers, FL) 59767
Toys R US (Hialeah, FL) 60015
Toys R US (Miami, FL) 61480
Toys R US (Tampa, FL) 63626
Toys R US (Oklahoma City, OK) 77631; 77633
Toys R US (Knoxville, TN) 81260
Toys R US (Austin, TX) 83049
Toys R US (Beaumont, TX) 83226
Toys R US (Houston, TX) 87031; 87032; 87033; 87034
Toys R US (Fairfax, VA) 90811
Toys R US (Falls Church, VA) 90872
Toys R US (Hampton, VA) 91057
Toys R US (Norfolk, VA) 91586

5651 Family Clothing Stores

August Max (Richmond, VA) 91739
Banana Republic (Birmingham, AL) 55159
Banana Republic (Boca Raton, FL) 58670; 58671
Banana Republic (Tampa, FL) 63333
Banana Republic (Winter Park, FL) 63961
Banana Republic (Winston-Salem, NC) 76708
Banana Republic (Tulsa, OK) 77885
Banana Republic (Memphis, TN) 81466
Banana Republic (Austin, TX) 82822; 82823
Banana Republic (Dallas, TX) 83869

Banana Republic (San Antonio, TX) 88923; 88924
Burlington Coat Factory (Little Rock, AR) 57263
Burlington Coat Factory (Savannah, GA) 67457
Burlington Coat Factory (Greensboro, NC) 74792
Burlington Coat Factory (Oklahoma City, OK) 77315
Burlington Coat Factory (Memphis, TN) 81488
Burlington Coat Factory Warehouse (Burlington, NC) 73745
Burlington Coat Factory Warehouse (Nashville, TN) 81912
Cacique (Greenville, SC) 79323; 79323
Capezio (Virginia Beach, VA) 92443
Career Image (Gainesville, FL) 59865
Career Image (Jacksonville, FL) 60236
Career Image (Oklahoma City, OK) 77317; 77318
Career Image (Abilene, TX) 82429
Career Image (Austin, TX) 82835
Career Image (Dallas, TX) 83895
Casual Corner (Birmingham, AL) 55181; 55182; 55183
Casual Corner (Enterprise, AL) 55680
Casual Corner (Gadsden, AL) 55777
Casual Corner (Huntsville, AL) 55898
Casual Corner (Montgomery, AL) 56288
Casual Corner (Tuscaloosa, AL) 56637
Casual Corner (Fort Smith, AR) 57035
Casual Corner (Jonesboro, AR) 57210
Casual Corner (Boca Raton, FL) 58688
Casual Corner (Boynton Beach, FL) 58768
Casual Corner (Bradenton, FL) 58812
Casual Corner (Clearwater, FL) 58982
Casual Corner (Daytona Beach, FL) 59168
Casual Corner (Fort Myers, FL) 59689
Casual Corner (Fort Pierce, FL) 59789
Casual Corner (Mary Esther, FL) 61014
Casual Corner (Merritt Island, FL) 61139
Casual Corner (Naples, FL) 61612
Casual Corner (Orlando, FL) 61944; 61945
Casual Corner (Panama City, FL) 62319
Casual Corner (Pensacola, FL) 62413
Casual Corner (Pinellas Park, FL) 62513
Casual Corner (Sarasota, FL) 62802
Casual Corner (Stuart, FL) 63161
Casual Corner (Tallahassee, FL) 63220
Casual Corner (Tampa, FL) 63378; 63380
Casual Corner (Valdosta, GA) 67943
Casual Corner (Bowling Green, KY) 68134
Casual Corner (Florence, KY) 68307
Casual Corner (Louisville, KY) 68728
Casual Corner (Owensboro, KY) 69161
Casual Corner (Baton Rouge, LA) 69479
Casual Corner (Bossier City, LA) 69712
Casual Corner (Kenner, LA) 69994
Casual Corner (Lafayette, LA) 70049
Casual Corner (Metairie, LA) 70255
Casual Corner (Monroe, LA) 70351
Casual Corner (Shreveport, LA) 70696
Casual Corner (Slidell, LA) 70817
Casual Corner (Greenville, MS) 72792
Casual Corner (Jackson, MS) 72956; 72957
Casual Corner (Ridgeland, MS) 73317
Casual Corner (Utica, MS) 73433
Casual Corner (Charlotte, NC) 73889
Casual Corner (High Point, NC) 75120
Casual Corner (Wilmington, NC) 76549
Casual Corner (Bartlesville, OK) 76831
Casual Corner (Enid, OK) 77044
Casual Corner (Oklahoma City, OK) 77319; 77320; 77325
Casual Corner (Tulsa, OK) 77898; 77899; 77900
Casual Corner (Columbia, SC) 78997; 78998; 78999
Casual Corner (Greenville, SC) 79325; 79326
Casual Corner (Spartanburg, SC) 79886
Casual Corner (Antioch, TN) 80166
Casual Corner (Memphis, TN) 81494
Casual Corner (Nashville, TN) 81914; 81915
Casual Corner (Abilene, TX) 82431
Casual Corner (Amarillo, TX) 82538
Casual Corner (Arlington, TX) 82639
Casual Corner (Austin, TX) 82836; 82837
Casual Corner (Baytown, TX) 83108
Casual Corner (Beaumont, TX) 83148
Casual Corner (Clute, TX) 83596
Casual Corner (College Station, TX) 83616
Casual Corner (Dallas, TX) 83896; 83897
Casual Corner (El Paso, TX) 84779
Casual Corner (Fort Worth, TX) 85076; 85078
Casual Corner (Houston, TX) 85925; 85927; 85930
Casual Corner (Humble, TX) 87217
Casual Corner (Hurst, TX) 87269
Casual Corner (Killeen, TX) 87507
Casual Corner (Lake Jackson, TX) 87579
Casual Corner (Longview, TX) 87707
Casual Corner (Midland, TX) 88026
Casual Corner (Port Arthur, TX) 88629
Casual Corner (San Angelo, TX) 88870
Casual Corner (San Antonio, TX) 88947; 88949; 88951
Casual Corner (Sherman, TX) 89392
Casual Corner (Temple, TX) 89608
Casual Corner (Texarkana, TX) 89670
Casual Corner (Victoria, TX) 89879
Casual Corner (Wichita Falls, TX) 90069
Casual Corner (Chesapeake, VA) 90559
Casual Corner (Fredericksburg, VA) 90913
Casual Corner (Hampton, VA) 91018
Casual Corner (Newport News, VA) 91453
Casual Corner (Richmond, VA) 91751; 91752
Casual Corner (Roanoke, VA) 92107
Casual Corner (Virginia Beach, VA) 92444
Casual Corner (Barboursville, WV) 92668
Casual Corners (Tampa, FL) 63381
Decorp (Dallas, TX) 83969
Express (Mobile, AL) 56159
Express (Boca Raton, FL) 58695
Express (Boynton Beach, FL) 58770
Express (Bradenton, FL) 58813
Express (Alexandria, LA) 69375
Express (Oklahoma City, OK) 77353
Express (Charleston, SC) 78810
Express (Columbia, SC) 79010
Express (Hurst, TX) 87273
Express Ltd. (Lakeland, FL) 60719
First Choice (Laredo, TX) 87610
The Gap (Birmingham, AL) 55274
The Gap (Enterprise, AL) 55685
The Gap (Huntsville, AL) 55946
The Gap (Altamonte Springs, FL) 58556
The Gap (Boynton Beach, FL) 58775
The Gap (Clearwater, FL) 59017
The Gap (Daytona Beach, FL) 59181
The Gap (Fort Myers, FL) 59699
The Gap (Jacksonville, FL) 60315
The Gap (Merritt is, FL) 61128
The Gap (Orange Park, FL) 61886
The Gap (Orlando, FL) 61992
The Gap (Pinellas Park, FL) 62520
The Gap (Sarasota, FL) 62836
The Gap (Tallahassee, FL) 63243
The Gap (Tampa, FL) 63438; 63438; 63440; 63441
The Gap (Winter Park, FL) 63979
The Gap (Savannah, GA) 67476
The Gap (Baton Rouge, LA) 69539
The Gap (Bossier City, LA) 69715
The Gap (Marrero, LA) 70227
The Gap (Metairie, LA) 70264
The Gap (Slidell, LA) 70825
The Gap (Ridgeland, MS) 73318
The Gap (Utica, MS) 73434
The Gap (Oklahoma City, OK) 77368
The Gap (Tulsa, OK) 77944; 77945; 77946
The Gap (Charleston, SC) 78818
The Gap (Austin, TX) 82880; 82881
The Gap (Beaumont, TX) 83153
The Gap (Dallas, TX) 84083; 84084
The Gap (Fort Worth, TX) 85123; 85124
The Gap (Galveston, TX) 85439
The Gap (Houston, TX) 86217; 86226; 86229
The Gap (San Antonio, TX) 89015
Gap the (Chesapeake, VA) 90581
The Gap (Fredericksbrg, VA) 90911
Gap the (Hampton, VA) 91037
The Gap Kids (Baton Rouge, LA) 69540
The Gap Kids (Metairie, LA) 70265
The Gap Kids (Dallas, TX) 84085
Gap Store the (Oklahoma City, OK) 77371
Gap Stores (Houston, TX) 86240; 86243
Gayfers (Dothan, AL) 55649
Hit or Miss (Birmingham, AL) 55282
Hit or Miss (Huntsville, AL) 55952
Hit or Miss (Brandon, FL) 58873
Hit or Miss (Clearwater, FL) 59019
Hit or Miss (Jacksonville, FL) 60328
Hit or Miss (Melbourne, FL) 61068
Hit or Miss (Pensacola, FL) 62435
Hit or Miss (W Palm Beach, FL) 63792
Hit or Miss (Lexington, KY) 68558
Hit or Miss (Louisville, KY) 68774
Hit or Miss (Baton Rouge, LA) 69556
Hit or Miss (Lafayette, LA) 70061
Hit or Miss (Metairie, LA) 70274
Hit or Miss (New Orleans, LA) 70506
Hit or Miss (Charlotte, NC) 74035; 74036; 74037; 74039; 74040
Hit or Miss (Greensboro, NC) 74852
Hit or Miss (Morrisville, NC) 75667
Hit or Miss (Raleigh, NC) 75915
Hit or Miss (Oklahoma City, OK) 77383; 77384
Hit or Miss (Cayce, SC) 78776
Hit or Miss (Greenville, SC) 79368
Hit or Miss (Goodlettsville, TN) 80864
Hit or Miss (Memphis, TN) 81627
Hit or Miss (Murfreesboro, TN) 81852; 81852
Hit or Miss (Amarillo, TX) 82551
Hit or Miss (Arlington, TX) 82662; 82663
Hit or Miss (Austin, TX) 82889; 82892
Hit or Miss (Beaumont, TX) 83160
Hit or Miss (College Station, TX) 83619
Hit or Miss (Dallas, TX) 84124; 84126; 84127
Hit or Miss (El Paso, TX) 84811
Hit or Miss (San Antonio, TX) 89028; 89029; 89030
Hit or Miss (Chesapeake, VA) 90584
Hit or Miss (Norfolk, VA) 91545
Hit or Miss (Richmond, VA) 91903; 91904; 91905
Hit or Miss (Virginia Beach, VA) 92486; 92487
Hit or Miss (Williamsburg, VA) 92574
Hit or Miss Clothes (Jacksonville, FL) 60329
Hit or Miss No 327 (Birmingham, AL) 55283
Kayser-Roth Corp. (Greensboro, NC) 74856
Kids R US (Birmingham, AL) 55300
Kids R US (Norfolk, VA) 91548
Kids R US (Virginia Beach, VA) 92489
Kmart (Florence, AL) 55738
Lane Bryant (Auburn, AL) 55064
Lane Bryant (Birmingham, AL) 55301; 55302; 55303; 55304
Lane Bryant (Huntsville, AL) 55964; 55965
Lane Bryant (Mobile, AL) 56194; 56195
Lane Bryant (Montgomery, AL) 56350; 56351
Lane Bryant (Fort Smith, AR) 57067
Lane Bryant (Boca Raton, FL) 58716
Lane Bryant (Boynton Beach, FL) 58782
Lane Bryant (Bradenton, FL) 58830
Lane Bryant (Clearwater, FL) 59027
Lane Bryant (Daytona Beach, FL) 59190
Lane Bryant (Gainesville, FL) 59890
Lane Bryant (Mary Esther, FL) 61017
Lane Bryant (Merritt Island, FL) 61142
Lane Bryant (Orange Park, FL) 61889
Lane Bryant (Pensacola, FL) 62443; 62444
Lane Bryant (St Petersburg, FL) 62989
Lane Bryant (Stuart, FL) 63172
Lane Bryant (Tallahassee, FL) 63249
Lane Bryant (Tampa, FL) 63480
Lane Bryant (West Palm Beach, FL) 63879
Lane Bryant (Gainesville, GA) 66280
Lane Bryant (Valdosta, GA) 67965
Lane Bryant (Alexandria, LA) 69389
Lane Bryant (Baton Rouge, LA) 69575; 69576
Lane Bryant (Bossier City, LA) 69722
Lane Bryant (Lafayette, LA) 70068
Lane Bryant (Marrero, LA) 70228
Lane Bryant (Shreveport, LA) 70747
Lane Bryant (Slidell, LA) 70832
Lane Bryant (Biloxi, MS) 72628
Lane Bryant (Escatawpa, MS) 72757
Lane Bryant (Ridgeland, MS) 73322
Lane Bryant (Utica, MS) 73437
Lane Bryant (Charlotte, NC) 74069
Lane Bryant (Jacksonville, NC) 75219; 75220
Lane Bryant (Lawton, OK) 77164
Lane Bryant (Muskogee, OK) 77224
Lane Bryant (Oklahoma City, OK) 77415; 77416
Lane Bryant (Tulsa, OK) 77987; 77988
Lane Bryant (Anderson, SC) 78679
Lane Bryant (Columbia, SC) 79043
Lane Bryant (Myrtle Beach, SC) 79705
Lane Bryant (Abilene, TX) 82441
Lane Bryant (Amarillo, TX) 82560
Lane Bryant (Arlington, TX) 82683; 82684
Lane Bryant (Austin, TX) 82916; 82917
Lane Bryant (Beaumont, TX) 83168
Lane Bryant (Dallas, TX) 84192; 84193; 84195
Lane Bryant (Denton, TX) 84618
Lane Bryant (El Paso, TX) 84828; 84829; 84830
Lane Bryant (Fort Worth, TX) 85165; 85166; 85167
Lane Bryant (Galveston, TX) 85447
Lane Bryant (Hurst, TX) 87278
Lane Bryant (Killeen, TX) 87515
Lane Bryant (Port Arthur, TX) 88634
Lane Bryant (San Angelo, TX) 88881
Lane Bryant (San Antonio, TX) 89063; 89064; 89065; 89066; 89067; 89068; 89069
Lane Bryant (Sherman, TX) 89409
Lane Bryant (Temple, TX) 89621
Lane Bryant (Texarkana, TX) 89684
Lane Bryant (Tyler, TX) 89811
Lane Bryant (Victoria, TX) 89894
Lerner Shop (Birmingham, AL) 55306; 55307
Lerner Shop (Dothan, AL) 55655
Lerner Shop (Fairfield, AL) 55714
Lerner Shop (Mobile, AL) 56197; 56198
Lerner Shop (Montgomery, AL) 56352
Lerner Shop (Tuscaloosa, AL) 56661
Lerner Shop (Hot Springs National Park, AR) 57175
Lerner Shop (N Little Rock, AR) 57412
Lerner Shop (Boca Raton, FL) 58717
Lerner Shop (Boynton Beach, FL) 58784
Lerner Shop (Bradenton, FL) 58831
Lerner Shop (Fort Myers, FL) 59716
Lerner Shop (Gainesville, FL) 59891; 59891
Lerner Shop (Jacksonville, FL) 60362; 60363; 60364
Lerner Shop (Lakeland, FL) 60744
Lerner Shop (Leesburg, FL) 60884
Lerner Shop (Mary Esther, FL) 61018
Lerner Shop (Orlando, FL) 62036; 62037
Lerner Shop (Panama City, FL) 62329
Lerner Shop (St Augustine, FL) 62943; 62944
Lerner Shop (St Petersburg, FL) 62991; 62991; 62992
Lerner Shop (Stuart, FL) 63173
Lerner Shop (Tallahassee, FL) 63250
Lerner Shop (Tampa, FL) 63482; 63483
Lerner Shop (Titusville, FL) 63694
Lerner Shop (West Palm Beach, FL) 63880
Lerner Shop (Winter Haven, FL) 63944
Lerner Shop (Alexandria, LA) 69391
Lerner Shop (Baton Rouge, LA) 69578
Lerner Shop (Gretna, LA) 69905
Lerner Shop (Lafayette, LA) 70070; 70071; 70071
Lerner Shop (Marrero, LA) 70229
Lerner Shop (Metairie, LA) 70285
Lerner Shop (Shreveport, LA) 70748
Lerner Shop (Gulfport, MS) 72862
Lerner Shop (Jackson, MS) 73016
Lerner Shop (Laurel, MS) 73103
Lerner Shop (Meridian, MS) 73169
Lerner Shop (Ridgeland, MS) 73323
Lerner Shop (Utica, MS) 73439
Lerner Shop (Vicksburg, MS) 73458
Lerner Shop (Charlotte, NC) 74070
Lerner Shop (High Point, NC) 75148
Lerner Shop (Jacksonville, NC) 75221; 75222
Lerner Shop (Rocky Mount, NC) 76096; 76097
Lerner Shop (Oklahoma City, OK) 77421; 77422; 77423
Lerner Shop (Tulsa, OK) 77990; 77991
Lerner Shop (Anderson, SC) 78680
Lerner Shop (Charleston, SC) 78834
Lerner Shop (Greenville, SC) 79385
Lerner Shop (Abilene, TX) 82443
Lerner Shop (Amarillo, TX) 82561
Lerner Shop (Arlington, TX) 82689
Lerner Shop (Austin, TX) 82920; 82921
Lerner Shop (Beaumont, TX) 83170
Lerner Shop (Clute, TX) 83600
Lerner Shop (Dallas, TX) 84199
Lerner Shop (El Paso, TX) 84832; 84832; 84833; 84834; 84835
Lerner Shop (Fort Worth, TX) 85169; 85171
Lerner Shop (Longview, TX) 87719
Lerner Shop (Lufkin, TX) 87807
Lerner Shop (Port Arthur, TX) 88635
Lerner Shop (San Antonio, TX) 89072; 89075; 89077; 89078
Lerner Shop (Texarkana, TX) 89686
Lerner Shop (Victoria, TX) 89895
The Limited (Birmingham, AL) 55308; 55309
The Limited (Huntsville, AL) 55967
The Limited (Mobile, AL) 56199; 56200
The Limited (Tuscaloosa, AL) 56662
The Limited (N Little Rock, AR) 57413
The Limited (Altamonte Spg, FL) 58541
The Limited (Boynton Beach, FL) 58785
The Limited (Daytona Beach, FL) 59191
The Limited (Fort Myers, FL) 59717
The Limited (Jacksonville, FL) 60366
The Limited (Mary Esther, FL) 61019
The Limited (Melbourne, FL) 61076
The Limited (Orange Park, FL) 61891
The Limited (Pensacola, FL) 62446
The Limited (Stuart, FL) 63174
The Limited (Tallahassee, FL) 63251; 63251

The Limited (Tampa, FL) 63486; 63488
The Limited (Gainesville, GA) 66282
The Limited (Alexandria, LA) 69392
The Limited (Baton Rouge, LA) 69581; 69582
The Limited (Bossier City, LA) 69723
The Limited (Gretna, LA) 69906
The Limited (Marrero, LA) 70230
The Limited (Metairie, LA) 70288
The Limited (Monroe, LA) 70358
The Limited (Shreveport, LA) 70750
The Limited (Slidell, LA) 70833
The Limited (Biloxi, MS) 72630
The Limited (Jackson, MS) 73019; 73020
The Limited (Ridgeland, MS) 73324
The Limited (Charlotte, NC) 74072; 74073; 74074
The Limited (Oklahoma City, OK) 77425; 77427; 77428
The Limited (Tulsa, OK) 77994; 77995; 77996; 77997
The Limited (Charleston, SC) 78836; 78837; 78838
The Limited (Columbia, SC) 79047
The Limited (Greenville, SC) 79387
The Limited (Abilene, TX) 82444
The Limited (Amarillo, TX) 82563
The Limited (Arlington, TX) 82690; 82691
The Limited (Austin, TX) 82926; 82927
The Limited (Beaumont, TX) 83172
The Limited (Clute, TX) 83601
The Limited (Dallas, TX) 84201; 84202; 84203
The Limited (El Paso, TX) 84838; 84839; 84840
The Limited (Fort Worth, TX) 85172; 85173; 85174; 85175
The Limited (Galveston, TX) 85448
The Limited (Hurst, TX) 87279
The Limited (Lake Jackson, TX) 87582
The Limited (Plano, TX) 88581
The Limited (San Antonio, TX) 89082; 89083; 89084
The Limited (Sherman, TX) 89410
The Limited Express (Birmingham, AL) 55310
The Limited Express (Huntsville, AL) 55968
The Limited Express (Mobile, AL) 56201
The Limited Express (Montgomery, AL) 56353
The Limited Express (Naples, FL) 61638
The Limited Express (Pensacola, FL) 62447
The Limited Express (St Petersburg, FL) 62993
The Limited Express (Stuart, FL) 63175
The Limited Express (Kenner, LA) 69998
The Limited Express (Metairie, LA) 70289
The Limited Express (Monroe, LA) 70359
The Limited Express (Slidell, LA) 70834
The Limited Express (Jackson, MS) 73022
The Limited Express (Ridgeland, MS) 73325
The Limited Express (Utica, MS) 73440
The Limited Express (Charlotte, NC) 74076; 74077
The Limited Express (Greensboro, NC) 74865
The Limited Express (Oklahoma City, OK) 77429
The Limited Express (Tulsa, OK) 77998; 77999; 78000
The Limited Express (Charleston, SC) 78839
The Limited Express (Greenville, SC) 79389
The Limited Express (Arlington, TX) 82692
The Limited Express (Austin, TX) 82928
The Limited Express (Beaumont, TX) 83173
The Limited Express (Dallas, TX) 84208
The Limited Express (El Paso, TX) 84843
The Limited Express (Fort Worth, TX) 85177
The Limited Express (San Antonio, TX) 89086; 89087; 89088; 89090
Liz Claiborne (Boaz, AL) 55470
Lowe's (Texas City, TX) 89724
Maison Blanche Goudchaux De (New Orleans, LA) 70525
Marshalls (Charleston, SC) 78844
Marshalls Department Store (Tampa, FL) 63492
Marshalls Department Store (Pittsburg, TX) 88518
Marshalls Inc. (Mesquite, TX) 87978
Pappagallo (Dothan, AL) 55657
Pappagallo (Louisville, KY) 68935
Pappagallo (Austin, TX) 82951
Pappagallo (Dallas, TX) 84291
Petite Sophisticate (Birmingham, AL) 55329; 55330
Petite Sophisticate (Dothan, AL) 55658
Petite Sophisticate (Boynton Beach, FL) 58786
Petite Sophisticate (Clearwater, FL) 59035
Petite Sophisticate (Fort Myers, FL) 59731
Petite Sophisticate (Gainesville, FL) 59898
Petite Sophisticate (Jacksonville, FL) 60390
Petite Sophisticate (Lakeland, FL) 60760
Petite Sophisticate (Orange Park, FL) 61892
Petite Sophisticate (Orlando, FL) 62078
Petite Sophisticate (Pensacola, FL) 62455
Petite Sophisticate (Sarasota, FL) 62854
Petite Sophisticate (St Petersburg, FL) 63001
Petite Sophisticate (Stuart, FL) 63176
Petite Sophisticate (Louisville, KY) 68946
Petite Sophisticate (Kenner, LA) 70002
Petite Sophisticate (Metairie, LA) 70298
Petite Sophisticate (Oklahoma City, OK) 77485; 77487
Petite Sophisticate (Charleston, SC) 78851
Petite Sophisticate (Columbia, SC) 79061
Petite Sophisticate (Arlington, TX) 82721; 82722
Petite Sophisticate (Austin, TX) 82956; 82957
Petite Sophisticate (Beaumont, TX) 83198
Petite Sophisticate (Dallas, TX) 84302; 84303
Petite Sophisticate (Fort Worth, TX) 85218; 85219
Petite Sophisticate (San Antonio, TX) 89145; 89146
Petite Sophisticate (Richmond, VA) 91942
Sam's Wholesale Club (Jacksonville, FL) 60452
T J Maxx (Birmingham, AL) 55402
T J Maxx (Pensacola, FL) 62475
T J Maxx (Baton Rouge, LA) 69661
T J Maxx (Oklahoma City, OK) 77568
T J Maxx (Spartanburg, SC) 79954
T J Maxx (Houston, TX) 86930
T J Maxx Clothes Store (Austin, TX) 83010
T J Maxx Regional Office (Dallas, TX) 84406
T J Maxx Store (Savannah, GA) 67516
T J Maxx Store (Tulsa, OK) 78121
Tj Maxx (Melbourne, FL) 61112
Tj Maxx (Tampa, FL) 63623
US Shoe Corp. (Arlington, TX) 82776
Victoria's Secret (Birmingham, AL) 55446
Victoria's Secret (Mobile, AL) 56251; 56252
Victoria's Secret (N Little Rock, AR) 57433
Victoria's Secret (Boynton Beach, FL) 58796
Victoria's Secret (Clearwater, FL) 59051
Victoria's Secret (Gainesville, FL) 59923
Victoria's Secret (Pensacola, FL) 62485
Victoria's Secret (Punta Gorda, FL) 62723
Victoria's Secret (Stuart, FL) 63181
Victoria's Secret (Tallahassee, FL) 63285
Victoria's Secret (Tampa, FL) 63646
Victoria's Secret (Winter Park, FL) 63999
Victoria's Secret (Kenner, LA) 70022
Victoria's Secret (Metairie, LA) 70325
Victoria's Secret (Jackson, MS) 73088
Victoria's Secret (Ridgeland, MS) 73329
Victoria's Secret (Utica, MS) 73442
Victoria's Secret (Charlotte, NC) 74195
Victoria's Secret (Oklahoma City, OK) 77648; 77649
Victoria's Secret (Tulsa, OK) 78188
Victoria's Secret (Charleston, SC) 78909
Victoria's Secret (Columbia, SC) 79120
Victoria's Secret (Greenville, SC) 79443
Victoria's Secret (Arlington, TX) 82777; 82778
Victoria's Secret (Dallas, TX) 84489; 84490
Victoria's Secret (El Paso, TX) 84960
Victoria's Secret (Fort Worth, TX) 85347
Victoria's Secret (San Antonio, TX) 89292; 89293; 89294

5661 Shoe Stores

Banister Outlet Store (Knoxville, TN) 81144
Banister Shoe (Chester, MD) 71516
Banister Shoe (Woodbridge, VA) 92608
Banister Shoe Factory Outlet (Roanoke, VA) 92103
Banister Shoe Factory Outlet (Williamsburg, VA) 92560
Banister Shoes (Memphis, TN) 81467; 81468
Burdines Department Stores (Miami, FL) 61213
Burlington Coat Factory (Columbia, SC) 78992
Burlington Coat Factory (Memphis, TN) 81488
Burlington Coat Factory Warehouse (Jacksonville, FL) 60235
Burlington Coat Factory Warehouse (Marietta, GA) 66758
Burlington Coat Factory Warehouse (Burlington, NC) 73745
Burlington Coat Factory Warehouse (Antioch, TN) 80165
Burlington Coat Factory Warehouse (Nashville, TN) 81912
Burlington Shoe Outlet (Burlington, NC) 73750
Burlington Shoes (Burlington, NC) 73751
Capezio (Smithfield, NC) 76258
Capezio Factory Direct (Lake Park, GA) 66496
Capezio Shoes (Houston, TX) 85916
Capezio Shoes (Humble, TX) 87216
Cincinnati Shoe Co. (Mc Kinney, TX) 87908
Foot Action (Mobile, AL) 56180
Foot Action (Daytona Beach, FL) 59180
Foot Action (Alexandria, LA) 69379
Foot Action (Monroe, LA) 70354
Foot Action (Shawnee, OK) 77818
Foot Action (Abilene, TX) 82436
Foot Action (Amarillo, TX) 82548
Foot Action (Austin, TX) 82877; 82878
Foot Action (Brownsville, TX) 83358
Foot Action (Clute, TX) 83598
Foot Action (Fort Worth, TX) 85119
Foot Action (Harlingen, TX) 85700
Foot Action (Houston, TX) 86202; 86203
Foot Action (Killeen, TX) 87511; 87512
Foot Action (Lake Jackson, TX) 87580
Foot Action (Laredo, TX) 87611
Foot Action (Odessa, TX) 88244
Foot Action (Plano, TX) 88568
Foot Action (San Angelo, TX) 88873
Foot Action (San Antonio, TX) 89009; 89010; 89011
Foot Action (Temple, TX) 89617
Foot Action (Texarkana, TX) 89675
Foot Action Inc. (Norman, OK) 77252
Foot Action for Kids (Shawnee, OK) 77819
Foot Action for Kids (El Paso, TX) 84802
Foot Action for Kids (San Angelo, TX) 88874
Foot Action No 8036 (Plant City, FL) 62545
Foot Action No 8025 (Eagle Pass, TX) 84716
Foot Action No 8023 (Austin, TX) 82879
Foot Action U S a (Pinellas Park, FL) 62518
Foot Action U S a (Stuart, FL) 63167
Foot Action U S a (Dallas, TX) 84074; 84075
Foot Action U S a (El Paso, TX) 84803
Foot Action U S a (Lufkin, TX) 87803
Foot Action U S a (San Antonio, TX) 89012
Foot Action U S a (Sherman, TX) 89397
Footaction (Dothan, AL) 55648
Footaction U S a (Dallas, TX) 84076
Footaction U S a (Fort Worth, TX) 85120
Footaction U S a (Longview, TX) 87716
Footaction U S a (San Antonio, TX) 89013
Footaction USA (Bradenton, FL) 58825
Pappagallo (Birmingham, AL) 55328
Pappagallo (Mobile, AL) 56218
Pappagallo (Montgomery, AL) 56362
Pappagallo (Point Clear, AL) 56484
Pappagallo (West Memphis, AR) 57728
Pappagallo (Delray Beach, FL) 59325
Pappagallo (Fort Lauderdale, FL) 59551
Pappagallo (Miami, FL) 61387
Pappagallo (Greenville, MS) 72810
Pappagallo (Pinehurst, NC) 75805
Pappagallo (Oklahoma City, OK) 77462; 77463
Pappagallo (Sumter, SC) 80026
Pappagallo (Houston, TX) 86636; 86637
Pappagallo (Lexington, VA) 91210
Pappagallo (Virginia Beach, VA) 92494
Pappagallo (Charleston, WV) 92772; 92773
Payless Shoe Source (Bowling Green, KY) 68157; 68158
Payless Shoe Source (Covington, KY) 68229
Payless Shoe Source (Elizabethtown, KY) 68288
Payless Shoe Source (Florence, KY) 68324; 68325
Payless Shoe Source (Frankfort, KY) 68365
Payless Shoe Source (Henderson, KY) 68453
Payless Shoe Source (Lexington, KY) 68598; 68599
Payless Shoe Source (London, KY) 68664
Payless Shoe Source (Louisville, KY) 68936; 68937; 68938; 68939; 68940; 68941
Payless Shoe Source (Newport, KY) 69139
Payless Shoe Source (Owensboro, KY) 69189
Payless Shoe Source (Paducah, KY) 69210
Payless Shoe Source (Athens, TN) 80193
Payless Shoe Source (Chattanooga, TN) 80459; 80460; 80461; 80462; 80463
Payless Shoe Source (Columbia, TN) 80637
Payless Shoe Source (Dickson, TN) 80734
Payless Shoe Source (Dyersburg, TN) 80756
Payless Shoe Source (Fort Oglethorpe, TN) 80802
Payless Shoe Source (Franklin, TN) 80821
Payless Shoe Source (Jackson, TN) 80993
Payless Shoe Source (Knoxville, TN) 81233; 81234
Payless Shoe Source (Lebanon, TN) 81306
Payless Shoe Source (Manchester, TN) 81394
Payless Shoe Source (Maryville, TN) 81418; 81419
Payless Shoe Source (Memphis, TN) 81663
Payless Shoe Source (Millington, TN) 81778
Payless Shoe Source (Murfreesboro, TN) 81862
Payless Shoe Source (Nashville, TN) 82075; 82076; 82077; 82078
Payless Shoe Source (Charleston, WV) 92774; 92775; 92776
Payless Shoe Source (Fairmont, WV) 92845
Payless Shoe Source (Martinsburg, WV) 92933
Payless Shoe Source (Parkersburg, WV) 92994
Payless Shoesource (Hot Springs National Park, AR) 57177
Payless Shoesource (Jonesboro, AR) 57226
Payless Shoesource (North Little Rock, AR) 57470
Payless Shoesource (Pinellas Park, FL) 62524
Payless Shoesource (Punta Gorda, FL) 62713
Payless Shoesource (Dublin, GA) 66011
Payless Shoesource (Florence, KY) 68326
Payless Shoesource (Frankfort, KY) 68366
Payless Shoesource (Lexington, KY) 68600
Payless Shoesource (Louisville, KY) 68942
Payless Shoesource (Paducah, KY) 69211
Payless Shoesource (Metairie, LA) 70297
Payless Shoesource (New Orleans, LA) 70545; 70546
Payless Shoesource (Baltimore, MD) 71215; 71216; 71217; 71218
Payless Shoesource (Natchez, MS) 73205
Payless Shoesource (Ardmore, OK) 76816
Payless Shoesource (Chickasha, OK) 76933
Payless Shoesource (Claremore, OK) 76954
Payless Shoesource (Edmond, OK) 77010
Payless Shoesource (Enid, OK) 77058
Payless Shoesource (Guymon, OK) 77106
Payless Shoesource (Lawton, OK) 77168; 77169
Payless Shoesource (Miami, OK) 77207
Payless Shoesource (Oklahoma City, OK) 77467; 77468; 77469; 77471; 77472; 77473; 77474; 77475; 77476; 77478; 77479; 77480; 77481; 77482
Payless Shoesource (Ponca City, OK) 77710
Payless Shoesource (Poteau, OK) 77725
Payless Shoesource (Sand Springs, OK) 77782
Payless Shoesource (Sapulpa, OK) 77795
Payless Shoesource (Stillwater, OK) 77842
Payless Shoesource (Tulsa, OK) 78044; 78046; 78048; 78049; 78050; 78051; 78052; 78053
Payless Shoesource (Woodward, OK) 78263
Payless Shoesource (Charleston, SC) 78849; 78850
Payless Shoesource (Athens, TN) 80194
Payless Shoesource (Dickson, TN) 80735
Payless Shoesource (Dyersburg, TN) 80757
Payless Shoesource (Knoxville, TN) 81235
Payless Shoesource (Maryville, TN) 81420; 81421
Payless Shoesource (Murfreesboro, TN) 81863
Payless Shoesource (Alvin, TX) 82513
Payless Shoesource (Amarillo, TX) 82573; 82574
Payless Shoesource (Angleton, TX) 82611
Payless Shoesource (Arlington, TX) 82715
Payless Shoesource (Austin, TX) 82952; 82953
Payless Shoesource (Borger, TX) 83320
Payless Shoesource (Brenham, TX) 83338
Payless Shoesource (Brownsville, TX) 83372
Payless Shoesource (Carrollton, TX) 83496; 83497
Payless Shoesource (Corsicana, TX) 83786
Payless Shoesource (Dallas, TX) 84294
Payless Shoesource (El Paso, TX) 84862; 84863; 84864; 84865; 84866; 84867; 84868; 84869; 84870; 84871; 84872
Payless Shoesource (Fort Worth, TX) 85215

Payless Shoesource (Galveston, TX) 85459
Payless Shoesource (Garland, TX) 85520
Payless Shoesource (Houston, TX) 86640; 86641; 86643; 86647; 86650; 86651; 86653; 86654; 86655; 86657; 86658; 86663
Payless Shoesource (Hurst, TX) 87289
Payless Shoesource (Irving, TX) 87388; 87389
Payless Shoesource (Liberty, TX) 87677
Payless Shoesource (Mcallen, TX) 87935
Payless Shoesource (Midland, TX) 88063; 88064
Payless Shoesource (New Braunfels, TX) 88217
Payless Shoesource (Paris, TX) 88374
Payless Shoesource (Pasadena, TX) 88452; 88453; 88454; 88455
Payless Shoesource (Pearland, TX) 88484
Payless Shoesource (Portland, TX) 88690
Payless Shoesource (Rosenberg, TX) 88831
Payless Shoesource (San Angelo, TX) 88890; 88891
Payless Shoesource (San Antonio, TX) 89124; 89125; 89126; 89127; 89128; 89129; 89130; 89131; 89132; 89133; 89134; 89135; 89136; 89137; 89139; 89140; 89141; 89142
Payless Shoesource (Temple, TX) 89628; 89629
Payless Shoesource (Victoria, TX) 89899; 89900
Payless Shoesource (Arlington, VA) 90366
Payless Shoesource No. 2191 (Poteau, OK) 77726
Payless Shoesource No. 2132 (Portland, TX) 88691
Texas Boot Co. (Hartsville, TN) 80905
Texas Boot Co. (Lebanon, TN) 81309
Thom Mcan (Hialeah, FL) 60013
Thom Mcan (Miami, FL) 61477
Thom Mcan Factory Outlet (Boone, NC) 73718
Thom Mcan Family Shoe Store (El Paso, TX) 84948
Thom Mcan Family Shoes (Spring, TX) 89495
Thom Mcan Shoe (Hollywood, FL) 60099
Thom Mcan Shoe Store (Homestead, FL) 60123
Thom Mcan Shoe Store (Orlando, FL) 62168
Thom Mcan Shoe Store (Alamo, TX) 82480
Thom Mcan Shoe Store (Laredo, TX) 87625
Thom Mcan Shoe Store (Mesquite, TX) 88008
Thom Mcan Shoe Store (San Antonio, TX) 89275
Thom Mcan Shoe Store No 141 (Mc Allen, TX) 87901
Thom Mcan Shoe Stores (Fort Lauderdale, FL) 59620; 59621
Thom Mcan Shoe Stores (Houston, TX) 87024
Thom Mcan Shoe Stores (Richardson, TX) 88783; 88784
Thom Mcan Shoes (Daytona Beach, FL) 59219; 59220
Thom Mcan Shoes (Orlando, FL) 62169
Thom Mcan Shoes (Midland, TX) 88088
Thom Mcan Store No 7141 (Houston, TX) 87025

5699 Miscellaneous Apparel & Accessory Stores

Banana Republic (Jacksonville, FL) 60189
Banana Republic (Miami, FL) 61170
Bermans the Leather Experts (Arlington, TX) 82636
Capezio Dance Theatre Shop (Miami, FL) 61222
Capezio Factory (Galveston, TX) 85436
Casual Corner (Jacksonville, FL) 60237
Casual Corner (Pompano Beach, FL) 62589
Casual Corner (Baltimore, MD) 71077
Casual Corner (Clarksville, TN) 80538
Casual Corner 095 (Dallas, TX) 83898
Foot Action (Baytown, TX) 83123
Foot Action 8099 (Tupelo, MS) 73403
The Gap (Boca Raton, FL) 58705
The Gap (Fort Lauderdale, FL) 59496
The Gap (Miami, FL) 61315
The Gap (Orlando, FL) 61991
The Gap (Palm Beach Gardens, FL) 62272
The Gap (Pompano Beach, FL) 62598
The Gap (Baltimore, MD) 71156; 71157; 71158
The Gap (Charlotte, NC) 74025
The Gap (Hickory, NC) 75075
The Gap (Raleigh, NC) 75911
The Gap 1410 (Cpe St Claire, MD) 71611
The Gap 1024 (Alexandria, VA) 90222
Gap Stores (Charlotte, NC) 74026
Gap Stores the (Hickory, NC) 75076
The Gap Stores (Annandale, VA) 90267
Gap Stores (Fairfax, VA) 90787; 90788
Hewlett-Packard Co. (San Antonio, TX) 89026
Hit or Miss (Boca Raton, FL) 58711
Hit or Miss (Clearwater, FL) 59020
Hit or Miss (Alexandria, VA) 90225
Hit or Miss (Sterling, VA) 92345
Lane Bryant (Orlando, FL) 62029
Lerner Shop (Shreveport, LA) 70748
Petite Sophisticate (Jacksonville, FL) 60389
Petite Sophisticate (Salisbury, MD) 72358
Thom Mcan Shoe Store (Miami, FL) 61478
Thom Mcan Shoe Stores (Fort Lauderdale, FL) 59622
Toys R US (Orlando, FL) 62171
Victoria's Secret (Clearwater, FL) 59052
Victoria's Secret (Hialeah, FL) 60016
Victoria's Secret (Jacksonville, FL) 60491
Victoria's Secret (Lakeland, FL) 60791
Victoria's Secret (Miami, FL) 61492
Victoria's Secret (Orlando, FL) 62178
Victoria's Secret (Tampa, FL) 63645
Victoria's Secret (West Palm Beach, FL) 63906

5712 Furniture Stores

Aaron Rents (Atlanta, GA) 64187
Burdines (Longwood, FL) 60928
Burlington Coat Factory (Greenbelt, MD) 71855
Dixon Hardware & Furniture Co. Inc. (Camilla, GA) 65478
Foster Production Corp. (Miami, FL) 61314
Radio Shack (Fort Smith, AR) 57090
Sealy Mattress Co. (Bluefield, VA) 90462
This End Up (Lakeland, FL) 60789
This End Up (Naples, FL) 61666
This End Up (Orlando, FL) 62165
This End Up (Tampa, FL) 63622
This End Up (Marrero, LA) 70236
This End Up (Metairie, LA) 70321
This End Up (Charlotte, NC) 74171
This End Up (Durham, NC) 74430
This End Up (Raleigh, NC) 75963
This End Up Furn Co. (Fort Smith, AR) 57104
This End Up Furniture (Melbourne, FL) 61111
This End Up Furniture (Miami, FL) 61476
This End Up Furniture (Orlando, FL) 62166; 62167
This End Up Furniture Co. (Huntsville, AL) 56038
This End Up Furniture Co. (Stuart, FL) 63180
This End Up Furniture Co. (Charlotte, NC) 74172
This End Up Furniture Co. (Wilmington, NC) 76600
This End Up Furniture Co. (Winston Salem, NC) 76687
This End Up Furniture Co. (Columbia, SC) 79107

5713 Floor Covering Stores

Gap (Laurel, MD) 72076
Lees Carpets (Aberdeen, MS) 72577
Winston Carpet (Fort Lauderdale, FL) 59643

5714 Drapery & Upholstery Stores

Burlington Industries William G. Lord (Belmont, NC) 73673
Prelude Co. (High Point, NC) 75156
Virginia Natural Gas Co. Inc. (Norfolk, VA) 91593

5719 Miscellaneous Home Furnishings Stores

Ace Hardware (Severn, MD) 72369
Ace Hardware (Hayes, VA) 91111
Anchor Hocking Corp. (Memphis, TN) 81458
Bed & Bath Etc (Mohawk, TN) 81780
Circuit City (Altamonte Springs, FL) 58552
Circuit City (Clearwater, FL) 58984
Circuit City (Port Richey, FL) 62670
Circuit City (Arlington, TX) 82641
Circuit City (Doswell, VA) 90727
Kitchen Collection Inc. (Fort Lauderdale, FL) 59520
Kitchen Collection Inc. (Houston, TX) 86373
Lenox China (Oxford, NC) 75782
Linens N Things (Clearwater, FL) 59031
Linens 'n Things (Deerfield Beach, FL) 59283
Linens N Things (Orlando, FL) 62039
Linens N Things (Tampa, FL) 63490; 63490
Linens N Things (Charlotte, NC) 74078
Linens N Things (Raleigh Nc, NC) 75985
Linens N Things (Broken Arrow, OK) 76885
Linens N Things Inc. (Hallandale, FL) 59961
Lowe's (Warner Robins, GA) 68017
Mcduff Appliance & Electron (Tampa, FL) 63501
Mcduff Electronics (Bradenton, FL) 58836; 58837
Prints Plus (Melbourne, FL) 61089
Radio Shack (Mammoth Spg, AR) 57346
Radio Shack (Bradenton, FL) 58847
Radio Shack (De Land, FL) 59256
Radio Shack (Gainesville, FL) 59908
Radio Shack (Jacksonville, FL) 60429
Radio Shack (Lakeland, FL) 60774
Radio Shack (Melbourne, FL) 61098
Radio Shack (N Fort Myers, FL) 61589; 61590
Radio Shack (New Smyrna, FL) 61696
Radio Shack (Ocala, FL) 61817
Radio Shack (Sanford, FL) 62775
Radio Shack (St Augstn Beach, FL) 62937
Radio Shack (St Petersburg, FL) 63022; 63024; 63024; 63026
Radio Shack (Tampa, FL) 63559; 63564; 63568; 63571
Radio Shack (Titusville, FL) 63702
Radio Shack (Valdosta, GA) 67971
Radio Shack (Buras, LA) 69747
Radio Shack (Columbia, MS) 72700
Radio Shack (Clayton, NC) 74266
Radio Shack (Elizabethtown, NC) 74491
Radio Shack (Morehead City, NC) 75627
Radio Shack (S Brunswick, NC) 76151
Radio Shack (Woodward, OK) 78265
Radio Shack (Myrtle Beach, SC) 79712
Radio Shack (Garland, TX) 85528
Radio Shack (Richardson, TX) 88762
Radio Shack (Falls Church, VA) 90865
Radio Shack (Fredericksburg, VA) 90935
Radio Shack (Woodbridge, VA) 92621; 92624
Tandy Electronics (Alexandria, VA) 90240
Zippy Mart Inc. (Jacksonville, FL) 60516

5722 Household Appliance Stores

Aaron Rents (Atlanta, GA) 64187
Ace Hardware (Claxton, GA) 65564
Albertson's Sew & Vacuum (Fort Worth, TX) 85058
Baltimore Gas & Electric Co. (Glen Burnie, MD) 71835
Black & Decker Housewares Group (Asheboro, NC) 73580
Browning Ferris Industries Service Group Inc. (Mobile, AL) 56145
Circuit City (Birmingham, AL) 55187; 55188
Circuit City (Mobile, AL) 56149
Circuit City (Orlando, FL) 61948
Circuit City (Pensacola, FL) 62414
Circuit City (St Petersburg, FL) 62967
Circuit City (Louisville, KY) 68731
Circuit City (Charlotte, NC) 73896
Circuit City (Nashville, TN) 81923
Circuit City (Portsmouth, VA) 91642
Circuit City (Richmond, VA) 91771; 91772
Coast to Coast (Arkadelphia, AR) 56716
Coast to Coast Home & Auto (Sandersville, GA) 67428
Dixon Hardware & Furniture Co. Inc. (Camilla, GA) 65478
Duke Power Co. Inc. (Charlotte, NC) 73940
Home Products Co. (Knoxville, TN) 81217
Lowe's (Atkins, VA) 90409
Lowe's (Lynchburg, VA) 91267
Radio Shack (Pryor, OK) 77748
Sale James J III (Madison, FL) 60968
Sun Refining & Marketing Co. (De Valls Bluff, AR) 56901
Sunbeam Appliance Co. (Houston, TX) 86921
Vision Energy (Sarasota, FL) 62864
West Texas Utilities Co. (Abilene, TX) 82468
West Texas Utilities Co. (Childress, TX) 83563
West Texas Utilities Co. (Paducah, TX) 88339
West Texas Utilities Co. (Quanah, TX) 88702
West Texas Utilities Co. (San Angelo, TX) 88906

5731 Radio, Television & Electronics Stores

Aaron Rents (Atlanta, GA) 64187
Ace Hardware of Del Rio Inc. (Del Rio, TX) 84578
Associated Milk Producers Inc. (San Antonio, TX) 88919
Circuit City (Huntsville, AL) 55899
Circuit City (Lexington, KY) 68533
Circuit City (Louisville, KY) 68729; 68730; 68731
Circuit City (Charlotte, NC) 73893; 73895; 73896
Circuit City (Charleston, SC) 78797
Circuit City (Columbia, SC) 79002
Circuit City (Goodlettsville, TN) 80861
Circuit City (Knoxville, TN) 81155
Circuit City (Nashville, TN) 81922; 81923
Circuit City (Fairfax, VA) 90759
Circuit City (Falls Church, VA) 90821
Circuit City (Hampton, VA) 91019; 91020
Circuit City (Norfolk, VA) 91502; 91503
Circuit City (Charleston, WV) 92732
Circuit City Superstore (Jacksonville, FL) 60244
Circuit City Superstore (Greensboro, NC) 74799
Coast to Coast Store (Fairview, OK) 77077
Lane Bryant (Pt Charlotte, FL) 62699
Publix Super Market (Miami, FL) 61411
Radio Shack (Albertville, AL) 54970
Radio Shack (Anniston, AL) 55010
Radio Shack (Bessemer, AL) 55101; 55102
Radio Shack (Birmingham, AL) 55357; 55364
Radio Shack (Camden, AL) 55500
Radio Shack (Cullman, AL) 55549
Radio Shack (Dothan, AL) 55664; 55665
Radio Shack (Enterprise, AL) 55692
Radio Shack (Fairfield, AL) 55715
Radio Shack (Gadsden, AL) 55786
Radio Shack (Gilbertown, AL) 55809
Radio Shack (Huntsville, AL) 56003; 56004; 56005; 56006; 56008
Radio Shack (Leeds, AL) 56108
Radio Shack (Mobile, AL) 56228; 56231; 56232
Radio Shack (Opelika, AL) 56423
Radio Shack (Phenix City, AL) 56471
Radio Shack (Selma, AL) 56535; 56536
Radio Shack (Thomasville, AL) 56610
Radio Shack (Bentonville, AR) 56788
Radio Shack (Camden, AR) 56840
Radio Shack (Conway, AR) 56869
Radio Shack (Crossett, AR) 56886
Radio Shack (Forrest City, AR) 57012
Radio Shack (H Spg Nat Pk, AR) 57129; 57131
Radio Shack (N Little Rock, AR) 57419
Radio Shack (Pine Bluff, AR) 57528
Radio Shack (Rogers, AR) 57569
Radio Shack (Siloam Springs, AR) 57622
Radio Shack (Stuttgart, AR) 57665
Radio Shack (Trumann, AR) 57687
Radio Shack (Wynne, AR) 57744
Radio Shack (Wilmington, DE) 58099
Radio Shack (Altamonte Spg, FL) 58545
Radio Shack (Auburndale, FL) 58601
Radio Shack (Avon Park, FL) 58610
Radio Shack (Boca Raton, FL) 58734; 58735; 58736; 58737
Radio Shack (Boynton Beach, FL) 58788; 58789
Radio Shack (Bradenton, FL) 58848
Radio Shack (Brandon, FL) 58879
Radio Shack (Brooksville, FL) 58895
Radio Shack (Casselberry, FL) 58940
Radio Shack (Clearwater, FL) 59042; 59044
Radio Shack (Cocoa, FL) 59071
Radio Shack (Cocoa Beach, FL) 59083
Radio Shack (Daytona Beach, FL) 59207; 59208
Radio Shack (De Bary, FL) 59237
Radio Shack (De Land, FL) 59256
Radio Shack (Delray Beach, FL) 59327; 59328
Radio Shack (Fort Lauderdale, FL) 59579; 59581
Radio Shack (Fort Myers, FL) 59747; 59754
Radio Shack (Fort Pierce, FL) 59803; 59805
Radio Shack (Fort Walton Beach, FL) 59836
Radio Shack (Gainesville, FL) 59909; 59910
Radio Shack (Hollywood, FL) 60089
Radio Shack (Homosassa, FL) 60126
Radio Shack (Jacksonville, FL) 60423; 60424; 60425; 60427; 60428; 60430
Radio Shack (Jupiter, FL) 60547
Radio Shack (Lake City, FL) 60626
Radio Shack (Lake Wales, FL) 60657; 60658
Radio Shack (Lake Worth, FL) 60690; 60691; 60692
Radio Shack (Lakeland, FL) 60775; 60776; 60777
Radio Shack (Largo, FL) 60861
Radio Shack (Miami, FL) 61432; 61433; 61438
Radio Shack (Milton, FL) 61551
Radio Shack (Mount Dora, FL) 61568
Radio Shack (Niceville, FL) 61716
Radio Shack (Ocala, FL) 61816
Radio Shack (Ocoee, FL) 61837
Radio Shack (Okeechobee, FL) 61844
Radio Shack (Orange Park, FL) 61895
Radio Shack (Orlando, FL) 62122; 62123; 62124; 62125; 62129
Radio Shack (Ormond Beach, FL) 62209
Radio Shack (Pensacola, FL) 62463; 62464; 62465; 62466
Radio Shack (Pompano Beach, FL) 62626; 62628
Radio Shack (Sarasota, FL) 62857; 62858; 62859
Radio Shack (Seffner, FL) 62899

Radio Shack (St Petersburg, FL) 63022; 63024; 63027; 63028
Radio Shack (Tallahassee, FL) 63263; 63265
Radio Shack (Tampa, FL) 63558; 63560; 63561; 63563; 63566; 63570; 63571
Radio Shack (Venice, FL) 63734
Radio Shack (W Palm Beach, FL) 63808; 63809; 63810; 63812
Radio Shack (Wildwood, FL) 63917
Radio Shack (Winter Garden, FL) 63923
Radio Shack (Winter Haven, FL) 63949
Radio Shack (Winter Park, FL) 63993
Radio Shack (Zephyrhills, FL) 64026; 64027
Radio Shack (Bowdon, GA) 65390
Radio Shack (Brunswick, GA) 65423; 65424
Radio Shack (Covington, GA) 65740
Radio Shack (Douglas, GA) 65974
Radio Shack (Gainesville, GA) 66288
Radio Shack (Nashville, GA) 67069
Radio Shack (Oakwood, GA) 67216
Radio Shack (Quitman, GA) 67291
Radio Shack (Swainsboro, GA) 67757
Radio Shack (Valdosta, GA) 67971; 67973
Radio Shack (Vidalia, GA) 67993
Radio Shack (Baker, LA) 69437
Radio Shack (Baton Rouge, LA) 69638; 69639; 69642; 69643; 69644; 69646
Radio Shack (Donaldsonvl, LA) 69845
Radio Shack (Greenwell Spg, LA) 69902
Radio Shack (Kenner, LA) 70009
Radio Shack (Lake Charles, LA) 70169
Radio Shack (Lockport, LA) 70195
Radio Shack (Mandeville, LA) 70210
Radio Shack (Marrero, LA) 70234
Radio Shack (Metairie, LA) 70306; 70307; 70308
Radio Shack (Baltimore, MD) 71224
Radio Shack (Columbia, MD) 71599
Radio Shack (Cumberland, MD) 71633; 71635
Radio Shack (Frederick, MD) 71744
Radio Shack (Hagerstown, MD) 71892
Radio Shack (Odenton, MD) 72170
Radio Shack (Prince Frederick, MD) 72241
Radio Shack (Randallstown, MD) 72245
Radio Shack (Reisterstown, MD) 72247
Radio Shack (Sykesville, MD) 72485; 72486
Radio Shack (Biloxi, MS) 72638
Radio Shack (Columbus, MS) 72726
Radio Shack (Escatawpa, MS) 72759
Radio Shack (Gulfport, MS) 72872
Radio Shack (Jackson, MS) 73039; 73042; 73046; 73048; 73049; 73050; 73051; 73052; 73053
Radio Shack (Mc Comb, MS) 73149
Radio Shack (Meridian, MS) 73177
Radio Shack (New Albany, MS) 73217
Radio Shack (Pascagoula, MS) 73270
Radio Shack (Philadelphia, MS) 73281
Radio Shack (Port Gibson, MS) 73306
Radio Shack (Raymond, MS) 73313
Radio Shack (Aberdeen, NC) 73518
Radio Shack (Charlotte, NC) 74130; 74132; 74134; 74136; 74137; 74140; 74142
Radio Shack (Concord, NC) 74321
Radio Shack (Dunn, NC) 74377
Radio Shack (Fayetteville, NC) 74574
Radio Shack (Garner, NC) 74648
Radio Shack (Goldsboro, NC) 74733
Radio Shack (Greensboro, NC) 74885; 74887; 74888
Radio Shack (Greenville, NC) 74974; 74975
Radio Shack (High Point, NC) 75157; 75158
Radio Shack (Jacksonville, NC) 75227; 75228
Radio Shack (Kannapolis, NC) 75267; 75267
Radio Shack (Kernersville, NC) 75284
Radio Shack (Matthews, NC) 75529
Radio Shack (Mooresville, NC) 75608
Radio Shack (Murphy, NC) 75708
Radio Shack (New Bern, NC) 75734
Radio Shack (Pineville, NC) 75821
Radio Shack (Raleigh, NC) 75946
Radio Shack (Reidsville, NC) 76010
Radio Shack (Rockingham, NC) 76067
Radio Shack (Rocky Mount, NC) 76101
Radio Shack (S Brunswick, NC) 76151
Radio Shack (Skyland, NC) 76252
Radio Shack (Smithfield, NC) 76268
Radio Shack (Wake Forest, NC) 76432
Radio Shack (Washington, NC) 76459
Radio Shack (Wilmington, NC) 76591; 76592; 76593
Radio Shack (Wilson, NC) 76641; 76641
Radio Shack (Ardmore, OK) 76818
Radio Shack (Claremore, OK) 76956
Radio Shack (Enid, OK) 77065; 77067
Radio Shack (Guymon, OK) 77110
Radio Shack (Muskogee, OK) 77228
Radio Shack (Oklahoma City, OK) 77511; 77520; 77523; 77528; 77532
Radio Shack (Okmulgee, OK) 77684
Radio Shack (Pawhuska, OK) 77696
Radio Shack (Pryor, OK) 77748
Radio Shack (Sapulpa, OK) 77797
Radio Shack (Sayre, OK) 77800
Radio Shack (Tulsa, OK) 78073; 78076; 78077; 78078; 78080; 78083; 78086; 78090; 78093
Radio Shack (Vinita, OK) 78227
Radio Shack (Woodward, OK) 78265
Radio Shack (Anderson, SC) 78687; 78688
Radio Shack (Charleston, SC) 78875; 78876; 78877; 78878; 78879
Radio Shack (Clinton, SC) 78962
Radio Shack (Columbia, SC) 79079; 79080; 79081
Radio Shack (Conway, SC) 79137
Radio Shack (Greenville, SC) 79415; 79417; 79418
Radio Shack (Hiltn Head is, SC) 79507
Radio Shack (Mt Pleasant, SC) 79679
Radio Shack (Myrtle Beach, SC) 79711
Radio Shack (Rock Hill, SC) 79838
Radio Shack (Spartanburg, SC) 79933; 79934
Radio Shack (Abilene, TX) 82453
Radio Shack (Amarillo, TX) 82577
Radio Shack (Arlington, TX) 82736; 82737; 82742
Radio Shack (Atlanta, TX) 82797
Radio Shack (Austin, TX) 82980; 82987; 82988
Radio Shack (Baytown, TX) 83133
Radio Shack (Beaumont, TX) 83208
Radio Shack (Bedford, TX) 83249
Radio Shack (Bowie, TX) 83327
Radio Shack (Brady, TX) 83331
Radio Shack (Brenham, TX) 83340
Radio Shack (Bryan, TX) 83406
Radio Shack (Carrollton, TX) 83501
Radio Shack (College Sta, TX) 83613
Radio Shack (Colorado City, TX) 83640
Radio Shack (Cuero, TX) 83825
Radio Shack (Dallas, TX) 84328; 84334; 84335; 84339; 84345; 84348
Radio Shack (Decatur, TX) 84544
Radio Shack (Denton, TX) 84635
Radio Shack (El Paso, TX) 84897; 84900; 84901; 84902
Radio Shack (Fort Worth, TX) 85249; 85251; 85254
Radio Shack (Garland, TX) 85531
Radio Shack (Hearne, TX) 85726
Radio Shack (Houston, TX) 86773; 86775; 86785
Radio Shack (Irving, TX) 87397
Radio Shack (La Marque, TX) 87545
Radio Shack (Lewisville, TX) 87662
Radio Shack (Liberty, TX) 87679
Radio Shack (Mexia, TX) 88015
Radio Shack (Ozona, TX) 88336
Radio Shack (Port Arthur, TX) 88644
Radio Shack (Port Isabel, TX) 88664
Radio Shack (San Antonio, TX) 89189; 89191; 89192; 89198; 89199; 89202
Radio Shack (Seminole, TX) 89385
Radio Shack (Stephenville, TX) 89523
Radio Shack (Sulphur Springs, TX) 89563
Radio Shack (Temple, TX) 89634
Radio Shack (Vidor, TX) 89918
Radio Shack (Weatherford, TX) 90011
Radio Shack (West Columbia, TX) 90046
Radio Shack (Alexandria, VA) 90230; 90236
Radio Shack (Blackstone, VA) 90454
Radio Shack (Bristol, VA) 90485
Radio Shack (Charlottesville, VA) 90547
Radio Shack (Chesapeake, VA) 90592; 90593
Radio Shack (Covington, VA) 90664
Radio Shack (Danville, VA) 90713; 90715
Radio Shack (Fredericksburg, VA) 90934; 90935; 90936
Radio Shack (Front Royal, VA) 90953
Radio Shack (Galax, VA) 90963
Radio Shack (Hampton, VA) 91047; 91048; 91049
Radio Shack (Harrisonburg, VA) 91097
Radio Shack (Hopewell, VA) 91162; 91163
Radio Shack (Lexington, VA) 91211; 91212
Radio Shack (Lynchburg, VA) 91278; 91279; 91281; 91282
Radio Shack (Madison Heights, VA) 91301
Radio Shack (Marion, VA) 91338
Radio Shack (Midlothian, VA) 91421; 91423
Radio Shack (Newport News, VA) 91478; 91480; 91482
Radio Shack (Norfolk, VA) 91568; 91569; 91571
Radio Shack (Norton, VA) 91608; 91609
Radio Shack (Orange, VA) 91619; 91620
Radio Shack (Portsmouth, VA) 91664; 91666
Radio Shack (Radford, VA) 91701
Radio Shack (Richmond, VA) 91955; 91956; 91960; 91961; 91962; 91964; 91965; 91966; 91969; 91971; 91973; 91974; 91976
Radio Shack (Roanoke, VA) 92178; 92180; 92182; 92183
Radio Shack (South Boston, VA) 92257; 92258
Radio Shack (Springfield, VA) 92290; 92291
Radio Shack (Suffolk, VA) 92372
Radio Shack (Virginia Beach, VA) 92497; 92498; 92499; 92501; 92502; 92503
Radio Shack (Williamsburg, VA) 92578
Radio Shack (Woodbridge, VA) 92622; 92623
Radio Shack (Yorktown, VA) 92655
Tandy Consumer Products Ser (Tulsa, OK) 78131
Tandy Corp. (Newport News, VA) 91489

5734 Computer & Software Stores

Business Systems & Service Inc. (Vienna, WV) 93077
Digital Equip Corp. (Fort Worth, TX) 85102
Digital Equipment Corporati (Pensacola, FL) 62419
Digital Equipment Corp. (Birmingham, AL) 55223
Digital Equipment Corp. (Jacksonville, FL) 60263
Digital Equipment Corp. (Kernersville, NC) 75277
Exxon (Bentonville, AR) 56784
Hewlett Packard Co. (Tulsa, OK) 77955
Ibm Corp. (Lake City, FL) 60622
Ibm Corp. (Clarksdale, MS) 72675
Ibm Corp. (Burlington, NC) 73757
Ibm Corp. (Wilkesboro, NC) 76516
International Computer Service Inc. (Hialeah, FL) 59989
Radio Shack (Mc Gehee, AR) 57358
Radio Shack (Springdale, AR) 57641
Radio Shack (Apopka, FL) 58575
Radio Shack (Fort Lauderdale, FL) 59577; 59578; 59582; 59588; 59590; 59591
Radio Shack (Fort Myers, FL) 59748; 59749
Radio Shack (Hialeah, FL) 60007
Radio Shack (Hialeah Gdns, FL) 60022
Radio Shack (Jacksonville, FL) 60431
Radio Shack (Melbourne, FL) 61099
Radio Shack (Miami, FL) 61423; 61425; 61427
Radio Shack (N Bay Village, FL) 61584
Radio Shack (N Miami Beach, FL) 61594
Radio Shack (Ocala, FL) 61816
Radio Shack (Olympia Heights, FL) 61855
Radio Shack (Palm Beach, FL) 62261
Radio Shack (Sanford, FL) 62776
Radio Shack (Tampa, FL) 63562
Radio Shack (Titusville, FL) 63702
Radio Shack (W Palm Beach, FL) 63811
Radio Shack (Bowdon, GA) 65391
Radio Shack (Georgia South, GA) 66302
Radio Shack (Griffin, GA) 66322
Radio Shack (Milledgeville, GA) 66984
Radio Shack (Houma, LA) 69968
Radio Shack (Larose, LA) 70187
Radio Shack (Pineville, LA) 70627
Radio Shack (Baltimore, MD) 71225; 71227; 71228
Radio Shack (Cambridge, MD) 71487
Radio Shack (Chestertown, MD) 71524
Radio Shack (Frederick, MD) 71741; 71745
Radio Shack (Waldorf, MD) 72534; 72536
Radio Shack (Greenwood, MS) 72840
Radio Shack (Vicksburg, MS) 73460
Radio Shack (Aberdeen, NC) 73517
Radio Shack (Charlotte, NC) 74133; 74139
Radio Shack (Lenoir, NC) 75386
Radio Shack (Nags Head, NC) 75715
Radio Shack (Raleigh, NC) 75945
Radio Shack (Bartlesville, OK) 76850
Radio Shack (Edmond, OK) 77014
Radio Shack (Shawnee, OK) 77823
Radio Shack (Piedmont, SC) 79796
Radio Shack (Seneca, SC) 79863
Radio Shack (Alamo, TX) 82478
Radio Shack (Carrollton, TX) 83502
Radio Shack (Duncanville, TX) 84708
Radio Shack (El Paso, TX) 84911
Radio Shack (Fort Worth, TX) 85254; 85262
Radio Shack (Groves, TX) 85683
Radio Shack (Houston, TX) 86732; 86745
Radio Shack (Humble, TX) 87243
Radio Shack (Laredo, TX) 87621
Radio Shack (Mcallen, TX) 87938
Radio Shack (Mesquite, TX) 87990
Radio Shack (Porter, TX) 88683
Radio Shack (San Antonio, TX) 89203
Radio Shack (Waco, TX) 89970
Radio Shack (Arlington, VA) 90367; 90373; 90374
Radio Shack (Manassas, VA) 91318
Radio Shack (Norfolk, VA) 91574
Radio Shack (Vienna, VA) 92413; 92416
Radio Shack (Warrenton, VA) 92528
Texas Instruments (Fairfax, VA) 90809

5735 Record & Prerecorded Tape Stores

Radio Shack (H Spg Nat Pk, AR) 57130
Radio Shack (Dripping Springs, TX) 84682

5736 Musical Instruments Stores

Radio Shack (Douglas, GA) 65974
Radio Shack (Crowley, LA) 69802

5800 Eating & Drinking Places

Snap-On Tools Corp. (Elizabethton, TN) 80770

5812 Eating Places

Canteen Corp. (Covington, KY) 68215
Canteen Corp. (La Vergne, TN) 81281
Circuit City (Winston Salem, NC) 76665
Coast to Coast (Lighthouse Point, FL) 60901
Coca Cola Bottling Co. (Key West, FL) 60571
Coca Cola Bottling Co. (Pahokee, FL) 62221
Coca Cola Bottling Co. (Fort Worth, TX) 85085; 85086
Coca-Cola Bottling Co. of Memphis Tennessee Inc. (Memphis, TN) 81497
Courtyard by Marriott (Greenville, SC) 79332
Denny's, Inc. (Spartanburg, SC) 79890
Denny's Restaurant (Louisville, KY) 68751; 68752
Denny's Restaurant (Nashville, TN) 81931; 81932
Denny's Restaurant (Charles Town, WV) 92720
Exxon (Hot Springs National Park, AR) 57168
Flagstar Companies (Spartanburg, SC) 79895
Flagstar Co. Volume Services (Jacksonville, FL) 60302
Flagstar Corp. (Spartanburg, SC) 79898
Flagstar Corp. Canteen Corp. (Spartanburg, SC) 79899
Flagstar Corp. Recreation Services Group (Spartanburg, SC) 79900
Flagstar Corp. Spartan Food Systems Div. (Spartanburg, SC) 79901
Flagstar Corp. Volume Services (Spartanburg, SC) 79903
General Mills Restaurants Inc. (Orlando, FL) 61996
Giant Food Deli (Memphis, TN) 81615
Greyhound Bus Lines (Baton Rouge, LA) 69541
Hertz Rent-A-Car (Dallas, TX) 84115
Intel Corp. (Roanoke, VA) 92159
Kentucky Fried Chicken (Alabaster, AL) 54954
Kentucky Fried Chicken (Alex City, AL) 54972
Kentucky Fried Chicken (Anniston, AL) 55002; 55003
Kentucky Fried Chicken (Athens, AL) 55041
Kentucky Fried Chicken (Attalla, AL) 55055
Kentucky Fried Chicken (Auburn, AL) 55062
Kentucky Fried Chicken (Bessemer, AL) 55096; 55097
Kentucky Fried Chicken (Birmingham, AL) 55291; 55292; 55293; 55294; 55295; 55296; 55297; 55298; 55299
Kentucky Fried Chicken (Boaz, AL) 55468
Kentucky Fried Chicken (Brewton, AL) 55482
Kentucky Fried Chicken (Childersburg, AL) 55514
Kentucky Fried Chicken (Cullman, AL) 55545
Kentucky Fried Chicken (Daleville, AL) 55562
Kentucky Fried Chicken (Dothan, AL) 55654
Kentucky Fried Chicken (Evergreen, AL) 55708
Kentucky Fried Chicken (Fairhope, AL) 55723
Kentucky Fried Chicken (Fayette, AL) 55731
Kentucky Fried Chicken (Gadsden, AL) 55784
Kentucky Fried Chicken (Gardendale, AL) 55799
Kentucky Fried Chicken (Greenville, AL) 55818
Kentucky Fried Chicken (Guntersville, AL) 55829
Kentucky Fried Chicken (Haleyville, AL) 55842

Kentucky Fried Chicken (Hamilton, AL) 55848

Kentucky Fried Chicken (Hartselle, AL) 55856

Kentucky Fried Chicken (Huntsville, AL) 55956; 55957; 55958

Kentucky Fried Chicken (Jacksonville, AL) 56071

Kentucky Fried Chicken (Jasper, AL) 56088

Kentucky Fried Chicken (Leeds, AL) 56106

Kentucky Fried Chicken (Mobile, AL) 56191; 56192; 56193

Kentucky Fried Chicken (Montevallo, AL) 56274

Kentucky Fried Chicken (Montgomery, AL) 56347

Kentucky Fried Chicken (Phenix City, AL) 56462

Kentucky Fried Chicken (Roanoke, AL) 56500

Kentucky Fried Chicken (Russellville, AL) 56508

Kentucky Fried Chicken (Talladega, AL) 56594; 56594

Kentucky Fried Chicken (Tuscaloosa, AL) 56659; 56660

Kentucky Fried Chicken (Valley, AL) 56689

Kentucky Fried Chicken (Alma, AR) 56714

Kentucky Fried Chicken (Arkadelphia, AR) 56717

Kentucky Fried Chicken (Ashdown, AR) 56728

Kentucky Fried Chicken (Bentonville, AR) 56785

Kentucky Fried Chicken (Blytheville, AR) 56807

Kentucky Fried Chicken (Booneville, AR) 56818

Kentucky Fried Chicken (Brinkley, AR) 56820

Kentucky Fried Chicken (Conway, AR) 56864

Kentucky Fried Chicken (Dumas, AR) 56912

Kentucky Fried Chicken (El Dorado, AR) 56950; 56950

Kentucky Fried Chicken (Fayetteville, AR) 56981; 56982

Kentucky Fried Chicken (Forrest City, AR) 57009

Kentucky Fried Chicken (Fort Smith, AR) 57062; 57063; 57064; 57065

Kentucky Fried Chicken (Heber Springs, AR) 57150

Kentucky Fried Chicken (Hope, AR) 57157

Kentucky Fried Chicken (Hot Springs, AR) 57163

Kentucky Fried Chicken (Hot Springs National Park, AR) 57171

Kentucky Fried Chicken (Jonesboro, AR) 57223; 57224

Kentucky Fried Chicken (Malvern, AR) 57340

Kentucky Fried Chicken (Mc Gehee, AR) 57356

Kentucky Fried Chicken (Mena, AR) 57365

Kentucky Fried Chicken (Mountain Home, AR) 57387

Kentucky Fried Chicken (Mountain View, AR) 57396

Kentucky Fried Chicken (N Little Rock, AR) 57405; 57406; 57407; 57408

Kentucky Fried Chicken (Newport, AR) 57449

Kentucky Fried Chicken (Paragould, AR) 57492

Kentucky Fried Chicken (Paris, AR) 57499

Kentucky Fried Chicken (Pine Bluff, AR) 57523

Kentucky Fried Chicken (Pocahontas, AR) 57541

Kentucky Fried Chicken (Searcy, AR) 57603; 57604

Kentucky Fried Chicken (Siloam Springs, AR) 57618

Kentucky Fried Chicken (Springdale, AR) 57636; 57637

Kentucky Fried Chicken (Trumann, AR) 57684

Kentucky Fried Chicken (West Helena, AR) 57713

Kentucky Fried Chicken (West Memphis, AR) 57724

Kentucky Fried Chicken (Wynne, AR) 57741

Kentucky Fried Chicken (Altamonte Spg, FL) 58538

Kentucky Fried Chicken (Apopka, FL) 58572

Kentucky Fried Chicken (Arcadia, FL) 58584

Kentucky Fried Chicken (Auburndale, FL) 58599

Kentucky Fried Chicken (Avon Park, FL) 58608

Kentucky Fried Chicken (Bartow, FL) 58628

Kentucky Fried Chicken (Belle Glade, FL) 58644; 58645

Kentucky Fried Chicken (Bonita Springs, FL) 58759

Kentucky Fried Chicken (Boynton Beach, FL) 58781

Kentucky Fried Chicken (Bradenton, FL) 58827; 58828

Kentucky Fried Chicken (Brooksville, FL) 58891

Kentucky Fried Chicken (Casselberry, FL) 58934; 58935

Kentucky Fried Chicken (Clearwater, FL) 59025; 59025; 59026

Kentucky Fried Chicken (Clewiston, FL) 59060

Kentucky Fried Chicken (Crestview, FL) 59124

Kentucky Fried Chicken (Dade City, FL) 59141

Kentucky Fried Chicken (Dania, FL) 59148

Kentucky Fried Chicken (Daytona Beach, FL) 59187; 59188; 59189

Kentucky Fried Chicken (De Land, FL) 59251; 59252

Kentucky Fried Chicken (Deerfield Beach, FL) 59281; 59282

Kentucky Fried Chicken (Delray Beach, FL) 59320

Kentucky Fried Chicken (Dunedin, FL) 59363

Kentucky Fried Chicken (Fernandina Beach, FL) 59412

Kentucky Fried Chicken (Fort Lauderdale, FL) 59516; 59517; 59518; 59519

Kentucky Fried Chicken (Fort Myers, FL) 59709; 59710; 59711; 59712; 59713

Kentucky Fried Chicken (Gainesville, FL) 59885; 59886; 59887; 59888

Kentucky Fried Chicken (Green Cove Springs, FL) 59932

Kentucky Fried Chicken (Haines City, FL) 59950

Kentucky Fried Chicken (Hallandale, FL) 59960

Kentucky Fried Chicken (Hawthorne, FL) 59972

Kentucky Fried Chicken (Hialeah, FL) 59992; 59993; 59994; 59995

Kentucky Fried Chicken (Hollywood, FL) 60068; 60069; 60070; 60071

Kentucky Fried Chicken (Homestead, FL) 60116

Kentucky Fried Chicken (Inverness, FL) 60150

Kentucky Fried Chicken (Jacksonville, FL) 60344; 60345; 60346; 60347; 60348; 60349; 60350; 60351; 60352; 60353; 60354; 60355; 60356; 60357

Kentucky Fried Chicken (Jasper, FL) 60521

Kentucky Fried Chicken (Jaxville Beach, FL) 60522

Kentucky Fried Chicken (Jupiter, FL) 60542

Kentucky Fried Chicken (Kissimmee, FL) 60590

Kentucky Fried Chicken (Lake City, FL) 60623

Kentucky Fried Chicken (Lake Placid, FL) 60646

Kentucky Fried Chicken (Lake Wales, FL) 60655

Kentucky Fried Chicken (Lake Worth, FL) 60678; 60679

Kentucky Fried Chicken (Lakeland, FL) 60738; 60739; 60740; 60741

Kentucky Fried Chicken (Largo, FL) 60842; 60843

Kentucky Fried Chicken (Live Oak, FL) 60915

Kentucky Fried Chicken (Longwood, FL) 60932

Kentucky Fried Chicken (MacClenny, FL) 60961

Kentucky Fried Chicken (Maitland, FL) 60980

Kentucky Fried Chicken (Marianna, FL) 61004

Kentucky Fried Chicken (Meadows Village, FL) 61028

Kentucky Fried Chicken (Melbourne, FL) 61073; 61074; 61075

Kentucky Fried Chicken (Merritt Island, FL) 61141

Kentucky Fried Chicken (Miami, FL) 61339; 61340; 61341; 61342; 61343; 61344; 61345; 61346; 61347; 61348; 61349; 61350; 61351

Kentucky Fried Chicken (Milton, FL) 61548

Kentucky Fried Chicken (Mount Dora, FL) 61566

Kentucky Fried Chicken (Naples, FL) 61634; 61635; 61636; 61637

Kentucky Fried Chicken (Niceville, FL) 61710

Kentucky Fried Chicken (Nokomis, FL) 61725

Kentucky Fried Chicken (Ocala, FL) 61803

Kentucky Fried Chicken (Opa Locka, FL) 61859; 61860

Kentucky Fried Chicken (Orange Park, FL) 61888

Kentucky Fried Chicken (Orlando, FL) 62018; 62019; 62020; 62021; 62022; 62023; 62024; 62025; 62026

Kentucky Fried Chicken (Ormond Beach, FL) 62206

Kentucky Fried Chicken (Palmetto, FL) 62309

Kentucky Fried Chicken (Panama City, FL) 62325; 62326; 62327; 62328

Kentucky Fried Chicken (Pensacola, FL) 62438; 62439; 62440; 62441; 62442

Kentucky Fried Chicken (Perry, FL) 62500

Kentucky Fried Chicken (Pinellas Park, FL) 62521

Kentucky Fried Chicken (Plant City, FL) 62548; 62549

Kentucky Fried Chicken (Port Richey, FL) 62677

Kentucky Fried Chicken (Punta Gorda, FL) 62710

Kentucky Fried Chicken (Quincy, FL) 62729

Kentucky Fried Chicken (Ruskin, FL) 62758

Kentucky Fried Chicken (Sarasota, FL) 62839; 62840

Kentucky Fried Chicken (Sebring, FL) 62889

Kentucky Fried Chicken (Seffner, FL) 62898

Kentucky Fried Chicken (Smyrna Beach, FL) 62919

Kentucky Fried Chicken (Spring Hill, FL) 62935

Kentucky Fried Chicken (St Augustine, FL) 62941; 62942

Kentucky Fried Chicken (St Petersburg, FL) 62982; 62983; 62984; 62985; 62986

Kentucky Fried Chicken (St. Augustine, FL) 63062

Kentucky Fried Chicken (St. Cloud, FL) 63066

Kentucky Fried Chicken (Starke, FL) 63148

Kentucky Fried Chicken (Tallahassee, FL) 63245; 63246; 63247; 63248

Kentucky Fried Chicken (Tampa, FL) 63466; 63467; 63468; 63469; 63470; 63471; 63472; 63473; 63474; 63475; 63476; 63477

Kentucky Fried Chicken (Titusville, FL) 63692; 63693

Kentucky Fried Chicken (W Palm Beach, FL) 63793; 63794

Kentucky Fried Chicken (West Palm Beach, FL) 63874; 63875; 63876; 63877; 63878

Kentucky Fried Chicken (Winter Garden, FL) 63922

Kentucky Fried Chicken (Winter Haven, FL) 63942; 63943; 63943

Kentucky Fried Chicken (Winter Park, FL) 63984; 63985

Kentucky Fried Chicken (Zephyrhills, FL) 64013; 64014; 64015

Kentucky Fried Chicken (Albany, GA) 64077

Kentucky Fried Chicken (Americus, GA) 64141

Kentucky Fried Chicken (Bainbridge, GA) 65367

Kentucky Fried Chicken (Baxley Georgi, GA) 65381

Kentucky Fried Chicken (Brunswick, GA) 65415; 65416

Kentucky Fried Chicken (Carrollton, GA) 65496

Kentucky Fried Chicken (Cedartown, GA) 65512

Kentucky Fried Chicken (Covington, GA) 65730

Kentucky Fried Chicken (Cumming, GA) 65747

Kentucky Fried Chicken (Douglas, GA) 65971

Kentucky Fried Chicken (Eastman, GA) 66158

Kentucky Fried Chicken (Gainesville, GA) 66278

Kentucky Fried Chicken (Griffin, GA) 66318

Kentucky Fried Chicken (Macon, GA) 66695

Kentucky Fried Chicken (Milledgeville, GA) 66980

Kentucky Fried Chicken (Monroe, GA) 66991

Kentucky Fried Chicken (Perry, GA) 67266

Kentucky Fried Chicken (Quitman, GA) 67288

Kentucky Fried Chicken (St Simons is, GA) 67620

Kentucky Fried Chicken (Statesboro, GA) 67638

Kentucky Fried Chicken (Stone Mountain, GA) 67695

Kentucky Fried Chicken (Swainsboro, GA) 67753

Kentucky Fried Chicken (Thomasville, GA) 67800

Kentucky Fried Chicken (Valdosta, GA) 67961; 67962; 67963; 67964

Kentucky Fried Chicken (Vidalia, GA) 67987

Kentucky Fried Chicken (Waycross, GA) 68034

Kentucky Fried Chicken (Alexandria, LA) 69386; 69387

Kentucky Fried Chicken (Baker, LA) 69436

Kentucky Fried Chicken (Baton Rouge, LA) 69567; 69568; 69569; 69570; 69571; 69572; 69573; 69574

Kentucky Fried Chicken (Bossier City, LA) 69718; 69719; 69720

Kentucky Fried Chicken (De Ridder, LA) 69815

Kentucky Fried Chicken (Denham Springs, LA) 69829

Kentucky Fried Chicken (Gonzales, LA) 69891

Kentucky Fried Chicken (Hammond, LA) 69930

Kentucky Fried Chicken (Houma, LA) 69959

Kentucky Fried Chicken (Jonesboro, LA) 69983

Kentucky Fried Chicken (Lafayette, LA) 70066

Kentucky Fried Chicken (Lake Charles, LA) 70143

Kentucky Fried Chicken (Mansfield, LA) 70214

Kentucky Fried Chicken (Metairie, LA) 70280; 70281

Kentucky Fried Chicken (Minden, LA) 70342

Kentucky Fried Chicken (Monroe, LA) 70356; 70357

Kentucky Fried Chicken (Natchitoches, LA) 70401

Kentucky Fried Chicken (New Orleans, LA) 70509; 70510; 70511; 70512

Kentucky Fried Chicken (Pineville, LA) 70621

Kentucky Fried Chicken (Ruston, LA) 70669

Kentucky Fried Chicken (Shreveport, LA) 70737; 70738; 70738; 70739; 70740; 70740; 70741; 70742

Kentucky Fried Chicken (Slidell, LA) 70830

Kentucky Fried Chicken (Springhill, LA) 70851

Kentucky Fried Chicken (Tallulah, LA) 70906

Kentucky Fried Chicken (Winnfield, LA) 70977

Kentucky Fried Chicken (Belzoni, MS) 72613

Kentucky Fried Chicken (Biloxi, MS) 72623; 72624

Kentucky Fried Chicken (Booneville, MS) 72644

Kentucky Fried Chicken (Brookhaven, MS) 72657

Kentucky Fried Chicken (Carthage, MS) 72661

Kentucky Fried Chicken (Clarksdale, MS) 72676

Kentucky Fried Chicken (Clinton, MS) 72685

Kentucky Fried Chicken (Columbus, MS) 72715; 72716

Kentucky Fried Chicken (Corinth, MS) 72739

Kentucky Fried Chicken (Crystal Springs, MS) 72749

Kentucky Fried Chicken (Forest, MS) 72773

Kentucky Fried Chicken (Greenville, MS) 72803; 72804; 72805

Kentucky Fried Chicken (Greenwood, MS) 72836

Kentucky Fried Chicken (Grenada, MS) 72841

Kentucky Fried Chicken (Gulfport, MS) 72858; 72859

Kentucky Fried Chicken (Holly Springs, MS) 72909

Kentucky Fried Chicken (Indianola, MS) 72928

Kentucky Fried Chicken (Jackson, MS) 72996; 72997; 72998; 72999; 73000; 73001; 73002; 73003

Kentucky Fried Chicken (Kosciusko, MS) 73096

Kentucky Fried Chicken (Mc Comb, MS) 73145; 73146

Kentucky Fried Chicken (Meridian, MS) 73165; 73166; 73167

Kentucky Fried Chicken (Moss Point, MS) 73194

Kentucky Fried Chicken (Natchez, MS) 73202

Kentucky Fried Chicken (New Albany, MS) 73215

Kentucky Fried Chicken (Oxford, MS) 73240

Kentucky Fried Chicken (Pontotoc, MS) 73302

Kentucky Fried Chicken (Ridgeland, MS) 73320

Kentucky Fried Chicken (Senatobia, MS) 73339

Kentucky Fried Chicken (Southaven, MS) 73348

Kentucky Fried Chicken (Starkville, MS) 73365

Kentucky Fried Chicken (Tupelo, MS) 73407

Kentucky Fried Chicken (Vicksburg, MS) 73455; 73456; 73457

Kentucky Fried Chicken (Waynesboro, MS) 73473

Kentucky Fried Chicken (West Point, MS) 73483

Kentucky Fried Chicken (Albemarle, NC) 73538; 73539

Kentucky Fried Chicken (Asheboro, NC) 73589

Kentucky Fried Chicken (Black Mountain, NC) 73698

Kentucky Fried Chicken (Boone, NC) 73714

Kentucky Fried Chicken (Burlington, NC) 73758

Kentucky Fried Chicken (Canton, NC) 73780

Kentucky Fried Chicken (Carrboro, NC) 73784

Kentucky Fried Chicken (Charlotte, NC) 74053; 74054; 74055; 74056; 74057; 74058; 74059; 74060; 74061

Kentucky Fried Chicken (Cherokee, NC) 74234

Kentucky Fried Chicken (Cherryville, NC) 74247

Kentucky Fried Chicken (Clinton, NC) 74292

Kentucky Fried Chicken (Conover, NC) 74334

Kentucky Fried Chicken (Durham, NC) 74410; 74411

Kentucky Fried Chicken (Eden, NC) 74460

Kentucky Fried Chicken (Elizabeth City, NC) 74482

Kentucky Fried Chicken (Fayetteville, NC) 74562

Kentucky Fried Chicken (Forest City, NC) 74607

Kentucky Fried Chicken (Fuquay Varina, NC) 74638

Kentucky Fried Chicken (Greensboro, NC) 74858; 74859; 74860

Kentucky Fried Chicken (Hickory, NC) 75083; 75084

Kentucky Fried Chicken (High Point, NC) 75139; 75140; 75141; 75142

Kentucky Fried Chicken (Jacksonville, NC) 75218

Kentucky Fried Chicken (Kannapolis, NC) 75264

Kentucky Fried Chicken (Kernersville, NC) 75281

Kentucky Fried Chicken (Kill Devil Hills, NC) 75287

Kentucky Fried Chicken (Kings Mountain, NC) 75305

Kentucky Fried Chicken (Lenoir, NC) 75381

Kentucky Fried Chicken (Lewisville, NC) 75395

Kentucky Fried Chicken (Lexington, NC) 75405

Kentucky Fried Chicken (Lumberton, NC) 75467; 75468

Kentucky Fried Chicken (Matthews, NC) 75525

Kentucky Fried Chicken (Morehead City, NC) 75622

Kentucky Fried Chicken (Morganton, NC) 75651

Kentucky Fried Chicken (Morgantown, NC) 75661

Kentucky Fried Chicken (Mount Airy, NC) 75680

McDonald's Hamburgers (Lexington, KY) 68577
McDonald's Hamburgers (Louisville, KY) 68882
McDonald's Hamburgers (Madisonville, KY) 69066
McDonald's Hamburgers (Mayfield, KY) 69079
McDonald's Hamburgers (Paducah, KY) 69209
McDonald's Hamburgers (Versailles, KY) 69329
McDonald's Hamburgers (Winchester, KY) 69348
McDonalds Hamburgers (Bossier City, LA) 69724
McDonalds Hamburgers (Mandeville, LA) 70209
McDonalds Hamburgers (New Orleans, LA) 70531; 70532
McDonald's Hamburgers (Baltimore, MD) 71189; 71190; 71191; 71192; 71193; 71194; 71195; 71196; 71197
McDonald's Hamburgers (Clinton, MD) 71541
McDonald's Hamburgers (Glen Burnie, MD) 71846
McDonald's Hamburgers (Pocomoke City, MD) 72222
McDonald's Hamburgers (Salisbury, MD) 72349; 72350
McDonald's Hamburgers (Severna Park, MD) 72375
McDonalds Hamburgers (Fayetteville, NC) 74565; 74566
McDonalds Hamburgers (Goldsboro, NC) 74725
McDonalds Hamburgers (Owasso, OK) 77685
McDonald's Hamburgers (Chattanooga, TN) 80426; 80427; 80428; 80429; 80430; 80431; 80432; 80433; 80434
McDonald's Hamburgers (Clarksville, TN) 80557
McDonald's Hamburgers (Cleveland, TN) 80594
McDonald's Hamburgers (Cookeville, TN) 80661
McDonald's Hamburgers (Fort Oglethorpe, TN) 80801
McDonald's Hamburgers (Jackson, TN) 80990
McDonald's Hamburgers (Kingsport, TN) 81111
McDonald's Hamburgers (Lawrenceburg, TN) 81291
McDonald's Hamburgers (Manchester, TN) 81393
McDonald's Hamburgers (Nashville, TN) 82061
McDonald's Hamburgers (Union City, TN) 82386
McDonald's Hamburgers (Abilene, TX) 82448
McDonald's Hamburgers (Garland, TX) 85508
McDonald's Hamburgers (Arlington, VA) 90358
McDonald's Hamburgers (Belle Haven, VA) 90428
McDonald's Hamburgers (Charlottesville, VA) 90543
McDonald's Hamburgers (Chester, VA) 90620
McDonald's Hamburgers (Hampton, VA) 91045
McDonald's Hamburgers (Leesburg, VA) 91195
McDonald's Hamburgers (Newport News, VA) 91473
McDonald's Hamburgers (Norton, VA) 91605
McDonald's Hamburgers (Richmond, VA) 91929
McDonald's Hamburgers (Williamsburg, VA) 92576
McDonald's Hamburgers (Barboursville, WV) 92671
McDonald's Hamburgers (Ripley, WV) 93028
McDonald's Hamburgers Office (Proctor, WV) 93014
McDonalds of King (King, NC) 75290
McDonalds of Mckinney (Mc Kinney, TX) 87916
McDonalds of Miners Plaza (Fort Myers, FL) 59722
McDonalds No 6574 (Panama City, FL) 62334
McDonalds Office (West Palm Beach, FL) 63885
McDonalds Ofifce (Midland, TX) 88049
McDonalds of Red Bluff (Pasadena, TX) 88440
McDonald's Restaurant (Alabaster, AL) 54955
McDonald's Restaurant (Davenport, FL) 59151
McDonalds Restaurant (Destin, FL) 59345

McDonalds Restaurant (Fort Lauderdale, FL) 59535; 59536; 59537
McDonalds Restaurant (Miami, FL) 61371; 61372
McDonalds Restaurant (Pompano Beach, FL) 62611
McDonalds Restaurant (Columbus, MS) 72718; 72719
McDonalds Restaurant (Yazoo City, MS) 73504
McDonalds Restaurant (Durant, OK) 77001
McDonalds Restaurant (Henrietta, OK) 77126
McDonalds Restaurant (Hardeeville, SC) 79496
McDonalds Restaurant (Alief, TX) 82492
McDonalds Restaurant (Azle, TX) 83080
McDonalds Restaurant (Brenham, TX) 83337
McDonalds Restaurant (Channelview, TX) 83551
McDonalds Restaurant (Cleburne, TX) 83577
McDonalds Restaurant (Houston, TX) 86547; 86549; 86550; 86551; 86552; 86553; 86554; 86555; 86556; 86557; 86558; 86559; 86560; 86561; 86562; 86563; 86564; 86565; 86566; 86567; 86568; 86569
McDonalds Restaurant (Odessa, TX) 88255
McDonalds Restaurant (Pasadena, TX) 88441; 88442
McDonalds Restaurant (Richardson, TX) 88749
McDonalds Restaurant (Stafford, TX) 89502
McDonalds Restaurant (Weslaco, TX) 90035
McDonalds Restaurants (Bessemer, AL) 55098
McDonalds Restaurants (Apopka, FL) 58574
McDonalds Restaurants (Bradenton, FL) 58834; 58835
McDonalds Restaurants (Brandon, FL) 58874
McDonald's Restaurants (Clearwater, FL) 59034
McDonalds Restaurants (Kissimmee, FL) 60593; 60594
McDonalds Restaurants (Lakeland, FL) 60749; 60750; 60751; 60752
McDonalds Restaurants (Melbourne, FL) 61079
McDonald's Restaurants (Miami, FL) 61373; 61374
McDonalds Restaurants (New Port Richey, FL) 61688
McDonald's Restaurants (Orlando, FL) 62055; 62056; 62057; 62058; 62059
McDonalds Restaurants (St Petersburg, FL) 62995; 62996; 62997
McDonalds Restaurants (Tampa, FL) 63497; 63498; 63499; 63500
McDonalds Restaurants (Temple Ter, FL) 63674
McDonalds Restaurants (Winter Haven, FL) 63946
McDonalds Restaurants (Duncan, OK) 76994
McDonalds Restaurants (Corpus Christi, TX) 83732
McDonalds Restaurants (Houston, TX) 86570; 86571
McDonalds Restaurants (Irving, TX) 87376
McDonalds Restaurants (San Antonio, TX) 89101
McDonalds Restaurants (Wichita Falls, TX) 90083
McDonalds of Seneca (Seneca, SC) 79862
McDonalds of Wallace (Wallace, NC) 76441
McDonalds of Wynne (Wynne, AR) 57742
Piggly Wiggly (Aliceville, AL) 54983
Piggly Wiggly (Daleville, AL) 55563
Piggly Wiggly (Goodwater, AL) 55810
Piggly Wiggly (Niceville, FL) 61714
Piggly Wiggly (Tifton, GA) 67827
Pizza Hut (Albertville, AL) 54969
Pizza Hut (Andalusia, AL) 54988
Pizza Hut (Anniston, AL) 55007; 55008
Pizza Hut (Arab, AL) 55026
Pizza Hut (Athens, AL) 55045
Pizza Hut (Atmore, AL) 55052
Pizza Hut (Attalla, AL) 55057
Pizza Hut (Auburn, AL) 55068; 55069
Pizza Hut (Bay Minette, AL) 55077
Pizza Hut (Bessemer, AL) 55099; 55100

Pizza Hut (Birmingham, AL) 55337; 55338; 55339; 55340; 55341; 55342; 55343; 55344; 55345; 55346; 55347; 55348; 55349; 55350; 55351; 55352
Pizza Hut (Boaz, AL) 55474
Pizza Hut (Cullman, AL) 55548
Pizza Hut (Daphne, AL) 55568
Pizza Hut (Decatur, AL) 55602; 55603
Pizza Hut (Dothan, AL) 55661; 55662
Pizza Hut (Enterprise, AL) 55690
Pizza Hut (Fairhope, AL) 55724
Pizza Hut (Fayette, AL) 55732
Pizza Hut (Foley, AL) 55750
Pizza Hut (Greenville, AL) 55819
Pizza Hut (Guntersville, AL) 55832
Pizza Hut (Haleyville, AL) 55845
Pizza Hut (Hamilton, AL) 55850
Pizza Hut (Huntsville, AL) 55994; 55995; 55996; 55997; 55998; 55999
Pizza Hut (Jackson, AL) 56069
Pizza Hut (Jacksonville, AL) 56075
Pizza Hut (Leeds, AL) 56107
Pizza Hut (Mobile, AL) 56220; 56221; 56222; 56223; 56224; 56225; 56226; 56227
Pizza Hut (Monroeville, AL) 56268
Pizza Hut (Montgomery, AL) 56364; 56365; 56366; 56367; 56368; 56369
Pizza Hut (Northport, AL) 56409
Pizza Hut (Opelika, AL) 56422
Pizza Hut (Opp, AL) 56435
Pizza Hut (Ozark, AL) 56445
Pizza Hut (Phenix City, AL) 56470
Pizza Hut (Prattville, AL) 56490
Pizza Hut (Russellville, AL) 56510
Pizza Hut (Scottsboro, AL) 56522
Pizza Hut (Sylacauga, AL) 56587
Pizza Hut (Talladega, AL) 56597
Pizza Hut (Trussville, AL) 56629
Pizza Hut (Tuscaloosa, AL) 56668; 56669
Pizza Hut (Wetumpka, AL) 56704
Pizza Hut (Arkadelphia, AR) 56720
Pizza Hut (Ash Flat, AR) 56726
Pizza Hut (Ashdown, AR) 56729
Pizza Hut (Batesville, AR) 56760; 56760
Pizza Hut (Beebe, AR) 56768
Pizza Hut (Benton, AR) 56773
Pizza Hut (Blytheville, AR) 56813
Pizza Hut (Brinkley, AR) 56821
Pizza Hut (Bryant, AR) 56824
Pizza Hut (Camden, AR) 56839
Pizza Hut (Clarksville, AR) 56850
Pizza Hut (Clinton, AR) 56858
Pizza Hut (Conway, AR) 56868
Pizza Hut (Dardanelle, AR) 56888
Pizza Hut (De Queen, AR) 56895
Pizza Hut (El Dorado, AR) 56956
Pizza Hut (Fayetteville, AR) 56986; 56987; 56988
Pizza Hut (Forrest City, AR) 57011
Pizza Hut (Fort Smith, AR) 57083; 57084; 57085
Pizza Hut (H Spg Nat Pk, AR) 57127
Pizza Hut (Harrison, AR) 57140
Pizza Hut (Heber Springs, AR) 57151
Pizza Hut (Hot Springs National Park, AR) 57182; 57183
Pizza Hut (Jacksonville, AR) 57199
Pizza Hut (Little Rock, AR) 57297; 57298
Pizza Hut (Mena, AR) 57366
Pizza Hut (Mountain Home, AR) 57388
Pizza Hut (N Little Rock, AR) 57416; 57416
Pizza Hut (Nashville, AR) 57441
Pizza Hut (Newport, AR) 57450; 57451
Pizza Hut (Ozark, AR) 57487
Pizza Hut (Pea Ridge, AR) 57504
Pizza Hut (Pine Bluff, AR) 57527
Pizza Hut (Pocahontas, AR) 57543
Pizza Hut (Prescott, AR) 57552
Pizza Hut (Russellville, AR) 57585
Pizza Hut (Searcy, AR) 57606; 57607
Pizza Hut (Springdale, AR) 57640
Pizza Hut (Stuttgart, AR) 57663
Pizza Hut (Trumann, AR) 57686
Pizza Hut (Van Buren, AR) 57691
Pizza Hut (Warren, AR) 57709
Pizza Hut (West Helena, AR) 57714
Pizza Hut (West Memphis, AR) 57730
Pizza Hut (Alachua, FL) 58532
Pizza Hut (Altamonte Springs, FL) 58562
Pizza Hut (Arcadia, FL) 58585
Pizza Hut (Avon Park, FL) 58609
Pizza Hut (Belleview, FL) 58656
Pizza Hut (Boca Raton, FL) 58727; 58729; 58730
Pizza Hut (Boynton Beach, FL) 58787

Pizza Hut (Bradenton, FL) 58839; 58840; 58841; 58842
Pizza Hut (Brandon, FL) 58876
Pizza Hut (Brooksville, FL) 58893
Pizza Hut (Casselberry, FL) 58939
Pizza Hut (Clearwater, FL) 59037; 59038
Pizza Hut (Clermont, FL) 59057
Pizza Hut (Cocoa Beach, FL) 59082
Pizza Hut (Dade City, FL) 59142
Pizza Hut (Dania, FL) 59149
Pizza Hut (Daytona Beach, FL) 59197; 59198; 59199; 59200; 59201; 59202
Pizza Hut (De Funiak Springs, FL) 59244
Pizza Hut (De Land, FL) 59254; 59255
Pizza Hut (Destin, FL) 59347; 59348
Pizza Hut (Dunedin, FL) 59365
Pizza Hut (Eustis, FL) 59401
Pizza Hut (Fernandina Beach, FL) 59413
Pizza Hut (Flagler Beach, FL) 59418
Pizza Hut (Fort Lauderdale, FL) 59553; 59554; 59555; 59556; 59557; 59558; 59559; 59560
Pizza Hut (Fort Myers, FL) 59732; 59733; 59734; 59735; 59736; 59737; 59738; 59739; 59740
Pizza Hut (Fort Pierce, FL) 59799; 59800; 59801
Pizza Hut (Fort Walton Beach, FL) 59833; 59834; 59835
Pizza Hut (Gainesville, FL) 59899; 59900; 59901; 59902; 59903; 59904
Pizza Hut (Gulf Breeze, FL) 59938
Pizza Hut (Haines City, FL) 59951
Pizza Hut (Hialeah, FL) 60000; 60001; 60002
Pizza Hut (Hollywood, FL) 60080; 60081; 60082; 60083
Pizza Hut (Homestead, FL) 60118
Pizza Hut (Homosassa, FL) 60125
Pizza Hut (Inverness, FL) 60151
Pizza Hut (Jacksonville, FL) 60392; 60393; 60394; 60395; 60396; 60397; 60398; 60399; 60400; 60401; 60402; 60403; 60404; 60405; 60406; 60408; 60409; 60410; 60411; 60412
Pizza Hut (Jupiter, FL) 60545
Pizza Hut (Key Largo, FL) 60567
Pizza Hut (Key West, FL) 60577
Pizza Hut (Kissimmee, FL) 60595; 60596; 60597
Pizza Hut (Lake City, FL) 60624; 60625
Pizza Hut (Lake Placid, FL) 60647
Pizza Hut (Lake Wales, FL) 60656
Pizza Hut (Lake Worth, FL) 60685; 60686; 60687
Pizza Hut (Lakeland, FL) 60762; 60763; 60764; 60765; 60766
Pizza Hut (Largo, FL) 60849; 60850; 60851; 60852; 60853
Pizza Hut (Lehigh Acres, FL) 60895
Pizza Hut (Live Oak, FL) 60916
Pizza Hut (Longwood, FL) 60943; 60944
Pizza Hut (Maitland, FL) 60983
Pizza Hut (Marianna, FL) 61006; 61007
Pizza Hut (Mary Esther, FL) 61021
Pizza Hut (Meadows Village, FL) 61029
Pizza Hut (Melbourne, FL) 61084; 61085; 61086; 61087; 61088
Pizza Hut (Merritt Island, FL) 61143
Pizza Hut (Miami, FL) 61391; 61392; 61393; 61394; 61395; 61396; 61397; 61398; 61399
Pizza Hut (Milton, FL) 61550
Pizza Hut (N Bay Village, FL) 61583
Pizza Hut (Naples, FL) 61651; 61652
Pizza Hut (Niceville, FL) 61715
Pizza Hut (No Palm Beach, FL) 61723
Pizza Hut (Ocala, FL) 61811; 61812
Pizza Hut (Ocoee, FL) 61836
Pizza Hut (Okeechobee, FL) 61843
Pizza Hut (Opa Locka, FL) 61862
Pizza Hut (Orange Park, FL) 61893; 61894
Pizza Hut (Orlando, FL) 62082; 62084; 62085; 62086; 62087; 62088; 62089; 62090; 62091; 62092; 62093; 62095; 62096; 62097; 62099
Pizza Hut (Ormond Beach, FL) 62207
Pizza Hut (Palm Bay, FL) 62243
Pizza Hut (Palm Springs, FL) 62305

Pizza Hut (Panama City, FL) 62338; 62339; 62340; 62341; 62342; 62343; 62344
Pizza Hut (Pensacola, FL) 62456; 62457; 62458; 62459; 62460; 62461; 62462
Pizza Hut (Perry, FL) 62501
Pizza Hut (Pinellas Park, FL) 62525; 62526
Pizza Hut (Plant City, FL) 62551
Pizza Hut (Pompano Beach, FL) 62614; 62616; 62617
Pizza Hut (Port Richey, FL) 62679
Pizza Hut (Port St Lucie, FL) 62689
Pizza Hut (Punta Gorda, FL) 62714
Pizza Hut (Quincy, FL) 62731
Pizza Hut (Rockledge, FL) 62747
Pizza Hut (Ruskin, FL) 62759
Pizza Hut (Sanford, FL) 62771; 62772
Pizza Hut (Sarasota, FL) 62855; 62856
Pizza Hut (Sebring, FL) 62891
Pizza Hut (Smyrna Beach, FL) 62920
Pizza Hut (St Augustine, FL) 62946; 62947; 62948; 62949; 62960
Pizza Hut (St Petersburg, FL) 63002; 63003; 63004; 63005; 63006; 63007; 63008; 63009; 63010; 63011
Pizza Hut (St. Cloud, FL) 63069
Pizza Hut (Starke, FL) 63150
Pizza Hut (Stuart, FL) 63177
Pizza Hut (Sunrise, FL) 63195
Pizza Hut (Tallahassee, FL) 63255; 63256; 63257; 63258
Pizza Hut (Tampa, FL) 63520; 63521; 63522; 63523; 63524; 63525; 63526; 63527; 63528; 63529; 63530; 63531; 63532; 63533; 63534; 63535
Pizza Hut (Titusville, FL) 63698
Pizza Hut (Valrico, FL) 63716
Pizza Hut (Venice, FL) 63730
Pizza Hut (Vero Beach, FL) 63767
Pizza Hut (W Palm Beach, FL) 63799; 63800
Pizza Hut (West Palm Beach, FL) 63891; 63892; 63893
Pizza Hut (Winter Haven, FL) 63948
Pizza Hut (Winter Park, FL) 63988; 63989; 63990
Pizza Hut (Winter Springs, FL) 64003
Pizza Hut (Zephyrhills, FL) 64017; 64018; 64019
Pizza Hut (Albany, GA) 64086
Pizza Hut (Alma, GA) 64101
Pizza Hut (Americus, GA) 64143
Pizza Hut (Bainbridge, GA) 65369
Pizza Hut (Brunswick, GA) 65421; 65422
Pizza Hut (Cairo, GA) 65448
Pizza Hut (Camilla, GA) 65482
Pizza Hut (Canton, GA) 65485
Pizza Hut (Cartersville, GA) 65505
Pizza Hut (Cordele, GA) 65717
Pizza Hut (Covington, GA) 65739
Pizza Hut (Cumming, GA) 65748
Pizza Hut (Dawson, GA) 65793
Pizza Hut (Douglas, GA) 65973
Pizza Hut (Dublin, GA) 66014
Pizza Hut (Fitzgerald, GA) 66212
Pizza Hut (Gainesville, GA) 66286; 66287
Pizza Hut (Hinesville, GA) 66356
Pizza Hut (Jackson, GA) 66366
Pizza Hut (Jesup, GA) 66372
Pizza Hut (Macon, GA) 66705
Pizza Hut (Moultrie, GA) 67062
Pizza Hut (Perry, GA) 67267
Pizza Hut (Quitman, GA) 67290
Pizza Hut (Statesboro, GA) 67642
Pizza Hut (Swainsboro, GA) 67756
Pizza Hut (Sylvester, GA) 67776
Pizza Hut (Thomasville, GA) 67802; 67803
Pizza Hut (Valdosta, GA) 67967; 67968; 67969; 67970
Pizza Hut (Vidalia, GA) 67992
Pizza Hut (Warner Robins, GA) 68019
Pizza Hut (Alexandria, LA) 69397; 69398
Pizza Hut (Bastrop, LA) 69445
Pizza Hut (Baton Rouge, LA) 69600; 69601; 69602; 69603; 69604; 69605; 69606; 69607; 69609
Pizza Hut (Bogalusa, LA) 69707
Pizza Hut (Bossier City, LA) 69725; 69726; 69727
Pizza Hut (Chalmette, LA) 69767
Pizza Hut (Covington, LA) 69797
Pizza Hut (Cut Off, LA) 69806
Pizza Hut (De Ridder, LA) 69817
Pizza Hut (Denham Springs, LA) 69830
Pizza Hut (Donaldsonville, LA) 69841
Pizza Hut (Galliano, LA) 69861

Pizza Hut (Spearman, TX) 89461
Pizza Hut (Spring, TX) 89481; 89482; 89483
Pizza Hut (Stafford, TX) 89503
Pizza Hut (Stamford, TX) 89512
Pizza Hut (Stephenville, TX) 89522
Pizza Hut (Sulphur Springs, TX) 89562
Pizza Hut (Sweetwater, TX) 89589
Pizza Hut (Taylor, TX) 89600
Pizza Hut (Temple, TX) 89631; 89633
Pizza Hut (Terrell, TX) 89660
Pizza Hut (Texas City, TX) 89731
Pizza Hut (Tomball, TX) 89775
Pizza Hut (Tulia, TX) 89786
Pizza Hut (Tyler, TX) 89822; 89823
Pizza Hut (Universal Cty, TX) 89846
Pizza Hut (Uvalde, TX) 89854
Pizza Hut (Vernon, TX) 89868
Pizza Hut (Victoria, TX) 89901
Pizza Hut (Vidor, TX) 89917
Pizza Hut (Weatherford, TX) 90010
Pizza Hut (Weslaco, TX) 90036
Pizza Hut (Whitesboro, TX) 90061
Pizza Hut (Wichita Falls, TX) 90088; 90089; 90090; 90092
Pizza Hut (Yoakum, TX) 90136
Pizza Hut (Zapata, TX) 90138
Pizza Hut Area Office (Abilene, TX) 82452
Pizza Hut District Office (Rural Hall, NC) 76134
Pizza Hut District Office (Tulsa, OK) 78069
Pizza Hut Hearne Office (Hearne, TX) 85725
Pizza Hut Inc. (Hammond, LA) 69932
Pizza Hut Inc. (Gulfport, MS) 72869
Pizza Hut Inc. (Midland, TX) 88069
Pizza Hut Inc. (San Antonio, TX) 89184
Pizza Hut Region Training (Tampa, FL) 63536
Publix Super Market (St Petersburg, FL) 63015
Publix Super Market (Zephyrhills, FL) 64020; 64021
Publix Super Markets (Plant City, FL) 62553
Publix Super Markets (St Petersburg, FL) 63018
Publix Super Markets (Zephyrhills, FL) 64023
Publix Super Markets Inc. (Zephyrhills, FL) 64024
Quincy Family Steak House (Spartanburg, SC) 79929
Quincy Family Steakhouse (Maryville, TN) 81422
Quincy Family Steakhouse (Nashville, TN) 82085

Shell Oil (Louisville, KY) 69005
Shell Pipeline Corp. (El Paso, TX) 84928; 84929
Shell Super Stop (Magnolia, AR) 57336
Shell Truck Stop (Bastrop, LA) 69450
Taco Bell (Anniston, AL) 55015
Taco Bell (Auburn, AL) 55072
Taco Bell (Bessemer, AL) 55103
Taco Bell (Birmingham, AL) 55404; 55405; 55406; 55407; 55408; 55410; 55411; 55412; 55413; 55414; 55415; 55416; 55417
Taco Bell (Boaz, AL) 55476
Taco Bell (Brewton, AL) 55484
Taco Bell (Cullman, AL) 55552
Taco Bell (Decatur, AL) 55605; 55606
Taco Bell (Dothan, AL) 55671
Taco Bell (Gadsden, AL) 55791; 55792
Taco Bell (Huntsville, AL) 56025; 56026; 56027; 56028; 56029; 56030
Taco Bell (Mobile, AL) 56242; 56243; 56244
Taco Bell (Scottsboro, AL) 56524
Taco Bell (Selma, AL) 56539
Taco Bell (Tuscaloosa, AL) 56676
Taco Bell (Benton, AR) 56778
Taco Bell (Conway, AR) 56872
Taco Bell (El Dorado, AR) 56959
Taco Bell (Fayetteville, AR) 56995; 56996
Taco Bell (Fort Smith, AR) 57100; 57101; 57103
Taco Bell (H Spg Nat Pk, AR) 57133; 57134
Taco Bell (Jacksonville, AR) 57203
Taco Bell (Jonesboro, AR) 57231
Taco Bell (Monticello, AR) 57374; 57374
Taco Bell (N Little Rock, AR) 57424; 57425; 57426; 57427; 57428
Taco Bell (Pine Bluff, AR) 57531
Taco Bell (Van Buren, AR) 57694
Taco Bell (West Memphis, AR) 57736
Taco Bell (Altamonte Spg, FL) 58546
Taco Bell (Boca Raton, FL) 58745
Taco Bell (Casselberry, FL) 58943
Taco Bell (Clearwater, FL) 59048
Taco Bell (Daytona Beach, FL) 59215; 59216
Taco Bell (Fernandina Beach, FL) 59414
Taco Bell (Fort Lauderdale, FL) 59615; 59616
Taco Bell (Fort Myers, FL) 59763; 59764; 59765
Taco Bell (Fort Walton Beach, FL) 59839
Taco Bell (Gainesville, FL) 59920; 59921
Taco Bell (Hialeah, FL) 60011
Taco Bell (Hollywood, FL) 60097; 60098
Taco Bell (Jacksonville, FL) 60460; 60461; 60462; 60463; 60464; 60465; 60466; 60467; 60468; 60469; 60470
Taco Bell (Jupiter, FL) 60552
Taco Bell (Kissimmee, FL) 60602
Taco Bell (Lake City, FL) 60629; 60630
Taco Bell (Lake Mary, FL) 60639
Taco Bell (Lakeland, FL) 60785
Taco Bell (Largo, FL) 60864
Taco Bell (Leesburg, FL) 60887
Taco Bell (Longwood, FL) 60949
Taco Bell (Mary Esther, FL) 61023
Taco Bell (Melbourne, FL) 61107; 61108; 61109
Taco Bell (Merritt is, FL) 61133
Taco Bell (Miami, FL) 61469; 61470; 61471
Taco Bell (Naples, FL) 61665
Taco Bell (North Fort Myers, FL) 61729
Taco Bell (Orange Park, FL) 61898
Taco Bell (Orlando, FL) 62153; 62154; 62155; 62156; 62157
Taco Bell (Panama City, FL) 62352
Taco Bell (Pensacola, FL) 62476; 62477; 62478; 62479; 62480
Taco Bell (Pinellas Park, FL) 62528
Taco Bell (Sanford, FL) 62781
Taco Bell (St Petersburg, FL) 63035
Taco Bell (Starke, FL) 63152
Taco Bell (Tallahassee, FL) 63272; 63273; 63274
Taco Bell (Tampa, FL) 63607; 63608; 63609; 63610
Taco Bell (Titusville, FL) 63705
Taco Bell (W Palm Beach, FL) 63815
Taco Bell (West Palm Beach, FL) 63902; 63903
Taco Bell (Winter Garden, FL) 63924
Taco Bell (Winter Haven, FL) 63953
Taco Bell (Winter Park, FL) 63995
Taco Bell (Winter Springs, FL) 64004
Taco Bell (Zephyrhills, FL) 64028
Taco Bell (Bainbridge, GA) 65370
Taco Bell (Griffin, GA) 66326
Taco Bell (Macon, GA) 66714
Taco Bell (Alexandria, LA) 69411
Taco Bell (Baton Rouge, LA) 69662; 69663; 69664; 69665; 69666; 69667; 69668; 69669
Taco Bell (Bossier City, LA) 69733
Taco Bell (Chalmette, LA) 69768; 69769
Taco Bell (Eunice, LA) 69848
Taco Bell (Hammond, LA) 69934
Taco Bell (Jennings, LA) 69981
Taco Bell (Kenner, LA) 70018; 70019; 70020
Taco Bell (Lafayette, LA) 70107; 70108; 70109; 70110; 70111; 70112; 70113
Taco Bell (Lake Charles, LA) 70173; 70174; 70175
Taco Bell (Marrero, LA) 70235
Taco Bell (Metairie, LA) 70314; 70315; 70316
Taco Bell (Monroe, LA) 70379
Taco Bell (Morgan City, LA) 70394
Taco Bell (Natchitoches, LA) 70404
Taco Bell (New Orleans, LA) 70565
Taco Bell (Pineville, LA) 70632
Taco Bell (Shreveport, LA) 70787; 70788; 70789; 70790
Taco Bell (Slidell, LA) 70840; 70841; 70842
Taco Bell (Sulphur, LA) 70892
Taco Bell (Westwego, LA) 70973; 70973
Taco Bell (Biloxi, MS) 72640
Taco Bell (Gautier, MS) 72787
Taco Bell (Greenville, MS) 72821
Taco Bell (Grenada, MS) 72848
Taco Bell (Gulfport, MS) 72878; 72879
Taco Bell (Jackson, MS) 73069; 73070; 73071; 73072
Taco Bell (Meridian, MS) 73179
Taco Bell (Ocean Springs, MS) 73223
Taco Bell (Pascagoula, MS) 73272
Taco Bell (Southaven, MS) 73356
Taco Bell (Albemarle, NC) 73542
Taco Bell (Boone, NC) 73717
Taco Bell (Chapel Hill, NC) 73821
Taco Bell (Charlotte, NC) 74166; 74167; 74168
Taco Bell (Concord, NC) 74323
Taco Bell (Greensboro, NC) 74916; 74917; 74918; 74919
Taco Bell (Greenville, NC) 74978
Taco Bell (High Point, NC) 75172
Taco Bell (Jacksonville, NC) 75230; 75231
Taco Bell (Kannapolis, NC) 75268
Taco Bell (Lewisville, NC) 75396
Taco Bell (Raleigh, NC) 75958; 75959; 75960
Taco Bell (Roanoke Rpds, NC) 76044
Taco Bell (Rocky Mount, NC) 76105
Taco Bell (Southern Pnes, NC) 76280
Taco Bell (Wake Forest, NC) 76435
Taco Bell (Wilmington, NC) 76597; 76598
Taco Bell (Wilson, NC) 76647
Taco Bell (Ardmore, OK) 76821
Taco Bell (Del City, OK) 76988
Taco Bell (Edmond, OK) 77021
Taco Bell (Lawton, OK) 77174; 77175
Taco Bell (Muskogee, OK) 77229
Taco Bell (Norman, OK) 77275; 77277
Taco Bell (Oklahoma City, OK) 77569; 77570; 77571; 77572; 77573; 77574; 77575; 77576; 77577; 77578; 77579; 77580; 77582; 77583; 77584; 77585; 77586; 77587; 77588; 77589; 77590; 77591; 77593
Taco Bell (Sand Springs, OK) 77786
Taco Bell (Tulsa, OK) 78122; 78123; 78125; 78126; 78127
Taco Bell (Beaufort, SC) 78719
Taco Bell (Cayce, SC) 78780
Taco Bell (Charleston, SC) 78897; 78898; 78899; 78900; 78901
Taco Bell (Columbia, SC) 79103; 79104; 79105; 79106
Taco Bell (Greer, SC) 79483
Taco Bell (Mt Pleasant, SC) 79682
Taco Bell (Myrtle Beach, SC) 79714; 79715
Taco Bell (Rock Hill, SC) 79842
Taco Bell (Spartanburg, SC) 79955; 79956
Taco Bell (Sumter, SC) 80032
Taco Bell (Alief, TX) 82494
Taco Bell (Allen, TX) 82497
Taco Bell (Angleton, TX) 82613
Taco Bell (Arlington, TX) 82755; 82756; 82757; 82758; 82759; 82760
Taco Bell (Austin, TX) 83013; 83014; 83015; 83016; 83017; 83018; 83019; 83020; 83021; 83022; 83023
Taco Bell (Baytown, TX) 83139; 83140
Taco Bell (Beaumont, TX) 83215; 83216; 83217; 83218
Taco Bell (Bedford, TX) 83252; 83254
Taco Bell (Brownwood, TX) 83389
Taco Bell (Bryan, TX) 83409
Taco Bell (Burleson, TX) 83426
Taco Bell (Carrollton, TX) 83508
Taco Bell (Channelview, TX) 83556
Taco Bell (Cleburne, TX) 83589
Taco Bell (Conroe, TX) 83685
Taco Bell (Corpus Chrsti, TX) 83773
Taco Bell (Crp Christi, TX) 83815
Taco Bell (Dallas, TX) 84408; 84409; 84410; 84411; 84412; 84414; 84415; 84416; 84417; 84418; 84420
Taco Bell (Del Rio, TX) 84586
Taco Bell (Dickinson, TX) 84672
Taco Bell (Duncanville, TX) 84711; 84712
Taco Bell (El Paso, TX) 84936; 84937; 84938; 84939; 84940; 84941; 84942; 84943; 84944; 84945
Taco Bell (Euless, TX) 85020
Taco Bell (Fort Worth, TX) 85285; 85286; 85287; 85288; 85289; 85290; 85291; 85292; 85293; 85294; 85296; 85297; 85297; 85298; 85299; 85300; 85301; 85302; 85303; 85304; 85305
Taco Bell (Galveston, TX) 85467; 85468
Taco Bell (Garland, TX) 85538; 85539; 85540; 85541
Taco Bell (Grand Prairie, TX) 85640
Taco Bell (Houston, TX) 86932; 86933; 86934; 86935; 86936; 86937; 86938; 86939; 86940; 86941; 86942; 86943; 86944; 86945; 86946; 86947; 86949; 86951; 86952; 86953; 86954; 86956; 86957; 86958; 86959; 86961; 86962
Taco Bell (Huntsville, TX) 87265
Taco Bell (Hurst, TX) 87298
Taco Bell (Irving, TX) 87404; 87405; 87406; 87408; 87409; 87410
Taco Bell (Killeen, TX) 87524; 87525; 87526
Taco Bell (Lewisville, TX) 87666
Taco Bell (Lubbock, TX) 87783; 87784
Taco Bell (Mesquite, TX) 87999; 88002
Taco Bell (Mineral Wells, TX) 88119
Taco Bell (Nacogdoches, TX) 88175
Taco Bell (Nederland, TX) 88194
Taco Bell (Odessa, TX) 88280; 88281
Taco Bell (Orange, TX) 88330
Taco Bell (Paris, TX) 88379
Taco Bell (Pasadena, TX) 88470; 88471; 88472
Taco Bell (Plainview, TX) 88534
Taco Bell (Port Arthur, TX) 88646
Taco Bell (Richardson, TX) 88779; 88781
Taco Bell (Rosenberg, TX) 88838
Taco Bell (San Angelo, TX) 88902
Taco Bell (San Antonio, TX) 89239; 89240; 89241; 89242; 89244; 89245; 89245; 89246; 89247; 89248; 89249; 89250; 89251; 89252
Taco Bell (San Marcos, TX) 89342
Taco Bell (Seguin, TX) 89376
Taco Bell (Stafford, TX) 89506
Taco Bell (Temple, TX) 89646
Taco Bell (Texarkana, TX) 89710
Taco Bell (Texas City, TX) 89738
Taco Bell (Tyler, TX) 89830; 89831; 89832
Taco Bell (Victoria, TX) 89906
Taco Bell (Vidor, TX) 89919
Taco Bell (Weatherford, TX) 90014
Taco Bell (Wichita Falls, TX) 90104; 90105
Taco Bell Executive Office (Birmingham, AL) 55418
Texaco Truck Stop (Guymon, OK) 77114
Texaco Truck Terminal Cafe (Guymon, OK) 77115

Trailways Food Services Inc. (Corpus Christi, TX) 83762
Trailways Restaurnat (Texarkana, AR) 57682
Wal Mart (Cafeteria) (Birmingham, AL) 55451
Walgreen Drug Stores (Tallahassee, FL) 63287
Walgreen Drug Stores (West Palm Beach, FL) 63907
Walgreen Drug Stores (Winter Haven, FL) 63956
Walgreen Drug Stores (Lafayette, LA) 70125
Walgreen Drug Stores (Tulsa, OK) 78205
Walgreen Drug Stores (El Paso, TX) 84971; 84972
Woodhaven Foods (Birmingham, AL) 55459
Wrangler (Nashville, TN) 82145

5813 Drinking Places

Burdines (Yazoo City, MS) 73498

Pizza Hut (Orlando, FL) 62083; 62094; 62098

5912 Drug Stores & Proprietary Stores

Albertson's (Fort Walton Beach, FL) 59820
Albertson's (Bossier City, LA) 69711
Albertson's (Lafayette, LA) 70039
Albertson's (Slidell, LA) 70815; 70816
Albertson's (San Angelo, TX) 88866
Albertson's Drug & Food (Victoria, TX) 89876
Albertson's Drug Store (San Antonio, TX) 88912; 88913
Albertson's Inc. (Alexandria, LA) 69367
Albertson's Pharmacy (Jupiter, FL) 60530
Albertson's Pharmacy (Largo, FL) 60808
Albertson's Pharmacy (Melbourne, FL) 61034
Albertson's Pharmacy (Pensacola, FL) 62378
Bi-Lo Pharmacy (Charlotte, NC) 73861
Bi-Lo Pharmacy (Pineville, NC) 75808
Bruno S Inc. (Birmingham, AL) 55172
Durr-Fillauer Medical Inc. (Shreveport, LA) 70717
Eckerd Corp. (Largo, FL) 60829
Eckerd Corp. Eckerd Drug Co. (Deerfield, FL) 59263
Eckerd Corp. Eckerd Drug Co. (Largo, FL) 60833
Eckerd Corp. Eckerd Drug Co. (Orlando, FL) 61963
Eckerd Corp. Eckerd Drug Co. (Newnan, GA) 67080
Eckerd Corp. Eckerd Drug Co. (Charlotte, NC) 73941
Eckerd Corp. Eckerd Drug Co. (Conroe, TX) 83658
Eckerd Corp. Eckerd Drug Co. (Garland, TX) 85483
Jack Eckerd Corp. (Largo, FL) 60834
Eckerd Drug Co. (Birmingham, AL) 55229
Eckerd Drug Co. (Valley, AL) 56688
Eckerd Drug Co. (Hendersonville, TN) 80911
Eckerd Drug Co. (Hermitage, TN) 80924
Eckerd Drug Co. (Carthage, TX) 83515
Eckerd Drug Co. (Dallas, TX) 83998; 83999
Eckerd Drug Co. (Humble, TX) 87219
Eckerd Drug Co. (Roanoke, VA) 92137
Eckerd Drug Co. No. 848 (Dallas, TX) 84000
Eckerd Drug Co. No. 827 (Dallas, TX) 84001
Eckerd Drug Co. No. 21 (Dallas, TX) 84002
Eckerd Drugs (Claymont, DE) 57762
Eckerd Drugs (New Castle, DE) 57863
Eckerd Drugs (Newark, DE) 57902
Eckerd Drugs (Wilmington, DE) 58057
Eckerd Drugs (North East, MD) 72155
Eckerd Drugs (Antioch, TN) 80167
Eckerd Drugs (Bristol, TN) 80239
Eckerd Drugs (Chattanooga, TN) 80359; 80360; 80361; 80362; 80364; 80365; 80366
Eckerd Drugs (Cleveland, TN) 80580
Eckerd Drugs (Dayton, TN) 80717
Eckerd Drugs (Hendersonville, TN) 80912
Eckerd Drugs (Hermitage, TN) 80925
Eckerd Drugs (Johnson City, TN) 81028
Eckerd Drugs (Johonson City, TN) 81062
Eckerd Drugs (Kingsport, TN) 81078; 81079; 81080; 81081
Eckerd Drugs (Knoxville, TN) 81166; 81167
Eckerd Drugs (Madison, TN) 81373; 81374
Eckerd Drugs (Maryville, TN) 81402
Eckerd Drugs (Murfressboro, TN) 81875
Eckerd Drugs (Nashville, TN) 81943; 81944; 81945; 81946; 81947; 81948; 81949; 81950; 81951; 81952
Eckerd Drugs (Oak Ridge, TN) 82185
Eckerd Drugs (Shelbyville, TN) 82303
Eckerd Drugs (Bristol, VA) 90472
Eckerd Drugs (Danville, VA) 90690; 90691
Eckerd Drugs (Harrisonburg, VA) 91077; 91078
Eckerd Drugs (Madison Heights, VA) 91296
Eckerd Drugs (Norton, VA) 91602
Eckerd Drugs (Radford, VA) 91696

Rite Aid Drugs (Gainesville, FL) 59914
Rite Aid Drugs (Homestead, FL) 60121
Rite Aid Drugs (Lake Placid, FL) 60649
Rite Aid Drugs (Lakeland, FL) 60779
Rite Aid Drugs (Pompano Beach, FL) 62629
Rite-Aid Drugs (Nashville, GA) 67070
Rite Aid Drugs (Charleston, SC) 78886
Rite Aid Drugs (Greenville, SC) 79427; 79428
Rite Aid Drugs Store (St Petersburg, FL) 63030
Rite Aid Inc. (Catlettsburg, KY) 68197
Rite Aid of N C Inc. (Laurinburg, NC) 75356
Rite Aid No 1045 (Spartanburg, SC) 79945
Rite Aid No 1110 (Spartanburg, SC) 79946
Rite Aid of North Carolina (Greenville, NC) 74976
Rite Aid of North Carolina (Reidsville, NC) 76012
Rite Aid Pharm (Tampa, FL) 63580
Rite Aid Pharm Prescription (Darlington, SC) 79157
Rite Aid Pharmacy (Enterprise, AL) 55694
Rite Aid Pharmacy (Apopka, FL) 58576
Rite Aid Pharmacy (Boynton Beach, FL) 58790
Rite-Aid Pharmacy (Bradenton, FL) 58849
Rite Aid Pharmacy (De Land, FL) 59258
Rite Aid Pharmacy (Fort Myers, FL) 59759
Rite-Aid Pharmacy (Jupiter, FL) 60550; 60551
Rite Aid Pharmacy (Kenneth City, FL) 60561
Rite Aid Pharmacy (Kissimmee, FL) 60601
Rite Aid Pharmacy (Lutz, FL) 60954
Rite Aid Pharmacy (Melbourne, FL) 61104
Rite-Aid Pharmacy (Naples, FL) 61662; 61663
Rite-Aid Pharmacy (Orlando, FL) 62135
Rite Aid Pharmacy (Punta Gorda, FL) 62720
Rite Aid Pharmacy (St Petersburg, FL) 63031
Rite Aid Pharmacy (Tampa, FL) 63581
Rite Aid Pharmacy (Adel, GA) 64056
Rite Aid Pharmacy (Glennville, GA) 66304
Rite-Aid Pharmacy (Quitman, GA) 67292
Rite Aid Pharmacy (Statesboro, GA) 67645
Rite Aid Pharmacy (Waycross, GA) 68038
Rite Aid Pharmacy (Burgaw, NC) 73737
Rite Aid Pharmacy (Charlotte, NC) 74147; 74148
Rite Aid Pharmacy (Greensboro, NC) 74899
Rite Aid Pharmacy (High Point, NC) 75164
Rite Aid Pharmacy (Madison, NC) 75484
Rite Aid Pharmacy (Sanford, NC) 76204
Rite Aid Pharmacy (Greenville, SC) 79429
Rite-Aid Pharmacy (Irmo, SC) 79540
Rite Aid Pharmacy (Marion, SC) 79643
Rite-Aid Pharmacy (Mt Pleasant, SC) 79681
Rite-Aid Pharmacy (Sumter, SC) 80030; 80030
Rite Aid Pharmacy (West Columbia, SC) 80107
Rite Aid Pharmacy No 1224 (High Point, NC) 75165
Rite Aid Store No 1220 (High Point, NC) 75166
Rite Aid Store Number Two Z (Gainesville, FL) 59915
Rite Aide (Spartanburg, SC) 79947
Rite Aide Discount Pharmacy (Washington, NC) 76460
Rite Aide Drug Store (Lake Worth, FL) 60695
Rite Aide Drugs (Fort Walton Beach, FL) 59837
Rite Aide Pharmacy (Rockingham, NC) 76068
Riteaid (Baltimore, MD) 71268
Sav on Food & Drug (Roanoke, VA) 92184
Sav-On-Drugs of Okolona (Okolona, MS) 73225
Sentry Drugs (Columbia, SC) 79095
Texaco Food Mart (Fort Worth, TX) 85325
Thrift Drug (New Castle, DE) 57876
Thrift Drug (Cumberland, MD) 71637
Thrift Drug (Denton, MD) 71644
Thrift Drug (Salisbury, MD) 72363
Thrift Drug (Covington, VA) 90665
Thrift Drugs (Ashland, KY) 68108
Thrift Drugs (Russell, KY) 69255
Thrift Drugs (Mc Comb, MS) 73151
Thrift Drugs (Bluefield, WV) 92704
Thrift Drugs (Fairmont, WV) 92848
Thrift Drugs (Huntington, WV) 92897; 92898
Thrift Drugs (Parkersburg, WV) 92997
Thrift Drugs (Weirton, WV) 93101; 93102
Trailways Bus System (Marked Tree, AR) 57348
Wal Mart (Attalla, AL) 55059
Wal Mart (Gadsden, AL) 55796
Wal Mart (Fernandina Beach, FL) 59415
Wal Mart (Pensacola, FL) 62487
Wal Mart (Kingfisher, OK) 77153
Wal Mart (Allen, TX) 82498
Wal Mart (Crockett, TX) 83803
Wal Mart (Lewisville, TX) 87669
Wal Mart Discount Cities (Fort Smith, AR) 57118
Wal Mart Discount Cities (Haines City, FL) 59956
Wal Mart Discount Cities (Meridian, MS) 73185
Wal Mart Discount Cities (Lincolnton, NC) 75443
Wal Mart Discount Cities (Rutherfordton, NC) 76150
Wal Mart Discount Cities (Vinita, OK) 78230
Wal Mart Discount Cities (Denton, TX) 84645
Wal Mart Discount City (Oklahoma City, OK) 77654
Wal Mart Discount City (Humble, TX) 87254
Wal Mart Discount City (Jasper, TX) 87435
Wal Mart Discount Pharmacy (Jonesboro, AR) 57235
Wal Mart Discount Pharmacy (Lakeland, FL) 60794
Wal Mart Discount Pharmacy (Lake Charles, LA) 70182; 70183
Wal Mart Discount Pharmacy (Atoka, OK) 76829
Wal Mart Discount Pharmacy (Bartlesville, OK) 76854
Wal Mart Discount Pharmacy (Cleveland, OK) 76963
Wal Mart Discount Pharmacy (Idabel, OK) 77147
Wal Mart Discount Pharmacy (Miami, OK) 77212
Wal Mart Discount Pharmacy (Skiatook, OK) 77828
Wal Mart Discount Pharmacy (Ennis, TX) 85004
Wal Mart Discount Pharmacy (Gainesville, TX) 85429
Wal Mart Discount Pharmacy (Gonzales, TX) 85596
Wal Mart Discount Pharmacy (Mt Pleasant, TX) 88162
Wal Mart Discount Pharmacy (Plainview, TX) 88536
Wal Mart Discount Pharmacy (Port Neches, TX) 88680
Wal Mart Discount Pharmacy (Victoria, TX) 89910
Wal Mart Discount Pharmacy (Waxahachie, TX) 90000
Wal Mart Discount Store (El Paso, TX) 84962
Wal Mart Drug Stores (Siloam Springs, AR) 57624
Wal Mart Pharmacy (Benton, AR) 56783
Wal Mart Pharmacy (Fayetteville, AR) 57002; 57003
Wal Mart Pharmacy (Harrison, AR) 57144
Wal Mart Pharmacy (Hot Springs National Park, AR) 57186; 57187
Wal Mart Pharmacy (Magnolia, AR) 57338
Wal Mart Pharmacy (Malvern, AR) 57343
Wal Mart Pharmacy (Mountain Home, AR) 57393
Wal Mart Pharmacy (Osceola, AR) 57485
Wal Mart Pharmacy (Springdale, AR) 57658
Wal Mart Pharmacy (Plant City, FL) 62558
Wal Mart Pharmacy (Lafayette, LA) 70124
Wal Mart Pharmacy (Mansfield, LA) 70218
Wal Mart Pharmacy (Sulphur, LA) 70896
Wal Mart Pharmacy (Ada, OK) 76791
Wal Mart Pharmacy (Bristow, OK) 76876
Wal Mart Pharmacy (Broken Arrow, OK) 76891
Wal Mart Pharmacy (Chickasha, OK) 76940
Wal Mart Pharmacy (Cushing, OK) 76983
Wal Mart Pharmacy (El Reno, OK) 77036
Wal Mart Pharmacy (Grove, OK) 77094
Wal Mart Pharmacy (Hugo, OK) 77141
Wal Mart Pharmacy (Marlow, OK) 77186
Wal Mart Pharmacy (Mc Alester, OK) 77202
Wal Mart Pharmacy (Poteau, OK) 77730
Wal Mart Pharmacy (Sallisaw, OK) 77777
Wal Mart Pharmacy (Sapulpa, OK) 77799
Wal Mart Pharmacy (Tahlequah, OK) 77863
Wal Mart Pharmacy (Tulsa, OK) 78197; 78198
Wal Mart Pharmacy (Weatherford, OK) 78245
Wal Mart Pharmacy (Decatur, TX) 84545
Wal Mart Pharmacy (Fort Worth, TX) 85355
Wal Mart Pharmacy (Iowa Park, TX) 87310
Wal Mart Pharmacy (Jasper, TX) 87436
Wal Mart Pharmacy (Kenedy, TX) 87467
Wal Mart Pharmacy (Mc Kinney, TX) 87926
Wal Mart Pharmacy (Vidor, TX) 89922
Wal Mart Prescriptions (Claremore, OK) 76958
Wal Mart Prescriptions (Wagoner, OK) 78235
Wal Mart Pro Pharmacy (Broken Bow, OK) 76900
Wal-Mart Stores Inc. (Franklin, TN) 80829
Wal-Mart Stores Inc. (Mc Minnville, TN) 81440
Wal-Mart Stores Inc. (Nashville, TN) 82137
Walgreen (Bartow, FL) 58634
Walgreen (Boynton Beach, FL) 58798
Walgreen (Cocoa Beach, FL) 59085
Walgreen (Daytona Beach, FL) 59225
Walgreen (Fort Lauderdale, FL) 59628
Walgreen (Hollywood, FL) 60104
Walgreen (Inverness, FL) 60152
Walgreen (Jacksonville, FL) 60499
Walgreen (Lehigh Acres, FL) 60896
Walgreen (Melbourne, FL) 61117
Walgreen (Northwest Smyrna Beach, FL) 61760
Walgreen (Ocala, FL) 61825; 61826
Walgreen (Kenner, LA) 70024
Walgreen (Metairie, LA) 70327
Walgreen (Southaven, MS) 73360
Walgreen (Tupelo, MS) 73428
Walgreen (El Paso, TX) 84967
Walgreen (Houston, TX) 87102
Walgreen (Killeen, TX) 87530
Walgreen (Odessa, TX) 88292
Walgreen (San Antonio, TX) 89306
Walgreen Co. (Altamonte Springs, FL) 58566
Walgreen Drug Store (Avon Park, FL) 58612
Walgreen Drug Store (Fort Pierce, FL) 59816
Walgreen Drug Store (Jacksonville, FL) 60501
Walgreen Drug Store (Marathon, FL) 60994
Walgreen Drug Store (Mandeville, LA) 70211
Walgreen Drug Store (Sugar Land, TX) 89546
Walgreen Drug Stores (Hot Springs National Park, AR) 57190; 57191
Walgreen Drug Stores (West Memphis, AR) 57738; 57739
Walgreen Drug Stores (Apopka, FL) 58578
Walgreen Drug Stores (Auburndale, FL) 58604
Walgreen Drug Stores (Boca Raton, FL) 58751; 58752; 58753
Walgreen Drug Stores (Bradenton, FL) 58860; 58861
Walgreen Drug Stores (Bradenton Beach, FL) 58862
Walgreen Drug Stores (Brandon, FL) 58882
Walgreen Drug Stores (Brooksville, FL) 58899
Walgreen Drug Stores (Casselberry, FL) 58945
Walgreen Drug Stores (Clearwater, FL) 59054
Walgreen Drug Stores (Cocoa, FL) 59076
Walgreen Drug Stores (Daytona Beach, FL) 59227; 59228; 59229; 59230; 59231; 59232
Walgreen Drug Stores (De Land, FL) 59262
Walgreen Drug Stores (Deerfield Beach, FL) 59290
Walgreen Drug Stores (Dunedin, FL) 59368
Walgreen Drug Stores (Fort Lauderdale, FL) 59630; 59631; 59632; 59633; 59634; 59635; 59636; 59640
Walgreen Drug Stores (Fort Myers, FL) 59776; 59777; 59778; 59779
Walgreen Drug Stores (Hialeah, FL) 60018
Walgreen Drug Stores (Hollywood, FL) 60105
Walgreen Drug Stores (Homosassa Springs, FL) 60128
Walgreen Drug Stores (Jacksonville, FL) 60502; 60503; 60504; 60505; 60506
Walgreen Drug Stores (Jupiter, FL) 60554
Walgreen Drug Stores (Lake Worth, FL) 60701
Walgreen Drug Stores (Lakeland, FL) 60796; 60797; 60798; 60799
Walgreen Drug Stores (Largo, FL) 60867; 60868; 60869
Walgreen Drug Stores (Leesburg, FL) 60888
Walgreen Drug Stores (Melbourne, FL) 61118; 61119; 61120; 61121
Walgreen Drug Stores (Merritt Island, FL) 61150
Walgreen Drug Stores (Miami, FL) 61502; 61504; 61508; 61509; 61511
Walgreen Drug Stores (New Port Richey, FL) 61693; 61694
Walgreen Drug Stores (Ocala, FL) 61827
Walgreen Drug Stores (Orlando, FL) 62182; 62183; 62184; 62185; 62186; 62187
Walgreen Drug Stores (Ormond Beach, FL) 62212
Walgreen Drug Stores (Palm City, FL) 62280
Walgreen Drug Stores (Pinellas Park, FL) 62530
Walgreen Drug Stores (Pompano Beach, FL) 62642; 62643; 62644; 62645
Walgreen Drug Stores (Punta Gorda, FL) 62725
Walgreen Drug Stores (Ruskin, FL) 62760
Walgreen Drug Stores (Sarasota, FL) 62866; 62867
Walgreen Drug Stores (Sebastian, FL) 62876
Walgreen Drug Stores (St Pete, FL) 62961
Walgreen Drug Stores (St Petersburg, FL) 63043; 63044; 63045; 63046
Walgreen Drug Stores (Stuart, FL) 63183
Walgreen Drug Stores (Tallahassee, FL) 63288; 63289
Walgreen Drug Stores (Tampa, FL) 63651; 63652; 63653; 63654; 63655; 63656; 63657; 63658
Walgreen Drug Stores (Vero Beach, FL) 63771
Walgreen Drug Stores (W Palm Beach, FL) 63822
Walgreen Drug Stores (West Palm Beach, FL) 63908; 63909
Walgreen Drug Stores (Winter Garden, FL) 63926
Walgreen Drug Stores (Winter Haven, FL) 63956; 63957
Walgreen Drug Stores (Zephyrhills, FL) 64030; 64031
Walgreen Drug Stores (Chalmette, LA) 69773
Walgreen Drug Stores (Hammond, LA) 69935
Walgreen Drug Stores (Lake Charles, LA) 70185
Walgreen Drug Stores (Marrero, LA) 70238
Walgreen Drug Stores (Metairie, LA) 70328; 70329; 70330; 70331
Walgreen Drug Stores (New Orleans, LA) 70585; 70586; 70587; 70588
Walgreen Drug Stores (Slidell, LA) 70846
Walgreen Drug Stores (Escatawpa, MS) 72763
Walgreen Drug Stores (Austin, TX) 83060; 83061; 83062; 83063; 83064
Walgreen Drug Stores (Beaumont, TX) 83235; 83236
Walgreen Drug Stores (Brownsville, TX) 83385
Walgreen Drug Stores (Collinsville, TX) 83637
Walgreen Drug Stores (Corpus Christi, TX) 83766
Walgreen Drug Stores (El Paso, TX) 84968; 84969; 84970; 84972
Walgreen Drug Stores (Galveston, TX) 85471; 85472
Walgreen Drug Stores (Groves, TX) 85687
Walgreen Drug Stores (Houston, TX) 87105; 87106; 87107; 87108; 87109; 87110; 87111; 87112; 87113; 87114; 87117; 87120; 87126; 87127; 87142; 87143; 87144; 87146; 87147; 87148; 87149; 87150; 87151; 87152; 87153; 87154; 87155; 87156; 87157; 87158; 87159; 87160; 87161; 87162; 87163; 87164; 87165; 87166; 87167; 87168
Walgreen Drug Stores (Humble, TX) 87257
Walgreen Drug Stores (La Porte, TX) 87573
Walgreen Drug Stores (Missouri City, TX) 88134
Walgreen Drug Stores (Nederland, TX) 88198
Walgreen Drug Stores (Orange, TX) 88332
Walgreen Drug Stores (Pasadena, TX) 88476; 88477; 88478; 88479
Walgreen Drug Stores (Pearland, TX) 88491
Walgreen Drug Stores (Port Arthur, TX) 88659; 88660; 88661
Walgreen Drug Stores (San Antonio, TX) 89308; 89310; 89311; 89312; 89313; 89314; 89315; 89316; 89317; 89318; 89319; 89320; 89321; 89322; 89323; 89324
Walgreen Drug Stores (Tomball, TX) 89781; 89782
Walgreen Drug Stores (Victoria, TX) 89913
Walgreen Drugs (Clearwater, FL) 59055
Walgreen Drugs (Crystal River, FL) 59135
Walgreen Drugs (Fort Myers, FL) 59780
Walgreen Drugs (Jupiter, FL) 60555
Walgreen Drugs (Kissimmee, FL) 60607
Walgreen Drugs (Lake Wales, FL) 60659
Walgreen Drugs (St Augustine, FL) 62960
Walgreen Drugs (Metairie, LA) 70332
Walgreen Drugs (Clute, TX) 83605
Walgreen Drugs (La Marque, TX) 87551
Walgreen Louisiana Co. (Lafayette, LA) 70126
Walgreen Pharmacy (Naples, FL) 61670
Walgreen Pharmacy (Northwest Smyrna Beach, FL) 61761
Walgreen Pharmacy (Palm City, FL) 62281
Walgreen Pharmacy (El Paso, TX) 84974; 84975

5921 Liquor Stores

Albertson's Liquor Store (Bradenton, FL) 58800
Coca Cola Bottling Co. (Marion, NC) 75498
Coca Cola Bottling Co. Whse (Brownfield, TX) 83351
Eckerd Drugs (Murfreesboro, TN) 81839
Kroger Family Center (College Sta, TX) 83610
Sam's Wholesale Liquor Store (Oklahoma City, OK) 77550
Stop & Shop Liquors (Pensacola, FL) 62473
Texaco Food Mart (Bainbridge, GA) 65371

Walgreen Drug Stores (Punta Gorda, FL) 62725
Walgreen Drug Stores (Stuart, FL) 63183
Walgreen Drug Stores (Tampa, FL) 63655
Walgreen Drug Stores (Vero Beach, FL) 63771
Wilsons (Ringgold, LA) 70666; 70667

5932 Used Merchandise Stores

Aaron Rents (Atlanta, GA) 64187

5941 Sporting Goods & Bicycle Shops

Ace Hardware & Marine (Atl Beach, NC) 73642
Coast to Coast (Lonoke, AR) 57322
Coast to Coast (Mena, AR) 57363
Coast to Coast Hardware (Church Hill, TN) 80529
Coast to Coast Home & Auto (Port Richey F, FL) 62684
Foot Action (El Paso, TX) 84801
Foot Action U S a (Tampa, FL) 63434
Footaction USA (Humble, TX) 87221
Hudson's (Culpeper, VA) 90676
Kmart Auto Accessories & Sporting Goods (Mount Airy, NC) 75681
Kmart Discount Stores (Southaven, MS) 73349
Kmart Sporting Goods (Pompano Beach, FL) 62603
Mini Mart & Bait Shop (Monroeville, AL) 56263

Toys R US (Hollywood, FL) 60100
Toys R US (Tulsa, OK) 78176

5942 Book Stores

Richards S P Co. (Jacksonville, FL) 60438
Waldenbooks (Birmingham, AL) 55452
Waldenbooks (Dothan, AL) 55675
Waldenbooks (Enterprise, AL) 55700
Waldenbooks (Huntsville, AL) 56054; 56055
Waldenbooks (Jasper, AL) 56090
Waldenbooks (Mobile, AL) 56256
Waldenbooks (Tuscaloosa, AL) 56681; 56682
Waldenbooks (Hot Springs National Park, AR) 57188; 57189
Waldenbooks (Jonesboro, AR) 57236
Waldenbooks (Little Rock, AR) 57319
Waldenbooks (N Little Rock, AR) 57436
Waldenbooks (Dover, DE) 57811; 57812
Waldenbooks (Wilmington, DE) 58119
Waldenbooks (Altamonte Springs, FL) 58565
Waldenbooks (Boynton Beach, FL) 58797
Waldenbooks (Bradenton, FL) 58857
Waldenbooks (Clearwater, FL) 59053
Waldenbooks (Fort Lauderdale, FL) 59625
Waldenbooks (Fort Myers, FL) 59774
Waldenbooks (Hialeah, FL) 60017
Waldenbooks (Lakeland, FL) 60795
Waldenbooks (Mary Esther, FL) 61026
Waldenbooks (Melbourne, FL) 61115; 61116
Waldenbooks (Merritt Island, FL) 61149
Waldenbooks (Miami, FL) 61493; 61494; 61495; 61496; 61497; 61498
Waldenbooks (Orlando, FL) 62180; 62181
Waldenbooks (Panama City, FL) 62358

Waldenbooks (Pinellas Park, FL) 62529
Waldenbooks (Plant City, FL) 62559
Waldenbooks (Pompano Beach, FL) 62639
Waldenbooks (Punta Gorda, FL) 62724
Waldenbooks (St Augustine, FL) 62958; 62959
Waldenbooks (Stuart, FL) 63182
Waldenbooks (Tampa, FL) 63648; 63649; 63650
Waldenbooks (Titusville, FL) 63708
Waldenbooks (W Palm Beach, FL) 63820
Waldenbooks (Winter Haven, FL) 63955
Waldenbooks (Brunswick, GA) 65430
Waldenbooks (Milledgeville, GA) 66986
Waldenbooks (Valdosta, GA) 67980
Waldenbooks (Alexandria, LA) 69417
Waldenbooks (Baton Rouge, LA) 69685
Waldenbooks (Bossier City, LA) 69735
Waldenbooks (Gretna, LA) 69919
Waldenbooks (Kenner, LA) 70023
Waldenbooks (Lake Charles, LA) 70184
Waldenbooks (Marrero, LA) 70237
Waldenbooks (Metairie, LA) 70326
Waldenbooks (Monroe, LA) 70383
Waldenbooks (Shreveport, LA) 70805; 70806
Waldenbooks (Baltimore, MD) 71325; 71326
Waldenbooks (Cape St. Claire, MD) 71496
Waldenbooks (Cockeysville, MD) 71556
Waldenbooks (Frederick, MD) 71752; 71753
Waldenbooks (Escatawpa, MS) 72762
Waldenbooks (Jackson, MS) 73091; 73092; 73093
Waldenbooks (Oxford, MS) 73248
Waldenbooks (Ridgeland, MS) 73331
Waldenbooks (Utica, MS) 73443
Waldenbooks (Vicksburg, MS) 73464
Waldenbooks (Boone, NC) 73720
Waldenbooks (Charlotte, NC) 74218; 74219; 74220
Waldenbooks (Concord, NC) 74326
Waldenbooks (Greenville, NC) 74989
Waldenbooks (Hendersonville, NC) 75047
Waldenbooks (Jacksonville, NC) 75235
Waldenbooks (Kinston, NC) 75332
Waldenbooks (Monroe, NC) 75595
Waldenbooks (Raleigh, NC) 75982; 75983
Waldenbooks (Roanoke Rapids, NC) 76040
Waldenbooks (Rocky Mount, NC) 76111
Waldenbooks (Wilmington, NC) 76612
Waldenbooks (Bartlesville, OK) 76855
Waldenbooks (Muskogee, OK) 77236
Waldenbooks (Norman, OK) 77280
Waldenbooks (Oklahoma City, OK) 77655; 77656; 77657; 77658; 77659; 77660; 77661
Waldenbooks (Tulsa, OK) 78199; 78200; 78201; 78202; 78203
Waldenbooks (Charleston, SC) 78910; 78911; 78912; 78913
Waldenbooks (Columbia, SC) 79122
Waldenbooks (Greenville, SC) 79447; 79448
Waldenbooks (Greenwood, SC) 79465
Waldenbooks (Myrtle Beach, SC) 79717; 79718
Waldenbooks (Spartanburg, SC) 79967
Waldenbooks (Abilene, TX) 82466
Waldenbooks (Amarillo, TX) 82589
Waldenbooks (Arlington, TX) 82780; 82781; 82782; 82783
Waldenbooks (Austin, TX) 83055
Waldenbooks (Baytown, TX) 83141
Waldenbooks (Beaumont, TX) 83234
Waldenbooks (Brownsville, TX) 83384
Waldenbooks (Clute, TX) 83604
Waldenbooks (Corsicana, TX) 83797
Waldenbooks (Dallas, TX) 84492

Waldenbooks (El Paso, TX) 84963; 84964; 84965
Waldenbooks (Fort Worth, TX) 85356; 85357; 85358
Waldenbooks (Harlingen, TX) 85720
Waldenbooks (Houston, TX) 87089; 87090; 87091; 87093; 87094; 87095; 87097; 87098; 87099; 87100; 87101
Waldenbooks (Killeen, TX) 87528; 87529
Waldenbooks (Lake Jackson, TX) 87588
Waldenbooks (Longview, TX) 87745
Waldenbooks (Lufkin, TX) 87821
Waldenbooks (Marshall, TX) 87871
Waldenbooks (Mc Allen, TX) 87904
Waldenbooks (Mesquite, TX) 88012
Waldenbooks (Odessa, TX) 88291
Waldenbooks (Pampa, TX) 88359
Waldenbooks (Pasadena, TX) 88475
Waldenbooks (Plano, TX) 88618
Waldenbooks (Port Arthur, TX) 88658
Waldenbooks (Richardson, TX) 88789
Waldenbooks (San Angelo, TX) 88905
Waldenbooks (San Antonio, TX) 89300; 89301; 89302; 89303; 89304; 89305
Waldenbooks (Temple, TX) 89651; 89652
Waldenbooks (Texarkana, TX) 89715
Waldenbooks (Victoria, TX) 89911; 89912
Waldenbooks (Arlington, VA) 90392
Waldenbooks (Chesapeake, VA) 90608; 90609
Waldenbooks (Fredericksburg, VA) 90945
Waldenbooks (Norfolk, VA) 91595; 91596
Waldenbooks (Portsmouth, VA) 91673
Waldenbooks (Richmond, VA) 92079; 92080
Waldenbooks (Staunton, VA) 92332
Waldenbooks (Winchester, VA) 92606
Waldenbooks Co. (Charlotte, NC) 74221
Waldenbooks Deerbrook (Humble, TX) 87255
Waldenbooks Inc. (Br) (Roanoke, VA) 92198
Waldenbooks & More (Fort Lauderdale, FL) 59626
Waldenbooks & More (Charlotte, NC) 74222
Waldenbooks & More (Carrollton, TX) 83512
World Book Childcraft (Fairhope, AL) 55726
World Book Childcraft (Abilene, TX) 82469
World Book Childcraft (Newport News, VA) 91492
World Book Educational Products (Fayetteville, NC) 74587
World Book, Inc. (Orlando, FL) 62194
World Book, Inc. (North Augusta, SC) 79742

5943 Stationery Stores

Garrett-Buchanan Co. (Jessup, MD) 71984
Graphic Systems (Burlington, NC) 73756
Innovative Office Systems, Inc. (Dallas, TX) 84133; 84134
Nationwide Papers (Hanover, MD) 71912
Owens Corning Fiberglass (Charlotte, NC) 74101; 74101
Perma Products Co. (Duncanville, TX) 84702
Scoot-Rice Co. Inc. (Tulsa, OK) 78074
Sonoco Products Co. (Morganfield, KY) 69107
Sonoco Products Co. (Newport, TN) 82173
Westvaco Corp. (Herndon, VA) 91136

5944 Jewelry Stores

Kirk Stieff Co. (Baltimore, MD) 71174
Maison Blanche (Boca Raton, FL) 58719

Service Merchandise (Birmingham, AL) 55386; 55387
Service Merchandise (Mobile, AL) 56238
Service Merchandise (North Little Rock, AR) 57471
Service Merchandise (Clearwater, FL) 59047
Service Merchandise (Hollywood, FL) 60096
Service Merchandise (Tampa, FL) 63588
Service Merchandise (Louisville, KY) 69002
Service Merchandise (Shreveport, LA) 70782
Service Merchandise (Jackson, MS) 73060
Service Merchandise (Oklahoma City, OK) 77555; 77556
Service Merchandise (Tulsa, OK) 78109
Service Merchandise (Sumter, SC) 80031
Service Merchandise (Goodlettsville, TN) 80871
Service Merchandise (Kingsport, TN) 81118
Service Merchandise (Knoxville, TN) 81251
Service Merchandise (Beaumont, TX) 83213
Service Merchandise (College Station, TX) 83623
Service Merchandise (Longview, TX) 87735
Service Merchandise (Midland, TX) 88074

5945 Hobby, Toy & Game Shops

Circus World (Birmingham, AL) 55189; 55190; 55191
Circus World (Dothan, AL) 55630
Circus World (Huntsville, AL) 55900
Circus World (Mobile, AL) 56150
Circus World (Montgomery, AL) 56293
Circus World (Daytona Beach, FL) 59169
Circus World (Fort Myers, FL) 59690
Circus World (Fort Pierce, FL) 59790
Circus World (Gainesville, FL) 59866
Circus World (Mary Esther, FL) 61015
Circus World (Miami, FL) 61232
Circus World (Naples, FL) 61615
Circus World (Orange Park, FL) 61878
Circus World (Orlando, FL) 61949
Circus World (St Petersburg, FL) 62968
Circus World (Tallahassee, FL) 63221
Circus World (Tampa, FL) 63390
Circus World (Alexandria, LA) 69371
Circus World (Monroe, LA) 70352
Circus World (Escatawpa, MS) 72756
Circus World (Pascagoula, MS) 73255
Circus World (Charlotte, NC) 73897; 73898
Circus World (Greenville, NC) 74954
Circus World (Bartlesville, OK) 76832
Circus World (Abilene, TX) 82432
Circus World (Clute, TX) 83597
Circus World (Collinsville, TX) 83632
Circus World (Dallas, TX) 83912; 83913
Circus World (Del Rio, TX) 84579
Circus World (Hurst, TX) 87270
Circus World (Lufkin, TX) 87801
Circus World (San Angelo, TX) 88871
Circus World (San Antonio, TX) 88953
Circus World (Sherman, TX) 89393
Circus World (Texarkana, TX) 89672
Circus World (Victoria, TX) 89880
Circus World Inc. (Durham, NC) 74390
Circus World No 7329 (Tulsa, OK) 77902
Circus World Toy Store (Lakeland, FL) 60718
Circus World Toy Store (Pinellas Park, FL) 62515
Circus World Toy Store (Jackson, MS) 72960; 72961
Circus World Toy Store (Sumter, SC) 80016
Circus World Toy Store (Killeen, TX) 87508

Circus World Toy Store (Plano, TX) 88546
Circus World Toy Store Inc. (Altamonte Spg, FL) 58535
Circus World Toy Stores (Tuscaloosa, AL) 56638
Circus World Toy Stores (Orlando, FL) 61950
Circus World Toy Stores (Columbus, MS) 72706
Circus World Toy Stores (Norman, OK) 77248
Circus World Toy Stores (Oklahoma City, OK) 77327
Circus World Toy Stores (Greenwood, SC) 79453
Circus World Toy Stores (Houston, TX) 85944; 85945; 85946; 85947; 85948; 85949; 85950; 85951; 85952; 85953; 85954
Circus World Toy Stores (Pasadena, TX) 88396
Circus World Toy Stores (Richardson, TX) 88727
Circus World Toy Stores Inc. (Tampa, FL) 63391
Circus World Toy Stores Inc. (Macon, GA) 66680
Circus World Toy Stores Inc. (Raleigh, NC) 75883
Circus World Toy Stores Inc. (Dallas, TX) 83914
Circus World Toy Stores Inc. (Longview, TX) 87708
Circus World Toys (Hollywood, FL) 60049
Circus World Toys (Enid, OK) 77045
Circus World Toys (Tulsa, OK) 77903
Circus World Toys (Florence, SC) 79197
Circus World Toys (Myrtle Beach, SC) 79695
Circus World Toys (Eagle Pass, TX) 84714
Circus World Toys (El Paso, TX) 84784
Circus World Toys Inc. (Irving, TX) 87330
Circus World Toys Store (Tampa, FL) 63392; 63393
Kay-Bee Toy & Hobby (Birmingham, AL) 55288
Kay Bee Toy & Hobby (Enterprise, AL) 55687
Kay-Bee Toy & Hobby (Boynton Beach, FL) 58780
Kay Bee Toy & Hobby (Orlando, FL) 62017
Kay-Bee Toy & Hobby (Alexandria, LA) 69385
Kay-Bee Toy & Hobby (Kenner, LA) 69996
Kay Bee Toy & Hobby (Ridgeland, MS) 73319
Kay Bee Toy & Hobby (Utica, MS) 73435
Kay-Bee Toy & Hobby (Tulsa, OK) 77970
Kay-Bee Toy & Hobby (Arlington, TX) 82670
Kay Bee Toy & Hobby (Fort Worth, TX) 85137
Kay Bee Toy & Hobby (Victoria, TX) 89889
Kay-Bee Toy & Hobby Inc. (N Little Rock, AR) 57404
Kay-Bee Toy & Hobby Shop (Fort Smith, AR) 57061
Kay-Bee Toy & Hobby Shop (Pompano Beach, FL) 62601
Kay-Bee Toy & Hobby Shop (Greenville, MS) 72801
Kay-Bee Toy & Hobby Shop (Jackson, MS) 72994
Kay-Bee Toy & Hobby Shop (Oklahoma City, OK) 77396; 77397
Kay-Bee Toy & Hobby Shop (Greenville, SC) 79377; 79378
Kay Bee Toy & Hobby Shop (Abilene, TX) 82440
Kay-Bee Toy & Hobby Shop (Killeen, TX) 87513
Kay Bee Toy & Hobby Shop (San Antonio, TX) 89037; 89038; 89039; 89040
Kay Bee Toy Inc. (W Palm Beach Fl, FL) 63824
Kay Bee Toy Shop (Baytown, TX) 83129
Kay Bee Toy Store (Amarillo, TX) 82555
Kay Bee Toy Store (Temple, TX) 89620
Kay Bee Toy&Hobby Inc. (Rocky Mount, NC) 76093
Kay Bee Toy&Hobby Shop (Birmingham, AL) 55289
Kay Bee Toy&Hobby Shop (Huntsville, AL) 55955
Kay Bee Toy&Hobby Shop (Fayetteville, AR) 56980

Kay Bee Toy&Hobby Shop (Melbourne, FL) 61072
Kay Bee Toy&Hobby Shop (Miami, FL) 61337; 61338
Kay Bee Toy&Hobby Shop (Pompano Beach, FL) 62602
Kay Bee Toy&Hobby Shop (Lafayette, LA) 70064; 70065
Kay Bee Toy&Hobby Shop (Lake Charles, LA) 70142
Kay Bee Toy&Hobby Shop (Shreveport, LA) 70736
Kay Bee Toy&Hobby Shop (Lawton, OK) 77161
Kay Bee Toy&Hobby Shop (Greenville, SC) 79379
Kay Bee Toy&Hobby Shop (Austin, TX) 82899
Kay Bee Toy&Hobby Shop (Dallas, TX) 84154
Kay Bee Toy&Hobby Shop (Humble, TX) 87227
Kay Bee Toy&Hobby Shop (San Antonio, TX) 89041; 89042
Kay Bee Toy&Hobby Shop (Victoria, TX) 89890
Kay Bee Toy&Hobby Shop Etal (Amarillo, TX) 82556
Kay Bee Toy&Hobby Shops (Greenville, MS) 72802
Kay Bee Toy&Hobby Shops (Jackson, MS) 72995
Kay Bee Toys (Conway, AR) 56863
Kay Bee Toys (Orange Park, FL) 61887
Kay Bee Toys (Baton Rouge, LA) 69566
Kay Bee Toys (Eden, NC) 74459
Kay Bee Toys (Shawnee, OK) 77820
Kay Bee Toys (Tulsa, OK) 77971; 77972
Kay Bee Toys (Charleston, SC) 78823
Kay Bee Toys (Corsicana, TX) 83780
Kay Bee Toys (El Paso, TX) 84814; 84815
Kay Bee Toys (Sherman, TX) 89402
Kay Bee Toys & Hobby (Tampa, FL) 63465
Kay Bee Toys & Hobby (Beaumont, TX) 83163
Kay Bee Toys & Hobby Shop (Pine Bluff, AR) 57522
Kids-R-US (Bradenton, FL) 58829
Radio Shack (Bowling Green, VA) 90464
Tandy Corp. Del (Houston, TX) 86963
Toys R US (Birmingham, AL) 55431; 55432
Toys R US (Huntsville, AL) 56040
Toys R US (Newark, DE) 57933
Toys R US (Clearwater, FL) 59050
Toys R US (Fort Myers, FL) 59767
Toys R US (Jacksonville, FL) 60477
Toys R US (Orange Park, FL) 61899
Toys R US (Pensacola, FL) 62482
Toys R US (St Petersburg, FL) 63037
Toys R US (Tallahassee, FL) 63280
Toys R US (Tampa, FL) 63626
Toys R US (Louisville, KY) 69022
Toys R US (Monroe, LA) 70380
Toys R US (Shreveport, LA) 70796
Toys R US (Frederick, MD) 71751
Toys R US (Jackson, MS) 73076
Toys R US (Charlotte, NC) 74175
Toys R US (Wilmington, NC) 76601
Toys R US (Oklahoma City, OK) 77631; 77632
Toys R US (Tulsa, OK) 78176
Toys R US (Spartanburg, SC) 79959
Toys R US (Austin, TX) 83050; 83051
Toys R US (Beaumont, TX) 83226
Toys R US (Webster, TX) 90026
Toys R US (Hampton, VA) 91057
Toys R US (Norfolk, VA) 91586
Toys R US (Richmond, VA) 92057

5946 Camera & Photographic Supply Stores

Casual Corner (Wilmington, DE) 58030
Eastman Kodak Co. (Louisville, KY) 68757
Eastman Kodak Co. (Memphis, TN) 81515; 81516
Reneer Films Corp. (Charlotte, NC) 74145
Rite Aid Discount Pharmacy (Clarksburg, WV) 92818
Wal Mart (Tahlequah, OK) 77862

Walgreen (Tulsa, OK) 78204

5947 Gift, Novelty & Souvenir Shops

Acme Markets (Washington, DC) 58122
American Greeting Corp. (Danville, KY) 68252
Capezio Dance Shop (Charlotte, NC) 73887
Courtyard (Lexington, KY) 68539
Exxon Party Shoppe (Gastonia, NC) 74675
McDonald's Hamburgers (Cross Junction, VA) 90670
Shell Service (Savannah, GA) 67513; 67513
Texaco (Houston, TX) 86985
Union Bank (N Little Rock, AR) 57432
Walt Disney World Co. (Orlando, FL) 62191

5948 Luggage & Leather Goods Stores

Bermans the Leather Experts (Oklahoma City, OK) 77308
Tandy (Wichita Falls, TX) 90106

5949 Sewing, Needlework & Piece Goods

BASF Fibers Corp. (Greensboro, NC) 74788
The Limited Express (Clearwater, FL) 59030
The Limited Express (Oklahoma City, OK) 77430
Linens N Things (Orlando, FL) 62038
Springs Industries Inc. (Lancaster, SC) 79049
Stop & Shop (Floyd, VA) 90882
Wilsons (Maben, MS) 73133

5961 Catalog & Mail-Order Houses

Dell Computer Corp. (Austin, TX) 82847
J C Penney Catalog Center (Newport News, VA) 91470
J C Penney Catalog Sales (Danville, VA) 90700
Ring Around Products (Prattville, AL) 56492
Service Merchandise (Montgomery, AL) 56378
Service Merchandise (Daytona Beach, FL) 59212
Service Merchandise (Fort Lauderdale, FL) 59611
Service Merchandise (Hialeah, FL) 60009
Service Merchandise (Miami, FL) 61458
Service Merchandise (Tampa, FL) 63589
Service Merchandise (Gulfport, MS) 72875
Service Merchandise (Jackson, MS) 73059
Service Merchandise (Memphis, TN) 81692
Service Merchandise (Nashville, TN) 82095
Service Merchandise (Arlington, TX) 82749
Service Merchandise Catalog (Jackson, MS) 73061
Sysco Food Services (Mcallen, TX) 87941

5962 Merchandising Machine Operators

Canteen Corp. (La Vergne, TN) 81281
Coca-Cola Bottling Co. of Memphis Tennessee Inc. (Memphis, TN) 81497
Coca-Cola Bottling Co. of Shreveprot Inc. (Atlanta, GA) 64373
Pepsi-Cola General Bottlers (Covington, KY) 68230

5963 Direct Selling Establishments

Mary Kay Cosmetics (Longwood, FL) 60934
World Book Childcraft (Fairhope, AL) 55726
World Book Childcraft (Tampa, FL) 63663
World Book Childcraft (Macon, GA) 66726; 66727

World Book Childcraft (Abilene, TX) 82469
World Book Childcraft (Newport News, VA) 91491; 91492
World Book Childcraft (Staunton, VA) 92334
World Book Educational Products (Fayetteville, NC) 74587

5983 Fuel Oil Dealers

Amerada Hess Corp. (Belton, SC) 78722
Citgo Petroleum Corp. (Fairfax, VA) 90760; 90761
Clark Gas & Oil Co. (Stuart, VA) 92351
Coastal Fuels Marketing Inc. (Miami, FL) 61267
Cosbel Petroleum Corp. (Houston, TX) 86015
Edwards Co., Inc. (Newport News, VA) 91460
Exxon Co. (Whitley City, KY) 69338
Exxon Co. U S a (Cleveland, TN) 80582
Exxon Co. U S a (Crossville, TN) 80693
Exxon Co. USA (Ruskin, FL) 62757
Exxon Corp. (Baltimore, MD) 71116
Marathon Fuels Inc. (Hartford, KY) 68418
Mobil Oil Corp. (Morgan City, LA) 70389
Quaker State Oil Refining (Fairmont, WV) 92846
Shell Mart (Vansant, VA) 92390
Shell Oil Co. (Starke, FL) 63151
Tesoro Petroleum Distrib Co. (Cameron, LA) 69754
Tesoro Petroleum Distribution (Venice, LA) 70925
Tesoro Petroleum Distribution Co. (Laurel, MS) 73108
Union Oil Co. (Wheeling, WV) 93121

5984 Liquefied Petroleum Gas Dealers

Ace Hareware (Sanford, FL) 62763
Columbia Propane Corp. (Richmond, VA) 91785
Enron Corp. (Houston, TX) 86062
Exxon L P Gas Co. (Greenville, NC) 74959
Mapco Inc. (Tulsa, OK) 78009
Mapco Natural Gas Liquids Inc. (Tulsa, OK) 78010
Shell Oil Co. (Ballinger, TX) 83091
Sun Refining & Marketing Co. (Rison, AR) 57556
Union Texas Petroleum (Breaux Bridge, LA) 69741
Vision Energy (Fort Myers, FL) 59771; 59771
Vision Energy (Sarasota, FL) 62864
Warren Petroleum Co. (Louisville, KY) 69036
Warren Petroleum Co. (Jackson, MS) 73094
Warren Petroleum Co. (Elmore City, OK) 77040
Warren Petroleum Co. (Tulsa, OK) 78206
Warren Petroleum Co. (Houston, TX) 87170

5989 Fuel Dealers Nec

Leslie Coal Mining Co. (Stone, KY) 69311
Mapco Coal Inc. (Richmond, VA) 91921

5992 Florists

Ace Hardware (Newberry, FL) 61705
Ace Hardware Co. Inc. (Cornelius, NC) 74346
Ace Hardware Store (Bartow, FL) 58620
Casual Corner (Columbia, SC) 78997
Kroger Sav on Food&Drugs (Columbia, SC) 79041
Lone Star Gas Co. (Arlington, TX) 82697
Lone Star Gas Co. (Fort Worth, TX) 85181
Piggly Wiggly (Dothan, AL) 55659
Warren Petroleum Co. (Fort Worth, TX) 85359

5993 Tobacco Stores & Stands

Philip Morris Inc. (Louisville, KY) 68947

RJ Reynolds Tobacco Co. (Birmingham, AL) 55372

5995 Optical Goods Stores

Allergan Optical (Hurst, TX) 87268
Burdines Beauty Salon (Hollywood, FL) 60045
Burdines Optical (Altamonte Spg, FL) 58533
Burdines Optical Dept (Fort Myers, FL) 59686
Jack Eckerd Corp. (Largo, FL) 60834
Lens Crafters (Mobile, AL) 56196
Lens Crafters (Jacksonville, FL) 60360; 60361
Lens Crafters (Orlando, FL) 62034
Lens Crafters (St Petersburg, FL) 62990
Lens Crafters (Baton Rouge, LA) 69577
Lens Crafters (Kenner, LA) 69997
Lens Crafters (Utica, MS) 73438
Lens Crafters (Greensboro, NC) 74863
Lens Crafters (Charleston, SC) 78832
Lens Crafters (Columbia, SC) 79044
Lens Crafters (Greenville, SC) 79384
Lens Crafters (Austin, TX) 82918
Lens Crafters (Dallas, TX) 84197
Lens Crafters (El Paso, TX) 84831
Lens Crafters (San Antonio, TX) 89070
Lenscrafters (Chesapeake, VA) 90586
Lenscrafters (Richmond, VA) 91916; 91917

5999 Miscellaneous Retail Stores Nec

ABM Graphics (Birmingham, AL) 55109
Ace Hardware (New Port Richey, FL) 61672
Ace Hardware (Ville Platte, LA) 70932
Ace Hareware (Sanford, FL) 62763
ACME Business Products (Athens, GA) 64152
ACME Business Products (Brunswick, GA) 65399; 65400
ACME Business Products (Valdosta, GA) 67938
Avery Dennison (Clinton, SC) 78957
Avon Products (Radford, VA) 91689
Avon Products Business Office (Plant City, FL) 62536
Avon Products Inc. (Sheffield, AL) 56547
Avon Products Inc. (Fort Smith, AR) 57025
Avon Products Inc. (Little Rock, AR) 57256
Avon Products Inc. (Newark, DE) 57890
Avon Products Inc. (Washington, DC) 58130
Avon Products, Inc. (Melrose, FL) 61126
Avon Products Inc. (Ocala, FL) 61772
Avon Products Inc. (Suwanee, GA) 67741
Avon Products, Inc. (Tifton, GA) 67818
Avon Products, Inc. (Lafayette, LA) 70043
Avon Products Inc. (Carnegie, OK) 76905
Avon Products Inc. (Oklahoma City, OK) 77302
Avon Products Inc. (Bath, SC) 78705
Avon Products Inc. (Charleston, SC) 78789
Avon Products Inc. (Corpus Christi, TX) 83702
Avon Products Inc. (El Paso, TX) 84764
Avon Products Inc. (Grand Prairie, TX) 85605
Avon Products Inc. (Houston, TX) 85826
Avon Products Inc. (Odessa, TX) 88237
Avon Products Inc. (San Antonio, TX) 88922
Avon Products Inc. (Tyler, TX) 89790
Avon Products Inc. (Hampton, VA) 91015
Avon Products Inc. (Portsmouth, VA) 91641
Avon Products Inc. (Richmond, VA) 91740

Avon Products Inc. (Virginia Beach, VA) 92433
Bell Atlantic Metro Mobile (Greenville, SC) 79300
Bell Atlantic Mobile (El Paso, TX) 84767
BellSouth Communication Systems (Norcross, GA) 67105
Bellsouth Communication Systems Inc. (Irving, TX) 87322
Bellsouth Communications Systems, Inc. (Roanoke, VA) 92106
BellSouth Mobility (Huntsville, AL) 55889
BellSouth Services Inc. (Birmingham, AL) 55166
Burlington Coat Factory (Augusta, GA) 65316
Business Systems & Service Inc. (Vienna, WV) 93077
Centel Cellular Inc. (Atlanta, GA) 64348
Circuit City Inc. (Fort Lauderdale, FL) 59469
Circuit City Stores Inc. (Fort Lauderdale, FL) 59470
Copy Van Inc. (Richmond, VA) 91790
Costco Wholesale (Miami, FL) 61269
Delta Business Systems (Orlando, FL) 61960
Diebold Inc. (Charlotte, NC) 73930
Diebold, Inc. (Oklahoma City, OK) 77345
Dow Corning Corp. (Arlington, TN) 80180
Electronic Systems Inc. (Virginia Beach, VA) 92459
Gold Kist Inc. (Atlanta, GA) 64511
GTE Communications Corp. (Tampa, FL) 63445
GTE Mobile Communications Inc. (Atlanta, GA) 64525
House of Fragrance (Louisville, KY) 68776
Ibm Corp. (Gainesville, FL) 59881
Ibm Corp. (Columbus, MS) 72714
Ibm Corp. (Bartlesville, OK) 76833
Ibm Corp. (Tulsa, OK) 77957
Ibm Corp. (Kerrville, TX) 87473
Innovative Office Systems, Inc. (Dallas, TX) 84133; 84134
Jafra Cosmetics (Richmond, VA) 91909
Kay Bee Toys (Beaumont, TX) 83162
Kitchen Collection Inc. (Kannapolis, NC) 75265
Lens Crafters (Altamonte Springs, FL) 58557
Lens Crafters (Fort Lauderdale, FL) 59523
Lens Crafters (Orange Park, FL) 61890
Lens Crafters (Tampa, FL) 63481
Lens Crafters (Florence, SC) 79215
The Limited (Russellville, AR) 57584
Linvatec (Largo, FL) 60844
Magnetek (Palmetto, FL) 62310
Maison Blanche Optical Dept (Baton Rouge, LA) 69586
Mary Kay Cos Ind Sales Dir (Copperas Cove, TX) 83694
Mary Kay Cosm (Tampa, FL) 63493
Mary Kay Cosmet Ind Sls Dir (Longwood, FL) 60933
Mary Kay Cosmet Indep Sales (Harlingen, TX) 85705
Mary Kay Cosmet Independ Sl (Hobart, OK) 77133
Mary Kay Cosmet Independent (Big Spring, TX) 83290
Mary Kay Cosmetic (Radcliff, KY) 69240
Mary Kay Cosmetic (Midland, TX) 88048
Mary Kay Cosmetic Director (Gainesville, TX) 85423
Mary Kay Cosmetic Indpnt Sl (Starke, FL) 63149
Mary Kay Cosmetics (Alexander City, AL) 54975
Mary Kay Cosmetics (Auburn, AL) 55065
Mary Kay Cosmetics (Birmingham, AL) 55314; 55315; 55316; 55317; 55318
Mary Kay Cosmetics (Demopolis, AL) 55617
Mary Kay Cosmetics (Enterprise, AL) 55688
Mary Kay Cosmetics (Hartselle, AL) 55858
Mary Kay Cosmetics (Huntsville, AL) 55971
Mary Kay Cosmetics (Mobile, AL) 56203
Mary Kay Cosmetics (Quinton, AL) 56496

Mary Kay Cosmetics (Talladega, AL) 56595; 56596
Mary Kay Cosmetics (Mountainburg, AR) 57397
Mary Kay Cosmetics (North Little Rock, AR) 57468
Mary Kay Cosmetics (Pine Bluff, AR) 57525
Mary Kay Cosmetics (Thornton, AR) 57683
Mary Kay Cosmetics (Bridgeville, DE) 57753
Mary Kay Cosmetics (Boca Raton, FL) 58720
Mary Kay Cosmetics (Crystal River, FL) 59134
Mary Kay Cosmetics (Fort Myers, FL) 59718
Mary Kay Cosmetics (Fort Walton Beach, FL) 59830
Mary Kay Cosmetics (Gainesville, FL) 59892
Mary Kay Cosmetics (Hialeah, FL) 59998
Mary Kay Cosmetics (Hollywood, FL) 60075
Mary Kay Cosmetics (Indian Rocks, FL) 60139
Mary Kay Cosmetics (Lake Worth, FL) 60680; 60681
Mary Kay Cosmetics (Maitland, FL) 60981
Mary Kay Cosmetics (Miami, FL) 61367; 61368; 61369
Mary Kay Cosmetics (Niceville, FL) 61711
Mary Kay Cosmetics (Ocala, FL) 61808
Mary Kay Cosmetics (Orlando, FL) 62053; 62054
Mary Kay Cosmetics (Panama City, FL) 62332
Mary Kay Cosmetics (Pensacola, FL) 62448
Mary Kay Cosmetics (Ponte Vedra Beach, FL) 62651
Mary Kay Cosmetics (Shalimar, FL) 62913
Mary Kay Cosmetics (Tampa, FL) 63494
Mary Kay Cosmetics (West Palm Beach, FL) 63883
Mary Kay Cosmetics (Winter Springs, FL) 64001
Mary Kay Cosmetics (Benton, KY) 68125
Mary Kay Cosmetics (Danville, KY) 68260
Mary Kay Cosmetics (Elizabethtown, KY) 68287
Mary Kay Cosmetics (Hopkinsville, KY) 68481
Mary Kay Cosmetics (Louisville, KY) 68881
Mary Kay Cosmetics (Shepherdsville, KY) 69282
Mary Kay Cosmetics (Somerset, KY) 69296
Mary Kay Cosmetics (Baton Rouge, LA) 69587
Mary Kay Cosmetics (Lafayette, LA) 70075
Mary Kay Cosmetics (Monroe, LA) 70360
Mary Kay Cosmetics (New Iberia, LA) 70412
Mary Kay Cosmetics (Pineville, LA) 70623
Mary Kay Cosmetics (Robeline, LA) 70668
Mary Kay Cosmetics (Baltimore, MD) 71187
Mary Kay Cosmetics (Bethesda, MD) 71410
Mary Kay Cosmetics (Hagerstown, MD) 71884
Mary Kay Cosmetics (Ocean City, MD) 72161
Mary Kay Cosmetics (Taneytown, MD) 72490
Mary Kay Cosmetics (Southaven, MS) 73353
Mary Kay Cosmetics (Charlotte, NC) 74081
Mary Kay Cosmetics (Fayetteville, NC) 74564
Mary Kay Cosmetics (Morehead City, NC) 75625
Mary Kay Cosmetics (Pineville, NC) 75818
Mary Kay Cosmetics (Raleigh, NC) 75930
Mary Kay Cosmetics (Roanoke Rapids, NC) 76037
Mary Kay Cosmetics (Winston Salem, NC) 76675
Mary Kay Cosmetics (Altus, OK) 76794
Mary Kay Cosmetics (Chickasha, OK) 76931
Mary Kay Cosmetics (Clinton, OK) 76965
Mary Kay Cosmetics (Lawton, OK) 77165
Mary Kay Cosmetics (Miami, OK) 77206
Mary Kay Cosmetics (Ponca City, OK) 77707
Mary Kay Cosmetics (Woodward, OK) 78261
Mary Kay Cosmetics (Chesnee, SC) 78930
Mary Kay Cosmetics (Columbia, SC) 79051; 79053; 79054
Mary Kay Cosmetics (Greenville, SC) 79393
Mary Kay Cosmetics (Taylors, SC) 80038
Mary Kay Cosmetics (Bruceton, TN) 80262
Mary Kay Cosmetics (Delano, TN) 80730
Mary Kay Cosmetics (Knoxville, TN) 81229
Mary Kay Cosmetics (Memphis, TN) 81656
Mary Kay Cosmetics (Strawberry Plains, TN) 82363
Mary Kay Cosmetics (Arlington, TX) 82699
Mary Kay Cosmetics (Austin, TX) 82934
Mary Kay Cosmetics (Colleyville, TX) 83629
Mary Kay Cosmetics (Dallas, TX) 84218; 84220
Mary Kay Cosmetics (El Paso, TX) 84846; 84847
Mary Kay Cosmetics (Garland, TX) 85506; 85507
Mary Kay Cosmetics (Houston, TX) 86517; 86518
Mary Kay Cosmetics (Hurst, TX) 87281
Mary Kay Cosmetics (Kerrville, TX) 87475
Mary Kay Cosmetics (La Marque, TX) 87544
Mary Kay Cosmetics (Levelland, TX) 87639
Mary Kay Cosmetics (Livingston, TX) 87687
Mary Kay Cosmetics (Lubbock, TX) 87772
Mary Kay Cosmetics (Lufkin, TX) 87810
Mary Kay Cosmetics (Montgomery, TX) 88147
Mary Kay Cosmetics (Muenster, TX) 88164
Mary Kay Cosmetics (Port Arthur, TX) 88637
Mary Kay Cosmetics (San Antonio, TX) 89093
Mary Kay Cosmetics (Waco, TX) 89950
Mary Kay Cosmetics (Wichita Falls, TX) 90081
Mary Kay Cosmetics (Arlington, VA) 90357
Mary Kay Cosmetics (Burke, VA) 90505; 90506
Mary Kay Cosmetics (Charlottesville, VA) 90542
Mary Kay Cosmetics (Chesapeake, VA) 90587
Mary Kay Cosmetics (Falls Church, VA) 90859
Mary Kay Cosmetics (Front Royal, VA) 90951; 90952
Mary Kay Cosmetics (Hampton Virgi, VA) 91059
Mary Kay Cosmetics (Hillsville, VA) 91142
Mary Kay Cosmetics (Madison Heights, VA) 91299
Mary Kay Cosmetics (Mc Lean, VA) 91370
Mary Kay Cosmetic's (Midlothian, VA) 91419
Mary Kay Cosmetics (Norfolk, VA) 91552; 91553; 91554
Mary Kay Cosmetics (Petersburg, VA) 91633
Mary Kay Cosmetics (Richmond, VA) 91923
Mary Kay Cosmetics (Charleston, WV) 92768
Mary Kay Cosmetics (Parkersburg, WV) 92992
Mary Kay Cosmetics Sales (Jacksonville, AR) 57195
Mary Kay Cosmetics Sales (Mount Holly, NC) 75693
Mary Kay Cosmetics Sales Div. (Fort Myers, FL) 59719
Mary Kay Cosmetics Director (Austin, TX) 82935
Mary Kay Cosmetics Dist. (Roanoke, VA) 92172
Mary Kay Cosmetics, Inc. (Durham, NC) 74416
Mary Kay Cosmetics, Inc. (Broken Bow, OK) 76893
Mary Kay Cosmetics, Inc. (Dallas, TX) 84221; 84222
Mary Kay Cosmetics Independ (Fairfax, VA) 90794
Mary Kay Cosmetics Independent (Mobile, AL) 56205
Mary Kay Cosmetics Independent (Cary, NC) 73799
Mary Kay Cosmetics Independent (Marble Falls, TX) 87839
Mary Kay Cosmetics Independent (New Braunfels, TX) 88216
Mary Kay Cosmetics Sr Direc (Richmond, VA) 91927
Mary Kay Cosmitcs (Houston, TX) 86520
Mary Kay Costmetics (Florence, SC) 79217
Mobil Chemical Co. (Norcross, GA) 67153
Mobilecomm of Austin Inc. (Austin, TX) 82944
Modern Business Systems (Harrison, AR) 57139
Noxell Corp. (Hurst, TX) 87287
Radio Shack (Huntsville, AL) 56002
Radio Shack (Orlando, FL) 62128
Radio Shack (Tallahassee, FL) 63266
Radio Shack (Littleton, NC) 75450
Radio Shack (Henryetta, OK) 77130
Ring Around Products Inc. (Plainview, TX) 88532
Rite Aid (Westminster, MD) 72544
Rite Aid (Centreville, VA) 90518
Rite Aid Discount Pharmacy (Whitesville, WV) 93128
Rite Aid 2012 (Fort Lauderdale, FL) 59598
Service Merchandise (Corpus Christi, TX) 83749
Southern Copy Machines Inc. (Atlanta, GA) 65162; 65163
Southern Cotton Oil Co. (Quann, TX) 88703
Specialty Products Co. (Griffin, GA) 66325
Sports Authority (Miami, FL) 61465
Stop & Shop Pawn (Ocala, FL) 61822
Texaco Food Mart (Orlando, FL) 62162
Texaco Mini Mart Ii (Daytona Beach, FL) 59218
Wal Mart (Rogers, AR)·57577
Waldenbooks (Hollywood, FL) 60103
Waldenbooks (Westminster, MD) 72546
Waldenbooks (Dallas, TX) 84491
Waldenbooks (Friendswood, TX) 85408
Walgreen (Bradenton, FL) 58858
Walgreen (Fort Lauderdale, FL) 59629
Walgreen (Jacksonville, FL) 60500
Walgreen (Sarasota, FL) 62865
Walgreen (St. Petersburg, FL) 63137
Walgreen Co. (Daytona Beach, FL) 59226
Walgreen Drug Stores (Bradenton, FL) 58859
Walgreen Drug Stores (Miami, FL) 61506; 61510
Walgreen Drug Stores (Ocala, FL) 61828
Walgreen Drug Stores (Vero Beach, FL) 63770
Walgreen Drug Stores (Houston, TX) 87122
Walgreen Drug Stores (Wichita Falls, TX) 90121
Walgreen Pharmacy (Venice, FL) 63738
Western Geophysical Co. (Jackson, TN) 81018
Xomox Corp. (Tampa, FL) 63664
Zeno Systems of Georgia Inc. (Norcross, GA) 67214

6020 Commercial Banks

First Alabama Bank (Mobile, AL) 56173; 56177

6021 National Commercial Banks

American Express Bank International (Miami, FL) 61156
American Express Credit Corp. (Wilmington, DE) 57978
American General Finance Inc. (Concord, NC) 74305
American National Bank (Union Springs, AL) 56686
American National Bank (Ardmore, OK) 76808
American National Bank (Bristow, OK) 76869
American National Bank (Woodward, OK) 78255
American National Bank (Corpus Christi, TX) 83699
American National Bank (Gonzales, TX) 85586
American National Bank (Terell, TX) 89657
American National Bank (Texarkana, TX) 89667
American National Bank (Wichita Falls, TX) 90065
American Savings of FL FSB (Boca Raton, FL) 58664
American Savings of FL FSB (Deerfield Beach, FL) 59264
American Savings of FL FSB (Ft. Lauderdale, FL) 59847; 59848
American Savings of FL FSB (Hallandale, FL) 59957
American Savings of FL FSB (Hollywood, FL) 60036
American Savings of FL FSB (Miami, FL) 61157; 61158; 61159; 61160; 61161
American Savings of FL FSB (Miami Beach, FL) 61518
American Savings of FL FSB (Pompano Beach, FL) 62581; 62582; 62583
American Savings of FL FSB (West Palm Beach, FL) 63837
American Savings of Florida (Boca Raton, FL) 58665
American Savings of Florida (Ft. Lauderdale, FL) 59849
American Savings of Florida (Hollywood, FL) 60037
American Savings of Florida (Lake Worth, FL) 60662
American Savings of Florida (Miami, FL) 61162; 61163; 61164; 61165
AmSouth Bancorp (Birmingham, AL) 55127
AmSouth Bank (Alabaster, AL) 54953
AmSouth Bank (Bessemer, AL) 55085
AmSouth Bank (Fairfield, AL) 55711
AmSouth Bank (Fultondale, AL) 55771
AmSouth Bank (Montevallo, AL) 56271
AmSouth Bank NA (Birmingham, AL) 55130
AmSouth Bank NA (Dothan, AL) 55625
AmSouth Bank NA (Huntsville, AL) 55880
AmSouth Bank NA (Mobile, AL) 56140
AmSouth Bank National Association (Talladega, AL) 56591
AmSouth of Louisiana, Inc. (New Orleans, LA) 70432
AmSouth Mortgage Co. (Birmingham, AL) 55156
Anchor Bank (Murrells Inlet, SC) 79688
Anchor Bank (Myrtle Beach, SC) 79689
Anchor Bank, Inc. (Myrtle Beach, SC) 79692
Anchor Savings (Largo, FL) 60813
Anchor Savings Bank (Largo, FL) 60814
Anchor Savings Bank (St. Petersburg, FL) 63079
Anchor Savings Bank Sun (Tampa, FL) 63325
Anchor Savings Bank, FSB (Callahan, FL) 58903
Anchor Savings Bank, FSB (Deerfield Beach, FL) 59266
Anchor Savings Bank, FSB (Fort Meyers, FL) 59655
Anchor Savings Bank, FSB (Jacksonville Beach, FL) 60517
Anchor Savings Bank, FSB (Naples, FL) 61600
Anchor Savings Bank, FSB (New Port Richey, FL) 61674
Anchor Savings Bank, FSB (St. Augustine Beach, FL) 63064
Anchor Savings Bank, FSB (Tampa, FL) 63327
Annapolis Banking & Trust Co. (Annapolis, MD) 71001; 71002; 71003; 71004; 71005; 71006; 71007
Annapolis Banking & Trust Co. (Cape St. Claire, MD) 71492
Annapolis Banking & Trust Co. (Edgewater, MD) 71663
Annapolis Banking & Trust Co. (Pasadena, MD) 72211
Annapolis Banking & Trust Co. (Riva, MD) 72250
Annapolis Banking & Trust Co. (Severna Park, MD) 72370
Athens First Bank & First (Athens, GA) 64153
Athens First Bank & Trust (Athens, GA) 64154; 64155; 64156; 64157; 64158; 64159
Athens First Bank & Trust (Bogart, GA) 65384
Athens First Bank & Trust (Hartwell, GA) 66341
Athens First Bank & Trust (Lavonia, GA) 66498
Athens First Bank & Trust (Monroe, GA) 66988
Athens First Bank & Trust (Watkinsville, GA) 68023
Baltimore Trust Co. (Bethany Beach, DE) 57751
Baltimore Trust Co. (Bridgeville, DE) 57752
Baltimore Trust Co. (Fenwick Island, DE) 57816
Baltimore Trust Co. (Rehoboth Beach, DE) 57942
Baltimore Trust Co. (Selbyville, DE) 57955; 57956
Banco Popular de Puerto Rico (Ciales, PR) 78389
Banco Popular de Puerto Rico (San Juan, PR) 78552; 78561; 78569
Bank of Boston Corp. (Dallas, TX) 83870
Bank of Boston-Florida (Palm Beach, FL) 62245
Bank of Boston-Florida N.A. (Palm Beach, FL) 62246
Bank of Boston International (Miami, FL) 61172
Bank of Commerce (Auburn Town, TN) 80197
Bank of Commerce (Woodbury, TN) 82422; 82423
Bank of Coweta (Luthersville, GA) 66629
Bank of Coweta (Newman, GA) 67071; 67072; 67073; 67074
Bank of Coweta (Newnan, GA) 67076; 67077
Bank of Coweta (Senoia, GA) 67536
Bank of Delaware (Bear, DE) 57748
Bank of Delaware (Claymont, DE) 57760
Bank of Delaware (Dover, DE) 57781; 57782; 57783
Bank of Delaware (Elsmere, DE) 57813
Bank of Delaware (Greenville, DE) 57819
Bank of Delaware (Henry Clay, DE) 57822
Bank of Delaware (Hockessin, DE) 57823
Bank of Delaware (Middletown, DE) 57831
Bank of Delaware (Milford, DE) 57838; 57839
Bank of Delaware (New Castle, DE) 57855
Bank of Delaware (Newar, DE) 57879
Bank of Delaware (Newark, DE) 57892; 57893; 57894
Bank of Delaware (Odessa, DE) 57939
Bank of Delaware (Ogletown, DE) 57940; 57941
Bank of Delaware (Rehoboth Beach, DE) 57943
Bank of Delaware (Seaford, DE) 57949; 57950
Bank of Delaware (Smyrna, DE) 57959
Bank of Delaware (Wilmington, DE) 57990; 57991; 57992; 57993; 57994; 57995; 57996; 57997; 57998; 57999; 58000; 58001
Bank of East Tennessee (Morristown, TN) 81784; 81785; 81786; 81787; 81788
Bank of East Tennessee (Talbott, TN) 82367
Bank of Hazelhurst (Hazelhurst, GA) 66343; 66344
Bank of Hazelurst (Hazelhurst, GA) 66345
Bank of New York Trust Co. of Florida National Association (Miami, FL) 61176
Bank of Pensacola (Pensacola, FL) 62393; 62394; 62395; 62396
Bank of Rector (Rector, AR) 57554; 57555
Bank of Roane County (Harriman, TN) 80898
Bank of Roane County (Harrimen, TN) 80904
Bank of Roane County (Kingston, TN) 81124
Bank of Roane County (Oliver Springs, TN) 82208
Bank of Roane County (Rockwood, TN) 82267
Bank South (Athens, GA) 64160
Bank South (Atlanta, GA) 64250
Bank South (Conyers, GA) 65667; 65668
Bank South (Macon, GA) 66654
Bank South (Monticello, GA) 66997
Bank South (Riverdale, GA) 67304

Bank South (Smyrna, GA) 67541; 67542
Bank South (Tennille, GA) 67782
Bank South (Waycross, GA) 68026; 68027
Bank South Corp. (Atlanta, GA) 64253
Bank South-Douglas (Douglas, GA) 65964
Bank South Houston Co. (Perry, GA) 67259
Bank South Macon (Macon, GA) 66655
Bank South Macon Wesleyan Sta (Macon, GA) 66656
Bank South Mortgate Inc. (Atlanta, GA) 64260
Bank South, NA (Alpharetta, GA) 64104; 64105; 64106; 64107
Bank South, NA (Athens, GA) 64161; 64162
Bank South NA (Atlanta, GA) 64261; 64262; 64263; 64264; 64265; 64266; 64267; 64268; 64269; 64270; 64271; 64272; 64273; 64274; 64275; 64276; 64277; 64278; 64279; 64280; 64281; 64282; 64283; 64284; 64285; 64286; 64287
Bank South, NA (Auburn, GA) 65309
Bank South, NA (Buford, GA) 65432
Bank South, NA (Centerville, GA) 65514
Bank South, NA (Chamblee, GA) 65519; 65520; 65521
Bank South, NA (College Park, GA) 65577
Bank South NA (Conyers, GA) 65669; 65670; 65671; 65672; 65673; 65674
Bank South, NA (Cumming, GA) 65744; 65745
Bank South, NA (Decatur, GA) 65799; 65800
Bank South, NA (Doraville, GA) 65920
Bank South, NA (Douglas, GA) 65965
Bank South, NA (Duluth, GA) 66021; 66022; 66023; 66024; 66025; 66026
Bank South, NA (Dunwoody, GA) 66100; 66101; 66102
Bank South, NA (East Point, GA) 66141; 66142
Bank South, NA (Fayetteville, GA) 66187; 66188; 66189
Bank South, NA (Fitzgerald, GA) 66206; 66207
Bank South, NA (Forest Park, GA) 66228
Bank South, NA (Forsyth, GA) 66253
Bank South NA (Griffin, GA) 66309
Bank South, NA (Jonesboro, GA) 66376; 66377
Bank South, NA (Kennesaw, GA) 66407
Bank South, NA (Lake City, GA) 66495
Bank South NA (Lawrenceville, GA) 66501; 66502; 66503; 66504; 66505
Bank South, NA (Lilburn, GA) 66553; 66554; 66555
Bank South, NA (Macon, GA) 66658; 66659; 66660; 66661; 66662; 66663; 66664; 66665; 66666; 66667; 66668
Bank South, NA (Marietta, GA) 66740; 66741; 66742; 66743; 66744; 66745; 66746; 66747; 66748; 66749; 66750; 66751; 66752; 66753; 66754
Bank South, NA (Monticello, GA) 66998
Bank South, NA (Morrow, GA) 67003
Bank South, NA (Norcross, GA) 67101; 67102; 67103
Bank South, NA (Palmetto, GA) 67222
Bank South, NA (Perry, GA) 67260
Bank South NA (Riverdale, GA) 67305; 67306; 67307
Bank South NA (Roswell, GA) 67359; 67360; 67361; 67362; 67363
Bank South, NA (Sandy Springs, GA) 67433; 67434
Bank South, NA (Savannah, GA) 67447; 67448; 67449; 67450; 67451; 67452
Bank South, NA (Smyrna, GA) 67543; 67544
Bank South, NA (Snellville, GA) 67588
Bank South NA (St. Marys, GA) 67622
Bank South, NA (Stockbridge, GA) 67656
Bank South, NA (Stone Mountain, GA) 67681; 67682; 67683; 67684
Bank South, NA (Tennille, GA) 67783
Bank South, NA (Tucker, GA) 67845
Bank South NA (Union City, GA) 67911
Bank South, NA (Warner Robins, GA) 68007; 68008
Bank South, NA (Waycross, GA) 68028; 68029; 68030
Bank South NA (Winder, GA) 68055; 68056; 68057
Bank South NA (Columbia, SC) 78974
Bank South NA/Athens Main Office (Athens, GA) 64163
Bank South NA/Buckhead (Atlanta, GA) 64288
Bank South NA/Centerville (Centerville, GA) 65515
Bank South NA/College Park (College Park, GA) 65578
Bank South NA Conyers (Conyers, GA) 65675
Bank South NA/Cumming (Cumming, GA) 65746
Bank South NA/Douglas (Dougals, GA) 65963
Bank South NA/Dunwoody (Dunwoody, GA) 66103
Bank South NA/East Point (East Point, GA) 66143
Bank South NA/Folkston (Folkston, GA) 66222
Bank South NA/Forest Park (Forest Park, GA) 66229
Bank South NA/Forsyth (Forsyth, GA) 66254
Bank South NA/Fulton Industrial (Atlanta, GA) 64289
Bank South NA/Fulton Industries (Atlanta, GA) 64290
Bank South NA/Griffin (Griffin, GA) 66310
Bank South NA/Houston County (Perry, GA) 67261
Bank South NA/Houston-Warner Robbins (Warner Robbins, GA) 68004
Bank South NA/Jasper (Monticello, GA) 66999
Bank South NA Lake Harbin (Morrow, GA) 67004
Bank South NA/Lenox (Atlanta, GA) 64291
Bank South NA/Macon (Macon, GA) 66669
Bank South NA/Midtown (Atlanta, GA) 64292
Bank South NA/Peachtree Park (Doreville, GA) 65962
Bank South NA/Pensacola Main Office (Pensacola, FL) 62397
Bank South NA/Riverdale (Riverdale, GA) 67308
Bank South NA/Roswell (Roswell, GA) 67364
Bank South NA/St. Mary's (St. Marys, GA) 67623
Bank South NA/Sandy Springs (Atlanta, GA) 64293
Bank South NA/Savannah Main Office (Savannah, GA) 67454
Bank South NA/Smyrna (Smyrna, GA) 67545
Bank South NA/Sprayberry (Marietta, GA) 66755
Bank South NA/Stone Mountain (Stone Mountain, GA) 67685
Bank South NA/Waycross Main Office (401 Carswell Ave., GA) 64033
Bank South NA/Winder Main Office (Winder, GA) 68058
Bank South NA/Windy Hill (Marietta, GA) 66756
Bank of Southern Maryland (Hughesville, MD) 71923
Bank of Southern Maryland (La Plata, MD) 72003; 72004
Bank of Tokyo (Dallas, TX) 83871
Bank of Tokyo Ltd. (Miami, FL) 61177
Bank of Trenton & Trust Co. (Trenton, TN) 82373; 82374
Bank of Tuscaloosa (Tuscaloosa, AL) 56631; 56632; 56633
Bankers Trust (Huntsville, AL) 55887
Bankers Trust (Wilmington, DE) 58002
Bankers Trust (Houston, TX) 85863
Bankers Trust Co. (West Palm Beach, FL) 63839
Bankers Trust Co. of Florida NA (West Palm Beach, FL) 63840
Bankers Trust Delaware (Wilmington, DE) 58003
Bankers Trust International (Miami, FL) 61178
Bankers Trust of Madison (Ardmore, AL) 55029
Bankers Trust of Madison (Madison, AL) 56118
Bankers Trust of North Carolina (Asheboro, NC) 73577
Bankers Trust of North Carolina (Greensboro, NC) 74783; 74784; 74785; 74786; 74787
Barnett Bank of Alachua County, NA (Archer, FL) 58587
Barnett Bank of Alachua County, NA (Gainesville, FL) 59857; 59858; 59859; 59860; 59861
Barnett Bank of Alachua County, NA (High Springs, FL) 60024
Barnett Bank of Alachua County, NA (Newberry, FL) 61706
Barnett Bank of Broward County, NA (Coconut Creek, FL) 59087
Barnett Bank of Broward County, NA (Cooper City, FL) 59090
Barnett Bank of Broward County, NA (Coral Springs, FL) 59107; 59108; 59109
Barnett Bank of Broward County, NA (Dania, FL) 59145
Barnett Bank of Broward County, NA (Davie, FL) 59154
Barnett Bank of Broward County, NA (Deerfield Beach, FL) 59268; 59269; 59270; 59271
Barnett Bank of Broward County, NA (Fort Lauderdale, FL) 59444; 59445; 59446; 59447; 59448; 59449; 59450; 59451; 59452; 59453; 59454; 59455
Barnett Bank of Broward County, NA (Hallandale, FL) 59958
Barnett Bank of Broward County, NA (Hollywood, FL) 60039; 60040; 60041; 60042
Barnett Bank of Broward County, NA (Lighthouse Point, FL) 60899
Barnett Bank of Broward County, NA (Margate, FL) 60999; 61000
Barnett Bank of Broward County, NA (Miramar, FL) 61557
Barnett Bank of Broward County, NA (Pembroke Pines, FL) 62364; 62365; 62366
Barnett Bank of Broward County, NA (Plantation, FL) 62562; 62563; 62564
Barnett Bank of Broward County, NA (Pompano Beach, FL) 62584; 62585; 62586
Barnett Bank of Broward County, NA (Sunrise, FL) 63191
Barnett Bank of Broward County, NA (Tamarac, FL) 63295
Barnett Bank of Broward County, NA (West Hollywood, FL) 63832
Barnett Bank of Central Florida (Orlando, FL) 61921
Barnett Bank of Central Florida, NA (Altamonte Springs, FL) 58549
Barnett Bank of Central Florida, NA (Apopka, FL) 58568; 58569
Barnett Bank of Central Florida, NA (Casselberry, FL) 58927; 58928
Barnett Bank of Central Florida, NA (Cocoa, FL) 59065
Barnett Bank of Central Florida, NA (Cocoa Beach, FL) 59078
Barnett Bank of Central Florida, NA (Goldenrod, FL) 59928
Barnett Bank of Central Florida, NA (Indian Harbour Beach, FL) 60136
Barnett Bank of Central Florida, NA (Kissimmee, FL) 60582; 60583; 60584; 60585; 60586
Barnett Bank of Central Florida, NA (Longwood, FL) 60926; 60927
Barnett Bank of Central Florida, NA (Maitland, FL) 60973
Barnett Bank of Central Florida, NA (Melbourne, FL) 61035; 61036; 61037; 61038
Barnett Bank of Central Florida, NA (Merritt Island, FL) 61137
Barnett Bank of Central Florida, NA (Ocoee, FL) 61832
Barnett Bank of Central Florida, NA (Orlando, FL) 61922; 61923; 61924; 61925; 61926; 61927; 61928; 61929; 61930; 61931; 61932; 61933; 61934; 61935
Barnett Bank of Central Florida, NA (Oviedo, FL) 62214
Barnett Bank of Central Florida, NA (Palm Bay, FL) 62230; 62231; 62232
Barnett Bank of Central Florida, NA (Patrick Air Force Base, FL) 62361
Barnett Bank of Central Florida, NA (Rockledge, FL) 62742
Barnett Bank of Central Florida, NA (Sanford, FL) 62764
Barnett Bank of Central Florida, NA (St. Cloud, FL) 63065
Barnett Bank of Central Florida, NA (Titusville, FL) 63684
Barnett Bank of Central Florida, NA (West Melbourne, FL) 63833
Barnett Bank of Central Florida, NA (Winter Park, FL) 63962; 63963; 63964
Barnett Bank of Central Florida, NA (Zellwood, FL) 64006
Barnett Bank of Jacksonville, NA (Jacksonville, FL) 60191; 60192; 60193; 60194; 60195; 60196; 60197; 60198; 60199; 60200; 60201; 60202; 60203; 60204; 60205; 60206; 60207; 60208; 60209; 60210; 60211; 60212; 60213; 60214; 60215; 60216; 60217; 60218; 60219; 60220; 60221; 60222
Barnett Bank of Lake County, NA (Eustis, FL) 59396; 59397
Barnett Bank of Lake County, NA (Leesburg, FL) 60876; 60877; 60878; 60879
Barnett Bank of Lake County, NA (Mount Dora, FL) 61561; 61562
Barnett Bank of Lake County, NA (Tavares, FL) 63668
Barnett Bank of Lake County, NA (Umatilla, FL) 63711; 63712
Barnett Bank of Lee County, NA (Fort Myers, FL) 59663; 59664; 59665; 59666; 59667; 59668; 59669; 59670; 59671; 59672; 59673; 59674; 59675; 59676; 59677; 59678; 59679; 59680; 59681; 59682; 59683; 59684
Barnett Bank of Manatee County, NA (Bradenton, FL) 58802; 58803; 58804; 58805; 58806; 58807; 58808; 58809; 58810; 58811
Barnett Bank of Manatee County, NA (Ellenton, FL) 59385
Barnett Bank of Manatee County, NA (Holmes Beach, FL) 60110
Barnett Bank of Manatee County, NA (Oneco, FL) 61857
Barnett Bank of Manatee County, NA (Palmetto, FL) 62306
Barnett Bank of Manatee County, NA (Sarasota, FL) 62788
Barnett Bank of Marion County, NA (Belleview, FL) 58654
Barnett Bank of Marion County, NA (Dunnellon, FL) 59371
Barnett Bank of Marion County, NA (Ocala, FL) 61773; 61774; 61775; 61776; 61777; 61778; 61779; 61780; 61781
Barnett Bank of Marion County, NA (Silver Springs, FL) 62916; 62917
Barnett Bank of Martin County, NA (Hobe Sound, FL) 60026
Barnett Bank of Martin County, NA (Palm City, FL) 62276
Barnett Bank of Martin County, NA (Stuart, FL) 63155; 63156; 63157; 63158; 63159; 63160
Barnett Bank of South Florida, NA (Bay Harbor Islands, FL) 58636
Barnett Bank of South Florida, NA (Coral Gables, FL) 59093; 59094; 59095
Barnett Bank of South Florida, NA (Hialeah, FL) 59974; 59975; 59976
Barnett Bank of South Florida, NA (Homestead, FL) 60113
Barnett Bank of South Florida, NA (Key Biscayne, FL) 60562
Barnett Bank of South Florida, NA (Key Largo, FL) 60565
Barnett Bank of South Florida, NA (Miami, FL) 61179; 61180; 61181; 61182; 61183; 61184; 61185; 61186; 61187; 61188; 61189; 61190; 61191; 61192; 61193; 61194; 61195; 61196; 61197; 61198
Barnett Bank of South Florida, NA (Miami Beach, FL) 61524; 61525; 61526
Barnett Bank of South Florida, NA (Miami Lakes, FL) 61532; 61533
Barnett Bank of South Florida, NA (Miami Shores, FL) 61536
Barnett Bank of South Florida, NA (North Miami, FL) 61731; 61732; 61733
Barnett Bank of South Florida, NA (North Miami Beach, FL) 61741; 61742
Barnett Bank of South Florida, NA (Perrine, FL) 62494
Barnett Bank of Southeast Georgia, NA (Brunswick, GA) 65402; 65403
Barnett Bank of Southeast Georgia, NA (Jekyll Island, GA) 66367
Barnett Bank of Southeast Georgia, NA (Jessup, GA) 66368
Barnett Bank of Southeast Georgia, NA (Kingsland, GA) 66466
Barnett Bank of Southeast Georgia, NA (St. Marys, GA) 67624
Barnett Bank of Southeast Georgia, NA (St. Simons Island, GA) 67626
Barnett Bank of Southwest Florida (Charlotte Harbor, FL) 58948
Barnett Bank of Southwest Florida (Englewood, FL) 59390; 59391; 59392
Barnett Bank of Southwest Florida (Longboat Key, FL) 60923
Barnett Bank of Southwest Florida (Nokomis, FL) 61724
Barnett Bank of Southwest Florida (North Port, FL) 61753
Barnett Bank of Southwest Florida (Port Charlotte, FL) 62653; 62654
Barnett Bank of Southwest Florida (Sarasota, FL) 62789; 62790; 62791; 62792; 62795; 62796; 62798
Barnett Bank of Southwest Florida (Venice, FL) 63717; 63718; 63719; 63720
Barnett Bank of the Suncoast, NA (Beverly Hills, FL) 58659
Barnett Bank of the Suncoast, NA (Brooksville, FL) 58885; 58886; 58887
Barnett Bank of the Suncoast, NA (Citrus Springs, FL) 58955
Barnett Bank of the Suncoast, NA (Crystal River, FL) 59130
Barnett Bank of the Suncoast, NA (Homosassa Springs, FL) 60127
Barnett Bank of the Suncoast, NA (Inverness, FL) 60145; 60146; 60147
Barnett Bank of the Suncoast, NA (Spring Hill, FL) 62928; 62929; 62930; 62931; 62932
Barnett Bank of the Treasure Coast (Fort Pierce, FL) 59786; 59787; 59788
Barnett Bank of the Treasure Coast (Port St. Lucie, FL) 62696
Barnett Bank of Volusia County (Daytona Beach, FL) 59166
Barnett Bank of Volusia County (New Smyrna Beach, FL) 61698; 61699; 61700
Barnett Bank of Volusia County (Ormond Beach, FL) 62195; 62197; 62198; 62199
Barnett Bank of Volusia County (Palm Coast, FL) 62282; 62283
Barnett Bank of Volusia County (Port Orange, FL) 62659; 62660; 62661
Barnett Bank of West Florida (Cantonment, FL) 58907
Barnett Bank of West Florida (Gulf Breeze, FL) 59935
Barnett Bank of West Florida (Milton, FL) 61545; 61546
Barnett Bank of West Florida (Pace, FL) 62220
Barnett Bank of West Florida (Pensacola, FL) 62398; 62399; 62400; 62401; 62402; 62403; 62404; 62405; 62406; 62407; 62408
Barnett Banks Trust Co., NA (Jacksonville, FL) 60225; 60226
Barnett Banks of Volusia County (Orange City, FL) 61868
Beneficial Corp. (Wilmington, DE) 58015; 58017
Beneficial National Bank (Bear, DE) 57749
Beneficial National Bank (Dover, DE) 57785
Beneficial National Bank (New Castle, DE) 57856
Beneficial National Bank (Newark, DE) 57898
Beneficial National Bank (Talleyville, DE) 57963
Beneficial National Bank (Wilmington, DE) 58019; 58020; 58021; 58022; 58023; 58024
Beneficial National Bank USA (Wilmington, DE) 58025; 58026; 58029
Beneficial Savings Bank, FSB (Orlando, FL) 61937
Beneficial Savings Bank, FSB (Tampa, FL) 63365
Branch Banking & Trust (Orangeburg, SC) 79768
Branch Banking & Trust Co. (Aberdeen, NC) 73509; 73510; 73511
Branch Banking & Trust Co. (Angier, NC) 73551
Branch Banking & Trust Co. (Apex, NC) 73553
Branch Banking & Trust Co. (Asheville, NC) 73607; 73608

Citibank International (Houston, TX) 85960
Citibank, NA (Coconut Creek, FL) 59089
Citibank, NA (Dania, FL) 59146
Citibank, NA (Davie, FL) 59156
Citibank, NA (Deerfield Beach, FL) 59275
Citizens Bank (Byron, GA) 65446
Citizens Bank (Ft. Valley, GA) 66263
Citizens Bank (Algood, TN) 80161
Citizens Bank (Baxter, TN) 80201
Citizens Bank (Cookeville, TN) 80644; 80645; 80646
Citizens Bank (Cookville, TN) 80672
Citizens Bank (Monterey, TN) 81782
Citizens Bank & Trust (Oliver Springs, TN) 82209
Citizens Bank & Trust Co. (Sunbright, TN) 82364
Citizens Bank & Trust Co. (Wartburg, TN) 82399; 82400
Citizens Bank & Trust of West Georgia (Carrollton, GA) 65490; 65491; 65493; 65494
Citizens Bank & Trust of West Georgia (Tallapposa, GA) 67779
Citizens Bank & Trust of West Georgia (Temple, GA) 67781
Citizens Bank & Trust of West Georgia (Villa Rica, GA) 68002
Citizens Bank & Trust of West Georgia (Whitesburg, GA) 68050
Citizens Federal Bank, AFSB (Boca Raton, FL) 58691
Citizens Federal Bank, AFSB (Boynton Beach, FL) 58769
Citizens Federal Bank, AFSB (Clearwater, FL) 58987
Citizens Federal Bank, AFSB (DeLand, FL) 59299
Citizens Federal Bank, AFSB (Deltona, FL) 59334
Citizens Federal Bank, FSB (Hialeah, FL) 59981; 59982
Citizens Federal Bank, FSB (Holly Hill, FL) 60032
Citizens Federal Bank, FSB (Hollywood, FL) 60052
Citizens Federal Bank, FSB (Lehigh Acres, FL) 60891
Citizens Federal Bank, FSB (Miami, FL) 61247; 61249
Citizens Federal Bank, FSB (Miami Beach, FL) 61529
Citizens Federal Bank, FSB (Ocala, FL) 61788; 61789
Citizens Federal Bank, FSB (Ormond Beach, FL) 62200
Citizens Federal Bank, FSB (Palm Harbor, FL) 62296
Citizens Federal Bank, FSB (Pembroke Pines, FL) 62368
Citizens Federal Bank, FSB (Pinellas Park, FL) 62516
Citizens Federal Bank, FSB (Port Charlotte, FL) 62655
Citizens Federal Bank, FSB (Sarasota, FL) 62803; 62804
Citizens Federal Bank, FSB (South Miami, FL) 62922
Citizens Federal Bank, FSB (St. Petersburg, FL) 63098
Citizens Federal Bank, FSB (Sun City, FL) 63185
Citizens Federal Bank, FSB (Vero Beach, FL) 63745
Citizens First Bank (Rome, GA) 67335; 67336
Citizens Naitonal Bank (Fort George G. Meade, MD) 71705
Citizens National Bank (Beltsville, MD) 71349
Citizens National Bank (Bowie, MD) 71457; 71458
Citizens National Bank (Burtonsville, MD) 71480
Citizens National Bank (Clarksville, MD) 71536
Citizens National Bank (Crofton, MD) 71614
Citizens National Bank (Ellicott City, MD) 71677
Citizens National Bank (Glenelg, MD) 71850
Citizens National Bank (Jessup, MD) 71983
Citizens National Bank (Laurel, MD) 72065; 72066; 72067; 72068
Citizens National Bank (Odenton, MD) 72166
Citizens National Bank (Simpsonville, MD) 72450
Citizens Savings Bank, SSB (Claremont, NC) 74254
Citizens Savings Bank, SSB (Hickory, NC) 75063; 75064; 75065
Citizens Savings Bank, SSB (Lincolnton, NC) 75436; 75437
Citizens Savings Bank, SSB (Maiden, NC) 75489
Citizens Savings Bank, SSB (Stanley, NC) 76310
Citizens Savings Bank, SSB (Formerly Citizens S&L) (Mooresville, NC) 75601; 75602
Citizens Savings Bank, SSB (Formerly Citizens Savings Bank, Inc.) (Newton, NC) 75743; 75744; 75745
City National Bank (Fort Smith, AR) 57038
City National Bank (Miami, FL) 61250; 61251; 61252; 61255
City National Bank (Tallahassee, FL) 63222; 63223; 63224
City National Bank (Fulton, KY) 68374
City National Bank (Baton Rouge, LA) 69480; 69481; 69482; 69483; 69484
City National Bank (Amarillo, TX) 82539
City National Bank (Taylor, TX) 89597
City National Bank (Weslaco, TX) 90032; 90033
City National Bank (Whitehouse, TX) 90057; 90058
City National Bank (Winnsboro, TX) 90125
City National Bank (Charleston, WV) 92733
City National Bank Carrollton (Carrollton, TX) 83459
City National Bank of Carrollton (Dallas, TX) 83916
City National Bank of Charleston (Charleston, WV) 92736
City National Bank of Fairmont (Fairmont, WV) 92837
City National Bank of Fairmont (Farmington, WV) 92851
City National Bank of Florida (Fort Lauderdale, FL) 59475
City National Bank of Florida (Miami, FL) 61259
City National Bank of Fulton (Fulton, KY) 68375
City National Bank of Irvin (Irving, TX) 87331
City National Bank of Irving (Irving, TX) 87332; 87333
City National Bank of Kilgore (Kilgore, TX) 87486
City National Bank Mignon Branch (Sylacauga, AL) 56578
City National Bank of San Saba (San Saba, TX) 89346
City National Bank of Sulphur Spring (Sulphur Spring, TX) 89549; 89550
City National Bank Sylacauga (Sylacauga, AL) 56579; 56581; 56582
City National Bank of Taylor (Taylor, TX) 89598
City National Bank & Trust (Guymon, OK) 77100
City National Bank of Washi (Atlanta, GA) 64364
City National Bank of Weath (Weatherford, OK) 78239
City National Corp. (Sylacauga, AL) 56583
Clavert Bank & Trust Co. (Chaneyville, MD) 71509
Coastal Bank of Georgia (Brunswick, GA) 65404; 65405; 65406
Coastal Bank of Georgia (Kings Bay, GA) 66465
Coastal Bank of Georgia (St. Mary's, GA) 67621
Coastal Bank of Georgia (St. Simons Island, GA) 67627; 67628
Cohutta Banking Co. (Chatsworth, GA) 65554; 65555
Cohutta Banking Co. (Chickamauga, GA) 65560
Cohutta Banking Co. (Eton, GA) 66171
Cohutta Banking Co. (La Fayette, GA) 66469
Collective Federal Savings Bank (Wilmington, DE) 58040
Colmbus Bank & Trust Co. (Columbus, GA) 65623
Columbia First Bank, A Federal Savings Bank (Washington, DC) 58168; 58169; 58170; 58171; 58172; 58173; 58174; 58175; 58176; 58177; 58178; 58179; 58180
Columbia First Bank, FSB (Alexandria, VA) 90168
Columbia First Bank, FSB (Annandale, VA) 90255
Columbus Bank & Trust (Columbus, GA) 65624
Columbus Bank & Trust Co. (Columbus, GA) 65625; 65626; 65627; 65628; 65629; 65630; 65631; 65632; 65633; 65634; 65635; 65636; 65637
Comerica Bank-Texas (Addison, TX) 82471
Comerica Bank-Texas (Arlington, TX) 82642; 82643
Comerica Bank-Texas (Austin, TX) 82841; 82842; 82843; 82844
Comerica Bank-Texas (Balch Springs, TX) 83085
Comerica Bank-Texas (Carrollton, TX) 83460
Comerica Bank-Texas (Cleveland, TX) 83591
Comerica Bank-Texas (Coppell, TX) 83690
Comerica Bank-Texas (Dallas, TX) 83926; 83927; 83928; 83929; 83930; 83931; 83932; 83933; 83934; 83935; 83936; 83937; 83938; 83939; 83940; 83941; 83942; 83943
Comerica Bank-Texas (De Soto, TX) 84532
Comerica Bank-Texas (Farmers Branch, TX) 85031; 85032
Comerica Bank-Texas (Fort Worth, TX) 85089; 85090
Comerica Bank-Texas (Frisco, TX) 85410
Comerica Bank-Texas (Houston, TX) 85988; 85989; 85990
Comerica Bank-Texas (Humble, TX) 87218
Comerica Bank-Texas (Irving, TX) 87334
Comerica Bank-Texas (Kingwood, TX) 87536
Comerica Bank-Texas (Lewisville, TX) 87648
Comerica Bank-Texas (Pflugerville, TX) 88506
Comerica Bank-Texas (Plano, TX) 88547
Comerica Bank-Texas (Richardson, TX) 88728; 88729; 88730
Comerica Bank-Texas (San Antoino, TX) 88908
Comerica Bank-Texas (San Antonio, TX) 88960; 88961
Comerica Bank-Texas (Sugar Land, TX) 89529
Comerica Bank-Texas (Waxahochie, TX) 90003
Comerica Bank & Trust, FSB (Baco Raton, FL) 58614
Comerica Bank & Trust, FSB (Clearwater, FL) 58990
Comerica Bank Trust, FSB (Naples, FL) 61617
Comerica Bank & Trust, FSB (Palm Beach Gardens, FL) 62269
Commerce Banc Corp. (Charleston, WV) 92740
Commerce Bank & Trust Co. of Troup County (La Grange, GA) 66473
Commercial Bank (Boston, GA) 65387
Commercial Bank (Thomasville, GA) 67789; 67790; 67791; 67792
Commercial Bank & Trust Co. of Troup County (La Grange, GA) 66474; 66475; 66476
Commercial National Bank in Shreveport (Shreveport, LA) 70701; 70702; 70703; 70704; 70705; 70706; 70707; 70708; 70709; 70710; 70711
Community Bank & Trust National Association (Fairmont, WV) 92838
Compass Bank (Huntsville, AL) 55901; 55902; 55903; 55904; 55905; 55906
Compass Bank-Dallas (Carrollton, TX) 83461; 83462; 83463
Compass Bank-Dallas (Dallas, TX) 83948; 83949; 83950; 83951; 83952; 83953; 83954; 83955
Compass Bank-Dallas (Frisco, TX) 85411
Compass Bank-Dallas (Irving, TX) 87335
Compass Bank-Dallas (Mertzon, TX) 87954
Compass Bank-Dallas (Plano, TX) 88548; 88549; 88550; 88551; 88552; 88553; 88554; 88555
Compass Bank-Dallas (Richardson, TX) 88732
Compass Bank-Houston (Crosley, TX) 83810
Compass Bank-Houston (Houston, TX) 85997; 85998; 85999; 86000; 86001; 86002; 86003; 86004; 86005; 86006
Compass Bank-Houston (Kingwood, TX) 87537
Compass Bank-Houston (Spring, TX) 89464
Compass Bank-Houston (Sugar Land, TX) 89530
Continental Illinois Trust Co. of Florida, NA (Boca Raton, FL) 58693
Continental Illinois Trust Co. of Florida, NA (Sarasota, FL) 62807
County Banking & Trust Co. (Aberdeen, MD) 70992
County Banking & Trust Co. (Cecilton, MD) 71507
County Banking & Trust Co. (Chesapeake City, MD) 71515
County Banking & Trust Co. (Elkton, MD) 71671; 71672
County Banking & Trust Co. (Elton, MD) 71681
County Banking & Trust Co. (Havre De Grace, MD) 71916; 71917
County Banking & Trust Co. (North East, MD) 72154
County Banking & Trust Co. (Rising Sun, MD) 72248
Crestar Bank (, VA) 90151
Crestar Bank (Accomac, VA) 90162
Crestar Bank (Alexandria, VA) 90169; 90170; 90171; 90172; 90173; 90174; 90175; 90176; 90177; 90178
Crestar Bank (Annandale, VA) 90257; 90258
Crestar Bank (Arlington, VA) 90286; 90287; 90288; 90289; 90290; 90291; 90292; 90293; 90294; 90295
Crestar Bank (Ashland, VA) 90401
Crestar Bank (Beaverdam, VA) 90417
Crestar Bank (Burke, VA) 90499
Crestar Bank (Centreville, VA) 90514
Crestar Bank (Chantilly, VA) 90519; 90520
Crestar Bank (Charlottesville, VA) 90528; 90529; 90530; 90531; 90532; 90533; 90534
Crestar Bank (Cheriton, VA) 90555
Crestar Bank (Chesapeake, VA) 90565; 90566; 90567; 90568; 90569; 90570
Crestar Bank (Chester, VA) 90618
Crestar Bank (Clifton Forge, VA) 90640; 90641
Crestar Bank (Collinsville, VA) 90647
Crestar Bank (Dale City, VA) 90681
Crestar Bank (Doswell, VA) 90728
Crestar Bank (Edinberg, VA) 90739
Crestar Bank (Fairfax, VA) 90762; 90763; 90764; 90765
Crestar Bank (Fairfax Station, VA) 90815
Crestar Bank (Falls Church, VA) 90827; 90828
Crestar Bank (Fieldale, VA) 90878
Crestar Bank (Fort Belvoir, VA) 90886; 90887
Crestar Bank (Fort Lee, VA) 90888
Crestar Bank (Franklin, VA) 90892
Crestar Bank (Fredericksburg, VA) 90915
Crestar Bank (Fredricksberg, VA) 90946
Crestar Bank (Gloucester, VA) 90990
Crestar Bank (Gloucester Point, VA) 90993
Crestar Bank (Grafton, VA) 90995
Crestar Bank (Great Falls, VA) 90998
Crestar Bank (Gretna, VA) 91002
Crestar Bank (Hampton, VA) 91021; 91022; 91023; 91024
Crestar Bank (Harrisonburg, VA) 91072; 91073; 91074
Crestar Bank (Herndon, VA) 91119
Crestar Bank (Hopewell, VA) 91160
Crestar Bank (Keller, VA) 91174
Crestar Bank (Keysville, VA) 91176
Crestar Bank (Langley AFB, VA) 91183
Crestar Bank (Lexington, VA) 91198; 91199; 91200
Crestar Bank (Lynchburg, VA) 91228; 91229; 91230; 91231; 91232; 91233
Crestar Bank (Madison Heights, VA) 91295
Crestar Bank (Manassas, VA) 91305; 91306
Crestar Bank (Martinsville, VA) 91345; 91346; 91347; 91348; 91349
Crestar Bank (McLean, VA) 91378; 91379; 91380; 91381
Crestar Bank (Mechanicsville, VA) 91400
Crestar Bank (Midlothian, VA) 91412; 91413
Crestar Bank (Nassawa Dox, VA) 91440
Crestar Bank (New Market, VA) 91441
Crestar Bank (Newport News, VA) 91456; 91457; 91458; 91459
Crestar Bank (Newprot News, VA) 91495
Crestar Bank (Norfolk, VA) 91505; 91506; 91507; 91508; 91509; 91510; 91511; 91512
Crestar Bank (Onancock, VA) 91614
Crestar Bank (Orange, VA) 91617
Crestar Bank (Painter, VA) 91621
Crestar Bank (Petersburg, VA) 91630; 91631
Crestar Bank (Portsmouth, VA) 91643; 91644; 91645
Crestar Bank (Radford, VA) 91693; 91694; 91695
Crestar Bank (Ranoke, VA) 91702
Crestar Bank (Reston, VA) 91704; 91705; 91706
Crestar Bank (Richmond, VA) 91794; 91795; 91796; 91797; 91798; 91799; 91800; 91801; 91802; 91803; 91804; 91805; 91806; 91807; 91808; 91809; 91810; 91811; 91813; 91814; 91815; 91816; 91817; 91818; 91819; 91820; 91821; 91822; 91823; 91824; 91825; 91826; 91827; 91828; 91829; 91830
Crestar Bank (Roanoke, VA) 92121; 92122; 92123; 92124; 92125; 92126; 92127; 92128; 92129; 92130; 92131; 92132
Crestar Bank (Salem, VA) 92208
Crestar Bank (South Boston, VA) 92247; 92248
Crestar Bank (Spotsylvania, VA) 92271
Crestar Bank (Springfield, VA) 92274; 92275; 92276; 92277
Crestar Bank (Staunton, VA) 92310; 92311; 92312; 92313
Crestar Bank (Sterling, VA) 92338; 92339
Crestar Bank (Stuart, VA) 92352
Crestar Bank (Suffolk, VA) 92362; 92363
Crestar Bank (Vienna, VA) 92396; 92397; 92398
Crestar Bank (Vinton, VA) 92424
Crestar Bank (Virgilina, VA) 92428
Crestar Bank (Virginia Beach, VA) 92448; 92449; 92450; 92451; 92452; 92453; 92454; 92455; 92456
Crestar Bank (Waynesboro, VA) 92532; 92533
Crestar Bank (West Point, VA) 92540
Crestar Bank (Williamsberg, VA) 92546; 92547; 92548; 92549; 92550
Crestar Bank (Williamsburg, VA) 92567; 92568
Crestar Bank (Woodbridge, VA) 92610; 92611
Crestar Bank MD (Bethesda, MD) 71379; 71380; 71381; 71382; 71383
Crestar Bank MD (District Heights, MD) 71652
Crestar Bank MD (Gaithersburg, MD) 71768; 71769
Crestar Bank MD (Germantown, MD) 71825
Crestar Bank MD (Greenbelt, MD) 71857
Crestar Bank MD (Hyattsville, MD) 71956
Crestar Bank MD (Kensington, MD) 71992
Crestar Bank MD (Largo, MD) 72062
Crestar Bank MD (Laurel, MD) 72070
Crestar Bank MD (Potomac, MD) 72226; 72227
Crestar Bank MD (Rockville, MD) 72264; 72265
Crestar Bank MD (Silver Spring, MD) 72387; 72388; 72389
Crestar Bank MD (Waldorf, MD) 72527
Crestar Bank MD (Wheaton, MD) 72552
Crestar Bank, NA (Washington, DC) 58182; 58183; 58184; 58185; 58186; 58187; 58188; 58189; 58190; 58191; 58192; 58193; 58194; 58195; 58196; 58197; 58198; 58199; 58200; 58201; 58202; 58203; 58204; 58206
Crestview Bank, NA (Washington, DC) 58208
Crestwood State Bank (Crestwood, KY) 68245
Crestwood State Bank (La Grange, KY) 68502
Crestwood State Bank (Prospect, KY) 69232
Cretar Bank (Arlington, VA) 90296

First-Citizens Bank & Trust Co. (Hendersonville, NC) 75033; 75034; 75035; 75036; 75037; 75038; 75039
First-Citizens Bank & Trust Co. (Hickory, NC) 75069; 75070; 75071; 75072; 75073
First-Citizens Bank & Trust Co. (High Point, NC) 75125; 75126; 75127; 75128; 75129
First-Citizens Bank & Trust Co. (Highlands, NC) 75184
First-Citizens Bank & Trust Co. (Hudson, NC) 75199
First-Citizens Bank & Trust Co. (Jacksonville, NC) 75210; 75211; 75212; 75213; 75214
First-Citizens Bank & Trust Co. (Kernersville, NC) 75278
First-Citizens Bank & Trust Co. (Kill Devil Hills, NC) 75286
First-Citizens Bank & Trust Co. (Kings Mountain, NC) 75303
First-Citizens Bank & Trust Co. (Kinston, NC) 75319; 75320; 75321; 75322; 75323
First-Citizens Bank & Trust Co. (Lansing, NC) 75343
First-Citizens Bank & Trust Co. (Lenior, NC) 75362
First-Citizens Bank & Trust Co. (Lenoir, NC) 75377
First-Citizens Bank & Trust Co. (Lincolnton, NC) 75438
First-Citizens Bank & Trust Co. (Littleton, NC) 75449
First-Citizens Bank & Trust Co. (Louisburg, NC) 75454
First-Citizens Bank & Trust Co. (Madison, NC) 75481; 75482
First-Citizens Bank & Trust Co. (Maiden, NC) 75493
First-Citizens Bank & Trust Co. (Marion, NC) 75504
First-Citizens Bank & Trust Co. (Marshall, NC) 75513
First-Citizens Bank & Trust Co. (Maysville, NC) 75541
First-Citizens Bank & Trust Co. (Monroe, NC) 75575; 75576
First-Citizens Bank & Trust Co. (Morehead City, NC) 75616; 75617; 75618; 75619; 75620
First-Citizens Bank & Trust Co. (Morganton, NC) 75646; 75647
First-Citizens Bank & Trust Co. (Mount Airy, NC) 75676
First-Citizens Bank & Trust Co. (Murphy, NC) 75703; 75704
First-Citizens Bank & Trust Co. (Nashville, NC) 75716
First-Citizens Bank & Trust Co. (New Bern, NC) 75723; 75724; 75725; 75726; 75727; 75728
First-Citizens Bank & Trust Co. (Newport, NC) 75740; 75741
First-Citizens Bank & Trust Co. (Newton, NC) 75746; 75747
First-Citizens Bank & Trust Co. (Newton Grove, NC) 75757
First-Citizens Bank & Trust Co. (North Wilkesboro, NC) 75760; 75761
First-Citizens Bank & Trust Co. (Pilot Mountain, NC) 75799
First-Citizens Bank & Trust Co. (Pink Hill, NC) 75829
First-Citizens Bank & Trust Co. (Pittsboro, NC) 75830
First-Citizens Bank & Trust Co. (Princeton, NC) 75844
First-Citizens Bank & Trust Co. (Raleigh, NC) 75892; 75893; 75894; 75895; 75896; 75897; 75898; 75899; 75900; 75901; 75902; 75903; 75904; 75905; 75906
First-Citizens Bank & Trust Co. (Ramseur, NC) 75987
First-Citizens Bank & Trust Co. (Research Triangle Park, NC) 76019
First-Citizens Bank & Trust Co. (Richlands, NC) 76025
First-Citizens Bank & Trust Co. (Roanoke Rapids, NC) 76034; 76035; 76036
First-Citizens Bank & Trust Co. (Rocky Mount, NC) 76083; 76084; 76085; 76086; 76087
First-Citizens Bank & Trust Co. (Rural Hill, NC) 76137; 76138; 76139
First-Citizens Bank & Trust Co. (Rutherford College, NC) 76140
First-Citizens Bank & Trust Co. (Salisbury, NC) 76158
First-Citizens Bank & Trust Co. (Sanford, NC) 76192
First-Citizens Bank & Trust Co. (Scotland Neck, NC) 76212
First-Citizens Bank & Trust Co. (Selma, NC) 76222
First-Citizens Bank & Trust Co. (Shallote, NC) 76228
First-Citizens Bank & Trust Co. (Shelby, NC) 76238
First-Citizens Bank & Trust Co. (Snow Hill, NC) 76270; 76271; 76272
First-Citizens Bank & Trust Co. (Southern Pines, NC) 76276
First-Citizens Bank & Trust Co. (Southport, NC) 76284; 76285
First-Citizens Bank & Trust Co. (Sparta, NC) 76291
First-Citizens Bank & Trust Co. (Spring Hope, NC) 76295
First-Citizens Bank & Trust Co. (Statesville, NC) 76326; 76327; 76328
First-Citizens Bank & Trust Co. (Stedman, NC) 76342
First-Citizens Bank & Trust Co. (Stokesdale, NC) 76343
First-Citizens Bank & Trust Co. (Sunbury, NC) 76347; 76348
First-Citizens Bank & Trust Co. (Swansboro, NC) 76352; 76353
First-Citizens Bank & Trust Co. (Sylva, NC) 76356
First-Citizens Bank & Trust Co. (Tarboro, NC) 76363
First-Citizens Bank & Trust Co. (Thomasville, NC) 76376; 76377
First-Citizens Bank & Trust Co. (Tryon, NC) 76411
First-Citizens Bank & Trust Co. (Walnut Cove, NC) 76446
First-Citizens Bank & Trust Co. (Warrenton, NC) 76448
First-Citizens Bank & Trust Co. (Washington, NC) 76455; 76456
First-Citizens Bank & Trust Co. (Waynesville, NC) 76466; 76467; 76468; 76469
First-Citizens Bank & Trust Co. (Weldon, NC) 76480; 76481
First-Citizens Bank & Trust Co. (West Jefferson, NC) 76486; 76487
First-Citizens Bank & Trust Co. (Whiteville, NC) 76499
First-Citizens Bank & Trust Co. (Wilkesboro, NC) 76506
First-Citizens Bank & Trust Co. (Williamston, NC) 76528; 76529
First-Citizens Bank & Trust Co. (Wilmington, NC) 76559; 76560; 76561; 76562; 76563; 76564; 76565
First-Citizens Bank & Trust Co. (Wilson, NC) 76629; 76630; 76631
First-Citizens Bank & Trust Co. (Windsor, NC) 76656
First-Citizens Bank & Trust Co. (Winston-Salem, NC) 76725; 76726; 76727; 76728; 76729; 76730
First-Citizens Bnak & Trust Co. (Reidsville, NC) 75998
First Coast Community Bank (Fernandina Beach, FL) 59408
First Coast Community Bank (Fernandino Beach, FL) 59416
First Commercial Bank (Birmingham, AL) 55263; 55264; 55265; 55266; 55267; 55268; 55269; 55270; 55271
First Commercial Bank (Huntsville, AL) 55937; 55938; 55939; 55940; 55941; 55942
First Community Bank of Tifton (Tifton, GA) 67821; 67822; 67823; 67824
First Federal S & L (Cullman, AL) 55544
First Federal S & L (Florence, AL) 55736
First Federal S & L (Sheffield, AL) 56549
First Federal S & L (Sylacauga, AL) 56586
First Federal S & L (Talladega, AL) 56593
First Federal S & L (Harrison, AR) 57137
First Federal S & L (Mountain Home, AR) 57386
First Federal S & L (Cape Coral, FL) 58919
First Federal S & L (Milledgeville, GA) 66975
First Federal S & L. (Lexington, KY) 68549; 68550; 68551
First Federal S & L (Durham, NC) 74398
First Federal S & L (Darlington, SC) 79146
First Federal S & L (Columbia, TN) 80627
First Federal Savings Bank (Hopkinsville, KY) 68477; 68478
First Federal Savings Bank of Maryville (Maryville, TN) 81408; 81409
First Fidelity Bancorp (Oklahoma City, OK) 77358
First FSB of Maryville (Alcoa, TN) 80153
First National Bank (Jasper, AL) 56080; 56082; 56083; 56084; 56085
First National Bank (Montgomery, AL) 56335
First National Bank (Crossville, TN) 80697; 80698; 80699; 80700
First National Bank (Fairfield Glade, TN) 80784
First National Bank (Monteagle, TN) 81781
First National Bank (Shelbyville, TN) 82307; 82308; 82309; 82310
First National Bank (Tracy City, TN) 82372
First National Bank of Atlanta (New Castle, DE) 57864
First National Bank of Atlanta (Wilmington, DE) 58062
First National Bank of Birmingham Alabama (Wylam, AL) 56711
First National Bank of Florida (Eagle Lake, FL) 59374
First National Bank of Georgia (College Park, GA) 65584
First National Bank of Georgia (Marietta, GA) 66770
First National Bank of Jasper (Carbon Hill, AL) 55501
First National Bank of Jasper (Cordova, AL) 55530
First National Bank of Jasper (Dora, AL) 55622
First National Bank of Jasper (Oakman, AL) 56411
First National Bank of Maryland (Baltimore, MD) 71122; 71123; 71124; 71125; 71126; 71127; 71128; 71129; 71130; 71131; 71132; 71133; 71134; 71135; 71136; 71137; 71138; 71139; 71140; 71141; 71142; 71143; 71144; 71145; 71146; 71147; 71148; 71149
First National Bank of Maryland (Dorsey, MD) 71654
First National Bank of Maryland, DC (Washington, DC) 58246
First National Bank of St. Mary's (Charlotte Hall, MD) 71510
First National Bank of St. Mary's (Hollywood, MD) 71921
First National Bank of St. Mary's (Leonardtown, MD) 72099; 72100
First National Bank of St. Mary's (Lexington Park, MD) 72101; 72102
First National Bank of St. Mary's (Patuxent River, MD) 72214
First National Bank & Trust (Crestview, FL) 59123
First National Bank & Trust (Fort Walton Beach, FL) 59825
First National Bank & Trust (Blackwell, OK) 76864
First National Bank & Trust (Chickasha, OK) 76925
First National Bank & Trust (Frederick, OK) 77081
First National Bank & Trust (Perry, OK) 77702
First National Bank of Tuscaloosa (Tuscaloosa, AL) 56653
First Omni Bank, NA (Millsboro, DE) 57846; 57847
First Omni Bank National as (Millsboro, DE) 57848
First State Bank of Fayette County (Somerville, TN) 82334; 82335
First State Bank & Trust Co. (Bay City, TX) 83098
First State Bank & Trust Co. (Port Lavaca, TX) 88666; 88667
First State Bank & Trust Co. of Valdosta (Lake Park, GA) 66497
First State Bank & Trust Co. of Valdosta (Valdosta, GA) 67949; 67950; 67951; 67952; 67953; 67954
First Teneseee Bank NA (Greenville, TN) 80895
First Tennesee Bank NA (Madison, TN) 81376
First Tennessee Bank NA (Alcoa, TN) 80154; 80155
First Tennessee Bank NA (Antioch, TN) 80169
First Tennessee Bank NA (Bartlett, TN) 80198
First Tennessee Bank NA (Blountville, TN) 80204
First Tennessee Bank NA (Brentwood, TN) 80227; 80228
First Tennessee Bank NA (Bristol, TN) 80244; 80245
First Tennessee Bank NA (Chattanooga, TN) 80376; 80377; 80378; 80379; 80380; 80381; 80382; 80383; 80384; 80385; 80386; 80387; 80388; 80389; 80390; 80391; 80392
First Tennessee Bank NA (Cookeville, TN) 80654; 80655; 80656
First Tennessee Bank NA (Cordova, TN) 80675; 80676
First Tennessee Bank NA (Dandridge, TN) 80710
First Tennessee Bank NA (Dyersburg, TN) 80747; 80748
First Tennessee Bank NA (Erwin, TN) 80775
First Tennessee Bank NA (Fall Branch, TN) 80788
First Tennessee Bank NA (Franklin, TN) 80813; 80814; 80815; 80816
First Tennessee Bank NA (Gallatin, TN) 80845; 80846
First Tennessee Bank NA (Gray, TN) 80874
First Tennessee Bank NA (Greenville, TN) 80896
First Tennessee Bank NA (Hendersonville, TN) 80914
First Tennessee Bank NA (Jackson, TN) 80978; 80979; 80980; 80981; 80982; 80983
First Tennessee Bank NA (Johnson City, TN) 81033; 81034; 81035; 81036
First Tennessee Bank NA (Jonesborough, TN) 81066
First Tennessee Bank NA (Kingsport, TN) 81090; 81091; 81092; 81093
First Tennessee Bank NA (Knoxville, TN) 81185; 81186; 81187; 81188; 81189; 81190; 81191; 81192; 81193; 81194; 81195; 81196; 81197; 81198; 81199; 81200; 81201; 81202; 81203; 81204; 81205; 81206; 81207; 81208; 81209; 81210; 81211
First Tennessee Bank NA (LaVergne, TN) 81287
First Tennessee Bank NA (Lebanon, TN) 81297; 81298; 81299
First Tennessee Bank NA (Maryville, TN) 81410; 81411; 81412; 81413; 81414; 81415
First Tennessee Bank NA (Memphis, TN) 81566; 81567; 81568; 81569; 81570; 81571; 81572; 81573; 81574; 81575; 81576; 81577; 81578; 81579; 81580; 81581; 81582; 81583; 81584; 81585; 81586; 81587; 81588; 81589; 81590; 81591; 81592; 81593; 81594; 81595; 81596; 81597; 81598; 81599; 81600; 81601; 81602; 81603; 81604
First Tennessee Bank NA (Morristown, TN) 81794; 81795; 81796; 81797
First Tennessee Bank NA (Mosheim, TN) 81820
First Tennessee Bank NA (Mt. Juliet, TN) 81829
First Tennessee Bank NA (Murfreesboro, TN) 81843; 81844; 81845
First Tennessee Bank NA (Nashville, TN) 81988; 81989; 81990; 81991; 81992
First Tennessee Bank NA (Nolensville, TN) 82177
First Tennessee Bank NA (Rogersville, TN) 82274
First Tennessee Bank NA (Unicol, TN) 82380
First Tennessee Bank NA (White Creek, TN) 82414
First Tennessee Bank NA (White Pine, TN) 82416
First Tennessee National Corp. (Memphis, TN) 81605
First Trust Savings Bank, FSB (Jacksonville, FL) 60269
First Union Bank of Florida (Apopka, FL) 58570
First Union Corp. (Charlotte, NC) 73980
First Union Naitonal Bank of Maryland (Frederick, MD) 71725
First Union Naitonal Bank of Maryland (Landover, MD) 72015
First Union Natinal Bank of Virginia (Arlington, VA) 90322
First Union Nationa Bank of Tennessee (Dickson, TN) 80732
First Union National Bak of Virginia (Grafton, VA) 90996
First Union National Bank of Florida (, FL) 58531
First Union National Bank of Florida (Altamonte Springs, FL) 58554
First Union National Bank of Florida (Auburndale, FL) 58596
First Union National Bank of Florida (Barefoot Bay, FL) 58617
First Union National Bank of Florida (Barton, FL) 58619
First Union National Bank of Florida (Belle Glade, FL) 58643
First Union National Bank of Florida (Belleair Bluff, FL) 58647
First Union National Bank of Florida (Boca Raton, FL) 58697; 58698; 58699; 58700; 58701; 58702; 58703; 58704
First Union National Bank of Florida (Boynton Beach, FL) 58771; 58772; 58773; 58774
First Union National Bank of Florida (Bradenton, FL) 58818; 58819; 58820; 58821; 58822; 58823
First Union National Bank of Florida (Brandon, FL) 58869
First Union National Bank of Florida (Bushnell, FL) 58901
First Union National Bank of Florida (Callahan, FL) 58906
First Union National Bank of Florida (Cape Canaveral, FL) 58912; 58913
First Union National Bank of Florida (Cape Coral, FL) 58920; 58921
First Union National Bank of Florida (Chipley, FL) 58953
First Union National Bank of Florida (Clearwater, FL) 58996; 58997; 58998; 58999; 59000; 59001; 59002; 59003
First Union National Bank of Florida (Clermont, FL) 59056
First Union National Bank of Florida (Cocoa, FL) 59068
First Union National Bank of Florida (Cocoa Beach, FL) 59080
First Union National Bank of Florida (Cooper City, FL) 59091
First Union National Bank of Florida (Coral Gables, FL) 59100; 59101
First Union National Bank of Florida (Coral Springs, FL) 59113; 59114
First Union National Bank of Florida (Crystal River, FL) 59131
First Union National Bank of Florida (Dade City, FL) 59138
First Union National Bank of Florida (Davie, FL) 59157; 59158
First Union National Bank of Florida (Daytona Beach, FL) 59174; 59175; 59176; 59177; 59178
First Union National Bank of Florida (Daytonna Beach, FL) 59235
First Union National Bank of Florida (Deerfield Beach, FL) 59277; 59278
First Union National Bank of Florida (DeLand, FL) 59301; 59302
First Union National Bank of Florida (Delray Beach, FL) 59316; 59317
First Union National Bank of Florida (Deltona, FL) 59335; 59336
First Union National Bank of Florida (Dundee, FL) 59353
First Union NAtional Bank of Florida (Dunedin, FL) 59360; 59361
First Union National Bank of Florida (Edgewater, FL) 59377
First Union National Bank of Florida (Englewood, FL) 59394; 59395
First Union National Bank of FLorida (Eustis, FL) 59398; 59399
First Union National Bank of Florida (Fernandina Beach, FL) 59409; 59410
First Union National Bank of Florida (For Lauderdale, FL) 59420
First Union National Bank of Florida (For Myers, FL) 59421
First Union National Bank of Florida (Fort Lauderdale, FL) 59484; 59485; 59486; 59487; 59488; 59489; 59490; 59491; 59492; 59493; 59494; 59495
First Union National Bank of Florida (Fort Meade, FL) 59649
First Union National Bank of Florida (Fort Myers, FL) 59696; 59697
First Union National Bank of Florida (Fort Pierce, FL) 59795; 59796; 59797
First Union National Bank of Florida (Gainesville, FL) 59869; 59870; 59871; 59872; 59873; 59874; 59875; 59876

First Union National Bank of Florida (Green Cove Springs, FL) 59931

First Union National Bank of Florida (Haines City, FL) 59944; 59945

First Union National Bank of Florida (Hialeah, FL) 59984; 59985

First Union National Bank of Florida (Hollywood, FL) 60057; 60058; 60059

First Union National Bank of Florida (Holmes Beach, FL) 60112

First Union National Bank of Florida (Indialantic, FL) 60135

First Union National Bank of Florida (Indian Harbour Beach, FL) 60137; 60138

First Union National Bank of Florida (Jacksonville, FL) 60270; 60271; 60272; 60273; 60274; 60275; 60276; 60277; 60278; 60279; 60280; 60281; 60282; 60283; 60284; 60285; 60286; 60287; 60288; 60289; 60290; 60291; 60292; 60293; 60294; 60295; 60296; 60297; 60298; 60299; 60300

First Union National Bank of Florida (Jacksonville Beach, FL) 60518; 60519

First Union National Bank of Florida (Jensen Beach, FL) 60525; 60526

First Union National Bank of Florida (Juno Beach, FL) 60528

First Union National Bank of Florida (Jupiter, FL) 60535; 60536; 60537; 60538

First Union National Bank of Florida (Key Largo, FL) 60566

First Union National Bank of Florida (Key West, FL) 60572; 60573

First Union National Bank of Florida (Keystone Heights, FL) 60580

First Union National Bank of Florida (Kissimmee, FL) 60587

First Union National Bank of Florida (Lake Alfred, FL) 60609

First Union National Bank of Florida (Lake Panasoffkee, FL) 60640

First Union National Bank of Florida (Lake Wales, FL) 60652

First Union National Bank of Florida (Lake Worth, FL) 60668; 60669

First Union National Bank of Florida (Lakeland, FL) 60720; 60721; 60723; 60724

First Union National Bank of Florida (Lakewood, FL) 60801

First Union National Bank of Florida (Lantana, FL) 60804; 60805

First Union National Bank of Florida (Lauderdale Lakes, FL) 60872

First Union National Bank of Florida (Lauderhill, FL) 60875

First Union National Bank of Florida (Leesburg, FL) 60883

First Union National Bank of Florida (Lehigh Acres, FL) 60894

First Union National Bank of Florida (Lessburg, FL) 60897

First Union National Bank of Florida (Lighthouse Point, FL) 60903

First Union National Bank of Florida (Longwood, FL) 60929; 60930; 60931

First Union National Bank of Florida (Madeira Beach, FL) 60965

First Union National Bank of Florida (Madison, FL) 60966

First Union National Bank of Florida (Maitland, FL) 60977

First Union National Bank of Florida (Margate, FL) 61001

First Union National Bank of Florida (Melbourne, FL) 61054; 61055

First Union National Bank of Florida (Merritt Island, FL) 61140

First Union National Bank of Florida (Miami, FL) 61283; 61284; 61285; 61286; 61287; 61288; 61289; 61290; 61291; 61292; 61293; 61294; 61295; 61296; 61297; 61298; 61299; 61300; 61301; 61302; 61303; 61304; 61305; 61306; 61307; 61308; 61309; 61310

First Union National Bank of Florida (Miami Lakes, FL) 61535

First Union National Bank of Florida (Miami Springs, FL) 61538

First Union National Bank of Florida (Middleburg, FL) 61539

First Union National Bank of Florida (Miramar, FL) 61558

First Union National Bank of Florida (Mount Dora, FL) 61564

First Union National Bank of Florida (Naples, FL) 61618; 61619; 61620; 61621

First Union National Bank of Florida (New Port Richey, FL) 61683; 61684; 61685

First Union National Bank of Florida (New Smyrna Beach, FL) 61701; 61702; 61703

First Union National Bank of Florida (North Fort Myers, FL) 61728

First Union National Bank of Florida (North Miami, FL) 61734; 61735

First Union National Bank of Florida (North Palm Beach, FL) 61749; 61750

First Union National Bank of Florida (North Port, FL) 61755

First Union National Bank of Florida (Ocala, FL) 61794; 61795; 61796; 61797; 61798

First Union National Bank of Florida (Oldsmar, FL) 61847

First Union National Bank of Florida (Opa Locka, FL) 61858

First Union National Bank of Florida (Orange Park, FL) 61880; 61881; 61882; 61883

First Union National Bank of Florida (Orlanda, FL) 61901

First Union National Bank of Florida (Orlando, FL) 61970; 61971; 61972; 61973; 61974; 61975; 61976; 61977; 61978; 61979; 61980; 61981; 61982; 61983; 61984; 61985

First Union National Bank of Florida (Ormond Beach, FL) 62201; 62202; 62203

First Union National Bank of Florida (Pahokee, FL) 62222

First Union National Bank of Florida (Palatka, FL) 62225; 62226

First Union National Bank of Florida (Palm Bay, FL) 62233; 62234

First Union National Bank of Florida (Palm Beach, FL) 62252; 62253; 62254; 62255; 62256; 62257

First Union National Bank of Florida (Palm Beach Garden, FL) 62262

First Union National Bank of Florida (Palm Beach Gardens, FL) 62270; 62271

First Union National Bank of Florida (Palm City, FL) 62277; 62278

First Union National Bank of Florida (Palm Harbor, FL) 62297

First Union National Bank of Florida (Palm Springs, FL) 62303

First Union National Bank of Florida (Panama City, FL) 62320; 62321

First Union National Bank of Florida (Panama City Beach, FL) 62359

First Union National Bank of Florida (Pembroke Pines, FL) 62369

First Union National Bank of Florida (Pensacola, FL) 62424; 62425; 62426; 62427; 62428; 62429; 62430

First Union National Bank of Florida (Perrine, FL) 62495

First Union National Bank of Florida (Perry, FL) 62499

First Union National Bank of Florida (Plantation, FL) 62568; 62569; 62570

First Union National Bank of Florida (Pompano Beach, FL) 62594; 62595; 62596; 62597

First Union National Bank of Florida (Ponte Vedra Beach, FL) 62650

First Union National Bank of Florida (Port Orange, FL) 62662; 62663

First Union National Bank of Florida (Port Richey, FL) 62671; 62672

First Union National Bank of Florida (Port St. Lucie, FL) 62698

First Union National Bank of Florida (Punta Gorda, FL) 62707

First Union National Bank of Florida (Redington Shores, FL) 62735

First Union National Bank of Florida (Riviera Beach, FL) 62738

First Union National Bank of Florida (Rockledge, FL) 62744

First Union National Bank of Florida (Royal Palm Beach, FL) 62754; 62755

First Union National Bank of Florida (Sanford, FL) 62766; 62767

First Union National Bank of Florida (Sarasota, FL) 62825; 62826; 62827; 62828; 62829; 62830; 62831

First Union National Bank of Florida (Satellite Beach, FL) 62870

First Union National Bank of Florida (Sebastian, FL) 62873

First Union National Bank of Florida (Sebring, FL) 62880; 62881

First Union National Bank of Florida (Seminole, FL) 62905; 62906; 62907

First Union National Bank of Florida (South Miami, FL) 62923

First Union National Bank of Florida (St. Augustine, FL) 63055; 63056; 63057

First Union National Bank of Florida (St. Petersburg, FL) 63108; 63109; 63110; 63111; 63112; 63113; 63114

First Union National Bank of Florida (St. Petersburg Beach, FL) 63140

First Union National Bank of Florida (Starke, FL) 63143; 63144

First Union National Bank of Florida (Stuart, FL) 63163; 63164; 63165; 63166

First Union National Bank of Florida (Sun City Center, FL) 63187

First Union National Bank of Florida (Tallahassee, FL) 63237; 63238; 63239; 63240; 63241

First Union National Bank of Florida (Tamarac, FL) 63299

First Union National Bank of Florida (Tampa, FL) 63417; 63418; 63419; 63420; 63421; 63422; 63423; 63424; 63425; 63426; 63427; 63428; 63429; 63430; 63431

First Union National Bank of Florida (Tavares, FL) 63669; 63670

First Union National Bank of Florida (Titusville, FL) 63685; 63686; 63687

First Union National Bank of Florida (Venice, FL) 63723; 63724; 63725

First Union National Bank of Florida (Vero Beach, FL) 63750; 63751; 63752; 63753; 63754; 63755

First Union National Bank of Florida (Webster, FL) 63829

First Union National Bank of Florida (Wellington, FL) 63831

First Union National Bank of Florida (West Melbourne, FL) 63834; 63835

First Union National Bank of Florida (West Miami, FL) 63836

First Union National Bank of Florida (West Palm Beach, FL) 63856; 63857; 63858; 63859; 63860; 63861; 63862; 63863

First Union National Bank of Florida (Wildwood, FL) 63916

First Union National Bank of Florida (Winter Garden, FL) 63921

First Union National Bank of Florida (Winter Haven, FL) 63934; 63935; 63936; 63937; 63938; 63939

First Union National Bank of Florida (Winter Park, FL) 63974; 63975; 63976; 63977; 63978

First Union National Bank of Florida (Zephyrhills, FL) 64010; 64011

First Union National Bank of Forida (Vero Beach, FL) 63756

First Union National Bank of Georgia (Kenneth City, FL) 60560

First Union National Bank of Georgia (Melbourne, FL) 61056

First Union National Bank of Georgia (Albany, GA) 64072; 64073

First Union National Bank of Georgia (Alpharetta, GA) 64110; 64111

First Union National Bank of Georgia (Atlanta, GA) 64451; 64452; 64453; 64454; 64455; 64456; 64457; 64458; 64459; 64460; 64461; 64462; 64463; 64464; 64465; 64466; 64467; 64468; 64469

First Union National Bank of Georgia (Augusta, GA) 65323; 65324; 65325; 65326; 65327; 65328; 65329; 65330

First Union National Bank of Georgia (Bremen, GA) 65394

First Union National Bank of Georgia (Chamblee, GA) 65523; 65524; 65525

First Union National Bank of Georgia (Chatsworth, GA) 65556

First Union National Bank of Georgia (Columbus, GA) 65640; 65641; 65642; 65643; 65644; 65645; 65646

First Union National Bank of Georgia (Conyers, GA) 65679

First Union National Bank of Georgia (Dalton, GA) 65783; 65784; 65785

First Union National Bank of Georgia (Decatur, GA) 65814; 65815; 65816; 65817; 65818; 65819; 65820

First Union National Bank of Georgia (Doraville, GA) 65928

First Union National Bank of Georgia (Douglasville, GA) 65985

First Union National Bank of Georgia (Dublin, GA) 66008

First Union National Bank of Georgia (Duluth, GA) 66036

First Union National Bank of Georgia (Dunwoody, GA) 66109

First Union National Bank of Georgia (East Point, GA) 66144

First Union National Bank of Georgia (Evans, GA) 66172

First Union National Bank of Georgia (Fayetteville, GA) 66190

First Union National Bank of Georgia (Fort Benning, GA) 66256; 66257

First Union National Bank of Georgia (Fort Gordon, GA) 66258

First Union National Bank of Georgia (Griffin, GA) 66315; 66316

First Union National Bank of Georgia (Hamilton, GA) 66329

First Union National Bank of Georgia (Hampton, GA) 66330

First Union National Bank of Georgia (Hapeville, GA) 66333

First Union National Bank of Georgia (Hinesville, GA) 66350

First Union National Bank of Georgia (Kennesaw, GA) 66413; 66414

First Union National Bank of Georgia (Lawrenceville, GA) 66513; 66514

First Union National Bank of Georgia (Lilburn, GA) 66558; 66559

First Union National Bank of Georgia (Lithonia, GA) 66594

First Union National Bank of Georgia (Mableton, GA) 66633

First Union National Bank of Georgia (Macon, GA) 66686; 66687; 66688; 66689; 66690

First Union National Bank of Georgia (Marietta, GA) 66771; 66772; 66773; 66774; 66775; 66776; 66777; 66778; 66779

First Union National Bank of Georgia (Martinez, GA) 66954

First Union National Bank of Georgia (Newnan, GA) 67081

First Union National Bank of Georgia (Norcross, GA) 67117; 67118; 67119

First Union National Bank of Georgia (Pine Mountain, GA) 67268

First Union National Bank of Georgia (Powder Springs, GA) 67286

First Union National Bank of Georgia (Riverdale, GA) 67311

First Union National Bank of Georgia (Rome, GA) 67337; 67338; 67339; 67340

First Union National Bank of Georgia (Roswell, GA) 67369; 67370; 67371; 67372; 67373

First Union National Bank of Georgia (Savannah, GA) 67467; 67468; 67469; 67470; 67471; 67472; 67473; 67475

First Union National Bank of Georgia (Smyrna, GA) 67550

First Union National Bank of Georgia (Snellville, GA) 67589

First Union National Bank of Georgia (Stockbridge, GA) 67658

First Union National Bank of Georgia (Stone Mountain, GA) 67689; 67690; 67691; 67692

First Union National Bank of Georgia (Sylvania, GA) 67769

First Union National Bank of Georgia (Tucker, GA) 67855

First Union National Bank of Georgia (Valdosta, GA) 67955; 67956

First Union National Bank of Georgia (Vidalia, GA) 67986

First Union National Bank of Georgia (Waycross, GA) 68032

First Union National Bank of Georgia (Waynesboro, GA) 68046

First Union National Bank of Georgia (Woodstock, GA) 68069

First Union National Bank of Maryland (Annapolis, MD) 71012; 71013

First Union National Bank of Maryland (Baltimore, MD) 71150; 71151

First Union National Bank of Maryland (Beltsville, MD) 71356

First Union National Bank of Maryland (Bethesda, MD) 71387; 71388; 71389; 71390; 71391

First Union National Bank of Maryland (Bowie, MD) 71461

First Union National Bank of Maryland (Chevy Chase, MD) 71529

First Union National Bank of Maryland (Clinton, MD) 71537

First Union National Bank of Maryland (Cockeysville, MD) 71549

First Union National Bank of Maryland (Columbia, MD) 71587; 71588; 71589

First Union National Bank of Maryland (Crofton, MD) 71615

First Union National Bank of Maryland (Ferestville, MD) 71684

First Union National Bank of Maryland (Frederick, MD) 71726

First Union National Bank of Maryland (Gaithersburg, MD) 71778; 71779; 71780

First Union National Bank of Maryland (Glen Burnie, MD) 71842

First Union National Bank of Maryland (Greenbelt, MD) 71861

First Union National Bank of Maryland (Kensington, MD) 71994; 71995

First Union National Bank of Maryland (Landover, MD) 72016

First Union National Bank of Maryland (Langley Park, MD) 72040

First Union National Bank of Maryland (Laurel, MD) 72073; 72074; 72075

First Union National Bank of Maryland (Olney, MD) 72174

First Union National Bank of Maryland (Owings Mills, MD) 72185

First Union National Bank of Maryland (Oxon Hill, MD) 72196

First Union National Bank of Maryland (Potomac, MD) 72229; 72230

First Union National Bank of Maryland (Rockville, MD) 72276; 72277; 72278; 72279; 72280; 72281; 72282

First Union National Bank of Maryland (Severna Park, MD) 72374

First Union National Bank of Maryland (Silver Spring, MD) 72402; 72403; 72404; 72405; 72406

First Union National Bank of Maryland (Towson, MD) 72507

First Union National Bank of Maryland (Waldorf, MD) 72528

First Union National Bank of Maryland (Wheaton, MD) 72554

First Union National Bank of North Carolina (Advance, NC) 73521

First Union National Bank of North Carolina (Albemarle, NC) 73534; 73535

First Union National Bank of North Carolina (Albermarle, NC) 73545

First Union National Bank of North Carolina (Andrews, NC) 73546

First Union National Bank of North Carolina (Archdale, NC) 73561

First Union National Bank of North Carolina (Arden, NC) 73569

First Union National Bank of North Carolina (Asheville, NC) 73622; 73623; 73624; 73625; 73626; 73627

First Union National Bank of North Carolina (Bakersville, NC) 73655

First Union National Bank of North Carolina (Banner Elk, NC) 73658
First Union National Bank of North Carolina (Bessemer City, NC) 73687
First Union National Bank of North Carolina (Bethlehem, NC) 73693
First Union National Bank of North Carolina (Black Mountain, NC) 73697
First Union National Bank of North Carolina (Blowing Rock, NC) 73702
First Union National Bank of North Carolina (Boone, NC) 73711; 73712; 73713
First Union National Bank of North Carolina (Bostic, NC) 73721
First Union National Bank of North Carolina (Brevard, NC) 73724; 73725
First Union National Bank of North Carolina (Burlington, NC) 73753; 73754
First Union National Bank of North Carolina (Burnsville, NC) 73766; 73767
First Union National Bank of North Carolina (Canton, NC) 73779
First Union National Bank of North Carolina (Cary, NC) 73796; 73797; 73798
First Union National Bank of North Carolina (Chapel Hill, NC) 73813; 73814
First Union National Bank of North Carolina (Charlotte, NC) 73985; 73986; 73987; 73988; 73989; 73990; 73991; 73992; 73993; 73994; 73995; 73996; 73997; 73998; 73999; 74000; 74001; 74002; 74003; 74004; 74005; 74006; 74007; 74008; 74009; 74010
First Union National Bank of North Carolina (China Grove, NC) 74251
First Union National Bank of North Carolina (Claremont, NC) 74255
First Union National Bank of North Carolina (Clemmons, NC) 74269
First Union National Bank of North Carolina (Clinton, NC) 74289; 74290
First Union National Bank Of Florida (Altamonte Springs, FL) 58555
First Union National Bank of South Carolian (Chapin, SC) 78785
First Union National Bank of South Carolian (Hollywood, SC) 79524
First Union National Bank of South Carolina (Anderson, SC) 78675
First Union National Bank of South Carolina (Beaufort, SC) 78707
First Union National Bank of South Carolina (Bennettsville, SC) 78726
First Union National Bank of South Carolina (Blacksburg, SC) 78746
First Union National Bank of South Carolina (Cayce, SC) 78775
First Union National Bank of South Carolina (Charleston, SC) 78813; 78814
First Union National Bank of South Carolina (Chester, SC) 78934; 78935
First Union National Bank of South Carolina (Clover, SC) 78964
First Union National Bank of South Carolina (Columbia, SC) 79012; 79013; 79014; 79015; 79016; 79017
First Union National Bank of South Carolina (Easley, SC) 79179
First Union National Bank of South Carolina (Florence, SC) 79200; 79201; 79202
First Union National Bank of South Carolina (Fountain Inn, SC) 79245
First Union National Bank of South Carolina (Ft. Mill, SC) 79256
First Union National Bank of South Carolina (Gaffney, SC) 79259
First Union National Bank of South Carolina (Greenville, SC) 79350; 79351; 79352; 79353; 79354; 79355; 79356; 79357; 79358; 79359; 79360
First Union National Bank of South Carolina (Hartsville, SC) 79497
First Union National Bank of South Carolina (Hilton Head Island, SC) 79514; 79515; 79516
First Union National Bank of South Carolina (Isle of Palms, SC) 79541
First Union National Bank of South Carolina (James Island, SC) 79542
First Union National Bank of South Carolina (Laurens, SC) 79590

First Union National Bank of South Carolina (Lugoff, SC) 79619
First Union National Bank of South Carolina (Manning, SC) 79631
First Union National Bank of South Carolina (Mt. Pleasant, SC) 79683; 79684
First Union National Bank of South Carolina (Myrtle Beach, SC) 79698
First Union National Bank of South Carolina (North Charleston, SC) 79749
First Union National Bank of South Carolina (Orangeburg, SC) 79772; 79773
First Union National Bank of South Carolina (Prosperity, SC) 79802
First Union National Bank of South Carolina (Rock Hill, SC) 79820; 79821; 79822; 79823
First Union National Bank of South Carolina (Spartanburg, SC) 79893; 79894
First Union National Bank of South Carolina (Summerville, SC) 79984
First Union National Bank of South Carolina (Sumter, SC) 80019
First Union National Bank of South Carolina (Travelers Rest, SC) 80044
First Union National Bank of South Carolina (Walhalla, SC) 80057
First Union National Bank of South Carolina (Williamston, SC) 80123
First Union National Bank of South Carolina (Winnsboro, SC) 80131
First Union National Bank of South Carolina (York, SC) 80139
First Union National Bank of Tennessee (Ashland City, TN) 80184
First Union National Bank of Tennessee (Brentwood, TN) 80229
First Union National Bank of Tennessee (Bulls Gap, TN) 80263
First Union National Bank of Tennessee (Church Hill, TN) 80530
First Union National Bank of Tennessee (Clarksville, TN) 80545; 80546; 80547; 80548; 80549
First Union National Bank of Tennessee (College Grove, TN) 80616
First Union National Bank of Tennessee (Cosby, TN) 80680
First Union National Bank of Tennessee (Dandridge, TN) 80711; 80712
First Union National Bank of Tennessee (Dechard, TN) 80728
First Union National Bank of Tennessee (Dickson, TN) 80733
First Union National Bank of Tennessee (Fayetteville, TN) 80793; 80794; 80795
First Union National Bank of Tennessee (Franklin, TN) 80817; 80818
First Union National Bank of Tennessee (Gallatin, TN) 80847
First Union National Bank of Tennessee (Goodlettsville, TN) 80863
First Union National Bank of Tennessee (Greenbrier, TN) 80881
First Union National Bank of Tennessee (Hendersonville, TN) 80915; 80916
First Union National Bank of Tennessee (Jefferson City, TN) 81022
First Union National Bank of Tennessee (Kingsport, TN) 81094; 81095
First Union National Bank of Tennessee (Murfreesboro, TN) 81846
First Union National Bank of Tennessee (Nashville, TN) 81993; 81994; 81995; 81996; 81997; 81998; 81999; 82000; 82001; 82002; 82003; 82004; 82005; 82006
First Union National Bank of Tennessee (Newport, TN) 82161; 82162; 82163
First Union National Bank of Tennessee (Parrottsville, TN) 82224
First Union National Bank of Tennessee (Pleasant View, TN) 82232
First Union National Bank of Tennessee (Portland, TN) 82234
First Union National Bank of Tennessee (Rogersville, TN) 82275; 82276; 82277

First Union National Bank of Tennessee (Shelbyville, TN) 82311; 82312; 82313
First Union National Bank of Tennessee (Sparta, TN) 82341; 82342
First Union National Bank of Tennessee (Springfield, TN) 82356; 82357
First Union National Bank of Tennessee (St. Bethlehem, TN) 82361
First Union National Bank of Tennessee (Westmoreland, TN) 82408
First Union National Bank of Tennessee (White Pine, TN) 82417
First Union National Bank of Tennessee (Whitehouse, TN) 82418
First Union National Bank of Tennessee (Winchester, TN) 82419
First Union National Bank of Virginia (Abingdon, VA) 90152
First Union National Bank of Virginia (Alexandria, VA) 90194; 90195; 90196; 90197; 90198; 90199; 90200; 90201; 90202; 90203; 90204; 90205; 90206; 90207; 90208; 90209
First Union National Bank of Virginia (Annandale, VA) 90263; 90264; 90265
First Union National Bank of Virginia (Arlington, VA) 90323; 90324; 90325; 90326; 90327; 90328; 90329; 90330
First Union National Bank of Virginia (Bassett, VA) 90415
First Union National Bank of Virginia (Bedford, VA) 90418; 90419
First Union National Bank of Virginia (Big Stone Gap, VA) 90432
First Union National Bank of Virginia (Blacksburg, VA) 90444
First Union National Bank of Virginia (Bluefield, VA) 90460
First Union National Bank of Virginia (Bridgewater, VA) 90467
First Union National Bank of Virginia (Bristol, VA) 90475; 90476; 90477; 90478
First Union National Bank of Virginia (Burke, VA) 90501
First Union National Bank of Virginia (Centreville, VA) 90515
First Union National Bank of Virginia (Chantilly, VA) 90522
First Union National Bank of Virginia (Chesapeake, VA) 90574; 90575; 90576
First Union National Bank of Virginia (Chesterfield, VA) 90630
First Union National Bank of Virginia (Christiansburg, VA) 90634
First Union National Bank of Virginia (Clintwood, VA) 90645
First Union National Bank of Virginia (Collinsville, VA) 90648
First Union National Bank of Virginia (Courtland, VA) 90654
First Union National Bank of Virginia (Covington, VA) 90656
First Union National Bank of Virginia (Culpeper, VA) 90674
First Union National Bank of Virginia (Dale City, VA) 90682
First Union National Bank of Virginia (Edinburg, VA) 90740
First Union National Bank of Virginia (Fairfax, VA) 90773; 90774; 90775; 90776; 90777; 90778
First Union National Bank of Virginia (Falls Church, VA) 90836; 90837; 90838
First Union National Bank of Virginia (Franklin, VA) 90893
First Union National Bank of Virginia (Fredericksburg, VA) 90917; 90918
First Union National Bank of Virginia (Front Royal, VA) 90950
First Union National Bank of Virginia (Gloucester, VA) 90991
First Union National Bank of Virginia (Grottoes, VA) 91004
First Union National Bank of Virginia (Grundy, VA) 91008
First Union National Bank of Virginia (Hampton, VA) 91031; 91032; 91033
First Union National Bank of Virginia (Harman Junction, VA) 91061
First Union National Bank of Virginia (Harrisonburg, VA) 91082; 91083; 91084; 91085; 91086; 91087

First Union National Bank of Virginia (Haysi, VA) 91113
First Union National Bank of Virginia (Herndon, VA) 91124; 91125
First Union National Bank of Virginia (Hollins, VA) 91146; 91147
First Union National Bank of Virginia (Lebanon, VA) 91188
First Union National Bank of Virginia (Leesburg, VA) 91192; 91193
First Union National Bank of Virginia (Lexington, VA) 91204; 91205; 91206
First Union National Bank of Virginia (Manassas, VA) 91309
First Union National Bank of Virginia (Marion, VA) 91332
First Union National Bank of Virginia (Martinsville, VA) 91350
First Union National Bank of Virginia (McLean, VA) 91386; 91387
First Union National Bank of Virginia (Mechanicsville, VA) 91402
First Union National Bank of Virginia (Moneta, VA) 91432
First Union National Bank of Virginia (Newport News, VA) 91464; 91465; 91466; 91467; 91468
First Union National Bank of Virginia (Newsoms, VA) 91496
First Union National Bank of Virginia (Norfolk, VA) 91522; 91523; 91524; 91525; 91526; 91527
First Union National Bank of Virginia (Norton, VA) 91603
First Union National Bank of Virginia (Oakwood, VA) 91613
First Union National Bank of Virginia (Pearisburg, VA) 91622
First Union National Bank of Virginia (Pembroke, VA) 91626
First Union National Bank of Virginia (Pocahontas, VA) 91637
First Union National Bank of Virginia (Portsmouth, VA) 91648; 91649; 91650; 91651
First Union National Bank of Virginia (Purcellville, VA) 91682
First Union National Bank of Virginia (Reston, VA) 91707; 91708
First Union National Bank of Virginia (Richlands, VA) 91719
First Union National Bank of Virginia (Richmond, VA) 91874; 91875; 91876; 91877; 91878; 91879; 91880; 91881
First Union National Bank of Virginia (Roanoke, VA) 92139; 92140; 92141; 92142; 92143; 92144; 92145; 92146; 92147; 92148; 92149; 92150
First Union National Bank of Virginia (Salem, VA) 92211; 92212
First Union National Bank of Virginia (Saluda, VA) 92229
First Union National Bank of Virginia (Smithfield, VA) 92237
First Union National Bank of Virginia (Springfield, VA) 92282; 92283; 92284; 92285
First Union National Bank of Virginia (St. Paul, VA) 92297
First Union National Bank of Virginia (Staunton, VA) 92317
First Union National Bank of Virginia (Stephens city, VA) 92335
First Union National Bank of Virginia (Sterling, VA) 92340; 92341; 92342
First Union National Bank of Virginia (Tappahannock, VA) 92374
First Union National Bank of Virginia (Verona, VA) 92392
First Union National Bank of Virginia (Vienna, VA) 92405; 92406
First Union National Bank of Virginia (Vinton, VA) 92425
First Union National Bank of Virginia (Virginia Beach, VA) 92468; 92469; 92470; 92471; 92472; 92473; 92474; 92475
First Union National Bank of Virginia (Waynesboro, VA) 92534
First Union National Bank of Virginia (West Point, VA) 92542
First Union National Bank of Virginia (Weyers Cave, VA) 92544
First Union National Bank of Virginia (Williamsburg, VA) 92569

First Union National Bank of Virginia (Winchester, VA) 92583; 92584; 92585; 92586; 92587; 92588
First Union National Bank of Virginia (Woodbridge, VA) 92613
First Union National Bank of Virginia (Woodstock, VA) 92629
First Union National Bank of Virginia (Wytheville, VA) 92639
First Union National Bank of Washington (Washington, DC) 58247
First Union National Bank of Washington DC (Washington, DC) 58248; 58249; 58250; 58251; 58252; 58253; 58254; 58255; 58256; 58257; 58258; 58259; 58260; 58261; 58262; 58263; 58264; 58265; 58266; 58267; 58268; 58269; 58270; 58271; 58272; 58273; 58274; 58275; 58276; 58277; 58278; 58279
First Union Nationl Bank of Virginia (Arlington, VA) 90331
First Union Natonal Bank of Florida (Casselberry, FL) 58932
First Virginia Bank (Alexandria, VA) 90210; 90211; 90212; 90213; 90214; 90215; 90216; 90217; 90218; 90220
First Virginia Bank (Annandale, VA) 90266
First Virginia Bank (Arlington, VA) 90332; 90333; 90334; 90335; 90336; 90337; 90338; 90339; 90340; 90341; 90342; 90343; 90344
First Virginia Bank (Bailey Crossroads, VA) 90412
First Virginia Bank (Burke, VA) 90502; 90503; 90504
First Virginia Bank (Callao, VA) 90508
First Virginia Bank (Centreville, VA) 90516
First Virginia Bank (Colonial Beach, VA) 90649
First Virginia Bank (Dahlgren, VA) 90680
First Virginia Bank (Fairfax, VA) 90779; 90780; 90781; 90782; 90783; 90784; 90785
First Virginia Bank (Falls Church, VA) 90840; 90841; 90842; 90843; 90844; 90845
First Virginia Bank (Fredericksburg, VA) 90919; 90920; 90921; 90922; 90923; 90924
First Virginia Bank (Great Falls, VA) 90999
First Virginia Bank (Hague, VA) 91009
First Virginia Bank (Haymarket, VA) 91112
First Virginia Bank (Heathsville, VA) 91114
First Virginia Bank (Herndon, VA) 91126; 91127; 91128
First Virginia Bank (King George, VA) 91180
First Virginia Bank (Leesburg, VA) 91194
First Virginia Bank (Manassas, VA) 91310; 91311; 91312; 91313
First Virginia Bank (McLean, VA) 91388; 91389
First Virginia Bank (Oakton, VA) 91611
First Virginia Bank (Purcellville, VA) 91683; 91684
First Virginia Bank (Reston, VA) 91709
First Virginia Bank (Springfield, VA) 92286
First Virginia Bank (Stafford, VA) 92299; 92300
First Virginia Bank (Sterling, VA) 92343; 92344
First Virginia Bank (Vienna, VA) 92407; 92408; 92409; 92410
First Virginia Bank (Warrenton, VA) 92523; 92524; 92525
First Virginia Bank (Woodbridge, VA) 92614; 92615; 92616
First Virginia Bank - Shenandoah Valley (Woodstock, VA) 92630
Firstar Trust Co. of Florida, NA (Sarasota, FL) 62832
Firstar Trust Co. of Florida, NA (West Palm Beach, FL) 63864
Firt-Citizens Bank & Trust Co. (Wilmington, NC) 76566
Fist Trust Savings Bank, FSB (Jacksonville, FL) 60301
Fist Union National Bank of Florida (Lake Worth, FL) 60670
Fleet Trust Co. of Florida, NA (Naples, FL) 61622
Forest Hill State Bank (Bel Air, MD) 71336; 71337
Forest Hill State Bank (Belcamp, MD) 71342

Forest Hill State Bank (Darlington, MD) 71641
Forest Hill State Bank (Forest Hill, MD) 71686
Forest Hill State Bank (Jarrettsville, MD) 71980
Forest Hill State Bank (Whiteford, MD) 72570
Fort Rucker Naitonal Bank (Fort Rucker, AL) 55765
Fort Rucker National Bank (Fort Rucker, AL) 55766; 55767; 55768
Fortuen Bank, ASB (New Port Richey, FL) 61686
Fortuen Bank, SB (St. Petersburg, FL) 63118
Fortune Bancorp. Inc. (Clearwater, FL) 59006; 59007
Fortune Bank, ASB (Cape Coral, FL) 58922
Fortune Bank, ASB (Clearwater, FL) 59010; 59011; 59012; 59013; 59014; 59015; 59016
Fortune Bank, ASB (Gulfport, FL) 59940
Fortune Bank, ASB (Hudson, FL) 60132; 60133
Fortune Bank, ASB (Largo, FL) 60838
Fortune Bank, ASB (Naples, FL) 61624; 61626; 61627
Fortune Bank, ASB (New Port Richey, FL) 61687
Fortune Bank, ASB (Palm Harbor, FL) 62298; 62299
Fortune Bank, ASB (Seminole, FL) 62908; 62909
Fortune Bank, ASB (Spring Hill, FL) 62934
Fortune Bank, ASB (St. Petersburg Beach, FL) 63141
Fortune Bank, ASB (Tampa, FL) 63436
Fortune Bank, ASB (Tarpon, FL) 63665
Fortune Bank, SB (Palm Harbor, FL) 62300
Fortune Bank, SB (Pinellas Park, FL) 62519
Fortune Bank, SB (Port Charlotte, FL) 62657
Fortune Bank, SB (Port Richey, FL) 62673
Fortune Bank, SB (Safety Harbor, FL) 62762
Fortune Bank, SB (Sarasota, FL) 62834; 62835
Fortune Bank, SB (St. Petersburg, FL) 63119; 63120; 63121; 63122; 63123; 63124; 63125
Fredericktown Bank & Trust Co. (Frederick, MD) 71727; 71728; 71729; 71730; 71731
Fredericktown Bank & Trust Co. (Walkersville, MD) 72539
Frist of America Bank (Arcadia, FL) 58583
Frist of America Bank (Cape Coral, FL) 58923
Frist American National Bank (Clarksville, TN) 80550
Frist American National Bank (Harriman, TN) 80901
Frist American National Bank (Jackson, TN) 80984
Frist American National Bank (Norris, TN) 82179
Frist-Citizens Bank & Trust CO. (Albemarle, NC) 73537
Frist National Bank (Shelbyville, TN) 82314
Frist Union National Bank of Florida (Brandon, FL) 58871
Frist Union National Bank of Florida (Charlotte Harbor, FL) 58949
Frist Union National Bank of Florida (Destin, FL) 59344
Hardin County Bank & Trust (Elizabethtown, KY) 68279
Hardin County Bank & Trust (Radcliff, KY) 69239
Hardin County Bank & Trust (Vine Grove, KY) 69333
Hibernia National Bank (Alexandria, LA) 69382; 69384
Hibernia National Bank (Baker, LA) 69435
Hibernia National Bank (Baton Rouge, LA) 69548
Hibernia National Bank (Covington, LA) 69795
Hibernia National Bank (Mandeville, LA) 70208
Hibernia National Bank (Metairie, LA) 70271; 70272; 70273
Hibernia National Bank (Shreveport, LA) 70730
Huntington Federal Savings Bank (Avon Park, FL) 58607
Huntington, FSB (Lake Placid, FL) 60645
Huntington, FSB (Naples, FL) 61631
Huntington, FSB (Sebring, FL) 62884; 62885; 62886; 62887; 62888
Huntington Trust Co. of Florida, NA (Naples, FL) 61633
J P Morgan Delaware (Wilmington, DE) 58076
Libert National of Madisonville (Madisonville, KY) 69061
Liberty National Bank of Madisonville (Hanson, KY) 68407
Liberty National Bank of Madisonville (Madisonville, KY) 69062; 69063; 69064; 69065
Liberty National Bank of Madisonville (Mortons Gap, KY) 69111
Liberty National Bank of Northern Kentucky (Bellevue, KY) 68123
Liberty National Bank of Northern Kentucky (Burlington, KY) 68173
Liberty National Bank of Northern Kentucky (Cold Spring, KY) 68205
Liberty National Bank of Northern Kentucky (Crescent Springs, KY) 68241
Liberty National Bank of Northern Kentucky (Dayton, KY) 68267
Liberty National Bank of Northern Kentucky (Edgewood, KY) 68269
Liberty National Bank of Northern Kentucky (Erlanger, KY) 68298
Liberty National Bank of Northern Kentucky (Florence, KY) 68315; 68316; 68317; 68318
Liberty National Bank of Northern Kentucky (Fort Thomas, KY) 68350; 68351
Liberty National Bank of Owensboro (Owensboro, KY) 69178; 69179; 69180; 69181; 69182; 69183
Liberty National Bank of Shelbyville (Shelbyville, KY) 69273; 69274
Liberty National Bank & Trust Co. of Hardin County (Elizabethtown, KY) 68286
Lockwood National Bank of Houston (Deer Park, TX) 84552
Lockwood National Bank of Houston (Friendswood, TX) 85402
Lockwood National Bank of Houston (Galena Park, TX) 85434
Lockwood National Bank of Houston (Houston, TX) 86486; 86487; 86488; 86489; 86490
Lockwood National Bank of Houston (Pasadena, TX) 88433; 88434
Marshall & Ilsley Trust Co. of Florida (Naples, FL) 61641
MBNA America Bank, NA (Newark, DE) 57917
Mellon Bank (DE) NA (Dover, DE) 57793; 57794; 57795; 57796
Mellon Bank (DE) NA (Georgetown, DE) 57818
Mellon Bank (DE) NA (Laurel, DE) 57826
Mellon Bank (DE) NA (Lewes, DE) 57828
Mellon Bank (DE) NA (New Castle, DE) 57870
Mellon Bank (DE) NA (Newark, DE) 57920; 57921; 57922
Mellon Bank (DE) NA (Rehoboth Beach, DE) 57946; 57947
Mellon Bank (DE) NA (Seaford, DE) 57951
Mellon Bank (DE) NA (Smyrna, DE) 57960
Mellon Bank (DE) NA (Wilmington, DE) 58081; 58082; 58083; 58084; 58085; 58086; 58087
Mellon Bank (MD) (Annapolis, MD) 71016
Mellon Bank (MD) (Bethesda, MD) 71414; 71415; 71416
Mellon Bank (MD) (Bowie, MD) 71468
Mellon Bank (MD) (Gaithersburg, MD) 71798; 71799
Mellon Bank (MD) (Greenbelt, MD) 71867
Mellon Bank (MD) (Langley Park, MD) 72041
Mellon Bank (MD) (Rockville, MD) 72298; 72299
Mellon Bank (MD) (Silver Spring, MD) 72418
Mellon Bank (MD) (Sivler Spring, MD) 72451
Mellon Bank (MD) (Wheaton, MD) 72558; 72559
Mellon Bank, NA (New Castle, DE) 57871
Mellon Bank(DE) NA (Dagsboro, DE) 57767
Mercantile-Safe Deposit & Trust Co. (Baltimore, MD) 71199; 71200; 71201; 71202; 71203; 71204; 71205; 71206
Merchants State Bank (Dyersburg, TN) 80754
Merchants State Bank (Humboldt, TN) 80954; 80955; 80956; 80957; 80958
Merchants State Bank (Martin, TN) 81397
Merchants State Bank (Ripley, TN) 82263
Merchants State Bank (Rutherford, TN) 82286
Merchants State Bank (Union City, TN) 82387; 82388
Merchants State Bank (Yorkville, TN) 82425
Morgan Trust Co. of Florida, NA (Palm Beach, FL) 62259
Mutual Savings & Loan Assoc (Durham, NC) 74420
Mutual Savings & Loan Assoc (Greensboro, NC) 74869
National Bank of Walton County (Loganville, GA) 66616
National Bank of Walton County (Monroe, GA) 66992; 66993
National City Bank, Ashland Kentucky (Ashland, KY) 68100; 68101; 68103; 68104; 68105
National City Bank, Ashland Kentucky (Catlettsburg, KY) 68196
National City Bank, Bowling Green (Bowling Green, KY) 68149; 68150; 68151; 68152; 68153
National City Bank, Bowling Green (Smiths Grove, KY) 69291
National City Bank, Kentucky (Jeffersontown, KY) 68494; 68495
National City Bank, Kentucky (Lexington, KY) 68579; 68580; 68581; 68582; 68583; 68584; 68585; 68586; 68587; 68588; 68589; 68590; 68591; 68592; 68593
National City Bank, Kentucky (Louisville, KY) 68890; 68891; 68892; 68893; 68894; 68895; 68896; 68897; 68898; 68899; 68900; 68901; 68902; 68903; 68904; 68905; 68906; 68907; 68908; 68909; 68910; 68911; 68912; 68913; 68914; 68915; 68916; 68917; 68918; 68919; 68920; 68921; 68922; 68923; 68924; 68925; 68926; 68927
National City Bank, Kentucky (Middletown, KY) 69095
National City Bank, Kentucky (Okolona, KY) 69154; 69155
National City Bank, Kentucky (Pleasure Ridge Park, KY) 69227
National City Bank, Kentucky (Prospect, KY) 69233
National City Bank, Kentucky (Rolling Hills, KY) 69252
National City Bank, Kentucky (Shively, KY) 69287; 69288; 69289
National City Bank, Kentucky (St. Matthews, KY) 69303; 69304; 69305
National City Bank, Kentucky (Valley Station, KY) 69321
National City Trust Co. (Naples, FL) 61647; 61648
National City Trust Co. (Vero Beach, FL) 63761
National City Trust Co. (West Palm Beach, FL) 63888
NationsBank of DC, NA (Washington, DC) 58380; 58381; 58382; 58383; 58384; 58385; 58386; 58388; 58389; 58390; 58391; 58392
NBD Bank, FSB (Boca Raton, FL) 58722
NBD Bank, FSB (Naples, FL) 61649
NBD Bank, FSB (North Palm Beach, FL) 61751
NBD Bank, FSB (Sarasota, FL) 62846
NBD Bank, FSB (Venice, FL) 63729
NBD Trust Co. of Florida, NA (Boca Raton, FL) 58723
NBD Trust Co. of Florida, NA (Naples, FL) 61650
NBD Trust Co. of Florida, NA (North Palm Beach, FL) 61752
Northern Trust Bank of Texas, NA (Dallas, TX) 84271; 84272; 84273
Northern Trust Bank of Texas, NA (Houston, TX) 86620; 86621
Peninsula Bank (Berlin, MD) 71365; 71366
Peninsula Bank (Crisfield, MD) 71612; 71613
Peninsula Bank (Marion Station, MD) 72124
Peninsula Bank (Ocean City, MD) 72164; 72165
Peninsula Bank (Pittsville, MD) 72217
Peninsula Bank (Pocomoke City, MD) 72223; 72224
Peninsula Bank (Princess Anne, MD) 72242
Peninsula Bank (Priness Anne, MD) 72243
Peninsula Bank (Salisbury, MD) 72354; 72355; 72356
Peoples Bank of Maryland (Denton, MD) 71642; 71643
Peoples & Union Bank (Lewisburg, TN) 81327; 81328; 81329; 81330
Pickett County Bank & Trust Co. (Byrdstown, TN) 80265; 80266
PNC Bank Corp.- Kentucky (Louisville, KY) 68949; 68950
PNC Bank Kentuck Inc. (Jeffersontown, KY) 68497
PNC Bank Kentucky Inc. (Buckner, KY) 68171
PNC Bank Kentucky Inc. (Buechel, KY) 68172
PNC Bank Kentucky Inc. (Crestwood, KY) 68246
PNC Bank Kentucky Inc. (Elizabethtown, KY) 68290; 68291; 68292
PNC Bank Kentucky Inc. (Fern Creek, KY) 68303; 68304
PNC Bank Kentucky Inc. (Glendale, KY) 68399
PNC Bank Kentucky Inc. (Harrodsburg, KY) 68414; 68415
PNC Bank Kentucky Inc. (Jeffersontown, KY) 68498
PNC Bank Kentucky Inc. (La Grange, KY) 68504
PNC Bank Kentucky Inc. (Lexington, KY) 68604; 68605; 68606; 68607; 68608; 68609; 68610; 68611
PNC Bank Kentucky Inc. (Louisville, KY) 68951; 68952; 68953; 68954; 68955; 68956; 68957; 68958; 68959; 68960; 68961; 68962; 68963; 68964; 68965; 68966; 68967; 68968; 68969; 68970; 68971; 68972; 68973; 68974; 68975; 68976; 68977; 68978; 68979
PNC Bank Kentucky, Inc. (Okolona, KY) 69156; 69157
PNC Bank Kentucky, Inc. (Pewee Valley, KY) 69222
PNC Bank of Kentucky, Inc. (Pleasure Ridge Park, KY) 69228
PNC Bank Kentucky, Inc. (Prospect, KY) 69234
PNC Bank Kentucky, Inc. (Radcliff, KY) 69241
PNC Bank Kentucky, Inc. (Richmond, KY) 69246; 69247
PNC Bank Kentucky, Inc. (Sonora, KY) 69299
PNC Bank Kentucky, Inc. (St. Matthews, KY) 69306; 69307; 69308
PNC Bank Kentucky, Inc. (Upton, KY) 69320
PNC Bank Kentucky, Inc. (Valley Station, KY) 69322; 69323
PNC Bank Kentucky, Inc. (Winchester, KY) 69350; 69351; 69352
PNC Bank Kentuky Inc. (Elizabethtown, KY) 68293
PNC Bank Northern Kentucky, NA (Covington, KY) 68231
PNC Bank Northern Kentucky, NA (Crescent Springs, KY) 68242
PNC Bank Northern Kentucky, NA (Edgewood, KY) 68270
PNC Bank Northern Kentucky, NA (Florence, KY) 68328
PNC Bank Northern Kentucky, NA (Fort Mitchell, KY) 68348
PNC Bank Northern Kentucky, NA (Fort Thomas, KY) 68352
PNC Bank Northern Kentucky, NA (Fort Wright, KY) 68354
PNC Bank Northern Kentucky, NA (Highland Heights, KY) 68468
PNC Bank Northern Kentucky, NA (Newport, KY) 69140
PNC Bank Northern Kentucky, NA (Taylor Mill, KY) 69312
PNC Bank, Northern Kentucky, NA (Union, KY) 69319
PNC National Bank (Wilmington, DE) 58093
PNC Trust Co. of Florida, NA (Tampa, FL) 63537
PNC Trust Co. of Florida, NA (Vero Beach, FL) 63768
PNCBank Kentucky Inc. (Louisville, KY) 68980
Potomac Valley Bank (Bethesda, MD) 71433
Potomac Valley Bank (Gaithersburg, MD) 71807
Potomac Valley Bank (Germantown, MD) 71829
Potomac Valley Bank (Potomac, MD) 72233
Potomac Valley Bank (Rockville, MD) 72313
Potomac Valley Bank (Sumner, MD) 72483
Provident Financial Corp. (Columbia, SC) 79077
Quincy State Bank (Chattahoochie, FL) 58950
Quincy State Bank (Havana, FL) 59969
Quincy State Bank (Quincy, FL) 62732; 62733
Riggs National Bank of Washington (Washington, DC) 58431; 58432; 58433; 58434; 58435; 58436; 58437; 58438; 58439; 58440; 58441; 58442; 58443; 58444; 58445; 58446; 58447; 58448; 58449; 58450; 58451; 58452; 58453; 58454; 58455; 58456; 58457; 58458
River Oaks Trust Co. (Houston, TX) 86799
St. Michaels Bank (Easton, MD) 71661; 71662
St. Michaels Bank (St. Michaels, MD) 72472; 72473
St. Michaels Bank (Tilghman, MD) 72501
Save Trust Federal Savings Bank (Dyersburg, TN) 80758; 80759; 80760
Save Trust Federal Savings Bank (Newbern, TN) 82158
Savings of America A Div. of Home Savings of America, FSB (Fort Myers, FL) 59762
Savings of America Home Savings of America, FSB (Lake Worth, FL) 60697
Savings of America Home Savings of America, FSB (Margate, FL) 61002
Savings of America Home Savings of America, FSB (Miami Beach, FL) 61530; 61531
Savings of America Home Savings of America, FSB (Miami Shores, FL) 61537
Savings of America Home Savings of America, FSB (Naples, FL) 61664
Savings of America Home Savings of America, FSB (North Miami Beach, FL) 61744
Savings of America Home Savings of America, FSB (Pembroke Pines, FL) 62372; 62373
Savings of America Home Savings of America, FSB (Pompano Beach, FL) 62634; 62635; 62636
Savings of America Home Savings of America, FSB (Port Charlotte, FL) 62658
Savings of America Home Savings of America, FSB (Port Richey, FL) 62680
Savings of America Home Savings of America, FSB (Sarasota, FL) 62861
Savings of America Home Savings of America, FSB (St. Petersburg, FL) 63133
Savings of America Home Savings of America, FSB (Sunrise, FL) 63199
Savings of America Home Savings of America, FSB (Surfside, FL) 63202
Savings of America Home Savings of America, FSB (Tamarac, FL) 63300
Savings of America Home Savings of America, FSB (Tequesta, FL) 63681
Savings of America Home Savings of America, FSB (Venice, FL) 63736
Savings of America Home Savings of America, FSB (Vero Beach, FL) 63769
Savings of America Home Savings of America, FSB (West Palm Beach, FL) 63900; 63901
Savings of America, A Div. of Home Savings of America, FSB (Delray Beach, FL) 59331
Savings of America, A Division of Home Savings of America (Altamonte Springs, FL) 58563
Savings of America, A Division of Home Savings of America (Deerfield Beach, FL) 59289
Savings of America, A Division of Home Savings of America, FSB (Boca Raton, FL) 58741

Savings of America, A Division of Home Savings of America, FSB (Boynton Beach, FL) 58792
Savings of America, A Division of Home Savings of America, FSB (Bradenton, FL) 58851; 58852
Savings of America, A Division of Home Savings of America, FSB (Clearwater, FL) 59046
Savings of America, A Division of Home Savings of America, FSB (Coral Gables, FL) 59104
Savings of America, A Division of Home Savings of America, FSB (Dunedin, FL) 59367
Savings of America, A Division of Home Savings of America, FSB (Fort Lauderdale, FL) 59608; 59609
Savings of America, A Division of Home Savings of America, FSB (Fort Pierce, FL) 59811
Savings of America, A Division of Home Savings of America FSB (Houston, TX) 86858; 86859; 86860
Savings of America, A Division of Home Savings of America, FSB (Humble, TX) 87244
Savings of America, A Division of Home Savings of America, FSB (Hurst, TX) 87296
Savings of America, A Division of Home Savings of America, FSB (Irving, TX) 87400
Savings of America, A Division of Home Savings of America, FSB (Nederland, TX) 88191
Savings of America, A Division of Home Savings of America, FSB (Pasadena, TX) 88468
Savings of America, A Division of Home Savings of America, FSB (Plano, TX) 88607
Savings of America, A Division of Home Savings of America, FSB (Richardson, TX) 88774; 88775
Savings of America, A Division of Home Savings of America, FSB (San Antonio, TX) 89223; 89224; 89225
Savings of America, A Division of Home Savings of America, FSB (Webster, TX) 90024
Savings of America, FSB (Beaumont, TX) 83212
Savings of America, FSB (Dallas, TX) 84376; 84377; 84378; 84379
Savings of America, FSB (Deer Park, TX) 84566
Savings of America, FSB (Dllas, TX) 84675
Savings of America, FSB (Ft. Worth, TX) 85415
Savings of America, FSB (Groves, TX) 85684
Savings of America, FSB (Houston, TX) 86861; 86862; 86863; 86864; 86865; 86866; 86867; 86868; 86869; 86870
Savings of America, FSB Home Savings of America (Hollandale, FL) 60031
Savings of America, FSB Home Savings of America (Hollywood, FL) 60094
Sea Island Bank (Stateboro, GA) 67631
Sea Island Bank (Statesboro, GA) 67646; 67647; 67648
Sea Island Park (Statesboro, GA) 67649
Security Bank & Trust Co. of Albany (Albany, GA) 64092; 64093; 64094; 64095; 64096
Security Bank & Trust Co. of Albany (Colquitt, GA) 65614
Security Trust Bypass (Greeneville, TN) 80888
Security Trust Federal S&L (Fulton, KY) 68377
Security Trust Federal S&L (Hickman, KY) 68461
Security Trust FS & LA (Clinton, TN) 80614
Security Trust FS & LA (Kingston, TN) 81128
Security Trust FS & LA (Knoxville, TN) 81249; 81250
Security Trust FS & LA (Morristown, TN) 81809
Security Trust FS & LA (Oak Ridge, TN) 82198
Shawmut National Trust Co. (Stuart, FL) 63179
Signet Bank (Herndon, VA) 91132
Signet Bank/Maryland (Baltimore, MD) 71280; 71281; 71282; 71283; 71284; 71285; 71286; 71287; 71288; 71289; 71290; 71291; 71292; 71293; 71294; 71295; 71296; 71297; 71298; 71299; 71300; 71301; 71302; 71303; 71304; 71305; 71306
Signet Bank, NA (Washington, DC) 58472; 58473; 58474; 58475; 58476; 58477; 58478; 58479; 58480; 58481; 58482; 58483; 58484; 58485; 58486; 58487; 58488
Signet Bank, VA (Danville, VA) 90716; 90717
Signet Bank, Virginia (Alexandra, VA) 90164
Signet Bank, Virginia (Alexandria, VA) 90239
Signet Bank, Virginia (Arlington, VA) 90382; 90383; 90384; 90385; 90386; 90387; 90388
Signet Bank, Virginia (Boydton, VA) 90465
Signet Bank, Virginia (Bristol, VA) 90488; 90489; 90490; 90491
Signet Bank, Virginia (Burgess, VA) 90498
Signet Bank, Virginia (Chesapeake, VA) 90602; 90603; 90604
Signet Bank, Virginia (Chester, VA) 90626
Signet Bank, Virginia (Chesterfield, VA) 90631
Signet Bank, Virginia (Colonial Beach, VA) 90650
Signet Bank, Virginia (Colonial Heights, VA) 90652
Signet Bank, Virginia (Danville, VA) 90718; 90719
Signet Bank, Virginia (Dinwiddie, VA) 90726
Signet Bank, Virginia (Dublin, VA) 90729
Signet Bank, Virginia (Dumfries, VA) 90731
Signet Bank, Virginia (Fairfax, VA) 90807
Signet Bank, Virginia (Falls Church, VA) 90869; 90870
Signet Bank, Virginia (Fredericksburg, VA) 90940; 90941; 90942
Signet Bank, Virginia (Front Royal, VA) 90955; 90956
Signet Bank, Virginia (Galax, VA) 90965; 90966
Signet Bank, Virginia (Gate City, VA) 90969
Signet Bank, Virginia (Glen Allen, VA) 90984
Signet Bank, Virginia (Grafton, VA) 90997
Signet Bank, Virginia (Great Falls, VA) 91001
Signet Bank, Virginia (Hampton, VA) 91056
Signet Bank, Virginia (Herndon, VA) 91133; 91134
Signet Bank, Virginia (Honaker, VA) 91150
Signet Bank, Virginia (Kilmarnock, VA) 91179
Signet Bank, Virginia (La Crosse, VA) 91182
Signet Bank, Virginia (Lebanon, VA) 91191
Signet Bank, Virginia (Leesburg, VA) 91197
Signet Bank, Virginia (Manassas, VA) 91324; 91325
Signet Bank, Virginia (Mappsville, VA) 91329
Signet Bank, Virginia (Mc Leen, VA) 91376
Signet Bank, Virginia (Mechanicsville, VA) 91403
Signet Bank, Virginia (Midlothian, VA) 91425; 91426; 91427
Signet Bank, Virginia (Montross, VA) 91433
Signet Bank, Virginia (Newport News, VA) 91483; 91484; 91485; 91486; 91487; 91488
Signet Bank, Virginia (Nokesville, VA) 91497
Signet Bank, Virginia (Norfolk, VA) 91578; 91579; 91580; 91581; 91582
Signet Bank, Virginia (Petersburg, VA) 91635; 91636
Signet Bank, Virginia (Portsmouth, VA) 91669; 91670; 91671
Signet Bank, Virginia (Pulaski, VA) 91678; 91679
Signet Bank, Virginia (Richmond, VA) 92013; 92014; 92015; 92016; 92017; 92018; 92019; 92020; 92021; 92022; 92023; 92024; 92025; 92026; 92027; 92028; 92029; 92030; 92031; 92032; 92033; 92034; 92035; 92036; 92037
Signet Bank, Virginia (Roanoke, VA) 92187; 92188; 92189; 92190
Signet Bank, Virginia (Salem, VA) 92224
Signet Bank, Virginia (South Hill, VA) 92267; 92268
Signet Bank, Virginia (Springfield, VA) 92292
Signet Bank, Virginia (St. Paul, VA) 92298
Signet Bank, Virginia (Vienna, VA) 92420; 92421
Signet Bank, Virginia (Vinton, VA) 92426
Signet Bank, Virginia (Virginia Beach, VA) 92511; 92512; 92513; 92514; 92515; 92516; 92517
Signet Bank, Virginia (Warsaw, VA) 92530
Signet Bank, Virginia (Weber City, VA) 92536
Signet Bank, Virginia (White Stone, VA) 92545
Signet Bank, Virginia (Woodbridge, VA) 92626; 92627
Signet Bank, Virginia (Yarina, VA) 92648
Signet Banking Corp. (Richmond, VA) 92038
Signet Trust Co. (Richmond, VA) 92040
Star Bank NA, Kentucky (Alexandria, KY) 68079
Star Bank NA, Kentucky (Carrollton, KY) 68192
Star Bank NA, Kentucky (Cold Spring, KY) 68206
Star Bank NA, Kentucky (Covington, KY) 68233; 68234; 68235; 68236; 68237
Star Bank NA, Kentucky (Crescent Springs, KY) 68243
Star Bank NA, Kentucky (Crestview Hills, KY) 68244
Star Bank NA, Kentucky (Elsemere, KY) 68295
Star Bank NA, Kentucky (Falmouth, KY) 68301; 68302
Star Bank NA, Kentucky (Florence, KY) 68337; 68338; 68339
Star Bank NA, Kentucky (Florene, KY) 68346
Star Bank NA, Kentucky (Fort Mitchell, KY) 68349
Star Bank NA, Kentucky (Fort Thomas, KY) 68353
Star Bank NA, Kentucky (Fort Wright, KY) 68355
Star Bank NA, Kentucky (Independence, KY) 68486
Star Bank NA, Kentucky (Lebanon, KY) 68510
Star Bank NA, Kentucky (Loretto, KY) 68673
Star Bank NA, Kentucky (Newport, KY) 69143; 69144
Star Bank NA, Kentucky (Taylor Mill, KY) 69313
Star Bank NA, Kentucky (Verona, KY) 69324
Star Bank NA, Kentucky (Walton, KY) 69335
Steiner Bank (Birmingham, AL) 55395; 55396
Sterling Bank (Montgomery, AL) 56381; 56382
Sumter Bank & Trust Co. (Americus, GA) 64144; 64145
Sumter Bank & Trust Co. (Leslie, GA) 66550
Superior Federal Bank, FSB (Arkadelphia, AR) 56721
Superior Federal Bank, FSB (Benton, AR) 56776; 56777
Superior Federal Bank, FSB (Brinkley, AR) 56822
Superior Federal Bank, FSB (Carlisle, AR) 56844
Superior Federal Bank, FSB (Danville, AR) 56887
Superior Federal Bank, FSB (England, AR) 56966
Superior Federal Bank, FSB (Fayetteville, AR) 56993; 56994
Superior Federal Bank, FSB (Marshall, AR) 57349
Superior Federal Bank, FSB (Paris, AR) 57500
Superior Federal Bank, FSB (Siloam Springs, AR) 57623
Tallahassee State Bank (Tallahassee, FL) 63275; 63276
Texas Commerce BancShares (Houston, TX) 87013
Texas Commerce Bank NA (Dallas, TX) 84443
Texas Commerce Bank National (Houston, TX) 87014; 87016; 87017; 87019; 87020
Texas Commerce Bank National (Humble, TX) 87251
Trust Co. Bank of Aujusta, N.A. (Thomson, GA) 67814; 67815
Trust Co. Bank of Coffee County (Douglas, GA) 65977; 65978; 65979
Trust Co. Bank of Columbus, N.A. (La Grange, GA) 66487; 66488
Trust Co. Bank of Middle Georgia, N.A. (Macon, GA) 66719
Trust Co. Bank of NE Georgia, N.A. (Madison, GA) 66729
Trust Co. Bank of North Georgia (Gainesville, GA) 66294; 66295; 66296; 66297; 66298
Trust Co. Bank of NW Georgia, N.A. (Rockmart, GA) 67334
Trust Co. Bank of NW Georgia, N.A. (Rome, GA) 67347; 67348; 67349; 67350; 67351; 67352
Trust Co. Bank of Savannah, N.A. (Savannah, GA) 67518
Trust Co. Bank of SE Georgia, N.A. (Screven, GA) 67535
Trust Co. Bank of SE Georgia, N.A. (St. Simons Island, GA) 67629; 67630
Trust Co. Bank of SE Georgia, N.A. (Waycross, GA) 68040; 68041
Trust Co. Bank of South Georgia (Thomasville, GA) 67807
Trust Co. Bank of South Georgia, N.A. (Pelham, GA) 67258
Trust Co. Bank of South Georgia, N.A. (Sylvester, GA) 67778
Trust Co. Bank of South Georgia, N.A. (Thomasville, GA) 67808; 67809
Trust Co. Bank of South Georgia, N.A. (Tifton, GA) 67832; 67833
Trust Co. Bank of South Georgia, National Assoc. (Albany, GA) 64097
Trust Co. Bank of Southeast Georgia, National Assoc. (Jesue, GA) 66369
Trust Co. of Georgia Bank of Savannah, N.A. (Savannah, GA) 67519; 67520; 67521; 67522; 67523; 67524; 67525; 67526; 67527; 67528
Turst Co. Bank of Columbus, N.A. (La Grange, GA) 66489
Union Planers National Bank (Chattanooga, TN) 80509
Union Planters National Bank (Antioch, TN) 80178
Union Planters National Bank (Bartlett, TN) 80199; 80200
Union Planters National Bank (Brentwood, TN) 80237
Union Planters National Bank (Chattanooga, TN) 80510; 80511; 80512; 80513
Union Planters National Bank (Clinton, TN) 80615
Union Planters National Bank (Cordova, TN) 80679
Union Planters National Bank (Dickson, TN) 80737
Union Planters National Bank (Eagleville, TN) 80765
Union Planters National Bank (Franklin, TN) 80825
Union Planters National Bank (Gallatin, TN) 80852
Union Planters National Bank (Germantown, TN) 80857; 80858
Union Planters National Bank (Goodlettsville, TN) 80872
Union Planters National Bank (Greenback, TN) 80880
Union Planters National Bank (Hendersonville, TN) 80920
Union Planters National Bank (Jackson, TN) 81004; 81005; 81006; 81007; 81008; 81009; 81010; 81011; 81012; 81013
Union Planters National Bank (Knoxville, TN) 81267; 81268; 81269; 81270; 81271; 81272
Union Planters National Bank (Lebanon, TN) 81314; 81315
Union Planters National Bank (Madison, TN) 81382; 81383
Union Planters National Bank (Maryville, TN) 81426; 81427
Union Planters National Bank (Memphis, TN) 81721; 81722; 81723; 81724; 81725; 81726; 81727; 81728; 81729; 81730; 81731; 81732; 81733; 81734; 81735; 81736; 81737; 81738; 81739; 81740; 81741; 81742; 81743; 81744; 81745; 81746; 81747; 81748
Union Planters National Bank (Milan, TN) 81772; 81773
Union Planters National Bank (Mt. Juliet, TN) 81830
Union Planters National Bank (Murfreesboro, TN) 81869; 81870; 81871
Union Planters National Bank (Nashville, TN) 82119; 82120; 82121; 82122; 82123; 82124; 82125; 82126; 82127; 82128
Union Planters National Bank (Oak Ridge, TN) 82199; 82200; 82200
Union Planters National Bank (Smyrna, TN) 82329
Union Planters National Bank (Townsend, TN) 82371
Union Plnaters National Bank (Memphis, TN) 81749
United Missouri Bank, USA (New Castle, DE) 57877
United Missouri Bank, USA (Wilmington, DE) 58118
Vaguard Bank & Trust Co. (Eglin AFB, FL) 59380
Vaguard Bank & Trust Co. (Fort Walton Beach, FL) 59843
Vanguard Bank & Trust Co. (Eglin AFB, FL) 59381
Vanguard Bank & Trust Co. (Mary Esther, FL) 61024
Vanguard Bank & Trust Co. (Niceville, FL) 61720; 61721
Vanguard Bank & Trust Co. (Valparaiso, FL) 63713
Wachovia Bank and Trust Com (Winston Salem, NC) 76694
Wachovia Bank & Trust Compa (Charlotte, NC) 74198
Wachovia Bank & Trust Compa (Hickory, NC) 75104
Wachovia Corp. (Winston-Salem, NC) 76776
Westminster Bank & Trust Co. (Gamber, MD) 71822
Westminster Bank & Trust Co. of Carroll County (Eldersburg, MD) 71668
Westminster Bank & Trust Co. of Carroll County (Manchester, MD) 72123
Westminster Bank & Trust Co. of Carroll County (Union Mills, MD) 72512
Westminster Bank & Trust Co. of Carroll County (Westminster, MD) 72547; 72548; 72549
Westminster Bank & Trust Co. of Carroll County (Winfield, MD) 72574
Westminster Bank & Trust Co. of Carroll County (Woodbine, MD) 72575
World S&L, A Federal S&L (Bayonet Point, FL) 58639
World S&L, A Federal S&L (Boca Raton, FL) 58754; 58756

6022 State Commercial Banks

American National Bank (Union Springs, AL) 56686
AmSouth Bank of Florida (Belleair Bluffs, FL) 58648
AmSouth Bank of Florida (Belleview, FL) 58653
AmSouth Bank of Florida (Beverly Hills, FL) 58658
AmSouth Bank of Florida (Brooksville, FL) 58883; 58884
AmSouth Bank of Florida (Bushnell, FL) 58900
AmSouth Bank of Florida (Clearwater, FL) 58961; 58962; 58963; 58964; 58966; 58967
AmSouth Bank of Florida (Crytal River, FL) 59136
AmSouth Bank of Florida (Destin, FL) 59338; 59339; 59340
AmSouth Bank of Florida (Dunedin, FL) 59354
AmSouth Bank of Florida (Dunnellon, FL) 59370
AmSouth Bank of Florida (Fern Park, FL) 59403
AmSouth Bank of Florida (Fort Walton Beach, FL) 59821; 59822
AmSouth Bank of Florida (Gulf Breeze, FL) 59933; 59934
AmSouth Bank of Florida (Gulfport, FL) 59939
AmSouth Bank of Florida (Holiday, FL) 60027
AmSouth Bank of Florida (Homosassa, FL) 60124
AmSouth Bank of Florida (Indian Shores, FL) 60140
AmSouth Bank of Florida (Inverness, FL) 60143; 60144
AmSouth Bank of Florida (Kissimmee, FL) 60581
AmSouth Bank of Florida (Largo, FL) 60812
AmSouth Bank of Florida (Mary Esther, FL) 61013
AmSouth Bank of Florida (Milton, FL) 61544
AmSouth Bank of Florida (Mims, FL) 61552
AmSouth Bank of Florida (Niceville, FL) 61707
AmSouth Bank of Florida (Ocala, FL) 61765; 61766; 61767; 61768; 61769; 61770; 61771
AmSouth Bank of Florida (Ocoee, FL) 61830; 61831
AmSouth Bank of Florida (Oldsmar, FL) 61845

Barnett Bank of Volusia County (Edgewater, FL) 59376
Barnett Bank of Volusia County (Flagler Beach, FL) 59417
Barnett Banks of Volusia County (Daytona Beach Shores, FL) 59234
Barnett Banks of Volusia County (DeLand, FL) 59296
Beneficial National Bank (Bear, DE) 57750
Beneficial National Bank (New Castle, DE) 57857
Beneficial National Bank (Wilmington, DE) 58019
Beneficial Savings Bank (Pinellas Park, FL) 62512
Beneficial Savings Bank FSB (Brandon, FL) 58866
Boatmen's Bank of Delaware (New Castle, DE) 57860
Boatmen's Bank of Tennessee (Memphis, TN) 81483
Branch Banking & Trust Co. (Black Creek, NC) 73694
Branch Banking & Trust Co. (Charlotte, NC) 73880; 73881; 73882
Branch Banking & Trust Co. (Cramerton, NC) 74350
Branch Banking & Trust Co. (Farmville, NC) 74519
Branch Banking & Trust Co. (Fountain, NC) 74620
Branch Banking & Trust Co. (Fremont, NC) 74633; 74634
Branch Banking & Trust Co. (Gastonia, NC) 74666
Branch Banking & Trust Co. (Goldsboro, NC) 74708
Branch Banking & Trust Co. (Greenville, NC) 74951; 74952
Branch Banking & Trust Co. (Halifax, NC) 74992
Branch Banking & Trust Co. (Jamesville, NC) 75247
Branch Banking & Trust Co. (Lexington, NC) 75398
Branch Banking & Trust Co. (Matthews, NC) 75522
Branch Banking & Trust Co. (Mocksville, NC) 75562
Branch Banking & Trust Co. (Mount Holly, NC) 75688
Branch Banking & Trust Co. (New Bern, NC) 75720
Branch Banking & Trust Co. (Pikeville, NC) 75796
Branch Banking & Trust Co. (Pinehurst, NC) 75801
Branch Banking & Trust Co. (Pineville, NC) 75809
Branch Banking & Trust Co. (Princeton, NC) 75842
Branch Banking & Trust Co. (Raleigh, NC) 75876
Branch Banking & Trust Co. (Saratoga, NC) 76209
Branch Banking & Trust Co. (Scotland Neck, NC) 76210
Branch Banking & Trust Co. (Shelby, NC) 76235; 76236
Branch Banking & Trust Co. (Stanley, NC) 76309
Branch Banking & Trust Co. (Stantonsburg, NC) 76313
Branch Banking & Trust Co. (Statesville, NC) 76318
Branch Banking & Trust Co. (Wallace, NC) 76437
Branch Banking & Trust Co. (Warrenton, NC) 76447
Branch Banking & Trust Co. (Weldon, NC) 76479
Branch Banking & Trust Co. (Williamston, NC) 76527
Branch Banking & Trust Co. (Wilson, NC) 76620; 76621; 76622; 76623
Branch Banking & Trust Co. (Greenville, SC) 79321
Branch Banking & Trust Co. (Spartanburg, SC) 79882
California Federal Bank (Plant City, FL) 62539
California Federal Bank (Tampa, FL) 63374
Calvert Village Professional Bldg. (, MD) 70991
Central Fidelity Banks Inc. (Richmond, VA) 91756
Chase Bank of Maryland (Baltimore, MD) 71078
Chase Manhatten Bank (USA) (Wilmington, DE) 58031; 58032
Chemical Bank Delaware (Wilmington, DE) 58036
Citibank Delaware (New Castle, DE) 57861
Citizens State Bank (Vernon, AL) 56697
Citizens State Bank (Bald Knob, AR) 56736
Citizens State Bank (Nashville, AR) 57439
Citizens State Bank (Kingsland, GA) 66467
Citizens State Bank (Maud, OK) 77188
Citizens State Bank (Anton, TX) 82621
Citizens State Bank (Buffalo, TX) 83413
Citizens State Bank (Cross Plains, TX) 83811
Citizens State Bank (Dickinson, TX) 84663
Citizens State Bank (Donna, TX) 84676
Citizens State Bank (Giddings, TX) 85575
Citizens State Bank (Gorman, TX) 85597
Citizens State Bank (Hempstead, TX) 85731
Citizens State Bank (Malakoff, TX) 87830
Citizens State Bank (Roby, TX) 88810
Citizens State Bank (Roma, TX) 88826
Citizens State Bank (San Antonio, TX) 88957
Citizens State Bank (Sealy, TX) 89364
Citizens State Bank (Somerville, TX) 89455
Citizens State Bank (Tenaha, TX) 89655
Citizens State Bank (Woodville, TX) 90130
Citizens State Bank Dalhart (Dalhart, TX) 83831
Citizens State Bank, Ganado (Ganado, TX) 85474
City National Bank (Dothan, AL) 55631
City National Bank (Sylacauga, AL) 56577
City National Bank (Fort Smith, AR) 57036; 57037; 57038; 57039; 57040; 57041; 57042
City National Bank (Miami, FL) 61251; 61252
City National Bank (Baton Rouge, LA) 69485; 69487; 69489; 69491; 69493; 69494; 69495; 69496; 69497
City National Bank (Charlotte, NC) 73902
City National Bank (Lawton, OK) 77156
City National Bank (Amarillo, TX) 82539
City National Bank (Corsicana, TX) 83778
City National Bank the (Mineral Wells, TX) 88108
City National Bank (Sulphur Springs, TX) 89555; 89556
City National Bank of Charleston (Charleston, WV) 92735
City National Bank of Dotha (Dothan, AL) 55632; 55633
City National Bank of Fairmont (Farmington, WV) 92851
City National Bank of Florida (Hallandale, FL) 59959
City National Bank of Florida (Miami, FL) 61259
City National Bank of Fort (Fort Smith, AR) 57043
City National Bank of Miami (Miami, FL) 61261; 61262
Comerica Trust Co. of Florid (Boca Raton, FL) 58692
Commerce Banc Corp. (Charleston, WV) 92740
Commercial Bank (Andalusia, AL) 54986
Commercial Bank (Roanoke, AL) 56499
Commercial Bank (Donalds, SC) 79167
Commercial National Bank (Shreveport, LA) 70700
Compass Bank (Dallas, TX) 83947
Compass Bank (Houston, TX) 85996
Compass Bank (Richardson, TX) 88731
Continental Bank (Metairie, LA) 70257; 70257
Crestar Bank (Richmond, VA) 91793
Crestar Bank Maryland (Bethesda, MD) 71378
Crestar Bank NA (Washington, DC) 58205
Eastville Banks (Eastville, VA) 90738
Farmers Bank & Trust Co. (Bardstown, KY) 68114
Farmers Bank & Trust Co. (Georgetown, KY) 68381
Farmers Bank & Trust Co. (Henderson, KY) 68447; 68448
Farmers Bank & Trust Co. (Madisonville, KY) 69048; 69049; 69050
Farmers Bank & Trust Co. (Marion, KY) 69076
Farmers Bank & Trust Co. (Princeton, KY) 69230
Farmers Merchants Bank-Eastern Shore (Onley, VA) 91616
First Alabama Bank (Anniston, AL) 54995
First Alabama Bank (Auburn, AL) 55060
First Alabama Bank (Birmingham, AL) 55241; 55243; 55244; 55245; 55246; 55247
First Alabama Bank (Cullman, AL) 55542
First Alabama Bank (Dothan, AL) 55636
First Alabama Bank (Fairfield, AL) 55712
First Alabama Bank (Gadsden, AL) 55779; 55780
First Alabama Bank (Gardendale, AL) 55797
First Alabama Bank (Guntersville, AL) 55824
First Alabama Bank (Huntsville, AL) 55924; 55926
First Alabama Bank (Killen, AL) 56095
First Alabama Bank (Mobile, AL) 56168; 56169; 56170; 56171; 56173; 56174; 56175; 56176; 56177
First Alabama Bank (Montgomery, AL) 56321; 56323; 56324; 56325; 56326; 56327; 56328; 56329; 56331
First Alabama Bank (Phenix City, AL) 56460; 56461
First Alabama Bank (Prattville, AL) 56488
First Alabama Bank (York, AL) 56712
First Alabama Bank of Birmi (Birmingham, AL) 55248; 55249; 55250; 55251; 55252; 55253
First Alabama Bank Birmingh (Birmingham, AL) 55254; 55255; 55256; 55257; 55258; 55259; 55260; 55261
First Alabama Bank of Birmingham (Bessemer, AL) 55089
First Alabama Bank of Birmingham (Birmingham, AL) 55262
First Alabama Bank Chilton (Thorsby, AL) 56611
First Alabama Bank Conecuh (Evergreen, AL) 55706
First Alabama Bank of Dotha (Dothan, AL) 55643; 55644; 55645; 55646
First Alabama Bank Dothan (Dothan, AL) 55647
First Alabama Bank of Hunts (Huntsville, AL) 55928
First Alabama Bank Huntsvil (Huntsville, AL) 55929; 55930; 55932; 55933
First Alabama Bank Huntsville (Huntsville, AL) 55935
First Alabama Bank of Montg (Montgomery, AL) 56332; 56333
First Alabama Bank of Selma (Selma, AL) 56528
First Alabama Bank Slema (Selma, AL) 56529
First Alabama Bank Talladeg (Munford, AL) 56402
First Alabama Bank of Tusca (Tuscaloosa, AL) 56650; 56651
First American Bank (Decatur, AL) 55581
First American Bank (Ashland, KY) 68095
First American Bank (Erick, OK) 77074
First American Bank (Stratford, OK) 77855
First American Bank (Bryan, TX) 83395
First American Bank (Front Royal, VA) 90948
First American Bank (Yorktown, VA) 92651
First American Bank Maryland (Baltimore, MD) 71118
First American Bank Maryland (Cockeysville, MD) 71548
First American Bank Maryland (Glen Burnie, MD) 71841
First American Bank Virginia (Alexandria, VA) 90185; 90186; 90187; 90188; 90189; 90190; 90191; 90192; 90193
First American Bank Virginia (Annandale, VA) 90260; 90261; 90262
First American Bank Virginia (Arlington, VA) 90308; 90309; 90310; 90311; 90312; 90313; 90314; 90315; 90316; 90317; 90318; 90319; 90320; 90321
First American Bank of Virginia (Fairfax, VA) 90770; 90771
First American Bank of Virginia (Falls Church, VA) 90833
First American Bank of Virginia (Harrisonburg, VA) 91079; 91080; 91081
First American Bank of Virginia (Herndon, VA) 91122; 91123
First American Bank of Virginia (Lexington, VA) 91202; 91203
First American Bank of Virginia (Norfolk, VA) 91518; 91519; 91520
First American Bank Virginia (Springfield, VA) 92280; 92281
First American Bank of Virginia (Staunton, VA) 92316
First American Bank of Virginia (Vienna, VA) 92403; 92404
First American Bank of Virginia (Virginia Beach, VA) 92464; 92465; 92466; 92467
First American Corp. (Washington, DC) 58245
First American National Bank (North Little Rock, AR) 57456; 57457; 57458; 57459; 57460; 57460; 57461; 57462
First American National Bank (Belmont, MS) 72608; 72609
First American National Bank (Golden, MS) 72788
First American National Bank (Iuka, MS) 72934
First American National Bank (Bristol, VA) 90474
First Bank (Slidell, LA) 70820; 70821; 70822; 70823
First Bank (Magnolia, MS) 73140
First Bank (Mc Comb, MS) 73143
First Bank (Albemarle, NC) 73529
First Bank (Concord, NC) 74311
First Bank (Kannapolis, NC) 75258
First Bank (Troy, NC) 76410
First Bank (Groveton, TX) 85689
First Bank (Houston, TX) 86195
First Bank (Mesquite, TX) 87962
First Bank (Navasota, TX) 88177
First Bank of Apache (Apache, OK) 76807
First Fidelity Bancorp (Fairmont, WV) 92839
First Financial Bank F S B (Kenner, LA) 69995
First Gibraltar Bank (Enid, OK) 77052
First Gibraltar Bank (Irving, TX) 87345
First Interstate Bank of Texas (Houston, TX) 86196
First National Bank & Trust (Crestview, FL) 59123
First National Bank & Trust (Destin, FL) 59343
First National Bank & Trust (Fort Pierce, FL) 59794
First National Bank & Trust (Immokalee, FL) 60134
First National Bank & Trust (Mary Esther, FL) 61016
First National Bank & Trust (Stuart, FL) 63162
First National Bank & Trust (Blackwell, OK) 76864
First National Bank & Trust (Mc Alester, OK) 77190
First National Bank & Trust (Muskogee, OK) 77218
First National Bank & Trust (Tulsa, OK) 77940
First National Bank & Trust Co. (Cumberland, MD) 71622
First National Bank of Tusk (Tuscaloosa, AL) 56654
First State Bank & Trust Co. (Conway, AR) 56860
First State Bank & Trust Co. (Greenbrier, AR) 57123
First State Bank & Trust Co. (Mayflower, AR) 57355
First State Bank & Trust Co. (Vilonia, AR) 57700
First State Bank & Trust Co. (Albany, GA) 64067
First State Bank & Trust Co. (Valdosta, GA) 67945
First State Bank & Trust Co. (Baton Rouge, LA) 69535
First State Bank & Trust Co. (Bogalusa, LA) 69701
First State Bank & Trust Co. (Hollis, OK) 77137
First State Bank & Trust Co. (Carthage, TX) 83517
First State Bank & Trust Co. (Edinburg, TX) 84732
First State Bank & Trust Co. (Mission, TX) 88122
First Union National Bank, Capital Area (McLean, VA) 91385
First Union National Bank of Tennessee (Nashville, TN) 82007
First Virginia Bank (Bel Air, MD) 71335
First Virginia Bank (Falls Church, VA) 90839; 90846
First Virginia Bank (Farmville, VA) 90875
First Virginia Bank (South Hill, VA) 92264; 92265
First Virginia Bank Augusta (Staunton, VA) 92318
First Virginia Bank Central (Charlottesville, VA) 90536
First Virginia Bank Clinch Valley (Richlands, VA) 91720
First Virginia Bank Colonial (Richmond, VA) 91882
First Virginia Bank Commonwealth (Williamsburg, VA) 92570
First Virginia Bank Franklin County (Rocky Mount, VA) 92199
First Virginia Bank Highlands (Covington, VA) 90657
First Virginia Bank Maryland (Upper Marlboro, MD) 72517
First Virginia Bank Mountain Empire (Damascus, VA) 90683
First Virginia Bank of Tidewater (Norfolk, VA) 91528
First Virginia Bank Piedmont (Lynchburg, VA) 91244
First Virginia Bank Planters (Bridgewater, VA) 90468
First Virginia Bank Southwest (Roanoke, VA) 92151
First Virginia Bank - Augusta (Staunton, VA) 92319
First Virginia Bank Central (Charlottesville, VA) 90537
First Virginia Bank Clinch Valley (Richlands, VA) 91721
First Virginia Bank - Colonial (Richmond, VA) 91883
First Virginia Bank Franklin County (Rocky Mount, VA) 92200
First Virginia Bank - Highlands (Covington, VA) 90658
First Virginia Bank - Maryland (Upper Marlboro, MD) 72518
First Virginia Bank - Moutain Empire (Danville, VA) 90692
First Virginia Bank - Piedmont (Lynchburg, VA) 91245
First Virginia Bank - Planters (Bridgewater, VA) 90469
First Virginia Bank - Southside (Farmville, VA) 90876
First Virginia Bank - Southwest (Roanoke, VA) 92152
First Virginia Banks Inc. (Falls Church, VA) 90848; 90849
Fortuen Bank, ASB (Dunedin, FL) 59362
Georgia Federal Bank F S B (Albany, GA) 64074
Georgia Federal Bank, F S B (Savannah, GA) 67477
Great Western Bank (Boca Raton, FL) 58708
Great Western Bank (Boynton Beach, FL) 58776
Great Western Bank (Fort Myers, FL) 59700
Great Western Bank (Lake Worth, FL) 60674; 60675
Great Western Bank (Lakeland, FL) 60731
Great Western Bank (Pensacola, FL) 62432; 62434
Great Western Bank (Port St Lucie, FL) 62686
Great Western Bank (Titusville, FL) 63688
Great Western Bank (W Palm Beach, FL) 63791
Hibernia National Bank (Alexandria, LA) 69382
Hibernia National Bank (Baker, LA) 69435
Hibernia National Bank (Baton Rouge, LA) 69546; 69547; 69548; 69549; 69553
Hibernia National Bank (Bossier City, LA) 69717
Hibernia National Bank (Covington, LA) 69795
Hibernia National Bank (Lafayette, LA) 70059
Hibernia National Bank (Mandeville, LA) 70208
Hibernia National Bank (Metairie, LA) 70268; 70270; 70271; 70272; 70273
Hibernia National Bank (New Orleans, LA) 70502; 70505
Hibernia National Bank (Shreveport, LA) 70729; 70730
Hibernia National Bank Inc. B (Baton Rouge, LA) 69555
Huntington Trust Co. (Naples, FL) 61632

J P Morgan Delaware (Wilmington, DE) 58076
Key Bank of Fla (Tampa, FL) 63478
Lebanon Bank (Lebanon, TN) 81303; 81304; 81305
Marshall & Ilsley Trust Com (Naples, FL) 61640
Merchants Bank-Eastern Shore; Farmers (Onley, VA) 91616
Mini Mart (West Columbia, TX) 90045
Mutual Federal S & L Association (Monticello, KY) 69100
People's Bank (Bagdad, KY) 68109
Peoples Bank (Louisville, KY) 68943; 68944
Peoples Bank (Olive Hill, KY) 69158
Peoples Bank (Paint Lick, KY) 69215
Peoples Bank (Shelbyville, KY) 69277
Peoples Bank (Shepherdsville, KY) 69283; 69284; 69285
People's Bank (Taylorsville, KY) 69314
Peoples Bank (Tompkinsville, KY) 69317
People's Bank (Gulfport, MS) 72864
Peoples Bank (Arlington, TN) 80183
People's Bank (Clifton, TN) 80610
Peoples Bank (Collierville, TN) 80620; 80621
People's Bank (Dresden, TN) 80741
People's Bank (Humboldt, TN) 80959
People's Bank (Lebanon, TN) 81307
Peoples Bank (Memphis, TN) 81664; 81665
Peoples Bank (Ridgely, TN) 82248
People's Bank (Vanleer, TN) 82391
Peoples Bank (Charles Town, WV) 92722; 92723
Peoples Bank Crossville (Crossville, TN) 80704
Peoples Bank Elk Valley (Fayetteville, TN) 80798
Peoples Bank Elk Valley (Kelso, TN) 81068
Peoples Bank Hustonville (Stanford, KY) 69310
Peoples Bank of Morehead (Morehead, KY) 69103
Peoples Bank of Mullens (Mullens, WV) 92956
Peoples Bank of Murray (Murray, KY) 69128
Peoples Bank of Richwood Inc. (Richwood, WV) 93025
Peoples Bank & Trust Co. (Berea, KY) 68128
People's Bank & Trust Co. (Earlington, KY) 68268
Peoples Bank & Trust Co. (Hazard, KY) 68427
Peoples Bank & Trust Co. (Madisonville, KY) 69067; 69068; 69069
Peoples Bank & Trust Co. (Owenton, KY) 69200; 69201
Potomac Valley Bank (Petersburg, WV) 93002; 93003
Rapides Bank & Trust (Alexandria, LA) 69401
Rapides Bank & Trust Compan (Alexandria, LA) 69402; 69403
Rapides Bank & Trust Co. (Alexandria, LA) 69405; 69406; 69407; 69408
Rapides Bank & Trust Co. (Leesville, LA) 70191
Rapides Bank & Trust Co. (Pineville, LA) 70630
Rapides Bank & Trust Co. (Tioga, LA) 70915
Security Bank & Trust Co. (Maysville, KY) 69090
Security Bank & Trust Co. (Paris, TN) 82223
St Michaels Bank (St Michaels, MD) 72469
Standard Federal S & L Association (Baltimore, MD) 71313
Standard Federal S&L (Laurel, MD) 72091
Sunwest Bank of El Paso (El Paso, TX) 84935
Texas Commerce Bank National (Houston, TX) 87014; 87016; 87017; 87019; 87020
Texas Commerce Bank National (Humble, TX) 87251
Tri-City Bank & Trust Co. (Blountville, TN) 80205; 80206; 80207
Tri City Bank & Trust Co. (Kingsport, TN) 81120

Tri City Bank & Trust Co. (Piney Flats, TN) 82230
Tri-City & Trust Co. (Blountville, TN) 80208
Trust Co. Bank of South Georgia (Thomasville, GA) 67807
U S Bancorp Inc. (St Petersburg, FL) 63039
Union Bank (Jellico, TN) 81024
Union Bank (San Antonio, TX) 89281
Wachovia Bank & Tr Co. N a B (Winston Salem, NC) 76692
Wachovia Bank & Trust (Belmont, NC) 73675; 73676; 73677
Wachovia Bank & Trust (Charlotte, NC) 74197
Wachovia Bank & Trust (Durham, NC) 74434
Wachovia Bank & Trust (Fayetteville, NC) 74580
Wachovia Bank & Trust (Matthews, NC) 75532
Wachovia Bank & Trust Compa (Charlotte, NC) 74198
Wachovia Bank & Trust Compa (Hickory, NC) 75104
Wachovia Bank & Trust Compa (Wilson, NC) 76651
Wachovia Bank & Trust Co. (Asheboro, NC) 73599
Wachovia Bank & Trust Co. (Asheville, NC) 73639
Wachovia Bank & Trust Co. (Charlotte, NC) 74199
Wachovia Bank & Trust Co. (Gastonia, NC) 74692
Wachovia Bank & Trust Co. (Harkers is, NC) 75003
Wachovia Bank & Trust Co. (Laurinburg, NC) 75358
Wachovia Bank & Trust Co. (Mars Hill, NC) 75511; 75512
Wachovia Bank & Trust Co. (Morganton, NC) 75657
Wachovia Bank & Trust Co. (Pineville, NC) 75828
Wachovia Bank & Trust Co. (Rural Hall, NC) 76135
Wachovia Bank & Trust Co. (Williamston, NC) 76535; 76536
Wachovia Bank & Trust Co. (Wilson, NC) 76652
Wachovia Bank & Trust Co. N (Arden, NC) 73572
Wachovia Bank & Trust Co. N (Aurora, NC) 73645
Wachovia Bank & Trust Co. N (Belhaven, NC) 73671
Wachovia Bank & Trust Co. N (Belmont, NC) 73678; 73679
Wachovia Bank & Trust Co. N (Bethel, NC) 73691
Wachovia Bank & Trust Co. N (Chapel Hill, NC) 73824
Wachovia Bank & Trust Co. N (Charlotte, NC) 74201; 74202; 74204; 74205; 74206; 74207
Wachovia Bank & Trust Co. N (Durham, NC) 74438; 74439; 74440; 74441
Wachovia Bank & Trust Co. N (Eden, NC) 74469
Wachovia Bank & Trust Co. N (Fayetteville, NC) 74581
Wachovia Bank & Trust Co. N (Goldsboro, NC) 74741
Wachovia Bank & Trust Co. N (Greensboro, NC) 74932; 74934; 74935
Wachovia Bank & Trust Co. N (Greenville, NC) 74985; 74986; 74987; 74988
Wachovia Bank & Trust Co. N (Hamilton, NC) 74994
Wachovia Bank & Trust Co. N (High Point, NC) 75181; 75182; 75183
Wachovia Bank & Trust Co. N (Hildebran, NC) 75188
Wachovia Bank & Trust Co. N (Jamestown, NC) 75246
Wachovia Bank & Trust Co. N (Kernersville, NC) 75285
Wachovia Bank & Trust Co. N (Lumberton, NC) 75475
Wachovia Bank & Trust Co. N (Maxton, NC) 75536
Wachovia Bank & Trust Co. N (Mc Leansville, NC) 75543
Wachovia Bank & Trust Co. N (Mebane, NC) 75553
Wachovia Bank & Trust Co. N (Morganton, NC) 75658
Wachovia Bank & Trust Co. N (Mount Olive, NC) 75697
Wachovia Bank & Trust Co. N (Murphy, NC) 75711
Wachovia Bank & Trust Co. N (New Bern, NC) 75738
Wachovia Bank & Trust Co. N (Raleigh, NC) 75978; 75979; 75980; 75981

Wachovia Bank & Trust Co. N (Salisbury, NC) 76182; 76183; 76184
Wachovia Bank & Trust Co. N (Sanford, NC) 76208
Wachovia Bank & Trust Co. N (Sealevel, NC) 76216
Wachovia Bank & Trust Co. N (Vanceboro, NC) 76415
Wachovia Bank & Trust Co. N (Wilmington, NC) 76607; 76608; 76610; 76611
Wachovia Bank & Trust Co. N (Winston Salem, NC) 76695; 76696; 76697; 76699
Wachovia Bank & Trust Co. Na (Charlotte, NC) 74210; 74216
Wachovia Bank & Trust Co. NA (Greensboro, NC) 74941
Wachovia Bank & Trust Co. Na (Reidsville, NC) 76017
Wachovia Bank & Trust Co. Na (Rocky Mount, NC) 76110

6029 Commercial Banks Nec

Bank of Boston International (Miami, FL) 61174
Branch Banking & Trust Co. (Kings Mountain, NC) 75294
Branch Banking & Trust Co. (Lawndale, NC) 75360
Branch Banking & Trust Co. (Raleigh, NC) 75875; 75877
Citizens State Bank (Bald Knob, AR) 56736
Citizens State Bank (Tenaha, TX) 89655
City National Bank (Birmingham, AL) 55194; 55195
City National Bank (Pleasant Grove, AL) 56483
City National Bank (Baton Rouge, LA) 69488
City National Bank (Charlotte, NC) 73900; 73901; 73903
City National Bank (Plainview, TX) 88527
City National Bank (Wichita Falls, TX) 90070
Continental Bank (Harvey, LA) 69939
First Alabama Bank (Montgomery, AL) 56322
First Alabama Bank Athens (Elkmont, AL) 55677
First Alabama Bank Huntsvil (Huntsville, AL) 55931
First Alabama Bank Lee Cnty (Opelika, AL) 56416
First American Bank Maryland (Columbia, MD) 71585
First American Bank of Virginia (Alexandria, VA) 90190
First American Bank of Virginia (Arlington, VA) 90314
First Virginia Bank - Tidewater (Norfolk, VA) 91529
Lebanon Bank (Mount Juliet, TN) 81823
Madison Bank & Trust Co. (Tallulah, LA) 70907
People's Bank (Bradfordsville, KY) 68166
People's Bank (Gravel Switch, KY) 68400
People's Bank (Lebanon Junction, KY) 68511
People's Bank (Mount Eden, KY) 69112
Peoples Bank (Petersburg, TN) 82227
Peoples Bank (Ridgely, TN) 82248
People's Bank (Waynesboro, TN) 82407
Peoples Bank (Richwood, WV) 93024
Peoples Bank (Weirton, WV) 93098
Rapides Bank & Trust Co. (Alexandria, LA) 69404
Republic New York Trust Co. (Miami, FL) 61441
Wachovia Bank & Trust Co. (Asheville, NC) 73640
Wachovia Bank&Trust Co. Libr (Winston Salem, NC) 76700

6035 Federal Savings Institutions

American Savings of FL FSB (Boca Raton, FL) 58664
American Savings of FL FSB (Deerfield Beach, FL) 59264
American Savings of FL FSB (Ft. Lauderdale, FL) 59847; 59848
American Savings of FL FSB (Hallandale, FL) 59957
American Savings of FL FSB (Hollywood, FL) 60035; 60036

American Savings of FL FSB (Miami, FL) 61157; 61158; 61159; 61160; 61161
American Savings of FL FSB (Miami Beach, FL) 61518
American Savings of FL FSB (Pompano Beach, FL) 62581; 62582
American Savings of FL FSB (West Palm Beach, FL) 63837
American Savings of Florida (Boca Raton, FL) 58665
American Savings of Florida (Delray Beach, FL) 59305
American Savings of Florida (Ft. Lauderdale, FL) 59849
American Savings of Florida (Hollywood, FL) 60037
American Savings of Florida (Lake Worth, FL) 60662
American Savings of Florida (Miami, FL) 61162; 61163; 61164; 61165
American Savings of Florida, FSB (Boca Raton, FL) 58666; 58667
American Savings of Florida, FSB (Coconut Creek, FL) 59086
American Savings of Florida, FSB (Coral Gables, FL) 59092
American Savings of Florida, FSB (Coral Springs, FL) 59106
American Savings of Florida, FSB (Davie, FL) 59153
American Savings of Florida, FSB (Deerfield Beach, FL) 59265
American Savings of Florida, FSB (Delray Beach, FL) 59306; 59307
American Savings of Florida, FSB (Hallendale, FL) 59967
American Savings of Florida, FSB (Hollywood, FL) 60038
American Savings of Florida, FSB (Lake Worth, FL) 60663
American Savings of Florida, FSB (Lauderhill, FL) 60873
American Savings of Florida, FSB (Margate, FL) 60998
American Savings of Florida FSB (Miami, FL) 61167; 61168
American Savings of Florida, FSB (Miami Beach, FL) 61520; 61521; 61522; 61523
American Savings of Florida, FSB (North Miami, FL) 61730
American Savings of Florida, FSB (North Miami Beach, FL) 61739; 61740
American Savings of Florida, FSB (Pembroke Pines, FL) 62362; 62363
American Savings of Florida, FSB (Sunrise, FL) 63189; 63190
American Savings of Florida, FSB (Tamarac, FL) 63294
American Savings of Florida, FSB (West Palm Beach, FL) 63838
AmSouth Bank of Florida (Clearwater, FL) 58967
AmSouth Bank, N.A. (Birmingham, AL) 55131; 55132; 55133; 55134; 55135; 55136; 55137; 55138; 55139; 55140; 55141; 55142; 55143; 55144; 55145; 55146; 55147; 55148; 55149; 55150; 55151
AmSouth Bank of Walker County (Jasper, AL) 56077
Anchor Savings (Largo, FL) 60813
Anchor Savings Bank (Largo, FL) 60814
Anchor Savings Bank (Live Oak, FL) 60907
Anchor Savings Bank (St. Petersburg, FL) 63080
Anchor Savings Bank (Tampa, FL) 63324
Anchor Savings Bank Sun (Tampa, FL) 63325
Anchor Savings Bank F S B (Jacksonville, FL) 60181
Anchor Savings Bank F S B (Tallahassee, FL) 63209
Anchor Savings Bank, FSB (Callahan, FL) 58903
Anchor Savings Bank, FSB (Deerfield Beach, FL) 59266
Anchor Savings Bank, FSB (Fort Meyers, FL) 59655
Anchor Savings Bank, FSB (Jacksonville Beach, FL) 60517
Anchor Savings Bank, FSB (Naples, FL) 61600
Anchor Savings Bank, FSB (New Port Richey, FL) 61674
Anchor Savings Bank, FSB (St. Augustine Beach, FL) 63064
Anchor Savings Bank, FSB (Tallahassee, FL) 63210
Anchor Savings Bank FSB (Tampa, FL) 63326; 63327
Beneficial Corp. (Wilmington, DE) 58015
Beneficial Savings Bank, FSB (Tampa, FL) 63366

C S F Holdings Inc. (Miami, FL) 61220
California Federal Bank (St Petersburg, FL) 62966
California Federal Bank, AFSB (Delray Beach, FL) 59313
California Federal Bank, AFSB (Dunnellon, FL) 59373
California Federal Bank, AFSB (Fort Lauderdale, FL) 59464
Citibank Federal Savings Bank (Washington, DC) 58151; 58152; 58153; 58154; 58155; 58156; 58157; 58158; 58159; 58160; 58161; 58162; 58163; 58164; 58165; 58166
Citibank Federal Savings Bank (Miami, FL) 61234
Citibank, FSB (Clearwater, FL) 58985
Citibank, FSB (Coral Springs, FL) 59111; 59112
Citizens Federal Bank (Fort Lauderdale, FL) 59474
Collective Federal Savings Bank (Wilmington, DE) 58040
Columbia First Bank, A Federal Savings Bank (Washington, DC) 58168; 58169; 58170; 58171; 58172; 58173; 58174; 58175; 58176; 58177; 58178; 58179; 58180
Columbia 1st Bank FSB (Arlington, VA) 90285
Farm & Home Savings Associa (Austin, TX) 82876
Farm & Home Savings Associa (San Antonio, TX) 89005; 89006
Farm & Home Savings Association (Corpus Christi, TX) 83717
Farm & Home Savings Association (Fort Worth, TX) 85117
Farm & Home Savings Association (Houston, TX) 86188; 86189; 86190; 86191; 86192
Farm & Home Savings Association (San Antonio, TX) 89007
First Alabama Bank (Birmingham, AL) 55242
First Federal S & L (Florence, AL) 55736
First Federal S & L (Guntersville, AL) 55826
First Federal S & L (Sheffield, AL) 56549
First Federal S & L (Sylacauga, AL) 56586
First Federal S & L (Talladega, AL) 56593
First Federal S & L (Camden, AR) 56830
First Federal S & L (Harrison, AR) 57137
First Federal S & L (Mountain Home, AR) 57386
First Federal S & L (Cape Coral, FL) 58919
First Federal S & L (Milledgeville, GA) 66975
First Federal S & L (Valdosta, GA) 67944
First Federal S & L (Ashland, KY) 68096
First Federal S & L (Hazard, KY) 68425
First Federal S & L. (Lexington, KY) 68549; 68550; 68551
First Federal S & L (Houma, LA) 69953; 69954
First Federal S & L (Charlotte, NC) 73976
First Federal S & L (Durham, NC) 74398
First Federal S & L (Lincolnton, NC) 75439
First Federal S & L (Rockingham, NC) 76060
First Federal S & L (Cheraw, SC) 78922
First Federal S & L (Darlington, SC) 79146
First Federal S & L (Columbia, TN) 80627
First Federal S & L (Paris, TX) 88366
First Federal S & L (Tyler, TX) 89801
First Federal S & L (Fairfax, VA) 90772
First Federal S & L (Ravenswood, WV) 93022
First Federal S&L of America (Front Royal, VA) 90949
First Federal S&L of America (Lynchburg, VA) 91242; 91242; 91243
First Federal S&L of America (South Boston, VA) 92249
First Gibraltar Bank (Enid, OK) 77052
Firstfed Bancorp Inc. (Bessemer, AL) 55090

Firstfed Northern Kentucky Bancorporation (Covington, KY) 68217
Firstfed Northern Kentucky Bancorporation Inc. (Covington, KY) 68218
Fortune Bank (Clearwater, FL) 59009
Fortune Bank (Punta Gorda, FL) 62708
Georgia Federal Bank F S B (Albany, GA) 64074
Georgia Federal Bank, FSB (Atlanta, GA) 64504
Georgia Federal Bank FSB (Savannah, GA) 67478
Great Western Bank (Fort Myers, FL) 59701
Great Western Bank (Lake Worth, FL) 60673
J P Morgan Services (Newark, DE) 57911
Metropolitan Federal Saving (Arlington, VA) 90360
Mutual Savings & Loan Assoc (Metairie, LA) 70294
Mutual Savings & Loan Assoc (Durham, NC) 74420
Mutual Savings & Loan Assoc (Greensboro, NC) 74869
Standard Federal Savings Bank (Columbia, SC) 79097
Standard Federal Savings Bank (West Columbia, SC) 80108; 80109
Star Bank NA, Kentucky (Verona, KY) 69324
Star Bank NA, Kentucky (Walton, KY) 69335
World Savings & Loan (Temple, TX) 89654

6036 Savings Institutions Except Federal

American Savings Bank (Livingston, TN) 81348
AmSouth Bank of Tennessee (Nashville, TN) 81892
Anchor Savings Bank (St. Petersburg, FL) 63080
Bank South Macon (Macon, GA) 66655
Columbia First Bank, FSB (Arlington, VA) 90284
Commercial Bank (Bowdon, GA) 65388
Community Bank & Trust of Randolph County (Elkins, WV) 92833
Farm & Home Savings Association (Bedford, TX) 83241
Farm & Home Savings Association (Dallas, TX) 84060
Farm & Home Savings Association (Plano, TX) 88567
Farmers Bank & Trust Co. (Marion, KY) 69076
First Financial Bank a Fsb (El Dorado, AR) 56942
Fortune Bancorp Inc. (Clearwater, FL) 59005
Fortune Bancorporation (Clearwater, FL) 59008
Georgia Federal Bank FSB (Savannah, GA) 67478
Peoples Bank & Trust Co. (Greensburg, KY) 68404
Peoples Bank & Trust Co. (Owenton, KY) 69200
Standard Federal S & L Association (Greenbelt, MD) 71878
Western Carolina Savings (Valdese, NC) 76414

6061 Federal Credit Unions

AFLAC Federal Credit Union (Columbus, GA) 65615
American Family Life Assurance Co. (Columbus, GA) 65617
American General Federal Credit Union (Baltimore, MD) 71038
American General Federal Credit Union (Nashville, TN) 81882
American General Federal Credit Union (Houston, TX) 85780
Arcadian Corp. (Memphis, TN) 81460
Arco Oil & Gas Co. (Dallas, TX) 83857
Arkansas Best Corp. (Fort Smith, AR) 57023
AT & T Family Federal Credit Union (Jacksonville, FL) 60183
AT & T Family Federal Credit Union (Asheboro, NC) 73576
AT & T Family Federal Credit Union (Burlington, NC) 73741
AT & T Family Federal Credit Union (Charlotte, NC) 73842
AT & T Family Federal Credit Union (Greensboro, NC) 74778; 74779
AT & T Family Federal Credit Union (McAdenville, NC) 75544
AT & T Family Federal Credit Union (Shelby, NC) 76231
AT & T Family Federal Credit Union (Winston-Salem, NC) 76704; 76705; 76706; 76707
AT & T Family Federal Credit Union (Martinsville, VA) 91342
AT & T Family Federal Credit Union (Radford, VA) 91688
AT & T Family Federal Credit Union (Richmond, VA) 91736
AT&T Family Federal Credit Union (Charlotte, NC) 73843
AT&T Family Federal Credit Union (McAdenville, NC) 75545
Atlantic Richfield Credit Union (Pasadena, TX) 88387
Ball-Incon Glass Packaging (Henderson, NC) 75018; 75019
BASF Corp. Fibers Division (Anderson, SC) 78664
BASF Federal Credit Union (Chattanooga, TN) 80330
Baxter Healthcare Corp. (Marion, NC) 75497
Bowater Inc. Carolina Div. (Catawba, SC) 78771
Bowaters Carolina Federal Credit Union (Lancaster, SC) 79567
Chesapeake & Potomac Telephone Co. (Richmond, VA) 91765
Mobil Alaska Pipeline Co. (Dallas, TX) 84238
Monsanto Anniston Empl Crdt Un (Anniston, AL) 55005
Monsanto Car Employees Cr (Greenwood, SC) 79458
Monsanto Co. (Nitro, WV) 92972
Monsanto Employees Cr Union (Pensacola, FL) 62451
Zebco Corp. (Tulsa, OK) 78214

6062 State Credit Unions

Aetna Financial Services Inc. (Gainesville, GA) 66264
AT & T Employees Credit Union (Dallas, TX) 83863
Ball Corp. (North Charleston, SC) 79744
Beneficial Texas Inc. (Austin, TX) 82825
Beneficial Texas Inc. (Midland, TX) 88023
Beneficial Texas Inc. (Plainview, TX) 88525
Beneficial Texas Inc. (Tyler, TX) 89791
Blazer Financial Services (Bristol, TN) 80238
Blazer Financial Services (Gallatin, TN) 80838
Blazer Financial Services (Memphis, TN) 81477
Blazer Financial Services (Murfreesboro, TN) 81836
Blazer Financial Services I (Virginia Beach, VA) 92441
Builders Square (San Antonio, TX) 88936
Crestar Mortgage Corp. (Lexington, KY) 68540
Exxon Credit Union (Overton, TX) 88335
First Federal S & L (Lexington, KY) 68550
Fleet Finance Inc. (Brandon, FL) 58870
Fleet Finance Inc. (Live Oak, FL) 60909
Fleet Finance Inc. (Alexandria, LA) 69378
Fleet Finance Inc. (Monroe, LA) 70353
Fleet Finance Inc. (New Orleans, LA) 70454
Fleet Finance Inc. (Jackson, MS) 72984
Great Western Bank (Daytona Beach, FL) 59183
Mellon Financial Services Corp. (West Palm Beach, FL) 63886
Mobil Credit Union (Electra, TX) 84985
Norwest Mortgage Inc. (Greensboro, NC) 74871
Student Loan Marketing Association (Antioch, TN) 80175
Texaco P a W Employees Fede (Port Arthur, TX) 88651
Textron Financial Corp. (Louisville, KY) 69020
Valley National Financial Service (Oklahoma City, OK) 77647
Valley National Financial Service (Fort Worth, TX) 85343
Valley National Financial Service (San Antonio, TX) 89291
Whirlpool Financial Corp. (Charlotte, NC) 74230

6081 Foreign Banks—Branches & Agencies

Bank of Boston International (Miami, FL) 61172
Citizens State Bank (Lometa, TX) 87698
First State Bank & Trust Co. (Lake Village, AR) 57240
Peoples Bank (Hustonville, KY) 68485
People's Bank (Clifton, TN) 80610

6082 Foreign Trade & International Banks

Bank of Boston International (Miami, FL) 61173

6091 Nondeposit Trust Facilities

Ameritrust Texas NA (Dallas, TX) 83851
Bank of Boston-Florida (Palm Beach, FL) 62245
Bank of Boston-Florida (Sarasota, FL) 62787
Bank of Boston-Florida N.A. (Palm Beach, FL) 62246
Bank South Macon (Macon, GA) 66655
Fleet Trust Co. of Florida, NA (Naples, FL) 61623

6099 Functions Related to Deposit Banking

American Savings of Florida (Clearwater, FL) 58960
American Savings of Florida (Delray Beach, FL) 59304
American Savings of Florida (Fort Lauderdale, FL) 59440
American Savings of Florida (Miami Beach, FL) 61519
American Savings of Florida (N Miami Beach, FL) 61591
American Savings of Florida (Sunrise, FL) 63188
AmSouth Bank, N.A. (Birmingham, AL) 55131; 55132; 55133; 55134; 55135; 55136; 55137; 55138; 55139; 55140; 55141; 55142; 55143; 55144; 55145; 55146; 55147; 55148; 55149; 55150; 55151
Anchor Savings Bank F S B (Macclenny, FL) 60959
Anchor Savings Bank FSB (Callahan, FL) 58904
Bank South NA-Savannah (Savannah, GA) 67453
Branch Banking & Trust Co. (Charlotte, NC) 73878; 73879
Branch Banking & Trust Co. (Fayetteville, NC) 74539
Branch Banking & Trust Co. (Gastonia, NC) 74665; 74667
Branch Banking & Trust Co. (Goldsboro, NC) 74707
Branch Banking & Trust Co. (Raleigh, NC) 75874
Branch Banking & Trust Co. (Columbia, SC) 78989
Branch Banking & Trust Co. (Greer, SC) 79471
California Federal Bank (Boca Raton, FL) 58682
California Federal Bank (Dunnellon, FL) 59372
California Federal Bank (Fort Lauderdale, FL) 59462
California Federal Bank (Orange City, FL) 61869
California Federal Bank (Spring Hill, FL) 62933
California Federal Bank (Tampa, FL) 63373
California Federal Bank (West Palm Beach, FL) 63851
Citizens State Bank (Reynolds, GA) 67295
Citizens State Bank (Georgetown, TX) 85565
Citizens State Bank-Edna of (Edna, TX) 84743
City National Bank (Fort Smith, AR) 57037
City National Bank (North Bay Village, FL) 61727
City National Bank (Baton Rouge, LA) 69486; 69490; 69492
City National Bank (Carrollton, TX) 83458
City National Bank (Charleston, WV) 92734
City National Bank of Fl (Miami, FL) 61256; 61257
City National Bank of Fl (N Miami Beach, FL) 61592
City National Bank of Flori (Miami, FL) 61258
City National Bank of Miami (Miami, FL) 61260
City National Bank & Trust (Lawton, OK) 77157
First Alabama Bank (Albertville, AL) 54963
First Alabama Bank (Cullman, AL) 55541
First Alabama Bank (Huntsville, AL) 55925; 55927
First Alabama Bank (Madison, AL) 56120
First Alabama Bank (Montgomery, AL) 56323; 56326
First Alabama Bank (Pennington, AL) 56454
First Alabama Bank (Selma, AL) 56527
First Alabama Bank (Tuscaloosa, AL) 56649
First Alabama Bank Huntsville (Huntsville, AL) 55934
First American Bank (Laurel, MD) 72071
First American Bank (Alexandria, VA) 90180; 90181; 90182; 90183; 90184
First American Bank (Annandale, VA) 90259
First American Bank (Arlington, VA) 90301; 90302; 90303; 90304; 90305; 90306; 90307
First American Bank (Bridgewater, VA) 90466
First American Bank (Burke, VA) 90500
First American Bank (Fairfax, VA) 90767; 90768; 90769
First American Bank (Falls Church, VA) 90832
First American Bank (Hampton, VA) 91025; 91026; 91027
First American Bank (Herndon, VA) 91121
First American Bank (Mc Lean, VA) 91365
First American Bank (Newport News, VA) 91462; 91463
First American Bank (Purcellville, VA) 91681
First American Bank (Springfield, VA) 92278; 92279
First American Bank (Staunton, VA) 92314; 92315
First American Bank (Vienna, VA) 92401; 92402
First American Bank Maryland (Baltimore, MD) 71119; 71120
First American Bank Maryland (Columbia, MD) 71586
First American Bank Maryland (Frederick, MD) 71723; 71724
First American Bank NA (Gaithersburg, MD) 71776
First American Bank NA (Laurel, MD) 72072
First American Bank of Virginia (Hampton, VA) 91030
First American Bank of Virginia (Norfolk, VA) 91521
First American National Bank (Golden, MS) 72788
First American National Bank (Bristol, VA) 90474
First Bank (Indiantown, FL) 60141
First Bank (Covington, LA) 69793
First Bank (Mandeville, LA) 70207
First Bank (Slidell, LA) 70824
First Bank (Brookhaven, MS) 72654
First Bank (Liberty, MS) 73117
First Bank (Albemarle, NC) 73528; 73530; 73531
First Bank (Chattanooga, OK) 76914
First Bank (Celeste, TX) 83535
First National Bank Maryland (Silver Spring, MD) 72401
First National Bank & Trust (Port St Lucie, FL) 62685
First National Bank & Trust Co. (Louisville, GA) 66619
First State Bank & Trust Co. (Albany, GA) 64068; 64069; 64070; 64071
First State Bank & Trust Co. (Valdosta, GA) 67946; 67948
Georgia Federal Bank F S B (Hinesville, GA) 66353
Georgia Federal Bank F S B (Marietta, GA) 66782
Georgia Federal Bank, F S B (Savannah, GA) 67477
Glendale Federal Bank F S B (West Palm Beach, FL) 63868
Great Western Bank (Boca Raton, FL) 58707; 58709
Great Western Bank (Coral Springs, FL) 59115
Great Western Bank (Gulf Breeze, FL) 59937
Great Western Bank (Lake Worth, FL) 60671; 60672
Great Western Bank (Orlando, FL) 61998
Great Western Bank (Pensacola, FL) 62433
Great Western Bank (Stuart, FL) 63168
Great Western Bank (West Palm Beach, FL) 63870
Hibernia National Bank (Alexandria, LA) 69380; 69381; 69383
Hibernia National Bank (Baton Rouge, LA) 69545; 69549; 69550; 69551; 69552
Hibernia National Bank (Lacombe, LA) 70037
Hibernia National Bank (Livingston, LA) 70193
Hibernia National Bank (Metairie, LA) 70269
Hibernia National Bank (New Orleans, LA) 70501; 70503; 70504; 70505
Hibernia National Bank (Pineville, LA) 70616; 70617
Hibernia National Bank (Reserve, LA) 70661
Hibernia National Bank (Carrollton, TX) 83468
Hibernia National Bank (Dallas, TX) 84123
Israel Discount Bank Ltd (Miami, FL) 61333
Lebanon Bank (Mount Juliet, TN) 81823
Mobil Oil Federal Credit Un (Beaumont, TX) 83184
People's Bank (Statham, GA) 67654
People's Bank (Morehead, KY) 69102
People's Bank (Alamo, TN) 80146
People's Bank (Brownsville, TN) 80260
People's Bank (Henning, TN) 80921
People's Bank (Norene, TN) 82178
People's Bank (Pointe Pleasant, WV) 93007
Peoples Bank & Trust (Cookeville, TN) 80662
Rapides Bank & Trust Co. (Pineville, LA) 70628; 70629
Standard Federal Savings Bank (Columbia, SC) 79096
Texaco Inc. (Bellaire, TX) 83267
Texas Commerce Bank National (Houston, TX) 87015; 87018
Union Bank (Lakeland, FL) 60790
Union Bank (Jamestown, TN) 81019
Wachovia Bank & Tr Co. N a B (Burlington, NC) 73763
Wachovia Bank & Tr Co. N a B (Winston Salem, NC) 76691; 76692
Wachovia Bank & Trust (Asheboro, NC) 73598
Wachovia Bank & Trust (Atlantic Beach, NC) 73643
Wachovia Bank & Trust (Bayboro, NC) 73665
Wachovia Bank & Trust (Beaufort, NC) 73670
Wachovia Bank & Trust (Bostic, NC) 73722
Wachovia Bank & Trust (Cary, NC) 73801
Wachovia Bank & Trust (Cashiers, NC) 73802
Wachovia Bank & Trust (Chapel Hill, NC) 73822; 73823
Wachovia Bank & Trust (Charlotte, NC) 74196
Wachovia Bank & Trust (Clemmons, NC) 74273
Wachovia Bank & Trust (Concord, NC) 74324
Wachovia Bank & Trust (Durham, NC) 74433
Wachovia Bank & Trust (E Fayettevlle, NC) 74445
Wachovia Bank & Trust (Elizabeth City, NC) 74485
Wachovia Bank & Trust (Gastonia, NC) 74691
Wachovia Bank & Trust (Greensboro, NC) 74930
Wachovia Bank & Trust (Hendersonville, NC) 75045
Wachovia Bank and Trust (High Point, NC) 75179; 75180
Wachovia Bank & Trust (Kill Devil Hills, NC) 75288
Wachovia Bank & Trust (New Bern, NC) 75737
Wachovia Bank & Trust (Raleigh, NC) 75973

Wachovia Bank & Trust (Winston Salem, NC) 76693
Wachovia Bank & Trust Compa (Albemarle, NC) 73543
Wachovia Bank & Trust Co. (Apex, NC) 73560
Wachovia Bank & Trust Co. (Asheboro, NC) 73600
Wachovia Bank & Trust Co. (Durham, NC) 74435; 74436; 74437
Wachovia Bank & Trust Co. (Greensboro, NC) 74931
Wachovia Bank & Trust Co. (Greenville, NC) 74984
Wachovia Bank & Trust Co. (Raleigh, NC) 75974; 75975
Wachovia Bank & Trust Co. (Thomasville, NC) 76403
Wachovia Bank & Trust Co. (Wilmington, NC) 76605
Wachovia Bank & Trust Co. N (Asheville, NC) 73641
Wachovia Bank & Trust Co. N (Greensboro, NC) 74933
Wachovia Bank & Trust Co. N (Jacksonville, NC) 75232
Wachovia Bank & Trust Co. N (Morehead City, NC) 75628
Wachovia Bank & Trust Co. N (Raleigh, NC) 75976; 75977
Wachovia Bank & Trust Co. N (Wilmington, NC) 76606; 76609
Wachovia Bank & Trust Co. N (Winston Salem, NC) 76698
Wachovia Bank & Trust Co. Na (Charlotte, NC) 74211; 74213; 74215
Wachovia Bank & Trust Co. Na (Greensboro, NC) 74936; 74937; 74939; 74940
Wachovia Bank & Trust Co. Na (Reidsville, NC) 76016

6100 Nondepository Institutions

Bank South Leasing, Inc. (Atlanta, GA) 64256

6111 Federal & Federally-Sponsored Credit

AmSouth Bank, N.A. (Birmingham, AL) 55131; 55132; 55133; 55134; 55135; 55136; 55137; 55138; 55139; 55140; 55141; 55142; 55143; 55144; 55145; 55146; 55147; 55148; 55149; 55150; 55151
Federal Home Loan Mortgage Corp. (McLean, VA) 91383
Federal Home Loan Mortgage Corp. (Freddic Mac)-Northeast Region (Arlington, VA) 90300
Federal Home Loan Mortgage Corp. (Freddie Mac)-Southeast/Southwest Region (Atlanta, GA) 64442

6141 Personal Credit Institutions

American Financial Service Inc. (Houston, TX) 85777
American General Corp. (Houston, TX) 85779
American General Finance (Bessemer, AL) 55082
American General Finance (Birmingham, AL) 55121; 55122
American General Finance (Decatur, AL) 55573
American General Finance (Gadsden, AL) 55772
American General Finance (Huntsville, AL) 55878
American General Finance (Mobile, AL) 56136
American General Finance (Montgomery, AL) 56277
American General Finance (Dover, DE) 57779
American General Finance (Laurel, DE) 57824
American General Finance (Milford, DE) 57836
American General Finance (Newark, DE) 57886
American General Finance (Smyrna, DE) 57957
American General Finance (Fort Lauderdale, FL) 59434; 59435; 59436
American General Finance (Hollywood, FL) 60033
American General Finance (Jacksonville, FL) 60164; 60165; 60166; 60167; 60168; 60169
American General Finance (Orlando, FL) 61908; 61909
American General Finance (Tallahassee, FL) 63204
American General Finance (Tampa, FL) 63310; 63311; 63312; 63313; 63314
American General Finance (Atlanta, GA) 64225; 64226; 64227; 64228
American General Finance (Columbus, GA) 65619
American General Finance (Macon, GA) 66648
American General Finance (Roswell, GA) 67357
American General Finance (Savannah, GA) 67441; 67442
American General Finance (Hazard, KY) 68422
American General Finance (Hopkinsville, KY) 68472
American General Finance (Lexington, KY) 68518
American General Finance (Louisville, KY) 68675; 68676; 68677; 68678; 68679; 68680
American General Finance (Radcliff, KY) 69237
American General Finance (Baton Rouge, LA) 69463; 69464; 69465
American General Finance (Metairie, LA) 70246
American General Finance (New Orleans, LA) 70429
American General Finance (Shreveport, LA) 70682
American General Finance (Owings Mills, MD) 72182
American General Finance (Jackson, MS) 72941
American General Finance (Burlington, NC) 73739
American General Finance (Charlotte, NC) 73837
American General Finance (Durham, NC) 74382; 74383
American General Finance (Fayetteville, NC) 74525; 74526
American General Finance (Goldsboro, NC) 74700
American General Finance (Greensboro, NC) 74763; 74764; 74765
American General Finance (Greenville, NC) 74947; 74948
American General Finance (Hendersonville, NC) 75030
American General Finance (Matthews, NC) 75517
American General Finance (Raleigh, NC) 75854; 75855; 75856
American General Finance (Wilson, NC) 76615
American General Finance (Winston Salem, NC) 76660
American General Finance (Oklahoma City, OK) 77296; 77297
American General Finance (Tulsa, OK) 77876
American General Finance (Antioch, TN) 80162
American General Finance (Chattanooga, TN) 80293; 80294
American General Finance (Cleveland, TN) 80566
American General Finance (Hermitage, TN) 80922
American General Finance (Hixson, TN) 80928
American General Finance (Knoxville, TN) 81135; 81136
American General Finance (Madison, TN) 81370
American General Finance (Memphis, TN) 81450; 81451; 81452
American General Finance (Nashville, TN) 81883; 81884
American General Finance (El Paso, TX) 84756
American General Finance (Falls Church, VA) 90816
American General Finance (Hampton, VA) 91011; 91012
American General Finance (Newport News, VA) 91450
American General Finance (Richmond, VA) 91728
American General Finance (Virginia Beach, VA) 92431
American General Finance Co. (Metairie, LA) 70247
American General Finance Co., Inc. (Mobile, AL) 56137
American General Finance Inc. (Bessemer, AL) 55083
American General Finance Inc. (Birmingham, AL) 55123; 55124; 55125
American General Finance Inc. (Decatur, AL) 55574
American General Finance Inc. (Gadsden, AL) 55773
American General Finance Inc. (Huntsville, AL) 55879
American General Finance Inc. (Mobile, AL) 56138; 56139
American General Finance Inc. (Montgomery, AL) 56278
American General Finance Inc. (Dover, DE) 57780
American General Finance Inc. (Laurel, DE) 57825
American General Finance Inc. (Milford, DE) 57837
American General Finance Inc. (Newark, DE) 57887
American General Finance Inc. (Smyrna, DE) 57958
American General Finance Inc. (Fort Lauderdale, FL) 59437; 59438; 59439
American General Finance Inc. (Hollywood, FL) 60034
American General Finance Inc. (Jacksonville, FL) 60170; 60171; 60172; 60173; 60174; 60175
American General Finance Inc. (Orlando, FL) 61910; 61911; 61912
American General Finance Inc. (Tallahassee, FL) 63205
American General Finance Inc. (Tampa, FL) 63315; 63316; 63317; 63318; 63319
American General Finance Inc. (Atlanta, GA) 64229; 64230; 64231; 64232
American General Finance Inc. (Columbus, GA) 65620; 65621; 65622
American General Finance Inc. (Macon, GA) 66649; 66650
American General Finance Inc. (Roswell, GA) 67358
American General Finance Inc. (Savannah, GA) 67443; 67444
American General Finance Inc. (Hazard, KY) 68423
American General Finance Inc. (Hopkinsville, KY) 68473
American General Finance Inc. (Lexington, KY) 68519
American General Finance Inc. (Louisville, KY) 68681; 68682; 68683; 68684; 68685; 68686
American General Finance Inc. (Radcliff, KY) 69238
American General Finance Inc. (Baton Rouge, LA) 69466; 69467; 69468
American General Finance Inc. (Metairie, LA) 70248; 70249
American General Finance Inc. (New Orleans, LA) 70430
American General Finance Inc. (Shreveport, LA) 70683; 70684; 70685; 70686; 70687; 70688; 70689
American General Finance Inc. (Owings Mills, MD) 72183
American General Finance Inc. (Jackson, MS) 72942; 72943; 72944
American General Finance Inc. (Burlington, NC) 73740
American General Finance Inc. (Charlotte, NC) 73838; 73839
American General Finance Inc. (Durham, NC) 74384; 74385
American General Finance Inc. (Fayetteville, NC) 74527; 74528
American General Finance Inc. (Goldsboro, NC) 74701
American General Finance Inc. (Greensboro, NC) 74766; 74767; 74768
American General Finance Inc. (Greenville, NC) 74949; 74950
American General Finance Inc. (Hendersonville, NC) 75031
American General Finance Inc. (Hickory, NC) 75057
American General Finance Inc. (Raleigh, NC) 75857; 75858; 75859
American General Finance Inc. (Wilson, NC) 76616
American General Finance Inc. (Winston Salem, NC) 76661; 76662; 76663
American General Finance Inc. (Oklahoma City, OK) 77298; 77299
American General Finance Inc. (Tulsa, OK) 77877; 77878
American General Finance Inc. (Tulso, OK) 78218
American General Finance Inc. (Columbia, SC) 78971; 78972
American General Finance Inc. (Antioch, TN) 80163
American General Finance Inc. (Chattanooga, TN) 80295; 80296
American General Finance Inc. (Cleveland, TN) 80567
American General Finance Inc. (Hermitage, TN) 80923
American General Finance Inc. (Hixson, TN) 80929
American General Finance Inc. (Knoxville, TN) 81137; 81138
American General Finance Inc. (Madison, TN) 81371
American General Finance Inc. (Memphis, TN) 81453; 81454; 81455; 81456; 81457
American General Finance Inc. (Nashville, TN) 81885; 81886
American General Finance Inc. (El Paso, TX) 84757
American General Finance Inc. (Falls Church, VA) 90817
American General Finance Inc. (Hampton, VA) 91013; 91014
American General Finance Inc. (Martinsville, VA) 91340; 91341
American General Finance Inc. (Newport News, VA) 91451
American General Finance Inc. (Norfolk, VA) 91498; 91499
American General Finance Inc. (Portsmouth, VA) 91639; 91640
American General Finance Inc. (Richmond, VA) 91729; 91730; 91731; 91732; 91733
American Savings of FL FSB (Miami, FL) 61161
American Savings of Florida (Tampa, FL) 63320; 63321
AmSouth Bank (Bessemer, AL) 55085
AmSouth Financial Corp. (Birmingham, AL) 55153
Anchor Mortgage Services Inc. (Tampa, FL) 63323
Anchor Savings Bank, FSB (Deerfield Beach, FL) 59266
Anchor Savings Bank, FSB (Fort Meyers, FL) 59655
Anchor Savings Bank, FSB (Naples, FL) 61600
Aristar Inc. (Cordova, TN) 80673
BancBoston Mortagage Corp. (Huntsville, AL) 55886
BancBoston Mortgage Corp. (Montgomery, AL) 56281
BancBoston Mortgage Corp. (Ft. Lauderdale, FL) 59850
BancBoston Mortgage Corp. (Tampa, FL) 63334
BancBoston Mortgage Corp. (Raleigh, NC) 75862
BancBoston Mortgage Corp. (Virginia Beach, VA) 92435
Bank of Boston Corp. (Dallas, TX) 83870
Bank South (Athens, GA) 64160
Bank South (Monticello, GA) 66997
Bank South (Smyrna, GA) 67542
Bank South (Tennille, GA) 67782
Bank South-Douglas (Douglas, GA) 65964
Bank South Houston Co. (Perry, GA) 67259
Bank South Macon (Macon, GA) 66655
Bank South Mortgate Inc. (Atlanta, GA) 64260
Bank South NA (Conyers, GA) 65669
Bank South NA (Griffin, GA) 66309
Bank South NA (Marietta, GA) 66753; 66754; 66754
Bank South NA (Riverdale, GA) 67305
Bank South NA (Roswell, GA) 67360
Bank South NA (Union City, GA) 67911
Bank South NA (Columbia, SC) 78974
Bankers Trust Co. (Houston, TX) 85864
Bankers Trust of Madison (Ardmore, AL) 55029
Bankers Trust of North Carolina (Asheboro, NC) 73577
Bankers Trust of North Carolina (Greensboro, NC) 74787
Bell Atlantic Tricon (Atlanta, GA) 64300
Bell Atlantic Tricon Lease Corp. (Tampa, FL) 63364
Bencharge Credit Service of America, Inc. (Wilmington, DE) 58013
Bencharge Credit Services LA Inc. (New Orleans, LA) 70434
Beneficial Corp. (Wilmington, DE) 58015
Beneficial Delaware Inc. (Dover, DE) 57784
Beneficial Delaware Inc. (Newark, DE) 57895
Beneficial Finance Co. (Columbia, SC) 78975
Beneficial Florida Inc. (Pensacola, FL) 62409
Beneficial Georgia Inc. (Kennesaw, GA) 66409
Beneficial Georgia Inc. (Tucker, GA) 67847
Beneficial Income Tax Service (Woodward, OK) 78259
Beneficial Management Corp. America (Fayetteville, NC) 74529
Beneficial Maryland Inc. (Baltimore, MD) 71064
Beneficial Mgmt Corp. (Jacksonville, FL) 60229
Beneficial Mississippi Inc. (Ocean Springs, MS) 73221
Beneficial Mortgage Co. of Maryland (Gaithersburg, MD) 71764
Beneficial Mortgage Co. of MD (California, MD) 71482
Beneficial Mortgage Co. of Oklahoma (Oklahoma City, OK) 77305
Beneficial North Carolina Inc. (Fayetteville, NC) 74530
Beneficial North Carolina Inc. (Raleigh, NC) 75864
Beneficial North Carolina Inc. (Rocky Mount, NC) 76074
Beneficial Oklahoma Inc. (Oklahoma City, OK) 77306; 77307
Beneficial Tennessee Inc. (Nashville, TN) 81902
Beneficial Texas Inc. (Carrollton, TX) 83453
Beneficial Texas Inc. (Dallas, TX) 83877; 83878
Beneficial Texas Inc. (El Paso, TX) 84768; 84769
Beneficial Texas Inc. (Garland, TX) 85477
Beneficial Texas Inc. (Houston, TX) 85869; 85870; 85871; 85872; 85873; 85874
Beneficial Texas, Inc. (Pasadena, TX) 88388; 88389
Beneficial Texas Inc. (Plainview, TX) 88525
Beneficial Texas Inc. (Portland, TX) 88686
Beneficial Texas Inc. (San Antonio, TX) 88926; 88927; 88928
Beneficial Virginia Inc. (Alexandra, VA) 90163
Beneficial Virginia Inc. (Chesapeake, VA) 90556
Beneficial Virginia Inc. (Fairfax, VA) 90754
Beneficial Virginia Inc. (Newport News, VA) 91452
Beneficial Virginia Inc. (Virginia Beach, VA) 92436
Beneficial Virgnia Inc. (Chesapeake, VA) 90557
Blazer Financial Services (Camden Wy, DE) 57757
Blazer Financial Services (Dover, DE) 57786
Blazer Financial Services (Milford, DE) 57840
Blazer Financial Services (New Castle, DE) 57858
Blazer Financial Services (Newark, DE) 57899
Blazer Financial Services (Baltimore, MD) 71067; 71068
Blazer Financial Services (Bristol, TN) 80238
Blazer Financial Services (Clarksville, TN) 80537
Blazer Financial Services (Cleveland, TN) 80571
Blazer Financial Services (Columbia, TN) 80625
Blazer Financial Services (Jackson, TN) 80965
Blazer Financial Services (Johnson City, TN) 81025
Blazer Financial Services (Memphis, TN) 81476; 81477; 81478
Blazer Financial Services (Murfreesboro, TN) 81836
Blazer Financial Services (Culpeper, VA) 90672
Blazer Financial Services (Danville, VA) 90685
Blazer Financial Services (Falls Church, VA) 90819
Blazer Financial Services (Petersburg, VA) 91628
Blazer Financial Services (Richmond, VA) 91746
Blazer Financial Services (Virginia Beach, VA) 92440
Blazer Financial Services Inc. (Cordova, TN) 80674
Capital Finance Group, Inc. (Charlotte, NC) 73888
Chase Home Mortgage Corp. (Orlando, FL) 61947
Chase Home Mortgage Corp. (Tampa, FL) 63383

Chase Home Mortgage Corp. (West Palm Beach, FL) 63852
Chase Home Mortgage Corp. (Winter Park, FL) 63965
Citizens State Bank (Nashville, AR) 57439
Citizens State Bank (Earth, TX) 84724
City National Bank (Sylacauga, AL) 56576
City National Bank (Fort Smith, AR) 57037
City National Bank (Miami, FL) 61250; 61251
City National Bank (Weslaco, TX) 90033
City National Bank of Fairmont (Fairmont, WV) 92837
City National Bank of Florida (Hallandale, FL) 59959
City National Bank of Fulton (Fulton, KY) 68375
City National Bank of Kilgore (Kilgore, TX) 87486
City National Bank Laredo (Laredo, TX) 87608
City National Bank of San Saba (San Saba, TX) 89346
City National Bank of Sulphur Spring (Sulphur Spring, TX) 89549
City National Bank Sylacauga (Sylacauga, AL) 56579
City National Bank of Taylor (Taylor, TX) 89598
Collective Mortgage Service (Winter Park, FL) 63968
Deposit Guaranty Mortgage C (Meridian, MS) 73162
Deposit Guaranty Mortgage C (Tupelo, MS) 73399
Finance Co. (Manassas, VA) 91308
First American Bank Maryland (Annapolis, MD) 71011
First Bank (Covington, LA) 69793
First Federal S & L (Guntersville, AL) 55826
First Federal S & L (Talladega, AL) 56593
First Federal S & L (Harrison, AR) 57137
First Federal S & L (Mountain Home, AR) 57386
First Federal S & L (Valdosta, GA) 67944
First Federal S & L (Ashland, KY) 68096
First Federal S & L (Durham, NC) 74398
First Federal S & L (Lincolnton, NC) 75439
First Federal S & L (Darlington, SC) 79146
First Federal S & L (Columbia, TN) 80627
First Federal S & L (Ravenswood, WV) 93022
First Louisiana Acceptance Corp. (Metairie, LA) 70261
First Mutual Financial Corp. (Houston, TX) 86197; 86198
First Mutual Investments (Knoxville, TN) 81184
First National Bank & Trust (Ponca City, OK) 77704
First Security Mortgage Cor (Metairie, LA) 70262
Fleet Finance Inc. (Brandon, FL) 58870
Fleet Finance Inc. (Live Oak, FL) 60909
Fleet Finance, Inc. (Atlanta, GA) 64470
Fleet Finance Inc. (Arabi, LA) 69425
Fleet Finance Inc. (Houma, LA) 69955
Fleet Finance Inc. (Lafayette, LA) 70055
Fleet Finance Inc. (Monroe, LA) 70353
Fleet Finance Inc. (New Iberia, LA) 70408
Fleet Finance Inc. (New Orleans, LA) 70455; 70457
Fleet Finance Inc. (Thibodaux, LA) 70912
Fleet Finance Inc. (Westwego, LA) 70970
Fleet Finance Inc. (Columbus, MS) 72709
Fleet Finance Inc. (Columbia, SC) 79018
Fleet Finance Inc. (Walterboro, SC) 80070
Geico Corp. (Washington, DC) 58289
Government Employees Insurance Co. (Washington, DC) 58292
Hibernia National Bank (Bossier City, LA) 69716
IDS Financial Services (Richardson, TX) 88741
IDS Financial Services Inc. (Atlanta, GA) 64547
Mellon Fin Services Corp. (Tampa, FL) 63502
Mellon Financial Service Corp. (Casselberry, FL) 58936
Mellon Financial Service Corp. (Miami, FL) 61375
Mellon Financial Service Corp. (Madison, MS) 73136
Mellon Financial Services Corp. (Fort Lauderdale, FL) 59538
Mellon Financial Services Corp. (West Palm Beach, FL) 63886
Metropolitan Financial Corp. (Monroe, NC) 75584
Monsanto Employees Cr Union (Pensacola, FL) 62451
Mutual Federal S & L Association (Russell Springs, KY) 69256
Mutual Savings & Loan Assoc (Durham, NC) 74420
Mutual Savings & Loan Assoc (Greensboro, NC) 74869
Norwest Mortgage Inc. (Maitland, FL) 60982
Norwest Mortgage Inc. (Oklahoma City, OK) 77455
Norwest Mortgage Inc. (Austin, TX) 82948
Norwest Mortgage Inc. (Corpus Christi, TX) 83743
Norwest Mortgage, Inc. (Fort Worth, TX) 85205
Peoples Bank (Hustonville, KY) 68485
People's Bank (Oliver Springs, TN) 82211
Peoples Bank of Polk County (Benton, TN) 80202
Peoples Bank & Trust Co. (Sunbright, TN) 82365
Personal Finance Co. (Batesville, MS) 72601
Personal Finance Co. (Columbus, MS) 72721
Personal Finance Co. (Corinth, MS) 72742
Personal Finance Co. (Eupora, MS) 72764
Personal Finance Co. (Iuka, MS) 72935
Personal Finance Co. (Pontotoc, MS) 73304
Personal Finance Co. (Starkville, MS) 73367
Personal Finance Co. (Tupelo, MS) 73417
Personal Finance Co. (West Point, MS) 73484; 73484
Pitney Bowes Credit Corp. (Charlotte, NC) 74106
Pitney Bowes Credit Corp. (Oklahoma City, OK) 77488
Provident Financial Corp. (Columbia, SC) 79077; 79078
Security Pacific Finance Corp. (Raleigh, NC) 75954
Security Pacific Financial Services (Greensboro, NC) 74905
Security Pacific Financial Services, Inc. (Lexington, KY) 68625; 68626
Security Pacific Financial Services, Inc. (Baltimore, MD) 71276
Security Pacific Financial Services Inc. (Oklahoma City, OK) 77553
Security Pacific Financial Services Inc. (Tulsa, OK) 78106
Security Pacific Housing Services, Inc. (Raleigh, NC) 75955
Third National Mortgage Co. (Knoxville, TN) 81259
Valley National Financial Service Co. (Farmers Branch, TX) 85036
Wachovia Bank & Trust (New Bern, NC) 75737
Wachovia Bank & Trust (Salisbury, NC) 76181
Wachovia Bank & Trust Co. (Charlotte, NC) 74200
Wachovia Bank & Trust Co. (Durham, NC) 74435
Wachovia Bank & Trust Co. (Goldsboro, NC) 74740
Wachovia Bank & Trust Co. (Hayesville, NC) 75015
Wachovia Bank & Trust Co. N (Andrews, NC) 73550
Wachovia Bank & Trust Co. N (Kernersville, NC) 75285
Wachovia Bank & Trust Co. N (Morganton, NC) 75659
Wachovia Bank & Trust Co. N (Washington, NC) 76462
Wachovia Bank & Trust Co. N (Waynesville, NC) 76474
Wachovia Bank & Trust Co. N (Wilmington, NC) 76608
Wachovia Bank & Trust Co. NA (Hendersonville, NC) 75046
Western Carolina Savings (Valdese, NC) 76414

6153 Short-Term Business Credit

American Express Credit Corp. (Wilmington, DE) 57977; 57979
American General Corp. (Houston, TX) 85779
AmSouth Bank (Bessemer, AL) 55085
AmSouth Bank, N.A. (Birmingham, AL) 55131; 55132; 55133; 55134; 55135; 55136; 55137; 55138; 55139; 55140; 55141; 55142; 55143; 55144; 55145; 55146; 55147; 55148; 55149; 55150; 55150; 55151
Aristar Inc. (Cordova, TN) 80673
Bank of Boston International (Miami, FL) 61172
Beneficial National Bank USA (Wilmington, DE) 58027
City National Bank of Fairmont (Fairmont, WV) 92837
Corestates Bank Of Delaware NA (Wilmington, DE) 58047
Dillard Investment Co., Inc. (Little Rock, AR) 57278
First Union Commercial Corp. (Charlotte, NC) 73978

6159 Miscellaneous Business Credit Institutions

Alco Capital Resource (Macon, GA) 66644
Alco Capital Resource Inc. (Macon, GA) 66645; 66646
ALLTEL Finance Corp. (Little Rock, AR) 57247
American Savings of Florida (St Petersburg, FL) 62964
Anchor Savings Bank (New Port Richey, FL) 61673
Anchor Savings Bank (St. Petersburg, FL) 63080
Anchor Savings Bank F S B (Lake City, FL) 60616
Anchor Savings Bank FSB (Callahan, FL) 58904
Armstrong Ventures, Inc. (Wilmington, DE) 57988
AT&T Commercial Finance (Dallas, TX) 83864
Autoparts Finance Co. Inc. (Houston, TX) 85825
Bank of Boston Corp. (Dallas, TX) 83870
Bank South Leasing Inc. (Atlanta, GA) 64255
Bankers Trust Co. (Houston, TX) 85865
Bear Stearns Secured Investors Inc. (Dallas, TX) 83874
Bell Atlantic Bus Syst Servs. (Louisville, KY) 68700
Bell Atlantic Business System Services (Birmingham, AL) 55161
Bell Atlantic Financial Svs. (Wilmington, DE) 58007
Bell Atlantic Tricon Lease Corp. (Ft. Lauderdale, FL) 59852
Bell Atlantic Tricon Lease Corp. (Tampa, FL) 63364
Bell Atlantic Tricon Lease Corp. (Atlanta, GA) 64301
Bell Atlantic Tricon Leasing (Deerfield Beach, FL) 59272
Beneficial Texas Inc. (Carrollton, TX) 83454
Blount Inc. (Montgomery, AL) 56284
California Federal Bank (Port Richey, FL) 62668
Capital Finance Group, Inc. (Charlotte, NC) 73888
Coast Federal Bank (Deland, FL) 59300
Columbia First Bank, FSB (Arlington, VA) 90284
Compass Bank (Crosby, TX) 83805
Congress Financial Corp. (Dallas, TX) 83957
Creditquick Inc. (Brunswick, GA) 65407
Csc Credit Services (Houston, TX) 86021
Dominion Capital Inc. (Richmond, VA) 91846
Dominion Financing Inc. (Richmond, VA) 91850
Federal Home Loan Mortgage (McLean, VA) 91382
First American Bank (Cape St. Claire, MD) 71494; 71495
First American Bank (Severna Park, MD) 72373
First Financial Bank-F S B (New Orleans, LA) 70453
First Security Mortgage (Jackson, TN) 80977
First Union Commercial Corp. (Charlotte, NC) 73978
Fleet Finance Inc. (Mt Pleasant, SC) 79673
Fleming Cos. Inc. (Oklahoma City, OK) 77362
General American Life Insurance (Orlando, FL) 61994
Georgia Federal Bank F S B (St Simons is, GA) 67619
Georgia Federal Bank FSB (Savannah, GA) 67478
Great Western Bank (Brandon, FL) 58872
Great Western Bank (Crystal River, FL) 59132
Great Western Bank (Fort Myers, FL) 59701
Great Western Bank (Largo, FL) 60840
Great Western Bank (Orlando, FL) 61997
Great Western Bank (Oviedo, FL) 62215
Great Western Bank Mtge Ofc (Port St Lucie, FL) 62687
Home Savings Bank (Hampton, VA) 91041
Liberty Business Credit Cor (Tampa, FL) 63484
Norwest Mortgage Inc. (Austin, TX) 82948
Norwest Mortgage Inc. (Duncanville, TX) 84701
Norwest Mortgage Inc. (Houston, TX) 86622
Personal Finance Co. Inc. (Dallas, TX) 84300
Pitney Bowes Credit Corp. (Farmers Branch, TX) 85034
Pizza Hut (Jacksonville, FL) 60407
Sponser's Plan Asset Management, Inc. (New Castle, DE) 57875
Standard Federal S & L (Crofton, MD) 71617
Verex Assurance Inc. (Tampa, FL) 63644
Whirlpool Financial Corp. (Metairie, LA) 70336
World Savings & Loan (Port Richey, FL) 62683
World Savings & Loan (Irving, TX) 87417

6162 Mortgage Bankers & Correspondents

Ahmanson Morgage Co. (Rockville, MD) 72255
American Financial Corp. of Tampa (Tampa, FL) 63309
American General Corp. (Houston, TX) 85779
American General Finance (Bessemer, AL) 55082
American General Finance (Birmingham, AL) 55121; 55122
American General Finance (Decatur, AL) 55573
American General Finance (Gadsden, AL) 55772
American General Finance (Huntsville, AL) 55878
American General Finance (Mobile, AL) 56136
American General Finance (Montgomery, AL) 56277
American General Finance (Dover, DE) 57779
American General Finance (Laurel, DE) 57824
American General Finance (Milford, DE) 57836
American General Finance (Newark, DE) 57886
American General Finance (Smyrna, DE) 57957
American General Finance (Fort Lauderdale, FL) 59434; 59435; 59436
American General Finance (Hollywood, FL) 60033
American General Finance (Jacksonville, FL) 60164; 60165; 60166; 60167; 60168; 60169
American General Finance (Orlando, FL) 61908; 61909
American General Finance (Tallahassee, FL) 63204
American General Finance (Tampa, FL) 63310; 63312; 63313; 63314
American General Finance (Atlanta, GA) 64225; 64226; 64227; 64228
American General Finance (Hazard, KY) 68422
American General Finance (Hopkinsville, KY) 68472
American General Finance (Lexington, KY) 68518
American General Finance (Louisville, KY) 68675; 68676; 68677; 68678; 68679
American General Finance (Baton Rouge, LA) 69463; 69465
American General Finance (Metairie, LA) 70246
American General Finance (New Orleans, LA) 70429
American General Finance (Shreveport, LA) 70682
American General Finance (Owings Mills, MD) 72182
American General Finance (Jackson, MS) 72941
American General Finance (Wilson, NC) 76615
American General Finance (Oklahoma City, OK) 77296; 77297
American General Finance (Tulsa, OK) 77876
American General Finance (Antioch, TN) 80162
American General Finance (Chattanooga, TN) 80293; 80294
American General Finance (Cleveland, TN) 80566
American General Finance (Hermitage, TN) 80922
American General Finance (Hixson, TN) 80928
American General Finance (Knoxville, TN) 81135; 81136
American General Finance (Madison, TN) 81370
American General Finance (Memphis, TN) 81450; 81451; 81452
American General Finance (Nashville, TN) 81883; 81884
American General Finance (Richmond, VA) 91728
American General Finance (Virginia Beach, VA) 92431
American General Finance Co. (Metairie, LA) 70247
American General Finance Co., Inc. (Mobile, AL) 56137
American General Finance Inc. (Bessemer, AL) 55083
American General Finance Inc. (Birmingham, AL) 55123; 55125
American General Finance Inc. (Decatur, AL) 55574
American General Finance Inc. (Gadsden, AL) 55773
American General Finance Inc. (Huntsville, AL) 55879
American General Finance Inc. (Mobile, AL) 56138; 56139
American General Finance Inc. (Montgomery, AL) 56278
American General Finance Inc. (Dover, DE) 57780
American General Finance Inc. (Laurel, DE) 57825
American General Finance Inc. (Milford, DE) 57837
American General Finance Inc. (Newark, DE) 57887
American General Finance Inc. (Smyrna, DE) 57958
American General Finance Inc. (Fort Lauderdale, FL) 59437; 59438; 59439
American General Finance Inc. (Hollywood, FL) 60034
American General Finance Inc. (Jacksonville, FL) 60170; 60171; 60172; 60173; 60174; 60175
American General Finance Inc. (Orlando, FL) 61910; 61911; 61912
American General Finance Inc. (Tallahassee, FL) 63205
American General Finance Inc. (Tampa, FL) 63315; 63317; 63318; 63319
American General Finance Inc. (Atlanta, GA) 64229; 64230; 64231; 64232
American General Finance Inc. (Hazard, KY) 68423
American General Finance Inc. (Hopkinsville, KY) 68473
American General Finance Inc. (Lexington, KY) 68519
American General Finance Inc. (Louisville, KY) 68681; 68682; 68683; 68685; 68686
American General Finance Inc. (Baton Rouge, LA) 69466; 69467
American General Finance Inc. (Metairie, LA) 70248; 70249
American General Finance Inc. (New Orleans, LA) 70430
American General Finance Inc. (Shreveport, LA) 70683; 70684; 70685; 70686; 70687; 70688; 70689
American General Finance Inc. (Owings Mills, MD) 72183
American General Finance Inc. (Jackson, MS) 72942; 72943; 72944

American General Finance Inc. (Wilson, NC) 76616
American General Finance Inc. (Oklahoma City, OK) 77298; 77299
American General Finance Inc. (Tulsa, OK) 77877; 77878
American General Finance Inc. (Tulso, OK) 78218
American General Finance Inc. (Antioch, TN) 80163
American General Finance Inc. (Chattanooga, TN) 80295; 80296
American General Finance Inc. (Cleveland, TN) 80567
American General Finance Inc. (Hermitage, TN) 80923
American General Finance Inc. (Hixson, TN) 80929
American General Finance Inc. (Knoxville, TN) 81137; 81138
American General Finance Inc. (Madison, TN) 81371
American General Finance Inc. (Memphis, TN) 81453; 81454; 81455; 81456; 81457
American General Finance Inc. (Nashville, TN) 81885; 81886
American General Finance Inc. (Norfolk, VA) 91498; 91499
American General Finance Inc. (Portsmouth, VA) 91639; 91640
American General Finance Inc. (Richmond, VA) 91729; 91730; 91731; 91732; 91733
American General Investment Corp. (Houston, TX) 85781; 85783
American General Mortgage Co. (Houston, TX) 85787; 85788; 85789
American Savings of FL FSB (Deerfield Beach, FL) 59264
American Savings of FL FSB (Ft. Lauderdale, FL) 59847
American Savings of FL FSB (Miami, FL) 61158; 61160; 61161
American Savings of Florida (Tampa, FL) 63321
AmSouth Bank (Bessemer, AL) 55085
AmSouth Bank, N.A. (Birmingham, AL) 55131; 55132; 55133; 55134; 55135; 55136; 55137; 55138; 55139; 55140; 55141; 55142; 55143; 55144; 55145; 55146; 55147; 55148; 55149; 55150; 55151
AmSouth Bank North America (Birmingham, AL) 55152
AmSouth Bank of Tennessee (Antioch, TN) 80164
AmSouth Bank of Tennessee (Brainerd, TN) 80210
AmSouth Bank of Tennessee (Chattanooga, TN) 80298; 80299; 80300; 80301; 80302; 80303; 80304; 80305; 80306; 80307; 80308
AmSouth Bank of Tennessee (Cleveland, TN) 80568
AmSouth Bank of Tennessee (Dayton, TN) 80716
AmSouth Bank of Tennessee (Fayetteville, TN) 80790
AmSouth Bank of Tennessee (Gallatin, TN) 80837
AmSouth Bank of Tennessee (Hendersonville, TN) 80910
AmSouth Bank of Tennessee (Nashville, TN) 81893; 81894
AmSouth Bank of Tennessee (South Pittsburg, TN) 82338
AmSouth Bank of Walker County (Jasper, AL) 56077
AmSouth Mortgage Co. (Birmingham, AL) 55155
Anchor Financial Group (Greensboro, NC) 74777
Anchor Mortgage Services Inc. (Jacksonville, FL) 60180
Anchor Mortgage Services Inc. (Tampa, FL) 63323
Anchor Savings Bank, FSB (Deerfield Beach, FL) 59266
Anchor Savings Bank, FSB (Fort Meyers, FL) 59655
Anchor Savings Bank, FSB (Naples, FL) 61600
Anchor Savings Bank Loan of (Waycross, GA) 68025
Banc One Mortgage Corp. (Virginia Beach, VA) 92434
BancBoston Mortagage Corp. (Huntsville, AL) 55886
BancBoston Mortgage Corp. (Montgomery, AL) 56281
BancBoston Mortgage Corp. (Ft. Lauderdale, FL) 59850
BancBoston Mortgage Corp. (Jacksonville, FL) 60190
BancBoston Mortgage Corp. (Tampa, FL) 63334
BancBoston Mortgage Corp. (Raleigh, NC) 75862
BancBoston Mortgage Corp. (Houston, TX) 85862
Bank South (Monticello, GA) 66997
Bank South (Smyrna, GA) 67542
Bank South (Tennille, GA) 67782
Bank South Corp. (Atlanta, GA) 64253
Bank South Home Equity (Atlanta, GA) 64254
Bank South Mortgage Inc. (Atlanta, GA) 64258; 64259
Bank South Mortgate Inc. (Atlanta, GA) 64260
Bank South NA (Atlanta, GA) 64263
Bank South NA (Griffin, GA) 66309
Bank South NA (Union City, GA) 67911
Bankers Trust of Madison (Ardmore, AL) 55029
Beneficial Corp. (Wilmington, DE) 58015
Beneficial Delaware Inc. (Dover, DE) 57784
Beneficial Delaware Inc. (Newark, DE) 57895
Beneficial Finance Co. (Columbia, SC) 78975
Beneficial Florida Inc. (Pensacola, FL) 62409
Beneficial Georgia Inc. (Kennesaw, GA) 66409
Beneficial Georgia Inc. (Tucker, GA) 67847
Beneficial Maryland Inc. (Baltimore, MD) 71064
Beneficial Mortgage Co. of Maryland (Gaithersburg, MD) 71764
Beneficial Mortgage Co. of MD (California, MD) 71482
Beneficial Mortgage Co. of Oklahoma (Oklahoma City, OK) 77305
Beneficial Mortgage Corp. (Newark, DE) 57896
Beneficial North Carolina Inc. (Fayetteville, NC) 74530
Beneficial North Carolina Inc. (Raleigh, NC) 75864
Beneficial North Carolina Inc. (Rocky Mount, NC) 76074
Beneficial Oklahoma Inc. (Oklahoma City, OK) 77306; 77307
Beneficial Tennessee Inc. (Nashville, TN) 81902
Beneficial Virginia Inc. (Alexandra, VA) 90163
Beneficial Virginia Inc. (Chesapeake, VA) 90556
Beneficial Virginia Inc. (Fairfax, VA) 90754
Beneficial Virginia Inc. (Newport News, VA) 91452
Beneficial Virginia Inc. (Virginia Beach, VA) 92436
Beneficial Virgnia Inc. (Chesapeake, VA) 90557
Chase Home Mortgage Corp. (Brandon, FL) 58867
Chase Home Mortgage Corp. (Miami, FL) 61226
Chase Home Mortgage Corp. (Winter Park, FL) 63965
Chase Home Mortgage Corp. (Grand Prairie, TX) 85614
City National Bank (Weslaco, TX) 90033
City National Bank of Fairmont (Fairmont, WV) 92837
City National Bank of Fulton (Fulton, KY) 68375
City National Bank of Kilgore (Kilgore, TX) 87486
City National Bank Sylacauga (Sylacauga, AL) 56579
Coast to Coast Mortgage Ser (Sarasota, FL) 62805
Collective Mortgage Service (Wilmington, DE) 58041
Collective Mortgage Service (Gainesville, FL) 59867
Collective Mortgage Service (Pensacola, FL) 62417
Collective Mortgage Service (Tampa, FL) 63397
Crestar Bank (Richmond, VA) 91793
Crestar Morgage Corp. (Richmond, VA) 91833
Crestar Mortgage Corp. (Maitland, FL) 60975
Crestar Mortgage Corp. (Louisville, KY) 68738
Crestar Mortgage Corp. (Metairie, LA) 70258
Crestar Mortgage Corp. (Greensboro, NC) 74806
Crestar Mortgage Corp. (Nashville, TN) 81927
Danaher Corp. (Washington, DC) 58209
Deposit Guaranty Mortgage C (Tampa, FL) 63407
Deposit Guaranty Mortgage C (Greenville, MS) 72796
Deposit Guaranty Mortgage C (Jackson, MS) 72971; 72972
Deposit Guaranty Mortgage C (Meridian, MS) 73162
Deposit Guaranty Mortgage C (Southaven, MS) 73347
Deposit Guaranty Mortgage Co. (Jackson, MS) 72973
Federal Home Loan Mortgage (Dallas, TX) 84062
First Federal S & L (Florence, AL) 55736
First Federal S & L (Guntersville, AL) 55826
First Federal S & L (Sylacauga, AL) 56586
First Federal S & L (Talladega, AL) 56593
First Federal S & L (Milledgeville, GA) 66975
First Federal S & L (Ashland, KY) 68096
First Federal S & L. (Lexington, KY) 68549; 68551
First Federal S & L (Durham, NC) 74398
First Federal S & L (Lincolnton, NC) 75439
First Federal S & L (Rockingham, NC) 76060
First Federal S & L (Cheraw, SC) 78922
First Federal S & L (Darlington, SC) 79146
First Federal S & L (Columbia, TN) 80627
First Federal S & L (Tyler, TX) 89801
First General Mortgage Co. (Falls Church, VA) 90834
First General Mortgage Co. Inc. (Falls Church, VA) 90835
First National Bank & Trust (Siler City, NC) 76248
First Security Mortgage Cor (Birmingham, AL) 55272
First Security Mortgage Cor (Metairie, LA) 70262
First Union Home Equity Corp. (Charlotte, NC) 73983
First Union Mortgage Corp. (Charlotte, NC) 73984
First Union National Bank of Florida (Jacksonville, FL) 60300
First Union National Bank of Georgia (Atlanta, GA) 64450
First Virginia Bank - Southside (Farmville, VA) 90876
First Virginia Mortgage Co. (Falls Church, VA) 90852; 90853
Fleet Finance Inc. (Mobile, AL) 56179
Fleet Finance Inc. (Gulfport, MS) 72855
Fleet Finance Inc. (Nashville, TN) 82010
Fleet Mortgage Group Inc. (Columbia, SC) 79019
General American Life Insurance (Orlando, FL) 61995
Great Western Bank (West Palm Beach, FL) 63869
Household Mortgage Services (Tampa, FL) 63459
Household Mortgage Services (Charlotte, NC) 74047
Huntington Mortgage Co. (Richmond, VA) 91907
Mellon Financial Service Corp. (New Orleans, LA) 70533; 70534
Mellon Financial Services Corp. (Miami, FL) 61376
Mercantile Mortgage Corp. (Austin, TX) 82938
Mercantile Mortgage Corp. (Grand Prairie, TX) 85629
Mutual Savings & Loan Assoc (Durham, NC) 74420
Mutual Savings & Loan Assoc (Greensboro, NC) 74869
National City Mortgage Co. (Virginia Beach, VA) 92492
Norwest Mortgage Inc. (Sarasota, FL) 62847
Norwest Mortgage Inc. (Tampa, FL) 63512
Norwest Mortgage Inc. (West Palm Beach, FL) 63889
Norwest Mortgage Inc. (Tulsa, OK) 78034
Norwest Mortgage Inc. (Charleston, SC) 78848
Norwest Mortgage Inc. (Dallas, TX) 84275
Provident Financial Corp. (Columbia, SC) 79077
Security Pacific Finance Corp. (Raleigh, NC) 75954
Security Pacific Financial Services, Inc. (Lexington, KY) 68626
Security Pacific Financial Services Inc. (Oklahoma City, OK) 77553
Security Pacific Financial Services Inc. (Tulsa, OK) 78106
Southtrust Mortgage (Brentwood, TN) 80236
St Michaels Bank (St Michaels, MD) 72470
Standard Federal Savings Bank (Frederick, MD) 71749
Third National Mortgage Co. (Nashville, TN) 82110

6163 Loan Brokers

American Financial Corp. of Tampa (Tampa, FL) 63309
AmSouth Bank, N.A. (Birmingham, AL) 55131; 55132; 55133; 55134; 55135; 55136; 55137; 55138; 55139; 55140; 55141; 55142; 55143; 55144; 55145; 55146; 55147; 55148; 55149; 55150; 55150; 55151
Equitable Agri-Business Inc. (Atlanta, GA) 64429

6211 Security Brokers & Dealers

AMBAC Indemnity Corp. (Tampa, FL) 63306
American General Finance (Wilson, NC) 76615
American General Finance Inc. (Wilson, NC) 76616
American General Securities Inc. (Houston, TX) 85791; 85792; 85793
American Savings of Florida, FSB (Boca Raton, FL) 58666; 58667
American Savings of Florida, FSB (Coconut Creek, FL) 59086
American Savings of Florida, FSB (Coral Gables, FL) 59092
American Savings of Florida, FSB (Coral Springs, FL) 59106
American Savings of Florida, FSB (Davie, FL) 59153
American Savings of Florida, FSB (Deerfield Beach, FL) 59265
American Savings of Florida, FSB (Delray Beach, FL) 59306
American Savings of Florida, FSB (Hallendale, FL) 59967
American Savings of Florida, FSB (Hollywood, FL) 60038
American Savings of Florida, FSB (Lake Worth, FL) 60663
American Savings of Florida, FSB (Lauderhill, FL) 60873
American Savings of Florida, FSB (Margate, FL) 60998
American Savings of Florida FSB (Miami, FL) 61167; 61168
American Savings of Florida, FSB (Miami Beach, FL) 61520; 61521; 61522; 61523
American Savings of Florida, FSB (North Miami, FL) 61730
American Savings of Florida, FSB (North Miami Beach, FL) 61739; 61740
American Savings of Florida, FSB (Pembroke Pines, FL) 62362; 62363
American Savings of Florida, FSB (Sunrise, FL) 63189; 63190
American Savings of Florida, FSB (Tamarac, FL) 63294
American Savings of Florida, FSB (West Palm Beach, FL) 63838
AmSouth Bank North America (Birmingham, AL) 55152
AmSouth Investment Services Inc. (Birmingham, AL) 55154
Anchor Savings Bank, FSB (Callahan, FL) 58903
Anchor Savings Bank, FSB (Deerfield Beach, FL) 59266
Anchor Savings Bank, FSB (Fort Meyers, FL) 59655
Anchor Savings Bank, FSB (Jacksonville Beach, FL) 60517
Anchor Savings Bank, FSB (Naples, FL) 61600
Anchor Savings Bank, FSB (New Port Richey, FL) 61674
Anchor Savings Bank, FSB (St. Augustine Beach, FL) 63064
Anchor Savings Bank, FSB (Tampa, FL) 63327
Bankers Trust (Houston, TX) 85863
Bear Stearns Companies Inc. (Atlanta, GA) 64296
Bear Stearns Companies Inc. (Dallas, TX) 83872
Bear Stearns & Co., Inc. (Atlanta, GA) 64297
Bear Stearns & Co., Inc. Atlanta (Atlanta, GA) 64298
Bear, Stearns & Co., Inc. Dallas (Dallas, TX) 83873
Bear Stearns Fiduciary Services Inc. (Washington, DC) 58136
Charles Schwab & Co. Inc. (Midland, TX) 88028
Charles Schwab&Co Inc. (Dallas, TX) 83909
Cigna Individual Financial Services Co. (Covington, KY) 68216
City National Bank (Fort Smith, AR) 57037
City National Bank of Florida (Hallandale, FL) 59959
City National Bank of Florida (Miami, FL) 61259
City National Bank of Taylor (Taylor, TX) 89598
Colony Insurance Co. (Richmond, VA) 91783
Crestar Securities Corp. (Richmond, VA) 91834
Dean Witter Reynolds Inc. (Louisville, KY) 68742
Dean Witter Reynolds Inc. (Jackson, TN) 80968
Dean Witter Reynolds Inc. (Madison, TN) 81372
Dean Witter Reynolds Inc. (Memphis, TN) 81503
Dean Witter Reynolds Inc. (Nashville, TN) 81928
Dean Witter Reynolds Inc. (Charleston, WV) 92741; 92742
Deposit Guaranty Investments; Inc. (Jackson, MS) 72970
Exxon (Lehigh Acres, FL) 60892
Federal Home Life Insurance Co. Inc. (Orlando, FL) 61969
Hamilton Insurance Co. (Glen Allen, VA) 90979
IDS Financial Services (Richardson, TX) 88741
IDS Financial Services Inc. (Montgomery, AL) 56345
IDS Financial Services Inc. (Washington, DC) 58306
IDS Financial Services Inc. (Miami, FL) 61332
IDS Financial Services Inc. (Atlanta, GA) 64547
IDS Financial Services Inc. (Slidell, LA) 70828
IDS Financial Services Inc. (Hickory, NC) 75082
IDS Financial Services Inc. (Tulsa, OK) 77958
IDS Financial Services Inc. (Memphis, TN) 81629
IDS Financial Services Inc. (Nashville, TN) 82028
Invest Financial Corporatio (Johnson City, TN) 81048
Lehman Brothers (Houston, TX) 86443
Louisiana Land & Exploratio (Houma, LA) 69960
Meridian Securities (Tulsa, OK) 78021
Mutual of New York Financial (Metairie, LA) 70293
Painewebber Inc. (Charlotte, NC) 74102
Salomon Brothers Inc. (Houston, TX) 86854
Schwab Charles & Co. Inc. (St Petersburg, FL) 63034
Schwab Charles & Co. Inc. (Tulsa, OK) 78104
Schwab Charles & Co. Inc. (Virginia Beach, VA) 92509
Schwab & Co. Inc/Charles (Oklahoma City, OK) 77551
Smith Barney Harris Upham & Co. (Washington, DC) 58121
Smith Barney Harris Upham & Co. (Washington, DC) 58489
Smith Barney Harris Upham & Co. (Miami, FL) 61462; 61463
Smith Barney Harris Upham & Co. (Atlanta, GA) 65158
Smith Barney Harris Upham & Co. (Bethesda, MD) 71441
Smith Barney Harris Upham & Co. (Durham, NC) 74428
Smith Barney Harris Upham & Co. (Winston Salem, NC) 76685
Smith Barney Harris Upham & Co. (Dallas, TX) 84387
Smith Barney Harris Upham & Co. (Houston, TX) 86896
Transamerica Occidental Life Insurance (Cedartown, GA) 65513
Waite Hill Holdings Inc. (Glen Allen, VA) 90988

6221 Commodity Contracts Brokers & Dealers

Bear Steam Co. Inc. (Houston, TX) 85866

Bear Stearns & Co., Inc. (Atlanta, GA) 64297
Dean Witter Reynolds Inc. (Memphis, TN) 81502; 81504; 81505
First Union Brokerage Services, Inc. (Charlotte, NC) 73977
First Union Futures Corp. (Charlotte, NC) 73982
Service Merchandise (Enid, OK) 77070
Smith Barney Harris Upham & Co. (Washington, DC) 58489
Smith Barney Harris Upham & Co. (Miami, FL) 61463
Smith Barney Harris Upham & Co. (Houston, TX) 86896

6231 Security & Commodity Exchanges

Life Insurance Co. of Virginia (Richmond, VA) 91919

6282 Investment Advice

AmSouth Bank of Florida (Clearwater, FL) 58967
AmSouth Bank, N.A. (Birmingham, AL) 55131; 55132; 55133; 55134; 55135; 55136; 55137; 55138; 55139; 55140; 55141; 55142; 55143; 55144; 55145; 55146; 55147; 55148; 55149; 55150; 55151
AmSouth Bank of Walker County (Jasper, AL) 56077
Bank of Boston-Florida (Palm Beach, FL) 62245
Bank of Boston-Florida (Sarasota, FL) 62787; 62787
Bank of Boston-Florida N.A. (Palm Beach, FL) 62246
Bank of Boston International (Miami, FL) 61172
Beneficial Virginia Inc. (Chesapeake, VA) 90556
Cigna Holdings Inc. (Wilmington, DE) 58038
Coast to Coast Investments (Elizabethtown, KY) 68274
Dauphin Investment Co. (Wilmington, DE) 58048
First American National Bank (Huntsville, AL) 55936
First Federal S & L (Lincolnton, NC) 75439
IDS Financial Services (Houston, TX) 86305
IDS Financial Services (Richardson, TX) 88741
IDS Financial Services Inc. (Montgomery, AL) 56345
IDS Financial Services Inc. (Miami, FL) 61332
IDS Financial Services Inc. (Atlanta, GA) 64547
IDS Financial Services Inc. (Slidell, LA) 70828
IDS Financial Services Inc. (Hickory, NC) 75082
IDS Financial Services Inc. (Tulsa, OK) 77958
IDS Financial Services Inc. (Memphis, TN) 81629
IDS Financial Services Inc. (Nashville, TN) 82028
IDS Financial Services Inc. (Harlingen, TX) 85702
IDS Financial Services Inc. (Houston, TX) 86306; 86307
Jiffy Lube (Oklahoma City, OK) 77390
Rincon Securities Inc. (Richmond, VA) 91996
Structured Shelt Richmond (Richmond, VA) 92054

6289 Security & Commodity Services Nec

American Transtech Inc. (Jacksonville, FL) 60177
IDS Financial Services Inc. (Montgomery, AL) 56345

6311 Life Insurance

AGC Life Insurance Co. (Nashville, TN) 81878; 81879; 81880
Albertson's (Fort Walton Beach, FL) 59820
ALG Life Insurance Co. (Wilmington, DE) 57975
American-Amicable Life Insurance Co. of Texas (Waco, TX) 89927
American Family Life Assurance Co. (Columbus, GA) 65617
American General Corp. (Houston, TX) 85779
American General Group Insurance Co. (Dallas, TX) 83846
American General Group Insurance Co. of Florida (Jacksonville, FL) 60176
American General Life & Accedent Insurance Co. (Nashville, TN) 81887
American General Life Insurance Co. (Houston, TX) 85784; 85785; 85786
American General Life Insurance Co. of Oklahoma (Oklahoma City, OK) 77300
Cigna Holdings Inc. (Wilmington, DE) 58038
Cigna Worldwide Insurance Co. Inc. (Wilmington, DE) 58039
Delaware American Life Insurance Co. (Wilmington, DE) 58049; 58050
Equitable Life Insurance Co. (Nashville, TN) 81954
Equitable Life Insurance Co. (Mc Lean, VA) 91364
Ethyl Corp. (Richmond, VA) 91862
First American Corp. (Atlanta, GA) 64445
First Colony Life (Richmond, VA) 91873
First Colony Life Insurance Co. (Lynchburg, VA) 91241
First Virginia Life Insurance Co. (Falls Church, VA) 90851
G & W Life Insurance Co. (Jackson, MS) 72985
Geico Corp. (Washington, DC) 58289
General Financial Agency, Inc. (Charlotte, NC) 74029
Gulf Life Insurance Co. (Nashville, TN) 82020; 82021
Harvest Life Insurance Co. (Orlando, FL) 62001
Harvest Life Insurance Co. Inc. (Orlando, FL) 62002
Life & Casvality Insurance Co. of Tennessee (Nashville, TN) 82054
Life Insurance Co. of Virginia (Richmond, VA) 91919
Mutual of New York (De Land, FL) 59253
National Public Service Isurance Co. (Waco, TX) 89954
New England Mutl Life Insurance C (Fort Lauderdale, FL) 59546
New York Life Insurance (Bassett, VA) 90416
New York Life Insurance (Charlottesville, VA) 90544
New York Life Insurance Agt (Martinsville, VA) 91355
Penn Mutual Life Insurance (Greensboro, NC) 74875
Penn Mutual Life Insurance (Spartanburg, SC) 79922
Penn Mutual Life Insurance (Knoxville, TN) 81236
Penn Mutual Life Insurance Co. (Meridian, MS) 73173
Pioneer Security Life Insurance (Waco, TX) 89966
Pioneer Security Life Insurance Co. (Waco, TX) 89967
Shenandoah Life Insurance Co. (Roanoke, VA) 92186
Variable Annuity Life Insurance C (Columbia, SC) 79118
Variable Annuity Life Insurance Co. (Columbia, SC) 79119
Variable Annuity Life Insurance Co. (Houston, TX) 87074; 87075

6321 Accident & Health Insurance

American Family Life Assurance Co. (Columbus, GA) 65617
American General Group Insurance Co. (Dallas, TX) 83846
American General Group Insurance Co. of Florida (Jacksonville, FL) 60176
American General Life & Accedent Insurance Co. (Nashville, TN) 81887
American General Life Insurance Co. (Houston, TX) 85784; 85786
Cigna Holdings Inc. (Wilmington, DE) 58038
Cigna Insurance Co. of Texas (Irving, TX) 87329
Federal Home Life Insurance Co. Inc. (Orlando, FL) 61969
First Colony Life Insurance Co. (Lynchburg, VA) 91241
Geico Corp. (Washington, DC) 58289
General Financial Agency, Inc. (Charlotte, NC) 74029
INA Financial Corp. (Wilmington, DE) 58075
Litton Clifton Precision South (Murphy, NC) 75705

6324 Hospital & Medical Service Plans

AFLAC (Shelby, NC) 76230
American Family Life Assurance Co. (Columbus, GA) 65617
Cigna Dental Health Inc. (Miami, FL) 61230
Cigna Health Plan of Florida Inc. (Tampa, FL) 63389
Cigna Healthplan of Georgia Inc. (Atlanta, GA) 64354
Cigna Healthplan Mid-Atlantic Inc. (Columbia, MD) 71580
Island Healthcare Inc. (Hato Rey, PR) 78456

6331 Fire, Marine & Casualty Insurance

AIG Aviation, Inc. (Atlanta, GA) 64208
American General Life & Accedent Insurance Co. (Nashville, TN) 81887
American General Property Insurance Co. (Nashville, TN) 81890; 81891
Atlanta Casualty Co. (Norcross, GA) 67100
Cigna Holdings Inc. (Wilmington, DE) 58038
Cigna Insurance Co. of Texas (Irving, TX) 87329
Cigna Worldwide Insurance Co. Inc. (Wilmington, DE) 58039
Colony Insurance Co. Inc. (Glen Allen, VA) 90977
Dixie Insurance Co. (Birmingham, AL) 55226
Enron Corp. (Houston, TX) 86062
First Virginia Insurance Services Inc. (Falls Church, VA) 90850
Geico Corp. (Washington, DC) 58289
Geico Indemnity Co., Inc. (Washington, DC) 58290
Government Employees Insurance Co. (Washington, DC) 58292
Halliburton Co. Inc. (Dallas, TX) 84110
Hamilton Insurance Co. Inc. (Washington, DC) 58296
Hanover Lloyd's Insurance Co. (Richardson, TX) 88737
INA Financial Corp. (Wilmington, DE) 58075
Interstate Fire Insurance Co. (Nashville, TN) 82036
Merastar Insurance Co. (Chattanooga, TN) 80436
Mid-Continent Casualty Co. (Tulsa, OK) 78025
Southern Heritage Insurance Co., Inc. (Tucker, GA) 67890
Stonewall Insurance Co. (Birmingham, AL) 55400
Transport Insurance Co. (Dallas, TX) 84464
Travelers Lloyds Insurance (Dallas, TX) 84465

6341 Insurance & Diversified Financial Companies

Bear Stearns Companies Inc. (Atlanta, GA) 64296
Bear Stearns Companies Inc. (Dallas, TX) 83872
Bear Stearns Fiduciary Services Inc. (Washington, DC) 58136

6351 Surety Insurance

American Credit Indemnity (Baltimore, MD) 71036; 71037
Aristar Inc. (Cordova, TN) 80673
Beneficial Corp. (Wilmington, DE) 58015
Cigna Insurance Co. of Texas (Irving, TX) 87329
GE Capital Mortgage Corp. (Raleigh, NC) 75912
INA Financial Corp. (Wilmington, DE) 58075
Rollins Burdick & Hunter (Oklahoma City, OK) 77538

6361 Title Insurance

Chicago Title Insurance Ticor (Birmingham, AL) 55185
Chicago Title Insurance Co. (Hickory, NC) 75062
Chicago Title Insurance Co. Memphis (Memphis, TN) 81495
Ticor Title Insurance (Birmingham, AL) 55428
Ticor Title Insurance (Nashville, TN) 82112

6371 Pension, Health & Welfare Funds

Bear, Stearns Fiduciary Services Inc. (Washington, DC) 58137
General American Life Insur (Tulsa, OK) 77948
New England Mutl Life Insur (Tampa, FL) 63506
New England Mutual Life Insurance (Tampa, FL) 63507
Penn Mutual Life Insurance (Dallas, TX) 84295
Principal Mutual Life Insurance Co. (Greenville, SC) 79408
Provident National Assurance (Atlanta, GA) 65044
Provident National Assurance (Chattanooga, TN) 80473

6399 Insurance Carriers Nec

American Family Life Assurance Co. (Columbus, GA) 65617
American Life Insurance Co. (Wilmington, DE) 57982
Mid-Continent Casualty Co. (Tulsa, OK) 78025
Standard Fire Insurance Co. (Birmingham, AL) 55394
United Services Auto Association (San Antonio, TX) 89287

6411 Insurance Agents, Brokers & Service

Aetna Financial Services Inc. (Jackson, MS) 72939
Aetna Life & Annuity Co. (Memphis, TN) 81445
Aid Association for Luthera (Orange, TX) 88300
AIG Aviation, Inc. (Atlanta, GA) 64207
AIG Marketing Inc. (Wilmington, DE) 57974
Albertson's (Austin, TX) 82808
Allstate Life Insurance Co. (Dallas, TX) 83842; 83843
Allstate Life Insurance Co. (Houston, TX) 85774
Allstate Life Insurance Co. (Kerrville, TX) 87471
American Family Life Assrnc (Greenwood, MS) 72831
American Family Life Assur (Pensacola, FL) 62379
American Family Life Assur (Statesboro, GA) 67632
American Family Life Assur (Hickory, NC) 75055
American Family Life Assurance (Atmore, AL) 55049
American Family Life Assurance (Birmingham, AL) 55120
American Family Life Assurance (Dothan, AL) 55624
American Family Life Assurance (Mobile, AL) 56135
American Family Life Assurance (Montgomery, AL) 56276
American Family Life Assurance (Tuscaloosa, AL) 56630
American Family Life Assurance (Fayetteville, AR) 56969
American Family Life Assurance (Fort Smith, AR) 57021
American Family Life Assurance (Altamonte Springs, FL) 58548
American Family Life Assurance (Crestview, FL) 59122
American Family Life Assurance (Fort Myers, FL) 59659
American Family Life Assurance (Pensacola, FL) 62380; 62381
American Family Life Assurance (Punta Gorda, FL) 62701
American Family Life Assurance (Tallahassee, FL) 63203
American Family Life Assurance (Macon, GA) 66647
American Family Life Assurance (Savannah, GA) 67440
American Family Life Assurance (Statesboro, GA) 67633
American Family Life Assurance (Valdosta, GA) 67940
American Family Life Assurance (Warner Robins, GA) 68005
American Family Life Assurance (Lafayette, LA) 70041
American Family Life Assurance (Greenwood, MS) 72832
American Family Life Assurance (Jackson, MS) 72940
American Family Life Assurance (Charlotte, NC) 73836
American Family Life Assurance (Clinton, NC) 74278
American Family Life Assurance (Fayetteville, NC) 74524
American Family Life Assurance (Hickory, NC) 75056
American Family Life Assurance (Spartanburg, SC) 79875
American Family Life Assurance (Dumas, TX) 84686
American Family Life Assurance (Hereford, TX) 85738
American Family Life Assurance (San Angelo, TX) 88867
American Family Life Assurance (Harrisonburg, VA) 91063
American Family Life Assurance (Lynchburg, VA) 91221
American Family Life Assurance (Richmond, VA) 91727
American Family Life Assurance (Virginia Beach, VA) 92429; 92430
American Family Life Assurance Co. (Columbus, GA) 65617
American General Property Insurance Co. (Nashville, TN) 81889
American Life Insurance (Wilmington, DE) 57981
Atlanta Group, Inc. (Atlanta, GA) 64243
Bank South Corp. (Atlanta, GA) 64253
Bank South Life Insurance Corp. (Atlanta, GA) 64257
Bayly Martin & Fay Inc. (W Palm Beach, FL) 63779
Cardinal Casualty Co. Inc. (Glen Allen, VA) 90975
Cigna Dental Health of Florida Inc. (Miami, FL) 61229
Cigna Dental Health of Texas Inc. (Miami, FL) 61231
Cincinnati Insurance Co. (Birmingham, AL) 55186
Cincinnati Insurance Co. (Naples, FL) 61613; 61614
Cincinnati Insurance Co. (St Simons is, GA) 67617
Cincinnati Insurance Co. (Columbia, SC) 79001
Cincinnati Insurance Co. (Charlottesville, VA) 90527
Cincinnati Insurance Co. (Roanoke, VA) 92109; 92110
Coast to Coast Adjusters (Dallas, TX) 83917
Coast to Coast Corp. (Dallas, TX) 83918
Coast to Coast Credit Servs (Fort Lauderdale, FL) 59477
Colony Insurance Co. Inc. (Glen Allen, VA) 90977
Commonwealth Mortgage Assurance (Annandale, VA) 90256
Dun & Bradstreet Dun & Bradstreet Plan Services, Inc. (Tampa, FL) 63408
Dun & Bradstreet Pension Services, Inc. (Tampa, FL) 63409
Dun & Bradstreet Plan Services (Tampa, FL) 63410
Equitable Life Insurance Co. (Dover, DE) 57788
Equitable Life Insurance Co. (Newark, DE) 57903
Equitable Life Insurance Co. (Wilmington, DE) 58059
Equitable Life Insurance Co. (Frederick, MD) 71720; 71721
Equitable Life Insurance Co. (Mc Lean, VA) 91364
Ffrl Re Corp. (Richmond, VA) 91872
First Colony Life (Lubbock, TX) 87763
First Colony Life Insurance (Lynchburg, VA) 91239
First Colony Life Insurance Co. (Mobile, AL) 56178
First Colony Life Insurance Co. (Chattanooga, TN) 80375
Forth Financial Resources Ltd. Inc. (Richmond, VA) 91893
General American Life Insur (Birmingham, AL) 55277
General American Life Insur (Metairie, LA) 70266
General American Life Insur (Columbia, SC) 79028
General American Life Insur (Richmond, VA) 91896
General American Life Insurance (Dallas, TX) 84086
General American Life Insurance C (Mobile, AL) 56183
General American Life Insurance C (Maitland, FL) 60978
General American Life Insurance C (Charlotte, NC) 74027
General American Life Insurance C (Dallas, TX) 84087; 84088
General American Life Insurance C (Houston, TX) 86244
General American Life Insurance Co. (Austin, TX) 82882

Globe Life Insurance Co. (Dublin, GA) 66009
Humana Health Care Plans (Richmond, VA) 91906
INA Financial Corp. (Wilmington, DE) 58075
ITT Life Insurance Corp. (Corpus Christi, TX) 83724
Itt Life Insurance Corp. (Richardson, TX) 88742
Jackson National Life Insur (St Petersburg, FL) 62977
Jackson National Life Insurance (Metairie, LA) 70275
Jackson National Life Insurance C (St Petersburg, FL) 62978
Jackson National Life Insurance C (Dallas, TX) 84136
John Hancock Property & Cas (Maitland, FL) 60979
Kroger Financial Center (Huntsville, AL) 55961
Kroger Financial Center (Grand Prairie, TX) 85621
Kroger Financial Centers (Richardson, TX) 88745
Kroger Financial Cetner (Decatur, AL) 55595
Kroger Financial Ctrs (Mesquite, TX) 87969
Kroger Food Store (Pineville, LA) 70622
Liberty Mutual Insur Co. (Dallas, TX) 84200
Liberty Mutual Insurance Companie (Gainesville, GA) 66281
Liberty Mutual Insurance Companie (Midland, TX) 88042
Liberty Mutual Insurance Co. (Fort Smith, AR) 57068
Liberty Mutual Insurance Co. (Wilmington, DE) 58078
Liberty Mutual Insurance Co. (Jacksonville, FL) 60365
Liberty Mutual Insurance Co. (Tampa, FL) 63485
Liberty Mutual Insurance Co. (Covington, LA) 69796
Liberty Mutual Insurance Co. (Metairie, LA) 70287
Liberty Mutual Insurance Co. (Charlotte, NC) 74071
Liberty Mutual Insurance Co. (Greensboro, NC) 74864
Liberty Mutual Insurance Co. (Matthews, NC) 75526
Liberty Mutual Insurance Co. (Raleigh, NC) 75925
Liberty Mutual Insurance Co. (Charleston, SC) 78835
Liberty Mutual Insurance Co. (Columbia, SC) 79046
Liberty Mutual Insurance Co. (Austin, TX) 82923
Liberty Mutual Insurance Co. (Beaumont, TX) 83171
Liberty Mutual Insurance Co. (Brownwood, TX) 83386
Liberty Mutual Insurance Co. (Corsicana, TX) 83782
Liberty Mutual Insurance Co. (El Paso, TX) 84837
Liberty Mutual Insurance Co. (Houston, TX) 86456; 86457
Liberty Mutual Insurance Co. (Lubbock, TX) 87769
Liberty Mutual Insurance Co. (Tyler, TX) 89812
Liberty Mutual Insurance Co. (Fairfax, VA) 90790
Liberty Mutual Insurance Co. (Lynchburg, VA) 91266
Liberty Mutual Insurance Co. (Norfolk, VA) 91549
Liberty Mutual Insurance Co. (Roanoke, VA) 92168
Liberty Mutual Insurance Cos (Miami, FL) 61359
Liberty Mutual Insurance Gr (Austin, TX) 82924
Life Insur Co. of Virginia (Staunton, VA) 92325
Life Insurance Co. of Va (Baltimore, MD) 71180
Life Insurance Co. of Va (Midlothian, VA) 91418
Life Insurance Co. of Va (Williamsburg, VA) 92575
Life Insurance Co. of Va (Winchester, VA) 92597
Life Insurance Co. of Va (Charleston, WV) 92764
Life Insurance Co. of Virgin (Bristol, TN) 80251
Life Insurance Co. of Virgin (Richmond, VA) 91918
Life Insurance Co. of Virgin (Roanoke, VA) 92169
Life Insurance Co. Virginia (Danville, VA) 90704
Life Insurance Co. of Virginia (Fairfax, VA) 90791
Life Insurance Co. of Virginia (Lawrenceville, VA) 91185
Life Insurance Co. of Virginia (Norfolk, VA) 91550
Life Insurance Co. of Virginia (Portsmouth, VA) 91661
Life Insurance Co. of Virginia (Richmond, VA) 91919
Life Insurance Co. of Virginia (Roanoke, VA) 92170
Massachusetts Mutual Life Insurance (Birmingham, AL) 55319
Massachusetts Mutual Life Insurance (Huntsville, AL) 55972
Massachusetts Mutual Life Insurance (Mobile, AL) 56206; 56207
Massachusetts Mutual Life Insurance (Gainesville, FL) 59893
Massachusetts Mutual Life Insurance (Naples, FL) 61643; 61644
Massachusetts Mutual Life Insurance (Sarasota, FL) 62845
Massachusetts Mutual Life Insurance (Tampa, FL) 63495
Massachusetts Mutual Life Insurance (Greenville, MS) 72808
Massachusetts Mutual Life Insurance (Charlotte, NC) 74082
Massachusetts Mutual Life Insurance (Eden, NC) 74461
Massachusetts Mutual Life Insurance (Williamston, NC) 76530
Massachusetts Mutual Life Insurance (Wilmington, NC) 76583
Massachusetts Mutual Life Insurance (Lawton, OK) 77166
Massachusetts Mutual Life Insurance (Greer, SC) 79480
Massachusetts Mutual Life Insurance (Spartanburg, SC) 79919
Massachusetts Mutual Life Insurance (Dallas, TX) 84223
Massachusetts Mutual Life Insurance (El Paso, TX) 84848
Massachusetts Mutual Life Insurance (Hurst, TX) 87282; 87283
Mid Continent Life Insuranc (Nashville, TN) 82063
Minnesota Mutual Life Insurance C (Roanoke, VA) 92173
Mutual of New York (Athens, AL) 55044
Mutual of New York (Eufaula, AL) 55702
Mutual of New York (Foley, AL) 55749
Mutual of New York (Mobile, AL) 56210
Mutual of New York (Tuscaloosa, AL) 56664
Mutual of New York (Fort Lauderdale, FL) 59544
Mutual of New York (Lakeland, FL) 60756
Mutual of New York (Naples, FL) 61646
Mutual of New York (Ocala, FL) 61809
Mutual of New York (Tallahassee, FL) 63252
Mutual of New York (W Palm Beach, FL) 63797
Mutual of New York (Albany, GA) 64084
Mutual of New York (Bogalusa, LA) 69706
Mutual of New York (Natchez, MS) 73204
Mutual of New York (Vicksburg, MS) 73459
Mutual of New York (Goldsboro, NC) 74726; 74727
Mutual of New York (Lexington, NC) 75420
Mutual of New York (Bartlesville, OK) 76836
Mutual of New York (Norman, OK) 77262
Mutual of New York (Myrtle Beach, SC) 79706
Mutual of New York (Cleveland, TN) 80595
Mutual of New York (Edna, TX) 84744
Mutual of New York (Harlingen, TX) 85707
Mutual of New York (Mc Allen, TX) 87891
Mutual of New York Insurance (Geneva, AL) 55803
Mutual of New York Insurance Co. (Leesburg, VA) 91196
Mutual of New York Money (El Paso, TX) 84854
National Home Life Assur Co. (Fayetteville, NC) 74569
National Home Life Assurancenc (Winston Salem, NC) 76677
Nationwide Life Insurance C (Arlington, TX) 82711
New England Mutl Life Insurance C (Fort Lauderdale, FL) 59545
New England Mutl Life Insurance C (Miami, FL) 61381
New England Mutl Life Insurance C (Pensacola, FL) 62452
New England Mutl Life Insurance C (Kenner, LA) 70001
New England Mutl Life Insurance C (El Paso, TX) 84858
New England Mutl Life Insurance C (Fort Worth, TX) 85203
New England Mutual Life (Alexandria, LA) 69395
New England Mutual Life Insurance (Huntsville, AL) 55978
New England Mutual Life Insurance (Monroeville, AL) 56266
New England Mutual Life Insurance (Orlando, FL) 62067
New England Mutual Life Insurance (Tampa, FL) 63507
New England Mutual Life Insurance (High Point, NC) 75153
New England Mutual Life Insurance (Tulsa, OK) 78031
New England Mutual Life Insurance (Greenville, SC) 79399
New England Mutual Life Insurance (Huntington, WV) 92885
New York Life (Altavista, VA) 90251
New York Life (Chester, VA) 90621
New York Life (Danville, VA) 90705
New York Life (Madison Heights, VA) 91300
New York Life (Newport News, VA) 91474
New York Life Insur Co. (Waynesboro, VA) 92535
New York Life Insurance (Lewes, DE) 57829
New York Life Insurance (Rehoboth Beach, DE) 57948
New York Life Insurance (Middletown, MD) 72135
New York Life Insurance (Rising Sun, MD) 72249
New York Life Insurance (Abingdon, VA) 90155
New York Life Insurance (Bassett, VA) 90416
New York Life Insurance (Lynchburg, VA) 91270
New York Life Insurance (Midlothian, VA) 91420
New York Life Insurance (Norfolk, VA) 91555
New York Life Insurance (Richmond, VA) 91935
New York Life Insurance (Verona, VA) 92394
New York Life Insurance Co. (Wilmington, DE) 58089
New York Life Insurance Co. (Cumberland, MD) 71631
New York Life Insurance Co. (Frederick, MD) 71738
New York Life Insurance Co. (Hagerstown, MD) 71886
New York Life Insurance Co. (Maugansville, MD) 72133
New York Life Insurance Co. (North East, MD) 72156
New York Life Insurance Co. (Rockville, MD) 72309
New York Life Insurance Co. (Silver Spring, MD) 72433
New York Life Insurance Co. (Union Bridge, MD) 72511
New York Life Insurance Co. (Amherst, VA) 90253
New York Life Insurance Co. (Arlington, VA) 90362; 90363
New York Life Insurance Co. (Chase City, VA) 90552
New York Life Insurance Co. (Covington, VA) 90663
New York Life Insurance Co. (Danville, VA) 90706
New York Life Insurance Co. (Franklin, VA) 90896
New York Life Insurance Co. (Fredericksburg, VA) 90932
New York Life Insurance Co. (Harrisonburg, VA) 91094
New York Life Insurance Co. (Lynchburg, VA) 91271; 91272; 91273
New York Life Insurance Co. (Manassas, VA) 91317
New York Life Insurance Co. (Marion, VA) 91335
New York Life Insurance Co. (Norfolk, VA) 91556; 91557
New York Life Insurance Co. (Pearisburg, VA) 91625
New York Life Insurance Co. (Portsmouth, VA) 91662
New York Life Insurance Co. (Prince George, VA) 91676
New York Life Insurance Co. (South Boston, VA) 92254
New York Life Insurance Co. (Staunton, VA) 92326
New York Life Insurance Co. (Virginia Beach, VA) 92493
New York Life Insurance Co. (Warrenton, VA) 92526
New York Life Insurance Co. (Yorktown, VA) 92654
New York Life Insurance Co. Gnl (Bethesda, MD) 71425
Northrop Inc. (New Orleans, LA) 70544
Northwestern Mutual Life (Dover, DE) 57797
Northwestern Mutual Life (Covington, KY) 68228
Northwestern Mutual Life (Johnson City, TN) 81051
Northwestern Mutual Life (Richmond, VA) 91937
Northwestern Mutual Life (Winchester, VA) 92599
Northwestern Mutual Life, Inc. (Bowling Green, KY) 68154
Northwestern Mutual Life Inc. (Danville, KY) 68261
Northwestern Mutual Life Inc. (Leitchfield, KY) 68513
Northwestern Mutual Life Inc. (Lexington, KY) 68595; 68596
Northwestern Mutual Life Inc. (Louisville, KY) 68932
Northwestern Mutual Life Inc. (Owensboro, KY) 69187
Northwestern Mutual Life Inc. (Baltimore, MD) 71213
Northwestern Mutual Life Inc. (Memphis, TN) 81661
Northwestern Mutual Life Inc. (Nashville, TN) 82071
Northwestern Mutual Life Inc. (Charlottesville, VA) 90545
Northwestern Mutual Life Inc. (Lexington, VA) 91209
Northwestern Mutual Life Inc. (Lynchburg, VA) 91274
Northwestern Mutual Life Inc. (South Boston, VA) 92255
Northwestern Mutual Life Inc. (Beckley, WV) 92679
Northwestern Mutual Life Inc. (Clarksburg, WV) 92813
Northwestern Mutual Life Inc. (Huntington, WV) 92886
Northwestern Mutual Life Inc. (Lewisburg, WV) 92917
Northwestern Mutual Life Inc. (Princeton, WV) 93011
Northwestern Mutual Life Inc. (Wheeling, WV) 93116
Penn Mutual Life Insurance (St Petersburg, FL) 63000
Penn Mutual Life Insurance (Jackson, MS) 73029
Penn Mutual Life Insurance (Greensboro, NC) 74875
Penn Mutual Life Insurance (Charleston, WV) 92777
Penn Mutual Life Insurance (Clarksburg, WV) 92815
Penn Mutual Life Insurance Co. (Fort Smith, AR) 57080
Penn Mutual Life Insurance Co. (Orlando, FL) 62073
Penn Mutual Life Insurance Co. (Thomasville, GA) 67801
Penn Mutual Life Insurance Co. (Baton Rouge, LA) 69594
Penn Mutual Life Insurance Co. (Johnson City, TN) 81052
Penn Mutual Life Insurance Co. (Nashville, TN) 82079
Penn Mutual Life Insurance Co. (Dallas, TX) 84296; 84297
Penn Mutual Life Insurance Co. (Clarksburg, WV) 92816
Phoenix Home Life Mutual Insurance Co. (Bethesda, MD) 71432
Principal Mutual Life Insurance (Birmingham, AL) 55353
Principal Mutual Life Insurance (Huntsville, AL) 56001
Principal Mutual Life Insurance Co. (Austin, TX) 82974
Progressive Casualty Insurance Co. (Baltimore, MD) 71221
Progressive Casualty Insurance Co. (Richmond, VA) 91952
Progressive Insurance Agency (Punta Gorda, FL) 62715
Provident National Assurance (Atlanta, GA) 65044
Recovery Services International (Tampa, FL) 63575
Recovery Services International (Metairie, LA) 70310
Recovery Services International (Charlotte, NC) 74144
Recovery Servies International (Dallas, TX) 84351
Reliance Insurance Co. (Birmingham, AL) 55369; 55370
Reliance Insurance Co. (Orlando, FL) 62132
Reliance Insurance Co. (Atlanta, GA) 65076
Reliance Insurance Co. (Louisville, KY) 68986
Reliance Insurance Co. (Shreveport, LA) 70777
Reliance Insurance Co. (Columbia, MD) 71600
Reliance Insurance Co. (Nashville, TN) 82086; 82087
Reliance Insurance Co. (Dallas, TX) 84355
Reliance Insurance Co. (Houston, TX) 86793
Reliance Insurance Co. (San Antonio, TX) 89212; 89213
Reliance Insurance Co. (Columbia, VA) 90653
Rollins Burdick & Hunter (Oklahoma City, OK) 77538
Rollins Burdick Hunter (San Antonio, TX) 89214
Rollins Burdick Hunter Agcy (Dallas, TX) 84357
Rollins Burdick Hunter Fla (Winter Haven, FL) 63951
Safeco Insurance Co. of America (Birmingham, AL) 55383
Safeco Insurance Co. of America (Montgomery, AL) 56376
Safeco Insurance Co. of America (Savannah, GA) 67510
Safeco Insurance Co. of America (Dallas, TX) 84372; 84373
Safeco Insurance Co. of America (Plano, TX) 88606
Safeco Insurance Co. of America (San Antonio, TX) 89219
Shelby Insurance Co. (Greensboro, NC) 74907
Shenandoah Life Insurance Co. (Roanoke, VA) 92186
State Mutual of America (Tampa, FL) 63603
State Mutual of America (Austin, TX) 83006
Superior Life Insurance (Monroe, LA) 70378
Title Insur Co. of Minn Titl (Jacksonville, FL) 60476
Title Insurance Co. Minnesot (Columbia, SC) 79109
Transamerica Occidental Lif (Greenville, MS) 72823
Transamerica Occidental Life Inc. (Altamonte Spg, FL) 58547
Transamerica Occidental Life Inc. (Maitland, FL) 60987
Transamerica Occidental Life Inc. (Louisville, KY) 69025
Transamerica Occidental Life Inc. (Nashville, TN) 82115
Transamerica Occidental Life Insurance (Destin, FL) 59350
Transamerica Occidental Life Insurance (Tallahassee, FL) 63282
Transamerica Occidental Life Insurance (Tampa, FL) 63631
Transamerica Occidental Life Insurance (W Palm Beach, FL) 63818
Transamerica Occidental Life Insurance (Valdosta, GA) 67975
Transamerica Occidental Life Insurance (Charlotte, NC) 74180; 74181
Transamerica Occidental Life Insurance (Tulsa, OK) 78181
Transamerica Occidental Life Insurance (Columbia, SC) 79111
Transamerica Occidental Life Insurance (Bristol, TN) 80257
Transamerica Occidental Life Insurance (Madison, TN) 81381
Transamerica Occidental Life Insurance (Dallas, TX) 84463
Transamerica Occidental Life Insurance (Houston, TX) 87041
Transamerica Occidental Life Insurance (Longview, TX) 87739
Transamerica Occidental Life Insurance (Midland, TX) 88090
Transamerica Occidental Life Insurance (Norfolk, VA) 91588
Transamerica Occidental Life Insurance (Charleston, WV) 92794
Travelers Insurance (Lynchburg, VA) 91290
Underwriters Adjusting Comp (Oklahoma City, OK) 77639
Underwriters Adjusting Co. (Huntsville, AL) 56044
Underwriters Adjusting Co. (Fort Smith, AR) 57112
Underwriters Adjusting Co. (Little Rock, AR) 57318

Underwriters Adjusting Co. (Jacksonville, FL) 60480
Underwriters Adjusting Co. (Miami, FL) 61486
Underwriters Adjusting Co. (Naples, FL) 61668
Underwriters Adjusting Co. (Pensacola, FL) 62484
Underwriters Adjusting Co. (Vidalia, GA) 67995
Underwriters Adjusting Co. (Bowling Green, KY) 68163
Underwriters Adjusting Co. (Lexington, KY) 68647
Underwriters Adjusting Co. (Baton Rouge, LA) 69678
Underwriters Adjusting Co. (Lafayette, LA) 70119
Underwriters Adjusting Co. (Shreveport, LA) 70798
Underwriters Adjusting Co. (Belmont, MS) 72611
Underwriters Adjusting Co. (Collins, MS) 72697
Underwriters Adjusting Co. (Jackson, MS) 73079
Underwriters Adjusting Co. (Mc Comb, MS) 73152
Underwriters Adjusting Co. (Asheville, NC) 73638
Underwriters Adjusting Co. (Charlotte, NC) 74182
Underwriters Adjusting Co. (Fayetteville, NC) 74578
Underwriters Adjusting Co. (Raleigh, NC) 75966
Underwriters Adjusting Co. (Wilmington, NC) 76602
Underwriters Adjusting Co. (Cyril, OK) 76984
Underwriters Adjusting Co. (Tulsa, OK) 78184
Underwriters Adjusting Co. (Greenville, SC) 79442
Underwriters Adjusting Co. (Cookeville, TN) 80669
Underwriters Adjusting Co. (Gibson, TN) 80859
Underwriters Adjusting Co. (Knoxville, TN) 81265
Underwriters Adjusting Co. (Martin, TN) 81399
Underwriters Adjusting Co. (Nashville, TN) 82117
Underwriters Adjusting Co. (Arlington, TX) 82772
Underwriters Adjusting Co. (Dallas, TX) 84468
Underwriters Adjusting Co. (El Paso, TX) 84954
Underwriters Adjusting Co. (Fort Worth, TX) 85338
Underwriters Adjusting Co. (Harlingen, TX) 85718
Underwriters Adjusting Co. (San Angelo, TX) 88904
Underwriters Adjusting Co. (San Antonio, TX) 89280
Underwriters Adjusting Co. (Temple, TX) 89650
Underwriters Adjusting Co. (Wichita Falls, TX) 90118
Underwriters Adjusting Co. (Norfolk, VA) 91589
Underwriters Adjusting Co. (Beckley, WV) 92687; 92688
Underwriters Adjusting Co. (Charleston, WV) 92795
Union Equity (Fort Worth, TX) 85339
Unum Life Insurance (Atlanta, GA) 65236
Unum Life Insurance Co. (Nashville, TN) 82131
US Fidelity (Birmingham, AL) 55442
US Fidelity (Fort Myers, FL) 59770
US Fidelity (Greenville, MS) 72824
US Fidelity (Charleston, SC) 78908
US Fidelity (Columbia, SC) 79117
US Fidelity (Commerce, TX) 83645
US Fidelity (Dallas, TX) 84478
US Fidelity (El Paso, TX) 84957
US Fidelity & Gu (Montgomery, AL) 56394
US Fidelity & Gu (Lafayette, LA) 70121
US Fidelity & Gu (Metairie, LA) 70323
US Fidelity & Gu (Gulfport, MS) 72881
US Fidelity & Gu (Jackson, MS) 73083
US Fidelity & Gu (Wilmington, NC) 76604
US Fidelity & Gu (Guymon, OK) 77117
US Fidelity & Gu (Muskogee, OK) 77232
US Fidelity & Gu (Tulsa, OK) 78187
US Fidelity & Gu (Houston, TX) 87063; 87064
US Fidelity & Gu (Midland, TX) 88094
US Fidelity & Gu (Richmond, VA) 92072
US Fidelity & Guaranty Insurance (Lexington, KY) 68650
US Fidelity & Guaranty Insurance (Louisville, KY) 69030
US Fidelity & Guaranty Insurance (Nashville, TN) 82132
Variable Annuity Life Insurance (Boca Raton, FL) 58747
Variable Annuity Life Insurance (Winter Park, FL) 63998
Variable Annuity Life Insurance (Dunwoody, GA) 66139
Variable Annuity Life Insurance (Metairie, LA) 70324
Variable Annuity Life Insurance (Montgomery, MD) 72138
Variable Annuity Life Insurance (Jackson, MS) 73084
Variable Annuity Life Insurance (Dallas, TX) 84485
Variable Annuity Life Insurance (Richmond, VA) 92074
Variable Annuity Life Insurance Co. (Boca Raton, FL) 58748
Variable Annuity Life Insurance Co. (Dallas, TX) 84486
Variable Annuity Life Insurance Co. (Houston, TX) 87074
Variable Annuity Marketing Co. (Houston, TX) 87076
Verex Assurance Inc. (Annapolis, MD) 71022
Verex Assurance Inc. (Charlotte, NC) 74194
Verex Assurance Inc. (Houston, TX) 87077
Verex Assurance Inc. (Mc Lean, VA) 91375
Volunteer State Life Insurance Co. (Beaumont, TX) 83232
Volunteer State Life Insurance Co. (San Antonio, TX) 89295
Wal Mart Insurance Agency (Tulsa, OK) 78196
West American Insurance Co. (Fort Lauderdale, FL) 59641
Western Life Insurance Co. (Maitland, FL) 60989
Western Life Insurance Co. (Metairie, LA) 70335
Western Life Insurance Co. (Baltimore, MD) 71327
Western Life Insurance Co. (Nashville, TN) 82144
Wetterau Inc. (Charleston, SC) 78915

6512 Nonresidential Building Operators

Arco Oil & Gas Co. (Dallas, TX) 83857
Arkansas Best (Fort Smith, AR) 57022
Bank South NA (Atlanta, GA) 64263
Builders Square Corporate Office (San Antonio, TX) 88941
Burlington Coat Factory (Greenbelt, MD) 71855
Burlington Manufactures Outlet Center (Burlington, NC) 73748
Burlington Outlet Mall (Burlington, NC) 73749
Career Image (Houston, TX) 85918
Casual Corner (Raleigh, NC) 75882
Cigna Holdings Inc. (Wilmington, DE) 58038
Coastal Corp. (Myrtle Beach, SC) 79696; 79697
Columbia Mall (Columbia, SC) 79007
Congen Properties Inc. (Wilmington, DE) 58046
Delta Air Lines (Dallas, TX) 83971
Delta Business Systems (Orlando, FL) 61960
First Federal S & L (Florence, AL) 55736
FPL Group Inc. (West Palm Beach, FL) 63866
Friendswood Development Co. (Houston, TX) 86212
Giant Food Market Inc. (Kingsport, TN) 81105
Hibernia National Bank (Alexandria, LA) 69384
Hibernia National Bank (Lafayette, LA) 70059
Intereal Co. (Nashville, TN) 82032
KMS Group, Inc. (Columbia, MD) 71595
Northrop Inc. (New Orleans, LA) 70543
Piggly Wiggly (Marion, VA) 91337
Publix Super Market (Lakeland, FL) 60770
Summit Corporate Center (Charleston, SC) 78893
Tyson Foods Inc. (Springdale, AR) 57651
US Fidelity & Gu (Jacksonville, FL) 60488
Volume Services Inc. (Baltimore, MD) 71322
Wachovia Bank Building (Fayetteville, NC) 74579
Wal Mart (Vinita, OK) 78229
Wal Mart Discount City (Bartow, FL) 58633
Wal Mart Plaza (Orange Park, FL) 61900
Wal Mart Properties Inc. (Bentonville, AR) 56796

6513 Apartment Building Operators

Citgo Service Station (Fort Pierce, FL) 59791
Courtyards (Memphis, TN) 81499
Kentucky Fried Chicken (Natchitoches, LA) 70402
KMS Group, Inc. (Columbia, MD) 71595
Oaks at Baymeadows the (Jacksonville, FL) 60382
Taco Bell (Titusville, FL) 63704

6514 Dwelling Operators Except Apartments

Cigna Holdings Inc. (Wilmington, DE) 58038
Congen Properties Inc. (Wilmington, DE) 58046
KMS Group, Inc. (Columbia, MD) 71595

6519 Real Property Lessors Nec

Blount Inc. (Montgomery, AL) 56284
Bowater Southern Div. (Newnan, GA) 67078
Bowater Southern (Newnan, GA) 67079
Champion International Corp. (Birmingham, AL) 55184
GTE Florida Inc. (Tampa, FL) 63447
GTE South Inc. (Tampa, FL) 63451
GTE Southwest Inc. (Irving, TX) 87351
Tredegar Industries Inc. (Richmond, VA) 92060

6531 Real Estate Agents & Managers

Ace Hardware (Solomons, MD) 72454
American Credit Services (Maitland, FL) 60972
American General Investment Corp. (Houston, TX) 85782
American General Mortgage Co. (Houston, TX) 85787
American General Realty Investment Corp. (Houston, TX) 85790
Appraisal Services Inc. (Baltimore, MD) 71039
Bank South Corp. (Atlanta, GA) 64253
Bank South NA (Atlanta, GA) 64263
Brookhollow Corp. (Richmond, VA) 91747
Casual Corner (Nashville, TN) 81915
Coast to Coast Real Estate (Jupiter, FL) 60533
Coast to Coast Realty (Punta Gorda, FL) 62703
Coast to Coast Realty & Inv (Ocala, FL) 61791
Constellation Holdings, Inc. (Baltimore, MD) 71097
Constellation Real Estate Group, Inc. (Baltimore, MD) 71102; 71103
Continental Indus Inc. (Winter Park, FL) 63969
Continental Industries Inc. (Winter Park, FL) 63970
CSX Realty Inc. (Richmond, VA) 91838
Danaher Corp. (Washington, DC) 58209
Dominion Lands Inc. (Richmond, VA) 91852
Equitable Real Estate Investment Management Inc. (Atlanta, GA) 64430
First American Bank (Cape St. Claire, MD) 71494
First Citizens Mortgage (High Point, NC) 75130
Firstmark Development Corp. (Charlotte, NC) 74013
Florida Power & Light Co., Inc. (West Palm Beach, FL) 63865
Friendswood Development Co. (Humble, TX) 87222
Great Western Bank (Boynton Beach, FL) 58777
Jiffy Lube (Greenville, SC) 79371
Jiffy Lube (Austin, TX) 82896
Kentucky Fried Chicken (Fort Myers Beach, FL) 59781
Kentucky Fried Chicken (Metairie, LA) 70279
Luhens Development Corp. (New Castle, DE) 57869
Marriott Ownership Resorts (Kissimmee, FL) 60592
Mary Kay Cosmetics (Port Richey, FL) 62678
Mary Kay Cosmetics (Zachary, LA) 70988
Mary Kay Cosmetics (Beaumont, TX) 83175
Meridian Properties Inc. (Charlotte, NC) 74083
Phillips Investments (Richmond, VA) 91949
Pizza Hut (Boca Raton, FL) 58728
Pizza Hut (Baton Rouge, LA) 69608
Pizza Hut (Darlington, SC) 79156
Pizza Hut (Conroe, TX) 83681
PRC Realty Systems Inc. (McLean, VA) 91397
Premier Bancorp (Houma, LA) 69965
Properties Inc. (Baltimore, MD) 71222
Pulte Home Corp. (Cary, NC) 73800
Record Data Inc. (Charlotte, NC) 74143
Safety Kleen Corp. (Kenner, LA) 70011
Shannon Properties (Charlotte, NC) 74155
Shell Co. Trust (Brunswick, GA) 65428
Sico Inc. (Tampa, FL) 63595
Signet Investment Corp. (Tampa, FL) 63597
South Padre Land Co. (Houston, TX) 86901
Southland Corp. (Laurel, MD) 72090
Southland Corp. (Ocean Springs, MS) 73222
Stop & Shop Bar B Q Inc. (Lafayette, LA) 70106
Sunrise Properties (Fort Worth, TX) 85284
Taco Bell (Winter Haven, FL) 63953
Taco Bell (Austin, TX) 83011
Talquin Corp. (St Petersburg, FL) 63036
Talquin Corp. (Tallahassee, FL) 63278
Tri-W Corp. (Nashville, TN) 82116
Turner Corp. (Oklahoma City, OK) 77638
Turner Corp. (Alexandria, VA) 90241
Turner Corp. (Newport News, VA) 91490
Turner Foods Corp. (Punta Gorda, FL) 62722
Walgreen Discount Store (Miami, FL) 61500
Winchester Homes Inc. (Pasadena, MD) 72213
Zebco (Alexandria, LA) 69418

6541 Title Abstract Offices

Chicago Title Insurance Co. (Baltimore, MD) 71086
Chicago Title Insurance Co. Maryland (Baltimore, MD) 71087
Chicago Title Insurance Co. Memphis (Memphis, TN) 81495
Title Insurance Co. of Minn (Dallas, TX) 84452
Title Insurance Co. of Minn (Fairfax, VA) 90810

6552 Subdividers & Developers Nec

American General Investment Corp. (Houston, TX) 85781; 85783
American General Life & Accedent Insurance Co. (Nashville, TN) 81887
Arkansas Best Corp. (Fort Smith, AR) 57023
Baltimore Gas & Electric Co. (Baltimore, MD) 71051
Beneficial Corp. (Wilmington, DE) 58015
Blount Inc. (Montgomery, AL) 56284
Bowater Inc. South Div. (Cullman, AL) 55538
Circuit City (Charlotte, NC) 73894
Constellation Energy Inc. (Baltimore, MD) 71092
Constellation Holdings, Inc. (Baltimore, MD) 71097
Constellation Real Estate Group, Inc. (Baltimore, MD) 71102; 71103
Continental Industries Inc. (Orlando, FL) 61956
Dominion Lands Inc. (Richmond, VA) 91853
Dominion Resources Inc. (Richmond, VA) 91858
Duke Power Co. Inc. (Charlotte, NC) 73940
Friendswood Development Co. (Houston, TX) 86210; 86212
Greystone Realty Corp. (Irving, TX) 87349
Harbour Island, Inc. (Tampa, FL) 63455
Intereal Co. (Houston, TX) 86309
KMS Group at Piney Orchard (Odenton, MD) 72168; 72169
Maxxam Inc. (Houston, TX) 86524
MAXXAM Property Co. (Houston, TX) 86526
Mitchell Energy Prod Corp. (Spring, TX) 89472
Pulte Home Corp. (Hialeah, FL) 60004
Talquin Corp. (St Petersburg, FL) 63036

6700 Holding & Other Investment Offices

Amax Metals Recovery Inc. (Braithwaite, LA) 69738

6712 Bank Holding Companies

AmSouth Bancorporation (Birmingham, AL) 55129
Bank South Corp. (Atlanta, GA) 64253
Bank South Macon (Macon, GA) 66655
Bank South NA (Atlanta, GA) 64263
Bank South NA/Macon (Macon, GA) 66669
BNY Holdings (Delaware) Corp. (Newark, DE) 57900
Deposit Guaranty Corp. (Jackson, MS) 72968
First Union Corp. (Charlotte, NC) 73979; 73980
First Union Corp. of Georgia (Atlanta, GA) 64449
First Union National Bank of Florida (Jacksonville, FL) 60300
First Virginia Banks Inc. (Falls Church, VA) 90848
Firstfed Bancorp Inc. (Bessemer, AL) 55090
Firstfed Northern Kentucky Bancorporation Inc. (Covington, KY) 68218
Fortune Bancorp Inc. (Clearwater, FL) 59005
Provident Financial Corp. (Columbia, SC) 79077

6719 Holding Companies Nec

ADP Automatic Data Processing (Wilmington, DE) 57973
ALLTEL Corp. (Little Rock, AR) 57245
Alumax Inc. (Norcross, GA) 67095
American Medical Holdings, Inc. (Dallas, TX) 83850
Arkansas Best Corp. (Fort Smith, AR) 57023
Armstrong Cork Finance Corp. (Wilmington, DE) 57987
Armstrong World Industries (DE), Inc. (Wilmington, DE) 57989
Bell Atlantic Bus Syst Servs. (Louisville, KY) 68700
Bell Atlantic Business System Services (Birmingham, AL) 55161
Bell Atlantic Tricon Lease Corp. (Ft. Lauderdale, FL) 59852
BellSouth Corp. (Atlanta, GA) 64317
BellSouth Enterprises Inc. (Atlanta, GA) 64318
Beneficial Corp. (Wilmington, DE) 58015
Blount Inc. (Montgomery, AL) 56284
Constellation Investments, Inc. (Baltimore, MD) 71100

Danaher Corp. (Washington, DC) 58209
Dominion Resources Inc. (Richmond, VA) 91856
Dominion Resources Inc. VA (Richmond, VA) 91859
First Colony Life (Richmond, VA) 91873
Flagstar Companies (Spartanburg, SC) 79895
Fleet Mortgage Group Inc. (Columbia, SC) 79019
GTE Mobile Communications Inc. (Atlanta, GA) 64526
J P Morgan Delaware (Wilmington, DE) 58076
Mobil Corp. (Fairfax, VA) 90797
Prodair Corp. (Wilmington, DE) 58095
Provident Financial Corp. (Columbia, SC) 79077
United Guaranty Corp. (Greensboro, NC) 74927

6722 Management Investment—Open-End
First Alabama Bank (Birmingham, AL) 55241
Southtrust Securities Inc. (Birmingham, AL) 55393

6726 Investment Offices Nec
Church Street Capital Corp. (Wilmington, DE) 58037

6733 Trusts Nec
J P Morgan Delaware (Wilmington, DE) 58076

6792 Oil Royalty Traders
Mitchell Energy Prod Corp. (Spring, TX) 89472

6794 Patent Owners & Lessors
Beneficial Business Brokers Inc. (Atlanta, GA) 64327
Dollar Rent-A-Car Systems Inc. (Tulsa, OK) 77932
Freeport-McMoran Resource Partners (New Orleans, LA) 70464
Piggly Wiggly Corp. (Memphis, TN) 81666
Thrifty Rent-A-Car System Inc. (Tulsa, OK) 78167
Tuner Broadcasting System, Inc. was Turner Communications Corp. (Atlanta, GA) 65225

6798 Real Estate Investment Trusts
American General Realty Investment Corp. (Houston, TX) 85790
First American Corp. (Greensboro, NC) 74820

6799 Investors Nec
Arcadian Corp. (Memphis, TN) 81461
Baltimore Gas & Electric Co. (Baltimore, MD) 71051
Constellation Investments, Inc. (Baltimore, MD) 71099
Dominion Resources Inc. (Richmond, VA) 91858
Duke Energy Corp. (Charlotte, NC) 73934
Duke Power Co. Inc. (Charlotte, NC) 73940
North Riverside Holding Inc. (Norcross, GA) 67165

7011 Hotels & Motels
American Family Life Assurance Co. (Columbus, GA) 65617
Courtyard (Memphis, TN) 81498
Courtyard by Marriott (Birmingham, AL) 55210
Courtyard by Marriott (West Palm Beach, FL) 63853
Courtyard by Marriott (Greenville, SC) 79332
Courtyard by Marriott (Chattanooga, TN) 80344
Courtyard by Marriott (San Antonio, TX) 88962; 88963
Courtyard by Marriott (Manassas, VA) 91304
Courtyard by Marriott (Richmond, VA) 91792

Courtyard by Marriott (Virginia Beach, VA) 92447
Fairfield Inn by Marriott (Birmingham, AL) 55234
Fairfield Inn by Marriott (Orlando, FL) 61965
Fairfield Inn by Marriott (Greensboro, NC) 74817
Fairfield Inn by Marriott (Florence, SC) 79199
Fairfield Inn by Marriott (Greenville, SC) 79348
Fairfield Inn by Marriott (Chattanooga, TN) 80371
Greyhound Bus Station (Titusville, FL) 63689
Marriott/Fairfield Inn (Washington, DC) 58317
Marriott Hotels (Salem, VA) 92217
Marriott Hotels, Resorts, & Suites (Washington, DC) 58323
Marriott Hotels Resorts Suites (Chattanooga, TN) 80422
Marriott International, Inc. (Washington, DC) 58323
Residence Inn by Marriott (Lexington, KY) 68613
Residence Inn by Marriott (Nashville, TN) 82088
Residence Inn by Marriott (Richmond, VA) 91978
Residence Inn by Marriott (Vienna, VA) 92419
Wal Mart Discount City (Cuero, TX) 83826
Walt Disney World Co. (Orlando, FL) 62191

7212 Garment Pressing & Cleaners' Agents
Trailway Laundry Inc. (Boone, NC) 73719

7213 Linen Supply
Springs Industries Inc. (Lancaster, SC) 79578

7217 Carpet & Upholstery Cleaning
Burdines Home Cleaning Service (W Palm Beach, FL) 63780
Burdines Home Clenaing Service (Orlando, FL) 61941
Rite Aid Discount Pharmacy (Owensboro, KY) 69191
Trailway Laundry Inc. (Boone, NC) 73719

7221 Photographic Studios—Portrait
Burdines Portrait Studio (Miami, FL) 61215; 61216
Burdines Portrait Studio (Pompano Beach, FL) 62587
Dillard Department Stores (Midland, TX) 88033
Foot Action (Killeen, TX) 87512
Wal Mart Portrait Studio (Alexandria, LA) 69415

7231 Beauty Shops
Ace Hardware (Concord, NC) 74303
Burdines Store Bty Salon (Miami, FL) 61217
Casual Corner (Frederick, MD) 71715
Casual Corner (Oklahoma City, OK) 77324
Casual Corner Beauty Shop (Taylorsville, NC) 76367
Coast to Coast Builders (Punta Gorda, FL) 62702
Exxon Co. (Kingsport, TN) 81082
Exxon Service Station (Norfolk, VA) 91516
Gayfers (Auburn, AL) 55061
Gayfers Department Store (Montgomery, AL) 56339
J C Penney Co. (White Marsh M, MD) 72569
J C Penney Co. (Fredericksbrg, VA) 90912
Kids R Us (Tyler, TX) 89808
Macy's Hair Design (Honea Path, SC) 79529
Mary Kay Cosmenics (Windsor, NC) 76657
Mary Kay Cosmetics (Van Buren, AR) 57690
Mary Kay Cosmetics (Columbia, SC) 79052
Mary Kay Cosmetics (Pflugerville, TX) 88507
Mary Kay Cosmetics (San Antonio, TX) 89096

Mary Kay Cosmetics (Waco, TX) 89952
Mary Kay Cosmetics (Marion, VA) 91334
Mary Kay Cosmetics (Charleston, WV) 92767; 92767
Mary Kay Cosmetics Dir (Mc Kinney, TX) 87915
Mary Kay Cosmetics Director (Austin, TX) 82935
Nike International (Huntsville, AL) 55979
Radio Shack (Van Horn, TX) 89861
Radio Shack (Exmore, VA) 90751; 90752

7241 Barber Shops
Taco Bell (Tuscaloosa, AL) 56676

7261 Funeral Services & Crematories
Exxon (Arcadia, LA) 69429

7291 Tax Return Preparation Services
Beneficial Florida Inc. (Pensacola, FL) 62409
Beneficial Income Tax Service (Baton Rouge, LA) 69473
Beneficial Income Tax Service (Killeen, TX) 87506
Beneficial Income Tax Service (Staunton, VA) 92308

7299 Miscellaneous Personal Services Nec
Air Products & Chemicals, Inc. (Tulsa, OK) 77874
Coast to Coast Bail Bond (New Port Richey, FL) 61680
Fitness Center (Athens, TN) 80188
Fitness Connection (Knoxville, TN) 81212
Fitness Factory (Cleveland, TN) 80586
Fitness World (Barboursville, WV) 92669
McDonalds (Plano, TX) 88586
McDonalds Hamburgers (St Augustine, FL) 62945
Thrift Drug (Wilmington, DE) 58114
Weight Watchers Internation (Hampton, VA) 91058

7300 Business Services
Bell Atlantic Bus Syst Servs. (Louisville, KY) 68700
Delta Air Systems Corp. (Birmingham, AL) 55216
US Doe Oak Ridge National Laboratory (Oak Ridge, TN) 82201

7311 Advertising Agencies
Bell South Enterprises, Inc. (Atlanta, GA) 64304
BellSouth Advertising & Publishing (Savannah, GA) 67456
Bellsouth Advertising & Publishing (Charlotte, NC) 73858
Berry L M & Co. (Nashville, TN) 81903
GTE National Marketing Services Inc. (Dallas, TX) 84106
L M Berry & Co. (Metairie, LA) 70283
Lorillard Inc. (Lexington, KY) 68574
Mast Advertising & Publishing (Fredericksburg, VA) 90930; 90931
Mast Advertising & Publishing (Woodbridge, VA) 92619
Sight & Sound (Laurens, SC) 79598
Springdale Advertising Agency Inc. (Falls Church, VA) 90871
Sterling Advertising (Birmingham, AL) 55597
U S Design (Tampa, FL) 63632
Westvaco Corp. Library (Charleston, SC) 78914

7312 Outdoor Advertising Services
Prints Plus (Kenner, LA) 70006
3M Advertising (Sanford, FL) 62783
3M Co. (Westminster, MD) 72545
3M National Advertising Co. (Nashville, TN) 82111

7313 Radio, T.V. & Publisher Representatives
BellSouth Advertising & Publishing (Savannah, GA) 67456
Donnelley Publishing (Houston, TX) 86045
L M Berry & Co. (Metairie, LA) 70283
L M Berry & Co. (Shreveport, LA) 70746
Mast Advertising & Publishing (Woodbridge, VA) 92619
Media Networks Inc. (Pompano Beach, FL) 62612
Media Networks Inc. (Tulsa, OK) 78020
Southwestern Bell Yellow Pages (Tulsa, OK) 78115
Southwestern Bell Yellow Pages (Fort Worth, TX) 85277
Union Recorder (Milledgeville, GA) 66985

7319 Advertising Nec
Donnelley Directory (Elm City, NC) 74502
Early Times Distillers Co. (Louisville, KY) 68756
Radio Shack (Charleston, SC) 78871
Stanhome Inc. (Charlotte, NC) 74164

7322 Adjustment & Collection Services
BellSouth Corp. (Atlanta, GA) 64317
Coast to Coast Credit Servs (Fort Lauderdale, FL) 59477
Mary Kay Cosmetics Representatives (Niceville, FL) 61712

7323 Credit Reporting Services
American Credit Services (Austin, TX) 82814
American General Finance (Greensboro, NC) 74763
American General Finance Inc. (Greensboro, NC) 74768
Beneficial Virginia Inc. (Virginia Beach, VA) 92436
Coast to Coast Cr Servs Inc. (Fort Lauderdale, FL) 59476
Pitney Bowes Credit Corp. (Metairie, LA) 70300

7331 Direct Mail Advertising Services
Southern Post (Nashville, TN) 82099

7335 Commercial Photography
Aero Service Corp. (Houston, TX) 85765

7336 Commercial Art & Graphic Design
Graphic Systems (Burlington, NC) 73756
International Computer Service Inc. (Hialeah, FL) 59989
Silicon Graphics Inc. (Dallas, TX) 84386

7338 Secretarial & Court Reporting
Manpower Inc. (Roanoke, VA) 92171
Ryder Truck Rental (Fairmont, WV) 92847

7342 Disinfecting & Pest Control Services
Edwards Co., Inc. (Newport News, VA) 91460
Pest Elimination Service (Fairview, TN) 80787
Wal Mart Discount Cities (Fort Smith, AR) 57116; 57117

7349 Building Maintenance Services Nec
Ace Hardware (Merritt Island, FL) 61136

Coast to Coast Janitor (Vero Beach, FL) 63746
Coast to Coast Janitor Service (Vero Beach, FL) 63747
Coast to Coast Pressure Clg (Fort Pierce, FL) 63747
Manpower Inc. (Norfolk, VA) 91551
Safety-Kleen Corp. (Chester, VA) 90625
Trailways Bus System (Terrell, TX) 89663

7353 Heavy Construction Equipment Rental
Bell Atl Syst Leasing International (Birmingham, AL) 55160
Grace Energy Corp. (Dallas, TX) 84094
Osca Inc. (Lafayette, LA) 70080
Ryder Truck Rental (Conway, AR) 56870
Ryder Truck Rental (Asheville, NC) 73637

7359 Equipment Rental & Leasing Nec
Aaron Rents (Atlanta, GA) 64187
Advanced Image Systems Inc. (Dallas, TX) 83837
Air Products & Chemicals Inc. (Albany, GA) 64061
,Albertson's (Maitland, FL) 60971
AMR Corp. (Fort Worth, TX) 85064
AmSouth Bank North America (Birmingham, AL) 55152
Ashland Services Co. (Lexington, KY) 68524
Baker Hughes Inc. (Houston, TX) 85835
BellSouth Corp. (Atlanta, GA) 64317
BellSouth Financial Services Corp. (Atlanta, GA) 64319
Central Products Inc. (Montgomery, AL) 56291; 56292
Elmco Inc. (Annapolis, MD) 71010
Fleet Financial Group Denrich Leasing Div. (Miami, FL) 61311
GTE Communications Corp. (Tampa, FL) 63445
GTE Leasing Corp. (Tampa, FL) 63450
Halliburton Resource Mgt (Robstown, TX) 88808
Hertz Rent-A-Car (Dallas, TX) 84115
Innovative Office Systems, Inc. (Dallas, TX) 84133
Liberty National Leasing Co. (Louisville, KY) 68864
Mobilecomm of Austin Inc. (Austin, TX) 82944
Modern Office Machines Inc. (Greenville, SC) 79396
Piggly Wiggly (Beaufort, SC) 78714
Ryder Truck Rental (Alabaster, AL) 54956
Ryder Truck Rental (Anniston, AL) 55012; 55013
Ryder Truck Rental (Birmingham, AL) 55375; 55376; 55377; 55378; 55379
Ryder Truck Rental (Cullman, AL) 55551
Ryder Truck Rental (Enterprise, AL) 55695
Ryder Truck Rental (Florence, AL) 55745
Ryder Truck Rental (Gardendale, AL) 55800
Ryder Truck Rental (Huntsville, AL) 56011
Ryder Truck Rental (Opelika, AL) 56424; 56425
Ryder Truck Rental (Selma, AL) 56538
Ryder Truck Rental (Tuscaloosa, AL) 56673; 56674
Ryder Truck Rental (Clarksville, AR) 56851
Ryder Truck Rental (De Queen, AR) 56896
Ryder Truck Rental (Dumas, AR) 56915
Ryder Truck Rental (Fayetteville, AR) 56990; 56991
Ryder Truck Rental (Fort Smith, AR) 57097; 57098
Ryder Truck Rental (H Spg Nat Pk, AR) 57132
Ryder Truck Rental (Little Rock, AR) 57308; 57310
Ryder Truck Rental (Morrilton, AR) 57380
Ryder Truck Rental (N Little Rock, AR) 57422
Ryder Truck Rental (Russellville, AR) 57588
Ryder Truck Rental (Searcy, AR) 57608

Ryder Truck Rental (Springdale, AR) 57642
Ryder Truck Rental (Van Buren, AR) 57693
Ryder Truck Rental (Apopka, FL) 58577
Ryder Truck Rental (Daytona Beach, FL) 59209
Ryder Truck Rental (De Funiak Spg, FL) 59239
Ryder Truck Rental (Fort Lauderdale, FL) 59600; 59601; 59602; 59603; 59604; 59605; 59606; 59607
Ryder Truck Rental (Gainesville, FL) 59917
Ryder Truck Rental (Hollywood, FL) 60093
Ryder Truck Rental (Homestead, FL) 60122
Ryder Truck Rental (Jacksonville, FL) 60440; 60441; 60443; 60448; 60449
Ryder Truck Rental (Lakeland, FL) 60781
Ryder Truck Rental (Miami, FL) 61453
Ryder Truck Rental (Ocala, FL) 61821
Ryder Truck Rental (Opa-Locka, FL) 61867
Ryder Truck Rental (Pensacola, FL) 62469
Ryder Truck Rental (Perry, FL) 62505
Ryder Truck Rental (Pompano Beach, FL) 62631; 62632
Ryder Truck Rental (Sanford, FL) 62780
Ryder Truck Rental (Tallahassee, FL) 63269
Ryder Truck Rental (Cartersville, GA) 65508
Ryder Truck Rental (Cordele, GA) 65720
Ryder Truck Rental (Gainesville, GA) 66290
Ryder Truck Rental (Macon, GA) 66709; 66710
Ryder Truck Rental (Moultrie, GA) 67064
Ryder Truck Rental (Thomasville, GA) 67804
Ryder Truck Rental (Valdosta, GA) 67974
Ryder Truck Rental (Warner Robins, GA) 68020
Ryder Truck Rental (Florence, KY) 68329
Ryder Truck Rental (Lexington, KY) 68623
Ryder Truck Rental (Versailles, KY) 69330
Ryder Truck Rental (Alexandria, LA) 69410
Ryder Truck Rental (Lafayette, LA) 70100; 70101; 70103
Ryder Truck Rental (New Iberia, LA) 70420
Ryder Truck Rental (New Orleans, LA) 70553; 70554
Ryder Truck Rental (West Monroe, LA) 70961
Ryder Truck Rental (Greenville, MS) 72820
Ryder Truck Rental (Jackson, MS) 73055
Ryder Truck Rental (Natchez, MS) 73211
Ryder Truck Rental (Vicksburg, MS) 73461
Ryder Truck Rental (Ahoskie, NC) 73525
Ryder Truck Rental (Asheboro, NC) 73596
Ryder Truck Rental (Charlotte, NC) 74153
Ryder Truck Rental (Dunn, NC) 74378
Ryder Truck Rental (Greensboro, NC) 74900; 74901; 74902; 74903
Ryder Truck Rental (Greenville, NC) 74977
Ryder Truck Rental (Havelock, NC) 75010
Ryder Truck Rental (Hope Mills, NC) 75195
Ryder Truck Rental (Laurinburg, NC) 75357
Ryder Truck Rental (Lenoir, NC) 75388
Ryder Truck Rental (Raleigh, NC) 75951; 75952; 75953
Ryder Truck Rental (Roanoke Rpds, NC) 76043
Ryder Truck Rental (Salisbury, NC) 76178
Ryder Truck Rental (Washington, NC) 76461; 76461
Ryder Truck Rental (Wilkesboro, NC) 76518
Ryder Truck Rental (Wilson, NC) 76642
Ryder Truck Rental (Altus, OK) 76796
Ryder Truck Rental (Ardmore, OK) 76819
Ryder Truck Rental (Bartlesville, OK) 76852
Ryder Truck Rental (Elk City, OK) 77038
Ryder Truck Rental (Grove, OK) 77093
Ryder Truck Rental (Guymon, OK) 77111
Ryder Truck Rental (Miami, OK) 77210; 77210
Ryder Truck Rental (Norman, OK) 77273
Ryder Truck Rental (Oklahoma City, OK) 77543
Ryder Truck Rental (Ponca City, OK) 77712
Ryder Truck Rental (Tulsa, OK) 78097; 78101
Ryder Truck Rental (Vinita, OK) 78228
Ryder Truck Rental (Watts, OK) 78238
Ryder Truck Rental (Aiken, SC) 78657
Ryder Truck Rental (Anderson, SC) 78692
Ryder Truck Rental (Camden, SC) 78762
Ryder Truck Rental (Florence, SC) 79223; 79224
Ryder Truck Rental (Greenville, SC) 79431
Ryder Truck Rental (Crossville, TN) 80705
Ryder Truck Rental (Abilene, TX) 82454; 82455; 82456
Ryder Truck Rental (Alpine, TX) 82501
Ryder Truck Rental (Amarillo, TX) 82578
Ryder Truck Rental (Austin, TX) 82996; 82997; 82998
Ryder Truck Rental (Bastrop, TX) 83097
Ryder Truck Rental (Big Spring, TX) 83294
Ryder Truck Rental (Brady, TX) 83332
Ryder Truck Rental (Brenham, TX) 83341
Ryder Truck Rental (Brownsville, TX) 83381
Ryder Truck Rental (Bryan, TX) 83408
Ryder Truck Rental (Channelview, TX) 83555
Ryder Truck Rental (Childress, TX) 83560
Ryder Truck Rental (Cleburne, TX) 83587
Ryder Truck Rental (Corpus Chrsti, TX) 83771; 83772
Ryder Truck Rental (Dalhart, TX) 83836
Ryder Truck Rental (Dallas, TX) 84359; 84362; 84364; 84371
Ryder Truck Rental (Denison, TX) 84607
Ryder Truck Rental (Duncanville, TX) 84710
Ryder Truck Rental (Eagle Pass, TX) 84722
Ryder Truck Rental (Fredericksbg, TX) 85373
Ryder Truck Rental (Garland, TX) 85532
Ryder Truck Rental (Georgetown, TX) 85573
Ryder Truck Rental (Harlingen, TX) 85714
Ryder Truck Rental (Houston, TX) 86800; 86801; 86802; 86803; 86804; 86805; 86806; 86809; 86810; 86811; 86812; 86813; 86815; 86816; 86817; 86818; 86823; 86824; 86826; 86827; 86829; 86829; 86830; 86831; 86832; 86833; 86834; 86835; 86836; 86837; 86839; 86841; 86842; 86844; 86846; 86851; 86853
Ryder Truck Rental (Irving, TX) 87398
Ryder Truck Rental (Kerrville, TX) 87483
Ryder Truck Rental (Levelland, TX) 87641
Ryder Truck Rental (Liberty, TX) 87680
Ryder Truck Rental (Lufkin, TX) 87817
Ryder Truck Rental (Mc Kinney, TX) 87920
Ryder Truck Rental (Mexia, TX) 88016
Ryder Truck Rental (Odessa, TX) 88270; 88271
Ryder Truck Rental (Pasadena, TX) 88466
Ryder Truck Rental (Pecos, TX) 88497
Ryder Truck Rental (Pharr, TX) 88512
Ryder Truck Rental (Plainview, TX) 88533
Ryder Truck Rental (Port Isabel, TX) 88665
Ryder Truck Rental (Portland, TX) 88694
Ryder Truck Rental (Richardson, TX) 88770; 88771
Ryder Truck Rental (San Angelo, TX) 88899; 88900
Ryder Truck Rental (Snyder, TX) 89452
Ryder Truck Rental (Spring, TX) 89486
Ryder Truck Rental (Stephenville, TX) 89525
Ryder Truck Rental (Taylor, TX) 89601
Ryder Truck Rental (Temple, TX) 89643; 89644
Ryder Truck Rental (Terrell, TX) 89661
Ryder Truck Rental (Tyler, TX) 89827
Ryder Truck Rental (Uvalde, TX) 89856
Ryder Truck Rental (Vernon, TX) 89871
Ryder Truck Rental (Weatherford, TX) 90013
Ryder Truck Rental (Wichita Falls, TX) 90099; 90100; 90101
Ryder Truck Rental (Charleston, WV) 92793
Ryder Truck Rental (Dunbar, WV) 92830
Ryder Truck Rental Inc. (New Castle, DE) 57874
Ryder Truck Rental Inc. (Newark, DE) 57930; 57931
Ryder Truck Rental Inc. (Richmond, VA) 92007
Ryder Truck Rental & Leasing (Nashville, TN) 82094
Ryder Truck Rental-One Way (Owensboro, KY) 69192
Ryder Truck Rental-One Way (Columbia, TN) 80639
Ryder Truck Rental-One Way (Lebanon, TN) 81308
Ryder Truck Rental One Way (Bluefield, WV) 92703
Ryder Truck Rental-Oneway (Bardstown, KY) 68119
Ryder Truck Rental-Oneway (Campbellsville, KY) 68183
Ryder Truck Rental-Oneway (Covington, KY) 68232
Ryder Truck Rental-Oneway (Danville, KY) 68262
Ryder Truck Rental-Oneway (Florence, KY) 68330
Ryder Truck Rental-Oneway (Greenville, KY) 68406
Ryder Truck Rental-Oneway (Henderson, KY) 68455
Ryder Truck Rental-Oneway (Madisonville, KY) 69070
Ryder Truck Rental-Oneway (Mayfield, KY) 69080
Ryder Truck Rental-Oneway (Richmond, KY) 69248
Ryder Truck Rental-Oneway (Johnson City, TN) 81055
Ryder Truck Rental-Oneway (Tullahoma, TN) 82379
Ryder Truck Rental-Oneway (Elkins, WV) 92834
Ryder Truck Rental Shop (Oklahoma City, OK) 77545
Safety Kleen Corp. (El Paso, TX) 84925
Security Pacific Housing (Greenville, SC) 79435
Short & Paulk Supply Co. Inc. (Tifton, GA) 67830
System Devices & Supplies Inc. (Miami, FL) 61467
Systems & Services (Greenville, SC) 79437
US Concord, Inc. (Houston, TX) 87062
Zeno Systems of Georgia Inc. (Atlanta, GA) 65299
Zeno Systems of Houston Inc. (Houston, TX) 87210
Zeno Systems of Oklahoma Inc. (Oklahoma City, OK) 77674

7361 Employment Agencies

Coast to Coast Services (Biloxi, MS) 72617
Human Affairs International (Baton Rouge, LA) 69558
Manpower, Inc. (Montgomery, AL) 56354
Manpower, Inc. (Jacksonville, FL) 60369
Manpower, Inc. (Panama City, FL) 62331
Manpower Inc. (Louisville, KY) 68874
Manpower, Inc. (Dallas, TX) 84216

7363 Help Supply Services

Manpower, Inc. (North Little Rock, AR) 57467
Manpower, Inc. (Jacksonville, FL) 60367; 60368; 60370
Manpower, Inc. (Albany, GA) 64081
Manpower, Inc. (Gulfport, MS) 72863
Manpower, Inc. (High Point, NC) 75152
Manpower, Inc. (Tulsa, OK) 78005
Manpower, Inc. (Beaumont, TX) 83174
Manpower, Inc. (Denton, TX) 84621
Manpower, Inc. (Temple, TX) 89623
Manpower, Inc. of Amarillo (Amarillo, TX) 82566
Manpower Inc. of Ce (Lexington, KY) 68576
Monarch Industries (Atlanta, GA) 64732
Reedy Creek Energy Services Inc. (Lake Buena Vista, FL) 60612

7371 Computer Programming Services

Advanced Micro Devices (Dallas, TX) 83838
Bell Atlantic Business System Services (Huntsville, AL) 55888
Bell Atlantic Corp. (San Antonio, TX) 88925
Bowater Computer Forms (Richardson, TX) 88723
Business Systems (Andrews, SC) 78698
Business Systems (Fairfax, VA) 90756
Business Systems Design Inc. (Orlando, FL) 61943
Business Systems Engineering (Myrtle Beach, SC) 79694
Business Systems Group (Pensacola, FL) 62412
Business Systems Inc. (Woodbridge, VA) 92609
Business Systems & Service Inc. (Vienna, WV) 93077
Business Systems Services (Atlantic Beach, FL) 58588
Business Systems & Software (Melbourne, FL) 61040
Business Systems Support Group Inc. (Rockville, MD) 72258
CSX Technology Inc. (Jacksonville, FL) 60248
Delta Business Systems (Bowie, MD) 71459
Dun & Bradstreet Software (Atlanta, GA) 64425
International Computer Service Inc. (Annapolis, MD) 71014
PRC (McLean, VA) 91394
PRC Inc. (McLean, VA) 91395
Radio Shack (Jacksonville, FL) 60435
Syscon Corp. (Washington, DC) 58499
Syscon Services Inc. (Washington, DC) 58500
Systems Engineering (Louisville, KY) 69012
Systems Engineering Associates International (Melbourne Beach, FL) 61124
Systems Engineering Solutions Inc. (Vienna, VA) 92423

7372 Prepackaged Software

Advanced Medical Systems (Clearwater, FL) 58958
Advanced Medical Systems (Houston, TX) 85762
Apple Computers Inc. (Nashville, TN) 81896
Boeing Co. Inc (Huntsville, AL) 55891
Compaq Computer Corp. (Dallas, TX) 83946
Critikon Inc. (Irving, TX) 87338
Digital Equipment Corporati (Little Rock, AR) 57273
Digital Equipment Corp. (Metairie, LA) 70260
Dun & Bradstreet Dun & Bradstreet Plan Services, Inc. (Tampa, FL) 63408
Dun & Bradstreet Software (Atlanta, GA) 64425
Dun & Bradstreet Software (Huntsville) (Huntsville, AL) 55909
Epsilon/Southwest (Dallas, TX) 84015
Inacomp Computer Centers (Baton Rouge, LA) 69560
Inacomp Computer Centers (Nashville, TN) 82030
Intergraph Corp. (Nashville, TN) 82034
Intergrated Technologies (Houston, TX) 86310
Johnson Controls Inc. (Tulsa, OK) 77969
Logistics Data System (Irving, TX) 87370
Martin Marietta Corp. Electonic Systems Co. (Orlando, FL) 62044
Martin Marietta Electronics Systems Co. (Orlando, FL) 62047
Martin Marietta Missile Systems (Orlando, FL) 62049
Martin Marietta Missile Systems Co. (Orlando, FL) 62050
Martin Marietta Ocala Operations (Ocala, FL) 61807
Microsoft Corp. (Houston, TX) 86580
Radio Shack (Jacksonville, FL) 60432; 60433
Sales Technologies (Atlanta, GA) 65138; 65139
Structured Management Syste (Richmond, VA) 92051
Sun Microsystems Inc. (Huntsville, AL) 56024
Syscon Corp. (Washington, DC) 58499
Syscon Corp. (Metairie, LA) 70313
Syscon Corp. (Williamsburg, VA) 92579
Systematics Information Services Inc. (Little Rock, AR) 57313
SYTECH Corp. (Houston, TX) 86928
Unisys Corp. (Tampa, FL) 63637
Unisys Corp. (Tyler, TX) 89838
Unisys Corp. (Clarksburg, WV) 92821
Universal Data Systems (Maitland, FL) 60988

7373 Computer Integrated Systems Design

Apple Computer (Austin, TX) 82818
Apple Computer Inc. (Nashville, TN) 81895
Apple Computers Inc. (Dallas, TX) 83856
AT&T Co. Software Solutions (Duluth, GA) 66020
Bell Atlantic Busn Sys Servs (Jackson, MS) 72949
Bell Atlantic Software & Systems Solutions, Inc. (Arlington, VA) 90279
Casi-Rusco Inc. (Boca Raton, FL) 58687
Computer Associates Inc. (Greenville, SC) 79331
Cray Research Inc. (Huntsville, AL) 55907
Cray Research Inc. (Tulsa, OK) 77925
DataServe (Louisville, KY) 68739
Diebold Inc. (Albany, GA) 64066
Digital Equipment Corporati (Fayetteville, AR) 56975
Digital Equipment Corporati (Melbourne, FL) 61049
Digital Equipment Corp. (Birmingham, AL) 55224
Digital Equipment Corp. (Fort Myers, FL) 59695
Digital Equipment Corp. (Tallahassee, FL) 63234
Digital Equipment Corp. (Lafayette, LA) 70051
Digital Equipment Corp. (Winston Salem, NC) 76667
Digital Equipment Corp. (Charleston, SC) 78807
Digital Equipment Corp. (Nashville, TN) 81934
Digital Equipment Corp. (Midland, TX) 88031
Digital Equipment Corporation (San Antonio, TX) 88971
Digital Equipment Corp. (Richmond, VA) 91844
Digital Equipment Corp. (Virginia Beach, VA) 92458
E-Systems Inc. (Dallas, TX) 83992
Electronic Data Systems Corp. (Tallahassee, FL) 63236
Engineering Research Associates Inc. (Vienna, VA) 92400

GTE Spacenet Corp. (McLean, VA) 91391
Hewlett-Packard Co. (Tulsa, OK) 77956
Hewlett-Packard Co. (San Antonio, TX) 89026
Inacomp Computer Centers (Melbourne, FL) 61070
Inacomp Computer Centers (Greensboro, NC) 74853
Intel Corp. (Oklahoma City, OK) 77388
Intel Corp. (Richmond, VA) 91908
Intergraph Corp. (Nashville, TN) 82033
Johnson Controls Inc. (Lubbock, TX) 87767
Maxtor Corp. (Austin, TX) 82936
Microage (Birmingham, AL) 55321
Microage (Mount Dora, FL) 61567
Microage (Greenville, NC) 74967
Mobil Oil Corp. (Longwood, FL) 60936
National Semiconductor Corp. (Austin, TX) 82946
Omni Business Systems (Melbourne, FL) 61081
PRC Public Sector Inc. (McLean, VA) 91396
Quotron Systems (Oklahoma City, OK) 77509
Radio Shack (Birmingham, AL) 55354
Radio Shack (West Memphis, AR) 57732
Radio Shack (Cocoa, FL) 59072
Radio Shack (Fort Myers, FL) 59753
Radio Shack (Fort Pierce, FL) 59806
Radio Shack (Jacksonville, FL) 60422
Radio Shack (Jupiter, FL) 60548
Radio Shack (Merritt is, FL) 61132
Radio Shack (Orlando, FL) 62128
Radio Shack (Sarasota, FL) 62860
Radio Shack (St Petersburg, FL) 63029
Radio Shack (Tampa, FL) 63573
Radio Shack (Gretna, LA) 69915
Radio Shack (Kenner, LA) 70010
Radio Shack (Monroe, LA) 70376
Radio Shack (Frederick, MD) 71741; 71745
Radio Shack (Goldsboro, NC) 74732
Radio Shack (Greensboro, NC) 74882
Radio Shack (Oklahoma City, OK) 77530
Radio Shack (North Augusta, SC) 79739
Radio Shack (Arlington, TX) 82741
Radio Shack (Austin, TX) 82990; 82991
Radio Shack (Fort Stockton, TX) 85047
Radio Shack (Galveston, TX) 85464
Radio Shack (Hurst, TX) 87292; 87294
Radio Shack (San Antonio, TX) 89196; 89201
Radio Shack (Danville, VA) 90710; 90711; 90712
Radio Shack (Richmond, VA) 91967; 91968; 91975
Radio Shack (Virginia Beach, VA) 92495; 92504
Southern Companies (Nashville, TN) 82098
Sun Microsystems Inc. (Tulsa, OK) 78116
Sun Microsystems Inc. (Austin, TX) 83008
Syscon Corp. (Tampa, FL) 63606
Tandy Computer Center (Charleston, SC) 78902
Ungermann-Bass Inc. (Longwood, FL) 60950
Unisys Corp. (Birmingham, AL) 55437
Unisys Corp. (Sarasota, FL) 62863
Unisys Corp. (Tampa, FL) 63637
Unisys Corp. (Baton Rouge, LA) 69681
Unisys Corp. (Jackson, MS) 73081
Unisys Corp. (Winston Salem, NC) 76688
Unisys Corp. (Bridgeport, WV) 92712
Wang Laboratories, Inc. (Nashville, TN) 82140
Western Digital (Greensboro, NC) 74942
Willamette Industries Inc. (Tulsa, OK) 78209

7374 Data Processing & Preparation

ADP Automatic Data Processing (Wilmington, DE) 57973
ADP-Automatic Data Processing (Tampa, FL) 63303
ADP Dealers Services (Newport News, VA) 91448
ADP Network Services (Washington, DC) 58123
AMR Corp. (Fort Worth, TX) 85064
AMR Information Services (Dallas-Fort Worth Airport, TX) 84513
Arkansas Best (Fort Smith, AR) 57022
Arkansas Best Corp. (Fort Smith, AR) 57023
Ashland Services Co. (Lexington, KY) 68524
AT&T Paradyne Corp. (Largo, FL) 60818
Automatic Data Processing (Newark, DE) 57889
Automatic Data Processing (Lexington, KY) 68527
Automatic Data Processing (Louisville, KY) 68694
Automatic Data Processing (San Antonio, TX) 88921
Boeing Co (Arlington, VA) 90280
Boeing Co. (Vienna, VA) 92395
Business Systems Tech. Inc. (Richardson, TX) 88724
Business Systems Technology Inc. (Richardson, TX) 88725
Centech Group (Arlington, VA) 90282
Critikon Inc. (Irving, TX) 87338
CSC Logic Inc. (Dallas, TX) 83960
CSX Technology Inc. (Jacksonville, FL) 60248
Data-Tronics Corp. (Fort Smith, AR) 57044; 57045; 57046
Davenport Data Processors, Inc. (Dallas, TX) 83968
Digital Equipment Corp. (Wilmington, DE) 58054
Digital Equipment Corp. (Daytona Beach, FL) 59173
Eastern Operations Center Inc. (Mechanicsville, VA) 91401
Electronic Data Systems (Winter Park, FL) 63971
Electronic Data Systems (Jackson, MS) 72978
Electronic Data Systems (Amarillo, TX) 82544
Electronic Data Systems (San Antonio, TX) 88976
Electronic Data Systems (Victoria, TX) 89885
Electronic Data Systems Cor (Herndon, VA) 91120
Electronic Data Systems Corp. (Charlotte, NC) 73942
Electronic Data Systems Corp. (Plano, TX) 88562
Electronic Data Systems Corp. (San Antonio, TX) 88977
First Data Corp. (Greensboro, NC) 74830
First Virginia Services Inc. (Falls Church, VA) 90854
GTE Data Services Inc. (Tampa, FL) 63446
GTE Data Services Inc. (Temple Terrace, FL) 63678
GTE Leasing Corp. (Tampa, FL) 63449
Intel Corp. (Annapolis Jct, MD) 71025
Intel Corp. (Tulsa, OK) 77959
International Computer Service Inc. (Hialeah, FL) 59989
Litton Computer Services-Eastern Regional Data Center (Reston, VA) 91713
Mead Data Central (Oklahoma City, OK) 77442
Mead Data Central (Austin, TX) 82937
NCR Corp. (Orlando, FL) 62066
Northern Operations Center Inc. (Falls Church, VA) 90862
Occupational Health Service (Nashville, TN) 82072
Payroll Data Service Inc. (Destin, FL) 59346
PRC (McLean, VA) 91394
PRC Inc. (McLean, VA) 91395
PRC Realty Systems Inc. (McLean, VA) 91397
Record Data Inc. (High Point, NC) 75159
Southwest Operations Center Inc. (Roanoke, VA) 92195
Structured Management Syste (Richmond, VA) 92052
Structured Mgt Systems Inc. (Richmond, VA) 92053
Syscon Corp. (Washington, DC) 58499
Syscon Corp. (King George, VA) 91181
Systematics Information Services Inc. (Little Rock, AR) 57313
Unisys Corp. (Huntsville, AL) 56047
Universal Data Systems (Brandon, FL) 58881
Washington Inventory Servic (Winter Park, FL) 64000
Washington Inventory Servic (Richmond, VA) 92081

7375 Information Retrieval Services

GTE Information Services (Dallas, TX) 84104

7376 Computer Facilities Management

Syscon Services Inc. (Washington, DC) 58500

7377 Computer Rental & Leasing

Bell Atl Syst Leasing International (Birmingham, AL) 55160
Butler Paper Co. (Amarillo, TX) 82534; 82535
Computer Associates Inc. (Greenville, SC) 79330
Modern Office Machines Inc. (Greenville, SC) 79395; 79396
Radio Shack (Ocala, FL) 61818
Systems Control Inc. (Springfield, VA) 92293

7378 Computer Maintenance & Repair

Amdahl Federal Service Corp. (Reston, VA) 91703
Automated Office Systems (Virginia Beach, VA) 92432
Bell Atlantic Bus Syst Servs. (Louisville, KY) 68700
Bell Atlantic Bus System Svc. (Tampa, FL) 63363
Bell Atlantic Bus Systems Svc. (Ft. Lauderdale, FL) 59851
Bell Atlantic Bus Systems Svc. (Jacksonville, FL) 60227
Bell Atlantic Bus Systems Svc. (Atlanta, GA) 64299
Bell Atlantic Bus Systems Svc (Baltimore, MD) 71062
Bell Atlantic Bus Systems Svc. (Lanham, MD) 72048
Bell Atlantic Bus Systems Svc. (Rockville, MD) 72257
Bell Atlantic Bus Systems Svc (Raleigh, NC) 75863
Bell Atlantic Business Services (El Paso, TX) 84766
Bell Atlantic Business System Services (Birmingham, AL) 55161
Bell Atlantic Business System Services (Huntsville, AL) 55888
Bell Atlantic Business Systems (Lubbock, TX) 87747
Bell Atlantic Business Systems Services (Memphis, TN) 81471
Bell Atlantic Business Systems Services (Austin, TX) 82824
Bell Atlantic Business Systems Services (Houston, TX) 85868
Bell Atlantic Business Systems Services (Richmond, VA) 91742
Bell Atlantic Business Systems Services (Roanoke, VA) 92104
Bell Atlantic Corp. (Dallas, TX) 83875
Bell Atlantic Corp. (San Antonio, TX) 88925
Bell Atlantic Services (Lynchburg, VA) 91224
Bell Atlantic Tricon Lease Corp. (Ft. Lauderdale, FL) 59852
Business Systems & Service Inc. (Vienna, WV) 93077
DataServe (Louisville, KY) 68739
Delta Business Systems (Orlando, FL) 61960; 61961
Digital Equipment Corp. (Nashville, TN) 81934
Digital Equipment Corp. (Webster, TX) 90018
First Data Resources (San Antonio, TX) 89008
Hewlett-Packard Co. (Oklahoma City, OK) 77382
Modern Office Machines Inc. (Greenville, SC) 79395
NCR Corp. (Hagerstown, MD) 71885
NCR Corp. (Olney, MD) 72177
Radio Shack (Tulsa, OK) 78072
Radio Shack (Greenville, SC) 79412
Radio Shack (Waco, TX) 89969
Sun Microsystems Inc. (Columbia, SC) 79099

7379 Computer Related Services Nec

Arkansas Best Corp. (Fort Smith, AR) 57023
Arnet Computer (Fort Lauderdale, FL) 59442
Arnet Computer (St. Petersburg, FL) 63081
Arnet Computer (Deluth, GA) 65915
Arnet Computer (Columbia, MD) 71576
Arnet Computer (Raleigh, NC) 75860
Arnet Computer (Addison, TX) 82470
Arnet Computer (Houston, TX) 85817
Data-Tronics Corp. (Fort Smith, AR) 57045
Digital Equipment Corp. (Tulsa, OK) 77929
Digital Equipment Corp. (North Parkers, WV) 92976
Ibm Corp. Nsd (Houston, TX) 86304
Inacomp Computer Centers (Louisville, KY) 68779
Intergraph Corp. (Nashville, TN) 82035
Logistics Data System (Irving, TX) 87370
PRC Inc. (McLean, VA) 91395
Radio Shack (Tampa, FL) 63574
Radio Shack (Richmond, VA) 91957
Syscon Services Inc. (Washington, DC) 58500
Systems Control Inc. (Houston, TX) 86927

7381 Detective & Armored Car Services

Advance Security Inc. (Atlanta, GA) 64202
Diebold Inc. (Memphis, TN) 81511
Diversified Claim Services (Birmingham, AL) 55225
Fleet Finance Inc. (New Orleans, LA) 70456
Fred Meyers Co. Inc. (Little Rock, AR) 57282; 57283
Wells Fargo Armored Services Corp. (Atlanta, GA) 65282
Wells Fargo Guard Service (Gainesville, FL) 59925
Wells Fargo Guard Service (Metairie, LA) 70333
Wells Fargo Guard Service (Tulsa, OK) 78207
Wells Fargo Guard Service Inc. (Miami, FL) 61515
Wells Fargo Guard Services (Casselberry, FL) 58946
Wells Fargo Guard Services (Jacksonville, FL) 60509
Wells Fargo Guard Services (W Palm Beach, FL) 63823
Wells Fargo Guard Servs (Tulsa, OK) 78208
Wells Fargo Guard Servs Co. (Houston, TX) 87173

7382 Security Systems Services

Diebold Inc. (Mobile, AL) 56155
Diebold Inc. (Montgomery, AL) 56301
Diebold Inc. (Jacksonville, FL) 60260
Diebold Inc. (Tallahassee, FL) 63233
Diebold Inc. (Vero Beach, FL) 63749
Diebold Inc. (Raymond, MS) 73312
Diebold, Inc. (San Antonio, TX) 88970
Diebold Inc. (Virginia Beach, VA) 92457

7383 News Syndicates

Kentucky Post the (Frankfort, KY) 68363
Press Inc. (Johnson City, TN) 81054
Wall Street Journal (Charlotte, NC) 74223

7384 Photofinishing Laboratories

Eckerd Corp. (Largo, FL) 60829
Jack Eckerd Corp. (Largo, FL) 60834
International Computer Service (Hialeah, FL) 59988
Kmart Photography Studio (Garland, TX) 85495
Qualex Inc. (Durham, NC) 74425
Radio Shack (Stilwell, OK) 77850
Rite Aid (Arlington, VA) 90381
Rite Aid Discount Pharmacy (St. Marys, WV) 93073
Shell Service Ctr (Mountain Home, AR) 57391
Wal Mart (Tulsa, OK) 78189
Walgreen (W Palm Beach, FL) 63821
Walgreen (El Paso, TX) 84966
Walgreen Drug Stores (Brandon, FL) 58882
Walgreen Drug Stores (Lake Worth, FL) 60702
Walgreen Drug Stores (Miami, FL) 61503; 61505; 61507
Walgreen Drug Stores (Tampa, FL) 63651; 63654
Walgreen Drug Stores (West Palm Beach, FL) 63908
Walgreen Drug Stores (Deer Park, TX) 84575
Walgreen Drug Stores (El Paso, TX) 84969; 84970
Walgreen Drug Stores (Huntsville, TX) 87267
Walgreen Drug Stores (San Antonio, TX) 89309; 89312; 89313; 89314; 89315; 89318; 89320; 89321; 89322; 89323; 89324

7389 Business Services Nec

Ace Hardware (Buna, TX) 83414
AMR Corp. (Fort Worth, TX) 85064
Avery Dennison (Meridian, MS) 73159
Baltimore Gas (Cockys Height Valley, MD) 71558
Beneficial Business Brokers Inc. (Atlanta, GA) 64327
Beneficial National Bank USA (Wilmington, DE) 58028
Burlington Industries Inc. (Dallas, TX) 83891
Capezio (Dallas, TX) 83893
Charles Schwab Co. Inc. (Nashville, TN) 81920
The Chesapeake & Potomac Telephone Co. of Virginia (Richmond, VA) 91768
Coast to Coast Express (Gulfport, MS) 72850
Coast to Coast Imprinted Sp (San Antonio, TX) 88958
Computer Assoc (Sanford, FL) 62765
Csc Credit Service (Metairie, LA) 70259
Delta Air Systems Corp. (Birmingham, AL) 55216
Digital Equipment Corp. (Greenville, SC) 79345
Electronic Data Systems (Elizabethtown, KY) 68277
Emery Worldwide (Baton Rouge, LA) 69511
Emery Worldwide (Dallas, TX) 84007
FCC National Bank (Wilmington, DE) 58060
Federal Express Corp. (Jonesboro, AR) 57215
Federal Express Corp. (Clearwater, FL) 58992
Federal Express Corp. (Orlando, FL) 61968
Federal Express Corp. (Pensacola, FL) 62423
Federal Express Corp. (Savannah, GA) 67466
Gannett Telemarketing (Nashville, TN) 82016
General Motors Corp. Pontiac Motor Division (Oklahoma City, OK) 77373
Greyhound Bus Lines (Georgetown, TX) 85567
Ibm Corp. (Savannah, GA) 67489
Innovative Office Systems, Inc. (Dallas, TX) 84133; 84134
Intel Corp. (Austin, TX) 82894
A & a International (Fort Worth, TX) 85131
International Computer Service Inc. (Hialeah, FL) 59989
Lapp Insulator Co. (Pineville, NC) 75817
McDonalds Office (Birmingham, AL) 55320
Metlife Capital Corp. (Houston, TX) 86578
Minnesota Mining&Mfg Co. Inc. (Louisville, KY) 68885
Mobil Oil Corp. (Chickasha, OK) 76932
Mobile Communications Corp. of America (Ridgeland, MS) 73326
Pittston Coal Export Co. (Norfolk, VA) 91565
Pizza Hut (Little Rock, AR) 57295
PRC Inc. (McLean, VA) 91395

Radio Shack (St Petersburg, FL) 63023

RJ Reynolds Tabacco Co. (Winston Salem, NC) 76683

Royal Manufacturing Inc. (Pompano Beach, FL) 62630

Ryder Truck Rental (Foley, AL) 55754

Ryder Truck Rental (Little Rock, AR) 57309

Ryder Truck Rental (Magnolia, AR) 57335

Ryder Truck Rental (Boca Raton, FL) 58739; 58740

Ryder Truck Rental (Deerfield Beach, FL) 59287

Ryder Truck Rental (Fort Myers, FL) 59760

Ryder Truck Rental (Gainesville, FL) 59916

Ryder Truck Rental (Hallandale, FL) 59965

Ryder Truck Rental (Hollywood, FL) 60092

Ryder Truck Rental (Jacksonville, FL) 60442

Ryder Truck Rental (Lake Worth, FL) 60696

Ryder Truck Rental (Largo, FL) 60862

Ryder Truck Rental (Melbourne Fl, FL) 61125

Ryder Truck Rental (Miami, FL) 61448; 61450; 61451

Ryder Truck Rental (N Bay Village, FL) 61585

Ryder Truck Rental (Ocala, FL) 61820

Ryder Truck Rental (Ormond Beach, FL) 62211

Ryder Truck Rental (Pensacola, FL) 62470

Ryder Truck Rental (W Palm Beach, FL) 63814

Ryder Truck Rental (West Palm Beach, FL) 63897; 63898

Ryder Truck Rental (Cordele, GA) 65719

Ryder Truck Rental (Douglas, GA) 65975

Ryder Truck Rental (Griffin, GA) 66323

Ryder Truck Rental (Savannah, GA) 67508

Ryder Truck Rental (Baton Rouge, LA) 69654

Ryder Truck Rental (Burlington, NC) 73761

Ryder Truck Rental (Jackson, TN) 81000

Ryder Truck Rental (Madisonville, TN) 81387

Ryder Truck Rental (Rogersville T, TN) 82283

Ryder Truck Rental (Cedar Hill, TX) 83531

Ryder Truck Rental (Dallas, TX) 84365

Ryder Truck Rental (Houston, TX) 86847; 86848; 86849; 86850

Ryder Truck Rental (La Marque, TX) 87546

Ryder Truck Rental (Moundsville, WV) 92954

Ryder Truck Rental Inc. (Wilmington, DE) 58108

Ryder Truck Rental Inc. (Martinsville, VA) 91356

Safety Kleen Corp. (Midland, TX) 88072

Service Merchandise (Miami, FL) 61459

Sparkletts Water Sys. Aqua Vend (North Miami, FL) 61736

Sparkletts Water Sys. Aqua Vend (St. Petersburg, FL) 63134

Sparkletts Water Sys. Aqua Vend (North Myrtle Beach, SC) 79764

Sparkletts Water Sys. Aqua Vend (Houston, TX) 86906

Sparkletts Water Sys. Auqa Vend (Kenner, LA) 70015

Sparkletts Water Systems Aqua Vend (Houston, TX) 86907

Sparkletts Water Systems Aquavend (North Miami, FL) 61737

Sparkletts Water Systems Aquavend (St. Petersburg, FL) 63135

Sparkletts Water Systems Aquavend (Kenner, LA) 70016

Sparkletts Water Systems Aquavend (North Myrtle Beach, SC) 79765

Sparkletts Water Systems Aquavend (Houston, TX) 86908

Sparkletts Water Sytems Aqua Vend (St. Petersburg, FL) 63136

Sparkletts Water Sytems Aquavend (North Miami, FL) 61738

Spartan Express Inc. (Charleston, SC) 78891

Texaco Refining & Marketing (Bellaire, TX) 83269

Texas Boot Company (Dallas, TX) 84442

Time Electronics (Charlotte, NC) 74173

Tj Maxx (Farmers Branch, TX) 85035

Union Camp Corp. (Rincon, GA) 67302

United Media Productions Inc. (Daytona Beach, FL) 59222

United Parcel Service (Fort Meade, FL) 59651; 59652

United Parcel Service (Jacksonville, FL) 60486

United Parcel Service (W Palm Beach, FL) 63819

United Parcel Service (Charleston, SC) 78907

United Parcel Service (Norfolk, VA) 91590

United Van Lines Inc. (De Land, FL) 59261

United Van Lines Inc. (Richmond, VA) 92070

US Sprint Communication Co. (Lufkin, TX) 87820

Walgreen Answering Service (Houston, TX) 87103

Walgreen Drug Stores (Deerfield Beach, FL) 59291; 59292

Walgreen Drug Stores (Fort Lauderda, FL) 59422

Walgreen Drug Stores (Fort Lauderdale, FL) 59637; 59638; 59639

Walgreen Drug Stores (Hallandale, FL) 59966

Walgreen Drug Stores (Hollywood, FL) 60106; 60107; 60108; 60109

Walgreen Drug Stores (Key Largo, FL) 60568

Walgreen Drug Stores (Lake Worth, FL) 60700

Walgreen Drug Stores (Miami, FL) 61501

Walgreen Drug Stores (Pompano Beach, FL) 62641

Walgreen Drug Stores (Port St Lucie, FL) 62691

Walgreen Drug Stores (Village of Golf, FL) 63772

Walgreen Drug Stores (West Palm Beach, FL) 63910; 63911

Walgreen Drug Stores (Zephyrhills, FL) 64029

Walgreen Drug Stores (Houston, TX) 87118; 87119; 87121; 87123; 87124; 87125; 87145

Walt Disney World (Hialeah, FL) 60019

Washington Inventory Servic (Fort Worth, TX) 85360

Western Union International (Memphis, TN) 81757

Wormald U S Inc. (Dallas, TX) 84499

7513 Truck Rental & Leasing Without Drivers

Citgo Service Station (Baltimore, MD) 71088

Exxon (Sylvania, GA) 67767

Kilgore Plumbing Products Inc. (Kilgore, TX) 87489

Ryder Truck Rental (Alexander Cy, AL) 54981

Ryder Truck Rental (Birmingham, AL) 55375; 55380; 55381

Ryder Truck Rental (Boaz, AL) 55475

Ryder Truck Rental (Cullman, AL) 55550

Ryder Truck Rental (Dothan, AL) 55667

Ryder Truck Rental (Enterprise, AL) 55696

Ryder Truck Rental (Eufaula, AL) 55703

Ryder Truck Rental (Fairfield, AL) 55716

Ryder Truck Rental (Gadsden, AL) 55788; 55789; 55790

Ryder Truck Rental (Huntsville, AL) 56010; 56011

Ryder Truck Rental (Madison, AL) 56123

Ryder Truck Rental (Mobile, AL) 56234; 56236

Ryder Truck Rental (Montgomery, AL) 56374; 56375

Ryder Truck Rental (Selma, AL) 56537

Ryder Truck Rental (Talladega, AL) 56599

Ryder Truck Rental (Tuscaloosa, AL) 56675

Ryder Truck Rental (Forrest City, AR) 57013

Ryder Truck Rental (Fort Smith, AR) 57096

Ryder Truck Rental (H Spg Nat Pk, AR) 57132

Ryder Truck Rental (Jonesboro, AR) 57230

Ryder Truck Rental (Little Rock, AR) 57305; 57306

Ryder Truck Rental (Magnolia, AR) 57334

Ryder Truck Rental (Stuttgart, AR) 57670

Ryder Truck Rental (West Memphis, AR) 57733

Ryder Truck Rental (Bartow, FL) 58629

Ryder Truck Rental (Boynton Beach, FL) 58791

Ryder Truck Rental (Bradenton, FL) 58850

Ryder Truck Rental (Brandon, FL) 58880

Ryder Truck Rental (Cape Coral, FL) 58926

Ryder Truck Rental (Cocoa, FL) 59073

Ryder Truck Rental (Cocoa Beach, FL) 59084

Ryder Truck Rental (Crestview, FL) 59127

Ryder Truck Rental (Daytona Beach, FL) 59209; 59210

Ryder Truck Rental (Deerfield Beach, FL) 59288

Ryder Truck Rental (Destin, FL) 59349

Ryder Truck Rental (Edgewater, FL) 59378; 59379

Ryder Truck Rental (Fort Lauderdale, FL) 59599

Ryder Truck Rental (Fort Myers, FL) 59761; 59761

Ryder Truck Rental (Fort Pierce, FL) 59808; 59810

Ryder Truck Rental (Fort Walton Beach, FL) 59838

Ryder Truck Rental (Gainesville, FL) 59917

Ryder Truck Rental (Haines City, FL) 59953

Ryder Truck Rental (Hialeah, FL) 60008

Ryder Truck Rental (Jacksonville, FL) 60439; 60443; 60444; 60446; 60447; 60450

Ryder Truck Rental (Lakeland, FL) 60780

Ryder Truck Rental (Leesburg, FL) 60886

Ryder Truck Rental (Live Oak, FL) 60920

Ryder Truck Rental (Marathon, FL) 60993

Ryder Truck Rental (Melbourne, FL) 61106

Ryder Truck Rental (Miami, FL) 61449; 61454

Ryder Truck Rental (Niceville, FL) 61718

Ryder Truck Rental (Nw Prt Richey, FL) 61762

Ryder Truck Rental (Ocala, FL) 61821

Ryder Truck Rental (Orange Park, FL) 61896

Ryder Truck Rental (Orlando, FL) 62136

Ryder Truck Rental (Panama City, FL) 62347

Ryder Truck Rental (Pensacola, FL) 62469

Ryder Truck Rental (Perry, FL) 62505

Ryder Truck Rental (Rockledge, FL) 62748

Ryder Truck Rental (Sanford, FL) 62779

Ryder Truck Rental (Seffner, FL) 62900

Ryder Truck Rental (St Augustine, FL) 62956

Ryder Truck Rental (St Petersburg, FL) 63032

Ryder Truck Rental (Stuart, FL) 63178

Ryder Truck Rental (Tallahassee, FL) 63269

Ryder Truck Rental (Tampa, FL) 63582; 63583; 63584; 63585; 63586

Ryder Truck Rental (Titusville, FL) 63703

Ryder Truck Rental (Winter Haven, FL) 63952

Ryder Truck Rental (Adel, GA) 64057

Ryder Truck Rental (Albany, GA) 64091

Ryder Truck Rental (Barnesville, GA) 65379

Ryder Truck Rental (Brunswick, GA) 65425

Ryder Truck Rental (Cairo, GA) 65454

Ryder Truck Rental (Canton, GA) 65486

Ryder Truck Rental (Dublin, GA) 66017

Ryder Truck Rental (Gainesville, GA) 66290

Ryder Truck Rental (Jesup, GA) 66373

Ryder Truck Rental (Macon, GA) 66711

Ryder Truck Rental (Savannah, GA) 67509

Ryder Truck Rental (Thomasville, GA) 67805

Ryder Truck Rental (Valdosta, GA) 67974

Ryder Truck Rental (Florence, KY) 68329

Ryder Truck Rental (Georgetown, KY) 68386

Ryder Truck Rental (Lexington, KY) 68622; 68623

Ryder Truck Rental (London, KY) 68667

Ryder Truck Rental (Alexandria, LA) 69409; 69410

Ryder Truck Rental (Bastrop, LA) 69449

Ryder Truck Rental (Baton Rouge, LA) 69653; 69656

Ryder Truck Rental (Bossier City, LA) 69730

Ryder Truck Rental (Lafayette, LA) 70101; 70102; 70104

Ryder Truck Rental (Port Allen, LA) 70648

Ryder Truck Rental (Shreveport, LA) 70778; 70779; 70780

Ryder Truck Rental (Sulphur, LA) 70890

Ryder Truck Rental (Gulfport, MS) 72874

Ryder Truck Rental (Hattiesburg, MS) 72896

Ryder Truck Rental (Jackson, MS) 73056

Ryder Truck Rental (Meridian, MS) 73178

Ryder Truck Rental (Pascagoula, MS) 73271

Ryder Truck Rental (Charlotte, NC) 74153; 74154

Ryder Truck Rental (Gastonia, NC) 74688

Ryder Truck Rental (Goldsboro, NC) 74734

Ryder Truck Rental (Greensboro, NC) 74900; 74901; 74904

Ryder Truck Rental (Hope Mills, NC) 75195

Ryder Truck Rental (Lexington, NC) 75423

Ryder Truck Rental (Mount Airy, NC) 75684

Ryder Truck Rental (Roxboro, NC) 76133

Ryder Truck Rental (Statesville, NC) 76337

Ryder Truck Rental (W Jefferson, NC) 76420

Ryder Truck Rental (Whiteville, NC) 76504

Ryder Truck Rental (Altus, OK) 76796

Ryder Truck Rental (Ardmore, OK) 76820

Ryder Truck Rental (Bristow, OK) 76874

Ryder Truck Rental (Chickasha, OK) 76937

Ryder Truck Rental (Edmond, OK) 77018

Ryder Truck Rental (El Reno, OK) 77034

Ryder Truck Rental (Elk City, OK) 77038

Ryder Truck Rental (Enid, OK) 77069

Ryder Truck Rental (Grove, OK) 77093

Ryder Truck Rental (Holdenville, OK) 77135

Ryder Truck Rental (Hugo, OK) 77140

Ryder Truck Rental (Mc Alester, OK) 77199

Ryder Truck Rental (Norman, OK) 77274

Ryder Truck Rental (Oklahoma, OK) 77289

Ryder Truck Rental (Oklahoma City, OK) 77540; 77541; 77542; 77543; 77544

Ryder Truck Rental (Sand Springs, OK) 77784

Ryder Truck Rental (Sayre, OK) 77801

Ryder Truck Rental (Tulsa, OK) 78095; 78098; 78099; 78100; 78101

Ryder Truck Rental (Anderson, SC) 78692

Ryder Truck Rental (Beaufort, SC) 78718

Ryder Truck Rental (Chester, SC) 78941

Ryder Truck Rental (Columbia, SC) 79093; 79094

Ryder Truck Rental (Kingstree, SC) 79559

Ryder Truck Rental (Moncks Corner, SC) 79666

Ryder Truck Rental (Myrtle Beach, SC) 79713

Ryder Truck Rental (Simpsonville, SC) 79869

Ryder Truck Rental (Spartanburg, SC) 79949; 79950

Ryder Truck Rental (Cookeville, TN) 80666

Ryder Truck Rental (Franklin, TN) 80822

Ryder Truck Rental (Memphis, TN) 81680; 81681; 81682

Ryder Truck Rental (Murfreesboro, TN) 81865

Ryder Truck Rental (Nashville, TN) 82093

Ryder Truck Rental (Union City, TN) 82389

Ryder Truck Rental (Andrews, TX) 82603

Ryder Truck Rental (Arlington, TX) 82743; 82744

Ryder Truck Rental (Austin, TX) 82996; 82998

Ryder Truck Rental (Baytown, TX) 83138

Ryder Truck Rental (Beaumont, TX) 83210

Ryder Truck Rental (Beeville, TX) 83261

Ryder Truck Rental (Big Spring, TX) 83295

Ryder Truck Rental (Borger, TX) 83325

Ryder Truck Rental (Bryan, TX) 83408

Ryder Truck Rental (Cameron, TX) 83438

Ryder Truck Rental (Cedar Hill, TX) 83530

Ryder Truck Rental (Childress, TX) 83561

Ryder Truck Rental (Clarksville, TX) 83573

Ryder Truck Rental (Corpus Chrsti, TX) 83770; 83771

Ryder Truck Rental (Corsicana, TX) 83790

Ryder Truck Rental (Dallas, TX) 84360; 84361; 84363; 84366; 84367; 84369

Ryder Truck Rental (El Paso, TX) 84919; 84920; 84921

Ryder Truck Rental (Farmers Brnch, TX) 85037

Ryder Truck Rental (Fort Worth, TX) 85266; 85268

Ryder Truck Rental (Gainesville, TX) 85427

Ryder Truck Rental (Grand Prairie, TX) 85638

Ryder Truck Rental (Harlingen, TX) 85715

Ryder Truck Rental (Houston, TX) 86802; 86825; 86828; 86838; 86840; 86843; 86845; 86852

Ryder Truck Rental (Irving, TX) 87398

Ryder Truck Rental (Lampasas, TX) 87594

Ryder Truck Rental (Lockhart, TX) 87696

Ryder Truck Rental (Marble Falls, TX) 87840

Ryder Truck Rental (Marshall, TX) 87866

Ryder Truck Rental (Mesquite, TX) 87995; 87996

Ryder Truck Rental (Mineral Wells, TX) 88117

Ryder Truck Rental (Monahans, TX) 88143

Ryder Truck Rental (Orange, TX) 88329

Ryder Truck Rental (Pasadena, TX) 88464

Ryder Truck Rental (Plano, TX) 88605

Ryder Truck Rental (Raymondville, TX) 88710

Ryder Truck Rental (Red Oak, TX) 88712

Ryder Truck Rental (Richardson, TX) 88769

Ryder Truck Rental (Rockport, TX) 88820

Ryder Truck Rental (Rosenberg, TX) 88836

Ryder Truck Rental (San Antonio, TX) 89215

Ryder Truck Rental (Temple, TX) 89643

Ryder Truck Rental (Tyler, TX) 89827

Ryder Truck Rental (Wichita Falls, TX) 90098

Ryder Truck Rental (Buckhannon, WV) 92717

Ryder Truck Rental (Charleston, WV) 92793
Ryder Truck Rental (Clarksburg, WV) 92819
Ryder Truck Rental (Fairmont, WV) 92847
Ryder Truck Rental (Holden Wv, WV) 92864
Ryder Truck Rental (Huntington, WV) 92896
Ryder Truck Rental (Petersburg, WV) 93004
Ryder Truck Rental (Summersville, WV) 93075
Ryder Truck Rental (Weston Wv, WV) 93109
Ryder Truck Rental Inc. (Milford, DE) 57845
Ryder Truck Rental Inc. (Wilmington, DE) 58107
Ryder Truck Rental Inc. (Baltimore, MD) 71271
Ryder Truck Rental Inc. (Chase, MD) 71513
Ryder Truck Rental Inc. (Abingdon, VA) 90158
Ryder Truck Rental Inc. (Chesapeake, VA) 90599
Ryder Truck Rental Inc. (Lynchburg, VA) 91287
Ryder Truck Rental Inc. (Manassas, VA) 91322
Ryder Truck Rental Inc. (Norfolk, VA) 91576
Ryder Truck Rental Inc. (Richmond, VA) 92007; 92008; 92009
Ryder Truck Rental Inc. (Virginia Beach, VA) 92508
Ryder Truck Rental & Leasing (Jackson, TN) 81001
Ryder Truck Rental & Leasing (Memphis, TN) 81683
Ryder Truck Rental & Leasing (Murfreesboro, TN) 81866
Ryder Truck Rental-One Way (Grayson, KY) 68403
Ryder Truck Rental-One Way (Lexington, KY) 68624
Ryder Truck Rental-One Way (Memphis, TN) 81684; 81685; 81686; 81687; 81688
Ryder Truck Rental-One Way (Murfreesboro, TN) 81867
Ryder Truck Rental-Oneway (Corbin, KY) 68213
Ryder Truck Rental-Oneway (Frankfort, KY) 68368
Ryder Truck Rental-Oneway (Glasgow, KY) 68397
Ryder Truck Rental-Oneway (Newport, KY) 69141
Ryder Truck Rental Shop (Oklahoma City, OK) 77545
Thrifty Rent-A-Car System Inc. (Tulsa, OK) 78167
Trans State Line Inc. (Memphis, TN) 81716
United Parcel Service (Fort Worth, TX) 85341
United Parcel Service (San Antonio, TX) 89283; 89284

7514 Passenger Car Rental

Dollar Rent-A-Car Systems Inc. (Tulsa, OK) 77932
Hertz Rent-A-Car Division (El Paso, TX) 84809
Hertz Rent-A-Car (Anniston, AL) 55001
Hertz Rent-A-Car (Birmingham, AL) 55280
Hertz Rent-A-Car (Dothan, AL) 55653
Hertz Rent-A-Car (Huntsville, AL) 55950
Hertz Rent-A-Car (Montgomery, AL) 56343
Hertz Rent-A-Car (Batesville, AR) 56757
Hertz Rent-A-Car (Fort Smith, AR) 57055
Hertz Rent-A-Car (Hot Springs National Park, AR) 57169
Hertz Rent-A-Car (Jonesboro, AR) 57221
Hertz Rent-A-Car (Dover, DE) 57791
Hertz Rent-A-Car (New Castle, DE) 57866
Hertz Rent-A-Car (Daytona Beach, FL) 59184; 59185
Hertz Rent-A-Car (Fort Lauderdale, FL) 59504; 59505
Hertz Rent-A-Car (Fort Myers, FL) 59705
Hertz Rent-A-Car (Gainesville, FL) 59880
Hertz Rent-A-Car (Jacksonville, FL) 60323; 60324; 60325
Hertz Rent-A-Car (Key West, FL) 60575

Hertz Rent-A-Car (Kissimmee, FL) 60588
Hertz Rent-A-Car (Lakeland, FL) 60733
Hertz Rent-A-Car (Marco Island, FL) 60997
Hertz Rent-A-Car (Miami, FL) 61326
Hertz Rent-A-Car (Naples, FL) 61629; 61630
Hertz Rent-A-Car (Orlando, FL) 62003; 62006
Hertz Rent-A-Car (Palm Beach, FL) 62258
Hertz Rent-A-Car (Panama City, FL) 62324
Hertz Rent-A-Car (Sarasota, FL) 62837
Hertz Rent-A-Car (Shalimar, FL) 62912
Hertz Rent-A-Car (St Petersburg, FL) 62975
Hertz Rent-A-Car (Stuart, FL) 63171
Hertz Rent-A-Car (Tallahassee, FL) 63244
Hertz Rent-A-Car (Tampa, FL) 63456
Hertz Rent-A-Car (Titusville, FL) 63691
Hertz Rent-A-Car (Winter Park, FL) 63981
Hertz Rent-A-Car (Macon, GA) 66691
Hertz Rent-A-Car (Milledgeville, GA) 66979
Hertz Rent-A-Car (Moultrie, GA) 67054
Hertz Rent-A-Car (Valdosta, GA) 67960
Hertz Rent-A-Car (Lafayette, LA) 70057
Hertz Rent-A-Car (Lake Charles, LA) 70140; 70141
Hertz Rent-A-Car (New Orleans, LA) 70472; 70473
Hertz Rent-A-Car (Shreveport, LA) 70725
Hertz Rent-A-Car (St. Bernard, LA) 70859
Hertz Rent-A-Car (Baltimore, MD) 71166
Hertz Rent-A-Car (California, MD) 71483
Hertz Rent-A-Car (Gaithersburg, MD) 71785
Hertz Rent-A-Car (Hagerstown, MD) 71883
Hertz Rent-A-Car (Laurel, MD) 72077
Hertz Rent-A-Car (Biloxi, MS) 72622
Hertz Rent-A-Car (Greenwood, MS) 72834
Hertz Rent-A-Car (Gulfport, MS) 72856; 72857
Hertz Rent-A-Car (Jackson, MS) 72988; 72989
Hertz Rent-A-Car (Pascagoula, MS) 73259
Hertz Rent-A-Car (Tupelo, MS) 73405
Hertz Rent-A-Car (Arden, NC) 73570
Hertz Rent-A-Car (Charlotte, NC) 74033; 74034
Hertz Rent-A-Car (Fayetteville, NC) 74559
Hertz Rent-A-Car (Greensboro, NC) 74850
Hertz Rent-A-Car (Hickory, NC) 75080
Hertz Rent-A-Car (Rocky Mount, NC) 76091; 76092
Hertz Rent-A-Car (Winston Salem, NC) 76672
Hertz Rent-A-Car (Lawton, OK) 77160
Hertz Rent-A-Car (Oklahoma City, OK) 77378; 77379
Hertz Rent-A-Car (Ponca City, OK) 77705
Hertz Rent-A-Car (Stillwater, OK) 77838
Hertz Rent-A-Car (Tulsa, OK) 77951; 77952
Hertz Rent-A-Car (Charleston, SC) 78820
Hertz Rent-A-Car (Hilton Head Island, SC) 79517
Hertz Rent-A-Car (Lyman, SC) 79625
Hertz Rent-A-Car (Spartanburg, SC) 79912
Hertz Rent-A-Car (Sumter, SC) 80021
Hertz Rent-A-Car (Abilene, TX) 82439
Hertz Rent-A-Car (Austin, TX) 82886; 82887
Hertz Rent-A-Car (Baytown, TX) 83125
Hertz Rent-A-Car (College Station, TX) 83618

Hertz Rent-A-Car (Corpus Christi, TX) 83720; 83721
Hertz Rent-A-Car (Dallas, TX) 84115; 84116; 84117; 84118; 84118; 84119; 84121; 84122
Hertz Rent-A-Car (Fort Worth, TX) 85128
Hertz Rent-A-Car (Galveston, TX) 85440
Hertz Rent-A-Car (Houston, TX) 86266; 86267; 86271; 86272
Hertz Rent-A-Car (Lubbock, TX) 87765
Hertz Rent-A-Car (Midland, TX) 88039
Hertz Rent-A-Car (San Angelo, TX) 88877
Hertz Rent-A-Car (San Antonio, TX) 89025
Hertz Rent-A-Car (Victoria, TX) 89887
Hertz Rent-A-Car (Waco, TX) 89938
Hertz Rent-A-Car (Charlottesville, VA) 90541
Hertz Rent-A-Car (Fredericksburg, VA) 90928
Hertz Rent-A-Car (Hot Springs, VA) 91167
Hertz Rent-A-Car (Lynchburg, VA) 91260
Hertz Rent-A-Car (Mc Lean, VA) 91368
Hertz Rent-A-Car (Norfolk, VA) 91543
Hertz Rent-A-Car (Richmond, VA) 91902
Hertz Rent-A-Car (Sandston, VA) 92232
Hertz Rent-A-Car (Williamsburg, VA) 92573
Hertz Rent-A-Car (Winchester, VA) 92595
Hertz Rent-A-Car Car Rental Lo (Atlanta, GA) 64532
Hertz Rent-A-Car Corp. (Savannah, GA) 67486
Hertz Rent-A-Car Dba (Pompano Beach, FL) 62600
Hertz Rent-A-Car Licensee (Huntsville, AL) 55951
Hertz Rent-A-Car Licensee (Madison, AL) 56122
Hertz Rent-A-Car Licensee (Northport, AL) 56407
Hertz Rent-A-Car Licensee (Hot Springs National Park, AR) 57170
Hertz Rent-A-Car Licensee (Cumberland, MD) 71624
Hertz Rent-A-Car Licensee (Salisbury, MD) 72347
Hertz Rent-A-Car Licensee (Hattiesburg, MS) 72891
Hertz Rent-A-Car Licensee (Oxford, MS) 73239
Hertz Rent-A-Car Licensee (Tupelo, MS) 73406
Hertz Rent-A-Car Licensee (Fayetteville, NC) 74560
Hertz Rent-A-Car Licensee (Goldsboro, NC) 74723
Hertz Rent-A-Car Licensee (Greenville, NC) 74964
Hertz Rent-A-Car Licensee (Raleigh, NC) 75914
Hertz Rent-A-Car Licensee (Richlands, NC) 76026
Hertz Rent-A-Car Licensee (Wilmington, NC) 76575
Hertz Rent-A-Car Licensee (Ponca City, OK) 77706
Hertz Rent-A-Car Licensee (Florence, SC) 79207
Hertz Rent-A-Car Licensee (Alice, TX) 82483
Hertz Rent-A-Car Licensee (College Sta, TX) 83609
Hertz Rent-A-Car Licensee (Kingsville, TX) 87533
Hertz Rent-A-Car Licensee (Laredo, TX) 87612; 87612
Hertz Rent-A-Car Licensee (Longview, TX) 87717
Hertz Rent-A-Car Licensee (Lufkin, TX) 87806
Hertz Rent-A-Car Licensee (Mc Allen, TX) 87883
Hertz Rent-A-Car Licensee (Orange, TX) 88315
Hertz Rent-A-Car Licensee (Waco, TX) 89939
Hertz Rent-A-Car Licensee (Wichita Falls, TX) 90073
Hertz Rent-A-Car Rental Statio (Washington, DC) 58300
Hertz Rent-A-Car Svc Dept (Mc Allen, TX) 87884
Hertz Rent-A-Car System (Meridian, MS) 73164
Hertz Rent-A-Car System (Norfolk, VA) 91544
Hertz Rent Car (Miami, FL) 61327; 61328

The Limited (Hilton Head Island, SC) 79518
Penske Truck Leasing (Ashland, VA) 90406
Pentastar Transportation Group Inc. (Tulsa, OK) 78054
Ryder Truck Rental (Birmingham, AL) 55374
Ryder Truck Rental (Lakeland, FL) 60780
Ryder Truck Rental (Dallas, TX) 84358; 84371
Ryder Truck Rental Inc. (Norfolk, VA) 91576
Snappy Car Rental Inc. (Tulsa, OK) 78113
Thrifty Rent-A-Car System Inc. (Tulsa, OK) 78167
Thrifty Rent a Car Systems, Inc. (Norman, OK) 77278
Thrifty Rent a Car Systems, Inc. (Tulsa, OK) 78168; 78169; 78170
US Fleet Leasing (Houston, TX) 87065

7515 Passenger Car Leasing

Thrifty Rent-A-Car System Inc. (Tulsa, OK) 78167

7519 Utility Trailer Rental

Fruehauf Trailer Corp. (Odessa, TX) 88245
Fruehauf Trailers (Odessa, TX) 88246
Ryder Truck Rental (Tulsa, OK) 78096

7530 Automotive Repair Shops

Jiffy Lube (Charleston, SC) 78822
Jiffy Lube (Greenville, SC) 79371
Jiffy Lube (Austin, TX) 82896

7532 Top & Body Repair & Paint Shops

Digital Equipment Corp. (Oklahoma City, OK) 77346
Jiffy Lube (Dallas, TX) 84145
Pizza Hut (Columbia, SC) 79070
Ryder Truck Rental Body Shop (Birmingham, AL) 55382
Texaco Express Lube (Tyler, TX) 89835

7534 Tire Retreading & Repair Shops

Air Treads Inc. (Atlanta, GA) 64211
Arkansas Best (Fort Smith, AR) 57022
Arkansas Best Corp. (Fort Smith, AR) 57023
Treadco (Lubbock, TX) 87791
Treadco, Inc. (Fort Smith, AR) 57109
Treadco, Inc. (Atlanta, GA) 65224
Washington Services (Greensburg, LA) 69901

7538 General Automotive Repair Shops

Burdines Body Shop (Yazoo City, MS) 73499
Burdines Upholstery Shop (Yazoo City, MS) 73500
Coast to Coast Shops (Pollok, TX) 88626
Exxon (Dallas, TX) 84024
Exxon (Fort Worth, TX) 85112
Exxon (Texas City, TX) 89717
Exxon Car Care Center (Memphis, TN) 81521
Exxon Car Care Center (Addison, TX) 82472
Exxon Car Care Center (Arlington, TX) 82648
Exxon Car Care Center (Dallas, TX) 84038; 84039; 84041; 84042; 84044; 84046; 84047
Exxon Car Care Center (Spring, TX) 89468
Exxon Car Care Center (Arlington, VA) 90297; 90298
Exxon Car Care Center (Richmond, VA) 91865
Exxon Car Care Center (Virginia Beach, VA) 92461
Exxon Car Care Centers (Nashville, TN) 81955; 81957
Exxon Co. USA (Houston, TX) 86130

Exxon Co. USA (San Antonio, TX) 89000
Exxon Service Center (Magee, MS) 73138
Exxon Truck Stop (Macclenny, FL) 60960
Jiffy Lube (Mobile, AL) 56189
Jiffy Lube (Fort Lauderdale, FL) 59511; 59512
Jiffy Lube (Homestead, FL) 60115
Jiffy Lube (Lighthouse Point, FL) 60904
Jiffy Lube (Miami, FL) 61335
Jiffy Lube (Orlando, FL) 62014
Jiffy Lube (Palm Springs, FL) 62304
Jiffy Lube (Macon, GA) 66692
Jiffy Lube (Baton Rouge, LA) 69561
Jiffy Lube (Metairie, LA) 70276
Jiffy Lube (Wilmington, NC) 76576
Jiffy Lube (Cayce, SC) 78777
Jiffy Lube (Charleston, SC) 78822
Jiffy Lube (Columbia, SC) 79031; 79034; 79035
Jiffy Lube (Greenville, SC) 79372
Jiffy Lube (Garland, TX) 85491
Jiffy Lube of Davie (Hollywood, FL) 60065
Jiffy Lube of Hallandale (Pembroke Pines, FL) 62370
Jiffy Lube of Hialeah (Hialeah, FL) 59990
Jiffy Lube International (Birmingham, AL) 55286
Jiffy Lube Miami Shores (Miami, FL) 61336
Jiffy Lube Oil Change (Louisville, KY) 68782; 68785
Jiffy Lube Oil Change (Kingsport, TN) 81107
Jiffy Lube Oil Change (Martinsburg, WV) 92932
Jiffy Lube Oil Change (Parkersburg, WV) 92986
Jiffy Lube of Pembroke (Hollywood, FL) 60066
Jiffy Lube of Sunrise (Fort Lauderdale, FL) 59513
Kentucky Fried Chicken (Alexandria, LA) 69386
Kmart Store (St Petersburg, FL) 62987
Mini Mart (Mars Hill, NC) 75510
Mobil Oil Corporation (St Petersburg, FL) 62999
Mobil Servcie Station (Opa Locka, FL) 61861
Mobil Service Center (Fort Lauderdale, FL) 59543
Pennzoil (Beaufort, SC) 78712
Ryder Truck Rental (Little Rock, AR) 57307
Ryder Truck Rental (Miami, FL) 61455
Safety Kleen Corp. (Casselberry, FL) 58941
Shell Service Station (New Windsor, MD) 72152
Stewart & Stevenson Service Inc. (San Juan, TX) 89335
Ten Minute Oil Change (Miami, FL) 61474
Texaco Auto Service (Troy, AL) 56621
Texaco Auto Service Ctr (Tyler, TX) 89834
Texaco Service Center (Dayton, TX) 84525
Texaco Service Staion (Winder, GA) 68064
Texaco Service Station (Wesleyan Col, NC) 76482
Texaco 62 (Yellville, AR) 57747
Total Auto Care (Lake City, FL) 60632
Wal Mart (Poteau, OK) 77729
Wal Mart Auto Center (Morgan City, LA) 70398
Wal Mart Auto Center (Tulsa, OK) 78191
Wal Mart Auto Center (Vidor, TX) 89921
Wal Mart Auto Repair (Waldron, AR) 57705
Wal Mart Auto Repair (Sulphur Springs, TX) 89565
Wal Mart Auto Repair (Texas City, TX) 89746
Wal Mart Automotive (Oklahoma City, OK) 77652
Wal Mart Automotive (Granbury, TX) 85603
Wal Mart Discount City (Alma, AR) 56715
Wal Mart Discount City (Cuero, TX) 83826
Wal Mart Discount City (Gonzales, TX) 85595
Wal Mart Tire (Port Arthur, TX) 88657
Wal Mart Tire & Auto Ctr (Rogers, AR) 57578

Wal Mart Tire & Auto Ctr (Grove, OK) 77095
Wal Mart Tire & Auto Ctr (Hearne, TX) 85728
Wal Mart Tire, Battery, & Auto Ctr (Alexandria, LA) 69416
Wal Mart Tire, Battery, & Auto Ctr (Opelousas, LA) 70605
Wal Mart Tire & Battery Ctr (Edmond, OK) 77028
Wal Mart Tire & Battery Ctr (Alvin, TX) 82518
Wal Mart Tire & Battery Ctr (El Campo, TX) 84753

7539 Automotive Repair Shops Nec

Coast to Coast Carriers (Fort Pierce, FL) 59792
Electronic Data Systems (Dallas, TX) 84004
Exxon Shop (Charleston, SC) 78811
Fruehauf Trailer Corp. (Shreveport, LA) 70722
Fruehauf Trailer Corp. (Greensboro, NC) 74840
Fruehauf Trailer Corp. (Odessa, TX) 88245
Fruehauf Trailers (Greensboro, NC) 74841
Fruehauf Trailers (Odessa, TX) 88246
Hertz Rent-A-Car (Delray Beach, FL) 59319
Hertz Rent-A-Car (Fort Lauderdale, FL) 59503; 59506
Hertz Rent-A-Car (Orlando, FL) 62004; 62005
Hertz Rent-A-Car (West Palm Beach, FL) 63871
Hertz Rent-A-Car (Winston Salem, NC) 76673
Hertz Rent-A-Car Lcns (Myrtle Beach, SC) 79700
Jiffy Lube (Birmingham, AL) 55285
Jiffy Lube (Montgomery, AL) 56346
Jiffy Lube (N Little Rock, AR) 57403
Jiffy Lube (Clearwater, FL) 59024
Jiffy Lube (Daytona Beach, FL) 59186
Jiffy Lube (Jacksonville, FL) 60340; 60341
Jiffy Lube (Orlando, FL) 62012
Jiffy Lube (St Petersburg, FL) 62979
Jiffy Lube (Tampa, FL) 63461
Jiffy Lube (Winter Park, FL) 63982
Jiffy Lube (Baton Rouge, LA) 69563; 69564
Jiffy Lube (Jackson, MS) 72992
Jiffy Lube (High Point, NC) 75138
Jiffy Lube (Wilmington, NC) 76576
Jiffy Lube (Oklahoma City, OK) 77389; 77391; 77392; 77393; 77394; 77395
Jiffy Lube (Tulsa, OK) 77960; 77962; 77963; 77964; 77965; 77966; 77967; 77968
Jiffy Lube (Anderson, SC) 78677
Jiffy Lube (Cayce, SC) 78777
Jiffy Lube (Charleston, SC) 78822
Jiffy Lube (Columbia, SC) 79031; 79032; 79033; 79034; 79035
Jiffy Lube (Arlington, TX) 82666; 82667; 82668
Jiffy Lube (Austin, TX) 82895; 82896
Jiffy Lube (Bedford, TX) 83242
Jiffy Lube (Carrollton, TX) 83473; 83474; 83475
Jiffy Lube (Dallas, TX) 84141; 84142; 84143; 84145; 84146; 84150; 84151
Jiffy Lube (Euless, TX) 85010
Jiffy Lube (Fort Worth, TX) 85132; 85134; 85135; 85136
Jiffy Lube (Mesquite, TX) 87965
Jiffy Lube of East Macon (Macon, GA) 66693
Jiffy Lube Oil Change (Lexington, KY) 68563
Jiffy Lube Oil Change (Louisville, KY) 68783
Jiffy Lube Oil Change (Antioch, TN) 80170
Jiffy Lube Oil Change (Charleston, WV) 92751
Jiffy Lube Oil Change (Huntington, WV) 92877
Jiffy Lube U S a (Dallas, TX) 84152
Quaker State Minituelube (Dallas, TX) 84327
Ryder Truck Rental (Enterprise, AL) 55696
Ryder Truck Rental (Cocoa, FL) 59074
Ryder Truck Rental (Daytona Beach, FL) 59211
Ryder Truck Rental (Fort Pierce, FL) 59809

Ryder Truck Rental (Orlando, FL) 62137; 62138
Ryder Truck Rental (Austin, TX) 82999
Ten Minute Oil Change (West Palm Beach, FL) 63904
Ten Minute Oil Change (Stafford, TX) 89507
Texaco Express Lube (Van Buren, AR) 57695
Texaco Express Lube (Douglas, GA) 65976
Texaco Express Lube (Tyler, TX) 89835
Texaco Instant Lube (Garland, TX) 85544
Texaco Service Center Inc. (Opelika, AL) 56426
United Brake Systems Inc. (Oklahoma City, OK) 77645
United Brake Systems Inc. (Columbia, SC) 79116
Valvoline Instant Oil Chang (Lexington, KY) 68653

7542 Car Washes

Exxon (Nederland, TX) 88185
Exxon Car Wash (Casselberry, FL) 58931
Exxon Car Wash (Winter Park, FL) 63972
Exxon Car Wash (Jackson, MS) 72982
Exxon Car Wash (Rock Hill, SC) 79819
Exxon Car Wash (Nashville, TN) 81958
Exxon Car Wash (Dallas, TX) 84048
Exxon Car Wash (Houston, TX) 86113; 86114
Exxon Car Wash (Texas City, TX) 89718
Exxon Car Wash (Arlington, VA) 90299
Exxon Co. USA (Houston, TX) 86132
Jiffy Lube (Dallas, TX) 84149
Lees Car Wash (Vienna, VA) 92412
Mobil Mart (St Petersburg, FL) 62998
Safety-Kleen Corp. (Louisville, KY) 69000
Shell Co. (Dallas, TX) 84381
Shell Co. (Houston, TX) 86875
Shell Oil Co. (Garland, TX) 85533
Shell Self Service (Midland, TX) 88077; 88078
Texaco (Baton Rouge, LA) 69670

7549 Automotive Services Nec

Cathodic Protection Services Co. (Houston, TX) 85936
Exxon Shop (Alexandria, LA) 69377
Jiffy Lube (Altamonte Spg, FL) 58537
Jiffy Lube (Casselberry, FL) 58933
Jiffy Lube (Metairie, LA) 70277
Jiffy Lube (Greensboro, NC) 74855
Jiffy Lube (San Antonio, TX) 89032
Mobil (Virginia Beach, VA) 92491

7600 Miscellaneous Repair Services

Randall Textron Inc. (Blytheville, AR) 56815

7622 Radio & T.V. Repair

B.F. Goodrich Aerospace Component Overhaul and Repair Inc. (Austin, TX) 82826
Circuit City (Jacksonville, FL) 60243
Circuit City (Richmond, VA) 91771
Coast to Coast Video (Jackson, MS) 72962
Hertz Rent-A-Car (Patterson, LA) 70611
Radio Shack (Russellville, AL) 56511; 56511
Radio Shack (Picayune, MS) 73294
Radio Shack (Roxboro, NC) 76132
Radio Shack (Lake Jackson, TX) 87585
Radio Shack (Liberty, TX) 87679
Walker Manufacturing (Plant City Fl, FL) 62561

7623 Refrigeration Services Repair

Baltimore Gas & Electric Co. (Baltimore, MD) 71056

Johnson Controls Inc. (Hollywood, FL) 60067
Johnson Controls Inc. (Columbia, SC) 79036
Trane Co. (Tulsa, OK) 78178

7629 Electrical Repair Shops Nec

Baltimore Gas & Electric Co. (Baltimore, MD) 71056
Bellsouth Mobility (Nashville, TN) 81901
B.F. Goodrich Aerospace Component Overhaul and Repair Inc. (Austin, TX) 82826
Circuit City (Richmond, VA) 91773
Electro Mechanical Devices Inc. (Cordova, AL) 55528
Electronic Systems Group Frienship Site (Linthicum Heights, MD) 72110
Electronic Systems Inc. (Virginia Beach, VA) 92459
GTE Communications Corp. (Tampa, FL) 63445
GTE Customer Networks Inc. (Atlanta, GA) 64524
GTE Florida Inc. (Tampa, FL) 63447
GTE Southwest Inc. (Irving, TX) 87351
Hercules Simmonds Precision Products Division (Miami, FL) 61325
Radio Shack (Haines City, FL) 59952
Radio Shack (Lakeland, FL) 60778
Radio Shack (Sanford, FL) 62775
Radio Shack (St Petersburg, FL) 63025
Radio Shack (Bastrop, LA) 69446
Radio Shack (Crowley, LA) 69803
Radio Shack (Marksville, LA) 70223
Radio Shack (Southaven, MS) 73355
Radio Shack (Staunton, VA) 92327
Raytheon Service Co. (El Paso, TX) 84913
Simmonds Precision Products (Miami, FL) 61461
Western Digital Corp. (Austin, TX) 83071
Westinghouse Electric Corp. Electronic Systems Group (Linthicum Heights, MD) 72113

7631 Watch, Clock & Jewelry Repair

Maison Blanche (New Orleans, LA) 70524

7641 Reupholstery & Furniture Repair

Pizza Hut (Tallahassee, FL) 63258

7692 Welding Repair

Air Products & Chemicals, Inc. (Valdosta, GA) 67939
Alliant Tech Systems (San Antonio, TX) 88917
Lewis Engineering Co. (Marshall, TX) 87857
Wal Mart (Walterboro, SC) 80078

7694 Armature Rewinding Shops

Magnetek National Elec Coil (Alcoa, TN) 80156
Magnetek/Ohio Transformer (Houston, TX) 86511
Tramco Inc. (Bristol, TN) 80256

7699 Repair Services Nec

Aero Technical Services (Fort Walton Beach, FL) 59818
Air Products & Chemicals Inc. (Jacksonville, FL) 60160
Brown & Root Industrial Services Inc. (Houston, TX) 85897
Browning Ferris Industries BFI (Baton Rouge, LA) 69477
Chrysler Technologies Airborne Systems Inc. (Waco, TX) 89932
Dover Elevator International Inc. (Memphis, TN) 81513
Footaction U S a (Irving, TX) 87346
Kwikset Corp. (Bristow, OK) 76872
Magnetek (Palmetto, FL) 62310
Mary Kay Cosemetics (West Palm Beach, FL) 63882
Mobil Diesel Service (Bandera, TX) 83094
Mobil Service (Austin, TX) 82943

Modern Office Machines Inc. (Greenville, SC) 79396
Ncr Corp. (Lakeland, FL) 60757
Piggly Wiggly (Americus, GA) 64142
Porter Cable Corp. (Hialeah, FL) 60003
Raytheon Service Co. (Oklahoma City, OK) 77536
Solar Turbines Inc. (Belle Chasse, LA) 69695
Solar Turbines Inc. (De Soto, TX) 84538

7832 Motion Picture Theaters Except Drive-In

Lorillard Inc. (Virginia Beach, VA) 92490

7841 Video Tape Rental

Circuit City (Roanoke, VA) 92111
Circuit City Stores Inc. (Roanoke, VA) 92112
Delta Air Lines (Mount Dora, FL) 61563
Radio Shack (Greenville, SC) 79414

7922 Theatrical Producers & Services

Delta Air Lines (Birmingham, AL) 55211
Delta Air Lines (Jacksonville, FL) 60255
Delta Air Lines (Jackson, MS) 72966
Delta Air Lines (Memphis, TN) 81507
Romper Room Enterprises Inc. (Baltimore, MD) 71269

7941 Sports Clubs, Managers & Promoters

Tuner Broadcasting System, Inc. was Turner Communications Corp. (Atlanta, GA) 65225

7991 Physical Fitness Facilities

Fitness Center (Glasgow, KY) 68395
Fitness Center (Irvine, KY) 68487
Fitness Center (Jackson, KY) 68489
Fitness Challenge (Covington, KY) 68219
Fitness Factory (Louisville, KY) 68763
Fitness Factory the (Paducah, KY) 69202
Fitness Pro (Lexington, KY) 68553
Fitness Spa for Men (Lexington, KY) 68554
Fitness World (Huntington, WV) 92873
Fitness World (Weirton, WV) 93087

7996 Amusement Parks

Busch Gardens (Tampa, FL) 63372
Busch Gardens Williamsburg (Williamsburg, VA) 92566
Sea World of Florida, Inc. (Orlando, FL) 62139
Walt Disney World Co. (Orlando, FL) 62191

7997 Membership Sports & Recreation Clubs

Fitness Concepts Hlth Club (Skelton, WV) 93045
Flagstar Corp. Recreation Services Group (Spartanburg, SC) 79900
Jonathan's Landing Inc. (Jupiter, FL) 60541
Racquet Club Wimbledon (Arlington, TX) 82732

7999 Amusement & Recreation Nec

Burdines Travel Bureau (Altamonte Spg, FL) 58534
Carnival Cruise Lines (Miami, FL) 61223
Flagstar Corp. TW Recreational Services Inc. (Spartanburg, SC) 79902

Florida Cypress Gardens, Inc. (Winter Haven, FL) 63940
Sea World of Texax, Inc. (San Antonio, TX) 89226
Water Country USA (Williamsburg, VA) 92580

8011 Offices & Clinics of Medical Doctors

Baxter Physical Therapy Center (West Columbia, SC) 80084
Cigna Health Plan of Florida Inc. (Tampa, FL) 63389
Humana Medical Plan (Dade City, FL) 59140
Linvatec (Largo, FL) 60844

8042 Offices & Clinics of Optometrists

Lens Crafters (Oklahoma City, OK) 77418
Lens Crafters (Austin, TX) 82918
Lens Crafters (San Antonio, TX) 89071
Lenscrafters (Hampton, VA) 91043

8049 Offices of Health Practitioners Nec

Baxter Physical Therapy Center (West Columbia, SC) 80084
Coast to Coast Collection (Maitland, FL) 60974
Coast to Coast Collection (Winter Park, FL) 63967

8051 Skilled Nursing Care Facilities

Baltimore Gas & Electric Co. (Baltimore, MD) 71051
Beverly Enterprises (Arlington, TX) 82637
Beverly Enterprises Inc. (Virginia Beach, VA) 92437; 92438; 92439
Cedars (Charlottesville, VA) 90526
Cedars Guest Homes The (Richmond, VA) 91753
Constellation Real Estate Group, Inc. (Baltimore, MD) 71102; 71103
Health Care Management Corp. (Baltimore, MD) 71165
Whispering Pines Nursing Home (Plain Dealing, LA) 70635
Whispering Pines Nursing Home (Winnsboro, TX) 90126

8052 Intermediate Care Facilities

Baltimore Gas & Electric Co. (Baltimore, MD) 71051
Constellation Health Service, Inc. (Baltimore, MD) 71093

8059 Nursing & Personal Care Nec

Allenbrook Healthcare Center (Baytown, TX) 83107
Beverly Enterprise (Wichita Falls, TX) 90067
Beverly Enterprises (Arlington, TX) 82637
Beverly Enterprises (Houston, TX) 85878
Beverly Enterprises (Paris, TX) 88361
Cedars (Charlottesville, VA) 90526
Cedars Guest Homes The (Richmond, VA) 91753
Constellation Holdings, Inc. (Baltimore, MD) 71097
Crown of Texas Hospice (Conroe, TX) 83656
Crown of Texas Hospice (Hereford, TX) 85740
Residential Services (Macon, GA) 66708

8062 General Medical & Surgical Hospitals

American Medical Holdings, Inc. (Dallas, TX) 83850
Brookwood Medical Center (Birmingham, AL) 55169
Brownsville Medical Center (Brownsville, TX) 83354
Central Arkansas Hospital (Searcy, AR) 57601
Central Carolina Hospital (Sanford, NC) 76191
Cincinnati Insurance Co. (Front Royal, VA) 90947
East Cooper Community Hospital (Mount Pleasant, SC) 79671
Fairfield Memorial Hospital (Fairfield, TX) 85029
Fryef Regional Medical Center (Hickory, NC) 75074
Memorial Hospital of Tampa (Tampa, FL) 63503
Mid-Jefferson County Hospital (Nederland, TX) 88187
Nacogdoches Medical Center (Nacogdoches, TX) 88173
National Park Medical Center (Hot Springs National Park, AR) 57176
North Fulton Regional Hospital (Roswell, GA) 67411
North Ridgef Medical Center (Fort Lauderdale, FL) 59548
Odesa Women's & Children's Hospital (Odessa, TX) 88258
Palm Beach Gardens Medical Center (Palm Beach Gardens, FL) 62273
Palmetto General Hospital (Hialeah, FL) 59999
Park Place Hospital (Port Arthur, TX) 88641
Park Plaza Hospital (Houston, TX) 86638
Piedmont Medical Center (Rock Hill, SC) 79836
St. Jude Medical Center (Kenner, LA) 70013
Saint Mary's Medical Center (Russellville, AR) 57589
Spalding Regional Hospital (Griffin, GA) 66324
St Jude Medical Center (Kenner, LA) 70017
Town & Country Medical Center (Tampa, FL) 63625
Twelve Oaks Hospital (Houston, TX) 87048
Twin Cities Hospital (Niceville, FL) 61719
Twin Lakes Hospital (Denton, TX) 84643
West Side Hospital (Nashville, TN) 82143
Wheeler County Hospital (Glenwood, GA) 66305

8063 Psychiatric Hospitals

American Medical Holdings, Inc. (Dallas, TX) 83850

8069 Specialty Hospitals Except Psychiatric

American Medical Holdings, Inc. (Dallas, TX) 83850

8082 Home Health Care Services

American Family Life Assurance (Lafayette, LA) 70041
Kelly Assisted Living Servi (Birmingham, AL) 55290
Kelly Assisted Living Servi (Charleston, SC) 78824

8093 Specialty Outpatient Facilities Nec

Fairfield Memorial Hospital (Fairfield, TX) 85029
Kentucky Fried Chicken (Yazoo City, MS) 73503
Ryder Truck Rental Inc. (Baltimore, MD) 71272

8099 Health & Allied Services Nec

Air Products & Chemicals, Inc. (Largo, FL) 60807
Fairfield Memorial Hospital (Fairfield, TX) 85029
Inland Gas Co. Inc. (Huntington, WV) 92875
Kelly Assisted Living Servi (Fort Myers, FL) 59707

Kelly Assisted Living Servi (St Petersburg, FL) 62981
Kelly Assisted Living Servi (Winter Park, FL) 63983
Kelly Assisted Living Service (Virginia Beach, VA) 92488
Miles Cutter Biological Division (Daphne, AL) 55567
Ncr Corp. (San Angelo, TX) 88888

8111 Legal Services

Ace Hardware (Miami, FL) 61151
Avon Products Inc. (Anderson, SC) 78662
Liberty Mutual Insurance Co. (Baltimore, MD) 71179
Trailways Bus Center (Harrison, AR) 57141
Trailways Inc. (Murfreesboro, AR) 57400

8211 Elementary & Secondary Schools

Greyhound Bus Lines (Dumas, TX) 84688
Kids R US (Jacksonville, TX) 87423
Wal Mart Shoes (Harrison, AR) 57145

8221 Colleges & Universities

The Limited Express (San Antonio, TX) 89089

8231 Libraries

Exxon Chemical Lab Library (Baton Rouge, LA) 69524
Exxon Chemical Plastics Library (Baton Rouge, LA) 69525
Exxon Co. Refinery Library (Baytown, TX) 83117
Martin Marietta Corp. Librar (Baltimore, MD) 71185
National Steel Corp. (Weirton, WV) 93097
Philip Morris USA (Richmond, VA) 91943
Shell Oil Legal Library (Houston, TX) 86887

8243 Data Processing Schools

Auto Data Processing, Inc. Dealer Services Div. (Irving, TX) 87321

8249 Vocational Schools Nec

Burdines Department Store (Miami, FL) 61212

8299 Schools & Educational Services Nec

Kroger,Genevieve Mrs (Mc Alester, OK) 77195
Pizza Hut Region Training (Tampa, FL) 63536

8322 Individual & Family Services

Human Affairs International (Boca Raton, FL) 58712
Human Affairs International (Charlotte, NC) 74048
Kelly Assisted Living Servi (Ormond Beach, FL) 62205
Mary Kay Cosmetics (Austin, TX) 82933

8331 Job Training & Related Services

Avon Products Business Office (Plant City, FL) 62536

8351 Child Day Care Services

Kids-R-US (Bradenton, FL) 58829
Kids R US (Lutz, FL) 60952; 60953
Kids R US (Frederick, OK) 77083
Kids R US (Tulsa, OK) 77985; 77986
Kids R US (Walters, OK) 78236
Kids R US (Austin, TX) 82912; 82913; 82914
Kids R US (El Paso, TX) 84827
Kids R US (Houston, TX) 86371
Kids R US (Paris, TX) 88368
Kids R US Inc. (Houston, TX) 86372

8361 Residential Care

Cedars (Charlottesville, VA) 90526
Cedars Guest Homes The (Richmond, VA) 91753

8412 Museums & Art Galleries

Prints Plus (Dallas, TX) 84324

8641 Civic & Social Associations

Coast to Coast Club (Oklahoma City, OK) 77337
Texaco Inc. (Houston, TX) 87001
TNI Inc. (Houston, TX) 87028
Wrangler (Huntsville, AL) 56056

8661 Religious Organizations

Avon Products Inc. (Waco, TX) 89929
Casual Corner (San Antonio, TX) 88948
Digital Equipment Corp. (Birmingham, AL) 55223
Hudson's (Amarillo, TX) 82553
Mary Kay Cosmetics (Houston, TX) 86519

8699 Membership Organizations Nec

Blount Inc. (Montgomery, AL) 56284
Human Affairs International (Chapel Hill, NC) 73816
Kelly Assisted Living Servi (Greensboro, NC) 74857

8711 Engineering Services

Brown & Root Holdings Inc. (Houston, TX) 85892
Brown & Root Inc. (Houston, TX) 85893
Brown & Root Industrial Services Inc. (Houston, TX) 85897
Dow Chemical Co. Engineering & Construction Services Division (Houston, TX) 86046
Duke Energy Corp. (Charlotte, NC) 73934
Duke Engineering & Services Inc. (Charlotte, NC) 73955
Duke/Fluor Daniel (Charlotte, NC) 73937
Engineering Research Associ (Pensacola, FL) 62421
Enserch Corp. (Dallas, TX) 84010; 84011
Entergy Services Inc. (New Orleans, LA) 70448
GTE Spacenet Corp. (McLean, VA) 91391
Halliburton Co. Inc. (Dallas, TX) 84110
Halliburton Holdings Inc. (Dallas, TX) 84111
Halliburton Nus Corp. (Houston, TX) 86263
Johnson Controls Inc. (Gainesville, FL) 59884
Johnson Controls Inc. (Memphis, TN) 81631
Lockheed Engineering & Services Co., Inc. (Houston, TX) 86483
Loral AeroSys (Lanham Seabrook, MD) 72060
Loral Space Information Systems (Houston, TX) 86497
Otis Elevator Co. (Tulsa, OK) 78037
Pentastar Support Services Inc. (Richardson, TX) 88755
PRC Engineering Systems, Inc. (Reston, VA) 91717
PRC Inc. (McLean, VA) 91395
Seagram Joseph E & Sons (Louisville, KY) 69001
Turner Foods Corp. (Punta Gorda, FL) 62722
Unisys Corp. (Beaumont, TX) 83228
Williams Brothers Engineeri (Tulsa, OK) 78210

8712 Architectural Services

Boeing Co (Houston, TX) 85884
Fluor Daniel Inc. (Richmond, VA) 91884
Foster Wheeler Corp. (Carrollton, KY) 68190
Hudson Eng Corp. Mcdermott C (Houston, TX) 86299

Safeco Insurance Co. of America (Manassas, VA) 91323
Southern Development Co. (Lexington, KY) 68629
Standard Fire Insurance Co. (Dallas, TX) 84398
Star Telegram (Fort Worth, TX) 85278
Unisys Corp. (Charleston, WV) 92796
Volunteer State Life Insurance Co. (Granbury, TX) 85602

8713 Surveying Services

Coast to Coast Assoc Inc. (Winter Park, FL) 63966
Systems Research Labs Inc. (San Antonio, TX) 89237
Western Geophysical Co. (Galveston, TX) 85473

8721 Accounting, Auditing & Bookkeeping

Beneficial Income Tax Service (Baltimore, MD) 71063
Centec (Metairie, LA) 70256
The Chesapeake & Potomac Telephone Co. (Washington, DC) 58150
GTE Florida Inc. (Tampa, FL) 63447
GTE South Inc. (Tampa, FL) 63451
GTE Southwest Inc. (Irving, TX) 87351
Kentucky Fried Chicken (Paris, TX) 88367
Mary Kay Cosmet Consultants (Ellisville, MS) 72754
Maxus Energy Corp. (Dallas, TX) 84228
Payroll Data Service Inc. (Destin, FL) 59346
Professional Accounting Ser (St Augustine, FL) 62951
Professional Accounting Ser (Venice, FL) 63731
Professional Accounting Ser (Statesboro, GA) 67643
Texaco Inc. (Shreveport, LA) 70793
Washington Inventory Servic (Fort Pierce, FL) 59817
Washington Inventory Servic (Jacksonville, FL) 60507
Washington Inventory Servic (Austin, TX) 83066
Washington Inventory Servic (Virginia Beach, VA) 92520
Washington Inventory Service (Austin, TX) 83067
Washington Inventory Service (Beaumont, TX) 83237
Zimmer Patient Care System (Charlotte, NC) 74231

8731 Commercial Physical Research

Alliant Tech Systems (San Antonio, TX) 88917
BASF Corp. (Greenville, MS) 72790
Betz Laboratories Inc. (Spring, TX) 89463
Boeing Co. the (El Paso, TX) 84770
Browning-Ferris Industries (Jackson, MS) 72955
Casi-Rusco Inc. (Boca Raton, FL) 58687
Dow Chemical Co. Texas Division (Freeport, TX) 85380
Duracell International Inc. (Lexington, NC) 75402
Exxon Production Research Co. (Houston, TX) 86180; 86182
General Dynamics Services C (Cape Canavral, FL) 58916
Hazleton Corp. (Vienna, VA) 92411
Martin Marietta Corp. (Hampton, VA) 91044
Pennzoil Products Co. (Spring, TX) 89479; 89480
Systems Research Laboratories (Pensacola, FL) 62474
Systems Research Labs Inc. (San Antonio, TX) 89235; 89236
W. R. Grace & Co. Washington Research Center (Columbia, MD) 71604
Westvaco Corp. (Laurel, MD) 72094
Whitby Inc. (Richmond, VA) 92094

8732 Commercial Nonphysical Research

Beneficial Management Corp. (Greenville, SC) 79301
Big Bear (Kenner, LA) 69993

Tandy Consumer Service (Pompano Beach, FL) 62637

8734 Testing Laboratories

Abbott Laboratories (Laurinburg, NC) 75347
Abbott Laboratories (Rocky Mountain, NC) 76112
Abbott Laboratories (Memphis, TN) 81444
Abbott Laboratories Diagnostic Div. (Metairie, LA) 70245
Associated Milk Producers Inc. (Martin, TN) 81396
Betz Laboratory (Midland, TX) 88024
Betz Labs (Macon, GA) 66673
Cutter Biological (Jackson, MS) 72963
Electro Mechanical Energy Corp. (Arnold, MD) 71028
Exxon Enterprises (Fountain Inn, SC) 79244
Halliburton Nus Corp. (Houston, TX) 86263
Maremont Exhaust Products, Inc. (Loudon, TN) 81354
Sterwin Laboratories (Gainesville, GA) 66292

8741 Management Services

A.H. Robins Co. Operations (Richmond, VA) 91724
American Family Life Assurance Co. (Columbus, GA) 65617
Baxter Healthcare (McDonough, GA) 66967
Bell atlantic Financial Services (Wilmington, DE) 58012
BellSouth Services Inc. (Birmingham, AL) 55166
Coast to Coast Food (W Palm Beach, FL) 63785
Criterion Catalyst Co. LP (Houston, TX) 86019
Dominion Resources Inc. (Richmond, VA) 91858
Duke Power Co. Inc. (Charlotte, NC) 73940
Enron Americas Inc. (Houston, TX) 86060
Enserch Exploration Inc. (Dallas, TX) 84014
Entergy Services Inc. (New Orleans, LA) 70448
First American Corp. (Greensboro, NC) 74820
Greenbrier Resort Management Co. Inc. (White Sulphur Springs, WV) 93126
Healthtrust, Inc. (Nashville, TN) 82023
Litton Industrial Contracting (Florence, KY) 68322
Litton Industrial Services (Erlanger, KY) 68299
Mil-Mor Media, Inc. (Richmond, VA) 91931
PRC Inc. (McLean, VA) 91395
A.H. Robins Finance (Richmond, VA) 92005
A.H. Robins Co. Administration (Richmond, VA) 92006
Value Added Service Corp. (Georgetown, KY) 68387
Wingfoot Ventures Seven Inc. (Houston, TX) 87199

8742 Management Consulting Services

Bell Atlantic Business Services (El Paso, TX) 84766
BFI-Richmond Landfill (Richmond, VA) 91745
Brown & Root Holdings Inc. (Houston, TX) 85892
Casi-Rusco Inc. (Boca Raton, FL) 58687
Coastal Power Production Co. (Houston, TX) 85979
Copier Consultants (Greensboro, NC) 74474
Courtyard by Marriott (San Antonio, TX) 88962
Jack Eckerd Corp. (Largo, FL) 60834
FPL Group Inc. (West Palm Beach, FL) 63866
GTE Directories Sales Corp. (Dallas, TX) 84102
Health Care Investment Analysts Inc. (Greenville, SC) 79367
Human Affairs International (Boca Raton, FL) 58712
Kentucky Fried Chicken (Birmingham, AL) 55296
Life Insurance Co. of Va (Suffolk, VA) 92370

Life Insurance Co. of Va
  (Huntington, WV) 92883
Life Insurance Co. of Virginia
  (Fredericksburg, VA) 90929
Logistics Data System (Irving, TX)
  87370
New York Life Insurance Co.
  (Williamsburg, VA) 92577
Personal Performance Consultants
  (Casselberry, FL) 58938
Personal Performance Consultants
  (Orlando, FL) 62077
Personal Performance Consultants
  (Houston, TX) 86675
Pizza Hut (Conroe, TX) 83679
PRC (McLean, VA) 91394
Pulte Home Corp. (Hanover, MD)
  71913
SABRE Travel Information Network
  (Fort Worth, TX) 85271
Southern Group Inc. (Greensboro,
  NC) 74914
Syscon Corp. (Virginia Beach, VA)
  92518
Syscon Corp. (Williamsburg, VA)
  92579
System Energy Resources Inc.
  (Jackson, MS) 73068
Systems Engineering Associates
  International (Melbourne Beach,
  FL) 61124
TNI Inc. (Middleburg, VA) 91406
Transamerica Occidental Life
  Insurance (Corpus Chrsti, TX)
  83774
Zenger-Miller (Fort Lauderdale, FL)
  59645
Zenger-Miller & Associates (Austin,
  TX) 83074
Zenger-Miller & Associates Inc.
  (Houston, TX) 87208

8743 Public Relations Services

Sterling Advertising (Birmingham,
  AL) 55397

8748 Business Consulting Services Nec

American Airlines Decision
  Technologies Inc. (Fort Worth,
  TX) 85061
Diablo Services Corp. (Jackson,
  MS) 72975
Enserch Corp. (Dallas, TX) 84011
Equicor Inc. (Nashville, TN) 81953
Innovative Logistics Inc. (Fort Mill,
  SC) 79234
Northrop Corp. (Huntsville, AL)
  55980
Osca Inc. (Lafayette, LA) 70080
Pizza Hut (Lghthouse Point, FL)
  60898
Rite Aid Corp. (Henderson, NC)
  75028
Syscon Corp. (Columbia, MD)
  71601
Universal Instruments Corp.
  (Shreveport, LA) 70800
Xetron Corp. (Devine, TX) 84650

8999 Services Nec

Engineering Research Assoc
  (Pensacola, FL) 62420
Forcum Lannon Associates
  (Dyersburg, TN) 80750
Halliburton Geophysical Services
  Inc. (Houston, TX) 86260
Jostens Learning Corporatio (Fort
  Lauderdale, FL) 59515
Peoples Bank & Trust Co.
  (Wartburg, TN) 82401
Western Geophysical Co.
  (Jackson, TN) 81018

9100 Executive, Legislative & General

American General Finance Inc.
  (Concord, NC) 74306

9111 Executive Offices

BFI Waste Systems (Gainesville,
  FL) 59862
Pizza Hut (Borger, TX) 83324

9131 Executive and Legislative Combined

Ace Hardware (Pearl River, LA)
  70614

9661 Space Research & Technology

Lockheed Corp. Austin Div. (Austin,
  TX) 82930

9711 National Security

General Electric Ndd Pinellas Plant
  (Largo, FL) 60839
Martin Marietta Speciality Co. US
  Doe Pinellas Plant (Largo, FL)
  60846

9721 International Affairs

Champion International Corp/Ne
  (Marietta, GA) 66759
Champion International Corp. Pr
  (Marietta, GA) 66760
Human Affairs International
  (Atlanta, GA) 64543
Schuller International Inc-Man
  (Washington, DC) 58468
Trans World Airlines Inc. (Houston,
  TX) 87040

9999 Nonclassifiable Establishments

Avon Products (Radford, VA)
  91689
Cape Canaveral Air Force Station
  (Cocoa Beach, FL) 59079
R. J. Reynolds Tobacco Co. -
  Downtown (Winston-Salem, NC)
  76741

Company Name Index

This index lists the companies profiled in this volume of the *American Business Locations Directory*. Index citations consist of company names, entry numbers, and geographic references. Entry numbers that appear in bold face indicate the entry is an ultimate parent company. All other types of entries are denoted by lightfaced numbers.

A

A. G. Industries, Inc. (Forest City, NC) 74595
A. O. Smith Automotive Prods. Co. (Bowling Green, KY) 68131
A. O. Smith Automotive Prods. Co. (Milan, TN) 81765
A. O. Smith Electrical Prods. Co. (Mount Sterling, KY) 69113
A. O. Smith Electrical Prods. Co. (Mebane, NC) 75547
A. O. Smith Water Prods. Co. (Mc Bee, SC) 79654
A. O. Smith Water Prods. Co. (El Paso, TX) 84754
A. O. Smith Water Products Co. (Mc Bee, SC) 79655; 79656
A. Schulman Inc. (Orange, TX) 88297; 88298
A. Schulman Inc. Dispersion (Orange, TX) 88299
AA Decision Technologies (Dallas-Fort Worth Airport, TX) 84511
AA Decision Technologies Inc. (Dallas-Fort Worth, TX) 84501
Aaron Rents (Atlanta, GA) 64187
Abb Power T&D Co. Inc. (Pinetops, NC) 75806
Abbott Chemical Inc. (Barceloneta, PR) 78319
Abbott Chemicals Inc. (Barceloneta, PR) 78320; 78321
Abbott Laboratories (Jackson, MS) 72937
Abbott Laboratories (Laurinburg, NC) 75347; 75348
Abbott Laboratories (Louisburg, NC) 75453
Abbott Laboratories (Rocky Mount, NC) 76071; 76072
Abbott Laboratories (Rocky Mountain, NC) 76112
Abbott Laboratories (Memphis, TN) 81444
Abbott Laboratories (Austin, TX) 82799
Abbott Laboratories Diagnostic Div. (Metairie, LA) 70245
Abbott Laboratories Diagnostic Div. (Irving, TX) 87315
Abbott Laboratories Diagnostics Division (Irving, TX) 87316
Abbott Laboratories International Co. (New Orleans, LA) 70423
Abbott Manufacturing Inc. (Irving, TX) 87317
Abercrombie & Fitch (Atlanta, GA) 64188
Abercrombie & Fitch (Houston, TX) 85757
ABF Cartage, Inc. (Fort Smith, AR) 57015
ABF Freight System (BC) Ltd. (Fort Smith, AR) 57016
ABF Freight System, Inc. (Fort Smith, AR) 57017
ABF Freight System Inc. (Daytona Beach, FL) 59161
ABF Freight System Inc. (Tampa, FL) 63301
ABF Freight System Inc. (Atlanta, GA) 64189
ABF Freight System Inc. (Baltimore, MD) 71029
ABF Freight System Inc. (Jackson, MS) 72938
ABF Freight System Inc. (Hickory, NC) 75052
ABF Freight System Inc. (Raleigh, NC) 75847
ABF Freight System Inc. (Oklahoma City, OK) 77290
ABF Freight System Inc. (North Charleston, SC) 79743
ABF Freight System Inc. (Chattanooga, TN) 80292
ABF Freight System Inc. (Knoxville, TN) 81129
ABF Freight System Inc. (Nashville, TN) 81876; 81877

ABF Freight System Inc. (Forthworth, TX) 85370
ABF Freight System Inc. (Houston, TX) 85758
ABF Freight System Inc. (Lubbock, TX) 87746
ABF Freight System Inc. (Texarkana, TX) 89664
ABF Freight System Inc. (Richmond, VA) 91723
ABF Freight Systems (Pecos, TX) 88493
ABF Freight Systems Inc. (Lynchburg, VA) 91219
Abitibi-Price Building Products (Roaring River, NC) 76045
Abitibi-Price Building Products (Lumberton, NC) 75457
Abitibi-Price Corp. (Lumberton, NC) 75458; 75459
Abitibi-Price Corp. (Roaring River, NC) 76046; 76047
Abitibi Price Sales Corp. (Atlanta, GA) 64190; 64191
ABM Graphics (Birmingham, AL) 55109
Acco Waste Paper (Houston, TX) 85759
Accuride Corp. (Henderson, KY) 68437
Ace Hardware (Birmingham, AL) 55110; 55111
Ace Hardware (Dothan, AL) 55623
Ace Hardware (Fort Smith, AR) 57018
Ace Hardware (Searcy, AR) 57600
Ace Hardware (Smackover, AR) 57625
Ace Hardware (Belleview, FL) 58652
Ace Hardware (Blountstown, FL) 58661
Ace Hardware (Bradenton, FL) 58799
Ace Hardware (Cocoa Beach, FL) 59077
Ace Hardware (Delray Beach, FL) 59303
Ace Hardware (Destin, FL) 59337
Ace Hardware (Fort Lauderdale, FL) 59423
Ace Hardware (Fort Myers, FL) 59657
Ace Hardware (Frnandina Beach, FL) 59844
Ace Hardware (Jacksonville, FL) 60156
Ace Hardware (Jensen Beach, FL) 60524
Ace Hardware (Lake Mary, FL) 60637
Ace Hardware (Lake Worth, FL) 60660; 60661
Ace Hardware (Lakeland, FL) 60703
Ace Hardware (Largo, FL) 60806
Ace Hardware (Longwood, FL) 60924; 60925
Ace Hardware (Melbourne, FL) 61031; 61032
Ace Hardware (Merritt Island, FL) 61136
Ace Hardware (Miami, FL) 61151
Ace Hardware (New Port Richey, FL) 61672
Ace Hardware (Newberry, FL) 61705
Ace Hardware (Palatka, FL) 62223
Ace Hardware (Panama City, FL) 62312
Ace Hardware (Perry, FL) 62496
Ace Hardware (Pinellas Park, FL) 62507
Ace Hardware (St Petersburg, FL) 62962; 62963
Ace Hardware (St. Petersburg, FL) 63075
Ace Hardware (W Palm Beach, FL) 63775
Ace Hardware (Acworth, GA) 64034

Ace Hardware (Alpharetta, GA) 64102; 64103
Ace Hardware (Atlanta, GA) 64192; 64193; 64194
Ace Hardware (Brunswick, GA) 65397
Ace Hardware (Buford, GA) 65431
Ace Hardware (Chamblee, GA) 65516
Ace Hardware (Claxton, GA) 65564
Ace Hardware (College Park, GA) 65574
Ace Hardware (Decatur, GA) 65796
Ace Hardware (Douglasville, GA) 65983
Ace Hardware (Dunwoody, GA) 66097; 66098
Ace Hardware (Fayetteville, GA) 66186
Ace Hardware (Gray, GA) 66308
Ace Hardware (Hapeville, GA) 66332
Ace Hardware (Hinesville, GA) 66349
Ace Hardware (Lilburn, GA) 66552
Ace Hardware (Marietta, GA) 66730; 66731; 66732; 66733
Ace Hardware (Norcross, GA) 67088; 67089
Ace Hardware (Peachtree Cit, GA) 67233
Ace Hardware (Roswell, GA) 67354
Ace Hardware (Snellville, GA) 67587
Ace Hardware (Breaux Bridge, LA) 69740
Ace Hardware (Eunice, LA) 69847
Ace Hardware (Folsom, LA) 69857
Ace Hardware (Monroe, LA) 70349
Ace Hardware (Pearl River, LA) 70614
Ace Hardware (Shreveport, LA) 70679
Ace Hardware (St. Martinville, LA) 70869
Ace Hardware (Ville Platte, LA) 70932
Ace Hardware (Edgewood, MD) 71664
Ace Hardware (Germantown, MD) 71823
Ace Hardware (Severn, MD) 72369
Ace Hardware (Solomons, MD) 72454
Ace Hardware (Madison, MS) 73135
Ace Hardware (Ahoskie, NC) 73522
Ace Hardware (Concord, NC) 74303
Ace Hardware (Greenville, NC) 74945
Ace Hardware (Hickory, NC) 75053
Ace Hardware (Lenoir, NC) 75363
Ace Hardware (Maxton, NC) 75553
Ace Hardware (Nags Head, NC) 75714
Ace Hardware (Raleigh, NC) 75848; 75849
Ace Hardware (Selma, NC) 76218
Ace Hardware (Bartlesville, OK) 76830
Ace Hardware (Enid, OK) 77041
Ace Hardware (Guymon, OK) 77099
Ace Hardware (Jenks, OK) 77148
Ace Hardware (Kingfisher, OK) 77149
Ace Hardware (Stillwater, OK) 77833
Ace Hardware (Tulsa, OK) 77871; 77872
Ace Hardware (Woodward, OK) 78254
Ace Hardware (Florence, SC) 79192
Ace Hardware (Georgetown, SC) 79270
Ace Hardware (Spartanburg, SC) 79873

Ace Hardware (West Columbia, SC) 80083
Ace Hardware (Aransas Pass, TX) 82622
Ace Hardware (Arlington, TX) 82628; 82629
Ace Hardware (Austin, TX) 82800; 82801
Ace Hardware (Bedford, TX) 83238
Ace Hardware (Buna, TX) 83414
Ace Hardware (Copperas Cove, TX) 83691
Ace Hardware (Crowley, TX) 83813
Ace Hardware (Denton, TX) 84614
Ace Hardware (Fort Worth, TX) 85053
Ace Hardware (Humble, TX) 87215
Ace Hardware (Irving, TX) 87318
Ace Hardware (Kemp, TX) 87464
Ace Hardware (Malakoff, TX) 87829
Ace Hardware (Rockwall, TX) 88822
Ace Hardware (The Woodlands, TX) 89749
Ace Hardware (Timpson, TX) 89764
Ace Hardware (Wellington, TX) 90029
Ace Hardware (Buena Vista, VA) 90497
Ace Hardware (Hayes, VA) 91111
Ace Hardware (Portsmouth, VA) 91638
Ace Hardware-Bates (Atlanta, GA) 64195
Ace Hardware & Building Sup (Clanton, AL) 55518
Ace Hardware & Building Sup (W Palm Beach, FL) 63776
Ace Hardware & Building Sup (Fort Mill, SC) 79231
Ace Hardware of Butler Inc. (Butler, AL) 55493
Ace Hardware-Butlers (Dallas, GA) 65756
Ace Hardware of Charlotte (Charlotte, NC) 73826
Ace Hardware Co. (Jackson, AL) 56061
Ace Hardware Co. (Opelika, AL) 56415
Ace Hardware Co. (Dunnellon, FL) 59369
Ace Hardware Co. (Atlanta, GA) 64196
Ace Hardware Co. (Forest Park, GA) 66225
Ace Hardware Co. (Riverdale, GA) 67303
Ace Hardware Co. Inc. (New Iberia, LA) 70407
Ace Hardware Co. Inc. (Cornelius, NC) 74346
Ace Hardware Co. Inc. (Greenwood, SC) 79451
Ace Hardware of Concord (Concord, NC) 74304
Ace Hardware Corp. (Arlington, TX) 82630
Ace Hardware of Del Rio Inc. (Del Rio, TX) 84578
Ace Hardware Downtown (Texarkana, TX) 89665
Ace Hardware & Farm Supply (Saluda, SC) 79849
Ace Hardware of Fayette (Atlanta, GA) 64197
Ace Hardware & Garden Cente (Starke, FL) 63142
Ace Hardware Garner (Jacksonville, FL) 60157
Ace Hardware Home Center (Chamblee, GA) 65517
Ace Hardware & Home Center (Raleigh, NC) 75850; 75851; 75852
Ace Hardware, Inc. (Ocala, FL) 61764
Ace Hardware Inc. (Brunswick, GA) 65398

Ace Hardware Inc. (Roswell, GA) 67355
Ace Hardware Lacombe (Lacombe, LA) 70036
Ace Hardware & Locksmith (Tampa, FL) 63302
Ace Hardware & Locksmith (Temple Ter, FL) 63673
Ace Hardware & Lumber (Pilot Point, TX) 88514
Ace Hardware Margate (Pompano Beach, FL) 62579
Ace Hardware & Marine (Atl Beach, NC) 73642
Ace Hardware & Marine (Morehead City, NC) 75610
Ace Hardware Marine Eqot (Fort Myers, FL) 59658
Ace Hardware at Newport (Rock Hill, SC) 79810
Ace Hardware of Noble (Noble, OK) 77245
Ace Hardware No. 679 (Forest Park, GA) 66226
Ace Hardware No. 2822a (Donaldsonvl, LA) 69844
Ace Hardware P P (Plant City, FL) 62533
Ace Hardware of Palm Bay (Palm Bay, FL) 62229
Ace Hardware Plus (Ennis, TX) 84993
Ace Hardware Proctor (Jacksonville, FL) 60158
Ace Hardware Ragsdale (Marietta, GA) 66734
Ace Hardware Reynolds Brothers (Foley, AL) 55747
Ace Hardware of Salisbury (Salisbury, NC) 76152
Ace Hardware of Screven (Screven, GA) 67534
Ace Hardware of Slidell Inc. (Slidell, LA) 70814
Ace Hardware-Smith (Atlanta, GA) 64198
Ace Hardware-Smith Open 7 Days (Decatur, GA) 65797
Ace Hardware Store (Conway, AR) 56859
Ace Hardware Store (Bartow, FL) 58620
Ace Hardware Store (Fort Lauderdale, FL) 59424
Ace Hardware Store (Newnan, GA) 67075
Ace Hardware Store (Winston Salem, NC) 76659
Ace Hardware Store (Hobart, OK) 77132
Ace Hardware Store (San Antonio, TX) 88910
Ace Hardware Store No. 540 (W Palm Beach, FL) 63777
Ace Hardware Stores (Hobe Sound, FL) 60025
Ace Hardware Stores (Houston, TX) 85760
Ace Hardware & Supply (Fultondale, AL) 55770
Ace Hardware Supply (Oklahoma City, OK) 77291
Ace Hardware Talbert Lumber (Roxboro, NC) 76119
Ace Hardware 3141 a (Pensacola, FL) 62376
Ace Hardware of Villa Rica (Villa Rica, GA) 68001
Ace Hardware-Workbench (Atlanta, GA) 64199; 64200
Ace Hardware-Workbench (Chamblee, GA) 65518
Ace Hardware Workbench (Peachtree, GA) 67223
Ace Hardware&Equipment Co. (Waynesboro, MS) 73472
Ace Hardware&Farm Supply (Rector, AR) 57553
Ace Hardware&Furniture Inc. (Fordyce, AR) 57004
Ace Hardware&Garden Center (Baton Rouge, LA) 69453

Ace Hardware&Hm Improvement (Edmond, OK) 77004
Ace Hardware&Hm Imprvmt Center (Angleton, TX) 82608
Ace Hardware&Home Center (Broken Arrow, OK) 76877
Ace Hardware&Home Center (Houston, TX) 85761
Ace Hardware&Home Center Inc. (Raleigh, NC) 75853
Ace Hardware&Home Center Inc. (Spring, TX) 89462
Ace Hardware&Locksmith (Brandon, FL) 58863
Ace Hardware&Lumber (Pompano Beach, FL) 62580
Ace Hareware (Sanford, FL) 62763
ACI (Benton, AR) 56770
Acme Business Product (Greenville, SC) 79290
Acme Business Products (Albany, GA) 64060
ACME Business Products (Athens, GA) 64152
ACME Business Products (Brunswick, GA) 65399; 65400
Acme Business Products (Macon, GA) 66643
ACME Business Products (Valdosta, GA) 67938
ACME Business Products (Asheville, NC) 73601
ACME Business Products (Anderson, SC) 78661
ACME Frame Products (Harrisburg, AR) 57135
ACME Frame Products of Mississippi (Tutwiler, MS) 73429
ACME Markets (Dover, DE) 57775; 57776; 57777; 57778
Acme Markets (Middletown, DE) 57830
Acme Markets (Milford, DE) 57835
ACME Markets (Newark, DE) 57880; 57881; 57882; 57883
Acme Markets (Wilmington, DE) 57965; 57966; 57967; 57968; 57969; 57970
Acme Markets (Washington, DC) 58122
Acme Markets (Cambridge, MD) 71484
ACME Markets (Easton, MD) 71657
Acme Markets (Elkton, MD) 71669
Acme Markets (Salisbury, MD) 72333; 72334
Acme Markets (North Tazewell, VA) 91599
ACME Markets (Radford, VA) 91687
Acme Markets (Tazewell, VA) 92378
Acme Markets (Martinsburg, WV) 92926
ACME Markets Inc. (Wilmington, DE) 57971; 57972
Acme Markets of Tazewell Va (Bluefield, WV) 92699
ACME Markets of Virginia Inc. (North Tazewell, VA) 91600
Action Industries Inc. (Tupelo, MS) 73384
Acustar Inc. Huntsville Electronics Plant (Huntsville, AL) 55872; 55873
Adams-Millis Drexel Knitting (Drexel, NC) 74363
Adams-Millis Hoisery (Hickory, NC) 75054
Adams-Millis Hoisery (Kernersville, NC) 75273
Adams-Millis Hoisery (Mount Airy, NC) 75671
Adams Millis Hoisery Corp. (Kernersville, NC) 75274
Adams Millis Hosiery Corp. (Mount Airy, NC) 75672
Adams-Millis Influential (High Point, NC) 75109
Adams Millis Influential (Mebane, NC) 75548
Adams-Millis Influential No. 2 (Mebane, NC) 75549
Adams-Millis Wrangler (High Point, NC) 75110
Adams Millis Wranlger (High Point, NC) 75111
Adcom Wire Co. (Jacksonville, FL) 60159
Adcom Wire Co. (Nicholasville, KY) 69147; 69148; 69149; 69150; 69151
Adhesive Technologies Corp. (Burlington, NC) 73738
Adm (Southport, NC) 76281
ADM Co. (Clarksdale, MS) 72665
ADM Miling Co. (Crowley, LA) 69799
ADM Miling Co. (Charlottte, NC) 74232
ADM Milling (Knobel, AR) 57237

Adm Milling Harvest Queen Mill & Elevator Div. (Plainview, TX) 88523
ADM Milling Co. (Weiner, AR) 57712
ADM Milling Co. (Destrehan, LA) 69836
ADM Milling Co. (Enid, OK) 77042
ADM Milling Co. (Chatanooga, TN) 80291
ADM Milling Co. (Cleveland, TN) 80563
Adm Milling Co. Harvest Queen Mill & Elevator Div. (Plainview, TX) 88524
Adm Milling Co. Interstate Div. (Charlotte, NC) 73827
ADM Milling Co. Inc. (North Little Rock, AR) 57452
ADM Milling Co. Otwell (Jonesboro, AR) 57209
ADM Specialty Grain (Muleshoe, TX) 88165
Adolph Coors Co. (Elkton, VA) 90743
ADP Automatic Data Processing (Wilmington, DE) 57973
ADP-Automatic Data Processing (Tampa, FL) 63303
ADP Dealers Services (Newport News, VA) 91448
ADP Network Services (Washington, DC) 58123
Advance Security (Atlanta, GA) 64201
Advance Security Inc. (Atlanta, GA) 64202
Advanced Image Systems Inc. (Dallas, TX) 83837
Advanced Medical Systems (Clearwater, FL) 58958
Advanced Medical Systems (Houston, TX) 85762
Advanced Medical Systems Inc. (Birmingham, AL) 55112; 55113
Advanced Medical Systems Inc. (Kenner, LA) 69992
Advanced Micro Devices (Austin, TX) 82802; 82803
Advanced Micro Devices (Dallas, TX) 83838
Advanced Micro Devices Inc. (Fort Lauderdale, FL) 59425
Advanced Micro Devices Inc. (Maitland, FL) 60970
Advanced Micro Devices Inc. (Norcross, GA) 67090
Advanced Micro Devices Inc. (Austin, TX) 82804
Advanced Micro Devices Inc. (Houston, TX) 85763; 85764
Advanced Micro Devices Inc. (San Antonio, TX) 88911
Advanced Seperation Technologies Inc. (Lakeland, FL) 60704
Advanced Technology Lab (Linthicum Heights, MD) 72106
Advanced Technology Labroatories (Linthicum, MD) 72104
Aero M Inc. (Huntsville, AL) 55874
Aero M Inc. (Glasgow, KY) 68390
Aero Service Corp. (Houston, TX) 85765
Aero Technical Services (Fort Walton Beach, FL) 59818
Aerojet Electrosystems Co. (Washington, DC) 58124
Aerojet Heavy Metals Co. (Jonesborough, TN) 81063
Aerojet Ordnance Co. (Washington, DC) 58125
Aeroquip Corp. (Heber Springs, AR) 57148; 57149
Aeroquip Corp. (Mountain Home, AR) 57381; 57382; 57383
Aeroquip Corp. (Fitzgerald, GA) 66205
Aeroquip Corp. (Toccoa, GA) 67835
Aeroquip Corp. (Henderson, KY) 68438
Aeroquip Corp. (Williamsport, MD) 72572
Aeroquip Corp. (Forest City, NC) 74596; 74597; 74598; 74599
Aeroquip Corp. (Middlesex, NC) 75557
Aeroquip Corp. (Mooresville, NC) 75596; 75597
Aeroquip Corp. (Norwood, NC) 75768; 75769
Aeroquip Corp. (Statesville, NC) 76315
Aeroquip Corp. (Lancaster, SC) 79566
Aeroquip Corp. (Franklin, TN) 80806
Aeroquip Corp. (Gainesboro, TN) 80831; 80832; 80833
Aeroquip Corp. (Livingston, TN) 81347
Aeroquip Corp. (Bassett, VA) 90414

Aeroquip Corp. Diversified Products Div. (Franklin, TN) 80807
Aeroquip Corp. Industrial Products Div. (Gainesboro, TN) 80834
Aeroquip Corp. Sterling Div. (Mooresville, NC) 75598
Aeroquip Corp. Industrial Products Group (Norwood, NC) 75770
Aeroquip Corp. Middlesex Plant (Middlesex, NC) 75558
Aerospace Products SE Inc. (Huntsville, AL) 55875
Aerospace Technologies Inc. (Fort Worth, TX) 85054; 85055; 85056
Aerovox Mallory (Huntsville, AL) 55876
Aetna Financial Services Inc. (Gainesville, GA) 66264
Aetna Financial Services Inc. (Jackson, MS) 72939
Aetna Life & Annuity Co. (Memphis, TN) 81445
AFLAC (Shelby, NC) 76230
AFLAC Federal Credit Union (Columbus, GA) 65615
AFLAC Inc. (Columbus, GA) 65616
A.G. Industries, Inc. (Forest City, NC) 74600
AGC Life Insurance Co. (Nashville, TN) 81878; 81879; 81880
AGR Co. (Charlotte, NC) 73828
Agra Tech Seeds Inc. (Atlanta, GA) 64203
Agra Trade Financing Inc. (Atlanta, GA) 64204
Agri-Bio Corp. (Gainesville, GA) 66265
Agri International Inc. (Atlanta, GA) 64205
Agri-Services of Harrisonburg (Harrisonburg, VA) 91062
Agri Services Inc. (Catlett, VA) 90511
Agrico Chemical Co. (Gibsonton, FL) 59926
Agrico Chemical Co. (Mulberry, FL) 61570
Agrico Chemical Co. (Polk City, FL) 62578
Agrico Chemical Co. (Cecilia, KY) 68199
Agrico Chemical Co. (Clay, KY) 68202
Agrico Chemical Co. (Henderson, KY) 68439
Agrico Chemical Co. (Melbourne, KY) 69093
Agrico Chemical Co. (Baltimore, MD) 71030
Agrico Chemical Co. (Catoosa, OK) 76907
Agrico Chemical Co. (Tulsa, OK) 77873
Agrico Chemical Co. (Union City, TN) 82381
Agrico Chemical Co., Inc. (Clarkson, KY) 68201
Agrico Chemical Co. Inc. (Madisonville, KY) 69046
Agrico Chemical Co. Inc. (Newport, KY) 69136
Agrico Chemical Co. S. Pierce (Mulberry, FL) 61571; 61572
Agrico Chemical Co. Taft Plant (Hahnville, LA) 69922
Agrico Chemical Co. Uncle Sam Plant (Uncle Sam, LA) 70916
Agricultural Products (Durham, NC) 74379
Agvestments Inc. (Atlanta, GA) 64206
A.H. Robins Co. Operations (Richmond, VA) 91724
A.H. Robins Co., Inc. (Richmond, VA) 91725
A.H. Robins Manufacturing Co. (Barceloneta, PR) 78322
Ahmanson Morgage Co. (Rockville, MD) 72255
Aid Association for Luthera (Orange, TX) 88300
AIG Aviation, Inc. (Atlanta, GA) 64207; 64208
AIG Marketing Inc. (Wilmington, DE) 57974
Air Control Products (Roxboro, NC) 76120
Air Products (Guayanilla, PR) 78430
Air Products & Chemicals (Decatur, AL) 55570
Air Products & Chemicals (Madison, AL) 56117
Air Products & Chemicals (Theodore, AL) 56605
Air Products & Chemicals (New Orleans, LA) 70424
Air Products & Chemicals (St. Gabriel, LA) 70862
Air Products & Chemicals (Beltsville, MD) 71347
Air Products & Chemicals (Sparrows Poin, MD) 72462

Air Products & Chemicals (Arden, NC) 73563
Air Products & Chemicals (Charlotte, NC) 73829
Air Products & Chemicals (Durham, NC) 74380; 74381
Air Products & Chemicals (Greenville, SC) 79291
Air Products & Chemicals (Seguin, TX) 89366
Air Products & Chemicals Co. (Orlando, FL) 61902
Air Products & Chemicals Inc. (Birmingham, AL) 55114
Air Products & Chemicals Inc. (Decatur, AL) 55571; 55572
Air Products & Chemicals Inc. (Sheffield, AL) 56543
Air Products & Chemicals Inc. (Fayetteville, AR) 56967; 56968
Air Products & Chemicals, Inc. (Fort Smith, AR) 57019; 57020
Air Products & Chemicals Inc. (Huntsville, AR) 57192
Air Products & Chemicals Inc. (Delaware City, DE) 57768
Air Products & Chemicals Inc. (New Castle, DE) 57853; 57854
Air Products & Chemicals Inc. (Newark, DE) 57884
Air Products & Chemicals, Inc. (Clearwater, FL) 58959
Air Products & Chemicals, Inc. (Fort Walton Beach, FL) 59819
Air Products & Chemicals, Inc. (Jacksonville, FL) 60160
Air Products & Chemicals, Inc. (Largo, FL) 60807
Air Products & Chemicals, Inc. (Milton, FL) 61540; 61541; 61542
Air Products & Chemicals, Inc. (Orlando, FL) 61903
Air Products & Chemicals, Inc. (Pace, FL) 62217; 62218; 62219
Air Products & Chemicals, Inc. (Pensacola, FL) 62377
Air Products & Chemicals, Inc. (Tampa, FL) 63304
Air Products & Chemicals Inc. (Albany, GA) 64061; 64062; 64063
Air Products & Chemicals, Inc. (Atlanta, GA) 64209; 64210
Air Products & Chemicals Inc. (Conyers, GA) 65666
Air Products & Chemicals, Inc. (Valdosta, GA) 67939
Air Products & Chemicals Inc. (Ashland, KY) 68083
Air Products & Chemicals Inc. (Calvert City, KY) 68174; 68175
Air Products & Chemicals Inc. (Addis, LA) 69364
Air Products & Chemicals Inc. (Convent, LA) 69781
Air Products & Chemicals Inc. (New Orleans, LA) 70425; 70426
Air Products & Chemicals Inc. (St. Gabriel, LA) 70863; 70864; 70865
Air Products & Chemicals Inc. (Baltimore, MD) 71031
Air Products & Chemicals, Inc. (Elkton, MD) 71670
Air Products & Chemicals Inc. (Hyattsville, MD) 71952
Air Products & Chemicals, Inc. (Clarksdale, MS) 72666
Air Products & Chemicals, Inc. (Tupelo, MS) 73385
Air Products & Chemicals Inc. (Greensboro, NC) 74759
Air Products & Chemicals, Inc. (Oklahoma City, OK) 77292
Air Products & Chemicals, Inc. (Pryor, OK) 77732; 77733; 77734; 77735; 77736
Air Products & Chemicals, Inc. (Tulsa, OK) 77874
Air Products & Chemicals, Inc. (Columbia, SC) 78965
Air Products & Chemicals, Inc. (Langley, SC) 79584; 79585
Air Products & Chemicals, Inc. (Piedmont, SC) 79792
Air Products & Chemicals, Inc. (Travelers Rest, SC) 80041; 80042
Air Products & Chemicals Inc. (Kingsport, TN) 81069; 81070; 81071; 81072
Air Products & Chemicals Inc. (Knoxville, TN) 81130
Air Products & Chemicals Inc. (Memphis, TN) 81446; 81447
Air Products & Chemicals Inc. (Nashville, TN) 81881
Air Products & Chemicals Inc. (Austin, TX) 82805
Air Products & Chemicals, Inc. (Baytown, TX) 83106
Air Products & Chemicals Inc. (Deer Park, TX) 84546

Air Products & Chemicals Inc. (Irving, TX) 87319
Air Products & Chemicals Inc. (La Porte, TX) 87552
Air Products & Chemicals, Inc. (Lone Star, TX) 87699
Air Products & Chemicals Inc. (Midlothian, TX) 88097; 88098
Air Products & Chemicals Inc. (Pasadena, TX) 88381
Air Products & Chemicals Inc. (Lynchburg, VA) 91220
Air Products & Chemicals Inc. (Roanoke, VA) 92099
Air Products & Chemicals Inc. (Weirton, WV) 93083; 93084
Air Products Manufacturing Corp. (Gruver, TX) 85691; 85692
Air Products Manufacturing Corp. (La Porte, TX) 87553; 87554
Air Products Manufacturing Corp. (LaPorte, TX) 87602
Air Products Manufacturing Corp. (Midlothian, TX) 88099
Air Products Manufacturing Corp. (Pasadena, TX) 88382; 88383; 88384
Air Products of Puerto Rico (Guayanilla, PR) 78431
Air Products World Trade, Inc. c/oChase Trade, Inc. (St. Thomas, VI) 90150
Air Treads Inc. (Atlanta, GA) 64211; 64212
Air Treads Inc. Atlanta Div. (Forest Park, GA) 66227
Air Treads Inc. Dallas Div. (Irving, TX) 87320
Airborne Freight Corp. (Fort Lauderdale, FL) 59426
Airborne Freight Corp. (Jacksonville, FL) 60161
Airborne Freight Corp. (Orlando, FL) 61904
Airborne Freight Corp. (Tampa, FL) 63305
Airborne Freight Corp. (Baton Rouge, LA) 69454; 69455
Airborne Freight Corp. (Shreveport, LA) 70680
Airborne Freight Corp. (Montgomery, MD) 72137
Airborne Freight Corp. (Greenville, NC) 74946
Airborne Freight Corp. (Oklahoma City, OK) 77293
Airborne Freight Corp. (Greer, SC) 79468
Airborne Freight Corp. (Hilton Head isLand, SC) 79510
Airborne Freight Corp. (Dallas, TX) 83839
Airborne Freight Corp. (Houston, TX) 85766
Airborne Freight Corp. (Richmond, VA) 91726
Aircraft Porous Media Inc. (Pinellas Park, FL) 62508; 62509
Airfoil Textron Inc. (Orlando, FL) 61905
Ajax-Superior Compressor Packaging Plant (Oklahoma City, OK) 77294
Aker Sulfur Recovery Plant (Streetman, TX) 89528
Alabama Reclamation Plant (Sheffield, AL) 56544; 56545
Alabama Reclamation Plant Alabama Reclamation Plant (Sheffield, AL) 56546
Alberto Culver (Dunwoody, GA) 66099
Alberto Culver Co. (Atlanta, GA) 64213
Albertson's (Fort Walton Beach, FL) 59820
Albertson's (Jupiter, FL) 60529
,Albertson's (Maitland, FL) 60971
Albertson's (Melbourne, FL) 61033
Albertson's (Mount Dora, FL) 61560
Albertson's (Winter Park, FL) 63958
Albertson's (Baton Rouge, LA) 69456
Albertson's (Bossier City, LA) 69711
Albertson's (Lafayette, LA) 70039
Albertson's (Slidell, LA) 70815; 70816
Albertson's (Austin, TX) 82806; 82807; 82808; 82809
Albertson's (Bedford, TX) 83239
Albertson's (Lewisville, TX) 87644; 87645
Albertson's (San Angelo, TX) 88866
Albertson's (Wichita Falls, TX) 90063; 90064
Albertson's Drug & Food (Victoria, TX) 89876
Albertson's Drug Store (San Antonio, TX) 88912; 88913

American Cyanamid Co. (Havre De Grace, MD) 71914; 71915
American Cyanamid Co. (Pearl, MS) 73274
American Cyanamid Co. (Charlotte, NC) 73834; 73835
American Cyanamid Co. (Memphis, TN) 81448; 81449
American Cyanamid Co. (Dallas, TX) 83845
American Cyanamid Co. (Richardson, TX) 88720
American Cyanamid Co. (Willow Island, WV) 93131; 93132
American Cyanamid Co. Lederle Laboratories Division (Atlanta, GA) 64224
American Cyanamid Co. Lederle Laboratories Division (Sanford, NC) 76186
American Cyanamid Co. Shulton (Pearl, MS) 73275
American Electric (Bainbridge, GA) 65363
American Electric (Southaven, MS) 73346
American Electric (Athens, TN) 80185
American Emblem Tool Co. (Shelbyville, KY) 69270
American Emulsions Co. Inc. (Dalton, GA) 65771
American Express Bank International (Miami, FL) 61156
American Express Centurion Bank (Wilmington, DE) 57976
American Express Credit Corp. (Wilmington, DE) 57977; 57978; 57979
American Family Life Assrnc (Greenwood, MS) 72831
American Family Life Assur (Pensacola, FL) 62379
American Family Life Assur (Statesboro, GA) 67632
American Family Life Assur (Hickory, NC) 75055
American Family Life Assurance (Atmore, AL) 55049
American Family Life Assurance (Birmingham, AL) 55120
American Family Life Assurance (Dothan, AL) 55624
American Family Life Assurance (Mobile, AL) 56135
American Family Life Assurance (Montgomery, AL) 56276
American Family Life Assurance (Tuscaloosa, AL) 56630
American Family Life Assurance (Fayetteville, AR) 56969
American Family Life Assurance (Fort Smith, AR) 57021
American Family Life Assurance (Altamonte Springs, FL) 58548
American Family Life Assurance (Crestview, FL) 59122
American Family Life Assurance (Fort Myers, FL) 59659
American Family Life Assurance (Pensacola, FL) 62380; 62381
American Family Life Assurance (Punta Gorda, FL) 62701
American Family Life Assurance (Tallahassee, FL) 63203
American Family Life Assurance (Macon, GA) 66647
American Family Life Assurance (Savannah, GA) 67440
American Family Life Assurance (Statesboro, GA) 67633
American Family Life Assurance (Valdosta, GA) 67940
American Family Life Assurance (Warner Robins, GA) 68005
American Family Life Assurance (Lafayette, LA) 70041
American Family Life Assurance (Greenwood, MS) 72832
American Family Life Assurance (Jackson, MS) 72940
American Family Life Assurance (Charlotte, NC) 73836
American Family Life Assurance (Clinton, NC) 74278
American Family Life Assurance (Fayetteville, NC) 74524
American Family Life Assurance (Hickory, NC) 75056
American Family Life Assurance (Spartanburg, SC) 79875
American Family Life Assurance (Dumas, TX) 84686
American Family Life Assurance (Hereford, TX) 85738
American Family Life Assurance (San Angelo, TX) 88867
American Family Life Assurance (Harrisonburg, VA) 91063
American Family Life Assurance (Lynchburg, VA) 91221
American Family Life Assurance (Richmond, VA) 91727
American Family Life Assurance (Virginia Beach, VA) 92429; 92430
American Family Life Assurance Co. (Columbus, GA) **65617**
American Family Life Assurance Co. Broadcast Div. (Columbus, GA) 65618
American Financial Corp. of Tampa (Tampa, FL) 63309
American Financial Service Inc. (Houston, TX) 85777
American General Corp. (Houston, TX) 85778; **85779**
American General Federal Credit Union (Baltimore, MD) 71038
American General Federal Credit Union (Nashville, TN) 81882
American General Federal Credit Union (Houston, TX) 85780
American General Finance (Bessemer, AL) 55082
American General Finance (Birmingham, AL) 55121; 55122
American General Finance (Decatur, AL) 55573
American General Finance (Gadsden, AL) 55772
American General Finance (Huntsville, AL) 55878
American General Finance (Mobile, AL) 56136
American General Finance (Montgomery, AL) 56277
American General Finance (Dover, DE) 57779
American General Finance (Laurel, DE) 57824
American General Finance (Milford, DE) 57836
American General Finance (Newark, DE) 57886
American General Finance (Smyrna, DE) 57957
American General Finance (Fort Lauderdale, FL) 59434; 59435; 59436
American General Finance (Hollywood, FL) 60033
American General Finance (Jacksonville, FL) 60164; 60165; 60166; 60167; 60168; 60169
American General Finance (Orlando, FL) 61908; 61909
American General Finance (Tallahassee, FL) 63204
American General Finance (Tampa, FL) 63310; 63311; 63312; 63313; 63314
American General Finance (Atlanta, GA) 64225; 64226; 64227; 64228
American General Finance (Columbus, GA) 65619
American General Finance (Macon, GA) 66648
American General Finance (Roswell, GA) 67357
American General Finance (Savannah, GA) 67441; 67442
American General Finance (Hazard, KY) 68422
American General Finance (Hopkinsville, KY) 68472
American General Finance (Lexington, KY) 68518
American General Finance (Louisville, KY) 68675; 68676; 68677; 68678; 68679; 68680
American General Finance (Radcliff, KY) 69237
American General Finance (Baton Rouge, LA) 69463; 69464; 69465
American General Finance (Metairie, LA) 70246
American General Finance (New Orleans, LA) 70429
American General Finance (Shreveport, LA) 70682
American General Finance (Owings Mills, MD) 72182
American General Finance (Jackson, MS) 72941
American General Finance (Burlington, NC) 73739
American General Finance (Charlotte, NC) 73837
American General Finance (Durham, NC) 74382; 74383
American General Finance (Fayetteville, NC) 74525; 74526
American General Finance (Goldsboro, NC) 74700
American General Finance (Greensboro, NC) 74763; 74764; 74765
American General Finance (Greenville, NC) 74947; 74948
American General Finance (Hendersonville, NC) 75030
American General Finance (Matthews, NC) 75517
American General Finance (Raleigh, NC) 75854; 75855; 75856
American General Finance (Wilson, NC) 76615
American General Finance (Winston Salem, NC) 76660
American General Finance (Oklahoma City, OK) 77296; 77297
American General Finance (Tulsa, OK) 77876
American General Finance (Antioch, TN) 80162
American General Finance (Chattanooga, TN) 80293; 80294
American General Finance (Cleveland, TN) 80566
American General Finance (Hermitage, TN) 80922
American General Finance (Hixson, TN) 80928
American General Finance (Knoxville, TN) 81135; 81136
American General Finance (Madison, TN) 81370
American General Finance (Memphis, TN) 81450; 81451; 81452
American General Finance (Nashville, TN) 81883; 81884
American General Finance (El Paso, TX) 84756
American General Finance (Falls Church, VA) 90816
American General Finance (Hampton, VA) 91011; 91012
American General Finance (Newport News, VA) 91450
American General Finance (Richmond, VA) 91728
American General Finance (Virginia Beach, VA) 92431
American General Finance Co. (Metairie, LA) 70247
American General Finance Co., Inc. (Mobile, AL) 56137
American General Finance Inc. (Bessemer, AL) 55083
American General Finance Inc. (Birmingham, AL) 55123; 55124; 55125
American General Finance Inc. (Decatur, AL) 55574
American General Finance Inc. (Gadsden, AL) 55773
American General Finance Inc. (Huntsville, AL) 55879
American General Finance Inc. (Mobile, AL) 56138; 56139
American General Finance Inc. (Montgomery, AL) 56278
American General Finance Inc. (Dover, DE) 57780
American General Finance Inc. (Laurel, DE) 57825
American General Finance Inc. (Milford, DE) 57837
American General Finance Inc. (Newark, DE) 57887
American General Finance Inc. (Smyrna, DE) 57958
American General Finance Inc. (Fort Lauderdale, FL) 59437; 59438; 59439
American General Finance Inc. (Hollywood, FL) 60034
American General Finance Inc. (Jacksonville, FL) 60170; 60171; 60172; 60173; 60174; 60175
American General Finance Inc. (Orlando, FL) 61910; 61911; 61912
American General Finance Inc. (Tallahassee, FL) 63205
American General Finance Inc. (Tampa, FL) 63315; 63316; 63317; 63318; 63319
American General Finance Inc. (Atlanta, GA) 64229; 64230; 64231; 64232
American General Finance Inc. (Columbus, GA) 65620; 65621; 65622
American General Finance Inc. (Macon, GA) 66649; 66650
American General Finance Inc. (Roswell, GA) 67358
American General Finance Inc. (Savannah, GA) 67443; 67444
American General Finance Inc. (Hazard, KY) 68423
American General Finance Inc. (Hopkinsville, KY) 68473
American General Finance Inc. (Lexington, KY) 68519
American General Finance Inc. (Louisville, KY) 68681; 68682; 68683; 68684; 68685; 68686
American General Finance Inc. (Radcliff, KY) 69238
American General Finance Inc. (Baton Rouge, LA) 69466; 69467; 69468
American General Finance Inc. (Metairie, LA) 70248; 70249
American General Finance Inc. (New Orleans, LA) 70430
American General Finance Inc. (Shreveport, LA) 70683; 70684; 70685; 70686; 70687; 70688; 70689
American General Finance Inc. (Owings Mills, MD) 72183
American General Finance Inc. (Jackson, MS) 72942; 72943; 72944
American General Finance Inc. (Burlington, NC) 73740
American General Finance Inc. (Charlotte, NC) 73838; 73839
American General Finance Inc. (Concord, NC) 74305; 74306
American General Finance Inc. (Durham, NC) 74384; 74385
American General Finance Inc. (Fayetteville, NC) 74527; 74528
American General Finance Inc. (Goldsboro, NC) 74701
American General Finance Inc. (Greensboro, NC) 74766; 74767; 74768
American General Finance Inc. (Greenville, NC) 74949; 74950
American General Finance Inc. (Hendersonville, NC) 75031
American General Finance Inc. (Hickory, NC) 75057
American General Finance Inc. (Raleigh, NC) 75857; 75858; 75859
American General Finance Inc. (Wilson, NC) 76616
American General Finance Inc. (Winston Salem, NC) 76661; 76662; 76663
American General Finance Inc. (Oklahoma City, OK) 77298; 77299
American General Finance Inc. (Tulsa, OK) 77877; 77878
American General Finance Inc. (Tulso, OK) 78218
American General Finance Inc. (Columbia, SC) 78971; 78972
American General Finance Inc. (Antioch, TN) 80163
American General Finance Inc. (Chattanooga, TN) 80295; 80296
American General Finance Inc. (Cleveland, TN) 80567
American General Finance Inc. (Hermitage, TN) 80923
American General Finance Inc. (Hixson, TN) 80929
American General Finance Inc. (Knoxville, TN) 81137; 81138
American General Finance Inc. (Madison, TN) 81371
American General Finance Inc. (Memphis, TN) 81453; 81454; 81455; 81456; 81457
American General Finance Inc. (Nashville, TN) 81885; 81886
American General Finance Inc. (El Paso, TX) 84757
American General Finance Inc. (Falls Church, VA) 90817
American General Finance Inc. (Hampton, VA) 91013; 91014
American General Finance Inc. (Martinsville, VA) 91340; 91341
American General Finance Inc. (Newport News, VA) 91451
American General Finance Inc. (Norfolk, VA) 91498; 91499
American General Finance Inc. (Portsmouth, VA) 91639; 91640
American General Finance Inc. (Richmond, VA) 91729; 91730; 91731; 91732; 91733
American General Group Insurance Co. (Dallas, TX) 83846
American General Group Insurance Co. of Florida (Jacksonville, FL) 60176
American General Investment Corp. (Houston, TX) 85781; 85782; 85783
American General Life & Accedent Insurance Co. (Nashville, TN) 81887
American General Life & Accident Insurance Co. (Nashville, TN) 81888
American General Life Insurance Co. (Houston, TX) 85784; 85785; 85786
American General Life Insurance Co. of Oklahoma (Oklahoma City, OK) 77300
American General Mortgage Co. (Houston, TX) 85787; 85788; 85789
American General Property Insurance Co. (Nashville, TN) 81889; 81890; 81891
American General Realty Investment Corp. (Houston, TX) 85790
American General Securities Inc. (Houston, TX) 85791; 85792; 85793
American Greeting Corp. (Danville, KY) 68252
American Greetings (Bardstown, KY) 68112
American Greetings Corp. (McCrory, AR) 57360
American Greetings Corp. (Osceola, AR) 57480; 57481
American Greetings Corp. (Norcross, GA) 67096
American Greetings Corp. (Bardstown, KY) 68113
American Greetings Corp. (Corbin, KY) 68208
American Greetings Corp. (Lafayette, TN) 81286
American Greetings Corp. (Carrollton, TX) 83447
American Greetings Inc. (McCrory, AR) 57361
American Home Food Prods, Inc. (Fort Worth, TX) 85062
American Home Food Products Inc. (Fort Worth, TX) 85063
American International Recover (Atlanta, GA) 64233
American La France (Bluefield, VA) 90457
American LaFrance (Bluefield, VA) 90458
American Life (Wilmington, DE) **57980**
American Life Insurance (Wilmington, DE) 57981
American Life Insurance Co. (Wilmington, DE) 57982
American Limestone Co. (Springfield, TN) 82353
American Limestone Co. Inc. (Knoxville, TN) 81139
American Limestone Co. Inc. (Pleasant View, TN) 82231
American Limestone Co. Inc. (Springfield, TN) 82354
American Limestone Co. Inc. (Watauga, TN) 82403
American Limestone Co. Inc. (Dallas, TX) 83847
American Medical Holdings (Dallas, TX) **83848**
American Medical Holdings, Inc. (Dallas, TX) 83849; 83850
American National Bank (Union Springs, AL) 56686
American National Bank (Ardmore, OK) 76808
American National Bank (Bristow, OK) 76869
American National Bank (Woodward, OK) 78255
American National Bank (Corpus Christi, TX) 83699
American National Bank (Gonzales, TX) 85586
American National Bank (Terell, TX) 89657
American National Bank (Texarkana, TX) 89667
American National Bank (Wichita Falls, TX) 90065
American Olean Tile Co. (Fayette, AL) 55727
American Olean Tile Co. (Lewisport, KY) 68516; 68517
American Olean Tile Co. (Jackson, TN) 80964
American Parts System Inc. (Houston, TX) 85794
American Ref-Fuel Co. (Houston, TX) 85795
American Savings Bank (Livingston, TN) 81348
American Savings of FL FSB (Boca Raton, FL) 58664
American Savings of FL FSB (Deerfield Beach, FL) 59264
American Savings of FL FSB (Ft. Lauderdale, FL) 59847; 59848
American Savings of FL FSB (Hallandale, FL) 59957
American Savings of FL FSB (Hollywood, FL) 60035; 60036
American Savings of FL FSB (Miami, FL) 61157; 61158; 61159; 61160; 61161
American Savings of FL FSB (Miami Beach, FL) 61518
American Savings of FL FSB (Pompano Beach, FL) 62581; 62582; 62583
American Savings of FL FSB (West Palm Beach, FL) 63837
American Savings of Florida (Boca Raton, FL) 58665
American Savings of Florida (Clearwater, FL) 58960
American Savings of Florida (Delray Beach, FL) 59304; 59305

Apple Computer (Austin, TX) 82818
Apple Computer Inc. (Nashville, TN) 81895
Apple Computers Inc. (Nashville, TN) 81896
Apple Computers Inc. (Dallas, TX) 83856
Appleton Electric Co. (Stephenville, TX) 89513
Appraisal Services Inc. (Baltimore, MD) 71039
APS Acquisition Corp. (Houston, TX) 85803
APS Holding Corp. (Houston, TX) 85804
APS Inc. (Houston, TX) 85805
Aqua Glass Corp. (Adamsville, TN) 80141
Aqua Glass Corp. Main Plant (Adamsville, TN) 80142
Aqualon Co. (Wilmington, DE) 57986
Aqualon Co. (Kenedy, TX) 87465
Aqualon Co. (Hopewell, VA) 91156
Arbrook Manufacturing Corp. (Caguas, PR) 78348
Arbrook Mfg. Corp. (Caguas, PR) 78349
Arcadian Corp. (Savannah, GA) 67446
Arcadian Corp. (Geismar, LA) 69872
Arcadian Corp. (Lake Charles, LA) 70127; 70128; 70129
Arcadian Corp. (Wilmington, NC) 76539; 76540
Arcadian Corp. (Wilson, NC) 76618
Arcadian Corp. (Memphis, TN) 81460; **81461;** 81462; 81463
Arcadian Corp. Augusta Plant (Augusta, GA) 65312
Arcadian Corp. Savannah Plant (Port Wentworth, GA) 67273; 67274
Arcadian Fertilizer LP (Augusta, GA) 65313
Arcadian Fertilizer L.P. (Geismar, LA) 69873
Arcadian Fertilizer, LP (Memphis, TN) 81464
Arcadian Fertilizer LP (Millington, TN) 81774
Arcadian Partners Ltd. Partnership (Memphis, TN) 81465
Archer Daniels Southern Cotton Oil Co. (North Little Rock, AR) 57453
Archer Daniels Midland (Destrehan, LA) 69837
Archer Daniels Midland (Houston, TX) 85806
Archer Daniels Midland Co. (Little Rock, AR) 57250; 57251
Archer Daniels Midland Co. (Augusta, GA) 65314
Archer Daniels Midland Co. (Macon, GA) 66651
Archer Daniels Midland Co. (Valdosta, GA) 67941; 67942
Archer Daniels Midland Co. (Clarksdale, MS) 72667
Archer Daniels Midland Co. (Southport, NC) 76282; 76283
Archer Daniels Midland Co. (Kershaw, SC) 79547
Archer Daniels Midland Co. (Chattanooga, TN) 80324
Archer Daniels Midland Co. (Sweetwater, TX) 89581
Archer Daniels Midland Co. (Adm) (Clarksdale, MS) 72668
Arco (Channelview, TX) 83545
Arco (Houston, TX) 85807
ARCO Channelview, Inc. (Houston, TX) 85808
Arco Chemical Co. (Channelview, TX) 83546; 83547
Arco Chemical Co. (Pasadena, TX) 88385
Arco Chemical Co. (South Charleston, WV) 93046
Arco Chemical Co. Bayport Div. (Pasadena, TX) 88386
Arco Chemical Co. Institute West Virginia Plant (Institute, WV) 92901
ARCO Lyondell, Inc. (Houston, TX) 85809
Arco Mini Market (Falls Church, VA) 90818
ARCO Mont Belview Corp. (Houston, TX) 85810
Arco Oil & Gas (Vencie, LA) 70921
Arco Oil & Gas Co. (Magnolia, AR) 57328
Arco Oil & Gas Co. (Abbeville, LA) 69360; 69361
Arco Oil & Gas Co. (Amelia, LA) 69419
Arco Oil & Gas Co. (Crowley, LA) 69800
Arco Oil & Gas Co. (Lafayette, LA) 70042
Arco Oil & Gas Co. (Venice, LA) 70922
Arco Oil & Gas Co. (Lindsay, OK) 77178
Arco Oil & Gas Co. (Woodward, OK) 78256
Arco Oil & Gas Co. (Alamo, TX) 82475
Arco Oil & Gas Co. (Andrews, TX) 82593
Arco Oil & Gas Co. (Dallas, TX) 83857
Arco Oil & Gas Co. (Denver City, TX) 84646
Arco Oil & Gas Co. (Edinburg, TX) 84731
Arco Oil & Gas Co. (Eldorado, TX) 84983
Arco Oil & Gas Co. (Gainesville, TX) 85419
Arco Oil & Gas Co. (Hemphill, TX) 85730
Arco Oil & Gas Co. (Henderson, TX) 85732
Arco Oil & Gas Co. (Ingleside, TX) 87303; 87304
Arco Oil & Gas Co. (Longview, TX) 87702; 87703
Arco Oil & Gas Co. (Midland, TX) 88020
Arco Oil & Gas Co. (Mirando City, TX) 88120
Arco Oil & Gas Co. (Mission, TX) 88121
Arco Oil & Gas Co. (Odessa, TX) 88236
Arco Oil & Gas Co. (Silsbee, TX) 89431
Arco Pipe Lie Vickers Station (Ardmore, OK) 76809
Arco Pipe Line (Maysville, OK) 77189
Arco Pipe Line (Yoakum, TX) 90135
Arco Pipe Line Co. (Natchitoches, LA) 70399
Arco Pipe Line Co. (Ardmore, OK) 76810; 76811
Arco Pipe Line Co. (Copan, OK) 76971; 76972
Arco Pipe Line Co. (Cushing, OK) 76975; 76976
Arco Pipe Line Co. (Pauls Valley, OK) 77687; 77688
Arco Pipe Line Co. (Ringling, OK) 77765; 77766
Arco Pipe Line Co. (Shawnee, OK) 77811; 77812; 77813
Arco Pipe Line Co. (Skiatook, OK) 77825; 77826
Arco Pipe Line Co. (Euless, TX) 85005; 85006
Arco Pipe Line Co. (Gainesville, TX) 85420; 85421
Arco Pipe Line Co. (Jacksboro, TX) 87420
Arco Pipe Line Co. (Lolita, TX) 87697
Arco Pipe Line Co. (Luling, TX) 87822; 87823
Arco Pipe Line Co. (Midland, TX) 88021
Arco Pipe Line Co. (Plantersville, TX) 88620
Arco Pipe Line Co. (Refugio, TX) 88714
Arco Pipe Line Co. (Teague, TX) 89604
Arco Pipe Line Co. (Wichita Falls, TX) 90066
Arco Pipe Line Co., Inc. (Houston, TX) 85811
Arco Pipe Line Vickers Station (Ardmore, OK) 76812
Arco Pipeline (Bryan, TX) 83392
Arco Pipeline Co. (Ratliff City, OK) 77764
Arco Pipeline Co. (Stratford, OK) 77853; 77854
Arco Pipeline Co. (Thackerville, OK) 77865
Arco Pipeline Co. (Corpus Christi, TX) 83700
Arco Pipeline Co. (Seminole, TX) 89381
Arco Pipline Co. (Seminole, TX) 89382
Ardmore Farms Inc. (De Land, FL) 59246
Aristar Inc. (Cordova, TN) 80673
Aristokraft Inc. (Crossville, TN) 80689
Arizona Chemical (Port St. Joe, FL) 62692
Arizona Chemical Co. (Panama City, FL) 62318
Arizona Chemical Co. (Springhill, LA) 70847; 70848; 70849
Arizona Chemical Co. (Picayune, MS) 73290; 73291
Arizona Chemical Co. Sylvachem Corp. (Port St. Joe, FL) 62693
Arkansas Best (Fort Smith, AR) **57022**
Arkansas Best Corp. (Fort Smith, AR) 57023; 57024
Arkansas Chemicals Inc. (El Dorado, AR) 56925; 56926
Arkansas Chemicals Inc. (Eldorado, AR) 56963
Arkansas Eastman Co. (Batesville, AR) 56740; 56741
Arkansas Power & Light Co. (Little Rock, AR) 57252
Armco Bowman Metal Deck Div. Cyclops (Nashville, TN) 81897
Armco Tex-Tube Div. (Fort Worth, TX) 85067
Armco Tex-Tube Div. (Houston, TX) 85812; 85813; 85814; 85815
Armco Advanced Materials Corp. (Wildwood, FL) 63914
Armco Ashland Works West Works (Ashland, KY) 68084
Armco Inc. Tex Tube Div. (Houston, TX) 85816
Armco Stainless & Alloy Prods. (Baltimore, MD) 71040
Armco Stainless & Alloy Products (Baltimore, MD) 71041; 71042
Armco Stainless & Alloy Products (Baltimore) (Baltimore, MD) 71043
Armco Steel Co. L.P. Coke Plant (Ashland, KY) 68085
Armco Steel Co. L.P. Grey Iron Foundry (Ashland, KY) 68086
Armco Steel Co. L.P. West Works (Ashland, KY) 68087; 68088
Armco Steel Co. LP (Ashland, KY) 68089
Armco Steel Co. LP (Dallas, TX) 83858
Armco Steel Corp. (Lexington, KY) 68523
Armco Steel Inc. (Brentwood, TN) 80215
Armour Dairy & Food Oils Co. (Springfield, KY) 69300
Armour Food Co. (Louisville, KY) 68692
Armour Food Ingredients Co. (Springfield, KY) 69301
Armour Swift-Eckrich (Huntsville, AR) 57193
Armour Swift-Eckrich (Wallace, NC) 76436
Armour Swift-Eckrich (El Paso, TX) 84758
Armstar (Lenoir City, TN) 81318; 81319
Armstrong Cork Finance Corp. (Wilmington, DE) 57987
Armstrong Furniture (Fort Union, VA) 90889
Armstrong Furniture Inc. (Appomattox, VA) 90271
Armstrong Ventures, Inc. (Wilmington, DE) 57988
Armstrong World Ind. Inc. (Macon, GA) 66652
Armstrong World Industries Furniture Div. (Thomasville, NC) 76371
Armstrong World Industries Stillwater Plant (Stillwater, OK) 77834
Armstrong World Industries (DE), Inc. (Wilmington, DE) 57989
Armstrong World Industries Inc. (Mobile, AL) 56141
Armstrong World Industries Inc. (Pensacola, FL) 62391
Armstrong World Industries Inc. (Dallas, GA) 65757
Armstrong World Industries Inc. (Macon, GA) 66653
Armstrong World Industries Inc. (Jackson, MS) 72946; 72947
Armstrong World Industries Inc. Jackson Plant (Jackson, MS) 72948
Armstrong Worldindustries Inc. (Pensacola, FL) 62392
Arnet Computer (Fort Lauderdale, FL) 59442
Arnet Computer (St. Petersburg, FL) 63081
Arnet Computer (Deluth, GA) 65915
Arnet Computer (Columbia, MD) 71576
Arnet Computer (Raleigh, NC) 75860
Arnet Computer (Addison, TX) 82470
Arnet Computer (Houston, TX) 85817
Arnold Engineering Development Center Operations (Tullahoma, TN) 82376
Arrow Electronics Commercial Systems Div. (Duluth, GA) 66018
Arrow Electronics MTI Systems Div. (Huntsville, AL) 55881
Arrow Electronics Inc. (Baltimore, MD) 71044
Arrow Electronics Inc. (Richmond, VA) 91735
Arrow Electronics Inc. Arrow/Ki (Atlanta, GA) 64237
Arrow Electronics Inc. Arrow-Ki (Gaithersburg, MD) 71761
Arrow Industries (Carrollton, TX) 83448
Arrow/Kierulff Electronics (Deerfield Beach, FL) 59267
Arrow/Kierulff Electronics (Lake Mary, FL) 60638
Arrow/Kierulff Electronics (Duluth, GA) 66019
Arrow/Kierulff Electronics (Carrollton, TX) 83449
Arrow/Kieulff Electronics (Huntsville, AL) 55882
Arrow/Kieulff Electronics (Columbia, MD) 71577
Arrow/Kieulff Electronics (Caparra Heights, PR) 78365
Arrow/Kieulft Electronics (Gaithersburg, MD) 71762
Arrow/Kieulft Electronics (Raleigh, NC) 75861
Arrow/Kieulft Electronics (Tulsa, OK) 77880
Arrow/Kieulft Electronics (Houston, TX) 85818
Arvin Industires Inc. Gabriel Ride Control Div. (Pulaski, TN) 82238
Arvin Industries Gabriel Div. (Pulaski, TN) 82239
Arvin Industries Inc. (Fayette, AL) 55728
Arvin Industries Inc. AVM Div. (Marion, SC) 79637
Arvin Industries Inc. Gabriel Ride Control Div. (Pulsaski, TN) 82246; 82247
Arvin Industries Inc. Gabriel Ride Control Products Div. (Brentwood, TN) 80216; 80217
Arvin Industries Inc. Gabriel Shock Absorber Plant (Chickasha, OK) 76920
Arvin Industries Inc. Maremount Exhaust Products Div. (Loudon, TN) 81350
Arvin Industries Inc. Maremount Exhaust Systems Product Div. (Loudon, TN) 81351
Arvin Industries Inc. Service Contracts Div. (Tullahoma, TN) 82377
Arvin North American Automotive (Fayette, AL) 55729
Asarco Inc. (Washington, DC) 58128
Asarco Inc. (Jefferson City, TN) 81020
Asarco Inc. (Knoxville, TN) 81143
Asarco Inc. (Maryville, TN) 81401
Asarco Inc. (Mascot, TN) 81430
Asarco Inc. (New Market, TN) 82152; 82153
Asarco Inc. (Straw Plains, TN) 82362
Asarco Inc. (Amarillo, TX) 82520
Asarco Inc. (Corpus Christi, TX) 83701
Asarco Inc. (El Paso, TX) 84759
Asarco Inc. Amarillo Copper Refinery (Amarillo, TX) 82521
Asarco Inc. Amarillo Plant (Amarillo, TX) 82522; 82523
Asarco Inc. El Paso (El Paso, TX) 84760; 84761
Asgrow Florida Co. (Belle Glade, FL) 58641
Asgrow Florida Co. (Plant City, FL) 62535
Asgrow Seed Co. (Doraville, GA) 65919
Asgrow Seed Co. (Uvalde, TX) 89848
Asgrow Seed Co. (Exmore, VA) 90750
Ashland Chemical Co. (Louisa/ Ivanhoe, LA) 70201
Ashland Chemical Co. (Dallas, TX) 83859
Ashland Chemical Co. (Neal, WV) 92959
Ashland Chemical Co. Carbon Black Div. (Aransas Pass, TX) 82623
Ashland Chemical E & Lp (Dallas, TX) 83860
Ashland Chemical Inc. (Plaquemine, LA) 70636
Ashland Chemical Inc. (Houston, TX) 85819
Ashland Chemical Inc. (Neal, WV) 92960
Ashland Chemical Inc. Drew Div. (Houston, TX) 85820
Ashland Coal, Inc. (Huntington, WV) 92867
Ashland Exploration, Inc. (Houston, TX) 85821; 85822
Ashland Oil (Russell, KY) **69253**
Ashland Oil Inc. (Ashland, KY) 68090; 68091
Ashland Petroleum Co. (Russell, KY) 69254
Ashland Petroleum Co. Catlettsburg Refinery (Ashland, KY) 68092
Ashland Petroleum Co. Catlettsburg Refinery (Catlettsburg, KY) 68195
Ashland Pipe Line Co. (Ashland, KY) 68093
Ashland Services Co. (Lexington, KY) 68524; 68525
Ashley Drew & Northern Railway (Crossett, AR) 56878
Ask. Coca-Cola Bottling Co. (Little Rock, AR) 57253
Associated Business Products (Warner Robins, GA) 68006
Associated Milk Producers Inc. (Lawton, OK) 77154
Associated Milk Producers Inc. (Shattuck, OK) 77808
Associated Milk Producers Inc. (Tulsa, OK) 77881; 77882
Associated Milk Producers Inc. (Martin, TN) 81396
Associated Milk Producers Inc. (Arlington, TX) 82633; 82634
Associated Milk Producers Inc. (Muenster, TX) 88163
Associated Milk Producers Inc. (San Angelo, TX) 88868
Associated Milk Producers Inc. (San Antonio, TX) **88918;** 88919
Associated Milk Producers Inc. (Sulphur Springs, TX) 89551; 89552
Associates Corp. of North America (Dallas, TX) 83861
Associates First Capital Corp. (Dallas, TX) 83862
Assured Castings Corp. (Rogersville, TN) 82270
AST Research Inc. (Atlanta, GA) 64238; 64239
Astro Industries Inc. Astro Industries Division (Morganton, NC) 75629
AT & T (Austin, TX) 82819
AT & T (Roanoke, VA) 92102
AT & T Employees Credit Union (Dallas, TX) 83863
AT & T Family Federal Credit Union (Jacksonville, FL) 60183
AT & T Family Federal Credit Union (Asheboro, NC) 73576
AT & T Family Federal Credit Union (Burlington, NC) 73741
AT & T Family Federal Credit Union (Charlotte, NC) 73842
AT & T Family Federal Credit Union (Greensboro, NC) 74778; 74779
AT & T Family Federal Credit Union (McAdenville, NC) 75544
AT & T Family Federal Credit Union (Shelby, NC) 76231
AT & T Family Federal Credit Union (Winston-Salem, NC) 76704; 76705; 76706; 76707
AT & T Family Federal Credit Union (Martinsville, VA) 91342
AT & T Family Federal Credit Union (Radford, VA) 91688
AT & T Family Federal Credit Union (Richmond, VA) 91736
AT & T Network Systems (Norcross, GA) 67097
AT & T Network Systems (Oklahoma City, OK) 77301
AT&T (Montgomery, AL) 56279
AT&T (Little Rock, AR) 57254; 57255
AT&T (Atlanta, GA) 64240
At&T (Norcross, GA) 67098
AT&T (Athens, LA) 69434
AT&T (Hornbeck, LA) 69949
AT&T (Welsh, LA) 70941
AT&T (West Monroe, LA) 70942
AT&T (Greensboro, NC) 74780
AT&T (Huntersville, NC) 75206
AT&T (McLeansville, NC) 75546
AT&T (Sweetwater, TN) 82366
AT&T (Caldwell, TX) 83431
AT&T (Temple, TX) 89605
AT&T (Richmond, VA) 91737
AT&T (Standardsville, VA) 92305
AT&T Capital Corp. Instr. Services (Baltimore, MD) 71045
AT&T Capital Small Business Lending (San Antonio, TX) 88920
AT&T Commercial Finance (Dallas, TX) 83864
AT&T Co. Software Solutions (Duluth, GA) 66020
AT&T Easylink Services (Nashville, TN) 81898
AT&T Family Federal Credit Union (Charlotte, NC) 73843
AT&T Family Federal Credit Union (McAdenville, NC) 75545

Baltimore American Business Locations Directory

Baltimore Gas & Electric Co. (Lutherville Timonium, MD) 72118
Baltimore Specialty Steele Corp. (Houston, TX) 85860
Baltimore Specialty Steele Corps. (Baltimore, MD) 71059
Baltimore Specialty Steels Corp. (Baltimore, MD) 71060
Baltimore Trust Co. (Bethany Beach, DE) 57751
Baltimore Trust Co. (Bridgeville, DE) 57752
Baltimore Trust Co. (Fenwick Island, DE) 57816
Baltimore Trust Co. (Rehoboth Beach, DE) 57942
Baltimore Trust Co. (Selbyville, DE) 57955; 57956
Baltimore Trust Co. Inc. (Tulsa, OK) 77883
Bama Food Products (Birmingham, AL) 55158
Bama Pies (Tulsa, OK) 77884
Banana Republic (Birmingham, AL) 55159
Banana Republic (Washington, DC) 58132; 58133; 58134
Banana Republic (Boca Raton, FL) 58670; 58671
Banana Republic (Fort Lauderdale, FL) 59443
Banana Republic (Jacksonville, FL) 60189
Banana Republic (Miami, FL) 61170
Banana Republic (Tampa, FL) 63333
Banana Republic (Winter Park, FL) 63961
Banana Republic (Bethesda, MD) 71371
Banana Republic (Chevy Chase, MD) 71528
Banana Republic (Rockville, MD) 72256
Banana Republic (Winston-Salem, NC) 76708
Banana Republic (Tulsa, OK) 77885
Banana Republic (Charleston, SC) 78790
Banana Republic (Memphis, TN) 81466
Banana Republic (Austin, TX) 82822; 82823
Banana Republic (Dallas, TX) 83869
Banana Republic (Houston, TX) 85861
Banana Republic (San Antonio, TX) 88923; 88924
Banana Republic Regional Office (Peachtree, GA) 67224
Banana Republic Retail Clothing (Atlanta, GA) 64249
Banc One Mortgage Corp. (Bethesda, MD) 71372; 71373
Banc One Mortgage Corp. (Greenbelt, MD) 71854
Banc One Mortgage Corp. (Severna Park, MD) 72371
Banc One Mortgage Corp. (Virginia Beach, VA) 92434
Banc One Mortgage Corp. Regional (Bethesda, MD) 71374
BancBoston Mortagage Corp. (Huntsville, AL) 55886
BancBoston Mortgage Corp. (Montgomery, AL) 56281
BancBoston Mortgage Corp. (Ft. Lauderdale, FL) 59850
BancBoston Mortgage Corp. (Jacksonville, FL) 60190
BancBoston Mortgage Corp. (Tampa, FL) 63334
BancBoston Mortgage Corp. (Raleigh, NC) 75862
BancBoston Mortgage Corp. (Houston, TX) 85862
BancBoston Mortgage Corp. (Virginia Beach, VA) 92435
Banco Popular de Puerto Rico (Adjuntas, PR) 78287
Banco Popular de Puerto Rico (Aguada, PR) 78288
Banco Popular de Puerto Rico (Aguadilla, PR) 78291; 78292; 78293
Banco Popular de Puerto Rico (Aguas Buenas, PR) 78296
Banco Popular de Puerto Rico (Aibonito, PR) 78302
Banco Popular de Puerto Rico (Arecibo, PR) 78308; 78309; 78310; 78311
Banco Popular de Puerto Rico (Arroyo, PR) 78317
Banco Popular de Puerto Rico (Barceloneta, PR) 78323; 78324
Banco Popular de Puerto Rico (Barranquitas, PR) 78335
Banco Popular de Puerto Rico (Cabo Rojo, PR) 78345; 78346
Banco Popular de Puerto Rico (Caguas, PR) 78350; 78351; 78352; 78353; 78354; 78355
Banco Popular de Puerto Rico (Camuy, PR) 78360
Banco Popular de Puerto Rico (Canovanas, PR) 78363
Banco Popular de Puerto Rico (Carolina, PR) 78366; 78367; 78368; 78369; 78370; 78371
Banco Popular de Puerto Rico (Cayey, PR) 78381; 78382
Banco Popular de Puerto Rico (Ceiba, PR) 78388
Banco Popular de Puerto Rico (Ciales, PR) 78389
Banco Popular de Puerto Rico (Cidra, PR) 78394
Banco Popular de Puerto Rico (Coamo, PR) 78401
Banco Popular de Puerto Rico (Comerio, PR) 78405
Banco Popular de Puerto Rico (Corozal, PR) 78406
Banco Popular de Puerto Rico (Dorado, PR) 78407
Banco Popular de Puerto Rico (Fajardo, PR) 78413
Banco Popular de Puerto Rico (Florida, PR) 78416
Banco Popular de Puerto Rico (Guayama, PR) 78422; 78423
Banco Popular de Puerto Rico (Guayanilla, PR) 78432
Banco Popular de Puerto Rico (Guaynabo, PR) 78434; 78435; 78436; 78437; 78438; 78439; 78440
Banco Popular de Puerto Rico (Gurabo, PR) 78441
Banco Popular de Puerto Rico (Hatillo, PR) 78445
Banco Popular de Puerto Rico (Hato Rey, PR) 78448; 78449; 78450; 78451; 78452; 78453
Banco Popular de Puerto Rico (Hormigueros, PR) 78458
Banco Popular de Puerto Rico (Humacao, PR) 78460
Banco Popular de Puerto Rico (Isabela, PR) 78464
Banco Popular de Puerto Rico (Jayuya, PR) 78465
Banco Popular de Puerto Rico (Juana Diaz, PR) 78467
Banco Popular de Puerto Rico (Lares, PR) 78474
Banco Popular de Puerto Rico (Las Marias, PR) 78475
Banco Popular de Puerto Rico (Luquillo, PR) 78489
Banco Popular de Puerto Rico (Manati, PR) 78492
Banco Popular de Puerto Rico (Maricao, PR) 78505
Banco Popular de Puerto Rico (Mayaguez, PR) 78506; 78507; 78508; 78509; 78510
Banco Popular de Puerto Rico (Moca, PR) 78520
Banco Popular de Puerto Rico (Morovis, PR) 78521
Banco Popular de Puerto Rico (Naranjito, PR) 78522
Banco Popular de Puerto Rico (Orocovis, PR) 78523
Banco Popular de Puerto Rico (Patillas, PR) 78525
Banco Popular de Puerto Rico (Penuelas, PR) 78526
Banco Popular de Puerto Rico (Ponce, PR) 78528; 78529; 78530; 78531; 78532; 78533; 78534
Banco Popular de Puerto Rico (Puerto Rico, PR) 78539
Banco Popular de Puerto Rico (Quebradillas, PR) 78540
Banco Popular de Puerto Rico (Rincon, PR) 78541
Banco Popular de Puerto Rico (Rio Grande, PR) 78543
Banco Popular de Puerto Rico (Salinas, PR) 78545
Banco Popular de Puerto Rico (San German, PR) 78547
Banco Popular de Puerto Rico (San Juan, PR) 78552; 78553; 78554; 78555; 78556; 78557; 78558; 78559; 78560; 78561; 78562; 78563; 78564; 78565; 78566; 78567; 78568; 78569; 78570; 78571; 78572; 78573; 78574
Banco Popular de Puerto Rico (San Lorenzo, PR) 78581
Banco Popular de Puerto Rico (San Sebastian, PR) 78585
Banco Popular de Puerto Rico (Santa Isabel, PR) 78587
Banco Popular de Puerto Rico (Santurce, PR) 78592; 78593; 78594; 78595; 78596; 78597; 78598; 78599; 78600; 78601; 78602
Banco Popular de Puerto Rico (Toa Alta, PR) 78604
Banco Popular de Puerto Rico (Toa Baja, PR) 78607
Banco Popular de Puerto Rico (Trujillo Alto, PR) 78615; 78616
Banco Popular de Puerto Rico (Utuado, PR) 78617
Banco Popular de Puerto Rico (Vega Alta, PR) 78618
Banco Popular de Puerto Rico (Vega Baja, PR) 78624; 78625
Banco Popular de Puerto Rico (Vieques, PR) 78632
Banco Popular de Puerto Rico (Villalba, PR) 78633
Banco Popular de Puerto Rico (Yabucoa, PR) 78638
Banco Popular de Puerto Rico (Yauco, PR) 78639; 78640
Banco Popular de Puerto Rico (Charlotte Amalie, VI) 90140; 90141; 90142; 90143; 90144
Banco Popular de Puerto Rico (Christiansted, VI) 90146; 90147
Banister Outlet Store (Knoxville, TN) 81144
Banister Shoe (Chester, MD) 71516
Banister Shoe (Woodbridge, VA) 92608
Banister Shoe Factory Outlet (Roanoke, VA) 92103
Banister Shoe Factory Outlet (Williamsburg, VA) 92560
Banister Shoes (Memphis, TN) 81467; 81468
Bank of Boston (Miami, FL) 61171
Bank of Boston Corp. (Dallas, TX) 83870
Bank of Boston-Florida (Palm Beach, FL) 62245
Bank of Boston-Florida (Sarasota, FL) 62787
Bank of Boston-Florida N.A. (Palm Beach, FL) 62246
Bank of Boston International (Miami, FL) 61172; 61173; 61174
Bank of Commerce (Auburn Town, TN) 80197
Bank of Commerce (Woodbury, TN) 82422; 82423
Bank of Coweta (Luthersville, GA) 66629
Bank of Coweta (Newman, GA) 67071; 67072; 67073; 67074
Bank of Coweta (Newnan, GA) 67076; 67077
Bank of Coweta (Senoia, GA) 67536
Bank of Delaware (Bear, DE) 57748
Bank of Delaware (Claymont, DE) 57760
Bank of Delaware (Dover, DE) 57781; 57782; 57783
Bank of Delaware (Elsmere, DE) 57813
Bank of Delaware (Greenville, DE) 57819
Bank of Delaware (Henry Clay, DE) 57822
Bank of Delaware (Hockessin, DE) 57823
Bank of Delaware (Middletown, DE) 57831
Bank of Delaware (Milford, DE) 57838; 57839
Bank of Delaware (New Castle, DE) 57855
Bank of Delaware (Newar, DE) 57879
Bank of Delaware (Newark, DE) 57892; 57893; 57894
Bank of Delaware (Odessa, DE) 57939
Bank of Delaware (Ogletown, DE) 57940; 57941
Bank of Delaware (Rehoboth Beach, DE) 57943
Bank of Delaware (Seaford, DE) 57949; 57950
Bank of Delaware (Smyrna, DE) 57959
Bank of Delaware (Wilmington, DE) 57990; 57991; 57992; 57993; 57994; 57995; 57996; 57997; 57998; 57999; 58000; 58001
Bank of East Tennessee (Morristown, TN) 81784; 81785; 81786; 81787; 81788
Bank of East Tennessee (Talbott, TN) 82367
Bank of Hazelhurst (Hazelhurst, GA) 66343; 66344
Bank of Hazelurst (Hazelhurst, GA) 66345
Bank of Hundred (Hundred, WV) 92866
Bank of Madisonville (Madisonville, TN) 81385; 81386
Bank of New York International Inc. (Miami, FL) 61175
Bank of New York Trust Co. of Florida National Association (Miami, FL) 61176
Bank of Pensacola (Pensacola, FL) 62393; 62394; 62395; 62396
Bank of Rector (Rector, AR) 57554; 57555
Bank of Roane County (Harriman, TN) 80898
Bank of Roane County (Harrimen, TN) 80904
Bank of Roane County (Kingston, TN) 81124
Bank of Roane County (Oliver Springs, TN) 82208
Bank of Roane County (Rockwood, TN) 82267
Bank South (Athens, GA) 64160
Bank South (Atlanta, GA) 64250
Bank South (Conyers, GA) 65667; 65668
Bank South (Macon, GA) 66654
Bank South (Monticello, GA) 66997
Bank South (Riverdale, GA) 67304
Bank South (Smyrna, GA) 67541; 67542
Bank South (Tennille, GA) 67782
Bank South (Waycross, GA) 68026; 68027
Bank South Corp. (Atlanta, GA) 64251; 64252; **64253**
Bank South-Douglas (Douglas, GA) 65964
Bank South Home Equity (Atlanta, GA) 64254
Bank South Houston Co. (Perry, GA) 67259
Bank South Leasing Inc. (Atlanta, GA) 64255; 64256
Bank South Life Insurance Corp. (Atlanta, GA) 64257
Bank South Macon (Macon, GA) 66655
Bank South Macon Wesleyan Sta (Macon, GA) 66656
Bank South Mortgage Inc. (Atlanta, GA) 64258; 64259
Bank South Mortgate Inc. (Atlanta, GA) 64260
Bank South, NA (Alpharetta, GA) 64104; 64105; 64106; 64107
Bank South, NA (Athens, GA) 64161; 64162
Bank South NA (Atlanta, GA) 64261; 64262; 64263; 64264; 64265; 64266; 64267; 64268; 64269; 64270; 64271; 64272; 64273; 64274; 64275; 64276; 64277; 64278; 64279; 64280; 64281; 64282; 64283; 64284; 64285; 64286; 64287
Bank South, NA (Auburn, GA) 65309
Bank South, NA (Buford, GA) 65432
Bank South, NA (Centerville, GA) 65514
Bank South, NA (Chamblee, GA) 65519; 65520; 65521
Bank South, NA (College Park, GA) 65577
Bank South NA (Conyers, GA) 65669; 65670; 65671; 65672; 65673; 65674
Bank South, NA (Cumming, GA) 65744; 65745
Bank South NA (Decatur, GA) 65798; 65799; 65800
Bank South, NA (Doraville, GA) 65920
Bank South, NA (Douglas, GA) 65965
Bank South, NA (Duluth, GA) 66021; 66022; 66023; 66024; 66025; 66026
Bank South, NA (Dunwoody, GA) 66100; 66101; 66102
Bank South, NA (East Point, GA) 66141; 66142
Bank South, NA (Fayetteville, GA) 66187; 66188; 66189
Bank South, NA (Fitzgerald, GA) 66206; 66207
Bank South, NA (Forest Park, GA) 66228
Bank South, NA (Forsyth, GA) 66253
Bank South NA (Griffin, GA) 66309
Bank South, NA (Jonesboro, GA) 66376; 66377
Bank South, NA (Kennesaw, GA) 66407
Bank South, NA (Lake City, GA) 66495
Bank South NA (Lawrenceville, GA) 66501; 66502; 66503; 66504; 66505
Bank South, NA (Lilburn, GA) 66553; 66554; 66555
Bank South NA (Macon, GA) 66657; 66658; 66659; 66660; 66661; 66662; 66663; 66664; 66665; 66666; 66667; 66668
Bank South, NA (Marietta, GA) 66740; 66741; 66742; 66743; 66744; 66745; 66746; 66747; 66748; 66749; 66750; 66751; 66752; 66753; 66754
Bank South, NA (Monticello, GA) 66998
Bank South, NA (Morrow, GA) 67003
Bank South, NA (Norcross, GA) 67101; 67102; 67103
Bank South, NA (Palmetto, GA) 67222
Bank South, NA (Perry, GA) 67260
Bank South NA (Riverdale, GA) 67305; 67306; 67307
Bank South NA (Roswell, GA) 67359; 67360; 67361; 67362; 67363
Bank South, NA (Sandy Springs, GA) 67433; 67434
Bank South, NA (Savannah, GA) 67447; 67448; 67449; 67450; 67451; 67452
Bank South, NA (Smyrna, GA) 67543; 67544
Bank South, NA (Snellville, GA) 67588
Bank South NA (St. Marys, GA) 67622
Bank South, NA (Stockbridge, GA) 67656
Bank South NA (Stone Mountain, GA) 67678; 67679; 67680; 67681; 67682; 67683; 67684
Bank South, NA (Tennille, GA) 67783
Bank South NA (Tucker, GA) 67844; 67845
Bank South NA (Union City, GA) 67911
Bank South, NA (Warner Robins, GA) 68007; 68008
Bank South, NA (Waycross, GA) 68028; 68029; 68030
Bank South NA (Winder, GA) 68055; 68056; 68057
Bank South NA (Columbia, SC) 78974
Bank South NA/Athens Main Office (Athens, GA) 64163
Bank South NA/Buckhead (Atlanta, GA) 64288
Bank South NA/Centerville (Centerville, GA) 65515
Bank South NA/College Park (College Park, GA) 65578
Bank South NA Conyers (Conyers, GA) 65675
Bank South NA/Cumming (Cumming, GA) 65746
Bank South NA/Douglas (Dougals, GA) 65963
Bank South NA/Dunwoody (Dunwoody, GA) 66103
Bank South NA/East Point (East Point, GA) 66143
Bank South NA/Fitzgerald (Fitzgerald, GA) 66208
Bank South NA/Folkston (Folkston, GA) 66222
Bank South NA/Forest Park (Forest Park, GA) 66229
Bank South NA/Forsyth (Forsyth, GA) 66254
Bank South NA/Fulton Industrial (Atlanta, GA) 64289
Bank South NA/Fulton Industries (Atlanta, GA) 64290
Bank South NA/Griffin (Griffin, GA) 66310
Bank South NA/Houston County (Perry, GA) 67261
Bank South NA/Houston-Warner Robbins (Warner Robbins, GA) 68004
Bank South NA/Jasper (Monticello, GA) 66999
Bank South NA Lake Harbin (Morrow, GA) 67004
Bank South NA/Lenox (Atlanta, GA) 64291
Bank South NA/Macon (Macon, GA) 66669
Bank South NA/Midtown (Atlanta, GA) 64292
Bank South NA/Peachtree Park (Doreville, GA) 65962
Bank South NA/Pensacola Main Office (Pensacola, FL) 62397
Bank South NA/Riverdale (Riverdale, GA) 67308
Bank South NA/Roswell (Roswell, GA) 67364
Bank South NA/St. Mary's (St. Marys, GA) 67623
Bank South NA/Sandy Springs (Atlanta, GA) 64293
Bank South NA-Savannah (Savannah, GA) 67453
Bank South NA/Savannah Main Office (Savannah, GA) 67454

Company Name Index
Barnett

Bank South NA/Smyrna (Smyrna, GA) 67545
Bank South NA/Sprayberry (Marietta, GA) 66755
Bank South NA/Stone Mountain (Stone Mountain, GA) 67685
Bank South NA/Tennille (Tennille, GA) 67784
Bank South NA/Waycross Main Office (401 Carswell Ave., GA) 64033
Bank South NA/Winder Main Office (Winder, GA) 68058
Bank South NA/Windy Hill (Marietta, GA) 66756
Bank of Southern Maryland (Hughesville, MD) 71923
Bank of Southern Maryland (La Plata, MD) 72003; 72004
Bank of Tokyo (Dallas, TX) 83871
Bank of Tokyo Ltd. (Miami, FL) 61177
Bank of Trenton & Trust Co. (Trenton, TN) 82373; 82374
Bank of Tuscaloosa (Tuscaloosa, AL) 56631; 56632; 56633
Bankers Trust (Huntsville, AL) 55887
Bankers Trust (Wilmington, DE) 58002
Bankers Trust (Houston, TX) 85863
Bankers Trust Co. (West Palm Beach, FL) 63839
Bankers Trust Co. (Houston, TX) 85864; 85865
Bankers Trust Co. of Florida NA (West Palm Beach, FL) 63840
Bankers Trust Delaware (Wilmington, DE) 58003
Bankers Trust International (Miami, FL) 61178
Bankers Trust of Madison (Ardmore, AL) 55029
Bankers Trust of Madison (Madison, AL) 56118
Bankers Trust of North Carolina (Asheboro, NC) 73577
Bankers Trust of North Carolina (Greensboro, NC) 74783; 74784; 74785; 74786; 74787
Banponce Corp. (San Juan, PR) **78575**
Banta Co. (Harrisonburg, VA) 91067
Banta Co., Inc. (Harrisonburg, VA) 91068
Banta Co., Inc. Harrisonburg (Harrisonburg, VA) 91069
Banta Corp. (Harrisonburg, VA) 91070
Banta Corp. Freuhauf Div. (Charlotte, NC) 73848
Barcroft Co. (Lewes, DE) 57827
Bard C R Inc. (Moncks Corner, SC) 79658
Bard Cardiopulmonary Inc. (Las Piedras, PR) 78476; 78477; 78478
Bard Urological (Covington, GA) 65723
Barfield Mfg Co. Inc. (Murfreesboro, TN) 81835
Barnett Bank of Alachua County, NA (Archer, FL) 58587
Barnett Bank of Alachua County, NA (Gainesville, FL) 59857; 59858; 59859; 59860; 59861
Barnett Bank of Alachua County, NA (High Springs, FL) 60024
Barnett Bank of Alachua County, NA (Newberry, FL) 61706
Barnett Bank of Broward County, NA (Coconut Creek, FL) 59087
Barnett Bank of Broward County, NA (Cooper City, FL) 59090
Barnett Bank of Broward County, NA (Coral Springs, FL) 59107; 59108; 59109
Barnett Bank of Broward County, NA (Dania, FL) 59145
Barnett Bank of Broward County, NA (Davie, FL) 59154
Barnett Bank of Broward County, NA (Deerfield Beach, FL) 59268; 59269; 59270; 59271
Barnett Bank of Broward County, NA (Fort Lauderdale, FL) 59444; 59445; 59446; 59447; 59448; 59449; 59450; 59451; 59452; 59453; 59454; 59455
Barnett Bank of Broward County, NA (Hallandale, FL) 59958
Barnett Bank of Broward County, NA (Hollywood, FL) 60039; 60040; 60041; 60042
Barnett Bank of Broward County, NA (Lighthouse Point, FL) 60899
Barnett Bank of Broward County, NA (Margate, FL) 60999; 61000
Barnett Bank of Broward County, NA (Miramar, FL) 61557
Barnett Bank of Broward County, NA (Pembroke Pines, FL) 62364; 62365; 62366
Barnett Bank of Broward County, NA (Plantation, FL) 62562; 62563; 62564
Barnett Bank of Broward County, NA (Pompano Beach, FL) 62584; 62585; 62586
Barnett Bank of Broward County, NA (Sunrise, FL) 63191
Barnett Bank of Broward County, NA (Tamarac, FL) 63295
Barnett Bank of Broward County, NA (West Hollywood, FL) 63832
Barnett Bank of Central Florida (Orlando, FL) 61921
Barnett Bank of Central Florida, NA (Altamonte Springs, FL) 58549
Barnett Bank of Central Florida, NA (Apopka, FL) 58568; 58569
Barnett Bank of Central Florida, NA (Casselberry, FL) 58927; 58928
Barnett Bank of Central Florida, NA (Cocoa, FL) 59065
Barnett Bank of Central Florida, NA (Cocoa Beach, FL) 59078
Barnett Bank of Central Florida, NA (Goldenrod, FL) 59928
Barnett Bank of Central Florida, NA (Indian Harbour Beach, FL) 60136
Barnett Bank of Central Florida, NA (Kissimmee, FL) 60582; 60583; 60584; 60585; 60586
Barnett Bank of Central Florida, NA (Longwood, FL) 60926; 60927
Barnett Bank of Central Florida, NA (Maitland, FL) 60973
Barnett Bank of Central Florida, NA (Melbourne, FL) 61035; 61036; 61037; 61038
Barnett Bank of Central Florida, NA (Merritt Island, FL) 61137
Barnett Bank of Central Florida, NA (Ocoee, FL) 61832
Barnett Bank of Central Florida, NA (Orlando, FL) 61922; 61923; 61924; 61925; 61926; 61927; 61928; 61929; 61930; 61931; 61932; 61933; 61934; 61935
Barnett Bank of Central Florida, NA (Oviedo, FL) 62214
Barnett Bank of Central Florida, NA (Palm Bay, FL) 62230; 62231; 62232
Barnett Bank of Central Florida, NA (Patrick Air Force Base, FL) 62361
Barnett Bank of Central Florida, NA (Rockledge, FL) 62742
Barnett Bank of Central Florida, NA (Sanford, FL) 62764
Barnett Bank of Central Florida, NA (St. Cloud, FL) 63065
Barnett Bank of Central Florida, NA (Titusville, FL) 63684
Barnett Bank of Central Florida, NA (West Melbourne, FL) 63833
Barnett Bank of Central Florida, NA (Winter Park, FL) 63962; 63963; 63964
Barnett Bank of Central Florida, NA (Zellwood, FL) 64006
Barnett Bank of Highlands County (Arcadia, FL) 58579
Barnett Bank of Highlands County (Avon Park, FL) 58605
Barnett Bank of Highlands County (Lake Placid, FL) 60641
Barnett Bank of Highlands County (Sebring, FL) 62877; 62878; 62879
Barnett Bank of Jacksonville, NA (Jacksonville, FL) 60191; 60192; 60193; 60194; 60195; 60196; 60197; 60198; 60199; 60200; 60201; 60202; 60203; 60204; 60205; 60206; 60207; 60208; 60209; 60210; 60211; 60212; 60213; 60214; 60215; 60216; 60217; 60218; 60219; 60220; 60221; 60222
Barnett Bank of the Keys (Big Pine Key, FL) 58660
Barnett Bank of the Keys (Islamorada, FL) 60153
Barnett Bank of the Keys (Key Largo, FL) 60564
Barnett Bank of the Keys (Key West, FL) 60569; 60570
Barnett Bank of the Keys (Marathon, FL) 60992
Barnett Bank of the Keys (Summerland Key, FL) 63184
Barnett Bank of the Keys (Tavernier, FL) 63672
Barnett Bank of Lake County, NA (Eustis, FL) 59396; 59397
Barnett Bank of Lake County, NA (Leesburg, FL) 60876; 60877; 60878; 60879
Barnett Bank of Lake County, NA (Mount Dora, FL) 61561; 61562
Barnett Bank of Lake County, NA (Tavares, FL) 63668
Barnett Bank of Lake County, NA (Umatilla, FL) 63711; 63712
Barnett Bank of Lake Okeechobee (Belle Glade, FL) 58642
Barnett Bank of Lake Okeechobee (Moore Haven, FL) 61559
Barnett Bank of Lake Okeechobee (Okeechobee, FL) 61840; 61841; 61842
Barnett Bank of Lee County, NA (Fort Myers, FL) 59663; 59664; 59665; 59666; 59667; 59668; 59669; 59670; 59671; 59672; 59673; 59674; 59675; 59676; 59677; 59678; 59679; 59680; 59681; 59682; 59683; 59684
Barnett Bank of Manatee County, NA (Bradenton, FL) 58802; 58803; 58804; 58805; 58806; 58807; 58808; 58809; 58810; 58811
Barnett Bank of Manatee County, NA (Ellenton, FL) 59385
Barnett Bank of Manatee County, NA (Holmes Beach, FL) 60110
Barnett Bank of Manatee County, NA (Oneco, FL) 61857
Barnett Bank of Manatee County, NA (Palmetto, FL) 62306
Barnett Bank of Manatee County, NA (Sarasota, FL) 62788
Barnett Bank of Marion County, NA (Belleview, FL) 58654
Barnett Bank of Marion County, NA (Dunnellon, FL) 59371
Barnett Bank of Marion County, NA (Ocala, FL) 61773; 61774; 61775; 61776; 61777; 61778; 61779; 61780; 61781
Barnett Bank of Marion County, NA (Silver Springs, FL) 62916; 62917
Barnett Bank of Martin County, NA (Hobe Sound, FL) 60026
Barnett Bank of Martin County, NA (Palm City, FL) 62276
Barnett Bank of Martin County, NA (Stuart, FL) 63155; 63156; 63157; 63158; 63159; 63160
Barnett Bank of Naples (Golden Gate, FL) 59927
Barnett Bank of Naples (Marco Island, FL) 60995
Barnett Bank of Naples (Naples, FL) 61601; 61602; 61603; 61604; 61605; 61606; 61607; 61608; 61609; 61610; 61611
Barnett Bank of Nassau County (Callahan, FL) 58905
Barnett Bank of Nassau County (Fernandina Beach, FL) 59406; 59407
Barnett Bank of North Central Florida (Dowling Park, FL) 59351
Barnett Bank of North Central Florida (Jasper, FL) 60520
Barnett Bank of North Central Florida (Lake City, FL) 60617; 60618; 60619
Barnett Bank of North Central Florida (Live Oak, FL) 60908
Barnett Bank of Northwest Florida (De Funiak Springs, FL) 59241
Barnett Bank of Northwest Florida (Destin, FL) 59341
Barnett Bank of Northwest Florida (Fort Walton Beach, FL) 59823; 59824
Barnett Bank of Northwest Florida (Niceville, FL) 61708; 61709
Barnett Bank of Northwest Florida (Shalimar, FL) 62911
Barnett Bank of Palm Beach County (Atlantis, FL) 58589
Barnett Bank of Palm Beach County (Boca Raton, FL) 58672; 58673; 58674; 58675; 58676; 58677; 58678; 58679; 58680; 58681
Barnett Bank of Palm Beach County (Boynton Beach, FL) 58762; 58763; 58764; 58765
Barnett Bank of Palm Beach County (Delray Beach, FL) 59308; 59309; 59310; 59311
Barnett Bank of Palm Beach County (Jupiter, FL) 60531; 60532
Barnett Bank of Palm Beach County (Lake Worth, FL) 60664; 60665; 60666; 60667
Barnett Bank of Palm Beach County (North Palm Beach, FL) 61745; 61746; 61747
Barnett Bank of Palm Beach County (Ocean Ridge, FL) 61829
Barnett Bank of Palm Beach County (Palm Beach, FL) 62247
Barnett Bank of Palm Beach County (Palm Beach Gardens, FL) 62263; 62264; 62265; 62266; 62267
Barnett Bank of Palm Beach County (Palm Springs, FL) 62302
Barnett Bank of Palm Beach County (Riviera Beach, FL) 62737
Barnett Bank of Palm Beach County (Royal Palm Beach, FL) 62753
Barnett Bank of Palm Beach County (Singer Island, FL) 62918
Barnett Bank of Palm Beach County (Tequesta, FL) 63680
Barnett Bank of Palm Beach County (West Palm Beach, FL) 63841; 63842; 63843; 63844; 63845; 63846; 63847
Barnett Bank of Pasco County (Bayonet Point, FL) 58637; 58638
Barnett Bank of Pasco County (Dade City, FL) 59137
Barnett Bank of Pasco County (Elfers, FL) 59383; 59384
Barnett Bank of Pasco County (Holiday, FL) 60028; 60029
Barnett Bank of Pasco County (Hudson, FL) 60129; 60130
Barnett Bank of Pasco County (Land O' Lakes, FL) 60802
Barnett Bank of Pasco County (New Port Richey, FL) 61675; 61676; 61677; 61678; 61679
Barnett Bank of Pasco County (Port Richey, FL) 62665; 62666; 62667
Barnett Bank of Pasco County (Zephyrhills, FL) 64008; 64009
Barnett Bank of Pinellas County (Belleair Bluffs, FL) 58649
Barnett Bank of Pinellas County (Clearwater, FL) 58968; 58969; 58970; 58971; 58972; 58973; 58974; 58975; 58976; 58977; 58978; 58979
Barnett Bank of Pinellas County (Dunedin, FL) 59355; 59356
Barnett Bank of Pinellas County (Largo, FL) 60819; 60820; 60821; 60822
Barnett Bank of Pinellas County (Madeira Beach, FL) 60963
Barnett Bank of Pinellas County (North Redington Beach, FL) 61756
Barnett Bank of Pinellas County (Oldsmar, FL) 61846
Barnett Bank of Pinellas County (Palm Harbor, FL) 62289; 62290; 62291; 62292; 62293; 62294; 62295
Barnett Bank of Pinellas County (Pinellas Park, FL) 62510; 62511
Barnett Bank of Pinellas County (Seminole, FL) 62901; 62902; 62903; 62904
Barnett Bank of Pinellas County (South Pasadena, FL) 62924
Barnett Bank of Pinellas County (St. Petersburg, FL) 63082; 63083; 63084; 63085; 63086; 63087; 63088; 63089; 63090; 63091; 63092; 63093; 63094; 63095; 63096
Barnett Bank of Pinellas County (St. Petersburg Beach, FL) 63138; 63139
Barnett Bank of Pinellas County (Tarpon Springs, FL) 63666; 63667
Barnett Bank of Pinellas County (Treasure Island, FL) 63709
Barnett Bank of Polk County (Auburndale, FL) 58590
Barnett Bank of Polk County (Dundee, FL) 59352
Barnett Bank of Polk County (Haines City, FL) 59941; 59942
Barnett Bank of Polk County (Lake Wales, FL) 60651
Barnett Bank of Polk County (Lakeland, FL) 60705; 60706; 60707; 60708; 60709; 60710; 60711; 60712; 60713; 60714; 60715
Barnett Bank of Polk County (Winter Haven, FL) 63928; 63929; 63930; 63931; 63932
Barnett Bank of the St. Johns (Crescent City, FL) 59120; 59121
Barnett Bank of the St. Johns (Palatka, FL) 62224
Barnett Bank of the St. Johns (St. Augustine, FL) 63047; 63048; 63049; 63050; 63051; 63052; 63053
Barnett Bank of the St. Johns (Welaka, FL) 63830
Barnett Bank of South Florida, NA (Bay Harbor Islands, FL) 58636
Barnett Bank of South Florida, NA (Coral Gables, FL) 59093; 59094; 59095
Barnett Bank of South Florida, NA (Hialeah, FL) 59974; 59975; 59976
Barnett Bank of South Florida, NA (Homestead, FL) 60113
Barnett Bank of South Florida, NA (Key Biscayne, FL) 60562
Barnett Bank of South Florida, NA (Key Largo, FL) 60565
Barnett Bank of South Florida, NA (Miami, FL) 61179; 61180; 61181; 61182; 61183; 61184; 61185; 61186; 61187; 61188; 61189; 61190; 61191; 61192; 61193; 61194; 61195; 61196; 61197; 61198
Barnett Bank of South Florida, NA (Miami Beach, FL) 61524; 61525; 61526
Barnett Bank of South Florida, NA (Miami Lakes, FL) 61532; 61533
Barnett Bank of South Florida, NA (Miami Shores, FL) 61536
Barnett Bank of South Florida, NA (North Miami, FL) 61731; 61732; 61733
Barnett Bank of South Florida, NA (North Miami Beach, FL) 61741; 61742
Barnett Bank of South Florida, NA (Perrine, FL) 62494
Barnett Bank of Southeast Georgia, NA (Brunswick, GA) 65401; 65402; 65403
Barnett Bank of Southeast Georgia, NA (Jekyll Island, GA) 66367
Barnett Bank of Southeast Georgia, NA (Jessup, GA) 66368
Barnett Bank of Southeast Georgia, NA (Kingsland, GA) 66466
Barnett Bank of Southeast Georgia, NA (St. Marys, GA) 67624
Barnett Bank of Southeast Georgia, NA (St. Simons Island, GA) 67626
Barnett Bank of Southwest Florida (Charlotte Harbor, FL) 58948
Barnett Bank of Southwest Florida (Englewood, FL) 59390; 59391; 59392
Barnett Bank of Southwest Florida (Longboat Key, FL) 60923
Barnett Bank of Southwest Florida (Nokomis, FL) 61724
Barnett Bank of Southwest Florida (North Port, FL) 61753
Barnett Bank of Southwest Florida (Port Charlotte, FL) 62653; 62654
Barnett Bank of Southwest Florida (Sarasota, FL) 62789; 62790; 62791; 62792; 62793; 62794; 62795; 62796; 62797; 62798
Barnett Bank of Southwest Florida (Venice, FL) 63717; 63718; 63719; 63720
Barnett Bank of the Suncoast, NA (Beverly Hills, FL) 58659
Barnett Bank of the Suncoast, NA (Brooksville, FL) 58885; 58886; 58887
Barnett Bank of the Suncoast, NA (Citrus Springs, FL) 58955
Barnett Bank of the Suncoast, NA (Crystal River, FL) 59130
Barnett Bank of the Suncoast, NA (Homosassa Springs, FL) 60127
Barnett Bank of the Suncoast, NA (Inverness, FL) 60145; 60146; 60147
Barnett Bank of the Suncoast, NA (Spring Hill, FL) 62928; 62929; 62930; 62931; 62932
Barnett Bank of Tallahassee (Quincy, FL) 62727; 62728
Barnett Bank of Tallahassee (Tallahassee, FL) 63211; 63212; 63213; 63214; 63215; 63216; 63217; 63218
Barnett Bank of Tampa (Apollo Beach, FL) 58567
Barnett Bank of Tampa (Brandon, FL) 58864; 58865
Barnett Bank of Tampa (Lutz, FL) 60951
Barnett Bank of Tampa (Mac Dill Air Force Base, FL) 60958
Barnett Bank of Tampa (Plant City, FL) 62537; 62538
Barnett Bank of Tampa (Riverview, FL) 62736
Barnett Bank of Tampa (Ruskin, FL) 62756
Barnett Bank of Tampa (Seffner, FL) 62897
Barnett Bank of Tampa (Sun City Center, FL) 63186
Barnett Bank of Tampa (Tampa, FL) 63335; 63336; 63337; 63338; 63339; 63340; 63341; 63342; 63343; 63344; 63345; 63346; 63347; 63348; 63349; 63350; 63351; 63352; 63353;

Company Name Index

63354; 63355; 63356; 63357; 63358; 63359; 63360
Barnett Bank of Tampa (Temple Terrace, FL) 63676
Barnett Bank of Tampa (Valrico, FL) 63714
Barnett Bank of the Treasure Coast (Fort Pierce, FL) 59786; 59787; 59788
Barnett Bank of the Treasure Coast (Port St. Lucie, FL) 62695; 62696; 62697
Barnett Bank of the Treasure Coast (Sebastian, FL) 62871; 62872
Barnett Bank of the Treasure Coast (Vero Beach, FL) 63739; 63740; 63741; 63742; 63743
Barnett Bank of Volusia County (Datona Beach Shores, FL) 59150
Barnett Bank of Volusia County (Daytona Beach, FL) 59164; 59165; 59166; 59167
Barnett Bank of Volusia County (Daytona Beach Shores, FL) 59233
Barnett Bank of Volusia County (De Bary, FL) 59236
Barnett Bank of Volusia County (De Land, FL) 59247; 59248
Barnett Bank of Volusia County (DeLand, FL) 59294; 59295
Barnett Bank of Volusia County (Deltona, FL) 59333
Barnett Bank of Volusia County (Edgewater, FL) 59376
Barnett Bank of Volusia County (Flagler Beach, FL) 59417
Barnett Bank of Volusia County (New Smyrna Beach, FL) 61698; 61699; 61700
Barnett Bank of Volusia County (Ormond Beach, FL) 62195; 62196; 62197; 62198; 62199
Barnett Bank of Volusia County (Palm Coast, FL) 62282; 62283
Barnett Bank of Volusia County (Port Orange, FL) 62659; 62660; 62661
Barnett Bank of West Florida (Cantonment, FL) 58907
Barnett Bank of West Florida (Gulf Breeze, FL) 59935
Barnett Bank of West Florida (Milton, FL) 61545; 61546
Barnett Bank of West Florida (Pace, FL) 62220
Barnett Bank of West Florida (Pensacola, FL) 62398; 62399; 62400; 62401; 62402; 62403; 62404; 62405; 62406; 62407; 62408
Barnett Banks (Jacksonville, FL) **60223**
Barnett Banks Inc. (Jacksonville, FL) 60224
Barnett Banks Trust Co., NA (Jacksonville, FL) 60225; 60226
Barnett Banks of Volusia County (Daytona Beach Shores, FL) 59234
Barnett Banks of Volusia County (DeLand, FL) 59296
Barnett Banks of Volusia County (Orange City, FL) 61868
Bartlett-Collins (Sapulpa, OK) 77788
BASF Corp. (College Park, GA) 65579
BASF Corp. (Dalton, GA) 65772
BASF Corp. (Doraville, GA) 65921
BASF Corp. (Stone Mountain, GA) 67686
BASF Corp. (Geismar, LA) 69874; 69875; 69876
BASF Corp. (Greenville, MS) 72790
BASF Corp. (Charlotte, NC) 73849; 73850; 73851
BASF Corp. (Durham, NC) 74386
BASF Corp. (Enka, NC) 74505
BASF Corp. (Morganton, NC) 75630
BASF Corp. (Morgantown, NC) 75660
BASF Corp. (Central, SC) 78781
BASF Corp. (Spartanburg, SC) 79876
BASF Corp. (Chattanooga, TN) 80325; 80326; 80327; 80328
BASF Corp. (Lowland, TN) 81358
BASF Corp. (Carrollton, TX) 83452
BASF Corp. (Freeport, TX) 85378
BASF Corp. (Richmond, VA) 91741
BASF Corp. (Williamsburg, VA) 92561
BASF Corp. (Huntington, WV) 92868; 92869
BASF Corp. Chemical (Charlotte, NC) 73852
BASF Corp. Chemical Division (Geidmar, LA) 69867
BASF Corp. Chemical Division (Geismar, LA) 69877
BASF Corp. Chemicals (Spartanburg, SC) 79877
BASF Corp. Chemicals (Chattanooga, TN) 80329
BASF Corp. Chemicals (Huntington, WV) 92870
BASF Corp. Chemicals Division (Spartanburg, SC) 79878
BASF Corp. Coatings & Inks (Louisville, KY) 68695; 68696
BASF Corp. Coatings & Inks (Charlotte, NC) 73853; 73854
BASF Corp. Coatings & Inks (Morganton, NC) 75631
BASF Corp. Fiber Products (Williamsburg, VA) 92562
BASF Corp. Fibers (Sylvania, GA) 67764
BASF Corp. Fibers (Enka, NC) 74506
BASF Corp. Fibers (Anderson, SC) 78663
BASF Corp. Fibers (Central, SC) 78782; 78783
BASF Corp. Fibers (Lowland, TN) 81359; 81360
BASF Corp. Fibers (Williamsburg, VA) 92563
BASF Corp. Fibers Div. (Williamsburg, VA) 92564
BASF Corp. Fibers Division (Dalton, GA) 65773
BASF Corp. Fibers Division (Anderson, SC) 78664
BASF Corp. Fibers Division (Lowland, TN) 81361; 81362
BASF Corp. Fibers & Products (Anderson, SC) 78665
BASF Corp. Industrial Coatings Morganton (Morganton, NC) 75632
BASF Corp.-Clemson Plant (Central, SC) 78784
BASF Corp. Engineering Plastics (Marietta, GA) 66757
BASF Corp. Engineering Plastics (Louisville, KY) 68697
BASF Corp. Urethanes (Memphis, TN) 81469
BASF Federal Credit Union (Chattanooga, TN) 80330
BASF Fibers (Sylvania, GA) 67765
BASF Fibers (Anderson, SC) 78666
BASF Fibers (Lowland, TN) 81363
BASF Fibers (Williamsburg, VA) 92565
BASF Fibers Corp. (Greensboro, NC) 74788
BASF Graphic Systems (Louisville, KY) 68698
BASF Inmont Corp. (Corinth, MS) 72734
BASF Structural Materials (Rock Hill, SC) 79811
BASF Structural Materials Inc. (Charlotte, NC) 73855; 73856
BASF Structural Materials Inc. (Rock Hill, SC) 79812
BASF Structural Materials Inc. Celion Carbon Fibers (Rock Hill, SC) 79813
BASF Tpu Marketing (Richmond, TX) 88793
Bassett-Walker Inc. (Martinsville, VA) 91343; 91344
Batesville Casket Co. (Campbellsville, KY) 68178
Batesville Casket Co. (Manchester, TN) 81390
Batesville Casket Co. Inc. (Campbellsville, KY) 68179
Batesville Casket Co. Inc. (Campbellsvl, KY) 68184
Batesville Casket Co. Inc. (Baltimore, MD) 71061
Batesville Casket Co. Inc. (Batesville, MS) 72593
Batesville Casket Co. Inc. (Knoxville, TN) 81145
Batesville Casket Co. Inc. (Manchester, TN) 81391
Batesville Casket Co. Inc. (Petersburg, VA) 91627
Bath & Body Works (Atlanta, GA) 64294; 64295
Bath & Body Works (Kennesaw, GA) 66408
Baton Rouge Coca-Cola Bottling Co. (Baton Rouge, LA) 69470
Bausch & Lomb Inc. (Sarasota, FL) 62799
Bausch & Lomb Inc. (Oakland, MD) 72157
Bausch & Lomb Inc. (Greenville, SC) 79297; 79298
Bausch & Lomb Inc. Oral Care Div. (Tucker, GA) 67846
Bausch & Lomb Inc. Pharmaceutical Div. (Tampa, FL) 63361
Bausch & Lomb Pharmaceuticals Inc. (Tampa, FL) 63362
Baxter Diagnostics Inc. (Miami, FL) 61199; 61200
Baxter Diagnostics Inc. Dade Div. (Miami, FL) 61201
Baxter Health Care (Largo, FL) 60823
Baxter Healthcare (Bessemer, AL) 55086
Baxter Healthcare (McDonough, GA) 66967
Baxter Healthcare (Marion, NC) 75496
Baxter Healthcare (Kingstree, SC) 79550
Baxter Healthcare Corp. (Mountain Home, AR) 57384
Baxter Healthcare Corp. (Largo, FL) 60824; 60825
Baxter Healthcare Corp. (Norcross, GA) 67104
Baxter Healthcare Corp. (Cleveland, MS) 72682
Baxter Healthcare Corp. (Marion, NC) 75497
Baxter Healthcare Corp. (Kingstree, SC) 79551; 79552
Baxter Healthcare Corp. (El Paso, TX) 84765
Baxter Healthcare Corp. (Grand Prairie, TX) 85609
Baxter Healthcare Corp. (Jacksonville, TX) 87421
Baxter Healthcare Corp. Dade (Miami, FL) 61202
Baxter Healthcare Corp. Hospital (Columbia, MD) 71578
Baxter Healthcare Corp. Prescr (Ashland, VA) 90398
Baxter Healthcare Corp. of Puerto Rico (Jayuya, PR) 78466
Baxter Hospital Supplies (Little Rock, AR) 57257
Baxter Hospital Supply (Memphis, TN) 81470
Baxter International Baxter Diagnostics Div. (Miami, FL) 61203
Baxter International Baxter Hospital Supply Div. (Destrehan, LA) 69838
Baxter International Scientific Products Division (Ocala, FL) 61782
Baxter International Scientific Products Division (Stone Mountain, GA) 67687
Baxter International Washington D.C. Government Affairs Office (Washington, DC) 58135
Baxter Physical Therapy Center (West Columbia, SC) 80084
Baxter Scientific Products (Charlotte, NC) 73857
Bayamon Can Co. (Toa Alta, PR) 78605; 78606
Bayly Martin & Fay Inc. (W Palm Beach, FL) 63779
BB&T Financial Corp. (Wilson, NC) 76619
BCT International Inc. (Fort Lauderdale, FL) 59456
BD Primary Care Diagnostics (Sparks, MD) 72458
Bea Fasteners Inc. (Hamlet, NC) 74996
Beaird Industries (Shreveport, LA) 70691
Bear Automotive Service Equipment (Louisville, KY) 68699
Bear Island Paper Co. (Ashland, VA) 90399; 90400
Bear Stearn Co. Inc. (Houston, TX) 85866
Bear Stearns Companies Inc. (Atlanta, GA) 64296
Bear Stearns Companies Inc. (Dallas, TX) 83872
Bear Stearns & Co., Inc. (Atlanta, GA) 64297
Bear Stearns & Co., Inc. Atlanta (Atlanta, GA) 64298
Bear, Stearns & Co., Inc. Dallas (Dallas, TX) 83873
Bear Stearns Fiduciary Services Inc. (Washington, DC) 58136; 58137
Bear Stearns Secured Investors Inc. (Dallas, TX) 83874
Beatrice/Hunt-Wesson Inc. Savannah Refinery (Savannah, GA) 67455
Beck/Arnley Worldparts Corp. (Nashville, TN) 81899
Beckman Instruments Inc. (Peachtree, GA) 67225
Beckman Instruments Inc. (Baton Rouge, LA) 69471
Beckman Instruments Inc. (Houston, TX) 85867
Becton Dickinson Advanced Diagnostics (Hunt Valley, MD) 71924
Becton Dickinson & Co. (Hunt Valley, MD) 71925
Becton Dickinson & Co. (Honea Path, SC) 79526
Becton Dickinson & Co. Vacutainer Systems (Sumter, SC) 80004
Becton Dickinson Diagnostic Instrument Systems (Sparks, MD) 72459
Becton Dickinson, Diagnostics Inc. (Cayey, PR) 78383; 78384
Becton Dickinson Microbiology Systems (Cockeysville, MD) 71545
Becton Dickinson Systems (Sumter, SC) 80005
Becton Dickinson Vacutainer Systems (Sumter, SC) 80006
Bed & Bath Etc (Mohawk, TN) 81780
Bed & Bath Home Fashions (Chattanooga, TN) 80331
Belcher Co. of Tennessee (West Memphis, AR) 57716
Belcher Refining Co. (Mobile, AL) 56142
Belden Automotive Wire & Cable (Dumas, AR) 56908; 56909; 56910
Belden/Cooper Industries Franklin Plant (Franklin, NC) 74622
Belden/Copper Industries Franklin Plant (Franklin, NC) 74623
Belden Wire & Cable (Clinton, AR) 56855
Belden Wire & Cable (Monticello, KY) 69096; 69097
Belden Wire & Cable (Jena, LA) 69977
Belden Wire & Cable Tompkinsville (Tompkinsville, KY) 69315
Bell Atl Syst Leasing International (Birmingham, AL) 55160
Bell Atlantic Argentina, Inc. (Arlington, VA) 90274
Bell Atlantic Asia, Inc. (Arlington, VA) 90275
Bell Atlantic Bus Syst Servs. (Louisville, KY) 68700
Bell Atlantic Bus System Svc. (Tampa, FL) 63363
Bell Atlantic Bus Systems Svc. (Ft. Lauderdale, FL) 59851
Bell Atlantic Bus Systems Svc. (Jacksonville, FL) 60227
Bell Atlantic Bus Systems Svc. (Atlanta, GA) 64299
Bell Atlantic Bus Systems Svc (Baltimore, MD) 71062
Bell Atlantic Bus Systems Svc. (Lanham, MD) 72048
Bell Atlantic Bus Systems Svc. (Rockville, MD) 72257
Bell Atlantic Bus Systems Svc (Raleigh, NC) 75863
Bell Atlantic Business Services (El Paso, TX) 84766
Bell Atlantic Business System Services (Birmingham, AL) 55161
Bell Atlantic Business System Services (Huntsville, AL) 55888
Bell Atlantic Business Systems (Greenville, SC) 79299
Bell Atlantic Business Systems (Lubbock, TX) 87747
Bell Atlantic Business Systems Services (Memphis, TN) 81471
Bell Atlantic Business Systems Services (Austin, TX) 82824
Bell Atlantic Business Systems Services (Houston, TX) 85868
Bell Atlantic Business Systems Services (Hampton, VA) 91016
Bell Atlantic Business Systems Services (Richmond, VA) 91742
Bell Atlantic Business Systems Services (Roanoke, VA) 92104
Bell Atlantic Busn Sys Servs (Jackson, MS) 72949
Bell Atlantic Capital Funding Corp. (Wilmington, DE) 58004
Bell Atlantic Capital Investments, Inc. (Wilmington, DE) 58005
Bell Atlantic Corp. (Dallas, TX) 83875
Bell Atlantic Corp. (Midland, TX) 88022
Bell Atlantic Corp. (San Antonio, TX) 88925
Bell Atlantic Financial Services (Wilmington, DE) 58006
Bell Atlantic Financial Svs. (Wilmington, DE) 58007
Bell Atlantic Foreign Sales Corp. (Charlotte Amalie, VI) 90145
Bell Atlantic International, Inc. (Arlington, VA) 90276
Bell Atlantic Investments, Inc. (Wilmington, DE) 58008
Bell Atlantic Metro Mobile (Greenville, SC) 79300
Bell Atlantic Mobile (Lanham, MD) 72049
Bell Atlantic Mobile (Westminster, MD) 72540
Bell Atlantic Mobile (Hickory, NC) 75058
Bell Atlantic Mobile (El Paso, TX) 84767
Bell Atlantic Mobile Systems (Wilmington, DE) 58009
Bell Atlantic Mobile Systems (Silver Spring, MD) 72384
Bell Atlantic Mobile Systems (Vienna, MD) 72526
Bell Atlantic Network Funding Corp. (Wilmington, DE) 58010
Bell Atlantic Network SErvices Inc. (Arlington, VA) 90277
Bell Atlantic New Zealand Investments, Inc. (Wilmington, DE) 58011
Bell Atlantic Paging (Richmond, VA) 91743
Bell Atlantic Puerto Rico, Inc. (Arlington, VA) 90278
Bell Atlantic Services (Lynchburg, VA) 91224
Bell Atlantic Software & Systems Solutions, Inc. (Arlington, VA) 90279
Bell Atlantic Systems Lease International (Dallas, TX) 83876
Bell Atlantic Tricon (Atlanta, GA) 64300
Bell Atlantic Tricon Lease Corp. (Ft. Lauderdale, FL) 59852
Bell Atlantic Tricon Lease Corp. (Tampa, FL) 63364
Bell Atlantic Tricon Lease Corp. (Atlanta, GA) 64301
Bell Atlantic Tricon Leasing (Deerfield Beach, FL) 59272
Bell Dairy Products Inc. (Lubbock, TX) 87748
Bell atlantic Financial Services (Wilmington, DE) 58012
Bell Helicopter Textron Inc. (Amarillo, TX) 82525
Bell Helicopter Textron Inc. (Fort Worth, TX) 85069
Bell Helicopter Textron Inc. (Grand Prairie, TX) 85610
Bell Helicopter Textron Inc. Plant I (Fort Worth, TX) 85070
Bell South Advanced Networks (Atlanta, GA) 64302
Bell South Advertising & Publishing Corp. (Atlanta, GA) 64303
Bell South Advertising & Publishing Corp. (Metairie, LA) 70251
Bell South Cellular Corp. (Atlantga, GA) 65304
Bell South Co. (Metairie, LA) 70252
Bell South Enterprises, Inc. (Atlanta, GA) 64304
Bell South Information Systems Inc. (Atlanta, GA) 64305
Bell South International Inc. (Atlanta, GA) 64306
Bell South Mobile Data Inc. (Atlanta, GA) 64307
Bell South Mobility (Tuscaloosa, AL) 56634
Bell South Mobility Inc. (Atlanta, GA) 64308
Bell South Mobility Inc. (Louisville, KY) 68701
Bell South Telecommunications (Atlanta, GA) 64309
Bellinger Shipyard (Jacksonville, FL) 60228
Bellsouth mobility (Baton rouge, LA) 69472
Bellsouth Adv & Publishing Corp. ALA (Birmingham, AL) 55162
BellSouth Advanced Networks, Inc. (Atlanta, GA) 64310
BellSouth Advertising & Publishing (Savannah, GA) 67456
Bellsouth Advertising & Publishing (Charlotte, NC) 73858; 73859
Bellsouth Advertising & Publishing Corp. (Atlanta, GA) 64311; 64312; 64313
BellSouth Business Systems, Inc. (Atlanta, GA) 64314
Bellsouth Cellular Corp. (Atlanta, GA) 64315
BellSouth Communication Systems (Norcross, GA) 67105
Bellsouth Communication Systems Inc. (Irving, TX) 87322
BellSouth Communication Systems, Inc. (Roanoke, VA) 92105
Bellsouth Communications (Birmingham, AL) 55163; 55164
BellSouth Communications, Inc. (Atlanta, GA) 64316
Bellsouth Communications Systems, Inc. (Roanoke, VA) 92106
Bellsouth Corp. (Washington, DC) 58138
BellSouth Corp. (Atlanta, GA) **64317**
BellSouth Enterprises Inc. (Atlanta, GA) 64318

BellSouth Financial Services Corp. (Atlanta, GA) 64319
BellSouth International, Inc. (Atlanta, GA) 64320
BellSouth Mobility (Birmingham, AL) 55165
BellSouth Mobility (Huntsville, AL) 55889
BellSouth Mobility (West Palm Beach, FL) 63848
BellSouth Mobility (Gainesville, GA) 66266
Bellsouth Mobility (Crowley, LA) 69801
Bellsouth Mobility (Metairie, LA) 70253
Bellsouth Mobility (Franklin, TN) 80808
Bellsouth Mobility (Nashville, TN) 81900; 81901
BellSouth Mobility, Inc. (Atlanta, GA) 64321; 64322
BellSouth Services Inc. (Birmingham, AL) 55166
BellSouth Systems Integration, Inc. (Atlanta, GA) 64323
BellSouth Telecom Inc. (Atlanta, GA) 64324
BellSouth Telecommunications Inc. (Atlanta, GA) 64325
BellSouth /telecommunictions Inc. (Atlanta, GA) 64326
Bellwood Printing Plant (Richmond, VA) 91744
Beloit Manhattan (Columbus, MS) 72703
Bemis Co. (Crossett, AR) 56879
Bemis Co. (Memphis, TN) 81472
Bemis Co. Custom Resins Div. (Henderson, KY) 68440
Bencharge Credit Service of America, Inc. (Wilmington, DE) 58013
Bencharge Credit Services LA Inc. (New Orleans, LA) 70434
Beneficial (Wilmington, DE) **58014**
Beneficial Business Brokers Inc. (Atlanta, GA) 64327
Beneficial Corp. (Wilmington, DE) 58015; 58016; 58017
Beneficial Delaware Inc. (Dover, DE) 57784
Beneficial Delaware Inc. (Newark, DE) 57895
Beneficial Finance Co. (Columbia, SC) 78975
Beneficial Florida Inc. (Pensacola, FL) 62409
Beneficial Georgia Inc. (Kennesaw, GA) 66409
Beneficial Georgia Inc. (Tucker, GA) 67847
Beneficial Income Tax Service (Baton Rouge, LA) 69473
Beneficial Income Tax Service (Baltimore, MD) 71063
Beneficial Income Tax Service (Woodward, OK) 78259
Beneficial Income Tax Service (Killeen, TX) 87506
Beneficial Income Tax Service (Staunton, VA) 92308
Beneficial Management Corp. (Greenville, SC) 79301
Beneficial Management Corp. America (Fayetteville, NC) 74529
Beneficial Management Corp. of America & Affiliated Corp. (Wilmington, DE) 58018
Beneficial Maryland Inc. (Baltimore, MD) 71064
Beneficial Mgmt Corp. (Jacksonville, FL) 60229
Beneficial Mississippi Inc. (Ocean Springs, MS) 73221
Beneficial Mortgage Co. of Maryland (Gaithersburg, MD) 71764
Beneficial Mortgage Co. of MD (California, MD) 71482
Beneficial Mortgage Co. of Oklahoma (Oklahoma City, OK) 77305
Beneficial Mortgage Corp. (Newark, DE) 57896; 57897
Beneficial National Bank (Bear, DE) 57749; 57750
Beneficial National Bank (Dover, DE) 57785
Beneficial National Bank (New Castle, DE) 57856; 57857
Beneficial National Bank (Newark, DE) 57898
Beneficial National Bank (Talleyville, DE) 57963
Beneficial National Bank (Wilmington, DE) 58019; 58020; 58021; 58022; 58023; 58024
Beneficial National Bank USA (Wilmington, DE) 58025; 58026; 58027; 58028; 58029
Beneficial North Carolina Inc. (Fayetteville, NC) 74530
Beneficial North Carolina Inc. (Raleigh, NC) 75864
Beneficial North Carolina Inc. (Rocky Mount, NC) 76074
Beneficial Oklahoma Inc. (Oklahoma City, OK) 77306; 77307
Beneficial Savings Bank (Pinellas Park, FL) 62512
Beneficial Savings Bank FSB (Brandon, FL) 58866
Beneficial Savings Bank, FSB (Orlando, FL) 61936; 61937
Beneficial Savings Bank, FSB (Tampa, FL) 63365; 63366
Beneficial Tennessee Inc. (Nashville, TN) 81902
Beneficial Texas (Irving, TX) 87323
Beneficial Texas (Plano, TX) 88537
Beneficial Texas Inc. (Austin, TX) 82825
Beneficial Texas Inc. (Carrollton, TX) 83453; 83454
Beneficial Texas Inc. (Dallas, TX) 83877; 83878
Beneficial Texas Inc. (El Paso, TX) 84768; 84769
Beneficial Texas Inc. (Garland, TX) 85477
Beneficial Texas Inc. (Houston, TX) 85869; 85870; 85871; 85872; 85873; 85874
Beneficial Texas Inc. (Midland, TX) 88023
Beneficial Texas, Inc. (Pasadena, TX) 88388; 88389
Beneficial Texas Inc. (Plainview, TX) 88525
Beneficial Texas Inc. (Portland, TX) 88686
Beneficial Texas Inc. (San Antonio, TX) 88926; 88927; 88928
Beneficial Texas Inc. (Tyler, TX) 89791
Beneficial Virginia Inc. (Alexandra, VA) 90163
Beneficial Virginia Inc. (Chesapeake, VA) 90556
Beneficial Virginia Inc. (Fairfax, VA) 90754
Beneficial Virginia Inc. (Newport News, VA) 91452
Beneficial Virginia Inc. (Virginia Beach, VA) 92436
Beneficial Virgnia Inc. (Chesapeake, VA) 90557
Bergen Brunswig Corp. (Suwanee, GA) 67742
Bergen Brunswig Corp. (Glen Allen, VA) 90974
Bergen Brunswig Drug Co. (Tulsa, OK) 77886
Bergen Brunswig Drug Co. (Carrollton, TX) 83455
Bergen Brunswig Drug Co. (San Antonio, TX) 88929
Berkeley Mills (Balfour, NC) 73656
Berkshire Hathaway France (Fairview, TN) 80785
Berkshire Hathaway Franee (Fairview, TN) 80786
Bermans the Leather Experts (Oklahoma City, OK) 77308
Bermans the Leather Experts (Arlington, TX) 82636
Berry L M & Co. (Louisville, KY) 68702
Berry L M & Co. (Nashville, TN) 81903
Best Foods Caribbean Inc. (San Juan, PR) 78576
Best Foods Grocery Products Group (Little Rock, AR) 57258
Bethelhem Steel Corp. Sales OFC (Jacksonville, FL) 60230
Bethlehem Steel Beth-Ship (Port Arthur, TX) 88627
Bethlehem Steel Corp. (Atlanta, GA) 64328
Bethlehem Steel Corp. (Baltimore, MD) 71065
Bethlehem Steel Corp. (Columbia, SC) 78976
Bethlehem Steel Corp. (Brentwood, TN) 80218
Bethlehem Steel Corp. (Dallas, TX) 83879
Bethlehem Steel Corp. (Houston, TX) 85875
Bethlehem Steel Corp. Baltimore Marine (Sparrows Point, MD) 72463
Bethlehem Steel Corp. Bethship Div. (Sparrows Point, MD) 72464
Bethlehem Steel Corp. Marine (Sparrows Point, MD) 72465
Bethlehem Steel Corp. Sabine Yard (Port Arthur, TX) 88628
Bethlehem Steel Corp. Sparrows Point Div. (Sparrows Point, MD) 72466
Bethlehem Steel Corp. Sparrows Point Division (Sparrows Point, MD) 72467
Bethlehem Steel Corp. Sparrows Point Plant (Sparrows Point, MD) 72468
Betts Baking Co. (Dallas, TX) 83880
Betz Laboratories (Macon, GA) 66670
Betz Laboratories Inc. (Macon, GA) 66671; 66672
Betz Laboratories Inc. (Reserve, LA) 70660
Betz Laboratories Inc. (Beaumont, TX) 83143; 83144
Betz Laboratories Inc. (Garland, TX) 85478; 85479
Betz Laboratories Inc. (Houston, TX) 85876; 85877
Betz Laboratories Inc. (Spring, TX) 89463
Betz Laboratories Inc. (West Orange, TX) 90048; 90049
Betz Laboratory (Midland, TX) 88024
Betz Labs (Macon, GA) 66673
Betz PaperChem Inc. (Huntsville, AL) 55890
Betz PaperChem, Inc. (Jacksonville, FL) 60231
Betz Process Chemicals (Sulphur, LA) 70881
Betz Process Chemicals (Longview, TX) 87704
Betz Process Chemicals Inc. (Beaumont, TX) 83145; 83146; 83147
Betz Process Chemicals, Inc. (Friendswood, TX) 85396
Betz Process Chemicals Inc. (The Woodlands, TX) 89750
Beverly Enterprise (Wichita Falls, TX) 90067
Beverly Enterprises (Fort Smith, AR) 57028; **57029**
Beverly Enterprises (Arlington, TX) 82637
Beverly Enterprises (Houston, TX) 85878
Beverly Enterprises (Paris, TX) 88361
Beverly Enterprises Inc. (Virginia Beach, VA) 92437; 92438; 92439
Beverly Enterprises Medical Equipment Corp. (Fort Smith, AR) 57030
Beverly Manor of Portsmouth (Fort Smith, AR) 57031
B.F. Goodrich Aerospace Component Overhaul and Repair Inc. (Austin, TX) 82826
BF Goodrich Co. (Jacksonville, FL) 60232
Bf Goodrich Co. Geon Vinyl Div. Deer Park Plant (Deer Park, TX) 84547
Bf Goodrich Co. Hattiesburg Plant (Hattiesburg, MS) 72888
BFI-Gulf West Landfill (Anahuac, TX) 82591
BFI International Inc. (Houston, TX) 85879; 85880
BFI Landfill (Tulsa, OK) 77887
BFI Medical Waste Systems (Houston, TX) 85881
BFI Medical Waste Systems (Nederland, TX) 88183
BFI-Memphis Recyclery Inc. (Memphis, TN) 81473
BFI-Model Fill Landfill (Little Rock, AR) 57259
BFI-Oklahoma Landfill (Wheatland, OK) 78249
BFI-Recyclery (Winston Salem, NC) 76664
BFI Recycling Systems (Rocky Mount, NC) 76075
BFI Recycling Systems (Wheatland, OK) 78250
BFI Recycling Systems (Summerville, SC) 79981
BFI Regional Landfill (Abilene, TX) 82427
BFI-Richmond Landfill (Richmond, VA) 91745
BFI Services Group (Jessup, MD) 71982
BFI Waste Systems (Cullman, AL) 55537
BFI Waste Systems (Gainesville, FL) 59862
BFI Waste Systems (Lakeland, FL) 60716
BFI Waste Systems (Lawrenceville, GA) 66506
BFI Waste Systems (Frederick, MD) 71714
BFI Waste Systems (Salisbury, MD) 72335
BFI Waste Systems (Durham, NC) 74387
BFI Waste Systems (Fayetteville, NC) 74531
BFI Waste Systems (Kinston, NC) 75312
BFI Waste Systems (Paw Creek, NC) 75790
BFI Waste Systems (Raleigh, NC) 75865
BFI Waste Systems (Tulsa, OK) 77888
BFI Waste Systems (Rock Hill, SC) 79814
BFI Waste Systems (Cleveland, TN) 80569; 80570
BFI Waste Systems (Memphis, TN) 81474; 81475
BFI Waste Systems (Millington, TN) 81775
BFI Waste Systems (Nashville, TN) 81904
BFI Waste Systems (Rogersville, TN) 82272
BFI Waste Systems (Harlingen, TX) 85697
BFI Waste Systems (Plano, TX) 88538
BFI Waste Systems (San Antonio, TX) 88930
BFI Waste Systems (Chesapeake, VA) 90558
BFI Waste Systems (Lynchburg, VA) 91225
BFI Waste Systems (Winchester, VA) 92581
Bi-Lo (Cartersville, GA) 65498
Bi-Lo (Cochran, GA) 65570
Bi-Lo (Charlotte, NC) 73860
Bi-Lo (Matthews, NC) 75518
Bi-Lo (Manning, SC) 79629
Bi-Lo (Mt Pleasant, SC) 79672
Bi-Lo (North Augusta, SC) 79731
Bi-Lo (Sumter, SC) 80007
Bi-Lo Food Stores (Chesnee, SC) 78929
Bi-Lo Food Warehouse (Sand Springs, OK) 77779
Bi-Lo Food Warehouse (Tulsa, OK) 77889
Bi-Lo Grocery (Concord, NC) 74307
Bi-Lo Grocery & Deli (Delray Beach, FL) 59312
Bi-Lo Inc. (Vidalia, GA) 67984
Bi-Lo Inc. (Kannapolis, NC) 75253
Bi-Lo Inc. (Anderson, SC) 78667
Bi-Lo Inc. (Greenville, SC) 79302; 79303
Bi-Lo Inc. (Lexington, SC) 79601
Bi-Lo Inc. (Taylors, SC) 80035
Bi-Lo Inc. No 196 (Columbia, SC) 78977
Bi-Lo Incorporation (Pelzer, SC) 79786
Bi-Lo No One Ninety-Five (Greenville, SC) 79304
Bi-Lo No 63 (Darlington, SC) 79143
Bi-Lo No 265 (Spartanburg, SC) 79879
Bi-Lo Pharmacy (Charlotte, NC) 73861
Bi-Lo Pharmacy (Pineville, NC) 75808
Bi-Lo Store (Franklin, NC) 74624
Bi-Lo Store (Rockingham, NC) 76055
Bi-Lo Store (Honea Path, SC) 79527
Bi-Lo Store (Inman, SC) 79533
Bi-Lo Store No 216 (Gainesville, GA) 66267
Bi-Lo Super Market (Beaufort, SC) 78706
Bi-Lo Super Market One-Hund (Asheville, NC) 73606
Bi-Lo Supermarket No 225 (Rock Hill, SC) 79815
Bi-Lo Wholesl Inc. (Denison, TX) 84593
Big A Auto Parts Inc. (Houston, TX) 85882
Big Bear (Tuskegee, AL) 56684
Big Bear (Haines City, FL) 59943
Big Bear (Kenner, LA) 69993
Big Bear (Spartanburg, SC) 79880
Big Bear Store (Prattville, AL) 56485
Big Bear Super Market (Enterprise, AL) 55679
Big Bear Super Market (Waller, TX) 89986
Bindley Western Drug (Austell, GA) 65349
Bindley Western Drug Co. (Dallas, TX) 83881
Bindley Western Drug Co. Dallas, Texas (Dallas, TX) 83882
Bindley Western Drug Co. Florida (Orlando, FL) 61938
Bindley Western Drug Co. Georgia (Austell, GA) 65350
Bindley Western Drug Co. Houston, Texas (Houston, TX) 85883
Bindley Western Drug Co. North Carolina (Charlotte, NC) 73862
Bindley-Western Industries, Inc. Charise Charles Division (Altamonte Springs, FL) 58550
Bio-Lab Inc. (Decatur, GA) 65801; 65802
Bio-Lab Inc./Hydrotech Chemical Corp. (Decator, GA) 65795
Biolab Inc. (Conyers, GA) 65676
Bird-Johnson Co. (Mobile, AL) 56143
Bird-Johnson Co. (Pascagoula, MS) 73251
Bird Machine Co. (Scott Depot, WV) 93039
Birmingham Coca-Cola (Birmingham, AL) 55167
Birmingham Coca-Cola Bottling Co. (Birmingham, AL) 55168
Black & Decker (Austin, TX) 82827
Black & Decker Co. (Franklin, TN) 80809
The Black & Decker Corp. (Hampstead, MD) 71899
Black & Decker Corp. (Towson, MD) **72506**
Black & Decker Corp. (Asheboro, NC) 73578
Black & Decker Corp. (Fayetteville, NC) 74532
Black & Decker Corp. (Tarboro, NC) 76362
Black & Decker Corp. Household Products Group (Asheboro, NC) 73579
Black & Decker Corp. PO Fastenr Division (Hopkinsville, KY) 68474
Black & Decker Corp. Pop Fasteners (Hopkinsville, KY) 68475
Black & Decker Corp. Pop Fastners Division (Coldwater, MS) 72691
Black & Decker Corp. Power Tools Group (Easton, MD) 71658
Black & Decker Corp. Power Tools Group (Fayetteville, NC) 74533
Black & Decker Corp. True Temper Sports (Amory, MS) 72583
Black & Decker Corp. True Temper Sports (Anderson, SC) 78668
Black & Decker Housewares Group (Asheboro, NC) 73580
Black & Decker Inc. Facilities Group (Hampstead, MD) 71900
Black & Decker Inc. Power Tools Group (Fayetteville, NC) 74534
Black & Decker U.S. Inc. (Baltimore, MD) 71066
Black & Decker US Distr Ctr (Charlotte, NC) 73863
Black & Decker US Inc. (Lutherville Timonium, MD) 72119
Black & Decker US Inc. (Winston-Salem, NC) 76709
Black & Decker USA (Easton, MD) 71659
Blanket Finishing (Eden, NC) 74449
Blazer Financial Services (Camden Wy, DE) 57757
Blazer Financial Services (Dover, DE) 57786
Blazer Financial Services (Milford, DE) 57840
Blazer Financial Services (New Castle, DE) 57858
Blazer Financial Services (Newark, DE) 57899
Blazer Financial Services (Baltimore, MD) 71067; 71068
Blazer Financial Services (Bristol, TN) 80238
Blazer Financial Services (Clarksville, TN) 80537
Blazer Financial Services (Cleveland, TN) 80571
Blazer Financial Services (Columbia, TN) 80625
Blazer Financial Services (Gallatin, TN) 80838
Blazer Financial Services (Jackson, TN) 80965
Blazer Financial Services (Johnson City, TN) 81025
Blazer Financial Services (Memphis, TN) 81476; 81477; 81478
Blazer Financial Services (Murfreesboro, TN) 81836
Blazer Financial Services (Culpeper, VA) 90672
Blazer Financial Services (Danville, VA) 90685
Blazer Financial Services (Falls Church, VA) 90819
Blazer Financial Services (Petersburg, VA) 91628
Blazer Financial Services (Richmond, VA) 91746
Blazer Financial Services (Virginia Beach, VA) 92440
Blazer Financial Services I (Virginia Beach, VA) 92441

Blazer Financial Services Inc. (Chattanooga, TN) 80332
Blazer Financial Services Inc. (Cordova, TN) 80674
Block Drug Co. (Memphis, TN) 81479
Block Drug Co. Inc. (Memphis, TN) 81480; 81481; 81482
Blount Construction Co. Inc. (Atlanta, GA) 64329
Blount Inc. (Montgomery, AL) 56282; 56283; 56284; **56285**
Blount Inc. (Zebulon, NC) 76783
Blount Inc. Construction Div. (Montgomery, AL) 56286
Blue Goose Growers Inc. (Vero Beach, FL) 63744
Blue Goose Growers Inc. (Cobbtown, GA) 65569
Blue Grass Cooperage Co. (Louisville, KY) 68703; 68704; 68705
Blue Grass Cooperage Co. (Byrdstown, TN) 80264
Blue Grass Cooperage Co., Inc. (Benton, KY) 68124
Blue Grass Cooperage Co., Inc. (Honenwald, TN) 80948
Bluegrass Coca-Cola Bottling Co., Inc. (Louisville, KY) 68706
Bluegrass Coca Cola Inc. (Louisville, KY) 68707
BNG, Inc. (Baltimore, MD) 71069; 71070; 71071; 71072
BNY Financial Corp. (Dunwoody, GA) 66104
BNY Holdings (Delaware) Corp. (Newark, DE) 57900
Boatman's Bank of Delaware (New Castle, DE) 57859
Boatmen's Bank of Delaware (New Castle, DE) 57860
Boatmen's Bank of Tennessee (Memphis, TN) 81483
Boeing Aerospace & Electronics (Oak Ridge, TN) 82180
Boeing Aerospace & Electronics (Lake Dallas, TX) 87576
Boeing Co (Houston, TX) 85884
Boeing Co (Arlington, VA) 90280
Boeing Co. (Miami, FL) 61204
Boeing Co. the (Atlanta, GA) 64330
Boeing Co. the (Forest Park, GA) 66230
Boeing Co. the (Warner Robins, GA) 68009
Boeing Co. the (El Paso, TX) 84770
Boeing Co. the (Hampton, VA) 91017
Boeing Co. (Mc Lean, VA) 91362
Boeing Co. (Vienna, VA) 92395
Boeing Co. Inc (Huntsville, AL) 55891
Boeing Co. Inc (Dallas, TX) 83883
Boeing Defense & Space Group (Oak Ridge, TN) 82181
Boeing Electronics Irving Co. (Irving, TX) 87324
Boeing Georgia Inc. (Macon, GA) 66674
Boeing Louisiana Inc. (Lake Charles, LA) 70130; 70131
Boeing Tennessee Inc. (Oak Ridge, TN) 82182
Boise Cascade (Jackson, AL) 56062
Boise Cascade Jackson Operations (Jackson, AL) 56063
Boise Cascade Office Products Division (Hialeah, FL) 59977
Boise Cascade Corp. (DeRidder, LA) 69834
Boise Cascade Corp. (Florien, LA) 69854
Boise Cascade Corp. (Oakdale, LA) 70597
Boise Cascade Corp. Container (West Memphis, AR) 57717
Boise Cascade Corp. Deridder Mill (De Ridder, LA) 69809
Boise Cascade Corp. White Paper (Jackson, AL) 56064
Boise Cascade Paper Group (Jackson, AL) 56065
Boise Southern Deridder Mill (De Ridder, LA) 69810
Boise Southern Deridder Paper Mill (De Ridder, LA) 69811
T. Talbott Bond (Baltimore, MD) 71073
Bonny Products Inc. (Washington, NC) 76452; 76453
Borden (Geismar, LA) 69878
Borden Chemical Inc. (Griffin, GA) 66311
Borden Chemicals & Plastics (Geismar, LA) 69879
Borden City Foods, Inc. (Fort Smith, AR) 57032
Borden Foodservice (Jackson, MS) 72950
Borden Inc. (Augusta, GA) 65315
Borden Inc. (Griffin, GA) 66312
Borden Inc. (Macon, GA) 66675
Borden Inc. (Shively, KY) 69286
Borden Inc. (Baton Rouge, LA) 69474
Borden Inc. (Lafayette, LA) 70044
Borden Inc. (Lake Charles, LA) 70132
Borden Inc. (Biloxi, MS) 72615
Borden Inc. (Jackson, MS) 72951
Borden Inc. (Meridian, MS) 73160
Borden Inc. (Starkville, MS) 73361
Borden Inc. (Oklahoma City, OK) 77309
Borden Inc. (Toa Baja, PR) 78608
Borden Inc. (Chester, SC) 78931
Borden Inc. (Amarillo, TX) 82526
Borden Inc. (Corpus Christi, TX) 83703
Borden Inc. (Dallas, TX) 83884
Borden Inc. (El Paso, TX) 84771
Borden Inc. (Fort Worth, TX) 85071
Borden Inc. (Garland, TX) 85480
Borden Inc. (Houston, TX) 85885
Borden Inc. (Lubbock, TX) 87749
Borden Inc. (San Antonio, TX) 88931
Borden Inc. (Suplhur Springs, TX) 89575
Borden Inc. (Texarkana, TX) 89668
Borden Inc. (Tyler, TX) 89792
Borden Inc. (Waco, TX) 89930
Borden Inc. (Charleston, WV) 92725
Borden Inc. Astro Industries Division (Morganton, NC) 75633
Borden Inc. Chemical (Demopolis, AL) 55613
Borden Inc. Chemical (Louisville, KY) 68708
Borden Inc. Chemical (Alexandria, LA) 69368
Borden Inc. Chemical (Fayetteville, NC) 74535
Borden Inc. Chemical (High Point, NC) 75112
Borden Inc. Chemical (Diboll, TX) 84652
Borden Inc. Dairy (Gadsden, AL) 55774; 55775
Borden Inc. Dairy (Huntsville, AL) 55892; 55893
Borden Inc. Dairy (Tuscaloosa, AL) 56635; 56636
Borden Inc. Dairy (Asher, AR) 56730
Borden Inc. Dairy (Little Rock, AR) 57260
Borden Inc. Dairy (Miami, FL) 61205; 61206
Borden Inc. Dairy (Pennsacola, FL) 62375
Borden Inc. Dairy (Tampa, FL) 63367; 63368
Borden Inc. Dairy (Macon, GA) 66676; 66677
Borden Inc. Dairy (Lexington, KY) 68528; 68529
Borden Inc. Dairy (Baton Rouge, LA) 69475
Borden Inc. Dairy (Lafayette, LA) 70045; 70046
Borden Inc. Dairy (Minden, LA) 70338; 70339
Borden Inc. Dairy (Tupelo, MS) 73386; 73387
Borden Inc. Dairy (High Point, NC) 75113; 75114
Borden Inc. Dairy (Oklahoma City, OK) 77310; 77311
Borden Inc. Dairy (Greenville, SC) 79305; 79306
Borden Inc. Dairy (Nashville, TN) 81905; 81906
Borden Inc. Dairy (Amarillo, TX) 82527; 82528; 82529; 82530
Borden Inc. Dairy (Austin, TX) 82828; 82829
Borden Inc. Dairy (Corpus Christi, TX) 83704
Borden Inc. Dairy (Dallas, TX) 83885
Borden Inc. Dairy (El Paso, TX) 84772; 84773
Borden Inc. Dairy (Houston, TX) 85886; 85887
Borden Inc. Dairy (San Antonio, TX) 88932; 88933
Borden Inc. Dairy (Sulphur Springs, TX) 89553
Borden Inc. Dairy (Strasburg, VA) 92348; 92349
Borden Inc. Dairy Div. (Miami, FL) 61207
Borden Inc. Dairy Div. (Metairie, LA) 70254
Borden Inc. Dairy Division (Dothan, AL) 55626
Borden Inc. Dairy Division (Orlando, FL) 61939
Borden Inc. Dairy Division (Jackson, MS) 72952
Borden Inc. Grocery (Starkville, MS) 73362
Borden Inc. Grocery Division (Sulphur Springs, TX) 89554
Borden Inc. Grocery & Specialty Products (Little Rock, AR) 57261
Borden Inc. Grocery & Specialty Products (Macon, GA) 66678
Borden Inc. Grocery & Specialty Products (Starkville, MS) 73363
Borden Inc. Grocery & Specialty Products (Tupelo, MS) 73388
Borden Inc. Grocery & Specialty Products (Corpus Christi, TX) 83705
Borden Inc. Grocery & Specialty Products (El Paso, TX) 84774
Borden Inc. Grocery & Specialty Products (San Antonio, TX) 88934
Borden Inc. Meadow Gold Dairy (Tulsa, OK) 77890
Borden Inc. North American Foods Div. (Starkville, MS) 73364
Borden Inc. North American Foods Div. (Chester, SC) 78932
Borden Inc. Package & Industrial Products (Fayetteville, NC) 74536; 74537
Borden Inc. Package & Industrial Products (High Point, NC) 75115
Borden Inc. Packaging & Industrial Products (Griffin, GA) 66313
Borden Inc. Packaging & Industrial Products (Alexandria, LA) 69369
Borden Inc. Packaging & Industrial Products (High Point, NC) 75116
Borden Inc. Snacks & International Products (Dallas, TX) 83886
Borden Inc. Southwest Snacks (Dallas, TX) 83887
Borden Inc. Wise Foods (St Augustine, FL) 62939
Borden Inc. Dairy (Dothan, AL) 55627
Borden Inc. Dairy (Gadsden, AL) 55776
Borden Inc. Dairy (Monroe, LA) 70350
Borden Inc. Dairy (Jackson, MS) 72953
Borden Inc. Diary (Dothan, AL) 55628
Borden Inc. Diary (Nashville, TN) 81907
Borden Inc. Foodservice (Jackson, MS) 72954
Borden Inc. Grocery & Speciality (Austin, TX) 82830
Borden Inc. Grocery & Speciality Prds. (Miami, FL) 61208
Borden Inc. Grocery & Speciality Prds. (Baton Rouge, LA) 69476
Borden Inc. Grocery & Speciality Prds. (Dallas, TX) 83888
Borden Inc. Grocery & Specialty Products (Conroe, TX) 83653
Borden Inc. Grocery & Specialty Prds. (Nashville, TN) 81908
Borden Inc. Grocery & Specialty Products (Oklahoma City, OK) 77312
Borden Inc. Grocery & Specialty Products (Nashville, TN) 81909
Borden Inc. Packaging & Industrial Prods. (Diboll, TX) 84653
Borden Inc. Refrigerated Products (Dothan, AL) 55629
Borden Inc. Valley Bell Dairy (Charleston, WV) 92726
Borden Milk & Ice Cream (Shreveport, LA) 70692
Borden Milk & Ice Cream (Tupelo, MS) 73389
Borden Packaging & Industrial Products (Demopolis, AL) 55614
Borden Packaging & Industrial Products (Louisville, KY) 68709
Borden Packaging & Industrial Products (Fayetteville, NC) 74538
Borden Packaging & Industrial Products (Diboll, TX) 84654
Borden Packaging & Industrial Products (Gainsville, TX) 85431
Borden Snacks Inc. (Spartanburg, SC) 79881
Borden Superior Dairies Inc. (Austin, TX) 82831
Borg Warner Automotive (Blytheville, AR) 56803
Borg Warner Automotive (Gary, NC) 74651
Boston Industrial Products (Paragould, AR) 57488; 57489
Boston Industrial Products (Brentwood, TN) 80219; 80220
Boston Industrial Products (Hohenwald, TN) 80939; 80940; 80941
Boston Industrial Products (Newbern, TN) 82155
Bowater (Greenville, SC) **79307**
Bowater Carolina Div. (Catawba, SC) 78768
Bowater Data Processing Division (Greenville, SC) 79308
Bowater Southern Div. (Newnan, GA) 67078
Bowater Carolina Co. (Catawba, SC) 78769
Bowater Communications Papers (Lakeland, FL) 60717
Bowater Computer Forms (Plano, TX) 88539
Bowater Computer Forms (Richardson, TX) 88723
Bowater Computer Forms Inc. (Plano, TX) 88540
Bowater Inc. (Albertville, AL) 54959
Bowater Inc. (Calhoun, GA) 65460
Bowater Inc. (Duluth, GA) 66027
Bowater Inc. (Lilesville, NC) 75430
Bowater Inc. (Aiken, SC) 78645
Bowater Inc. (Greenville, SC) 79309; 79310; 79311
Bowater Inc. (White Oak, SC) 80121
Bowater, Inc. (Etowah, TN) 80778
Bowater Inc. (Hixson, TN) 80931
Bowater Inc. (Kingston, TN) 81125
Bowater Inc. (Soddy-Daisy, TN) 82333
Bowater Inc. Carolina Div. (Catawba, SC) 78770; 70771
Bowater Inc. Carolina Div. Woodlands (Blythewood, SC) 78748
Bowater Inc. Carolina Division (Catawba, SC) 78772
Bowater Inc. South Div. (Cullman, AL) 55538
Bowater Inc. South Div. (Elgin, TN) 80767
Bowater Inc. Southern Div. (Albertville, AL) 54960
Bowater Inc. Southern Div. (Calhoun, TN) 80267; 80268; 80269
Bowater Inc. Southern Div. (Spring City, TN) 82349
Bowater Inc. Southern Division (Calhoun, TN) 80270; 80271
Bowater Lumber Co. (Albertville, AL) 54961; 54962
Bowater Southern (Newnan, GA) 67079
Bowater Southern Paper Co. (Calhoun, TN) 80272
Bowater Southern Paper Co. Southern Division (Calhoun, TN) 80273
Bowater Woodlands (Harriman, TN) 80899
Bowater Woodlands (Kingston, TN) 81126
Bowaters Carolina Federal Credit Union (Lancaster, SC) 79567
Boyle-Midway Household Products Inc. (Atlanta, GA) 64331
Brad Ragan, Inc. (Charlotte, NC) 73864
Brad Ragan Inc. (Radford, VA) 91690; 91691
Brad Regan Inc. Rubber Div. (Radford, VA) 91692
Braden Carco Gearmatic (Broken Arrow, OK) 76879
Branch Banking & Trust (Orangeburg, SC) 79768
Branch Banking & Trust Co. (Aberdeen, NC) 73509; 73510; 73511
Branch Banking & Trust Co. (Angier, NC) 73551
Branch Banking & Trust Co. (Apex, NC) 73553
Branch Banking & Trust Co. (Asheville, NC) 73607; 73608
Branch Banking & Trust Co. (Ayden, NC) 73647
Branch Banking & Trust Co. (Beaufort, NC) 73666
Branch Banking & Trust Co. (Benson, NC) 73680
Branch Banking & Trust Co. (Black Creek, NC) 73694
Branch Banking & Trust Co. (Boiling Springs, NC) 73704
Branch Banking & Trust Co. (Boone, NC) 73709
Branch Banking & Trust Co. (Broadway, NC) 73727
Branch Banking & Trust Co. (Burlington, NC) 73743; 73744
Branch Banking & Trust Co. (Butner, NC) 73771; 73772
Branch Banking & Trust Co. (Carolina Beach, NC) 73783
Branch Banking & Trust Co. (Carthage, NC) 73785; 73786
Branch Banking & Trust Co. (Cary, NC) 73787; 73788; 73789; 73790; 73791
Branch Banking & Trust Co. (Chadbourn, NC) 73807
Branch Banking & Trust Co. (Chapel Hill, NC) 73809; 73810
Branch Banking & Trust Co. (Charlotte, NC) 73865; 73866; 73867; 73868; 73869; 73870; 73871; 73872; 73873; 73874; 73875; 73876; 73877; 73878; 73879; 73880; 73881; 73882; 73883
Branch Banking & Trust Co. (Cherryville, NC) 74237
Branch Banking & Trust Co. (Clayton, NC) 74257
Branch Banking & Trust Co. (Clemmons, NC) 74267
Branch Banking & Trust Co. (Clinton, NC) 74279; 74280; 74281
Branch Banking & Trust Co. (Coats, NC) 74298
Branch Banking & Trust Co. (Cramerton, NC) 74349; 74350
Branch Banking & Trust Co. (Creedmoor, NC) 74353
Branch Banking & Trust Co. (Dallas, NC) 74357
Branch Banking & Trust Co. (Denver, NC) 74361
Branch Banking & Trust Co. (Eden, NC) 74450
Branch Banking & Trust Co. (Edenton, NC) 74470
Branch Banking & Trust Co. (Elizabeth City, NC) 74474; 74475
Branch Banking & Trust Co. (Elkin, NC) 74496
Branch Banking & Trust Co. (Ellenboro, NC) 74500
Branch Banking & Trust Co. (Elm City, NC) 74501
Branch Banking & Trust Co. (Enfield, NC) 74503
Branch Banking & Trust Co. (Eureka, NC) 74510
Branch Banking & Trust Co. (Fairmont, NC) 74511
Branch Banking & Trust Co. (Faison, NC) 74512
Branch Banking & Trust Co. (Fallston, NC) 74517
Branch Banking & Trust Co. (Farmville, NC) 74518; 74519
Branch Banking & Trust Co. (Fayetteville, NC) 74539; 74540; 74541; 74542; 74543
Branch Banking & Trust Co. (Fletcher, NC) 74588
Branch Banking & Trust Co. (Forest City, NC) 74601; 74602
Branch Banking & Trust Co. (Fountain, NC) 74619; 74620
Branch Banking & Trust Co. (Fremont, NC) 74632; 74633; 74634
Branch Banking & Trust Co. (Fuquay Varina, NC) 74635; 74636
Branch Banking & Trust Co. (Garner, NC) 74645
Branch Banking & Trust Co. (Gastonia, NC) 74657; 74658; 74659; 74660; 74661; 74662; 74663; 74664; 74665; 74666; 74667
Branch Banking & Trust Co. (Goldsboro, NC) 74702; 74703; 74704; 74705; 74706; 74707; 74708; 74709
Branch Banking & Trust Co. (Goldston, NC) 74743
Branch Banking & Trust Co. (Graham, NC) 74745; 74746
Branch Banking & Trust Co. (Greensboro, NC) 74789; 74790
Branch Banking & Trust Co. (Greenville, NC) 74951; 74952
Branch Banking & Trust Co. (Grifton, NC) 74990
Branch Banking & Trust Co. (Halifax, NC) 74992; 74993
Branch Banking & Trust Co. (Hamlet, NC) 74997
Branch Banking & Trust Co. (Havelock, NC) 75007
Branch Banking & Trust Co. (Henderson, NC) 75021; 75022
Branch Banking & Trust Co. (Hickory, NC) 75059; 75060; 75061
Branch Banking & Trust Co. (High Point, NC) 75117; 75118
Branch Banking & Trust Co. (Hope Mills, NC) 75192
Branch Banking & Trust Co. (Jamestown, NC) 75237
Branch Banking & Trust Co. (Jamesville, NC) 75247
Branch Banking & Trust Co. (Kernersville, NC) 75275; 75276
Branch Banking & Trust Co. (King, NC) 75289
Branch Banking & Trust Co. (Kings Mountain, NC) 75293; 75294
Branch Banking & Trust Co. (Kinston, NC) 75313; 75314; 75315; 75316; 75317
Branch Banking & Trust Co. (Kitty Hawk, NC) 75333; 75334

Branch Banking & Trust Co. (Knightdale, NC) 75335; 75336
Branch Banking & Trust Co. (LaGrange, NC) 75341
Branch Banking & Trust Co. (Laurinburg, NC) 75349; 75350
Branch Banking & Trust Co. (Lawndale, NC) 75359; 75360
Branch Banking & Trust Co. (Lewisville, NC) 75394
Branch Banking & Trust Co. (Lexington, NC) 75397; 75398
Branch Banking & Trust Co. (Liberty, NC) 75426
Branch Banking & Trust Co. (Lillington, NC) 75431
Branch Banking & Trust Co. (Littleton, NC) 75448
Branch Banking & Trust Co. (Lowell, NC) 75455
Branch Banking & Trust Co. (Lumberton, NC) 75460; 75461; 75462; 75463
Branch Banking & Trust Co. (Macksville, NC) 75478
Branch Banking & Trust Co. (Madison, NC) 75479; 75480
Branch Banking & Trust Co. (Maggic Valley, NC) 75487
Branch Banking & Trust Co. (Magnalia, NC) 75488
Branch Banking & Trust Co. (Matthews, NC) 75519; 75520; 75521; 75522
Branch Banking & Trust Co. (Micro, NC) 75556
Branch Banking & Trust Co. (Mint Hill, NC) 75561
Branch Banking & Trust Co. (Mocksville, NC) 75562
Branch Banking & Trust Co. (Morehead City, NC) 75611; 75612; 75613
Branch Banking & Trust Co. (Morven, NC) 75670
Branch Banking & Trust Co. (Mount Airy, NC) 75673; 75674
Branch Banking & Trust Co. (Mount Gilead, NC) 75687
Branch Banking & Trust Co. (Mount Holly, NC) 75688
Branch Banking & Trust Co. (New Bern, NC) 75717; 75718; 75719; 75720
Branch Banking & Trust Co. (North Wilkesboro, NC) 75759
Branch Banking & Trust Co. (Ocean Isle Beach, NC) 75771
Branch Banking & Trust Co. (Old Fort, NC) 75772
Branch Banking & Trust Co. (Oxford, NC) 75774; 75775
Branch Banking & Trust Co. (Pikeville, NC) 75795; 75796
Branch Banking & Trust Co. (Pilot Mountain, NC) 75798
Branch Banking & Trust Co. (Pinehurst, NC) 75801; 75802
Branch Banking & Trust Co. (Pineville, NC) 75809
Branch Banking & Trust Co. (Plymouth, NC) 75834; 75835
Branch Banking & Trust Co. (Princeton, NC) 75842; 75843
Branch Banking & Trust Co. (Raleigh, NC) 75866; 75867; 75868; 75869; 75870; 75871; 75872; 75873; 75874; 75875; 75876; 75877
Branch Banking & Trust Co. (Ramseur, NC) 75986
Branch Banking & Trust Co. (Ranlo, NC) 75991
Branch Banking & Trust Co. (Red Springs, NC) 75992
Branch Banking & Trust Co. (Reidsville, NC) 75996
Branch Banking & Trust Co. (Roanoke Rapids, NC) 76032; 76033
Branch Banking & Trust Co. (Rockingham, NC) 76056; 76057
Branch Banking & Trust Co. (Rocky Mount, NC) 76076; 76077
Branch Banking & Trust Co. (Roper, NC) 76115
Branch Banking & Trust Co. (Roseboro, NC) 76116
Branch Banking & Trust Co. (Rowland, NC) 76118
Branch Banking & Trust Co. (Roxboro, NC) 76121
Branch Banking & Trust Co. (Rutherfordton, NC) 76141
Branch Banking & Trust Co. (Sanford, NC) 76187; 76188; 76189; 76190
Branch Banking & Trust Co. (Saratoga, NC) 76209
Branch Banking & Trust Co. (Scotland Neck, NC) 76210
Branch Banking & Trust Co. (Selina, NC) 76217
Branch Banking & Trust Co. (Shallotte, NC) 76229
Branch Banking & Trust Co. (Shelby, NC) 76232; 76233; 76234; 76235; 76236
Branch Banking & Trust Co. (Silver City, NC) 76251
Branch Banking & Trust Co. (Southern Pines, NC) 76273; 76274
Branch Banking & Trust Co. (Sparta, NC) 76290
Branch Banking & Trust Co. (Spindale, NC) 76293
Branch Banking & Trust Co. (Spring Lake, NC) 76297
Branch Banking & Trust Co. (Stanley, NC) 76308; 76309
Branch Banking & Trust Co. (Stantonsburg, NC) 76312; 76313
Branch Banking & Trust Co. (Statesville, NC) 76316; 76317; 76318
Branch Banking & Trust Co. (Tabor City, NC) 76358
Branch Banking & Trust Co. (Tarbara, NC) 76359; 76360; 76361
Branch Banking & Trust Co. (Thomasville, NC) 76372; 76373; 76374
Branch Banking & Trust Co. (Trenton, NC) 76405
Branch Banking & Trust Co. (Vass, NC) 76417
Branch Banking & Trust Co. (Wadesboro, NC) 76422; 76423
Branch Banking & Trust Co. (Wallace, NC) 76437; 76438; 76439
Branch Banking & Trust Co. (Warrenton, NC) 76447
Branch Banking & Trust Co. (Warsaw, NC) 76450
Branch Banking & Trust Co. (Weldon, NC) 76479
Branch Banking & Trust Co. (West End, NC) 76484
Branch Banking & Trust Co. (Whiteville, NC) 76492; 76493; 76494
Branch Banking & Trust Co. (Wilkesboro, NC) 76505
Branch Banking & Trust Co. (Williamston, NC) 76525; 76526; 76527
Branch Banking & Trust Co. (Wilmington, NC) 76541; 76542; 76543; 76544; 76545
Branch Banking & Trust Co. (Wilson, NC) 76620; 76621; 76622; 76623; 76624; 76625; 76626; 76627
Branch Banking & Trust Co. (Winston-Salem, NC) 76710; 76711; 76712; 76713; 76714; 76715; 76716; 76717; 76718; 76719
Branch Banking & Trust Co. (Anderson, SC) 78669; 78670
Branch Banking & Trust Co. (Belton, SC) 78723; 78724
Branch Banking & Trust Co. (Camden, SC) 78758
Branch Banking & Trust Co. (Charleston, SC) 78791; 78792; 78793; 78794
Branch Banking & Trust Co. (Chester, SC) 78933
Branch Banking & Trust Co. (Clemson, SC) 78948; 78949
Branch Banking & Trust Co. (Columbia, SC) 78978; 78979; 78980; 78981; 78982; 78983; 78984; 78985; 78986; 78987; 78988; 78989
Branch Banking & Trust Co. (Easley, SC) 79178
Branch Banking & Trust Co. (Florence, SC) 79193; 79194
Branch Banking & Trust Co. (Goose Creek, SC) 79278
Branch Banking & Trust Co. (Greenville, SC) 79312; 79313; 79314; 79315; 79316; 79317; 79318; 79319; 79320; 79321
Branch Banking & Trust Co. (Greer, SC) 79470; 79471
Branch Banking & Trust Co. (Honea Path, SC) 79528
Branch Banking & Trust Co. (Irmo, SC) 79537
Branch Banking & Trust Co. (Johns Island, SC) 79543
Branch Banking & Trust Co. (Lancaster, SC) 79568; 79569
Branch Banking & Trust Co. (Lexington, SC) 79602; 79603
Branch Banking & Trust Co. (Little River, SC) 79614
Branch Banking & Trust Co. (Loris, SC) 79615
Branch Banking & Trust Co. (Lyman, SC) 79623
Branch Banking & Trust Co. (Mauldin, SC) 79646
Branch Banking & Trust Co. (Mount Pleasant, SC) 79669; 79670
Branch Banking & Trust Co. (Myrtle Beach, SC) 79693
Branch Banking & Trust Co. (Newberry, SC) 79722; 79723
Branch Banking & Trust Co. (North Charleston, SC) 79745; 79746; 79747; 79748
Branch Banking & Trust Co. (North Myrtle Beach, SC) 79761
Branch Banking & Trust Co. (Orangeburg, SC) 79769
Branch Banking & Trust Co. (Piedmont, SC) 79793
Branch Banking & Trust Co. (Rock Hill, SC) 79816; 79817
Branch Banking & Trust Co. (Socastee, SC) 79872
Branch Banking & Trust Co. (Spartanburg, SC) 79882; 79883; 79884
Branch Banking & Trust Co. (St. Matthews, SC) 79974
Branch Banking & Trust Co. (Summerville, SC) 79982
Branch Banking & Trust Co. (Sumter, SC) 80008; 80009; 80010
Branch Banking & Trust Co. (Taylors, SC) 80036
Branch Banking & Trust Co. (Walterboro, SC) 80066
Branch Banking & Trust Co. (West Columbia, SC) 80085; 80086; 80087
Branch Banking & Trust Co. (Williamston, SC) 80122
Branchh Banking & Trust Co. (Raeford, NC) 75845
Branck Banking & Trust Co. (Rutherfordton, NC) 76142
Brass Craft Western Co. (Lancaster, TX) 87596
Brazos Point, Inc. (Ft. Worth, TX) 85413
Briggs & Stratton Corp. (Perry, GA) 67262
Briggs & Stratton Corp. (Murray, KY) 69119; 69120; 69121
Brighton Corp. (Pine Bluff, AR) 57508
Bristol Compressors Inc. (Bristol, VA) 90470
Bristol Myers (Arlington, TX) 82638
Bristol-Myers Barceloneta Inc. (Barceloneta, PR) 78325
Bristol Myers Co. (Grand Prairie, TX) 85611
Bristol-Myers Products (Morrisville, NC) 75662; 75663
Bristol Myers Products Co. (Morrisville, NC) 75664
Bristol-Myers Squibb Zimmer Patient Care Div. (Statesville, NC) 76319
Bristol-Myers Squibb Co. (Atlanta, GA) 64332; 64333
Bristol Myers Squibb Co. (Morrow, GA) 67005
Bristol-Myers-Squibb Co. (Morrisville, NC) 75665
Bristol-Myers Squibb Co. (Irving, TX) 87325
Britt Airways Inc. (Houston, TX) 85888
Brnach Banking & Trust Co. (Charlotte, NC) 73884
Brnach Banking & Trust Co. (Cherryville, NC) 74238
Broadcasting Group (Memphis, TN) 81484
Brookhollow Corp. (Richmond, VA) 91747
Brookshore Lithographers (Cary, NC) 73792
Brookshore Lithographers Corp. (Cary, NC) 73793
Brookwood Medical Center (Birmingham, AL) 55169
Broward Hurricane Panel Co. (Fort Lauderdale, FL) 59457
Brown-Forman (Louisville, KY) **68710**
Brown-Forman Beverage Co. (Louisville, KY) 68711; 68712
Brown-Forman Corp. (Louisville, KY) 68713; 68714; 68715; 68716; 68717; 68718; 68719
Brown-Forman International Ltd. (Louisville, KY) 68720; 68721
Brown-Forman Production Co. (Louisville, KY) 68722; 68723
Brown & Root Civil (Houston, TX) 85889
Brown & Root Environmental (Houston, TX) 85890
Brown & Root Forest Products (Houston, TX) 85891
Brown & Root Holdings Inc. (Houston, TX) 85892
Brown & Root Inc. (Houston, TX) 85893; 85894
Brown & Root Inc. Marine Fabrication Yard (Houston, TX) 85895
Brown & Root Industrial Services Inc. (Houston, TX) 85896; 85897
Brown & Root Manufacturing & Process Industries (Houston, TX) 85898
Brown & Root Petroleum & Chemical (Houston, TX) 85899
Brown & Root Power (Houston, TX) 85900
Brown & Root Services Corp. (Houston, TX) 85901
Brownell Electro Inc. (Birmingham, AL) 55170
Brownell Electro Inc. (Mobile, AL) 56144
Brownell Electro Inc. (Little Rock, AR) 57262
Brownell Electro Inc. (Miami, FL) 61209
Brownell Electro Inc. (Orlando, FL) 61940
Brownell Electro Inc. (Forest Park, GA) 66231
Brownell Electro Inc. (Charlotte, NC) 73885
Brownell Electro Inc. (Raleigh, NC) 75878
Brownell Electro Inc. (Columbia, SC) 78990
Brownell Electro Inc. (Knoxville, TN) 81146
Brownell Electro Inc. (Memphis, TN) 81485
Brownell Electro Inc. (Nashville, TN) 81910
Brownell Electro Inc. (Grand Prairie, TX) 85612
Brownell Electro Inc. (Houston, TX) 85902
Brownell Electro Inc. (Lubbock, TX) 87750
Brownell Electro Inc. (Bluefield, VA) 90459
Brownell Electro Inc. (Norfolk, VA) 91500
Browning-Ferris Inc. (Salisbury, MD) 72336
Browning Ferris Inc. Waste System (San Antonio, TX) 88935
Browning-Ferris Industrial (Houston, TX) 85903; 85904
Browning-Ferris Industries (Huntsville, AL) 55894
Browning Ferris Industries (Washington, DC) 58139
Browning-Ferris Industries (Fort Lauderdale, FL) 59458
Browning Ferris Industries (Louisville, KY) 68724
Browning-Ferris Industries (Lake Charles, LA) 70133
Browning-Ferris Industries (Metarie, LA) 70337
Browning-Ferris Industries (Baltimore, MD) 71074; 71075
Browning-Ferris Industries (Capital Heights, MD) 71499
Browning-Ferris Industries (Capitol Heights, MD) 71504
Browning-Ferris Industries (Hyattsville, MD) 71954
Browning-Ferris Industries (Greenville, MS) 72791
Browning-Ferris Industries (Jackson, MS) 72955
Browning-Ferris Industries (Greensboro, NC) 74791
Browning-Ferris Industries (Rocky Mount, NC) 76078
Browning-Ferris Industries (Tulsa, OK) 77891
Browning-Ferris Industries (Chattanooga, TN) 80333
Browning-Ferris Industries (Knoxville, TN) 81147
Browning-Ferris Industries (Oak Ridge, TN) 82183
Browning-Ferris Industries (Alief, TX) 82489
Browning Ferris Industries (Amarillo, TX) 82531
Browning Ferris Industries (Harlingen, TX) 85698
Browning-Ferris Industries (Houston, TX) 85905; 85906; **85907**
Browning-Ferris Industries (Hutchins, TX) 87301
Browning-Ferris Industries (Lubbock, TX) 87751; 87752
Browning-Ferris Industries (Fairfax, VA) 90755
Browning-Ferris Industries (Hopewell, VA) 91157
Browning-Ferris Industries (Lorton, VA) 91215
Browning-Ferris Industries (Sterling, VA) 92337
Browning-Ferris Industries (Yorktown, VA) 92649
Browning Ferris Industries Alabama Inc. (Montgomery, AL) 56287
Browning Ferris Industries BFI (Baton Rouge, LA) 69477
Browning Ferris Industries of Fall Township Inc. (Houston, TX) 85908
Browning Ferris Industries Florida Inc. (Jacksonville, FL) 60233
Browning Ferris Industries Georgia Inc. (Atlanta, GA) 64334
Browning-Ferris Industries Inc. (Hyattsville, MD) 71955
Browning Ferris Industries Inc. (Houston, TX) 85909; 85910
Browning Ferris Industries Service Group Inc. (Mobile, AL) 56145
Browning Ferris Industries South Atl (Columbia, SC) 78991
Browning Manufacturing (Maysville, KY) 69083
Browning Mfg. Plant 1 (Maysville, KY) 69084
Browning Mfg. Plant 3 (Maysville, KY) 69085
Browning Mfg. Plant 2 (Maysville, KY) 69086
Brownsville Medical Center (Brownsville, TX) 83354
Broyhill Furniture Ind., Inc. Lenoir Furn. Plant (Lenoir, NC) 75365
Broyhill Furniture Ind. Inc. Complex (Lenoir, NC) 75366
Broyhill Furniture Ind. Inc. Conover Plant (Conover, NC) 74327
Broyhill Furniture Ind. Inc. Harper Plant (Lenoir, NC) 75367
Broyhill Furniture Ind. Inc. Newton Plant (Newton, NC) 75742
Broyhill Furniture Ind., Inc. P Pacemaker Plant (Lenoir, NC) 75368
Broyhill Furniture Ind. Inc. Rutherford Plant (Rutherfordton, NC) 76143
Broyhill Furniture Ind. Inc. Taylorsville Plant (Taylorsville, NC) 76366
Broyhill Furniture Ind. Inc. Wall Systems Plt. (Lenoir, NC) 75369
Broyhill Furniture Ind. Inc. Whitnel Plant (Lenoir, NC) 75370
Broyhill Furniture Industries Inc. (Lenoir, NC) 75371
Bruno Inc. Birmingham (Birmingham, AL) 55171
Bruno S Inc. (Birmingham, AL) 55172
Bruno's (Birmingham, AL) **55173**
Bruno's Sea Ray Division (Knoxville, TN) 81148
Bruno's Zebco Division (Tulsa, OK) 77892
Bruno's Inc. (Birmingham, AL) 55174
Brunswick Defense Div. (East Camden, AR) 56918
Brunswick Bowling & Billiards (Eminence, KY) 68296; 68297
Brunswick Composites Defense Div. (East Camden, AR) 56919
Brunswick Composites Defense Facility (Marion, VA) 91330
Brunswick Corp. (Camden, AR) 56827
Brunswick Corp. (DeLand, FL) 59297
Brunswick Corp. (Stillwater, OK) 77835
Brunswick Corp. (Marion, VA) 91331
Brunswick Corp. Defense Div. (East Camden, AR) 56920
Brunswick Corp. Defense Div. (De Land, FL) 59249
Brunswick Corp. Defense Div. (Deland, FL) 59298
Brunswick Corp. Defense Division (East Camden, AR) 56921
Brunswick Corp. Marine Div. (Delhi, LA) 69823
Brunswick Corp. Technetics Division (De Land, FL) 59250
Brunswick Corp. Zebco Division (Tulsa, OK) 77893
Brunswick Fishing Boat Div. (Murfreesboro, TN) 81837
Brunswick Marine (Murfreesboro, TN) 81838
Brunswick Marine/Fisher Plant (West Point, MS) 73476
Brunswick Mercury Marine Plant 14 (Stillwater, OK) 77836
Brunswick Sea Ray Div. (Knoxville, TN) 81149
Bryan Foods Inc. (West Point, MS) 73477; 73478; 73479
Bryloc Inc. (Aibonito, PR) 78303; 78304

Buckeye
American Business Locations Directory

Buckeye Cellulose Corp. (Perry, FL) 62497; 62498
Buckeye Cellulose Corp. (Oglethorpe, GA) 67218
Builders Square (Casselberry, FL) 58929; 58930
Builders Square (Pensacola, FL) 62410
Builders Square (Tampa, FL) 63369
Builders Square (Oklahoma City, OK) 77313; 77314
Builders Square (Tulsa, OK) 77894; 77895
Builders Square (Austin, TX) 82832
Builders Square (El Paso, TX) 84775
Builders Square (Houston, TX) 85911; 85912; 85913
Builders Square (Pasadena, TX) 88390
Builders Square (San Antonio, TX) 88936; 88937; 88938; 88939; 88940
Builders Square (Webster, TX) 90017
Builder's Square (Virginia Beach, VA) 92442
Builders Square Corporate Office (San Antonio, TX) 88941
Builders Square Inc. (Largo, FL) 60826
Builders Square Inc. (San Antonio, TX) 88942
Bunny Bread (New Orleans, LA) 70435
Bunny Bread Co. (New Orleans, LA) 70436
Burdines (Fort Lauderdale, FL) 59459; 59460
Burdines (Fort Myers, FL) 59685
Burdines (Hollywood, FL) 60043; 60044
Burdines (Longwood, FL) 60928
Burdines (Merritt Island, FL) 61138
Burdines (Miami, FL) 61210
Burdines (St Petersburg, FL) 62965
Burdines (West Palm Beach, FL) 63849; 63850
Burdines (Yazoo City, MS) 73498
Burdines Department Store Division (Miami, FL) 61211
Burdines Beauty Salon (Hollywood, FL) 60045
Burdines Body Shop (Yazoo City, MS) 73499
Burdines Department Store (Gainesville, FL) 59863
Burdines Department Store (Hollywood, FL) 60046
Burdines Department Store (Melbourne, FL) 61039
Burdines Department Store (Miami, FL) 61212
Burdines Department Store (Tampa, FL) 63370
Burdines Department Stores (Miami, FL) 61213
Burdines Dept Store (Miami, FL) 61214
Burdines Home Cleaning Service (W Palm Beach, FL) 63780
Burdines Home Clenaing Service (Orlando, FL) 61941
Burdines Optical (Altamonte Spg, FL) 58533
Burdines Optical Dept (Fort Myers, FL) 59686
Burdines Portrait Studio (Miami, FL) 61215; 61216
Burdines Portrait Studio (Pompano Beach, FL) 62587
Burdines Store Bty Salon (Miami, FL) 61217
Burdines Travel (Miami, FL) 61218
Burdines Travel Bureau (Altamonte Spg, FL) 58534
Burdines Travel Bureau (Gainesville, FL) 59864
Burdines Travel Bureau (Orlando, FL) 61942
Burdines Travel Bureau (W Palm Beach, FL) 63781
Burdines Upholstery Shop (Yazoo City, MS) 73500
Burdines Variety Store (W Palm Beach, FL) 63782
Buring Foods (Memphis, TN) 81486
Burlington Air Express (Birmingham, AL) 55175
Burlington Air Express (Mobile, AL) 56146
Burlington Air Express (Jacksonville, FL) 60234
Burlington Air Express (College Park, GA) 65580
Burlington Air Express (Lexington, KY) 68530
Burlington Air Express (Louisville, KY) 68725
Burlington Air Express (Shreveport, LA) 70693
Burlington Air Express (Charlotte, NC) 73886
Burlington Air Express (Tulsa, OK) 77896
Burlington Air Express (Chattanooga, TN) 80334
Burlington Air Express (Memphis, TN) 81487
Burlington Air Express (Nashville, TN) 81911
Burlington Air Express (Austin, TX) 82833
Burlington Air Express (El Paso, TX) 84776
Burlington Air Express (Midland, TX) 88025
Burlington Air Express (San Antonio, TX) 88943
Burlington Coat Factory (Little Rock, AR) 57263
Burlington Coat Factory (Augusta, GA) 65316
Burlington Coat Factory (Macon, GA) 66679
Burlington Coat Factory (Savannah, GA) 67457
Burlington Coat Factory (Columbia, MD) 71579
Burlington Coat Factory (Glen Burnie, MD) 71836
Burlington Coat Factory (Greenbelt, MD) 71855
Burlington Coat Factory (Greensboro, NC) 74792
Burlington Coat Factory (Oklahoma City, OK) 77315
Burlington Coat Factory (Columbia, SC) 78992
Burlington Coat Factory (Kingsport, TN) 81073
Burlington Coat Factory (Memphis, TN) 81488
Burlington Coat Factory (Plano, TX) 88541
Burlington Coat Factory Warehouse (Huntsville, AL) 55895
Burlington Coat Factory Warehouse (Jacksonville, FL) 60235
Burlington Coat Factory Warehouse (Duluth, GA) 66028
Burlington Coat Factory Warehouse (Marietta, GA) 66758
Burlington Coat Factory Warehouse (District Heights, MD) 71651
Burlington Coat Factory Warehouse (Burlington, NC) 73745
Burlington Coat Factory Warehouse (Antioch, TN) 80165
Burlington Coat Factory Warehouse (Nashville, TN) 81912
Burlington Coat Factory Warehouse (Corpis Christi, TX) 83697
Burlington Coat Factory Warehouse (Dallas, TX) 83889
Burlington Coat Factory Warehouse (El Paso, TX) 84777
Burlington Cotton Co. (Greenville, SC) 79322
Burlington Denim (Greensboro, NC) 74793
Burlington Handbag Factory Str. (Conway, SC) 79132
Burlington House Fabrics (Dallas, TX) 83890
Burlington House Upholstery (High Point, NC) 75119
Burlington Industries (Calhoun, GA) 65461
Burlington Industries (Denton, NC) 74359
Burlington Industries (Mount Olive, NC) 75694
Burlington Industries (Bishopville, SC) 78738
Burlington Industries, Equity (Greensboro, NC) **74794**
Burlington Industries Fabrics Inc. (Franklinton, NC) 74630
Burlington Industries Inc. (Monticello, AR) 57370
Burlington Industries Inc. (Atlanta, GA) 64335
Burlington Industries Inc. (Dahlonega, GA) 65753
Burlington Industries Inc. (Rahun Gap, GA) 67293
Burlington Industries Inc. (Asheboro, NC) 73581; 73582
Burlington Industries Inc. (Belmont, NC) 73672
Burlington Industries Inc. (Burlington, NC) 73746
Burlington Industries Inc. (Caroleen, NC) 73782
Burlington Industries Inc. (Cordova, NC) 74344
Burlington Industries Inc. (Denton, NC) 74360
Burlington Industries Inc. (Forest city, NC) 74603
Burlington Industries Inc. (Gastonia, NC) 74668; 74669
Burlington Industries Inc. (Gibsonville, NC) 74697
Burlington Industries Inc. (Graham, NC) 74747
Burlington Industries Inc. (Greensbor, NC) 74758
Burlington Industries Inc. (Greensboro, NC) 74795; 74796
Burlington Industries Inc. (Liberty, NC) 75427
Burlington Industries Inc. (Mooresville, NC) 75599
Burlington Industries Inc. (Mount Holly, NC) 75689; 75690
Burlington Industries Inc. (Mt. Holly, NC) 75699
Burlington Industries Inc. (Mt. Olive, NC) 75700
Burlington Industries Inc. (Oxford, NC) 75776; 75777
Burlington Industries Inc. (Reidsville, NC) 75997
Burlington Industries Inc. (Rocky Mount, NC) 76079; 76080
Burlington Industries Inc. (Smithfield, NC) 76256; 76257
Burlington Industries Inc. (St. Pauls, NC) 76305
Burlington Industries Inc. (Statesville, NC) 76320
Burlington Industries Inc. (Wake Forest, NC) 76430
Burlington Industries Inc. (Bishopville, SC) 78739
Burlington Industries Inc. (Johnson City, TN) 81026
Burlington Industries Inc. (Dallas, TX) 83891
Burlington Industries Inc. (Altavista, VA) 90245
Burlington Industries Inc. (Clarksville, VA) 90637
Burlington Industries Inc. (Hillsville, VA) 91139
Burlington Industries Inc. (Hurt, VA) 91168
Burlington Industries Inc. Pine (Dahlonega, GA) 65754
Burlington Industries/Lakewood Plant (Cramerton, NC) 74351
Burlington Industries/Pioneer Plant (Burlington, NC) 73747
Burlington Industries/Ranlo Plant (Gastonia, NC) 74670
Burlington Industries Richmond Plant (Cordova, NC) 74345
Burlington Industries/Sheffield Plant (Rocky Mount, NC) 76081
Burlington Industries William G. Lord (Belmont, NC) 73673
Burlington Klopman Fabrics (Bremen, GA) 65393
Burlington Klopman Fabrics (Greensboro, NC) 74797
Burlington Madison Yark Co. (Greensboro, NC) 74798
Burlington Madison Yarn Co. (Mayodan, NC) 75537
Burlington Madison Yarn Co. (St. Pauls, NC) 76306
Burlington Madison Yarn Co. (Chattanooga, TN) 80335
Burlington Maid Enterprises II (Haw River, NC) 75011
Burlington Manufactures Outlet Center (Burlington, NC) 73748
Burlington Menswear (Clarksville, VA) 90638
Burlington Menswear Halifax (Halifax, VA) 91010
Burlington Menswear/Plant 17 (Raeford, NC) 75846
Burlington Northern (Fort Worth, TX) **85072**
Burlington Northern Inc. (Fort Worth, TX) 85073
Burlington Northern R R (Sherman, TX) 89390
Burlington Northern R R Co. (Chandler, OK) 76913
Burlington Northern Rail Rd (Clarendon, TX) 83567
Burlington Northern Railroa (Aliceville, AL) 54982
Burlington Northern Railroa (Birmingham, AL) 55176; 55177
Burlington Northern Railroa (Jasper, AL) 56078
Burlington Northern Railroa (Monroeville, AL) 56258
Burlington Northern Railroa (Winfield, AL) 56707
Burlington Northern Railroa (Springdale, AR) 57627
Burlington Northern Railroa (Pensacola, FL) 62411
Burlington Northern Railroa (Tampa, FL) 63371
Burlington Northern Railroa (Amory, MS) 72584
Burlington Northern Railroa (Columbus, MS) 72704
Burlington Northern Railroa (Enid, OK) 77043
Burlington Northern Railroa (Henryetta, OK) 77127
Burlington Northern Railroa (Muskogee, OK) 77217
Burlington Northern Railroa (Pawnee, OK) 77699
Burlington Northern Railroa (Thomas, OK) 77866
Burlington Northern Railroa (Amarillo, TX) 82532
Burlington Northern Railroa (Frisco, TX) 85409
Burlington Northern Railroa (Henrietta, TX) 85735
Burlington Northern Railroa (Irving, TX) 87326
Burlington Northern Railroa (Lubbock, TX) 87753
Burlington Northern Railroa (Paris, TX) 88362
Burlington Northern Railroa (Plainview, TX) 88526
Burlington Northern Railroa (San Antonio, TX) 88944
Burlington Northern Railroa (Stamford, TX) 89510
Burlington Northern Railroa (Wichita Falls, TX) 90068
Burlington Northern Railroad (Thomaston, AL) 56607
Burlington Northern Railroad (Atlanta, GA) 64336
Burlington Northern Railroad (Okeene, OK) 77287
Burlington Northern Railroad (Valliant, OK) 78219
Burlington Northern Railroad (Amarillo, TX) 82533
Burlington Northern Railroad (Petersburg, TX) 88505
Burlington Northern Railroad Co. (Fort Worth, TX) 85074; 85075
Burlington Northern Railroad I (Atlanta, GA) 64337
Burlington Northern Railroad M (Atlanta, GA) 64338
Burlington Northern Railroad O (Atlanta, GA) 64339
Burlington Northern Railway (Sapulpa, OK) 77789
Burlington Northern Railway (Sherman, TX) 89391
Burlington Northern Rr (Tupelo, MS) 73390
Burlington Northern Rr (Galveston, TX) 85435
Burlington Outlet Mall (Burlington, NC) 73749
Burlington Resources (Houston, TX) **85914**
Burlington Shoe Outlet (Burlington, NC) 73750
Burlington Shoes (Burlington, NC) 73751
Burlington Sportswear (Stonewall, MS) 73373; 73374
Burton Rubber Processing Inc. (Jonesborough, TN) 81064
Busch Gardens (Tampa, FL) 63372
Busch Gardens Williamsburg (Williamsburg, VA) 92566
Business Systems (Decatur, AL) 55576
Business Systems (Andrews, SC) 78698
Business Systems (Fairfax, VA) 90756
Business Systems Design Inc. (Orlando, FL) 61943
Business Systems Engineering (Myrtle Beach, SC) 79694
Business Systems Group (Pensacola, FL) 62412
Business Systems Inc. (Shreveport, LA) 70694
Business Systems Inc. (Woodbridge, VA) 92609
Business Systems & Service Inc. (Vienna, WV) 93077
Business Systems Services (Atlantic Beach, FL) 58588
Business Systems & Software (Melbourne, FL) 61040
Business Systems Support Group Inc. (Rockville, MD) 72258
Business Systems Tech. Inc. (Richardson, TX) 88724
Business Systems Technology Inc. (Richardson, TX) 88725
Business Week (Houston, TX) 85915
Business Week-Corporate Circul (Washington, DC) 58140
Business Week Editorial (Washington, DC) 58141
Buster Brown Apparel Inc. (La Fayette, GA) 66468
Buster Brown Apparel Inc. (Chattanooga, TN) 80336
Butler Paper (Mobile, AL) 56147; 56148
Butler Paper (Fort Smith, AR) 57033; 57034
Butler Paper (Miami, FL) 61219
Butler Paper (Tallahassee, FL) 63219
Butler Paper (New Orleans, LA) 70437; 70438
Butler Paper (Tupelo, MS) 73391; 73392
Butler Paper (Tulsa, OK) 77897
Butler Paper (Knoxville, TN) 81150; 81151
Butler Paper (Memphis, TN) 81489; 81490
Butler Paper (Lufkin, TX) 87797
Butler Paper (Temple, TX) 89606; 89607
Butler Paper (Tyler, TX) 89793; 89794
Butler Paper Co. (Rogers, AR) 57558; 57559
Butler Paper Co. (Alexandria, LA) 69370
Butler Paper Co. (Baton Rouge, LA) 69478
Butler Paper Co. (Lafayette, LA) 70047; 70048
Butler Paper Co. (Shreveport, LA) 70695
Butler Paper Co. (West Monroe, LA) 70943
Butler Paper Co. (Upper Marlboro, MD) 72514; 72515
Butler Paper Co. (Abilene, TX) 82428
Butler Paper Co. (Amarillo, TX) 82534; 82535
Butler Paper Co. (Austin, TX) 82834
Butler Paper Co. (El Paso, TX) 84778
Butler Paper Co. (Longview, TX) 87705; 87706
Butler Paper Co. (Plano, TX) 88542; 88543
Butler Paper Co. (San Angelo, TX) 88869
Butler Paper Co. (San Antonio, TX) 88945; 88946
Butler Paper Co. (Victoria, TX) 89877; 89878
Butler Paper Co. (Suffolk, VA) 92359; 92360

C

C. F. Sauer Co. Inc. (Richmond, VA) 91748
C-K Co. (South Boston, VA) 92245
C. R. Bard Inc. (Moncks Corner, SC) 79659; 79660
C. R. Bard Inc. Bard Urological (Covington, GA) 65724
C S F Holdings Inc. (Miami, FL) 61220
Cabot Petroleum Corp. (Beaver, OK) 76856
Cacique (Greenville, SC) 79323
Cain Chemical Inc. (Orange, TX) 88307
Cain Chemical Inc. Bayport Site (Pasadena, TX) 88391
Cain Chemical Inc. Chocolate Bayou Plant (Alvin, TX) 82505
Cain Chemical Inc. Corpus Christi Plant (Corpus Christi, TX) 83706
Cain Chemical Inc. Matagorda Operation (Wadsworth, TX) 89983
Cain Chemical Inc. Matagorda Operations (Wadsworth, TX) 89984
Cake Products Group (Thomasville, GA) 67788
Cal-Compack Foods (Vinton, TX) 89923
Calgon Corp. (Pasadena, TX) 88392
Calhun Newsprint Co. (Calhoun, TN) 80274
California Federal Bank (Boca Raton, FL) 58682
California Federal Bank (Dunnellon, FL) 59372
California Federal Bank (Fort Lauderdale, FL) 59461; 59462
California Federal Bank (Orange City, FL) 61869
California Federal Bank (Plant City, FL) 62539
California Federal Bank (Port Richey, FL) 62668
California Federal Bank (Spring Hill, FL) 62933
California Federal Bank (St Petersburg, FL) 62966
California Federal Bank (Tampa, FL) 63373; 63374
California Federal Bank (West Palm Beach, FL) 63851

Casual Corner (Austin, TX) 82836; 82837
Casual Corner (Baytown, TX) 83108
Casual Corner (Beaumont, TX) 83148
Casual Corner (Clute, TX) 83596
Casual Corner (College Station, TX) 83616
Casual Corner (Dallas, TX) 83896; 83897
Casual Corner (Denton, TX) 84615
Casual Corner (Duncanville, TX) 84694
Casual Corner (El Paso, TX) 84779
Casual Corner (Fort Worth, TX) 85076; 85077; 85078
Casual Corner (Harlingen, TX) 85699
Casual Corner (Houston, TX) 85923; 85924; 85925; 85926; 85927; 85928; 85929; 85930; 85931; 85932; 85933; 85934; 85935
Casual Corner (Humble, TX) 87217
Casual Corner (Hurst, TX) 87269
Casual Corner (Irving, TX) 87328
Casual Corner (Killeen, TX) 87507
Casual Corner (Lake Jackson, TX) 87579
Casual Corner (Longview, TX) 87707
Casual Corner (McAllen, TX) 87928
Casual Corner (Mesquite, TX) 87956
Casual Corner (Midland, TX) 88026
Casual Corner (Pasadena, TX) 88394
Casual Corner (Plano, TX) 88544
Casual Corner (Port Arthur, TX) 88629
Casual Corner (Richardson, TX) 88726
Casual Corner (San Angelo, TX) 88870
Casual Corner (San Antonio, TX) 88947; 88948; 88949; 88950; 88951
Casual Corner (Sherman, TX) 89392
Casual Corner (Temple, TX) 89608; 89609
Casual Corner (Texarkana, TX) 89669; 89670
Casual Corner (Victoria, TX) 89879
Casual Corner (Wichita Falls, TX) 90069
Casual Corner (Annandale, VA) 90254
Casual Corner (Arlington, VA) 90281
Casual Corner (Chesapeake, VA) 90559
Casual Corner (Fredericksburg, VA) 90913
Casual Corner (Hampton, VA) 91018
Casual Corner (Lynchburg, VA) 91226
Casual Corner (Mc Lean, VA) 91363
Casual Corner (Newport News, VA) 91453
Casual Corner (Norfolk, VA) 91501
Casual Corner (Richmond, VA) 91751; 91752
Casual Corner (Roanoke, VA) 92107
Casual Corner (Virginia Beach, VA) 92444
Casual Corner (Barboursville, WV) 92668
Casual Corner (Bridgeport, WV) 92706
Casual Corner (Charleston, WV) 92727
Casual Corner (Huntington, WV) 92871
Casual Corner (Northfork, WV) 92977
Casual Corner Beauty Shop (Taylorsville, NC) 76367
Casual Corner Corp. (Charlotte, NC) 73890
Casual Corner Corp. (Durham, NC) 74389
Casual Corner District Office (Atlanta, GA) 64346
Casual Corner General Office (Decatur, GA) 65804
Casual Corner Inc. (Hialeah, FL) 59978
Casual Corner 095 (Dallas, TX) 83898
Casual Corners (Tampa, FL) 63381
Catalyst Resources Inc. (Pasadena, TX) 88395
Caterpillar Financial Servies Corp. (Nashville, TN) 81917
Caterpillar Inc. (Corinth, MS) 72735
Caterpillar Inc. (Brentwood, TN) 80221
Caterpillar Insurance Co. Ltd. (Nashville, TN) 81918
Caterpillar Remanufactured Products Group (Corinth, MS) 72736
Cates Charles F. & Sons Inc. (Faison, NC) 74513
Cathodic Protection Services Co. (Houston, TX) 85936
Cato Oil & Grease Co. (Atlanta, GA) 64347
Cato Oil & Grease Co. (Oklahoma City, OK) 77326
CB & T Bank of Middle Georgia (Warner Robins, GA) 68010; 68011
CB&T Bank of Middle Georgia (Perry, GA) 67263
CB&T Bank of Russell County (Hurtsboro, AL) 56058
CB&T Bank of Russell County (Phenix City, AL) 56456; 56457; 56458; 56459
CB&T of Middle Georgia (Warner Robins, GA) 68012
CBI Co. Ltd. (Houston, TX) 85937; 85938
Cbi Na-Con (Houston, TX) 85939
Cbi Na-Con_Inc. (Houston, TX) 85940
Cbs News (Alpharetta, GA) 64108
Ccpc Chemical Inc. (Corpus Christi, TX) 83707
Cd Medical Inc. (Miami Lakes, FL) 61534
Cecos International Inc. (Westlake, LA) 70962
Cedars (Charlottesville, VA) 90526
Cedars Guest Homes The (Richmond, VA) 91753
Celanese Engineering Resins Inc. (Bishop, TX) 83300
Celanese Engineering Resins Inc. Resins Div. (Bishop, TX) 83301
Celeron Corp. (Houston, TX) 85941
Cellulosic Products Inc. (Greensburg, LA) 69900
Cellwood Products (Gaffney, SC) 79257
Centec (Metairie, LA) 70256
Centech (Silver Spring, MD) 72385
Centech Group (Arlington, VA) 90282
Centel Cellular Inc. (Atlanta, GA) 64348
Centex (Dallas, TX) **83899**
Centex Bateson Construction Co., Inc. (Dallas, TX) 83900
Centex Cement Enterprises, Inc. (Dallas, TX) 83901
Centex Construction Group Inc. (Dallas, TX) 83902
Centex Corp. (Dallas, TX) 83903
Centex-Great Southwest Corp. (Orlando, FL) 61946
Centex-Hamby Construction, Inc. (Atlanta, GA) 64349
Centex Materials, Inc. (Austin, TX) 82838
Centex Real Estate Corp./Centex Homes (Dallas, TX) 83904
Centex Rodgers Construction Co. (Nashville, TN) 81919
Centex Rooney Construction Co., Inc. (Fort Lauderdale, FL) 59466
Centex-Rooney Enterprises, Inc. (Fort Lauderdale, FL) 59467
Centex-Simpson Construction Co., Inc. (Fairfax, VA) 90758
Centex Title & Escrow Operations (Dallas, TX) 83905
Central Arkansas Hospital (Searcy, AR) 57601
Central Bank & Trust Co. (Owensboro, KY) 69162; 69163; 69164; 69165; 69166; 69167; 69168
Central Carolina Hospital (Sanford, NC) 76191
Central Fidelity Bank (Richmond, VA) **91754**
Central Fidelity Bank NA (Richmond, VA) 91755
Central Fidelity Banks Inc. (Richmond, VA) 91756
Central Fidelity National Bank (Falls Church, VA) 90820
Central Fidelity National Bank (Farmerville, VA) 90874
Central Fidelity National Bank (Forest, VA) 90883
Central Fidelity National Bank (Fort Belvoir, VA) 90885
Central Fidelity National Bank (Franklin, VA) 90891
Central Fidelity National Bank (Fredericksburg, VA) 90914
Central Filter (Eden, NC) 74451
Central Moloney Transformer Div. (Pine Bluff, AR) 57509
Central Moloney Inc. Arcadia (Arcadia, FL) 58580
Central Moloney Transformer Arcadia (Arcadia, FL) 58581
Central Moloney Transformer Components Operation (Pine Bluff, AR) 57510
Central Phosphates Inc. (Plant City, FL) 62541; 62542
Central Power & Light Co. (Corpus Christi, TX) 83708
Central Products Co., Inc. (Montgomery, AL) 56289; 56290
Central Products Inc. (Montgomery, AL) 56291; 56292
Central & South West (Dallas, TX) **83906**
Central & South West Services (Washington, DC) 58147
Central & South West Services, Inc. (Dallas, TX) 83907
Central Soya Co. Inc. (Guntersville, AL) 55823
Central Soya Co. Inc. (Tifton, GA) 67819
Central Soya Co. Inc. (Charlotte, NC) 73891
Central Soya Co. Inc. (Wilson, NC) 76628
Central Soya Co. Inc. (Chattanooga, TN) 80338
Central Soya Del Norte Inc. (Hatillo, PR) 78446; 78447
Central Soya Feed Co. Inc. (Tifton, GA) 67820
Central Soya Feed Co. Inc. (Orangeburg, SC) 79770
Centri Marc (Houston, TX) 85942
Centrilift (Claremore, OK) 76948; 76949
Centrilift Cable (Claremore, OK) 76950
Centrilift Co. (Claremore, OK) 76951
Centrilift Co. (Midland, TX) 88027
Ceramic Cooling Tower Co. (Fort Worth, TX) 85079
Ceramx Corp. (Laurens, SC) 79588
Cf Chemicals Inc. (Bartow, FL) 58625
Cf Ind Inc. (Wauchula, FL) 63827
Cf Industries Inc. (Tampa, FL) 63382
Chace Precision Materials Group (Carolina, PR) 78372
Challenger Caribbean Corp. (Canovanas, PR) 78364
Challenger Electric Equipment Co. (Vidalia, GA) 67985
Challenger Electrical Equipment (Grand Prairie, TX) 85613
Challenger Electrical Equipment Corp. (Jackson, MS) 72959
Challenger Electrical Equipment Corp. (Pageland, SC) 79783
Challenger Electrical Equipment Corp. (Portland, TN) 82233
Challenger Electrical Equipment Corp. (Parkersburg, WV) 92981
Challenger Electrical Equipment Inc. (Pageland, SC) 79784
Champion Forest Products (Silverstreet, SC) 79867
Champion International Corp/Ne (Marietta, GA) 66759
Champion International Corp. (Birmingham, AL) 55184
Champion International Corp. (Courtland, AL) 55532
Champion International Corp. (Cullman, AL) 55539
Champion International Corp. (Monroeville, AL) 56259
Champion International Corp. (Cantonment, FL) 58908
Champion International Corp. (De Funiak Spg, FL) 59238
Champion International Corp. (Jacksonville, FL) 60239; 60240; 60241
Champion International Corp. (Nw Smyrna Beach, FL) 61763
Champion International Corp. (Athens, GA) 64165
Champion International Corp. (Waycross, GA) 68031
Champion International Corp. (Canton, NC) 73777
Champion International Corp. (Edgefield, SC) 79184
Champion International Corp. (Greenville, SC) 79327
Champion International Corp. (Newberry, SC) 79724
Champion International Corp. (Arlington, TX) 82640
Champion International Corp. (Camden, TX) 83434; 83435
Champion International Corp. (Corrigan, TX) 83775
Champion International Corp. (Dallas, TX) 83908
Champion International Corp. (Fort Worth, TX) 85080
Champion International Corp. (Lufkin, TX) 87798
Champion International Corp. (Sheldon, TX) 89389
Champion International Corp. (Temple, TX) 89610
Champion International Corp. Courtland Mill (Courtland, AL) 55533; 55534
Champion International Corp. Lufkin Newsprint Operations (Lufkin, TX) 87799
Champion International Corp. Pr (Marietta, GA) 66760
Champion International Courtland Mill (Courtland, AL) 55535
Champion International Lufkin Newsprint Operation (Lufkin, TX) 87800
Champion Laboratories Inc. (York, SC) 80138
Champion Products Inc. (Clayton, NC) 74258; 74259
Champion Products Inc. (Dunn, NC) 74370
Champlin Refining Co. (Corpus Christi, TX) 83709; 83710
Channel Master (Smithfield, NC) 76259
Chaparral Steel Co. (Midlothian, TX) 88100
Charles F. Cates & Son Inc. (Faison, NC) 74514
Charles F. Cates & Sons (Faison, NC) 74515
Charles Schwab & Co. (Atlanta, GA) 64350
Charles Schwab & Co. Inc. (Atlanta, GA) 64351; 64352; 64353
Charles Schwab & Co. Inc. (Peachtree, GA) 67228
Charles Schwab Co. Inc. (Nashville, TN) 81920
Charles Schwab & Co. Inc. (Midland, TX) 88028
Charles Schwab & Co. Inc. Bethes (Bethesda, MD) 71376
Charles Schwab & Co. Inc. Gaithe (Montgomery Co, MD) 72140
Charles Schwab Inc. (Little Rock, AR) 57264
Charles Schwab&Co Inc. (Dallas, TX) 83909
Charter Co. (Brenham, TX) 83334; 83335
Chase Bank International (Miami, FL) 61225
Chase Bank of Maryland (Baltimore, MD) 71078
Chase Home Mortgage Corp. (Brandon, FL) 58867
Chase Home Mortgage Corp. (Jacksonville, FL) 60242
Chase Home Mortgage Corp. (Miami, FL) 61226
Chase Home Mortgage Corp. (Orlando, FL) 61947
Chase Home Mortgage Corp. (Tampa, FL) 63383; 63384; 63385; 63386
Chase Home Mortgage Corp. (West Palm Beach, FL) 63852
Chase Home Mortgage Corp. (Winter Park, FL) 63965
Chase Home Mortgage Corp. (Grand Prairie, TX) 85614
Chase Manhatten Bank of Florida, NA (Baco Raton, FL) 58613
Chase Manhatten Bank of Florida, NA (Clearwater, FL) 58983
Chase Manhatten Bank of Florida, NA (Coral Gables, FL) 59097
Chase Manhatten Bank of Florida, NA (Fort Lauderdale, FL) 59468
Chase Manhatten Bank of Florida, NA (Miami, FL) 61227
Chase Manhatten Bank of Florida, NA (Palm Beach, FL) 62248
Chase Manhatten Bank of Florida, NA (Pinellas Park, FL) 62514
Chase Manhatten Bank of Florida, NA (St. Petersburg, FL) 63097
Chase Manhatten Bank of Florida, NA (Tampa, FL) 63387
Chase Manhatten Bank (USA) (Wilmington, DE) 58031; 58032
Chase Manhatten Overseas Banking Corp. (Wilmington, DE) 58033; 58034
Chase Packaging Corp. (Asheville, NC) 73609
Chemical Bank Delaware (Wilmington, DE) 58035; 58036
Chemical Bank Florida (Boca Raton, FL) 58689
Chemical Bank Florida, SB (Palm Beach, FL) 62249
Chemical Coatings Inc. (Hudson, NC) 75198
Chemical Specialties Manufacturing Corp. (Baltimore, MD) 71079
Chemspec Inc. (Baltimore, MD) 71080
Chemtronics Inc. (Swannanoa, NC) 76349
Cheraw Dyeing & Finishing Plant (Cheraw, SC) 78918
Chesapeak Corp. (Richmond, VA) 91757
Chesapeak Display & Packaging Co. Inc. (Winston-Salem, NC) 76720
The Chesapeak & Potomae Co. of West Virginia (Charleston, WV) 92728
Chesapeake (Richmond, VA) **91758**
Chesapeake Packaging (Richmond, VA) 91759
Chesapeake Consumer Products Co. (Richmond, VA) 91760
Chesapeake Corp. (Richmond, VA) 91761
Chesapeake Corp. Fredericksburg Wood Treating (New Post, VA) 91445
Chesapeake Corp. Wood Treating (Elizabeth City, NC) 74476
Chesapeake Display & Packaging Co. (Winston-Salem, NC) 76721
Chesapeake Forest Products Co. (Richmond, VA) 91762
Chesapeake Land Development Operations (West Point, VA) 92537
Chesapeake Packaging Co. (Richmond, VA) 91763
Chesapeake Paper Products Co. (West Point, VA) 92538
Chesapeake & Patomac Telephone Co. (Washington, DC) 58148
Chesapeake & Patomac Telephone Co. of Virginia (Richmond, VA) 91764
Chesapeake & Patomac Telephone Co. of West Virginia (Charleston, WV) 92729
Chesapeake & Patomic Telephone Co. of Maryland (Baltimore, MD) 71081
The Chesapeake & Potomac Co. of Maryland (Baltimore, MD) 71082
Chesapeake & Potomac Phone Co. (Leonardtown, MD) 72098
Chesapeake & Potomac Tel Co. (Washington, DC) 58149
Chesapeake & Potomac Tel Co. (Newport News, VA) 91454
Chesapeake & Potomac Tel Co. MD (Baltimore, MD) 71083
Chesapeake & Potomac Tel Co. MD (Cumberland, MD) 71620; 71621
Chesapeake & Potomac Tel Co. MD (Keedysville, MD) 71991
The Chesapeake & Potomac Telephone Co. (Washington, DC) 58150
Chesapeake & Potomac Telephone Co. (Culpeper, VA) 90673
Chesapeake & Potomac Telephone Co. (Hopewell, VA) 91159
Chesapeake & Potomac Telephone Co. (Richmond, VA) 91765; 91766; 91767
Chesapeake & Potomac Telephone Co. (Roanoke, VA) 92108
Chesapeake & Potomac Telephone Co. (Staunton, VA) 92309
Chesapeake & Potomac Telephone Co. (Suffolk, VA) 92361
Chesapeake & Potomac Telephone Co. (Beckley, WV) 92674
Chesapeake & Potomac Telephone Co. (Charleston, WV) 92730
Chesapeake & Potomac Telephone Co. (Clarksburg, WV) 92804
Chesapeake & Potomac Telephone Co. (Moundsville, WV) 92951
Chesapeake & Potomac Telephone Co. (Parkersburg, WV) 92982
Chesapeake & Potomac Telephone Co. (Salem, WV) 93037
Chesapeake & Potomac Telephone Co. of Maryland (Baltimore, MD) 71084
The Chesapeake & Potomac Telephone Co. of Virginia (Richmond, VA) 91768
The Chesapeake & Potomic Co. of Virginia (Richmond, VA) 91769
Chesapeake Wood Treating (Pocomoke City, MD) 72219; 72220
Chesapeake Wood Treating (Eutawville, SC) 79191
Chesapeake Wood Treating Co. (North East, MD) 72153
Chesapeake Wood Treating Co. (Pocomoke City, MD) 72221
Chesapeake Wood Treating Co. (Elizabeth City, NC) 74477
Chesapeake Wood Treating Co. (New Post, VA) 91446
Chesapeake Wood Treating Co. (Richmond, VA) 91770
Chesapeake Wood Treating Co. (West Point, VA) 92539
Chestertown Bank of Maryland (Chestertown, MD) 71520; 71521; 71522; 71523

Citibank, FSB (Coral Gables, FL) 59099
Citibank, FSB (Coral Springs, FL) 59111; 59112
Citibank, FSB (Davie, FL) 59155
Citibank, FSB (Deerfield Beach, FL) 59274
Citibank, FSB (Delray Beach, FL) 59314; 59315
Citibank, FSB (Hollywood, FL) 60051
Citibank, FSB (Key Biscayne, FL) 60563
Citibank, FSB (Madeira Beach, FL) 60964
Citibank, FSB (Marco Island, FL) 60996
Citibank, FSB (Miami, FL) 61239; 61240; 61241; 61242; 61243; 61244
Citibank FSB (Miami Beach, FL) 61527; 61528
Citibank, FSB (North Miami Beach, FL) 61743
Citibank, FSB (Palm Beach, FL) 62250
Citibank, FSB (Palm Beach Gardens, FL) 62268
Citibank, FSB (Pompano Beach, FL) 62591
Citibank, FSB (Surfside, FL) 63201
Citibank, FSB (Tamarac, FL) 63298
Citibank International (Miami, FL) 61245
Citibank International (Houston, TX) 85960
Citibank, NA (Coconut Creek, FL) 59089
Citibank, NA (Dania, FL) 59146
Citibank, NA (Davie, FL) 59156
Citibank, NA (Deerfield Beach, FL) 59275
Citicorp Holdings, Inc. (New Castle, DE) 57862
Citicorp Trust, NA (Palm Beach, FL) 62251
Citizens Bank (Byron, GA) 65446
Citizens Bank (Ft. Valley, GA) 66263
Citizens Bank (Algood, TN) 80161
Citizens Bank (Baxter, TN) 80201
Citizens Bank (Cookeville, TN) 80644; 80645; 80646
Citizens Bank (Cookville, TN) 80672
Citizens Bank (Monterey, TN) 81782
Citizens Bank & Trust (Oliver Springs, TN) 82209
Citizens Bank & Trust Co. (Sunbright, TN) 82364
Citizens Bank & Trust Co. (Wartburg, TN) 82399; 82400
Citizens Bank & Trust of West Georgia (Carrollton, GA) 65490; 65491; 65492; 65493; 65494
Citizens Bank & Trust of West Georgia (Tallapposa, GA) 67779
Citizens Bank & Trust of West Georgia (Temple, GA) 67781
Citizens Bank & Trust of West Georgia (Villa Rica, GA) 68002
Citizens Bank & Trust of West Georgia (Whitesburg, GA) 68050
Citizens Federal Bank (Fort Lauderdale, FL) 59474
Citizens Federal Bank, AFSB (Boca Raton, FL) 58691
Citizens Federal Bank, AFSB (Boynton Beach, FL) 58769
Citizens Federal Bank, AFSB (Clearwater, FL) 58986; 58987
Citizens Federal Bank, AFSB (Deerfield Beach, FL) 59276
Citizens Federal Bank, AFSB (DeLand, FL) 59299
Citizens Federal Bank, AFSB (Deltona, FL) 59334
Citizens Federal Bank, FSB (Hialeah, FL) 59981; 59982
Citizens Federal Bank, FSB (Holiday, FL) 60030
Citizens Federal Bank, FSB (Holly Hill, FL) 60032
Citizens Federal Bank, FSB (Hollywood, FL) 60052
Citizens Federal Bank, FSB (Lehigh Acres, FL) 60891
Citizens Federal Bank, FSB (Miami, FL) 61246; 61247; 61248; 61249
Citizens Federal Bank, FSB (Miami Beach, FL) 61529
Citizens Federal Bank, FSB (Naples, FL) 61616
Citizens Federal Bank, FSB (Ocala, FL) 61788; 61789
Citizens Federal Bank, FSB (Ormond Beach, FL) 62200
Citizens Federal Bank, FSB (Palm Harbor, FL) 62296
Citizens Federal Bank, FSB (Pembroke Pines, FL) 62368
Citizens Federal Bank, FSB (Pinellas Park, FL) 62516
Citizens Federal Bank, FSB (Port Charlotte, FL) 62655
Citizens Federal Bank, FSB (Sarasota, FL) 62803; 62804
Citizens Federal Bank, FSB (South Miami, FL) 62922
Citizens Federal Bank, FSB (St. Petersburg, FL) 63098
Citizens Federal Bank, FSB (Sun City, FL) 63185
Citizens Federal Bank, FSB (Venice, FL) 63721
Citizens Federal Bank, FSB (Vero Beach, FL) 63745
Citizens First Bank (Rome, GA) 67335; 67336
Citizens Naitonal Bank (Fort George G. Meade, MD) 71705
Citizens National Bank (Beltsville, MD) 71349
Citizens National Bank (Bowie, MD) 71457; 71458
Citizens National Bank (Burtonsville, MD) 71480
Citizens National Bank (Clarksville, MD) 71536
Citizens National Bank (Crofton, MD) 71614
Citizens National Bank (Ellicott City, MD) 71677
Citizens National Bank (Glenelg, MD) 71850
Citizens National Bank (Jessup, MD) 71983
Citizens National Bank (Laurel, MD) 72065; 72066; 72067; 72068
Citizens National Bank (Odenton, MD) 72166
Citizens National Bank (Simpsonville, MD) 72450
Citizens National Banks (Laurel, MD) 72069
Citizens Savings Bank, SSB (Claremont, NC) 74254
Citizens Savings Bank, SSB (Hickory, NC) 75063; 75064; 75065
Citizens Savings Bank, SSB (Lincolnton, NC) 75436; 75437
Citizens Savings Bank, SSB (Maiden, NC) 75489
Citizens Savings Bank, SSB (Stanley, NC) 76310
Citizens Savings Bank, SSB (Formerly Citizens S&L) (Mooresville, NC) 75601; 75602
Citizens Savings Bank, SSB (Formerly Citizens Savings Bank, Inc.) (Newton, NC) 75743; 75744; 75745
Citizens State Bank (Vernon, AL) 56697
Citizens State Bank (Bald Knob, AR) 56736
Citizens State Bank (Nashville, AR) 57439
Citizens State Bank (Kingsland, GA) 66467
Citizens State Bank (Reynolds, GA) 67295
Citizens State Bank (Maud, OK) 77188
Citizens State Bank (Anton, TX) 82621
Citizens State Bank (Buffalo, TX) 83413
Citizens State Bank (Cross Plains, TX) 83811
Citizens State Bank (Dickinson, TX) 84663
Citizens State Bank (Donna, TX) 84676
Citizens State Bank (Earth, TX) 84724
Citizens State Bank (Georgetown, TX) 85565
Citizens State Bank (Giddings, TX) 85575
Citizens State Bank (Gorman, TX) 85597
Citizens State Bank (Hempstead, TX) 85731
Citizens State Bank (Lometa, TX) 87698
Citizens State Bank (Malakoff, TX) 87830
Citizens State Bank (Roby, TX) 88810
Citizens State Bank (Roma, TX) 88826
Citizens State Bank (San Antonio, TX) 88957
Citizens State Bank (Sealy, TX) 89364
Citizens State Bank (Somerville, TX) 89455
Citizens State Bank (Tenaha, TX) 89655
Citizens State Bank (Woodville, TX) 90130
Citizens State Bank Dalhart (Dalhart, TX) 83831
Citizens State Bank-Edna of (Edna, TX) 84743
Citizens State Bank, Ganado (Ganado, TX) 85474
Citrus Corp. (Houston, TX) 85961
Citrus Corp. Florida Gas Transmission Co. (Houston, TX) 85962
Citrus Hill Manufacturing Co. (Frostproof, FL) 59845
Citrus Hill Mfg. Co. (Frostproof, FL) 59846
City National Bank (Birmingham, AL) 55194; 55195
City National Bank (Dothan, AL) 55631
City National Bank (Pleasant Grove, AL) 56483
City National Bank (Sylacauga, AL) 56576; 56577
City National Bank (Fort Smith, AR) 57036; 57037; 57038; 57039; 57040; 57041; 57042
City National Bank (Miami, FL) 61250; 61251; 61252; 61253; 61254; 61255
City National Bank (North Bay Village, FL) 61727
City National Bank (Tallahassee, FL) 63222; 63223; 63224; 63225
City National Bank (Fulton, KY) 68374
City National Bank (Baton Rouge, LA) 69480; 69481; 69482; 69483; 69484; 69485; 69486; 69487; 69488; 69489; 69490; 69491; 69492; 69493; 69494; 69495; 69496; 69497
City National Bank (Charlotte, NC) 73900; 73901; 73902; 73903
City National Bank (Lawton, OK) 77156
City National Bank (Amarillo, TX) 82539
City National Bank (Carrollton, TX) 83458
City National Bank (Corsicana, TX) 83778
City National Bank (Kilgore, TX) 87485
City National Bank the (Mineral Wells, TX) 88108
City National Bank (Plainview, TX) 88527
City National Bank (Sulphur Springs, TX) 89555; 89556
City National Bank (Taylor, TX) 89597
City National Bank (Weslaco, TX) 90032; 90033
City National Bank (Whitehouse, TX) 90057; 90058
City National Bank (Wichita Falls, TX) 90070
City National Bank (Winnsboro, TX) 90125
City National Bank (Charleston, WV) 92733; 92734
City National Bank of Baton (Baton Rouge, LA) 69498
City National Bank (Br) (Baton Rouge, LA) 69499
City National Bank Carrollton (Carrollton, TX) 83459
City National Bank of Carrollton (Dallas, TX) 83916
City National Bank of Charleston (Charleston, WV) 92735; 92736; 92737
City National Bank of Charleston (St. Albans, WV) 93066
City National Bank of Dotha (Dothan, AL) 55632; 55633
City National Bank of Fairmont (Fairmont, WV) 92837
City National Bank of Fairmont (Farmington, WV) 92851
City National Bank of Fl (Miami, FL) 61256; 61257
City National Bank of Fl (N Miami Beach, FL) 61592
City National Bank of Flori (Miami, FL) 61258
City National Bank of Florida (Fort Lauderdale, FL) 59475
City National Bank of Florida (Hallandale, FL) 59959
City National Bank of Florida (Miami, FL) 61259
City National Bank of Fort (Fort Smith, AR) 57043
City National Bank of Fulton (Fulton, KY) 68375
City National Bank of Irvin (Irving, TX) 87331
City National Bank of Irving (Irving, TX) 87332; 87333
City National Bank of Kilgore (Kilgore, TX) 87486
City National Bank Laredo (Laredo, TX) 87608
City National Bank of Miami (Miami, FL) 61260; 61261; 61262
City National Bank Mignon Branch (Sylacauga, AL) 56578
City National Bank of San Saba (San Saba, TX) 89346
City National Bank of Sulphur Spring (Sulphur Spring, TX) 89549; 89550
City National Bank Sylacauga (Sylacauga, AL) 56579; 56580; 56581; 56582
City National Bank of Taylor (Taylor, TX) 89598
City National Bank & Trust (Guymon, OK) 77100
City National Bank & Trust (Lawton, OK) 77157
City National Bank of Washi (Atlanta, GA) 64364
City National Bank of Weath (Weatherford, OK) 78239
City National Corp. (Sylacauga, AL) 56583; 56584
C.J. Gayfer & Co., Inc. (Mobile, AL) 56151
Clairson International Corp. (Ocala, FL) 61790
Claris Corp. (Atlanta, GA) 64365
Clark Equipment Co. (Miami, FL) 61263
Clark Equipment Co. (Statesville, NC) 76321
Clark Equipment Co. (Hurst, TX) 87271
Clark Equipment Co., Inc. (Winter Garden, FL) 63919
Clark Gas & Oil Co. (Stuart, VA) 92351
Clark-Hurth Components Box 38 (Statesville, NC) 76322
Clark-Hurth Components Co. (Statesville, NC) 76323
Clark Material Handling Co. (Danville, KY) 68253
Clark Material Handling Co. (Lexington, KY) 68534; 68535; 68536; 68537
Clark Printing Co. (Pine Bluff, AR) 57511
Clark Printing Co. (Louisville, KY) 68732
Clark Printing Co. (Shelbyville, KY) 69271
Clark Printing Co. (Marion, MS) 73141
Clark Printing Inc. (Oklahoma City, OK) 77336
Clark-Schwebel Fiber Glass Corp. (Statesville, NC) 76324
Clark-Schwebel Fiber Glass Corp. (Anderson, SC) 78672
Clark-Schwebel Fiberglas Corp. (Anderson, SC) 78673
Clark-Schwebel Fiberglass Corp. (Anderson, SC) 78674
Clavert Bank & Trust Co. (Chaneyville, MD) 71509
Clean Coal Research Center (Wilsonville, AL) 56705
Clean Coal Research Center Southern Co. Services Inc. (Wilsonville, AL) 56706
Clereon Corp. (Houston, TX) 85963
Cliffside Plant (Cliffside, NC) 74274
Clorox Co. (Forest Park, GA) 66232
Clorox Co. (Frederick, MD) 71717
Clorox Co. (Pearl, MS) 73276
Clorox Co. (Charlotte, NC) 73904
Clorox Co. Charlotte Plant (Charlotte, NC) 73905
Clorox Co. Dyersburg Plant (Dyersburg, TN) 80743
Clorox Co. Frederick Plant (Frederick, MD) 71718
Clorox Co. Household Products Co. (Houston, TX) 85964
Clorox Co. Houston Plant (Houston, TX) 85965
Clorox Co. Jackson Plant (Pearl, MS) 73277
Clorox Co. of Puerto Rico (Caguas, PR) 78356; 78357
Clorox Co., Tampa Plant (Tampa, FL) 63394
Cluett Hosiery Annedeen Hosiery Mill (Burlington, NC) 73752
CNG Producing Co. (New Orleans, LA) 70439
CNG Transmission Corp. (Clarksburg, WV) 92805
Coal-Mac, Inc. (Pikeville, KY) 69224
Coast to Coast (Brewton, AL) 55480
Coast to Coast (Cullman, AL) 55540
Coast to Coast (Arkadelphia, AR) 56716
Coast to Coast (Beebe, AR) 56767
Coast to Coast (Lonoke, AR) 57322
Coast to Coast (Mena, AR) 57363
Coast to Coast (Monticello, AR) 57371
Coast to Coast (Siloam Springs, AR) 57617
Coast to Coast (Lighthouse Point, FL) 60901
Coast to Coast (Covington, GA) 65725
Coast to Coast (Sterlington, LA) 70879
Coast to Coast (Baltimore, MD) 71089
Coast to Coast (Cushing, OK) 76977
Coast to Coast (Grove, OK) 77088
Coast to Coast (Hinton, OK) 77131
Coast to Coast (Lawton, OK) 77158
Coast to Coast (Pryor, OK) 77738
Coast to Coast (Yale, OK) 78275
Coast to Coast (Georgetown, SC) 79272
Coast to Coast (Rock Hill, SC) 79818
Coast to Coast (Covington, TN) 80683
Coast to Coast (Andrews, TX) 82594
Coast to Coast (Austin, TX) 82839
Coast to Coast (Borger, TX) 83316
Coast to Coast (Mineral Wells, TX) 88109
Coast to Coast (Whitesboro, TX) 90059
Coast to Coast Adj (Fort Worth, TX) 85083
Coast to Coast Adjusters (Dallas, TX) 83917
Coast to Coast Assoc Inc. (Winter Park, FL) 63966
Coast to Coast Auto (Butler, AL) 55494
Coast to Coast Auto (Alpine, TX) 82499
Coast to Coast Auto Sales (Pensacola, FL) 62415
Coast to Coast Bail Bond (New Port Richey, FL) 61680
Coast to Coast Bldg Maint (Corpus Chrsti, TX) 83767
Coast to Coast Builders (Punta Gorda, FL) 62702
Coast to Coast Cap Co. (Jacksonville, FL) 60245; 60246
Coast to Coast Car Sales (Pensacola, FL) 62416
Coast to Coast Carriers (Fort Pierce, FL) 59792
Coast to Coast Club (Oklahoma City, OK) 77337
Coast to Coast Coatings (Dothan, AL) 55634
Coast to Coast Collection (Maitland, FL) 60974
Coast to Coast Collection (Winter Park, FL) 63967
Coast to Coast Communications Inc. (Dania, FL) 59147
Coast to Coast Computers (Lawrenceville, GA) 66507
Coast to Coast Contractors (Pompano Beach, FL) 62592
Coast to Coast Corp. (Dallas, TX) 83918
Coast to Coast Cr Servs Inc. (Fort Lauderdale, FL) 59476
Coast to Coast Credit Servs (Fort Lauderdale, FL) 59477
Coast to Coast Engineering (Plain Dealing, LA) 70634
Coast to Coast Exc (Dallas, TX) 83919
Coast to Coast Express (Birmingham, AL) 55196
Coast to Coast Express (Montgomery, AL) 56294
Coast to Coast Express (Jacksonville, FL) 60247
Coast to Coast Express (Tampa, FL) 63395
Coast to Coast Express (Savannah, GA) 67459
Coast to Coast Express (Calhoun, LA) 69748
Coast to Coast Express (Gulfport, MS) 72850
Coast to Coast Express (Charlotte, NC) 73906
Coast to Coast Express (Fayetteville, NC) 74544
Coast to Coast Express (Greenville, SC) 79329
Coast to Coast Express (El Paso, TX) 84785
Coast to Coast Exteriors (Clearwater, FL) 58988
Coast to Coast Fence Co. (Fort Myers, FL) 59691
Coast to Coast Food (W Palm Beach, FL) 63785
Coast to Coast Hardware (Batesville, AR) 56742
Coast to Coast Hardware (Cynthiana, KY) 68248

Coast to Coast Hardware (Elizabethtown, KY) 68273
Coast to Coast Hardware (Frankfort, KY) 68359
Coast to Coast Hardware (Georgetown, KY) 68379; 68380
Coast to Coast Hardware (Leitchfield, KY) 68512
Coast to Coast Hardware (Maysville, KY) 69087
Coast to Coast Hardware (Murray, KY) 69122
Coast to Coast Hardware (Paris, KY) 69218
Coast to Coast Hardware (Whitesburg, KY) 69337
Coast to Coast Hardware (Winston Salem, NC) 76666
Coast to Coast Hardware (Ada, OK) 76784
Coast to Coast Hardware (Alva, OK) 76798
Coast to Coast Hardware (Church Hill, TN) 80529
Coast to Coast Hardware (Johnson City, TN) 81027
Coast to Coast Hardware (Mc Kenzie, TN) 81431
Coast to Coast Hardware (Mount Juliet, TN) 81821
Coast to Coast Hardware (Bedford, TX) 83240
Coast to Coast Hardware (Fort Worth, TX) 85084
Coast to Coast Home (Fort Gibson, OK) 77080
Coast to Coast Home (Liberty, TX) 87671
Coast to Coast Home & Aut (Centerville, TN) 80286
Coast to Coast Home & Auto (Carlisle, AR) 56843
Coast to Coast Home & Auto (Port Richey F, FL) 62684
Coast to Coast Home & Auto (Sandersville, GA) 67428
Coast to Coast Home & Auto (Oberlin, LA) 70602
Coast to Coast Home & Auto (Vidalia, LA) 70929
Coast to Coast Home & Auto (Indianola, MS) 72927
Coast to Coast Home & Auto (Cordell, OK) 76973
Coast to Coast Home & Auto (Lyles, TN) 81364
Coast to Coast Home & Auto (Hereford, TX) 85739
Coast to Coast Home&Auto (Alva, OK) 76799
Coast to Coast Imprinted Sp (San Antonio, TX) 88958
Coast to Coast Inc. Collision R (Peachtree, GA) 67229
Coast to Coast Investigative S (Atlanta, GA) 64366
Coast to Coast Investments (Elizabethtown, KY) 68274
Coast to Coast Janitor (Vero Beach, FL) 63746
Coast to Coast Janitor Service (Vero Beach, FL) 63747
Coast to Coast Limousine (Orlando, FL) 61952
Coast to Coast Lumber Co. Inc. (Louisville, KY) 68733
Coast to Coast of Monticell (Monticello, KY) 69098
Coast to Coast Mortgage Ser (Sarasota, FL) 62805
Coast to Coast Motel (Hinton, WV) 92862
Coast to Coast Pressure Clg (Fort Pierce, FL) 59793
Coast to Coast Real Estate (Jupiter, FL) 60533
Coast to Coast Realty (Punta Gorda, FL) 62703
Coast to Coast Realty & Inv (Ocala, FL) 61791
Coast to Coast Sales Inc. (Orlando, FL) 61953
Coast to Coast Seafood Inc. (Biloxi, MS) 72616
Coast to Coast Service Cent (Farmerville, LA) 69850
Coast to Coast Services (Biloxi, MS) 72617
Coast to Coast Sfd Sales Inc. (Miami, FL) 61264
Coast to Coast Shops (Pollok, TX) 88626
Coast to Coast Store (Mountain Home, AR) 57385
Coast to Coast Store (Fairview, OK) 77077
Coast to Coast Store (Perry, OK) 77701
Coast to Coast Store (Weatherford, OK) 78240
Coast to Coast Store (Mc Kinney, TX) 87909
Coast to Coast Suppliers Inc. (Rockledge, FL) 62743
Coast to Coast Tire & Wheel (Decatur, GA) 65809
Coast to Coast Total Hdwe (Vinita, OK) 78222
Coast to Coast Total Hdwe (Greeneville, TN) 80884
Coast to Coast Total Hdwe (Powell, TN) 82237
Coast to Coast Transmission (Tampa, FL) 63396
Coast to Coast Travel (Miami, FL) 61265
Coast to Coast Trucking Inc. (Searcy, AR) 57602
Coast to Coast Video (Jackson, MS) 72962
Coast to Coast Welding & Fa (Flatwoods, KY) 68306
Coast to Coast Yellow Pages (Alamo, TX) 82476
Coast to Coastsupply (Tishomingo, OK) 77869
Coast Federal Bank (Deland, FL) 59300
Coastal Bank of Georgia (Brunswick, GA) 65404; 65405; 65406
Coastal Bank of Georgia (Kings Bay, GA) 66465
Coastal Bank of Georgia (St. Mary's, GA) 67621
Coastal Bank of Georgia (St. Simons Island, GA) 67627; 67628
Coastal Catalyst Technology, Inc. (Houston, TX) 85966
Coastal Coal Sales, Inc. (Roanoke, VA) 92113
Coastal Corp. (Myrtle Beach, SC) 79696; 79697
Coastal Corp. (Houston, TX) 85967; **85968**
Coastal Dril, Inc. (Houston, TX) 85969
Coastal Finance Corp. (Houston, TX) 85970
Coastal Fuels Marketing, Inc. (Miami, FL) 61266; 61267
Coastal Gas Service Co. (Houston, TX) 85971
Coastal Holding Corp. (Houston, TX) 85972
Coastal Ltd. Ventures, Inc. (Houston, TX) 85973
Coastal Mart, Inc. (Houston, TX) 85974
Coastal Mobile Refining Co. (Chickasaw, AL) 55511
Coastal Multi-Fuels, Inc. (Houston, TX) 85975
Coastal Natural Gas Co. (Houston, TX) 85976
Coastal Oil & Gas Corp. (Houston, TX) 85977; 85978
Coastal Power Production Co. (Houston, TX) 85979
Coastal Power Production Co. (Roanoke, VA) 92114
Coastal Refining & Marketing Inc. (Corpus Christi, TX) 83711
Coastal Remediation Co. (Roanoke, VA) 92115
Coastal States Crude Gathering Co. (Corpus Christi, TX) 83712
Coastal States Gas Transmission Co. (Houston, TX) 85980; 85981
Coastal States Trading, Inc. (Houston, TX) 85982
Coastal Technology Inc. (Roanoke, VA) 92116; 92117
Coastal Unilube Inc. (West Memphis, AR) 57720; 57721; 57722; 57723
Coastal Unilube Inc. (Perryville, MD) 72215
Coastal Unilube Inc. (Charlotte, NC) 73907
Coated & Laminated Products (West Monroe, LA) 70944
Coca-Cola (Auburndale, FL) 58591
Coca-Cola (Atlanta, GA) **64367**
Coca Cola Bot Co. Laurens (Laurens, SC) 79589
Coca-Cola Botlg Co. (Amarillo, TX) 82540
Coca-Cola Botlg Co. (Odessa, TX) 88238
Coca-Cola Botting Co. of Bat (Baton Rouge, LA) 69500
Coca-Cola Botting Co. of Miami (Hollywood, FL) 60053
Coca-Cola Bottling (Atlanta, GA) 64368
Coca Cola Bottling Austin (Austin, TX) 82840
Coca-Cola Bottling Com Metro S (Atlanta, GA) 64369
Coca-Cola Bottling Com Metro S (College Park, GA) 65581
Coca-Cola Bottling Com Metro S (Decatur, GA) 65810
Coca-Cola Bottling Com Metro S (Lawrenceville, GA) 66508
Coca-Cola Bottling Co. (Andalusia, AL) 54985
Coca Cola Bottling Co. (Daleville, AL) 55561
Coca Cola Bottling Co. (Dothan, AL) 55635
Coca Cola Bottling Co. (Florence, AL) 55735
Coca Cola Bottling Co. (Sylacauga, AL) 56585
Coca Cola Bottling Co. (Batesville, AR) 56743
Coca Cola Bottling Co. (Camden, AR) 56828
Coca Cola Bottling Co. (Monticello, AR) 57372
Coca-Cola Bottling Co. of so (Pine Bluff, AR) 57512
Coca Cola Bottling Co. (Rogers, AR) 57561
Coca Cola Bottling Co. (Key West, FL) 60571
Coca Cola Bottling Co. (Leesburg, FL) 60880
Coca-Cola Bottling Co. (Ocala, FL) 61792
Coca Cola Bottling Co. (Pahokee, FL) 62221
Coca Cola Bottling Co. (Vero Beach, FL) 63748
Coca-Cola Bottling Co. the (Atlanta, GA) 64370; 64371; 64372
Coca-Cola Bottling Co. the (Austell, GA) 65351
Coca-Cola Bottling Co. (Sylvania, GA) 67766
Coca-Cola Bottling Co. (Warner Robins, GA) 68013
Coca Cola Bottling Co. (Jennings, LA) 69978
Coca Cola Bottling Co. (Lafayette, LA) 70050
Coca Cola Bottling Co. (Lake Charles, LA) 70137
Coca Cola Bottling Co. (Leesville, LA) 70189
Coca Cola Bottling Co. (Shreveport, LA) 70698
Coca Cola Bottling Co. (Winnsboro, LA) 70980
Coca Cola Bottling Co. (Asheville, NC) 73610
Coca Cola Bottling Co. (Bessemer City, NC) 73686
Coca Cola Bottling Co. (Goldsboro, NC) 74712
Coca Cola Bottling Co. (Greensboro, NC) 74800
Coca Cola Bottling Co. (Marion, NC) 75498
Coca-Cola Bottling Co. (Wesleyan College, NC) 76483
Coca-Cola Bottling Co. (Altus, OK) 76793
Coca Cola Bottling Co. (Guthrie, OK) 77096
Coca Cola Bottling Co. (Ripley, OK) 77767
Coca Cola Bottling Co. (Stillwater, OK) 77837
Coca-Cola Bottling Co. (Georgetown, SC) 79273
Coca Cola Bottling Co. (Lancaster, SC) 79570
Coca Cola Bottling Co. (Walterboro, SC) 80067
Coca Cola Bottling Co. (Amarillo, TX) 82541
Coca Cola Bottling Co. (Angleton, TX) 82609
Coca Cola Bottling Co. (Bryan, TX) 83394
Coca Cola Bottling Co. (Collinsville, TX) 83633
Coca Cola Bottling Co. (Conroe, TX) 83654
Coca Cola Bottling Co. (Cuero, TX) 83823
Coca Cola Bottling Co. (El Campo, TX) 84745
Coca Cola Bottling Co. (Fort Worth, TX) 85085; 85086
Coca Cola Bottling Co. (Jasper, TX) 87430
Coca Cola Bottling Co. (Longview, TX) 87709
Coca Cola Bottling Co. (Madisonville, TX) 87826
Coca Cola Bottling Co. (Midland, TX) 88030
Coca Cola Bottling Co. (Sweetwater, TX) 89582
Coca Cola Bottling Co. (Temple, TX) 89611
Coca Cola Bottling Co. (Tyler, TX) 89796
Coca Cola Bottling Co. (Victoria, TX) 89881; 89882
Coca-Cola Bottling Co. (Roanoke, VA) 92118
Coca Cola Bottling Co. of Ar (Morrilton, AR) 57376
Coca-Cola Bottling Co. of Arkansas (Little Rock, AR) 57265
Coca-Cola Bottling Co. of Arkansas (Morrilton, AR) 57377
Coca-Cola Bottling Co. Blue Grass (Louisville, KY) 68734
Coca-Cola Bottling Co. Bluegrass (Louisville, KY) 68735
Coca Cola Bottling Co. Conso (Gastonia, NC) 74672
Coca Cola Bottling Co. Conso (Statesville, NC) 76325
Coca Cola Bottling Co. Conso (South Boston, VA) 92246
Coca Cola Bottling Co. Consolidated (Mobile, AL) 56152
Coca-Cola Bottling Co. Consolidated (Charlotte, NC) 73908
Coca-Cola Bottling Co. Consolidated (Roanoke, VA) 92119
Coca Cola Bottling Co. of Fr (Frisco City, AL) 55769
Coca Cola Bottling Co. Inc. (Minden, LA) 70340
Coca Cola Bottling Co. Inc. (Lucedale, MS) 73127
Coca Cola Bottling Co. Inc. (Washington, NC) 76454
Coca Cola Bottling Co. Inc. (Pittsburg, TX) 88517
Coca-Cola Bottling Co. of Jackson Inc. (Jackson, TN) 80967
Coca-Cola Bottling Co. Johnston (Cleveland, TN) 80573
Coca-Cola Bottling Co. Louisiana Ltd. (New Orleans, LA) 70440
Coca-Cola Bottling Co. of Memphis (Memphis, TN) 81496
Coca-Cola Bottling Co. of Memphis Tennessee Inc. (Memphis, TN) 81497
Coca-Cola Bottling Co. of Miami (Hollywood, FL) 60054
Coca-Cola Bottling Co. of Miami Inc. (Hollywood, FL) 60055
Coca-Cola Bottling Co. Mid Atlantic (Alexandria, VA) 90167
Coca-Cola Bottling Co. N. Texas (Fort Worth, TX) 85087
Coca-Cola Bottling Co. of Nashville (Nashville, TN) 81924
Coca-Cola Bottling Co. of North Texas (Dallas, TX) 83920; 83921
Coca-Cola Bottling Co. of North Texas (Fort Worth, TX) 85088
Coca-Cola Bottling Co. Of Mobile Inc. (Mobile, AL) 56153
Coca-Cola Bottling Co. Of Nashville Inc. (Nashville, TN) 81925
Coca-Cola Bottling Co. Orlando (Orlando, FL) 61954
Coca-Cola Bottling Co. of Pl (Plainview, TX) 88528
Coca-Cola Bottling Co. of San Antonio (San Antonio, TX) 88959
Coca-Cola Bottling Co. of Sherveport (Shreveport, LA) 70699
Coca-Cola Bottling Co. of Shreveprot Inc. (Atlanta, GA) 64373
Coca-Cola Bottling Co. of South Arkansas (Monticello, AR) 57373
Coca-Cola Bottling Co. of Tu (Tulsa, OK) 77919
Coca Cola Bottling Co. Whse (Brownfield, TX) 83351
Coca-Cola Bottling Consol. (Charlotte, NC) **73909**
Coca-Cola Bottling of Miami Inc. (Hollywood, FL) 60056
Coca-Cola Co. (Atlanta, GA) 64374
Coca-Cola Enterprises (Atlanta, GA) **64375**
Coca-Cola Enterprises (Capital Heights, MD) 71500; 71501
Coca-Cola Enterprises (La Plata, MD) 72005
Coca-Cola Enterprises (Rockville, MD) 72261
Coca-Cola Enterprises Inc. (Atlanta, GA) 64376
Coca-Cola Financial Corp. (Atlanta, GA) 64377
Coca-Cola Foods (Auburndale, FL) 58592
Coca-Cola Foods (Leesburg, FL) 60881
Coca-Cola Foods (Houston, TX) 85983
Coca-Cola Foods Auburndale (Auburndale, FL) 58593
Coca-Cola Foods Auburndale Facility (Auburndale, FL) 58594
Coca-Cola Foods Food Service Group (Dunedin, FL) 59357
Coca-Cola Foods Foodservice Product Group (Dunedin, FL) 59358
Coca-Cola Foods Leesburg (Leesburg, FL) 60882
Coca-Cola Foods Plymouth (Plymouth, FL) 62572
Coca-Cola Foods Plymouth Chilled Juice (Plymouth, FL) 62573
Coca-Cola Foods Special Products Dept. (Plymouth, FL) 62574
Coca-Cola Plymouth (Plymouth, FL) 62575
Coca Cola U S a (Altamonte Spg, FL) 58536
Coca Cola U S a (Orlando, FL) 61955
Coca Cola U S a (Atlanta, GA) 64378
Coca-Cola U S a (New Orleans, LA) 70441
Coca Cola U S a (Dallas, TX) 83922
Coca Cola U S A (Dallas, TX) 83923
Coca Cola U S a Fnt Sales (Little Rock, AR) 57266
Coca Cola U S a Fountain Sl (Raleigh, NC) 75884
Coca-Cola USA (Atlanta, GA) 64379; 64380; 64381; 64382
Coca-Cola USA (Harahan, LA) 69936
Coca-Cola USA (Baltimore, MD) 71090
Coca-Cola USA (Dallas, TX) 83924
Coca Cola USA (Houston, TX) 85984
Coco Lopez Manufacturing (San Juan, PR) 78577
Cohutta Banking Co. (Chatsworth, GA) 65554; 65555
Cohutta Banking Co. (Chickamauga, GA) 65560
Cohutta Banking Co. (Eton, GA) 66171
Cohutta Banking Co. (La Fayette, GA) 66469
Cole Engineering (Gulfport, MS) 72851
Cole Engineering Corp. (Clearwater, FL) 58989
Coleman Co. (Lake City, SC) 79560
Coleman Co. (New Braunfels, TX) 88206
Colgate-Palmolive Co. (Bethune, SC) 78735
Colgate-Palmolive Co. Institutional Products Div. (Texarkana, TX) 89673
Collective Federal Savings Bank (Wilmington, DE) 58040
Collective Mortgage Service (Wilmington, DE) 58041
Collective Mortgage Service (Gainesville, FL) 59867
Collective Mortgage Service (Pensacola, FL) 62417
Collective Mortgage Service (Tampa, FL) 63397
Collective Mortgage Service (Winter Park, FL) 63968
Collier-Keyworth Co. (Liberty, NC) 75428; 75429
Collingwood Grain Inc. (Guymon, OK) 77101
Collins & Aiken Holding II Corp. (Charlotte, NC) 73910
Collins & Aikman (Charlotte, NC) 73911
Collins Aikman Corp. (Charlotte, NC) 73912
Collins & Aikman Corp. (Salisbury, NC) 76156
Collins & Aikman Corp. Auto Div. Clinton Plant (Clinton, OK) 76964
Collins & Aikman Corp. Cavel Div. (Roxboro, NC) 76122
Collins & Aikman Corp. Floor Covering Div. (Dalton, GA) 65774; 65775
Collins & Aikman Corp. Specialty Fabrics Div. (Farmville, NC) 74520
Collins & Aikman Corp. Albemarle Plant (Albemarle, NC) 73526; 73527
Collins & Aikman Corp. Old Fort Plant (Old Fort, NC) 75773
Collins & Aikman Group (Charlotte, NC) **73913**
Collins & Aikman Group, Inc. (Charlotte, NC) 73914
Collins & Aikman Holdings Corp. (Charlotte, NC) 73915
Collins General Aviation (Melbourne, FL) 61042; 61043; 61044
Collins International Service Co. (Herndon, VA) 91117
Colmbus Bank & Trust Co. (Columbus, GA) 65623
Colonial Baking Co. (Dallas, TX) 83925
Colonial Heights Packaging Inc. (Colonial Heights, VA) 90651
Colonial Pipeline (Anniston, AL) 54994

Colonial
American Business Locations Directory

Colonial Pipeline (Atlanta, GA) **64383**
Colonial Pipeline Atlanta Junc (Austell, GA) 65352
Colonial Pipeline Co. (Washington, DC) 58167
Colonial Pipeline Co. (Tallahassee, FL) 63226
Colonial Pipeline Co. (Bainbridge, GA) 65364
Colonial Pipeline Co. (Gaithrsbrg Md, MD) 71820
Colonial Pipeline Co. (Greensboro, NC) 74801
Colonial Pipeline Co. (Chattanooga, TN) 80340; 80341; 80342
Colonial Pipeline Co. (Nashville, TN) 81926
Colonial Pipeline Co. (Pasadena, TX) 88397
Colonial Pipeline Co. (Chesapeake, VA) 90563; 90564
Colonial Pipeline Co. (Richmond, VA) 91781
Colonial Pipeline Co. Chat (Atlanta, GA) 64384
Colonial Pipeline Co. Dacu (Dacula, GA) 65752
Colonial Pipeline Co. Dora (Doraville, GA) 65924
Colonial Pipeline Co. Hart (Atlanta, GA) 64385
Colonial Pipeline Co. Inc. (Atlanta, GA) 64386
Colonial Pipeline Co. Inc. (Richmond, VA) 91782
Colonial Pipeline Co. Main (Atlanta, GA) 64387
Colonial Pipeline Co. Main (Austell, GA) 65353
Colonial Pipeline Co. Main (Peachtree, GA) 67230
Colonial Pipeline Co. Smyr (Smyrna, GA) 67547
Colonial Pipeline Inc. (Collins, MS) 72694
Colonial Rubber Works Inc. (Kingstree, SC) 79553
Colonial Rubber Works Inc. (Dyersburg, TN) 80744; 80745
Colonial Sugars Inc. (Gramercy, LA) 69894; 69895; 69896; 69897
Colony Insurance Co. (Richmond, VA) 91783
Colony Insurance Co. Inc. (Glen Allen, VA) 90977
Color Response Inc. (Charlotte, NC) 73916; 73917
Color Response Inc. (Richmond, VA) 91784
Color-Tech Plant (Dalton, GA) 65776
Colt Industries Inc. Holley Automotive Div. (Water Valley, MS) 73466
Colt Industries Inc. Holley Replacement Parts Div. (Bowling Green, KY) 68135
Coltec Automotive Div. (Sallisaw, OK) 77768
Coltec Industries Delavan Commercial Products (Lexington, TN) 81335
Coltec Industries Menasco Aerospace (Euless, TX) 85008
Coltec Industries Stemco Truck Products (Longview, TX) 87710
Coltec Industries Inc. Holley Automotive Div. (Water Valley, MS) 73467
Columbia Atlantic Trading Corp. (Wilmington, DE) 58042
Columbia Coal Gasification Corp. (Ashland, KY) 68094
Columbia First Bank, A Federal Savings Bank (Washington, DC) 58168; 58169; 58170; 58171; 58172; 58173; 58174; 58175; 58176; 58177; 58178; 58179; 58180
Columbia First Bank, FSB (Alexandria, VA) 90168
Columbia First Bank, FSB (Annandale, VA) 90255
Columbia First Bank, FSB (Arlington, VA) **90284**
Columbia Gas Development Corp. (Houston, TX) 85985; 85986
Columbia Gas Dvlpmnt Corp. (Oklahoma City, OK) 77338
Columbia Gas System (Wilmington, DE) **58043**
Columbia Gas System Service Corp. (Wilmington, DE) 58044
Columbia Gas Transmission Corp. (Charleston, WV) 92738
Columbia Gulf Transmission Co. (Houston, TX) 85987
Columbia Healthcare Corp. (Louisville, KY) **68736**
Columbia LNG Corp. (Wilmington, DE) 58045
Columbia Mall (Columbia, SC) 79007
Columbia Natural Resources Inc. (Charleston, WV) 92739
Columbia 1st Bank FSB (Arlington, VA) 90285
Columbia Propane Corp. (Richmond, VA) 91785
Columbian Chemicals Co. (El Dorado, AR) 56927; 56928
Columbian Chemicals Co. (Atlanta, GA) 64388
Columbian Chemicals Co. (Centerville, LA) 69759
Columbian Chemicals Co. (Moundsville, WV) 92952
Columbian Chemicals Co. Inc. (Tulsa, OK) 77920
Columbus Bank & Trust (Columbus, GA) 65624
Columbus Bank & Trust Co. (Columbus, GA) 65625; 65626; 65627; 65628; 65629; 65630; 65631; 65632; 65633; 65634; 65635; 65636; 65637
Columbus Coca-Cola Bottling Inc. (Columbus, GA) 65638
Columbus Pulp & Paper Complex (Columbus, MS) 72707
Columbus Towel (Columbus, GA) 65639
Combustion Technologies Inc. (Flowery Branch, GA) 66217
Comdisco Resources Inc. (Tulsa, OK) 77921
Comerica Bank-Texas (Addison, TX) 82471
Comerica Bank-Texas (Arlington, TX) 82642; 82643
Comerica Bank-Texas (Austin, TX) 82841; 82842; 82843; 82844
Comerica Bank-Texas (Balch Springs, TX) 83085
Comerica Bank-Texas (Carrollton, TX) 83460
Comerica Bank-Texas (Cleveland, TX) 83591
Comerica Bank-Texas (Coppell, TX) 83690
Comerica Bank-Texas (Dallas, TX) 83926; 83927; 83928; 83929; 83930; 83931; 83932; 83933; 83934; 83935; 83936; 83937; 83938; 83939; 83940; 83941; 83942; 83943
Comerica Bank-Texas (De Soto, TX) 84532
Comerica Bank-Texas (Farmers Branch, TX) 85031; 85032
Comerica Bank-Texas (Fort Worth, TX) 85089; 85090
Comerica Bank-Texas (Frisco, TX) 85410
Comerica Bank-Texas (Houston, TX) 85988; 85989; 85990
Comerica Bank-Texas (Humble, TX) 87218
Comerica Bank-Texas (Irving, TX) 87334
Comerica Bank-Texas (Kingwood, TX) 87536
Comerica Bank-Texas (Lewisville, TX) 87648
Comerica Bank-Texas (Pflugerville, TX) 88506
Comerica Bank-Texas (Plano, TX) 88547
Comerica Bank-Texas (Richardson, TX) 88728; 88729; 88730
Comerica Bank-Texas (San Antoino, TX) 88908
Comerica Bank-Texas (San Antonio, TX) 88960; 88961
Comerica Bank-Texas (Sugar Land, TX) 89529
Comerica Bank-Texas (Waxahochie, TX) 90003
Comerica Bank & Trust, FSB (Baco Raton, FL) 58614
Comerica Bank & Trust, FSB (Clearwater, FL) 58990
Comerica Bank & Trust, FSB (Fort Lauderdale, FL) 59478
Comerica Bank Trust, FSB (Naples, FL) 61617
Comerica Bank & Trust, FSB (Palm Beach Gardens, FL) 62269
Comerica Trust Co. of Florid (Boca Raton, FL) 58692
Comm/Scope Inc. (Catawba, NC) 73806
Commerce Banc Corp. (Charleston, WV) 92740
Commerce Bank & Trust Co. of Troup County (La Grange, GA) 66473
Commercial Bank (Andalusia, AL) 54986
Commercial Bank (Roanoke, AL) 56499
Commercial Bank (Boston, GA) 65387
Commercial Bank (Bowdon, GA) 65388
Commercial Bank (Thomasville, GA) 67789; 67790; 67791; 67792
Commercial Bank (Donalds, SC) 79167
Commercial Bank & Trust Co. of Troup County (La Grange, GA) 66474; 66475; 66476
Commercial Metals (Dallas, TX) **83944; 83945**
Commercial National Bank (Shreveport, LA) 70700
Commercial National Bank in Shreveport (Shreveport, LA) 70701; 70702; 70703; 70704; 70705; 70706; 70707; 70708; 70709; 70710; 70711
Commonwealth Gas Services Inc. (Richmond, VA) 91786
Commonwealth Mortgage Assurance (Annandale, VA) 90256
Commonwealth Propane, Inc. (Richmond, VA) 91787
Commonwealth Tobacco Co. Inc. (Kenbridge, VA) 91175
Communications Inc. (Knoxville, TN) 81158
Community Bank & Trust National Association (Fairmont, WV) 92838
Community Bank & Trust of Randolph County (Elkins, WV) 92833
Community Bank & Trust of Ritchie County (Harrisville, WV) 92861
Compaq Computer (Houston, TX) **85991**
Compaq Computer Corp. (Washington, DC) 58181
Compaq Computer Corp. (Dunwoody, GA) 66106
Compaq Computer Corp. (Dallas, TX) 83946
Compaq Computer Corp. (Houston, TX) 85992; 85993; 85994; 85995
Compass Bancshares (Birmingham, AL) **55197**
Compass Bank (Birmingham, AL) 55198; 55199; 55200; 55201; 55202; 55203; 55204; 55205; 55206; 55207
Compass Bank (Huntsville, AL) 55901; 55902; 55903; 55904; 55905; 55906
Compass Bank (Crosby, TX) 83805
Compass Bank (Dallas, TX) 83947
Compass Bank (Houston, TX) 85996
Compass Bank (Richardson, TX) 88731
Compass Bank-Dallas (Carrollton, TX) 83461; 83462; 83463
Compass Bank-Dallas (Dallas, TX) 83948; 83949; 83950; 83951; 83952; 83953; 83954; 83955
Compass Bank-Dallas (Frisco, TX) 85411
Compass Bank-Dallas (Irving, TX) 87335
Compass Bank-Dallas (Mertzon, TX) 87954
Compass Bank-Dallas (Plano, TX) 88548; 88549; 88550; 88551; 88552; 88553; 88554; 88555
Compass Bank-Dallas (Richardson, TX) 88732
Compass Bank-Houston (Crosley, TX) 83810
Compass Bank-Houston (Houston, TX) 85997; 85998; 85999; 86000; 86001; 86002; 86003; 86004; 86005; 86006
Compass Bank-Houston (Kingwood, TX) 87537
Compass Bank-Houston (Spring, TX) 89464
Compass Bank-Houston (Sugar Land, TX) 89530
Compass Bank Na (Houston, TX) 86007; 86008; 86009
Complete Leasing Concepts, Inc. (Cherryville, NC) 74245
Composite Technologies Inc. (Fort Worth, TX) 85091
Composite Technology Polycel Div. (Fort Worth, TX) 85092
Composite Technology Inc. Conn (Fort Worth, TX) 85093
Compressor Components (Odessa, TX) 88239
Compressor Components Textron Inc. (Thomasville, GA) 67793
Computer Assoc (Sanford, FL) 62765
Computer Associates (Fayette, AL) 55730
Computer Associates (Dallas, TX) 83956
Computer Associates (Irving, TX) 87336
Computer Associates Inc. (Marietta, GA) 66764
Computer Associates Inc. (Greenville, SC) 79330; 79331
Computer Assocs (Austin, TX) 82845
Computer Sciences Applied Technology (Falls Church, VA) 90823
Computer Sciences Business Development (Falls Church, VA) 90824
Computer Sciences Health & Administrative Services (Lanham, MD) 72050
Computer Sciences Network Integration (Herndon, VA) 91118
Computer Sciences System Sciences (Falls Church, VA) 90825
Computer Sciences Technology Management (Falls Church, VA) 90826
Con-Way Intermodal Inc. (Fort Worth, TX) 85094
Con-Way Southern Express Inc. (Charlotte, NC) 73918
Con-Way Southwest Express Inc. (Fort Worth, TX) 85095
Conagra Delmarva Div. (Milford, DE) 57841
Conagra Delmarva Div. (Queenstown, MD) 72244
Conagra Broiler (El Dorado, AR) 56929
ConAgra Broiler Co. (Athens, AL) 55036
Conagra Broiler Co. (Enterprise, AL) 55681
Conagra Broiler Co. (El Dorado, AR) 56930; 56931; 56932; 56933
Conagra Broiler Co. (Dalton, GA) 65777
Conagra Broiler Co. (Gainesville, GA) 66270; 66271
Conagra Broiler Co. (Arcadia, LA) 69426
Conagra Broiler Co. (Farmerville, LA) 69851
Conagra Broiler Co. (Many, LA) 70219
Conagra Broiler Co. (Natchitoches, LA) 70400
Conagra Broiler Co. Arcadia Div. (Arcadia, LA) 69427
Conagra Broiler Co. Arcadia Feedmill (Arcadia, LA) 69428
Conagra Broiler Co. Feed Mill (Hurlock, MD) 71949
Conagra Broiler Co. Feedmill (Choudrant, LA) 69777; 69778
Conagra Broiler Co. Hurlock Processing Plant (Hurlock, MD) 71950
Conagra Broiler Co. Milford Processing Plant (Milford, DE) 57842
ConAgra Feed Co. (Augusta, GA) 65317
Conagra Feed Mill (Enterprise, AL) 55682
Conagra Feed Mill (Tunnel Hill, GA) 67910
ConAgra Fertilizer Co. (Knoxville, TN) 81159
Conagra Flour Mill (Macon, GA) 66681
Conagra Foodservice Companies (Birmingham, AL) 55208
Conagra Frozen Foods (Atkins, AR) 56732
ConAgra Frozen Foods (Batesville, AR) 56744
ConAgra Frozen Foods (Russellville, AR) 57579
ConAgra Frozen Foods (Atlanta, GA) 64389
ConAgra Frozen Foods (Crozet, VA) 90671
Conagra Frozen Foods Cooking Plant (Batesville, AR) 56745; 56746
Conagra Frozen Foods Feed Mill (Batesville, AR) 56747
Conagra Frozen Foods Feedmill (Batesville, AR) 56748
Conagra Frozen Foods Processing Plant (Batesville, AR) 56749
ConAgra Latin America (Miami, FL) 61268
Conagra Pet Products Co. (Richmond, VA) 91788
ConAgra Poultry Co. (El Dorado, AR) 56934; 56935
Conagra Poultry Co. (Dalton, GA) 65778
Conagra Poultry Co. (Gainesville, GA) 66272
ConAgra Shrimp Co./Singleton Seafood Co. (Tampa, FL) 63398
Conangra Poultry Co. (Dalton, GA) 65779
Concentrate Mfg. Co. Inc. (Cidra, PR) 78397
Conductor Products Inc. (Scottsville, TX) 89354
Cone Mills (Greensboro, NC) **74802**
Cone Mills Prelude Co. (Thomasville, NC) 76375
Cone Mills Corp. (Greensboro, NC) 74803
Cone Mills Corp. Cliffside Plant (Cliffside, NC) 74275
Cone Mills Corp. Granite Finishing Plant (Haw River, NC) 75012
Cone Mills Corp. Granite Plant (Haw River, NC) 75013
Cone Mills Corp. Salisbury Plant (Salisbury, NC) 76157
Cone Mills Corp. White Oak Plant (Greensboro, NC) 74804
Congen Properties Inc. (Wilmington, DE) 58046
Congress Financial Corp. (Atlanta, GA) 64390
Congress Financial Corp. (Dallas, TX) 83957
Conitron (Trinity, NC) 76406
Conitron Chemical Chair (Trinity, NC) 76407
Conoco In. (Ponca City, OK) 77703
Conoco Inc. (Westlake, LA) 70963
Conoco Inc. (Mertzon, TX) 87955
Conover Inc. Southern Furniture Co. Main Pl (Conover, NC) 74328
Conover Inc. Southern Furniture Co.-Plant 2 (Conover, NC) 74329
Consolidated Diesel Co. (Whitakers, NC) 76490; 76491
Consolidated Papers Inc. (Atlanta, GA) 64391
Constar International Inc. (Atlanta, GA) 64392
Constellation Energy (Baltimore, MD) 71091
Constellation Energy Inc. (Baltimore, MD) 71092
Constellation Health Service, Inc. (Baltimore, MD) 71093
Constellation Health Services (Baltimore, MD) 71094
Constellation Holding Inc. (Baltimore, MD) 71095
Constellation Holdings Inc. (Baltimore, MD) 71096; 71097
Constellation Investments (Baltimore, MD) 71098
Constellation Investments, Inc. (Baltimore, MD) 71099; 71100
Constellation Real Estate Group (Baltimore, MD) 71101
Constellation Real Estate Group, Inc. (Baltimore, MD) 71102; 71103
Constellation Real Estate Inc. (Columbia, MD) 71581
Container Corp. of America (Stone Mountain, GA) 67688
Contel Cellular Communications Inc. (Atlanta, GA) 64393
Continental Airlines (Houston, TX) **86010**
Continental Airlines Inc. (Houston, TX) 86011
Continental Bank (Atlanta, GA) 64394
Continental Bank (Harvey, LA) 69939
Continental Bank (Metairie, LA) 70257
Continental Banking Co. (Rockville, MD) 72262
Continental Express (Baltimore, MD) 71104
Continental Express (Gulfport, MS) 72852
Continental Express (Nederland, TX) 88184
Continental Express Airline (Sarasota, FL) 62806
Continental Express Inc. (Little Rock, AR) 57267
Continental Group Inc. (Birmingham, AL) 55209
Continental Group Inc. (Olive Branch, MS) 73226
Continental Group Inc. (Houston, TX) 86012
Continental Illinois Trust Co. of Florida, NA (Boca Raton, FL) 58693
Continental Illinois Trust Co. of Florida, NA (Sarasota, FL) 62807
Continental Ind Inc. (Houston, TX) 86013
Continental Indus Inc. (Winter Park, FL) 63969
Continental Industries (Broken Arrow, OK) 76880
Continental Industries Inc. (Orlando, FL) 61956
Continental Industries Inc. (Winter Park, FL) 63970
Continental Industries Inc. (Conyers, GA) 65677
Continental Industries Inc. (Broken Arrow, OK) 76881

Crown Cork & Seal Co. Inc. (Arlington, TX) 82644
Crown Cork & Seal Co., Inc. (Conroe, TX) 83655
Crown Cork & Seal Co. Inc. (Winchester, VA) 92582
Crown Cork & Seal Co. Inc. Metals Div. (Plymouth, FL) 62576
Crown Cork & Seal Co. Inc. Winter Garden Can Div. (Winter Garden, FL) 63920
Crown Cork & Seal Co. Inc. (Batesville, MS) 72596
Crown Metro Aerospace (Greenville, SC) 79333
Crown of Texas Hospice (Conroe, TX) 83656
Crown of Texas Hospice (Hereford, TX) 85740
Cryovac North America (Duncan, SC) 79171
Csc Credit Service (Metairie, LA) 70259
Csc Credit Services (Sandy Springs, GA) 67435
CSC Credit Services (Houston, TX) 86020; 86021; 86022
Csc Credit Svcs (Norman, OK) 77250
CSC Industry Services Group (Houston, TX) 86023
CSC Intelicom (Bethesda, MD) 71384
Csc Intelicom (Betheseda, MD) 71451
CSC Logic Inc. (Dallas, TX) 83960; 83961
CSC Systems Group (Falls Church, VA) 90829
CSF Holdings (Miami, FL) **61270**
CSF Holdings, Inc. (Miami, FL) 61271
CSW Credit, Inc. (Dallas, TX) 83962
CSW Energy, Inc. (Dallas, TX) 83963
CSW Leasing, Inc. (Dallas, TX) 83964
CSX Corp. (Richmond, VA) 91835; **91836**; 91837
CSX Intermodal Inc. (Hunt Valley, MD) 71926; 71927
CSX Realty Inc. (Richmond, VA) 91838
CSX Technology Inc. (Jacksonville, FL) 60248
CSX Transportation Inc. (Jacksonville, FL) 60249
Ctx Mortgage Co. (Rockville, MD) 72266
CTX Mortgage Co. (Dallas, TX) 83965
Culp Smelting & Refining Co. (Steele, AL) 56571
Cumberland City Bank (Cumberland, TN) 80707
Cumberland City Bank (Cumberland City, TN) 80708
Cumberland City Bank (Tennessee Ridge, TN) 82369
Cummins Engine Co. Inc. (Charleston, SC) 78798; 78799; 78800
Cummins Military Systems (Augusta, GA) 65318
Cummins Military Systems Co. (Augusta, GA) 65319
Custom Resins (Henderson, KY) 68441
Customized Transportation Inc. (Jacksonville, FL) 60250
Cutter Biological (Jackson, MS) 72963
Cyanamid Agricultural De Puerto Rico Inc. (Manati, PR) 78494; 78495; 78496
Cynamid Agricultural De Puerto Rico Inc. (Manati, PR) 78497
Cyprus Foote Mineral Co. (Kings Mountain, NC) 75295; 75296
Cyprus Foote Mineral Co. (New Johnsonville, TN) 82150
Cyprus Foote Mineral Co. (Duffield, VA) 90730
Cyprus Minerals (Houston, TX) 86024
Cyprus Mines Corp. (Gleason, TN) 80860
Cyprus Mountain Coals Corp. (Hazard, KY) 68424

D

D (Columbia, MD) 71582
D-Graphics Inc. (Jacksonville, FL) 60251
D. H. Compounding Co. (Clinton, TN) 80611
D Magazine (Dallas, TX) 83966
D & S Plastics International (Grand Prairie, TX) 85615; 85616
Dal-Tex Coal Co. (Sharples, WV) 93042
Dale Electronics Inc. (El Paso, TX) 84786
Dalton Plant (Dalton, GA) 65780
Dan-Co Bakery (Forest Park, GA) 66233
Dana Corp. (Montgomery, AL) 56295
Dana Corp. (Jonesboro, AR) 57211
Dana Corp. (Sarasota, FL) 62808
Dana Corp. (Hopkinsville, KY) 68476
Dana Corp. (Olive Branch, MS) 73227
Dana Corp. (Morganton, NC) 75634
Dana Corp. (Oklahoma City, OK) 77341; 77342
Dana Corp. (Dillon, SC) 79159
Dana Corp. (Gordonsville, TN) 80873
Dana Corp. (Lancaster, TX) 87597
Dana Corp. (Wichita Fall, TX) 90062
Dana Corp. Arab Hydraulic Plant (Arab, AL) 55019
Dana Corp. Boston Industrial Products Div. (Paragould, AR) 57490
Dana Corp. Boston Industrial Products Div. (Hohenwald, TN) 80942
Dana Corp. Boston Industrial Products Division (Brentwood, TN) 80224
Dana Corp. Corinth Plant (Corinth, MS) 72737
Dana Corp. Mobile Fluid (Greenville, SC) 79334
Dana Corp. Mobile Fluid Controls Div. (Sarasota, FL) 62809; 62810
Dana Corp. Mobile Fluid Products (Greenville, SC) 79335
Dana Corp. Mobile Fluid Products Div. (Corinth, MS) 72738
Dana Corp. Mobile Fluid Products Div. (Lancaster, TX) 87598
Dana Corp. Mobile Fluid Products Division (Greenville, SC) 79336
Dana Corp. Spicer Systems Assembly Div. (Lugoff, SC) 79617
Dana Corp. Spicer Transmission (Knoxville, TN) 81160
Dana Corp. Spicer Transmission Div. (Jonesboro, AR) 57212
Dana Corp. Spicer Transmission Div. Gear Plant (Jonesboro, AR) 57213
Dana Corp. Spicer Transmission Div. Jonesboro Gear Plant (Jonesboro, AR) 57214
Dana Corp. Spicer Universal (Charlotte, NC) 73922
Dana Corp. Spicer Universal Joint Div. (Bristol, VA) 90471
Dana Corp. Victor Products Div. (Danville, KY) 68254
Dana Corp. Weatherhead Div. (Vinita, OK) 78223
Dana Corp. Weatherhead Division (Kennesaw, GA) 66412
Dana Corp. Arab Hydraulics (Arab, AL) 55020; 55021
Dana Corp. Arab Hydraulics Plant (Arab, AL) 55022
Dana Corp. Camshaft Plant (Russellville, AR) 57580
Dana Corp., Spicer Trailer Axle Plant (Montgomery, AL) 56296
Dana Corp. Wix Corp. (Dillon, SC) 79160
Danaher Controls (Elizabethtown, NC) 74488
Danaher Corp. (Washington, DC) 58209; **58210**
Danaher Tool Group (Springdale, AR) 57628
Danaher Tool Group (Hanover, MD) 71909
Danaher Tool Group (Gastonia, NC) 74673
Danaher Tool Group Fayetteville Ar. Operation (Fayetteville, AR) 56974
Daniel Radiator Corp. (West Palm Beach, FL) 63854
Daniel Radiator Corp. (Atlanta, GA) 64402
Daniel Radiator Corp. (La Grange, GA) 66477
Daniel Radiator Corp. (Lexington, TN) 81336
Daniel Radiator Corp. (Houston, TX) 86025
Daniels Packaging Co. Inc. (Hendersonville, NC) 75032
DAP Inc. (Conyers, GA) 65678
Dap Inc. (Baltimore, MD) 71109
Dap Inc. (Dallas, TX) 83967
Data General Co. (Norcross, GA) 67110
Data General Corp. (Apex, NC) 73554; 73555
Data General Corp. (Clayton, NC) 74260; 74261; 74262; 74263
Data General Corp. (Raleigh, NC) 75885
Data General Corp. (Research Triangle Park, NC) 76018
Data General Puerto Rico Inc. (Hato Rey, PR) 78454
Data-Tronics Corp. (Fort Smith, AR) 57044; 57045; 57046
Datamyte Corp. (Lawrenceville, GA) 66509
DataServe (Louisville, KY) 68739
Dataserve Inc. (Killeen, TX) 87509
Dauphin Investment Co. (Wilmington, DE) 58048
Davenport Data Processors, Inc. (Dallas, TX) 83968
Davidson Exterior Trim Textron (Americus, GA) 64137; 64138
Davidson Interior Trim Textron (Athens, TN) 80186
Davies Can Co. (Fairdale, KY) 68300
Davis & Geck, Inc. (Manati, PR) 78498
Day-Brite Lighting Inc. (Tupelo, MS) 73395
Day International (Arden, NC) 73565
Day International Inc. (Arden, NC) 73566
Day International Textiles Products (Greenville, SC) 79337
Dayco Prods. Inc. (Waynesville, NC) 76463
Dayco Prods. Inc. (Walterboro, SC) 80068
Dayco Prods. Inc. (Williston, SC) 80125
Dayco Products Inc. (Ocala, FL) 61793
Dayco Products Inc. (Waynesville, NC) 76464
Dayco Products Inc. (Walterboro, SC) 80069
Dayco Products Inc. (Williston, SC) 80126
Dean Foods Co. (Louisville, KY) 68740
Dean Foods Co. (Memphis, TN) 81501
Dean Foods Co. (Richmond, VA) 91839
Dean Foods Co. (Sandston, VA) 92230
Dean Foods Vegetable Co. (Uvalde, TX) 89849
Dean Milk Co. (Louisville, KY) 68741
Dean Sausage Co. (Attalla, AL) 55054
Dean Witter Reynolds Inc. (Louisville, KY) 68742
Dean Witter Reynolds Inc. (Chattanooga, TN) 80346
Dean Witter Reynolds Inc. (Jackson, TN) 80968
Dean Witter Reynolds Inc. (Madison, TN) 81372
Dean Witter Reynolds Inc. (Memphis, TN) 81502; 81503; 81504; 81505
Dean Witter Reynolds Inc. (Nashville, TN) 81928
Dean Witter Reynolds Inc. (Charleston, WV) 92741; 92742
Dearborn Brass (Tyler, TX) 89797; 89798
Dearborn Brass East Texas Ctr. (Tyler, TX) 89799
Decatur Aluminum Co. (Decatur, AL) 55577
Decker Food Co. (San Antonio, TX) 88964
Decorp (Dallas, TX) 83969
Deer Park Spring Water Co., Inc. (Destin, FL) 59342
Deer Park Spring Water Inc. (Frederick, MD) 71719
DeKalb Country Bank & Trust Co. (Alexandria, TN) 80158; 80159
DeKalb Country Bank & Trust Co. (Celina, TN) 80281
Dekalb County Bank & Trust Co. (Alexandria, TN) 80160
DeKalb County Bank & Trust Co. (Dowelltown, TN) 80740
DeKalb County Bank & Trust Co. (Smithville, TN) 82324
Del Monte Corp. (Cambridge, MD) 71485
Del Monte Corp. (Columbia, MD) 71583
Del Monte Corp. (Crystal City, TX) 83817
Del Monte Foods Plant No. 250 (Crystal City, TX) 83818
Del Monte Foods Atlanta Sales (Tucker, GA) 67849
Del Monte Foods Midsouth Sales (Tucker, GA) 67850
Del Monte Foods Plants (Crystal City, TX) 83819
Del Monte Foods Plants 250 & 255 (Crystal City, TX) 83820
Del Monte Foods Southeast Regi (Tucker, GA) 67851
Delaware American Life Insurance Co. (Wilmington, DE) 58049; 58050
Delfield Co. (Covington, TN) 80684
Delight Prods. Co. (Springfield, TN) 82355
Dell Computer (Austin, TX) **82846**
Dell Computer Corp. (Austin, TX) 82847
Dell Computer Corp. (Dallas, TX) 83970
Dell Computer USA Corp. (Austin, TX) 82848
Dell Direct Sales L.P. (Austin, TX) 82849
Dell International Inc. (Austin, TX) 82850
Dell Marketing Corp. (Austin, TX) 82851; 82852
Dell Marketing LP (Austin, TX) 82853
Dell Products LP. (Austin, TX) 82854
Dell U S A (Austin, TX) 82855
Delmarva Properties, Inc. (West Point, VA) 92541
Delphax Systems (Baltimore, MD) 71110
Delta Air Cargo (Fort Myers, FL) 59692
Delta Air Cargo (Jacksonville, FL) 60252
Delta Air Cargo (Melbourne, FL) 61045
Delta Air Cargo (Tallahassee, FL) 63227
Delta Air Cargo (Atlanta, GA) 64403
Delta Air Cargo (Baton Rouge, LA) 69501
Delta Air Cargo (Charleston, SC) 78801
Delta Air Cargo (Greenville, SC) 79338
Delta Air Cargo (El Paso, TX) 84787
Delta Air Freight (Daytona Beach, FL) 59170
Delta Air Freight (Charlotte, NC) 73923
Delta Air Lines (Birmingham, AL) 55211; 55212; 55213; 55214
Delta Air Lines (Montgomery, AL) 56297; 56298
Delta Air Lines (Ozark, AL) 56442
Delta Air Lines (Little Rock, AR) 57268; 57269; 57270
Delta Air Lines (Hartly, DE) 57821
Delta Air Lines (Washington, DC) 58211
Delta Air Lines (Brandon, FL) 58868
Delta Air Lines (Daytona Beach, FL) 59171; 59172
Delta Air Lines (Fort Lauderdale, FL) 59479
Delta Air Lines (Fort Myers, FL) 59693; 59694
Delta Air Lines (Jacksonville, FL) 60253; 60254; 60255
Delta Air Lines (Melbourne, FL) 61046
Delta Air Lines (Miami, FL) 61272; 61273; 61274
Delta Air Lines (Mount Dora, FL) 61563
Delta Air Lines (Orange City, FL) 61870
Delta Air Lines (Orlando, FL) 61959
Delta Air Lines (Pensacola, FL) 62418
Delta Air Lines (Sarasota, FL) 62811
Delta Air Lines (St Petersburg, FL) 62969
Delta Air Lines (Tallahassee, FL) 63228; 63229; 63230; 63231
Delta Air Lines (Tampa, FL) 63399; 63400; 63401
Delta Air Lines (W Palm Beach, FL) 63786; 63787
Delta Air Lines (West Palm Beach, FL) 63855
Delta Air Lines (Atlanta, GA) 64404; 64405; 64406; 64407; 64408; 64409; 64410
Delta Air Lines (Dallas, GA) 65758
Delta Air Lines (Decatur, GA) 65811
Delta Air Lines (Duluth, GA) 66031
Delta Air Lines (Dunwoody, GA) 66107
Delta Air Lines (Lawrenceville, GA) 66510
Delta Air Lines (Macon, GA) 66682
Delta Air Lines (Savannah, GA) 67460; 67461; 67462
Delta Air Lines (Suwanee, GA) 67743
Delta Air Lines (Lexington, KY) 68541; 68542; 68543
Delta Air Lines (Louisville, KY) 68743; 68744; 68745; 68746
Delta Air Lines (Baton Rouge, LA) 69502; 69503; 69504
Delta Air Lines (New Orleans, LA) 70442
Delta Air Lines (Shreveport, LA) 70712; 70713; 70714
Delta Air Lines (Kensington, MD) 71993
Delta Air Lines (Jackson, MS) 72964; 72965; 72966
Delta Air Lines (Charlotte, NC) 73924
Delta Air Lines (Greensboro, NC) 74807; 74808
Delta Air Lines (Oklahoma City, OK) 77343; 77344
Delta Air Lines (Tulsa, OK) 77926; 77927
Delta Air Lines (Charleston, SC) 78802; 78803; 78804
Delta Air Lines (Columbia, SC) 79008
Delta Air Lines (Greenville, SC) 79339
Delta Air Lines (Greer, SC) 79472
Delta Air Lines (West Columbia, SC) 80088
Delta Air Lines (Chattanooga, TN) 80347; 80348; 80349
Delta Air Lines (Knoxville, TN) 81161
Delta Air Lines (Memphis, TN) 81506; 81507
Delta Air Lines (Nashville, TN) 81929
Delta Air Lines (Austin, TX) 82856
Delta Air Lines (Dallas, TX) 83971; 83972
Delta Air Lines (El Paso, TX) 84788
Delta Air Lines (Fort Worth, TX) 85096; 85097
Delta Air Lines (Houston, TX) 86026; 86027; 86028; 86029; 86030
Delta Air Lines (Hurst, TX) 87272
Delta Air Lines (Lubbock, TX) 87754
Delta Air Lines (San Antonio, TX) 88965; 88966; 88967
Delta Air Lines Air Cargo (Louisville, KY) 68747
Delta Air Lines Credit Union (Atlanta, GA) 64411
Delta Air Lines Inc. (Birmingham, AL) 55215
Delta Air Lines, Inc. (Montgomery, AL) 56299; 56300
Delta Air Lines Inc. (Ozark, AL) 56443
Delta Air Lines Inc. (Little Rock, AR) 57271
Delta Air Lines Inc. (Fort Lauderdale, FL) 59480
Delta Air Lines Inc. (Jacksonville, FL) 60256
Delta Air Lines Inc. (Melbourne, FL) 61047
Delta Air Lines Inc. (Miami, FL) 61275; 61276
Delta Air Lines Inc. (St Petersburg, FL) 62970
Delta Air Lines Inc. (Tallahassee, FL) 63232
Delta Air Lines Inc. (Tampa, FL) 63402
Delta Air Lines Inc. (W Palm Beach, FL) 63788
Delta Air Lines, Inc. (Atlanta, GA) **64412**
Delta Air Lines, Inc. (Duluth, GA) 66032
Delta Air Lines Inc. (Macon, GA) 66683
Delta Air Lines Inc. (Savannah, GA) 67463; 67464; 67465
Delta Air Lines Inc. (Lexington, KY) 68544; 68545
Delta Air Lines Inc. (Louisville, KY) 68748; 68749; 68750
Delta Air Lines Inc. (Baton Rouge, LA) 69505; 69506
Delta Air Lines Inc. (Shreveport, LA) 70715; 70716
Delta Air Lines Inc. (Glen Burnie, MD) 71838
Delta Air Lines Inc. (Linthicum Heights, MD) 72107; 72108
Delta Air Lines Inc. (Rockville, MD) 72267
Delta Air Lines Inc. (Jackson, MS) 72967
Delta Air Lines, Inc. (Charlotte, NC) 73925
Delta Air Lines Inc. (Greensboro, NC) 74809
Delta Air Lines Inc. (Charleston, SC) 78805; 78806
Delta Air Lines, Inc. (Columbia, SC) 79009

Dr. T.C. Smith Co. (Asheville, NC) 73611
Dole Foods of America (Houston, TX) 86044
Dole Fresh Fruit Co. (Marietta, GA) 66767
Dollar Rent-A-Car Systems Inc. (Tulsa, OK) 77932
Dolphin Construction (Dallas, TX) 83981
Dolphin Construction Co. (Melbourne, FL) 61051
Dolphin Construction Co. (Alexandria, LA) 69373; 69374
Dolphin Construction Co. (Pineville, LA) 70615
Dolphin Construction Co. Inc. (Melbourne, FL) 61052
Dominion Bankshare Corp. (Roanoke, VA) 92136
Dominion Capital Inc. (Richmond, VA) 91845; 91846
Dominion Energy Inc. (Richmond, VA) 91847; 91848
Dominion Energy Services Co. (Richmond, VA) 91849
Dominion Financing Inc. (Richmond, VA) 91850
Dominion Lands Inc. (Richmond, VA) 91851; 91852; 91853
Dominion Resources (Richmond, VA) 91854; **91855**
Dominion Resources Inc. (Richmond, VA) 91856; 91857; 91858
Dominion Resources Inc. VA (Richmond, VA) 91859
Donnelley Directory (Maitland, FL) 60976
Donnelley Directory (Tallahassee, FL) 63235
Donnelley Directory (Elm City, NC) 74502
Donnelley Printing Co. (Gallatin, TN) 80839
Donnelley Publishing (Houston, TX) 86045
R.R. Donnelley & Sons Co. Danville Manufacturing Div. (Danville, KY) 68255; 68256
R.R. Donnelley & Sons Co. Gallatin Manufacturing Div. (Gallatin, TN) 80840
R.R. Donnelley & Sons Co. Glasgow Manufacturing Div. (Glasgow, KY) 68391
R.R. Donnelley & Sons Co. Harrisonburg Manufacturing Div. (Harrisonburg, VA) 91075; 91076
R.R. Donnelley & Sons Co. Kentucky E. Manufacturing Div. (Danville, KY) 68257
R.R. Donnelley & Sons Co. Kentucky W. Div. (Glasgow, KY) 68392
Donzi Marine (Sarasota, FL) 62812; 62813
Donzi Marine (Tallevast, FL) 63291
Donzi Marine Inc. (Fort Lauderdale, FL) 59481
Doskocil (Oklahoma City, OK) **77347**
Douglas/Quikut (Walnut Ridge, AR) 57706
Douglas/Quikut (Germantown, TN) 80855
Dover Corp. Heil Bulk Trailer Div. (Athens, TN) 80187
Dover Elevator Co. (Louisville, KY) 68755
Dover Elevator Co. (Walnut, MS) 73465
Dover Elevator Co. (Charlotte, NC) 73932
Dover Elevator Co. (Greensboro, NC) 74812
Dover Elevator Co. (Raleigh, NC) 75887
Dover Elevator Co. (Knoxville, TN) 81165
Dover Elevator Co. (Middleton, TN) 81764
Dover Elevator Co. (Norfolk, VA) 91514
Dover Elevator International Inc. (Horn Lake, MS) 72913
Dover Elevator International Inc. (Memphis, TN) 81513
Dover Elevator Systems Inc. (Horn Lake, MS) 72914
Dow Chemical Co. (Magnolia, AR) 57329
Dow Chemical Co. (Russellville, AR) 57581
Dow Chemical Co. (Freeport, TX) 85379
Dow Chemical Co. (La Porte, TX) 87555
Dow Chemical Co. Engineering & Construction Services Division (Houston, TX) 86046
Dow Chemical Co. Louisiana Div. (Plaquemine, LA) 70637
Dow Chemical Co. Louisiana Division (Plaguemine, LA) 70633
Dow Chemical Co. Texas Division (Freeport, TX) 85380
Dow Chemical Co. Grand Bayou Plant (Paincourtville, LA) 70606; 70607
Dow Chemical Co. La Porte Plant (La Porte, TX) 87556
Dow Chemical Co. La Porte Site (La Porte, TX) 87557
Dow Chemical Co. Texas Operations (Freeport, TX) 85381; 85382
Dow Chemical Co. USA (Russellville, AR) 57582
Dow Chemical Dalton Site (Dalton, GA) 65781; 65782
Dow Chemical Grand Bayou Plant (Paincourtville, LA) 70608
Dow Chemical USA (Russellville, AR) 57583
Dow Consumer Products Inc. (Mauldin, SC) 79647
Dow Corning Corp. (Carrollton, KY) 68189
Dow Corning Corp. (Elizabethtown, KY) 68275
Dow Corning Corp. (Greensboro, NC) 74813
Dow Corning Corp. (Arlington, TN) 80180
Dow Corning Corp. Atlanta Plant (Norcross, GA) 67111
Dow Corning Corp. Elizabethtown Plant (Elizabethtown, KY) 68276
Dow Corning Corp. Norcross Plant (Norcross, GA) 67112
Dow Corning *Org Dow Corning Wright (Arlington, TN) 80181
Dow Corning Wright (Arlington, TN) 80182
Dow Jones Capital Markets Report (Washington Bureau) (Washington, DC) 58216
Dow Jones & Co. (Silver Spring, MD) 72391
Dow Jones & Co. (Charlotte, NC) 73933
Dow Jones & Co. (Beaumont, TX) 83149
Dow Jones & Co. (Dallas, TX) 83982
Dow Jones News Service (Washington Bureau) (Washington, DC) 58217
Dowbrands (Mauldin, SC) 79648
Dowbrands (Greenville, TX) 85664
Dowbrands Inc. (Mauldin, SC) 79649
Dowbrands Lp (Mauldin, SC) 79650
Dowbrands L.P. (Greenville, TX) 85665
Dowell Schlumberger Inc. (Tulsa, OK) 77933
Downhole Seismic Services (Houston, TX) 86047
Drake Beam Morin Inc. (Washington, DC) 58218
Dresser Industries Inc. (Dallas, TX) 83983; **83984**
Dresser Industries Inc. Guiberson Div. (Dallas, TX) 83985
Dresser Industries Inc. Security Division (Dallas, TX) 83986
Dresser Industries Inc. Trading Division (Houston, TX) 86048
Dresser Industries Inc. Valve & Controls Division (The Woodlands, TX) 89751
Dresser Industries Inc. Waukesha Engine Division (Houston, TX) 86049
Dresser Industries Inc. Wayne Div. (Salisbury, MD) 72341
Dresser Industries Inc. Wayne Division (Salisbury, MD) 72342
Dresser-Rand Compression Services (Broken Arrow, OK) 76883
Dresser Valve&Cntr (Spring, TX) 89466
Drew Chemical Corp. (Houston, TX) 86050
Drexel Heritage Furnishings Plant 6 (Morganton, NC) 75635
Drexel Heritage Furnishings Plant 33 (Morganton, NC) 75636
Drexel Heritage Furnishings Plant 3/5 (Morganton, NC) 75637
Drexel Heritage Furnishings Plant 2 (Marion, NC) 75501
Drexel Heritage Furnishings Inc. (Drexel, NC) 74365
Drexel Heritage Furnishings Inc. Plant 43 (Hildebran, NC) 75185
Drexel Heritage Furnishings Inc. Plant 6 (Morganton, NC) 75638
Drexel Heritage Furnishings Inc. Plant 33 (Morganton, NC) 75639
Drexel Heritage Furnishings Inc. Plant 3/5 (Morganton, NC) 75640
Drexel Heritage Furnishings Inc. Plant 2 (Marion, NC) 75502
Drexel Heritage Furniture Plant 45 (Hickory, NC) 75066
Drexel Heritage Furniture Plant 43 (Hildebran, NC) 75186
Drexel Heritage Furniture Plant 1 (Drexel, NC) 74366; 74367
Drexel Heritage Furniture Plant 6 (Morganton, NC) 75641
Drexel Heritage Furniture Plant 60 (Morganton, NC) 75642
Drexel Heritage Furniture Plant 33 (Morganton, NC) 75643
Drexel Heritage Furniture Plant 315 (Morganton, NC) 75644
Drexel Heritage Furniture Plant 2 (Marion, NC) 75503
Drilling Specialties Co. Alamo Plant (Conroe, TX) 83657
Drinnon Inc. (Milledgeville, GA) 66974
Drive Systems Operations (Salem, VA) 92209
DSC Communication Corp. (Plano, TX) 88556
DSC Communications (Plano, TX) **88557**
Dsc Communications Corp. (Atlanta, GA) 64424
DSC Internation Corp. (Plano, TX) 88558
Duck Head Apparel Co. (Baldwin, GA) 65375
Duck Head Apparel Co. (Monroe, GA) 66989; 66990
Duck Head Apparel Co. (Sandersville, GA) 67429
Duck Head Apparel Co. (Sparta, GA) 67616
Duck Head Apparel Co. (Washington, GA) 68021
Duck Head Apparel Co. (Winder, GA) 68059
Duck Head Apparel Co. (Maiden, NC) 75492
Duck Head Apparel Co. (Jellico, TN) 81023
Duck Head Outlet Stores (Greenville, SC) 79346
Duke Energy Corp. (Charlotte, NC) 73934
Duke Engineering & Services Inc. (Charlotte, NC) 73935; 73936
Duke/Fluor Daniel (Charlotte, NC) 73937
Duke Power (Charlotte, NC) **73938**
Duke Power Co. (Charlotte, NC) 73939
Duke Power Co. Inc. (Charlotte, NC) 73940
Dumaine Towel Mill (Fieldale, VA) 90879
Dun & Bradstreet Dun & Bradstreet Plan Services, Inc. (Tampa, FL) 63408
Dun & Bradstreet Pension Services, Inc. (Tampa, FL) 63409
Dun & Bradstreet Plan Services (Tampa, FL) 63410
Dun & Bradstreet Software (Atlanta, GA) 64425
Dun & Bradstreet Software (Huntsville) (Huntsville, AL) 55909
E.I. DuPont De Nemours (Wilmington, DE) **58055**
Dupont Publishing (Tampa, FL) 63411
Duracell International Inc. (Jacksonville, FL) 60264
Duracell International Inc. (Lexington, NC) 75402
Duracell International Inc. (Valdese, NC) 76412
Duracell USA (La Grange, GA) 66478
Duracell USA (Lexington, NC) 75403
Duracell USA (Lancaster, SC) 79571
Duracell USA (Cleveland, TN) 80574; 80575
Durr Drug Co., Inc. (Montgomery, AL) 56302
Durr-Fillauer Medical Inc. (Birmingham, AL) 55227
Durr-Fillauer Medical Inc. (Mobile, AL) 56158
Durr-Fillauer Medical, Inc. (Montgomery, AL) 56303; 56304; 56305
Durr-Fillauer Medical Inc. (Jacksonville, FL) 60265
Durr-Fillauer Medical Inc. (Tampa, FL) 63412
Durr-Fillauer Medical Inc. (Shreveport, LA) 70717
Durr-Fillauer Medical Inc. (Tulsa, OK) 77934; 77935
Durr-Fillauer Medical Inc. (West Columbia, SC) 80090
Durr-Fillauer Medical Inc. (Memphis, TN) 81514
Durr-Fillauer Medical Inc. (Dallas, TX) 83987
Durr Medical (Montgomery, AL) 56306
Durr Medical Corp. (Montgomery, AL) 56307
Durr Medical Corporation (Atlanta, GA) 64426
Durr Medical Corp. (Chattanooga, TN) 80355
Durr Medical Inc. (Chattanooga, TN) 80356; 80357
Dynapert (Roswell, GA) 67368
Dyno Merchandise Corp. (Pompano Beach, FL) 62593

E

E/M Corp. (Fort Worth, TX) 85106
E/M Corp. Fort Worth Div. Processing (Fort Worth, TX) 85107
E. R. Carpenter Co. (Texarkana, AR) 57675
E R Carpenter Co. (Oklahoma City, OK) 77348
E R Carpenter Co. (Dallas, TX) 83988
E R Carpenter Co. (New Braunfels, TX) 88207
E R Carpenter Co. (Temple, TX) 89613
E. R. Carpenter Co. Inc. (Birmingham, AL) 55228
E. R. Carpenter Co. Inc. (Fort Smith, AR) 57048
E. R. Carpenter Co. Inc. (Russellville, KY) 69258; 69259
E. R. Carpenter Co. Inc. (Booneville, MS) 72643
E. R. Carpenter Co. Inc. (Pontotoc, MS) 73299
E. R. Carpenter Co. Inc. (Saltillo, MS) 73335
E. R. Carpenter Co. Inc. (Conover, NC) 74330
E. R. Carpenter Co. Inc. (Hickory, NC) 75067; 75068
E. R. Carpenter Co. Inc. (High Point, NC) 75121; 75122
E. R. Carpenter Co. Inc. (Lenoir, NC) 75372; 75373; 75374
E. R. Carpenter Co. Inc. (Longview, NC) 75451
E. R. Carpenter Co. Inc. (Morganton, NC) 75645
E. R. Carpenter Co. Inc. (Taylorsville, NC) 76368
E. R. Carpenter Co. Inc. (Cleveland, TN) 80576
E. R. Carpenter Co. Inc. (Cookeville, TN) 80648; 80649
E. R. Carpenter Co. Inc. (Morristown, TN) 81792
E. R. Carpenter Co. Inc. (Niota, TN) 82176
E. R. Carpenter Co. Inc. (Dallas, TX) 83989
E. R. Carpenter Co. Inc. (Houston, TX) 86051; 86052; 86053
E. R. Carpenter Co. Inc. (Temple, TX) 89614
E. R. Carpenter Co. Inc. (Texarkana, TX) 89674
E. R. Carpenter Co. Inc. (Richmond, VA) 91860
E. R. Carpenter Co. Inc. New Braunfels (New Braunfels, TX) 88208
E. R. Carpenter Co. Inc. Tupelo (Verona, MS) 73445
E. R. Carpenter Co. of Texas (Temple, TX) 89615
E. R. Squibb & Sons Inc. (Kenly, NC) 75272
E-Systems ECI Div. (St. Petersburg, FL) 63099
E Systems Inc. (Dallas, TX) 83990; 83991; **83992**
E-Systems Inc. (Greenville, TX) 85666
E-Systems Inc. (Ashburn, VA) 90397
E-Systems Inc. C. M. Div. (St. Petersburg, FL) 63100
E-Systems Inc. C.M. Div. (St. Petersburg, FL) 63101
E-Systems Inc. ECI Div. (St. Petersburg, FL) 63102
E-Systems Inc. ECI Division (St. Petersburg, FL) 63103
E-Systems Inc. Garland Div. (Garland, TX) 85481; 85482
E-Systems Inc. Garland Division (Dallas, TX) 83993
E-Systems Inc. Go-Co. (Lexington, KY) 68547
E-Systems Inc. Greenville Div. (Greenville, TX) 85667
E-Systems Inc. Greenville Division (Greenville, TX) 85668
E-Systems Inc. Melpar Div. (Fairfax, VA) 90766
E-Systems Inc. Melpar Div. (Falls Church, VA) 90830; 90831
E-Systems Medical Electronics Inc. (Dallas, TX) 83994
Eagle Bus Mfg. Inc. (Brownsville, TX) 83355
Eagle Crest Foods, Inc. (Dallas, TX) 83995
Eagle Crest Inc. (Dallas, TX) 83996
Eagle-Picher Construction (Lubbock, TX) 87756
Eagle-Picher Ind. Inc. (Grove, OK) 77089
Eagle-Picher Ind. Inc. Construction Equipment Div. (Lubbock, TX) 87757
Eagle-Picher Ind. Inc. Boron Dept. (Quapaw, OK) 77753
Eagle Picher Ind. Inc. Electro-Optic Materials Dept. (Quapaw, OK) 77754
Eagle Picher Ind. Inc. Electro-Optics Mat. 1 (Quapaw, OK) 77755
Eagle-Picher Ind. Inc. Electro-Optics Materials Dept. (Quapaw, OK) 77756
Eagle-Picher Industries (Grove, OK) 77090
Eagle Picher Industries Construction Equipment Div. (Lubbock, TX) 87758
Eagle Picher Industries Specialty Materials Div. (Quapaw, OK) 77757
Eagle Picher Industries Inc. (Miami, OK) 77203
Eagle-Picher Industries Inc. (Quapaw, OK) 77758
Eagle Picher Industries Inc. (Mineola, TX) 88105
Eagle-Picher Industries Inc. Construction Equipment Div. (Lubbock, TX) 87759; 87760; 87761
Eagle-Picher Industries Inc. Molding Orthane Div. (Denton, TX) 84616
Eagle-Picher Industries Inc. Wolverine Gasket Div. (Lisbon, FL) 60905
Eagle-Picher Industries Inc. Wolverine Gasket Div. Blacksburg Div. (Blacksburg, VA) 90437
Eagle-Picher Industries Inc. Boron Dept. (Quapaw, OK) 77759; 77760; 77761
Eagle Picher Industries Inc. Boron Dept (Quapaw, OK) 77762
Eagle Picher Industry Inc. (Marietta, GA) 66768
Eagle-Picher Specialty Materials (Quapaw, OK) 77763
Eagle Signal Controls (Austin, TX) 82860
Eagle Snacks Inc. (Robersonville, NC) 76054
Eagle Snacks Inc. (Fayetteville, TN) 80792
Eagle Snacks Inc. (Dallas, TX) 83997
Early Times Distillers Co. (Louisville, KY) 68756
Easco Hand Tools Inc. (Springdale, AR) 57629
Easco Hand Tools Inc. (Gastonia, NC) 74674
East Cooper Community Hospital (Mount Pleasant, SC) 79671
Eastern Operations Center Inc. (Mechanicsville, VA) 91401
Eastern Stainless Corp. (Baltimore, MD) 71111
Eastman Chemical Co. (Kingsport, TN) 81074; 81075
Eastman Christensen (Oklahoma City, OK) 77349
Eastman Kodak (Owensboro, KY) 69169
Eastman Kodak Co. (Lexington, KY) 68548
Eastman Kodak Co. (Louisville, KY) 68757
Eastman Kodak Co. (Memphis, TN) 81515; 81516
Eastman Kodak Co. (Nashville, TN) 81938
Eastman Kodak Co. (Charleston, WV) 92743; 92744
Eastman Kodak Co. Arkansas Eastman Co. (Batesville, AR) 56752
Eastman Kodak Co. Arkansas Eastman Div. (Batesville, AR) 56753
Eastman Kodak Co. Tennessee Div. (Kingsport, TN) 81076
Eastman Kodak Co. Tennessee Eastman Div. (Kingsport, TN) 81077

Eastman Teleco (Oklahoma City, OK) 77350
Eastville Bank (Eastville, VA) 90736; 90737
Eastville Banks (Eastville, VA) 90738
Eaton Administration Corp. (Wilimington, DE) 57964
Eaton Air Controls Products (Roxboro, NC) 76123
Eaton Corp. (Arab, AL) 55023
Eaton Corp. (Athens, AL) 55037; 55038
Eaton Corp. (Sarasota, FL) 62814
Eaton Corp. (Athens, GA) 64166
Eaton Corp. (Doraville, GA) 65926
Eaton Corp. (Bowling Green, KY) 68136
Eaton Corp. (Glasgow, KY) 68393
Eaton Corp. (Harrodsburg, KY) 68411
Eaton Corp. (Henderson, KY) 68442; 68443
Eaton Corp. (Louisville, KY) 68758
Eaton Corp. (Arden, NC) 73567
Eaton Corp. (Fletcher, NC) 74589
Eaton Corp. (Laurinburg, NC) 75351
Eaton Corp. (Roxboro, NC) 76124; 76125
Eaton Corp. (Chattanooga, TN) 80358
Eaton Corp. (Cleveland, TN) 80577; 80578
Eaton Corp. (Humboldt, TN) 80950
Eaton Corp. (Memphis, TN) 81517
Eaton Corp. (Nashville, TN) 81939; 81940; 81941
Eaton Corp. (Shelbyville, TN) 82301
Eaton Corp. Aerospace & Commercial Controls Div. (Arab, AL) 55024
Eaton Corp. Aerospace Commercial Controls Div. (Sarasota, FL) 62815; 62816
Eaton Corp. Aerospace & Commercial Controls Div. (Selma, NC) 76221
Eaton Corp. Axel & Brake Div. (Henderson, KY) 68444
Eaton Corp. Axle & Brake Div. (Glasgow, KY) 68394
Eaton Corp. Axle & Brake Div. (Gallatin, TN) 80841
Eaton Corp. Axle & Brake Div. (Humboldt, TN) 80951
Eaton Corp. Condura (Brownsville, TX) 83356
Eaton Corp. Florida Commercial Controls Div. (Sarasota, FL) 62817
Eaton Corp. Fluid Power Div. (Fletcher, NC) 74590
Eaton Corp. Golf Grip Div. (Laurinburg, NC) 75352
Eaton Corp. Golf Group Div. (Laurinburg, NC) 75353
Eaton Corp. Heinemann Products (Salisbury, MD) 72343
Eaton Corp. Heinemann Products Commercial Controls Div. (Salisbury, MD) 72344
Eaton Corp. Hydraulics Div. (Shawnee, OK) 77816; 77817
Eaton Corp. Ion Beam Systems Div. (Austin, TX) 82861
Eaton Corp. Logic Control Div. (Arden, NC) 73568
Eaton Corp. Power Control Div. (Bowling Green, KY) 68137
Eaton Corp. Power Distribution Div. (Cleveland, TN) 80579
Eaton Corp. Semiconductor Equipment (Austin, TX) 82862
Eaton Corp. Supercharger Div. (Athens, GA) 64167
Eaton Corp. Transmission (Kings Mountain, NC) 75297
Eaton Corp. Transmission Div. (Kings Mountain, NC) 75298; 75299
Eaton Corp. Transmission Div. (Shelbyville, TN) 82302
Eaton Corp. Transmission Div. Kings Mountain (Kings Mountain, NC) 75300
Eaton Corp. Transmission Div. Kings Moutain Plant (Kings Mountain, NC) 75301
Eaton Corp. Bowling Green Plant (Bowling Green, KY) 68138
Eaton Corp. Heinemann Products (Salisbury, MD) 72345
Eaton Corp. Ion Beam (Houston, TX) 86054
Eaton Corp., U.S. Engine Valve Corp. (Westminister, SC) 80113
Eaton International Corp. (Wilmington, DE) 58056
Eaton Kenway Inc. (Claymont, DE) 57761
Eaton Laboratories, Inc. (Manati, PR) 78499
EBM Inc. (Gallatin, TN) 80842

EBM, Inc. (Nashville, TN) 81942
Ecco (Lynchburg, VA) 91234
Ecco Inc. (Morrow, GA) 67007
Ecco Inc. (High Point, NC) 75123
Ecco Inc. (Beaumont, TX) 83150
Echlin Ponce Inc. (Ponce, PR) 78535
Echota Cushion (Calhoun, GA) 65462
Echota Cushion Inc. (Calhoun, GA) 65463; 65464
Eckerd Corp. (Clearwater, FL) 58991
Eckerd Corp. (Largo, FL) 60829; 60830; 60831; **60832**
Eckerd Corp. Eckerd Drug Co. (Deerfield, FL) 59263
Eckerd Corp. Eckerd Drug Co. (Largo, FL) 60833
Eckerd Corp. Eckerd Drug Co. (Orlando, FL) 61963
Eckerd Corp. Eckerd Drug Co. (Newnan, GA) 67080
Eckerd Corp. Eckerd Drug Co. (Charlotte, NC) 73941
Eckerd Corp. Eckerd Drug Co. (Conroe, TX) 83658
Eckerd Corp. Eckerd Drug Co. (Garland, TX) 85483
Jack Eckerd Corp. (Largo, FL) 60834
Eckerd Drug Co. (Birmingham, AL) 55229
Eckerd Drug Co. (Valley, AL) 56688
Eckerd Drug Co. (Largo, FL) 60835
Eckerd Drug Co. (Hendersonville, TN) 80911
Eckerd Drug Co. (Hermitage, TN) 80924
Eckerd Drug Co. (Carthage, TX) 83515
Eckerd Drug Co. (Dallas, TX) 83998; 83999
Eckerd Drug Co. (Humble, TX) 87219
Eckerd Drug Co. (Roanoke, VA) 92137
Eckerd Drug Co. No. 848 (Dallas, TX) 84000
Eckerd Drug Co. No. 827 (Dallas, TX) 84001
Eckerd Drug Co. No. 21 (Dallas, TX) 84002
Eckerd Drugs (Claymont, DE) 57762
Eckerd Drugs (New Castle, DE) 57863
Eckerd Drugs (Newark, DE) 57902
Eckerd Drugs (Wilmington, DE) 58057
Eckerd Drugs (North East, MD) 72155
Eckerd Drugs (Antioch, TN) 80167
Eckerd Drugs (Bristol, TN) 80239
Eckerd Drugs (Chattanooga, TN) 80359; 80360; 80361; 80362; 80363; 80364; 80365; 80366
Eckerd Drugs (Cleveland, TN) 80580
Eckerd Drugs (Dayton, TN) 80717
Eckerd Drugs (Hendersonville, TN) 80912
Eckerd Drugs (Hermitage, TN) 80925
Eckerd Drugs (Johnson City, TN) 81028
Eckerd Drugs (Johonson City, TN) 81062
Eckerd Drugs (Kingsport, TN) 81078; 81079; 81080; 81081
Eckerd Drugs (Knoxville, TN) 81166; 81167
Eckerd Drugs (Madison, TN) 81373; 81374
Eckerd Drugs (Maryville, TN) 81402
Eckerd Drugs (Murfreesboro, TN) 81839
Eckerd Drugs (Murfressboro, TN) 81875
Eckerd Drugs (Nashville, TN) 81943; 81944; 81945; 81946; 81947; 81948; 81949; 81950; 81951; 81952
Eckerd Drugs (Oak Ridge, TN) 82185
Eckerd Drugs (Shelbyville, TN) 82303
Eckerd Drugs (Bristol, VA) 90472
Eckerd Drugs (Danville, VA) 90690; 90691
Eckerd Drugs (Harrisonburg, VA) 91077; 91078
Eckerd Drugs (Madison Heights, VA) 91296
Eckerd Drugs (Norton, VA) 91602
Eckerd Drugs (Radford, VA) 91696
Eckerd Drugs (Roanoke, VA) 92138
Eckerd Drugs (Salem, VA) 92210
Eckerd Drugs (Wytheville, VA) 92636

Eckerd Express Photo (Largo, FL) 60836
Eckerd Vision Group (Largo, FL) 60837
Ecolab Inc. (Dorado, PR) 78408
Ecolab, Inc. (Garland, TX) 85484
Ecolab Inc. Mc Donough Plant (Mc Donough, GA) 66955
Ecolab Manufacturing Inc. (Dorado, PR) 78409
Ecolab Manufacturing Inc. (Hato Tejas, PR) 78457
Eds (Atlanta, GA) 64427
Eds (Smyrna, GA) 67549
Eds (Plano, TX) 88559
Eds (Richardson, TX) 88733
EDUSA Corp. (El Paso, TX) 84792
Edwards Co., Inc. (Newport News, VA) 91460
EG & G Pressure Science Inc. (Beltsville, MD) 71351
EG & G Florida (Kennedy Space Center, FL) 60556
EG & G Florida (Cocoa) (Cocoa, FL) 59067
EG & G Instruments (Oak Ridge, TN) 82186
EG & G Instruments/Ortec (Oak Ridge, TN) 82187
EG & G Nuclear Instruments (Oak Ridge, TN) 82188
Eg & G Ortec (Oak Ridge, TN) 82189
EG & G Pressure Science (Beltsville, MD) 71352
EG & G Process Measurements/ Chandler Eng. (Tulsa, OK) 77936
EG & G Science Support Corp. (Dallas, TX) 84003
EG & G Washington Analytical Service Center (Morgantown, WV) 92943
EG & G Washington Analytical Servies Center (Rockville, MD) 72270
Egp Fuels Co. (La Porte, TX) 87558
Eimco Coal Machinery Inc. (Bolt, WV) 92705
El Campo Aluminum Co. (El Campo, TX) 84746; 84747
El Dorado Engineering Inc. (New Orleans, LA) 70444
El Paso Natural Gas Co. (Washington, DC) 58219
El Paso Natural Gas Inc. (El Paso, TX) 84793
El Paso Refining Inc. (El Paso, TX) 84794
Electric Fuels Corp. (St. Petersburg, FL) 63104
Electrical Specialty Prods. Co. (Montevallo, AL) 56272
Electro Mechanical Corp. (Knoxville, TN) 81168
Electro Mechanical Design Services (Gaithersburg, MD) 71770
Electro Mechanical Devices Inc. (Cordova, AL) 55528
Electro Mechanical Energy Corp. (Arnold, MD) 71028
Electro Mechanical Holding Inc. (Lynchburg, VA) 91235
Electro Mechanical Services (Miami, FL) 61279
Electronic Data Systems (Winter Park, FL) 63971
Electronic Data Systems (Clarkston, GA) 65562
Electronic Data Systems (Norcross, GA) 67113
Electronic Data Systems (Elizabethtown, KY) 68277
Electronic Data Systems (Jackson, MS) 72978
Electronic Data Systems (Amarillo, TX) 82544
Electronic Data Systems (Dallas, TX) 84004
Electronic Data Systems (Plano, TX) 88560; **88561**
Electronic Data Systems (San Antonio, TX) 88976
Electronic Data Systems (Victoria, TX) 89885
Electronic Data Systems (Alexandria, VA) 90179
Electronic Data Systems Cor (Herndon, VA) 91120
Electronic Data Systems Corp. (Tallahassee, FL) 63236
Electronic Data Systems Corp. (Charlotte, NC) 73942
Electronic Data Systems Corp. (Dalas, TX) 83830
Electronic Data Systems Corp. (Dallas, TX) 84005
Electronic Data Systems Corp. (Plano, TX) 88562
Electronic Data Systems Corp. (San Antonio, TX) 88977

Electronic Data Systems Dat (San Antonio, TX) 88978
Electronic Data Systems-Easter (Bethesda, MD) 71385
Electronic Data Systems Health (Gaithersburg, MD) 71771
Electronic Systems Group (Glen Burnie, MD) 71839
Electronic Systems Group Friendship Site (Linthicum, MD) 72105
Electronic Systems Group Frienship Site (Linthicum Heights, MD) 72110
Electronic Systems Group Materials Acquistion Center (Glen Burnie, MD) 71840
Electronic Systems Inc. (Virginia Beach, VA) 92459
Electronic Warfare Systems (Washington, DC) 58220
Electrospace Systems inc. (Richardson, TX) 88734
Eli Lilly & Co. (Washington, DC) 58221
Eli Lilly Ind. Inc. (Carolina, PR) 78376
Eli Lilly Ind. Inc. (Mayaguez, PR) 78511
Eli Lilly Industries, Inc. (Carolina, PR) 78377
Eli Lilly Industries, Inc. (Mayaguez, PR) 78512
Ellesse USA Inc. (Dallas, TX) 84006
Elmco Inc. (Annapolis, MD) 71010
Elographics Inc. (Woodstock, GA) 68068
Elographics Inc. (Oak Ridge, TN) 82190; 82191
EMB Corp. (Elizabethtown, KY) 68278
Emc (Washington, DC) 58222
Emc (St. Augustine, FL) 63054
Emc Corp. (Atlanta, GA) 64428
Emerson Electri Co. Inc. Emerson Motor Div. (Oxford, MS) 73235
Emerson Electric Co. (Paragould, AR) 57491
Emerson Electric Co. (Russellville, KY) 69260
Emerson Electric Co. (Newport, TN) 82160
Emerson Electric Co. (Paris, TN) 82216
Emerson Electric Co. Alco Controls Div. (Hazlehurst, GA) 66346
Emerson Electric Co. Alco Controls Div. (Wytheville, VA) 92637
Emerson Electric Co. Brooks Instrument Div. (Statesboro, GA) 67634
Emerson Electric Co. Chromalox Div. (Murfreesboro, TN) 81840
Emerson Electric Co. E. L. Wiegnd Div. (Vernon, AL) 56698
Emerson Electric Co. Emerson Motor Div. (Oxford, MS) 73236; 73237
Emerson Electric Co. Special Products Div. (Murphy, NC) 75701
Emerson Electric Co. Special Products Div. (Paris, TN) 82217; 82218
Emerson Electric Co. Terminal Products Div. (Hormigueros, PR) 78459
Emerson Electric Co. White-Rodger Div. (Harrison, AR) 57136
Emerson Electric Co. Wiegand Industrial Div. (Murfreesboro, TN) 81841
Emerson Electric Co. Inc. Alco Controls Div. (Hazlehurst, GA) 66347
Emerson Electric Co. Inc. Alco Controls Div. (Wytheville, VA) 92638
Emerson Electric Co. SPD (Murphy, NC) 75702
Emerson Motor Co. (Oxford, MS) 73238
Emerson Motor Co. (Humboldt, TN) 80952
Emerson Puerto Rico Inc. (Dorado, PR) 78410
Emery Worldwide (Birmingham, AL) 55230
Emery Worldwide (Madison, AL) 56119
Emery Worldwide (Montgomery, AL) 56308
Emery Worldwide (Fayetteville, AR) 56976
Emery Worldwide (Little Rock, AR) 57281
Emery Worldwide (Springdale, AR) 57630
Emery Worldwide (Fort Lauderdale, FL) 59482
Emery Worldwide (Jacksonville, FL) 60266

Emery Worldwide (Tampa, FL) 63413
Emery Worldwide (W Palm Beach, FL) 63789
Emery Worldwide (Macon, GA) 66684
Emery Worldwide (Baton Rouge, LA) 69511
Emery Worldwide (Lafayette, LA) 70053
Emery Worldwide (Lake Charles, LA) 70138
Emery Worldwide (Shreveport, LA) 70718
Emery Worldwide (Gulfport, MS) 72854
Emery Worldwide (Jackson, MS) 72979
Emery Worldwide (Charlotte, NC) 73943
Emery Worldwide (Fletcher, NC) 74591
Emery Worldwide (Greensboro, NC) 74814
Emery Worldwide (Raleigh, NC) 75888
Emery Worldwide (Wilmington, NC) 76551; 76552; 76553
Emery Worldwide (Oklahoma City, OK) 77351
Emery Worldwide (Charleston, SC) 78808
Emery Worldwide (Greer, SC) 79473
Emery Worldwide (N Myrtle Beach, SC) 79719
Emery Worldwide (West Columbia, SC) 80091
Emery Worldwide (Maryville, TN) 81403
Emery Worldwide (Memphis, TN) 81518
Emery Worldwide (Abilene, TX) 82435
Emery Worldwide (Austin, TX) 82863
Emery Worldwide (Dallas, TX) 84007
Emery Worldwide (El Paso, TX) 84795
Emery Worldwide (Fort Worth, TX) 85108
Emery Worldwide (Houston, TX) 86055
Emery Worldwide (Laredo, TX) 87609
Emery Worldwide (Lubbock, TX) 87762
Emery Worldwide (Sherman, TX) 89394
Emery Worldwide ACF Co. (Chattanooga, TN) 80367
Emery Worldwide (ACF Co.) (Wheeling, WV) 93111
Emhart Corp. (Baltimore, MD) 71112
Emhart Industries Inc. (Baltimore, MD) 71113
Empire Detroit Steel Div. (Cary, NC) 73794
Encoat-North Arlington, Inc. (Wilmington, DE) 58058
Enenco Inc. (Memphis, TN) 81519
Energy Coatings Co. (Houston, TX) 86056
Energy Development Corp. (Matewan, WV) 92938
Energy Service Co. Inc. (Dallas, TX) 84008
Engelhard Catalyst & Chemicals Div. (Huntsville, AL) 55910
Engelhard Corp. (Huntsville, AL) 55911
Engelhard Corp. (Attapulgus, GA) 65307; 65308
Engelhard Corp. (Gordon, GA) 66306
Engelhard Corp. (Mc Intyre, GA) 66960
Engelhard Corp. (Louisville, KY) 68759
Engelhard Corp. (Jackson, MS) 72980
Engelhard Corp. (Seneca, SC) 79856; 79857
Engelhard Corp. Catalysts & Chemicals Div. (Seneca, SC) 79858
Engelhard Corp. Environmental Catalysts Div. (Huntsville, AL) 55912
Engelhard Corp. McIntyre-Toddville Plant (McIntyre, GA) 66971
Engelhard Corp. Pigments & Additives Div. (Louisville, KY) 68760
Engelhard Corp. Catalyst & Chemical (Huntsville, AL) 55913
Engelhard Corp. Daveyville Plant (Mc Intyre, GA) 66961
Engelhard Corp. Dixie Mine (Toomsboro, GA) 67839
Engelhard Corp. Edgar Plant (Mc Intyre, GA) 66962

Engelhard Corp. Engelhard Di (Houston, TX) 86057
Engelhard Corp. Environmental Catalyst Group (Huntsville, AL) 55914
Engelhard Corp. Gardner Plant (Oconee, GA) 67217
Engelhard Corp. Gibraltar Mine (Toomsboro, GA) 67840
Engelhard Corp. Gordon Plant (Gordon, GA) 66307
Engelhard Corp. Klondyke Mine (Mc Intyre, GA) 66963
Engelhard Corp. Mcintyre-Edgars Plant (Mc Intyre, GA) 66964
Engelhard Corp. Toddville Plant (Mc Intyre, GA) 66965
Engelhard Corp. Washington Co. Mine (Deepstep, GA) 65913
Engelhard Kaolin Co. Griffin Mine (Dry Branch, GA) 66006
Engelhard Kaolin Co. Scott Mine (Deepstep, GA) 65914
Engelhard Kaolin Corp. Griffin Mine (Dry Branch, GA) 66007
Engelhard Specialty Chemicals (Huntsville, AL) 55915
Engineered Polymers (Winston-Salem, NC) 76724
Engineered Sintered Components Co. (Troutman, NC) 76408
Engineering & Industrial Group (New Orleans, LA) 70445
Engineering Research Assoc (Pensacola, FL) 62420
Engineering Research Associ (Pensacola, FL) 62421
Engineering Research Associates (Vienna, VA) 92399
Engineering Research Associates Inc. (Vienna, VA) 92400
Enron (Houston, TX) **86058**; 86059
Enron Americas Inc. (Houston, TX) 86060; 86061
Enron Corp. (Geismar, LA) 69880
Enron Corp. (Houston, TX) 86062; 86063; 86064
Enron Corp. (La Porte, TX) 87559
Enron Gas Gathering Inc. (Houston, TX) 86065
Enron Gas Liquids Inc. (Houston, TX) 86066; 86067
Enron Gas Marketing (Washington, DC) 58223
Enron Gas Processing (Houston, TX) 86068
Enron Gas Processing Co. (Houston, TX) 86069
Enron Gas Processing Co. Inc. (Houston, TX) 86070
Enron Gas Services Corp. (Houston, TX) 86071
Enron Gas Services Group (Houston, TX) 86072
Enron Interstate Pipeline Co. (Houston, TX) 86073
Enron Liquid Fuels (Houston, TX) 86074
Enron Liquids Pipeline Co. (Houston, TX) 86075
Enron Liquids Pipeline Group (Houston, TX) 86076
Enron Methanol Co. (Pasadena, TX) 88401
Enron Oil & Gas Co. (Houston, TX) 86077
Enron Oil & Gas Co. Inc. (Houston, TX) 86078
Enron Oil & Gas Marketing Inc. (Houston, TX) 86079
Enron Oil Trading & Transportation (Houston, TX) 86080
Enron Operating Co. (Houston, TX) 86081
Enron Operations Corp. (Houston, TX) 86082
Enron Power Corp. (Houston, TX) 86083
Enron Power Development Corp. (Houston, TX) 86084
Enserch (Dallas, TX) **84009**
Enserch Corp. (Dallas, TX) 84010; 84011; 84012
Enserch Exlporation Partners Ltd. (Dallas, TX) 84013
Enserch Exploration Inc. (Dallas, TX) 84014
Entergy (New Orleans, LA) **70446**
Entergy Corp. (New Orleans, LA) 70447
Entergy Operations Inc. (Jackson, MS) 72981
Entergy Services Inc. (New Orleans, LA) 70448
Enthone-OMI (Seagoville, TX) 89363
Epsilon/Southwest (Dallas, TX) 84015
Equicor Inc. (Nashville, TN) 81953
Equitable Halter Div. (New Orleans, LA) 70449
Equitable Agri-Business Inc. (Atlanta, GA) 64429

Equitable Life Insurance Co. (Dover, DE) 57788
Equitable Life Insurance Co. (Newark, DE) 57903
Equitable Life Insurance Co. (Wilmington, DE) 58059
Equitable Life Insurance Co. (Frederick, MD) 71720; 71721
Equitable Life Insurance Co. (Nashville, TN) 81954
Equitable Life Insurance Co. (Mc Lean, VA) 91364
Equitable Madisonville (Madisonville, LA) 70206
Equitable Real Estate Investment Management Inc. (Atlanta, GA) 64430
Equitable Variable Life Insurance (Atlanta, GA) 64431
Equity Country Inc. (Darrouzett, TX) 84518
Equity Export, Oil & Gas Inc. (Enid, OK) 77047
Equity Title Service Corp. (Bethesda, MD) 71386
E.R. Carpenter Co. Inc. (Birmingham, AL) 55231
E.R. Carpenter Co. Inc. (Pontotoc, MS) 73300
E.R. Carpenter Co., Inc. (Verona, MS) 73446
E.R. Carpenter Co. Inc. (Conover, NC) 74331
E.R. Carpenter Co. Inc. (Lenoir, NC) 75375; 75376
E.R. Carpenter Co. Inc. (Longview, NC) 75452
E.R. Carpenter Co. Inc. (Cleveland, TN) 80581
E.R. Carpenter Co. Inc. (Morristown, TN) 81793
E.R. Carpenter Co. Inc. (Dallas, TX) 84016
E.R. Carpenter Co. of Texas (Temple, TX) 89616
Erin Bank & Trust Co. (Erin, TN) 80772; 80773
Eron Exploration Co. (Houston, TX) 86085
Eron Gas Liquids International Ltd. (Houston, TX) 86086
Eron International Inc. (Houston, TX) 86087
Escod Industries (Morrisville, NC) 75666
ESI Inc. (Gainesville, GA) 66273
Esp Products (Oklahoma City, OK) 77352
Essex Group Inc. (Lithonia, GA) 66593
Essex Group Inc. (Bennettsville, SC) 78725
Essex Specialty Products (Griffin, GA) 66314
Essick Mayco (Charleston, SC) 78809
Esskay (Baltimore, MD) 71114
Ethicon, Inc. (Cornelia, GA) 65722
Ethicon Inc. (San Angelo, TX) 88872
Ethyl (Richmond, VA) **91861**
Ethyl Corp. (Magnolia, AR) 57330; 57331
Ethyl Corp. (Baton Rouge, LA) 69512
Ethyl Corp. (Orangeburg, SC) 79771
Ethyl Corp. (Pasadena, TX) 88402
Ethyl Corp. (Richmond, VA) 91862; 91863
Ethyl Corp. Houston Plant (Pasadena, TX) 88403
Ethyl Corp. Chemicals (Baton Rouge, LA) 69513
Ethyl Corp. Pao Facility (Deer Park, TX) 84549
Ethyl Petroleum Additives Inc. (Richmond, VA) 91864
Ethyl Process Development Center (Baton Rouge, LA) 69514
European Bakers, Ltd. (Tucker, GA) 67854
Eveready Battery Co. Inc. (Asheboro, NC) 73585; 73586
Eveready Battery Co. Inc. (Greenville, NC) 74957
Everglades Sugar Refinery Inc. (Clewiston, FL) 59059
Evodex (Birmingham, AL) 55232
Evtech (Charlotte, NC) 73944
Evtech a Kodak Co. (Charlotte, NC) 73945
Executive Airlines (San Juan, PR) 78578
Executive Airlines Inc. (Fort Lauderdale, FL) 59483
Express (Mobile, AL) 56159
Express (Boca Raton, FL) 58695
Express (Boynton Beach, FL) 58770
Express (Bradenton, FL) 58813
Express (Hialeah, FL) 59983
Express (Gainesville, GA) 66274
Express (Morrow, GA) 67008
Express (Alexandria, LA) 69375

Express (Oklahoma City, OK) 77353
Express (Charleston, SC) 78810
Express (Columbia, SC) 79010
Express (Chattanooga, TN) 80368
Express (El Paso, TX) 84796
Express (Fort Worth, TX) 85109
Express (Houston, TX) 86088
Express (Hurst, TX) 87273
Express Ltd. (Jacksonville, FL) 60267
Express Ltd. (Lakeland, FL) 60719
Express Ltd. (Tulsa, OK) 77937; 77938
Express Ltd. (Arlington, TX) 82647
Express Ltd. (El Paso, TX) 84797
Express Ltd. (Mesquite, TX) 87957
Exxon (Gilbertown, AL) 55807
Exxon (Huntsville, AL) 55916
Exxon (Montgomery, AL) 56309
Exxon (Somerville, AL) 56569
Exxon (Tuscaloosa, AL) 56639
Exxon (Bentonville, AR) 56784
Exxon (Camden, AR) 56829
Exxon (Dierks, AR) 56904
Exxon (Fort Smith, AR) 57049; 57050; 57051
Exxon (Hot Springs National Park, AR) 57168
Exxon (Mena, AR) 57364
Exxon (N Little Rock, AR) 57401
Exxon (Pine Bluff, AR) 57513
Exxon (Lehigh Acres, FL) 60892
Exxon (Lighthouse Point, FL) 60902
Exxon (Melbourne, FL) 61053
Exxon (Palmetto, FL) 62307
Exxon (Punta Gorda, FL) 62704
Exxon (Tampa, FL) 63414
Exxon (Atlanta, GA) 64432
Exxon (Macon, GA) 66685
Exxon (Norcross, GA) 67114
Exxon (Sylvania, GA) 67767
Exxon (Arcadia, LA) 69429
Exxon (Baton Rouge, LA) 69515; 69516; 69517; 69518
Exxon (Lafayette, LA) 70054
Exxon (Shreveport, LA) 70719
Exxon (Slidell, LA) 70818; 70819
Exxon (Clarksdale, MS) 72674
Exxon (Gautier, MS) 72784
Exxon (Greenville, MS) 72797; 72798
Exxon (Coinjock, NC) 74300
Exxon (Greensboro, NC) 74815
Exxon (Kinston, NC) 75318
Exxon (Matthews, NC) 75523; 75524
Exxon (Davis, OK) 76985
Exxon (Columbia, SC) 79011
Exxon (Greenville, SC) 79347
Exxon (Hilton Head Island, SC) 79513
Exxon (Lugoff, SC) 79618
Exxon (Travelers Rest, SC) 80043
Exxon (Austin, TX) 82864
Exxon (Bastrop, TX) 83095
Exxon (Baytown, TX) 83111
Exxon (Bellaire, TX) 83264
Exxon (Big Spring, TX) 83284
Exxon (Canyon, TX) 83442
Exxon (Cedar Hill, TX) 83527
Exxon (Corpus Christi, TX) 83714
Exxon (Cushing, TX) 83827
Exxon (Dallas, TX) 84017; 84018; 84019; 84020; 84021; 84022; 84023; 84024; 84025; 84026; 84027; 84028; 84029; 84030; 84031; 84032; 84033; 84034; 84035; 84036
Exxon (De Soto, TX) 84533
Exxon (El Paso, TX) 84798
Exxon (Fort Worth, TX) 85110; 85111; 85112
Exxon (Garland, TX) 85485
Exxon (Grand Prairie, TX) 85617
Exxon (Houston, TX) 86089; 86090; 86091; 86092; 86093; 86094; 86095; 86096; 86097; 86098; 86099; 86100; 86101; 86102; 86103; 86104; 86105; 86106; 86107; 86108; 86109; 86110; 86111; 86112
Exxon (Hutchins, TX) 87302
Exxon (Irving, TX) **87340**
Exxon (Killeen, TX) 87510
Exxon (Kingsville, TX) 87532
Exxon (Lufkin, TX) 87802
Exxon (Mc Queeney, TX) 87927
Exxon (Mesquite, TX) 87958; 87959
Exxon (Nederland, TX) 88185
Exxon (Orange, TX) 88311
Exxon (Pasadena, TX) 88404; 88405
Exxon (Plano, TX) 88563
Exxon (Poynor, TX) 88696
Exxon (Richardson, TX) 88735
Exxon (San Antonio, TX) 88979; 88980; 88981; 88982; 88983; 88984; 88985; 88986; 88987; 88988; 88989; 88990; 88991; 88992; 88993
Exxon (Spring, TX) 89467
Exxon (Texas City, TX) 89717

Exxon (Wichita Falls, TX) 90071
Exxon Auto Repair (Frederick, MD) 71722
Exxon Capital Holding Corp. (Irving, TX) 87341
Exxon Car Care (Malvern, AR) 57339
Exxon Car Care (Atlanta, GA) 64433
Exxon Car Care (Plano, TX) 88564
Exxon Car Care Center (Atlanta, GA) 64434
Exxon Car Care Center (New Orleans, LA) 70450
Exxon Car Care Center (Collierville, TN) 80618
Exxon Car Care Center (Memphis, TN) 81520; 81521
Exxon Car Care Center (Addison, TX) 82472
Exxon Car Care Center (Arlington, TX) 82648; 82649
Exxon Car Care Center (Dallas, TX) 84037; 84038; 84039; 84040; 84041; 84042; 84043; 84044; 84045; 84046; 84047
Exxon Car Care Center (Fort Worth, TX) 85113
Exxon Car Care Center (San Antonio, TX) 88994; 88995; 88996
Exxon Car Care Center (Spring, TX) 89468
Exxon Car Care Center (Arlington, VA) 90297; 90298
Exxon Car Care Center (Richmond, VA) 91865
Exxon Car Care Center (Virginia Beach, VA) 92460; 92461
Exxon Car Care Centers (Nashville, TN) 81955; 81956; 81957
Exxon Car Wash (Casselberry, FL) 58931
Exxon Car Wash (Winter Park, FL) 63972
Exxon Car Wash (Jackson, MS) 72982
Exxon Car Wash (Winston Salem, NC) 76668
Exxon Car Wash (Rock Hill, SC) 79819
Exxon Car Wash (Nashville, TN) 81958
Exxon Car Wash (Dallas, TX) 84048
Exxon Car Wash (Houston, TX) 86113; 86114
Exxon Car Wash (San Antonio, TX) 88997; 88998
Exxon Car Wash (Texas City, TX) 89718
Exxon Car Wash (Arlington, VA) 90299
Exxon Chemical Americas (Baytown, TX) 83112
Exxon Chemical Co. (Atlanta, GA) 64435
Exxon Chemical Co. (Baton Rouge, LA) 69519; 69520; 69521; 69522; 69523
Exxon Chemical Co. (New Orleans, LA) 70451
Exxon Chemical Co. (Oklahoma City, OK) 77354
Exxon Chemical Co. (Andrews, TX) 82595
Exxon Chemical Co. (Baytown, TX) 83113; 83114; 83115
Exxon Chemical Co. (Big Spring, TX) 83285
Exxon Chemical Co. (Dallas, TX) 84049
Exxon Chemical Co. (Houston, TX) 86115; 86116; 86117; 86118; 86119; 86120; 86121
Exxon Chemical Co. (Kilgore, TX) 87487
Exxon Chemical Co. (Midland, TX) 88034
Exxon Chemical Co. (Monahans, TX) 88137
Exxon Chemical Co. (Odessa, TX) 88240
Exxon Chemical Fertilizer Co. (Houston, TX) 86122
Exxon Chemical Lab Library (Baton Rouge, LA) 69524
Exxon Chemical Plant (Baytown, TX) 83116
Exxon Chemical Plastics Library (Baton Rouge, LA) 69525
Exxon Chemicals Americas (Charleston, WV) 92745
Exxon Coal & Minerals Co. (Houston, TX) 86123
Exxon Coal USA Inc. (Houston, TX) 86124
Exxon Co. (Batesville, AR) 56754
Exxon Co. (De Queen, AR) 56891
Exxon Co. (Washington, DC) 58224; 58225; 58226; 58227
Exxon Co. (Orange Park, FL) 61879

Exxon Co. (Whitley City, KY) 69338
Exxon Co. (Alexandria, LA) 69376
Exxon Co. (Baltimore, MD) 71115
Exxon Co. (Beltsville, MD) 71353; 71354
Exxon Co. (Bladensburg, MD) 71452
Exxon Co. (Bowie, MD) 71460
Exxon Co. (Bowie Md, MD) 71475
Exxon Co. (Capital Heigh, MD) 71497
Exxon Co. (Cockeysville, MD) 71547
Exxon Co. (College Park, MD) 71561; 71562
Exxon Co. (Gaithersburg, MD) 71772; 71773; 71774
Exxon Co. (Hillcrest Heights, MD) 71920
Exxon Co. (Silver Spring, MD) 72392; 72393
Exxon Co. (Suitland, MD) 72475
Exxon Co. (Florence, SC) 79198
Exxon Co. (Kingsport, TN) 81082
Exxon Co. (Austin, TX) 82865
Exxon Co. (Carthage, TX) 83516
Exxon Co. (Houston, TX) 86125
Exxon Co. (San Antonio, TX) 88999
Exxon Co. (Tomball, TX) 89768
Exxon Co. (Victoria, TX) 89886
Exxon Co. (Chesapeake, VA) 90571
Exxon Co. (Covington, VA) 90655
Exxon Co. (Lexington, VA) 91201
Exxon Co. (Lynchburg, VA) 91236
Exxon Co. (Richmond, VA) 91866
Exxon Co. (Charleston, WV) 92746
Exxon Co. (Ripley, WV) 93027
Exxon Co. Refinery Library (Baytown, TX) 83117
Exxon Co. Terminal (Collins, MS) 72695
Exxon Co. U S a (Henderson, KY) 68445
Exxon Co. U S a (Somerset, KY) 69292
Exxon Co. U S a (Chattanooga, TN) 80369; 80370
Exxon Co. U S a (Cleveland, TN) 80582
Exxon Co. U S a (Crossville, TN) 80693
Exxon Co. U S a (Kingsport, TN) 81083
Exxon Co. U S a (Memphis, TN) 81522
Exxon Co. U S a (Nashville, TN) 81959
Exxon Co. U S a (Charleston, WV) 92747
Exxon Co. U S A (Memphis, TN) 81523
Exxon Co. U S A (Nashville, TN) 81960
Exxon Co. U S a Marketing (Jackson, TN) 80970
Exxon Co. U S a Service Center (Nashville, TN) 81961
Exxon Co. USA (Atmore, AL) 55050
Exxon Co. USA (Mobile, AL) 56160
Exxon Co. USA (Tuscaloosa, AL) 56640
Exxon Co. USA (Booneville, AR) 56817
Exxon Co. USA (Newport, AR) 57448
Exxon Co. USA (Gulf Breeze, FL) 59936
Exxon Co. USA (Jay, FL) 60523
Exxon Co. USA (Meadows Village, FL) 61027
Exxon Co. USA (Pensacola, FL) 62422
Exxon Co. USA (Ruskin, FL) 62757
Exxon Co. USA (Tampa, FL) 63415
Exxon Co. USA (W Palm Beach, FL) 63790
Exxon Co. USA (Atlanta, GA) 64436; 64437
Exxon Co. USA (Doraville, GA) 65927
Exxon Co. USA (Marietta, GA) 66769
Exxon Co. USA (Sylvania, GA) 67768
Exxon Co. USA (Henderson, KY) 68446
Exxon Co. USA (Baton Rouge, LA) 69526; 69527; 69528; 69529
Exxon Co. USA (Centerville, LA) 69760; 69761; 69762
Exxon Co. USA (Columbia, LA) 69780
Exxon Co. USA (Houma, LA) 69951; 69952
Exxon Co. USA (Columbia, MS) 72698
Exxon Co. USA (Hattiesburg, MS) 72889

Federal Express Corp. (Atlanta, GA) 64441
Federal Express Corp. (Savannah, GA) 67466
Federal Express Corp. (Greensboro, NC) 74818
Federal Express Corp. (West Columbia, SC) 80092
Federal Express Corp. (Memphis, TN) 81533; 81534; 81535
Federal Express Corp. (Amarillo, TX) 82546
Federal Express Corp. (Dallas, TX) 84061
Federal Express Corp. (Houston, TX) 86193
Federal Express Europlex Inc. (Memphis, TN) 81536
Federal Express International Inc. (Memphis, TN) 81537; 81538; 81539
Federal Express Leasing Corp. (Memphis, TN) 81540; 81541
Federal Express Logistics Inc. (Memphis, TN) 81542; 81543
Federal Express Redevelopment Corp. (Memphis, TN) 81544; 81545
Federal Home Life Insurance Co. Inc. (Orlando, FL) 61969
Federal Home Loan Mortgage (Dallas, TX) 84062
Federal Home Loan Mortgage (McLean, VA) **91382**
Federal Home Loan Mortgage Cor (Washington, DC) 58239
Federal Home Loan Mortgage Corp. (McLean, VA) 91383
Federal Home Loan Mortgage Corp. (Freddic Mac)-Northeast Region (Arlington, VA) 90300
Federal Home Loan Mortgage Corp. (Freddie Mac)-Southeast/ Southwest Region (Atlanta, GA) 64442
Federal Metals Co. (Miami, FL) 61280
Federal Mogul (Summerton, SC) 79978
Federal Mogul (Blacksburg, VA) 90438
Federal Mogul Corp. (Atlanta, GA) 64443
Federal Mogul Corp. (Oklahoma City, OK) 77357
Federal Mogul Corp. (Manning, SC) 79630
Federal Mogul Corp. (Summerton, SC) 79979
Federal Mogul Corp. (Blacksburg, VA) 90439; 90440; 90441; 90442
Federal-Mogul Corp. Blacksburg Plant (Blacksburg, VA) 90443
Federal National Mortgage Asso (Washington, DC) 58240
Federal National Mortgage Association (Washington, DC) **58241**
Federal National Mortgage Association (Atlanta, GA) 64444
Federal Paper Board (Pineville, NC) 75814
Federal Paper Board Co. (Augusta, GA) 65320
Federal Paper Board Co. (Thomaston, GA) 67785
Federal Paper Board Co. (Washington, GA) 68022
Federal Paper Board Co. (Louisville, KY) 68762
Federal Paper Board Co. (Durham, NC) 74392
Federal Paper Board Co. (E Flat Rock, NC) 74446
Federal Paper Board Co. (East Flat Rock, NC) 74448
Federal Paper Board Co. (Four Oaks, NC) 74621
Federal Paper Board Co. (High Point, NC) 75124
Federal Paper Board Co. (Lumberton, NC) 75464
Federal Paper Board Co. (Rieglewood, NC) 76031
Federal Paper Board Co. (Wilmington, NC) 76556
Federal Paper Board Co. (Johnston, SC) 79545
Federal Paper Board Co. (Newberry, SC) 79725
Federal Paper Board Co. (Prosperity, SC) 79800; 79801
Federal Paper Board Co. Inc. (Norcross, GA) 67116
Federal Paper Board Co., Inc. (Bolton, NC) 73705
Federal Paper Board Co. Inc. (Charlotte, NC) 73950
Federal Paper Board Co. Inc. (Durham, NC) 74393
Federal Paper Board Co. Inc. (Riegelwood, NC) 76028; 76029
Federal Paper Board Co. Inc. (Wilmington, NC) 76557
Federal Paper Board Co. Inc. (Newberry, SC) 79726
Federal Paper Board Co. Inc. (Richmond, VA) 91871
Federal Paper Board Co. Inc. Augusta (Augusta, GA) 65321
Federal Paper Board Co. Inc.- Augusta Operations (Augusta, GA) 65322
Federal Paper Board Co. Inc. Plant 49 (Durham, NC) 74394
Federal Paper Board Co., Inc., Plant 24 (Wilmington, NC) 76558
Federal Paper Board Co. Inc. Riegelwood Operations (Riegelwood, NC) 76030
Federal Paperboard Co. Inc. (New Bern, NC) 75722
Federal Systems Advanced Technologies (Greensboro, NC) 74819
Federal Systems Group Inc. (Washington, DC) 58242
Federated Department Stores (Fort Worth, TX) 85118
Federated Dept Stores (Miami, FL) 61281
Federated Metals Corp. (Charlotte, NC) 73951
Federated Metals Corp. (Sand Springs, OK) 77780
FedEx Aeronautics Corp. (Memphis, TN) 81546
Fedex Customs Brokerage Corp. (Memphis, TN) 81547
Fedex International Transmission Corp. (Memphis, TN) 81548; 81549
Ferro Corp. (Miami, FL) 61282
Ferro Corp. (Wildwood, FL) 63915
Ferro Corp. (Duluth, GA) 66035
Ferro Corp. (Arlington, TX) 82652; 82653; 82654; 82655
Ferro Corp. (Houston, TX) 86194
Ferro Corp. (Tyler, TX) 89800
Ferro Corp. Coating Div. (Nashville, TN) 81962
Ferro Corp. Color Div. (Toccoa, GA) 67836
Ferro Corp. Grant Chemical (Baton Rouge, LA) 69534
Ferro Corp. Grant Chemical Div. (Zachary, LA) 70982
Ffrl Re Corp. (Richmond, VA) 91872
Fhp Inc. (Washington, DC) 58243
Fibers Business Unit (Fuquay Varina, NC) 74637
Fibertec Co. (Bethune, SC) 78736
FICON Corp. (Woodbridge, VA) 92612
Fidelity Bank (Frostburg, MD) 71754; 71755
Fieldale Towel Mill (Fieldale, VA) 90880
Fieldcrest Cannon (Pheonix City, AL) 56479
Fieldcrest Cannon (Scottsboro, AL) 56520
Fieldcrest Cannon (Eden, NC) **74452**
Fieldcrest Cannon Inc. (Eden, NC) 74453; 74454
Fieldcrest Cannon, Inc. (Kannapolis, NC) 75254; 75255; 75256
Fieldcrest Cannon Inc. Carpet & Rug (Calhoun Falls, SC) 78754
Fieldcrest Cannon Inc. Landrum Mills (Landrum, SC) 79583
Fieldcrest Cannon Inc. Non-Woven (Eden, NC) 74455
Fieldcrest Canon Inc. (Kannapolis, NC) 75257
Figgie Fire Protection Systems (Charlottesville, VA) 90535
Figgie Fire Protection Systems (Ranson, WV) 93021
Figgie Packaging Systems (Goose Creek, SC) 79279
Filterite, Plant 1 (Timonium, MD) 72502
Filterite, Plant 2 (Timonium, MD) 72503
Fina (Dallas, TX) **84063**
Fina Inc. (Dallas, TX) 84064; 84065
Fina Oil & Chemical Co. (Big Springs, TX) 83299
Fina Oil & Chemical Co. (Dallas, TX) 84066; 84067
Fina Oil & Chemical Co. (LaPorte, TX) 87603
Fina Oil & Chemical Co. (Pasadena, TX) 88407
Fina Oil & Chemical Co. La Porte Plant (La Porte, TX) 87560
Fina Technology Inc. (Deer Park, TX) 84550
Finance Co. (Manassas, VA) 91308
Fireside Books (Arlington, TX) 82656
First Alabama bank (Tuscaloosa, AL) 56641
First Alabama Bancshares (Birmingham, AL) **55235**
First Alabama Bancshares, Inc. (Birmingham, AL) 55236
First Alabama Bank (Alberta, AL) 54958
First Alabama Bank (Albertville, AL) 54963; 54964; 54965
First Alabama Bank (Alexander City, AL) 54974
First Alabama Bank (Andalusia, AL) 54987
First Alabama Bank (Anniston, AL) 54995; 54996; 54997
First Alabama Bank (Arab, AL) 55025
First Alabama Bank (Athens, AL) 55039; 55040
First Alabama Bank (Auburn, AL) 55060
First Alabama Bank (Bay Minette, AL) 55074
First Alabama Bank (Bayou La Batre, AL) 55078
First Alabama Bank (Bessemer, AL) 55087
First Alabama Bank (Birmingham, AL) 55237; 55238; 55239; 55240; 55241; 55242; 55243; 55244; 55245; 55246; 55247
First Alabama Bank (Blountsville, AL) 55463
First Alabama Bank (Butler, AL) 55495
First Alabama Bank (Cahaba Heights, AL) 55498
First Alabama Bank (Center Point, AL) 55502
First Alabama Bank (Centre, AL) 55503; 55504
First Alabama Bank (Citronelle, AL) 55516
First Alabama Bank (Clanton, AL) 55519; 55520
First Alabama Bank (Columbiana, AL) 55526
First Alabama Bank (Cordova, AL) 55529
First Alabama Bank (Cullman, AL) 55541; 55542; 55543
First Alabama Bank (Daphne, AL) 55565
First Alabama Bank (Decatur, AL) 55578; 55579; 55580
First Alabama Bank (Demopolis, AL) 55615
First Alabama Bank (Dothan, AL) 55636; 55637; 55638; 55639; 55640; 55641; 55642
First Alabama Bank (Ensley, AL) 55678
First Alabama Bank (Enterprise, AL) 55683; 55684
First Alabama Bank (Evergreen, AL) 55705
First Alabama Bank (Fairfield, AL) 55712
First Alabama Bank (Fairhope, AL) 55721; 55722
First Alabama Bank (Foley, AL) 55748
First Alabama Bank (Gadsden, AL) 55778; 55779; 55780
First Alabama Bank (Gardendale, AL) 55797; 55798
First Alabama Bank (Gilbertown, AL) 55808
First Alabama Bank (Gulf Shores, AL) 55822
First Alabama Bank (Guntersville, AL) 55824; 55825
First Alabama Bank (Hartselle, AL) 55855
First Alabama Bank (Homewood, AL) 55867; 55868
First Alabama Bank (Hoover, AL) 55870
First Alabama Bank (Huntsville, AL) 55917; 55918; 55919; 55920; 55921; 55922; 55923; 55924; 55925; 55926; 55927
First Alabama Bank (Jackson, AL) 56066
First Alabama Bank (Jemison, AL) 56091
First Alabama Bank (Killen, AL) 56094; 56095
First Alabama Bank (Lincoln, AL) 56112
First Alabama Bank (Livingston, AL) 56113
First Alabama Bank (Loxley, AL) 56115
First Alabama Bank (Madison, AL) 56120; 56121
First Alabama Bank (Mobile, AL) 56161; 56162; 56163; 56164; 56165; 56166; 56167; 56168; 56169; 56170; 56171; 56172; 56173; 56174; 56175; 56176; 56177
First Alabama Bank (Monroeville, AL) 56260
First Alabama Bank (Montevallo, AL) 56273
First Alabama Bank (Montgomery, AL) 56310; 56311; 56312; 56313; 56314; 56315; 56316; 56317; 56318; 56319; 56320; 56321; 56322; 56323; 56324; 56325; 56326; 56327; 56328; 56329; 56330; 56331
First Alabama Bank (Mountain Brook, AL) 56399
First Alabama Bank (North Port, AL) 56406
First Alabama Bank (Notasulga, AL) 56410
First Alabama Bank (Oneonta, AL) 56412
First Alabama Bank (Oxford, AL) 56439
First Alabama Bank (Pelham, AL) 56447; 56448
First Alabama Bank (Pennington, AL) 56453; 56454
First Alabama Bank (Phenix City, AL) 56460; 56461
First Alabama Bank (Prattville, AL) 56486; 56487; 56488
First Alabama Bank (Priceville, AL) 56495
First Alabama Bank (Robertsdale, AL) 56502
First Alabama Bank (Rogersville, AL) 56505
First Alabama Bank (Saraland, AL) 56513; 56514
First Alabama Bank (Selma, AL) 56525; 56526; 56527
First Alabama Bank (Semmes, AL) 56542
First Alabama Bank (Spanish Fort, AL) 56570
First Alabama Bank (Talladega, AL) 56592
First Alabama Bank (Thomasville, AL) 56608
First Alabama Bank (Trinity, AL) 56615
First Alabama Bank (Troy, AL) 56617; 56618; 56619
First Alabama Bank (Trussville, AL) 56627
First Alabama Bank (Tuscaloosa, AL) 56642; 56643; 56644; 56645; 56646; 56647; 56648; 56649
First Alabama Bank (Vestavia Hills, AL) 56702
First Alabama Bank (York, AL) 56712
First Alabama Bank Athens (Elkmont, AL) 55677
First Alabama Bank of Birmi (Bessemer, AL) 55088
First Alabama Bank of Birmi (Birmingham, AL) 55248; 55249; 55250; 55251; 55252; 55253
First Alabama Bank Birmingh (Birmingham, AL) 55254; 55255; 55256; 55257; 55258; 55259; 55260; 55261
First Alabama Bank of Birmingham (Bessemer, AL) 55089
First Alabama Bank of Birmingham (Birmingham, AL) 55262
First Alabama Bank Chilton (Thorsby, AL) 56611
First Alabama Bank Conecuh (Evergreen, AL) 55706
First Alabama Bank of Dotha (Dothan, AL) 55643; 55644; 55645; 55646
First Alabama Bank Dothan (Dothan, AL) 55647
First Alabama Bank of Hunts (Huntsville, AL) 55928
First Alabama Bank Huntsvil (Huntsville, AL) 55929; 55930; 55931; 55932; 55933
First Alabama Bank Huntsville (Huntsville, AL) 55934; 55935
First Alabama Bank Lee Cnty (Opelika, AL) 56416
First Alabama Bank of Montg (Montgomery, AL) 56332; 56333; 56334
First Alabama Bank of Selma (Selma, AL) 56528
First Alabama Bank Slema (Selma, AL) 56529
First Alabama Bank Talladeg (Munford, AL) 56402
First Alabama Bank of Tusca (Tuscaloosa, AL) 56650; 56651
First of America (Clearwater, FL) 58993
First of America (St. Petersburg, FL) 63105
First of America Banik (Rotunda, FL) 62752
First of America Bank (Arcadia, FL) 58582
First of America Bank (Bellaire Bluffs, FL) 58640
First of America Bank (Belleair Bluffs, FL) 58650
First of America Bank (Boca Raton, FL) 58696
First of America Bank (Bradenton, FL) 58814; 58815; 58816; 58817
First of America Bank (Cape Coral, FL) 58918
First of America Bank (Clearwater, FL) 58994; 58995
First of America Bank (Dunedin, FL) 59359
First of America Bank (El Jobean, FL) 59382
First of America Bank (Ellenton, FL) 59386; 59387; 59388; 59389
First of America Bank (Englewood, FL) 59393
First of America Bank (Foot Meyers, FL) 59419
First of America Bank (Fort Meyers, FL) 59656
First of America Bank (Holmes Beach, FL) 60111
First of America Bank (Hudson, FL) 60131
First of America Bank (Inverness, FL) 60149
First of America Bank (Lake Placid, FL) 60642
First of America Bank (Lehigh Acres, FL) 60893
First of America Bank (Murdock, FL) 61582
First of America Bank (N. Fort Meyers, FL) 61595
First of America Bank (New Port Richey, FL) 61681; 61682
First of America Bank (North Port, FL) 61754
First of America Bank (Osprey, FL) 62213
First of America Bank (Palmetto, FL) 62308
First of America Bank (Pinellas Park, FL) 62517
First of America Bank (Port Charlotte, FL) 62656
First of America Bank (Punta Gorda, FL) 62705; 62706
First of America Bank (Sarasota, FL) 62818; 62819; 62820; 62821; 62822; 62823; 62824
First of America Bank (Saratoga, FL) 62869
First of America Bank (St Petersburg, FL) 62971; 62972
First of America Bank (St. Petersburg, FL) 63106; 63107
First of America Bank (Treasure Island, FL) 63710
First of America Bank (Venice, FL) 63722
First of America Bank (W. Palm Beach, FL) 63825; 63826
First American Bank (Decatur, AL) 55581
First American Bank (Washington, DC) 58244
First American Bank (Ashland, KY) 68095
First American Bank (Cape St. Claire, MD) 71494; 71495
First American Bank (Laurel, MD) 72071
First American Bank (Severna Park, MD) 72373
First American Bank (Erick, OK) 77074
First American Bank (Stratford, OK) 77855
First American Bank (Bryan, TX) 83395
First American Bank (Alexandria, VA) 90180; 90181; 90182; 90183; 90184
First American Bank (Annandale, VA) 90259
First American Bank (Arlington, VA) 90301; 90302; 90303; 90304; 90305; 90306; 90307
First American Bank (Bridgewater, VA) 90466
First American Bank (Burke, VA) 90500
First American Bank (Chesapeake, VA) 90572
First American Bank (Fairfax, VA) 90767; 90768; 90769
First American Bank (Falls Church, VA) 90832
First American Bank (Front Royal, VA) 90948
First American Bank (Hampton, VA) 91025; 91026; 91027
First American Bank (Herndon, VA) 91121
First American Bank (Mc Lean, VA) 91365
First American Bank (Newport News, VA) 91462; 91463

First-Citizens Bank & Trust Co. (Sunbury, NC) 76347; 76348
First-Citizens Bank & Trust Co. (Swansboro, NC) 76352; 76353
First-Citizens Bank & Trust Co. (Sylva, NC) 76356
First-Citizens Bank & Trust Co. (Tarboro, NC) 76363
First-Citizens Bank & Trust Co. (Thomasville, NC) 76376; 76377
First-Citizens Bank & Trust Co. (Tryon, NC) 76411
First-Citizens Bank & Trust Co. (Walnut Cove, NC) 76446
First-Citizens Bank & Trust Co. (Warrenton, NC) 76448
First-Citizens Bank & Trust Co. (Washington, NC) 76455; 76456
First-Citizens Bank & Trust Co. (Waynesville, NC) 76466; 76467; 76468; 76469
First-Citizens Bank & Trust Co. (Weldon, NC) 76480; 76481
First-Citizens Bank & Trust Co. (West Jefferson, NC) 76486; 76487
First-Citizens Bank & Trust Co. (Whiteville, NC) 76499
First-Citizens Bank & Trust Co. (Wilkesboro, NC) 76506
First-Citizens Bank & Trust Co. (Williamston, NC) 76528; 76529
First-Citizens Bank & Trust Co. (Wilmington, NC) 76559; 76560; 76561; 76562; 76563; 76564; 76565
First-Citizens Bank & Trust Co. (Wilson, NC) 76629; 76630; 76631
First-Citizens Bank & Trust Co. (Windsor, NC) 76656
First-Citizens Bank & Trust Co. (Winston-Salem, NC) 76725; 76726; 76727; 76728; 76729; 76730
First-Citizens Bnak & Trust Co. (Reidsville, NC) 75998
First Citizens Mortgage (High Point, NC) 75130
First Citizens Mortgage Corp. (Silver Spring, MD) 72399; 72400
First Coast Community Bank (Fernandina Beach, FL) 59408
First Coast Community Bank (Fernandino Beach, FL) 59416
First Colony Life (Lubbock, TX) 87763
First Colony Life (Lynchburg, VA) 91238
First Colony Life (Richmond, VA) 91873
First Colony Life Insurance (Lynchburg, VA) 91239
First Colony Life Insurance Co. (Mobile, AL) 56178
First Colony Life Insurance Co. (Rockville, MD) 72275
First Colony Life Insurance Co. (Chattanooga, TN) 80375
First Colony Life Insurance Co. (Lynchburg, VA) 91240; 91241
First Commerce Corp. (New Orleans, LA) 70452
First Commercial Bank (Birmingham, AL) 55263; 55264; 55265; 55266; 55267; 55268; 55269; 55270; 55271
First Commercial Bank (Huntsville, AL) 55937; 55938; 55939; 55940; 55941; 55942
First Community Bank of Tifton (Tifton, GA) 67821; 67822; 67823; 67824
First Data Corp. (Greensboro, NC) 74830
First Data Corp. (Dallas, TX) 84068
First Data Resources (Atlanta, GA) 64447
First Data Resources (Chamblee, GA) 65522
First Data Resources (San Antonio, TX) 89008
First Federal S & L (Cullman, AL) 55544
First Federal S & L (Florence, AL) 55736
First Federal S & L (Guntersville, AL) 55826
First Federal S & L (Sheffield, AL) 56549
First Federal S & L (Sylacauga, AL) 56586
First Federal S & L (Talladega, AL) 56593
First Federal S & L (Camden, AR) 56830
First Federal S & L (Harrison, AR) 57137
First Federal S & L (Mountain Home, AR) 57386
First Federal S & L (Cape Coral, FL) 58919

First Federal S & L (Milledgeville, GA) 66975
First Federal S & L (Valdosta, GA) 67944
First Federal S & L (Ashland, KY) 68096
First Federal S & L (Hazard, KY) 68425
First Federal S & L. (Lexington, KY) 68549; 68550; 68551
First Federal S & L (Houma, LA) 69953; 69954
First Federal S & L (Charlotte, NC) 73976
First Federal S & L (Durham, NC) 74398
First Federal S & L (Lincolnton, NC) 75439
First Federal S & L (Rockingham, NC) 76060
First Federal S & L (Cheraw, SC) 78922
First Federal S & L (Darlington, SC) 79146
First Federal S & L (Columbia, TN) 80627
First Federal S & L (Paris, TX) 88366
First Federal S & L (Tyler, TX) 89801
First Federal S & L (Fairfax, VA) 90772
First Federal S & L (Ravenswood, WV) 93022
First Federal S&L of America (Front Royal, VA) 90949
First Federal S&L of America (Lynchburg, VA) 91242; 91243
First Federal S&L of America (South Boston, VA) 92249
First Federal Savings Bank (Hopkinsville, KY) 68477; 68478
First Federal Savings Bank of Maryville (Maryville, TN) 81408; 81409
First Fidelity Bancorp (Oklahoma City, OK) 77358
First Fidelity Bancorp (Fairmont, WV) 92839
First Financial Bank F S B (Kenner, LA) 69995
First Financial Bank-F S B (New Orleans, LA) 70453
First Financial Bank a Fsb (El Dorado, AR) 56942
First Financial Management Corp. (Atlanta, GA) 64448
First FSB of Maryville (Alcoa, TN) 80153
First General Mortgage Co. (Falls Church, VA) 90834
First General Mortgage Co. Inc. (Falls Church, VA) 90835
First Gibraltar Bank (Enid, OK) 77052
First Gibraltar Bank (Irving, TX) 87345
First Interstate Bank of Texas (Houston, TX) 86196
First Louisiana Acceptance Corp. (Metairie, LA) 70261
First Maryland Bancorp (Baltimore, MD) 71121
First Mutual Financial Corp. (Houston, TX) 86197; 86198
First Mutual Investments (Knoxville, TN) 81184
First National Bank (Jasper, AL) 56079; 56080; 56081; 56082; 56083; 56084; 56085
First National Bank (Montgomery, AL) 56335
First National Bank (Crossville, TN) 80697; 80698; 80699; 80700
First National Bank (Fairfield Glade, TN) 80784
First National Bank (Monteagle, TN) 81781
First National Bank (Shelbyville, TN) 82307; 82308; 82309; 82310
First National Bank (Tracy City, TN) 82372
First National Bank of Atlanta (New Castle, DE) 57864
First National Bank of Atlanta (Wilmington, DE) 58062
First National Bank of Birmingham Alabama (Wylam, AL) 56711
First National Bank of Florida (Eagle Lake, FL) 59374
First National Bank of Georgia (College Park, GA) 65584
First National Bank of Georgia (Marietta, GA) 66770
First National Bank of Jasper (Carbon Hill, AL) 55501
First National Bank of Jasper (Cordova, AL) 55530
First National Bank of Jasper (Dora, AL) 55622
First National Bank of Jasper (Oakman, AL) 56411
First National Bank of Maryland (Baltimore, MD) 71122; 71123;

71124; 71125; 71126; 71127; 71128; 71129; 71130; 71131; 71132; 71133; 71134; 71135; 71136; 71137; 71138; 71139; 71140; 71141; 71142; 71143; 71144; 71145; 71146; 71147; 71148; 71149
First National Bank of Maryland (Dorsey, MD) 71654
First National Bank Maryland (Silver Spring, MD) 72401
First National Bank of Maryland, DC (Washington, DC) 58246
First National Bank of St. Mary's (Charlotte Hall, MD) 71510
First National Bank of St. Mary's (Hollywood, MD) 71921
First National Bank of St. Mary's (Leonardtown, MD) 72099; 72100
First National Bank of St. Mary's (Lexington Park, MD) 72101; 72102
First National Bank of St. Mary's (Patuxent River, MD) 72214
First National Bank & Trust (Crestview, FL) 59123
First National Bank & Trust (Destin, FL) 59343
First National Bank & Trust (Fort Pierce, FL) 59794
First National Bank & Trust (Fort Walton Beach, FL) 59825; 59826
First National Bank & Trust (Immokalee, FL) 60134
First National Bank & Trust (Mary Esther, FL) 61016
First National Bank & Trust (Port St Lucie, FL) 62685
First National Bank & Trust (Stuart, FL) 63162
First National Bank & Trust (Siler City, NC) 76248
First National Bank & Trust (Blackwell, OK) 76864
First National Bank & Trust (Chickasha, OK) 76925
First National Bank & Trust (Frederick, OK) 77081
First National Bank & Trust (Mc Alester, OK) 77190
First National Bank & Trust (Muskogee, OK) 77218
First National Bank & Trust (Perry, OK) 77702
First National Bank & Trust (Ponca City, OK) 77704
First National Bank & Trust (Tulsa, OK) 77940
First National Bank & Trust Co. (Louisville, GA) 66619
First National Bank & Trust Co. (Cumberland, MD) 71622
First National Bank of Tuscaloosa (Tuscaloosa, AL) 56653
First National Bank of Tusk (Tuscaloosa, AL) 56654
First Omni Bank, NA (Millsboro, DE) 57846; 57847
First Omni Bank National as (Millsboro, DE) 57848
First Recovery (Lexington, KY) 68552
First Savings Bank (Greenville, SC) 79349
First Security Mortgage (Greenbelt, MD) 71860
First Security Mortgage (Temple Hills, MD) 72493
First Security Mortgage (Jackson, TN) 80977
First Security Mortgage Cor (Birmingham, AL) 55272
First Security Mortgage Cor (Metairie, LA) 70262
First Security Mortgage Inc. (Gaithersburg, MD) 71777
First State Bank of Fayette County (Somerville, TN) 82334; 82335
First State Bank & Trust Co. (Conway, AR) 56860
First State Bank & Trust Co. (Greenbrier, AR) 57123
First State Bank & Trust Co. (Lake Village, AR) 57240
First State Bank & Trust Co. (Mayflower, AR) 57355
First State Bank & Trust Co. (Vilonia, AR) 57700
First State Bank & Trust Co. (Albany, GA) 64067; 64068; 64069; 64070; 64071
First State Bank & Trust Co. (Valdosta, GA) 67945; 67946; 67947; 67948
First State Bank & Trust Co. (Baton Rouge, LA) 69535
First State Bank & Trust Co. (Bogalusa, LA) 69701
First State Bank & Trust Co. (Hollis, OK) 77137
First State Bank & Trust Co. (Bay City, TX) 83098

First State Bank & Trust Co. (Carthage, TX) 83517
First State Bank & Trust Co. (Edinburg, TX) 84732
First State Bank & Trust Co. (Mission, TX) 88122
First State Bank & Trust Co. (Port Lavaca, TX) 88666; 88667
First State Bank & Trust Co. of Valdosta (Lake Park, GA) 66497
First State Bank & Trust Co. of Valdosta (Valdosta, GA) 67949; 67950; 67951; 67952; 67953; 67954
First Tennesee Bank NA (Greenville, TN) 80895
First Tennesse Bank NA (Madison, TN) 81376
First Tennessee Bank NA (Alcoa, TN) 80154; 80155
First Tennessee Bank NA (Antioch, TN) 80169
First Tennessee Bank NA (Bartlett, TN) 80198
First Tennessee Bank NA (Blountville, TN) 80204
First Tennessee Bank NA (Brentwood, TN) 80227; 80228
First Tennessee Bank NA (Bristol, TN) 80244; 80245
First Tennessee Bank NA (Chattanooga, TN) 80376; 80377; 80378; 80379; 80380; 80381; 80382; 80383; 80384; 80385; 80386; 80387; 80388; 80389; 80390; 80391; 80392
First Tennessee Bank NA (Cookeville, TN) 80654; 80655; 80656
First Tennessee Bank NA (Cordova, TN) 80675; 80676
First Tennessee Bank NA (Dandridge, TN) 80710
First Tennessee Bank NA (Dyersburg, TN) 80747; 80748
First Tennessee Bank NA (Erwin, TN) 80775
First Tennessee Bank NA (Fall Branch, TN) 80788
First Tennessee Bank NA (Franklin, TN) 80813; 80814; 80815; 80816
First Tennessee Bank NA (Gallatin, TN) 80845; 80846
First Tennessee Bank NA (Gray, TN) 80874
First Tennessee Bank NA (Greenville, TN) 80896
First Tennessee Bank NA (Hendersonville, TN) 80914
First Tennessee Bank NA (Jackson, TN) 80978; 80979; 80980; 80981; 80982; 80983
First Tennessee Bank NA (Johnson City, TN) 81033; 81034; 81035; 81036
First Tennessee Bank NA (Jonesborough, TN) 81066
First Tennessee Bank NA (Kingsport, TN) 81090; 81091; 81092; 81093
First Tennessee Bank NA (Knoxville, TN) 81185; 81186; 81187; 81188; 81189; 81190; 81191; 81192; 81193; 81194; 81195; 81196; 81197; 81198; 81199; 81200; 81201; 81202; 81203; 81204; 81205; 81206; 81207; 81208; 81209; 81210; 81211
First Tennessee Bank NA (LaVergne, TN) 81287
First Tennessee Bank NA (Lebanon, TN) 81297; 81298; 81299
First Tennessee Bank NA (Maryville, TN) 81410; 81411; 81412; 81413; 81414; 81415
First Tennessee Bank NA (Memphis, TN) 81566; 81567; 81568; 81569; 81570; 81571; 81572; 81573; 81574; 81575; 81576; 81577; 81578; 81579; 81580; 81581; 81582; 81583; 81584; 81585; 81586; 81587; 81588; 81589; 81590; 81591; 81592; 81593; 81594; 81595; 81596; 81597; 81598; 81599; 81600; 81601; 81602; 81603; 81604
First Tennessee Bank NA (Morristown, TN) 81794; 81795; 81796; 81797
First Tennessee Bank NA (Mosheim, TN) 81820
First Tennessee Bank NA (Mt. Juliet, TN) 81829
First Tennessee Bank NA (Murfreesboro, TN) 81843; 81844; 81845
First Tennessee Bank NA (Nashville, TN) 81988; 81989; 81990; 81991; 81992

First Tennessee Bank NA (Nolensville, TN) 82177
First Tennessee Bank NA (Rogersville, TN) 82274
First Tennessee Bank NA (Unicol, TN) 82380
First Tennessee Bank NA (White Creek, TN) 82414
First Tennessee Bank NA (White Pine, TN) 82416
First Tennessee National Corp. (Memphis, TN) 81605; 81606
First Trust Savings Bank, FSB (Jacksonville, FL) 60269
First Union Bank of Florida (Apopka, FL) 58570
First Union Brokerage Services, Inc. (Charlotte, NC) 73977
First Union Commercial Corp. (Charlotte, NC) 73978
First Union Corp. (Charlotte, NC) 73979; 73980; 73981
First Union Corp. of Georgia (Atlanta, GA) 64449
First Union Futures Corp. (Charlotte, NC) 73982
First Union Home Equity Corp. (Charlotte, NC) 73983
First Union Mortgage Corp. (Charlotte, NC) 73984
First Union Naitonal Bank of Maryland (Frederick, MD) 71725
First Union Naitonal Bank of Maryland (Landover, MD) 72015
First Union Natinal Bank of Virginia (Arlington, VA) 90322
First Union Nationa Bank of Tennessee (Dickson, TN) 80732
First Union National Bak of Virginia (Grafton, VA) 90996
First Union National Bank, Capital Area (McLean, VA) 91385
First Union National Bank of Florida (, FL) 58531
First Union National Bank of Florida (Altamonte Springs, FL) 58554
First Union National Bank of Florida (Auburndale, FL) 58596
First Union National Bank of Florida (Barefoot Bay, FL) 58617
First Union National Bank of Florida (Barton, FL) 58619
First Union National Bank of Florida (Belle Glade, FL) 58643
First Union National Bank of Florida (Belleair Bluff, FL) 58647
First Union National Bank of Florida (Boca Raton, FL) 58697; 58698; 58699; 58700; 58701; 58702; 58703; 58704
First Union National Bank of Florida (Boynton Beach, FL) 58771; 58772; 58773; 58774
First Union National Bank of Florida (Bradenton, FL) 58818; 58819; 58820; 58821; 58822; 58823
First Union National Bank of Florida (Brandon, FL) 58869
First Union National Bank of Florida (Bushnell, FL) 58901
First Union National Bank of Florida (Callahan, FL) 58906
First Union National Bank of Florida (Cape Canaveral, FL) 58912; 58913
First Union National Bank of Florida (Cape Coral, FL) 58920; 58921
First Union National Bank of Florida (Chipley, FL) 58953
First Union National Bank of Florida (Clearwater, FL) 58996; 58997; 58998; 58999; 59000; 59001; 59002; 59003
First Union National Bank of Florida (Clermont, FL) 59056
First Union National Bank of Florida (Cocoa, FL) 59068
First Union National Bank of Florida (Cocoa Beach, FL) 59080
First Union National Bank of Florida (Cooper City, FL) 59091
First Union National Bank of Florida (Coral Gables, FL) 59100; 59101
First Union National Bank of Florida (Coral Springs, FL) 59113; 59114
First Union National Bank of Florida (Crystal River, FL) 59131
First Union National Bank of Florida (Dade City, FL) 59138
First Union National Bank of Florida (Davie, FL) 59157; 59158
First Union National Bank of Florida (Daytona Beach, FL) 59174; 59175; 59176; 59177; 59178
First Union National Bank of Florida (Daytonna Beach, FL) 59235

First Union National Bank of Florida (Deerfield Beach, FL) 59277; 59278
First Union National Bank of Florida (DeLand, FL) 59301; 59302
First Union National Bank of Florida (Delray Beach, FL) 59316; 59317
First Union National Bank of Florida (Deltona, FL) 59335; 59336
First Union National Bank of Florida (Dundee, FL) 59353
First Union NAtional Bank of Florida (Dunedin, FL) 59360; 59361
First Union National Bank of Florida (Edgewater, FL) 59377
First Union National Bank of Florida (Englewood, FL) 59394; 59395
First Union National Bank of FLorida (Eustis, FL) 59398; 59399
First Union National Bank of Florida (Fernandina Beach, FL) 59409; 59410
First Union National Bank of Florida (For Lauderdale, FL) 59420
First Union National Bank of Florida (For Myers, FL) 59421
First Union National Bank of Florida (Fort Lauderdale, FL) 59484; 59485; 59486; 59487; 59488; 59489; 59490; 59491; 59492; 59493; 59494; 59495
First Union National Bank of Florida (Fort Meade, FL) 59649
First Union National Bank of Florida (Fort Myers, FL) 59696; 59697
First Union National Bank of Florida (Fort Pierce, FL) 59795; 59796; 59797
First Union National Bank of Florida (Gainesville, FL) 59869; 59870; 59871; 59872; 59873; 59874; 59875; 59876
First Union National Bank of Florida (Green Cove Springs, FL) 59931
First Union National Bank of Florida (Haines City, FL) 59944; 59945
First Union National Bank of Florida (Hialeah, FL) 59984; 59985
First Union National Bank of Florida (Hollywood, FL) 60057; 60058; 60059
First Union National Bank of Florida (Holmes Beach, FL) 60112
First Union National Bank of Florida (Indialantic, FL) 60135
First Union National Bank of Florida (Indian Harbour Beach, FL) 60137; 60138
First Union National Bank of Florida (Jacksonville, FL) 60270; 60271; 60272; 60273; 60274; 60275; 60276; 60277; 60278; 60279; 60280; 60281; 60282; 60283; 60284; 60285; 60286; 60287; 60288; 60289; 60290; 60291; 60292; 60293; 60294; 60295; 60296; 60297; 60298; 60299; 60300
First Union National Bank of Florida (Jacksonville Beach, FL) 60518; 60519
First Union National Bank of Florida (Jensen Beach, FL) 60525; 60526
First Union National Bank of Florida (Juno Beach, FL) 60528
First Union National Bank of Florida (Jupiter, FL) 60535; 60536; 60537; 60538
First Union National Bank of Florida (Key Largo, FL) 60566
First Union National Bank of Florida (Key West, FL) 60572; 60573
First Union National Bank of Florida (Keystone Heights, FL) 60580
First Union National Bank of Florida (Kissimmee, FL) 60587
First Union National Bank of Florida (Lake Alfred, FL) 60609
First Union National Bank of Florida (Lake Panasoffkee, FL) 60640
First Union National Bank of Florida (Lake Wales, FL) 60652
First Union National Bank of Florida (Lake Worth, FL) 60668; 60669
First Union National Bank of Florida (Lakeland, FL) 60720; 60721; 60722; 60723; 60724
First Union National Bank of Florida (Lakewood, FL) 60801
First Union National Bank of Florida (Lantana, FL) 60804; 60805
First Union National Bank of Florida (Lauderdale Lakes, FL) 60872
First Union National Bank of Florida (Lauderhill, FL) 60875
First Union National Bank of Florida (Leesburg, FL) 60883
First Union National Bank of Florida (Lehigh Acres, FL) 60894
First Union National Bank of Florida (Lessburg, FL) 60897
First Union National Bank of Florida (Lighthouse Point, FL) 60903
First Union National Bank of Florida (Longwood, FL) 60929; 60930; 60931
First Union National Bank of Florida (Madeira Beach, FL) 60965
First Union National Bank of Florida (Madison, FL) 60966
First Union National Bank of Florida (Maitland, FL) 60977
First Union National Bank of Florida (Margate, FL) 61001
First Union National Bank of Florida (Melbourne, FL) 61054; 61055
First Union National Bank of Florida (Merritt Island, FL) 61140
First Union National Bank of Florida (Miami, FL) 61283; 61284; 61285; 61286; 61287; 61288; 61289; 61290; 61291; 61292; 61293; 61294; 61295; 61296; 61297; 61298; 61299; 61300; 61301; 61302; 61303; 61304; 61305; 61306; 61307; 61308; 61309; 61310
First Union National Bank of Florida (Miami Lakes, FL) 61535
First Union National Bank of Florida (Miami Springs, FL) 61538
First Union National Bank of Florida (Middleburg, FL) 61539
First Union National Bank of Florida (Miramar, FL) 61558
First Union National Bank of Florida (Mount Dora, FL) 61564
First Union National Bank of Florida (Naples, FL) 61618; 61619; 61620; 61621
First Union National Bank of Florida (New Port Richey, FL) 61683; 61684; 61685
First Union National Bank of Florida (New Smyrna Beach, FL) 61701; 61702; 61703
First Union National Bank of Florida (North Fort Myers, FL) 61728
First Union National Bank of Florida (North Miami, FL) 61734; 61735
First Union National Bank of Florida (North Palm Beach, FL) 61749; 61750
First Union National Bank of Florida (North Port, FL) 61755
First Union National Bank of Florida (Ocala, FL) 61794; 61795; 61796; 61797; 61798
First Union National Bank of Florida (Oldsmar, FL) 61847
First Union National Bank of Florida (Opa Locka, FL) 61858
First Union National Bank of Florida (Orange Park, FL) 61880; 61881; 61882; 61883
First Union National Bank of Florida (Orlanda, FL) 61901
First Union National Bank of Florida (Orlando, FL) 61970; 61971; 61972; 61973; 61974; 61975; 61976; 61977; 61978; 61979; 61980; 61981; 61982; 61983; 61984; 61985
First Union National Bank of Florida (Ormond Beach, FL) 62201; 62202; 62203
First Union National Bank of Florida (Pahokee, FL) 62222
First Union National Bank of Florida (Palatka, FL) 62225; 62226
First Union National Bank of Florida (Palm Bay, FL) 62233; 62234
First Union National Bank of Florida (Palm Beach, FL) 62252; 62253; 62254; 62255; 62256; 62257
First Union National Bank of Florida (Palm Beach Garden, FL) 62262
First Union National Bank of Florida (Palm Beach Gardens, FL) 62270; 62271
First Union National Bank of Florida (Palm City, FL) 62277; 62278
First Union National Bank of Florida (Palm Coast, FL) 62284
First Union National Bank of Florida (Palm Harbor, FL) 62297
First Union National Bank of Florida (Palm Springs, FL) 62303
First Union National Bank of Florida (Panama City, FL) 62320; 62321
First Union National Bank of Florida (Panama City Beach, FL) 62359
First Union National Bank of Florida (Pembroke Pines, FL) 62369
First Union National Bank of Florida (Pensacola, FL) 62424; 62425; 62426; 62427; 62428; 62429; 62430
First Union National Bank of Florida (Perrine, FL) 62495
First Union National Bank of Florida (Perry, FL) 62499
First Union National Bank of Florida (Plantation, FL) 62568; 62569; 62570
First Union National Bank of Florida (Pompano Beach, FL) 62594; 62595; 62596; 62597
First Union National Bank of Florida (Ponte Vedra Beach, FL) 62650
First Union National Bank of Florida (Port Orange, FL) 62662; 62663
First Union National Bank of Florida (Port Richey, FL) 62671; 62672
First Union National Bank of Florida (Port St. Lucie, FL) 62698
First Union National Bank of Florida (Punta Gorda, FL) 62707
First Union National Bank of Florida (Redington Shores, FL) 62735
First Union National Bank of Florida (Riviera Beach, FL) 62738
First Union National Bank of Florida (Rockledge, FL) 62744
First Union National Bank of Florida (Royal Palm Beach, FL) 62754; 62755
First Union National Bank of Florida (Sanford, FL) 62766; 62767
First Union National Bank of Florida (Sarasota, FL) 62825; 62826; 62827; 62828; 62829; 62830; 62831
First Union National Bank of Florida (Satellite Beach, FL) 62870
First Union National Bank of Florida (Sebastian, FL) 62873
First Union National Bank of Florida (Sebring, FL) 62880; 62881
First Union National Bank of Florida (Seminole, FL) 62905; 62906; 62907
First Union National Bank of Florida (South Miami, FL) 62923
First Union National Bank of Florida (St. Augustine, FL) 63055; 63056; 63057
First Union National Bank of Florida (St. Petersburg, FL) 63108; 63109; 63110; 63111; 63112; 63113; 63114
First Union National Bank of Florida (St. Petersburg Beach, FL) 63140
First Union National Bank of Florida (Starke, FL) 63143; 63144
First Union National Bank of Florida (Stuart, FL) 63163; 63164; 63165; 63166
First Union National Bank of Florida (Sun City Center, FL) 63187
First Union National Bank of Florida (Sunrise, FL) 63193
First Union National Bank of Florida (Tallahassee, FL) 63237; 63238; 63239; 63240; 63241
First Union National Bank of Florida (Tamarac, FL) 63299
First Union National Bank of Florida (Tampa, FL) 63417; 63418; 63419; 63420; 63421; 63422; 63423; 63424; 63425; 63426; 63427; 63428; 63429; 63430; 63431
First Union National Bank of Florida (Tavares, FL) 63669; 63670
First Union National Bank of Florida (Titusville, FL) 63685; 63686; 63687
First Union National Bank of Florida (Venice, FL) 63723; 63724; 63725
First Union National Bank of Florida (Vero Beach, FL) 63750; 63751; 63752; 63753; 63754; 63755
First Union National Bank of Florida (Webster, FL) 63829
First Union National Bank of Florida (Wellington, FL) 63831
First Union National Bank of Florida (West Melbourne, FL) 63834; 63835
First Union National Bank of Florida (West Miami, FL) 63836
First Union National Bank of Florida (West Palm Beach, FL) 63856; 63857; 63858; 63859; 63860; 63861; 63862; 63863
First Union National Bank of Florida (Wildwood, FL) 63916
First Union National Bank of Florida (Winter Garden, FL) 63921
First Union National Bank of Florida (Winter Haven, FL) 63934; 63935; 63936; 63937; 63938; 63939
First Union National Bank of Florida (Winter Park, FL) 63974; 63975; 63976; 63977; 63978
First Union National Bank of Florida (Zephyrhills, FL) 64010; 64011
First Union National Bank of Forida (Vero Beach, FL) 63756
First Union National Bank of Georgia (Kenneth City, FL) 60560
First Union National Bank of Georgia (Melbourne, FL) 61056
First Union National Bank of Georgia (Albany, GA) 64072; 64073
First Union National Bank of Georgia (Alpharetta, GA) 64110; 64111
First Union National Bank of Georgia (Atlanta, GA) 64450; 64451; 64452; 64453; 64454; 64455; 64456; 64457; 64458; 64459; 64460; 64461; 64462; 64463; 64464; 64465; 64466; 64467; 64468; 64469
First Union National Bank of Georgia (Augusta, GA) 65323; 65324; 65325; 65326; 65327; 65328; 65329; 65330
First Union National Bank of Georgia (Bremen, GA) 65394
First Union National Bank of Georgia (Chamblee, GA) 65523; 65524; 65525
First Union National Bank of Georgia (Chatsworth, GA) 65556
First Union National Bank of Georgia (Columbus, GA) 65640; 65641; 65642; 65643; 65644; 65645; 65646
First Union National Bank of Georgia (Conyers, GA) 65679
First Union National Bank of Georgia (Dalton, GA) 65783; 65784; 65785
First Union National Bank of Georgia (Decatur, GA) 65814; 65815; 65816; 65817; 65818; 65819; 65820
First Union National Bank of Georgia (Doraville, GA) 65928
First Union National Bank of Georgia (Douglasville, GA) 65985
First Union National Bank of Georgia (Dublin, GA) 66008
First Union National Bank of Georgia (Duluth, GA) 66036
First Union National Bank of Georgia (Dunwoody, GA) 66109
First Union National Bank of Georgia (East Point, GA) 66144
First Union National Bank of Georgia (Evans, GA) 66172
First Union National Bank of Georgia (Fayetteville, GA) 66190
First Union National Bank of Georgia (Fort Benning, GA) 66256; 66257
First Union National Bank of Georgia (Fort Gordon, GA) 66258
First Union National Bank of Georgia (Griffin, GA) 66315; 66316
First Union National Bank of Georgia (Hamilton, GA) 66329
First Union National Bank of Georgia (Hampton, GA) 66330
First Union National Bank of Georgia (Hapeville, GA) 66333
First Union National Bank of Georgia (Hinesville, GA) 66350
First Union National Bank of Georgia (Kennesaw, GA) 66413; 66414
First Union National Bank of Georgia (Lawrenceville, GA) 66513; 66514
First Union National Bank of Georgia (Lilburn, GA) 66558; 66559
First Union National Bank of Georgia (Lithonia, GA) 66594
First Union National Bank of Georgia (Mableton, GA) 66633
First Union National Bank of Georgia (Macon, GA) 66686; 66687; 66688; 66689; 66690
First Union National Bank of Georgia (Marietta, GA) 66771; 66772; 66773; 66774; 66775; 66776; 66777; 66778; 66779
First Union National Bank of Georgia (Martinez, GA) 66954
First Union National Bank of Georgia (Newnan, GA) 67081
First Union National Bank of Georgia (Norcross, GA) 67117; 67118; 67119
First Union National Bank of Georgia (Pine Mountain, GA) 67268
First Union National Bank of Georgia (Powder Springs, GA) 67286
First Union National Bank of Georgia (Riverdale, GA) 67311
First Union National Bank of Georgia (Rome, GA) 67337; 67338; 67339; 67340
First Union National Bank of Georgia (Roswell, GA) 67369; 67370; 67371; 67372; 67373
First Union National Bank of Georgia (Savannah, GA) 67467; 67468; 67469; 67470; 67471; 67472; 67473; 67474; 67475
First Union National Bank of Georgia (Smyrna, GA) 67550
First Union National Bank of Georgia (Snellville, GA) 67589
First Union National Bank of Georgia (Stockbridge, GA) 67658
First Union National Bank of Georgia (Stone Mountain, GA) 67689; 67690; 67691; 67692
First Union National Bank of Georgia (Sylvania, GA) 67769
First Union National Bank of Georgia (Tucker, GA) 67855
First Union National Bank of Georgia (Valdosta, GA) 67955; 67956
First Union National Bank of Georgia (Vidalia, GA) 67986
First Union National Bank of Georgia (Waycross, GA) 68032
First Union National Bank of Georgia (Waynesboro, GA) 68046
First Union National Bank of Georgia (Woodstock, GA) 68069
First Union National Bank of Maryland (Annapolis, MD) 71012; 71013
First Union National Bank of Maryland (Baltimore, MD) 71150; 71151
First Union National Bank of Maryland (Beltsville, MD) 71356
First Union National Bank of Maryland (Bethesda, MD) 71387; 71388; 71389; 71390; 71391
First Union National Bank of Maryland (Bowie, MD) 71461
First Union National Bank of Maryland (Chevy Chase, MD) 71529
First Union National Bank of Maryland (Clinton, MD) 71537
First Union National Bank of Maryland (Cockeysville, MD) 71549
First Union National Bank of Maryland (Columbia, MD) 71587; 71588; 71589
First Union National Bank of Maryland (Crofton, MD) 71615
First Union National Bank of Maryland (Ferestville, MD) 71684
First Union National Bank of Maryland (Frederick, MD) 71726
First Union National Bank of Maryland (Gaithersburg, MD) 71778; 71779; 71780
First Union National Bank of Maryland (Glen Burnie, MD) 71842
First Union National Bank of Maryland (Greenbelt, MD) 71861

First Union National Bank of Maryland (Kensington, MD) 71994; 71995
First Union National Bank of Maryland (Landover, MD) 72016
First Union National Bank of Maryland (Langley Park, MD) 72040
First Union National Bank of Maryland (Laurel, MD) 72073; 72074; 72075
First Union National Bank of Maryland (Olney, MD) 72174
First Union National Bank of Maryland (Owings Mills, MD) 72185
First Union National Bank of Maryland (Oxon Hill, MD) 72196
First Union National Bank of Maryland (Potomac, MD) 72229; 72230
First Union National Bank of Maryland (Rockville, MD) 72276; 72277; 72278; 72279; 72280; 72281; 72282
First Union National Bank of Maryland (Severna Park, MD) 72374
First Union National Bank of Maryland (Silver Spring, MD) 72402; 72403; 72404; 72405; 72406
First Union National Bank of Maryland (Towson, MD) 72507
First Union National Bank of Maryland (Waldorf, MD) 72528
First Union National Bank of Maryland (Wheaton, MD) 72554
First Union National Bank of North Carolina (Advance, NC) 73521
First Union National Bank of North Carolina (Albemarle, NC) 73534; 73535
First Union National Bank of North Carolina (Albermarle, NC) 73545
First Union National Bank of North Carolina (Andrews, NC) 73546
First Union National Bank of North Carolina (Archdale, NC) 73561
First Union National Bank of North Carolina (Arden, NC) 73569
First Union National Bank of North Carolina (Asheville, NC) 73622; 73623; 73624; 73625; 73626; 73627
First Union National Bank of North Carolina (Bakersville, NC) 73655
First Union National Bank of North Carolina (Banner Elk, NC) 73658
First Union National Bank of North Carolina (Bessemer City, NC) 73687
First Union National Bank of North Carolina (Bethlehem, NC) 73693
First Union National Bank of North Carolina (Black Mountain, NC) 73697
First Union National Bank of North Carolina (Blowing Rock, NC) 73702
First Union National Bank of North Carolina (Boone, NC) 73711; 73712; 73713
First Union National Bank of North Carolina (Bostic, NC) 73721
First Union National Bank of North Carolina (Brevard, NC) 73724; 73725
First Union National Bank of North Carolina (Burlington, NC) 73753; 73754
First Union National Bank of North Carolina (Burnsville, NC) 73766; 73767
First Union National Bank of North Carolina (Canton, NC) 73779
First Union National Bank of North Carolina (Cary, NC) 73796; 73797; 73798
First Union National Bank of North Carolina (Chapel Hill, NC) 73813; 73814
First Union National Bank of North Carolina (Charlotte, NC) 73985; 73986; 73987; 73988; 73989; 73990; 73991; 73992; 73993; 73994; 73995; 73996; 73997; 73998; 73999; 74000; 74001; 74002; 74003; 74004; 74005; 74006; 74007; 74008; 74009; 74010
First Union National Bank of North Carolina (China Grove, NC) 74251
First Union National Bank of North Carolina (Claremont, NC) 74255
First Union National Bank of North Carolina (Clemmons, NC) 74269
First Union National Bank of North Carolina (Clinton, NC) 74289; 74290
First Union National Bank Of Florida (Altamonte Springs, FL) 58555
First Union National Bank of South Carolian (Chapin, SC) 78785
First Union National Bank of South Carolian (Hollywood, SC) 79524
First Union National Bank of South Carolina (Anderson, SC) 78675
First Union National Bank of South Carolina (Beaufort, SC) 78707
First Union National Bank of South Carolina (Bennettsville, SC) 78726
First Union National Bank of South Carolina (Blacksburg, SC) 78746
First Union National Bank of South Carolina (Cayce, SC) 78775
First Union National Bank of South Carolina (Charleston, SC) 78813; 78814
First Union National Bank of South Carolina (Chester, SC) 78934; 78935
First Union National Bank of South Carolina (Clover, SC) 78964
First Union National Bank of South Carolina (Columbia, SC) 79012; 79013; 79014; 79015; 79016; 79017
First Union National Bank of South Carolina (Easley, SC) 79179
First Union National Bank of South Carolina (Florence, SC) 79200; 79201; 79202
First Union National Bank of South Carolina (Fountain Inn, SC) 79245
First Union National Bank of South Carolina (Ft. Mill, SC) 79256
First Union National Bank of South Carolina (Gaffney, SC) 79259
First Union National Bank of South Carolina (Greenville, SC) 79350; 79351; 79352; 79353; 79354; 79355; 79356; 79357; 79358; 79359; 79360
First Union National Bank of South Carolina (Hartsville, SC) 79497
First Union National Bank of South Carolina (Hilton Head Island, SC) 79514; 79515; 79516
First Union National Bank of South Carolina (Isle of Palms, SC) 79541
First Union National Bank of South Carolina (James Island, SC) 79542
First Union National Bank of South Carolina (Laurens, SC) 79590
First Union National Bank of South Carolina (Lugoff, SC) 79619
First Union National Bank of South Carolina (Manning, SC) 79631
First Union National Bank of South Carolina (Mt. Pleasant, SC) 79683; 79684
First Union National Bank of South Carolina (Myrtle Beach, SC) 79698
First Union National Bank of South Carolina (North Charleston, SC) 79749
First Union National Bank of South Carolina (Orangeburg, SC) 79772; 79773
First Union National Bank of South Carolina (Prosperity, SC) 79802
First Union National Bank of South Carolina (Rock Hill, SC) 79820; 79821; 79822; 79823
First Union National Bank of South Carolina (Spartanburg, SC) 79893; 79894
First Union National Bank of South Carolina (Summerville, SC) 79984
First Union National Bank of South Carolina (Sumter, SC) 80019
First Union National Bank of South Carolina (Travelers Rest, SC) 80044
First Union National Bank of South Carolina (Walhalla, SC) 80057
First Union National Bank of South Carolina (Williamston, SC) 80123
First Union National Bank of South Carolina (Winnsboro, SC) 80131
First Union National Bank of South Carolina (York, SC) 80139
First Union National Bank of Tennessee (Ashland City, TN) 80184
First Union National Bank of Tennessee (Brentwood, TN) 80229
First Union National Bank of Tennessee (Bulls Gap, TN) 80263
First Union National Bank of Tennessee (Church Hill, TN) 80530
First Union National Bank of Tennessee (Clarksville, TN) 80545; 80546; 80547; 80548; 80549
First Union National Bank of Tennessee (College Grove, TN) 80616
First Union National Bank of Tennessee (Cosby, TN) 80680
First Union National Bank of Tennessee (Dandridge, TN) 80711; 80712
First Union National Bank of Tennessee (Dechard, TN) 80728
First Union National Bank of Tennessee (Dickson, TN) 80733
First Union National Bank of Tennessee (Fayetteville, TN) 80793; 80794; 80795
First Union National Bank of Tennessee (Franklin, TN) 80817; 80818
First Union National Bank of Tennessee (Gallatin, TN) 80847
First Union National Bank of Tennessee (Goodlettsville, TN) 80863
First Union National Bank of Tennessee (Greenbrier, TN) 80881
First Union National Bank of Tennessee (Hendersonville, TN) 80915; 80916
First Union National Bank of Tennessee (Jefferson City, TN) 81022
First Union National Bank of Tennessee (Kingsport, TN) 81094; 81095
First Union National Bank of Tennessee (Murfreesboro, TN) 81846
First Union National Bank of Tennessee (Nashville, TN) 81993; 81994; 81995; 81996; 81997; 81998; 81999; 82000; 82001; 82002; 82003; 82004; 82005; 82006; 82007
First Union National Bank of Tennessee (Newport, TN) 82161; 82162; 82163
First Union National Bank of Tennessee (Parrottsville, TN) 82224
First Union National Bank of Tennessee (Pleasant View, TN) 82232
First Union National Bank of Tennessee (Portland, TN) 82234
First Union National Bank of Tennessee (Rogersville, TN) 82275; 82276; 82277
First Union National Bank of Tennessee (Shelbyville, TN) 82311; 82312; 82313
First Union National Bank of Tennessee (Sparta, TN) 82341; 82342
First Union National Bank of Tennessee (Springfield, TN) 82356; 82357
First Union National Bank of Tennessee (St. Bethlehem, TN) 82361
First Union National Bank of Tennessee (Westmoreland, TN) 82408
First Union National Bank of Tennessee (White Pine, TN) 82417
First Union National Bank of Tennessee (Whitehouse, TN) 82418
First Union National Bank of Tennessee (Winchester, TN) 82419
First Union National Bank of Virginia (Abingdon, VA) 90152
First Union National Bank of Virginia (Alexandria, VA) 90194; 90195; 90196; 90197; 90198; 90199; 90200; 90201; 90202; 90203; 90204; 90205; 90206; 90207; 90208; 90209
First Union National Bank of Virginia (Annandale, VA) 90263; 90264; 90265
First Union National Bank of Virginia (Arlington, VA) 90323; 90324; 90325; 90326; 90327; 90328; 90329; 90330
First Union National Bank of Virginia (Bassett, VA) 90415
First Union National Bank of Virginia (Bedford, VA) 90418; 90419
First Union National Bank of Virginia (Big Stone Gap, VA) 90432
First Union National Bank of Virginia (Blacksburg, VA) 90444
First Union National Bank of Virginia (Bluefield, VA) 90460
First Union National Bank of Virginia (Bridgewater, VA) 90467
First Union National Bank of Virginia (Bristol, VA) 90475; 90476; 90477; 90478
First Union National Bank of Virginia (Burke, VA) 90501
First Union National Bank of Virginia (Centreville, VA) 90515
First Union National Bank of Virginia (Chantilly, VA) 90522
First Union National Bank of Virginia (Chesapeake, VA) 90574; 90575; 90576
First Union National Bank of Virginia (Chesterfield, VA) 90630
First Union National Bank of Virginia (Christiansburg, VA) 90634
First Union National Bank of Virginia (Clintwood, VA) 90645
First Union National Bank of Virginia (Collinsville, VA) 90648
First Union National Bank of Virginia (Courtland, VA) 90654
First Union National Bank of Virginia (Covington, VA) 90656
First Union National Bank of Virginia (Culpeper, VA) 90674
First Union National Bank of Virginia (Dale City, VA) 90682
First Union National Bank of Virginia (Edinburg, VA) 90740
First Union National Bank of Virginia (Fairfax, VA) 90773; 90774; 90775; 90776; 90777; 90778
First Union National Bank of Virginia (Falls Church, VA) 90836; 90837; 90838
First Union National Bank of Virginia (Franklin, VA) 90893
First Union National Bank of Virginia (Fredericksburg, VA) 90917; 90918
First Union National Bank of Virginia (Front Royal, VA) 90950
First Union National Bank of Virginia (Gloucester, VA) 90991
First Union National Bank of Virginia (Grottoes, VA) 91004
First Union National Bank of Virginia (Grundy, VA) 91008
First Union National Bank of Virginia (Hampton, VA) 91031; 91032; 91033
First Union National Bank of Virginia (Harman Junction, VA) 91061
First Union National Bank of Virginia (Harrisonburg, VA) 91082; 91083; 91084; 91085; 91086; 91087
First Union National Bank of Virginia (Haysi, VA) 91113
First Union National Bank of Virginia (Herndon, VA) 91124; 91125
First Union National Bank of Virginia (Hollins, VA) 91146; 91147
First Union National Bank of Virginia (Lebanon, VA) 91188
First Union National Bank of Virginia (Leesburg, VA) 91192; 91193
First Union National Bank of Virginia (Lexington, VA) 91204; 91205; 91206
First Union National Bank of Virginia (Manassas, VA) 91309
First Union National Bank of Virginia (Marion, VA) 91332
First Union National Bank of Virginia (Martinsville, VA) 91350
First Union National Bank of Virginia (McLean, VA) 91386; 91387
First Union National Bank of Virginia (Mechanicsville, VA) 91402
First Union National Bank of Virginia (Moneta, VA) 91432
First Union National Bank of Virginia (Newport News, VA) 91464; 91465; 91466; 91467; 91468
First Union National Bank of Virginia (Newsoms, VA) 91496
First Union National Bank of Virginia (Norfolk, VA) 91522; 91523; 91524; 91525; 91526; 91527
First Union National Bank of Virginia (Norton, VA) 91603
First Union National Bank of Virginia (Oakwood, VA) 91613
First Union National Bank of Virginia (Pearisburg, VA) 91622
First Union National Bank of Virginia (Pembroke, VA) 91626
First Union National Bank of Virginia (Pocahontas, VA) 91637
First Union National Bank of Virginia (Portsmouth, VA) 91648; 91649; 91650; 91651
First Union National Bank of Virginia (Purcellville, VA) 91682
First Union National Bank of Virginia (Reston, VA) 91707; 91708
First Union National Bank of Virginia (Richlands, VA) 91719
First Union National Bank of Virginia (Richmond, VA) 91874; 91875; 91876; 91877; 91878; 91879; 91880; 91881
First Union National Bank of Virginia (Roanoke, VA) 92139; 92140; 92141; 92142; 92143; 92144; 92145; 92146; 92147; 92148; 92149; 92150
First Union National Bank of Virginia (Salem, VA) 92211; 92212
First Union National Bank of Virginia (Saluda, VA) 92229
First Union National Bank of Virginia (Smithfield, VA) 92237
First Union National Bank of Virginia (Springfield, VA) 92282; 92283; 92284; 92285
First Union National Bank of Virginia (St. Paul, VA) 92297
First Union National Bank of Virginia (Staunton, VA) 92317
First Union National Bank of Virginia (Stephens city, VA) 92335
First Union National Bank of Virginia (Sterling, VA) 92340; 92341; 92342
First Union National Bank of Virginia (Tappahannock, VA) 92374
First Union National Bank of Virginia (Verona, VA) 92392
First Union National Bank of Virginia (Vienna, VA) 92405; 92406
First Union National Bank of Virginia (Vinton, VA) 92425
First Union National Bank of Virginia (Virginia Beach, VA) 92468; 92469; 92470; 92471; 92472; 92473; 92474; 92475
First Union National Bank of Virginia (Waynesboro, VA) 92534
First Union National Bank of Virginia (West Point, VA) 92542
First Union National Bank of Virginia (Weyers Cave, VA) 92544
First Union National Bank of Virginia (Williamsburg, VA) 92569
First Union National Bank of Virginia (Winchester, VA) 92583; 92584; 92585; 92586; 92587; 92588
First Union National Bank of Virginia (Woodbridge, VA) 92613
First Union National Bank of Virginia (Woodstock, VA) 92629
First Union National Bank of Virginia (Wytheville, VA) 92639
First Union National Bank of Washington (Washington, DC) 58247
First Union National Bank of Washington DC (Washington, DC) 58248; 58249; 58250; 58251; 58252; 58253; 58254; 58255; 58256; 58257; 58258; 58259; 58260; 58261; 58262; 58263; 58264; 58265; 58266; 58267; 58268; 58269; 58270; 58271; 58272; 58273; 58274; 58275; 58276; 58277; 58278; 58279
First Union Nationl Bank of Virginia (Arlington, VA) 90331
First Union Natonal Bank of Florida (Casselberry, FL) 58932
First Union Securities Inc. (Charlotte, NC) 74011
First Union Transportation Services Inc. (Charlotte, NC) 74012
First United Financial Service (Dunwoody, GA) 66110
First Virginia Bank (Bel Air, MD) 71335
First Virginia Bank (Alexandria, VA) 90210; 90211; 90212; 90213; 90214; 90215; 90216; 90217; 90218; 90219; 90220
First Virginia Bank (Annandale, VA) 90266
First Virginia Bank (Arlington, VA) 90332; 90333; 90334; 90335; 90336; 90337; 90338; 90339; 90340; 90341; 90342; 90343; 90344
First Virginia Bank (Bailey Crossroads, VA) 90412
First Virginia Bank (Burke, VA) 90502; 90503; 90504
First Virginia Bank (Callao, VA) 90508
First Virginia Bank (Centreville, VA) 90516

Fmc Corp. Lakeland Facility (Lakeland, FL) 60729
Fmc Corp. Lakeland Plant (Lakeland, FL) 60730
Fmc Corp. Newark (Newark, DE) 57905
Fmc Corp.-Newark De. (Newark, DE) 57906
Fmc Corp. Newark Delaware Plant (Newark, DE) 57907
Fmc Corp. Nitro Plant (Nitro, WV) 92970; 92971
Fmc Corp. Orlando (Orlando, FL) 61990
Fmc Corp. Spring Hill Plant (South Charleston, WV) 93049
FMC Corp., Tupelo Plant (Tupelo, MS) 73401
FMC Energy & Transmission Equipment Group (Houston, TX) 86201
Fmc Fluid Control Stephenville (Stephenville, TX) 89515
FMP-Rauma Co. (Birmingham, AL) 55273
Foam Molding Co. of Arkansas (Rogers, AR) 57564
Foamax Products Inc. (Verona, MS) 73447
Foamex Foamex L.P. (Conover, NC) 74332
Foamex Kihi Foamex (Tupelo, MS) 73402
Foamex L.P. (Conyers, GA) 65681
Foamex L.P. (Conover, NC) 74333
Foamex LP (High Point, NC) 75131
Foamex LP (Cookeville, TN) 80658
Foamex LP (Milan, TN) 81768
Foamex LP (Morristown, TN) 81800
Foamex L.P. (Mesquite, TX) 87963
Foamex L.P. Curon (Tampa, FL) 63433
Foamex L.P. Foamex Division (Cornelius, NC) 74347
Foamex LP Kihi Foamex (Verona, MS) 73448; 73449
Foamex L.P. Vahala (Bogart, GA) 65385
Foamex L.P. Plant 1 (Morristown, TN) 81801
Foamex L.P. Plant 3 (Morristown, TN) 81802
Folger Coffee Co. (Sherman, TX) 89396
Food Lion (Rehoboth Beach, DE) 57944
Food Lion (Brooksville, FL) 58888
Food Lion (Daytona Beach, FL) 59179
Food Lion (Fernandina Beach, FL) 59411
Food Lion (Gainesville, FL) 59877
Food Lion (Jacksonville, FL) 60308; 60309; 60310; 60311; 60312
Food Lion (Lake Wales, FL) 60653
Food Lion (Live Oak, FL) 60910
Food Lion (Northwest Smyrna Beach, FL) 61757
Food Lion (Ocala, FL) 61799
Food Lion (Ocoee, FL) 61833
Food Lion (Orange Park, FL) 61884; 61885
Food Lion (Ormond Beach, FL) 62204
Food Lion (Plant City, FL) 62544
Food Lion (Ponte Vedra, FL) 62648
Food Lion (St Augustine, FL) 62940
Food Lion (St Petersburg, FL) 62973
Food Lion (Starke, FL) 63145
Food Lion (Tallahassee, FL) 63242
Food Lion (Temple Terrace, FL) 63677
Food Lion (Brunswick, GA) 65408
Food Lion (Hinesville, GA) 66351
Food Lion (Pooler, GA) 67270
Food Lion (Richmond Hill, GA) 67296
Food Lion (Snellville, GA) 67590
Food Lion (St Simons is, GA) 67618
Food Lion (Valdosta, GA) 67957; 67958
Food Lion (Hagerstown, MD) 71881
Food Lion (Aberdeen, NC) 73514; 73515
Food Lion (Albemarle, NC) 73536
Food Lion (Apex, NC) 73556
Food Lion (Asheville, NC) 73628
Food Lion (Belmont, NC) 73674
Food Lion (Benson, NC) 73683
Food Lion (Chapel Hill, NC) 73815
Food Lion (Charlotte, NC) 74014; 74015; 74016; 74017; 74018; 74019; 74020; 74021
Food Lion (China Grove, NC) 74252
Food Lion (Clemmons, NC) 74270
Food Lion (Clinton, NC) 74291
Food Lion (Columbus, NC) 74301
Food Lion (Concord, NC) 74314; 74315
Food Lion (Cornelius, NC) 74348
Food Lion (Cramerton, NC) 74352
Food Lion (Durham, NC) 74399; 74400; 74401
Food Lion (E Fayettevlle, NC) 74443
Food Lion (E Laurinburg, NC) 74447
Food Lion (Eden, NC) 74457
Food Lion (Edenton, NC) 74471
Food Lion (Elizabeth City, NC) 74480
Food Lion (Enka, NC) 74507
Food Lion (Fayetteville, NC) 74556
Food Lion (Gastonia, NC) 74681
Food Lion (Goldsboro, NC) 74718; 74719
Food Lion (Graham, NC) 74748
Food Lion (Greensboro, NC) 74831; 74832; 74833; 74834; 74835; 74836; 74837; 74838
Food Lion (Hamlet, NC) 74998
Food Lion (High Point, NC) 75132; 75133; 75134; 75135
Food Lion (Hope Mills, NC) 75193
Food Lion (Huntersville, NC) 75207
Food Lion (Indian Trail, NC) 75208
Food Lion (Jacksonville, NC) 75215; 75216
Food Lion (Jefferson, NC) 75248
Food Lion (Jonesville, NC) 75250
Food Lion (Kannapolis, NC) 75259; 75260; 75261; 75262; 75263
Food Lion (Kernersville, NC) 75279; 75280
Food Lion (Kings Mountain, NC) 75304
Food Lion (Lexington, NC) 75404
Food Lion (Lillington, NC) 75432
Food Lion (Lumberton, NC) 75465
Food Lion (Marshville, NC) 75514
Food Lion (Mayodan, NC) 75538
Food Lion (Mooresville, NC) 75603
Food Lion (Morehead City, NC) 75621
Food Lion (Mount Airy, NC) 75677
Food Lion (Mount Holly, NC) 75691
Food Lion (Oxford, NC) 75778
Food Lion (Pinehurst, NC) 75804
Food Lion (Pineville, NC) 75815
Food Lion (Raleigh, NC) 75907; 75908; 75909; 75910
Food Lion (Reidsville, NC) 75999
Food Lion (Rocky Mount, NC) 76088; 76089; 76090
Food Lion (Salisbury, NC) 76159; 76160; 76161; **76162**
Food Lion (Salisbury Nc, NC) 76185
Food Lion (Sanford, NC) 76193; 76194
Food Lion (Selma, NC) 76223
Food Lion (Shelby, NC) 76239
Food Lion (Siler City, NC) 76249
Food Lion (Smithfield, NC) 76260
Food Lion (Southern Pines, NC) 76277
Food Lion (Statesville, NC) 76329
Food Lion (Summerfield, NC) 76345
Food Lion (Whiteville, NC) 76500
Food Lion (Wilmington, NC) 76567; 76568; 76569; 76570
Food Lion (Wilson, NC) 76632; 76633
Food Lion (Winston Salem, NC) 76669; 76670; 76671
Food Lion (Winston-Salem, NC) 76731
Food Lion (Aiken, SC) 78648
Food Lion (Ballentine, SC) 78700
Food Lion (Barnwell, SC) 78701
Food Lion (Beaufort, SC) 78708
Food Lion (Bennettsville, SC) 78727
Food Lion (Bishopville, SC) 78742
Food Lion (Bucksport, SC) 78751
Food Lion (Camden, SC) 78759
Food Lion (Charleston, SC) 78815; 78816
Food Lion (Chester, SC) 78936
Food Lion (Columbia, SC) 79020; 79021; 79022; 79023; 79024; 79025; 79026
Food Lion (Darlington, SC) 79147
Food Lion (Easley, SC) 79180
Food Lion (Edgemoor, SC) 79187
Food Lion (Elloree, SC) 79190
Food Lion (Florence, SC) 79203; 79204; 79205
Food Lion (Fort Mill, SC) 79232
Food Lion (Goose Creek, SC) 79280
Food Lion (Greer, SC) 79474
Food Lion (Johns Island, SC) 79544
Food Lion (Kingstree, SC) 79554
Food Lion (Laurens, SC) 79591
Food Lion (Lugoff, SC) 79620
Food Lion (Manning, SC) 79632
Food Lion (Marion, SC) 79640
Food Lion (Mt. Pleasant, SC) 79685
Food Lion (Myrtle Beach, SC) 79699
Food Lion (North Augusta, SC) 79732
Food Lion (Orangeburg, SC) 79774
Food Lion (Rock Hill, SC) 79824; 79825; 79826
Food Lion (Santee, SC) 79852
Food Lion (St. George, SC) 79972
Food Lion (Summerville, SC) 79985
Food Lion (West Columbia, SC) 80093; 80094
Food Lion (Abingdon, VA) 90153
Food Lion (Ashland, VA) 90402
Food Lion (Bedford, VA) 90420
Food Lion (Big Stone Gap, VA) 90434
Food Lion (Blacksburg, VA) 90445; 90446
Food Lion (Bristol, VA) 90479
Food Lion (Charlottesvle, VA) 90551
Food Lion (Chesapeake, VA) 90577; 90578; 90579; 90580
Food Lion (Christiansburg, VA) 90635
Food Lion (Covington, VA) 90659
Food Lion (Culpeper, VA) 90675
Food Lion (Danville, VA) 90694; 90695; 90696
Food Lion (Fredericksbrg, VA) 90907; 90908
Food Lion (Fredericksburg, VA) 90925
Food Lion (Gate City, VA) 90967
Food Lion (Hampton, VA) 91034; 91035; 91036
Food Lion (Harrisonburg, VA) 91088; 91089
Food Lion (Hillsville, VA) 91140
Food Lion (Lynchburg, VA) 91250; 91251; 91252
Food Lion (Madison Heights, VA) 91297
Food Lion (Martinsville, VA) 91351
Food Lion (Mechanicsvl, VA) 91405
Food Lion (Midlothian, VA) 91414
Food Lion (N Tazewell, VA) 91437
Food Lion (Norfolk, VA) 91532; 91533; 91534; 91535
Food Lion (Orange, VA) 91618
Food Lion (Pearisburg, VA) 91623
Food Lion (Portsmouth, VA) 91652; 91653; 91654; 91655; 91656
Food Lion (Richmond, VA) 91885; 91886; 91887; 91888; 91889; 91890; 91891
Food Lion (Roanoke, VA) 92154
Food Lion (South Boston, VA) 92250
Food Lion (Staunton, VA) 92320; 92321
Food Lion (Suffolk, VA) 92367; 92368
Food Lion (Tappahannock, VA) 92375
Food Lion (Tazewell, VA) 92379
Food Lion (Verona, VA) 92393
Food Lion (Virginia Beach, VA) 92476; 92477; 92478; 92479; 92480; 92481; 92482; 92483
Food Lion (Williamsburg, VA) 92571
Food Lion (Winchester, VA) 92591
Food Lion (Woodstock, VA) 92631
Food Lion (Yorktown, VA) 92652
Food Lion Inc. (Rehoboth Beach, DE) 57945
Food Lion Inc. (Brooksville, FL) 58889
Food Lion Inc. (Gainesville, FL) 59878
Food Lion Inc. (Jacksonville, FL) 60313
Food Lion Inc. (Ocoee, FL) 61834
Food Lion Inc. (Ponte Vedra, FL) 62649
Food Lion Inc. (Hinesville, GA) 66352
Food Lion Inc. (Pooler, GA) 67271
Food Lion Inc. (Snellville, GA) 67591
Food Lion Inc. (Benson, NC) 73684
Food Lion Inc. (Charlotte, NC) 74022; 74023
Food Lion Inc. (Columbus, NC) 74302
Food Lion Inc. (E Fayettevlle, NC) 74444
Food Lion Inc. (Enka, NC) 74508
Food Lion Inc. (Goldsboro, NC) 74720
Food Lion Inc. (Greensboro, NC) 74839
Food Lion Inc. (High Point, NC) 75136
Food Lion Inc. (Indian Trail, NC) 75209
Food Lion Inc. (Jefferson, NC) 75249
Food Lion Inc. (Jonesville, NC) 75251
Food Lion, Inc. (Lillington, NC) 75433
Food Lion Inc. (Mooresville, NC) 75604
Food Lion, Inc. (Mount Airy, NC) 75678
Food Lion Inc. (Salisbury, NC) 76163; 76164; 76165
Food Lion Inc. (Siler City, NC) 76250
Food Lion Inc. (Summerfield, NC) 76346
Food Lion Inc. (Wilmington, NC) 76571
Food Lion Inc. (Goose Creek, SC) 79281
Food Lion Inc. (Kingstree, SC) 79555
Food Lion Inc. (Laurens, SC) 79592
Food Lion Inc. (Manning, SC) 79633
Food Lion Inc. (Fort Oglethorpe, TN) 80800
Food Lion Inc. (Johnson City, TN) 81039; 81040
Food Lion Inc. (Kingsport, TN) 81096; 81097; 81098; 81099
Food Lion Inc. (Ashland, VA) 90403
Food Lion Inc. (Bedford, VA) 90421
Food Lion Inc. (Fredericksbrg, VA) 90909
Food Lion Inc. (Gate City, VA) 90968
Food Lion Inc. (Harrisonburg, VA) 91090
Food Lion Inc. (Madison Heights, VA) 91298
Food Lion Inc. (Martinsville, VA) 91352
Food Lion Inc. (Richmond, VA) 91892
Food Lion Inc. (Tappahannock, VA) 92376
Food Lion Inc. (Virginia Beach, VA) 92484
Food Lion Inc. (Winchester, VA) 92592
Food Lion Inc. Store (Marshville, NC) 75515
Food Lion Inc. Store (Bristol, TN) 80246; 80247
Food Lion Inc. Store (Chattanooga, TN) 80396; 80397; 80398; 80399; 80400; 80401; 80402
Food Lion Inc. Store (Fort Oglthorpe, TN) 80805
Food Lion Inc. Store (Hixson, TN) 80934
Food Lion Inc. Store (Johnson City, TN) 81041; 81042
Food Lion Inc. Store (Kingsport, TN) 81100; 81101; 81102
Food Lion Inc. Store (Murfreesboro, TN) 81847
Food Lion Inc. Store 851 (Chattanooga, TN) 80403
Food Lion Inc. Store 846 (Chattanooga, TN) 80404
Food Lion Inc. Store No. 519 (Asheville, NC) 73629
Food Lion Inc. Store No. 425 (Blacksburg, VA) 90447
Food Lion Inc. Store No. 358 (Fredericksbrg, VA) 90910
Food Lion Inc. Store 661 (Chattanooga, TN) 80405
Food Lion Inc. Store 630 (Chattanooga, TN) 80406
Food Lion Inc. Store 634 (Chattanooga, TN) 80407
Food Lion Inc. Store 629 (Chattanooga, TN) 80408
Food Lion Inc. Store 623 (Midlothian, VA) 91415
Food Lion Inc. 256 (Midlothian, VA) 91416
Food & Services Management (Washington, DC) 58280
Foot Action (Mobile, AL) 56180
Foot Action (Daytona Beach, FL) 59180
Foot Action (Atlanta, GA) 64472
Foot Action (Alexandria, LA) 69379
Foot Action (Monroe, LA) 70354
Foot Action (Shawnee, OK) 77818
Foot Action (Abilene, TX) 82436
Foot Action (Amarillo, TX) 82548
Foot Action (Arlington, TX) 82657
Foot Action (Austin, TX) 82877; 82878
Foot Action (Baytown, TX) 83123
Foot Action (Brownsville, TX) 83358
Foot Action (Clute, TX) 83598
Foot Action (Dallas, TX) 84073
Foot Action (El Paso, TX) 84801
Foot Action (Fort Worth, TX) 85119
Foot Action (Harlingen, TX) 85700
Foot Action (Houston, TX) 86202; 86203
Foot Action (Killeen, TX) 87511; 87512
Foot Action (Lake Jackson, TX) 87580
Foot Action (Laredo, TX) 87611
Foot Action (Odessa, TX) 88244
Foot Action (Plano, TX) 88568
Foot Action (San Angelo, TX) 88873
Foot Action (San Antonio, TX) 89009; 89010; 89011
Foot Action (Temple, TX) 89617
Foot Action (Texarkana, TX) 89675
Foot Action 8099 (Tupelo, MS) 73403
Foot Action Inc. (Norman, OK) 77252
Foot Action Inc. (Houston, TX) 86204; 86205
Foot Action for Kids (Shawnee, OK) 77819
Foot Action for Kids (El Paso, TX) 84802
Foot Action for Kids (San Angelo, TX) 88874
Foot Action No 8036 (Plant City, FL) 62545
Foot Action No 8025 (Eagle Pass, TX) 84716
Foot Action No 8023 (Austin, TX) 82879
Foot Action U S a (Pinellas Park, FL) 62518
Foot Action U S a (Stuart, FL) 63167
Foot Action U S a (Tampa, FL) 63434
Foot Action U S a (Dallas, TX) 84074; 84075
Foot Action U S a (El Paso, TX) 84803
Foot Action U S a (Lufkin, TX) 87803
Foot Action U S a (San Antonio, TX) 89012
Foot Action U S a (Sherman, TX) 89397
Foot Action USA (Morrow, GA) 67010
Foot Action USA (Houston, TX) 86206
Foot Action USA (Mcallen, TX) 87930
Footaction (Dothan, AL) 55648
Footaction U S a (Dallas, TX) 84076
Footaction U S a (Fort Worth, TX) 85120
Footaction U S a (Irving, TX) 87346
Footaction U S a (Longview, TX) 87716
Footaction U S a (San Antonio, TX) 89013
Footaction USA (Bradenton, FL) 58825
Footaction USA (Oklahoma City, OK) 77363
Footaction USA (Humble, TX) 87221
Forcum-Lannom Associates Inc. (Dyersburg, TN) 80749
Forcum Lannon Associates (Dyersburg, TN) 80750
Ford Motor Co. (Nashville, TN) 82012
Ford Motor Co., Atlanta Assembly Plant (Hapeville, GA) 66334
Ford Motor Co. Kentucky Truck Plant (Louisville, KY) 68764
Ford Motor Co., Louisville Assembly Plant (Louisville, KY) 68765
Ford Motor Co. Nashville Glass (Nashville, TN) 82013
Ford Motor Co. Norfolk Assembly Plant (Norfolk, VA) 91536
Ford Motor Co., Tulsa Glass Plant (Tulsa, OK) 77941
Fordyce & Princeton Railroad (Crossett, AR) 56880
Forest Hill State Bank (Bel Air, MD) 71336; 71337
Forest Hill State Bank (Belcamp, MD) 71342
Forest Hill State Bank (Darlington, MD) 71641
Forest Hill State Bank (Forest Hill, MD) 71686
Forest Hill State Bank (Jarrettsville, MD) 71980
Forest Hill State Bank (Whiteford, MD) 72570
Fort Bend Letilities (Sugarland, TX) 89547
Fort Howard Corp. (Kennesaw, GA) 66415
Fort Howard Corp. (Rincon, GA) 67299; 67300
Fort Howard Corp. (Owings Mills, MD) 72186
Fort Howard Corp. (Muskogee, OK) 77219; 77220

Fort Howard Cup Corp. (Owings Mills, MD) 72187
Fort Howard Paper Co. (Muskogee, OK) 77221
Fort Howard Paper Corp. (Rincon, GA) 67301
Fort Rucker Naitonal Bank (Fort Rucker, AL) 55765
Fort Rucker National Bank (Fort Rucker, AL) 55766; 55767; 55768
Forth Financial Resources Ltd. Inc. (Richmond, VA) 91893
Fortuen Bank, ASB (Dunedin, FL) 59362
Fortuen Bank, ASB (New Port Richey, FL) 61686
Fortuen Bank, SB (St. Petersburg, FL) 63118
Fortune Bancorp (Clearwater, FL) **59004**
Fortune Bancorp Inc. (Clearwater, FL) 59005; 59006; 59007
Fortune Bancorporation (Clearwater, FL) 59008
Fortune Bank (Clearwater, FL) 59009
Fortune Bank (Punta Gorda, FL) 62708
Fortune Bank, A Savings Bank (Belleair Bluffs, FL) 58651
Fortune Bank, ASB (Cape Coral, FL) 58922
Fortune Bank, ASB (Clearwater, FL) 59010; 59011; 59012; 59013; 59014; 59015; 59016
Fortune Bank, ASB (Fort Myers, FL) 59698
Fortune Bank, ASB (Gulfport, FL) 59940
Fortune Bank, ASB (Hudson, FL) 60132; 60133
Fortune Bank, ASB (Largo, FL) 60838
Fortune Bank, ASB (Naples, FL) 61624; 61625; 61626; 61627
Fortune Bank, ASB (New Port Richey, FL) 61687
Fortune Bank, ASB (Palm Harbor, FL) 62298; 62299
Fortune Bank, ASB (Sarasota, FL) 62833
Fortune Bank, ASB (Seminole, FL) 62908; 62909
Fortune Bank, ASB (Spring Hill, FL) 62934
Fortune Bank, ASB (St. Petersburg Beach, FL) 63141
Fortune Bank, ASB (Tampa, FL) 63435; 63436
Fortune Bank, ASB (Tarpon, FL) 63665
Fortune Bank, SB (Palm Harbor, FL) 62300
Fortune Bank, SB (Pinellas Park, FL) 62519
Fortune Bank, SB (Port Charlotte, FL) 62657
Fortune Bank, SB (Port Richey, FL) 62673
Fortune Bank, SB (Safety Harbor, FL) 62762
Fortune Bank, SB (Sarasota, FL) 62834; 62835
Fortune Bank, SB (St. Petersburg, FL) 63119; 63120; 63121; 63122; 63123; 63124; 63125
Foster Prods. Corp. (Houston, TX) 86207
Foster Production Corp. (Miami, FL) 61314
Foster Products Corp. (Houston, TX) 86208
Foster Wheeler Corp. (Carrollton, KY) 68190
Foster Wheeler Enviresponse Inc. (Washington, DC) 58281
Foundation Health Pharmaceutic (Duluth, GA) 66037
Four Seasons (Grapevine, TX) 85657
Four Winns of Texas (Athens, TX) 82787
Four Winns of Texas Inc. (Athens, TX) 82788
Fox Meyer Corp. (Carrollton, TX) 83466
FPL Group (Jacksonville, FL) **60314**
FPL Group Inc. (West Palm Beach, FL) 63866
Fred Meyers Co. Inc. (Little Rock, AR) 57282; 57283
Fredericktown Bank & Trust Co. (Frederick, MD) 71727; 71728; 71729; 71730; 71731
Fredericktown Bank & Trust Co. (Walkersville, MD) 72539
Freeman Resins (Marshall, TX) 87853
Freeman Resins (Chatham, VA) 90553
P. T. Freeport Indonesia Co. (New Orleans, LA) 70458
Freeport-McMoran (New Orleans, LA) **70459**
Freeport Mcmoran Agrico Chemical Co. Div. (Blytheville, AR) 56804
Freeport Mcmoran Agrico Chemical Co. Div. (Uncle Sam, LA) 70917
Freeport-McMoran Copper & Gold Co. (New Orleans, LA) 70460
Freeport-McMoran Copper & Gold Co., Inc. (New Orleans, LA) 70461
Freeport-McMoran Inc. (New Orleans, LA) 70462
Freeport-McMoran Oil & Gas Co. (New Orleans, LA) 70463
Freeport-McMoran Resource Partners (New Orleans, LA) 70464
Freeport-McMoran Resource Partners Ltd. (New Orleans, LA) 70465
Freeport Sulphur Co. (New Orleans, LA) 70466
Fresh Foods (Irving, TX) 87347
Friction, Inc. (Dallas, TX) 84077; 84078
Friction Inc. (Fredericksburg, VA) 90926
Friendswood Dev Co. (Fairfax, VA) 90786
Friendswood Development Com (Houston, TX) 86209
Friendswood Development Co. (Houston, TX) 86210; 86211; 86212
Friendswood Development Co. (Humble, TX) 87222
Frio Foods Inc. (Uvalde, TX) 89851
Frist of America Bank (Arcadia, FL) 58583
Frist of America Bank (Cape Coral, FL) 58923
Frist American National Bank (Clarksville, TN) 80550
Frist American National Bank (Harriman, TN) 80901
Frist American National Bank (Jackson, TN) 80984
Frist American National Bank (Norris, TN) 82179
Frist-Citizens Bank & Trust CO. (Albemarle, NC) 73537
Frist National Bank (Shelbyville, TN) 82314
Frist Union National Bank of Florida (Brandon, FL) 58871
Frist Union National Bank of Florida (Charlotte Harbor, FL) 58949
Frist Union National Bank of Florida (Destin, FL) 59344
Frito-Lay, Inc. (Plano, TX) 88569
Fruehauf Corp. (Richmond, VA) 91894
Fruehauf Inc. (Nashville, TN) 82014
Fruehauf Trailer Corp. (Decatur, AL) 55582; 55583; 55584
Fruehauf Trailer Corp. (Little Rock, AR) 57284
Fruehauf Trailer Corp. (Shreveport, LA) 70722
Fruehauf Trailer Corp. (Charlotte, NC) 74024
Fruehauf Trailer Corp. (Greensboro, NC) 74840
Fruehauf Trailer Corp. (Tulsa, OK) 77942
Fruehauf Trailer Corp. (Huntsville, TN) 80961
Fruehauf Trailer Corp. (Memphis, TN) 81608; 81609
Fruehauf Trailer Corp. (Odessa, TX) 88245
Fruehauf Trailer Corp. (Richmond, VA) 91895
Fruehauf Trailers (Greensboro, NC) 74841
Fruehauf Trailers (Tulsa, OK) 77943
Fruehauf Trailers (Odessa, TX) 88246
Fruit Growers Express Co. Inc. (Alexandria, VA) 90221
Fruit of the Loom (Campbellsvlle, KY) 68185; 68186; 68187
Fruit of the Loom General Management (Bowling Green, KY) 68142
Fruit of the Loom Hosiery Star Div. (Star, NC) 76314
Fruit of the Loom Inc. (Jamestown, KY) 68490
Fruit of the Loom Inc. Arkansas (Osceola, AR) 57482
Fruit of the Loom Inc. Martin Mills Inc. (St. Martinville, LA) 70870
Fruit of the Loom Inc. Richmond Apparel (Rockingham, NC) 76061
Fruit of the Loom Inc. Union Underwear (Campbellsville, KY) 68180
Fryef Regional Medical Center (Hickory, NC) 75074
Fuel Management Systems Inc. (College Pk, MD) 71567
Full Circle (Fayetteville, NC) 74557
H.B. Fuller Co. Foster Div. (Houston, TX) 86213
Funk Manufacturing Inc/O D (N Little Rock, AR) 57402

G

G. D. Searle & Co. (Augusta, GA) 65331
A G Industries Inc. (Forest City, NC) 74606
G & W Life Insurance Co. (Jackson, MS) 72985
Gabriel Ride Control Products Inc. (Brentwood, TN) 80230
GAF Building Materials Corp. (Mobile, AL) 56181
GAF Building Materials Corp. (Garden City, GA) 66301
GAF Building Materials Corp. (Baltimore, MD) 71155
GAF Building Materials Corp. (Chester, SC) 78937
GAF Building Materials Corp. (Nashville, TN) 82015
GAF Building Materials Corp. (Dallas, TX) 84079
Gaf Chemical Corp. (Huntsville, AL) 55943
Gaf Chemical Corp. (Spartanburg, SC) 79907
Gaf Chemicals Corp. (Huntsville, AL) 55944; 55945
GAF Chemicals Corp. (Calvert City, KY) 68176
Gaf Chemicals Corp. (Spartanburg, SC) 79908
Gaf Chemicals Corp. (Texas City, TX) 89720
Gaf Chemicals Corp. Seadrift Plant (Long Mott, TX) 87700
GAF Corp. (Tampa, FL) 63437
Gaf Corp. (Chester, SC) 78938
Gamco Prods. Co. (Henderson, KY) 68449
Gamco Products Co. (Henderson, KY) 68450
Gandy's Dairies (San Angelo, TX) 88875
Gandy's Dairies Inc. (San Angelo, TX) 88876
Gannett (Arlington, VA) **90345**
Gannett Newspaper Division (Arlington, VA) 90346
Gannett Broadcasting (Arlington, VA) 90347
Gannett Co., Inc. (Arlington, VA) 90348
Gannett Direct Marketing Services Inc. (Louisville, KY) 68766
Gannett New Media Services (Arlington, VA) 90349
Gannett News Service (Arlington, VA) 90350
Gannett Supply Corp. (Arlington, VA) 90351
Gannett Telemarketing (Nashville, TN) 82016
Gannett Telemarketing Inc. (Arlington, VA) 90352
Gannett Television (Arlington, VA) 90353
The Gap (Birmingham, AL) 55274; 55275
The Gap (Enterprise, AL) 55685
The Gap (Huntsville, AL) 55946
The Gap (Newark, DE) 57908
Gap the (Wilmington, DE) 58063
The Gap (Washington, DC) 58282; 58283
The Gap (Altamonte Springs, FL) 58556
The Gap (Boca Raton, FL) 58705
The Gap (Boynton Beach, FL) 58775
The Gap (Clearwater, FL) 59017
The Gap (Daytona Beach, FL) 59181
The Gap (Fort Lauderdale, FL) 59496
The Gap (Fort Myers, FL) 59699
The Gap (Hollywood, FL) 60061
The Gap (Jacksonville, FL) 60315; 60316
The Gap (Merritt is, FL) 61128
The Gap (Miami, FL) 61315
The Gap (Orange Park, FL) 61886
The Gap (Orlando, FL) 61991; 61992
The Gap (Palm Beach Gardens, FL) 62272
The Gap (Pinellas Park, FL) 62520
The Gap (Pompano Beach, FL) 62598
The Gap (Sarasota, FL) 62836
The Gap (Tallahassee, FL) 63243
The Gap (Tampa, FL) 63438; 63439; 63440; 63441
The Gap (West Palm Beach, FL) 63867
The Gap (Winter Park, FL) 63979
The Gap (Atlanta, GA) 64473; 64474; 64475; 64476; 64477; 64478; 64479; 64480; 64481; 64482
The Gap (Marietta, GA) 66780
The Gap (Morrow, GA) 67011
The Gap (Savannah, GA) 67476
The Gap (Union City, GA) 67913
The Gap (Baton Rouge, LA) 69539
The Gap (Bossier City, LA) 69715
The Gap (Marrero, LA) 70227
The Gap (Metairie, LA) 70264
The Gap (Slidell, LA) 70825
The Gap (Baltimore, MD) 71156; 71157; 71158
Gap the (Chevy Chase, MD) 71530
Gap (Laurel, MD) 72076
The Gap (Potomac, MD) 72231
The Gap (Jackson, MS) 72986
The Gap (Ridgeland, MS) 73318
The Gap (Utica, MS) 73434
The Gap (Charlotte, NC) 74025
The Gap (Hickory, NC) 75075
The Gap (Raleigh, NC) 75911
The Gap (Oklahoma City, OK) 77364; 77365; 77366; 77367; 77368
The Gap (Tulsa, OK) 77944; 77945; 77946
The Gap (Charleston, SC) 78817; 78818
The Gap (Arlington, TX) 82658
The Gap (Austin, TX) 82880; 82881
The Gap (Baytown, TX) 83124
The Gap (Beaumont, TX) 83152; 83153
The Gap (Corpus Christi, TX) 83718
The Gap (Dallas, TX) 84080; 84081; 84082; 84083; 84084
The Gap (El Paso, TX) 84804; 84805
The Gap (Fort Worth, TX) 85121; 85122; 85123; 85124
The Gap (Friendswood, TX) 85398
The Gap (Galveston, TX) 85439
The Gap (Houston, TX) 86214; 86215; 86216; 86217; 86218; 86219; 86220; 86221; 86222; 86223; 86224; 86225; 86226; 86227; 86228; 86229
The Gap (Humble, TX) 87223; 87224
The Gap (Irving, TX) 87348
The Gap (Mesquite, TX) 87964
The Gap (Pasadena, TX) 88411; 88412
The Gap (Plano, TX) 88570
The Gap (San Antonio, TX) 89014; 89015; 89016; 89017
The Gap (Waco, TX) 89936
Gap the (Chesapeake, VA) 90581
The Gap (Fredericksbrg, VA) 90911
Gap the (Hampton, VA) 91037
Gap the (Midlothian Vi, VA) 91428
Gap Kids (Washington, DC) 58284
The Gap Kids (Orlando, FL) 61993
The Gap Kids (Atlanta, GA) 64483
The Gap Kids (Kennesaw, GA) 66416
The Gap Kids (Baton Rouge, LA) 69540
The Gap Kids (Metairie, LA) 70265
Gap Kids (Bethesda, MD) 71392
Gap Kids (Chevy Chase, MD) 71531
The Gap Kids (Gaithersburg, MD) 71781
Gap Kids (Chattanooga, TN) 80409
The Gap Kids (Dallas, TX) 84085
The Gap Kids (Houston, TX) 86230
The Gap Kids (Plano, TX) 88571
The Gap Kids (San Antonio, TX) 89018
The Gap 1410 (Cpe St Claire, MD) 71611
The Gap 1024 (Alexandria, VA) 90222
The Gap Store (Washington, DC) 58285
Gap Store (Oklahoma City, OK) 77369; 77370; 77371; 77372
Gap Store Inc. Maryland Stores (Bethesda, MD) 71393; 71394
Gap Stores (Washington, DC) 58286
Gap Stores (Jacksonville, FL) 60317
Gap Stores the (Atl, GA) 64180
Gap Stores the (Atlanta, GA) 64484; 64485; 64486; 64487; 64488
Gap Stores the (Marietta, GA) 66781
Gap Stores (Morrow, GA) 67012
Gap Stores (Union City, GA) 67914; 67915
Gap Stores (Forestville, MD) 71688
Gap Stores (Landover, MD) 72017
Gap Stores (Wheaton, MD) 72555
Gap Stores (Charlotte, NC) 74026
Gap Stores the (Hickory, NC) 75076
Gap Stores (El Paso, TX) 84806
Gap Stores (Houston, TX) 86231; 86232; 86233; 86234; 86235; 86236; 86237; 86238; 86239; 86240; 86241; 86242; 86243
Gap Stores (Pasadena, TX) 88413
Gap Stores (San Antonio, TX) 89019; 89020
The Gap Stores (Annandale, VA) 90267
Gap Stores (Fairfax, VA) 90787; 90788
Gap Stores (Mc Lean, VA) 91366; 91367
Gap Stores the District Store (Washington, DC) 58287
Gap Stores Inc (Birmingham, AL) 55276
Gap Stores Inc. (Hollywood, FL) 60062
Gap Stores Inc. (Gaithersburg, MD) 71782
Gap Stores Inc. (Hyattsville, MD) 71958
Gap Stores Inc. (Rockville, MD) 72283
Gap Stores Inc. (Norfolk, VA) 91537; 91538
Gap Stores Inc. Maryland Stores (Gaithersburg, MD) 71783
Gap Stores Inc. Maryland Stores (Hyattsville, MD) 71959
Gap Stores Inc. Mayland Stores (Rockville, MD) 72284
Gap Stores the Marlyand Stores (Forestville, MD) 71689
Gap Stores the Maryland Stores (Greenbelt, MD) 71862
Gap Stores the Maryland Stores (Landover, MD) 72018
Gap Stores the Maryland Stores (Wheaton, MD) 72556
Gap Stores the Regional Office (Atlanta, GA) 64489
Gap Stores the Underground Atl (Atlanta, GA) 64490
Gardner Denver Mc (Roanoke, VA) 92155
Garland Beverage Co. (Garland, TX) 85486
Garrett Airlines Repair (Anniston, AL) 55000
Garrett Airlines Service (Miami, FL) 61316
Garrett-Buchanan Co. (Jessup, MD) 71984
Gate City Oil Equipment Co., Inc. (Rosewell, GA) 67353
GATX Logistics Inc. (Jacksonville, FL) 60318
Gayfers (Auburn, AL) 55061
Gayfers (Dothan, AL) 55649
Gayfers (Fort Walton Beach, FL) 59827
Gayfers (Jackson, MS) 72987
Gayfers Cordova Mall (Pensacola, FL) 62431
Gayfers Department Store (Montgomery, AL) 56339
Gayfers Department Store (Tuscaloosa, AL) 56655
Gayfers Department Str (Daphne, AL) 55566
Gayfers Dept Store (Mobile, AL) 56182
Gayfer's Montgomery Fair Co. (Montgomery, AL) 56340
Gaylord Chemical Corp. (Bogalusa, LA) 69702
Gaylord Chemical Corp. (Slidell, LA) 70826
Gaylord Container Corp. (Pine Bluff, AR) 57514; 57515
Gaylord Container Corp. (Newark, DE) 57909
Gaylord Container Corp. (Bogalusa, LA) 69703; 69704
Gaylord Container Corp. (Weslaco, TX) 90034
Gaylord Container Corp. Formerly Known as Mid-America (Pine Bluff, AR) 57516
Gaylords National Corp. (Newark, DE) 57910
GB Labels (Burlington, NC) 73755
GE Appliances Manufacturing Division (Decatur, AL) 55585
GE Aircraft Engines (Madisonville, KY) 69051
GE Appliances (Louisville, KY) 68767
GE Capital Mortgage Corp. (Raleigh, NC) 75912
GE Capital Railcar Service (Camden, AR) 56831
GE Capital Railcar Service (Ranger, TX) 88706
GE Capital Railcar Service (Texarkana, TX) 89676
GE Chemicals Inc. (Washington, WV) 93080

GE Co. Component Products Operation (Greeneville, TN) 80885
GE Co. Medium Transformer Operation (Rome, GA) 67341
GE Co. Plastics (Sparta, TN) 82343
GE Consumer Service (New Orleans, LA) 70467
GE Consumer Service (Columbia, SC) 79027
GE Electrial Distribution & Control (Morristown, TN) 81803
GE Electrical Distribution (Jacksonville, FL) 60319
GE Electrical Distribution & Control (Morristown, TN) 81804
GE Fanuc (Charlottesville, VA) 90539
GE Fanuc Automation North America (Charlottesville, VA) 90540
GE Information Services (Rockville, MD) 72285
GE Lighting (3010 Spartanburg Hwy., NC) 73508
GE Lighting (Memphis, TN) 81610
GE Medical Systems (Fort Lauderdale, FL) 59497
GE Medical Systems (St. Rose, LA) 70873
GE Medical Systems (Hanover, MD) 71911
GE Medical Systems (Fort Mill, SC) 79233
GE Microelectronics Center (Research Triangle Park, NC) 76020
GE Plastics (Pearlington, MS) 73278
GE Plastics (Parkersburg, WV) 92984
GE Plastics Burkville Div. (Lowndesboro, AL) 56114
GE Plastics-Burkville Operation (Burkville, AL) 55491
GE Specialty Chemicals (Morgantown, WV) 92944
GE Specialty Chemicals North Plant (Morgantown, WV) 92945
Gear Products Inc. (Catoosa, OK) 76909
Gear Products Inc. (Tulsa, OK) 77947
Geico (Washington, DC) **58288**
Geico Corp. (Washington, DC) 58289
Geico Indemnity Co., Inc. (Washington, DC) 58290
Gemoco (Houma, LA) 69956
GemStone Gasket Co. (Danville, KY) 68258
Gencorp Aerojet (Jonesborough, TN) 81067
Gencorp Automotive Dba Gencorp Automotive (Batesville, AR) 56755
Gencorp Automotive Inc. Dba Gencorp Automotive (Batesville, AR) 56756
Gencorp Inc. (Columbus, MS) 72710
Gencorp Polymer Prods. (Fort Smith, AR) 57052
Gencorp Polymer Prods. (Columbus, MS) 72711
Gencorp Polymer Products (Fort Smith, AR) 57053
Gencorp Polymer Products (Columbus, MS) 72712
General American Life Insur (Birmingham, AL) 55277
General American Life Insur (Metairie, LA) 70266
General American Life Insur (Tulsa, OK) 77948
General American Life Insur (Columbia, SC) 79028
General American Life Insur (Richmond, VA) 91896
General American Life Insuranc (Atlanta, GA) 64491; 64492
General American Life Insurance (Orlando, FL) 61994; 61995
General American Life Insurance (Dallas, TX) 84086
General American Life Insurance C (Mobile, AL) 56183
General American Life Insurance C (Maitland, FL) 60978
General American Life Insurance C (Charlotte, NC) 74027
General American Life Insurance C (Dallas, TX) 84087; 84088
General American Life Insurance C (Houston, TX) 86244
General American Life Insurance Co. (Austin, TX) 82882
General Cable Consumer Products Group (Highland Heights, KY) 68463
General Cable Corp. (Highland Heights, KY) **68464**
General Cable Corp. (Lawrenceburg, KY) 68505
General Cable Corp. (Bonham, TX) 83312
General Cable Electrical Group (Highland Heights, KY) 68465
General Cable Manufacturing Group (Highland Heights, KY) 68466
General Cable Telecommunications & Electronics Group (Highland Heights, KY) 68467
General Dynamics (East Camden, AR) 56922; 56923
General Dynamics (Falls Church, VA) **90855**
General Dynamics Corp. (Goose Creek, SC) 79282
General Dynamics Corp. (Arlington, VA) 90354
General Dynamics Corp. (Falls Church, VA) 90856
General Dynamics Corp. Abilene Facility (Abilene, TX) 82437
General Dynamics Corp. Space Sys. (Cape Canaveral, FL) 58914
General Dynamics Services C (Cape Canavral, FL) 58916
General Dynamics Space Systems (Huntsville, AL) 55947
General Dynamics Space Systems (Cocoa Beach, FL) 59081
General Electric Carolina Products Plant (Goldsboro, NC) 74721
General Electric Ceramics Inc. (Laurens, SC) 79593
General Electric Ceramics Inc. (Chattanooga, TN) 80410
General Electric Co. (Birmingham, AL) 55278
General Electric Co. (Burkville, AL) 55492
General Electric Co. (Decatur, AL) 55586
General Electric Co. (Dothan, AL) 55650
General Electric Co. (Homewood, AL) 55869
General Electric Co. (Jonesboro, AR) 57219; 57220
General Electric Co. (Tampa, FL) 63442
General Electric Co. (Norcross, GA) 67120
General Electric Co. (Rome, GA) 67342
General Electric Co. (Lexington, KY) 68555; 68556
General Electric Co. (Louisville, KY) 68768
General Electric Co. (Madisonville, KY) 69052
General Electric Co. (Owensboro, KY) 69170
General Electric Co. (Scottsville, KY) 69266
General Electric Co. (Somerset, KY) 69293
General Electric Co. (New Orleans, LA) 70468
General Electric Co. (Shreveport, LA) 70723; 70724
General Electric Co. (Baltimore, MD) 71159
General Electric Co. (Columbia, MD) 71590; 71591
General Electric Co. (Charlotte, NC) 74028
General Electric Co. (Durham, NC) 74402
General Electric Co. (Goldsboro, NC) 74722
General Electric Co. (Hickory, NC) 75077
General Electric Co. (Mebane, NC) 75550; 75551
General Electric Co. (Salisbury, NC) 76166
General Electric Co. (Wilmington, NC) 76572; 76573
General Electric Co. (Greenville, SC) 79361
General Electric Co. (Columbia, TN) 80628; 80629
General Electric Co. (Hendersonville, TN) 80917
General Electric Co. (Morristown, TN) 81805
General Electric Co. (Murfreesboro, TN) 81848
General Electric Co. (Selmer, TN) 82291; 82292; 82293
General Electric Co. (Dallas, TX) 84089; 84090; 84091
General Electric Co. (Houston, TX) 86245; 86246; 86247
General Electric Co. (San Antonio, TX) 89021
General Electric Co. (Hampton, VA) 91038
General Electric Co. (Lynchburg, VA) 91253
General Electric Co. (Richmond, VA) 91897
General Electric Co. (Winchester, VA) 92593
General Electric Co. Columbia Plant Operations (Columbia, MD) 71592
General Electric Co. Frankfort Plant (Frankfort, KY) 68360
General Electric Co. Mobile Communications (Lynchburg, VA) 91254
General Electric Co. Mobile Communications Business (Lynchburg, VA) 91255
General Electric Co. Transformer Bus. Dept. (Hickory, NC) 75078
General Electric Co. Transformer Business Dept. (Hickory, NC) 75079
General Electric Co. Winchester Lamp Plant (Winchester, VA) 92594
General Electric Drive Systems (Salem, VA) 92213
General Electric Ed&C (Houston, TX) 86248
General Electric Lighting Systems (Hendersonville, NC) 75040
General Electric Medical Sy (Richmond, VA) 91898
General Electric Memphis Lamp Plant (Memphis, TN) 81611
General Electric Motor Plant (Owensboro, KY) 69171
General Electric Ndd Pinellas Plant (Largo, FL) 60839
General Electric Plastics Baymar (Bay St. Louis, MS) 72607
General Electric Simulation & Control Systems (Daytona Beach, FL) 59182
General Financial Agency, Inc. (Charlotte, NC) 74029
General Foods Corp. Maxwell House Div. (Houston, TX) 86249
General Foods Mfg. Corp. Maxwell Div. (Houston, TX) 86250
General Foods USA (Dover, DE) 57789
General Instrument Corp. (Brownsville, TX) 83359
General Instrument Corp. Comm/ Scope Cable Division (Atlanta, GA) 64493
General Instrument Corp. Puerto Rico (Barceloneta, PR) 78327
General Mills Inc. (Washington, DC) 58291
General Mills Inc. (Johnson City, TN) 81043
General Mills Restaurants Inc. (Orlando, FL) 61996
General Motors Corp. Pontiac Motor Division (Oklahoma City, OK) 77373
General Polymers (Charlotte, NC) 74030
General Processors Inc. (Oxford, NC) 75779
Genesis Underwriting Mgt Co. 7 (Atlanta, GA) 64494
Genuine Parts (Atlanta, GA) **64495**
Genuine Parts Mid-South Division (Atlanta, GA) 64496
Genuine Parts Piedmont Division (Atlanta, GA) 64497
Genuine Parts Rayloc Div. (Atlanta, GA) 64498
Genuine Parts Southeast Division (Atlanta, GA) 64499
Genuine Parts Southwest Division (Dallas, TX) 84092
Genuine Parts Co. (Atlanta, GA) 64500
Genuine Parts Co. (Wheeling, WV) 93112
Genuine Parts Co. Rayloc Div. (Atlanta, GA) 64501; 64502
Genuine Parts Co. Rayloc Div. (Morganfield, KY) 69104
Genuine Parts Co. Rayloc Div. (Hancock, MD) 71903; 71904
Genuine Parts Co. Rayloc Div. (Memphis, TN) 81612; 81613
Genuine Parts Co. Rayloc Div. (Stephenville, TX) 89516
Genuine Parts Co., Inc. (Atlanta, GA) 64503
Geo. A. Hormel & Co. (Oklahoma City, OK) 77374
Georgia Boot Inc. Blairsville Plant (Blairsville, GA) 65382
Georgia Boot Inc. Franklin Plant (Franklin, TN) 80819
Georgia Federal Bank F S B (Albany, GA) 64074
Georgia Federal Bank F S B (Hinesville, GA) 66353
Georgia Federal Bank F S B (Marietta, GA) 66782
Georgia Federal Bank, F S B (Savannah, GA) 67477
Georgia Federal Bank F S B (St Simons is, GA) 67619
Georgia Federal Bank, FSB (Atlanta, GA) 64504
Georgia Federal Bank FSB (Savannah, GA) 67478
Georgia Gulf (Atlanta, GA) **64505**
Georgia Gulf Corp. (Delaware City, DE) 57769; 57770; 57771
Georgia Gulf Corp. (Atlanta, GA) 64506; 64507
Georgia Gulf Corp. (Plaquemine, LA) 70639; 70640
Georgia Gulf Corp. (Gallman, MS) 72781
Georgia Gulf Corp. (Tiptonville, TN) 82370
Georgia Gulf Corp. (Houston, TX) 86251
Georgia-Pacific (Atlanta, GA) **64508**
Georgia Pacific Corp. (Belk, AL) 55079; 55080
Georgia Pacific Corp. (Bellamy, AL) 55081
Georgia Pacific Corp. (Monroeville, AL) 56261
Georgia Pacific Corp. (Ashdown, AR) 56727
Georgia Pacific Corp. (El Dorado, AR) 56943
Georgia Pacific Corp. (Fordyce, AR) 57005
Georgia-Pacific Corp. (Little Rock, AR) 57285
Georgia Pacific Corp. (North Little Rock, AR) 57463; 57464
Georgia Pacific Corp. (Wilmington, DE) 58064
Georgia Pacific Corp. (Cross City, FL) 59128
Georgia Pacific Corp. (Hawthorne, FL) 59970
Georgia Pacific Corp. (Lake City, FL) 60620
Georgia Pacific Corp. (Lake Placid, FL) 60643
Georgia Pacific Corp. (Miami, FL) 61317
Georgia Pacific Corp. (Ocala, FL) 61800
Georgia-Pacific Corp. (Palatka, FL) 62227; 62228
Georgia Pacific Corp. (Tampa, FL) 63443
Georgia-Pacific Corp. (Albany, GA) 64075
Georgia-Pacific Corp. (Atlantic, GA) 65305
Georgia Pacific Corp. (Augusta, GA) 65332
Georgia Pacific Corp. (Brunswick, GA) 65409; 65410
Georgia Pacific Corp. (Cedar Springs, GA) 65509
Georgia Pacific Corp. (Claxton, GA) 65565
Georgia Pacific Corp. (Doraville, GA) 65930
Georgia Pacific Corp. (Ellabell, GA) 66167
Georgia Pacific Corp. (Hagan, GA) 66328
Georgia Pacific Corp. (Hampton, GA) 66331
Georgia-Pacific Corp. (Monticello, MS) 73186; 73187
Georgia-Pacific Corp. (Pryor, OK) 77739
Georgia-Pacific Corp. (Plano, TX) 88572
Georgia-Pacific Corp. Packaging Div. (Asheboro, NC) 73587
Georgia-Pacific Corp. Resins Div. (Taylorsville, MS) 73376
Georgia-Pacific Corp. Warm Springs Pine Plywood (Warm Springs, GA) 68003
Georgia-Pacific Corp. Brunswick Operations (Brunswick, GA) 65411
Georgia-Pacific Corp. Catawba Hardboard (Catawba, SC) 78773; 78774
Georgia-Pacific Corp. Conway Hardboard (Conway, NC) 74341
Georgia-Pacific Corp. Dudley Comply (Dudley, NC) 74368
Georgia-Pacific Corp. Emporia Pine Plywood (Emporia, VA) 90748
Georgia-Pacific Corp. Hawthorne Plywood (Hawthorne, FL) 59971
Georgia-Pacific Corp. Holly Hill Fiberboard (Holly Hill, SC) 79522
Georgia-Pacific Corp. Jarratt Softboard (Jarratt, VA) 91172
Georgia-Pacific Corp. Madison Plywood (Madison, GA) 66728
Georgia Pacific Corp. Monticello Mill (Monticello, MS) 73188
Georgia-Pacific Corp. Monticello Panelboard (Monticello, GA) 67000
Georgia-Pacific Corp. Monticello Pine Plywood (Monticello, GA) 67001
Georgia-Pacific Corp. Monticello Plywood (Monticello, GA) 67002
Georgia-Pacific Corp. Ocala Wood-I-Beam (Ocala, FL) 61801
Georgia-Pacific Corp. Paper Operations (Crossett, AR) 56881
Georgia-Pacific Corp. Paper Ops. (Crossett, AR) 56882
Georgia-Pacific Corp. Particleboard (Taylorsville, MS) 73377
Georgia-Pacific Corp. Pearson Sawmill (Pearson, GA) 67255
Georgia Pacific Corp. Peterman Pine Plywood (Monroeville, AL) 56262
Georgia-Pacific Corp. Plywood (Crossett, AR) 56883
Georgia-Pacific Corp. Plywood Plant (Louisville, MS) 73119
Georgia-Pacific Corp. Port Hudson (Zachary, LA) 70983
Georgia-Pacific Corp. Port Hudson Operations (Zachary, LA) 70984; 70985
Georgia-Pacific Corp. Prosperity Pine Plywood (Prosperity, SC) 79803
Georgia-Pacific Corp. Prosperity Plywood (Prosperity, SC) 79804
Georgia-Pacific Corp. Resins Plant (Louisville, MS) 73120
Georgia- Pacific Corp. Russellville Particleboard (Russellville, SC) 79844
Georgia Pacific Corp. Russellville Pine Plywood (Russellville, SC) 79845
Georgia-Pacific Corp. Russellville Plywood (Russellville, SC) 79846
Georgia-Pacific Corp. S. Boston Particleboard (South Boston, VA) 92251
Georgia-Pacific Corp. Savannah Plywood (Savannah, GA) 67479
Georgia-Pacific Corp. Skippers Osb (Skippers, VA) 92236
Georgia Pacific Corp. South Boston Particleboard (South Boston, VA) 92252
Georgia-Pacific Corp. Sterling Sawmill (Brunswick, GA) 65412
Georgia-Pacific Corp. Sterling Sawmill (Sterling, GA) 67655
Georgia-Pacific Corp. Vienna Particleboard (Vienna, GA) 67998
Georgia-Pacific Corp. Whiteville Plywood (Whiteville, NC) 76501
Georgia Pacific Resins Inc. (Crossett, AR) 56884
Georgia-Pacific Resins Inc. (Peachtree City, GA) 67243
Georgia-Pacific Resins Inc. (Port Wentworth, GA) 67275
Georgia-Pacific Resins Inc. (Vienna, GA) 67999
Georgia Pacific Resins Inc. (Louisville, MS) 73121
Georgia Pacific Resins Inc. (Conway, NC) 74342
Georgia-Pacific Resins Inc. (Hampton, SC) 79492
Georgia-Pacific Resins Inc. (Russellville, SC) 79847; 79848
Georgia-Pacific Resins Inc. (Houston, TX) 86252
Georgia Pacific Resins Inc. (Lufkin, TX) 87804; 87805
Georgia-Pacific Resins Inc. Conway Hardboard (Conway, NC) 74343
Georgia-Pacific Resins Inc. Particleboard (Taylorsville, MS) 73378
Georgia-Pacific Resins Inc. Resins (Crossett, AR) 56885
Georgia-Pacific Resins Inc. Resins Plant (Louisville, MS) 73122
Georgia Rug Mill (Summerville, GA) 67737
Gerber Childrenswear Inc. (Greenville, SC) 79362
GFS (Landover, MD) 72019
Giant Food (Landover, MD) **72020**
Giant Food Dairy (Landover, MD) 72021
Giant Food Deli (Memphis, TN) 81614; 81615
Giant Food Inc. (Landover, MD) 72022
Giant Food Inc. (Columbia, TN) 80630
Giant Food Market Inc. (Bristol, TN) 80248
Giant Food Market Inc. (Centerville, TN) 80287
Giant Food Market Inc. (Greeneville, TN) 80886
Giant Food Market Inc. (Johnson City, TN) 81044; 81045

Greyhound American Business Locations Directory

Greyhound Bus Lines (Henderson, KY) 68451
Greyhound Bus Lines (Hopkinsville, KY) 68479
Greyhound Bus Lines (Lexington, KY) 68557
Greyhound Bus Lines (Louisville, KY) 68769
Greyhound Bus Lines (Madisonville, KY) 69055
Greyhound Bus Lines (Middlesboro, KY) 69094
Greyhound Bus Lines (Morehead, KY) 69101
Greyhound Bus Lines (Mt Sterling, KY) 69117
Greyhound Bus Lines (Pikeville, KY) 69225
Greyhound Bus Lines (Richmond, KY) 69242
Greyhound Bus Lines (Shelbyville, KY) 69272
Greyhound Bus Lines (Whitley City, KY) 69339
Greyhound Bus Lines (Amite, LA) 69424
Greyhound Bus Lines (Baton Rouge, LA) 69541
Greyhound Bus Lines (Covington, LA) 69794
Greyhound Bus Lines (Grambling, LA) 69893
Greyhound Bus Lines (Hammond, LA) 69929
Greyhound Bus Lines (Jennings, LA) 69979
Greyhound Bus Lines (Lafayette, LA) 70056
Greyhound Bus Lines (Metairie, LA) 70267
Greyhound Bus Lines (New Orleans, LA) 70470; 70471
Greyhound Bus Lines (Ponchatoula, LA) 70647
Greyhound Bus Lines (Thibodaux, LA) 70913
Greyhound Bus Lines (Baltimore, MD) 71161; 71162; 71163
Greyhound Bus Lines (Cumberland, MD) 71623
Greyhound Bus Lines (Fork, MD) 71701
Greyhound Bus Lines (Frostburg, MD) 71756
Greyhound Bus Lines (Hagerstown, MD) 71882
Greyhound Bus Lines (Salisbury, MD) 72346
Greyhound Bus Lines (Silver Spring, MD) 72407; 72408
Greyhound Bus Lines (Waldorf, MD) 72529
Greyhound Bus Lines (Belzoni, MS) 72612
Greyhound Bus Lines (Brookhaven, MS) 72655
Greyhound Bus Lines (Cleveland, MS) 72683
Greyhound Bus Lines (Crystal Springs, MS) 72748
Greyhound Bus Lines (Greenville, MS) 72800
Greyhound Bus Lines (Greenwood, MS) 72833
Greyhound Bus Lines (Holly Springs, MS) 72908
Greyhound Bus Lines (Laurel, MS) 73101
Greyhound Bus Lines (Leland, MS) 73111
Greyhound Bus Lines (Meridian, MS) 73163
Greyhound Bus Lines (Natchez, MS) 73198
Greyhound Bus Lines (Pascagoula, MS) 73256
Greyhound Bus Lines (Picayune, MS) 73292
Greyhound Bus Lines (Ruleville, MS) 73333
Greyhound Bus Lines (Shaw, MS) 73342
Greyhound Bus Lines (Shelby, MS) 73343
Greyhound Bus Lines (Tchula, MS) 73380
Greyhound Bus Lines (Tupelo, MS) 73404
Greyhound Bus Lines (Vicksburg, MS) 73452
Greyhound Bus Lines (Charlotte, NC) 74032
Greyhound Bus Lines (Fayetteville, NC) 74558
Greyhound Bus Lines (Fort Bragg, NC) 74618
Greyhound Bus Lines (Gastonia, NC) 74682
Greyhound Bus Lines (Hendersonville, NC) 75041
Greyhound Bus Lines (High Point, NC) 75137
Greyhound Bus Lines (Mocksville, NC) 75563
Greyhound Bus Lines (Mount Airy, NC) 75679
Greyhound Bus Lines (Mount Olive, NC) 75695
Greyhound Bus Lines (Reidsville, NC) 76003
Greyhound Bus Lines (Wallace, NC) 76440
Greyhound Bus Lines (Warsaw, NC) 76451
Greyhound Bus Lines (Wilmington, NC) 76574
Greyhound Bus Lines (Claremore, OK) 76952
Greyhound Bus Lines (El Reno, OK) 77031
Greyhound Bus Lines (Elk City, OK) 77037
Greyhound Bus Lines (Henryetta, OK) 77128
Greyhound Bus Lines (Mc Alester, OK) 77191
Greyhound Bus Lines (Miami, OK) 77204
Greyhound Bus Lines (Mustang, OK) 77237
Greyhound Bus Lines (Norman, OK) 77255
Greyhound Bus Lines (Oklahoma City, OK) 77377
Greyhound Bus Lines (Okmulgee, OK) 77680
Greyhound Bus Lines (Weatherford, OK) 78241
Greyhound Bus Lines (Anderson, SC) 78676
Greyhound Bus Lines (Cheraw, SC) 78923
Greyhound Bus Lines (Florence, SC) 79206
Greyhound Bus Lines (Greenville, SC) 79366
Greyhound Bus Lines (Kingstree, SC) 79556
Greyhound Bus Lines (Lake City, SC) 79561; 79562
Greyhound Bus Lines (Rock Hill, SC) 79827
Greyhound Bus Lines (Spartanburg, SC) 79910; 79911
Greyhound Bus Lines (St Stephen, SC) 79971
Greyhound Bus Lines (Summerville, SC) 79986
Greyhound Bus Lines (Sumter, SC) 80020
Greyhound Bus Lines (Walterboro, SC) 80071
Greyhound Bus Lines (Bristol, TN) 80249
Greyhound Bus Lines (Brownsville, TN) 80258
Greyhound Bus Lines (Chattanooga, TN) 80412
Greyhound Bus Lines (Clarksville, TN) 80551
Greyhound Bus Lines (Cleveland, TN) 80587
Greyhound Bus Lines (Columbia, TN) 80631
Greyhound Bus Lines (Dyersburg, TN) 80752
Greyhound Bus Lines (Fayetteville, TN) 80796
Greyhound Bus Lines (Kingsport, TN) 81106
Greyhound Bus Lines (Knoxville, TN) 81215; 81216
Greyhound Bus Lines (Manchester, TN) 81392
Greyhound Bus Lines (Mc Minnville, TN) 81435
Greyhound Bus Lines (Memphis, TN) 81619; 81620; 81621; 81622; 81623
Greyhound Bus Lines (Milan, TN) 81769
Greyhound Bus Lines (Millington, TN) 81776
Greyhound Bus Lines (Murfreesboro, TN) 81850
Greyhound Bus Lines (Nashville, TN) 82017; 82018
Greyhound Bus Lines (Newport, TN) 82168
Greyhound Bus Lines (Oak Ridge, TN) 82193
Greyhound Bus Lines (Pulaski, TN) 82242
Greyhound Bus Lines (Ripley, TN) 82253
Greyhound Bus Lines (Springfield, TN) 82359
Greyhound Bus Lines (Tullahoma, TN) 82378
Greyhound Bus Lines (Union City, TN) 82384
Greyhound Bus Lines (Winchester, TN) 82420
Greyhound Bus Lines (Addison, TX) 82473
Greyhound Bus Lines (Amarillo, TX) 82549
Greyhound Bus Lines (Austin, TX) 82884
Greyhound Bus Lines (Beaumont, TX) 83156
Greyhound Bus Lines (Big Spring, TX) 83287
Greyhound Bus Lines (Bryan, TX) 83396
Greyhound Bus Lines (Cisco, TX) 83564
Greyhound Bus Lines (Corpus Christi, TX) 83719
Greyhound Bus Lines (Cotulla, TX) 83800
Greyhound Bus Lines (Dalhart, TX) 83832
Greyhound Bus Lines (Dallas, TX) 84096; 84097; 84098; 84099
Greyhound Bus Lines (Denison, TX) 84596
Greyhound Bus Lines (Dumas, TX) 84688
Greyhound Bus Lines (Eastland, TX) 84728
Greyhound Bus Lines (El Paso, TX) 84807; 84808
Greyhound Bus Lines (Fort Worth, TX) 85126
Greyhound Bus Lines (Garland, TX) 85487
Greyhound Bus Lines (Georgetown, TX) 85567
Greyhound Bus Lines (Hearne, TX) 85722
Greyhound Bus Lines (Hillsboro, TX) 85750
Greyhound Bus Lines (Houston, TX) 86254; 86255; 86256
Greyhound Bus Lines (Liberty, TX) 87672
Greyhound Bus Lines (Mc Kinney, TX) 87912
Greyhound Bus Lines (Monahans, TX) 88139
Greyhound Bus Lines (New Braunfels, TX) 88209
Greyhound Bus Lines (Odessa, TX) 88247
Greyhound Bus Lines (Orange, TX) 88313
Greyhound Bus Lines (Port Arthur, TX) 88632
Greyhound Bus Lines (Richardson, TX) 88736
Greyhound Bus Lines (San Antonio, TX) 89022; 89023
Greyhound Bus Lines (Seguin, TX) 89367
Greyhound Bus Lines (Temple, TX) 89618
Greyhound Bus Lines (Texarkana, TX) 89677
Greyhound Bus Lines (Van Horn, TX) 89860
Greyhound Bus Lines (Waco, TX) 89937
Greyhound Bus Lines (Alexandria, VA) 90223
Greyhound Bus Lines (Burkeville, VA) 90507
Greyhound Bus Lines (Clifton Forge, VA) 90642
Greyhound Bus Lines (Covington, VA) 90660
Greyhound Bus Lines (Fredericksburg, VA) 90927
Greyhound Bus Lines (Hampton, VA) 91039
Greyhound Bus Lines (Hillsville, VA) 91141
Greyhound Bus Lines (Lexington, VA) 91207
Greyhound Bus Lines (Marion, VA) 91333
Greyhound Bus Lines (Norfolk, VA) 91539; 91540; 91541
Greyhound Bus Lines (Portsmouth, VA) 91657
Greyhound Bus Lines (Radford, VA) 91697
Greyhound Bus Lines (Richmond, VA) 91900; 91901
Greyhound Bus Lines (Roanoke, VA) 92156
Greyhound Bus Lines (South Boston, VA) 92253
Greyhound Bus Lines (Springfield, VA) 92287
Greyhound Bus Lines (Tappahannock, VA) 92377
Greyhound Bus Lines (Triangle, VA) 92387
Greyhound Bus Lines (Virginia Beach, VA) 92485
Greyhound Bus Lines (Williamsburg, VA) 92572
Greyhound Bus Lines (Woodbridge, VA) 92617
Greyhound Bus Lines (Wytheville, VA) 92640
Greyhound Bus Lines (Yorktown, VA) 92653
Greyhound Bus Lines (Bluefield, WV) 92702
Greyhound Bus Lines (Charleston, WV) 92748
Greyhound Bus Lines (Fairmont, WV) 92840
Greyhound Bus Lines (Gauley Bridge, WV) 92855
Greyhound Bus Lines (Lewisburg, WV) 92915; 92916
Greyhound Bus Lines (Martinsburg, WV) 92931
Greyhound Bus Lines (Rainelle, WV) 93017
Greyhound Bus Lines (Weirton, WV) 93088
Greyhound Bus Lines (Wheeling, WV) 93113
Greyhound Bus Lines District O (Atlanta, GA) 64516
Greyhound Bus Lines E (Rayne, LA) 70656
Greyhound Bus Lines Inc. (Thomasville, AL) 56609
Greyhound Bus Lines Inc. (Crystal River, FL) 59133
Greyhound Bus Lines Inc. (Monroe, LA) 70355
Greyhound Bus Lines Inc. (Taft, TX) 89594
Greyhound Bus Lines Local Info (Atlanta, GA) 64517; 64518
Greyhound Bus Lines Local Info (Decatur, GA) 65822
Greyhound Bus Lines Local Info (Doraville, GA) 65931
Greyhound Bus Lines Local Info (Hapeville, GA) 66336
Greyhound Bus Lines Local Info (Marietta, GA) 66783
Greyhound Bus Lines Transporta (Atlanta, GA) 64519
Greyhound Bus Lins (Amarillo, TX) 82550
Greyhound Bus Lins (Dickinson, TX) 84665
Greyhound Bus Lins (Odessa, TX) 88248
Greyhound Bus Lins (Sweetwater, TX) 89584
Greyhound Bus Lins (Tyler, TX) 89804
Greyhound Bus Liwes (Tulsa, OK) 77949
Greyhound Bus Lnes (Carrollton, TX) 83467
Greyhound Bus Lnes (Sherman, TX) 89398
Greyhound Bus Sta (Floresville, TX) 85038
Greyhound Bus Station (Flomaton, AL) 55733
Greyhound Bus Station (Greenville, AL) 55817
Greyhound Bus Station (Lanett, AL) 56101
Greyhound Bus Station (Pine Bluff, AR) 57517
Greyhound Bus Station (Boynton Beach, FL) 58778
Greyhound Bus Station (Brooksville, FL) 58890
Greyhound Bus Station (Eastpoint, FL) 59375
Greyhound Bus Station (Haines City, FL) 59949
Greyhound Bus Station (Homestead, FL) 60114
Greyhound Bus Station (Jacksonville, FL) 60322
Greyhound Bus Station (Lake Placid, FL) 60644
Greyhound Bus Station (Live Oak, FL) 60913
Greyhound Bus Station (Panama City, FL) 62323
Greyhound Bus Station (Starke, FL) 63147
Greyhound Bus Station (Titusville, FL) 63689
Greyhound Bus Station (Adel, GA) 64055
Greyhound Bus Station (Nashville, GA) 67068
Greyhound Bus Station (Quitman, GA) 67287
Greyhound Bus Station (De Ridder, LA) 69812
Greyhound Bus Station (Gonzales, LA) 69890
Greyhound Bus Station (New Iberia, LA) 70409
Greyhound Bus Station (Sulphur, LA) 70884
Greyhound Bus Station (Asheville, NC) 73630
Greyhound Bus Station (Oxford, NC) 75780
Greyhound Bus Station (Aiken, SC) 78650
Greyhound Bus Station (Beaufort, SC) 78709
Greyhound Bus Station (Bishopville, SC) 78743
Greyhound Bus Station (Arlington, TX) 82660
Greyhound Bus Station (Carthage, TX) 83518
Greyhound Bus Station (College Station, TX) 83617
Greyhound Bus Station (Fabens, TX) 85027
Greyhound Bus Station (Sherman, TX) 89399
Greyhound Bus Stop (Evergreen, AL) 55707
Greyhound Bus Stop (Mooresville, NC) 75605
Greyhound Bus System (Rockingham, NC) 76062
Greyhound Bus Terminal (Avon Park, FL) 58606
Greyhound Bus Terminal (Fort Myers, FL) 59702
Greyhound Bus Terminal (Gainesville, FL) 59879
Greyhound Bus Terminal (Marianna, FL) 61003
Greyhound Bus Terminal (Houma, LA) 69957
Greyhound Bus Terminal (Yazoo City, MS) 73502
Greyhound Bus Terminal (Midland, TX) 88038
Greyhound Bus Terminial (Dublin, GA) 66010
Greyhound Lines Inc. (Covington, KY) 68221
Greyhound Lines Inc. (Memphis, TN) 81624
Greyhound Lines Inc. (Nashville, TN) 82019
Greyhound Lines Inc. (Dallas, TX) **84100**
Greyhound Lines Inc. (Charleston, WV) 92749
Greystone Realty Corp. (Atlanta, GA) 64520
Greystone Realty Corp. (Irving, TX) 87349
Gribetz International, Inc. (Sunrise, FL) 63194
Griffin Pie Co. (London, KY) 68660
Griffin Pie Co. Inc. (London, KY) 68661
Griffin Pipe Products Co. (Lynchburg, VA) 91256; 91257; 91258
Griffin Wheel Co. (Bessemer, AL) 55092; 55093
Griffin Wheel Co. Bessemer Plant (Bessemer, AL) 55094
Grinnell Corp. (Henderson, TN) 80907
Grinnell Corp. (Houston, TX) 86257
GroAgriseed Co. (Lubbock, TX) 87764
Grocery USA (Chickasha, OK) 76926
Groupamerica Insurance Co. (Atlanta, GA) 64521
Grumman Aircraft Systems Div. (Milledgeville, GA) 66976; 66977
Grumman Melbourne Systems Division (Melbourne, FL) 61057
Grumman Space Station Integration Division (Reston, VA) 91710
Grumman Aerospace & Electronics (Milledgeville, GA) 66978
Grumman Corp. (Arlington, VA) 90355
Grumman Corp. Aircraft Systems Div. (Stuart, FL) 63170
Grumman Corp. St. Augustine (St. Augustine, FL) 63058
Grumman Houston Corp. (Webster, TX) 90019
Grumman St. Augustine Corp. (St. Augustine, FL) 63059; 63060; 63061
Grumman Systems Support (Chamblee, GA) 65528
Grumman Technical Services Corp. (Titusville, FL) 63690
GSC Leasing Dr. (Claymont, DE) 57763
GTE Technical Products Div. (Reidsville, NC) 76004
GTE Cellular Communications Corp. (Atlanta, GA) 64522
GTE Center (League City, TX) 87627
GTE Center (Martindale, TX) 87877
GTE Center (Robstown, TX) 88807
GTE Communications Corp. (Tampa, FL) 63445
GTE Customer Networks, Inc. (Atlanta, GA) 64523; 64524
GTE Data Services Inc. (Tampa, FL) 63446
GTE Data Services Inc. (Temple Terrace, FL) 63678
GTE Directories Corp. (Dallas, TX) 84101
GTE Directories Sales Corp. (Dallas, TX) 84102
GTE Directories Service Corp. (Dallas, TX) 84103

Hertz Rent-A-Car (Palm Beach, FL) 62258
Hertz Rent-A-Car (Panama City, FL) 62324
Hertz Rent-A-Car (Sarasota, FL) 62837
Hertz Rent-A-Car (Shalimar, FL) 62912
Hertz Rent-A-Car (St Petersburg, FL) 62975
Hertz Rent-A-Car (Stuart, FL) 63171
Hertz Rent-A-Car (Tallahassee, FL) 63244
Hertz Rent-A-Car (Tampa, FL) 63456
Hertz Rent-A-Car (Titusville, FL) 63691
Hertz Rent-A-Car (West Palm Beach, FL) 63871
Hertz Rent-A-Car (Winter Park, FL) 63981
Hertz Rent-A-Car (Atlanta, GA) 64531
Hertz Rent-A-Car (Macon, GA) 66691
Hertz Rent-A-Car (Milledgeville, GA) 66979
Hertz Rent-A-Car (Moultrie, GA) 67054
Hertz Rent-A-Car (Valdosta, GA) 67960
Hertz Rent-A-Car (Houma, LA) 69958
Hertz Rent-A-Car (Lafayette, LA) 70057
Hertz Rent-A-Car (Lake Charles, LA) 70140; 70141
Hertz Rent-A-Car (New Orleans, LA) 70472; 70473
Hertz Rent-A-Car (Patterson, LA) 70611
Hertz Rent-A-Car (Shreveport, LA) 70725
Hertz Rent-A-Car (St. Bernard, LA) 70859
Hertz Rent-A-Car (Baltimore, MD) 71166
Hertz Rent-A-Car (California, MD) 71483
Hertz Rent-A-Car (Cambridge, MD) 71486
Hertz Rent-A-Car (Gaithersburg, MD) 71785
Hertz Rent-A-Car (Hagerstown, MD) 71883
Hertz Rent-A-Car (Laurel, MD) 72077
Hertz Rent-A-Car (Ocean City, MD) 72160
Hertz Rent-A-Car (Biloxi, MS) 72622
Hertz Rent-A-Car (Greenwood, MS) 72834
Hertz Rent-A-Car (Gulfport, MS) 72856; 72857
Hertz Rent-A-Car (Jackson, MS) 72988; 72989
Hertz Rent-A-Car (Pascagoula, MS) 73259
Hertz Rent-A-Car (Tupelo, MS) 73405
Hertz Rent-A-Car (Arden, NC) 73570
Hertz Rent-A-Car (Charlotte, NC) 74033; 74034
Hertz Rent-A-Car (Fayetteville, NC) 74559
Hertz Rent-A-Car (Greensboro, NC) 74850
Hertz Rent-A-Car (Hickory, NC) 75080
Hertz Rent-A-Car (Rocky Mount, NC) 76091; 76092
Hertz Rent-A-Car (Winston Salem, NC) 76672; 76673
Hertz Rent-A-Car (Enid, OK) 77054
Hertz Rent-A-Car (Lawton, OK) 77160
Hertz Rent-A-Car (Oklahoma City, OK) 77378; 77379; 77380
Hertz Rent-A-Car (Ponca City, OK) 77705
Hertz Rent-A-Car (Stillwater, OK) 77838
Hertz Rent-A-Car (Tulsa, OK) 77951; 77952; 77953
Hertz Rent-A-Car (Charleston, SC) 78820
Hertz Rent-A-Car (Hilton Head Island, SC) 79517
Hertz Rent-A-Car (Lyman, SC) 79625
Hertz Rent-A-Car (Spartanburg, SC) 79912
Hertz Rent-A-Car (Sumter, SC) 80021
Hertz Rent-A-Car (Abilene, TX) 82439
Hertz Rent-A-Car (Austin, TX) 82886; 82887
Hertz Rent-A-Car (Baytown, TX) 83125
Hertz Rent-A-Car (College Station, TX) 83618
Hertz Rent-A-Car (Corpus Christi, TX) 83720; 83721
Hertz Rent-A-Car (Dallas, TX) 84115; 84116; 84117; 84118; 84119; 84120; 84121; 84122
Hertz Rent-A-Car (Fort Worth, TX) 85128
Hertz Rent-A-Car (Galveston, TX) 85440
Hertz Rent-A-Car (Houston, TX) 86266; 86267; 86268; 86269; 86270; 86271; 86272; 86273
Hertz Rent-A-Car (Lubbock, TX) 87765
Hertz Rent-A-Car (Midland, TX) 88039
Hertz Rent-A-Car (San Angelo, TX) 88877
Hertz Rent-A-Car (San Antonio, TX) 89025
Hertz Rent-A-Car (Temple, TX) 89619
Hertz Rent-A-Car (Victoria, TX) 89887
Hertz Rent-A-Car (Waco, TX) 89938
Hertz Rent-A-Car (Charlottesville, VA) 90541
Hertz Rent-A-Car (Fredericksburg, VA) 90928
Hertz Rent-A-Car (Hot Springs, VA) 91167
Hertz Rent-A-Car (Lynchburg, VA) 91260
Hertz Rent-A-Car (Mc Lean, VA) 91368
Hertz Rent-A-Car (Norfolk, VA) 91543
Hertz Rent-A-Car (Richmond, VA) 91902
Hertz Rent-A-Car (Sandston, VA) 92232
Hertz Rent-A-Car (Williamsburg, VA) 92573
Hertz Rent-A-Car (Winchester, VA) 92595
Hertz Rent-A-Car Car Rental Lo (Atlanta, GA) 64532
Hertz Rent-A-Car Car Rental Lo (Marietta, GA) 66784
Hertz Rent-A-Car Corp. (Savannah, GA) 67486
Hertz Rent-A-Car Dba (Pompano Beach, FL) 62600
Hertz Rent-A-Car Lcns (Myrtle Beach, SC) 79700
Hertz Rent-A-Car Licensee (Huntsville, AL) 55951
Hertz Rent-A-Car Licensee (Madison, AL) 56122
Hertz Rent-A-Car Licensee (Northport, AL) 56407
Hertz Rent-A-Car Licensee (Hot Springs National Park, AR) 57170
Hertz Rent-A-Car Licensee (Cumberland, MD) 71624
Hertz Rent-A-Car Licensee (Salisbury, MD) 72347
Hertz Rent-A-Car Licensee (Columbus, MS) 72713
Hertz Rent-A-Car Licensee (Hattiesburg, MS) 72891
Hertz Rent-A-Car Licensee (Oxford, MS) 73239
Hertz Rent-A-Car Licensee (Tupelo, MS) 73406
Hertz Rent-A-Car Licensee (Fayetteville, NC) 74560
Hertz Rent-A-Car Licensee (Goldsboro, NC) 74723
Hertz Rent-A-Car Licensee (Greenville, NC) 74964
Hertz Rent-A-Car Licensee (Raleigh, NC) 75914
Hertz Rent-A-Car Licensee (Richlands, NC) 76026
Hertz Rent-A-Car Licensee (Wilmington, NC) 76575
Hertz Rent-A-Car Licensee (Oklahoma City, OK) 77381
Hertz Rent-A-Car Licensee (Ponca City, OK) 77706
Hertz Rent-A-Car Licensee (Florence, SC) 79207
Hertz Rent-A-Car Licensee (Alice, TX) 82483
Hertz Rent-A-Car Licensee (College Sta, TX) 83609
Hertz Rent-A-Car Licensee (Kingsville, TX) 87533
Hertz Rent-A-Car Licensee (Laredo, TX) 87612
Hertz Rent-A-Car Licensee (Longview, TX) 87717
Hertz Rent-A-Car Licensee (Lufkin, TX) 87806
Hertz Rent-A-Car Licensee (Mc Allen, TX) 87883
Hertz Rent-A-Car Licensee (Orange, TX) 88315
Hertz Rent-A-Car Licensee (Waco, TX) 89939
Hertz Rent-A-Car Licensee (Wichita Falls, TX) 90073
Hertz Rent-A-Car Local Rese (Houston, TX) 86274
Hertz Rent-A-Car Regional Travel (College Park, GA) 65585
Hertz Rent-A-Car Rental Locati (Atlanta, GA) 64533; 64534; 64535
Hertz Rent-A-Car Rental Statio (Washington, DC) 58300
Hertz Rent-A-Car Svc Dept (Mc Allen, TX) 87884
Hertz Rent-A-Car System (Meridian, MS) 73164
Hertz Rent-A-Car System (Norfolk, VA) 91544
Hertz Rent Car (Miami, FL) 61327; 61328
Hertz Rental Trucks (Houston, TX) 86275
Hess Oil Virgin Islands Corp. (Hovic) (Kingshill, VI) 90148
Hess Oil Virgin Islands Corp. (Hovic) (St. Croix, VI) 90149
Hevi Duty Electric (Goldsbora, NC) 74699
Hevi Duty Electric (Celina, TN) 80282; 80283
Hevi-Duty Electric Co. (Goldsboro, NC) 74724
Hevi-Duty Electric Co. (Celina, TN) 80284
Hevi Duty Nelson (Tulsa, OK) 77954
Hewlett Packard Co. (Little Rock, AR) 57287
Hewlett-Packard Co. (Fort Lauderdale, FL) 59507
Hewlett Packard Co. (Melbourne, FL) 61067
Hewlett Packard Co. (Marietta, GA) 66785
Hewlett Packard Co. (Norcross, GA) 67123
Hewlett Packard Co. (Bethany, OK) 76858
Hewlett-Packard Co. (Oklahoma City, OK) 77382
Hewlett Packard Co. (Tulsa, OK) 77955; 77956
Hewlett-Packard Co. (Aguadilla, PR) 78294
Hewlett-Packard Co. (Columbia, SC) 79029
Hewlett Packard Co. (Austin, TX) 82888
Hewlett-Packard Co. (Mc Allen, TX) 87885
Hewlett-Packard Co. (San Antonio, TX) 89026
Hewlett Packard Co. Inc. (Jacksonville, FL) 60326
Hewlett-Packard Co. Sales (Norcross, GA) 67124
Hewlett-Packard Oki Printed Circuits (Aguadilla, PR) 78295
Hi-Tek Polymers Inc. Plant 2700 (Louisville, KY) 68772
Hi-Tek Polymers Inc. Vernon Plant (Vernon, TX) 89865
Hibernia Corp. (New Orleans, LA) **70474**
Hibernia Corp. Holding Co. (New Orleans, LA) 70475; 70476
Hibernia National Bank (Alexandria, LA) 69380; 69381; 69382; 69383; 69384
Hibernia National Bank (Baker, LA) 69435
Hibernia National Bank (Baton Rouge, LA) 69544; 69545; 69546; 69547; 69548; 69549; 69550; 69551; 69552; 69553; 69554
Hibernia National Bank (Bossier City, LA) 69716; 69717
Hibernia National Bank (Covington, LA) 69795
Hibernia National Bank (Lacombe, LA) 70037
Hibernia National Bank (Lafayette, LA) 70058; 70059; 70060
Hibernia National Bank (Livingston, LA) 70193
Hibernia National Bank (Mandeville, LA) 70208
Hibernia National Bank (Metairie, LA) 70268; 70269; 70270; 70271; 70272; 70273
Hibernia National Bank (New Orleans, LA) 70477; 70478; 70479; 70480; 70481; 70482; 70483; 70484; 70485; 70486; 70487; 70488; 70489; 70490; 70491; 70492; 70493; 70494; 70495; 70496; 70497; 70498; 70499; 70500; 70501; 70502; 70503; 70504; 70505
Hibernia National Bank (Pineville, LA) 70616; 70617
Hibernia National Bank (Reserve, LA) 70661
Hibernia National Bank (Shreveport, LA) 70726; 70727; 70728; 70729; 70730
Hibernia National Bank (Slidell, LA) 70827
Hibernia National Bank (Carrollton, TX) 83468
Hibernia National Bank (Dallas, TX) 84123
Hibernia National Bank (San Antonio, TX) 89027
Hibernia National Bank Inc. B (Baton Rouge, LA) 69555
Hickorycraft, Inc. (Hickory, NC) 75081
Highlands Insurance Co. (Houston, TX) 86276
Hiland Dairy Co. (Springdale, AR) 57634
Hill Petroleum Co. Krotz Springs Refinery (Krotz Springs, LA) 70028
Hill Petroleum Co. St. Rose Refinery (St. Rose, LA) 70874
Hill-Rom Co. Inc. (Birmingham, AL) 55281
Hill's Pet Nutrition Inc. (Bowling Green, KY) 68144
Hill's Pet Nutrition Inc. Pet S (Duluth, GA) 66038
Hills Pet Products (Bowling Green, KY) 68145
Hillshire Farm & Kahn's Co. (Alexandria, KY) 68078
Hispan Corp. (Decatur, AL) 55592
Hit or Miss (Birmingham, AL) 55282
Hit or Miss (Huntsville, AL) 55952
Hit or Miss (Washington, DC) 58301; 58302
Hit or Miss (Boca Raton, FL) 58711
Hit or Miss (Boynton Beach, FL) 58779
Hit or Miss (Brandon, FL) 58873
Hit or Miss (Clearwater, FL) 59019; 59020
Hit or Miss (Deerfield Beach, FL) 59279; 59280
Hit or Miss (Fort Lauderdale, FL) 59508; 59509
Hit or Miss (Hollywood, FL) 60064
Hit or Miss (Jacksonville, FL) 60327; 60328
Hit or Miss (Lake Worth, FL) 60677
Hit or Miss (Largo, FL) 60841
Hit or Miss (Melbourne, FL) 61068
Hit or Miss (Miami, FL) 61329; 61330
Hit or Miss (Orlando, FL) 62007
Hit or Miss (Pensacola, FL) 62435
Hit or Miss (Sarasota, FL) 62838
Hit or Miss (W Palm Beach, FL) 63792
Hit or Miss (Morrow, GA) 67013
Hit or Miss (Covington, KY) 68222
Hit or Miss (Lexington, KY) 68558
Hit or Miss (Louisville, KY) 68773; 68774; 68775
Hit or Miss (Baton Rouge, LA) 69556
Hit or Miss (Lafayette, LA) 70061
Hit or Miss (Metairie, LA) 70274
Hit or Miss (New Orleans, LA) 70506
Hit or Miss (Baltimore, MD) 71167; 71168
Hit or Miss (Gaithersburg, MD) 71786
Hit or Miss (Germantown, MD) 71826
Hit or Miss (Greenbelt, MD) 71863
Hit or Miss (Langley Pk, MD) 72046
Hit or Miss (Marlow Heights, MD) 72127
Hit or Miss (Owings Mills, MD) 72188
Hit or Miss (Rockville, MD) 72288
Hit or Miss (Silver Spring, MD) 72409; 72410
Hit or Miss (Charlotte, NC) 74035; 74036; 74037; 74038; 74039; 74040
Hit or Miss (Greensboro, NC) 74851; 74852
Hit or Miss (Morrisville, NC) 75667
Hit or Miss (Raleigh, NC) 75915
Hit or Miss (Oklahoma City, OK) 77383; 77384; 77385
Hit or Miss (Cayce, SC) 78776
Hit or Miss (Columbia, SC) 79030
Hit or Miss (Greenville, SC) 79368
Hit or Miss (Goodlettsville, TN) 80864
Hit or Miss (Memphis, TN) 81627
Hit or Miss (Murfreesboro, TN) 81852
Hit or Miss (Nashville, TN) 82024
Hit or Miss (Amarillo, TX) 82551; 82552
Hit or Miss (Arlington, TX) 82662; 82663
Hit or Miss (Austin, TX) 82889; 82890; 82891; 82892
Hit or Miss (Beaumont, TX) 83160
Hit or Miss (Carrollton, TX) 83469
Hit or Miss (College Station, TX) 83619; 83620
Hit or Miss (Dallas, TX) 84124; 84125; 84126; 84127; 84128
Hit or Miss (El Paso, TX) 84810; 84811
Hit or Miss (Fort Worth, TX) 85129
Hit or Miss (Harlingen, TX) 85701
Hit or Miss (Houston, TX) 86277; 86278; 86279; 86280; 86281; 86282; 86283; 86284; 86285; 86286
Hit or Miss (Irving, TX) 87354
Hit or Miss (Mc Allen, TX) 87886
Hit or Miss (Midland, TX) 88040
Hit or Miss (Plano, TX) 88573
Hit or Miss (San Antonio, TX) 89028; 89029; 89030
Hit or Miss (Alexandria, VA) 90225
Hit or Miss (Chesapeake, VA) 90583; 90584
Hit or Miss (Fairfax, VA) 90789
Hit or Miss (Falls Church, VA) 90857
Hit or Miss (Hampton, VA) 91040
Hit or Miss (Manassas, VA) 91314
Hit or Miss (Norfolk, VA) 91545
Hit or Miss (Richmond, VA) 91903; 91904; 91905
Hit or Miss (Roanoke, VA) 92157
Hit or Miss (Spotsylvania, VA) 92272
Hit or Miss (Sterling, VA) 92345
Hit or Miss (Virginia Beach, VA) 92486; 92487
Hit or Miss (Williamsburg, VA) 92574
Hit or Miss (Huntington, WV) 92874
Hit or Miss (Parkersburg, WV) 92985
Hit or Miss Austin (Round Rock, TX) 88848
Hit or Miss Clothes (Jacksonville, FL) 60329
Hit or Miss No 327 (Birmingham, AL) 55283
Hit or Miss Wms Apparel Distri (Atlanta, GA) 64536
Hit or Miss Wms Apparel Region (Decatur, GA) 65823
Hit or Miss Wms Apparel Retail (Atlanta, GA) 64537; 64538
Hit or Miss Wms Apparel Retail (Decatur, GA) 65824; 65825
Hit or Miss Wms Apparel Retail (Duluth, GA) 66039
Hit or Miss Wms Apparel Retail (Marietta, GA) 66786; 66787
Hit or Miss Wms Apparel Retail (Roswell, GA) 67374
Hit or Miss Womens Apparel (Orlando, FL) 62008
H.K. Porter/Wiss (Statesboro, GA) 67637
HMO National Network (Austin, TX) 82893
Hobart Corp. Pmi Food Equipment Group (Richmond Hill, GA) 67297
Hobert Mining, Inc. (Madison, WV) 92921
Hoechst Celanese (Shelby, NC) 76240
Hoechst Celanese (Carlisle, SC) 78766
Hoechst Celanese (Narrows, VA) 91438
Hoechst Celanese (Portsmouth, VA) 91659
Hoechst Celanese Engineering Plastics Div. (Florence, KY) 68308
Hoechst Celanese Seperations Products Div. (Charlotte, NC) 74041
Hoechst Celanese Celriver Plant (Rock Hill, SC) 79828
Hoechst Celanese Chamical Group Inc. Clear Lake Plant (Pasadena, TX) 88417
Hoechst-Celanese Charlotte Specialty Chemicals Group (Charlotte, NC) 74042
Hoechst Celanese Charlotte Spg (Charlotte, NC) 74043
Hoechst-Celanese Chemical Group Inc. (Bay City, TX) 83099; 83100
Hoechst Celanese Chemical Group Inc. Bayport (Seabrook, TX) 89357
Hoechst Celanese Chemical Group Inc. Bayport Terminal (Seabrook, TX) 89358
Hoechst-Celanese Chemical Group Inc. Clear Lake Plant (Pasadena, TX) 88418
Hoechst-Celanese Corp. (Bucks, AL) 55489
Hoechst-Celanese Corp. (Greer, SC) 79475; 79476

Hoechst Celanese Corp. (Spartanburg, SC) 79913
Hoechst Celanese Corp. (Bishop, TX) 83302
Hoechst-Celanese Corp. (Narrows, VA) 91439
Hoechst-Celanese Corp. (Portsmouth, VA) 91660
Hoechst-Celanese Corp. Bayport Works (Pasadena, TX) 88419
Hoechst-Celanese Corp. Seperations Products Div. (Charlotte, NC) 74044
Hoechst Celanese Corp. Baton Rouge Works (Baton Rouge, LA) 69557
Hoechst-Celanese Corp. Celriver Plant (Rock Hill, SC) 79829
Hoechst Celanese Corp. Corpus Christi Technical Ctr. (Corpus Christi, TX) 83722
Hoechst-Celanese Corp. Dreyfus Research Park (Charlotte, NC) 74045
Hoechst-Celanese Corp. Greenville Plant (Greenville, SC) 79369
Hoechst-Celanese Corp. Leeds Plant (Leeds, SC) 79599
Hoechst-Celanese Corp. Pampa Plant (Pampa, TX) 88350
Hoechst-Celanese Corp. Salisbury Plant (Salisbury, NC) 76167
Hoechst-Celanese Corp. Shelby Plant (Shelby, NC) 76241
Hoechst Celanese Corp. Sou-Tex Works (Mount Holly, NC) 75692
Hoechst-Celanese Corp. Spartanburg (Spartanburg, SC) 79914
Hoechst Celanese Corp. Spartanburg Plant (Spartanburg, SC) 79915
Hoechst-Celanese Corp. Specialty Prods. Facility (Florence, KY) 68309
Hoechst-Celanese Corp. Technical Center (Corpus Christi, TX) 83723
Hoechst Celanese Corp. Virginia Chemicals Co. (Bucks, AL) 55490
Hoechst Celanese Corp. Virginia Chemicals Co. (Bishop, TX) 83303
Hoechst Celanese Dreyfus Research Park (Charlotte, NC) 74046
Hoechst Celanese Eng. Plastics (Florence, KY) 68310
Hoechst Celanese - Pampa Plant (Pampa, TX) 88351; 88352
Hoechst Celanese Salisbury Plant (Salisbury, NC) 76168
Hoechst Celanese Shelby Plant (Shelby, NC) 76242
Hoechst Celanese Specialty Chemicals Group (Bishop, TX) 83304
Hoechst Roussel Pharmaceutc (Hurst, TX) 87274
Hoechst Roussel Pharmaceuti (Tampa, FL) 63457
Hoechst Roussel Pharmaceutical (Dunwoody, GA) 66111
Hoechst-Roussel Pharmaceutical (Chevy Chase, MD) 71532
Holly Corp. (Dallas, TX) 84129; **84130**
Holly Farms Food Service Inc. (Wilkesboro, NC) 76507
Holly Farms Foods Inc. (Harmony, NC) 75004
Holly Farms Foods Inc. (Roaring River, NC) 76048
Holly Farms Foods Inc. (Wilkesboro, NC) 76508; 76509
Holly Farms Foods Inc. (Glen Allen, VA) 90980
Holly Farms Foods Inc. (Harrisonburg, VA) 91091
Holly Farms Foods Inc. (Jetersville, VA) 91173
Holly Farms Foods Inc. Center Texas Plant (Center, TX) 83536
Holly Farms Foods Inc. Harmony Rendering (Harmony, NC) 75005
Holly Farms Foods Inc. Monroe Plant (Monroe, NC) 75577
Holly Farms Foods Inc. New Market Feed Mill (New Market, VA) 91442
Holly Farms Foods Inc. Richmond Plant (Glen Allen, VA) 90981
Holly Farms Foods Inc. Roaring River Mill (Roaring River, NC) 76049
Holly Farms Foods Inc. Sequin Texas Plant (Sequin, TX) 89386
Holly Farms Foods Inc. Temperanceville Plant (Temperanceville, VA) 92380
Holly Farms Foods Inc. Cooked Products Plant (Wilkesboro, NC) 76510
Holly Farms Foods Inc. Seguin Plant (New Berlin, TX) 88199
Holly Farms Foods, Inc.-Snow Hill Feed Mill (Snow Hill, MD) 72452
Holly Farms Foods Inc. Tyson Foods Inc. Feed Mill (Gonzales, TX) 85587
Holly Farms Foods Inc. Tyson Foods Pretreatment Plant (Wilkesboro, NC) 76511
Holly Farms Foods Inc. Tyson Foods Processing Plant (Monroe, NC) 75578
Holly Farms Foods Inc. Waste Water Treatment Plant (Glen Allen, VA) 90982
Holly Farms Foods Inc. Wastewater Processing Plant (Harrisonburg, VA) 91092
Holly Farms of Texas Nacogdoches Feed Mill (Nacogdoches, TX) 88167
Holly Farms of Texas Inc. Center Texas Plant (Center, TX) 83537
Holly Farms of Texas, Inc. Gonzales Feed Mill (Gonzales, TX) 85588
Holly Farms of Texas Inc. Sequin Texas Plant (Seguin, TX) 89368
Holly Farms of Texas Inc. Nacogdoches Mill (Nacogdoches, TX) 88168
Holly Farms/Tyson Foods Inc. Pre-Treatment Plant (Wilkesboro, NC) 76512
Holly Farms/Tyson Foods Inc. Processing Plant (Wilkesboro, NC) 76513
Holly Farms/Tyson Foods Inc. Processing Plant (Center, TX) 83538
Holly Farms/Tyson Foods Inc. Roaring River Feed Mill (Roaring River, NC) 76050
Holly Farms/Tyson Foods Inc. Tyson Foods Inc. (Temperanceville, VA) 92381
Holly Farms/Tyson Foods Inc. Tyson Foods Pretreatment Plant (Wilkesboro, NC) 76514
Holly Farms/Tyson Foods Inc. Tyson Foods Processing Plant (Monroe, NC) 75579
Holly Farms/Tyson Foods Inc. Waste Water Treatment (Wilkesboro, NC) 76515
Holly Sugar Corp. Hereford Factory (Hereford, TX) 85742
Holsum Bakers of Puerto Rico (Toa Baja, PR) 78609
Holsum Foods (Navasota, TX) 88178
Holt Rinehart & Winston Inc. (Orlando, FL) 62009
Home Depot (Atlanta, GA) **64539**
Home Depot (Gaithersburg, MD) 71787
Home Depot (Madison, TN) 81377
Home Depot Inc (St Petersburg, FL) 62976
Home Depot Inc. (Clearwater, FL) 59021
Home Depot Inc. (Fort Lauderdale, FL) 59510
Home Depot Inc. the (Jacksonville, FL) 60330
Home Depot Inc. (Port Richey, FL) 62674
Home Depot Inc. (West Palm Beach, FL) 63872
Home Depot, Inc. (Atlanta, GA) 64540
Home Depot Inc. (Gaithersburg, MD) 71788
Home Depot Inc. (Carrollton, TX) 83470
Home Depot Inc. the Stores Atla (Atlanta, GA) 64541
Home Depot Inc. the Stores Deca (Decatur, GA) 65826
Home Products Co. (Knoxville, TN) 81217
Home Savings Bank (Hampton, VA) 91041
Homelite (Gastonia, NC) 74683
Homelite (Greer, SC) 79477
Homelite Homelite Division (Greer, SC) 79478
Hon Co. (Cedartown, GA) 65511
Hon Co. (Owensboro, KY) 69172
Hon Co. (Sulphur Springs, TX) 89557
Hon Co. (Chester, VA) 90619
Honeywell Micro Switch Div. (Mars Hill, NC) 75508
Honeywell Inc. (Clearwater, FL) 59022; 59023
Honeywell Inc. (St. Petersburg, FL) 63126
Honeywell Inc. (Durham, NC) 74406; 74407
Honeywell Inc. Micro Switch Div. (Mars Hill, NC) 75509
Honeywell Inc. Dcpd (Tampa, FL) 63458
Honeywell Inc. Electro Components (Durham, NC) 74408
Honeywell Inc. Optoelectronics (Richardson, TX) 88739
Honeywell Optoelectronics (Richardson, TX) 88740
Hoov-R-Line (Providence, KY) 69235
Hoover Treated Wood Prods. Inc. (Pine Bluff, AR) 57518
Hoover Treated Wood Prods. Inc. (Thomson, GA) 67810
Hoover Treated Wood Prods. Inc. (Milford, VA) 91430
Hoover Treated Wood Products (Pine Bluff, AR) 57519
Hoover Treated Wood Products (Thomson, GA) 67811
Hoover Treated Wood Products (Milford, VA) 91431
Hoover Treated Wood Products, Inc. (Thomson, GA) 67812
Hope Gas, Inc. (Clarksburg, WV) 92806
Horchow Mail Order Inc. (Dallas, TX) 84131
Hormel & Co/Geo (Baltimore, MD) 71169
Hormel Foods Corp. (Tucker, GA) 67857
Hormel Foods Corp. (Oklahoma City, OK) 77386
Hormel Foods Corp. (Houston, TX) 86287
Hormel&Co/George a (Midlothian, VA) 91417
Hospital Corp. of America (Nashville, TN) **82025**
Host Marriott (Washington, DC) **58303**
Host Marriott Corp. (Washington, DC) 58304
Hosuton Industries Energy Inc. (Houston, TX) 86288
Hot Shoppes Cafeterias (Bethesda, MD) 71395
Hot Shoppes Cafeterias (Marland Area, MD) 72125
Hot Shoppes Cafeterias (Maryland Area, MD) 72129; 72130; 72131; 72132
Hot Shoppes Cafeterias & Restaurants (Washington, DC) 58305
Hot Spring Continuous Rolling Plant (Jones Mills, AR) 57204
House of Fragrance (Louisville, KY) 68776
House of Seagram (Lawrenceburg, KY) 68506
Household Mortgage Services (Tampa, FL) 63459
Household Mortgage Services (Atlanta, GA) 64542
Household Mortgage Services (Charlotte, NC) 74047
Housing Supply Inc. (Americus, GA) 64139
Houston Coca-Cola Bottling Co. (Houston, TX) 86289; 86290; 86291; 86292
Houston Industries (Houston, TX) **86293**
Houston Industries Inc. (Houston, TX) 86294
Houston Lighting & Power Co. (Houston, TX) 86295
Houston Pipe Line Co. (Houston, TX) 86296
Houston Pipe Line Co. Inc. (Houston, TX) 86297
Howard Industries Inc. (Miami, FL) 61331
Howmedica Inc. (Orlando, FL) 62010
Hta Aerostructures Inc. (San Marcos, TX) 89337
Hubbell Lighting Division (Christiansburg, VA) 90636
Huck International (Waco, TX) 89940
Huck International Inc. (Waco, TX) 89941; 89942
Huck Manufacturing Co. (Waco, TX) 89943
Huck Mfg. Co. (Waco, TX) 89944
Hudson Co. (Houston, TX) 86298
Hudson Eng Corp. Mcdermott C (Houston, TX) 86299
Hudson Farms Inc. (Albertville, AL) 54966
Hudson Farms Inc. (Muskogee, OK) 77222
Hudson Foods (Rogers, AR) **57565**
Hudson Foods Inc. (Albertville, AL) 54967
Hudson Foods Inc. (Rogers, AR) 57566
Hudson Foods Inc. (Springdale, AR) 57635
Hudson Foods Inc. (Stilwell, OK) 77849
Hudson Foods Inc. National Egg Products Div. (Social Circle, GA) 67615
Hudson Foods Inc. Feedmill (Westville, OK) 78246
Hudson International Conductors (Trenton, GA) 67842
Hudson International Conductors (Inman, SC) 79534
Hudson Products Corp. (Beasley, TX) 83142
Hudson's (Live Oak, FL) 60914
Hudson's (Pensacola, FL) 62436
Hudson's (Port Richey, FL) 62675; 62676
Hudson's (Pickens, MS) 73297
Hudson's (Hendersonville, NC) 75042
Hudsons (Nashville, TN) 82026
Hudson's (Amarillo, TX) 82553
Hudson's (Dallas, TX) 84132
Hudson's (Culpeper, VA) 90676
Hudsons (S Charleston, WV) 93036
Hughes Christensen Co. Hughes Tool Co. (Houston, TX) 86300
Hughes Diamond Products (Houston, TX) 86301
Hughes Missile Sys. Co. (East Camden, AR) 56924
Hughes-Mpd (Houston, TX) 86302
Human Affairs International (Boca Raton, FL) 58712
Human Affairs International (Atlanta, GA) 64543
Human Affairs International (Baton Rouge, LA) 69558
Human Affairs International (Chapel Hill, NC) 73816
Human Affairs International (Charlotte, NC) 74048
Human Affairs International Inc. (Atlanta, GA) 64544
Human Affairs Int'l Inc. (Houston, TX) 86303
Humana (Louisville, KY) **68777**
Humana Health Care Plans (Richmond, VA) 91906
Humana Inc. (Louisville, KY) 68778
Humana Medical Plan (Dade City, FL) 59140
Hunt Transport Inc/J B (Lowell, AR) 57324
J. B. Hunt Transport (Lowell, AR) **57325**
Hunt-Wesson Inc. (Savannah, GA) 67487
Hunt-Wesson Inc. (Sylvester, GA) 67774
Hunt-Wesson, Inc. (Memphis, TN) 81628
Hunt-Wesson Inc. Savannah Refinery (Savannah, GA) 67488
Hunter Zep (Baton Rouge, LA) 69559
Huntington Federal Savings Bank (Avon Park, FL) 58607
Huntington, FSB (Lake Placid, FL) 60645
Huntington, FSB (Naples, FL) 61631
Huntington, FSB (Sebring, FL) 62884; 62885; 62886; 62887; 62888
Huntington Mortgage Co. (Greenbelt, MD) 71864
Huntington Mortgage Co. (Richmond, VA) 91907
Huntington Trust Co. (Naples, FL) 61632
Huntington Trust Co. of Florida, NA (Naples, FL) 61633
Huntsman Chemical (Norfolk, VA) 91546
Huntsman Chemical Corp. (Chesapeake, VA) 90585
Hussmann Corp. (Montgomery, AL) 56344
Hussmann Corp. (Dumas, AR) 56911
Huval Bakeries Inc. (Lafayette, LA) 70062
Huval Baking Co. (Lafayette, LA) 70063
Hydra-Sports Inc. (Nashville, TN) 82027
Hygeia Coca-Cola Bottling Co. (Pensacola, FL) 62437
Hyster Co. (Berea, KY) 68127

I

IBM (Boca Raton, FL) 58713
IBM (Atlanta, GA) 64545
IBM Corp. (Fort Smith, AR) 57056
IBM Corp. (Little Rock, AR) 57288
IBM Corp. (Boca Raton, FL) 58714
IBM Corp. (Fort Myers, FL) 59706
IBM Corp. (Gainesville, FL) 59881
IBM Corp. (Lake City, FL) 60622
IBM Corp. (Melbourne, FL) 61069
IBM Corp. (N Fort Myers, FL) 61586
IBM Corp. (Orlando, FL) 62011
IBM Corp. (Tampa, FL) 63460
IBM Corp. (Marietta, GA) 66788
IBM Corp. (Savannah, GA) 67489
IBM Corp. (Clarksdale, MS) 72675
IBM Corp. (Columbus, MS) 72714
IBM Corp. (Greenwood, MS) 72835
IBM Corp. (Burlington, NC) 73757
IBM Corp. (Durham, NC) 74409
IBM Corp. (Wilkesboro, NC) 76516
IBM Corp. (Bartlesville, OK) 76833
IBM Corp. (Tulsa, OK) 77957
IBM Corp. (Florence, SC) 79208
IBM Corp. (Beaumont, TX) 83161
IBM Corp. (Big Spring, TX) 83288
IBM Corp. (Huntsville, TX) 87260
IBM Corp. (Kerrville, TX) 87473
IBM Corp. (Wichita Falls, TX) 90074
IBM Corp. Nsd (Houston, TX) 86304
IBM Corp. Sales (Atlanta, GA) 64546
IBP Inc. (Amarillo, TX) 82554
IDS Financial Services (Houston, TX) 86305
IDS Financial Services (Richardson, TX) 88741
IDS Financial Services Inc. (Montgomery, AL) 56345
IDS Financial Services Inc. (Washington, DC) 58306
IDS Financial Services Inc. (Miami, FL) 61332
IDS Financial Services Inc. (Atlanta, GA) 64547
IDS Financial Services Inc. (Savannah, GA) 67490
IDS Financial Services Inc. (Slidell, LA) 70828
IDS Financial Services Inc. (Hickory, NC) 75082
IDS Financial Services Inc. (Tulsa, OK) 77958
IDS Financial Services Inc. (Memphis, TN) 81629
IDS Financial Services Inc. (Nashville, TN) 82028
IDS Financial Services Inc. (Harlingen, TX) 85702
IDS Financial Services Inc. (Houston, TX) 86306; 86307
Ikg Industries (Nashville, TN) 82029
Illinois Central R R Co. (Aberdeen, MS) 72576
Illinois Central Railroad (Reserve, LA) 70662
Illinois Central Railroad (Brookhaven, MS) 72656
Illinois Central Railroad (Jackson, MS) 72990
Illinois Central Railroad (Mc Comb, MS) 73144
Illinois Central Railroad C (New Orleans, LA) 70507
Illinois Power (Washington, DC) 58307
Illinois Tool Works Devilbiss Spray Booth Div. (Atlanta, GA) 64548
Illinois Tool Works Inc. Shakeproof Div. (Russellville, KY) 69261
IMC Development Corp. (Bartow, FL) 58626
Imc Fertilizer (Fort Meade, FL) 59650
Imc Fertilizer Inc. (Florence, AL) 55737
IMC Fertilizer Inc. (Bartow, FL) 58627
Imc Fertilizer Inc. (Indiantown, FL) 60142
Imc Fertilizer Inc. (Mulberry, FL) 61573
Imc Fertilizer Inc. (Americus, GA) 64140
Imc Fertilizer Inc. (Sterlington, LA) 70880
Imc Fertilizer Inc. (Winston-Salem, NC) 76733
Imc Fertilizer Inc. (Hartsville, SC) 79498
IMC Fertilizer Inc. New Wales Operation (Mulberry, FL) 61574
Imc Fertilizer Inc. Plant City Uranium Recovery (Plant City, FL) 62546; 62547
Imo Delaval Inc. (Monroe, NC) 75580
IMO Pumps (Monroe, NC) 75581
Imperial Bondware (Lafayette, GA) 66492
Imperial Holly (Sugar Land, TX) **89532**
Imperial Holly Corp. (Sugarland, TX) 89548
Imprimis Technology Inc. (Oklahoma City, OK) 77387
INA Financial Corp. (Wilmington, DE) 58075
Inacomp Computer Centers (Melbourne, FL) 61070
Inacomp Computer Centers (Roswell, GA) 67375; 67376

Inacomp Computer Centers (Louisville, KY) 68779
Inacomp Computer Centers (Baton Rouge, LA) 69560
Inacomp Computer Centers (Greensboro, NC) 74853
Inacomp Computer Centers (Nashville, TN) 82030
Inacomp Computer Centers Advan (Atlanta, GA) 64549
Indiana Glass Co. (Sapulpa, OK) 77791
Indiana Glass Co. Bartlett-Collins (Sapulpa, OK) 77792
Indiana Glass Sapulpa (Sapulpa, OK) 77793
Indland Towing Co. (Ashland, KY) 68097
Industrial Automation Systems Group (Hebron, KY) 68429
Industrial Lubricants Co. (San Antonio, TX) 89031
Industrial & Specialty Chemicals Plant (Mulberry, FL) 61575
Industrial Systems (Birmingham, AL) 55284
Industrial Systems (Goodlettsville, TN) 80865
Industrial Systems Associates (Raleigh, NC) 75916
Industrial Systems Associates Inc. (Lenoir, NC) 75380
Industrial Systems Inc. (Nashville, TN) 82031
Industrias La Famosa (Toa Baja, PR) 78610; 78611
Inexco Oil Co. (New Orleans, LA) 70508
Information Systems & Services Inc. (Silver Spring, MD) 72411
Ingalls Shipbuilding (Pascagoula, MS) 73260
Ingalls Shipbuilding Inc. (Pascagoula, MS) 73261; 73262
Ingersoll Rand (Mocksville, NC) 75564
Ingersoll-Rand Centrifugal Compressor Div. (Mayfield, KY) 69077
Ingersoll Rand Small Compressor Div. (Davidson, NC) 74358
Ingersoll-Rand Co. (Mayfield, KY) 69078
Ingersoll-Rand Co. (Roanoke, VA) 92158
Ingersoll-Rand Co. Portable Compressor Div. (Mocksville, NC) 75565
Ingram Plywoods Inc. (Thomasville, NC) 76378
Inland Container Corp. (Rome, GA) 67343
Inland Container Corp. (Louisville, KY) 68780
Inland Container Corp. (Minden, LA) 70341
Inland Container Corp. (Hattiesburg, MS) 72892
Inland Container Corp. (Vega Alta, PR) 78622
Inland Container Corp. (Carrollton, TX) 83471
Inland Container Corp. No. 33 (Fort Smith, AR) 57057
Inland Container Corp. No. 24 (Hattiesburg, MS) 72893
Inland Gas Co. Inc. (Ashland, KY) 68098
Inland Gas Co. Inc. (Huntington, WV) 92875
Inland Materials Distribution Group Inc. (Norcross, GA) 67125
Inland-Orange Inc. (Orange, TX) 88316
Inland-Rome, Inc. (Rome, GA) 67344
Innivative Logistics Inc. (Cherryville, NC) 74246
Innovative Logistics Inc. (Fort Mill, SC) 79234
Innovative Office Systems (Shreveport, LA) 70731
Innovative Office Systems, Inc. (Dallas, TX) 84133; 84134
Innovative Office Systems Inc. (Fort Worth, TX) 85130
Integris (Atlanta, GA) 64550
Intel Corp. (Annapolis Jct, MD) 71025
Intel Corp. (Oklahoma City, OK) 77388
Intel Corp. (Tulsa, OK) 77959
Intel Corp. (Austin, TX) 82894
Intel Corp. (Dallas, TX) 84135
Intel Corp. (Houston, TX) 86308
Intel Corp. (Richmond, VA) 91908
Intel Corp. (Roanoke, VA) 92159
Intel Puerto Rico Inc. (Las Piedras, PR) 78479
Intelligent Media Ventures, Inc. (Atlanta, GA) 64551
Intercontinental Mfg. Co. (Garland, TX) 85489
Intercraft Co., Inc. (Taylor, TX) 89599
Intereal Co. (Nashville, TN) 82032
Intereal Co. (Houston, TX) 86309
Interface Flooring Sys. Inc. Inc. (La Grange, GA) 66479
Interface Flooring Systems Inc. (Washington, DC) 58308
Interface Flooring Systems Inc. (La Grange, GA) 66480; 66481
Interface Inc. (La Grange, GA) 66482
Interface Inc. (LaGrange, GA) **66493**
Interface Research Corp. (Kennesaw, GA) 66417
Intergraph (Huntsville, AL) **55953**
Intergraph Corp. (Huntsville, AL) 55954
Intergraph Corp. (Nashville, TN) 82033; 82034; 82035
Intergrated Technologies (Houston, TX) 86310
Interlake Packaging Corp. (Smyrna, GA) 67552
Intermarine USA (Savannah, GA) 67491
A & a International (Fort Worth, TX) 85131
International Business Machines Corp. (Boca Raton, FL) 58715
International Computer Service (Hialeah, FL) 59988
International Computer Service Inc. (Hialeah, FL) 59989
International Computer Service Inc. (Annapolis, MD) 71014
International Paper (Bay Minette, AL) 55075
International Paper (Mobile, AL) 56185
International Paper (East Point, GA) 66145
International Paper (Wiggins, MS) 73489; 73490; 73491
International Paper (Edinburg, TX) 84733
International Paper (El Paso, TX) 84812
International Paper (Nacogdoches, TX) 88169
International Paper Container Div. (Shreveport, LA) 70732
International Paper Container Div. (Carrollton, TX) 83472
International Paper Kraft Packaging Div. (Mobile, AL) 56186
International Paper Liquid Packaging Div. (Bastrop, LA) 69440
International Paper Uniwood Div. (Statesville, NC) 76330
International Paper Aerated Stabilization Basins (Bastrop, LA) 69441
International Paper Camden Facility (Camden, AR) 56833
International Paper Clarifiers & Fiber Reclaimer (Bastrop, LA) 69442
International Paper Cmpany Natchez Mill (Natchez, MS) 73199
International Paper Co. (Decatur, GA) 65827
International Paper Co. (Mineola, TX) 88106
International Paper Co. Container Div. (Statesville, NC) 76331
International Paper Co. Container Div. (Georgetown, SC) 79274
International Paper Co. Gurdon Wood Products (Gurdon, AR) 57124
International Paper Co. Nevamar Div. (Odenton, MD) 72167
International Paper Co. Nevamar Div. (Memphis, TN) 81630
International Paper Co. Uniwood Div. (Statesville, NC) 76332
International Paper Co. Camden Mill (Camden, AR) 56834
International Paper Co. De Ridder (De Ridder, LA) 69813
International Paper Co. Mansfield Mill (Mansfield, LA) 70212
International Paper Co. Moss Point Mill (Moss Point, MS) 73192
International Paper Co. Pine Bluff Mill (Pine Bluff, AR) 57520
International Paper Co. Pineville Mill (Pineville, LA) 70618
International Paper Co. Richmond Gravure (Raleigh, NC) 75917
International Paper Co. Vicksburg Mill (Vicksburg, MS) 73453
International Paper De Ridder (De Ridder, LA) 69814
International Paper Georgetown Mill (Georgetown, SC) 79275; 79276
International Paper Gurdon Wood Products (Gurdon, AR) 57125
International Paper Hammermill Riverdale Mill (Selma, AL) 56532
International Paper Louisiana Mill (Bastrop, LA) 69443; 69444
International Paper Mansfield Mill (Mansfield, LA) 70213
International Paper Masonite Plant (Sellers, SC) 79854
International Paper Mobile Mill (Mobile, AL) 56187
International Paper-Moss Point Mill (Moss Point, MS) 73193
International Paper Natchez Mill (Natchez, MS) 73200; 73201
International Paper - Pine Bluff Mill (Pine Bluff, AR) 57521
International Paper Pineville Mill (Pineville, LA) 70619; 70620
International Paper Richmond Gravure (Raleigh, NC) 75918
International Paper Springhill Wood Products Plt. (Springhill, LA) 70850
International Paper Texarkana Mill (Texarkana, TX) 89678
International Paper Vicksburg Mill (Redwood, MS) 73314
International Paper Vicksburg Mill (Vicksburg, MS) 73454
International Seafood Traders (Chauvin, LA) 69775
International Turbine Corp. (Grapevine, TX) 85658
Interpublic Group of Companies (Atlanta, GA) 64552
Interstate Fire Insurance Co. (Nashville, TN) 82036
Intertel, Inc. (Houston, TX) 86311
Intertrade Corp. (Lakeland, FL) 60734
Intro-Europe, Inc. (Greensboro, NC) 74854
Invest Financial Corporatio (Johnson City, TN) 81048
Ipc Avery Dennison (Rogersville, TN) 82278
IRI International Corp. (Pampa, TX) 88353
Island Healthcare Inc. (Hato Rey, PR) 78456
Israel Discount Bank Ltd (Miami, FL) 61333
ITT Life Insurance Corp. (Corpus Christi, TX) 83724
Itt Life Insurance Corp. (Richardson, TX) 88742
Itt Rayonier (Fernandina, FL) 59404
ITT Rayonier Inc.. Jessup Div. (Jesup, GA) 66370
ITT Rayonier Inc. Jesup Pulp Div. (Jesup, GA) 66371
ITW Dynatec (Hendersonville, TN) 80918
ITW Electronic Component Packaging (Arlington, TX) 82664
ITW Fluid Products (Norcross, GA) 67126
ITW Meritex (Arlington, TX) 82665
ITW Pactron (Lynchburgh, VA) 91293
Itw Paslode (Augusta, AR) 56735
Itw Paslode (Pontotoc, MS) 73301
Itw Paslode (Covington, TN) 80685
Itw Shakeproof Indl. Prods. Products (Mineral Wells, TX) 88110
ITW Shakeproof Industrial Products (Mineral Wells, TX) 88111
ITW Shippers Paper Products/ Airbags (Mt. Pleasant, TN) 81832
ITW Southern Gage Co. (Erin, TN) 80774
Ivac Co. (Creedmoor, NC) 74354
Ivac Corp. (Creedmoor, NC) 74355; 74356
IVAX (Miami, FL) **61334**
Ivax Industries Inc. Textile Products (Rock Hill, SC) 79830; 79831
Ivax Industry Inc. Textile Products (Rock Hill, SC) 79832

J

J B Hunt Transport Inc. (Houston, TX) 86312
J B Hunt Transport Services Inc. (Lowell, AR) 57326
J. Bacon & Sons (Louisville, KY) 68781
J C Penney Catalog Center (Newport News, VA) 91470
J C Penney Catalog Sales (Elizabethtown, KY) 68280
J C Penney Catalog Sales (Georgetown, KY) 68382
J C Penney Catalog Sales (Danville, VA) 90700
J C Penney Co. (Laurel, MD) 72078
J C Penney Co. (Westminster, MD) 72541
J C Penney Co. (White Marsh M, MD) 72569
J C Penney Co. (Bristol, VA) 90480
J C Penney Co. (Fredericksbrg, VA) 90912
J C Penney Co. (Hampton, VA) 91042
J C Penney Co. (Lynchburg, VA) 91261
J C Penney Co. (Martinsville, VA) 91353
J C Penney Co. (Newport News, VA) 91471
J C Penney Co. (Norfolk, VA) 91547
J C Penney Co. (Roanoke, VA) 92160
J C Penney Co. (Staunton, VA) 92322
J C Penney Co. (Winchester, VA) 92596
J C Penney Co. Inc. (Elizabethtown, KY) 68281
J C Penney Co. Inc. (Clarksville, TN) 80552
J C Penney Co. Inc. (Cleveland, TN) 80588
J C Penney Co. Inc. (Dyersburg, TN) 80753
J C Penney Co. Inc. (Charleston, WV) 92750
J C Penney Insurance (Nashville, TN) 82037
J. H. Fletcher & Co. (Huntington, WV) 92876
J. Hungerford Smith Co. (Humboldt, TN) 80953
J. L. Anderson Co. Inc. Palmetto Brick Co. (Wallace, SC) 80064
J. M. Huber Corp. (Commerce, GA) 65661; 65662
J. M. Huber Corp. (Etowah, TN) 80779
J. M. Huber Corp. Baytown Carbon Plant (Baytown, TX) 83126
J. M. Huber Corp. Borger Carbon Plant (Borger, TX) 83317
J. M. Huber Corp. Echo Carbon Plant (Orange, TX) 88317
J P Morgan Delaware (Wilmington, DE) 58076
J P Morgan Services (Newark, DE) 57911
J. P. Stevens & Co. (Clemson, SC) 78950
J. P. Stevens & Co. Bob Stevens Plant (Wagram, NC) 76428
J. P. Stevens & Co. Inc. Seneca Plant (Seneca, SC) 79861
J. Schoeneman Wiltex (Wilmington, DE) 58077
Jack Daniel Distillery (Lynchburg, TN) 81365; 81366; 81367
Jack Daniel Distillery (Nashville, TN) 82038
Jack Daniel Distillery Lem Motlow Prop. (Lynchburg, TN) 81368
Jack Daniel Distillery Lem Motlow Prop. Inc. (Lynchburg, TN) 81369
Jackson Coca-Cola Bottling Co. (Jackson, MS) 72991
Jackson National Life Insur (St Petersburg, FL) 62977
Jackson National Life Insurance (Metairie, LA) 70275
Jackson National Life Insurance C (St Petersburg, FL) 62978
Jackson National Life Insurance C (Dallas, TX) 84136
Jackson National Life Insurance Co. (Atlanta, GA) 64553
Jacksonville Coca-Cola Bottling Co. (Jacksonville, FL) 60331
Jacksonville Shipyards Inc. (Jacksonville, FL) 60332
Jacksonville Shipyards, Inc. Electro Lube Devices (Jacksonville, FL) 60333
Jacksonville Shipyards, Inc.-Electro Lube Devices (Jacksonville, FL) 60334
Jacksonville Shipyards, Inc.-Key Houston & Bellinger (Jacksonville, FL) 60335
Jacksonville Welder Sup (Jacksonville, FL) 60336
Jacobs Chuck Manufacturing Co. (Clemson, SC) 78951; 78952
Jacobs Chuck Mfg. Co. (Clemson, SC) 78953
Jacobs Man Jacobs Chuck Manufacturing (Clemson, SC) 78954
Jacobs Manufacturing Co. (Bridgeport, AL) 55485
Jafra Cosmetics (Richmond, VA) 91909
James River Co. (Lexington, KY) 68559
James River Corp Advance Film Div. (New Castle, DE) 57867
James River Corp. (Cantonment, FL) 58909
James River Corp. (Newnan, GA) 67082
James River Corp. (Lexington, KY) 68560
James River Corp. (Shreveport, LA) 70733
James River Corp. (Jackson, TN) 80986
James River Corp. Advanced Film Div. (New Castle, DE) 57868
James River Corp. Curtis Div. (Newark, DE) 57912; 57913
James River Corp. Dixie Products (Darlington, SC) 79148
James River Corp. Filtration Products Div. Richmond (Richmond, VA) 91910; 91911
James River Corp. Flexible Packaging Group (Orange, TX) 88318
James River Corp. Dixie Products Group (Fort Smith, AR) 57058
James River Corp. Naheola Mill (Pennington, AL) 56455
James River Corp.-Naheola Mill (Silas, AL) 56568
James River Corp. of Virginia (Richmond, VA) **91912**
James River Dixie Products (Darlington, SC) 79149
James River Paper Co. (Lexington, KY) 68561
James River Paper Co. Dixie Products (Fort Smith, AR) 57059
James River Paper Co. Inc. (Jackson, TN) 80987
James River Paper Co. Inc. Curtis Div. (Newark, DE) 57914
James River Paper Co. Inc. Dixie Products (Fort Smith, AR) 57060
James River Paper Co. Inc. Dixie Products (Darlington, SC) 79150
James River Paper Co. Inc. St. Francisville (St. Francisville, LA) 70861
James River Paper Products Inc. (Darlington, SC) 79151; 79152
Jamieson Film Co. (Dallas, TX) 84137
Javelin Boats (Murfreesboro, TN) 81853
JB White & Co. (Augusta, GA) 65333
J.C. Penney (Plano, TX) **88574**
J.C. Penney Business Services, Inc. (Dallas, TX) 84138
J.C. Penney Co., Inc. (Dallas, TX) 84139
J.C. Penney Life Insurance Co. (Plano, TX) 88575
JCP Realty, Inc. (Dallas, TX) 84140
JCPenney National Bank (Harrington, DE) 57820
Jefferson Smurfit Corp. (Bryant, AR) 56823
Jefferson Smurfit Corp. (Jacksonville, FL) 60337
Jefferson Smurfit Corp. (Chattanooga, TN) 80416
Jefferson Smurfit Corp. Containerboard Mill Div. (Jacksonville, FL) 60338
Jet Research Center Inc. Defense & Aerospace Div. (Swannanoa, NC) 76350
Jetco Chemicals (Corsicana, TX) 83779
Jiffy Lube (Birmingham, AL) 55285
Jiffy Lube (Mobile, AL) 56188; 56189
Jiffy Lube (Montgomery, AL) 56346
Jiffy Lube (Prattville, AL) 56489
Jiffy Lube (N Little Rock, AR) 57403
Jiffy Lube (Altamonte Spg, FL) 58537
Jiffy Lube (Bradenton, FL) 58826
Jiffy Lube (Casselberry, FL) 58933
Jiffy Lube (Clearwater, FL) 59024
Jiffy Lube (Daytona Beach, FL) 59186
Jiffy Lube (Fort Lauderdale, FL) 59511; 59512
Jiffy Lube (Gainesville, FL) 59882; 59883
Jiffy Lube (Homestead, FL) 60115
Jiffy Lube (Jacksonville, FL) 60339; 60340; 60341
Jiffy Lube (Kissimmee, FL) 60589
Jiffy Lube (Lighthouse Point, FL) 60904
Jiffy Lube (Melbourne, FL) 61071
Jiffy Lube (Miami, FL) 61335
Jiffy Lube (Orlando, FL) 62012; 62013; 62014
Jiffy Lube (Palm Springs, FL) 62304
Jiffy Lube (St Petersburg, FL) 62979; 62980
Jiffy Lube (Tampa, FL) 63461; 63462; 63463
Jiffy Lube (Winter Park, FL) 63982
Jiffy Lube (Atlanta, GA) 64554
Jiffy Lube (Dunwoody, GA) 66112

Kelly Assisted Living Servi (Charleston, SC) 78824
Kelly Assisted Living Service (Virginia Beach, VA) 92488
Kelly Springfield Tire (Hialeah, FL) 59991
Kelly Springfield Tire Co. (Morrow, GA) 67016; 67017
Kelly-Springfield Tire Co. (Cumberland, MD) 71625; 71626
Kelly-Springfield Tire Co. (Fayetteville, NC) 74561
Kelly Springfield Tire Co. (Tyler, TX) 89805
Kelly Springfield Tire Co. Associate Brands Div. (Cumberland, MD) 71627
Kelly-Springfield Tire Co. Custom Brands Div. (Cumberland, MD) 71628
Kelly-Springfield Tire Co. Inc. (Cumberland, MD) 71629
Kelly Springfield Tire Co. T (Cumberland, MD) 71630
Kelly-Springfield Tire Co. T (Tyler, TX) 89806
Kelly-Sprngfld Tr (Carrollton, TX) 83477
Kemper Securities Inc. (Atlanta, GA) 64569
Kendall Co. (Augusta, GA) 65334
Kentucky Fried Chicken (Alabaster, AL) 54954
Kentucky Fried Chicken (Alex City, AL) 54972
Kentucky Fried Chicken (Anniston, AL) 55002; 55003
Kentucky Fried Chicken (Athens, AL) 55041
Kentucky Fried Chicken (Attalla, AL) 55055
Kentucky Fried Chicken (Auburn, AL) 55062
Kentucky Fried Chicken (Bessemer, AL) 55096; 55097
Kentucky Fried Chicken (Birmingham, AL) 55291; 55292; 55293; 55294; 55295; 55296; 55297; 55298; 55299
Kentucky Fried Chicken (Boaz, AL) 55468
Kentucky Fried Chicken (Brewton, AL) 55482
Kentucky Fried Chicken (Childersburg, AL) 55514
Kentucky Fried Chicken (Cullman, AL) 55545
Kentucky Fried Chicken (Daleville, AL) 55562
Kentucky Fried Chicken (Dothan, AL) 55654
Kentucky Fried Chicken (Evergreen, AL) 55708
Kentucky Fried Chicken (Fairhope, AL) 55723
Kentucky Fried Chicken (Fayette, AL) 55731
Kentucky Fried Chicken (Gadsden, AL) 55784
Kentucky Fried Chicken (Gardendale, AL) 55799
Kentucky Fried Chicken (Greenville, AL) 55818
Kentucky Fried Chicken (Guntersville, AL) 55829
Kentucky Fried Chicken (Haleyville, AL) 55842
Kentucky Fried Chicken (Hamilton, AL) 55848
Kentucky Fried Chicken (Hartselle, AL) 55856
Kentucky Fried Chicken (Huntsville, AL) 55956; 55957; 55958
Kentucky Fried Chicken (Jacksonville, AL) 56071
Kentucky Fried Chicken (Jasper, AL) 56088
Kentucky Fried Chicken (Leeds, AL) 56106
Kentucky Fried Chicken (Mobile, AL) 56191; 56192; 56193
Kentucky Fried Chicken (Montevallo, AL) 56274
Kentucky Fried Chicken (Montgomery, AL) 56347
Kentucky Fried Chicken (Phenix City, AL) 56462
Kentucky Fried Chicken (Roanoke, AL) 56500
Kentucky Fried Chicken (Russellville, AL) 56508
Kentucky Fried Chicken (Talladega, AL) 56594
Kentucky Fried Chicken (Tuscaloosa, AL) 56659; 56660
Kentucky Fried Chicken (Valley, AL) 56689
Kentucky Fried Chicken (Alma, AR) 56714
Kentucky Fried Chicken (Arkadelphia, AR) 56717
Kentucky Fried Chicken (Ashdown, AR) 56728
Kentucky Fried Chicken (Bentonville, AR) 56785
Kentucky Fried Chicken (Blytheville, AR) 56807
Kentucky Fried Chicken (Booneville, AR) 56818
Kentucky Fried Chicken (Brinkley, AR) 56820
Kentucky Fried Chicken (Conway, AR) 56864
Kentucky Fried Chicken (Dumas, AR) 56912
Kentucky Fried Chicken (El Dorado, AR) 56950
Kentucky Fried Chicken (Fayetteville, AR) 56981; 56982
Kentucky Fried Chicken (Forrest City, AR) 57009
Kentucky Fried Chicken (Fort Smith, AR) 57062; 57063; 57064; 57065
Kentucky Fried Chicken (Heber Springs, AR) 57150
Kentucky Fried Chicken (Hope, AR) 57157
Kentucky Fried Chicken (Hot Springs, AR) 57163
Kentucky Fried Chicken (Hot Springs National Park, AR) 57171
Kentucky Fried Chicken (Jonesboro, AR) 57223; 57224
Kentucky Fried Chicken (Malvern, AR) 57340
Kentucky Fried Chicken (Mc Gehee, AR) 57356
Kentucky Fried Chicken (Mena, AR) 57365
Kentucky Fried Chicken (Mountain Home, AR) 57387
Kentucky Fried Chicken (Mountain View, AR) 57396
Kentucky Fried Chicken (N Little Rock, AR) 57405; 57406; 57407; 57408
Kentucky Fried Chicken (Newport, AR) 57449
Kentucky Fried Chicken (Paragould, AR) 57492
Kentucky Fried Chicken (Paris, AR) 57499
Kentucky Fried Chicken (Pine Bluff, AR) 57523
Kentucky Fried Chicken (Pocahontas, AR) 57541
Kentucky Fried Chicken (Searcy, AR) 57603; 57604
Kentucky Fried Chicken (Siloam Springs, AR) 57618
Kentucky Fried Chicken (Springdale, AR) 57636; 57637
Kentucky Fried Chicken (Trumann, AR) 57684
Kentucky Fried Chicken (West Helena, AR) 57713
Kentucky Fried Chicken (West Memphis, AR) 57724
Kentucky Fried Chicken (Wynne, AR) 57741
Kentucky Fried Chicken (Altamonte Spg, FL) 58538
Kentucky Fried Chicken (Apopka, FL) 58572
Kentucky Fried Chicken (Arcadia, FL) 58584
Kentucky Fried Chicken (Auburndale, FL) 58599
Kentucky Fried Chicken (Avon Park, FL) 58608
Kentucky Fried Chicken (Bartow, FL) 58628
Kentucky Fried Chicken (Belle Glade, FL) 58644; 58645
Kentucky Fried Chicken (Bonita Springs, FL) 58759
Kentucky Fried Chicken (Boynton Beach, FL) 58781
Kentucky Fried Chicken (Bradenton, FL) 58827; 58828
Kentucky Fried Chicken (Brooksville, FL) 58891
Kentucky Fried Chicken (Casselberry, FL) 58934; 58935
Kentucky Fried Chicken (Clearwater, FL) 59025; 59026
Kentucky Fried Chicken (Clewiston, FL) 59060
Kentucky Fried Chicken (Crestview, FL) 59124
Kentucky Fried Chicken (Dade City, FL) 59141
Kentucky Fried Chicken (Dania, FL) 59148
Kentucky Fried Chicken (Daytona Beach, FL) 59187; 59188; 59189
Kentucky Fried Chicken (De Land, FL) 59251; 59252
Kentucky Fried Chicken (Deerfield Beach, FL) 59281; 59282
Kentucky Fried Chicken (Delray Beach, FL) 59320
Kentucky Fried Chicken (Dunedin, FL) 59363
Kentucky Fried Chicken (Fernandina Beach, FL) 59412
Kentucky Fried Chicken (Fort Lauderdale, FL) 59516; 59517; 59518; 59519
Kentucky Fried Chicken (Fort Myers, FL) 59708; 59709; 59710; 59711; 59712; 59713
Kentucky Fried Chicken (Fort Myers Beach, FL) 59781
Kentucky Fried Chicken (Gainesville, FL) 59885; 59886; 59887; 59888
Kentucky Fried Chicken (Green Cove Springs, FL) 59932
Kentucky Fried Chicken (Haines City, FL) 59950
Kentucky Fried Chicken (Hallandale, FL) 59960
Kentucky Fried Chicken (Hawthorne, FL) 59972
Kentucky Fried Chicken (Hialeah, FL) 59992; 59993; 59994; 59995
Kentucky Fried Chicken (Hollywood, FL) 60068; 60069; 60070; 60071
Kentucky Fried Chicken (Homestead, FL) 60116
Kentucky Fried Chicken (Inverness, FL) 60150
Kentucky Fried Chicken (Jacksonville, FL) 60344; 60345; 60346; 60347; 60348; 60349; 60350; 60351; 60352; 60353; 60354; 60355; 60356; 60357
Kentucky Fried Chicken (Jasper, FL) 60521
Kentucky Fried Chicken (Jaxville Beach, FL) 60522
Kentucky Fried Chicken (Jupiter, FL) 60542
Kentucky Fried Chicken (Kissimmee, FL) 60590
Kentucky Fried Chicken (Lake City, FL) 60623
Kentucky Fried Chicken (Lake Placid, FL) 60646
Kentucky Fried Chicken (Lake Wales, FL) 60655
Kentucky Fried Chicken (Lake Worth, FL) 60678; 60679
Kentucky Fried Chicken (Lakeland, FL) 60738; 60739; 60740; 60741
Kentucky Fried Chicken (Largo, FL) 60842; 60843
Kentucky Fried Chicken (Live Oak, FL) 60915
Kentucky Fried Chicken (Longwood, FL) 60932
Kentucky Fried Chicken (MacClenny, FL) 60961
Kentucky Fried Chicken (Maitland, FL) 60980
Kentucky Fried Chicken (Marianna, FL) 61004
Kentucky Fried Chicken (Meadows Village, FL) 61028
Kentucky Fried Chicken (Melbourne, FL) 61073; 61074; 61075
Kentucky Fried Chicken (Merritt Island, FL) 61141
Kentucky Fried Chicken (Miami, FL) 61339; 61340; 61341; 61342; 61343; 61344; 61345; 61346; 61347; 61348; 61349; 61350; 61351
Kentucky Fried Chicken (Milton, FL) 61548
Kentucky Fried Chicken (Mount Dora, FL) 61566
Kentucky Fried Chicken (Naples, FL) 61634; 61635; 61636; 61637
Kentucky Fried Chicken (Niceville, FL) 61710
Kentucky Fried Chicken (Nokomis, FL) 61725
Kentucky Fried Chicken (Ocala, FL) 61803
Kentucky Fried Chicken (Opa Locka, FL) 61859; 61860
Kentucky Fried Chicken (Orange Park, FL) 61888
Kentucky Fried Chicken (Orlando, FL) 62018; 62019; 62020; 62021; 62022; 62023; 62024; 62025; 62026
Kentucky Fried Chicken (Ormond Beach, FL) 62206
Kentucky Fried Chicken (Palmetto, FL) 62309
Kentucky Fried Chicken (Panama City, FL) 62325; 62326; 62327; 62328
Kentucky Fried Chicken (Pensacola, FL) 62438; 62439; 62440; 62441; 62442
Kentucky Fried Chicken (Perry, FL) 62500
Kentucky Fried Chicken (Pinellas Park, FL) 62521
Kentucky Fried Chicken (Plant City, FL) 62548; 62549
Kentucky Fried Chicken (Port Richey, FL) 62677
Kentucky Fried Chicken (Punta Gorda, FL) 62710
Kentucky Fried Chicken (Quincy, FL) 62729
Kentucky Fried Chicken (Ruskin, FL) 62758
Kentucky Fried Chicken (Sarasota, FL) 62839; 62840
Kentucky Fried Chicken (Sebring, FL) 62889
Kentucky Fried Chicken (Seffner, FL) 62898
Kentucky Fried Chicken (Smyrna Beach, FL) 62919
Kentucky Fried Chicken (Spring Hill, FL) 62935
Kentucky Fried Chicken (St Augustine, FL) 62941; 62942
Kentucky Fried Chicken (St Petersburg, FL) 62982; 62983; 62984; 62985; 62986
Kentucky Fried Chicken (St. Augustine, FL) 63062
Kentucky Fried Chicken (St. Cloud, FL) 63066
Kentucky Fried Chicken (Starke, FL) 63148
Kentucky Fried Chicken (Tallahassee, FL) 63245; 63246; 63247; 63248
Kentucky Fried Chicken (Tampa, FL) 63466; 63467; 63468; 63469; 63470; 63471; 63472; 63473; 63474; 63475; 63476; 63477
Kentucky Fried Chicken (Titusville, FL) 63692; 63693
Kentucky Fried Chicken (W Palm Beach, FL) 63793; 63794
Kentucky Fried Chicken (West Palm Beach, FL) 63874; 63875; 63876; 63877; 63878
Kentucky Fried Chicken (Winter Garden, FL) 63922
Kentucky Fried Chicken (Winter Haven, FL) 63942; 63943
Kentucky Fried Chicken (Winter Park, FL) 63984; 63985
Kentucky Fried Chicken (Zephyrhills, FL) 64013; 64014; 64015
Kentucky Fried Chicken (Acworth, GA) 64037
Kentucky Fried Chicken (Albany, GA) 64077
Kentucky Fried Chicken (Alpharetta, GA) 64113
Kentucky Fried Chicken (Americus, GA) 64141
Kentucky Fried Chicken (Atlanta, GA) 64570; 64571; 64572; 64573; 64574; 64575; 64576; 64577; 64578; 64579; 64580; 64581; 64582; 64583; 64584; 64585; 64586; 64587
Kentucky Fried Chicken (Bainbridge, GA) 65367
Kentucky Fried Chicken (Baxley Georgi, GA) 65381
Kentucky Fried Chicken (Brunswick, GA) 65415; 65416
Kentucky Fried Chicken (Buford, GA) 65433
Kentucky Fried Chicken (Carrollton, GA) 65496
Kentucky Fried Chicken (Cedartown, GA) 65512
Kentucky Fried Chicken (Chamblee, GA) 65530; 65531
Kentucky Fried Chicken (Clarkston, GA) 65563
Kentucky Fried Chicken (College Park, GA) 65586
Kentucky Fried Chicken (Conyers, GA) 65684
Kentucky Fried Chicken (Covington, GA) 65730
Kentucky Fried Chicken (Cumming, GA) 65747
Kentucky Fried Chicken (Dallas, GA) 65761
Kentucky Fried Chicken (Decatur, GA) 65830; 65831; 65832; 65833; 65834; 65835; 65836
Kentucky Fried Chicken (Doraville, GA) 65933; 65934
Kentucky Fried Chicken (Douglas, GA) 65971
Kentucky Fried Chicken (Douglasville, GA) 65986; 65987
Kentucky Fried Chicken (Duluth, GA) 66041
Kentucky Fried Chicken (East Point, GA) 66146; 66147
Kentucky Fried Chicken (Eastman, GA) 66158
Kentucky Fried Chicken (Fayetteville, GA) 66191
Kentucky Fried Chicken (Forest Park, GA) 66238
Kentucky Fried Chicken (Gainesville, GA) 66278
Kentucky Fried Chicken (Griffin, GA) 66318
Kentucky Fried Chicken (Jonesboro, GA) 66381; 66382
Kentucky Fried Chicken (Kennesaw, GA) 66420
Kentucky Fried Chicken (Lawrenceville, GA) 66516; 66517
Kentucky Fried Chicken (Lilburn, GA) 66561
Kentucky Fried Chicken (Lithonia, GA) 66595
Kentucky Fried Chicken (Loganville, GA) 66614
Kentucky Fried Chicken (Mableton, GA) 66634
Kentucky Fried Chicken (Macon, GA) 66695
Kentucky Fried Chicken (Marietta, GA) 66792; 66793; 66794; 66795; 66796; 66797; 66798
Kentucky Fried Chicken (Mcdonough, GA) 66968
Kentucky Fried Chicken (Milledgeville, GA) 66980
Kentucky Fried Chicken (Monroe, GA) 66991
Kentucky Fried Chicken (Morrow, GA) 67018
Kentucky Fried Chicken (Norcross, GA) 67131; 67132
Kentucky Fried Chicken (Peachtree Cit, GA) 67234
Kentucky Fried Chicken (Perry, GA) 67266
Kentucky Fried Chicken (Powder Spring, GA) 67279
Kentucky Fried Chicken (Quitman, GA) 67288
Kentucky Fried Chicken (Riverdale, GA) 67313
Kentucky Fried Chicken (Roswell, GA) 67377
Kentucky Fried Chicken (Sandy Springs, GA) 67436
Kentucky Fried Chicken (Smyrna, GA) 67553; 67554
Kentucky Fried Chicken (Snellville, GA) 67593
Kentucky Fried Chicken (St Simons is, GA) 67620
Kentucky Fried Chicken (Statesboro, GA) 67638
Kentucky Fried Chicken (Stockbridge, GA) 67659
Kentucky Fried Chicken (Stone Mountain, GA) 67694; 67695; 67696; 67697
Kentucky Fried Chicken (Swainsboro, GA) 67753
Kentucky Fried Chicken (Thomasville, GA) 67800
Kentucky Fried Chicken (Tucker, GA) 67861
Kentucky Fried Chicken (Union City, GA) 67918
Kentucky Fried Chicken (Valdosta, GA) 67961; 67962; 67963; 67964
Kentucky Fried Chicken (Vidalia, GA) 67987
Kentucky Fried Chicken (Waycross, GA) 68034
Kentucky Fried Chicken (Woodstock, GA) 68070
Kentucky Fried Chicken (Alexandria, LA) 69386; 69387
Kentucky Fried Chicken (Baker, LA) 69436
Kentucky Fried Chicken (Baton Rouge, LA) 69567; 69568; 69569; 69570; 69571; 69572; 69573; 69574
Kentucky Fried Chicken (Bossier City, LA) 69718; 69719; 69720
Kentucky Fried Chicken (De Ridder, LA) 69815
Kentucky Fried Chicken (Denham Springs, LA) 69829
Kentucky Fried Chicken (Gonzales, LA) 69891
Kentucky Fried Chicken (Hammond, LA) 69930
Kentucky Fried Chicken (Houma, LA) 69959
Kentucky Fried Chicken (Jonesboro, LA) 69983
Kentucky Fried Chicken (Lafayette, LA) 70066
Kentucky Fried Chicken (Lake Charles, LA) 70143
Kentucky Fried Chicken (Mansfield, LA) 70214
Kentucky Fried Chicken (Metairie, LA) 70279; 70280; 70281
Kentucky Fried Chicken (Minden, LA) 70342
Kentucky Fried Chicken (Monroe, LA) 70356; 70357
Kentucky Fried Chicken (Natchitoches, LA) 70401; 70402

Kentucky Fried Chicken (New Orleans, LA) 70509; 70510; 70511; 70512

Kentucky Fried Chicken (Pineville, LA) 70621

Kentucky Fried Chicken (Ruston, LA) 70669

Kentucky Fried Chicken (Shreveport, LA) 70737; 70738; 70739; 70740; 70741; 70742

Kentucky Fried Chicken (Slidell, LA) 70830

Kentucky Fried Chicken (Springhill, LA) 70851

Kentucky Fried Chicken (Tallulah, LA) 70906

Kentucky Fried Chicken (Winnfield, LA) 70977

Kentucky Fried Chicken (Belzoni, MS) 72613

Kentucky Fried Chicken (Biloxi, MS) 72623; 72624

Kentucky Fried Chicken (Booneville, MS) 72644

Kentucky Fried Chicken (Brookhaven, MS) 72657

Kentucky Fried Chicken (Carthage, MS) 72661

Kentucky Fried Chicken (Clarksdale, MS) 72676

Kentucky Fried Chicken (Clinton, MS) 72685

Kentucky Fried Chicken (Columbus, MS) 72715; 72716

Kentucky Fried Chicken (Corinth, MS) 72739

Kentucky Fried Chicken (Crystal Springs, MS) 72749

Kentucky Fried Chicken (Forest, MS) 72773

Kentucky Fried Chicken (Greenville, MS) 72803; 72804; 72805

Kentucky Fried Chicken (Greenwood, MS) 72836

Kentucky Fried Chicken (Grenada, MS) 72841

Kentucky Fried Chicken (Gulfport, MS) 72858; 72859

Kentucky Fried Chicken (Holly Springs, MS) 72909

Kentucky Fried Chicken (Indianola, MS) 72928

Kentucky Fried Chicken (Jackson, MS) 72996; 72997; 72998; 72999; 73000; 73001; 73002; 73003

Kentucky Fried Chicken (Kosciusko, MS) 73096

Kentucky Fried Chicken (Mc Comb, MS) 73145; 73146

Kentucky Fried Chicken (Meridian, MS) 73165; 73166; 73167

Kentucky Fried Chicken (Moss Point, MS) 73194

Kentucky Fried Chicken (Natchez, MS) 73202

Kentucky Fried Chicken (New Albany, MS) 73215

Kentucky Fried Chicken (Oxford, MS) 73240

Kentucky Fried Chicken (Pontotoc, MS) 73302

Kentucky Fried Chicken (Ridgeland, MS) 73320

Kentucky Fried Chicken (Senatobia, MS) 73339

Kentucky Fried Chicken (Southaven, MS) 73348

Kentucky Fried Chicken (Starkville, MS) 73365

Kentucky Fried Chicken (Tupelo, MS) 73407

Kentucky Fried Chicken (Vicksburg, MS) 73455; 73456; 73457

Kentucky Fried Chicken (Waynesboro, MS) 73473

Kentucky Fried Chicken (West Point, MS) 73483

Kentucky Fried Chicken (Yazoo City, MS) 73503

Kentucky Fried Chicken (Albemarle, NC) 73538; 73539

Kentucky Fried Chicken (Asheboro, NC) 73589

Kentucky Fried Chicken (Black Mountain, NC) 73698

Kentucky Fried Chicken (Boone, NC) 73714

Kentucky Fried Chicken (Burlington, NC) 73758

Kentucky Fried Chicken (Canton, NC) 73780

Kentucky Fried Chicken (Carrboro, NC) 73784

Kentucky Fried Chicken (Charlotte, NC) 74053; 74054; 74055; 74056; 74057; 74058; 74059; 74060; 74061

Kentucky Fried Chicken (Cherokee, NC) 74234

Kentucky Fried Chicken (Cherryville, NC) 74247

Kentucky Fried Chicken (Clinton, NC) 74292

Kentucky Fried Chicken (Conover, NC) 74334

Kentucky Fried Chicken (Durham, NC) 74410; 74411

Kentucky Fried Chicken (Eden, NC) 74460

Kentucky Fried Chicken (Elizabeth City, NC) 74482

Kentucky Fried Chicken (Fayetteville, NC) 74562

Kentucky Fried Chicken (Forest City, NC) 74607

Kentucky Fried Chicken (Fuquay Varina, NC) 74638

Kentucky Fried Chicken (Greensboro, NC) 74858; 74859; 74860

Kentucky Fried Chicken (Hickory, NC) 75083; 75084

Kentucky Fried Chicken (High Point, NC) 75139; 75140; 75141; 75142

Kentucky Fried Chicken (Jacksonville, NC) 75218

Kentucky Fried Chicken (Kannapolis, NC) 75264

Kentucky Fried Chicken (Kernersville, NC) 75281

Kentucky Fried Chicken (Kill Devil Hills, NC) 75287

Kentucky Fried Chicken (Kings Mountain, NC) 75305

Kentucky Fried Chicken (Lenoir, NC) 75381

Kentucky Fried Chicken (Lewisville, NC) 75395

Kentucky Fried Chicken (Lexington, NC) 75405

Kentucky Fried Chicken (Lumberton, NC) 75467; 75468

Kentucky Fried Chicken (Matthews, NC) 75525

Kentucky Fried Chicken (Monroe, NC) 75582

Kentucky Fried Chicken (Morehead City, NC) 75622

Kentucky Fried Chicken (Morganton, NC) 75651

Kentucky Fried Chicken (Morgantown, NC) 75661

Kentucky Fried Chicken (Mount Airy, NC) 75680

Kentucky Fried Chicken (Oxford, NC) 75781

Kentucky Fried Chicken (Pineville, NC) 75816

Kentucky Fried Chicken (Raleigh, NC) 75919; 75920; 75921; 75922

Kentucky Fried Chicken (Reidsville, NC) 76005

Kentucky Fried Chicken (Rockingham, NC) 76063

Kentucky Fried Chicken (Rocky Mount, NC) 76094; 76095

Kentucky Fried Chicken (Roxboro, NC) 76129

Kentucky Fried Chicken (Rutherfordton, NC) 76144

Kentucky Fried Chicken (Selma, NC) 76224

Kentucky Fried Chicken (Smithfield, NC) 76261; 76262

Kentucky Fried Chicken (Southport, NC) 76286

Kentucky Fried Chicken (Sylva, NC) 76357

Kentucky Fried Chicken (W Jefferson, NC) 76418

Kentucky Fried Chicken (Washington, NC) 76457

Kentucky Fried Chicken (Waynesville, NC) 76470

Kentucky Fried Chicken (Whiteville, NC) 76502

Kentucky Fried Chicken (Wilmington, NC) 76577; 76578; 76579; 76580; 76581

Kentucky Fried Chicken (Wilson, NC) 76634

Kentucky Fried Chicken (Yadkinville, NC) 76779

Kentucky Fried Chicken (Ada, OK) 76785

Kentucky Fried Chicken (Ardmore, OK) 76813; 76814

Kentucky Fried Chicken (Bartlesville, OK) 76834

Kentucky Fried Chicken (Bixby, OK) 76861

Kentucky Fried Chicken (Blackwell, OK) 76865

Kentucky Fried Chicken (Bristow, OK) 76870

Kentucky Fried Chicken (Broken Arrow, OK) 76884

Kentucky Fried Chicken (Chickasha, OK) 76928

Kentucky Fried Chicken (Cleveland, OK) 76961

Kentucky Fried Chicken (Cushing, OK) 76979

Kentucky Fried Chicken (Duncan, OK) 76993

Kentucky Fried Chicken (Edmond, OK) 77006

Kentucky Fried Chicken (El Reno, OK) 77032

Kentucky Fried Chicken (Enid, OK) 77055; 77056

Kentucky Fried Chicken (Frederick, OK) 77082

Kentucky Fried Chicken (Grove, OK) 77091

Kentucky Fried Chicken (Guthrie, OK) 77097

Kentucky Fried Chicken (Guymon, OK) 77103

Kentucky Fried Chicken (Henryetta, OK) 77129

Kentucky Fried Chicken (Kingfisher, OK) 77150

Kentucky Fried Chicken (Lawton, OK) 77162; 77163

Kentucky Fried Chicken (Madill, OK) 77181

Kentucky Fried Chicken (Marlow, OK) 77185

Kentucky Fried Chicken (Mc Alester, OK) 77192; 77193; 77194

Kentucky Fried Chicken (Miami, OK) 77205

Kentucky Fried Chicken (Muskogee, OK) 77223

Kentucky Fried Chicken (Norman, OK) 77257; 77258

Kentucky Fried Chicken (Oklahoma City, OK) 77398; 77399; 77400; 77401; 77402; 77403; 77404; 77405; 77406; 77407; 77408; 77409; 77410; 77411; 77412; 77413

Kentucky Fried Chicken (Pauls Valley, OK) 77689

Kentucky Fried Chicken (Pryor, OK) 77740

Kentucky Fried Chicken (Sallisaw, OK) 77769

Kentucky Fried Chicken (Sand Springs, OK) 77781

Kentucky Fried Chicken (Sapulpa, OK) 77794

Kentucky Fried Chicken (Skiatook Ok, OK) 77829

Kentucky Fried Chicken (Sulphur, OK) 77856

Kentucky Fried Chicken (Tulsa, OK) 77973; 77974; 77975; 77976; 77977; 77978; 77979; 77980; 77981; 77982; 77983; 77984

Kentucky Fried Chicken (Vinita, OK) 78225

Kentucky Fried Chicken (Watonga, OK) 78237

Kentucky Fried Chicken (Weatherford, OK) 78242

Kentucky Fried Chicken (Wilburton, OK) 78252

Kentucky Fried Chicken (Woodward, OK) 78260

Kentucky Fried Chicken (Yukon, OK) 78276

Kentucky Fried Chicken (Abbeville, SC) 78642

Kentucky Fried Chicken (Aiken, SC) 78651; 78652

Kentucky Fried Chicken (Anderson, SC) 78678

Kentucky Fried Chicken (Batesburg, SC) 78703

Kentucky Fried Chicken (Beaufort, SC) 78710; 78711

Kentucky Fried Chicken (Bennettsville, SC) 78728

Kentucky Fried Chicken (Bucksport, SC) 78752

Kentucky Fried Chicken (Camden, SC) 78760

Kentucky Fried Chicken (Charleston, SC) 78825; 78826; 78827; 78828; 78829; 78830; 78831

Kentucky Fried Chicken (Clemson, SC) 78955

Kentucky Fried Chicken (Clinton, SC) 78960

Kentucky Fried Chicken (Columbia, SC) 79037; 79038; 79039; 79040

Kentucky Fried Chicken (Columbia Sc, SC) 79129

Kentucky Fried Chicken (Darlington, SC) 79153

Kentucky Fried Chicken (Dillon, SC) 79161

Kentucky Fried Chicken (Florence, SC) 79209; 79210; 79211

Kentucky Fried Chicken (Fort Mill, SC) 79235

Kentucky Fried Chicken (Gaffney, SC) 79260

Kentucky Fried Chicken (Georgetown, SC) 79277

Kentucky Fried Chicken (Goose Creek, SC) 79284

Kentucky Fried Chicken (Greenville, SC) 79380; 79381; 79382; 79383

Kentucky Fried Chicken (Greenwood, SC) 79456; 79457

Kentucky Fried Chicken (Greer, SC) 79479

Kentucky Fried Chicken (Hilton Head, SC) 79508

Kentucky Fried Chicken (Irmo, SC) 79538

Kentucky Fried Chicken (Lancaster, SC) 79572

Kentucky Fried Chicken (Lexington, SC) 79605

Kentucky Fried Chicken (Lugoff, SC) 79621

Kentucky Fried Chicken (Manning, SC) 79634

Kentucky Fried Chicken (Moncks Corner, SC) 79662; 79663

Kentucky Fried Chicken (Myrtle Beach, SC) 79701; 79702

Kentucky Fried Chicken (North Augusta, SC) 79733

Kentucky Fried Chicken (North Myrtle Beach, SC) 79762

Kentucky Fried Chicken (Orangeburg, SC) 79775

Kentucky Fried Chicken (Rock Hill, SC) 79833; 79834

Kentucky Fried Chicken (Santee, SC) 79853

Kentucky Fried Chicken (Spartanburg, SC) 79916; 79917

Kentucky Fried Chicken (Summerville, SC) 79987

Kentucky Fried Chicken (Taylors, SC) 80037

Kentucky Fried Chicken (Union, SC) 80048

Kentucky Fried Chicken (Walterboro, SC) 80072; 80073

Kentucky Fried Chicken (West Columbia, SC) 80095; 80096

Kentucky Fried Chicken (Winnsboro, SC) 80132

Kentucky Fried Chicken (Alief, TX) 82490

Kentucky Fried Chicken (Allen, TX) 82495

Kentucky Fried Chicken (Alvin, TX) 82506

Kentucky Fried Chicken (Amarillo, TX) 82557; 82558

Kentucky Fried Chicken (Andrews, TX) 82598

Kentucky Fried Chicken (Arlington, TX) 82671; 82672; 82673

Kentucky Fried Chicken (Athens, TX) 82789

Kentucky Fried Chicken (Atlanta, TX) 82796

Kentucky Fried Chicken (Austin, TX) 82900; 82901; 82902; 82903; 82904; 82905; 82906; 82907; 82908; 82909; 82910

Kentucky Fried Chicken (Austin Texas, TX) 83076

Kentucky Fried Chicken (Bay City, TX) 83101

Kentucky Fried Chicken (Baytown, TX) 83130

Kentucky Fried Chicken (Beaumont, TX) 83164; 83165; 83166

Kentucky Fried Chicken (Beeville, TX) 83258

Kentucky Fried Chicken (Belton, TX) 83276

Kentucky Fried Chicken (Borger, TX) 83319

Kentucky Fried Chicken (Brady, TX) 83329

Kentucky Fried Chicken (Brenham, TX) 83336

Kentucky Fried Chicken (Brownfield, TX) 83352

Kentucky Fried Chicken (Brownsville, TX) 83360; 83361

Kentucky Fried Chicken (Burkburnett, TX) 83415

Kentucky Fried Chicken (Burleson, TX) 83421

Kentucky Fried Chicken (Canyon, TX) 83443

Kentucky Fried Chicken (Channelview, TX) 83549

Kentucky Fried Chicken (Childress, TX) 83558

Kentucky Fried Chicken (Cleburne, TX) 83575

Kentucky Fried Chicken (Cleveland, TX) 83592

Kentucky Fried Chicken (Conroe, TX) 83663; 83664

Kentucky Fried Chicken (Copperas Cove, TX) 83692

Kentucky Fried Chicken (Corpus Christi, TX) 83725

Kentucky Fried Chicken (Corsicana, TX) 83781

Kentucky Fried Chicken (Dalhart, TX) 83833

Kentucky Fried Chicken (Dallas, TX) 84155; 84156; 84157; 84158; 84159; 84160; 84161; 84162; 84163; 84164; 84165; 84166; 84167; 84168; 84169; 84170

Kentucky Fried Chicken (Del Rio, TX) 84580

Kentucky Fried Chicken (Denison, TX) 84598

Kentucky Fried Chicken (Eagle Pass, TX) 84717

Kentucky Fried Chicken (Edinburg, TX) 84734

Kentucky Fried Chicken (El Paso, TX) 84816; 84817; 84818; 84819; 84820; 84821; 84822; 84823; 84824; 84825; 84826

Kentucky Fried Chicken (Euless, TX) 85012

Kentucky Fried Chicken (Fort Stockton, TX) 85045

Kentucky Fried Chicken (Fort Worth, TX) 85138; 85139; 85140; 85141; 85142; 85143; 85144; 85145; 85146; 85147; 85148; 85149

Kentucky Fried Chicken (Freeport, TX) 85385

Kentucky Fried Chicken (Gainesville, TX) 85422

Kentucky Fried Chicken (Galena Park, TX) 85433

Kentucky Fried Chicken (Galveston, TX) 85442; 85443; 85444

Kentucky Fried Chicken (Garland, TX) 85493; 85494

Kentucky Fried Chicken (Georgetown, TX) 85569

Kentucky Fried Chicken (Grand Prairie, TX) 85619

Kentucky Fried Chicken (Harlingen, TX) 85703

Kentucky Fried Chicken (Henderson, TX) 85733

Kentucky Fried Chicken (Hereford, TX) 85743

Kentucky Fried Chicken (Houston, TX) 86325; 86326; 86327; 86328; 86329; 86330; 86331; 86332; 86333; 86334; 86335; 86336; 86337; 86338; 86339; 86340; 86341; 86342; 86343; 86344; 86345; 86346; 86347; 86348; 86349; 86350; 86351; 86352; 86353; 86354; 86355; 86356; 86357; 86358; 86359; 86360; 86361; 86362; 86363; 86364; 86365; 86366; 86367; 86368; 86369

Kentucky Fried Chicken (Humble, TX) 87228; 87229

Kentucky Fried Chicken (Huntsville, TX) 87261

Kentucky Fried Chicken (Hurst, TX) 87275; 87276; 87277

Kentucky Fried Chicken (Irving, TX) 87356; 87357; 87358

Kentucky Fried Chicken (Jacksonville, TX) 87422

Kentucky Fried Chicken (Jasper, TX) 87432

Kentucky Fried Chicken (Katy, TX) 87449

Kentucky Fried Chicken (Kerrville, TX) 87474

Kentucky Fried Chicken (Kilgore, TX) 87488

Kentucky Fried Chicken (Killeen, TX) 87514

Kentucky Fried Chicken (Lamesa, TX) 87590

Kentucky Fried Chicken (League City, TX) 87628

Kentucky Fried Chicken (Liberty, TX) 87673

Kentucky Fried Chicken (Livingston, TX) 87686

Kentucky Fried Chicken (Longview, TX) 87718

Kentucky Fried Chicken (Marshall, TX) 87854

Kentucky Fried Chicken (Mc Allen, TX) 87887

Kentucky Fried Chicken (Mc Kinney, TX) 87913

Kentucky Fried Chicken (Midland, TX) 88041

Kentucky Fried Chicken (Mineral Wells, TX) 88112

Kentucky Fried Chicken (Mission, TX) 88123

Kentucky Fried Chicken (Mt Pleasant, TX) 88157

Kentucky Fried Chicken (Nacogdoches, TX) 88170

Kentucky Fried Chicken (Nederland, TX) 88186

Kentucky Fried Chicken (New Braunfels, TX) 88210

Kentucky Fried Chicken (Odessa, TX) 88251; 88252

Kentucky Fried Chicken (Orange, TX) 88321
Kentucky Fried Chicken (Palestine, TX) 88341
Kentucky Fried Chicken (Paris, TX) 88367
Kentucky Fried Chicken (Pasadena, TX) 88420; 88421; 88422; 88423
Kentucky Fried Chicken (Pearland, TX) 88481
Kentucky Fried Chicken (Pecos, TX) 88495
Kentucky Fried Chicken (Perryton, TX) 88500
Kentucky Fried Chicken (Pharr, TX) 88508
Kentucky Fried Chicken (Plainview, TX) 88530
Kentucky Fried Chicken (Port Arthur, TX) 88633
Kentucky Fried Chicken (Portland, TX) 88689
Kentucky Fried Chicken (Rosenberg, TX) 88828
Kentucky Fried Chicken (San Angelo, TX) 88878; 88879; 88880
Kentucky Fried Chicken (San Antonio, TX) 89043; 89044; 89045; 89046; 89047; 89048; 89049; 89050; 89051; 89052; 89053; 89054; 89055
Kentucky Fried Chicken (San Marcos, TX) 89338
Kentucky Fried Chicken (Seguin, TX) 89369
Kentucky Fried Chicken (Sherman, TX) 89403
Kentucky Fried Chicken (Silsbee, TX) 89432
Kentucky Fried Chicken (Stephenville, TX) 89517
Kentucky Fried Chicken (Sulphur Springs, TX) 89558
Kentucky Fried Chicken (Sweetwater, TX) 89585
Kentucky Fried Chicken (Terrell, TX) 89658
Kentucky Fried Chicken (Texarkana, TX) 89679; 89680
Kentucky Fried Chicken (Texas City, TX) 89721
Kentucky Fried Chicken (Tomball, TX) 89770
Kentucky Fried Chicken (Tyler, TX) 89807
Kentucky Fried Chicken (Uvalde, TX) 89852
Kentucky Fried Chicken (Vernon, TX) 89866
Kentucky Fried Chicken (Victoria, TX) 89891
Kentucky Fried Chicken (Vidor, TX) 89916
Kentucky Fried Chicken (Weatherford, TX) 90007
Kentucky Fried Chicken (Wichita Falls, TX) 90075; 90076; 90077
Kentucky Fried Chicken Regional (Acworth, GA) 64038
Kentucky Fried Chicken Regional (Norcross, GA) 67133
Kentucky Fried Chicken Regional (Roswell, GA) 67378
Kentucky Glass Plant - General Electric (Lexington, KY) 68564
Kentucky Post (Covington, KY) 68223; 68224
Kentucky Post the (Frankfort, KY) 68363
Kerox Business Services (Austin, TX) 82911
Kerr-McGee (Oklahoma City, OK) **77414**
Kerr-Mcgee Chemical Corp. (Theodore, AL) 56606
Kerr-Mcgee Chemical Corp. (Columbus, MS) 72717
Kerr-Mcgee Chemical Corp. (Hamilton, MS) 72884; 72885
Kerr-Mcgee Chemical Corp. (Texarkana, TX) 89681; 89682
Kerr-Mcgee Chemical Corp. Electrolytic Plant (Hamilton, MS) 72886
Kerr-Mcgee Chemical Corp. Pigment Plant (Hamilton, MS) 72887
Kerr-Mcgee Refining Corp. (Cotton Valley, LA) 69785; 69786
Kerr-Mcgee Refining Corp. (Wynnewood, OK) 78272; 78273
Kerr Mcgee Refining Corp. (Lubbock, TX) 87768
Kerr-Mcgee Refining Corp. Corp. (Cotton Valley, LA) 69787
Key Bank of Fla (Tampa, FL) 63478
Key Pharmaceuticals Puerto Rico Inc. (Las Piedras, PR) 78482
Keystone Indernational Inc. (Houston, TX) 86370
KFC (Louisville, KY) 68788
Kids R US (Birmingham, AL) 55300
Kids-R-US (Bradenton, FL) 58829
Kids R US (Lutz, FL) 60952; 60953
Kids R US (Duluth, GA) 66042
Kids R US (Kennesaw, GA) 66421
Kids R US (Tucker, GA) 67862
Kids R US (Hyattsville, MD) 71960
Kids R US (Rockville, MD) 72289; 72290
Kids R US (Frederick, OK) 77083
Kids R US (Tulsa, OK) 77985; 77986
Kids R US (Walters, OK) 78236
Kids R US (Chattanooga, TN) 80417
Kids R US (Austin, TX) 82912; 82913; 82914
Kids R US (Dallas, TX) 84171; 84172
Kids R US (El Paso, TX) 84827
Kids R US (Houston, TX) 86371
Kids R US (Jacksonville, TX) 87423
Kids R US (Paris, TX) 88368
Kids R US (Tyler, TX) 89808
Kids R US (Norfolk, VA) 91548
Kids R US (Virginia Beach, VA) 92489
Kids R US Employment Office (Wheaton, MD) 72557
Kids R US Inc. (Houston, TX) 86372
Kids R US No. 1240 (Kennesaw, GA) 66422
Kids R US No. 1241 (Duluth, GA) 66043
Kilgore Plumbing Products Inc. (Kilgore, TX) 87489
Kilpatrick's Bakeries, Inc. (Dallas, TX) 84173
Kim Products (Clarksville, AR) 56848
Kimball Furniture Reproductions (Montgomery, AL) 56348
Kimball Furniture Reproductions Inc. (Montgomery, AL) 56349
Kimberly-Clark (La Grange, GA) 66483
Kimberly-Clark (Irving, TX) **87359**
Kimberly-Clark Corp. (Corinth, MS) 72740
Kimberly-Clark Corp. (Lexington, NC) 75406
Kimberly-Clark Corp. Beech Island Mill (Beech Island, SC) 78721
Kimberly-Clark Corp. Lagrange Mill (La Grange, GA) 66484
Kimberly-Clark Corp. Lexington Mill (Lexington, NC) 75407
Kimberly-Clark Corp. Paris Tx Plant (Paris, TX) 88369
Kincaid Furniture Co. (Hudson, NC) 75200; 75201
Kincaid Furniture Co. Inc. Plant 8 (Lenoir, NC) 75382
Kincaid Furniture Co. Inc. Plant 1 (Hudson, NC) 75202; 75203
Kincaid Furniture Co. Inc. Plant 6 (Hudson, NC) 75204; 75205
Kincaid Furniture Co. Plant 8 (Gamewell, NC) 74643
Kinder-Harris, Inc. (Stuttgart, AR) 57660
Kingston-Warren Corp. (Church Hill, TN) 80531; 80532
Kingston-Warren Corp. (Wytheville, VA) 92641
Kirby Forest Ind. Inc. Bon Wier Plywood (Bon Wier, TX) 83308
Kirby Forest Industries Inc. Trt./Osb (Silsbee, TX) 89433
Kirby Forest Industries Plywood (Bon Wier, TX) 83309
Kirby Forest Industries Plywood (Cleveland, TX) 83593
Kirk Steiff Co. (Baltimore, MD) 71173
Kirk Stieff Co. (Baltimore, MD) 71174
Kirk Stieff Co. Kirk Stieff Division (Baltimore, MD) 71175
Kirsch (Scottsville, KY) 69267
Kit Chemicals Inc. (Carrollton, TX) 83478
Kitchen Aid Inc. (Mount Sterling, KY) 69115
Kitchen Collection Inc. (Boaz, AL) 55469
Kitchen Collection Inc. (Fort Lauderdale, FL) 59520
Kitchen Collection Inc. (Kannapolis, NC) 75265
Kitchen Collection Inc. (Houston, TX) 86373
Kitchenaid Inc. (Mount Sterling, KY) 69116
Klopman Burlington Fabrics (Rockingham, NC) 76064
Kmart (Florence, AL) 55738
Kmart (Fort Myers, FL) 59714
Kmart (Adelphi, MD) 70997
Kmart (Clinton, MD) 71539
Kmart (Forestville, MD) 71690
Kmart (Greenbelt, MD) 71865
Kmart (Hyattsville, MD) 71961
Kmart (Oxon Hill, MD) 72197
Kmart (Silver Spring, MD) 72412
Kmart (Suitland, MD) 72476
Kmart (Waldorf, MD) 72530
Kmart (Arlington, TX) 82674
Kmart (Burleson, TX) 83422
Kmart (Corpus Christi, TX) 83726; 83727
Kmart (Dallas, TX) 84174
Kmart (Euless, TX) 85013
Kmart Apparel Corp. (Mesquite, TX) 87967
Kmart Auto Accessories & Sporting Goods (Mount Airy, NC) 75681
Kmart Automotive Center (Fort Lauderdale, FL) 59521
Kmart Corp. (Waco, TX) 89946; 89947
Kmart Discount Store (Slidell, LA) 70831
Kmart Discount Store (Tyler, TX) 89809
Kmart Discount Stores (Sanford, FL) 62768
Kmart Discount Stores (Zephyrhills, FL) 64016
Kmart Discount Stores (Albany, GA) 64078; 64079
Kmart Discount Stores (Metairie, LA) 70282
Kmart Discount Stores (New Orleans, LA) 70513
Kmart Discount Stores (Southaven, MS) 73349
Kmart Discount Stores (Durham, NC) 74412
Kmart Discount Stores (Austin, TX) 82915
Kmart Discount Stores (Beaumont, TX) 83167
Kmart Discount Stores (Brownsville, TX) 83362
Kmart Discount Stores (Cedar Hill, TX) 83528
Kmart Discount Stores (Conroe, TX) 83665
Kmart Discount Stores (Dallas, TX) 84175; 84176
Kmart Discount Stores (De Soto, TX) 84534; 84535
Kmart Discount Stores (Grand Prairie, TX) 85620
Kmart Discount Stores (Houston, TX) 86374; 86375; 86376; 86377; 86378; 86379; 86380; 86381; 86382; 86383
Kmart Discount Stores (Mesquite, TX) 87968
Kmart Discount Stores (Mission, TX) 88124
Kmart Discount Stores (Pearland, TX) 88482
Kmart Discount Stores (Rosenberg, TX) 88829
Kmart Discount Stores (South Houston, TX) 89459
Kmart Pharmacy (Fort Walton Beach, FL) 59828
Kmart Pharmacy (Savannah, GA) 67493
Kmart Pharmacy (Bartlesville, OK) 76835
Kmart Pharmacy (Corpus Christi, TX) 83728
Kmart Pharmacy (Mc Allen, TX) 87888
Kmart Photography Studio (Fort Worth, TX) 85150
Kmart Photography Studio (Garland, TX) 85495
Kmart Portrait Studio (Fort Worth, TX) 85151
Kmart Sporting Goods (Pompano Beach, FL) 62603
Kmart Store (St Petersburg, FL) 62987
Kmart Store (Moultrie, GA) 67055
Kmart Store (Smyrna, GA) 67555
Kmart Store (Garland, TX) 85496; 85497
Kmart Store Auto Service (Moncks Corner, SC) 79664
Kmart Stores (Acworth, GA) 64039; 64040
Kmart Stores (Atlanta, GA) 64588; 64589; 64590; 64591; 64592
Kmart Stores (Buford, GA) 65434
Kmart Stores (Conyers, GA) 65685
Kmart Stores (Covington, GA) 65731
Kmart Stores (Decatur, GA) 65837
Kmart Stores (Duluth, GA) 66044
Kmart Stores (Fayetteville, GA) 66192
Kmart Stores (Hiram, GA) 66358
Kmart Stores (Jonesboro, GA) 66383
Kmart Stores (Lawrenceville, GA) 66518; 66519
Kmart Stores (Mableton, GA) 66635
Kmart Stores (Marietta, GA) 66799; 66800; 66801
Kmart Stores (Norcross, GA) 67134
Kmart Stores (Peachtree Cit, GA) 67235
Kmart Stores (Roswell, GA) 67379
Kmart Stores (Sandy Springs, GA) 67437
Kmart Stores (Snellville, GA) 67594
Kmart Stores (Stockbridge, GA) 67660
Kmart Stores (Stone Mountain, GA) 67698; 67699; 67700
Kmart Stores Automotive (Atlanta, GA) 64593; 64594; 64595
Kmart Stores Automotive (Austell, GA) 65354
Kmart Stores Automotive (Decatur, GA) 65838
Kmart Stores Automotive (Doraville, GA) 65935
Kmart Stores Automotive (Forest Park, GA) 66239
Kmart Stores Automotive (Lilburn, GA) 66562
Kmart Stores Automotive (Marietta, GA) 66802; 66803
Kmart Stores Automotive (Norcross, GA) 67135
Kmart Stores Automotive (Roswell, GA) 67380
Kmart Stores Automotive (Stone Mountain, GA) 67701
Kmart Stores Pharmacy (Acworth, GA) 64041
Kmart Stores Pharmacy (Atlanta, GA) 64596; 64597
Kmart Stores Pharmacy (Buford, GA) 65435
Kmart Stores Pharmacy (Conyers, GA) 65686
Kmart Stores Pharmacy (Covington, GA) 65732
Kmart Stores Pharmacy (Decatur, GA) 65839
Kmart Stores Pharmacy (Doraville, GA) 65936
Kmart Stores Pharmacy (Douglasville, GA) 65988
Kmart Stores Pharmacy (Duluth, GA) 66045
Kmart Stores Pharmacy (Fayetteville, GA) 66193
Kmart Stores Pharmacy (Forest Park, GA) 66240
Kmart Stores Pharmacy (Hiram, GA) 66359
Kmart Stores Pharmacy (Jonesboro, GA) 66384
Kmart Stores Pharmacy (Kennesaw, GA) 66423
Kmart Stores Pharmacy (Lawrenceille, GA) 66499
Kmart Stores Pharmacy (Lilburn, GA) 66563; 66564
Kmart Stores Pharmacy (Mableton, GA) 66636
Kmart Stores Pharmacy (Marietta, GA) 66804; 66805; 66806
Kmart Stores Pharmacy (Norcross, GA) 67136
Kmart Stores Pharmacy (Peachtree Cit, GA) 67236
Kmart Stores Pharmacy (Roswell, GA) 67381
Kmart Stores Pharmacy (Sandy Springs, GA) 67438
Kmart Stores Pharmacy (Smyrna, GA) 67556
Kmart Stores Pharmacy (Snellville, GA) 67595
Kmart Stores Pharmacy (Stockbridge, GA) 67661
Kmart Stores Pharmacy (Stone Mountain, GA) 67702; 67703
Kmart Stores Pharmacy (Woodstock, GA) 68071
Kmart Stores Portrait Studio (Covington, GA) 65733
Kmart Stores Portrait Studio (Roswell, GA) 67382
Kmart Tire & Service Center (St Petersburg, FL) 62988
KMS Group (Columbia, MD) 71594
KMS Group, Inc. (Columbia, MD) 71595
KMS Group at Piney Orchard (Odenton, MD) 72168; 72169
Knight-Ridder (Miami, FL) **61352**
Knoll International Holdings Foames L.P. (Orlando, FL) 62027
Knoll International Holdings Foamex LP (Opa-Locka, FL) 61864; 61865
Kraft Food Ingredients Corp. (Sherman, TX) 89404; 89405
Kraft General Foods (Charlotte, NC) 74062
Kraft General Foods Frozen Foods Div. (Richmond, VA) 91913
Kraft General Foods Frozen Products (Charlotte, NC) 74063
Kraft General Foods Inc. (Decatur, GA) 65840
Kraft General Foods Inc. (Lawrenceburg, KY) 68507
Kraft General Foods Inc. Frozen Dairy Group (Memphis, TN) 81634
Kraft General Foods Inc. National Dairy Products Corp. (Richmond, VA) 91914
Kraft Inc. (Bentonville, AR) 56786
Kraft Inc. (Decatur, GA) 65841
Kraft Inc. (Garland, TX) 85498
Kraft USA Fayetteville (Fayetteville, TN) 80797
Kroger (El Dorado, AR) 56951
Kroger (West Memphis, AR) 57725
Kroger (Savannah, GA) 67494
Kroger (Waycross, GA) 68035
Kroger (Lafayette, LA) 70067
Kroger (Greenville, MS) 72806
Kroger (Fort Worth, TX) 85152
Kroger (Houston, TX) 86384; 86385
Kroger (La Porte, TX) 87561
Kroger (Mc Kinney, TX) 87914
Kroger (Tomball, TX) 89771
Kroger Bakery Division Sales Office (Doraville, GA) 65937
Kroger Dairy Division (Doraville, GA) 65938
Kroger Bakery (Houston, TX) 86386
Kroger Co (Decatur, AL) 55594
Kroger Co (Huntsville, AL) 55959; 55960
Kroger Co (Hot Springs National Park, AR) 57172; 57173
Kroger Co (Little Rock, AR) 57289
Kroger Co (Newnan, GA) 67083
Kroger Co (Southaven, MS) 73350
Kroger Co (North Augusta, SC) 79734
Kroger Co (Denton, TX) 84617
Kroger Co (Fort Worth, TX) 85153
Kroger Co (Greenville, TX) 85672
Kroger Co Retail Stores (Lilburn, GA) 66565
Kroger Co Retail Stores (Tucker, GA) 67863
Kroger Comapny No 289 (Houston, TX) 86387
Kroger Co. (Auburn, AL) 55063
Kroger Co. (Guntersville, AL) 55830
Kroger Co. (Lanett, AL) 56102
Kroger Co. (Camden, AR) 56835
Kroger Company the (Conway, AR) 56865
Kroger Co. (Helena, AR) 57156
Kroger Company the (Little Rock, AR) 57290
Kroger Co. the (North Little Rock, AR) 57466
Kroger Co. (Covington, GA) 65734
Kroger Co. (Gainesville, GA) 66279
Kroger Co. (Macon, GA) 66696
Kroger Company (Snellville, GA) 67596
Kroger Co. (Bowling Green, KY) 68146
Kroger Co. (Carrollton, KY) 68191
Kroger Co. (Covington, KY) 68225; 68226
Kroger Co. (Elizabethtown, KY) 68282; 68283; 68284
Kroger Co. (Frankfort, KY) 68364
Kroger Co. (Georgetown, KY) 68384
Kroger Co. (Harrodsburg, KY) 68413
Kroger Co. (Hopkinsville, KY) 68480
Kroger Co. (La Grange, KY) 68503
Kroger Co. (Lebanon, KY) 68509
Kroger Co. (Lexington, KY) 68565; 68566; 68567; 68568; 68569; 68570
Kroger Co. (London, KY) 68662
Kroger Co. (Louisville, KY) 68789; 68790; 68791; 68792; 68793; 68794; 68795; 68796; 68797; 68798; 68799; 68800; 68801; 68802; 68803; 68804; 68805; 68806; 68807; 68808; 68809; 68810; 68811; 68812; 68813
Kroger Co. (Madisonville, KY) 69060
Kroger Co. (Maysville, KY) 69088
Kroger Co. (Murray, KY) 69126; 69127
Kroger Co. (Newport, KY) 69137; 69138
Kroger Co. (Nicholasville, KY) 69152
Kroger Co. (Owensboro, KY) 69173; 69174; 69175; 69176
Kroger Co. (Paducah, KY) 69204; 69205
Kroger Co. (Pikeville, KY) 69226
Kroger Co. (Richmond, KY) 69243
Kroger Co. (Shepherdsville, KY) 69281
Kroger Co. (Somerset, KY) 69294; 69295
Kroger Co. (St. Matthews, KY) 69302

Kroger Sav-On (Myrtle Beach, SC) 79703
Kroger Sav-On (Summerville, SC) 79989
Kroger Sav-On Food & Drugs (Myrtle Beach, SC) 79704
Kroger Sav-On Pharmacy Dept (Savannah, GA) 67496
Kroger Savon Food&Drug (Savannah, GA) 67497
Kroger Savon Food&Drugs (Sumter, SC) 80023
Kroger Snack Bar (New Iberia, LA) 70411
Kroger Store (Sulphur, LA) 70885
Kroger Store (Galveston, TX) 85445
Kroger Store (Houston, TX) 86427; 86428; 86429
Kroger Store No 542 (Pine Bluff, AR) 57524
Kroger Store No 108 (Texas City, TX) 89723
Kroger Store No 632 (Dallas, TX) 84186
Kroger Stores (Monroe, NC) 75583
Kroger Stores (Dallas, TX) 84187
Kroger Stores (Duncanville, TX) 84698
Kroger Stores (Garland, TX) 85500
Kroger Stores (Mesquite, TX) 87972
Kroger Stores (Richardson, TX) 88747
Kroger Stores No 421 (Dallas, TX) 84188
Kroger Super Market (Bossier City, LA) 69721
Kroger Super Market (Shreveport, LA) 70743; 70744
Kroger Super Markets (Shreveport, LA) 70745
Kroger Supermarket (Savannah, GA) 67498
Kroger Supermarket (Jackson, MS) 73011
Kroger Supermarket (Dallas, TX) 84189
Kroger 377 (Clinton, MS) 72687
Kroger 325 (Starkville, MS) 73366
Kroger Transportation (Houston, TX) 86430
Kroger Vo the Atlanta Executiv (Atlanta, GA) 64624
Kroger Vot the Retail Stores (Acworth, GA) 64043
Kroger Warehouse (Jackson, MS) 73012
Kroger Warehouse (Dallas, TX) 84190
Kroger Wesco Foods Co. (Pompano Beach, FL) 62604
Kroger Wesco Foods Co. (Vero Beach, FL) 63760
Kroger Zone Office (Roanoke, VA) 92167
Krogerco (Winchester, KY) 69345
Kroger,Genevieve Mrs (Mc Alester, OK) 77195
Krogers (Hartselle, AL) 55857
Kroger's (Paragould, AR) 57493
Kroger's (West Memphis, AR) 57726
Kroger's (Macon, GA) 66697
Krogers (Lake Charles, LA) 70146
Kroger's (Grenada, MS) 72842
Kroger's (Gulfport, MS) 72861
Krogers (High Point, NC) 75143
Krogers (Shelbyville, TN) 82316
Krogers (League City, TX) 87629
Krogers Co. the Retail Sotres (Chamblee, GA) 65533
Kroger's Co. the Retail Stores (Atlanta, GA) 64625
Krogers Pharmacy (Lake Charles, LA) 70147
Krogers Pharmacy (Ridgeland, MS) 73321
Kroger's Pharmacy (Galveston, TX) 85446
Krogers Pharmacy Kroger Co. the (Atlanta, GA) 64626
Kti Chemicals Inc. (Carrollton, TX) 83480
Kuppenheimer Manufacturing Co., Inc. (Norcross, GA) 67142
Kurfees Coatings Inc. (Louisville, KY) 68816
Kwikset Corp. (Bristow, OK) 76871; 76872
Kwikset Corp. (Denison, TX) 84600; 84601

L

L L & E Petroleum Marketing Inc. (Saraland, AL) 56515
L L & E Petroleum Mtg. Inc. (Saraland, AL) 56516
L M Berry & Co. (Metairie, LA) 70283
L M Berry & Co. (Shreveport, LA) 70746
L & P Foam Inc. (Tupelo, MS) 73409
La Gloria Oil & Gas Co. (Tyler, TX) 89810
La Gloria Oil & Gas Co. Inc. (Bellaire, TX) 83265
La-Z-Boy Arkansas (Siloam Springs, AR) 57619
La-Z-Boy Chair Co. (Siloam Springs, AR) 57620
La-Z-Boy Chair Co. Chair Co. (Siloam Springs, AR) 57621
La-Z-Boy East (Florence, SC) 79212; 79213
La-Z-Boy East East (Florence, SC) 79214
La-Z-Boy Leland (Leland, MS) 73112; 73113
La-Z-Boy Lincolnton (Lincolnton, NC) 75440
La-Z-Boy S. South (Newton, MS) 73219
La-Z-Boy South (Newton, MS) 73220
La-Z-Boy Tennessee (Dayton, TN) 80721; 80722
Label Systems International (Jacksonville, FL) 60358
Lafarge (Reston, VA) **91711**
Lafarge Corp. (Demopolis, AL) 55616
Lafarge Corp. (Dallas, TX) 84191
Lafarge Corp. (Fort Worth, TX) 85162; 85163
Lafarge Corp. (Houston, TX) 86431
Lafarge Corp. (Reston, VA) 91712
Lafarge Corp. -Balcones (New Braunfels, TX) 88213
Lafarge Corp. Balcones Cement Plant (New Braunfels, TX) 88214
Lafarge Corp. Balcones Plant (New Braunfels, TX) 88215
Lagrange Molded Products Inc. (La Grange, GA) 66485; 66486
LaGrange Molded Products, Inc. (LaGrange, GA) 66494
Lakeland Indl. Center & Bakery & Bakery (Lakeland, FL) 60742
Land Marine Cargo Inc. (Fort Smith, AR) 57066
Land-Marine Cargo Inc. (Jacksonville, FL) 60359
Land O'lakes Inc. (Lilburn, GA) 66569
Land O'lakes Inc. (Norcross, GA) 67143
L&P Foam Inc. (Tupelo, MS) 73410
L&P Foam Inc. (High Point, NC) 75144
L&P Foam Inc. (Newton, NC) 75748
Lane Bryant (Auburn, AL) 55064
Lane Bryant (Birmingham, AL) 55301; 55302; 55303; 55304
Lane Bryant (Huntsville, AL) 55964; 55965
Lane Bryant (Mobile, AL) 56194; 56195
Lane Bryant (Montgomery, AL) 56350; 56351
Lane Bryant (Fort Smith, AR) 57067
Lane Bryant (Altamonte Spg, FL) 58539
Lane Bryant (Boca Raton, FL) 58716
Lane Bryant (Boynton Beach, FL) 58782
Lane Bryant (Bradenton, FL) 58830
Lane Bryant (Clearwater, FL) 59027
Lane Bryant (Daytona Beach, FL) 59190
Lane Bryant (Fort Lauderdale, FL) 59522
Lane Bryant (Gainesville, FL) 59889; 59890
Lane Bryant (Hollywood, FL) 60072
Lane Bryant (Kissimmee, FL) 60591
Lane Bryant (Lakeland, FL) 60743
Lane Bryant (Mary Esther, FL) 61017
Lane Bryant (Merritt Island, FL) 61142
Lane Bryant (Miami, FL) 61353; 61354; 61355
Lane Bryant (Orange Park, FL) 61889
Lane Bryant (Orlando, FL) 62029; 62030; 62031
Lane Bryant (Pensacola, FL) 62443; 62444
Lane Bryant (Plant City, FL) 62550
Lane Bryant (Pt Charlotte, FL) 62699
Lane Bryant (St Petersburg, FL) 62989
Lane Bryant (Stuart, FL) 63172
Lane Bryant (Tallahassee, FL) 63249
Lane Bryant (Tampa, FL) 63479; 63480
Lane Bryant (West Palm Beach, FL) 63879
Lane Bryant (Atlanta, GA) 64627; 64628; 64629; 64630; 64631; 64632
Lane Bryant (Decatur, GA) 65849
Lane Bryant (Duluth, GA) 66049
Lane Bryant (Fairburn, GA) 66174
Lane Bryant (Gainesville, GA) 66280
Lane Bryant (Morrow, GA) 67021
Lane Bryant (Valdosta, GA) 67965
Lane Bryant (Elizabethtown, KY) 68285
Lane Bryant (Florence, KY) 68313
Lane Bryant (Lexington, KY) 68571
Lane Bryant (Louisville, KY) 68817
Lane Bryant (Owensboro, KY) 69177
Lane Bryant (Alexandria, LA) 69389
Lane Bryant (Baton Rouge, LA) 69575; 69576
Lane Bryant (Bossier City, LA) 69722
Lane Bryant (Lafayette, LA) 70068
Lane Bryant (Marrero, LA) 70228
Lane Bryant (Metairie, LA) 70284
Lane Bryant (Shreveport, LA) 70747
Lane Bryant (Slidell, LA) 70832
Lane Bryant (Biloxi, MS) 72628
Lane Bryant (Escatawpa, MS) 72757
Lane Bryant (Jackson, MS) 73013; 73014
Lane Bryant (Ridgeland, MS) 73322
Lane Bryant (Utica, MS) 73437
Lane Bryant (Charlotte, NC) 74068; 74069
Lane Bryant (Hickory, NC) 75086
Lane Bryant (Jacksonville, NC) 75219; 75220
Lane Bryant (Raleigh, NC) 75924
Lane Bryant (Lawton, OK) 77164
Lane Bryant (Muskogee, OK) 77224
Lane Bryant (Norman, OK) 77259
Lane Bryant (Oklahoma City, OK) 77415; 77416; 77417
Lane Bryant (Shawnee, OK) 77821
Lane Bryant (Tulsa, OK) 77987; 77988
Lane Bryant (Anderson, SC) 78679
Lane Bryant (Columbia, SC) 79042; 79043
Lane Bryant (Myrtle Beach, SC) 79705
Lane Bryant (Antioch, TN) 80171
Lane Bryant (Chattanooga, TN) 80418
Lane Bryant (Clarksville, TN) 80554
Lane Bryant (Goodlettsville, TN) 80866
Lane Bryant (Abilene, TX) 82441
Lane Bryant (Amarillo, TX) 82559; 82560
Lane Bryant (Arlington, TX) 82683; 82684; 82685
Lane Bryant (Austin, TX) 82916; 82917
Lane Bryant (Beaumont, TX) 83168
Lane Bryant (Brownsville, TX) 83364
Lane Bryant (Dallas, TX) 84192; 84193; 84194; 84195
Lane Bryant (Denton, TX) 84618
Lane Bryant (El Paso, TX) 84828; 84829; 84830
Lane Bryant (Fort Worth, TX) 85164; 85165; 85166; 85167
Lane Bryant (Galveston, TX) 85447
Lane Bryant (Houston, TX) 86432; 86433; 86434; 86435; 86436; 86437; 86438; 86439; 86440; 86441; 86442
Lane Bryant (Hurst, TX) 87278
Lane Bryant (Irving, TX) 87366
Lane Bryant (Killeen, TX) 87515
Lane Bryant (Mcallen, TX) 87931
Lane Bryant (Mesquite, TX) 87973
Lane Bryant (Odessa, TX) 88253
Lane Bryant (Pasadena, TX) 88429
Lane Bryant (Plano, TX) 88578
Lane Bryant (Port Arthur, TX) 88634
Lane Bryant (San Angelo, TX) 88881
Lane Bryant (San Antonio, TX) 89063; 89064; 89065; 89066; 89067; 89068; 89069
Lane Bryant (Sherman, TX) 89409
Lane Bryant (Temple, TX) 89621
Lane Bryant (Texarkana, TX) 89683; 89684
Lane Bryant (Tyler, TX) 89811
Lane Bryant (Victoria, TX) 89894
Lane Bryant (Charleston, WV) 92760; 92761
Lane Bryant (Parkersburg, WV) 92990
Lane Co. Inc. (Altavista, VA) 90246; 90247
Lane Co. Inc. (Rocky Mount, VA) 92203
Lanier International Operations (Atlanta, GA) 64633
Lanier Worldwide Strategic Marketing (Atlantic, GA) 65306
Lanier Worldwide Inc. (Atlanta, GA) 64634
Lapp Insulator Co. (Birmingham, AL) 55305
Lapp Insulator Co. (Dunwoody, GA) 66119
Lapp Insulator Co. (Pineville, NC) 75817
Larsen Co. Dba Frio Foods (Uvalde, TX) 89853
Las Palmas Mexican Restaurant (Burkburnett, TX) 83416
Lasalle National Bank (Atlanta, GA) 64635
Latas De Aluminio Reynolds Inc. Reynolds Metals Co. (Guayama, PR) 78424
Latco, Inc.- Pro AG (Lincoln, AR) 57243
Laurel Hill Carpet Mill (Laurel Hill, NC) 75345
Lawn Boy (Morehead City, NC) 75623
Lawn-Boy Oxford (Oxford, MS) 73242
Lawyers Title Corp. (Richmond, VA) 91915
Layne & Bowler Inc. (Memphis, TN) 81642
Layne Bryant (Memphis, TN) 81643
Layne Bryant (Barboursville, WV) 92670
Layne Bryant (Huntington, WV) 92880
Leader Financial Corp. (Memphis, TN) **81644**
Lebanon Bank (Lebanon, TN) 81303; 81304; 81305
Lebanon Bank (Mount Juliet, TN) 81823
Lederle Parentelas Lederle Piperacillin Inc. (Carolina, PR) 78378
Lederle Parenterals Inc.-Lederle Piperacillin Inc. (Carolina, PR) 78379
Lederle Parenterals & Lederle Piperacillin Inc. (Carolina, PR) 78380
Lederle Piperacillin Inc.; Lederle Parenterals Inc.- (Carolina, PR) 78379
Lederle-Praxis Biologics Inc. (Sanford, NC) 76198
T. G. Lee Foods, Inc. (Orange City, FL) 61871
T. G. Lee Foods Inc. (Orlando, FL) 62032
T.G. Lee Foods, Inc. (Orange City, FL) 61872
T. G. Lee Foods (Fort Myers, FL) 59715
T. G. Lee Foods (Orange City, FL) 61873
T. G. Lee Foods (Orlando, FL) 62033
Lee Laboratories, Inc. (Petersburg, VA) 91632
T. G. Lee Lifestyle (Orange City, FL) 61874
Leeds & Northrup Instruments (St. Petersburg, FL) 63127
Lees Car Wash (Vienna, VA) 92412
Lees Carpet (Glasgow, VA) 90972
Lees Carpet Burlington (Glasgow, VA) 90973
Lees Carpets (Aberdeen, MS) 72577
Lees Carpets (Greensboro, NC) 74862
Lees Carpets (Dallas, TX) 84196
Lees Carry out (Baltimore, MD) 71176; 71177; 71178
Leggett & Platt Foam Inc. (High Point, NC) 75145
Leggett & Platt Inc. (Simpsonville, KY) 69290
Leggett & Platt Inc. (Winchester, KY) 69346; 69347
Leggett & Platt Inc. (Lexington, NC) 75408
Leggett & Platt Inc. (Linwood, NC) 75445
Leggett & Platt Inc. (Newton, NC) 75749
Leggett & Platt Inc. Masterack Div. (Atlanta, GA) 64636; 64637; 64638
Leggett & Platt Inc. Urethane Foam Div. (Tupelo, MS) 73411
Leggett & Platt Inc. Cotton Grove Plant (Lexington, NC) 75409
Leggett & Platt Inc. 0700 (Linwood, NC) 75446
Leggett & Platt Inc. 0701 (Lexington, NC) 75410
Leggett & Platt Sleeper Comp-O Nents (High Point, NC) 75146
Leggett & Platt Sleeper Components (High Point, NC) 75147
Lehman Brothers (Atlanta, GA) 64639; 64640
Lehman Brothers (Houston, TX) 86443
Lehman Brothers Institutional Fund (Roswell, GA) 67389
Lenox China (Kinston, NC) 75324
Lenox China (Oxford, NC) 75782; 75783
Lenox China Shop (Kinston, NC) 75325
Lenox China Shop (Oxford, NC) 75784; 75785
Lens Crafters (Mobile, AL) 56196
Lens Crafters (Altamonte Springs, FL) 58557
Lens Crafters (Fort Lauderdale, FL) 59523
Lens Crafters (Jacksonville, FL) 60360; 60361
Lens Crafters (Orange Park, FL) 61890
Lens Crafters (Orlando, FL) 62034
Lens Crafters (St Petersburg, FL) 62990
Lens Crafters (Tampa, FL) 63481
Lens Crafters (Atlanta, GA) 64641; 64642
Lens Crafters (Baton Rouge, LA) 69577
Lens Crafters (Kenner, LA) 69997
Lens Crafters (Lafayette, LA) 70069
Lens Crafters (Utica, MS) 73438
Lens Crafters (Greensboro, NC) 74863
Lens Crafters (Oklahoma City, OK) 77418
Lens Crafters (Tulsa, OK) 77989
Lens Crafters (Charleston, SC) 78832
Lens Crafters (Columbia, SC) 79044
Lens Crafters (Florence, SC) 79215
Lens Crafters (Greenville, SC) 79384
Lens Crafters (Austin, TX) 82918; 82919
Lens Crafters (Dallas, TX) 84197; 84198
Lens Crafters (El Paso, TX) 84831
Lens Crafters (San Antonio, TX) 89070; 89071
Lens Crafters Regional Office (Arlington, TX) 82686
Lenscrafters (Bethesda, MD) 71396
Lenscrafters (Hyattsville, MD) 71962; 71963
Lenscrafters (Kensington, MD) 71996; 71997
Lenscrafters (Montgomery Co, MD) 72143; 72144
Lenscrafters (Rockville, MD) 72291
Lenscrafters (Chesapeake, VA) 90586
Lenscrafters (Hampton, VA) 91043
Lenscrafters (Richmond, VA) 91916; 91917
Lerner the (Chattanooga, TN) 80419
Lerner Shop (Birmingham, AL) 55306; 55307
Lerner Shop (Decatur, AL) 55596
Lerner Shop (Dothan, AL) 55655
Lerner Shop (Fairfield, AL) 55714
Lerner Shop (Huntsville, AL) 55966
Lerner Shop (Mobile, AL) 56197; 56198
Lerner Shop (Montgomery, AL) 56352
Lerner Shop (Tuscaloosa, AL) 56661
Lerner Shop (Hot Springs National Park, AR) 57174; 57175
Lerner Shop (N Little Rock, AR) 57412
Lerner Shop (Altamonte Spg, FL) 58540
Lerner Shop (Boca Raton, FL) 58717
Lerner Shop (Boynton Beach, FL) 58783; 58784
Lerner Shop (Bradenton, FL) 58831; 58832
Lerner Shop (Clearwater, FL) 59028
Lerner Shop (Fort Myers, FL) 59716
Lerner Shop (Fort Walton Beach, FL) 59829
Lerner Shop (Gainesville, FL) 59891
Lerner Shop (Hialeah, FL) 59996
Lerner Shop (Hollywood, FL) 60073; 60074

Lerner Shop (Jacksonville, FL) 60362; 60363; 60364
Lerner Shop (Lakeland, FL) 60744
Lerner Shop (Leesburg, FL) 60884
Lerner Shop (Mary Esther, FL) 61018
Lerner Shop (Miami, FL) 61356; 61357; 61358
Lerner Shop (Ocala, FL) 61804
Lerner Shop (Orlando, FL) 62035; 62036; 62037
Lerner Shop (Panama City, FL) 62329
Lerner Shop (Pensacola, FL) 62445
Lerner Shop (Pompano Beach, FL) 62605
Lerner Shop (St Augustine, FL) 62943; 62944
Lerner Shop (St Petersburg, FL) 62991; 62992
Lerner Shop (Stuart, FL) 63173
Lerner Shop (Tallahassee, FL) 63250
Lerner Shop (Tampa, FL) 63482; 63483
Lerner Shop (Titusville, FL) 63694
Lerner Shop (West Palm Beach, FL) 63880
Lerner Shop (Winter Haven, FL) 63944
Lerner Shop (Winter Park, FL) 63986
Lerner Shop (Atlanta, GA) 64643; 64644; 64645; 64646
Lerner Shop (Decatur, GA) 65850
Lerner Shop (Fairburn, GA) 66175
Lerner Shop (Kennesaw, GA) 66426
Lerner Shop (Morrow, GA) 67022
Lerner Shop (Smyrna, GA) 67559
Lerner Shop (Alexandria, LA) 69390; 69391
Lerner Shop (Baton Rouge, LA) 69578; 69579
Lerner Shop (Gretna, LA) 69904; 69905
Lerner Shop (Hammond, LA) 69931
Lerner Shop (Lafayette, LA) 70070; 70071
Lerner Shop (Lake Charles, LA) 70148
Lerner Shop (Marrero, LA) 70229
Lerner Shop (Metairie, LA) 70285; 70286
Lerner Shop (Shreveport, LA) 70748
Lerner Shop (Biloxi, MS) 72629
Lerner Shop (Gulfport, MS) 72862
Lerner Shop (Jackson, MS) 73015; 73016; 73017
Lerner Shop (Laurel, MS) 73103
Lerner Shop (Meridian, MS) 73169
Lerner Shop (Pascagoula, MS) 73263
Lerner Shop (Ridgeland, MS) 73323
Lerner Shop (Utica, MS) 73439
Lerner Shop (Vicksburg, MS) 73458
Lerner Shop (Charlotte, NC) 74070
Lerner Shop (Greenville, NC) 74966
Lerner Shop (High Point, NC) 75148; 75149
Lerner Shop (Jacksonville, NC) 75221; 75222
Lerner Shop (Rocky Mount, NC) 76096; 76097
Lerner Shop (Wilmington, NC) 76582
Lerner Shop (Norman, OK) 77260
Lerner Shop (Oklahoma City, OK) 77419; 77420; 77421; 77422; 77423
Lerner Shop (Tulsa, OK) 77990; 77991; 77992
Lerner Shop (Anderson, SC) 78680
Lerner Shop (Charleston, SC) 78833; 78834
Lerner Shop (Columbia, SC) 79045
Lerner Shop (Florence, SC) 79216
Lerner Shop (Greenville, SC) 79385; 79386
Lerner Shop (Sumter, SC) 80024
Lerner Shop (Abilene, TX) 82442; 82443
Lerner Shop (Amarillo, TX) 82561; 82562
Lerner Shop (Arlington, TX) 82687; 82688; 82689
Lerner Shop (Austin, TX) 82920; 82921; 82922
Lerner Shop (Baytown, TX) 83131
Lerner Shop (Beaumont, TX) 83169; 83170
Lerner Shop (Brownsville, TX) 83365; 83366
Lerner Shop (Clute, TX) 83600
Lerner Shop (Dallas, TX) 84199
Lerner Shop (Denton, TX) 84619
Lerner Shop (Duncanville, TX) 84699
Lerner Shop (Eagle Pass, TX) 84718
Lerner Shop (El Paso, TX) 84832; 84833; 84834; 84835; 84836
Lerner Shop (Fort Worth, TX) 85168; 85169; 85170; 85171
Lerner Shop (Friendswood, TX) 85401
Lerner Shop (Harlingen, TX) 85704
Lerner Shop (Houston, TX) 86444; 86445; 86446; 86447; 86448; 86449; 86450; 86451; 86452; 86453; 86454; 86455
Lerner Shop (Humble, TX) 87231
Lerner Shop (Irving, TX) 87367
Lerner Shop (Killeen, TX) 87516
Lerner Shop (Lake Jackson, TX) 87581
Lerner Shop (Laredo, TX) 87613
Lerner Shop (Longview, TX) 87719
Lerner Shop (Lufkin, TX) 87807
Lerner Shop (Mcallen, TX) 87932
Lerner Shop (Mesquite, TX) 87974; 87975
Lerner Shop (Odessa, TX) 88254
Lerner Shop (Pasadena, TX) 88430; 88431
Lerner Shop (Plano, TX) 88579
Lerner Shop (Port Arthur, TX) 88635
Lerner Shop (San Antonio, TX) 89072; 89073; 89074; 89075; 89076; 89077; 89078; 89079
Lerner Shop (Texarkana, TX) 89685; 89686
Lerner Shop (Victoria, TX) 89895
Lerner Shop (Wichita Falls, TX) 90078
Lerner Shops (Covington, KY) 68227
Lerner Shops (Florence, KY) 68314
Lerner Shops (Louisville, KY) 68818; 68819; 68820
Lerner Shops (Chattanooga, TN) 80420
Lerner Shops (Clarksville, TN) 80555
Lerner Shops (Johnson City, TN) 81050
Lerner Shops (Kingsport, TN) 81110
Lerner Shops (Knoxville, TN) 81224; 81225
Lerner Shops (Maryville, TN) 81417
Lerner Shops (Memphis, TN) 81645; 81646; 81647
Lerner Shops (Nashville, TN) 82052; 82053
Lerner Shops (Beckley, WV) 92677
Lerner Shops (Charleston, WV) 92762; 92763
Lerner Shops (Clarksburg, WV) 92809
Lerner Shops (Huntington, WV) 92881; 92882
Lerner Shops (Parkersburg, WV) 92991
Lerner Woman (Paducah, KY) 69206
Lerner Woman (Clarksville, TN) 80556
Lerner Woman (Goodlettsville, TN) 80867
Lerner Woman (Memphis, TN) 81648
Leslie Coal Mining Co. (Stone, KY) 69311
Leucadia National Corp. (Washington, DC) 58311
Levelland Vegetable Oil (Levelland, TX) 87638
Lewis Engineering Co. (Marshall, TX) 87857
Lexington Furniture Ind. Plant 8 (Lexington, NC) 75411
Lexington Furniture Ind. Plant 11 (Mocksville, NC) 75566
Lexington Furniture Ind. Plant 1 (Lexington, NC) 75412
Lexington Furniture Ind. Plant 10 (Hildebran, NC) 75187
Lexington Furniture Ind. Plant 3 (Lexington, NC) 75413
Lexington Furniture Ind. Plant 12 (Lexington, NC) 75414
Lexington Furniture Ind. Plant 2 (Linwood, NC) 75447
Lexington Furniture Ind. Plants 4 & 5 (Lexington, NC) 75415
Lexington Furniture Ind. Inc. Plant 9 (Lexington, NC) 75416
Lexington Furniture Ind. Inc. Plant 7 (Lexington, NC) 75417
Lexington Furniture Industries (Lexington, NC) 75418
Lexington Furniture Industries Plant Plant 2 (Lexington, NC) 75419
Lexington Lamp Plant (Lexington, KY) 68572
Lexington Tube Co. (Lexington, TN) 81339
LF Corp. (North Wilkesboro, NC) 75762
LFE Corp. Traffic Control Division (Decatur, GA) 65851; 65852; 65853
Libbey Glass Co. (Shreveport, LA) 70749
Libert National of Madisonville (Madisonville, KY) 69061
Liberty Business Credit Cor (Tampa, FL) 63484
Liberty Financial Services Inc. (Rockville, MD) 72292
Liberty Mutual Insco (Olden, TX) 88293
Liberty Mutual Insur Co. (Dallas, TX) 84200
Liberty Mutual Insurance Companie (Gainesville, GA) 66281
Liberty Mutual Insurance Companie (Midland, TX) 88042
Liberty Mutual Insurance Co. (Fort Smith, AR) 57068
Liberty Mutual Insurance Co. (Wilmington, DE) 58078
Liberty Mutual Insurance Co. (Jacksonville, FL) 60365
Liberty Mutual Insurance Co. (Tampa, FL) 63485
Liberty Mutual Insurance Co. (Covington, LA) 69796
Liberty Mutual Insurance Co. (Metairie, LA) 70287
Liberty Mutual Insurance Co. (Baltimore, MD) 71179
Liberty Mutual Insurance Co. (Charlotte, NC) 74071
Liberty Mutual Insurance Co. (Greensboro, NC) 74864
Liberty Mutual Insurance Co. (Matthews, NC) 75526
Liberty Mutual Insurance Co. (Raleigh, NC) 75925
Liberty Mutual Insurance Co. (Charleston, SC) 78835
Liberty Mutual Insurance Co. (Columbia, SC) 79046
Liberty Mutual Insurance Co. (Austin, TX) 82923
Liberty Mutual Insurance Co. (Beaumont, TX) 83171
Liberty Mutual Insurance Co. (Brownwood, TX) 83386
Liberty Mutual Insurance Co. (Corsicana, TX) 83782
Liberty Mutual Insurance Co. (El Paso, TX) 84837
Liberty Mutual Insurance Co. (Houston, TX) 86456; 86457
Liberty Mutual Insurance Co. (Lubbock, TX) 87769
Liberty Mutual Insurance Co. (Tyler, TX) 89812
Liberty Mutual Insurance Co. (Fairfax, VA) 90790
Liberty Mutual Insurance Co. (Lynchburg, VA) 91266
Liberty Mutual Insurance Co. (Norfolk, VA) 91549
Liberty Mutual Insurance Co. (Roanoke, VA) 92168
Liberty Mutual Insurance Cos (Miami, FL) 61359
Liberty Mutual Insurance Gr (Austin, TX) 82924
Liberty National Bak & Trust Co. Of Kentucky (Louisville, KY) 68821
Liberty National Bancorp (Louisville, KY) **68822**
Liberty National Bancorp, Inc. (Louisville, KY) 68823
Liberty National Bank & Braodcast Co. of Kentucky (Louisville, KY) 68824
Liberty National Bank & Broadcast Co. of Kentucky (Louisville, KY) 68825; 68826; 68827; 68828; 68829; 68830; 68831; 68832; 68833; 68834; 68835; 68836
Liberty National Bank of Madisonville (Hanson, KY) 68407
Liberty National Bank of Madisonville (Madisonville, KY) 69062; 69063; 69064; 69065
Liberty National Bank of Madisonville (Mortons Gap, KY) 69111
Liberty National Bank of Northern Kentucky (Bellevue, KY) 68123
Liberty National Bank of Northern Kentucky (Burlington, KY) 68173
Liberty National Bank of Northern Kentucky (Cold Spring, KY) 68205
Liberty National Bank of Northern Kentucky (Crescent Springs, KY) 68241
Liberty National Bank of Northern Kentucky (Dayton, KY) 68267
Liberty National Bank of Northern Kentucky (Edgewood, KY) 68269
Liberty National Bank of Northern Kentucky (Erlanger, KY) 68298
Liberty National Bank of Northern Kentucky (Florence, KY) 68315; 68316; 68317; 68318
Liberty National Bank of Northern Kentucky (Fort Thomas, KY) 68350; 68351
Liberty National Bank of Owensboro (Owensboro, KY) 69178; 69179; 69180; 69181; 69182; 69183
Liberty National Bank & Proadcast Co. of Kentucky (Louisville, KY) 68837
Liberty National Bank of Shelbyville (Shelbyville, KY) 69273; 69274
Liberty National Bank & Trust Co. of Hardin County (Elizabethtown, KY) 68286
Liberty National Bank & Trust Co. of Kentucky (Louisville, KY) 68838; 68839; 68840; 68841; 68842; 68843; 68844; 68845; 68846; 68847; 68848; 68849; 68850; 68851; 68852; 68853; 68854; 68855; 68856; 68857; 68858; 68859; 68860; 68861
Liberty National Bankcorp., Inc. Holding Co. (Louisville, KY) 68862; 68863
Liberty National Leasing Co. (Louisville, KY) 68864
Life & Casvality Insurance Co. of Tennessee (Nashville, TN) 82054
Life Insur Co. of Virginia (Staunton, VA) 92325
Life Insurance Co. of Va (Baltimore, MD) 71180
Life Insurance Co. of Va (Midlothian, VA) 91418
Life Insurance Co. of Va (Suffolk, VA) 92370
Life Insurance Co. of Va (Williamsburg, VA) 92575
Life Insurance Co. of Va (Winchester, VA) 92597
Life Insurance Co. of Va (Charleston, WV) 92764
Life Insurance Co. of Va (Huntington, WV) 92883
Life Insurance Co. of Virgin (Bristol, TN) 80251
Life Insurance Co. of Virgin (Richmond, VA) 91918
Life Insurance Co. of Virgin (Roanoke, VA) 92169
Life Insurance Co. Virginia (Danville, VA) 90704
Life Insurance Co. of Virginia (Fairfax, VA) 90791
Life Insurance Co. of Virginia (Fredericksburg, VA) 90929
Life Insurance Co. of Virginia (Lawrenceville, VA) 91185
Life Insurance Co. of Virginia (Norfolk, VA) 91550
Life Insurance Co. of Virginia (Portsmouth, VA) 91661
Life Insurance Co. of Virginia (Richmond, VA) **91919**
Life Insurance Co. of Virginia (Roanoke, VA) 92170
Life Savers Inc. (Las Piedras, PR) 78483
Life Savers Mfg. Inc. (Las Piedras, PR) 78484
Lifeco/American Express (Houston, TX) 86458
Lifeco/American Express Corp. (Houston, TX) 86459
Lika Southwest (Azle, TX) 83079
Lilly Research Laboratories (Shellman, GA) 67537
The Limited (Birmingham, AL) 55308; 55309
The Limited (Huntsville, AL) 55967
The Limited (Mobile, AL) 56199; 56200
The Limited (Tuscaloosa, AL) 56662
The Limited (Fort Smith, AR) 57069
The Limited (N Little Rock, AR) 57413; 57414
The Limited (Russellville, AR) 57584
The Limited (Altamonte Spg, FL) 58541
The Limited (Boca Raton, FL) 58718
The Limited (Boynton Beach, FL) 58785
The Limited (Bradenton, FL) 58833
The Limited (Clearwater, FL) 59029
The Limited (Daytona Beach, FL) 59191
The Limited (Fort Lauderdale, FL) 59524; 59525
The Limited (Fort Myers, FL) 59717
The Limited (Hialeah, FL) 59997
The Limited (Jacksonville, FL) 60366
The Limited (Lakeland, FL) 60745
The Limited (Mary Esther, FL) 61019
The Limited (Melbourne, FL) 61076
The Limited (Miami, FL) 61360; 61361
The Limited (Orange Park, FL) 61891
The Limited (Pensacola, FL) 62446
The Limited (Pompano Beach, FL) 62606
The Limited (Stuart, FL) 63174
The Limited (Tallahassee, FL) 63251
The Limited (Tampa, FL) 63486; 63487; 63488
The Limited (Atlanta, GA) 64647; 64648; 64649; 64650; 64651; 64652; 64653; 64654
The Limited (Duluth, GA) 66050; 66051
The Limited (Gainesville, GA) 66282
The Limited (Marietta, GA) 66819
The Limited (Morrow, GA) 67023
Limited the (Bowling Green, KY) 68147
Limited the (Florence, KY) 68319
Limited the (Lexington, KY) 68573
The Limited (Louisville, KY) 68865; 68866; 68867
The Limited (Alexandria, LA) 69392
The Limited (Baton Rouge, LA) 69580; 69581; 69582
The Limited (Bossier City, LA) 69723
The Limited (Gretna, LA) 69906
The Limited (Marrero, LA) 70230
The Limited (Metairie, LA) 70288
The Limited (Monroe, LA) 70358
The Limited (Shreveport, LA) 70750
The Limited (Slidell, LA) 70833
The Limited (Biloxi, MS) 72630
The Limited (Jackson, MS) 73018; 73019; 73020
The Limited (Ridgeland, MS) 73324
The Limited (Charlotte, NC) 74072; 74073; 74074; 74075
The Limited (Durham, NC) 74414
The Limited (Hickory, NC) 75087
The Limited (Raleigh, NC) 75926
The Limited (Oklahoma City, OK) 77424; 77425; 77426; 77427; 77428
The Limited (Tulsa, OK) 77993; 77994; 77995; 77996; 77997
The Limited (Charleston, SC) 78836; 78837; 78838
The Limited (Columbia, SC) 79047; 79048
The Limited (Greenville, SC) 79387; 79388
The Limited (Hilton Head Island, SC) 79518
Limited the (Chattanooga, TN) 80421
Limited (Knoxville, TN) 81226
Limited the (Memphis, TN) 81649; 81650
Limited (Nashville, TN) 82055; 82056; 82057
The Limited (Abilene, TX) 82444; 82445
The Limited (Amarillo, TX) 82563; 82564
The Limited (Arlington, TX) 82690; 82691
The Limited (Austin, TX) 82925; 82926; 82927
The Limited (Beaumont, TX) 83172
The Limited (Clute, TX) 83601
The Limited (Dallas, TX) 84201; 84202; 84203; 84204; 84205; 84206; 84207
The Limited (El Paso, TX) 84838; 84839; 84840; 84841
The Limited (Fort Worth, TX) 85172; 85173; 85174; 85175; 85176
The Limited (Galveston, TX) 85448; 85449
The Limited (Houston, TX) 86460; 86461; 86462; 86463; 86464; 86465; 86466; 86467; 86468; 86469; 86470; 86471
The Limited (Humble, TX) 87232
The Limited (Hurst, TX) 87279
The Limited (Irving, TX) 87368
The Limited (Lake Jackson, TX) 87582
The Limited (Lubbock, TX) 87770
The Limited (Mesquite, TX) 87976
The Limited (Plano, TX) 88580; 88581
The Limited (Richardson, TX) 88748
The Limited (San Antonio, TX) 89080; 89081; 89082; 89083; 89084; 89085
The Limited (Sherman, TX) 89410
The Limited (Tyler, TX) 89813
The Limited (Charleston, WV) 92765; 92766
Limited (Huntington, WV) 92884
The Limited Express (Birmingham, AL) 55310

The Limited Express (Huntsville, AL) 55968
The Limited Express (Mobile, AL) 56201
The Limited Express (Montgomery, AL) 56353
The Limited Express (Altamonte Spg, FL) 58542
The Limited Express (Clearwater, FL) 59030
The Limited Express (Miami, FL) 61362
The Limited Express (Naples, FL) 61638
The Limited Express (Pensacola, FL) 62447
The Limited Express (St Petersburg, FL) 62993
The Limited Express (Stuart, FL) 63175
The Limited Express (Tampa, FL) 63489
The Limited Express (Atlanta, GA) 64655; 64656; 64657; 64658; 64659
The Limited Express (Duluth, GA) 66052
The Limited Express (Kennesaw, GA) 66427
The Limited Express (Union City, GA) 67921
Limited Express (Florence, KY) 68320
Limited Express (Paducah, KY) 69207
The Limited Express (Kenner, LA) 69998
The Limited Express (Lafayette, LA) 70072
The Limited Express (Marrero, LA) 70231
The Limited Express (Metairie, LA) 70289
The Limited Express (Monroe, LA) 70359
The Limited Express (Slidell, LA) 70834
The Limited Express (Jackson, MS) 73021; 73022
The Limited Express (Ridgeland, MS) 73325
The Limited Express (Utica, MS) 73440
The Limited Express (Charlotte, NC) 74076; 74077
The Limited Express (Durham, NC) 74415
The Limited Express (Greensboro, NC) 74865
The Limited Express (Oklahoma City, OK) 77429; 77430
The Limited Express (Tulsa, OK) 77998; 77999; 78000
The Limited Express (Charleston, SC) 78839
The Limited Express (Columbia, SC) 79049
The Limited Express (Greenville, SC) 79389
Limited Express (Antioch, TN) 80172
Limited Express (Goodlettsville, TN) 80868
Limited Express the (Memphis, TN) 81651
Limited Express (Nashville, TN) 82058
The Limited Express (Arlington, TX) 82692
The Limited Express (Austin, TX) 82928
The Limited Express (Beaumont, TX) 83173
The Limited Express (Dallas, TX) 84208; 84209
The Limited Express (El Paso, TX) 84842; 84843
The Limited Express (Fort Worth, TX) 85177
The Limited Express (Houston, TX) 86472; 86473; 86474; 86475; 86476; 86477; 86478; 86479; 86480; 86481
The Limited Express (Humble, TX) 87233
The Limited Express (Irving, TX) 87369
The Limited Express (Plano, TX) 88582
The Limited Express (San Antonio, TX) 89086; 89087; 89088; 89089; 89090
The Limited Regional Office (Atlanta, GA) 64660
Lincoln (Jonesboro, AR) 57225
Lincoln Electric Co. (Fairfax, VA) 90792
Lincoln Electric Co. Harris Calorific Div. (Gainesville, GA) 66283
Lineage Home Furnishings (High Point, NC) 75150
Linens N Things (Little Rock, AR) 57292
Linens N Things (Altamonte Springs, FL) 58558
Linens N Things (Clearwater, FL) 59031
Linens 'n Things (Deerfield Beach, FL) 59283
Linens N Things (Orlando, FL) 62038; 62039
Linens N Things (Tampa, FL) 63490
Linens N Things (Charlotte, NC) 74078
Linens 'n Things (Morrisville, NC) 75668
Linens N Things (Raleigh Nc, NC) 75985
Linens N Things (Broken Arrow, OK) 76885
Linens 'n Things Cobb Place (Kennesaw, GA) 66428
Linens N Things Duluth Store (Duluth, GA) 66053
Linens N Things Inc. (Hallandale, FL) 59961
Linens 'n Things Kings Market (Roswell, GA) 67390
Linens 'n Things Marietta Stor (Marietta, GA) 66820
Linens 'n Things Sandy Springs (Atlanta, GA) 64661
Linens 'n Things Shannon Mall (Union City, GA) 67922
Linens 'n Things Snellville St (Snellville, GA) 67601
Linens 'n Things Southlake/She (Morrow, GA) 67024
Linens 'n Things Stone Mountai (Stone Mountain, GA) 67710; 67711
Linvatec (Largo, FL) 60844
Linvatec Corp. (Largo, FL) 60845
Liqui Dri Foods Inc. (Louisville, KY) 68868; 68869
Liquid Carbonic Carbon Dioxide Corp. (Loudon, TN) 81352
Liquid Carbonic Carbon Dioxide Corp. (Hopewell, VA) 91161
Liquid Carbonic Specialty Gas Corp. (Orlando, FL) 62040
Liquid Carbonic Specialty Gas Corp. (Gonzales, LA) 69892
Liquid Carbonic Specialty Gas Corp. (Pasadena, TX) 88432
Lithium Corp. of America (Bessemer City, NC) 73689
Lithium Corp. of America FMC Lithium Div. (Bessemer City, NC) 73690
Lithonia Lighting Co. (Conyers, GA) 65689
Little Giant Pump Co. (Oklahoma City, OK) 77431
Litton Ingalls Shipbuilding Div. (Pascagoula, MS) 73264
Litton Clifton Precision (Blacksburg, VA) 90449
Litton Clifton Precision South (Murphy, NC) 75705
Litton Computer Services-Eastern Regional Data Center (Reston, VA) 91713
Litton Industrial Unit Handling Systems Div. (Hebron, KY) 68430
Litton Industrial Automation Disc Abrasives Grinders (Calhoun, GA) 65468
Litton Industrial Automation Disc Grinders & Abrasives (Calhoun, GA) 65469
Litton Industrial Automation Systems Automated Systems Div. (Hebron, KY) 68431
Litton Industrial Automation Systems Engineered Systems Div. (Florence, KY) 68321
Litton Industrial Automation Systems Inc. (Hebron, KY) 68432
Litton Industrial Automation Systems Inc. (Disc Grinders & Abrasives) (Calhoun, GA) 65470
Litton Industrial Automation Systems (Unit Handling Systems) (Hebron, KY) 68433
Litton Industrial Contracting (Florence, KY) 68322
Litton Industrial Services (Erlanger, KY) 68299
Litton Industries Advanced Circuit Design Div. (Austin, TX) 82929
Litton Industries C. Plath North American Div. (Annapolis, MD) 71015
Litton Industries Integrated Systems Div. (Hebron, KY) 68434
Litton Industries Poly-Scientific Div. (Blacksburg, VA) 90450
Litton Industries Disc Grinders & Abrasives Div. (Calhoun, GA) 65471
Litton Industries, Inc. Amercom Div. (College Park, MD) 71563
Litton Industries, Inc. Laser Systems (Apopka, FL) 58573
Litton Material Handling Systems (Hebron, KY) 68435
Litton UHS Conveyor Systems (Hebron, KY) 68436
Liz Claiborne (Boaz, AL) 55470
Liz Claiborne Inc. (Atlanta, GA) 64662
Ll & E Petroleum Mtg. Inc. (Saraland, AL) 56517
LL& E Petroleum Marketing , Inc. (New Orleans, LA) 70514
LL&E Gas Marketing, Inc. (New Orleans, LA) 70515
Ll&E Mobile River Terminal (Mobile, AL) 56202
Ll&E Petroleum Marketing Inc. Mobile Refinery (Saraland, AL) 56518
Lockheed Abilene Facility (Abilene, TX) 82446
Lockheed Aeromod Center, Inc. (Greenville, SC) 79390
Lockheed Aeromod Centers Inc. (Greenville, SC) 79391
Lockheed Aeronautical Sys. Co. Charleston Adhesive Bond Plan (Charleston, SC) 78840
Lockheed Aeronautical Systems Co. (Marietta, GA) 66821
Lockheed Aeronautical Systems Co. (Charleston, SC) 78841
Lockheed Aeronautical Systems Co. (Clarksburg, WV) 92810
Lockheed Aeronautical Systems Co.-Charleston (Charleston, SC) 78842
Lockheed Aeronautical Systems Co.-Georgia (Afp 6) (Marietta, GA) 66822
Lockheed Corp. Austin Div. (Austin, TX) 82930
Lockheed Engineering & Sciences Co. (Houston, TX) 86482
Lockheed Engineering & Services Co., Inc. (Houston, TX) 86483
Lockheed Environmental Systems & Technologies Co. (Houston, TX) 86484; 86485
Lockheed Fort Worth Co. (Fort Worth, TX) 85178; 85179
Lockheed-Latin America (Atlanta, GA) 64663
Lockheed Missiles & Space Co. Austin Div. (Austin, TX) 82931
Lockheed Space Operations Co. (Titusville, FL) 63695
Lockheed Support Systems, Inc. (Arlington, TX) 82693; 82694; 82695
Lockheed Systems Corp. Lasc-Georgia Div. (Meridian, MS) 73170
Lockheed Technical Operations (Greentbelt, MD) 71880
Lockwood National Bank of Houston (Deer Park, TX) 84552
Lockwood National Bank of Houston (Friendswood, TX) 85402
Lockwood National Bank of Houston (Galena Park, TX) 85434
Lockwood National Bank of Houston (Houston, TX) 86486; 86487; 86488; 86489; 86490
Lockwood National Bank of Houston (Pasadena, TX) 88433; 88434
Logan Guildepath (Louisville, KY) 68870
Logistics Data System (Irving, TX) 87370
Logistics Management System (Greensboro, NC) 74866
Lone Star Gas Co. (Durant, OK) 77000
Lone Star Gas Co. (Idabel, OK) 77142
Lone Star Gas Co. (Marietta, OK) 77183
Lone Star Gas Co. (Pauls Valley, OK) 77690
Lone Star Gas Co. (Purcell, OK) 77749
Lone Star Gas Co. (Tulsa, OK) 78001
Lone Star Gas Co. (Abilene, TX) 82447
Lone Star Gas Co. (Archer City, TX) 82627
Lone Star Gas Co. (Arlington, TX) 82696; 82697
Lone Star Gas Co. (Athens, TX) 82790; 82791
Lone Star Gas Co. (Ballinger, TX) 83086; 83087; 83088
Lone Star Gas Co. (Bedford, TX) 83244
Lone Star Gas Co. (Belton, TX) 83277
Lone Star Gas Co. (Bryan, TX) 83397
Lone Star Gas Co. (Calvert, TX) 83433
Lone Star Gas Co. (Cameron, TX) 83436
Lone Star Gas Co. (Carrollton, TX) 83481
Lone Star Gas Co. (Clarksville, TX) 83568
Lone Star Gas Co. (Clifton, TX) 83595
Lone Star Gas Co. (Coleman, TX) 83606
Lone Star Gas Co. (Collinsville, TX) 83635
Lone Star Gas Co. (Comanche, TX) 83642
Lone Star Gas Co. (Copperas Cove, TX) 83693
Lone Star Gas Co. (Corsicana, TX) 83783
Lone Star Gas Co. (Dallas, TX) 84210
Lone Star Gas Co. (Denton, TX) 84620
Lone Star Gas Co. (Duncanville, TX) 84700
Lone Star Gas Co. (Eastland, TX) 84729
Lone Star Gas Co. (Electra, TX) 84984
Lone Star Gas Co. (Ennis, TX) 84994
Lone Star Gas Co. (Fort Worth, TX) 85180; 85181
Lone Star Gas Co. (Fredericksbg, TX) 85372
Lone Star Gas Co. (Garland, TX) 85501
Lone Star Gas Co. (Greenville, TX) 85673
Lone Star Gas Co. (Hamilton, TX) 85694
Lone Star Gas Co. (Hearne, TX) 85723
Lone Star Gas Co. (Henrietta, TX) 85736
Lone Star Gas Co. (Houston, TX) 86491; 86492
Lone Star Gas Co. (Iowa Park, TX) 87306
Lone Star Gas Co. (Irving, TX) 87371; 87372
Lone Star Gas Co. (Katy, TX) 87450
Lone Star Gas Co. (Killeen, TX) 87517
Lone Star Gas Co. (Lampasas, TX) 87592
Lone Star Gas Co. (Lancaster, TX) 87600
Lone Star Gas Co. (Longview, TX) 87720
Lone Star Gas Co. (Marlin, TX) 87850
Lone Star Gas Co. (Memphis, TX) 87948
Lone Star Gas Co. (Mesquite, TX) 87977
Lone Star Gas Co. (Midland, TX) 88043; 88044
Lone Star Gas Co. (Midlothian, TX) 88101
Lone Star Gas Co. (Midway, TX) 88103
Lone Star Gas Co. (Monahans, TX) 88140
Lone Star Gas Co. (Nocona, TX) 88228
Lone Star Gas Co. (Normangee, TX) 88231
Lone Star Gas Co. (North Zulch, TX) 88232
Lone Star Gas Co. (Olney, TX) 88294; 88295
Lone Star Gas Co. (Paducah, TX) 88338
Lone Star Gas Co. (Paris, TX) 88371
Lone Star Gas Co. (Plano, TX) 88583
Lone Star Gas Co. (Refugio, TX) 88716
Lone Star Gas Co. (Rockdale, TX) 88817
Lone Star Gas Co. (San Angelo, TX) 88882
Lone Star Gas Co. (Santa Anna, TX) 89349
Lone Star Gas Co. (Sherman, TX) 89411
Lone Star Gas Co. (Snyder, TX) 89446; 89447
Lone Star Gas Co. (Sonora, TX) 89456
Lone Star Gas Co. (Springtown, TX) 89497
Lone Star Gas Co. (Stephenville, TX) 89518; 89519
Lone Star Gas Co. (Sweetwater, TX) 89586
Lone Star Gas Co. (Temple, TX) 89622
Lone Star Gas Co. (Vernon, TX) 89867
Lone Star Gas Co. (Victoria, TX) 89896
Lone Star Gas Co. (Waco, TX) 89948
Lone Star Gas Co. (Waxahachie, TX) 89996
Lone Star Gas Co. (Wellington, TX) 90030
Lone Star Gas Co. (West, TX) 90043
Lone Star Gas Co. (Whitesboro, TX) 90060
Lone Star Gas Co. (Wichita Falls, TX) 90079; 90080
Lone Star Gas Co. Trans Division (Iowa Park, TX) 87307
Lone Star Gas Co. Texas Inc. (Cisco, TX) 83565
Lone Star Gas Co. Transmissi (Waco, TX) 89949
Lone Star Industries Inc. (Pryor, OK) 77741
Lone Star Industries Inc. (Maryneal, TX) 87878
Lone Star Lead Construction (Houston, TX) 86493
Lone Star Lead Construction Co. Inc. (Houston, TX) 86494
Lone Star Lead Construction Corp. (Houston, TX) 86495
Long Mile Rubber Co. (Miami, FL) 61363
Long Mile Rubber Co. (Spartanburg, SC) 79918
Long Mile Rubber Co. (Dallas, TX) 84211
Longs Drug Store (Belzoni, MS) 72614
Longs Drug Store (Knoxville, TN) 81227
Longs Drugs (Baxley, GA) 65380
Loral Advanced Projects (Reston, VA) 91714
Loral AeroSys (Lanham Seabrook, MD) 72060
Loral AeroSys (Seabrook, MD) 72366
Loral American Beryllium (Tallevast, FL) 63292
Loral American Beryllium Corp. (Tallevast, FL) 63293
Loral Data Systems (Sarasota, FL) 62841
Loral Engineered Fabrics (Rockmart, GA) 67332
Loral Fairchild Corp. Loral Data Systems Div. (Sarasota, FL) 62842
Loral Information Display Systems (Atlanta, GA) 64664
Loral Instrumentation (Orlando, FL) 62041
Loral Space Information Stysems (Houston, TX) 86496
Loral Space Information Systems (Houston, TX) 86497
Loral Vought Stytems (Dallas, TX) 84212
Loral Vought Systems (Camden, AR) 56836
Loral Vought Systems (Grand Prairie, TX) 85623
Loral Vought Systems Corp. Missiles & Electronics Div. (Camden, AR) 56837
Lord & Taylor (Washington, DC) 58312
Lord & Taylor (Falls Church, VA) 90858
Lorillard Inc. (Huntsville, AL) 55969
Lorillard Inc. (Statesboro, GA) 67639
Lorillard Inc. (Lexington, KY) 68574
Lorillard Inc. (Baton Rouge, LA) 69583
Lorillard Inc. (Greensboro, NC) 74867
Lorillard Inc. (Tulsa, OK) 78002
Lorillard Inc. (Virginia Beach, VA) 92490
Lorillard Tobacco Co. (Greensboro, NC) 74868
Louie Glass Co. Inc. (Weston, WV) 93107
Louis Rich Co. (Newberry, SC) 79727
Louisiana Coca-Cola Bottling Co. (New Orleans, LA) 70516
Louisiana Coca-Cola Bottling Co. Ltd. (Gretna, LA) 69907
Louisiana Coca-Cola Bottling Co. Ltd. (New Orleans, LA) 70517
Louisiana Land & Exploratio (Houma, LA) 69960
Louisiana Land & Exploratio (Oklahoma City, OK) 77432
Louisiana Land & Exploration (Washington, DC) 58313
Louisiana Land & Exploration (New Orleans, LA) **70518**
Louisiana Land & Exploration Houston Div. (Houston, TX) 86498

Marathon Petroleum Co. (Tampa, FL) 63491
Marathon Petroleum Co. (Charleston, SC) 78843
Marathon Petroleum Co. (Houston, TX) 86514
Marathon Petroleum Co. (Midland, TX) 88047
Marathon Petroleum Co. (Texas City, TX) 89727
Marathon Petroleum Co. Southern (Chamblee, GA) 65534
Marathon Pipeline Co. (Zachary, LA) 70987
Marathon Pipeline Co. (Pasadena, TX) 88439
Marathon Service Station (London, KY) 68663
Marathon Service Station (Louisville, KY) 68880
Maremont Corp. (Chickasha, OK) 76929
Maremont Corp. (Brentwood, TN) 80231
Maremont Corp. (Loudon, TN) 81353
Maremont Corp. (Pulaski, TN) 82244
Maremont Corp. (Ripley, TN) 82262
Maremont Corp. Pulaski Plant (Pulaski, TN) 82245
Maremont Exhaust Products, Inc. (Loudon, TN) 81354
Maremont Exhaust System (Loudon, TN) 81355
Maremont Exhaust Systems (Loudon, TN) 81356
Maremount Corp. Shock Absorber (Chickasha, OK) 76930
Marine Engineering & Production (Pascagoula, MS) 73265
Marine Group (Murfreesboro, TN) 81857
Marine Group Inc. (Murfreesboro, TN) 81858; 81859
Marine Terminal Shipping Co. (Enid, OK) 77057
Mark Vii Transportation (Jacksonville, FL) 60371; 60372
Marketing Services (Dalton, GA) 65786
Marriott/Fairfield Inn (Washington, DC) 58317
Marriott Hotels (Washington, DC) 58318; 58319
Marriott Hotels (Bethesda, MD) 71400; 71401
Marriott Hotels (Gaithersburg, MD) 71789
Marriott Hotels (Salem, VA) 92217
Marriott Hotels, Resorts, & Suites (Washington, DC) 58320; 58321
Marriott Hotels, Resorts Suites (Atlanta, GA) 64670; 64671; 64672; 64673; 64674
Marriott Hotels, Resorts Suites (College Park, GA) 65589
Marriott Hotels, Resorts Suites (Norcross, GA) 67145
Marriott Hotels Resorts Suites (Bethesda, MD) 71402; 71403
Marriott Hotels Resorts Suites (Gaithersburg, MD) 71790
Marriott Hotels Resorts Suites (Chattanooga, TN) 80422
Marriott International (Washington, DC) **58322**
Marriott International, Inc. (Washington, DC) 58323
Marriott Management Services (Atlanta, GA) 64675
Marriott Ownership Resorts (Kissimmee, FL) 60592
Marriott Senior Living Service (Bethesda, MD) 71404; 71405
Marshall Field (Georgetown, KY) 68385
Marshall & Ilsley Trust Com (Naples, FL) 61640
Marshall & Ilsley Trust Co. of Florida (Naples, FL) 61641
Marshalls (Birmingham, AL) 55313
Marshalls (Daytona Beach, FL) 59192
Marshalls (Atlanta, GA) 64676; 64677
Marshalls (Austell, GA) 65355
Marshalls (Decatur, GA) 65855
Marshalls (Duluth, GA) 66055
Marshalls (Kennesaw, GA) 66429
Marshalls (Marietta, GA) 66823
Marshalls (Morrow, GA) 67026
Marshalls (Stone Mountain, GA) 67712; 67713
Marshalls (Charleston, SC) 78844
Marshalls (Carrollton, TX) 83482
Marshalls (Colorado City, TX) 83638
Marshalls (Fort Worth, TX) 85183
Marshalls (San Antonio, TX) 89091
Marshalls (Tyler, TX) 89814
Marshalls Department Store (Delray Beach, FL) 59321
Marshalls Department Store (Lakeland, FL) 60747
Marshalls Department Store (Melbourne, FL) 61077
Marshalls Department Store (Sarasota, FL) 62843
Marshalls Department Store (St Petersburg, FL) 62994
Marshalls Department Store (Tampa, FL) 63492
Marshalls Department Store (Gretna, LA) 69908
Marshalls Department Store (Lafayette, LA) 70074
Marshalls Department Store (New Orleans, LA) 70526
Marshalls Department Store (Gilmer, TX) 85578
Marshalls Department Store (Pittsburg, TX) 88518
Marshalls Dept Str (Humble, TX) 87234
Marshalls Inc. (Miami, FL) 61365
Marshalls Inc. (Pompano Beach, FL) 62607
Marshalls Inc. (Tulsa, OK) 78012
Marshalls Inc. (Houston, TX) 86515; 86516
Marshalls Inc. (Hurst, TX) 87280
Marshalls Inc. (Mesquite, TX) 87978
Marshalls Inc. (Sugar Land, TX) 89534
Marshalls Incorporation (Tulsa, OK) 78013
Martin Marietta (Bethesda, MD) **71406**
Martin Marietta Milan Army Ammunition Plant (Milan, TN) 81770
Martin Marietta Oak Ridge Y-12 Plant Dept. of Energy (Oak Ridge, TN) 82194
Martin Marietta Paducah Gaseous Diffusion Plant (Paducah, KY) 69208
Martin Marietta US Doe Oak Ridge Y-12 Palnt (Oak Ridge, TN) 82195
Martin Marietta US Doe Y-12 Plant (Oak Ridge, TN) 82196
Martin Marietta Aero & Naval Systems (Baltimore, MD) 71183; 71184
Martin Marietta Aggregates (Atlanta, GA) 64678
Martin Marietta Aggregates (Auburn, GA) 65310
Martin Marietta Aggregates (Leesburg, GA) 66549
Martin Marietta Aggregates (Charlotte, NC) 74079; 74080
Martin Marietta Aggregates (Hickory, NC) 75088
Martin Marietta Aggregates (Jamestown, NC) 75240
Martin Marietta Aggregates (Lemon Springs, NC) 75361
Martin Marietta Aggregates (Maysville, NC) 75542
Martin Marietta Aggregates (New Bern, NC) 75729
Martin Marietta Aggregates (Raleigh, NC) 75927
Martin Marietta Aggregates (West Columbia, SC) 80098
Martin Marietta Aggreghates Fo (Suwanee, GA) 67745
Martin Marietta Air Traffic Systems (Washington, DC) 58324
Martin Marietta Corp. (Bethesda, MD) 71407
Martin Marietta Corp. (Hampton, VA) 91044
Martin Marietta Corp. (North Garden, VA) 91598
Martin Marietta Corp. Air Traff (Washington, DC) 58325
Martin Marietta Corp. Electonic Systems Co. (Orlando, FL) 62044
Martin Marietta Corp. En (Washington, DC) 58326
Martin Marietta Corp. Inc. (Lanham, MD) 72051
Martin Marietta Corp. Librar (Baltimore, MD) 71185
Martin Marietta Corp. Ov (Bethesda, MD) 71408
Martin Marietta Corp. Services Inc. (Landover, MD) 72023
Martin Marietta Corp. Srvcs Inc. (Rockville, MD) 72294
Martin Marietta Corp. Washingto (Washington, DC) 58327
Martin Marietta Electronic Systems (Orlando, FL) 62045
Martin Marietta Electronics Information & Missile Systems (Ocala, FL) 61805
Martin Marietta Electronics & Missiles (Orlando, FL) 62046
Martin Marietta Electronics Systems Co. (Orlando, FL) 62047
Martin Marietta Energy Systems, Inc. (Oak Ridge, TN) 82197
Martin Marietta Information Systems (Bethesda, MD) 71409
Martin Marietta Laboratories (Baltimore, MD) 71186
Martin Marietta Magnesia (Knoxville, TN) 81228
Martin Marietta Magnesia Specialities, Inc. (Cockeysville Hunt Valley, MD) 71557
Martin Marietta Manned Space Systems (New Orleans, LA) 70527
Martin Marietta Materials Group (Raleigh, NC) 75928
Martin Marietta Missile Systems (Orlando, FL) 62048; 62049
Martin Marietta Missile Systems Building 7 Ocala (Ocala, FL) 61806
Martin Marietta Missile Systems Co. (Orlando, FL) 62050
Martin Marietta Ocala Operations (Ocala, FL) 61807
Martin Marietta Ocean Systems Operations (Glen Burnie, MD) 71844
Martin Marietta Ordnance Systems, Inc. (Orlando, FL) 62051
Martin Marietta Space Launch Systems (Cape Canaveral, FL) 58915
Martin Marietta Speciality Co. US Doe Pinellas Plant (Largo, FL) 60846
Martin Marietta Specialty Components, Inc. (Largo, FL) 60847
Martin Marietta Technologies Inc. (Orlando, FL) 62052
Mary Kay Cos (Kinards, SC) 79549
Mary Kay Cos Ind Sales Dir (Copperas Cove, TX) 83694
Mary Kay Cosemetics (West Palm Beach, FL) 63882
Mary Kay Cosemtics Indep Sales (Morrow, GA) 67027
Mary Kay Cosm (Tampa, FL) 63493
Mary Kay Cosmenics (Windsor, NC) 76657
Mary Kay Cosmestics (Fort Lauderdale, FL) 59529
Mary Kay Cosmet Consultants (Ellisville, MS) 72754
Mary Kay Cosmet Ind Sls Dir (Longwood, FL) 60933
Mary Kay Cosmet Indep Sales (Harlingen, TX) 85705
Mary Kay Cosmet Independ Sl (Hobart, OK) 77133
Mary Kay Cosmet Independent (Big Spring, TX) 83290
Mary Kay Cosmetic (Radcliff, KY) 69240
Mary Kay Cosmetic (Midland, TX) 88048
Mary Kay Cosmetic Director (Gainesville, TX) 85423
Mary Kay Cosmetic Indpnt Sl (Starke, FL) 63149
Mary Kay Cosmetics (Alexander City, AL) 54975
Mary Kay Cosmetics (Auburn, AL) 55065
Mary Kay Cosmetics (Birmingham, AL) 55314; 55315; 55316; 55317; 55318
Mary Kay Cosmetics (Demopolis, AL) 55617
Mary Kay Cosmetics (Enterprise, AL) 55688
Mary Kay Cosmetics (Hartselle, AL) 55858
Mary Kay Cosmetics (Huntsville, AL) 55970; 55971
Mary Kay Cosmetics (Mobile, AL) 56203; 56204
Mary Kay Cosmetics (Quinton, AL) 56496
Mary Kay Cosmetics (Talladega, AL) 56595; 56596
Mary Kay Cosmetics (Tuscaloosa, AL) 56663
Mary Kay Cosmetics (Bull Shoals, AR) 56825
Mary Kay Cosmetics (Mountainburg, AR) 57397
Mary Kay Cosmetics (North Little Rock, AR) 57468
Mary Kay Cosmetics (Pine Bluff, AR) 57525
Mary Kay Cosmetics (Thornton, AR) 57683
Mary Kay Cosmetics (Van Buren, AR) 57690
Mary Kay Cosmetics (Bridgeville, DE) 57753
Mary Kay Cosmetics (Dover, DE) 57792
Mary Kay Cosmetics (Boca Raton, FL) 58720
Mary Kay Cosmetics (Brooksville, FL) 58892
Mary Kay Cosmetics (Clearwater, FL) 59033
Mary Kay Cosmetics (Crystal River, FL) 59134
Mary Kay Cosmetics (Fort Myers, FL) 59718
Mary Kay Cosmetics (Fort Walton Beach, FL) 59830
Mary Kay Cosmetics (Gainesville, FL) 59892
Mary Kay Cosmetics (Hialeah, FL) 59998
Mary Kay Cosmetics (Hollywood, FL) 60075
Mary Kay Cosmetics (Homestead, FL) 60117
Mary Kay Cosmetics (Indian Rocks, FL) 60139
Mary Kay Cosmetics (Jensen Beach, FL) 60527
Mary Kay Cosmetics (Lake Worth, FL) 60680; 60681
Mary Kay Cosmetics (Lakeland, FL) 60748
Mary Kay Cosmetics (Longwood, FL) 60934
Mary Kay Cosmetics (Maitland, FL) 60981
Mary Kay Cosmetics (Melbourne, FL) 61078
Mary Kay Cosmetics (Miami, FL) 61366; 61367; 61368; 61369
Mary Kay Cosmetics (Naples, FL) 61642
Mary Kay Cosmetics (Niceville, FL) 61711
Mary Kay Cosmetics (Ocala, FL) 61808
Mary Kay Cosmetics (Orlando, FL) 62053; 62054
Mary Kay Cosmetics (Panama City, FL) 62332
Mary Kay Cosmetics (Pensacola, FL) 62448
Mary Kay Cosmetics (Pompano Beach, FL) 62608; 62609
Mary Kay Cosmetics (Ponte Vedra Beach, FL) 62651
Mary Kay Cosmetics (Port Richey, FL) 62678
Mary Kay Cosmetics (Punta Gorda, FL) 62711
Mary Kay Cosmetics (Quincy, FL) 62730
Mary Kay Cosmetics (Rotonda West, FL) 62751
Mary Kay Cosmetics (Sarasota, FL) 62844
Mary Kay Cosmetics (Sebring, FL) 62890
Mary Kay Cosmetics (Shalimar, FL) 62913
Mary Kay Cosmetics (Tampa, FL) 63494
Mary Kay Cosmetics (West Palm Beach, FL) 63883
Mary Kay Cosmetics (Winter Haven, FL) 63945
Mary Kay Cosmetics (Winter Springs, FL) 64001
Mary Kay Cosmetics (Andersonville, GA) 64148
Mary Kay Cosmetics (Buford, GA) 65438
Mary Kay Cosmetics (Duluth, GA) 66056
Mary Kay Cosmetics (Benton, KY) 68125
Mary Kay Cosmetics (Danville, KY) 68260
Mary Kay Cosmetics (Elizabethtown, KY) 68287
Mary Kay Cosmetics (Hodgenville, KY) 68469; 68470
Mary Kay Cosmetics (Hopkinsville, KY) 68481
Mary Kay Cosmetics (Louisville, KY) 68881
Mary Kay Cosmetics (Shepherdsville, KY) 69282
Mary Kay Cosmetics (Somerset, KY) 69296
Mary Kay Cosmetics (Baton Rouge, LA) 69587
Mary Kay Cosmetics (Lafayette, LA) 70075
Mary Kay Cosmetics (Monroe, LA) 70360
Mary Kay Cosmetics (New Iberia, LA) 70412
Mary Kay Cosmetics (New Orleans, LA) 70528
Mary Kay Cosmetics (Pineville, LA) 70623
Mary Kay Cosmetics (Robeline, LA) 70668
Mary Kay Cosmetics (Zachary, LA) 70988
Mary Kay Cosmetics (Baltimore, MD) 71187
Mary Kay Cosmetics (Bethesda, MD) 71410
Mary Kay Cosmetics (Ellicott City, MD) 71678
Mary Kay Cosmetics (Hagerstown, MD) 71884
Mary Kay Cosmetics (Hollywood, MD) 71922
Mary Kay Cosmetics (Hyattsville, MD) 71964
Mary Kay Cosmetics (Ocean City, MD) 72161
Mary Kay Cosmetics (Taneytown, MD) 72490
Mary Kay Cosmetics (Flora, MS) 72770
Mary Kay Cosmetics (Jackson, MS) 73024
Mary Kay Cosmetics (Southaven, MS) 73353
Mary Kay Cosmetics (Charlotte, NC) 74081
Mary Kay Cosmetics (Fayetteville, NC) 74564
Mary Kay Cosmetics (Morehead City, NC) 75625
Mary Kay Cosmetics (Pineville, NC) 75818
Mary Kay Cosmetics (Raleigh, NC) 75929; 75930
Mary Kay Cosmetics (Roanoke Rapids, NC) 76037
Mary Kay Cosmetics (Winston Salem, NC) 76675
Mary Kay Cosmetics (Altus, OK) 76794
Mary Kay Cosmetics (Broken Bow, OK) 76892
Mary Kay Cosmetics (Chickasha, OK) 76931
Mary Kay Cosmetics (Clinton, OK) 76965
Mary Kay Cosmetics (Lawton, OK) 77165
Mary Kay Cosmetics (Miami, OK) 77206
Mary Kay Cosmetics (Oklahoma City, OK) 77435
Mary Kay Cosmetics (Ponca City, OK) 77707
Mary Kay Cosmetics (Tulsa, OK) 78014; 78015
Mary Kay Cosmetics (Woodward, OK) 78261
Mary Kay Cosmetics (Charleston, SC) 78845
Mary Kay Cosmetics (Chesnee, SC) 78930
Mary Kay Cosmetics (Columbia, SC) 79051; 79052; 79053; 79054
Mary Kay Cosmetics (Greenville, SC) 79393
Mary Kay Cosmetics (North Myrtle Beach, SC) 79763
Mary Kay Cosmetics (Taylors, SC) 80038
Mary Kay Cosmetics (Bruceton, TN) 80262
Mary Kay Cosmetics (Delano, TN) 80730
Mary Kay Cosmetics (Knoxville, TN) 81229
Mary Kay Cosmetics (Memphis, TN) 81656
Mary Kay Cosmetics (Strawberry Plains, TN) 82363
Mary Kay Cosmetics (Arlington, TX) 82698; 82699
Mary Kay Cosmetics (Austin, TX) 82932; 82933; 82934
Mary Kay Cosmetics (Beaumont, TX) 83175
Mary Kay Cosmetics (Colleyville, TX) 83629
Mary Kay Cosmetics (Dallas, TX) **84217**; 84218; 84219; 84220
Mary Kay Cosmetics (El Paso, TX) 84846; 84847
Mary Kay Cosmetics (Fort Worth, TX) 85184; 85185
Mary Kay Cosmetics (Garland, TX) 85506; 85507
Mary Kay Cosmetics (Houston, TX) 86517; 86518; 86519
Mary Kay Cosmetics (Hurst, TX) 87281
Mary Kay Cosmetics (Irving, TX) 87373
Mary Kay Cosmetics (Kerrville, TX) 87475
Mary Kay Cosmetics (La Marque, TX) 87544
Mary Kay Cosmetics (Levelland, TX) 87639
Mary Kay Cosmetics (Lewisville, TX) 87653
Mary Kay Cosmetics (Livingston, TX) 87687
Mary Kay Cosmetics (Lubbock, TX) 87772
Mary Kay Cosmetics (Lufkin, TX) 87810
Mary Kay Cosmetics (Missouri City, TX) 88129

McDonald's Hamburgers (Colmar Manor, MD) 71571
McDonald's Hamburgers (Coral Hills, MD) 71609
McDonald's Hamburgers (Damascus, MD) 71640
McDonald's Hamburgers (Derwood, MD) 71646
McDonald's Hamburgers (Forestville, MD) 71692
McDonald's Hamburgers (Forrest Heights, MD) 71702
McDonald's Hamburgers (Frederick, MD) 71732
McDonald's Hamburgers (Gaithersburg, MD) 71794; 71795; 71796; 71797
McDonald's Hamburgers (Germantown, MD) 71827
McDonald's Hamburgers (Glen Burnie, MD) 71846; 71847
McDonald's Hamburgers (Hyattsville, MD) 71966; 71967
McDonald's Hamburgers (Kensington, MD) 71998
McDonald's Hamburgers (La Plata, MD) 72006
McDonald's Hamburgers (Landover, MD) 72025; 72026
McDonald's Hamburgers (Landover Hill, MD) 72039
McDonald's Hamburgers (Lanham, MD) 72053
McDonald's Hamburgers (Laurel, MD) 72080
McDonald's Hamburgers (Ocean City, MD) 72162
McDonald's Hamburgers (Oxon Hill, MD) 72198; 72199; 72200; 72201; 72202; 72203
McDonald's Hamburgers (Pocomoke City, MD) 72222
McDonald's Hamburgers (Poolesville, MD) 72225
McDonald's Hamburgers (Riverdale, MD) 72251; 72252
McDonald's Hamburgers (Rockville, MD) 72297
McDonald's Hamburgers (Salisbury, MD) 72349; 72350
McDonald's Hamburgers (Severna Park, MD) 72375
McDonald's Hamburgers (Silver Spring, MD) 72415; 72416; 72417
McDonald's Hamburgers (South Capital Heights, MD) 72456
McDonald's Hamburgers (Suitland, MD) 72477; 72478
McDonald's Hamburgers (Takoma Park, MD) 72489
McDonald's Hamburgers (Waldorf, MD) 72531; 72532
McDonalds Hamburgers (Fayetteville, NC) 74565; 74566
McDonalds Hamburgers (Goldsboro, NC) 74725
McDonalds Hamburgers (Edmond, OK) 77008
McDonalds Hamburgers (Glenpool, OK) 77087
McDonalds Hamburgers (Mustang, OK) 77238
McDonalds Hamburgers (Norman, OK) 77261
McDonalds Hamburgers (Oklahoma City, OK) 77437; 77438; 77439
McDonalds Hamburgers (Owasso, OK) 77685
McDonalds Hamburgers (Yukon, OK) 78277
McDonald's Hamburgers (Chattanooga, TN) 80426; 80427; 80428; 80429; 80430; 80431; 80432; 80433; 80434
McDonald's Hamburgers (Clarksville, TN) 80557
McDonald's Hamburgers (Cleveland, TN) 80594
McDonald's Hamburgers (Cookeville, TN) 80661
McDonald's Hamburgers (Fort Oglethorpe, TN) 80801
McDonald's Hamburgers (Jackson, TN) 80990
McDonald's Hamburgers (Kingsport, TN) 81111
McDonald's Hamburgers (Lawrenceburg, TN) 81291
McDonald's Hamburgers (Manchester, TN) 81393
McDonald's Hamburgers (Nashville, TN) 82061
McDonald's Hamburgers (Union City, TN) 82386
McDonalds Hamburgers (Abilene, TX) 82448
McDonalds Hamburgers (Garland, TX) 85508
McDonalds Hamburgers (Texarkana, TX) 89688; 89689
McDonald's Hamburgers (Arlington, VA) 90358
McDonald's Hamburgers (Belle Haven, VA) 90428
McDonald's Hamburgers (Charlottesville, VA) 90543
McDonald's Hamburgers (Chester, VA) 90620
McDonald's Hamburgers (Cross Junction, VA) 90670
McDonald's Hamburgers (Great Falls, VA) 91000
McDonald's Hamburgers (Hampton, VA) 91045
McDonald's Hamburgers (Leesburg, VA) 91195
McDonald's Hamburgers (Newport News, VA) 91473
McDonald's Hamburgers (Norton, VA) 91605
McDonald's Hamburgers (Richmond, VA) 91928; 91929
McDonald's Hamburgers (Williamsburg, VA) 92576
McDonald's Hamburgers (Barboursville, WV) 92671
McDonald's Hamburgers (Ripley, WV) 93028
McDonald's Hamburgers Office (Salem, VA) 92218
McDonald's Hamburgers Office (Proctor, WV) 93014
McDonalds of King (King, NC) 75290
McDonalds of Mckinney (Mc Kinney, TX) 87916
McDonalds of Miners Plaza (Fort Myers, FL) 59722
McDonalds No 6574 (Panama City, FL) 62334
McDonalds Office (Birmingham, AL) 55320
McDonalds Office (West Palm Beach, FL) 63885
McDonalds Ofifce (Midland, TX) 88049
McDonalds of Plano (Plano, TX) 88587
McDonalds of Porter (Porter, TX) 88681
McDonalds of Red Bluff (Pasadena, TX) 88440
McDonalds Restaurant (Alabaster, AL) 54955
McDonalds Restaurant (Texarkana, AR) 57677
McDonald's Restaurant (Davenport, FL) 59151
McDonalds Restaurant (Destin, FL) 59345
McDonalds Restaurant (Fort Lauderdale, FL) 59535; 59536; 59537
McDonalds Restaurant (Miami, FL) 61371; 61372
McDonalds Restaurant (Pompano Beach, FL) 62611
McDonald's Restaurant (Atlanta, GA) 64693
McDonald's Restaurant (Buford, GA) 65439
McDonald's Restaurant (Peachtree Cit, GA) 67238
McDonalds Restaurant (Columbus, MS) 72718; 72719
McDonalds Restaurant (Yazoo City, MS) 73504
McDonalds Restaurant (Taylorsville, NC) 76369
McDonalds Restaurant (Claremore, OK) 76953
McDonalds Restaurant (Durant, OK) 77001
McDonalds Restaurant (Henrietta, OK) 77126
McDonalds Restaurant (Sallisaw, OK) 77770
McDonalds Restaurant (Tulsa, OK) 78016
McDonalds Restaurant (Hardeeville, SC) 79496
McDonalds Restaurant (Alief, TX) 82492
McDonalds Restaurant (Arlington, TX) 82700; 82701
McDonalds Restaurant (Athens, TX) 82792
McDonalds Restaurant (Azle, TX) 83080
McDonalds Restaurant (Bastrop, TX) 83096
McDonalds Restaurant (Bedford, TX) 83245
McDonalds Restaurant (Belton, TX) 83278
McDonalds Restaurant (Brenham, TX) 83337
McDonalds Restaurant (Carrollton, TX) 83485; 83486
McDonalds Restaurant (Cedar Park, TX) 83533
McDonalds Restaurant (Channelview, TX) 83551
McDonalds Restaurant (Cleburne, TX) 83577
McDonalds Restaurant (Corpus Christi, TX) 83731
McDonalds Restaurant (Denison, TX) 84602
McDonalds Restaurant (Fort Worth, TX) 85186
McDonalds Restaurant (Friendswood, TX) 85403
McDonalds Restaurant (Galveston, TX) 85452
McDonalds Restaurant (Garland, TX) 85509; 85510
McDonalds Restaurant (Houston, TX) 86530; 86531; 86532; 86533; 86534; 86535; 86536; 86537; 86538; 86539; 86540; 86541; 86542; 86543; 86544; 86545; 86546; 86547; 86548; 86549; 86550; 86551; 86552; 86553; 86554; 86555; 86556; 86557; 86558; 86559; 86560; 86561; 86562; 86563; 86564; 86565; 86566; 86567; 86568; 86569
McDonalds Restaurant (Hurst, TX) 87284
McDonalds Restaurant (Kilgore, TX) 87490
McDonalds Restaurant (Laredo, TX) 87615
McDonalds Restaurant (Longview, TX) 87721; 87722
McDonalds Restaurant (Mansfield, TX) 87833
McDonalds Restaurant (Odessa, TX) 88255; 88256
McDonalds Restaurant (Pasadena, TX) 88441; 88442
McDonalds Restaurant (Raymondville, TX) 88707
McDonalds Restaurant (Richardson, TX) 88749
McDonalds Restaurant (Rockwall, TX) 88823
McDonalds Restaurant (San Antonio, TX) 89097; 89098; 89099; 89100
McDonalds Restaurant (Sherman, TX) 89412
McDonalds Restaurant (Spring, TX) 89471
McDonalds Restaurant (Stafford, TX) 89502
McDonalds Restaurant (Sugar Land, TX) 89536
McDonalds Restaurant (Texarkana, TX) 89690
McDonalds Restaurant (Tyler, TX) 89815; 89816
McDonalds Restaurant (Weatherford, TX) 90009
McDonalds Restaurant (Weslaco, TX) 90035
McDonalds Restaurant (Wichita Falls, TX) 90082
McDonalds Restaurant (Wylie, TX) 90133
McDonalds Restaurants (Bessemer, AL) 55098
McDonalds Restaurants (Apopka, FL) 58574
McDonalds Restaurants (Bradenton, FL) 58834; 58835
McDonalds Restaurants (Brandon, FL) 58874
McDonald's Restaurants (Clearwater, FL) 59034
McDonalds Restaurants (Kissimmee, FL) 60593; 60594
McDonalds Restaurants (Lakeland, FL) 60749; 60750; 60751; 60752
McDonalds Restaurants (Melbourne, FL) 61079
McDonald's Restaurants (Miami, FL) 61373; 61374
McDonalds Restaurants (New Port Richey, FL) 61688
McDonald's Restaurants (Orlando, FL) 62055; 62056; 62057; 62058; 62059
McDonalds Restaurants (St Petersburg, FL) 62995; 62996; 62997
McDonalds Restaurants (Tampa, FL) 63497; 63498; 63499; 63500
McDonalds Restaurants (Temple Ter, FL) 63674
McDonalds Restaurants (Winter Haven, FL) 63946
McDonald's Restaurants (Acworth, GA) 64046
McDonald's Restaurants (Alpharetta, GA) 64120; 64121; 64122
McDonald's Restaurants (Atlanta, GA) 64694; 64695; 64696; 64697; 64698; 64699; 64700; 64701; 64702; 64703; 64704; 64705; 64706; 64707; 64708; 64709; 64710; 64711; 64712; 64713; 64714; 64715
McDonald's Restaurants (College Park, GA) 65590; 65591
McDonald's Restaurants (Conyers, GA) 65692
McDonald's Restaurants (Dallas, GA) 65763
McDonald's Restaurants (Decatur, GA) 65858; 65859; 65860; 65861; 65862
McDonalds Restaurants (Douglasville, GA) 65991
McDonald's Restaurants (Duluth, GA) 66058; 66059
McDonald's Restaurants (Dunwoody, GA) 66121; 66122
McDonald's Restaurants (East Point, GA) 66149; 66150
McDonald's Restaurants (Fairburn, GA) 66176
McDonald's Restaurants (Forest Park, GA) 66241; 66242
McDonald's Restaurants (Jonesboro, GA) 66386; 66387; 66388
McDonald's Restaurants (Kennesaw, GA) 66431; 66432
McDonald's Restaurants (Lawrenceville, GA) 66526; 66527
McDonald's Restaurants (Lilburn, GA) 66571
McDonald's Restaurants (Lithonia, GA) 66597; 66598
McDonald's Restaurants (Loganville, GA) 66615
McDonald's Restaurants (Marietta, GA) 66832; 66833; 66834; 66835; 66836; 66837; 66838; 66839; 66840
McDonald's Restaurants (Mc Donough, GA) 66956
McDonald's Restaurants (Morrow, GA) 67028
McDonald's Restaurants (Norcross, GA) 67147; 67148; 67149; 67150; 67151
McDonald's Restaurants (Peachtree Cit, GA) 67239
McDonald's Restaurants (Powder Spring, GA) 67283
McDonald's Restaurants (Roswell, GA) 67394
McDonald's Restaurants (Snellville, GA) 67605
McDonald's Restaurants (Stone Mountai, GA) 67672
McDonald's Restaurants (Stone Mountain, GA) 67717; 67718; 67719; 67720
McDonald's Restaurants (Suwanee, GA) 67746
McDonald's Restaurants (Union City, GA) 67923
McDonald's Restaurants (Woodstock, GA) 68073
McDonalds Restaurants (Duncan, OK) 76994
McDonalds Restaurants (Corpus Christi, TX) 83732
McDonalds Restaurants (Houston, TX) 86570; 86571
McDonalds Restaurants (Irving, TX) 87376
McDonalds Restaurants (San Antonio, TX) 89101
McDonalds Restaurants (Wichita Falls, TX) 90083
McDonald's Restaurants Regional (Atlanta, GA) 64716
McDonalds of Seneca (Seneca, SC) 79862
McDonalds of Wallace (Wallace, NC) 76441
McDonalds of Wynne (Wynne, AR) 57742
McDonnell Douglas (Tulsa, OK) 78017
McDonnell Douglas Tulsa (Tulsa, OK) 78018
McDonnell Douglas Astronautics Co. (Titusville, FL) 63696
McDonnell Douglas Helicopter Co. (Dunwoody, GA) 66123
McDonnell Douglas Missile Systems Co. (Titusville, FL) 63697
Mcduff Appliance & Electron (Tampa, FL) 63501
Mcduff Elctrncs (Mcallen, TX) 87934
Mcduff Elctrncs Ct (Lewisville, TX) 87656
Mcduff Elec Applnc (Sherman, TX) 89413
Mcduff Electrncs (San Antonio, TX) 89102; 89103
Mcduff Electrncs (Webster, TX) 90021
Mcduff Electronics (Bradenton, FL) 58836; 58837
Mcduff Electronics (Abilene, TX) 82449
Mcduff Electronics (El Paso, TX) 84851; 84852
Mcduff Electronics (Houston, TX) 86572; 86573; 86574; 86575
Mcduff Electronics (Humble, TX) 87236
Mcduff Electronics (Irving, TX) 87377
Mcduff Electronics (Pasadena, TX) 88443
Mcduff Electronics (Richardson, TX) 88750
Mcgraw Edison (Lumberton, MS) 73131
MCI Business Services (Atlanta, GA) 64717
MCI Communications (Washington, DC) **58361**
MCI Communications Corp. (Washington, DC) 58362
MCI Consumer Markets (Arlington, VA) 90359
McKesson Service Merchandising Div. (Harrison, AR) 57138
Mckesson Drg Co. (Oklahoma City, OK) 77440
Mckesson Drug Co. (Landover, MD) 72027
Mcneil Consumer Products Co. (Round Rock, TX) 88850
Mcneil Pharmaceutical (Arlington, TX) 82702
Mcneil Pharmaceutical Co. (Dorado, PR) 78411; 78412
Mead Coated Board Div. (Atlanta, GA) 64718
Mead Packaging Div. Atlanta Plant (Atlanta, GA) 64719; 64720
Mead Packaging Division (Richmond, VA) 91930
Mead Coated Board Inc. (Cottonton, AL) 55531
Mead Containerboard (Stevenson, AL) 56572
Mead Containerboard (Atlanta, GA) 64721
Mead Corp (Oklahoma City, OK) 77441
Mead Corp. (Covington, GA) 65735
Mead Corp. Kingsport Mill (Kingsport, TN) 81112
Mead Data Central (Oklahoma City, OK) 77442
Mead Data Central (Austin, TX) 82937
Mead Data Central Inc. (Houston, TX) 86576
Mead Ink Products (Anniston, AL) 55004
Mead Ink Products (Atlanta, GA) 64722
Mead Packaging (Atlanta, GA) 64723
Mead Paper (Kingsport, TN) 81113
Mead Paperboard Products (Lynchburg, VA) 91268
Meadow Gold Dairy (Dothan, AL) 55656
Meadow Gold Dairy (Huntsville, AL) 55974
Meadow Gold Dairy (Lexington, KY) 68578
Meadow Gold Dairy (Nashville, TN) 82062
Meadow Gold Dairy Inc. (Tulsa, OK) 78019
Meadow Gold Dairy Products (Gadsden, AL) 55785
Meadowland Creamery (Conroe, TX) 83668
Med Rel, Inc. (Humacao, PR) 78462
Medeco Security Locks Inc. (Salem, VA) 92219; 92220; 92221
Media Networks Inc. (Pompano Beach, FL) 62612
Media Networks Inc. (Tulsa, OK) 78020
Medtronic Neuro Div. (Tucker, GA) 67868
Medtronic Inc. (Louisville, KY) 68883; 68884
Medtronic Inc. Puerto Rico (Villalba, PR) 78634
Medtronic Pr Inc. (Villalba, PR) 78635
Medtronic Puerto Rico Inc. (Villalba, PR) 78636
Mellon Bank (DE) NA (Dover, DE) 57793; 57794; 57795; 57796
Mellon Bank (DE) NA (Georgetown, DE) 57818
Mellon Bank (DE) NA (Laurel, DE) 57826
Mellon Bank (DE) NA (Lewes, DE) 57828
Mellon Bank (DE) NA (New Castle, DE) 57870
Mellon Bank (DE) NA (Newark, DE) 57920; 57921; 57922
Mellon Bank (DE) NA (Rehoboth Beach, DE) 57946; 57947
Mellon Bank (DE) NA (Seaford, DE) 57951
Mellon Bank (DE) NA (Smyrna, DE) 57960

Mobil Mining & Minerals Co. (Wauchula, FL) 63828
Mobil Mining & Minerals Co. (Pasadena, TX) 88444
Mobil Natural Gas, Inc. (Houston, TX) 86591; 86592
Mobil Oil (Lake Worth, FL) 60682
Mobil Oil (Longwood, FL) 60935
Mobil Oil (Orlando, FL) 62062
Mobil Oil (West Palm Beach, FL) 63887
Mobil Oil (Atlanta, GA) 64731
Mobil Oil (Louisville, KY) 68886
Mobil Oil (Houma, LA) 69962
Mobil Oil (Metairie, LA) 70292
Mobil Oil (Poteau, OK) 77723
Mobil Oil (Keller, TX) 87461
Mobil Oil (Plano, TX) 88588; 88589
Mobil Oil (San Saba, TX) 89347
Mobil Oil Beaumont Refinery (Beaumont, TX) 83181
Mobil Oil Bulk Plant (Galveston, TX) 85456
Mobil Oil Chalmette Refinery (Chalmette, LA) 69765
Mobil Oil Co. (Texarkana, AR) 57678
Mobil Oil Co. (Bogalusa, LA) 69705
Mobil Oil Company (Springhill, LA) 70852
Mobil Oil Co. (Altair, TX) 82503
Mobil Oil Co. (Anson, TX) 82616
Mobil Oil Co. (Corsicana, TX) 83784
Mobil Oil Co. (Crosbyton, TX) 83809
Mobil Oil Co. (Del Rio, TX) 84581
Mobil Oil Co. (Galveston, TX) 85457
Mobil Oil Co. (Georgetown, TX) 85570
Mobil Oil Co. (Grand Prairie, TX) 85630
Mobil Oil Co. (Nacogdoches, TX) 88172
Mobil Oil Co. (Seguin, TX) 89370
Mobil Oil Co. (Snyder, TX) 89448
Mobil Oil Co. (Thorndale, TX) 89758
Mobil Oil Co. (Three Rivers, TX) 89762
Mobil Oil Co. (Waxahachie, TX) 89997
Mobil Oil Co. Consignee (Memphis, TX) 87949
Mobil Oil Co. Inc. (Midland, TX) 88052
Mobil Oil Co. Products (Cameron, TX) 83437
Mobil Oil Co. Terminal (Port Neches, TX) 88675
Mobil Oil Co. Wholesale Dept (Electra, TX) 84986
Mobil Oil Consignee (Freeport, TX) 85387
Mobil Oil Consignee (Tomball, TX) 89773
Mobil Oil Corp-10 Aer (Fort Lauderdale, FL) 59539
Mobil Oil Corp. (Little Rock, AR) 57293
Mobil Oil Corp. (Washington, DC) 58367; 58368
Mobil Oil Corp. (Bonita Springs, FL) 58760
Mobil Oil Corp. (Delray Beach, FL) 59322; 59323; 59324
Mobil Oil Corp. (Fort Lauderdale, FL) 59540; 59541; 59542
Mobil Oil Corp. (Hollywood, FL) 60078; 60079
Mobil Oil Corp. (Jacksonville, FL) 60379
Mobil Oil Corp. (Lake Worth, FL) 60683; 60684
Mobil Oil Corp. (Longwood, FL) 60936; 60937
Mobil Oil Corp. (Naples, FL) 61645
Mobil Oil Corp. (Orlando, FL) 62063
Mobil Oil Corporation (Palm Harbor, FL) 62301
Mobil Oil Corporation (St Petersburg, FL) 62999
Mobil Oil Corp. (Winter Springs, FL) 64002
Mobil Oil Corp. (Covington, GA) 65738
Mobil Oil Corp. (Louisville, KY) 68887
Mobil Oil Corp. (Morgan City, LA) 70389
Mobil Oil Corp. (Baltimore, MD) 71210
Mobil Oil Corp. (Charlotte, NC) 74085
Mobil Oil Corp. (Cement, OK) 76912
Mobil Oil Corp. (Chickasha, OK) 76932
Mobil Oil Corporation (Chickasha Ok, OK) 76942
Mobil Oil Corp. (Lindsay, OK) 77179
Mobil Oil Corp. (Oklahoma City, OK) 77447; 77448
Mobil Oil Corp. (Thomas, OK) 77867; 77868
Mobil Oil Corp. (Alvin, TX) 82508
Mobil Oil Corp. (Arlington, TX) 82705
Mobil Oil Corp. (Austin, TX) 82942
Mobil Oil Corp. (Avinger, TX) 83078
Mobil Oil Corp. (Beaumont, TX) 83182; 83183
Mobil Oil Corp. (Bedford, TX) 83246
Mobil Oil Corp. (Carrollton, TX) 83487; 83488; 83489
Mobil Oil Corp. (Corpus Christi, TX) 83736
Mobil Oil Corporation (Dallas, TX) 84246; 84247; 84248
Mobil Oil Corp. (Dayton, TX) 84522
Mobil Oil Corp. (Eagle Pass, TX) 84719
Mobil Oil Corp. (Garland, TX) 85511
Mobil Oil Corp. (Highlands, TX) 85749
Mobil Oil Corp. (Houston, TX) 86593; 86594
Mobil Oil Corp. (Humble, TX) 87237
Mobil Oil Corp. (Kilgore, TX) 87492
Mobil Oil Corp. (Midland, TX) 88053
Mobil Oil Corp. (Richardson, TX) 88751
Mobil Oil Corp. (Rowlett, TX) 88860
Mobil Oil Corp. (Waskom, TX) 89988
Mobil Oil Corp. (Annandale, VA) 90268
Mobil Oil Corp. (Arlington, VA) 90361
Mobil Oil Corp. (Fairfax, VA) 90799; 90800
Mobil Oil Corp. (Falls Church, VA) 90860
Mobil Oil Corp. (Manassas, VA) 91315; 91316
Mobil Oil Corp. Chalmette Refinery (Chalmette, LA) 69766
Mobil Oil Corp. Chitwood Gas (Ninnekah, OK) 77244
Mobil Oil Corp. Eagle Lake P (Altair, TX) 82504
Mobil Oil Corp. Field Office (Corpus Christi, TX) 83737
Mobil Oil Corp. Offshore Production (Cameron, LA) 69752
Mobil Oil Corp. S a Terminal (San Antonio, TX) 89113
Mobil Oil Corp. (Terminal) (Fort Worth, TX) 85194
Mobil Oil Distrbtr (Odessa, TX) 88257
Mobil Oil Distributor (Henrietta, TX) 85737
Mobil Oil Drilling Department (Jayton, TX) 87438
Mobil Oil Explor&Produc Se (Natchez, MS) 73203
Mobil Oil Exploration & Pro (Dallas, TX) 84249
Mobil Oil Exploring & Producing (Cameron, LA) 69753
Mobil Oil Exploring & Producing SE (Kaplan, LA) 69990
Mobil Oil Exploring & Producing SE (Lake Charles, LA) 70150
Mobil Oil Federal Credit Un (Beaumont, TX) 83184
Mobil Oil Gas Station (W Palm Beach, FL) 63796
Mobil Oil Hughes Station (Alex, OK) 76792
Mobil Oil Inc/E&P S (Kaplan, LA) 69991
Mobil Oil Inc. (Lakeland, FL) 60754
Mobil Oil L B J Midway (Dallas, TX) 84250
Mobil Oil No H Four-D (Altamonte Spg, FL) 58544
Mobil Oil No 12 (Fort Worth, TX) 85195
Mobil Oil Products (Lake Village, AR) 57241
Mobil Oil Products (Montgomery, WV) 92939
Mobil Oil Refining Div (Beaumont, TX) 83185
Mobil Oil Self Serve (San Antonio, TX) 89114
Mobil Oil Self Sv (Sugar Land, TX) 89537
Mobil Oil Service Sta (Port St Lucie, FL) 62688
Mobil Oil Service Station (Allen, KY) 68081; 68082
Mobil Oil Service Station (Arlington, TX) 82706
Mobil Oil Service Station N (San Antonio, TX) 89115
Mobil Oil 12jna (Dallas, TX) 84251
Mobil Oils Distributor (Mc Allen, TX) 87890
Mobil Petroleum Co. (Gonzales, TX) 85589
Mobil Petroleum Products (Freeport, TX) 85388
Mobil Pipe Line (Andrews, TX) 82599
Mobil Pipe Line (Beaumont, TX) 83186
Mobil Pipe Line (Midland, TX) 88054
Mobil Pipe Line (Perryton, TX) 88501
Mobil Pipe Line Co. (Foreman, AR) 57007
Mobil Pipe Line Co. (Glenwood, AR) 57120
Mobil Pipe Line Co. (Saffell, AR) 57597
Mobil Pipe Line Co. (Guymon, OK) 77104
Mobil Pipe Line Co. (Beaumont, TX) 83187; 83188
Mobil Pipe Line Co. (Corpus Christi, TX) 83738; 83739
Mobil Pipe Line Co. (Corsicana, TX) 83785
Mobil Pipe Line Co. (Electra, TX) 84987; 84988; 84989
Mobil Pipe Line Co. (Gainesville, TX) 85424
Mobil Pipe Line Co. (Groveton, TX) 85690
Mobil Pipe Line Co. (Houston, TX) 86595
Mobil Pipe Line Co. (Hull, TX) 87213
Mobil Pipe Line Co. (Keller, TX) 87462
Mobil Pipe Line Co. (Kilgore, TX) 87493
Mobil Pipe Line Co. (Longview, TX) 87723
Mobil Pipe Line Co. (Luling, TX) 87824
Mobil Pipe Line Co. (Midland, TX) 88055
Mobil Pipe Line Co. (Mont Belvieu, TX) 88146
Mobil Pipe Line Co. (Mount Vernon, TX) 88155
Mobil Pipe Line Co. (Nederland, TX) 88188
Mobil Pipe Line Co. (Poynor, TX) 88697
Mobil Pipe Line Co. (Quitman, TX) 88704
Mobil Pipe Line Co. (Ringgold, TX) 88799
Mobil Pipe Line Co. (Schulenburg, TX) 89353
Mobil Pipe Line Co. (Seminole, TX) 89383
Mobil Pipe Line Co. (Sweetwater, TX) 89587
Mobil Pipe Line Co. (Vanderbilt, TX) 89863
Mobil Pipe Line Co. (Walnut Springs, TX) 89987
Mobil Pipe Line Co. (Waskom, TX) 89989
Mobil Pipe Line Co. Inc. (Houston, TX) 86596
Mobil Pipe Line Co. Sohio Plant (Elmore City, OK) 77039
Mobil Pipeline (Midland, TX) 88056
Mobil Pipeline (Saratoga, TX) 89351
Mobil Pipeline Co. (Healdton, OK) 77120
Mobil Pipeline Co. (Center, TX) 83539
Mobil Pipeline Co. (Grapeland, TX) 85654
Mobil Pipeline Co. (Kermit, TX) 87468
Mobil Pipeline Co. (Midland, TX) 88057; 88058
Mobil Pipeline Co. (Navasota, TX) 88179
Mobil Pipeline Co. (Pineland, TX) 88515
Mobil Pipeline Co. Tec Techn (Alice, TX) 82486
Mobil Pipeline Sta. (Liberty, TX) 87674; 87675
Mobil Pipeline Stations (Dayton, TX) 84523
Mobil Prdcng. TX & New Mex Inc. (Wichita Falls, TX) 90084
Mobil Producing TX & New (Vanderbilt, TX) 89864
Mobil Producing TX & New Mex (Andrews, TX) 82600
Mobil Producing TX & New Mex (Sunray, TX) 89572
Mobil Producing TX & NM (Kilgore, TX) 87494
Mobil Producing TX & NM Inc. (Taft, TX) 89595
Mobil Research Devlpmnt Cor (Addison, TX) 82474
Mobil Self Serv (Dallas, TX) 84252
Mobil Self Serv Co. (Texas City, TX) 89728
Mobil Self Serve (Carrollton, TX) 83490; 83491
Mobil Self Serve (Garland, TX) 85512; 85513; 85514
Mobil Self Serve (Houston, TX) 86597; 86598; 86599; 86600; 86601; 86602
Mobil Self Serve (Hurst, TX) 87285
Mobil Self Service (Winter Park, FL) 63987
Mobil Self Service (Arlington, TX) 82707; 82708
Mobil Self-Service (Dallas, TX) 84253
Mobil Self Service (Garland, TX) 85515; 85516
Mobil Self Service (Irving, TX) 87379
Mobil Self Service (Lewisville, TX) 87657
Mobil Self Service (Plano, TX) 88590
Mobil Selv Serv (Dallas, TX) 84254
Mobil Servcie Station (Opa Locka, FL) 61861
Mobil Service (Orlando, FL) 62064
Mobil Service (Austin, TX) 82943
Mobil Service Center (Daytona Beach, FL) 59193
Mobil Service Center (Fort Lauderdale, FL) 59543
Mobil Service Center (Punta Gorda, FL) 62712
Mobil Service Center (Shreveport, LA) 70751
Mobil Service Center (Fairfax, VA) 90801
Mobil Service Center (Winchester, VA) 92598
Mobil Service Sta (Seguin, TX) 89371
Mobil Service Station (Daytona Beach, FL) 59194
Mobil Service Station (Arlington, TX) 82709
Mobil Service Station (Dallas, TX) 84255
Mobil Service Station (Fort Worth, TX) 85196; 85197; 85198
Mobil Service Station (Hurst, TX) 87286
Mobil Service Station (Chesapeake, VA) 90588; 90589
Mobil Service Station (Weirton, WV) 93095
Mobil Servicenter Venice (Venice, FL) 63728
Mobil Slf Srv (Fort Worth, TX) 85199
Mobil Station (Melbourne, FL) 61080
Mobil Station (Pensacola, FL) 62449
Mobil Station (Colbert, OK) 76966
Mobil Station (Dallas, TX) 84256; 84257
Mobil Station No 12468 (Spring, TX) 89476
Mobil Steel Corp. (Houston, TX) 86603
Mobil Tech Inc. (Sanford, FL) 62769
Mobil Tire Service (Campton, KY) 68188
Mobile Asphalt Terminal (Mobile, AL) 56208
Mobile Communications Corp. of America (Ridgeland, MS) 73326
Mobile River Terminal (Mobile, AL) 56209
Mobilecomm of Austin Inc. (Austin, TX) 82944
Mobilecomm of Nashville Inc. (Nashville, TN) 82064
Mobilecomm of Ohio Inc. (Ridgeland, MS) 73327
Modern Business Systems (Harrison, AR) 57139
Modern Office Machines Inc. (Greenville, SC) 79395; 79396
Moen Inc. (Durham, NC) 74419
Moen Inc. (New Bern, NC) 75730
Moen Inc. (Sanford, NC) 76199
Moen Inc. (Trent Woods, NC) 76404
Molex-ETC Inc. (Pinellas Park, FL) 62523
Molex-Etc Inc. (Pinellas Pk., FL) 62532
Molex-Etc Inc. (St. Petersburg, FL) 63128
Molex-Etc Inc. (Roswell, GA) 67395
Molex Inc. (Huntsville, AL) 55976
Molex Inc. (N. Little Rock, AR) 57438
Molex Inc. (Roswell, GA) 67396
Molex Inc. (Louisville, KY) 68888
Molex Inc. (Tulsa, OK) 78027
Molex Inc. (Austin, TX) 82945
Molex Inc. (Houston, TX) 86604
Monarch Crown Corp. (San Antonio, TX) 89116
Monarch Industries (Atlanta, GA) 64732
Monarch Industries Inc. (Orlando, FL) 62065
Monarch Industries Inc. (Br) (Dallas, TX) 84258
Monarch Paper Co. (Fort Worth, TX) 85200
Monarch Paper Co. (Houston, TX) 86605
Monfort Beef Dumas Plant Fka-Sipco-D-B-A (Cactus, TX) 83430
Monfort Inc. (Louisville, KY) 68889
Monogahela Power Co. (Fairmont, WV) 92842
Monogahela Power Co. (Parkersburg, WV) 92993
Monongahela Power Co. (Clarksburg, WV) 92812
Monongahela Power Co. (Fairmont, WV) 92843; 92844
Monongahela Power Co. (Franklin, WV) 92853
Monongahela Power Co. (Marlinton, WV) 92925
Monongahela Power Co. (Morgantown, WV) 92946
Monongahela Power Co. (Parsons, WV) 93001
Monongahela Power Co. (Weirton, WV) 93096
Monroe Auto Equipment Co. (Paragould, AR) 57494; 57495
Monroe Auto Equipment Co. (Hartwell, GA) 66342
Monroe Industries Inc. (Greenville, SC) 79397
Monroeville Particleboard Plant (Monroeville, AL) 56264; 56265
Monsanto Agricultural Co. (Marietta, GA) 66841
Monsanto Anniston Empl Crdt Un (Anniston, AL) 55005
Monsanto Car Employees Cr (Greenwood, SC) 79458
Monsanto Chemical Group-Fibers (Greenwood, SC) 79459
Monsanto Co. (Anniston, AL) 55006
Monsanto Co. (Decatur, AL) 55597; 55598
Monsanto Co. (Wilmington, DE) 58088
Monsanto Co. (Washington, DC) 58369
Monsanto Co. (Cantonment, FL) 58910
Monsanto Co. (Pensacola, FL) 62450
Monsanto Co. (Atlanta, GA) 64733
Monsanto Co. (Augusta, GA) 65336; 65337
Monsanto Co. (Luling, LA) 70202; 70203; 70204
Monsanto Co. (Fayetteville, NC) 74567
Monsanto Co. (Greenwood, SC) 79460
Monsanto Co. (Moore, SC) 79667; 79668
Monsanto Co. (Columbia, TN) 80632; 80633
Monsanto Co. (Alvin, TX) 82509
Monsanto Co. (Nitro, WV) 92972
Monsanto Co. Chemical Group (Decatur, AL) 55599
Monsanto Co./Agricultural Grp (Fayetteville, NC) 74568
Monsanto Employees Cr Union (Pensacola, FL) 62451
Montgomery Food Processing Inc. (Montgomery, AL) 56356
Monumental Paper Co. (Baltimore, MD) 71211
Moore's Quality Snack Food Inc. (Bristol, VA) 90482
Morgan Trust Co. of Florida, NA (Palm Beach, FL) 62259
Morgantown Plastics Co. (Morgantown, KY) 69110
Morrison Molded Fiber Glass Co. (Bristol, VA) 90483
Morton International Arspc Polymer (Lilburn, GA) 66572
Morton International Inc. (Decatur, AL) 55600
Morton International Inc. (Weeks Island, LA) 70940
Morton International Inc. (Wytheville, VA) 92643; 92644; 92645
Morton International Inc. Morton Salt Div. (New Iberia, LA) 70413
Morton International Ind Chemls (Tucker, GA) 67869
Morton International Polmer Systems (Moss Point, MS) 73195
Morton International Specialty (Greenville, SC) 79398
Morton Salt (Roswell, GA) 67397
Morton Salt (Conroe, TX) 83670
Morton Salt Co. (Plano, TX) 88591

Moss Point Marine (Escatawpa, MS) 72758
Motion Industries Inc. (Birmingham, AL) 55322; 55323
Motion Industries Midwest, Inc. (Birmingham, AL) 55324
Motor Carrier Insurance, Ltd. (Cherryville, NC) 74248
Motorola De Puerto Rico (Vega Baja, PR) 78626
Motorola Inc. Portable Products Div. (Plantation, FL) 62571
Motorola P.R. Operations (Vega Baja, PR) 78627
Mott's Blue Coach (Water Valley, MS) 73468
Mott's - Blue Coach Foods (Water Valley, MS) 73469
Mott's Prepared Foods (Talmo, GA) 67780
Mountain Pass Canning (Anthony, TX) 82617
Mountain Pass Canning Co. (Anthony, TX) 82618
Mountain State Telephone Co. (Masontown, WV) 92937
Mpi Inc. (Lakeland, FL) 60755
Mpi Inc. (Coldwater, MS) 72692
Mpi Inc. (Houston, MS) 72919
MPI, Inc. (Fort Worth, TX) 85201
MPI, Inc. (Ft. Worth, TX) 85414
Mrs Smith's Frozen Foods (Atlanta, GA) 64734; 64735
Mrs. Smith's Frozen Foods Co. (Atlanta, GA) 64736
Mrs. Smith's Frozen Foods Co. (Rossville, TN) 82285
Mueller Co. (Albertville, AL) 54968
Mueller Co. & ORG Chattanooga Plant (Chattanooga, TN) 80438
Murdock Engineering Co. (Grand Prairie, TX) 85631
Murdock Engineering Co. (Irving, TX) 87380; 87381
Murphy Exploration & Production Co. (New Orleans, LA) 70539
Murphy Oil (El Dorado, AR) **56953**
Murphy Oil Corp. (El Dorado, AR) 56954
Murphy Oil Corp. (Nashville, TN) 82065; 82066
Murphy Oil USA, Inc. (El Dorado, AR) 56955
Murphy Oil USA Inc. Meraux Louisiana Refinery (Meraux, LA) 70241
Murphy Oil USA Inc. Meraux Refinery (Meraux, LA) 70242; 70243
Murray Machinery (Florence, AL) 55739
Mutual Federal S & L Association (Monticello, KY) 69100
Mutual Federal S & L Association (Russell Springs, KY) 69256
Mutual of New York (Athens, AL) 55044
Mutual of New York (Eufaula, AL) 55702
Mutual of New York (Foley, AL) 55749
Mutual of New York (Mobile, AL) 56210
Mutual of New York (Tuscaloosa, AL) 56664
Mutual of New York (De Land, FL) 59253
Mutual of New York (Fort Lauderdale, FL) 59544
Mutual of New York (Lakeland, FL) 60756
Mutual of New York (Naples, FL) 61646
Mutual of New York (Ocala, FL) 61809
Mutual of New York (Tallahassee, FL) 63252
Mutual of New York (W Palm Beach, FL) 63797
Mutual of New York (Albany, GA) 64084
Mutual of New York (Bogalusa, LA) 69706
Mutual of New York (Natchez, MS) 73204
Mutual of New York (Vicksburg, MS) 73459
Mutual of New York (Goldsboro, NC) 74726; 74727
Mutual of New York (Lexington, NC) 75420
Mutual of New York (Bartlesville, OK) 76836
Mutual of New York (Norman, OK) 77262
Mutual of New York (Myrtle Beach, SC) 79706
Mutual of New York (Cleveland, TN) 80595
Mutual of New York (Edna, TX) 84744
Mutual of New York (Harlingen, TX) 85707
Mutual of New York (Mc Allen, TX) 87891
Mutual of New York (San Angelo, TX) 88887
Mutual of New York (Waco, TX) 89953
Mutual of New York Financial (Metairie, LA) 70293
Mutual of New York Insurance (Geneva, AL) 55803
Mutual of New York Insurance Co. (Leesburg, VA) 91196
Mutual of New York Money (El Paso, TX) 84854
Mutual of New York/ Mony (Atlanta, GA) 64737
Mutual of New York/Mony Atlant (Atlanta, GA) 64738
Mutual of New York/Mony Atlant (Snellville, GA) 67606
Mutual of New York/Mony Region (Atlanta, GA) 64739
Mutual Savings & Loan Assoc (Metairie, LA) 70294
Mutual Savings & Loan Assoc (Durham, NC) 74420
Mutual Savings & Loan Assoc (Greensboro, NC) 74869
MW Kellogg Co. (Houston, TX) 86606

N

N W Ball & Roller (Walterboro, SC) 80074
Nabanco (Rockville, MD) 72302
Nabisco Biscuit Co. (Richmond, VA) 91933
Nabisco Brands Inc. (Atlanta, GA) 64740
Nabisco Foods Group (Atlanta, GA) 64741; 64742; 64743
Nabisco Foods Group Bakery (Atlanta, GA) 64744
Nabisco Inc. Nabisco Biscuit Co. (Houston, TX) 86607
Nacogdoches Medical Center (Nacogdoches, TX) 88173
Nadco Inc. (Nashville, TN) 82067
Nalco Chemical (Duncan, OK) 76995
Nalco Chemical (Corpus Christi, TX) 83740
Nalco Chemical (Sugar Land, TX) 89538
Nalco Chemical Co. (Mobile, AL) 56211; 56212
Nalco Chemical Co. (Jacksonville, FL) 60380
Nalco Chemical Co. (Longwood, FL) 60938
Nalco Chemical Co. (Jonesboro, GA) 66389
Nalco Chemical Co. (Baton Rouge, LA) 69590
Nalco Chemical Co. (Garyville, LA) 69865; 69866
Nalco Chemical Co. (Kenner, LA) 70000
Nalco Chemical Co. (Lake Charles, LA) 70151
Nalco Chemical Co. (Charlotte, NC) 74086
Nalco Chemical Co. (Guymon, OK) 77105
Nalco Chemical Co. (Oklahoma City, OK) 77449
Nalco Chemical Co. (Mt Pleasant, SC) 79675; 79676
Nalco Chemical Co. (Corpus Christi, TX) 83741
Nalco Chemical Co. (Freeport, TX) 85389
Nalco Chemical Co. (Kilgore, TX) 87495
Nalco Chemical Co. (Liberty, TX) 87676
Nalco Chemical Co. (Plano, TX) 88592
Nalco Chemical Co. (Sugar Land, TX) 89539
Nalco Chemical Co. Water Division (Atlanta, GA) 64745
Nalco Chemical Co. Inc. (Shreveport, LA) 70752
Nalco Chemical Co. Inc. (Tulsa, OK) 78028
Nalco Chemical Co. Unisolve (Atlanta, GA) 64746
Nalco Chemical Co. Utility Chem (Atlanta, GA) 64747
Nalco Chemical Co. Warehouse (Jonesboro, GA) 66390
Nantahala Power & Light Co. (Bryson City, NC) 73732
Nantahala Power & Light Co. (Franklin, NC) 74627; 74628; 74629
Napa Auto Parts (Ocala, FL) 61810
Nashville Foam (Nashville, TN) 82068
National Bank of Walton County (Loganville, GA) 66616
National Bank of Walton County (Monroe, GA) 66992; 66993
National Cabinet Lock (Mauldin, SC) 79651
National Chemsearch (Atlanta, GA) 64748
National Chemsearch (San Antonio, TX) 89117
National Chemsearch Corp. (Houston, TX) 86608
National City Bank, Ashland Kentucky (Ashland, KY) 68100; 68101; 68102; 68103; 68104; 68105
National City Bank, Ashland Kentucky (Catlettsburg, KY) 68196
National City Bank, Bowling Green (Bowling Green, KY) 68149; 68150; 68151; 68152; 68153
National City Bank, Bowling Green (Smiths Grove, KY) 69291
National City Bank, Kentucky (Jeffersontown, KY) 68494; 68495
National City Bank, Kentucky (Lexington, KY) 68579; 68580; 68581; 68582; 68583; 68584; 68585; 68586; 68587; 68588; 68589; 68590; 68591; 68592; 68593
National City Bank, Kentucky (Louisville, KY) 68890; 68891; 68892; 68893; 68894; 68895; 68896; 68897; 68898; 68899; 68900; 68901; 68902; 68903; 68904; 68905; 68906; 68907; 68908; 68909; 68910; 68911; 68912; 68913; 68914; 68915; 68916; 68917; 68918; 68919; 68920; 68921; 68922; 68923; 68924; 68925; 68926; 68927
National City Bank, Kentucky (Middletown, KY) 69095
National City Bank, Kentucky (Okolona, KY) 69154; 69155
National City Bank, Kentucky (Pleasure Ridge Park, KY) 69227
National City Bank, Kentucky (Prospect, KY) 69233
National City Bank, Kentucky (Rolling Hills, KY) 69252
National City Bank, Kentucky (Shively, KY) 69287; 69288; 69289
National City Bank, Kentucky (St. Matthews, KY) 69303; 69304; 69305
National City Bank, Kentucky (Valley Station, KY) 69321
National City Mortgage Co. (South Wheaton, MD) 72457
National City Mortgage Co. (Virginia Beach, VA) 92492
National City Trust Co. (Naples, FL) 61647; 61648
National City Trust Co. (Vero Beach, FL) 63761
National City Trust Co. (West Palm Beach, FL) 63888
National Coop Refinery Association (Oklahoma City, OK) 77450
National Dairy Products Corp. (Charlotte, NC) 74087
National Hand Tool Mechanics Tool Division (Farmers Branch, TX) 85033
National Home Life Assur Co. (Fayetteville, NC) 74569
National Home Life Assurancenc (Winston Salem, NC) 76677
National Intergroup (Carrollton, TX) **83492**
National Intergroup, Inc. (Carrollton, TX) 83493
National Linen Service (Atlanta, GA) 64749
National Medical Care Medical Products Div. (Mc Allen, TX) 87892
National Medical Care Inc. Medical Products Div. (Mc Allen, TX) 87893
National Mines Corp. (Wayland, KY) 69336
National Mines Corp. (Pineville, WV) 93006
National-Oilwell (Shreveport, LA) 70753
National-Oilwell (Woodward, OK) 78262
National-Oilwell (Houston, TX) 86609; 86610
National Packing Co. (Playa Ponce, PR) 78527
National Park Medical Center (Hot Springs National Park, AR) 57176
National Projects Inc. (Key West, FL) 60576
National Projects Inc. (Dallas, TX) 84259
National Public Service Isurance Co. (Waco, TX) 89954
National Rx Services Inc. (Tampa) (Tampa, FL) 63505
National Seating Co. (Vonore, TN) 82395
National Semiconductor (Huntsville, AL) 55977
National Semiconductor (Norcross, GA) 67154
National Semiconductor Corp. (Kennesaw, GA) 66433; 66434
National Semiconductor Corp. (Arlington, TX) 82710
National Semiconductor Corp. (Austin, TX) 82946
National Service Industries (Atlanta, GA) **64750**
National Service Industries, Inc. (Atlanta, GA) 64751
National Services Ind. Lithonia Lighting Div. (Cochran, GA) 65571
National Services Ind. Lithonia Lighting Div. (Conyers, GA) 65693
National Steel Corp. (Washington, DC) 58370
National Steel Corp. (Chester, SC) 78939
National Steel Corp. (Houston, TX) 86611
National Steel Corp. (Weirton, WV) 93097
National Vendors (Tucker, GA) 67870
National Vendors (Richmond, VA) 91934
Nationsbank (Atlanta, GA) 64752; 64753; 64754; 64755; 64756; 64757; 64758; 64759
Nationsbank (Balto, MD) 71332; 71333
Nationsbank (Bethesda, MD) 71418; 71419; 71420; 71421; 71422; 71423
Nationsbank (Frederick, MD) 71734
Nationsbank (Greenbelt, MD) 71868
Nationsbank (Silver Spring, MD) 72420
Nationsbank (Wheaton, MD) 72560
Nationsbank Account Activity I (Marietta, GA) 66842
Nationsbank Acct Activity Inf (Atlanta, GA) 64760
Nationsbank Acct Activity Inf (Decatur, GA) 65863
Nationsbank Acct Activity Inf (Jonesboro, GA) 66391
Nationsbank Acct Activity Inf (Marietta, GA) 66843
Nationsbank Acct Activity Inf (Morrow, GA) 67029
Nationsbank Acct Activity Inf (Smyrna, GA) 67560
Nationsbank Acct Activity Inf (Snellville, GA) 67607
Nationsbank Acct Activity Inf (Union City, GA) 67924
Nationsbank ATM Div. (Atlanta, GA) 64761
Nationsbank Atm Honor-Cirrus L (Atlanta, GA) 64762; 64763; 64764; 64765; 64766
Nationsbank Atm Honor-Cirrus L (Chamblee, GA) 65535
Nationsbank Atm Honor-Cirrus L (Decatur, GA) 65864
Nationsbank Atm Honor-Cirrus L (Hapeville, GA) 66337
Nationsbank Atm Honor-Cirrus L (Norcross, GA) 67155
Nationsbank Banking Centers (Baltimore, MD) 71212
Nationsbank Banking Centers (Beltsville, MD) 71360
Nationsbank Banking Centers (Bethesda, MD) 71424
Nationsbank Banking Centers (Bowie, MD) 71469; 71470
Nationsbank Banking Centers (Centers Clint, MD) 71508
Nationsbank Banking Centers (Chevy Chase, MD) 71533
Nationsbank Banking Centers (College Park, MD) 71564
Nationsbank Banking Centers (Coral Hills, MD) 71610
Nationsbank Banking Centers (Derwood, MD) 71647
Nationsbank Banking Centers (East Riverdale, MD) 71656
Nationsbank Banking Centers (Frederick, MD) 71735; 71736
Nationsbank Banking Centers (Gaithersburg, MD) 71800; 71801; 71802
Nationsbank Banking Centers (Greenbelt, MD) 71869; 71870; 71871
Nationsbank Banking Centers (Hyattsville, MD) 71968; 71969
Nationsbank Banking Centers (Langley Park, MD) 72042
Nationsbank Banking Centers (Laurel, MD) 72081; 72082
Nationsbank Banking Centers (Lutherville, MD) 72117
Nationsbank Banking Centers (Middle Brook, MD) 72134
Nationsbank Banking Centers (Mitchellville, MD) 72136
Nationsbank Banking Centers (Mt Rainer, MD) 72151
Nationsbank Banking Centers (Olney, MD) 72176
Nationsbank Banking Centers (Oxon Hill, MD) 72204
Nationsbank Banking Centers (Potomac, MD) 72232
Nationsbank Banking Centers (Rockville, MD) 72303; 72304; 72305; 72306; 72307
Nationsbank Banking Centers (Silver Spring, MD) 72421; 72422; 72423; 72424; 72425
Nationsbank Banking Centers (St. Charles, MD) 72471
Nationsbank Banking Centers (Suitland, MD) 72479; 72480
Nationsbank Banking Centers (Temple Hills, MD) 72494; 72495
Nationsbank Banking Centers (Towson, MD) 72508
Nationsbank Banking Centers (Upper Marlboro, MD) 72519
Nationsbank Banking Centers (Wheaton, MD) 72561
Nationsbank Banking Centers Ch (Chattanooga, TN) 80439; 80440; 80441; 80442; 80443; 80444; 80445
Nationsbank Banking Centers Co. (Columbia, MD) 71597
Nationsbank Banking Centers Ev (Frederick, MD) 71737
Nationsbank Banking Centers Fo (Forrestville, MD) 71704
Nationsbank Banking Centers Ga (Gaithersburg, MD) 71803
Nationsbank Banking Centers Ge (Germantown, MD) 71828
Nationsbank Banking Centers Hy (Hyattsville, MD) 71970
Nationsbank Banking Centers La (Hyattsville, MD) 71971
Nationsbank Banking Centers Si (Silver Spring, MD) 72426; 72427; 72428
Nationsbank Banking Centers Up (Upper Marlboro, MD) 72520
Nationsbank Banking Centers We (Hyattsville, MD) 71972
Nationsbank Banking Cneters (Hyattsville, MD) 71973
Nationsbank Banking Ctrs Rockv (Rockville, MD) 72308
Nationsbank Cash Flow Cards (Silver Spring, MD) 72429
Nationsbank Check Verification (Atlanta, GA) 64767; 64768
Nationsbank Commercial Account Information (Atlanta, GA) 64769
Nationsbank Commercial Departments (Chattanooga, TN) 80446
Nationsbank Community Departments (Chattanooga, TN) 80447
Nationsbank Consumer Departments (Chattanooga, TN) 80448
Nationsbank Corporate Customer Office (Atlanta, GA) 64770
Nationsbank Corp. (Charlotte, NC) **74088**
Nationsbank Customer Cash Flow Cards (Silver Spring, MD) 72430
Nationsbank Customer Service (Silver Spring, MD) 72431
Nationsbank Customer Service Dept. (Silver Spring, MD) 72432
Nationsbank-Dc Area Branch Ofc (Washington, DC) 58371; 58372; 58373; 58374; 58375; 58376; 58377; 58378; 58379
NationsBank of DC, NA (Washington, DC) 58380; 58381; 58382; 58383; 58384; 58385; 58386; 58387; 58388; 58389; 58390; 58391; 58392
Nationsbank Departments (Atlanta, GA) 64771
Nationsbank Departments Atm in (Atlanta, GA) 64772; 64773
Nationsbank Departments Commer (Chattanooga, TN) 80449
Nationsbank Departments Employ (College Park, GA) 65592
Nationsbank Departments Nation (Forest Park, GA) 66244
Nationsbank Departments Nation (Lilburn, GA) 66573
Nationsbank Departments Nation (Marietta, GA) 66844
Nationsbank Departments Nation (Tucker, GA) 67871

Nationsbank Departments Non-Pr (Atlanta, GA) 64774
Nationsbank Departments Person (Atlanta, GA) 64775
Nationsbank Departments Person (College Park, GA) 65593
Nationsbank Departments Person (Tucker, GA) 67872
Nationsbank Departments Privat (Atlanta, GA) 64776
Nationsbank Departments Prof&E (Atlanta, GA) 64777; 64778; 64779
Nationsbank Departments Real E (Atlanta, GA) 64780; 64781
Nationsbank Executive Departments (Chattanooga, TN) 80450
Nationsbank Homnor-Cirrus L Un (Atlanta, GA) 64782
Nationsbank Honor-Ccirrus L Sn (Atlanta, GA) 64783
Nationsbank Honor-Cirrus (Atlanta, GA) 64784
Nationsbank Honor-Cirrus Fulto (Atlanta, GA) 64785
Nationsbank Honor-Cirrus L (Atlanta, GA) 64786
Nationsbank Honor-Cirrus L Gle (Peachtree Cty, GA) 67251
Nationsbank Honor-Cirrus L Hai (Stone Mountain, GA) 67721
Nationsbank Honor-Cirrus L Hig (Douglasville, GA) 65992
Nationsbank Honor-Cirrus L Hol (Roswell, GA) 67398
Nationsbank Honor-Cirrus L Hor (Atlanta, GA) 64787
Nationsbank Honor-Cirrus L How (Atlanta, GA) 64788
Nationsbank Honor-Cirrus L How (Duluth, GA) 66061
Nationsbank Honor-Cirrus L Ind (Norcross, GA) 67156
Nationsbank Honor-Cirrus L Jim (Norcross, GA) 67157
Nationsbank Honor-Cirrus L Law (Atlanta, GA) 64789
Nationsbank Honor-Cirrus L Len (Atlanta, GA) 64790
Nationsbank Honor-Cirrus L Lil (Atlanta, GA) 64791
Nationsbank Honor-Cirrus L Lin (Atlanta, GA) 64792
Nationsbank Honor-Cirrus L Lit (Atlanta, GA) 64793
Nationsbank Honor-Cirrus L Mar (Atlanta, GA) 64794
Nationsbank Honor-Cirrus L Mar (Marietta, GA) 66845
Nationsbank Honor-Cirrus L Pan (Lithonia, GA) 66599
Nationsbank Honor-Cirrus L Par (Marietta, GA) 66846
Nationsbank Honor-Cirrus L Pea (Atlanta, GA) 64795
Nationsbank Honor-Cirrus L Per (Atlanta, GA) 64796
Nationsbank Honor-Cirrus L Pie (Atlanta, GA) 64797
Nationsbank Honor-Cirrus L Pla (Atlanta, GA) 64798
Nationsbank Honor-Cirrus L Pow (Atlanta, GA) 64799
Nationsbank Honor-Cirrus L Pow (Marietta, GA) 66847
Nationsbank Honor-Cirrus L Ros (Atlanta, GA) 64800
Nationsbank Honor-Cirrus L Ros (Roswell, GA) 67399; 67400
Nationsbank Honor-Cirrus L San (Atlanta, GA) 64801
Nationsbank Honor-Cirrus L San (Roswell, GA) 67401
Nationsbank Honor-Cirrus L Smy (Atlanta, GA) 64802
Nationsbank Honor-Cirrus L Sou (Atlanta, GA) 64803
Nationsbank Honor-Cirrus L Sou (Decatur, GA) 65865
Nationsbank Honor-Cirrus L Sou (Jonesboro, GA) 66392
Nationsbank Honor-Cirrus L Spr (Marietta, GA) 66848
Nationsbank Honor-Cirrus L Sta (Alpharetta, GA) 64123
Nationsbank Honor-Cirrus L Sto (Atlanta, GA) 64804
Nationsbank Honor-Cirrus L Toc (Atlanta, GA) 64805
Nationsbank Honor-Cirrus L Twi (Atlanta, GA) 64806
Nationsbank Honor-Cirrus L Wad (Kennesaw, GA) 66435
Nationsbank Honor-Cirrus L Wes (Atlanta, GA) 64807
Nationsbank Honor-Cirrus L Win (Marietta, GA) 66849
Nationsbank Honor-Cirrus Marke (Atlanta, GA) 64808
Nationsbank Honor-Cirrus Midto (Atlanta, GA) 64809
Nationsbank Honor-Cirrus Mitch (Atlanta, GA) 64810
Nationsbank Honor-Cirrus Mount (Stone Mountain, GA) 67722
Nationsbank Honor-Cirrus North (Atlanta, GA) 64811
Nationsbank Honor-Cirrus North (Chamblee, GA) 65536
Nationsbank Honor-Cirrus North (Tucker, GA) 67873
Nationsbank Honor-Cirrus Palis (Atlanta, GA) 64812
Nationsbank Honor-Cirrus Peach (Atlanta, GA) 64813; 64814; 64815
Nationsbank Honor-Cirrus Perim (Atlanta, GA) 64816
Nationsbank Honor-Cirrus Point (Riverdale, GA) 67316
Nationsbank Honor-Cirrus Power (Atlanta, GA) 64817
Nationsbank Honor-Cirrus River (Atlanta, GA) 64818
Nationsbank Honor-Cirrus Russe (Atlanta, GA) 64819
Nationsbank Honor-Cirrus Shall (Atlanta, GA) 64820
Nationsbank Honor-Cirrus South (Atlanta, GA) 64821
Nationsbank Honor-Cirrus South (College Park, GA) 65594
Nationsbank Honor-Cirrus Spelm (Atlanta, GA) 64822
Nationsbank Honor-Cirrus Tenth (Atlanta, GA) 64823
Nationsbank Honor-Cirrus Tri-C (Atlanta, GA) 64824
Nationsbank Honor-Cirrus Tucke (Tucker, GA) 67874
Nationsbank Honor-Cirrus Villa (Marietta, GA) 66850
Nationsbank Honor-Crrus Mablet (Atlanta, GA) 64825
Nationsbank Honorcirrus Pharr (Atlanta, GA) 64826
Nationsbank Honr-Cirrus L Shan (Atlanta, GA) 64827
Nationsbank Instant Check Information (Atlanta, GA) 64828
Nationsbank Instant Check Information Div. (Atlanta, GA) 64829
Nationsbank International Banking Dept. (Atlanta, GA) 64830
Nationsbank International Banking Departments (Atlanta, GA) 64831; 64832
Nationsbank Marketing Departments (Atlanta, GA) 64833
Nationsbank Mortgage Departments (Chattanooga, TN) 80451
Nationsbank New Accounts Rates Div. (Kensington, MD) 71999
Nationsbank Ofc Atl Area Accou (Marietta, GA) 66851
Nationsbank Ofc Atlana Area Co. (Atlanta, GA) 64834
Nationsbank Ofc Atlanta Area a (Atlanta, GA) 64835; 64836; 64837
Nationsbank Ofc Atlanta Area a (Decatur, GA) 65866
Nationsbank Ofc Atlanta Area a (Dunwoody, GA) 66124
Nationsbank Ofc Atlanta Area C (Atlanta, GA) 64838; 64839; 64840; 64841; 64842
Nationsbank Ofc Atlanta Area C (Conyers, GA) 65694
Nationsbank Ofc Atlanta Area C (Decatur, GA) 65867
Nationsbank Ofc Atlanta Area C (Dunwoody, GA) 66125
Nationsbank Ofc Atlanta Area C (Kennesaw, GA) 66436
Nationsbank Ofc Atlanta Area L (Atlanta, GA) 64843
Nationsbank Ofc Atlanta Area L (Decatur, GA) 65868
Nationsbank Ofc Atlanta Area L (Marietta, GA) 66852
Nationsbank Ofc Atlanta Area N (Atlanta, GA) 64844
Nationsbank Ofc Atlanta Area N (Decatur, GA) 65869; 65870
Nationsbank Ofc Atlanta Area N (Douglasville, GA) 65993
Nationsbank Ofc Atlanta Area N (Dunwoody, GA) 66126
Nationsbank Ofc Atlanta Area N (Marietta, GA) 66853
Nationsbank Ofc Atlanta Area P (Atlanta, GA) 64845
Nationsbank Ofcs Alanta Area a (Atlanta, GA) 64846
Nationsbank Ofcs Atl Acc Activ (Atlanta, GA) 64847
Nationsbank Ofcs Atl Area Acc (Avondale Esta, GA) 65361
Nationsbank Ofcs Atla Area Acc (Atlanta, GA) 64848
Nationsbank Ofcs Atla Area Act (Roswell, GA) 67402
Nationsbank Ofcs Atla Area Alp (Roswell, GA) 67403
Nationsbank Ofcs Atla T Area L (Atlanta, GA) 64849
Nationsbank Ofcs Atlaanta Area (Roswell, GA) 67404
Nationsbank Ofcs Atlanta Acc a (Atlanta, GA) 64850
Nationsbank Ofcs Atlanta Area (Atlanta, GA) 64851; 64852; 64853; 64854; 64855; 64856; 64857; 64858; 64859; 64860; 64861; 64862; 64863; 64864
Nationsbank Ofcs Atlanta Area (Avondale Esta, GA) 65362
Nationsbank Ofcs Atlanta Area (Chamblee, GA) 65537
Nationsbank Ofcs Atlanta Area (Decatur, GA) 65871
Nationsbank Ofcs Atlanta Area (Kennesaw, GA) 66437
Nationsbank Ofcs Atlanta Area (Marietta, GA) 66854
Nationsbank Ofcs Atlanta Area (Norcross, GA) 67158
Nationsbank Ofcs Atlanta Area (Peachtree City, GA) 67246
Nationsbank Ofcs Atlnta Area C (Atlanta, GA) 64865
Nationsbank Offices Atlanta Area (Suwanee, GA) 67747
Nationsbank Offices Atlanta Area (Roswell, GA) 67405
Nationsbank Offices Atlanta Area (Stone Mountain, GA) 67723
Nationsbank Offices Atlanta Area (Roswell, GA) 67406
Nationsbank Offices Atlanta Area (Atlanta, GA) 64866; 64867
Nationsbank Offices Atlanta Area (Marietta, GA) 66855
Nationsbank Offices Atlanta Area (Norcross, GA) 67159
Nationsbank Offices Atlanta Area (Stone Mountain, GA) 67724
Nationsbank Offices Atanta Are (Norcross, GA) 67160
Nationsbank Offices Atlant Are (Atlanta, GA) 64868; 64869
Nationsbank Offices Atlanta (Atlanta, GA) 64870
Nationsbank Offices Atlanta Ac (Atlanta, GA) 64871
Nationsbank Offices Atlanta Ar (Alpharetta, GA) 64124
Nationsbank Offices Atlanta Ar (Atlanta, GA) 64872; 64873; 64874; 64875; 64876; 64877; 64878; 64879; 64880; 64881; 64882; 64883; 64884; 64885; 64886; 64887; 64888; 64889; 64890; 64891; 64892; 64893; 64894; 64895; 64896; 64897; 64898; 64899; 64900; 64901; 64902; 64903; 64904; 64905; 64906; 64907; 64908; 64909; 64910; 64911; 64912; 64913; 64914; 64915; 64916; 64917; 64918; 64919; 64920; 64921
Nationsbank Offices Atlanta Ar (College Park, GA) 65595
Nationsbank Offices Atlanta Ar (Decatur, GA) 65872
Nationsbank Offices Atlanta Ar (Douglasville, GA) 65994
Nationsbank Offices Atlanta Ar (Duluth, GA) 66062; 66063; 66064
Nationsbank Offices Atlanta Ar (Jonesboro, GA) 66393
Nationsbank Offices Atlanta Ar (Kennesaw, GA) 66438; 66439
Nationsbank Offices Atlanta Ar (Lawrenceville, GA) 66528
Nationsbank Offices Atlanta Ar (Lilburn, GA) 66574
Nationsbank Offices Atlanta Ar (Lithonia, GA) 66600; 66601
Nationsbank Offices Atlanta Ar (Marietta, GA) 66856; 66857; 66858; 66859; 66860; 66861; 66862; 66863; 66864; 66865; 66866; 66867; 66868
Nationsbank Offices Atlanta Ar (Mc Donough, GA) 66957
Nationsbank Offices Atlanta Ar (Morrow, GA) 67030
Nationsbank Offices Atlanta Ar (Norcross, GA) 67161; 67162; 67163
Nationsbank Offices Atlanta Ar (Peachtree City, GA) 67247
Nationsbank Offices Atlanta Ar (Riverdale, GA) 67317; 67318; 67319
Nationsbank Offices Atlanta Ar (Roswell, GA) 67407; 67408; 67409
Nationsbank Offices Atlanta Ar (Sandy Springs, GA) 67439
Nationsbank Offices Atlanta Ar (Smyrna, GA) 67561
Nationsbank Offices Atlanta Ar (Snellville, GA) 67608
Nationsbank Offices Atlanta Ar (Stockbridge, GA) 67664
Nationsbank Offices Atlanta Ar (Stone Mountain, GA) 67725; 67726
Nationsbank Offices Atlanta Ar (Suwanee, GA) 67748
Nationsbank Offices Atlanta Ar (Tucker, GA) 67875; 67876
Nationsbank Offices Atlanta Ar (Union City, GA) 67925
Nationsbank Offices Atlanta Lo (Atlanta, GA) 64922
Nationsbank Offices Atlanta Ne (Atlanta, GA) 64923
Nationsbank Offices Atlata Are (Duluth, GA) 66065
Nationsbank Offices Attlanta a (Tucker, GA) 67877
Nationsbank Offices Tlanta Are (Atlanta, GA) 64924
Nationsbank Officess Atlanta a (Atlanta, GA) 64925
Nationsbank Offies Atlanta Are (Atlanta, GA) 64926; 64927; 64928
Nationsbank Oldd National Hwy (College Park, GA) 65596
Nationsbank Orrices Atlanta Ar (Atlanta, GA) 64929
Nationsbank Personal Account Informaiton (Atlanta, GA) 64930
Nationsbank Personal Accounts Department (Atlanta, GA) 64931
Nationsbank Personal Accounts Departments (Chattanooga, TN) 80452
Nationsbank Professional Accounts Departments (Chattanooga, TN) 80453
Nationsbank Real Estate Departments (Cartersville, GA) 65503
Nationsbank Real Estate Departments (Conyers, GA) 65695
Nationsbank Real Estate Departments (Douglasville, GA) 65995
Nationsbank Real Estate Departments (East Point, GA) 66151
Nationsbank Real Estate Departments (Fayetteville, GA) 66197
Nationsbank Real Estate Departments (Lawrenceville, GA) 66529
Nationsbank Real Estate Departments (Marietta, GA) 66869
Nationsbank Saturday Banking O (Atlanta, GA) 64932; 64933; 64934; 64935; 64936; 64937; 64938; 64939; 64940; 64941; 64942; 64943
Nationsbank Saturday Banking O (Chamblee, GA) 65538
Nationsbank Saturday Banking O (Decatur, GA) 65873
Nationsbank Saturday Banking O (Douglasville, GA) 65996
Nationsbank Saturday Banking O (Marietta, GA) 66870; 66871
Nationsbank Saturday Banking O (Peachtree City, GA) 67248
Nationsbank Saturday Banking O (Roswell, GA) 67410
Nationsbank Saturday Banking O (Stone Mountain, GA) 67727
Nationsbank Saturday Bk Ofcs D (Atlanta, GA) 64944
Nationsbank Savings Account Departments (Atlanta, GA) 64945; 64946
Nationsbank Securities Departments (Atlanta, GA) 64947
Nationsbank Security Emergency Office (Atlanta, GA) 64948
Nationsbank Services Inc. (Charlotte, NC) 74089
Nationsbank Sough Pittsburg Wh (Chattanooga, TN) 80454
Nationsbank South Pittsburg (South Pittsburg, TN) 82339
Nationsbank South Pittsburg Ja (Chattanooga, TN) 80455
Nationsbank Stop Payments Departments (Atlanta, GA) 64949; 64950
Nationsbank Student Loan Departments (Atlanta, GA) 64951
Nationsbank Swaturday Banking (Mc Donough, GA) 66958
Nationsbank for Those Areas No (Atlanta, GA) 64952
Nationsbank Training Departments (Atlanta, GA) 64953
Nationsbank Trust Div. (Atlanta, GA) 64954; 64955; 64956; 64957; 64958; 64959; 64960; 64961; 64962; 64963; 64964
Nationsbank 24 Hour Departments (Atlanta, GA) 64965
Nationsbank 24 Hour Jobline (Atlanta, GA) 64966
Nationsbankdc Area Branch Ofc (Washington, DC) 58393
Nationwide Life Insurance C (Arlington, TX) 82711
Nationwide Papers (Hanover, MD) 71912
Natkin Service Co. (Tucker, GA) 67878
Natural Gas Pipeline Co. of Ame (Washington, DC) 58394
Nautilis International (Independence, VA) 91169
Navajo Refing Co. (El Paso, TX) 84855
Navajo Refining Co. (El Paso, TX) 84856; 84857
Navistar International Tran (Charlotte, NC) 74090
Navistar International Transpo (Atlanta, GA) 64967
Navistar International Transpo (Conley, GA) 65663
Navistar International Transportation C (Decatur, GA) 65874
NBD Bank, FSB (Boca Raton, FL) 58722
NBD Bank, FSB (Naples, FL) 61649
NBD Bank, FSB (North Palm Beach, FL) 61751
NBD Bank, FSB (Sarasota, FL) 62846
NBD Bank, FSB (Venice, FL) 63729
NBD Trust Co. of Florida, NA (Boca Raton, FL) 58723
NBD Trust Co. of Florida, NA (Naples, FL) 61650
NBD Trust Co. of Florida, NA (North Palm Beach, FL) 61752
NCH (Irving, TX) **87382**
NCH Corp. (Irving, TX) 87383
NCH Corp. Mohawk Labratories Div. (Irving, TX) 87384; 87385
NCR Corp. (Springdale, AR) 57638
Ncr Corp. (Lakeland, FL) 60757
NCR Corp. (Orlando, FL) 62066
NCR Corp. (Atlanta, GA) 64968
Ncr Corp. (Doraville, GA) 65943
NCR Corp. (Peachtree City, GA) 67249
NCR Corp. (Corbin, KY) 68209
NCR Corp. (Louisville, KY) 68928
NCR Corp. (Metairie, LA) 70295
NCR Corp. (Columbia, MD) 71598
NCR Corp. (Hagerstown, MD) 71885
NCR Corp. (Olney, MD) 72177
Ncr Corp. (Charlotte, NC) 74091
Ncr Corp. (Greenville, NC) 74968; 74969
Ncr Corp. (Oklahoma City, OK) 77451
Ncr Corp. (Tulsa, OK) 78029
NCR Corp. (Brentwood, TN) 80232
NCR Corp. (Jackson, TN) 80991
NCR Corp. (Morristown, TN) 81806
Ncr Corp. (Arlington, TX) 82712
NCR Corp. (Dallas, TX) 84260
Ncr Corp. (Fort Worth, TX) 85202
NCR Corp. (Harlingen, TX) 85708
Ncr Corp. (Houston, TX) 86612
Ncr Corp. (Longview, TX) 87724
Ncr Corp. (Richardson, TX) 88752
Ncr Corp. (San Angelo, TX) 88888
NCR Corp. (Charleston, WV) 92769
Ncr Corp. Atlanta Distri (Atlanta, GA) 64969
Neches River Treatment Corp. Lower Neches Valley Authority (Beaumont, TX) 83189
Nekoosa Packaging (Winter Haven, FL) 63947
Nekoosa Packaging (Big Island, VA) 90431
Nelson Electric (Tulsa, OK) 78030
New England Mutl Life Insur (Tampa, FL) 63506
New England Mutl Life Insurance C (Fort Lauderdale, FL) 59545; 59546
New England Mutl Life Insurance C (Miami, FL) 61381
New England Mutl Life Insurance C (Pensacola, FL) 62452
New England Mutl Life Insurance C (Kenner, LA) 70001
New England Mutl Life Insurance C (El Paso, TX) 84858
New England Mutl Life Insurance C (Fort Worth, TX) 85203
New England Mutual Life (Alexandria, LA) 69395
New England Mutual Life Insurance (Huntsville, AL) 55978
New England Mutual Life Insurance (Monroeville, AL) 56266
New England Mutual Life Insurance (Orlando, FL) 62067
New England Mutual Life Insurance (Tampa, FL) 63507

New England Mutual Life Insurance (High Point, NC) 75153
New England Mutual Life Insurance (Tulsa, OK) 78031
New England Mutual Life Insurance (Greenville, SC) 79399
New England Mutual Life Insurance (Huntington, WV) 92885
New Hope Plant (Scroggins, TX) 89356
New Industrial Techniques, Inc. (Coral Springs, FL) 59116
New Orleans Public Service Inc. (New Orleans, LA) 70540
New Woman Magazine (Hendersonville, NC) 75043
New York Life (Atlanta, GA) 64970
New York Life (Altavista, VA) 90251
New York Life (Chester, VA) 90621
New York Life (Danville, VA) 90705
New York Life (Madison Heights, VA) 91300
New York Life (Newport News, VA) 91474
New York Life Southeastern Agencies (Tampa, FL) 63508
New York Life Acadian Sales Office Western Agencies (New Orleans, LA) 70541
New York Life Annapolis Sales Office Baltimore General Office (Annopolis, MD) 71027
New York Life Arkansas General Office (Little Rock, AR) 57294
New York Life Atlanta Central Service Office (Tucker, GA) 67879
New York Life Atlanta Group Claims Office Western Group Claims Region (Atlanta, GA) 64971
New York Life Atlanta Group Claims Office Western Group Claims Region (Norcross, GA) 67164
New York Life Atlanta Group Sales Office Central Group Marketing Zone Office (Atlanta, GA) 64972
New York Life Austin General Office (Austin, TX) 82947
New York Life Baltimore General Office (Towson, MD) 72509
New York Life Baton Rouge General Office (Baton Rouge, LA) 69591
New York Life Beaumont Sales Office Houston General Office (Beaumont, TX) 83190
New York Life Birmingham General Office (Birmingham, AL) 55325
New York Life Boca Raton Southeastern Agencies (Boca Raton, FL) 58724
New York Life Central Atlantic Pension Reg. Eatern Pension Zone (Reston, VA) 91715
New York Life Charleston General Office Southeastern Agencies (Charleston, SC) 78846; 78847
New York Life Charlotte General Office Southeastern Agencies (Charlotte, NC) 74092
New York Life Charlotte Group Sales Office Eastern Group Marketing Zone (Charlotte, NC) 74093
New York Life Chattanooga Knoxville General Office (Chattanooga, TN) 80456
New York Life Chevy Chase General Office Southeastern Agencies (Dethesda, MD) 71650
New York Life Columbia General Office Southeastern Agencies (Columbia, SC) 79056; 79057
New York Life Corpus Christi General Office Western Agencies (Corpus Christi, TX) 83742
New York Life Dalla Service Center (Dallas, TX) 84261
New York Life Dallas General Office Western Agencies (Dallas, TX) 84262
New York Life Dallas Group Claims Office Western Group Claims Region (Dallas, TX) 84263
New York Life Dallas Group Claims Office Western Groups Claims Office (Dallas, TX) 84264
New York Life Dallas Group Sales Office Western Group Marketing Zone Office (Dallas, TX) 84265
New York Life Dallas Service Center (Dallas, TX) 84266
New York Life El Paso General Office Western Agencies (El Paso, TX) 84859
New York Life Fairfax General Office Southeastern Agencies (Falls Church, VA) 90861
New York Life Fort Lauderdale General Office Southeastern Agencies (Fort Lauderdale, FL) 59547
New York Life Fort Smith Sales Office Arkansas General Office (Fayetteville, AR) 56984
New York Life Fort Worth General Office Western Agencies (Fort Worth, TX) 85204
New York Life Greater Atlanta Office Southeasten Agencies (Atlanta, GA) 64973
New York Life Greenville General Office Southeastern Agenices (Greenville, SC) 79400
New York Life Gulf Coast Houston General Office Western Agencies (Houston, TX) 86613
New York Life Houston General Office Western Agencies (Houston, TX) 86614
New York Life Houston Group Sales Office Western Group Marketing Zone Office (Houston, TX) 86615
New York Life Insur Co. (Waynesboro, VA) 92535
New York Life Insurance (Lewes, DE) 57829
New York Life Insurance (Rehoboth Beach, DE) 57948
New York Life Insurance (Middletown, MD) 72135
New York Life Insurance (Rising Sun, MD) 72249
New York Life Insurance (Seabrook, MD) 72367
New York Life Insurance (Abingdon, VA) 90155
New York Life Insurance (Bassett, VA) 90416
New York Life Insurance (Charlottesville, VA) 90544
New York Life Insurance (Lynchburg, VA) 91270
New York Life Insurance (Midlothian, VA) 91420
New York Life Insurance (Norfolk, VA) 91555
New York Life Insurance (Richmond, VA) 91935
New York Life Insurance (Verona, VA) 92394
New York Life Insurance Agt (Martinsville, VA) 91355
New York Life Insurance Co. (Wilmington, DE) 58089
New York Life Insurance Co. (Cumberland, MD) 71631
New York Life Insurance Co. (Frederick, MD) 71738
New York Life Insurance Co. (Gaithersburg, MD) 71804
New York Life Insurance Co. (Hagerstown, MD) 71886
New York Life Insurance Co. (Maugansville, MD) 72133
New York Life Insurance Co. (North East, MD) 72156
New York Life Insurance Co. (Rockville, MD) 72309
New York Life Insurance Co. (Silver Spring, MD) 72433
New York Life Insurance Co. (Union Bridge, MD) 72511
New York Life Insurance Co. (Amherst, VA) 90253
New York Life Insurance Co. (Arlington, VA) 90362; 90363
New York Life Insurance Co. (Chase City, VA) 90552
New York Life Insurance Co. (Covington, VA) 90663
New York Life Insurance Co. (Danville, VA) 90706
New York Life Insurance Co. (Franklin, VA) 90896
New York Life Insurance Co. (Fredericksburg, VA) 90932
New York Life Insurance Co. (Harrisonburg, VA) 91094
New York Life Insurance Co. (Lynchburg, VA) 91271; 91272; 91273
New York Life Insurance Co. (Manassas, VA) 91317
New York Life Insurance Co. (Marion, VA) 91335
New York Life Insurance Co. (Norfolk, VA) 91556; 91557
New York Life Insurance Co. (Pearisburg, VA) 91625
New York Life Insurance Co. (Portsmouth, VA) 91662
New York Life Insurance Co. (Prince George, VA) 91676
New York Life Insurance Co. (South Boston, VA) 92254
New York Life Insurance Co. (Staunton, VA) 92326
New York Life Insurance Co. (Virginia Beach, VA) 92493
New York Life Insurance Co. (Warrenton, VA) 92526
New York Life Insurance Co. (Williamsburg, VA) 92577
New York Life Insurance Co. (Yorktown, VA) 92654
New York Life Insurance Co. Fede (Washington, DC) 58395
New York Life Insurance Co. Gnl (Bethesda, MD) 71425
New York Life Jackson General Office Southeastern Agencies (Jacksonville, FL) 60381
New York Life Knoxville General Office Southeasten Agnecies (Knoxville, TN) 81231
New York Life Lafayette General Office Western Agencies (Lafayette, LA) 70076; 70077
New York Life Lexington General Office Southeastern Agencies (Lexington, KY) 68594
New York Life Louisville General Office Southeastern Agencies (Louisville, KY) 68929
New York Life Louisville Group Claims Office Western Group Claims Region (Louisville, KY) 68930; 68931
New York Life Macon General Office Southeastern Agencies (Macon, GA) 66699; 66700
New York Life Memphis General Office Southeastern Agencies (Memphis, TN) 81658
New York Life Miami General Office Southeastern Agencies (Coral Gables, FL) 59102
New York Life Mobile General Office Southeastern Agencies (Mobile, AL) 56213; 56214
New York Life Monroe General Office Western Agencies (Monroe, LA) 70362
New York Life Montgomery General Office Southeastern Agencies (Montgomery, AL) 56357
New York Life Nashville General Office Southeastern Agencies (Nashville, TN) 82069; 82070
New York Life New Orleans General Office Western Agencies (New Orleans, LA) 70542
New York Life New Orleans Group Claims Office Western Group Calims Region (Gretna, LA) 69910
New York Life New Orleans Group Claims Office Western Group Claims Region (Gretna, LA) 69911
New York Life Norfolk General Office Southeastern Agencies (Norfolk, VA) 91558; 91559
New York Life Northern Virginia General Office Southeastern Agencies (Mclean, VA) 91393
New York Life Oklahoma City General Office Western Agencies (Oklahoma City, OK) 77452
New York Life Oklahoma City Group Sales Central Group Marketing Zone Office (Oklahoma City, OK) 77453
New York Life Orlando General Office Southeastern Agencies (Orlando, FL) 62068
New York Life Piedmont Triad General Office Southeastern Agencies (Greensboro, NC) 74870
New York Life Raleigh General Office Southeastern Agencies (Raleigh, NC) 75931; 75932
New York Life Richmond General Office Southeastern Agencies (Richmond, VA) 91936
New York Life Roanoke General Office Southeasten Agnecies (Roanoke, VA) 92174
New York Life Roanoke General Office Southeastern Agencies (Roanoke, VA) 92175
New York Life San Antonio General Office Western Agencies (San Antonio, TX) 89118
New York Life Savannah General Office Southeastern Agencies (Savannah, GA) 67500; 67501
New York Life Shreveport General Office Western Agencies (Shreveport, LA) 70754
New York Life Silver Springs Office Southeastern Agencies (Silver Springs, MD) 72449
New York Life South Atlantic Pension Region Eastern Pension Zone (Atlanta, GA) 64974
New York Life South Cenntral Pension Region Central Pension Zone (Dallas, TX) 84267
New York Life Southeastern Agencies (Atlanta, GA) 64975
New York Life Tampa Group Sales Office Eastern Group Marketing Zone (Tampa, FL) 63509
New York Life Tulsa General Office Western Agencies (Tulsa, OK) 78032
New York Life Tyler Sales Office Dallas General Office (Tyler, TX) 89818
New York Life Washington General Office Southeastern Agencies (Rosslyn, VA) 92207
New York Life Washington Group Claims Office Eastern Group Claims (Lanham, MD) 72054
New York Life Washington Group Sales Office Eastern Group Marketing Zone (Rockville, MD) 72310
New York Life West Texas General Office Western Agencies (Midland, TX) 88059; 88060
New York Life West Virgina General Office Southeastern Agencies (Charleston, WV) 92770
New York Life West Virginia General Office Southeastern Agencies (Charleston, WV) 92771
New York Life Westen Group Claims Region (Dallas, TX) 84268
New York Life Western Agencies (Dallas, TX) 84269
New York Life Western Group Claims Region (Dallas, TX) 84270
New York Life Wilmington General Office Northeasten Agencies (Wilmington, DE) 58090
New York Life World Bank Group Claims Office Eastern Group Claims Region (Washinton, DC) 58530
New York Lifestyle Inc. (Gaithersburg, MD) 71805
New York Lifestyle Inc. (Rockville, MD) 72311
New York State Electric & Gas (Washington, DC) 58396
New York life Tampa General Office Southeastern Agencies (Tampa, FL) 63510
Newark Assembly Plant (Newark, DE) 57923; 57924
Newell Home Hardware Co. (Memphis, TN) 81659
Newell Ind. Inc. (San Antonio, TX) 89119
Newell Window Furnishing (Atlanta, GA) 64976
Newport News Shipbuilding & Dry Dock Co. (Newport News, VA) 91475
Newport News Shipbuilding & Drydock Co. (Newport News, VA) 91476
Nichols Wire Inc. (Florence, AL) 55740
Nicholson File (Cullman, AL) 55546
Nicholson Saw (Greenville, MS) 72809
Nike Inc. (Memphis, TN) 81660
Nike International (Huntsville, AL) 55979
Nike International (Houston, TX) 86616
Nn Ball & Roller Inc. (Walterboro, SC) 80075
Noramco of Delaware Inc. (Wilmington, DE) 58091
Noramco Inc. (Athens, GA) 64172
Nordstrom (Bethesda, MD) 71426
Nordstrom (Upper Marlborough, MD) 72525
Nordstrom (Arlington, VA) 90364
Norfolk Southern (Norfolk, VA) **91560**
Norfolk Southern Corp. (Norfolk, VA) 91561
Norfolk Southern Railway Co. (Norfolk, VA) 91562
Norfolk & Western Railway Co. (Norfolk, VA) 91563
Norris & O'Bannon (Tulsa, OK) 78033
North American Stainless (Chent, KY) 68200
North American Stainless (Ghent, KY) 68388; 68389
North American Van Lines (Severna Park, MD) 72376
North American Van Lines Agenc (Washington, DC) 58397
North American Van Lines Agent (Bethesda, MD) 71427
North American Van Lines Inc. (Atlanta, GA) 64977
North American Van Lines Inc. (Hickory, NC) 75089
North American Van Lines Inc. (San Antonio, TX) 89120
North American Van Lines International (Hyattsville, MD) 71974
North Arkansas Wholesale Co. (Laurens, SC) 79594; 79595
North Bros. Co. (Atlanta, GA) 64978
North Carolina Finishing Co. (Salisbury, NC) 76169
North End Houston Avenue (Port Arthur, TX) 88640
North Fulton Regional Hospital (Roswell, GA) 67411
North Ridgef Medical Center (Fort Lauderdale, FL) 59548
North Riverside Holding Inc. (Norcross, GA) 67165
Northern Mich Exploration Co. (Houston, TX) 86617
Northern National Gas Co. (Houston, TX) 86618
Northern Natural Gas Co. (Jackson, TN) 80992
Northern Natural Gas Co. (Houston, TX) 86619
Northern Operations Center Inc. (Falls Church, VA) 90862
Northern Trust Bank of Texas, NA (Dallas, TX) 84271; 84272; 84273
Northern Trust Bank of Texas, NA (Houston, TX) 86620; 86621
Northrop Aircraft Inc. (Dierks, AR) 56905
Northrop Corp. (Huntsville, AL) 55980; 55981
Northrop Corp. (Shalimar, FL) 62914
Northrop Corp. (Jackson, MS) 73026
Northrop Corp. (Oklahoma City, OK) 77454
Northrop Inc. (New Orleans, LA) 70543; 70544
Northrop Worldwide Aircraft Services, Inc. (NWASI) (Lawton, OK) 77167
Northwest Airlines Inc. (Birmingham, AL) 55326
Northwest Airlines Inc. (Fort Lauderdale, FL) 59549; 59550
Northwest Airlines Inc. (Fort Myers, FL) 59725
Northwest Airlines Inc. (Miami, FL) 61382; 61383
Northwest Airlines Inc. (Tampa, FL) 63511
Northwest Airlines Inc. (Dallas, TX) 84274
Northwest Fabrics & Crafts (Charlotte, NC) 74094
Northwest Industries Inc. (Newcastle, OK) 77242
Northwestern Mutual Life (Dover, DE) 57797
Northwestern Mutual Life (Covington, KY) 68228
Northwestern Mutual Life (Johnson City, TN) 81051
Northwestern Mutual Life (Richmond, VA) 91937
Northwestern Mutual Life (Winchester, VA) 92599
Northwestern Mutual Life, Inc. (Bowling Green, KY) 68154
Northwestern Mutual Life Inc. (Danville, KY) 68261
Northwestern Mutual Life Inc. (Leitchfield, KY) 68513
Northwestern Mutual Life Inc. (Lexington, KY) 68595; 68596
Northwestern Mutual Life Inc. (Louisville, KY) 68932
Northwestern Mutual Life Inc. (Owensboro, KY) 69187
Northwestern Mutual Life Inc. (Baltimore, MD) 71213
Northwestern Mutual Life Inc. (Memphis, TN) 81661
Northwestern Mutual Life Inc. (Nashville, TN) 82071
Northwestern Mutual Life Inc. (Charlottesville, VA) 90545
Northwestern Mutual Life Inc. (Lexington, VA) 91209
Northwestern Mutual Life Inc. (Lynchburg, VA) 91274
Northwestern Mutual Life Inc. (South Boston, VA) 92255
Northwestern Mutual Life Inc. (Beckley, WV) 92679
Northwestern Mutual Life Inc. (Clarksburg, WV) 92813
Northwestern Mutual Life Inc. (Huntington, WV) 92886
Northwestern Mutual Life Inc. (Lewisburg, WV) 92917
Northwestern Mutual Life Inc. (Princeton, WV) 93011
Northwestern Mutual Life Inc. (Wheeling, WV) 93116
Northwestern Mutual Life Inusr (Bethesda, MD) 71428

Norwest Mortgage Inc. (Maitland, FL) 60982
Norwest Mortgage Inc. (Sarasota, FL) 62847
Norwest Mortgage Inc. (Tampa, FL) 63512
Norwest Mortgage Inc. (West Palm Beach, FL) 63889
Norwest Mortgage Inc. (Alpharetta, GA) 64125
Norwest Mortgage Inc. (Atlanta, GA) 64979
Norwest Mortgage Inc. (Dunwoody, GA) 66127
Norwest Mortgage Inc. (Fayetteville, GA) 66198
Norwest Mortgage Inc. (Lilburn, GA) 66575
Norwest Mortgage Inc. (Greensboro, NC) 74871
Norwest Mortgage Inc. (Oklahoma City, OK) 77455
Norwest Mortgage Inc. (Tulsa, OK) 78034
Norwest Mortgage Inc. (Charleston, SC) 78848
Norwest Mortgage Inc. (Austin, TX) 82948
Norwest Mortgage Inc. (Corpus Christi, TX) 83743
Norwest Mortgage Inc. (Dallas, TX) 84275
Norwest Mortgage Inc. (Duncanville, TX) 84701
Norwest Mortgage, Inc. (Fort Worth, TX) 85205
Norwest Mortgage Inc. (Houston, TX) 86622
Novacor Chemicals Inc. (Forest City, NC) 74608
Noxell Corp. (Hunt Valley, MD) 71939; 71940
Noxell Corp. (Hurst, TX) 87287
Nsi Inc. Lithonia Lighting Div. (Cochran, GA) 65572
NTS (Fort Worth, TX) 85206
Nucor Bearing Prods. (Wilson, NC) 76635
Nucor Bearing Products, Inc. (Wilson, NC) 76636
Nucor Corp. (Charlotte, NC) **74095**
Nucor Corp. (Darlington Sc, SC) 79158
Nucor Corp. Cold Finish Div. (Charlotte, NC) 74096
Nucor Corp. Nucor Steel Div. (Jewett, TX) 87441
Nucor Corp. Steel Div. (Charlotte, NC) 74097
Nucor Corp. Vulcraft Al. Div. (Fort Payne, AL) 55758
Nucor Corp. Vulcraft Div. (Fort Payne, AL) 55759; 55760
Nucor Corp. Vulcraft Div. (Charlotte, NC) 74098
Nucor Corp. Vulcraft Div. (Grapeland, TX) 85655
Nucor Corp. Wire Div. (Charlotte, NC) 74099
Nucor Steel (Darlington, SC) 79154
Nucor Steel Texas Div. (Jewett, TX) 87442
Nucor Steel Arkansas (Blytheville, AR) 56810
Nucor-Yamato Steel Co. (Armorel, AR) 56725
Nucor-Yamato Steel Co. (Barfield, AR) 56739
Nucor-Yamato Steel Co. (Blytheville, AR) 56811; 56812
Number One Building Supply Inc. (Mount Olive, NC) 75696
Nutrasweet Co. (Augusta, GA) 65338
Nutrasweet Co. (Morrow, GA) 67031
Nutri Basics Co. (Chattanooga, TN) 80457

O

O/C Tanks Corp. (Conroe, TX) 83671
O-I Brockway Glass Inc. Plant 13 (Montgomery, AL) 56358
O-I Brockway Glass Inc. Plant 3 (Muskogee, OK) 77225
O-I Brockway Glass Inc. Plant 29 (Ringgold, VA) 92096
O & M Manufacturing Co. (Houston, TX) 86623; 86624; 86625
Oak Farms Dairy (Dallas, TX) 84276
Oak Farms Inc. (Houston, TX) 86626
Oakdale Plywood Plant (Oakdale, LA) 70598
Oaks at Baymeadows the (Jacksonville, FL) 60382
Ocapi Houston Ammonia Terminal (Pasadena, TX) 88445; 88446
Occidental Chemical (Salisbury, MD) 72351
Occidental Chemical Co. (Victoria, TX) 89897
Occidental Chemical Corp. (Mobile, AL) 56215
Occidental Chemical Corp. (Muscle Shoals, AL) 56403
Occidental Chemical Corp. (Sheffield, AL) 56553
Occidental Chemical Corp. (Delaware City, DE) 57772
Occidental Chemical Corp. (White Springs, FL) 63912
Occidental Chemical Corp. (Addis, LA) 69365; 69366
Occidental Chemical Corp. (Convent, LA) 69782; 69783
Occidental Chemical Corp. (Taft, LA) 70898
Occidental Chemical Corp. (Salisbury, MD) 72352; 72353
Occidental Chemical Corp. (Columbia, TN) 80634; 80635; 80636
Occidental Chemical Corp. (Alvin, TX) 82510
Occidental Chemical Corp. (Dallas, TX) 84277; 84278; 84279
Occidental Chemical Corp. (Deer Park, TX) 84557
Occidental Chemical Corp. (Orange, TX) 88325
Occidental Chemical Corp. (Pasadena, TX) 88447; 88448
Occidental Chemical Corp. (Victoria, TX) 89898
Occidental Chemical Corp. (Wadsworth, TX) 89985
Occidental Chemical Corp. (Belle, WV) 92694; 92695
Occidental Chemical Corp. Agricultural Products (White Springs, FL) 63913
Occidental Chemical Corp. Battleground Site (La Porte, TX) 87562
Occidental Chemical Corp. Castle Hayne Plant (Castle Hayne, NC) 73803; 73804
Occidental Chemical Corp. Corpus Christi Plant (Gregory, TX) 85681
Occidental Chemical Corp. Deer Park (Deer Park, TX) 84558
Occidental Chemical Corp. Houston Ammonia Terminal (Pasadena, TX) 88449
Occidental Chemical Corp. Taft Ammonia Terminal (Taft, LA) 70899
Occidental Chemical Corp. Vcm Plant (Deer Park, TX) 84559
Occidental International Corp. (Washington, DC) 58398
Occidental Oil & Gas Corp. (Tulsa, OK) 78035
Occidental Petroleum Corp. Alathon Polymers Div. (Ponca City, OK) 77708
Occidental Petroleum Corp. Alathon Polymers Div. Technology Dept. (Ponca City, OK) 77709
Occupational Health Service (Nashville, TN) 82072
Occupational Health Services Inc. (Washington, DC) 58399
Ocean Spray Cranberries Inc. (Vero Beach, FL) 63762
Ocean Spray Cranberries Inc. (Sulphur Springs, TX) 89559; 89560; 89561
Ochoa Fertilizer Co., Inc. (Guanica, PR) 78417
Odesa Women's & Children's Hospital (Odessa, TX) 88258
O'Donnell-Usen USA (Tampa, FL) 63513
Office Products Inc. (Harrisonburg, VA) 91095
Ogden Project Inc. (Tulsa, OK) 78036
Oglethorpe Power (Tucker, GA) **67880**
Oglethorpe Power Corp. (Tucker, GA) 67881
Oglethorpe Power Corp. E (Atlanta, GA) 64980
Oglethorpe Power Corp. Ga Elect (Atlanta, GA) 64981
Ohio Rubber Co. Orthane Div. (Denton, TX) 84624
Ohio Valley-Clarksburg Inc. (Wheeling, WV) 93117
Oilfield Service Corp. of Am (Lafayette, LA) 70078
Oilfield Service Corp. Amer (Oklahoma City, OK) 77456
Oilfield Service Corp. Amer (Houston, TX) 86627
Okla Homer Smith Furniture Co. Inc. (Fort Smith, AR) 57070
Oklahoma ALLTEL Inc. (Poteau, OK) 77724
Oklahoma Canning Co. (Oklahoma City, OK) 77457
Oklahoma Executive Office (Oklahoma City, OK) 77458
Olay Co. Inc. (Cayey, PR) 78385; 78386; 78387
Old El Paso Foods Mountain Pass Canning (Anthony, TX) 82619
Olga (Checotah, OK) 76915
Olin Augusta Plant (Augusta, GA) 65339; 65340
Olin Chemicals Group (Charleston, TN) 80289
Olin Chemicals Group (Beaumont, TX) 83191
Olin Corp. (Mc Intosh, AL) 56125; 56126; 56127
Olin Corp. (St. Marks, FL) 63072; 63073
Olin Corp. (Augusta, GA) 65341
Olin Corp. (Brandenburg, KY) 68169; 68170
Olin Corp. (Shreveport, LA) 70755
Olin Corp. (Westlake, LA) 70966
Olin Corp. (Beaumont, TX) 83192
Olin Corp. (South Charleston, WV) 93051; 93052
Olin Corp. Augusta Plant (Augusta, GA) 65342; 65343
Olin Corp. Beaumont Plant (Beaumont, TX) 83193
Olin Corp. Charleston Facility (Charleston, TN) 80290
Olin Corp. Hackberry Plant (Hackberry, LA) 69921
Olin Corp. Lake Charles Plant (Lake Charles, LA) 70152; 70153
Olin Corp. Shreveport Plant (Shreveport, LA) 70756; 70757; 70758
Olin Ordance Div. (St. Petersburg, FL) 63129
Olive Garden (Orlando, FL) 62069
Oliver Rubber Co. (Athens, GA) 64173
Oliver Rubber Co. (Asheboro, NC) 73590
Oliver Rubber Co. (Dallas, TX) 84280
Oliver Rubber Co. (Paris, TX) 88372; 88373
Oliver Rubber Co. Asheboro (Asheboro, NC) 73591
Oliver Rubber Co. Athens (Athens, GA) 64174
Olympic Homecare Products Co. (Louisville, KY) 68933
Olympic Prods. Co. (Tupelo, MS) 73414
Olympic Prods. Co. (Greensboro, NC) 74872
Olympic Prods. Co. Rebond Plant (Greensboro, NC) 74873
Olympic Products Co. (Tupelo, MS) 73415
Olympic Products Co. (Pleasant Garden, NC) 75832
Olympic Rebond Plant (Greensboro, NC) 74874
Omb Pharmaceutical Partners (Gurabo, PR) 78444
Omc Fishing Boat Group Engineering (Murfreesboro, TN) 81860
Omc Fishing Boat Group Inc. (Murfreesboro, TN) 81861
Omc Fishing Boat Group Inc. (Nashville, TN) 82073
OMC Andrews (Andrews, NC) 73547; 73548
OMC Burnsville (Burnsville, NC) 73768; 73769; 73770
Omc Calhoun (Calhoun, GA) 65472
Omc Chris Craft (Sarasota, FL) 62848; 62849
Omc Chris Craft Inc. (Sarasota, FL) 62850; 62851
Omc Chris-Craft Inc. (Hubert, NC) 75196
Omc Fishing Boat Group Inc. (Old Hickory, TN) 82205
Omc Inc. Boat Development Center (Sarasota, FL) 62852
OMC Industries Inc. (Bryan, TX) 83399
Omc Lexington (Lexington, TN) 81342; 81343
OMC Recreational Boat Group (Sarasota, FL) 62853
Omc Rutherfordton (Rutherfordton, NC) 76145
Omc Spruce Pine (Spruce Pine, NC) 76303
Omc-Stratos Boats Inc. (Old Hickory, TN) 82206
Ome Hydra-Sports (Hubert, NC) 75197
Omni Business Systems (Melbourne, FL) 61081
Omni Business Systems, Inc. (Fort Myers, FL) 59726; 59727
Omni Business Systems, Inc. (Fort Pierce, FL) 59798
Omni Business Systems, Inc. (Melbourne, FL) 61082
ONAN Corp. (Huntsville, AL) 55982
1 P Forest Resources Co. (Dallas, TX) 84281
Broyhill Furniture Ind. Inc. Lenoir Furniture & Occ.1 Plts (Lenoir, NC) 75383
Optic-Electronic Ni-Tec Div. (Garland, TX) 85517
Oracle Complex Systems Corp. (Arlington, VA) 90365
Orchard Decorative Prods. (Blythewood, SC) 78749
Orchard Decorative Products (Blythewood, SC) 78750
Ore-Ida Inc. (Atlanta, GA) 64982
Orlando Coca-Cola Bottling Co. (Orlando, FL) 62070
Ortho Biologics, Inc. (Manati, PR) 78500
Ortho Pharmaceuticals Inc. (Manati, PR) 78501
Oryx Energy (Oklahoma City, OK) 77459
Oryx Energy (Dallas, TX) 84282; **84283**
Oryx Energy Co. (Washington, DC) 58400
Oryx Energy Co. (Andrews, TX) 82601
Oryx Energy Co. (Big Spring, TX) 83291
Oryx Energy Co. (Dallas, TX) 84284
Oryx Energy Co. (Kermit, TX) 87469
Oryx Energy Co. (Premont, TX) 88699
Oryx Energy Co. (Sabine Pass, TX) 88862
Oryx Energy Co. (Tyler, TX) 89819
Oryx Energy Co. Dgn Non (Seminole, OK) 77804
OSCA (Lafayette, LA) 70079
Osca Inc. (Lafayette, LA) 70080; 70081
Oscar Mayer Foods Corp. (Goodlettsville, TN) 80870
Oscar Mayer Foods Corp. (Sherman, TX) 89415
Osco Drug (Fort Smith, AR) 57071; 57072; 57073
Osco Drug (N Little Rock, AR) 57415
Osco Drug (Norman, OK) 77263
Osco Drug (Denton, TX) 84625
Osco Drug Inc. (Jacksonville, AR) 57197
Osco Drug Store (Bowling Green, KY) 68155; 68156
Osco Drug Store (Owensboro, KY) 69188
Oshkosh Trailer Div. (Bradenton, FL) 58838
Oshkosh Truck Corp. (Alvin, TX) 82511
Oshkosh Truck Corp. Chassis Div. (Gaffney, SC) 79261
Oster Specialty Prods. (Mc Minnville, TN) 81438
O'sullivan Ind. Inc. of Virginia (South Boston, VA) 92256
OTC Co. (Houston, TX) 86628
Otis Elevator Co. (Birmingham, AL) 55327
Otis Elevator Co. (Huntsville, AL) 55983
Otis Elevator Co. (Mobile, AL) 56216
Otis Elevator Co. (Montgomery, AL) 56359
Otis Elevator Co. (Sheffield, AL) 56554
Otis Elevator Co. (Fayetteville, AR) 56985
Otis Elevator Co. (Fort Smith, AR) 57074
Otis Elevator Co. (Daytona Beach, FL) 59195
Otis Elevator Co. (Fort Myers, FL) 59728
Otis Elevator Co. (Jacksonville, FL) 60383
Otis Elevator Co. (Miami, FL) 61384; 61385
Otis Elevator Co. (Orlando, FL) 62071
Otis Elevator Co. (Pensacola, FL) 62453
Otis Elevator Co. (Tallahassee, FL) 63253
Otis Elevator Co. (Tampa, FL) 63514
Otis Elevator Co. (Atlanta, GA) 64983
Otis Elevator Co. (Macon, GA) 66701
Otis Elevator Co. (Savannah, GA) 67502
Otis Elevator Co. (Louisville, KY) 68934
Otis Elevator Co. (Alexandria, LA) 69396
Otis Elevator Co. (Baton Rouge, LA) 69592
Otis Elevator Co. (Lake Charles, LA) 70154
Otis Elevator Co. (Metairie, LA) 70296
Otis Elevator Co. (Monroe, LA) 70363
Otis Elevator Co. (Hagerstown, MD) 71887
Otis Elevator Co. (Ocean City, MD) 72163
Otis Elevator Co. (Jackson, MS) 73027
Otis Elevator Co. (Long Beach, MS) 73118
Otis Elevator Co. (Kernersville, NC) 75282
Otis Elevator Co. (Raleigh, NC) 75933
Otis Elevator Co. (Wilmington, NC) 76584
Otis Elevator Co. (Oklahoma City, OK) 77460
Otis Elevator Co. (Tulsa, OK) 78037
Otis Elevator Co. (Anderson, SC) 78681
Otis Elevator Co. (Columbia, SC) 79058
Otis Elevator Co. (Spartanburg, SC) 79921
Otis Elevator Co. (Chattanooga, TN) 80458
Otis Elevator Co. (Kingsport, TN) 81114
Otis Elevator Co. (Knoxville, TN) 81232
Otis Elevator Co. (Nashville, TN) 82074
Otis Elevator Co. (Amarillo, TX) 82570
Otis Elevator Co. (Austin, TX) 82949; 82950
Otis Elevator Co. (Corpus Chrsti, TX) 83768
Otis Elevator Co. (Dallas, TX) 84285; 84286; 84287
Otis Elevator Co. (El Paso, TX) 84860; 84861
Otis Elevator Co. (Galveston, TX) 85458
Otis Elevator Co. (Houston, TX) 86629
Otis Elevator Co. (Midland, TX) 88061
Otis Elevator Co. (Odessa, TX) 88259
Otis Elevator Co. (San Angelo, TX) 88889
Otis Elevator Co. (Texarkana, TX) 89692
Otis Elevator Co. (Tyler, TX) 89820
Otis Elevator Co. (Wichita Falls, TX) 90085
Otis Elevator Co. (Alexandria, VA) 90228
Otis Elevator Co. (Norfolk, VA) 91564
Otis Elevator Co. (Clarksburg, WV) 92814
Otis Elevator Co. (Huntington, WV) 92887
Otis Elevator Co. Inc. (Fort Worth, TX) 85207
Otis Elevator Co. Inc. (San Antonio, TX) 89121
Otis Elevator Co. Inc. (Chesapeake, VA) 90590
Otis Elevator Construction (Atlanta, GA) 64984
Otis Engineering Corp. (Carrollton, TX) 83494; 83495
Ouachita Coca-Cola Bottling Co. Inc. (Monroe, LA) 70364
Outboard Marine Corp. (Oxford, MS) 73243
Outboard Marine Corp. (Andrews, NC) 73549
Outboard Marine Corp. (Rutherfordton, NC) 76146
Outboard Marine Corp. Four Winds Yacht Div. (Tampa, FL) 63515
Overnite Transportation Co. (Federalsburg, MD) 71682
Overnite Transportation Co. (Landover, MD) 72028
Overnite Transportation Co. (Abingdon, VA) 90156
Overnite Transportation Co. (Chesapeake, VA) 90591
Overnite Transportation Co. (Danville, VA) 90707; 90708
Overnite Transportation Co. (Lynchburg, VA) 91275
Overnite Transportation Co. (Richmond, VA) 91938
Overnite Transportation Co. (Roanoke, VA) 92176
Owens-Brockway Glass Container (Montgomery, AL) 56360

Payless Shoesource (Enid, OK) 77058
Payless Shoesource (Guymon, OK) 77106
Payless Shoesource (Lawton, OK) 77168; 77169
Payless Shoesource (Miami, OK) 77207
Payless Shoesource (Norman, OK) 77267
Payless Shoesource (Oklahoma City, OK) 77467; 77468; 77469; 77470; 77471; 77472; 77473; 77474; 77475; 77476; 77477; 77478; 77479; 77480; 77481; 77482
Payless Shoesource (Ponca City, OK) 77710
Payless Shoesource (Poteau, OK) 77725
Payless Shoesource (Sand Springs, OK) 77782
Payless Shoesource (Sapulpa, OK) 77795
Payless Shoesource (Stillwater, OK) 77842
Payless Shoesource (Tulsa, OK) 78044; 78045; 78046; 78047; 78048; 78049; 78050; 78051; 78052; 78053
Payless Shoesource (Woodward, OK) 78263
Payless Shoesource (Charleston, SC) 78849; 78850
Payless Shoesource (Athens, TN) 80194
Payless Shoesource (Chattanooga, TN) 80464; 80465; 80466; 80467
Payless Shoesource (Dickson, TN) 80735
Payless Shoesource (Dyersburg, TN) 80757
Payless Shoesource (Fort Oglethorpe, TN) 80803
Payless Shoesource (Knoxville, TN) 81235
Payless Shoesource (Maryville, TN) 81420; 81421
Payless Shoesource (Murfreesboro, TN) 81863
Payless Shoesource (Alvin, TX) 82513
Payless Shoesource (Amarillo, TX) 82573; 82574
Payless Shoesource (Angleton, TX) 82611
Payless Shoesource (Arlington, TX) 82715; 82716
Payless Shoesource (Athens, TX) 82793
Payless Shoesource (Austin, TX) 82952; 82953; 82954
Payless Shoesource (Borger, TX) 83320
Payless Shoesource (Brenham, TX) 83338
Payless Shoesource (Brownsville, TX) 83372
Payless Shoesource (Carrollton, TX) 83496; 83497
Payless Shoesource (Cleburne, TX) 83580
Payless Shoesource (Corsicana, TX) 83786
Payless Shoesource (Dallas, TX) 84293; 84294
Payless Shoesource (El Paso, TX) 84862; 84863; 84864; 84865; 84866; 84867; 84868; 84869; 84870; 84871; 84872
Payless Shoesource (Fort Worth, TX) 85213; 85214; 85215
Payless Shoesource (Friendswood, TX) 85405
Payless Shoesource (Galveston, TX) 85459; 85460
Payless Shoesource (Garland, TX) 85520; 85521
Payless Shoesource (Houston, TX) 86640; 86641; 86642; 86643; 86644; 86645; 86646; 86647; 86648; 86649; 86650; 86651; 86652; 86653; 86654; 86655; 86656; 86657; 86658; 86659; 86660; 86661; 86662; 86663
Payless Shoesource (Hurst, TX) 87288; 87289
Payless Shoesource (Irving, TX) 87388; 87389
Payless Shoesource (Katy, TX) 87452
Payless Shoesource (Liberty, TX) 87677
Payless Shoesource (Lubbock, TX) 87774
Payless Shoesource (Mcallen, TX) 87935
Payless Shoesource (Midland, TX) 88063; 88064
Payless Shoesource (New Braunfels, TX) 88217
Payless Shoesource (Odessa, TX) 88260; 88261
Payless Shoesource (Paris, TX) 88374
Payless Shoesource (Pasadena, TX) 88451; 88452; 88453; 88454; 88455
Payless Shoesource (Pearland, TX) 88484
Payless Shoesource (Portland, TX) 88690
Payless Shoesource (Richardson, TX) 88754
Payless Shoesource (Rosenberg, TX) 88831
Payless Shoesource (San Angelo, TX) 88890; 88891
Payless Shoesource (San Antonio, TX) 89124; 89125; 89126; 89127; 89128; 89129; 89130; 89131; 89132; 89133; 89134; 89135; 89136; 89137; 89138; 89139; 89140; 89141; 89142
Payless Shoesource (Spring, TX) 89477
Payless Shoesource (Temple, TX) 89628; 89629
Payless Shoesource (Tomball, TX) 89774
Payless Shoesource (Victoria, TX) 89899; 89900
Payless Shoesource (Webster, TX) 90022
Payless Shoesource (Arlington, VA) 90366
Payless Shoesource No. 2191 (Poteau, OK) 77726
Payless Shoesource No. 2132 (Portland, TX) 88691
Payment Services Co. (Atlanta, GA) 65002
Payment Services Co. (Houston, TX) 86664
Payroll Data Service Inc. (Destin, FL) 59346
PCI Industries Inc. (Riviera Beach, FL) 62740
Pci Industries Inc. (West Palm Beach, FL) 63890
Pd Glycol (Beaumont, TX) 83195
Pearland Lumber Co. Inc. (Pearland, TX) 88485
Peco (Huntsville, AL) 55989
Peco Inc. (Jupiter, FL) 60544
Peninsula Bank (Berlin, MD) 71365; 71366
Peninsula Bank (Crisfield, MD) 71612; 71613
Peninsula Bank (Marion Station, MD) 72124
Peninsula Bank (Ocean City, MD) 72164; 72165
Peninsula Bank (Pittsville, MD) 72217
Peninsula Bank (Pocomoke City, MD) 72223; 72224
Peninsula Bank (Princess Anne, MD) 72242
Peninsula Bank (Priness Anne, MD) 72243
Peninsula Bank (Salisbury, MD) 72354; 72355; 72356
Penn Mutual Life Insurance (St Petersburg, FL) 63000
Penn Mutual Life Insurance (Jackson, MS) 73029
Penn Mutual Life Insurance (Greensboro, NC) 74875
Penn Mutual Life Insurance (Spartanburg, SC) 79922
Penn Mutual Life Insurance (Chattanooga, TN) 80468
Penn Mutual Life Insurance (Knoxville, TN) 81236
Penn Mutual Life Insurance (Dallas, TX) 84295
Penn Mutual Life Insurance (Charleston, WV) 92777
Penn Mutual Life Insurance (Clarksburg, WV) 92815
Penn Mutual Life Insurance Co. (Fort Smith, AR) 57080
Penn Mutual Life Insurance Co. (Orlando, FL) 62073
Penn Mutual Life Insurance Co. (Dunwoody, GA) 66128
Penn Mutual Life Insurance Co. (Thomasville, GA) 67801
Penn Mutual Life Insurance Co. (Baton Rouge, LA) 69594
Penn Mutual Life Insurance Co. (Meridian, MS) 73173
Penn Mutual Life Insurance Co. (Johnson City, TN) 81052
Penn Mutual Life Insurance Co. (Nashville, TN) 82079
Penn Mutual Life Insurance Co. (Dallas, TX) 84296; 84297
Penn Mutual Life Insurance Co. (Clarksburg, WV) 92816
Penney J C (Frankfort, KY) 68367
Penney J C (Antioch, TN) 80173
Penney J C (Murfreesboro, TN) 81864
Pennzoil (Beaufort, SC) 78712
Pennzoil (Houston, TX) **86665**; 86666; 86667
Pennzoil Co. (Jacksonville, FL) 60387
Pennzoil Co. (Lexington, KY) 68601
Pennzoil Co. (Abbeville, LA) 69362
Pennzoil Co. (Baton Rouge, LA) 69595
Pennzoil Co. (Houma, LA) 69963
Pennzoil Co. (New Orleans, LA) 70547
Pennzoil Co. (Beaumont, TX) 83196
Pennzoil Co. (Carthage, TX) 83520
Pennzoil Co. (Houston, TX) 86668
Pennzoil Co. (Midland, TX) 88065
Pennzoil Co. (Spring, TX) 89478
Pennzoil Co. (Waco, TX) 89959
Pennzoil Co. (Arnoldsburg, WV) 92665
Pennzoil Co. (Falling Rock, WV) 92850
Pennzoil Co. (Mannington, WV) 92924
Pennzoil Co. (Morgantown, WV) 92947
Pennzoil Co. (Parkersburg, WV) 92995
Pennzoil Co. (Spencer, WV) 93063; 93064
Pennzoil Co. (Tariff, WV) 93076
Pennzoil Corp. (Houston, TX) 86669
Pennzoil Explor&Prod Co. (Corpus Christi, TX) 83746
Pennzoil Exploration (Portland, TX) 88692
Pennzoil Exploration & Production Co. (Houston, TX) 86670
Pennzoil Lube Stop (Nashville, TN) 82080
Pennzoil Oil Change Center (Beckley, WV) 92680
Pennzoil Prodcts Co. (Vero Beach, FL) 63764
Pennzoil Producing Co. (Monroe, LA) 70365
Pennzoil Producing Co. (Tylertown, MS) 73430
Pennzoil Producing Co. (Refugio, TX) 88717
Pennzoil Producing Co. Inc. (Mc Allen, TX) 87894
Pennzoil Product Co. (Savannah, GA) 67503; 67504
Pennzoil Products (Gainesville, FL) 59896
Pennzoil Products (Fredericksburg, VA) 90933
Pennzoil Products Co. (Longwood, FL) 60941; 60942
Pennzoil Products Co. (Vero Beach, FL) 63765
Pennzoil Products Co. (Atlanta, GA) 65003; 65004; 65005
Pennzoil Products Co. (Shreveport, LA) 70760
Pennzoil Products Co. (Tinsley, MS) 73381
Pennzoil Products Co. (Chattanooga, TN) 80469
Pennzoil Products Co. (Arlington, TX) 82717; 82718
Pennzoil Products Co. (Houston, TX) 86671
Pennzoil Products Co. (Spring, TX) 89479; 89480
Pennzoil Products Co. (Charleston, WV) 92778; 92779
Pennzoil Products Co. Dickinson (Dickinson, TX) 84667
Pennzoil Products Co. Dickinson Plant (Penreco) (Dickinson, TX) 84668
Pennzoil Products Co. Shreveport Packaging Plant (Shreveport, LA) 70761
Pennzoil Self Service Station (Beckley, WV) 92681
Pennzoil Sulphur Co. (Houston, TX) 86672
Pennzoil Swifty Lube Center (Panama City, FL) 62336
Pennzoil Ten Minute Oil Change (Casselberry, FL) 58937
Pennzoil Ten Minute Oil Change (Melbourne, FL) 61083
Pennzoil 10 Minute Oil Change (Charleston, WV) 92780
Pennzoil-Zippy Lube (Fort Worth, TX) 85216
Penreco Dickinson Pennzoil Products Co. (Dickinson, TX) 84669
Penske Truck Leasing (Ashland, VA) 90406
Pentastar Electronics Inc. (Huntsville, AL) 55990; 55991
Pentastar Support Services Inc. (Richardson, TX) 88755
Pentastar Transportation Group Inc. (Tulsa, OK) 78054
Penton Publishing (Atlanta, GA) 65006
People's Bank (Statham, GA) 67654
People's Bank (Bagdad, KY) 68109
People's Bank (Bradfordsville, KY) 68166
People's Bank (Gravel Switch, KY) 68400
Peoples Bank (Hustonville, KY) 68485
People's Bank (Lebanon Junction, KY) 68511
Peoples Bank (Louisville, KY) 68943; 68944
People's Bank (Morehead, KY) 69102
People's Bank (Mount Eden, KY) 69112
Peoples Bank (Olive Hill, KY) 69158
Peoples Bank (Paint Lick, KY) 69215
Peoples Bank (Shelbyville, KY) 69277
Peoples Bank (Shepherdsville, KY) 69283; 69284; 69285
People's Bank (Taylorsville, KY) 69314
Peoples Bank (Tompkinsville, KY) 69317
People's Bank (Gulfport, MS) 72864
People's Bank (Alamo, TN) 80146
Peoples Bank (Arlington, TN) 80183
People's Bank (Brownsville, TN) 80260
People's Bank (Clifton, TN) 80610
Peoples Bank (Collierville, TN) 80620; 80621
People's Bank (Dresden, TN) 80741
People's Bank (Henning, TN) 80921
People's Bank (Humboldt, TN) 80959
People's Bank (Lebanon, TN) 81307
Peoples Bank (Memphis, TN) 81664; 81665
People's Bank (Norene, TN) 82178
People's Bank (Oliver Springs, TN) 82211
Peoples Bank (Petersburg, TN) 82227
Peoples Bank (Ridgely, TN) 82248
People's Bank (Vanleer, TN) 82391
People's Bank (Waynesboro, TN) 82407
Peoples Bank (Charles Town, WV) 92722; 92723
People's Bank (Pointe Pleasant, WV) 93007
Peoples Bank (Richwood, WV) 93024
Peoples Bank (Weirton, WV) 93098
Peoples Bank Crossville (Crossville, TN) 80704
Peoples Bank Elk Valley (Fayetteville, TN) 80798
Peoples Bank Elk Valley (Kelso, TN) 81068
Peoples Bank Hustonville (Stanford, KY) 69310
Peoples Bank of Maryland (Denton, MD) 71642; 71643
Peoples Bank of Morehead (Morehead, KY) 69103
Peoples Bank of Mullens (Mullens, WV) 92956
Peoples Bank of Murray (Murray, KY) 69128
Peoples Bank of Polk County (Benton, TN) 80202
Peoples Bank of Richwood Inc. (Richwood, WV) 93025
Peoples Bank & Trust (Cookeville, TN) 80662
Peoples Bank & Trust Co. (Berea, KY) 68128
People's Bank & Trust Co. (Earlington, KY) 68268
Peoples Bank & Trust Co. (Greensburg, KY) 68404
Peoples Bank & Trust Co. (Hazard, KY) 68427
Peoples Bank & Trust Co. (Madisonville, KY) 69067; 69068; 69069
Peoples Bank & Trust Co. (Owenton, KY) 69200; 69201
Peoples Bank & Trust Co. (Sunbright, TN) 82365
Peoples Bank & Trust Co. (Wartburg, TN) 82401
Peoples Drug Store (Lutcher, LA) 70205
Peoples Drug Store (Oxford, NC) 75786
Peoples Drug Store (Taylorsville, NC) 76370
Peoples Drug Store (W Jefferson, NC) 76419
Peoples Drug Store (Williamston, NC) 76531
Peoples Drug Store (Wilmington, NC) 76585
Peoples Drug Store (Saluda, SC) 79850
Peoples Drug Store Inc. (Lenoir, NC) 75384
Peoples Drug Stores Inc. (Hickory, NC) 75090
Peoples Natural Gas Co. (Texline, TX) 89748
Peoples & Union Bank (Lewisburg, TN) 81327; 81328; 81329; 81330
Pepsi-Cola Knoxville (Knoxville, TN) 81237
Pepsi-Cola South North America (Conroe, TX) 83676
Pepsi-Cola Bottlers of Miami (Miami, FL) 61388
Pepsi-Cola Bottling (Asheville, NC) 73631
Pepsi-Cola Bottling Co. (Decatur, AL) 55601
Pepsi-Cola Bottling Co. (Huntsville, AL) 55992
Pepsi-Cola Bottling Co. (Luverne, AL) 56116
Pepsi-Cola Bottling Co. (Selma, AL) 56533
Pepsi-Cola Bottling Co. (Tuscaloosa, AL) 56665
Pepsi-Cola Bottling Co. (Batesville, AR) 56759
Pepsi-Cola Bottling Co. (Jonesboro, AR) 57227
Pepsi-Cola Bottling Co. (Springdale, AR) 57639
Pepsi-Cola Bottling Co. (Wilmington, DE) 58092
Pepsi-Cola Bottling Co. (Fort Walton Beach, FL) 59832
Pepsi-Cola Bottling Co. (Gainesville, FL) 59897
Pepsi-Cola Bottling Co. (Jacksonville, FL) 60388
Pepsi-Cola Bottling Co. (Orlando, FL) 62074; 62075
Pepsi-Cola Bottling Co. (Riviera Beach, FL) 62741
Pepsi-Cola Bottling Co. (Atlanta, GA) 65007
Pepsi-Cola Bottling Co. (Augusta, GA) 65344
Pepsi-Cola Bottling Co. (Bainbridge, GA) 65368
Pepsi-Cola Bottling Co. (Bogart, GA) 65386
Pepsi-Cola Bottling Co. (Gainsville, GA) 66300
Pepsi-Cola Bottling Co. (Macon, GA) 66702
Pepsi-Cola Bottling Co. (Newnan, GA) 67084
Pepsi-Cola Bottling Co. (Savannah, GA) 67505
Pepsi-Cola Bottling Co. (Valdosta, GA) 67966
Pepsi-Cola Bottling Co. (Corbin, KY) 68210; 68211
Pepsi-Cola Bottling Co. (Hazard, KY) 68428
Pepsi-Cola Bottling Co. (Lexington, KY) 68602
Pepsi-Cola Bottling Co. (Winchester, KY) 69349
Pepsi-Cola Bottling Co. (Lake Charles, LA) 70155
Pepsi-Cola Bottling Co. (Cheverly, MD) 71526
Pepsi-Cola Bottling Co. (Havre DeGrace, MD) 71918
Pepsi-Cola Bottling Co. (Salisbury, MD) 72357
Pepsi-Cola Bottling Co. (Columbus, MS) 72720
Pepsi-Cola Bottling Co. (Greenville, MS) 72811
Pepsi-Cola Bottling Co. (Jackson, MS) 73030
Pepsi Cola Bottling Co. (McComb, MS) 73155
Pepsi-Cola Bottling Co. (Tupelo, MS) 73416
Pepsi-Cola Bottling Co. (Charlette, NC) 73825
Pepsi-Cola Bottling Co. (Cherryville, NC) 74249
Pepsi-Cola Bottling Co. (Durham, NC) 74421
Pepsi-Cola Bottling Co. (Elizabeth City, NC) 74483
Pepsi-Cola Bottling Co. (Goldsboro, NC) 74728
Pepsi-Cola Bottling Co. (Greenville, NC) 74970
Pepsi-Cola Bottling Co. (Hickory, NC) 75091
Pepsi-Cola Bottling Co. (Jonesville, NC) 75252
Pepsi-Cola Bottling Co. (Kinston, NC) 75326
Pepsi-Cola Bottling Co. (Lumberton, NC) 75469

Pepsi-Cola Bottling Co. (Marion, NC) 75506
Pepsi-Cola Bottling Co. (Midland, NC) 75559
Pepsi-Cola Bottling Co. (New Bern, NC) 75731
Pepsi-Cola Bottling Co. (Rockingham, NC) 76065
Pepsi-Cola Bottling Co. (Rocky Mountain, NC) 76113
Pepsi-Cola Bottling Co. (Roxboro, NC) 76130
Pepsi-Cola Bottling Co. (Enid, OK) 77059
Pepsi-Cola Bottling Co. (Lawton, OK) 77170
Pepsi-Cola Bottling Co. (Oklahoma City, OK) 77483
Pepsi-Cola Bottling Co. (Tulsa, OK) 78055
Pepsi-Cola Bottling Co. (Anderson, SC) 78685
Pepsi-Cola Bottling Co. (Bennettsville, SC) 78729
Pepsi-Cola Bottling Co. (Conway, SC) 79133
Pepsi-Cola Bottling Co. (Greenville, SC) 79401
Pepsi-Cola Bottling Co. (Kingstree, SC) 79557
Pepsi-Cola Bottling Co. (Jackson, TN) 80994
Pepsi-Cola Bottling Co. (Knoxville, TN) 81238
Pepsi-Cola Bottling Co. (Nashville, TN) 82081
Pepsi-Cola Bottling Co. (Austin, TX) 82955
Pepsi-Cola Bottling Co. (Beaumont, TX) 83197
Pepsi Cola Bottling Co. (Corpus Christi, TX) 83747
Pepsi-Cola Bottling Co. (El Paso, TX) 84873
Pepsi-Cola Bottling Co. (Fort Worth, TX) 85217
Pepsi-Cola Bottling Co. (San Antonio, TX) 89143
Pepsi-Cola Bottling Co. (Charlottesville, VA) 90546
Pepsi-Cola Bottling Co. (Hollins, VA) 91148
Pepsi-Cola Bottling Co. (Newport News, VA) 91477
Pepsi-Cola Bottling Co. (Petersburg, VA) 91634
Pepsi-Cola Bottling Co. (Richmond, VA) 91941
Pepsi-Cola Bottling Co. (Warrenton, VA) 92527
Pepsi-Cola Bottling Co. Knoxville (Knoxville, TN) 81239
Pepsi-Cola Bottling Co. Tampa (Tampa, FL) 63516
Pepsi-Cola Bottling Co. Winston-Salem (Winston-Salem, NC) 76737
Pepsi-Cola Co. (Mobile, AL) 56219
Pepsi-Cola Co. (Fort Smith, AR) 57081
Pepsi-Cola Co. (Daytona Beach, FL) 59196
Pepsi-Cola Co. (Tallahassee, FL) 63254
Pepsi-Cola Co. (Tampa, FL) 63517
Pepsi-Cola Co. (Codele, GA) 65573
Pepsi-Cola Co. (Columbus, GA) 65647
Pepsi-Cola Co. (Rome, GA) 67345
Pepsi-Cola Co. (Vidalia, GA) 67988
Pepsi-Cola Co. (Louisville, KY) 68945
Pepsi-Cola Co. (Shreveport, LA) 70762
Pepsi-Cola Co. (Baltimore, MD) 71219
Pepsi-Cola Co. (Hattiesburg, MS) 72894
Pepsi-Cola Co. (Wilmington, NC) 76586
Pepsi-Cola Co. (Columbia, SC) 79060
Pepsi-Cola Co. (Summerville, SC) 79990
Pepsi-Cola Co. (Chattanooga, TN) 80470
Pepsi-Cola Co. (Cookeville, TN) 80663
Pepsi-Cola Co. (Bryan, TX) 83400
Pepsi-Cola Co. (Conroe, TX) 83677
Pepsi-Cola Co. (Houston, TX) 86673
Pepsi-Cola Co. (Longview, TX) 87727
Pepsi-Cola Co. (Lubbock, TX) 87775
Pepsi-Cola Co. (Mesquite, TX) 87982
Pepsi-Cola Co. (San Antonio, TX) 89144
Pepsi-Cola Co. (Waco, TX) 89960
Pepsi-Cola Co. (Huntington, WV) 92890
Pepsi-Cola Co. (Nitor, WV) 92968
Pepsi-Cola Co. South (Mesquite, TX) 87983
Pepsi-Cola Co. West Columbia Plant (West Columbia, SC) 80099
Pepsi-Cola Distributing Co. (Albany, GA) 64085
Pepsi-Cola Distributing Co. (Corinth, MS) 72741
Pepsi-Cola Distributing Co. (Washington, NC) 76458
Pepsi Cola General Bottlers (Bowling Green, KY) 68159; 68160
Pepsi-Cola General Bottlers (Covington, KY) 68230
Pepsi-Cola General Bottlers (Elizabethtown, KY) 68289
Pepsi Cola General Bottlers (Hopkinsville, KY) 68482
Pepsi Cola General Bottlers (Owensboro, KY) 69190
Pepsi Cola General Bottlers (Marion, VA) 91336
Pepsi Cola General Bottlers (Princeton, WV) 93012
Pepsi-Cola Manufacturing (Arlington, TX) 82719
Pepsi Cola Manufacturing Co. Inc. (Cidra, PR) 78398
Pepsi-Cola Mfg. Co. Inc. (Cidra, PR) 78399
Pepsi-Cola Seven-Up (Fayetteville, NC) 74570
Pepsi-Cola Seven-Up Bottling (Montgomery, AL) 56363
Pepsi-Cola Seven-Up Bottling (Monroe, LA) 70366
Pepsi-Cola Seven-Up Bottling (Pineville, LA) 70624
Pepsi-Cola Seven-Up Bottling (Batesville, MS) 72600
Pepsi-Cola Seven-Up Group (Baton Rouge, LA) 69596
Pepsi-Cola South (Bay City, TX) 83104
Pepsi-Cola South (Dallas, TX) 84298
Pepsi-Cola South (Houston, TX) 86674
Pepsi-Cola South Bottling Co. (Burton, SC) 78753
Pepsi South (Johnson City, TN) 81053
Pepsico Food Systems Inc. (Oklahoma City, OK) 77484
PepsiCo Food Systems Worldwide (Dallas, TX) 84299
PepsiCo Foods International (Plano, TX) 88595
Pepsico Inc. (Arlington, TX) 82720
Pepsico Worldwide Foods (Plano, TX) 88596
Performance Friction Products (Longview, TX) 87728
Performance Plastics Business Unit (Kingsport, TN) 81115
Perkin Elmer Corp. (Orlando, FL) 62076
Perkin Elmer Corp. Inc. (Tulsa, OK) 78056
Perma Products (Atlanta, GA) 65008
Perma Products Co. (Duncanville, TX) 84702
Perma Products Co., Inc. (Duncanville, TX) 84703; 84704
Perma Products Inc. (Atlanta, GA) 65009
Perma Products Inc. (Duncanville, TX) 84705
Permatech (Charlotte, NC) 74104
Permatech Inc. (Graham, NC) 74750; 74751
Personal Finance Co. (Batesville, MS) 72601
Personal Finance Co. (Columbus, MS) 72721
Personal Finance Co. (Corinth, MS) 72742
Personal Finance Co. (Eupora, MS) 72764
Personal Finance Co. (Iuka, MS) 72935
Personal Finance Co. (Pontotoc, MS) 73304
Personal Finance Co. (Starkville, MS) 73367
Personal Finance Co. (Tupelo, MS) 73417
Personal Finance Co. (West Point, MS) 73484
Personal Finance Co. Inc. (Dallas, TX) 84300
Personal Performance Consultan (Decatur, GA) 65879
Personal Performance Consultants (Casselberry, FL) 58938
Personal Performance Consultants (Orlando, FL) 62077
Personal Performance Consultants (Atlanta, GA) 65010
Personal Performance Consultants (Chamblee, GA) 65539
Personal Performance Consultants (Decatur, GA) 65880
Personal Performance Consultants (Houston, TX) 86675
Personal Sportswear (Dallas, TX) 84301
Personal Systems (Washington, DC) 58404
Pest Elimination Service (Fairview, TN) 80787
Pest Elimination Services (Houston, TX) 86676
Pet Bakery (Rome, GA) 67346
Pet Dairy (Charlotte, NC) 74105
Pet Dairy (Hickory, NC) 75092
Pet Inc. (Atlanta, GA) 65011
Pet, Inc. (Lithonia, GA) 66602
Pet Inc. (Federalsburg, MD) 71683
Pet, Inc. (Chickasha, OK) 76934
Pet, Inc. (Greeneville, TN) 80887
Pet Inc. Frozen Foods Div. (Chickasha, OK) 76935
Pet Inc. Grocery Operations (Lithonia, GA) 66603
Pet Inc. Pet Dairy Group (Greenville, SC) 79402
Pet Inc. Dairy (Portsmouth, VA) 91663
Pet Inc. Mountain Pass Canning (Anthony, TX) 82620
Pet Poultry Products Inc. (Bridgeville, DE) 57754
Pet Specialties Inc. (Hanceville, AL) 55851
Peterbilt Motors Co. (Madison, TN) 81379
Peterbilt Motors Co. (Denton, TX) 84626
Petite Sophisticate (Birmingham, AL) 55329; 55330
Petite Sophisticate (Dothan, AL) 55658
Petite Sophisticate (Newark, DE) 57925
Petite Sophisticate (Altamonte Springs, FL) 58561
Petite Sophisticate (Boca Raton, FL) 58726
Petite Sophisticate (Boynton Beach, FL) 58786
Petite Sophisticate (Clearwater, FL) 59035
Petite Sophisticate (Fort Lauderdale, FL) 59552
Petite Sophisticate (Fort Myers, FL) 59731
Petite Sophisticate (Gainesville, FL) 59898
Petite Sophisticate (Jacksonville, FL) 60389; 60390
Petite Sophisticate (Lakeland, FL) 60760
Petite Sophisticate (Miami, FL) 61389
Petite Sophisticate (Orange Park, FL) 61892
Petite Sophisticate (Orlando, FL) 62078; 62079
Petite Sophisticate (Pensacola, FL) 62455
Petite Sophisticate (Sarasota, FL) 62854
Petite Sophisticate (St Petersburg, FL) 63001
Petite Sophisticate (Stuart, FL) 63176
Petite Sophisticate (Tampa, FL) 63518
Petite Sophisticate (Atlanta, GA) 65012; 65013; 65014; 65015; 65016
Petite Sophisticate (Kennesaw, GA) 66441
Petite Sophisticate (Morrow, GA) 67033
Petite Sophisticate (Louisville, KY) 68946
Petite Sophisticate (Kenner, LA) 70002
Petite Sophisticate (Metairie, LA) 70298
Petite Sophisticate (Bethesda, MD) 71429; 71430
Petite Sophisticate (Salisbury, MD) 72358
Petite Sophisticate (Wheaton, MD) 72562
Petite Sophisticate (Durham, NC) 74422
Petite Sophisticate (Oklahoma City, OK) 77485; 77486; 77487
Petite Sophisticate (Charleston, SC) 78851
Petite Sophisticate (Columbia, SC) 79061
Petite Sophisticate (Chattanooga, TN) 80471
Petite Sophisticate (Arlington, TX) 82721; 82722
Petite Sophisticate (Austin, TX) 82956; 82957
Petite Sophisticate (Beaumont, TX) 83198
Petite Sophisticate (Dallas, TX) 84302; 84303
Petite Sophisticate (Fort Worth, TX) 85218; 85219
Petite Sophisticate (Houston, TX) 86677; 86678; 86679; 86680
Petite Sophisticate (Humble, TX) 87238
Petite Sophisticate (San Antonio, TX) 89145; 89146
Petite Sophisticate (Richmond, VA) 91942
Petrocorp (Houston, TX) 86681
Peyton Packing Co. (El Paso, TX) 84874
Peyton Packing Co. Inc. (El Paso, TX) 84875
Pfizer Inc. (Southport, NC) 76287
Pfizer Inc. Coty Div. (Sanford, NC) 76200
Pfizer Pharmaceuticals Inc. (Barceloneta, PR) 78330
Pfizer Specialty Minerals Inc. (Chickasaw, AL) 55512
PG&E Resources Co. (Dallas, TX) 84304
Pgg Industries Inc. (Wichita Falls, TX) 90087
Pharmacy Corp. of America (Fort Smith, AR) 57082
Phelps Dodge Copper Products (El Paso, TX) 84876
Phelps Dodge International Corp. (Coral Gables, FL) 59103
Phelps Dodge Magnet Wire Co. (Hopkinsville, KY) 68483; 68484
Phelps Dodge Refining Corp. (El Paso, TX) 84877
Phelps Dodge Refining Corp. El Paso Works (El Paso, TX) 84878
PHH (Hunt Valley, MD) **71941**
PHH Corp. (Hunt Valley, MD) 71942
PHH Fleet America (Hunt Valley, MD) 71943
PHH US Mortgage (Atlanta, GA) 65017
PHH US Mortgage Corp. (Jonesboro, GA) 66394
Phibro Energy USA Inc. (Houston, TX) 86682
Phibro Energy USA Inc. (Texas City, TX) 89729
Phibro Refinery Krotz Springs Refinery (Krotz Springs, LA) 70029
Phibro Refining (Krotz Springs, LA) 70030
Phibro Refining St. Rose Refinery (St. Rose, LA) 70875; 70876
Phibro Refining Inc. (Houston, TX) 86683
Phibro Refining Inc. (Texas City, TX) 89730
Phibro Refining Inc. St. Rose Refinery (St. Rose, LA) 70877
Philip Morris Inc. (Louisville, KY) 68947
Philip Morris USA (Richmond, VA) 91943
Philip Morris USA Bl Plant (Richmond, VA) 91944
Philip Morris USA Cabarrus Manufacturing Center (Concord, NC) 74317
Philip Morris USA MS Complex (Louisville, KY) 68948
Philip Morris USA Park 500 (Chester, VA) 90622
Philip Morris USA Mfg. Center (Richmond, VA) 91945
Philips P. R. Core Inc. Durand/ Learned Plant (Guayama, PR) 78425
Philips P.R. Core Inc. Durand/ Learned Plant (Guayama, PR) 78426
Phillip Morris USA Bl Plant (Richmond, VA) 91946
Phillip Morris USA Cabarrus (Concord, NC) 74318
Phillip Morris USA Park 500 (Chester, VA) 90623
Phillip Morris USA Westab Annex (Richmond, VA) 91947
Phillip Morris USA Manufacturing Center (Richmond, VA) 91948
Phillips Alaska Pipeline Corp. (Bartlesville, OK) 76837
Phillips Coal Co. (Richardson, TX) 88756
Phillips Driscopipe Inc. (Richardson, TX) 88757
Phillips Fibers Corp. Spartanburg Plant (Spartanburg, SC) 79923
Phillips Fruitland Gas Corp. (Houston, TX) 86684
Phillips Gas Co. (Houston, TX) 86685
Phillips Investments (Richmond, VA) 91949
Phillips Natrual Gas Co. (Bartlesville, OK) 76838
Phillips P. R. Core Inc. Phillips Paraxylene Inc. (Guayama, PR) 78427
Phillips Petroleum (Bartlesville, OK) **76839**
Phillips Petroleum Co. (Bartlesville, OK) 76840
Phillips Petroleum Co. Houston Chemical Complex (Pasadena, TX) 88456
Phillips Petroleum Co. United Kingdom Ltd. (Bartlesville, OK) 76841
Phillips Pipe Line Co. (Doraville, GA) 65944
Phillips Pipe Line Co. (Bartlesville, OK) 76842
Phillips P.R. Core Inc. Phillips Paraxylene Inc. (Guayama, PR) 78428
Phillips P.R. Core/P.P. Inc. Duran/ Learned Plant (Guayama, PR) 78429
Phillips Puerto Rico Core Inc. (Bartlesville, OK) 76843
Phillips Research Center (Bartlesville, OK) 76844
Phillips Research Ctr. (Bartlesville, OK) 76845
Phillips 66 Freeport Terminal Ii (Sweeny, TX) 89576
Phillips 66 Jones Creek Terminal (Jones Creek, TX) 87445
Phillips 66 Co. (Borger, TX) 83321
Phillips 66 Co. (Sweeny, TX) 89577
Phillips 66 Co. Clemens Terminal (Brazoria, TX) 83333
Phillips 66 Co. Freeport Ii Terminal (Sweeny, TX) 89578
Phillips 66 Co. Freeport Terminal (Sweeny, TX) 89579
Phillips 66 Co. Jones Creek Terminal (Jones Creek, TX) 87446
Phillips 66 Co. Philtex/Ryton Complex (Borger, TX) 83322
Phillips 66 Co. San Bernard Terminal (Sweeny, TX) 89580
Philtankers Inc. (Bartlesville, OK) 76846
Phoenix Home Life Mutual Inc. (Bethesda, MD) 71431
Phoenix Home Life Mutual Insurance Co. (Bethesda, MD) 71432
Phoenix Packaging (Dallas, TX) 84305
Phoenix Packaging (Plano, TX) 88597
Phoenix Packaging Inc. (Winston-Salem, NC) 76738
Pickett County Bank & Trust Co. (Byrdstown, TN) 80265; 80266
Piedmont Medical Center (Rock Hill, SC) 79836
Piggly Wiggly (Abbeville, AL) 54951
Piggly Wiggly (Aliceville, AL) 54983
Piggly Wiggly (Atmore, AL) 55051
Piggly Wiggly (Attalla, AL) 55056
Piggly Wiggly (Auburn, AL) 55067
Piggly Wiggly (Bay Minette, AL) 55076
Piggly Wiggly (Birmingham, AL) 55331; 55332; 55333; 55334; 55335
Piggly Wiggly (Boaz, AL) 55473
Piggly Wiggly (Brewton, AL) 55483
Piggly Wiggly (Butler, AL) 55496
Piggly Wiggly (Centre, AL) 55505
Piggly Wiggly (Chatom, AL) 55509
Piggly Wiggly (Citronelle, AL) 55517
Piggly Wiggly (Courtland, AL) 55536
Piggly Wiggly (Cullman, AL) 55547
Piggly Wiggly (Dadeville, AL) 55558; 55559
Piggly Wiggly (Daleville, AL) 55563
Piggly Wiggly (Dothan, AL) 55659; 55660
Piggly Wiggly (Elba, AL) 55676
Piggly Wiggly (Enterprise, AL) 55689
Piggly Wiggly (Evergreen, AL) 55710
Piggly Wiggly (Florala, AL) 55734
Piggly Wiggly (Florence, AL) 55741
Piggly Wiggly (Geneva, AL) 55804
Piggly Wiggly (Goodwater, AL) 55810
Piggly Wiggly (Greensboro, AL) 55812
Piggly Wiggly (Grove Hill, AL) 55820
Piggly Wiggly (Guntersville, AL) 55831
Piggly Wiggly (Gurley, AL) 55838

Piggly American Business Locations Directory

Piggly Wiggly (Haleyville, AL) 55843; 55844
Piggly Wiggly (Hamilton, AL) 55849
Piggly Wiggly (Hartford, AL) 55853
Piggly Wiggly (Hartselle, AL) 55860
Piggly Wiggly (Headland, AL) 55862
Piggly Wiggly (Huntsville, AL) 55993
Piggly Wiggly (Jackson, AL) 56068
Piggly Wiggly (Jemison, AL) 56093
Piggly Wiggly (Killen, AL) 56096
Piggly Wiggly (Lanett, AL) 56104
Piggly Wiggly (Monroeville, AL) 56267
Piggly Wiggly (Montevallo, AL) 56275
Piggly Wiggly (Moulton, AL) 56397; 56398
Piggly Wiggly (Opp, AL) 56434
Piggly Wiggly (Parrish, AL) 56446
Piggly Wiggly (Phenix City, AL) 56463; 56464; 56465; 56466; 56467; 56468; 56469
Piggly Wiggly (Phil Campbell, AL) 56480
Piggly Wiggly (Roanoke, AL) 56501
Piggly Wiggly (Rogersville, AL) 56506
Piggly Wiggly (Russellville, AL) 56509
Piggly Wiggly (Samson, AL) 56512
Piggly Wiggly (Selma, AL) 56534
Piggly Wiggly (Shelby, AL) 56567
Piggly Wiggly (Sulligent, AL) 56574
Piggly Wiggly (Tuscaloosa, AL) 56666; 56667
Piggly Wiggly (Union Springs, AL) 56687
Piggly Wiggly (Winfield, AL) 56709; 56710
Piggly Wiggly (Arkadelphia, AR) 56718; 56719
Piggly Wiggly (Bald Knob, AR) 56737
Piggly Wiggly (Camden, AR) 56838
Piggly Wiggly (Clarksville, AR) 56849
Piggly Wiggly (Conway, AR) 56867
Piggly Wiggly (De Queen, AR) 56892
Piggly Wiggly (Gurdon, AR) 57126
Piggly Wiggly (Hot Springs National Park, AR) 57178; 57179; 57180; 57181
Piggly Wiggly (Morrilton, AR) 57379
Piggly Wiggly (Mulberry, AR) 57398
Piggly Wiggly (Murfreesboro, AR) 57399
Piggly Wiggly (Osceola, AR) 57484
Piggly Wiggly (Ozark, AR) 57486
Piggly Wiggly (Stuttgart, AR) 57662
Piggly Wiggly (Wynne, AR) 57743
Piggly Wiggly (Brandon, FL) 58875
Piggly Wiggly (Cantonment, FL) 58911
Piggly Wiggly (Century, FL) 58947
Piggly Wiggly (Clearwater, FL) 59036
Piggly Wiggly (Cross City, FL) 59129
Piggly Wiggly (De Funiak Spring, FL) 59240
Piggly Wiggly (Dunedin, FL) 59364
Piggly Wiggly (Havana, FL) 59968
Piggly Wiggly (Lakeland, FL) 60761
Piggly Wiggly (Lynn Haven, FL) 60956
Piggly Wiggly (Marianna, FL) 61005
Piggly Wiggly (Miami, FL) 61390
Piggly Wiggly (Milton, FL) 61549
Piggly Wiggly (Niceville, FL) 61714
Piggly Wiggly (Ocoee, FL) 61835
Piggly Wiggly (Orlando, FL) 62080
Piggly Wiggly (Panama City, FL) 62337
Piggly Wiggly (Vero Beach, FL) 63766
Piggly Wiggly (Americus, GA) 64142
Piggly Wiggly (Atlanta, GA) 65018; 65019
Piggly Wiggly (Bowdon, GA) 65389
Piggly Wiggly (Brunswick, GA) 65420
Piggly Wiggly (Cairo, GA) 65447
Piggly-Wiggly (Calhoun, GA) 65473
Piggly Wiggly (Camilla, GA) 65481
Piggly Wiggly (Colquitt, GA) 65613
Piggly Wiggly (Cordele, GA) 65714; 65715
Piggly Wiggly (Decatur, GA) 65881
Piggly Wiggly (Donalsonville, GA) 65917
Piggly Wiggly (Douglas, GA) 65972
Piggly Wiggly (Dublin, GA) 66012
Piggly Wiggly (Eastman, GA) 66159
Piggly Wiggly (Fitzgerald, GA) 66211
Piggly Wiggly (Forest Park, GA) 66245
Piggly Wiggly (Fort Valley, GA) 66259
Piggly Wiggly (Griffin, GA) 66319
Piggly Wiggly (Hazlehurst, GA) 66348
Piggly Wiggly (Hinesville, GA) 66355
Piggly Wiggly (Louisville, GA) 66620; 66621; 66622
Piggly Wiggly (Lyons, GA) 66632
Piggly Wiggly (Macon, GA) 66703; 66704
Piggly Wiggly (Milledgeville, GA) 66981; 66982
Piggly Wiggly (Moultrie, GA) 67059; 67060; 67061
Piggly Wiggly (Pelham, GA) 67257
Piggly Wiggly (Quitman, GA) 67289
Piggly Wiggly (Sandersville, GA) 67430
Piggly Wiggly (Savannah, GA) 67506; 67507
Piggly Wiggly (Statesboro, GA) 67641
Piggly Wiggly (Stone Mountain, GA) 67729
Piggly Wiggly (Swainsboro, GA) 67755
Piggly Wiggly (Sylvania, GA) 67770
Piggly Wiggly (Sylvester, GA) 67775
Piggly Wiggly (Tifton, GA) 67827
Piggly Wiggly (Vidalia, GA) 67989; 67990
Piggly Wiggly (Warner Robins, GA) 68018
Piggly Wiggly (Waycross, GA) 68036
Piggly Wiggly (Ball, LA) 69439
Piggly Wiggly (Baton Rouge, LA) 69597; 69598
Piggly Wiggly (Bernice, LA) 69696
Piggly Wiggly (De Ridder, LA) 69816
Piggly Wiggly (Ferriday, LA) 69853
Piggly Wiggly (Haynesville, LA) 69945
Piggly Wiggly (Homer, LA) 69948
Piggly Wiggly (Jennings, LA) 69980
Piggly Wiggly (Jonesboro, LA) 69984
Piggly Wiggly (Jonesville, LA) 69986
Piggly Wiggly (Lafayette, LA) 70082; 70083
Piggly Wiggly (Mansfield, LA) 70215
Piggly Wiggly (Minden, LA) 70343; 70344
Piggly Wiggly (Oakdale, LA) 70599
Piggly Wiggly (Plaquemine, LA) 70641
Piggly Wiggly (Ringgold, LA) 70665
Piggly Wiggly (Ruston, LA) 70670
Piggly Wiggly (Shreveport, LA) 70763; 70764
Piggly Wiggly (Springhill, LA) 70853; 70854; 70855
Piggly Wiggly (Tallulah, LA) 70908
Piggly Wiggly (Vidalia, LA) 70930
Piggly Wiggly (Vivian, LA) 70936
Piggly Wiggly (West Monroe, LA) 70955
Piggly Wiggly (Amory, MS) 72585
Piggly Wiggly (Ashland, MS) 72591
Piggly Wiggly (Bay Springs, MS) 72604
Piggly Wiggly (Belmont, MS) 72610
Piggly Wiggly (Biloxi, MS) 72631
Piggly Wiggly (Booneville, MS) 72646
Piggly Wiggly (Carthage, MS) 72662
Piggly Wiggly (Charleston, MS) 72664
Piggly Wiggly (Clarksdale, MS) 72677
Piggly Wiggly (Collins, MS) 72696
Piggly Wiggly (Columbia, MS) 72699
Piggly Wiggly (Crystal Springs, MS) 72750
Piggly Wiggly (Dennis, MS) 72751
Piggly Wiggly (Durant, MS) 72752
Piggly Wiggly (Eupora, MS) 72765
Piggly Wiggly (Fulton, MS) 72779
Piggly Wiggly (Greenwood, MS) 72837; 72838
Piggly Wiggly (Houston, MS) 72920
Piggly Wiggly (Indianola, MS) 72929
Piggly Wiggly (Laurel, MS) 73106
Piggly Wiggly (Leakesville, MS) 73110
Piggly Wiggly (Lexington, MS) 73115
Piggly Wiggly (Louisville, MS) 73124
Piggly Wiggly (Lucedale, MS) 73128
Piggly Wiggly (Morton, MS) 73190
Piggly Wiggly (Natchez, MS) 73206; 73207; 73208
Piggly Wiggly (Poplarville, MS) 73305
Piggly Wiggly (Prentiss, MS) 73307
Piggly Wiggly (Ruleville, MS) 73334
Piggly Wiggly (Sardis, MS) 73338
Piggly Wiggly (Smithville, MS) 73345
Piggly Wiggly (Starkville, MS) 73368
Piggly Wiggly (Sumrall, MS) 73375
Piggly Wiggly (Taylorsville, MS) 73379
Piggly Wiggly (Tunica, MS) 73383
Piggly Wiggly (Tylertown, MS) 73431
Piggly Wiggly (Union, MS) 73432
Piggly Wiggly (Vaiden, MS) 73444
Piggly Wiggly (Water Valley, MS) 73470
Piggly Wiggly (Wiggins, MS) 73492
Piggly Wiggly (Winona, MS) 73494
Piggly Wiggly (Benson, NC) 73685
Piggly Wiggly (Castle Hayne, NC) 73805
Piggly Wiggly (Clinton, NC) 74293; 74294; 74295
Piggly Wiggly (Dunn, NC) 74376
Piggly Wiggly (Faison, NC) 74516
Piggly Wiggly (Fayetteville, NC) 74571
Piggly Wiggly (Fuquay-Varina, NC) 74640
Piggly Wiggly (Garland, NC) 74644
Piggly Wiggly (Goldsboro, NC) 74729; 74730
Piggly Wiggly (Grantsboro, NC) 74756
Piggly Wiggly (Greenville, NC) 74971
Piggly Wiggly (Jacksonville, NC) 75223
Piggly Wiggly (Kinston, NC) 75327
Piggly Wiggly (Lumberton, NC) 75470
Piggly Wiggly (Maxton, NC) 75535
Piggly Wiggly (Midway Park, NC) 75560
Piggly Wiggly (Murphy, NC) 75706
Piggly Wiggly (Newton Grove, NC) 75758
Piggly Wiggly (Pembroke, NC) 75794
Piggly Wiggly (Pikeville, NC) 75797
Piggly Wiggly (Pittsboro, NC) 75831
Piggly Wiggly (Red Springs, NC) 75993
Piggly Wiggly (Reidsville, NC) 76008
Piggly Wiggly (Richlands, NC) 76027
Piggly Wiggly (Rocky Mount, NC) 76098
Piggly Wiggly (Roseboro, NC) 76117
Piggly Wiggly (Selma, NC) 76226
Piggly Wiggly (Smithfield, NC) 76264
Piggly Wiggly (St. Pauls, NC) 76307
Piggly Wiggly (Swansboro, NC) 76354; 76355
Piggly Wiggly (Tarboro, NC) 76364
Piggly Wiggly (Wallace, NC) 76442; 76443
Piggly Wiggly (Williamston, NC) 76532
Piggly Wiggly (Wilson, NC) 76637; 76638; 76639
Piggly Wiggly (Broken Arrow, OK) 76887
Piggly Wiggly (Broken Bow, OK) 76894
Piggly Wiggly (Durant, OK) 77002
Piggly Wiggly (Idabel, OK) 77143; 77144
Piggly Wiggly (Muldrow, OK) 77216
Piggly Wiggly (Pawnee, OK) 77700
Piggly Wiggly (Aiken, SC) 78655
Piggly Wiggly (Andrews, SC) 78699
Piggly Wiggly (Barnwell, SC) 78702
Piggly Wiggly (Beaufort, SC) 78713; 78714; 78715
Piggly Wiggly (Bishopville, SC) 78744
Piggly Wiggly (Camden, SC) 78761
Piggly Wiggly (Charleston, SC) 78852; 78853; 78854; 78855; 78856; 78857; 78858; 78859; 78860; 78861; 78862; 78863
Piggly Wiggly (Columbia, SC) 79062; 79063; 79064; 79065; 79066; 79067; 79068; 79069
Piggly Wiggly (Conway, SC) 79134
Piggly Wiggly (Darlington, SC) 79155
Piggly Wiggly (Florence, SC) 79218
Piggly Wiggly (Fountain Inn, SC) 79248
Piggly Wiggly (Goose Creek, SC) 79286
Piggly Wiggly (Great Falls, SC) 79289
Piggly Wiggly (Greenwood, SC) 79461
Piggly Wiggly (Hampton, SC) 79493
Piggly Wiggly (Hartsville, SC) 79499
Piggly Wiggly (Holly Hill, SC) 79523
Piggly Wiggly (Hollywood, SC) 79525
Piggly Wiggly (Johnston, SC) 79546
Piggly Wiggly (Kingstree, SC) 79558
Piggly Wiggly (Lake City, SC) 79563
Piggly Wiggly (Loris, SC) 79616
Piggly Wiggly (Lugoff, SC) 79622
Piggly Wiggly (Manning, SC) 79635
Piggly Wiggly (Mt Pleasant, SC) 79677
Piggly Wiggly (Mt. Pleasant, SC) 79686
Piggly Wiggly (Myrtle Beach, SC) 79707; 79708
Piggly Wiggly (N Myrtle Beach, SC) 79720
Piggly Wiggly (North Augusta, SC) 79736
Piggly Wiggly (Orangeburg, SC) 79776
Piggly Wiggly (Prosperity, SC) 79806
Piggly Wiggly (Ridgeland, SC) 79809
Piggly Wiggly (Saluda, SC) 79851
Piggly Wiggly (Spartanburg, SC) 79924
Piggly Wiggly (St Matthews, SC) 79970
Piggly Wiggly (St. George, SC) 79973
Piggly Wiggly (Summerville, SC) 79991
Piggly Wiggly (Sumter, SC) 80027
Piggly Wiggly (Walterboro, SC) 80076
Piggly Wiggly (West Columbia, SC) 80100; 80101; 80102
Piggly Wiggly (Nashville, TN) 82082
Piggly Wiggly (Abilene, TX) 82450; 82451
Piggly Wiggly (Aspermont, TX) 82785
Piggly Wiggly (Ballinger, TX) 83089
Piggly Wiggly (Beaumont, TX) 83199
Piggly Wiggly (Bonham, TX) 83313
Piggly Wiggly (Bryan, TX) 83401
Piggly Wiggly (Clarksville, TX) 83569
Piggly Wiggly (Cleburne, TX) 83581
Piggly Wiggly (College Station, TX) 83621
Piggly Wiggly (Conroe, TX) 83678
Piggly Wiggly (Copperas Cove, TX) 83695
Piggly Wiggly (De Kalb, TX) 84526
Piggly Wiggly (Denton, TX) 84627; 84628
Piggly Wiggly (Emory, TX) 84992
Piggly Wiggly (Ennis, TX) 84996
Piggly Wiggly (Fort Worth, TX) 85220; 85221
Piggly Wiggly (Gainesville, TX) 85425
Piggly Wiggly (Georgetown, TX) 85571
Piggly Wiggly (Gilmer, TX) 85579
Piggly Wiggly (Grand Saline, TX) 85648
Piggly Wiggly (Hearne, TX) 85724
Piggly Wiggly (Honey Grove, TX) 85756
Piggly Wiggly (Hughes Springs, TX) 87212
Piggly Wiggly (Jefferson, TX) 87439
Piggly Wiggly (Joaquin, TX) 87443
Piggly Wiggly (Lewisville, TX) 87659
Piggly Wiggly (Lindale, TX) 87683
Piggly Wiggly (Linden, TX) 87684
Piggly Wiggly (Livingston, TX) 87689
Piggly Wiggly (Llano, TX) 87693
Piggly Wiggly (Mc Kinney, TX) 87917
Piggly Wiggly (Mineral Wells, TX) 88113
Piggly Wiggly (Mt Pleasant, TX) 88158
Piggly Wiggly (New Boston, TX) 88201
Piggly Wiggly (Nocona, TX) 88229
Piggly Wiggly (San Juan, TX) 89334
Piggly Wiggly (Sherman, TX) 89417; 89418
Piggly Wiggly (Slaton, TX) 89443
Piggly Wiggly (Snyder, TX) 89449
Piggly Wiggly (Spur, TX) 89498
Piggly Wiggly (Stamford, TX) 89511
Piggly Wiggly (Stephenville, TX) 89521
Piggly Wiggly (Sweetwater, TX) 89588
Piggly Wiggly (Temple, TX) 89630
Piggly Wiggly (Texarkana, TX) 89694; 89695; 89696; 89697; 89698
Piggly Wiggly (Waco, TX) 89961; 89962; 89963; 89964; 89965
Piggly Wiggly (Winters, TX) 90128
Piggly Wiggly (Abingdon, VA) 90157
Piggly Wiggly (Bristol, VA) 90484
Piggly Wiggly (Coeburn, VA) 90646
Piggly Wiggly (Danville, VA) 90709
Piggly Wiggly (Galax, VA) 90962
Piggly Wiggly (Glade Spring, VA) 90970
Piggly Wiggly (Honaker, VA) 91149
Piggly Wiggly (Lebanon, VA) 91189
Piggly Wiggly (Marion, VA) 91337
Piggly Wiggly (Norton, VA) 91606; 91607
Piggly Wiggly (Pulaski, VA) 91677
Piggly Wiggly (Rose Hill, VA) 92206
Piggly Wiggly (Saltville, VA) 92226; 92227
Piggly Wiggly Alabama Distribution (Birmingham, AL) 55336
Piggly Wiggly of Atlanta (Forest Park, GA) 66246
Piggly Wiggly Central Office (Monroe, LA) 70367; 70368
Piggly Wiggly of Coffeeville (Coffeeville, MS) 72690
Piggly Wiggly Corp. (Northport, AL) 56408
Piggly Wiggly Corp. (Sanford, NC) 76201
Piggly Wiggly Corp. (Memphis, TN) 81666
Piggly Wiggly Corp. (Sherman, TX) 89419
Piggly Wiggly Employees Federal Credit Union (West Monroe, LA) 70956
Piggly Wiggly Food Store (Corbin, KY) 68212
Piggly Wiggly Interstate (Houston, MS) 72921
Piggly Wiggly Memphis Inc. (Memphis, TN) 81667
Piggly-Wiggly OFC (Clarksville, TX) 83570
Piggly Wiggly of Rocky Mount Inc. (Rocky Mount, NC) 76099
Piggly Wiggly Southern (Cordele, GA) 65716
Piggly Wiggly Southern Inc. (Dublin, GA) 66013
Piggly Wiggly Southern Inc. (Eastman, GA) 66160
Piggly Wiggly Southern Inc. (Fort Valley, GA) 66260
Piggly Wiggly Southern Inc. (Griffin, GA) 66320
Piggly Wiggly Southern Inc. (Louisville, GA) 66623
Piggly Wiggly Southern Inc. (Milledgeville, GA) 66983
Piggly Wiggly Southern Inc. (Sandersville, GA) 67431
Piggly Wiggly Southern Inc. (Vidalia, GA) 67991
Piggly Wiggly 255 (Itta Bena, MS) 72933
Pilgrim Farms, Inc. (Sanford, FL) 62770
Pilgrim's Pride Corp. (De Queen, AR) 56893
Pilgrim's Pride Corp. (Dallas, TX) 84306
Pilgrim's Pride Corp. (Lufkin, TX) 87811; 87812
Pilgrim's Pride Corp. (Mount Pleasant, TX) 88148; 88149
Pilgrim's Pride Corp. (Mt Pleasant, TX) 88159
Pilgrim's Pride Corp. (Pittsburg, TX) **88519;** 88520
Pilgrim's Pride Corp. Dallas Processing (Dallas, TX) 84307
Pilgrim's Pride Corp. Dequeen Processing (De Queen, AR) 56894
Pilgrim's Pride Corp. East Processing Plant (Mount Pleasant, TX) 88150
Pilgrim's Pride Corp. Hope Feed Mill (Hope, AR) 57158
Pilgrim's Pride Corp. Lufkin Processing (Lufkin, TX) 87813
Pilgrim's Pride Corp. Nacogdoches Feed Nill (Nacogdoches, TX) 88174

Pilgrim's Pride Corp. Nashville Feed Mill (Nashville, AR) 57440
Pilgrim's Pride Corp. Pittsburg Feed Mill (Pittsburg, TX) 88521
Pilgrim's Pride Corp. Protein Conversion (Mount Pleasant, TX) 88151
Pilgrim's Pride Corp. Wastewater Treatment (Mount Pleasant, TX) 88152
Pilgrim's Pride Corp. West Processing Plant (Mount Pleasant, TX) 88153
Pilgrim's Pride Corp. Prepared Foods (Mount Pleasant, TX) 88154
Pineland (Diboll, TX) 84657
Pinnacle West Capital Corporate (Washington, DC) 58405
Pioneer Security Life Insurance (Waco, TX) 89966
Pioneer Security Life Insurance Co. (Waco, TX) 89967
Piper/Casepro (Clarendon, AR) 56847
Pitney Bowes (Washington, DC) 58406
Pitney Bowes (Jacksonville, FL) 60391
Pitney Bowes (Tampa, FL) 63519
Pitney Bowes (Norcross, GA) 67166
Pitney Bowes (Jeffersontown, KY) 68496
Pitney Bowes (Lexington, KY) 68603
Pitney Bowes (Baton Rouge, LA) 69599
Pitney Bowes (Shreveport, LA) 70765
Pitney Bowes (St. Rose, LA) 70878
Pitney Bowes (Tulsa, OK) 78057
Pitney Bowes (West Columbia, SC) 80103
Pitney Bowes (Memphis, TN) 81668
Pitney Bowes (Nashville, TN) 82083
Pitney Bowes (Austin, TX) 82958
Pitney Bowes (Richmond, VA) 91950
Pitney Bowes (Roanoke, VA) 92177
Pitney Bowes (Springfield, VA) 92289
Pitney Bowes (South Charleston, WV) 93053
Pitney Bowes Credit Corp. (Atlanta, GA) 65020
Pitney Bowes Credit Corp. (Metairie, LA) 70299; 70300
Pitney Bowes Credit Corp. (Charlotte, NC) 74106
Pitney Bowes Credit Corp. (Oklahoma City, OK) 77488
Pitney Bowes Credit Corp. (Farmers Branch, TX) 85034
Pitney Bowes Facsimile Systems (Brimingham, AL) 55487
Pitney Bowes Facsimile Systems (Orlando, FL) 62081
Pitney Bowes Management Services (Dallas, TX) 84308
Pitney Bowes Management Services (Houston, TX) 86686
Pittston Coal Export Co. (Norfolk, VA) 91565
Pizza Hut (Albertville, AL) 54969
Pizza Hut (Andalusia, AL) 54988
Pizza Hut (Anniston, AL) 55007; 55008
Pizza Hut (Arab, AL) 55026
Pizza Hut (Athens, AL) 55045
Pizza Hut (Atmore, AL) 55052
Pizza Hut (Attalla, AL) 55057
Pizza Hut (Auburn, AL) 55068; 55069
Pizza Hut (Bay Minette, AL) 55077
Pizza Hut (Bessemer, AL) 55099; 55100
Pizza Hut (Birmingham, AL) 55337; 55338; 55339; 55340; 55341; 55342; 55343; 55344; 55345; 55346; 55347; 55348; 55349; 55350; 55351; 55352
Pizza Hut (Boaz, AL) 55474
Pizza Hut (Cullman, AL) 55548
Pizza Hut (Daphne, AL) 55568
Pizza Hut (Decatur, AL) 55602; 55603
Pizza Hut (Dothan, AL) 55661; 55662
Pizza Hut (Enterprise, AL) 55690
Pizza Hut (Fairhope, AL) 55724
Pizza Hut (Fayette, AL) 55732
Pizza Hut (Florence, AL) 55742
Pizza Hut (Foley, AL) 55750
Pizza Hut (Greenville, AL) 55819
Pizza Hut (Guntersville, AL) 55832
Pizza Hut (Haleyville, AL) 55845
Pizza Hut (Hamilton, AL) 55850
Pizza Hut (Huntsville, AL) 55994; 55995; 55996; 55997; 55998; 55999
Pizza Hut (Jackson, AL) 56069

Pizza Hut (Jacksonville, AL) 56075
Pizza Hut (Leeds, AL) 56107
Pizza Hut (Mobile, AL) 56220; 56221; 56222; 56223; 56224; 56225; 56226; 56227
Pizza Hut (Monroeville, AL) 56268
Pizza Hut (Montgomery, AL) 56364; 56365; 56366; 56367; 56368; 56369
Pizza Hut (Northport, AL) 56409
Pizza Hut (Opelika, AL) 56422
Pizza Hut (Opp, AL) 56435
Pizza Hut (Ozark, AL) 56445
Pizza Hut (Phenix City, AL) 56470
Pizza Hut (Prattville, AL) 56490
Pizza Hut (Russellville, AL) 56510
Pizza Hut (Scottsboro, AL) 56522
Pizza Hut (Sylacauga, AL) 56587
Pizza Hut (Talladega, AL) 56597
Pizza Hut (Trussville, AL) 56629
Pizza Hut (Tuscaloosa, AL) 56668; 56669
Pizza Hut (Wetumpka, AL) 56704
Pizza Hut (Arkadelphia, AR) 56720
Pizza Hut (Ash Flat, AR) 56726
Pizza Hut (Ashdown, AR) 56729
Pizza Hut (Batesville, AR) 56760
Pizza Hut (Beebe, AR) 56768
Pizza Hut (Benton, AR) 56773
Pizza Hut (Blytheville, AR) 56813
Pizza Hut (Brinkley, AR) 56821
Pizza Hut (Bryant, AR) 56824
Pizza Hut (Camden, AR) 56839
Pizza Hut (Clarksville, AR) 56850
Pizza Hut (Clinton, AR) 56858
Pizza Hut (Conway, AR) 56868
Pizza Hut (Dardanelle, AR) 56888
Pizza Hut (De Queen, AR) 56895
Pizza Hut (El Dorado, AR) 56956
Pizza Hut (Fayetteville, AR) 56986; 56987; 56988
Pizza Hut (Forrest City, AR) 57011
Pizza Hut (Fort Smith, AR) 57083; 57084; 57085
Pizza Hut (H Spg Nat Pk, AR) 57127
Pizza Hut (Harrison, AR) 57140
Pizza Hut (Heber Springs, AR) 57151
Pizza Hut (Hot Springs National Park, AR) 57182; 57183
Pizza Hut (Jacksonville, AR) 57198; 57199
Pizza Hut (Little Rock, AR) 57295; 57296; 57297; 57298
Pizza Hut (Mabelvale, AR) 57327
Pizza Hut (Malvern, AR) 57341
Pizza Hut (Mena, AR) 57366
Pizza Hut (Mountain Home, AR) 57388
Pizza Hut (N Little Rock, AR) 57416; 57417
Pizza Hut (Nashville, AR) 57441
Pizza Hut (Newport, AR) 57450; 57451
Pizza Hut (Ozark, AR) 57487
Pizza Hut (Pea Ridge, AR) 57504
Pizza Hut (Pine Bluff, AR) 57527
Pizza Hut (Pocahontas, AR) 57543
Pizza Hut (Prescott, AR) 57551; 57552
Pizza Hut (Rogers, AR) 57567; 57568
Pizza Hut (Russellville, AR) 57585
Pizza Hut (Searcy, AR) 57606; 57607
Pizza Hut (Springdale, AR) 57640
Pizza Hut (Stuttgart, AR) 57663
Pizza Hut (Trumann, AR) 57686
Pizza Hut (Van Buren, AR) 57691
Pizza Hut (Warren, AR) 57709
Pizza Hut (West Helena, AR) 57714
Pizza Hut (West Memphis, AR) 57730
Pizza Hut (Alachua, FL) 58532
Pizza Hut (Altamonte Springs, FL) 58562
Pizza Hut (Arcadia, FL) 58585
Pizza Hut (Avon Park, FL) 58609
Pizza Hut (Belleview, FL) 58656
Pizza Hut (Boca Raton, FL) 58727; 58728; 58729; 58730
Pizza Hut (Boynton Beach, FL) 58787
Pizza Hut (Bradenton, FL) 58839; 58840; 58841; 58842
Pizza Hut (Brandon, FL) 58876
Pizza Hut (Brooksville, FL) 58893
Pizza Hut (Casselberry, FL) 58939
Pizza Hut (Clearwater, FL) 59037; 59038
Pizza Hut (Clermont, FL) 59057
Pizza Hut (Cocoa Beach, FL) 59082
Pizza Hut (Dade City, FL) 59142
Pizza Hut (Dania, FL) 59149
Pizza Hut (Daytona Beach, FL) 59197; 59198; 59199; 59200; 59201; 59202
Pizza Hut (De Funiak Springs, FL) 59244
Pizza Hut (De Land, FL) 59254; 59255

Pizza Hut (Destin, FL) 59347; 59348
Pizza Hut (Dunedin, FL) 59365
Pizza Hut (Eustis, FL) 59401
Pizza Hut (Fernandina Beach, FL) 59413
Pizza Hut (Flagler Beach, FL) 59418
Pizza Hut (Fort Lauderdale, FL) 59553; 59554; 59555; 59556; 59557; 59558; 59559; 59560
Pizza Hut (Fort Myers, FL) 59732; 59733; 59734; 59735; 59736; 59737; 59738; 59739; 59740
Pizza Hut (Fort Pierce, FL) 59799; 59800; 59801
Pizza Hut (Fort Walton Beach, FL) 59833; 59834; 59835
Pizza Hut (Gainesville, FL) 59899; 59900; 59901; 59902; 59903; 59904
Pizza Hut (Gulf Breeze, FL) 59938
Pizza Hut (Haines City, FL) 59951
Pizza Hut (Hialeah, FL) 60000; 60001; 60002
Pizza Hut (Hollywood, FL) 60080; 60081; 60082; 60083
Pizza Hut (Homestead, FL) 60118
Pizza Hut (Homosassa, FL) 60125
Pizza Hut (Inverness, FL) 60151
Pizza Hut (Jacksonville, FL) 60392; 60393; 60394; 60395; 60396; 60397; 60398; 60399; 60400; 60401; 60402; 60403; 60404; 60405; 60406; 60407; 60408; 60409; 60410; 60411; 60412
Pizza Hut (Jupiter, FL) 60545
Pizza Hut (Key Largo, FL) 60567
Pizza Hut (Key West, FL) 60577
Pizza Hut (Kissimmee, FL) 60595; 60596; 60597
Pizza Hut (Lake City, FL) 60624; 60625
Pizza Hut (Lake Placid, FL) 60647
Pizza Hut (Lake Wales, FL) 60656
Pizza Hut (Lake Worth, FL) 60685; 60686; 60687
Pizza Hut (Lakeland, FL) 60762; 60763; 60764; 60765; 60766
Pizza Hut (Largo, FL) 60849; 60850; 60851; 60852; 60853
Pizza Hut (Lehigh Acres, FL) 60895
Pizza Hut (Lghthouse Point, FL) 60898
Pizza Hut (Live Oak, FL) 60916
Pizza Hut (Longwood, FL) 60943; 60944
Pizza Hut (Maitland, FL) 60983
Pizza Hut (Marianna, FL) 61006; 61007
Pizza Hut (Mary Esther, FL) 61021
Pizza Hut (Meadows Village, FL) 61029
Pizza Hut (Melbourne, FL) 61084; 61085; 61086; 61087; 61088
Pizza Hut (Merritt Island, FL) 61143
Pizza Hut (Miami, FL) 61391; 61392; 61393; 61394; 61395; 61396; 61397; 61398; 61399
Pizza Hut (Milton, FL) 61550
Pizza Hut (N Bay Village, FL) 61583
Pizza Hut (Naples, FL) 61651; 61652
Pizza Hut (Niceville, FL) 61715
Pizza Hut (No Palm Beach, FL) 61723
Pizza Hut (Ocala, FL) 61811; 61812
Pizza Hut (Ocoee, FL) 61836
Pizza Hut (Okeechobee, FL) 61843
Pizza Hut (Opa Locka, FL) 61862
Pizza Hut (Orange Park, FL) 61893; 61894
Pizza Hut (Orlando, FL) 62082; 62083; 62084; 62085; 62086; 62087; 62088; 62089; 62090; 62091; 62092; 62093; 62094; 62095; 62096; 62097; 62098; 62099
Pizza Hut (Ormond Beach, FL) 62207
Pizza Hut (Palm Bay, FL) 62243
Pizza Hut (Palm Springs, FL) 62305
Pizza Hut (Panama City, FL) 62338; 62339; 62340; 62341; 62342; 62343; 62344
Pizza Hut (Pensacola, FL) 62456; 62457; 62458; 62459; 62460; 62461; 62462
Pizza Hut (Perry, FL) 62501
Pizza Hut (Pinellas Park, FL) 62525; 62526
Pizza Hut (Plant City, FL) 62551
Pizza Hut (Pompano Beach, FL) 62614; 62615; 62616; 62617
Pizza Hut (Port Richey, FL) 62679
Pizza Hut (Port St Lucie, FL) 62689
Pizza Hut (Punta Gorda, FL) 62714
Pizza Hut (Quincy, FL) 62731
Pizza Hut (Rockledge, FL) 62747

Pizza Hut (Ruskin, FL) 62759
Pizza Hut (Sanford, FL) 62771; 62772
Pizza Hut (Sarasota, FL) 62855; 62856
Pizza Hut (Sebring, FL) 62891
Pizza Hut (Smyrna Beach, FL) 62920
Pizza Hut (St Augustine, FL) 62946; 62947; 62948; 62949; 62950
Pizza Hut (St Petersburg, FL) 63002; 63003; 63004; 63005; 63006; 63007; 63008; 63009; 63010; 63011
Pizza Hut (St. Cloud, FL) 63069
Pizza Hut (Starke, FL) 63150
Pizza Hut (Stuart, FL) 63177
Pizza Hut (Sunrise, FL) 63195
Pizza Hut (Tallahassee, FL) 63255; 63256; 63257; 63258
Pizza Hut (Tampa, FL) 63520; 63521; 63522; 63523; 63524; 63525; 63526; 63527; 63528; 63529; 63530; 63531; 63532; 63533; 63534; 63535
Pizza Hut (Titusville, FL) 63698
Pizza Hut (Valrico, FL) 63716
Pizza Hut (Venice, FL) 63730
Pizza Hut (Vero Beach, FL) 63767
Pizza Hut (W Palm Beach, FL) 63799; 63800
Pizza Hut (West Palm Beach, FL) 63891; 63892; 63893
Pizza Hut (Winter Haven, FL) 63948
Pizza Hut (Winter Park, FL) 63988; 63989; 63990
Pizza Hut (Winter Springs, FL) 64003
Pizza Hut (Zephyrhills, FL) 64017; 64018; 64019
Pizza Hut (Acworth, GA) 64047; 64048
Pizza Hut (Albany, GA) 64086
Pizza Hut (Alma, GA) 64101
Pizza Hut (Alpharetta, GA) 64126; 64127; 64128
Pizza Hut (Americus, GA) 64143
Pizza Hut (Atlanta, GA) 65021; 65022; 65023; 65024; 65025; 65026; 65027; 65028; 65029; 65030; 65031; 65032; 65033; 65034; 65035; 65036; 65037
Pizza Hut (Bainbridge, GA) 65369
Pizza Hut (Brunswick, GA) 65421; 65422
Pizza Hut (Buford, GA) 65440
Pizza Hut (Cairo, GA) 65448
Pizza Hut (Camilla, GA) 65482
Pizza Hut (Canton, GA) 65484; 65485
Pizza Hut (Carrollton, GA) 65497
Pizza Hut (Cartersville, GA) 65505
Pizza Hut (Chamblee, GA) 65540
Pizza Hut (College Park, GA) 65598; 65599
Pizza Hut (Conyers, GA) 65696; 65697
Pizza Hut (Cordele, GA) 65717
Pizza Hut (Covington, GA) 65739
Pizza Hut (Cumming, GA) 65748
Pizza Hut (Dallas, GA) 65764; 65765
Pizza Hut (Dawson, GA) 65793
Pizza Hut (Decatur, GA) 65882; 65883; 65884; 65885; 65886
Pizza Hut (Doraville, GA) 65945
Pizza Hut (Douglas, GA) 65973
Pizza Hut (Douglasville, GA) 65997; 65998
Pizza Hut (Dublin, GA) 66014
Pizza Hut (Duluth, GA) 66068; 66069; 66070
Pizza Hut (Dunwoody, GA) 66129; 66130
Pizza Hut (East Point, GA) 66152
Pizza Hut (Ellenwood, GA) 66169
Pizza Hut (Fayetteville, GA) 66200
Pizza Hut (Fitzgerald, GA) 66212
Pizza Hut (Forest Park, GA) 66247
Pizza Hut (Gainesville, GA) 66286; 66287
Pizza Hut (Griffin, GA) 66321
Pizza Hut (Hapeville, GA) 66338
Pizza Hut (Hinesville, GA) 66356
Pizza Hut (Jackson, GA) 66366
Pizza Hut (Jesup, GA) 66372
Pizza Hut (Jonesboro, GA) 66395
Pizza Hut (Kennesaw, GA) 66442; 66443; 66444
Pizza Hut (Lawrenceville, GA) 66530; 66531; 66532
Pizza Hut (Lilburn, GA) 66576; 66577
Pizza Hut (Lithia Spring, GA) 66585
Pizza Hut (Lithonia, GA) 66604; 66605
Pizza Hut (Loganville, GA) 66617
Pizza Hut (Mableton, GA) 66640
Pizza Hut (Macon, GA) 66705
Pizza Hut (Marietta, GA) 66873; 66874; 66875; 66876; 66877;

66878; 66879; 66880; 66881; 66882; 66883
Pizza Hut (McDonough, GA) 66969
Pizza Hut (Morrow, GA) 67034; 67035; 67036
Pizza Hut (Moultrie, GA) 67062
Pizza Hut (Norcross, GA) 67167; 67168
Pizza Hut (Peachtree Cty, GA) 67252
Pizza Hut (Perry, GA) 67267
Pizza Hut (Powder Spring, GA) 67284
Pizza Hut (Quitman, GA) 67290
Pizza Hut (Riverdale, GA) 67321; 67322; 67323
Pizza Hut (Roswell, GA) 67412; 67413; 67414; 67415; 67416
Pizza Hut (Smyrna, GA) 67563; 67564; 67565; 67566
Pizza Hut (Snellville, GA) 67609; 67610
Pizza Hut (Statesboro, GA) 67642
Pizza Hut (Stockbridge, GA) 67665; 67666
Pizza Hut (Stone Mountain, GA) 67730; 67731; 67732
Pizza Hut (Suwanee, GA) 67749
Pizza Hut (Swainsboro, GA) 67756
Pizza Hut (Sylvester, GA) 67776
Pizza Hut (Thomasville, GA) 67802; 67803
Pizza Hut (Tucker, GA) 67883; 67884
Pizza Hut (Union City, GA) 67926
Pizza Hut (Valdosta, GA) 67967; 67968; 67969; 67970
Pizza Hut (Vidalia, GA) 67992
Pizza Hut (Warner Robins, GA) 68019
Pizza Hut (Woodstock, GA) 68074
Pizza Hut (Alexandria, LA) 69397; 69398
Pizza Hut (Bastrop, LA) 69445
Pizza Hut (Baton Rouge, LA) 69600; 69601; 69602; 69603; 69604; 69605; 69606; 69607; 69608; 69609
Pizza Hut (Bogalusa, LA) 69707
Pizza Hut (Bossier City, LA) 69725; 69726; 69727
Pizza Hut (Chalmette, LA) 69767
Pizza Hut (Covington, LA) 69797
Pizza Hut (Cut Off, LA) 69806
Pizza Hut (De Ridder, LA) 69817
Pizza Hut (Denham Springs, LA) 69830
Pizza Hut (Donaldsonville, LA) 69841
Pizza Hut (Galliano, LA) 69861
Pizza Hut (Gretna, LA) 69912; 69913
Pizza Hut (Houma, LA) 69964
Pizza Hut (Jonesboro, LA) 69985
Pizza Hut (Kenner, LA) 70003; 70004; 70005
Pizza Hut (La Place, LA) 70031
Pizza Hut (Lafayette, LA) 70084; 70085; 70086; 70087
Pizza Hut (Lake Charles, LA) 70156; 70157; 70158
Pizza Hut (Leesville, LA) 70190
Pizza Hut (Mansfield, LA) 70216
Pizza Hut (Many, LA) 70220
Pizza Hut (Marksville, LA) 70222
Pizza Hut (Marrero, LA) 70232
Pizza Hut (Meraux, LA) 70244
Pizza Hut (Metairie, LA) 70301; 70302; 70303; 70304
Pizza Hut (Minden, LA) 70345
Pizza Hut (Monroe, LA) 70369
Pizza Hut (Morgan City, LA) 70390; 70391
Pizza Hut (Natchitoches, LA) 70403
Pizza Hut (New Orleans, LA) 70548
Pizza Hut (Oakdale, LA) 70600
Pizza Hut (Patterson, LA) 70612
Pizza Hut (Plaquemine, LA) 70642
Pizza Hut (Raceland, LA) 70654
Pizza Hut (Ruston, LA) 70671
Pizza Hut (Shreveport, LA) 70766; 70767; 70768; 70769; 70770; 70771
Pizza Hut (Slidell, LA) 70836
Pizza Hut (Springhill, LA) 70856
Pizza Hut (Sulphur, LA) 70888
Pizza Hut (Tallulah, LA) 70909
Pizza Hut (Thibodaux, LA) 70914
Pizza Hut (Vidalia, LA) 70931
Pizza Hut (Vivian, LA) 70937
Pizza Hut (Westlake, LA) 70967
Pizza Hut (Westwego, LA) 70971
Pizza Hut (Winnsboro, LA) 70981
Pizza Hut (Aberdeen, MS) 72578
Pizza Hut (Bay St Louis, MS) 72605
Pizza Hut (Biloxi, MS) 72632; 72633; 72634; 72635; 72636; 72637
Pizza Hut (Booneville, MS) 72647
Pizza Hut (Brandon, MS) 72651; 72652

Pizza Hut (Clarksdale, MS) 72678; 72679
Pizza Hut (Columbus, MS) 72722; 72723; 72724
Pizza Hut (Corinth, MS) 72743; 72744
Pizza Hut (Ellisville, MS) 72755
Pizza Hut (Forest, MS) 72774
Pizza Hut (Gautier, MS) 72785
Pizza Hut (Greenville, MS) 72812; 72813; 72814; 72815
Pizza Hut (Greenwood, MS) 72839
Pizza Hut (Grenada, MS) 72844
Pizza Hut (Gulfport, MS) 72865; 72866; 72867; 72868
Pizza Hut (Houston, MS) 72922
Pizza Hut (Indianola, MS) 72930
Pizza Hut (Jackson, MS) 73031; 73032; 73033; 73034; 73035; 73036; 73037; 73038
Pizza Hut (Kosciusko, MS) 73097
Pizza Hut (Laurel, MS) 73107
Pizza Hut (Mc Comb, MS) 73148
Pizza Hut (Meridian, MS) 73174; 73175; 73176
Pizza Hut (Natchez, MS) 73209; 73210
Pizza Hut (New Albany, MS) 73216
Pizza Hut (Oxford, MS) 73244; 73245
Pizza Hut (Pascagoula, MS) 73266; 73267; 73268; 73269
Pizza Hut (Philadelphia, MS) 73280
Pizza Hut (Picayune, MS) 73293
Pizza Hut (Ripley, MS) 73332
Pizza Hut (Senatobia, MS) 73340
Pizza Hut (Southaven, MS) 73354
Pizza Hut (Starkville, MS) 73369; 73370
Pizza Hut (Tupelo, MS) 73418; 73419; 73420
Pizza Hut (Water Valley, MS) 73471
Pizza Hut (West Point, MS) 73485
Pizza Hut (Yazoo City, MS) 73505
Pizza Hut (Aberdeen, NC) 73516
Pizza Hut (Asheboro, NC) 73592
Pizza Hut (Asheville, NC) 73632; 73633
Pizza Hut (Blowing Rock, NC) 73703
Pizza Hut (Boone, NC) 73715
Pizza Hut (Brevard, NC) 73726
Pizza Hut (Burlington, NC) 73759
Pizza Hut (Canton, NC) 73781
Pizza Hut (Chapel Hill, NC) 73818; 73819
Pizza Hut (Charlotte, NC) 74107; 74108; 74109; 74110; 74111; 74112; 74113; 74114; 74115; 74116; 74117
Pizza Hut (Clemmons, NC) 74271
Pizza Hut (Clinton, NC) 74296; 74297
Pizza Hut (Concord, NC) 74319; 74320
Pizza Hut (Durham, NC) 74423; 74424
Pizza Hut (Eden, NC) 74464
Pizza Hut (Edenton, NC) 74472
Pizza Hut (Elizabeth Cit, NC) 74473
Pizza Hut (Enka, NC) 74509
Pizza Hut (Farmville, NC) 74521
Pizza Hut (Fayetteville, NC) 74572
Pizza Hut (Garner, NC) 74647
Pizza Hut (Goldsboro, NC) 74731
Pizza Hut (Greensboro, NC) 74876; 74877; 74878; 74879; 74880; 74881
Pizza Hut (Greenville, NC) 74972; 74973
Pizza Hut (Havelock, NC) 75009
Pizza Hut (Henderson, NC) 75025
Pizza Hut (Hendersonvl, NC) 75048; 75049
Pizza Hut (Hickory, NC) 75093; 75094
Pizza Hut (High Point, NC) 75154; 75155
Pizza Hut (Hope Mills, NC) 75194
Pizza Hut (Jacksonville, NC) 75224; 75225; 75226
Pizza Hut (Jamestown, NC) 75241; 75242
Pizza Hut (Kannapolis, NC) 75266
Pizza Hut (Kernersville, NC) 75283
Pizza Hut (King, NC) 75291
Pizza Hut (Kings Mountain, NC) 75306
Pizza Hut (Lenoir, NC) 75385
Pizza Hut (Lexington, NC) 75421
Pizza Hut (Lumberton, NC) 75471
Pizza Hut (Madison, NC) 75483
Pizza Hut (Matthews, NC) 75527
Pizza Hut (Monroe, NC) 75585; 75586
Pizza Hut (Mooresville, NC) 75607
Pizza Hut (Morehead City, NC) 75626
Pizza Hut (Morganton, NC) 75652
Pizza Hut (Mt. Airy, NC) 75698
Pizza Hut (Murphy, NC) 75707
Pizza Hut (N Wilkesboro, NC) 75712
Pizza Hut (Newton, NC) 75751
Pizza Hut (Pineville, NC) 75819; 75820
Pizza Hut (Plymouth, NC) 75836
Pizza Hut (Raleigh, NC) 75935; 75936; 75937; 75938; 75939; 75940; 75941
Pizza Hut (Reidsville, NC) 76009
Pizza Hut (Roanoke Rapids, NC) 76038
Pizza Hut (Rockingham, NC) 76066
Pizza Hut (Rocky Mount, NC) 76100
Pizza Hut (Roxboro, NC) 76131
Pizza Hut (Salisbury, NC) 76170; 76171
Pizza Hut (Sanford, NC) 76202
Pizza Hut (Selma, NC) 76227
Pizza Hut (Shelby, NC) 76243
Pizza Hut (Smithfield, NC) 76265; 76266; 76267
Pizza Hut (Spring Lake, NC) 76298
Pizza Hut (Statesville, NC) 76333
Pizza Hut (Thomasville, NC) 76381
Pizza Hut (Wadesboro, NC) 76426
Pizza Hut (Wake Forest, NC) 76431
Pizza Hut (Waynesville, NC) 76471
Pizza Hut (Weaverville, NC) 76475
Pizza Hut (Whiteville, NC) 76503
Pizza Hut (Wilkesboro, NC) 76517
Pizza Hut (Williamston, NC) 76533; 76534
Pizza Hut (Wilmington, NC) 76587; 76588
Pizza Hut (Wilson, NC) 76640
Pizza Hut (Winston Salem, NC) 76679
Pizza Hut (Wrightsville Beach, NC) 76778
Pizza Hut (Ada, OK) 76787
Pizza Hut (Altus, OK) 76795
Pizza Hut (Anadarko, OK) 76805
Pizza Hut (Ardmore, OK) 76817
Pizza Hut (Atoka, OK) 76827
Pizza Hut (Bartlesville, OK) 76847; 76848
Pizza Hut (Beaver, OK) 76857
Pizza Hut (Bethany, OK) 76859
Pizza Hut (Bixby, OK) 76862
Pizza Hut (Bristow, OK) 76873
Pizza Hut (Broken Arrow, OK) 76888
Pizza Hut (Carnegie, OK) 76906
Pizza Hut (Catoosa, OK) 76910
Pizza Hut (Checotah, OK) 76916
Pizza Hut (Cherokee, OK) 76918
Pizza Hut (Chickasha, OK) 76936
Pizza Hut (Choctaw, OK) 76943
Pizza Hut (Claremore, OK) 76955
Pizza Hut (Cushing, OK) 76981
Pizza Hut (Dewey, OK) 76989
Pizza Hut (Duncan, OK) 76996
Pizza Hut (Durant, OK) 77003
Pizza Hut (Edmond, OK) 77011; 77012; 77013
Pizza Hut (El Reno, OK) 77033
Pizza Hut (Enid, OK) 77060; 77061; 77062
Pizza Hut (Fairview, OK) 77079
Pizza Hut (Frederick, OK) 77084; 77085
Pizza Hut (Grove, OK) 77092
Pizza Hut (Guthrie, OK) 77098
Pizza Hut (Guymon, OK) 77107; 77108; 77109
Pizza Hut (Hennessey, OK) 77124
Pizza Hut (Holdenville, OK) 77134
Pizza Hut (Hollis, OK) 77138
Pizza Hut (Hugo, OK) 77139
Pizza Hut (Idabel, OK) 77145
Pizza Hut (Kingfisher, OK) 77151
Pizza Hut (Lawton, OK) 77171; 77172
Pizza Hut (Lindsay, OK) 77180
Pizza Hut (Madill, OK) 77182
Pizza Hut (Marietta, OK) 77184
Pizza Hut (Mc Alester, OK) 77197
Pizza Hut (Miami, OK) 77208; 77209
Pizza Hut (Norman, OK) 77268; 77269
Pizza Hut (Nowata, OK) 77284
Pizza Hut (Oklahoma City, OK) 77489; 77490; 77491; 77492; 77493; 77494; 77495; 77496; 77497; 77498; 77499; 77500; 77501; 77502; 77503; 77504; 77505; 77506; 77507
Pizza Hut (Okmulgee, OK) 77683
Pizza Hut (Pauls Valley, OK) 77693
Pizza Hut (Pawhuska, OK) 77695
Pizza Hut (Ponca City, OK) 77711
Pizza Hut (Poteau, OK) 77727
Pizza Hut (Pryor, OK) 77742
Pizza Hut (Purcell, OK) 77750
Pizza Hut (Sallisaw, OK) 77773
Pizza Hut (Sand Springs, OK) 77783
Pizza Hut (Sapulpa, OK) 77796
Pizza Hut (Seminole, OK) 77805
Pizza Hut (Shattuck, OK) 77809
Pizza Hut (Stigler, OK) 77831
Pizza Hut (Stillwater, OK) 77843; 77844
Pizza Hut (Sulphur, OK) 77857
Pizza Hut (Tahlequah, OK) 77858
Pizza Hut (Tishomingo, OK) 77870
Pizza Hut (Tulsa, OK) 78058; 78059; 78060; 78061; 78062; 78063; 78064; 78065; 78066; 78067; 78068
Pizza Hut (Vinita, OK) 78226
Pizza Hut (Wagoner, OK) 78231
Pizza Hut (Weatherford, OK) 78243
Pizza Hut (Wewoka, OK) 78248
Pizza Hut (Wilburton, OK) 78253
Pizza Hut (Woodward, OK) 78264
Pizza Hut (Yukon, OK) 78278; 78279
Pizza Hut (Anderson, SC) 78686
Pizza Hut (Batesburg, SC) 78704
Pizza Hut (Beaufort, SC) 78716; 78717
Pizza Hut (Bennettsville, SC) 78730
Pizza Hut (Bishopville, SC) 78745
Pizza Hut (Cayce, SC) 78778
Pizza Hut (Charleston, SC) 78864; 78865; 78866; 78867; 78868; 78869; 78870
Pizza Hut (Chester, SC) 78940
Pizza Hut (Clemson, SC) 78956
Pizza Hut (Clinton, SC) 78961
Pizza Hut (Columbia, SC) 79070; 79071; 79072; 79073; 79074; 79075; 79076
Pizza Hut (Conway, SC) 79135; 79136
Pizza Hut (Darlington, SC) 79156
Pizza Hut (Dillon, SC) 79163; 79164
Pizza Hut (Florence, SC) 79219; 79220; 79221
Pizza Hut (Gaffney, SC) 79262
Pizza Hut (Greenville, SC) 79403; 79404; 79405; 79406; 79407
Pizza Hut (Greenwood, SC) 79462; 79463
Pizza Hut (Hartsville, SC) 79500
Pizza Hut (Hilton Head Island, SC) 79520; 79521
Pizza Hut (Inman, SC) 79535
Pizza Hut (Lake City, SC) 79564
Pizza Hut (Laurens, SC) 79596
Pizza Hut (Lexington, SC) 79606; 79607
Pizza Hut (Marion, SC) 79641
Pizza Hut (Mauldin, SC) 79652
Pizza Hut (Mt Pleasant, SC) 79678
Pizza Hut (Myrtle Beach, SC) 79709
Pizza Hut (North Augusta, SC) 79737; 79738
Pizza Hut (Rock Hill, SC) 79837
Pizza Hut (Spartanburg, SC) 79925; 79926
Pizza Hut (Summerville, SC) 79992
Pizza Hut (Sumter, SC) 80028; 80029
Pizza Hut (Taylors, SC) 80039
Pizza Hut (West Columbia, SC) 80104
Pizza Hut (Woodruff, SC) 80136
Pizza Hut (Alpine, TX) 82500
Pizza Hut (Alvin, TX) 82514
Pizza Hut (Amarillo, TX) 82575; 82576
Pizza Hut (Andrews, TX) 82602
Pizza Hut (Angleton, TX) 82612
Pizza Hut (Aransas Pass, TX) 82624
Pizza Hut (Arlington, TX) 82723; 82724; 82725; 82726; 82727; 82728; 82729; 82730; 82731
Pizza Hut (Austin, TX) 82959; 82960; 82961; 82962; 82963; 82964; 82965; 82966; 82967; 82968; 82969; 82970; 82971; 82972; 82973
Pizza Hut (Baytown, TX) 83132
Pizza Hut (Beaumont, TX) 83200; 83201; 83202; 83203
Pizza Hut (Beeville, TX) 83259
Pizza Hut (Belton, TX) 83279
Pizza Hut (Big Spring, TX) 83292
Pizza Hut (Borger, TX) 83323; 83324
Pizza Hut (Bowie, TX) 83326
Pizza Hut (Brady, TX) 83330
Pizza Hut (Brenham, TX) 83339
Pizza Hut (Bridge City, TX) 83346
Pizza Hut (Brownfield, TX) 83353
Pizza Hut (Brownsville, TX) 83373; 83374; 83375; 83376
Pizza Hut (Brownwood, TX) 83387
Pizza Hut (Bryan, TX) 83402; 83403; 83404; 83405
Pizza Hut (Burkburnett, TX) 83417
Pizza Hut (Burleson, TX) 83423
Pizza Hut (Burnet, TX) 83428
Pizza Hut (Canadian, TX) 83441
Pizza Hut (Carrizo Springs, TX) 83446
Pizza Hut (Carrollton, TX) 83498; 83499
Pizza Hut (Carthage, TX) 83521
Pizza Hut (Cedar Park, TX) 83534
Pizza Hut (Center, TX) 83540
Pizza Hut (Channelview, TX) 83552
Pizza Hut (Childress, TX) 83559
Pizza Hut (Clarksville, TX) 83571
Pizza Hut (Cleburne, TX) 83582
Pizza Hut (Coleman, TX) 83607
Pizza Hut (College Station, TX) 83622
Pizza Hut (Colorado City, TX) 83639
Pizza Hut (Conroe, TX) 83679; 83680; 83681
Pizza Hut (Copperas Cove, TX) 83696
Pizza Hut (Corpus Christi, TX) 83748
Pizza Hut (Corsicana, TX) 83787
Pizza Hut (Crosby, TX) 83806
Pizza Hut (Crystal City, TX) 83821
Pizza Hut (Cuero, TX) 83824
Pizza Hut (Dalhart, TX) 83834
Pizza Hut (Dallas, TX) 84309; 84310; 84311; 84312; 84313; 84314; 84315; 84316; 84317; 84318; 84319; 84320
Pizza Hut (De Soto, TX) 84536
Pizza Hut (Decatur, TX) 84543
Pizza Hut (Del Rio, TX) 84582; 84583; 84584
Pizza Hut (Denison, TX) 84604; 84605
Pizza Hut (Denton, TX) 84629; 84630
Pizza Hut (Denver City, TX) 84647
Pizza Hut (Dickinson, TX) 84670
Pizza Hut (Dimmitt, TX) 84674
Pizza Hut (Donna, TX) 84677; 84678
Pizza Hut (Dumas, TX) 84689
Pizza Hut (Duncanville, TX) 84706
Pizza Hut (Eagle Pass, TX) 84720; 84721
Pizza Hut (Edinburg, TX) 84735; 84736
Pizza Hut (El Campo, TX) 84749
Pizza Hut (El Paso, TX) 84879; 84880; 84881; 84882; 84883; 84884; 84885; 84886; 84887; 84888; 84889; 84890; 84891; 84892; 84893; 84894
Pizza Hut (Ennis, TX) 84997
Pizza Hut (Euless, TX) 85016; 85017
Pizza Hut (Falfurrias, TX) 85030
Pizza Hut (Fort Stockton, TX) 85046
Pizza Hut (Fort Worth, TX) 85222; 85223; 85224; 85225; 85226; 85227; 85228; 85229; 85230; 85231; 85232; 85233; 85234; 85235
Pizza Hut (Fredericksburg, TX) 85377
Pizza Hut (Friendswood, TX) 85406
Pizza Hut (Gainesville, TX) 85426
Pizza Hut (Galveston, TX) 85461
Pizza Hut (Garland, TX) 85522; 85523
Pizza Hut (Georgetown, TX) 85572
Pizza Hut (Giddings, TX) 85576
Pizza Hut (Gladewater, TX) 85581
Pizza Hut (Gonzales, TX) 85590; 85591
Pizza Hut (Granbury, TX) 85598
Pizza Hut (Grand Prairie, TX) 85632
Pizza Hut (Grapevine, TX) 85659
Pizza Hut (Greenville, TX) 85674
Pizza Hut (Harlingen, TX) 85709; 85710; 85711
Pizza Hut (Hereford, TX) 85744; 85745
Pizza Hut (Hillsboro, TX) 85751
Pizza Hut (Hondo, TX) 85752
Pizza Hut (Houston, TX) 86687; 86688; 86689; 86690; 86691; 86692; 86693; 86694; 86695; 86696; 86697; 86698; 86699; 86700; 86701; 86702; 86703; 86704; 86705; 86706; 86707; 86708; 86709; 86710; 86711; 86712; 86713; 86714; 86715; 86716
Pizza Hut (Humble, TX) 87239; 87240
Pizza Hut (Huntsville, TX) 87263; 87264
Pizza Hut (Hurst, TX) 87290
Pizza Hut (Irving, TX) 87390; 87391; 87392
Pizza Hut (Jacksonville, TX) 87424
Pizza Hut (Jasper, TX) 87434
Pizza Hut (Katy, TX) 87453
Pizza Hut (Kaufman, TX) 87459
Pizza Hut (Kenedy, TX) 87466
Pizza Hut (Kermit, TX) 87470
Pizza Hut (Kerrville, TX) 87481
Pizza Hut (Kilgore, TX) 87496
Pizza Hut (Killeen, TX) 87518; 87519; 87520; 87521
Pizza Hut (Lake Jackson, TX) 87583
Pizza Hut (Lamesa, TX) 87591
Pizza Hut (Lampasas, TX) 87593
Pizza Hut (Laredo, TX) 87616; 87617; 87618; 87619; 87620
Pizza Hut (Lewisville, TX) 87660
Pizza Hut (Liberty, TX) 87678
Pizza Hut (Livingston, TX) 87690
Pizza Hut (Llano, TX) 87694
Pizza Hut (Lockhart, TX) 87695
Pizza Hut (Longview, TX) 87729; 87730; 87731
Pizza Hut (Lubbock, TX) 87776; 87777
Pizza Hut (Lufkin, TX) 87814
Pizza Hut (Mansfield, TX) 87835
Pizza Hut (Marlin, TX) 87851
Pizza Hut (Marshall, TX) 87860
Pizza Hut (Mathis, TX) 87879; 87880
Pizza Hut (Mc Allen, TX) 87895
Pizza Hut (Mc Kinney, TX) 87918
Pizza Hut (McAllen, TX) 87936
Pizza Hut (Mercedes, TX) 87953
Pizza Hut (Mesquite, TX) 87984; 87985; 87986; 87987
Pizza Hut (Mexia, TX) 88014
Pizza Hut (Midland, TX) 88066; 88067; 88068
Pizza Hut (Mineral Wells, TX) 88114
Pizza Hut (Mission, TX) 88125
Pizza Hut (Missouri City, TX) 88130
Pizza Hut (Monahans, TX) 88142
Pizza Hut (Mt Pleasant, TX) 88160
Pizza Hut (Muleshoe, TX) 88166
Pizza Hut (Navasota, TX) 88180; 88181
Pizza Hut (Nederland, TX) 88189
Pizza Hut (New Boston, TX) 88202
Pizza Hut (New Braunfels, TX) 88218
Pizza Hut (Odessa, TX) 88262; 88263; 88264; 88265
Pizza Hut (Orange, TX) 88326
Pizza Hut (Palestine, TX) 88344
Pizza Hut (Pampa, TX) 88354; 88355
Pizza Hut (Paris, TX) 88375
Pizza Hut (Pasadena, TX) 88457; 88458; 88459
Pizza Hut (Pearland, TX) 88486
Pizza Hut (Pearsall, TX) 88492
Pizza Hut (Pecos, TX) 88496
Pizza Hut (Perryton, TX) 88502
Pizza Hut (Pharr, TX) 88509
Pizza Hut (Plainview, TX) 88531
Pizza Hut (Plano, TX) 88598; 88599; 88600
Pizza Hut (Pleasanton, TX) 88622
Pizza Hut (Port Arthur, TX) 88642; 88643
Pizza Hut (Port Isabel, TX) 88662; 88663
Pizza Hut (Port Lavaca, TX) 88669
Pizza Hut (Porter, TX) 88682
Pizza Hut (Portland, TX) 88693
Pizza Hut (Quanah, TX) 88700
Pizza Hut (Raymondville, TX) 88708
Pizza Hut (Refugio, TX) 88718
Pizza Hut (Richardson, TX) 88758; 88759; 88760
Pizza Hut (Rio Grande City, TX) 88800; 88801; 88802
Pizza Hut (Robinson Plz, TX) 88804
Pizza Hut (Robstown, TX) 88809
Pizza Hut (Rockdale, TX) 88818
Pizza Hut (Rockport, TX) 88819
Pizza Hut (Rockwall, TX) 88824
Pizza Hut (Rosenberg, TX) 88832
Pizza Hut (Round Rock, TX) 88851
Pizza Hut (San Angelo, TX) 88892; 88893; 88894; 88895
Pizza Hut (San Antonio, TX) 89147; 89148; 89149; 89150; 89151; 89152; 89153; 89154; 89155; 89156; 89157; 89158; 89159; 89160; 89161; 89162; 89163; 89164; 89165; 89166; 89167; 89168; 89169; 89170; 89171; 89172; 89173; 89174; 89175; 89176; 89177; 89178; 89179; 89180; 89181; 89182; 89183
Pizza Hut (San Benito, TX) 89331
Pizza Hut (San Marcos, TX) 89339; 89340
Pizza Hut (Seguin, TX) 89372
Pizza Hut (Seminole, TX) 89384
Pizza Hut (Sherman, TX) 89420; 89421
Pizza Hut (Silsbee, TX) 89434
Pizza Hut (Sinton, TX) 89441
Pizza Hut (Slaton, TX) 89444
Pizza Hut (Snyder, TX) 89450
Pizza Hut (Spearman, TX) 89461
Pizza Hut (Spring, TX) 89481; 89482; 89483
Pizza Hut (Stafford, TX) 89503

Pizza Hut (Stamford, TX) 89512
Pizza Hut (Stephenville, TX) 89522
Pizza Hut (Sugar Land, TX) 89540
Pizza Hut (Sulphur Springs, TX) 89562
Pizza Hut (Sweetwater, TX) 89589
Pizza Hut (Taylor, TX) 89600
Pizza Hut (Temple, TX) 89631; 89632; 89633
Pizza Hut (Terrell, TX) 89660
Pizza Hut (Texarkana, TX) 89699
Pizza Hut (Texas City, TX) 89731
Pizza Hut (Tomball, TX) 89775
Pizza Hut (Tulia, TX) 89786
Pizza Hut (Tyler, TX) 89822; 89823
Pizza Hut (Universal City, TX) 89844
Pizza Hut (Universal Cty, TX) 89846
Pizza Hut (Uvalde, TX) 89854
Pizza Hut (Vernon, TX) 89868
Pizza Hut (Victoria, TX) 89901
Pizza Hut (Vidor, TX) 89917
Pizza Hut (Waxahachie, TX) 89999
Pizza Hut (Weatherford, TX) 90010
Pizza Hut (Weslaco, TX) 90036
Pizza Hut (Whitesboro, TX) 90061
Pizza Hut (Wichita Falls, TX) 90088; 90089; 90090; 90091; 90092
Pizza Hut (Winters, TX) 90129
Pizza Hut (Yoakum, TX) 90136
Pizza Hut (Zapata, TX) 90138
Pizza Hut Area Office (Abilene, TX) 82452
Pizza Hut District Office (Rural Hall, NC) 76134
Pizza Hut District Office (Tulsa, OK) 78069
Pizza Hut Hearne Office (Hearne, TX) 85725
Pizza Hut Inc. (Atlanta, GA) 65038
Pizza Hut Inc. (Hammond, LA) 69932
Pizza Hut Inc. (Gulfport, MS) 72869
Pizza Hut Inc. (Midland, TX) 88069
Pizza Hut Inc. (San Antonio, TX) 89184
Pizza Hut Office (San Angelo, TX) 88896
Pizza Hut Region Training (Tampa, FL) 63536
Plant City Steel Co. (Plant City, FL) 62552
Plantation Pipe Line (Newington, VA) 91447
Planters Lifesavers Co. (Suffolk, VA) 92371
Plastic Packaging Inc. (Hickory, NC) 75095
Plastics Inc. (Greensboro, AL) 55813
Plastics Inc. (Rayne, LA) 70657
Plastics, Inc. (Jacksonville, TX) 87425
Plastics Inc. Seadrift Plant; Union Carbide Chemicals (Port Lavaca, TX) 88672
Platte Chemical Co. (Greenville, MS) 72816; 72817
Playtex Apparel Inc. (Dover, DE) 57798
Plexco (Abbeville, SC) 78643
Plexco (Knoxville, TN) 81240
Plexco (Corsicana, TX) 83788
Plough Inc. (Memphis, TN) 81669; 81670
Plough Inc. Printing Plant (Memphis, TN) 81671
Plough Printing Plant (Memphis, TN) 81672
Plus Mark (Norcross, GA) 67169
Plus Mark, Inc. (Afton, TN) 80144; 80145
Plus Mark, Inc. (Greenville, TN) 80897
Pmi Food Equipment Group Hobart Corp. (Richmond Hill, GA) 67298
PMS Consolidated (Buford, GA) 65441
PMS Consolidated (Swanee Mission, GA) 67762
PMS Consolidated (Florence, KY) 68327
PMS Consolidated (Gastonia, NC) 74684
PMS Consolidated (Fort Worth, TX) 85236; 85237
Pms Consolidated Corporate Hea (Suwanee, GA) 67750
Pms Consolidated Fiber Service (Buford, GA) 65442
PNC Bank Corp.- Kentucky (Louisville, KY) 68949; 68950
PNC Bank Kentuck Inc. (Jeffersontown, KY) 68497
PNC Bank Kentucky Inc. (Buckner, KY) 68171
PNC Bank Kentucky Inc. (Buechel, KY) 68172
PNC Bank Kentucky Inc. (Crestwood, KY) 68246
PNC Bank Kentucky Inc. (Elizabethtown, KY) 68290; 68291; 68292
PNC Bank Kentucky Inc. (Fern Creek, KY) 68303; 68304
PNC Bank Kentucky Inc. (Glendale, KY) 68399
PNC Bank Kentucky Inc. (Harrodsburg, KY) 68414; 68415
PNC Bank Kentucky Inc. (Jeffersontown, KY) 68498
PNC Bank Kentucky Inc. (La Grange, KY) 68504
PNC Bank Kentucky Inc. (Lexington, KY) 68604; 68605; 68606; 68607; 68608; 68609; 68610; 68611
PNC Bank Kentucky Inc. (Louisville, KY) 68951; 68952; 68953; 68954; 68955; 68956; 68957; 68958; 68959; 68960; 68961; 68962; 68963; 68964; 68965; 68966; 68967; 68968; 68969; 68970; 68971; 68972; 68973; 68974; 68975; 68976; 68977; 68978; 68979
PNC Bank Kentucky, Inc. (Okolona, KY) 69156; 69157
PNC Bank Kentucky, Inc. (Pewee Valley, KY) 69222
PNC Bank of Kentucky, Inc. (Pleasure Ridge Park, KY) 69228
PNC Bank Kentucky, Inc. (Prospect, KY) 69234
PNC Bank Kentucky, Inc. (Radcliff, KY) 69241
PNC Bank Kentucky, Inc. (Richmond, KY) 69246; 69247
PNC Bank Kentucky, Inc. (Sonora, KY) 69299
PNC Bank Kentucky, Inc. (St. Matthews, KY) 69306; 69307; 69308
PNC Bank Kentucky, Inc. (Upton, KY) 69320
PNC Bank Kentucky, Inc. (Valley Station, KY) 69322; 69323
PNC Bank Kentucky, Inc. (Winchester, KY) 69350; 69351; 69352
PNC Bank Kentuky Inc. (Elizabethtown, KY) 68293
PNC Bank Northern Kentucky, NA (Covington, KY) 68231
PNC Bank Northern Kentucky, NA (Crescent Springs, KY) 68242
PNC Bank Northern Kentucky, NA (Edgewood, KY) 68270
PNC Bank Northern Kentucky, NA (Florence, KY) 68328
PNC Bank Northern Kentucky, NA (Fort Mitchell, KY) 68348
PNC Bank Northern Kentucky, NA (Fort Thomas, KY) 68352
PNC Bank Northern Kentucky, NA (Fort Wright, KY) 68354
PNC Bank Northern Kentucky, NA (Highland Heights, KY) 68468
PNC Bank Northern Kentucky, NA (Newport, KY) 69140
PNC Bank Northern Kentucky, NA (Taylor Mill, KY) 69312
PNC Bank, Northern Kentucky, NA (Union, KY) 69319
PNC National Bank (Wilmington, DE) 58093; 58094
PNC Trust Co. of Florida, NA (Tampa, FL) 63537
PNC Trust Co. of Florida, NA (Vero Beach, FL) 63768
PNCBank Kentucky Inc. (Louisville, KY) 68980
Polar Ice Co. (Fort Worth, TX) 85238
Polaroid Corp. (Miami, FL) 61400
Polaroid Corp. (Atlanta, GA) 65039
Polymer Technology (Charlotte, NC) 74118
Pony Express Courier Corp. (Charlotte, NC) 74119; 74120
Porelon Inc. (Cookeville, TN) 80664
Porex Technologies Corp. (Fairburn, GA) 66179
Porex Technologies Corp. of Georgia (Fairburn, GA) 66180
Porocel Corp. (Little Rock, AR) 57299
Porter Cable Corp. (Hialeah, FL) 60003
Porter Cable Corp. (Charlotte, NC) 74121
Porter-Cable Corp. (Jackson, TN) 80995; 80996
Porter-Cable Corp. (Richmond, VA) 91951
Portion Pac, Inc. (Dallas, TX) 84321
Potlatch Corp. (Arkansas City, AR) 56724
Potlatch Corp. (Mc Gehee, AR) 57357
Potlatch Corp. (McGehee, AR) 57362
Potlatch Corp. (Warren, AR) 57710
Potlatch Corp. (Atlanta, GA) 65040
Potlatch Corp. Southern Unit (Warren, AR) 57711
Potlatch Corp. Townsend Unit (Stuttgart, AR) 57664
Potlatch Corp. Dairy (Dallas, TX) 84322
Potomac Capital Investment Corp. (Washington, DC) 58407
Potomac Edison Co. (Cumberland, MD) 71632
Potomac Edison Co. (Frederick, MD) 71739; 71740
The Potomac Edison Co. (Hagerstown, MD) 71888; 71889; 71890
Potomac Edison Co. (Oakland, MD) 72158
Potomac Edison Co. (Gordonsville, VA) 90994
Potomac Edison Co. (Luray, VA) 91216
Potomac Edison Co. (Winchester, VA) 92600
Potomac Edison Co. (Augusta, WV) 92666
Potomac Edison Co. (Martinsburg, WV) 92934
Potomac Electric Power (Washington, DC) **58408**
Potomac Valley Bank (Bethesda, MD) 71433
Potomac Valley Bank (Gaithersburg, MD) 71807
Potomac Valley Bank (Germantown, MD) 71829
Potomac Valley Bank (Potomac, MD) 72233
Potomac Valley Bank (Rockville, MD) 72313
Potomac Valley Bank (Sumner, MD) 72483
Potomac Valley Bank (Petersburg, WV) 93002; 93003
Powell Valley Foods Co. (Caryville, TN) 80280
Power Systems (Lancaster, TX) 87601
Power Systems Diesel Inc. (Belle Chasse, LA) 69693
Power Tools & Accessories (Towson, MD) 72510
Ppg Architectural Finishes (East Point, GA) 66153
Ppg Architectural Finishes (Louisville, KY) 68981
PPG Industries (Hunt Valley, MD) 71944
Ppg Industries (Lattimore, NC) 75344
Ppg Industries (La Porte, TX) 87563
PPG Industries (Lewisville, TX) 87661
PPG Industries Inc. (Huntsville, AL) 56000
Ppg Industries Inc. (N Little Rock, AR) 57418
PPG Industries Inc. (Dover, DE) 57799
Ppg Industries Inc. (Orlando, FL) 62100
Ppg Industries Inc. (Atlanta, GA) 65041; 65042; 65043
PPG Industries Inc. (Lawrenceville, GA) 66533
PPG Industries Inc. (Smyrna, GA) 67567
PPG Industries Inc. (Lake Charles, LA) 70159
PPG Industries Inc. (Hagerstown, MD) 71891
PPG Industries Inc. (Hyattsville, MD) 71975
Ppg Industries Inc. (Shelby, NC) 76244; 76245
Ppg Industries Inc. (Oklahoma City, OK) 77508
Ppg Industries Inc. (Spartanburg, SC) 79927
PPG Industries Inc. (Knoxville, TN) 81241; 81242
PPG Industries Inc. (Nashville, TN) 82084
Ppg Industries Inc. (Beaumont, TX) 83204
Ppg Industries Inc. (Houston, TX) 86717; 86718
PPG Industries Inc. (LaPorte, TX) 87604
PPG Industries Inc. (Wichita Falls, TX) 90093; 90094; 90095
PPG Industries Inc. (Norfolk, VA) 91566
PPG Industries Inc. (Salem, VA) 92222
PPG Industries Inc. (N. Martinsville, WV) 92958
Ppg Industries Inc. (New Martinsville, WV) 92962; 92963
Ppg Printing Inks (Spartanburg, SC) 79928
Ppm Inc. (Tucker, GA) 67885
Pratt & Whitney (Columbus, GA) 65648
Pratt & Whitney Aircraft of West Virginia (Bridgeport, WV) 92709
Prattville Mfg. Inc. (Prattville, AL) 56491
Praxair Inc. (Mims, FL) 61553
Praxair Inc. (Deer Park, TX) 84560
Praxair Inc. (Garland, TX) 85524
Praxair Inc. (Texas City, TX) 89732
Praxair Inc. Linde (La Porte, TX) 87564
Praxair Inc. Linde Div. (Garland, TX) 85525
PRC (McLean, VA) 91394
PRC Engineering Systems, Inc. (Reston, VA) 91717
PRC Inc. (McLean, VA) 91395
PRC Public Sector Inc. (McLean, VA) 91396
PRC Realty Systems Inc. (McLean, VA) 91397
Precise Hard Chrome (Waco, TX) 89968
Precision Fabrication Center (Columbus, GA) 65649
Precision Interconnect (Grapevine, TX) 85660
Precision Microblenders Inc. (Ciales, PR) 78390
Precision Steel Warehouse (Charlotte, NC) 74122
Precoat Metals (Channelview, TX) 83553
Prelude Co. (High Point, NC) 75156
Prelude Co. (Thomasville, NC) 76382
Premark International (Montgomery, AL) 56370
Premier Bancorp (Baton Rouge, LA) **69610**
Premier Bancorp (Houma, LA) 69965
Premier Bancorp, Inc. Holding Co. (Baton Rouge, LA) 69611; 69612
Premier Bank, NA (Baton Rouge, LA) 69613; 69614; 69615; 69616; 69617; 69618; 69619; 69620; 69621; 69622; 69623; 69624; 69625; 69626; 69627; 69628; 69629; 69630; 69631; 69632; 69633; 69634; 69635; 69636; 69637
Premier Bank, NA (Lafayett, LA) 70038
Premier Bank, NA (Lafayette, LA) 70088; 70089; 70090; 70091; 70092; 70093; 70094; 70095; 70096; 70097
Premier Bank, NA (Lake Charles, LA) 70160; 70161; 70162; 70163; 70164
Premier Bank, NA (Monroe, LA) 70370; 70371; 70372; 70373; 70374; 70375
Premier Bank, NA (New Iberia, LA) 70414; 70415; 70416
Premier Bank, National Assoc. (Lake Charles, LA) 70165; 70166; 70167; 70168
Premier Bank, National Assoc. (Lake Shore Dr., LA) 70186
Premier Bank, National Assoc. (New Iberia, LA) 70417; 70418; 70419
Premier Beverage Co. (Dallas, TX) 84323
Prescolite (El Dorado, AR) 56957
Press (Hilton Head, SC) 79509
Press (Ennis, TX) 84998
Press (Waxahacie, TX) 90001
Press Inc. (Johnson City, TN) 81054
Press Inc. (Ennis, TX) 84999
Press Inc. (Waxahacie, TX) 90002
Preston Corp. (Preston, MD) 72237
Preston Trucking Co., Inc. (Preston, MD) 72238
Price Club (Beltsville, MD) 71361
Price Club (Suitland, MD) 72481
Price Club (Glen Allen, VA) 90983
Price Club (Hampton, VA) 91046
Price Club (Norfolk, VA) 91567
Price Club of Gaithersburg (Gaithersburg, MD) 71808
Price Club Hearing Aid Departm (Gaithersburg, MD) 71809
Price Club 218 (Sterling, VA) 92346
Price Pfister, Inc. (Morrow, GA) 67037
Price Pfister Inc. (Irving, TX) 87393
Price's Creameries (El Paso, TX) 84895
Principal Mutual Life (Macon, GA) 66706
Principal Mutual Life Insurance (Birmingham, AL) 55353
Principal Mutual Life Insurance (Huntsville, AL) 56001
Principal Mutual Life Insurance Co. (Greenville, SC) 79408
Principal Mutual Life Insurance Co. (Austin, TX) 82974
Prints Plus (Melbourne, FL) 61089
Prints Plus (Duluth, GA) 66071
Prints Plus (Kenner, LA) 70006
Prints Plus (Dallas, TX) 84324
Process Conveyors (Salisbury, NC) 76172
Procter & Gamble Cellulose Co. (Perry, FL) 62502; 62503; 62504
Procter & Gamble Cellulose Co. (Oglethorpe, GA) 67219
Procter & Gamble Cellulose Co. Memphis Plant (Memphis, TN) 81673
Procter & Gamble Co. Paper Products (Albany, GA) 64087
Procter & Gamble Manuf. Co. (Augusta, GA) 65345
Procter & Gamble Manufacturing (Lexington, KY) 68612
Procter & Gamble Manufacturing Co. (Browns Summit, NC) 73729
Procter & Gamble Mfg. Co. (Augusta, GA) 65346
Procter & Gamble Mfg. Co. (Pineville, LA) 70625
Procter & Gamble Mfg. Co. (Baltimore, MD) 71220
Procter & Gamble Mfg. Co. (Browns Summit, NC) 73730
Procter & Gamble Mfg. Co. (Greenville, SC) 79409; 79410
Procter & Gamble Mfg. Co. (Jackson, TN) 80997
Procter & Gamble Mfg. Co. (Dallas, TX) 84325
Procter & Gamble Mfg. Co. Co. (Pineville, LA) 70626
Procter & Gamble Oilseed Products Co. (Levelland, TX) 87640
Procter & Gamble Paper Product Co. (Albany, GA) 64088
Proctor & Gamble Pharmaceuticals Pr Inc. (Manati, PR) 78502
Prodair Corp. (Wilmington, DE) 58095
Productos Borden Can Division (San Juan, PR) 78579
Productos Circuitos De P.R. (Juana Diaz, PR) 78468
Professional Accounting Ser (St Augustine, FL) 62951
Professional Accounting Ser (Venice, FL) 63731
Professional Accounting Ser (Statesboro, GA) 67643
Professional Accounting Servuc (Dunwoody, GA) 66131
Professional Assistance, Inc. (McLean, VA) 91398
Professional Dental Inc. (Batesville, AR) 56761
Professional Food Systems (El Dorado, AR) 56958
Progress Credit Corp. (St. Petersburg, FL) 63130
Progressive Casualty Insurance Co. (Baltimore, MD) 71221
Progressive Casualty Insurance Co. (Camp Springs, MD) 71489
Progressive Casualty Insurance Co. (Richmond, VA) 91952
Progressive Insurance Agency (Punta Gorda, FL) 62715
Properties Inc. (Baltimore, MD) 71222
Protein Tech. International International (Louisville, KY) 68982
Protein Tech. International International (Pryor, OK) 77743
Protein Tech. International International (Memphis, TN) 81674
Protein Technologies Intern. (Louisville, KY) 68983
Protein Technologies International (Louisville, KY) 68984
Protein Technologies International (Pryor, OK) 77744; 77745
Protein Technologies International (Memphis, TN) 81675
Provident Financial Corp. (Columbia, SC) 79077; 79078
Provident Life & Accident (Chattanooga, TN) **80472**
Provident National Assurance (Atlanta, GA) 65044
Provident National Assurance (Chattanooga, TN) 80473
Provident National Assurance (Houston, TX) 86719
Provident National Assurance Co. (Chattanooga, TN) 80474; 80475
Prudential Secruities Inc. (Atlanta, GA) 65045
Prudential Securities Inc. (Washington, DC) 58409
Prudential Securities Inc. (Atlanta, GA) 65046
Prudential Securities Inc. (Bethesda, MD) 71434
Pryor Fndy. Inc. (Pryor, OK) 77746

Pryor Foundry Inc. (Pryor, OK) 77747
PTS Liquidation, Co. (Owings Mills, MD) 72190
Public Service Co. of Oklahoma (Tulsa, OK) 78070
Publix Deerfield Beach Facility (Deerfield Beach, FL) 59284
Publix Super Market (Boca Raton, FL) 58731; 58732
Publix Super Market (Bradenton, FL) 58843; 58844; 58845; 58846
Publix Super Market (Brandon, FL) 58877; 58878
Publix Super Market (Clearwater, FL) 59039; 59040
Publix Super Market (Clermont, FL) 59058
Publix Super Market (Cocoa, FL) 59069
Publix Super Market (Daytona Beach, FL) 59203; 59204; 59205
Publix Super Market (Delray Beach, FL) 59326
Publix Super Market (Dunedin, FL) 59366
Publix Super Market (Fort Lauderdale, FL) 59561; 59562; 59563; 59564; 59565; 59566; 59567; 59568
Publix Super Market (Fort Myers, FL) 59741; 59742; 59743; 59744
Publix Super Market (Fort Myers Beach, FL) 59782
Publix Super Market (Fort Myers Fl, FL) 59784
Publix Super Market (Fort Pierce, FL) 59802
Publix Super Market (Gainesville, FL) 59905; 59906
Publix Super Market (Hollywood, FL) 60084; 60085; 60086
Publix Super Market (Jacksonville, FL) 60413; 60414; 60415; 60416; 60417; 60418; 60419; 60420
Publix Super Market (Jupiter, FL) 60546
Publix Super Market (Kissimmee, FL) 60598
Publix Super Market (Lake Worth, FL) 60688
Publix Super Market (Lakeland, FL) 60767; 60768; 60769; 60770
Publix Super Market (Largo, FL) 60854; 60855; 60856; 60857
Publix Super Market (Live Oak, FL) 60917
Publix Super Market (Longwood, FL) 60945
Publix Super Market (Melbourne, FL) 61090; 61091; 61092; 61093
Publix Super Market (Merritt is, FL) 61129
Publix Super Market (Miami, FL) 61401; 61402; 61403; 61404; 61405; 61406; 61407; 61408; 61409; 61410; 61411; 61412
Publix Super Market (Naples, FL) 61653; 61654; 61655; 61656
Publix Super Market (Nokomis, FL) 61726
Publix Super Market (Northwest Smyrna Beach, FL) 61758
Publix Super Market (Ocala, FL) 61813; 61814
Publix Super Market (Orlando, FL) 62101; 62102; 62103; 62104; 62105; 62106; 62107; 62108; 62109; 62110; 62111; 62112
Publix Super Market (Ormond Beach, FL) 62208
Publix Super Market (Palm Beach, FL) 62260
Publix Super Market (Palm City, FL) 62279
Publix Super Market (Palm Coast, FL) 62285
Publix Super Market (Pinellas Park, FL) 62527
Publix Super Market (Pompano Beach, FL) 62618; 62619; 62620; 62621
Publix Super Market (Port St Lucie, FL) 62690
Publix Super Market (Punta Gorda, FL) 62716
Publix Super Market (Sanford, FL) 62773
Publix Super Market (Sarasota Sq, FL) 62868
Publix Super Market (Sebastian, FL) 62874
Publix Super Market (Sebring, FL) 62892
Publix Super Market (St Augustine, FL) 62952; 62953
Publix Super Market (St Petersburg, FL) 63012; 63013; 63014; 63015; 63016; 63017
Publix Super Market (St. Cloud, FL) 63070
Publix Super Market (Sunrise, FL) 63196
Publix Super Market (Tallahassee, FL) 63259
Publix Super Market (Tampa, FL) 63538; 63539; 63540; 63541; 63542; 63543; 63544; 63545; 63546; 63547; 63548
Publix Super Market (Temple Ter, FL) 63675
Publix Super Market (Titusville, FL) 63699; 63700
Publix Super Market (Venice, FL) 63732
Publix Super Market (Vlg of Golf, FL) 63773
Publix Super Market (W Palm Beach, FL) 63801; 63802; 63803; 63804; 63805
Publix Super Market (West Palm Beach, FL) 63894
Publix Super Market (Winter Park, FL) 63991
Publix Super Market (Zephyrhills, FL) 64020; 64021; 64022
Publix Super Market (Atlanta, GA) 65047
Publix Super Market (Marietta, GA) 66884; 66885; 66886
Publix Super Market (Norcross, GA) 67170
Publix Super Market (Kenner, LA) 70007
Publix Super Markets (Boca Raton, FL) 58733
Publix Super Markets (Clearwater, FL) 59041
Publix Super Markets (Cocoa, FL) 59070
Publix Super Markets (Fort Lauderdale, FL) 59569; 59570; 59571; 59572; 59573; 59574; 59575; 59576
Publix Super Markets (Fort Myers, FL) 59745; 59746
Publix Super Markets (Fort Myers Beach, FL) 59783
Publix Super Markets (Fort Myers Fl, FL) 59785
Publix Super Markets (Gainesville, FL) 59907
Publix Super Markets (Hollywood, FL) 60087
Publix Super Markets (Jacksonville, FL) 60421
Publix Super Markets (Kissimmee, FL) 60599
Publix Super Markets (Lake Worth, FL) 60689
Publix Super Markets (Lakeland, FL) 60771; **60772**
Publix Super Markets (Largo, FL) 60858; 60859
Publix Super Markets (Live Oak, FL) 60918
Publix Super Markets (Longwood, FL) 60946
Publix Super Markets (Melbourne, FL) 61094; 61095; 61096; 61097
Publix Super Markets (Miami, FL) 61413; 61414; 61415; 61416; 61417; 61418; 61419
Publix Super Markets (Naples, FL) 61657
Publix Super Markets (New Smyrna Beach, FL) 61704
Publix Super Markets (Ocala, FL) 61815
Publix Super Markets (Orlando, FL) 62113; 62114; 62115; 62116; 62117; 62118; 62119; 62120; 62121
Publix Super Markets (Plant City, FL) 62553
Publix Super Markets (Pompano Beach, FL) 62622; 62623; 62624; 62625
Publix Super Markets (Sanford, FL) 62774
Publix Super Markets (Sebastian, FL) 62875
Publix Super Markets (St Augustine, FL) 62954
Publix Super Markets (St Petersburg, FL) 63018; 63019; 63020
Publix Super Markets (St. Petersburg, FL) 63131
Publix Super Markets (Sunrise, FL) 63197
Publix Super Markets (Tampa, FL) 63549; 63550
Publix Super Markets (Titusville, FL) 63701
Publix Super Markets (Venice, FL) 63733
Publix Super Markets (W Palm Beach, FL) 63806; 63807
Publix Super Markets (West Palm Beach, FL) 63895
Publix Super Markets (Zephyrhills, FL) 64023
Publix Super Markets (Marietta, GA) 66887; 66888; 66889; 66890; 66891; 66892; 66893; 66894; 66895; 66896; 66897
Publix Super Markets (Mreat, GA) 67066
Publix Super Markets (Norcross, GA) 67171; 67172; 67173
Publix Super Markets Atlanta D (Atlanta, GA) 65048
Publix Super Markets Inc. (Naples, FL) 61658
Publix Super Markets Inc. (Tampa, FL) 63551; 63552; 63553
Publix Super Markets Inc. (Vlg of Golf, FL) 63774
Publix Super Markets Inc. (Zephyrhills, FL) 64024
Pulp & Paperboard Operations (Evadale, TX) 85024
Pulse Communications Inc/Subsi (Duluth, GA) 66072
Pulse Communications Inc. (Herndon, VA) 91129
Pulte Home Corp. (Clg Pkwy, FL) 59064
Pulte Home Corp. (Hialeah, FL) 60004
Pulte Home Corp. (Tampa, FL) 63554; 63555; 63556; 63557
Pulte Home Corp. (Atlanta, GA) 65049
Pulte Home Corp. (Dunwoody, GA) 66132
Pulte Home Corp. (Lawrenceville, GA) 66534
Pulte Home Corp. (Germantown, MD) 71830
Pulte Home Corp. (Hanover, MD) 71913
Pulte Home Corp. (Hyattsville, MD) 71976
Pulte Home Corp. (Laurel, MD) 72083
Pulte Home Corp. (Rockville, MD) 72314
Pulte Home Corp. (Cary, NC) 73800
Pulte Home Corp. (Matthews, NC) 75528
Pulte Home Corp. (Carrollton, TX) 83500
Pulte Home Corp. (Cypress, TX) 83828
Pulte Home Corp. (Fort Worth, TX) 85239
Pulte Home Corp. (Grand Prairie, TX) 85633
Pulte Home Corp. (Houston, TX) 86720; 86721; 86722; 86723; 86724; 86725
Pulte Home Corp. (La Porte, TX) 87565; 87566
Pulte Home Corp. (Mesquite, TX) 87988
Pulte Home Corp. (Missouri City, TX) 88131
Pulte Home Corp. (Pearland, TX) 88487; 88488
Pulte Home Corp. (Sugar Land, TX) 89541
Pulte Home Corp. (Tomball, TX) 89776
Pulte Home Corp. (Woodbridge, VA) 92620
Pulte Home Corp. Cons (Houston, TX) 86726
Pulte Home Corp.s Georgi (Alpharetta, GA) 64129
Pulte Home Corp. Georgia (Alpharetta, GA) 64130
Pulte Home Corp. Georgia (Duluth, GA) 66073; 66074
Pulte Home Corp. Georgia (Lawrenceville, GA) 66535
Pulte Home Corp. I C M Mortg (Maitland, FL) 60984
Pulte Home Corp. Model Home (Duluth, GA) 66075
Pulte Home Corp. Potomac (Gaithersburg, MD) 71810
Pulte Home Corp. Quail Hollo (Bedford, TX) 83247
Puritan Sportswear (Houston, TX) 86727
Purolator Products Co. Air Filtration Co. (Henderson, NC) 75026
Putnam Investments (Chattanooga, TN) 80476
PYA Monarch Inc. (Greenville, SC) 79411
Pyro Chem Inc. (Louisville, KY) 68985
Pyroil Performance Products (Hernando, MS) 72903

Q

Qo Chemicals Inc. (Memphis, TN) 81676
QO Chemicals Inc. Belle Glade Plant (Belle Glade, FL) 58646
Quaker Oats Co. (Jackson, TN) 80998; 80999
Quaker Oats Co. (Newport, TN) 82170
Quaker Oats Co. (Dallas, TX) 84326
Quaker State Corp. Congo Plant (Congo, WV) 92823
Quaker State Corp. Congo Plant (Newell, WV) 92964; 92965
Quaker State Minit Lube Inc. (Lawrenceville, GA) 66536
Quaker State Minitueube (Dallas, TX) 84327
Quaker State Oil Refining (Chester, WV) 92802
Quaker State Oil Refining (Fairmont, WV) 92846
Quaker State Oil Refining Co. (Joppa, MD) 71990
Quaker State Oil Refining Co. (Alma, WV) 92657
Quaker State Oil Refining Co. (Newell, WV) 92966
Quaker State Oil Refining Co. (St. Marys, WV) 93072
Qualex Inc. (Charlotte, NC) 74123
Qualex Inc. (Durham, NC) 74425
Qualex Inc. (Fayetteville, NC) 74573
Qualex Inc. (Memphis, TN) 81677
Quality Bakery (Enid, OK) 77063
Quality Care Dialysis Center (Temple Hills, MD) 72496
Quality Mills Inc. Cloth Plant (Mount Airy, NC) 75682
Quality Park Product (Atlanta, GA) 65050; 65051
Quality Park Products (Atlanta, GA) 65052
Qualtec Quality Service Inc. (Washington, DC) 58410
Qualtec Quality Services (Washington, DC) 58411
Quanex (Houston, TX) **86728**
Quanex Co. Macsteel Division (Fort Smith, AR) 57086
Quanex Corp. Gulf States Tube (Rosenberg, TX) 88833
Quanex Corp. Macsteel Div. (Fort Smith, AR) 57087; 57088
Quanex Gulf States Tube (Rosenberg, TX) 88834
Quantum (Duncanville, TX) 84707
Quantum Corp. (Marietta, GA) 66898
Quarles Drilling Corp. (Belle Chasse, LA) 69694
Quarles Drilling & Exploration, Inc. (Tulsa, OK) 78071
Quazite (Lenoir City, TN) 81322; 81323
Quick-To-Fix Foods (Garland, TX) 85526
Quincy Compressor Colt Indu (Houston, TX) 86729
Quincy Family Steak House (Spartanburg, SC) 79929
Quincy Family Steakhouse (Maryville, TN) 81422
Quincy Family Steakhouse (Nashville, TN) 82085
Quincy State Bank (Chattahoochie, FL) 58950
Quincy State Bank (Havana, FL) 59969
Quincy State Bank (Quincy, FL) 62732; 62733
Quinton Instrument Co. (Gaithersburg, MD) 71811
Quintus Corp. (Dunwoody, GA) 66133
Quotron Systems (Beaver, AR) 56766
Quotron Systems (Atlanta, GA) 65053
Quotron Systems (Oklahoma City, OK) 77509

R

R. J. Reynolds Tobacco Co. Archer 200 (Winston-Salem, NC) 76739
R. J. Reynolds Tobacco Co. Downtown (Winston-Salem, NC) 76740; 76741
R. J. Reynolds Tobacco Co. Downtown 91-1 (Winston-Salem, NC) 76742
R. J. Reynolds Tobacco Co. Downtown 93-7 (Winston-Salem, NC) 76743
R. J. Reynolds Tobacco Co. Downtown 92-2 (Winston-Salem, NC) 76744; 76745
R. J. Reynolds Tobacco Co. Downtown 64 (Winston-Salem, NC) 76746
R. J. Reynolds Tobacco Co. Downtown 26 (Winston-Salem, NC) 76747
R. J. Reynolds Tobacco Co. Downtown 23-1 (Winston-Salem, NC) 76748; 76749
R. J. Reynolds Tobacco Co. Dt 95-1 (Winston-Salem, NC) 76750
R. J. Reynolds Tobacco Co. Dt 90-3 (Winston-Salem, NC) 76751
R. J. Reynolds Tobacco Co. Dt 63-1 (Winston-Salem, NC) 76752
R. J. Reynolds Tobacco Co. Tobaccoville (King, NC) 75292
R. J. Reynolds Tobacco Co. Whitaker Park (Winston-Salem, NC) 76753
R. J. Reynolds Tobacco Co. Whitaker Park 605-1 (Winston-Salem, NC) 76754
R. J. Reynolds Tobacco Co. Whitaker Park 641 (Winston-Salem, NC) 76755
R. J. Reynolds Tobacco Co. Whitaker Park 604 (Winston-Salem, NC) 76756
R. J. Reynolds Tobacco Co. Whitaker Park 604-1 (Winston-Salem, NC) 76757
R. J. Reynolds Tobacco Co. Wp 631-1 (Winston-Salem, NC) 76758
R R Donnelley Financial (Atlanta, GA) 65054
R. R. Donnelley Printing (Lynchburg, VA) 91276
R. R. Donnelley Printing Co. (Newton, NC) 75752
R. R. Donnelley Printing Co. (Lynchburg, VA) 91277
R R Donnelley & Sons Co. (Atlanta, GA) 65055
R R Donnelley & Sons Co. (Charlotte, NC) 74124
R. R. Donnelley & Sons Co. (Spartanburg, SC) 79930
R. R. Donnelley & Sons Co. (Gallatin, TN) 80850
R R Donnelley & Sons Co. (Fort Worth, TX) 85240
R. R. Donnelley & Sons Co. Lakeside Press (Spartanburg, SC) 79931
R-Tec Systems (Bedford, TX) 83248
R. W. Snyder Co. Inc. (Marshall, TX) 87861
Raceland Sugars Inc. (Raceland, LA) 70655
Raco Inc. (Gretna, VA) 91003
Racquet Club Wimbledon (Arlington, TX) 82732
Radford Army Ammunition Plant (Radford, VA) 91699; 91700
Radio Shack (Albertville, AL) 54970
Radio Shack (Anniston, AL) 55009; 55010
Radio Shack (Auburn, AL) 55070
Radio Shack (Bessemer, AL) 55101; 55102
Radio Shack (Birmingham, AL) 55354; 55355; 55356; 55357; 55358; 55359; 55360; 55361; 55362; 55363; 55364; 55365; 55366; 55367
Radio Shack (Camden, AL) 55500
Radio Shack (Cullman, AL) 55549
Radio Shack (Dothan, AL) 55663; 55664; 55665
Radio Shack (Enterprise, AL) 55691; 55692
Radio Shack (Fairfield, AL) 55715
Radio Shack (Florence, AL) 55743
Radio Shack (Gadsden, AL) 55786; 55787
Radio Shack (Gilbertown, AL) 55809
Radio Shack (Huntsville, AL) 56002; 56003; 56004; 56005; 56006; 56007; 56008
Radio Shack (Jasper, AL) 56089
Radio Shack (Leeds, AL) 56108
Radio Shack (Mobile, AL) 56228; 56229; 56230; 56231; 56232
Radio Shack (Montgomery, AL) 56371; 56372
Radio Shack (Opelika, AL) 56423
Radio Shack (Pelham, AL) 56450
Radio Shack (Pell City, AL) 56452
Radio Shack (Phenix City, AL) 56471
Radio Shack (Piedmont, AL) 56481
Radio Shack (Russellville, AL) 56511
Radio Shack (Selma, AL) 56535; 56536
Radio Shack (Sylacauga, AL) 56588
Radio Shack (Talladega, AL) 56598
Radio Shack (Thomasville, AL) 56610
Radio Shack (Tuscaloosa, AL) 56670; 56671; 56672
Radio Shack (Valley, AL) 56690
Radio Shack (Benton, AR) 56774
Radio Shack (Bentonville, AR) 56788
Radio Shack (Camden, AR) 56840
Radio Shack (Conway, AR) 56869
Radio Shack (Crossett, AR) 56886

Radio Shack (Charlotte, NC) 74125; 74126; 74127; 74128; 74129; 74130; 74131; 74132; 74133; 74134; 74135; 74136; 74137; 74138; 74139; 74140; 74141; 74142
Radio Shack (Clayton, NC) 74266
Radio Shack (Concord, NC) 74321; 74322
Radio Shack (Conover, NC) 74335
Radio Shack (Dunn, NC) 74377
Radio Shack (Durham, NC) 74426; 74427
Radio Shack (Eden, NC) 74465
Radio Shack (Elizabeth Cy, NC) 74487
Radio Shack (Elizabethtown, NC) 74491
Radio Shack (Fayetteville, NC) 74574; 74575
Radio Shack (Garner, NC) 74648
Radio Shack (Goldsboro, NC) 74732; 74733
Radio Shack (Greensboro, NC) 74882; 74883; 74884; 74885; 74886; 74887; 74888; 74889; 74890
Radio Shack (Greenville, NC) 74974; 74975
Radio Shack (Henderson, NC) 75027
Radio Shack (Hickory, NC) 75096; 75097; 75098
Radio Shack (High Point, NC) 75157; 75158
Radio Shack (Jacksonville, NC) 75227; 75228; 75229
Radio Shack (Kannapolis, NC) 75267
Radio Shack (Kernersville, NC) 75284
Radio Shack (Lenoir, NC) 75386
Radio Shack (Lexington, NC) 75422
Radio Shack (Lincolnton, NC) 75441
Radio Shack (Littleton, NC) 75450
Radio Shack (Matthews, NC) 75529
Radio Shack (Monroe, NC) 75587
Radio Shack (Mooresville, NC) 75608
Radio Shack (Morehead City, NC) 75627
Radio Shack (Morganton, NC) 75653
Radio Shack (Mount Airy, NC) 75683
Radio Shack (Murphy, NC) 75708
Radio Shack (N Wilkesboro, NC) 75713
Radio Shack (Nags Head, NC) 75715
Radio Shack (New Bern, NC) 75732; 75733; 75734
Radio Shack (Pineville, NC) 75821
Radio Shack (Raleigh, NC) 75942; 75943; 75944; 75945; 75946; 75947; 75948
Radio Shack (Reidsville, NC) 76010
Radio Shack (Roanoke Rpds, NC) 76041; 76042
Radio Shack (Rockingham, NC) 76067
Radio Shack (Rocky Mount, NC) 76101
Radio Shack (Roxboro, NC) 76132
Radio Shack (S Brunswick, NC) 76151
Radio Shack (Shelby, NC) 76246; 76247
Radio Shack (Skyland, NC) 76252
Radio Shack (Smithfield, NC) 76268
Radio Shack (Southport, NC) 76288
Radio Shack (Spring Lake, NC) 76299
Radio Shack (Statesville, NC) 76334
Radio Shack (Wake Forest, NC) 76432
Radio Shack (Washington, NC) 76459
Radio Shack (Waynesville, NC) 76472
Radio Shack (Wilmington, NC) 76589; 76590; 76591; 76592; 76593
Radio Shack (Wilson, NC) 76641
Radio Shack (Winston Salem, NC) 76680; 76681; 76682
Radio Shack (Ardmore, OK) 76818
Radio Shack (Bartlesville, OK) 76849; 76850; 76851
Radio Shack (Bethany, OK) 76860
Radio Shack (Claremore, OK) 76956
Radio Shack (Duncan, OK) 76997
Radio Shack (Edmond, OK) 77014; 77015
Radio Shack (Enid, OK) 77064; 77065; 77066; 77067
Radio Shack (Frederick, OK) 77086
Radio Shack (Guymon, OK) 77110
Radio Shack (Henryetta, OK) 77130
Radio Shack (Kingfisher, OK) 77152
Radio Shack (Mc Alester, OK) 77198
Radio Shack (Muskogee, OK) 77228
Radio Shack (Mustang, OK) 77239
Radio Shack (Norman, OK) 77270; 77271; 77272
Radio Shack (Oklahoma City, OK) 77510; 77511; 77512; 77513; 77514; 77515; 77516; 77517; 77518; 77519; 77520; 77521; 77522; 77523; 77524; 77525; 77526; 77527; 77528; 77529; 77530; 77531; 77532; 77533; 77534; 77535
Radio Shack (Okmulgee, OK) 77684
Radio Shack (Pawhuska, OK) 77696
Radio Shack (Pryor, OK) 77748
Radio Shack (Purcell, OK) 77751
Radio Shack (Sapulpa, OK) 77797
Radio Shack (Sayre, OK) 77800
Radio Shack (Shattuck, OK) 77810
Radio Shack (Shawnee, OK) 77823
Radio Shack (Skiatook, OK) 77827
Radio Shack (Stilwell, OK) 77850
Radio Shack (Tahlequah, OK) 77859
Radio Shack (Tulsa, OK) 78072; 78073; 78074; 78075; 78076; 78077; 78078; 78079; 78080; 78081; 78082; 78083; 78084; 78085; 78086; 78087; 78088; 78089; 78090; 78091; 78092; 78093
Radio Shack (Vinita, OK) 78227
Radio Shack (Wagoner, OK) 78232
Radio Shack (Woodward, OK) 78265
Radio Shack (Yukon, OK) 78280
Radio Shack (Aiken, SC) 78656
Radio Shack (Anderson, SC) 78687; 78688; 78689; 78690
Radio Shack (Charleston, SC) 78871; 78872; 78873; 78874; 78875; 78876; 78877; 78878; 78879
Radio Shack (Clinton, SC) 78962
Radio Shack (Columbia, SC) 79079; 79080; 79081; 79082; 79083; 79084
Radio Shack (Conway, SC) 79137
Radio Shack (Dillon, SC) 79165
Radio Shack (Florence, SC) 79222
Radio Shack (Greenville, SC) 79412; 79413; 79414; 79415; 79416; 79417; 79418
Radio Shack (Greenwood, SC) 79464
Radio Shack (Hartsville, SC) 79501
Radio Shack (Hiltn Head is, SC) 79507
Radio Shack (Mauldin, SC) 79653
Radio Shack (Mt Pleasant, SC) 79679
Radio Shack (Myrtle Beach, SC) 79710; 79711; 79712
Radio Shack (North Augusta, SC) 79739
Radio Shack (Orangeburg, SC) 79777
Radio Shack (Piedmont, SC) 79796
Radio Shack (Rock Hill, SC) 79838
Radio Shack (Seneca, SC) 79863
Radio Shack (Spartanburg, SC) 79932; 79933; 79934; 79935
Radio Shack (West Columbia, SC) 80105; 80106
Radio Shack (Abilene, TX) 82453
Radio Shack (Alamo, TX) 82478
Radio Shack (Alice, TX) 82487
Radio Shack (Alief, TX) 82493
Radio Shack (Alvin, TX) 82515
Radio Shack (Amarillo, TX) 82577
Radio Shack (Arlington, TX) 82733; 82734; 82735; 82736; 82737; 82738; 82739; 82740; 82741; 82742
Radio Shack (Arlington Tex, TX) 82784
Radio Shack (Atlanta, TX) 82797
Radio Shack (Austin, TX) 82975; 82976; 82977; 82978; 82979; 82980; 82981; 82982; 82983; 82984; 82985; 82986; 82987; 82988; 82989; 82990; 82991
Radio Shack (Azle, TX) 83081
Radio Shack (Baytown, TX) 83133; 83134; 83135
Radio Shack (Beaumont, TX) 83205; 83206; 83207; 83208; 83209
Radio Shack (Bedford, TX) 83249; 83250
Radio Shack (Beeville, TX) 83260
Radio Shack (Bellaire, TX) 83266
Radio Shack (Big Spring, TX) 83293
Radio Shack (Boerne, TX) 83306
Radio Shack (Bowie, TX) 83327
Radio Shack (Brady, TX) 83331
Radio Shack (Brenham, TX) 83340
Radio Shack (Brownsville, TX) 83377; 83378; 83379; 83380
Radio Shack (Brownwood, TX) 83388
Radio Shack (Bryan, TX) 83406; 83407
Radio Shack (Burleson, TX) 83424
Radio Shack (Canyon, TX) 83444
Radio Shack (Carrollton, TX) 83501; 83502; 83503
Radio Shack (Channelview, TX) 83554
Radio Shack (College Sta, TX) 83611; 83612; 83613
Radio Shack (Colorado City, TX) 83640
Radio Shack (Conroe, TX) 83682; 83683
Radio Shack (Corpus Chrsti, TX) 83769
Radio Shack (Corsicana, TX) 83789
Radio Shack (Crosby, TX) 83807
Radio Shack (Cuero, TX) 83825
Radio Shack (Cypress, TX) 83829
Radio Shack (Dalhart, TX) 83835
Radio Shack (Dallas, TX) 84328; 84329; 84330; 84331; 84332; 84333; 84334; 84335; 84336; 84337; 84338; 84339; 84340; 84341; 84342; 84343; 84344; 84345; 84346; 84347; 84348
Radio Shack (Dayton, TX) 84524
Radio Shack (De Soto, TX) 84537
Radio Shack (Decatur, TX) 84544
Radio Shack (Deer Park, TX) 84561; 84562
Radio Shack (Del Rio, TX) 84585
Radio Shack (Denison, TX) 84606
Radio Shack (Denton, TX) 84631; 84632; 84633; 84634; 84635
Radio Shack (Dickinson, TX) 84671
Radio Shack (Dripping Springs, TX) 84682
Radio Shack (Dumas, TX) 84690
Radio Shack (Duncanville, TX) 84708; 84709
Radio Shack (El Paso, TX) 84896; 84897; 84898; 84899; 84900; 84901; 84902; 84903; 84904; 84905; 84906; 84907; 84908; 84909; 84910; 84911; 84912
Radio Shack (Euless, TX) 85018
Radio Shack (Fort Stockton, TX) 85047
Radio Shack (Fort Worth, TX) 85241; 85242; 85243; 85244; 85245; 85246; 85247; 85248; 85249; 85250; 85251; 85252; 85253; 85254; 85255; 85256; 85257; 85258; 85259; 85260; 85261; 85262; 85263; 85264
Radio Shack (Fortworth, TX) 85371
Radio Shack (Friendswood, TX) 85407
Radio Shack (Galveston, TX) 85462; 85463; 85464
Radio Shack (Garland, TX) 85527; 85528; 85529; 85530; 85531
Radio Shack (Glen Rose, TX) 85583
Radio Shack (Grand Prairie, TX) 85634; 85635
Radio Shack (Greenville, TX) 85675
Radio Shack (Groves, TX) 85683
Radio Shack (Harlingen, TX) 85712; 85713
Radio Shack (Hearne, TX) 85726
Radio Shack (Houston, TX) 86730; 86731; 86732; 86733; 86734; 86735; 86736; 86737; 86738; 86739; 86740; 86741; 86742; 86743; 86744; 86745; 86746; 86747; 86748; 86749; 86750; 86751; 86752; 86753; 86754; 86755; 86756; 86757; 86758; 86759; 86760; 86761; 86762; 86763; 86764; 86765; 86766; 86767; 86768; 86769; 86770; 86771; 86772; 86773; 86774; 86775; 86776; 86777; 86778; 86779; 86780; 86781; 86782; 86783; 86784; 86785; 86786; 86787; 86788; 86789; 86790; 86791
Radio Shack (Humble, TX) 87241; 87242; 87243
Radio Shack (Hurst, TX) 87291; 87292; 87293; 87294
Radio Shack (Irving, TX) 87394; 87395; 87396; 87397
Radio Shack (Katy, TX) 87454; 87455
Radio Shack (Kerrville, TX) 87482
Radio Shack (Kilgore, TX) 87497
Radio Shack (Killeen, TX) 87522; 87523
Radio Shack (La Marque, TX) 87545
Radio Shack (La Porte, TX) 87567
Radio Shack (Lake Jackson, TX) 87584; 87585
Radio Shack (Laredo, TX) 87621; 87622; 87623
Radio Shack (League City, TX) 87630
Radio Shack (Lewisville, TX) 87662; 87663
Radio Shack (Liberty, TX) 87679
Radio Shack (Longview, TX) 87732
Radio Shack (Lubbock, TX) 87778; 87779
Radio Shack (Lufkin, TX) 87815; 87816
Radio Shack (Marshall, TX) 87862; 87863; 87864; 87865
Radio Shack (Mc Kinney, TX) 87919
Radio Shack (Mcallen, TX) 87937; 87938; 87939
Radio Shack (Mesquite, TX) 87989; 87990; 87991; 87992; 87993; 87994
Radio Shack (Mexia, TX) 88015
Radio Shack (Midland, TX) 88070; 88071
Radio Shack (Mineral Wells, TX) 88115
Radio Shack (Mission, TX) 88126
Radio Shack (Missouri City, TX) 88132
Radio Shack (Nederland, TX) 88190
Radio Shack (New Braunfels, TX) 88219
Radio Shack (Odessa, TX) 88266; 88267; 88268; 88269
Radio Shack (Orange, TX) 88327; 88328
Radio Shack (Ozona, TX) 88336
Radio Shack (Palestine, TX) 88345
Radio Shack (Pampa, TX) 88356
Radio Shack (Paris, TX) 88376
Radio Shack (Pasadena, TX) 88460; 88461; 88462
Radio Shack (Pearland, TX) 88489
Radio Shack (Perryton, TX) 88503
Radio Shack (Pharr, TX) 88510; 88511
Radio Shack (Plano, TX) 88601; 88602; 88603; 88604
Radio Shack (Port Arthur, TX) 88644; 88645
Radio Shack (Port Isabel, TX) 88664
Radio Shack (Porter, TX) 88683
Radio Shack (Richardson, TX) 88761; 88762
Radio Shack (Rockwall, TX) 88825
Radio Shack (Rosenberg, TX) 88835
Radio Shack (Round Rock, TX) 88852
Radio Shack (San Angelo, TX) 88897; 88898
Radio Shack (San Antonio, TX) 89185; 89186; 89187; 89188; 89189; 89190; 89191; 89192; 89193; 89194; 89195; 89196; 89197; 89198; 89199; 89200; 89201; 89202; 89203; 89204; 89205; 89206; 89207; 89208; 89209; 89210; 89211
Radio Shack (Santa Fe, TX) 89350
Radio Shack (Seabrook, TX) 89359
Radio Shack (Seguin, TX) 89373
Radio Shack (Seminole, TX) 89385
Radio Shack (Sherman, TX) 89422; 89423
Radio Shack (Silsbee, TX) 89435
Radio Shack (Snyder, TX) 89451
Radio Shack (South Houston, TX) 89460
Radio Shack (Spring, TX) 89484; 89485
Radio Shack (Stafford, TX) 89504
Radio Shack (Stephenville, TX) 89523
Radio Shack (Sugar Land, TX) 89542
Radio Shack (Sulphur Springs, TX) 89563
Radio Shack (Sweetwater, TX) 89590
Radio Shack (Temple, TX) 89634; 89635
Radio Shack (Texarkana, TX) 89700; 89701; 89702; 89703; 89704; 89705
Radio Shack (Texas City, TX) 89733
Radio Shack (Tomball, TX) 89777
Radio Shack (Trinity, TX) 89784
Radio Shack (Tyler, TX) 89824
Radio Shack (Universal Cty, TX) 89847
Radio Shack (Uvalde, TX) 89855
Radio Shack (Van Horn, TX) 89861
Radio Shack (Victoria, TX) 89902; 89903
Radio Shack (Vidor, TX) 89918
Radio Shack (Waco, TX) 89969; 89970
Radio Shack (Weatherford, TX) 90011
Radio Shack (West, TX) 90044
Radio Shack (West Columbia, TX) 90046
Radio Shack (Wichita Falls, TX) 90096; 90097
Radio Shack (Winnie, TX) 90123
Radio Shack (Woodville, TX) 90131
Radio Shack (Alexandria, VA) 90229; 90230; 90231; 90232; 90233; 90234; 90235; 90236; 90237
Radio Shack (Annandale, VA) 90269; 90270
Radio Shack (Arlington, VA) 90367; 90368; 90369; 90370; 90371; 90372; 90373; 90374; 90375; 90376; 90377
Radio Shack (Ashland, VA) 90407
Radio Shack (Berryville, VA) 90429
Radio Shack (Blackstone, VA) 90454; 90455; 90456
Radio Shack (Bowling Green, VA) 90464
Radio Shack (Bristol, VA) 90485
Radio Shack (Charlottesville, VA) 90547
Radio Shack (Chesapeake, VA) 90592; 90593; 90594; 90595; 90596
Radio Shack (Covington, VA) 90664
Radio Shack (Culpeper, VA) 90677
Radio Shack (Danville, VA) 90710; 90711; 90712; 90713; 90714; 90715
Radio Shack (Exmore, VA) 90751; 90752
Radio Shack (Fairfax, VA) 90802; 90803; 90804; 90805
Radio Shack (Falls Church, VA) 90863; 90864; 90865; 90866; 90867; 90868
Radio Shack (Franklin, VA) 90897; 90898
Radio Shack (Fredericksburg, VA) 90934; 90935; 90936
Radio Shack (Front Royal, VA) 90953
Radio Shack (Galax, VA) 90963
Radio Shack (Hampton, VA) 91047; 91048; 91049; 91050; 91051
Radio Shack (Harrisonburg, VA) 91097; 91098
Radio Shack (Herndon, VA) 91130; 91131
Radio Shack (Hopewell, VA) 91162; 91163
Radio Shack (Lexington, VA) 91211; 91212
Radio Shack (Lynchburg, VA) 91278; 91279; 91280; 91281; 91282
Radio Shack (Madison Heights, VA) 91301
Radio Shack (Manassas, VA) 91318; 91319; 91320
Radio Shack (Marion, VA) 91338
Radio Shack (Mc Lean, VA) 91371; 91372; 91373; 91374
Radio Shack (Midlothian, VA) 91421; 91422; 91423
Radio Shack (Newport News, VA) 91478; 91479; 91480; 91481; 91482
Radio Shack (Norfolk, VA) 91568; 91569; 91570; 91571; 91572; 91573; 91574
Radio Shack (Norton, VA) 91608; 91609
Radio Shack (Orange, VA) 91619; 91620
Radio Shack (Portsmouth, VA) 91664; 91665; 91666
Radio Shack (Radford, VA) 91701
Radio Shack (Richmond, VA) 91953; 91954; 91955; 91956; 91957; 91958; 91959; 91960; 91961; 91962; 91963; 91964; 91965; 91966; 91967; 91968; 91969; 91970; 91971; 91972; 91973; 91974; 91975; 91976; 91977
Radio Shack (Roanoke, VA) 92178; 92179; 92180; 92181; 92182; 92183
Radio Shack (Smithfield, VA) 92239; 92240
Radio Shack (South Boston, VA) 92257; 92258
Radio Shack (Springfield, VA) 92290; 92291
Radio Shack (Staunton, VA) 92327
Radio Shack (Suffolk, VA) 92372
Radio Shack (Triangle, VA) 92388; 92389

Rincon Securities Inc. (Richmond, VA) 91996
Ring Around Prdts Inc. (East Bernard, TX) 84725
Ring Around Products (Prattville, AL) 56492
Ring Around Products Inc. (N Little Rock, AR) 57421
Ring Around Products Inc. (Sebree, KY) 69269
Ring Around Products Inc. (Houston, TX) 86798
Ring Around Products Inc. (Plainview, TX) 88532
Rio Grande Foods (McAllen, TX) 87940
Rio Grande Foods Inc. (Mc Allen, TX) 87897
Rio Grande Valley Gas Co. (Alamo, TX) 82479
Rio Grande Valley Gas Co. (Donna, TX) 84679
Rio Grande Valley Gas Co. (Raymondville, TX) 88709
Rio Grande Valley Gas Co. (Weslaco, TX) 90037; 90038
Ripley Graphies (Ripley, TN) 82264
Rite Aid (Dothan, AL) 55666
Rite-Aid (Enterprise, AL) 55693
Rite Aid (Claymont, DE) 57765; 57766
Rite Aid (Newark, DE) 57929
Rite Aid (Newcastle, DE) 57937; 57938
Rite Aid (Seaford, DE) 57953
Rite Aid (Wilmington, DE) 58100; 58101; 58102; 58103; 58104; 58105; 58106
Rite Aid (Washington, DC) 58460; 58461; 58462; 58463; 58464; 58465; 58466
Rite Aid (Clewiston, FL) 59061
Rite Aid (De Land, FL) 59257
Rite Aid (Fort Myers, FL) 59755; 59756; 59757
Rite Aid (Fort Pierce, FL) 59807
Rite Aid (Kissimmee, FL) 60600
Rite Aid (Lake City, FL) 60627
Rite Aid (Lake Worth, FL) 60694
Rite Aid (Leesburg, FL) 60885
Rite Aid (Live Oak, FL) 60919
Rite Aid (Naples, FL) 61661
Rite-Aid (Ormond Beach, FL) 62210
Rite Aid (Panama City, FL) 62346
Rite Aid (Tampa, FL) 63578
Rite-Aid (Tavares, FL) 63671
Rite-Aid (W Palm Beach, FL) 63813
Rite Aid (Covington, GA) 65741
Rite Aid (Aberdeen, MD) 70993
Rite Aid (Adelphi, MD) 70998; 70999
Rite Aid (Annapolis, MD) 71020
Rite Aid (Baltimore, MD) 71241; 71242; 71243; 71244; 71245; 71246; 71247; 71248; 71249; 71250; 71251; 71252; 71253; 71254; 71255; 71256; 71257; 71258; 71259; 71260; 71261; 71262; 71263; 71264; 71265; 71266; 71267
Rite Aid (Belair, MD) 71341
Rite Aid (Belotsville, MD) 71346
Rite Aid (Beltsville, MD) 71364
Rite Aid (Berlin, MD) 71368
Rite Aid (Bethesda, MD) 71440
Rite Aid (Bladensburg, MD) 71455
Rite Aid (Capital Heights, MD) 71503
Rite Aid (Chestertown, MD) 71525
Rite Aid (Chillum, MD) 71534
Rite Aid (Cockeysville, MD) 71555
Rite Aid (College Park, MD) 71566
Rite Aid (Collegepark, MD) 71570
Rite Aid (Cumberland, MD) 71636
Rite Aid (Elkton, MD) 71674
Rite Aid (Fort Washington, MD) 71713
Rite Aid (Frederick, MD) 71746
Rite Aid (Frostburg, MD) 71757
Rite Aid (Gaithersburg, MD) 71815
Rite Aid (Germantown, MD) 71831
Rite Aid (Grantsville, MD) 71852
Rite Aid (Hagerstown, MD) 71895
Rite Aid (Landover, MD) 72032
Rite Aid (Langley Park, MD) 72045
Rite Aid (Largo, MD) 72063
Rite Aid (Laurel, MD) 72087; 72088; 72089
Rite Aid (Lutherville-Timnum, MD) 72121
Rite Aid (Owingsmills, MD) 72192
Rite Aid (Oxon Hill, MD) 72208
Rite Aid (Pasadena, MD) 72212
Rite Aid (Phoenix, MD) 72216
Rite Aid (Potomac, MD) 72236
Rite Aid (Randallstown, MD) 72246
Rite Aid (Riverdale, MD) 72253
Rite Aid (Rockville, MD) 72319; 72320; 72321
Rite Aid (Salisbury, MD) 72361
Rite Aid (Seabrook, MD) 72368
Rite Aid (Severnapark, MD) 72380; 72381
Rite Aid (Silver Spring, MD) 72440; 72441; 72442
Rite Aid (Suitland, MD) 72482
Rite Aid (Sykesville, MD) 72487
Rite Aid (Temple Hills, MD) 72498; 72499
Rite Aid (Upper Marlboro, MD) 72521
Rite Aid (Westminster, MD) 72544
Rite Aid (Cherryville, NC) 74250
Rite-Aid (Gastonia, NC) 74686
Rite Aid (Hamlet, NC) 75000
Rite Aid (Reidsville, NC) 76011
Rite Aid (Charleston, SC) 78880
Rite Aid (Alexandria, VA) 90238
Rite Aid (Arlington, VA) 90380; 90381
Rite Aid (Baileys Crossroad, VA) 90413
Rite Aid (Big Stonegap, VA) 90436
Rite Aid (Blacksburg, VA) 90451
Rite Aid (Bluefield, VA) 90461
Rite Aid (Centreville, VA) 90518
Rite Aid (Chantilly, VA) 90523; 90524
Rite Aid (Chesapeake, VA) 90597; 90598
Rite Aid (Chester, VA) 90624
Rite Aid (Culpeper, VA) 90678
Rite Aid (Elkton, VA) 90747
Rite Aid (Fairfax, VA) 90806
Rite Aid (Fortbelvoir, VA) 90890
Rite Aid (Fredericksburg, VA) 90937; 90938; 90939
Rite Aid (Front Royal, VA) 90954
Rite Aid (Frontroyal, VA) 90959
Rite Aid (Hampton, VA) 91052; 91053; 91054
Rite Aid (Harrisonburg, VA) 91099
Rite Aid (Hopewell, VA) 91164
Rite Aid (Lebanon, VA) 91190
Rite Aid (Luray, VA) 91217
Rite Aid (Lynchburg, VA) 91283; 91284; 91285
Rite Aid (Madison Heights, VA) 91302
Rite Aid (Manassas, VA) 91321
Rite Aid (Mclean, VA) 91399
Rite Aid (Midlothian, VA) 91424
Rite Aid (Newportnews, VA) 91493; 91494
Rite Aid (Norfolk, VA) 91575
Rite Aid (Portsmouth, VA) 91667; 91668
Rite Aid (Pound, VA) 91674
Rite Aid (Purcellville, VA) 91685
Rite Aid (Richmond, VA) 91997; 91998; 91999; 92000; 92001; 92002; 92003; 92004
Rite Aid (Saltville, VA) 92228
Rite Aid (South Hill, VA) 92266
Rite Aid (Southboston, VA) 92270
Rite Aid (Staunton, VA) 92328
Rite Aid (Stephens City, VA) 92336
Rite Aid (Stuart, VA) 92354; 92355
Rite Aid (Suffolk, VA) 92373
Rite Aid (Virginia Beach, VA) 92505; 92506; 92507
Rite Aid (Woodbridge, VA) 92625
Rite Aid (Woodstock, VA) 92632
Rite Aid (Yorktown, VA) 92656
Rite Aid of so Carolina Inc. (Goose Creek, SC) 79287
Rite Aid Center (Wilmington, NC) 76594
Rite Aid Corp. (Venice, FL) 63735
Rite Aid Corp. (Atlanta, GA) 65079
Rite Aid Corp. (Henderson, NC) 75028
Rite Aid Corp. (Hendersonvl, NC) 75050
Rite Aid Corp. (Duncan, SC) 79174
Rite Aid Corp. (Spartanburg, SC) 79939; 79940
Rite Aid Disc Pharm (Woodruff, SC) 80137
Rite Aid Disc Pharmacies (Boca Raton, FL) 58738
Rite Aid Disc Pharmacies (Hallandale, FL) 59964
Rite Aid Disc Pharmacies (Melbourne, FL) 61102
Rite Aid Disc Pharmacies (Gastonia, NC) 74687
Rite Aid Disc Pharmacy (Homerville, GA) 66364
Rite Aid Disc Pharmacy (Swainsboro, GA) 67758
Rite Aid Discount Center (Greenville, SC) 79421
Rite Aid Discount Drugs (Ocoee, FL) 61838
Rite Aid Discount Pahrmacie (Morganton, NC) 75654
Rite Aid Discount Phar (Laurens, SC) 79597
Rite Aid Discount Pharamacy (Huntington, WV) 92891
Rite Aid Discount Pharm (Miami, FL) 61442
Rite Aid Discount Pharm (Southport, NC) 76289
Rite Aid Discount Pharmacie (Delray Beach, FL) 59329
Rite Aid Discount Pharmacie (Fort Lauderdale, FL) 59595
Rite Aid Discount Pharmacie (Fort Myers, FL) 59758
Rite Aid Discount Pharmacie (Hialeah Gdns, FL) 60023
Rite Aid Discount Pharmacie (Jupiter, FL) 60549
Rite Aid Discount Pharmacie (Miami, FL) 61443; 61444
Rite Aid Discount Pharmacie (Sunrise, FL) 63198
Rite Aid Discount Pharmacie (West Palm Beach, FL) 63896
Rite Aid Discount Pharmacie (Arden, NC) 73571
Rite Aid Discount Pharmacie (Asheboro, NC) 73594; 73595
Rite Aid Discount Pharmacie (Asheville, NC) 73635; 73636
Rite Aid Discount Pharmacie (Eden, NC) 74466
Rite Aid Discount Pharmacie (High Point, NC) 75161
Rite Aid Discount Pharmacie (Kinston, NC) 75328
Rite Aid Discount Pharmacie (Lenoir, NC) 75387
Rite Aid Discount Pharmacie (Murphy, NC) 75709
Rite Aid Discount Pharmacie (New Bern, NC) 75735; 75736
Rite Aid Discount Pharmacie (Raleigh, NC) 75949; 75950
Rite Aid Discount Pharmacie (Sanford, NC) 76203
Rite Aid Discount Pharmacie (Sparta, NC) 76292
Rite Aid Discount Pharmacie (Statesville, NC) 76335
Rite Aid Discount Pharmacie (Valdese, NC) 76413
Rite Aid Discount Pharmacie (Warrenton, NC) 76449
Rite Aid Discount Pharmacie (Anderson, SC) 78691
Rite Aid Discount Pharmacie (Charleston, SC) 78881
Rite Aid Discount Pharmacie (Columbia, SC) 79085; 79086; 79087
Rite Aid Discount Pharmacie (Gaffney, SC) 79263
Rite Aid Discount Pharmacie (Greenville, SC) 79422; 79423; 79424; 79425
Rite Aid Discount Pharmacie (Greer, SC) 79481
Rite Aid Discount Pharmacie (Lyman, SC) 79626
Rite Aid Discount Pharmacie (Marion, SC) 79642
Rite Aid Discount Pharmacie (Mt Pleasant, SC) 79680
Rite Aid Discount Pharmacie (Spartanburg, SC) 79941
Rite Aid Discount Pharmacie (Travelers Rst, SC) 80045
Rite Aid Discount Pharmacie (Walterboro, SC) 80077
Rite Aid Discount Pharmacie (Williamston, SC) 80124
Rite Aid Discount Pharmacy (Brooksville, FL) 58896
Rite Aid Discount Pharmacy (Melbourne, FL) 61103
Rite Aid Discount Pharmacy (Orlando, FL) 62133; 62134
Rite Aid Discount Pharmacy (Sanford, FL) 62777; 62778
Rite Aid Discount Pharmacy (Tampa, FL) 63579
Rite Aid Discount Pharmacy (Bowdon, GA) 65392
Rite Aid Discount Pharmacy (Bowling Green, KY) 68161
Rite Aid Discount Pharmacy (Grayson, KY) 68402
Rite Aid Discount Pharmacy (Henderson, KY) 68454
Rite Aid Discount Pharmacy (Hodgenville, KY) 68471
Rite Aid Discount Pharmacy (Leitchfield, KY) 68514
Rite Aid Discount Pharmacy (Lexington, KY) 68614; 68615; 68616; 68617; 68618; 68619; 68620; 68621
Rite Aid Discount Pharmacy (London, KY) 68665; 68666
Rite Aid Discount Pharmacy (Louisa, KY) 68674
Rite Aid Discount Pharmacy (Mt Washington, KY) 69118
Rite Aid Discount Pharmacy (Olive Hill, KY) 69159
Rite Aid Discount Pharmacy (Owensboro, KY) 69191
Rite Aid Discount Pharmacy (Salyersville, KY) 69265
Rite Aid Discount Pharmacy (Scottsville, KY) 69268
Rite Aid Discount Pharmacy (Somerset, KY) 69297
Rite Aid Discount Pharmacy (Aberdeen, NC) 73519
Rite Aid Discount Pharmacy (Chapel Hill, NC) 73820
Rite Aid Discount Pharmacy (Charlotte, NC) 74146
Rite Aid Discount Pharmacy (Eden, NC) 74467
Rite Aid Discount Pharmacy (Greensboro, NC) 74894; 74895; 74896; 74897
Rite Aid Discount Pharmacy (High Point, NC) 75162
Rite Aid Discount Pharmacy (Lumberton, NC) 75472
Rite Aid Discount Pharmacy (Maiden, NC) 75494
Rite Aid Discount Pharmacy (Oxford, NC) 75787
Rite Aid Discount Pharmacy (Charleston, SC) 78882; 78883; 78884; 78885
Rite Aid Discount Pharmacy (Columbia, SC) 79088; 79089
Rite Aid Discount Pharmacy (Cowpens, SC) 79141
Rite Aid Discount Pharmacy (Moncks Corner, SC) 79665
Rite Aid Discount Pharmacy (Piedmont, SC) 79797
Rite Aid Discount Pharmacy (Rock Hill, SC) 79840
Rite Aid Discount Pharmacy (Simpsonville, SC) 79868
Rite Aid Discount Pharmacy (Spartanburg, SC) 79942
Rite Aid Discount Pharmacy (Bristol, TN) 80254
Rite Aid Discount Pharmacy (Celina, TN) 80285
Rite Aid Discount Pharmacy (Cleveland, TN) 80596; 80597
Rite Aid Discount Pharmacy (Clinton, TN) 80613
Rite Aid Discount Pharmacy (Columbia, TN) 80638
Rite Aid Discount Pharmacy (Kingsport, TN) 81116; 81117
Rite Aid Discount Pharmacy (Loudon, TN) 81357
Rite Aid Discount Pharmacy (Mc Kenzie, TN) 81432; 81433
Rite Aid Discount Pharmacy (Milan, TN) 81771
Rite Aid Discount Pharmacy (Oliver Springs, TN) 82212
Rite Aid Discount Pharmacy (Selmer, TN) 82294
Rite Aid Discount Pharmacy (Smithville, TN) 82325
Rite Aid Discount Pharmacy (Smyrna, TN) 82328
Rite Aid Discount Pharmacy (Ansted, WV) 92661
Rite Aid Discount Pharmacy (Beckley, WV) 92682; 92683; 92684; 92685; 92686
Rite Aid Discount Pharmacy (Belle, WV) 92696
Rite Aid Discount Pharmacy (Bridgeport, WV) 92710; 92711
Rite Aid Discount Pharmacy (Buckhannon, WV) 92714; 92715
Rite Aid Discount Pharmacy (Charleston, WV) 92781; 92782; 92783; 92784; 92785; 92786; 92787; 92788; 92789; 92790; 92791; 92792
Rite Aid Discount Pharmacy (Clarksburg, WV) 92817; 92818
Rite Aid Discount Pharmacy (Dorothy, WV) 92825
Rite Aid Discount Pharmacy (Dunbar, WV) 92829
Rite Aid Discount Pharmacy (Eleanor, WV) 92831; 92832
Rite Aid Discount Pharmacy (Elkview, WV) 92835; 92836
Rite Aid Discount Pharmacy (Glenville, WV) 92857
Rite Aid Discount Pharmacy (Grafton, WV) 92858; 92859
Rite Aid Discount Pharmacy (Hinton, WV) 92863
Rite Aid Discount Pharmacy (Huntington, WV) 92892; 92893; 92894; 92895
Rite Aid Discount Pharmacy (Keyser, WV) 92912
Rite Aid Discount Pharmacy (Le Roy, WV) 92914
Rite Aid Discount Pharmacy (Lewisburg, WV) 92918; 92919
Rite Aid Discount Pharmacy (Madison, WV) 92923
Rite Aid Discount Pharmacy (Martinsburg, WV) 92935
Rite Aid Discount Pharmacy (Montgomery, WV) 92940
Rite Aid Discount Pharmacy (Morgantown, WV) 92948; 92949; 92950
Rite Aid Discount Pharmacy (Moundsville, WV) 92953
Rite Aid Discount Pharmacy (Mullens, WV) 92957
Rite Aid Discount Pharmacy (Nitro, WV) 92973; 92974
Rite Aid Discount Pharmacy (Oak Hill, WV) 92978
Rite Aid Discount Pharmacy (Parkersburg, WV) 92996
Rite Aid Discount Pharmacy (Philippi, WV) 93005
Rite Aid Discount Pharmacy (Princeton, WV) 93013
Rite Aid Discount Pharmacy (Pt Pleasant, WV) 93015
Rite Aid Discount Pharmacy (Rainelle, WV) 93018
Rite Aid Discount Pharmacy (Ravenswood, WV) 93023
Rite Aid Discount Pharmacy (Richwood, WV) 93026
Rite Aid Discount Pharmacy (Ripley, WV) 93029; 93030; 93031
Rite Aid Discount Pharmacy (Romney, WV) 93033; 93034
Rite Aid Discount Pharmacy (Ronceverte, WV) 93035
Rite Aid Discount Pharmacy (Shinnston, WV) 93043
Rite Aid Discount Pharmacy (Spencer, WV) 93065
Rite Aid Discount Pharmacy (St. Albans, WV) 93069
Rite Aid Discount Pharmacy (St. Marys, WV) 93073
Rite Aid Discount Pharmacy (Summersville, WV) 93074
Rite Aid Discount Pharmacy (Webster Springs, WV) 93082
Rite Aid Discount Pharmacy (Weston, WV) 93108
Rite Aid Discount Pharmacy (Wheeling, WV) 93118; 93119
Rite Aid Discount Pharmacy (Whitesville, WV) 93128
Rite Aid Discount Pharmacy (Williamson, WV) 93130
Rite Aid Discount Pharms (Fort Lauderdale, FL) 59596; 59597
Rite Aid Discount Pharms (Miami, FL) 61445
Rite Aid Discount Phrmcy (Lake City, FL) 60628
Rite Aid Discount Phrmcy (Dublin, GA) 66016
Rite Aid Discount Phrmcy (Folkston, GA) 66223
Rite Aid Discount Phrmcy (Mebane, NC) 75552
Rite Aid Discount Phrmcy (Columbia, SC) 79090; 79091
Rite Aid Discount Phrmcy (Ninety Six, SC) 79730
Rite Aid Discoutn Pharmacie (Thomasville, NC) 76383; 76384
Rite-Aid Drug (Greensboro, NC) 74898
Rite Aid Drug (Spartanburg, SC) 79943
Rite Aid Drug Store (Punta Gorda, FL) 62719
Rite Aid Drug Store (Columbia, SC) 79092
Rite Aid Drug Store (Greenville, SC) 79426
Rite Aid Drug Store No 4 (Spartanburg, SC) 79944
Rite Aid Drug Store No 1219 (High Point, NC) 75163
Rite Aid Drugs (Clearwater, FL) 59045
Rite Aid Drugs (Eustis, FL) 59402
Rite Aid Drugs (Gainesville, FL) 59914
Rite Aid Drugs (Homestead, FL) 60121
Rite Aid Drugs (Lake Placid, FL) 60649
Rite Aid Drugs (Lakeland, FL) 60779
Rite Aid Drugs (Pompano Beach, FL) 62629
Rite-Aid Drugs (Nashville, GA) 67070
Rite Aid Drugs (Charleston, SC) 78886
Rite Aid Drugs (Greenville, SC) 79427; 79428
Rite Aid Drugs Store (St Petersburg, FL) 63030
Rite Aid Inc. (Catlettsburg, KY) 68197
Rite Aid of N C Inc. (Laurinburg, NC) 75356
Rite Aid No 1045 (Spartanburg, SC) 79945
Rite Aid No 1110 (Spartanburg, SC) 79946
Rite Aid of North Carolina (Greenville, NC) 74976
Rite Aid of North Carolina (Reidsville, NC) 76012
Rite Aid Pharm (Tampa, FL) 63580

Rite Aid Pharm Prescription (Darlington, SC) 79157
Rite Aid Pharmacy (Enterprise, AL) 55694
Rite Aid Pharmacy (Apopka, FL) 58576
Rite Aid Pharmacy (Boynton Beach, FL) 58790
Rite-Aid Pharmacy (Bradenton, FL) 58849
Rite Aid Pharmacy (De Land, FL) 59258
Rite Aid Pharmacy (Fort Myers, FL) 59759
Rite-Aid Pharmacy (Jupiter, FL) 60550; 60551
Rite Aid Pharmacy (Kenneth City, FL) 60561
Rite Aid Pharmacy (Kissimmee, FL) 60601
Rite Aid Pharmacy (Lutz, FL) 60954
Rite Aid Pharmacy (Melbourne, FL) 61104
Rite-Aid Pharmacy (Naples, FL) 61662; 61663
Rite-Aid Pharmacy (Orlando, FL) 62135
Rite Aid Pharmacy (Punta Gorda, FL) 62720
Rite Aid Pharmacy (St Petersburg, FL) 63031
Rite Aid Pharmacy (Tampa, FL) 63581
Rite Aid Pharmacy (Adel, GA) 64056
Rite Aid Pharmacy (Glennville, GA) 66304
Rite-Aid Pharmacy (Quitman, GA) 67292
Rite Aid Pharmacy (Statesboro, GA) 67645
Rite Aid Pharmacy (Waycross, GA) 68038
Rite Aid Pharmacy (Burgaw, NC) 73737
Rite Aid Pharmacy (Charlotte, NC) 74147; 74148
Rite Aid Pharmacy (Greensboro, NC) 74899
Rite Aid Pharmacy (High Point, NC) 75164
Rite Aid Pharmacy (Madison, NC) 75484
Rite Aid Pharmacy (Sanford, NC) 76204
Rite Aid Pharmacy (Greenville, SC) 79429
Rite-Aid Pharmacy (Irmo, SC) 79540
Rite Aid Pharmacy (Marion, SC) 79643
Rite-Aid Pharmacy (Mt Pleasant, SC) 79681
Rite-Aid Pharmacy (Sumter, SC) 80030
Rite Aid Pharmacy (West Columbia, SC) 80107
Rite Aid Pharmacy No 1224 (High Point, NC) 75165
Rite Aid Store No 1220 (High Point, NC) 75166
Rite Aid Store Number Two Z (Gainesville, FL) 59915
Rite Aid 2012 (Fort Lauderdale, FL) 59598
Rite Aide (Spartanburg, SC) 79947
Rite Aide Discount Pharmacy (Washington, NC) 76460
Rite Aide Drug Store (Lake Worth, FL) 60695
Rite Aide Drugs (Fort Walton Beach, FL) 59837
Rite Aide Pharmacy (Rockingham, NC) 76068
Riteaid (Baltimore, MD) 71268
River Oaks Trust Co. (Houston, TX) 86799
River Valley By-Products (Scranton, AR) 57598; 57599
Riverside Furniture (Russellville, AR) 57586
Riverside Furniture (Atlanta, GA) 65080
Riverside Furniture Plant 4 (Fort Smith, AR) 57092
Riverside Furniture Plant 1 (Fort Smith, AR) 57093
Riverside Furniture Plants 2, 6, & 7 (Fort Smith, AR) 57094
Riverside Furniture Corp. (Fort Smith, AR) 57095
Riverside Grocery (Bee, VA) 90426
Riverside Grocery (Clinchco, VA) 90644
Riverside Market (Buckeystown, MD) 71479
Riverwood International Corp. (Atlanta, GA) 65081; 65082
Riverwood International USA Inc. (West Monroe, LA) 70957; 70958; 70959; 70960
RJ Reynolds Tabacco Co. (Winston Salem, NC) 76683
RJ Reynolds Tobacco (Edmond, OK) 77017
RJ Reynolds Tobacco Co. (Birmingham, AL) 55372
RJ Reynolds Tobacco Co. (Mobile, AL) 56233
RJ Reynolds Tobacco Co. (Lafayette, LA) 70099
RJ Reynolds Tobacco Co. (Oxford, NC) 75788
R.J. Reynolds Tobacco Co. (Winston-Salem, NC) 76759
RJ Reynolds Tobacco Co. (Greenville, SC) 79430
R.J. Reynolds Tobacco Co. Avoca Div. (Merry Hill, NC) 75555
RJ Reynolds Tobacco Co. Inc. (Vidalia, GA) 67994
RJ Reynolds Tobacco Co. Inc. (New Orleans, LA) 70552
RJ Reynolds Tobacco Co. Inc. (Winston Salem, NC) 76684
Rmc Corp. Anniston Plant (Anniston, AL) 55011
Roaring River Feed Mill Holly Farms Foods/Tyson Foods Inc. (Roaring River, NC) 76051
A.H. Robins Finance (Richmond, VA) 92005
A.H. Robins Co. Administration (Richmond, VA) 92006
Rock Hill Printing & Finishing (Rock Hill, SC) 79841
Rockingham Poultry Inc. (Stanley, VA) 92306
Rockingham Poultry Inc. (Timberville, VA) 92383
Rockingham Poultry Inc. (Moorefield, WV) 92942
Rockland React-Rite Inc. (Chatom, AL) 55510
Rockland React-Rite Inc. (Cartersville, GA) 65506; 65507
Rockland React-Rite Inc. (Rockmart, GA) 67333
Rockwell (El Paso, TX) 84914
Rockwell International (Winchester, KY) 69353
Rockwell International (Tulsa, OK) 78094
Rockwell International (York, SC) 80140
Rockwell International (El Paso, TX) 84915
Rockwell International (Richardson, TX) 88764
Rockwell International Corp. (Texarkana, AR) 57679
Rockwell International Corp. (Morristown, TN) 81807
Rockwell International Corp. (El Paso, TX) 84916
Rockwell International Corp. (Richardson, TX) 88765
Rockwell International Corp. Collins General Aviation Div. (Melbourne, FL) 61105
Rockwell International Corp. MF&C Div. (Sulphur Springs, TX) 89564
Rockwell International Corp. NTSD Div. (Richardson, TX) 88766
Rockwell International Corp. Plastics Div. (Louisville, KY) 68996
Rockwell International Corp. R.I. Plastics Div. Louisville Plastics Plant (Louisville, KY) 68997
Rockwell International Corp. Autonetic Electronics System (El Paso, TX) 84917
Rockwell International Corp. Msd (Duluth) (Duluth, GA) 66077
Rockwell International Corp. Russelville Plant Measurement (Russellville, KY) 69262
Rockwell International Corp. Winchester Facility (Winchester, KY) 69354
Rockwell International Msd (Duluth) (Duluth, GA) 66078
Rockwell International Ntsd (Richardson, TX) 88767
Rockwell Int'l Spd/Ntsd (El Paso, TX) 84918
W. B. Roddenbery Co., Inc. (Cairo, GA) 65450
W. B. Roddenbery Co., Inc. Peanut Butter Division (Cairo, GA) 65451
W. B. Roddenbery Co., Inc. Pickle Division (Cairo, GA) 65452
W. B. Roddenbery Co., Inc. Syrup Division (Cairo, GA) 65453
Roddy Coca-Cola Bottling Co. Inc. (Knoxville, TN) 81243
Rohm &. Haas Inc. Texas (Deer Park, TX) 84563
Rohm & Haas Unocal Chemical Div. (Charlotte, NC) 74149; 74150; 74151
Rohm & Haas Bayport Inc. (La Porte, TX) 87569
Rohm & Haas Co. (Charlotte, NC) 74152
Rohm & Haas Co. Latin America (Corel Gables, FL) 59118
Rohm & Haas Inc. Bayport (La Porte, TX) 87570
Rohm & Haas Inc. Kentucky (Louisville, KY) 68998
Rohm & Haas Inc. Tennessee (Knoxville, TN) 81244
Rohm & Haas Inc. Texas (Deer Park, TX) 84564
Rohm & Haas Kentucky Inc. (Louisville, KY) 68999
Rohm & Haas Tennessee Inc. (Knoxville, TN) 81245
Rohm & Haas of Texas Inc. (Deer Park, TX) 84565
Rohne Poulenc Ag Co. (Research Triangle Pk., NC) 76024
Rohne Poulenc Inc. (Winder, GA) 68063
Rohr Aero Service Inc. (Fairhope, AL) 55725
Rohr Inc. (Hagerstown, MD) 71896
Rohr Inc. Foley Facility (Foley, AL) 55751
Rohr Ind. Inc. (Heber Springs, AR) 57152
Rohr Ind. Inc. (Sheridan, AR) 57612
Rohr Industries Foley Plant (Foley, AL) 55752
Rohr Industries Inc. (Foley, AL) 55753
Rohr Industries Inc. (Heber Springs, AR) 57153; 57154
Rohr Industries Inc. (Sheridan, AR) 57613
Rohr Industries Inc. (Hagerstown, MD) 71897; 71898
Rollins Burdick Hunter (Atlanta, GA) 65083
Rollins Burdick & Hunter (Oklahoma City, OK) 77538
Rollins Burdick Hunter (San Antonio, TX) 89214
Rollins Burdick Hunter Agcy (Dallas, TX) 84357
Rollins Burdick Hunter Fla (Winter Haven, FL) 63951
Romper Room Enterprises Inc. (Baltimore, MD) 71269
Rooftop Systems Inc. (Carrollton, TX) 83504
Roper Corp. (La Fayette, GA) 66471
Roper Corp. (Swainsboro, GA) 67759
Roper Corp. (Chattanooga, TN) 80478
Roper Corp. Outdoor Power Equipment (Mc Rae, GA) 66966
Ross Laboratories (Altavista, VA) 90252
Royal Crown Cola Co. (Columbus, GA) 65650
Royal Development Co. (High Point, NC) 75167; 75168; 75169
Royal Manufacturing Inc. (Pompano Beach, FL) 62630
R.R. Donnelley Printing Co. (Newton, NC) 75753
R.R. Donnelley Printing Co. (Lynchburg, VA) 91286
R.R. Donnelley & Sons Co. (Spartanburg, SC) 79948
Rubbermaid Commercial Prods. Inc. (Cleburne, TX) 83583
Rubbermaid Commercial Products (Marietta, GA) 66907
Rubbermaid Commercial Products (Cleburne, TX) 83584
Rubbermaid Commercial Products (Winchester, VA) 92603
Rubbermaid Commercial Products Inc. (Cleburne, TX) 83585
Rubbermaid Commercial Proudcts (Cleveland, TN) 80598
Rubbermaid Inc. Commercial Products (Winchester, VA) 92604
Rubbermaid Office Products Inc. (Statesville, NC) 76336
Rubbermaid Office Products Inc. (Maryville, TN) 81423
Rubbermaid Office Products Inc. (Greenville, TX) 85676
Rubbermaid Specialty Products Inc. (Stanley, NC) 76311
Rudys Farm (Florence, AL) 55744
Rudys Farm Co. (Nashville, TN) 82091
Rudys Farm Co. (Newbern, TN) 82156
Russell (Alexander City, AL) **54976**
Russell Associates Inc. (Plant City, FL) 62555
Russell Associates Inc. (Winter Park, FL) 63994
Russell Associates Inc. (Richardson, TX) 88768
Russell Corp. (Alexander City, AL) 54977; 54978; 54979; 54980
Russell Corp. (Ashland, AL) 55031
Russell Corp. (Columbia, AL) 55525
Russell Corp. (Dadeville, AL) 55560
Russell Corp. (Lafayette, AL) 56099; 56100
Russell Corp. (Montgomery, AL) 56373
Russell Corp. (Sylacauga, AL) 56589
Russell Corp. (Crestview, FL) 59125
Russell Corp. (Marianna, FL) 61008; 61009; 61010
Russell Corp. (Niceville, FL) 61717
Russell Corp. (Cumming, GA) 65749
Russell Corp. (Norcross, GA) 67175
Russell Corp. (Nashville, TN) 82092
Russell Corp. D.C. & Ind. Park (Marianna, FL) 61011
Russellville Distribution Center (Russellville, AR) 57587
Rust International Inc. (Birmingham, AL) 55373
Rutland Plastics (Pineville, NC) 75826
Ryan Milk Co. (Murray, KY) 69129; 69130; 69131; 69132
Ryan Milk Co. Inc. (Murray, KY) 69133
Ryder Airline Services Mcallen (Mc Allen, TX) 87898
Ryder System (Miami, FL) **61446**
Ryder Systems Inc. (Miami, FL) 61447
Ryder Truck Rental (Alabaster, AL) 54956
Ryder Truck Rental (Alexander Cy, AL) 54981
Ryder Truck Rental (Anniston, AL) 55012; 55013
Ryder Truck Rental (Birmingham, AL) 55374; 55375; 55376; 55377; 55378; 55379; 55380; 55381
Ryder Truck Rental (Boaz, AL) 55475
Ryder Truck Rental (Cullman, AL) 55550; 55551
Ryder Truck Rental (Daphne, AL) 55569
Ryder Truck Rental (Dothan, AL) 55667; 55668
Ryder Truck Rental (Enterprise, AL) 55695; 55696
Ryder Truck Rental (Eufaula, AL) 55703
Ryder Truck Rental (Fairfield, AL) 55716
Ryder Truck Rental (Florence, AL) 55745
Ryder Truck Rental (Foley, AL) 55754
Ryder Truck Rental (Gadsden, AL) 55788; 55789; 55790
Ryder Truck Rental (Gardendale, AL) 55800
Ryder Truck Rental (Huntsville, AL) 56010; 56011; 56012
Ryder Truck Rental (Madison, AL) 56123
Ryder Truck Rental (Mobile, AL) 56234; 56235; 56236
Ryder Truck Rental (Montgomery, AL) 56374; 56375
Ryder Truck Rental (Opelika, AL) 56424; 56425
Ryder Truck Rental (Selma, AL) 56537; 56538
Ryder Truck Rental (Talladega, AL) 56599
Ryder Truck Rental (Tuscaloosa, AL) 56673; 56674; 56675
Ryder Truck Rental (Batesville, AR) 56762
Ryder Truck Rental (Bentonville, AR) 56789
Ryder Truck Rental (Blytheville, AR) 56816
Ryder Truck Rental (Clarksville, AR) 56851
Ryder Truck Rental (Conway, AR) 56870
Ryder Truck Rental (De Queen, AR) 56896
Ryder Truck Rental (Dumas, AR) 56915
Ryder Truck Rental (Fayetteville, AR) 56990; 56991
Ryder Truck Rental (Forrest City, AR) 57013
Ryder Truck Rental (Fort Smith, AR) 57096; 57097; 57098
Ryder Truck Rental (H Spg Nat Pk, AR) 57132
Ryder Truck Rental (Jacksonville, AR) 57201
Ryder Truck Rental (Jonesboro, AR) 57230
Ryder Truck Rental (Little Rock, AR) 57305; 57306; 57307; 57308; 57309; 57310
Ryder Truck Rental (Magnolia, AR) 57334; 57335
Ryder Truck Rental (Malvern, AR) 57342
Ryder Truck Rental (Morrilton, AR) 57380
Ryder Truck Rental (Mountain Home, AR) 57390
Ryder Truck Rental (N Little Rock, AR) 57422
Ryder Truck Rental (Russellville, AR) 57588
Ryder Truck Rental (Searcy, AR) 57608
Ryder Truck Rental (Springdale, AR) 57642
Ryder Truck Rental (Stuttgart, AR) 57670
Ryder Truck Rental (Texarkana, AR) 57680; 57681
Ryder Truck Rental (Van Buren, AR) 57693
Ryder Truck Rental (West Memphis, AR) 57733; 57734
Ryder Truck Rental (Apopka, FL) 58577
Ryder Truck Rental (Bartow, FL) 58629
Ryder Truck Rental (Boca Raton, FL) 58739; 58740
Ryder Truck Rental (Boynton Beach, FL) 58791
Ryder Truck Rental (Bradenton, FL) 58850
Ryder Truck Rental (Brandon, FL) 58880
Ryder Truck Rental (Cape Coral, FL) 58926
Ryder Truck Rental (Cocoa, FL) 59073; 59074
Ryder Truck Rental (Cocoa Beach, FL) 59084
Ryder Truck Rental (Crestview, FL) 59126; 59127
Ryder Truck Rental (Daytona Beach, FL) 59209; 59210; 59211
Ryder Truck Rental (De Funiak Spg, FL) 59239
Ryder Truck Rental (Deerfield Beach, FL) 59287; 59288
Ryder Truck Rental (Delray Beach, FL) 59330
Ryder Truck Rental (Destin, FL) 59349
Ryder Truck Rental (Edgewater, FL) 59378; 59379
Ryder Truck Rental (Fort Lauderdale, FL) 59599; 59600; 59601; 59602; 59603; 59604; 59605; 59606; 59607
Ryder Truck Rental (Fort Myers, FL) 59760; 59761
Ryder Truck Rental (Fort Pierce, FL) 59808; 59809; 59810
Ryder Truck Rental (Fort Walton Beach, FL) 59838
Ryder Truck Rental (Gainesville, FL) 59916; 59917
Ryder Truck Rental (Haines City, FL) 59953
Ryder Truck Rental (Hallandale, FL) 59965
Ryder Truck Rental (Hialeah, FL) 60008
Ryder Truck Rental (Hollywood, FL) 60092; 60093
Ryder Truck Rental (Homestead, FL) 60122
Ryder Truck Rental (Jacksonville, FL) 60439; 60440; 60441; 60442; 60443; 60444; 60445; 60446; 60447; 60448; 60449; 60450
Ryder Truck Rental (Lake Placid, FL) 60650
Ryder Truck Rental (Lake Worth, FL) 60696
Ryder Truck Rental (Lakeland, FL) 60780; 60781
Ryder Truck Rental (Largo, FL) 60862
Ryder Truck Rental (Leesburg, FL) 60886
Ryder Truck Rental (Live Oak, FL) 60920
Ryder Truck Rental (Marathon, FL) 60993
Ryder Truck Rental (Melbourne, FL) 61106
Ryder Truck Rental (Melbourne Fl, FL) 61125
Ryder Truck Rental (Miami, FL) 61448; 61449; 61450; 61451; 61452; 61453; 61454; 61455
Ryder Truck Rental (N Bay Village, FL) 61585
Ryder Truck Rental (Niceville, FL) 61718
Ryder Truck Rental (Nw Prt Richey, FL) 61762
Ryder Truck Rental (Ocala, FL) 61820; 61821
Ryder Truck Rental (Opa-Locka, FL) 61867

Ryder Truck Rental (Orange Park, FL) 61896

Ryder Truck Rental (Orlando, FL) 62136; 62137; 62138

Ryder Truck Rental (Ormond Beach, FL) 62211

Ryder Truck Rental (Panama City, FL) 62347; 62348

Ryder Truck Rental (Pensacola, FL) 62468; 62469; 62470

Ryder Truck Rental (Perry, FL) 62505

Ryder Truck Rental (Pompano Beach, FL) 62631; 62632; 62633

Ryder Truck Rental (Punta Gorda, FL) 62721

Ryder Truck Rental (Rockledge, FL) 62748

Ryder Truck Rental (Sanford, FL) 62779; 62780

Ryder Truck Rental (Sebring, FL) 62894

Ryder Truck Rental (Seffner, FL) 62900

Ryder Truck Rental (St Augustine, FL) 62956

Ryder Truck Rental (St Petersburg, FL) 63032; 63033

Ryder Truck Rental (Stuart, FL) 63178

Ryder Truck Rental (Tallahassee, FL) 63269

Ryder Truck Rental (Tampa, FL) 63582; 63583; 63584; 63585; 63586

Ryder Truck Rental (Titusville, FL) 63703

Ryder Truck Rental (W Palm Beach, FL) 63814

Ryder Truck Rental (West Palm Beach, FL) 63897; 63898

Ryder Truck Rental (Winter Haven, FL) 63952

Ryder Truck Rental (Acworth, GA) 64051; 64052

Ryder Truck Rental (Adel, GA) 64057

Ryder Truck Rental (Albany, GA) 64091

Ryder Truck Rental (Alpharetta, GA) 64132; 64133; 64134

Ryder Truck Rental (Atl, GA) 64181

Ryder Truck Rental (Atl Ga, GA) 64186

Ryder Truck Rental (Atlanta, GA) 65084; 65085; 65086; 65087; 65088; 65089; 65090; 65091; 65092; 65093; 65094; 65095; 65096; 65097; 65098; 65099; 65100; 65101; 65102; 65103; 65104; 65105; 65106; 65107; 65108; 65109; 65110; 65111; 65112; 65113; 65114; 65115; 65116; 65117; 65118; 65119; 65120; 65121; 65122; 65123; 65124; 65125; 65126; 65127; 65128; 65129; 65130; 65131; 65132; 65133; 65134; 65135; 65136

Ryder Truck Rental (Austell, GA) 65357

Ryder Truck Rental (Barnesville, GA) 65379

Ryder Truck Rental (Brunswick, GA) 65425

Ryder Truck Rental (Buford, GA) 65444

Ryder Truck Rental (Cairo, GA) 65454

Ryder Truck Rental (Canton, GA) 65486

Ryder Truck Rental (Cartersville, GA) 65508

Ryder Truck Rental (Chamblee, GA) 65542; 65543

Ryder Truck Rental (College Park, GA) 65601; 65602

Ryder Truck Rental (Conyers, GA) 65700; 65701; 65702; 65703

Ryder Truck Rental (Cordele, GA) 65719; 65720

Ryder Truck Rental (Cumming, GA) 65750

Ryder Truck Rental (Dallas, GA) 65766

Ryder Truck Rental (Decatur, GA) 65893; 65894

Ryder Truck Rental (Doraville, GA) 65947; 65948

Ryder Truck Rental (Douglas, GA) 65975

Ryder Truck Rental (Douglasville, GA) 66000; 66001

Ryder Truck Rental (Dublin, GA) 66017

Ryder Truck Rental (Duluth, GA) 66079

Ryder Truck Rental (Dunwoody, GA) 66135

Ryder Truck Rental (Fairburn, GA) 66182

Ryder Truck Rental (Fayetteville, GA) 66202; 66203

Ryder Truck Rental (Gainesville, GA) 66290

Ryder Truck Rental (Griffin, GA) 66323

Ryder Truck Rental (Hapeville, GA) 66339; 66340

Ryder Truck Rental (Hinesville, GA) 66357

Ryder Truck Rental (Jesup, GA) 66373

Ryder Truck Rental (Jonesboro, GA) 66396; 66397

Ryder Truck Rental (Kennesaw, GA) 66447

Ryder Truck Rental (Lithonia, GA) 66607; 66608

Ryder Truck Rental (Macon, GA) 66709; 66710; 66711

Ryder Truck Rental (Marietta, GA) 66908; 66909; 66910; 66911; 66912; 66913; 66914; 66915

Ryder Truck Rental (Morrow, GA) 67040; 67041; 67042

Ryder Truck Rental (Moultrie, GA) 67064

Ryder Truck Rental (Norcross, GA) 67176; 67177; 67178; 67179

Ryder Truck Rental (Nroc, GA) 67215

Ryder Truck Rental (Peachtrr City, GA) 67253

Ryder Truck Rental (Savannah, GA) 67508; 67509

Ryder Truck Rental (Smyrna, GA) 67572; 67573

Ryder Truck Rental (Stockbridge, GA) 67668

Ryder Truck Rental (Stone Mountain, GA) 67734

Ryder Truck Rental (Thomasville, GA) 67804; 67805

Ryder Truck Rental (Tucker, GA) 67886

Ryder Truck Rental (Union City, GA) 67928

Ryder Truck Rental (Valdosta, GA) 67974

Ryder Truck Rental (Warner Robins, GA) 68020

Ryder Truck Rental (Florence, KY) 68329

Ryder Truck Rental (Georgetown, KY) 68386

Ryder Truck Rental (Lexington, KY) 68622; 68623

Ryder Truck Rental (London, KY) 68667

Ryder Truck Rental (Versailles, KY) 69330

Ryder Truck Rental (Alexandria, LA) 69409; 69410

Ryder Truck Rental (Bastrop, LA) 69449

Ryder Truck Rental (Baton Rouge, LA) 69652; 69653; 69654; 69655; 69656

Ryder Truck Rental (Bossier City, LA) 69730

Ryder Truck Rental (Lafayette, LA) 70100; 70101; 70102; 70103; 70104; 70105

Ryder Truck Rental (New Iberia, LA) 70420

Ryder Truck Rental (New Orleans, LA) 70553; 70554

Ryder Truck Rental (Port Allen, LA) 70648

Ryder Truck Rental (Shreveport, LA) 70778; 70779; 70780

Ryder Truck Rental (Sulphur, LA) 70890

Ryder Truck Rental (West Monroe, LA) 70961

Ryder Truck Rental (Brookhaven, MS) 72658

Ryder Truck Rental (Greenville, MS) 72820

Ryder Truck Rental (Gulfport, MS) 72874

Ryder Truck Rental (Hattiesburg, MS) 72896; 72897

Ryder Truck Rental (Jackson, MS) 73054; 73055; 73056

Ryder Truck Rental (Meridian, MS) 73178

Ryder Truck Rental (Natchez, MS) 73211

Ryder Truck Rental (Pascagoula, MS) 73271

Ryder Truck Rental (Tupelo, MS) 73424; 73425

Ryder Truck Rental (Vicksburg, MS) 73461

Ryder Truck Rental (Ahoskie, NC) 73525

Ryder Truck Rental (Asheboro, NC) 73596

Ryder Truck Rental (Asheville, NC) 73637

Ryder Truck Rental (Burlington, NC) 73761

Ryder Truck Rental (Charlotte, NC) 74153; 74154

Ryder Truck Rental (Dunn, NC) 74378

Ryder Truck Rental (Gastonia, NC) 74688

Ryder Truck Rental (Goldsboro, NC) 74734

Ryder Truck Rental (Greensboro, NC) 74900; 74901; 74902; 74903; 74904

Ryder Truck Rental (Greenville, NC) 74977

Ryder Truck Rental (Havelock, NC) 75010

Ryder Truck Rental (Hickory, NC) 75099

Ryder Truck Rental (Hope Mills, NC) 75195

Ryder Truck Rental (Laurinburg, NC) 75357

Ryder Truck Rental (Lenoir, NC) 75388

Ryder Truck Rental (Lexington, NC) 75423

Ryder Truck Rental (Mount Airy, NC) 75684

Ryder Truck Rental (Raleigh, NC) 75951; 75952; 75953

Ryder Truck Rental (Reidsville, NC) 76013

Ryder Truck Rental (Roanoke Rpds, NC) 76043

Ryder Truck Rental (Roxboro, NC) 76133

Ryder Truck Rental (Salisbury, NC) 76178

Ryder Truck Rental (Statesville, NC) 76337

Ryder Truck Rental (Swannanoa, NC) 76351

Ryder Truck Rental (W Jefferson, NC) 76420

Ryder Truck Rental (Washington, NC) 76461

Ryder Truck Rental (Whiteville, NC) 76504

Ryder Truck Rental (Wilkesboro, NC) 76518

Ryder Truck Rental (Wilson, NC) 76642

Ryder Truck Rental (Altus, OK) 76796

Ryder Truck Rental (Ardmore, OK) 76819; 76820

Ryder Truck Rental (Bartlesville, OK) 76852

Ryder Truck Rental (Bristow, OK) 76874

Ryder Truck Rental (Chickasha, OK) 76937

Ryder Truck Rental (Cushing, OK) 76982

Ryder Truck Rental (Edmond, OK) 77018

Ryder Truck Rental (El Reno, OK) 77034

Ryder Truck Rental (Elk City, OK) 77038

Ryder Truck Rental (Enid, OK) 77068; 77069

Ryder Truck Rental (Grove, OK) 77093

Ryder Truck Rental (Guymon, OK) 77111

Ryder Truck Rental (Holdenville, OK) 77135

Ryder Truck Rental (Hugo, OK) 77140

Ryder Truck Rental (Lawton, OK) 77173

Ryder Truck Rental (Mc Alester, OK) 77199

Ryder Truck Rental (Miami, OK) 77210

Ryder Truck Rental (Norman, OK) 77273; 77274

Ryder Truck Rental (Oklahoma, OK) 77289

Ryder Truck Rental (Oklahoma City, OK) 77539; 77540; 77541; 77542; 77543; 77544

Ryder Truck Rental (Ponca City, OK) 77712

Ryder Truck Rental (Poteau, OK) 77728

Ryder Truck Rental (Sallisaw, OK) 77774

Ryder Truck Rental (Sand Springs, OK) 77784

Ryder Truck Rental (Sayre, OK) 77801

Ryder Truck Rental (Tahlequah, OK) 77860

Ryder Truck Rental (Tulsa, OK) 78095; 78096; 78097; 78098; 78099; 78100; 78101; 78102

Ryder Truck Rental (Vinita, OK) 78228

Ryder Truck Rental (Watts, OK) 78238

Ryder Truck Rental (Woodward, OK) 78266

Ryder Truck Rental (Aiken, SC) 78657

Ryder Truck Rental (Anderson, SC) 78692

Ryder Truck Rental (Beaufort, SC) 78718

Ryder Truck Rental (Camden, SC) 78762

Ryder Truck Rental (Cayce, SC) 78779

Ryder Truck Rental (Charleston, SC) 78887

Ryder Truck Rental (Chester, SC) 78941

Ryder Truck Rental (Columbia, SC) 79093; 79094

Ryder Truck Rental (Florence, SC) 79223; 79224

Ryder Truck Rental (Greenville, SC) 79431

Ryder Truck Rental (Kingstree, SC) 79559

Ryder Truck Rental (Moncks Corner, SC) 79666

Ryder Truck Rental (Myrtle Beach, SC) 79713

Ryder Truck Rental (Simpsonville, SC) 79869

Ryder Truck Rental (Spartanburg, SC) 79949; 79950

Ryder Truck Rental (Summerville, SC) 79993

Ryder Truck Rental (Wallace, SC) 80065

Ryder Truck Rental (Cookeville, TN) 80666

Ryder Truck Rental (Crossville, TN) 80705

Ryder Truck Rental (Franklin, TN) 80822

Ryder Truck Rental (Jackson, TN) 81000

Ryder Truck Rental (Madisonville, TN) 81387

Ryder Truck Rental (Memphis, TN) 81680; 81681; 81682

Ryder Truck Rental (Murfreesboro, TN) 81865

Ryder Truck Rental (Nashville, TN) 82093

Ryder Truck Rental (Rogersville T, TN) 82283

Ryder Truck Rental (Union City, TN) 82389

Ryder Truck Rental (Abilene, TX) 82454; 82455; 82456

Ryder Truck Rental (Allen, TX) 82496

Ryder Truck Rental (Alpine, TX) 82501

Ryder Truck Rental (Alvin, TX) 82516

Ryder Truck Rental (Amarillo, TX) 82578

Ryder Truck Rental (Andrews, TX) 82603

Ryder Truck Rental (Arlington, TX) 82743; 82744; 82745; 82746; 82747

Ryder Truck Rental (Austin, TX) 82993; 82994; 82995; 82996; 82997; 82998; 82999

Ryder Truck Rental (Ballinger, TX) 83090

Ryder Truck Rental (Bastrop, TX) 83097

Ryder Truck Rental (Baytown, TX) 83138

Ryder Truck Rental (Beaumont, TX) 83210

Ryder Truck Rental (Bedford, TX) 83251

Ryder Truck Rental (Beeville, TX) 83261

Ryder Truck Rental (Big Spring, TX) 83294; 83295

Ryder Truck Rental (Borger, TX) 83325

Ryder Truck Rental (Brady, TX) 83332

Ryder Truck Rental (Brenham, TX) 83341

Ryder Truck Rental (Brownsville, TX) 83381

Ryder Truck Rental (Bryan, TX) 83408

Ryder Truck Rental (Burkburnett, TX) 83418

Ryder Truck Rental (Burleson, TX) 83425

Ryder Truck Rental (Cameron, TX) 83438

Ryder Truck Rental (Cedar Hill, TX) 83530; 83531

Ryder Truck Rental (Channelview, TX) 83555

Ryder Truck Rental (Childress, TX) 83560; 83561

Ryder Truck Rental (Clarksville, TX) 83573

Ryder Truck Rental (Cleburne, TX) 83586; 83587

Ryder Truck Rental (Conroe, TX) 83684

Ryder Truck Rental (Corpus Chrsti, TX) 83770; 83771; 83772

Ryder Truck Rental (Corsicana, TX) 83790

Ryder Truck Rental (Crowley, TX) 83814

Ryder Truck Rental (Dalhart, TX) 83836

Ryder Truck Rental (Dallas, TX) 84358; 84359; 84360; 84361; 84362; 84363; 84364; 84365; 84366; 84367; 84368; 84369; 84370; 84371

Ryder Truck Rental (Denison, TX) 84607; 84608

Ryder Truck Rental (Dumas, TX) 84691

Ryder Truck Rental (Duncanville, TX) 84710

Ryder Truck Rental (Eagle Pass, TX) 84722

Ryder Truck Rental (El Paso, TX) 84919; 84920; 84921; 84922; 84923; 84924

Ryder Truck Rental (Ennis, TX) 85000

Ryder Truck Rental (Euless, TX) 85019

Ryder Truck Rental (Farmers Brnch, TX) 85037

Ryder Truck Rental (Fort Worth, TX) 85265; 85266; 85267; 85268; 85269; 85270

Ryder Truck Rental (Fredericksbg, TX) 85373

Ryder Truck Rental (Gainesville, TX) 85427

Ryder Truck Rental (Garland, TX) 85532

Ryder Truck Rental (Georgetown, TX) 85573

Ryder Truck Rental (Grand Prairie, TX) 85637; 85638

Ryder Truck Rental (Grand Saline, TX) 85649

Ryder Truck Rental (Grapevine, TX) 85661; 85662; 85663

Ryder Truck Rental (Harlingen, TX) 85714; 85715

Ryder Truck Rental (Hewitt, TX) 85747

Ryder Truck Rental (Houston, TX) 86800; 86801; 86802; 86803; 86804; 86805; 86806; 86807; 86808; 86809; 86810; 86811; 86812; 86813; 86814; 86815; 86816; 86817; 86818; 86819; 86820; 86821; 86822; 86823; 86824; 86825; 86826; 86827; 86828; 86829; 86830; 86831; 86832; 86833; 86834; 86835; 86836; 86837; 86838; 86839; 86840; 86841; 86842; 86843; 86844; 86845; 86846; 86847; 86848; 86849; 86850; 86851; 86852; 86853

Ryder Truck Rental (Hurst, TX) 87295

Ryder Truck Rental (Irving, TX) 87398; 87399

Ryder Truck Rental (Jacksonville, TX) 87426

Ryder Truck Rental (Kerrville, TX) 87483

Ryder Truck Rental (La Marque, TX) 87546

Ryder Truck Rental (Lampasas, TX) 87594; 87595

Ryder Truck Rental (League City, TX) 87631

Ryder Truck Rental (Levelland, TX) 87641

Ryder Truck Rental (Lewisville, TX) 87664

Ryder Truck Rental (Liberty, TX) 87680

Ryder Truck Rental (Lockhart, TX) 87696

Ryder Truck Rental (Longview, TX) 87733; 87734

Ryder Truck Rental (Lubbock, TX) 87780

Ryder Truck Rental (Lufkin, TX) 87817

Ryder Truck Rental (Mansfield, TX) 87836

Ryder Truck Rental (Marble Falls, TX) 87840

Ryder Truck Rental (Marshall, TX) 87866; 87867

Ryder Truck Rental (Mc Kinney, TX) 87920

Ryder Truck Rental (Mesquite, TX) 87995; 87996

Ryder Truck Rental (Mexia, TX) 88016

Ryder Truck Rental (Mineral Wells, TX) 88116; 88117; 88118

Ryder Truck Rental (Monahans, TX) 88143

Ryder Truck Rental (Odessa, TX) 88270; 88271

Ryder Truck Rental (Orange, TX) 88329

Ryder Truck Rental (Pasadena, TX) 88464; 88465; 88466

Company Name Index Savings

Ryder Truck Rental (Pecos, TX) 88497
Ryder Truck Rental (Pharr, TX) 88512
Ryder Truck Rental (Plainview, TX) 88533
Ryder Truck Rental (Plano, TX) 88605
Ryder Truck Rental (Port Isabel, TX) 88665
Ryder Truck Rental (Portland, TX) 88694
Ryder Truck Rental (Raymondville, TX) 88710
Ryder Truck Rental (Red Oak, TX) 88712
Ryder Truck Rental (Richardson, TX) 88769; 88770; 88771; 88772; 88773
Ryder Truck Rental (Rockport, TX) 88820
Ryder Truck Rental (Rosenberg, TX) 88836
Ryder Truck Rental (Round Rock, TX) 88853
Ryder Truck Rental (San Angelo, TX) 88899; 88900
Ryder Truck Rental (San Antonio, TX) 89215; 89216; 89217; 89218
Ryder Truck Rental (San Marcos, TX) 89341
Ryder Truck Rental (Seguin, TX) 89374
Ryder Truck Rental (Snyder, TX) 89452
Ryder Truck Rental (Spring, TX) 89486; 89487; 89488
Ryder Truck Rental (Stephenville, TX) 89525
Ryder Truck Rental (Taylor, TX) 89601
Ryder Truck Rental (Temple, TX) 89643; 89644
Ryder Truck Rental (Terrell, TX) 89661
Ryder Truck Rental (Texarkana, TX) 89706; 89707
Ryder Truck Rental (Tomball, TX) 89778
Ryder Truck Rental (Tyler, TX) 89825; 89826; 89827
Ryder Truck Rental (Uvalde, TX) 89856
Ryder Truck Rental (Vernon, TX) 89871
Ryder Truck Rental (Waco, TX) 89972; 89973; 89974; 89975
Ryder Truck Rental (Weatherford, TX) 90012; 90013
Ryder Truck Rental (Webster, TX) 90023
Ryder Truck Rental (Wichita Falls, TX) 90098; 90099; 90100; 90101
Ryder Truck Rental (Buckhannon, WV) 92716; 92717
Ryder Truck Rental (Charleston, WV) 92793
Ryder Truck Rental (Clarksburg, WV) 92819
Ryder Truck Rental (Dunbar, WV) 92830
Ryder Truck Rental (Fairmont, WV) 92847
Ryder Truck Rental (Holden Wv, WV) 92864
Ryder Truck Rental (Huntington, WV) 92896
Ryder Truck Rental (Moundsville, WV) 92954
Ryder Truck Rental (Petersburg, WV) 93004
Ryder Truck Rental (Summersville, WV) 93075
Ryder Truck Rental (Weston Wv, WV) 93109
Ryder Truck Rental Body Shop (Birmingham, AL) 55382
Ryder Truck Rental Inc. (Milford, DE) 57845
Ryder Truck Rental Inc. (New Castle, DE) 57874
Ryder Truck Rental Inc. (Newark, DE) 57930; 57931
Ryder Truck Rental Inc. (Wilmington, DE) 58107; 58108
Ryder Truck Rental Inc. (Baltimore, MD) 71270; 71271; 71272
Ryder Truck Rental Inc. (Chase, MD) 71513
Ryder Truck Rental Inc. (Olney, MD) 72180
Ryder Truck Rental Inc. (Silver Spring, MD) 72443
Ryder Truck Rental Inc. (Abingdon, VA) 90158
Ryder Truck Rental Inc. (Chesapeake, VA) 90599
Ryder Truck Rental Inc. (Lynchburg, VA) 91287
Ryder Truck Rental Inc. (Manassas, VA) 91322
Ryder Truck Rental Inc. (Martinsville, VA) 91356
Ryder Truck Rental Inc. (Norfolk, VA) 91576
Ryder Truck Rental Inc. (Richmond, VA) 92007; 92008; 92009
Ryder Truck Rental Inc. (Virginia Beach, VA) 92508
Ryder Truck Rental & Leasing (Chattanooga, TN) 80479
Ryder Truck Rental & Leasing (Jackson, TN) 81001
Ryder Truck Rental & Leasing (Memphis, TN) 81683
Ryder Truck Rental & Leasing (Morristown, TN) 81808
Ryder Truck Rental & Leasing (Murfreesboro, TN) 81866
Ryder Truck Rental & Leasing (Nashville, TN) 82094
Ryder Truck Rental-One Way (Grayson, KY) 68403
Ryder Truck Rental-One Way (Lexington, KY) 68624
Ryder Truck Rental-One Way (Owensboro, KY) 69192
Ryder Truck Rental-One Way (Chattanooga, TN) 80480; 80481; 80482; 80483; 80484; 80485
Ryder Truck Rental-One Way (Columbia, TN) 80639
Ryder Truck Rental-One Way (Henderson, TN) 80908
Ryder Truck Rental-One Way (Hixson, TN) 80936
Ryder Truck Rental-One Way (Lebanon, TN) 81308
Ryder Truck Rental-One Way (Memphis, TN) 81684; 81685; 81686; 81687; 81688
Ryder Truck Rental-One Way (Murfreesboro, TN) 81867
Ryder Truck Rental One Way (Bluefield, WV) 92703
Ryder Truck Rental-Oneway (Bardstown, KY) 68119
Ryder Truck Rental-Oneway (Campbellsville, KY) 68183
Ryder Truck Rental-Oneway (Corbin, KY) 68213
Ryder Truck Rental-Oneway (Covington, KY) 68232
Ryder Truck Rental-Oneway (Danville, KY) 68262
Ryder Truck Rental-Oneway (Florence, KY) 68330
Ryder Truck Rental-Oneway (Frankfort, KY) 68368
Ryder Truck Rental-Oneway (Glasgow, KY) 68397
Ryder Truck Rental-Oneway (Greenville, KY) 68406
Ryder Truck Rental-Oneway (Harrodsburg, KY) 68416
Ryder Truck Rental-Oneway (Henderson, KY) 68455
Ryder Truck Rental-Oneway (Madisonville, KY) 69070
Ryder Truck Rental-Oneway (Mayfield, KY) 69080
Ryder Truck Rental-Oneway (Newport, KY) 69141
Ryder Truck Rental-Oneway (Richmond, KY) 69248
Ryder Truck Rental-Oneway (Cleveland, TN) 80599
Ryder Truck Rental-Oneway (Johnson City, TN) 81055
Ryder Truck Rental-Oneway (Tullahoma, TN) 82379
Ryder Truck Rental-Oneway (Elkins, WV) 92834
Ryder Truck Rental Shop (Oklahoma City, OK) 77545

S

S. P. Richards Co. (Smyrna, GA) 67574
S. P. Richards Co., Inc. (Smyrna, GA) 67575
SABRE Computer Services (Forth Worth, TX) 85369
SABRE Development Services (Dallas-Fort Worth, TX) 84507
SABRE Technology Group (Dallas-Fort Worth, TX) 84508
Sabre Textron (Pontiac, SC) 79799
Sabre Travel Information Network (Baton Rouge, LA) 69657
SABRE Travel Information Network (Dallas-Fort Worth, TX) 84509
SABRE Travel Information Network (Fort Worth, TX) 85271
Safeco Insurance Co. of America (Birmingham, AL) 55383
Safeco Insurance Co. of America (Montgomery, AL) 56376
Safeco Insurance Co. of America (Savannah, GA) 67510
Safeco Insurance Co. of America (Dallas, TX) 84372; 84373
Safeco Insurance Co. of America (Plano, TX) 88606
Safeco Insurance Co. of America (San Antonio, TX) 89219
Safeco Insurance Co. of America (Manassas, VA) 91323
Safety Kleen Corp. (Birmingham, AL) 55384
Safety Kleen Corp. (Montgomery, AL) 56377
Safety Kleen Corp. (West Memphis, AR) 57735
Safety Kleen Corp. (Casselberry, FL) 58941
Safety Kleen Corp. (Clair Mel City, FL) 58956
Safety Kleen Corp. (Jacksonville, FL) 60451
Safety Kleen Corp. (Macon, GA) 66712
Safety-Kleen Corp. (Louisville, KY) 69000
Safety Kleen Corp. (Kenner, LA) 70011; 70012
Safety Kleen Corp. (Pineville, LA) 70631
Safety Kleen Corp. (Catoosa, OK) 76911
Safety Kleen Corp. (Oklahoma City, OK) 77546
Safety Kleen Corp. (Wheatland, OK) 78251
Safety Kleen Corp. (Lexington, SC) 79608
Safety Kleen Corp. (Denton, TX) 84636
Safety Kleen Corp. (El Paso, TX) 84925
Safety Kleen Corp. (Mc Allen, TX) 87899
Safety Kleen Corp. (Midland, TX) 88072
Safety Kleen Corp. (Missouri City, TX) 88133
Safety Kleen Corp. (Pasadena, TX) 88467
Safety Kleen Corp. (San Antonio, TX) 89220
Safety Kleen Corp. (Waco, TX) 89976
Safety-Kleen Corp. (Chester, VA) 90625
Safety-Kleen Corp. (Wheeling, WV) 93120
Safeway Inc. (Texas City, TX) 89734
Saia Motor Freight Line, Inc. (Houma, LA) 69969
St. Jude Medical Center (Kenner, LA) 70013
Saint Mary's Medical Center (Russellville, AR) 57589
St. Michaels Bank (Easton, MD) 71661; 71662
St. Michaels Bank (St. Michaels, MD) 72472; 72473
St. Michaels Bank (Tilghman, MD) 72501
Sale James J III (Madison, FL) 60968
Salem Carpet Mills Inc. (S Pittsburg, TN) 82287
Sales, Marketing, Manufaturing, Finance & Administration (Bowling Green, KY) 68162
Sales Technologies (Atlanta, GA) 65137; 65138; 65139
Sally Beauty Co., Inc. (Denton, TX) 84637
Salomon Brothers Inc. (Washington, DC) 58467
Salomon Brothers Inc. (Atlanta, GA) 65140
Salomon Brothers Inc. (Houston, TX) 86854
Sam's Wholesale Club (Birmingham, AL) 55385
Sam's Wholesale Club (Huntsville, AL) 56013
Sam's Wholesale Club (Fort Smith, AR) 57099
Sam's Wholesale Club (Springdale, AR) 57643
Sam's Wholesale Club (Casselberry, FL) 58942
Sam's Wholesale Club (Jacksonville, FL) 60452; 60453
Sam's Wholesale Club (Lakeland, FL) 60782
Sam's Wholesale Club (Pensacola, FL) 62471
Sam's Wholesale Club (Tallahassee, FL) 63270
Sam's Wholesale Club (Macon, GA) 66713
Sam's Wholesale Club (Savannah, GA) 67511
Sam's Wholesale Club (Shreveport, LA) 70781
Sam's Wholesale Club (Jackson, MS) 73057
Sam's Wholesale Club (Oklahoma City, OK) 77547; 77548; 77549
Sam's Wholesale Club (Tulsa, OK) 78103
Sam's Wholesale Club (Charleston, SC) 78888
Sam's Wholesale Club (Greenville, SC) 79432
Sam's Wholesale Club (Austin, TX) 83000
Sam's Wholesale Club (Beaumont, TX) 83211
Sam's Wholesale Club (Dallas, TX) 84374
Sam's Wholesale Club (El Paso, TX) 84926
Sam's Wholesale Club (Fort Worth, TX) 85272; 85273
Sam's Wholesale Club (Houston, TX) 86855; 86856; 86857
Sam's Wholesale Club (Mesquite, TX) 87997
Sam's Wholesale Club (Midland, TX) 88073
Sam's Wholesale Club (San Antonio, TX) 89221
Sam's Wholesale Club (Texarkana, TX) 89708
Sam's Wholesale Club (Tyler, TX) 89828
Sam's Wholesale Liquor Store (Oklahoma City, OK) 77550
Sam's Wholesale Warehouse (West Palm Beach, FL) 63899
Sandhill Telephone Co. (Aberdeen, NC) 73520
Sani-Fresh International (San Antonio, TX) 89222
Sara Lee Bakery (Forest, MS) 72776; 72777
Sara Lee Bakery (Tarboro, NC) 76365
Sara Lee Bakery (Greenville, SC) 79433
Sara Lee Corp. (Athens, AL) 55046
Sara Lee Corp. (West Point, MS) 73486
Sara Lee Corp. (High Point, NC) 75170
Sara Lee Corp. (Winston-Salem, NC) 76760; 76761
Sara Lee Corp. (Greenville, SC) 79434
Sara Lee Corp. (Cordova, TN) 80677
Sara Lee Corp. (Memphis, TN) 81689
Sara Lee Corp. (Dallas, TX) 84375
Sara Lee Direct (Winston-Salem, NC) 76762
Sara Lee Graphics (Winston-Salem, NC) 76763
Sara Lee Hosiery (Lumberton, NC) 75473
Sara Lee Hosiery (Rockingham, NC) 76069
Sara Lee Hosiery (Winston-Salem, NC) 76764; 76765
Sara Lee Hosiery (Yadkinville, NC) 76781
Sara Lee Hosiery (Bennettsville, SC) 78731; 78732
Sara Lee Hosiery (Florence, SC) 79225
Sara Lee Hosiery (Hartsville, SC) 79502
Sara Lee Hosiery (Marion, SC) 79644
Sara Lee Intimates (Winston-Salem, NC) 76766
Sara Lee Intimates (BALI) (Winston-Salem, NC) 76767
Sara Lee Knit Products (Asheboro, NC) 73597
Sara Lee Knit Products (Forest City, NC) 74611
Sara Lee Knit Products (Gastonia, NC) 74689
Sara Lee Knit Products (Lumberton, NC) 75474
Sara Lee Knit Products (Morganton, NC) 75655
Sara Lee Knit Products (Winston-Salem, NC) 76768; 76769
Sara Lee Knit Products (Martinsville, VA) 91357; 91358
Sara Lee Knit Products Dyeing & Finishing Plant (Eden, NC) 74468
Sara Lee Knit Products Galax Plant (Galax, VA) 90964
Sara Lee Knit Products Hanes Menswear (Ponce, PR) 78537
Sara Lee Meats (Cordova, TN) 80678
Sara Lee Personal Products (Winston-Salem, NC) 76770
Sara Lee Sausage Newbern Facility (Newbern, TN) 82157
Saturn Corp. (Cheverly, MD) 71527
Sav on Food & Drug (Roanoke, VA) 92184; 92185
Sav-On (Fort Worth, TX) 85274
Sav-On-Drugs of Okolona (Okolona, MS) 73225
Savannah Foods & Industries, Inc. (Savannah, GA) **67512**
Savannah Sugar Refinery (Port Wentworth, GA) 67276
Save Trust Federal Savings Bank (Dyersburg, TN) 80758; 80759; 80760
Save Trust Federal Savings Bank (Newbern, TN) 82158
Savings of America A Div. of Home Savings of America, FSB (Fort Myers, FL) 59762
Savings of America Home Savings of America, FSB (Lake Worth, FL) 60697
Savings of America Home Savings of America, FSB (Margate, FL) 61002
Savings of America Home Savings of America, FSB (Miami Beach, FL) 61530; 61531
Savings of America Home Savings of America, FSB (Miami Shores, FL) 61537
Savings of America Home Savings of America, FSB (Naples, FL) 61664
Savings of America Home Savings of America, FSB (North Miami Beach, FL) 61744
Savings of America Home Savings of America, FSB (Pembroke Pines, FL) 62372; 62373
Savings of America Home Savings of America, FSB (Pompano Beach, FL) 62634; 62635; 62636
Savings of America Home Savings of America, FSB (Port Charlotte, FL) 62658
Savings of America Home Savings of America, FSB (Port Richey, FL) 62680
Savings of America Home Savings of America, FSB (Sarasota, FL) 62861
Savings of America Home Savings of America, FSB (St. Petersburg, FL) 63133
Savings of America Home Savings of America, FSB (Sunrise, FL) 63199
Savings of America Home Savings of America, FSB (Surfside, FL) 63202
Savings of America Home Savings of America, FSB (Tamarac, FL) 63300
Savings of America Home Savings of America, FSB (Tequesta, FL) 63681
Savings of America Home Savings of America, FSB (Venice, FL) 63736
Savings of America Home Savings of America, FSB (Vero Beach, FL) 63769
Savings of America Home Savings of America, FSB (West Palm Beach, FL) 63900; 63901
Savings of America, A Div. of Home Savings of America, FSB (Delray Beach, FL) 59331
Savings of America, A Division of Home Savings of America (Altamonte Springs, FL) 58563
Savings of America, A Division of Home Savings of America (Deerfield Beach, FL) 59289
Savings of America, A Division of Home Savings of America, FSB (Boca Raton, FL) 58741
Savings of America, A Division of Home Savings of America, FSB (Boynton Beach, FL) 58792
Savings of America, A Division of Home Savings of America, FSB (Bradenton, FL) 58851; 58852
Savings of America, A Division of Home Savings of America, FSB (Clearwater, FL) 59046
Savings of America, A Division of Home Savings of America, FSB (Coral Gables, FL) 59104
Savings of America, A Division of Home Savings of America, FSB (Dunedin, FL) 59367
Savings of America, A Division of Home Savings of America, FSB (Fort Lauderdale, FL) 59608; 59609
Savings of America, A Division of Home Savings of America, FSB (Fort Pierce, FL) 59811
Savings of America, A Division of Home Savings of America FSB (Houston, TX) 86858; 86859; 86860
Savings of America, A Division of Home Savings of America, FSB (Humble, TX) 87244
Savings of America, A Division of Home Savings of America, FSB (Hurst, TX) 87296

Company Name Index

Savings of America, A Division of Home Savings of America, FSB (Irving, TX) 87400
Savings of America, A Division of Home Savings of America, FSB (Nederland, TX) 88191
Savings of America, A Division of Home Savings of America, FSB (Pasadena, TX) 88468
Savings of America, A Division of Home Savings of America, FSB (Plano, TX) 88607
Savings of America, A Division of Home Savings of America, FSB (Richardson, TX) 88774; 88775
Savings of America, A Division of Home Savings of America, FSB (San Antonio, TX) 89223; 89224; 89225
Savings of America, A Division of Home Savings of America, FSB (Webster, TX) 90024
Savings of America, FSB (Beaumont, TX) 83212
Savings of America, FSB (Dallas, TX) 84376; 84377; 84378; 84379
Savings of America, FSB (Deer Park, TX) 84566
Savings of America, FSB (Dllas, TX) 84675
Savings of America, FSB (Ft. Worth, TX) 85415
Savings of America, FSB (Groves, TX) 85684
Savings of America, FSB (Houston, TX) 86861; 86862; 86863; 86864; 86865; 86866; 86867; 86868; 86869; 86870
Savings of America, FSB Home Savings of America (Hollandale, FL) 60031
Savings of America, FSB Home Savings of America (Hollywood, FL) 60094
Saxon Paper Florida (Hollywood, FL) 60095
Saxon Paper-Florida (Miami, FL) 61456
Schering Industrial Development Corp. (Manati, PR) 78503
Schering Lab (Miami, FL) 61457
Schering-Plough Healthcare Products (Chatsworth, GA) 65557
Schering-Plough Healthcare Products (Cleveland, TN) 80600
Schering-Plough Healthcare Products Inc. (Memphis, TN) 81690
Schering-Plough Inc. El Jibaro Incustrial (Cidra, PR) 78400
Schering-Plough Prodsucts Inc. Key Pharmaceuticals (Las Piedras, PR) 78487
Schering-Plough Products Inc. Development (Manati, PR) 78504
Schering-Plough Products Inc. Key Pharmaceuticals (Las Piedras, PR) 78488
Schlage Lock Co. (Rocky Mount, NC) 76102
Scholl Inc. (Cleveland, TN) 80601
Schott's Bakery (Stafford, TX) 89505
Schott's Bakery Inc. (Houston, TX) 86871
Schrader Automotive Inc. (Monroe, NC) 75588; 75589; 75590
Schrader Bellows (Wake Forest, NC) 76433; 76434
Schuller International Inc-Man (Washington, DC) 58468
Schuller International Inc/Manville Fib (Atlanta, GA) 65141
Schuller International Inc/Manville Fib (Norcross, GA) 67180
Schuller International Inc. (Etowah, TN) 80783
Schuller International Inc. (Cleburne, TX) 83588
Schuller International Inc. (Ennis, TX) 85001
Schuller International Inc. (Richmond, VA) 92010
Schuller International Inc./Manville Fib (Atlanta, GA) 65142
Schuller Manufacturing Corp. (Vienna, WV) 93079
A Schulman Inc. (Arlington, TX) 82748
Schuylkill Metals Corp. (Baton Rouge, LA) 69658
Schwab Charles & Co. Inc. (St Petersburg, FL) 63034
Schwab Charles & Co. Inc. (Atlanta, GA) 65143
Schwab Charles & Co. Inc. (Tulsa, OK) 78104
Schwab Charles & Co. Inc. (Virginia Beach, VA) 92509
Schwab & Co. Inc/Charles (Washington, DC) 58469
Schwab & Co. Inc/Charles (Oklahoma City, OK) 77551
SCI Manufacturing (Graham, NC) 74752
SCI Manufacturing Inc. (Huntsville, AL) 56014; 56015
SCI Manufacturing Inc. (Laceys Spring, AL) 56097; 56098
SCI Systems, Inc. (Huntsville, AL) **56016**
SCI Systems Inc. (Graham, NC) 74753
SCI Technology Inc. (Huntsville, AL) 56017; 56018
Scientific-Atla Inc. Network Sy (Norcross, GA) 67181
Scientific-Atlanta (Signal Mounta, TN) 82323
Scientific-Atlanta, Inc. (Atlanta, GA) **65144**
Scientific Atlanta Inc. (Odenton, MD) 72171
Scientific-Atlanta Inc. Nwtwork (Norcross, GA) 67182
Scm Chemicals (Baltimore, MD) 71273
SCM Chemicals Inc. (Baltimore, MD) 71274
Scm Glidco Organics Corp. (Jacksonville, FL) 60454
Scm Glidco Organics Corp. (Brunswick, GA) 65426; 65427
Scm Glidco Organics Corp. (Baltimore, MD) 71275
Scm Metal Products Inc. (Research Triangle Park, NC) 76023
Scoot-Rice Co. Inc. (Tulsa, OK) 78105
Scott Aviation (Monroe, NC) 75591
Scott Paper Co. (Mobile, AL) 56237
Scott Paper Co. (Dover, DE) 57808
Scott Polymers Inc. (Fort Worth, TX) 85275
Scott Polymers Inc. (Saginaw, TX) 88863; 88864
Scottsboro Rug Mill (Scottsboro, AL) 56523
Scurlock Permian Corp. (Houston, TX) 86872
Sea Island Bank (Stateboro, GA) 67631
Sea Island Bank (Statesboro, GA) 67646; 67647; 67648
Sea Island Park (Statesboro, GA) 67649
Sea Ray Boats Florida Corp. (Palm Coast, FL) 62286
Sea Ray Boats Inc. (Merritt Island, FL) 61144; 61145
Sea Ray Boats Inc. (Fort Mill, SC) 79236
Sea Ray Boats Inc. (Knoxville, TN) 81246; 81247
Sea Ray Boats Inc. (Vonore, TN) 82396
Sea Ray Boats Inc. Cherokee Cove (Madisonville, TN) 81388
Sea Ray Boats Inc. Product Development (Merritt Island, FL) 61146
Sea Ray Boats Inc. Riverview (Knoxville, TN) 81248
Sea World of Florida, Inc. (Orlando, FL) 62139
Sea World of Texax, Inc. (San Antonio, TX) 89226
Seaboard Farms of Athens Inc. Feed Mill (Athens, GA) 64176
Seaboard Farms of Athens Inc. Processing Plant (Athens, GA) 64177
Seaboard Farms of Canton Inc. (Canton, GA) 65487
Seaboard Farms of Canton Inc. Feedmill (Canton, GA) 65488
Seaboard Farms of Chattanooga Inc. (Chattanooga, TN) 80486; 80487
Seaboard Farms of Chattanooga Inc. Processing Plant (Chattanooga, TN) 80488
Seaboard Farms of KY Inc. (Hickory, KY) 68462
Seaboard Farms of KY Inc. (Mayfield, KY) 69081
Seabury & Smith (Washington, DC) 58470
Seabury & Smith Inc. (Atlanta, GA) 65145
Seadrift Plant (Port Lavaca, TX) 88670
Seagate Technology (Atlanta, GA) 65146
Seagate Technology Inc. (Oklahoma City, OK) 77552
Seagram Joseph E & Sons (Louisville, KY) 69001
Seagram Sons Inc/Joseph E (Tampa, FL) 63587
Seagram Sons Inc. Joseph E (Lawrenceburg, KY) 68508
Sealy Mattress Co. (Orlando, FL) 62140
Sealy Mattress Co. (Lexington, NC) 75424
Sealy Mattress Co. (Memphis, TN) 81691
Sealy Mattress Co. (Brenham, TX) 83342
Sealy Mattress Co. (Bluefield, VA) 90462
Sealy Stearns & Foster Bedding (Conyers, GA) 65704
Searle & Co. (Caguas, PR) 78358; 78359
Sears Mortgage Co. (Victoria, TX) 89904
Sears Roebuck & Co. (Fort Lauderdale, FL) 59610
Seco Electronic (Lancaster, SC) 79575
Security Bank & Trust Co. (Maysville, KY) 69090
Security Bank & Trust Co. (Paris, TN) 82223
Security Bank & Trust Co. of Albany (Albany, GA) 64092; 64093; 64094; 64095; 64096
Security Bank & Trust Co. of Albany (Colquitt, GA) 65614
Security Connecticut Life Insu (Roswell, GA) 67418
Security Pacific Finance Corp. (Raleigh, NC) 75954
Security Pacific Financial Services (Greensboro, NC) 74905
Security Pacific Financial Services, Inc. (Lexington, KY) 68625; 68626
Security Pacific Financial Services, Inc. (Baltimore, MD) 71276
Security Pacific Financial Services Inc. (Oklahoma City, OK) 77553
Security Pacific Financial Services Inc. (Tulsa, OK) 78106
Security Pacific Housing (Greenville, SC) 79435
Security Pacific Housing Services, Inc. (Raleigh, NC) 75955
Security Trust Bypass (Greeneville, TN) 80888
Security Trust Federal S&L (Fulton, KY) 68377
Security Trust Federal S&L (Hickman, KY) 68461
Security Trust FS & LA (Clinton, TN) 80614
Security Trust FS & LA (Kingston, TN) 81128
Security Trust FS & LA (Knoxville, TN) 81249; 81250
Security Trust FS & LA (Morristown, TN) 81809
Security Trust FS & LA (Oak Ridge, TN) 82198
Sedgefield Specialties (Greensboro, NC) 74906
Seiscor Tech. Inc. (Tulsa, OK) 78107
Sekin Transport Internation (Houston, TX) 86873
Sekin Transport International (Tulsa, OK) 78108
Sekin Transport International (Dallas, TX) 84380
Selig Chemical Ind. (Atlanta, GA) 65147
Selig Chemical Industries (Atlanta, GA) 65148
Seminole Fertilizer Corp. (Bartow, FL) 58630
Seminole Kraft Corp. (Jacksonville, FL) 60455
Sentry Drugs (Columbia, SC) 79095
Sentry Polymers Inc. (Freeport, TX) 85392
Septem Energy Resources Inc. (Jackson, MS) 73058
Sequa Chemicals (Chester, SC) 78942
Sequa Chemicals Inc. (Chester, SC) 78943
Sequa Corp. Chromalloy (Midwest City, OK) 77213; 77214
Sequa Corp. Chromalloy (Oklahoma City, OK) 77554
Sequa Corp. Gemoco (Houma, LA) 69970; 69971
Sermatech International Inc. (Boynton Beach, FL) 58793
Sermatech International Inc. (Sugar Land, TX) 89543
Serv - Air Inc. (Greenville, TX) 85677; 85678
Serv Air Inc. (Norfolk, VA) 91577
Service Merchandise (Birmingham, AL) 55386; 55387
Service Merchandise (Huntsville, AL) 56019
Service Merchandise (Mobile, AL) 56238
Service Merchandise (Montgomery, AL) 56378
Service Merchandise (North Little Rock, AR) 57471
Service Merchandise (Wilmington, DE) 58109
Service Merchandise (Clearwater, FL) 59047
Service Merchandise (Daytona Beach, FL) 59212
Service Merchandise (Fort Lauderdale, FL) 59611
Service Merchandise (Fort Pierce, FL) 59812
Service Merchandise (Gainesville, FL) 59918
Service Merchandise (Hialeah, FL) 60009
Service Merchandise (Hollywood, FL) 60096
Service Merchandise (Jacksonville, FL) 60456; 60457
Service Merchandise (Lakeland, FL) 60783
Service Merchandise (Largo, FL) 60863
Service Merchandise (Miami, FL) 61458; 61459
Service Merchandise (Orlando, FL) 62141
Service Merchandise (Pensacola, FL) 62472
Service Merchandise (Port Richey, FL) 62681
Service Merchandise (Tallahassee, FL) 63271
Service Merchandise (Tampa, FL) 63588; 63589
Service Merchandise (Atlanta, GA) 65149; 65150; 65151
Service Merchandise (College Park, GA) 65603
Service Merchandise (Decatur, GA) 65895; 65896
Service Merchandise (Doraville, GA) 65949
Service Merchandise (Duluth, GA) 66080
Service Merchandise (Dunwoody, GA) 66136
Service Merchandise (Kennesaw, GA) 66448
Service Merchandise (Morrow, GA) 67043
Service Merchandise (Tucker, GA) 67887
Service Merchandise (Louisville, KY) 69002; 69003
Service Merchandise (Owensboro, KY) 69193
Service Merchandise (Baton Rouge, LA) 69659
Service Merchandise (Bossier City, LA) 69731
Service Merchandise (Lake Charles, LA) 70171
Service Merchandise (Shreveport, LA) 70782
Service Merchandise (Forestville, MD) 71699
Service Merchandise (Frederick, MD) 71747
Service Merchandise (Escatawpa, MS) 72760
Service Merchandise (Gulfport, MS) 72875
Service Merchandise (Jackson, MS) 73059; 73060
Service Merchandise (Enid, OK) 77070
Service Merchandise (Oklahoma City, OK) 77555; 77556; 77557
Service Merchandise (Tulsa, OK) 78109; 78110
Service Merchandise (Charleston, SC) 78889
Service Merchandise (Sumter, SC) 80031
Service Merchandise (Brentwood, TN) 80233; 80234
Service Merchandise (Chattanooga, TN) 80489; 80490
Service Merchandise (Goodlettsville, TN) 80871
Service Merchandise (Kingsport, TN) 81118
Service Merchandise (Knoxville, TN) 81251
Service Merchandise (Madison, TN) 81380
Service Merchandise (Memphis, TN) 81692
Service Merchandise (Nashville, TN) 82095; 82096; 82097
Service Merchandise (Arlington, TX) 82749
Service Merchandise (Beaumont, TX) 83213
Service Merchandise (Clute, TX) 83602
Service Merchandise (College Station, TX) 83623
Service Merchandise (Corpus Christi, TX) 83749
Service Merchandise (Fort Worth, TX) 85276
Service Merchandise (Hurst, TX) 87297
Service Merchandise (Lake Jackson, TX) 87586
Service Merchandise (Longview, TX) 87735
Service Merchandise (Midland, TX) 88074
Service Merchandise (San Angelo, TX) 88901
Service Merchandise (San Antonio, TX) 89227; 89228
Service Merchandise (Temple, TX) 89645
Service Merchandise (Hampton, VA) 91055
Service Merchandise Catalog (Florence, KY) 68331
Service Merchandise Catalog (Lexington, KY) 68627
Service Merchandise Catalog (Jackson, MS) 73061
Service Merchandise Catalog Sales (Florence, KY) 68332
Service Merchandise Catalog Sales (Lexington, KY) 68628
Service Merchandise Co., Inc. (Brentwood, TN) **80235**
Sesame Prods. Inc. (Paris, TX) 88377
Sesame Products Inc. (Paris, TX) 88378
Seven-Up Bottling Co. (Bayamon, PR) 78340
Seven-Up Bottling Co. (Union City, TN) 82390
Seven-Up Bottling Co. (Salem, VA) 92223
Seven Up Bottling Co. Inc. (Bayamon, PR) 78341
Seven-Up-RC-Big Red Bottling (Austin, TX) 83001
Seven-Up Royal Crown Cola (Tulsa, OK) 78111
Seven Up U S a Inc. (San Antonio, TX) 89229
Shannon Group (Parsons, TN) 82225
Shannon Industries Inc. (Knoxville, TN) 81252
Shannon Properties (Charlotte, NC) 74155
Shannon Properties Inc. (Charlotte, NC) 74156
Shaw Co/Benjamin F (Wilmington, DE) 58110
Shaw Industries Co. (Millendgeville, GA) 66987
Shaw Industries Inc. (Stevenson, AL) 56573
Shaw Industries Inc. (Valley Head, AL) 56696
Shaw Industries Inc. (Blue Ridge, GA) 65383
Shaw Industries Inc. (Calhoun, GA) 65474
Shaw Industries Inc. (Chatsworth, GA) 65558; 65559
Shaw Industries Inc. (Dallas, GA) 65767
Shaw Industries Inc. (Dalton, GA) 65788; 65789; **65790**
Shaw Industries Inc. (Fitzgerald, GA) 66213
Shaw Industries Inc. (La Fayette, GA) 66472
Shaw Industries Inc. (Newnan, GA) 67085
Shaw Industries Inc. (Tifton, GA) 67829
Shaw Industries Inc. (Toccoa, GA) 67838
Shaw Industries Inc. (Trenton, GA) 67843
Shaw Industries Inc. (Prairieville, LA) 70651
Shaw Industries Inc. (Trenton, SC) 80046
Shaw Industries Inc. (Decatur, TN) 80727
Shaw Industries Inc. (South Pittsburg, TN) 82340
Shaw Industries Inc. (Winchester, TN) 82421
Shaw Industries Plant (Charlotte, NC) 74157
Shawmut National Trust Co. (Stuart, FL) 63179
Shelby Insurance Co. (Greensboro, NC) 74907
Shell Chemical Co. (Memphis, TN) 81693
Shell Chemical Co. Geismar (Geismar, LA) 69883
Shell Chemical Co. Geismar Plant (Geismar, LA) 69884
Shell Chemical Co. Point Pleasure Polyester Plant (Apple Grove, WV) 92664
Shell Chemical Co. Reserve Plant (Reserve, LA) 70664
Shell Chemical Co. Taft Plant (Taft, LA) 70900; 70901
Shell Co. (Miami, FL) 61460
Shell Co. (Dallas, TX) 84381; 84382; 84383

Company Name Index Smith

Shell Co. (Houston, TX) 86874; 86875; 86876; 86877; 86878; 86879; 86880
Shell Co. (Spring, TX) 89489
Shell Co. (Tomball, TX) 89779
Shell Co. (Richmond, VA) 92011
Shell Co. Trust (Brunswick, GA) 65428
Shell Food Mart (Dothan, AL) 55669
Shell Food Mart (Huntsville, AL) 56020; 56021; 56022
Shell Food Mart (Phenix City, AL) 56472
Shell Food Mart (Newark, DE) 57932
Shell Food Mart (Daytona Beach, FL) 59213
Shell Food Mart (Panama City, FL) 62349; 62350
Shell Food Mart (Atlanta, GA) 65152; 65153
Shell Food Mart (College Park, GA) 65604
Shell Food Mart (Jonesboro, GA) 66398
Shell Food Mart (Riverdale, GA) 67325
Shell Food Mart (Metairie, LA) 70311
Shell Food Mart (Clarksdale, MS) 72680
Shell Food Mart (Antioch, TN) 80174
Shell Food Mart (Arlington, TX) 82750
Shell Food Mart (Corsicana, TX) 83791; 83792
Shell Food Mart (Nederland, TX) 88192
Shell Gas Park (Lake Charles, LA) 70172
Shell Gas Station (Pine Bluff, AR) 57530
Shell Gas Station (Lake Worth, FL) 60698
Shell Gas Station (Kenner, LA) 70014
Shell Hammond Oil (Fort Stockton, TX) 85048
Shell Interstate Service Station (Richmond, KY) 69249
Shell Mart (Vansant, VA) 92390
Shell Mini Mart (Jonesboro, GA) 66399
Shell Mini Mart (Jackson, MS) 73062
Shell Oil (Florence, KY) 68333; 68334
Shell Oil (Louisville, KY) 69004; 69005
Shell Oil (Charlotte, NC) 74158
Shell Oil (Charleston, SC) 78890
Shell Oil (Chattanooga, TN) 80491
Shell Oil (Freeport, TX) 85393
Shell Oil (Pasadena, TX) 88469
Shell Oil Co. (Birmingham, AL) 55388
Shell Oil Co. (Guntersville, AL) 55833
Shell Oil Co. (Mobile, AL) 56239
Shell Oil Co. (Washington, DC) 58471
Shell Oil Co. (De Funiak Springs, FL) 59245
Shell Oil Co. (Orlando, FL) 62142
Shell Oil Co. (Starke, FL) 63151
Shell Oil Co. (Tampa, FL) 63590; 63591
Shell Oil Co. (Doraville, GA) 65950
Shell Oil Co. (Cheneyville, LA) 69776
Shell Oil Co. (Donaldsonville, LA) 69842
Shell Oil Co. (Gibson, LA) 69887; 69888
Shell Oil Co. (Jefferson, LA) 69975
Shell Oil Co. (Morgan City, LA) 70393
Shell Oil Co. (New Orleans, LA) 70555
Shell Oil Co. (Norco, LA) 70592
Shell Oil Co. (Baltimore, MD) 71277; 71278
Shell Oil Co. (Rockville, MD) 72322; 72323
Shell Oil Co. (Florence, MS) 72772
Shell Oil Co. (Mc Comb, MS) 73150
Shell Oil Co. (Greensboro, NC) 74908
Shell Oil Co. (Tulsa, OK) 78112
Shell Oil Co. (Yukon, OK) 78281
Shell Oil Co. (Ballinger, TX) 83091
Shell Oil Co. (Corpus Christi, TX) 83750; 83751
Shell Oil Co. (Deer Park, TX) 84567
Shell Oil Co. (Douglassville, TX) 84681
Shell Oil Co. (Edinburg, TX) 84737
Shell Oil Co. (El Paso, TX) 84927
Shell Oil Co. (Garland, TX) 85533
Shell Oil Co. (Houston, TX) 86881; 86882; 86883; 86884; 86885; **86886**
Shell Oil Co. (Irving, TX) 87401
Shell Oil Co. (Kilgore, TX) 87498
Shell Oil Co. (Marietta, TX) 87844
Shell Oil Co. (Mt Pleasant, TX) 88161
Shell Oil Co. (Nordheim, TX) 88230
Shell Oil Co. (Odessa, TX) 88272; 88273; 88274
Shell Oil Co. (Sugar Land, TX) 89544
Shell Oil Co. (Tilden, TX) 89763
Shell Oil Co. (Chesapeake, VA) 90600; 90601
Shell Oil Co. Deer Park Manufacturing Complex (Deer Park, TX) 84568; 84569
Shell Oil Co. Metairie Plant (Jefferson, LA) 69976
Shell Oil Co. Norco Manufacturing Complex (Norco, LA) 70593; 70594; 70595; 70596
Shell Oil Co. Odessa Refinery (Odessa, TX) 88275; 88276
Shell Oil Company Asphalt Sale (Atlanta, GA) 65154
Shell Oil Company Eastern Dist (Atlanta, GA) 65155
Shell Oil Company Jobber Sales (Atlanta, GA) 65156
Shell Oil Co. Library (Deer Park, TX) 84570
Shell Oil Company Lubricant Sa (Atlanta, GA) 65157
Shell Oil Legal Library (Houston, TX) 86887
Shell Oil Marketing (Abilene, TX) 82457
Shell Oil Offshore Inc. (Golden Meadow, LA) 69889
Shell Oil Self Service (Guntersville, AL) 55834
Shell Oil Self Service (Gautier, MS) 72786
Shell Oil Service Station (Orange Park, FL) 61897
Shell Oil Service Station (Baton Rouge, LA) 69660
Shell One Stop (Frankfort, KY) 68369
Shell Petroleum Inc. (Wilmington, DE) 58111
Shell Pipe Line Corp. (Houston, TX) 86888
Shell Pipe Line Corp. Centra (Midland, TX) 88075
Shell Pipeline Corp. (Donaldsonville, LA) 69843
Shell Pipeline Corp. (Donaldsonvl, LA) 69846
Shell Pipeline Corp. (Montegut, LA) 70384; 70385
Shell Pipeline Corp. (New Orleans, LA) 70556
Shell Pipeline Corp. (Austin, TX) 83002
Shell Pipeline Corp. (Denver City, TX) 84648; 84649
Shell Pipeline Corp. (El Paso, TX) 84928; 84929
Shell Pipeline Corp. (Houston, TX) 86889; 86890; 86891
Shell Pipeline Corp. (Livingston, TX) 87691
Shell Pipeline Corp. (Midland, TX) 88076
Shell Pipeline Corp. (Odessa, TX) 88277; 88278
Shell Pipeline Corp. (Texas City, TX) 89735; 89736
Shell Pipeline Corp. (Ofc) (New Orleans, LA) 70557
Shell Self Serve (El Paso, TX) 84930
Shell Self Serve (Garland, TX) 85534
Shell Self Serve (Houston, TX) 86892
Shell Self Serve Food Mart (Cocoa, FL) 59075
Shell Self Service (Senatobia, MS) 73341
Shell Self Service (Vicksburg, MS) 73462
Shell Self Service (Mesquite, TX) 87998
Shell Self Service (Midland, TX) 88077; 88078
Shell Self Service Station (Mobile, AL) 56240
Shell Self Service Station (Louisville, KY) 69006; 69007; 69008
Shell Self Service Station (Newport, KY) 69142
Shell Self Service Station (Rosenberg, TX) 88837
Shell Service (Savannah, GA) 67513
Shell Service (Elizabeth City, NC) 74484
Shell Service (Wylie, TX) 90134
Shell Service Ctr (Dothan, AL) 55670
Shell Service Ctr (Mountain Home, AR) 57391
Shell Service Food Mart (Tampa, FL) 63592
Shell Service Station (Hartselle, AL) 55861
Shell Service Station (Hialeah, FL) 60010
Shell Service Station (Gainesville, GA) 66291
Shell Service Station (New Orleans, LA) 70558
Shell Service Station (New Windsor, MD) 72152
Shell Service Station (Dallas, TX) 84384; 84385
Shell Service Station (Lufkin, TX) 87818
Shell Service Station (Richardson, TX) 88776
Shell Station (Tampa, FL) 63593
Shell Station (Ellaville, GA) 66168
Shell Station & Car Wash (Boca Raton, FL) 58742
Shell Super Service (Cleveland, TN) 80602
Shell Super Stop (Camden, AR) 56841
Shell Super Stop (Magnolia, AR) 57336
Shell Super Stop (Wheatley, AR) 57740
Shell Super Stop (Wynne, AR) 57745
Shell Super Stop (Cumberland Gap, TN) 80709
Shell Super Stop (Sevierville, TN) 82297
Shell Truck Stop (Bastrop, LA) 69450
Shell Truck Stop (Jackson, MS) 73063
Shenandoah Life Insurance Co. (Roanoke, VA) 92186
Sherman County Grain Co. (Texhoma, OK) 77864
Sherwin-Williams Co. (Orlando, FL) 62143
Sherwin-Williams Co. (Morrow, GA) 67044
Sherwin-Williams Co. (Tucker, GA) 67888
Sherwin-Williams Co. (Richmond, KY) 69250
Sherwin-Williams Co. (Baltimore, MD) 71279
Sherwin-Williams Co. (Greensboro, NC) 74909; 74910
Sherwin-Williams Co. (Garland, TX) 85535
Sherwin Williams Paint Stor (Fernandina, FL) 59405
Sherwin Williams Paint Stor (Fort Pierce, FL) 59813
Sherwin Williams Paint Stor (Bossier City, LA) 69732
Sherwin Williams Paint Stor (Greensboro, NC) 74911
Sherwin Williams Paint Stor (Sanford, NC) 76205
Sherwin Williams Paint Stor (Virginia Beach, VA) 92510
Sherwood Medical Co. (De Land, FL) 59259
Sherwood Medical Co. (Commerce, TX) 83644
Shipley Co. (Carrollton, TX) 83505
Shipley Co. Inc. (Irving, TX) 87402
Shipley Co. Inc. (Richmond, VA) 92012
Short & Paulk Supply Co. Inc. (Tifton, GA) 67830
Sico Inc. (Conway, AR) 56871
Sico Inc. (Tampa, FL) 63594; 63595; 63596
Sico Inc. (Ruston, LA) 70672; 70673
Siecor Corp. (Hickory, NC) 75100
Siecor Corp. Rocky Mount Plant (Rocky Mount, NC) 76103
Sierra Industries Inc. (Uvalde, TX) 89857
Sight & Sound (Laurens, SC) 79598
Sigma Coatings Inc. (Harvey, LA) 69941
Sigma Coatings Inc. (Houston, TX) 86893; 86894
Sigma Diagnostics (Marietta, GA) 66916
Sigma Diagnostics (Farmerville, LA) 69852
Sigmaform Corp. (Vicksburg, MS) 73463
Signal Caribe Inc. (St. Just, PR) 78603
Signature Travel (Rockville, MD) 72324
Signature Travel Inc. (Houston, TX) 86895
Signet Bank (Herndon, VA) 91132
Signet Bank/Maryland (Baltimore, MD) 71280; 71281; 71282; 71283; 71284; 71285; 71286; 71287; 71288; 71289; 71290; 71291; 71292; 71293; 71294; 71295; 71296; 71297; 71298; 71299; 71300; 71301; 71302; 71303; 71304; 71305; 71306
Signet Bank, NA (Washington, DC) 58472; 58473; 58474; 58475; 58476; 58477; 58478; 58479; 58480; 58481; 58482; **58483**; 58484; 58485; 58486; 58487; 58488
Signet Bank, VA (Danville, VA) 90716; 90717
Signet Bank, Virginia (Alexandra, VA) 90164
Signet Bank, Virginia (Alexandria, VA) 90239
Signet Bank, Virginia (Arlington, VA) 90382; 90383; 90384; 90385; 90386; 90387; 90388
Signet Bank, Virginia (Boydton, VA) 90465
Signet Bank, Virginia (Bristol, VA) 90488; 90489; 90490; 90491
Signet Bank, Virginia (Burgess, VA) 90498
Signet Bank, Virginia (Chesapeake, VA) 90602; 90603; 90604
Signet Bank, Virginia (Chester, VA) 90626
Signet Bank, Virginia (Chesterfield, VA) 90631
Signet Bank, Virginia (Colonial Beach, VA) 90650
Signet Bank, Virginia (Colonial Heights, VA) 90652
Signet Bank, Virginia (Danville, VA) 90718; 90719
Signet Bank, Virginia (Dinwiddie, VA) 90726
Signet Bank, Virginia (Dublin, VA) 90729
Signet Bank, Virginia (Dumfries, VA) 90731
Signet Bank, Virginia (Fairfax, VA) 90807
Signet Bank, Virginia (Falls Church, VA) 90869; 90870
Signet Bank, Virginia (Fredericksburg, VA) 90940; 90941; 90942
Signet Bank, Virginia (Front Royal, VA) 90955; 90956
Signet Bank, Virginia (Galax, VA) 90965; 90966
Signet Bank, Virginia (Gate City, VA) 90969
Signet Bank, Virginia (Glen Allen, VA) 90984
Signet Bank, Virginia (Grafton, VA) 90997
Signet Bank, Virginia (Great Falls, VA) 91001
Signet Bank, Virginia (Hampton, VA) 91056
Signet Bank, Virginia (Herndon, VA) 91133; 91134
Signet Bank, Virginia (Honaker, VA) 91150
Signet Bank, Virginia (Kilmarnock, VA) 91179
Signet Bank, Virginia (La Crosse, VA) 91182
Signet Bank, Virginia (Lebanon, VA) 91191
Signet Bank, Virginia (Leesburg, VA) 91197
Signet Bank, Virginia (Manassas, VA) 91324; 91325
Signet Bank, Virginia (Mappsville, VA) 91329
Signet Bank, Virginia (Mc Leen, VA) 91376
Signet Bank, Virginia (Mechanicsville, VA) 91403
Signet Bank, Virginia (Midlothian, VA) 91425; 91426; 91427
Signet Bank, Virginia (Montross, VA) 91433
Signet Bank, Virginia (Newport News, VA) 91483; 91484; 91485; 91486; 91487; 91488
Signet Bank, Virginia (Nokesville, VA) 91497
Signet Bank, Virginia (Norfolk, VA) 91578; 91579; 91580; 91581; 91582
Signet Bank, Virginia (Petersburg, VA) 91635; 91636
Signet Bank, Virginia (Portsmouth, VA) 91669; 91670; 91671
Signet Bank, Virginia (Pulaski, VA) 91678; 91679
Signet Bank, Virginia (Richmond, VA) 92013; 92014; 92015; 92016; 92017; 92018; 92019; 92020; 92021; 92022; 92023; 92024; 92025; 92026; 92027; 92028; 92029; 92030; 92031; 92032; 92033; 92034; 92035; 92036; 92037
Signet Bank, Virginia (Roanoke, VA) 92187; 92188; 92189; 92190
Signet Bank, Virginia (Salem, VA) 92224
Signet Bank, Virginia (South Hill, VA) 92267; 92268
Signet Bank, Virginia (Springfield, VA) 92292
Signet Bank, Virginia (St. Paul, VA) 92298
Signet Bank, Virginia (Vienna, VA) 92420; 92421
Signet Bank, Virginia (Vinton, VA) 92426
Signet Bank, Virginia (Virginia Beach, VA) 92511; 92512; 92513; 92514; 92515; 92516; 92517
Signet Bank, Virginia (Warsaw, VA) 92530
Signet Bank, Virginia (Weber City, VA) 92536
Signet Bank, Virginia (White Stone, VA) 92545
Signet Bank, Virginia (Woodbridge, VA) 92626; 92627
Signet Bank, Virginia (Yarina, VA) 92648
Signet Banking Corp. (Richmond, VA) 92038; **92039**
Signet Investment Corp. (Tampa, FL) 63597
Signet Trust Co. (Richmond, VA) 92040
Signode Corp. (Baltimore, MD) 71307
Signode Corp. (Bel Air, MD) 71339
Signode Eastern Ops. (Baltimore, MD) 71308
Signode Supply Corp. (Baltimore, MD) 71309
Signode Supply Corp. (Weirton, WV) 93099
Silicon Graphics Inc. (Dallas, TX) 84386
Silicon Materials Service (Garland, TX) 85536
Silicon Materials Service Inc. (Garland, TX) 85537
Silver Knit Industries, Inc. (High Point, NC) 75171
Simco Co. Inc. (Plano, TX) 88608
Simmonds Precision Products (Miami, FL) 61461
Simmonds Precision Products Su (Norcross, GA) 67183
Simmons-Rand Co. (Cedar Bluff, VA) 90512
Simulation & Automated Systems (Daytona Beach, FL) 59214
Singleton Seafood Co. (Tampa, FL) 63598
Skil Corp. (Heber Springs, AR) 57155
Skil Dremel Corp. (Walnut Ridge, AR) 57707
Skinner Macaroni Co. (Charlotte, NC) 74159
Skinner Macroni Co. (La Vernia, TX) 87575
Skylark Inc. (Franklin, TN) 80823
Skyline Coal Co. (Roanoke, VA) 92191
Sloan Paper Co. (Birmingham, AL) 55389
Sloan Paper Co. (Huntsville, AL) 56023
Sloan Paper Co. (Tampa, FL) 63599
Sloan Paper Co. (Doraville, GA) 65951
Sloan Paper Co. (Jackson, MS) 73064
Sloan Paper Co. (Knoxville, TN) 81253
Sloan Paper Co. Inc. (Birmingham, AL) 55390
Slocomb Industries Inc. (Wilmington, DE) 58112
Sloss Industries Corp. Ariton Facility (Ariton, AL) 55030
Sloss Industries Corp. Birmingham Facility (Birmingham, AL) 55391
Smalley Transportation Co. (Tampa, FL) 63600
Smith Barney Harris Upham & Co. (Washington, DC) 58121
Smith Barney Harris Upham & Co. (Washington, DC) 58489
Smith Barney Harris Upham & Co. (Miami, FL) 61462; 61463
Smith Barney Harris Upham & Co. (Atlanta, GA) 65158
Smith Barney Harris Upham & Co. (Bethesda, MD) 71441
Smith Barney Harris Upham & Co. (Durham, NC) 74428
Smith Barney Harris Upham & Co. (Winston Salem, NC) 76685
Smith Barney Harris Upham & Co. (Dallas, TX) 84387
Smith Barney Harris Upham & Co. (Houston, TX) 86896

Company Name Index

Smith Corona Corp. (Arlington, TX) 82751
A.O. Smith Corp. P.C. Div. (Florence, KY) 68335
A.O. Smith Corp. Protective Coatings Div. (Florence, KY) 68336
Smith Fiberglass Products Inc. (Little Rock, AR) 57311
Smithfield Foods Inc. (Smithfield, VA) **92241**
Smithfield Ham Products (Smithfield, VA) 92242
Smithfield Packing Co. (Kinston, NC) 75329
Smithfield Packing Co. (Wilson, NC) 76643
Smithfield Packing Co. (Norfolk, VA) 91583
Smithfield Packing Co. (Smithfield, VA) 92243
Smithfield Packing Co. Inc. (Bowie, MD) 71473
Smithfield Packing Co. Inc. (Kinston, NC) 75330
Smithfield Packing Co. Inc. (Norfolk, VA) 91584
Smithfield Packing Co. Inc. (Smithfield, VA) 92244
Smoky Hollow Foods (Little Rock, AR) 57312
Snap-On Tools (Johnson City, TN) 81056
Snap On Tools Corp. (Elizabethton, TN) 80769; 80770
Snap On Tools Corp. (Johnson City, TN) 81057
Snap On Tools Corp. (Richmond, VA) 92041
Snappy Car Rental Inc. (Tulsa, OK) 78113
Snyder Production Center Consolidated (Charlotte, NC) 74160
Soabar Group Soabar Graphics Div. (Greensboro, NC) 74912
Soabar Group Soabar Products Group (Charlotte, NC) 74161
Solar Turbines Inc. (Washington, DC) 58490
Solar Turbines Inc. (Belle Chasse, LA) 69695
Solar Turbines Inc. (New Orleans, LA) 70559
Solar Turbines Inc. (Scott, LA) 70678
Solar Turbines Inc. (De Soto, TX) 84538
Solar Turbines Inc. (Houston, TX) 86897; 86898
Solar Turbines Inc. (Odessa, TX) 88279
Solarex Corp. (Frederick, MD) 71748
Solem Ind. (Fairmount, GA) 66184
Solem Industries Inc. (Benton, AR) 56775
Solem Industries Inc. (Fairmount, GA) 66185
Sonoco Fibre Drum Co. (Culloden, WV) 92824
Sonoco Fibre Drum Inc. (Charlotte, NC) 74162
Sonoco Products (Hartsville, SC) **79503**
Sonoco Products Co. (Canden, AR) 56842
Sonoco Products Co. (Orlando, FL) 62144
Sonoco Products Co. (Atlanta, GA) 65159
Sonoco Products Co. (Forest Park, GA) 66249
Sonoco Products Co. (Marietta, GA) 66917
Sonoco Products Co. (Henderson, KY) 68456
Sonoco Products Co. (Morganfield, KY) 69107
Sonoco Products Co. (Lincolnton, NC) 75442
Sonoco Products Co. (Broken Arrow, OK) 76889
Sonoco Products Co. (Fountain Inn, SC) 79249
Sonoco Products Co. (Greenville, SC) 79436
Sonoco Products Co. (Hartsville, SC) 79504; 79505
Sonoco Products Co. (Chattanooga, TN) 80492; 80493
Sonoco Products Co. (Henderson, TN) 80909
Sonoco Products Co. (Jackson, TN) 81002
Sonoco Products Co. (Memphis, TN) 81694; 81695
Sonoco Products Co. (Newport, TN) 82171; 82172; 82173
Sonoco Products Co. (Arlington, TX) 82752
Sonoco Products Co. (Denison, TX) 84609
Sonoco Products Co. (Victoria, TX) 89905
Sonoco Products Co. (Chester, VA) 90627
Sonoco Products Co. (Richmond, VA) 92042
Sonoco Products Co. Hartsville (Hartsville, SC) 79506
Sonoco Semi-Bulk Packaging (Saraland, AL) 56519
Sonoco Semi-Bulk Packaging (Marietta, GA) 66918
Sonoco Semi-Bulk Packaging (Houston, TX) 86899; 86900
South Central Florida Railroad (Clewiston, FL) 59062
South Padre Land Co. (Houston, TX) 86901
Southeast Vinyl Co. (Lynchburg, VA) 91288
Southern (Atlanta, GA) **65160**
Southern California Edison Co. (Washington, DC) 58491
Southern California Gas Co. (Washington, DC) 58492
Southern Companies (Nashville, TN) 82098
Southern Co. (North Little Rock, AR) 57472
The Southern Co. (Atlanta, GA) 65161
Southern Co. (Memphis, TN) 81696
Southern Controls (Montgomery, AL) 56379
Southern Copy Machines Inc. (Atlanta, GA) 65162; 65163
Southern Copy Machines, Inc. (Norcross, GA) 67184; 67185
Southern Cotton Oil (Montgomery, AL) 56380
Southern Cotton Oil Co. (North Little Rock, AR) 57473; 57474
Southern Cotton Oil Co. (Memphis, TN) 81697; 81698
Southern Cotton Oil Co. (Ft. Worth, TX) 85416
Southern Cotton Oil Co. (Levelland, TX) 87642
Southern Cotton Oil Co. (Quann, TX) 88703
Southern Cotton Oil Co. (Richmond, TX) 88797
Southern Cotton Oil Co. (Thorndale, TX) 89759
Southern Cotton Oil Co. INc. (Sweetwater, TX) 89591
Southern Cotton Oil Co. Inc. (North Little Rock, AR) 57475
Southern Cotton Oil Co. Inc. (Memphis, TN) 81699
Southern Cotton Oil Co. Inc. (Levelland, TX) 87643
Southern Cotton Oil Co. Inc. (Lubbock, TX) 87781
Southern Cotton Oil Co. Inc. (Quanah, TX) 88701
Southern Cotton Oil Co. Inc. (Richmond, TX) 88798
Southern Development Co. (Lexington, KY) 68629
Southern Electric Corp. (Staunton, VA) 92329
Southern Electric International (Atl, GA) 64182
Southern Food Inc. (Greensboro, NC) 74913
Southern Furniture Co. Conover Inc. (Conover, NC) 74336; 74337
Southern Furniture Co. of Conover Inc. -Catawba Plant (Claremont, NC) 74256
Southern Gas Co. Inc. (Owensboro, KY) 69194
Southern Gas Co. Inc. (Versailles, KY) 69331
Southern Gravure Service (Richmond, VA) 92043
Southern Gravure Service Inc. (Louisville, KY) 69009
Southern Gravure Service Inc. (Wilmington, NC) 76595
Southern Group Inc. (Greensboro, NC) 74914
Southern Heritage Insurance Co. (Tucker, GA) 67889
Southern Heritage Insurance Co., Inc. (Tucker, GA) 67890
Southern Ice Cream Specialties (Marietta, GA) 66919
Southern International Corp. (Washington, DC) 58493
Southern National Corp. (Winston-Salem, NC) **76771**
Southern Pacific Railroad (Bacliff, TX) 83084
Southern Pacific Railroad (Sherman, TX) 89424; 89425
Southern Pacific Railroad (Sierra Blanca, TX) 89430
Southern Phenix Textiles Inc. (Phenix City, AL) 56473; 56474
Southern Post (Nashville, TN) 82099
Southern Processors Inc. (Danville, VA) 90720
Southern Reclamation Co. (Sheffield, AL) 56563
Southern States Asphalt Co. (Nashville, TN) 82100
Southern States Co-Op. Inc. (Harrisonburg, VA) 91100
Southern States Co-Op. Inc. Feed Div. (Park City, KY) 69221
Southern States Co-Op. Inc. Feed Div. (Baltimore, MD) 71310
Southern States Co-Op. Inc. Barber Feed Mill (Barber, NC) 73661
Southern States Co-Op Inc. Feed Mill (Winchester, KY) 69355
Southern States Co-Op. Inc. Feed Mill (Durham, NC) 74429
Southern States Co-Op. Inc. Feed Mill (Farmville, NC) 74522
Southern States Co-Op. Inc. Inc. (Baltimore, MD) 71311
Southern States Co-Op. Inc. Inc. (Statesville, NC) 76338
Southern States Co-Op. Inc. Inc. (Chesapeake, VA) 90605
Southern States Co-Op. Inc. Richmond Feed Mill (Richmond, VA) 92044
Southern States Co-Op. Inc. Roanoke Feed Mill (Vinton, VA) 92427
Southern Utah Fuel Co. (Roanoke, VA) 92192
Southern Utah Fuel Co. Inc. (Roanoke, VA) 92193; 92194
Southern Wood Piedmont Co. (Baldwin, FL) 58616
Southern Wood Piedmont Co. (Augusta, GA) 65347
Southern Wood Piedmont Co. (Inman, SC) 79536
Southern Wood Piedmont Co. (Spartanburg, SC) 79951
Southern Wood Piedmont Co. (Chattanooga, TN) 80494
Southland (Haleyville, AL) 55846
Southland (Plymouth, FL) 62577
Southland (Dallas, TX) 84388
Southland Corp. (Wilmington, DE) 58113
Southland Corp. (Fort Lauderdale, FL) 59612
Southland Corp. (Orlando, FL) 62145; 62146; 62147
Southland Corp. (Shreveport, LA) 70783
Southland Corp. (Baltimore, MD) 71312
Southland Corp. (Clinton, MD) 71543
Southland Corp. (Greenbelt, MD) 71876
Southland Corp. (Laurel, MD) 72090
Southland Corp. (Silver Spring, MD) 72444
Southland Corp. (Temple Hills, MD) 72500
Southland Corp. (Ocean Springs, MS) 73222
Southland Corp. (Austin, TX) 83003
Southland Corp. (College Sta, TX) 83614
Southland Corp. (Dallas, TX) 84389; 84390; 84391; **84392;** 84393
Southland Corp. (Houston, TX) 86902
Southland Corp. (Lubbock, TX) 87782
Southland Corp. (Fairfax, VA) 90808
Southland Corp. (Manassas, VA) 91326
Southland Corp. (Richmond, VA) 92045; 92046
Southland Corp. (Winchester, VA) 92605
Southland Corp. (Woodbridge, VA) 92628
Southland Oil Co. (Jackson, MS) 73065
Southland Oil Co. (Sandersville, MS) 73336
Southland Oil Co. Lumberton (Lumberton, MS) 73132
Southland Oil Co. Sandersville (Sandersville, MS) 73337
Southland Royalty Co. (Vernon, AL) 56700; 56701
Southland Royalty Co. (Oklahoma City, OK) 77558
Southland Royalty Co. (Seiling, OK) 77802; 77803
Southland Royalty Co. (Woodward, OK) 78267
Southland Royalty Co. (Midland, TX) 88079
Southland Royalty Co. (Novice, TX) 88233; 88234
Southland Royalty Co. Inc. (Houston, TX) 86903
Southren Cotton Oil Co. (Sweetwater, TX) 89592
Southtrust Corp. (Birmingham, AL) **55392**
Southtrust Mortgage (Brentwood, TN) 80236
Southtrust Securities Inc. (Birmingham, AL) 55393
Southwest Airlines (Dallas, TX) 84394; **84395**
Southwest Airlines Co. (Oklahoma City, OK) 77559; 77560
Southwest Airlines Co. (Tulsa, OK) 78114
Southwest Airlines Co. (Amarillo, TX) 82579
Southwest Airlines Co. (Austin, TX) 83004
Southwest Airlines Co. (El Paso, TX) 84931
Southwest Airlines Co. (Houston, TX) 86904
Southwest Airlines Co. (Midland, TX) 88080
Southwest Airlines Co. (San Antonio, TX) 89230
Southwest Chemical Services (Seabrook, TX) 89360
Southwest Chemical Services Inc. (Seabrook, TX) 89361; 89362
Southwest Coca Cola (Abilene, TX) 82458
Southwest Coca-Cola Bottling Co. (Amarillo, TX) 82580
Southwest Operations Center Inc. (Roanoke, VA) 92195
Southwestern Bell (San Antonio, TX) **89231**
Southwestern Bell Corp. (San Antonio, TX) 89232
Southwestern Bell Printing Co. (Houston, TX) 86905
Southwestern Bell Yellow Pages (Tulsa, OK) 78115
Southwestern Bell Yellow Pages (Amarillo, TX) 82581
Southwestern Bell Yellow Pages (Austin, TX) 83005
Southwestern Bell Yellow Pages (Fort Worth, TX) 85277
Southwestern Electric Power Co. (Shreveport, LA) 70784
Southwestern Refining Co. Inc. (Corpus Christi, TX) 83752
Southwestern Refining Co. Inc. Inc. (Corpus Christi, TX) 83753
Southwestern Tobacco Co. (Lexington, KY) 68630
Space Industries International (League City, TX) 87632
Spalding Regional Hospital (Griffin, GA) 66324
Sparkletts Drinking Water (Amarillo, TX) 82582
Sparkletts Drinking Water Corp. (Dallas, TX) 84396
Sparkletts Water Sys. Aqua Vend (North Miami, FL) 61736
Sparkletts Water Sys. Aqua Vend (St. Petersburg, FL) 63134
Sparkletts Water Sys. Aqua Vend (North Myrtle Beach, SC) 79764
Sparkletts Water Sys. Aqua Vend (Houston, TX) 86906
Sparkletts Water Sys. Auqa Vend (Kenner, LA) 70015
Sparkletts Water Systems Aqua Vend (Houston, TX) 86907
Sparkletts Water Systems Aquavend (North Miami, FL) 61737
Sparkletts Water Systems Aquavend (St. Petersburg, FL) 63135
Sparkletts Water Systems Aquavend (Kenner, LA) 70016
Sparkletts Water Systems Aquavend (North Myrtle Beach, SC) 79765
Sparkletts Water Systems Aquavend (Houston, TX) 86908
Sparkletts Water Sytems Aqua Vend (St. Petersburg, FL) 63136
Sparkletts Water Sytems Aquavend (North Miami, FL) 61738
Spartan Express Inc. (Decatur, AL) 55604
Spartan Express Inc. (Atlanta, GA) 65164
Spartan Express Inc. (Conover, NC) 74338
Spartan Express Inc. (Wilson, NC) 76644
Spartan Express Inc. (Charleston, SC) 78891
Spartan Express Inc. (Florence, SC) 79226
Spartan Express Inc. (Chattanooga, TN) 80495
Spartan Express Inc. (Knoxville, TN) 81254
Spartan Express Inc. (Chesapeake, VA) 90606
Spartan Food Systems Inc. (Spartanburg, SC) 79952
Spd Magnet Wire Co. (Edmonton, KY) 68271
Speciality Products Group (Tucker, GA) 67891
Specialized Transportation Inc. (Houston, TX) 86909
Specialty Food Products (Jackson, MS) 73066
Specialty Metal Products (Houston, TX) 86910
Specialty Products (Tampa, FL) 63601
Specialty Products (Wynnewood, OK) 78274
Specialty Products of America (Miami, FL) 61464
Specialty Products Co. (Griffin, GA) 66325
Specialty Products Inc. (Norfolk, VA) 91585
Specialty Products & Installation (Greensboro, NC) 74915
Specialty Products & Insulation (Savannah, GA) 67514
Specialty Products International (Camden, TN) 80275
Speed Queen Co. (Searcy, AR) 57609
Speed Queen Co. (Madisonville, KY) 69071; 69072
Spenco Medical Corp. (Waco, TX) 89977; 89978; 89979
Sperry Marine Inc. (Charlottesville, VA) 90549
Sponser's Plan Asset Management, Inc. (New Castle, DE) 57875
Sports Authority (Miami, FL) 61465
Sports Authority (Atlanta, GA) 65165; 65166
Sports Authority (Duluth, GA) 66081
Sports Authority (Kennesaw, GA) 66449
Sports Authority (Morrow, GA) 67045
Sports Authority (Greenbelt, MD) 71877
Sports Authority (Rockville, MD) 72325
Spring City Knitting Co. (Gaffney, SC) 79264
Springdale Advertising Agency Inc. (Falls Church, VA) 90871
Springs Industires Inc. (Fort Lawn, SC) 79229
Springs Industrial Products (Honea Path, SC) 79530
Springs Industries (Dunwoody, GA) 66137
Springs Industries (Marietta, GA) 66920
Springs Industries (Fort Mill, SC) **79237**
Springs Industries (Lancaster, SC) 79576
Springs Industries Bath Fashions (Calhoun, GA) 65475
Springs Industries Grace Finishing (Lancaster, SC) 79577
Springs Industries, Inc. (Piedmont, AL) 56482
Springs Industries, Inc. (Calhoun, GA) 65476
Springs Industries, Inc. (Dalton, GA) 65791
Springs Industries, Inc. (Laurel Hill, NC) 75346
Springs Industries, Inc. (Anderson, SC) 78693
Springs Industries, Inc. (Chester, SC) 78944
Springs Industries, Inc. (Fort Lawn, SC) 79230
Springs Industries, Inc. (Fort Mill, SC) 79238
Springs Industries, Inc. (Gaffney, SC) 79265
Springs Industries, Inc. (Kershaw, SC) 79548
Springs Industries Inc. (Lancaster, SC) 79578
Springs Industries, Inc. (Lyman, SC) 79627
Springs Industries Inc. (Dallas, TX) 84397
Springs Industries, Inc. Eureka (Chester, SC) 78945
Springs Industries Lyman Filter Plant (Lyman, SC) 79628
Springs Industries Marketing Materials (Lancaster, SC) 79579
Sprint (Reston, VA) 91718
SPX Corp. Sealed Power Div. (Franklin, KY) 68372
Squibb Mfg. Inc. (Humacao, PR) 78463
Srb Assembly & Refurbishment Facility (Kennedy Space Center, FL) 60557

SSI Medical Services Inc. (Charleston, SC) 78892
St Jude Medical Center (Kenner, LA) 70017
St Michaels Bank (St Michaels, MD) 72469; 72470
Standard Cap & Seal Inc. (Norcross, GA) 67186
Standard Commercial (Wilson, NC) **76645**
Standard Commercial Corp. (Wilson, NC) 76646
Standard Federal S & L (Crofton, MD) 71617
Standard Federal S & L Association (Baltimore, MD) 71313
Standard Federal S & L Association (Greenbelt, MD) 71878
Standard Federal S & L Bank (Crofton, MD) 71618
Standard Federal S&L (Laurel, MD) 72091
Standard Federal Savings Bank (Bethesda, MD) 71442
Standard Federal Savings Bank (Briggs Chaney, MD) 71476
Standard Federal Savings Bank (Chillum, MD) 71535
Standard Federal Savings Bank (Forestville, MD) 71700
Standard Federal Savings Bank (Frederick, MD) 71749
Standard Federal Savings Bank (Gaithersburg, MD) 71816
Standard Federal Savings Bank (Germantown, MD) 71832
Standard Federal Savings Bank (Laurel, MD) 72092
Standard Federal Savings Bank (Marlow Height, MD) 72126
Standard Federal Savings Bank (Montgomery Co, MD) 72146; 72147
Standard Federal Savings Bank (Olney, MD) 72181
Standard Federal Savings Bank (Oxon Hill, MD) 72209
Standard Federal Savings Bank (Rockville, MD) 72326
Standard Federal Savings Bank (Columbia, SC) 79096; 79097
Standard Federal Savings Bank (West Columbia, SC) 80108; 80109
Standard Fire Insurance Co. (Birmingham, AL) 55394
Standard Fire Insurance Co. (Dallas, TX) 84398
Standard Office Systems, Inc. (Norcross, GA) 67187; 67188
Standard Products Co. (Lexington, KY) 68631
Standard Products Co. (Goldsboro, NC) 74735
Standard Products Co. (Rocky Mountain, NC) 76114
Standard Products Co. (Spartanburg, SC) 79953
Standard Products Co. (Winnsboro, SC) 80133
Standard Products Co. Goldsboro Division (Goldsboro, NC) 74736
Standard Register Business (Raleigh, NC) 75956
Standard Register Co. (Fayetteville, AR) 56992
Standard Register Co. (Tampa, FL) 63602
Standard Register Co. (Atlanta, GA) 65167
Standard Register Co. (St. Matthews, KY) 69309
Standard Register Co. (Cockysville Hunt Valley, MD) 71559
Standard Register Co. (Salisbury, MD) 72362
Standard Register Co. (Charlotte, NC) 74163
Standard Register Co. (Murfreesboro, TN) 81868
Standard Register Co. (Beaumont, TX) 83214
Standard Register Co. (Rocky Mount, VA) 92204
Standard Register Houston Div. (Houston, TX) 86911
Stanfast Inc. (Carrollton, TX) 83506
Stanhome Inc. (Charlotte, NC) 74164
Stanhome Inc. (San Antonio, TX) 89233
Stanley-Bostitch Inc. (Atlanta, GA) 65168
Stanley-Bostitch Inc. Hamlet Plant (Hamlet, NC) 75001
Stanley Door Systems (Orlando, FL) 62148
Stanley Hardware Wondura Products (Tupelo, MS) 73426
Stanley Proto Industrial Tools (Wichita Falls, TX) 90102
Stanley Tools (Cheraw, SC) 78924
Stanley Tools (Shelbyville, TN) 82317
Stanley Works (Cheraw, SC) 78925
Stanley Works Mechanics Tool Division (Wichita Falls, TX) 90103
Stanley Works Stanley Hardware Division (Richmond, VA) 92047
Stanley Works Stanley Tools Division (Cheraw, SC) 78926
Stanric Inc. (Puerto Real, PR) 78538
Stanric Inc. Pto. Real Industrial Park (Fajardo, PR) 78414; 78415
Star Bank NA, Kentucky (Alexandria, KY) 68079
Star Bank NA, Kentucky (Carrollton, KY) 68192
Star Bank NA, Kentucky (Cold Spring, KY) 68206
Star Bank NA, Kentucky (Covington, KY) 68233; 68234; 68235; 68236; 68237
Star Bank NA, Kentucky (Crescent Springs, KY) 68243
Star Bank NA, Kentucky (Crestview Hills, KY) 68244
Star Bank NA, Kentucky (Elsemere, KY) 68295
Star Bank NA, Kentucky (Falmouth, KY) 68301; 68302
Star Bank NA, Kentucky (Florence, KY) 68337; 68338; 68339
Star Bank NA, Kentucky (Florene, KY) 68346
Star Bank NA, Kentucky (Fort Mitchell, KY) 68349
Star Bank NA, Kentucky (Fort Thomas, KY) 68353
Star Bank NA, Kentucky (Fort Wright, KY) 68355
Star Bank NA, Kentucky (Independence, KY) 68486
Star Bank NA, Kentucky (Lebanon, KY) 68510
Star Bank NA, Kentucky (Loretto, KY) 68673
Star Bank NA, Kentucky (Newport, KY) 69143; 69144
Star Bank NA, Kentucky (Taylor Mill, KY) 69313
Star Bank NA, Kentucky (Verona, KY) 69324
Star Bank NA, Kentucky (Walton, KY) 69335
Star Enterprise Delaware City Refinery (Delaware City, DE) 57773
Star Kist Caribe Inc. (Mayaguez, PR) 78513; 78514
Star-Kist Caribe Inc. (Mayaquez, PR) 78518
Star-Kist Foods, Inc. (Newport, KY) 69145
Star-Kist Foods, Inc. (Biloxi, MS) 72639
Star-Kist Foods, Inc. (El Paso, TX) 84932
Star Manufacturing Co. (Doraville, GA) 65952
Star Manufacturing Co. (Tucker, GA) 67892
Star Manufacturing Co. (Oklahoma City, OK) 77561
Star Market (Columbia, SC) 79098
Star Market (Strasburg, VA) 92350
Star Market Inc. (Miami, FL) 61466
Star Marketing Co. (Dallas, TX) 84399
Star Telegram (Fort Worth, TX) 85278; 85279
Starkist Foods Inc. Pet Food Div. (Weirton, WV) 93100
Starmark of Virginia (Lynchburg, VA) 91289
State Fair Foods Inc. (Dallas, TX) 84400; 84401
State Mutual of America (Tampa, FL) 63603
State Mutual of America (Austin, TX) 83006
State Street Bank & Trust Co. (Atlanta, GA) 65169
Stauffer Chemical Co. (Bastrop, LA) 69451
Stauffer Chemical Co. Furnace Plant (Mount Pleasant, TN) 81828
Stearns & Foster Co. (Brenham, TX) 83343
Steiner Bank (Birmingham, AL) 55395; 55396
Steiner Liff Textile Produc (Nashville, TN) 82101
Steiner Liff Textile Products Co. (Nashville, TN) 82102
Stemco Inc. (Longview, TX) 87736
Sterling Advertising (Birmingham, AL) 55397
Sterling Advertising (Lawrenceville, GA) 66538
Sterling Advertising, Ltd. (North Wilkesboro, NC) 75766
Sterling Bank (Montgomery, AL) 56381; 56382
Sterling Chemicals Inc. (Texas City, TX) 89737
Sterling Drug Inc. (Gulfport, MS) 72876
Sterling Eng. Prods. Inc. (Franklin, TN) 80824
Sterling Engineered Products (Mooresville, NC) 75609
Sterling Engineered Products (Morristown, TN) 81810
Sterling Health (Gulfport, MS) 72877
Sterling Pharmaceuticals Inc. (Barceloneta, PR) 78331
Sterwin Laboratories (Millsboro, DE) 57849
Sterwin Laboratories (Gainesville, GA) 66292
Sterwin Laboratories Inc. (Auburn, AL) 55071
Sterwin Labs Imc (Springdale, AR) 57644
Stevcoknit Fabric Co. Maiden (Maiden, NC) 75495
Stevcoknit Fabrics Co. (Fayetteville, NC) 74576
Stevcoknit Fabrics Co. (Wallace, NC) 76444
Stevcoknit Fabrics Co. (Edgefield, SC) 79185
Stevcoknit Fabrics Co. (Greer, SC) 79482
Stevcoknit Fabrics Co. Carter Plant (Wallace, NC) 76445
Stevens Graphics (richmond, VA) 92048
Stevens Graphics Business (Green Springs, FL) 59930
Stevens Graphics Corp. (Fort Worth, TX) 85280
Stevens Graphics Inc. (Birmingham, AL) 55398
Stevens Graphics Inc. (Atlanta, GA) 65170; 65171; 65172
Stewart & Stevenson (Houston, TX) **86912**
Stewart & Stevenson Inc. (Houston, TX) 86913
Stewart & Stevenson Service Inc. (San Juan, TX) 89335
Stewart & Stevenson Services (Austin, TX) 83007
Stewart & Stevenson Services Inc. (Houston, TX) 86914
Stewart & Stevenson SVC (Harvey, LA) 69942
Stewart & Stevenson SVC (Dallas, TX) 84402
Stewart & Stevenson SVC (Houston, TX) 86915; 86916; 86917
Stillwell Foods Inc. (Stillwell, OK) 77848
Stilwell Foods Inc. (Stilwell, OK) 77851
Stock Equipment Co. (Lynn Haven, FL) 60957
Stockholder Systems Inc. (Norcross, GA) 67189
Stokely USA Inc. (Mc Allen, TX) 87900
Stone Container Corp. (Birmingham, AL) 55399
Stone Container Corp. (Jacksonville, AR) 57202
Stone Container Corp. (Sheridan, AR) 57614
Stone Container Corp. (Orlando, FL) 62149
Stone Container Corp. (Panama City, FL) 62351
Stone Container Corp. (Yulee, FL) 64005
Stone Container Corp. (Lithonia, GA) 66609
Stone Container Corp. (Port Wentworth, GA) 67277
Stone Container Corp. (Savannah, GA) 67515
Stone Container Corp. (Jeffersontown, KY) 68500
Stone Container Corp. (Louisville, KY) 69010
Stone Container Corp. (Arcadia, LA) 69430
Stone Container Corp. (Hodge, LA) 69946
Stone Container Corp. (Tupelo, MS) 73427
Stone Container Corp. (Lexington, NC) 75425
Stone Container Corp. (Sand Springs, OK) 77785
Stone Container Corp. (Florence, SC) 79227
Stone Container Corp. (Orangeburg, SC) 79778
Stone Container Corp. (Collierville, TN) 80622
Stone Container Corp. (Nashville, TN) 82103
Stone Container Corp. (Hopewell, VA) 91165
Stone Container Corp. (Martinsville, VA) 91359
Stone Container Corp. (Moseley, VA) 91434
Stone Container Corp. (Richmond, VA) 92049; 92050
Stone Container Corp. (Wellsburg, WV) 93104
Stone Container Corp. Containerboard & Paper Division (Florence, SC) 79228
Stone Container Corp. Corrugated Container Div. (Pineville, NC) 75827
Stone Container Corp. Corrugate (Atlanta, GA) 65173; 65174
Stone Container Corp. Corrugate (Lithonia, GA) 66610
Stone Hodge Inc. (Hodge, LA) 69947
Stone Hopewell Inc. (Hopewell, VA) 91166
Stone Savannah River Pulp & Paper (Port Wentworth, GA) 67278
Stonehouse Inc. (West Point, VA) 92543
Stonewall Insurance Co. (Birmingham, AL) 55400
Stop & Shop (Mobile, AL) 56241
Stop & Shop (Avon Park, FL) 58611
Stop & Shop (Clewiston, FL) 59063
Stop & Shop (Jacksonville, FL) 60458; 60459
Stop & Shop (Tampa, FL) 63604
Stop & Shop (Statesboro, GA) 67650
Stop & Shop (Irvine, KY) 68488
Stop & Shop (Prestonsburg, KY) 69229
Stop & Shop (Shreveport, LA) 70785
Stop & Shop (Baltimore, MD) 71314
Stop & Shop (Lucedale, MS) 73129
Stop & Shop (Lillington, NC) 75435
Stop & Shop (Reidsville, NC) 76014
Stop & Shop (Rocky Mount, NC) 76104
Stop & Shop (Oklahoma City, OK) 77562
Stop & Shop (Greenfield, TN) 80894
Stop & Shop (Morristown, TN) 81811
Stop & Shop (Ripley, TN) 82265
Stop & Shop (Fort Stockton, TX) 85049
Stop & Shop (Fort Worth, TX) 85281
Stop & Shop (Galveston, TX) 85466
Stop & Shop (Houston, TX) 86918
Stop & Shop (Clarksville, VA) 90639
Stop & Shop (Floyd, VA) 90882
Stop & Shop (Fredericksburg, VA) 90943
Stop & Shop (Kopperston, WV) 92913
Stop & Shop (Seth, WV) 93041
Stop & Shop Bar B Q Inc. (Lafayette, LA) 70106
Stop & Shop Food Mart (Elizabethtown, NC) 74492
Stop & Shop Food Store (Sunrise, FL) 63200
Stop & Shop Food Store Inc. (Boca Raton, FL) 58743
Stop & Shop Grocery (Mer Rouge, LA) 70240
Stop & Shop Grocery (Monroe, LA) 70377
Stop & Shop Grocery (Montegut, LA) 70386
Stop & Shop Grocery (Center, TX) 83541
Stop & Shop Grocery (El Paso, TX) 84933
Stop & Shop Grocery (Goldthwaite, TX) 85585
Stop & Shop Grocery (Newcastle, TX) 88226
Stop & Shop Liquors (Pensacola, FL) 62473
Stop & Shop No. 1645 (Colbert, OK) 76967
Stop & Shop Pawn (Ocala, FL) 61822
Stop & Shop Store (Anniston, AL) 55014
Stop & Shop Superette (Castlewood, VA) 90509
Stop & Shop Supermarket (Castlewood, VA) 90510
Stop & Shop Whitesburg (Whitesburg, GA) 68051
Storage Tek Printer Operations (Palm Bay, FL) 62244
Stratoflex Inc. Aerospace & Military Div. (Fort Worth, TX) 85282
Stratos Boats Inc. (Old Hickory, TN) 82207
Stratton Field Office (Bishop, TX) 83305
Structural Metals Inc. (Seguin, TX) 89375
Structure (Washington, DC) 58494
Structure (Atl, GA) 64183
Structure (Atlanta, GA) 65175; 65176; 65177; 65178
Structure (Kennesaw, GA) 66450
Structure (Morrow, GA) 67046
Structure (Bethesda, MD) 71443
Structure (Kensington, MD) 72002
Structure (Montgomery Co, MD) 72148
Structure (Fort Worth, TX) 85283
Structure Corp. (Huntingtown, MD) 71948
Structure Tone Interior Design (Washington, DC) 58495
Structured Management Syste (Richmond, VA) 92051; 92052
Structured Mgt Systems Inc. (Richmond, VA) 92053
Structured Shelt Richmond (Richmond, VA) 92054
Structures Inc. (Baltimore, MD) 71315
Structures Unlimited (Forest, VA) 90884
Structures Unlimited (Fredericksburg, VA) 90944
Strunk Lumberyard Inc. (Key West, FL) 60579
Sts-Klock (Palm Beach Gardens, FL) 62274
Student Loan Marketing Association (Washington, DC) **58496**; 58497; 58498
Student Loan Marketing Association (Antioch, TN) 80175
Studio W (Nashville, TN) 82104
Stylelander Metal Stamping Inc. (Verona, MS) 73450
Subsea Venture Inc. (Houston, TX) 86919
Sullivan Graphics (Dallas, TX) 84403
Sullivan Graphics (San Antonio, TX) 89234
Sullivan Graphics Inc. (Decatur, GA) 65897
Sullivan Graphics Inc. (Lufkin, TX) 87819
Summit Corporate Center (Charleston, SC) 78893
Summit Corp. (Ashland, KY) 68106
Summit Corp. (St. Albans, WV) 93070
Summitt Insulators Pc (Memphis, TN) 81700
Sumter Bank & Trust Co. (Americus, GA) 64144; 64145
Sumter Bank & Trust Co. (Leslie, GA) 66550
Sun Diamond Growers (Robertsdale, AL) 56503
Sun Diamond Growers (Richardson, TX) 88777
Sun Microsystems Inc. (Huntsville, AL) 56024
Sun Microsystems Inc. (Tulsa, OK) 78116
Sun Microsystems Inc. (Columbia, SC) 79099
Sun Microsystems Inc. (Austin, TX) 83008
Sun Microsystems Inc. (Dallas, TX) 84404
Sun Microsystems Inc. (Vienna, VA) 92422
Sun Refining & Marketing (Tulsa, OK) 78117
Sun Refining & Marketing (Corpus Christi, TX) 83754
Sun Refining & Marketing (Midland, TX) 88081
Sun Refining & Marketing Co. (De Valls Bluff, AR) 56901
Sun Refining & Marketing Co. (Rison, AR) 57556
Sun Refining & Marketing Co. (Tampa, FL) 63605
Sun Refining & Marketing Co. (Henderson, KY) 68457
Sun Refining & Marketing Co. (Chickasha, OK) 76938
Sun Refining & Marketing Co. (Tulsa, OK) 78118; 78119
Sun Refining & Marketing Co. (Houston, TX) 86920
Sun Refining & Marketing Co. (Nederland, TX) 88193
Sun Trust Bank Inc. (Atlanta, GA) 65179
Sunbeam Appliance Co. (Houston, TX) 86921
Sunbeam/Oster (Fort Lauderdale, FL) **59613**
Sunbeam Oster (Shubuta, MS) 73344

Sunbeam Oster Co. Inc. (Ft. Lauderdale, FL) 59855
Sunbeam-Oster Corp. (Coushatta, LA) 69792
Sunbeam-Oster Household Products (Holly Springs, MS) 72910; 72911
Sunbeam Outdoor Products (Paragould, AR) 57496
Sunbeam Outdoor Products (Waynesboro, GA) 68047
Sunbeam Outdoor Products (Portland, TN) 82235
Sunbean Outdoor Prods. (Paragould, AR) 57497
Sunbird Boat Co. (Columbia, SC) 79100
Sunbird Boat Co. Inc. (Columbia, SC) 79101; 79102
Sundstrand Service Corp. (Oklahoma City, OK) 77563
Sunlink Corp. (Atlanta, GA) 65180
Sunoco Products Co. (Orlando, FL) 62150
Sunrise Properties (Fort Worth, TX) 85284
Sunrise Properties (Glen Rose, TX) 85584
Suntrust Banks (Atlanta, GA) **65181**
Sunwest Bank of El Paso (El Paso, TX) 84934; 84935
Super America Group, Inc. (Lexington, KY) 68632
Super G Inc. (Landover, MD) 72033
Super Saver (Hot Springs National Park, AR) 57184
Super Saver (New Orleans, LA) 70560
Super Saver (Sulphur, LA) 70891
Super Saver (Aberdeen, MS) 72579
Super Saver (Columbus, MS) 72728
Super Saver (Pickens, MS) 73298
Super Saver (Woodville, MS) 73497
Super Saver (Wilmington, NC) 76596
Super Saver (Ada, OK) 76788; 76789
Super Saver (Katy, TX) 87456
Super Saver Station (Oklahoma City, OK) 77564; 77565; 77566; 77567
Super Saver Station (Tulsa, OK) 78120
Super Saver Warehouse Foods (Lakeland, FL) 60784
Super Saver Wholesale Club (Shreveport, LA) 70786
Superamerica (Ashland, KY) 68107
Superamerica (Bardstown, KY) 68120
Superamerica (Covington, KY) 68238
Superamerica (Lexington, KY) 68633; 68634; 68635; 68636; 68637; 68638
Superamerica (Maysville, KY) 69091
Superamerica (Newport, KY) 69146
Superamerica (Buckhannon, WV) 92718
Superamerica (Pt Pleasant, WV) 93016
Superamerica Design & Const (Louisville, KY) 69011
Superamerica 5086 (Belle, WV) 92697
SuperAmerica Group, Inc. (Lexington, KY) 68639
Superamerica No 5677 (Lexington, KY) 68640
Superamerica Store 5675 (Lexington, KY) 68641
Superior Coffee & Foods (Norcross, GA) 67190
Superior Coffee & Foods (New Orleans, LA) 70561
Superior Federal Bank, FSB (Arkadelphia, AR) 56721
Superior Federal Bank, FSB (Benton, AR) 56776; 56777
Superior Federal Bank, FSB (Brinkley, AR) 56822
Superior Federal Bank, FSB (Carlisle, AR) 56844
Superior Federal Bank, FSB (Danville, AR) 56887
Superior Federal Bank, FSB (England, AR) 56966
Superior Federal Bank, FSB (Fayetteville, AR) 56993; 56994
Superior Federal Bank, FSB (Marshall, AR) 57349
Superior Federal Bank, FSB (Paris, AR) 57500
Superior Federal Bank, FSB (Siloam Springs, AR) 57623
Superior Life Insurance (Monroe, LA) 70378
Superior Pools Products Inc. (Fort Pierce, FL) 59814
Superwood Corp. (North Little Rock, AR) 57476
Supreme Sugar Co. (New Orleans, LA) 70562
Supreme Sugar Co., Inc. (Labadieville, LA) 70032; 70033; 70034; 70035
Supreme Sugar Co., Inc. (Metairie, LA) 70312
Supreme Sugar Co. Inc. (New Orleans, LA) 70563; 70564
Surgikos (Arlington, TX) 82753
Sutter Corp. (College Pk, MD) 71569
Swaco Geolograph Operations (Houston, TX) 86922
SWECO Inc. (Florence, KY) 68340; 68341; 68342
Sweet Sue Kitchens (Athens, AL) 55047
Sweet Sue Kitchens Inc. (Athens, AL) 55048
Swift Independent Packing Co. (Morristown, TN) 81812
Swift Independent Packing Co. (Nashville, TN) 82105
Sybra Inc. (Clair Mel City, FL) 58957
Syltron Inc. Lighting Products (Luquillo, PR) 78491
Sylvachem Corp. (Port St. Joe, FL) 62694
Sylvachem Corp. (Picayune, MS) 73295
Synovus Financial Corp. (Columbus, GA) **65651**; 65652
Sysco (Houston, TX) **86923**
Sysco Corp. (Houston, TX) 86924
Sysco Food Service (Ocoee, FL) 61839
Sysco Food Services (Palm Beach Gardens, FL) 62275
Sysco Food Services (Mcallen, TX) 87941
Sysco Food Services of Atlanta (College Park, GA) 65605
Sysco Food Services Inc. (Austin, TX) 83009
Sysco Food Services Inc. (Houston, TX) 86925
Syscon Corp. (Washington, DC) 58499
Syscon Corp. (Tampa, FL) 63606
Syscon Corp. (Metairie, LA) 70313
Syscon Corp. (Columbia, MD) 71601
Syscon Corp. (Assawoman, VA) 90408
Syscon Corp. (King George, VA) 91181
Syscon Corp. (Virginia Beach, VA) 92518
Syscon Corp. (Williamsburg, VA) 92579
Syscon Services Inc. (Washington, DC) 58500
Systech Corp. (Demopolis, AL) 55618
Systech Environmental Corp. (Demopolis, AL) 55619
System Devices & Supplies Inc. (Miami, FL) 61467
System Energy Resources Inc. (Jackson, MS) 73067; 73068
System One Information Management Inc. (Houston, TX) 86926
Systematics Information Services Inc. (Little Rock, AR) 57313
Systems Control Inc. (Houston, TX) 86927
Systems Control Inc. (Springfield, VA) 92293
Systems Engineering (Louisville, KY) 69012
Systems Engineering Associates International (Melbourne Beach, FL) 61124
Systems Engineering Solutions Inc. (Vienna, VA) 92423
Systems Research Laboratories (Pensacola, FL) 62474
Systems Research Labs Inc. (San Antonio, TX) 89235; 89236; 89237
Systems & Services (Greenville, SC) 79437
SYTECH Corp. (Charleston, SC) 78894
SYTECH Corp. (Houston, TX) 86928

T

T. G. Lee Foods Inc. (Orange City, FL) 61875
T. G. Lee Foods Inc. (Orlando, FL) 62151; 62152
T J Maxx (Birmingham, AL) 55401; 55402; 55403
T J Maxx (Montgomery, AL) 56383
T J Maxx (Boca Raton, FL) 58744
T J Maxx (Fort Lauderdale, FL) 59614
T J Maxx (Gainesville, FL) 59919
T J Maxx (Miami, FL) 61468
T J Maxx (Pensacola, FL) 62475
T J Maxx (Alpharetta, GA) 64135
T J Maxx (Atlanta, GA) 65182
T J Maxx (Decatur, GA) 65898
T J Maxx (Doraville, GA) 65953
T J Maxx (Duluth, GA) 66082
T J Maxx (Kennesaw, GA) 66451
T J Maxx (Marietta, GA) 66921; 66922
T J Maxx (Morrow, GA) 67047
T J Maxx (Stone Mountain, GA) 67735
T J Maxx (Baton Rouge, LA) 69661
T J Maxx (Charlotte, NC) 74165
T J Maxx (Oklahoma City, OK) 77568
T J Maxx (Charleston, SC) 78895; 78896
T J Maxx (Spartanburg, SC) 79954
T J Maxx (Arlington, TX) 82754
T J Maxx (Dallas, TX) 84405
T J Maxx (Houston, TX) 86929; 86930
T J Maxx (Irving, TX) 87403
T J Maxx (Richardson, TX) 88778
T J Maxx Clothes Store (Austin, TX) 83010
T J Maxx Dept Stor (Plano, TX) 88609
T J Maxx No Two Seventy Fiv (Houston, TX) 86931
T J Maxx Real Estate Ofc (Atlanta, GA) 65183
T J Maxx Regional Office (Atlanta, GA) 65184
T J Maxx Regional Office (Dallas, TX) 84406
T J Maxx Store (Savannah, GA) 67516
T J Maxx Store (Raleigh, NC) 75957
T J Maxx Store (Winston Salem, NC) 76686
T J Maxx Store (Tulsa, OK) 78121
T J Maxx Store (Carrollton, TX) 83507
A T Massey Coal Co. Inc. (Richmond, VA) 92055
T X T Mortgage Co. (Dallas, TX) 84407
Table Pride Inc. (Chamblee, GA) 65544
Taco Bell (Anniston, AL) 55015
Taco Bell (Auburn, AL) 55072
Taco Bell (Bessemer, AL) 55103
Taco Bell (Birmingham, AL) 55404; 55405; 55406; 55407; 55408; 55409; 55410; 55411; 55412; 55413; 55414; 55415; 55416; 55417
Taco Bell (Boaz, AL) 55476
Taco Bell (Brewton, AL) 55484
Taco Bell (Cullman, AL) 55552
Taco Bell (Decatur, AL) 55605; 55606
Taco Bell (Dothan, AL) 55671
Taco Bell (Gadsden, AL) 55791; 55792
Taco Bell (Huntsville, AL) 56025; 56026; 56027; 56028; 56029; 56030
Taco Bell (Mobile, AL) 56242; 56243; 56244
Taco Bell (Scottsboro, AL) 56524
Taco Bell (Selma, AL) 56539
Taco Bell (Tuscaloosa, AL) 56676
Taco Bell (Benton, AR) 56778
Taco Bell (Conway, AR) 56872
Taco Bell (El Dorado, AR) 56959
Taco Bell (Fayetteville, AR) 56995; 56996
Taco Bell (Fort Smith, AR) 57100; 57101; 57102; 57103
Taco Bell (H Spg Nat Pk, AR) 57133; 57134
Taco Bell (Jacksonville, AR) 57203
Taco Bell (Jonesboro, AR) 57231
Taco Bell (Monticello, AR) 57374
Taco Bell (N Little Rock, AR) 57423; 57424; 57425; 57426; 57427; 57428
Taco Bell (Pine Bluff, AR) 57531
Taco Bell (Rogers, AR) 57570
Taco Bell (Russellville, AR) 57590
Taco Bell (Van Buren, AR) 57694
Taco Bell (West Memphis, AR) 57736
Taco Bell (Altamonte Spg, FL) 58546
Taco Bell (Boca Raton, FL) 58745
Taco Bell (Casselberry, FL) 58943
Taco Bell (Clearwater, FL) 59048
Taco Bell (Daytona Beach, FL) 59215; 59216
Taco Bell (Fernandina Beach, FL) 59414
Taco Bell (Fort Lauderdale, FL) 59615; 59616
Taco Bell (Fort Myers, FL) 59763; 59764; 59765; 59766
Taco Bell (Fort Walton Beach, FL) 59839
Taco Bell (Gainesville, FL) 59920; 59921
Taco Bell (Hialeah, FL) 60011
Taco Bell (Hollywood, FL) 60097; 60098
Taco Bell (Jacksonville, FL) 60460; 60461; 60462; 60463; 60464; 60465; 60466; 60467; 60468; 60469; 60470
Taco Bell (Jupiter, FL) 60552
Taco Bell (Kissimmee, FL) 60602
Taco Bell (Lake City, FL) 60629; 60630
Taco Bell (Lake Mary, FL) 60639
Taco Bell (Lakeland, FL) 60785
Taco Bell (Largo, FL) 60864
Taco Bell (Leesburg, FL) 60887
Taco Bell (Longwood, FL) 60949
Taco Bell (Mary Esther, FL) 61023
Taco Bell (Melbourne, FL) 61107; 61108; 61109
Taco Bell (Merritt is, FL) 61133
Taco Bell (Miami, FL) 61469; 61470; 61471
Taco Bell (Naples, FL) 61665
Taco Bell (North Fort Myers, FL) 61729
Taco Bell (Orange Park, FL) 61898
Taco Bell (Orlando, FL) 62153; 62154; 62155; 62156; 62157
Taco Bell (Panama City, FL) 62352
Taco Bell (Pensacola, FL) 62476; 62477; 62478; 62479; 62480
Taco Bell (Pinellas Park, FL) 62528
Taco Bell (Sanford, FL) 62781
Taco Bell (St Petersburg, FL) 63035
Taco Bell (Starke, FL) 63152
Taco Bell (Tallahassee, FL) 63272; 63273; 63274
Taco Bell (Tampa, FL) 63607; 63608; 63609; 63610
Taco Bell (Titusville, FL) 63704; 63705
Taco Bell (W Palm Beach, FL) 63815
Taco Bell (West Palm Beach, FL) 63902; 63903
Taco Bell (Winter Garden, FL) 63924
Taco Bell (Winter Haven, FL) 63953
Taco Bell (Winter Park, FL) 63995
Taco Bell (Winter Springs, FL) 64004
Taco Bell (Zephyrhills, FL) 64028
Taco Bell (Acworth, GA) 64053
Taco Bell (Alpharetta, GA) 64136
Taco Bell (Atlanta, GA) 65185; 65186; 65187; 65188; 65189; 65190; 65191; 65192; 65193; 65194
Taco Bell (Austell, GA) 65358
Taco Bell (Bainbridge, GA) 65370
Taco Bell (Buford, GA) 65445
Taco Bell (Chamblee, GA) 65545
Taco Bell (Conyers, GA) 65705
Taco Bell (Decatur, GA) 65899; 65900; 65901
Taco Bell (Doraville, GA) 65954
Taco Bell (Douglasville, GA) 66002; 66003
Taco Bell (Duluth, GA) 66083; 66084
Taco Bell (East Point, GA) 66154
Taco Bell (Fayetteville, GA) 66204
Taco Bell (Forest Park, GA) 66250
Taco Bell (Griffin, GA) 66326
Taco Bell (Jonesboro, GA) 66400; 66401
Taco Bell (Kennesaw, GA) 66452; 66453
Taco Bell (Lawrenceville, GA) 66539; 66540
Taco Bell (Lilburn, GA) 66579
Taco Bell (Lithia Spring, GA) 66586
Taco Bell (Mableton, GA) 66642
Taco Bell (Macon, GA) 66714
Taco Bell (Marietta, GA) 66923; 66924; 66925; 66926; 66927; 66928; 66929
Taco Bell (Mcdonough, GA) 66970
Taco Bell (Morrow, GA) 67048
Taco Bell (Norcross, GA) 67191; 67192; 67193
Taco Bell (Peachtree Cit, GA) 67240
Taco Bell (Powder Spring, GA) 67285
Taco Bell (Riverdale, GA) 67326
Taco Bell (Roswell, GA) 67419
Taco Bell (Smyrna, GA) 67576; 67577; 67578
Taco Bell (Snellville, GA) 67612
Taco Bell (Stockbridge, GA) 67669
Taco Bell (Stone Mountai, GA) 67674; 67675
Taco Bell (Suwanee, GA) 67751
Taco Bell (Tucker, GA) 67893; 67894
Taco Bell (Union City, GA) 67929; 67930
Taco Bell (Woodstock, GA) 68075
Taco Bell (Alexandria, LA) 69411
Taco Bell (Baton Rouge, LA) 69662; 69663; 69664; 69665; 69666; 69667; 69668; 69669
Taco Bell (Bossier City, LA) 69733
Taco Bell (Chalmette, LA) 69768; 69769
Taco Bell (Eunice, LA) 69848
Taco Bell (Hammond, LA) 69934
Taco Bell (Jennings, LA) 69981
Taco Bell (Kenner, LA) 70018; 70019; 70020
Taco Bell (Lafayette, LA) 70107; 70108; 70109; 70110; 70111; 70112; 70113
Taco Bell (Lake Charles, LA) 70173; 70174; 70175
Taco Bell (Marrero, LA) 70235
Taco Bell (Metairie, LA) 70314; 70315; 70316
Taco Bell (Monroe, LA) 70379
Taco Bell (Morgan City, LA) 70394
Taco Bell (Natchitoches, LA) 70404
Taco Bell (New Orleans, LA) 70565
Taco Bell (Pineville, LA) 70632
Taco Bell (Shreveport, LA) 70787; 70788; 70789; 70790
Taco Bell (Slidell, LA) 70840; 70841; 70842
Taco Bell (Sulphur, LA) 70892
Taco Bell (Westwego, LA) 70973
Taco Bell (Biloxi, MS) 72640
Taco Bell (Gautier, MS) 72787
Taco Bell (Greenville, MS) 72821
Taco Bell (Grenada, MS) 72848
Taco Bell (Gulfport, MS) 72878; 72879
Taco Bell (Jackson, MS) 73069; 73070; 73071; 73072
Taco Bell (Meridian, MS) 73179
Taco Bell (Ocean Springs, MS) 73223
Taco Bell (Pascagoula, MS) 73272
Taco Bell (Southaven, MS) 73356
Taco Bell (Albemarle, NC) 73542
Taco Bell (Boone, NC) 73717
Taco Bell (Chapel Hill, NC) 73821
Taco Bell (Charlotte, NC) 74166; 74167; 74168
Taco Bell (Concord, NC) 74323
Taco Bell (Elizabeth Cty, NC) 74486
Taco Bell (Greensboro, NC) 74916; 74917; 74918; 74919
Taco Bell (Greenville, NC) 74978; 74979
Taco Bell (High Point, NC) 75172
Taco Bell (Jacksonville, NC) 75230; 75231
Taco Bell (Kannapolis, NC) 75268
Taco Bell (Lewisville, NC) 75396
Taco Bell (Raleigh, NC) 75958; 75959; 75960
Taco Bell (Roanoke Rpds, NC) 76044
Taco Bell (Rocky Mount, NC) 76105
Taco Bell (Southern Pnes, NC) 76280
Taco Bell (Wake Forest, NC) 76435
Taco Bell (Wilmington, NC) 76597; 76598
Taco Bell (Wilson, NC) 76647
Taco Bell (Ardmore, OK) 76821
Taco Bell (Claremore, OK) 76957
Taco Bell (Del City, OK) 76988
Taco Bell (Duncan, OK) 76998
Taco Bell (Edmond, OK) 77019; 77020; 77021
Taco Bell (Lawton, OK) 77174; 77175
Taco Bell (Muskogee, OK) 77229
Taco Bell (Mustang, OK) 77240
Taco Bell (Norman, OK) 77275; 77276; 77277
Taco Bell (Oklahoma City, OK) 77569; 77570; 77571; 77572; 77573; 77574; 77575; 77576; 77577; 77578; 77579; 77580; 77581; 77582; 77583; 77584; 77585; 77586; 77587; 77588; 77589; 77590; 77591; 77592; 77593
Taco Bell (Ponca City, OK) 77713
Taco Bell (Sand Springs, OK) 77786
Taco Bell (Tulsa, OK) 78122; 78123; 78124; 78125; 78126; 78127; 78128; 78129
Taco Bell (Yukon, OK) 78282
Taco Bell (Beaufort, SC) 78719
Taco Bell (Cayce, SC) 78780
Taco Bell (Charleston, SC) 78897; 78898; 78899; 78900; 78901
Taco Bell (Columbia, SC) 79103; 79104; 79105; 79106
Taco Bell (Greer, SC) 79483
Taco Bell (Mt Pleasant, SC) 79682
Taco Bell (Myrtle Beach, SC) 79714; 79715
Taco Bell (Rock Hill, SC) 79842
Taco Bell (Spartanburg, SC) 79955; 79956
Taco Bell (Sumter, SC) 80032

Texaco (Corpus Christi, TX) 83755; 83756; 83757; 83758; 83759
Texaco (El Paso, TX) 84946
Texaco (Houston, TX) 86981; 86982; 86983; 86984; 86985; 86986; 86987
Texaco (Johnson City, TX) 87444
Texaco (Liberty, TX) 87681
Texaco (McAllen, TX) 87942
Texaco (Mesquite, TX) 88006
Texaco (Midland, TX) 88082
Texaco (Richardson, TX) 88782
Texaco (San Antonio, TX) 89257
Texaco (Sour Lake, TX) 89457
Texaco (Terrell, TX) 89662
Texaco (Vernon, TX) 89872
Texaco Auto Service (Troy, AL) 56621
Texaco Auto Service (Wynne, AR) 57746
Texaco Auto Service Ctr (Tyler, TX) 89834
Texaco Auto Truck Stop (Lk Panasoffke, FL) 60922
Texaco Bulk Plant (Murray, KY) 69134
Texaco Car Care Center (Houston, TX) 86988
Texaco Chemical Co. (Austin, TX) 83027
Texaco Chemical Co. (Conroe, TX) 83686
Texaco Chemical Co. (Port Neches, TX) 88676
Texaco Chemical Co. Port Arthur Chemical Plant (Port Arthur, TX) 88647
Texaco Corporate Library (New Orleans, LA) 70567
Texaco Corp. (Hawthorne, FL) 59973
Texaco Delaware City Plant (Delaware City, DE) 57774
Texaco Dist (Plaquemine, LA) 70643
Texaco Distbtr (Benton, AR) 56779
Texaco Distrbtr (Fredericksbrg, TX) 85375
Texaco Distribution (Hearne, TX) 85727
Texaco Distributor (Pawhuska, OK) 77697
Texaco Distributor (Greeneville, TN) 80889
Texaco Distributor (Caldwell, TX) 83432
Texaco Distributor (Madisonville, TX) 87828
Texaco Distributors (Aberdeen, MS) 72580
Texaco Express Lub (Little Rock, AR) 57314
Texaco Express Lub (Arlington, TX) 82765
Texaco Express Lub (Carrollton, TX) 83510
Texaco Express Lub (Port Arthur, TX) 88648
Texaco Express Lube (Dolomite, AL) 55621
Texaco Express Lube (Van Buren, AR) 57695
Texaco Express Lube (Jacksonville, FL) 60473; 60474
Texaco Express Lube (Atlanta, GA) 65204; 65205
Texaco Express Lube (Douglas, GA) 65976
Texaco Express Lube (Douglasville, GA) 66005
Texaco Express Lube (Duluth, GA) 66089
Texaco Express Lube (Marietta, GA) 66939
Texaco Express Lube (Tucker, GA) 67897
Texaco Express Lube (Lancaster, SC) 79580
Texaco Express Lube (Chattanooga, TN) 80503
Texaco Express Lube (Del Rio, TX) 84588
Texaco Express Lube (Tyler, TX) 89835
Texaco Express Lube Auto Serv (Duluth, GA) 66090
Texaco Express Lube Sandy Plai (Marietta, GA) 66940
Texaco Express Lube & Tune (Jonesboro, GA) 66404
Texaco Exprss Lube (Moore, OK) 77215
Texaco Exprss Lube (Oklahoma City, OK) 77601
Texaco Exprss Lube (Denton, TX) 84638
Texaco Exprss Lube (Humble, TX) 87247
Texaco Exprss Tube (Granbury, TX) 85599
Texaco Fastop (N Little Rock, AR) 57429
Texaco Fd Mart 1 (Andrews, TX) 82604

Texaco & Food Gas Mart (San Antonio, TX) 89258
Texaco Food Mart (Bessemer, AL) 55104
Texaco Food Mart (Birmingham, AL) 55419
Texaco Food Mart (Guntersville, AL) 55835
Texaco Food Mart (York, AL) 56713
Texaco Food Mart (Beebe, AR) 56769
Texaco Food Mart (Fort Walton Beach, FL) 59840
Texaco Food Mart (Haines City, FL) 59954; 59955
Texaco Food Mart (Kissimmee, FL) 60604; 60605
Texaco Food Mart (Lake City, FL) 60631
Texaco Food Mart (Lakeland, FL) 60786
Texaco Food Mart (Live Oak, FL) 60921
Texaco Food Mart (New Port Richey, FL) 61692
Texaco Food Mart (New Smyrna, FL) 61697
Texaco Food Mart (Orlando, FL) 62162
Texaco Food Mart (Oviedo, FL) 62216
Texaco Food Mart (Sanford, FL) 62782
Texaco Food Mart (Sebring, FL) 62895
Texaco Food Mart (Starke, FL) 63153
Texaco Food Mart (Tallahassee, FL) 63279
Texaco Food Mart (Tampa, FL) 63612; 63613; 63614; 63615
Texaco Food Mart (Winter Garden, FL) 63925
Texaco Food Mart (Winter Haven, FL) 63954
Texaco Food Mart (Winter Park, FL) 63996
Texaco Food Mart (Atlanta, GA) 65206
Texaco Food Mart (Bainbridge, GA) 65371
Texaco Food Mart (College Park, GA) 65607
Texaco Food Mart (Conyers, GA) 65709
Texaco Food Mart (Decatur, GA) 65906
Texaco Food Mart (Doraville, GA) 65957; 65958
Texaco Food Mart (East Point, GA) 66155
Texaco Food Mart (Jonesboro, GA) 66405
Texaco Food Mart (Lawrenceville, GA) 66542
Texaco Food Mart (Macon, GA) 66715
Texaco Food Mart (Riverdale, GA) 67327; 67328
Texaco Food Mart (Hattiesburg, MS) 72898
Texaco Food Mart (Greensboro, NC) 74920; 74921
Texaco Food Mart (Raleigh, NC) 75962
Texaco Food Mart (Robbinsville, NC) 76053
Texaco-Food Mart (Smithfield, NC) 76269
Texaco Food Mart (Wilmington, NC) 76599
Texaco Food Mart (Guymon, OK) 77112
Texaco Food Mart (Oklahoma City, OK) 77602
Texaco Food Mart (Tulsa, OK) 78141; 78142; 78143
Texaco Food Mart (North Augusta, SC) 79740
Texaco Food Mart (Dyersburg, TN) 80761
Texaco Food Mart (Arlington, TX) 82766; 82767; 82768; 82769
Texaco Food Mart (Austin, TX) 83028; 83029
Texaco Food Mart (Beaumont, TX) 83220; 83221; 83222
Texaco Food Mart (Bedford, TX) 83255
Texaco Food Mart (Dallas, TX) 84425; 84426; 84427
Texaco Food Mart (Denton, TX) 84639; 84640
Texaco Food Mart (Fort Worth, TX) 85323; 85324; 85325; 85326; 85327; 85328
Texaco Food Mart (Grand Prairie, TX) 85641
Texaco Food Mart (Houston, TX) 86989; 86990; 86991; 86992; 86993; 86994; 86995; 86996; 86997; 86998; 86999

Texaco Food Mart (Humble, TX) 87248
Texaco Food Mart (Irving, TX) 87412
Texaco Food Mart (Lewisville, TX) 87668
Texaco Food Mart (Lubbock, TX) 87785
Texaco Food Mart (Mesquite, TX) 88007
Texaco Food Mart (Plano, TX) 88613; 88614
Texaco Food Mart (Rosenberg, TX) 88839
Texaco Food Mart (San Antonio, TX) 89259; 89260; 89261
Texaco Food Mart (Spring, TX) 89492; 89493; 89494
Texaco Food Mart (Stafford, TX) 89508
Texaco Food Mart (Tyler, TX) 89836
Texaco Food Mart (Vidor, TX) 89920
Texaco Food Mart (Wichita Falls, TX) 90108; 90109; 90110
Texaco Food Mart & Car Wash (Oklahoma City, OK) 77603
Texaco Food Mart & Gas Stat (Tampa, FL) 63616
Texaco Food Mart Hiram (Hiram, GA) 66363
Texaco Food Mart No 4 (Jamestown, NC) 75243
Texaco Food Mart No One (Temple, TX) 89647
Texaco Food Mart No 7 (Huntsville, AL) 56035
Texaco Food Mart No 71 (San Antonio, TX) 89262
Texaco Food Mart No 6 (Sheffield, AL) 56564
Texaco Food Mart No 2 (Beaumont, TX) 83223
Texaco Food Mart No 2048 (East Point, GA) 66156
Texaco Food Mart 119 (New Port Rich, FL) 61671
Texaco Food Mart 160 (Tulsa, OK) 78144
Texaco Food Mart 2 (Temple, TX) 89648
Texaco Food Marts (Lubbock, TX) 87786
Texaco Food Mrt (Irving, TX) 87413
Texaco Food Shop (College Park, GA) 65608
Texaco Food Shop (Decatur, GA) 65907
Texaco Foodmart (Temple Terrace, FL) 63679
Texaco Foodmart (Stockbridge, GA) 67670
Texaco Foodmart (Arlington, TX) 82770
Texaco Foods (Tampa, FL) 63617
Texaco Fuel Man (Shreveport, LA) 70791
Texaco Full Service (Oklahoma City, OK) 77604
Texaco Gas Bar (Oklahoma City, OK) 77605; 77606
Texaco Gas Bar & Food Mart (Oklahoma City, OK) 77607
Texaco Gas Mart (Montgomery, AL) 56385
Texaco Gas Sta (New Orleans, LA) 70568
Texaco Gas Station (Russellville, KY) 69263
Texaco Gas Station (Oklahoma City, OK) 77608
Texaco Gas Station (College Station, TX) 83624
Texaco Gas Station (Hurst, TX) 87299
Texaco Gas Station & Food M (Daytona Beach, FL) 59217
Texaco Gas Station South (Dallas, TX) 84428
Texaco Gasoline Plant (Ozona, TX) 88337
Texaco Gasoline Station (Dallas, TX) 84429
Texaco Gass Barr (Tulsa, OK) 78145
Texaco-Hanson Hank's (Fort Worth, TX) 85329
Texaco Inc. (Birmingham, AL) 55420
Texaco Inc. (Mobile, AL) 56247; 56248
Texaco Inc. (Conway, AR) 56873
Texaco Inc. (Marvell, AR) 57350
Texaco Inc. (Russellville, AR) 57591
Texaco Inc. (Dade City, FL) 59143
Texaco Inc. (Fort Lauderdale, FL) 59619
Texaco Inc. (Jacksonville, FL) 60475
Texaco Inc. (Lakeland, FL) 60787
Texaco Inc. (Orlando, FL) 62163
Texaco Inc. (Tampa, FL) 63618

Texaco Inc. (Frankfort, KY) 68370
Texaco Inc. (Louisville, KY) 69019
Texaco Inc. (Morganfield, KY) 69108
Texaco Inc. (Owensboro, KY) 69195
Texaco Inc. (Paducah, KY) 69212
Texaco Inc. (Baton Rouge, LA) 69672
Texaco Inc. (Bossier City, LA) 69734
Texaco Inc. (Centerville, LA) 69763
Texaco Inc. (Houma, LA) 69972
Texaco Inc. (Lafayette, LA) 70114
Texaco Inc. (Loreauville, LA) 70200
Texaco Inc. (Morgan City, LA) 70396
Texaco Inc. (New Iberia, LA) 70421
Texaco Inc. (Paradis, LA) 70609; 70610
Texaco Incorporated (Shreveport, LA) 70792; 70793; 70794
Texaco Inc. (Venice, LA) 70926
Texaco Inc. (Yazoo City, MS) 73507
Texaco Inc. (Charlotte, NC) 74169
Texaco Inc. (Greensboro, NC) 74922
Texaco Inc. (Paw Creek, NC) 75791
Texaco Inc. (Ardmore, OK) 76822
Texaco Inc. (Drumright, OK) 76990
Texaco Inc. (Enid, OK) 77071
Texaco Incorporated (Oklahoma City, OK) 77609; 77610; 77611; 77612
Texaco Inc. (Seminole, OK) 77806
Texaco Inc. (Stillwater, OK) 77845
Texaco Incorporated (Tulsa, OK) 78146; 78147; 78148; 78149; 78150
Texaco Inc. (Charleston, SC) 78903
Texaco Inc. (Spartanburg, SC) 79957
Texaco Inc. (Knoxville, TN) 81258
Texaco Inc. (Memphis, TN) 81706
Texaco Inc. (Abilene, TX) 82460
Texaco Inc. (Amarillo, TX) 82583
Texaco Inc. (Andrews, TX) 82605
Texaco Inc. (Aransas Pass, TX) 82625
Texaco Inc. (Ballinger, TX) 83092
Texaco Inc. (Bellaire, TX) 83267
Texaco Inc. (Benavides, TX) 83281
Texaco Inc. (Bogata, TX) 83307
Texaco Inc. (Corpus Christi, TX) 83760
Texaco Inc. (Dallas, TX) 84430
Texaco Inc. (De Kalb, TX) 84527
Texaco Inc. (Electra, TX) 84990
Texaco Inc. (Gainesville, TX) 85428
Texaco Inc. (Georgetown, TX) 85574
Texaco Inc. (Hamilton, TX) 85695
Texaco Inc. (Houston, TX) 87000; 87001; 87002; 87003; 87004
Texaco Inc. (Hull, TX) 87214
Texaco Inc. (Humble, TX) 87249
Texaco Incorporated (Kilgore, TX) 87500
Texaco Inc. (Kingsbury, TX) 87531
Texaco Inc. (Laredo, TX) 87624
Texaco Inc. (Marfa, TX) 87842
Texaco Inc. (Midland, TX) 88083
Texaco Inc. (Mount Vernon, TX) 88156
Texaco Inc. (Odem, TX) 88235
Texaco Inc. (Odessa, TX) 88282; 88283
Texaco Inc. (Olney, TX) 88296
Texaco Inc. (Orla, TX) 88333
Texaco Inc. (Pecos, TX) 88498
Texaco Inc. (Port Arthur, TX) 88649
Texaco Inc. (Port Neches, TX) 88677
Texaco Inc. (Sabinal, TX) 88861
Texaco Inc. (San Isidro, TX) 89333
Texaco Inc. (Seymour, TX) 89388
Texaco Inc. (Snyder, TX) 89453
Texaco Inc. (Sundown, TX) 89568
Texaco Inc. (Sweetwater, TX) 89593
Texaco Inc. (Taylor, TX) 89602
Texaco Inc. (Texarkana, TX) 89712
Texaco Incorporated (Vernon, TX) 89873
Texaco Inc. (Waco, TX) 89980
Texaco Inc. (Waskom, TX) 89990
Texaco Inc. (Weimar, TX) 90028
Texaco Inc. (Weslaco, TX) 90039
Texaco Inc. (Hugheston, WV) 92865
Texaco Inc. (St. Albans, WV) 93071
Texaco Inc. Distributor (Hope, AR) 57159
Texaco Inc. Marketing Dept (Lake Charles, LA) 70176
Texaco Inc. (Ofc) (Tulsa, OK) 78151

Texaco Inc. Prod Dept (Edinburg, TX) 84738
Texaco Inc. Prod Dept (West Columbia, TX) 90047
Texaco Inc. Prod Dept (Winnie, TX) 90124
Texaco Inc. Producing Dept (Gladewater, TX) 85582
Texaco Inc. Producingdepartm (Odessa, TX) 88284
Texaco Inc. Production Dept (Danevang, TX) 84517
Texaco Inc. Research & Development (Port Arthur, TX) 88650
Texaco Incorporated Sales (Abilene, TX) 82461
Texaco Inc. Sales Office (Nashville, TN) 82106
Texaco Incorporated Service (Oklahoma City, OK) 77613
Texaco Inc. Warehouse (Cameron, TX) 83439
Texaco Inc. Warhse (Aransas Pass, TX) 82626
Texaco Industries Inc. (Guayanilla, PR) 78433
Texaco Instant Lube (Garland, TX) 85544
Texaco & J & L Snacks (San Antonio, TX) 89263
Texaco Jobber Warehouse (Jefferson, TX) 87440
Texaco Jpep (Odessa, TX) 88285
Texaco Kwik Mart No 19 (Goldsboro, NC) 74738
Texaco Kwik Trip (Shreveport, LA) 70795
Texaco Latin Amer W African (Miami, FL) 61475
Texaco Lubracants Co. (Houston, TX) 87005
Texaco Lubricants (Houston, TX) 87006
Texaco Lubricants (Irving, TX) 87414
Texaco Lubricants Companies (Doraville, GA) 65959
Texaco Lubricants Co. (North Charleston, SC) 79750
Texaco Lubricants Co. Inc. (Chesapeake, VA) 90607
Texaco Mart (Sheffield, AL) 56565
Texaco Mart (Tulsa, OK) 78152
Texaco Mini Mart (Aliceville, AL) 54984
Texaco Mini-Mart (Fairfax, OK) 77075
Texaco Mini Mart (Tulsa, OK) 78153
Texaco Mini Mart Ii (Daytona Beach, FL) 59218
Texaco Mini Mart & Serv Sta (Metairie, LA) 70317
Texaco Mortor Tune Center Dora (Doraville, GA) 65960
Texaco No 5 (Florence, AL) 55746
Texaco No 411 (Kissimmee, FL) 60606
Texaco No 320 (Largo, FL) 60865
Texaco No 208 (Tampa, FL) 63619
Texaco Northpk Svc (Dallas, TX) 84431
Texaco-Nrthrn Oil (Benton, AR) 56780
Texaco Number One (Seguin, TX) 89377
Texaco Nw Hills (Austin, TX) 83030
Texaco Oil Co. (Merritt is, FL) 61134
Texaco Oil Company (Opa Locka, FL) 61863
Texaco Oil Co. (Guymon, OK) 77113
Texaco Oil Co. (Weatherford, TX) 90015
Texaco Oil Distributors (Houston, MS) 72923
Texaco Oil & Gas (Jackson, MS) 73074
Texaco 134 (Lakeland, FL) 60788
Texaco One Stop (Austin, TX) 83031; 83032
Texaco P a W Employees Fede (Port Arthur, TX) 88651
Texaco Pep Stop (Forney, TX) 85041
Texaco Pep Stop (Humble, TX) 87250
Texaco Pep Stop (Rosenberg, TX) 88840
Texaco Petroleum (El Dorado, AR) 56960
Texaco Petroleum Prod Dist (Palestine, TX) 88346
Texaco/Philadelphia (Bellaire, TX) 83268
Texaco Pipeline (Ponca City, OK) 77714
Texaco Pipeline (Wichita Falls, TX) 90111
Texaco Pipeline Inc. (Houston, TX) 87007

Thomas Mfg. Co. Inc. (Thomasville, NC) 76385
Thomasville Forest Prods. (Thomasville, NC) 76386
Thomasville Forest Products (Thomasville, NC) 76387
Thomasville Furniture Ind. Inc. (Lenoir, NC) 75389
Thomasville Furniture Ind. Inc. (Pleasant Garden, NC) 75833
Thomasville Furniture Ind. Inc. (Thomasville, NC) 76388
Thomasville Furniture Ind. Inc. (West Jefferson, NC) 76489
Thomasville Furniture Ind. Inc. (Brookneal, VA) 90496
Thomasville Furniture Ind. Inc. Plant A (Thomasville, NC) 76389
Thomasville Furniture Ind. Inc. Plant B (Thomasville, NC) 76390
Thomasville Furniture Ind. Inc. Plant C (Thomasville, NC) 76391
Thomasville Furniture Ind. Inc. Plant D (Thomasville, NC) 76392
Thomasville Furniture Ind. Inc. Plant H (Winston-Salem, NC) 76772
Thomasville Furniture Industries Inc. (Lenoir, NC) 75390; 75391
Thomasville Furniture Industries Inc. (Thomasville, NC) 76393; 76394; 76395; 76396
Thomasville Furniture Industries Inc. (Winston-Salem, NC) 76773
Thomasville Furniture Industries, Inc. Plant A (Thomasville, NC) 76397
Thomasville Furniture Industries, Inc. Plant B (Thomasville, NC) 76398
Thomasville Furniture Industries Inc. Plant C (Thomasville, NC) 76399
Thomasville Furniture Industries Inc. Plant D (Thomasville, NC) 76400
Thomasville Furniture Industries Inc. Plant E (Thomasville, NC) 76401
Thomasville Furniture Industries Inc. Plant H (Winston-Salem, NC) 76774
Thomasville Furniture Industries Inc. Plant L (Thomasville, NC) 76402
Thomasville Upholstery, Inc. (Conover, NC) 74339
Thomasville Upholstery, Inc. (Hickory, NC) 75102
Thomasville Upholstery, Inc. (Statesville, NC) 76339
Thomasville Upholstery, Inc. (Troutman, NC) 76409
Thomasville Upholstry Inc. (Statesville, NC) 76340
Thompson & Formby Inc. (Olive Branch, MS) 73230
Thompson & Formby Inc. (Memphis, TN) 81709
Thompson & Formby's Inc. (Olive Branch, MS) 73231
Thompson & Formby's Inc. (Memphis, TN) 81710
Thorn Apple Valley Inc. Carolina Div. (Holly Ridge, NC) 75191
Thoroughbred Plastics Corp. (Jonesboro, GA) 66406
Thoroughbred Plastics Corp. (Louisville, KY) 69021
3 Com (Atlanta, GA) 65212
GTE Valenite Corp. Plant 3 (Westminster, SC) 80118
Three Rivers Timber Co. Inc. (Simmesport, LA) 70810
3M (Atlanta, GA) 65213
3M (Dallas, TX) 84451
3M Adhesive Technology Corp. (Burlington, NC) 73762
3M Advertising (Sanford, FL) 62783
3M Co. (Decatur, AL) 55607
3M Co. (Guin, AL) 55821
3M Co. (Little Rock, AR) 57316
3M Co. (Cynthiana, KY) 68250
3M Co. (Westminster, MD) 72545
3M Co. (High Point, NC) 75173
3M Co. (Brownwood, TX) 83390
3M Co. (Kearneysville, WV) 92909
3M Co. Tape Manufacturing Div. (Greenville, SC) 79440
3M Co. Telecom Markets Div. (Austin, TX) 83046
3M & D Inc. (Hialeah, FL) 60014
3M National Advertising Co. (Nashville, TN) 82111
3M Scotchtint Window Film (Norcross, GA) 67202
Thrift Drug (Dover, DE) 57809; 57810
Thrift Drug (New Castle, DE) 57876
Thrift Drug (Seaford, DE) 57954
Thrift Drug (Wilmington, DE) 58114; 58115
Thrift Drug (Morrow, GA) 67050

Thrift Drug (Bel Air, MD) 71340
Thrift Drug (Cumberland, MD) 71637; 71638
Thrift Drug (Denton, MD) 71644
Thrift Drug (Salisbury, MD) 72363
Thrift Drug (Covington, VA) 90665
Thrift Drug (Danville, VA) 90721
Thrift Drug Express Pharmacy (Atlanta, GA) 65214
Thrift Drugs (Ashland, KY) 68108
Thrift Drugs (Russell, KY) 69255
Thrift Drugs (Mc Comb, MS) 73151
Thrift Drugs (Bluefield, WV) 92704
Thrift Drugs (Fairmont, WV) 92848
Thrift Drugs (Huntington, WV) 92897; 92898
Thrift Drugs (Parkersburg, WV) 92997
Thrift Drugs (Weirton, WV) 93101; 93102
Thrifty Rent-A-Car System Inc. (Tulsa, OK) 78167
Thrifty Rent a Car Systems, Inc. (Norman, OK) 77278
Thrifty Rent a Car Systems, Inc. (Tulsa, OK) 78168; 78169; 78170
Tibbals Flooring Co. (Oneida, TN) 82213
Tibbals Flooring Co. East Plant (Oneida, TN) 82214
Tibbals Flooring Co. West Plant (Oneida, TN) 82215
Ticor Title Insurance (Birmingham, AL) 55428
Ticor Title Insurance (Nashville, TN) 82112
Tifpc Bleached Paperboard Pulp & Paperboard Operations (Evadale, TX) 85026
Tifton Aluminum Co., Inc. (Tifton, GA) 67831
Tifton Aluminum Co., Inc. (Delhi, LA) 69825
Timberlake Grocery Co. (Thomasville, GA) 67806
Time Electronics (Huntsville, AL) 56039
Time Electronics (Ft. Lauderdale, FL) 59856
Time Electronics (Orlando, FL) 62170
Time Electronics (Atlanta, GA) 65215
Time Electronics (Norcross, GA) 67203
Time Electronics (Smyrna, GA) 67582
Time Electronics (Columbia, MD) 71603
Time Electronics (Charlotte, NC) 74173
Time Electronics (Oxford, NC) 75789
Time Electronics (Raleigh, NC) 75965
Time Electronics (Austin, TX) 83047; 83048
Time Electronics (Houston, TX) 87027
Time Electronics (Richardson, TX) 88785
Timeplex Caribe Ltd. (Juncos, PR) 78472; 78473
Tip-Transport International Po (Atlanta, GA) 65216
Tip-Transport International Po (Austell, GA) 65360
Tipper Tie Inc. (Apex, NC) 73558; 73559
Title Insur Co. of Minn Titl (Jacksonville, FL) 60476
Title Insurance Co. of Minn (Dallas, TX) 84452
Title Insurance Co. of Minn (Fairfax, VA) 90810
Title Insurance Co. Minnesot (Columbia, SC) 79109
Tj Maxx (Melbourne, FL) 61112
Tj Maxx (Tampa, FL) 63623
Tj Maxx (Rockville, MD) 72328
Tj Maxx (Farmers Branch, TX) 85035
Tj Maxx (Lubbock, TX) 87790
Tj Maxx District Office (Kennesaw, GA) 66458
Tn Tech. Inc. (Round Rock, TX) 88855
TNI Inc. (Houston, TX) 87028
TNI Inc. (Middleburg, VA) 91406
Tobacco Processors, Inc. (Wilson, NC) 76649
Tombstone Pizza Corp. (College Park, GA) 65609
Tonka Corp. (El Paso, TX) 84949
Tonka Toys (El Paso, TX) 84950
Torrington Co (Charlotte, NC) 74174
Torrington Co (Tulsa, OK) 78171
Torrington Co. (Houston, TX) 87029
Torrington Co. the (Birmingham, AL) 55429; 55430
Torrington Co. the (Tampa, FL) 63624
Torrington Co. (Cairo, GA) 65455

Torrington Co. (Sylvania, GA) 67771
Torrington Co. (Clinton, SC) 78963
Torrington Co. (Honea Path, SC) 79531
Torrington Co. (Union, SC) 80049
Torrington Co. (Walhalla, SC) 80058
Torrington Co. Bearing Div. (Dahlonega, GA) 65755
Torrington Co. Shiloh Plant (Rutherfordton, NC) 76147
Torrington Co. Inc (Honea Path, SC) 79532
Torrington Co. Inc. (Sylvania, GA) 67772
Torrington Co. Shiloh Plant (Rutherfordton, NC) 76148
Torrington Co. Tyger River (Union, SC) 80050
Torrington Co. Tyger River Plant (Union, SC) 80051; 80052; 80053
Tosco Corp. (Memphis, TN) 81711
Tosco Corp. (Nashville, TN) 82113
Total Auto Care (Fort Lauderdale, FL) 59623
Total Auto Care (Lake City, FL) 60632
Total Petroleum Inc. (New Orleans, LA) 70576; 70577
Total Petroleum Inc. (Ardmore, OK) 76823; 76824; 76825
Total Petroleum Inc. (Healdton, OK) 77121; 77122
Total Petroleum Inc. (Oklahoma City, OK) 77629; 77630
Total Petroleum Inc. (Tulsa, OK) 78172; 78173; 78174; 78175
Total Petroleum Inc. (Yukon, OK) 78283; 78284
Total Petroleum Inc. (Memphis, TN) 81712
Total Petroleum Inc. (Dallas, TX) 84453; 84454
Total Petroleum Inc. (Euless, TX) 85021; 85022
Total Service Station (Memphis, TN) 81713
Total System Services Inc. (Columbus, GA) 65654
Town & Country Medical Center (Tampa, FL) 63625
Toys R US (Birmingham, AL) 55431; 55432
Toys R US (Huntsville, AL) 56040
Toys R US (Fort Smith, AR) 57105
Toys R US (Newark, DE) 57933
Toys R US (Clearwater, FL) 59050
Toys R US (Fort Myers, FL) 59767
Toys R US (Hialeah, FL) 60015
Toys R US (Hollywood, FL) 60100
Toys R US (Jacksonville, FL) 60477
Toys R US (Miami, FL) 61479; 61480
Toys R US (Orange Park, FL) 61899
Toys R US (Orlando, FL) 62171
Toys R US (Pensacola, FL) 62482
Toys R US (St Petersburg, FL) 63037
Toys R US (Tallahassee, FL) 63280
Toys R US (Tampa, FL) 63626
Toys R US (Atlanta, GA) 65217
Toys R US (Decatur, GA) 65908
Toys R US (Duluth, GA) 66092
Toys R US (Kennesaw, GA) 66459
Toys R US (Morrow, GA) 67051
Toys R US (Tucker, GA) 67898
Toys R US (Union City, GA) 67932
Toys R US (Louisville, KY) 69022
Toys R US (Monroe, LA) 70380
Toys R US (Shreveport, LA) 70796
Toys R US (Frederick, MD) 71751
Toys R US (Landover, MD) 72034
Toys R US (Langley Pk, MD) 72047
Toys R US (Lanham, MD) 72058
Toys R US (Marlow Heights, MD) 72128
Toys R US (Rockville, MD) 72329
Toys R US (Salisbury, MD) 72364
Toys R US (Jackson, MS) 73076
Toys R US (Charlotte, NC) 74175
Toys R US (Wilmington, NC) 76601
Toys R US (Oklahoma City, OK) 77631; 77632; 77633
Toys R US (Tulsa, OK) 78176
Toys R US (Spartanburg, SC) 79959
Toys R US (Chattanooga, TN) 80505
Toys R US (Knoxville, TN) 81260
Toys R US (Arlington, TX) 82771
Toys R US (Austin, TX) 83049; 83050; 83051
Toys R US (Beaumont, TX) 83226
Toys R US (Dallas, TX) 84455
Toys R US (El Paso, TX) 84951
Toys R US (Fort Worth, TX) 85336

Toys R US (Houston, TX) 87030; 87031; 87032; 87033; 87034
Toys R US (Midland, TX) 88089
Toys R US (Webster, TX) 90026
Toys R US (Fairfax, VA) 90811
Toys R US (Falls Church, VA) 90872
Toys R US (Hampton, VA) 91057
Toys R US (Norfolk, VA) 91586
Toys R US (Richmond, VA) 92057; 92058
Tracy-Locke, A DDB Needham Agency (Dallas, TX) 84456
Tracy Locke Inc. (Atlanta, GA) 65218
Trailer Train Co. Hamburg Di (North Augusta, SC) 79741
Trailway Bus Station (Arab, AL) 55027
Trailway Bus Station (Enterprise, AL) 55697
Trailway Bus Station (Kinder, LA) 70026
Trailway Bus Station (Corinth, MS) 72746
Trailway Bus Station (Laurel, MS) 73109
Trailway Bus Station (Roanoke Rapids, NC) 76039
Trailway Bus Terminal (Dawson, GA) 65794
Trailway Enterprises (Bay St Louis, MS) 72606
Trailway Laundry Inc. (Boone, NC) 73719
Trailway Tours Inc. (Irving, TX) 87415
Trailways (Monticello, AR) 57375
Trailways (Gulfport, MS) 72880
Trailways (Murphy, NC) 75710
Trailways (Wilson, NC) 76650
Trailways (Amarillo, TX) 82586
Trailways (New Braunfels, TX) 88221
Trailways American Bus Line (Oklahoma City, OK) 77634
Trailways Bu System (Birmingham, AL) 55433
Trailways Bus (Alpine, TX) 82502
Trailways Bus Center (Harrison, AR) 57141
Trailways Bus Depot (Clarksville, AR) 56852
Trailways Bus Depot (Bainbridge, GA) 65373
Trailways Bus Depot (De Quincy, LA) 69808
Trailways Bus Depot (Delhi, LA) 69826
Trailways Bus Depot (Winona, MS) 73495
Trailways Bus Depot (Center, TX) 83542
Trailways Bus Depot (Palestine, TX) 88347
Trailways Bus Inc. (Carthage, TX) 83522
Trailways Bus Line (Rocky Mount, NC) 76106
Trailways Bus Lines (Haleyville, AL) 55847
Trailways Bus Lines (Ocala, FL) 61824
Trailways Bus Lines (Lexington, KY) 68643
Trailways Bus Lines (London, KY) 68669
Trailways Bus Lines (Louisville, KY) 69023
Trailways Bus Lines (Williamsburg, KY) 69341
Trailways Bus Lines (Black Mountain, NC) 73699
Trailways Bus Lines (Bristol, TN) 80255
Trailways Bus Lines (Cookeville, TN) 80668
Trailways Bus Lines (Crossville, TN) 80706
Trailways Bus Lines (Elizabethton, TN) 80771
Trailways Bus Lines (Fayetteville, TN) 80799
Trailways Bus Lines (Gallatin, TN) 80851
Trailways Bus Lines (Jackson, TN) 81003
Trailways Bus Lines (Kingsport, TN) 81119
Trailways Bus Lines (Knoxville, TN) 81261
Trailways Bus Lines (Lebanon, TN) 81310
Trailways Bus Lines (Lenoir City, TN) 81324
Trailways Bus Lines (Lewisburg, TN) 81333
Trailways Bus Lines (Martin, TN) 81398
Trailways Bus Lines (Memphis, TN) 81714; 81715
Trailways Bus Lines (Morristown, TN) 81813

Trailways Bus Lines (Nashville, TN) 82114
Trailways Bus Lines (Shelbyville, TN) 82318
Trailways Bus Lines (Logan, WV) 92920
Trailways Bus Lines Carolin (Sanford, NC) 76206
Trailways Bus Linescarolina (Greensboro, NC) 74924
Trailways Bus Station (Albertville, AL) 54971
Trailways Bus Station (Enterprise, AL) 55698
Trailways Bus Station (Reform, AL) 56498
Trailways Bus Station (Sylacauga, AL) 56590
Trailways Bus Station (Talladega, AL) 56600
Trailways Bus Station (Arkadelphia, AR) 56722
Trailways Bus Station (Bald Knob, AR) 56738
Trailways Bus Station (El Dorado, AR) 56961
Trailways Bus Station (Hope, AR) 57160
Trailways Bus Station (Nashville, AR) 57442
Trailways Bus Station (Pocahontas, AR) 57544
Trailways Bus Station (Lake City, FL) 60633
Trailways Bus Station (Cairo, GA) 65456
Trailways Bus Station (Camilla, GA) 65483
Trailways Bus Station (Claxton, GA) 65566
Trailways Bus Station (Jesup, GA) 66374
Trailways Bus Station (Pearson, GA) 67256
Trailways Bus Station (Bogalusa, LA) 69709
Trailways Bus Station (Forest, MS) 72778
Trailways Bus Station (Greenville, MS) 72822
Trailways Bus Station (Oxford, MS) 73246
Trailways Bus Station (Spindale, NC) 76294
Trailways Bus Station (Aiken, SC) 78658
Trailways Bus Station (Manning, SC) 79636
Trailways Bus Station (Abilene, TX) 82464
Trailways Bus Station (Euless, TX) 85023
Trailways Bus Station (Palacios, TX) 88340
Trailways Bus Station (Rio Grande City, TX) 88803
Trailways Bus Station (Seguin, TX) 89378
Trailways Bus Station (Silsbee, TX) 89436
Trailways Bus Station (Wharton, TX) 90051
Trailways Bus Stop (Livingston, TX) 87692
Trailways Bus Sys (Granbury, TX) 85600
Trailways Bus System (Decatur, AL) 55608
Trailways Bus System (Huntsville, AL) 56041
Trailways Bus System (Tuscaloosa, AL) 56678
Trailways Bus System (Conway, AR) 56874
Trailways Bus System (Little Rock, AR) 57317
Trailways Bus System (Marked Tree, AR) 57348
Trailways Bus System (Mc Gehee, AR) 57359
Trailways Bus System (Russellville, AR) 57592
Trailways Bus System (Arcadia, FL) 58586
Trailways Bus System (Blountstown, FL) 58663
Trailways Bus System (Daytona Beach, FL) 59221
Trailways Bus System (Fort Myers, FL) 59768
Trailways Bus System (Fort Walton Beach, FL) 59841
Trailways Bus System (Hollywood, FL) 60101
Trailways Bus System (Jacksonville, FL) 60478
Trailways Bus System (Miami, FL) 61481
Trailways Bus System (Naples, FL) 61667
Trailways Bus System (Orlando, FL) 62172
Trailways Bus System (Panama City, FL) 62354

Trailways Bus System (Pensacola, FL) 62483
Trailways Bus System (St Petersburg, FL) 63038
Trailways Bus System (Tallahassee, FL) 63281
Trailways Bus System (W Palm Beach, FL) 63816
Trailways Bus System (Americus, GA) 64146
Trailways Bus System (Savannah, GA) 67517
Trailways Bus System (Waycross, GA) 68039
Trailways Bus System (Alexandria, LA) 69412
Trailways Bus System (Arcadia, LA) 69431
Trailways Bus System (Bunkie, LA) 69746
Trailways Bus System (Many, LA) 70221
Trailways Bus System (New Orleans, LA) 70578
Trailways Bus System (Oakdale, LA) 70601
Trailways Bus System (Opelousas, LA) 70603
Trailways Bus System (Ruston, LA) 70674
Trailways Bus System (Shreveport, LA) 70797
Trailways Bus System (Biloxi, MS) 72641
Trailways Bus System (Booneville, MS) 72649
Trailways Bus System (Carthage, MS) 72663
Trailways Bus System (Columbus, MS) 72730
Trailways Bus System (Grenada, MS) 72849
Trailways Bus System (Hattiesburg, MS) 72899
Trailways Bus System (Meridian, MS) 73182
Trailways Bus System (Hamlet, NC) 75002
Trailways Bus System (High Point, NC) 75174
Trailways Bus System (Morganton, NC) 75656
Trailways Bus System (Newton, NC) 75755
Trailways Bus System (Spring Lake, NC) 76300
Trailways Bus System (Waynesville, NC) 76473
Trailways Bus System (Charleston, SC) 78905
Trailways Bus System (Greenville, SC) 79441
Trailways Bus System (Alice, TX) 82488
Trailways Bus System (Bowie, TX) 83328
Trailways Bus System (Brownsville, TX) 83382
Trailways Bus System (Childress, TX) 83562
Trailways Bus System (Cisco, TX) 83566
Trailways Bus System (Colorado City, TX) 83641
Trailways Bus System (Corsicana, TX) 83794
Trailways Bus System (Dallas, TX) 84457; 84458; 84459
Trailways Bus System (Del Rio, TX) 84589
Trailways Bus System (Denton, TX) 84641
Trailways Bus System (Donna, TX) 84680
Trailways Bus System (Eastland, TX) 84730
Trailways Bus System (Edinburg, TX) 84741
Trailways Bus System (El Campo, TX) 84751
Trailways Bus System (El Paso, TX) 84952
Trailways Bus System (Greenville, TX) 85679
Trailways Bus System (Harlingen, TX) 85716
Trailways Bus System (Houston, TX) 87035; 87036; 87037
Trailways Bus System (Kilgore, TX) 87501
Trailways Bus System (Mathis, TX) 87881
Trailways Bus System (Mc Kinney, TX) 87924
Trailways Bus System (Memphis, TX) 87951
Trailways Bus System (Mesquite, TX) 88009
Trailways Bus System (Mineola, TX) 88107
Trailways Bus System (Monahans, TX) 88144
Trailways Bus System (Pampa, TX) 88357
Trailways Bus System (Pecos, TX) 88499
Trailways Bus System (Pharr, TX) 88513
Trailways Bus System (Taylor, TX) 89603
Trailways Bus System (Terrell, TX) 89663
Trailways Bus System (Waskom, TX) 89991
Trailways Bus System (Weslaco, TX) 90040
Trailways Bus System Inc. (Dallas, TX) 84460
Trailways Bus System Inc. (Huntsville, TX) 87266
Trailways Bus Systemm (Macon, GA) 66716
Trailways Bus Systems (Dothan, AL) 55672
Trailways Bus Systems (Pine Bluff, AR) 57532
Trailways Bus Systems (Miami, FL) 61482
Trailways Bus Systems (Panama City, FL) 62355
Trailways Bus Systems (Sanford, FL) 62784
Trailways Bus Systems (Tampa, FL) 63627
Trailways Bus Systems (Sandersville, GA) 67432
Trailways Bus Systems (Sylvester, GA) 67777
Trailways Bus Systems (De Ridder, LA) 69819
Trailways Bus Systems (Mansfield, LA) 70217
Trailways Bus Systems (Durant, MS) 72753
Trailways Bus Systems (Waynesboro, MS) 73474
Trailways Bus Systems (Fayetteville, NC) 74577
Trailways Bus Systems (Lenoir, NC) 75392
Trailways Bus Systems (Monroe, NC) 75593
Trailways Bus Systems (Rutherfordton, NC) 76149
Trailways Bus Systems (Muskogee, OK) 77230
Trailways Bus Systems (Tulsa, OK) 78177
Trailways Bus Systems (Wagoner, OK) 78233
Trailways Bus Systems (Charleston, SC) 78906
Trailways Bus Systems (Union, SC) 80054
Trailways Bus Systems (Abilene, TX) 82465
Trailways Bus Systems (Beaumont, TX) 83227
Trailways Bus Systems (Crockett, TX) 83802
Trailways Bus Systems (Mc Allen, TX) 87902
Trailways Bus Systems (Odessa, TX) 88286
Trailways Bus Systems (San Antonio, TX) 89276
Trailways Bus Systems (Sherman, TX) 89428
Trailways Bus Systems (Wichita Falls, TX) 90115
Trailways Bus Terminal (Tampa, FL) 63628
Trailways Bus Terminal (Columbia, SC) 79110
Trailways Bus Terminal (Marshall, TX) 87869
Trailways Bus Terminal of D (Dallas, TX) 84461
Trailways Bus Terminal Inc. (Wadesboro, NC) 76427
Trailways Bus Terminal&Gril (Winnsboro, SC) 80134
Trailways Business Systems (Houston, TX) 87038
Trailways Communter Transit (Dallas, TX) 84462
Trailways Food Services Inc. (Corpus Christi, TX) 83762
Trailways Greyhound Bus Lines (Cleveland, TN) 80603
Trailways & Greyhounds Bus (Corsicana, TX) 83795
Trailways Group Travel (Grand Prairie, TX) 85644
Trailways Hickory Bus Sta (Hickory, NC) 75103
Trailways Inc. (Birmingham, AL) 55434
Trailways Inc. (Murfreesboro, AR) 57400
Trailways Inc. (Macon, GA) 66717
Trailways Incorporated (Monroe, LA) 70381
Trailways Inc. (Rayville, LA) 70659
Trailways Inc. (Charlotte, NC) 74176
Trailways Inc. (Marion, NC) 75507
Trailways Inc. (Bay City, TX) 83105
Trailways Inc. (El Paso, TX) 84953
Trailways Inc. (Fort Worth, TX) 85337
Trailways Inc. (Houston, TX) 87039
Trailways Inc. (Refugio, TX) 88719
Trailways Inc. (Vernon, TX) 89874
Trailways Inc. Bus Station (Tahlequah, OK) 77861
Trailways Manufacturing Inc. (Harlingen, TX) 85717
Trailways Package Express (San Antonio, TX) 89277
Trailways Package Xpress (Lafayette, LA) 70118
Trailways Restaurnat (Texarkana, AR) 57682
Trailways Southern Lines in (Lake Charles, LA) 70177
Trailways Southern Lines in (New Orleans, LA) 70579
Trailways Texas Inc. (San Antonio, TX) 89278
Trailways Texas Inc. (Stephenville, TX) 89526
Trailways Transportation (Universal City, TX) 89845
Tramco Inc. (Bristol, TN) 80256
Tramco Inc. (Chattaroy, WV) 92801
Trane Air Handling Systems Business Unit (Lexington, KY) 68644
Trane Commercial Self-Contained Systems Business Unit (Macon, GA) 66718
Trane Co. (Mobile, AL) 56250
Trane Co. (Fort Smith, AR) 57106; 57107
Trane Co. (Miami, FL) 61483; 61484
Trane Co. (Lexington, KY) 68645
Trane Co. (Jessup, MD) 71986
Trane Co. (Jackson, MS) 73077
Trane Co. (Tulsa, OK) 78178
Trane Co. (Clarksville, TN) 80558
Trane Co. (Tyler, TX) 89837
Trane Co. Wshpbu (Mc Gregor, TX) 87907
Trane/Service First (Charlotte, NC) 74177
Trane/Servicefirst Service First (Charlotte, NC) 74178
Tranmission Systems Inc. (Fort Stockton, TX) 85050
Trans State Line Inc. (Memphis, TN) 81716
Trans State Lines, Inc. (Fort Smith, AR) 57108
Trans Unitary Products Group Commercial (Clarksville, TN) 80559
Trans World Airlines (Washington, DC) 58505; 58506
Trans World Airlines (Fort Myers, FL) 59769
Trans World Airlines (W Palm Beach, FL) 63817
Trans World Airlines (Lexington, KY) 68646
Trans World Airlines (Charlotte, NC) 74179
Trans World Airlines (Tulsa, OK) 78179; 78180
Trans World Airlines (Memphis, TN) 81717
Trans World Airlines, Inc. (Washington, DC) 58507; 58508
Trans World Airlines Inc. (Tampa, FL) 63629; 63630
Trans World Airlines Inc. (Atlanta, GA) 65219; 65220; 65221
Trans World Airlines Inc. (Louisville, KY) 69024
Trans World Airlines Inc. (Oklahoma City, OK) 77635
Trans World Airlines Inc. (Memphis, TN) 81718
Trans World Airlines Inc. (Houston, TX) 87040
Trans World Airlines, Inc. (Chantilly, VA) 90525
Trans World Airlines, Inc. (Norfolk, VA) 91587
Transamerica Occidental Lif (Greenville, MS) 72823
Transamerica Occidental Life Inc. (Altamonte Spg, FL) 58547
Transamerica Occidental Life Inc. (Maitland, FL) 60987
Transamerica Occidental Life Inc. (Louisville, KY) 69025
Transamerica Occidental Life Inc. (Nashville, TN) 82115
Transamerica Occidental Life Insurance (Destin, FL) 59350
Transamerica Occidental Life Insurance (Tallahassee, FL) 63282
Transamerica Occidental Life Insurance (Tampa, FL) 63631
Transamerica Occidental Life Insurance (W Palm Beach, FL) 63818
Transamerica Occidental Life Insurance (Atlanta, GA) 65222
Transamerica Occidental Life Insurance (Cedartown, GA) 65513
Transamerica Occidental Life Insurance (Valdosta, GA) 67975
Transamerica Occidental Life Insurance (Silver Spring, MD) 72445
Transamerica Occidental Life Insurance (Charlotte, NC) 74180; 74181
Transamerica Occidental Life Insurance (Tulsa, OK) 78181
Transamerica Occidental Life Insurance (Columbia, SC) 79111
Transamerica Occidental Life Insurance (Bristol, TN) 80257
Transamerica Occidental Life Insurance (Madison, TN) 81381
Transamerica Occidental Life Insurance (Corpus Chrsti, TX) 83774
Transamerica Occidental Life Insurance (Dallas, TX) 84463
Transamerica Occidental Life Insurance (Houston, TX) 87041
Transamerica Occidental Life Insurance (Longview, TX) 87739
Transamerica Occidental Life Insurance (Midland, TX) 88090
Transamerica Occidental Life Insurance (Norfolk, VA) 91588
Transamerica Occidental Life Insurance (Charleston, WV) 92794
Transamerica Premier Insurance (Atlanta, GA) 65223
Transamerica Real Estate (Bowie, MD) 71474
Transco Coal Co. (Richmond, VA) 92059
Transco Energy Co. (Houston, TX) **87042**
Transco Exploration Co. (New Orleans, LA) 70580
Transok, Inc. (Tulsa, OK) 78182
Transport Insurance Co. (Dallas, TX) 84464
Transwestern Pipeline Co. (Fort Stockton, TX) 85051
Transwestern Pipeline Co. (Houston, TX) 87043
Transwestern Pipeline Co. (Perryton, TX) 88504
Transwestern Pipeline Co. Inc. (Houston, TX) 87044
Tranter Inc. (Edgefield, SC) 79186
Tranter Inc. (Wichita Falls, TX) 90116
Travel Publications Inc. (Miami, FL) 61485
Travelers Insurance (Lynchburg, VA) 91290
Travelers Lloyds Insurance (Dallas, TX) 84465
Treadco (Lubbock, TX) 87791
Treadco, Inc. (Fort Smith, AR) 57109
Treadco, Inc. (Atlanta, GA) 65224
Treadco Inc. (Norcross, GA) 67204
Tredegar Industries Inc. (Richmond, VA) 92060
Tremco Inc. (Barbourville, KY) 68110
Tri-City Bank & Trust Co. (Blountville, TN) 80205; 80206; 80207
Tri City Bank & Trust Co. (Kingsport, TN) 81120
Tri City Bank & Trust Co. (Piney Flats, TN) 82230
Tri-City & Trust Co. (Blountville, TN) 80208
Tri Valley Growers (Kennesaw, GA) 66460
Tri-W Corp. (Nashville, TN) 82116
Triarc (West Palm Beach, FL) **63905**
Trico Ind. Inc. (Greenville, TX) 85680
Trico Ind. Inc. (Odessa, TX) 88287
Trico Industries Inc. (Oklahoma City, OK) 77636
Trico Industries Inc. (Woodward, OK) 78268
Trico Industries Inc. (Andrews, TX) 82606
Trico Industries Inc. (Big Spring, TX) 83296
Trico Industries Inc. (Houston, TX) 87045
Trico Industries Inc. (Ira, TX) 87312
Trico Industries Inc. (Knox City, TX) 87538
Trico Industries Inc. (Midland, TX) 88091
Trico Industries Inc. (Odessa, TX) 88288
Trico Industries Inc. (San Antonio, TX) 89279
Trico Industries Inc. (Wichita Falls, TX) 90117
Trico Industries Inc. (Wickett, TX) 90122
Trico Submersible System (Oklahoma City, OK) 77637
Trim Masters Inc. (Bardstown, KY) 68121
Trinity Ind. Inc. (Longview, TX) 87740
Trinity Industries (Dallas, TX) **84466**
Trinity Industries Equitable Div. (New Orleans, LA) 70581
Trinity Industries Halter Marine Lockport Div. (Lockport, LA) 70196
Trinity Industries Halter Marine Moss Point Div. (Moss Point, MS) 73196
Trinity Industries Moss Point Marine Div. (Escatawpa, MS) 72761
Trinity Industries Structural Steel Div. No. 32 (Montgomery, AL) 56389
Trinity Industries Trinity Structural Div. (Montgomery, AL) 56390
Trinity Industries Inc. (Bessemer, AL) 55107
Trinity Industries Inc. (Jacksonville, FL) 60479
Trinity Industries Inc. (Rocky Mount, NC) 76107
Trinity Industries Inc. (Denton, TX) 84642
Trinity Industries Inc. (Longview, TX) 87741
Trinity Industries Inc. Lockport Div. (Lockport, LA) 70197
Trinity Industries Inc. East (Longview, TX) 87742
Trinity Industries Inc. Plant 32 (Montgomery, AL) 56391
Trinity Industries, Plant 77 Structural Steel Div. (Montgomery, AL) 56392
Trinity Industries Transport (Montgomery, AL) 56393
Trinity Industries_Inc. Structural Steel Plant 64 (Bainbridge, GA) 65374
TriStar Capital Corp. (Wilmington, DE) 58116
TriStar Ventures Corp. (Wilmington, DE) 58117
Tropicana Products Inc. (Bradenton, FL) 58853
Tropicana Products Inc. (Pierce, FL) 62506
True Temper Sports Division (Amory, MS) 72589
True Temper Sports Division (Olive Branch, MS) 73232
True Temper Sports Division (Seneca, SC) 79864
True Temper Sports Division (Memphis, TN) 81719
True Temper Sports (Olive Branch, MS) 73233
True Temper Sports (Seneca, SC) 79865; 79866
Trugreen Chemlawn (College Park, GA) 65610
Trugreen Chemlawn (Norcross, GA) 67205
Trugreen-Chemlawn (Gaithersburg, MD) 71817
Trugreen-Chemlawn (Landover, MD) 72035
Trugreen-Chemlawn (Chattanooga, TN) 80506
Trugreen-Chemlawn Commercial D (Gaithersburg, MD) 71818
Trunkline Gas Co. (Houston, TX) 87046
Trust Co. Bank of Aujusta, N.A. (Thomson, GA) 67814; 67815
Trust Co. Bank of Coffee County (Douglas, GA) 65977; 65978; 65979
Trust Co. Bank of Columbus, N.A. (La Grange, GA) 66487; 66488
Trust Co. Bank of Middle Georgia, N.A. (Macon, GA) 66719
Trust Co. Bank of NE Georgia, N.A. (Madison, GA) 66729
Trust Co. Bank of North Georgia (Gainesville, GA) 66294; 66295; 66296; 66297; 66298
Trust Co. Bank of NW Georgia, N.A. (Rockmart, GA) 67334
Trust Co. Bank of NW Georgia, N.A. (Rome, GA) 67347; 67348; 67349; 67350; 67351; 67352
Trust Co. Bank of Savannah, N.A. (Savannah, GA) 67518
Trust Co. Bank of SE Georgia, N.A. (Screven, GA) 67535
Trust Co. Bank of SE Georgia, N.A. (St. Simons Island, GA) 67629; 67630
Trust Co. Bank of SE Georgia, N.A. (Waycross, GA) 68040; 68041
Trust Co. Bank of South Georgia (Thomasville, GA) 67807

Trust Co. Bank of South Georgia, N.A. (Pelham, GA) 67258
Trust Co. Bank of South Georgia, N.A. (Sylvester, GA) 67778
Trust Co. Bank of South Georgia, N.A. (Thomasville, GA) 67808; 67809
Trust Co. Bank of South Georgia, N.A. (Tifton, GA) 67832; 67833
Trust Co. Bank of South Georgia, National Assoc. (Albany, GA) 64097
Trust Co. Bank of Southeast Georgia, National Assoc. (Jesue, GA) 66369
Trust Co. of Georgia Bank of Savannah, N.A. (Savannah, GA) 67519; 67520; 67521; 67522; 67523; 67524; 67525; 67526; 67527; 67528
TRW Automotive Products Remfg. (McAllen, TX) 87943
TRW Commercial Steering (Lebanon, TN) 81311
TRW Inc. (Huntsville, AL) 56042
TRW Inc. (Greensboro, NC) 74925
TRW Inc. (Greenville, NC) 74980
TRW Inc. (Rogersville, TN) 82282
TRW Inc. Commercial Steering Div. (Greeneville, TN) 80890
TRW Inc. Commercial Steering Div. (Lebanon, TN) 81312
TRW Inc. Fuji Valve Div. (Sevierville, TN) 82298
TRW Inc. Reda Pump Div. (Bartlesville, OK) 76853
TRW Inc. Ross Gear Div. (Greeneville, TN) 80891
TRW Inc. Ross Gear Inc. (Lebanon, TN) 81313
TRW Inc. Station Plant Steering & Suspension Div. (Greenville, NC) 74981
TRW Inc. Transportation Electronics Div. (Knoxville, TN) 81262; 81263
Trw Inc. Carr Knoxville (Knoxville, TN) 81264
Trw Inc. Koyo Steering Sys. Co. (Vonore, TN) 82397
Trw Inc. Mission Drilling Products (Houston, TX) 87047
TRW Inc. Redi Property Data (Fort Lauderdale, FL) 59624
Trw Inc. Station Plant (Greenville, NC) 74982
Trw Inc. Staton (Greenville, NC) 74983
TRW Information Svc. (Arlington, VA) 90389
TRW Koyo Steering System (Vonove, TN) 82398
TRW Seat Belt Systems (Louisville, MS) 73125
TRW System Integration Group (Fairfax, VA) 90812
TRW Vehicle Safety Systems (McAllen, TX) 87944
Trylon Corp. Inc. (San Marcos, TX) 89344
Tuco, Inc. (Amarillo, TX) 82587
Tuner Broadcasting System, Inc. (was Turner Communications Corp.) (Atlanta, GA) 65225
Turner Broadcasting System, Inc. (Atlanta, GA) **65226**
Turner Corp. (Oklahoma City, OK) 77638
Turner Corp. (Alexandria, VA) 90241
Turner Corp. (Newport News, VA) 91490
Turner Food Corp. (Parrish, FL) 62360
Turner Foods Corp. (Punta Gorda, FL) 62722
Turner Home Entertainment (Atlanta, GA) 65227
Turst Co. Bank of Columbus, N.A. (La Grange, GA) 66489
Twb Inc. (Jackson, MS) 73078
Twelve Oaks Hospital (Houston, TX) 87048
Twentieth Century Companies Inc. Hoov-R-Line (Providence, KY) 69236
Twin Cities Hospital (Niceville, FL) 61719
Twin Lakes Hospital (Denton, TX) 84643
Del Monte Foods USA Plant 255 (Crystal City, TX) 83822
Txt a Brunswick Co. (Houston, TX) 87049
Tyler Refrigeration Corp. (Olive Branch, MS) 73234
Tylor Publishing Co. (Dallas, TX) 84467
Tyson Distribution Center (Rogers, AR) 57571
Tyson E. Feed Mill (Springdale, AR) 57645
Tyson Feed Mill (Attalla, AL) 55058
Tyson Feed Mill (Cullman, AL) 55553
Tyson Feed Mill (Estill Springs, TN) 80777
Tyson Feed Mills (Roaring River, NC) 76052
Tyson Fods Inc. (Cullman, AL) 55554
Tyson Food Chick'n Quick (Rogers, AR) 57572
Tyson Food Service (Wilkesboro, NC) 76521
Tyson Foods (Boaz, AL) 55478
Tyson Foods (Waldron, AR) 57701
Tyson Foods (Shelbyville, TN) 82319
Tyson Foods of Bentonville (Bentonville, AR) 56790
Tyson Foods Bloomer Plant (Charleston, AR) 56845
Tyson Foods Cornish Cornish Plant (Springdale, AR) 57646
Tyson Foods Feed Mill (Springdale, AR) 57647
Tyson Foods Feed Mill (Gonzales, TX) 85592
Tyson Foods Inc. (Ashland, AL) 55032; 55033; 55034
Tyson Foods, Inc. (Blountsville, AL) 55464
Tyson Foods Inc. (Gadsden, AL) 55793
Tyson Foods Inc. (Heflin, AL) 55863; 55864; 55865
Tyson Foods Inc. (Oxford, AL) 56440; 56441
Tyson Foods Inc. (Bentonville, AR) 56791
Tyson Foods Inc. (Berryville, AR) 56799
Tyson Foods Inc. (Clarksville, AR) 56853; 56854
Tyson Foods Inc. (Dardanelle, AR) 56889
Tyson Foods Inc. (Fayetteville, AR) 56997; 56998
Tyson Foods Inc. (Fort Smith, AR) 57110; 57111
Tyson Foods Inc. (Grannis, AR) 57121
Tyson Foods, Inc. (Green Forest, AR) 57122
Tyson Foods Inc. (Nashville, AR) 57443
Tyson Foods Inc. (North Little Rock, AR) 57478
Tyson Foods Inc. (Paris, AR) 57501; 57502; 57503
Tyson Foods Inc. (Pine Bluff, AR) 57533; 57534
Tyson Foods Inc. (Rison, AR) 57557
Tyson Foods Inc. (Rogers, AR) 57573
Tyson Foods, Inc. (Spingdale, AR) **57626**
Tyson Foods Inc. (Springdale, AR) 57648; 57649; 57650; 57651; 57652
Tyson Foods Inc. (Van Buren, AR) 57696; 57697
Tyson Foods Inc. (Waldron, AR) 57702; 57703; 57704
Tyson Foods Inc. (Ball Ground, GA) 65377; 65378
Tyson Foods Inc. (Cumming, GA) 65751
Tyson Foods Inc. (Springhill, LA) 70858
Tyson Foods Inc. (Snow Hills, MD) 72453
Tyson Foods Inc. (Harmony, NC) 75006
Tyson Foods Inc. (Monroe, NC) 75594
Tyson Foods Inc. (Wilkesboro, NC) 76522
Tyson Foods Inc. (Broken Bow, OK) 76895; 76896
Tyson Foods Inc. (Decherd, TN) 80729
Tyson Foods Inc. (Shelbyville, TN) 82320; 82321; 82322
Tyson Foods Inc. (Carthage, TX) 83523; 83524
Tyson Foods Inc. (Garland, TX) 85545
Tyson Foods Inc. (Humble, TX) 87252
Tyson Foods Inc. (Sequin, TX) 89387
Tyson Foods Inc. (Crewe, VA) 90669
Tyson Foods Inc. (Glen Allen, VA) 90985
Tyson Foods Inc. (Harrisonburg, VA) 91101
Tyson Foods Inc. (Temperanceville, VA) 92382
Tyson Foods Inc. Cooked Products Div. (Wilkesboro, NC) 76523
Tyson Foods Inc. Entree Div. (Fayetteville, AR) 56999
Tyson Foods Inc. of Bentonville (Bentonville, AR) 56792
Tyson Foods Inc. Bergman Feed Mill (Bergman, AR) 56798
Tyson Foods, Inc.- Berry St. Plant (Springdale, AR) 57653
Tyson Foods Inc. of Berryville (Berryville, AR) 56800
Tyson Foods Inc. Berryville of Berryville (Berryville, AR) 56801
Tyson Foods Inc. Blountsville Plant (Blountsville, AL) 55465
Tyson Foods Inc. Broken Bow Processing (Broken Bow, OK) 76897
Tyson Foods Inc. Cornish Plant-Protein (Springdale, AR) 57654
Tyson Foods Inc. Craig Feed Mill (Broken Bow, OK) 76898
Tyson Foods Inc. Dardanelle Complex (Dardanelle, AR) 56890
Tyson Foods Inc. Feed Mill (Pine Bluff, AR) 57535
Tyson Foods Inc. Feed Mill (New Market, VA) 91443; 91444
Tyson Foods Inc. Feedmill (Tenaha, TX) 89656
Tyson Foods Inc. Gadsden Processing Plant (Gadsden, AL) 55794
Tyson Foods Inc. Gonzales Feed Mill (Gonzales, TX) 85593; 85594
Tyson Foods Inc. Krispy Kitchens (Bentonville, AR) 56793
Tyson Foods Inc. N. Litle Rock Plant (North Little Rock, AR) 57479
Tyson Foods Inc. Nacogdoches Mill (Nacogdoches, TX) 88176
Tyson Foods Inc. Nashville Feed Mill (Nashville, AR) 57444
Tyson Foods Inc. Pine Bluff Feed Mill (Pine Bluff, AR) 57536
Tyson Foods Inc. Pine Bluff Further Processing (Pine Bluff, AR) 57537
Tyson Foods Inc. Processing Plant (Carthage, TX) 83525
Tyson Foods Inc. (Quik-To-Fix) (Garland, TX) 85546
Tyson Foods Inc. Seguin Plant (Seguin, TX) 89379
Tyson Foods Inc. Shenandoah Valley Complex (Harrisonburg, VA) 91102
Tyson Foods Inc. Tyler Rd. Plant (Russellville, AR) 57593
Tyson Foods Inc. Tyler Road Plant (Russellville, AR) 57594
Tyson Foods Inc. Tyson Feed Mill (Cullman, AL) 55555
Tyson Foods Inc. (was Tysons Foods Inc.) (Springdale, AR) 57655
Tyson Foods Inc. Wastewater Treatment Plant (Harrisonburg, VA) 91103
Tyson Foods Longhaul Shop (Springdale, AR) 57656
Tyson Garrett Plant (Rogers, AR) 57574
Tyson/Holly Farms Foods Inc. Waste Water Treatment Plant (Glen Allen, VA) 90986
Tyson Johnson Rd. Mill (Springdale, AR) 57657
Tyson Mexican Original (Sanford, NC) 76207
Tyson of Nashville (Nashville, AR) 57445
Tyson & ORG Holly Farms Inc. (Center, TX) 83543
Tyson Valley Distribution Center (Russellville, AR) 57595
Tyson's Chick'n Quick (Rogers, AR) 57575
Tyson's of Fayetteville Entree (Fayetteville, AR) 57000
Tyson's & ORG Rogers (Rogers, AR) 57576

U

U S Bancorp Inc. (St Petersburg, FL) 63039
U S Design (Tampa, FL) 63632
U S Design (Tulsa, OK) 78183
Ucar Carbon Co. Inc. (Columbia, TN) 80640
Ucar Carbon Co. Inc. (Lawrenceburg, TN) 81292
Ucar Carbon Co. Inc. (Anmoore, WV) 92659
Ucar Emulsion Systems (Garland, TX) 85547
Ucar Pipeline Inc. (Groves, TX) 85685
Ucar Resinas Caribe Inc. (Bayamon, PR) 78342
UCIG Inc. Linde Div. (Big Spring, TX) 83297
Uds/Motorola (Huntsville, AL) 56043
Underwriters Adjusting Comp (Oklahoma City, OK) 77639
Underwriters Adjusting Co. (Huntsville, AL) 56044
Underwriters Adjusting Co. (Fort Smith, AR) 57112
Underwriters Adjusting Co. (Little Rock, AR) 57318
Underwriters Adjusting Co. (Jacksonville, FL) 60480; 60481
Underwriters Adjusting Co. (Miami, FL) 61486
Underwriters Adjusting Co. (Naples, FL) 61668
Underwriters Adjusting Co. (Pensacola, FL) 62484
Underwriters Adjusting Co. (Vidalia, GA) 67995
Underwriters Adjusting Co. (Bowling Green, KY) 68163
Underwriters Adjusting Co. (Lexington, KY) 68647
Underwriters Adjusting Co. (Baton Rouge, LA) 69678
Underwriters Adjusting Co. (Lafayette, LA) 70119
Underwriters Adjusting Co. (Shreveport, LA) 70798
Underwriters Adjusting Co. (Belmont, MS) 72611
Underwriters Adjusting Co. (Collins, MS) 72697
Underwriters Adjusting Co. (Jackson, MS) 73079
Underwriters Adjusting Co. (Mc Comb, MS) 73152
Underwriters Adjusting Co. (Asheville, NC) 73638
Underwriters Adjusting Co. (Charlotte, NC) 74182
Underwriters Adjusting Co. (Fayetteville, NC) 74578
Underwriters Adjusting Co. (Raleigh, NC) 75966
Underwriters Adjusting Co. (Wilmington, NC) 76602
Underwriters Adjusting Co. (Cyril, OK) 76984
Underwriters Adjusting Co. (Tulsa, OK) 78184
Underwriters Adjusting Co. (Greenville, SC) 79442
Underwriters Adjusting Co. (Cookeville, TN) 80669
Underwriters Adjusting Co. (Gibson, TN) 80859
Underwriters Adjusting Co. (Knoxville, TN) 81265
Underwriters Adjusting Co. (Martin, TN) 81399
Underwriters Adjusting Co. (Nashville, TN) 82117
Underwriters Adjusting Co. (Arlington, TX) 82772
Underwriters Adjusting Co. (Dallas, TX) 84468
Underwriters Adjusting Co. (El Paso, TX) 84954
Underwriters Adjusting Co. (Fort Worth, TX) 85338
Underwriters Adjusting Co. (Harlingen, TX) 85718
Underwriters Adjusting Co. (Hurst, TX) 87300
Underwriters Adjusting Co. (San Angelo, TX) 88904
Underwriters Adjusting Co. (San Antonio, TX) 89280
Underwriters Adjusting Co. (Temple, TX) 89650
Underwriters Adjusting Co. (Wichita Falls, TX) 90118
Underwriters Adjusting Co. (Norfolk, VA) 91589
Underwriters Adjusting Co. (Beckley, WV) 92687; 92688
Underwriters Adjusting Co. (Charleston, WV) 92795
Ungermann-Bass Inc. (Longwood, FL) 60950
Ungermann-Bass Inc. (Atlanta, GA) 65228
Ungermann-Bass Inc. (Houston, TX) 87050
Uni-Copy Corp. (Morrisville, NC) 75669
Uni-Copy Corp. of North Carolina (Raleigh, NC) 75967
Unicopy Corp. of North Carolina (Durham, NC) 74431
UNIFI (Madison, NC) 75485
UNIFI (Staunton, VA) 92330
UNIFI, Inc. (Archdale, NC) 73562
UNIFI, Inc. (Greensboro, NC) **74926**
UNIFI, Inc. (Madison, NC) 75486
UNIFI, Inc. (Mayodan, NC) 75539
UNIFI, Inc. (Reidsville, NC) 76015
UNIFI, Inc. (Stoneville, NC) 76344
Unifi, Inc. (Yadkinville, NC) 76782
Unifi Inc. (Chattanooga, TN) 80507
Unifi Inc. (Staunton, VA) 92331
Unifi Inc. Plant 1 (Mayodan, NC) 75540
Unijax, Inc. (Jacksonville, FL) 60482
Unijax Inc. (Miami, FL) 61487; 61488
Unijax Inc. (Tampa, FL) 63633
Unijax Inc. (Atlanta, GA) 65229
Unijax Inc. (Columbus, GA) 65655; 65656
Unijax Inc. (Macon, GA) 66720
Unijax Inc. (Savannah, GA) 67529
Unijax Inc. (Valdosta, GA) 67976; 67977
Unijax, Inc. (Charlotte, NC) 74183; 74184
Unijax Inc. (Garner, NC) 74649
Unijax Inc. (Columbia, SC) 79112; 79113
Unijax Inc. (Alexandria, VA) 90242
Unijax Inc. (Huntington, WV) 92899; 92900
Unijax Sloan Paper (Hollywood, FL) 60102
Unimark Plastics (Greer, SC) 79491
Union Bank (N Little Rock, AR) 57432
Union Bank (Lakeland, FL) 60790
Union Bank (Jamestown, TN) 81019
Union Bank (Jellico, TN) 81024
Union Bank (San Antonio, TX) 89281
Union/Butterfield Straight Line (Gaffney, SC) 79267
Union Camp Corp. (Brent, AL) 55479
Union Camp Corp. (Chapman, AL) 55506; 55507; 55508
Union Camp Corp. (Decatur, AL) 55609; 55610
Union Camp Corp. (Georgiana, AL) 55806
Union Camp Corp. (Opelika, AL) 56427; 56428; 56429
Union Camp Corp. (Prattville, AL) 56493
Union Camp Corp. (Thorsby, AL) 56612; 56613; 56614
Union Camp Corp. (Conway, AR) 56875
Union Camp Corp. (Van Buren, AR) 57698
Union Camp Corp. (Jacksonville, FL) 60483
Union Camp Corp. (Folkston, GA) 66224
Union Camp Corp. (Forest Park, GA) 66251
Union Camp Corp. (Griffin, GA) 66327
Union Camp Corp. (La Grange, GA) 66490
Union Camp Corp. (Lifton, GA) 66551
Union Camp Corp. (Louisville, GA) 66625; 66626
Union Camp Corp. (Marietta, GA) 66942
Union Camp Corp. (Pooler, GA) 67272
Union Camp Corp. (Rincon, GA) 67302
Union Camp Corp. (Savannah, GA) 67530; 67531
Union Camp Corp. (Statesboro, GA) 67651
Union Camp Corp. (Swainsboro, GA) 67760
Union Camp Corp. (Tifton Georgi, GA) 67834
Union Camp Corp. (Townsend, GA) 67841
Union Camp Corp. (Tucker, GA) 67899; 67900
Union Camp Corp. (Valdosta, GA) 67978
Union Camp Corp. (Vidalia, GA) 67996
Union Camp Corp. (Waycross, GA) 68042
Union Camp Corp. (Shelbyville, KY) 69278
Union Camp Corp. (Broussard, LA) 69745
Union Camp Corp. (Houston, MS) 72924; 72925
Union Camp Corp. (Jamestown, NC) 75244; 75245
Union Camp Corp. (Seaboard, NC) 76214
Union Camp Corp. (Eastover, SC) 79182; 79183
Union Camp Corp. (Gray Court, SC) 79288
Union Camp Corp. (Spartanburg, SC) 79960; 79961
Union Camp Corp. (Spartenburg, SC) 79969
Union Camp Corp. (Wellford, SC) 80082
Union Camp Corp. (Morristown, TN) 81814

United Parcel Service (Guymon, OK) 77116
United Parcel Service (Lawton, OK) 77176
United Parcel Service (Mc Alester, OK) 77200
United Parcel Service (Muskogee, OK) 77231
United Parcel Service (Oklahoma City, OK) 77646
United Parcel Service (Ponca City, OK) 77715
United Parcel Service (Tulsa, OK) 78185; 78186
United Parcel Service (Anderson, SC) 78694; 78695
United Parcel Service (Charleston, SC) 78907
United Parcel Service (Spartanburg, SC) 79963
United Parcel Service (West Columbia, SC) 80110
United Parcel Service (Dyersburg, TN) 80762
United Parcel Service (Nashville, TN) 82130
United Parcel Service (Arlington, TX) 82775
United Parcel Service (Austin, TX) 83052
United Parcel Service (Beaumont, TX) 83229
United Parcel Service (Bryan, TX) 83410
United Parcel Service (Dallas, TX) 84471; 84472; 84473
United Parcel Service (Denton, TX) 84644
United Parcel Service (El Paso, TX) 84956
United Parcel Service (Fort Worth, TX) 85341
United Parcel Service (Granbury, TX) 85601
United Parcel Service (La Marque, TX) 87547; 87548
United Parcel Service (Longview, TX) 87743
United Parcel Service (Lubbock, TX) 87792; 87793
United Parcel Service (Midland, TX) 88093
United Parcel Service (San Antonio, TX) 89283; 89284; 89285; 89286
United Parcel Service (Stafford, TX) 89509
United Parcel Service (Tyler, TX) 89840
United Parcel Service (Vernon, TX) 89875
United Parcel Service (Victoria, TX) 89908
United Parcel Service (Wichita Falls, TX) 90119
United Parcel Service (Alexandria, VA) 90243
United Parcel Service (Cedar Bluff, VA) 90513
United Parcel Service (Danville, VA) 90722
United Parcel Service (Fredericksbg, VA) 90906
United Parcel Service (Front Royal, VA) 90957; 90958
United Parcel Service (Lynchburg, VA) 91291
United Parcel Service (Norfolk, VA) 91590
United Parcel Service (Richmond, VA) 92065; 92066; 92067; 92068; 92069
United Parcel Service (Virginia Beach, VA) 92519
United Parcel Service (Beckley, WV) 92689
United Parcel Service (Caldwell, WV) 92719
United Parcel Service (Charleston, WV) 92797; 92798
United Parcel Service (Clarksburg, WV) 92822
United Parcel Service (Fairmont, WV) 92849
United Parcel Service (Parkersburg, WV) 92998
United Parcel Service Air (Birmingham, AL) 55441
United Parcel Service of America (Atlanta, GA) **65234**
United Parcel Service Inc. (Lexington, KY) 68649
United Parcel Service Inc. (La Marque, TX) 87549; 87550
United Parcel Service/UPS Customer Service (Atlanta, GA) 65235
United Parcel Services (Spartanburg, SC) 79964
United Parcel Services Inc. (Orlando, FL) 62174
United Services Auto Association (San Antonio, TX) 89287
United Services Automobile (Annapolis, MD) 71021
United Services Automobile (Alexandria, VA) 90244
United State Lime & Minerals, Inc. (Fairfax, VA) 90813
U.S. Engine Valve Corp. (Westminister, SC) 80114
United Technologies Advanced Systems Div. (Huntsville, AL) 56048
United Technologies Automotive Engineered Systems Div. (Dayton, TN) 80723
United Technologies Automotive Engineered Systems Div. (Lexington, TN) 81344
United Technologies Auto (Washington, DC) 58510
United Technologies Auto (Tampa, FL) 63640
United Technologies Auto (Thomson, GA) 67816
United Technologies Auto (Manfield, KY) 69075
United Technologies Auto (Columbus, MS) 72731
United Technologies Auto (Bennettsville, SC) 78733
United Technologies Auto (St. Matthews, SC) 79975
United Technologies Automative Inc. (Mount Airy, NC) 75685
United Technologies Automotive (Tampa, FL) 63641
United Technologies Automotive Inc. (Mount Airy, NC) 75686
United Technologies Automotive Inc. (Lexington, TN) 81345
United Technologies Automotive Thomson Plant (Thomson, GA) 67817
United Technologies Corp. Advanced Systems Div. (Huntsville, AL) 56049
United Technologies Corp. Srb Assembly & Refurb. Fac. (Kennedy Space Center, FL) 60558
United Technologies Electro Systems (Columbus, MS) 72732
United Technologies Optical (Jupiter, FL) 60553
United Van Lines Inc. (De Land, FL) 59261
United Van Lines Inc. (High Point, NC) 75175
United Van Lines Inc. (Rocky Mount, NC) 76109
United Van Lines Inc. (Richmond, VA) 92070
Unitron Inc. (Dallas, TX) 84474
Universal Bedroom Furniture Ltd. (Morristown, TN) 81815
Universal Corp. (Richmond, VA) **92071**
Universal Data Systems (Huntsville, AL) 56050
Universal Data Systems (Brandon, FL) 58881
Universal Data Systems (Maitland, FL) 60988
Universal Data Systems (Roswell, GA) 67425
Universal Data Systems (Winston Salem, NC) 76689
Universal Foods Corp. (Baltimore, MD) 71318
Universal Foods Corp. (Dallas, TX) 84475; 84476
Universal Foods Corp. (Houston, TX) 87061
Universal Foods Corp. (San Antonio, TX) 89288
Universal Forest Prod (Grandview, TX) 85651
Universal Forest Prods Inc. (Moultrie, GA) 67065
Universal Forest Products (Union City, GA) 67933
Universal Forest Products (Grandview, TX) 85652
Universal Forest Products, Inc. (Auburndale, FL) 58603
Universal Forest Products, Inc. (Mouetrie, GA) 67053
Universal Forest Products, Inc. (Salisbury, NC) 76180
Universal Furniture (High Point, NC) 75176
Universal Instruments Corp. (Lawrenceville, GA) 66543
Universal Instruments Corp. (Shreveport, LA) 70800
Universal Instruments Corp. (Raleigh, NC) 75972
Universal-Rundle Corp. (Lawrenceville, GA) 66544
Universal Rundle Corp. (Monroe, GA) 66994; 66995
Universal Rundle Corp. (Union Point, GA) 67935; 67936
Universal Rundle Corp. (Hondo, TX) 85753; 85754; 85755
Universal-Rundle Corp. Fiberglass Div. (Union Point, GA) 67937
Unocal Corp. (Chunchula, AL) 55515
Unocal Corp. Unocal Chemicals Div. (Charlotte, NC) 74191; 74192
Unum Life (Dallas, TX) 84477
Unum Life Insurance (Atlanta, GA) 65236
Unum Life Insurance Co. (Nashville, TN) 82131
UOP Inc. (Blanchard, LA) 69700
UOP Inc. (Shreveport, LA) 70801
Upjohn Co. (Barceloneta, PR) 78332
Upjohn Manufacturing Co. (Barceloneta, PR) 78333
Upjohn Mfg. Co. (Barceloneta, PR) 78334
US Agri-Chemicals Bartow Facility (Bartow, FL) 58631
US Agri-Chemicals Bartow Plant (Bartow, FL) 58632
US Agri-Chemicals Fort Meade Chemical Plant (Fort Meade, FL) 59653
US Agri-Chemicals Ft. Meade Facility (Fort Meade, FL) 59654
US Clinical Prods. Inc. (Richardson, TX) 88786
US Clinical Products, Inc. (Plano, TX) 88615
US Concord, Inc. (Houston, TX) 87062
US Design Corp. (Lanham Seabrook, MD) 72061
US Doe Oak Ridge National Laboratory (Oak Ridge, TN) 82201
US Electrical Motors (Mena, AR) 57367; 57368
US Electrical Motors (Philadelphia, MS) 73282
US Engine Valve Co. (Westminster, SC) 80119; 80120
US Fidelity (Birmingham, AL) 55442
US Fidelity (Fort Myers, FL) 59770
US Fidelity (Greenville, MS) 72824
US Fidelity (Charleston, SC) 78908
US Fidelity (Columbia, SC) 79117
US Fidelity (Commerce, TX) 83645
US Fidelity (Dallas, TX) 84478
US Fidelity (El Paso, TX) 84957
US Fidelity & Gu (Montgomery, AL) 56394
US Fidelity & Gu (Jacksonville, FL) 60488
US Fidelity & Gu (Lafayette, LA) 70121
US Fidelity & Gu (Metairie, LA) 70323
US Fidelity & Gu (Gulfport, MS) 72881
US Fidelity & Gu (Jackson, MS) 73083
US Fidelity & Gu (Wilmington, NC) 76604
US Fidelity & Gu (Guymon, OK) 77117
US Fidelity & Gu (Muskogee, OK) 77232
US Fidelity & Gu (Tulsa, OK) 78187
US Fidelity & Gu (Houston, TX) 87063; 87064
US Fidelity & Gu (Midland, TX) 88094
US Fidelity & Gu (Richmond, VA) 92072
US Fidelity & Guaranty Insurance (Lexington, KY) 68650
US Fidelity & Guaranty Insurance (Louisville, KY) 69030
US Fidelity & Guaranty Insurance (Chattanooga, TN) 80514
US Fidelity & Guaranty Insurance (Nashville, TN) 82132
US Fleet Leasing (Marietta, GA) 66944
US Fleet Leasing (Houston, TX) 87065
US Gypsum Co. (Birmingham, AL) 55443
US Gypsum Co. (Jacksonville, FL) 60489
US Gypsum Co. (Miami, FL) 61491
US Gypsum Co. (Atlanta, GA) 65237; 65238
US Gypsum Co. (Chamblee, GA) 65549; 65550
US Gypsum Co. (Louisville, KY) 69031
US Gypsum Co. (Baltimore, MD) 71319
US Gypsum Co. (Kings Mountain, NC) 75311
US Gypsum Co. (Spruce Pine, NC) 76304
US Gypsum Co. (Nashville, TN) 82133
US Gypsum Co. (Bellaire, TX) 83272
US Gypsum Co. (Dallas, TX) 84479; 84480
US Gypsum Co. (New Braunfels, TX) 88222
US Gypsum Co. (Norfolk, VA) 91591
US Gypsum Co. Inc. (Heflin, AL) 55866
US Leasing Internat (Bethesda, MD) 71445
US Leasing International (Bethesda, MD) 71446
US Marine/Bayliner (Tallahassee, FL) 63284
US Marine/Bayliner (Salisbury, MD) 72365
US Marine/Bayliner (Dandridge, TN) 80714
US Motors (Philadelphia, MS) 73283
US Navy Naval Weapons Industrial Reserve Plant (Dallas, TX) 84481
US Pipe & Foundry Co. (Chattanooga, TN) 80515
US Pipe & Foundry Co. Chattanooga Valve & Fittings (Chattanooga, TN) 80516
US Pulp & Newsprint (Coosa Pines, AL) 55527
US Shoe Corp. (Arlington, TX) 82776
US Sprint Communication Co. (Fort Worth, TX) 85342
US Sprint Communication Co. (Lufkin, TX) 87820
USA Today (Arlington, VA) 90390
USAA (San Antonio, TX) **89289**
USAIR Group (Arlington, VA) **90391**
Uscar Carbon Co. Inc. (Clarksville, TN) 80560
USF&G Corp. (Baltimore, MD) **71320**
USG Interiors Inc. (Birmingham, AL) 55444
Uss Fairfield Works Fairfield Works (Fairfield, AL) 55717
UST Inc. (Norcross, GA) 67206
USX Fairfield Works (Fairfield, AL) 55718
Utah Fuel Co. Inc. (Roanoke, VA) 92196
Utility Fuels Inc. (Washington, DC) 58511
Utility Fuels Inc. (Houston, TX) 87066
UTL Corp. (Dallas, TX) 84482

V

Vaguard Bank & Trust Co. (Eglin AFB, FL) 59380
Vaguard Bank & Trust Co. (Fort Walton Beach, FL) 59843
Valaspar Corp. (High Point, NC) 75177
Valentec Dayron (Orlando, FL) 62175
Valentec Dayron Inc. (Orlando, FL) 62176
Valentec International Corp. Valentec Dayron Div. (Orlando, FL) 62177
Valentine Paper Co. Lockport Div. (Lockport, LA) 70198
Valero Energy Corp. (San Antonio, TX) **89290**
Valero Refining Co. (Corpus Christi, TX) 83763
Valero Refining & Marketing Co. (Houston, TX) 87067
Valhi Inc. (Dallas, TX) **84483;** 84484
Valley Coca-Cola Bottling Co. (Mc Allen, TX) 87903
Valley Coca-Cola Bottling Co., Inc. (McAllen, TX) 87945
Valley Line Co. Inc (Houston, TX) 87068
Valley National Financial Service (Atlanta, GA) 65239
Valley National Financial Service (Oklahoma City, OK) 77647
Valley National Financial Service (Fort Worth, TX) 85343
Valley National Financial Service (San Antonio, TX) 89291
Valley National Financial Service Co. (Farmers Branch, TX) 85036
Valleydale Inc. (Salem, VA) 92225
Valspar Corp (Houston, TX) 87069
Valspar Corp. (Tampa, FL) 63642
Valspar Corp. (Covington, GA) 65742
Valspar Corp. (Louisville, KY) 69032
Valspar Corp. (New Orleans, LA) 70583
Valspar Corp. (Baltimore, MD) 71321
Valspar Corp. (High Point, NC) 75178
Valspar Corp. (Beaumont, TX) 83230
Valspar Corp. (Garland, TX) 85554; 85555
Valspar Corp. (Houston, TX) 87070
Valspar Corp. Beaumont (Beaumont, TX) 83231
Valspar Corp. Fed (Tampa, FL) 63643
Valspar Corp. Garland (Garland, TX) 85556
Valspar Corp. Jackson (Jackson, TN) 81014
Value Added Service Corp. (Georgetown, KY) 68387
Valvoline Inc. (College Park, GA) 65611
Valvoline Inc. (Lexington, KY) 68651; 68652
Valvoline Instant Oil Chang (Lexington, KY) 68653; 68654
Valvoline Instant Oil Chang (Nashville, TN) 82134
Valvoline Instant Oil Change (Atlanta, GA) 65240
Valvoline Instant Oil Change (Decatur, GA) 65909; 65910; 65911
Valvoline Instant Oil Change (Lawrenceville, GA) 66545; 66546
Valvoline Instant Oil Change (Lilburn, GA) 66582; 66583
Valvoline Instant Oil Change (Lithia Spring, GA) 66588
Valvoline Instant Oil Change (Peachtree City, GA) 67250
Valvoline Instant Oil Change (Riverdale, GA) 67329; 67330
Valvoline Instant Oil Change (Smyrna, GA) 67583; 67584
Valvoline Instant Oil Change (Chattanooga, TN) 80517; 80518; 80519
Valvoline Instant Oil Change (East Ridge, TN) 80766
Valvoline Instant Oil Change (Hixson, TN) 80937
Valvoline Instant Oil Change, Inc. (Lexington, KY) 68655
Valvoline Oil Change (Madison, TN) 81384
Valvoline Oil Co. (Lexington, KY) 68656
Van Dorn Co. (Fountain Inn, SC) 79250
Van Waters & Rogers Inc. (Birmingham, AL) 55445
Van Waters & Rogers Inc. (New Orleans, LA) 70584
Van Waters & Rogers Inc. (Charlotte, NC) 74193
Van Waters & Rogers Inc. (Murfreesboro, TN) 81872
Van Waters & Rogers Inc. (Amarillo, TX) 82588
Van Waters & Rogers Inc. (Houston, TX) 87071
Van Waters & Rogers Inc. (Richmond, VA) 92073
Vandervoort (Fort Worth, TX) 85344
Vandervoort Dairy Foods Co. (Fort Worth, TX) 85345
Vandervoort's (Fort Worth, TX) 85346
Vanguard Bank & Trust Co. (Eglin AFB, FL) 59381
Vanguard Bank & Trust Co. (Mary Esther, FL) 61024
Vanguard Bank & Trust Co. (Niceville, FL) 61720; 61721
Vanguard Bank & Trust Co. (Valparaiso, FL) 63713
Vanguard Financial Services Inc. (Norcross, GA) 67207
Vanity Fair Mills Inc. (Atmore, AL) 55053
Vanity Fair Mills Inc. (Butler, AL) 55497
Vanity Fair Mills Inc. (Jackson, AL) 56070
Vanity Fair Mills Inc. (Monroeville, AL) 56269
Vanity Fair Mills Inc. (Robertsdale, AL) 56504
Vanity Fair Mills Inc. Plant 6 (Monroeville, AL) 56270
Vapor Corp. (Montgomery, AL) 56395
Variable Annuity Life (Houston, TX) **87072**
Variable Annuity Life Insur (Houston, TX) 87073
Variable Annuity Life Insurance (Boca Raton, FL) 58747
Variable Annuity Life Insurance (Winter Park, FL) 63998
Variable Annuity Life Insurance (Dunwoody, GA) 66139
Variable Annuity Life Insurance (Metairie, LA) 70324
Variable Annuity Life Insurance (Montgomery, MD) 72138

Wachovia Bank & Trust Co. N (Maxton, NC) 75536
Wachovia Bank & Trust Co. N (Mc Leansville, NC) 75543
Wachovia Bank & Trust Co. N (Mebane, NC) 75553
Wachovia Bank & Trust Co. N (Morehead City, NC) 75628
Wachovia Bank & Trust Co. N (Morganton, NC) 75658; 75659
Wachovia Bank & Trust Co. N (Mount Olive, NC) 75697
Wachovia Bank & Trust Co. N (Murphy, NC) 75711
Wachovia Bank & Trust Co. N (New Bern, NC) 75738
Wachovia Bank & Trust Co. N (Raleigh, NC) 75976; 75977; 75978; 75979; 75980; 75981
Wachovia Bank & Trust Co. N (Salisbury, NC) 76182; 76183; 76184
Wachovia Bank & Trust Co. N (Sanford, NC) 76208
Wachovia Bank & Trust Co. N (Sealevel, NC) 76216
Wachovia Bank & Trust Co. N (Vanceboro, NC) 76415
Wachovia Bank & Trust Co. N (Washington, NC) 76462
Wachovia Bank & Trust Co. N (Waynesville, NC) 76474
Wachovia Bank & Trust Co. N (Wilmington, NC) 76606; 76607; 76608; 76609; 76610; 76611
Wachovia Bank & Trust Co. N (Winston Salem, NC) 76695; 76696; 76697; 76698; 76699
Wachovia Bank & Trust Co. Na (Charlotte, NC) 74208; 74209; 74210; 74211; 74212; 74213; 74214; 74215; 74216; 74217
Wachovia Bank & Trust Co. Na (Greensboro, NC) 74936; 74937; 74938; 74939; 74940; 74941
Wachovia Bank & Trust Co. NA (Hendersonville, NC) 75046
Wachovia Bank & Trust Co. Na (Reidsville, NC) 76016; 76017
Wachovia Bank & Trust Co. Na (Rocky Mount, NC) 76110
Wachovia Bank&Trust Co. Libr (Winston Salem, NC) 76700
Wachovia Corp. (Winston-Salem, NC) **76775**; 76776
Wadsworth/Alert Laboratories Inc. (Atlanta, GA) 65253
Wagner Brake Co. (Fort Worth, TX) 85349
Wagner Brake Subsidiary (Memphis, TN) 81752
Wagner Electric Corp. (Memphis, TN) 81753
Wagner Electric Corp. (Fort Worth, TX) 85350
Waite Hill Holdings Inc. (Glen Allen, VA) 90987; 90988; 90989
Wal Mart (Alex City, AL) 54973
Wal Mart (Anniston, AL) 55018
Wal Mart (Attalla, AL) 55059
Wal Mart (Birmingham, AL) 55449; 55450
Wal Mart (Demopolis, AL) 55620
Wal Mart (Gadsden, AL) 55796
Wal Mart (Gardendale, AL) 55801
Wal Mart (Geneva, AL) 55805
Wal Mart (Huntsville, AL) 56051
Wal Mart (Leeds, AL) 56110
Wal Mart (Oneonta, AL) 56413
Wal Mart (Opelika, AL) 56431
Wal Mart (Prattville, AL) 56494
Wal Mart (Sheffield, AL) 56566
Wal Mart (Tuscaloosa, AL) 56679
Wal Mart (Benton, AR) 56781; 56782
Wal Mart (Bentonville, AR) 56794
Wal Mart (Conway, AR) 56877
Wal Mart (De Queen, AR) 56897
Wal Mart (Fayetteville, AR) 57001
Wal Mart (Harrison, AR) 57142; 57143
Wal Mart (Hot Springs National Park, AR) 57185
Wal Mart (Mountain Home, AR) 57392
Wal Mart (Paragould, AR) 57498
Wal Mart (Rogers, AR) 57577
Wal Mart (Walnut Ridge, AR) 57708
Wal Mart (West Memphis, AR) 57737
Wal Mart (Bradenton, FL) 58855
Wal Mart (Casselberry, FL) 58944
Wal Mart (Daytona Beach, FL) 59224
Wal Mart (Fernandina Beach, FL) 59415
Wal Mart (Fort Myers, FL) 59772
Wal Mart (Gainesville, FL) 59924
Wal Mart (Jacksonville, FL) 60495; 60496
Wal Mart (Lake City, FL) 60636
Wal Mart (Marianna, FL) 61012
Wal Mart (Mary Esther, FL) 61025
Wal Mart (Melbourne, FL) 61114
Wal Mart (Mount Dora, FL) 61569
Wal Mart (Northwest Smyrna Beach, FL) 61759
Wal Mart (Panama City, FL) 62356; 62357
Wal Mart (Pensacola, FL) 62486; 62487
Wal Mart (Sebring, FL) 62896
Wal Mart (St. Cloud, FL) 63071
Wal Mart (Starke, FL) 63154
Wal Mart (Tampa, FL) 63647
Wal Mart (Cairo, GA) 65459
Wal Mart (Covington, GA) 65743
Wal Mart (Douglas, GA) 65980
Wal Mart (Statesboro, GA) 67652
Wal Mart (Vidalia, GA) 67997
Wal Mart (Waycross, GA) 68043
Wal Mart (Abbeville, LA) 69363
Wal Mart (Bastrop, LA) 69452
Wal Mart (Baton Rouge, LA) 69683; 69684
Wal Mart (Bogalusa, LA) 69710
Wal Mart (Chalmette, LA) 69772
Wal Mart (De Ridder, LA) 69820
Wal Mart (Eunice, LA) 69849
Wal Mart (Franklin, LA) 69860
Wal Mart (Gretna, LA) 69918
Wal Mart (Lafayette, LA) 70123
Wal Mart (Lake Charles, LA) 70179; 70180
Wal Mart (Port Allen, LA) 70650
Wal Mart (Slidell, LA) 70845
Wal Mart (Clarksdale, MS) 72681
Wal Mart (Columbia, MS) 72701
Wal Mart (Greenville, MS) 72828; 72829
Wal Mart (Gulfport, MS) 72882
Wal Mart (Holly Springs, MS) 72912
Wal Mart (Mc Comb, MS) 73153
Wal Mart (Meridian, MS) 73183; 73184
Wal Mart (Pascagoula, MS) 73273
Wal Mart (Ridgeland, MS) 73330
Wal Mart (Southaven, MS) 73359
Wal Mart (Winona, MS) 73496
Wal Mart (Albemarle, NC) 73544
Wal Mart (Fayetteville, NC) 74582
Wal Mart (Goldsboro, NC) 74742
Wal Mart (Jacksonville, NC) 75234
Wal Mart (Kinston, NC) 75331
Wal Mart (Blackwell, OK) 76866
Wal Mart (Checotah, OK) 76917
Wal Mart (Duncan, OK) 76999
Wal Mart (Edmond, OK) 77026
Wal Mart (Kingfisher, OK) 77153
Wal Mart (Miami, OK) 77211
Wal Mart (Newcastle, OK) 77243
Wal Mart (Norman, OK) 77279
Wal Mart (Nowata, OK) 77285
Wal Mart (Oklahoma City, OK) 77650; 77651
Wal Mart (Poteau, OK) 77729
Wal Mart (Shawnee, OK) 77824
Wal Mart (Tahlequah, OK) 77862
Wal Mart (Tulsa, OK) 78189; 78190
Wal Mart (Vinita, OK) 78229
Wal Mart (Yukon, OK) 78285
Wal Mart (Aiken, SC) 78659
Wal Mart (Camden, SC) 78763
Wal Mart (Cheraw, SC) 78927; 78928
Wal Mart (Conway, SC) 79139
Wal Mart (Dillon, SC) 79166
Wal Mart (Gaffney, SC) 79268; 79269
Wal Mart (Greenville, SC) 79444; 79445
Wal Mart (Lake City, SC) 79565
Wal Mart (Lancaster, SC) 79582
Wal Mart (Lexington, SC) 79609
Wal Mart (Myrtle Beach, SC) 79716
Wal Mart (Newberry, SC) 79728; 79729
Wal Mart (Orangeburg, SC) 79779
Wal Mart (Spartanburg, SC) 79965; 79966
Wal Mart (Summerville, SC) 79994
Wal Mart (Taylors, SC) 80040
Wal Mart (Union, SC) 80055
Wal Mart (Walterboro, SC) 80078
Wal Mart (West Columbia, SC) 80111
Wal Mart (Allen, TX) 82498
Wal Mart (Athens, TX) 82794
Wal Mart (Austin, TX) 83053
Wal Mart (Ballinger, TX) 83093
Wal Mart (Carthage, TX) 83526
Wal Mart (Center, TX) 83544
Wal Mart (Clute, TX) 83603
Wal Mart (Conroe, TX) 83687; 83688
Wal Mart (Corsicana, TX) 83796
Wal Mart (Crockett, TX) 83803
Wal Mart (Denison, TX) 84611
Wal Mart (Dumas, TX) 84692
Wal Mart (Fort Stockton, TX) 85052
Wal Mart (Fort Worth, TX) 85351; 85352
Wal Mart (Fredericksbg, TX) 85374
Wal Mart (Henderson, TX) 85734
Wal Mart (Kilgore, TX) 87502
Wal Mart (Lewisville, TX) 87669
Wal Mart (Liberty, TX) 87682
Wal Mart (Mc Kinney, TX) 87925
Wal Mart (Mesquite, TX) 88010
Wal Mart (Pearland, TX) 88490
Wal Mart (Rosenberg, TX) 88841
Wal Mart (San Antonio, TX) 89297
Wal Mart (Seguin, TX) 89380
Wal Mart (Uvalde, TX) 89859
Wal Mart (Victoria, TX) 89909
Wal Mart Auto Center (Morgan City, LA) 70398
Wal Mart Auto Center (Tulsa, OK) 78191
Wal Mart Auto Center (Vidor, TX) 89921
Wal Mart Auto Ctr (Fort Smith, AR) 57115
Wal Mart Auto Repair (Waldron, AR) 57705
Wal Mart Auto Repair (Sulphur Springs, TX) 89565
Wal Mart Auto Repair (Texas City, TX) 89746
Wal Mart Automotive (Oklahoma City, OK) 77652
Wal Mart Automotive (Sallisaw, OK) 77775
Wal Mart Automotive (Granbury, TX) 85603
Wal Mart (Cafeteria) (Birmingham, AL) 55451
Wal Mart Cities (Tulsa, OK) 78192
Wal Mart Corp. (Tallahassee, FL) 63286
Wal Mart Department Store (Magee, MS) 73139
Wal Mart Department Store N (Mobile, AL) 56253
Wal Mart Dept Store (Guymon, OK) 77119
Wal Mart Dict Cty (Weslaco, TX) 90041
Wal Mart Disc (Marion, AR) 57347
Wal Mart Disc (Edinburg, TX) 84742
Wal Mart Disc Cits (Owasso, OK) 77686
Wal Mart Disc Cits (Sand Springs, OK) 77787
Wal Mart Disc Cits (Tulsa, OK) 78193
Wal Mart Disc Cits (Marshall, TX) 87870
Wal Mart Disc City (Austin, TX) 83054
Wal Mart Discnt (Jacksonville, TX) 87427
Wal Mart Discnt (Kerrville, TX) 87484
Wal Mart Discnt (San Benito, TX) 89332
Wal Mart Discnt (Weatherford, TX) 90016
Wal Mart Discnt Cy (Houston, TX) 87082
Wal Mart Discount (Pine Bluff, AR) 57538
Wal Mart Discount (Mustang, OK) 77241
Wal Mart Discount (Oklahoma City, OK) 77653
Wal Mart Discount (Belton, TX) 83280
Wal Mart Discount (Carrollton, TX) 83511
Wal Mart Discount (Denison, TX) 84612
Wal Mart Discount (El Paso, TX) 84961
Wal Mart Discount (Kilgore, TX) 87503
Wal Mart Discount (New Boston, TX) 88203
Wal Mart Discount (Plano, TX) 88617
Wal Mart Discount Center (Jacksonville, TX) 87428
Wal Mart Discount Cities (Mobile, AL) 56254
Wal Mart Discount Cities (Batesville, AR) 56763
Wal Mart Discount Cities (Forrest City, AR) 57014
Wal Mart Discount Cities (Fort Smith, AR) 57116; 57117; 57118
Wal Mart Discount Cities (Magnolia, AR) 57337
Wal Mart Discount Cities (Mena, AR) 57369
Wal Mart Discount Cities (N Little Rock, AR) 57434
Wal Mart Discount Cities (Nashville, AR) 57446
Wal Mart Discount Cities (Pocahontas, AR) 57545
Wal Mart Discount Cities (Van Buren, AR) 57699
Wal Mart Discount Cities (Bushnell, FL) 58902
Wal Mart Discount Cities (Chiefland, FL) 58952
Wal Mart Discount Cities (Haines City, FL) 59956
Wal Mart Discount Cities (Jacksonville, FL) 60497
Wal Mart Discount Cities (Lakeland, FL) 60792
Wal Mart Discount Cities (MacClenny, FL) 60962
Wal Mart Discount Cities (Spring Hill, FL) 62936
Wal Mart Discount Cities (Atlanta, GA) 65254; 65255; 65256; 65257; 65258; 65259; 65260; 65261; 65262; 65263; 65264; 65265; 65266; 65267; 65268; 65269; 65270
Wal Mart Discount Cities (Cordele, GA) 65721
Wal Mart Discount Cities (Decatur, GA) 65912
Wal Mart Discount Cities (Eastman, GA) 66163
Wal Mart Discount Cities (Forsyth, GA) 66255
Wal Mart Discount Cities (Kennesaw, GA) 66463
Wal Mart Discount Cities (Macon, GA) 66723
Wal Mart Discount Cities (Swainsboro, GA) 67761
Wal Mart Discount Cities (Woodstock, GA) 68076
Wal Mart Discount Cities (Jennings, LA) 69982
Wal Mart Discount Cities (Minden, LA) 70347
Wal Mart Discount Cities (Ruston, LA) 70675
Wal Mart Discount Cities (Vivian, LA) 70938
Wal Mart Discount Cities (Corinth, MS) 72747
Wal Mart Discount Cities (Houston, MS) 72926
Wal Mart Discount Cities (Meridian, MS) 73185
Wal Mart Discount Cities (Natchez, MS) 73213
Wal Mart Discount Cities (Picayune, MS) 73296
Wal Mart Discount Cities (West Point, MS) 73487
Wal Mart Discount Cities (Hickory, NC) 75105
Wal Mart Discount Cities (Lincolnton, NC) 75443
Wal Mart Discount Cities (Rutherfordton, NC) 76150
Wal Mart Discount Cities (Southern Pines, NC) 76278
Wal Mart Discount Cities (Ada, OK) 76790
Wal Mart Discount Cities (Ardmore, OK) 76826
Wal Mart Discount Cities (Bixby, OK) 76863
Wal Mart Discount Cities (Broken Arrow, OK) 76890
Wal Mart Discount Cities (Chickasha, OK) 76939
Wal Mart Discount Cities (Idabel, OK) 77146
Wal Mart Discount Cities (Muskogee, OK) 77233
Wal Mart Discount Cities (Pawhuska, OK) 77698
Wal Mart Discount Cities (Sallisaw, OK) 77776
Wal Mart Discount Cities (Vinita, OK) 78230
Wal Mart Discount Cities (Wagoner, OK) 78234
Wal Mart Discount Cities (Woodward, OK) 78269
Wal Mart Discount Cities (Yukon, OK) 78286
Wal Mart Discount Cities (Alvin, TX) 82517
Wal Mart Discount Cities (Bonham, TX) 83314
Wal Mart Discount Cities (Canyon, TX) 83445
Wal Mart Discount Cities (Conroe, TX) 83689
Wal Mart Discount Cities (Corpus Christi, TX) 83764
Wal Mart Discount Cities (Denton, TX) 84645
Wal Mart Discount Cities (Dickinson, TX) 84673
Wal Mart Discount Cities (Floresville, TX) 85039
Wal Mart Discount Cities (Fort Worth, TX) 85353; 85354
Wal Mart Discount Cities (Galveston, TX) 85470
Wal Mart Discount Cities (Giddings, TX) 85577
Wal Mart Discount Cities (Grand Prairie, TX) 85645
Wal Mart Discount Cities (Harlingen, TX) 85719
Wal Mart Discount Cities (Houston, TX) 87083
Wal Mart Discount Cities (La Grange, TX) 87539
Wal Mart Discount Cities (Lake Jackson, TX) 87587
Wal Mart Discount Cities (Lewisville, TX) 87670
Wal Mart Discount Cities (Lubbock, TX) 87794
Wal Mart Discount Cities (Marble Falls, TX) 87841
Wal Mart Discount Cities (Mesquite, TX) 88011
Wal Mart Discount Cities (Nederland, TX) 88197
Wal Mart Discount Cities (Paris, TX) 88380
Wal Mart Discount Cities (San Antonio, TX) 89298
Wal Mart Discount Cities (Sealy, TX) 89365
Wal Mart Discount Cities (Sherman, TX) 89429
Wal Mart Discount Cities (Sulphur Springs, TX) 89566
Wal Mart Discount Cities (Webster, TX) 90027
Wal Mart Discount Cities (Big Stone Gap, VA) 90435
Wal-Mart Discount Cities (Lexington, VA) 91213
Wal Mart Discount Cities Stock (Atlanta, GA) 65271
Wal Mart Discount City (Alabaster, AL) 54957
Wal Mart Discount City (Cullman, AL) 55556
Wal Mart Discount City (Decatur, AL) 55612
Wal Mart Discount City (Dothan, AL) 55674
Wal Mart Discount City (Fairfield, AL) 55720
Wal Mart Discount City (Guntersville, AL) 55836
Wal Mart Discount City (Huntsville, AL) 56052; 56053
Wal Mart Discount City (Mobile, AL) 56255
Wal Mart Discount City (Phenix City, AL) 56475
Wal Mart Discount City (Talladega, AL) 56603
Wal Mart Discount City (Tuscaloosa, AL) 56680
Wal Mart Discount City (Alma, AR) 56715
Wal Mart Discount City (Arkadelphia, AR) 56723
Wal Mart Discount City (El Dorado, AR) 56962
Wal Mart Discount City (Hot Springs, AR) 57166
Wal Mart Discount City (Huntsville, AR) 57194
Wal Mart Discount City (N Little Rock, AR) 57435
Wal Mart Discount City (Pine Bluff, AR) 57539
Wal Mart Discount City (Bartow, FL) 58633
Wal Mart Discount City (Bradenton, FL) 58856
Wal Mart Discount City (Dade City, FL) 59144
Wal Mart Discount City (Fort Myers, FL) 59773
Wal Mart Discount City (Lakeland, FL) 60793
Wal Mart Discount City (Merritt Island, FL) 61147; 61148
Wal Mart Discount City (Orlando, FL) 62179
Wal Mart Discount City (Port Richey, FL) 62682
Wal Mart Discount City (Brunswick, GA) 65429
Wal Mart Discount City (Savannah, GA) 67533
Wal Mart Discount City (Alexandria, LA) 69414
Wal Mart Discount City (Breaux Bridge, LA) 69742
Wal Mart Discount City (Kinder, LA) 70027
Wal Mart Discount City (Lake Charles, LA) 70181
Wal Mart Discount City (Natchitoches, LA) 70406
Wal Mart Discount City (New Iberia, LA) 70422
Wal Mart Discount City (Plaquemine, LA) 70644
Wal Mart Discount City (Shreveport, LA) 70802; 70803; 70804
Wal Mart Discount City (St. Martinville, LA) 70872
Wal Mart Discount City (Sulphur, LA) 70895
Wal Mart Discount City (Winnfield, LA) 70979
Wal Mart Discount City (Zachary, LA) 70989
Wal Mart Discount City (Booneville, MS) 72650

Waldenbooks (Valdosta, GA) 67980
Waldenbooks (Alexandria, LA) 69417
Waldenbooks (Baton Rouge, LA) 69685
Waldenbooks (Bossier City, LA) 69735
Waldenbooks (Gretna, LA) 69919
Waldenbooks (Kenner, LA) 70023
Waldenbooks (Lake Charles, LA) 70184
Waldenbooks (Marrero, LA) 70237
Waldenbooks (Metairie, LA) 70326
Waldenbooks (Monroe, LA) 70383
Waldenbooks (Shreveport, LA) 70805; 70806
Waldenbooks (Baltimore, MD) 71325; 71326
Waldenbooks (Cape St. Claire, MD) 71496
Waldenbooks (Cockeysville, MD) 71556
Waldenbooks (Frederick, MD) 71752; 71753
Waldenbooks (Westminster, MD) 72546
Waldenbooks (Escatawpa, MS) 72762
Waldenbooks (Jackson, MS) 73091; 73092; 73093
Waldenbooks (Oxford, MS) 73248
Waldenbooks (Ridgeland, MS) 73331
Waldenbooks (Utica, MS) 73443
Waldenbooks (Vicksburg, MS) 73464
Waldenbooks (Boone, NC) 73720
Waldenbooks (Charlotte, NC) 74218; 74219; 74220
Waldenbooks (Concord, NC) 74326
Waldenbooks (Greenville, NC) 74989
Waldenbooks (Hendersonville, NC) 75047
Waldenbooks (Jacksonville, NC) 75235
Waldenbooks (Kinston, NC) 75332
Waldenbooks (Monroe, NC) 75595
Waldenbooks (Raleigh, NC) 75982; 75983
Waldenbooks (Roanoke Rapids, NC) 76040
Waldenbooks (Rocky Mount, NC) 76111
Waldenbooks (Wilkesboro, NC) 76524
Waldenbooks (Wilmington, NC) 76612
Waldenbooks (Bartlesville, OK) 76855
Waldenbooks (Muskogee, OK) 77236
Waldenbooks (Norman, OK) 77280
Waldenbooks (Oklahoma City, OK) 77655; 77656; 77657; 77658; 77659; 77660; 77661
Waldenbooks (Tulsa, OK) 78199; 78200; 78201; 78202; 78203
Waldenbooks (Charleston, SC) 78910; 78911; 78912; 78913
Waldenbooks (Columbia, SC) 79122
Waldenbooks (Greenville, SC) 79447; 79448
Waldenbooks (Greenwood, SC) 79465
Waldenbooks (Myrtle Beach, SC) 79717; 79718
Waldenbooks (Spartanburg, SC) 79967
Waldenbooks (Abilene, TX) 82466
Waldenbooks (Amarillo, TX) 82589
Waldenbooks (Arlington, TX) 82780; 82781; 82782; 82783
Waldenbooks (Austin, TX) 83055
Waldenbooks (Baytown, TX) 83141
Waldenbooks (Beaumont, TX) 83234
Waldenbooks (Brownsville, TX) 83384
Waldenbooks (Clute, TX) 83604
Waldenbooks (Corsicana, TX) 83797
Waldenbooks (Dallas, TX) 84491; 84492
Waldenbooks (El Paso, TX) 84963; 84964; 84965
Waldenbooks (Fort Worth, TX) 85356; 85357; 85358
Waldenbooks (Friendswood, TX) 85408
Waldenbooks (Harlingen, TX) 85720
Waldenbooks (Houston, TX) 87089; 87090; 87091; 87092; 87093; 87094; 87095; 87096; 87097; 87098; 87099; 87100; 87101
Waldenbooks (Killeen, TX) 87528; 87529
Waldenbooks (Lake Jackson, TX) 87588

Waldenbooks (Longview, TX) 87745
Waldenbooks (Lufkin, TX) 87821
Waldenbooks (Marshall, TX) 87871
Waldenbooks (Mc Allen, TX) 87904
Waldenbooks (Mesquite, TX) 88012
Waldenbooks (Odessa, TX) 88291
Waldenbooks (Pampa, TX) 88359
Waldenbooks (Pasadena, TX) 88475
Waldenbooks (Plano, TX) 88618
Waldenbooks (Port Arthur, TX) 88658
Waldenbooks (Richardson, TX) 88789
Waldenbooks (San Angelo, TX) 88905
Waldenbooks (San Antonio, TX) 89300; 89301; 89302; 89303; 89304; 89305
Waldenbooks (Temple, TX) 89651; 89652
Waldenbooks (Texarkana, TX) 89715
Waldenbooks (Victoria, TX) 89911; 89912
Waldenbooks (Arlington, VA) 90392
Waldenbooks (Chesapeake, VA) 90608; 90609
Waldenbooks (Fredericksburg, VA) 90945
Waldenbooks (Norfolk, VA) 91595; 91596
Waldenbooks (Portsmouth, VA) 91673
Waldenbooks (Richmond, VA) 92079; 92080
Waldenbooks (Staunton, VA) 92332
Waldenbooks (Winchester, VA) 92606
Waldenbooks Co. (Charlotte, NC) 74221
Waldenbooks Deerbrook (Humble, TX) 87255
Waldenbooks Inc. (Br) (Roanoke, VA) 92198
Waldenbooks Maryland Stores (Bethesda, MD) 71447
Waldenbooks Maryland Stores (Forrest Village, MD) 71703
Waldenbooks Maryland Stores (Landover, MD) 72036
Waldenbooks Maryland Stores (Laurel, MD) 72093
Waldenbooks Maryland Stores (Rockville, MD) 72330
Waldenbooks Maryland Stores (Wheaton, MD) 72567
Waldenbooks & More (Fort Lauderdale, FL) 59626
Waldenbooks & More (Marietta, GA) 66950
Waldenbooks & More (Stone Mountain, GA) 67736
Waldenbooks & More (Charlotte, NC) 74222
Waldenbooks & More (Austin, TX) 83056
Waldenbooks & More (Carrollton, TX) 83512
Waldenbooks & More (Plano, TX) 88619
Waldenbooks Wa Spring Valley S (Washington, DC) 58514
Waldenbooks Wa Stores Spring V (Washington, DC) 58515
Walgreen (Bartow, FL) 58634
Walgreen (Belleview, FL) 58657
Walgreen (Boynton Beach, FL) 58798
Walgreen (Bradenton, FL) 58858
Walgreen (Brooksville, FL) 58898
Walgreen (Cocoa Beach, FL) 59085
Walgreen (Daytona Beach, FL) 59225
Walgreen (Fort Lauderdale, FL) 59627; 59628; 59629
Walgreen (Fort Myers, FL) 59775
Walgreen (Hollywood, FL) 60104
Walgreen (Inverness, FL) 60152
Walgreen (Jacksonville, FL) 60499; 60500
Walgreen (Lehigh Acres, FL) 60896
Walgreen (Melbourne, FL) 61117
Walgreen (Naples, FL) 61669
Walgreen (Northwest Smyrna Beach, FL) 61760
Walgreen (Ocala, FL) 61825; 61826
Walgreen (Sarasota, FL) 62865
Walgreen (St. Petersburg, FL) 63137
Walgreen (W Palm Beach, FL) 63821
Walgreen (Kenner, LA) 70024
Walgreen (Metairie, LA) 70327
Walgreen (Southaven, MS) 73360
Walgreen (Tupelo, MS) 73428
Walgreen (Tulsa, OK) 78204

Walgreen (Austin, TX) 83057; 83058
Walgreen (El Paso, TX) 84966; 84967
Walgreen (Houston, TX) 87102
Walgreen (Killeen, TX) 87530
Walgreen (Odessa, TX) 88292
Walgreen (San Antonio, TX) 89306
Walgreen Answering Service (Houston, TX) 87103
Walgreen Co. (Altamonte Springs, FL) 58566
Walgreen Co. (Daytona Beach, FL) 59226
Walgreen Construction Co. in (Houston, TX) 87104
Walgreen Data Terminal (San Antonio, TX) 89307
Walgreen Discount Store (Miami, FL) 61500
Walgreen Drug Store (Avon Park, FL) 58612
Walgreen Drug Store (Fort Pierce, FL) 59816
Walgreen Drug Store (Jacksonville, FL) 60501
Walgreen Drug Store (Marathon, FL) 60994
Walgreen Drug Store (Mandeville, LA) 70211
Walgreen Drug Store (Sugar Land, TX) 89546
Walgreen Drug Stores (Hot Springs National Park, AR) 57190; 57191
Walgreen Drug Stores (West Memphis, AR) 57738; 57739
Walgreen Drug Stores (Apopka, FL) 58578
Walgreen Drug Stores (Auburndale, FL) 58604
Walgreen Drug Stores (Boca Raton, FL) 58751; 58752; 58753
Walgreen Drug Stores (Bradenton, FL) 58859; 58860; 58861
Walgreen Drug Stores (Bradenton Beach, FL) 58862
Walgreen Drug Stores (Brandon, FL) 58882
Walgreen Drug Stores (Brooksville, FL) 58899
Walgreen Drug Stores (Casselberry, FL) 58945
Walgreen Drug Stores (Clearwater, FL) 59054
Walgreen Drug Stores (Cocoa, FL) 59076
Walgreen Drug Stores (Daytona Beach, FL) 59227; 59228; 59229; 59230; 59231; 59232
Walgreen Drug Stores (De Land, FL) 59262
Walgreen Drug Stores (Deerfield Beach, FL) 59290; 59291; 59292
Walgreen Drug Stores (Dunedin, FL) 59368
Walgreen Drug Stores (Fort Lauderda, FL) 59422
Walgreen Drug Stores (Fort Lauderdale, FL) 59630; 59631; 59632; 59633; 59634; 59635; 59636; 59637; 59638; 59639; 59640
Walgreen Drug Stores (Fort Myers, FL) 59776; 59777; 59778; 59779
Walgreen Drug Stores (Hallandale, FL) 59966
Walgreen Drug Stores (Hialeah, FL) 60018
Walgreen Drug Stores (Hollywood, FL) 60105; 60106; 60107; 60108; 60109
Walgreen Drug Stores (Homosassa Springs, FL) 60128
Walgreen Drug Stores (Jacksonville, FL) 60502; 60503; 60504; 60505; 60506
Walgreen Drug Stores (Jupiter, FL) 60554
Walgreen Drug Stores (Key Largo, FL) 60568
Walgreen Drug Stores (Lake Worth, FL) 60700; 60701; 60702
Walgreen Drug Stores (Lakeland, FL) 60796; 60797; 60798; 60799
Walgreen Drug Stores (Largo, FL) 60867; 60868; 60869
Walgreen Drug Stores (Leesburg, FL) 60888
Walgreen Drug Stores (Melbourne, FL) 61118; 61119; 61120; 61121
Walgreen Drug Stores (Merritt Island, FL) 61150
Walgreen Drug Stores (Miami, FL) 61501; 61502; 61503; 61504; 61505; 61506; 61507; 61508; 61509; 61510; 61511
Walgreen Drug Stores (New Port Richey, FL) 61693; 61694
Walgreen Drug Stores (Ocala, FL) 61827; 61828
Walgreen Drug Stores (Orlando, FL) 62182; 62183; 62184; 62185; 62186; 62187

Walgreen Drug Stores (Ormond Beach, FL) 62212
Walgreen Drug Stores (Palm City, FL) 62280
Walgreen Drug Stores (Pinellas Park, FL) 62530
Walgreen Drug Stores (Pompano Beach, FL) 62641; 62642; 62643; 62644; 62645
Walgreen Drug Stores (Port St Lucie, FL) 62691
Walgreen Drug Stores (Punta Gorda, FL) 62725
Walgreen Drug Stores (Ruskin, FL) 62760
Walgreen Drug Stores (Sarasota, FL) 62866; 62867
Walgreen Drug Stores (Sebastian, FL) 62876
Walgreen Drug Stores (St Pete, FL) 62961
Walgreen Drug Stores (St Petersburg, FL) 63043; 63044; 63045; 63046
Walgreen Drug Stores (Stuart, FL) 63183
Walgreen Drug Stores (Tallahassee, FL) 63287; 63288; 63289
Walgreen Drug Stores (Tampa, FL) 63651; 63652; 63653; 63654; 63655; 63656; 63657; 63658
Walgreen Drug Stores (Vero Beach, FL) 63770; 63771
Walgreen Drug Stores (Village of Golf, FL) 63772
Walgreen Drug Stores (W Palm Beach, FL) 63822
Walgreen Drug Stores (West Palm Beach, FL) 63907; 63908; 63909; 63910; 63911
Walgreen Drug Stores (Winter Garden, FL) 63926
Walgreen Drug Stores (Winter Haven, FL) 63956; 63957
Walgreen Drug Stores (Zephyrhills, FL) 64029; 64030; 64031
Walgreen Drug Stores (Bossier City, LA) 69736
Walgreen Drug Stores (Chalmette, LA) 69773
Walgreen Drug Stores (Hammond, LA) 69935
Walgreen Drug Stores (Lafayette, LA) 70125
Walgreen Drug Stores (Lake Charles, LA) 70185
Walgreen Drug Stores (Marrero, LA) 70238
Walgreen Drug Stores (Metairie, LA) 70328; 70329; 70330; 70331
Walgreen Drug Stores (New Orleans, LA) 70585; 70586; 70587; 70588
Walgreen Drug Stores (Slidell, LA) 70846
Walgreen Drug Stores (Escatawpa, MS) 72763
Walgreen Drug Stores (Tulsa, OK) 78205
Walgreen Drug Stores (Austin, TX) 83059; 83060; 83061; 83062; 83063; 83064; 83065
Walgreen Drug Stores (Beaumont, TX) 83235; 83236
Walgreen Drug Stores (Bellaire, TX) 83273
Walgreen Drug Stores (Brownsville, TX) 83385
Walgreen Drug Stores (Collinsville, TX) 83637
Walgreen Drug Stores (Corpus Christi, TX) 83766
Walgreen Drug Stores (Deer Park, TX) 84575
Walgreen Drug Stores (El Paso, TX) 84968; 84969; 84970; 84971; 84972; 84973
Walgreen Drug Stores (Galveston, TX) 85471; 85472
Walgreen Drug Stores (Groves, TX) 85687
Walgreen Drug Stores (Houston, TX) 87105; 87106; 87107; 87108; 87109; 87110; 87111; 87112; 87113; 87114; 87115; 87116; 87117; 87118; 87119; 87120; 87121; 87122; 87123; 87124; 87125; 87126; 87127; 87128; 87129; 87130; 87131; 87132; 87133; 87134; 87135; 87136; 87137; 87138; 87139; 87140; 87141; 87142; 87143; 87144; 87145; 87146; 87147; 87148; 87149; 87150; 87151; 87152; 87153; 87154; 87155; 87156; 87157; 87158; 87159; 87160; 87161; 87162; 87163; 87164; 87165; 87166; 87167; 87168
Walgreen Drug Stores (Humble, TX) 87256; 87257
Walgreen Drug Stores (Huntsville, TX) 87267

Walgreen Drug Stores (Katy, TX) 87458
Walgreen Drug Stores (La Porte, TX) 87573
Walgreen Drug Stores (League City, TX) 87635
Walgreen Drug Stores (Missouri City, TX) 88134
Walgreen Drug Stores (Nederland, TX) 88198
Walgreen Drug Stores (Orange, TX) 88332
Walgreen Drug Stores (Pasadena, TX) 88476; 88477; 88478; 88479
Walgreen Drug Stores (Pearland, TX) 88491
Walgreen Drug Stores (Port Arthur, TX) 88659; 88660; 88661
Walgreen Drug Stores (San Antonio, TX) 89308; 89309; 89310; 89311; 89312; 89313; 89314; 89315; 89316; 89317; 89318; 89319; 89320; 89321; 89322; 89323; 89324
Walgreen Drug Stores (Spring, TX) 89496
Walgreen Drug Stores (Tomball, TX) 89781; 89782
Walgreen Drug Stores (Victoria, TX) 89913
Walgreen Drug Stores (Wichita Falls, TX) 90121
Walgreen Drugs (Clearwater, FL) 59055
Walgreen Drugs (Crystal River, FL) 59135
Walgreen Drugs (Fort Myers, FL) 59780
Walgreen Drugs (Jupiter, FL) 60555
Walgreen Drugs (Kissimmee, FL) 60607
Walgreen Drugs (Lake Wales, FL) 60659
Walgreen Drugs (St Augustine, FL) 62960
Walgreen Drugs (Metairie, LA) 70332
Walgreen Drugs (Clute, TX) 83605
Walgreen Drugs (La Marque, TX) 87551
Walgreen Louisiana Co. (Lafayette, LA) 70126
Walgreen Pharmacy (Naples, FL) 61670
Walgreen Pharmacy (Northwest Smyrna Beach, FL) 61761
Walgreen Pharmacy (Palm City, FL) 62281
Walgreen Pharmacy (Venice, FL) 63738
Walgreen Pharmacy (El Paso, TX) 84974; 84975
Walker Manufacturing (Plant City Fl, FL) 62561
Walker Manufacturing (Punta Gorda, FL) 62726
Walker Manufacturing Co. (Pocahontas, AR) 57546
Walker Manufacturing Co. (Norcross, GA) 67211
Walker Manufacturing Co. (Aberdeen, MS) 72581
Walker Manufacturing Co. (Harrisonburg, VA) 91104
Walker Manufacturing Inc. (Walker, LA) 70939
Walker Mfg. Co. (Harrisonburg, VA) 91105
Wall Street Journal (Birmingham, AL) 55453
Wall Street Journal (Washington, DC) 58516; 58517
Wall Street Journal (Miami, FL) 61512; 61513
Wall Street Journal (Orlando, FL) 62188
Wall Street Journal (Atlanta, GA) 65276; 65277; 65278; 65279
Wall Street Journal (Chalmette, LA) 69774
Wall Street Journal the (Silver Spring, MD) 72446
Wall Street Journal (Charlotte, NC) 74223
Wall Street Journal the (Oklahoma City, OK) 77662
Wall Street Journal (Memphis, TN) 81755
Wall Street Journal (Bellaire, TX) 83274
Wall Street Journal (Houston, TX) 87169
Wall Street Journal (Arlington Vir, VA) 90396
Wall Street Journal (Charlottesville, VA) 90550
Wall Street Journal the All Ot (Silver Spring, MD) 72447
Wall Street Journal the Classi (Silver Spring, MD) 72448
Wall Street Journal the News B (Montgomery Co, MD) 72149

Westinghouse Electric Corp. Electronic Systems Group (Linthicum Heights, MD) 72113
Westinghouse Electric Corp. Integrated Logistics Support (Hunt Valley, MD) 71945; 71946; 71947
Westinghouse Electric Corp. Micarta Div. (Pendleton, SC) 79789
Westinghouse Electric Corp. Oceanic Div. (Annapolis, MD) 71024
Westinghouse Electric Corp. Pensacola (Pensacola, FL) 62491
Westinghouse Electric Corp. Productos Electronic (Santa Isabel, PR) 78588
Westinghouse Electric Corp. Productos Electronicos (Santa Isabel, PR) 78589
Westinghouse Electric Corp. Thermo King Carribean (Ciales, PR) 78393
Westinghouse Electric Corp. Thermo King Corp. (Montgomery, AL) 56396
Westinghouse Electric Corp. Thermo King Corp. (Louisville, GA) 66627; 66628
Westinghouse Electric Corp. Thermo King De Puerto Rico (Arecibo, PR) 78316
Westinghouse Electric Corp. Turbine Generator (Charlotte, NC) 74227
Westinghouse Electric Corp. Wire Div. (Abingdon, VA) 90161
Westinghouse Electric Corp. Electrical Components Plant Electrical Componets (Fort Payne, AL) 55763
Westinghouse Motor Co. (Round Rock, TX) 88857
Westinghouse Power Systems (Round Rock, TX) 88858
Westinghouse Productos (Mayaguez, PR) 78516
Westinghouse de Puerto Rico Productos Circuitos De Puerto Rico (Juana Diaz, PR) 78470
Westinghouse de Puerto Rico Productos Electronicos Industriales (Santa Isabel, PR) 78590
Westinghouse de Puerto Rico Productos Westinghouse (Mayaguez, PR) 78517
Westinghouse Puerto Rico Inc. Breakers Div. (Aguas Buenas, PR) 78301
Westinghouse de Purerto Rico Productos Electronicos Industriales (Santa Isabel, PR) 78591
Westinghouse Specialty (Round Rock, TX) 88859
Westminster Bank & Trust Co. (Gamber, MD) 71822
Westminster Bank & Trust Co. of Carroll County (Eldersburg, MD) 71668
Westminster Bank & Trust Co. of Carroll County (Manchester, MD) 72123
Westminster Bank & Trust Co. of Carroll County (Union Mills, MD) 72512
Westminster Bank & Trust Co. of Carroll County (Westminster, MD) 72547; 72548; 72549
Westminster Bank & Trust Co. of Carroll County (Winfield, MD) 72574
Westminster Bank & Trust Co. of Carroll County (Woodbine, MD) 72575
Westover Dairy (Lynchburg, VA) 91292
Westpoint Pepperell (Elizabethtown, NC) 74495
Westpoint Pepperell (Hamilton, NC) 74995
Westpoint Pepperell (Lumberton, NC) 75477
Westpoint Pepperell (Keysville, VA) 91178
Westronics (Fort Worth, TX) 85362
Westronics Inc. (Fort Worth, TX) 85363
Westvaco (Richmond, VA) 92082; 92083
Westvaco Folding Box Div. (Cleveland, TN) 80605
Westvaco Folding Carton (Richmond, VA) 92084; 92085
Westvaco Corp. (Newark, DE) 57934
Westvaco Corp. (Mulberry, FL) 61577
Westvaco Corp. (Chamblee, GA) 65552
Westvaco Corp. (De Ridder, LA) 69821
Westvaco Corp. (Jessup, MD) 71987
Westvaco Corp. (Laurel, MD) 72094; 72095
Westvaco Corp. (Luke, MD) 72115
Westvaco Corp. (Burlington, NC) 73764
Westvaco Corp. (Charlotte, NC) 74228
Westvaco Corp. (Gastonia, NC) 74693
Westvaco Corp. (Summerville, SC) 79995; 79996
Westvaco Corp. (Walterboro, SC) 80079
Westvaco Corp. (Winnsboro, SC) 80135
Westvaco Corp. (Camden, TN) 80277
Westvaco Corp. (Cleveland, TN) 80606; 80607; 80608
Westvaco Corp. (Dallas, TX) 84494; 84495
Westvaco Corp. (Houston, TX) 87193; 87194
Westvaco Corp. (Bedford, VA) 90425
Westvaco Corp. (Chatham, VA) 90554
Westvaco Corp. (Herndon, VA) 91136; 91137
Westvaco Corp. (Ivy, VA) 91171
Westvaco Corp. (Lexington, VA) 91214
Westvaco Corp. (Richmond, VA) 92086; 92087; 92088; 92089
Westvaco Corp. (Staunton, VA) 92333
Westvaco Corp. (Winchester, VA) 92607
Westvaco Corp. (Parkersburg, WV) 92999; 93000
Westvaco Corp. (Washington, WV) 93081
Westvaco Corp. (Wellsburg, WV) 93105
Westvaco Corp. Bleached Board (Covington, VA) 90666
Westvaco Corp. Charleston Chemical (North Charleston, SC) 79753
Westvaco Corp. Chemical Div. (North Charleston, SC) 79754
Westvaco Corp. Chemicals (Mulberry, FL) 61578; 61579; 61580
Westvaco Corp. Chemicals (De Ridder, LA) 69822
Westvaco Corp. Chemicals (Covington, VA) 90667
Westvaco Corp. Container (Chattanooga, TN) 80527
Westvaco Corp. Envelope (Dallas, TX) 84496
Westvaco Corp. Fine Paper (Luke, MD) 72116
Westvaco Corp. Fine Papers Div. (Wickliffe, KY) 69340
Westvaco Corp. Folding Carton (Newark, DE) 57935
Westvaco Corp. Folding Carton (Cleveland, TN) 80609
WestVaco Corp. Folding Carton Div. (Newark, DE) 57936
WestVaco Corp. Kraft Div. (North Charleston, SC) 79755; 79756
Westvaco Corp. Liquid Packaging (Richmond, VA) 92090
Westvaco Corp. Milk Carton (Richmond, VA) 92091
Westvaco Corp. Polychemicals (North Charleston, SC) 79757; 79758
Westvaco Corp. Carbon Dept. (Covington, VA) 90668
Westvaco Corp. Chemical (Mulberry, FL) 61581
Westvaco Corp. Envelope (Chamblee, GA) 65553
Westvaco Corp. Fine Pape (Atlanta, GA) 65286
Westvaco Corp. Library (Charleston, SC) 78914
Westvaco Corp. Research (Laurel, MD) 72096
Westvaco Corp. Research (Ravenel, SC) 79807
Westvaco Lumber (Summerville, SC) 79997
Wetterau Inc. (Charleston, SC) 78915
Wetterau Inc. West Virginia (Nitro, WV) 92975
Wewstern Publishing Co. (Fayetteville, NC) 74586
Weyeerhaeuser Co. (Plymouth, NC) 75837
Weyerhaeuser (Oglethorpe, GA) 67220
Weyerhaeuser Co. (Millport, AL) 56128; 56129
Weyerhaeuser Co. (De Queen, AR) 56898
Weyerhaeuser Co. (Dierks, AR) 56906; 56907
Weyerhaeuser Co. (Hot Springs, AR) 57167
Weyerhaeuser Co. (Mountain Pine, AR) 57394; 57395
Weyerhaeuser Co. (Adel, GA) 64058
Weyerhaeuser Co. (Atlanta, GA) 65287
Weyerhaeuser Co. (Oglethorpe, GA) 67221
Weyerhaeuser Co. (Bruce, MS) 72659; 72660
Weyerhaeuser Co. (Columbus, MS) 72733
Weyerhaeuser Co. (Philadelphia, MS) 73285; 73286
Weyerhaeuser Co. (Elkin, NC) 74498; 74499
Weyerhaeuser Co. (Jacksonville, NC) 75236
Weyerhaeuser Co. (Moncure, NC) 75569; 75570
Weyerhaeuser Co. (Broken Bow, OK) 76901
Weyerhaeuser Co. (Wright City, OK) 78271
Weyerhaeuser Co. (Memphis, TN) 81758
Weyerhaeuser Co. (Waco, TX) 89982
Weyerhaeuser Co. (Chesapeake, VA) 90611; 90612
Weyerhaeuser Co. Bowling Green (Bowling Green, KY) 68165
Weyerhaeuser Co. Plymouth Mill (Plymouth, NC) 75838
Weyerhaeuser Co. Wood Treating Plant (De Queen, AR) 56899
Weyerhaeuser Forest Prods. Co. (Plymouth, NC) 75839
Weyerhaeuser Forest Products Co. (Plymouth, NC) 75840; 75841
Weyerhaeuser Paper (Carrollton, TX) 83513
Weyerhaeuser Paper (McAllen, TX) 87947
Weyerhaeuser Paper (San Antonio, TX) 89326
Weyerhaeuser Paper Co. (Jacksonville, FL) 60510
Weyerhaeuser Paper Co. (Lithonia, GA) 66613
Weyerhaeuser Paper Co. (Richland, MS) 73315
Weyerhaeuser Paper Co. (Charlotte, NC) 74229
Weyerhaeuser Paper Co. (New Bern, NC) 75739
Weyerhaeuser Paper Co. (Vanceboro, NC) 76416
Weyerhaeuser Paper Co. (Valliant, OK) 78220; 78221
Weyerhaeuser Paper Co. (Memphis, TN) 81759
Weyerhaeuser Paper Co. (Amarillo, TX) 82590
Weyerhaeuser Paper Co. (Richmond, VA) 92092
Weyerhaeuser Paper Co. Inc. (Franklin, KY) 68373
Weyerhaeuser Particleboard Mill (Adel, GA) 64059
Weyerhaeuser Wood Treating Plant (De Queen, AR) 56900
WGNX-Channel 46 News (Atlanta, GA) 65288
Wheelabrator Corp. (Newnan, GA) 67086
Wheelabrator Corp. (Walterboro, SC) 80080
Wheeler County Hospital (Glenwood, GA) 66305
Wheeling Corrugating Co. (Fort Payne, AL) 55764
Wheeling Corrugating Co. (Statesville, NC) 76341
Wheeling Corrugating Co. (Wilmington, NC) 76614
Wheeling Corrugating Co. (Houston, TX) 87195
Wheeling Corrugating Co. (Wheeling, WV) 93122
Wheeling Corrugating Co. Inc. (Louisville, KY) 69040
Wheeling Corrugating Co. Inc. (Houston, TX) 87196
Wheeling Machine Products (Birmingham, AL) 55457
Wheeling Machine Products (Houston, TX) 87197
Wheeling-Machine Products Cooper Industries (Pine Bluff, AR) 57540
Wheeling-Pittsburgh Steel (Beech Bottom, WV) 92690
Wheeling-Pittsburgh Steel (Follansbee, WV) 92852
Wheeling-Pittsburgh Steel Corp. (Beech Bottom, WV) 92691; 92692
Wheeling Pittsburgh Steel Corp. (Wheeling, WV) 93123
Wheeling-Pittsburgh Steel Corp. Labelle (Wheeling, WV) 93124
Whirlpool Corp. (Fort Smith, AR) 57119
Whirlpool Corp. (Danville, KY) 68264; 68265
Whirlpool Corp. (Oxford, MS) 73249; 73250
Whirlpool Corp. (Columbia, SC) 79127
Whirlpool Corp. (La Vergne, TN) 81285
Whirlpool Corp. Danville Div. (Danville, KY) 68266
Whirlpool Financial Corp. (Duluth, GA) 66095
Whirlpool Financial Corp. (Metairie, LA) 70336
Whirlpool Financial Corp. (Charlotte, NC) 74230
Whispering Pines Nursing Home (Plain Dealing, LA) 70635
Whispering Pines Nursing Home (Winnsboro, TX) 90126
Whitby Inc. (Richmond, VA) 92093; 92094
White County Industries Inc. (Sparta, TN) 82348
White-Rodgers (Harrison, AR) 57146
White Rodgers Co. (Batesville, AR) 56764
White-Rodgers Harrison Air (Harrison, AR) 57147
Whitle Communications LP (Knoxville, TN) 81275
Whittle Communications (Knoxville, TN) 81276
Wichita Eagle-Beacon the (Washington, DC) 58521
Wika Instrument Corp. (Lawrenceville, GA) 66548
Willamette Ind. Lillie (Lillie, LA) 70192
Willamette Industries, Inc. (Emerson, AR) 56964
Willamette Industries Inc. (Marietta, GA) 66953
Willamette Industries Inc. (Hawesville, KY) 68419; 68420; 68421
Willamette Industries Inc. (Campti, LA) 69755
Willamette Industries Inc. (Simsboro, LA) 70811
Willamette Industries Inc. (Taylor, LA) 70910
Willamette Industries Inc. (Columbia, MD) 71607
Willamette Industries, Inc. (Moncure, NC) 75571
Willamette Industries Inc. (Tulsa, OK) 78209
Willamette Industries Inc. (Bennettsville, SC) 78734
Willamette Industries Inc. (Chester, SC) 78946
Willamette Industries Inc. (Grand Prairie, TX) 85647
Willamette Industries Inc. (Irving, TX) 87416
Willamette Industries, Inc. Chester (Chester, SC) 78947
Willamette Industries, Inc. Dodson (Dodson, LA) 69839; 69840
Willamette Industries Inc. Emerson (Emerson, AR) 56965
Willamette Industries, Inc. Malvern (Malvern, AR) 57344
Willamette Industries, Inc. Moncure (Moncure, NC) 75572
Willamette Industries Inc. Ruston (Ruston, LA) 70676; 70677
Willamette Industries Inc. Surepine (Simsboro, LA) 70812; 70813
Willamette Industries Inc. Taylor (Taylor, LA) 70911
Willamette Industries Inc. Zwolle (Zwolle, LA) 70990
William L. Bonnell Co. Inc. (Newnan, GA) 67087
William L. Bonnell Co., Inc. (Carthage, TN) 80279
William Wrigley Co. (Flowery Branch, GA) 66221
Williamette Industries Inc. Malvern (Malvern, AR) 57345
Williams Brothers Engineeri (Tulsa, OK) 78210
Williams Brothers Engineering (Pensacola Fl, FL) 62493
Williams Companies, Inc. (Tulsa, OK) **78211**
Wilmer Service Line (Kemah, TX) 87463
Wilmington Plant (New Castle, DE) 57878
Wilson Brands Corp. (Birmingham, AL) 55458
Wilson Brands Corp. (Oklahoma City, OK) 77664
Wilson Foods Corp. (Fort Lauderdale, FL) 59642
Wilson Foods Corp. (Shreveport, LA) 70807
Wilson Foods Corp. (Wilson, NC) 76654
Wilson Foods Corp. (Edmond, OK) 77030
Wilson Foods Corp. (Oklahoma City, OK) 77665; 77666; 77667; 77668
Wilsonart (Dallas, TX) 84497
Wilsonart (Houston, TX) 87198
Wilsons (Quincy, FL) 62734
Wilsons (Ringgold, LA) 70666; 70667
Wilsons (Maben, MS) 73133
Wilsons (Durham, NC) 74442
Wilsons (Hickory, NC) 75106; 75107
Wilsons (Lexington, OK) 77177
Wilsons (Conway, SC) 79140
Wilsons Department Store (Delhi, LA) 69827
Wilsons Dept Store (Eupora, MS) 72767
Wiltel Communications Systems (Kennesaw, GA) 66464
Wiltel Inc. (Rockville, MD) 72331
Winchester Farms Dairy (Winchester, KY) 69356
Winchester Homes Incorporat (Rockville, MD) 72332
Winchester Homes Inc. (Accokeek, MD) 70995; 70996
Winchester Homes Inc. (Bethesda, MD) 71449
Winchester Homes Inc. (Cavetown, MD) 71506
Winchester Homes Inc. (Clinton, MD) 71544
Winchester Homes Inc. (Fort George Mead, MD) 71707
Winchester Homes Inc. (Laurel, MD) 72097
Winchester Homes Inc. (Pasadena, MD) 72213
Winchester Homes Inc. (Severna Park, MD) 72379
Windsor Insurance Co. (Atlanta, GA) 65289
Wingfoot Ventures Seven Inc. (Houston, TX) 87199
Winmar Co. Inc. (Louisville, KY) 69041
Winn-Dixie Louisville Inc. (Louisville, KY) 69042
Winn-Dixie Stores (Danville, VA) 90723; 90724
Winn-Dixie Stores, Inc. (Jacksonville, FL) **60511**
Winn-Dixie Texas Inc. No. 248 (San Angelo, TX) 88907
Winstead Co. Inc. (Lothian, MD) 72114
Winston Carpet (Fort Lauderdale, FL) 59643
Wisconsin Tissue Mills (Louisville, KY) 69043
Wisconsin Tissue Mills Inc. (Woodstock, GA) 68077
Wise Foods (St. Augustine, FL) 63063
Wise Foods (Atlanta, GA) 65290
Witco Corp. (Phenix City, AL) 56476
Witco Corp. (Hahnville, LA) 69926
Witco Corp. (Harvey, LA) 69943
Witco Corp. (New Orleans, LA) 70590
Witco Corp. (Philadelphia, MS) 73287
Witco Corp. (Fort Worth, TX) 85364
Witco Corp. (Houston, TX) 87200
Witco Corp. (LaPorte, TX) 87605
Witco Corp. (Marshall, TX) 87872; 87873
Witco Corp. Argus (Hahnville, LA) 69927
Witco Corp. Argus (La Porte, TX) 87574
Witco Corp. Argus (Marshall, TX) 87874; 87875
Witco Corp. Argus Chemcial Div. (Marshall, TX) 87876
Witco Corp. Argus Chemical (Taft, LA) 70904
Witco Corp. Concarb (Phenix City, AL) 56477; 56478
Witco Corp. Concarb (Ponca City, OK) 77717; 77718; 77719
Witco Corp. Concarb (Sunray, TX) 89573
Witco Corp. Concarb Div. (Sunray, TX) 89574
Witco Corp. Concarb Division (Duluth, GA) 66096
Witco Corp. Harahan (Harahan, LA) 69937
Witco Corp. Humko Chemical (Memphis, TN) 81760; 81761
Witco Corp. Humko Chemical Div. (Memphis, TN) 81762; 81763

Witco Corp. Kendall-Amalie (Jacksonville, FL) 60512
Witco Corp. Kendall-Amalie (East Houston, TX) 84726
Witco Corp. Oleo-Surfactant Organics (Houston, TX) 87201
Witco Corp. Organics (Houston, TX) 87202
Witco Corp. Polymer Additives (Taft, LA) 70905
Witco Corp. Richardson Battery Parts (Philadelphia, MS) 73288; 73289
Wix Corp. (Gustonia, NC) 74991
Wix Dana Corp. Air Refiner Div. Perry Plant (Oklahoma City, OK) 77669
Wix/Dana Corp. Allen Plant (Gastonia, NC) 74694
Wix/Dana Corp. Dixon Plant (Gastonia, NC) 74695
Wix/Dana Corp. (Dixow Plant) (Gastonia, NC) 74696
Wix Dana Corp. Perry Plant (Oklahoma City, OK) 77670
Wjz-Tv Television Station (Baltimore, MD) 71328
WLR Foods (Timberville, VA) **92385**
Wolf Brand Product (Richardson, TX) 88791
Wolf Brand Products Inc. (Corsicana, TX) 83798
Wolf Brand Products Inc. (Dallas, TX) 84498
Wolverine Gasket Co. (Leesburg, FL) 60889; 60890
Wolverine Gasket Co. Blacksburg Div. (Blacksburg, VA) 90452
Wolverine Gasket & Mfg Co. (Blacksburg, VA) 90453
Wood Fiber Industries (Danville, VA) 90725
Wood Products Co. (Newport, TN) 82175
Wood Products Inc. (Oakland, MD) 72159
Woodhaven Foods (Birmingham, AL) 55459
Woodlands Corp. (The Woodlands, TX) 89757
Woodside Mills Inc. (Anderson, SC) 78696
Woodside Mills Inc. (Fountain Inn, SC) 79251
Woodside Mills Inc. Beattie Plant (Fountain Inn, SC) 79252; 79253
Woodside Mills Inc. Furman Plant (Fountain Inn, SC) 79254; 79255
Woodside Mills Inc. Haynsworth Plant (Anderson, SC) 78697
Woodtek/Textone (North Charleston, SC) 79759
Woodtek/Textone Inc. (Charleston, SC) 78916
World Book Childcraft (Fairhope, AL) 55726
World Book Childcraft (Tampa, FL) 63663
World Book Childcraft (Macon, GA) 66726; 66727
World Book Childcraft (Abilene, TX) 82469
World Book Childcraft (Newport News, VA) 91491; 91492
World Book Childcraft (Staunton, VA) 92334
World Book Educational Products (Fayetteville, NC) 74587
World Book, Inc. (Orlando, FL) 62194
World Book, Inc. (North Augusta, SC) 79742
World S&L, A Federal S&L (Bayonet Point, FL) 58639
World S&L, A Federal S&L (Boca Raton, FL) 58754; 58755; 58756
World Savings & Loan (Port Richey, FL) 62683
World Savings & Loan (Irving, TX) 87417
World Savings & Loan (Temple, TX) 89654
Wormald U S Inc. (Dallas, TX) 84499
Worthington Cylinder Corp. (Claremore, OK) 76959
Worthington Cylinders Corp. (Columbus, GA) 65658
Worthington Cylinders Corp. (Claremore, OK) 76960
Worthington Steel Co. (Baltimore, MD) 71329
W.R. Grace InterAmerican Division (Boca Raton, FL) 58757
W.R. Grace Research Division (Columbia, MD) 71608
W.R. Grace & Co. (Atlanta, GA) 65291
W.R. Grace & Co. (Owensboro, KY) 69199
W.R. Grace & Co. (Sulphur, LA) 70897

W.R. Grace & Co. (Morristown, TN) 81819
W.R. Grace & Co. Bartow Chemical Complex (Bartow, FL) 58635
W.R. Grace & Co. Construction Production Div. (Houston, TX) 87203
W.R. Grace & Co. Construction Products Div. (Pompano Beach, FL) 62646
W.R. Grace & Co. Cryovac Div. (Simpsonville, SC) 79871
W.R. Grace & Co. Cryovac Div. (Iowa Park, TX) 87311
W.R. Grace & Co. Davison Chemical Div. (Baltimore, MD) 71330
W.R. Grace & Co. Dewey & Almy Chemical Div. (Atlanta, GA) 65292
W.R. Grace & Co. Conn (Fort Worth, TX) 85365
W.R. Grace & Co.-Conn. Cpd (Pompano Beach, FL) 62647
W.R. Grace & Co. -Deer Park (Deer Park, TX) 84576
W.R. Grace & Co. Deer Park Facility (Deer Park, TX) 84577
Wrangler (Arab, AL) 55028
Wrangler (Hackleburg, AL) 55840
Wrangler (Hanceville, AL) 55852
Wrangler (Huntsville, AL) 56056
Wrangler (Oneonta, AL) 56414
Wrangler (Red Bay, AL) 56497
Wrangler (Miami, FL) 61516
Wrangler (Greensboro, NC) 74943; 74944
Wrangler (Wilson, NC) 76655
Wrangler (Windsor, NC) 76658
Wrangler (Colgate, OK) 76968
Wrangler (Okemah, OK) 77288
Wrangler (Prague, OK) 77731
Wrangler (Seminole, OK) 77807
Wrangler (Greenville, SC) 79449
Wrangler (Nashville, TN) 82145
Wrangler (Newbern, TN) 82159
Wrangler (Troy, TN) 82375
Wrangler (Fabens, TX) 85028
Wrangler (Luray, VA) 91218
Wrangler (Madison, VA) 91294
Wrangler (Shenandoah, VA) 92235
Wrangler (Woodstock, VA) 92633
Wrangler Menswear (El Paso, TX) 84979
Wrigley W M Jr Co. (Atlanta, GA) 65293
WSA (Falls Church, VA) 90873
Wusa-Tv Channel Job Inquiries (Washington, DC) 58522
WUSA-TV Channel 9 (Washington, DC) 58523; 58524
WUSA-TV Channel 9 Community Affairs (Washington, DC) 58525
WUSA-TV Channel 9 News (Washington, DC) 58526
WUSA-TV Channel 9 Personnel (Washington, DC) 58527
Wusa-Tv Channel 9 Program Info (Washington, DC) 58528
Wusa-Tv Channel 9 Sales (Washington, DC) 58529
Ww Henry Co. (Dallas, GA) 65768
WXIA TV-11 (Atlanta, GA) 65294
WXIA TV-11 Alive 11 Alive Data (Atlanta, GA) 65295
WXIA TV-11 Alive News Hotline (Atlanta, GA) 65296
Wyeth-Ayerst Laboratories Inc. (Atlanta, GA) 65297

X

X-Chem Inc. (Harahan, LA) 69938
Xeroc Corp. (Miami, FL) 61517
Xerox Business Services (Birmingham, AL) 55460
Xerox Business Services (New Orleans, LA) 70591
Xerox Business Services (Austin, TX) 83072
Xerox Computer Services (College Park, GA) 65612
Xerox Corp. (Huntsville, AL) 56057
Xerox Corp. (Mobile, AL) 56257
Xerox Corp. (Little Rock, AR) 57321
Xerox Corp. (Wilmington, DE) 58120
Xerox Corp. (Coral Gables, FL) 59105
Xerox Corp. (Fort Lauderdale, FL) 59644
Xerox Corp. (Jacksonville, FL) 60513
Xerox Corp. (Pensacola, FL) 62492
Xerox Corp. (Tallahassee, FL) 63290
Xerox Corp. (Baton Rouge, LA) 69688
Xerox Corp. (Shreveport, LA) 70808
Xerox Corp. (Baltimore, MD) 71331
Xerox Corp. (Rideland, MS) 73316

Xerox Corp. (Oklahoma City, OK) 77671; 77672
Xerox Corp. (Tulsa, OK) 78212
Xerox Corp. (Charleston, SC) 78917
Xerox Corp. (Columbia, SC) 79128
Xerox Corp. (Greenville, SC) 79450
Xerox Corp. (Chattanooga, TN) 80528
Xerox Corp. (Knoxville, TN) 81277
Xerox Corp. (Nashville, TN) 82146
Xerox Corp. (Austin, TX) 83073
Xerox Corp. (El Paso, TX) 84980
Xerox Corp. (Fort Worth, TX) 85366
Xerox Corp. (Houston, TX) 87204
Xerox Corp. (San Antonio, TX) 89327; 89328
Xerox Corp. (Arlington, VA) 90394; 90395
Xerox Corp. (Herndon, VA) 91138
Xerox Corp. (Richmond, VA) 92095
Xerox Corp. (Charleston, WV) 92800
Xetron Corp. (Devine, TX) 84650
XI Datacomp (Houston, TX) 87205
XI Datacomp (Midlothian Vi, VA) 91429
Xomed Inc. (Jacksonville, FL) 60514
Xomed-Treace Inc. (Jacksonville, FL) 60515
Xomox Corp. (Tampa, FL) 63664
Xomox Corp. (Tucker, GA) 67909
Xomox Corp. (Houston, TX) 87206

Y

Yadkin, Inc. (Badin, NC) 73654
Yale Materials Handling Corp. (Lenoir, NC) 75393
Yescor Telephony Cable Plant (Hickory, NC) 75108
Yoplait USA Inc. (Richardson, TX) 88792
York Air Conditioning (Fort Worth, TX) 85367
York Heating & Air Conditioning (Norman, OK) 77281
York International Corp. (Norcross, GA) 67213
York International Corp. (Madisonville, KY) 69074
York International Corp. (Norman, OK) 77282; 77283

Z

Zeagen Inc. (Winchester, KY) 69357
Zebco (Alexandria, LA) 69418
Zebco Corp-A Brunswick Co. (Tulsa, OK) 78213
Zebco Corp. (Tulsa, OK) 78214; 78215; 78216
Zenger-Miller (Fort Lauderdale, FL) 59645
Zenger-Miller (Bethesda, MD) 71450
Zenger-Miller Associates (Atlanta, GA) 65298
Zenger-Miller & Associates (Austin, TX) 83074
Zenger-Miller & Associates (Houston, TX) 87207
Zenger-Miller & Associates Inc. (Houston, TX) 87208
Zenith Electronic Corp. of T (El Paso, TX) 84981
Zenith Electronics (El Paso, TX) 84982
Zeno Systems (Oklahoma City, OK) 77673
Zeno Systems of Georgia Inc. (Atlanta, GA) 65299
Zeno Systems of Georgia Inc. (Norcross, GA) 67214
Zeno Systems of Houston (Houston, TX) 87209
Zeno Systems of Houston Inc. (Houston, TX) 87210
Zeno Systems Inc. (Carrollton, TX) 83514
Zeno Systems Inc. (Irving, TX) 87418; 87419
Zeno Systems of Oklahoma Inc. (Oklahoma City, OK) 77674
Zep Manuf Co. (Birmingham, AL) 55461
Zep Manufacturing (San Antonio, TX) 89329
ZEP Manufacturing Co. (Hialeah, FL) 60021
Zep Manufacturing Co. (Atlanta, GA) 65300; 65301
ZEP Manufacturing Co. (Smyrna, GA) 67585
Zep Manufacturing Co. (Louisville, KY) 69044
ZEP Manufacturing Co. (Baton Rouge, LA) 69689

Zep Manufacturing Co. (Minden, LA) 70348
ZEP Manufacturing Co. (Jessup, MD) 71988; 71989
Zep Manufacturing Co. (Oklahoma City, OK) 77675
Zep Manufacturing Co. (Tulsa, OK) 78217
Zep Manufacturing Co. (Austin, TX) 83075
Zep Manufacturing Co. (De Soto, TX) 84540; 84541
ZEP Manufacturing Co. (Houston, TX) 87211
Zep Manufacturing Co. Atlanta S (Smyrna, GA) 67586
Zep Manufacturing Co. Executive (Atlanta, GA) 65302
Zep Mfg. Co. (Atlanta, GA) 65303
Zep Mfg. Co. (De Soto, TX) 84542
Zimmer Patient Care System (Charlotte, NC) 74231
Zippy Mart (Chesapeake, VA) 90613
Zippy Mart Inc. (Birmingham, AL) 55462
Zippy Mart Inc. (Grant, FL) 59929
Zippy Mart Inc. (Jacksonville, FL) 60516
Zippy Mart Inc. (Melbourne, FL) 61122; 61123
Zippy Mart Inc. (Rockledge, FL) 62750
Zippy Mart Inc. (Jesup, GA) 66375
Zippy Mart Inc. (Valdosta, GA) 67981; 67982; 67983
Zippy Mart Inc. (Allendale, SC) 78660
Zippy Mart Inc. (Beaufort, SC) 78720
Zippy Mart Inc. (Summerton, SC) 79980
Zippy Mart Inc. (West Columbia, SC) 80112
Zippy Mart Inc. No. 883 (Walterboro, SC) 80081
Zippy Mart Inc. No. 515 (Adamsville, AL) 54952
Zippy Mart Inc. No. 516 (Bessemer, AL) 55108